THE NEW OXFORD ANNOTATED BIBLE

THIRD EDITION

MICHAEL D. COOGAN

EDITOR

Marc Z. Brettler, Carol A. Newsom, Pheme Perkins

ASSOCIATE EDITORS

New Revised Standard Version

OXFORD
UNIVERSITY PRESS

OXFORD
UNIVERSITY PRESS

Oxford New York

Athens Auckland Bangkok Bogota Buenos Aires Calcutta
Cape Town Chennai Dar es Salaam Delhi Florence Hong Kong Istanbul
Karachi Kuala Lumpur Madrid Melbourne Mexico City Mumbai
Nairobi Paris Sao Paulo Shanghai Singapore Taipei Tokyo Toronto Warsaw
and associated companies in
Berlin Ibadan

Published by Oxford University Press, Inc.
198 Madison Avenue, New York, New York 10016
http://www.oup-usa.org
Oxford is a registered trademark of Oxford University Press

3 5 7 9 10 8 6 4

Printed in the United States of America

Contributors

Mark E. Biddle: *Jeremiah* Joseph Blenkinsopp: *Isaiah* M. Eugene Boring: *1 Peter*

Sheila Briggs: *Galatians* David M. Carr: *Genesis*

Stephen L. Cook: *Ezekiel* F.W. Dobbs-Allsopp: *Lamentations, Song of Solomon*

Neil Elliott: *Romans* Tamara Cohn Eskenazi: *Ezra-Nehemiah*

Cain Hope Felder: *James* Obery M. Hendricks, Jr.: *John*

Richard A. Horsley: *Mark, 1 Corinthians*

Cynthia Briggs Kittredge: *Hebrews* Gary Knoppers: *1 and 2 Chronicles*

John S. Kselman: *Psalms* Mary Joan Winn Leith: *Ruth, Esther, Jonah*

Amy-Jill Levine: *Daniel* Bernard M. Levinson: *Deuteronomy*

Jennifer K. Berenson Maclean: *Ephesians, Colossians*

Christopher R. Matthews: *Acts* Steven L. McKenzie: *1 and 2 Samuel*

Margaret M. Mitchell: *1 and 2 Timothy, Titus, Philemon*

Gregory Mobley: *Book of the Twelve (except Jonah)*

Carolyn Osiek: *Philippians* J. Andrew Overman: *Matthew*

Pheme Perkins: *1, 2, 3 John* Iain W. Provan: *1 and 2 Kings*

Jean-Pierre Ruiz: *Revelation* Judith E. Sanderson: *Exodus*

Leong Seow: *Job, Ecclesiastes* Abraham Smith: *1 and 2 Thessalonians*

Marion Lloyd Soards: *Luke* Patrick A. Tiller: *2 Peter, Jude*

Sze-kar Wan: *2 Corinthians* Harold C. Washington: *Proverbs*

David P. Wright: *Leviticus, Numbers* K. Lawson Younger: *Joshua, Judges*

Marc Z. Brettler: *The Pentateuch; The Historical Books; The Poetical and Wisdom Books, The Canons of the Bible* [with Pheme Perkins]; *The Hebrew Bible's Interpretation of Itself; Jewish Interpretation in the Premodern Era*

Michael D. Coogan: *Textual Criticism* [with Pheme Perkins]; *The Interpretation of the Bible: From the Nineteenth to the Mid-twentieth Centuries; The Geography of the Bible; The Ancient Near East*

Carol A. Newsom: *The Prophetic Books; Christian Interpretation in the Premodern Era; Contemporary Methods in Biblical Study; The Persian and Hellenistic Periods*

Pheme Perkins: *The Gospels; Letters/Epistles in the New Testament; The Canons of the Bible [with Marc Z. Brettler]; Textual Criticism* [with Michael D. Coogan]; *Translation of the Bible into English; The New Testament Interprets the Jewish Scriptures; The Roman Period*

Contents

Note: In accordance with traditional practice, the pages of the separate Testaments are numbered independently. Thus, the Introductions to the Pentateuch and the Gospels are respectively the first page of the Hebrew Bible and the first page of the New Testament. As an aid to the reader the page numbers in the lists of contents are distinguished by the abbreviations HB and NT. The essay and reference material at the back of the book continue the numbering of the New Testament and carry the abbreviation ES.

List of Maps and Diagrams

List of Maps and Diagrams

OLD TESTAMENT

NEW TESTAMENT

COLOR MAPS

following the last page of text

The Editors' Preface

For nearly four decades *The Oxford Annotated Bible* has served generations of readers and students as a study Bible. That extraordinary longevity alone is eloquent testimony to its success. This new edition retains the format and features that have proven so attractive. At the same time, the field of biblical studies has not been static, and this edition is a thoroughgoing revision of the previous ones. In particular, the editors have recruited contributors from a wide diversity of backgrounds and of scholarly approaches to the biblical traditions. In order to present this diversity more fully, the space devoted to introductions to the biblical books, to the annotations, and to the study materials at the end of the book has been increased by over 30 percent.

We recognize that no single interpretation or approach is sufficient for informed reading of these ancient texts, and have aimed at inclusivity of interpretive strategies. On a great number of issues there is a consensus among scholars, and the contributors have been encouraged to present such consensus when it exists. Where it has broken down, and has not yet re-formed, alternatives are mentioned. Moreover, in order to respect the canonical status of various parts of the Bible for different communities, and to avoid privileging any book or part of the Bible, we have kept both introductions and annotations roughly proportionate to the length of the books, while recognizing that some parts require more elaboration than others.

The editorial process was collaborative. Each contribution was read in its entirety by at least three of the editors, and revised with a view toward consistency of tone, coherence of approach, and completeness of coverage. We have also wanted to allow the contributors' own voices to be heard, and we have avoided imposing a superficial uniformity of style and approach. Throughout, we have kept the needs of the general audience firmly in mind during the editorial stages, and our aim has been a congruity of experience as a reader turns from book to book and from section to section of the finished volume.

CONTENTS OF THE ANNOTATED BIBLE

The biblical text stands apart from any editorial contributions, in both placement and format. This will enable anyone who wishes to do so to read the text unprejudiced by editorial judgments.

The footnotes that are part of the New Revised Standard Version (indicated by an italic superscript letter after the word or phrase in question) are printed at the bottom of the right-hand column of the biblical text on each page where they occur. In these notes, divergent textual readings and alternate translations are printed in italics. The phrase "Other ancient authorities read" means that the reading (i.e., the wording) of the passage is different in various manuscripts and early versions, and the word "Or" signifies that the Hebrew, Aramaic, Greek, or Latin text permits an alternate rendering besides the one given in the text. (See "Textual Criticism," p. 460 ES.)

Discussion of larger units in the Bible is provided by essays introducing each of them: "The Pentateuch," "The Historical Books," "The Poetical and Wisdom Books," "The Prophetic Books," "The Gospels," and "Letters/Epistles in the New Testament."

Each book is preceded by its own introduction, which sketches the book's structure, main themes, literary history, and historical context, as well as broad lines of interpretation. As mentioned above, these introductions are in most cases considerably longer than in previous editions; they therefore present a clear overview and guide to reading.

At the bottom of each page of the biblical text, in a different font from it and in a single column, are the annotations. The annotations are just that, notes rather than paraphrase or commentary, although these genres admittedly overlap. They are intended to enhance the reader's understanding of the text, providing essential information, background, and interpretation, rather than only summarizing what it says. The boldface headings delineate the larger units of the book, and provide a detailed consecutive outline of its contents. The word or phrase being glossed is given in italics. Quotation marks are used for words quoted from elsewhere in the Bible as well as for transliterations of ancient languages. Since we desire each book to stand on its own, as much as possible the annotations are self-contained. We have thus tried to avoid both cross-references to fuller discussions elsewhere, and the misconception that a book or larger part of the Bible is merely a perfunctory reworking of other material, or that a particular passage can only be understood fully in the light of later biblical traditions. At the same time, we recognize that the Bible is often a progressive text, and that later parts of the Bible often contain the oldest interpretations of earlier traditions. The best starting point for interpreting a particular passage is often another passage, and we have encouraged contributors to point out interconnections in the biblical material by means of cross-references. (The cross-references that end with "n." refer to the annotation as well as to the biblical text.)

A listing of abbreviations for the books of the Bible used in this edition is found on p. xxv below. The chapter and verse divisions in a reference are separated by a period; thus, Gen 3.8 refers to the book of Genesis, chapter 3, verse 8. Inclusive references are used for both chapters and verses; thus, Ex 1–15 refers to the first fifteen chapters of the book of Exodus; Rom 11.33–36 to verses 33 through 36 of chapter 11 of the letter to the Romans; and so forth. When a book of the Bible is referred to within an annotation on that book, the name of the book is not repeated unless there is ambiguity.

In keeping with our general desire to take account of the diversity of the users of this study Bible, we have adopted two widely accepted conventions: We have referred to the first portion of the text as "the Hebrew Bible," since it is a collection preserved by the Jewish community and that is how Jews regard it; and we have cited all dates in the notes as BCE or CE ("Before the Common Era" and "Common Era") instead of BC or AD ("Before Christ" and "Anno Domini" ["in the year of the Lord"]), which imply a Christian view of the status of Jesus of Nazareth. Use of the title "Old Testament" for those books here designated as "the Hebrew Bible" is confined to instances expressing the historical view of various Christian interpreters. These conventions are followed in the study materials that we have produced; the translation has its own conventions which we are not at liberty to alter.

Because this Bible is published in editions with and without the Apocryphal/Deuterocanonical Books, it is necessary to number each major portion separately. The portions are distinguished by short titles in small capitals following the page numbers. The Hebrew Bible therefore begins with the introduction to the Pentateuch on the first page of the HEBREW BIBLE; the Apocryphal/Deuterocanonical Books begin with the introduction to the Apocrypha on the first page of the APOCRYPHA; the New Testament begins with the introduction to the Gospels on the first page of the NEW TESTAMENT.

The general essays at the back of the volume continue the pagination from the end of the New Testament, but designate their pages by ESSAYS. Abbreviations of these designations—HB, AP, NT, and ES—serve to identify the page numbers in the index.

Several dozen maps and plans are interspersed in the biblical text. These will assist readers to locate important places mentioned in the text or to clarify the prose descriptions of such structures as the Tabernacle and the Temple.

The study materials at the end of the volume are a series of interconnected essays that provide background information for understanding the Bible, the processes by which it was formed, the contexts in which it was produced, and the ways in which it has been interpreted through the ages. These essays are followed by tables of rulers, of weights and measures, of the calendar, and of parallel passages in the biblical traditions. A select chronology provides a quick reference for major events, rulers, and other persons contemporaneous with the biblical accounts.

At the end of the book is a comprehensive subject index to all of the study materials, including the annotations. Finally, there is a separate set of fourteen color maps, with a separate index to them, that constitute a brief historical atlas to the Bible.

ACKNOWLEDGMENTS

It remains to express our gratitude, first and above all to the contributors, whose learning has made this a work of which we are immensely proud, and whose uncommon patience with the editorial process made our task light. Allen D. Callahan was of assistance early in the development of the edition. Donald Kraus, Executive Editor in the Bible department at Oxford University Press, U.S.A., has guided this edition from its inception with wisdom and tact. Deborah Darcy, Michele McEnroe, Penelope Anderson, and Jennifer Grady, the editorial staff at the Press, have been meticulous in dealing with the complexities of an editorial process that went through many stages. Katrina Gettman carefully and conscientiously prepared the edited materials for the compositor. Leslie Phillips created the page design and oversaw every detail of the entire typesetting process, as well as providing the maps within the text. Peachtree Editorial and Proofreading Service proofread the entire text with extraordinary care and speed. The Scriptorium prepared the very useful index. We thank them all.

MICHAEL D. COOGAN
MARC Z. BRETTLER
CAROL A. NEWSOM
PHEME PERKINS
August, 2000

To the Reader

[The following prefatory essay, "To the Reader," is part of the New Revised Standard Version Bible translation (NRSV), and is reprinted here in accordance with the requirements of the National Council of the Churches of Christ in the U.S.A., which holds copyright to the NRSV.]

This preface is addressed to you by the Committee of translators, who wish to explain, as briefly as possible, the origin and character of our work. The publication of our revision is yet another step in the long, continual process of making the Bible available in the form of the English language that is most widely current in our day. To summarize in a single sentence: the New Revised Standard Version of the Bible is an authorized revision of the Revised Standard Version, published in 1952, which was a revision of the American Standard Version, published in 1901, which, in turn, embodied earlier revisions of the King James Version, published in 1611.

In the course of time, the King James Version came to be regarded as "the Authorized Version." With good reason it has been termed "the noblest monument of English prose," and it has entered, as no other book has, into the making of the personal character and the public institutions of the English-speaking peoples. We owe to it an incalculable debt.

Yet the King James Version has serious defects. By the middle of the nineteenth century, the development of biblical studies and the discovery of many biblical manuscripts more ancient than those on which the King James Version was based made it apparent that these defects were so many as to call for revision. The task was begun, by authority of the Church of England, in 1870. The (British) Revised Version of the Bible was published in 1881–1885; and the American Standard Version, its variant embodying the preferences of the American scholars associated with the work, was published, as was mentioned above, in 1901. In 1928 the copyright of the latter was acquired by the International Council of Religious Education and thus passed into the ownership of the churches of the United States and Canada that were associated in this Council through their boards of education and publication.

The Council appointed a committee of scholars to have charge of the text of the American Standard Version and to undertake inquiry concerning the need for further revision. After studying the questions whether or not revision should be undertaken, and if so, what its nature and extent should be, in 1937 the Council authorized a revision. The scholars who served as members of the Committee worked in two sections, one dealing with the Old Testament and one with the New Testament. In 1946 the Revised Standard Version of the New Testament was published. The publication of the Revised Standard Version of the Bible, containing the Old and New Testaments, took place on September 30, 1952. A translation of the Apocryphal/Deuterocanonical Books of the Old Testament followed in 1957. In 1977 this collection was issued in an expanded edition, containing three additional texts received by Eastern Orthodox communions (3 and 4 Maccabees and Psalm 151). Thereafter the Revised Standard Version gained the distinction of being officially authorized for use by all major Christian churches: Protestant, Anglican, Roman Catholic, and Eastern Orthodox.

The Revised Standard Version Bible Committee is a continuing body, comprising about thirty members, both men and women. Ecumenical in representation, it includes scholars affiliated with various Protestant denominations, as well as several Roman Catholic members, an Eastern Orthodox member, and a Jewish member who serves in the Old Testament section. For a period of time the Committee included several members from Canada and from England.

Because no translation of the Bible is perfect or is acceptable to all groups of readers, and because discoveries of older manuscripts and further investigation of linguistic features of the text continue to become available, renderings of the Bible have proliferated. During the years following the publication of the Revised Standard Version, twenty-six other English translations and revisions of the Bible were produced by committees and by individual scholars—not to mention twenty-five other translations and revisions of the New Testament alone. One of the latter was the second edition of the RSV New Testament, issued in 1971, twenty-five years after its initial publication.

Following the publication of the RSV Old Testament in 1952, significant advances were made in the discovery and interpretation of documents in Semitic languages related to Hebrew. In addition to the information that had become available in the late 1940s from the Dead Sea texts of Isaiah and Habakkuk, subsequent acquisitions from the same area brought to light many other early copies of all the books of the Hebrew Scriptures (except Esther), though most of these copies are fragmentary. During the same period early Greek manuscript copies of books of the New Testament also became available.

In order to take these discoveries into account, along with recent studies of documents in Semitic languages related to Hebrew, in 1974 the Policies Committee of the Revised Standard Version, which is a standing committee of the National Council of the Churches of Christ in the U.S.A., authorized the preparation of a revision of the entire RSV Bible.

For the Old Testament the Committee has made use of the *Biblia Hebraica Stuttgartensia* (1977; ed. sec. emendata, 1983). This is an edition of the Hebrew and Aramaic text as current early in the Christian era and fixed by Jewish scholars (the "Masoretes") of the sixth to the ninth centuries. The vowel signs, which were added by the Masoretes, are accepted in the main, but where a more probable and convincing reading can be obtained by assuming different vowels, this has been done. No notes are given in such cases, because the vowel points are less ancient and reliable than the consonants. When an alternative reading given by the Masoretes is translated in a footnote, this is identified by the words "Another reading is."

Departures from the consonantal text of the best manuscripts have been made only where it seems clear that errors in copying had been made before the text was standardized. Most of the corrections adopted are based on the ancient versions (translations into Greek, Aramaic, Syriac, and Latin), which were made prior to the time of the work of the Masoretes and which therefore may reflect earlier forms of the Hebrew text. In such instances a footnote specifies the version or versions from which the correction has been derived and also gives a translation of the Masoretic Text. Where it was deemed appropriate to do so, information is supplied in footnotes from subsidiary Jewish traditions concerning other textual readings (the *Tiqqune Sopherim*, "emendations of the scribes"). These are identified in the footnotes as "Ancient Heb tradition."

Occasionally it is evident that the text has suffered in transmission and that none of the versions provides a satisfactory restoration. Here we can only follow the best judgment of competent scholars as to the most probable reconstruction of the original text. Such reconstructions are indicated in footnotes by the abbreviation Cn ("Correction"), and a translation of the Masoretic Text is added.

For the New Testament the Committee has based its work on the most recent edition of *The Greek New Testament*, prepared by an interconfessional and international committee and published by the United Bible Societies (1966; 3rd ed. corrected, 1983; information concerning changes to be introduced into the critical apparatus of the forthcoming 4th edition was available to the Committee). As in that edition, double brackets are used to enclose a few passages that are generally regarded to be later additions to the text, but which we have retained because of their evident antiquity and their importance in the textual tradition. Only in very rare instances have we replaced the text or the punctuation of the Bible Societies' edition by an alternative that seemed to us to be superior. Here and there in the footnotes the phrase, "Other ancient authorities read," identifies alternative readings preserved by Greek manuscripts and early versions. In both Testaments, alternative renderings of the text are indicated by the word "Or."

As for the style of English adopted for the present revision, among the mandates given to the Committee in 1980 by the Division of Education and Ministry of the National Council of Churches of Christ (which now holds the copyright of the RSV Bible) was the directive to continue in the tradition of the King James Bible, but to introduce such changes as are warranted on the basis of accuracy, clarity, euphony, and current English usage. Within the constraints set by the original texts and by the mandates of the Division, the Committee has followed the maxim, "As literal as possible, as free as necessary." As a consequence, the New Revised Standard Version (NRSV) remains essentially a literal translation. Paraphrastic renderings have been adopted only sparingly, and then chiefly to compensate for a deficiency in the English language—the lack of a common gender third person singular pronoun.

During the almost half a century since the publication of the RSV, many in the churches have become sensitive to the danger of linguistic sexism arising from the inherent bias of the English language towards the masculine gender, a bias that in the case of the Bible has often restricted or obscured the meaning of the original text. The mandates from the Division specified that, in references to men and women, masculine-oriented language should be eliminated as far as this can be done without altering passages that reflect the historical situation of ancient patriarchal culture. As can be appreciated, more than once the Committee found that the several mandates stood in tension and even in conflict. The various concerns had to be balanced case by case in order to provide a faithful and acceptable rendering without using contrived English. Only very occasionally has the pronoun "he" or "him" been retained in passages where the reference may have been to a woman as well as to a man; for example, in several legal texts in Leviticus and Deuteronomy. In such instances of formal, legal language, the options of either putting the passage in the plural or of introducing additional nouns to avoid masculine pronouns in English seemed to the Committee to obscure the historic structure and literary character of the original. In the vast majority of cases, however, inclusiveness has been attained by simple rephrasing or by introducing plural forms when this does not distort the meaning of the passage. Of course, in narrative and in parable no attempt was made to generalize the sex of individual persons.

Another aspect of style will be detected by readers who compare the more stately English rendering of the Old Testament with the less formal rendering adopted for the New Testament. For example, the traditional distinction between *shall* and *will* in English has been retained in the Old Testament as appropriate in rendering a document that embodies what may be termed the classic form of Hebrew, while in the New Testament the abandonment of such distinctions in the usage of the future tense in English reflects the more colloquial nature of the koine Greek used by most New Testament authors except when they are quoting the Old Testament.

Careful readers will notice that here and there in the Old Testament the word LORD (or in certain cases GOD) is printed in capital letters. This represents the traditional manner in English versions of rendering the Divine Name, the "Tetragrammaton" (see the translators' notes on Exodus 3.14, 15), following the precedent of the ancient Greek and Latin translators and the long established practice in the reading of the Hebrew Scriptures in the synagogue. While it is almost if not quite certain that the Name was originally pronounced "Yahweh," this pronunciation was not indicated when the Masoretes added vowel sounds to the consonantal Hebrew text. To the four consonants YHWH of the Name, which had come to be regarded as too sacred to be pronounced, they attached vowel signs indicating that in its place should be read the Hebrew word *Adonai* meaning "Lord" (or *Elohim* meaning "God"). Ancient Greek translators employed the word *Kyrios* ("Lord") for the Name. The Vulgate likewise used the Latin word *Dominus* ("Lord"). The form "Jehovah" is of late medieval origin; it is a combination of the consonants of the Divine Name and the vowels attached to it by the Masoretes but belonging to an entirely different word. Although the American Standard Version (1901) had used "Jehovah" to render the Tetragrammaton (the sound of Y being represented by J and the sound of W by V, as in Latin), for two reasons the Committees that produced the RSV and the NRSV returned to the more familiar usage of the King James Version. (1) The word "Jehovah" does not accurately represent any form of the Name ever used in Hebrew. (2) The use of any proper name for the one and only God, as though there were other gods from whom the true God had to be distinguished, began to be discontinued in Judaism before the Christian era and is inappropriate for the universal faith of the Christian Church.

It will be seen that in the Psalms and in other prayers addressed to God the archaic second person singular pronouns *thee, thou, thine*) and verb forms *(art, hast, hadst)* are no longer used. Although some readers may regret this change, it should be pointed out that in the original languages neither the Old Testament nor the New makes any linguistic distinction between addressing a human being and addressing the Deity. Furthermore, in the tradition of the King James Version one will not expect to find the use of capital letters for pronouns that refer to the Deity—such capitalization is an unnecessary innovation that has only recently been introduced into a few English translations of the Bible. Finally, we have left to the discretion of the licensed publishers such matters as section headings, cross-references, and clues to the pronunciation of proper names.

This new version seeks to preserve all that is best in the English Bible as it has been known and used through the years. It is intended for use in public reading and congregational worship, as well as in private study, instruction, and meditation. We have resisted the temptation to introduce terms and phrases that merely reflect current moods, and have tried to put the message of the Scriptures in simple, enduring words and expressions that are worthy to stand in the great tradition of the King James Bible and its predecessors.

In traditional Judaism and Christianity, the Bible has been more than a historical document to be preserved or a classic of literature to be cherished and admired; it is recognized as the unique record of God's dealings with people over the ages. The Old Testament sets forth the call of a special people to enter into covenant relation with the God of justice and steadfast love and to bring God's law to the nations. The New Testament records the life and work of Jesus Christ, the one in whom "the Word became flesh," as well as describes the rise and spread of the early Christian Church. The Bible carries its full message, not to those who regard it simply as a noble literary heritage of the past or who wish to use it to enhance political purposes and advance otherwise desirable goals, but to all persons and communities who read it so that they may discern and understand what God is saying to them. That message must not be disguised in phrases that are no longer clear, or hidden under words that have changed or lost their meaning; it must be presented in language that is direct and plain and meaningful to people today. It is the hope and prayer of the translators that this version of the Bible may continue to hold a large place in congregational life and to speak to all readers, young and old alike, helping them to understand and believe and respond to its message.

For the Committee,
BRUCE M. METZGER

Alphabetical Listing of the Books of the Bible

HB = Hebrew Bible NT = New Testament

List of Abbreviations

The following abbreviations are used for the books of the Bible:

OLD TESTAMENT

Gen	Genesis	2 Chr	2 Chronicles	Dan	Daniel
Ex	Exodus	Ezra	Ezra	Hos	Hosea
Lev	Leviticus	Neh	Nehemiah	Joel	Joel
Num	Numbers	Esth	Esther	Am	Amos
Deut	Deuteronomy	Job	Job	Ob	Obadiah
Josh	Joshua	Ps	Psalms	Jon	Jonah
Judg	Judges	Prov	Proverbs	Mic	Micah
Ruth	Ruth	Eccl	Ecclesiastes	Nah	Nahum
1 Sam	1 Samuel	Song	Song of Solomon	Hab	Habakkuk
2 Sam	2 Samuel	Isa	Isaiah	Zeph	Zephaniah
1 Kings	1 Kings	Jer	Jeremiah	Hag	Haggai
2 Kings	2 Kings	Lam	Lamentations	Zech	Zechariah
1 Chr	1 Chronicles	Ezek	Ezekiel	Mal	Malachi

NEW TESTAMENT

Mt	Matthew	Eph	Ephesians	Heb	Hebrews
Mk	Mark	Phil	Philippians	Jas	James
Lk	Luke	Col	Colossians	1 Pet	1 Peter
Jn	John	1 Thess	1 Thessalonians	2 Pet	2 Peter
Acts	Acts of the Apostles	2 Thess	2 Thessalonians	1 Jn	1 John
Rom	Romans	1 Tim	1 Timothy	2 Jn	2 John
1 Cor	1 Corinthians	2 Tim	2 Timothy	3 Jn	3 John
2 Cor	2 Corinthians	Titus	Titus	Jude	Jude
Gal	Galatians	Philem	Philemon	Rev	Revelation

In the notes to the books of the Hebrew Bible the following abbreviations are used:

Ant.	Josephus, *Antiquities of the Jews*
Aram	Aramaic
Ch, chs	Chapter, chapters
Cn	Correction; made where the text has suffered in transmission and the versions provide no satisfactory restoration but where the Standard Bible Committee agrees with the judgment of competent scholars as to the most probable reconstruction of the original text.
Gk	Septuagint, Greek version of the Old Testament
Heb	Hebrew of the consonantal Masoretic Text of the Old Testament
Josephus	Flavius Josephus (Jewish historian, ca. 37–95 CE)

Macc	The book(s) of the Maccabees
Ms(s)	Manuscript(s)
MT	The Hebrew of the pointed Masoretic Text of the Old Testament
OL	Old Latin
Q Ms(s)	Manuscript(s) found at Qumran by the Dead Sea
Sam	Samaritan Hebrew text of the Old Testament
Syr	Syriac Version of the Old Testament
Syr H	Syriac Version of Origen's Hexapla
Tg	Targum
Vg	Vulgate, Latin Version of the Old Testament

For a detailed discussion of these terms, see "Textual Criticism," p. 460 ES.

The following abbreviations of additional ancient works are used in the introductions and annotations to the biblical books, and in the General Essays at the end of the volume:

Ag. Ap.	Josephus, *Against Apion*
Apoc. Bar.	*Apocalypse of Baruch*
Apoc. Zeph.	*Apocalypse of Zephaniah*
b. Ber.	Babylonian Talmud, Tractate *Berakot*
b. Eruv.	Babylonian Talmud, Tractate *Eruvim*
b. Git.	Babylonian Talmud, Tractate *Gittin*
b. Ned.	Babylonian Talmud, Tractate *Nedarim*
b. San.	Babylonian Talmud, Tractate *Sanhedrin*
b. Shabb	Babylonian Talmud, Tractate *Shabbat*
b. Yoma	Babylonian Talmud, Tractate *Yoma*
b. Meg.	Babylonian Talmud, Tractate *Megillah*
CD	Cairo Genizah, Damascus Document
1 Clem	*1 Clement (*First Epistle of Clement)
Ep. Arist.	*Letter of Aristeas*
Gen. Rab.	*Genesis Rabbah*
Hermas, *Mand.*	*Shepherd of Hermas, Mandate*
Ignatius, *Philad.*	Ignatius, *Epistle to the Philadelphians*
Irenaeus, *Adv. Haer.*	Irenaeus, *Adversus omnes Haereses*
Jer. Sot.	Jerusalem Talmud, *Sotah* (see *y. Sot.*)
Josephus, *Ag. Ap.*	Josephus, *Against Apion*
Jub.	*Jubilees*
Lam. Rab.	*Lamentations Rabbah*
m. Ketub.	*Mishnah Ketubim*
m. Ned.	*Mishnah Nedarim*
m. Ohalot	*Mishnah Ohalot*
Midr.	*Midrash*
Midr. Pss.	*Midrash Psalms*
P. Oxy.	*Oxyrhynchus Papyri*
Philo, *De Conf.Ling.*	Philo, *De Confusione Linguarum*
Philo, *De spec. leg.*	Philo, *De specialibus Legibus*
Philo, *Leg. all.*	Philo, *Legum allegoriae*
Philo, *Leg. Gai.*	Philo, *Legatio ad Gaium*

Philo, *Rer. div. her.*	Philo, *Quis rerum divinarum heres sit*
Pliny, *Nat. Hist.*	Pliny, *Naturalis Historia*
11QTemple	The Temple Scroll from Qumran Cave 11 (11Q19)
1QH	Hodayot (Thanksgiving Hymns) from Qumran Cave 1
1QM	Milhamah (War Scroll) from Qumran Cave 1
11QMelch	Melchizedek Scroll from Qumran Cave 11 (11Q13)
1QpHab	Pesher to Habakkuk from Qumran Cave 1
11QPs[a]	The Psalms[a] Scroll from Qumran Cave 11 (11Q5)
1QS	Rule of the Community (Serek Hayahd) from Qumran Cave 1
Seder Olam R.	*Seder Olam Rabbah*
Shab.	*Shabbat*
Sifre Num.	*Sifre Numbers*
Sib. Or.	*Sibylline Oracles*
T. Jud. (Test. Jud.)	*Testament of Judah*
T. Moses	*Testament of Moses*
T. Reuben	*Testament of Reuben*
Tr. Eruv.	Babylonian Talmud, *Tractate Eruvim* (see *b. Eruv.*)
y.	Jerusalem Talmud
y. Sot.	Jerusalem Talmud, *Sotah*

Note: The abbreviation "Q," unless specified as "Quelle" ("Source") for the posited New Testament document of non-Markan common material in Matthew and Luke, refers to Qumran, and manuscripts from Qumran are identified by the cave number, which precedes the Q, and the official manuscript number, which follows it; thus, 1Q34 = Manuscript 34 from Cave 1 at Qumran; 4Q174 = Manuscript 174 from Cave 4; etc.

THE NEW OXFORD

ANNOTATED BIBLE

THIRD EDITION

THE HEBREW BIBLE

THE HEBREW SCRIPTURES

COMMONLY CALLED THE OLD TESTAMENT

New Revised Standard Version

INTRODUCTION
to the Pentateuch

TERMINOLOGY, CONTENTS, AND TRADITIONAL VIEWS OF AUTHORSHIP

THE WORD "PENTATEUCH," from the Greek for "five (*penta*) books (*teuchos*)," has entered English by way of Latin as the designation for the first group of books in the Hebrew Bible, comprising Genesis, Exodus, Leviticus, Numbers, and Deuteronomy. Unlike other canonical divisions, where there is significant debate within and between different religious traditions, both Jewish and Christian tradition view these five books in this order as a single unit, introducing the Bible. The unanimity of tradition and the initial placement of these five books reflect their significant place within both Judaism and Christianity.

Despite this unanimity of tradition, it is not so obvious how these five books cohere. They certainly do not form a single book in the modern sense, with a single author; modern scholarship has persuasively argued that each of these books is composite, reflecting many traditions and sources (see below). Nor is there complete coherence of plot among them. Without any question, Moses is the central human character of much of the Pentateuch, but he is only introduced in ch 2 of Exodus, the second book. Nor is the early development of Israel as a people the Pentateuch's unifying theme, as may be seen from the first eleven chapters of the Bible, which are concerned with the world from creation to the birth of Abraham (Gen 11.27). Various other suggested unifying themes for the Pentateuch, such as covenant, are also incorrect, since they do not really appear at the beginning of the Pentateuch and are continued well beyond it. The suggestion that the promise of the land unifies the Pentateuch is especially problematic, since this theme, though introduced in Gen 12, is only fulfilled with the conquest of the land in Joshua, in which case the Hexateuch ("six books": the Pentateuch plus Joshua) rather than the Pentateuch should be seen as the decisive unit.

The Hebrew terms *torah* and *torat moshe* ("the Torah of Moses"), already in use in late biblical literature to describe what is later called the Pentateuch, offer a better clue to the nature and unity of these books. *Torah* is often understood as "law," and indeed this is one of its frequent meanings in the Bible, as in Ex 12.49; "There shall be one law [Heb *torah*] for the native and for the alien who resides among you." Law is a predominant genre of the Pentateuch, which contains not only the Ten Commandments in Ex 20 and Deut 5, but extensive legal collections in Ex 21–23, Lev 17–26, and Deut 12–26, as well as selected laws within various narratives, such as the law of circumcision in the narrative about Abraham in Gen 17 and the law concerning inheritance of the land by women in Num 36, embedded within a section about the possession of the land. Many narrative sections also contain material that is of legal significance. For example, the first creation story in Genesis culminates with the "creation" of the sabbath (Gen 2.2–3), though this would only be legislated in Exodus, first in ch 16, and then as part of the Ten Commandments, in Ex 20.8–11. Similarly, the story of the construction of the tabernacle (Ex 25–40), a temporary temple for God in the wilderness, is not narrated for its own sake, but as an introduction to the various laws of sacrifice, narrated at the beginning of Leviticus, the book that immediately follows these chapters.

Yet "law" is not the only possible translation of *torah*, and the Pentateuch should not be typified as a book of law. The Hebrew term *torah* also means "instruction" or "teaching," as in Prov 1.8, "Hear, my child, your father's instruction, and do not reject your mother's teaching [Heb *torah*]." Teaching is not confined to law; indeed narratives or stories are as effective a medium of instruction. Thus, given the predominance of narrative in significant portions of the Pentateuch, especially in Genesis, the beginning of Exodus, and Numbers, it is best to understand the biblical term *torat moshe*, the earliest extant term for these five books, as "the instruction of Moses." This instruction was realized through narratives and laws, which together elucidate the proper norms of living and the relationship between God and the world.

The term *torat moshe*, found predominantly in various late biblical sections and books, such as Ezra, Nehemiah, and Chronicles, refers to the Pentateuch more or less as it now exists, but it is not found in the Pentateuch itself. In fact, the Torah does not explicitly suggest that it was compiled by Moses himself. (The phrase "the Torah" in passages such as Deut 4.44, "This is the law [Heb *torah*] that Moses set before the Israelites," never refers to the complete Pentateuch.) It is easy to see how the tradition ascribing these five books as a whole to Moses developed. In several places, the Hebrew Scriptures suggest that Moses stayed on Mount Sinai for forty days and forty nights (Ex 24.18; 34.28; Deut 9.9; 10.10). Clearly, this was too long a time for short legal collections such as Ex 21–23 to have been conveyed to him, and thus traditions developed that Moses received the entire written Torah from God at that point. According to the classical rabbis, Moses simultaneously received the oral law, which served as the authoritative interpretation of the written law. The written Torah would include, according to all rabbinic sources (which are followed by the early church), even the book of Genesis, which thus represents God's narration to Moses of the early history of the world and of Abraham and his family. Some rabbinic sources even suggest that the final chapter of the Torah, Deut 34, which narrates the death of Moses, was dictated by God to Moses, who wrote them with his tears. The view that the Torah should be understood as the divine word mediated by Moses was the standard view of church and synagogue through the Renaissance.

This view is explicitly contradicted by the Torah's narrative, as was sometimes (though rarely) recognized in the Middle Ages. Thus, Abraham ibn (son of) Ezra, active in the twelfth century CE, noted that Gen 12.6 states in reference to Abraham that "at that time the Canaanites were in the land." The words "at that time" suggest that for the author, the Canaanites were no longer in the land; in other words, it appears that the text was written after the time of Moses, because during his time the Canaanites were still in the land. A small number of other places that suggest authorship later than Moses were pointed out by a few medieval scholars, but these were not systematized into a thesis that could challenge the dominant view concerning Moses' authorship of the Torah.

MODERN SOURCE THEORIES

Slowly, with the rise of rationalism, particularly as associated with figures such as Thomas Hobbes (1588–1679) and Benedict (Baruch) Spinoza (1632–1677), the view that the Torah was a unified whole, written by Moses, began to be questioned. (For additional information on this development, see the essays on "The Interpretation of the Bible," pp. 471–497 ESSAYS.) This culminated in the development of the model of the Documentary Hypothesis in the nineteenth century, according to which the Pentateuch (or Hexateuch) is composed of four main sources or documents that were edited or redacted together: J, E, P, and D. Each of these sources or documents is embedded in a (relatively) complete form in the current Pentateuch, and is typified by both vocabulary and theological perspective.

J and E are so called after the names for God that each of them uses in Genesis: J uses the name "Yahweh" (German "Jahwe," hence "J"), translated in the NRSV as "LORD," though it is really a personal name, whose exact meaning is unknown, from the root "to be"; E prefers to call the deity "Elohim" (translated "God"), an epithet that also serves as the generic term for God or gods in the Bible. P, which also uses "Elohim," is an abbreviation for the Priestly material, and D refers to Deuteronomy.

The difference in divine names, however, is not the main criterion used by scholars for suggesting that the Torah is not a unified composition. Much more significant are doublets and contradictions, in both narrative and legal material. For example, it has long been noted that chs 1–3 of Genesis twice narrate the creation of the world. People are created first in 1.27—"So God created humankind in his image, in the image of God he created them; male and female he created them"—and then again in 2.7—"Then the LORD God formed man from the dust of the ground, and breathed into his nostrils the breath of life; and the man became a living being." Furthermore, the second creation account does not simply mirror or repeat the first, but differs from the first in both outline and detail. Gen 1.1–2.3, the first account, narrates the creation of a highly symmetrical world by a very powerful deity who creates through the word. In this story, for example, man and woman are created together (1.27) after the creation of the land animals (1.25). In contrast, the second story, in Gen 2.4–3.24, suggests that man was created (2.7), then the animals (2.19), and then woman (2.21–22). Its focus is on the creation of humanity, not of the entire physical world, and God anthropomorphically "forms" various beings, rather than creating them with the word. Thus, these are two separate stories, written by two authors, representing different worldviews about the nature of creation, humanity, and God.

The two creation stories appear as two totally separate blocks of material in Gen 1.1–2.3 and 2.4–3.24. In several cases, however, such a clear-cut division of sources is impossible for narrative reasons. For example, the flood story culminates in a tradition that God will never again bring a flood on the land (Gen 9.11); for this reason, the J and P narratives cannot appear as separate and complete narratives, so they are intertwined. Similarly, the story of the plague of blood (Ex 7.14–24) contains two intertwined accounts; in one (J), Moses is the protagonist, and the blood only affects the Nile (e.g., vv. 17–18), while in the other (P), Aaron appears as well, and the flood affects all Egyptian water sources (e.g., vv. 19,24). In such cases, the narratives are combined with great skill, though careful attention to plot and vocabulary help to discern the original building blocks or sources of the story.

In addition to narrative, the legal material in the Torah is also the product of several sources. For example, slave laws concerning the Hebrew or Israelite slave are found in the Torah in Ex 21.1–6, Lev 25.39–46, and Deut 15.12–18. These laws cannot be reconciled in a straightforward fashion since they represent three different notions of slavery. Most significant is the way in which Exodus differentiates between the treatment of a male and female slave, whereas Deuteronomy insists that they should both be treated similarly. While Exodus and Deuteronomy agree that a slave who loves his master may opt to remain a slave "for life" (Ex 21.6) or "forever" (Deut 15.17), Lev 25 insists that slavery does not really exist, since slaves must be treated "as hired or bound laborers," and they may only serve "until the year of the jubilee" (v. 40). Such legal differences are not surprising once we are open to the hypotheses that the Bible is composite, and the different legal collections reflect norms or ideals of different groups living in different time periods.

In fact, it is possible to trace distinctive styles and theological notions that typify individual Pentateuchal sources. For example, the J source is well-known for its highly anthropomorphic God, who has a close relationship with humans, as seen in Gen 2.4–3.24, which includes, for example, a description of God "walking in the garden" (3.8) and says that God "made garments of skins for the man and for his wife, and clothed them" (3.21). On the other hand, in E, the Elohist source, God is more distant from people, typically communicating with them by dreams or via intermediaries, such as heavenly messengers (NRSV "angels") and prophets. The P or Priestly source is characterized by a strong interest in order and boundaries (see Gen 1), as well as an overriding concern with the priestly family of Aaron and the Temple-based religious system. D, or Deuteronomy, is characterized by a unique hortatory or preaching style, and insists strongly that God cannot be seen, as in this source's description of revelation: "Then the LORD spoke to you out of the fire. You heard the sound of words but saw no form; there was only a voice" (Deut 4.12). This explains why this source, uniquely, insists that God does not physically dwell in the temple or tabernacle; rather, the temple is "the place that the LORD your God will choose as a dwelling for his name" (Deut 12.11). D also emphasizes that this one God must be worshiped in one place only (see especially Deut 12); this place is later understood to be Jerusalem.

The narrative sources J, E, P, and D also have legal collections associated with them. The Covenant Collection (see Ex 24.7) in Ex 20.22–23.33 is associated with J or E. The Holiness Collection of Lev 17–26 is so named because of its central injunction, "You shall be holy, for I the LORD your God am holy" (Lev 19.2). Though not composed by the Priestly author (P), it represents Priestly theology. The Deuteronomic law collection appears in Deut 12–26. These blocks of material were called "codes" by earlier scholars; since the blocks are neither complete nor organized for the law court, however, as a "code" might be, the term "collection" is more suitable.

Critical biblical scholarship, through the latter part of the twentieth century, was quite confident in dating each of these Pentateuchal sources along with the legal collections they incorporated. Thus, J was seen as the earliest collection, often dated to the period of David and Solomon in the tenth century BCE, followed by E, which was often associated with the Northern Kingdom. D was connected to the reform of King Josiah in the late seventh century, and P was seen as deriving from the sixth century. Scholars now agree that the reasons usually given for assigning these dates are problematic, and a lively debate has developed concerning such fundamental issues as the relative order of these sources and the extent to which any of them are as early as previous scholars had suggested. The existence of E as a complete source has been questioned as well, especially since E first appears well after the beginning of the Torah and is very difficult to disentangle from J after the beginning of Exodus. Thus, many scholars now talk of JE together as an early narrative source, incorporating diverse traditions. Additionally, most scholars now do not see each source as representative of a single author writing at one particular time but recognize that each may reflect a long historical period within a single group or "school." Thus, it is best to speak of streams or strands of tradition and to contrast their basic underpinnings, rather than to speak of sources reflecting a single author, period, and locale. For example, despite the unraveling of a consensus on the exact date of the sources, it is still valid to contrast the Deuteronomic view of Israel's fundamental, intrinsic holiness—as seen, for example, in Deut 7.6, "For you are a people holy to the LORD your God"—with the Priestly view, articulated most clearly in the Holiness Collection (HC), which suggests that Israel must aspire to holiness—as in Lev 19.2, "You shall be holy."

COMPILATION AND REDACTION OF THE PENTATEUCH

It is unclear how these various sources and legal collections, which now comprise the Torah, came together to form a single book. Scholars posit an editor or series of editors or redactors, conveniently called R, who combined the various sources, perhaps in several stages, over a long time. Certainly not all ancient Israelite legal and narrative traditions were collected and redacted as part of the Torah. Much was certainly lost. Without access to this lost material, it is impossible to suggest in detail how and why the redactor(s), R, functioned in a particular way. It is sufficient to notice that in contrast to modern editing, which is fundamentally interested in articulating a single viewpoint, the redaction of the Torah, like the editing of other ancient works, was not interested in creating a purely consistent, singular perspective but incorporated a variety of voices and perspectives.

The ultimate result of this redaction, which most likely took place during the Babylonian exile (586–538 BCE) or soon thereafter in the early Persian period, was the creation of a very long book, narrating what must have been felt to be the formative period of Israel, from the period of the creation of the world through the death of Moses. Perhaps the events narrated in Gen 1–11 were included as a type of introduction to the choosing of Abraham, describing in detail the failures of humanity, as seen especially in the flood narrative (Gen 6–9) and the Tower of Babel episode (Gen 11.1–9), which necessitated the choosing of a particular nation by God.

No other work of comparable length or inclusiveness, both in terms of the time covered or the sources systematically incorporated, was produced in the ancient Near Eastern world. This extensive, inclusive nature of the Torah has created a fundamental and interesting problem with which all serious biblical interpreters have either consciously or subconsciously grappled: Do we concentrate on interpreting the individual sources, on hearing the voices of the component parts of the text before redaction took place? Or do we focus on the final product, an approach that has been called holistic reading? The annotations of the following books will highlight this issue, showing how meaning may be uncovered by looking both at the early building blocks of the text, and at the text in its final, redacted form.

GENESIS

Genesis, meaning "origin" (genealogical), covers the time from creation to the descent of Jacob and his sons into Egypt. The book is generally divided into a "primeval history" focusing on all of humanity (chs 1–11) and an "ancestral history" focusing on Abraham and his descendants (chs 12–50).

The primeval history has two major sections that parallel each other: (1) the creation of the cosmos and stories of the first humans (1.1–6.4); and (2) the flood and dispersal of post-flood humanity (6.5–11.9). It features universal traditions similar to myths in other cultures, particularly in the ancient Near East and Greece. For example, the Mesopotamian Atrahasis epic was written hundreds of years before chs 1–11, yet it parallels numerous particulars of the biblical narrative as it describes the creation of the world, a flood, and the vow of the gods (here plural) not to destroy life with a flood again.

The ancestral history picks up where the primeval history left off and tells the story of God's choice of Abraham and the transmission of the promise (12.1–3) down to the twelve sons of Jacob/Israel, the progenitors of the people of Israel. These stories are closest to oral folklore, so it is often difficult to find ancient textual parallels to chs 12–50. Nevertheless, recent scholarship has found similarities between Israelite tales about the matriarchs and patriarchs and modern legends told in oral cultures. For example, there are some striking parallels between the depiction of the clever deceptions of Jacob and others (e.g., 25.27–34; 27.1–45) and the celebration of wily "tricksters" in Native American and other traditions.

These different parts of Genesis are united by a set of "toledot" ("descendants") headings, each of which guides the reader in the major focus of the section that follows it (2.4; 5.1; 6.9; 10.1; 11.10; 11.27; 25.12; 25.19; 36.1,9; 37.2). They lead from a focus on the world at the outset to the final focus of the book on the twelve sons born to Jacob. In addition, other patterns also characterize these genealogically defined sections, such as the parallels between the pre-flood and flood/post-flood stories of chs 1–11 that were noted above. Using these kinds of guides, we can outline Genesis as follows. The narrative opens with the pre-flood primeval history, creation and its aftermath (including Adam and Eve, Cain and Abel, etc.): 2.4–6.8. It then moves to the flood and post-flood primeval history, the re-creation of the world and replay of destructive patterns from before the flood (Noah and his sons, Tower of Babel): 6.9–11.9. Then follows a genealogical bridge to the ancestral history: 11.10–26. The longest part of the narrative is the ancestral history, the giving of the promise to the sons of Jacob/Israel: 11.28–50.26. This is in three parts: First, the gift of the promise to Abraham and divine designation of Isaac (not Ishmael) as heir of the promise (11.28–25.11); second, the divergent destinies of the descendants of Ishmael (25.12–18) and Isaac (Esau and Jacob in 25.19–35.29); third, the divergent destinies of the descendants of Esau (36.1–43) and the sons of Jacob/Israel (Joseph and his brothers in 37.1–50.26).

Genesis has been a major focus of study for almost every approach in biblical scholarship. Two hundred and fifty years of historical-critical scholarship have established that Genesis was written over a long period of time, using oral and written traditions. In particular, most scholars now recognize that Genesis is a postexilic combination of two bodies of material: (1) a "Priestly" editorial layer or source (P) beginning with the seven-day creation account in 1.1–2.3, and (2) a "non-Priestly" source beginning with the garden of Eden story in 2.4–3.24. In addition to 1.1–2.3, the Priestly layer encompasses most of the genealogies in Genesis, the above discussed genealogical headings, a version of the flood narrative that culminated in the Noah covenant of 9.7–17, the covenant of circumcision with Abraham in 17.1–27, and related promise texts in 26.34–35; 27.46–28.9; 35.9–15; and 48.3–6. The non-Priestly layer encompasses almost everything else. In its present form the Priestly layer is integrally related to the non-Priestly material and forms an editorial framework for much of it. Scholars continue to debate, however, the exact relationship between the Priestly and non-Priestly material, and whether a large portion of the present Priestly layer in Genesis once may have been part of a Priestly source that originally stood separate from the non-Priestly material and had even been designed to replace it.

Ever since the work of Graf and Wellhausen in the late nineteenth century, most scholars have recognized that the earliest origins of Genesis probably are to be found in the non-Priestly material. Nevertheless, there is considerable debate about the history of the formation of that material. Over the last hundred years most scholars have maintained that the bulk of the non-Priestly material of Genesis was formed out of the combination of materials from two hypothesized Pentateuchal sources: a "Yahwistic" document (J) written in the South during the reign of David or Solomon and an "Elohistic" document (E) written one or two centuries later in the Northern kingdom of Israel. Recently, however, many would date crucial elements of the hypothesized "Yahwistic" document four hundred years later to the time of exile. Moreover, many specialists working with Genesis no longer think there was an "Elohistic" source. Rather than non-Priestly material being formed out of interwoven "Yahwistic" and "Elohistic" documents, some scholars think that the earliest written origins of the non-Priestly material are to be found in hypothesized preexilic independent documents focusing on different parts of the story: for instance, a separate, Atrahasis-like "primeval history" or separate Jacob and Joseph stories. Thus, the early history of the written formation of Genesis and other Pentateuchal books remains an unresolved problem in Pentateuchal research.

Recent years have seen a proliferation of other approaches to Genesis, particularly literary studies of Genesis in its present form and feminist rereadings of the plentiful narratives in Genesis featuring women. For example, some feminist scholars have questioned whether the garden of Eden story in 2.4–3.24 is as critical of women as it has often been seen to be. Others have highlighted the crucial role of the matriarchs as actors in the Genesis drama, especially as determiners of which son of a given patriarch will inherit the promise (e.g., Sarah and Rebekah) or as influencers of the levels of privilege among brothers (e.g., Rachel).

Because of the mythic and legendary character of much material in Genesis, it is less often used now than it once was as a reliable source of historical information. Yet, perhaps partly as a result of its long process of formation, the book of Genesis has proven its ability to speak to people of varying cultures and times. It is not just a story about things happening in a bygone age. It is a crystallization of Israel's most fervent beliefs and hopes as expressed in genealogy and vivid narrative.

1 In the beginning when God created[a]
the heavens and the earth, 2 the earth
was a formless void and darkness covered
the face of the deep, while a wind from
God[b] swept over the face of the waters.
3 Then God said, "Let there be light"; and
there was light. 4 And God saw that the
light was good; and God separated the light
from the darkness. 5 God called the light
Day, and the darkness he called Night. And
there was evening and there was morning,
the first day.
6 And God said, "Let there be a dome in
the midst of the waters, and let it separate
the waters from the waters." 7 So God
made the dome and separated the waters
that were under the dome from the waters
that were above the dome. And it was so.
8 God called the dome Sky. And there was
evening and there was morning, the second
day.
9 And God said, "Let the waters under
the sky be gathered together into one place,
and let the dry land appear." And it was so.
10 God called the dry land Earth, and the
waters that were gathered together he
called Seas. And God saw that it was good.
11 Then God said, "Let the earth put forth
vegetation: plants yielding seed, and fruit
trees of every kind on earth that bear fruit
with the seed in it." And it was so. 12 The
earth brought forth vegetation: plants
yielding seed of every kind, and trees of
every kind bearing fruit with the seed in it.
And God saw that it was good. 13 And there
was evening and there was morning, the
third day.
14 And God said, "Let there be lights in

a Or *when God began to create* or *In the beginning God created* *b* Or *while the spirit of God* or *while a mighty wind*

1.1–11.26: The primeval history. From creation to the birth of Abraham. This unit is composed of two principal layers, a Priestly source that also provides an editorial framework, and a non-Priestly narrative, identified by many scholars as belonging to J (the Yahwist).

1.1–2.3: Creation culminating in sabbath. This Priestly account of creation presents God as a divine ruler, creating the universe by decree in six days and resting on the seventh. **1.1:** Scholars differ on whether this verse is to be translated as an independent sentence summarizing what follows (e.g., "In the beginning God created") or as a temporal phrase describing what things were like when God started (e.g., "When God began to create . . . the earth was a formless void"; cf. 2.4–6). In either case, the text does not describe creation out of nothing (contrast 2 Macc 7.28). Instead, the story emphasizes how God creates order from a watery chaos. **2:** As elsewhere in the Bible, *the deep* (Heb "tehom") has no definite article ("the") attached to it in the Heb. Some see "tehom" here to be related to the Babylonian goddess Tiamat, a divinity representing oceanic chaos, whom the head god, Marduk, defeated in *Enuma Elish,* a major Babylonian creation story. Christian interpreters have tended to see the "Spirit" of the Trinity later in this verse. *Wind* fits the ancient context better (see 8.1). **3:** The first of eight acts of creation through decree. Like a divine king God pronounces his will and it is accomplished. **4–5:** These verses introduce two other themes crucial to this account: the goodness of creation and the idea that creation is accomplished through God's separating, ordering, and naming elements of the universe. The seven-day scheme of 1.1–2.3 requires the creation of light, day, and night at the outset. Since in some traditions the Jewish day began with sundown, the order is *evening* and *morning.* **6–8:** The *dome/Sky* made on the second day separates an upper ocean (Ps 148.4; see Gen 7.11) from a lower one. This creates a space in which subsequent creation can take place. **9–13:** Two creative acts: creation of dry land and command of that land to bring forth vegetation. *Earth* is a feminine noun in Heb. The text thus echoes other ancient mythologies and the life cycle in having a feminine earth bring forth the first life in the universe (cf. Job 1.21). God is only involved indirectly here, commanding the earth to *put forth.* **14–19:** There is a correspondence between days one to three and days four to six (1 ‖ 4, 2 ‖ 5, 3 ‖ 6), which heightens the symmetry and order of God's creation. Here, God's creation of heavenly *lights* on the fourth day corresponds to creation of light, day, and night on the first. In a critical response to non-Israelite cultures who worshiped these heavenly bodies, the bodies are not named and are identified as mere timekeepers. **20–23:** See vv. 14–19n.

the dome of the sky to separate the day
from the night; and let them be for signs
and for seasons and for days and years,
15 and let them be lights in the dome of the
sky to give light upon the earth." And it
was so. 16 God made the two great lights—
the greater light to rule the day and the
lesser light to rule the night—and the stars.
17 God set them in the dome of the sky to
give light upon the earth, 18 to rule over the
day and over the night, and to separate the
light from the darkness. And God saw that
it was good. 19 And there was evening and
there was morning, the fourth day.
20 And God said, "Let the waters bring
forth swarms of living creatures, and let
birds fly above the earth across the dome of
the sky." 21 So God created the great sea
monsters and every living creature that
moves, of every kind, with which the wa-
ters swarm, and every winged bird of every
kind. And God saw that it was good.
22 God blessed them, saying, "Be fruitful
and multiply and fill the waters in the seas,
and let birds multiply on the earth." 23 And
there was evening and there was morning,
the fifth day.
24 And God said, "Let the earth bring
forth living creatures of every kind: cattle
and creeping things and wild animals of the
earth of every kind." And it was so. 25 God
made the wild animals of the earth of every
kind, and the cattle of every kind, and ev-
erything that creeps upon the ground of ev-
ery kind. And God saw that it was good.
26 Then God said, "Let us make hu-
mankind[a] in our image, according to our
likeness; and let them have dominion over
the fish of the sea, and over the birds of the
air, and over the cattle,[b] and over all the
wild animals of the earth,[b] and over every
creeping thing that creeps upon the earth."
27 So God created humankind[a] in his
image,
in the image of God he created
them;[c]
male and female he created them.
28 God blessed them, and God said to them,
"Be fruitful and multiply, and fill the earth
and subdue it; and have dominion over the
fish of the sea and over the birds of the
air and over every living thing that moves
upon the earth." 29 God said, "See, I have
given you every plant yielding seed that is
upon the face of all the earth, and every tree
with seed in its fruit; you shall have them
for food. 30 And to every beast of the earth,
and to every bird of the air, and to every-
thing that creeps on the earth, everything
that has the breath of life, I have given ev-
ery green plant for food." And it was so.
31 God saw everything that he had made,
and indeed, it was very good. And there

a Heb *adam* b Syr: Heb *and over all the earth*
c Heb *him*

Where the second day featured the dome separating upper and lower oceans, the fifth day features the creation of birds to fly *across the dome* and ocean creatures, including sea monsters (Ps 104.25–26). God's blessing of the swarming creatures (1.22) anticipates a similar blessing that God will give humanity (1.28). **24–30:** See vv. 14–19n. Where the third day involved creation of land and plants in turn, this sixth day involves the creation of two types of plant-eating land-dwellers: animals and then humans. **24–25:** Again, earth is involved in bringing forth life (see 1.9–13n.). **26:** The plural *us, our* (3.22; 11.7) probably refers to the divine beings who compose God's heavenly court (1 Kings 22.19; Job 1.6). *Image, likeness* is often interpreted to be a spiritual likeness between God and humanity. Another view is that this text builds on ancient concepts of the king physically resembling the god and thus bearing a bodily stamp of his authority to rule. Here this idea is democratized, as all of humanity appears godlike. This appearance equips humans for godlike rule over the fish, birds, and animals. **27–28:** The text stresses the creation of humanity as simultaneously male and female. This leads to the emphasis in the blessing of v. 28 and the book of Genesis as a whole on the multiplication of humanity in general (6.1; 9.1–7) and Israel in particular (17.2–6; 47.27). **29–30:** The text envisions an ancient mythological time before violence disturbs God's perfect order (cf. 6.11). **31:** Where individual elements of creation were "good" (vv. 4,10, etc.), the whole is *very good,* perfectly corresponding to God's intention. **2.1–3:** This day is the point to which the whole

was evening and there was morning, the
sixth day.

2 Thus the heavens and the earth were
finished, and all their multitude. 2 And
on the seventh day God finished the work
that he had done, and he rested on the sev-
enth day from all the work that he had
done. 3 So God blessed the seventh day and
hallowed it, because on it God rested from
all the work that he had done in creation.

4 These are the generations of the heav-
ens and the earth when they were created.

In the day that the LORD[a] God made the
earth and the heavens, 5 when no plant of
the field was yet in the earth and no herb of
the field had yet sprung up—for the LORD
God had not caused it to rain upon the
earth, and there was no one to till the
ground; 6 but a stream would rise from the
earth, and water the whole face of
the ground— 7 then the LORD God formed
man from the dust of the ground,[b] and
breathed into his nostrils the breath of life;
and the man became a living being. 8 And
the LORD God planted a garden in Eden, in
the east; and there he put the man whom he
had formed. 9 Out of the ground the LORD
God made to grow every tree that is pleas-
ant to the sight and good for food, the tree
of life also in the midst of the garden, and
the tree of the knowledge of good and evil.

10 A river flows out of Eden to water
the garden, and from there it divides and
becomes four branches. 11 The name of the
first is Pishon; it is the one that flows
around the whole land of Havilah, where
there is gold; 12 and the gold of that land is
good; bdellium and onyx stone are there.
13 The name of the second river is Gihon; it
is the one that flows around the whole land
of Cush. 14 The name of the third river is
Tigris, which flows east of Assyria. And the
fourth river is the Euphrates.

15 The LORD God took the man and put
him in the garden of Eden to till it and keep
it. 16 And the LORD God commanded the
man, "You may freely eat of every tree of

a Heb YHWH, as in other places where "LORD" is spelled with capital letters (see also Exod 3.14-15 with notes). *b* Or *formed a man* (Heb *adam*) *of dust from the ground* (Heb *adamah*)

seven-day scheme has led. God does not command the sabbath, but does rest (Heb "shabat") on the seventh day and bless it, weaving the seven-day rhythm into creation. The "creation" of institutions is found in other ancient creation stories as well.

2.4a: Probably not the conclusion of the Priestly creation story, but a separate superscription introducing the following material, as elsewhere in Genesis (e.g., 5.1; 6.9; 10.1).

2.4b–25: Creation in a garden. This tradition, often identified as J, is different from 1.1–2.3, as evidenced by the different style and order of events. Though distinct from the Priestly account of 1.1–2.3, it nevertheless reflects ancient temple imagery. **4b–6:** A description of how things were prior to creation (cf. 1.1–2) is common in ancient Near Eastern creation stories. **7:** The word play on Heb "'adam" (human being; here translated "man" [cf. 1.26]) and "'adamah" (arable land; here *ground*) introduces a motif characteristic of this tradition: the relation of humankind to the soil from which it was *formed*. Human nature is not a duality of body and soul; rather God's *breath* animates the *dust* and it becomes a single *living being* (Ps 104.29; Job 34.14–15). **8–9:** *Eden* means "delight." This divine garden recalls the "garden of God/the LORD" mentioned elsewhere in the Hebrew Bible (13.10; Ezek 28.13–16; 31.8–9; Isa 51.3; Joel 2.3), and such sacred gardens are known in other ancient Near Eastern temple traditions. In addition, ancient Near Eastern art and texts feature a prominent focus on trees, often associated with feminine powers of fertility. Usually such trees symbolize life, as in the *tree of life* here (3.22; see Prov 3.18; Rev 22.2,14,19). But this story focuses more on the *tree of the knowledge of good and evil*, symbolizing wisdom (2 Sam 14.17; 1 Kings 3.9). See 12.6–8n. **10–14:** This section, along with the preceding one describing the "stream" rising up to water the ground (2.6), may draw on the ancient tradition that a temple is built on a primal mountain of creation from which the waters of the earth flow. The rivers mentioned here combine world rivers like the *Tigris* and *Euphrates* (both in Mesopotamia) with the local *Gihon* that flowed from Mount Zion in Jerusalem (Ps 46.4; Isa 7.6; Zech 14.8), although *Cush* is generally either Ethiopia or in Arabia. *Pishon* is unknown; *Havilah* is probably in Arabia. **16–17:** The speech

the garden; 17 but of the tree of the knowl-
edge of good and evil you shall not eat,
for in the day that you eat of it you shall
die."
18 Then the LORD God said, "It is not
good that the man should be alone; I will
make him a helper as his partner." 19 So out
of the ground the LORD God formed every
animal of the field and every bird of the air,
and brought them to the man to see what
he would call them; and whatever the man
called every living creature, that was its
name. 20 The man gave names to all cattle,
and to the birds of the air, and to every
animal of the field; but for the man[a] there
was not found a helper as his partner. 21 So
the LORD God caused a deep sleep to fall
upon the man, and he slept; then he took
one of his ribs and closed up its place with
flesh. 22 And the rib that the LORD God had
taken from the man he made into a woman
and brought her to the man. 23 Then the
man said,

"This at last is bone of my bones
and flesh of my flesh;
this one shall be called Woman,[b]
for out of Man[c] this one was
taken."

24 Therefore a man leaves his father and his
mother and clings to his wife, and they be-
come one flesh. 25 And the man and his wife
were both naked, and were not ashamed.

3 Now the serpent was more crafty than
any other wild animal that the LORD
God had made. He said to the woman,
"Did God say, 'You shall not eat from any
tree in the garden'?" 2 The woman said to
the serpent, "We may eat of the fruit of the
trees in the garden; 3 but God said, 'You
shall not eat of the fruit of the tree that is in
the middle of the garden, nor shall you
touch it, or you shall die.'" 4 But the ser-
pent said to the woman, "You will not die;
5 for God knows that when you eat of it
your eyes will be opened, and you will be
like God,[d] knowing good and evil." 6 So
when the woman saw that the tree was

a Or *for Adam* *b* Heb *ishshah* *c* Heb *ish*
d Or *gods*

concludes with a legal prohibition using technical death-penalty language (see Lev 20.9,11,12, etc.). **18–20:** Animals are created after the first human rather than before (cf. 1.24–25). The human's naming of the animals implies a dominion over them analogous to that seen in 1.26–28. Yet the LORD God here contrasts with the all-powerful deity depicted in ch 1. The LORD God creates the animals in a comical, failed attempt to make a *helper* for the human that "corresponds to him" (compare *as his partner* in the NRSV of vv. 18,20). **21–23:** Just as the connection of humanity to the ground is affirmed in the making of the first human ("'adam") from earthy "humus" ("'adamah") (2.7), so also the connection of men and women is affirmed here through the crowning event of creation: the making of the woman from a part of the man (2.21–22). The man affirms this connection in a jubilant poem (2.23) featuring a word play on "man" ("'ish") and "woman" ("'ishah"). This concluding song of praise of the woman corresponds to God's concluding affirmation of all of creation as "very good" in 1.31. **24–25:** Sex between a *man* and *his wife* is regarded here as reflecting the essence of the connection God created between men and women. The unashamed nakedness of the man and woman indicates their still uncivilized status.

3.1–24: Garden disobedience and punishment. Though this story is often taken by Christians as an account of "original sin," the word "sin" never occurs in it. Instead, it describes how the maturing of humans into civilized life involved damage of connections established in 2.4–25 between the LORD God, man, woman, and earth. **1:** This characterization of the snake emphasizes his wise craftiness (Heb "'arum"), a characteristic that contrasts with the innocent nakedness ("'arum") of the man and woman. Snakes were a symbol in the ancient world of wisdom, fertility, and immortality. Only later was the snake in this story seen by interpreters as the devil. **4–5:** The snake introduces doubt through rightly predicting the consequences of eating the fruit—the humans will not be put to death as implied in the language of 2.17 and their eyes will be *opened* (see v. 7) so they gain wisdom, *knowing good and evil.* **6–7:** The woman sees that the pleasant fruit of the tree is desirable *to make one wise;* she eats it and shares it with her husband. The result is enlightenment, *the eyes of both were opened.* Such wisdom takes them from

good for food, and that it was a delight to
the eyes, and that the tree was to be desired
to make one wise, she took of its fruit and
ate; and she also gave some to her husband,
who was with her, and he ate. 7 Then the
eyes of both were opened, and they knew
that they were naked; and they sewed fig
leaves together and made loincloths for
themselves.

8 They heard the sound of the LORD
God walking in the garden at the time of
the evening breeze, and the man and his
wife hid themselves from the presence of
the LORD God among the trees of the gar-
den. 9 But the LORD God called to the man,
and said to him, "Where are you?" 10 He
said, "I heard the sound of you in the gar-
den, and I was afraid, because I was naked;
and I hid myself." 11 He said, "Who told
you that you were naked? Have you eaten
from the tree of which I commanded you
not to eat?" 12 The man said, "The woman
whom you gave to be with me, she gave me
fruit from the tree, and I ate." 13 Then the
LORD God said to the woman, "What is
this that you have done?" The woman said,
"The serpent tricked me, and I ate." 14 The
LORD God said to the serpent,

"Because you have done this,
cursed are you among all animals
and among all wild creatures;
upon your belly you shall go,
and dust you shall eat
all the days of your life.
15 I will put enmity between you and the
woman,
and between your offspring and
hers;
he will strike your head,
and you will strike his heel."

16 To the woman he said,
"I will greatly increase your pangs in
childbearing;
in pain you shall bring forth
children,
yet your desire shall be for your
husband,
and he shall rule over you."

17 And to the man[a] he said,
"Because you have listened to the
voice of your wife,
and have eaten of the tree
about which I commanded you,
'You shall not eat of it,'
cursed is the ground because of you;
in toil you shall eat of it all the
days of your life;
18 thorns and thistles it shall bring forth
for you;
and you shall eat the plants of the
field.
19 By the sweat of your face
you shall eat bread
until you return to the ground,
for out of it you were taken;
you are dust,
and to dust you shall return."

20 The man named his wife Eve,[b] be-
cause she was the mother of all living.

a Or *to Adam*   b In Heb *Eve* resembles the word for *living*

the unashamed nakedness of before (2.25) to clothing, a mark of civilization in nonbiblical primeval narratives. **8–13:** Legal forms again predominate as the LORD God interrogates first the man and then the woman (see 2.16–17n.). The disintegration of earlier connectedness is shown by the hiding of the humans from the LORD God and the tendency of the man to blame the woman (and implicitly the LORD God) for his action. Later interpreters of the story have shown a similar tendency to blame the woman. **14–19:** A proclamation of sentence follows the interrogation, starting with the snake and concluding with the man. **14–15:** Here the crawl of the snake is linked to the LORD God's punishing curse. As a result, later audiences can look to the crawling snake as a reminder of the story and testimony to its truth. **16–19:** Though this is often understood as a "curse" of the woman to pain in childbirth, the word "curse" is not used in these verses. Others have suggested that this text sentences the woman to endless "toil" (not *pain*) of reproduction, much as the man is condemned in vv. 17–19 to endless toil in food production. The man's *rule* over the woman here is a tragic reflection of the disintegration of original connectedness between them. **21:** The LORD God's clothing of the

21 And the LORD God made garments of
skins for the man[a] and for his wife, and
clothed them.
22 Then the LORD God said, "See, the
man has become like one of us, knowing
good and evil; and now, he might reach out
his hand and take also from the tree of life,
and eat, and live forever"— 23 therefore the
LORD God sent him forth from the garden
of Eden, to till the ground from which he
was taken. 24 He drove out the man; and at
the east of the garden of Eden he placed the
cherubim, and a sword flaming and turning
to guard the way to the tree of life.

4 Now the man knew his wife Eve, and
she conceived and bore Cain, saying, "I
have produced[b] a man with the help of the
LORD." 2 Next she bore his brother Abel.
Now Abel was a keeper of sheep, and Cain
a tiller of the ground. 3 In the course of time
Cain brought to the LORD an offering of
the fruit of the ground, 4 and Abel for his
part brought of the firstlings of his flock,
their fat portions. And the LORD had re-
gard for Abel and his offering, 5 but for
Cain and his offering he had no regard. So
Cain was very angry, and his countenance
fell. 6 The LORD said to Cain, "Why are you
angry, and why has your countenance fall-
en? 7 If you do well, will you not be accept-
ed? And if you do not do well, sin is lurking
at the door; its desire is for you, but you
must master it."
8 Cain said to his brother Abel, "Let us
go out to the field."[c] And when they were
in the field, Cain rose up against his brother
Abel, and killed him. 9 Then the LORD said
to Cain, "Where is your brother Abel?" He
said, "I do not know; am I my brother's
keeper?" 10 And the LORD said, "What
have you done? Listen; your brother's
blood is crying out to me from the ground!
11 And now you are cursed from the
ground, which has opened its mouth to re-
ceive your brother's blood from your hand.
12 When you till the ground, it will no lon-
ger yield to you its strength; you will be a
fugitive and a wanderer on the earth."
13 Cain said to the LORD, "My punishment
is greater than I can bear! 14 Today you
have driven me away from the soil, and I
shall be hidden from your face; I shall be a
fugitive and a wanderer on the earth, and

a Or *for Adam* *b* The verb in Heb resembles the word for *Cain* *c* Sam Gk Syr Compare Vg: MT lacks *Let us go out to the field*

humans here reflects care for them in the process of becoming civilized, even though that process involved disobedience. **22:** As elsewhere in the ancient Near East, humans here are depicted as having a brief opportunity for immortality. The LORD God's fear of humans becoming godlike (cf. 1.26–27) recalls the serpent's assertions in 3.4–5. The term "us" probably refers to the heavenly court (see 1.26n.). **24:** Cf. Ezek 28.13–16. The last echoes of temple imagery occur here. *The cherubim* are winged creatures like the Sphinx of Egypt, half human and half lion. Statues of them guarded sanctuaries like the one in Jerusalem (1 Kings 6.23–28,32,35). The gate to the garden of Eden is in the east, like the processional gate to the Temple (Ezek 10.19).

4.1–16: Cain and Abel. While 2.4–3.24 featured relations between men and women, 4.1–16 turns to relations between brothers, paralleling 3.1–24 in many respects. **1:** This first verse emphasizes the wonder of creative power in the first birth of a child. The child's name, "Cain," resembles a Hebrew word for create, "qanah." Ancient Israelites may have associated this Cain with the Kenite tribe (Num 24.21–22). **2:** The name "Abel" is the same word translated as "vanity" (or "emptiness") in Ecclesiastes. His name anticipates his destiny. The distinction between Cain and Abel's occupations implies a further step toward culture. **3–5:** The story pointedly does not explain why the LORD *had regard for Abel and his offering,* but did not have regard *for Cain and his offering.* Instead, it focuses on Cain's reaction to this unexplained divine preference for the sacrifice of his brother. **6–7:** This is the first mention of "sin" in the Bible. It is depicted as a predatory animal, *lurking at the door.* **10–11:** Blood is sacred, for it is the seat of life (9.4; Deut 12.23), and blood of unpunished murders pollutes the ground (Num 35.30–34). **13–14:** The importance of arable ground in these chapters can be seen in Cain's conclusion that expulsion from the *soil* means being *hidden* from the LORD's *face.* **16:** See 11.1–9n.

anyone who meets me may kill me."
15 Then the LORD said to him, "Not so![a]
Whoever kills Cain will suffer a sevenfold
vengeance." And the LORD put a mark on
Cain, so that no one who came upon him
would kill him. 16 Then Cain went away
from the presence of the LORD, and settled
in the land of Nod,[b] east of Eden.
17 Cain knew his wife, and she con-
ceived and bore Enoch; and he built a city,
and named it Enoch after his son Enoch.
18 To Enoch was born Irad; and Irad was
the father of Mehujael, and Mehujael the
father of Methushael, and Methushael the
father of Lamech. 19 Lamech took two
wives; the name of the one was Adah, and
the name of the other Zillah. 20 Adah bore
Jabal; he was the ancestor of those who live
in tents and have livestock. 21 His brother's
name was Jubal; he was the ancestor of all
those who play the lyre and pipe. 22 Zillah
bore Tubal-cain, who made all kinds of
bronze and iron tools. The sister of Tubal-
cain was Naamah.
23 Lamech said to his wives:
"Adah and Zillah, hear my voice;
you wives of Lamech, listen to
what I say:
I have killed a man for wounding me,
a young man for striking me.
24 If Cain is avenged sevenfold,
truly Lamech seventy-sevenfold."
25 Adam knew his wife again, and she
bore a son and named him Seth, for she
said, "God has appointed[c] for me another
child instead of Abel, because Cain killed
him." 26 To Seth also a son was born, and
he named him Enosh. At that time people
began to invoke the name of the LORD.

5 This is the list of the descendants of
Adam. When God created human-
kind,[d] he made them[e] in the likeness of
God. 2 Male and female he created them,
and he blessed them and named them "Hu-
mankind"[d] when they were created.
3 When Adam had lived one hundred
thirty years, he became the father of a son
in his likeness, according to his image, and
named him Seth. 4 The days of Adam after
he became the father of Seth were eight
hundred years; and he had other sons and
daughters. 5 Thus all the days that Adam

a Gk Syr Vg: Heb *Therefore* *b* That is *Wandering*
c The verb in Heb resembles the word for *Seth*
d Heb *adam* *e* Heb *him*

4.17–26: First overview of generations from creation to flood. Though the order is different, the names here are variants of those in 5.1–32. **17:** Cain's marriage, along with his fear of others (4.14) presume the presence of a broader population, indicating that the stories about him were once not connected with creation. **19–22:** The emphasis on civilization seen in 3.1–24 emerges again here in the depiction of the occupations of Lamech's sons. This tradition does not anticipate a flood narrative. **23–24:** The first half of this song may once have been used to brag about the ability of Lamech and his family to avenge their honor. Placed where it is and including v. 24, it now functions to demonstrate a major consequence of the expansion of civilization: a corresponding expansion of the violence with which the family tree began (see 4.1–16). **25:** A parallel to 4.1, introducing a new line of Seth. **26:** This tradition locates the beginning of use of the divine name "Yahweh" (*LORD*) in the primeval period, in contrast to the Priestly tradition, which does not see the divine name as used until the time of Moses (Ex 6.2–6).

5.1–32: Second overview of generations from creation to flood. This Priestly genealogy parallels 4.1–26, building from the P creation story (1.1–2.3) to the Priestly strand of the flood narrative. **1a:** *The list of descendants of Adam* (lit. "the scroll of descendants") was evidently a separate source which the Priestly writer drew upon for this chapter and used as a model for later notices (6.9; 10.1; etc.). **1b–2:** The Priestly writer uses this reprise of 1.26–28 to bind his genealogical source (where "'adam" designates a particular person) to 1.1–2.3 (where "'adam" designates humanity as a whole). **3:** The divine *likeness* (v. 1; see 1.26n.) was continued in Adam's son Seth and thus transmitted to succeeding generations (9.6). **4–32:** Ancient Babylonian lists similarly survey a series of heroes before the flood, each of which lived fantastically long times. Like those lists, the list in 5.4–32 postulates extraordinary ages to pre-flood figures, with ages declining over time to the 100–200 years of Israel's ancestors. The names of the figures in this list resemble those of 4.17–26 (see 4.17–26n.). **24:** Babylonian traditions also report that certain

lived were nine hundred thirty years; and
he died.
6 When Seth had lived one hundred five
years, he became the father of Enosh. 7 Seth
lived after the birth of Enosh eight hundred
seven years, and had other sons and daugh-
ters. 8 Thus all the days of Seth were nine
hundred twelve years; and he died.
9 When Enosh had lived ninety years, he
became the father of Kenan. 10 Enosh lived
after the birth of Kenan eight hundred fif-
teen years, and had other sons and daugh-
ters. 11 Thus all the days of Enosh were nine
hundred five years; and he died.
12 When Kenan had lived seventy years,
he became the father of Mahalalel. 13 Ke-
nan lived after the birth of Mahalalel eight
hundred and forty years, and had other
sons and daughters. 14 Thus all the days of
Kenan were nine hundred and ten years;
and he died.
15 When Mahalalel had lived sixty-five
years, he became the father of Jared. 16 Ma-
halalel lived after the birth of Jared eight
hundred thirty years, and had other sons
and daughters. 17 Thus all the days of Ma-
halalel were eight hundred ninety-five
years; and he died.
18 When Jared had lived one hundred
sixty-two years he became the father of
Enoch. 19 Jared lived after the birth of
Enoch eight hundred years, and had other
sons and daughters. 20 Thus all the days of
Jared were nine hundred sixty-two years;
and he died.
21 When Enoch had lived sixty-five
years, he became the father of Methuselah.
22 Enoch walked with God after the birth of
Methuselah three hundred years, and had
other sons and daughters. 23 Thus all the
days of Enoch were three hundred sixty-
five years. 24 Enoch walked with God; then
he was no more, because God took him.
25 When Methuselah had lived one hun-
dred eighty-seven years, he became the fa-
ther of Lamech. 26 Methuselah lived after
the birth of Lamech seven hundred eighty-
two years, and had other sons and daugh-
ters. 27 Thus all the days of Methuselah
were nine hundred sixty-nine years; and he
died.
28 When Lamech had lived one hundred
eighty-two years, he became the father of a
son; 29 he named him Noah, saying, "Out
of the ground that the LORD has cursed this
one shall bring us relief from our work and
from the toil of our hands." 30 Lamech lived
after the birth of Noah five hundred ninety-
five years, and had other sons and daugh-
ters. 31 Thus all the days of Lamech were
seven hundred seventy-seven years; and he
died.
32 After Noah was five hundred years
old, Noah became the father of Shem,
Ham, and Japheth.

6 When people began to multiply on the
face of the ground, and daughters were
born to them, 2 the sons of God saw that
they were fair; and they took wives for
themselves of all that they chose. 3 Then the
LORD said, "My spirit shall not abide[a] in
mortals forever, for they are flesh; their
days shall be one hundred twenty years."
4 The Nephilim were on the earth in those
days—and also afterward—when the sons
of God went in to the daughters of humans,

a Meaning of Heb uncertain

figures—e.g., Emmeduranki (a pre-flood figure), Etana, and Adapa—were taken up into heaven by God. Later Jewish tradition speculated at length on Enoch's travels. **29:** This (non-Priestly) verse links the curse of the ground in 3.17–19 and viniculture, which was inaugurated by Noah (9.20).

6.1–4: Divine-human reproduction illustrates the kind of breaching of the divine-human boundary which the LORD God feared in 3.22. There the LORD God drove humans away from the tree of life. Here, in an abbreviated narrative often attributed to J, the LORD God limits their life-span to *one hundred twenty* years; others suggest that the *one hundred twenty* years refer to a reprieve from punishment for several generations. Nothing appears to happen to the *sons of God* (see the "heavenly court" in 1.26n.) who started it all. **4:** The products of divine-human intercourse are legendary *warriors of renown.* They are distinguished here from the *Nephilim,* a race of giants said to exist both prior to and after those times (cf. Num 13.33; Deut 2.10–11).

who bore children to them. These were the
heroes that were of old, warriors of re-
nown.
5 The LORD saw that the wickedness of
humankind was great in the earth, and that
every inclination of the thoughts of their
hearts was only evil continually. 6 And the
LORD was sorry that he had made human-
kind on the earth, and it grieved him to his
heart. 7 So the LORD said, "I will blot out
from the earth the human beings I have cre-
ated—people together with animals and
creeping things and birds of the air, for I
am sorry that I have made them." 8 But
Noah found favor in the sight of the LORD.
9 These are the descendants of Noah.
Noah was a righteous man, blameless in his
generation; Noah walked with God. 10 And
Noah had three sons, Shem, Ham, and Ja-
pheth.
11 Now the earth was corrupt in God's
sight, and the earth was filled with vio-
lence. 12 And God saw that the earth was
corrupt; for all flesh had corrupted its ways
upon the earth. 13 And God said to Noah,
"I have determined to make an end of all
flesh, for the earth is filled with violence
because of them; now I am going to destroy
them along with the earth. 14 Make yourself
an ark of cypress[a] wood; make rooms in
the ark, and cover it inside and out with
pitch. 15 This is how you are to make it: the
length of the ark three hundred cubits, its
width fifty cubits, and its height thirty cu-
bits. 16 Make a roof[b] for the ark, and finish
it to a cubit above; and put the door of the
ark in its side; make it with lower, second,
and third decks. 17 For my part, I am going
to bring a flood of waters on the earth,
to destroy from under heaven all flesh in
which is the breath of life; everything that is
on the earth shall die. 18 But I will establish
my covenant with you; and you shall come
into the ark, you, your sons, your wife, and
your sons' wives with you. 19 And of every
living thing, of all flesh, you shall bring two
of every kind into the ark, to keep them
alive with you; they shall be male and fe-
male. 20 Of the birds according to their
kinds, and of the animals according to their
kinds, of every creeping thing of the ground
according to its kind, two of every kind
shall come in to you, to keep them alive.
21 Also take with you every kind of food
that is eaten, and store it up; and it shall
serve as food for you and for them."
22 Noah did this; he did all that God com-
manded him.
7 Then the LORD said to Noah, "Go into
the ark, you and all your household, for
I have seen that you alone are righteous
before me in this generation. 2 Take with

a Meaning of Heb uncertain *b* Or *window*

6.5–8.19: The great flood. This story describes God's un-creation and re-creation of the world. The version preserved here is an interweaving of parallel accounts, one of which links with the Priestly traditions of 1.1–2.3; 5.1–32 and the other of which links with the non-Priestly traditions, often identified as J, of 2.4b–4.26. This type of intertwining of traditions is less usual, but is necessary here, to avoid describing two consecutive floods. **6.5–8:** This introduction links with the non-Priestly material, particularly 2.7 (compare 6.7). **5:** Though the biblical account is quite close in many respects to Mesopotamian flood stories, one significant difference is that this text attributes the flood to God's judgment on *the wickedness of humankind* rather than divine frustration with human overpopulation and noise. **9–22:** This section begins the Priestly account of the flood. **11–13:** Here the Priestly writers attribute the flood to corruption of the earth and *violence* filling it (see 4.8,10,23–24). **14–16:** In the Babylonian epic of Gilgamesh, the hero is told to build a similar houseboat, sealing it with pitch. The description of a three-leveled ark may be based on an ancient idea that the ark reflects the three-part structure of both universe and temple. It is about 133 x 22 x 13 m (437 x 73 x 44 ft). **19–20:** See 7.2–3n. **7.1–5:** This non-Priestly text parallels P in 6.11–22 and continues the tradition seen in 6.5–8. **2–3:** The provision of extra *clean* animals allows for the sacrifice that will occur in 8.20. If only one pair of each animal were taken, every sacrifice would eliminate a species. In contrast, the Priestly tradition presumes that sacrifice and the distinction between clean and unclean animals (see Lev 11) was not introduced until Sinai. Therefore only one pair of each species is taken in that tradition (6.19–20; 7.14–15; cf. 7.9), and

you seven pairs of all clean animals, the
male and its mate; and a pair of the animals
that are not clean, the male and its mate;
3 and seven pairs of the birds of the air also,
male and female, to keep their kind alive on
the face of all the earth. 4 For in seven days
I will send rain on the earth for forty days
and forty nights; and every living thing that
I have made I will blot out from the face of
the ground." 5 And Noah did all that the
LORD had commanded him.

6 Noah was six hundred years old when
the flood of waters came on the earth.
7 And Noah with his sons and his wife and
his sons' wives went into the ark to escape
the waters of the flood. 8 Of clean animals,
and of animals that are not clean, and of
birds, and of everything that creeps on the
ground, 9 two and two, male and female,
went into the ark with Noah, as God
had commanded Noah. 10 And after seven
days the waters of the flood came on the
earth.

11 In the six hundredth year of Noah's
life, in the second month, on the seven-
teenth day of the month, on that day all the
fountains of the great deep burst forth, and
the windows of the heavens were opened.
12 The rain fell on the earth forty days and
forty nights. 13 On the very same day Noah
with his sons, Shem and Ham and Japheth,
and Noah's wife and the three wives of his
sons entered the ark, 14 they and every wild
animal of every kind, and all domestic ani-
mals of every kind, and every creeping
thing that creeps on the earth, and every
bird of every kind—every bird, every
winged creature. 15 They went into the ark
with Noah, two and two of all flesh in
which there was the breath of life. 16 And
those that entered, male and female of all
flesh, went in as God had commanded him;
and the LORD shut him in.

17 The flood continued forty days on
the earth; and the waters increased, and
bore up the ark, and it rose high above the
earth. 18 The waters swelled and increased
greatly on the earth; and the ark floated on
the face of the waters. 19 The waters swelled
so mightily on the earth that all the high
mountains under the whole heaven were
covered; 20 the waters swelled above the
mountains, covering them fifteen cubits
deep. 21 And all flesh died that moved on
the earth, birds, domestic animals, wild an-
imals, all swarming creatures that swarm
on the earth, and all human beings; 22 ev-
erything on dry land in whose nostrils was
the breath of life died. 23 He blotted out
every living thing that was on the face of
the ground, human beings and animals and
creeping things and birds of the air; they
were blotted out from the earth. Only
Noah was left, and those that were with
him in the ark. 24 And the waters swelled on
the earth for one hundred fifty days.

8 But God remembered Noah and all the
wild animals and all the domestic ani-
mals that were with him in the ark. And
God made a wind blow over the earth, and
the waters subsided; 2 the fountains of the
deep and the windows of the heavens were
closed, the rain from the heavens was re-
strained, 3 and the waters gradually receded

there is no concluding sacrifice (9.1–17). **6–16:** Noah, his family, and the animals enter the ark twice (7.7–9 || 7.13–16), reflecting the interweaving of the two flood accounts discussed above. Whereas the non-Priestly account has the flood caused by forty days of rain (7.12; 7.4), the Priestly account attributes the flood to God's opening of the protective dome created on the second day (1.6–8), thus allowing the upper and lower oceans to meet (7.11). **17–24:** The P and non-P strands are thoroughly interwoven in this description of the flood itself, including multiple descriptions of the extinction of life outside the ark (7.21–23). Such flood imagery seems to have been a powerful image of chaos worldwide. Though many world traditions speak of floods, there is no geological evidence of a global flood of the sort described here. **8.1–5:** With the exception of 8.2b–3a, this unit comes from the Priestly writer. **1–2a:** God's wind echoes the first creation (1.2) in the process of starting the re-creation process. The closing of the *fountains of the deep and the windows of the heavens* reestablishes the space for life that was first created on the second day (1.6–8). **4:** In the Mesopotamian Gilgamesh epic the boat also rested on a mountain.

from the earth. At the end of one hundred
fifty days the waters had abated; [4]and in
the seventh month, on the seventeenth day
of the month, the ark came to rest on the
mountains of Ararat. [5]The waters contin-
ued to abate until the tenth month; in the
tenth month, on the first day of the month,
the tops of the mountains appeared.
6 At the end of forty days Noah opened
the window of the ark that he had made
[7]and sent out the raven; and it went to and
fro until the waters were dried up from the
earth. [8]Then he sent out the dove from
him, to see if the waters had subsided from
the face of the ground; [9]but the dove found
no place to set its foot, and it returned to
him to the ark, for the waters were still on
the face of the whole earth. So he put out
his hand and took it and brought it into the
ark with him. [10]He waited another seven
days, and again he sent out the dove from
the ark; [11]and the dove came back to him
in the evening, and there in its beak was a
freshly plucked olive leaf; so Noah knew
that the waters had subsided from the
earth. [12]Then he waited another seven
days, and sent out the dove; and it did not
return to him any more.
13 In the six hundred first year, in the
first month, on the first day of the month,
the waters were dried up from the earth;
and Noah removed the covering of the ark,
and looked, and saw that the face of the
ground was drying. [14]In the second month,
on the twenty-seventh day of the month,
the earth was dry. [15]Then God said to
Noah, [16]"Go out of the ark, you and your
wife, and your sons and your sons' wives
with you. [17]Bring out with you every living
thing that is with you of all flesh—birds
and animals and every creeping thing that
creeps on the earth—so that they may
abound on the earth, and be fruitful and
multiply on the earth." [18]So Noah went
out with his sons and his wife and his sons'
wives. [19]And every animal, every creeping
thing, and every bird, everything that
moves on the earth, went out of the ark by
families.
20 Then Noah built an altar to the
LORD, and took of every clean animal and
of every clean bird, and offered burnt offer-
ings on the altar. [21]And when the LORD
smelled the pleasing odor, the LORD said
in his heart, "I will never again curse the
ground because of humankind, for the in-
clination of the human heart is evil from
youth; nor will I ever again destroy every
living creature as I have done.
22 As long as the earth endures,
seedtime and harvest, cold and
heat,
summer and winter, day and night,
shall not cease."
9 God blessed Noah and his sons, and
said to them, "Be fruitful and multiply,

Ararat, a region in Armenia. **6–12:** Part of the non-Priestly account. In the Gilgamesh epic (see v. 4) the hero sent out two birds, a dove and a swallow, each of which came back; the third, a raven, did not return. **13–19:** The Priestly account resumes here with a description of the exit from the ark of Noah, his family, and the animals.

8.20–9.17: Divine commitments after the flood. This section features two accounts of God's commitments after the flood (8.20–22 non-P; 9.1–17 P), both of which include God's promise not to destroy life through such a flood ever again. **8.20–22:** The non-Priestly tradition describes Noah's *burnt offerings* of clean animals (see 7.2–3n.). In the Gilgamesh epic (see 8.4n.; 8.6–12n.) the hero offered sacrifices and "the gods smelled the pleasant fragrance" and repented of their decision to destroy humanity. Here the LORD smells the *pleasing odor* of Noah's offering and resolves never again to curse the ground or destroy all creatures (v. 21). The LORD does this despite full recognition that the human heart has not changed (cf. 6.5–7). The final result of Noah's sacrifice is the LORD's promise to preserve the cycle of agricultural seasons (v. 22). A central aim of temple sacrifice in Israel and elsewhere was to preserve that cycle. The echo of that idea here is yet another way in which the "non-Priestly" primeval history reflects temple concerns (see also the focus on responses to sacrifice in 4.1–8 and notes on 2.8–9,10–14; 3.24). **9.1–17:** The Priestly tradition lacks an account of sacrifice (see 7.2–3n.). Instead it focuses on affirmations of some aspects of the creation in 1.1–31 and revisions of others. **1–7:** This section begins and ends

and fill the earth. 2The fear and dread of
you shall rest on every animal of the earth,
and on every bird of the air, on everything
that creeps on the ground, and on all the
fish of the sea; into your hand they are de-
livered. 3Every moving thing that lives shall
be food for you; and just as I gave you the
green plants, I give you everything. 4Only,
you shall not eat flesh with its life, that is,
its blood. 5For your own lifeblood I will
surely require a reckoning: from every ani-
mal I will require it and from human be-
ings, each one for the blood of another, I
will require a reckoning for human life.

6 Whoever sheds the blood of a human,
by a human shall that person's
blood be shed;
for in his own image
God made humankind.

7And you, be fruitful and multiply, abound
on the earth and multiply in it."

8 Then God said to Noah and to his
sons with him, 9"As for me, I am establish-
ing my covenant with you and your descen-
dants after you, 10and with every living
creature that is with you, the birds, the do-
mestic animals, and every animal of the
earth with you, as many as came out of the
ark.[a] 11I establish my covenant with you,
that never again shall all flesh be cut off by
the waters of a flood, and never again shall
there be a flood to destroy the earth."
12God said, "This is the sign of the cove-
nant that I make between me and you and
every living creature that is with you, for all
future generations: 13I have set my bow in
the clouds, and it shall be a sign of the cove-
nant between me and the earth. 14When I
bring clouds over the earth and the bow is
seen in the clouds, 15I will remember my
covenant that is between me and you and
every living creature of all flesh; and the
waters shall never again become a flood to
destroy all flesh. 16When the bow is in the
clouds, I will see it and remember the ever-
lasting covenant between God and every
living creature of all flesh that is on the
earth." 17God said to Noah, "This is the
sign of the covenant that I have established
between me and all flesh that is on the
earth."

18 The sons of Noah who went out of
the ark were Shem, Ham, and Japheth.
Ham was the father of Canaan. 19These
three were the sons of Noah; and from
these the whole earth was peopled.

20 Noah, a man of the soil, was the first
to plant a vineyard. 21He drank some of
the wine and became drunk, and he lay un-
covered in his tent. 22And Ham, the father

a Gk: Heb adds *every animal of the earth*

with a reaffirmation of the fertility blessing (vv. 1,7; cf. 1.28). **2–6:** Here God revises the earlier command of vegetarianism (1.29–30). This is a partial concession to the "violence" observed prior to the flood (6.11,13) and an extension of the human dominion over creation described in 1.26–28. At the same time, God regulates this violence through stipulating that humans may not eat the blood in which life resides (see 4.10–11n.) and that humans as bearers of God's image (1.26–27) may not be killed. Since these laws are given to Noah and his sons, the ancestors of all post-flood humanity, they were used in later Jewish tradition as the basis for a set of Noachide laws that were seen as binding upon Gentiles as well as Jews (see Acts 15.20; 21.25). **8–17:** This is the first "covenant" explicitly described as such in the Bible, and it encompasses all of humanity. Indeed, the animal world (vv. 10,12,15) and even the earth (v. 13) are included as well. A "covenant" is a formal agreement, often between a superior and inferior party, the former "making" or "establishing" (vv. 9,11) the bond with the latter. This agreement is often sealed through ceremonies. In this case, God sets his weapon, the bow (Ps 7.12–13; Hab 3.9–11), in the sky facing away from humanity as a sign of God's commitment not to flood the earth again.

9.18–27: Noah and his sons. Aside from P in vv. 18–19, this text is a non-Priestly narrative, often attributed to J, that repeats major themes from the pre-flood period: farming (see 3.17; 5.29), nakedness, alienation in the family, curse, and domination. **22–23:** Some have speculated that Ham had sex with his father, since seeing nakedness refers to incestuous behavior in Lev 20.17. Nevertheless, a more common expression for sexual intercourse in Leviticus is "uncover nakedness" (e.g., 18.6; 20.18) or "lie with"

of Canaan, saw the nakedness of his father,
and told his two brothers outside. 23 Then
Shem and Japheth took a garment, laid it
on both their shoulders, and walked back-
ward and covered the nakedness of their
father; their faces were turned away, and
they did not see their father's nakedness.
24 When Noah awoke from his wine and
knew what his youngest son had done to
him, 25 he said,

"Cursed be Canaan;
lowest of slaves shall he be to his
brothers."

26 He also said,

"Blessed by the LORD my God be
Shem;
and let Canaan be his slave.
27 May God make space for[a] Japheth,
and let him live in the tents of
Shem;
and let Canaan be his slave."

28 After the flood Noah lived three hun-
dred fifty years. 29 All the days of Noah
were nine hundred fifty years; and he died.

10 These are the descendants of Noah's
sons, Shem, Ham, and Japheth; chil-
dren were born to them after the flood.
2 The descendants of Japheth: Gomer,
Magog, Madai, Javan, Tubal, Meshech,
and Tiras. 3 The descendants of Gomer:
Ashkenaz, Riphath, and Togarmah. 4 The
descendants of Javan: Elishah, Tarshish,
Kittim, and Rodanim.[b] 5 From these the
coastland peoples spread. These are the de-
scendants of Japheth[c] in their lands, with
their own language, by their families, in
their nations.

6 The descendants of Ham: Cush,
Egypt, Put, and Canaan. 7 The descendants
of Cush: Seba, Havilah, Sabtah, Raamah,
and Sabteca. The descendants of Raamah:
Sheba and Dedan. 8 Cush became the father
of Nimrod; he was the first on earth to be-
come a mighty warrior. 9 He was a mighty
hunter before the LORD; therefore it is said,
"Like Nimrod a mighty hunter before the
LORD." 10 The beginning of his kingdom
was Babel, Erech, and Accad, all of them in
the land of Shinar. 11 From that land he
went into Assyria, and built Nineveh,
Rehoboth-ir, Calah, and 12 Resen between
Nineveh and Calah; that is the great city.
13 Egypt became the father of Ludim, Ana-
mim, Lehabim, Naphtuhim, 14 Pathrusim,
Casluhim, and Caphtorim, from which the
Philistines come.[d]

15 Canaan became the father of Sidon
his firstborn, and Heth, 16 and the Jebu-
sites, the Amorites, the Girgashites, 17 the

a Heb *yapht*, a play on *Japheth* *b* Heb Mss Sam Gk See 1 Chr 1.7: MT *Dodanim* *c* Compare verses 20, 31. Heb lacks *These are the descendants of Japheth* *d* Cn: Heb *Casluhim, from which the Philistines come, and Caphtorim*

(e.g., 20.11–12). Moreover, the description of Ham's brothers' contrasting behavior in v. 23 (*their faces were turned away*) makes clear that the problem with Ham's behavior was that he did not look away. In the ancient Near East, sons were expected to protect the honor of their father through caring for him when he was drunk (with no negative judgment being attached to getting drunk). Ham here does the opposite, both looking upon his father naked and telling his brothers about it. Such behavior is an example of the same kind of breakdown of family relationships that was seen in ch 3 (see 3.8–13,16–19n.) and ch 4 (see 4.1–16n.). **24–27:** Many have puzzled over why Canaan is cursed for his father, Ham's, misdeed (9.25–26). Some speculate that a story originally focusing on Canaan was modified to focus on the Ham featured in the broader context. Yet it is more likely that a later editor redirected an earlier curse on Ham toward Canaan, so that the curse could then anticipate later traditions about the conquest of the land of Canaan (see 10.16–18a; 14.1–12,13–16n.).

10.1–32: The table of nations. See Map on p. 24 HB. This is a (largely Priestly) survey of the world of the Israelites. Like many ancient peoples, they depicted the relations between national groups in kinship terms. **2–5:** *The descendants of Japheth* had their center in Asia Minor (present day Turkey). **6–20:** *The descendants of Ham* lived in the Egyptian orbit. **8–15:** A fragment of the non-Priestly primeval history. It features a legend regarding Nimrod's building a kingdom in *Shinar* (Babylonia) and Assyria (vv. 8–12). Canaan is the father of two sons, *Heth* (representing the Hittites originally of Asia Minor) and *Sidon* (who represents the Phoenician coastal cities). **14:** See Jer 47.4; Amos 9.7. **16–18a:** This survey of Canaanite

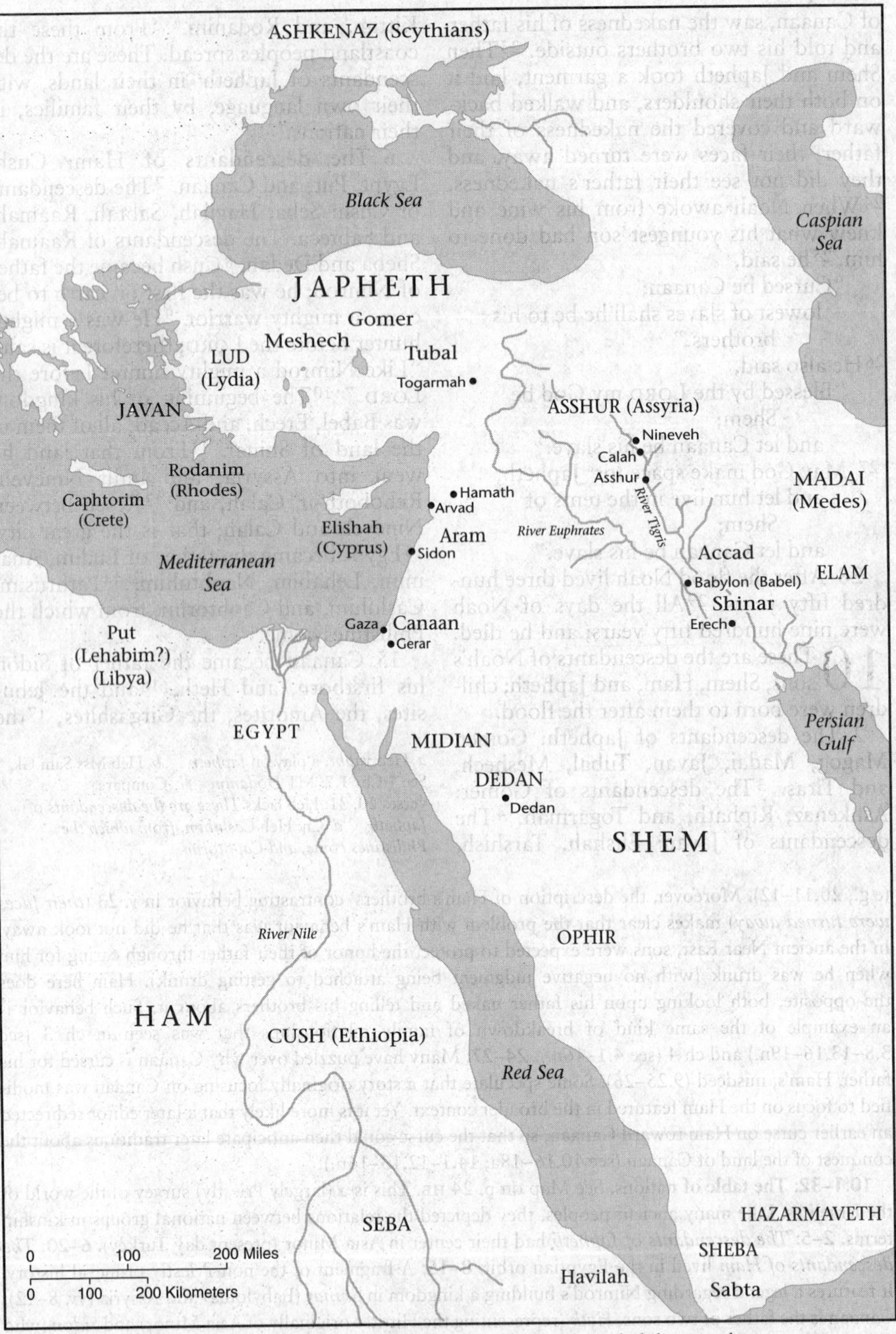

Ch 10: **The table of nations.** Only places that can be identified with probability are shown.

Hivites, the Arkites, the Sinites, 18 the Ar-
vadites, the Zemarites, and the Hamathites.
Afterward the families of the Canaanites
spread abroad. 19 And the territory of the
Canaanites extended from Sidon, in the di-
rection of Gerar, as far as Gaza, and in the
direction of Sodom, Gomorrah, Admah,
and Zeboiim, as far as Lasha. 20 These are
the descendants of Ham, by their families,
their languages, their lands, and their na-
tions.
21 To Shem also, the father of all the
children of Eber, the elder brother of Ja-
pheth, children were born. 22 The descen-
dants of Shem: Elam, Asshur, Arpachshad,
Lud, and Aram. 23 The descendants of
Aram: Uz, Hul, Gether, and Mash. 24 Ar-
pachshad became the father of Shelah; and
Shelah became the father of Eber. 25 To
Eber were born two sons: the name of the
one was Peleg,[a] for in his days the earth
was divided, and his brother's name was
Joktan. 26 Joktan became the father of Al-
modad, Sheleph, Hazarmaveth, Jerah,
27 Hadoram, Uzal, Diklah, 28 Obal, Abima-
el, Sheba, 29 Ophir, Havilah, and Jobab;
all these were the descendants of Joktan.
30 The territory in which they lived extend-
ed from Mesha in the direction of Sephar,
the hill country of the east. 31 These are the
descendants of Shem, by their families,
their languages, their lands, and their na-
tions.
32 These are the families of Noah's
sons, according to their genealogies, in
their nations; and from these the nations
spread abroad on the earth after the flood.
11 Now the whole earth had one lan-
guage and the same words. 2 And as
they migrated from the east,[b] they came
upon a plain in the land of Shinar and set-
tled there. 3 And they said to one another,
"Come, let us make bricks, and burn them
thoroughly." And they had brick for stone,
and bitumen for mortar. 4 Then they said,
"Come, let us build ourselves a city, and a
tower with its top in the heavens, and let us
make a name for ourselves; otherwise we
shall be scattered abroad upon the face of
the whole earth." 5 The LORD came down
to see the city and the tower, which mortals
had built. 6 And the LORD said, "Look, they
are one people, and they have all one lan-
guage; and this is only the beginning of
what they will do; nothing that they pro-
pose to do will now be impossible for them.
7 Come, let us go down, and confuse their
language there, so that they will not under-
stand one another's speech." 8 So the LORD
scattered them abroad from there over the

a That is *Division* *b* Or *migrated eastward*

peoples lists ethnic groups rather than ancestors, including the *Jebusites* (centered in Jerusalem), *Amorites* (natives of the hill country); and the *Hivites* (a tribe in central Palestine). The list resembles later lists of peoples displaced by Israel (e.g., 15.19–21; Deut 7.1) and may be an addition from the same hand that directed Noah's curse toward Canaan (see 9.18–27n.). **21–31:** *Shem* is the father of the Semitic peoples, including Israel. Another pair of fragments of the non-Priestly primeval history (vv. 21,24–30) feature a focus on the *children of Eber.* The name *Eber* may be related to "Hebrew." If so, then this text postulates a wider group of *children of Eber* of which the Israelites are a part.

11.1–9: The tower of Babel. This narrative (from the non-Priestly or J source) revisits the theme of preservation of the divine-human boundary. The threat to that boundary, self-reflective speech by the LORD, and act of divine prevention all parallel 3.22–24 and 6.1–4. With 11.2 the human family completes the eastward movement begun in 3.22–24 (cf. 4.16). Yet this story will focus on a scattering of the human family into different ethnic, linguistic, and territorial groups. As such, it now gives background for the table of nations in ch 10, although it was not originally written with that in view. **2:** *Shinar,* see 10.8–12n. **4:** The humans are depicted as fearful of being scattered and thus aiming to make a name for themselves through a tower reaching into heaven. The humans' intention here to stay together contradicts the divine imperative to "fill the earth" now found in Priestly traditions (1.28; 9.1,7). **6:** The LORD is described here as fearing the human power that might result from ethnic and linguistic unity (see 3.22). **7:** *Let us,* see 1.26n. **8–9:** The LORD's scattering of humanity and confusing of language is the final step in creation of civilized humanity, with its multiple territorial and linguistic groups. The movement toward cultural

face of all the earth, and they left off build-
ing the city. 9 Therefore it was called Babel,
because there the LORD confused[a] the lan-
guage of all the earth; and from there the
LORD scattered them abroad over the face
of all the earth.
10 These are the descendants of Shem.
When Shem was one hundred years old, he
became the father of Arpachshad two years
after the flood; 11 and Shem lived after the
birth of Arpachshad five hundred years,
and had other sons and daughters.
12 When Arpachshad had lived thirty-
five years, he became the father of Shelah;
13 and Arpachshad lived after the birth of
Shelah four hundred three years, and had
other sons and daughters.
14 When Shelah had lived thirty years,
he became the father of Eber; 15 and Shelah
lived after the birth of Eber four hundred
three years, and had other sons and daugh-
ters.
16 When Eber had lived thirty-four
years, he became the father of Peleg; 17 and
Eber lived after the birth of Peleg four hun-
dred thirty years, and had other sons and
daughters.
18 When Peleg had lived thirty years, he
became the father of Reu; 19 and Peleg lived
after the birth of Reu two hundred nine
years, and had other sons and daughters.
20 When Reu had lived thirty-two
years, he became the father of Serug; 21 and
Reu lived after the birth of Serug two hun-
dred seven years, and had other sons and
daughters.
22 When Serug had lived thirty years, he
became the father of Nahor; 23 and Serug
lived after the birth of Nahor two hundred
years, and had other sons and daughters.
24 When Nahor had lived twenty-nine
years, he became the father of Terah; 25 and
Nahor lived after the birth of Terah one
hundred nineteen years, and had other sons
and daughters.
26 When Terah had lived seventy years,
he became the father of Abram, Nahor, and
Haran.
27 Now these are the descendants of Te-
rah. Terah was the father of Abram, Na-
hor, and Haran; and Haran was the father
of Lot. 28 Haran died before his father Te-
rah in the land of his birth, in Ur of the
Chaldeans. 29 Abram and Nahor took
wives; the name of Abram's wife was Sarai,
and the name of Nahor's wife was Milcah.
She was the daughter of Haran the father of
Milcah and Iscah. 30 Now Sarai was barren;
she had no child.
31 Terah took his son Abram and his

a Heb *balal*, meaning *to confuse*

maturity begun in ch 3 is complete. Each step toward this end has been fraught with conflict and loss. The name "Babel," interpreted here as "confusion," serves as a final testimony to the ambiguous results of this process.

11.20–26: The descendants of Shem. This genealogy from the Priestly tradition closely parallels 5.1–32 (though it lacks death notices). It builds a genealogical bridge from Shem to Terah, the father of Abraham. Parts of the genealogy of Shem (10.21–31) are repeated, but now the text focuses exclusively on those descendants who will lead to Abraham. The text implies that all these descendants are firstborn sons, thus setting up Abraham as the firstborn heir of Shem, the eldest of Noah's sons.

11.27–32: Introduction of the Abraham story. The genealogical heading (v. 27) and the concluding notices regarding Terah's travels and death (vv. 31–32) are Priestly materials, whereas many attribute vv. 28–30 to the non-Priestly source. **27:** *Abram,* see 17.5n. The designation "Abraham" is used here in the annotations as the better-known name of Abra(ha)m. Aside from his birth, nothing is told about the early life of Abraham; this lack is filled in by later tradition. **29–30:** *Sarai,* see 17.15n. This is the first appearance of the theme of barrenness of the three most central matriarchs: Sarai/Sarah, Rebekah (25.21), and Rachel (29.31). Their initial barrenness helps highlight God's power to provide heirs of the promise. **31:** *Haran,* in northwest Mesopotamia, was Abraham's ancestral home, according to 24.10 (cf. 29.4). Nonbiblical sources show that several of the names of Abraham's ancestors in the preceding genealogy were place names in Haran; e.g., Peleg (vv. 16–19; also 10.25), Serug (vv. 20–23), Nahor (vv. 24–25; cf. 26), and Terah (vv. 24–26).

grandson Lot son of Haran, and his
daughter-in-law Sarai, his son Abram's
wife, and they went out together from Ur of
the Chaldeans to go into the land of Ca-
naan; but when they came to Haran, they
settled there. 32 The days of Terah were two
hundred five years; and Terah died in Ha-
ran.

12 Now the LORD said to Abram, "Go
from your country and your kin-
dred and your father's house to the land
that I will show you. 2 I will make of you a
great nation, and I will bless you, and make
your name great, so that you will be a bless-
ing. 3 I will bless those who bless you, and
the one who curses you I will curse; and in
you all the families of the earth shall be
blessed."[a]

4 So Abram went, as the LORD had told
him; and Lot went with him. Abram was
seventy-five years old when he departed
from Haran. 5 Abram took his wife Sarai
and his brother's son Lot, and all the pos-
sessions that they had gathered, and the
persons whom they had acquired in Haran;
and they set forth to go to the land of Ca-
naan. When they had come to the land of
Canaan, 6 Abram passed through the land
to the place at Shechem, to the oak[b] of

a Or *by you all the families of the earth shall bless themselves* *b* Or *terebinth*

12.1–3: The LORD's call and promise to Abraham initiates a major new movement in the story of Genesis. This is the first of three divine speeches in which a patriarch is given travel directions and promises of blessing (12.1–3; 26.2–5; 46.1–4; see also 31.3,13). The combination of command (v. 1) and promise (vv. 2–3) implies that the LORD's fulfillment of the promise will follow upon Abraham's fulfillment of the command. **1:** This command to Abraham is similar to, and may have been modeled on, the later divine command for Jacob to return to the "land of your ancestors and to your kindred" (31.3) and to "the land of your birth" (31.13). **2:** The promise that *a great nation* will come from Abraham stands in tension with Sarah's barrenness in 11.30. Much of the following narrative revolves around this tension. *Nation* implies not just a numerous people (cf. 13.16; 15.5; etc.), but a politically independent social group. *I will bless you,* involves giving Abraham the power to flourish in flocks, other riches, and offspring (12.16; 13.2,5,16; etc.; cf. Job 42.12–13). *And make your name great,* to have one's *name* made *great* is to become famous. The LORD promises Abraham a fame similar to that promised to Israelite kings (2 Sam 7.9; 1 Kings 1.47). Thus Abraham, as heir of Shem (see 11.20–26n.)—which means "name" in Hebrew—gains the great "name" that the peoples at Babel had futilely sought for themselves (cf. 11.4). *So that you will be a blessing,* implies that those associated with Abraham and his heirs will flourish as well. Later Laban (30.27–30) and Potiphar (39.5) will both gain blessing through their association with Abraham's heirs. **3:** Though obscured in the translation, the promise to curse *the one who curses* Abraham is a slight modification of a similar formula. Whereas the parallel texts (e.g., 27.29; Num 24.9) speak of God cursing the one who curses, the LORD in this text promises to curse anyone who even "treats [Abraham] lightly." *In you all the families of the earth shall be blessed* has been a particularly important passage in the Christian tradition. Building on the ancient Greek translation of the Hebrew Bible, the Septuagint, Paul interpreted this as a blessing of the Gentiles through Abraham (Gal 3.8). Yet the closest analogies to this promise suggest that the alternate translation, *by you all the families of the earth shall bless themselves,* i.e., they will say "may we be like Abraham," is probably closer to the meaning of the Hebrew. Like 48.20, it envisions other nations of the world looking to Abraham's great blessing and wishing a similar one on themselves (see Ps 72.17). Later in the narrative we see this kind of recognition of Abraham and his heirs' special blessing by foreigners like Abimelech (26.28), Laban (30.27), Potiphar (39.3–5), Joseph's jailer (39.21–23), Pharaoh (Ex 1.9), Jethro (Ex 18.10–12), and Balaam (24.1).

12.4–9: Abraham's first journey to the land. 4b–5: Part of the Priestly Abraham narrative. **6–8:** This brief report of Abraham's journey anticipates the much longer story of Jacob's travels through similar places: Shechem with its oak (cf. 33.18–35.4) and Bethel (cf. 35.1,9–16; see Map on p. 28 HB). Sacred trees like the *oak of Moreh* ("oracle giver"; cf. 13.18; 18.1; 35.4; Deut 11.30; Josh 24.26; Judg 9.37) occur elsewhere in Genesis (e.g., 21.33; 35.8) and seem to have played an important role in the religion of the ancient Israelites and surrounding peoples (see 2.8–9n.).

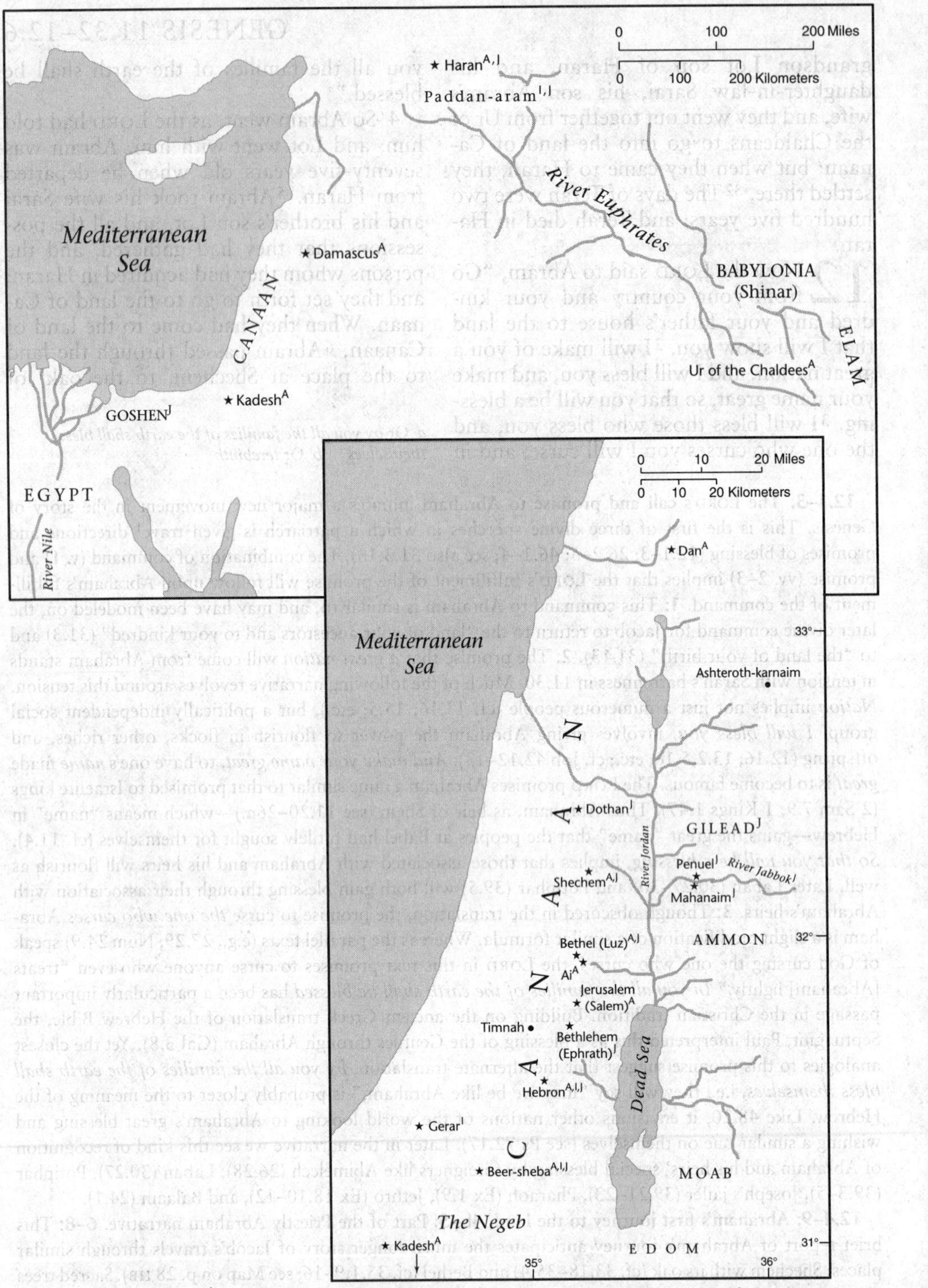

Chs 12–50: The geography of the ancestral narratives. Places associated with a particular ancestor are highlighted with a star, and the initial of the ancestor follows the place name: A(braham), I(saac), or J(acob).

Moreh. At that time the Canaanites were
in the land. 7 Then the LORD appeared to
Abram, and said, "To your offspring[a] I
will give this land." So he built there an
altar to the LORD, who had appeared to
him. 8 From there he moved on to the hill
country on the east of Bethel, and pitched
his tent, with Bethel on the west and Ai on
the east; and there he built an altar to the
LORD and invoked the name of the LORD.
9 And Abram journeyed on by stages to-
ward the Negeb.

10 Now there was a famine in the land.
So Abram went down to Egypt to reside
there as an alien, for the famine was severe
in the land. 11 When he was about to enter
Egypt, he said to his wife Sarai, "I know
well that you are a woman beautiful in ap-
pearance; 12 and when the Egyptians see
you, they will say, 'This is his wife'; then
they will kill me, but they will let you live.
13 Say you are my sister, so that it may go
well with me because of you, and that my
life may be spared on your account."
14 When Abram entered Egypt the Egyp-
tians saw that the woman was very beauti-
ful. 15 When the officials of Pharaoh saw
her, they praised her to Pharaoh. And the
woman was taken into Pharaoh's house.
16 And for her sake he dealt well with
Abram; and he had sheep, oxen, male don-
keys, male and female slaves, female don-
keys, and camels.

17 But the LORD afflicted Pharaoh and
his house with great plagues because of
Sarai, Abram's wife. 18 So Pharaoh called
Abram, and said, "What is this you have
done to me? Why did you not tell me that
she was your wife? 19 Why did you say, 'She
is my sister,' so that I took her for my wife?
Now then, here is your wife, take her, and
be gone." 20 And Pharaoh gave his men or-
ders concerning him; and they set him on
the way, with his wife and all that he had.

13 So Abram went up from Egypt, he
and his wife, and all that he had,
and Lot with him, into the Negeb.

2 Now Abram was very rich in live-
stock, in silver, and in gold. 3 He journeyed
on by stages from the Negeb as far as Beth-
el, to the place where his tent had been at
the beginning, between Bethel and Ai, 4 to
the place where he had made an altar at the
first; and there Abram called on the name
of the LORD. 5 Now Lot, who went with
Abram, also had flocks and herds and
tents, 6 so that the land could not support
both of them living together; for their pos-
sessions were so great that they could not
live together, 7 and there was strife between
the herders of Abram's livestock and the
herders of Lot's livestock. At that time the
Canaanites and the Perizzites lived in the
land.

8 Then Abram said to Lot, "Let there be
no strife between you and me, and between
your herders and my herders; for we are
kindred. 9 Is not the whole land before you?
Separate yourself from me. If you take the
left hand, then I will go to the right; or if
you take the right hand, then I will go to
the left." 10 Lot looked about him, and saw
that the plain of the Jordan was well wa-
tered everywhere like the garden of the
LORD, like the land of Egypt, in the direc-
tion of Zoar; this was before the LORD had
destroyed Sodom and Gomorrah. 11 So Lot
chose for himself all the plain of the Jordan,

a Heb *seed*

12.10–13.1: First story of endangerment of the matriarch (cf. ch 20; 26.6–11). Through putting Sarah in jeopardy to protect himself, Abraham appears not to trust the promise of protection just offered him. On Abraham's later claim to be Sarah's half-brother, see 20.12n. Overall, this story of descent into Egypt because of famine and rescue through plagues anticipates many aspects of the later narrative about Israel's descent into Egypt and Exodus from it (Gen 45–Ex 14).

13.2–18: Split of Abraham and Lot. 2–7: This narrative describing huge flocks and riches in Abraham's household testifies to the preliminary fulfillment of the promises of blessing in 12.2–3. *Lot,* see 11.27,31. **8–13:** The narrative anticipates the Sodom and Gomorrah narrative (ch 19) through mention of those cities, the wickedness of their inhabitants (13.13), and references to *Zoar* (19.19–23). It also notes that Lot, the heir apparent, does not choose to stay in the land of Canaan (vv. 10–12). **14–17:** Only after

and Lot journeyed eastward; thus they sep-
arated from each other. 12 Abram settled
in the land of Canaan, while Lot settled
among the cities of the Plain and moved his
tent as far as Sodom. 13 Now the people of
Sodom were wicked, great sinners against
the LORD.

14 The LORD said to Abram, after Lot
had separated from him, "Raise your eyes
now, and look from the place where you
are, northward and southward and east-
ward and westward; 15 for all the land that
you see I will give to you and to your off-
spring[a] forever. 16 I will make your off-
spring like the dust of the earth; so that if
one can count the dust of the earth, your
offspring also can be counted. 17 Rise up,
walk through the length and the breadth of
the land, for I will give it to you." 18 So
Abram moved his tent, and came and set-
tled by the oaks[b] of Mamre, which are at
Hebron; and there he built an altar to the
LORD.

14 In the days of King Amraphel of Shi-
nar, King Arioch of Ellasar, King
Chedorlaomer of Elam, and King Tidal of
Goiim, 2 these kings made war with King
Bera of Sodom, King Birsha of Gomorrah,
King Shinab of Admah, King Shemeber of
Zeboiim, and the king of Bela (that is,
Zoar). 3 All these joined forces in the Valley
of Siddim (that is, the Dead Sea).[c] 4 Twelve
years they had served Chedorlaomer, but in
the thirteenth year they rebelled. 5 In the
fourteenth year Chedorlaomer and the
kings who were with him came and sub-
dued the Rephaim in Ashteroth-karnaim,
the Zuzim in Ham, the Emim in Shaveh-
kiriathaim, 6 and the Horites in the hill
country of Seir as far as El-paran on the
edge of the wilderness; 7 then they turned
back and came to En-mishpat (that is, Ka-
desh), and subdued all the country of the
Amalekites, and also the Amorites who
lived in Hazazon-tamar. 8 Then the king of
Sodom, the king of Gomorrah, the king of
Admah, the king of Zeboiim, and the king
of Bela (that is, Zoar) went out, and they
joined battle in the Valley of Siddim 9 with
King Chedorlaomer of Elam, King Tidal of
Goiim, King Amraphel of Shinar, and King
Arioch of Ellasar, four kings against five.
10 Now the Valley of Siddim was full of bi-
tumen pits; and as the kings of Sodom and
Gomorrah fled, some fell into them, and
the rest fled to the hill country. 11 So the
enemy took all the goods of Sodom and
Gomorrah, and all their provisions, and
went their way; 12 they also took Lot, the
son of Abram's brother, who lived in Sod-
om, and his goods, and departed.

13 Then one who had escaped came and
told Abram the Hebrew, who was living by
the oaks[b] of Mamre the Amorite, brother
of Eshcol and of Aner; these were allies
of Abram. 14 When Abram heard that his

a Heb *seed* *b* Or *terebinths* *c* Heb *Salt Sea*

Abraham has split from Lot and settled in *Canaan* does God show him the land (cf. 12.7). This certifies that Abraham has fulfilled God's command to go to the land that God "will show" him (12.1). Similarly, Jacob is promised the land after he has split from Esau (28.13–14). **18:** *Mamre* was an ancient Southern sacred place, slightly north of Hebron, with which Abraham was associated (see ch 23).

14.1–24: Abraham's rescue of Lot from the eastern kings. This and ch 15 relate closely to each other and link in multiple ways with late layers of the primeval history (see 9.18–27n.; 10.16–18a n.). **1–12:** Here an alliance of four eastern kings conquers five Canaanite kings associated with the Dead Sea region where Lot is said to have settled. In a fulfillment of the curse of Noah predicting the enslavement of Canaan by Shem (9.25–26), these Canaanite kings had been subject for twelve years to an eastern alliance of kings headed by the Shemite king, *Chedorlaomer* (cf. 10.22). When the Canaanite kings rebel, the eastern kings crush the revolt and seize Lot and his household and take them back toward their home. Neither the battle nor any of the kings can be identified in nonbiblical sources. **13–16:** Abraham's ability to pursue and overcome the Shemite conquerors testifies to his status as heir of Shem and recipient of Shem's blessing (9.25–27). Moreover, this demonstrates the fulfillment of the divine promise to protect Abraham and his household (12.3). **13:** *Hebrew,* probably meaning an outsider, as often in the Hebrew Bible (see 39.14; Ex 1.15; 1 Sam 29.3; Jon 1.9). **17–20:** This is the only section of Genesis associating

nephew had been taken captive, he led
forth his trained men, born in his house,
three hundred eighteen of them, and went
in pursuit as far as Dan. 15 He divided his
forces against them by night, he and his
servants, and routed them and pursued
them to Hobah, north of Damascus.
16 Then he brought back all the goods, and
also brought back his nephew Lot with his
goods, and the women and the people.

17 After his return from the defeat of
Chedorlaomer and the kings who were
with him, the king of Sodom went out to
meet him at the Valley of Shaveh (that is,
the King's Valley). 18 And King Melchize-
dek of Salem brought out bread and wine;
he was priest of God Most High.[a] 19 He
blessed him and said,

"Blessed be Abram by God Most
High,[a]
maker of heaven and earth;
20 and blessed be God Most High,[a]
who has delivered your enemies
into your hand!"

And Abram gave him one-tenth of every-
thing. 21 Then the king of Sodom said to
Abram, "Give me the persons, but take the
goods for yourself." 22 But Abram said to
the king of Sodom, "I have sworn to the
LORD, God Most High,[a] maker of heaven
and earth, 23 that I would not take a thread
or a sandal-thong or anything that is yours,
so that you might not say, 'I have made
Abram rich.' 24 I will take nothing but what
the young men have eaten, and the share of
the men who went with me—Aner, Eshcol,
and Mamre. Let them take their share."

15 After these things the word of the
LORD came to Abram in a vision,
"Do not be afraid, Abram, I am your
shield; your reward shall be very great."
2 But Abram said, "O Lord GOD, what will
you give me, for I continue childless, and
the heir of my house is Eliezer of Damas-
cus?"[b] 3 And Abram said, "You have given
me no offspring, and so a slave born in my
house is to be my heir." 4 But the word of
the LORD came to him, "This man shall not
be your heir; no one but your very own
issue shall be your heir." 5 He brought him
outside and said, "Look toward heaven
and count the stars, if you are able to count
them." Then he said to him, "So shall your
descendants be." 6 And he believed the
LORD; and the LORD[c] reckoned it to him
as righteousness.

7 Then he said to him, "I am the LORD

a Heb *El Elyon* *b* Meaning of Heb uncertain
c Heb *he*

a patriarch with Jerusalem; indeed, it is the only place in the entire Torah where Jerusalem is referred to by name. As heir of Shem, Abraham now receives the blessing of the priest in what will become Israel's royal and religious center. *Salem* is a name for Jerusalem (Ps 76.2), where the ancient high god of the Canaanite pantheon, El (*God Most High*), was worshiped in pre- and early Israelite times. The *King's Valley* is near Jerusalem (2 Sam 18.18), and the priest *Melchizedek* appears as the founder of a royal priesthood in an ancient Jerusalemite Psalm (110.4). This mysterious Melchizedek was later interpreted eschatologically at Qumran and typologically by the early church (Heb 7.1–17).

15.1–21: The first covenant with Abraham. The LORD promises Abraham protection, reward, and an heir in the wake of his recent military encounter with the eastern kings. **1:** The promise to be a *shield* (Heb "magen") for Abraham echoes Melchizedek's praise of the god who "delivered" ("miggen") Abraham (14.20), and the *reward* replaces the goods he had refused from the king of Sodom (14.21–24). **2–5:** Some scholars view the parallel objections from Abraham (vv. 2 and 3) and divine responses (vv. 4 and 5) as the first indicators of the existence of parallel non-Priestly sources (J and E) that were interwoven here and in the rest of the Pentateuch (see the Introduction). **6:** This verse indicates that Abraham considered his objections answered. Though later tradition has generally understood God to be the one who reckoned righteousness to Abraham (e.g., Rom 4.9; Gal 3.6), the subject is not specified in Hebrew. *Righteousness* is being true to one's social obligations and commitments. It is possible that it is Abraham here who reckons righteousness to the LORD, certifying that he now believes that the LORD will be true to his commitments in 15.1 (cf. 15.2–3). **7–21:** This section parallels the promise-objection-reassurance pattern of 15.1–6, but with the added component of a covenant ceremony sealing God's promise to give

who brought you from Ur of the Chalde-
ans, to give you this land to possess." 8 But
he said, "O Lord GOD, how am I to know
that I shall possess it?" 9 He said to him,
"Bring me a heifer three years old, a female
goat three years old, a ram three years old,
a turtledove, and a young pigeon." 10 He
brought him all these and cut them in two,
laying each half over against the other; but
he did not cut the birds in two. 11 And when
birds of prey came down on the carcasses,
Abram drove them away.

12 As the sun was going down, a deep
sleep fell upon Abram, and a deep and ter-
rifying darkness descended upon him.
13 Then the LORD[a] said to Abram, "Know
this for certain, that your offspring shall be
aliens in a land that is not theirs, and shall
be slaves there, and they shall be oppressed
for four hundred years; 14 but I will bring
judgment on the nation that they serve, and
afterward they shall come out with great
possessions. 15 As for yourself, you shall go
to your ancestors in peace; you shall be
buried in a good old age. 16 And they shall
come back here in the fourth generation;
for the iniquity of the Amorites is not yet
complete."

17 When the sun had gone down and it
was dark, a smoking fire pot and a flaming
torch passed between these pieces. 18 On
that day the LORD made a covenant with
Abram, saying, "To your descendants I
give this land, from the river of Egypt to the
great river, the river Euphrates, 19 the land
of the Kenites, the Kenizzites, the Kadmon-
ites, 20 the Hittites, the Perizzites, the Reph-
aim, 21 the Amorites, the Canaanites, the
Girgashites, and the Jebusites."

16 Now Sarai, Abram's wife, bore him
no children. She had an Egyptian

a Heb *he*

Abraham the land. **9–17:** The ceremony (9–11,17) reflects an ancient practice in which the participants in a covenant oath passed through the dismembered parts of an animal and proclaimed a similar fate on themselves if they disobeyed the terms of the agreement (cf. Jer 34.18). Perhaps because of this, the Heb word for "making" a covenant is literally to "cut" a covenant (found in 15.18). In this case, God passes between the pieces in the form of fire (see Ex 3.2; 13.21). A speech (15.12–16) has been inserted into this ceremony that echoes Abraham's earlier triumph over the eastern kings at "Dan" and return from there with "goods" (Heb "rekush"; 14.14–16). Here in v. 14 God promises a future *judgment* (Heb "dan") on Egypt and escape of Abraham's descendants from there with yet more goods (again "rekush" in 15.14; see Ex 3.21–22; 12.33–36). Though this is promised in four generations at the end of the speech (15.16), a Priestly editor may have modified this in v. 13 to four hundred years in order to better match Priestly material in Exodus (Ex 12.40). **16:** *The iniquity of the Amorites,* see Lev 20.23; Deut 9.4. **18–21:** The ceremony is concluded with God's promise to give the land of the Canaanite peoples (cf. 10.16–18) to Abraham. **18:** The boundaries given here are the broadest definition of the promised land in the Hebrew Bible. They correspond to similarly broad, ideal descriptions of the land in the Deuteronomistic History (e.g., 2 Sam 8.3; 1 Kings 4.21; cf. Deut 1.7; 11.24; Josh 1.4). The phrase *river of Egypt* occurs only here, and may refer to the Nile. But elsewhere in the Hebrew Bible (e.g., Num 34.5; 2 Kings 24.7; Isa 27.12) and in other sources, the "Wadi of Egypt" is apparently either the Wadi Besor or the Wadi el-Arish, both south of Gaza. **19–21:** The list of ten nations here resembles similar such lists of Canaanite peoples in the Tetrateuch (e.g., Ex 3.8,17; 13.5) and Deuteronomistic history (e.g., Deut 7.1; 20.17; Josh 3.10). This list, however, is significantly longer than others. Though it is missing the "Hivites" (see 10.16–18a n.), who occur on most other lists, this list is unique in including the *Kenites, Kenizzites, Kadmonites,* and *Rephaim.*

16.1–16: Hagar's encounter with God and the birth of Ishmael stand at the heart of the Abraham story, enveloped by parallel traditions dealing with covenant (chs 15 and 17), Lot and Abraham (chs 13–14 and 18–19), the endangerment of Sarah (12.10–20 and ch 20), and the promise (12.1–6 and 22.1–19). This story echoes the story of Abraham's endangerment of Sarah in 12.10–20 in describing the complications resulting from human attempts to fulfill the promise, in this case the promise of offspring. In addition,

slave-girl whose name was Hagar, 2 and Sa-
rai said to Abram, "You see that the LORD
has prevented me from bearing children; go
in to my slave-girl; it may be that I shall
obtain children by her." And Abram lis-
tened to the voice of Sarai. 3 So, after
Abram had lived ten years in the land of
Canaan, Sarai, Abram's wife, took Hagar
the Egyptian, her slave-girl, and gave her to
her husband Abram as a wife. 4 He went in
to Hagar, and she conceived; and when she
saw that she had conceived, she looked
with contempt on her mistress. 5 Then Sarai
said to Abram, "May the wrong done to
me be on you! I gave my slave-girl to your
embrace, and when she saw that she had
conceived, she looked on me with con-
tempt. May the LORD judge between you
and me!" 6 But Abram said to Sarai, "Your
slave-girl is in your power; do to her as you
please." Then Sarai dealt harshly with her,
and she ran away from her.

7 The angel of the LORD found her by a
spring of water in the wilderness, the spring
on the way to Shur. 8 And he said, "Hagar,
slave-girl of Sarai, where have you come
from and where are you going?" She said,
"I am running away from my mistress Sa-
rai." 9 The angel of the LORD said to her,
"Return to your mistress, and submit to
her." 10 The angel of the LORD also said to
her, "I will so greatly multiply your off-
spring that they cannot be counted for mul-
titude." 11 And the angel of the LORD said
to her,

"Now you have conceived and shall
bear a son;
you shall call him Ishmael,[a]
for the LORD has given heed to
your affliction.
12 He shall be a wild ass of a man,
with his hand against everyone,
and everyone's hand against him;
and he shall live at odds with all his
kin."

13 So she named the LORD who spoke to
her, "You are El-roi";[b] for she said, "Have
I really seen God and remained alive after
seeing him?"[c] 14 Therefore the well was
called Beer-lahai-roi;[d] it lies between Ka-
desh and Bered.

15 Hagar bore Abram a son; and Abram
named his son, whom Hagar bore, Ishmael.
16 Abram was eighty-six years old when
Hagar bore him[e] Ishmael.

17 When Abram was ninety-nine years
old, the LORD appeared to Abram,
and said to him, "I am God Almighty;[f]
walk before me, and be blameless. 2 And I

a That is *God hears* *b* Perhaps *God of seeing* or *God who sees* *c* Meaning of Heb uncertain *d* That is *the Well of the Living One who sees me* *e* Heb *Abram* *f* Traditional rendering of Heb *El Shaddai*

like that story, this one links with the Exodus. In this case, however, it is an Egyptian, Hagar, who is "oppressed" (Heb "ʿanah"; "dealt harshly with" in the NRSV of v. 6), flees, and meets God in the wilderness. **2:** According to ancient surrogate motherhood customs, a wife could give her maid to her husband and claim the child as her own (30.3,9). **4–5:** The translation *looked with contempt* implies that Hagar disdained her mistress, whereas the Heb verb ("qll," "to treat lightly") only implies that Hagar did not look up to her mistress the way she once did. Having had a child, Hagar is now derisively seen by her mistress as an "uppity slave." **7:** Here *the angel of the LORD* is not a heavenly being subordinate to God but the LORD (Yahweh) in earthly manifestation, as is clear from v. 13 (cf. 21.17,19; Ex 14.19). **11:** *The LORD has given heed,* lit., "The LORD has heard," an explanation of the name Ishmael (see note *a* and 21.17n.). **13:** *God of seeing* (see note *b*) was the name of the deity at the Beer-lahai-roi well, now identified with Israel's God. On Hagar's question, cf. 32.30; Ex 33.20; Judg 6.22–23; 13.22. **15–16:** Priestly material focusing more on Ishmael than Hagar.

17.1–27: The everlasting covenant and sign of circumcision. This account from the Priestly tradition is parallel to that in 15.1–21 and links to the Priestly Noachic covenant in 9.8–17. See 9.8–17n. on "covenant." **1:** The phrase translated as *God Almighty* is variously understood as "God, the one of the Mountains," "God of the Shadday [deities]," or even "God with breasts" (= "fertile God," see 49.25). Whatever its original meaning, the Priestly tradition understands this epithet to be what the early ancestors of Israel called God before they learned the name Yahweh during the Exodus (Ex 6.2–8). **2–6:** In a

will make my covenant between me and
you, and will make you exceedingly numer-
ous." 3 Then Abram fell on his face; and
God said to him, 4 "As for me, this is my
covenant with you: You shall be the ances-
tor of a multitude of nations. 5 No longer
shall your name be Abram,[a] but your
name shall be Abraham;[b] for I have made
you the ancestor of a multitude of nations.
6 I will make you exceedingly fruitful; and I
will make nations of you, and kings shall
come from you. 7 I will establish my cove-
nant between me and you, and your off-
spring after you throughout their genera-
tions, for an everlasting covenant, to be
God to you and to your offspring[c] after
you. 8 And I will give to you, and to your
offspring after you, the land where you are
now an alien, all the land of Canaan, for a
perpetual holding; and I will be their God."
9 God said to Abraham, "As for you,
you shall keep my covenant, you and your
offspring after you throughout their gener-
ations. 10 This is my covenant, which you
shall keep, between me and you and your
offspring after you: Every male among you
shall be circumcised. 11 You shall circum-
cise the flesh of your foreskins, and it shall
be a sign of the covenant between me and
you. 12 Throughout your generations every
male among you shall be circumcised when
he is eight days old, including the slave
born in your house and the one bought
with your money from any foreigner who is
not of your offspring. 13 Both the slave born
in your house and the one bought with
your money must be circumcised. So shall
my covenant be in your flesh an everlasting
covenant. 14 Any uncircumcised male who
is not circumcised in the flesh of his fore-
skin shall be cut off from his people; he has
broken my covenant."
15 God said to Abraham, "As for Sarai
your wife, you shall not call her Sarai, but
Sarah shall be her name. 16 I will bless her,
and moreover I will give you a son by her.
I will bless her, and she shall give rise to
nations; kings of peoples shall come from
her." 17 Then Abraham fell on his face and
laughed, and said to himself, "Can a child
be born to a man who is a hundred years
old? Can Sarah, who is ninety years old,
bear a child?" 18 And Abraham said to
God, "O that Ishmael might live in your
sight!" 19 God said, "No, but your wife Sar-
ah shall bear you a son, and you shall name
him Isaac.[d] I will establish my covenant
with him as an everlasting covenant for his
offspring after him. 20 As for Ishmael, I
have heard you; I will bless him and make

a That is *exalted ancestor* *b* Here taken to mean *ancestor of a multitude* *c* Heb *seed* *d* That is *he laughs*

parallel to 15.1–6 this text includes the promise of offspring in the covenant. **5:** A new name signifies a new relationship or status (see 32.28). *Abraham,* a dialectical variant of *Abram,* means "the [divine] ancestor is exalted." Here the name is explained by its similarity to the Hebrew for *ancestor of a multitude,* referring to nations whose ancestry was traced to Abraham (v. 16; 28.3; 35.11; 48.4), such as Edomites and Ishmaelites. The promise to make Abraham "exceedingly numerous" (v. 2) and *exceedingly fruitful* (v. 6) echoes the broader fertility blessing given animals (1.22; 8.17) and humanity (1.28; 9.1,7) in the primeval history. **7:** Within the Priestly tradition, the promise to be God to Abraham and his offspring leads to the divine provision of religious laws and a tabernacle sanctuary into which God comes to dwell in Israel's midst (Ex 25–31,35–40). Like the covenant with Noah (9.8–17), this covenant to be bound to Israel is *an everlasting covenant* (vv. 13,19) because it is grounded in the will of God, not human behavior. **9–14:** Circumcision was an ancient rite, perhaps originally connected to marriage (see 34.14–17), probably having to do with warding off demons (see Ex 4.24–26). Here, however, it is moved to early childhood and reinterpreted as a sign of God's everlasting covenant with Israel, a mark of membership in the covenant community. Unlike the Noachic covenant (9.1–17), this one pertains only to the household and heirs of Abraham. **15:** *Sarah,* meaning "princess," is a variant of *Sarai;* see v. 5n. **17:** Abraham's laughter here in the Priestly tradition anticipates Sarah's laughter in the non-Priestly (J) account (18.9–15n.).

him fruitful and exceedingly numerous; he
shall be the father of twelve princes, and I
will make him a great nation. 21 But my
covenant I will establish with Isaac, whom
Sarah shall bear to you at this season next
year." 22 And when he had finished talking
with him, God went up from Abraham.

23 Then Abraham took his son Ishmael
and all the slaves born in his house or
bought with his money, every male among
the men of Abraham's house, and he cir-
cumcised the flesh of their foreskins that
very day, as God had said to him. 24 Abra-
ham was ninety-nine years old when he
was circumcised in the flesh of his foreskin.
25 And his son Ishmael was thirteen years
old when he was circumcised in the flesh of
his foreskin. 26 That very day Abraham and
his son Ishmael were circumcised; 27 and all
the men of his house, slaves born in the
house and those bought with money from a
foreigner, were circumcised with him.

18 The LORD appeared to Abraham[a]
by the oaks[b] of Mamre, as he sat at
the entrance of his tent in the heat of the
day. 2 He looked up and saw three men
standing near him. When he saw them, he
ran from the tent entrance to meet them,
and bowed down to the ground. 3 He said,
"My lord, if I find favor with you, do not
pass by your servant. 4 Let a little water be
brought, and wash your feet, and rest your-
selves under the tree. 5 Let me bring a little
bread, that you may refresh yourselves, and
after that you may pass on—since you have
come to your servant." So they said, "Do as
you have said." 6 And Abraham hastened
into the tent to Sarah, and said, "Make
ready quickly three measures[c] of choice
flour, knead it, and make cakes." 7 Abra-
ham ran to the herd, and took a calf, tender
and good, and gave it to the servant, who
hastened to prepare it. 8 Then he took curds
and milk and the calf that he had prepared,
and set it before them; and he stood by
them under the tree while they ate.

9 They said to him, "Where is your wife
Sarah?" And he said, "There, in the tent."
10 Then one said, "I will surely return to
you in due season, and your wife Sarah
shall have a son." And Sarah was listening
at the tent entrance behind him. 11 Now
Abraham and Sarah were old, advanced in
age; it had ceased to be with Sarah after the
manner of women. 12 So Sarah laughed to
herself, saying, "After I have grown old,
and my husband is old, shall I have plea-
sure?" 13 The LORD said to Abraham,
"Why did Sarah laugh, and say, 'Shall I
indeed bear a child, now that I am old?'
14 Is anything too wonderful for the LORD?
At the set time I will return to you, in due
season, and Sarah shall have a son." 15 But
Sarah denied, saying, "I did not laugh"; for
she was afraid. He said, "Oh yes, you did
laugh."

16 Then the men set out from there, and
they looked toward Sodom; and Abraham
went with them to set them on their way.
17 The LORD said, "Shall I hide from Abra-
ham what I am about to do, 18 seeing that
Abraham shall become a great and mighty

[a] Heb *him* [b] Or *terebinths* [c] Heb *seahs*

18.1–15: The LORD's visit to Abraham and Sarah. 1: The *oaks of Mamre,* see 12.6–8n.; 13.18n. **2–8:** A description of ideal hospitality of Abraham parallel to that of Lot in 19.1–11. This motif of secretly divine visitors is widespread in folklore. The relation between the three visitors and the LORD (v. 1) is unclear. The narrative fluidly shifts from speaking of them as a group (e.g., v. 9) to having "the LORD" speak alone (e.g., v. 13; cf. v. 10). Later materials in v. 22 and 19.1 conceive of "the LORD" as one of the three angels (see 16.7n.), though this is not specified in the preceding narrative ("one" in the NRSV of v. 10 is a translator's addition). **9–15:** The narrator uses the theme of Sarah's laughter (cf. 17.17) to stress the incredibility of God's promise of a son (eventually Isaac, 21.1–3). **11:** *Ceased . . . after the manner of women,* a circumlocution for menopause. **12:** Isaac's name means "he laughs," and other traditions develop the link with laughter as well (17.17–19; 21.6,8; 26.8).

18.16–33: Abraham's intercession for Sodom and Gomorrah. 17–19: This first speech by the LORD stresses that he speaks to Abraham because he chose him to teach his household the ways of righteousness. In vv. 22–32 the LORD will model such righteousness in his responsiveness to Abraham. **18:** See 12.3n.

nation, and all the nations of the earth shall
be blessed in him?[a] 19 No, for I have cho-
sen[b] him, that he may charge his children
and his household after him to keep the
way of the LORD by doing righteousness
and justice; so that the LORD may bring
about for Abraham what he has promised
him." 20 Then the LORD said, "How great
is the outcry against Sodom and Gomorrah
and how very grave their sin! 21 I must go
down and see whether they have done alto-
gether according to the outcry that has
come to me; and if not, I will know."

22 So the men turned from there, and
went toward Sodom, while Abraham re-
mained standing before the LORD.[c]
23 Then Abraham came near and said,
"Will you indeed sweep away the righteous
with the wicked? 24 Suppose there are fifty
righteous within the city; will you then
sweep away the place and not forgive it for
the fifty righteous who are in it? 25 Far be it
from you to do such a thing, to slay the
righteous with the wicked, so that the righ-
teous fare as the wicked! Far be that from
you! Shall not the Judge of all the earth do
what is just?" 26 And the LORD said, "If I
find at Sodom fifty righteous in the city, I
will forgive the whole place for their sake."
27 Abraham answered, "Let me take it upon
myself to speak to the Lord, I who am but
dust and ashes. 28 Suppose five of the fifty
righteous are lacking? Will you destroy the
whole city for lack of five?" And he said, "I
will not destroy it if I find forty-five there."
29 Again he spoke to him, "Suppose forty
are found there." He answered, "For the
sake of forty I will not do it." 30 Then he
said, "Oh do not let the Lord be angry if I
speak. Suppose thirty are found there." He
answered, "I will not do it, if I find thirty
there." 31 He said, "Let me take it upon
myself to speak to the Lord. Suppose twen-
ty are found there." He answered, "For
the sake of twenty I will not destroy it."
32 Then he said, "Oh do not let the Lord be
angry if I speak just once more. Suppose ten
are found there." He answered, "For the
sake of ten I will not destroy it." 33 And the
LORD went his way, when he had finished
speaking to Abraham; and Abraham re-
turned to his place.

19 The two angels came to Sodom in
the evening, and Lot was sitting in
the gateway of Sodom. When Lot saw
them, he rose to meet them, and bowed
down with his face to the ground. 2 He said,
"Please, my lords, turn aside to your ser-

a Or *and all the nations of the earth shall bless themselves by him* b Heb *known* c Another ancient tradition reads *while the LORD remained standing before Abraham*

20–21: This second speech by the LORD echoes his decision at Babel to *go down* and *see* what was going on there (11.5; cf. divine self-reflection in 3.22; 6.3,5–7; 11.6–7). Unlike vv. 17–19, this speech suggests that the LORD has not yet decided what to do. **22–33:** Like Moses (e.g., Ex 32.9–14), Abraham negotiates with an angry God, appealing to God's righteousness. In this case, however, the terms he ends up winning—aversion of disaster if ten righteous people can be found—does not avert destruction. Thus, this text appears to be a theoretical reflection on God's righteousness and how many righteous people are required to save a broader group; cf. Ezek 14.12–23.

19.1–38: The rescue of Lot and his family from the destruction of Sodom and Gomorrah. The destruction of Sodom and Gomorrah was a prominent example in Israelite tradition of God's total judgment (Deut 29.23; Isa 1.9; Jer 49.18; Am 4.11). **1:** *Two angels,* see 18.2–8n. **1–11:** As in the case of 18.1–8, the main issue here is hospitality to secretly divine visitors. Here, however, the sanctity of hospitality is threatened by *the men of the city* who wish to rape (*know*) the guests (cf. Judg 19.22–30). Though disapproval of male homosexual rape is assumed here, the primary point of this text is how this threat by the townspeople violates the value of hospitality (contrast 18.1–16). Hospitality is valued so strongly in this context that this text positively portrays Lot's offer of his virgin daughters in place of his guests. Though the text presupposes that a father would have extreme difficulty offering his daughters to such violence, Lot's virtue is demonstrated by his willingness to go to such a length—and put his own body in danger (vv. 9–10)—to avoid violation of his guests. As a result of his protection of his guests, he, like Noah, "finds favor" with God (v. 19; cf. 6.8) and he and his household are rescued out of destruction.

vant's house and spend the night, and wash your feet; then you can rise early and go on your way." They said, "No; we will spend the night in the square." 3 But he urged them strongly; so they turned aside to him and entered his house; and he made them a feast, and baked unleavened bread, and they ate. 4 But before they lay down, the men of the city, the men of Sodom, both young and old, all the people to the last man, surrounded the house; 5 and they called to Lot, "Where are the men who came to you tonight? Bring them out to us, so that we may know them." 6 Lot went out of the door to the men, shut the door after him, 7 and said, "I beg you, my brothers, do not act so wickedly. 8 Look, I have two daughters who have not known a man; let me bring them out to you, and do to them as you please; only do nothing to these men, for they have come under the shelter of my roof." 9 But they replied, "Stand back!" And they said, "This fellow came here as an alien, and he would play the judge! Now we will deal worse with you than with them." Then they pressed hard against the man Lot, and came near the door to break it down. 10 But the men inside reached out their hands and brought Lot into the house with them, and shut the door. 11 And they struck with blindness the men who were at the door of the house, both small and great, so that they were unable to find the door.

12 Then the men said to Lot, "Have you anyone else here? Sons-in-law, sons, daughters, or anyone you have in the city—bring them out of the place. 13 For we are about to destroy this place, because the outcry against its people has become great before the LORD, and the LORD has sent us to destroy it." 14 So Lot went out and said to his sons-in-law, who were to marry his daughters, "Up, get out of this place; for the LORD is about to destroy the city." But he seemed to his sons-in-law to be jesting.

15 When morning dawned, the angels urged Lot, saying, "Get up, take your wife and your two daughters who are here, or else you will be consumed in the punishment of the city." 16 But he lingered; so the men seized him and his wife and his two daughters by the hand, the LORD being merciful to him, and they brought him out and left him outside the city. 17 When they had brought them outside, they[a] said, "Flee for your life; do not look back or stop anywhere in the Plain; flee to the hills, or else you will be consumed." 18 And Lot said to them, "Oh, no, my lords; 19 your servant has found favor with you, and you have shown me great kindness in saving my life; but I cannot flee to the hills, for fear the disaster will overtake me and I die. 20 Look, that city is near enough to flee to, and it is a little one. Let me escape there—is it not a little one?—and my life will be saved!" 21 He said to him, "Very well, I grant you this favor too, and will not overthrow the city of which you have spoken. 22 Hurry, escape there, for I can do nothing until you arrive there." Therefore the city was called Zoar.[b] 23 The sun had risen on the earth when Lot came to Zoar.

24 Then the LORD rained on Sodom and Gomorrah sulfur and fire from the LORD out of heaven; 25 and he overthrew those cities, and all the Plain, and all the inhabitants of the cities, and what grew on the ground. 26 But Lot's wife, behind him, looked back, and she became a pillar of salt.

a Gk Syr Vg: Heb *he*   *b* That is *Little*

12–14: In place of Sarah's laughter (Heb "tshq") in the preceding hospitality scene (18.11–14), we have here the Sodomite *sons-in-law* assuming that Lot is *jesting* (Heb "tshq"). **15–23:** Although Lot has been positively portrayed up to this point, his repeated lingering here compares negatively with Noah's immediate compliance with God's commands. **20–23:** *That city, Zoar,* the name means "little"; see note *b* and v. 20. **24–25:** The *rain* of destruction continues the echoes of the Noah story. **26:** This text turns salt formations in the Dead Sea area into a testimony to the truth of the story, asserting that one of those formations was Lot's wife, who disobediently looked back at the cities God was destroying. **29:** This is

27 Abraham went early in the morning
to the place where he had stood before the
LORD; 28 and he looked down toward Sod-
om and Gomorrah and toward all the land
of the Plain and saw the smoke of the land
going up like the smoke of a furnace.

29 So it was that, when God destroyed
the cities of the Plain, God remembered
Abraham, and sent Lot out of the midst of
the overthrow, when he overthrew the cit-
ies in which Lot had settled.

30 Now Lot went up out of Zoar and
settled in the hills with his two daughters,
for he was afraid to stay in Zoar; so he
lived in a cave with his two daughters.
31 And the firstborn said to the younger,
"Our father is old, and there is not a man
on earth to come in to us after the manner
of all the world. 32 Come, let us make our
father drink wine, and we will lie with him,
so that we may preserve offspring through
our father." 33 So they made their father
drink wine that night; and the firstborn
went in, and lay with her father; he did not
know when she lay down or when she rose.
34 On the next day, the firstborn said to the
younger, "Look, I lay last night with my
father; let us make him drink wine tonight
also; then you go in and lie with him, so
that we may preserve offspring through our
father." 35 So they made their father drink
wine that night also; and the younger rose,
and lay with him; and he did not know
when she lay down or when she rose.
36 Thus both the daughters of Lot became
pregnant by their father. 37 The firstborn
bore a son, and named him Moab; he is the
ancestor of the Moabites to this day. 38 The
younger also bore a son and named him
Ben-ammi; he is the ancestor of the Am-
monites to this day.

20 From there Abraham journeyed to-
ward the region of the Negeb, and
settled between Kadesh and Shur. While re-
siding in Gerar as an alien, 2 Abraham said
of his wife Sarah, "She is my sister." And
King Abimelech of Gerar sent and took
Sarah. 3 But God came to Abimelech in a
dream by night, and said to him, "You are
about to die because of the woman whom
you have taken; for she is a married wom-
an." 4 Now Abimelech had not approached
her; so he said, "Lord, will you destroy an
innocent people? 5 Did he not himself say to
me, 'She is my sister'? And she herself said,
'He is my brother.' I did this in the integrity
of my heart and the innocence of my
hands." 6 Then God said to him in the
dream, "Yes, I know that you did this in
the integrity of your heart; furthermore it
was I who kept you from sinning against
me. Therefore I did not let you touch her.
7 Now then, return the man's wife; for he is
a prophet, and he will pray for you and you
shall live. But if you do not restore her,
know that you shall surely die, you and all
that are yours."

8 So Abimelech rose early in the morn-
ing, and called all his servants and told
them all these things; and the men were

a Priestly summary of the story, echoing 8.1 and attributing Lot's rescue to his relation with Abraham. **37–38:** This story suggests that two of Israel's closest neighbors, the Moabites and Ammonites in Transjordan, originated in incest. Mistakenly assuming that the destruction of Sodom and Gomorrah was so total that there is no one else on earth by whom to have children (19.31), Lot's daughters get their father drunk so that he will conceive with them. The themes of drunkenness and (implicit) nakedness are reminiscent of the story of Noah and his sons (9.20–27).

20.1–18: The second story of endangerment of the matriarch (cf. 12.10–20; 26.6–11). Many scholars have argued that chs 20–22 contain the first major block of an Elohistic (E) source parallel to the Yahwistic (J) source found in chs 12–19 and extending through the rest of the Pentateuch (cf. 15.2–5n. and the Introduction). Nevertheless, Abraham's brief request in 20.2 that Sarah claim to be his sister would not make sense without the explanation of a similar request in 12.11–13 (often attributed to J). Thus the present version of ch 20 probably is not part of a separate "Elohistic" source. **3–7:** The depiction of Abimelech is far more detailed and sympathetic than that of the foreign king in either of the parallel accounts (cf. 12.15–19; 26.9–10). **7:** To Abraham is attributed the intercessory role of *prophet;* this is the only designation of Abraham as a prophet in the Torah (but see Ps 105.15). **12:** The narrator never asserts

very much afraid. 9 Then Abimelech called
Abraham, and said to him, "What have
you done to us? How have I sinned against
you, that you have brought such great guilt
on me and my kingdom? You have done
things to me that ought not to be done."
10 And Abimelech said to Abraham, "What
were you thinking of, that you did this
thing?" 11 Abraham said, "I did it because I
thought, There is no fear of God at all in
this place, and they will kill me because of
my wife. 12 Besides, she is indeed my sister,
the daughter of my father but not the
daughter of my mother; and she became my
wife. 13 And when God caused me to wan-
der from my father's house, I said to her,
'This is the kindness you must do me: at
every place to which we come, say of me,
He is my brother.' " 14 Then Abimelech
took sheep and oxen, and male and female
slaves, and gave them to Abraham, and re-
stored his wife Sarah to him. 15 Abimelech
said, "My land is before you; settle where it
pleases you." 16 To Sarah he said, "Look, I
have given your brother a thousand pieces
of silver; it is your exoneration before all
who are with you; you are completely vin-
dicated." 17 Then Abraham prayed to God;
and God healed Abimelech, and also healed
his wife and female slaves so that they bore
children. 18 For the LORD had closed fast all
the wombs of the house of Abimelech be-
cause of Sarah, Abraham's wife.

21 The LORD dealt with Sarah as he
had said, and the LORD did for Sar-
ah as he had promised. 2 Sarah conceived
and bore Abraham a son in his old age, at
the time of which God had spoken to him.
3 Abraham gave the name Isaac to his son
whom Sarah bore him. 4 And Abraham cir-
cumcised his son Isaac when he was eight
days old, as God had commanded him.
5 Abraham was a hundred years old when
his son Isaac was born to him. 6 Now Sarah
said, "God has brought laughter for me;
everyone who hears will laugh with me."
7 And she said, "Who would ever have said
to Abraham that Sarah would nurse chil-
dren? Yet I have borne him a son in his old
age."

8 The child grew, and was weaned; and
Abraham made a great feast on the day that
Isaac was weaned. 9 But Sarah saw the son
of Hagar the Egyptian, whom she had
borne to Abraham, playing with her son
Isaac.[a] 10 So she said to Abraham, "Cast
out this slave woman with her son; for the
son of this slave woman shall not inherit
along with my son Isaac." 11 The matter
was very distressing to Abraham on ac-
count of his son. 12 But God said to Abra-
ham, "Do not be distressed because of the
boy and because of your slave woman;
whatever Sarah says to you, do as she tells
you, for it is through Isaac that offspring
shall be named for you. 13 As for the son of
the slave woman, I will make a nation of
him also, because he is your offspring."
14 So Abraham rose early in the morning,
and took bread and a skin of water, and
gave it to Hagar, putting it on her shoulder,
along with the child, and sent her away.
And she departed, and wandered about in
the wilderness of Beer-sheba.

15 When the water in the skin was gone,
she cast the child under one of the bushes.
16 Then she went and sat down opposite
him a good way off, about the distance of

a Gk Vg: Heb lacks *with her son Isaac*

that Sarah is Terah's daughter (cf. 11.27–30). Nevertheless, faced with Abimelech's passionate questioning, Abraham claims to be her half-brother by way of his father. Though many have taken his assertion at face-value, it is read by others as an attempt to provide as many excuses for his behavior as possible (cf. 20.11).

21.1–21: Isaac and Ishmael. 6: See 18.9–15n. **8–21:** This story of endangerment of Ishmael parallels the following one of endangerment of Isaac. After God gives Abraham the command to let his child go (v. 12; 22.2), he rises *early in the morning* to fulfill it (v. 14 ‖ 22.3), the child is delivered when an *angel of God/the LORD* cries out from heaven (v. 17; 22.11–12), and Hagar and Abraham both see a way to save the child (v. 19 ‖ 22.13). **9:** *Playing with,* literally "making [him] laugh," another reference to Isaac's

a bowshot; for she said, "Do not let me
look on the death of the child." And as she
sat opposite him, she lifted up her voice and
wept. 17 And God heard the voice of the
boy; and the angel of God called to Hagar
from heaven, and said to her, "What trou-
bles you, Hagar? Do not be afraid; for God
has heard the voice of the boy where he is.
18 Come, lift up the boy and hold him fast
with your hand, for I will make a great
nation of him." 19 Then God opened her
eyes and she saw a well of water. She went,
and filled the skin with water, and gave the
boy a drink.

20 God was with the boy, and he grew
up; he lived in the wilderness, and became
an expert with the bow. 21 He lived in the
wilderness of Paran; and his mother got a
wife for him from the land of Egypt.

22 At that time Abimelech, with Phicol
the commander of his army, said to Abra-
ham, "God is with you in all that you do;
23 now therefore swear to me here by God
that you will not deal falsely with me or
with my offspring or with my posterity, but
as I have dealt loyally with you, you will
deal with me and with the land where you
have resided as an alien." 24 And Abraham
said, "I swear it."

25 When Abraham complained to
Abimelech about a well of water that
Abimelech's servants had seized, 26 Abime-
lech said, "I do not know who has done
this; you did not tell me, and I have not
heard of it until today." 27 So Abraham
took sheep and oxen and gave them to
Abimelech, and the two men made a cove-
nant. 28 Abraham set apart seven ewe lambs
of the flock. 29 And Abimelech said to
Abraham, "What is the meaning of these
seven ewe lambs that you have set apart?"
30 He said, "These seven ewe lambs you
shall accept from my hand, in order that
you may be a witness for me that I dug this
well." 31 Therefore that place was called
Beer-sheba;[a] because there both of them
swore an oath. 32 When they had made a
covenant at Beer-sheba, Abimelech, with
Phicol the commander of his army, left and
returned to the land of the Philistines.
33 Abraham[b] planted a tamarisk tree in
Beer-sheba, and called there on the name of
the LORD, the Everlasting God.[c] 34 And
Abraham resided as an alien many days in
the land of the Philistines.

22 After these things God tested Abra-
ham. He said to him, "Abraham!"
And he said, "Here I am." 2 He said, "Take
your son, your only son Isaac, whom you

a That is *Well of seven* or *Well of the oath*
b Heb *He* *c* Or *the* LORD, *El Olam*

name; see 18.12n. **17:** See 16.7n. *God has heard,* a play on the name Ishmael, which means "God hears" (see 16.11n.).

21.22–34: Abraham's dispute with Abimelech. This text continues the story about Abraham and Abimelech that was begun in ch 20. Together, the stories about Abraham's sojourn in Gerar in ch 20 and 21.22–34 resemble stories about Isaac's sojourn in Gerar in 26.6–33, and they may have a common oral background. This story combines a tradition that explains the name *Beer-sheba* as meaning "well of seven" (see 22.28–30) with an explanation (parallel to 26.31–33) that it means "well of oath." **33:** On the tamarisk tree, see 12.6–8n. *Everlasting God* ("El Olam") may be an ancient divine name once associated with the sanctuary at Beer-sheba.

22.1–19: The testing of Abraham. 1a: The narrative begins by informing the reader of something that Abraham does not know, that *God tested Abraham.* Abraham's "fear" of God is not proven (v. 12) until he has reached out his hand to slaughter his son (v. 10). **1b–2:** After giving up Ishmael earlier (see 21.8–21n.), Abraham must prepare to give up Isaac, his promised heir, as well. The story echoes the opening of the Abraham story. Just as he was once asked to *go* (Heb "lek leka") from his family of origin and travel to a land God would show him (12.1), so now he must *go* ("lek leka") and sacrifice his future family on a mountain that God will show him (v. 2). The way the command is stated (*your only son . . . whom you love*), which parallels the syntax of 12.1, presupposes that what is being asked of Abraham is extraordinary and extremely difficult. The story does not presuppose a general practice of sacrifice of the firstborn, but does suggest that such a practice could be performed under extraordinary circumstances

love, and go to the land of Moriah, and
offer him there as a burnt offering on one
of the mountains that I shall show you."
3 So Abraham rose early in the morning,
saddled his donkey, and took two of his
young men with him, and his son Isaac; he
cut the wood for the burnt offering, and set
out and went to the place in the distance
that God had shown him. 4 On the third
day Abraham looked up and saw the place
far away. 5 Then Abraham said to his
young men, "Stay here with the donkey;
the boy and I will go over there; we will
worship, and then we will come back to
you." 6 Abraham took the wood of the
burnt offering and laid it on his son Isaac,
and he himself carried the fire and the
knife. So the two of them walked on to-
gether. 7 Isaac said to his father Abraham,
"Father!" And he said, "Here I am, my
son." He said, "The fire and the wood are
here, but where is the lamb for a burnt
offering?" 8 Abraham said, "God himself
will provide the lamb for a burnt offering,
my son." So the two of them walked on
together.

9 When they came to the place that God
had shown him, Abraham built an altar
there and laid the wood in order. He bound
his son Isaac, and laid him on the altar, on
top of the wood. 10 Then Abraham reached
out his hand and took the knife to kill[a] his
son. 11 But the angel of the LORD called
to him from heaven, and said, "Abraham,
Abraham!" And he said, "Here I am."
12 He said, "Do not lay your hand on the
boy or do anything to him; for now I know
that you fear God, since you have not with-
held your son, your only son, from me."
13 And Abraham looked up and saw a ram,
caught in a thicket by its horns. Abraham
went and took the ram and offered it up as
a burnt offering instead of his son. 14 So
Abraham called that place "The LORD will
provide";[b] as it is said to this day, "On the
mount of the LORD it shall be provided."[c]

15 The angel of the LORD called to
Abraham a second time from heaven,
16 and said, "By myself I have sworn, says
the LORD: Because you have done this, and
have not withheld your son, your only son,
17 I will indeed bless you, and I will make
your offspring as numerous as the stars of
heaven and as the sand that is on the sea-
shore. And your offspring shall possess the
gate of their enemies, 18 and by your off-
spring shall all the nations of the earth gain
blessing for themselves, because you have
obeyed my voice." 19 So Abraham returned
to his young men, and they arose and went
together to Beer-sheba; and Abraham lived
at Beer-sheba.

20 Now after these things it was told
Abraham, "Milcah also has borne children,
to your brother Nahor: 21 Uz the firstborn,
Buz his brother, Kemuel the father of
Aram, 22 Chesed, Hazo, Pildash, Jidlaph,
and Bethuel." 23 Bethuel became the father
of Rebekah. These eight Milcah bore to
Nahor, Abraham's brother. 24 Moreover,
his concubine, whose name was Reumah,
bore Tebah, Gaham, Tahash, and Maacah.

a Or *to slaughter* *b* Or *will see*; Heb traditionally transliterated *Jehovah Jireh* *c* Or *he shall be seen*

(see 2 Kings 3.27). **3:** As in 12.4–6 Abraham obeys the command immediately. **5:** Abraham's promise that he and Isaac will return may suggest a faith that God will work out an alternative sacrifice (see v. 8). **9–13:** The narration slows down here, showing how close Abraham came to fulfilling the command. Some later Jewish traditions understood Abraham to have actually sacrificed (an obedient) Isaac, making both men models for later generations of Jewish martyrs. A similar image stands behind the Christian understanding of Isaac as a prefiguration of Christ. **12:** See 22.1a n. **14:** Like other characters in Genesis (e.g., Jacob in 28.19 and 32.2,30), Abraham names the place in response to his encounter with God (see 22.8; cf. 28.19; 32.30). The name *The LORD will provide* is not attested elsewhere as a place name. The mention of *Moriah* in v. 2 and of *the mount of the LORD* in v. 14 may be allusions to Jerusalem (see 1 Chr 3.1). **15–18:** This second divine call stands out as an additional divine response to his obedience (cf. vv. 11–12), this time providing a reward for Abraham's passing of the "test." **18:** See 12.3n.

22.20–24: The descendants of Abraham's brother Nahor. See ch 24.

23 Sarah lived one hundred twenty-
seven years; this was the length of
Sarah's life. 2 And Sarah died at Kiriath-
arba (that is, Hebron) in the land of Ca-
naan; and Abraham went in to mourn for
Sarah and to weep for her. 3 Abraham rose
up from beside his dead, and said to the
Hittites, 4 "I am a stranger and an alien re-
siding among you; give me property among
you for a burying place, so that I may bury
my dead out of my sight." 5 The Hittites
answered Abraham, 6 "Hear us, my lord;
you are a mighty prince among us. Bury
your dead in the choicest of our burial
places; none of us will withhold from you
any burial ground for burying your dead."
7 Abraham rose and bowed to the Hittites,
the people of the land. 8 He said to them,
"If you are willing that I should bury my
dead out of my sight, hear me, and entreat
for me Ephron son of Zohar, 9 so that he
may give me the cave of Machpelah, which
he owns; it is at the end of his field. For the
full price let him give it to me in your pres-
ence as a possession for a burying place."
10 Now Ephron was sitting among the Hit-
tites; and Ephron the Hittite answered
Abraham in the hearing of the Hittites, of
all who went in at the gate of his city,
11 "No, my lord, hear me; I give you the
field, and I give you the cave that is in it; in
the presence of my people I give it to you;
bury your dead." 12 Then Abraham bowed
down before the people of the land. 13 He
said to Ephron in the hearing of the people
of the land, "If you only will listen to me!
I will give the price of the field; accept it
from me, so that I may bury my dead
there." 14 Ephron answered Abraham,
15 "My lord, listen to me; a piece of land
worth four hundred shekels of silver—
what is that between you and me? Bury
your dead." 16 Abraham agreed with
Ephron; and Abraham weighed out for
Ephron the silver that he had named in the
hearing of the Hittites, four hundred shek-
els of silver, according to the weights cur-
rent among the merchants.

17 So the field of Ephron in Machpelah,
which was to the east of Mamre, the field
with the cave that was in it and all the trees
that were in the field, throughout its whole
area, passed 18 to Abraham as a possession
in the presence of the Hittites, in the pres-
ence of all who went in at the gate of his
city. 19 After this, Abraham buried Sarah
his wife in the cave of the field of Machpe-
lah facing Mamre (that is, Hebron) in the
land of Canaan. 20 The field and the cave
that is in it passed from the Hittites into
Abraham's possession as a burying place.

24 Now Abraham was old, well ad-
vanced in years; and the LORD had
blessed Abraham in all things. 2 Abraham
said to his servant, the oldest of his house,
who had charge of all that he had, "Put
your hand under my thigh 3 and I will make
you swear by the LORD, the God of heaven
and earth, that you will not get a wife for
my son from the daughters of the Canaan-
ites, among whom I live, 4 but will go to my
country and to my kindred and get a wife

23.1–20: Abraham's purchase of a family burial place. A late Priestly tradition. **2:** *Kiriath-arba,* the older name of Hebron (Josh 14.15; 15.13; Judg 1.10). **3:** The *Hittites* are considered at this point to be among the Canaanite peoples (see v. 7 and 10.15). **4–16:** The narrative stresses the legitimacy of the Israelites' claim to this burial plot. **10:** Legal transactions often took place at the city gate; see 34.20; Deut 20.19; 25.7; Ruth 4.1–11; 2 Sam 15.2; etc.). **15:** *Four hundred shekels,* about 4.5 kg (10 lb). **17–20:** As in many ancient cultures, the Israelites believed that burial of ancestors in a plot of land gave their heirs a sacred claim to it. The Priestly notices of the Genesis story indicate that descendants of Abraham who did not inherit the promise ended up outside Canaan (e.g., Ishmael in 25.12–18 and Esau in 36.1–43; cf. 25.1–6), while Israel's early patriarchs and matriarchs were buried in the land (25.9–10; 35.27–29; 49.29–32; 50.12–13; etc.; cf. non-Priestly traditions in 35.19–20; 50.5,25).

24.1–67: Finding a wife for Isaac among kinfolk in Haran. **2:** Putting the hand under the thigh, an old form of oath taking (47.29), reflected the view that reproductive organs were sacred. **3:** The text describes a concern in Abraham about intermarriage with Canaanites that is otherwise seen primarily in late materials from Deuteronomy (e.g., Deut 7.3–4) and texts influenced by Deuteronomy. **10:** *Aram-*

for my son Isaac." 5 The servant said to
him, "Perhaps the woman may not be will-
ing to follow me to this land; must I then
take your son back to the land from which
you came?" 6 Abraham said to him, "See to
it that you do not take my son back there.
7 The LORD, the God of heaven, who took
me from my father's house and from the
land of my birth, and who spoke to me and
swore to me, 'To your offspring I will give
this land,' he will send his angel before you,
and you shall take a wife for my son from
there. 8 But if the woman is not willing to
follow you, then you will be free from this
oath of mine; only you must not take my
son back there." 9 So the servant put his
hand under the thigh of Abraham his mas-
ter and swore to him concerning this mat-
ter.

10 Then the servant took ten of his mas-
ter's camels and departed, taking all kinds
of choice gifts from his master; and he set
out and went to Aram-naharaim, to the
city of Nahor. 11 He made the camels kneel
down outside the city by the well of water;
it was toward evening, the time when wom-
en go out to draw water. 12 And he said,
"O LORD, God of my master Abraham,
please grant me success today and show
steadfast love to my master Abraham. 13 I
am standing here by the spring of water,
and the daughters of the townspeople are
coming out to draw water. 14 Let the girl to
whom I shall say, 'Please offer your jar that
I may drink,' and who shall say, 'Drink,
and I will water your camels'—let her be
the one whom you have appointed for your
servant Isaac. By this I shall know that you
have shown steadfast love to my master."

15 Before he had finished speaking,
there was Rebekah, who was born to Be-
thuel son of Milcah, the wife of Nahor,
Abraham's brother, coming out with her
water jar on her shoulder. 16 The girl was
very fair to look upon, a virgin, whom no
man had known. She went down to the
spring, filled her jar, and came up. 17 Then
the servant ran to meet her and said,
"Please let me sip a little water from your
jar." 18 "Drink, my lord," she said, and
quickly lowered her jar upon her hand and
gave him a drink. 19 When she had finished
giving him a drink, she said, "I will draw
for your camels also, until they have fin-
ished drinking." 20 So she quickly emptied
her jar into the trough and ran again to the
well to draw, and she drew for all his cam-
els. 21 The man gazed at her in silence to
learn whether or not the LORD had made
his journey successful.

22 When the camels had finished drink-
ing, the man took a gold nose-ring weigh-
ing a half shekel, and two bracelets for her
arms weighing ten gold shekels, 23 and said,
"Tell me whose daughter you are. Is there
room in your father's house for us to spend
the night?" 24 She said to him, "I am the
daughter of Bethuel son of Milcah, whom
she bore to Nahor." 25 She added, "We
have plenty of straw and fodder and a place
to spend the night." 26 The man bowed his
head and worshiped the LORD 27 and said,
"Blessed be the LORD, the God of my mas-
ter Abraham, who has not forsaken his
steadfast love and his faithfulness toward
my master. As for me, the LORD has led me
on the way to the house of my master's
kin."

28 Then the girl ran and told her moth-
er's household about these things. 29 Re-
bekah had a brother whose name was La-
ban; and Laban ran out to the man, to the
spring. 30 As soon as he had seen the nose-
ring, and the bracelets on his sister's arms,
and when he heard the words of his sister
Rebekah, "Thus the man spoke to me," he
went to the man; and there he was, stand-
ing by the camels at the spring. 31 He said,
"Come in, O blessed of the LORD. Why do
you stand outside when I have prepared the
house and a place for the camels?" 32 So the
man came into the house; and Laban un-

naharaim, the upper Euphrates region of northern Syria. **12:** *Steadfast love,* NRSV's translation of a Heb term ("ḥesed") that signifies the loyalty arising from a relationship (e.g., friendship; see 1 Sam 20.8). Applied to God, it means benevolent action, loyalty manifest in deeds. **15:** See 22.20–23. **22:** A *shekel* weighed about 11.5 gr (.4 oz). **62:** *Beer-lahai-roi,* see 16.14; 25.11.

loaded the camels, and gave him straw and
fodder for the camels, and water to wash
his feet and the feet of the men who were
with him. 33 Then food was set before
him to eat; but he said, "I will not eat un-
til I have told my errand." He said,
"Speak on."
34 So he said, "I am Abraham's servant.
35 The LORD has greatly blessed my master,
and he has become wealthy; he has given
him flocks and herds, silver and gold, male
and female slaves, camels and donkeys.
36 And Sarah my master's wife bore a son to
my master when she was old; and he has
given him all that he has. 37 My master
made me swear, saying, 'You shall not take
a wife for my son from the daughters of the
Canaanites, in whose land I live; 38 but you
shall go to my father's house, to my kin-
dred, and get a wife for my son.' 39 I said to
my master, 'Perhaps the woman will not
follow me.' 40 But he said to me, 'The
LORD, before whom I walk, will send his
angel with you and make your way success-
ful. You shall get a wife for my son from
my kindred, from my father's house.
41 Then you will be free from my oath,
when you come to my kindred; even if they
will not give her to you, you will be free
from my oath.'
42 "I came today to the spring, and said,
'O LORD, the God of my master Abraham,
if now you will only make successful the
way I am going! 43 I am standing here by
the spring of water; let the young woman
who comes out to draw, to whom I shall
say, "Please give me a little water from
your jar to drink," 44 and who will say to
me, "Drink, and I will draw for your cam-
els also"—let her be the woman whom the
LORD has appointed for my master's son.'
45 "Before I had finished speaking in my
heart, there was Rebekah coming out with
her water jar on her shoulder; and she went
down to the spring, and drew. I said to her,
'Please let me drink.' 46 She quickly let
down her jar from her shoulder, and said,
'Drink, and I will also water your camels.'
So I drank, and she also watered the cam-
els. 47 Then I asked her, 'Whose daughter
are you?' She said, 'The daughter of Bethu-
el, Nahor's son, whom Milcah bore to
him.' So I put the ring on her nose, and the
bracelets on her arms. 48 Then I bowed my
head and worshiped the LORD, and blessed
the LORD, the God of my master Abraham,
who had led me by the right way to obtain
the daughter of my master's kinsman for
his son. 49 Now then, if you will deal loyally
and truly with my master, tell me; and if
not, tell me, so that I may turn either to the
right hand or to the left."
50 Then Laban and Bethuel answered,
"The thing comes from the LORD; we can-
not speak to you anything bad or good.
51 Look, Rebekah is before you, take her
and go, and let her be the wife of your mas-
ter's son, as the LORD has spoken."
52 When Abraham's servant heard their
words, he bowed himself to the ground be-
fore the LORD. 53 And the servant brought
out jewelry of silver and of gold, and gar-
ments, and gave them to Rebekah; he also
gave to her brother and to her mother cost-
ly ornaments. 54 Then he and the men who
were with him ate and drank, and they
spent the night there. When they rose in the
morning, he said, "Send me back to my
master." 55 Her brother and her mother
said, "Let the girl remain with us a while, at
least ten days; after that she may go." 56 But
he said to them, "Do not delay me, since
the LORD has made my journey successful;
let me go that I may go to my master."
57 They said, "We will call the girl, and ask
her." 58 And they called Rebekah, and said
to her, "Will you go with this man?" She
said, "I will." 59 So they sent away their
sister Rebekah and her nurse along with
Abraham's servant and his men. 60 And
they blessed Rebekah and said to her,

"May you, our sister, become
thousands of myriads;
may your offspring gain possession
of the gates of their foes."

61 Then Rebekah and her maids rose up,
mounted the camels, and followed the man;
thus the servant took Rebekah, and went
his way.
62 Now Isaac had come from[a] Beer-

a Syr Tg: Heb *from coming to*

lahai-roi, and was settled in the Negeb.
63 Isaac went out in the evening to walk[a] in
the field; and looking up, he saw camels
coming. 64 And Rebekah looked up, and
when she saw Isaac, she slipped quickly
from the camel, 65 and said to the servant,
"Who is the man over there, walking in the
field to meet us?" The servant said, "It is
my master." So she took her veil and cov-
ered herself. 66 And the servant told Isaac
all the things that he had done. 67 Then
Isaac brought her into his mother Sarah's
tent. He took Rebekah, and she became his
wife; and he loved her. So Isaac was com-
forted after his mother's death.

25 Abraham took another wife, whose
name was Keturah. 2 She bore him
Zimran, Jokshan, Medan, Midian, Ishbak,
and Shuah. 3 Jokshan was the father of She-
ba and Dedan. The sons of Dedan were
Asshurim, Letushim, and Leummim. 4 The
sons of Midian were Ephah, Epher, Ha-
noch, Abida, and Eldaah. All these were the
children of Keturah. 5 Abraham gave all he
had to Isaac. 6 But to the sons of his concu-
bines Abraham gave gifts, while he was still
living, and he sent them away from his son
Isaac, eastward to the east country.

7 This is the length of Abraham's life,
one hundred seventy-five years. 8 Abraham
breathed his last and died in a good old age,
an old man and full of years, and was gath-
ered to his people. 9 His sons Isaac and Ish-
mael buried him in the cave of Machpelah,
in the field of Ephron son of Zohar the
Hittite, east of Mamre, 10 the field that
Abraham purchased from the Hittites.
There Abraham was buried, with his wife
Sarah. 11 After the death of Abraham God
blessed his son Isaac. And Isaac settled at
Beer-lahai-roi.

12 These are the descendants of Ishmael,
Abraham's son, whom Hagar the Egyptian,
Sarah's slave-girl, bore to Abraham.
13 These are the names of the sons of Ishma-
el, named in the order of their birth: Neba-
ioth, the firstborn of Ishmael; and Kedar,
Adbeel, Mibsam, 14 Mishma, Dumah, Mas-
sa, 15 Hadad, Tema, Jetur, Naphish, and
Kedemah. 16 These are the sons of Ishmael
and these are their names, by their villages
and by their encampments, twelve princes
according to their tribes. 17 (This is the
length of the life of Ishmael, one hundred
thirty-seven years; he breathed his last and
died, and was gathered to his people.)
18 They settled from Havilah to Shur, which
is opposite Egypt in the direction of Assyr-
ia; he settled down[b] alongside of[c] all his
people.

19 These are the descendants of Isaac,
Abraham's son: Abraham was the father of
Isaac, 20 and Isaac was forty years old when
he married Rebekah, daughter of Bethuel
the Aramean of Paddan-aram, sister of La-
ban the Aramean. 21 Isaac prayed to the
LORD for his wife, because she was barren;
and the LORD granted his prayer, and his
wife Rebekah conceived. 22 The children
struggled together within her; and she said,
"If it is to be this way, why do I live?"[d] So
she went to inquire of the LORD. 23 And the
LORD said to her,

"Two nations are in your womb,
and two peoples born of you shall
be divided;

a Meaning of Heb word is uncertain *b* Heb *he fell*
c Or *down in opposition to* *d* Syr: Meaning of Heb
uncertain

25.1–11: The death of Abraham. 1–6: The ancestry of Arabian tribes, including Midian (Ex 2.15b–22; 18.1–27), is traced to Abraham through his other wife, Keturah. **9–11:** See ch 23. **11:** *Beer-lahai-roi,* see 16.14; 24.62.

25.12–18: Overview of the descendants of Ishmael (cf. 36.1–43). Before the narrative discusses the descendants of Isaac (25.19–35.29), it gives an overview of the descendants of Ishmael, the firstborn son of Abraham. **16:** Like Israel, the Ishmaelites are said to have twelve tribes. **18:** The Ishmaelites are placed in the desert on either side of the Red Sea. See Map on p. 24 HB.

25.19–28: Introduction of the descendants of Isaac. 19–20: Introductory Priestly material. **22–23:** The narrative presupposes an ancient practice of seeking a divine oracle at a local sanctuary. **25:** The Heb

the one shall be stronger than the
other,
the elder shall serve the younger."
24 When her time to give birth was at hand,
there were twins in her womb. 25 The first
came out red, all his body like a hairy man-
tle; so they named him Esau. 26 Afterward
his brother came out, with his hand grip-
ping Esau's heel; so he was named Jacob.[a]
Isaac was sixty years old when she bore
them.
27 When the boys grew up, Esau was a
skillful hunter, a man of the field, while
Jacob was a quiet man, living in tents.
28 Isaac loved Esau, because he was fond of
game; but Rebekah loved Jacob.
29 Once when Jacob was cooking a
stew, Esau came in from the field, and he
was famished. 30 Esau said to Jacob, "Let
me eat some of that red stuff, for I am fam-
ished!" (Therefore he was called Edom.[b])
31 Jacob said, "First sell me your birth-
right." 32 Esau said, "I am about to die; of
what use is a birthright to me?" 33 Jacob
said, "Swear to me first."[c] So he swore
to him, and sold his birthright to Jacob.
34 Then Jacob gave Esau bread and lentil
stew, and he ate and drank, and rose and
went his way. Thus Esau despised his birth-
right.

26 Now there was a famine in the land,
besides the former famine that had
occurred in the days of Abraham. And
Isaac went to Gerar, to King Abimelech
of the Philistines. 2 The LORD appeared to
Isaac[d] and said, "Do not go down to
Egypt; settle in the land that I shall show
you. 3 Reside in this land as an alien, and I
will be with you, and will bless you; for to
you and to your descendants I will give all
these lands, and I will fulfill the oath that
I swore to your father Abraham. 4 I will
make your offspring as numerous as the
stars of heaven, and will give to your off-
spring all these lands; and all the nations of
the earth shall gain blessing for themselves
through your offspring, 5 because Abraham
obeyed my voice and kept my charge, my
commandments, my statutes, and my laws."
6 So Isaac settled in Gerar. 7 When the
men of the place asked him about his wife,
he said, "She is my sister"; for he was
afraid to say, "My wife," thinking, "or else
the men of the place might kill me for the
sake of Rebekah, because she is attractive
in appearance." 8 When Isaac had been
there a long time, King Abimelech of the

a That is *He takes by the heel* or *He supplants*
b That is *Red* *c* Heb *today* *d* Heb *him*

word for *red* ("ʾadmoni") is a play on the word "Edom" ("ʾedom"; v. 30); *hairy* ("seʿar") is a play on Seir, the region of the Edomites (32.3). **26:** *Jacob* is interpreted by a play on the Hebrew word for "heel," i.e., "he takes by the heel" or "he supplants"; see Hos 12.3. **27–28:** As in the Cain and Abel story, this narrative plays on the tension between the hunter and the shepherd (4.2).

25.29–34: Jacob buys Esau's birthright. 30: See 25.25n. **31–34:** The *birthright* refers to the extra rights that normally go to the eldest son: leadership of the family and a double share of the inheritance (Deut 21.15–17). This caricature of Esau as a dull person, outwitted on an empty stomach, is intended to explain Israel's domination of Edom during the time of David and Solomon (2 Sam 8.9–14; 1 Kings 11.14–22) and/or later (1 Kings 3.9–12; 8.20–22).

26.1–33: Interlude on Isaac. Whereas the surrounding sections focus primarily on Isaac's descendants, this chapter focuses on Isaac apart from his children. Although relatively little is told about Isaac, it is significant that each element makes him parallel to his father Abraham: the initial note linking his trip to Gerar with Abraham's initial journey to Egypt (v. 1; cf. 12.10), the travel command and promise (vv. 2–5; see 12.1–3n.; 22.18n.), the story of endangerment of the matriarch (vv. 6–11; cf. 12.10–13.1 and 20.1–18), the manifestation of blessing on Isaac (vv. 12–14; cf. 12.16; 20.14), the recognition of that blessing by Abimelech (v. 28; cf. 21.22), and the well stories (vv. 17–33; see 21.22–34n.). By the end of the chapter it is clear that Isaac has successfully inherited Abraham's blessing and is thus prepared to pass it on to one of his sons (see ch 27). **8:** *Fondling,* Heb "metsaheq," another reference to Isaac's name; see 18.12n. **33:** Another explanation of the name "Beer-sheba"; see 21.22–34n.

Philistines looked out of a window and saw
him fondling his wife Rebekah. 9 So Abime-
lech called for Isaac, and said, "So she is
your wife! Why then did you say, 'She is
my sister'?" Isaac said to him, "Because I
thought I might die because of her."
10 Abimelech said, "What is this you have
done to us? One of the people might easily
have lain with your wife, and you would
have brought guilt upon us." 11 So Abime-
lech warned all the people, saying, "Who-
ever touches this man or his wife shall be
put to death."

12 Isaac sowed seed in that land, and in
the same year reaped a hundredfold. The
LORD blessed him, 13 and the man became
rich; he prospered more and more until he
became very wealthy. 14 He had possessions
of flocks and herds, and a great household,
so that the Philistines envied him. 15 (Now
the Philistines had stopped up and filled
with earth all the wells that his father's ser-
vants had dug in the days of his father
Abraham.) 16 And Abimelech said to Isaac,
"Go away from us; you have become too
powerful for us."

17 So Isaac departed from there and
camped in the valley of Gerar and settled
there. 18 Isaac dug again the wells of water
that had been dug in the days of his father
Abraham; for the Philistines had stopped
them up after the death of Abraham; and
he gave them the names that his father had
given them. 19 But when Isaac's servants
dug in the valley and found there a well of
spring water, 20 the herders of Gerar quar-
reled with Isaac's herders, saying, "The wa-
ter is ours." So he called the well Esek,[a]
because they contended with him. 21 Then
they dug another well, and they quarreled
over that one also; so he called it Sitnah.[b]
22 He moved from there and dug another
well, and they did not quarrel over it; so he
called it Rehoboth,[c] saying, "Now the
LORD has made room for us, and we shall
be fruitful in the land."

23 From there he went up to Beer-sheba.
24 And that very night the LORD appeared
to him and said, "I am the God of your
father Abraham; do not be afraid, for I am
with you and will bless you and make your
offspring numerous for my servant Abra-
ham's sake." 25 So he built an altar there,
called on the name of the LORD, and
pitched his tent there. And there Isaac's ser-
vants dug a well.

26 Then Abimelech went to him from
Gerar, with Ahuzzath his adviser and Phi-
col the commander of his army. 27 Isaac
said to them, "Why have you come to me,
seeing that you hate me and have sent me
away from you?" 28 They said, "We see
plainly that the LORD has been with you; so
we say, let there be an oath between you
and us, and let us make a covenant with
you 29 so that you will do us no harm, just
as we have not touched you and have done
to you nothing but good and have sent you
away in peace. You are now the blessed of
the LORD." 30 So he made them a feast, and
they ate and drank. 31 In the morning they
rose early and exchanged oaths; and Isaac
set them on their way, and they departed
from him in peace. 32 That same day Isaac's
servants came and told him about the well
that they had dug, and said to him, "We
have found water!" 33 He called it Shibah;[d]
therefore the name of the city is Beer-
sheba[e] to this day.

34 When Esau was forty years old, he
married Judith daughter of Beeri the Hit-
tite, and Basemath daughter of Elon the
Hittite; 35 and they made life bitter for Isaac
and Rebekah.

27 When Isaac was old and his eyes
were dim so that he could not see,
he called his elder son Esau and said to him,
"My son"; and he answered, "Here I am."

a That is *Contention* *b* That is *Enmity* *c* That is *Broad places* or *Room* *d* A word resembling the word for *oath* *e* That is *Well of the oath* or *Well of seven*

26.34–28.4: The transfer of blessing to Jacob and not Esau. 26.34–35 (cf. 28.8–9 and 36.2–3): This Priestly note on Esau's difficult marriages was originally connected with 27.46–28.9 (P). Now, however, it helps legitimate the following story about how he was tricked out of his father's blessing. **27.1–45:** This non-Priestly (J) story of Rebekah and Jacob's cunning resembles "trickster" traditions in

2 He said, "See, I am old; I do not know the
day of my death. 3 Now then, take your
weapons, your quiver and your bow, and
go out to the field, and hunt game for me.
4 Then prepare for me savory food, such as
I like, and bring it to me to eat, so that I
may bless you before I die."

5 Now Rebekah was listening when
Isaac spoke to his son Esau. So when Esau
went to the field to hunt for game and bring
it, 6 Rebekah said to her son Jacob, "I heard
your father say to your brother Esau,
7 'Bring me game, and prepare for me sa-
vory food to eat, that I may bless you be-
fore the LORD before I die.' 8 Now there-
fore, my son, obey my word as I command
you. 9 Go to the flock, and get me two
choice kids, so that I may prepare from
them savory food for your father, such as
he likes; 10 and you shall take it to your
father to eat, so that he may bless you be-
fore he dies." 11 But Jacob said to his moth-
er Rebekah, "Look, my brother Esau is a
hairy man, and I am a man of smooth skin.
12 Perhaps my father will feel me, and I shall
seem to be mocking him, and bring a curse
on myself and not a blessing." 13 His moth-
er said to him, "Let your curse be on me,
my son; only obey my word, and go, get
them for me." 14 So he went and got them
and brought them to his mother; and his
mother prepared savory food, such as his
father loved. 15 Then Rebekah took the best
garments of her elder son Esau, which were
with her in the house, and put them on her
younger son Jacob; 16 and she put the skins
of the kids on his hands and on the smooth
part of his neck. 17 Then she handed the
savory food, and the bread that she had
prepared, to her son Jacob.

18 So he went in to his father, and said,
"My father"; and he said, "Here I am; who
are you, my son?" 19 Jacob said to his fa-
ther, "I am Esau your firstborn. I have done
as you told me; now sit up and eat of my
game, so that you may bless me." 20 But
Isaac said to his son, "How is it that you
have found it so quickly, my son?" He an-
swered, "Because the LORD your God
granted me success." 21 Then Isaac said to
Jacob, "Come near, that I may feel you, my
son, to know whether you are really my son
Esau or not." 22 So Jacob went up to his
father Isaac, who felt him and said, "The
voice is Jacob's voice, but the hands are the
hands of Esau." 23 He did not recognize
him, because his hands were hairy like his
brother Esau's hands; so he blessed him.
24 He said, "Are you really my son Esau?"
He answered, "I am." 25 Then he said,
"Bring it to me, that I may eat of my son's
game and bless you." So he brought it to
him, and he ate; and he brought him wine,
and he drank. 26 Then his father Isaac said
to him, "Come near and kiss me, my son."
27 So he came near and kissed him; and
he smelled the smell of his garments, and
blessed him, and said,

"Ah, the smell of my son
  is like the smell of a field that the
    LORD has blessed.
28 May God give you of the dew of
    heaven,
  and of the fatness of the earth,
  and plenty of grain and wine.
29 Let peoples serve you,
  and nations bow down to you.
Be lord over your brothers,
  and may your mother's sons bow
    down to you.
Cursed be everyone who curses you,
  and blessed be everyone who
    blesses you!"

30 As soon as Isaac had finished blessing
Jacob, when Jacob had scarcely gone out
from the presence of his father Isaac, his
brother Esau came in from his hunting.
31 He also prepared savory food, and

other cultures, where a culture hero flourishes through underhanded tactics (cf. 29.23–25; 31.19–35; 34.1–31; 38.1–30). **4:** Death-bed blessings (and curses) were important in the life and literature of ancient peoples (48.8–20; 49.1–28; etc.). It was believed that such blessings irrevocably released a tangible power that determined the character and destiny of the recipient. Ch 27 itself focuses exclusively on Isaac's blessing, but the preceding chapter (ch 26) makes clear that this is Isaac's transfer of a divine blessing first given to Abraham (12.1–3, etc.). **11:** See 25.25n. **34–35:** The blessing was believed to release a power that

brought it to his father. And he said to his
father, "Let my father sit up and eat of his
son's game, so that you may bless me."
32 His father Isaac said to him, "Who are
you?" He answered, "I am your firstborn
son, Esau." 33 Then Isaac trembled violent-
ly, and said, "Who was it then that hunted
game and brought it to me, and I ate it all[a]
before you came, and I have blessed him?—
yes, and blessed he shall be!" 34 When Esau
heard his father's words, he cried out with
an exceedingly great and bitter cry, and
said to his father, "Bless me, me also, fa-
ther!" 35 But he said, "Your brother came
deceitfully, and he has taken away your
blessing." 36 Esau said, "Is he not rightly
named Jacob?[b] For he has supplanted me
these two times. He took away my birth-
right; and look, now he has taken away my
blessing." Then he said, "Have you not
reserved a blessing for me?" 37 Isaac an-
swered Esau, "I have already made him
your lord, and I have given him all his
brothers as servants, and with grain and
wine I have sustained him. What then can I
do for you, my son?" 38 Esau said to his
father, "Have you only one blessing, fa-
ther? Bless me, me also, father!" And Esau
lifted up his voice and wept.

39 Then his father Isaac answered him:
"See, away from[c] the fatness of the
earth shall your home be,
and away from[d] the dew of heaven
on high.
40 By your sword you shall live,
and you shall serve your brother;
but when you break loose,[e]
you shall break his yoke from your
neck."

41 Now Esau hated Jacob because of the
blessing with which his father had blessed
him, and Esau said to himself, "The days of
mourning for my father are approaching;
then I will kill my brother Jacob." 42 But the
words of her elder son Esau were told to
Rebekah; so she sent and called her youn-
ger son Jacob and said to him, "Your
brother Esau is consoling himself by plan-
ning to kill you. 43 Now therefore, my son,
obey my voice; flee at once to my brother
Laban in Haran, 44 and stay with him a
while, until your brother's fury turns
away— 45 until your brother's anger
against you turns away, and he forgets
what you have done to him; then I will
send, and bring you back from there. Why
should I lose both of you in one day?"

46 Then Rebekah said to Isaac, "I am
weary of my life because of the Hittite
women. If Jacob marries one of the Hittite
women such as these, one of the women of
the land, what good will my life be to me?"

28 Then Isaac called Jacob and blessed
him, and charged him, "You shall
not marry one of the Canaanite women.
2 Go at once to Paddan-aram to the house
of Bethuel, your mother's father; and take
as wife from there one of the daughters of
Laban, your mother's brother. 3 May God
Almighty[f] bless you and make you fruitful
and numerous, that you may become a
company of peoples. 4 May he give to you
the blessing of Abraham, to you and to
your offspring with you, so that you may
take possession of the land where you now
live as an alien—land that God gave to
Abraham." 5 Thus Isaac sent Jacob away;
and he went to Paddan-aram, to Laban son
of Bethuel the Aramean, the brother of Re-
bekah, Jacob's and Esau's mother.

a Cn: Heb *of all* *b* That is *He supplants* or *He takes by the heel* *c* Or *See, of* *d* Or *and of* *e* Meaning of Heb uncertain *f* Traditional rendering of Heb *El Shaddai*

could not be retracted (see v. 4n.). **36:** See 25.26n.; 25.29–34. There is a word play in the Heb words for *my birthright* ("bekorati") and *my blessing* ("birkati"). **39:** An inversion of the same words in v. 28. **40:** See 25.31–34n. Edom repeatedly revolted from subjection by Judah (1 Kings 11.14–22; 2 Kings 8.20–22). **43:** See 24.4,29. **46:** See 26.34–35n. **27.46–28.1:** On foreign intermarriage, see 24.3n. **28.1–4:** A Priestly parallel to the preceding story (27.27–29). Compare with P in 17.1–8; 35.11–12; 48.3–4. **3:** *God Almighty,* see 17.1n.

28.5–22: The split between Jacob and Esau occurs twice here, the Priestly version in 28.5–9 and the non-Priestly account (J) in 28.10–22. **8–9:** See 26.34–35 and compare 36.2–3. **10–11:** Bethel (see

6 Now Esau saw that Isaac had blessed
Jacob and sent him away to Paddan-aram
to take a wife from there, and that as he
blessed him he charged him, “You shall not
marry one of the Canaanite women,” 7 and
that Jacob had obeyed his father and his
mother and gone to Paddan-aram. 8 So
when Esau saw that the Canaanite women
did not please his father Isaac, 9 Esau went
to Ishmael and took Mahalath daughter of
Abraham’s son Ishmael, and sister of Neba-
ioth, to be his wife in addition to the wives
he had.

10 Jacob left Beer-sheba and went to-
ward Haran. 11 He came to a certain place
and stayed there for the night, because the
sun had set. Taking one of the stones of the
place, he put it under his head and lay
down in that place. 12 And he dreamed that
there was a ladder[a] set up on the earth, the
top of it reaching to heaven; and the angels
of God were ascending and descending on
it. 13 And the LORD stood beside him[b] and
said, “I am the LORD, the God of Abraham
your father and the God of Isaac; the land
on which you lie I will give to you and to
your offspring; 14 and your offspring shall
be like the dust of the earth, and you shall
spread abroad to the west and to the east
and to the north and to the south; and all
the families of the earth shall be blessed[c] in
you and in your offspring. 15 Know that I
am with you and will keep you wherever
you go, and will bring you back to this
land; for I will not leave you until I have
done what I have promised you.” 16 Then
Jacob woke from his sleep and said, “Sure-
ly the LORD is in this place—and I did not
know it!” 17 And he was afraid, and said,
“How awesome is this place! This is none
other than the house of God, and this is the
gate of heaven.”

18 So Jacob rose early in the morning,
and he took the stone that he had put under
his head and set it up for a pillar and
poured oil on the top of it. 19 He called that
place Bethel;[d] but the name of the city was
Luz at the first. 20 Then Jacob made a vow,
saying, “If God will be with me, and will
keep me in this way that I go, and will give
me bread to eat and clothing to wear, 21 so
that I come again to my father’s house in
peace, then the LORD shall be my God,
22 and this stone, which I have set up for a
pillar, shall be God’s house; and of all that
you give me I will surely give one-tenth to
you.”

29 Then Jacob went on his journey,
and came to the land of the people
of the east. 2 As he looked, he saw a well in
the field and three flocks of sheep lying

a Or *stairway* or *ramp* *b* Or *stood above it*
c Or *shall bless themselves* *d* That is *House of God*

12.6–8n.; Map on p. 28 HB) is depicted as an unsettled place. **12:** The earliest version of this oracle described angels ascending and descending a stairway (a better translation than NRSV’s *ladder*) to heaven. This is reflected in v. 17. **13–15:** God’s appearance here is awkwardly linked to the preceding stairway vision. Therefore, many have seen another author’s hand here, either the J source (see Introduction) or a later editor. **13–14:** The promise to Jacob here after his split from Esau is similar to the promise to Abraham in 13.14–17 just after his split from Lot. On the formulation of these promises, see 12.1–3n. **15:** This portion of the divine promise relates specifically to Jacob’s journey and anticipates both his vow (vv. 20–22) and later references to this event (35.3; cf. 31.13). It may be the earliest layer of the promise speech. **16–17:** Some have seen a doubled response here by Jacob, a response to God’s appearance and speech in v. 16 and a (possibly earlier) response to the vision of the stairway in v. 17 (see v. 12n.). V. 17 explains the name “Bethel” (“house of El”) as *house of God. Gate of heaven* suggests the ancient view that a sanctuary was a place where the god came to earth, like “Babel” or “gate of God” (11.1–9). **18:** Ancient Israelite local sanctuaries featured sacred pillars, perhaps signifying male powers of fertility (see v. 22; 31.13,45–54; 35.14,20). For feminine tree imagery, see 2.8–9n. **19:** *Bethel,* see vv. 16–17n. **20–22:** This text looks toward both Jacob’s immediate trip to Haran and the longer range future of the sanctuary at Bethel. Bethel was one of the two royal sanctuaries of the Northern Kingdom (1 Kings 12.26–29; cf. 2 Kings 23.15).

29.1–30: Jacob’s marriages to Laban’s daughters. 2–12: Wells often serve as meeting places for men

there beside it; for out of that well the
flocks were watered. The stone on the
well's mouth was large, 3 and when all the
flocks were gathered there, the shepherds
would roll the stone from the mouth of the
well, and water the sheep, and put the stone
back in its place on the mouth of the well.
4 Jacob said to them, "My brothers,
where do you come from?" They said, "We
are from Haran." 5 He said to them, "Do
you know Laban son of Nahor?" They
said, "We do." 6 He said to them, "Is it well
with him?" "Yes," they replied, "and here
is his daughter Rachel, coming with the
sheep." 7 He said, "Look, it is still broad
daylight; it is not time for the animals to be
gathered together. Water the sheep, and go,
pasture them." 8 But they said, "We cannot
until all the flocks are gathered together,
and the stone is rolled from the mouth of
the well; then we water the sheep."
9 While he was still speaking with them,
Rachel came with her father's sheep; for
she kept them. 10 Now when Jacob saw Ra-
chel, the daughter of his mother's brother
Laban, and the sheep of his mother's broth-
er Laban, Jacob went up and rolled the
stone from the well's mouth, and watered
the flock of his mother's brother Laban.
11 Then Jacob kissed Rachel, and wept
aloud. 12 And Jacob told Rachel that he was
her father's kinsman, and that he was Re-
bekah's son; and she ran and told her fa-
ther.
13 When Laban heard the news about
his sister's son Jacob, he ran to meet him;
he embraced him and kissed him, and
brought him to his house. Jacob[a] told La-
ban all these things, 14 and Laban said to
him, "Surely you are my bone and my
flesh!" And he stayed with him a month.
15 Then Laban said to Jacob, "Because
you are my kinsman, should you therefore
serve me for nothing? Tell me, what shall
your wages be?" 16 Now Laban had two
daughters; the name of the elder was Leah,
and the name of the younger was Rachel.
17 Leah's eyes were lovely,[b] and Rachel
was graceful and beautiful. 18 Jacob loved
Rachel; so he said, "I will serve you seven
years for your younger daughter Rachel."
19 Laban said, "It is better that I give her to
you than that I should give her to any other
man; stay with me." 20 So Jacob served sev-
en years for Rachel, and they seemed to
him but a few days because of the love he
had for her.
21 Then Jacob said to Laban, "Give me
my wife that I may go in to her, for my time
is completed." 22 So Laban gathered togeth-
er all the people of the place, and made a
feast. 23 But in the evening he took his
daughter Leah and brought her to Jacob;
and he went in to her. 24 (Laban gave his
maid Zilpah to his daughter Leah to be her
maid.) 25 When morning came, it was Leah!
And Jacob said to Laban, "What is this you
have done to me? Did I not serve with you
for Rachel? Why then have you deceived
me?" 26 Laban said, "This is not done in
our country—giving the younger before the
firstborn. 27 Complete the week of this one,
and we will give you the other also in re-
turn for serving me another seven years."
28 Jacob did so, and completed her week;
then Laban gave him his daughter Rachel
as a wife. 29 (Laban gave his maid Bilhah to
his daughter Rachel to be her maid.) 30 So
Jacob went in to Rachel also, and he loved
Rachel more than Leah. He served Laban[c]
for another seven years.
31 When the LORD saw that Leah was

a Heb *He* *b* Meaning of Heb uncertain
c Heb *him*

and women in the cultures of the Near East. The Bible describes many such well scenes (e.g., 24.10–27; Ex 2.15–22; etc.). **10:** Jacob, the folk hero, has superhuman strength (see v. 3). **18:** Jacob asks for Rachel as a reward for service (cf. Josh 15.16–17; 1 Sam 17.25; 18.17) instead of paying the usual marriage price (34.12; Ex 22.16–17; Deut 22.29). **23–25:** Here Jacob the trickster (see 27.1–45n.) is tricked; this motive will continue throughout the Jacob story. The exchange could be made because the bride was brought veiled to the bridegroom (24.65). **27:** *The week* refers to the week of marriage festivity (Judg 14.12).

29.31–30.24: The birth of eleven of Jacob's sons and Dinah (for Benjamin's birth, see 35.16–18). This

unloved, he opened her womb; but Rachel
was barren. 32 Leah conceived and bore a
son, and she named him Reuben;[a] for she
said, "Because the LORD has looked on my
affliction; surely now my husband will love
me." 33 She conceived again and bore a son,
and said, "Because the LORD has heard[b]
that I am hated, he has given me this son
also"; and she named him Simeon. 34 Again
she conceived and bore a son, and said,
"Now this time my husband will be
joined[c] to me, because I have borne him
three sons"; therefore he was named Levi.
35 She conceived again and bore a son, and
said, "This time I will praise[d] the LORD";
therefore she named him Judah; then she
ceased bearing.

30 When Rachel saw that she bore Ja-
cob no children, she envied her sis-
ter; and she said to Jacob, "Give me chil-
dren, or I shall die!" 2 Jacob became very
angry with Rachel and said, "Am I in the
place of God, who has withheld from you
the fruit of the womb?" 3 Then she said,
"Here is my maid Bilhah; go in to her, that
she may bear upon my knees and that I too
may have children through her." 4 So she
gave him her maid Bilhah as a wife; and
Jacob went in to her. 5 And Bilhah con-
ceived and bore Jacob a son. 6 Then Rachel
said, "God has judged me, and has also
heard my voice and given me a son"; there-
fore she named him Dan.[e] 7 Rachel's maid
Bilhah conceived again and bore Jacob a
second son. 8 Then Rachel said, "With
mighty wrestlings I have wrestled[f] with
my sister, and have prevailed"; so she
named him Naphtali.

9 When Leah saw that she had ceased
bearing children, she took her maid Zilpah
and gave her to Jacob as a wife. 10 Then
Leah's maid Zilpah bore Jacob a son.
11 And Leah said, "Good fortune!" so she
named him Gad.[g] 12 Leah's maid Zilpah
bore Jacob a second son. 13 And Leah said,
"Happy am I! For the women will call me
happy"; so she named him Asher.[h]

14 In the days of wheat harvest Reuben
went and found mandrakes in the field, and
brought them to his mother Leah. Then Ra-
chel said to Leah, "Please give me some of
your son's mandrakes." 15 But she said to
her, "Is it a small matter that you have tak-
en away my husband? Would you take
away my son's mandrakes also?" Rachel
said, "Then he may lie with you tonight for
your son's mandrakes." 16 When Jacob
came from the field in the evening, Leah
went out to meet him, and said, "You must
come in to me; for I have hired you with my
son's mandrakes." So he lay with her that
night. 17 And God heeded Leah, and she
conceived and bore Jacob a fifth son.
18 Leah said, "God has given me my hire[i]
because I gave my maid to my husband"; so
she named him Issachar. 19 And Leah con-
ceived again, and she bore Jacob a sixth
son. 20 Then Leah said, "God has endowed
me with a good dowry; now my husband
will honor[j] me, because I have borne him
six sons"; so she named him Zebulun.
21 Afterwards she bore a daughter, and
named her Dinah.

22 Then God remembered Rachel, and
God heeded her and opened her womb.
23 She conceived and bore a son, and said,
"God has taken away my reproach"; 24 and
she named him Joseph,[k] saying, "May the
LORD add to me another son!"

25 When Rachel had borne Joseph, Ja-
cob said to Laban, "Send me away, that I
may go to my own home and country.
26 Give me my wives and my children for
whom I have served you, and let me go; for
you know very well the service I have given
you." 27 But Laban said to him, "If you will

a That is *See, a son* *b* Heb *shama* *c* Heb *lawah*
d Heb *hodah* *e* That is *He judged* *f* Heb *niphtal*
g That is *Fortune* *h* That is *Happy* *i* Heb *sakar*
j Heb *zabal* *k* That is *He adds*

birth of children and the later birth of flocks (30.25–43) stand at the heart of the Jacob story. The pathos of the conflict between women is expressed through folk-explanations of the names (see notes *a* to *k*). **30.14:** *Mandrakes,* roots of a potato-like plant, were thought to have aphrodisiac properties.

30.25–43: The birth of Jacob's flocks. Since striped or speckled coloration was unusual, Laban seemingly had nothing to lose. **37–40:** Ancient breeders believed that the female, at the time of conception,

allow me to say so, I have learned by divi-
nation that the LORD has blessed me be-
cause of you; 28 name your wages, and I will
give it." 29 Jacob said to him, "You yourself
know how I have served you, and how your
cattle have fared with me. 30 For you had
little before I came, and it has increased
abundantly; and the LORD has blessed you
wherever I turned. But now when shall I
provide for my own household also?" 31 He
said, "What shall I give you?" Jacob said,
"You shall not give me anything; if you will
do this for me, I will again feed your flock
and keep it: 32 let me pass through all your
flock today, removing from it every speck-
led and spotted sheep and every black
lamb, and the spotted and speckled among
the goats; and such shall be my wages. 33 So
my honesty will answer for me later, when
you come to look into my wages with you.
Every one that is not speckled and spotted
among the goats and black among the
lambs, if found with me, shall be counted
stolen." 34 Laban said, "Good! Let it be as
you have said." 35 But that day Laban re-
moved the male goats that were striped and
spotted, and all the female goats that were
speckled and spotted, every one that had
white on it, and every lamb that was black,
and put them in charge of his sons; 36 and
he set a distance of three days' journey be-
tween himself and Jacob, while Jacob was
pasturing the rest of Laban's flock.

37 Then Jacob took fresh rods of poplar
and almond and plane, and peeled white
streaks in them, exposing the white of the
rods. 38 He set the rods that he had peeled
in front of the flocks in the troughs, that is,
the watering places, where the flocks came
to drink. And since they bred when they
came to drink, 39 the flocks bred in front of
the rods, and so the flocks produced young
that were striped, speckled, and spotted.
40 Jacob separated the lambs, and set the
faces of the flocks toward the striped and
the completely black animals in the flock of
Laban; and he put his own droves apart,
and did not put them with Laban's flock.
41 Whenever the stronger of the flock were
breeding, Jacob laid the rods in the troughs
before the eyes of the flock, that they might
breed among the rods, 42 but for the feebler
of the flock he did not lay them there; so
the feebler were Laban's, and the stronger
Jacob's. 43 Thus the man grew exceedingly
rich, and had large flocks, and male and
female slaves, and camels and donkeys.

31 Now Jacob heard that the sons of
Laban were saying, "Jacob has tak-
en all that was our father's; he has gained
all this wealth from what belonged to our
father." 2 And Jacob saw that Laban did
not regard him as favorably as he did be-
fore. 3 Then the LORD said to Jacob, "Re-
turn to the land of your ancestors and to
your kindred, and I will be with you." 4 So
Jacob sent and called Rachel and Leah into
the field where his flock was, 5 and said to
them, "I see that your father does not re-
gard me as favorably as he did before. But
the God of my father has been with me.
6 You know that I have served your father
with all my strength; 7 yet your father has
cheated me and changed my wages ten
times, but God did not permit him to harm
me. 8 If he said, 'The speckled shall be your
wages,' then all the flock bore speckled;
and if he said, 'The striped shall be your
wages,' then all the flock bore striped.
9 Thus God has taken away the livestock of
your father, and given them to me.

10 "During the mating of the flock I
once had a dream in which I looked up and
saw that the male goats that leaped upon
the flock were striped, speckled, and mot-
tled. 11 Then the angel of God said to me in
the dream, 'Jacob,' and I said, 'Here I am!'
12 And he said, 'Look up and see that all the
goats that leap on the flock are striped,
speckled, and mottled; for I have seen all

was influenced by visual impressions that affect the color of the offspring. Jacob produced striped animals by putting striped sticks before the females' eyes while they were breeding.

31.1–55: Jacob's departure from Laban's family. 4–16: This speech by Jacob and reply by his wives is often assigned by scholars to a different author than the surrounding verses, generally identified as J. In it Jacob presents to his wives a particular perspective on the previously narrated events (cf. 30.25–43).

that Laban is doing to you. 13I am the God
of Bethel,[a] where you anointed a pillar and
made a vow to me. Now leave this land at
once and return to the land of your birth.' "
14Then Rachel and Leah answered him, "Is
there any portion or inheritance left to us in
our father's house? 15Are we not regarded
by him as foreigners? For he has sold us,
and he has been using up the money given
for us. 16All the property that God has tak-
en away from our father belongs to us and
to our children; now then, do whatever
God has said to you."

17 So Jacob arose, and set his children
and his wives on camels; 18and he drove
away all his livestock, all the property that
he had gained, the livestock in his posses-
sion that he had acquired in Paddan-aram,
to go to his father Isaac in the land of Ca-
naan.

19 Now Laban had gone to shear his
sheep, and Rachel stole her father's house-
hold gods. 20And Jacob deceived Laban the
Aramean, in that he did not tell him that he
intended to flee. 21So he fled with all that
he had; starting out he crossed the Euphra-
tes,[b] and set his face toward the hill coun-
try of Gilead.

22 On the third day Laban was told that
Jacob had fled. 23So he took his kinsfolk
with him and pursued him for seven days
until he caught up with him in the hill
country of Gilead. 24But God came to La-
ban the Aramean in a dream by night, and
said to him, "Take heed that you say not a
word to Jacob, either good or bad."

25 Laban overtook Jacob. Now Jacob
had pitched his tent in the hill country, and
Laban with his kinsfolk camped in the hill
country of Gilead. 26Laban said to Jacob,
"What have you done? You have deceived
me, and carried away my daughters like
captives of the sword. 27Why did you flee
secretly and deceive me and not tell me? I
would have sent you away with mirth and
songs, with tambourine and lyre. 28And
why did you not permit me to kiss my sons
and my daughters farewell? What you have
done is foolish. 29It is in my power to do
you harm; but the God of your father spoke
to me last night, saying, 'Take heed that
you speak to Jacob neither good nor bad.'
30Even though you had to go because you
longed greatly for your father's house, why
did you steal my gods?" 31Jacob answered
Laban, "Because I was afraid, for I thought
that you would take your daughters from
me by force. 32But anyone with whom you
find your gods shall not live. In the pres-
ence of our kinsfolk, point out what I have
that is yours, and take it." Now Jacob did
not know that Rachel had stolen the
gods.[c]

33 So Laban went into Jacob's tent, and
into Leah's tent, and into the tent of the
two maids, but he did not find them. And
he went out of Leah's tent, and entered Ra-
chel's. 34Now Rachel had taken the house-
hold gods and put them in the camel's sad-
dle, and sat on them. Laban felt all about in
the tent, but did not find them. 35And she
said to her father, "Let not my lord be an-
gry that I cannot rise before you, for the
way of women is upon me." So he
searched, but did not find the household
gods.

36 Then Jacob became angry, and up-
braided Laban. Jacob said to Laban,
"What is my offense? What is my sin, that
you have hotly pursued me? 37Although
you have felt about through all my goods,
what have you found of all your household
goods? Set it here before my kinsfolk and
your kinsfolk, so that they may decide be-
tween us two. 38These twenty years I have
been with you; your ewes and your female
goats have not miscarried, and I have not
eaten the rams of your flocks. 39That which
was torn by wild beasts I did not bring to
you; I bore the loss of it myself; of my hand
you required it, whether stolen by day or

a Cn: Meaning of Heb uncertain *b* Heb *the river*
c Heb *them*

13: See 28.18–22. **19–35:** The *household gods* (see 1 Sam 19.13–17) may have been figures representing ancestral deities. Possession of them ensured leadership of the family and legitimated property claims. Here Jacob's favored wife, Rachel, is the trickster (see 27.1–45n.). **35:** *The way of women,* menstruation.

stolen by night. 40 It was like this with me:
by day the heat consumed me, and the cold
by night, and my sleep fled from my eyes.
41 These twenty years I have been in your
house; I served you fourteen years for your
two daughters, and six years for your flock,
and you have changed my wages ten times.
42 If the God of my father, the God of Abra-
ham and the Fear[a] of Isaac, had not been
on my side, surely now you would have
sent me away empty-handed. God saw my
affliction and the labor of my hands, and
rebuked you last night."
43 Then Laban answered and said to Ja-
cob, "The daughters are my daughters, the
children are my children, the flocks are my
flocks, and all that you see is mine. But
what can I do today about these daughters
of mine, or about their children whom they
have borne? 44 Come now, let us make a
covenant, you and I; and let it be a witness
between you and me." 45 So Jacob took a
stone, and set it up as a pillar. 46 And Jacob
said to his kinsfolk, "Gather stones," and
they took stones, and made a heap; and
they ate there by the heap. 47 Laban called
it Jegar-sahadutha:[b] but Jacob called it
Galeed.[c] 48 Laban said, "This heap is a
witness between you and me today."
Therefore he called it Galeed, 49 and the pil-
lar[d] Mizpah,[e] for he said, "The LORD
watch between you and me, when we are
absent one from the other. 50 If you ill-treat
my daughters, or if you take wives in addi-
tion to my daughters, though no one else is
with us, remember that God is witness be-
tween you and me."
51 Then Laban said to Jacob, "See this
heap and see the pillar, which I have set
between you and me. 52 This heap is a wit-
ness, and the pillar is a witness, that I will
not pass beyond this heap to you, and you
will not pass beyond this heap and this pil-
lar to me, for harm. 53 May the God of
Abraham and the God of Nahor"—the
God of their father—"judge between us."
So Jacob swore by the Fear[a] of his father
Isaac, 54 and Jacob offered a sacrifice on the
height and called his kinsfolk to eat bread;
and they ate bread and tarried all night in
the hill country.
55[f] Early in the morning Laban rose up,
and kissed his grandchildren and his
daughters and blessed them; then he de-
parted and returned home.

32 Jacob went on his way and the an-
gels of God met him; 2 and when
Jacob saw them he said, "This is God's
camp!" So he called that place Maha-
naim.[g]
3 Jacob sent messengers before him to
his brother Esau in the land of Seir, the
country of Edom, 4 instructing them, "Thus
you shall say to my lord Esau: Thus says
your servant Jacob, 'I have lived with La-
ban as an alien, and stayed until now; 5 and
I have oxen, donkeys, flocks, male and fe-
male slaves; and I have sent to tell my lord,
in order that I may find favor in your
sight.'"
6 The messengers returned to Jacob,

a Meaning of Heb uncertain *b* In Aramaic *The heap of witness* *c* In Hebrew *The heap of witness* *d* Compare Sam: MT lacks *the pillar* *e* That is *Watchpost* *f* Ch 32.1 in Heb *g* Here taken to mean *Two camps*

42: The Heb word rendered as *Fear* in *Fear of Isaac,* is different from the Heb word usually used to speak of "fear" of the LORD. The same word clearly means "terror" or "dread" elsewhere, as in the "terror of the LORD" refrain in Isa 2.10,19,21. Some, however, have proposed alternative understandings of the word in this context, such as "refuge" of Isaac. **43–54:** The story is built around an older tradition regarding a boundary covenant between Arameans and Israelites (v. 52), both of whom laid claim to the region of Gilead in Transjordan. On the *pillar,* see 28.18n. **47:** The stone heap is given two names (see notes *b* and *c*), one in Laban's language (Aramaic) and one in Jacob's (Hebrew).

32.1–32: Journey toward Esau. 1–2: The Transjordanian town of Mahanaim was the site of important events (2 Sam 2.8–9; 17.24–29) and an administrative center in the time of Solomon (1 Kings 4.14). *Angels,* see 28.12n. **3–21:** The ever clever Jacob develops multiple strategies to appease his brother: dividing his camp (vv. 6–8), praying for divine help (vv. 9–12), and then sending several waves of livestock as a gift to Esau (vv. 13–21). **22–32:** Where Abraham unknowingly hosted divine visitors

saying, "We came to your brother Esau,
and he is coming to meet you, and four
hundred men are with him." 7 Then Jacob
was greatly afraid and distressed; and he
divided the people that were with him, and
the flocks and herds and camels, into two
companies, 8 thinking, "If Esau comes to
the one company and destroys it, then the
company that is left will escape."

9 And Jacob said, "O God of my father
Abraham and God of my father Isaac,
O LORD who said to me, 'Return to your
country and to your kindred, and I will do
you good,' 10 I am not worthy of the least of
all the steadfast love and all the faithfulness
that you have shown to your servant, for
with only my staff I crossed this Jordan;
and now I have become two companies.
11 Deliver me, please, from the hand of my
brother, from the hand of Esau, for I am
afraid of him; he may come and kill us all,
the mothers with the children. 12 Yet you
have said, 'I will surely do you good, and
make your offspring as the sand of the sea,
which cannot be counted because of their
number.'"

13 So he spent that night there, and
from what he had with him he took a
present for his brother Esau, 14 two hun-
dred female goats and twenty male goats,
two hundred ewes and twenty rams, 15 thir-
ty milch camels and their colts, forty cows
and ten bulls, twenty female donkeys and
ten male donkeys. 16 These he delivered into
the hand of his servants, every drove by
itself, and said to his servants, "Pass on
ahead of me, and put a space between
drove and drove." 17 He instructed the fore-
most, "When Esau my brother meets you,
and asks you, 'To whom do you belong?
Where are you going? And whose are these
ahead of you?' 18 then you shall say, 'They
belong to your servant Jacob; they are a
present sent to my lord Esau; and moreover
he is behind us.'" 19 He likewise instructed
the second and the third and all who fol-
lowed the droves, "You shall say the same
thing to Esau when you meet him, 20 and
you shall say, 'Moreover your servant Ja-
cob is behind us.'" For he thought, "I may
appease him with the present that goes
ahead of me, and afterwards I shall see his
face; perhaps he will accept me." 21 So the
present passed on ahead of him; and he
himself spent that night in the camp.

22 The same night he got up and took
his two wives, his two maids, and his eleven
children, and crossed the ford of the Jab-
bok. 23 He took them and sent them across
the stream, and likewise everything that he
had. 24 Jacob was left alone; and a man
wrestled with him until daybreak. 25 When
the man saw that he did not prevail against
Jacob, he struck him on the hip socket; and
Jacob's hip was put out of joint as he wres-
tled with him. 26 Then he said, "Let me go,
for the day is breaking." But Jacob said, "I
will not let you go, unless you bless me."
27 So he said to him, "What is your name?"
And he said, "Jacob." 28 Then the man[a]
said, "You shall no longer be called Jacob,
but Israel,[b] for you have striven with God
and with humans,[c] and have prevailed."
29 Then Jacob asked him, "Please tell me
your name." But he said, "Why is it that

a Heb *he* *b* That is *The one who strives with God* or *God strives* *c* Or *with divine and human beings*

(18.1–15), Jacob unknowingly fights with God (Ex 4.24–26). The narrative includes a complicated word play on the names of Jacob (Heb "yaʿaqob"), the river Jabbok ("yabboq"; modern Nahr ez-Zerqa) and *wrestled* ("wayye'abeq"; v. 24). **25:** Jacob is so strong (29.10) that he is winning the contest until his divine opponent pulls Jacob's hip out of joint. **26:** The divine being had to vanish before sunrise—a mark of the antiquity of the tradition on which this story is based. **28:** Jacob's new name reflects a new self: no longer was he the "supplanter" (25.26; 27.36), but *Israel* (35.10), which probably originally meant "El rules" (with El being the head of the Northwest Semitic pantheon). Here, however, it is interpreted to mean "the one who strives with God" (cf. Hos 12.3–4). *And with humans* refers to Jacob's strife with Esau and Laban. In this way, the community of Israel, as descendants of this god-wrestler, is depicted as a group that successfully strives with God and humans. **29:** The divine being refuses lest Jacob, by possessing the name, gain power over him. **30:** Jacob had feared to see Esau's face (v. 20), but instead you ask my name?" And there he blessed him. 30 So Jacob called the place Peniel,[a] saying, "For I have seen God face to face, and yet my life is preserved." 31 The sun rose upon him as he passed Penuel, limping because of his hip. 32 Therefore to this day the Israelites do not eat the thigh muscle that is on the hip socket, because he struck Jacob on the hip socket at the thigh muscle.

33 Now Jacob looked up and saw Esau coming, and four hundred men with him. So he divided the children among Leah and Rachel and the two maids. 2 He put the maids with their children in front, then Leah with her children, and Rachel and Joseph last of all. 3 He himself went on ahead of them, bowing himself to the ground seven times, until he came near his brother.

4 But Esau ran to meet him, and embraced him, and fell on his neck and kissed him, and they wept. 5 When Esau looked up and saw the women and children, he said, "Who are these with you?" Jacob said, "The children whom God has graciously given your servant." 6 Then the maids drew near, they and their children, and bowed down; 7 Leah likewise and her children drew near and bowed down; and finally Joseph and Rachel drew near, and they bowed down. 8 Esau said, "What do you mean by all this company that I met?" Jacob answered, "To find favor with my lord." 9 But Esau said, "I have enough, my brother; keep what you have for yourself." 10 Jacob said, "No, please; if I find favor with you, then accept my present from my hand; for truly to see your face is like seeing the face of God—since you have received me with such favor. 11 Please accept my gift that is brought to you, because God has dealt graciously with me, and because I have everything I want." So he urged him, and he took it.

12 Then Esau said, "Let us journey on our way, and I will go alongside you." 13 But Jacob said to him, "My lord knows that the children are frail and that the flocks and herds, which are nursing, are a care to me; and if they are overdriven for one day, all the flocks will die. 14 Let my lord pass on ahead of his servant, and I will lead on slowly, according to the pace of the cattle that are before me and according to the pace of the children, until I come to my lord in Seir."

15 So Esau said, "Let me leave with you some of the people who are with me." But he said, "Why should my lord be so kind to me?" 16 So Esau returned that day on his way to Seir. 17 But Jacob journeyed to Succoth,[b] and built himself a house, and made booths for his cattle; therefore the place is called Succoth.

18 Jacob came safely to the city of Shechem, which is in the land of Canaan, on his way from Paddan-aram; and he camped before the city. 19 And from the sons of Hamor, Shechem's father, he bought for one hundred pieces of money[c] the plot of land on which he had pitched his tent. 20 There

a That is *The face of God* *b* That is *Booths*
c Heb *one hundred qesitah*

saw God *face to face* and lived (see 16.13n.). **30–31:** The story is located at Penuel/Peniel ("face of El"), one of the first capitals of the Northern Kingdom (1 Kings 12.25). **32:** An Israelite prohibition against eating the thigh muscle of an animal is cited as testimony to the truth of the story. This prohibition is reflected nowhere else in the Bible.

33.1–17: Partial reunion with Esau. 10: *Like seeing the face of God,* who at Penuel (or Peniel) also proved to be gracious (32.30–31). **12–17:** Esau proposes to stay with Jacob, but Jacob sends him ahead, promising to join with him (v. 14). Jacob does not join him, however (v. 17), perhaps noting that Esau had always planned to wait to kill him until their father died (27.41; cf. 35.29). **17:** *Succoth* means "booths." Its precise location is uncertain.

33.18–35.5: The stay in Shechem and the rape of Dinah. 33.18: *Shechem,* see 12.6–8n. **19:** Here and in the following chapter *Shechem* is a personal name. As elsewhere in Genesis, the story portrays, in the guise of individuals, relations between Israel and non-Israelite groups. **20:** The name of the altar ("El is

he erected an altar and called it El-Elohe-
Israel.[a]

34 Now Dinah the daughter of Leah,
whom she had borne to Jacob, went
out to visit the women of the region.
2 When Shechem son of Hamor the Hivite,
prince of the region, saw her, he seized her
and lay with her by force. 3 And his soul
was drawn to Dinah daughter of Jacob; he
loved the girl, and spoke tenderly to her.
4 So Shechem spoke to his father Hamor,
saying, "Get me this girl to be my wife."
5 Now Jacob heard that Shechem[b] had
defiled his daughter Dinah; but his sons
were with his cattle in the field, so Jacob
held his peace until they came. 6 And Ha-
mor the father of Shechem went out to Ja-
cob to speak with him, 7 just as the sons of
Jacob came in from the field. When they
heard of it, the men were indignant and
very angry, because he had committed an
outrage in Israel by lying with Jacob's
daughter, for such a thing ought not to be
done.
8 But Hamor spoke with them, saying,
"The heart of my son Shechem longs for
your daughter; please give her to him in
marriage. 9 Make marriages with us; give
your daughters to us, and take our daugh-
ters for yourselves. 10 You shall live with us;
and the land shall be open to you; live and
trade in it, and get property in it." 11 She-
chem also said to her father and to her
brothers, "Let me find favor with you, and
whatever you say to me I will give. 12 Put
the marriage present and gift as high as you
like, and I will give whatever you ask me;
only give me the girl to be my wife."
13 The sons of Jacob answered Shechem
and his father Hamor deceitfully, because
he had defiled their sister Dinah. 14 They
said to them, "We cannot do this thing, to
give our sister to one who is uncircumcised,
for that would be a disgrace to us. 15 Only
on this condition will we consent to you:
that you will become as we are and every
male among you be circumcised. 16 Then
we will give our daughters to you, and we
will take your daughters for ourselves, and
we will live among you and become one
people. 17 But if you will not listen to us
and be circumcised, then we will take our
daughter and be gone."
18 Their words pleased Hamor and Ha-
mor's son Shechem. 19 And the young man
did not delay to do the thing, because he
was delighted with Jacob's daughter. Now
he was the most honored of all his family.
20 So Hamor and his son Shechem came to
the gate of their city and spoke to the men
of their city, saying, 21 "These people are
friendly with us; let them live in the land
and trade in it, for the land is large enough
for them; let us take their daughters in mar-
riage, and let us give them our daughters.
22 Only on this condition will they agree to
live among us, to become one people: that
every male among us be circumcised as they
are circumcised. 23 Will not their livestock,
their property, and all their animals be
ours? Only let us agree with them, and they
will live among us." 24 And all who went
out of the city gate heeded Hamor and his
son Shechem; and every male was circum-

a That is *God, the God of Israel* *b* Heb *he*

the God of Israel") may be another reflection of the worship of El in early Israel (see 28.16–17n.; 32.28,31–32n.). **34.1–31:** See 49.1–28n. **2:** See 33.19n. *Lay with her by force,* raped her. **7:** *Committed an outrage in Israel* is an old expression for ultimate offenses, such as violations of the sexual honor of the tribal group (here), the ban on booty in holy war (Josh 7.15), and the sanctity of hospitality (Judg 19.23–24; 20.6,10). **8–12:** Israelite law stipulates that a man who has sex with an unbetrothed woman must retroactively marry her by paying her father a high marriage price (Ex 22.16–17; Deut 22.28–29). This narrative seems to assume that this law does not apply outside the people of Israel. **13–17:** Jacob's sons now are the tricksters (see 27.1–45n.). On circumcision see 17.9–14n. **21–23:** In contrast to Hamor's proposal to the Israelites of intermarriage and acquisition of land (vv. 8–10), his speech to his countrymen here betrays an interest in impoverishing the Israelites through assimilating them. On concern about intermarriage, see 24.3n. **25–26:** Simeon and Levi lead the killing and recapture of Dinah because, as older full brothers of Dinah (29.33–34; 30.21), they were responsible for avenging the violation of

cised, all who went out of the gate of his
city.
25 On the third day, when they were
still in pain, two of the sons of Jacob, Sime-
on and Levi, Dinah's brothers, took their
swords and came against the city unawares,
and killed all the males. 26 They killed Ha-
mor and his son Shechem with the sword,
and took Dinah out of Shechem's house,
and went away. 27 And the other sons of
Jacob came upon the slain, and plundered
the city, because their sister had been de-
filed. 28 They took their flocks and their
herds, their donkeys, and whatever was in
the city and in the field. 29 All their wealth,
all their little ones and their wives, all that
was in the houses, they captured and made
their prey. 30 Then Jacob said to Simeon
and Levi, "You have brought trouble on
me by making me odious to the inhabitants
of the land, the Canaanites and the Periz-
zites; my numbers are few, and if they gath-
er themselves against me and attack me, I
shall be destroyed, both I and my house-
hold." 31 But they said, "Should our sister
be treated like a whore?"

35 God said to Jacob, "Arise, go up to
Bethel, and settle there. Make an al-
tar there to the God who appeared to you
when you fled from your brother Esau."
2 So Jacob said to his household and to all
who were with him, "Put away the foreign
gods that are among you, and purify your-
selves, and change your clothes; 3 then
come, let us go up to Bethel, that I may
make an altar there to the God who an-
swered me in the day of my distress and has
been with me wherever I have gone." 4 So
they gave to Jacob all the foreign gods that
they had, and the rings that were in their
ears; and Jacob hid them under the oak that
was near Shechem.
5 As they journeyed, a terror from God
fell upon the cities all around them, so that
no one pursued them. 6 Jacob came to Luz
(that is, Bethel), which is in the land of Ca-
naan, he and all the people who were with
him, 7 and there he built an altar and called
the place El-bethel,[a] because it was there
that God had revealed himself to him when
he fled from his brother. 8 And Deborah,
Rebekah's nurse, died, and she was buried
under an oak below Bethel. So it was called
Allon-bacuth.[b]
9 God appeared to Jacob again when he
came from Paddan-aram, and he blessed
him. 10 God said to him, "Your name is
Jacob; no longer shall you be called Jacob,
but Israel shall be your name." So he was
called Israel. 11 God said to him, "I am God
Almighty:[c] be fruitful and multiply; a na-
tion and a company of nations shall come
from you, and kings shall spring from you.
12 The land that I gave to Abraham and
Isaac I will give to you, and I will give the
land to your offspring after you." 13 Then
God went up from him at the place where

a That is *God of Bethel* *b* That is *Oak of weeping*
c Traditional rendering of Heb *El Shaddai*

the family's honor through her. **27–29:** In a reversal of what the Shechemites had planned for them (vv. 21–23), the Israelites take all the Shechemites' possessions. **30–31:** Jacob is depicted here as less concerned about family honor than about good relations with the Canaanites (see 35.5). His sons' question is left unanswered at the end of the story (cf. Jon 4.11), but is ultimately addressed in 49.5–7. **35.1–4:** The present narrative reflects a negative judgment on non-Yahwistic cult objects that developed later in Israel. It and its parallels (Josh 24.23; Judg 10.16; 1 Sam 7.3) may presuppose, however, a more ancient practice of burial of divine images in sacred places, i.e., by a sacred tree (see 12.6–8n.). **5:** Jacob's fears (see 34.30) prove to be unfounded.

35.6–15: Jacob's return to Bethel (cf. 28.10–22). **6–7:** In the ancient world deities had local manifestations (e.g., Yahweh of Samaria, Yahweh of Teman). Jacob honors the local manifestation of El at Bethel by calling the sanctuary there "El of Bethel." **8:** Once again a tree is associated with a revered sanctuary (see 12.6–8n.). **9–15:** A Priestly parallel to the non-Priestly renaming tradition in 32.28 and the Bethel tradition in 28.10–22. **10:** Cf. 32.28. **11–12:** Cf. non-P, 28.13–15. The divine fulfillment of Isaac's wish (28.3–4) that God bestow Abraham's blessing (17.1–8) on Jacob. **11:** *God Almighty,* see 17.1n.

he had spoken with him. 14 Jacob set up a
pillar in the place where he had spoken
with him, a pillar of stone; and he poured
out a drink offering on it, and poured oil on
it. 15 So Jacob called the place where God
had spoken with him Bethel.

16 Then they journeyed from Bethel;
and when they were still some distance
from Ephrath, Rachel was in childbirth,
and she had hard labor. 17 When she was in
her hard labor, the midwife said to her,
"Do not be afraid; for now you will have
another son." 18 As her soul was departing
(for she died), she named him Ben-oni;[a]
but his father called him Benjamin.[b] 19 So
Rachel died, and she was buried on the way
to Ephrath (that is, Bethlehem), 20 and Ja-
cob set up a pillar at her grave; it is the
pillar of Rachel's tomb, which is there to
this day. 21 Israel journeyed on, and pitched
his tent beyond the tower of Eder.

22 While Israel lived in that land, Reu-
ben went and lay with Bilhah his father's
concubine; and Israel heard of it.

Now the sons of Jacob were twelve.
23 The sons of Leah: Reuben (Jacob's first-
born), Simeon, Levi, Judah, Issachar, and
Zebulun. 24 The sons of Rachel: Joseph and
Benjamin. 25 The sons of Bilhah, Rachel's
maid: Dan and Naphtali. 26 The sons of Zil-
pah, Leah's maid: Gad and Asher. These
were the sons of Jacob who were born to
him in Paddan-aram.

27 Jacob came to his father Isaac at
Mamre, or Kiriath-arba (that is, Hebron),
where Abraham and Isaac had resided as
aliens. 28 Now the days of Isaac were one
hundred eighty years. 29 And Isaac breathed
his last; he died and was gathered to his
people, old and full of days; and his sons
Esau and Jacob buried him.

36 These are the descendants of Esau
(that is, Edom). 2 Esau took his
wives from the Canaanites: Adah daughter
of Elon the Hittite, Oholibamah daughter
of Anah son[c] of Zibeon the Hivite, 3 and
Basemath, Ishmael's daughter, sister of Ne-
baioth. 4 Adah bore Eliphaz to Esau; Base-
math bore Reuel; 5 and Oholibamah bore
Jeush, Jalam, and Korah. These are the
sons of Esau who were born to him in the
land of Canaan.

6 Then Esau took his wives, his sons,
his daughters, and all the members of his
household, his cattle, all his livestock, and
all the property he had acquired in the land
of Canaan; and he moved to a land some
distance from his brother Jacob. 7 For their

a That is *Son of my sorrow* *b* That is *Son of the right hand* or *Son of the South* *c* Sam Gk Syr: Heb *daughter*

13: P stresses that God is not bound to Bethel in the way asserted in the non-Priestly Bethel narratives (28.10–22; 32.6–7). God merely spoke there and left. **14:** In a P doublet of 28.18–19, Jacob sets up a pillar at Bethel (see 28.18n.) and (re)names the place.

35.16–21: The birth of Benjamin and death of Rachel. 18: Dying in childbirth, Rachel gives an ominous name ("son of my sorrow") to the baby. In this instance (cf. 29.31–30.24) the father overrules his wife's naming and gives him a more propitious one. *Benjamin* (see note *b*) refers either to the right hand as a symbol of power or to the tribe's position south ("right") of Ephraim. **19:** Here and in 48.7 the tomb of Rachel is located near Bethlehem (south of Jerusalem). Compare 1 Sam 10.2 and Jer 31.15. **20:** On pillars, see 28.18n. **21:** From this point on the name *Israel* is often used to refer to Jacob (32.28).

35.22–26: Concluding materials on Jacob's sons and Isaac's death and burial. 22a: This aside describes how Reuben violated his father's honor by sleeping with Jacob's concubine, the servant of recently deceased Rachel, Bilhah (29.29; 30.3–8). Later he will be cursed for this act (see 49.3–4n.). **22b–29:** A Priestly listing of Jacob's sons and the death and burial notice of Isaac.

36.1–43: Overview of the descendants of Esau and prior inhabitants of Edom/Seir. Cf. 25.12–18. Before the narrative goes into detail on the descendants of Jacob (37.2–50.26), it gives an overview (largely Priestly) of the descendants of Esau, the firstborn son of Isaac. **2–3:** Though this note agrees with other Priestly material in stressing his intermarriage with foreigners, the names and/or parentage of Esau's wives is different here (cf. 26.34–35; 28.8–9). **6–8:** Echoes the (non-Priestly) story of Abraham's split from Lot (13.2–13). **9–14:** A list of Esau's descendants organized by the mother (cf. 35.23–26). **9:** The

possessions were too great for them to live
together; the land where they were staying
could not support them because of their
livestock. 8So Esau settled in the hill coun-
try of Seir; Esau is Edom.
9 These are the descendants of Esau, an-
cestor of the Edomites, in the hill country
of Seir. 10These are the names of Esau's
sons: Eliphaz son of Adah the wife of Esau;
Reuel, the son of Esau's wife Basemath.
11The sons of Eliphaz were Teman, Omar,
Zepho, Gatam, and Kenaz. 12(Timna was a
concubine of Eliphaz, Esau's son; she bore
Amalek to Eliphaz.) These were the sons of
Adah, Esau's wife. 13These were the sons of
Reuel: Nahath, Zerah, Shammah, and Miz-
zah. These were the sons of Esau's wife,
Basemath. 14These were the sons of Esau's
wife Oholibamah, daughter of Anah son[a]
of Zibeon: she bore to Esau Jeush, Jalam,
and Korah.
15 These are the clans[b] of the sons of
Esau. The sons of Eliphaz the firstborn of
Esau: the clans[b] Teman, Omar, Zepho,
Kenaz, 16Korah, Gatam, and Amalek; these
are the clans[b] of Eliphaz in the land of
Edom; they are the sons of Adah. 17These
are the sons of Esau's son Reuel: the clans[b]
Nahath, Zerah, Shammah, and Mizzah;
these are the clans[b] of Reuel in the land of
Edom; they are the sons of Esau's wife Bas-
emath. 18These are the sons of Esau's wife
Oholibamah: the clans[b] Jeush, Jalam, and
Korah; these are the clans[b] born of Esau's
wife Oholibamah, the daughter of Anah.
19These are the sons of Esau (that is,
Edom), and these are their clans.[b]
20 These are the sons of Seir the Horite,
the inhabitants of the land: Lotan, Shobal,
Zibeon, Anah, 21Dishon, Ezer, and Dishan;
these are the clans[b] of the Horites, the sons
of Seir in the land of Edom. 22The sons of
Lotan were Hori and Heman; and Lotan's
sister was Timna. 23These are the sons of
Shobal: Alvan, Manahath, Ebal, Shepho,
and Onam. 24These are the sons of Zibeon:
Aiah and Anah; he is the Anah who found
the springs[c] in the wilderness, as he pas-
tured the donkeys of his father Zibeon.
25These are the children of Anah: Dishon
and Oholibamah daughter of Anah.
26These are the sons of Dishon: Hemdan,
Eshban, Ithran, and Cheran. 27These are
the sons of Ezer: Bilhan, Zaavan, and
Akan. 28These are the sons of Dishan: Uz
and Aran. 29These are the clans[b] of the
Horites: the clans[b] Lotan, Shobal, Zibeon,
Anah, 30Dishon, Ezer, and Dishan; these
are the clans[b] of the Horites, clan by clan[d]
in the land of Seir.
31 These are the kings who reigned in
the land of Edom, before any king reigned
over the Israelites. 32Bela son of Beor
reigned in Edom, the name of his city being
Dinhabah. 33Bela died, and Jobab son of
Zerah of Bozrah succeeded him as king.
34Jobab died, and Husham of the land of
the Temanites succeeded him as king.
35Husham died, and Hadad son of Bedad,
who defeated Midian in the country of
Moab, succeeded him as king, the name of
his city being Avith. 36Hadad died, and
Samlah of Masrekah succeeded him as
king. 37Samlah died, and Shaul of Reho-
both on the Euphrates succeeded him as
king. 38Shaul died, and Baal-hanan son of
Achbor succeeded him as king. 39Baal-
hanan son of Achbor died, and Hadar suc-
ceeded him as king, the name of his city
being Pau; his wife's name was Mehetabel,
the daughter of Matred, daughter of Me-
zahab.
40 These are the names of the clans[b] of

a Gk Syr: Heb *daughter* *b* Or *chiefs* *c* Meaning of Heb uncertain *d* Or *chief by chief*

extra label (cf. 36.1) may indicate that an earlier Priestly overview of Esau's descendants began here. **15–19:** A list of clans of the sons of Esau that diverges slightly from vv. 9–14 in its list of offspring of Eliphaz (cf. 36.11 and 15–16). **20–30:** A list of clans of *Horite* inhabitants of *Seir* (see 14.6), which may have been originally understood as a region in Transjordan different from Edom. In Deut 2.12,22 Esau (Edom) is described as having expelled the Horites from Seir. **31–39:** A list of early kings of Edom (see Num 20.14). **40–43:** A list of a slightly different kind of clan group (Heb "'aluph") in Edom that partially overlaps with names occurring in 36.9–19.

Esau, according to their families and their
localities by their names: the clans[a] Timna,
Alvah, Jetheth, 41 Oholibamah, Elah, Pi-
non, 42 Kenaz, Teman, Mibzar, 43 Magdiel,
and Iram; these are the clans[a] of Edom
(that is, Esau, the father of Edom), accord-
ing to their settlements in the land that they
held.

37 Jacob settled in the land where his
father had lived as an alien, the land
of Canaan. 2 This is the story of the family
of Jacob.

Joseph, being seventeen years old, was
shepherding the flock with his brothers; he
was a helper to the sons of Bilhah and Zil-
pah, his father's wives; and Joseph brought
a bad report of them to their father. 3 Now
Israel loved Joseph more than any other of
his children, because he was the son of his
old age; and he had made him a long robe
with sleeves.[b] 4 But when his brothers saw
that their father loved him more than all his
brothers, they hated him, and could not
speak peaceably to him.

5 Once Joseph had a dream, and when
he told it to his brothers, they hated him
even more. 6 He said to them, "Listen to
this dream that I dreamed. 7 There we were,
binding sheaves in the field. Suddenly my
sheaf rose and stood upright; then your
sheaves gathered around it, and bowed
down to my sheaf." 8 His brothers said to
him, "Are you indeed to reign over us? Are
you indeed to have dominion over us?" So
they hated him even more because of his
dreams and his words.

9 He had another dream, and told it to
his brothers, saying, "Look, I have had an-
other dream: the sun, the moon, and eleven
stars were bowing down to me." 10 But
when he told it to his father and to his
brothers, his father rebuked him, and said
to him, "What kind of dream is this that
you have had? Shall we indeed come, I and
your mother and your brothers, and bow to
the ground before you?" 11 So his brothers
were jealous of him, but his father kept the
matter in mind.

12 Now his brothers went to pasture
their father's flock near Shechem. 13 And Is-
rael said to Joseph, "Are not your brothers
pasturing the flock at Shechem? Come, I
will send you to them." He answered,
"Here I am." 14 So he said to him, "Go
now, see if it is well with your brothers and

a Or *chiefs* *b* Traditional rendering (compare Gk): *a coat of many colors*; meaning of Heb uncertain

37.1–11: Joseph's dreams of power. These narratives open the remarkably cohesive story of Joseph and his brothers in chs 37–50. Source critics have attempted to trace strands of the hypothesized Yahwistic and Elohistic source documents (see Introduction) through the Joseph story; thus sections focusing on Reuben and Midianites (e.g., 37.22–24,28–36) were assigned to E, while sections focusing on Judah and the Ishmaelites (e.g., 37.25–28) were assigned to J. Others suggested that an early Joseph story focused on Reuben was revised by an author who focused on Judah and referred to Jacob as "Israel." Despite the presence of some additions and modifications (e.g., 37.2a; 41.46), however, the essential unity of the Joseph story is clear. **2a:** Despite the different translation here in the NRSV, this label is identical with those in 5.1; 6.9; 10.1; 11.27; 25.12,18; 36.1,9 that refer to the "descendants" of a given figure. This label identifies the following as concerning the "descendants of Jacob," that is Joseph and his brothers. **2b–4:** According to the Priestly narrative (vv. 1–2), Joseph tattled on his brothers. The non-Priestly narrative (vv. 3–4) explains his brothers' antagonism toward him as resulting from jealousy about Jacob's love. Joseph is favored as the eldest of the children of Jacob and his favorite wife, Rachel (30.22–24). The *long robe with sleeves* (v. 3; see note *b*) is a royal garment (2 Sam 13.18–19) anticipating Joseph's future status. **5–8:** This first dream report predicts Joseph's domination of his brothers (43.26; 50.18; cf. 42.6). The story may intend to predict the future rule of Jeroboam, a member of the Joseph tribe of Ephraim, over the other tribes of northern Israel (1 Kings 11.26; 12.1–14.20). **9–11:** Jacob sees this dream as predicting that he and Joseph's mother, Rachel, will join the brothers in submitting to Joseph. This episode was probably part of an independent Joseph story that originally did not follow an account of Rachel's death (see 35.16–20).

37.12–36: Joseph is sold into slavery. 17: Dothan is a few miles north of Shechem and lay along a trade

with the flock; and bring word back to
me." So he sent him from the valley of He-
bron.

He came to Shechem, 15 and a man found
him wandering in the fields; the man asked
him, "What are you seeking?" 16 "I am
seeking my brothers," he said; "tell me,
please, where they are pasturing the flock."
17 The man said, "They have gone away,
for I heard them say, 'Let us go to Do-
than.' " So Joseph went after his brothers,
and found them at Dothan. 18 They saw
him from a distance, and before he came
near to them, they conspired to kill him.
19 They said to one another, "Here comes
this dreamer. 20 Come now, let us kill him
and throw him into one of the pits; then we
shall say that a wild animal has devoured
him, and we shall see what will become of
his dreams." 21 But when Reuben heard it,
he delivered him out of their hands, saying,
"Let us not take his life." 22 Reuben said to
them, "Shed no blood; throw him into this
pit here in the wilderness, but lay no hand
on him"—that he might rescue him out of
their hand and restore him to his father.
23 So when Joseph came to his brothers,
they stripped him of his robe, the long robe
with sleeves[a] that he wore; 24 and they
took him and threw him into a pit. The pit
was empty; there was no water in it.

25 Then they sat down to eat; and look-
ing up they saw a caravan of Ishmaelites
coming from Gilead, with their camels car-
rying gum, balm, and resin, on their way to
carry it down to Egypt. 26 Then Judah said
to his brothers, "What profit is it if we
kill our brother and conceal his blood?
27 Come, let us sell him to the Ishmaelites,
and not lay our hands on him, for he is our
brother, our own flesh." And his brothers
agreed. 28 When some Midianite traders
passed by, they drew Joseph up, lifting him
out of the pit, and sold him to the Ishmael-
ites for twenty pieces of silver. And they
took Joseph to Egypt.

29 When Reuben returned to the pit and
saw that Joseph was not in the pit, he tore
his clothes. 30 He returned to his brothers,
and said, "The boy is gone; and I, where
can I turn?" 31 Then they took Joseph's
robe, slaughtered a goat, and dipped the
robe in the blood. 32 They had the long robe
with sleeves[a] taken to their father, and
they said, "This we have found; see now
whether it is your son's robe or not." 33 He
recognized it, and said, "It is my son's robe!
A wild animal has devoured him; Joseph is
without doubt torn to pieces." 34 Then Ja-
cob tore his garments, and put sackcloth on
his loins, and mourned for his son many
days. 35 All his sons and all his daughters
sought to comfort him; but he refused to be
comforted, and said, "No, I shall go down
to Sheol to my son, mourning." Thus his
father bewailed him. 36 Meanwhile the
Midianites had sold him in Egypt to Poti-
phar, one of Pharaoh's officials, the captain
of the guard.

a See note on 37.3

route from Syria to Egypt. **20:** *The pits* were cisterns for storing rain water and sometimes used to imprison people (Jer 38.6). **22–27:** The advice of Reuben and Judah reflects the ancient idea that blood cannot be "concealed" (v. 26), but cries out for requital (see 4.10–11n.). **25–36:** Most agree that some combination or modification of traditions has occurred here. Though the brothers decide here to sell Joseph (v. 27) and Joseph later says that they did so (45.4–5), this narrative describes the *Midianites* as drawing him out and selling him to the *Ishmaelites* (v. 28). Later, both the *Midianites* (37.36) and the *Ishmaelites* (39.1; cf. 37.25) are identified as the ones who sold Joseph to Potiphar. **26–27:** On the role of Judah, see 44.18–34n. **31–34:** Now Jacob is tricked by an article of clothing (contrast 27.15; see 29.23–25n.). **35:** *Sheol,* the underworld to which a person went at death. Since this afterlife was at best a shadowy existence (see Ps 6.5; Eccl 9.10), Jacob's going to his son there was not a comforting expectation. **36:** Multiple traditions testify to some kind of connection between Joseph and an Egyptian *Potiphar*/"Potiphera." *Potiphar* is a form of "Potiphera," the name of the Egyptian priest who is Joseph's father-in-law in 41.45 and 46.20.

38 It happened at that time that Judah
went down from his brothers and
settled near a certain Adullamite whose
name was Hirah. 2 There Judah saw the
daughter of a certain Canaanite whose
name was Shua; he married her and went in
to her. 3 She conceived and bore a son; and
he named him Er. 4 Again she conceived
and bore a son whom she named Onan.
5 Yet again she bore a son, and she named
him Shelah. She[a] was in Chezib when she
bore him. 6 Judah took a wife for Er his
firstborn; her name was Tamar. 7 But Er,
Judah's firstborn, was wicked in the sight
of the LORD, and the LORD put him to
death. 8 Then Judah said to Onan, "Go in
to your brother's wife and perform the duty
of a brother-in-law to her; raise up off-
spring for your brother." 9 But since Onan
knew that the offspring would not be his,
he spilled his semen on the ground whenev-
er he went in to his brother's wife, so that
he would not give offspring to his brother.
10 What he did was displeasing in the sight
of the LORD, and he put him to death also.
11 Then Judah said to his daughter-in-law
Tamar, "Remain a widow in your father's
house until my son Shelah grows up"—for
he feared that he too would die, like his
brothers. So Tamar went to live in her fa-
ther's house.

12 In course of time the wife of Judah,
Shua's daughter, died; when Judah's time
of mourning was over,[b] he went up to
Timnah to his sheepshearers, he and his
friend Hirah the Adullamite. 13 When Ta-
mar was told, "Your father-in-law is going
up to Timnah to shear his sheep," 14 she put
off her widow's garments, put on a veil,
wrapped herself up, and sat down at the
entrance to Enaim, which is on the road to
Timnah. She saw that Shelah was grown
up, yet she had not been given to him in
marriage. 15 When Judah saw her, he
thought her to be a prostitute, for she had
covered her face. 16 He went over to her at
the roadside, and said, "Come, let me come
in to you," for he did not know that she
was his daughter-in-law. She said, "What
will you give me, that you may come in to
me?" 17 He answered, "I will send you a kid
from the flock." And she said, "Only if you
give me a pledge, until you send it." 18 He
said, "What pledge shall I give you?" She
replied, "Your signet and your cord, and
the staff that is in your hand." So he gave
them to her, and went in to her, and she
conceived by him. 19 Then she got up and
went away, and taking off her veil she put
on the garments of her widowhood.

20 When Judah sent the kid by his friend
the Adullamite, to recover the pledge from
the woman, he could not find her. 21 He
asked the townspeople, "Where is the tem-

a Gk: Heb *He* *b* Heb *when Judah was comforted*

38.1–30: Judah and Tamar. Though an apparent interlude in the Joseph story, this chapter echoes elements of ch 37 and anticipates themes from the upcoming Joseph story. **1–2:** Adullam was a village near Bethlehem where David later built up his mercenary army (1 Sam 22.1; 2 Sam 23.13). The locales in this narrative are appropriately in the territory of the tribe of Judah. Judah's wife, the daughter of Shua (Heb "Bat Shu'a"), anticipates the later "Bathsheba" of the David and Solomon narratives (2 Sam 11; cf. 1 Chr 3.5). **6:** Links to the David and Solomon story continue with mention of "Tamar" (see 2 Sam 13). **8–10:** According to the ancient custom of levirate marriage (Deut 25.5–10), *the duty of the brother-in-law* was to father a male descendant for his deceased brother and thus perpetuate his name and inheritance. Onan's death is attributed to his refusal to perform this duty (thus endangering Judah's line), probably by coitus interruptus (rather than "onanism," masturbation). **11:** Judah apparently fears that the death of his sons resulted from Tamar's sinister power. **12–19:** Tamar tricks Judah into playing the role of the brother-in-law by dressing as a prostitute and allowing him to hire her to have sex (see 27.1–45n.). **18:** The *signet* was a seal, often suspended from the neck with a *cord,* used to sign documents. **20–22:** Though some interpret the Heb here for "holy woman" ("qedeshah") as referring to a *temple prostitute/prostitute* (so NRSV), it is unclear whether there was an institution of sacred prostitution in ancient Israel. Some propose that Judah's Adullamite friend is just delicately referring to the missing "prostitute" as a similarly unattached, "holy woman." **24:** Stoning was the usual punishment for adultery

ple prostitute who was at Enaim by the
wayside?" But they said, "No prostitute
has been here." 22 So he returned to Judah,
and said, "I have not found her; moreover
the townspeople said, 'No prostitute has
been here.' " 23 Judah replied, "Let her
keep the things as her own, otherwise we
will be laughed at; you see, I sent this kid,
and you could not find her."

24 About three months later Judah was
told, "Your daughter-in-law Tamar has
played the whore; moreover she is pregnant
as a result of whoredom." And Judah said,
"Bring her out, and let her be burned."
25 As she was being brought out, she sent
word to her father-in-law, "It was the own-
er of these who made me pregnant." And
she said, "Take note, please, whose these
are, the signet and the cord and the staff."
26 Then Judah acknowledged them and
said, "She is more in the right than I, since
I did not give her to my son Shelah." And
he did not lie with her again.

27 When the time of her delivery came,
there were twins in her womb. 28 While she
was in labor, one put out a hand; and the
midwife took and bound on his hand a
crimson thread, saying, "This one came
out first." 29 But just then he drew back
his hand, and out came his brother; and
she said, "What a breach you have made
for yourself!" Therefore he was named
Perez.[a] 30 Afterward his brother came out
with the crimson thread on his hand; and
he was named Zerah.[b]

39 Now Joseph was taken down to
Egypt, and Potiphar, an officer of
Pharaoh, the captain of the guard, an Egyp-
tian, bought him from the Ishmaelites who
had brought him down there. 2 The LORD
was with Joseph, and he became a success-
ful man; he was in the house of his Egyp-
tian master. 3 His master saw that the LORD
was with him, and that the LORD caused all
that he did to prosper in his hands. 4 So
Joseph found favor in his sight and attend-
ed him; he made him overseer of his house
and put him in charge of all that he had.
5 From the time that he made him overseer
in his house and over all that he had, the
LORD blessed the Egyptian's house for Jo-
seph's sake; the blessing of the LORD was
on all that he had, in house and field. 6 So
he left all that he had in Joseph's charge;
and, with him there, he had no concern for
anything but the food that he ate.

Now Joseph was handsome and good-
looking. 7 And after a time his master's wife
cast her eyes on Joseph and said, "Lie with
me." 8 But he refused and said to his mas-
ter's wife, "Look, with me here, my master
has no concern about anything in the
house, and he has put everything that he
has in my hand. 9 He is not greater in this
house than I am, nor has he kept back any-
thing from me except yourself, because you
are his wife. How then could I do this great
wickedness, and sin against God?" 10 And
although she spoke to Joseph day after day,
he would not consent to lie beside her or to
be with her. 11 One day, however, when he
went into the house to do his work, and
while no one else was in the house, 12 she
caught hold of his garment, saying, "Lie
with me!" But he left his garment in her
hand, and fled and ran outside. 13 When
she saw that he had left his garment in her

a That is *A breach* *b* That is *Brightness*; perhaps alluding to the crimson thread

(Deut 22.23–24; cf. Jn 8.5), although burning was prescribed for exceptional cases (Lev 21.9). **25–26:** The presentation of evidence to Judah here echoes the presentation of the bloody robe to Jacob in 37.32–33. **27–30:** The birth of Judah's twins is depicted in terms similar to that of Jacob and Esau (21.21–26). The final link of this chapter to the David story (see 38.1–2,6n.) occurs with Perez, the first-born and ancestor of David (Ruth 4.18–22; see 49.1–28 and 8–12n.).

39.1–23: Joseph's success, temptation, and imprisonment. 1–6: Joseph's enjoyment of blessing and Potiphar's recognition of it are an outgrowth of the promise to Abraham in 12.1–3 (see 12.2n.). **7–20:** A parallel Egyptian "Tale of Two Brothers" also tells a tale of how a man rejected the advances of another's wife, who then laid false accusations against him and almost brought about his death.

hand and had fled outside, 14 she called out to the members of her household and said to them, "See, my husband[a] has brought among us a Hebrew to insult us! He came in to me to lie with me, and I cried out with a loud voice; 15 and when he heard me raise my voice and cry out, he left his garment beside me, and fled outside." 16 Then she kept his garment by her until his master came home, 17 and she told him the same story, saying, "The Hebrew servant, whom you have brought among us, came in to me to insult me; 18 but as soon as I raised my voice and cried out, he left his garment beside me, and fled outside."

19 When his master heard the words that his wife spoke to him, saying, "This is the way your servant treated me," he became enraged. 20 And Joseph's master took him and put him into the prison, the place where the king's prisoners were confined; he remained there in prison. 21 But the LORD was with Joseph and showed him steadfast love; he gave him favor in the sight of the chief jailer. 22 The chief jailer committed to Joseph's care all the prisoners who were in the prison, and whatever was done there, he was the one who did it. 23 The chief jailer paid no heed to anything that was in Joseph's care, because the LORD was with him; and whatever he did, the LORD made it prosper.

40 Some time after this, the cupbearer of the king of Egypt and his baker offended their lord the king of Egypt. 2 Pharaoh was angry with his two officers, the chief cupbearer and the chief baker, 3 and he put them in custody in the house of the captain of the guard, in the prison where Joseph was confined. 4 The captain of the guard charged Joseph with them, and he waited on them; and they continued for some time in custody. 5 One night they both dreamed—the cupbearer and the baker of the king of Egypt, who were confined in the prison—each his own dream, and each dream with its own meaning. 6 When Joseph came to them in the morning, he saw that they were troubled. 7 So he asked Pharaoh's officers, who were with him in custody in his master's house, "Why are your faces downcast today?" 8 They said to him, "We have had dreams, and there is no one to interpret them." And Joseph said to them, "Do not interpretations belong to God? Please tell them to me."

9 So the chief cupbearer told his dream to Joseph, and said to him, "In my dream there was a vine before me, 10 and on the vine there were three branches. As soon as it budded, its blossoms came out and the clusters ripened into grapes. 11 Pharaoh's cup was in my hand; and I took the grapes and pressed them into Pharaoh's cup, and placed the cup in Pharaoh's hand." 12 Then Joseph said to him, "This is its interpretation: the three branches are three days; 13 within three days Pharaoh will lift up your head and restore you to your office; and you shall place Pharaoh's cup in his hand, just as you used to do when you were his cupbearer. 14 But remember me when it is well with you; please do me the kindness to make mention of me to Pharaoh, and so get me out of this place. 15 For in fact I was stolen out of the land of the Hebrews; and here also I have done nothing that they should have put me into the dungeon."

16 When the chief baker saw that the interpretation was favorable, he said to Joseph, "I also had a dream: there were three cake baskets on my head, 17 and in the uppermost basket there were all sorts of baked food for Pharaoh, but the birds were eating it out of the basket on my head." 18 And Joseph answered, "This is its interpretation: the three baskets are three days; 19 within three days Pharaoh will lift up

a Heb *he*

12–15: Again (see 37.31–33), Joseph's *garment* is used as misleading evidence. **14:** *Hebrew,* see 14.13n. **21–23:** Abraham's blessing is again evident here.

40.1–23: Joseph establishes his expertise as dream interpreter. Dreams are a recurring motif in the Joseph narrative (see 37.5–10; 42.9). **13:** *Lift up your head,* i.e., graciously free you from prison (2 Kings 25.27). The same expression, with extreme irony, is applied to the baker's fate in v. 19. **15:** *Stolen,* 37.28.

your head—from you!—and hang you on a
pole; and the birds will eat the flesh from
you."
20 On the third day, which was Phar-
aoh's birthday, he made a feast for all his
servants, and lifted up the head of the chief
cupbearer and the head of the chief baker
among his servants. 21 He restored the chief
cupbearer to his cupbearing, and he placed
the cup in Pharaoh's hand; 22 but the chief
baker he hanged, just as Joseph had inter-
preted to them. 23 Yet the chief cupbearer
did not remember Joseph, but forgot him.
41 After two whole years, Pharaoh
dreamed that he was standing by
the Nile, 2 and there came up out of the Nile
seven sleek and fat cows, and they grazed in
the reed grass. 3 Then seven other cows,
ugly and thin, came up out of the Nile after
them, and stood by the other cows on the
bank of the Nile. 4 The ugly and thin cows
ate up the seven sleek and fat cows. And
Pharaoh awoke. 5 Then he fell asleep and
dreamed a second time; seven ears of grain,
plump and good, were growing on one
stalk. 6 Then seven ears, thin and blighted
by the east wind, sprouted after them. 7 The
thin ears swallowed up the seven plump
and full ears. Pharaoh awoke, and it was a
dream. 8 In the morning his spirit was trou-
bled; so he sent and called for all the magi-
cians of Egypt and all its wise men. Phar-
aoh told them his dreams, but there was no
one who could interpret them to Pharaoh.
9 Then the chief cupbearer said to Phar-
aoh, "I remember my faults today. 10 Once
Pharaoh was angry with his servants, and
put me and the chief baker in custody in the
house of the captain of the guard. 11 We
dreamed on the same night, he and I, each
having a dream with its own meaning. 12 A
young Hebrew was there with us, a servant
of the captain of the guard. When we told
him, he interpreted our dreams to us, giving
an interpretation to each according to his
dream. 13 As he interpreted to us, so it
turned out; I was restored to my office, and
the baker was hanged."
14 Then Pharaoh sent for Joseph, and he
was hurriedly brought out of the dungeon.
When he had shaved himself and changed
his clothes, he came in before Pharaoh.
15 And Pharaoh said to Joseph, "I have had
a dream, and there is no one who can inter-
pret it. I have heard it said of you that when
you hear a dream you can interpret it."
16 Joseph answered Pharaoh, "It is not I;
God will give Pharaoh a favorable an-
swer." 17 Then Pharaoh said to Joseph, "In
my dream I was standing on the banks of
the Nile; 18 and seven cows, fat and sleek,
came up out of the Nile and fed in the reed
grass. 19 Then seven other cows came up
after them, poor, very ugly, and thin. Never
had I seen such ugly ones in all the land of
Egypt. 20 The thin and ugly cows ate up the
first seven fat cows, 21 but when they had
eaten them no one would have known that
they had done so, for they were still as ugly
as before. Then I awoke. 22 I fell asleep a
second time[a] and I saw in my dream seven
ears of grain, full and good, growing on
one stalk, 23 and seven ears, withered, thin,
and blighted by the east wind, sprouting
after them; 24 and the thin ears swallowed
up the seven good ears. But when I told it
to the magicians, there was no one who
could explain it to me."
25 Then Joseph said to Pharaoh, "Phar-
aoh's dreams are one and the same; God
has revealed to Pharaoh what he is about to
do. 26 The seven good cows are seven years,
and the seven good ears are seven years; the
dreams are one. 27 The seven lean and ugly
cows that came up after them are seven
years, as are the seven empty ears blighted
by the east wind. They are seven years of
famine. 28 It is as I told Pharaoh; God has
shown to Pharaoh what he is about to do.
29 There will come seven years of great

a Gk Syr Vg: Heb lacks *I fell asleep a second time*

41.1–57: Joseph's elevation as the result of successful dream interpretation. **8:** The narrator intends to demonstrate the superiority of Israel's God over Egyptian magic and wisdom (cf. Ex 8.18–19; 9.11; Dan 2.2–19; 5.8,15–28). **16:** Joseph denies having any occult art and ascribes his skill solely to God. **42:** *His*

plenty throughout all the land of Egypt.
30 After them there will arise seven years of
famine, and all the plenty will be forgotten
in the land of Egypt; the famine will con-
sume the land. 31 The plenty will no longer
be known in the land because of the famine
that will follow, for it will be very grievous.
32 And the doubling of Pharaoh's dream
means that the thing is fixed by God, and
God will shortly bring it about. 33 Now
therefore let Pharaoh select a man who is
discerning and wise, and set him over the
land of Egypt. 34 Let Pharaoh proceed to
appoint overseers over the land, and take
one-fifth of the produce of the land of
Egypt during the seven plenteous years.
35 Let them gather all the food of these good
years that are coming, and lay up grain un-
der the authority of Pharaoh for food in the
cities, and let them keep it. 36 That food
shall be a reserve for the land against the
seven years of famine that are to befall the
land of Egypt, so that the land may not
perish through the famine."
37 The proposal pleased Pharaoh and
all his servants. 38 Pharaoh said to his ser-
vants, "Can we find anyone else like this—
one in whom is the spirit of God?" 39 So
Pharaoh said to Joseph, "Since God has
shown you all this, there is no one so dis-
cerning and wise as you. 40 You shall be
over my house, and all my people shall or-
der themselves as you command; only with
regard to the throne will I be greater than
you." 41 And Pharaoh said to Joseph, "See,
I have set you over all the land of Egypt."
42 Removing his signet ring from his hand,
Pharaoh put it on Joseph's hand; he ar-
rayed him in garments of fine linen, and put
a gold chain around his neck. 43 He had
him ride in the chariot of his second-in-
command; and they cried out in front of
him, "Bow the knee!"[a] Thus he set him
over all the land of Egypt. 44 Moreover
Pharaoh said to Joseph, "I am Pharaoh,
and without your consent no one shall
lift up hand or foot in all the land of
Egypt." 45 Pharaoh gave Joseph the name
Zaphenath-paneah; and he gave him Ase-
nath daughter of Potiphera, priest of On, as
his wife. Thus Joseph gained authority over
the land of Egypt.
46 Joseph was thirty years old when he
entered the service of Pharaoh king of
Egypt. And Joseph went out from the pres-
ence of Pharaoh, and went through all the
land of Egypt. 47 During the seven plente-
ous years the earth produced abundantly.
48 He gathered up all the food of the seven
years when there was plenty[b] in the land of
Egypt, and stored up food in the cities; he
stored up in every city the food from the
fields around it. 49 So Joseph stored up
grain in such abundance—like the sand of
the sea—that he stopped measuring it; it
was beyond measure.
50 Before the years of famine came, Jo-
seph had two sons, whom Asenath daugh-
ter of Potiphera, priest of On, bore to him.
51 Joseph named the firstborn Manasseh,[c]
"For," he said, "God has made me forget
all my hardship and all my father's house."
52 The second he named Ephraim,[d] "For
God has made me fruitful in the land of my
misfortunes."
53 The seven years of plenty that pre-
vailed in the land of Egypt came to an end;
54 and the seven years of famine began to
come, just as Joseph had said. There was
famine in every country, but throughout
the land of Egypt there was bread. 55 When
all the land of Egypt was famished, the peo-
ple cried to Pharaoh for bread. Pharaoh

a *Abrek*, apparently an Egyptian word similar in sound to the Hebrew word meaning *to kneel*
b Sam Gk: MT *the seven years that were*
c That is *Making to forget*
d From a Hebrew word meaning *to be fruitful*

signet ring (see 38.18n.) empowered Joseph to act as Pharaoh's representative. **45:** The installation rites culminate in the bestowal of an Egyptian name on Joseph. Joseph's adoption into the Egyptian court is further indicated by his marriage into the priesthood of *On* or Heliopolis. No judgment is attached to this intermarriage with an Egyptian foreigner (see Deut 23.8–9). *Potiphera,* see 37.36n. **46:** This is the first Priestly notice since the outset of the Joseph story (37.2). **50–52:** The birth of Joseph's two sons; see 46.20; ch 48.

said to all the Egyptians, "Go to Joseph;
what he says to you, do." 56 And since the
famine had spread over all the land, Joseph
opened all the storehouses,[a] and sold to
the Egyptians, for the famine was severe
in the land of Egypt. 57 Moreover, all the
world came to Joseph in Egypt to buy
grain, because the famine became severe
throughout the world.

42 When Jacob learned that there was
grain in Egypt, he said to his sons,
"Why do you keep looking at one another?
2 I have heard," he said, "that there is grain
in Egypt; go down and buy grain for us
there, that we may live and not die." 3 So
ten of Joseph's brothers went down to buy
grain in Egypt. 4 But Jacob did not send Jo-
seph's brother Benjamin with his brothers,
for he feared that harm might come to him.
5 Thus the sons of Israel were among the
other people who came to buy grain, for
the famine had reached the land of Canaan.

6 Now Joseph was governor over the
land; it was he who sold to all the people of
the land. And Joseph's brothers came and
bowed themselves before him with their
faces to the ground. 7 When Joseph saw his
brothers, he recognized them, but he treat-
ed them like strangers and spoke harshly to
them. "Where do you come from?" he said.
They said, "From the land of Canaan, to
buy food." 8 Although Joseph had recog-
nized his brothers, they did not recognize
him. 9 Joseph also remembered the dreams
that he had dreamed about them. He said
to them, "You are spies; you have come to
see the nakedness of the land!" 10 They said
to him, "No, my lord; your servants have
come to buy food. 11 We are all sons of one
man; we are honest men; your servants
have never been spies." 12 But he said to
them, "No, you have come to see the na-
kedness of the land!" 13 They said, "We,
your servants, are twelve brothers, the sons
of a certain man in the land of Canaan; the
youngest, however, is now with our father,
and one is no more." 14 But Joseph said to
them, "It is just as I have said to you; you
are spies! 15 Here is how you shall be tested:
as Pharaoh lives, you shall not leave this
place unless your youngest brother comes
here! 16 Let one of you go and bring your
brother, while the rest of you remain in
prison, in order that your words may be
tested, whether there is truth in you; or else,
as Pharaoh lives, surely you are spies."
17 And he put them all together in prison for
three days.

18 On the third day Joseph said to them,
"Do this and you will live, for I fear God:
19 if you are honest men, let one of your
brothers stay here where you are impris-
oned. The rest of you shall go and carry
grain for the famine of your households,
20 and bring your youngest brother to me.
Thus your words will be verified, and you
shall not die." And they agreed to do so.
21 They said to one another, "Alas, we are
paying the penalty for what we did to our
brother; we saw his anguish when he plead-
ed with us, but we would not listen. That
is why this anguish has come upon us."
22 Then Reuben answered them, "Did I not
tell you not to wrong the boy? But you
would not listen. So now there comes a
reckoning for his blood." 23 They did not
know that Joseph understood them, since
he spoke with them through an interpreter.
24 He turned away from them and wept;
then he returned and spoke to them. And
he picked out Simeon and had him bound

a Gk Vg Compare Syr: Heb *opened all that was in* (or, *among*) *them*

42.1–38: Joseph's brothers' first journey to Egypt. 5: See 12.10; 26.1. **6:** *Bowed themselves before him,* since all but Benjamin are present, Joseph's first dream (37.5–8) is almost fulfilled (cf. 43.26). **9–14:** The charge of spying is natural, since Egypt's frontier, facing Canaan, was vulnerable to attack (Ex 1.10). Nevertheless, the narrator (v. 9) explains Joseph's accusation as related to his memory of his dreams (37.5–11). **15–17:** Though Joseph claims to be "testing" whether his brothers are spies, he actually seems to be "testing" whether they will betray his full brother and father's favorite (v. 4), Benjamin, the way they once betrayed him (see chs 43–44). **21–23:** The brothers' expression of guilt at their earlier betrayal of Joseph hints at the change of heart for which Joseph is looking. **38:** *Sheol,* see 37.35n.

before their eyes. 25 Joseph then gave orders
to fill their bags with grain, to return every
man's money to his sack, and to give them
provisions for their journey. This was done
for them.

26 They loaded their donkeys with their
grain, and departed. 27 When one of them
opened his sack to give his donkey fodder
at the lodging place, he saw his money at
the top of the sack. 28 He said to his broth-
ers, "My money has been put back; here it
is in my sack!" At this they lost heart and
turned trembling to one another, saying,
"What is this that God has done to us?"

29 When they came to their father Jacob
in the land of Canaan, they told him all that
had happened to them, saying, 30 "The
man, the lord of the land, spoke harshly to
us, and charged us with spying on the land.
31 But we said to him, 'We are honest men,
we are not spies. 32 We are twelve brothers,
sons of our father; one is no more, and the
youngest is now with our father in the land
of Canaan.' 33 Then the man, the lord of the
land, said to us, 'By this I shall know that
you are honest men: leave one of your
brothers with me, take grain for the famine
of your households, and go your way.
34 Bring your youngest brother to me, and I
shall know that you are not spies but hon-
est men. Then I will release your brother to
you, and you may trade in the land.' "

35 As they were emptying their sacks,
there in each one's sack was his bag of
money. When they and their father saw
their bundles of money, they were dis-
mayed. 36 And their father Jacob said to
them, "I am the one you have bereaved of
children: Joseph is no more, and Simeon is
no more, and now you would take Benja-
min. All this has happened to me!" 37 Then
Reuben said to his father, "You may kill
my two sons if I do not bring him back to
you. Put him in my hands, and I will bring
him back to you." 38 But he said, "My son
shall not go down with you, for his brother
is dead, and he alone is left. If harm should
come to him on the journey that you are to
make, you would bring down my gray hairs
with sorrow to Sheol."

43 Now the famine was severe in the
land. 2 And when they had eaten up
the grain that they had brought from
Egypt, their father said to them, "Go again,
buy us a little more food." 3 But Judah said
to him, "The man solemnly warned us, say-
ing, 'You shall not see my face unless your
brother is with you.' 4 If you will send our
brother with us, we will go down and buy
you food; 5 but if you will not send him, we
will not go down, for the man said to us,
'You shall not see my face, unless your
brother is with you.' " 6 Israel said, "Why
did you treat me so badly as to tell the man
that you had another brother?" 7 They re-
plied, "The man questioned us carefully
about ourselves and our kindred, saying, 'Is
your father still alive? Have you another
brother?' What we told him was in answer
to these questions. Could we in any way
know that he would say, 'Bring your broth-
er down'?" 8 Then Judah said to his father
Israel, "Send the boy with me, and let us be
on our way, so that we may live and not
die—you and we and also our little ones. 9 I
myself will be surety for him; you can hold
me accountable for him. If I do not bring
him back to you and set him before you,
then let me bear the blame forever. 10 If we
had not delayed, we would now have re-
turned twice."

11 Then their father Israel said to them,
"If it must be so, then do this: take some of
the choice fruits of the land in your bags,
and carry them down as a present to the
man—a little balm and a little honey, gum,
resin, pistachio nuts, and almonds. 12 Take
double the money with you. Carry back
with you the money that was returned in
the top of your sacks; perhaps it was an
oversight. 13 Take your brother also, and be
on your way again to the man; 14 may God

43.1–34: **Joseph's brothers' second journey to Egypt.** **1–2**: Simeon, left as a hostage in Egypt (vv. 14,23), is apparently forgotten, for the brothers return only when more grain is needed. **3–7**: Cf. 42.29–34. **8–10**: Again (see 37.26–27) *Judah* is depicted as the hero; see 44.18–34n. **14**: *God Almighty,* see 17.1n. **23**: The Egyptian steward anticipates the emphasis of the story on divine providence

Almighty[a] grant you mercy before the
man, so that he may send back your other
brother and Benjamin. As for me, if I am
bereaved of my children, I am bereaved."
15 So the men took the present, and they
took double the money with them, as well
as Benjamin. Then they went on their way
down to Egypt, and stood before Joseph.
16 When Joseph saw Benjamin with
them, he said to the steward of his house,
"Bring the men into the house, and slaughter
an animal and make ready, for the men
are to dine with me at noon." 17 The man
did as Joseph said, and brought the men to
Joseph's house. 18 Now the men were afraid
because they were brought to Joseph's
house, and they said, "It is because of the
money, replaced in our sacks the first time,
that we have been brought in, so that he
may have an opportunity to fall upon us, to
make slaves of us and take our donkeys."
19 So they went up to the steward of Joseph's
house and spoke with him at the entrance
to the house. 20 They said, "Oh, my
lord, we came down the first time to buy
food; 21 and when we came to the lodging
place we opened our sacks, and there was
each one's money in the top of his sack, our
money in full weight. So we have brought it
back with us. 22 Moreover we have brought
down with us additional money to buy
food. We do not know who put our money
in our sacks." 23 He replied, "Rest assured,
do not be afraid; your God and the God of
your father must have put treasure in your
sacks for you; I received your money."
Then he brought Simeon out to them.
24 When the steward[b] had brought the men
into Joseph's house, and given them water,
and they had washed their feet, and when
he had given their donkeys fodder, 25 they
made the present ready for Joseph's coming
at noon, for they had heard that they would
dine there.
26 When Joseph came home, they
brought him the present that they had carried
into the house, and bowed to the
ground before him. 27 He inquired about
their welfare, and said, "Is your father well,
the old man of whom you spoke? Is he still
alive?" 28 They said, "Your servant our father
is well; he is still alive." And they
bowed their heads and did obeisance.
29 Then he looked up and saw his brother
Benjamin, his mother's son, and said, "Is
this your youngest brother, of whom you
spoke to me? God be gracious to you, my
son!" 30 With that, Joseph hurried out, because
he was overcome with affection for
his brother, and he was about to weep.
So he went into a private room and wept
there. 31 Then he washed his face and came
out; and controlling himself he said, "Serve
the meal." 32 They served him by himself,
and them by themselves, and the Egyptians
who ate with him by themselves, because
the Egyptians could not eat with the Hebrews,
for that is an abomination to the
Egyptians. 33 When they were seated before
him, the firstborn according to his birthright
and the youngest according to his
youth, the men looked at one another in
amazement. 34 Portions were taken to them
from Joseph's table, but Benjamin's portion
was five times as much as any of theirs. So
they drank and were merry with him.

44 Then he commanded the steward of
his house, "Fill the men's sacks with
food, as much as they can carry, and put

a Traditional rendering of Heb *El Shaddai*
b Heb *the man*

(44.16; 45.5–8; 50.20). **26:** With all eleven brothers now bowing down (cf. v. 15), they unknowingly fulfill the first dream in 37.5–8 (see 50.18n.). **29–30:** Joseph *was overcome with affection* for Benjamin, his only full brother through Rachel. **34:** Just as Benjamin (42.4,38; 43.6–14) and before him Joseph (37.3–4) was favored by Jacob, so here—through Joseph's actions—the brothers watch a son of Rachel enjoy special privilege in the Egyptian court.

44.1–34: Joseph's final test of his brothers. 1–5: Here the focus is on Joseph's cup, a sacred vessel for divination, that is, magical prediction of the future (cf. 42.25–28). The brothers' (unknowing) taking of the cup and pronouncement of a death penalty on the thief (v. 9) echo the earlier story of Rachel's stealing of Laban's household gods (31.19) and Jacob's pronouncement of the death penalty on the thief (31.32).

each man's money in the top of his sack.
2 Put my cup, the silver cup, in the top of
the sack of the youngest, with his money
for the grain." And he did as Joseph told
him. 3 As soon as the morning was light, the
men were sent away with their donkeys.
4 When they had gone only a short distance
from the city, Joseph said to his steward,
"Go, follow after the men; and when you
overtake them, say to them, 'Why have you
returned evil for good? Why have you sto-
len my silver cup?[a] 5 Is it not from this that
my lord drinks? Does he not indeed use it
for divination? You have done wrong in
doing this.' "

6 When he overtook them, he repeated
these words to them. 7 They said to him,
"Why does my lord speak such words as
these? Far be it from your servants that
they should do such a thing! 8 Look, the
money that we found at the top of our
sacks, we brought back to you from the
land of Canaan; why then would we steal
silver or gold from your lord's house?
9 Should it be found with any one of your
servants, let him die; moreover the rest of
us will become my lord's slaves." 10 He
said, "Even so; in accordance with your
words, let it be: he with whom it is found
shall become my slave, but the rest of you
shall go free." 11 Then each one quickly
lowered his sack to the ground, and each
opened his sack. 12 He searched, beginning
with the eldest and ending with the youn-
gest; and the cup was found in Benjamin's
sack. 13 At this they tore their clothes. Then
each one loaded his donkey, and they re-
turned to the city.

14 Judah and his brothers came to Jo-
seph's house while he was still there; and
they fell to the ground before him. 15 Joseph
said to them, "What deed is this that you
have done? Do you not know that one such
as I can practice divination?" 16 And Judah
said, "What can we say to my lord? What
can we speak? How can we clear ourselves?
God has found out the guilt of your ser-
vants; here we are then, my lord's slaves,
both we and also the one in whose posses-
sion the cup has been found." 17 But he
said, "Far be it from me that I should do so!
Only the one in whose possession the cup
was found shall be my slave; but as for you,
go up in peace to your father."

18 Then Judah stepped up to him and
said, "O my lord, let your servant please
speak a word in my lord's ears, and do not
be angry with your servant; for you are like
Pharaoh himself. 19 My lord asked his ser-
vants, saying, 'Have you a father or a
brother?' 20 And we said to my lord, 'We
have a father, an old man, and a young
brother, the child of his old age. His broth-
er is dead; he alone is left of his mother's
children, and his father loves him.' 21 Then
you said to your servants, 'Bring him down
to me, so that I may set my eyes on him.'
22 We said to my lord, 'The boy cannot
leave his father, for if he should leave his
father, his father would die.' 23 Then you
said to your servants, 'Unless your youn-
gest brother comes down with you, you
shall see my face no more.' 24 When we
went back to your servant my father we
told him the words of my lord. 25 And when
our father said, 'Go again, buy us a little
food,' 26 we said, 'We cannot go down.
Only if our youngest brother goes with us,
will we go down; for we cannot see the
man's face unless our youngest brother is
with us.' 27 Then your servant my father

a Gk Compare Vg: Heb lacks *Why have you stolen my silver cup?*

9: See vv. 1–5n. **17:** Joseph tests his brothers (see 42.15–17) to see whether they will let Benjamin go into slavery as they once did with him (37.25–35). **18–34:** Judah had secured Jacob's release of Benjamin through offering himself as collateral (43.8–10; see v. 32). Now he steps forth to express a respect for their father's bond to Rachel's son(s) that had not been evident among the brothers before (cf. 37.19–35). This is a prime example of a text in the Joseph story where Judah, rather than the elder Reuben, plays the role of the most powerful and prominent son (see also 37.26–27; ch 38; 43.3–5,8–10; 46.28). Such texts have typically been assigned to the early Yahwist or a Judah-Israel layer of the story (see Introduction and 37.1–11n.).

said to us, 'You know that my wife bore me
two sons; 28 one left me, and I said, Surely
he has been torn to pieces; and I have never
seen him since. 29 If you take this one also
from me, and harm comes to him, you will
bring down my gray hairs in sorrow to
Sheol.' 30 Now therefore, when I come to
your servant my father and the boy is not
with us, then, as his life is bound up in the
boy's life, 31 when he sees that the boy is
not with us, he will die; and your servants
will bring down the gray hairs of your ser-
vant our father with sorrow to Sheol. 32 For
your servant became surety for the boy to
my father, saying, 'If I do not bring him
back to you, then I will bear the blame in
the sight of my father all my life.' 33 Now
therefore, please let your servant remain as
a slave to my lord in place of the boy; and
let the boy go back with his brothers. 34 For
how can I go back to my father if the boy
is not with me? I fear to see the suffering
that would come upon my father."

45 Then Joseph could no longer con-
trol himself before all those who
stood by him, and he cried out, "Send ev-
eryone away from me." So no one stayed
with him when Joseph made himself
known to his brothers. 2 And he wept so
loudly that the Egyptians heard it, and the
household of Pharaoh heard it. 3 Joseph
said to his brothers, "I am Joseph. Is my
father still alive?" But his brothers could
not answer him, so dismayed were they at
his presence.

4 Then Joseph said to his brothers,
"Come closer to me." And they came clos-
er. He said, "I am your brother, Joseph,
whom you sold into Egypt. 5 And now do
not be distressed, or angry with yourselves,
because you sold me here; for God sent me
before you to preserve life. 6 For the famine
has been in the land these two years; and
there are five more years in which there will
be neither plowing nor harvest. 7 God sent
me before you to preserve for you a rem-
nant on earth, and to keep alive for you
many survivors. 8 So it was not you who
sent me here, but God; he has made me a
father to Pharaoh, and lord of all his house
and ruler over all the land of Egypt. 9 Hurry
and go up to my father and say to him,
'Thus says your son Joseph, God has made
me lord of all Egypt; come down to me, do
not delay. 10 You shall settle in the land of
Goshen, and you shall be near me, you and
your children and your children's children,
as well as your flocks, your herds, and all
that you have. 11 I will provide for you
there—since there are five more years of
famine to come—so that you and your
household, and all that you have, will not
come to poverty.' 12 And now your eyes and
the eyes of my brother Benjamin see that
it is my own mouth that speaks to you.
13 You must tell my father how greatly I am
honored in Egypt, and all that you have
seen. Hurry and bring my father down
here." 14 Then he fell upon his brother Ben-
jamin's neck and wept, while Benjamin
wept upon his neck. 15 And he kissed all his
brothers and wept upon them; and after
that his brothers talked with him.

16 When the report was heard in Phar-
aoh's house, "Joseph's brothers have
come," Pharaoh and his servants were
pleased. 17 Pharaoh said to Joseph, "Say to
your brothers, 'Do this: load your animals
and go back to the land of Canaan. 18 Take
your father and your households and come
to me, so that I may give you the best of the
land of Egypt, and you may enjoy the fat of
the land.' 19 You are further charged to say,
'Do this: take wagons from the land of
Egypt for your little ones and for your
wives, and bring your father, and come.
20 Give no thought to your possessions, for
the best of all the land of Egypt is yours.' "

21 The sons of Israel did so. Joseph gave
them wagons according to the instruction

45.1–28: Joseph makes himself known to his brothers and father. 1–3: The brothers initially react with shock to the knowledge that they face the brother whom they sold into slavery. **4–13:** Joseph reassures his brothers by telling them that God—not they—sent him into slavery. God sent him there so that he might feed his family in the famine. **10:** *The land of Goshen,* probably located in the eastern Nile delta. **16–20:** Asiatics are frequently attested as living in Egypt.

of Pharaoh, and he gave them provisions
for the journey. 22 To each one of them he
gave a set of garments; but to Benjamin he
gave three hundred pieces of silver and five
sets of garments. 23 To his father he sent the
following: ten donkeys loaded with the
good things of Egypt, and ten female don-
keys loaded with grain, bread, and provi-
sion for his father on the journey. 24 Then
he sent his brothers on their way, and as
they were leaving he said to them, "Do not
quarrel[a] along the way."

25 So they went up out of Egypt and
came to their father Jacob in the land of
Canaan. 26 And they told him, "Joseph is
still alive! He is even ruler over all the land
of Egypt." He was stunned; he could not
believe them. 27 But when they told him all
the words of Joseph that he had said to
them, and when he saw the wagons that
Joseph had sent to carry him, the spirit of
their father Jacob revived. 28 Israel said,
"Enough! My son Joseph is still alive. I
must go and see him before I die."

46 When Israel set out on his journey
with all that he had and came to
Beer-sheba, he offered sacrifices to the God
of his father Isaac. 2 God spoke to Israel in
visions of the night, and said, "Jacob, Ja-
cob." And he said, "Here I am." 3 Then he
said, "I am God,[b] the God of your father;
do not be afraid to go down to Egypt, for
I will make of you a great nation there. 4 I
myself will go down with you to Egypt, and
I will also bring you up again; and Joseph's
own hand shall close your eyes."

5 Then Jacob set out from Beer-sheba;
and the sons of Israel carried their father
Jacob, their little ones, and their wives, in
the wagons that Pharaoh had sent to carry
him. 6 They also took their livestock and
the goods that they had acquired in the
land of Canaan, and they came into Egypt,
Jacob and all his offspring with him, 7 his
sons, and his sons' sons with him, his
daughters, and his sons' daughters; all his
offspring he brought with him into Egypt.

8 Now these are the names of the Israel-
ites, Jacob and his offspring, who came to
Egypt. Reuben, Jacob's firstborn, 9 and the
children of Reuben: Hanoch, Pallu, Hez-
ron, and Carmi. 10 The children of Simeon:
Jemuel, Jamin, Ohad, Jachin, Zohar, and
Shaul,[c] the son of a Canaanite woman.
11 The children of Levi: Gershon, Kohath,
and Merari. 12 The children of Judah: Er,
Onan, Shelah, Perez, and Zerah (but Er and
Onan died in the land of Canaan); and the
children of Perez were Hezron and Hamul.
13 The children of Issachar: Tola, Puvah,
Jashub,[d] and Shimron. 14 The children of
Zebulun: Sered, Elon, and Jahleel 15 (these
are the sons of Leah, whom she bore to
Jacob in Paddan-aram, together with his
daughter Dinah; in all his sons and his
daughters numbered thirty-three). 16 The
children of Gad: Ziphion, Haggi, Shuni,
Ezbon, Eri, Arodi, and Areli. 17 The chil-
dren of Asher: Imnah, Ishvah, Ishvi, Beriah,
and their sister Serah. The children of Beri-
ah: Heber and Malchiel 18 (these are the
children of Zilpah, whom Laban gave to
his daughter Leah; and these she bore to
Jacob—sixteen persons). 19 The children of
Jacob's wife Rachel: Joseph and Benjamin.
20 To Joseph in the land of Egypt were born
Manasseh and Ephraim, whom Asenath
daughter of Potiphera, priest of On, bore to
him. 21 The children of Benjamin: Bela, Be-
cher, Ashbel, Gera, Naaman, Ehi, Rosh,
Muppim, Huppim, and Ard 22 (these are
the children of Rachel, who were born to
Jacob—fourteen persons in all). 23 The chil-

a Or *be agitated* *b* Heb *the God* *c* Or *Saul*
d Compare Sam Gk Num 26.24; 1 Chr 7.1: MT *Iob*

46.1–27: Jacob's migration to Egypt. 1–4: Jacob's first stop on the way out of the land is *Beer-sheba,* where the same God who told Isaac to stay in the land (26.2–3) now tells his son, Jacob, to proceed in leaving the land for Egypt (see 12.1–3n.; 28.13–15n.). Now, God expands the earlier promise that Abraham would be a *great nation* (see 12.2n.) by saying that God will make Jacob a great nation in *Egypt* (v. 3; see 47.27; Ex 1.7,9). **8–27:** A Priestly section listing Jacob's descendants using the traditional number seventy (v. 27; Ex 1.5; Deut 10.22). Most names of the clan leaders are in the priestly list in Num 26. **12:** See ch 38.

dren of Dan: Hashum.[a] 24 The children of
Naphtali: Jahzeel, Guni, Jezer, and Shillem
25 (these are the children of Bilhah, whom
Laban gave to his daughter Rachel, and
these she bore to Jacob—seven persons in
all). 26 All the persons belonging to Jacob
who came into Egypt, who were his own
offspring, not including the wives of his
sons, were sixty-six persons in all. 27 The
children of Joseph, who were born to him
in Egypt, were two; all the persons of the
house of Jacob who came into Egypt were
seventy.

28 Israel[b] sent Judah ahead to Joseph
to lead the way before him into Goshen.
When they came to the land of Goshen,
29 Joseph made ready his chariot and went
up to meet his father Israel in Goshen. He
presented himself to him, fell on his neck,
and wept on his neck a good while. 30 Israel
said to Joseph, "I can die now, having seen
for myself that you are still alive." 31 Joseph
said to his brothers and to his father's
household, "I will go up and tell Pharaoh,
and will say to him, 'My brothers and my
father's household, who were in the land of
Canaan, have come to me. 32 The men are
shepherds, for they have been keepers of
livestock; and they have brought their
flocks, and their herds, and all that they
have.' 33 When Pharaoh calls you, and says,
'What is your occupation?' 34 you shall say,
'Your servants have been keepers of live-
stock from our youth even until now, both
we and our ancestors'—in order that you
may settle in the land of Goshen, because
all shepherds are abhorrent to the Egyp-
tians."

47 So Joseph went and told Pharaoh,
"My father and my brothers, with
their flocks and herds and all that they pos-
sess, have come from the land of Canaan;
they are now in the land of Goshen."
2 From among his brothers he took five men
and presented them to Pharaoh. 3 Pharaoh
said to his brothers, "What is your occupa-
tion?" And they said to Pharaoh, "Your
servants are shepherds, as our ancestors
were." 4 They said to Pharaoh, "We have
come to reside as aliens in the land; for
there is no pasture for your servants' flocks
because the famine is severe in the land of
Canaan. Now, we ask you, let your ser-
vants settle in the land of Goshen." 5 Then
Pharaoh said to Joseph, "Your father and
your brothers have come to you. 6 The land
of Egypt is before you; settle your father
and your brothers in the best part of the
land; let them live in the land of Goshen;
and if you know that there are capable men
among them, put them in charge of my live-
stock."

7 Then Joseph brought in his father Ja-
cob, and presented him before Pharaoh,
and Jacob blessed Pharaoh. 8 Pharaoh said
to Jacob, "How many are the years of your
life?" 9 Jacob said to Pharaoh, "The years
of my earthly sojourn are one hundred thir-
ty; few and hard have been the years of my
life. They do not compare with the years of
the life of my ancestors during their long
sojourn." 10 Then Jacob blessed Pharaoh,
and went out from the presence of Phar-
aoh. 11 Joseph settled his father and his
brothers, and granted them a holding in the
land of Egypt, in the best part of the land,
in the land of Rameses, as Pharaoh had in-
structed. 12 And Joseph provided his father,
his brothers, and all his father's household
with food, according to the number of their
dependents.

13 Now there was no food in all the
land, for the famine was very severe. The
land of Egypt and the land of Canaan lan-
guished because of the famine. 14 Joseph
collected all the money to be found in the
land of Egypt and in the land of Canaan, in
exchange for the grain that they bought;
and Joseph brought the money into Phar-
aoh's house. 15 When the money from the

a Gk: Heb *Hushim* *b* Heb *He*

46.28–47.28: **Jacob's family settles in Egypt.** **46.34:** *All shepherds are abhorrent,* there is no nonbiblical evidence for this assertion. **47.7–12:** According to this Priestly tradition, *Jacob blessed Pharaoh.* **11:** *The land of Rameses* cannot be identified with certainty. The first Egyptian pharaoh with that name ruled at the beginning of the thirteenth century BCE. **13–26:** Joseph's clever impoverishment of the Egyptians

land of Egypt and from the land of Canaan
was spent, all the Egyptians came to Jo-
seph, and said, "Give us food! Why should
we die before your eyes? For our money is
gone." 16 And Joseph answered, "Give me
your livestock, and I will give you food in
exchange for your livestock, if your money
is gone." 17 So they brought their livestock
to Joseph; and Joseph gave them food in
exchange for the horses, the flocks, the
herds, and the donkeys. That year he sup-
plied them with food in exchange for all
their livestock. 18 When that year was end-
ed, they came to him the following year,
and said to him, "We can not hide from my
lord that our money is all spent; and the
herds of cattle are my lord's. There is noth-
ing left in the sight of my lord but our bod-
ies and our lands. 19 Shall we die before
your eyes, both we and our land? Buy us
and our land in exchange for food. We with
our land will become slaves to Pharaoh;
just give us seed, so that we may live and
not die, and that the land may not become
desolate."

20 So Joseph bought all the land of
Egypt for Pharaoh. All the Egyptians sold
their fields, because the famine was severe
upon them; and the land became Phar-
aoh's. 21 As for the people, he made slaves
of them[a] from one end of Egypt to the
other. 22 Only the land of the priests he did
not buy; for the priests had a fixed allow-
ance from Pharaoh, and lived on the allow-
ance that Pharaoh gave them; therefore
they did not sell their land. 23 Then Joseph
said to the people, "Now that I have this
day bought you and your land for Pharaoh,
here is seed for you; sow the land. 24 And
at the harvests you shall give one-fifth to
Pharaoh, and four-fifths shall be your own,
as seed for the field and as food for your-
selves and your households, and as food for
your little ones." 25 They said, "You have
saved our lives; may it please my lord, we
will be slaves to Pharaoh." 26 So Joseph
made it a statute concerning the land of
Egypt, and it stands to this day, that Phar-
aoh should have the fifth. The land of the
priests alone did not become Pharaoh's.

27 Thus Israel settled in the land of
Egypt, in the region of Goshen; and they
gained possessions in it, and were fruitful
and multiplied exceedingly. 28 Jacob lived
in the land of Egypt seventeen years; so the
days of Jacob, the years of his life, were one
hundred forty-seven years.

29 When the time of Israel's death drew
near, he called his son Joseph and said to
him, "If I have found favor with you, put
your hand under my thigh and promise to
deal loyally and truly with me. Do not bury
me in Egypt. 30 When I lie down with my
ancestors, carry me out of Egypt and bury
me in their burial place." He answered, "I
will do as you have said." 31 And he said,
"Swear to me"; and he swore to him. Then
Israel bowed himself on the head of his bed.

48 After this Joseph was told, "Your
father is ill." So he took with him
his two sons, Manasseh and Ephraim.
2 When Jacob was told, "Your son Joseph
has come to you," he[b] summoned his
strength and sat up in bed. 3 And Jacob said

a Sam Gk Compare Vg: MT *He removed them to the cities* *b* Heb *Israel*

here contrasts with his beneficent provision for his own family (see 45.5–11; 50.20–21). **27:** The Priestly fertility promise to Abraham (17.2,6; cf. 1.28; 9.1,7) is fulfilled in Egypt.

47.29–49.33: Jacob's preparations for death, including the adoption and blessing of Ephraim and Manasseh. This section is viewed by many scholars as a series of later insertions into the Joseph story, linking it back to the Jacob story and forward to the story of the Israelites. **47.29:** *Put your hand under my thigh,* see 24.2n. **30–31:** Joseph binds himself by oath to bury Jacob in an ancestral burial place, perhaps in Transjordan (see 50.10n.). This non-Priestly (J) notice parallels the Priestly notice where Jacob orders his sons to bury him in the cave at Machpelah (49.29–32; see ch 23). **48.3–6:** This Priestly narrative refers to the Priestly Bethel (Luz) account (35.9–13) in describing Jacob's adoption of his two Josephite grandsons. The narrative accounts for the division of the "house of Joseph" (Josh 17.17; 18.5; Judg 1.23,35) into two tribes, Manasseh and Ephraim. **7:** 35.16–20. **8–14:** In having Jacob favor the younger son,

to Joseph, "God Almighty[a] appeared to
me at Luz in the land of Canaan, and he
blessed me, 4 and said to me, 'I am going to
make you fruitful and increase your num-
bers; I will make of you a company of peo-
ples, and will give this land to your off-
spring after you for a perpetual holding.'
5 Therefore your two sons, who were born
to you in the land of Egypt before I came to
you in Egypt, are now mine; Ephraim and
Manasseh shall be mine, just as Reuben
and Simeon are. 6 As for the offspring born
to you after them, they shall be yours. They
shall be recorded under the names of their
brothers with regard to their inheritance.
7 For when I came from Paddan, Rachel,
alas, died in the land of Canaan on the way,
while there was still some distance to go to
Ephrath; and I buried her there on the way
to Ephrath" (that is, Bethlehem).

8 When Israel saw Joseph's sons, he
said, "Who are these?" 9 Joseph said to his
father, "They are my sons, whom God has
given me here." And he said, "Bring them
to me, please, that I may bless them."
10 Now the eyes of Israel were dim with
age, and he could not see well. So Joseph
brought them near him; and he kissed them
and embraced them. 11 Israel said to Joseph,
"I did not expect to see your face; and here
God has let me see your children also."
12 Then Joseph removed them from his fa-
ther's knees,[b] and he bowed himself with
his face to the earth. 13 Joseph took them
both, Ephraim in his right hand toward Is-
rael's left, and Manasseh in his left hand
toward Israel's right, and brought them
near him. 14 But Israel stretched out his
right hand and laid it on the head of Ephra-
im, who was the younger, and his left hand
on the head of Manasseh, crossing his
hands, for Manasseh was the firstborn.
15 He blessed Joseph, and said,

"The God before whom my ancestors
Abraham and Isaac walked,
the God who has been my shepherd
all my life to this day,
16 the angel who has redeemed me from
all harm, bless the boys;
and in them let my name be
perpetuated, and the name of
my ancestors Abraham and
Isaac;
and let them grow into a multitude
on the earth."

17 When Joseph saw that his father laid
his right hand on the head of Ephraim, it
displeased him; so he took his father's
hand, to remove it from Ephraim's head to
Manasseh's head. 18 Joseph said to his fa-
ther, "Not so, my father! Since this one is
the firstborn, put your right hand on his
head." 19 But his father refused, and said, "I
know, my son, I know; he also shall be-
come a people, and he also shall be great.
Nevertheless his younger brother shall be
greater than he, and his offspring shall be-
come a multitude of nations." 20 So he
blessed them that day, saying,

"By you[c] Israel will invoke blessings,
saying,
'God make you[c] like Ephraim and
like Manasseh.' "

So he put Ephraim ahead of Manasseh.
21 Then Israel said to Joseph, "I am about
to die, but God will be with you and will
bring you again to the land of your ances-
tors. 22 I now give to you one portion[d]

a Traditional rendering of Heb *El Shaddai*
b Heb *from his knees* *c* *you* here is singular in Heb
d Or *mountain slope* (Heb *shekem*, a play on the name of the town and district of Shechem)

Ephraim, over the older, Manasseh, this non-Priestly narrative echoes the earlier stories of Jacob's achievement of ascendancy over Esau (25.22–34; 27.1–45). Like the older Joseph story into which this scene is inserted (see 47.28–49.33n.), this section may intend to predict the Ephraimite Jeroboam's ascendancy over the Northern Kingdom (1 Kings 11.26; 12.1–14.20; see 37.5–8n.). **15–16:** Jacob passes onto the Joseph tribes the special blessing of Abraham and Isaac (12.1–3; 26.2–5; etc.). **17–19:** See 8–14n. **20:** This older version of the blessing on Ephraim and Manasseh (cf. vv. 15–16) is an example of people "blessing themselves by" another (see 12.3n.). **22:** In Hebrew *one portion* (or "shoulder," Heb "shekem") is a play on the name "Shechem" (see 12.6n.). *With my sword and with my bow,* cf. 33.19–34.31. *Amorites,* see 10.16–18a n.

more than to your brothers, the portion[a]
that I took from the hand of the Amorites
with my sword and with my bow."

49 Then Jacob called his sons, and
said: "Gather around, that I may
tell you what will happen to you in days to
come.
2 Assemble and hear, O sons of Jacob;
listen to Israel your father.

3 Reuben, you are my firstborn,
my might and the first fruits of my
vigor,
excelling in rank and excelling in
power.
4 Unstable as water, you shall no longer
excel
because you went up onto your
father's bed;
then you defiled it—you[b] went up
onto my couch!

5 Simeon and Levi are brothers;
weapons of violence are their
swords.
6 May I never come into their council;
may I not be joined to their
company—
for in their anger they killed men,
and at their whim they hamstrung
oxen.
7 Cursed be their anger, for it is fierce,
and their wrath, for it is cruel!
I will divide them in Jacob,
and scatter them in Israel.

8 Judah, your brothers shall praise you;
your hand shall be on the neck of
your enemies;
your father's sons shall bow down
before you.
9 Judah is a lion's whelp;
from the prey, my son, you have
gone up.
He crouches down, he stretches out
like a lion,
like a lioness—who dares rouse him
up?
10 The scepter shall not depart from
Judah,
nor the ruler's staff from between
his feet,
until tribute comes to him;[c]
and the obedience of the peoples is
his.
11 Binding his foal to the vine
and his donkey's colt to the choice
vine,
he washes his garments in wine
and his robe in the blood of grapes;

a Or *mountain slope* (Heb *shekem*, a play on the name of the town and district of Shechem) *b* Gk Syr Tg: Heb *he* *c* Or *until Shiloh comes* or *until he comes to Shiloh* or (with Syr) *until he comes to whom it belongs*

49.1–28: Jacob's blessing on his twelve sons. Though the poem is depicted as a deathbed *blessing* by the text following it (49.28; cf. 27.4 and n.), this poem seems to have been originally designed as a prediction of the destiny, good and bad, of the tribes of Israel. Many have argued that the poem is ancient on the basis of its language and resemblance to tribal poems in Deut 33 and Judg 5. Nevertheless, the present form of the poem appears to have been modified to fit the narrative context in which it has been put. Its first part follows the birth order of 29.31–35 and legitimates rule for Judah and—by extension—the Davidic dynasty. The author of these changes may be responsible for inserting the whole poem into its present context, as well as for the addition to the Jacob-Joseph story of the narratives referred to in 48.3–7 (30.21; 34.1–31; 35.21–22a; cf. 37.36–38.30). **3–4:** This section justifies Reuben's ejection from favor as firstborn by recalling the story of his sleeping with his father's concubine (see 35.22n.). **5–7:** Judah's older brothers, Simeon and Levi, fail to take Reuben's place because of their role in the despoiling of Shechem (34.25–31). **8–12:** With his three older brothers out of favor (vv. 3–7), Judah receives the greatest part of his father's blessing. The story of the succession to David features a similar displacement of older sons: Amnon (2 Sam 13), Absalom (2 Sam 15–18), and Adonijah (1 Kings 1–2). See 38.27–30n. **10:** The *scepter* and *staff* are representations of sovereignty. The latter part of the verse, however, is obscure (see note *c*). It appears to predict rule for Judean royalty until Judah's Davidic descendants achieve universal dominion (Num 24.17; Ps 2; 110) and must be preexilic. **13–27:** This latter part of the blessing

12 his eyes are darker than wine,
and his teeth whiter than milk.
13 Zebulun shall settle at the shore of the sea;
he shall be a haven for ships,
and his border shall be at Sidon.

14 Issachar is a strong donkey,
lying down between the sheepfolds;
15 he saw that a resting place was good,
and that the land was pleasant;
so he bowed his shoulder to the burden,
and became a slave at forced labor.

16 Dan shall judge his people
as one of the tribes of Israel.
17 Dan shall be a snake by the roadside,
a viper along the path,
that bites the horse's heels
so that its rider falls backward.

18 I wait for your salvation, O LORD.

19 Gad shall be raided by raiders,
but he shall raid at their heels.

20 Asher's[a] food shall be rich,
and he shall provide royal delicacies.

21 Naphtali is a doe let loose
that bears lovely fawns.[b]

22 Joseph is a fruitful bough,
a fruitful bough by a spring;
his branches run over the wall.[c]
23 The archers fiercely attacked him;
they shot at him and pressed him hard.
24 Yet his bow remained taut,
and his arms[d] were made agile
by the hands of the Mighty One of Jacob,
by the name of the Shepherd, the Rock of Israel,
25 by the God of your father, who will help you,
by the Almighty[e] who will bless you
with blessings of heaven above,
blessings of the deep that lies beneath,
blessings of the breasts and of the womb.
26 The blessings of your father
are stronger than the blessings of the eternal mountains,
the bounties[f] of the everlasting hills;
may they be on the head of Joseph,
on the brow of him who was set apart from his brothers.

27 Benjamin is a ravenous wolf,
in the morning devouring the prey,
and at evening dividing the spoil."

28 All these are the twelve tribes of Isra-
el, and this is what their father said to them
when he blessed them, blessing each one of
them with a suitable blessing.
29 Then he charged them, saying to
them, "I am about to be gathered to my
people. Bury me with my ancestors—in the
cave in the field of Ephron the Hittite, 30 in
the cave in the field at Machpelah, near
Mamre, in the land of Canaan, in the field
that Abraham bought from Ephron the

a Gk Vg Syr: Heb *From Asher* *b* Or *that gives beautiful words* *c* Meaning of Heb uncertain *d* Heb *the arms of his hands* *e* Traditional rendering of Heb *Shaddai* *f* Cn Compare Gk: Heb *of my progenitors to the boundaries*

(vv. 13–27) diverges from the birth order of 30.1–24. This section appears to predate placement into its present context in the story of Jacob and Joseph. **16:** The tribal name *Dan* is derived from the Heb verb for "judge" ("dan"). **22–26:** The lengthy blessing on Joseph and its triumphant conclusion (v. 26) suggest that he may have been the original focus of the early blessing (see 49.1–28n.). **25:** *The Almighty,* see 17.1n. *Blessings of heaven,* i.e., rain, dew, sun. *The deep that lies beneath,* an allusion to the subterranean ocean (see 1.6; 2.6). Compare Deut 33.13.

49.29–33: This Priestly section includes an order to bury Jacob at Machpelah (see ch 23) that parallels the earlier non-Priestly burial order (47.29–31).

Hittite as a burial site. 31 There Abraham
and his wife Sarah were buried; there Isaac
and his wife Rebekah were buried; and
there I buried Leah— 32 the field and the
cave that is in it were purchased from the
Hittites." 33 When Jacob ended his charge
to his sons, he drew up his feet into the bed,
breathed his last, and was gathered to his
people.

50 Then Joseph threw himself on his
father's face and wept over him and
kissed him. 2 Joseph commanded the physi-
cians in his service to embalm his father. So
the physicians embalmed Israel; 3 they spent
forty days in doing this, for that is the time
required for embalming. And the Egyptians
wept for him seventy days.

4 When the days of weeping for him
were past, Joseph addressed the household
of Pharaoh, "If now I have found favor
with you, please speak to Pharaoh as fol-
lows: 5 My father made me swear an oath;
he said, 'I am about to die. In the tomb that
I hewed out for myself in the land of Ca-
naan, there you shall bury me.' Now there-
fore let me go up, so that I may bury my
father; then I will return." 6 Pharaoh an-
swered, "Go up, and bury your father, as
he made you swear to do."

7 So Joseph went up to bury his father.
With him went up all the servants of Phar-
aoh, the elders of his household, and all the
elders of the land of Egypt, 8 as well as all
the household of Joseph, his brothers, and
his father's household. Only their children,
their flocks, and their herds were left in the
land of Goshen. 9 Both chariots and chario-
teers went up with him. It was a very great
company. 10 When they came to the thresh-
ing floor of Atad, which is beyond the Jor-
dan, they held there a very great and sor-
rowful lamentation; and he observed a time
of mourning for his father seven days.
11 When the Canaanite inhabitants of the
land saw the mourning on the threshing
floor of Atad, they said, "This is a grievous
mourning on the part of the Egyptians."
Therefore the place was named Abel-
mizraim;[a] it is beyond the Jordan. 12 Thus
his sons did for him as he had instructed
them. 13 They carried him to the land of
Canaan and buried him in the cave of the
field at Machpelah, the field near Mamre,
which Abraham bought as a burial site
from Ephron the Hittite. 14 After he had
buried his father, Joseph returned to Egypt
with his brothers and all who had gone up
with him to bury his father.

15 Realizing that their father was dead,
Joseph's brothers said, "What if Joseph still
bears a grudge against us and pays us back
in full for all the wrong that we did to
him?" 16 So they approached[b] Joseph, say-
ing, "Your father gave this instruction be-
fore he died, 17 'Say to Joseph: I beg you,
forgive the crime of your brothers and the
wrong they did in harming you.' Now
therefore please forgive the crime of the ser-
vants of the God of your father." Joseph
wept when they spoke to him. 18 Then his

a That is *mourning* (or *meadow*) *of Egypt*
b Gk Syr: Heb *they commanded*

50.1–26: Burial of Jacob and final days of Joseph. 2–3: Jacob is provided with Egyptian honors: embalming and lengthy mourning. **5:** This speech by Joseph links to the non-Priestly order to bury him at an ancestral burial place,here a tomb that Jacob had hewn out for himself. **10:** Hebron/Mamre is much closer to Egypt than this unidentified location in Transjordan. This non-Priestly narrative (vv. 1–11) seems to presuppose that the burial and mourning occurred in Transjordan, not at the cave at Machpelah (23.1,19). **12–13:** The Priestly narrative. **15–16:** In fear now that their father is dead (cf. 27.41 and 33.12–17n.), Joseph's brothers attempt to protect themselves through reporting that Jacob had ordered Joseph to forgive them (vv. 16–17). The text is ambiguous; it is unclear whether or not they are fabricating this instruction. **18–21:** For the first time, the brothers knowingly subject themselves to Joseph (cf. 43.26), fulfill Joseph's first dream (37.5–7), and thus refute their own challenge of his destiny (37.8). Since they had just spoken of themselves as God's slaves (v. 17; translated in the NRSV as *servants*), their description of themselves here as Joseph's slaves implicitly equates him with God. Echoing his father's words to Rachel (30.2), Joseph rejects this equation, attributing his dominion over his brothers as

brothers also wept,[a] fell down before him,
and said, "We are here as your slaves."
19 But Joseph said to them, "Do not be
afraid! Am I in the place of God? 20 Even
though you intended to do harm to me,
God intended it for good, in order to pre-
serve a numerous people, as he is doing to-
day. 21 So have no fear; I myself will pro-
vide for you and your little ones." In this
way he reassured them, speaking kindly to
them.
22 So Joseph remained in Egypt, he and
his father's household; and Joseph lived
one hundred ten years. 23 Joseph saw
Ephraim's children of the third generation;
the children of Machir son of Manasseh
were also born on Joseph's knees.
24 Then Joseph said to his brothers, "I
am about to die; but God will surely come
to you, and bring you up out of this land
to the land that he swore to Abraham, to
Isaac, and to Jacob." 25 So Joseph made the
Israelites swear, saying, "When God comes
to you, you shall carry up my bones from
here." 26 And Joseph died, being one hun-
dred ten years old; he was embalmed and
placed in a coffin in Egypt.

a Cn: Heb *also came*

resulting from God's plan for him to provide for them. **23:** *Machir* was an early tribal group (Judg 5.14) later seen as a clan within Manasseh that laid claim to Gilead (Num 32.39–40; Deut 3.15). *Born on Joseph's knees,* see 30.3. **24:** A reference to God's covenant oath to give the land to Abraham (15.9–17n.; 22.15–18). It closely resembles similar texts in Deut 1.8; 6.10 and related materials. **25–26:** See Ex 13.19; Josh 24.32.

EXODUS

The book of Exodus is named after the focus of the first fifteen chapters of the book: the liberation of Israel from Egypt by "the God of Abraham . . . Isaac, and . . . Jacob" (3.15). The Exodus, however, is not a goal unto itself; the book continues with various laws which distinguish the community (chs 20–23,34), as well as the instructions for the construction of the tabernacle (chs 25–40), which are narrated in great detail, and assure that a holy God will reside among the people.

It is impossible to discern what historical events lie behind the book of Exodus. Given the lack of contemporaneous evidence outside the Bible, we can hope only to attain a plausible reconstruction. Reconstructions run the gamut from identifying the Pharaoh of the plagues with Rameses II (1279–1213 BCE) to asserting that the entire story is metaphorical, and Israel was never in Egypt. Those favoring a historical reading of the book have noted that no nation is likely to make up a story that its ancestors had been slaves. Those favoring a metaphorical reading have suggested that the tyranny experienced reflects Egypt's political and economic domination of the land of Canaan in the Late Bronze Age. They emphasize the continuity of Israelite culture with Canaanite (rather than Egyptian) culture in architecture, crafts, language, and worship. There is also uncertainty about most of the place names in the book, even about the location of Mount Sinai. Nor is there a consensus on the authorship and date of the various parts of this complex work. Some sections are Priestly (compare 20.8–11 with Gen 2.1–3, and note the interest in the priestly tabernacle in chs 25–40), other sections are clearly reminiscent of Deuteronomy (compare 23.23–33 with Deuteronomy 7), and some contain material usually ascribed to JE, traditionally considered to be the earliest sources of the Pentateuch. Underlying the final form of the book is a complicated literary prehistory, in which the sources or "documents" of the Pentateuch (J, E, and P) have been combined in a way that values the preservation of divergent traditions more than a superficial consistency. The book also includes an often bewildering variety of smaller units from various stages of Israel's history. These include hymns and hymnic fragments, itineraries, ritual traditions, and legal codifications, along with elements of myth and folklore and birth and contest narratives. Some of these traditions are relatively ancient and may well reflect authentic historical memory.

In the absence of a consensus concerning the book's historicity and composition, it is best to read Exodus as a finished narrative, a story—though never forgetting that it has a pre-history, and that in its final form within the larger story of the Torah or Pentateuch, it is the definitive story of the establishment of Israel as a people freed from human tyranny who became slaves to their own loving God.

God's purpose in liberating Israel is expressed in several similar ways: in order to establish an exclusive relationship ("I will take you as my people, and I will be your God," 6.7; "I . . . brought you to myself," 19.4), to make them unique ("my treasured possession out of all the peoples, . . . a priestly kingdom and a holy nation," 19.5–6), and to "dwell among them" (29.46). Indeed, the Exodus is inextricably tied to the provisions of the covenant by providing reason and motivation for much of what God expects of the people. In worship, the experience of liberation from slavery prompts the Israelites to reinterpret ancient festivals, instilling them with completely new meaning: passover (12.1–13n.), unleavened bread (12.14–20n.), and sacrifice of firstborn (13.1–2n.). Likewise, in late biblical legislation, the festival of booths comes to commemorate the wilderness wandering (Lev 23.39–43), and in post-biblical Judaism, the festival of weeks celebrates the giving of the covenant at Sinai (19.1n.). The central commandment, "you shall have no other gods before me," is immediately preceded by the identification of God as the one "who brought you out of the land of Egypt" (20.1–3). An important component of the upbringing of children is to be explanation of customs on the basis of liberation (12.24–27n.). Ethically, God uses the experience of oppression to motivate the covenant partner: Israel's memory of being aliens in Egypt gives them empathy for aliens within Israel (22.21; 23.9). Thus, the Exodus is truly the central, unifying focus of the book.

One way to express the movement in Exodus is to say that chs 1–15 tell the story of freedom *from* while chs 16–40 tell the story of freedom *to*: liberation *from* slavery is followed by liberation *to* accomplish a new thing. This is explicitly reflected in 7.16, where the LORD sent Moses to demand of the Pharaoh: "Let *my* people go, so that they may worship [serve/be slaves to] *me*" (emphasis added; cf. 4.23). The people are still servants, but the change of masters makes all the difference. Additionally, Israel was forced to serve Pharaoh, while it freely decides to serve the LORD (24.3,7).

Another way to understand the book is to visualize its geographical movement. Chapters 1–15 tell the story of leaving the city where the evil Pharaoh reigns and enslaves the Hebrews; chs 16–40 tell the story of arriving at the mountain where a holy God reigns and creates the people of Israel. In Egypt a royal construction program enslaves Hebrews; Hebrew boys are killed, and in the end God claims the lives of all the firstborn of Egypt, human and animal alike. At Sinai all the firstborn males of Israel, human and animal alike, are equally claimed by God. A new royal construction program is inaugurated, for building the portable tabernacle that assures the continuing presence of God among the new people as they travel to the promised land.

Indeed, this geographical movement can be understood more specifically as a pilgrimage undertaken first by Moses alone (chs 2–4), then by all the people (chs 13–40). Each pilgrimage proceeds from the evil land where Pharaoh reigns through the desert to the holy mountain where the God of Sinai reigns. The goal of each pilgrimage is experiencing God through a theophany and receiving a commission. The first theophany is for Moses alone (3.1–6), the second is for all Israel (19.16–19) but is too much for them to bear (20.18–21), so the third is for the leaders only (24.9–11), and the fourth is for Moses alone as covenant mediator (24.15–18). While Moses' commission is to act as God's agent in freeing the people (chs 3–4), Israel's commission is to act as God's holy people in all areas of life (chs 19–24) and to build a shrine so that God may dwell in their presence (chs 25–31). The first effort to fulfill each commission fails: Moses' first appearance before Pharaoh only makes the oppression worse (ch 5), and Israel's first impatient attempt to ensure God's continuing presence among them, the construction of the calf, almost brings complete destruction (ch 32). But after each commission is restated (6.2–7.7; 34.10–28 after the fifth theophany, again for Moses alone, 33.17–34.9), the second attempt is successful. Moses finally leads the slaves to freedom (chs 7–15), and Israel finally builds the tabernacle so that God may dwell among them (chs 35–40).

There is more than one way to outline the book, since many of the stories it narrates point both backward and forward. For example, the hymn in ch 15 points backward to celebrate the victories of the divine warrior, while it also points ahead to anticipate the terror of the other peoples and the march forward to God's mountain. Thus, the following suggested structure of the book is necessarily one-dimensional.

- 1.1–15.21. God liberates Israel from slavery by defeating Pharaoh
- 15.22–18.27. God journeys with Israel to Mount Sinai
- 19.1–31.18. God establishes the covenant with Israel
- 32.1–34.35. Israel breaks the covenant, but God reestablishes it
- 35.1–40.38. Israel obeys instructions, and God takes up residence with them

Many recurrent words and themes tie the book's different parts together. For example, some of the themes that frame the first part of the story, that of liberation, are women's activities (15.19–21n.), a life-threatening body of water with reeds (2.3n.), a loud cry (2.23n.), the plundering of Egypt (3.21–22n.), God's claim on the firstborn son (4.22–23n.), and ritual with blood (as protection against death at God's hand, 4.24–26n.).

The Hebrew word for heaviness (5.9), referring not only to the "hardening" of Pharaoh's heart (7.14; 8.15,32; 9.7,34; 10.1) but also to God's "glory" (14.4,17–18; 16.7,10; 24.16–17; 29.43; 33.18,22; 40.34–35), unifies the book. Other themes tie the parts of the story together: knowledge, or better, acknowledgment of God (5.2n.); the distinction between Israel and other peoples (Egypt, 8.22–23n.; other peoples, 15.13–18n.); and proper service/worship: first the right object of service, not the Pharaoh but God; second, the right means of worship, not a golden calf (ch 32) but a tabernacle (chs 25–31; 35–40). Several of the themes that frame the first part of the story, liberation, recur in the second half, covenant, thus linking the two sections together: the treasures from Egypt used both to break and to keep the covenant (3.21–22n.); the firstborn (4.22–23n.); and ritual with blood (now sealing the covenant between God and Israel, 24.3–8n.; and consecrating the priests, 29.20–21n.).

Another predominant pattern is God's precise command followed by Moses' exact obedience. It can be seen (7.6n.) in Moses' two commissions, the plagues, the victory at the sea, several incidents during the journey, and preeminently the instructions for making the tabernacle (chs 25–31). The one case of disobedience, the construction of the golden calf (ch 32), disrupts this theme. Moses must intercede four times, many Israelites must die, and three chapters are required before the story can get back on track. Finally the commands of chs 25–31 are carried out in chs 35–40, and God indeed takes up residence among the people.

1 These are the names of the sons of Isra-
el who came to Egypt with Jacob, each
with his household: 2 Reuben, Simeon,
Levi, and Judah, 3 Issachar, Zebulun, and
Benjamin, 4 Dan and Naphtali, Gad and
Asher. 5 The total number of people born to
Jacob was seventy. Joseph was already in
Egypt. 6 Then Joseph died, and all his
brothers, and that whole generation. 7 But
the Israelites were fruitful and prolific; they
multiplied and grew exceedingly strong, so
that the land was filled with them.

8 Now a new king arose over Egypt,
who did not know Joseph. 9 He said to
his people, "Look, the Israelite people are
more numerous and more powerful than

1.1–15.21: God liberates Israel from slavery by defeating Pharaoh.

1.1–22: The Israelites suffer oppression in Egypt. In spite of their suffering, the descendants of Jacob (Israel) multiply and prosper, in fulfillment of the divine promise repeated to Abraham, Isaac, and Jacob (Gen 12.2; 15.5; 22.17; 26.4; 28.14). V. 7 echoes the Priestly Gen 1.28, suggesting that the growth of Israel fulfills the divine blessing of creation as well. **1–7:** An abbreviated version of Gen 46.8–27, serving as a transition from Jacob's family in Genesis to the people Israel in Exodus. **1–5:** The sons are listed according to their mothers: Leah's six, Rachel's second, Bilhah's two, and Zilpah's two (Gen 29.31–30.24; 35.16–20,23–26). Rachel's firstborn, *Joseph,* whose story has been told in Gen 37–50, is mentioned in v. 5. Daughters such as Dinah (Gen 30.21; 34) are not counted in this list of heads of households (v. 1). **5:** *Total number of people . . . was seventy,* Gen 46.8–27; Deut 10.22. **6:** Gen 50.26. According to Ex 12.40 (cf. Gen 15.13) over four centuries have elapsed since Joseph's death. **7:** *The land* of Goshen in northeastern Egypt (8.22; Gen 45.10; Map on p. 28 HB). **8–14:** The *new king* attempts to counter the growth of the Israelite people by subjecting them to *forced labor* (Gen 15.13). **8:** *Know,* does not ac*know*ledge any obligation to Joseph's descendants. **9–10:** The presence of the Israelites on Egypt's frontier is regarded as a security risk. **11:** *Pithom* and *Rameses* are presumably in Goshen, though their

we. 10 Come, let us deal shrewdly with
them, or they will increase and, in the event
of war, join our enemies and fight against
us and escape from the land." 11 Therefore
they set taskmasters over them to oppress
them with forced labor. They built supply
cities, Pithom and Rameses, for Pharaoh.
12 But the more they were oppressed, the
more they multiplied and spread, so that
the Egyptians came to dread the Israelites.
13 The Egyptians became ruthless in impos-
ing tasks on the Israelites, 14 and made their
lives bitter with hard service in mortar and
brick and in every kind of field labor. They
were ruthless in all the tasks that they im-
posed on them.
15 The king of Egypt said to the Hebrew
midwives, one of whom was named Shiph-
rah and the other Puah, 16 "When you act
as midwives to the Hebrew women, and see
them on the birthstool, if it is a boy, kill
him; but if it is a girl, she shall live." 17 But
the midwives feared God; they did not do
as the king of Egypt commanded them, but
they let the boys live. 18 So the king of Egypt
summoned the midwives and said to them,
"Why have you done this, and allowed the
boys to live?" 19 The midwives said to Phar-
aoh, "Because the Hebrew women are not
like the Egyptian women; for they are vig-
orous and give birth before the midwife
comes to them." 20 So God dealt well with
the midwives; and the people multiplied
and became very strong. 21 And because the
midwives feared God, he gave them fami-
lies. 22 Then Pharaoh commanded all his
people, "Every boy that is born to the He-
brews[a] you shall throw into the Nile, but
you shall let every girl live."

2 Now a man from the house of Levi
went and married a Levite woman.
2 The woman conceived and bore a son;
and when she saw that he was a fine baby,
she hid him three months. 3 When she could
hide him no longer she got a papyrus bas-
ket for him, and plastered it with bitumen
and pitch; she put the child in it and placed
it among the reeds on the bank of the river.
4 His sister stood at a distance, to see what
would happen to him.
5 The daughter of Pharaoh came down
to bathe at the river, while her attendants
walked beside the river. She saw the basket
among the reeds and sent her maid to bring
it. 6 When she opened it, she saw the child.
He was crying, and she took pity on him.
"This must be one of the Hebrews' chil-
dren," she said. 7 Then his sister said to
Pharaoh's daughter, "Shall I go and get you
a nurse from the Hebrew women to nurse
the child for you?" 8 Pharaoh's daughter
said to her, "Yes." So the girl went and
called the child's mother. 9 Pharaoh's
daughter said to her, "Take this child and
nurse it for me, and I will give you your
wages." So the woman took the child and
nursed it. 10 When the child grew up, she
brought him to Pharaoh's daughter, and

a Sam Gk Tg: Heb lacks *to the Hebrews*

precise locations are disputed. **15–22:** Forced labor having failed, the king now attempts genocide. **15:** The term *Hebrew* probably refers to displaced persons rather than to a specific ethnic group. In Exodus the word occurs about a dozen times in chs 1–9, but afterward only once (21.2). *Hebrew midwives,* alternatively "midwives of the Hebrews," in which case *Shiphrah* and *Puah* may be Egyptians, the first outsiders to rescue Hebrews (another "righteous Gentile" appears in 2.5–10). Their names, however, are Semitic. **16:** The killing of *boys* rather than *girls* reflects a patrilineal society. **17:** *Feared God,* better, reverenced God. **22:** Unable to rely on the midwives, the Pharaoh turns to all of the Egyptians to carry out his genocide.

2.1–22: The early life of Moses. 1–10: Moses is born and adopted. **1:** *Levi,* the third son of Jacob (1.2). The parents' names are given in 6.20, Amram and Jochebed. **2–3:** *Saw that he was a fine baby,* lit. "saw that he was good," as in the creation story in Gen 1. The meaning here is "healthy." The *basket* occurs elsewhere only concerning Noah's ark (Gen 6–9). As Noah's ark rescued humankind, Moses' "ark" will rescue the future liberator of Israel. Since Moses will bring a new beginning, parallels with creation and flood are especially fitting. *The reeds* point ahead to the rescue of Israel at the Reed Sea (chs 14–15). **4:** The sister is elsewhere identified as Miriam in 15.20; Num 26.59. **6:** *Hebrews,* 1.15n. **10:** The name

she took him as her son. She named him
Moses,[a] "because," she said, "I drew him
out[b] of the water."
11 One day, after Moses had grown up,
he went out to his people and saw their
forced labor. He saw an Egyptian beating a
Hebrew, one of his kinsfolk. 12He looked
this way and that, and seeing no one he
killed the Egyptian and hid him in the sand.
13When he went out the next day, he saw
two Hebrews fighting; and he said to the
one who was in the wrong, "Why do you
strike your fellow Hebrew?" 14He an-
swered, "Who made you a ruler and judge
over us? Do you mean to kill me as you
killed the Egyptian?" Then Moses was
afraid and thought, "Surely the thing is
known." 15When Pharaoh heard of it, he
sought to kill Moses.
But Moses fled from Pharaoh. He settled
in the land of Midian, and sat down by a
well. 16The priest of Midian had seven
daughters. They came to draw water, and
filled the troughs to water their father's
flock. 17But some shepherds came and
drove them away. Moses got up and came
to their defense and watered their flock.
18When they returned to their father Reuel,
he said, "How is it that you have come
back so soon today?" 19They said, "An
Egyptian helped us against the shepherds;
he even drew water for us and watered the
flock." 20He said to his daughters, "Where
is he? Why did you leave the man? Invite
him to break bread." 21Moses agreed to
stay with the man, and he gave Moses his
daughter Zipporah in marriage. 22She bore
a son, and he named him Gershom; for he
said, "I have been an alien[c] residing in a
foreign land."
23 After a long time the king of Egypt
died. The Israelites groaned under their
slavery, and cried out. Out of the slavery
their cry for help rose up to God. 24God
heard their groaning, and God remembered
his covenant with Abraham, Isaac, and Ja-
cob. 25God looked upon the Israelites, and
God took notice of them.

3 Moses was keeping the flock of his
father-in-law Jethro, the priest of Midi-
an; he led his flock beyond the wilderness,
and came to Horeb, the mountain of God.
2There the angel of the LORD appeared to
him in a flame of fire out of a bush; he

[a] Heb *Mosheh* [b] Heb *mashah* [c] Heb *ger*

Moses, from an Egyptian word meaning "to beget a child" and perhaps once joined with the name of an Egyptian deity (cf. the name Thut-mose), is given a Hebrew etymology, "he who draws out"; as an adult Moses will live up to his name by drawing the Hebrews out of the Red Sea. **11–15a:** Despite his Egyptian upbringing and appearance (vv. 10,19), Moses identifies with his own people when he sees their suffering. His first attempt to help them fails, however, as both Hebrews and Pharaoh turn against him. **15b–22:** Moses flees and marries. **15:** Gen 25.2 identifies the Midianites as descendants of Abraham and Keturah, and thus relatives of Israel (contrast Judg 4.11). Their homeland was in northwestern Arabia (Map on p. 24 HB). **17:** Having been rescued by the daughter of the Egyptian king, Moses now rescues the seven daughters of a Midianite priest. Zipporah (v. 21) will later return the favor (4.24–26). **18:** Moses' father-in-law (v. 21) is elsewhere called either Jethro (3.1; 4.18; 18.1) or Hobab (Judg 4.11), while *Reuel* is Zipporah's grandfather (Num 10.29).

2.23–4.17: God calls Moses. In Midian the God of Israel's ancestors appears to Moses and summons him to take the lead in delivering Israel. **2.23–25:** The transition to the next king does not improve conditions for the Israelites, but it will make possible Moses' return to Egypt (4.19). Though it is not stated that the Israelites cry out to God, nonetheless God hears them and is moved to the first overt divine action on behalf of all the slaves (cf. 1.20–21). Israel's *cry* will be echoed by Egypt's "loud cry" at the end (11.6; 12.30). **24:** *Remembered,* or "focused attention on." *Covenant,* Gen 12.1–3; 17; 26.2–5. **3.1–6:** God appears for the first time at Horeb (or Sinai). This theophany, or divine appearance, to Moses alone, prefigures the second, beginning in ch 19, to all Israel. **1:** *The mountain of God,* called both Horeb (as here) and Sinai (19.11), is probably a Midianite sacred place. Its location is unknown, but three poems support the notion here that it is southeast of Israel rather than in what we now call the Sinai Peninsula (Deut 33.2; Judg 5.4; Hab 3.3,7; see Midian on color Map 2 at end of book). **2:** The *angel* (lit. "messen-

looked, and the bush was blazing, yet it
was not consumed. 3Then Moses said, "I
must turn aside and look at this great sight,
and see why the bush is not burned up."
4When the LORD saw that he had turned
aside to see, God called to him out of the
bush, "Moses, Moses!" And he said, "Here
I am." 5Then he said, "Come no closer!
Remove the sandals from your feet, for the
place on which you are standing is holy
ground." 6He said further, "I am the God
of your father, the God of Abraham, the
God of Isaac, and the God of Jacob." And
Moses hid his face, for he was afraid to
look at God.
7 Then the LORD said, "I have observed
the misery of my people who are in Egypt;
I have heard their cry on account of their
taskmasters. Indeed, I know their suffer-
ings, 8and I have come down to deliver
them from the Egyptians, and to bring
them up out of that land to a good and
broad land, a land flowing with milk and
honey, to the country of the Canaanites,
the Hittites, the Amorites, the Perizzites,
the Hivites, and the Jebusites. 9The cry of
the Israelites has now come to me; I have
also seen how the Egyptians oppress them.
10So come, I will send you to Pharaoh to
bring my people, the Israelites, out of
Egypt." 11But Moses said to God, "Who
am I that I should go to Pharaoh, and bring
the Israelites out of Egypt?" 12He said, "I
will be with you; and this shall be the sign
for you that it is I who sent you: when you
have brought the people out of Egypt, you
shall worship God on this mountain."
13 But Moses said to God, "If I come to
the Israelites and say to them, 'The God of
your ancestors has sent me to you,' and
they ask me, 'What is his name?' what shall
I say to them?" 14God said to Moses, "I AM
WHO I AM."[a] He said further, "Thus you
shall say to the Israelites, 'I AM has sent me
to you.' " 15God also said to Moses, "Thus
you shall say to the Israelites, 'The LORD,[b]
the God of your ancestors, the God of
Abraham, the God of Isaac, and the God of
Jacob, has sent me to you':

This is my name forever,
and this my title for all generations.

16Go and assemble the elders of Israel, and
say to them, 'The LORD, the God of your
ancestors, the God of Abraham, of Isaac,
and of Jacob, has appeared to me, saying: I
have given heed to you and to what has
been done to you in Egypt. 17I declare that
I will bring you up out of the misery of

a Or *I AM WHAT I AM* or *I WILL BE WHAT I WILL BE*
b The word "LORD" when spelled with capital letters stands for the divine name, *YHWH,* which is here connected with the verb *hayah,* "to be"

ger") will turn out to be the presence of the divine (vv. 4–6). *Fire* is often a form of the divine appearance (Gen 15.17; Ex 13.21; 19.18; 24.17; 40.38; Ps 104.3–4; Ezek 1.27). **5:** Moses unexpectedly finds himself in a *holy* place (3.1n.; Gen 28.16–17); cf. Josh 5.15. **6:** *The God of your father,* Gen 26.24. An alternate textual tradition reads: "the God of your ancestors" (cf. 3.15). The vision of God veiled in fire arouses dread (33.20), for divine holiness is experienced as a mysterious power that threatens human existence (19.10–13). **7–10:** God commissions Moses. **8:** *A land flowing with milk and honey,* a description with mythological overtones. The *honey* was probably a thick syrup made from grapes or dates. *The Canaanites . . .* , Similar lists of the peoples living in Canaan appear in Gen 10.15–20; 15.18–21; Ex 3.17; 13.5; Num 13.29; Deut 7.1. **11–12:** The first of Moses' four objections (v. 13; 4.1,10). God's promise will be confirmed retrospectively by a *sign:* The Israelites will follow Moses to worship at Mount Horeb/Sinai (v. 1; ch 19). **13–15:** Moses' second question: He must know which of all the gods in his world is commissioning him. See Gen 32.27–29. **14–15:** God provides three forms of the divine name: "ehyeh asher ehyeh," (one meaning of which is *I AM WHO I AM*); "ehyeh," (*I AM*); and "yhwh"(probably pronounced Yahweh, it may mean "he who causes to be"; see translators' notes and To the Reader, p. xvii). All three names are ambiguous, as is appropriate to the mysteriousness of Israel's God, though they may emphasize God's immanence. The structure of the longer name, *I AM WHO I AM,* is similar to that of another of God's self-disclosures in connection with the name "YHWH": "I will be gracious to whom I will be gracious" (33.19; cf. Ezek 12.25a). The name "YHWH" is here introduced as if for the first time

Egypt, to the land of the Canaanites, the
Hittites, the Amorites, the Perizzites, the
Hivites, and the Jebusites, a land flowing
with milk and honey.' 18They will listen to
your voice; and you and the elders of Israel
shall go to the king of Egypt and say to
him, 'The LORD, the God of the Hebrews,
has met with us; let us now go a three days'
journey into the wilderness, so that we may
sacrifice to the LORD our God.' 19I know,
however, that the king of Egypt will not
let you go unless compelled by a mighty
hand.[a] 20So I will stretch out my hand and
strike Egypt with all my wonders that I will
perform in it; after that he will let you go.
21I will bring this people into such favor
with the Egyptians that, when you go, you
will not go empty-handed; 22each woman
shall ask her neighbor and any woman liv-
ing in the neighbor's house for jewelry of
silver and of gold, and clothing, and you
shall put them on your sons and on your
daughters; and so you shall plunder the
Egyptians."

4 Then Moses answered, "But suppose
they do not believe me or listen to me,
but say, 'The LORD did not appear to
you.' " 2The LORD said to him, "What is
that in your hand?" He said, "A staff."
3And he said, "Throw it on the ground."
So he threw the staff on the ground, and
it became a snake; and Moses drew back
from it. 4Then the LORD said to Moses,
"Reach out your hand, and seize it by the
tail"—so he reached out his hand and
grasped it, and it became a staff in his
hand— 5"so that they may believe that the
LORD, the God of their ancestors, the God
of Abraham, the God of Isaac, and the God
of Jacob, has appeared to you."

6 Again, the LORD said to him, "Put
your hand inside your cloak." He put his
hand into his cloak; and when he took it
out, his hand was leprous,[b] as white as
snow. 7Then God said, "Put your hand
back into your cloak"—so he put his hand
back into his cloak, and when he took it
out, it was restored like the rest of his
body— 8"If they will not believe you or
heed the first sign, they may believe the sec-
ond sign. 9If they will not believe even these
two signs or heed you, you shall take some
water from the Nile and pour it on the dry
ground; and the water that you shall take
from the Nile will become blood on the dry
ground."

10 But Moses said to the LORD, "O my
Lord, I have never been eloquent, neither in
the past nor even now that you have spo-
ken to your servant; but I am slow of
speech and slow of tongue." 11Then the
LORD said to him, "Who gives speech to
mortals? Who makes them mute or deaf,
seeing or blind? Is it not I, the LORD?
12Now go, and I will be with your mouth
and teach you what you are to speak."
13But he said, "O my Lord, please send
someone else." 14Then the anger of the
LORD was kindled against Moses and he

a Gk Vg: Heb *no, not by a mighty hand* *b* A term for several skin diseases; precise meaning uncertain

(6.2–3; contrast Gen 4.26; 13.4). **16–22:** God restates Moses' commission (cf. vv. 7–10). **18:** *God of the Hebrews,* God does not hesitate to identify the divine self with displaced people (1.15n.). **19–20:** 5.2n. **21–22:** *Not . . . empty-handed,* suggesting freed slaves (23.15; Deut 15.13). *Plunder,* suggesting victors after battle. The *jewelry* and *clothing* are received when Moses carries out his commission (11.2–3; 12.35–36). These play a fateful role at Sinai: Desired by God to build the shrine by which the divine presence can accompany Israel on its travels (25.1–9; 35.4–29), they will first be used in the people's own plan to force God's presence (32.1–4; 33.4–6). **4.1–9:** In response to Moses' third objection he receives three more signs: *staff* to *snake* (vv. 2–5); diseased *hand* (vv. 6–8); and *water* to *blood* (v. 9). They differ from the first sign (3.12) since they are meant for persuasion in advance. The first of these signs anticipates the preface to the ten plagues (7.8–13), and the third will produce the first plague (7.14–24). **10–17:** God counters Moses' fourth objection by designating Aaron as Moses' aide. **10:** *Slow of speech,* may indicate a speech impediment, or metaphorically reflect Moses' reluctance to accept the divine commission. See also 6.12,30. **11:** In biblical thought human conditions are ascribed directly to God (Gen 16.2;

said, "What of your brother Aaron the Le-
vite? I know that he can speak fluently;
even now he is coming out to meet you, and
when he sees you his heart will be glad.
15 You shall speak to him and put the
words in his mouth; and I will be with your
mouth and with his mouth, and will teach
you what you shall do. 16 He indeed shall
speak for you to the people; he shall serve
as a mouth for you, and you shall serve as
God for him. 17 Take in your hand this
staff, with which you shall perform the
signs."

18 Moses went back to his father-in-law
Jethro and said to him, "Please let me go
back to my kindred in Egypt and see
whether they are still living." And Jethro
said to Moses, "Go in peace." 19 The LORD
said to Moses in Midian, "Go back to
Egypt; for all those who were seeking your
life are dead." 20 So Moses took his wife
and his sons, put them on a donkey, and
went back to the land of Egypt; and Moses
carried the staff of God in his hand.

21 And the LORD said to Moses, "When
you go back to Egypt, see that you perform
before Pharaoh all the wonders that I have
put in your power; but I will harden his
heart, so that he will not let the people go.
22 Then you shall say to Pharaoh, 'Thus
says the LORD: Israel is my firstborn son.
23 I said to you, "Let my son go that he may
worship me." But you refused to let him go;
now I will kill your firstborn son.' "

24 On the way, at a place where they
spent the night, the LORD met him and
tried to kill him. 25 But Zipporah took a
flint and cut off her son's foreskin, and
touched Moses'[a] feet with it, and said,
"Truly you are a bridegroom of blood to
me!" 26 So he let him alone. It was then she
said, "A bridegroom of blood by circum-
cision."

27 The LORD said to Aaron, "Go into
the wilderness to meet Moses." So he went;
and he met him at the mountain of God
and kissed him. 28 Moses told Aaron all the
words of the LORD with which he had sent
him, and all the signs with which he had
charged him. 29 Then Moses and Aaron
went and assembled all the elders of the
Israelites. 30 Aaron spoke all the words that
the LORD had spoken to Moses, and per-
formed the signs in the sight of the people.
31 The people believed; and when they
heard that the LORD had given heed to the
Israelites and that he had seen their misery,
they bowed down and worshiped.

a Heb *his*

Deut 32.39). **14:** *Aaron* is here mentioned for the first time. **15–16:** The relation between God and God's prophetic spokesperson is analogous to the relation between Moses and Aaron (7.1; cf. 4.28–30; 16.9–10).

4.18–31: Moses returns to Egypt to prepare the people for liberation. 18–20: Moses begins the trip back to Egypt. **19:** 2.23. **20:** Only one of Moses' *sons* has been mentioned so far (2.22); see 18.3–4. **21–23:** Two major themes are introduced: the hard heart and the firstborn son. **21:** Pharaoh's hard heart, or stubbornness, will play a major role in the liberation story. At first Pharaoh will harden his own heart (8.15,32; 9.34; cf. 7.13–14,22; 8.19; 9.7,35), but toward the end God will respond by hardening it for him (9.12; 10.1,20,27; 11.10; 14.4,8; cf. 14.17). In this introductory statement (cf. 7.3) God takes credit for the entire process. Pharaoh's stubbornness will give God ample opportunity to display the *wonders* that will force him to acknowledge the superior power of Israel's God (5.2n.). **22–23:** *Firstborn son,* a major theme of the entire book (vv. 24–26; 11.4–5; 12.12,29–34; 13.2,11–16; 22.29–30; 34.19–20). Since Pharaoh will not let God's firstborn go, his own firstborn and all the firstborn of Egypt will die. Henceforth all the firstborn of Israel will belong to God. (For Israel as God's firstborn son, see Jer 31.9; cf. Hos 11.1). **24–26:** God attacks Moses to prevent his attempting to carry out the divine commission while his household is uncircumcised despite God's requirement for Israelites (Gen 17.9–14). *Feet,* a euphemism for the genitals (Isa 7.20). Zipporah's quick action and the application of the blood of circumcision save Moses' life at the beginning of the story, as the blood of the passover will save all Israel at the end (12.7,13,22–27; cf. 12.43–49). **26:** *Bridegroom of blood,* the expression may reflect an ancient association of marriage and circumcision (cf. Gen 34.14–24). **27–31:** Aaron joins Moses and begins acting as his spokesman. **27:** *The mountain of God,* 3.1.

5 Afterward Moses and Aaron went to
Pharaoh and said, "Thus says the
LORD, the God of Israel, 'Let my people go,
so that they may celebrate a festival to me
in the wilderness.' " 2 But Pharaoh said,
"Who is the LORD, that I should heed him
and let Israel go? I do not know the LORD,
and I will not let Israel go." 3 Then they
said, "The God of the Hebrews has re-
vealed himself to us; let us go a three days'
journey into the wilderness to sacrifice to
the LORD our God, or he will fall upon us
with pestilence or sword." 4 But the king of
Egypt said to them, "Moses and Aaron,
why are you taking the people away from
their work? Get to your labors!" 5 Pharaoh
continued, "Now they are more numerous
than the people of the land[a] and yet you
want them to stop working!" 6 That same
day Pharaoh commanded the taskmasters
of the people, as well as their supervisors,
7 "You shall no longer give the people straw
to make bricks, as before; let them go and
gather straw for themselves. 8 But you shall
require of them the same quantity of bricks
as they have made previously; do not di-
minish it, for they are lazy; that is why they
cry, 'Let us go and offer sacrifice to our
God.' 9 Let heavier work be laid on them;
then they will labor at it and pay no atten-
tion to deceptive words."

10 So the taskmasters and the supervi-
sors of the people went out and said to the
people, "Thus says Pharaoh, 'I will not give
you straw. 11 Go and get straw yourselves,
wherever you can find it; but your work
will not be lessened in the least.' " 12 So the
people scattered throughout the land of
Egypt, to gather stubble for straw. 13 The
taskmasters were urgent, saying, "Com-
plete your work, the same daily assignment
as when you were given straw." 14 And the
supervisors of the Israelites, whom Phar-
aoh's taskmasters had set over them, were
beaten, and were asked, "Why did you not
finish the required quantity of bricks yes-
terday and today, as you did before?"

15 Then the Israelite supervisors came
to Pharaoh and cried, "Why do you treat
your servants like this? 16 No straw is given
to your servants, yet they say to us, 'Make
bricks!' Look how your servants are beat-
en! You are unjust to your own people."[b]
17 He said, "You are lazy, lazy; that is why
you say, 'Let us go and sacrifice to the
LORD.' 18 Go now, and work; for no straw
shall be given you, but you shall still deliver
the same number of bricks." 19 The Israelite
supervisors saw that they were in trouble
when they were told, "You shall not lessen
your daily number of bricks." 20 As they left
Pharaoh, they came upon Moses and Aar-
on who were waiting to meet them. 21 They
said to them, "The LORD look upon you
and judge! You have brought us into bad
odor with Pharaoh and his officials, and
have put a sword in their hand to kill us."

22 Then Moses turned again to the
LORD and said, "O LORD, why have you
mistreated this people? Why did you ever
send me? 23 Since I first came to Pharaoh to
speak in your name, he has mistreated this
people, and you have done nothing at all to
deliver your people."

6 Then the LORD said to Moses, "Now
you shall see what I will do to Pharaoh:

a Sam: Heb *The people of the land are now many*
b Gk Compare Syr Vg: Heb *beaten, and the sin of your people*

5.1–6.1: The first audience with Pharaoh fails. 5.1,3: The petition is for a leave of absence to make a pilgrimage to the sacred mountain (3.18). God has already predicted Pharaoh's refusal (3.19). **2:** Pharaoh knows many gods, and in Egyptian religion he himself was deified, but he has never heard of or does not acknowledge the authority of *the LORD* (YHWH). The question of the knowledge, or acknowledgment, of Israel's God is one of the dominant themes of the book (6.7; 7.5; 9.14,29; 14.4; 16.12; 18.11; 29.46; 31.13; 33.13). Only a very public contest in which God shows a "mighty hand," "signs and wonders," and "great acts of judgment" (3.19–20; 6.1,6; 7.3–4) will bring Pharaoh, the Egyptians, and the Israelites to an acknowledgment of Israel's God. **3:** *God of the Hebrews,* 3.18n. **4–9:** 1.8–14. **20–23:** As happened the first time Moses tried to help (2.11–15), this time Moses and Aaron together have only succeeded in angering both Pharaoh and Israel. **6.1:** 3.19–20.

Indeed, by a mighty hand he will let them
go; by a mighty hand he will drive them out
of his land."
2 God also spoke to Moses and said to
him: "I am the LORD. 3 I appeared to Abra-
ham, Isaac, and Jacob as God Almighty,[a]
but by my name 'The LORD'[b] I did not
make myself known to them. 4 I also estab-
lished my covenant with them, to give them
the land of Canaan, the land in which they
resided as aliens. 5 I have also heard the
groaning of the Israelites whom the Egyp-
tians are holding as slaves, and I have re-
membered my covenant. 6 Say therefore to
the Israelites, 'I am the LORD, and I will
free you from the burdens of the Egyptians
and deliver you from slavery to them. I will
redeem you with an outstretched arm and
with mighty acts of judgment. 7 I will take
you as my people, and I will be your God.
You shall know that I am the LORD your
God, who has freed you from the burdens
of the Egyptians. 8 I will bring you into the
land that I swore to give to Abraham, Isaac,
and Jacob; I will give it to you for a posses-
sion. I am the LORD.' " 9 Moses told this to
the Israelites; but they would not listen to
Moses, because of their broken spirit and
their cruel slavery.
10 Then the LORD spoke to Moses,
11 "Go and tell Pharaoh king of Egypt to let
the Israelites go out of his land." 12 But Mo-
ses spoke to the LORD, "The Israelites have
not listened to me; how then shall Pharaoh
listen to me, poor speaker that I am?"[c]
13 Thus the LORD spoke to Moses and Aar-
on, and gave them orders regarding the Is-
raelites and Pharaoh king of Egypt, charg-
ing them to free the Israelites from the land
of Egypt.
14 The following are the heads of their
ancestral houses: the sons of Reuben, the
firstborn of Israel: Hanoch, Pallu, Hezron,
and Carmi; these are the families of Reu-
ben. 15 The sons of Simeon: Jemuel, Jamin,
Ohad, Jachin, Zohar, and Shaul,[d] the son
of a Canaanite woman; these are the fami-
lies of Simeon. 16 The following are the
names of the sons of Levi according to their
genealogies: Gershon,[e] Kohath, and Mera-
ri, and the length of Levi's life was one hun-
dred thirty-seven years. 17 The sons of Ger-
shon:[e] Libni and Shimei, by their families.
18 The sons of Kohath: Amram, Izhar, He-
bron, and Uzziel, and the length of Ko-
hath's life was one hundred thirty-three
years. 19 The sons of Merari: Mahli and
Mushi. These are the families of the Levites
according to their genealogies. 20 Amram
married Jochebed his father's sister and she
bore him Aaron and Moses, and the length
of Amram's life was one hundred thirty-
seven years. 21 The sons of Izhar: Korah,
Nepheg, and Zichri. 22 The sons of Uzziel:
Mishael, Elzaphan, and Sithri. 23 Aaron
married Elisheba, daughter of Amminadab
and sister of Nahshon, and she bore him
Nadab, Abihu, Eleazar, and Ithamar.

a Traditional rendering of Heb *El Shaddai*
b Heb *YHWH*; see note at 3.15 *c* Heb *me? I am uncircumcised of lips* *d* Or *Saul* *e* Also spelled *Gershom*; see 2.22

6.2–7.7: God repeats the call of Moses and the appointment of Aaron (cf. 2.23–4.17) after their first attempt has only made things worse. **6.2–13:** After the divine self-introduction (vv. 2–5), God sends Moses to the Israelites (vv. 6–8) and then to Pharaoh (vv. 10–11). **2–3:** 3.14–15n. *The LORD* ("YHWH"), the same God who led Israel's ancestors, was known to them by another name, "El Shaddai" (Gen 17.1n.; 35.11). This section is the Priestly introduction of the name YHWH. **4:** God's *covenant* with Abraham (Gen 15.18–21; 17.7–8) promised possession of the land of Canaan (v. 8). **5:** 2.23–25. **6–8:** *I am the LORD* ("YHWH"), God's introductory statement in v. 2, is repeated at the beginning, middle, and end of this promise. God's personal name is tied to the fulfillment of this solemn promise of freedom and land. **7:** *My people . . . your God,* a succinct statement of the meaning of the covenant relationship (Hos 2.23; Jer 31.33). *Know,* or acknowledge; 5.2n. **12:** *Poor speaker* (also v. 30), see textual note *c;* a variant of the expression in 4.10 (n.). **12:** 4.10–16. After vv. 13–27 interrupt the flow of the story, Moses' question will be restated in v. 30 and answered in 7.1–2. **14–27:** The purpose of the genealogy of Aaron and Moses is to trace priestly lineage from *Levi,* Jacob's son, to *Aaron* and through Aaron's third son, *Eleazar,* to *Phinehas* (Num 3; 25.10–13). **14–16:** Gen 46.8–11. **20:** *Aaron* is the older brother (7.7). **6.28–7.7:** The

24 The sons of Korah: Assir, Elkanah, and
Abiasaph; these are the families of the Ko-
rahites. 25 Aaron's son Eleazar married one
of the daughters of Putiel, and she bore him
Phinehas. These are the heads of the ances-
tral houses of the Levites by their families.
26 It was this same Aaron and Moses to
whom the LORD said, "Bring the Israelites
out of the land of Egypt, company by com-
pany." 27 It was they who spoke to Pharaoh
king of Egypt to bring the Israelites out of
Egypt, the same Moses and Aaron.
28 On the day when the LORD spoke to
Moses in the land of Egypt, 29 he said to
him, "I am the LORD; tell Pharaoh king of
Egypt all that I am speaking to you." 30 But
Moses said in the LORD's presence, "Since
I am a poor speaker,[a] why would Pharaoh
listen to me?"

7 The LORD said to Moses, "See, I have
made you like God to Pharaoh, and
your brother Aaron shall be your prophet.
2 You shall speak all that I command you,
and your brother Aaron shall tell Pharaoh
to let the Israelites go out of his land. 3 But
I will harden Pharaoh's heart, and I will
multiply my signs and wonders in the land
of Egypt. 4 When Pharaoh does not listen to
you, I will lay my hand upon Egypt and
bring my people the Israelites, company by
company, out of the land of Egypt by great
acts of judgment. 5 The Egyptians shall
know that I am the LORD, when I stretch
out my hand against Egypt and bring the
Israelites out from among them." 6 Moses
and Aaron did so; they did just as the LORD
commanded them. 7 Moses was eighty
years old and Aaron eighty-three when
they spoke to Pharaoh.
8 The LORD said to Moses and Aaron,
9 "When Pharaoh says to you, 'Perform a
wonder,' then you shall say to Aaron,
'Take your staff and throw it down before
Pharaoh, and it will become a snake.' "
10 So Moses and Aaron went to Pharaoh
and did as the LORD had commanded; Aar-
on threw down his staff before Pharaoh
and his officials, and it became a snake.
11 Then Pharaoh summoned the wise men
and the sorcerers; and they also, the magi-
cians of Egypt, did the same by their secret
arts. 12 Each one threw down his staff, and
they became snakes; but Aaron's staff swal-
lowed up theirs. 13 Still Pharaoh's heart was
hardened, and he would not listen to them,
as the LORD had said.

a Heb *am uncircumcised of lips*; see 6.12

story continues from 6.12. **7.1–2:** 4.15–16n. **3–5:** *Harden,* 4.21n. *Signs and wonders, great acts of judgment, know,* 5.2n. **4:** *Company by company,* 12.37n. **6:** *Did just as . . . commanded,* an overarching pattern of the book (for instance, vv. 10,20; 8.17; 12.28,35,50; 17.10; 18.24; 24.3,7; 34.4; 39.1,5,7,21,26,29,31,32,42; 40.16,32).

7.8–11.10: The ten plagues. The number "ten" is nowhere explicitly stated, and the ten plagues are the result of the combination of several overlapping plague accounts, none of which narrated all ten plagues. Alternative traditions, with fewer plagues, in a different order, are preserved in Ps 78.44–51; 105.28–36. Some of the plagues could be natural phenomena. Yet for the biblical writers they are clearly extraordinary manifestations of divine power (see 9.18,24; 10.6,14; 11.6). The predictability, the timing of both beginning and ending, the intensity, the contest between Aaron and the magicians, the distinction between Egyptians and Israelites, and the emphasis on Pharaoh's knowing (acknowledging) God all point to combat on two interrelated levels: between Israel's God and Egypt's gods (12.12), including the deified Pharaoh, and between their human representatives, Moses and Aaron, and Pharaoh, his officials, and his magicians. Whereas plagues one, three, five, and six evoke no positive response from Pharaoh, the others prompt him to promise that they may go as soon as Moses' intercession causes the plague to leave (8.8; a short distance, 8.25–28; 9.27; only the men, 10.11; even the children, 10.24; flocks and herds, 12.31–32). Twice he will even admit that he has sinned (9.27; 10.10), but he will renege on his promise five times. Finally, after the tenth plague Pharaoh will let God's people go.

7.8–13: The preface to the sequence of plagues (cf. 4.1–5) features a contest between Aaron and Pharaoh's magicians. **9–10:** Aaron plays a prominent role in this episode and in the first three plagues, using his own staff rather than Moses'. **11–12:** The contest with the magicians will continue through

14 Then the LORD said to Moses, "Phar-
aoh's heart is hardened; he refuses to let the
people go. 15 Go to Pharaoh in the morn-
ing, as he is going out to the water; stand by
at the river bank to meet him, and take in
your hand the staff that was turned into a
snake. 16 Say to him, 'The LORD, the God
of the Hebrews, sent me to you to say, "Let
my people go, so that they may worship me
in the wilderness." But until now you have
not listened. 17 Thus says the LORD, "By
this you shall know that I am the LORD."
See, with the staff that is in my hand I will
strike the water that is in the Nile, and it
shall be turned to blood. 18 The fish in the
river shall die, the river itself shall stink,
and the Egyptians shall be unable to drink
water from the Nile.' " 19 The LORD said to
Moses, "Say to Aaron, 'Take your staff and
stretch out your hand over the waters of
Egypt—over its rivers, its canals, and its
ponds, and all its pools of water—so that
they may become blood; and there shall be
blood throughout the whole land of Egypt,
even in vessels of wood and in vessels of
stone.' "

20 Moses and Aaron did just as the
LORD commanded. In the sight of Pharaoh
and of his officials he lifted up the staff and
struck the water in the river, and all the
water in the river was turned into blood,
21 and the fish in the river died. The river
stank so that the Egyptians could not drink
its water, and there was blood throughout
the whole land of Egypt. 22 But the magi-
cians of Egypt did the same by their secret
arts; so Pharaoh's heart remained hard-
ened, and he would not listen to them, as
the LORD had said. 23 Pharaoh turned and
went into his house, and he did not take
even this to heart. 24 And all the Egyptians
had to dig along the Nile for water to
drink, for they could not drink the water of
the river.

25 Seven days passed after the LORD
had struck the Nile.

8 [a]Then the LORD said to Moses, "Go to
Pharaoh and say to him, 'Thus says the
LORD: Let my people go, so that they may
worship me. 2 If you refuse to let them go,
I will plague your whole country with
frogs. 3 The river shall swarm with frogs;
they shall come up into your palace, into
your bedchamber and your bed, and into
the houses of your officials and of your
people,[b] and into your ovens and your
kneading bowls. 4 The frogs shall come up
on you and on your people and on all your
officials.' " 5 [c] And the LORD said to Mo-
ses, "Say to Aaron, 'Stretch out your hand
with your staff over the rivers, the canals,
and the pools, and make frogs come up on
the land of Egypt.' " 6 So Aaron stretched
out his hand over the waters of Egypt; and
the frogs came up and covered the land of
Egypt. 7 But the magicians did the same by
their secret arts, and brought frogs up on
the land of Egypt.

8 Then Pharaoh called Moses and Aar-

a Ch 7.26 in Heb *b* Gk: Heb *upon your people*
c Ch 8.1 in Heb

several plagues (7.22; 8.7,18–19; 9.11). **13:** *Hardened,* 4.21n. *As . . . said,* almost every plague story will end similarly, emphasizing the accuracy of God's predictions.

7.14–24: First plague: blood. As in some other plague narratives, two sources are combined here. One depicts Moses as the sole actor, with only the Nile afflicted; the second, Priestly source adds Aaron, and suggests that all Egyptian water turned to blood. **15:** Moses is to meet Pharaoh *at the river bank* with a challenge to Egypt's very existence, for the Nile is the source of life and fertility. **16:** *God of the Hebrews,* 3.18n. **17–18:** Some suggest that the plague of *blood* represents an intensification of the naturally reddish color of the Nile from red particles of earth or minute organisms. **18:** *The Egyptians,* implicit here (and in vv. 21,24; 8.3–4,9–11) is the distinction between the Egyptians and the Israelites that will become explicit later (8.22–23n.). **19:** The beginning of the Priestly narrative, where Aaron's rather than Moses' staff (v. 17) is used. **22:** The magicians' ability to duplicate the event only makes things worse. *Hardened,* 4.21n.

7.25–8.15: Second plague: frogs. 8.5: *Your staff,* 7.9,19. **7:** 7.22n. **8:** *Pray to the LORD*, for the first time Pharaoh momentarily recognizes Israel's God (contrast 5.2). **9–11:** To enhance the wonder and

on, and said, "Pray to the LORD to take
away the frogs from me and my people,
and I will let the people go to sacrifice to
the LORD." 9 Moses said to Pharaoh,
"Kindly tell me when I am to pray for you
and for your officials and for your people,
that the frogs may be removed from you
and your houses and be left only in the
Nile." 10 And he said, "Tomorrow." Moses
said, "As you say! So that you may know
that there is no one like the LORD our God,
11 the frogs shall leave you and your houses
and your officials and your people; they
shall be left only in the Nile." 12 Then Mo-
ses and Aaron went out from Pharaoh; and
Moses cried out to the LORD concerning
the frogs that he had brought upon Phar-
aoh.[a] 13 And the LORD did as Moses re-
quested: the frogs died in the houses, the
courtyards, and the fields. 14 And they gath-
ered them together in heaps, and the land
stank. 15 But when Pharaoh saw that there
was a respite, he hardened his heart, and
would not listen to them, just as the LORD
had said.

16 Then the LORD said to Moses, "Say
to Aaron, 'Stretch out your staff and strike
the dust of the earth, so that it may become
gnats throughout the whole land of
Egypt.'" 17 And they did so; Aaron
stretched out his hand with his staff and
struck the dust of the earth, and gnats came
on humans and animals alike; all the dust
of the earth turned into gnats throughout
the whole land of Egypt. 18 The magicians
tried to produce gnats by their secret arts,
but they could not. There were gnats on
both humans and animals. 19 And the magi-
cians said to Pharaoh, "This is the finger of
God!" But Pharaoh's heart was hardened,
and he would not listen to them, just as the
LORD had said.

20 Then the LORD said to Moses, "Rise
early in the morning and present yourself
before Pharaoh, as he goes out to the water,
and say to him, 'Thus says the LORD: Let
my people go, so that they may worship
me. 21 For if you will not let my people go,
I will send swarms of flies on you, your
officials, and your people, and into your
houses; and the houses of the Egyptians
shall be filled with swarms of flies; so also
the land where they live. 22 But on that day
I will set apart the land of Goshen, where
my people live, so that no swarms of flies
shall be there, that you may know that I the
LORD am in this land. 23 Thus I will make a
distinction[b] between my people and your
people. This sign shall appear tomorrow.'"
24 The LORD did so, and great swarms of
flies came into the house of Pharaoh and
into his officials' houses; in all of Egypt the
land was ruined because of the flies.

25 Then Pharaoh summoned Moses and
Aaron, and said, "Go, sacrifice to your
God within the land." 26 But Moses said,
"It would not be right to do so; for the
sacrifices that we offer to the LORD our
God are offensive to the Egyptians. If we
offer in the sight of the Egyptians sacrifices
that are offensive to them, will they not
stone us? 27 We must go a three days' jour-
ney into the wilderness and sacrifice to the
LORD our God as he commands us." 28 So
Pharaoh said, "I will let you go to sacrifice

a Or *frogs, as he had agreed with Pharaoh*
b Gk Vg: Heb *will set redemption*

encourage Pharaoh's acknowledgment of Israel's God, Moses promises to pray that the plague stop at a designated time. **15:** *Hardened,* 4.21n.

8.16–19: Third plague: gnats or mosquitoes. **16:** *Your staff,* 7.9,19; 8.5. **18–19:** This time the magicians are unable to match the feat and confess that *this is the finger of God.* **19:** *Hardened,* 4.21n.

8.20–32: Fourth plague: flies, a parallel to gnats. **20:** This time *Moses* takes center stage. Aaron is mentioned only in v. 25. Moses will be the chief speaker and actor in each plague from now on. If Aaron is mentioned at all, he will remain passive (v. 25) or secondary (9.10). **22–23:** A new *sign* appears, an explicit *distinction* between Egyptians and Israelites (7.18n.; 9.4,6–7,26; 10.23; 11.7; 12.12–13; 14.13–14). **23:** For the first time Pharaoh is given a day's advance notice. The same will occur in 9.5,18; 10.4; cf. 11.4. **26:** For the Egyptian attitude toward foreign practices, see Gen 43.32. **27:** 3.18. **32:** *Hardened,* 4. 21n.

to the LORD your God in the wilderness,
provided you do not go very far away. Pray
for me." 29 Then Moses said, "As soon as I
leave you, I will pray to the LORD that the
swarms of flies may depart tomorrow from
Pharaoh, from his officials, and from his
people; only do not let Pharaoh again deal
falsely by not letting the people go to sacri-
fice to the LORD."

30 So Moses went out from Pharaoh
and prayed to the LORD. 31 And the LORD
did as Moses asked: he removed the
swarms of flies from Pharaoh, from his of-
ficials, and from his people; not one re-
mained. 32 But Pharaoh hardened his heart
this time also, and would not let the peo-
ple go.

9 Then the LORD said to Moses, "Go to
Pharaoh, and say to him, 'Thus says the
LORD, the God of the Hebrews: Let my
people go, so that they may worship me.
2 For if you refuse to let them go and still
hold them, 3 the hand of the LORD will
strike with a deadly pestilence your live-
stock in the field: the horses, the donkeys,
the camels, the herds, and the flocks. 4 But
the LORD will make a distinction between
the livestock of Israel and the livestock of
Egypt, so that nothing shall die of all that
belongs to the Israelites.'" 5 The LORD set
a time, saying, "Tomorrow the LORD will
do this thing in the land." 6 And on the next
day the LORD did so; all the livestock of the
Egyptians died, but of the livestock of the
Israelites not one died. 7 Pharaoh inquired
and found that not one of the livestock of
the Israelites was dead. But the heart of
Pharaoh was hardened, and he would not
let the people go.

8 Then the LORD said to Moses and
Aaron, "Take handfuls of soot from the
kiln, and let Moses throw it in the air in the
sight of Pharaoh. 9 It shall become fine dust
all over the land of Egypt, and shall cause
festering boils on humans and animals
throughout the whole land of Egypt." 10 So
they took soot from the kiln, and stood be-
fore Pharaoh, and Moses threw it in the air,
and it caused festering boils on humans and
animals. 11 The magicians could not stand
before Moses because of the boils, for the
boils afflicted the magicians as well as all
the Egyptians. 12 But the LORD hardened
the heart of Pharaoh, and he would not
listen to them, just as the LORD had spoken
to Moses.

13 Then the LORD said to Moses, "Rise
up early in the morning and present your-
self before Pharaoh, and say to him, 'Thus
says the LORD, the God of the Hebrews:
Let my people go, so that they may worship
me. 14 For this time I will send all my
plagues upon you yourself, and upon your
officials, and upon your people, so that you
may know that there is no one like me in
all the earth. 15 For by now I could have
stretched out my hand and struck you and
your people with pestilence, and you would
have been cut off from the earth. 16 But this
is why I have let you live: to show you my
power, and to make my name resound
through all the earth. 17 You are still exalt-
ing yourself against my people, and will not
let them go. 18 Tomorrow at this time I will
cause the heaviest hail to fall that has ever
fallen in Egypt from the day it was founded
until now. 19 Send, therefore, and have your
livestock and everything that you have in
the open field brought to a secure place;
every human or animal that is in the open

9.1–7: Fifth plague: livestock disease. 1: Again Moses is the speaker (8.20n.). *God of the Hebrews,* 3.18n. **4:** 8.22–23n. **5:** *Tomorrow,* 8.23n. **7:** *Hardened,* 4.21n.

9.8–12: Sixth plague: boils. 8–10: Though Aaron assists, it is Moses who acts in Pharaoh's presence (8.20n.). **11:** The magicians have not only lost the contest, they are themselves victims (contrast 7.11,22; 8.7,18–19). **12:** For the first time in the plague sequence God is said to be the one who hardens Pharaoh's heart (4.21n.).

9.13–35: Seventh plague: hail and thunderstorm. 13: The fourth plague in which Moses takes center stage (8.20n.). *God of the Hebrews,* 3.18n. **16:** *Name,* cf. 5.2. **18:** *Tomorrow,* 8.23n. The uniqueness of the plague of hail will be emphasized again (v. 24; see 10.6,14; 11.6). **19:** For the first time God suggests protective measures. **23:** *His staff,* this time Moses uses his own staff (contrast 7.9,19; 8.5,16).

field and is not brought under shelter will
die when the hail comes down upon
them.' " 20 Those officials of Pharaoh who
feared the word of the LORD hurried their
slaves and livestock off to a secure place.
21 Those who did not regard the word of
the LORD left their slaves and livestock in
the open field.

22 The LORD said to Moses, "Stretch
out your hand toward heaven so that hail
may fall on the whole land of Egypt, on
humans and animals and all the plants of
the field in the land of Egypt." 23 Then Mo-
ses stretched out his staff toward heaven,
and the LORD sent thunder and hail, and
fire came down on the earth. And the LORD
rained hail on the land of Egypt; 24 there
was hail with fire flashing continually in
the midst of it, such heavy hail as had never
fallen in all the land of Egypt since it be-
came a nation. 25 The hail struck down ev-
erything that was in the open field through-
out all the land of Egypt, both human and
animal; the hail also struck down all the
plants of the field, and shattered every tree
in the field. 26 Only in the land of Goshen,
where the Israelites were, there was no hail.

27 Then Pharaoh summoned Moses and
Aaron, and said to them, "This time I have
sinned; the LORD is in the right, and I and
my people are in the wrong. 28 Pray to the
LORD! Enough of God's thunder and hail!
I will let you go; you need stay no longer."
29 Moses said to him, "As soon as I have
gone out of the city, I will stretch out my
hands to the LORD; the thunder will cease,
and there will be no more hail, so that you
may know that the earth is the LORD's.
30 But as for you and your officials, I know
that you do not yet fear the LORD God."
31 (Now the flax and the barley were ru-
ined, for the barley was in the ear and the
flax was in bud. 32 But the wheat and the
spelt were not ruined, for they are late in
coming up.) 33 So Moses left Pharaoh, went
out of the city, and stretched out his hands
to the LORD; then the thunder and the hail
ceased, and the rain no longer poured
down on the earth. 34 But when Pharaoh
saw that the rain and the hail and the thun-
der had ceased, he sinned once more and
hardened his heart, he and his officials.
35 So the heart of Pharaoh was hardened,
and he would not let the Israelites go, just
as the LORD had spoken through Moses.

10 Then the LORD said to Moses, "Go
to Pharaoh; for I have hardened his
heart and the heart of his officials, in order
that I may show these signs of mine among
them, 2 and that you may tell your children
and grandchildren how I have made fools
of the Egyptians and what signs I have done
among them—so that you may know that I
am the LORD."

3 So Moses and Aaron went to Pharaoh,
and said to him, "Thus says the LORD, the
God of the Hebrews, 'How long will you
refuse to humble yourself before me? Let
my people go, so that they may worship
me. 4 For if you refuse to let my people go,
tomorrow I will bring locusts into your
country. 5 They shall cover the surface of
the land, so that no one will be able to see
the land. They shall devour the last rem-
nant left you after the hail, and they shall
devour every tree of yours that grows in the
field. 6 They shall fill your houses, and the
houses of all your officials and of all the
Egyptians—something that neither your
parents nor your grandparents have seen,
from the day they came on earth to this
day.' " Then he turned and went out from
Pharaoh.

7 Pharaoh's officials said to him, "How

26: 8.22–23n. **27:** For the first time Pharaoh confesses that he is beaten (contrast 5.2). **28:** 8.8,28. **29:** *The earth is the LORD's,* 19.5; Ps 24.1. **31–32:** This parenthetical remark explains why there are still plants for the locusts to eat during the next plague and, incidentally, places the seventh plague around the middle of January, when the crops begin to mature (cf. 12.2n.). **35:** *Hardened,* 4.21n.

10.1–20: Eighth plague: locusts. 1–2: One of the fullest statements of God's complex purpose, to be compared with 9.14–16. It offers a crucial transition, suggesting that not only Pharaoh, but also the Israelites of each generation, are to learn who their God is from the plagues (6.7). **3:** *God of the Hebrews,* 3.18n. **4:** *Tomorrow,* 8.23n. **6:** 9.18n. **7–11:** At the insistence of his awed courtiers, Pharaoh attempts

long shall this fellow be a snare to us? Let
the people go, so that they may worship the
LORD their God; do you not yet understand
that Egypt is ruined?" 8 So Moses and Aar-
on were brought back to Pharaoh, and he
said to them, "Go, worship the LORD your
God! But which ones are to go?" 9 Moses
said, "We will go with our young and our
old; we will go with our sons and daughters
and with our flocks and herds, because we
have the LORD's festival to celebrate."
10 He said to them, "The LORD indeed will
be with you, if ever I let your little ones go
with you! Plainly, you have some evil pur-
pose in mind. 11 No, never! Your men may
go and worship the LORD, for that is what
you are asking." And they were driven out
from Pharaoh's presence.

12 Then the LORD said to Moses,
"Stretch out your hand over the land of
Egypt, so that the locusts may come upon it
and eat every plant in the land, all that the
hail has left." 13 So Moses stretched out his
staff over the land of Egypt, and the LORD
brought an east wind upon the land all that
day and all that night; when morning came,
the east wind had brought the locusts.
14 The locusts came upon all the land of
Egypt and settled on the whole country of
Egypt, such a dense swarm of locusts as
had never been before, nor ever shall be
again. 15 They covered the surface of the
whole land, so that the land was black; and
they ate all the plants in the land and all the
fruit of the trees that the hail had left; noth-
ing green was left, no tree, no plant in the
field, in all the land of Egypt. 16 Pharaoh
hurriedly summoned Moses and Aaron and
said, "I have sinned against the LORD your
God, and against you. 17 Do forgive my sin
just this once, and pray to the LORD your
God that at the least he remove this deadly
thing from me." 18 So he went out from
Pharaoh and prayed to the LORD. 19 The
LORD changed the wind into a very strong
west wind, which lifted the locusts and
drove them into the Red Sea;[a] not a single
locust was left in all the country of Egypt.
20 But the LORD hardened Pharaoh's heart,
and he would not let the Israelites go.

21 Then the LORD said to Moses,
"Stretch out your hand toward heaven so
that there may be darkness over the land of
Egypt, a darkness that can be felt." 22 So
Moses stretched out his hand toward heav-
en, and there was dense darkness in all
the land of Egypt for three days. 23 People
could not see one another, and for three
days they could not move from where they
were; but all the Israelites had light where
they lived. 24 Then Pharaoh summoned
Moses, and said, "Go, worship the LORD.
Only your flocks and your herds shall re-
main behind. Even your children may go
with you." 25 But Moses said, "You must
also let us have sacrifices and burnt offer-
ings to sacrifice to the LORD our God.
26 Our livestock also must go with us; not
a hoof shall be left behind, for we must
choose some of them for the worship of the
LORD our God, and we will not know what
to use to worship the LORD until we arrive
there." 27 But the LORD hardened Phar-
aoh's heart, and he was unwilling to let
them go. 28 Then Pharaoh said to him, "Get
away from me! Take care that you do not
see my face again, for on the day you see
my face you shall die." 29 Moses said, "Just
as you say! I will never see your face
again."

11 The LORD said to Moses, "I will
bring one more plague upon Phar-
aoh and upon Egypt; afterwards he will let
you go from here; indeed, when he lets you

a Or *Sea of Reeds*

to negotiate (10.4). **13:** Again Moses uses his own staff (9.23n.). **14:** 9.18n. **16–17:** 8.8,28; 9.27–28. **19:** *Red Sea,* see 13.18n. **20:** *Hardened,* 4.21n.

10.21–29: Ninth plague: dense darkness. 21: *A darkness that can be felt* aptly describes conditions created by the hot wind, the "khamsin," which blows in from the desert during the spring (March–May), bringing with it so much dust and sand that the air is darkened and breathing becomes difficult. **23b:** 8.22–23n. **24:** *Your children,* contrast 10.7–11. **27:** *Hardened,* 4.21n.

11.1–10: The announcement of the final plague, the death of the firstborn (carried out in 12.29–36).

go, he will drive you away. 2 Tell the people
that every man is to ask his neighbor and
every woman is to ask her neighbor for ob-
jects of silver and gold." 3 The LORD gave
the people favor in the sight of the Egyp-
tians. Moreover, Moses himself was a man
of great importance in the land of Egypt, in
the sight of Pharaoh's officials and in the
sight of the people.

4 Moses said, "Thus says the LORD:
About midnight I will go out through
Egypt. 5 Every firstborn in the land of Egypt
shall die, from the firstborn of Pharaoh
who sits on his throne to the firstborn of
the female slave who is behind the hand-
mill, and all the firstborn of the livestock.
6 Then there will be a loud cry throughout
the whole land of Egypt, such as has never
been or will ever be again. 7 But not a dog
shall growl at any of the Israelites—not at
people, not at animals—so that you may
know that the LORD makes a distinction
between Egypt and Israel. 8 Then all these
officials of yours shall come down to me,
and bow low to me, saying, 'Leave us, you
and all the people who follow you.' After
that I will leave." And in hot anger he left
Pharaoh.

9 The LORD said to Moses, "Pharaoh
will not listen to you, in order that my
wonders may be multiplied in the land of
Egypt." 10 Moses and Aaron performed all
these wonders before Pharaoh; but the
LORD hardened Pharaoh's heart, and he
did not let the people of Israel go out of his
land.

12 The LORD said to Moses and Aaron
in the land of Egypt: 2 This month
shall mark for you the beginning of
months; it shall be the first month of the
year for you. 3 Tell the whole congregation
of Israel that on the tenth of this month
they are to take a lamb for each family, a
lamb for each household. 4 If a household is
too small for a whole lamb, it shall join its
closest neighbor in obtaining one; the lamb
shall be divided in proportion to the num-
ber of people who eat of it. 5 Your lamb
shall be without blemish, a year-old male;
you may take it from the sheep or from the
goats. 6 You shall keep it until the four-
teenth day of this month; then the whole
assembled congregation of Israel shall
slaughter it at twilight. 7 They shall take
some of the blood and put it on the two
doorposts and the lintel of the houses in
which they eat it. 8 They shall eat the lamb
that same night; they shall eat it roasted
over the fire with unleavened bread and bit-
ter herbs. 9 Do not eat any of it raw or
boiled in water, but roasted over the fire,
with its head, legs, and inner organs. 10 You
shall let none of it remain until the morn-
ing; anything that remains until the morn-
ing you shall burn. 11 This is how you shall
eat it: your loins girded, your sandals on
your feet, and your staff in your hand; and
you shall eat it hurriedly. It is the passover

2–3: This was first predicted in 3.21–22 (see note there) and will be fulfilled in 12.35–36. **4:** Once again Pharaoh is given advance notice (8.23n.). **5:** *Firstborn,* 4.22–23n. **6:** 2.23–25n.; 9.18n. **7:** 8.22–23n. **10:** *Hardened,* 4.21n.

12.1–28: The festivals of Passover and unleavened bread. 12.1–13 (and vv. 43–49): God gives instructions concerning the *passover,* an ancient nomadic herders' spring festival which Israel reinterprets as a celebration of liberation (Deut 16.1–8; Num 9.1–14; Ezek 45.21–25). **1:** It is important that God address Moses *and Aaron* (vv. 28,43,50), since this is priestly instruction. **2:** *This month* refers to Nisan (March-April) which in Israel's Priestly ritual calendar will be *the beginning of months* (Lev 23.5,23–25). According to the older agricultural calendar, the new year begins in the autumn (Ex 23.16; 34.22). **6:** The passover is celebrated here at night during full moon (v. 8; Isa 30.29). **7:** *Blood* (which had saved Moses' life at the beginning of the story, 4.24–26) is now smeared on the doorposts and lintel to save all Israelites from the destroyer (vv. 22–23). **11:** As they eat the feast the people must be ready to travel, in commemoration of Israel's hasty departure. **11–13:** *Passover* ("pesaḥ"), despite the traditional understanding of "passing over," it more likely means "have compassion on" or "protect" ("spare," Isa 31.5). Reading "protect" instead of "pass over" before "you" (v. 13), "door" (v. 23), and "houses" (v. 27) gives a more authentic sense. **12:** This statement of the divine purpose does not deny the existence of other gods, but

of the LORD. 12 For I will pass through the
land of Egypt that night, and I will strike
down every firstborn in the land of Egypt,
both human beings and animals; on all the
gods of Egypt I will execute judgments: I
am the LORD. 13 The blood shall be a sign
for you on the houses where you live: when
I see the blood, I will pass over you, and no
plague shall destroy you when I strike the
land of Egypt.
14 This day shall be a day of remem-
brance for you. You shall celebrate it as a
festival to the LORD; throughout your gen-
erations you shall observe it as a perpetual
ordinance. 15 Seven days you shall eat un-
leavened bread; on the first day you shall
remove leaven from your houses, for who-
ever eats leavened bread from the first day
until the seventh day shall be cut off from
Israel. 16 On the first day you shall hold a
solemn assembly, and on the seventh day a
solemn assembly; no work shall be done on
those days; only what everyone must eat,
that alone may be prepared by you. 17 You
shall observe the festival of unleavened
bread, for on this very day I brought your
companies out of the land of Egypt: you
shall observe this day throughout your gen-
erations as a perpetual ordinance. 18 In the
first month, from the evening of the four-
teenth day until the evening of the twenty-
first day, you shall eat unleavened bread.
19 For seven days no leaven shall be found
in your houses; for whoever eats what is
leavened shall be cut off from the congrega-
tion of Israel, whether an alien or a native
of the land. 20 You shall eat nothing leav-
ened; in all your settlements you shall eat
unleavened bread.
21 Then Moses called all the elders of
Israel and said to them, "Go, select lambs
for your families, and slaughter the pass-
over lamb. 22 Take a bunch of hyssop, dip it
in the blood that is in the basin, and touch
the lintel and the two doorposts with the
blood in the basin. None of you shall go
outside the door of your house until morn-
ing. 23 For the LORD will pass through to
strike down the Egyptians; when he sees the
blood on the lintel and on the two door-
posts, the LORD will pass over that door
and will not allow the destroyer to enter
your houses to strike you down. 24 You
shall observe this rite as a perpetual ordi-
nance for you and your children. 25 When
you come to the land that the LORD will
give you, as he has promised, you shall
keep this observance. 26 And when your
children ask you, 'What do you mean by
this observance?' 27 you shall say, 'It is the
passover sacrifice to the LORD, for he
passed over the houses of the Israelites in
Egypt, when he struck down the Egyptians
but spared our houses.' " And the people
bowed down and worshiped.
28 The Israelites went and did just as the
LORD had commanded Moses and Aaron.
29 At midnight the LORD struck down

rather declares war on them (15.11). **14–20:** God continues with instructions concerning the festival of *unleavened bread.* Originally an agricultural festival held at the time of barley harvest in spring, this festival is also converted into a historical commemoration and is ultimately combined with the passover (Deut 16.1–8; Ezek 45.21–25). **14:** The passover is celebrated on the 14th of Nisan (v. 6); *this day* refers to the 15th (Lev 23.6; Num 28.17). The seven-day festival is regarded as a continuation of the passover. **15:** The absence of leaven (yeast) is later interpreted as due to hasty preparations for flight (v. 39; cf. vv. 11,33–34,39; Deut 16.3). In the original spring harvest festival leaven was likely avoided because it was from last year's harvest, and thus inappropriate to a celebration of the new harvest. **17:** *Companies,* v. 37n. **18:** So closely is the festival combined with the passover that it is said to begin on the evening of the 14th, i.e., the night of the passover (v. 14). **21–28:** Moses passes the instructions concerning the passover on to *the elders* (4.29). **22:** *Hyssop,* the foliage of an aromatic wild bush, used for sprinkling liquids in religious rituals (Lev 14.4; Num 19.6,18; Ps 51.7). **23:** *The destroyer,* or the angel of death, is a manifestation of the divine power (2 Sam 24.16; Isa 37.36). **24–27:** The importance of teaching the traditions to each new generation is also emphasized in 10.2; 13.8–9,14–16; Deut 6.6–9.

12.29–51: The Israelites leave Egypt. 29–36: The conclusion of the tenth plague, the death of the firstborn (11.1–10). **29:** *Firstborn,* 4.22–23n. **30:** The *cry* at the beginning of the story (2.23) was that all the firstborn in the land of Egypt, from the firstborn of Pharaoh who sat on his throne to the firstborn of the prisoner who was in the dungeon, and all the firstborn of the livestock. 30 Pharaoh arose in the night, he and all his officials and all the Egyptians; and there was a loud cry in Egypt, for there was not a house without someone dead. 31 Then he summoned Moses and Aaron in the night, and said, "Rise up, go away from my people, both you and the Israelites! Go, worship the LORD, as you said. 32 Take your flocks and your herds, as you said, and be gone. And bring a blessing on me too!"

33 The Egyptians urged the people to hasten their departure from the land, for they said, "We shall all be dead." 34 So the people took their dough before it was leavened, with their kneading bowls wrapped up in their cloaks on their shoulders. 35 The Israelites had done as Moses told them; they had asked the Egyptians for jewelry of silver and gold, and for clothing, 36 and the LORD had given the people favor in the sight of the Egyptians, so that they let them have what they asked. And so they plundered the Egyptians.

37 The Israelites journeyed from Rameses to Succoth, about six hundred thousand men on foot, besides children. 38 A mixed crowd also went up with them, and livestock in great numbers, both flocks and herds. 39 They baked unleavened cakes of the dough that they had brought out of Egypt; it was not leavened, because they were driven out of Egypt and could not wait, nor had they prepared any provisions for themselves.

40 The time that the Israelites had lived in Egypt was four hundred thirty years. 41 At the end of four hundred thirty years, on that very day, all the companies of the LORD went out from the land of Egypt. 42 That was for the LORD a night of vigil, to bring them out of the land of Egypt. That same night is a vigil to be kept for the LORD by all the Israelites throughout their generations.

43 The LORD said to Moses and Aaron: This is the ordinance for the passover: no foreigner shall eat of it, 44 but any slave who has been purchased may eat of it after he has been circumcised; 45 no bound or hired servant may eat of it. 46 It shall be eaten in one house; you shall not take any of the animal outside the house, and you shall not break any of its bones. 47 The whole congregation of Israel shall celebrate it. 48 If an alien who resides with you wants to celebrate the passover to the LORD, all his males shall be circumcised; then he may draw near to celebrate it; he shall be regarded as a native of the land. But no uncir-

of the Israelites. Now it is the Egyptians who cry out. **32:** Contrast 10.24. **33–36:** The Egyptians urge them to leave (Ps 105.37–38). *Before it was leavened,* v. 15n. The *jewelry* and *clothing* will be used both to break and to obey the covenant (3.21–22n.).

12.37–42: The first stage of the journey. 37: Rameses (1.11) is the starting place of Israel's journey, and Succoth (13.20) is their first stop (Num 33.5). Neither can be identified with certainty. *Six hundred thousand men on foot, besides children* (Num 11.21), the number reflects the census list in Num 1.17–46. Children are mentioned but not counted, and women are completely ignored. The departing group is enormous, organized in "companies" (vv. 17,41,51; 7.4), and "prepared for battle" (13.18), and its size is inconsistent both with historical data and with other details in the narrative (e.g., 1.15; 14.7). **38:** The *mixed crowd* (Num 11.4) includes other "Hebrews" or displaced persons (1.15n.). **39:** V. 15n. **40–41:** *Four hundred thirty years,* Gen 15.13; contrast Gen 15.16. **41:** *On that very day,* the fifteenth day of the first month (v. 6; Num 33.3). *Companies,* v. 37n. **42:** The *night of vigil* is the passover. **43–49:** God gives further instructions for the celebration of *passover* when the Israelites are in their own land (cf. 12.1–13). A *foreigner* (v. 43) and a *bound or hired servant* (v. 45) are excluded from the celebration because they are related to other gods. However, the purchased *slave* who becomes a part of the family (v. 44) and the *alien who resides* permanently within Israel (v. 48) may eat the passover, if they are circumcised (vv. 48–49; Gen 17.9–14). **50–51:** This summary emphasizes the Israelites' obedience and military organization. **51:** V. 37n.

cumcised person shall eat of it; 49 there shall
be one law for the native and for the alien
who resides among you.
50 All the Israelites did just as the LORD
had commanded Moses and Aaron. 51 That
very day the LORD brought the Israelites
out of the land of Egypt, company by com-
pany.
13 The LORD said to Moses: 2 Conse-
crate to me all the firstborn; whatev-
er is the first to open the womb among the
Israelites, of human beings and animals, is
mine.
3 Moses said to the people, "Remember
this day on which you came out of Egypt,
out of the house of slavery, because the
LORD brought you out from there by
strength of hand; no leavened bread shall
be eaten. 4 Today, in the month of Abib,
you are going out. 5 When the LORD brings
you into the land of the Canaanites, the
Hittites, the Amorites, the Hivites, and the
Jebusites, which he swore to your ancestors
to give you, a land flowing with milk and
honey, you shall keep this observance in
this month. 6 Seven days you shall eat un-
leavened bread, and on the seventh day
there shall be a festival to the LORD. 7 Un-
leavened bread shall be eaten for seven
days; no leavened bread shall be seen in
your possession, and no leaven shall be
seen among you in all your territory. 8 You
shall tell your child on that day, 'It is be-
cause of what the LORD did for me when I
came out of Egypt.' 9 It shall serve for you
as a sign on your hand and as a reminder
on your forehead, so that the teaching of
the LORD may be on your lips; for with a
strong hand the LORD brought you out of
Egypt. 10 You shall keep this ordinance at
its proper time from year to year.
11 "When the LORD has brought you
into the land of the Canaanites, as he swore
to you and your ancestors, and has given it
to you, 12 you shall set apart to the LORD all
that first opens the womb. All the firstborn
of your livestock that are males shall be the
LORD's. 13 But every firstborn donkey you
shall redeem with a sheep; if you do not
redeem it, you must break its neck. Every
firstborn male among your children you
shall redeem. 14 When in the future your
child asks you, 'What does this mean?' you
shall answer, 'By strength of hand the
LORD brought us out of Egypt, from the
house of slavery. 15 When Pharaoh stub-
bornly refused to let us go, the LORD killed
all the firstborn in the land of Egypt, from
human firstborn to the firstborn of ani-
mals. Therefore I sacrifice to the LORD ev-
ery male that first opens the womb, but
every firstborn of my sons I redeem.' 16 It
shall serve as a sign on your hand and as
an emblem[a] on your forehead that by
strength of hand the LORD brought us out
of Egypt."
17 When Pharaoh let the people go, God

a Or *as a frontlet*; meaning of Heb uncertain

13.1–16: Consecration of the firstborn and Festival of Unleavened Bread. 1–2: Consecration of *the firstborn* (continued in vv. 11–16). The devotion of the firstborn of humans and of animals to God, the giver of fertility, assures continuing increase and well-being (22.29–30; Lev 27.26–27; Num 18.15). Because of the liberation, Israelite firstborn belong to God just as the Egyptian firstborn do (4.22–23n.; Num 3.13; 8.17–18). **3–10:** Festival of *unleavened bread.* Moses gives further instructions (cf. 12.14–20n.). **4:** *Abib,* the older name for the month of the Exodus (23.15; 12.2n.). **5:** 3.8n. **8:** *Tell your child,* 12.24–27n. Later generations can tell what God *did for me when I came out of Egypt,* since ritual makes the liberation present again to the worshipers (Deut 5.2–3). **9:** V. 16; Deut 6.8. **11–16:** Consecration of *the firstborn* (resuming the instructions begun in vv. 1–2). For the first time firstborn of animals and humans that belong to God are specified as male; cf. 11.5; 12.29–30. **13:** Unclean animals, of which the *donkey* is typical (Lev 11; Deut 14.3–21), and *male . . . children* may be redeemed by substituting a *sheep* (34.19–20; cf. Gen 22.13). In Num 3.12–13 the service of the Levites is a substitute for the firstborn of the other Israelites. **14–15:** *Your child,* 12.24–27n.

13.17–15.21: God rescues Israel at the sea (Ps 78.13–14,52–53; 106.7–12).

13.17–14.31: The story of the rescue is first told in prose. 13.17–14.4: God plans one more stubborn

did not lead them by way of the land of the
Philistines, although that was nearer; for
God thought, "If the people face war, they
may change their minds and return to
Egypt." 18 So God led the people by the
roundabout way of the wilderness toward
the Red Sea.[a] The Israelites went up out
of the land of Egypt prepared for battle.
19 And Moses took with him the bones of
Joseph who had required a solemn oath of
the Israelites, saying, "God will surely take
notice of you, and then you must carry my
bones with you from here." 20 They set out
from Succoth, and camped at Etham, on
the edge of the wilderness. 21 The LORD
went in front of them in a pillar of cloud by
day, to lead them along the way, and in a
pillar of fire by night, to give them light, so
that they might travel by day and by night.
22 Neither the pillar of cloud by day nor the
pillar of fire by night left its place in front
of the people.

14 Then the LORD said to Moses: 2 Tell
the Israelites to turn back and camp
in front of Pi-hahiroth, between Migdol
and the sea, in front of Baal-zephon; you
shall camp opposite it, by the sea. 3 Pharaoh
will say of the Israelites, "They are wander-
ing aimlessly in the land; the wilderness has
closed in on them." 4 I will harden Phar-
aoh's heart, and he will pursue them, so
that I will gain glory for myself over Phar-
aoh and all his army; and the Egyptians
shall know that I am the LORD. And they
did so.

5 When the king of Egypt was told that
the people had fled, the minds of Pharaoh
and his officials were changed toward the
people, and they said, "What have we
done, letting Israel leave our service?" 6 So
he had his chariot made ready, and took
his army with him; 7 he took six hundred
picked chariots and all the other chariots of
Egypt with officers over all of them. 8 The
LORD hardened the heart of Pharaoh king
of Egypt and he pursued the Israelites, who
were going out boldly. 9 The Egyptians pur-
sued them, all Pharaoh's horses and chari-
ots, his chariot drivers and his army; they
overtook them camped by the sea, by Pi-
hahiroth, in front of Baal-zephon.

10 As Pharaoh drew near, the Israelites
looked back, and there were the Egyptians
advancing on them. In great fear the Israel-
ites cried out to the LORD. 11 They said to
Moses, "Was it because there were no
graves in Egypt that you have taken us
away to die in the wilderness? What have
you done to us, bringing us out of Egypt?
12 Is this not the very thing we told you in

a Or *Sea of Reeds*

act from Pharaoh. **17:** *Philistines,* one of the "Sea Peoples," who came to Canaan's southwestern coast from the Aegean Sea around 1200 BCE. The rejected route is the main coastal road into Canaan (color Map 2 at back of book). **18:** The Hebrew name for the *Red Sea* is "yam suf," which can mean both Sea of Reeds (2.3n.) and Sea of the End (that is, distant). Some retain the traditional meaning, the Red Sea, while others think a shallow body of water farther north, perhaps in the area of Lake Timsah, is meant. It seems more fitting contextually that the climax of the liberating process should involve a miraculous splitting of a great and distant sea rather than a storm in a shallow lake. On this view the rescue is set in the northern part of the Gulf of Suez, the northwestern "rabbit ear" of the Red Sea. It should be noted, however, that underlying the narrative are several traditions, which may not be fully consistent. **19:** Gen 50.25–26. **20:** The second stage of the journey (Num 33.6). *Succoth,* 12.37. The precise locations of *Etham,* and of Pi-hahiroth, Migdol, and Baal-zephon (14.2) are unknown. **21–22:** The *pillar of cloud* and the *pillar of fire* are signs of God's presence to guide their travels while shielding them from the sun by day and giving them light and warmth at night (3.2n.; 19.9; 33.9; 40.34–38; 1 Kings 8.10–11; Ps 78.14; 105.39). **14.1:** Moses is the sole human leader; Aaron does not reappear in this role until 16.2 (but see 15.20). **2–4:** The third stage of the journey (see 13.20n.; Num 33.7). God tells the Israelites to *turn back* so that Pharaoh will stubbornly try to defeat Israel's God after all. **2:** *The sea,* 13.18n. **4:** *Harden,* 4.21n. *Know,* 5.2n. **5–12:** Pharaoh takes the bait, and the pursuing Egyptian army terrifies the Israelites. **8:** *Hardened,* 4.21n. **11–12:** 15.24n. The statement quoted in v. 12 has not appeared, but a similar attitude is evident in 5.21; 6.9. **13–31:** God the warrior fights for Israel. **13–14:** V. 25; 15.3; Ps 24.8. **17–18:** *Harden,* 4.21n. In this

Egypt, 'Let us alone and let us serve the
Egyptians'? For it would have been better
for us to serve the Egyptians than to die in
the wilderness." 13 But Moses said to the
people, "Do not be afraid, stand firm, and
see the deliverance that the LORD will ac-
complish for you today; for the Egyptians
whom you see today you shall never see
again. 14 The LORD will fight for you, and
you have only to keep still."
15 Then the LORD said to Moses, "Why
do you cry out to me? Tell the Israelites to
go forward. 16 But you lift up your staff,
and stretch out your hand over the sea and
divide it, that the Israelites may go into the
sea on dry ground. 17 Then I will harden the
hearts of the Egyptians so that they will go
in after them; and so I will gain glory for
myself over Pharaoh and all his army, his
chariots, and his chariot drivers. 18 And the
Egyptians shall know that I am the LORD,
when I have gained glory for myself over
Pharaoh, his chariots, and his chariot driv-
ers."
19 The angel of God who was going be-
fore the Israelite army moved and went be-
hind them; and the pillar of cloud moved
from in front of them and took its place
behind them. 20 It came between the army
of Egypt and the army of Israel. And so the
cloud was there with the darkness, and it lit
up the night; one did not come near the
other all night.
21 Then Moses stretched out his hand
over the sea. The LORD drove the sea back
by a strong east wind all night, and turned
the sea into dry land; and the waters were
divided. 22 The Israelites went into the sea
on dry ground, the waters forming a wall
for them on their right and on their left.
23 The Egyptians pursued, and went into
the sea after them, all of Pharaoh's horses,
chariots, and chariot drivers. 24 At the
morning watch the LORD in the pillar of
fire and cloud looked down upon the Egyp-
tian army, and threw the Egyptian army
into panic. 25 He clogged[a] their chariot
wheels so that they turned with difficulty.
The Egyptians said, "Let us flee from the
Israelites, for the LORD is fighting for them
against Egypt."
26 Then the LORD said to Moses,
"Stretch out your hand over the sea, so that
the water may come back upon the Egyp-
tians, upon their chariots and chariot driv-
ers." 27 So Moses stretched out his hand
over the sea, and at dawn the sea returned
to its normal depth. As the Egyptians fled
before it, the LORD tossed the Egyptians
into the sea. 28 The waters returned and
covered the chariots and the chariot driv-
ers, the entire army of Pharaoh that had
followed them into the sea; not one of them
remained. 29 But the Israelites walked on
dry ground through the sea, the waters
forming a wall for them on their right and
on their left.
30 Thus the LORD saved Israel that day
from the Egyptians; and Israel saw the
Egyptians dead on the seashore. 31 Israel
saw the great work that the LORD did
against the Egyptians. So the people feared
the LORD and believed in the LORD and in
his servant Moses.

15 Then Moses and the Israelites sang
this song to the LORD:

a Sam Gk Syr: MT *removed*

episode God hardens the hearts not only of Pharaoh, but also of all the Egyptian army. The goal is the same, namely that the divine reputation be enhanced and they *know,* that is, acknowledge, Israel's God (v. 4; 5.2n.). **19–20:** The divine presence is symbolized in two ways here: both as *the angel of God* (3.2n.) and *the pillar of cloud* (v. 24; 13.21–22n.). God's presence is needed now as shield against the pursuing army. **21–22:** In this Priestly summary, the *east wind* blowing over the waters and causing *dry ground* recalls Gen 1.2,9; 8.1 (also P). **24–25a:** An alternate tradition, according to which the Egyptians in chariots got stuck in the mud as the Israelites escaped on foot. **25b:** The Egyptians acknowledge God (vv. 17–18), but it is too late. **31:** God's purpose as far as the Israelites are concerned is fulfilled.

15.1–21: The story of the rescue is told in poetry. The poetic rendition does not agree in all details with the prose traditions. **1–18:** The song of Moses, celebrating God as warrior-king, may be one of the oldest compositions in the Bible. **1b–12:** The divine warrior defeats Pharaoh finally at the sea (Ps 78.12–13,53;

"I will sing to the LORD, for he has
triumphed gloriously;
horse and rider he has thrown into
the sea.
2 The LORD is my strength and my
might,[a]
and he has become my salvation;
this is my God, and I will praise
him,
my father's God, and I will exalt
him.
3 The LORD is a warrior;
the LORD is his name.

4 "Pharaoh's chariots and his army he
cast into the sea;
his picked officers were sunk in the
Red Sea.[b]
5 The floods covered them;
they went down into the depths like
a stone.
6 Your right hand, O LORD, glorious in
power—
your right hand, O LORD, shattered
the enemy.
7 In the greatness of your majesty you
overthrew your adversaries;
you sent out your fury, it consumed
them like stubble.
8 At the blast of your nostrils the
waters piled up,
the floods stood up in a heap;
the deeps congealed in the heart of
the sea.
9 The enemy said, 'I will pursue, I will
overtake,
I will divide the spoil, my desire
shall have its fill of them.
I will draw my sword, my hand
shall destroy them.'
10 You blew with your wind, the sea
covered them;
they sank like lead in the mighty
waters.

11 "Who is like you, O LORD, among
the gods?
Who is like you, majestic in
holiness,
awesome in splendor, doing
wonders?
12 You stretched out your right hand,
the earth swallowed them.

13 "In your steadfast love you led the
people whom you redeemed;
you guided them by your strength
to your holy abode.
14 The peoples heard, they trembled;
pangs seized the inhabitants of
Philistia.
15 Then the chiefs of Edom were
dismayed;
trembling seized the leaders of
Moab;
all the inhabitants of Canaan
melted away.
16 Terror and dread fell upon them;
by the might of your arm, they
became still as a stone
until your people, O LORD, passed
by,
until the people whom you
acquired passed by.

a Or *song* *b* Or *Sea of Reeds*

106.9–11). The language is influenced by the ancient myth of the storm god's battle against Sea, the chaotic power hostile to God's rule (Ps 77.16–19; 114.3–6; Hab 3.8). Here Sea is no longer God's enemy but rather the weapon with which the Egyptians are defeated. **2:** *My father's God* refers to "the God of the ancestors" (3.6,15). **3:** 14.13–14n. **4:** *Red Sea,* 13.18n. **11:** Israel's God is incomparable *among the gods* who compose the heavenly council (Ps 82.1; 86.8; 89.5–8; cf. Ex 12.12). **13–18:** The loving God guides Israel into Canaan and becomes king (Ps 78.54–55; 105.43–44). The neighbors of Israel hear of God's victory at the sea and are so paralyzed with dread at the divine power that Israel can travel safely to the promised land. As God treats Israel differently from other peoples (6.7–8; 17.14–15; 19.3–6; 23.22; 33.16; 34.10), so Israel will be expected to keep itself separate and different from other peoples (23.23–33; 34.11–17). **13:** *Your holy abode,* Canaan or one of its hills. **14:** *Philistia,* see 13.17n. **15:** *Edom* and *Moab* were kingdoms in southern Transjordan; cf. Num 20.21; 22.3. *Canaan* refers to the land west of the Jordan; cf. Josh 5.1. **17:** Canaan, or one of its hills, is described in terms reminiscent of Baal's

17 You brought them in and planted
them on the mountain of your
own possession,
the place, O LORD, that you made
your abode,
the sanctuary, O LORD, that your
hands have established.
18 The LORD will reign forever and
ever."

19 When the horses of Pharaoh with his chariots and his chariot drivers went into the sea, the LORD brought back the waters of the sea upon them; but the Israelites walked through the sea on dry ground.
20 Then the prophet Miriam, Aaron's sister, took a tambourine in her hand; and all the women went out after her with tambourines and with dancing.
21 And Miriam sang to them:

"Sing to the LORD, for he has
triumphed gloriously;
horse and rider he has thrown into
the sea."

22 Then Moses ordered Israel to set out from the Red Sea,[a] and they went into the wilderness of Shur. They went three days in the wilderness and found no water.
23 When they came to Marah, they could not drink the water of Marah because it was bitter. That is why it was called Marah.[b]
24 And the people complained against Moses, saying, "What shall we drink?"
25 He cried out to the LORD; and the LORD showed him a piece of wood;[c] he threw it into the water, and the water became sweet.

There the LORD[d] made for them a statute and an ordinance and there he put them to the test.
26 He said, "If you will listen carefully to the voice of the LORD your God, and do what is right in his sight, and give heed to his commandments and keep all his statutes, I will not bring upon you any of the diseases that I brought upon the Egyptians; for I am the LORD who heals you."
27 Then they came to Elim, where there were twelve springs of water and seventy palm trees; and they camped there by the water.

16 The whole congregation of the Israelites set out from Elim; and Israel came to the wilderness of Sin, which is between Elim and Sinai, on the fifteenth day of the second month after they had departed from the land of Egypt.
2 The whole congregation of the Israelites complained

a Or *Sea of Reeds* b That is *Bitterness* c Or *a tree* d Heb *he*

mountain, Zaphon (Ps 48.1–3). God's *abode* and *sanctuary* have moved from Mount Sinai/Horeb (3.1; 19.1–3) to Canaan (Ps 114.1–2); cf. Ps 78.54–55. **18:** The God who fights for Israel (v. 3) has earned the right to rule Israel forever. **19–21:** In song and dance, Miriam leads all the women in praising God for liberation. Women typically lead victory songs and dancing in celebration of victories (Judg 5.1; 11.34; 1 Sam 18.7; 2 Sam 1.20). As women were the first to resist Pharaoh and save Moses' life (1.15–2.10; 4.24–26), it is especially fitting that women also get the last word in the story of liberation. **20:** Miriam (Num 26.59; Mic 6.4), doubtless a dominant figure in early tradition, is named for the first time (contrast 2.4,7) and is called a *prophet* because of her ecstatic rousing of devotion to God (cf. Deborah in Judg 4.4–16; 5.1,12).

15.22–18.27: God journeys with Israel to Mount Sinai. Israel will remember this journey from slavery to covenant as a time of complete dependence on God and simultaneous complaining, despite having experienced rescue and provision at every stage (contrast 14.31; 15.1–21).

15.22–27: God makes the water drinkable at Marah. 22–23: The fourth stage of the journey. *The wilderness of Shur* is called the wilderness of Etham in Num 33.8. **24:** Israel's continual complaining is a dominant theme of the wilderness story (16.2–3,6–9; 17.3; Num 11.1,4–6; 14.2–3; 16.13–14; 20.2–5; 21.4–5). **25b:** *Test,* Deut 8.2,15–16. **26:** *Diseases,* the plagues (7.8–11.10). *Who heals you,* 23.25–26; Num 21.4–9; Deut 7.15; Ps 103.3. **27:** The fifth stage of the journey (Num 33.9).

16.1–36: God provides manna and quails (Num 11; Ps 78.17–31; 105.40). Two originally separate traditions are likely combined here. **1:** It is now one month since the Israelites began their journey (12.37; Num 33.3,10–11). *Sinai,* see 3.1n. **2:** *Complained,* 15.24n. *Aaron* reappears for the first time since 12.50

against Moses and Aaron in the wilderness.
3The Israelites said to them, "If only we
had died by the hand of the LORD in the
land of Egypt, when we sat by the fleshpots
and ate our fill of bread; for you have
brought us out into this wilderness to kill
this whole assembly with hunger."

4 Then the LORD said to Moses, "I am
going to rain bread from heaven for you,
and each day the people shall go out and
gather enough for that day. In that way I
will test them, whether they will follow my
instruction or not. 5On the sixth day, when
they prepare what they bring in, it will be
twice as much as they gather on other
days." 6So Moses and Aaron said to all the
Israelites, "In the evening you shall know
that it was the LORD who brought you out
of the land of Egypt, 7and in the morning
you shall see the glory of the LORD, because
he has heard your complaining against the
LORD. For what are we, that you complain
against us?" 8And Moses said, "When the
LORD gives you meat to eat in the evening
and your fill of bread in the morning, be-
cause the LORD has heard the complaining
that you utter against him—what are we?
Your complaining is not against us but
against the LORD."

9 Then Moses said to Aaron, "Say to the
whole congregation of the Israelites, 'Draw
near to the LORD, for he has heard your
complaining.' " 10And as Aaron spoke to
the whole congregation of the Israelites,
they looked toward the wilderness, and the
glory of the LORD appeared in the cloud.
11The LORD spoke to Moses and said, 12"I
have heard the complaining of the Israel-
ites; say to them, 'At twilight you shall eat
meat, and in the morning you shall have
your fill of bread; then you shall know that
I am the LORD your God.' "

13 In the evening quails came up and
covered the camp; and in the morning there
was a layer of dew around the camp.
14When the layer of dew lifted, there on the
surface of the wilderness was a fine flaky
substance, as fine as frost on the ground.
15When the Israelites saw it, they said to
one another, "What is it?"[a] For they did
not know what it was. Moses said to them,
"It is the bread that the LORD has given you
to eat. 16This is what the LORD has com-
manded: 'Gather as much of it as each of
you needs, an omer to a person according
to the number of persons, all providing for
those in their own tents.' " 17The Israelites
did so, some gathering more, some less.
18But when they measured it with an omer,
those who gathered much had nothing
over, and those who gathered little had no
shortage; they gathered as much as each of
them needed. 19And Moses said to them,
"Let no one leave any of it over until morn-
ing." 20But they did not listen to Moses;
some left part of it until morning, and it
bred worms and became foul. And Moses
was angry with them. 21Morning by morn-
ing they gathered it, as much as each need-
ed; but when the sun grew hot, it melted.

22 On the sixth day they gathered twice
as much food, two omers apiece. When all
the leaders of the congregation came and
told Moses, 23he said to them, "This is

a Or *"It is manna"* (Heb *man hu*, see verse 31)

(but see 15.20). **4:** *Test,* Deut 8.3,16. **6–7:** *In the evening* when the quails come; *in the morning* when the manna is found (vv. 8,12,13). *Know,* 5.2n. In the Priestly view expressed here, the divine *glory* is an envelope of light (associated with the pillar of cloud and fire; v. 10; 13.21–22n.) which veils God's being. Though human beings cannot see the deity, they can perceive the glory that signifies God's presence (40.34–35; Num 14.10b,22; 16.19; 1 Kings 8.10–11). **9–10:** *Aaron* again acts as Moses' spokesman (4.16 and note there). **12:** *Know,* 5. 2n. **13:** *Quails,* Num 11.1–35. **14:** The description here (see also v. 31n.) corresponds fairly closely to the carbohydrate-rich excretion of two scale-insects that feed on the twigs of the tamarisk tree. **15:** The name of the food, *manna* (v. 31), is explained by an expression meaning "What is it?" **16:** *Omer,* about 2.3 l (2 qt). **22–30:** The provision of manna is an occasion for instruction concerning the *sabbath,* or seventh day of the week, *a day of solemn rest* (20.8–11; 23.12; 31.12–17; 34.21; 35.1–3). Already established in Gen 2.2–3, the sabbath is explicitly found in the natural order, and thus occurs here, even before its mention in the Decalogue (20.8–11). **31:** A different description is found

what the LORD has commanded: 'Tomor-
row is a day of solemn rest, a holy sabbath
to the LORD; bake what you want to bake
and boil what you want to boil, and all that
is left over put aside to be kept until morn-
ing.' " 24 So they put it aside until morning,
as Moses commanded them; and it did not
become foul, and there were no worms in
it. 25 Moses said, "Eat it today, for today is
a sabbath to the LORD; today you will not
find it in the field. 26 Six days you shall
gather it; but on the seventh day, which is
a sabbath, there will be none."
27 On the seventh day some of the peo-
ple went out to gather, and they found
none. 28 The LORD said to Moses, "How
long will you refuse to keep my command-
ments and instructions? 29 See! The LORD
has given you the sabbath, therefore on the
sixth day he gives you food for two days;
each of you stay where you are; do not
leave your place on the seventh day." 30 So
the people rested on the seventh day.
31 The house of Israel called it manna;
it was like coriander seed, white, and the
taste of it was like wafers made with honey.
32 Moses said, "This is what the LORD has
commanded: 'Let an omer of it be kept
throughout your generations, in order that
they may see the food with which I fed you
in the wilderness, when I brought you out
of the land of Egypt.' " 33 And Moses said
to Aaron, "Take a jar, and put an omer of
manna in it, and place it before the LORD,
to be kept throughout your generations."
34 As the LORD commanded Moses, so Aar-
on placed it before the covenant,[a] for safe-
keeping. 35 The Israelites ate manna forty
years, until they came to a habitable land;
they ate manna, until they came to the bor-
der of the land of Canaan. 36 An omer is a
tenth of an ephah.

17 From the wilderness of Sin the
whole congregation of the Israelites
journeyed by stages, as the LORD com-
manded. They camped at Rephidim, but
there was no water for the people to drink.
2 The people quarreled with Moses, and
said, "Give us water to drink." Moses said
to them, "Why do you quarrel with me?
Why do you test the LORD?" 3 But the peo-
ple thirsted there for water; and the people
complained against Moses and said, "Why
did you bring us out of Egypt, to kill us and
our children and livestock with thirst?" 4 So
Moses cried out to the LORD, "What shall
I do with this people? They are almost
ready to stone me." 5 The LORD said to
Moses, "Go on ahead of the people, and
take some of the elders of Israel with you;
take in your hand the staff with which you
struck the Nile, and go. 6 I will be standing
there in front of you on the rock at Horeb.
Strike the rock, and water will come out of
it, so that the people may drink." Moses
did so, in the sight of the elders of Israel.
7 He called the place Massah[b] and Meri-
bah,[c] because the Israelites quarreled and
tested the LORD, saying, "Is the LORD
among us or not?"
8 Then Amalek came and fought with

a Or *treaty* or *testimony*; Heb *eduth* *b* That is *Test*
c That is *Quarrel*

in Num 11.7–9, giving rise to the early legend that the taste of *manna* varied according to the eater's preference. **33–34:** *Before the* LORD, *before the covenant,* that is, before the ark of the covenant (25.10–22). **35:** Josh 5.11–12.

17.1–7: Water flows out of the rock at Massah and Meribah (cf. Num 20.2–13; Ps 78.15–16; 105.41). **1:** The journey continues (Num 33.12–14). *The wilderness of Sin,* 16.1. *By stages,* Num 33.1–2. **2–3:** 15.24n. *Test,* demand proof that God is in their midst (v. 7b). **5–6:** In contrast to the story in ch 16, the sole leader in this episode is *Moses,* who carries out God's instructions with his own staff, but this time accompanied by *elders* as witnesses. **7:** The place receives two appropriate names, "Test" and "Quarrel," which will become reminders of Israel's lack of trust (Deut 6.16; 9.22; 33.8; Ps 95.8). *Meribah* is one of the springs at Kadesh(-barnea), an oasis on the border between the wilderness of Paran and the wilderness of Zin (color Map 2 at end of book; Num 27.14).

17.8–16: God defeats the Amalekites. 8: The Amalekites, a widespread semi-nomadic group, claim control of the wilderness in the region of Kadesh, where Meribah is (Gen 14.7). *Rephidim,* v. 1.

Israel at Rephidim. 9 Moses said to Joshua,
"Choose some men for us and go out, fight
with Amalek. Tomorrow I will stand on the
top of the hill with the staff of God in my
hand." 10 So Joshua did as Moses told him,
and fought with Amalek, while Moses,
Aaron, and Hur went up to the top of the
hill. 11 Whenever Moses held up his hand,
Israel prevailed; and whenever he lowered
his hand, Amalek prevailed. 12 But Moses'
hands grew weary; so they took a stone and
put it under him, and he sat on it. Aaron
and Hur held up his hands, one on one side,
and the other on the other side; so his
hands were steady until the sun set. 13 And
Joshua defeated Amalek and his people
with the sword.

14 Then the LORD said to Moses,
"Write this as a reminder in a book and
recite it in the hearing of Joshua: I will ut-
terly blot out the remembrance of Amalek
from under heaven." 15 And Moses built an
altar and called it, The LORD is my banner.
16 He said, "A hand upon the banner of the
LORD![a] The LORD will have war with Am-
alek from generation to generation."

18 Jethro, the priest of Midian, Moses'
father-in-law, heard of all that God
had done for Moses and for his people Isra-
el, how the LORD had brought Israel out of
Egypt. 2 After Moses had sent away his wife
Zipporah, his father-in-law Jethro took her
back, 3 along with her two sons. The name
of the one was Gershom (for he said, "I
have been an alien[b] in a foreign land"),
4 and the name of the other, Eliezer[c] (for
he said, "The God of my father was my
help, and delivered me from the sword of
Pharaoh"). 5 Jethro, Moses' father-in-law,
came into the wilderness where Moses was
encamped at the mountain of God, bring-
ing Moses' sons and wife to him. 6 He sent
word to Moses, "I, your father-in-law Jeth-
ro, am coming to you, with your wife and
her two sons." 7 Moses went out to meet his
father-in-law; he bowed down and kissed
him; each asked after the other's welfare,
and they went into the tent. 8 Then Moses
told his father-in-law all that the LORD had
done to Pharaoh and to the Egyptians for
Israel's sake, all the hardship that had beset
them on the way, and how the LORD had
delivered them. 9 Jethro rejoiced for all the
good that the LORD had done to Israel, in
delivering them from the Egyptians.

10 Jethro said, "Blessed be the LORD,
who has delivered you from the Egyptians
and from Pharaoh. 11 Now I know that the
LORD is greater than all gods, because he
delivered the people from the Egyptians,[d]
when they dealt arrogantly with them."
12 And Jethro, Moses' father-in-law,
brought a burnt offering and sacrifices to
God; and Aaron came with all the elders of
Israel to eat bread with Moses' father-in-
law in the presence of God.

13 The next day Moses sat as judge for

a Cn: Meaning of Heb uncertain *b* Heb *ger*
c Heb *Eli,* my God; *ezer,* help *d* The clause
because . . . Egyptians has been transposed from
verse 10

9–13: *Choose some men for us* implies "holy war" (v. 16) with a select group (cf. Judg ch 7). The unidentified young warrior, *Joshua,* leads the Israelite army. He is later identified as Moses' "assistant" (24.13; 32.17), and ultimately his successor (e.g., Deut 34.9). Moses ensures victory by the power of *the staff of God* (4.17) in his outstretched hands. **10:** *Hur,* elsewhere mentioned only in 24.14, also with Aaron. **16:** The bitter feud with the Amalekites will persist (Num 24.20; Deut 25.17–19; 1 Sam 15.2,7–8,32–33; 27.8; ch 30) until they are exterminated during the reign of Hezekiah (1 Chr 4.41–43).

18.1–27: Jethro visits. The priest of Midian celebrates a sacred meal and counsels Moses about the administration of justice. **1:** *Jethro,* 2.18n. **2–4:** Zipporah and her sons (2.21–22; 4.20) apparently were sent back from Egypt to Midian. **5:** The narrative is out of order, for Israel reaches *the mountain of God* later (19.2; 3.1n.; but see 17.6); Deut 1.9–18 places it later. **7–9:** The story focuses exclusively on Moses' welcome of and conversations with Jethro. The arrival of Zipporah and the two sons is not even mentioned. **9–12:** Even non-Israelites recognize God's greatness, as in 14.25, and later, in Josh 2.9–11; 9.3–27. **11:** *Greater than all gods,* 12.12; 15.11. **12:** *Aaron* and *the elders* join in a sacred meal *in the presence of God* (24.9–11). **13–27:** This episode, in which Jethro suggests a reorganization of the

the people, while the people stood around
him from morning until evening. 14 When
Moses' father-in-law saw all that he was
doing for the people, he said, "What is this
that you are doing for the people? Why do
you sit alone, while all the people stand
around you from morning until evening?"
15 Moses said to his father-in-law, "Be-
cause the people come to me to inquire of
God. 16 When they have a dispute, they
come to me and I decide between one per-
son and another, and I make known to
them the statutes and instructions of God."
17 Moses' father-in-law said to him, "What
you are doing is not good. 18 You will sure-
ly wear yourself out, both you and these
people with you. For the task is too heavy
for you; you cannot do it alone. 19 Now
listen to me. I will give you counsel, and
God be with you! You should represent the
people before God, and you should bring
their cases before God; 20 teach them the
statutes and instructions and make known
to them the way they are to go and the
things they are to do. 21 You should also
look for able men among all the people,
men who fear God, are trustworthy, and
hate dishonest gain; set such men over them
as officers over thousands, hundreds, fif-
ties, and tens. 22 Let them sit as judges for
the people at all times; let them bring every
important case to you, but decide every mi-
nor case themselves. So it will be easier for
you, and they will bear the burden with
you. 23 If you do this, and God so com-
mands you, then you will be able to endure,
and all these people will go to their home in
peace."
24 So Moses listened to his father-in-
law and did all that he had said. 25 Moses
chose able men from all Israel and appoint-
ed them as heads over the people, as offi-
cers over thousands, hundreds, fifties, and
tens. 26 And they judged the people at all
times; hard cases they brought to Moses,
but any minor case they decided them-
selves. 27 Then Moses let his father-in-law
depart, and he went off to his own country.

19 On the third new moon after the Is-
raelites had gone out of the land of
Egypt, on that very day, they came into the
wilderness of Sinai. 2 They had journeyed
from Rephidim, entered the wilderness of
Sinai, and camped in the wilderness; Israel
camped there in front of the mountain.
3 Then Moses went up to God; the LORD
called to him from the mountain, saying,
"Thus you shall say to the house of Jacob,
and tell the Israelites: 4 You have seen what
I did to the Egyptians, and how I bore you
on eagles' wings and brought you to my-
self. 5 Now therefore, if you obey my voice
and keep my covenant, you shall be my
treasured possession out of all the peoples.
Indeed, the whole earth is mine, 6 but you
shall be for me a priestly kingdom and a
holy nation. These are the words that you
shall speak to the Israelites."
7 So Moses came, summoned the elders
of the people, and set before them all these
words that the LORD had commanded him.
8 The people all answered as one: "Every-

administration of justice, is retold with significant differences in Deut 1.9–18. **15–16:** *Inquire of God,* seek a verdict by oracle (Judg 4.4–5). **21–22:** Cf. Num 11.16–17,24–25; Deut 16.18–20; 17.8–13.

Chs 19–31: God establishes the covenant with Israel.

19.1–25: God appears for the second time at Sinai/Horeb (continued in 20.18–21). God has already appeared to Moses at the sacred mountain and promised that all the people would follow him here to worship (3.12). This chapter incorporates a wide diversity of traditions, reflecting different understandings of God and the divine relationship with Israel. **1–2:** They have now reached the first goal of their journey, *Sinai,* also called Horeb (3.1n.). In rabbinic Judaism, the festival of weeks (Pentecost, 23.16) celebrates this arrival and the gift of the covenant. *Rephidim,* 17.1,8. **3–6:** The liturgical style expresses the solemnity of the occasion. **4:** *Eagles' wings,* Deut 32.11–12. **5:** *If you obey my voice,* the covenant is here conditional. The God to whom *the whole earth* belongs (9.29; Ps 24.1) has chosen Israel for a special role as *my treasured possession,* as "the people of God" (6.7; Deut 7.6; 14.2; 26.18). **6:** Israel is to be *a priestly kingdom,* consecrated for service to God (Isa 61.6), a *holy nation* set apart as belonging to the holy God. **7–8:** Cf. 24.7. **9:** This verse stresses Moses' role as the covenant mediator who represents

thing that the LORD has spoken we will
do." Moses reported the words of the peo-
ple to the LORD. 9 Then the LORD said to
Moses, "I am going to come to you in a
dense cloud, in order that the people may
hear when I speak with you and so trust
you ever after."

When Moses had told the words of the
people to the LORD, 10 the LORD said to
Moses: "Go to the people and consecrate
them today and tomorrow. Have them
wash their clothes 11 and prepare for the
third day, because on the third day the
LORD will come down upon Mount Sinai in
the sight of all the people. 12 You shall set
limits for the people all around, saying, 'Be
careful not to go up the mountain or to
touch the edge of it. Any who touch the
mountain shall be put to death. 13 No hand
shall touch them, but they shall be stoned
or shot with arrows;[a] whether animal or
human being, they shall not live.' When the
trumpet sounds a long blast, they may go
up on the mountain." 14 So Moses went
down from the mountain to the people. He
consecrated the people, and they washed
their clothes. 15 And he said to the people,
"Prepare for the third day; do not go near
a woman."

16 On the morning of the third day
there was thunder and lightning, as well as
a thick cloud on the mountain, and a blast
of a trumpet so loud that all the people
who were in the camp trembled. 17 Moses
brought the people out of the camp to meet
God. They took their stand at the foot of
the mountain. 18 Now Mount Sinai was
wrapped in smoke, because the LORD had
descended upon it in fire; the smoke went
up like the smoke of a kiln, while the whole
mountain shook violently. 19 As the blast of
the trumpet grew louder and louder, Moses
would speak and God would answer him
in thunder. 20 When the LORD descended
upon Mount Sinai, to the top of the moun-
tain, the LORD summoned Moses to the
top of the mountain, and Moses went up.
21 Then the LORD said to Moses, "Go down
and warn the people not to break through
to the LORD to look; otherwise many of
them will perish. 22 Even the priests who
approach the LORD must consecrate them-
selves or the LORD will break out against
them." 23 Moses said to the LORD, "The
people are not permitted to come up to
Mount Sinai; for you yourself warned us,
saying, 'Set limits around the mountain and
keep it holy.' " 24 The LORD said to him,
"Go down, and come up bringing Aaron
with you; but do not let either the priests or
the people break through to come up to the
LORD; otherwise he will break out against
them." 25 So Moses went down to the peo-
ple and told them.

20 Then God spoke all these words:
2 I am the LORD your God, who

a Heb lacks *with arrows*

God to the people and the people to God (20.19; 24.1–2; 34.27; Deut 5). **10–15:** In this paragraph, on the other hand, all the people are to prepare to take part in the covenant ceremony (24.3–8). **12–13:** These *limits* reflect the understanding of holiness as a mysterious, threatening power with which the mountain is charged (3.6n.; 2 Sam 6.6–9). No hand may touch the offender who has become affected with the contagion of holiness (Lev 6.27–28). **14–15:** Washing or changing of clothing (Gen 35.2) and sexual abstinence (1 Sam 21.4–6) are forms of ceremonial purification. *The people, ". . . a woman,"* the address betrays the narrator's androcentric view: He equates the Israelite people with the men. Deut 31.12 offers a more inclusive view. **16–19:** The theophany, or divine appearance, is portrayed this time as a violent thunderstorm and earthquake (Judg 5.4–5; Ps 18.7–15; 29.3–9). **16:** The trumpet (v. 13) sounds on ritual occasions (2 Sam 6.15). **20–25:** The three zones of increasing holiness must be carefully respected: All Israel must remain at the foot of the mountain (vv. 12,17), and the leaders may go up partway (24.1–2,9–11), but only Moses may ascend to the top where God is (v. 20; 20.21).

20.1–17: The Ten Commandments, the epitome of the covenant obligations toward God and neighbor (Deut 5.6–21). All are in unconditional and absolute (apodictic) second-person masculine singular form. **1:** *These words,* "the ten words" or the Decalogue (34.28; Deut 4.13; 10.4). "Words" is more suitable than commandments. Nowhere does the Bible establish how these ten should be enumerated, and there

brought you out of the land of Egypt, out
of the house of slavery; 3 you shall have no
other gods before[a] me.
4 You shall not make for yourself an
idol, whether in the form of anything that is
in heaven above, or that is on the earth
beneath, or that is in the water under the
earth. 5 You shall not bow down to them or
worship them; for I the LORD your God am
a jealous God, punishing children for the
iniquity of parents, to the third and the
fourth generation of those who reject me,
6 but showing steadfast love to the thou-
sandth generation[b] of those who love me
and keep my commandments.
7 You shall not make wrongful use of
the name of the LORD your God, for the
LORD will not acquit anyone who misuses
his name.
8 Remember the sabbath day, and keep
it holy. 9 Six days you shall labor and do all
your work. 10 But the seventh day is a sab-
bath to the LORD your God; you shall not
do any work—you, your son or your
daughter, your male or female slave, your
livestock, or the alien resident in your
towns. 11 For in six days the LORD made
heaven and earth, the sea, and all that is in
them, but rested the seventh day; therefore
the LORD blessed the sabbath day and con-
secrated it.
12 Honor your father and your mother,
so that your days may be long in the land
that the LORD your God is giving you.
13 You shall not murder.[c]
14 You shall not commit adultery.
15 You shall not steal.
16 You shall not bear false witness
against your neighbor.
17 You shall not covet your neighbor's
house; you shall not covet your neighbor's
wife, or male or female slave, or ox, or
donkey, or anything that belongs to your
neighbor.
18 When all the people witnessed the
thunder and lightning, the sound of the
trumpet, and the mountain smoking, they
were afraid[d] and trembled and stood at a
distance, 19 and said to Moses, "You speak
to us, and we will listen; but do not let God
speak to us, or we will die." 20 Moses said
to the people, "Do not be afraid; for God
has come only to test you and to put the

a Or *besides* *b* Or *to thousands* *c* Or *kill*
d Sam Gk Syr Vg: MT *they saw*

was a diversity of views on this already in antiquity. **2:** This self-identification summarizes the meaning of the Exodus, thereby setting command within the context of God's liberating action. In Jewish tradition this is the first "word." **3:** This "word," the first commandment in Christian tradition, does not deny the existence of other gods, but asserts that Israel shall acknowledge *no other gods* than the God who has liberated them (5.2n.; 12.12; 15.11). **4–6:** Imageless worship of God (20.23) distinguishes Israel's religion from those of its neighbors, where deities were typically depicted in animal or human form. Some consider vv. 3–6 as one commandment. **5:** *A jealous God* who will tolerate no rivals for Israel's devotion (34.14). **7:** A prohibition of the misuse of the divine *name* in magic, divination, or false swearing (Lev 19.12). **8–11:** Keeping *the sabbath,* or seventh day of the week, *holy* means to observe it as a day separated from others, a segment of time belonging especially to God. Since v. 11 refers to the Priestly creation story (Gen 1.1–2.3), this version of the ten words is often called the Priestly Decalogue. **10:** 16.22–30n. Since the Ten Commandments are in the masculine singular and addressed to individual males, wives are absent here (contrast v. 12). **11:** Compare the reasons in 23.12; Deut 5.15. **12:** In contrast to vv. 10 and 17, the woman is treated equally, precisely because she is a *mother* (21.15,17; Deut 27.16). **13:** This commandment forbids *murder,* not the forms of killing authorized for Israel, such as war and capital punishment. **15:** *Steal,* the same word is translated "kidnap" in 21.16. **17:** Some see two commandments here. However, *neighbor's house,* or household, introduces what is named in the second part of the verse: *wife, male or female slave,* etc. This final command shows most clearly that the commandments address the adult male.

20.18–21: The people request that Moses be the covenant mediator (19.9n.) so that they need not hear God's voice directly (Deut 5.4–5). The fear of the people is interpreted positively in Deut 5.22–23; 18.15–18, which view this as the beginning of institutionalized prophecy.

fear of him upon you so that you do not
sin." 21 Then the people stood at a distance,
while Moses drew near to the thick dark-
ness where God was.
22 The LORD said to Moses: Thus you
shall say to the Israelites: "You have seen
for yourselves that I spoke with you from
heaven. 23 You shall not make gods of silver
alongside me, nor shall you make for your-
selves gods of gold. 24 You need make for
me only an altar of earth and sacrifice on it
your burnt offerings and your offerings of
well-being, your sheep and your oxen; in
every place where I cause my name to be
remembered I will come to you and bless
you. 25 But if you make for me an altar of
stone, do not build it of hewn stones; for if
you use a chisel upon it you profane it.
26 You shall not go up by steps to my altar,
so that your nakedness may not be exposed
on it."

21 These are the ordinances that you
shall set before them:
2 When you buy a male Hebrew slave,
he shall serve six years, but in the seventh
he shall go out a free person, without debt.
3 If he comes in single, he shall go out sin-
gle; if he comes in married, then his wife
shall go out with him. 4 If his master gives
him a wife and she bears him sons or
daughters, the wife and her children shall
be her master's and he shall go out alone.
5 But if the slave declares, "I love my mas-
ter, my wife, and my children; I will not go
out a free person," 6 then his master shall
bring him before God.[a] He shall be
brought to the door or the doorpost; and
his master shall pierce his ear with an awl;
and he shall serve him for life.
7 When a man sells his daughter as a
slave, she shall not go out as the male slaves
do. 8 If she does not please her master, who
designated her for himself, then he shall let
her be redeemed; he shall have no right to
sell her to a foreign people, since he has
dealt unfairly with her. 9 If he designates
her for his son, he shall deal with her as
with a daughter. 10 If he takes another wife
to himself, he shall not diminish the food,
clothing, or marital rights of the first
wife.[b] 11 And if he does not do these three
things for her, she shall go out without
debt, without payment of money.
12 Whoever strikes a person mortally

a Or *to the judges* *b* Heb *of her*

20.22–23.19: The Covenant Collection, or Book of the Covenant (see 24.7). This legislation begins and ends with commands regarding ritual (20.22–26; 23.10–19), so that worship surrounds social legislation. The laws presuppose a settled agricultural society (22.5–6). They reflect Israelite life in Canaan, when laws of the surrounding culture were borrowed and adapted to the covenant tradition. Most scholars see this as the earliest of the biblical law collections.

20.22–26: Regulations for worship, in unconditional second-person style (like the Ten Commandments, 20.2–17), continued in 22.18–23.19. **22–23:** 20.4–6n.; Deut 4.15–40. **24–26:** On the types of *offerings,* see Lev 1; 3. The Israelite *altar* is to be built wherever *I cause my name to be remembered,* in other words, choose to reveal my presence. Contrast the reform of centralized worship demanded in Deut 12.5–14.

21.1–22.17: Case laws. 1: *Ordinances* are laws formulated (usually in the third person) to deal with various cases (casuistic law), in contrast to unconditional laws such as the Ten Commandments. These case laws are similar in style and content to other legal codes of the ancient Near East.

21.2–11: The rights of slaves (cf. Deut 15.12–18; Lev 25.39–55). **2–6:** Male slaves. **2:** *Hebrew* may refer here to displaced persons generally (1.15n.), though even some Israelites will go into servitude because of debt and poverty (22.1; Lev 25.39; 2 Kings 4.1). **6:** The pierced ear will be a lifelong symbol of the slave's status. **7–11:** Female slaves sold because of their fathers' poverty and taken as wives. **8:** *Redeemed* by a relative who pays the purchase price. *A foreign people,* better, anyone outside her family of origin.

21.12–32: Laws protecting human beings. 12–17: Capital offenses (22.18–20). **12–14:** A distinction between intentional and unintentional homicide. The asylum is at the *altar* (1 Kings 2.28–34), rather than at a city of refuge (Num 35.12; Deut 4.41–43; 19.1–13; Josh 20). **17:** Lev 20.9. The curse is understood

shall be put to death. 13 If it was not pre-
meditated, but came about by an act of
God, then I will appoint for you a place to
which the killer may flee. 14 But if someone
willfully attacks and kills another by
treachery, you shall take the killer from my
altar for execution.
15 Whoever strikes father or mother
shall be put to death.
16 Whoever kidnaps a person, whether
that person has been sold or is still held in
possession, shall be put to death.
17 Whoever curses father or mother
shall be put to death.
18 When individuals quarrel and one
strikes the other with a stone or fist so that
the injured party, though not dead, is con-
fined to bed, 19 but recovers and walks
around outside with the help of a staff, then
the assailant shall be free of liability, except
to pay for the loss of time, and to arrange
for full recovery.
20 When a slaveowner strikes a male or
female slave with a rod and the slave dies
immediately, the owner shall be punished.
21 But if the slave survives a day or two,
there is no punishment; for the slave is the
owner's property.
22 When people who are fighting injure
a pregnant woman so that there is a miscar-
riage, and yet no further harm follows, the
one responsible shall be fined what the
woman's husband demands, paying as
much as the judges determine. 23 If any
harm follows, then you shall give life for
life, 24 eye for eye, tooth for tooth, hand
for hand, foot for foot, 25 burn for burn,
wound for wound, stripe for stripe.
26 When a slaveowner strikes the eye of
a male or female slave, destroying it, the
owner shall let the slave go, a free person,
to compensate for the eye. 27 If the owner
knocks out a tooth of a male or female
slave, the slave shall be let go, a free person,
to compensate for the tooth.
28 When an ox gores a man or a woman
to death, the ox shall be stoned, and its
flesh shall not be eaten; but the owner of
the ox shall not be liable. 29 If the ox has
been accustomed to gore in the past, and its
owner has been warned but has not re-
strained it, and it kills a man or a woman,
the ox shall be stoned, and its owner also
shall be put to death. 30 If a ransom is im-
posed on the owner, then the owner shall
pay whatever is imposed for the redemp-
tion of the victim's life. 31 If it gores a boy
or a girl, the owner shall be dealt with ac-
cording to this same rule. 32 If the ox gores
a male or female slave, the owner shall pay
to the slaveowner thirty shekels of silver,
and the ox shall be stoned.
33 If someone leaves a pit open, or digs
a pit and does not cover it, and an ox or a
donkey falls into it, 34 the owner of the pit
shall make restitution, giving money to its
owner, but keeping the dead animal.
35 If someone's ox hurts the ox of an-
other, so that it dies, then they shall sell the
live ox and divide the price of it; and the
dead animal they shall also divide. 36 But if
it was known that the ox was accustomed
to gore in the past, and its owner has not
restrained it, the owner shall restore ox for
ox, but keep the dead animal.

22 [a]When someone steals an ox or a
sheep, and slaughters it or sells it,
the thief shall pay five oxen for an ox, and
four sheep for a sheep.[b] The thief shall

a Ch 21.37 in Heb *b* Verses 2, 3, and 4 rearranged thus: 3b, 4, 2, 3a

to release an inexorable power (Num 22.6), thus making it as serious to curse parents as to strike them (v. 15). The verb can also mean "humiliate" or "treat with contempt," the opposite of what is commanded in 20.12. **22–25:** This "lex talionis," or "law of retaliation" (Lev 24.19–20) is not a warrant for unrestrained vengeance but precisely a limitation on revenge: Only the equivalent of the damage may be taken. **28–32:** The goring ox is used as a paradigmatic case here, as in other ancient Near Eastern legal collections, for indirect manslaughter and negligent homicide. Biblical law is more stringent than the laws of the surrounding societies.

21.33–22.17: Laws dealing with property and compensation. 21.33–36: Responsibility in cases of negligence. **22.1–4:** Cases of stealing. **2–3:** These verses may mean that an intruder caught in the act at night

make restitution, but if unable to do so,
shall be sold for the theft. 4 When the ani-
mal, whether ox or donkey or sheep, is
found alive in the thief's possession, the
thief shall pay double.
2[a] If a thief is found breaking in, and is
beaten to death, no bloodguilt is incurred;
3 but if it happens after sunrise, bloodguilt
is incurred.
5 When someone causes a field or vine-
yard to be grazed over, or lets livestock
loose to graze in someone else's field, resti-
tution shall be made from the best in the
owner's field or vineyard.
6 When fire breaks out and catches in
thorns so that the stacked grain or the
standing grain or the field is consumed, the
one who started the fire shall make full res-
titution.
7 When someone delivers to a neighbor
money or goods for safekeeping, and they
are stolen from the neighbor's house, then
the thief, if caught, shall pay double. 8 If the
thief is not caught, the owner of the house
shall be brought before God,[b] to deter-
mine whether or not the owner had laid
hands on the neighbor's goods.
9 In any case of disputed ownership in-
volving ox, donkey, sheep, clothing, or any
other loss, of which one party says, "This is
mine," the case of both parties shall come
before God;[b] the one whom God con-
demns[c] shall pay double to the other.
10 When someone delivers to another a
donkey, ox, sheep, or any other animal for
safekeeping, and it dies or is injured or is
carried off, without anyone seeing it, 11 an
oath before the LORD shall decide between
the two of them that the one has not laid
hands on the property of the other; the
owner shall accept the oath, and no restitu-
tion shall be made. 12 But if it was stolen,
restitution shall be made to its owner. 13 If
it was mangled by beasts, let it be brought
as evidence; restitution shall not be made
for the mangled remains.
14 When someone borrows an animal
from another and it is injured or dies, the
owner not being present, full restitution
shall be made. 15 If the owner was present,
there shall be no restitution; if it was hired,
only the hiring fee is due.
16 When a man seduces a virgin who is
not engaged to be married, and lies with
her, he shall give the bride-price for her and
make her his wife. 17 But if her father re-
fuses to give her to him, he shall pay an
amount equal to the bride-price for virgins.
18 You shall not permit a female sorcer-
er to live.
19 Whoever lies with an animal shall be
put to death.
20 Whoever sacrifices to any god, other
than the LORD alone, shall be devoted to
destruction.
21 You shall not wrong or oppress a res-
ident alien, for you were aliens in the land
of Egypt. 22 You shall not abuse any widow
or orphan. 23 If you do abuse them, when
they cry out to me, I will surely heed their
cry; 24 my wrath will burn, and I will kill
you with the sword, and your wives shall
become widows and your children or-
phans.
25 If you lend money to my people, to

a Ch 22.1 in Heb *b* Or *before the judges*
c Or *the judges condemn*

may be killed with impunity, but not in broad daylight. **5–6:** More cases of negligence. **7–15:** Cases involving property entrusted to another. **8–9:** *Before God,* for an oracular decision or the sacred oath (v. 11; 1 Kings 8.31–32). **9:** *Whom God condemns,* alternatively, "whom the gods condemn," perhaps derived from pre-Israelite tradition. **16–17:** The case of consensual sexual relations with a virgin not promised to another is included here because it requires compensation for damage to property, *the bride-price.* Cf. Deut 22.13–30.

22.18–23.9: Social and religious commands, mostly in unconditional second-person style, continuing 20.22–26. **22.18–20:** Capital offenses (21.12–17). **20:** 20.3; Deut 13.12–18. **21–27:** In a society based on land ownership, patrilineality, and patriarchy, God is the protector of the legally and economically defenseless: resident aliens, widows, fatherless (*orphan*), and poor. **21:** Memory of the experience in Egypt creates empathy for aliens within Israel (23.9). **25:** Cf. Lev 25.35–38. **26–27:** A lender can keep a garment

the poor among you, you shall not deal
with them as a creditor; you shall not exact
interest from them. 26 If you take your
neighbor's cloak in pawn, you shall restore
it before the sun goes down; 27 for it may be
your neighbor's only clothing to use as cov-
er; in what else shall that person sleep? And
if your neighbor cries out to me, I will lis-
ten, for I am compassionate.
28 You shall not revile God, or curse a
leader of your people.
29 You shall not delay to make offerings
from the fullness of your harvest and from
the outflow of your presses.[a]
The firstborn of your sons you shall give
to me. 30 You shall do the same with your
oxen and with your sheep: seven days it
shall remain with its mother; on the eighth
day you shall give it to me.
31 You shall be people consecrated to
me; therefore you shall not eat any meat
that is mangled by beasts in the field; you
shall throw it to the dogs.
23 You shall not spread a false report.
You shall not join hands with the
wicked to act as a malicious witness. 2 You
shall not follow a majority in wrongdoing;
when you bear witness in a lawsuit, you
shall not side with the majority so as to
pervert justice; 3 nor shall you be partial to
the poor in a lawsuit.
4 When you come upon your enemy's
ox or donkey going astray, you shall bring
it back.
5 When you see the donkey of one who
hates you lying under its burden and you
would hold back from setting it free, you
must help to set it free.[a]
6 You shall not pervert the justice due to
your poor in their lawsuits. 7 Keep far from
a false charge, and do not kill the innocent
and those in the right, for I will not acquit
the guilty. 8 You shall take no bribe, for a
bribe blinds the officials, and subverts the
cause of those who are in the right.
9 You shall not oppress a resident alien;
you know the heart of an alien, for you
were aliens in the land of Egypt.
10 For six years you shall sow your land
and gather in its yield; 11 but the seventh
year you shall let it rest and lie fallow, so
that the poor of your people may eat; and
what they leave the wild animals may eat.
You shall do the same with your vineyard,
and with your olive orchard.
12 Six days you shall do your work, but
on the seventh day you shall rest, so that
your ox and your donkey may have relief,
and your homeborn slave and the resident
alien may be refreshed. 13 Be attentive to all
that I have said to you. Do not invoke the
names of other gods; do not let them be
heard on your lips.
14 Three times in the year you shall hold
a festival for me. 15 You shall observe the
festival of unleavened bread; as I com-
manded you, you shall eat unleavened
bread for seven days at the appointed time
in the month of Abib, for in it you came out
of Egypt.
No one shall appear before me empty-
handed.
16 You shall observe the festival of har-
vest, of the first fruits of your labor, of

a Meaning of Heb uncertain

as security only for the day, since a poor borrower needs it at night (Deut 24.12–13; Am 2.8). **28:** Lev 24.15–16; 2 Sam 16.9; 1 Kings 2.8–9; 21.10. **29–30:** 2.22–23n.; 13.1–2,11–16, and notes. However, it is uncertain if the redemption of the firstborn is recognized here. **31:** Flesh torn by beasts is regarded as unclean because it is not properly drained of blood (Lev 7.24; 17.15). **23.1–9:** Equal justice for all. **1–3:** 20.16. **4–5:** Justice extends even to helping *your enemy* (contrast Deut 22.1–4). **9:** 22.21.

23.10–19: A ritual calendar (34.18–24; Lev 23; Deut 16.1–17) concludes the Covenant Collection, so that social laws are framed by worship (20.22–26). **10–11:** Fallow land (Lev 25.2–7). The land, the poor, and wild animals are all objects of concern. **12:** Here the observance of *the seventh day,* not here called the sabbath, is based upon concern for the needs of exploitable humans and animals (cf. 20.11; 16.22–30n.; Deut 5.14–15). **13:** 20.3. **14–17:** Three annual pilgrimage festivals to a major sanctuary (1 Sam 1.3,21). **15:** *Unleavened bread,* 12.14–20n.; 13.3–10. *Abib,* 13.4n. *Empty-handed,* without a sacrificial offering. **16:** *The festival of harvest,* later called Shavuot, the festival of weeks, or Pentecost, celebrated in May-

what you sow in the field. You shall ob-
serve the festival of ingathering at the end
of the year, when you gather in from the
field the fruit of your labor. 17 Three times
in the year all your males shall appear be-
fore the Lord GOD.

18 You shall not offer the blood of my
sacrifice with anything leavened, or let the
fat of my festival remain until the morning.

19 The choicest of the first fruits of your
ground you shall bring into the house of the
LORD your God.

You shall not boil a kid in its mother's
milk.

20 I am going to send an angel in front
of you, to guard you on the way and to
bring you to the place that I have prepared.
21 Be attentive to him and listen to his voice;
do not rebel against him, for he will not
pardon your transgression; for my name is
in him.

22 But if you listen attentively to his
voice and do all that I say, then I will be an
enemy to your enemies and a foe to your
foes.

23 When my angel goes in front of you,
and brings you to the Amorites, the Hit-
tites, the Perizzites, the Canaanites, the Hi-
vites, and the Jebusites, and I blot them out,
24 you shall not bow down to their gods, or
worship them, or follow their practices, but
you shall utterly demolish them and break
their pillars in pieces. 25 You shall worship
the LORD your God, and I[a] will bless your
bread and your water; and I will take sick-
ness away from among you. 26 No one shall
miscarry or be barren in your land; I will
fulfill the number of your days. 27 I will
send my terror in front of you, and will
throw into confusion all the people against
whom you shall come, and I will make
all your enemies turn their backs to you.
28 And I will send the pestilence[b] in front
of you, which shall drive out the Hivites,
the Canaanites, and the Hittites from be-
fore you. 29 I will not drive them out from
before you in one year, or the land would
become desolate and the wild animals
would multiply against you. 30 Little by lit-
tle I will drive them out from before you,
until you have increased and possess the
land. 31 I will set your borders from the Red
Sea[c] to the sea of the Philistines, and from
the wilderness to the Euphrates; for I will
hand over to you the inhabitants of the
land, and you shall drive them out before
you. 32 You shall make no covenant with
them and their gods. 33 They shall not live
in your land, or they will make you sin
against me; for if you worship their gods, it
will surely be a snare to you.

24 Then he said to Moses, "Come up
to the LORD, you and Aaron, Na-
dab, and Abihu, and seventy of the elders
of Israel, and worship at a distance. 2 Moses

a Gk Vg: Heb *he* *b* Or *hornets*: Meaning of Heb uncertain *c* Or *Sea of Reeds*

June at the time of the wheat harvest (19.1n.; Lev 23.15–21; Deut 16.9–12). The third festival, *the festival of ingathering,* later called Sukkot, the festival of booths (Lev 23.33–43; Deut 16.13–15), celebrated *at the end of the year* (autumn), according to the old agricultural calendar (12.2n.), when fruit, grapes, and olives are harvested. **17:** Women and young children are not obligated to make the pilgrimage. They do make the pilgrimage, however, in 1 Sam 1; 2.19; cf. Ex 10.9. **18–19:** 34.25–26. *Fat,* see Lev 3.3–4. The ancient meaning of the prohibition against boiling *a kid in its mother's milk* (Deut 14.21) is disputed.

23.20–33: The divine warrior will conquer the promised land for Israel, and in return Israel is to keep separate from other peoples and their gods (Deut 7). **20–21:** The *angel* represents God's own presence (14.19). **23,28:** 3.8n. **25–26:** 15.26. **27–28:** *Terror* (Gen 35.5; Josh 10.10) and *pestilence* (Deut 7.20) are frequent weapons of "holy war." **31:** *Red Sea,* the Gulf of Eilat/Aqaba, the eastern arm of the Red Sea; *sea of the Philistines,* the Mediterranean; *the wilderness,* the desert south of Israel. For these boundaries, cf. Gen 15.18; Deut 11.24.

24.1–11: The covenant is ratified in two ceremonies: a theophany (the third divine appearance of the book) and sacred meal for a chosen few (vv. 1–2,9–11), and a ritual of blood for all Israel (vv. 3–8). This chapter too is an amalgam of traditions. **1–2:** This part of the story continues in vv. 9–11. **2:** *Moses alone,* an indication of Moses' special role as covenant mediator (19.9; 20.19). **3–8:** This ceremony stresses the

alone shall come near the LORD; but the
others shall not come near, and the people
shall not come up with him."
3 Moses came and told the people all the
words of the LORD and all the ordinances;
and all the people answered with one voice,
and said, "All the words that the LORD has
spoken we will do." 4 And Moses wrote
down all the words of the LORD. He rose
early in the morning, and built an altar at
the foot of the mountain, and set up twelve
pillars, corresponding to the twelve tribes
of Israel. 5 He sent young men of the people
of Israel, who offered burnt offerings and
sacrificed oxen as offerings of well-being to
the LORD. 6 Moses took half of the blood
and put it in basins, and half of the blood
he dashed against the altar. 7 Then he took
the book of the covenant, and read it in the
hearing of the people; and they said, "All
that the LORD has spoken we will do, and
we will be obedient." 8 Moses took the
blood and dashed it on the people, and
said, "See the blood of the covenant that
the LORD has made with you in accordance
with all these words."
9 Then Moses and Aaron, Nadab, and
Abihu, and seventy of the elders of Israel
went up, 10 and they saw the God of Israel.
Under his feet there was something like a
pavement of sapphire stone, like the very
heaven for clearness. 11 God[a] did not lay
his hand on the chief men of the people of
Israel; also they beheld God, and they ate
and drank.
12 The LORD said to Moses, "Come up
to me on the mountain, and wait there; and
I will give you the tablets of stone, with the
law and the commandment, which I have
written for their instruction." 13 So Moses
set out with his assistant Joshua, and Mo-
ses went up into the mountain of God.
14 To the elders he had said, "Wait here for
us, until we come to you again; for Aaron
and Hur are with you; whoever has a dis-
pute may go to them."

a Heb *He*

participation of all Israel (19.10–15). The *twelve pillars,* one for each tribe, symbolize Israel, while the *altar* represents God's presence. Since *blood* stands for life (and therefore death), throwing half the blood on the altar and half on the people obligates both parties to keep their side of the obligations of the covenant on pain of death (cf. Gen 15). Israel enters into the covenant knowing the conditions and willingly accepting them (vv. 3,7). **3:** *The words,* the Ten Commandments (20.1). *The ordinances,* the case laws of the Covenant Collection (21.1n.). **5:** On the types of *offerings,* see Lev 1; 3. **7:** *The book of the covenant* (Josh 24.25–26) contains the covenant laws, and here is implicitly identified with "the words" and "the ordinances" (v. 3). **9–11:** In this ceremony (continuing vv. 1–2), the chosen few see God and eat a sacred meal. **9:** The people do not take part in this theophany (contrast 19.16–19; 20.18–21), but are represented by the seventy *elders* or chief men (4.29). *Moses,* the covenant mediator, is accompanied by the priestly family, *Aaron, Nadab, and Abihu* (6.23; Lev 10.1–3). **10–11:** The description of the leaders' experience is extremely unusual; they actually see God and yet remain unharmed (contrast 3.6; 19.21; 33.18–23).

24.12–31.18: Instructions for worship. Now that the covenant has established a long-term relationship between the God of Sinai and the people of Israel, God tells Moses what must be done so that both parties can leave the mountain and travel together to the promised land. There must be a portable shrine ("tabernacle") and priests to officiate. The detailed instructions of chs 25–31 will be carried out in chs 35–40. This extensive material reflects the importance of building a physical house for God, ensuring God's presence among Israel.

24.12–18: Moses meets God on the mountain. Moses goes alone *up on the mountain* to meet God *for forty days and forty nights.* Moses' ascent and the theophany (vv. 15–18) introduce the Priestly instructions of chs 25–31, and his prolonged absence from the people, leaving Aaron in charge (vv. 14,18), sets the stage for the episode of the golden calf in ch 32. **12:** According to the first and last verses of this section (24.12 and 31.18), it is God who has written *the law and the commandment* on *tablets of stone* (32.15–19; 34.1,4,28–29; Deut 9.9–11; contrast Ex 24.4). **13:** *Joshua* appears for the second time (17.9). **14:** *Hur* appears for the second and final time (17.10). **15–18:** This fourth theophany, or divine appear-

15 Then Moses went up on the moun-
tain, and the cloud covered the mountain.
16 The glory of the LORD settled on Mount
Sinai, and the cloud covered it for six days;
on the seventh day he called to Moses out
of the cloud. 17 Now the appearance of the
glory of the LORD was like a devouring fire
on the top of the mountain in the sight of
the people of Israel. 18 Moses entered the
cloud, and went up on the mountain. Mo-
ses was on the mountain for forty days and
forty nights.

25 The LORD said to Moses: 2 Tell the
Israelites to take for me an offering;
from all whose hearts prompt them to give
you shall receive the offering for me. 3 This
is the offering that you shall receive from
them: gold, silver, and bronze, 4 blue, pur-
ple, and crimson yarns and fine linen,
goats' hair, 5 tanned rams' skins, fine leath-
er,[a] acacia wood, 6 oil for the lamps, spices
for the anointing oil and for the fragrant
incense, 7 onyx stones and gems to be set in
the ephod and for the breastpiece. 8 And
have them make me a sanctuary, so that I
may dwell among them. 9 In accordance

a Meaning of Heb uncertain

ance (19.16–19), follows the pattern of *six days* and a *seventh,* which began in ch 16. *The glory,* 16.6–7n.

25.1–27.21: The tabernacle and its furnishings (See Diagram below). The Israelites are to build a portable shrine so that God can leave Mount Sinai to travel with them and live among them. Like Mount Sinai (19.20–25n.), the shrine will have three carefully delimited zones of descending holiness. In these chapters the instructions move from the most holy place through the holy place to the surrounding court. The metals used will mark the level of holiness.

25.1–40: The offering, the ark, the table, and the lampstand. The three items described in this chapter, destined for the most holy place and the holy place, are made of or overlaid with gold.

25.1–9: A voluntary offering will supply the materials to make the tabernacle and its equipment (3.21–22n.; 35.4–29; 36.2–7). **7:** *Ephod* and *breastpiece,* 28.6–30n. **8–9:** The Israelites must make the

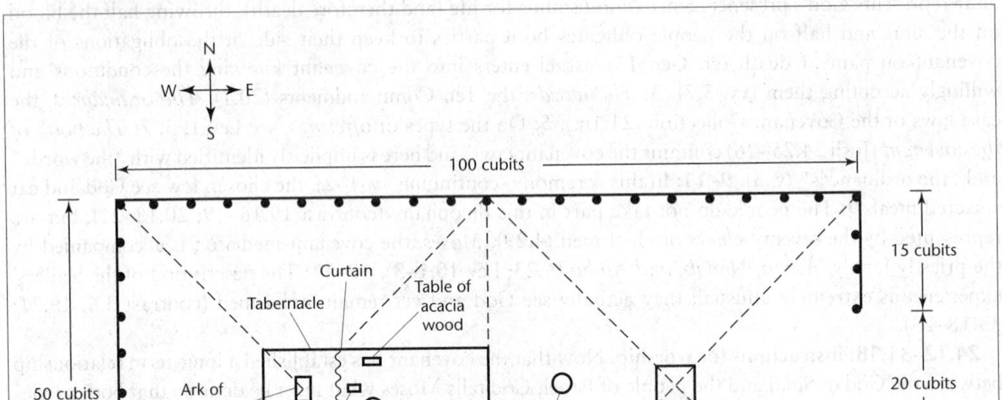

Chs 25–31, 36–39: The structure of the Tabernacle.

with all that I show you concerning the pattern of the tabernacle and of all its furniture, so you shall make it.

10 They shall make an ark of acacia wood; it shall be two and a half cubits long, a cubit and a half wide, and a cubit and a half high. 11 You shall overlay it with pure gold, inside and outside you shall overlay it, and you shall make a molding of gold upon it all around. 12 You shall cast four rings of gold for it and put them on its four feet, two rings on the one side of it, and two rings on the other side. 13 You shall make poles of acacia wood, and overlay them with gold. 14 And you shall put the poles into the rings on the sides of the ark, by which to carry the ark. 15 The poles shall remain in the rings of the ark; they shall not be taken from it. 16 You shall put into the ark the covenant[a] that I shall give you.

17 Then you shall make a mercy seat[b] of pure gold; two cubits and a half shall be its length, and a cubit and a half its width. 18 You shall make two cherubim of gold; you shall make them of hammered work, at the two ends of the mercy seat.[c] 19 Make one cherub at the one end, and one cherub at the other; of one piece with the mercy seat[c] you shall make the cherubim at its two ends. 20 The cherubim shall spread out their wings above, overshadowing the mercy seat[c] with their wings. They shall face one to another; the faces of the cherubim shall be turned toward the mercy seat.[c] 21 You shall put the mercy seat[c] on the top of the ark; and in the ark you shall put the covenant[a] that I shall give you. 22 There I will meet with you, and from above the mercy seat,[c] from between the two cherubim that are on the ark of the covenant,[a] I will deliver to you all my commands for the Israelites.

23 You shall make a table of acacia wood, two cubits long, one cubit wide, and a cubit and a half high. 24 You shall overlay it with pure gold, and make a molding of gold around it. 25 You shall make around it a rim a handbreadth wide, and a molding of gold around the rim. 26 You shall make for it four rings of gold, and fasten the rings to the four corners at its four legs. 27 The rings that hold the poles used for carrying the table shall be close to the rim. 28 You shall make the poles of acacia wood, and overlay them with gold, and the table shall be carried with these. 29 You shall make its plates and dishes for incense, and its flagons and bowls with which to pour drink offerings; you shall make them of pure gold. 30 And you shall set the bread of the Presence on the table before me always.

31 You shall make a lampstand of pure gold. The base and the shaft of the lamp-

a Or *treaty*, or *testimony*; Heb *eduth* *b* Or *a cover*
c Or *the cover*

sanctuary, or *tabernacle,* with its ritual equipment, as an exact replica of the *pattern* shown to Moses (v. 40; 26.30; 27.8) so that the God of heaven may reside on earth among them.

25.10–22: The ark (37.1–9), the only item in the most holy place, is a portable wooden chest that will serve to guide Israel in the wilderness (Num 10.33), to lead in war (Num 10.35–36), and to be a medium for oracles (1 Sam 3). It is both a container for the covenant documents (v. 16) and a footstool above which God is invisibly enthroned (1 Sam 4.4; 2 Sam 6.2; 2 Kings 19.15). By means of the ark the God of Sinai will go with Israel on the journey to the promised land. **10:** The dimensions are about 110 x 66 x 66 cm (44 x 26 x 26 in). **16:** *The covenant,* that is, the tablets of the law (24.12; 32.15). The chest is called "the ark of the covenant" (v. 22) after its chief contents. **17–22:** The *mercy seat* (Lev 16.2,13–15) is the cover of the ark. As the footstool of God's throne (1 Chr 28.2; Ps 132.7), it is the place where God meets Moses (v. 22). Winged *cherubim* (26.1; Gen 3.24) typically guard royal thrones.

25.23–30: The table for the sacred vessels and the holy *bread,* to stand in the holy place (26.35; 37.10–16; 1 Kings 7.48). **30:** The *bread of the Presence* or "holy bread" (1 Sam 21.4,6), twelve loaves placed before God as a sacrificial offering every sabbath, to be eaten only by priests (Num 4.7; Lev 24.5–9; 1 Sam 21.4–6; 1 Chr 9.32).

25.31–40: The seven-branched lampstand, depicted as a stylized tree of life, is to illuminate the interior of the holy place (26.35; 30.7–8; 37.17–24; 1 Kings 7.49). **40:** Vv. 8–9n.

stand shall be made of hammered work; its
cups, its calyxes, and its petals shall be of
one piece with it; 32 and there shall be six
branches going out of its sides, three
branches of the lampstand out of one side
of it and three branches of the lampstand
out of the other side of it; 33 three cups
shaped like almond blossoms, each with ca-
lyx and petals, on one branch, and three
cups shaped like almond blossoms, each
with calyx and petals, on the other
branch—so for the six branches going out
of the lampstand. 34 On the lampstand itself
there shall be four cups shaped like almond
blossoms, each with its calyxes and petals.
35 There shall be a calyx of one piece with it
under the first pair of branches, a calyx of
one piece with it under the next pair of
branches, and a calyx of one piece with it
under the last pair of branches—so for the
six branches that go out of the lampstand.
36 Their calyxes and their branches shall be
of one piece with it, the whole of it one
hammered piece of pure gold. 37 You shall
make the seven lamps for it; and the lamps
shall be set up so as to give light on the
space in front of it. 38 Its snuffers and trays
shall be of pure gold. 39 It, and all these
utensils, shall be made from a talent of pure
gold. 40 And see that you make them ac-
cording to the pattern for them, which is
being shown you on the mountain.

26 Moreover you shall make the taber-
nacle with ten curtains of fine twist-
ed linen, and blue, purple, and crimson
yarns; you shall make them with cherubim
skillfully worked into them. 2 The length of
each curtain shall be twenty-eight cubits,
and the width of each curtain four cubits;
all the curtains shall be of the same size.
3 Five curtains shall be joined to one anoth-
er; and the other five curtains shall be
joined to one another. 4 You shall make
loops of blue on the edge of the outermost
curtain in the first set; and likewise you
shall make loops on the edge of the outer-
most curtain in the second set. 5 You shall
make fifty loops on the one curtain, and
you shall make fifty loops on the edge of
the curtain that is in the second set; the
loops shall be opposite one another. 6 You
shall make fifty clasps of gold, and join the
curtains to one another with the clasps, so
that the tabernacle may be one whole.
7 You shall also make curtains of goats'
hair for a tent over the tabernacle; you shall
make eleven curtains. 8 The length of each
curtain shall be thirty cubits, and the width
of each curtain four cubits; the eleven cur-
tains shall be of the same size. 9 You shall
join five curtains by themselves, and six
curtains by themselves, and the sixth cur-
tain you shall double over at the front of
the tent. 10 You shall make fifty loops on
the edge of the curtain that is outermost in
one set, and fifty loops on the edge of the
curtain that is outermost in the second set.
11 You shall make fifty clasps of bronze,
and put the clasps into the loops, and join
the tent together, so that it may be one
whole. 12 The part that remains of the cur-
tains of the tent, the half curtain that re-
mains, shall hang over the back of the tab-
ernacle. 13 The cubit on the one side, and
the cubit on the other side, of what remains
in the length of the curtains of the tent,
shall hang over the sides of the tabernacle,
on this side and that side, to cover it. 14 You
shall make for the tent a covering of tanned
rams' skins and an outer covering of fine
leather.[a]
15 You shall make upright frames of
acacia wood for the tabernacle. 16 Ten cu-
bits shall be the length of a frame, and a
cubit and a half the width of each frame.
17 There shall be two pegs in each frame
to fit the frames together; you shall make
these for all the frames of the tabernacle.

a Meaning of Heb uncertain

26.1–37: The tabernacle, the structure holding the most holy place and the holy place (36.8–38). **1–6:** The interior is formed by ten richly decorated *curtains* (cf. 1 Kings 6.29). *Cherubim,* 25.17–22n. **7–14:** Over the curtains with cherubim will be placed curtains of *goats' hair* (v. 7) and reddened *rams' skins* (v. 14) as *a tent over the tabernacle* (v. 7; 39.33–34; 40.19). **15–30:** The framework of desert *acacia wood* is about 13 x 4.4 x 4.4 m (44 x 15 x 15 ft) (1 Kings 6.2). **30:** *Plan,* 25.8–9n. **31–37:** A richly decorated

18 You shall make the frames for the taber-
nacle: twenty frames for the south side;
19 and you shall make forty bases of silver
under the twenty frames, two bases under
the first frame for its two pegs, and two
bases under the next frame for its two pegs;
20 and for the second side of the tabernacle,
on the north side twenty frames, 21 and
their forty bases of silver, two bases under
the first frame, and two bases under the
next frame; 22 and for the rear of the taber-
nacle westward you shall make six frames.
23 You shall make two frames for corners of
the tabernacle in the rear; 24 they shall be
separate beneath, but joined at the top, at
the first ring; it shall be the same with both
of them; they shall form the two corners.
25 And so there shall be eight frames, with
their bases of silver, sixteen bases; two
bases under the first frame, and two bases
under the next frame.
26 You shall make bars of acacia wood,
five for the frames of the one side of the
tabernacle, 27 and five bars for the frames of
the other side of the tabernacle, and five
bars for the frames of the side of the taber-
nacle at the rear westward. 28 The middle
bar, halfway up the frames, shall pass
through from end to end. 29 You shall over-
lay the frames with gold, and shall make
their rings of gold to hold the bars; and you
shall overlay the bars with gold. 30 Then
you shall erect the tabernacle according to
the plan for it that you were shown on the
mountain.
31 You shall make a curtain of blue,
purple, and crimson yarns, and of fine
twisted linen; it shall be made with cheru-
bim skillfully worked into it. 32 You shall
hang it on four pillars of acacia overlaid
with gold, which have hooks of gold and
rest on four bases of silver. 33 You shall
hang the curtain under the clasps, and
bring the ark of the covenant[a] in there,
within the curtain; and the curtain shall
separate for you the holy place from the
most holy. 34 You shall put the mercy seat[b]
on the ark of the covenant[a] in the most
holy place. 35 You shall set the table outside
the curtain, and the lampstand on the south
side of the tabernacle opposite the table;
and you shall put the table on the north
side.
36 You shall make a screen for the en-
trance of the tent, of blue, purple, and crim-
son yarns, and of fine twisted linen, em-
broidered with needlework. 37 You shall
make for the screen five pillars of acacia,
and overlay them with gold; their hooks
shall be of gold, and you shall cast five
bases of bronze for them.

27 You shall make the altar of acacia
wood, five cubits long and five cu-
bits wide; the altar shall be square, and it
shall be three cubits high. 2 You shall make
horns for it on its four corners; its horns
shall be of one piece with it, and you shall
overlay it with bronze. 3 You shall make
pots for it to receive its ashes, and shovels
and basins and forks and firepans; you
shall make all its utensils of bronze. 4 You
shall also make for it a grating, a network
of bronze; and on the net you shall make
four bronze rings at its four corners. 5 You
shall set it under the ledge of the altar so
that the net shall extend halfway down the
altar. 6 You shall make poles for the altar,
poles of acacia wood, and overlay them
with bronze; 7 the poles shall be put
through the rings, so that the poles shall be
on the two sides of the altar when it is
carried. 8 You shall make it hollow, with

a Or *treaty*, or *testimony*; Heb *eduth*   *b* Or *the cover*

curtain (v. 1) separates the *most holy* place (holy of holies) and the *holy place* (sanctuary). A similarly ornate *screen*, though without cherubim, is to serve as *the entrance* from the court to the holy place.

27.1–21: The altar and the court. From the tabernacle, the writer turns to the surrounding, less sacred area. **1–8:** The central object in the court is the sacrificial *altar* (38.1–7; 1 Kings 8.64), about 2 x 2 x 1.3 m (7 x 7 x 4 ft). In contrast both to the simple altars of earth or unhewn stones in 20.24–25 and to the gold furnishings inside the tabernacle, this altar is overlaid with bronze. **2:** *Horns,* upward projections at the four top corners (29.12n.); these quarter-round projections have been recovered in various excavated altars. **8:** *Shown,* 25.8–9n. **9–19:** *The court of the tabernacle* is the sacred enclosure (about 44 x 22 m [146

boards. They shall be made just as you
were shown on the mountain.
9 You shall make the court of the taber-
nacle. On the south side the court shall
have hangings of fine twisted linen one
hundred cubits long for that side; 10 its
twenty pillars and their twenty bases shall
be of bronze, but the hooks of the pillars
and their bands shall be of silver. 11 Like-
wise for its length on the north side there
shall be hangings one hundred cubits long,
their pillars twenty and their bases twenty,
of bronze, but the hooks of the pillars and
their bands shall be of silver. 12 For the
width of the court on the west side there
shall be fifty cubits of hangings, with ten
pillars and ten bases. 13 The width of the
court on the front to the east shall be fifty
cubits. 14 There shall be fifteen cubits of
hangings on the one side, with three pillars
and three bases. 15 There shall be fifteen cu-
bits of hangings on the other side, with
three pillars and three bases. 16 For the gate
of the court there shall be a screen twenty
cubits long, of blue, purple, and crimson
yarns, and of fine twisted linen, embroi-
dered with needlework; it shall have four
pillars and with them four bases. 17 All the
pillars around the court shall be banded
with silver; their hooks shall be of silver,
and their bases of bronze. 18 The length of
the court shall be one hundred cubits, the
width fifty, and the height five cubits, with
hangings of fine twisted linen and bases of
bronze. 19 All the utensils of the tabernacle
for every use, and all its pegs and all the
pegs of the court, shall be of bronze.
20 You shall further command the Isra-
elites to bring you pure oil of beaten olives
for the light, so that a lamp may be set up
to burn regularly. 21 In the tent of meeting,
outside the curtain that is before the cove-
nant,[a] Aaron and his sons shall tend it
from evening to morning before the LORD.
It shall be a perpetual ordinance to be ob-
served throughout their generations by the
Israelites.

28 Then bring near to you your brother
Aaron, and his sons with him, from
among the Israelites, to serve me as
priests—Aaron and Aaron's sons, Nadab
and Abihu, Eleazar and Ithamar. 2 You
shall make sacred vestments for the glori-
ous adornment of your brother Aaron.
3 And you shall speak to all who have abili-
ty, whom I have endowed with skill, that
they make Aaron's vestments to consecrate
him for my priesthood. 4 These are the vest-
ments that they shall make: a breastpiece,
an ephod, a robe, a checkered tunic, a tur-
ban, and a sash. When they make these sa-
cred vestments for your brother Aaron and
his sons to serve me as priests, 5 they shall
use gold, blue, purple, and crimson yarns,
and fine linen.
6 They shall make the ephod of gold, of
blue, purple, and crimson yarns, and of fine
twisted linen, skillfully worked. 7 It shall
have two shoulder-pieces attached to its
two edges, so that it may be joined togeth-
er. 8 The decorated band on it shall be of
the same workmanship and materials, of
gold, of blue, purple, and crimson yarns,
and of fine twisted linen. 9 You shall take

a Or *treaty*, or *testimony*; Heb *edhuth*

x 76 ft]) surrounding it, where the altar and basin stand (30.17–21; 38.9–20). **16:** The entrance *screen* is made of the same material as the screen to the holy place (26.36). **20–21:** The *oil* is to keep the lamp burning continually as a sign of God's presence (25.31–40; Lev 24.2–4; Num 8.2–4). *The covenant,* 16.33–34n.

28.1–29.42: The priests. 28.1–43: The priests' vestments, special garments worn when acting in their official capacity (vv. 2,4,40,43; 39.1–31). **1–5:** A hereditary office of priest is established to officiate at the tabernacle. Beginning with Aaron (6.16–25, esp. v. 23) there is to be one high priest in each generation, though the actual term does not appear here. **6–39:** Aaron's vestments. **6–12:** The *ephod* is a garment similar to an apron (26.1; 1 Sam 2.28) used in connection with the sacred lot (v. 30). The engraved stones on each shoulder-piece (vv. 9–12) symbolize the high priest's intercessory role on behalf of the twelve tribes (v. 29). **15–30:** Hanging from the shoulder-pieces is the *breastpiece of judgment,* a pouch that contains

two onyx stones, and engrave on them the
names of the sons of Israel, 10 six of their
names on the one stone, and the names of
the remaining six on the other stone, in the
order of their birth. 11 As a gem-cutter en-
graves signets, so you shall engrave the two
stones with the names of the sons of Israel;
you shall mount them in settings of gold
filigree. 12 You shall set the two stones on
the shoulder-pieces of the ephod, as stones
of remembrance for the sons of Israel; and
Aaron shall bear their names before the
LORD on his two shoulders for remem-
brance. 13 You shall make settings of gold
filigree, 14 and two chains of pure gold,
twisted like cords; and you shall attach the
corded chains to the settings.

15 You shall make a breastpiece of judg-
ment, in skilled work; you shall make it in
the style of the ephod; of gold, of blue and
purple and crimson yarns, and of fine twist-
ed linen you shall make it. 16 It shall be
square and doubled, a span in length and a
span in width. 17 You shall set in it four
rows of stones. A row of carnelian,[a] chrys-
olite, and emerald shall be the first row;
18 and the second row a turquoise, a sap-
phire,[b] and a moonstone; 19 and the third
row a jacinth, an agate, and an amethyst;
20 and the fourth row a beryl, an onyx, and
a jasper; they shall be set in gold filigree.
21 There shall be twelve stones with names
corresponding to the names of the sons of
Israel; they shall be like signets, each en-
graved with its name, for the twelve tribes.
22 You shall make for the breastpiece chains
of pure gold, twisted like cords; 23 and you
shall make for the breastpiece two rings of
gold, and put the two rings on the two
edges of the breastpiece. 24 You shall put
the two cords of gold in the two rings at the
edges of the breastpiece; 25 the two ends of
the two cords you shall attach to the two
settings, and so attach it in front to the
shoulder-pieces of the ephod. 26 You shall
make two rings of gold, and put them at the
two ends of the breastpiece, on its inside
edge next to the ephod. 27 You shall make
two rings of gold, and attach them in front
to the lower part of the two shoulder-pieces
of the ephod, at its joining above the deco-
rated band of the ephod. 28 The breastpiece
shall be bound by its rings to the rings of
the ephod with a blue cord, so that it may
lie on the decorated band of the ephod, and
so that the breastpiece shall not come loose
from the ephod. 29 So Aaron shall bear the
names of the sons of Israel in the breast-
piece of judgment on his heart when he
goes into the holy place, for a continual
remembrance before the LORD. 30 In the
breastpiece of judgment you shall put the
Urim and the Thummim, and they shall be
on Aaron's heart when he goes in before
the LORD; thus Aaron shall bear the judg-
ment of the Israelites on his heart before the
LORD continually.

31 You shall make the robe of the ephod
all of blue. 32 It shall have an opening for
the head in the middle of it, with a woven
binding around the opening, like the open-
ing in a coat of mail,[c] so that it may not be
torn. 33 On its lower hem you shall make
pomegranates of blue, purple, and crimson
yarns, all around the lower hem, with bells
of gold between them all around—34 a
golden bell and a pomegranate alternating
all around the lower hem of the robe.
35 Aaron shall wear it when he ministers,
and its sound shall be heard when he goes
into the holy place before the LORD, and
when he comes out, so that he may not die.

36 You shall make a rosette of pure

a The identity of several of these stones is uncertain
b Or *lapis lazuli* *c* Meaning of Heb uncertain

the sacred lots, *Urim and Thummim* (v. 30), used to obtain oracular decisions (Lev 8.8; Num 27.21; Deut 33.8; 1 Sam 14.41–42; 23.6–13); it was about 22 cm (8.75 in) square. Like the ephod, the breastpiece also bears the names of the tribes *for a continual remembrance* before God (v. 29). **31–34:** A short garment, the blue *robe of the ephod,* is worn under the ephod. The bells will identify the high priest *so that he may not die* when he enters or leaves the holy place (v. 35). **36–39:** The *turban,* bearing an engraved *rosette of pure gold,* symbolizes the regal splendor of the high priest (Ezek 21.26; Zech 3.5) and his being set apart (*holy*) to God's service. **40–43:** Vestments for all the priests. **42:** 20.26.

gold, and engrave on it, like the engraving
of a signet, "Holy to the LORD." 37 You
shall fasten it on the turban with a blue
cord; it shall be on the front of the turban.
38 It shall be on Aaron's forehead, and Aar-
on shall take on himself any guilt incurred
in the holy offering that the Israelites conse-
crate as their sacred donations; it shall al-
ways be on his forehead, in order that they
may find favor before the LORD.
39 You shall make the checkered tunic
of fine linen, and you shall make a turban
of fine linen, and you shall make a sash
embroidered with needlework.
40 For Aaron's sons you shall make tu-
nics and sashes and headdresses; you shall
make them for their glorious adornment.
41 You shall put them on your brother Aar-
on, and on his sons with him, and shall
anoint them and ordain them and conse-
crate them, so that they may serve me as
priests. 42 You shall make for them linen
undergarments to cover their naked flesh;
they shall reach from the hips to the thighs;
43 Aaron and his sons shall wear them when
they go into the tent of meeting, or when
they come near the altar to minister in the
holy place; or they will bring guilt on them-
selves and die. This shall be a perpetual or-
dinance for him and for his descendants af-
ter him.

29 Now this is what you shall do to
them to consecrate them, so that
they may serve me as priests. Take one
young bull and two rams without blemish,
2 and unleavened bread, unleavened cakes
mixed with oil, and unleavened wafers
spread with oil. You shall make them of
choice wheat flour. 3 You shall put them in
one basket and bring them in the basket,
and bring the bull and the two rams. 4 You
shall bring Aaron and his sons to the en-
trance of the tent of meeting, and wash
them with water. 5 Then you shall take the
vestments, and put on Aaron the tunic and
the robe of the ephod, and the ephod, and
the breastpiece, and gird him with the deco-
rated band of the ephod; 6 and you shall set
the turban on his head, and put the holy
diadem on the turban. 7 You shall take the
anointing oil, and pour it on his head and
anoint him. 8 Then you shall bring his sons,
and put tunics on them, 9 and you shall gird
them with sashes[a] and tie headdresses on
them; and the priesthood shall be theirs by
a perpetual ordinance. You shall then or-
dain Aaron and his sons.
10 You shall bring the bull in front of
the tent of meeting. Aaron and his sons
shall lay their hands on the head of the bull,
11 and you shall slaughter the bull before
the LORD, at the entrance of the tent of
meeting, 12 and shall take some of the blood
of the bull and put it on the horns of the
altar with your finger, and all the rest of
the blood you shall pour out at the base of
the altar. 13 You shall take all the fat that
covers the entrails, and the appendage of the
liver, and the two kidneys with the fat that
is on them, and turn them into smoke on
the altar. 14 But the flesh of the bull, and its
skin, and its dung, you shall burn with fire
outside the camp; it is a sin offering.
15 Then you shall take one of the rams,
and Aaron and his sons shall lay their
hands on the head of the ram, 16 and you
shall slaughter the ram, and shall take its
blood and dash it against all sides of the
altar. 17 Then you shall cut the ram into its
parts, and wash its entrails and its legs, and
put them with its parts and its head, 18 and
turn the whole ram into smoke on the altar;
it is a burnt offering to the LORD; it is a

a Gk: Heb *sashes, Aaron and his sons*

29.1–37: The ordination service for the priests (Lev 8). Moses acts as priest throughout this ceremony until the first priests are installed. **1–9:** All the priests are to be washed, clothed in the garments described in ch 28, and ordained, but only Aaron, the high priest, is to be anointed on the head with oil (v. 7; Lev 16.32; Ps 133.2; the king will also be anointed, 1 Sam 24.6; Ps 2.2). **10–14:** The *sin* (or purification) *offering* (Lev 4.1–12), the *bull* of v. 1. **12:** The *horns* of the altar (27.2n.; 30.10) are its most sacred parts (1 Kings 1.50; Am 3.14). **15–18:** The *burnt offering* (Lev 1), one of the rams (v. 1). *Pleasing odor,* as God sees, hears, and speaks, so God smells the smoke (Gen 8.21; Lev 1.9). **19–34:** The *ordination* sacrifice of

pleasing odor, an offering by fire to the
LORD.
19 You shall take the other ram; and
Aaron and his sons shall lay their hands
on the head of the ram, 20 and you shall
slaughter the ram, and take some of its
blood and put it on the lobe of Aaron's
right ear and on the lobes of the right ears
of his sons, and on the thumbs of their right
hands, and on the big toes of their right
feet, and dash the rest of the blood against
all sides of the altar. 21 Then you shall take
some of the blood that is on the altar, and
some of the anointing oil, and sprinkle it on
Aaron and his vestments and on his sons
and his sons' vestments with him; then he
and his vestments shall be holy, as well as
his sons and his sons' vestments.
22 You shall also take the fat of the ram,
the fat tail, the fat that covers the entrails,
the appendage of the liver, the two kidneys
with the fat that is on them, and the right
thigh (for it is a ram of ordination), 23 and
one loaf of bread, one cake of bread made
with oil, and one wafer, out of the basket of
unleavened bread that is before the LORD;
24 and you shall place all these on the palms
of Aaron and on the palms of his sons, and
raise them as an elevation offering before
the LORD. 25 Then you shall take them from
their hands, and turn them into smoke on
the altar on top of the burnt offering of
pleasing odor before the LORD; it is an
offering by fire to the LORD.
26 You shall take the breast of the ram
of Aaron's ordination and raise it as an
elevation offering before the LORD; and it
shall be your portion. 27 You shall conse-
crate the breast that was raised as an eleva-
tion offering and the thigh that was raised
as an elevation offering from the ram of
ordination, from that which belonged to
Aaron and his sons. 28 These things shall be
a perpetual ordinance for Aaron and his
sons from the Israelites, for this is an offer-
ing; and it shall be an offering by the Israel-
ites from their sacrifice of offerings of well-
being, their offering to the LORD.
29 The sacred vestments of Aaron shall
be passed on to his sons after him; they
shall be anointed in them and ordained in
them. 30 The son who is priest in his place
shall wear them seven days, when he comes
into the tent of meeting to minister in the
holy place.
31 You shall take the ram of ordination,
and boil its flesh in a holy place; 32 and Aar-
on and his sons shall eat the flesh of the
ram and the bread that is in the basket, at
the entrance of the tent of meeting. 33 They
themselves shall eat the food by which
atonement is made, to ordain and conse-
crate them, but no one else shall eat of
them, because they are holy. 34 If any of the
flesh for the ordination, or of the bread,
remains until the morning, then you shall
burn the remainder with fire; it shall not be
eaten, because it is holy.
35 Thus you shall do to Aaron and to
his sons, just as I have commanded you;
through seven days you shall ordain them.
36 Also every day you shall offer a bull as a
sin offering for atonement. Also you shall
offer a sin offering for the altar, when you
make atonement for it, and shall anoint
it, to consecrate it. 37 Seven days you shall
make atonement for the altar, and conse-
crate it, and the altar shall be most holy;
whatever touches the altar shall become
holy.

the second ram is essentially an offering of well-being (Lev 3). **20–21:** Touching blood on the earlobe, thumb, and big toe consecrates the whole person for the office. Putting blood on both the priests and the altar (symbolizing God's presence) brings both parties together in this sacrifice celebrating the covenant relationship (24.6). **24:** Putting these things in the hands of the priests signifies that they are authorized to receive their portions of the offerings. The phrase translated in Judg 17.5 and 1 Kings 13.33 as "install" or "consecrate" is literally "fill the hand," in other words, invest with priestly prerogatives. The *elevation offering* (vv. 24,26–27; Lev 7.29–36) is the act of moving the sacrifice toward and away from the altar, to symbolize presenting the gift to God and receiving it back as the portion allotted to the priests. **35–37:** The ordination ceremony lasts seven days.

38 Now this is what you shall offer on
the altar: two lambs a year old regularly
each day. 39 One lamb you shall offer in the
morning, and the other lamb you shall offer
in the evening; 40 and with the first lamb
one-tenth of a measure of choice flour
mixed with one-fourth of a hin of beaten
oil, and one-fourth of a hin of wine for a
drink offering. 41 And the other lamb you
shall offer in the evening, and shall offer
with it a grain offering and its drink offer-
ing, as in the morning, for a pleasing odor,
an offering by fire to the LORD. 42 It shall be
a regular burnt offering throughout your
generations at the entrance of the tent of
meeting before the LORD, where I will meet
with you, to speak to you there. 43 I will
meet with the Israelites there, and it shall be
sanctified by my glory; 44 I will consecrate
the tent of meeting and the altar; Aaron
also and his sons I will consecrate, to serve
me as priests. 45 I will dwell among the Isra-
elites, and I will be their God. 46 And they
shall know that I am the LORD their God,
who brought them out of the land of Egypt
that I might dwell among them; I am the
LORD their God.

30 You shall make an altar on which to
offer incense; you shall make it of
acacia wood. 2 It shall be one cubit long,
and one cubit wide; it shall be square, and
shall be two cubits high; its horns shall be
of one piece with it. 3 You shall overlay it
with pure gold, its top, and its sides all
around and its horns; and you shall make
for it a molding of gold all around. 4 And
you shall make two golden rings for it; un-
der its molding on two opposite sides of it
you shall make them, and they shall hold
the poles with which to carry it. 5 You shall
make the poles of acacia wood, and overlay
them with gold. 6 You shall place it in front
of the curtain that is above the ark of the
covenant,[a] in front of the mercy seat[b] that
is over the covenant,[a] where I will meet
with you. 7 Aaron shall offer fragrant in-
cense on it; every morning when he dresses
the lamps he shall offer it, 8 and when Aar-
on sets up the lamps in the evening, he shall
offer it, a regular incense offering before
the LORD throughout your generations.
9 You shall not offer unholy incense on it,
or a burnt offering, or a grain offering; and
you shall not pour a drink offering on it.
10 Once a year Aaron shall perform the rite
of atonement on its horns. Throughout
your generations he shall perform the
atonement for it once a year with the blood
of the atoning sin offering. It is most holy
to the LORD.

11 The LORD spoke to Moses: 12 When
you take a census of the Israelites to register
them, at registration all of them shall give a
ransom for their lives to the LORD, so that
no plague may come upon them for being
registered. 13 This is what each one who is

a Or *treaty*, or *testimony*; Heb *eduth*   *b* Or *the cover*

29.38–41: The regular burnt offering to be offered every morning and evening (Num 28.3–8). *One tenth of a measure,* a tenth of an ephah (Num 15.2–10), about 2.3 l (2 qt). *Hin,* about 3.8 l (3.3 qt).

29.42–46: The purpose of the entire story—liberation from slavery, construction of the tabernacle and its furnishings, and consecration of the priests—is that God might *dwell among the Israelites* and be acknowledged as the LORD their God (3.14–15n.; 5.2n.). This is reflected in the Heb term for the tabernacle, "mishkan," the dwelling-place (of God). These five verses state the point of the entire book of Exodus. **43:** *Glory,* 16.6–7n. **45:** 6.7n.; 25.8; 40.34.

30.1–31.18: Concluding instructions.

30.1–10: The incense altar (about 44 x 44 x 88 cm [17.5 x 17.5 x 35 in]) is to stand in the holy place just outside the most holy place, thus it is to be overlaid with *gold* (37.25–28). The smoke will protect the priests from the divine presence above the mercy seat (Lev 16.3). **3:** *Horns,* 27.2n. **10:** *Atonement,* purification, through the ritual performed. *Once a year,* on the Day of Atonement (Lev 16).

30.11–16: The tax for the support of the sanctuary. Elsewhere the *census* is for military purposes (Num 1.2–3). So that the census will not anger God (2 Sam 24), the people pay a tax (2 Chr 24.6,9; Mt 17.24) as a *ransom* or *atonement* (v. 16). Rich and poor pay the same amount because each life is equally valuable. **13:** *The shekel of the sanctuary* (Lev 5.15; 27.25; Num 3.47; 18.16), based on the older registered shall give: half a shekel according to the shekel of the sanctuary (the shekel is twenty gerahs), half a shekel as an offering to the LORD. 14 Each one who is registered, from twenty years old and upward, shall give the LORD's offering. 15 The rich shall not give more, and the poor shall not give less, than the half shekel, when you bring this offering to the LORD to make atonement for your lives. 16 You shall take the atonement money from the Israelites and shall designate it for the service of the tent of meeting; before the LORD it will be a reminder to the Israelites of the ransom given for your lives.

17 The LORD spoke to Moses: 18 You shall make a bronze basin with a bronze stand for washing. You shall put it between the tent of meeting and the altar, and you shall put water in it; 19 with the water[a] Aaron and his sons shall wash their hands and their feet. 20 When they go into the tent of meeting, or when they come near the altar to minister, to make an offering by fire to the LORD, they shall wash with water, so that they may not die. 21 They shall wash their hands and their feet, so that they may not die: it shall be a perpetual ordinance for them, for him and for his descendants throughout their generations.

22 The LORD spoke to Moses: 23 Take the finest spices: of liquid myrrh five hundred shekels, and of sweet-smelling cinnamon half as much, that is, two hundred fifty, and two hundred fifty of aromatic cane, 24 and five hundred of cassia—measured by the sanctuary shekel—and a hin of olive oil; 25 and you shall make of these a sacred anointing oil blended as by the perfumer; it shall be a holy anointing oil. 26 With it you shall anoint the tent of meeting and the ark of the covenant,[b] 27 and the table and all its utensils, and the lampstand and its utensils, and the altar of incense, 28 and the altar of burnt offering with all its utensils, and the basin with its stand; 29 you shall consecrate them, so that they may be most holy; whatever touches them will become holy. 30 You shall anoint Aaron and his sons, and consecrate them, in order that they may serve me as priests. 31 You shall say to the Israelites, "This shall be my holy anointing oil throughout your generations. 32 It shall not be used in any ordinary anointing of the body, and you shall make no other like it in composition; it is holy, and it shall be holy to you. 33 Whoever compounds any like it or whoever puts any of it on an unqualified person shall be cut off from the people."

34 The LORD said to Moses: Take sweet spices, stacte, and onycha, and galbanum, sweet spices with pure frankincense (an equal part of each), 35 and make an incense blended as by the perfumer, seasoned with salt, pure and holy; 36 and you shall beat some of it into powder, and put part of it before the covenant[b] in the tent of meeting where I shall meet with you; it shall be for you most holy. 37 When you make incense according to this composition, you shall not make it for yourselves; it shall be regarded by you as holy to the LORD. 38 Whoever makes any like it to use as perfume shall be cut off from the people.

a Heb *it* *b* Or *treaty*, or *testimony*; Heb *eduth*

Phoenician or Hebrew measurement, weighed about 11.4 gr (.4 oz) and was heavier than the Babylonian shekel used in postexilic times. Here it is explained that the sanctuary tax is to be paid in the older weight. **16:** *Tent of meeting,* 27.21n.

30.17–21: The bronze basin for ritual cleansing (38.8; 1 Kings 7.38).

30.22–33: The recipe for the holy anointing oil and that for the incense (vv. 34–38) is fundamentally holy, and may not be used for any purpose other than the service of tabernacle and priests. **23–25:** About 17 kg (38 lb) of spices, including *myrrh,* an aromatic resin, and *cassia,* a variety of cinnamon, were *blended* with 3.8 l (1 gal) of *olive oil.*

30.34–38: The recipe for the incense (37.29). *Stacte,* an aromatic resin. *Onycha,* a perfume from a mollusk found in the Red Sea. *Galbanum,* an aromatic resin from Asiatic plants. *Frankincense,* a fragrant gum resin from shrubs found in Arabia and East Africa. **36:** 27.21n.

31 The LORD spoke to Moses: 2 See, I
have called by name Bezalel son of
Uri son of Hur, of the tribe of Judah: 3 and
I have filled him with divine spirit,[a] with
ability, intelligence, and knowledge in ev-
ery kind of craft, 4 to devise artistic designs,
to work in gold, silver, and bronze, 5 in
cutting stones for setting, and in carving
wood, in every kind of craft. 6 Moreover, I
have appointed with him Oholiab son of
Ahisamach, of the tribe of Dan; and I have
given skill to all the skillful, so that they
may make all that I have commanded you:
7 the tent of meeting, and the ark of the
covenant,[b] and the mercy seat[c] that is on
it, and all the furnishings of the tent, 8 the
table and its utensils, and the pure lamp-
stand with all its utensils, and the altar of
incense, 9 and the altar of burnt offering
with all its utensils, and the basin with its
stand, 10 and the finely worked vestments,
the holy vestments for the priest Aaron and
the vestments of his sons, for their service
as priests, 11 and the anointing oil and the
fragrant incense for the holy place. They
shall do just as I have commanded you.

12 The LORD said to Moses: 13 You
yourself are to speak to the Israelites: "You
shall keep my sabbaths, for this is a sign
between me and you throughout your gen-
erations, given in order that you may know
that I, the LORD, sanctify you. 14 You shall
keep the sabbath, because it is holy for you;
everyone who profanes it shall be put to
death; whoever does any work on it shall
be cut off from among the people. 15 Six
days shall work be done, but the seventh
day is a sabbath of solemn rest, holy to the
LORD; whoever does any work on the sab-
bath day shall be put to death. 16 Therefore
the Israelites shall keep the sabbath, ob-
serving the sabbath throughout their gener-
ations, as a perpetual covenant. 17 It is a
sign forever between me and the people of
Israel that in six days the LORD made heav-
en and earth, and on the seventh day he
rested, and was refreshed."

18 When God[d] finished speaking with
Moses on Mount Sinai, he gave him the
two tablets of the covenant,[b] tablets of
stone, written with the finger of God.

32 When the people saw that Moses
delayed to come down from the
mountain, the people gathered around Aar-
on, and said to him, "Come, make gods for
us, who shall go before us; as for this Mo-
ses, the man who brought us up out of the
land of Egypt, we do not know what has
become of him." 2 Aaron said to them,

a Or *with the spirit of God* b Or *treaty*, or *testimony*; Heb *eduth* c Or *the cover* d Heb *he*

31.1–11: The appointment of two leaders of the artisans (35.30–36.1). *Bezalel,* 1 Chr 2.18–20. *Oholiab* is otherwise unknown. *All the skillful* (v. 6), including women (35.25–26), will work with the two named men.

31.12–17: The sabbath command (16.22–30n.). The author has divided the instructions in chs 25–31 into seven sections introduced by *The LORD said to Moses* (25.1; 30.11,17,22,34; 31.1,12), with the sabbath command as the seventh, climactic section. The holiness of the seventh day supercedes even the importance of the work on God's dwelling, as it does the urgency of plowing and harvesting (34.21). As circumcision is the sign of the covenant with Abraham (Gen 17.11), so the sabbath is the *sign* of the covenant with all Israel; by observing the sabbath, Israel acknowledges YHWH as their God.

31.18: God's gift of the tablets to Moses closes the section on instructions for worship by resuming the theme of the opening verse (24.12) and leading into the episode of the golden calf (ch 32).

Chs 32–34: Israel breaks the covenant, but God reestablishes it.

32.1–35: The Israelites break the covenant. Even as God is giving Moses the instructions for establishing covenant worship, the Israelites impatiently begin worshiping in their own unacceptable way (contrast 24.7; cf. 15.22–17.16). **1–6:** During Moses' absence the people, becoming anxious, speak disrespectfully of Moses, choose Aaron as their new leader, and demand a tangible sign of God's presence immediately. **1:** Moses has stayed on the mountain forty days and forty nights (24.18). *Gods . . . who shall go before us,* ironically, they want visible symbols of the divine presence, which are exactly what God is even now telling Moses how to create. **2–3:** *Gold* earrings, 3.21–22n.; Gen 35.4; Judg 8.24. **4–6:** The *calf,* or young

"Take off the gold rings that are on the ears
of your wives, your sons, and your daugh-
ters, and bring them to me." 3 So all the
people took off the gold rings from their
ears, and brought them to Aaron. 4 He took
the gold from them, formed it in a mold,[a]
and cast an image of a calf; and they said,
"These are your gods, O Israel, who
brought you up out of the land of Egypt!"
5 When Aaron saw this, he built an altar
before it; and Aaron made proclamation
and said, "Tomorrow shall be a festival to
the LORD." 6 They rose early the next day,
and offered burnt offerings and brought
sacrifices of well-being; and the people sat
down to eat and drink, and rose up to revel.

7 The LORD said to Moses, "Go down
at once! Your people, whom you brought
up out of the land of Egypt, have acted
perversely; 8 they have been quick to turn
aside from the way that I commanded
them; they have cast for themselves an im-
age of a calf, and have worshiped it and
sacrificed to it, and said, 'These are your
gods, O Israel, who brought you up out of
the land of Egypt!' " 9 The LORD said to
Moses, "I have seen this people, how stiff-
necked they are. 10 Now let me alone, so
that my wrath may burn hot against them
and I may consume them; and of you I will
make a great nation."

11 But Moses implored the LORD his
God, and said, "O LORD, why does your
wrath burn hot against your people, whom
you brought out of the land of Egypt with
great power and with a mighty hand?
12 Why should the Egyptians say, 'It was
with evil intent that he brought them out to
kill them in the mountains, and to consume
them from the face of the earth'? Turn from
your fierce wrath; change your mind and
do not bring disaster on your people. 13 Re-
member Abraham, Isaac, and Israel, your
servants, how you swore to them by your
own self, saying to them, 'I will multiply
your descendants like the stars of heaven,
and all this land that I have promised I will
give to your descendants, and they shall in-
herit it forever.' " 14 And the LORD changed
his mind about the disaster that he planned
to bring on his people.

15 Then Moses turned and went down
from the mountain, carrying the two tab-
lets of the covenant[b] in his hands, tablets
that were written on both sides, written on
the front and on the back. 16 The tablets
were the work of God, and the writing was
the writing of God, engraved upon the tab-
lets. 17 When Joshua heard the noise of the
people as they shouted, he said to Moses,
"There is a noise of war in the camp."
18 But he said,

"It is not the sound made by victors,
or the sound made by losers;
it is the sound of revelers that I
hear."

19 As soon as he came near the camp and

[a] Or *fashioned it with a graving tool*; Meaning of Heb uncertain [b] Or *treaty*, or *testimony*; Heb *eduth*

bull, symbolizing strength and fertility, is an illegitimate way of depicting God's throne in contrast with the cherubim of 25.17–22. The calf was probably understood originally as a pedestal or divine throne, like the cherubim, but at some stages in the complex literary history of the passage it is understood as an idol. The use of two calves by King Jeroboam I (1 Kings 12.25–33) has influenced this narrative, including the plural form *gods* (vv. 4,8,31; contrast Neh 9.18). God intends Aaron's leadership, *gold, altar, festival, offerings,* eating, and drinking all to be part of the worship of the tabernacle. The people, however, in their impatience, use all of these to dedicate a *calf,* a worship symbol with which God will have nothing to do. **6:** *Revel,* with overtones of an orgy. **7–10:** God angrily resolves to destroy the Israelites and start over with Moses. **7:** *Your people, whom you brought up,* God disowns both the people and the divine role in the liberation. **11–14:** Moses' first intercession succeeds. *Your people, whom you brought out,* Moses insists on God's continuing relationship and uses God's liberating triumph (v. 11), reputation with the Egyptians (v. 12; 5.2n.), and covenant with the ancestors (v. 13) to persuade God to relent. **14:** *Changed his mind,* Gen 6.5–6; Am 7.3,6. **15–20:** Moses angrily responds to the people. **15–16:** 24.12n. **17:** *Joshua,* 17.9–13n. **19:** By breaking the tablets Moses is not only venting his anger, but also symbolizing that the covenant relationship has been broken (v. 15). **20:** Moses subjects the people to a

saw the calf and the dancing, Moses' anger
burned hot, and he threw the tablets from
his hands and broke them at the foot of the
mountain. 20 He took the calf that they had
made, burned it with fire, ground it to pow-
der, scattered it on the water, and made the
Israelites drink it.
21 Moses said to Aaron, "What did this
people do to you that you have brought so
great a sin upon them?" 22 And Aaron said,
"Do not let the anger of my lord burn hot;
you know the people, that they are bent on
evil. 23 They said to me, 'Make us gods,
who shall go before us; as for this Moses,
the man who brought us up out of the land
of Egypt, we do not know what has become
of him.' 24 So I said to them, 'Whoever has
gold, take it off'; so they gave it to me, and
I threw it into the fire, and out came this
calf!"
25 When Moses saw that the people
were running wild (for Aaron had let them
run wild, to the derision of their enemies),
26 then Moses stood in the gate of the camp,
and said, "Who is on the LORD's side?
Come to me!" And all the sons of Levi
gathered around him. 27 He said to them,
"Thus says the LORD, the God of Israel,
'Put your sword on your side, each of you!
Go back and forth from gate to gate
throughout the camp, and each of you kill
your brother, your friend, and your neigh-
bor.'" 28 The sons of Levi did as Moses
commanded, and about three thousand of
the people fell on that day. 29 Moses said,
"Today you have ordained yourselves[a] for
the service of the LORD, each one at the
cost of a son or a brother, and so have
brought a blessing on yourselves this day."
30 On the next day Moses said to the
people, "You have sinned a great sin. But
now I will go up to the LORD; perhaps I can
make atonement for your sin." 31 So Moses
returned to the LORD and said, "Alas, this
people has sinned a great sin; they have
made for themselves gods of gold. 32 But
now, if you will only forgive their sin—but
if not, blot me out of the book that you
have written." 33 But the LORD said to Mo-
ses, "Whoever has sinned against me I will
blot out of my book. 34 But now go, lead
the people to the place about which I have
spoken to you; see, my angel shall go in
front of you. Nevertheless, when the day
comes for punishment, I will punish them
for their sin."
35 Then the LORD sent a plague on the
people, because they made the calf—the
one that Aaron made.

33 The LORD said to Moses, "Go,
leave this place, you and the people
whom you have brought up out of the land

a Gk Vg Compare Tg: Heb *Today ordain yourselves*

trial by ordeal (Num 5.16–28). Those who suffer ill effects from drinking the water and pulverized metal are regarded as guilty and fall in a plague (v. 35). **21–24:** Moses' rebuke of Aaron contrasts starkly with his priestly prestige and intercessory role as described in chs 28–30. Aaron feebly disclaims responsibility by shifting the blame both to the people and to the calf. **25–29:** The Levites, Moses' and Aaron's own tribe, respond to Moses' challenge by killing three thousand; Aaron, however, remains unpunished, as he does in Num 12. In return Moses declares them *ordained* to God's service. Instead of being consecrated by a ceremony such as that prescribed in ch 29, the Levites have *ordained* themselves by their passionate loyalty to God despite social and family ties (Deut 33.8–11). Underlying this passage is probably rivalry between two priestly groups. **30–35:** Moses' second intercession, for complete forgiveness, is asking too much. **30:** *Make atonement,* that is, obtain forgiveness (v. 32). **32:** *The book,* following Mesopotamian ideas, is the register of the members of the covenant community destined for life (Ps 69.28; Isa 4.3; Dan 12.1; Mal 3.16). **34:** *Angel,* 23.20–21. **35:** The *plague* attacks those who have failed the ordeal (v. 20).

33.1–23: Will God be with Israel or not? Moses seeks assurance that God will accompany the people despite their attempt to force God to be present on their own terms. **1–3:** The *angel* is God's representative (32.34), showing that the people will not be completely forsaken by the deity. God will not, however, accompany the stubborn people directly, as was true from Egypt to Sinai (13.21–22; 17.1,6), so that divine holiness does not *consume* them. Perhaps God is (temporarily) canceling the instructions to build the tabernacle. **1:** *You have brought up,* 32.7n. **2:** 3.8n. **4–6:** The people remove their *ornaments,* their

of Egypt, and go to the land of which I
swore to Abraham, Isaac, and Jacob, say-
ing, 'To your descendants I will give it.' 2 I
will send an angel before you, and I will
drive out the Canaanites, the Amorites, the
Hittites, the Perizzites, the Hivites, and the
Jebusites. 3 Go up to a land flowing with
milk and honey; but I will not go up among
you, or I would consume you on the way,
for you are a stiff-necked people."
4 When the people heard these harsh
words, they mourned, and no one put on
ornaments. 5 For the LORD had said to Mo-
ses, "Say to the Israelites, 'You are a stiff-
necked people; if for a single moment I
should go up among you, I would consume
you. So now take off your ornaments, and
I will decide what to do to you.' " 6 There-
fore the Israelites stripped themselves of
their ornaments, from Mount Horeb on-
ward.
7 Now Moses used to take the tent and
pitch it outside the camp, far off from the
camp; he called it the tent of meeting. And
everyone who sought the LORD would go
out to the tent of meeting, which was out-
side the camp. 8 Whenever Moses went out
to the tent, all the people would rise and
stand, each of them, at the entrance of their
tents and watch Moses until he had gone
into the tent. 9 When Moses entered the
tent, the pillar of cloud would descend and
stand at the entrance of the tent, and the
LORD would speak with Moses. 10 When all
the people saw the pillar of cloud standing
at the entrance of the tent, all the people
would rise and bow down, all of them, at
the entrance of their tent. 11 Thus the LORD
used to speak to Moses face to face, as one
speaks to a friend. Then he would return to
the camp; but his young assistant, Joshua
son of Nun, would not leave the tent.
12 Moses said to the LORD, "See, you
have said to me, 'Bring up this people'; but
you have not let me know whom you will
send with me. Yet you have said, 'I know
you by name, and you have also found fa-
vor in my sight.' 13 Now if I have found
favor in your sight, show me your ways, so
that I may know you and find favor in your
sight. Consider too that this nation is your
people." 14 He said, "My presence will go
with you, and I will give you rest." 15 And
he said to him, "If your presence will not
go, do not carry us up from here. 16 For
how shall it be known that I have found
favor in your sight, I and your people, un-
less you go with us? In this way, we shall be
distinct, I and your people, from every peo-
ple on the face of the earth."
17 The LORD said to Moses, "I will do
the very thing that you have asked; for you
have found favor in my sight, and I know
you by name." 18 Moses said, "Show me
your glory, I pray." 19 And he said, "I will
make all my goodness pass before you, and

victors' plunder, to show contrition and try to persuade God to *decide* favorably (3.21–22n.). **7–11:** *The tent of meeting,* the depiction of the tent here contrasts sharply with the elaborate structure of chs 25–31, and it functions chiefly as a place where God speaks to Moses (Num 11.16–17,24–26; 12.1–8; Deut 31.14–15). Since God has now refused to be present among the people (v. 3), Moses pitches a tent *far off from the camp.* There is no priest or ritual. Instead, Moses and his *assistant, Joshua* (v. 11; 17.9–13n.) are in charge, and anyone can come to seek an oracle from God. **8:** The people's disrespect for Moses (32.1) is gone completely. **9–10:** *Pillar of cloud,* 13.21–22n. Even though God's presence is now distant and intermittent, it commands utter respect from the people. **11:** Moses' role as mediator (19.9; 20.19) is indicated by the fact that God speaks to him *face to face, as one speaks to a friend* (Num 12.7–8; Deut 34.10–12). **12–16:** Because of the people's change of heart (vv. 4–6,8,10) Moses intercedes a third time, and because of his special relationship with God, he succeeds. **13:** *Your people* (and twice in v. 16), in contrast to v. 1 (32.11–14n.). **16:** Israel is a unique people because they undertake a special journey with God leading them into the future (15.13–18n.). **17–23:** This paragraph anticipates the theophany of 34.5–7, the fifth divine appearance of the book. **18:** Having asked for a display of God's "ways" (v. 13; Ps 103.7–14) or manner of action in the world, Moses now asks for more: a manifestation of God's *glory,* the visible radiance and majesty of God (16.6–7n.). **19:** As God knows Moses "by name" (vv. 12,17), God will proclaim to him the divine name, "YHWH" (3.14n.), which is tantamount to disclosing the

will proclaim before you the name, 'The
LORD';[a] and I will be gracious to whom I
will be gracious, and will show mercy on
whom I will show mercy. 20 But," he said,
"you cannot see my face; for no one shall
see me and live." 21 And the LORD contin-
ued, "See, there is a place by me where you
shall stand on the rock; 22 and while my
glory passes by I will put you in a cleft of
the rock, and I will cover you with my hand
until I have passed by; 23 then I will take
away my hand, and you shall see my back;
but my face shall not be seen."

34 The LORD said to Moses, "Cut two
tablets of stone like the former ones,
and I will write on the tablets the words
that were on the former tablets, which you
broke. 2 Be ready in the morning, and come
up in the morning to Mount Sinai and
present yourself there to me, on the top of
the mountain. 3 No one shall come up with
you, and do not let anyone be seen
throughout all the mountain; and do not let
flocks or herds graze in front of that moun-
tain." 4 So Moses cut two tablets of stone
like the former ones; and he rose early in
the morning and went up on Mount Sinai,
as the LORD had commanded him, and
took in his hand the two tablets of stone.
5 The LORD descended in the cloud and
stood with him there, and proclaimed the
name, "The LORD."[a] 6 The LORD passed
before him, and proclaimed,

"The LORD, the LORD,
a God merciful and gracious,
slow to anger,
and abounding in steadfast love and
faithfulness,
7 keeping steadfast love for the
thousandth generation,[b]
forgiving iniquity and transgression
and sin,
yet by no means clearing the guilty,
but visiting the iniquity of the parents
upon the children
and the children's children,
to the third and the fourth
generation."

8 And Moses quickly bowed his head to-
ward the earth, and worshiped. 9 He said,
"If now I have found favor in your sight,
O Lord, I pray, let the Lord go with us.
Although this is a stiff-necked people, par-
don our iniquity and our sin, and take us
for your inheritance."

10 He said: I hereby make a covenant.
Before all your people I will perform mar-
vels, such as have not been performed in all

a Heb *YHWH*; see note at 3.15 *b* Or *for thousands*

character or identity of God (Gen 32.27–29). *I will be gracious to whom I will be gracious,* the structure of the sentence is similar to that of "I AM WHO I AM" (3.14), emphasizing divine freedom. God's actions, while free, are not capricious, however, but express divine "goodness" (34.6–7). **23:** Although using bold anthropomorphisms (the LORD's *hand* and *back*), the narrator stresses that God remains hidden (v. 20), even when most palpably present.

34.1–35: God renews the covenant by writing the commands again. The narrator here inserts a different version of the Ten Commandments (see v. 28), since the first version (20.2–17) has already been recorded. Scholars call this version (vv. 11–26) the "Ritual Decalogue." **1–4:** 24.12; 31.18; 32.15–19; Deut 10.1–5. **5–9:** The theophany, the fifth divine appearance in Exodus, is anticipated in 33.17–23 (cf. 19.20). **6–7:** While God passes before him (33.22), Moses hears the self-disclosure of the divine identity: "YHWH" (3.14) is above all the *merciful and gracious* God of *steadfast love* (the loyalty to Israel based on the covenant), though that does not exclude divine judgment upon sin. This description of the complexity of God's character as both forgiving and judging is echoed elsewhere (e.g., Num 14.18; Ps 103.7–14; Jer 32.18), while other texts quote the divine attributes of Exodus, but cut the section concerning intergenerational punishment (e.g., Deut 7.9–10; Jon 4.2; Neh 9.17,31). **8–9:** That Moses' fourth intercession succeeds will become clear in the climax of the book (40.34–38). **10–28:** God reestablishes the covenant after it has been broken by the people (ch 32). Whereas God looked back to the liberation the first time (19.3–6; 20.1–3), this time the words point forward to the promised land. Some of the commands resemble the first four of the Ten Commandments (20.2–11), and the festival laws from the Covenant Collection (23.14–19). All of the laws here relate to worship. **11–16:** Intolerance of the

the earth or in any nation; and all the peo-
ple among whom you live shall see the
work of the LORD; for it is an awesome
thing that I will do with you.
11 Observe what I command you today.
See, I will drive out before you the Amo-
rites, the Canaanites, the Hittites, the Periz-
zites, the Hivites, and the Jebusites. 12 Take
care not to make a covenant with the in-
habitants of the land to which you are go-
ing, or it will become a snare among you.
13 You shall tear down their altars, break
their pillars, and cut down their sacred
poles[a] 14 (for you shall worship no other
god, because the LORD, whose name is Jeal-
ous, is a jealous God). 15 You shall not
make a covenant with the inhabitants of
the land, for when they prostitute them-
selves to their gods and sacrifice to their
gods, someone among them will invite you,
and you will eat of the sacrifice. 16 And you
will take wives from among their daughters
for your sons, and their daughters who
prostitute themselves to their gods will
make your sons also prostitute themselves
to their gods.
17 You shall not make cast idols.
18 You shall keep the festival of unleav-
ened bread. Seven days you shall eat un-
leavened bread, as I commanded you, at the
time appointed in the month of Abib; for
in the month of Abib you came out from
Egypt.
19 All that first opens the womb is mine,
all your male[b] livestock, the firstborn of
cow and sheep. 20 The firstborn of a donkey
you shall redeem with a lamb, or if you will
not redeem it you shall break its neck. All
the firstborn of your sons you shall redeem.
No one shall appear before me empty-
handed.
21 Six days you shall work, but on the
seventh day you shall rest; even in plowing
time and in harvest time you shall rest.
22 You shall observe the festival of weeks,
the first fruits of wheat harvest, and the
festival of ingathering at the turn of the
year. 23 Three times in the year all your
males shall appear before the LORD God,
the God of Israel. 24 For I will cast out na-
tions before you, and enlarge your borders;
no one shall covet your land when you go
up to appear before the LORD your God
three times in the year.
25 You shall not offer the blood of my
sacrifice with leaven, and the sacrifice of
the festival of the passover shall not be left
until the morning.
26 The best of the first fruits of your
ground you shall bring to the house of the
LORD your God.
You shall not boil a kid in its mother's
milk.
27 The LORD said to Moses: Write these
words; in accordance with these words I
have made a covenant with you and with
Israel. 28 He was there with the LORD forty
days and forty nights; he neither ate bread
nor drank water. And he wrote on the tab-
lets the words of the covenant, the ten com-
mandments.[c]

a Heb *Asherim* *b* Gk Theodotion Vg Tg: Meaning of Heb uncertain *c* Heb *words*

forms of worship of the other peoples of Canaan (3.8) is motivated by fear of their seductive power (23.24,32–33). These laws are found in a more radical fashion in Deut 7.1–6; 20.16–18. **11:** See 3.8n. **13:** *Pillars,* upright stones associated with Baal shrines; the *sacred poles* (or "Asherim") symbolize Asherah, one of the major female deities of Canaanite religion. **14:** Religious exclusivism is derived from the total claim of Israel's God upon the people's loyalty (20.3). God's *name* (or character) is *Jealous,* that is, God will tolerate no rivals for Israel's devotion (20.5; Deut 4.24). **15–16:** *Prostitute themselves,* sexual metaphors are often used in the Bible for covenant loyalty and disloyalty (see esp. Ezek 16; 23; Hos 1–3). **18–24:** A ritual calendar. The instructions concerning the three annual pilgrimage festivals (vv. 18,22–23) largely parallel 23.14–17. The redemption of *the firstborn* (vv. 19–20), see 13.13n. **21:** 31.12–17n. **24:** The property will be protected while the pilgrims are on their way to the sanctuary. **25–26:** 23.18–19n. **27–28:** Moses' special role as covenant mediator (19.9n.) is shown by the fact that the covenant is made with him and, through him, with Israel. *These words,* a reference to the preceding ritual laws. *Forty days and forty nights,* 24.18.

29 Moses came down from Mount Si-
nai. As he came down from the mountain
with the two tablets of the covenant[a] in his
hand, Moses did not know that the skin of
his face shone because he had been talking
with God. 30 When Aaron and all the Israel-
ites saw Moses, the skin of his face was
shining, and they were afraid to come near
him. 31 But Moses called to them; and Aar-
on and all the leaders of the congregation
returned to him, and Moses spoke with
them. 32 Afterward all the Israelites came
near, and he gave them in commandment
all that the LORD had spoken with him on
Mount Sinai. 33 When Moses had finished
speaking with them, he put a veil on his
face; 34 but whenever Moses went in before
the LORD to speak with him, he would take
the veil off, until he came out; and when he
came out, and told the Israelites what he
had been commanded, 35 the Israelites
would see the face of Moses, that the skin
of his face was shining; and Moses would
put the veil on his face again, until he went
in to speak with him.

35 Moses assembled all the congrega-
tion of the Israelites and said to
them: These are the things that the LORD
has commanded you to do:

2 Six days shall work be done, but on
the seventh day you shall have a holy sab-
bath of solemn rest to the LORD; whoever
does any work on it shall be put to death.
3 You shall kindle no fire in all your dwell-
ings on the sabbath day.

4 Moses said to all the congregation of
the Israelites: This is the thing that the
LORD has commanded: 5 Take from among
you an offering to the LORD; let whoever is
of a generous heart bring the LORD's offer-
ing: gold, silver, and bronze; 6 blue, purple,
and crimson yarns, and fine linen; goats'
hair, 7 tanned rams' skins, and fine leath-
er;[b] acacia wood, 8 oil for the light, spices
for the anointing oil and for the fragrant
incense, 9 and onyx stones and gems to be
set in the ephod and the breastpiece.

10 All who are skillful among you shall
come and make all that the LORD has com-
manded: the tabernacle, 11 its tent and its
covering, its clasps and its frames, its bars,
its pillars, and its bases; 12 the ark with its
poles, the mercy seat,[c] and the curtain for
the screen; 13 the table with its poles and all
its utensils, and the bread of the Presence;
14 the lampstand also for the light, with its
utensils and its lamps, and the oil for the
light; 15 and the altar of incense, with its
poles, and the anointing oil and the fra-
grant incense, and the screen for the en-
trance, the entrance of the tabernacle; 16 the
altar of burnt offering, with its grating of
bronze, its poles, and all its utensils, the
basin with its stand; 17 the hangings of the
court, its pillars and its bases, and the
screen for the gate of the court; 18 the pegs
of the tabernacle and the pegs of the court,
and their cords; 19 the finely worked vest-
ments for ministering in the holy place, the
holy vestments for the priest Aaron, and
the vestments of his sons, for their service
as priests.

20 Then all the congregation of the Isra-
elites withdrew from the presence of Mo-
ses. 21 And they came, everyone whose
heart was stirred, and everyone whose spir-
it was willing, and brought the LORD's
offering to be used for the tent of meeting,
and for all its service, and for the sacred
vestments. 22 So they came, both men and
women; all who were of a willing heart
brought brooches and earrings and signet

a Or *treaty*, or *testimony*; Heb *eduth* b Meaning of Heb uncertain c Or *the cover*

Chs 35–40: Israel obeys instructions, and God takes up residence with them. Now that God has renewed the covenant broken in ch 32, Moses exactly carries out all the details of chs 25–31.

35.1–3: The sabbath command, which was the climax of God's instructions to Moses (31.12–17n.), is the first thing Moses says to Israel, to restrict work on the tabernacle.

35.4–29: The offering (25.1–9) **and the skillful craftspeople** (31.6). This time women are explicitly included among those who contribute (vv. 22,29), and they also do the spinning (vv. 25–26). The jewelry and clothing given by the Egyptians (3.21–22n.) are now used to obey rather than to break the covenant.

rings and pendants, all sorts of gold ob-
jects, everyone bringing an offering of gold
to the LORD. 23 And everyone who pos-
sessed blue or purple or crimson yarn or
fine linen or goats' hair or tanned rams'
skins or fine leather,[a] brought them. 24 Ev-
eryone who could make an offering of sil-
ver or bronze brought it as the LORD's
offering; and everyone who possessed aca-
cia wood of any use in the work, brought it.
25 All the skillful women spun with their
hands, and brought what they had spun in
blue and purple and crimson yarns and fine
linen; 26 all the women whose hearts moved
them to use their skill spun the goats' hair.
27 And the leaders brought onyx stones and
gems to be set in the ephod and the breast-
piece, 28 and spices and oil for the light, and
for the anointing oil, and for the fragrant
incense. 29 All the Israelite men and women
whose hearts made them willing to bring
anything for the work that the LORD had
commanded by Moses to be done, brought
it as a freewill offering to the LORD.

30 Then Moses said to the Israelites:
See, the LORD has called by name Bezalel
son of Uri son of Hur, of the tribe of Judah;
31 he has filled him with divine spirit,[b] with
skill, intelligence, and knowledge in every
kind of craft, 32 to devise artistic designs, to
work in gold, silver, and bronze, 33 in cut-
ting stones for setting, and in carving
wood, in every kind of craft. 34 And he has
inspired him to teach, both him and Oholi-
ab son of Ahisamach, of the tribe of Dan.
35 He has filled them with skill to do every
kind of work done by an artisan or by a
designer or by an embroiderer in blue, pur-
ple, and crimson yarns, and in fine linen, or
by a weaver—by any sort of artisan or
skilled designer.

36 Bezalel and Oholiab and every skill-
ful one to whom the LORD has given
skill and understanding to know how to do
any work in the construction of the sanctu-
ary shall work in accordance with all that
the LORD has commanded.

2 Moses then called Bezalel and Oholiab
and every skillful one to whom the LORD
had given skill, everyone whose heart was
stirred to come to do the work; 3 and they
received from Moses all the freewill offer-
ings that the Israelites had brought for do-
ing the work on the sanctuary. They still
kept bringing him freewill offerings every
morning, 4 so that all the artisans who were
doing every sort of task on the sanctuary
came, each from the task being performed,
5 and said to Moses, "The people are bring-
ing much more than enough for doing the
work that the LORD has commanded us to
do." 6 So Moses gave command, and word
was proclaimed throughout the camp: "No
man or woman is to make anything else as
an offering for the sanctuary." So the peo-
ple were restrained from bringing; 7 for
what they had already brought was more
than enough to do all the work.

8 All those with skill among the workers
made the tabernacle with ten curtains; they
were made of fine twisted linen, and blue,
purple, and crimson yarns, with cherubim
skillfully worked into them. 9 The length of
each curtain was twenty-eight cubits, and
the width of each curtain four cubits; all the
curtains were of the same size.

10 He joined five curtains to one anoth-
er, and the other five curtains he joined to
one another. 11 He made loops of blue on
the edge of the outermost curtain of the
first set; likewise he made them on the edge
of the outermost curtain of the second set;
12 he made fifty loops on the one curtain,
and he made fifty loops on the edge of the
curtain that was in the second set; the loops
were opposite one another. 13 And he made
fifty clasps of gold, and joined the curtains

a Meaning of Heb uncertain *b* Or *the spirit of God*

35.30–36.1: The artisans (31.1–11). Bezalel and Oholiab are not only craftsmen and designers but also teachers (v. 34).

36.2–7: The freewill offerings continue. The Israelites must be *restrained from bringing* an overflow of gifts.

36.8–38: The tabernacle (26.1–37; see Diagram on p. 118 HB).

one to the other with clasps; so the taberna-
cle was one whole.
14 He also made curtains of goats' hair
for a tent over the tabernacle; he made elev-
en curtains. 15The length of each curtain
was thirty cubits, and the width of each
curtain four cubits; the eleven curtains were
of the same size. 16He joined five curtains
by themselves, and six curtains by them-
selves. 17He made fifty loops on the edge of
the outermost curtain of the one set, and
fifty loops on the edge of the other connect-
ing curtain. 18He made fifty clasps of
bronze to join the tent together so that it
might be one whole. 19And he made for the
tent a covering of tanned rams' skins and
an outer covering of fine leather.[a]
20 Then he made the upright frames for
the tabernacle of acacia wood. 21Ten cubits
was the length of a frame, and a cubit and
a half the width of each frame. 22Each
frame had two pegs for fitting together; he
did this for all the frames of the tabernacle.
23The frames for the tabernacle he made in
this way: twenty frames for the south side;
24and he made forty bases of silver under
the twenty frames, two bases under the first
frame for its two pegs, and two bases under
the next frame for its two pegs. 25For the
second side of the tabernacle, on the north
side, he made twenty frames 26and their
forty bases of silver, two bases under the
first frame and two bases under the next
frame. 27For the rear of the tabernacle
westward he made six frames. 28He made
two frames for corners of the tabernacle in
the rear. 29They were separate beneath, but
joined at the top, at the first ring; he made
two of them in this way, for the two cor-
ners. 30There were eight frames with their
bases of silver: sixteen bases, under every
frame two bases.
31 He made bars of acacia wood, five
for the frames of the one side of the taber-
nacle, 32and five bars for the frames of the
other side of the tabernacle, and five bars
for the frames of the tabernacle at the rear
westward. 33He made the middle bar to
pass through from end to end halfway up
the frames. 34And he overlaid the frames
with gold, and made rings of gold for them
to hold the bars, and overlaid the bars with
gold.
35 He made the curtain of blue, purple,
and crimson yarns, and fine twisted linen,
with cherubim skillfully worked into it.
36For it he made four pillars of acacia, and
overlaid them with gold; their hooks were
of gold, and he cast for them four bases of
silver. 37He also made a screen for the en-
trance to the tent, of blue, purple, and crim-
son yarns, and fine twisted linen, embroi-
dered with needlework; 38and its five
pillars with their hooks. He overlaid their
capitals and their bases with gold, but their
five bases were of bronze.

37 Bezalel made the ark of acacia
wood; it was two and a half cubits
long, a cubit and a half wide, and a cubit
and a half high. 2He overlaid it with pure
gold inside and outside, and made a mold-
ing of gold around it. 3He cast for it four
rings of gold for its four feet, two rings on
its one side and two rings on its other side.
4He made poles of acacia wood, and over-
laid them with gold, 5and put the poles into
the rings on the sides of the ark, to carry the
ark. 6He made a mercy seat[b] of pure gold;
two cubits and a half was its length, and a
cubit and a half its width. 7He made two
cherubim of hammered gold; at the two
ends of the mercy seat[c] he made them,
8one cherub at the one end, and one cherub
at the other end; of one piece with the mer-
cy seat[c] he made the cherubim at its two
ends. 9The cherubim spread out their wings
above, overshadowing the mercy seat[c]
with their wings. They faced one another;
the faces of the cherubim were turned to-
ward the mercy seat.[c]
10 He also made the table of acacia
wood, two cubits long, one cubit wide, and
a cubit and a half high. 11He overlaid it

a Meaning of Heb uncertain *b* Or *a cover*
c Or *the cover*

37.1–9: The ark (25.10–22).
37.10–16: The table (25.23–30).

with pure gold, and made a molding of
gold around it. 12 He made around it a rim
a handbreadth wide, and made a molding
of gold around the rim. 13 He cast for it
four rings of gold, and fastened the rings to
the four corners at its four legs. 14 The rings
that held the poles used for carrying the
table were close to the rim. 15 He made the
poles of acacia wood to carry the table, and
overlaid them with gold. 16 And he made
the vessels of pure gold that were to be on
the table, its plates and dishes for incense,
and its bowls and flagons with which to
pour drink offerings.

17 He also made the lampstand of pure
gold. The base and the shaft of the lamp-
stand were made of hammered work; its
cups, its calyxes, and its petals were of one
piece with it. 18 There were six branches go-
ing out of its sides, three branches of the
lampstand out of one side of it and three
branches of the lampstand out of the other
side of it; 19 three cups shaped like almond
blossoms, each with calyx and petals, on
one branch, and three cups shaped like al-
mond blossoms, each with calyx and pet-
als, on the other branch—so for the six
branches going out of the lampstand. 20 On
the lampstand itself there were four cups
shaped like almond blossoms, each with its
calyxes and petals. 21 There was a calyx of
one piece with it under the first pair of
branches, a calyx of one piece with it under
the next pair of branches, and a calyx of
one piece with it under the last pair of
branches. 22 Their calyxes and their
branches were of one piece with it, the
whole of it one hammered piece of pure
gold. 23 He made its seven lamps and its
snuffers and its trays of pure gold. 24 He
made it and all its utensils of a talent of
pure gold.

25 He made the altar of incense of aca-
cia wood, one cubit long, and one cubit
wide; it was square, and was two cubits
high; its horns were of one piece with it.
26 He overlaid it with pure gold, its top, and
its sides all around, and its horns; and he
made for it a molding of gold all around,
27 and made two golden rings for it under
its molding, on two opposite sides of it,
to hold the poles with which to carry it.
28 And he made the poles of acacia wood,
and overlaid them with gold.

29 He made the holy anointing oil also,
and the pure fragrant incense, blended as
by the perfumer.

38 He made the altar of burnt offering
also of acacia wood; it was five cu-
bits long, and five cubits wide; it was
square, and three cubits high. 2 He made
horns for it on its four corners; its horns
were of one piece with it, and he overlaid it
with bronze. 3 He made all the utensils of
the altar, the pots, the shovels, the basins,
the forks, and the firepans: all its utensils he
made of bronze. 4 He made for the altar a
grating, a network of bronze, under its
ledge, extending halfway down. 5 He cast
four rings on the four corners of the bronze
grating to hold the poles; 6 he made the
poles of acacia wood, and overlaid them
with bronze. 7 And he put the poles through
the rings on the sides of the altar, to carry
it with them; he made it hollow, with
boards.

8 He made the basin of bronze with its
stand of bronze, from the mirrors of the
women who served at the entrance to the
tent of meeting.

9 He made the court; for the south side
the hangings of the court were of fine twist-
ed linen, one hundred cubits long; 10 its
twenty pillars and their twenty bases were
of bronze, but the hooks of the pillars and
their bands were of silver. 11 For the north

37.17–24: **The lampstand** (25.31–40).

37.25–28: **The incense altar** (30.1–10).

37.29: **The anointing oil and incense** (30.22–38).

38.1–7: **The sacrificial altar** (27.1–8).

38.8: **The basin** (30.17–21). *The women who served at the entrance to the tent of meeting* are also mentioned in 1 Sam 2.22, but nowhere is their role described.

38.9–20: **The court** (27.9–19).

side there were hangings one hundred cu-
bits long; its twenty pillars and their twenty
bases were of bronze, but the hooks of the
pillars and their bands were of silver. 12 For
the west side there were hangings fifty cu-
bits long, with ten pillars and ten bases; the
hooks of the pillars and their bands were of
silver. 13 And for the front to the east, fifty
cubits. 14 The hangings for one side of the
gate were fifteen cubits, with three pillars
and three bases. 15 And so for the other
side; on each side of the gate of the court
were hangings of fifteen cubits, with three
pillars and three bases. 16 All the hangings
around the court were of fine twisted linen.
17 The bases for the pillars were of bronze,
but the hooks of the pillars and their bands
were of silver; the overlaying of their capi-
tals was also of silver, and all the pillars of
the court were banded with silver. 18 The
screen for the entrance to the court was
embroidered with needlework in blue, pur-
ple, and crimson yarns and fine twisted lin-
en. It was twenty cubits long and, along the
width of it, five cubits high, corresponding
to the hangings of the court. 19 There were
four pillars; their four bases were of
bronze, their hooks of silver, and the over-
laying of their capitals and their bands of
silver. 20 All the pegs for the tabernacle and
for the court all around were of bronze.

21 These are the records of the taberna-
cle, the tabernacle of the covenant,[a] which
were drawn up at the commandment of
Moses, the work of the Levites being under
the direction of Ithamar son of the priest
Aaron. 22 Bezalel son of Uri son of Hur, of
the tribe of Judah, made all that the LORD
commanded Moses; 23 and with him was
Oholiab son of Ahisamach, of the tribe of
Dan, engraver, designer, and embroiderer
in blue, purple, and crimson yarns, and in
fine linen.

24 All the gold that was used for the
work, in all the construction of the sanctu-
ary, the gold from the offering, was twenty-
nine talents and seven hundred thirty shek-
els, measured by the sanctuary shekel.
25 The silver from those of the congregation
who were counted was one hundred talents
and one thousand seven hundred seventy-
five shekels, measured by the sanctuary
shekel; 26 a beka a head (that is, half a shek-
el, measured by the sanctuary shekel), for
everyone who was counted in the census,
from twenty years old and upward, for six
hundred three thousand, five hundred fifty
men. 27 The hundred talents of silver were
for casting the bases of the sanctuary, and
the bases of the curtain; one hundred bases
for the hundred talents, a talent for a base.
28 Of the thousand seven hundred seventy-
five shekels he made hooks for the pillars,
and overlaid their capitals and made bands
for them. 29 The bronze that was contribut-
ed was seventy talents, and two thousand
four hundred shekels; 30 with it he made the
bases for the entrance of the tent of meet-
ing, the bronze altar and the bronze grating
for it and all the utensils of the altar, 31 the
bases all around the court, and the bases of
the gate of the court, all the pegs of the
tabernacle, and all the pegs around the
court.

39 Of the blue, purple, and crimson
yarns they made finely worked vest-
ments, for ministering in the holy place;
they made the sacred vestments for Aaron;
as the LORD had commanded Moses.

2 He made the ephod of gold, of blue,

a Or *treaty*, or *testimony*; Heb *eduth*

38.21–31: The records of the amount of each metal contributed and how each has been used presuppose the appointment of *Ithamar* as head of the Levites (Num 3; 4.33) and the Israelite census (Num 1). **21:** *The tabernacle of the covenant,* a phrase indicating that the sanctuary contains the ark and Ten Commandments. **24–26:** The silver tax is computed at the rate set forth in 30.11–16 and with the figures of the census in mind (Num 1.46). A *talent* weighed ca. 34 kg (75 lb), a *shekel* ca. 11.4 gr (.4 oz).

39.1–43: According to God's instructions. Every paragraph in this chapter ends with the statement that all is being done according to God's instructions (see also v. 32; 40.16,19,21,23,25,27,29,32).

39.1–31: The priests' garments (28.1–43).

purple, and crimson yarns, and of fine
twisted linen. 3 Gold leaf was hammered
out and cut into threads to work into the
blue, purple, and crimson yarns and into
the fine twisted linen, in skilled design.
4 They made for the ephod shoulder-pieces,
joined to it at its two edges. 5 The decorated
band on it was of the same materials and
workmanship, of gold, of blue, purple, and
crimson yarns, and of fine twisted linen; as
the LORD had commanded Moses.

6 The onyx stones were prepared, en-
closed in settings of gold filigree and en-
graved like the engravings of a signet, ac-
cording to the names of the sons of Israel.
7 He set them on the shoulder-pieces of the
ephod, to be stones of remembrance for the
sons of Israel; as the LORD had commanded
Moses.

8 He made the breastpiece, in skilled
work, like the work of the ephod, of gold,
of blue, purple, and crimson yarns, and
of fine twisted linen. 9 It was square; the
breastpiece was made double, a span in
length and a span in width when doubled.
10 They set in it four rows of stones. A row
of carnelian,[a] chrysolite, and emerald was
the first row; 11 and the second row, a tur-
quoise, a sapphire,[b] and a moonstone;
12 and the third row, a jacinth, an agate,
and an amethyst; 13 and the fourth row, a
beryl, an onyx, and a jasper; they were en-
closed in settings of gold filigree. 14 There
were twelve stones with names correspond-
ing to the names of the sons of Israel; they
were like signets, each engraved with its
name, for the twelve tribes. 15 They made
on the breastpiece chains of pure gold,
twisted like cords; 16 and they made two
settings of gold filigree and two gold rings,
and put the two rings on the two edges
of the breastpiece; 17 and they put the two
cords of gold in the two rings at the edges
of the breastpiece. 18 Two ends of the two
cords they had attached to the two settings
of filigree; in this way they attached it in
front to the shoulder-pieces of the ephod.
19 Then they made two rings of gold, and
put them at the two ends of the breastpiece,
on its inside edge next to the ephod. 20 They
made two rings of gold, and attached them
in front to the lower part of the two
shoulder-pieces of the ephod, at its joining
above the decorated band of the ephod.
21 They bound the breastpiece by its rings
to the rings of the ephod with a blue cord,
so that it should lie on the decorated band
of the ephod, and that the breastpiece
should not come loose from the ephod; as
the LORD had commanded Moses.

22 He also made the robe of the ephod
woven all of blue yarn; 23 and the opening
of the robe in the middle of it was like the
opening in a coat of mail,[c] with a binding
around the opening, so that it might not be
torn. 24 On the lower hem of the robe they
made pomegranates of blue, purple, and
crimson yarns, and of fine twisted linen.
25 They also made bells of pure gold, and
put the bells between the pomegranates on
the lower hem of the robe all around, be-
tween the pomegranates; 26 a bell and a
pomegranate, a bell and a pomegranate all
around on the lower hem of the robe for
ministering; as the LORD had commanded
Moses.

27 They also made the tunics, woven of
fine linen, for Aaron and his sons, 28 and
the turban of fine linen, and the head-
dresses of fine linen, and the linen under-
garments of fine twisted linen, 29 and the
sash of fine twisted linen, and of blue, pur-
ple, and crimson yarns, embroidered with
needlework; as the LORD had commanded
Moses.

30 They made the rosette of the holy di-
adem of pure gold, and wrote on it an in-
scription, like the engraving of a signet,
"Holy to the LORD." 31 They tied to it a
blue cord, to fasten it on the turban above;
as the LORD had commanded Moses.

a The identification of several of these stones is uncertain *b* Or *lapis lazuli* *c* Meaning of Heb uncertain

39.32–43: Inspection. When everything has been made, each item is brought to Moses. He confirms that all of God's instructions have been followed and therefore blesses the craftspeople. **33,40:** *Tabernacle* and *tent*, 26.7–14n.

32 In this way all the work of the taber-
nacle of the tent of meeting was finished;
the Israelites had done everything just as
the LORD had commanded Moses. 33 Then
they brought the tabernacle to Moses, the
tent and all its utensils, its hooks, its
frames, its bars, its pillars, and its bases;
34 the covering of tanned rams' skins and
the covering of fine leather,[a] and the cur-
tain for the screen; 35 the ark of the cove-
nant[b] with its poles and the mercy seat;[c]
36 the table with all its utensils, and the
bread of the Presence; 37 the pure lamp-
stand with its lamps set on it and all its
utensils, and the oil for the light; 38 the
golden altar, the anointing oil and the fra-
grant incense, and the screen for the en-
trance of the tent; 39 the bronze altar, and
its grating of bronze, its poles, and all its
utensils; the basin with its stand; 40 the
hangings of the court, its pillars, and its
bases, and the screen for the gate of the
court, its cords, and its pegs; and all the
utensils for the service of the tabernacle, for
the tent of meeting; 41 the finely worked
vestments for ministering in the holy place,
the sacred vestments for the priest Aaron,
and the vestments of his sons to serve as
priests. 42 The Israelites had done all of the
work just as the LORD had commanded
Moses. 43 When Moses saw that they had
done all the work just as the LORD had
commanded, he blessed them.

40 The LORD spoke to Moses: 2 On the
first day of the first month you shall
set up the tabernacle of the tent of meeting.
3 You shall put in it the ark of the cove-
nant,[b] and you shall screen the ark with
the curtain. 4 You shall bring in the table,
and arrange its setting; and you shall bring
in the lampstand, and set up its lamps.
5 You shall put the golden altar for incense
before the ark of the covenant,[b] and set up
the screen for the entrance of the taberna-
cle. 6 You shall set the altar of burnt offer-
ing before the entrance of the tabernacle of
the tent of meeting, 7 and place the basin
between the tent of meeting and the altar,
and put water in it. 8 You shall set up the
court all around, and hang up the screen
for the gate of the court. 9 Then you shall
take the anointing oil, and anoint the taber-
nacle and all that is in it, and consecrate it
and all its furniture, so that it shall become
holy. 10 You shall also anoint the altar of
burnt offering and all its utensils, and con-
secrate the altar, so that the altar shall be
most holy. 11 You shall also anoint the ba-
sin with its stand, and consecrate it. 12 Then
you shall bring Aaron and his sons to the
entrance of the tent of meeting, and shall
wash them with water, 13 and put on Aaron
the sacred vestments, and you shall anoint
him and consecrate him, so that he may
serve me as priest. 14 You shall bring his
sons also and put tunics on them, 15 and
anoint them, as you anointed their father,
that they may serve me as priests: and their
anointing shall admit them to a perpetual
priesthood throughout all generations to
come.

16 Moses did everything just as the
LORD had commanded him. 17 In the first
month in the second year, on the first day
of the month, the tabernacle was set up.
18 Moses set up the tabernacle; he laid its
bases, and set up its frames, and put in its
poles, and raised up its pillars; 19 and he
spread the tent over the tabernacle, and put
the covering of the tent over it; as the LORD
had commanded Moses. 20 He took the
covenant[b] and put it into the ark, and put
the poles on the ark, and set the mercy
seat[c] above the ark; 21 and he brought the
ark into the tabernacle, and set up the cur-

a Meaning of Heb uncertain *b* Or *treaty*, or *testimony*; Heb *eduth* *c* Or *the cover*

40.1–33: The tabernacle and its furnishings are set up and anointed, and the priests are washed, clothed, and anointed. **1–15:** God gives complete instructions for the final arrangements, which Moses will carry out in vv. 16–33. **9–15:** 30.26–30.

40.16–33: Moses personally sets up and places each item. Eight times the narrator emphasizes that Moses does everything exactly as God has commanded (39.1–43n.). **17:** It is nine months after the arrival at Sinai (19.1).

tain for screening, and screened the ark of
the covenant;[a] as the LORD had command-
ed Moses. 22 He put the table in the tent of
meeting, on the north side of the taberna-
cle, outside the curtain, 23 and set the bread
in order on it before the LORD; as the LORD
had commanded Moses. 24 He put the
lampstand in the tent of meeting, opposite
the table on the south side of the taberna-
cle, 25 and set up the lamps before the
LORD; as the LORD had commanded Mo-
ses. 26 He put the golden altar in the tent of
meeting before the curtain, 27 and offered
fragrant incense on it; as the LORD had
commanded Moses. 28 He also put in place
the screen for the entrance of the taberna-
cle. 29 He set the altar of burnt offering at
the entrance of the tabernacle of the tent of
meeting, and offered on it the burnt offer-
ing and the grain offering as the LORD had
commanded Moses. 30 He set the basin be-
tween the tent of meeting and the altar, and
put water in it for washing, 31 with which
Moses and Aaron and his sons washed
their hands and their feet. 32 When they
went into the tent of meeting, and when
they approached the altar, they washed; as
the LORD had commanded Moses. 33 He set
up the court around the tabernacle and the
altar, and put up the screen at the gate of
the court. So Moses finished the work.

34 Then the cloud covered the tent of
meeting, and the glory of the LORD filled
the tabernacle. 35 Moses was not able to en-
ter the tent of meeting because the cloud
settled upon it, and the glory of the LORD
filled the tabernacle. 36 Whenever the cloud
was taken up from the tabernacle, the Isra-
elites would set out on each stage of their
journey; 37 but if the cloud was not taken
up, then they did not set out until the day
that it was taken up. 38 For the cloud of the
LORD was on the tabernacle by day, and
fire was in the cloud[b] by night, before the
eyes of all the house of Israel at each stage
of their journey.

a Or *treaty*, or *testimony*; Heb *eduth* *b* Heb *it*

40.34–38: The climax of the book. Now that Moses has carried out all of God's instructions (v. 33), everything is finally ready so that God may reside among the people (25.8; 29.42–46). *The cloud* and *the glory* are signs of God's presence "tabernacling," that is, dwelling, with Israel (16.6–7n.). **35:** 1 Kings 8.10–11; Isa 6.3–4. **36–38:** The pillar of *cloud* by day and the pillar of *fire* by night that have led Israel thus far (13.21–22) take their place over the tabernacle, since it will accompany Israel on the rest of its journey (Num 9.15–23). As the cloud covered the top of Mount Sinai (24.15–18), so it now covers the tabernacle and will guide Israel to the promised land. God is on the march.

LEVITICUS

The third book of the Torah or Pentateuch is chiefly concerned with the matters surrounding the worship of God at his sanctuary. Its English name, Leviticus, which characterizes the book as having to do with matters associated with priests, who are of the tribe of Levi, derives from the early Greek translation.

Leviticus is part of the Priestly writings of the Pentateuch. These writings are not from a single hand or tradition. The two main components of the Priestly source in Leviticus are the "Priestly Torah" and the materials from the "Holiness School," which are largely found in chs 17–26, the "Holiness Code," or "Holiness Collection." Material from the Holiness School is found interspersed occasionally in chs 1–16 and to a lesser or greater extent in chapters attributed to the Priestly source in the other books of the Torah. While many scholars have viewed the Holiness School materials as earlier than the Priestly Torah, recent work suggests that Holiness School material often supplements the Priestly Torah material, and therefore postdates it. Though the specific dates of these works are disputed, it is reasonable to assume that the Holiness Collection was produced at the end of the exile (538 BCE) or soon thereafter. The Priestly Torah must have existed before this, and may have been edited in the form taken up by the Holiness School in the early exile (after 586 BCE). These dates refer to the editing of these works; in part, they both incorporate earlier, preexilic traditions.

Inasmuch as Holiness School supplements Priestly Torah, it depends upon it and accepts its basic perspectives. But it is novel, especially in laying out rationalizations for matters such as sacrifice, holiness, the relationship of God to the people, and the relationship of God and the people to the land. It thus explains many issues that were present, but not explained in the Priestly Torah. The Holiness School updates the Priestly Torah, systematizes it further, and endows it with theological dynamism. (See further the Introduction to the book of Numbers.)

Leviticus has four main sections and displays a logical development.

(1) Sacrifice (chs 1–7). This is subdivided into (a) basic prescriptions (1.1–6.7) and (b) a recapitulation with elements pertinent to priests (6.8–7.38). This entire section interrupts the narrative flow between the end of the book of Exodus and Leviticus 8–9 in order to outline the customs that the priests and people are about to undertake at the sanctuary.

(2) The priestly consecration ceremony and its aftermath (chs 8–16). It has four subdivisions: (a) the seven-day consecration and eighth-day concluding ceremony (chs 8–9), which resumes the narrative at the end of the book of Exodus; (b) the sin of Aaron's sons and rules for priests (ch 10); (c) impurity laws (chs 11–15), which interrupt the narrative flow between chs 10 and 16 to provide background on impurity, the central concern of the ceremony in ch 16; and (d) the Day of Atonement sanctuary purification ceremony (ch 16).

(3) The "Holiness Code" or "Holiness Collection" (chs 17–26). This has five subdivisions: (a) sacrificial law (ch 17), which follows from the subject of ch 16; (b) moral and ethical laws (chs 18–20); (c) priestly and sacrificial rules (chs 21–22); (d) holy occasions (chs 23–25; ch 24 interrupts this, giving miscellaneous ritual laws and resuming the narrative left off in chs 10 and 16); and (e) blessings and curses (ch 26; these conclude the "Holiness Collection"). Chapters 17–26 roughly

follow the outline of chs 1–16: sacrifice (chs 1–7; 17), priestly duties (chs 8–9; 21–22), and holy occasions (chs 16; 23; 25).

(4) An appendix dealing with vows and dedications (ch 27).

Leviticus is difficult to understand and appreciate since it is technical and presumes knowledge of its ritual system almost at every turn. As the outline above indicates, although there is a narrative that runs through it, this is meager. Most of the book consists of blocks of laws. A first reading might include exemplary chapters: chs 16–17 on sacrifice, ch 8 on the priesthood, chs 11–12 on impurity, ch 23 on festivals, ch 25 on economic laws, and ch 19 on ethical concerns. From here, a reader can go on to focus on a particular topic or group of laws, as indicated in the outline. A careful and concentrated exploration of a chapter or group of related chapters, which tries to discover the system inherent in it, can provide the reader with knowledge and a sense of how to read the material that will then elucidate almost any other chapter of Leviticus, as well as similar chapters in Exodus, Numbers, and Deuteronomy.

1 The LORD summoned Moses and spoke
to him from the tent of meeting, saying:
2 Speak to the people of Israel and say to
them: When any of you bring an offering of
livestock to the LORD, you shall bring your
offering from the herd or from the flock.
3 If the offering is a burnt offering from
the herd, you shall offer a male without
blemish; you shall bring it to the entrance
of the tent of meeting, for acceptance in
your behalf before the LORD. 4 You shall
lay your hand on the head of the burnt
offering, and it shall be acceptable in your
behalf as atonement for you. 5 The bull
shall be slaughtered before the LORD; and
Aaron's sons the priests shall offer the
blood, dashing the blood against all sides of
the altar that is at the entrance of the tent
of meeting. 6 The burnt offering shall be
flayed and cut up into its parts. 7 The sons
of the priest Aaron shall put fire on the
altar and arrange wood on the fire. 8 Aar-
on's sons the priests shall arrange the parts,
with the head and the suet, on the wood
that is on the fire on the altar; 9 but its en-
trails and its legs shall be washed with wa-
ter. Then the priest shall turn the whole
into smoke on the altar as a burnt offering,
an offering by fire of pleasing odor to the
LORD.
10 If your gift for a burnt offering is
from the flock, from the sheep or goats,
your offering shall be a male without blem-
ish. 11 It shall be slaughtered on the north

1.1–6.7: Basic sacrificial prescriptions. The main sacrificial prescriptions are in chs 1–7, which is divided into two sections, 1.1–6.7 and 6.8–7.38. The first section gives the basic description of performance (see 6.8–7.38n.).

1.1–17: The burnt offering. Chapter 1 deals with three types of animals for the burnt offering, in descending order of economic worth: a bull (vv. 3–9), a male sheep or goat (vv. 10–13), and birds (vv. 14–17). **1:** *Tent of meeting,* see Ex 26; 33.9. **2:** This is a general introduction to the burnt offering here and the well-being offering in ch 3. Ch 2 secondarily interrupts the flow between chs 1 and 3 (see 2.1–16n.). **3:** Burnt offerings are brought for vows and freewill offerings (22.18–20), for purification rites (e.g., 12.6–8), daily offerings (6.8–13), and festivals (Num 28–29). *The entrance of the tent of meeting* is the forecourt area in front of the tent (Ex 29.9–19 and diagram on p. 118 HB). The *burnt offering* is unusual in that it is totally consumed by fire, and neither the priest nor the worshiper partakes of it. As such, it is considered most holy, as are the cereal (Lev 2.3,10; 6.17; 10.12; cf. the bread of Presence, 24.9), sin (6.25,29; 10.17; 14.13), and guilt (7.1,6; 14.13) offerings, and probably the priestly ordination offering (8.22–32n.). See Num 18.8–10. The well-being sacrifice (3.1–17; 7.11–36) has a lesser degree of holiness. **4:** *Lay your hand,* one hand only; see 16.21n. **5:** Dashing blood on the altar (Ex 27.1) is also found with the well-being offering (Lev 3.2,8,13) and the guilt offering (7.2); cf. Ex 24.6; 29.16. This in part ransoms the offerer for killing the animal (17.4,10–11n.), and may also have an expiatory effect (see 16.6–19n.). The sin offering has a different blood ritual (ch 4). **9:** *Pleasing odor,* Gen 8.21; Ex 29.18.

side of the altar before the LORD, and Aar-
on's sons the priests shall dash its blood
against all sides of the altar. 12 It shall be cut
up into its parts, with its head and its suet,
and the priest shall arrange them on the
wood that is on the fire on the altar; 13 but
the entrails and the legs shall be washed
with water. Then the priest shall offer the
whole and turn it into smoke on the altar;
it is a burnt offering, an offering by fire of
pleasing odor to the LORD.
14 If your offering to the LORD is a
burnt offering of birds, you shall choose
your offering from turtledoves or pigeons.
15 The priest shall bring it to the altar and
wring off its head, and turn it into smoke
on the altar; and its blood shall be drained
out against the side of the altar. 16 He shall
remove its crop with its contents[a] and
throw it at the east side of the altar, in the
place for ashes. 17 He shall tear it open by
its wings without severing it. Then the
priest shall turn it into smoke on the altar,
on the wood that is on the fire; it is a burnt
offering, an offering by fire of pleasing
odor to the LORD.

2 When anyone presents a grain offering
to the LORD, the offering shall be of
choice flour; the worshiper shall pour oil
on it, and put frankincense on it, 2 and
bring it to Aaron's sons the priests. After
taking from it a handful of the choice flour
and oil, with all its frankincense, the priest
shall turn this token portion into smoke on
the altar, an offering by fire of pleasing
odor to the LORD. 3 And what is left of the
grain offering shall be for Aaron and his
sons, a most holy part of the offerings by
fire to the LORD.
4 When you present a grain offering
baked in the oven, it shall be of choice
flour: unleavened cakes mixed with oil, or
unleavened wafers spread with oil. 5 If your
offering is grain prepared on a griddle, it
shall be of choice flour mixed with oil, un-
leavened; 6 break it in pieces, and pour oil
on it; it is a grain offering. 7 If your offering
is grain prepared in a pan, it shall be made
of choice flour in oil. 8 You shall bring to
the LORD the grain offering that is prepared
in any of these ways; and when it is present-
ed to the priest, he shall take it to the altar.
9 The priest shall remove from the grain
offering its token portion and turn this into
smoke on the altar, an offering by fire of
pleasing odor to the LORD. 10 And what is
left of the grain offering shall be for Aaron
and his sons; it is a most holy part of the
offerings by fire to the LORD.
11 No grain offering that you bring to
the LORD shall be made with leaven, for
you must not turn any leaven or honey into
smoke as an offering by fire to the LORD.
12 You may bring them to the LORD as an
offering of choice products, but they shall
not be offered on the altar for a pleasing

a Meaning of Heb uncertain

2.1–16: The grain offering. The position of this chapter after the burnt offering is probably based on the idea that the grain offering can serve as a substitute for that animal offering. This then continues the descending value of offerings from animal offerings of descending value (cf. 5.1–13) to grain offerings, of still less value. Grain offerings can also be offered independently (6.19–23; 7.12–14; Num 5.15–26; 6.19–21) and may accompany animal offerings (Num 15.1–12). Ch 2 discusses raw (vv. 1–3) and cooked (vv. 4–10) grain offerings. Both of these have oil; frankincense is used on only the raw type. The lack of incense with the cooked type may be a concession to the poor, who could not afford it. Oil and frankincense are apparently signs of joy, and are omitted from other uncooked grain offerings that are associated with wrongdoing (Lev 5.11; Num 5.15). **1:** *Frankincense,* an aromatic resin from shrubs found in Arabia and East Africa. **2:** *Pleasing odor,* see 1.9n. **3:** The priests' consumption of many sacrifices is ordained in Num 18.8–10. Not all grain offerings were eaten (cf. Lev 6.23). *Most holy,* see 1.3. **11–12:** The prohibition of leaven and fruit syrup ("honey," typically made from dates or grapes) may have to do with keeping fermenting or fermented materials away from the altar. Wine (or beer) libations accompanying offerings are not necessarily an exception since these are not burned on the altar. See Num 15.2–16n.; 28.5–7n. **12:** *Choice products,* i.e., first processed products, including oil, wine, grain, mixed bread or dough (Num 15.20–21; 18.12–13,27) presumably as well as leavened bread and fruit syrup (Lev 2.12). **13:** *Salt of the*

odor. 13 You shall not omit from your grain
offerings the salt of the covenant with your
God; with all your offerings you shall offer
salt.
14 If you bring a grain offering of first
fruits to the LORD, you shall bring as the
grain offering of your first fruits coarse new
grain from fresh ears, parched with fire.
15 You shall add oil to it and lay frankin-
cense on it; it is a grain offering. 16 And the
priest shall turn a token portion of it into
smoke—some of the coarse grain and oil
with all its frankincense; it is an offering by
fire to the LORD.

3 If the offering is a sacrifice of well-
being, if you offer an animal of the
herd, whether male or female, you shall of-
fer one without blemish before the LORD.
2 You shall lay your hand on the head of the
offering and slaughter it at the entrance of
the tent of meeting; and Aaron's sons the
priests shall dash the blood against all sides
of the altar. 3 You shall offer from the sacri-
fice of well-being, as an offering by fire to
the LORD, the fat that covers the entrails
and all the fat that is around the entrails;
4 the two kidneys with the fat that is on
them at the loins, and the appendage of the
liver, which he shall remove with the kid-
neys. 5 Then Aaron's sons shall turn these
into smoke on the altar, with the burnt
offering that is on the wood on the fire, as
an offering by fire of pleasing odor to the
LORD.
6 If your offering for a sacrifice of well-
being to the LORD is from the flock, male
or female, you shall offer one without
blemish. 7 If you present a sheep as your
offering, you shall bring it before the LORD
8 and lay your hand on the head of the
offering. It shall be slaughtered before the
tent of meeting, and Aaron's sons shall
dash its blood against all sides of the altar.
9 You shall present its fat from the sacrifice
of well-being, as an offering by fire to the
LORD: the whole broad tail, which shall be
removed close to the backbone, the fat that
covers the entrails, and all the fat that is
around the entrails; 10 the two kidneys with
the fat that is on them at the loins, and the
appendage of the liver, which you shall re-
move with the kidneys. 11 Then the priest
shall turn these into smoke on the altar as
a food offering by fire to the LORD.
12 If your offering is a goat, you shall
bring it before the LORD 13 and lay your
hand on its head; it shall be slaughtered
before the tent of meeting; and the sons of
Aaron shall dash its blood against all sides
of the altar. 14 You shall present as your
offering from it, as an offering by fire to the
LORD, the fat that covers the entrails, and
all the fat that is around the entrails; 15 the
two kidneys with the fat that is on them at
the loins, and the appendage of the liver,
which you shall remove with the kidneys.
16 Then the priest shall turn these into
smoke on the altar as a food offering by fire
for a pleasing odor.
All fat is the LORD's. 17 It shall be a per-

covenant, salt, as a preservative, symbolized the perpetuity of the covenant; cf. Num 18.19; 2 Chr 13.5. **14:** The offering of first fruits may be a form of the offering found in 23.10–11.

3.1–17: The well-being offering. This is a lesser holy offering (see 1.3n.). It can fulfill a vow or be used as a freewill offering (22.21). According to the Priestly system, an Israelite could not eat domesticated animals unless they were sacrificed at a sanctuary (see 17.3–4n.). The well-being offering is thus a sacrifice that an individual would bring in order to partake of meat. Most of the meat goes to the lay person who brings the offering (7.15–21; 19.6–8). Some portions of the offering go to the priests (7.28–36), and, since eating meat is understood as a sacral act, the deity receives some of the visceral fat and organs (3.9–10,14–15). The Heb term for the offering, "shelamim," has also been translated "gift," "payment," "peace," "communion," and "covenant" offering. The animal offered can be either male or female, as opposed to the burnt and guilt offerings, which must be male (1.3,10; 5.15,18,25), or the sin offering, where the gender differs according to the offerer's status in the community (4.3,14,23,28,32). Poorer individuals were more likely to own female animals because they provided milk. **2:** On the hand placement and blood dashing, see 16.21n. and 1.5n. **5:** *Pleasing odor,* see 1.9n. **9:** *Broad tail,* the predominant

petual statute throughout your generations,
in all your settlements: you must not eat
any fat or any blood.

4 The LORD spoke to Moses, saying,
2 Speak to the people of Israel, saying:
When anyone sins unintentionally in any of
the LORD's commandments about things
not to be done, and does any one of
them:

3 If it is the anointed priest who sins,
thus bringing guilt on the people, he shall
offer for the sin that he has committed a
bull of the herd without blemish as a sin
offering to the LORD. 4 He shall bring the
bull to the entrance of the tent of meeting
before the LORD and lay his hand on the
head of the bull; the bull shall be slaugh-
tered before the LORD. 5 The anointed
priest shall take some of the blood of the
bull and bring it into the tent of meeting.
6 The priest shall dip his finger in the blood
and sprinkle some of the blood seven times
before the LORD in front of the curtain of
the sanctuary. 7 The priest shall put some of
the blood on the horns of the altar of fra-
grant incense that is in the tent of meeting
before the LORD; and the rest of the blood
of the bull he shall pour out at the base of
the altar of burnt offering, which is at the
entrance of the tent of meeting. 8 He shall
remove all the fat from the bull of sin offer-
ing: the fat that covers the entrails and all
the fat that is around the entrails; 9 the two
kidneys with the fat that is on them at the
loins; and the appendage of the liver, which
he shall remove with the kidneys, 10 just as
these are removed from the ox of the sacri-
fice of well-being. The priest shall turn
them into smoke upon the altar of burnt
offering. 11 But the skin of the bull and all
its flesh, as well as its head, its legs, its en-
trails, and its dung— 12 all the rest of the
bull—he shall carry out to a clean place
outside the camp, to the ash heap, and shall
burn it on a wood fire; at the ash heap it
shall be burned.

13 If the whole congregation of Israel
errs unintentionally and the matter escapes
the notice of the assembly, and they do any
one of the things that by the LORD's com-
mandments ought not to be done and incur
guilt; 14 when the sin that they have com-
mitted becomes known, the assembly shall
offer a bull of the herd for a sin offering
and bring it before the tent of meeting.
15 The elders of the congregation shall lay
their hands on the head of the bull before
the LORD, and the bull shall be slaughtered
before the LORD. 16 The anointed priest
shall bring some of the blood of the bull

species of sheep in the Levant has a fatty area surrounding the tail that can weigh up to 15 kg (33 lb). **17:** Cf. 17.10–14n.

4.1–35: The sin offering. Sins and severe personal impurities pollute the sanctuary furniture and rooms in various ways. The blood of the sin offering purifies these places and objects. Hence the underlying Heb term for the offering should be translated "purification offering," since the focus is on the purification of the sanctuary, not the sin of the individual. Ch 4 is concerned with purifying pollution arising from inadvertently transgressing divine prohibitions. Numbers 15.22 expands the sins covered to include inadvertent violation of positive commandments; see Num 15.30 for deliberate transgressions. Ch 4 shows a two-tiered gradation in pollution effect, based on where the sacrificial blood, which serves as a ritual detergent, is applied (contrast 1.5). Inadvertent transgressions by the high priest or the people as a whole pollute or make impure the outer room of the tent (vv. 5–7,16–18). Sins by clan leaders or individuals pollute the sacrificial altar in the courtyard (vv. 25,30,34). Ch 16 adds a third tier to this gradation: the impurity of deliberate sins penetrate to the inner room of the tent (16.11–17). In ch 4, the animals brought correlate with the people's status: The high priest and community bring a bull; the clan leader, a male goat; and the lay person, a female goat or lamb (3.1–17). **3–12:** Offering for the high priest. **4:** *Entrance of the tent of meeting,* see 1.3n. *Lay his hand,* see 16.21n. **6:** *Curtain,* Ex 26.31–33. **6,17:** The sprinkling purges the entire room. **7:** *Horns,* see Ex 27.2n. *The altar of fragrant incense* was inside the tabernacle (Ex 30.1–10); see plan on p. 118 HB. **10:** 3.3–5. **11–12:** On the disposal of the carcass, see 6.24–30. **13–21:** Offering for the whole congregation. **13:** This probably gives the people's requirements in case the high priest errs and "brings guilt on the people" (v. 3), i.e., causes them to sin. **20:** *Make*

into the tent of meeting, 17 and the priest
shall dip his finger in the blood and sprin-
kle it seven times before the LORD, in front
of the curtain. 18 He shall put some of the
blood on the horns of the altar that is be-
fore the LORD in the tent of meeting; and
the rest of the blood he shall pour out at the
base of the altar of burnt offering that is at
the entrance of the tent of meeting. 19 He
shall remove all its fat and turn it into
smoke on the altar. 20 He shall do with the
bull just as is done with the bull of sin offer-
ing; he shall do the same with this. The
priest shall make atonement for them, and
they shall be forgiven. 21 He shall carry the
bull outside the camp, and burn it as he
burned the first bull; it is the sin offering for
the assembly.

22 When a ruler sins, doing unintention-
ally any one of all the things that by com-
mandments of the LORD his God ought not
to be done and incurs guilt, 23 once the sin
that he has committed is made known to
him, he shall bring as his offering a male
goat without blemish. 24 He shall lay his
hand on the head of the goat; it shall be
slaughtered at the spot where the burnt
offering is slaughtered before the LORD; it
is a sin offering. 25 The priest shall take
some of the blood of the sin offering with
his finger and put it on the horns of the
altar of burnt offering, and pour out the
rest of its blood at the base of the altar of
burnt offering. 26 All its fat he shall turn
into smoke on the altar, like the fat of the
sacrifice of well-being. Thus the priest shall
make atonement on his behalf for his sin,
and he shall be forgiven.

27 If anyone of the ordinary people
among you sins unintentionally in doing
any one of the things that by the LORD's
commandments ought not to be done and
incurs guilt, 28 when the sin that you have
committed is made known to you, you shall
bring a female goat without blemish as
your offering, for the sin that you have
committed. 29 You shall lay your hand on
the head of the sin offering; and the sin
offering shall be slaughtered at the place of
the burnt offering. 30 The priest shall take
some of its blood with his finger and put it
on the horns of the altar of burnt offering,
and he shall pour out the rest of its blood at
the base of the altar. 31 He shall remove all
its fat, as the fat is removed from the offer-
ing of well-being, and the priest shall turn
it into smoke on the altar for a pleasing
odor to the LORD. Thus the priest shall
make atonement on your behalf, and you
shall be forgiven.

32 If the offering you bring as a sin
offering is a sheep, you shall bring a female
without blemish. 33 You shall lay your hand
on the head of the sin offering; and it shall
be slaughtered as a sin offering at the spot
where the burnt offering is slaughtered.
34 The priest shall take some of the blood of
the sin offering with his finger and put it on
the horns of the altar of burnt offering, and
pour out the rest of its blood at the base of
the altar. 35 You shall remove all its fat, as
the fat of the sheep is removed from the
sacrifice of well-being, and the priest shall
turn it into smoke on the altar, with the
offerings by fire to the LORD. Thus the
priest shall make atonement on your behalf
for the sin that you have committed, and
you shall be forgiven.

5 When any of you sin in that you have
heard a public adjuration to testify
and—though able to testify as one who
has seen or learned of the matter—do not

atonement, this verb is primarily used of the cleansing effect of the sin offering; see 16.6–19n. **22–26:** Offering for the ruler. **22:** *Ruler* (Heb "nasi'") here probably means "chieftain" or "clan leader" (see Num 1.16). **27–35:** Offering for an ordinary person. **31:** *Pleasing odor,* see 1.9n.

5.1–13: The graded sin offering. This first part of ch 5 continues the "sin" or "purification offering" of ch 4, but differs from it in listing four specific wrongs for which a sin offering is brought. The offenses are not violations of prohibitions as in ch 4 but involve required actions left undone. In three of the cases, inadvertence is involved (vv. 2–5), and all of the cases are characterized by recognition of guilt. Since these are compared to ch 4—lesser offenses of an individual—birds or grain offerings may in case of need suffice. **2–3:** For laws about uncleanness, see chs 11–15. **7–13:** Other sacrifices with graded versions for

speak up, you are subject to punishment.
2 Or when any of you touch any unclean
thing—whether the carcass of an unclean
beast or the carcass of unclean livestock or
the carcass of an unclean swarming thing—
and are unaware of it, you have become
unclean, and are guilty. 3 Or when you
touch human uncleanness—any unclean-
ness by which one can become unclean—
and are unaware of it, when you come to
know it, you shall be guilty. 4 Or when any
of you utter aloud a rash oath for a bad or
a good purpose, whatever people utter in
an oath, and are unaware of it, when you
come to know it, you shall in any of these
be guilty. 5 When you realize your guilt in
any of these, you shall confess the sin that
you have committed. 6 And you shall bring
to the LORD, as your penalty for the sin
that you have committed, a female from the
flock, a sheep or a goat, as a sin offering;
and the priest shall make atonement on
your behalf for your sin.

7 But if you cannot afford a sheep, you
shall bring to the LORD, as your penalty for
the sin that you have committed, two tur-
tledoves or two pigeons, one for a sin offer-
ing and the other for a burnt offering. 8 You
shall bring them to the priest, who shall
offer first the one for the sin offering,
wringing its head at the nape without sever-
ing it. 9 He shall sprinkle some of the blood
of the sin offering on the side of the altar,
while the rest of the blood shall be drained
out at the base of the altar; it is a sin offer-
ing. 10 And the second he shall offer for a
burnt offering according to the regulation.
Thus the priest shall make atonement on
your behalf for the sin that you have com-
mitted, and you shall be forgiven.

11 But if you cannot afford two turtle-
doves or two pigeons, you shall bring as
your offering for the sin that you have com-
mitted one-tenth of an ephah of choice
flour for a sin offering; you shall not put oil
on it or lay frankincense on it, for it is a sin
offering. 12 You shall bring it to the priest,
and the priest shall scoop up a handful of it
as its memorial portion, and turn this into
smoke on the altar, with the offerings by
fire to the LORD; it is a sin offering. 13 Thus
the priest shall make atonement on your
behalf for whichever of these sins you have
committed, and you shall be forgiven. Like
the grain offering, the rest shall be for the
priest.

14 The LORD spoke to Moses, saying:
15 When any of you commit a trespass and
sin unintentionally in any of the holy things
of the LORD, you shall bring, as your guilt
offering to the LORD, a ram without blem-
ish from the flock, convertible into silver by
the sanctuary shekel; it is a guilt offering.
16 And you shall make restitution for the
holy thing in which you were remiss, and
shall add one-fifth to it and give it to the
priest. The priest shall make atonement on
your behalf with the ram of the guilt offer-
ing, and you shall be forgiven.

17 If any of you sin without knowing it,

the poor include that for childbirth (12.8) and that for the purification from surface affliction (14.21–32). Cf. 2.1–16n. **7:** Two birds are brought for the purification offering (for the terminology, see 4.1–35n.). One acts as the purification offering per se, supplying the blood to purify the altar. The bird offered as a burnt offering provides the equivalent of the fat pieces of the purgation offering, which are burned on the altar as a gift to God (see ch 4). It is offered according to the procedure outlined in 1.14–17. **11:** On grain offerings, see ch 2. *One-tenth of an ephah* was about 2.3 l (2 qt). *Frankincense,* see 2.1n.

5.14–6.7: The guilt offering. Alternatively, "reparation" or "compensation" offering; this is different from the "sin" or "purification offering" just described. This passage describes three cases requiring this offering: sacrilege committed against holy items (vv. 14–16); when a person senses he or she has done wrong but the error is not known (vv. 17–19; the "unknown sin" is a common motif in Near Eastern texts); and a false oath wherein one lies to a neighbor about his or her property, a type of sacrilege (6.1–7). Num 5.6–8 requires a guilt offering for sacrilege. The sacrifice alone is not sufficient; where appropriate, compensation and a twenty percent fine must be returned before offering the sacrifice; cf. 22.14. The sacrificial procedure concerning this "most holy" offering is found in 7.1–6. **5.15,18; 6.6:** *Convertible into silver/the equivalent,* a person could bring the silver equivalent in value to a ram instead of an actual

doing any of the things that by the LORD's
commandments ought not to be done, you
have incurred guilt, and are subject to pun-
ishment. 18 You shall bring to the priest a
ram without blemish from the flock, or
the equivalent, as a guilt offering; and the
priest shall make atonement on your behalf
for the error that you committed uninten-
tionally, and you shall be forgiven. 19 It is a
guilt offering; you have incurred guilt be-
fore the LORD.

6 [a]The LORD spoke to Moses, saying:
2 When any of you sin and commit a
trespass against the LORD by deceiving a
neighbor in a matter of a deposit or a
pledge, or by robbery, or if you have de-
frauded a neighbor, 3 or have found some-
thing lost and lied about it—if you swear
falsely regarding any of the various things
that one may do and sin thereby— 4 when
you have sinned and realize your guilt, and
would restore what you took by robbery or
by fraud or the deposit that was committed
to you, or the lost thing that you found, 5 or
anything else about which you have sworn
falsely, you shall repay the principal
amount and shall add one-fifth to it. You
shall pay it to its owner when you realize
your guilt. 6 And you shall bring to the
priest, as your guilt offering to the LORD, a
ram without blemish from the flock, or its
equivalent, for a guilt offering. 7 The priest
shall make atonement on your behalf be-
fore the LORD, and you shall be forgiven
for any of the things that one may do and
incur guilt thereby.

8 [b]The LORD spoke to Moses, saying:
9 Command Aaron and his sons, saying:
This is the ritual of the burnt offering. The
burnt offering itself shall remain on the
hearth upon the altar all night until the
morning, while the fire on the altar shall be
kept burning. 10 The priest shall put on his
linen vestments after putting on his linen
undergarments next to his body; and he
shall take up the ashes to which the fire has
reduced the burnt offering on the altar, and
place them beside the altar. 11 Then he shall
take off his vestments and put on other gar-
ments, and carry the ashes out to a clean
place outside the camp. 12 The fire on the
altar shall be kept burning; it shall not go
out. Every morning the priest shall add
wood to it, lay out the burnt offering on it,
and turn into smoke the fat pieces of the
offerings of well-being. 13 A perpetual fire
shall be kept burning on the altar; it shall
not go out.

14 This is the ritual of the grain offering:
The sons of Aaron shall offer it before the
LORD, in front of the altar. 15 They shall
take from it a handful of the choice flour
and oil of the grain offering, with all the
frankincense that is on the offering, and
they shall turn its memorial portion into
smoke on the altar as a pleasing odor to the
LORD. 16 Aaron and his sons shall eat what
is left of it; it shall be eaten as unleavened
cakes in a holy place; in the court of the
tent of meeting they shall eat it. 17 It shall
not be baked with leaven. I have given it as
their portion of my offerings by fire; it is
most holy, like the sin offering and the guilt
offering. 18 Every male among the descen-
dants of Aaron shall eat of it, as their per-
petual due throughout your generations,

a Ch 5.20 in Heb *b* Ch 6.1 in Heb

animal. **5.15:** A *shekel* weighed about 11.4 gr (.4 oz); see Ex 30.13n. **6.1–7:** Cf. Ex 22.7–15; Num 5.5–10.

6.8–7.38: Reprise of sacrificial prescriptions. This section treats again the sacrifices of 1.1–6.7, adding details about particular types, often from the point of view of the priests (see 1.1–6.7n.; 7.37–38n.). It likely derives from a torah ("teaching") to train priests to perform these rituals.

6.8–13: The burnt offering. Cf. 1.1–14. **9–13:** This may refer specifically to the daily burnt offering, offered in the morning and early evening (cf. Ex 29.38–42; Num 28.3–8). The evening offering is apparently the last offering of the day and is left burning all night (v. 13). The morning offering appears to begin the day's ritual activity (v. 12). **10:** The priestly garb is described in Ex 28.39–43.

6.14–23: Grain offerings. 14–18: This deals with the independent grain offering of 2.1–3. In contrast, the entirety of the grain offering which accompanies the daily regular burnt offering of vv. 8–13 is burned (Ex 29.38–42; 40.29; Num 28.3–8). **15:** *Frankincense,* see 2.1n. *Pleasing odor,* see 1.9n. **16–17:** *Unleav-*

from the LORD's offerings by fire; anything
that touches them shall become holy.
19 The LORD spoke to Moses, saying:
20 This is the offering that Aaron and his
sons shall offer to the LORD on the day
when he is anointed: one-tenth of an ephah
of choice flour as a regular offering, half of
it in the morning and half in the evening.
21 It shall be made with oil on a griddle; you
shall bring it well soaked, as a grain offer-
ing of baked[a] pieces, and you shall present
it as a pleasing odor to the LORD. 22 And so
the priest, anointed from among Aaron's
descendants as a successor, shall prepare it;
it is the LORD's—a perpetual due—to be
turned entirely into smoke. 23 Every grain
offering of a priest shall be wholly burned;
it shall not be eaten.
24 The LORD spoke to Moses, saying:
25 Speak to Aaron and his sons, saying: This
is the ritual of the sin offering. The sin
offering shall be slaughtered before the
LORD at the spot where the burnt offering
is slaughtered; it is most holy. 26 The priest
who offers it as a sin offering shall eat of it;
it shall be eaten in a holy place, in the court
of the tent of meeting. 27 Whatever touches
its flesh shall become holy; and when any
of its blood is spattered on a garment, you
shall wash the bespattered part in a holy
place. 28 An earthen vessel in which it was
boiled shall be broken; but if it is boiled in
a bronze vessel, that shall be scoured and
rinsed in water. 29 Every male among the
priests shall eat of it; it is most holy. 30 But
no sin offering shall be eaten from which
any blood is brought into the tent of meet-
ing for atonement in the holy place; it shall
be burned with fire.

7 This is the ritual of the guilt offering. It
is most holy; 2 at the spot where the
burnt offering is slaughtered, they shall
slaughter the guilt offering, and its blood
shall be dashed against all sides of the altar.
3 All its fat shall be offered: the broad tail,
the fat that covers the entrails, 4 the two
kidneys with the fat that is on them at the
loins, and the appendage of the liver, which
shall be removed with the kidneys. 5 The
priest shall turn them into smoke on the
altar as an offering by fire to the LORD; it
is a guilt offering. 6 Every male among the
priests shall eat of it; it shall be eaten in a
holy place; it is most holy.
7 The guilt offering is like the sin offer-
ing, there is the same ritual for them; the
priest who makes atonement with it shall
have it. 8 So, too, the priest who offers any-
one's burnt offering shall keep the skin of
the burnt offering that he has offered. 9 And
every grain offering baked in the oven, and
all that is prepared in a pan or on a griddle,
shall belong to the priest who offers it.
10 But every other grain offering, mixed
with oil or dry, shall belong to all the sons
of Aaron equally.
11 This is the ritual of the sacrifice of the
offering of well-being that one may offer to
the LORD. 12 If you offer it for thanksgiv-
ing, you shall offer with the thank offering

a Meaning of Heb uncertain

ened, see 2.11–12n. **19–23:** This is a different grain offering, offered morning and evening by the high priest (cf. Num 4.16; cf. Neh 10.34). **20:** *Ephah,* see 5.11n.

6.24–30: The sin offering. 24–29: This treats one type of sin/purification offering (see 4.1–35n.) whose blood is only used at the outer altar (4.22–26,27–31, 32–35) and whose flesh may be eaten by priests (6.26; 10.16–20). **26:** *Court,* see Ex 27.9–19n. **30:** This refers to another type of sin/purification offering for more serious sins. Its blood is used inside the tent (4.1–12,13–21), and its flesh must be disposed of (Ex 29.14; Lev 4.11–12,21; 6.23; 8.17; 9.11; 16.27). The flesh of sin offerings brought by priests is also discarded (8.14–17; 9.8–11).

7.1–10: The guilt offering. Cf. 5.14–26. Though brought for sins as is the sin/purification offering (see 4.1–35n.), the performance of the guilt offering is similar to the procedures for the burnt and well-being offerings (chs 1 and 3). **3:** *Broad tail,* see 3.9n. **6–10:** These verses summarize some of the rightful proceeds (prebends) that priests receive from various offerings.

7.11–38: The well-being offering. Cf. ch 3. This passage treats two categories of well-being offerings: the thanksgiving offering (vv. 12–15) and the vow and the freewill offering (vv. 16–18). **12–14:** The unleavened cakes mixed with oil, unleavened wafers spread with oil, and cakes of choice flour well soaked in oil. 13 With your thanksgiving sacrifice of well-being you shall bring your offering with cakes of leavened bread. 14 From this you shall offer one cake from each offering, as a gift to the LORD; it shall belong to the priest who dashes the blood of the offering of well-being. 15 And the flesh of your thanksgiving sacrifice of well-being shall be eaten on the day it is offered; you shall not leave any of it until morning. 16 But if the sacrifice you offer is a votive offering or a freewill offering, it shall be eaten on the day that you offer your sacrifice, and what is left of it shall be eaten the next day; 17 but what is left of the flesh of the sacrifice shall be burned up on the third day. 18 If any of the flesh of your sacrifice of well-being is eaten on the third day, it shall not be acceptable, nor shall it be credited to the one who offers it; it shall be an abomination, and the one who eats of it shall incur guilt.

19 Flesh that touches any unclean thing shall not be eaten; it shall be burned up. As for other flesh, all who are clean may eat such flesh. 20 But those who eat flesh from the LORD's sacrifice of well-being while in a state of uncleanness shall be cut off from their kin. 21 When any one of you touches any unclean thing—human uncleanness or an unclean animal or any unclean creature—and then eats flesh from the LORD's sacrifice of well-being, you shall be cut off from your kin.

22 The LORD spoke to Moses, saying: 23 Speak to the people of Israel, saying: You shall eat no fat of ox or sheep or goat. 24 The fat of an animal that died or was torn by wild animals may be put to any other use, but you must not eat it. 25 If any one of you eats the fat from an animal of which an offering by fire may be made to the LORD, you who eat it shall be cut off from your kin. 26 You must not eat any blood whatever, either of bird or of animal, in any of your settlements. 27 Any one of you who eats any blood shall be cut off from your kin.

28 The LORD spoke to Moses, saying: 29 Speak to the people of Israel, saying: Any one of you who would offer to the LORD your sacrifice of well-being must yourself bring to the LORD your offering from your sacrifice of well-being. 30 Your own hands shall bring the LORD's offering by fire; you shall bring the fat with the breast, so that the breast may be raised as an elevation offering before the LORD. 31 The priest shall turn the fat into smoke on the altar, but the breast shall belong to Aaron and his sons. 32 And the right thigh from your sacrifices of well-being you shall give to the priest as an offering; 33 the one among the sons of Aaron who offers the blood and fat of the offering of well-being shall have the right thigh for a portion. 34 For I have taken the breast of the elevation offering, and the thigh that is offered, from the people of Israel, from their sacrifices of well-being, and have given them to Aaron the priest and to his sons, as a perpetual due from the people of Israel. 35 This is the portion allotted to Aaron and to his sons from the offerings made by fire to the LORD, once they have been brought forward to serve the LORD as priests; 36 these the LORD commanded to be given them, when he anointed them, as a perpetual due from the people of Israel throughout their generations.

37 This is the ritual of the burnt offer-

thanksgiving offering has accompaniments and strictures that the other well-being offerings do not have. Three different kinds of grain offerings (cf. 2.4–10) as well as some unleavened bread are brought with the offering (see 2.11–12n.). One of each type of bread is given to the officiating priest. The rest of the loaves or cakes are presumably eaten by the offerer and the offerer's party, as part of the sacrificial meal. **15–18:** As opposed to the vow or freewill offering, which may be eaten over two days, the thanksgiving offering can only be eaten for one day. Cf. 19.5–8; 22.30. **19–21:** On eating sacrifices in purity, see 12.2–5n.; 22.1–9n.; Num 9.1–14n. **22–27:** Particular parts of animals may only be used for sacrificial purposes, and may not be consumed by the laity. **28–36:** The priests' portion of the well-being offering. **30:** *Elevation offering,* see Num 18.11n. **37–38:** These verses close 6.8–7.36, summarizing what

ing, the grain offering, the sin offering, the
guilt offering, the offering of ordination,
and the sacrifice of well-being, 38 which the
LORD commanded Moses on Mount Sinai,
when he commanded the people of Israel to
bring their offerings to the LORD, in the
wilderness of Sinai.

8 The LORD spoke to Moses, saying:
2 Take Aaron and his sons with him, the
vestments, the anointing oil, the bull of sin
offering, the two rams, and the basket of
unleavened bread; 3 and assemble the whole
congregation at the entrance of the tent
of meeting. 4 And Moses did as the LORD
commanded him. When the congregation
was assembled at the entrance of the tent of
meeting, 5 Moses said to the congregation,
"This is what the LORD has commanded to
be done."

6 Then Moses brought Aaron and his
sons forward, and washed them with wa-
ter. 7 He put the tunic on him, fastened the
sash around him, clothed him with the
robe, and put the ephod on him. He then
put the decorated band of the ephod
around him, tying the ephod to him with it.
8 He placed the breastpiece on him, and in
the breastpiece he put the Urim and the
Thummim. 9 And he set the turban on his
head, and on the turban, in front, he set the
golden ornament, the holy crown, as the
LORD commanded Moses.

10 Then Moses took the anointing oil
and anointed the tabernacle and all that
was in it, and consecrated them. 11 He
sprinkled some of it on the altar seven
times, and anointed the altar and all its
utensils, and the basin and its base, to con-
secrate them. 12 He poured some of the
anointing oil on Aaron's head and anointed
him, to consecrate him. 13 And Moses
brought forward Aaron's sons, and clothed
them with tunics, and fastened sashes
around them, and tied headdresses on
them, as the LORD commanded Moses.

14 He led forward the bull of sin offer-
ing; and Aaron and his sons laid their
hands upon the head of the bull of sin offer-
ing, 15 and it was slaughtered. Moses took
the blood and with his finger put some on
each of the horns of the altar, purifying the
altar; then he poured out the blood at the
base of the altar. Thus he consecrated it, to
make atonement for it. 16 Moses took all
the fat that was around the entrails, and the
appendage of the liver, and the two kidneys
with their fat, and turned them into smoke
on the altar. 17 But the bull itself, its skin
and flesh and its dung, he burned with fire
outside the camp, as the LORD commanded
Moses.

18 Then he brought forward the ram
of burnt offering. Aaron and his sons laid
their hands on the head of the ram, 19 and
it was slaughtered. Moses dashed the blood
against all sides of the altar. 20 The ram was
cut into its parts, and Moses turned into
smoke the head and the parts and the suet.
21 And after the entrails and the legs were
washed with water, Moses turned into
smoke the whole ram on the altar; it was a
burnt offering for a pleasing odor, an offer-

preceded, as is typical in Leviticus. The *ordination* offering has not yet been discussed (but see ch 8).
8.1–36: The consecration of the sanctuary and priests. This chapter fulfills Ex 28–29; 30.26–30; 40.9–15. In the flow of the narrative, it follows the setting up of the tent of meeting in Ex 40. The sacrificial laws in Lev 1–7 intervene to provide the legal background for the initiation of worship at the sanctuary. Once initiated, the priests may begin to officiate at the sacrifices just outlined. **2:** *Vestments,* Ex 39.1–31; *anointing oil,* Ex 30.22–31; *bull,* Lev 4.3; Ex 29.1; *the two rams, and the basket of unleavened bread,* Ex 29.1–3. **3:** *Entrance of the tent of meeting,* 1.3n. **6:** The washing is for purification and prepares for the ensuing sanctification of the priests. **7–9,13:** The high priest's clothing differs from that of regular priests (cf. v. 13; Ex 28; 39). It marks his higher ritual status and holiness. On the vestments, see notes to Ex 28. The *holy crown* (v. 9) is mentioned in Ex 29.6 ("holy diadem"). **10–12:** Anointing was used throughout the ancient Near Eastern world to change the status of a person or object, in this case, as part of a ritual making them holy. It was also used in Israel to change the status of a commoner to king (e.g., 1 Sam 10.1; 16.13). *On Aaron's head,* see Ps 133.2. **14–17:** 4.1–12. **18–21:** 1.10–13. **21:** *Pleasing odor,* see 1.9n. **22–32:** The ordination offering (Ex 29.29–37) is in many respects similar to the well-being

ing by fire to the LORD, as the LORD com-
manded Moses.
22 Then he brought forward the second
ram, the ram of ordination. Aaron and his
sons laid their hands on the head of the
ram, 23 and it was slaughtered. Moses took
some of its blood and put it on the lobe of
Aaron's right ear and on the thumb of his
right hand and on the big toe of his right
foot. 24 After Aaron's sons were brought
forward, Moses put some of the blood on
the lobes of their right ears and on the
thumbs of their right hands and on the big
toes of their right feet; and Moses dashed
the rest of the blood against all sides of the
altar. 25 He took the fat—the broad tail, all
the fat that was around the entrails, the
appendage of the liver, and the two kidneys
with their fat—and the right thigh. 26 From
the basket of unleavened bread that was
before the LORD, he took one cake of un-
leavened bread, one cake of bread with oil,
and one wafer, and placed them on the fat
and on the right thigh. 27 He placed all
these on the palms of Aaron and on the
palms of his sons, and raised them as an
elevation offering before the LORD. 28 Then
Moses took them from their hands and
turned them into smoke on the altar with
the burnt offering. This was an ordination
offering for a pleasing odor, an offering by
fire to the LORD. 29 Moses took the breast
and raised it as an elevation offering before
the LORD; it was Moses' portion of the ram
of ordination, as the LORD commanded
Moses.
30 Then Moses took some of the anoint-
ing oil and some of the blood that was on
the altar and sprinkled them on Aaron and
his vestments, and also on his sons and
their vestments. Thus he consecrated Aaron
and his vestments, and also his sons and
their vestments.
31 And Moses said to Aaron and his
sons, "Boil the flesh at the entrance of the
tent of meeting, and eat it there with the
bread that is in the basket of ordination
offerings, as I was commanded, 'Aaron and
his sons shall eat it'; 32 and what remains of
the flesh and the bread you shall burn with
fire. 33 You shall not go outside the en-
trance of the tent of meeting for seven days,
until the day when your period of ordina-
tion is completed. For it will take seven
days to ordain you; 34 as has been done to-
day, the LORD has commanded to be done
to make atonement for you. 35 You shall
remain at the entrance of the tent of meet-
ing day and night for seven days, keeping
the LORD's charge so that you do not die;
for so I am commanded." 36 Aaron and his
sons did all the things that the LORD com-
manded through Moses.
9 On the eighth day Moses summoned
Aaron and his sons and the elders of
Israel. 2 He said to Aaron, "Take a bull calf
for a sin offering and a ram for a burnt
offering, without blemish, and offer them
before the LORD. 3 And say to the people of
Israel, 'Take a male goat for a sin offering;
a calf and a lamb, yearlings without blem-
ish, for a burnt offering; 4 and an ox and a
ram for an offering of well-being to sacri-
fice before the LORD; and a grain offering
mixed with oil. For today the LORD will
appear to you.' " 5 They brought what Mo-

offering: Its fat is elevated (Lev 8.25–27; cf. 7.30); the breast is given to the priestly officiant (8.29; cf. 7.31); the offerers may eat of the meat (8.32; cf. 7.15–18); and the right thigh is singled out for special attention (8.26–28; cf. 7.32–34). Though similar to the well-being offering, it is probably to be considered most holy (see 1.3n.). **23–24:** Three basic acts sanctify the priests: clothing them (vv. 6–9,13), applying ordination offering blood to their extremities (vv. 23–24; cf. 14.14–17n.), and sprinkling them with oil and blood from the altar (v. 30). A fourth act, pouring oil on the head, further sanctifies Aaron, the high priest (see vv. 10–12n.). **25:** *Broad tail,* see 3.9n. **33–35:** The consecration rites are to be performed every day for seven days (cf. Ex 29.30,35–37), and so the priests must remain in the sanctuary.

9.1–24: Conclusion of the priestly consecration. The seven-day priestly consecration rites (8.33–35n.) are capped by an eighth-day ceremony in which communal sacrifices in addition to priestly sacrifices are offered. The goal of the ceremony is the revelation of God's glory (9.6,22–24), continuing the theme of Ex 40.34–35. **6–21:** In ch 8 Moses acted as the priest, manipulating sacrificial blood and portions. Now

ses commanded to the front of the tent of
meeting; and the whole congregation drew
near and stood before the LORD. 6 And Mo-
ses said, "This is the thing that the LORD
commanded you to do, so that the glory of
the LORD may appear to you." 7 Then Mo-
ses said to Aaron, "Draw near to the altar
and sacrifice your sin offering and your
burnt offering, and make atonement for
yourself and for the people; and sacrifice
the offering of the people, and make atone-
ment for them; as the LORD has com-
manded."
8 Aaron drew near to the altar, and
slaughtered the calf of the sin offering,
which was for himself. 9 The sons of Aaron
presented the blood to him, and he dipped
his finger in the blood and put it on the
horns of the altar; and the rest of the blood
he poured out at the base of the altar. 10 But
the fat, the kidneys, and the appendage of
the liver from the sin offering he turned
into smoke on the altar, as the LORD com-
manded Moses; 11 and the flesh and the
skin he burned with fire outside the camp.
12 Then he slaughtered the burnt offer-
ing. Aaron's sons brought him the blood,
and he dashed it against all sides of the
altar. 13 And they brought him the burnt
offering piece by piece, and the head, which
he turned into smoke on the altar. 14 He
washed the entrails and the legs and, with
the burnt offering, turned them into smoke
on the altar.
15 Next he presented the people's offer-
ing. He took the goat of the sin offering
that was for the people, and slaughtered it,
and presented it as a sin offering like the
first one. 16 He presented the burnt offer-
ing, and sacrificed it according to regula-
tion. 17 He presented the grain offering,
and, taking a handful of it, he turned it into
smoke on the altar, in addition to the burnt
offering of the morning.
18 He slaughtered the ox and the ram
as a sacrifice of well-being for the people.
Aaron's sons brought him the blood, which
he dashed against all sides of the altar,
19 and the fat of the ox and of the ram—the
broad tail, the fat that covers the entrails,
the two kidneys and the fat on them,[a] and
the appendage of the liver. 20 They first laid
the fat on the breasts, and the fat was
turned into smoke on the altar; 21 and the
breasts and the right thigh Aaron raised as
an elevation offering before the LORD, as
Moses had commanded.
22 Aaron lifted his hands toward the
people and blessed them; and he came
down after sacrificing the sin offering, the
burnt offering, and the offering of well-
being. 23 Moses and Aaron entered the tent
of meeting, and then came out and blessed
the people; and the glory of the LORD ap-
peared to all the people. 24 Fire came out
from the LORD and consumed the burnt
offering and the fat on the altar; and when
all the people saw it, they shouted and fell
on their faces.
10 Now Aaron's sons, Nadab and Abi-
hu, each took his censer, put fire in

a Gk: Heb *the broad tail, and that which covers, and the kidneys*

for the first time Aaron and his sons, fully installed as priests, officiate at the various types of sacrifice described in chs 1–5. **19:** *Broad tail,* see 3.9n. **22–23:** The people receive two blessings (cf. 1 Kings 8.14–21,55–61). The first time Aaron, standing on the altar where he had been arranging the sacrifices, holds out his hands over the people and blesses them. The second time both Moses and Aaron bless the people, after coming out of the tent of meeting. For a priestly blessing, see Num 6.22–27. **23–24:** God's presence is manifest, indicating that the priestly consecration has been performed correctly; cf. Judg 6.21; 1 Kings 18.38; 2 Chr 7.1. **24:** In other stories this fire is lethal (10.2; Num 16.35). The theophany or divine appearance is therefore not only a manifestation of the divine presence but of divine power and its accompanying danger. Hence the people fall in awe and in fear. God's fiery glory is also manifested in the cloud and fire pillar that led the Israelites and rested over the meeting tent (Ex 40.38; Num 9.15–23n.; 10.11). See also Ex 24.17; Ezek 1.27–28.

10.1–20: The aftermath of the priestly consecration. All has proceeded well with the consecration of the sanctuary and priests in chs 8–9. The new system of worship is, however, now threatened by priestly

it, and laid incense on it; and they offered
unholy fire before the LORD, such as he had
not commanded them. 2 And fire came out
from the presence of the LORD and con-
sumed them, and they died before the
LORD. 3 Then Moses said to Aaron, "This is
what the LORD meant when he said,

'Through those who are near me
I will show myself holy,
and before all the people
I will be glorified.' "

And Aaron was silent.
4 Moses summoned Mishael and Elza-
phan, sons of Uzziel the uncle of Aaron,
and said to them, "Come forward, and car-
ry your kinsmen away from the front of the
sanctuary to a place outside the camp."
5 They came forward and carried them by
their tunics out of the camp, as Moses had
ordered. 6 And Moses said to Aaron and to
his sons Eleazar and Ithamar, "Do not di-
shevel your hair, and do not tear your vest-
ments, or you will die and wrath will strike
all the congregation; but your kindred, the
whole house of Israel, may mourn the
burning that the LORD has sent. 7 You shall
not go outside the entrance of the tent of
meeting, or you will die; for the anointing
oil of the LORD is on you." And they did as
Moses had ordered.
8 And the LORD spoke to Aaron: 9 Drink
no wine or strong drink, neither you nor
your sons, when you enter the tent of meet-
ing, that you may not die; it is a statute
forever throughout your generations.
10 You are to distinguish between the holy
and the common, and between the unclean
and the clean; 11 and you are to teach the
people of Israel all the statutes that the
LORD has spoken to them through Moses.
12 Moses spoke to Aaron and to his re-
maining sons, Eleazar and Ithamar: Take
the grain offering that is left from the
LORD's offerings by fire, and eat it unleav-
ened beside the altar, for it is most holy;
13 you shall eat it in a holy place, because it
is your due and your sons' due, from the
offerings by fire to the LORD; for so I am
commanded. 14 But the breast that is elevat-
ed and the thigh that is raised, you and
your sons and daughters as well may eat in
any clean place; for they have been assigned
to you and your children from the sacrifices
of the offerings of well-being of the people
of Israel. 15 The thigh that is raised and the
breast that is elevated they shall bring, to-
gether with the offerings by fire of the fat,
to raise for an elevation offering before the
LORD; they are to be your due and that
of your children forever, as the LORD has
commanded.
16 Then Moses made inquiry about the
goat of the sin offering, and—it had al-
ready been burned! He was angry with Ele-

malfeasance. **1–3:** *Nadab and Abihu*, Aaron's older sons (Ex 6.23–24), offer incense, apparently using coals from an illicit source (cf. Lev 16.12). The punishment is measure for measure: They are destroyed with fire because they offered illicit fire. The fire that destroys them is that which had just manifested itself to the people (9.24n.). The story is similar to Korah's rebellion in Num 16, and may reflect a controversy in priesthood circles in later biblical history. The story also illustrates the necessity of strict adherence to ritual requirements. **4–5:** With others removing the corpses, the priests remain pure from corpse contamination (cf. 21.1–12n.) and can thus continue with their priestly duties. **6–7:** The priests are not to mourn for their relatives and are to avoid all activities associated with mourning (cf. 21.1–6,10–12). Mourning increases their chance of becoming contaminated by a corpse. **8–11:** Stating restrictions on mourning allows for raising other restrictions and duties of the priests. **10:** *Holy and . . . common, . . . unclean and . . . clean,* these two pairs, which are not identical, describe the status of every object, place, or person. All objects, places, or people have at the same time one quality of each pair. They may be holy and clean (e.g., the properly functioning sanctuary), common and clean (e.g., the "default" status of lay Israelites before suffering impurity such as found in chs 11–15 or Num 19), common and impure (e.g., lay Israelites after suffering an impurity), and, less frequently, holy and impure (this includes holy ritual items that become impure when used for purification, e.g., sin offering carcasses, cf. 6.27–30; 16.26–28). See 11.1–15.33n. **12–15:** 7.28–36. The grain offering (v. 12) accompanied the offering of well-being (7.11–14). **16–20:** The priests were to have eaten the flesh of the people's sin-offering goat offered on the

azar and Ithamar, Aaron's remaining sons,
and said, 17 "Why did you not eat the sin
offering in the sacred area? For it is most
holy, and God[a] has given it to you that
you may remove the guilt of the congrega-
tion, to make atonement on their behalf be-
fore the LORD. 18 Its blood was not brought
into the inner part of the sanctuary. You
should certainly have eaten it in the sanctu-
ary, as I commanded." 19 And Aaron spoke
to Moses, "See, today they offered their sin
offering and their burnt offering before the
LORD; and yet such things as these have
befallen me! If I had eaten the sin offering
today, would it have been agreeable to the
LORD?" 20 And when Moses heard that, he
agreed.

11 The LORD spoke to Moses and Aar-
on, saying to them: 2 Speak to the
people of Israel, saying:

From among all the land animals, these
are the creatures that you may eat. 3 Any
animal that has divided hoofs and is cleft-
footed and chews the cud—such you may
eat. 4 But among those that chew the cud or
have divided hoofs, you shall not eat the
following: the camel, for even though it
chews the cud, it does not have divided
hoofs; it is unclean for you. 5 The rock bad-
ger, for even though it chews the cud, it
does not have divided hoofs; it is unclean
for you. 6 The hare, for even though it
chews the cud, it does not have divided
hoofs; it is unclean for you. 7 The pig, for
even though it has divided hoofs and is
cleft-footed, it does not chew the cud; it is
unclean for you. 8 Of their flesh you shall
not eat, and their carcasses you shall not
touch; they are unclean for you.

9 These you may eat, of all that are in
the waters. Everything in the waters that
has fins and scales, whether in the seas or in
the streams—such you may eat. 10 But any-
thing in the seas or the streams that does
not have fins and scales, of the swarming
creatures in the waters and among all the
other living creatures that are in the wa-
ters—they are detestable to you 11 and de-
testable they shall remain. Of their flesh
you shall not eat, and their carcasses you
shall regard as detestable. 12 Everything in
the waters that does not have fins and
scales is detestable to you.

13 These you shall regard as detestable
among the birds. They shall not be eaten;
they are an abomination: the eagle, the vul-

a Heb *he*

eighth-day ceremony (9.3,15; cf. 6.24–30n.). Aaron's explanation of their failure to do so is tantalizingly vague, but is apparently accepted by Moses.

11.1–15.33: Impurity rules. These chapters interrupt the narrative flow between chs 10 and 16 (cf. 16.1). They do so to provide legislation pertaining to impurity, a central subject of chs 10 and 16. Cf. 8.1–36n. Chs 11–15, along with Num 19, which is related, deal with cases of natural and often necessary, hence tolerated, impurity, whose basic sources are human and certain animal dead bodies (ch 11; Num 19), normal and abnormal genital discharges (chs 12; 15), and a disease, "surface affliction," often mistranslated as leprosy (chs 13–14). Impurities may also arise from rites that remove these impurities; as such they are only a subsidiary source of impurity (10.10n.). Priestly legislation treats tolerated impurities in a rather abstract fashion, understanding impurity as that condition which is contrary to holiness (10.10n.). A common denominator of most tolerated impurities is a connection with death or threatening life processes. As such, impurity was part of everyday life, though priests were expected to minimize their contact with it. Certain types of impurity, however, were absolutely prohibited; cf. chs 4; 16; 18.24–30n.

11.1–47: Animal impurities and the diet. This chapter details rules against eating certain land, water, and air animals (vv. 2b–23), the impure effect of contact with various animal carcasses (vv. 24–41), and rules against eating small land animals (vv. 41–45). Deut 14.3–21 parallels vv. 2b–23, adding rules from Ex 22.30; 23.19. The permitted diet is limited to land animals with split hooves and that chew the cud (e.g., bovines and ovines), fish that have fins and scales, flying insects with jumping legs, and birds other than those expressly prohibited in the list. Cf. 13.1–46n. Though various rationales have been suggested for the prohibition of particular animals, none is explicit in the text. **39–40:** Though impure, the Israelites

ture, the osprey, 14 the buzzard, the kite of
any kind; 15 every raven of any kind; 16 the
ostrich, the nighthawk, the sea gull, the
hawk of any kind; 17 the little owl, the cor-
morant, the great owl, 18 the water hen, the
desert owl,[a] the carrion vulture, 19 the
stork, the heron of any kind, the hoopoe,
and the bat.[b]
20 All winged insects that walk upon all
fours are detestable to you. 21 But among
the winged insects that walk on all fours
you may eat those that have jointed legs
above their feet, with which to leap on the
ground. 22 Of them you may eat: the locust
according to its kind, the bald locust ac-
cording to its kind, the cricket according to
its kind, and the grasshopper according to
its kind. 23 But all other winged insects that
have four feet are detestable to you.
24 By these you shall become unclean;
whoever touches the carcass of any of them
shall be unclean until the evening, 25 and
whoever carries any part of the carcass of
any of them shall wash his clothes and be
unclean until the evening. 26 Every animal
that has divided hoofs but is not cleft-
footed or does not chew the cud is unclean
for you; everyone who touches one of them
shall be unclean. 27 All that walk on their
paws, among the animals that walk on all
fours, are unclean for you; whoever
touches the carcass of any of them shall be
unclean until the evening, 28 and the one
who carries the carcass shall wash his
clothes and be unclean until the evening;
they are unclean for you.
29 These are unclean for you among the
creatures that swarm upon the earth: the
weasel, the mouse, the great lizard accord-
ing to its kind, 30 the gecko, the land croco-
dile, the lizard, the sand lizard, and the
chameleon. 31 These are unclean for you
among all that swarm; whoever touches
one of them when they are dead shall be
unclean until the evening. 32 And anything
upon which any of them falls when they are
dead shall be unclean, whether an article of
wood or cloth or skin or sacking, any arti-
cle that is used for any purpose; it shall be
dipped into water, and it shall be unclean
until the evening, and then it shall be clean.
33 And if any of them falls into any earthen
vessel, all that is in it shall be unclean, and
you shall break the vessel. 34 Any food that
could be eaten shall be unclean if water
from any such vessel comes upon it; and
any liquid that could be drunk shall be un-
clean if it was in any such vessel. 35 Every-
thing on which any part of the carcass falls
shall be unclean; whether an oven or stove,
it shall be broken in pieces; they are un-
clean, and shall remain unclean for you.
36 But a spring or a cistern holding water
shall be clean, while whatever touches the
carcass in it shall be unclean. 37 If any part
of their carcass falls upon any seed set aside
for sowing, it is clean; 38 but if water is put
on the seed and any part of their carcass
falls on it, it is unclean for you.
39 If an animal of which you may eat
dies, anyone who touches its carcass shall
be unclean until the evening. 40 Those who
eat of its carcass shall wash their clothes
and be unclean until the evening; and those
who carry the carcass shall wash their
clothes and be unclean until the evening.
41 All creatures that swarm upon the
earth are detestable; they shall not be eaten.
42 Whatever moves on its belly, and what-
ever moves on all fours, or whatever has
many feet, all the creatures that swarm
upon the earth, you shall not eat; for they
are detestable. 43 You shall not make your-
selves detestable with any creature that
swarms; you shall not defile yourselves
with them, and so become unclean. 44 For I

a Or *pelican* *b* Identification of several of the birds in verses 13-19 is uncertain

may eat these animals (cf. 17.15–16). Priests may not eat them (22.8). Other legal traditions in the Pentateuch do not make this distinction between priests and non-priests, and prohibit all from eating these animals (Ex 22.30; Deut 14.21). **44–45:** Cf. 20.25–26, which indicates that the dietary laws have a political-symbolic purpose.

am the LORD your God; sanctify yourselves
therefore, and be holy, for I am holy. You
shall not defile yourselves with any swarm-
ing creature that moves on the earth. 45 For
I am the LORD who brought you up from
the land of Egypt, to be your God; you shall
be holy, for I am holy.
46 This is the law pertaining to land ani-
mal and bird and every living creature that
moves through the waters and every crea-
ture that swarms upon the earth, 47 to make
a distinction between the unclean and the
clean, and between the living creature that
may be eaten and the living creature that
may not be eaten.

12 The LORD spoke to Moses, saying:
2 Speak to the people of Israel, say-
ing:
If a woman conceives and bears a male
child, she shall be ceremonially unclean
seven days; as at the time of her menstrua-
tion, she shall be unclean. 3 On the eighth
day the flesh of his foreskin shall be circum-
cised. 4 Her time of blood purification shall
be thirty-three days; she shall not touch any
holy thing, or come into the sanctuary, un-
til the days of her purification are complet-
ed. 5 If she bears a female child, she shall be
unclean two weeks, as in her menstruation;
her time of blood purification shall be
sixty-six days.
6 When the days of her purification are
completed, whether for a son or for a
daughter, she shall bring to the priest at the
entrance of the tent of meeting a lamb in its
first year for a burnt offering, and a pigeon
or a turtledove for a sin offering. 7 He shall
offer it before the LORD, and make atone-
ment on her behalf; then she shall be clean
from her flow of blood. This is the law for
her who bears a child, male or female. 8 If
she cannot afford a sheep, she shall take
two turtledoves or two pigeons, one for a
burnt offering and the other for a sin offer-
ing; and the priest shall make atonement on
her behalf, and she shall be clean.

13 The LORD spoke to Moses and Aar-
on, saying:
2 When a person has on the skin of his
body a swelling or an eruption or a spot,

12.1–8. Childbirth. According to its content this fits better next to ch 15, which concerns genital discharges. It may be placed here because the length of purification is longer than that for surface affliction and abnormal genital discharges (14.1–10; 15.13,19,28). **2–5:** The mother's first stage of impurity is like that of menstrual impurity; she can pollute other common persons and things (cf. 15.19–24). After seven or fourteen days, depending on the gender of the newborn, her impurity is lighter and she can only pollute what is holy, and is therefore restricted from that (cf. 7.20–21; 22.1–9). The double length of impurity for a female child probably has to do with the social position women were viewed as having (cf. 27.2–8; Num 30; 36). **3:** On circumcision, cf. Gen 17.1–27. **6–8:** Even though the woman has not sinned, her impurity has polluted the sanctuary altar (see 4.1–35n.). Hence she must bring a sin/purification offering.

13.1–14.57: Surface affliction. These chapters deal with afflictions of human skin, fabrics, and walls of houses. Because of its appearance on fabrics and walls, because in humans it actually entails several conditions (see below), and because actual leprosy, Hansen's disease, is not clearly attested in the Near East when this text was written, the translation of the Heb term "tsar ʿat" as *leprous* is incorrect. Instead, it should be rendered "surface affliction." These conditions, especially in humans, may have been considered impure because they were unsightly and connected with death (cf. Num 12.9–12).

13.1–46: Surface affliction in humans. Some of the cases described in these verses seem to be unreal, such as the combination of "deepness" and white hair (cf. v. 3) in the same lesion. This may be the result of abstract systematizing on the basis of various real skin diseases. Similar systematizing is found in the criteria for pure animals in 11.2–23. The lesions that can be considered impure include apparently such conditions such as psoriasis, eczema, and fungal infections. Systematizing extends to the literary level. The main cases that deal with possible cases of surface affliction (excluding vv. 9–17, an extension of vv. 2–8) manifest a chiastic or inverted arrangement: A: a lesion on the skin, two possible quarantine periods (vv. 2–8); B: a healing boil, one quarantine period (vv. 18–23); B′: a healing burn, one quarantine period (vv. 24–28); A′: a lesion on the head or in the beard, two possible quarantine periods (vv. 29–37). A similar structure is found in ch 15 (see 15.1–32n.). **38–44:** These verses are mainly concerned to show and it turns into a leprous[a] disease on the skin of his body, he shall be brought to Aaron the priest or to one of his sons the priests. 3 The priest shall examine the disease on the skin of his body, and if the hair in the diseased area has turned white and the disease appears to be deeper than the skin of his body, it is a leprous[a] disease; after the priest has examined him he shall pronounce him ceremonially unclean. 4 But if the spot is white in the skin of his body, and appears no deeper than the skin, and the hair in it has not turned white, the priest shall confine the diseased person for seven days. 5 The priest shall examine him on the seventh day, and if he sees that the disease is checked and the disease has not spread in the skin, then the priest shall confine him seven days more. 6 The priest shall examine him again on the seventh day, and if the disease has abated and the disease has not spread in the skin, the priest shall pronounce him clean; it is only an eruption; and he shall wash his clothes, and be clean. 7 But if the eruption spreads in the skin after he has shown himself to the priest for his cleansing, he shall appear again before the priest. 8 The priest shall make an examination, and if the eruption has spread in the skin, the priest shall pronounce him unclean; it is a leprous[a] disease.

9 When a person contracts a leprous[a] disease, he shall be brought to the priest. 10 The priest shall make an examination, and if there is a white swelling in the skin that has turned the hair white, and there is quick raw flesh in the swelling, 11 it is a chronic leprous[a] disease in the skin of his body. The priest shall pronounce him unclean; he shall not confine him, for he is unclean. 12 But if the disease breaks out in the skin, so that it covers all the skin of the diseased person from head to foot, so far as the priest can see, 13 then the priest shall make an examination, and if the disease has covered all his body, he shall pronounce him clean of the disease; since it has all turned white, he is clean. 14 But if raw flesh ever appears on him, he shall be unclean; 15 the priest shall examine the raw flesh and pronounce him unclean. Raw flesh is unclean, for it is a leprous[a] disease. 16 But if the raw flesh again turns white, he shall come to the priest; 17 the priest shall examine him, and if the disease has turned white, the priest shall pronounce the diseased person clean. He is clean.

18 When there is on the skin of one's body a boil that has healed, 19 and in the place of the boil there appears a white swelling or a reddish-white spot, it shall be shown to the priest. 20 The priest shall make an examination, and if it appears deeper than the skin and its hair has turned white, the priest shall pronounce him unclean; this is a leprous[a] disease, broken out in the boil. 21 But if the priest examines it and the hair on it is not white, nor is it deeper than the skin but has abated, the priest shall confine him seven days. 22 If it spreads in the skin, the priest shall pronounce him unclean; it is diseased. 23 But if the spot remains in one place and does not spread, it is the scar of the boil; the priest shall pronounce him clean.

24 Or, when the body has a burn on the skin and the raw flesh of the burn becomes a spot, reddish-white or white, 25 the priest shall examine it. If the hair in the spot has turned white and it appears deeper than the skin, it is a leprous[a] disease; it has broken out in the burn, and the priest shall pronounce him unclean. This is a leprous[a] disease. 26 But if the priest examines it and the hair in the spot is not white, and it is no deeper than the skin but has abated, the priest shall confine him seven days. 27 The priest shall examine him the seventh day; if it is spreading in the skin, the priest shall pronounce him unclean. This is a leprous[a] disease. 28 But if the spot remains in one place and does not spread in the skin but has abated, it is a swelling from the burn, and the priest shall pronounce him clean; for it is the scar of the burn.

29 When a man or woman has a disease on the head or in the beard, 30 the priest shall examine the disease. If it appears deeper than the skin and the hair in it is

a A term for several skin diseases; precise meaning uncertain

yellow and thin, the priest shall pronounce
him unclean; it is an itch, a leprous[a] dis-
ease of the head or the beard. 31 If the priest
examines the itching disease, and it appears
no deeper than the skin and there is no
black hair in it, the priest shall confine the
person with the itching disease for seven
days. 32 On the seventh day the priest shall
examine the itch; if the itch has not spread,
and there is no yellow hair in it, and the
itch appears to be no deeper than the skin,
33 he shall shave, but the itch he shall not
shave. The priest shall confine the person
with the itch for seven days more. 34 On the
seventh day the priest shall examine the
itch; if the itch has not spread in the skin
and it appears to be no deeper than the
skin, the priest shall pronounce him clean.
He shall wash his clothes and be clean.
35 But if the itch spreads in the skin after he
was pronounced clean, 36 the priest shall
examine him. If the itch has spread in the
skin, the priest need not seek for the yellow
hair; he is unclean. 37 But if in his eyes the
itch is checked, and black hair has grown in
it, the itch is healed, he is clean; and the
priest shall pronounce him clean.

38 When a man or a woman has spots
on the skin of the body, white spots, 39 the
priest shall make an examination, and if the
spots on the skin of the body are of a dull
white, it is a rash that has broken out on
the skin; he is clean.

40 If anyone loses the hair from his
head, he is bald but he is clean. 41 If he loses
the hair from his forehead and temples, he
has baldness of the forehead but he is clean.
42 But if there is on the bald head or the
bald forehead a reddish-white diseased
spot, it is a leprous[a] disease breaking out
on his bald head or his bald forehead.
43 The priest shall examine him; if the dis-
eased swelling is reddish-white on his bald
head or on his bald forehead, which resem-
bles a leprous[a] disease in the skin of the
body, 44 he is leprous,[a] he is unclean. The
priest shall pronounce him unclean; the dis-
ease is on his head.

45 The person who has the leprous[a]
disease shall wear torn clothes and let the
hair of his head be disheveled; and he shall
cover his upper lip and cry out, "Unclean,
unclean." 46 He shall remain unclean as
long as he has the disease; he is unclean. He
shall live alone; his dwelling shall be out-
side the camp.

47 Concerning clothing: when a lep-
rous[a] disease appears in it, in woolen or
linen cloth, 48 in warp or woof of linen or
wool, or in a skin or in anything made of
skin, 49 if the disease shows greenish or red-
dish in the garment, whether in warp or
woof or in skin or in anything made of
skin, it is a leprous[a] disease and shall be
shown to the priest. 50 The priest shall ex-
amine the disease, and put the diseased arti-
cle aside for seven days. 51 He shall examine
the disease on the seventh day. If the dis-
ease has spread in the cloth, in warp or
woof, or in the skin, whatever be the use of
the skin, this is a spreading leprous[a] dis-
ease; it is unclean. 52 He shall burn the
clothing, whether diseased in warp or
woof, woolen or linen, or anything of skin,
for it is a spreading leprous[a] disease; it
shall be burned in fire.

53 If the priest makes an examination,
and the disease has not spread in the cloth-
ing, in warp or woof or in anything of skin,
54 the priest shall command them to wash
the article in which the disease appears, and
he shall put it aside seven days more. 55 The
priest shall examine the diseased article af-

a A term for several skin diseases; precise meaning uncertain

what skin conditions are not surface affliction. They supplement the main section in vv. 2–37. **45–46:** Other texts suggest that this legislation concerning the exclusion of surface-afflicted people from the habitation was carried out; cf. Num 5.1–4n.; 12.14–15; 2 Kings 7.3–10; 15.5; 2 Chr 26.21; Lk 17.12.

13.47–59: Surface affliction in fabrics. The legislation is set out in a way similar to the discussion of human surface affliction, with use of similar terminology, inspections, quarantine periods, and washings. It thus displays the systematization of priestly thinking (see 13.1–46n.). The surface affliction includes various forms of mold, fungus, and mildew.

ter it has been washed. If the diseased spot
has not changed color, though the disease
has not spread, it is unclean; you shall burn
it in fire, whether the leprous[a] spot is on
the inside or on the outside.
56 If the priest makes an examination,
and the disease has abated after it is
washed, he shall tear the spot out of the
cloth, in warp or woof, or out of skin. 57 If
it appears again in the garment, in warp or
woof, or in anything of skin, it is spreading;
you shall burn with fire that in which the
disease appears. 58 But the cloth, warp or
woof, or anything of skin from which the
disease disappears when you have washed
it, shall then be washed a second time, and
it shall be clean.
59 This is the ritual for a leprous[a] dis-
ease in a cloth of wool or linen, either in
warp or woof, or in anything of skin, to
decide whether it is clean or unclean.

14 The LORD spoke to Moses, saying:
2 This shall be the ritual for the lep-
rous[a] person at the time of his cleansing:
He shall be brought to the priest; 3 the
priest shall go out of the camp, and the
priest shall make an examination. If the dis-
ease is healed in the leprous[a] person, 4 the
priest shall command that two living clean
birds and cedarwood and crimson yarn and
hyssop be brought for the one who is to be
cleansed. 5 The priest shall command that
one of the birds be slaughtered over fresh
water in an earthen vessel. 6 He shall take
the living bird with the cedarwood and the
crimson yarn and the hyssop, and dip them
and the living bird in the blood of the bird
that was slaughtered over the fresh water.
7 He shall sprinkle it seven times upon the
one who is to be cleansed of the leprous[a]
disease; then he shall pronounce him clean,
and he shall let the living bird go into the
open field. 8 The one who is to be cleansed
shall wash his clothes, and shave off all his
hair, and bathe himself in water, and he
shall be clean. After that he shall come into
the camp, but shall live outside his tent sev-
en days. 9 On the seventh day he shall shave
all his hair: of head, beard, eyebrows; he
shall shave all his hair. Then he shall wash
his clothes, and bathe his body in water,
and he shall be clean.
10 On the eighth day he shall take two
male lambs without blemish, and one ewe
lamb in its first year without blemish, and
a grain offering of three-tenths of an ephah
of choice flour mixed with oil, and one
log[b] of oil. 11 The priest who cleanses shall
set the person to be cleansed, along with
these things, before the LORD, at the en-
trance of the tent of meeting. 12 The priest
shall take one of the lambs, and offer it as
a guilt offering, along with the log[b] of oil,
and raise them as an elevation offering be-
fore the LORD. 13 He shall slaughter the
lamb in the place where the sin offering and
the burnt offering are slaughtered in the
holy place; for the guilt offering, like the sin
offering, belongs to the priest: it is most
holy. 14 The priest shall take some of the
blood of the guilt offering and put it on
the lobe of the right ear of the one to be
cleansed, and on the thumb of the right

a A term for several skin diseases; precise meaning uncertain *b* A liquid measure

14.1–32: Purifying after recovery. The rites here do not heal, only purify after recovery by other means (contrast 2 Kings 5.10–14). **4–7:** The same rite is found in vv. 49–53 for houses. Like the goat sent to Azazel in 16.21–22, the bird carries the impurity away. **4:** Many of the materials in this verse (cf. Num 19.6) probably have symbolic significance. Cedar wood may signify the lack of decay. Crimson yarn may be associated with blood, which is a purifying detergent, though it also may have been used for tying the materials together. Hyssop is a small wild shrub whose branches were used as a ritual brush or aspergillum (sprinkler) for applying liquids in rituals (Ex 12.22; Job 9.19). In Ps 51.7, it carries a connotation of purification (perhaps because of its use in rites such as the one described here). **5–7:** The blood removes impurity as does the blood of the sin offering (see ch 4). **10–20:** While the individual's person is apparently pure, his or her impurity has affected the sanctuary, so it must be purged with sacrifices (see 4.1–35n.). **10:** *Ephah,* see 5.11n. *Log,* about .3 l (11 oz). **12:** *Elevation offering,* see Num 18.11n. **14–17:** Cf. 8.23–24. The application of blood and oil helps to lead the person from impure to pure status.

hand, and on the big toe of the right foot.
15 The priest shall take some of the log[a] of
oil and pour it into the palm of his own left
hand, 16 and dip his right finger in the oil
that is in his left hand and sprinkle some
oil with his finger seven times before the
LORD. 17 Some of the oil that remains in his
hand the priest shall put on the lobe of the
right ear of the one to be cleansed, and on
the thumb of the right hand, and on the big
toe of the right foot, on top of the blood of
the guilt offering. 18 The rest of the oil that
is in the priest's hand he shall put on the
head of the one to be cleansed. Then the
priest shall make atonement on his behalf
before the LORD: 19 the priest shall offer the
sin offering, to make atonement for the one
to be cleansed from his uncleanness. After-
ward he shall slaughter the burnt offering;
20 and the priest shall offer the burnt offer-
ing and the grain offering on the altar. Thus
the priest shall make atonement on his be-
half and he shall be clean.

21 But if he is poor and cannot afford so
much, he shall take one male lamb for a
guilt offering to be elevated, to make atone-
ment on his behalf, and one-tenth of an
ephah of choice flour mixed with oil for a
grain offering and a log[a] of oil; 22 also two
turtledoves or two pigeons, such as he can
afford, one for a sin offering and the other
for a burnt offering. 23 On the eighth day he
shall bring them for his cleansing to the
priest, to the entrance of the tent of meet-
ing, before the LORD; 24 and the priest shall
take the lamb of the guilt offering and the
log[a] of oil, and the priest shall raise them
as an elevation offering before the LORD.
25 The priest shall slaughter the lamb of the
guilt offering and shall take some of the
blood of the guilt offering, and put it on
the lobe of the right ear of the one to be
cleansed, and on the thumb of the right
hand, and on the big toe of the right foot.
26 The priest shall pour some of the oil into
the palm of his own left hand, 27 and shall
sprinkle with his right finger some of the oil
that is in his left hand seven times before
the LORD. 28 The priest shall put some of
the oil that is in his hand on the lobe of the
right ear of the one to be cleansed, and on
the thumb of the right hand, and the big toe
of the right foot, where the blood of the
guilt offering was placed. 29 The rest of the
oil that is in the priest's hand he shall put
on the head of the one to be cleansed, to
make atonement on his behalf before the
LORD. 30 And he shall offer, of the turtle-
doves or pigeons such as he can afford,
31 one[b] for a sin offering and the other for
a burnt offering, along with a grain offer-
ing; and the priest shall make atonement
before the LORD on behalf of the one being
cleansed. 32 This is the ritual for the one
who has a leprous[c] disease, who cannot
afford the offerings for his cleansing.

33 The LORD spoke to Moses and Aar-
on, saying:

34 When you come into the land of Ca-
naan, which I give you for a possession,
and I put a leprous[c] disease in a house in
the land of your possession, 35 the owner of
the house shall come and tell the priest, say-
ing, "There seems to me to be some sort of
disease in my house." 36 The priest shall
command that they empty the house before
the priest goes to examine the disease, or all
that is in the house will become unclean;
and afterward the priest shall go in to in-
spect the house. 37 He shall examine the dis-
ease; if the disease is in the walls of the
house with greenish or reddish spots, and if
it appears to be deeper than the surface,
38 the priest shall go outside to the door of

a A liquid measure *b* Gk Syr: Heb *afford, 31such as he can afford, one* *c* A term for several skin diseases; precise meaning uncertain

21–32: As in other cases (see ch 1), provisions are made so that all, including the poor, may perform the necessary ritual.

14.33–53: Surface affliction in houses. 34: *I put,* surface affliction, both in houses, such as a fungus, and especially in humans, is thought to be God's punishment (Num 12.10; Deut 28.27,35; 2 Sam 3.29; 2 Kings 5.26–27, 2 Chr 26.16–21). **36:** The house is only impure when the priest declares it so. Hence, removal of household effects before inspection saves them from becoming impure. **40–41,45:** Disposal

the house and shut up the house seven days.
39 The priest shall come again on the sev-
enth day and make an inspection; if the dis-
ease has spread in the walls of the house,
40 the priest shall command that the stones
in which the disease appears be taken out
and thrown into an unclean place outside
the city. 41 He shall have the inside of the
house scraped thoroughly, and the plaster
that is scraped off shall be dumped in an
unclean place outside the city. 42 They shall
take other stones and put them in the place
of those stones, and take other plaster and
plaster the house.

43 If the disease breaks out again in the
house, after he has taken out the stones and
scraped the house and plastered it, 44 the
priest shall go and make inspection; if the
disease has spread in the house, it is a
spreading leprous[a] disease in the house; it
is unclean. 45 He shall have the house torn
down, its stones and timber and all the
plaster of the house, and taken outside the
city to an unclean place. 46 All who enter
the house while it is shut up shall be un-
clean until the evening; 47 and all who sleep
in the house shall wash their clothes; and
all who eat in the house shall wash their
clothes.

48 If the priest comes and makes an in-
spection, and the disease has not spread in
the house after the house was plastered, the
priest shall pronounce the house clean; the
disease is healed. 49 For the cleansing of the
house he shall take two birds, with cedar-
wood and crimson yarn and hyssop, 50 and
shall slaughter one of the birds over fresh
water in an earthen vessel, 51 and shall take
the cedarwood and the hyssop and the
crimson yarn, along with the living bird,
and dip them in the blood of the slaugh-
tered bird and the fresh water, and sprinkle
the house seven times. 52 Thus he shall
cleanse the house with the blood of the
bird, and with the fresh water, and with the
living bird, and with the cedarwood and
hyssop and crimson yarn; 53 and he shall let
the living bird go out of the city into the
open field; so he shall make atonement for
the house, and it shall be clean.

54 This is the ritual for any leprous[a]
disease: for an itch, 55 for leprous[a] diseases
in clothing and houses, 56 and for a swelling
or an eruption or a spot, 57 to determine
when it is unclean and when it is clean. This
is the ritual for leprous[a] diseases.

15 The LORD spoke to Moses and Aar-
on, saying: 2 Speak to the people of
Israel and say to them:

When any man has a discharge from his
member,[b] his discharge makes him cere-
monially unclean. 3 The uncleanness of his
discharge is this: whether his member[b]
flows with his discharge, or his member[b] is
stopped from discharging, it is uncleanness
for him. 4 Every bed on which the one with
the discharge lies shall be unclean; and ev-
erything on which he sits shall be unclean.
5 Anyone who touches his bed shall wash
his clothes, and bathe in water, and be un-
clean until the evening. 6 All who sit on any-
thing on which the one with the discharge
has sat shall wash their clothes, and bathe
in water, and be unclean until the evening.
7 All who touch the body of the one with

a A term for several skin diseases; precise meaning uncertain *b* Heb *flesh*

outside the city parallels the exclusion of surface-afflicted humans outside the camp (13.45–46). **48–53:** See 14.4–7n. **54–57:** A typical Priestly conclusion formula to both chapters, though the items in the summary are ordered differently from the chapters.

15.1–32: Sexual discharges. The chapter has a chiastic or inverted structure: A: abnormal male discharge (vv. 2–15); B: normal male discharge (vv. 16–18); B′: normal female discharge (vv. 19–24); A′: abnormal female discharge (vv. 25–30). See 13.1–46n. The impurity of blood at childbirth is dealt with in ch 12 (see 12.1–8n.). Sexual fluxes may have been considered impure because they involve both the loss of life fluids and sexuality, a matter of shame and mystery in many societies. **2–3:** This probably refers to a purulent discharge due to urethral infection. **3:** *Stopped,* this may refer to an inability to urinate because of swelling from urethritis. **4–12:** The impurity is communicated to any person or object that has had contact with the man with the discharge. **13:** As with surface affliction, the purification rite is

the discharge shall wash their clothes, and
bathe in water, and be unclean until the
evening. 8 If the one with the discharge spits
on persons who are clean, then they shall
wash their clothes, and bathe in water, and
be unclean until the evening. 9 Any saddle
on which the one with the discharge rides
shall be unclean. 10 All who touch anything
that was under him shall be unclean until
the evening, and all who carry such a thing
shall wash their clothes, and bathe in wa-
ter, and be unclean until the evening. 11 All
those whom the one with the discharge
touches without his having rinsed his hands
in water shall wash their clothes, and bathe
in water, and be unclean until the evening.
12 Any earthen vessel that the one with the
discharge touches shall be broken; and ev-
ery vessel of wood shall be rinsed in water.

13 When the one with a discharge is
cleansed of his discharge, he shall count
seven days for his cleansing; he shall wash
his clothes and bathe his body in fresh wa-
ter, and he shall be clean. 14 On the eighth
day he shall take two turtledoves or two
pigeons and come before the LORD to the
entrance of the tent of meeting and give
them to the priest. 15 The priest shall offer
them, one for a sin offering and the other
for a burnt offering; and the priest shall
make atonement on his behalf before the
LORD for his discharge.

16 If a man has an emission of semen, he
shall bathe his whole body in water, and
be unclean until the evening. 17 Everything
made of cloth or of skin on which the se-
men falls shall be washed with water, and
be unclean until the evening. 18 If a man lies
with a woman and has an emission of se-
men, both of them shall bathe in water, and
be unclean until the evening.

19 When a woman has a discharge of
blood that is her regular discharge from her
body, she shall be in her impurity for seven
days, and whoever touches her shall be un-
clean until the evening. 20 Everything upon
which she lies during her impurity shall be
unclean; everything also upon which she
sits shall be unclean. 21 Whoever touches
her bed shall wash his clothes, and bathe in
water, and be unclean until the evening.
22 Whoever touches anything upon which
she sits shall wash his clothes, and bathe in
water, and be unclean until the evening;
23 whether it is the bed or anything upon
which she sits, when he touches it he shall
be unclean until the evening. 24 If any man
lies with her, and her impurity falls on him,
he shall be unclean seven days; and every
bed on which he lies shall be unclean.

25 If a woman has a discharge of blood
for many days, not at the time of her impu-
rity, or if she has a discharge beyond the
time of her impurity, all the days of the
discharge she shall continue in uncleanness;
as in the days of her impurity, she shall be
unclean. 26 Every bed on which she lies dur-
ing all the days of her discharge shall be
treated as the bed of her impurity; and ev-
erything on which she sits shall be unclean,
as in the uncleanness of her impurity.
27 Whoever touches these things shall be
unclean, and shall wash his clothes, and
bathe in water, and be unclean until the
evening. 28 If she is cleansed of her dis-
charge, she shall count seven days, and af-
ter that she shall be clean. 29 On the eighth
day she shall take two turtledoves or two
pigeons and bring them to the priest at
the entrance of the tent of meeting. 30 The
priest shall offer one for a sin offering and
the other for a burnt offering; and the priest

performed after recovery (14.1–32n.; cf. 5.7–10). **16–18:** These verses stand in the middle of the chapter, joining the section focusing on men with that focusing on women. Intercourse by itself is not defiling, only semen is. **19–24:** In the structure of the chapter, regular menstruation here parallels a seminal emission in a male (see 15.1–32n.). But its impurity is greater, similar to that in the cases of abnormal male and female flows (vv. 4–12,25–27). The prophets could thus use menstrual impurity as a strong, negative image (e.g., Ezek 36.17). No rules for purification are given; it must be assumed that the woman bathes and launders on the seventh day, and waits until evening (2 Sam 11.2,4; cf. Num 19.19). **25–30:** The polluting force of an irregular blood flow is the same as in normal menstruation (vv. 19–24), but unlike it, purification requires sacrifices, as in the case of a male with an abnormal discharge (vv. 13–15).

shall make atonement on her behalf before
the LORD for her unclean discharge.
31 Thus you shall keep the people of
Israel separate from their uncleanness, so
that they do not die in their uncleanness by
defiling my tabernacle that is in their midst.
32 This is the ritual for those who have
a discharge: for him who has an emission of
semen, becoming unclean thereby, 33 for
her who is in the infirmity of her period, for
anyone, male or female, who has a dis-
charge, and for the man who lies with a
woman who is unclean.

16 The LORD spoke to Moses after the
death of the two sons of Aaron,
when they drew near before the LORD and
died. 2 The LORD said to Moses:
Tell your brother Aaron not to come just
at any time into the sanctuary inside the
curtain before the mercy seat[a] that is upon
the ark, or he will die; for I appear in the
cloud upon the mercy seat.[a] 3 Thus shall
Aaron come into the holy place: with a
young bull for a sin offering and a ram for
a burnt offering. 4 He shall put on the holy
linen tunic, and shall have the linen under-
garments next to his body, fasten the linen
sash, and wear the linen turban; these are
the holy vestments. He shall bathe his body
in water, and then put them on. 5 He shall
take from the congregation of the people of
Israel two male goats for a sin offering, and
one ram for a burnt offering.
6 Aaron shall offer the bull as a sin
offering for himself, and shall make atone-
ment for himself and for his house. 7 He
shall take the two goats and set them before
the LORD at the entrance of the tent of
meeting; 8 and Aaron shall cast lots on the
two goats, one lot for the LORD and the
other lot for Azazel.[b] 9 Aaron shall present
the goat on which the lot fell for the LORD,
and offer it as a sin offering; 10 but the goat
on which the lot fell for Azazel[b] shall be
presented alive before the LORD to make
atonement over it, that it may be sent away
into the wilderness to Azazel.[b]
11 Aaron shall present the bull as a sin
offering for himself, and shall make atone-
ment for himself and for his house; he shall
slaughter the bull as a sin offering for him-
self. 12 He shall take a censer full of coals of
fire from the altar before the LORD, and
two handfuls of crushed sweet incense, and

a Or *the cover* *b* Traditionally rendered *a scapegoat*

16.1–34: The Day of Atonement. In its present context this chapter describes an annual sanctuary purification rite that occurs every fall, on the tenth day of the seventh month (September-October), accompanied by the people's fasting (v. 29; 23.26–32). It may have originally been a sanctuary purification rite, not connected to a particular day nor requiring fasting (16.29–34 are not original to the chapter, and are part of the Holiness tradition found mainly in chs 17–26). Thus it makes sense that the ceremony, in vv. 1–28, is prescribed immediately after, and contains a reference to, the death of Aaron's sons in Lev 10.1–7 (cf. 16.1; see 11.1–15.33n.; Num 7.1–89n.). The sanctuary needed purification because the priests' corpses had polluted it (cf. Lev 10.4–5; Num 19). Cf. Ezek 45.18–20. **2:** *Mercy seat,* see Ex 25.17–22n. *Cloud,* see Ex 40.34–38n. **3:** 4.3. **4:** See 8.6–7. **6–19:** The primary goal of the sin offering is to achieve "atonement" (Heb "kipper"; cf. the noun "kippûr," "atonement," as in the later Jewish term for the occasion, "Yom Kippur," based on a similar term in 23.27–28; 25.9). With the sin/purification offering, the Heb verb refers to the removal of impurity from certain sanctuary furniture and locales caused by sin and severe personal pollution (Ex 30.10; Lev 6.23; 8.15; 16.16,18,20,27,33; cf. Ezek 43.20, 26; 45.20; see Lev 4.1–35n.). The focus of the chapter is thus on the purification of the sanctuary, not, as in later times, on repentance of the individual. "Kipper" should therefore be translated as "purify" or "make purification on behalf of." When used in a summary fashion in sacrificial contexts, the term appears to indicate that all negative effects of the sin or personal pollution have been resolved, and thus carries the notion of "appeasement" (Num 17.11; 25.13; cf. Ex 30.15–16; Lev 17.11; Num 31.50). Other sacrifices, except for the well-being offering, may also achieve atonement (the burnt offering, Lev 1.4; cf. 14.31; 15.15; Num 6.11; the guilt offering, Lev 5.16; 14.21; 19.22; Num 5.8). **7:** *Tent of meeting,* see 1.1n. **8:** *Azazel,* meaning "angry/fierce god," probably a demonic figure (cf. 17.7), in contrast to the LORD, i.e., Yahweh. This is the "scapegoat" of older translations. **16:** The first part of the verse might

he shall bring it inside the curtain 13 and put
the incense on the fire before the LORD,
that the cloud of the incense may cover the
mercy seat[a] that is upon the covenant,[b] or
he will die. 14 He shall take some of the
blood of the bull, and sprinkle it with his
finger on the front of the mercy seat,[a] and
before the mercy seat[a] he shall sprinkle the
blood with his finger seven times.
15 He shall slaughter the goat of the sin
offering that is for the people and bring its
blood inside the curtain, and do with its
blood as he did with the blood of the bull,
sprinkling it upon the mercy seat[a] and be-
fore the mercy seat.[a] 16 Thus he shall make
atonement for the sanctuary, because of the
uncleannesses of the people of Israel, and
because of their transgressions, all their
sins; and so he shall do for the tent of meet-
ing, which remains with them in the midst
of their uncleannesses. 17 No one shall be in
the tent of meeting from the time he enters
to make atonement in the sanctuary until
he comes out and has made atonement for
himself and for his house and for all the
assembly of Israel. 18 Then he shall go out
to the altar that is before the LORD and
make atonement on its behalf, and shall
take some of the blood of the bull and of
the blood of the goat, and put it on each of
the horns of the altar. 19 He shall sprinkle
some of the blood on it with his finger sev-
en times, and cleanse it and hallow it from
the uncleannesses of the people of Israel.
20 When he has finished atoning for the
holy place and the tent of meeting and the
altar, he shall present the live goat. 21 Then
Aaron shall lay both his hands on the head
of the live goat, and confess over it all the
iniquities of the people of Israel, and all
their transgressions, all their sins, putting
them on the head of the goat, and sending
it away into the wilderness by means of
someone designated for the task.[c] 22 The
goat shall bear on itself all their iniquities
to a barren region; and the goat shall be set
free in the wilderness.
23 Then Aaron shall enter the tent of
meeting, and shall take off the linen vest-
ments that he put on when he went into the
holy place, and shall leave them there. 24 He
shall bathe his body in water in a holy
place, and put on his vestments; then he
shall come out and offer his burnt offering
and the burnt offering of the people, mak-
ing atonement for himself and for the peo-
ple. 25 The fat of the sin offering he shall
turn into smoke on the altar. 26 The one
who sets the goat free for Azazel[d] shall
wash his clothes and bathe his body in wa-
ter, and afterward may come into the
camp. 27 The bull of the sin offering and the
goat of the sin offering, whose blood was
brought in to make atonement in the holy
place, shall be taken outside the camp; their
skin and their flesh and their dung shall be

a Or *the cover* *b* Or *treaty*, or *testament*; Heb *eduth*
c Meaning of Heb uncertain *d* Traditionally
rendered *a scapegoat*

be alternatively rendered: "Thus shall he purify the sanctuary from the impurities of the people of Israel and from their rebellious acts, including all their sins." On rebellious acts, i.e., deliberate sins, in the scheme of the sin offering system, see 4.1–35n.; cf. Num 15.30–31n. *And so he shall do for the tent of meeting,* now that the inner room of the tent has been purified (vv. 11–16a), its outer room is purified. The procedure is not spelled out, but is probably similar to that in 4.5–7,16–18 (cf. Ex 30.10). **18–19:** The open-air altar, a third locale of the sanctuary area, is here purified. *Horns,* see Ex 27.2n. **21:** *Both his hands,* this gesture transfers sins to the head of the scapegoat (cf. 24.14; Num 27.18,23, where apparently two hands are used for transfer). This differs in form and meaning from the one-handed gesture that precedes the slaughtering of sacrificial animals (see 1.4; 3.2; 4.4; this gesture is not found with birds or grain offerings), which may seek to identify the animal as belonging to the offerer who brings it (cf. Num 8.5–26n.). This scapegoat ritual is somewhat redundant with the earlier purification rituals, but the purity of the sanctuary was so significant that redundancy was sensible. Though the goat to Azazel is part of a purgation offering complex (cf. Lev 16.5), it is not sacrificed or killed according to the biblical text, though further development of this ritual in early rabbinic literature assured that the scapegoat would die, so it could not return with the sins. **29,31:** *Deny yourselves,* in addition to abstaining from

consumed in fire. 28The one who burns
them shall wash his clothes and bathe his
body in water, and afterward may come
into the camp.
29 This shall be a statute to you forever:
In the seventh month, on the tenth day of
the month, you shall deny yourselves,[a] and
shall do no work, neither the citizen nor the
alien who resides among you. 30For on this
day atonement shall be made for you, to
cleanse you; from all your sins you shall be
clean before the LORD. 31It is a sabbath of
complete rest to you, and you shall deny
yourselves;[a] it is a statute forever. 32The
priest who is anointed and consecrated as
priest in his father's place shall make atone-
ment, wearing the linen vestments, the holy
vestments. 33He shall make atonement for
the sanctuary, and he shall make atone-
ment for the tent of meeting and for the
altar, and he shall make atonement for the
priests and for all the people of the assem-
bly. 34This shall be an everlasting statute
for you, to make atonement for the people
of Israel once in the year for all their sins.
And Moses did as the LORD had command-
ed him.

17 The LORD spoke to Moses:
2 Speak to Aaron and his sons and
to all the people of Israel and say to them:
This is what the LORD has commanded. 3If
anyone of the house of Israel slaughters an
ox or a lamb or a goat in the camp, or
slaughters it outside the camp, 4and does
not bring it to the entrance of the tent of
meeting, to present it as an offering to the
LORD before the tabernacle of the LORD, he
shall be held guilty of bloodshed; he has
shed blood, and he shall be cut off from the
people. 5This is in order that the people of
Israel may bring their sacrifices that they
offer in the open field, that they may bring
them to the LORD, to the priest at the en-
trance of the tent of meeting, and offer
them as sacrifices of well-being to the
LORD. 6The priest shall dash the blood
against the altar of the LORD at the en-
trance of the tent of meeting, and turn the
fat into smoke as a pleasing odor to the
LORD, 7so that they may no longer offer
their sacrifices for goat-demons, to whom
they prostitute themselves. This shall be a
statute forever to them throughout their
generations.
8 And say to them further: Anyone of
the house of Israel or of the aliens who re-
side among them who offers a burnt offer-
ing or sacrifice, 9and does not bring it to
the entrance of the tent of meeting, to sacri-
fice it to the LORD, shall be cut off from the
people.
10 If anyone of the house of Israel or of

a Or *shall fast*

food and anointing (Dan 10.12), sexual intercourse may be prohibited (2 Sam 12.15–24). These verses derive from the Holiness School (see Introduction), which viewed Yom Kippur in terms that are broader than the Priestly Torah described in vv. 1–28.

17.1–16: Slaughter at the sanctuary. Chs 1–16 in large part dealt with sacrificial matters. This chapter, which introduces the Holiness Collection (chs 17–26; see Introduction), augments these chapters by giving the requirement that sacrifices be offered only at the tent of meeting. **3–4:** Slaughtering of all sacrificial animals is to be done at the sanctuary. Contrast Deut 12.15–28, which allows for slaughter of these animals (not as sacrifices) outside the sanctuary (also Num 19.9n.). If the chapter implicitly allows for the existence of multiple sanctuaries, or if the prescriptions are formulated with only the wilderness situation with a single central sanctuary in view, the apparent stricture of ch 17 may be avoided. The tenor of the chapter, however, suggests there is only one legitimate sanctuary. **4:** The idea that illicit killing of animals brings blood guilt is used to enforce sanctuary slaughter. Cf. Gen 9.5–6. **5:** *Sacrifices,* i.e., well-being sacrifices (ch 3; 7.11–36). The reason this offering, as opposed to other types from chs 1–7, is singled out is probably because this sacrifice was used to allow meat to be eaten, so the individual might think it need not be brought to the sanctuary. The blood prohibitions in vv. 10–14 have well-being offerings mainly in mind. **6:** *Pleasing odor,* see 1.9n. **7:** *Goat-demons,* cf. 16.8n.; 2 Chr 11.15; Isa 13.21; 34.14. Prostitution is a frequent metaphor for idolatry. **10–14:** Blood is prohibited since it is seen as the animating force of the animals (vv. 11,14; cf. Gen 9.4; Deut 12.23). Once it is removed the flesh may be

the aliens who reside among them eats any
blood, I will set my face against that person
who eats blood, and will cut that person off
from the people. 11 For the life of the flesh
is in the blood; and I have given it to you
for making atonement for your lives on the
altar; for, as life, it is the blood that makes
atonement. 12 Therefore I have said to the
people of Israel: No person among you
shall eat blood, nor shall any alien who re-
sides among you eat blood. 13 And anyone
of the people of Israel, or of the aliens who
reside among them, who hunts down an
animal or bird that may be eaten shall pour
out its blood and cover it with earth.

14 For the life of every creature—its
blood is its life; therefore I have said to the
people of Israel: You shall not eat the blood
of any creature, for the life of every crea-
ture is its blood; whoever eats it shall be cut
off. 15 All persons, citizens or aliens, who
eat what dies of itself or what has been torn
by wild animals, shall wash their clothes,
and bathe themselves in water, and be un-
clean until the evening; then they shall be
clean. 16 But if they do not wash themselves
or bathe their body, they shall bear their
guilt.

18 The LORD spoke to Moses, saying:
2 Speak to the people of Israel and
say to them: I am the LORD your God.
3 You shall not do as they do in the land of
Egypt, where you lived, and you shall not
do as they do in the land of Canaan, to
which I am bringing you. You shall not
follow their statutes. 4 My ordinances you
shall observe and my statutes you shall
keep, following them: I am the LORD your
God. 5 You shall keep my statutes and my
ordinances; by doing so one shall live: I am
the LORD.

6 None of you shall approach anyone
near of kin to uncover nakedness: I am the
LORD. 7 You shall not uncover the naked-
ness of your father, which is the nakedness
of your mother; she is your mother, you
shall not uncover her nakedness. 8 You
shall not uncover the nakedness of your fa-
ther's wife; it is the nakedness of your fa-
ther. 9 You shall not uncover the nakedness
of your sister, your father's daughter or
your mother's daughter, whether born at
home or born abroad. 10 You shall not un-
cover the nakedness of your son's daughter
or of your daughter's daughter, for their
nakedness is your own nakedness. 11 You
shall not uncover the nakedness of your fa-
ther's wife's daughter, begotten by your fa-
ther, since she is your sister. 12 You shall
not uncover the nakedness of your father's
sister; she is your father's flesh. 13 You shall
not uncover the nakedness of your moth-
er's sister, for she is your mother's flesh.
14 You shall not uncover the nakedness of
your father's brother, that is, you shall not
approach his wife; she is your aunt. 15 You
shall not uncover the nakedness of your
daughter-in-law: she is your son's wife; you
shall not uncover her nakedness. 16 You
shall not uncover the nakedness of your

eaten. **11:** Placing blood on the altar ransoms (Heb "kipper") the offerer from shedding the animal's blood (cf. v. 4). Compare the payment of a ransom in Ex 30.11–16 and Num 31.48–50 to appease divine wrath. See also 16.6–19n. **13:** Game animals may be eaten in nonsacrificial contexts; cf. Deut 12.16,24. **15–16:** The eating of these is not prohibited; cf. 11.39–40n.

18.1–30: Sexual prohibitions. 1–5: The introduction is structured similarly to the conclusion (vv. 24–30), with a general prohibition followed by an admonition. **6–23:** These laws prohibit various cases of incestuous relationships, intercourse with a menstruating wife, adultery, male homosexuality, and intercourse with animals. The incest laws prohibit intercourse with mothers and aunts, sisters of any type, daughters, and granddaughters. 20.10–21 enumerates punishments. Cf. Deut 27.15–26; Ezek 22.7–12. In Lev 18 blood relatives are listed first (vv. 6–13), then those related by marriage (vv. 14–18), then other cases (vv. 19–23). **6:** This general introduction covers relations with any close family member not explicitly stated in the following (e.g., one's own daughter; a full sister). *Nakedness* refers specifically to the genitals; to *uncover nakedness* was a euphemism for sexual intercourse. **7–8:** Cf. Reuben and Bilhah, Gen 35.22; 49.4. **9,11:** Cf. Abraham and Sarah, Gen 20.12; Amnon and Tamar, 2 Sam 13.13. **10:** Cf. Lot and his daughters, Gen 19.30–38. **15:** Cf. Judah and Tamar, Gen 38. **16:** Contrast the levirate marriage law

brother's wife; it is your brother's naked-
ness. 17 You shall not uncover the naked-
ness of a woman and her daughter, and you
shall not take[a] her son's daughter or her
daughter's daughter to uncover her naked-
ness; they are your[b] flesh; it is depravity.
18 And you shall not take[a] a woman as a
rival to her sister, uncovering her naked-
ness while her sister is still alive.

19 You shall not approach a woman to
uncover her nakedness while she is in her
menstrual uncleanness. 20 You shall not
have sexual relations with your kinsman's
wife, and defile yourself with her. 21 You
shall not give any of your offspring to sacri-
fice them[c] to Molech, and so profane the
name of your God: I am the LORD. 22 You
shall not lie with a male as with a woman;
it is an abomination. 23 You shall not have
sexual relations with any animal and defile
yourself with it, nor shall any woman give
herself to an animal to have sexual rela-
tions with it: it is perversion.

24 Do not defile yourselves in any of
these ways, for by all these practices the
nations I am casting out before you have
defiled themselves. 25 Thus the land became
defiled; and I punished it for its iniquity,
and the land vomited out its inhabitants.
26 But you shall keep my statutes and my
ordinances and commit none of these
abominations, either the citizen or the alien
who resides among you 27 (for the inhabi-
tants of the land, who were before you,
committed all of these abominations, and
the land became defiled); 28 otherwise the
land will vomit you out for defiling it, as
it vomited out the nation that was before
you. 29 For whoever commits any of these
abominations shall be cut off from their
people. 30 So keep my charge not to commit
any of these abominations that were done
before you, and not to defile yourselves by
them: I am the LORD your God.

19 The LORD spoke to Moses, saying:
2 Speak to all the congregation of
the people of Israel and say to them: You
shall be holy, for I the LORD your God am
holy. 3 You shall each revere your mother
and father, and you shall keep my sab-
baths: I am the LORD your God. 4 Do not
turn to idols or make cast images for your-
selves: I am the LORD your God.

5 When you offer a sacrifice of well-
being to the LORD, offer it in such a way
that it is acceptable in your behalf. 6 It shall
be eaten on the same day you offer it, or on
the next day; and anything left over until
the third day shall be consumed in fire. 7 If
it is eaten at all on the third day, it is an
abomination; it will not be acceptable. 8 All
who eat it shall be subject to punishment,
because they have profaned what is holy to
the LORD; and any such person shall be cut
off from the people.

9 When you reap the harvest of your
land, you shall not reap to the very edges of
your field, or gather the gleanings of your
harvest. 10 You shall not strip your vine-

a Or *marry* *b* Gk: Heb lacks *your* *c* Heb *to pass them over*

in Deut 25.5–10. **19:** Cf. 15.24,33. **20:** Cf. Deut 22.22–29. **21:** *Molech,* a Canaanite deity associated with child sacrifice; see 20.2–5n. This prohibition may have been included here because it involved the abuse of family members. **22:** Cf. Gen 19.4–11; Judg 19.22–30. **23:** Cf. Ex 22.18; Deut 27.21. **24–30:** For crimes and sins polluting the land, see Num 35.33–34; Isa 24.5–7; Ezek 22.24; Ezra 9.11. These impurities are fundamentally different from the impurities noted in 11.1–15.33 (see note there). Punishment for sinful impurity is often exile or other destruction (Isa 64.4–11; Ezek 20.38; 22.2–16; 39.23–24; cf. Lev 26.33–39).

19.1–37: Various laws. Many of these laws display ethical concerns. **2:** The people become holy by keeping God's commandments (11.44–45; 20.7–8,24–26; Num 15.40–41). Cf. Ex 19.6; Deut 14.2,21; 26.19; 28.6. The "Holiness School" and "Holiness Collection" (see Introduction) derive their names from this verse. **3–4:** Cf. the Decalogue, Ex 20.12,8–11,2–6. Some have suggested that the Decalogue is elsewhere reflected in this chapter. **5–8:** Cf. 7.15–18. In contrast to the earlier Priestly Torah treatment of sacrifices at the beginning of Leviticus, the focus here, in the Holiness Collection, is on the lay Israelite. **9–10:** Cf. 23.22; 25.2–7; Ruth 2.1–10. **11–13:** Cf. the Decalogue, Ex 20.15,7,16. **14:** Cf. Deut 27.18.

yard bare, or gather the fallen grapes of
your vineyard; you shall leave them for the
poor and the alien: I am the LORD your
God.
11 You shall not steal; you shall not deal
falsely; and you shall not lie to one another.
12 And you shall not swear falsely by my
name, profaning the name of your God: I
am the LORD.
13 You shall not defraud your neighbor;
you shall not steal; and you shall not keep
for yourself the wages of a laborer until
morning. 14 You shall not revile the deaf or
put a stumbling block before the blind; you
shall fear your God: I am the LORD.
15 You shall not render an unjust judgment;
you shall not be partial to the poor or
defer to the great: with justice you shall
judge your neighbor. 16 You shall not go
around as a slanderer[a] among your people,
and you shall not profit by the blood[b]
of your neighbor: I am the LORD.
17 You shall not hate in your heart anyone
of your kin; you shall reprove your
neighbor, or you will incur guilt yourself.
18 You shall not take vengeance or bear a
grudge against any of your people, but you
shall love your neighbor as yourself: I am
the LORD.
19 You shall keep my statutes. You shall
not let your animals breed with a different
kind; you shall not sow your field with two
kinds of seed; nor shall you put on a garment
made of two different materials.
20 If a man has sexual relations with a
woman who is a slave, designated for another
man but not ransomed or given her
freedom, an inquiry shall be held. They
shall not be put to death, since she has not
been freed; 21 but he shall bring a guilt
offering for himself to the LORD, at the entrance
of the tent of meeting, a ram as guilt
offering. 22 And the priest shall make atonement
for him with the ram of guilt offering
before the LORD for his sin that he committed;
and the sin he committed shall be forgiven
him.
23 When you come into the land and
plant all kinds of trees for food, then you
shall regard their fruit as forbidden;[c] three
years it shall be forbidden[d] to you, it must
not be eaten. 24 In the fourth year all their
fruit shall be set apart for rejoicing in the
LORD. 25 But in the fifth year you may eat
of their fruit, that their yield may be increased
for you: I am the LORD your God.
26 You shall not eat anything with its
blood. You shall not practice augury or
witchcraft. 27 You shall not round off the
hair on your temples or mar the edges of
your beard. 28 You shall not make any
gashes in your flesh for the dead or tattoo
any marks upon you: I am the LORD.
29 Do not profane your daughter by
making her a prostitute, that the land not
become prostituted and full of depravity.
30 You shall keep my sabbaths and reverence
my sanctuary: I am the LORD.
31 Do not turn to mediums or wizards;
do not seek them out, to be defiled by them:
I am the LORD your God.
32 You shall rise before the aged, and
defer to the old; and you shall fear your
God: I am the LORD.
33 When an alien resides with you in
your land, you shall not oppress the alien.

a Meaning of Heb uncertain *b* Heb *stand against the blood* *c* Heb *as their uncircumcision* *d* Heb *uncircumcision*

17–18: For attitudes and actions toward aliens, as opposed to one's kin or people as discussed here, see vv. 33–34. Cf. 25.39–46. **18b:** This verse, along with Deut 6.5, is quoted in Mt 22.37–40 (cf. Mk 12.28–33; Lk 10.27; Rom 13.9; Gal 5.14). **19:** One reason mixtures are prohibited is that such prohibitions are reminders that the people, keeping themselves distinct, are holy (cf. Deut 22.9–11). See Num 15.37–41n. **20–22:** If the woman here were free and betrothed, the couple would have been put to death (20.10; cf. Deut 22.23–27). **23–25:** *Forbidden,* perhaps a remnant of fertility propitiation. The fruit of the *fourth year* is given to God, a type of first-fruits offering. After God receives his share, the people can use the fruit (23.14). Cf. Num 18.32n. **26:** *Blood,* 3.17n. *Augury or witchcraft,* forms of divination (cf. v. 31; Gen 44.5,15; Isa 2.6; Ezek 21.26–28; see Num 22.3). **27–28:** Cf. 21.5n. **29:** A father might force his daughter to prostitution for economic reasons. Cf. 21.9. **32:** Cf. v. 3; Isa 3.5. **33–34:**

34 The alien who resides with you shall be
to you as the citizen among you; you shall
love the alien as yourself, for you were
aliens in the land of Egypt: I am the LORD
your God.

35 You shall not cheat in measuring
length, weight, or quantity. 36 You shall
have honest balances, honest weights, an
honest ephah, and an honest hin: I am the
LORD your God, who brought you out of
the land of Egypt. 37 You shall keep all my
statutes and all my ordinances, and observe
them: I am the LORD.

20 The LORD spoke to Moses, saying:
2 Say further to the people of Israel:
Any of the people of Israel, or of the
aliens who reside in Israel, who give any of
their offspring to Molech shall be put to
death; the people of the land shall stone
them to death. 3 I myself will set my face
against them, and will cut them off from
the people, because they have given of their
offspring to Molech, defiling my sanctuary
and profaning my holy name. 4 And if the
people of the land should ever close their
eyes to them, when they give of their off-
spring to Molech, and do not put them to
death, 5 I myself will set my face against
them and against their family, and will cut
them off from among their people, them
and all who follow them in prostituting
themselves to Molech.

6 If any turn to mediums and wizards,
prostituting themselves to them, I will set
my face against them, and will cut them off
from the people. 7 Consecrate yourselves
therefore, and be holy; for I am the LORD
your God. 8 Keep my statutes, and observe
them; I am the LORD; I sanctify you. 9 All
who curse father or mother shall be put to
death; having cursed father or mother, their
blood is upon them.

10 If a man commits adultery with the
wife of[a] his neighbor, both the adulterer
and the adulteress shall be put to death.
11 The man who lies with his father's wife
has uncovered his father's nakedness; both
of them shall be put to death; their blood
is upon them. 12 If a man lies with his
daughter-in-law, both of them shall be put
to death; they have committed perversion,
their blood is upon them. 13 If a man lies
with a male as with a woman, both of them
have committed an abomination; they shall
be put to death; their blood is upon them.
14 If a man takes a wife and her mother
also, it is depravity; they shall be burned to
death, both he and they, that there may be
no depravity among you. 15 If a man has
sexual relations with an animal, he shall be
put to death; and you shall kill the animal.
16 If a woman approaches any animal and
has sexual relations with it, you shall kill
the woman and the animal; they shall be
put to death, their blood is upon them.

17 If a man takes his sister, a daughter
of his father or a daughter of his mother,
and sees her nakedness, and she sees his
nakedness, it is a disgrace, and they shall be
cut off in the sight of their people; he has
uncovered his sister's nakedness, he shall be

a Heb repeats *if a man commits adultery with the wife of*

Cf. vv. 17–18. **35–36:** Deut 25.13–16; Am 8.5; Mic 6.10–11. An *ephah* was a dry measure equivalent to ca. 23 l (21 qt); a *hin* was a liquid measure equivalent to ca. 3.8 l (1 gal).

20.1–27: Sexual and other prohibitions. This chapter recapitulates some of the laws found in chs 18–19, and adds penalties. **2–5:** The worship of *Molech,* a Canaanite deity, was practiced in the Valley of Hinnom near Jerusalem (2 Kings 23.10; Jer 32.35). The term may refer to a type of offering, or child sacrifice (see 18.21n.). V. 6 may indicate that the act is associated with divination. (Cf. Deut 18.10, which is similarly followed by prohibitions of necromancy and other divinatory acts.) Though all Molech worship as understood by the Bible might involve child sacrifice, not every case of child sacrifice in the Bible is Molech worship (e.g., 2 Kings 3.27; Isa 66.3). **5:** Prostitution is a frequent metaphor for idolatry. **9:** Ex 21.17. **10–21:** See 18.6–23n. The relationships in vv. 10–16 require execution by humans; those in vv. 17–21 require a penalty by the deity. The reason the latter offenses do not require execution is that they may have been viewed as less serious or less controllable or witnessable. **15–16:** On killing the animal, cf. Ex 21.28–32. **22–26:** *You shall keep all my statutes* and similar phrases function as a refrain

subject to punishment. 18 If a man lies with
a woman having her sickness and uncovers
her nakedness, he has laid bare her flow
and she has laid bare her flow of blood;
both of them shall be cut off from their
people. 19 You shall not uncover the naked-
ness of your mother's sister or of your fa-
ther's sister, for that is to lay bare one's
own flesh; they shall be subject to punish-
ment. 20 If a man lies with his uncle's wife,
he has uncovered his uncle's nakedness;
they shall be subject to punishment; they
shall die childless. 21 If a man takes his
brother's wife, it is impurity; he has uncov-
ered his brother's nakedness; they shall be
childless.

22 You shall keep all my statutes and all
my ordinances, and observe them, so that
the land to which I bring you to settle in
may not vomit you out. 23 You shall not
follow the practices of the nation that I am
driving out before you. Because they did all
these things, I abhorred them. 24 But I have
said to you: You shall inherit their land,
and I will give it to you to possess, a land
flowing with milk and honey. I am the
LORD your God; I have separated you from
the peoples. 25 You shall therefore make a
distinction between the clean animal and
the unclean, and between the unclean bird
and the clean; you shall not bring abomina-
tion on yourselves by animal or by bird or
by anything with which the ground teems,
which I have set apart for you to hold un-
clean. 26 You shall be holy to me; for I the
LORD am holy, and I have separated you
from the other peoples to be mine.

27 A man or a woman who is a medium
or a wizard shall be put to death; they shall
be stoned to death, their blood is upon
them.

21 The LORD said to Moses: Speak to
the priests, the sons of Aaron, and
say to them:

No one shall defile himself for a dead
person among his relatives, 2 except for his
nearest kin: his mother, his father, his son,
his daughter, his brother; 3 likewise, for a
virgin sister, close to him because she has
had no husband, he may defile himself for
her. 4 But he shall not defile himself as a
husband among his people and so profane
himself. 5 They shall not make bald spots
upon their heads, or shave off the edges of
their beards, or make any gashes in their
flesh. 6 They shall be holy to their God, and
not profane the name of their God; for they
offer the LORD's offerings by fire, the food
of their God; therefore they shall be holy.
7 They shall not marry a prostitute or a

for this chapter (see v. 8), and more broadly, for the Holiness Collection as a whole (18.5,26,30; 19.37; 22.31). The conclusion to this chapter is similar to 18.24–30. **24:** *Flowing with milk and honey,* a description with mythological overtones. The honey was probably a thick syrup made from grapes or dates. **27:** See 19.31.

21.1–22.33: Priestly restrictions and sacrificial requirements. Chs 18–20 gave commands whose observance leads to the people's holiness (cf. 19.2; 20.7,26); the text now gives commands to ensure the priests' holiness, which had been granted to them through their ordination (see ch 8). **21.1–12:** Besides having marriage and mourning restrictions, priests are restricted from corpse contamination; because of their holiness, they are expected to maintain their ritual purity. The high priest (vv. 10–15) is restricted from all corpses; regular priests may become impure by corpses of close relatives (cf. 10.6–7; Ezek 44.25–27). This contrasts with the rule for Israelites, who may become corpse contaminated as long as they purify on time (cf. Num 19) and do not contact what is holy (cf. Deut 26.14). The holiness of an Israelite under a nazirite vow is similar to a priest's; therefore the nazirite cannot come in contact with corpses (Num 6.1–21n.). For another impurity restriction of priests, cf. Lev 11.39–40n. **5:** Apparently mourning rituals, also prohibited to non-priests (19.27–28); cf. Deut 14.1–2; Isa 22.12; Jer 16.6. **6:** *Food of their God,* sacrifice is a metaphorical meal offered to the deity based in part on the analogy of presenting feasts to chieftains and kings (3.11; 21.8,17,21–22; 22.25; Num 28.2,24; Ezek 44.7; Mal 1.7). According to the priestly view, God does not eat this food, but smells its "pleasing odor" (Gen 8.21; Lev 1.9 and often elsewhere). Offerings consist of the main ingredients found in meals and feasts: meats, grains, and wine (cf. Num 15.2–16n.). On the metaphor, cf. Mal 1.8; Ps 50.7–14. **10:** See 8.10–12n. **16–23:** Bodily defects

woman who has been defiled; neither shall
they marry a woman divorced from her
husband. For they are holy to their God,
8 and you shall treat them as holy, since
they offer the food of your God; they shall
be holy to you, for I the LORD, I who sanc-
tify you, am holy. 9 When the daughter of
a priest profanes herself through prostitu-
tion, she profanes her father; she shall be
burned to death.

10 The priest who is exalted above his
fellows, on whose head the anointing oil
has been poured and who has been conse-
crated to wear the vestments, shall not di-
shevel his hair, nor tear his vestments. 11 He
shall not go where there is a dead body; he
shall not defile himself even for his father
or mother. 12 He shall not go outside the
sanctuary and thus profane the sanctuary
of his God; for the consecration of the
anointing oil of his God is upon him: I am
the LORD. 13 He shall marry only a woman
who is a virgin. 14 A widow, or a divorced
woman, or a woman who has been defiled,
a prostitute, these he shall not marry. He
shall marry a virgin of his own kin, 15 that
he may not profane his offspring among his
kin; for I am the LORD; I sanctify him.

16 The LORD spoke to Moses, saying:
17 Speak to Aaron and say: No one of your
offspring throughout their generations who
has a blemish may approach to offer the
food of his God. 18 For no one who has a
blemish shall draw near, one who is blind
or lame, or one who has a mutilated face or
a limb too long, 19 or one who has a broken
foot or a broken hand, 20 or a hunchback,
or a dwarf, or a man with a blemish in
his eyes or an itching disease or scabs or
crushed testicles. 21 No descendant of Aar-
on the priest who has a blemish shall come
near to offer the LORD's offerings by fire;
since he has a blemish, he shall not come
near to offer the food of his God. 22 He may
eat the food of his God, of the most holy as
well as of the holy. 23 But he shall not come
near the curtain or approach the altar, be-
cause he has a blemish, that he may not
profane my sanctuaries; for I am the LORD;
I sanctify them. 24 Thus Moses spoke to
Aaron and to his sons and to all the people
of Israel.

22 The LORD spoke to Moses, saying:
2 Direct Aaron and his sons to deal
carefully with the sacred donations of the
people of Israel, which they dedicate to me,
so that they may not profane my holy
name; I am the LORD. 3 Say to them: If any-
one among all your offspring throughout
your generations comes near the sacred do-
nations, which the people of Israel dedicate
to the LORD, while he is in a state of un-
cleanness, that person shall be cut off from
my presence: I am the LORD. 4 No one of
Aaron's offspring who has a leprous[a] dis-
ease or suffers a discharge may eat of the
sacred donations until he is clean. Whoever
touches anything made unclean by a corpse
or a man who has had an emission of se-
men, 5 and whoever touches any swarming
thing by which he may be made unclean
or any human being by whom he may be
made unclean—whatever his uncleanness
may be— 6 the person who touches any
such shall be unclean until evening and
shall not eat of the sacred donations unless
he has washed his body in water. 7 When
the sun sets he shall be clean; and afterward
he may eat of the sacred donations, for they
are his food. 8 That which died or was torn
by wild animals he shall not eat, becoming
unclean by it: I am the LORD. 9 They shall
keep my charge, so that they may not incur
guilt and die in the sanctuary[b] for having
profaned it: I am the LORD; I sanctify them.

10 No lay person shall eat of the sacred
donations. No bound or hired servant of

a A term for several skin diseases; precise meaning uncertain *b* Vg: Heb *incur guilt for it and die in it*

prevent priests from working at the altar (vv. 18–20), but they do not render them impure. These priests may still eat of the most holy offerings in the sanctuary (v. 22; cf. Num 18.8–10n.). Cf. 22.17–25. **22.1–16:** A continuation of the previous unit: Priests with impurity, which is a temporary state, as opposed to bodily imperfections (21.16–23), cannot eat any sacrifices or holy donations (cf. 11.1–15.33n.; 12.2–5n.). **8:** See 11.39–40n. **10–13:** On the priest's family consuming lesser holy offerings, see Num

the priest shall eat of the sacred donations;
[11]but if a priest acquires anyone by pur-
chase, the person may eat of them; and
those that are born in his house may eat of
his food. [12]If a priest's daughter marries a
layman, she shall not eat of the offering
of the sacred donations; [13]but if a priest's
daughter is widowed or divorced, without
offspring, and returns to her father's house,
as in her youth, she may eat of her father's
food. No lay person shall eat of it. [14]If a
man eats of the sacred donation uninten-
tionally, he shall add one-fifth of its value
to it, and give the sacred donation to the
priest. [15]No one shall profane the sacred
donations of the people of Israel, which
they offer to the LORD, [16]causing them to
bear guilt requiring a guilt offering, by eat-
ing their sacred donations: for I am the
LORD; I sanctify them.

17 The LORD spoke to Moses, saying:
[18]Speak to Aaron and his sons and all the
people of Israel and say to them: When
anyone of the house of Israel or of the
aliens residing in Israel presents an offering,
whether in payment of a vow or as a free-
will offering that is offered to the LORD as
a burnt offering, [19]to be acceptable in your
behalf it shall be a male without blemish, of
the cattle or the sheep or the goats. [20]You
shall not offer anything that has a blemish,
for it will not be acceptable in your behalf.

21 When anyone offers a sacrifice of
well-being to the LORD, in fulfillment of a
vow or as a freewill offering, from the herd
or from the flock, to be acceptable it must
be perfect; there shall be no blemish in it.
[22]Anything blind, or injured, or maimed,
or having a discharge or an itch or scabs—
these you shall not offer to the LORD or put
any of them on the altar as offerings by fire
to the LORD. [23]An ox or a lamb that has a
limb too long or too short you may present
for a freewill offering; but it will not be
accepted for a vow. [24]Any animal that has
its testicles bruised or crushed or torn or
cut, you shall not offer to the LORD; such
you shall not do within your land, [25]nor
shall you accept any such animals from a
foreigner to offer as food to your God;
since they are mutilated, with a blemish in
them, they shall not be accepted in your
behalf.

26 The LORD spoke to Moses, saying:
[27]When an ox or a sheep or a goat is born,
it shall remain seven days with its mother,
and from the eighth day on it shall be ac-
ceptable as the LORD's offering by fire.
[28]But you shall not slaughter, from the
herd or the flock, an animal with its young
on the same day. [29]When you sacrifice a
thanksgiving offering to the LORD, you
shall sacrifice it so that it may be acceptable
in your behalf. [30]It shall be eaten on the
same day; you shall not leave any of it until
morning: I am the LORD.

31 Thus you shall keep my command-
ments and observe them: I am the LORD.
[32]You shall not profane my holy name,
that I may be sanctified among the people
of Israel: I am the LORD; I sanctify you, [33]I
who brought you out of the land of Egypt
to be your God: I am the LORD.

23 The LORD spoke to Moses, saying:
[2]Speak to the people of Israel and
say to them: These are the appointed festi-
vals of the LORD that you shall proclaim as
holy convocations, my appointed festivals.

3 Six days shall work be done; but the
seventh day is a sabbath of complete rest, a

18.20. The priest's family was his immediate household, which included slaves but not servants. **14:** *One fifth,* according to 5.14–16, inadvertent misuse of sacred items similarly requires restoration of the item plus a payment of one-fifth its cost. **17–30:** The focus shifts from the person who makes the offering (an unmaimed, pure priest) to the type of animal that may be offered. **17–25:** Compare this passage to the rules on priestly defects in 21.16–23. Anything or anyone contacting the altar must be without defect. Cf. Mal 1.6–14. **30:** 7.15. **31–33:** God's holiness in the midst of Israel, assured by Israel's proper behavior, assures the divine presence in Israel.

23.1–44: The ritual calendar. For another calendar from the priestly tradition, see Num 28–29 (and the notes there); for non-priestly calendars, see Ex 23.10–17; 34.18–24; Deut 16. **2:** *Proclaim as holy convocations,* better, "proclaim as holy occasions." **3:** The sabbath, though central to priestly material,

holy convocation; you shall do no work: it
is a sabbath to the LORD throughout your
settlements.
4 These are the appointed festivals of the
LORD, the holy convocations, which you
shall celebrate at the time appointed for
them. 5 In the first month, on the fourteenth
day of the month, at twilight,[a] there shall
be a passover offering to the LORD, 6 and
on the fifteenth day of the same month is
the festival of unleavened bread to the
LORD; seven days you shall eat unleavened
bread. 7 On the first day you shall have a
holy convocation; you shall not work at
your occupations. 8 For seven days you
shall present the LORD's offerings by fire;
on the seventh day there shall be a holy
convocation: you shall not work at your
occupations.
9 The LORD spoke to Moses: 10 Speak to
the people of Israel and say to them: When
you enter the land that I am giving you and
you reap its harvest, you shall bring the
sheaf of the first fruits of your harvest to
the priest. 11 He shall raise the sheaf before
the LORD, that you may find acceptance;
on the day after the sabbath the priest shall
raise it. 12 On the day when you raise the
sheaf, you shall offer a lamb a year old,
without blemish, as a burnt offering to the
LORD. 13 And the grain offering with it
shall be two-tenths of an ephah of choice
flour mixed with oil, an offering by fire of
pleasing odor to the LORD; and the drink
offering with it shall be of wine, one-fourth
of a hin. 14 You shall eat no bread or
parched grain or fresh ears until that very
day, until you have brought the offering of
your God: it is a statute forever throughout
your generations in all your settlements.
15 And from the day after the sabbath,
from the day on which you bring the sheaf
of the elevation offering, you shall count
off seven weeks; they shall be complete.
16 You shall count until the day after the
seventh sabbath, fifty days; then you shall
present an offering of new grain to the
LORD. 17 You shall bring from your settle-
ments two loaves of bread as an elevation
offering, each made of two-tenths of an
ephah; they shall be of choice flour, baked
with leaven, as first fruits to the LORD.
18 You shall present with the bread seven
lambs a year old without blemish, one
young bull, and two rams; they shall be a
burnt offering to the LORD, along with
their grain offering and their drink offer-
ings, an offering by fire of pleasing odor to
the LORD. 19 You shall also offer one male
goat for a sin offering, and two male lambs
a year old as a sacrifice of well-being.
20 The priest shall raise them with the bread
of the first fruits as an elevation offering
before the LORD, together with the two
lambs; they shall be holy to the LORD for
the priest. 21 On that same day you shall
make proclamation; you shall hold a holy
convocation; you shall not work at your

a Heb *between the two evenings*

is not elsewhere considered an "appointed festival," a term usually reserved for annual events. The term *sabbath of complete rest* is used only for the sabbath and the Day of Atonement (Ex 16.23; 31.15; 35.2; Lev 16.31; 23.32). This refers to the prohibition of all work on these days (23.3,28; Num 29.7). Other holy occasions prohibit only laborious work, but not light work such as food preparation (23.7–8,21,25,35–36; Num 28.18,25–26; 29.1,12,35). Cf. Num 15.32–36n. **4–8:** As in the other calendars, the festivals are ordered according to the agricultural year; the combined spring festivals of Passover and the Festival of Unleavened Bread begin the celebration of the harvests; cf. Ex 12.1–20,43–49; Num 9.1–14n.; 28.16–25. **5:** *The first month,* March-April. **9–14:** The sheaf of first fruits is of barley, the first spring crop (cf. 2.14n.). **11:** The day meant by *after the sabbath* was fiercely debated in early Judaism. **13:** *Two-tenths of an ephah,* ca. 4.6 l (2 qt). *Pleasing odor,* see 1.9n. **14:** Cf. 19.23–25. **15–21:** The Festival of Weeks (also called "Pentecost," from the Gk for "fifty"), roughly fifty days after the Festival of Unleavened Bread, celebrates the wheat harvest. Though early Judaism connects this festival to the giving of the Torah, it is a purely agricultural festival in all of the Bible's calendars. Cf. Ex 23.16; 34.22; Num 28.26; Deut 16.10,16. **17:** *Elevation offering,* see Num 18.11n. **18–19:** On the various types of offerings, see chs 1–4. **22:** 19.9–10n. **23–25:** The first day of the seventh month became the new year in

occupations. This is a statute forever in all
your settlements throughout your genera-
tions.
22 When you reap the harvest of your
land, you shall not reap to the very edges of
your field, or gather the gleanings of your
harvest; you shall leave them for the poor
and for the alien: I am the LORD your God.
23 The LORD spoke to Moses, saying:
24 Speak to the people of Israel, saying: In
the seventh month, on the first day of the
month, you shall observe a day of complete
rest, a holy convocation commemorated
with trumpet blasts. 25 You shall not work
at your occupations; and you shall present
the LORD's offering by fire.
26 The LORD spoke to Moses, saying:
27 Now, the tenth day of this seventh month
is the day of atonement; it shall be a holy
convocation for you: you shall deny your-
selves[a] and present the LORD's offering by
fire; 28 and you shall do no work during
that entire day; for it is a day of atonement,
to make atonement on your behalf before
the LORD your God. 29 For anyone who
does not practice self-denial[b] during that
entire day shall be cut off from the people.
30 And anyone who does any work during
that entire day, such a one I will destroy
from the midst of the people. 31 You shall
do no work: it is a statute forever through-
out your generations in all your settle-
ments. 32 It shall be to you a sabbath of
complete rest, and you shall deny your-
selves;[a] on the ninth day of the month at
evening, from evening to evening you shall
keep your sabbath.
33 The LORD spoke to Moses, saying:
34 Speak to the people of Israel, saying: On
the fifteenth day of this seventh month, and
lasting seven days, there shall be the festival
of booths[c] to the LORD. 35 The first day
shall be a holy convocation; you shall not
work at your occupations. 36 Seven days
you shall present the LORD's offerings by
fire; on the eighth day you shall observe a
holy convocation and present the LORD's
offerings by fire; it is a solemn assembly;
you shall not work at your occupations.
37 These are the appointed festivals of
the LORD, which you shall celebrate as
times of holy convocation, for presenting to
the LORD offerings by fire—burnt offerings
and grain offerings, sacrifices and drink
offerings, each on its proper day— 38 apart
from the sabbaths of the LORD, and apart
from your gifts, and apart from all your
votive offerings, and apart from all your
freewill offerings, which you give to the
LORD.
39 Now, the fifteenth day of the seventh
month, when you have gathered in the pro-
duce of the land, you shall keep the festival
of the LORD, lasting seven days; a complete
rest on the first day, and a complete rest on
the eighth day. 40 On the first day you shall
take the fruit of majestic[d] trees, branches
of palm trees, boughs of leafy trees, and
willows of the brook; and you shall rejoice
before the LORD your God for seven days.
41 You shall keep it as a festival to the LORD
seven days in the year; you shall keep it
in the seventh month as a statute forever
throughout your generations. 42 You shall
live in booths for seven days; all that are
citizens in Israel shall live in booths, 43 so
that your generations may know that I
made the people of Israel live in booths
when I brought them out of the land of
Egypt: I am the LORD your God.

a Or *shall fast* *b* Or *does not fast*
c Or *tabernacles*: Heb *succoth* *d* Meaning of Heb uncertain

later Jewish tradition. The seventh month (September-October) is preeminent because of the holy occasions that occur in it. **26–32:** See ch 16 for the Day of Atonement. In contrast to the description of ch 16, from the Priestly Torah, the focus here in the Holiness Collection is on lay observance of this day. **33–36:** The seven-day festival of booths (or "tabernacles"), with an eighth-day conclusion, celebrates the final harvest; cf. Ex 23.16; 34.22; Deut 16.13; 1 Kings 8.65. **37–38:** The chapter's original conclusion. **39–43:** This is an addition to the calendar dealing with the festival of booths. **40:** In Neh 8.14–15, these branches are used to construct booths. **43:** Only here is the festival of booths historicized; nowhere else in the Bible is a tradition of living specifically in booths after the Exodus recorded.

44 Thus Moses declared to the people of
Israel the appointed festivals of the LORD.
24 The LORD spoke to Moses, saying:
2 Command the people of Israel to
bring you pure oil of beaten olives for the
lamp, that a light may be kept burning reg-
ularly. 3 Aaron shall set it up in the tent of
meeting, outside the curtain of the cove-
nant,[a] to burn from evening to morning
before the LORD regularly; it shall be a stat-
ute forever throughout your generations.
4 He shall set up the lamps on the lamp-
stand of pure gold[b] before the LORD regu-
larly.
5 You shall take choice flour, and bake
twelve loaves of it; two-tenths of an ephah
shall be in each loaf. 6 You shall place them
in two rows, six in a row, on the table of
pure gold.[c] 7 You shall put pure frankin-
cense with each row, to be a token offering
for the bread, as an offering by fire to the
LORD. 8 Every sabbath day Aaron shall set
them in order before the LORD regularly as
a commitment of the people of Israel, as a
covenant forever. 9 They shall be for Aaron
and his descendants, who shall eat them in
a holy place, for they are most holy por-
tions for him from the offerings by fire to
the LORD, a perpetual due.
10 A man whose mother was an Israelite
and whose father was an Egyptian came
out among the people of Israel; and the Is-
raelite woman's son and a certain Israelite
began fighting in the camp. 11 The Israelite
woman's son blasphemed the Name in a
curse. And they brought him to Moses—
now his mother's name was Shelomith,
daughter of Dibri, of the tribe of Dan—
12 and they put him in custody, until the
decision of the LORD should be made clear
to them.
13 The LORD said to Moses, saying:
14 Take the blasphemer outside the camp;
and let all who were within hearing lay
their hands on his head, and let the whole
congregation stone him. 15 And speak to the
people of Israel, saying: Anyone who curses
God shall bear the sin. 16 One who blas-
phemes the name of the LORD shall be put
to death; the whole congregation shall
stone the blasphemer. Aliens as well as citi-
zens, when they blaspheme the Name, shall
be put to death. 17 Anyone who kills a hu-
man being shall be put to death. 18 Anyone
who kills an animal shall make restitution
for it, life for life. 19 Anyone who maims
another shall suffer the same injury in re-
turn: 20 fracture for fracture, eye for eye,
tooth for tooth; the injury inflicted is the
injury to be suffered. 21 One who kills an
animal shall make restitution for it; but one
who kills a human being shall be put to
death. 22 You shall have one law for the
alien and for the citizen: for I am the LORD
your God. 23 Moses spoke thus to the peo-
ple of Israel; and they took the blasphemer
outside the camp, and stoned him to death.

a Or *treaty*, or *testament*; Heb *eduth* *b* Heb *pure lampstand* *c* Heb *pure table*

24.1–23: Various laws. 1–4: *Lamp,* Cf. Ex 25.31–40; 26.35; 27.20–21; 37.17–24; 40.24–25; Num 8.1–3. **3:** Just as the high priest is responsible for the rites in the inner room (see 16.2n.), so he is responsible for the rites in the forward room (24.8; cf. Ex 25.37; 27.20–21; 30.7–8,10; Lev 4.3–12, 13–21; 16.16; Num 8.1–3). Regular priests are allowed to enter this room to aid the high priest or to perform their own responsibilities (Ex 27.21; 28.43; 16.17; Num 4.5–20). **5–9:** On this bread and its table, see Ex 25.23–29; 26.35; 37.10–16; 40.22–23. **5:** *Two-tenths of an ephah,* 23.13n. **9:** The bread is eaten by the priests, perhaps to indicate that it is not really food for God. **10–22:** Here a case of blasphemy (cf. Ex 20.7; 22.28) leads to a legal amendment. For similar cases, see Num 9.6–14; 15.32–36; 27.5–11; and cf. Lev 10.1–8 and 16.1–34. **11:** *The Name,* a circumlocution for Yahweh (the LORD); see v. 16. **14:** On hand-laying, see 16.21n. The blasphemy appears to pollute the ones who hear it; by this gesture they return the pollution to the head of the culprit. **17–22:** The talion laws here are generally understood literally, while the earlier formulation in Ex 21.23–35 may intend compensation through money or property as long as it is equal to the damages. Cf. Deut 19.21. **17:** On homicide, see Num 35.9–34. **18,21:** The phrase *life for life* is not understood literally, but apparently maintains the earlier tradition allowing monetary compensation (vv. 17–22n.).

The people of Israel did as the LORD had
commanded Moses.

25 The LORD spoke to Moses on
Mount Sinai, saying: 2 Speak to the
people of Israel and say to them: When you
enter the land that I am giving you, the land
shall observe a sabbath for the LORD. 3 Six
years you shall sow your field, and six years
you shall prune your vineyard, and gather
in their yield; 4 but in the seventh year there
shall be a sabbath of complete rest for the
land, a sabbath for the LORD: you shall not
sow your field or prune your vineyard.
5 You shall not reap the aftergrowth of your
harvest or gather the grapes of your un-
pruned vine: it shall be a year of complete
rest for the land. 6 You may eat what the
land yields during its sabbath—you, your
male and female slaves, your hired and
your bound laborers who live with you;
7 for your livestock also, and for the wild
animals in your land all its yield shall be for
food.

8 You shall count off seven weeks[a] of
years, seven times seven years, so that the
period of seven weeks of years gives forty-
nine years. 9 Then you shall have the trum-
pet sounded loud; on the tenth day of the
seventh month—on the day of atone-
ment—you shall have the trumpet sounded
throughout all your land. 10 And you shall
hallow the fiftieth year and you shall pro-
claim liberty throughout the land to all its
inhabitants. It shall be a jubilee for you:
you shall return, every one of you, to your
property and every one of you to your fam-
ily. 11 That fiftieth year shall be a jubilee for
you: you shall not sow, or reap the after-
growth, or harvest the unpruned vines.
12 For it is a jubilee; it shall be holy to you:
you shall eat only what the field itself pro-
duces.

13 In this year of jubilee you shall re-
turn, every one of you, to your property.
14 When you make a sale to your neighbor
or buy from your neighbor, you shall not
cheat one another. 15 When you buy from
your neighbor, you shall pay only for the
number of years since the jubilee; the seller
shall charge you only for the remaining
crop years. 16 If the years are more, you
shall increase the price, and if the years are
fewer, you shall diminish the price; for it is
a certain number of harvests that are being
sold to you. 17 You shall not cheat one an-
other, but you shall fear your God; for I am
the LORD your God.

18 You shall observe my statutes and
faithfully keep my ordinances, so that you
may live on the land securely. 19 The land
will yield its fruit, and you will eat your fill
and live on it securely. 20 Should you ask,
"What shall we eat in the seventh year, if
we may not sow or gather in our crop?" 21 I
will order my blessing for you in the sixth
year, so that it will yield a crop for three
years. 22 When you sow in the eighth year,
you will be eating from the old crop; until
the ninth year, when its produce comes in,
you shall eat the old. 23 The land shall not
be sold in perpetuity, for the land is mine;
with me you are but aliens and tenants.
24 Throughout the land that you hold, you
shall provide for the redemption of the
land.

25 If anyone of your kin falls into diffi-

a Or *sabbaths*

25.1–55: The sabbatical and jubilee years. 2–7: Agricultural work is suspended in every seventh year. The people live off what grows on its own in the field. The phrase *sabbath of complete rest* (v. 4) indicates that this is observed by all simultaneously. As in early material (Ex 23.10–11) there is a social element to this institution, but it is also a religious institution—*a sabbath for the LORD* (v. 2). **8–17:** Every fifty years is a holy jubilee year. Land that has been sold reverts to its original owners and indentured Israelites return to their own households and land. Contrast Ex 21.1–6; Deut 15.1–3,12–18; Jer 34.8–22, which suggest that for others the seventh year had this function. **23–28:** In the theological economy expressed here the land belongs to God and Israelites are tenants upon it. Thus the holdings are to remain with the families and tribes to which they were originally assigned (cf. Num 27.1–11; 36.1–13). **25–55:** How impoverished Israelites should be treated within the context of this theological economy. **25:** For examples of redemption, see Jer 32.6–15; Ruth 4.3–6. Cf. Deut 25.5–10; cf. Ruth 3.13. **29–31:** A house in a walled

culty and sells a piece of property, then the
next of kin shall come and redeem what the
relative has sold. 26 If the person has no one
to redeem it, but then prospers and finds
sufficient means to do so, 27 the years since
its sale shall be computed and the differ-
ence shall be refunded to the person to
whom it was sold, and the property shall be
returned. 28 But if there are not sufficient
means to recover it, what was sold shall
remain with the purchaser until the year of
jubilee; in the jubilee it shall be released,
and the property shall be returned.
29 If anyone sells a dwelling house in a
walled city, it may be redeemed until a year
has elapsed since its sale; the right of re-
demption shall be one year. 30 If it is not
redeemed before a full year has elapsed, a
house that is in a walled city shall pass in
perpetuity to the purchaser, throughout the
generations; it shall not be released in the
jubilee. 31 But houses in villages that have
no walls around them shall be classed as
open country; they may be redeemed, and
they shall be released in the jubilee. 32 As
for the cities of the Levites, the Levites shall
forever have the right of redemption of the
houses in the cities belonging to them.
33 Such property as may be redeemed from
the Levites—houses sold in a city belonging
to them—shall be released in the jubilee;
because the houses in the cities of the Le-
vites are their possession among the people
of Israel. 34 But the open land around their
cities may not be sold; for that is their pos-
session for all time.
35 If any of your kin fall into difficulty
and become dependent on you,[a] you shall
support them; they shall live with you as
though resident aliens. 36 Do not take inter-
est in advance or otherwise make a profit
from them, but fear your God; let them live
with you. 37 You shall not lend them your
money at interest taken in advance, or pro-
vide them food at a profit. 38 I am the LORD
your God, who brought you out of the land
of Egypt, to give you the land of Canaan, to
be your God.
39 If any who are dependent on you be-
come so impoverished that they sell them-
selves to you, you shall not make them
serve as slaves. 40 They shall remain with
you as hired or bound laborers. They shall
serve with you until the year of the jubilee.
41 Then they and their children with them
shall be free from your authority; they shall
go back to their own family and return to
their ancestral property. 42 For they are my
servants, whom I brought out of the land of
Egypt; they shall not be sold as slaves are
sold. 43 You shall not rule over them with
harshness, but shall fear your God. 44 As
for the male and female slaves whom you
may have, it is from the nations around you
that you may acquire male and female
slaves. 45 You may also acquire them from
among the aliens residing with you, and
from their families that are with you, who
have been born in your land; and they may
be your property. 46 You may keep them as
a possession for your children after you, for
them to inherit as property. These you may
treat as slaves, but as for your fellow Israel-
ites, no one shall rule over the other with
harshness.
47 If resident aliens among you prosper,
and if any of your kin fall into difficulty
with one of them and sell themselves to an
alien, or to a branch of the alien's family,
48 after they have sold themselves they shall
have the right of redemption; one of their
brothers may redeem them, 49 or their uncle
or their uncle's son may redeem them, or
anyone of their family who is of their own

a Meaning of Heb uncertain

city is not redeemed, probably because of the unique economic and demographic situation there. **32:** *Cities of the Levites,* see Num 35.1–8; Josh 21.1–42. **35–38:** Interest on loans to the poor, which are charitable in nature, is prohibited. Cf. Ex 22.24; Deut 23.21. **39–43:** An Israelite who has become indentured to another Israelite is to be treated without harshness (as opposed to permanent non-Israelite slaves, cf. vv. 44–46) and is to be released in the jubilee year. Cf. 19.17–18,33–34. **42:** In Hebrew, the same word is used for "servants" and "slaves." **44–46:** Foreigners may be held as permanent non-Israelite slaves (contrast vv. 39–43,47–55) and may be treated harshly (cf. Ex 21.20–21). **55:** The metaphor of flesh may redeem them; or if they prosper they may redeem themselves. 50 They shall compute with the purchaser the total from the year when they sold themselves to the alien until the jubilee year; the price of the sale shall be applied to the number of years: the time they were with the owner shall be rated as the time of a hired laborer. 51 If many years remain, they shall pay for their redemption in proportion to the purchase price; 52 and if few years remain until the jubilee year, they shall compute thus: according to the years involved they shall make payment for their redemption. 53 As a laborer hired by the year they shall be under the alien's authority, who shall not, however, rule with harshness over them in your sight. 54 And if they have not been redeemed in any of these ways, they and their children with them shall go free in the jubilee year. 55 For to me the people of Israel are servants; they are my servants whom I brought out from the land of Egypt: I am the LORD your God.

26 You shall make for yourselves no idols and erect no carved images or pillars, and you shall not place figured stones in your land, to worship at them; for I am the LORD your God. 2 You shall keep my sabbaths and reverence my sanctuary: I am the LORD.

3 If you follow my statutes and keep my commandments and observe them faithfully, 4 I will give you your rains in their season, and the land shall yield its produce, and the trees of the field shall yield their fruit. 5 Your threshing shall overtake the vintage, and the vintage shall overtake the sowing; you shall eat your bread to the full, and live securely in your land. 6 And I will grant peace in the land, and you shall lie down, and no one shall make you afraid; I will remove dangerous animals from the land, and no sword shall go through your land. 7 You shall give chase to your enemies, and they shall fall before you by the sword. 8 Five of you shall give chase to a hundred, and a hundred of you shall give chase to ten thousand; your enemies shall fall before you by the sword. 9 I will look with favor upon you and make you fruitful and multiply you; and I will maintain my covenant with you. 10 You shall eat old grain long stored, and you shall have to clear out the old to make way for the new. 11 I will place my dwelling in your midst, and I shall not abhor you. 12 And I will walk among you, and will be your God, and you shall be my people. 13 I am the LORD your God who brought you out of the land of Egypt, to be their slaves no more; I have broken the bars of your yoke and made you walk erect.

14 But if you will not obey me, and do not observe all these commandments, 15 if you spurn my statutes, and abhor my ordi-

Israel as God's slaves (see also v. 42n.) in the priestly conception has literal, economic repercussions: No Israelite may enslave another Israelite.

26.1–46: Blessings and curses. This is the conclusion to chs 17–25. **1–2:** These verses are thematically independent of the economic laws before and the blessing and punishments that follow. Nonetheless the command to observe the sabbaths has resonances with the sabbatical year law in 25.2–7 (and see 26.43), and the command to avoid idols, with the destruction of illicit worship in 26.30. **3–46:** Deuteronomy also contains blessings and curses near its conclusion (Deut 28). The general format and tenor of the blessings and curses is similar to what is found in Near Eastern treaties. Treaties in the human political world were a model for describing the treaty or covenant relationship between God and his people (cf. Lev 25.25n.). The same Heb word, "berit," encompasses both secular political treaties, and covenants, which are understood as theologized political treaties. **3–13:** The focus of the blessings is the land, its people, its security, and its fertility. **11–12:** The ultimate reward for observance is the divine presence in Israel. Cf. Ex 6.7; Jer 7.23; 30.22. **14–46:** The punishments deal with the reverse of the topics mentioned in the blessings. The punishments are enumerated in cyclic fashion and in greater detail than the blessings in order to paint a picture of the people's incorrigibility. In contrast to Deut 28, these verses, which are characterized by the phrase "continue hostile to me," depict Israel's ever worsening behavior, despite divine punishment. **30:** *High places,* local shrines, often for the worship of other gods (see 1 Kings 11.7;

nances, so that you will not observe all my
commandments, and you break my cove-
nant, 16 I in turn will do this to you: I will
bring terror on you; consumption and fever
that waste the eyes and cause life to pine
away. You shall sow your seed in vain, for
your enemies shall eat it. 17 I will set my
face against you, and you shall be struck
down by your enemies; your foes shall rule
over you, and you shall flee though no one
pursues you. 18 And if in spite of this you
will not obey me, I will continue to punish
you sevenfold for your sins. 19 I will break
your proud glory, and I will make your
sky like iron and your earth like copper.
20 Your strength shall be spent to no pur-
pose: your land shall not yield its produce,
and the trees of the land shall not yield their
fruit.

21 If you continue hostile to me, and
will not obey me, I will continue to plague
you sevenfold for your sins. 22 I will let
loose wild animals against you, and they
shall bereave you of your children and de-
stroy your livestock; they shall make you
few in number, and your roads shall be de-
serted.

23 If in spite of these punishments you
have not turned back to me, but continue
hostile to me, 24 then I too will continue
hostile to you: I myself will strike you sev-
enfold for your sins. 25 I will bring the
sword against you, executing vengeance for
the covenant; and if you withdraw within
your cities, I will send pestilence among
you, and you shall be delivered into enemy
hands. 26 When I break your staff of bread,
ten women shall bake your bread in a single
oven, and they shall dole out your bread by
weight; and though you eat, you shall not
be satisfied.

27 But if, despite this, you disobey me,
and continue hostile to me, 28 I will contin-
ue hostile to you in fury; I in turn will pun-
ish you myself sevenfold for your sins.
29 You shall eat the flesh of your sons, and
you shall eat the flesh of your daughters.
30 I will destroy your high places and cut
down your incense altars; I will heap your
carcasses on the carcasses of your idols. I
will abhor you. 31 I will lay your cities
waste, will make your sanctuaries desolate,
and I will not smell your pleasing odors. 32 I
will devastate the land, so that your ene-
mies who come to settle in it shall be ap-
palled at it. 33 And you I will scatter among
the nations, and I will unsheathe the sword
against you; your land shall be a desola-
tion, and your cities a waste.

34 Then the land shall enjoy[a] its sab-
bath years as long as it lies desolate, while
you are in the land of your enemies; then
the land shall rest, and enjoy[a] its sabbath
years. 35 As long as it lies desolate, it shall
have the rest it did not have on your sab-
baths when you were living on it. 36 And as
for those of you who survive, I will send
faintness into their hearts in the lands of
their enemies; the sound of a driven leaf
shall put them to flight, and they shall flee
as one flees from the sword, and they shall
fall though no one pursues. 37 They shall
stumble over one another, as if to escape a
sword, though no one pursues; and you
shall have no power to stand against your
enemies. 38 You shall perish among the na-
tions, and the land of your enemies shall
devour you. 39 And those of you who sur-
vive shall languish in the land of your ene-
mies because of their iniquities; also they
shall languish because of the iniquities of
their ancestors.

40 But if they confess their iniquity and
the iniquity of their ancestors, in that they
committed treachery against me and, more-
over, that they continued hostile to me—
41 so that I, in turn, continued hostile to
them and brought them into the land of

a Or *make up for*

Ps 78.58; Jer 32.35). **33–45:** These verses, almost half of those devoted to punishments, deal with exile. This may indicate that the chapter was written or redacted after Babylonian conquest of Judah in 586 BCE. **34:** See 2 Chr 36.20, for exile offering the land an opportunity to enjoy its sabbath. **41:** *Uncircumcised heart,* a heart that is sealed or unresponsive to divine commands; cf. Deut 10.16; 30.6; Jer 4.4. **42,44–45:** Unlike secular treaties, God's treaty with Israel may not be abrogated by God. **45:** This

their enemies; if then their uncircumcised
heart is humbled and they make amends for
their iniquity, 42 then will I remember my
covenant with Jacob; I will remember also
my covenant with Isaac and also my cove-
nant with Abraham, and I will remember
the land. 43 For the land shall be deserted by
them, and enjoy[a] its sabbath years by lying
desolate without them, while they shall
make amends for their iniquity, because
they dared to spurn my ordinances, and
they abhorred my statutes. 44 Yet for all
that, when they are in the land of their ene-
mies, I will not spurn them, or abhor them
so as to destroy them utterly and break my
covenant with them; for I am the LORD
their God; 45 but I will remember in their
favor the covenant with their ancestors
whom I brought out of the land of Egypt in
the sight of the nations, to be their God: I
am the LORD.

46 These are the statutes and ordinances
and laws that the LORD established be-
tween himself and the people of Israel on
Mount Sinai through Moses.

27 The LORD spoke to Moses, saying:
2 Speak to the people of Israel and
say to them: When a person makes an ex-
plicit vow to the LORD concerning the
equivalent for a human being, 3 the equiva-
lent for a male shall be: from twenty to
sixty years of age the equivalent shall be
fifty shekels of silver by the sanctuary shek-
el. 4 If the person is a female, the equivalent
is thirty shekels. 5 If the age is from five to
twenty years of age, the equivalent is twen-
ty shekels for a male and ten shekels for a
female. 6 If the age is from one month to
five years, the equivalent for a male is five
shekels of silver, and for a female the equiv-
alent is three shekels of silver. 7 And if the
person is sixty years old or over, then the
equivalent for a male is fifteen shekels, and
for a female ten shekels. 8 If any cannot af-
ford the equivalent, they shall be brought
before the priest and the priest shall assess
them; the priest shall assess them according
to what each one making a vow can afford.

9 If it concerns an animal that may be
brought as an offering to the LORD, any
such that may be given to the LORD shall be
holy. 10 Another shall not be exchanged or
substituted for it, either good for bad or
bad for good; and if one animal is substitut-
ed for another, both that one and its substi-
tute shall be holy. 11 If it concerns any un-
clean animal that may not be brought as an
offering to the LORD, the animal shall be
presented before the priest. 12 The priest
shall assess it: whether good or bad, ac-
cording to the assessment of the priest, so it
shall be. 13 But if it is to be redeemed, one-
fifth must be added to the assessment.

14 If a person consecrates a house to the
LORD, the priest shall assess it: whether
good or bad, as the priest assesses it, so it
shall stand. 15 And if the one who conse-
crates the house wishes to redeem it, one-
fifth shall be added to its assessed value,
and it shall revert to the original owner.

16 If a person consecrates to the LORD
any inherited landholding, its assessment
shall be in accordance with its seed require-
ments: fifty shekels of silver to a homer of
barley seed. 17 If the person consecrates the
field as of the year of jubilee, that assess-

a Or *make up for*

leaves the people in exile, which may point to composition before 538 BCE, when the return to Judah began. **46:** This appears to apply only to chs 17–26; the legislation at the beginning of the book was given "from the tent of meeting" (1.1).

27.1–34: Dedications and holy gifts. An appendix to the foregoing (cf. 26.46). **2–13:** On vows, see Num 30.1–16n. **2–8:** Since human sacrifice is not allowed here, one substitutes a monetary equivalent when vowing a human (cf. Judg 11.30–31,34–40; 1 Sam 1.11,24–28), according to the economic and social position of the person vowed. **3:** A *shekel* weighed about 11.4 gr (.4 oz). **9–13:** This continues vv. 2–8, but now speaks of animals. **9:** *Be holy,* the vow is the means of consecrating the animal. **14–24:** The dedications in these verses are not conditional and are effective when uttered, in contrast to vows. Houses, hereditary land, and nonhereditary land are also concerns of 25.23–31. **16:** A *homer* was about 230 l (6.5 bu). **17–24:** *Jubilee,* see 25.8–17n. **25:** *Shekel,* see v. 3n. **26–27:** An exception to the foregoing:

ment shall stand; 18 but if the field is conse-
crated after the jubilee, the priest shall com-
pute the price for it according to the years
that remain until the year of jubilee, and
the assessment shall be reduced. 19 And if
the one who consecrates the field wishes to
redeem it, then one-fifth shall be added to
its assessed value, and it shall revert to the
original owner; 20 but if the field is not re-
deemed, or if it has been sold to someone
else, it shall no longer be redeemable. 21 But
when the field is released in the jubilee, it
shall be holy to the LORD as a devoted field;
it becomes the priest's holding. 22 If some-
one consecrates to the LORD a field that has
been purchased, which is not a part of the
inherited landholding, 23 the priest shall
compute for it the proportionate assess-
ment up to the year of jubilee, and the as-
sessment shall be paid as of that day, a sa-
cred donation to the LORD. 24 In the year of
jubilee the field shall return to the one from
whom it was bought, whose holding the
land is. 25 All assessments shall be by the
sanctuary shekel: twenty gerahs shall make
a shekel.

26 A firstling of animals, however,
which as a firstling belongs to the LORD,
cannot be consecrated by anyone; whether
ox or sheep, it is the LORD's. 27 If it is an
unclean animal, it shall be ransomed at its
assessment, with one-fifth added; if it is not
redeemed, it shall be sold at its assessment.

28 Nothing that a person owns that has
been devoted to destruction for the LORD,
be it human or animal, or inherited land-
holding, may be sold or redeemed; every
devoted thing is most holy to the LORD.
29 No human beings who have been devot-
ed to destruction can be ransomed; they
shall be put to death.

30 All tithes from the land, whether the
seed from the ground or the fruit from the
tree, are the LORD's; they are holy to the
LORD. 31 If persons wish to redeem any of
their tithes, they must add one-fifth to
them. 32 All tithes of herd and flock, every
tenth one that passes under the shepherd's
staff, shall be holy to the LORD. 33 Let no
one inquire whether it is good or bad, or
make substitution for it; if one makes sub-
stitution for it, then both it and the substi-
tute shall be holy and cannot be redeemed.

34 These are the commandments that
the LORD gave to Moses for the people of
Israel on Mount Sinai.

Firstborn animals and humans by nature belong to God (cf. Ex 13.1–2,12; 34.19) and therefore cannot be dedicated or vowed. Impure animals (v. 27) and humans must be redeemed (Num 18.15). **28**: Anything *devoted to destruction* cannot be redeemed or sold. Though this type of dedication is found mostly in war (e.g., Num 21.2; Josh 6.17–21; 8.26; 10.1,28; cf. Ex 22.20; Deut 13.15), v. 28 shows that proscription can apply to one's own property. This "herem" or dedication through destruction is a major theme of the first half of Joshua. *Most holy,* cf. Num 18.11–20,18n.; Lev 1.3n. **30–31**: That the produce tithe is called sacred indicates that it belongs to the priests (cf. Mal 3.10). Contrast Num 18.21–32n. **32–33**: On the animal tithe, cf. Gen 14.20; 28.22; 1 Sam 8.15–17; 2 Chr 31.5–6. **34**: A second conclusion to chs 17–26 (see 26.46).

NUMBERS

Numbers, the fourth book of the Torah or Pentateuch, is concerned with events during the Israelites' travels in the wilderness. Its English name, which derives from that of the early Greek translation, refers to the censuses that occur at the beginning and end of the wilderness period (chs 1 and 26).

The book consists of prescriptions woven around a narrative thread. It has two main sources: the Priestly writings (chs 1–9; 15; 17–19; 26–31; 34–36; and parts of 10; 13–14; 16; 20; 25; 32–33), mostly legal in character but having their own basic narrative; and a non-Priestly narrative source (the remaining portions). Neither of these is a single, unified body of work. The Priestly materials consist of the "Priestly Torah" (PT) and the "Holiness School" (HS). Of the two, HS largely predominates. Some of the chief concerns of the HS include the centrality of the sanctuary and, with this, God's presence among the people, and the installation of the Levites as sanctuary servants. The non-Priestly narrative sections have been ascribed to a combination of the Yahwist (Jahwist) and Elohist sources (JE), which are not easily distinguished in Numbers. For possible dates of PT and HS, see the Introduction to Leviticus. Though the date and extent of the non-Priestly material is debated by scholars, it predates the Priestly Torah/Holiness School portions.

The book has three main sections.

(1) Preparations for travel in the wilderness (chs 1–10). This section is mainly prescriptive. Its focus is the census and camp arrangement of the Israelites (chs 1–2; 5.1–4); the census, camp arrangement, duties, and consecration of the Levites (chs 3–4; 7–8); and the arrangement of the tribes and sanctuary while on the march (9.15–10.36). Interspersed in this are various prescriptions or descriptions concerning the guilt offering, suspected adultery, the nazirite vow, and the priestly blessing (5.5–6.27); and the delayed passover (9.1–4). It is not always clear why these laws are placed where they are now found. The section is almost entirely Priestly in origin.

(2) Travels in the wilderness (chs 11–25). This is mostly narrative, and combines Priestly and non-Priestly material. The narrative elements include rebellions and complaints by Israelites, Miriam and Aaron, and the scouts (chs 11–14); the rebellion of Korah, Dathan, and Abiram (chs 16–17); and Israel's encounters with various enemies, Balaam's blessing, and the Baal-peor incident (chs 20–25). Sections of prescription interspersed among these chapters include rules on offerings, sabbath violation (in a narrative context), and wearing fringes (ch 15); priesthood and Levitical duties (ch 18); and corpse contamination (ch 19).

(3) The end of the wilderness travels and preparations for entering the land of Canaan (chs 26–36). This section is mostly prescriptive. Portions that are closely connected with the narrative flow or the topic of acquiring the land of Canaan include the second census (ch 26); laws on female inheritance (27.1–11); the transfer of civil leadership to Joshua (27.12–23); revenge against the Midianites (ch 31); the distribution of the Transjordan land (ch 32); a summary of wilderness travels (ch 33); the boundaries of the land of Canaan (ch 34); Levitical cities and homicide laws (ch 35); and a supplement to laws of female inheritance (ch 36). Portions less visibly connected with the narrative context are the ritual calendar (chs 28–29); and rules about women's vows (ch 30). This section is almost entirely Priestly in origin.

At first reading the book might begin with the main narrative, chs 1; 10–14; 16–17; 20–27; 31–33. The legal sections are more difficult to understand, and may best be read according to different topics: the Levites (chs 3–4; 7–8; 18; 35); priestly and Levitical duties (chs 3–4; 16–17; 18; 35); the arrangement of camp (chs 2–3; 10); laws pertaining to women (ch 5; 27.1–11; chs 30; 36); holy days (9.1–14; 15.32–36; chs 28–29); impurity and holiness (5.1–4; chs 6; 16–17; 19; 35); sacrifices and offerings (chs 7; 15; 28–29); and distribution of the land (27.1–11; chs 32; 34–36). For suggestions on reading the legal sections, see the Introduction to the book of Leviticus. Any reading of the legal material in Numbers must ultimately be done in the larger context of the Priestly writings in Leviticus and Exodus. Numbers also contains a few poetic passages. Some of these are especially difficult, and might be studied together and in connection with the style of the Psalms (6.24–26; 10.35–36; 20.14–15,17–18,27–30; 23.7–10,18–24; 24.3–9,15–24).

1 The LORD spoke to Moses in the wil-
derness of Sinai, in the tent of meeting,
on the first day of the second month, in the
second year after they had come out of the
land of Egypt, saying: 2 Take a census of the
whole congregation of Israelites, in their
clans, by ancestral houses, according to the
number of names, every male individually;
3 from twenty years old and upward, every-
one in Israel able to go to war. You and
Aaron shall enroll them, company by com-
pany. 4 A man from each tribe shall be with
you, each man the head of his ancestral
house. 5 These are the names of the men
who shall assist you:
From Reuben, Elizur son of Shedeur.
6 From Simeon, Shelumiel son of
Zurishaddai.
7 From Judah, Nahshon son of
Amminadab.
8 From Issachar, Nethanel son of Zuar.
9 From Zebulun, Eliab son of Helon.
10 From the sons of Joseph:
from Ephraim, Elishama son of
Ammihud;
from Manasseh, Gamaliel son of
Pedahzur.
11 From Benjamin, Abidan son of
Gideoni.
12 From Dan, Ahiezer son of
Ammishaddai.
13 From Asher, Pagiel son of Ochran.
14 From Gad, Eliasaph son of Deuel.
15 From Naphtali, Ahira son of Enan.
16 These were the ones chosen from the con-
gregation, the leaders of their ancestral
tribes, the heads of the divisions of Is-
rael.
17 Moses and Aaron took these men
who had been designated by name, 18 and
on the first day of the second month they
assembled the whole congregation togeth-
er. They registered themselves in their
clans, by their ancestral houses, according
to the number of names from twenty years
old and upward, individually, 19 as the

1.1–54: The first Israelite census. The end of the book of Exodus dealt with the plan and construction of the wilderness sanctuary, and Leviticus in large part dealt with the ceremonies that take place in the sanctuary and the priesthood. Numbers opens (chs 1–10) with stories and laws pertaining more broadly to the people and their relationship to the sanctuary, still in the period soon after the Exodus and the revelation on Sinai. Ch 1 tells of a census taken of the twelve tribes. It omits the tribe of Levi and subdivides the tribe of Joseph into Ephraim and Manasseh, Joseph's sons (see Gen 48), to maintain the twelve-tribe structure (cf. 17.2–3). Two censuses of the Levites appear separately in chs 3 and 4. Ch 26 describes a further census of both the twelve tribes and the Levites. The two countings of the Israelites (chs 1 and 26) appear roughly at the beginning and end of the forty-year wilderness period. **1:** *Tent of meeting,* see Ex 26; 33.9. See also Num 7.89n. **3:** The wilderness camp and march has a military character (cf. 33.1), and the census seeks in part to determine the military capability of the people. Hence it counts only males twenty or more years old. **5–42:** For some of the principles influencing the order of the tribal lists, see 2.3–31n. **5–15:** Most of the individuals named do not occur elsewhere in the Bible outside of the book of Numbers (see also chs 2; 7; 10). **27:** The largest tribe is Judah; this likely reflects the political

LORD commanded Moses. So he enrolled
them in the wilderness of Sinai.
20 The descendants of Reuben, Israel's
firstborn, their lineage, in their clans, by
their ancestral houses, according to the
number of names, individually, every male
from twenty years old and upward, every-
one able to go to war: 21 those enrolled of
the tribe of Reuben were forty-six thou-
sand five hundred.
22 The descendants of Simeon, their lin-
eage, in their clans, by their ancestral
houses, those of them that were numbered,
according to the number of names, individ-
ually, every male from twenty years old
and upward, everyone able to go to war:
23 those enrolled of the tribe of Simeon were
fifty-nine thousand three hundred.
24 The descendants of Gad, their lin-
eage, in their clans, by their ancestral
houses, according to the number of the
names, from twenty years old and upward,
everyone able to go to war: 25 those en-
rolled of the tribe of Gad were forty-five
thousand six hundred fifty.
26 The descendants of Judah, their lin-
eage, in their clans, by their ancestral
houses, according to the number of names,
from twenty years old and upward, every-
one able to go to war: 27 those enrolled of
the tribe of Judah were seventy-four thou-
sand six hundred.
28 The descendants of Issachar, their
lineage, in their clans, by their ancestral
houses, according to the number of names,
from twenty years old and upward, every-
one able to go to war: 29 those enrolled of
the tribe of Issachar were fifty-four thou-
sand four hundred.
30 The descendants of Zebulun, their
lineage, in their clans, by their ancestral
houses, according to the number of names,
from twenty years old and upward, every-
one able to go to war: 31 those enrolled of
the tribe of Zebulun were fifty-seven thou-
sand four hundred.
32 The descendants of Joseph, namely,
the descendants of Ephraim, their lineage,
in their clans, by their ancestral houses,
according to the number of names, from
twenty years old and upward, everyone
able to go to war: 33 those enrolled of the
tribe of Ephraim were forty thousand five
hundred.
34 The descendants of Manasseh, their
lineage, in their clans, by their ancestral
houses, according to the number of names,
from twenty years old and upward, every-
one able to go to war: 35 those enrolled of
the tribe of Manasseh were thirty-two
thousand two hundred.
36 The descendants of Benjamin, their
lineage, in their clans, by their ancestral
houses, according to the number of names,
from twenty years old and upward, every-
one able to go to war: 37 those enrolled of
the tribe of Benjamin were thirty-five thou-
sand four hundred.
38 The descendants of Dan, their lin-
eage, in their clans, by their ancestral
houses, according to the number of names,
from twenty years old and upward, every-
one able to go to war: 39 those enrolled of
the tribe of Dan were sixty-two thousand
seven hundred.
40 The descendants of Asher, their lin-
eage, in their clans, by their ancestral
houses, according to the number of names,
from twenty years old and upward, every-
one able to go to war: 41 those enrolled of
the tribe of Asher were forty-one thousand
five hundred.
42 The descendants of Naphtali, their
lineage, in their clans, by their ancestral
houses, according to the number of names,
from twenty years old and upward, every-
one able to go to war: 43 those enrolled of
the tribe of Naphtali were fifty-three thou-
sand four hundred.
44 These are those who were enrolled,
whom Moses and Aaron enrolled with the
help of the leaders of Israel, twelve men,

importance of the tribe to the author. **46:** This high number is a reflection of the story's legendary rather than historical nature; see also Ex 12.37n. **47–53:** This is the first mention of the Levites as sanctuary servants, a theme that is continued in chs 3; 4; 8. Previously in the Priestly literature, only priests, the descendants of Aaron, have been of concern (e.g., Ex 29; Lev 8).

each representing his ancestral house. 45 So
the whole number of the Israelites, by their
ancestral houses, from twenty years old
and upward, everyone able to go to war in
Israel— 46 their whole number was six hun-
dred three thousand five hundred fifty.
47 The Levites, however, were not num-
bered by their ancestral tribe along with
them.

48 The LORD had said to Moses: 49 Only
the tribe of Levi you shall not enroll, and
you shall not take a census of them with the
other Israelites. 50 Rather you shall appoint
the Levites over the tabernacle of the cove-
nant,[a] and over all its equipment, and over
all that belongs to it; they are to carry the
tabernacle and all its equipment, and they
shall tend it, and shall camp around the
tabernacle. 51 When the tabernacle is to set
out, the Levites shall take it down; and
when the tabernacle is to be pitched, the
Levites shall set it up. And any outsider
who comes near shall be put to death.
52 The other Israelites shall camp in their
respective regimental camps, by companies;
53 but the Levites shall camp around the
tabernacle of the covenant,[a] that there
may be no wrath on the congregation of the
Israelites; and the Levites shall perform the
guard duty of the tabernacle of the cove-
nant.[a] 54 The Israelites did so; they did just
as the LORD commanded Moses.

2 The LORD spoke to Moses and Aaron,
saying: 2 The Israelites shall camp each
in their respective regiments, under ensigns
by their ancestral houses; they shall camp
facing the tent of meeting on every side.
3 Those to camp on the east side toward the
sunrise shall be of the regimental encamp-
ment of Judah by companies. The leader of
the people of Judah shall be Nahshon son
of Amminadab, 4 with a company as en-
rolled of seventy-four thousand six hun-
dred. 5 Those to camp next to him shall be
the tribe of Issachar. The leader of the Issa-
charites shall be Nethanel son of Zuar,
6 with a company as enrolled of fifty-four
thousand four hundred. 7 Then the tribe of
Zebulun: The leader of the Zebulunites
shall be Eliab son of Helon, 8 with a compa-
ny as enrolled of fifty-seven thousand four
hundred. 9 The total enrollment of the
camp of Judah, by companies, is one hun-
dred eighty-six thousand four hundred.
They shall set out first on the march.

10 On the south side shall be the regi-
mental encampment of Reuben by compa-
nies. The leader of the Reubenites shall be
Elizur son of Shedeur, 11 with a company as
enrolled of forty-six thousand five hun-
dred. 12 And those to camp next to him
shall be the tribe of Simeon. The leader of

a Or *treaty*, or *testimony*; Heb *eduth*

2.1–34: The plan of the wilderness camp. This is an idealized plan, with the sanctuary in the center of the community (contrast 11.26n.). Ch 2 prescribes the positions of the twelve tribes, and ch 3 sets out the positions of the Levites and priests (cf. 1.53; 3.23,29,35). **3–31:** The twelve tribes are divided into four divisions, each with three tribes. A combination of genealogical (Gen 29.31–30.24; 35.16–18) and geographical principles (see Josh 13–19; see color Map 3 at end of book) influences their positions around the wilderness sanctuary. Tribes that descend from Rachel (Ephraim, Manasseh, Benjamin) and are centrally located in the traditional apportionment of the land of Israel form a division on the west, the central axis of the camp (2.18–24). Tribes that descend from Rachel's and Leah's maidservants Bilhah (Dan, Naphtali) and Zilpah (Asher) and are the northernmost tribes in the land form a division on the north of the sanctuary (vv. 25–31). Two tribes that descend from Leah (Simeon and Reuben) and are southernmost tribes, together with Gad, a son of Zilpah, but who adjoins Reuben's inheritance in the land, form a division on the south of the sanctuary (vv. 10–16). Finally, three other tribes that descend from Leah (Judah, Issachar, and Zebulun) form a division on the east of the sanctuary. The geographical principle is less clear here since Judah is a southern tribe, and Issachar and Zebulun are northern tribes. However, these tribes fall together when one subtracts the northernmost and southernmost tribes, as well as the central Rachel tribes. Judah's placement in the distinguished position on the east, the location of the sanctuary's entrance, appears to be due in part to its position as the royal tribe of the southern kingdom. See 10.14–28n.; 34.16–19n. **9,17,24,31:** On the marching formation of the camp see 10.14–28n.

the Simeonites shall be Shelumiel son of
Zurishaddai, 13 with a company as enrolled
of fifty-nine thousand three hundred.
14 Then the tribe of Gad: The leader of the
Gadites shall be Eliasaph son of Reuel,
15 with a company as enrolled of forty-five
thousand six hundred fifty. 16 The total en-
rollment of the camp of Reuben, by compa-
nies, is one hundred fifty-one thousand
four hundred fifty. They shall set out sec-
ond.

17 The tent of meeting, with the camp of
the Levites, shall set out in the center of the
camps; they shall set out just as they camp,
each in position, by their regiments.

18 On the west side shall be the regi-
mental encampment of Ephraim by compa-
nies. The leader of the people of Ephraim
shall be Elishama son of Ammihud, 19 with
a company as enrolled of forty thousand
five hundred. 20 Next to him shall be the
tribe of Manasseh. The leader of the people
of Manasseh shall be Gamaliel son of Pe-
dahzur, 21 with a company as enrolled of
thirty-two thousand two hundred. 22 Then
the tribe of Benjamin: The leader of the
Benjaminites shall be Abidan son of Gideo-
ni, 23 with a company as enrolled of thirty-
five thousand four hundred. 24 The total
enrollment of the camp of Ephraim, by
companies, is one hundred eight thousand
one hundred. They shall set out third on the
march.

25 On the north side shall be the regi-
mental encampment of Dan by companies.
The leader of the Danites shall be Ahiezer
son of Ammishaddai, 26 with a company as
enrolled of sixty-two thousand seven hun-
dred. 27 Those to camp next to him shall be
the tribe of Asher. The leader of the Asher-
ites shall be Pagiel son of Ochran, 28 with a
company as enrolled of forty-one thousand
five hundred. 29 Then the tribe of Naphtali:
The leader of the Naphtalites shall be Ahira
son of Enan, 30 with a company as enrolled
of fifty-three thousand four hundred.
31 The total enrollment of the camp of Dan
is one hundred fifty-seven thousand six
hundred. They shall set out last, by compa-
nies.[a]

32 This was the enrollment of the Israel-
ites by their ancestral houses; the total en-
rollment in the camps by their companies
was six hundred three thousand five hun-
dred fifty. 33 Just as the LORD had com-
manded Moses, the Levites were not en-
rolled among the other Israelites.

34 The Israelites did just as the LORD
had commanded Moses: They camped by
regiments, and they set out the same way,
everyone by clans, according to ancestral
houses.

3 This is the lineage of Aaron and Moses
at the time when the LORD spoke with
Moses on Mount Sinai. 2 These are the
names of the sons of Aaron: Nadab the
firstborn, and Abihu, Eleazar, and Ithamar;
3 these are the names of the sons of Aaron,
the anointed priests, whom he ordained to
minister as priests. 4 Nadab and Abihu died
before the LORD when they offered unholy
fire before the LORD in the wilderness of
Sinai, and they had no children. Eleazar
and Ithamar served as priests in the lifetime
of their father Aaron.

5 Then the LORD spoke to Moses, say-
ing: 6 Bring the tribe of Levi near, and set
them before Aaron the priest, so that they

a Compare verses 9, 16, 24: Heb *by their regiments*

3.1–44: The first Levitical census. A second Levitical census appears in ch 4, and a third in 26.57–62. **1–4:** The Aaronides constitute the priestly line within the larger tribe of Levi. **4:** See Lev 10.1–7. **5–10:** The Levites are assistants to the priests. Their duties include "guarding" (translated as *perform duties, be in charge of* in vv. 7–8; cf. 1.53) the sanctuary, that is making certain that no one inappropriate enters it, and performing "labor" (translated *doing service,* v. 7), such as transporting the sanctuary and its furnishings (see ch 4). The Aaronides, for their part, are to "guard their priesthood" (v. 10; translated *attend to the priesthood*), i.e., make sure that only they perform priestly duties, such as working at the altar or in the tent of meeting. Non-priests, including even Levites, who encroach on these locales and prerogatives are to be put to death (cf. vv. 10,38; 1.51; 18.1–7). This highly ordered, hierarchical, border-conscious system is typical of priestly thinking. **11–13:** The Israelites are to devote the firstborn,

may assist him. 7They shall perform duties
for him and for the whole congregation in
front of the tent of meeting, doing service at
the tabernacle; 8they shall be in charge of
all the furnishings of the tent of meeting,
and attend to the duties for the Israelites
as they do service at the tabernacle. 9You
shall give the Levites to Aaron and his de-
scendants; they are unreservedly given to
him from among the Israelites. 10But you
shall make a register of Aaron and his de-
scendants; it is they who shall attend to the
priesthood, and any outsider who comes
near shall be put to death.

11 Then the LORD spoke to Moses, say-
ing: 12I hereby accept the Levites from
among the Israelites as substitutes for all
the firstborn that open the womb among
the Israelites. The Levites shall be mine,
13for all the firstborn are mine; when I
killed all the firstborn in the land of Egypt,
I consecrated for my own all the firstborn
in Israel, both human and animal; they
shall be mine. I am the LORD.

14 Then the LORD spoke to Moses in the
wilderness of Sinai, saying: 15Enroll the Le-
vites by ancestral houses and by clans. You
shall enroll every male from a month old
and upward. 16So Moses enrolled them ac-
cording to the word of the LORD, as he was
commanded. 17The following were the
sons of Levi, by their names: Gershon, Ko-
hath, and Merari. 18These are the names of
the sons of Gershon by their clans: Libni
and Shimei. 19The sons of Kohath by their
clans: Amram, Izhar, Hebron, and Uzziel.
20The sons of Merari by their clans: Mahli
and Mushi. These are the clans of the Le-
vites, by their ancestral houses.

21 To Gershon belonged the clan of the
Libnites and the clan of the Shimeites; these
were the clans of the Gershonites. 22Their
enrollment, counting all the males from a
month old and upward, was seven thou-
sand five hundred. 23The clans of the Ger-
shonites were to camp behind the taberna-
cle on the west, 24with Eliasaph son of Lael
as head of the ancestral house of the Ger-
shonites. 25The responsibility of the sons of
Gershon in the tent of meeting was to be
the tabernacle, the tent with its covering,
the screen for the entrance of the tent of
meeting, 26the hangings of the court, the
screen for the entrance of the court that is
around the tabernacle and the altar, and its
cords—all the service pertaining to these.

27 To Kohath belonged the clan of the
Amramites, the clan of the Izharites, the
clan of the Hebronites, and the clan of the
Uzzielites; these are the clans of the Ko-
hathites. 28Counting all the males, from a
month old and upward, there were eight
thousand six hundred, attending to the du-
ties of the sanctuary. 29The clans of the
Kohathites were to camp on the south side
of the tabernacle, 30with Elizaphan son of
Uzziel as head of the ancestral house of the
clans of the Kohathites. 31Their responsi-
bility was to be the ark, the table, the lamp-
stand, the altars, the vessels of the sanctu-
ary with which the priests minister, and the
screen—all the service pertaining to these.
32Eleazar son of Aaron the priest was to be
chief over the leaders of the Levites, and to
have oversight of those who had charge of
the sanctuary.

33 To Merari belonged the clan of the
Mahlites and the clan of the Mushites:
these are the clans of Merari. 34Their en-
rollment, counting all the males from a

of animals and humans, to God (Ex 13.2; Lev 27.26–27; Num 8.17; 18.15–16). Animals are sacrificed. Firstborn children would theoretically become temple servants (cf. 1 Sam 1.10–11,24–28). But the Levites are substitutes for the firstborn children and serve in the sanctuary in their place (see 3.40–51). **14–39:** The passage identifies three Levitical clans and notes their duties (see also the notes on ch 4). They camp on the west, south, and north of the sanctuary. They, together with the priests (and Moses, the inaugural priest and prophet and Aaron's brother) who camp on the east, form a ring around the sanctuary that protects it from encroachers (see 1.53; 2.1–34n.; 3.5–10n.). **25–26:** *The tabernacle,* Ex 26.7–14; *the screen,* Ex 26.36–37. **26:** *Hangings,* Ex 27.9; *screen,* Ex 27.16. **31:** *The ark, the table, the lampstand,* Ex 25.10–40; *the altars,* Ex 27.1–8; 30.1–10; *the vessels,* Ex 37.16; 38.3; cf. Num 4.7,14; *the screen,* Ex 26.31–35. **36–37:** Ex 26.15–31. **40–51:** The excess firstborn children are redeemed;

month old and upward, was six thousand
two hundred. 35 The head of the ancestral
house of the clans of Merari was Zuriel son
of Abihail; they were to camp on the north
side of the tabernacle. 36 The responsibility
assigned to the sons of Merari was to be the
frames of the tabernacle, the bars, the pil-
lars, the bases, and all their accessories—all
the service pertaining to these; 37 also the
pillars of the court all around, with their
bases and pegs and cords.

38 Those who were to camp in front of
the tabernacle on the east—in front of the
tent of meeting toward the east—were Mo-
ses and Aaron and Aaron's sons, having
charge of the rites within the sanctuary,
whatever had to be done for the Israelites;
and any outsider who came near was to be
put to death. 39 The total enrollment of the
Levites whom Moses and Aaron enrolled at
the commandment of the LORD, by their
clans, all the males from a month old and
upward, was twenty-two thousand.

40 Then the LORD said to Moses: Enroll
all the firstborn males of the Israelites, from
a month old and upward, and count their
names. 41 But you shall accept the Levites
for me—I am the LORD—as substitutes for
all the firstborn among the Israelites, and
the livestock of the Levites as substitutes
for all the firstborn among the livestock of
the Israelites. 42 So Moses enrolled all the
firstborn among the Israelites, as the LORD
commanded him. 43 The total enrollment,
all the firstborn males from a month old
and upward, counting the number of
names, was twenty-two thousand two hun-
dred seventy-three.

44 Then the LORD spoke to Moses, say-
ing: 45 Accept the Levites as substitutes for
all the firstborn among the Israelites, and
the livestock of the Levites as substitutes
for their livestock; and the Levites shall be
mine. I am the LORD. 46 As the price of re-
demption of the two hundred seventy-three
of the firstborn of the Israelites, over and
above the number of the Levites, 47 you
shall accept five shekels apiece, reckoning
by the shekel of the sanctuary, a shekel of
twenty gerahs. 48 Give to Aaron and his
sons the money by which the excess num-
ber of them is redeemed. 49 So Moses took
the redemption money from those who
were over and above those redeemed by the
Levites; 50 from the firstborn of the Israel-
ites he took the money, one thousand three
hundred sixty-five shekels, reckoned by the
shekel of the sanctuary; 51 and Moses gave
the redemption money to Aaron and his
sons, according to the word of the LORD, as
the LORD had commanded Moses.

4 The LORD spoke to Moses and Aaron,
saying: 2 Take a census of the Kohath-
ites separate from the other Levites, by
their clans and their ancestral houses,
3 from thirty years old up to fifty years old,
all who qualify to do work relating to the
tent of meeting. 4 The service of the Ko-
hathites relating to the tent of meeting con-
cerns the most holy things.

5 When the camp is to set out, Aaron
and his sons shall go in and take down the
screening curtain, and cover the ark of the
covenant[a] with it; 6 then they shall put on
it a covering of fine leather,[b] and spread
over that a cloth all of blue, and shall put
its poles in place. 7 Over the table of the
bread of the Presence they shall spread a
blue cloth, and put on it the plates, the

a Or *treaty*, or *testimony*; Heb *eduth* *b* Meaning of Heb uncertain

the redemption money becomes holy and goes to the priesthood. **47:** A *shekel* weighed about 11.4 gr (.4 oz); see Ex 30.13n.

4.1–49: The second Levitical census. This differs from the census in ch 3 by its detailed delineation of the Levites' duties in transporting the sanctuary and a limitation to those most fit for this service, i.e., thirty to fifty years of age (cf. 3.15). Moreover, ch 4 lists the Kohathites first, probably because they carried the most important and hazardous items of the sanctuary. Ch 3 lists the clans in their traditional birth order (cf. Gen 46.11; Ex 6.16). **5–20:** Since they are not holy like priests (see 8.5–26n.), the Kohathites may not contact or even look at the sanctuary furniture so they will not die by divine wrath (vv. 15,19–20). The priests first wrap up the holy items (see 3.31n.) for transport. **16:** *Oil for the light,*

dishes for incense, the bowls, and the flag-
ons for the drink offering; the regular bread
also shall be on it; 8 then they shall spread
over them a crimson cloth, and cover it
with a covering of fine leather,[a] and shall
put its poles in place. 9 They shall take a
blue cloth, and cover the lampstand for the
light, with its lamps, its snuffers, its trays,
and all the vessels for oil with which it is
supplied; 10 and they shall put it with all its
utensils in a covering of fine leather,[a] and
put it on the carrying frame. 11 Over the
golden altar they shall spread a blue cloth,
and cover it with a covering of fine leath-
er,[a] and shall put its poles in place; 12 and
they shall take all the utensils of the service
that are used in the sanctuary, and put
them in a blue cloth, and cover them with
a covering of fine leather,[a] and put them
on the carrying frame. 13 They shall take
away the ashes from the altar, and spread a
purple cloth over it; 14 and they shall put on
it all the utensils of the altar, which are
used for the service there, the firepans, the
forks, the shovels, and the basins, all the
utensils of the altar; and they shall spread
on it a covering of fine leather,[a] and shall
put its poles in place. 15 When Aaron and
his sons have finished covering the sanctu-
ary and all the furnishings of the sanctuary,
as the camp sets out, after that the Kohath-
ites shall come to carry these, but they must
not touch the holy things, or they will die.
These are the things of the tent of meeting
that the Kohathites are to carry.

16 Eleazar son of Aaron the priest shall
have charge of the oil for the light, the fra-
grant incense, the regular grain offering,
and the anointing oil, the oversight of all
the tabernacle and all that is in it, in the
sanctuary and in its utensils.

17 Then the LORD spoke to Moses and
Aaron, saying: 18 You must not let the tribe
of the clans of the Kohathites be destroyed
from among the Levites. 19 This is how you
must deal with them in order that they may
live and not die when they come near to the
most holy things: Aaron and his sons shall
go in and assign each to a particular task or
burden. 20 But the Kohathites[b] must not go
in to look on the holy things even for a
moment; otherwise they will die.

21 Then the LORD spoke to Moses, say-
ing: 22 Take a census of the Gershonites
also, by their ancestral houses and by their
clans; 23 from thirty years old up to fifty
years old you shall enroll them, all who
qualify to do work in the tent of meeting.
24 This is the service of the clans of the Ger-
shonites, in serving and bearing burdens:
25 They shall carry the curtains of the taber-
nacle, and the tent of meeting with its cov-
ering, and the outer covering of fine leath-
er[a] that is on top of it, and the screen for
the entrance of the tent of meeting, 26 and
the hangings of the court, and the screen
for the entrance of the gate of the court that
is around the tabernacle and the altar, and
their cords, and all the equipment for their
service; and they shall do all that needs to
be done with regard to them. 27 All the ser-
vice of the Gershonites shall be at the com-
mand of Aaron and his sons, in all that they
are to carry, and in all that they have to do;
and you shall assign to their charge all that
they are to carry. 28 This is the service of the
clans of the Gershonites relating to the tent
of meeting, and their responsibilities are to
be under the oversight of Ithamar son of
Aaron the priest.

29 As for the Merarites, you shall enroll
them by their clans and their ancestral
houses; 30 from thirty years old up to fifty
years old you shall enroll them, everyone
who qualifies to do the work of the tent of
meeting. 31 This is what they are charged to
carry, as the whole of their service in the
tent of meeting: the frames of the taberna-

a Meaning of Heb uncertain *b* Heb *they*

Ex 27.20; *incense,* Ex 30.7; *grain offering,* Lev 6.14–18; *anointing oil,* Ex 30.22–34. **21–28:** The Gershonites are in charge of transporting the tent's four layers, the fabric wall that surrounds the court, the hangings to the entrances of the tent and court, and their appurtenances (cf. Ex 26–27). **29–33:** The Merarites carry the framework of the sanctuary that supports the various layers and hangings (cf. Ex 26–27). **34–49:** A summary of the numbers of Levites, which differs from the previous chapter where all

cle, with its bars, pillars, and bases, 32 and
the pillars of the court all around with their
bases, pegs, and cords, with all their equip-
ment and all their related service; and you
shall assign by name the objects that they
are required to carry. 33 This is the service
of the clans of the Merarites, the whole of
their service relating to the tent of meeting,
under the hand of Ithamar son of Aaron the
priest.
34 So Moses and Aaron and the leaders
of the congregation enrolled the Kohath-
ites, by their clans and their ancestral
houses, 35 from thirty years old up to fifty
years old, everyone who qualified for work
relating to the tent of meeting; 36 and their
enrollment by clans was two thousand sev-
en hundred fifty. 37 This was the enrollment
of the clans of the Kohathites, all who
served at the tent of meeting, whom Moses
and Aaron enrolled according to the com-
mandment of the LORD by Moses.
38 The enrollment of the Gershonites,
by their clans and their ancestral houses,
39 from thirty years old up to fifty years old,
everyone who qualified for work relating to
the tent of meeting— 40 their enrollment by
their clans and their ancestral houses was
two thousand six hundred thirty. 41 This
was the enrollment of the clans of the Ger-
shonites, all who served at the tent of meet-
ing, whom Moses and Aaron enrolled ac-
cording to the commandment of the LORD.
42 The enrollment of the clans of the
Merarites, by their clans and their ancestral
houses, 43 from thirty years old up to fifty
years old, everyone who qualified for work
relating to the tent of meeting— 44 their en-
rollment by their clans was three thousand
two hundred. 45 This is the enrollment of
the clans of the Merarites, whom Moses
and Aaron enrolled according to the com-
mandment of the LORD by Moses.
46 All those who were enrolled of the
Levites, whom Moses and Aaron and the
leaders of Israel enrolled, by their clans and
their ancestral houses, 47 from thirty years
old up to fifty years old, everyone who
qualified to do the work of service and the
work of bearing burdens relating to the tent
of meeting, 48 their enrollment was eight
thousand five hundred eighty. 49 According
to the commandment of the LORD through
Moses they were appointed to their several
tasks of serving or carrying; thus they were
enrolled by him, as the LORD commanded
Moses.

5 The LORD spoke to Moses, saying:
2 Command the Israelites to put out of
the camp everyone who is leprous,[a] or has
a discharge, and everyone who is unclean
through contact with a corpse; 3 you shall
put out both male and female, putting them
outside the camp; they must not defile their
camp, where I dwell among them. 4 The Is-
raelites did so, putting them outside the
camp; as the LORD had spoken to Moses,
so the Israelites did.
5 The LORD spoke to Moses, saying:
6 Speak to the Israelites: When a man or a
woman wrongs another, breaking faith

a A term for several skin diseases; precise meaning uncertain

one month or older (3.15) were counted. This chapter focuses on physical labor, so a smaller number, aged thirty and above, is given.

5.1–6.27: Various laws. These rules are connected by an implicit common requirement of priestly supervision.

5.1–4: Expulsion of impure persons. This passage contextually relates to the plan for the sanctuary camp in chs 2–3. The Israelites are to exclude from it those with the severest impurities: surface affliction (rather than leprosy; see Lev 13.1–14.57n.), abnormal sexual flows (perhaps including menstruating women and those who have just given birth; Lev 12; 15), and corpse contamination (ch 19). These impurities can be communicated to others and threaten directly the holiness of the sanctuary, and may cause God to depart from the midst of the camp (cf. Deut 23.9–14). Other severe impurities are similarly excluded from the camp (Lev 13.52–57; 14.40–45; 16.22,27–28).

5.5–10: The guilt offering. This supplements Lev 5.14–6.7 (see the notes there). Reparation payment is made to the officiating priest when the injured party or a relative is not alive or available.

with the LORD, that person incurs guilt
7 and shall confess the sin that has been
committed. The person shall make full restitution for the wrong, adding one-fifth to
it, and giving it to the one who was
wronged. 8 If the injured party has no next
of kin to whom restitution may be made for
the wrong, the restitution for wrong shall
go to the LORD for the priest, in addition to
the ram of atonement with which atonement is made for the guilty party. 9 Among
all the sacred donations of the Israelites,
every gift that they bring to the priest shall
be his. 10 The sacred donations of all are
their own; whatever anyone gives to the
priest shall be his.

11 The LORD spoke to Moses, saying:
12 Speak to the Israelites and say to them: If
any man's wife goes astray and is unfaithful
to him, 13 if a man has had intercourse with
her but it is hidden from her husband, so
that she is undetected though she has defiled herself, and there is no witness against
her since she was not caught in the act; 14 if
a spirit of jealousy comes on him, and he is
jealous of his wife who has defiled herself;
or if a spirit of jealousy comes on him, and
he is jealous of his wife, though she has not
defiled herself; 15 then the man shall bring
his wife to the priest. And he shall bring the
offering required for her, one-tenth of an
ephah of barley flour. He shall pour no oil
on it and put no frankincense on it, for it is
a grain offering of jealousy, a grain offering
of remembrance, bringing iniquity to remembrance.

16 Then the priest shall bring her near,
and set her before the LORD; 17 the priest
shall take holy water in an earthen vessel,
and take some of the dust that is on the
floor of the tabernacle and put it into the
water. 18 The priest shall set the woman before the LORD, dishevel the woman's hair,
and place in her hands the grain offering of
remembrance, which is the grain offering of
jealousy. In his own hand the priest shall
have the water of bitterness that brings the
curse. 19 Then the priest shall make her take
an oath, saying, "If no man has lain with
you, if you have not turned aside to uncleanness while under your husband's authority, be immune to this water of bitterness that brings the curse. 20 But if you have
gone astray while under your husband's authority, if you have defiled yourself and
some man other than your husband has
had intercourse with you," 21—let the
priest make the woman take the oath of the
curse and say to the woman—"the LORD
make you an execration and an oath
among your people, when the LORD makes
your uterus drop, your womb discharge;
22 now may this water that brings the curse
enter your bowels and make your womb
discharge, your uterus drop!" And the
woman shall say, "Amen. Amen."

23 Then the priest shall put these curses
in writing, and wash them off into the water of bitterness. 24 He shall make the woman drink the water of bitterness that brings
the curse, and the water that brings the
curse shall enter her and cause bitter pain.
25 The priest shall take the grain offering
of jealousy out of the woman's hand, and
shall elevate the grain offering before the
LORD and bring it to the altar; 26 and the
priest shall take a handful of the grain
offering, as its memorial portion, and turn
it into smoke on the altar, and afterward
shall make the woman drink the water.
27 When he has made her drink the water,
then, if she has defiled herself and has been
unfaithful to her husband, the water that
brings the curse shall enter into her and

5.11–31: A suspected adulteress. A man who questions his wife's fidelity brings her to the sanctuary for an ordeal in which she drinks a mixture of water, dust, and ink to determine if she is culpable (cf. Ex 32.20). A guilty woman suffers what appears to be a miscarriage (if pregnant from adultery) or perhaps a distended uterus (vv. 22,27). God blesses an innocent woman with fertility (v. 28). Since Israel was a polygamous society, in which a man may have many wives, but a woman may not have many husbands, only women were subject to this ritual. Ordeals to determine culpability are found in other societies of the ancient Near East (e.g., Hammurabi's Laws §132). **15:** *One-tenth of an ephah* was about 2.3 l (2 qt). *Frankincense,* an aromatic resin from shrubs found in Arabia and East Africa.

cause bitter pain, and her womb shall dis-
charge, her uterus drop, and the woman
shall become an execration among her peo-
ple. 28 But if the woman has not defiled her-
self and is clean, then she shall be immune
and be able to conceive children.
29 This is the law in cases of jealousy,
when a wife, while under her husband's au-
thority, goes astray and defiles herself, 30 or
when a spirit of jealousy comes on a man
and he is jealous of his wife; then he shall
set the woman before the LORD, and the
priest shall apply this entire law to her.
31 The man shall be free from iniquity, but
the woman shall bear her iniquity.

6 The LORD spoke to Moses, saying:
2 Speak to the Israelites and say to
them: When either men or women make a
special vow, the vow of a nazirite,[a] to sep-
arate themselves to the LORD, 3 they shall
separate themselves from wine and strong
drink; they shall drink no wine vinegar or
other vinegar, and shall not drink any
grape juice or eat grapes, fresh or dried.
4 All their days as nazirites[b] they shall eat
nothing that is produced by the grapevine,
not even the seeds or the skins.
5 All the days of their nazirite vow no
razor shall come upon the head; until the
time is completed for which they separate
themselves to the LORD, they shall be holy;
they shall let the locks of the head grow
long.
6 All the days that they separate them-
selves to the LORD they shall not go near
a corpse. 7 Even if their father or mother,
brother or sister, should die, they may not
defile themselves; because their consecra-
tion to God is upon the head. 8 All their
days as nazirites[b] they are holy to the
LORD.
9 If someone dies very suddenly nearby,
defiling the consecrated head, then they
shall shave the head on the day of their
cleansing; on the seventh day they shall
shave it. 10 On the eighth day they shall
bring two turtledoves or two young pi-
geons to the priest at the entrance of the
tent of meeting, 11 and the priest shall offer
one as a sin offering and the other as a
burnt offering, and make atonement for
them, because they incurred guilt by reason
of the corpse. They shall sanctify the head
that same day, 12 and separate themselves
to the LORD for their days as nazirites,[b]
and bring a male lamb a year old as a guilt
offering. The former time shall be void, be-
cause the consecrated head was defiled.
13 This is the law for the nazirites[b]
when the time of their consecration has
been completed: they shall be brought to
the entrance of the tent of meeting, 14 and
they shall offer their gift to the LORD, one
male lamb a year old without blemish as a
burnt offering, one ewe lamb a year old
without blemish as a sin offering, one ram
without blemish as an offering of well-
being, 15 and a basket of unleavened bread,
cakes of choice flour mixed with oil and
unleavened wafers spread with oil, with
their grain offering and their drink offer-
ings. 16 The priest shall present them before
the LORD and offer their sin offering and
burnt offering, 17 and shall offer the ram as
a sacrifice of well-being to the LORD, with

a That is *one separated* or *one consecrated* *b* That is *those separated* or *those consecrated*

6.1–21: The nazirite vow. An Israelite may take upon him or herself a temporary vow of holiness (for lifetime nazirites, see Judg 13.4–7; 16.17; Am 2.11–12). Nazirites are to abstain from all grape products (cf. Jer 35.5–19); allow the hair, the focus of the vow's holiness, to grow unrestricted; and avoid corpse contamination. Some of the restrictions accompanying the vow are similar to those for priests (Lev 10.9–11; 21.1–12n.; also compare Judg 13.4,7 with Lev 22.8; Ezek 44.31). Hence, a nazirite enters a state of holiness similar to that of priests, albeit for a circumscribed time period. **9–12:** After becoming accidentally polluted by a corpse, the nazirite presumably follows the purification prescriptions in ch 19 and then brings the offerings listed here (see Lev 1; 4–5) to rectify the consequences of impurity and restart the vow. **13–20:** This is a sacrificial rite of passage which returns the individual to a profane state (cf. Lev 10.10n.); the shearing and burning of the hair (v. 18) is clearly symbolic of this return to lay status.

the basket of unleavened bread; the priest
also shall make the accompanying grain
offering and drink offering. 18 Then the
nazirites[a] shall shave the consecrated head
at the entrance of the tent of meeting, and
shall take the hair from the consecrated
head and put it on the fire under the sacri-
fice of well-being. 19 The priest shall take
the shoulder of the ram, when it is boiled,
and one unleavened cake out of the basket,
and one unleavened wafer, and shall put
them in the palms of the nazirites,[a] after
they have shaved the consecrated head.
20 Then the priest shall elevate them as an
elevation offering before the LORD; they
are a holy portion for the priest, together
with the breast that is elevated and the
thigh that is offered. After that the naz-
irites[a] may drink wine.

21 This is the law for the nazirites[a] who
take a vow. Their offering to the LORD
must be in accordance with the nazirite[b]
vow, apart from what else they can afford.
In accordance with whatever vow they
take, so they shall do, following the law for
their consecration.

22 The LORD spoke to Moses, saying:
23 Speak to Aaron and his sons, saying,
Thus you shall bless the Israelites: You
shall say to them,

24 The LORD bless you and keep you;
25 the LORD make his face to shine upon
you, and be gracious to you;
26 the LORD lift up his countenance
upon you, and give you peace.

27 So they shall put my name on the Is-
raelites, and I will bless them.

7 On the day when Moses had finished
setting up the tabernacle, and had
anointed and consecrated it with all its fur-
nishings, and had anointed and consecrated
the altar with all its utensils, 2 the leaders of
Israel, heads of their ancestral houses, the
leaders of the tribes, who were over those
who were enrolled, made offerings. 3 They
brought their offerings before the LORD,
six covered wagons and twelve oxen, a
wagon for every two of the leaders, and for
each one an ox; they presented them before
the tabernacle. 4 Then the LORD said to
Moses: 5 Accept these from them, that they
may be used in doing the service of the tent
of meeting, and give them to the Levites, to
each according to his service. 6 So Moses
took the wagons and the oxen, and gave
them to the Levites. 7 Two wagons and four
oxen he gave to the Gershonites, according
to their service; 8 and four wagons and eight
oxen he gave to the Merarites, according to
their service, under the direction of Ithamar
son of Aaron the priest. 9 But to the Ko-
hathites he gave none, because they were
charged with the care of the holy things
that had to be carried on the shoulders.

10 The leaders also presented offerings
for the dedication of the altar at the time
when it was anointed; the leaders presented
their offering before the altar. 11 The LORD
said to Moses: They shall present their
offerings, one leader each day, for the dedi-
cation of the altar.

a That is *those separated* or *those consecrated*
b That is *one separated* or *one consecrated*

Compare the ceremony that raises the priests from a profane to a holy state (Lev 8). **17:** *Sacrifice of well-being,* see Lev 3.1–17n. **20:** *Elevation offering,* see 18.11n.

6.22–27: The priestly blessing. This strikingly anthropomorphic blessing, in poetic style, was probably to be delivered at public gatherings at the sanctuary (cf. Lev 9.22–23; see Num 7.1–88n.). Two silver plaques from the seventh to sixth century BCE, found just outside Jerusalem, contain versions of this blessing, attesting to its traditional usage. For the language, cf. Ps 4.6; 67.1; Mal 1.8–10.

7.1–89: Sanctuary dedication offerings. The chieftains of the tribes contribute carts and oxen as well as dedication offerings of animals, incense, and precious vessels just after the sanctuary is consecrated (Lev 8–9). In the immediate context the passage tells how the Levitical clans of Gershon and Merari obtained carts on which to carry the sanctuary tent and frames, a duty outlined in chs 3–4. The Kohathites did not use carts for the holy furniture, which required more cautious transport by hand (v. 9; a change from cart to shoulder transport is implied in 2 Sam 6.3,6,13). In the larger context, the passage continues the narrative from the consecration of the sanctuary in Lev 8–9 (but cf. Lev 16.1–34n.). In view of this, the

12 The one who presented his offering
the first day was Nahshon son of Ammina-
dab, of the tribe of Judah; 13 his offering
was one silver plate weighing one hundred
thirty shekels, one silver basin weighing
seventy shekels, according to the shekel of
the sanctuary, both of them full of choice
flour mixed with oil for a grain offering;
14 one golden dish weighing ten shekels, full
of incense; 15 one young bull, one ram, one
male lamb a year old, for a burnt offering;
16 one male goat for a sin offering; 17 and
for the sacrifice of well-being, two oxen,
five rams, five male goats, and five male
lambs a year old. This was the offering of
Nahshon son of Amminadab.

18 On the second day Nethanel son of
Zuar, the leader of Issachar, presented an
offering; 19 he presented for his offering one
silver plate weighing one hundred thirty
shekels, one silver basin weighing seventy
shekels, according to the shekel of the sanc-
tuary, both of them full of choice flour
mixed with oil for a grain offering; 20 one
golden dish weighing ten shekels, full of in-
cense; 21 one young bull, one ram, one male
lamb a year old, as a burnt offering; 22 one
male goat as a sin offering; 23 and for the
sacrifice of well-being, two oxen, five rams,
five male goats, and five male lambs a year
old. This was the offering of Nethanel son
of Zuar.

24 On the third day Eliab son of Helon,
the leader of the Zebulunites: 25 his offering
was one silver plate weighing one hundred
thirty shekels, one silver basin weighing
seventy shekels, according to the shekel of
the sanctuary, both of them full of choice
flour mixed with oil for a grain offering;
26 one golden dish weighing ten shekels, full
of incense; 27 one young bull, one ram, one
male lamb a year old, for a burnt offering;
28 one male goat for a sin offering; 29 and
for the sacrifice of well-being, two oxen,
five rams, five male goats, and five male
lambs a year old. This was the offering of
Eliab son of Helon.

30 On the fourth day Elizur son of Shed-
eur, the leader of the Reubenites: 31 his
offering was one silver plate weighing one
hundred thirty shekels, one silver basin
weighing seventy shekels, according to the
shekel of the sanctuary, both of them full
of choice flour mixed with oil for a grain
offering; 32 one golden dish weighing ten
shekels, full of incense; 33 one young bull,
one ram, one male lamb a year old, for a
burnt offering; 34 one male goat for a sin
offering; 35 and for the sacrifice of well-
being, two oxen, five rams, five male goats,
and five male lambs a year old. This was
the offering of Elizur son of Shedeur.

36 On the fifth day Shelumiel son of
Zurishaddai, the leader of the Simeonites:
37 his offering was one silver plate weighing
one hundred thirty shekels, one silver basin
weighing seventy shekels, according to the
shekel of the sanctuary, both of them full
of choice flour mixed with oil for a grain
offering; 38 one golden dish weighing ten
shekels, full of incense; 39 one young bull,
one ram, one male lamb a year old, for a
burnt offering; 40 one male goat for a sin
offering; 41 and for the sacrifice of well-
being, two oxen, five rams, five male goats,
and five male lambs a year old. This was
the offering of Shelumiel son of Zurishad-
dai.

42 On the sixth day Eliasaph son of
Deuel, the leader of the Gadites: 43 his offer-
ing was one silver plate weighing one hun-
dred thirty shekels, one silver basin weigh-
ing seventy shekels, according to the shekel
of the sanctuary, both of them full of choice
flour mixed with oil for a grain offering;
44 one golden dish weighing ten shekels, full
of incense; 45 one young bull, one ram, one
male lamb a year old, for a burnt offering;
46 one male goat for a sin offering; 47 and
for the sacrifice of well-being, two oxen,
five rams, five male goats, and five male
lambs a year old. This was the offering of
Eliasaph son of Deuel.

48 On the seventh day Elishama son of

editor may have intended the priestly blessing in 6.22–27 as part of this narrative resumption, giving the blessing that Aaron gave the people in Lev 9.22–23. **12–83:** The names are the same as in 1.5–15, but the order of the tribes is different, with Judah first; see 1.27n.; 2.3–31n. **13:** *Shekel*, see 3.47n. **89:** This

Ammihud, the leader of the Ephraimites:
49 his offering was one silver plate weighing
one hundred thirty shekels, one silver basin
weighing seventy shekels, according to the
shekel of the sanctuary, both of them full
of choice flour mixed with oil for a grain
offering; 50 one golden dish weighing ten
shekels, full of incense; 51 one young bull,
one ram, one male lamb a year old, for a
burnt offering; 52 one male goat for a sin
offering; 53 and for the sacrifice of well-
being, two oxen, five rams, five male goats,
and five male lambs a year old. This was
the offering of Elishama son of Ammihud.
54 On the eighth day Gamaliel son of
Pedahzur, the leader of the Manassites:
55 his offering was one silver plate weighing
one hundred thirty shekels, one silver basin
weighing seventy shekels, according to the
shekel of the sanctuary, both of them full
of choice flour mixed with oil for a grain
offering; 56 one golden dish weighing ten
shekels, full of incense; 57 one young bull,
one ram, one male lamb a year old, for a
burnt offering; 58 one male goat for a sin
offering; 59 and for the sacrifice of well-
being, two oxen, five rams, five male goats,
and five male lambs a year old. This was
the offering of Gamaliel son of Pedahzur.
60 On the ninth day Abidan son of Gid-
eoni, the leader of the Benjaminites: 61 his
offering was one silver plate weighing one
hundred thirty shekels, one silver basin
weighing seventy shekels, according to the
shekel of the sanctuary, both of them full
of choice flour mixed with oil for a grain
offering; 62 one golden dish weighing ten
shekels, full of incense; 63 one young bull,
one ram, one male lamb a year old, for a
burnt offering; 64 one male goat for a sin
offering; 65 and for the sacrifice of well-
being, two oxen, five rams, five male goats,
and five male lambs a year old. This was
the offering of Abidan son of Gideoni.
66 On the tenth day Ahiezer son of Am-
mishaddai, the leader of the Danites: 67 his
offering was one silver plate weighing one
hundred thirty shekels, one silver basin
weighing seventy shekels, according to the
shekel of the sanctuary, both of them full
of choice flour mixed with oil for a grain
offering; 68 one golden dish weighing ten
shekels, full of incense; 69 one young bull,
one ram, one male lamb a year old, for a
burnt offering; 70 one male goat for a sin
offering; 71 and for the sacrifice of well-
being, two oxen, five rams, five male goats,
and five male lambs a year old. This was
the offering of Ahiezer son of Ammishad-
dai.
72 On the eleventh day Pagiel son of
Ochran, the leader of the Asherites: 73 his
offering was one silver plate weighing one
hundred thirty shekels, one silver basin
weighing seventy shekels, according to the
shekel of the sanctuary, both of them full
of choice flour mixed with oil for a grain
offering; 74 one golden dish weighing ten
shekels, full of incense; 75 one young bull,
one ram, one male lamb a year old, for a
burnt offering; 76 one male goat for a sin
offering; 77 and for the sacrifice of well-
being, two oxen, five rams, five male goats,
and five male lambs a year old. This was
the offering of Pagiel son of Ochran.
78 On the twelfth day Ahira son of
Enan, the leader of the Naphtalites: 79 his
offering was one silver plate weighing one
hundred thirty shekels, one silver basin
weighing seventy shekels, according to the
shekel of the sanctuary, both of them full
of choice flour mixed with oil for a grain
offering; 80 one golden dish weighing ten
shekels, full of incense; 81 one young bull,
one ram, one male lamb a year old, for a
burnt offering; 82 one male goat for a sin
offering; 83 and for the sacrifice of well-
being, two oxen, five rams, five male goats,
and five male lambs a year old. This was
the offering of Ahira son of Enan.
84 This was the dedication offering for
the altar, at the time when it was anointed,
from the leaders of Israel: twelve silver
plates, twelve silver basins, twelve golden
dishes, 85 each silver plate weighing one
hundred thirty shekels and each basin sev-
enty, all the silver of the vessels two thou-
sand four hundred shekels according to the
shekel of the sanctuary, 86 the twelve golden
dishes, full of incense, weighing ten shekels
apiece according to the shekel of the sanc-
tuary, all the gold of the dishes being one

hundred twenty shekels; 87 all the livestock
for the burnt offering twelve bulls, twelve
rams, twelve male lambs a year old, with
their grain offering; and twelve male goats
for a sin offering; 88 and all the livestock
for the sacrifice of well-being twenty-four
bulls, the rams sixty, the male goats sixty,
the male lambs a year old sixty. This was
the dedication offering for the altar, after it
was anointed.

89 When Moses went into the tent of
meeting to speak with the LORD,[a] he
would hear the voice speaking to him from
above the mercy seat[b] that was on the ark
of the covenant[c] from between the two
cherubim; thus it spoke to him.

8 The LORD spoke to Moses, saying:
2 Speak to Aaron and say to him: When
you set up the lamps, the seven lamps shall
give light in front of the lampstand. 3 Aaron
did so; he set up its lamps to give light in
front of the lampstand, as the LORD had
commanded Moses. 4 Now this was how
the lampstand was made, out of hammered
work of gold. From its base to its flowers,
it was hammered work; according to the
pattern that the LORD had shown Moses,
so he made the lampstand.

5 The LORD spoke to Moses, saying:
6 Take the Levites from among the Israelites
and cleanse them. 7 Thus you shall do to
them, to cleanse them: sprinkle the water of
purification on them, have them shave their
whole body with a razor and wash their
clothes, and so cleanse themselves. 8 Then
let them take a young bull and its grain
offering of choice flour mixed with oil, and
you shall take another young bull for a sin
offering. 9 You shall bring the Levites be-
fore the tent of meeting, and assemble the
whole congregation of the Israelites.
10 When you bring the Levites before the
LORD, the Israelites shall lay their hands on
the Levites, 11 and Aaron shall present the
Levites before the LORD as an elevation
offering from the Israelites, that they may
do the service of the LORD. 12 The Levites
shall lay their hands on the heads of the
bulls, and he shall offer the one for a sin
offering and the other for a burnt offering
to the LORD, to make atonement for the
Levites. 13 Then you shall have the Levites
stand before Aaron and his sons, and you
shall present them as an elevation offering
to the LORD.

14 Thus you shall separate the Levites
from among the other Israelites, and the
Levites shall be mine. 15 Thereafter the Le-
vites may go in to do service at the tent of
meeting, once you have cleansed them and
presented them as an elevation offering.
16 For they are unreservedly given to me
from among the Israelites; I have taken
them for myself, in place of all that open
the womb, the firstborn of all the Israelites.
17 For all the firstborn among the Israelites
are mine, both human and animal. On the
day that I struck down all the firstborn in
the land of Egypt I consecrated them for

a Heb *him* *b* Or *the cover* *c* Or *treaty*, or *testimony*; Heb *eduth*

also provides a connection with Lev 9.23, which says that Moses entered the tent of meeting. Only after the sanctuary is consecrated does Moses enter the tent to receive revelation (Ex 25.22; 40.34–35; cf. Lev 1.1; Num 1.1; 9.15–23n.).

8.1–4: The lampstand. This fulfills the command given in Ex 25.37. It may appear here because of the mention of Moses' entering the tent in 7.89. See also Ex 25.31–40; 27.20–21; 30.7–8; 40.4; Lev 24.1–3.

8.5–26: The dedication of the Levites. After detailing their duties in chs 1–4 and 7, Numbers now prescribes the rite for setting the Levites apart as sanctuary servants. They are prepared by being sprinkled with water and shaving (cf. Lev 8.6). The Israelites, probably represented by their chieftains, lay their hands on the Levites' heads to designate them as their representatives. This gesture is similar to that used on offerings in sacrifice (see Lev 16.21n.). After sacrifices, Aaron presents the Levites in an elevation rite to God (see 18.11n.), which delivers them into God's service. These rites do not appear to make the Levites holy, even though it advances their status and though the Levites are substitutes for the Israelite firstborn, who are theoretically holy (cf. 3.11–13n.). In contrast to priests, the Pentateuch does not call the Levites holy, and they are restricted from contacting the holy furniture as are lay persons (see

myself, 18 but I have taken the Levites in
place of all the firstborn among the Israel-
ites. 19 Moreover, I have given the Levites as
a gift to Aaron and his sons from among
the Israelites, to do the service for the Isra-
elites at the tent of meeting, and to make
atonement for the Israelites, in order that
there may be no plague among the Israelites
for coming too close to the sanctuary.

20 Moses and Aaron and the whole con-
gregation of the Israelites did with the Le-
vites accordingly; the Israelites did with the
Levites just as the LORD had commanded
Moses concerning them. 21 The Levites pu-
rified themselves from sin and washed their
clothes; then Aaron presented them as an
elevation offering before the LORD, and
Aaron made atonement for them to cleanse
them. 22 Thereafter the Levites went in to
do their service in the tent of meeting in
attendance on Aaron and his sons. As the
LORD had commanded Moses concerning
the Levites, so they did with them.

23 The LORD spoke to Moses, saying:
24 This applies to the Levites: from twenty-
five years old and upward they shall begin
to do duty in the service of the tent of meet-
ing; 25 and from the age of fifty years they
shall retire from the duty of the service and
serve no more. 26 They may assist their
brothers in the tent of meeting in carrying
out their duties, but they shall perform no
service. Thus you shall do with the Levites
in assigning their duties.

9 The LORD spoke to Moses in the wil-
derness of Sinai, in the first month of
the second year after they had come out of
the land of Egypt, saying: 2 Let the Israelites
keep the passover at its appointed time.
3 On the fourteenth day of this month, at
twilight,[a] you shall keep it at its appointed
time; according to all its statutes and all its
regulations you shall keep it. 4 So Moses
told the Israelites that they should keep the
passover. 5 They kept the passover in the
first month, on the fourteenth day of the
month, at twilight,[a] in the wilderness of
Sinai. Just as the LORD had commanded
Moses, so the Israelites did. 6 Now there
were certain people who were unclean
through touching a corpse, so that they
could not keep the passover on that day.
They came before Moses and Aaron on
that day, 7 and said to him, "Although we
are unclean through touching a corpse,
why must we be kept from presenting the
LORD's offering at its appointed time
among the Israelites?" 8 Moses spoke to
them, "Wait, so that I may hear what the
LORD will command concerning you."

9 The LORD spoke to Moses, saying:
10 Speak to the Israelites, saying: Anyone of
you or your descendants who is unclean
through touching a corpse, or is away on a
journey, shall still keep the passover to the
LORD. 11 In the second month on the four-
teenth day, at twilight,[a] they shall keep it;
they shall eat it with unleavened bread and
bitter herbs. 12 They shall leave none of it
until morning, nor break a bone of it; ac-
cording to all the statute for the passover
they shall keep it. 13 But anyone who is

a Heb *between the two evenings*

4.5–20n.). Contrast 2 Chr 23.6; 35.3. **12:** *Sin offering,* see Lev 4; *burnt offering,* see Lev 1. **23–26:** *Duty of the service,* see 3.5–10n.

9.1–14: The passover. For the first passover, see Ex 12. The passover is immediately followed by the seven-day Festival of Unleavened Bread (Ex 12.14–20; Lev 23.4–7). This festival is not mentioned here because the passage is concerned with how personal impurity affects performance of the sole sanctuary-related obligation of all the people for the two-part celebration, i.e., eating the passover animal. Impurity was not a concern at the first passover, since the sanctuary had not been built and therefore the slaughter was not sacrificial. But now with the sanctuary erected, the passover animal must be slaughtered there as a sacrifice (cf. Lev 17.3–7), and impure people may not consume it (cf. Lev 7.19–21; 12.4). These persons, as well as those absent from the community, may defer the festival's performance to the next month. This unique dispensation reflects the crucial importance of the passover offering to members of the community. **1:** Here, as contrasted with 1.1, the date is the same as in Ex 40.17. **3:** *This month,* i.e., the first month, March-April. **6:** On corpse contamination, see 19.1–22n. **14:** Ex 12.48.

clean and is not on a journey, and yet re-
frains from keeping the passover, shall be
cut off from the people for not presenting
the LORD's offering at its appointed time;
such a one shall bear the consequences for
the sin. 14 Any alien residing among you
who wishes to keep the passover to the
LORD shall do so according to the statute of
the passover and according to its regula-
tion; you shall have one statute for both the
resident alien and the native.

15 On the day the tabernacle was set up,
the cloud covered the tabernacle, the tent
of the covenant;[a] and from evening until
morning it was over the tabernacle, having
the appearance of fire. 16 It was always so:
the cloud covered it by day[b] and the ap-
pearance of fire by night. 17 Whenever the
cloud lifted from over the tent, then the
Israelites would set out; and in the place
where the cloud settled down, there the Is-
raelites would camp. 18 At the command of
the LORD the Israelites would set out, and
at the command of the LORD they would
camp. As long as the cloud rested over the
tabernacle, they would remain in camp.
19 Even when the cloud continued over the
tabernacle many days, the Israelites would
keep the charge of the LORD, and would
not set out. 20 Sometimes the cloud would
remain a few days over the tabernacle, and
according to the command of the LORD
they would remain in camp; then according
to the command of the LORD they would
set out. 21 Sometimes the cloud would re-
main from evening until morning; and
when the cloud lifted in the morning, they
would set out, or if it continued for a day
and a night, when the cloud lifted they
would set out. 22 Whether it was two days,
or a month, or a longer time, that the cloud
continued over the tabernacle, resting upon
it, the Israelites would remain in camp and
would not set out; but when it lifted they
would set out. 23 At the command of the
LORD they would camp, and at the com-
mand of the LORD they would set out. They
kept the charge of the LORD, at the com-
mand of the LORD by Moses.

10 The LORD spoke to Moses, saying:
2 Make two silver trumpets; you
shall make them of hammered work; and
you shall use them for summoning the con-
gregation, and for breaking camp. 3 When
both are blown, the whole congregation
shall assemble before you at the entrance of
the tent of meeting. 4 But if only one is
blown, then the leaders, the heads of the
tribes of Israel, shall assemble before you.
5 When you blow an alarm, the camps on
the east side shall set out; 6 when you blow
a second alarm, the camps on the south side
shall set out. An alarm is to be blown
whenever they are to set out. 7 But when the
assembly is to be gathered, you shall blow,
but you shall not sound an alarm. 8 The
sons of Aaron, the priests, shall blow the
trumpets; this shall be a perpetual institu-
tion for you throughout your generations.
9 When you go to war in your land against
the adversary who oppresses you, you shall

a Or *treaty*, or *testimony*; Heb *eduth* *b* Gk Syr Vg: Heb lacks *by day*

9.15–23: The divine fire cloud. This echoes Ex 40.34–38 and reintroduces (along with Num 10.1–10) the narrative about the journey in the wilderness (see Ex 15–18). God's glory manifests itself in a fire which can be seen at night, but which is enshrouded in a cloud at day though it may become visible at times (cf. Ex 24.15–18; Num 20.6). The fiery cloud moves from place to place as a signal when to break camp and when and where to set up camp. This conception of God as fire is developed by the priest Ezekiel in the elaborate vision of the divine glory in Ezek 1.

10.1–10: Signal trumpets. Animal horns and trumpets in the Bible and in traditional societies are primarily used for signaling rather than music-making (Lev 25.9; Judg 3.27; 2 Sam 15.10; 20.1; Isa 27.13), though the latter is a secondary use (2 Sam 6.15; 2 Chr 5.11–13). The two trumpets in ch 10, perhaps of different pitches, are played individually or together and with notes of different lengths (cf. *blow an alarm* versus merely *blow* in vv. 4–7) to signal assembly, breaking camp, going to war, and the beginning of festivals. The trumpets also draw God's beneficent attention to the people's activities. Since a significant function of these trumpets is breaking camp, this unit is placed here.

sound an alarm with the trumpets, so that
you may be remembered before the LORD
your God and be saved from your enemies.
10 Also on your days of rejoicing, at your
appointed festivals, and at the beginnings
of your months, you shall blow the trum-
pets over your burnt offerings and over
your sacrifices of well-being; they shall
serve as a reminder on your behalf before
the LORD your God: I am the LORD your
God.

11 In the second year, in the second
month, on the twentieth day of the month,
the cloud lifted from over the tabernacle of
the covenant.[a] 12 Then the Israelites set out
by stages from the wilderness of Sinai, and
the cloud settled down in the wilderness of
Paran. 13 They set out for the first time at
the command of the LORD by Moses. 14 The
standard of the camp of Judah set out first,
company by company, and over the whole
company was Nahshon son of Ammina-
dab. 15 Over the company of the tribe of
Issachar was Nethanel son of Zuar; 16 and
over the company of the tribe of Zebulun
was Eliab son of Helon.

17 Then the tabernacle was taken down,
and the Gershonites and the Merarites,
who carried the tabernacle, set out. 18 Next
the standard of the camp of Reuben set out,
company by company; and over the whole
company was Elizur son of Shedeur.
19 Over the company of the tribe of Simeon
was Shelumiel son of Zurishaddai, 20 and
over the company of the tribe of Gad was
Eliasaph son of Deuel.

21 Then the Kohathites, who carried the
holy things, set out; and the tabernacle was
set up before their arrival. 22 Next the
standard of the Ephraimite camp set out,
company by company, and over the whole
company was Elishama son of Ammihud.
23 Over the company of the tribe of Manas-
seh was Gamaliel son of Pedahzur, 24 and
over the company of the tribe of Benjamin
was Abidan son of Gideoni.

25 Then the standard of the camp of
Dan, acting as the rear guard of all the
camps, set out, company by company, and
over the whole company was Ahiezer son
of Ammishaddai. 26 Over the company of
the tribe of Asher was Pagiel son of Och-
ran, 27 and over the company of the tribe of
Naphtali was Ahira son of Enan. 28 This
was the order of march of the Israelites,
company by company, when they set out.

29 Moses said to Hobab son of Reuel
the Midianite, Moses' father-in-law, "We
are setting out for the place of which the
LORD said, 'I will give it to you'; come with
us, and we will treat you well; for the LORD
has promised good to Israel." 30 But he said
to him, "I will not go, but I will go back to
my own land and to my kindred." 31 He
said, "Do not leave us, for you know where
we should camp in the wilderness, and you
will serve as eyes for us. 32 Moreover, if you
go with us, whatever good the LORD does
for us, the same we will do for you."

33 So they set out from the mount of the
LORD three days' journey with the ark of
the covenant of the LORD going before
them three days' journey, to seek out a rest-
ing place for them, 34 the cloud of the LORD
being over them by day when they set out
from the camp.

35 Whenever the ark set out, Moses
would say,

a Or *treaty*, or *testimony*; Heb *eduth*

10.11–36: Breaking camp and traveling. The narrative of the wilderness journeys resumes here (cf. 9.15–23n.). **11:** *The second month,* as in 1.1 (contrast 9.1). **12:** *The wilderness of Paran,* the arid region between Israel and the southern Sinai peninsula. **14–28:** The tribes travel according to their four camp divisions (see 2.3–31n.). The sanctuary furniture—the ark, altars, lampstand, and bread table—travels with two divisions in front and behind. This parallels the placement of the sanctuary in the center of the pitched camp (see 2.3–31n.). The tent and its hangings and frames, which are supplemental to the more ceremonially significant sanctuary furniture, travel after the first division so they may be set up when the furniture arrives. The central placement of the sanctuary and its furnishings also protects it. On the Levites' duties, see 3.5–10n.; 4.1–33n. **29–32:** *Hobab,* Moses' father-in-law, earlier named Reuel (Ex 2.18) and Jethro (Ex 18). **35–36:** This song reflects the use of the ark in military activities (14.44;

"Arise, O LORD, let your enemies be
scattered,
and your foes flee before you."
36 And whenever it came to rest, he would
say,
"Return, O LORD of the ten thousand
thousands of Israel."[a]

11 Now when the people complained
in the hearing of the LORD about
their misfortunes, the LORD heard it and
his anger was kindled. Then the fire of the
LORD burned against them, and consumed
some outlying parts of the camp. 2 But the
people cried out to Moses; and Moses
prayed to the LORD, and the fire abated.
3 So that place was called Taberah,[b] be-
cause the fire of the LORD burned against
them.

4 The rabble among them had a strong
craving; and the Israelites also wept again,
and said, "If only we had meat to eat! 5 We
remember the fish we used to eat in Egypt
for nothing, the cucumbers, the melons, the
leeks, the onions, and the garlic; 6 but now
our strength is dried up, and there is noth-
ing at all but this manna to look at."

7 Now the manna was like coriander
seed, and its color was like the color of gum
resin. 8 The people went around and gath-
ered it, ground it in mills or beat it in mor-
tars, then boiled it in pots and made cakes
of it; and the taste of it was like the taste of
cakes baked with oil. 9 When the dew fell
on the camp in the night, the manna would
fall with it.

10 Moses heard the people weeping
throughout their families, all at the en-
trances of their tents. Then the LORD be-
came very angry, and Moses was dis-
pleased. 11 So Moses said to the LORD,
"Why have you treated your servant so
badly? Why have I not found favor in your
sight, that you lay the burden of all this
people on me? 12 Did I conceive all this peo-
ple? Did I give birth to them, that you
should say to me, 'Carry them in your bo-
som, as a nurse carries a sucking child,' to
the land that you promised on oath to their
ancestors? 13 Where am I to get meat to give
to all this people? For they come weeping
to me and say, 'Give us meat to eat!' 14 I am
not able to carry all this people alone, for
they are too heavy for me. 15 If this is the
way you are going to treat me, put me to
death at once—if I have found favor in
your sight—and do not let me see my mis-
ery."

16 So the LORD said to Moses, "Gather
for me seventy of the elders of Israel, whom
you know to be the elders of the people and

a Meaning of Heb uncertain *b* That is *Burning*

31.6; 1 Sam 4.3–11). Its presence in battle is a symbol of the deity's aiding presence. Cf. Ps 68.1; 132.8.

11.1–35: Two complaint stories. This is one of several stories of rebellion or sin in the wilderness. Many of these share a pattern of rebellion or sin, followed by divine punishment, and often by the successful intercession of Moses for the people or rebels; see Ex 16.1–17.7; 32.1–33.23; Lev 10.1–4; 24.10–23; Num 11.1–14.45; 16.1–17.12; 20.2–13; 21.4–9; 25.1–15; cf. 32.14–15. The stories are doublets of incidents in Ex 16. **1–3:** The reason for this first complaint is not clear. The impression is that the people begin to complain as soon as they begin their journey (see ch 10). God uses fire elsewhere for punishment (Lev 9.24n.), but here it does not come from the sanctuary since it burns the outskirts of the camp. **4–35:** This second complaint is about the lack of luxurious food; cf. Ex 16.2–3. **6–9:** On *manna,* see Ex 16, where it is, however, described in slightly different terms (Ex 16.31; Num 11.8). These differences gave rise to the postbiblical tradition that the taste of manna differed, suiting the palate of each individual. **10–15:** Moses here preempts God's punishment for the moment by intercession. But he himself complains about his burden of leadership (cf. Ex 18). **12:** The image of God as the one who gave birth to Israel is also found in Deut 32.18; cf. Isa 42.14; 66.13. **14:** Cf. Ex 18.17–18. **15:** Cf. Ex 32.32; 1 Kings 19.4. **16–34:** Moses' intercession here is not successful, and God's solutions to the people's and Moses' complaints are ultimately negative. He imparts some of Moses' *spirit* (leadership capacity and responsibility) to seventy elders (cf. Ex 24.1,9) so that they prophesy. But they do so only this once (v. 25). They do not continue to aid Moses in the future. God also sends quails (cf. Ex 16.13), but so much that the people gag (v. 20). He also strikes them with a plague (v. 33). **26:** This represents the tradition

officers over them; bring them to the tent of
meeting, and have them take their place
there with you. 17 I will come down and
talk with you there; and I will take some of
the spirit that is on you and put it on them;
and they shall bear the burden of the people
along with you so that you will not bear it
all by yourself. 18 And say to the people:
Consecrate yourselves for tomorrow, and
you shall eat meat; for you have wailed in
the hearing of the LORD, saying, 'If only we
had meat to eat! Surely it was better for us
in Egypt.' Therefore the LORD will give you
meat, and you shall eat. 19 You shall eat not
only one day, or two days, or five days, or
ten days, or twenty days, 20 but for a whole
month—until it comes out of your nostrils
and becomes loathsome to you—because
you have rejected the LORD who is among
you, and have wailed before him, saying,
'Why did we ever leave Egypt?' " 21 But
Moses said, "The people I am with number
six hundred thousand on foot; and you say,
'I will give them meat, that they may eat for
a whole month'! 22 Are there enough flocks
and herds to slaughter for them? Are there
enough fish in the sea to catch for them?"
23 The LORD said to Moses, "Is the LORD's
power limited?[a] Now you shall see wheth-
er my word will come true for you or not."

24 So Moses went out and told the peo-
ple the words of the LORD; and he gathered
seventy elders of the people, and placed
them all around the tent. 25 Then the LORD
came down in the cloud and spoke to him,
and took some of the spirit that was on him
and put it on the seventy elders; and when
the spirit rested upon them, they proph-
esied. But they did not do so again.

26 Two men remained in the camp, one
named Eldad, and the other named Medad,
and the spirit rested on them; they were
among those registered, but they had not
gone out to the tent, and so they prophesied
in the camp. 27 And a young man ran and
told Moses, "Eldad and Medad are proph-
esying in the camp." 28 And Joshua son of
Nun, the assistant of Moses, one of his cho-
sen men,[b] said, "My lord Moses, stop
them!" 29 But Moses said to him, "Are you
jealous for my sake? Would that all the
LORD's people were prophets, and that the
LORD would put his spirit on them!"
30 And Moses and the elders of Israel re-
turned to the camp.

31 Then a wind went out from the
LORD, and it brought quails from the sea
and let them fall beside the camp, about a
day's journey on this side and a day's jour-
ney on the other side, all around the camp,
about two cubits deep on the ground. 32 So
the people worked all that day and night
and all the next day, gathering the quails;
the least anyone gathered was ten homers;
and they spread them out for themselves all
around the camp. 33 But while the meat was
still between their teeth, before it was con-
sumed, the anger of the LORD was kindled
against the people, and the LORD struck the
people with a very great plague. 34 So that
place was called Kibroth-hattaavah,[c] be-
cause there they buried the people who had
the craving. 35 From Kibroth-hattaavah the
people journeyed to Hazeroth.

12 While they were at Hazeroth, Miri-
am and Aaron spoke against Moses
because of the Cushite woman whom he

a Heb *LORD's hand too short?* *b* Or *of Moses from his youth* *c* That is *Graves of craving*

that the sanctuary is located outside the camp (also Ex 33.7; Num 12.4). Num 2 differs by placing the sanctuary in the middle of the camp. **26–29:** These verses reflect ambivalence seen elsewhere in the Bible concerning prophecy as a broad-based institution. **31:** A *cubit* was about 44 cm (17.5 in). **32:** A *homer* was about 230 l (6.5 bu). *Spread them out,* to dry. **34–35:** The places cannot be identified.

12.1–9: Miriam's and Aaron's complaint. This continues the theme of Moses' prophetic status from the previous chapter. Miriam and Aaron complain about Moses' marrying a woman outside of the Israelite group (cf. 25.1–18n.). On the relationship of Moses, Aaron, and Miriam, contrast Ex 15.20 and Num 26.59. **1:** *Cush* may be part of Midian (Hab 3.7), in southern Transjordan. Hence Moses' wife Zipporah, a Midianite, could be the subject of the complaint (Ex 2.15,21; for an implicit ban on marrying Midianite women, cf. Num 25.1–11). The complaint about Moses' wife comes very soon after Zipporah joins the

had married (for he had indeed married a
Cushite woman); 2 and they said, "Has the
LORD spoken only through Moses? Has
he not spoken through us also?" And the
LORD heard it. 3 Now the man Moses was
very humble,[a] more so than anyone else on
the face of the earth. 4 Suddenly the LORD
said to Moses, Aaron, and Miriam, "Come
out, you three, to the tent of meeting."
So the three of them came out. 5 Then the
LORD came down in a pillar of cloud, and
stood at the entrance of the tent, and called
Aaron and Miriam; and they both came
forward. 6 And he said, "Hear my words:

When there are prophets among you,
I the LORD make myself known to
them in visions;
I speak to them in dreams.
7 Not so with my servant Moses;
he is entrusted with all my house.
8 With him I speak face to face—
clearly, not in riddles;
and he beholds the form of the
LORD.

Why then were you not afraid to speak
against my servant Moses?" 9 And the an-
ger of the LORD was kindled against them,
and he departed.

10 When the cloud went away from
over the tent, Miriam had become lep-
rous,[b] as white as snow. And Aaron
turned towards Miriam and saw that she
was leprous. 11 Then Aaron said to Moses,
"Oh, my lord, do not punish us[c] for a sin
that we have so foolishly committed. 12 Do
not let her be like one stillborn, whose flesh
is half consumed when it comes out of its
mother's womb." 13 And Moses cried to the
LORD, "O God, please heal her." 14 But the
LORD said to Moses, "If her father had but
spit in her face, would she not bear her
shame for seven days? Let her be shut out
of the camp for seven days, and after that
she may be brought in again." 15 So Miriam
was shut out of the camp for seven days;
and the people did not set out on the march
until Miriam had been brought in again.
16 After that the people set out from Haze-
roth, and camped in the wilderness of Pa-
ran.

13 The LORD said to Moses, 2 "Send
men to spy out the land of Canaan,

a Or *devout* *b* A term for several skin diseases; precise meaning uncertain *c* Heb *do not lay sin upon us*

Israelites in Ex 18.5–6, if the intervening legislative chapters (most of Ex 19–Num 10) are bracketed out. **3:** *Humble,* better, "devout, trusting." The comment may refer to Moses' leaving the response to God. **4:** On the tent's location, see 11.26n. **6–8:** Though Miriam and Aaron are prophets in their own right (v. 2; Ex 4.16; 15.20; Mic 6.4), Moses is the preeminent prophet since he is the only one to whom God speaks plainly and visibly (Ex 33.11; Deut 18.15; 34.10). Other forms of revelation, such as dreams, visions, and riddles, are of a lesser quality (cf. Jer 23.28), and are more widely available. **10–16:** Miriam, not Aaron, is punished, perhaps because she is the instigator ("spoke" in v. 1 agrees specifically with Miriam); but note that Aaron is also unpunished in the golden calf episode (Ex 32). **10:** Cf. Lev 13.1–14.57n. **14–15:** This may refer to an otherwise unknown custom, applied analogically to Miriam, where a father could shame a child for seven days by spitting in his or her face (cf. Deut 25.9). Miriam's exclusion from the camp is similar to rules in Lev 13.46 and Num 5.1–4 concerning the skin disease as surface affliction (see textual note *b* and Lev 13.1–14.57n.).

13.1–14.45: Scouting the land of Canaan. This story is incorporated here as a long complaint narrative. This complaint narrative about conquering the land of Canaan exhibits two layers, as may be seen in tension concerning the extent of the trip, and the roles of Caleb and Joshua. In an earlier (JE) version of the story, scouts are sent only to the southern half of the land, and only Caleb urges its conquest (13.17b–20,22–24,26b–31; 14.1b,4,11–25,26–45). This was augmented with elements (some attributed to P, others hard to identify) telling about a larger scouting expedition covering the entire land of Canaan. In this, Joshua adds an affirmative voice (13.1–3,4–17a,21,25–26a,32–14.1a,2–3,5–10,26–38). The earlier version is reflected in Josh 14.6–9. The combined account is reflected in Num 26.64–65; 32.8–13; Deut 1.19–46 (cf. also Ps 95.10–11; 106.24–26; Neh 9.21). **13: 2:** *Spy out,* better, "scout out," since the mission is not strictly military or covert. For similar episodes, cf. 21.32; Josh 2.1–22; 7.2–3; Judg 1.23;

which I am giving to the Israelites; from
each of their ancestral tribes you shall send
a man, every one a leader among them."
3 So Moses sent them from the wilderness
of Paran, according to the command of the
LORD, all of them leading men among the
Israelites. 4 These were their names: From
the tribe of Reuben, Shammua son of Zac-
cur; 5 from the tribe of Simeon, Shaphat son
of Hori; 6 from the tribe of Judah, Caleb
son of Jephunneh; 7 from the tribe of Issa-
char, Igal son of Joseph; 8 from the tribe of
Ephraim, Hoshea son of Nun; 9 from the
tribe of Benjamin, Palti son of Raphu;
10 from the tribe of Zebulun, Gaddiel son of
Sodi; 11 from the tribe of Joseph (that is,
from the tribe of Manasseh), Gaddi son of
Susi; 12 from the tribe of Dan, Ammiel son
of Gemalli; 13 from the tribe of Asher, Se-
thur son of Michael; 14 from the tribe of
Naphtali, Nahbi son of Vophsi; 15 from the
tribe of Gad, Geuel son of Machi. 16 These
were the names of the men whom Moses
sent to spy out the land. And Moses
changed the name of Hoshea son of Nun to
Joshua.

17 Moses sent them to spy out the land
of Canaan, and said to them, "Go up there
into the Negeb, and go up into the hill
country, 18 and see what the land is like,
and whether the people who live in it are
strong or weak, whether they are few or
many, 19 and whether the land they live in is
good or bad, and whether the towns that
they live in are unwalled or fortified, 20 and
whether the land is rich or poor, and
whether there are trees in it or not. Be bold,
and bring some of the fruit of the land."
Now it was the season of the first ripe
grapes.

21 So they went up and spied out the
land from the wilderness of Zin to Rehob,
near Lebo-hamath. 22 They went up into
the Negeb, and came to Hebron; and Ahi-
man, Sheshai, and Talmai, the Anakites,
were there. (Hebron was built seven years
before Zoan in Egypt.) 23 And they came to
the Wadi Eshcol, and cut down from there
a branch with a single cluster of grapes, and
they carried it on a pole between two of
them. They also brought some pomegran-
ates and figs. 24 That place was called the
Wadi Eshcol,[a] because of the cluster that
the Israelites cut down from there.

25 At the end of forty days they returned
from spying out the land. 26 And they came
to Moses and Aaron and to all the congre-
gation of the Israelites in the wilderness of
Paran, at Kadesh; they brought back word
to them and to all the congregation, and
showed them the fruit of the land. 27 And
they told him, "We came to the land to
which you sent us; it flows with milk and
honey, and this is its fruit. 28 Yet the people
who live in the land are strong, and the
towns are fortified and very large; and be-
sides, we saw the descendants of Anak
there. 29 The Amalekites live in the land
of the Negeb; the Hittites, the Jebusites,
and the Amorites live in the hill country;
and the Canaanites live by the sea, and
along the Jordan."

a That is *Cluster*

18.1–30. **3:** *Wilderness of Paran,* in the south central Sinai (see color Map at end of book). **4–15:** Most of the individuals named here do not occur elsewhere. **6:** In other places (e.g., 32.12), Caleb is considered a Kenizzite, a group eventually incorporated into Judah. **17:** *The Negeb,* the southern region of Israel. **20:** Grapes ripen in late summer. **21:** *Wilderness of Zin,* just north of Paran (v. 3). For *Lebo-hamath,* in the North, see 34.8n. and color Map 6. **22:** *Hebron,* a major city in the southern part of the land (see Map on p. 28 HB). For the *Anakites,* see v. 33n. (cf. Josh 15.13–14). **23:** *Wadi Eshcol,* near Hebron. *Eshcol* means "grape cluster." **26:** *Kadesh*(-barnea), an oasis between the wildernesses of Paran and Zin (see color Map 2), where the Israelites will stay until 20.22. **27:** *Flows with milk and honey,* a description with mythological overtones. The *honey* was probably a thick syrup made from grapes or dates. **29:** *Amalekites,* a widespread semi-nomadic group often at war with Israel; see Gen 14.9; Ex 17.8–16; Judg 6.3; 1 Sam 15.2–8. The other groups in this verse form part of a traditional list of the inhabitants of the land; see Gen 10.16–18n.; 15.19–21; Ex 3.8; Josh 3.10n. **33:** *Nephilim,* cf. Gen 6.1–4. Like the Anakites (v. 22), their size and strength were legendary (cf. Deut 1.28). **14.1–10:** The negative reports of the

30 But Caleb quieted the people before
Moses, and said, "Let us go up at once and
occupy it, for we are well able to overcome
it." 31 Then the men who had gone up with
him said, "We are not able to go up against
this people, for they are stronger than we."
32 So they brought to the Israelites an unfa-
vorable report of the land that they had
spied out, saying, "The land that we have
gone through as spies is a land that devours
its inhabitants; and all the people that we
saw in it are of great size. 33 There we saw
the Nephilim (the Anakites come from the
Nephilim); and to ourselves we seemed like
grasshoppers, and so we seemed to them."

14 Then all the congregation raised a
loud cry, and the people wept that
night. 2 And all the Israelites complained
against Moses and Aaron; the whole con-
gregation said to them, "Would that we
had died in the land of Egypt! Or would
that we had died in this wilderness! 3 Why
is the LORD bringing us into this land to fall
by the sword? Our wives and our little ones
will become booty; would it not be better
for us to go back to Egypt?" 4 So they said
to one another, "Let us choose a captain,
and go back to Egypt."

5 Then Moses and Aaron fell on their
faces before all the assembly of the congre-
gation of the Israelites. 6 And Joshua son
of Nun and Caleb son of Jephunneh, who
were among those who had spied out the
land, tore their clothes 7 and said to all the
congregation of the Israelites, "The land
that we went through as spies is an exceed-
ingly good land. 8 If the LORD is pleased
with us, he will bring us into this land and
give it to us, a land that flows with milk
and honey. 9 Only, do not rebel against the
LORD; and do not fear the people of the
land, for they are no more than bread for
us; their protection is removed from them,
and the LORD is with us; do not fear them."
10 But the whole congregation threatened to
stone them.

Then the glory of the LORD appeared
at the tent of meeting to all the Israelites.
11 And the LORD said to Moses, "How long
will this people despise me? And how long
will they refuse to believe in me, in spite of
all the signs that I have done among them?
12 I will strike them with pestilence and dis-
inherit them, and I will make of you a na-
tion greater and mightier than they."

13 But Moses said to the LORD, "Then
the Egyptians will hear of it, for in your
might you brought up this people from
among them, 14 and they will tell the inhab-
itants of this land. They have heard that
you, O LORD, are in the midst of this peo-
ple; for you, O LORD, are seen face to face,
and your cloud stands over them and you
go in front of them, in a pillar of cloud by
day and in a pillar of fire by night. 15 Now
if you kill this people all at one time, then
the nations who have heard about you will
say, 16 'It is because the LORD was not able
to bring this people into the land he swore
to give them that he has slaughtered them
in the wilderness.' 17 And now, therefore,
let the power of the LORD be great in the
way that you promised when you spoke,
saying,

18 'The LORD is slow to anger,
and abounding in steadfast love,
forgiving iniquity and transgression,
but by no means clearing the guilty,
visiting the iniquity of the parents
upon the children
to the third and the fourth
generation.'

scouts (13.28–29,31–33) lead to the people's complaint. **5–6:** *Fell on their faces,* in order to beseech the people. Joshua and Caleb tear their clothing in distress (Gen 37.29) and deliver a positive report (cf. Caleb already in 13.30). **9:** *Bread for us,* cf. Ps 14.4. **10:** Stoning may be legal (15.36) or extra-legal (Ex 17.4), as here. *The glory of the LORD* was the visible manifestation of the divine presence; see Ex 16.6–7n. **12:** God was ready to make Moses' posterity his chosen people also in Ex 32.10 (Deut 9.14). **13–19:** Moses defends the people in two ways: He says that God's reputation will suffer if he destroys them (vv. 13–16) and that God has before promised to be patient and forgiving (vv. 17–19; cf. Ex 34.5–8). The first argument had been used previously with success in Ex 32.12. On the *cloud,* see 9.15–23n. **20–45:** God imposes lesser punishments, some of which are ironic: The people will die in the wilderness as they wished

19 Forgive the iniquity of this people ac-
cording to the greatness of your steadfast
love, just as you have pardoned this people,
from Egypt even until now."
20 Then the LORD said, "I do forgive,
just as you have asked; 21 nevertheless—as I
live, and as all the earth shall be filled with
the glory of the LORD— 22 none of the peo-
ple who have seen my glory and the signs
that I did in Egypt and in the wilderness,
and yet have tested me these ten times and
have not obeyed my voice, 23 shall see the
land that I swore to give to their ancestors;
none of those who despised me shall see it.
24 But my servant Caleb, because he has a
different spirit and has followed me whole-
heartedly, I will bring into the land into
which he went, and his descendants shall
possess it. 25 Now, since the Amalekites and
the Canaanites live in the valleys, turn to-
morrow and set out for the wilderness by
the way to the Red Sea."[a]
26 And the LORD spoke to Moses and to
Aaron, saying: 27 How long shall this wick-
ed congregation complain against me? I
have heard the complaints of the Israelites,
which they complain against me. 28 Say to
them, "As I live," says the LORD, "I will do
to you the very things I heard you say:
29 your dead bodies shall fall in this very
wilderness; and of all your number, includ-
ed in the census, from twenty years old and
upward, who have complained against me,
30 not one of you shall come into the land in
which I swore to settle you, except Caleb
son of Jephunneh and Joshua son of Nun.
31 But your little ones, who you said would
become booty, I will bring in, and they
shall know the land that you have despised.
32 But as for you, your dead bodies shall fall
in this wilderness. 33 And your children
shall be shepherds in the wilderness for for-
ty years, and shall suffer for your faithless-
ness, until the last of your dead bodies lies
in the wilderness. 34 According to the num-
ber of the days in which you spied out the
land, forty days, for every day a year, you
shall bear your iniquity, forty years, and
you shall know my displeasure." 35 I the
LORD have spoken; surely I will do thus to
all this wicked congregation gathered to-
gether against me: in this wilderness they
shall come to a full end, and there they shall
die.
36 And the men whom Moses sent to
spy out the land, who returned and made
all the congregation complain against him
by bringing a bad report about the land—
37 the men who brought an unfavorable re-
port about the land died by a plague before
the LORD. 38 But Joshua son of Nun and
Caleb son of Jephunneh alone remained
alive, of those men who went to spy out the
land.
39 When Moses told these words to all
the Israelites, the people mourned greatly.
40 They rose early in the morning and went
up to the heights of the hill country, saying,
"Here we are. We will go up to the place
that the LORD has promised, for we have
sinned." 41 But Moses said, "Why do you
continue to transgress the command of the
LORD? That will not succeed. 42 Do not go
up, for the LORD is not with you; do not let
yourselves be struck down before your ene-
mies. 43 For the Amalekites and the Ca-
naanites will confront you there, and you
shall fall by the sword; because you have
turned back from following the LORD, the
LORD will not be with you." 44 But they
presumed to go up to the heights of the hill
country, even though the ark of the cove-
nant of the LORD, and Moses, had not left
the camp. 45 Then the Amalekites and the
Canaanites who lived in that hill country

a Or *Sea of Reeds*

(14.2,28–32), yet their children will enter the land contrary to their fear (14.3,31); the people will be allowed to journey in the direction of Egypt (*the way to the Red Sea*) as they wished, but only to die on the way (14.4,25,28–29); some die by the sword as they feared (14.3,43); they seek to take the land but fail as they said they would (13.28–29,31–33; 14.40–45). **34:** Cf. Ezek 4.6. **36–37:** The scouts who gave a discouraging report are killed in a plague, though the people in general are spared (cf. 14.12). **39–45:** The people cannot escape punishment by performing the original command, since God is not with them.

came down and defeated them, pursuing
them as far as Hormah.

15 The LORD spoke to Moses, saying:
2 Speak to the Israelites and say to
them: When you come into the land you are
to inhabit, which I am giving you, 3 and you
make an offering by fire to the LORD from
the herd or from the flock—whether a
burnt offering or a sacrifice, to fulfill a vow
or as a freewill offering or at your appoint-
ed festivals—to make a pleasing odor for
the LORD, 4 then whoever presents such an
offering to the LORD shall present also a
grain offering, one-tenth of an ephah of
choice flour, mixed with one-fourth of a
hin of oil. 5 Moreover, you shall offer one-
fourth of a hin of wine as a drink offering
with the burnt offering or the sacrifice, for
each lamb. 6 For a ram, you shall offer a
grain offering, two-tenths of an ephah of
choice flour mixed with one-third of a hin
of oil; 7 and as a drink offering you shall
offer one-third of a hin of wine, a pleasing
odor to the LORD. 8 When you offer a bull
as a burnt offering or a sacrifice, to fulfill a
vow or as an offering of well-being to the
LORD, 9 then you shall present with the bull
a grain offering, three-tenths of an ephah of
choice flour, mixed with half a hin of oil,
10 and you shall present as a drink offering
half a hin of wine, as an offering by fire, a
pleasing odor to the LORD.

11 Thus it shall be done for each ox or
ram, or for each of the male lambs or the
kids. 12 According to the number that you
offer, so you shall do with each and every
one. 13 Every native Israelite shall do these
things in this way, in presenting an offering
by fire, a pleasing odor to the LORD. 14 An
alien who lives with you, or who takes
up permanent residence among you, and
wishes to offer an offering by fire, a pleas-
ing odor to the LORD, shall do as you do.
15 As for the assembly, there shall be for
both you and the resident alien a single
statute, a perpetual statute throughout
your generations; you and the alien shall be
alike before the LORD. 16 You and the alien
who resides with you shall have the same
law and the same ordinance.

17 The LORD spoke to Moses, saying:
18 Speak to the Israelites and say to them:
After you come into the land to which I am
bringing you, 19 whenever you eat of the
bread of the land, you shall present a dona-
tion to the LORD. 20 From your first batch
of dough you shall present a loaf as a dona-
tion; you shall present it just as you present
a donation from the threshing floor.
21 Throughout your generations you shall
give to the LORD a donation from the first
of your batch of dough.

22 But if you unintentionally fail to ob-
serve all these commandments that the
LORD has spoken to Moses— 23 everything
that the LORD has commanded you by
Moses, from the day the LORD gave com-
mandment and thereafter, throughout your
generations— 24 then if it was done un-
intentionally without the knowledge of
the congregation, the whole congregation
shall offer one young bull for a burnt offer-
ing, a pleasing odor to the LORD, together
with its grain offering and its drink offer-
ing, according to the ordinance, and one
male goat for a sin offering. 25 The priest

44: On the ark representing God in battle, see 10.25–26n. **45:** *Hormah,* a city in the Negeb near Beer-sheba; see 21.2–3n.

15.1–31: Various offerings. 2–16: Grain and wine offerings accompany the burnt offering (Lev 1) and the well-being sacrifice (Lev 3). These elements, with sacrificial flesh, make a complete meal for the deity (cf. Lev 21.6n.). The grain offering is burned on the altar (Lev 2), and the wine is perhaps poured out at the base of the altar (but cf. 28.5–7n.). These offerings are loosely connected to the preceding narrative by noting that they are to be performed (v. 2) *when you come into the land you are to inhabit.* **3:** *Pleasing odor,* Gen 8.29; Ex 29.18; Lev 1.9. **4:** *Ephah,* 5.15n. A *hin* was about 3.8 l (1 gal). **17–21:** A loaf from the first mixed dough is given to the LORD, probably going specifically to the priests (as in Ezek 44.30). **22–31:** The sin purification offering is more fully described in Lev 4. **22:** *All these commandments,* both prohibitions and positive requirements as opposed to Lev 4, which is concerned only with inadvertent trespass of prohibitions. **30–31:** Intentional sins (cf. Lev 16.16n.) bring "cutting off," generally a divine

shall make atonement for all the congrega-
tion of the Israelites, and they shall be for-
given; it was unintentional, and they have
brought their offering, an offering by fire to
the LORD, and their sin offering before the
LORD, for their error. 26 All the congrega-
tion of the Israelites shall be forgiven, as
well as the aliens residing among them, be-
cause the whole people was involved in the
error.
27 An individual who sins unintention-
ally shall present a female goat a year old
for a sin offering. 28 And the priest shall
make atonement before the LORD for the
one who commits an error, when it is unin-
tentional, to make atonement for the per-
son, who then shall be forgiven. 29 For both
the native among the Israelites and the alien
residing among them—you shall have the
same law for anyone who acts in error.
30 But whoever acts high-handedly, wheth-
er a native or an alien, affronts the LORD,
and shall be cut off from among the people.
31 Because of having despised the word of
the LORD and broken his commandment,
such a person shall be utterly cut off and
bear the guilt.
32 When the Israelites were in the wil-
derness, they found a man gathering sticks
on the sabbath day. 33 Those who found
him gathering sticks brought him to Moses,
Aaron, and to the whole congregation.
34 They put him in custody, because it was
not clear what should be done to him.
35 Then the LORD said to Moses, "The man
shall be put to death; all the congregation
shall stone him outside the camp." 36 The
whole congregation brought him outside
the camp and stoned him to death, just as
the LORD had commanded Moses.
37 The LORD said to Moses: 38 Speak to
the Israelites, and tell them to make fringes
on the corners of their garments through-
out their generations and to put a blue cord
on the fringe at each corner. 39 You have
the fringe so that, when you see it, you will
remember all the commandments of the
LORD and do them, and not follow the lust
of your own heart and your own eyes. 40 So
you shall remember and do all my com-
mandments, and you shall be holy to your
God. 41 I am the LORD your God, who
brought you out of the land of Egypt, to be
your God: I am the LORD your God.
16 Now Korah son of Izhar son of Ko-
hath son of Levi, along with Dathan

punishment leading to the offender's early death or at least the termination of the person's family line (Mal 2.12; Ps 109.13; Ruth 4.10; cf. Lev 20.20–21). Some cases may include execution by human agency (cf. vv. 32–36; Lev 20.2–5).

15.32–36: A sabbath violation. This illustrates vv. 30–31. Sabbath work requires execution or cutting off (Ex 31.14; 35.2–3; Lev 23.3–4n.). Given the ambiguity of this term (see 15.30–31n.), a special ruling is needed. For other cases of legal amendment arising from specific cases, see Lev 24.10–22; Num 9.6–14; 27.5–11.

15.37–41: Wearing fringes. The blue (or violet) cord was presumably made of wool and placed on a garment with fringes made of linen, a mixture that was forbidden except in priestly clothing and sanctuary hangings (Deut 22.9–12; Lev 19.19n.; cf. Ex 26.1,31,36; 28.6,37,39). The people's clothing is thus a reminder of their holiness and metaphorical priestly status (Ex 19.6; cf. Num 16.3). Laity, however, do not wear full priestly garb, or have the same type of sanctity as priests.

16.1–35: The rebellion of Korah, Dathan, and Abiram. Stories of two rebellions have been woven together. One (JE) involves Dathan and Abiram (vv. 1b–2a), who complain about Moses (vv. 12–15). The ground swallows them, proving the legitimacy of his leadership (vv. 25–26,27b–32a,33–35). The other story (which itself is probably composite but mostly P) involves the Levite Korah and two-hundred fifty men, apparently Levites (1a,2b,8,35). They complain mainly about Aaron and demand a share in his priesthood (vv. 3–11). The ordeal of making an incense offering at the tent of meeting reveals whom God has chosen to serve as priests (vv. 16–24). Though v. 32 has Korah suffering the fate of Dathan and Abiram, the original story probably had him dying by God's fire (vv. 27a,35; cf. Lev 9.24; 10.2), an implication of vv. 36–40 (but cf. Num 26.10). The Korah story likely reflects a controversy over priesthood rights occurring in later history (cf. Ezek 43.9–31). **3:** Korah's group argues that all the people,

and Abiram sons of Eliab, and On son of
Peleth—descendants of Reuben—took
2 two hundred fifty Israelite men, leaders of
the congregation, chosen from the assem-
bly, well-known men,[a] and they confront-
ed Moses. 3 They assembled against Moses
and against Aaron, and said to them, "You
have gone too far! All the congregation are
holy, every one of them, and the LORD is
among them. So why then do you exalt
yourselves above the assembly of the
LORD?" 4 When Moses heard it, he fell on
his face. 5 Then he said to Korah and all his
company, "In the morning the LORD will
make known who is his, and who is holy,
and who will be allowed to approach him;
the one whom he will choose he will allow
to approach him. 6 Do this: take censers,
Korah and all your[b] company, 7 and to-
morrow put fire in them, and lay incense on
them before the LORD; and the man whom
the LORD chooses shall be the holy one.
You Levites have gone too far!" 8 Then
Moses said to Korah, "Hear now, you Le-
vites! 9 Is it too little for you that the God of
Israel has separated you from the congrega-
tion of Israel, to allow you to approach
him in order to perform the duties of the
LORD's tabernacle, and to stand before the
congregation and serve them? 10 He has al-
lowed you to approach him, and all your
brother Levites with you; yet you seek the
priesthood as well! 11 Therefore you and
all your company have gathered together
against the LORD. What is Aaron that you
rail against him?"

12 Moses sent for Dathan and Abiram
sons of Eliab; but they said, "We will not
come! 13 Is it too little that you have
brought us up out of a land flowing with
milk and honey to kill us in the wilderness,
that you must also lord it over us? 14 It is
clear you have not brought us into a land
flowing with milk and honey, or given us
an inheritance of fields and vineyards.
Would you put out the eyes of these men?
We will not come!"

15 Moses was very angry and said to the
LORD, "Pay no attention to their offering. I
have not taken one donkey from them, and
I have not harmed any one of them." 16 And
Moses said to Korah, "As for you and all
your company, be present tomorrow before
the LORD, you and they and Aaron; 17 and
let each one of you take his censer, and put
incense on it, and each one of you present
his censer before the LORD, two hundred
fifty censers; you also, and Aaron, each his
censer." 18 So each man took his censer,
and they put fire in the censers and laid
incense on them, and they stood at the en-
trance of the tent of meeting with Moses
and Aaron. 19 Then Korah assembled the
whole congregation against them at the en-
trance of the tent of meeting. And the glory
of the LORD appeared to the whole congre-
gation.

20 Then the LORD spoke to Moses and
to Aaron, saying: 21 Separate yourselves
from this congregation, so that I may con-
sume them in a moment. 22 They fell on
their faces, and said, "O God, the God of
the spirits of all flesh, shall one person sin
and you become angry with the whole con-
gregation?"

23 And the LORD spoke to Moses, say-
ing: 24 Say to the congregation: Get away
from the dwellings of Korah, Dathan, and
Abiram. 25 So Moses got up and went to
Dathan and Abiram; the elders of Israel fol-
lowed him. 26 He said to the congregation,
"Turn away from the tents of these wicked
men, and touch nothing of theirs, or you
will be swept away for all their sins." 27 So
they got away from the dwellings of Korah,

a Cn: Heb *and they confronted Moses, and two hundred fifty men . . . well-known men* b Heb *his*

which includes themselves, are as holy as the Aaronides since God is among the people (note also the popular holiness associated with wearing fringes in the preceding passage, 15.37–41n.). This contradicts the theology of the larger tradition, out of which the Korah story comes, whose view is that the people are not intrinsically holy, but are holy only insofar as they keep the commandments (see Lev 19.2; for a contrasting idea see Deut 7.6). **4:** *Fell on his face,* see 14.5–6n. **9:** On Levitical responsibilities, see 3.5–10; 4.2–39. **15:** Cf. 1 Sam 12.3. **19:** *Glory of the LORD,* see 14.10n. **30:** *Sheol,* the underworld abode of

Dathan, and Abiram; and Dathan and Abi-
ram came out and stood at the entrance of
their tents, together with their wives, their
children, and their little ones. 28 And Moses
said, "This is how you shall know that the
LORD has sent me to do all these works; it
has not been of my own accord: 29 If these
people die a natural death, or if a natural
fate comes on them, then the LORD has not
sent me. 30 But if the LORD creates some-
thing new, and the ground opens its mouth
and swallows them up, with all that be-
longs to them, and they go down alive into
Sheol, then you shall know that these men
have despised the LORD."

31 As soon as he finished speaking all
these words, the ground under them was
split apart. 32 The earth opened its mouth
and swallowed them up, along with their
households—everyone who belonged to
Korah and all their goods. 33 So they with
all that belonged to them went down alive
into Sheol; the earth closed over them, and
they perished from the midst of the assem-
bly. 34 All Israel around them fled at their
outcry, for they said, "The earth will swal-
low us too!" 35 And fire came out from the
LORD and consumed the two hundred fifty
men offering the incense.

36[a] Then the LORD spoke to Moses, say-
ing: 37 Tell Eleazar son of Aaron the priest
to take the censers out of the blaze; then
scatter the fire far and wide. 38 For the cen-
sers of these sinners have become holy at
the cost of their lives. Make them into ham-
mered plates as a covering for the altar, for
they presented them before the LORD and
they became holy. Thus they shall be a sign
to the Israelites. 39 So Eleazar the priest
took the bronze censers that had been pre-
sented by those who were burned; and they
were hammered out as a covering for the
altar— 40 a reminder to the Israelites that
no outsider, who is not of the descendants
of Aaron, shall approach to offer incense
before the LORD, so as not to become like
Korah and his company—just as the LORD
had said to him through Moses.

41 On the next day, however, the whole
congregation of the Israelites rebelled
against Moses and against Aaron, saying,
"You have killed the people of the LORD."
42 And when the congregation had assem-
bled against them, Moses and Aaron
turned toward the tent of meeting; the
cloud had covered it and the glory of the
LORD appeared. 43 Then Moses and Aaron
came to the front of the tent of meeting,
44 and the LORD spoke to Moses, saying,
45 "Get away from this congregation, so
that I may consume them in a moment."
And they fell on their faces. 46 Moses said to
Aaron, "Take your censer, put fire on it
from the altar and lay incense on it, and
carry it quickly to the congregation and
make atonement for them. For wrath has
gone out from the LORD; the plague has
begun." 47 So Aaron took it as Moses had
ordered, and ran into the middle of the as-
sembly, where the plague had already be-
gun among the people. He put on the in-
cense, and made atonement for the people.
48 He stood between the dead and the liv-
ing; and the plague was stopped. 49 Those
who died by the plague were fourteen thou-
sand seven hundred, besides those who
died in the affair of Korah. 50 When the
plague was stopped, Aaron returned to
Moses at the entrance of the tent of meet-
ing.

a Ch 17.1 in Heb

all dead (Isa 14.15–20; Ps 88.3–6). The Hebrew Bible has no conception of a separate heaven and hell.

16.36–40: The aftermath. These verses and ch 17 continue the story of Korah's rebellion in the foregoing combination of two stories (see 16.1–35n.). **40:** This cover, placed on the sacrificial altar in the court, will visibly warn unauthorized people who may come into the area (e.g., Lev 1.3) from undertaking priestly duties. **41–50:** All the people now complain against Moses and Aaron. **41:** The people, in addition to Korah and his group, also dispute the nature and theology of the priesthood. *People of the LORD*, i.e., the Levites. **42:** *Cloud,* see 9.15–23n. **47–48:** In contrast to the effects of Korah's incense offering, Aaron's offering has the power to stop God's plague.

17 [a]The LORD spoke to Moses, saying:
2 Speak to the Israelites, and get
twelve staffs from them, one for each an-
cestral house, from all the leaders of their
ancestral houses. Write each man's name
on his staff, 3 and write Aaron's name on
the staff of Levi. For there shall be one staff
for the head of each ancestral house. 4 Place
them in the tent of meeting before the cove-
nant,[b] where I meet with you. 5 And the
staff of the man whom I choose shall
sprout; thus I will put a stop to the com-
plaints of the Israelites that they continual-
ly make against you. 6 Moses spoke to the
Israelites; and all their leaders gave him
staffs, one for each leader, according to
their ancestral houses, twelve staffs; and
the staff of Aaron was among theirs. 7 So
Moses placed the staffs before the LORD in
the tent of the covenant.[b]

8 When Moses went into the tent of the
covenant[b] on the next day, the staff of
Aaron for the house of Levi had sprouted.
It put forth buds, produced blossoms, and
bore ripe almonds. 9 Then Moses brought
out all the staffs from before the LORD to
all the Israelites; and they looked, and each
man took his staff. 10 And the LORD said to
Moses, "Put back the staff of Aaron before
the covenant,[b] to be kept as a warning to
rebels, so that you may make an end of
their complaints against me, or else they
will die." 11 Moses did so; just as the LORD
commanded him, so he did.

12 The Israelites said to Moses, "We are
perishing; we are lost, all of us are lost!
13 Everyone who approaches the tabernacle
of the LORD will die. Are we all to perish?"

18 The LORD said to Aaron: You and
your sons and your ancestral house
with you shall bear responsibility for of-
fenses connected with the sanctuary, while
you and your sons alone shall bear respon-
sibility for offenses connected with the
priesthood. 2 So bring with you also your
brothers of the tribe of Levi, your ancestral
tribe, in order that they may be joined to
you, and serve you while you and your sons
with you are in front of the tent of the cove-
nant.[b] 3 They shall perform duties for you
and for the whole tent. But they must not
approach either the utensils of the sanctu-
ary or the altar, otherwise both they and
you will die. 4 They are attached to you in
order to perform the duties of the tent of
meeting, for all the service of the tent; no
outsider shall approach you. 5 You your-
selves shall perform the duties of the sanc-
tuary and the duties of the altar, so that
wrath may never again come upon the Isra-
elites. 6 It is I who now take your brother
Levites from among the Israelites; they are
now yours as a gift, dedicated to the LORD,
to perform the service of the tent of meet-
ing. 7 But you and your sons with you shall
diligently perform your priestly duties in all
that concerns the altar and the area behind
the curtain. I give your priesthood as a
gift;[c] any outsider who approaches shall
be put to death.

8 The LORD spoke to Aaron: I have giv-

a Ch 17.16 in Heb *b* Or *treaty*, or *testimony*; Heb *edut*h *c* Heb *as a service of gift*

17.1–12: Aaron's sprouting rod. Aaron's priesthood is affirmed after Korah's rebellion (ch 16). **2–3,6,8:** In contrast to other chapters in Numbers, the Levites (Aaron's tribe) are counted as one of the twelve tribes (see 1.1–54n.). Here the term *ancestral house,* a smaller unit, is used for "tribe." **5:** This is another ordeal-like event in which the deity shows whom he has chosen (cf. 16.5,7). **8:** A rod of Aaron is elsewhere associated with the miraculous (Ex 7.8–10,19; 8.5). **12–13:** This ends in a complaint, as did the ordeal with Korah (cf. 16.41–42). But this is answered, not with a plague, but with priesthood and Levitical provisions protecting the sanctuary and implicitly the people (18.1–7,22). Thus, this final complaint narrative, unlike the earlier ones (see 11.1–35n.), leads to positive results.

18.1–32: Priesthood and Levitical duties and dues. This builds on chs 16–17. **1–7:** For the duties outlined here, see 3.5–10,14–39; 4.1–49. **3,4,5:** *Perform duties,* perform guard duty. **6:** *Perform service,* do the work of transporting the tabernacle (also vv. 21,23,31). **8–20:** The priests receive offerings (prebends) for their work. **8–10:** The priests eat the portions of the most holy offerings (see Lev 2.3n.) in the sanctuary court (Lev 6.16,26; 7.6; 10.13,17; 24.9). **11–20:** The whole priestly family, including females,

en you charge of the offerings made to me,
all the holy gifts of the Israelites; I have
given them to you and your sons as a priest-
ly portion due you in perpetuity. [9]This
shall be yours from the most holy things,
reserved from the fire: every offering of
theirs that they render to me as a most holy
thing, whether grain offering, sin offering,
or guilt offering, shall belong to you and
your sons. [10]As a most holy thing you shall
eat it; every male may eat it; it shall be holy
to you. [11]This also is yours: I have given to
you, together with your sons and daugh-
ters, as a perpetual due, whatever is set
aside from the gifts of all the elevation
offerings of the Israelites; everyone who is
clean in your house may eat them. [12]All the
best of the oil and all the best of the wine
and of the grain, the choice produce that
they give to the LORD, I have given to you.
[13]The first fruits of all that is in their land,
which they bring to the LORD, shall be
yours; everyone who is clean in your house
may eat of it. [14]Every devoted thing in Isra-
el shall be yours. [15]The first issue of the
womb of all creatures, human and animal,
which is offered to the LORD, shall be
yours; but the firstborn of human beings
you shall redeem, and the firstborn of un-
clean animals you shall redeem. [16]Their re-
demption price, reckoned from one month
of age, you shall fix at five shekels of silver,
according to the shekel of the sanctuary
(that is, twenty gerahs). [17]But the firstborn
of a cow, or the firstborn of a sheep, or the
firstborn of a goat, you shall not redeem;
they are holy. You shall dash their blood on
the altar, and shall turn their fat into smoke
as an offering by fire for a pleasing odor to
the LORD; [18]but their flesh shall be yours,
just as the breast that is elevated and as the
right thigh are yours. [19]All the holy offer-
ings that the Israelites present to the LORD
I have given to you, together with your sons
and daughters, as a perpetual due; it is a
covenant of salt forever before the LORD
for you and your descendants as well.
[20]Then the LORD said to Aaron: You shall
have no allotment in their land, nor shall
you have any share among them; I am your
share and your possession among the Isra-
elites.

21 To the Levites I have given every tithe
in Israel for a possession in return for the
service that they perform, the service in the
tent of meeting. [22]From now on the Israel-
ites shall no longer approach the tent of
meeting, or else they will incur guilt and
die. [23]But the Levites shall perform the ser-
vice of the tent of meeting, and they shall
bear responsibility for their own offenses;
it shall be a perpetual statute throughout
your generations. But among the Israelites
they shall have no allotment, [24]because I
have given to the Levites as their portion
the tithe of the Israelites, which they set
apart as an offering to the LORD. Therefore
I have said of them that they shall have no
allotment among the Israelites.

25 Then the LORD spoke to Moses, say-
ing: [26]You shall speak to the Levites, say-
ing: When you receive from the Israelites
the tithe that I have given you from them
for your portion, you shall set apart an
offering from it to the LORD, a tithe of the
tithe. [27]It shall be reckoned to you as your
gift, the same as the grain of the threshing
floor and the fullness of the wine press.

may eat of lesser holy offerings (10.14–15; 22.10–14). This may be done outside the sanctuary, but must be done in a state of ritual purity. **11:** *Gifts of all the elevation offerings,* rather, "gifts including all the elevation offerings." Elevation, done in the sanctuary, specially consecrates portions of offerings (Ex 29.27–28; Lev 7.30; 10.14–15; 23.17–20; Num 6.19–20). *Gifts* include these and other items dedicated outside the sanctuary. **12–13:** For first produce and first fruits, cf. Ex 23.19; Lev 2.12; 19.24; Num 15.17–20; Deut 18.4. **14:** *Devoted thing,* see Lev 27.28n. **15–18:** Firstborn animals, cf. Lev 27.26; Num 1.11–13. **16:** *Shekel,* see 3.47n. **17:** *Pleasing odor,* see 15.3n. **19:** *Covenant of salt,* see Lev 2.13n. **21–32:** The Levites receive the produce tithe (cf. vv. 27,30; cf. Neh 10.38–39). This amends Lev 27.30–33, where produce and animal tithes appear to go to the priests. **25–32:** Even Levites are not exempt from supporting the priests. The tenth of the Levitical tithe that goes to the priests is holy (vv. 28–29) while the remaining nine-tenths is not (vv. 31–32).

28 Thus you also shall set apart an offering
to the LORD from all the tithes that you
receive from the Israelites; and from them
you shall give the LORD's offering to the
priest Aaron. 29 Out of all the gifts to you,
you shall set apart every offering due to the
LORD; the best of all of them is the part to
be consecrated. 30 Say also to them: When
you have set apart the best of it, then the
rest shall be reckoned to the Levites as pro-
duce of the threshing floor, and as produce
of the wine press. 31 You may eat it in any
place, you and your households; for it is
your payment for your service in the tent of
meeting. 32 You shall incur no guilt by rea-
son of it, when you have offered the best of
it. But you shall not profane the holy gifts
of the Israelites, on pain of death.

19 The LORD spoke to Moses and Aar-
on, saying: 2 This is a statute of the
law that the LORD has commanded: Tell
the Israelites to bring you a red heifer with-
out defect, in which there is no blemish and
on which no yoke has been laid. 3 You shall
give it to the priest Eleazar, and it shall be
taken outside the camp and slaughtered in
his presence. 4 The priest Eleazar shall take
some of its blood with his finger and sprin-
kle it seven times towards the front of the
tent of meeting. 5 Then the heifer shall be
burned in his sight; its skin, its flesh, and its
blood, with its dung, shall be burned. 6 The
priest shall take cedarwood, hyssop, and
crimson material, and throw them into the
fire in which the heifer is burning. 7 Then
the priest shall wash his clothes and bathe
his body in water, and afterwards he may
come into the camp; but the priest shall
remain unclean until evening. 8 The one
who burns the heifer[a] shall wash his
clothes in water and bathe his body in wa-
ter; he shall remain unclean until evening.
9 Then someone who is clean shall gather
up the ashes of the heifer, and deposit them
outside the camp in a clean place; and they
shall be kept for the congregation of the
Israelites for the water for cleansing. It is a
purification offering. 10 The one who gath-
ers the ashes of the heifer shall wash his
clothes and be unclean until evening.

This shall be a perpetual statute for the
Israelites and for the alien residing among
them. 11 Those who touch the dead body of
any human being shall be unclean seven
days. 12 They shall purify themselves with
the water on the third day and on the sev-
enth day, and so be clean; but if they do not
purify themselves on the third day and on
the seventh day, they will not become
clean. 13 All who touch a corpse, the body
of a human being who has died, and do not
purify themselves, defile the tabernacle of
the LORD; such persons shall be cut off

a Heb *it*

19.1–22: The red cow and corpse contamination. A human corpse causes impurity in another person or object by contact (vv. 11,16) or by being in the same enclosure with the person or object (v. 14). The impurity lasts seven days. To become ritually clean, a person or object is sprinkled, on the third and seventh days of the impurity, with water that has been mixed with the ashes prepared according to vv. 2–10 (vv. 12,17–19). This is followed by ritual bath on the seventh day (v. 19). This chapter fits better with the rituals described in Lev 11–15, which deal with other impurities (see Lev 11.1–15.33n.). It is placed here in part perhaps because of the death in Korah's rebellion and the mortal plague of chs 16–17. Ch 19 is supplemented by 31.19–24. **2:** *Heifer,* meaning a cow that has not had a calf, is more precise than the Heb word, which simply means "cow." **6:** On the materials, cf. Lev 14.4n. **7–10:** The process has made the participants impure (also v. 21); this explains why it is performed outside the camp (cf. 5.1–4n.). **9:** *Purification offering,* translated properly here. Elsewhere (e.g., Lev 4; Num 15.22–31), this is mistranslated as "sin offering." It is not an offering in the true sense, since it is slaughtered outside the camp and its blood is not used on the altar (despite the law in Lev 17.1–16). **12:** *Purify themselves,* better, "be purified." Someone else does the rite (vv. 18–19,21). **13,20:** For lay Israelites, corpse contamination itself is not a sin, though delay of purification is. The delay pollutes the sanctuary (Lev 5.2–3; 21.1–12n.; cf. Lev 4.1–35n.). Priests have restrictions from corpse contamination (Lev 21.1–12n.; Lev 10.4–5n.).

from Israel. Since water for cleansing was
not dashed on them, they remain unclean;
their uncleanness is still on them.
14 This is the law when someone dies in
a tent: everyone who comes into the tent,
and everyone who is in the tent, shall be
unclean seven days. 15 And every open ves-
sel with no cover fastened on it is unclean.
16 Whoever in the open field touches one
who has been killed by a sword, or who has
died naturally,[a] or a human bone, or a
grave, shall be unclean seven days. 17 For
the unclean they shall take some ashes of
the burnt purification offering, and running
water shall be added in a vessel; 18 then a
clean person shall take hyssop, dip it in the
water, and sprinkle it on the tent, on all the
furnishings, on the persons who were there,
and on whoever touched the bone, the
slain, the corpse, or the grave. 19 The clean
person shall sprinkle the unclean ones on
the third day and on the seventh day, thus
purifying them on the seventh day. Then
they shall wash their clothes and bathe
themselves in water, and at evening they
shall be clean. 20 Any who are unclean but
do not purify themselves, those persons
shall be cut off from the assembly, for they
have defiled the sanctuary of the LORD.
Since the water for cleansing has not been
dashed on them, they are unclean.
21 It shall be a perpetual statute for
them. The one who sprinkles the water for
cleansing shall wash his clothes, and who-
ever touches the water for cleansing shall
be unclean until evening. 22 Whatever the
unclean person touches shall be unclean,
and anyone who touches it shall be unclean
until evening.

20 The Israelites, the whole congrega-
tion, came into the wilderness of
Zin in the first month, and the people
stayed in Kadesh. Miriam died there, and
was buried there.
2 Now there was no water for the con-
gregation; so they gathered together against
Moses and against Aaron. 3 The people
quarreled with Moses and said, "Would
that we had died when our kindred died
before the LORD! 4 Why have you brought
the assembly of the LORD into this wilder-
ness for us and our livestock to die here?
5 Why have you brought us up out of Egypt,
to bring us to this wretched place? It is no
place for grain, or figs, or vines, or pome-
granates; and there is no water to drink."
6 Then Moses and Aaron went away from
the assembly to the entrance of the tent of
meeting; they fell on their faces, and the
glory of the LORD appeared to them. 7 The
LORD spoke to Moses, saying: 8 Take the
staff, and assemble the congregation, you
and your brother Aaron, and command the
rock before their eyes to yield its water.
Thus you shall bring water out of the rock
for them; thus you shall provide drink for
the congregation and their livestock.
9 So Moses took the staff from before
the LORD, as he had commanded him.
10 Moses and Aaron gathered the assembly
together before the rock, and he said to
them, "Listen, you rebels, shall we bring
water for you out of this rock?" 11 Then
Moses lifted up his hand and struck the
rock twice with his staff; water came out
abundantly, and the congregation and their

a Heb lacks *naturally*

20.1–29: Near the end of the wilderness period. This chapter telescopes many years, from the second to the fortieth year of wandering. **1:** The arrival at Zin and Kadesh apparently occurs early in the forty-year period of wandering. Vv. 4–5 are the complaint of the first generation, and 13.26 places the Israelites at Kadesh at the very beginning of the period (cf. Deut 2.14; Num 33.36–38). The Israelites appear to have stayed here a long time (see v. 14n.). The leading figures of the first generation begin to die in this chapter. See vv. 22–29. On *Miriam,* see 12.1–9; Ex 15.20. **2–13:** This resumes the stories of complaint and rebellion, interrupted at ch 15 (see 11.1–35n.). The present story of bringing water from a rock with a rod is a doublet, with significant variations, of Ex 17.1–7. **3:** *Our kindred died,* see ch 16. **9–13:** Moses and Aaron apparently sin by not clearly attributing the miracle to God (v. 12). Deut 3.26 preserves an alternate tradition for why Moses did not enter the land. On the pair's punishment, cf. vv. 22–29; Deut 34 (cf. Num 27.12–17n.). **14–21:** The events from this point on appear to occur near

livestock drank. 12 But the LORD said to
Moses and Aaron, "Because you did not
trust in me, to show my holiness before the
eyes of the Israelites, therefore you shall not
bring this assembly into the land that I have
given them." 13 These are the waters of
Meribah,[a] where the people of Israel quar-
reled with the LORD, and by which he
showed his holiness.

14 Moses sent messengers from Kadesh
to the king of Edom, "Thus says your
brother Israel: You know all the adversity
that has befallen us: 15 how our ancestors
went down to Egypt, and we lived in Egypt
a long time; and the Egyptians oppressed us
and our ancestors; 16 and when we cried to
the LORD, he heard our voice, and sent an
angel and brought us out of Egypt; and
here we are in Kadesh, a town on the edge
of your territory. 17 Now let us pass
through your land. We will not pass
through field or vineyard, or drink water
from any well; we will go along the King's
Highway, not turning aside to the right
hand or to the left until we have passed
through your territory."

18 But Edom said to him, "You shall
not pass through, or we will come out with
the sword against you." 19 The Israelites
said to him, "We will stay on the highway;
and if we drink of your water, we and our
livestock, then we will pay for it. It is only
a small matter; just let us pass through on
foot." 20 But he said, "You shall not pass
through." And Edom came out against
them with a large force, heavily armed.
21 Thus Edom refused to give Israel passage
through their territory; so Israel turned
away from them.

22 They set out from Kadesh, and the
Israelites, the whole congregation, came to
Mount Hor. 23 Then the LORD said to Mo-
ses and Aaron at Mount Hor, on the border
of the land of Edom, 24 "Let Aaron be gath-
ered to his people. For he shall not enter the
land that I have given to the Israelites, be-
cause you rebelled against my command at
the waters of Meribah. 25 Take Aaron and
his son Eleazar, and bring them up Mount
Hor; 26 strip Aaron of his vestments, and
put them on his son Eleazar. But Aaron
shall be gathered to his people,[b] and shall
die there." 27 Moses did as the LORD had
commanded; they went up Mount Hor in
the sight of the whole congregation. 28 Mo-
ses stripped Aaron of his vestments, and
put them on his son Eleazar; and Aaron
died there on the top of the mountain. Mo-
ses and Eleazar came down from the moun-
tain. 29 When all the congregation saw that
Aaron had died, all the house of Israel
mourned for Aaron thirty days.

21 When the Canaanite, the king of
Arad, who lived in the Negeb, heard
that Israel was coming by the way of Atha-
rim, he fought against Israel and took some
of them captive. 2 Then Israel made a vow
to the LORD and said, "If you will indeed
give this people into our hands, then we
will utterly destroy their towns." 3 The
LORD listened to the voice of Israel, and
handed over the Canaanites; and they ut-
terly destroyed them and their towns; so
the place was called Hormah.[c]

4 From Mount Hor they set out by the

a That is *Quarrel* *b* Heb lacks *to his people*
c Heb *Destruction*

the end of the forty-year wilderness period. See v. 1n. Passing through Edom would give a more direct route to Transjordan via the King's Highway (a term used only here in v. 17 and in 21.22), the primary north-south route through Transjordan (see Map on p. 28 HB). **21:** The Israelites need to turn south, toward the Red Sea, in order to avoid Edom (cf. 21.4). The Israelites are not meant to conquer Edom, so they may not engage them in battle. **22–29:** Cf. 33.38–39; Deut 32.50; contrast Deut 10.6. **24:** This refers to vv. 2–13. **26:** Aaron's priestly clothes are put on Eleazar. One would expect this investiture to occur at the sanctuary with a consecration rite (cf. Lev 8). **29:** *Thirty days,* cf. Deut 34.8.

21.1–35: Conflicts in the Negeb and Transjordan. The Israelites encounter other enemies as they move toward Transjordan (cf. 20.14–21). **1–3:** *Arad,* west of the Dead Sea and east of Beer-sheba. *Atharim* is unknown. **2–3:** *Utterly destroy,* cf. Lev 27.28n. The name *Hormah,* "Destruction," echoes the Heb word "ḥerem" for *utterly destroy;* cf. Judg 1.17. **4–9:** Another complaint, see 11.1–35n. **8–9:** This story,

way to the Red Sea,[a] to go around the land
of Edom; but the people became impatient
on the way. 5 The people spoke against God
and against Moses, "Why have you
brought us up out of Egypt to die in the
wilderness? For there is no food and no
water, and we detest this miserable food."
6 Then the LORD sent poisonous[b] serpents
among the people, and they bit the people,
so that many Israelites died. 7 The people
came to Moses and said, "We have sinned
by speaking against the LORD and against
you; pray to the LORD to take away the
serpents from us." So Moses prayed for the
people. 8 And the LORD said to Moses,
"Make a poisonous[c] serpent, and set it on
a pole; and everyone who is bitten shall
look at it and live." 9 So Moses made a ser-
pent of bronze, and put it upon a pole; and
whenever a serpent bit someone, that per-
son would look at the serpent of bronze
and live.

10 The Israelites set out, and camped in
Oboth. 11 They set out from Oboth, and
camped at Iye-abarim, in the wilderness
bordering Moab toward the sunrise.
12 From there they set out, and camped in
the Wadi Zered. 13 From there they set out,
and camped on the other side of the Arnon,
in[d] the wilderness that extends from the
boundary of the Amorites; for the Arnon is
the boundary of Moab, between Moab and
the Amorites. 14 Wherefore it is said in the
Book of the Wars of the LORD,

"Waheb in Suphah and the wadis.
The Arnon 15 and the slopes of the
wadis
that extend to the seat of Ar,
and lie along the border of Moab."[e]

16 From there they continued to Beer;[f]
that is the well of which the LORD said to
Moses, "Gather the people together, and I
will give them water." 17 Then Israel sang
this song:

"Spring up, O well!—Sing to it!—
18 the well that the leaders sank,
that the nobles of the people dug,
with the scepter, with the staff."

From the wilderness to Mattanah, 19 from
Mattanah to Nahaliel, from Nahaliel to Ba-
moth, 20 and from Bamoth to the valley ly-
ing in the region of Moab by the top of
Pisgah that overlooks the wasteland.[g]

21 Then Israel sent messengers to King
Sihon of the Amorites, saying, 22 "Let me
pass through your land; we will not turn
aside into field or vineyard; we will not
drink the water of any well; we will go by
the King's Highway until we have passed
through your territory." 23 But Sihon
would not allow Israel to pass through his
territory. Sihon gathered all his people to-
gether, and went out against Israel to the
wilderness; he came to Jahaz, and fought
against Israel. 24 Israel put him to the
sword, and took possession of his land
from the Arnon to the Jabbok, as far as to
the Ammonites; for the boundary of the
Ammonites was strong. 25 Israel took all
these towns, and Israel settled in all the

a Or *Sea of Reeds* *b* Or *fiery*; Heb *seraphim*
c Or *fiery*; Heb *seraph* *d* Gk: Heb *which is in*
e Meaning of Heb uncertain *f* That is *Well*
g Or *Jeshimon*

describing a kind of sympathetic magic, may give the etiology for a snake image in the Temple (cf. 2 Kings 18.4). **10–20:** This is a short itinerary of travels in Transjordan; cf. 33.41–49. It comes from different sources, and many of the places named cannot be identified. **12–13:** The *Wadi Zered,* probably the modern Wadi el-Hasa, and the *Arnon,* modern Wadi Mujib, southeast and east of the Dead Sea respectively, were the traditional boundaries of Moab. The *Amorites* were one of the groups identified as inhabitants of Canaan and Transjordan; see 13.29n. **14:** *Book of the Wars of the LORD,* an early nonbiblical work, perhaps poetic, from which the citation in vv. 14–15 was taken. Long poetic narratives are known from Ugarit (Syria) ca. 1400 BCE. Other poetic citations, though not necessarily coming from the book of v. 14, are found in vv. 16–18,27–30. Cf. Balaam's oracles in chs 23–24. **20:** *Pisgah,* a ridge overlooking the northeast of the Dead Sea, associated with Mount Nebo; see Deut 34.1. **21–31:** In contrast to Edom, the Israelites engage Sihon in battle and win (cf. 20.14–21). Sihon's land was north of Moab, between the Arnon and Jabbok rivers (see color Map 3 at end of book). **22:** *King's Highway,* see 20.14–21n. **25:** *Heshbon,* probably Tell Hesban, ca. 20 km (12 mi) southwest of Amman. **29:** *Chemosh,* the Moabite

towns of the Amorites, in Heshbon, and in
all its villages. 26 For Heshbon was the city
of King Sihon of the Amorites, who had
fought against the former king of Moab
and captured all his land as far as the Ar-
non. 27 Therefore the ballad singers say,

"Come to Heshbon, let it be built;
let the city of Sihon be established.

28 For fire came out from Heshbon,
flame from the city of Sihon.
It devoured Ar of Moab,
and swallowed up[a] the heights of
the Arnon.

29 Woe to you, O Moab!
You are undone, O people of
Chemosh!
He has made his sons fugitives,
and his daughters captives,
to an Amorite king, Sihon.

30 So their posterity perished
from Heshbon[b] to Dibon,
and we laid waste until fire spread
to Medeba."[c]

31 Thus Israel settled in the land of the
Amorites. 32 Moses sent to spy out Jazer;
and they captured its villages, and dispos-
sessed the Amorites who were there.

33 Then they turned and went up the
road to Bashan; and King Og of Bashan
came out against them, he and all his peo-
ple, to battle at Edrei. 34 But the LORD said
to Moses, "Do not be afraid of him; for I
have given him into your hand, with all his
people, and all his land. You shall do to
him as you did to King Sihon of the Amo-
rites, who ruled in Heshbon." 35 So they
killed him, his sons, and all his people, until
there was no survivor left; and they took
possession of his land.

22 The Israelites set out, and camped in
the plains of Moab across the Jor-
dan from Jericho. 2 Now Balak son of Zip-
por saw all that Israel had done to the Am-
orites. 3 Moab was in great dread of the
people, because they were so numerous;
Moab was overcome with fear of the peo-
ple of Israel. 4 And Moab said to the elders
of Midian, "This horde will now lick up all
that is around us, as an ox licks up the grass
of the field." Now Balak son of Zippor was
king of Moab at that time. 5 He sent mes-
sengers to Balaam son of Beor at Pethor,
which is on the Euphrates, in the land of
Amaw,[d] to summon him, saying, "A peo-
ple has come out of Egypt; they have spread

a Gk: Heb *and the lords of* *b* Gk: Heb *we have shot at them; Heshbon has perished* *c* Compare Sam Gk: Meaning of MT uncertain *d* Or *land of his kinsfolk*

national god. **30:** *Dibon,* modern Dhiban, ca. 55 km (34 mi) south-southwest of Amman. *Medeba,* between Heshbon and Dibon. **33–35:** Og's land was north of Sihon's, roughly in the Golan region east of Galilee. Sihon's and Og's land become the inheritance for the tribes of Gad, Reuben, and half of Manasseh (cf. 32.33). *Edrei,* modern Derʿa, 105 km (65 mi) south of Damascus.

22.1–24.5: The story of Balaam. Balak, king of Moab, hires the seer Balaam to curse the invading Israelites. But Balaam blesses them, speaking only what God will tell him (22.18,20,35,38, etc.). The character Balaam is also known from a fragmentary eighth-century BCE text written on plaster walls at a temple at Deir Allah, on the east side of the Jordan where the Jabbok joins the Jordan. It portrays him as a seer who has a night vision (cf. 22.8–9,20) and gives an interpretation. This and the biblical story indicate that Balaam was a relatively well-known legendary visionary associated with Transjordan. In fact, the biblical story here is composite, combining variant traditions about Balaam. The biblical stories reflect the belief that prophecy is not unique to Israel, and those distant from the people of Israel may also be subject to divine inspiration. Specifically, this may reflect Israelite knowledge of the phenomenon of prophecy in Mesopotamia.

22.1–40: Balak hires Balaam. 1–2: The Israelites have finished their wilderness journeys and are now opposite *across the Jordan from Jericho,* where their entrance to the land is to begin (33.48; Josh 2.1). *Amorites,* 21.21–35. **4:** Moab and Midian are also associated in 25.1,6. **5:** If *Pethor* is Pitru (on the Sajur river, a tributary of the Euphrates), then Balaam lives some 650 km (400 mi) northeast of where the Israelites are. The story thus has Balak taking pains to find a prophet whose words are effective and to his liking. **7–21:** Without much hesitation, God gives Balaam permission to go to Balak after Balaam's

over the face of the earth, and they have
settled next to me. 6 Come now, curse this
people for me, since they are stronger than
I; perhaps I shall be able to defeat them and
drive them from the land; for I know that
whomever you bless is blessed, and whom-
ever you curse is cursed."

7 So the elders of Moab and the elders of
Midian departed with the fees for divina-
tion in their hand; and they came to Ba-
laam, and gave him Balak's message. 8 He
said to them, "Stay here tonight, and I will
bring back word to you, just as the LORD
speaks to me"; so the officials of Moab
stayed with Balaam. 9 God came to Balaam
and said, "Who are these men with you?"
10 Balaam said to God, "King Balak son of
Zippor of Moab, has sent me this message:
11 'A people has come out of Egypt and has
spread over the face of the earth; now
come, curse them for me; perhaps I shall be
able to fight against them and drive them
out.' " 12 God said to Balaam, "You shall
not go with them; you shall not curse the
people, for they are blessed." 13 So Balaam
rose in the morning, and said to the offi-
cials of Balak, "Go to your own land, for
the LORD has refused to let me go with
you." 14 So the officials of Moab rose and
went to Balak, and said, "Balaam refuses to
come with us."

15 Once again Balak sent officials, more
numerous and more distinguished than
these. 16 They came to Balaam and said to
him, "Thus says Balak son of Zippor: 'Do
not let anything hinder you from coming to
me; 17 for I will surely do you great honor,
and whatever you say to me I will do;
come, curse this people for me.' " 18 But Ba-
laam replied to the servants of Balak, "Al-
though Balak were to give me his house full
of silver and gold, I could not go beyond
the command of the LORD my God, to do
less or more. 19 You remain here, as the oth-
ers did, so that I may learn what more the
LORD may say to me." 20 That night God
came to Balaam and said to him, "If the
men have come to summon you, get up and
go with them; but do only what I tell you to
do." 21 So Balaam got up in the morning,
saddled his donkey, and went with the offi-
cials of Moab.

22 God's anger was kindled because he
was going, and the angel of the LORD took
his stand in the road as his adversary. Now
he was riding on the donkey, and his two
servants were with him. 23 The donkey saw
the angel of the LORD standing in the road,
with a drawn sword in his hand; so the
donkey turned off the road, and went into
the field; and Balaam struck the donkey, to
turn it back onto the road. 24 Then the an-
gel of the LORD stood in a narrow path
between the vineyards, with a wall on ei-
ther side. 25 When the donkey saw the angel
of the LORD, it scraped against the wall,
and scraped Balaam's foot against the wall;
so he struck it again. 26 Then the angel of
the LORD went ahead, and stood in a nar-
row place, where there was no way to turn
either to the right or to the left. 27 When the
donkey saw the angel of the LORD, it lay
down under Balaam; and Balaam's anger
was kindled, and he struck the donkey with
his staff. 28 Then the LORD opened the
mouth of the donkey, and it said to Ba-
laam, "What have I done to you, that you
have struck me these three times?" 29 Ba-
laam said to the donkey, "Because you
have made a fool of me! I wish I had a
sword in my hand! I would kill you right
now!" 30 But the donkey said to Balaam,
"Am I not your donkey, which you have
ridden all your life to this day? Have I been

second request. **22–35**: These verses come from a tradition different from the foregoing, as indicated by God's anger at Balaam (v. 22) after having given permission to go (v. 20), by the seer's apparent blindness to divine will which was not the case in vv. 7–21, and the redundancy in vv. 20 and 35. In this version of the story, his donkey is smarter than he (cf. Isa 1.3). This version, which is only partly incorporated in the larger context of chs 22–24, may have first recounted that Balaam went without consulting the deity. Except for 22.22–35, chs 22–24 present Balaam in a positive light (cf. Mic 6.5). Other biblical passages portray him negatively (31.8,16; Deut 23.5; Josh 13.22; 24.10; Neh 13.2). **23,31:** *Drawn sword,* cf. Josh 5.13; 1 Chr 21.16.

in the habit of treating you this way?" And
he said, "No."
31 Then the LORD opened the eyes of
Balaam, and he saw the angel of the LORD
standing in the road, with his drawn sword
in his hand; and he bowed down, falling on
his face. 32 The angel of the LORD said to
him, "Why have you struck your donkey
these three times? I have come out as an
adversary, because your way is perverse[a]
before me. 33 The donkey saw me, and
turned away from me these three times. If it
had not turned away from me, surely just
now I would have killed you and let it live."
34 Then Balaam said to the angel of the
LORD, "I have sinned, for I did not know
that you were standing in the road to op-
pose me. Now therefore, if it is displeasing
to you, I will return home." 35 The angel of
the LORD said to Balaam, "Go with the
men; but speak only what I tell you to
speak." So Balaam went on with the offi-
cials of Balak.
36 When Balak heard that Balaam had
come, he went out to meet him at Ir-moab,
on the boundary formed by the Arnon, at
the farthest point of the boundary. 37 Balak
said to Balaam, "Did I not send to summon
you? Why did you not come to me? Am I
not able to honor you?" 38 Balaam said to
Balak, "I have come to you now, but do I
have power to say just anything? The word
God puts in my mouth, that is what I must
say." 39 Then Balaam went with Balak, and
they came to Kiriath-huzoth. 40 Balak sacri-
ficed oxen and sheep, and sent them to Ba-
laam and to the officials who were with
him.
41 On the next day Balak took Balaam
and brought him up to Bamoth-baal; and
from there he could see part of the people
23 of Israel.[b] 1 Then Balaam said to
Balak, "Build me seven altars here,
and prepare seven bulls and seven rams for
me." 2 Balak did as Balaam had said; and
Balak and Balaam offered a bull and a ram
on each altar. 3 Then Balaam said to Balak,
"Stay here beside your burnt offerings
while I go aside. Perhaps the LORD will
come to meet me. Whatever he shows me I
will tell you." And he went to a bare height.
4 Then God met Balaam; and Balaam
said to him, "I have arranged the seven al-
tars, and have offered a bull and a ram on
each altar." 5 The LORD put a word in Ba-
laam's mouth, and said, "Return to Balak,
and this is what you must say." 6 So he re-
turned to Balak,[c] who was standing beside
his burnt offerings with all the officials of
Moab. 7 Then Balaam[d] uttered his oracle,
saying:

"Balak has brought me from Aram,
the king of Moab from the eastern
mountains:
'Come, curse Jacob for me;
Come, denounce Israel!'
8 How can I curse whom God has not
cursed?
How can I denounce those whom
the LORD has not denounced?
9 For from the top of the crags I see
him,
from the hills I behold him.
Here is a people living alone,
and not reckoning itself among the
nations!
10 Who can count the dust of Jacob,
or number the dust-cloud[e] of
Israel?
Let me die the death of the upright,
and let my end be like his!"

11 Then Balak said to Balaam, "What
have you done to me? I brought you to

a Meaning of Heb uncertain *b* Heb lacks *of Israel*
c Heb *him* *d* Heb *he* *e* Or *fourth part*

22.41–23.11: The first oracle. 23.1: The offering presumably engages the deity's attention and favor so that he will reveal his will. **3:** In 24.1 Balaam's going aside is described as seeking omens. Hence his prophetic activity is specifically connected with divination of some sort. This may have in part given rise to negative assessments of his character (cf. Lev 19.26; Deut 18.10–13). **7–10:** The poetic oracle he recites is a blessing, not a curse. The meaning of this oracle is clear; some of the later oracles are poorly preserved and extremely unclear. **7:** *Aram,* Syria; see 22.5n. **10:** *Dust of Jacob,* see Gen 13.16; 28.14.

curse my enemies, but now you have done
nothing but bless them." 12 He answered,
"Must I not take care to say what the LORD
puts into my mouth?"
13 So Balak said to him, "Come with me
to another place from which you may see
them; you shall see only part of them, and
shall not see them all; then curse them for
me from there." 14 So he took him to the
field of Zophim, to the top of Pisgah. He
built seven altars, and offered a bull and a
ram on each altar. 15 Balaam said to Balak,
"Stand here beside your burnt offerings,
while I meet the LORD over there." 16 The
LORD met Balaam, put a word into his
mouth, and said, "Return to Balak, and
this is what you shall say." 17 When he
came to him, he was standing beside his
burnt offerings with the officials of Moab.
Balak said to him, "What has the LORD
said?" 18 Then Balaam uttered his oracle,
saying:

"Rise, Balak, and hear;
listen to me, O son of Zippor:
19 God is not a human being, that he should lie,
or a mortal, that he should change his mind.
Has he promised, and will he not do it?
Has he spoken, and will he not fulfill it?
20 See, I received a command to bless;
he has blessed, and I cannot revoke it.
21 He has not beheld misfortune in Jacob;
nor has he seen trouble in Israel.
The LORD their God is with them,
acclaimed as a king among them.
22 God, who brings them out of Egypt,
is like the horns of a wild ox for them.
23 Surely there is no enchantment against Jacob,
no divination against Israel;
now it shall be said of Jacob and Israel,
'See what God has done!'
24 Look, a people rising up like a lioness,
and rousing itself like a lion!
It does not lie down until it has eaten the prey
and drunk the blood of the slain."

25 Then Balak said to Balaam, "Do not
curse them at all, and do not bless them at
all." 26 But Balaam answered Balak, "Did I
not tell you, 'Whatever the LORD says, that
is what I must do'?"
27 So Balak said to Balaam, "Come
now, I will take you to another place; per-
haps it will please God that you may curse
them for me from there." 28 So Balak took
Balaam to the top of Peor, which overlooks
the wasteland.[a] 29 Balaam said to Balak,
"Build me seven altars here, and prepare
seven bulls and seven rams for me." 30 So
Balak did as Balaam had said, and offered
a bull and a ram on each altar.

24 Now Balaam saw that it pleased the
LORD to bless Israel, so he did not
go, as at other times, to look for omens, but
set his face toward the wilderness. 2 Balaam

a Or *overlooks Jeshimon*

23.13–25: The second oracle. Balak thinks that Balaam will curse Israel if he views them from another location. In describing the scene this way, the biblical author is mocking Balak. **14:** *Pisgah,* see 21.20n. **18–24:** The oracle is again positive, even more so than the first. **22:** *The horns of a wild ox,* a symbol of strength. **23:** *No enchantment against . . . ,* i.e., omens (cf. 24.1) do not portend any evil for the people. **24:** This addresses the military aspect of the people, anticipating the conquest of the land. *Like a lion,* see 24.9; Gen 49.9; Ezek 19.2–6.

23.27–24.9: The third oracle. Again Balak moves Balaam to yet another location (cf. 23.13). **23.28:** *Peor,* cf. Baal-peor, 25.3; 31.16. **24.1:** This follows a folkloric pattern in which the third in a series of similar events is different to some degree from the previous two (cf. 22.28). In this third oracle, Balaam dispenses with preparatory omens that tell him that he should bless Israel, since he knows God's intentions (cf. 23.23). **2:** In the first two oracles, Balaam saw only part of the people (22.41; 23.13). Apparently now he can see all of them. **3–9:** This oracle has more poetic lines than the first two, marking it as the climax.

looked up and saw Israel camping tribe by
tribe. Then the spirit of God came upon
him, 3 and he uttered his oracle, saying:

"The oracle of Balaam son of Beor,
the oracle of the man whose eye is clear,[a]
4 the oracle of one who hears the words of God,
who sees the vision of the Almighty,[b]
who falls down, but with eyes uncovered:
5 how fair are your tents, O Jacob,
your encampments, O Israel!
6 Like palm groves that stretch far away,
like gardens beside a river,
like aloes that the LORD has planted,
like cedar trees beside the waters.
7 Water shall flow from his buckets,
and his seed shall have abundant water,
his king shall be higher than Agag,
and his kingdom shall be exalted.
8 God who brings him out of Egypt,
is like the horns of a wild ox for him;
he shall devour the nations that are his foes
and break their bones.
He shall strike with his arrows.[c]
9 He crouched, he lay down like a lion,
and like a lioness; who will rouse him up?
Blessed is everyone who blesses you,
and cursed is everyone who curses you."

10 Then Balak's anger was kindled
against Balaam, and he struck his hands
together. Balak said to Balaam, "I sum-
moned you to curse my enemies, but in-
stead you have blessed them these three
times. 11 Now be off with you! Go home!
I said, 'I will reward you richly,' but the
LORD has denied you any reward." 12 And
Balaam said to Balak, "Did I not tell your
messengers whom you sent to me, 13 'If Ba-
lak should give me his house full of silver
and gold, I would not be able to go beyond
the word of the LORD, to do either good or
bad of my own will; what the LORD says,
that is what I will say'? 14 So now, I am
going to my people; let me advise you what
this people will do to your people in days to
come."
15 So he uttered his oracle, saying:

"The oracle of Balaam son of Beor,
the oracle of the man whose eye is clear,[a]
16 the oracle of one who hears the words of God,
and knows the knowledge of the Most High,[d]
who sees the vision of the Almighty,[b]
who falls down, but with his eyes uncovered:
17 I see him, but not now;
I behold him, but not near—
a star shall come out of Jacob,
and a scepter shall rise out of Israel;
it shall crush the borderlands[e] of Moab,
and the territory[f] of all the Shethites.
18 Edom will become a possession,
Seir a possession of its enemies,[g]
while Israel does valiantly.
19 One out of Jacob shall rule,
and destroy the survivors of Ir."

20 Then he looked on Amalek, and ut-
tered his oracle, saying:

a Or *closed* or *open* *b* Traditional rendering of Heb *Shaddai* *c* Meaning of Heb uncertain *d* Or *of Elyon* *e* Or *forehead* *f* Some Mss read *skull* *g* Heb *Seir, its enemies, a possession*

3–4: Each oracle begins with a statement reflecting on Balaam's prophetic knowledge or obligation, authenticating him as a prophet; after that follow the words of blessing. **7:** The mention of the king reflects the monarchic period. Agag, moreover, is the later king of Amalek (1 Sam 15.8). **8:** *Wild ox,* see 23.22n. **9:** See 23.24; Gen 49.9; 12.3.

24.10–25: The fourth oracle. This, actually a collection of short oracles, supplements the first three directed at Israel. It emphasizes the blessing of Israel by cursing Moab as well as other nations and groups. **17:** *Star . . . scepter,* royal symbols (see Gen 49.10). *Shethites,* uncertain. **18:** *Seir,* a synonym for Edom.

"First among the nations was
Amalek,
but its end is to perish forever."
21 Then he looked on the Kenite, and
uttered his oracle, saying:
"Enduring is your dwelling place,
and your nest is set in the rock;
22 yet Kain is destined for burning.
How long shall Asshur take you
away captive?"
23 Again he uttered his oracle, saying:
"Alas, who shall live when God does
this?
24 But ships shall come from Kittim
and shall afflict Asshur and Eber;
and he also shall perish forever."
25 Then Balaam got up and went back
to his place, and Balak also went his way.

25 While Israel was staying at Shittim,
the people began to have sexual re-
lations with the women of Moab. 2 These
invited the people to the sacrifices of their
gods, and the people ate and bowed down
to their gods. 3 Thus Israel yoked itself to
the Baal of Peor, and the LORD's anger was
kindled against Israel. 4 The LORD said to
Moses, "Take all the chiefs of the people,
and impale them in the sun before the
LORD, in order that the fierce anger of the
LORD may turn away from Israel." 5 And
Moses said to the judges of Israel, "Each of
you shall kill any of your people who have
yoked themselves to the Baal of Peor."
6 Just then one of the Israelites came and
brought a Midianite woman into his fami-
ly, in the sight of Moses and in the sight of
the whole congregation of the Israelites,
while they were weeping at the entrance of
the tent of meeting. 7 When Phinehas son of
Eleazar, son of Aaron the priest, saw it, he
got up and left the congregation. Taking a
spear in his hand, 8 he went after the Israel-
ite man into the tent, and pierced the two of
them, the Israelite and the woman, through
the belly. So the plague was stopped among
the people of Israel. 9 Nevertheless those
that died by the plague were twenty-four
thousand.
10 The LORD spoke to Moses, saying:
11 "Phinehas son of Eleazar, son of Aaron
the priest, has turned back my wrath from
the Israelites by manifesting such zeal
among them on my behalf that in my jeal-
ousy I did not consume the Israelites.
12 Therefore say, 'I hereby grant him my
covenant of peace. 13 It shall be for him and
for his descendants after him a covenant of
perpetual priesthood, because he was zeal-
ous for his God, and made atonement for
the Israelites.' "

20: *Amalek,* see 13.29n. **21:** *Kenite,* lit. "descendant of Kain" (or Cain; v. 22; cf. Gen 4). The Kenites were a group associated with the Midianites; see 22.4; compare 10.29 with Judg 1.16. **22:** *Asshur* may mean Assyria. **24:** *Kittim,* inhabitants of the Aegean Sea, or Cyprus; see Gen 10.4. *Eber,* perhaps a designation of Mesopotamia; cf. also Gen 10.25. **25:** A typical anticlimactic ending to the biblical story.

25.1–18: Moabite and Midianite women. Israelite men engage in illicit sexual activity, perhaps intermarriage, with foreign women in the context of idolatrous feasting (cf. Ps 106.28–31; Hos 9.10). Moabites are associated from their very beginning with illicit sexual activity (Gen 19.29–37). Contradictions (e.g., Moabites versus Midianites) are due to the joining of at least two different stories (vv. 1–5 [JE] and 6–18 [P]). **1:** *Shittim* is the last wilderness stop (cf. 33.49); its precise location is uncertain. **1–2:** Ex 34.15–16 presents a similar sequence of actions. **3:** *Baal of Peor,* the Baal deity associated with the place Peor (23.28; Deut 3.29). **4:** The leaders, as representatives of the people, are to be executed. Impalement (also in 2 Sam 21.6–10) perhaps deters the public from such actions, but here it also appeases the deity. It is presumably performed after execution by other means (cf. v. 5; Deut 21.21–23). **6:** Contrast Moses' marriage with a Midianite woman, Ex 2.15–22. **7–8:** Phinehas, who becomes high priest after his father Eleazar (cf. 20.22–29), spears the man and woman, apparently in a single thrust (v. 14), which suggests that they were having intercourse. This halts a plague (cf. vv. 5,11; 16.46–48). **10–12:** Phinehas's *zeal* is compared to God's *jealousy* (both terms are from the same Heb root). He receives a *covenant of peace* (cf. Isa 54.10; Ezek 34.25) assuring him and his descendants of the priesthood. This may refer to the ascendancy of the priesthood of Zadok, which at some point viewed itself as a descendant of Phinehas (1 Chr 6.50–54). **13:** Atonement here is appeasement of the deity (Ex 30.12,15; 2 Sam 21.3; cf. Lev

14 The name of the slain Israelite man,
who was killed with the Midianite woman,
was Zimri son of Salu, head of an ancestral
house belonging to the Simeonites. 15 The
name of the Midianite woman who was
killed was Cozbi daughter of Zur, who was
the head of a clan, an ancestral house in
Midian.

16 The LORD said to Moses, 17 "Harass
the Midianites, and defeat them; 18 for they
have harassed you by the trickery with
which they deceived you in the affair of
Peor, and in the affair of Cozbi, the daugh-
ter of a leader of Midian, their sister; she
was killed on the day of the plague that
resulted from Peor."

26 After the plague the LORD said to
Moses and to Eleazar son of Aaron
the priest, 2 "Take a census of the whole
congregation of the Israelites, from twenty
years old and upward, by their ancestral
houses, everyone in Israel able to go to
war." 3 Moses and Eleazar the priest spoke
with them in the plains of Moab by the
Jordan opposite Jericho, saying, 4 "Take a
census of the people,[a] from twenty years
old and upward," as the LORD commanded
Moses.

The Israelites, who came out of the land
of Egypt, were:

5 Reuben, the firstborn of Israel. The de-
scendants of Reuben: of Hanoch, the clan
of the Hanochites; of Pallu, the clan of the
Palluites; 6 of Hezron, the clan of the Hez-
ronites; of Carmi, the clan of the Carmites.
7 These are the clans of the Reubenites; the
number of those enrolled was forty-three
thousand seven hundred thirty. 8 And the
descendants of Pallu: Eliab. 9 The descen-
dants of Eliab: Nemuel, Dathan, and Abi-
ram. These are the same Dathan and Abi-
ram, chosen from the congregation, who
rebelled against Moses and Aaron in the
company of Korah, when they rebelled
against the LORD, 10 and the earth opened
its mouth and swallowed them up along
with Korah, when that company died,
when the fire devoured two hundred fifty
men; and they became a warning. 11 Not-
withstanding, the sons of Korah did not
die.

12 The descendants of Simeon by their
clans: of Nemuel, the clan of the Nemuel-
ites; of Jamin, the clan of the Jaminites; of
Jachin, the clan of the Jachinites; 13 of Ze-
rah, the clan of the Zerahites; of Shaul, the
clan of the Shaulites.[b] 14 These are the
clans of the Simeonites, twenty-two thou-
sand two hundred.

15 The children of Gad by their clans:
of Zephon, the clan of the Zephonites; of
Haggi, the clan of the Haggites; of Shuni,
the clan of the Shunites; 16 of Ozni, the clan
of the Oznites; of Eri, the clan of the Erites;
17 of Arod, the clan of the Arodites; of Are-
li, the clan of the Arelites. 18 These are the
clans of the Gadites: the number of those
enrolled was forty thousand five hundred.

19 The sons of Judah: Er and Onan; Er
and Onan died in the land of Canaan.
20 The descendants of Judah by their clans
were: of Shelah, the clan of the Shelanites;
of Perez, the clan of the Perezites; of Zerah,
the clan of the Zerahites. 21 The descen-
dants of Perez were: of Hezron, the clan of
the Hezronites; of Hamul, the clan of the
Hamulites. 22 These are the clans of Judah:
the number of those enrolled was seventy-
six thousand five hundred.

23 The descendants of Issachar by their
clans: of Tola, the clan of the Tolaites; of

a Heb lacks *take a census of the people*: Compare verse 2 *b* Or *Saul . . . Saulites*

16.6–19n.). **16–18:** This command is executed in ch 31. As elsewhere in the Bible, the growth of biblical books through the assimilation of new material has disrupted the flow of the narrative.

26.1–65: The second census. The people were first counted at the beginning of the forty-year wilderness period (chs 1; 3; 4). They are counted now again because the period is nearing its end (cf. vv. 64–65). **1–56:** Levi is not included among the twelve tribes (see vv. 57–62; 1.1–54n.). The sizes of the tribes in this list differ from those in ch 1. **2:** The census, in anticipation of entrance to the land, in part prepares for military actions (cf. ch 31; Josh 1–12; see Num 1.3n.). **9–11:** *Dathan* and *Abiram,* cf. ch 16. **11:** The Korahites are Temple singers and guards in other traditions (Ps 42.1; 1 Chr 9.19). **19:** See Gen 38.1–10.

Puvah, the clan of the Punites; 24 of Jashub,
the clan of the Jashubites; of Shimron, the
clan of the Shimronites. 25 These are the
clans of Issachar: sixty-four thousand three
hundred enrolled.
26 The descendants of Zebulun by their
clans: of Sered, the clan of the Seredites; of
Elon, the clan of the Elonites; of Jahleel, the
clan of the Jahleelites. 27 These are the clans
of the Zebulunites; the number of those en-
rolled was sixty thousand five hundred.
28 The sons of Joseph by their clans:
Manasseh and Ephraim. 29 The descen-
dants of Manasseh: of Machir, the clan of
the Machirites; and Machir was the father
of Gilead; of Gilead, the clan of the Gilead-
ites. 30 These are the descendants of Gilead:
of Iezer, the clan of the Iezerites; of Helek,
the clan of the Helekites; 31 and of Asriel,
the clan of the Asrielites; and of Shechem,
the clan of the Shechemites; 32 and of She-
mida, the clan of the Shemidaites; and of
Hepher, the clan of the Hepherites. 33 Now
Zelophehad son of Hepher had no sons,
but daughters: and the names of the daugh-
ters of Zelophehad were Mahlah, Noah,
Hoglah, Milcah, and Tirzah. 34 These are
the clans of Manasseh; the number of those
enrolled was fifty-two thousand seven hun-
dred.
35 These are the descendants of Ephra-
im according to their clans: of Shuthelah,
the clan of the Shuthelahites; of Becher, the
clan of the Becherites; of Tahan, the clan of
the Tahanites. 36 And these are the descen-
dants of Shuthelah: of Eran, the clan of
the Eranites. 37 These are the clans of the
Ephraimites: the number of those enrolled
was thirty-two thousand five hundred.
These are the descendants of Joseph by
their clans.
38 The descendants of Benjamin by their
clans: of Bela, the clan of the Belaites; of
Ashbel, the clan of the Ashbelites; of Ahi-
ram, the clan of the Ahiramites; 39 of She-
phupham, the clan of the Shuphamites; of
Hupham, the clan of the Huphamites.
40 And the sons of Bela were Ard and Naa-
man: of Ard, the clan of the Ardites; of
Naaman, the clan of the Naamites. 41 These
are the descendants of Benjamin by their
clans; the number of those enrolled was
forty-five thousand six hundred.
42 These are the descendants of Dan by
their clans: of Shuham, the clan of the Shu-
hamites. These are the clans of Dan by their
clans. 43 All the clans of the Shuhamites:
sixty-four thousand four hundred enrolled.
44 The descendants of Asher by their
families: of Imnah, the clan of the Imnites;
of Ishvi, the clan of the Ishvites; of Beriah,
the clan of the Beriites. 45 Of the descen-
dants of Beriah: of Heber, the clan of the
Heberites; of Malchiel, the clan of the Mal-
chielites. 46 And the name of the daughter
of Asher was Serah. 47 These are the clans
of the Asherites: the number of those en-
rolled was fifty-three thousand four hun-
dred.
48 The descendants of Naphtali by their
clans: of Jahzeel, the clan of the Jahzeelites;
of Guni, the clan of the Gunites; 49 of Jezer,
the clan of the Jezerites; of Shillem, the clan
of the Shillemites. 50 These are the Naphta-
lites[a] by their clans: the number of those
enrolled was forty-five thousand four hun-
dred.
51 This was the number of the Israelites
enrolled: six hundred and one thousand
seven hundred thirty.
52 The LORD spoke to Moses, saying:
53 To these the land shall be apportioned
for inheritance according to the number of
names. 54 To a large tribe you shall give a
large inheritance, and to a small tribe you
shall give a small inheritance; every tribe
shall be given its inheritance according to
its enrollment. 55 But the land shall be ap-

a Heb *clans of Naphtali*

33: On Zelophehad's daughters and inheritance by females, see 27.1–11; 36.1–12. **51:** 1,820 less than the first census total; cf. 1.46n. **52–56:** The census is also for determining the size of the tribal holdings in the land of Canaan (cf. Josh 14–19). **55–56:** Casting lots is a form of divination to determine the divine will (Lev 16.6–10; 1 Sam 10.19–21). This method of apportioning land was at times used in ancient Mesopotamia. **57–62:** This is the third census of the Levites, the first two occurring together in chs 3 and portioned by lot; according to the names of their ancestral tribes they shall inherit. 56 Their inheritance shall be apportioned according to lot between the larger and the smaller.

57 This is the enrollment of the Levites by their clans: of Gershon, the clan of the Gershonites; of Kohath, the clan of the Kohathites; of Merari, the clan of the Merarites. 58 These are the clans of Levi: the clan of the Libnites, the clan of the Hebronites, the clan of the Mahlites, the clan of the Mushites, the clan of the Korahites. Now Kohath was the father of Amram. 59 The name of Amram's wife was Jochebed daughter of Levi, who was born to Levi in Egypt; and she bore to Amram: Aaron, Moses, and their sister Miriam. 60 To Aaron were born Nadab, Abihu, Eleazar, and Ithamar. 61 But Nadab and Abihu died when they offered unholy fire before the LORD. 62 The number of those enrolled was twenty-three thousand, every male one month old and upward; for they were not enrolled among the Israelites because there was no allotment given to them among the Israelites.

63 These were those enrolled by Moses and Eleazar the priest, who enrolled the Israelites in the plains of Moab by the Jordan opposite Jericho. 64 Among these there was not one of those enrolled by Moses and Aaron the priest, who had enrolled the Israelites in the wilderness of Sinai. 65 For the LORD had said of them, "They shall die in the wilderness." Not one of them was left, except Caleb son of Jephunneh and Joshua son of Nun.

27 Then the daughters of Zelophehad came forward. Zelophehad was son of Hepher son of Gilead son of Machir son of Manasseh son of Joseph, a member of the Manassite clans. The names of his daughters were: Mahlah, Noah, Hoglah, Milcah, and Tirzah. 2 They stood before Moses, Eleazar the priest, the leaders, and all the congregation, at the entrance of the tent of meeting, and they said, 3 "Our father died in the wilderness; he was not among the company of those who gathered themselves together against the LORD in the company of Korah, but died for his own sin; and he had no sons. 4 Why should the name of our father be taken away from his clan because he had no son? Give to us a possession among our father's brothers."

5 Moses brought their case before the LORD. 6 And the LORD spoke to Moses, saying: 7 The daughters of Zelophehad are right in what they are saying; you shall indeed let them possess an inheritance among their father's brothers and pass the inheritance of their father on to them. 8 You shall also say to the Israelites, "If a man dies, and has no son, then you shall pass his inheritance on to his daughter. 9 If he has no daughter, then you shall give his inheritance to his brothers. 10 If he has no brothers, then you shall give his inheritance to his father's brothers. 11 And if his father has no brothers, then you shall give his inheritance to the nearest kinsman of his clan, and he shall possess it. It shall be for the Israelites a statute and ordinance, as the LORD commanded Moses."

4 (see 4.1–49n.). This census is separate from that of the twelve tribes because the Levites do not receive shares in the land (cf. ch 35). **61:** See Lev 10.1–3. **62:** Cf. 3.43. **64–65:** Cf. 14.20–35.

27.1–11: The daughters of Zelophehad. These women make a plea to inherit their father's land since they have no brothers. The passage assumes the following: Land is to remain in a family's possession (cf. Lev 25.25–34); sons customarily inherit land from their father; the father's name is associated with the land (Num 27.4); in the absence of sons, daughters (or other extended family members, cf. vv. 8–11) can hold the land for the father, and the father's land and name continues to his grandsons, who would receive the land from their mothers. Thus, as in the book of Ruth, land is held by male heirs. **3:** *Korah,* see ch 16. *His own sin,* see 14.29. **5–11:** A legal problem leads to inquiry of God as in Lev 24.10–22; Num 9.6–14; 15.32–36. The law goes beyond the case at hand, delineating a priority of heirs. A significant loophole left in the law presented here is corrected in 36.1–12, and the command is fulfilled in Josh 17.3–6.

12 The LORD said to Moses, "Go up this
mountain of the Abarim range, and see the
land that I have given to the Israelites.
13 When you have seen it, you also shall be
gathered to your people, as your brother
Aaron was, 14 because you rebelled against
my word in the wilderness of Zin when the
congregation quarreled with me.[a] You did
not show my holiness before their eyes at
the waters." (These are the waters of
Meribath-kadesh in the wilderness of Zin.)
15 Moses spoke to the LORD, saying, 16 "Let
the LORD, the God of the spirits of all flesh,
appoint someone over the congregation
17 who shall go out before them and come
in before them, who shall lead them out
and bring them in, so that the congregation
of the LORD may not be like sheep without
a shepherd." 18 So the LORD said to Moses,
"Take Joshua son of Nun, a man in whom
is the spirit, and lay your hand upon him;
19 have him stand before Eleazar the priest
and all the congregation, and commission
him in their sight. 20 You shall give him
some of your authority, so that all the con-
gregation of the Israelites may obey. 21 But
he shall stand before Eleazar the priest,
who shall inquire for him by the decision of
the Urim before the LORD; at his word they
shall go out, and at his word they shall
come in, both he and all the Israelites with
him, the whole congregation." 22 So Moses
did as the LORD commanded him. He took
Joshua and had him stand before Eleazar
the priest and the whole congregation; 23 he
laid his hands on him and commissioned
him—as the LORD had directed through
Moses.

28 The LORD spoke to Moses, saying:
2 Command the Israelites, and say to
them: My offering, the food for my offer-
ings by fire, my pleasing odor, you shall
take care to offer to me at its appointed
time. 3 And you shall say to them, This is
the offering by fire that you shall offer to
the LORD: two male lambs a year old with-
out blemish, daily, as a regular offering.
4 One lamb you shall offer in the morning,
and the other lamb you shall offer at twi-
light;[b] 5 also one-tenth of an ephah of
choice flour for a grain offering, mixed
with one-fourth of a hin of beaten oil. 6 It
is a regular burnt offering, ordained at
Mount Sinai for a pleasing odor, an offer-
ing by fire to the LORD. 7 Its drink offering
shall be one-fourth of a hin for each lamb;
in the sanctuary you shall pour out a drink

[a] Heb lacks *with me* [b] Heb *between the two evenings*

27.12–23: National leadership is transferred to Joshua. Earlier sanctuary leadership was transferred from Aaron to Eleazar (20.22–29). **12–17:** Moses appears to forestall his death (cf. Deut 32.48–52; 34.1–12) by asking God to appoint his successor. **12:** *Abarim,* elsewhere specified as Mount Nebo (Deut 32.49; cf. Num 33.47). **13:** 20.22–29. **14:** 20.12–13. **16:** *God . . . of all flesh,* see 16.22. **18–23:** Joshua, who with Caleb refused to deliver a negative report about the land the people were to acquire (chs 13–14), is designated successor, primarily in Moses' role as military leader. Moses imparts his authority to Joshua by laying his *hand* (v. 18; *hands* in v. 23) on him (see Lev 16.21n.). The installation is witnessed, and hence validated, by the priesthood and the congregation. **21:** While Moses directed the priesthood and received revelation personally, Joshua is subordinated to the priesthood's oracular authority. *Urim,* Ex 28.30; Lev 8.8.

28.1–29.40: The ritual calendar. For another calendar from the Priestly tradition, see Lev 23 (and the notes there). Num 28–29, in contrast to Lev 23, is concerned with prescribing sacrifices to be presented on the festivals (on the various sacrifices, see Lev 1–7). The emphasis of the verse, typifying priestly concerns, is that all offerings must be offered at their *appointed time* (v. 2). **28.2:** On sacrifices as divine food, see Lev 21.6n.; Num 15.2–16n. *Pleasing odor,* see 15.3n. **3–8:** The daily burnt offering treated here is not listed in Lev 23 since that calendar is interested in special holy occasions (cf. Lev 23.2n.). See Lev 6.9–13n. **5–7:** The offerings in this calendar are accompanied by grain and wine; see 15.2–16n. The *strong drink* in v. 7 may refer to old wine, as opposed to freshly pressed juice or regular wine, or may refer to beer or ale (cf. 6.3). The offering was poured out *in the sanctuary,* perhaps using the cups on the table for the bread of the Presence (Ex 25.29; 37.16). **9–10:** For the sabbath, cf. Lev 23.3–4n. **11–15:** Lev

offering of strong drink to the LORD. 8 The
other lamb you shall offer at twilight[a] with
a grain offering and a drink offering like
the one in the morning; you shall offer it as
an offering by fire, a pleasing odor to the
LORD.

9 On the sabbath day: two male lambs a
year old without blemish, and two-tenths
of an ephah of choice flour for a grain
offering, mixed with oil, and its drink offer-
ing— 10 this is the burnt offering for every
sabbath, in addition to the regular burnt
offering and its drink offering.

11 At the beginnings of your months
you shall offer a burnt offering to the
LORD: two young bulls, one ram, seven
male lambs a year old without blemish;
12 also three-tenths of an ephah of choice
flour for a grain offering, mixed with oil,
for each bull; and two-tenths of choice
flour for a grain offering, mixed with oil,
for the one ram; 13 and one-tenth of choice
flour mixed with oil as a grain offering for
every lamb—a burnt offering of pleasing
odor, an offering by fire to the LORD.
14 Their drink offerings shall be half a hin
of wine for a bull, one-third of a hin for a
ram, and one-fourth of a hin for a lamb.
This is the burnt offering of every month
throughout the months of the year. 15 And
there shall be one male goat for a sin offer-
ing to the LORD; it shall be offered in addi-
tion to the regular burnt offering and its
drink offering.

16 On the fourteenth day of the first
month there shall be a passover offering to
the LORD. 17 And on the fifteenth day of
this month is a festival; seven days shall
unleavened bread be eaten. 18 On the first
day there shall be a holy convocation. You
shall not work at your occupations. 19 You
shall offer an offering by fire, a burnt offer-
ing to the LORD: two young bulls, one ram,
and seven male lambs a year old; see that
they are without blemish. 20 Their grain
offering shall be of choice flour mixed with
oil: three-tenths of an ephah shall you offer
for a bull, and two-tenths for a ram; 21 one-
tenth shall you offer for each of the seven
lambs; 22 also one male goat for a sin offer-
ing, to make atonement for you. 23 You
shall offer these in addition to the burnt
offering of the morning, which belongs to
the regular burnt offering. 24 In the same
way you shall offer daily, for seven days,
the food of an offering by fire, a pleasing
odor to the LORD; it shall be offered in ad-
dition to the regular burnt offering and its
drink offering. 25 And on the seventh day
you shall have a holy convocation; you
shall not work at your occupations.

26 On the day of the first fruits, when
you offer a grain offering of new grain to
the LORD at your festival of weeks, you
shall have a holy convocation; you shall not
work at your occupations. 27 You shall of-
fer a burnt offering, a pleasing odor to the
LORD: two young bulls, one ram, seven
male lambs a year old. 28 Their grain offer-
ing shall be of choice flour mixed with oil,
three-tenths of an ephah for each bull, two-
tenths for one ram, 29 one-tenth for each of
the seven lambs; 30 with one male goat, to
make atonement for you. 31 In addition to
the regular burnt offering with its grain
offering, you shall offer them and their
drink offering. They shall be without blem-
ish.

29 On the first day of the seventh
month you shall have a holy convo-

a Heb *between the two evenings*

23 does not mention the first days of the months since these are not among the holy occasions. This calendar, however, lists them because special offerings are made on these days. Many other texts (e.g., 1 Sam 20.5; Isa 1.13; Am 8.5) suggest that the first day of the month was celebrated as a significant day. **16–25:** For the Passover and Festival of Unleavened Bread, see Lev 23.4–8. **18,25:** *Holy convocation,* see Lev 23.2n. On the work prohibition, cf. Lev 23.3–4n. **26–31:** For the Festival of Weeks, cf. Lev 23.15–21. **26:** *Grain offering of new grain,* see Lev 23.16–17. **29.1–6:** For the first day of the seventh month, cf. Lev 23.23–25. As in Lev 23, this day is not viewed as a new year festival. **1:** *Trumpets,* the instruments are not actually specified, and may be animal horns and other noise-making devices, rather than the metal trumpets prescribed in 10.2–10. The text does not clarify their significance in this context. **7–10:** For the

cation; you shall not work at your occupations. It is a day for you to blow the trumpets, 2 and you shall offer a burnt offering, a pleasing odor to the LORD: one young bull, one ram, seven male lambs a year old without blemish. 3 Their grain offering shall be of choice flour mixed with oil, three-tenths of one ephah for the bull, two-tenths for the ram, 4 and one-tenth for each of the seven lambs; 5 with one male goat for a sin offering, to make atonement for you. 6 These are in addition to the burnt offering of the new moon and its grain offering, and the regular burnt offering and its grain offering, and their drink offerings, according to the ordinance for them, a pleasing odor, an offering by fire to the LORD.

7 On the tenth day of this seventh month you shall have a holy convocation, and deny yourselves;[a] you shall do no work. 8 You shall offer a burnt offering to the LORD, a pleasing odor: one young bull, one ram, seven male lambs a year old. They shall be without blemish. 9 Their grain offering shall be of choice flour mixed with oil, three-tenths of an ephah for the bull, two-tenths for the one ram, 10 one-tenth for each of the seven lambs; 11 with one male goat for a sin offering, in addition to the sin offering of atonement, and the regular burnt offering and its grain offering, and their drink offerings.

12 On the fifteenth day of the seventh month you shall have a holy convocation; you shall not work at your occupations. You shall celebrate a festival to the LORD seven days. 13 You shall offer a burnt offering, an offering by fire, a pleasing odor to the LORD: thirteen young bulls, two rams, fourteen male lambs a year old. They shall be without blemish. 14 Their grain offering shall be of choice flour mixed with oil, three-tenths of an ephah for each of the thirteen bulls, two-tenths for each of the two rams, 15 and one-tenth for each of the fourteen lambs; 16 also one male goat for a sin offering, in addition to the regular burnt offering, its grain offering and its drink offering.

17 On the second day: twelve young bulls, two rams, fourteen male lambs a year old without blemish, 18 with the grain offering and the drink offerings for the bulls, for the rams, and for the lambs, as prescribed in accordance with their number; 19 also one male goat for a sin offering, in addition to the regular burnt offering and its grain offering, and their drink offerings.

20 On the third day: eleven bulls, two rams, fourteen male lambs a year old without blemish, 21 with the grain offering and the drink offerings for the bulls, for the rams, and for the lambs, as prescribed in accordance with their number; 22 also one male goat for a sin offering, in addition to the regular burnt offering and its grain offering and its drink offering.

23 On the fourth day: ten bulls, two rams, fourteen male lambs a year old without blemish, 24 with the grain offering and the drink offerings for the bulls, for the rams, and for the lambs, as prescribed in accordance with their number; 25 also one male goat for a sin offering, in addition to the regular burnt offering, its grain offering and its drink offering.

26 On the fifth day: nine bulls, two rams, fourteen male lambs a year old without blemish, 27 with the grain offering and the drink offerings for the bulls, for the rams, and for the lambs, as prescribed in accordance with their number; 28 also one male goat for a sin offering, in addition to the regular burnt offering and its grain offering and its drink offering.

29 On the sixth day: eight bulls, two rams, fourteen male lambs a year old without blemish, 30 with the grain offering and

a Or *and fast*

Day of Atonement, see Lev 16.1–34n.; 23.26–32. **11:** *Sin offering of atonement,* the sin/purification offerings prescribed in Lev 16. **12–38:** For the festival of booths treated in these verses, see Lev 23.33–36,39–43. Num 29 here lays out an extensive list of sacrifices, with a decreasing number of bulls for the burnt offering (a total of seventy) for each of the eight days of the festival. In terms of sacrifices, this is the major festival, a rank reflected in Neh 8.13–18.

the drink offerings for the bulls, for the
rams, and for the lambs, as prescribed in
accordance with their number; 31 also one
male goat for a sin offering, in addition to
the regular burnt offering, its grain offer-
ing, and its drink offerings.
32 On the seventh day: seven bulls, two
rams, fourteen male lambs a year old with-
out blemish, 33 with the grain offering and
the drink offerings for the bulls, for the
rams, and for the lambs, as prescribed in
accordance with their number; 34 also one
male goat for a sin offering, besides the reg-
ular burnt offering, its grain offering, and
its drink offering.
35 On the eighth day you shall have a
solemn assembly; you shall not work at
your occupations. 36 You shall offer a burnt
offering, an offering by fire, a pleasing odor
to the LORD: one bull, one ram, seven male
lambs a year old without blemish, 37 and
the grain offering and the drink offerings
for the bull, for the ram, and for the lambs,
as prescribed in accordance with their num-
ber; 38 also one male goat for a sin offering,
in addition to the regular burnt offering
and its grain offering and its drink offer-
ing.
39 These you shall offer to the LORD
at your appointed festivals, in addition to
your votive offerings and your freewill
offerings, as your burnt offerings, your
grain offerings, your drink offerings, and
your offerings of well-being.
40[a] So Moses told the Israelites every-
thing just as the LORD had commanded
Moses.

30 Then Moses said to the heads of the
tribes of the Israelites: This is what
the LORD has commanded. 2 When a man
makes a vow to the LORD, or swears an
oath to bind himself by a pledge, he shall
not break his word; he shall do according
to all that proceeds out of his mouth.
3 When a woman makes a vow to the
LORD, or binds herself by a pledge, while
within her father's house, in her youth,
4 and her father hears of her vow or her
pledge by which she has bound herself, and
says nothing to her; then all her vows shall
stand, and any pledge by which she has
bound herself shall stand. 5 But if her father
expresses disapproval to her at the time
that he hears of it, no vow of hers, and no
pledge by which she has bound herself,
shall stand; and the LORD will forgive her,
because her father had expressed to her his
disapproval.
6 If she marries, while obligated by her
vows or any thoughtless utterance of her
lips by which she has bound herself, 7 and
her husband hears of it and says nothing to
her at the time that he hears, then her vows
shall stand, and her pledges by which she
has bound herself shall stand. 8 But if, at the
time that her husband hears of it, he ex-
presses disapproval to her, then he shall
nullify the vow by which she was obligated,

a Ch 30.1 in Heb

30.1–16: Women's vows. Males have the right to affirm or nullify the vows and obligations (an oath or pledge by which a person is bound) made by women under their social and economic authority. Vows involve promising a sacrifice or some other gift to God in anticipation of divine blessing (cf. 21.2–3; Gen 28.20–21; Judg 11.30–31; Lev 22.17–23; 27.1–13; 1 Sam 1.11; 2 Sam 15.7–8; Ps 56.13–14). Obligations impose positive requirements or restrictions on a person (cf. v. 13; 6.2). These various promises must be fulfilled (v. 2; cf. Lev 5.4; Deut 23.21–23; Judg 11.29–40; Eccl 5.4; Ps 66.13–15). **2–15:** After presenting the simple case, of a male vow (v. 2), the chapter presents three cases where nullification is possible: A father may nullify his daughter's vows and obligations (vv. 3–5), a husband may nullify those his wife may have made before marriage (vv. 6–8), and a husband may nullify those that his wife makes after marriage (vv. 10–15). Nullification must occur on the day that the male *hears* (probably meaning "learns about") the vow or obligation. A woman is not liable for any nullified—and hence unfulfilled—vow or obligation (vv. 5,8,12). Nor is the male who nullifies. The male is only liable when he nullifies the vow or obligation some time after he learns about it (v. 15). In contrast to the foregoing cases, vows and obligations of widows and divorcees are binding, reflecting the fact that these women are economically and socially independent (v. 9). For women in other legal contexts, see Lev 27.1–8; Num 27.1–11.

or the thoughtless utterance of her lips, by
which she bound herself; and the LORD will
forgive her. 9 (But every vow of a widow or
of a divorced woman, by which she has
bound herself, shall be binding upon her.)
10 And if she made a vow in her husband's
house, or bound herself by a pledge with an
oath, 11 and her husband heard it and said
nothing to her, and did not express disap-
proval to her, then all her vows shall stand,
and any pledge by which she bound herself
shall stand. 12 But if her husband nullifies
them at the time that he hears them, then
whatever proceeds out of her lips concern-
ing her vows, or concerning her pledge of
herself, shall not stand. Her husband has
nullified them, and the LORD will forgive
her. 13 Any vow or any binding oath to
deny herself,[a] her husband may allow to
stand, or her husband may nullify. 14 But if
her husband says nothing to her from day
to day,[b] then he validates all her vows, or
all her pledges, by which she is obligated;
he has validated them, because he said
nothing to her at the time that he heard of
them. 15 But if he nullifies them some time
after he has heard of them, then he shall
bear her guilt.

16 These are the statutes that the LORD
commanded Moses concerning a husband
and his wife, and a father and his daughter
while she is still young and in her father's
house.

31 The LORD spoke to Moses, saying,
2 "Avenge the Israelites on the Midi-
anites; afterward you shall be gathered to
your people." 3 So Moses said to the peo-
ple, "Arm some of your number for the
war, so that they may go against Midian, to
execute the LORD's vengeance on Midian.
4 You shall send a thousand from each of
the tribes of Israel to the war." 5 So out of
the thousands of Israel, a thousand from
each tribe were conscripted, twelve thou-
sand armed for battle. 6 Moses sent them to
the war, a thousand from each tribe, along
with Phinehas son of Eleazar the priest,[c]
with the vessels of the sanctuary and the
trumpets for sounding the alarm in his
hand. 7 They did battle against Midian, as
the LORD had commanded Moses, and
killed every male. 8 They killed the kings of
Midian: Evi, Rekem, Zur, Hur, and Reba,
the five kings of Midian, in addition to oth-
ers who were slain by them; and they also
killed Balaam son of Beor with the sword.
9 The Israelites took the women of Midian
and their little ones captive; and they took
all their cattle, their flocks, and all their
goods as booty. 10 All their towns where
they had settled, and all their encamp-
ments, they burned, 11 but they took all the
spoil and all the booty, both people and
animals. 12 Then they brought the captives
and the booty and the spoil to Moses, to
Eleazar the priest, and to the congregation
of the Israelites, at the camp on the plains
of Moab by the Jordan at Jericho.

13 Moses, Eleazar the priest, and all the
leaders of the congregation went to meet
them outside the camp. 14 Moses became
angry with the officers of the army, the
commanders of thousands and the com-
manders of hundreds, who had come from
service in the war. 15 Moses said to them,
"Have you allowed all the women to live?
16 These women here, on Balaam's advice,
made the Israelites act treacherously
against the LORD in the affair of Peor, so

a Or *to fast* *b* Or *from that day to the next*
c Gk: Heb adds *to the war*

31.1–54: War against Midian. After various interludes, the command to attack Midian in 25.17 is turned to. **6:** On the priesthood, ark, and trumpets in battle, see 10.1–10n.; 10.35–36n.; 27.21. *Phinehas,* 25.7–13. **8:** Balaam (cf. chs 22–24) is implicated in the Baal-peor episode in v. 16. See 22.22–35n. **13:** The chief leaders do not go into war (cf. v. 6); this in part protects the high priest Eleazar from corpse contamination (cf. Lev 10.4; 21.12; 16.37). **14–18:** Moses is disturbed that the Midianite women had been allowed to live, since, according to this passage, they had seduced Israelite men in the Baal-peor episode in ch 25. He therefore orders the killing of non-virgin women and all male children. The remaining thirty-two thousand virgin girls and women (v. 35) presumably become slaves and slave wives (cf. Deut 21.10–14). **19–24:** Moses orders purification from corpse contamination, implicitly following

that the plague came among the congrega-
tion of the LORD. 17 Now therefore, kill ev-
ery male among the little ones, and kill
every woman who has known a man by
sleeping with him. 18 But all the young girls
who have not known a man by sleeping
with him, keep alive for yourselves.
19 Camp outside the camp seven days; who-
ever of you has killed any person or
touched a corpse, purify yourselves and
your captives on the third and on the sev-
enth day. 20 You shall purify every garment,
every article of skin, everything made of
goats' hair, and every article of wood."
21 Eleazar the priest said to the troops
who had gone to battle: "This is the statute
of the law that the LORD has commanded
Moses: 22 gold, silver, bronze, iron, tin, and
lead— 23 everything that can withstand
fire, shall be passed through fire, and it
shall be clean. Nevertheless it shall also be
purified with the water for purification;
and whatever cannot withstand fire, shall
be passed through the water. 24 You must
wash your clothes on the seventh day, and
you shall be clean; afterward you may
come into the camp."
25 The LORD spoke to Moses, saying,
26 "You and Eleazar the priest and the
heads of the ancestral houses of the congre-
gation make an inventory of the booty cap-
tured, both human and animal. 27 Divide
the booty into two parts, between the war-
riors who went out to battle and all the
congregation. 28 From the share of the war-
riors who went out to battle, set aside as
tribute for the LORD, one item out of every
five hundred, whether persons, oxen, don-
keys, sheep, or goats. 29 Take it from their
half and give it to Eleazar the priest as an
offering to the LORD. 30 But from the Israel-
ites' half you shall take one out of every
fifty, whether persons, oxen, donkeys,
sheep, or goats—all the animals—and give
them to the Levites who have charge of the
tabernacle of the LORD."
31 Then Moses and Eleazar the priest
did as the LORD had commanded Moses:
32 The booty remaining from the spoil
that the troops had taken totaled six
hundred seventy-five thousand sheep,
33 seventy-two thousand oxen, 34 sixty-one
thousand donkeys, 35 and thirty-two thou-
sand persons in all, women who had not
known a man by sleeping with him.
36 The half-share, the portion of those
who had gone out to war, was in number
three hundred thirty-seven thousand five
hundred sheep and goats, 37 and the LORD's
tribute of sheep and goats was six hundred
seventy-five. 38 The oxen were thirty-six
thousand, of which the LORD's tribute was
seventy-two. 39 The donkeys were thirty
thousand five hundred, of which the
LORD's tribute was sixty-one. 40 The per-
sons were sixteen thousand, of which the
LORD's tribute was thirty-two persons.
41 Moses gave the tribute, the offering for
the LORD, to Eleazar the priest, as the
LORD had commanded Moses.
42 As for the Israelites' half, which Mo-
ses separated from that of the troops, 43 the
congregation's half was three hundred
thirty-seven thousand five hundred sheep
and goats, 44 thirty-six thousand oxen,
45 thirty thousand five hundred donkeys,
46 and sixteen thousand persons. 47 From
the Israelites' half Moses took one of every
fifty, both of persons and of animals, and
gave them to the Levites who had charge of
the tabernacle of the LORD; as the LORD
had commanded Moses.
48 Then the officers who were over the
thousands of the army, the commanders of
thousands and the commanders of hun-
dreds, approached Moses, 49 and said to
Moses, "Your servants have counted the
warriors who are under our command, and

the laws of ch 19. Eleazar adds a novel element: Objects that can endure it must be passed through fire. **25–37:** Half the booty is to be given to those who did not go into battle, as in 1 Sam 30.24. Only animals and persons are so distributed; all objects may remain in the possession of the warriors (cf. vv. 48–54). **28:** *For the LORD*, as in sacrifices, this is accomplished by giving this to the priests (v. 41); this portion parallels that given to the Levites (vv. 30,47). **48–54:** The warriors give an offering from the objects they had plundered. Since this follows a census, the contribution may be to appease divine anger, similar to

not one of us is missing. 50 And we have
brought the LORD's offering, what each of
us found, articles of gold, armlets and
bracelets, signet rings, earrings, and pen-
dants, to make atonement for ourselves be-
fore the LORD." 51 Moses and Eleazar the
priest received the gold from them, all in
the form of crafted articles. 52 And all the
gold of the offering that they offered to the
LORD, from the commanders of thousands
and the commanders of hundreds, was six-
teen thousand seven hundred fifty shekels.
53 (The troops had all taken plunder for
themselves.) 54 So Moses and Eleazar the
priest received the gold from the command-
ers of thousands and of hundreds, and
brought it into the tent of meeting as a me-
morial for the Israelites before the LORD.

32 Now the Reubenites and the Gad-
ites owned a very great number of
cattle. When they saw that the land of Jazer
and the land of Gilead was a good place for
cattle, 2 the Gadites and the Reubenites
came and spoke to Moses, to Eleazar the
priest, and to the leaders of the congrega-
tion, saying, 3 "Ataroth, Dibon, Jazer, Nim-
rah, Heshbon, Elealeh, Sebam, Nebo, and
Beon— 4 the land that the LORD subdued
before the congregation of Israel—is a land
for cattle; and your servants have cattle."
5 They continued, "If we have found favor
in your sight, let this land be given to your
servants for a possession; do not make us
cross the Jordan."

6 But Moses said to the Gadites and to
the Reubenites, "Shall your brothers go to
war while you sit here? 7 Why will you dis-
courage the hearts of the Israelites from go-
ing over into the land that the LORD has
given them? 8 Your fathers did this, when I
sent them from Kadesh-barnea to see the
land. 9 When they went up to the Wadi Esh-
col and saw the land, they discouraged the
hearts of the Israelites from going into the
land that the LORD had given them. 10 The
LORD's anger was kindled on that day and
he swore, saying, 11 'Surely none of the peo-
ple who came up out of Egypt, from twenty
years old and upward, shall see the land
that I swore to give to Abraham, to Isaac,
and to Jacob, because they have not unre-
servedly followed me— 12 none except Ca-
leb son of Jephunneh the Kenizzite and
Joshua son of Nun, for they have unreserv-
edly followed the LORD.' 13 And the LORD's
anger was kindled against Israel, and he
made them wander in the wilderness for
forty years, until all the generation that had
done evil in the sight of the LORD had dis-
appeared. 14 And now you, a brood of sin-
ners, have risen in place of your fathers, to
increase the LORD's fierce anger against Is-
rael! 15 If you turn away from following
him, he will again abandon them in the wil-
derness; and you will destroy all this peo-
ple."

16 Then they came up to him and said,
"We will build sheepfolds here for our
flocks, and towns for our little ones, 17 but
we will take up arms as a vanguard[a] be-
fore the Israelites, until we have brought
them to their place. Meanwhile our little
ones will stay in the fortified towns because
of the inhabitants of the land. 18 We will
not return to our homes until all the Israel-
ites have obtained their inheritance. 19 We
will not inherit with them on the other side
of the Jordan and beyond, because our in-

a Cn: Heb *hurrying*

the half shekel paid after a census according to Ex 30.11–16 (cf. 2 Sam 24.10–14). **52:** A *shekel* weighed about 11.4 gr (.5 oz).

32.1–42: Distribution of land in Transjordan. Reuben, Gad, and half the tribe of Manasseh receive unanticipated inheritances in the land east of the Jordan River before the conquest of the land of Canaan west of the Jordan (for this, see the book of Joshua). In return, they must lead Israel into battle for the land. **3:** See these cities (with some variant forms) in vv. 34–38n. **4:** See 21.21–35 for this conquest. **6–15:** All the tribes are necessary for the conquest; note the fear of weakness in 13.31,33. **8–13:** On scouting the land, cf. chs 13–14. **14–15:** Moses initially takes the tribes' request as another complaint (cf. 11.1–35n.). See Josh 22.16–20; Judg 5.16–17 for other critiques of the Transjordan tribes. **16:** The tribes negotiate with a promise to be in the front line of the assault on the land of Canaan. **31–32:**

heritance has come to us on this side of the
Jordan to the east."
20 So Moses said to them, "If you do
this—if you take up arms to go before the
LORD for the war, 21 and all those of you
who bear arms cross the Jordan before the
LORD, until he has driven out his enemies
from before him 22 and the land is subdued
before the LORD—then after that you may
return and be free of obligation to the
LORD and to Israel, and this land shall be
your possession before the LORD. 23 But if
you do not do this, you have sinned against
the LORD; and be sure your sin will find
you out. 24 Build towns for your little ones,
and folds for your flocks; but do what you
have promised."
25 Then the Gadites and the Reubenites
said to Moses, "Your servants will do as
my lord commands. 26 Our little ones, our
wives, our flocks, and all our livestock shall
remain there in the towns of Gilead; 27 but
your servants will cross over, everyone
armed for war, to do battle for the LORD,
just as my lord orders."
28 So Moses gave command concerning
them to Eleazar the priest, to Joshua son
of Nun, and to the heads of the ancestral
houses of the Israelite tribes. 29 And Moses
said to them, "If the Gadites and the Reu-
benites, everyone armed for battle before
the LORD, will cross over the Jordan with
you and the land shall be subdued before
you, then you shall give them the land of
Gilead for a possession; 30 but if they will
not cross over with you armed, they shall
have possessions among you in the land of
Canaan." 31 The Gadites and the Reuben-
ites answered, "As the LORD has spoken to
your servants, so we will do. 32 We will
cross over armed before the LORD into the
land of Canaan, but the possession of our
inheritance shall remain with us on this side
of[a] the Jordan."
33 Moses gave to them—to the Gadites
and to the Reubenites and to the half-tribe
of Manasseh son of Joseph—the kingdom
of King Sihon of the Amorites and the king-
dom of King Og of Bashan, the land and its
towns, with the territories of the surround-
ing towns. 34 And the Gadites rebuilt Di-
bon, Ataroth, Aroer, 35 Atroth-shophan,
Jazer, Jogbehah, 36 Beth-nimrah, and Beth-
haran, fortified cities, and folds for sheep.
37 And the Reubenites rebuilt Heshbon,
Elealeh, Kiriathaim, 38 Nebo, and Baal-
meon (some names being changed), and
Sibmah; and they gave names to the towns
that they rebuilt. 39 The descendants of Ma-
chir son of Manasseh went to Gilead, cap-
tured it, and dispossessed the Amorites
who were there; 40 so Moses gave Gilead to
Machir son of Manasseh, and he settled
there. 41 Jair son of Manasseh went and
captured their villages, and renamed them
Havvoth-jair.[b] 42 And Nobah went and
captured Kenath and its villages, and re-
named it Nobah after himself.

33 These are the stages by which the
Israelites went out of the land of
Egypt in military formation under the lead-
ership of Moses and Aaron. 2 Moses wrote

a Heb *beyond* *b* That is *the villages of Jair*

The tribes repeat their promise (cf. vv. 25–27), now in a public, and perhaps ceremonial, context (cf. vv. 28–30). **33–42:** The mention of Manasseh, whose land holdings were split across both sides of the Jordan, only at the end of the story (vv. 33,39–42) is probably secondary to an original story that dealt with just Reuben and Gad. **33:** *Sihon . . . Og,* 21.21–35. **34–38:** These towns are east of the Dead Sea and Jordan, between the Arnon and Jabbok Rivers. According to the towns' distribution, Gad's holdings roughly form a C-shaped area around Reuben's (see color Map 1 at end of book). This contrasts with another tradition that places Reuben in the south and Gad north, in the Gilead area (Deut 4.43; Josh 20.8). **39–42:** The Gadites and Reubenites receive land already conquered; Manasseh has to conquer part of its area. Its holding is north of Gad's.

33.1–56: The wilderness travels. This itinerary, brought in now since the travels are complete, varies at points with the narrative. At points it summarizes earlier narratives, but at points it offers new information, suggesting that the extant Torah narratives were not its only source. See color Map 2 for some of these places; many cannot be identified with certainty. For another summary, cf. Deut 1.1–3.28.

down their starting points, stage by stage,
by command of the LORD; and these are
their stages according to their starting
places. 3 They set out from Rameses in the
first month, on the fifteenth day of the first
month; on the day after the passover the
Israelites went out boldly in the sight of all
the Egyptians, 4 while the Egyptians were
burying all their firstborn, whom the LORD
had struck down among them. The LORD
executed judgments even against their
gods.

5 So the Israelites set out from Rameses,
and camped at Succoth. 6 They set out from
Succoth, and camped at Etham, which is on
the edge of the wilderness. 7 They set out
from Etham, and turned back to Pi-
hahiroth, which faces Baal-zephon; and
they camped before Migdol. 8 They set out
from Pi-hahiroth, passed through the sea
into the wilderness, went a three days' jour-
ney in the wilderness of Etham, and
camped at Marah. 9 They set out from Ma-
rah and came to Elim; at Elim there were
twelve springs of water and seventy palm
trees, and they camped there. 10 They set
out from Elim and camped by the Red
Sea.[a] 11 They set out from the Red Sea[a]
and camped in the wilderness of Sin.
12 They set out from the wilderness of Sin
and camped at Dophkah. 13 They set out
from Dophkah and camped at Alush.
14 They set out from Alush and camped at
Rephidim, where there was no water for
the people to drink. 15 They set out from
Rephidim and camped in the wilderness of
Sinai. 16 They set out from the wilderness of
Sinai and camped at Kibroth-hattaavah.
17 They set out from Kibroth-hattaavah
and camped at Hazeroth. 18 They set out
from Hazeroth and camped at Rithmah.
19 They set out from Rithmah and camped
at Rimmon-perez. 20 They set out from
Rimmon-perez and camped at Libnah.
21 They set out from Libnah and camped at
Rissah. 22 They set out from Rissah and
camped at Kehelathah. 23 They set out from
Kehelathah and camped at Mount Shepher.
24 They set out from Mount Shepher and
camped at Haradah. 25 They set out from
Haradah and camped at Makheloth.
26 They set out from Makheloth and
camped at Tahath. 27 They set out from Ta-
hath and camped at Terah. 28 They set out
from Terah and camped at Mithkah.
29 They set out from Mithkah and camped
at Hashmonah. 30 They set out from Hash-
monah and camped at Moseroth. 31 They
set out from Moseroth and camped at
Bene-jaakan. 32 They set out from Bene-
jaakan and camped at Hor-haggidgad.
33 They set out from Hor-haggidgad and
camped at Jotbathah. 34 They set out from
Jotbathah and camped at Abronah. 35 They
set out from Abronah and camped at
Ezion-geber. 36 They set out from Ezion-
geber and camped in the wilderness of Zin
(that is, Kadesh). 37 They set out from Ka-
desh and camped at Mount Hor, on the
edge of the land of Edom.

38 Aaron the priest went up Mount Hor
at the command of the LORD and died there
in the fortieth year after the Israelites had
come out of the land of Egypt, on the first
day of the fifth month. 39 Aaron was one
hundred twenty-three years old when he
died on Mount Hor.

40 The Canaanite, the king of Arad,
who lived in the Negeb in the land of Ca-
naan, heard of the coming of the Israelites.

41 They set out from Mount Hor and
camped at Zalmonah. 42 They set out from

a Or *Sea of Reeds*

3–4: For *Rameses* in the narrative, cf. Ex 12.37. *Against their gods,* Ex 12.12. **5–6:** Cf. Ex 13.20. **7:** Cf. Ex 14.2. **8:** Cf. Ex 15.22–23. **9:** Cf. Ex 15.27. **10:** *Red Sea,* see Ex 13.18n.; 15.22. **11:** Cf. Ex 16.1. **12–13:** *Dophkah* and *Alush,* perhaps implied in the "stages" of Ex 17.1. **14:** Cf. Ex 17.1. **15:** Cf. Ex 19.1–2. **16:** Cf. 11.34. **17:** Cf. 11.35; 12.16. **18–34:** These stops are not mentioned in the narrative. **30–34:** Cf. Deut 10.6–7. **35:** *Ezion-geber,* not in the narrative; it may not be identical with the place of the same name in 1 Kings 9.26; 22.49. **36:** Cf. 13.26; 20.1n. **37:** *Mount Hor,* see 20.22. *Edom,* see 20.14; 21.4. **38–39:** Cf. 20.23–29. **40:** Cf. 21.1–3. **41–42:** *Zalmonah* and *Punon,* perhaps stops in circumventing Edom (cf. 21.4). **43:** Cf. 21.10–11. **45–47:** *Iyim,* Iye-abarim (v. 44). The other locales here are not

Zalmonah and camped at Punon. 43 They
set out from Punon and camped at Oboth.
44 They set out from Oboth and camped
at Iye-abarim, in the territory of Moab.
45 They set out from Iyim and camped at
Dibon-gad. 46 They set out from Dibon-gad
and camped at Almon-diblathaim. 47 They
set out from Almon-diblathaim and
camped in the mountains of Abarim, before
Nebo. 48 They set out from the mountains
of Abarim and camped in the plains of
Moab by the Jordan at Jericho; 49 they
camped by the Jordan from Beth-jeshimoth
as far as Abel-shittim in the plains of
Moab.

50 In the plains of Moab by the Jordan
at Jericho, the LORD spoke to Moses, say-
ing: 51 Speak to the Israelites, and say to
them: When you cross over the Jordan into
the land of Canaan, 52 you shall drive out
all the inhabitants of the land from before
you, destroy all their figured stones, de-
stroy all their cast images, and demolish all
their high places. 53 You shall take posses-
sion of the land and settle in it, for I have
given you the land to possess. 54 You shall
apportion the land by lot according to your
clans; to a large one you shall give a large
inheritance, and to a small one you shall
give a small inheritance; the inheritance
shall belong to the person on whom the lot
falls; according to your ancestral tribes you
shall inherit. 55 But if you do not drive out
the inhabitants of the land from before you,
then those whom you let remain shall be as
barbs in your eyes and thorns in your sides;
they shall trouble you in the land where
you are settling. 56 And I will do to you as
I thought to do to them.

34 The LORD spoke to Moses, saying:
2 Command the Israelites, and say to
them: When you enter the land of Canaan
(this is the land that shall fall to you for an
inheritance, the land of Canaan, defined by
its boundaries), 3 your south sector shall ex-
tend from the wilderness of Zin along the
side of Edom. Your southern boundary
shall begin from the end of the Dead Sea[a]
on the east; 4 your boundary shall turn
south of the ascent of Akrabbim, and cross
to Zin, and its outer limit shall be south
of Kadesh-barnea; then it shall go on to
Hazar-addar, and cross to Azmon; 5 the
boundary shall turn from Azmon to the
Wadi of Egypt, and its termination shall be
at the Sea.

6 For the western boundary, you shall
have the Great Sea and its[b] coast; this shall
be your western boundary.

7 This shall be your northern boundary:
from the Great Sea you shall mark out your
line to Mount Hor; 8 from Mount Hor you
shall mark it out to Lebo-hamath, and the
outer limit of the boundary shall be at Ze-
dad; 9 then the boundary shall extend to
Ziphron, and its end shall be at Hazar-
enan; this shall be your northern boundary.

10 You shall mark out your eastern

a Heb *Salt Sea* *b* Syr: Heb lacks *its*

mentioned as stops in the narratives, but see 32.34 for *Dibon* possessed by Gad, 27.12 for *Abarim,* and 32.38 for *Nebo.* **48:** Cf. 22.1. **49:** *Beth-jeshimoth* is not in the narrative. *Abel-shittim* is Shittim of 25.1 (cf. Josh 2.1; 3.1). **50–56:** Numbers now gives laws pertaining to the conquest and administration of the land of Canaan (33.50–36.13). **52:** *You shall drive out,* which is more extreme, insisting that these inhabitants be killed. Cf. Deut 7. *High places,* perhaps open-air altars; see Lev 26.30n. **54:** Cf. 26.52–56. **55:** Cf. Josh 23.13 (Ex 23.33; 34.12; Deut 7.16).

34.1–28: The boundaries of the land of Canaan. 1–12: This passage charts the land's ideal boundaries, and probably represents the extent of the land (actual or perceived) thought to obtain at the time of David (2 Sam 8.3–14; 1 Kings 8.65). See also Josh 13–19; Ezek 47.13–20. **3–5:** For these locales, see color Map 2 at end of book. **5:** *Wadi of Egypt,* or the Brook of Egypt. **5–7:** *The Wadi of Egypt,* either the Wadi Besor or the Wadi el-Arish, both south of Gaza. *The Great Sea,* i.e., the Mediterranean. **7:** This is not the Mount Hor near Edom (e.g., 20.22–29), but one north in the Lebanese mountains. **8:** *Lebo-hamath* is just south of Riblah between the Lebanon and Anti-Lebanon ranges (see color Map 6; cf. 1 Kings 8.65; 2 Kings 14.25). *Zedad* is northeast of Lebo-hamath. **9:** *Ziphron* and *Hazar-enan,* location unknown. **10–11:** *Shepham, Riblah* (not that in Lebanon valley), and *Ain,* location unknown. *Sea of Chinnereth,* i.e., Sea of

boundary from Hazar-enan to Shepham;
11 and the boundary shall continue down
from Shepham to Riblah on the east side of
Ain; and the boundary shall go down, and
reach the eastern slope of the sea of Chin-
nereth; 12 and the boundary shall go down
to the Jordan, and its end shall be at the
Dead Sea.[a] This shall be your land with its
boundaries all around.

13 Moses commanded the Israelites,
saying: This is the land that you shall inher-
it by lot, which the LORD has commanded
to give to the nine tribes and to the half-
tribe; 14 for the tribe of the Reubenites by
their ancestral houses and the tribe of the
Gadites by their ancestral houses have tak-
en their inheritance, and also the half-tribe
of Manasseh; 15 the two tribes and the half-
tribe have taken their inheritance beyond
the Jordan at Jericho eastward, toward the
sunrise.

16 The LORD spoke to Moses, saying:
17 These are the names of the men who shall
apportion the land to you for inheritance:
the priest Eleazar and Joshua son of Nun.
18 You shall take one leader of every tribe to
apportion the land for inheritance. 19 These
are the names of the men: Of the tribe of
Judah, Caleb son of Jephunneh. 20 Of the
tribe of the Simeonites, Shemuel son of Am-
mihud. 21 Of the tribe of Benjamin, Elidad
son of Chislon. 22 Of the tribe of the Dan-
ites a leader, Bukki son of Jogli. 23 Of the
Josephites: of the tribe of the Manassites a
leader, Hanniel son of Ephod, 24 and of the
tribe of the Ephraimites a leader, Kemuel
son of Shiphtan. 25 Of the tribe of the Zebu-
lunites a leader, Eli-zaphan son of Parnach.
26 Of the tribe of the Issacharites a leader,
Paltiel son of Azzan. 27 And of the tribe of
the Asherites a leader, Ahihud son of Shelo-
mi. 28 Of the tribe of the Naphtalites a lead-
er, Pedahel son of Ammihud. 29 These were
the ones whom the LORD commanded to
apportion the inheritance for the Israelites
in the land of Canaan.

35 In the plains of Moab by the Jordan
at Jericho, the LORD spoke to Mo-
ses, saying: 2 Command the Israelites to
give, from the inheritance that they possess,
towns for the Levites to live in; you shall
also give to the Levites pasture lands sur-
rounding the towns. 3 The towns shall be
theirs to live in, and their pasture lands
shall be for their cattle, for their livestock,
and for all their animals. 4 The pasture
lands of the towns, which you shall give to
the Levites, shall reach from the wall of
the town outward a thousand cubits all
around. 5 You shall measure, outside the
town, for the east side two thousand cubits,
for the south side two thousand cubits, for
the west side two thousand cubits, and for
the north side two thousand cubits, with
the town in the middle; this shall belong to
them as pasture land for their towns.

6 The towns that you give to the Levites
shall include the six cities of refuge, where
you shall permit a slayer to flee, and in
addition to them you shall give forty-two
towns. 7 The towns that you give to the Le-
vites shall total forty-eight, with their pas-
ture lands. 8 And as for the towns that you
shall give from the possession of the Israel-
ites, from the larger tribes you shall take
many, and from the smaller tribes you shall
take few; each, in proportion to the inheri-

a Heb *Salt Sea*

Galilee. **13–15:** Gad, Reuben, and half the tribe of Manasseh received their lands in ch 32. **16–29:** For other lists of tribal leaders or chieftains, cf. 1.4–16; 2.3–31; 13.3–16. The order of the tribes roughly follows their south to north distribution in the land of Canaan (see color Map 3 at end of book; see 2.3–31n.). With the exception of Caleb (v. 19), these tribal leaders differ from those given in 13.2–15, emphasizing that the generation of the wilderness has died out (14.22–23), and a new generation is ready to enter the land.

35.1–8: Levitical cities and cities of refuge. This continues the context of apportioning the land, begun in ch 32. Since the Levites have no specific geographical inheritance (see 18.23–24), they are to be given forty-eight towns from throughout the land; see Lev 25.32–34; Josh 21.1–42; 1 Chr 6.54–81. **4–5:** Each town is to have pasture area for the Levites' animals. *A thousand cubits,* about 433 m (1,457 ft). **6:** Refuge

tance that it obtains, shall give of its towns
to the Levites.
9 The LORD spoke to Moses, saying:
10 Speak to the Israelites, and say to them:
When you cross the Jordan into the land of
Canaan, 11 then you shall select cities to be
cities of refuge for you, so that a slayer who
kills a person without intent may flee there.
12 The cities shall be for you a refuge from
the avenger, so that the slayer may not die
until there is a trial before the congregation.
13 The cities that you designate shall be
six cities of refuge for you: 14 you shall designate three cities beyond the Jordan, and
three cities in the land of Canaan, to be
cities of refuge. 15 These six cities shall serve
as refuge for the Israelites, for the resident
or transient alien among them, so that anyone who kills a person without intent may
flee there.
16 But anyone who strikes another with
an iron object, and death ensues, is a murderer; the murderer shall be put to death.
17 Or anyone who strikes another with a
stone in hand that could cause death, and
death ensues, is a murderer; the murderer
shall be put to death. 18 Or anyone who
strikes another with a weapon of wood in
hand that could cause death, and death ensues, is a murderer; the murderer shall be
put to death. 19 The avenger of blood is the
one who shall put the murderer to death;
when they meet, the avenger of blood shall
execute the sentence. 20 Likewise, if someone pushes another from hatred, or hurls
something at another, lying in wait, and
death ensues, 21 or in enmity strikes another
with the hand, and death ensues, then the
one who struck the blow shall be put to
death; that person is a murderer; the avenger of blood shall put the murderer to death,
when they meet.
22 But if someone pushes another suddenly without enmity, or hurls any object
without lying in wait, 23 or, while handling
any stone that could cause death, unintentionally[a] drops it on another and death ensues, though they were not enemies, and no
harm was intended, 24 then the congregation shall judge between the slayer and the
avenger of blood, in accordance with these
ordinances; 25 and the congregation shall
rescue the slayer from the avenger of blood.
Then the congregation shall send the slayer
back to the original city of refuge. The slayer shall live in it until the death of the high
priest who was anointed with the holy oil.
26 But if the slayer shall at any time go outside the bounds of the original city of refuge, 27 and is found by the avenger of blood
outside the bounds of the city of refuge,
and is killed by the avenger, no bloodguilt
shall be incurred. 28 For the slayer must remain in the city of refuge until the death of
the high priest; but after the death of the
high priest the slayer may return home.
29 These things shall be a statute and
ordinance for you throughout your generations wherever you live.
30 If anyone kills another, the murderer
shall be put to death on the evidence of
witnesses; but no one shall be put to death
on the testimony of a single witness.
31 Moreover you shall accept no ransom for

a Heb *without seeing*

cities, see vv. 9–34n. **9–34:** In the ancient Near East the prosecution of homicide was often left to the victim's family. The law in ch 35 tempers the immediacy and severity of the family's vengeance by providing for judicial review (vv. 24–25) and designating cities to which one who has accidentally killed a person may flee and reside for protection against the victim's family. Cf. Gen 4.14–15; 9.5–6; Ex 21.12–14; Deut 4.41–43; 19.1–13; Josh 20. **12:** *Avenger,* a close relative responsible for vengeance. **16–23:** Intention is illustrated by example rather than by a purely theoretical statement. Illustration of an abstract principle through concrete examples is typical of ancient Near Eastern law. **25:** *The original city of refuge,* lit. "his refuge city." This verse indicates that judicial review is held outside the city. The definition of the high priest in this verse as the one *anointed with the holy oil* indicates that this is likely the chief priest of the national sanctuary. His death cancels the blood guilt of the killer (cf. v. 28). **26–27:** Even one who kills accidentally is guilty to a degree and liable to execution by the victim's kin before the

the life of a murderer who is subject to the
death penalty; a murderer must be put to
death. 32 Nor shall you accept ransom for
one who has fled to a city of refuge, en-
abling the fugitive to return to live in the
land before the death of the high priest.
33 You shall not pollute the land in which
you live; for blood pollutes the land, and no
expiation can be made for the land, for the
blood that is shed in it, except by the blood
of the one who shed it. 34 You shall not
defile the land in which you live, in which
I also dwell; for I the LORD dwell among
the Israelites.

36 The heads of the ancestral houses of
the clans of the descendants of Gile-
ad son of Machir son of Manasseh, of the
Josephite clans, came forward and spoke in
the presence of Moses and the leaders, the
heads of the ancestral houses of the Israel-
ites; 2 they said, "The LORD commanded
my lord to give the land for inheritance by
lot to the Israelites; and my lord was com-
manded by the LORD to give the inheri-
tance of our brother Zelophehad to his
daughters. 3 But if they are married into an-
other Israelite tribe, then their inheritance
will be taken from the inheritance of our
ancestors and added to the inheritance of
the tribe into which they marry; so it will be
taken away from the allotted portion of our
inheritance. 4 And when the jubilee of the
Israelites comes, then their inheritance will
be added to the inheritance of the tribe into
which they have married; and their inheri-
tance will be taken from the inheritance of
our ancestral tribe."

5 Then Moses commanded the Israelites
according to the word of the LORD, saying,
"The descendants of the tribe of Joseph are
right in what they are saying. 6 This is what
the LORD commands concerning the
daughters of Zelophehad, 'Let them marry
whom they think best; only it must be into
a clan of their father's tribe that they are
married, 7 so that no inheritance of the Isra-
elites shall be transferred from one tribe to
another; for all Israelites shall retain the in-
heritance of their ancestral tribes. 8 Every
daughter who possesses an inheritance in
any tribe of the Israelites shall marry one
from the clan of her father's tribe, so that
all Israelites may continue to possess their
ancestral inheritance. 9 No inheritance shall
be transferred from one tribe to another;
for each of the tribes of the Israelites shall
retain its own inheritance.' "

10 The daughters of Zelophehad did as
the LORD had commanded Moses. 11 Mah-
lah, Tirzah, Hoglah, Milcah, and Noah, the
daughters of Zelophehad, married sons of
their father's brothers. 12 They were mar-
ried into the clans of the descendants of
Manasseh son of Joseph, and their inheri-
tance remained in the tribe of their father's
clan.

13 These are the commandments and
the ordinances that the LORD commanded
through Moses to the Israelites in the plains
of Moab by the Jordan at Jericho.

death of the priest. **30:** On witnesses, cf. Deut 19.15. **31–32:** The victim's family may not accept monetary payment in place of execution because of the severe blood guilt associated with murder (cf. Gen 9.5–6). Murder is thus understood as a religious, and not merely a civil, crime. **33–34:** The blood guilt of murder is powerful enough to pollute the entire land. This can adversely affect agricultural production (Gen 4.10–12; 2 Sam 21.1–14; Ps 106.38; Hos 4.2–3). Deut 21.1–9 contains a rite for relocating the pollution of murder away from human habitation.

36.1–13: Marriage of Zelophehad's daughters. This corrects a deficiency in 27.1–11. The fear is that if the daughters marry into another tribe, the land will become the permanent possession of that tribe. **4:** *Jubilee,* cf. Lev 25.10–34, which implies that every fiftieth year, only sold land, but not inherited land, returns to the original owner. **6–9:** With the restriction that the daughters must marry within their tribe, the land will not be alienated. **13:** A concluding verse, which parallels the conclusion(s) of Leviticus (26.46; 27.34).

DEUTERONOMY

Deuteronomy directly addresses the problem of the historical distance between past and present, between tradition and the needs of the contemporary generation, between revelation and interpretation. In that way, it is a remarkably modern text that instructs its audience how to become more thoughtful readers of scripture. In narrative terms, Deuteronomy comes just as the Israelites, encamped on the plains of Moab, finally stand poised to enter the promised land. This entry into Canaan would provide the long-awaited climax of the story that had begun with the promises to the ancestors in Genesis, and whose fulfillment had been delayed by the enslavement in Egypt and the wandering in the wilderness. Now, on the eve both of his death and of the nation's entry into the land without him, Moses, as Deuteronomy's speaker, arrests the narrative action in order to deliver a series of three speeches, grouped together as a long valedictory address. He reviews the nation's history, expounds upon their laws, and instructs them about the importance of loyalty to God. He also requires that the nation swear upon oath to uphold this combination of law and theological instruction as a covenant upon the plains of Moab, one that supplements the prior covenant of Horeb (Deuteronomy's name for Sinai; 28.69). Only after the conclusion of these discourses and a following appendix (chs 31–34) does the overall narrative line resume with the account of the nation's entry into Canaan in Joshua and Judges.

The English name of the book, based on the Septuagint (see 17.18n.), means "second law." That title reflects the early Jewish perspective that Deuteronomy is Moses' rehearsal of the earlier legal sections of the Torah. Despite this perspective and the text's own self-presentation, Deuteronomy is likely not Mosaic but originates in the seventh century BCE. It has long been recognized that there are striking similarities between the distinctive religious and legal requirements of Deuteronomy and the account of the major religious reform carried out by King Josiah in 622 BCE (2 Kings 22–23). That reform had been inspired by the discovery in the Temple of a "scroll of the Torah" (2 Kings 22.8). Josiah's reform restricted all sacrificial worship of God to Jerusalem and removed foreign elements from the system of worship; it culminated in the celebration of the first nationally centralized Passover at the Temple in Jerusalem (2 Kings 23.21–23). So strongly do these royal initiatives correspond to the distinctive requirements of Deuteronomy that scholars, both traditional and critical, have long identified the "scroll of the Torah" discovered in Josiah's Temple as Deuteronomy.

Josiah's reform, with Deuteronomy as its catalyst, was much more a revolution than a simple return to older forms of worship. Previously, it was entirely legitimate to sacrifice to God throughout the land, as did Abraham at Shechem and near Bethel (Gen 12.7–8); Jacob at Bethel (Gen 35.1–7); Samuel at Mizpah, Ramah, Gilgal, and Bethlehem (1 Sam 7.9,17; 9.11–14; 10.8; 16.1–5); and Elijah upon Mount Carmel (1 Kings 18.20–46). Indeed, earlier biblical law stipulated that God would grant blessing "in every place where I cause my name to be remembered" (Ex 20.24). Deuteronomy challenged that older norm, prohibiting sacrifice "at any place" (lit. "in every place") and restricting it to a single site, implicitly Jerusalem (Deut 12.13–14). In this way, Deuteronomy's self-presentation as a rehearsal or explication of prior law (1.1–5) or as a simple supplement to the prior covenant (29.1) does not address the extent to which Deuteronomy actually challenges and revises earlier law in support of its new religious vision.

The historical background of Josiah's reforms was the increasing threat of imperial domination. The Northern Kingdom of Israel had fallen under Assyrian invasion a scant century before (722 BCE; 2 Kings 17). Continuing Assyrian incursions down the coastal littoral had all but reduced Judah to a rump-state (2 Kings 18.13). In a desperate bid to preserve the nation's autonomy, Hezekiah had already made a pact with Assyria (2 Kings 18.13–18). Subsequently, Judah's political and religious independence seemed to hover uncertainly between the threats presented by Assyria and resurgent Babylon (2 Kings 20.12–15). The resulting military allegiances led to religious syncretism, as forms of worship related to the Assyrian state religion (2 Kings 16.10–20) or other foreign forms of worship (2 Kings 21.1–6) were introduced into the Temple by Hezekiah.

In this context, Josiah's religious reforms represented an important bid for Judean cultural, political, and religious autonomy. The monarch extended his reforms into the area of the former Northern Kingdom of Israel (2 Kings 23.15–20), territory under Assyrian control. Deuteronomy, apparently written sometime during this historical crisis, likewise reflects the desire to preserve Judean cultural and religious integrity. Its authors had the conviction that older conventions of worship and social organization were no longer viable. If the religion of the LORD was to survive the crisis, renewal and adaptation were necessary. Deuteronomy's legal corpus (chs 12–26) provides a remarkably comprehensive program for cultural renewal. It addresses worship; the festival calendar; the major institutions of public life (justice, kingship, priesthood, prophecy); criminal, family, and civil law; and ethics. The law is presented as a covenant between God and nation, which the people take an oath to uphold, upon penalty of sanctions, while maintaining unconditional loyalty to their God. That covenant structure closely corresponds to Neo-Assyrian state treaties that have been recovered from this period, the most famous of which is the *Vassal Treaty of Esarhaddon* (672 BCE). At a number of points, the authors of Deuteronomy seem consciously to have patterned their covenant after this treaty tradition, whether known directly or in Aramaic translation. From this perspective, Deuteronomy is a counter-treaty: Its authors turned the weapon of imperialism into a bid for freedom, shifting its oath of loyalty from the Assyrian overlord to their divine sovereign.

The authors of Deuteronomy were thus tutored in international treaty conventions, and elsewhere reveal their knowledge of the literary traditions of ancient Near Eastern law (15.1–18n.; 17.8–13n.,14–20n.; 22.13–30n.) and wisdom literature (1.13n.; 4.2n.). The authors of Deuteronomy made use of another common ancient Near Eastern convention as well. They did not directly attach their name to their composition or write in their own voice; instead, they attributed their composition to a prestigious figure from the past. By employing "Moses" as their spokesperson, they established a link with tradition at precisely the time when tradition, for the sake of survival, had to be transformed. This convention of ascribing a text to an ancient personage, technically called "pseudepigraphy," is particularly well known in the later literature of the intertestamental or Second Temple period; examples include *Jubilees*, *4 Ezra*, the *Testament of Abraham*, and (among the Dead Sea Scrolls) the *Temple Scroll*.

Deuteronomy preserves several layers of tradition within itself: The structure of three different discourses with an appendix already suggests a process of literary growth. That growth is closely connected to the gradual formation of the Hebrew Bible. To appreciate what is involved, it helps imaginatively to turn the clock back to the time before the Bible achieved its present form.

When Deuteronomy was first promulgated, it would not have been part of any larger whole. Instead, it would have been complete by itself as a "scroll of the Torah" (i.e., the "book of the law" in 2 Kings 22.8). It would have consisted of most of the laws of chs 12–26, framed by a relatively simple introduction and conclusion. This form of Deuteronomy presented itself as a treaty concluded between the nation and its God in a formal ceremony whereby each citizen took an oath of loyalty under penalty of strict sanctions (28.1–46). This was very likely the preexilic form of Deuteronomy.

At a later stage, presumably sometime during the exile in the mid-sixth century BCE, Deuteronomy would have been incorporated into the Deuteronomistic History (Joshua through 2 Kings) to serve as its introduction. At this point, the "Deuteronomistic" editors would have given the book its present literary frame (1.1–4.40; chs 31–34), while also adding to the legal corpus, selectively tying its promises or expectations to the later historical material (see 12.8n.). Expansions in Deuteronomy that reflect the Babylonian exile may derive from this stage (i.e., 4.25–31; 28.47–56; 30.1–10).

At a still later point, in the exilic or postexilic period, Priestly editors appended Deuteronomy to the newly formed Pentateuch, to serve as its conclusion. Ironically, the decision to conclude the Pentateuch with Deuteronomy separated the overall narrative plan of Genesis through Numbers from its logical fulfillment in an account of the conquest of the land. This narrative climax was delayed to Joshua and Judges.

In the final chapters of Deuteronomy, these three viewpoints operate simultaneously, creating a complex interplay of perspectives. The legal corpus is brought to its conclusion with a formal ratification ceremony involving the swearing of an oath to assume the penalties for transgressing the covenant (chs 29–31). At the same time, other editors work to embed Deuteronomy in the Deuteronomistic History. Still other editors tie the book to Genesis-Numbers and thus make the creation of Torah—no longer the occupation of the land—the climax of the newly created Pentateuch. The three perspectives operate concurrently, spinning like Ezekiel's vision of "a wheel within a wheel" (1.16).

Part of the continuing relevance of Deuteronomy is that it does not permit itself to be read literally or passively. It challenges its readers actively to confront the problem of the relation between revelation and interpretation and breaks down conventional boundaries between scripture and tradition. It makes paradox central to its structure: The book distinctively narrates the process of its own formation (31.1–12) while also anticipating its existence and completion (17.18; 28.58; 30.10). Interpretation is directly and indirectly a theme of Deuteronomy (see 1.5). At many points, the authors of Deuteronomy reinterpret earlier narratives (see 6.1n.) and laws (particularly from the Covenant Collection in Ex 20–23). Moreover, the process of the book's editing intentionally preserves conflicting perspectives on a full range of key issues central to Israelite religion: on whether the revelation of the Decalogue at Sinai/Horeb was direct or required the mediation of Moses (5.5n.); on the stature of Moses relative to other prophets (34.10n.); on the nature of divine punishment for sin (5.9–10n.; 7.10n.); on whether God rules as head of a pantheon or is the only God who exists (4.7–8n., 15–31n., 35n.; 32.8n.); and even on Deuteronomy's own setting in time and place (1.1n.; 2.12n.; 3.11n.). These mutually exclusive positions preserve an ongoing ancient debate about fundamental religious assumptions. The editors of Deuteronomy opted against closure: They preserved these different schools of thought in their full integrity. Accordingly, there is for Deuteronomy no access to God in the covenant without entering into this debate. The modern reader of Deuteronomy must become, like the authors of Deuteronomy, an interpreter.

1 These are the words that Moses spoke
to all Israel beyond the Jordan—in the
wilderness, on the plain opposite Suph, be-
tween Paran and Tophel, Laban, Hazeroth,
and Di-zahab. 2 (By the way of Mount Seir
it takes eleven days to reach Kadesh-barnea
from Horeb.) 3 In the fortieth year, on the
first day of the eleventh month, Moses
spoke to the Israelites just as the LORD had
commanded him to speak to them. 4 This
was after he had defeated King Sihon of the
Amorites, who reigned in Heshbon, and
King Og of Bashan, who reigned in Ashta-
roth and[a] in Edrei. 5 Beyond the Jordan in
the land of Moab, Moses undertook to ex-
pound this law as follows:
6 The LORD our God spoke to us at Ho-
reb, saying, "You have stayed long enough
at this mountain. 7 Resume your journey,
and go into the hill country of the Amorites
as well as into the neighboring regions—
the Arabah, the hill country, the Shephe-
lah, the Negeb, and the seacoast—the land
of the Canaanites and the Lebanon, as far
as the great river, the river Euphrates. 8 See,
I have set the land before you; go in and
take possession of the land that I[b] swore to
your ancestors, to Abraham, to Isaac, and
to Jacob, to give to them and to their de-
scendants after them."
9 At that time I said to you, "I am un-

a Gk Syr Vg Compare Josh 12.4: Heb lacks *and*
b Sam Gk: MT *the LORD*

1.1–4.43: The first discourse of Moses has two subsections: a historical retrospective (1.6–3.29) and a sermon on the importance of obeying Torah (4.1–40). An editorial headnote (1.1–5) and appendix (4.41–43) frame the discourse. **1.1–5: Editorial headnote. 1:** *Beyond the Jordan,* the land east of the Jordan river (Transjordan), where the Israelites have stopped, awaiting entry to the land. The reference places the editor west of the Jordan, in Canaan. According to the narrative line, however, the Israelites have not yet reached the promised land, and Moses never does. From this and similar anachronisms, medieval Jewish commentators already recognized that not all of the Pentateuch could be attributed to Moses (see also 2.12; 3.11n.; 20.15; 34.5; Gen 12.6). *The plain* (lit. "the Arabah"), the rift valley that includes the Jordan River and stretches south from the Dead Sea through Eilat and the Red Sea into Africa. The places mentioned cannot be identified with certainty. **2:** *Eleven days* implies a scathing indictment of the nation. As a result of their rebellion in the desert (Num 13–14), it actually took them thirty-eight years, eight months, and twenty days to reach this point after they first broke camp (Num 10.11). *Horeb* (Ex 3.1; 17.6; 33.6) is Deuteronomy's term for the mount of revelation. "(Mount) Sinai," in contrast, is the more standard term used by the Yahwistic and Priestly writers (see Ex 19.11; 34.29); it occurs in Deuteronomy only at 33.1, where it refers more generally to a mountainous region in the south. **4:** Num 21.21–35. **5:** *Expound* seems intentionally ambiguous about whether Moses here proclaims new religious teachings or simply explicates material already proclaimed. *This law,* better, "this Torah" or "this teaching" (4.8,44; 27.3,8,26; 28.58,61; 29.20,28; 30.10; 31.9,11–12; 32.46). The word designates not only the combination of ritual, civil, family, and ethical law found in chs 12–26, but also the religious instruction of chs 5–11. For later editors, as here, the same word seems to refer to the entire book of Deuteronomy.

1.6–3.29: Historical review. Moses rehearses the Exodus, revelation at Horeb/Sinai, and rebellion in the desert for the generation who arose after these events, so that they may understand what brought them to the present moment. At a number of points, this narrative diverges from that of Exodus-Numbers. **1.6:** The original of the divine command quoted has not been preserved (cf. Num 10). **7:** *Amorites,* as at Gen 15.16, seems to be used generically for the family of nations who are the original inhabitants of Canaan, rather than technically to designate one of those nations (contrast Gen 15.19–21; Ex 3.8,17). *The Shephelah* is the region of foothills between the hill country on the east and the *seacoast* on the west. *The Negeb* is the semi-arid region south of the hill country. *Great river,* the ideal borders of the Israelite empire extended to the Euphrates (Gen 15.18), the northern limit of David's conquests (2 Sam 8.3). **8:** *See . . . set the land before you,* God symbolically displays the land and transfers its legal title to Israel (similarly, Gen 13.14–15). **9–18:** This account combines and reinterprets two previous accounts of the creation of a military-judicial system to share the burden of leadership (compare vv. 9–12 with

able by myself to bear you. 10The LORD
your God has multiplied you, so that today
you are as numerous as the stars of heaven.
11May the LORD, the God of your ances-
tors, increase you a thousand times more
and bless you, as he has promised you!
12But how can I bear the heavy burden of
your disputes all by myself? 13Choose for
each of your tribes individuals who are
wise, discerning, and reputable to be your
leaders." 14You answered me, "The plan
you have proposed is a good one." 15So I
took the leaders of your tribes, wise and
reputable individuals, and installed them
as leaders over you, commanders of thou-
sands, commanders of hundreds, com-
manders of fifties, commanders of tens, and
officials, throughout your tribes. 16I
charged your judges at that time: "Give the
members of your community a fair hearing,
and judge rightly between one person and
another, whether citizen or resident alien.
17You must not be partial in judging: hear
out the small and the great alike; you shall
not be intimidated by anyone, for the judg-
ment is God's. Any case that is too hard for
you, bring to me, and I will hear it." 18So
I charged you at that time with all the
things that you should do.

19 Then, just as the LORD our God had
ordered us, we set out from Horeb and
went through all that great and terrible wil-
derness that you saw, on the way to the hill
country of the Amorites, until we reached
Kadesh-barnea. 20I said to you, "You have
reached the hill country of the Amorites,
which the LORD our God is giving us.
21See, the LORD your God has given the
land to you; go up, take possession, as the
LORD, the God of your ancestors, has
promised you; do not fear or be dismayed."

22 All of you came to me and said, "Let
us send men ahead of us to explore the land
for us and bring back a report to us regard-
ing the route by which we should go up and
the cities we will come to." 23The plan
seemed good to me, and I selected twelve of
you, one from each tribe. 24They set out
and went up into the hill country, and
when they reached the Valley of Eshcol
they spied it out 25and gathered some of the
land's produce, which they brought down
to us. They brought back a report to us,
and said, "It is a good land that the LORD
our God is giving us."

26 But you were unwilling to go up. You
rebelled against the command of the LORD
your God; 27you grumbled in your tents
and said, "It is because the LORD hates us
that he has brought us out of the land of
Egypt, to hand us over to the Amorites to
destroy us. 28Where are we headed? Our
kindred have made our hearts melt by re-
porting, 'The people are stronger and taller
than we; the cities are large and fortified up
to heaven! We actually saw there the off-
spring of the Anakim!'" 29I said to you,
"Have no dread or fear of them. 30The

Num 11.14–17 and vv. 13–17 with Ex 18.13–27), placing the institutionalization of leadership after the departure from Sinai rather than before it and omitting the advisory role of Jethro, the non-Israelite (contrast Ex 18). **10:** *Stars of heaven,* fulfilling the promises made to the ancestors (Gen 15.5; 22.17; 26.4; Ex 32.13). **11:** *God of your ancestors,* Deuteronomy's normal phrase is "the LORD your/our God" (i.e., vv. 6,10). This departure from that formula ties this new generation to its past by recalling God's earlier promises (Gen 26.24; 32.9; Ex 3.6). **13:** *Wise* (contrast Ex 18.21), an attribute regularly stressed by Deuteronomy (4.6; 16.19; 32.29), suggesting the influence of wisdom literature upon its authors. *Reputable* (lit. "knowing"), continuing the emphasis upon wisdom as a criterion for leadership. **16:** *Resident alien,* the non-Israelite who lives in the community without title to land and who is therefore economically vulnerable; Deuteronomy insists upon a single law that applies to Israelite and non-Israelite alike (5.14; 10.18–19; 14.29; 16.11; 24.14,17,19–21). **17:** Similarly, 16.18–20.

1.19–46: From Horeb to Kadesh. A retelling, with significant variations, of the spies' reconnaissance of the land (Num 13), the people's complaining of God's inability to fulfill the promises made to Israel's ancestors (Num 14.1–38), and the abortive attempt to penetrate Canaan from the south despite the divine command not to do so (Num 14.39–45; cf. 21.1–3). **19:** *Kadesh-barnea,* see Num 13.26n. **28:** *Anakim,* see Num 13.22,33n. **30:** Ex 14.14. **33:** *Fire . . . cloud,* see Ex 13.21–22n. **34–35:** See Num 14.28–30. **37:**

LORD your God, who goes before you, is
the one who will fight for you, just as he
did for you in Egypt before your very eyes,
31 and in the wilderness, where you saw
how the LORD your God carried you, just
as one carries a child, all the way that you
traveled until you reached this place. 32 But
in spite of this, you have no trust in the
LORD your God, 33 who goes before you on
the way to seek out a place for you to
camp, in fire by night, and in the cloud by
day, to show you the route you should
take."

34 When the LORD heard your words,
he was wrathful and swore: 35 "Not one of
these—not one of this evil generation—
shall see the good land that I swore to give
to your ancestors, 36 except Caleb son of
Jephunneh. He shall see it, and to him and
to his descendants I will give the land on
which he set foot, because of his complete
fidelity to the LORD." 37 Even with me the
LORD was angry on your account, saying,
"You also shall not enter there. 38 Joshua
son of Nun, your assistant, shall enter
there; encourage him, for he is the one who
will secure Israel's possession of it. 39 And
as for your little ones, who you thought
would become booty, your children, who
today do not yet know right from wrong,
they shall enter there; to them I will give it,
and they shall take possession of it. 40 But
as for you, journey back into the wilder-
ness, in the direction of the Red Sea."[a]

41 You answered me, "We have sinned
against the LORD! We are ready to go up
and fight, just as the LORD our God com-
manded us." So all of you strapped on your
battle gear, and thought it easy to go up
into the hill country. 42 The LORD said to
me, "Say to them, 'Do not go up and do not
fight, for I am not in the midst of you; oth-
erwise you will be defeated by your ene-
mies.' " 43 Although I told you, you would
not listen. You rebelled against the com-
mand of the LORD and presumptuously
went up into the hill country. 44 The Amo-
rites who lived in that hill country then
came out against you and chased you as
bees do. They beat you down in Seir as
far as Hormah. 45 When you returned and
wept before the LORD, the LORD would
neither heed your voice nor pay you any
attention.

46 After you had stayed at Kadesh as

2 many days as you did, 1 we journeyed
back into the wilderness, in the direc-
tion of the Red Sea,[a] as the LORD had told
me and skirted Mount Seir for many days.
2 Then the LORD said to me: 3 "You have
been skirting this hill country long enough.
Head north, 4 and charge the people as fol-
lows: You are about to pass through the
territory of your kindred, the descendants
of Esau, who live in Seir. They will be
afraid of you, so, be very careful 5 not to
engage in battle with them, for I will not
give you even so much as a foot's length of
their land, since I have given Mount Seir to
Esau as a possession. 6 You shall purchase
food from them for money, so that you
may eat; and you shall also buy water from
them for money, so that you may drink.
7 Surely the LORD your God has blessed you
in all your undertakings; he knows your
going through this great wilderness. These
forty years the LORD your God has been
with you; you have lacked nothing." 8 So
we passed by our kin, the descendants of
Esau who live in Seir, leaving behind the
route of the Arabah, and leaving behind
Elath and Ezion-geber.

a Or *Sea of Reeds*

Here Moses is not punished for his own sin (contrast Num 20.10–13; 27.12–23). Instead, the narrator presents Moses as innocent and as vicariously bearing the punishment due Israel for its sin (see 3.24–28).

2.1–25: The circuit via Transjordan. 1–8a: Num 20.14–21. From Kadesh, Israel turned south through the Arabah to the Gulf of Aqaba in order to go around Edom (Num 21.4; cf. 33.47–49). **4:** *Descendants of Esau,* see Gen 36.1. **8a:** *Elath,* see 1 Kings 9.26. *Ezion-geber,* see Num 33.35. **8b–25:** Num 21.4–20, significantly revised. Turning along the brook Zered (modern Wadi el-Hasa), which formed Edom's southern boundary, Israel detoured through the wilderness of Moab toward the Amorite kingdom of Sihon. **9:** Moab and Ammon (v. 19) were traditionally related through Lot (Gen 19.36–38). **10–12:**

When we had headed out along the route
of the wilderness of Moab, 9 the LORD said
to me: "Do not harass Moab or engage
them in battle, for I will not give you any of
its land as a possession, since I have given
Ar as a possession to the descendants of
Lot." 10 (The Emim—a large and numerous
people, as tall as the Anakim—had former-
ly inhabited it. 11 Like the Anakim, they are
usually reckoned as Rephaim, though the
Moabites call them Emim. 12 Moreover, the
Horim had formerly inhabited Seir, but the
descendants of Esau dispossessed them, de-
stroying them and settling in their place, as
Israel has done in the land that the LORD
gave them as a possession.) 13 "Now then,
proceed to cross over the Wadi Zered."

So we crossed over the Wadi Zered.
14 And the length of time we had traveled
from Kadesh-barnea until we crossed the
Wadi Zered was thirty-eight years, until
the entire generation of warriors had per-
ished from the camp, as the LORD had
sworn concerning them. 15 Indeed, the
LORD's own hand was against them, to
root them out from the camp, until all had
perished.

16 Just as soon as all the warriors had
died off from among the people, 17 the
LORD spoke to me, saying, 18 "Today you
are going to cross the boundary of Moab at
Ar. 19 When you approach the frontier of
the Ammonites, do not harass them or en-
gage them in battle, for I will not give the
land of the Ammonites to you as a posses-
sion, because I have given it to the descen-
dants of Lot." 20 (It also is usually reckoned
as a land of Rephaim. Rephaim formerly
inhabited it, though the Ammonites call
them Zamzummim, 21 a strong and numer-
ous people, as tall as the Anakim. But the
LORD destroyed them from before the Am-
monites so that they could dispossess them
and settle in their place. 22 He did the same
for the descendants of Esau, who live in
Seir, by destroying the Horim before them
so that they could dispossess them and set-
tle in their place even to this day. 23 As for
the Avvim, who had lived in settlements in
the vicinity of Gaza, the Caphtorim, who
came from Caphtor, destroyed them and
settled in their place.) 24 "Proceed on your
journey and cross the Wadi Arnon. See, I
have handed over to you King Sihon the
Amorite of Heshbon, and his land. Begin to
take possession by engaging him in battle.
25 This day I will begin to put the dread and
fear of you upon the peoples everywhere
under heaven; when they hear report of
you, they will tremble and be in anguish
because of you."

26 So I sent messengers from the wilder-
ness of Kedemoth to King Sihon of Hesh-
bon with the following terms of peace:
27 "If you let me pass through your land, I
will travel only along the road; I will turn
aside neither to the right nor to the left.
28 You shall sell me food for money, so that
I may eat, and supply me water for money,
so that I may drink. Only allow me to pass
through on foot— 29 just as the descen-
dants of Esau who live in Seir have done for
me and likewise the Moabites who live in
Ar—until I cross the Jordan into the land
that the LORD our God is giving us." 30 But
King Sihon of Heshbon was not willing to

NRSV attempts to mitigate the anachronistic post-conquest perspective by confining it to parentheses (see v. 12n.). **10–11:** *Emim, Rephaim* (cf. v. 20; 3.11–13), names reflecting the legendary view that the aboriginal inhabitants of the land were fearsome giants. **12:** *Horim,* see Gen 36.20–30n. *As Israel has done . . . possession,* the conquest is represented anachronistically as already having been completed (see 1.1n.; 3.11n.). **13:** *Wadi,* a seasonal river. **14:** Fulfilling God's angry oath (1.34–35; Num 14.28–30). Without the death of the generation of the Exodus, here marked as accomplished, there can be no entry into the promised land. **15:** *LORD's own hand,* they did not die of natural causes. The imagery inverts the standard idea of holy war: God had turned against Israel rather than fighting on its behalf (see 3.22; 7.1–5; 12.29–31; 20.1–20). **20:** Cf. vv. 10–12n.; Gen 14.5. **23:** *Caphtor,* Crete, referring to the conquest of the coastal plain by "Sea Peoples" such as Philistines shortly after 1200 BCE (see Gen 10.2–5,14; Am 9.7). **24:** *Arnon,* see Num 21.12–13. **26–37:** The victory over Sihon, whose capital was at Heshbon. The earlier source in Num 21.21–32 is here supplemented and revised. **30:** See Ex 4.21n. **34:** *Utterly destroyed,* see

let us pass through, for the LORD your God
had hardened his spirit and made his heart
defiant in order to hand him over to you, as
he has now done.
31 The LORD said to me, "See, I have
begun to give Sihon and his land over to
you. Begin now to take possession of his
land." 32 So when Sihon came out against
us, he and all his people for battle at Jahaz,
33 the LORD our God gave him over to us;
and we struck him down, along with his
offspring and all his people. 34 At that time
we captured all his towns, and in each town
we utterly destroyed men, women, and
children. We left not a single survivor.
35 Only the livestock we kept as spoil for
ourselves, as well as the plunder of the
towns that we had captured. 36 From Aroer
on the edge of the Wadi Arnon (including
the town that is in the wadi itself) as far as
Gilead, there was no citadel too high for us.
The LORD our God gave everything to us.
37 You did not encroach, however, on the
land of the Ammonites, avoiding the whole
upper region of the Wadi Jabbok as well as
the towns of the hill country, just as[a] the
LORD our God had charged.

3 When we headed up the road to Ba-
shan, King Og of Bashan came out
against us, he and all his people, for battle
at Edrei. 2 The LORD said to me, "Do not
fear him, for I have handed him over to
you, along with his people and his land. Do
to him as you did to King Sihon of the Am-
orites, who reigned in Heshbon." 3 So the
LORD our God also handed over to us King
Og of Bashan and all his people. We struck
him down until not a single survivor was
left. 4 At that time we captured all his
towns; there was no citadel that we did not
take from them—sixty towns, the whole re-
gion of Argob, the kingdom of Og in Ba-
shan. 5 All these were fortress towns with
high walls, double gates, and bars, besides
a great many villages. 6 And we utterly de-
stroyed them, as we had done to King Si-
hon of Heshbon, in each city utterly de-
stroying men, women, and children. 7 But
all the livestock and the plunder of the
towns we kept as spoil for ourselves.
8 So at that time we took from the two
kings of the Amorites the land beyond the
Jordan, from the Wadi Arnon to Mount
Hermon 9 (the Sidonians call Hermon Siri-
on, while the Amorites call it Senir), 10 all
the towns of the tableland, the whole of
Gilead, and all of Bashan, as far as Salecah
and Edrei, towns of Og's kingdom in Ba-
shan. 11 (Now only King Og of Bashan was
left of the remnant of the Rephaim. In fact
his bed, an iron bed, can still be seen in
Rabbah of the Ammonites. By the common
cubit it is nine cubits long and four cubits
wide.) 12 As for the land that we took pos-
session of at that time, I gave to the Reu-
benites and Gadites the territory north of
Aroer,[b] that is on the edge of the Wadi
Arnon, as well as half the hill country of
Gilead with its towns, 13 and I gave to the
half-tribe of Manasseh the rest of Gilead
and all of Bashan, Og's kingdom. (The
whole region of Argob: all that portion of
Bashan used to be called a land of Repha-
im; 14 Jair the Manassite acquired the whole
region of Argob as far as the border of the
Geshurites and the Maacathites, and he
named them—that is, Bashan—after him-
self, Havvoth-jair,[c] as it is to this day.)
15 To Machir I gave Gilead. 16 And to the
Reubenites and the Gadites I gave the terri-
tory from Gilead as far as the Wadi Arnon,
with the middle of the wadi as a boundary,
and up to the Jabbok, the wadi being

a Gk Tg: Heb *and all* *b* Heb *territory from Aroer*
c That is *Settlement of Jair*

7.2n. **37:** The river Jabbok makes a wide bend south and thus forms the western border of Ammon (3.16). **3.1–11:** The victory over Bashan (Num 21.33–35). **1:** *Edrei,* on the extreme south border of *Bashan;* see Num 21.33–35n. **11:** The oversized bed of Og, one of the legendary Rephaim (2.10–11), was a "museum piece" in Rabbah, a city on the Ammonite border. The emphasis that this bed *can still be seen* there places the historical perspective of the narrator, and thus of Deuteronomy's composition, long after the events here recounted (1.1n.; 2.12n.). A *cubit* was about 44 cm (17.5 in). **12–22:** The allotment of tribal territories in Transjordan (Num 32; Josh 13). **14:** Num 32.41. **17:** The territory included the eastern part

boundary of the Ammonites; 17 the Arabah
also, with the Jordan and its banks, from
Chinnereth down to the sea of the Arabah,
the Dead Sea,[a] with the lower slopes of
Pisgah on the east.

18 At that time, I charged you as fol-
lows: "Although the LORD your God has
given you this land to occupy, all your
troops shall cross over armed as the van-
guard of your Israelite kin. 19 Only your
wives, your children, and your livestock—I
know that you have much livestock—shall
stay behind in the towns that I have given
to you. 20 When the LORD gives rest to your
kindred, as to you, and they too have occu-
pied the land that the LORD your God is
giving them beyond the Jordan, then each
of you may return to the property that I
have given to you." 21 And I charged Josh-
ua as well at that time, saying: "Your own
eyes have seen everything that the LORD
your God has done to these two kings; so
the LORD will do to all the kingdoms into
which you are about to cross. 22 Do not fear
them, for it is the LORD your God who
fights for you."

23 At that time, too, I entreated the
LORD, saying: 24 "O Lord GOD, you have
only begun to show your servant your
greatness and your might; what god in
heaven or on earth can perform deeds and
mighty acts like yours! 25 Let me cross over
to see the good land beyond the Jordan,
that good hill country and the Lebanon."
26 But the LORD was angry with me on your
account and would not heed me. The LORD
said to me, "Enough from you! Never
speak to me of this matter again! 27 Go up
to the top of Pisgah and look around you to
the west, to the north, to the south, and to
the east. Look well, for you shall not cross
over this Jordan. 28 But charge Joshua, and
encourage and strengthen him, because it is
he who shall cross over at the head of this
people and who shall secure their posses-
sion of the land that you will see." 29 So we
remained in the valley opposite Beth-peor.

4 So now, Israel, give heed to the statutes
and ordinances that I am teaching you
to observe, so that you may live to enter
and occupy the land that the LORD, the
God of your ancestors, is giving you. 2 You
must neither add anything to what I com-
mand you nor take away anything from it,
but keep the commandments of the LORD
your God with which I am charging you.

[a] Heb *Salt Sea*

of the Jordan Valley or Arabah. **22:** The whole story of the Exodus, wilderness journey, and invasion of Canaan is governed by the convictions of holy war, whereby God is a divine warrior who engages in battle on behalf of Israel. **23–29:** Num 27.12–23. **24:** *What god . . . can perform,* the assertion of God's superior power, relative to other gods *in heaven,* assumes the existence of other gods (5.7n.; 6.4n.; 32.8n.; Ex 15.11; Ps 89.5–8). For the later perspective of monotheism, see 4.35n. **26:** See 1.37n. **27:** Mount *Pisgah,* see 34.1n.

4.1–40: Exhortation to obey the Torah. While preceding the Decalogue (5.6–21), this unit provides a later theological reflection upon it, focusing on the second commandment and broadening its significance. Admonitions to obedience (vv. 1,40) frame the unit, which systematically contrasts obedience (vv. 5–24)/disobedience (vv. 25–31); remembering/forgetting (vv. 9,23); the LORD/other gods (vv. 7,34); Israel's revealed Torah/the laws of other nations (vv. 8,28); and God/idols (vv. 12–20). The correct worship of God is aniconic: Images (whether of God or of natural phenomena) should play no role in Israelite religion. This becomes so strong a theme that idolatry by itself is asserted to be the cause of the nation's exile from its land (vv. 25–31). The explicit reference to exile suggests that the unit is a late theological explanation for the Babylonian exile. The focus on idolatry as the basis for the divine punishment diverges significantly from the perspective elsewhere that views failure to heed "all his [God's] commandments and decrees" as the cause of exile (28.15; cf. 28.1,45,58–59). **1–4:** The incident at Peor (Num 25.1–9) is recalled to emphasize the importance of fidelity to God and the dire consequences of worshiping other gods. **2:** This admonition not to alter the Torah, whether by addition or subtraction (cf. 12.32), parallels similar admonitions in wisdom literature (Prov 30.6; Eccl 3.14; 12.12–13; Sir 42.21; cf. Rev 22.18–19) and in ancient Near Eastern legal traditions. **5–8:** The author here challenges the

3 You have seen for yourselves what the
LORD did with regard to the Baal of Peor—
how the LORD your God destroyed from
among you everyone who followed the
Baal of Peor, 4 while those of you who held
fast to the LORD your God are all alive to-
day.
5 See, just as the LORD my God has
charged me, I now teach you statutes and
ordinances for you to observe in the land
that you are about to enter and occupy.
6 You must observe them diligently, for this
will show your wisdom and discernment to
the peoples, who, when they hear all these
statutes, will say, "Surely this great nation
is a wise and discerning people!" 7 For what
other great nation has a god so near to it as
the LORD our God is whenever we call to
him? 8 And what other great nation has
statutes and ordinances as just as this entire
law that I am setting before you today?
9 But take care and watch yourselves
closely, so as neither to forget the things
that your eyes have seen nor to let them slip
from your mind all the days of your life;
make them known to your children and
your children's children— 10 how you once
stood before the LORD your God at Horeb,
when the LORD said to me, "Assemble the
people for me, and I will let them hear my
words, so that they may learn to fear me as
long as they live on the earth, and may
teach their children so"; 11 you approached
and stood at the foot of the mountain while
the mountain was blazing up to the very
heavens, shrouded in dark clouds. 12 Then
the LORD spoke to you out of the fire. You
heard the sound of words but saw no form;
there was only a voice. 13 He declared to
you his covenant, which he charged you to
observe, that is, the ten commandments;[a]
and he wrote them on two stone tablets.
14 And the LORD charged me at that time to
teach you statutes and ordinances for you
to observe in the land that you are about to
cross into and occupy.

a Heb *the ten words*

prevailing Near Eastern idea that wisdom was a royal prerogative. Whereas, for example, the ancient Babylonian *Laws of Hammurabi* (ca. 1755 BCE) praised the "just decisions" of its "wise" king (cols 47.1; 4.7), here it is the nation Israel who will be internationally renowned as "wise" for its "just" laws (vv. 6,8). See also 29.29n.; 30.11–14n. **7–8:** Israel is distinguished both by its God and by its law: The two ideas are interlocked. God is *near,* both in having entered history on behalf of Israel and in revealing his will as Torah (30.14). The laws are *just* (better, "righteous"), not only in their morality but also as embodying the will of God. **9–14:** The revelation at Sinai/Horeb (Ex 19–20; Deut 5) is recalled in order to instruct this generation, who did not experience it. **9:** The paired injunctions not to *forget* the powerful experience of God's actions and to educate *your children,* so that the past becomes "present" also to them, represent a prominent aim of Deuteronomy: to overcome the distance of the past and maintain it as a source of identity (vv. 23,25; 6.2,7,20–25; 8.11; 9.7; 31.13; 32.18). *Your eyes have seen,* as well as the following "how you once stood" (v. 10), are highly paradoxical assertions. Neither is literally true: The actual generation of the Exodus had died off (2.14–15n.). This paradoxical structure of thought, whereby Moses addresses those who had not witnessed the events as if they had, while insisting that they inculcate the events to posterity, is central to Deuteronomy's theology of history (5.3–4,23; 11.7; 29.16–17). **10:** *My words,* the Decalogue ("ten commandments"; v. 13; 5.22; 9.10; 10.2,4). Elsewhere, however, the phrase refers comprehensively to the legal corpus of chs 12–26 (12.28). *Fear,* respectful reverence, not intimidation (see Job 28.28; Prov 1.7). **11:** The manifestation of a god ("theophany") was often associated with disturbances of nature in Ugaritic (Canaanite) literature. This motif was taken over by Israelite writers and applied to God (Ex 19.16–19; 20.21; Ps 18.7–15; 29.3–9). **12:** *Form* (also vv. 15–16,23,25), directly alluding to the second commandment of the Decalogue (5.8 = Ex 20.4). **13:** A subtle reinterpretation of Sinai: The specification of that event as one where God proclaimed *ten commandments* occurs only here, at 10.4, and at Ex 34.28. There is no special number of or name for the commandments (lit. "words") in Ex 19–20 or Deut 5. The rationale for *two stone tablets* (as at 5.22) derives from ancient Near Eastern treaties, whereby both sovereign and vassal would retain a separate complete copy of the treaty. **15–31:** Reinterpretation of the second commandment. The Decalogue concedes the existence of

15 Since you saw no form when the
LORD spoke to you at Horeb out of the fire,
take care and watch yourselves closely,
16 so that you do not act corruptly by mak-
ing an idol for yourselves, in the form of
any figure—the likeness of male or female,
17 the likeness of any animal that is on the
earth, the likeness of any winged bird that
flies in the air, 18 the likeness of anything
that creeps on the ground, the likeness of
any fish that is in the water under the earth.
19 And when you look up to the heavens
and see the sun, the moon, and the stars, all
the host of heaven, do not be led astray and
bow down to them and serve them, things
that the LORD your God has allotted to
all the peoples everywhere under heaven.
20 But the LORD has taken you and brought
you out of the iron-smelter, out of Egypt,
to become a people of his very own posses-
sion, as you are now.

21 The LORD was angry with me be-
cause of you, and he vowed that I should
not cross the Jordan and that I should not
enter the good land that the LORD your
God is giving for your possession. 22 For I
am going to die in this land without cross-
ing over the Jordan, but you are going to
cross over to take possession of that good
land. 23 So be careful not to forget the cove-
nant that the LORD your God made with
you, and not to make for yourselves an idol
in the form of anything that the LORD your
God has forbidden you. 24 For the LORD
your God is a devouring fire, a jealous
God.

25 When you have had children and
children's children, and become compla-
cent in the land, if you act corruptly by
making an idol in the form of anything,
thus doing what is evil in the sight of the
LORD your God, and provoking him to an-
ger, 26 I call heaven and earth to witness
against you today that you will soon utterly
perish from the land that you are crossing
the Jordan to occupy; you will not live long
on it, but will be utterly destroyed. 27 The
LORD will scatter you among the peoples;
only a few of you will be left among the
nations where the LORD will lead you.
28 There you will serve other gods made by
human hands, objects of wood and stone
that neither see, nor hear, nor eat, nor
smell. 29 From there you will seek the LORD
your God, and you will find him if you
search after him with all your heart and
soul. 30 In your distress, when all these
things have happened to you in time to
come, you will return to the LORD your
God and heed him. 31 Because the LORD
your God is a merciful God, he will neither
abandon you nor destroy you; he will not

other gods, while prohibiting Israel from worshiping them (5.7; cf. 32.8; Ex 15.11; Ps 82.1). It then separately prohibits the making of images (5.8). The distinction between those two commandments is dissolved here. The existence of other gods is no longer conceivable; the sole focus is the prohibition against idols. Here and elsewhere (see v. 19n.) key ideas in Deuteronomy are reinterpreted from a later theological perspective; such passages therefore represent a later textual layer that dates to the exilic period. **16b–19a:** This catalogue follows the order of creation in Gen 1 in reverse order, consistent with ancient scribal practice when quoting an earlier text. **18:** *Water under the earth,* seas, rivers, and lakes. Ancient cosmology conceived the earth to be a disk floating on such waters (cf. Gen 1.9). **19:** *Sun . . . host of heaven* may reflect images derived from the Neo-Assyrian pantheon brought into the Jerusalem Temple by Manasseh but removed by Josiah (2 Kings 21.5; 23.4–5; Jer 8.2). The idea of idols or of celestial phenomena literally being worshiped sharply distorts ancient Near Eastern religion, which regarded such phenomena as visible manifestations or emblems of a deity, not as themselves divine. This polemic, with the idea that God *allotted* the celestial phenomena to other nations while reserving Israel as "his very own possession" (v. 20; cf. 7.6n.), reinterprets the earlier idea that God, as head of the pantheon, assigned other nations to the supervision of lesser gods but retained Israel as "his allotted share" (lit. "his very own possession"; 32.8–9). The author de-animates those gods, reducing them to lifeless celestial objects. **21:** See 1.37n. **26:** *Heaven . . . witness,* similarly, 30.19; 31.28; 32.1; Isa 1.2; 44.23; Ps 69.34; 96.11. **27–28:** These verses allude to the exile of conquered populations, a policy used effectively by the Assyrians and the Babylonians. **32–40:** Continuation of the double focus on the uniqueness of God's revelation to Israel

forget the covenant with your ancestors
that he swore to them.
32 For ask now about former ages, long
before your own, ever since the day that
God created human beings on the earth;
ask from one end of heaven to the other:
has anything so great as this ever happened
or has its like ever been heard of? 33 Has
any people ever heard the voice of a god
speaking out of a fire, as you have heard,
and lived? 34 Or has any god ever attempted
to go and take a nation for himself from the
midst of another nation, by trials, by signs
and wonders, by war, by a mighty hand
and an outstretched arm, and by terrifying
displays of power, as the LORD your God
did for you in Egypt before your very eyes?
35 To you it was shown so that you would
acknowledge that the LORD is God; there is
no other besides him. 36 From heaven he
made you hear his voice to discipline you.
On earth he showed you his great fire,
while you heard his words coming out of
the fire. 37 And because he loved your an-
cestors, he chose their descendants after
them. He brought you out of Egypt with his
own presence, by his great power, 38 driv-
ing out before you nations greater and
mightier than yourselves, to bring you in,
giving you their land for a possession, as it
is still today. 39 So acknowledge today and
take to heart that the LORD is God in heav-
en above and on the earth beneath; there is
no other. 40 Keep his statutes and his com-
mandments, which I am commanding you
today for your own well-being and that of
your descendants after you, so that you
may long remain in the land that the LORD
your God is giving you for all time.
41 Then Moses set apart on the east side
of the Jordan three cities 42 to which a ho-
micide could flee, someone who uninten-
tionally kills another person, the two not
having been at enmity before; the homicide
could flee to one of these cities and live:
43 Bezer in the wilderness on the tableland
belonging to the Reubenites, Ramoth in
Gilead belonging to the Gadites, and Golan
in Bashan belonging to the Manassites.

44 This is the law that Moses set before
the Israelites. 45 These are the decrees and
the statutes and ordinances that Moses
spoke to the Israelites when they had come
out of Egypt, 46 beyond the Jordan in the
valley opposite Beth-peor, in the land of
King Sihon of the Amorites, who reigned at
Heshbon, whom Moses and the Israelites
defeated when they came out of Egypt.
47 They occupied his land and the land of
King Og of Bashan, the two kings of the
Amorites on the eastern side of the Jordan:
48 from Aroer, which is on the edge of the
Wadi Arnon, as far as Mount Sirion[a] (that
is, Hermon), 49 together with all the Arabah
on the east side of the Jordan as far as the
Sea of the Arabah, under the slopes of Pis-
gah.

5 Moses convened all Israel, and said to
them:

a Syr: Heb *Sion*

and of the covenant he made with the nation. Several passages fit best in the historical context of the Babylonian exile (see v. 35n.). **33:** Alludes to the normal expectation that no human can look directly upon God and survive (Gen 16.13; 32.30; Ex 3.6; 19.21; 33.20). **34:** *Attempted,* better, "ventured" (as at 28.56). *Trials . . . wonders* refers to the signs performed by Moses and Aaron in Egypt, including the plagues, to persuade Pharaoh to release Israel (Ex 7.3; 8.23; 10.1–2; 11.9–10). **35:** *There is no other,* this affirmation of full monotheism (contrast v. 7; 5.7) corresponds to the thought of the exilic Second Isaiah (Isa 43.10–13; 44.6–8; 45.6–7,22).

4.41–43: An appendix. The cities of refuge to be established in Transjordan. Since the law concerned with these cities (ch 19) does not refer to this passage, these verses are most likely an editorial appendix composed after the completion of ch 19 (cf. Num 35.9–15; Josh 20.8). Similar disconnected appendices often appear in the Bible at the conclusion of longer literary units (e.g., Lev 27).

4.44–28.68: The second discourse of Moses.

4.44–49: Introduction. Cf. 1.1–5. **49:** *Sea of the Arabah,* the Dead Sea.

5.1–33: The revelation at Sinai/Horeb. Ostensibly a retelling of Ex 19–20, this version introduces

Hear, O Israel, the statutes and ordi-
nances that I am addressing to you today;
you shall learn them and observe them dili-
gently. 2 The LORD our God made a cove-
nant with us at Horeb. 3 Not with our an-
cestors did the LORD make this covenant,
but with us, who are all of us here alive
today. 4 The LORD spoke with you face to
face at the mountain, out of the fire. 5 (At
that time I was standing between the LORD
and you to declare to you the words[a] of
the LORD; for you were afraid because of
the fire and did not go up the mountain.)
And he said:

6 I am the LORD your God, who
brought you out of the land of Egypt, out
of the house of slavery; 7 you shall have no
other gods before[b] me.

8 You shall not make for yourself an
idol, whether in the form of anything that is
in heaven above, or that is on the earth
beneath, or that is in the water under the
earth. 9 You shall not bow down to them or
worship them; for I the LORD your God am
a jealous God, punishing children for the
iniquity of parents, to the third and fourth
generation of those who reject me, 10 but
showing steadfast love to the thousandth
generation[c] of those who love me and
keep my commandments.

11 You shall not make wrongful use of
the name of the LORD your God, for the
LORD will not acquit anyone who misuses
his name.

12 Observe the sabbath day and keep it

a Q Mss Sam Gk Syr Vg Tg: MT *word*
b Or *besides* *c* Or *to thousands*

significant changes in both detail and theology. The central idea is that God publicly reveals the law to the entire nation across boundaries of gender, race, and class, including non-Israelites (Ex 12.38). Near Eastern legal collections, in contrast, were attributed to a human monarch and were concerned to preserve class distinctions. Moreover, a deity disclosing himself to an entire nation was unprecedented. The Decalogue has God address each Israelite individually as a grammatically masculine singular "you," rather than the expected plural. In contrast to Near Eastern law, the prohibitions are universal and absolute: The aim of the law is to transform society by creating a moral community in which murder, theft, etc. will no longer exist. Obedience to God's will (vv. 6–16) demands active respect for the integrity of the neighbor (vv. 17–21). The editing drives home the point that there is no access to God or revelation without mediation and interpretation (vv. 5,28–32), preserving two mutually independent viewpoints about whether God spoke directly to the people (v. 4) or only through the mediation of Moses (v. 5n.). Similarly, the editing retains a debate about the terror involved in hearing directly the divine voice (vv. 24–25).

5.1–5: Making the past present. 3: *Not with our ancestors . . . but with us,* inconsistent with the earlier emphasis that the generation who experienced these events has now died off (2.14–15). The aim is to overcome the limits of historical time and place through participation in the covenant, which makes revelation "present" (see 4.9n.; 29.14–15n.). *Our ancestors* may refer either to the Exodus generation (2.14–15n.) or to the patriarchs Abraham, Isaac, and Jacob (1.11n.). **5:** NRSV suggests that the first sentence intends merely to clarify v. 4. More likely, it presents an independent view that challenges the assumption of v. 4. *I was standing between . . . you,* contrast "face to face" (v. 4). *You . . . did not go up the mountain,* contradicting v. 4, "with you . . . at the mountain" (Heb). *And he said,* in Hebrew, the original transition from the end of v. 4 directly to the Decalogue.

5.6–21: The Decalogue. This version differs at several points from that in Ex 20.2–17. **7–10:** See 4.15–31n. **9:** Punishment for sins against God extends across three generations. This principle of vicarious punishment contrasts sharply with the Israelite norm for civil and criminal law, which restricts punishment to the agent alone (24.16). Later layers of tradition challenged this theological principle of divine justice (see 7.10n.; Jer 31.29–30; Ezek 18). **10:** *Steadfast love* or "grace," loyalty of action as an expectation of the covenant (2 Sam 7.15; Hos 6.6). *Who love me,* technical language of Near Eastern treaties, whereby "love" refers to the loyalty of action that the vassal owes the sovereign. **11:** The intent is to prohibit careless use of the divine name in the context of swearing an oath ("May God do X to me unless I do Y"); such oaths were viewed as legally binding (see Judg 11.29–40). **12:** *Observe,* contrast Ex 20.8.

holy, as the LORD your God commanded
you. 13 Six days you shall labor and do all
your work. 14 But the seventh day is a sab-
bath to the LORD your God; you shall not do any work—you, or your son or your daughter, or your male or female slave, or your ox or your donkey, or any of your livestock, or the resident alien in your towns, so that your male and female slave
may rest as well as you. 15 Remember that
you were a slave in the land of Egypt, and the LORD your God brought you out from there with a mighty hand and an outstretched arm; therefore the LORD your God commanded you to keep the sabbath day.

16 Honor your father and your mother, as the LORD your God commanded you, so that your days may be long and that it may go well with you in the land that the LORD your God is giving you.

17 You shall not murder.[a]

18 Neither shall you commit adultery.

19 Neither shall you steal.

20 Neither shall you bear false witness against your neighbor.

21 Neither shall you covet your neighbor's wife.

Neither shall you desire your neighbor's house, or field, or male or female slave, or ox, or donkey, or anything that belongs to your neighbor.

22 These words the LORD spoke with a
loud voice to your whole assembly at the mountain, out of the fire, the cloud, and the thick darkness, and he added no more. He wrote them on two stone tablets, and gave
them to me. 23 When you heard the voice
out of the darkness, while the mountain was burning with fire, you approached me, all the heads of your tribes and your elders;
24 and you said, "Look, the LORD our God
has shown us his glory and greatness, and we have heard his voice out of the fire. Today we have seen that God may speak to
someone and the person may still live. 25 So
now why should we die? For this great fire will consume us; if we hear the voice of the LORD our God any longer, we shall die.
26 For who is there of all flesh that has
heard the voice of the living God speaking out of fire, as we have, and remained alive?
27 Go near, you yourself, and hear all that
the LORD our God will say. Then tell us everything that the LORD our God tells you, and we will listen and do it."

28 The LORD heard your words when you spoke to me, and the LORD said to me: "I have heard the words of this people, which they have spoken to you; they are
right in all that they have spoken. 29 If only
they had such a mind as this, to fear me and to keep all my commandments always, so that it might go well with them and with

a Or *kill*

14: The law equally benefits slaves and non-Israelites (1.16n.; 15.15; 16.11; 24.17). **15:** Contrast the rationale provided for the sabbath at Ex 20.11. Deuteronomy here, as elsewhere, emphasizes the Exodus as a central motivation for religious and social practices. **16:** *As . . . commanded you,* the ostensible precise repetition of the Decalogue here diverges from the original (Ex 20.12) by shifting to the perspective of Moses as speaker, whose annotation is now included in the revelation. **17:** *Murder* is correct; text note *a* is an inaccurate translation ("kill," as a global prohibition). **18:** The absolute prohibition of adultery transforms it from the breach of the contractual rights of the woman's husband into an offense against both God and the larger community. Near Eastern law normally granted the husband the sole right of deciding whether to execute or otherwise punish the wife for adultery (see *Laws of Hammurabi* § 129). Biblical law here removes the wife from the disposal of the husband and grants her the status of legal person (see 22.22n.). **21:** *Wife . . . house,* contrast the sequence of Ex 20.17.

5.22–33: Moses as mediator. While the Decalogue was given directly to the people (v. 4; 4.10–13), the rest of the laws were mediated to the people by Moses, at their plea (v. 27; 4.14). **23–27:** 4.33; cf. Ex 20.18–21. **24–25:** An awkward juxtaposition; v. 24 may be an insertion reflecting 4.33. The anxiety explains the request that Moses serve as mediator. **28–31:** The idea that Moses mediates between God and the people will be used in two ways: to justify the laws that Moses subsequently propounds as revelation (chs 12–26), and to justify the institution of "Mosaic" prophecy (18.15–22).

their children forever! 30 Go say to them,
'Return to your tents.' 31 But you, stand
here by me, and I will tell you all the com-
mandments, the statutes and the ordi-
nances, that you shall teach them, so that
they may do them in the land that I am
giving them to possess." 32 You must there-
fore be careful to do as the LORD your God
has commanded you; you shall not turn to
the right or to the left. 33 You must follow
exactly the path that the LORD your God
has commanded you, so that you may live,
and that it may go well with you, and that
you may live long in the land that you are
to possess.

6 Now this is the commandment—the
statutes and the ordinances—that the
LORD your God charged me to teach you to
observe in the land that you are about to
cross into and occupy, 2 so that you and
your children and your children's children
may fear the LORD your God all the days of
your life, and keep all his decrees and his
commandments that I am commanding
you, so that your days may be long. 3 Hear
therefore, O Israel, and observe them dili-
gently, so that it may go well with you, and
so that you may multiply greatly in a land
flowing with milk and honey, as the LORD,
the God of your ancestors, has promised
you.

4 Hear, O Israel: The LORD is our God,
the LORD alone.[a] 5 You shall love the
LORD your God with all your heart, and
with all your soul, and with all your might.
6 Keep these words that I am commanding
you today in your heart. 7 Recite them to
your children and talk about them when
you are at home and when you are away,
when you lie down and when you rise.
8 Bind them as a sign on your hand, fix
them as an emblem[b] on your forehead,
9 and write them on the doorposts of your
house and on your gates.

a Or *The LORD our God is one LORD,* or *The LORD our God, the LORD is one,* or *The LORD is our God, the LORD is one* *b* Or *as a frontlet*

6.1–11.32: The requirement of loyalty to God. A sermonic preamble to the laws of chs 12–26. **6.1–3:** Introduction, stressing the rewards of obedience to the covenant. **1:** *The commandment . . . occupy,* the Hebrew is nearly identical to 5.31. The precise repetition of terminology legitimates the entire second discourse—both *the commandment* (chs 6–11) and *the statutes and ordinances* (the legal corpus of chs 12–26; see 12.1)—as originating in direct divine revelation from God on Horeb (5.31). The Book of the Covenant (Ex 21–23), with its "ordinances" (Ex 21.1), and the "statutes and ordinances" of Deuteronomic law (6.1; 12.1), now in implicit tension, are independently presented as God's words to Moses on the mountain immediately following the Decalogue (Ex 20.21; 24.3,12). **2:** *Fear,* better, "revere" (see 4.10n.). **4–25:** A sermon on the first commandment of the Decalogue, incorporating direct allusions to it: vv. 4 and 14 refer to 5.7; vv. 12,21,23 refer to 5.6; v. 15 ("jealous God") refers to 5.9; vv. 5,17 refer to 5.10. **4–9:** In Jewish tradition these verses begin the important prayer known as the Shema ("Hear!"). **4–5:** This "first" commandment (Mk 12.29–30) restates the first Decalogue commandment in positive form. *Hear, O Israel* (5.1; 9.1; 20.3; 27.9), an imperative modeled on a wisdom teacher's call for attention (Prov 1.8; 4.1,10; 5.7; 7.24; 23.19). *The LORD . . . alone,* as text note *a* indicates, the Hebrew is difficult; the translation selected makes most sense historically. The focus is not on God's nature in the abstract but on the quality of Israel's relationship to God. The proclamation, like 5.7, does not deny the existence of other gods but is concerned with the exclusivity of Israel's loyalty to God (as in ch 13). This vision is universalized in later prophecy (Zech 14.9). **5:** *Love,* see 5.10n. The paradox of commanding a feeling (as in Lev 19.17–18) is resolved with the recognition that covenantal "love" is not private emotion but loyalty of action toward both deity and neighbor (see 5.1–33n.). **7:** *At home . . . away,* using paired opposites as a merism (28.3–6n.) to indicate totality: One should always *talk about* the commandments. **8:** *Bind them,* based on the wisdom teacher's symbolically urging his students to focus on the lesson (Prov 3.3; 6.21; 7.3). This law, literally interpreted, provides the basis for the Jewish convention of binding phylacteries, containing an abstract of biblical law, upon the arm and forehead. **9:** *Doorposts,* important transitional spaces in which religious-legal ceremonies were performed and where divine images might be stored (see Ex 12.7,21–23; 21.6; Isa 57.8). Perhaps partially reacting against a formerly magical back-

10 When the LORD your God has
brought you into the land that he swore to
your ancestors, to Abraham, to Isaac, and
to Jacob, to give you—a land with fine,
large cities that you did not build, 11 houses
filled with all sorts of goods that you did
not fill, hewn cisterns that you did not hew,
vineyards and olive groves that you did not
plant—and when you have eaten your fill,
12 take care that you do not forget the
LORD, who brought you out of the land of
Egypt, out of the house of slavery. 13 The
LORD your God you shall fear; him you
shall serve, and by his name alone you shall
swear. 14 Do not follow other gods, any of
the gods of the peoples who are all around
you, 15 because the LORD your God, who is
present with you, is a jealous God. The an-
ger of the LORD your God would be kin-
dled against you and he would destroy you
from the face of the earth.

16 Do not put the LORD your God to the
test, as you tested him at Massah. 17 You
must diligently keep the commandments of
the LORD your God, and his decrees, and
his statutes that he has commanded you.
18 Do what is right and good in the sight of
the LORD, so that it may go well with you,
and so that you may go in and occupy the
good land that the LORD swore to your an-
cestors to give you, 19 thrusting out all your
enemies from before you, as the LORD has
promised.

20 When your children ask you in time
to come, "What is the meaning of the de-
crees and the statutes and the ordinances
that the LORD our God has commanded
you?" 21 then you shall say to your chil-
dren, "We were Pharaoh's slaves in Egypt,
but the LORD brought us out of Egypt with
a mighty hand. 22 The LORD displayed be-
fore our eyes great and awesome signs and
wonders against Egypt, against Pharaoh
and all his household. 23 He brought us out
from there in order to bring us in, to give us
the land that he promised on oath to our
ancestors. 24 Then the LORD commanded us
to observe all these statutes, to fear the
LORD our God, for our lasting good, so as
to keep us alive, as is now the case. 25 If we
diligently observe this entire command-
ment before the LORD our God, as he has
commanded us, we will be in the right."

7 When the LORD your God brings you
into the land that you are about to enter
and occupy, and he clears away many na-

ground, this law devotes that space to Torah. The law provides the basis for the Jewish convention of placing a small box containing this and related texts upon the upper portion of the right doorpost (Heb "mezuzah"). **10–11:** The list, *land . . . houses . . . cisterns . . . olive groves* (cf. Josh 24.13; Neh 9.24–25), defines the elements of an established civilization, which Israel is about to both inherit and become. **12:** The threat of forgetting and the risk of apostasy are repeatedly stressed (4.9–14n.; 8.11–20; 32.18; cf. 5.29; Hos 2.5–13). **16:** *Test . . . Massah,* for the incident and the Hebrew pun, see Ex 17.2–7; see also Mt 4.7. **20:** The Jewish Passover text ("Haggadah") includes this and similar didactic questions (Ex 12.21–27; 13.1–10,11–16). **22:** See 4.34n.

7.1–10.11: Risks to covenantal faith upon entry to the land. The first issue is that Israel enters an already inhabited land, whose greater population and worship apparatus it must confront (ch 7). Thereafter, successful habitation carries its own risks: complacency and loss of historical memory (ch 8).

7.1–26: The war of conquest. Two topics are treated: the command to destroy the original occupants of Canaan (vv. 1–3,6,17–24); and the command not to worship their gods (vv. 4–5,7–15,25–26). The editors join the two themes at v. 16. **1:** An after-the-fact literary compilation more than a historical portrayal: The peoples included in the "table of nations" vary considerably (Gen 15.19–21; Ex 3.8,17; 13.5; 23.23; 33.2; 34.11; Deut 20.17; Josh 3.10; 9.1; 11.3; 12.8; 24.11; Judg 3.5; 1 Kings 9.20; Ezra 9.1; Neh 9.8; 2 Chr 8.7). *Hittites* (Gen 23.10; 25.9; 49.29–30; 50.13; Num 13.29, etc.), the Hittite Empire (ca. 1700–1200 BCE) in fact flourished not in Canaan but in Anatolia, in central Turkey. The *Jebusites,* the pre-Israelite inhabitants of Jerusalem, retained control of the city until conquered by David several centuries after the conquest (2 Sam 5.6–7). The latter narrative implies the nonimplementation of this law. The ideal number *seven,* which signifies completion or totality (28.7; Gen 1; the plague list of Ps 78.44–51 and 105.28–36 in contrast to Ex 7–12), suggests that the enumeration may be artificial. **2:** This

tions before you—the Hittites, the Girga-
shites, the Amorites, the Canaanites, the
Perizzites, the Hivites, and the Jebusites,
seven nations mightier and more numerous
than you— 2 and when the LORD your God
gives them over to you and you defeat
them, then you must utterly destroy them.
Make no covenant with them and show
them no mercy. 3 Do not intermarry with
them, giving your daughters to their sons or
taking their daughters for your sons, 4 for
that would turn away your children from
following me, to serve other gods. Then
the anger of the LORD would be kindled
against you, and he would destroy you
quickly. 5 But this is how you must deal
with them: break down their altars, smash
their pillars, hew down their sacred poles,[a]
and burn their idols with fire. 6 For you are
a people holy to the LORD your God; the
LORD your God has chosen you out of all
the peoples on earth to be his people, his
treasured possession.
7 It was not because you were more nu-
merous than any other people that the
LORD set his heart on you and chose you—
for you were the fewest of all peoples. 8 It
was because the LORD loved you and kept
the oath that he swore to your ancestors,
that the LORD has brought you out with a
mighty hand, and redeemed you from the
house of slavery, from the hand of Pharaoh
king of Egypt. 9 Know therefore that the
LORD your God is God, the faithful God
who maintains covenant loyalty with those
who love him and keep his command-

a Heb *Asherim*

requirement for destruction is anomalous: Earlier sources contemplate only expulsion (Ex 23.23–33; cf. 34.11). The definition and requirements of the "ban" vary considerably throughout the Bible: total destruction of people and property (here; 13.15–17; 20.16–17; 1 Sam 15.3); sparing of property (2.34–35; 3.6–7); sparing of women, children, and property (20.10–14). Finally, other narratives more realistically speak of the failure of conquest except in limited areas and the use of conquered populations for labor (Josh 15–17; Judg 1; 3.1–6). These factors suggest that the law of the ban is an anachronistic literary formulation. It first arose centuries after the settlement; it was never implemented because there was no population extant against whom it could be implemented. Its polemic is directed at internal issues of religious purity in sixth-century Judah. Often the authors of Deuteronomy stigmatize as "Canaanite" older forms of Israelite religion that they no longer accept (see v. 5n.; 16.22n.; 18.9–14n.). *Utterly destroy,* or "place under the ban," or "devote." That which is "devoted" is set aside for divine use and denied to humans. The war of conquest, as a holy war, should not be one where the individual profits through plunder (see 12.29–31n.; 13.15n.; 20.1–20n.; Josh 7). The law addresses apostasy as opposed to ethnicity; it is directed against apostate Israelites in 8.20; 13.15–17. **3:** This prohibition against intermarriage does not fit easily after v. 2, suggesting several layers of editing. It is also inconsistent with 21.10–14, which seems more likely to reflect the original policy. **5:** See Ex 34.13. *Pillars,* stone monuments that marked places where God appeared and were thus originally legitimate in worship (Gen 35.14; Ex 24.4; Hos 3.4). Only subsequently were they prohibited as alien (Ex 23.24; 34.13; Lev 26.1; Deut 12.3; 16.22; 2 Kings 18.4). *Sacred poles,* or, with text note *a, Asherim.* The singular, "Asherah," preserves the name of an important Canaanite goddess (1 Kings 18.19) known from Ugarit; here the word designates merely the wooden pole, tree, or image that represented her (16.21; Judg 6.25–26,28). **6–16:** The meaning of Israel's covenantal relationship to God. **6:** *For* suggests that the verse (also 14.2) originally continued v. 3, since it provides the rationale for total separation from the Canaanites, not for the destruction of their cult sites. This verse summarizes Deuteronomy's view of Israel's relation to God. *Holy,* lit. "set aside as separate," as is clear here. *Chosen,* the precondition of Israel's elected status. *His treasured possession* (14.2; 26.18; Ex 19.5; Ps 135.4; Mal 3.17), designating Israel as the exclusive property of God; cf. 4.20n., where a different Heb word is used. Just as the monarch is entitled to private "treasure" not in the public domain (1 Chr 29.3), so does God single Israel out for a special relationship. **9–11:** A sermon on the second commandment that radically revises its meaning. The reuse of key phrases and inversion of the order of punishment and blessing in 5.9–10 mark the citation. **9:** *Covenant loyalty,* NRSV translates the same word as "steadfast love" at 5.10 (see note). **10:** *In their own person,* individually or personally.

ments, to a thousand generations, 10and
who repays in their own person those who
reject him. He does not delay but repays
in their own person those who reject him.
11Therefore, observe diligently the com-
mandment—the statutes and the ordi-
nances—that I am commanding you today.
12 If you heed these ordinances, by dili-
gently observing them, the LORD your God
will maintain with you the covenant loyalty
that he swore to your ancestors; 13he will
love you, bless you, and multiply you; he
will bless the fruit of your womb and the
fruit of your ground, your grain and your
wine and your oil, the increase of your cat-
tle and the issue of your flock, in the land
that he swore to your ancestors to give you.
14You shall be the most blessed of peoples,
with neither sterility nor barrenness among
you or your livestock. 15The LORD will
turn away from you every illness; all the
dread diseases of Egypt that you experi-
enced, he will not inflict on you, but he will
lay them on all who hate you. 16You shall
devour all the peoples that the LORD your
God is giving over to you, showing them no
pity; you shall not serve their gods, for that
would be a snare to you.
17 If you say to yourself, "These nations
are more numerous than I; how can I dis-
possess them?" 18do not be afraid of them.
Just remember what the LORD your God
did to Pharaoh and to all Egypt, 19the great
trials that your eyes saw, the signs and
wonders, the mighty hand and the out-
stretched arm by which the LORD your God
brought you out. The LORD your God will
do the same to all the peoples of whom you
are afraid. 20Moreover, the LORD your
God will send the pestilence[a] against them,
until even the survivors and the fugitives
are destroyed. 21Have no dread of them,
for the LORD your God, who is present
with you, is a great and awesome God.
22The LORD your God will clear away
these nations before you little by little; you
will not be able to make a quick end of
them, otherwise the wild animals would
become too numerous for you. 23But the
LORD your God will give them over to you,
and throw them into great panic, until they
are destroyed. 24He will hand their kings
over to you and you shall blot out their
name from under heaven; no one will be
able to stand against you, until you have
destroyed them. 25The images of their gods
you shall burn with fire. Do not covet the
silver or the gold that is on them and take
it for yourself, because you could be en-
snared by it; for it is abhorrent to the LORD
your God. 26Do not bring an abhorrent
thing into your house, or you will be set
apart for destruction like it. You must ut-
terly detest and abhor it, for it is set apart
for destruction.

8 This entire commandment that I com-
mand you today you must diligently
observe, so that you may live and increase,
and go in and occupy the land that the
LORD promised on oath to your ancestors.

a Or *hornets*: Meaning of Heb uncertain

The repetition of the phrase, bracketing the key idea that God *does not delay,* highlights the rejection of vicarious punishment (5.9n.; Ex 34.7). Instead, the sermon argues for individual retribution, as in criminal law (24.16), while deleting any reference to the transmission of punishment across generations. **12–14:** The blessings of fertility do not come from the nature gods of Canaan but from Israel's God (see Hos 2). Natural fertility is here made contingent upon obedience to the covenant. **13:** *Increase . . . issue* (28.4,18,51), originally two Ugaritic fertility deities; the second, "Astarte," is named at 1 Kings 11.5. **15:** Cf. Ex 15.26. **17–26:** Israel need not fear nations more powerful than it since, according to the idea of the holy war, God "is present with you" in battle (v. 21; 6.15; cf. 20.1–4). These verses echo ideas found in Ex 23.20–33. **20:** *Pestilence,* see Ex 23.27–28n.; Josh 24.12. **22:** Abbreviating Ex 23.29–30; contrast 9.3.

8.1–20: The temptation to pride and self-sufficiency in the land. Moses warns the people that success in Canaan will tempt them to forget the wilderness lesson of complete dependence upon God. **1–10:** An appeal to Israel's memory: In the wilderness God sustained the people daily (Ex 12.37–17.16; Num 11–14). **3:** *Manna,* see Ex 16; Num 11.7–8. **5:** Suffering is here interpreted as discipline, as in a parent's

2 Remember the long way that the LORD
your God has led you these forty years in
the wilderness, in order to humble you,
testing you to know what was in your
heart, whether or not you would keep his
commandments. 3 He humbled you by let-
ting you hunger, then by feeding you with
manna, with which neither you nor your
ancestors were acquainted, in order to
make you understand that one does not live
by bread alone, but by every word that
comes from the mouth of the LORD.[a] 4 The
clothes on your back did not wear out and
your feet did not swell these forty years.
5 Know then in your heart that as a parent
disciplines a child so the LORD your God
disciplines you. 6 Therefore keep the com-
mandments of the LORD your God, by
walking in his ways and by fearing him.
7 For the LORD your God is bringing you
into a good land, a land with flowing
streams, with springs and underground wa-
ters welling up in valleys and hills, 8 a land
of wheat and barley, of vines and fig trees
and pomegranates, a land of olive trees and
honey, 9 a land where you may eat bread
without scarcity, where you will lack noth-
ing, a land whose stones are iron and from
whose hills you may mine copper. 10 You
shall eat your fill and bless the LORD your
God for the good land that he has given
you.

11 Take care that you do not forget the
LORD your God, by failing to keep his com-
mandments, his ordinances, and his stat-
utes, which I am commanding you today.
12 When you have eaten your fill and have
built fine houses and live in them, 13 and
when your herds and flocks have multi-
plied, and your silver and gold is multi-
plied, and all that you have is multiplied,
14 then do not exalt yourself, forgetting the
LORD your God, who brought you out of
the land of Egypt, out of the house of slav-
ery, 15 who led you through the great and
terrible wilderness, an arid wasteland with
poisonous[b] snakes and scorpions. He
made water flow for you from flint rock,
16 and fed you in the wilderness with man-
na that your ancestors did not know, to
humble you and to test you, and in the end
to do you good. 17 Do not say to yourself,
"My power and the might of my own hand
have gotten me this wealth." 18 But remem-
ber the LORD your God, for it is he who
gives you power to get wealth, so that he
may confirm his covenant that he swore to
your ancestors, as he is doing today. 19 If
you do forget the LORD your God and fol-
low other gods to serve and worship them,
I solemnly warn you today that you shall
surely perish. 20 Like the nations that the
LORD is destroying before you, so shall you
perish, because you would not obey the
voice of the LORD your God.

9 Hear, O Israel! You are about to cross
the Jordan today, to go in and dispos-
sess nations larger and mightier than you,
great cities, fortified to the heavens, 2 a

a Or *by anything that the* LORD *decrees* *b* Or *fiery;* Heb *seraph*

correction of a child (Hos 11); this metaphor reflects the influence of wisdom literature (see Prov 3.11–12; cf. 1.13n.; 4.2n.; 4.5–8n.; 4.10n.; 6.4n.; 11.2).

8.11–20: The peril of prosperity. 11: A bold equation between *the* LORD and the legal corpus (*his commandments . . . ordinances . . . statutes . . . today*). Disobedience of Deuteronomy's laws becomes tantamount to forgetting God and transgressing the first commandment (see v. 19n.). **15:** *Poisonous snakes,* Num 21.6–9. *Water . . . from flint rock,* Ex 17.1–7; Num 20.2–13; Ps 114.8. **16:** *Manna,* see v. 3n. **19:** *Other gods . . . serve . . . worship,* citing the first and second commandments (5.7,9). *Worship,* translated "bow down to" at 5.9. **20:** *Like the nations,* here Israel is itself placed under the ban if it commits apostasy (see 7.1–26n.). *Destroying . . . perish,* in Hebrew, the same word is used to underscore the precise "measure for measure" nature of the punishment. Israel's election (7.6n.) grants no exemption from upholding the law. Rightful habitation in the promised land, like its fertility (7.12–14n.), depends upon covenantal obedience, not ethnic identity (7.2n.).

9.1–10.11: The already broken and renewed covenant. God does not give the land to the people as a reward for righteousness, for in the wilderness they acted rebelliously. **9.2:** See Num 13.22, 33n. **4–5:**

strong and tall people, the offspring of the
Anakim, whom you know. You have heard
it said of them, "Who can stand up to
the Anakim?" 3Know then today that the
LORD your God is the one who crosses over
before you as a devouring fire; he will de-
feat them and subdue them before you, so
that you may dispossess and destroy them
quickly, as the LORD has promised you.
4 When the LORD your God thrusts
them out before you, do not say to yourself,
"It is because of my righteousness that the
LORD has brought me in to occupy this
land"; it is rather because of the wickedness
of these nations that the LORD is dispos-
sessing them before you. 5It is not because
of your righteousness or the uprightness of
your heart that you are going in to occupy
their land; but because of the wickedness of
these nations the LORD your God is dispos-
sessing them before you, in order to fulfill
the promise that the LORD made on oath to
your ancestors, to Abraham, to Isaac, and
to Jacob.
6 Know, then, that the LORD your God
is not giving you this good land to occupy
because of your righteousness; for you are
a stubborn people. 7Remember and do not
forget how you provoked the LORD your
God to wrath in the wilderness; you have
been rebellious against the LORD from the
day you came out of the land of Egypt until
you came to this place.
8 Even at Horeb you provoked the
LORD to wrath, and the LORD was so angry
with you that he was ready to destroy you.
9When I went up the mountain to receive
the stone tablets, the tablets of the covenant
that the LORD made with you, I remained
on the mountain forty days and forty
nights; I neither ate bread nor drank water.
10And the LORD gave me the two stone tab-
lets written with the finger of God; on them
were all the words that the LORD had spo-
ken to you at the mountain out of the fire
on the day of the assembly. 11At the end of
forty days and forty nights the LORD gave
me the two stone tablets, the tablets of the
covenant. 12Then the LORD said to me,
"Get up, go down quickly from here, for
your people whom you have brought from
Egypt have acted corruptly. They have been
quick to turn from the way that I com-
manded them; they have cast an image for
themselves." 13Furthermore the LORD said
to me, "I have seen that this people is in-
deed a stubborn people. 14Let me alone
that I may destroy them and blot out their
name from under heaven; and I will make
of you a nation mightier and more numer-
ous than they."
15 So I turned and went down from the
mountain, while the mountain was ablaze;
the two tablets of the covenant were in my
two hands. 16Then I saw that you had in-
deed sinned against the LORD your God, by
casting for yourselves an image of a calf;
you had been quick to turn from the way
that the LORD had commanded you. 17So I
took hold of the two tablets and flung them
from my two hands, smashing them before
your eyes. 18Then I lay prostrate before
the LORD as before, forty days and forty
nights; I neither ate bread nor drank water,
because of all the sin you had committed,
provoking the LORD by doing what was
evil in his sight. 19For I was afraid that the
anger that the LORD bore against you was
so fierce that he would destroy you. But the
LORD listened to me that time also. 20The
LORD was so angry with Aaron that he was
ready to destroy him, but I interceded also
on behalf of Aaron at that same time.
21Then I took the sinful thing you had
made, the calf, and burned it with fire and
crushed it, grinding it thoroughly, until it
was reduced to dust; and I threw the dust of
it into the stream that runs down the moun-
tain.
22 At Taberah also, and at Massah, and

Victory will be given in the holy war because (negatively) Canaan has been irrevocably corrupted by the actions of its present occupants and because (positively) of God's enduring commitment to the promises made to Israel's ancestors. **6–24:** The historical record shows that Israel has been rebellious since the Exodus (Ezek 20.5–8; contrast Hos 2.14–20; Jer 2.2–3). **8–10:** Ex 24.12–18; 31.18. **11–21:** Ex 32, revised. **17:** *Smashing them,* not simple anger but a legal ceremony to confirm breach of treaty. **22:** Num

at Kibroth-hattaavah, you provoked the
LORD to wrath. 23 And when the LORD sent
you from Kadesh-barnea, saying, “Go up
and occupy the land that I have given you,”
you rebelled against the command of the
LORD your God, neither trusting him nor
obeying him. 24 You have been rebellious
against the LORD as long as he has[a] known
you.

25 Throughout the forty days and forty
nights that I lay prostrate before the LORD
when the LORD intended to destroy you,
26 I prayed to the LORD and said, “Lord
GOD, do not destroy the people who are
your very own possession, whom you re-
deemed in your greatness, whom you
brought out of Egypt with a mighty hand.
27 Remember your servants, Abraham,
Isaac, and Jacob; pay no attention to the
stubbornness of this people, their wicked-
ness and their sin, 28 otherwise the land
from which you have brought us might say,
‘Because the LORD was not able to bring
them into the land that he promised them,
and because he hated them, he has brought
them out to let them die in the wilderness.’
29 For they are the people of your very own
possession, whom you brought out by your
great power and by your outstretched
arm.”

10 At that time the LORD said to me,
“Carve out two tablets of stone like
the former ones, and come up to me on the
mountain, and make an ark of wood. 2 I
will write on the tablets the words that
were on the former tablets, which you
smashed, and you shall put them in the
ark.” 3 So I made an ark of acacia wood,
cut two tablets of stone like the former
ones, and went up the mountain with the
two tablets in my hand. 4 Then he wrote on
the tablets the same words as before, the
ten commandments[b] that the LORD had
spoken to you on the mountain out of the
fire on the day of the assembly; and the
LORD gave them to me. 5 So I turned and
came down from the mountain, and put the
tablets in the ark that I had made; and there
they are, as the LORD commanded me.

6 (The Israelites journeyed from
Beeroth-bene-jaakan[c] to Moserah. There
Aaron died, and there he was buried; his
son Eleazar succeeded him as priest. 7 From
there they journeyed to Gudgodah, and
from Gudgodah to Jotbathah, a land with
flowing streams. 8 At that time the LORD set
apart the tribe of Levi to carry the ark of
the covenant of the LORD, to stand before
the LORD to minister to him, and to bless in
his name, to this day. 9 Therefore Levi has
no allotment or inheritance with his kin-
dred; the LORD is his inheritance, as the
LORD your God promised him.)

10 I stayed on the mountain forty days
and forty nights, as I had done the first
time. And once again the LORD listened to
me. The LORD was unwilling to destroy
you. 11 The LORD said to me, “Get up, go
on your journey at the head of the people,
that they may go in and occupy the land
that I swore to their ancestors to give
them.”

12 So now, O Israel, what does the

a Sam Gk: MT *I have* *b* Heb *the ten words*
c Or *the wells of the Bene-jaakan*

11.1–3; Ex 17.1–7; Num 11.31–34. **23:** Num 13–14. **25–29:** A paraphrase of Ex 32.11–14. Deuteronomy portrays Moses as the ideal prophet (34.10–12); he intercedes for the people and vicariously suffers for them (1.37n.; cf. Isa 53).

10.1–11: The second ascent of the mountain (cf. Ex 34.1–4,27–28). **1–3:** These verses reflect a tradition that Moses made the ark and put the stone tablets in it (1 Kings 8.9). **6–9:** An editorial insertion; vv. 6–7 seem to quote a wilderness itinerary from the Priestly literature (cf. Num 33.30–38). **6:** Num 20.22–29. **8:** Ex 32.25–29. The Levites' role is to bear the ark (Num 4.4–15), to *minister,* i.e., conduct the sacrificial services (Num 18), and to *bless* the people (Num 6.22–27). **9:** See 12.12n.; 18.2n.

10.12–11.32: Obedience as the condition for prosperity in the land. This section provides the climax and conclusion of the historical review found in 8.1–10.11. **10.12–13:** A striking transformation of the Decalogue. Earlier, breach of the first and second commandments, with their focus specifically on God, had been redefined and equated with “failing to keep his commandments . . . ordinances . . . and . . .

LORD your God require of you? Only to
fear the LORD your God, to walk in all his
ways, to love him, to serve the LORD your
God with all your heart and with all your
soul, 13 and to keep the commandments of
the LORD your God[a] and his decrees that
I am commanding you today, for your own
well-being. 14 Although heaven and the
heaven of heavens belong to the LORD your
God, the earth with all that is in it, 15 yet the
LORD set his heart in love on your ances-
tors alone and chose you, their descendants
after them, out of all the peoples, as it is
today. 16 Circumcise, then, the foreskin of
your heart, and do not be stubborn any
longer. 17 For the LORD your God is God of
gods and Lord of lords, the great God,
mighty and awesome, who is not partial
and takes no bribe, 18 who executes justice
for the orphan and the widow, and who
loves the strangers, providing them food
and clothing. 19 You shall also love the
stranger, for you were strangers in the land
of Egypt. 20 You shall fear the LORD your
God; him alone you shall worship; to him
you shall hold fast, and by his name you
shall swear. 21 He is your praise; he is your
God, who has done for you these great and
awesome things that your own eyes have
seen. 22 Your ancestors went down to Egypt
seventy persons; and now the LORD your
God has made you as numerous as the stars
in heaven.

11 You shall love the LORD your God,
therefore, and keep his charge, his
decrees, his ordinances, and his command-
ments always. 2 Remember today that it
was not your children (who have not
known or seen the discipline of the LORD
your God), but it is you who must ac-
knowledge his greatness, his mighty hand
and his outstretched arm, 3 his signs and his
deeds that he did in Egypt to Pharaoh, the
king of Egypt, and to all his land; 4 what he
did to the Egyptian army, to their horses
and chariots, how he made the water of the
Red Sea[b] flow over them as they pursued
you, so that the LORD has destroyed them
to this day; 5 what he did to you in the wil-
derness, until you came to this place; 6 and
what he did to Dathan and Abiram, sons of

a Q Ms Gk Syr: MT lacks *your God* *b* Or *Sea of Reeds*

statutes" (8.11n.). Now obedience to God is similarly redefined as compliance with the fixed *commandments . . . and . . . decrees* (v. 13) of Deuteronomy, i.e., the laws of chs 12–26 (see 28.15,45). For a similar catechism that does not extend the traditional focus upon God to law, see Mic 6.8. *And to keep* (lit. "by keeping") the precise antithesis of 8.11. The sequence *love . . . keep . . . commandments* cites 5.10. **16:** *Circumcise . . . the . . . heart* means to open oneself to God (Lev 26.41); no distinction is intended between mind, will, and emotion. The metaphorical formulation, which challenges any attempt to reduce Deuteronomy to narrow "legalism," corresponds to prophetic ideals (cf. Jer 4.4; 31.33). **17–18:** Integrity in the administration of court justice (v. 17; cf. 1.17; 16.19) and protection of the marginalized (v. 18) are given a theological foundation, making the remarkable argument that human social ethics amounts to "imitatio dei." Responsibility for ensuring justice in court and for defending the marginalized were conventional royal prerogatives (*Laws of Hammurabi* prologue; Ps 72.4). Deuteronomy contemplates no such role for the monarch (17.14–20n.). Instead, here it is God who protects the rights of the marginalized, entering history to do so (cf. Ex 3.7–10; Phil 2.6–7). Love of neighbor thus originates in divine action. **18–19:** *Strangers . . . stranger,* better, the legal term "resident alien" in both cases. Just as justice must be rendered to Israelite and alien alike (see 1.16n.), so must "love" reach across national or ethnic lines (cf. Lev 19.33–34). **18:** *Loves . . . providing,* note love's concrete expression in action and service (see 5.10n.; 6.5n.). **19:** *For you were,* see Ex 22.21; 23.9. **22:** *Seventy persons* (Gen 46.27; Ex 1.5) comes first in the Hebrew, emphasizing Israel's miraculous transformation into a nation. *Stars in heaven,* see 1.10n.

11.1–32: Loyalty to the covenant provides the condition for life in Canaan. The punishments and rewards noted in this section are predominantly addressed to a plural "you," stressing communal rather than individual responsibility. **2:** The frequent word *today* in Deuteronomy emphasizes the contemporaneity of the covenant (see 5.3n.). *Discipline,* see 8.5n. **4:** See Ex 14. **6:** The address is based upon the early tradition of the revolt of Dathan and Abiram (Num 16). There is no mention of Korah's rebellion

Eliab son of Reuben, how in the midst of all
Israel the earth opened its mouth and swal-
lowed them up, along with their house-
holds, their tents, and every living being in
their company; 7 for it is your own eyes that
have seen every great deed that the LORD
did.
8 Keep, then, this entire commandment
that I am commanding you today, so that
you may have strength to go in and occupy
the land that you are crossing over to occu-
py, 9 and so that you may live long in the
land that the LORD swore to your ancestors
to give them and to their descendants, a
land flowing with milk and honey. 10 For
the land that you are about to enter to oc-
cupy is not like the land of Egypt, from
which you have come, where you sow your
seed and irrigate by foot like a vegetable
garden. 11 But the land that you are cross-
ing over to occupy is a land of hills and
valleys, watered by rain from the sky, 12 a
land that the LORD your God looks after.
The eyes of the LORD your God are always
on it, from the beginning of the year to the
end of the year.
13 If you will only heed his every com-
mandment[a] that I am commanding you to-
day—loving the LORD your God, and serv-
ing him with all your heart and with all
your soul— 14 then he[b] will give the rain
for your land in its season, the early rain
and the later rain, and you will gather in
your grain, your wine, and your oil; 15 and
he[b] will give grass in your fields for your
livestock, and you will eat your fill. 16 Take
care, or you will be seduced into turning
away, serving other gods and worshiping
them, 17 for then the anger of the LORD will
be kindled against you and he will shut up
the heavens, so that there will be no rain
and the land will yield no fruit; then you
will perish quickly off the good land that
the LORD is giving you.
18 You shall put these words of mine in
your heart and soul, and you shall bind
them as a sign on your hand, and fix them
as an emblem[c] on your forehead. 19 Teach
them to your children, talking about them
when you are at home and when you are
away, when you lie down and when you
rise. 20 Write them on the doorposts of your
house and on your gates, 21 so that your
days and the days of your children may be
multiplied in the land that the LORD swore
to your ancestors to give them, as long as
the heavens are above the earth.
22 If you will diligently observe this en-
tire commandment that I am commanding
you, loving the LORD your God, walking
in all his ways, and holding fast to him,
23 then the LORD will drive out all these
nations before you, and you will dispossess
nations larger and mightier than your-
selves. 24 Every place on which you set foot
shall be yours; your territory shall extend
from the wilderness to the Lebanon and
from the River, the river Euphrates, to the
Western Sea. 25 No one will be able to stand
against you; the LORD your God will put
the fear and dread of you on all the land on
which you set foot, as he promised you.
26 See, I am setting before you today a
blessing and a curse: 27 the blessing, if you
obey the commandments of the LORD your
God that I am commanding you today;
28 and the curse, if you do not obey the

a Compare Gk: Heb *my commandments* *b* Sam Gk Vg: MT *I* *c* Or *as a frontlet*

(Num 16.3–11), which was very likely added by the Priestly school after this abstract was made. **10–12:** The Nile valley must be irrigated through human effort; Canaan depends upon seasonal rainfall. The difference is mentioned to stress Israel's dependence upon God, who gives and withholds rain (Am 4.7–8), as well as the fundamental sanctity of the land of Israel. **14:** The *early rain* comes at the end of the summer drought (October-November); the *later rain* comes in the spring (March-April). **16–17:** See 7.12–14n. **18–21:** See 6.6–9. **24:** *Every place . . . yours,* a legal ritual that effected transfer of title by pacing out the perimeter of the territory (see 25.9n.; Gen 13.17). The territory is described in terms of the ideal limits of David's empire (see 1.7n.). *The Western Sea,* the Mediterranean. **26–32:** The two ways (see ch 28; 30.15–20). **26:** *Curse,* the sanctions for violating a treaty, which a vassal assumes in a sworn oath (see 28.15–68). **29–30:** These verses represent an editorial intrusion. Previously, *blessing . . . and the curse*

commandments of the LORD your God, but
turn from the way that I am commanding
you today, to follow other gods that you
have not known.
29 When the LORD your God has
brought you into the land that you are en-
tering to occupy, you shall set the blessing
on Mount Gerizim and the curse on Mount
Ebal. 30 As you know, they are beyond the
Jordan, some distance to the west, in the
land of the Canaanites who live in the Ara-
bah, opposite Gilgal, beside the oak[a] of
Moreh.
31 When you cross the Jordan to go in
to occupy the land that the LORD your God
is giving you, and when you occupy it and
live in it, 32 you must diligently observe all
the statutes and ordinances that I am set-
ting before you today.

12 These are the statutes and ordi-
nances that you must diligently ob-
serve in the land that the LORD, the God of
your ancestors, has given you to occupy all
the days that you live on the earth.
2 You must demolish completely all the
places where the nations whom you are
about to dispossess served their gods, on
the mountain heights, on the hills, and un-
der every leafy tree. 3 Break down their al-
tars, smash their pillars, burn their sacred
poles[b] with fire, and hew down the idols of
their gods, and thus blot out their name
from their places. 4 You shall not worship
the LORD your God in such ways. 5 But you
shall seek the place that the LORD your
God will choose out of all your tribes as his
habitation to put his name there. You shall
go there, 6 bringing there your burnt offer-
ings and your sacrifices, your tithes and
your donations, your votive gifts, your free-
will offerings, and the firstlings of your
herds and flocks. 7 And you shall eat there
in the presence of the LORD your God, you
and your households together, rejoicing in
all the undertakings in which the LORD
your God has blessed you.

a Gk Syr: Compare Gen 12.6; Heb *oaks* or *terebinths*
b Heb *Asherim*

identify the benefits of covenantal obedience and the sanctions for breach of covenant (vv. 26–28; 28.2,15). That theme is the expected climax of this chapter. Here they are restricted to a series of positive and negative sayings shouted from mounts *Gerizim and . . . Ebal,* in anticipation of ch 27. *Gerizim,* on the south, and *Ebal,* on the north, flank the pass guarded by the city of Shechem in the central hill country. This geographic restriction fits poorly in a chapter otherwise directed to the entire land (vv. 22–25,31–32). **30:** *The oak of Moreh,* at Shechem (see Gen 12.6). **31–32:** Transition to the legal corpus. **32:** *Diligently observe . . . statutes and ordinances,* cited in reverse order at 12.1 to effect the transition from the literary frame of Deuteronomy (chs 1–11) into the laws (chs 12–26).

12.1–26.15: The legal corpus, Deuteronomy's transformation of Israelite religion.

12.1–32: Centralization of worship. Centralization and purification of worship, restriction to a single sanctuary, and removal of foreign influence distinguish Deuteronomy. Four paragraphs (vv. 2–7,8–12,13–19,20–28) command centralization; a fifth (vv. 29–31) warns against alien worship. **1:** An editorial superscription. *Earth,* more accurately, "land (of Israel)." **2–7:** Israel must reject the Canaanite precedent of multiple sanctuaries. **2:** *You,* The chapter alternates between plural (vv. 1–12) and singular (vv. 13–31), which, combined with six repetitions of the centralization command (vv. 5,11,14,18,21,26), suggests a long compositional history. *Demolish,* see Ex 23.23–24; 34.11–14; Deut 7.5. *Heights . . . leafy tree,* Canaanite sanctuaries, "high places" (1 Kings 3.2; 2 Kings 16.4), but used to worship God as well (1 Kings 3.4). **3:** See 7.5n. **5:** *The place that the LORD . . . will choose,* Jerusalem played no role in Israel's history until the period of David. Consequently the city cannot be named explicitly without undermining the literary form of Deuteronomy as a Mosaic address. *As his habitation,* better, "to establish it" (the divine name), indicating possession and special relationship. *Put his name there,* Deuteronomy rejects the idea that a nation's God would inhabit the Temple (contrast 1 Kings 8.12–13). **6:** *Burnt offerings,* in which all of the flesh was burnt on the altar (v. 27; Lev 1.3–17). *Sacrifices,* other offerings where portions of the animal were assigned to the priests or shared by worshipers (v. 27; 18.1–3; Lev 3; 7.29–36). **8–12:** That worship at multiple sanctuaries was to have limited

8 You shall not act as we are acting here
today, all of us according to our own de-
sires, 9 for you have not yet come into the
rest and the possession that the LORD your
God is giving you. 10 When you cross over
the Jordan and live in the land that the
LORD your God is allotting to you, and
when he gives you rest from your enemies
all around so that you live in safety, 11 then
you shall bring everything that I command
you to the place that the LORD your God
will choose as a dwelling for his name: your
burnt offerings and your sacrifices, your
tithes and your donations, and all your
choice votive gifts that you vow to the
LORD. 12 And you shall rejoice before the
LORD your God, you together with your
sons and your daughters, your male and
female slaves, and the Levites who reside in
your towns (since they have no allotment
or inheritance with you).

13 Take care that you do not offer your
burnt offerings at any place you happen to
see. 14 But only at the place that the LORD
will choose in one of your tribes—there
you shall offer your burnt offerings and
there you shall do everything I command
you.

15 Yet whenever you desire you may
slaughter and eat meat within any of your
towns, according to the blessing that the
LORD your God has given you; the unclean
and the clean may eat of it, as they would
of gazelle or deer. 16 The blood, however,
you must not eat; you shall pour it out on
the ground like water. 17 Nor may you eat
within your towns the tithe of your grain,
your wine, and your oil, the firstlings of
your herds and your flocks, any of your
votive gifts that you vow, your freewill
offerings, or your donations; 18 these you
shall eat in the presence of the LORD your
God at the place that the LORD your God
will choose, you together with your son
and your daughter, your male and female
slaves, and the Levites resident in your
towns, rejoicing in the presence of the
LORD your God in all your undertakings.
19 Take care that you do not neglect the
Levite as long as you live in your land.

20 When the LORD your God enlarges
your territory, as he has promised you, and

temporal validity differs from Ex 20.24. **8:** *Our own desires,* a negative judgment, as in Judg 17.6; 21.25. **9–10:** *Rest and . . . possession,* territorial security (Josh 21.44) would allow centralization. This was fulfilled with David's conquest of Jerusalem, which allowed the construction of the Temple (2 Sam 7.1,11; 1 Kings 8.56). **12:** Since *the Levites* were not assigned land (see Josh 13.14; cf. Ezek 44.28), they had to depend upon voluntary offerings (see 10.9; 18.1–2). **13–19:** The earliest of the chapter's five paragraphs is concentrically arranged in a chiasm to structure diverse material in an ABC:C′B′A′ pattern.

(13) *Take care that* A
(14) *but only* (Heb "ki 'im") + centralization B
(15) *yet* ("raq") + secular slaughter C
(16) *however* ("raq") + secular slaughter C′
(18) *rather* ("ki 'im" [untranslated in NRSV]) + centralization B′
(19) *Take care that* A′

13–16: Two important, revolutionary distinctions: First, between sacrificial worship at random sites, *any place,* rejected as illegitimate, and legitimate sacrifice performed at a single sanctuary, *the place that the LORD will choose.* This contrasts with previous norms, when altars were common throughout the land (Gen 12.7; 35.1–7; 1 Sam 3.1; 7.17; 1 Kings 18.20–46). Second, between ritual sacrifice and secular slaughter of domestic animals for food. Prior to Deuteronomy, all slaughter, even for food, was sacrificial and took place at an altar. With altars throughout the land, that rule imposed no burden upon Israelites. The prohibition of all local altars, however, created a real difficulty for those without easy access to the central sanctuary. The permission granted here for local, secular slaughter answers that need. By analogy to the rules for hunting wild game (*gazelle or deer*), domestic animals may be slaughtered throughout the land, on condition that their blood is poured out *on the ground like water* (cf. Lev 17.13). Blood symbolizes "life" (v. 23; 15.23; Gen 9.4–5; Lev 17.14; 19.26). **17:** *Tithe,* see 14.22–29n. **20–28:** Permission for secular slaughter is now justified by the expansion of Israel's boundaries. **30:** Elsewhere, the corruption of Israelite religion

you say, "I am going to eat some meat,"
because you wish to eat meat, you may eat
meat whenever you have the desire. 21 If
the place where the LORD your God will
choose to put his name is too far from you,
and you slaughter as I have commanded
you any of your herd or flock that the
LORD has given you, then you may eat
within your towns whenever you desire.
22 Indeed, just as gazelle or deer is eaten, so
you may eat it; the unclean and the clean
alike may eat it. 23 Only be sure that you do
not eat the blood; for the blood is the life,
and you shall not eat the life with the meat.
24 Do not eat it; you shall pour it out on the
ground like water. 25 Do not eat it, so that
all may go well with you and your children
after you, because you do what is right in
the sight of the LORD. 26 But the sacred do-
nations that are due from you, and your
votive gifts, you shall bring to the place that
the LORD will choose. 27 You shall present
your burnt offerings, both the meat and the
blood, on the altar of the LORD your God;
the blood of your other sacrifices shall be
poured out beside[a] the altar of the LORD
your God, but the meat you may eat.

28 Be careful to obey all these words
that I command you today,[b] so that it may
go well with you and with your children
after you forever, because you will be doing
what is good and right in the sight of the
LORD your God.

29 When the LORD your God has cut off
before you the nations whom you are about
to enter to dispossess them, when you have
dispossessed them and live in their land,
30 take care that you are not snared into
imitating them, after they have been de-
stroyed before you: do not inquire concern-
ing their gods, saying, "How did these na-
tions worship their gods? I also want to do
the same." 31 You must not do the same for
the LORD your God, because every abhor-
rent thing that the LORD hates they have
done for their gods. They would even burn
their sons and their daughters in the fire to
their gods. 32 [c] You must diligently observe
everything that I command you; do not add
to it or take anything from it.

13 [d]If prophets or those who divine
by dreams appear among you and
promise you omens or portents, 2 and the
omens or the portents declared by them

a Or *on* *b* Gk Sam Syr: MT lacks *today*
c Ch 13.1 in Heb *d* Ch 13.2 in Heb

is presented as resulting from the attractions of marital contract (7.1–5,25) or political treaty (Ex 23.33; 34.12). **31:** *Burn their sons and their daughters,* the Canaanites are accused of child sacrifice (see 2 Kings 3.27; 23.10; Jer 19.5–6; ch 31), elsewhere associated with the deity Molech (Lev 18.21; 20.2–5). **32:** An exhortation to preserve the law unchanged. *Diligently observe,* the same idiom found at 12.1 (also 11.32) frames the unit with an inclusio. *Do not add to it or take anything from it,* an ancient Near Eastern scribal formula often included in the epilogue of treaties, inscriptions, or law collections to protect them from being defaced, altered, or written over (see 4.2n.).

13.1–18: Unconditional loyalty to God. Various hypothetical situations involving conflict of covenant loyalty to God, treated analogously to ancient Near Eastern suzerainty treaties, which stipulated absolute loyalty. **1–5:** A prophet or diviner invites listeners to commit idolatry. While Deuteronomy presents Moses as the founder of Israelite prophecy, establishing both its standard (18.15–22) and its pinnacle (34.10–12), Deuteronomy nonetheless regulates prophecy, requiring the execution of the prophet who contravenes Deuteronomy's Torah (vv. 1–5; 18.19–22) and subordinating prophecy to covenantal law. No longer is the power to perform signs the test of a prophet's legitimacy (contrast v. 2 with 34.11–12; Ex 4.1–9,21; 1 Kings 18.20–40). The true prophet proclaims Torah (18.18). **1:** The religious stature of prophets makes it difficult to resist their incitement to commit apostasy. *Dreams,* the two sources of religious authority correspond to the nearly contemporary Neo-Assyrian *Vassal Treaty of Esarhaddon* (672 BCE), which requires loyalty even in the face of conspiracy from "your brothers, your sons, your daughters, or from the mouth of a prophet, an ecstatic, or an inquirer of oracles" (§ 10). *Omens or portents* were used by legitimate prophets to authenticate their proclamations (34.11; Ex 4.1–9,21; 7.9; Judg 6.17). **5:** *Treason,* as betrayal of the divine suzerain. *Purge the evil from your midst,* a formula

take place, and they say, "Let us follow
other gods" (whom you have not known)
"and let us serve them," 3you must not
heed the words of those prophets or those
who divine by dreams; for the LORD your
God is testing you, to know whether you
indeed love the LORD your God with all
your heart and soul. 4The LORD your God
you shall follow, him alone you shall fear,
his commandments you shall keep, his
voice you shall obey, him you shall serve,
and to him you shall hold fast. 5But those
prophets or those who divine by dreams
shall be put to death for having spoken
treason against the LORD your God—who
brought you out of the land of Egypt and
redeemed you from the house of slavery—
to turn you from the way in which the
LORD your God commanded you to walk.
So you shall purge the evil from your midst.
6 If anyone secretly entices you—even if
it is your brother, your father's son or[a]
your mother's son, or your own son or
daughter, or the wife you embrace, or your
most intimate friend—saying, "Let us go
worship other gods," whom neither you
nor your ancestors have known, 7any of
the gods of the peoples that are around
you, whether near you or far away from
you, from one end of the earth to the other,
8you must not yield to or heed any such
persons. Show them no pity or compassion
and do not shield them. 9But you shall
surely kill them; your own hand shall be
first against them to execute them, and af-
terwards the hand of all the people. 10Stone
them to death for trying to turn you away
from the LORD your God, who brought
you out of the land of Egypt, out of the
house of slavery. 11Then all Israel shall
hear and be afraid, and never again do any
such wickedness.
12 If you hear it said about one of the
towns that the LORD your God is giving
you to live in, 13that scoundrels from
among you have gone out and led the in-
habitants of the town astray, saying, "Let
us go and worship other gods," whom you
have not known, 14then you shall inquire
and make a thorough investigation. If the
charge is established that such an abhorrent
thing has been done among you, 15you
shall put the inhabitants of that town to the
sword, utterly destroying it and everything
in it—even putting its livestock to the
sword. 16All of its spoil you shall gather
into its public square; then burn the town
and all its spoil with fire, as a whole burnt
offering to the LORD your God. It shall re-
main a perpetual ruin, never to be rebuilt.
17Do not let anything devoted to destruc-
tion stick to your hand, so that the LORD
may turn from his fierce anger and show
you compassion, and in his compassion
multiply you, as he swore to your ances-
tors, 18if you obey the voice of the LORD
your God by keeping all his command-
ments that I am commanding you today,
doing what is right in the sight of the LORD
your God.

a Sam Gk Compare Tg: MT lacks *your father's son or*

emphasizing the obligation to eliminate particularly offensive religious transgressions (17.7,12; 19.19; 21.21; etc.). **6–11:** Conflict between family love, marriage, or friendship and covenantal fidelity (cf. Lk 14.26). **6:** *Secretly,* i.e., there are no witnesses. *Father's son,* this addition of the half-brother (see text note *b*) provides a poor reading. The Heb deliberately selects the most intimate of human relations in this verse; thus the full brother (*mother's son*). **9:** *But you shall surely kill them,* i.e., summary execution. The absence of witnesses and a trial conflicts with Deuteronomy's own requirements elsewhere (17.4,6; 19.15), but arises from the grave threat to the covenant (Ex 32.25–27; Num 25.6–9). **10:** *Stone,* the penalty carried out by the community for violations of its fundamental values or sources of authority: apostasy or treason (see 17.2–7; Lev 20.2; Josh 7.10–26; 1 Kings 21.8–14), blasphemy (Lev 24.13–23), defying parental authority (21.18–21; 22.20–21), and betraying marriage (22.23–24). Each is prohibited by the Decalogue (5.6,11,16,18). **13:** *Scoundrels,* lit. "sons of worthlessness," or "children of Belial" (KJV). **15–17:** The infidelity of the Israelite town requires that its entire population be placed under the same ban as that used for the Canaanites (7.1–6,25–26; 12.29–30; 20.16–18). **16:** Normally new occupants would rebuild cities after destruction right on top of the *ruin* (Heb "tel").

14 You are children of the LORD your
God. You must not lacerate your-
selves or shave your forelocks for the dead.
2 For you are a people holy to the LORD
your God; it is you the LORD has chosen
out of all the peoples on earth to be his
people, his treasured possession.
3 You shall not eat any abhorrent thing.
4 These are the animals you may eat: the ox,
the sheep, the goat, 5 the deer, the gazelle,
the roebuck, the wild goat, the ibex, the
antelope, and the mountain-sheep. 6 Any
animal that divides the hoof and has the
hoof cleft in two, and chews the cud,
among the animals, you may eat. 7 Yet of
those that chew the cud or have the hoof
cleft you shall not eat these: the camel, the
hare, and the rock badger, because they
chew the cud but do not divide the hoof;
they are unclean for you. 8 And the pig, be-
cause it divides the hoof but does not chew
the cud, is unclean for you. You shall not
eat their meat, and you shall not touch their
carcasses.
9 Of all that live in water you may eat
these: whatever has fins and scales you may
eat. 10 And whatever does not have fins and
scales you shall not eat; it is unclean for
you.
11 You may eat any clean birds. 12 But
these are the ones that you shall not eat: the
eagle, the vulture, the osprey, 13 the buz-
zard, the kite of any kind; 14 every raven of
any kind; 15 the ostrich, the nighthawk, the
sea gull, the hawk of any kind; 16 the little
owl and the great owl, the water hen 17 and
the desert owl,[a] the carrion vulture and the
cormorant, 18 the stork, the heron of any
kind; the hoopoe and the bat.[b] 19 And all
winged insects are unclean for you; they
shall not be eaten. 20 You may eat any clean
winged creature.
21 You shall not eat anything that dies
of itself; you may give it to aliens residing in
your towns for them to eat, or you may sell
it to a foreigner. For you are a people holy
to the LORD your God.
You shall not boil a kid in its mother's
milk.
22 Set apart a tithe of all the yield of
your seed that is brought in yearly from the
field. 23 In the presence of the LORD your

a Or *pelican* *b* Identification of several of the birds in verses 12-18 is uncertain

14.1–29: The obligations of holiness. 1–22: Special status entails special obligations, one of which is dietary. The affirmation of holiness (vv. 2,21) therefore frames the list of permitted and prohibited foods. **1:** *Children of the LORD,* the first of three metaphors to emphasize the special relation between God and Israel. The divine parent has special custody for the child (Ex 2.22–23; Hos 1.10) but, equally, special indignation at wrongdoing (32.5–6,19–20; Isa 1.2). *Lacerate . . . shave . . . dead,* laceration and head shaving, common mourning rituals, were associated with Canaanite customs and perhaps with ancestor worship (Lev 19.27–28; 1 Kings 18.28; Jer 16.6–7; 41.4–5; 47.5; Am 8.10). **2:** *Holy,* Israel must distinguish itself from other nations by observing the special requirements of the Torah. *Treasured possession,* see 7.6n. **3–21:** Deuteronomy's dietary restrictions abridge and revise the more detailed list of permitted and prohibited foods provided by the Priestly source (Lev 11.2–23). A binary classification system, permitted vs. forbidden, is systematically applied to each of the three basic divisions of species within creation (Gen 1.20–25; 9.2–3), which are grouped according to their habitat as creatures of the land (vv. 1–8), water (vv. 9–10), or air (vv. 11–20). Animals that do not satisfy the defining characteristics for their group are not to be eaten: the pig (v. 8) and shellfish (v. 10). The terms *unclean* (v. 8) and *clean* (v. 11) do not refer to hygiene. Ritually "impure" and "pure" convey the idea more clearly. Not all of the species mentioned can be identified. **21:** *Anything that dies of itself,* carrion (Ex 22.31) or any animal not slaughtered so that the blood can be drained (12.16,23–25). *Boil a kid,* Deuteronomy extends an older law specifically connected to the pilgrimage festival offerings (Ex 23.19; 34.26) into a general dietary rule. Some view it as directed against Canaanite religious rituals; others view it as concerned to prevent the abuse of animals. **22–29:** An annual *tithe* of ten percent of crops and livestock was a common tax or honorarium paid to a monarch (Gen 14.20; 28.22; 1 Sam 8.15,17). Here the rule signifies that Israel is God's steward, working but not owning the land. **23:** The standard rules of the tithe (Lev

God, in the place that he will choose as a
dwelling for his name, you shall eat the
tithe of your grain, your wine, and your oil,
as well as the firstlings of your herd and
flock, so that you may learn to fear the
LORD your God always. 24 But if, when the
LORD your God has blessed you, the dis-
tance is so great that you are unable to
transport it, because the place where the
LORD your God will choose to set his name
is too far away from you, 25 then you may
turn it into money. With the money secure
in hand, go to the place that the LORD your
God will choose; 26 spend the money for
whatever you wish—oxen, sheep, wine,
strong drink, or whatever you desire. And
you shall eat there in the presence of the
LORD your God, you and your household
rejoicing together. 27 As for the Levites resi-
dent in your towns, do not neglect them,
because they have no allotment or inheri-
tance with you.

28 Every third year you shall bring out
the full tithe of your produce for that year,
and store it within your towns; 29 the Le-
vites, because they have no allotment or in-
heritance with you, as well as the resident
aliens, the orphans, and the widows in your
towns, may come and eat their fill so that
the LORD your God may bless you in all the
work that you undertake.

15 Every seventh year you shall grant a
remission of debts. 2 And this is the
manner of the remission: every creditor
shall remit the claim that is held against a
neighbor, not exacting it of a neighbor who
is a member of the community, because the
LORD's remission has been proclaimed.
3 Of a foreigner you may exact it, but you
must remit your claim on whatever any
member of your community owes you.
4 There will, however, be no one in need
among you, because the LORD is sure to
bless you in the land that the LORD your
God is giving you as a possession to occu-
py, 5 if only you will obey the LORD your
God by diligently observing this entire
commandment that I command you today.
6 When the LORD your God has blessed
you, as he promised you, you will lend to
many nations, but you will not borrow;
you will rule over many nations, but they
will not rule over you.

7 If there is among you anyone in need,
a member of your community in any of
your towns within the land that the LORD

27.30–33; Num 18.21–32; cf. Ex 22.30) are revised to direct offerings to the single sanctuary (12.17). *You shall eat,* whereas Deuteronomy assigns the tithe to the landholder, Lev 27.30 assigns it to the sanctuary and Num 18.21 to the Levites. **24–25:** In light of centralization, the sanctified crops (designated for the sanctuary) may be converted *into money,* to facilitate the journey. That "firstlings" (v. 23) may also be sold for cash is at variance with Lev 27.32. *Too far,* as in 12.21. **27:** *Levites,* see 12.12n. **28–29:** One out of every three years the tithe law is shifted away from the central sanctuary to focus on the needs of the disadvantaged and the marginalized in the local community, to ensure they too may *eat their fill.*

15.1–18: Remission of debts (vv. 1–11) **and manumission of slaves** (vv. 12–18). On accession to the throne, ancient Near Eastern rulers would sometimes grant one-time cancellation of debts, return land confiscated by the crown, and free indentured slaves. That custom, Akkadian "duraru," is reflected in the Heb "deror," "jubilee" or "release," of Lev 25.10; Isa 61.1; Jer 34.15,17. Deuteronomy's conception of the covenant between Israel and God entails a similar fresh start as a covenantal obligation that recurs every seven years, adjusting earlier laws in the Book of the Covenant (Ex 21–23) to the innovation of centralization of worship. The sequence reflects increasingly severe stages of financial distress: from debt to indentured servitude, an ancient form of bankruptcy (see Lev 25.13–55 for a similar sequence).

15.1–6: Cancellation of debts. 1: *Seventh year,* this law presupposes Ex 23.10–11, which stipulates that agricultural land should be permitted to lie fallow each "seventh year." **2:** *Remission,* the same verb in Ex 23.11, "lie fallow," now means cancellation of debts. **3:** In not canceling debts of foreigners, the legislator makes a concession to the pragmatic concerns of the creditor. **4:** *There will . . . be no one in need,* or, "no poor." Contrast the pragmatism of v. 7.

15.7–11: An appeal to conscience, anticipating the problem of implementing and enforcing such a law. **9:** *Cry . . . guilt,* the law has no judicial penalty or sanction (similarly 24.15; Ex 22.23–24).

your God is giving you, do not be hard-
hearted or tight-fisted toward your needy
neighbor. 8 You should rather open your
hand, willingly lending enough to meet the
need, whatever it may be. 9 Be careful that
you do not entertain a mean thought,
thinking, "The seventh year, the year of re-
mission, is near," and therefore view your
needy neighbor with hostility and give
nothing; your neighbor might cry to the
LORD against you, and you would incur
guilt. 10 Give liberally and be ungrudging
when you do so, for on this account the
LORD your God will bless you in all your
work and in all that you undertake. 11 Since
there will never cease to be some in need on
the earth, I therefore command you, "Open
your hand to the poor and needy neighbor
in your land."

12 If a member of your community,
whether a Hebrew man or a Hebrew wom-
an, is sold[a] to you and works for you six
years, in the seventh year you shall set that
person free. 13 And when you send a male
slave[b] out from you a free person, you
shall not send him out empty-handed.
14 Provide liberally out of your flock, your
threshing floor, and your wine press, thus
giving to him some of the bounty with
which the LORD your God has blessed you.
15 Remember that you were a slave in the
land of Egypt, and the LORD your God re-
deemed you; for this reason I lay this com-
mand upon you today. 16 But if he says to
you, "I will not go out from you," because
he loves you and your household, since he
is well off with you, 17 then you shall take
an awl and thrust it through his earlobe
into the door, and he shall be your slave[c]
forever.

You shall do the same with regard to
your female slave.[d]

18 Do not consider it a hardship when
you send them out from you free persons,
because for six years they have given you
services worth the wages of hired laborers;
and the LORD your God will bless you in all
that you do.

19 Every firstling male born of your
herd and flock you shall consecrate to the
LORD your God; you shall not do work
with your firstling ox nor shear the firstling
of your flock. 20 You shall eat it, you to-
gether with your household, in the presence
of the LORD your God year by year at the
place that the LORD will choose. 21 But if it
has any defect—any serious defect, such as

a Or *sells himself or herself* *b* Heb *him*
c Or *bondman* *d* Or *bondwoman*

15.12–18: Manumission. This adjusts the older laws regulating male (Ex 21.2–6) and female (Ex 21.7–11) slaves in four ways: (1) A single law applies to both genders, abrogating the older law (contrast v. 17b with Ex 21.7b); (2) the ceremony where the slave relinquishes freedom is secularized (vv. 16–17), so that it now takes place at the house rather than at a local sanctuary (Ex 21.6); (3) the master must now grant the slave a gift (vv. 13–14; contrast Ex 21.2); (4) by conjoining the Covenant Collection's manumission (Ex 21.2–6) and land sabbatical (Ex 23.6–7) laws, Deuteronomy creates a single year of release and transforms manumission, formerly based in the individual household, into a year of universal liberty. The delay of manumission to the fiftieth year by the Holiness Collection may reflect the difficulty of implementing this idealistic law (Lev 25.39–44). **12:** *Hebrew,* see Ex 21.2n. *Is sold* and "sells himself" (see text note *a*), a court might require a thief, unable to repay a theft, to indenture his labor as compensation (Ex 22.1–4); or, overcome by debt, a serf might assign his labor to repay a loan (Lev 25.39–44). **14–15:** The gift provided the manumitted slave recalls and reenacts the nation's own manumission by God from slavery in Egypt. **18:** As in vv. 8–10, an appeal to conscience that anticipates the difficulty of enforcing a law that lacks judicial sanction.

15.19–23: Sacrifice: Older convention required that each firstborn male domestic animal be offered as a sacrifice to God at one of the local sanctuaries (Ex 13.1–2,11–16; 22.29–30; 34.19–20). The author now adjusts that law to the new one stipulating a single sanctuary. **19:** *Not do work,* thereby reserving the animal for God. **20:** *In the presence of the LORD,* at the central sanctuary in Jerusalem. **21–23:** Blemished firstborn livestock need not be taken to the central sanctuary. They may be slaughtered locally, following the requirements for secular slaughter (12.15–16,21–25).

lameness or blindness—you shall not sacri-
fice it to the LORD your God; 22 within your
towns you may eat it, the unclean and the
clean alike, as you would a gazelle or deer.
23 Its blood, however, you must not eat;
you shall pour it out on the ground like
water.

16 Observe the month[a] of Abib by
keeping the passover to the LORD
your God, for in the month of Abib the
LORD your God brought you out of Egypt
by night. 2 You shall offer the passover sac-
rifice to the LORD your God, from the flock
and the herd, at the place that the LORD
will choose as a dwelling for his name.
3 You must not eat with it anything leav-
ened. For seven days you shall eat unleav-
ened bread with it—the bread of afflic-
tion—because you came out of the land of
Egypt in great haste, so that all the days of
your life you may remember the day of
your departure from the land of Egypt.
4 No leaven shall be seen with you in all
your territory for seven days; and none of
the meat of what you slaughter on the eve-
ning of the first day shall remain until
morning. 5 You are not permitted to offer
the passover sacrifice within any of your
towns that the LORD your God is giving
you. 6 But at the place that the LORD your
God will choose as a dwelling for his name,
only there shall you offer the passover sac-
rifice, in the evening at sunset, the time of
day when you departed from Egypt. 7 You
shall cook it and eat it at the place that
the LORD your God will choose; the next
morning you may go back to your tents.
8 For six days you shall continue to eat un-
leavened bread, and on the seventh day
there shall be a solemn assembly for the
LORD your God, when you shall do no
work.

9 You shall count seven weeks; begin to
count the seven weeks from the time the

a Or *new moon*

16.1–17: The festival calendar. Previously, each male Israelite was commanded to undertake three pilgrimages to "appear before the LORD": to make an offering at one of the multiple local sanctuaries (v. 16; Ex 23.14–18). These occasions, which Deuteronomy redirects to the central sanctuary, were called "pilgrimage festivals" (v. 16; Ex 23.14). The three festivals were Unleavened Bread (Heb "mazzot"), harvest, and ingathering (Ex 23.14–17; 34.18,23). Deuteronomy renames the latter two "weeks" (v. 10) and "booths" (Heb "sukkoth," v. 13), their current names. **1–8:** Passover was originally a separate, family observance (Ex 12.1–13,21–23), involving a nighttime slaughter of a sheep or goat in the doorway of the house, where the blood was smeared to mark the house as Israelite. Deuteronomy's centralization of worship necessitated the redirection of the paschal slaughter to the central sanctuary (vv. 2,6–7). The older blood ritual then merges with the Festival of Unleavened Bread, also celebrated in early spring. In contrast to Deuteronomy, the festivals of Passover and Unleavened Bread remain distinct in Lev 23.5–6; Num 28.16,17–25. **1:** *Abib* (lit. "new ear" of grain), in early spring, when ears of barley, the first crop, began to ripen (Ex 13.4; 23.15; 34.18). Originally the first month of the Hebrew calendar (Ex 12.2), later called "Nisan." **2:** *From the flock and the herd,* earlier the offering was restricted to the flock only (Ex 12.4–5,21). **3:** *For seven days,* combining the seven-day observance of the Festival of Unleavened Bread (Ex 12.14–20; 23.15) and the one-day observance of Passover (vv. 1–3a,4b–7). **7:** *Cook,* more accurately, "boil," like other standard sacrifices (Ex 29.1; Lev 6.28; 8.31; Num 6.19; Zech 14.21). This provision conflicts with the stipulation that the paschal offering be "roasted over the fire," not "boiled in water" (Ex 12.8–9). The two inconsistent requirements for preparing the Passover are harmonized at 2 Chr 35.13. **8:** The Heb reads simply, "For six days you shall eat Unleavened Bread." The NRSV's addition, *continue,* results in an eight-day total for the festivals of Passover and Unleavened Bread, modeled after the Priestly version of the calendar: 1 day (Passover) + 6 days (unleavened bread) + 1 day (the solemn assembly); see Lev 23.3–8. In contrast, Deuteronomy intended to fuse the two holidays into a single seven-day observance. **9–12:** The Festival of Weeks (34.22; Lev 23.15–16; Num 28.26), Heb "shavuot," originally, a "festival of harvest" (Ex 23.16) celebrated in June. In postbiblical Judaism, the festival came to be associated with the revelation at Mount Sinai (Ex 19–20); in the New Testament it is called Pentecost because it begins on the fiftieth day after Passover (Acts 2.1; 20.16; 1 Cor 16.8). **9:**

sickle is first put to the standing grain.
10 Then you shall keep the festival of weeks
to the LORD your God, contributing a free-
will offering in proportion to the blessing
that you have received from the LORD your
God. 11 Rejoice before the LORD your
God—you and your sons and your daugh-
ters, your male and female slaves, the Le-
vites resident in your towns, as well as the
strangers, the orphans, and the widows
who are among you—at the place that the
LORD your God will choose as a dwelling
for his name. 12 Remember that you were a
slave in Egypt, and diligently observe these
statutes.
13 You shall keep the festival of
booths[a] for seven days, when you have
gathered in the produce from your thresh-
ing floor and your wine press. 14 Rejoice
during your festival, you and your sons and
your daughters, your male and female
slaves, as well as the Levites, the strangers,
the orphans, and the widows resident in
your towns. 15 Seven days you shall keep
the festival to the LORD your God at the
place that the LORD will choose; for the
LORD your God will bless you in all your
produce and in all your undertakings, and
you shall surely celebrate.
16 Three times a year all your males
shall appear before the LORD your God at
the place that he will choose: at the festival
of unleavened bread, at the festival of
weeks, and at the festival of booths.[a] They
shall not appear before the LORD empty-
handed; 17 all shall give as they are able,
according to the blessing of the LORD your
God that he has given you.
18 You shall appoint judges and offi-
cials throughout your tribes, in all your
towns that the LORD your God is giving
you, and they shall render just decisions for
the people. 19 You must not distort justice;
you must not show partiality; and you must

a Or *tabernacles*; Heb *succoth*

Begin to count . . . from the time the sickle is first put to the standing grain, the seven weeks begin when the grain is ripe, delaying the celebration until the conclusion of the harvest. The Holiness Collection offers a slightly different date for this festival (Lev 23.15). **11:** *You and your sons and your daughters,* the command to rejoice specifies the inclusion of women (as v. 14; 12.12,18). *Slaves . . . widows,* the marginalized and the disadvantaged are also included. *Stranger,* better, "resident alien"; see 1.16n. **13–15:** *The festival of booths,* originally the fall harvest festival, called "ingathering" (Ex 23.16; 34.22; cf. Lev 23.33–43). **16–17:** The formulaic summary ("colophon") reuses the conclusion of the older festival calendar in the Book of the Covenant (Ex 23.17). Two elements, however, reflect older assumptions inconsistent with the rest of this chapter: Passover (vv. 1–8) is not mentioned, and the pilgrimage requirement is directed to *all your males* (as Ex 23.17).

16.18–18.22: Laws of public officials. The proposed government has judicial, executive, and religious branches: local and central courts (16.18–17.13), kingship (17.14–20), Levitical priesthood (18.1–8), and prophecy (18.9–22). Each relates to the others and is subordinated to the authority of the word of God, the Torah of Deuteronomy. Even institutions that might claim absolute authority, such as king or prophet, are integrated into a comprehensive vision. The continual concern with centralization of worship connects this section with the preceding legislation on the sacrificial system. The ritual laws (16.21–17.1) seem to intrude between two paragraphs each concerned with justice (16.18–20; 17.2–7), but the repetition provides a transition into the new section, while establishing the underlying unity of both areas of community life: (A) worship (12.1–16.17); (B) justice (16.18–20); (A′) worship (16.21–17.1); (B′) justice (17.2–7,8–13).

16.18–17.13: The organization of justice. 16.18–20: Deuteronomy here establishes a professionalized local judiciary. **18:** *Towns* (lit. "gates"), the local sphere (12.15,17,21; 16.5), as distinguished from the central sanctuary; also the traditional place where the village elders dispensed justice (Job 29.7; Ruth 4.1,11; Lam 5.14). By leaving the elders unmentioned, Deuteronomy contracts or eliminates their authority, though they are mentioned elsewhere in older sections of Deuteronomy (e.g., 19.12; 21.2; 22.15). **19:** *You must not distort justice,* an admonition, quoting Ex 23.6a (where the same verb is translated "pervert"). *For a bribe blinds the eyes of the wise,* the older law in Ex 23.8, whose reference to "those

not accept bribes, for a bribe blinds the eyes
of the wise and subverts the cause of those
who are in the right. 20 Justice, and only
justice, you shall pursue, so that you may
live and occupy the land that the LORD
your God is giving you.

21 You shall not plant any tree as a sa-
cred pole[a] beside the altar that you make
for the LORD your God; 22 nor shall you set
up a stone pillar—things that the LORD
your God hates.

17 You must not sacrifice to the LORD
your God an ox or a sheep that has
a defect, anything seriously wrong; for that
is abhorrent to the LORD your God.

2 If there is found among you, in one of
your towns that the LORD your God is giv-
ing you, a man or woman who does what is
evil in the sight of the LORD your God, and
transgresses his covenant 3 by going to serve
other gods and worshiping them—whether
the sun or the moon or any of the host of
heaven, which I have forbidden— 4 and if it
is reported to you or you hear of it, and you
make a thorough inquiry, and the charge is
proved true that such an abhorrent thing
has occurred in Israel, 5 then you shall bring
out to your gates that man or that woman
who has committed this crime and you
shall stone the man or woman to death.
6 On the evidence of two or three witnesses
the death sentence shall be executed; a per-
son must not be put to death on the evi-
dence of only one witness. 7 The hands of
the witnesses shall be the first raised against
the person to execute the death penalty,
and afterward the hands of all the people.
So you shall purge the evil from your midst.

8 If a judicial decision is too difficult for
you to make between one kind of blood-
shed and another, one kind of legal right
and another, or one kind of assault and
another—any such matters of dispute in
your towns—then you shall immediately
go up to the place that the LORD your God
will choose, 9 where you shall consult with
the levitical priests and the judge who is in
office in those days; they shall announce to
you the decision in the case. 10 Carry out
exactly the decision that they announce to
you from the place that the LORD will
choose, diligently observing everything

a Heb *Asherah*

with sight" (NRSV's "officials" is not correct) is revised in light of Deuteronomy's stress upon wisdom (see notes on 1.13; 34.9).

16.21–17.1: Prohibitions against Canaanite cultic objects (7.5; 12.3; Ex 34.13). **16.21:** *Sacred pole,* see 7.5n. **22:** *Stone pillar,* see 7.5n. **17.1:** See 15.21, here broadened into a general law of sacrifice.

17.2–7: Local justice. This law overlaps with 13.6–11, but is placed here because it deals with the procedures and jurisdiction of the local courts. The law grants the local courts maximum autonomy (see 16.8), provided that a trial is conducted according to rational standards that assure empirical proof. **2:** *A man or woman,* the law views the woman as a legally responsible individual. The viewpoint in marriage and family law differs, however (see 22.13–29). **3:** Contravening the Decalogue (5.8–9). **6:** *Two or three witnesses,* the condition for establishing proof. The prohibition against execution on the basis of testimony by *one witness* is also found at 19.15–16; Num 35.30.

17.8–13: Justice at the central sanctuary. In the pre-Deuteronomic period, legal cases in which there was an absence of physical evidence or of witnesses were remanded to the local sanctuary, where the parties to the dispute would swear a judicial oath at the altar (19.17; Ex 22.7–11; 1 Kings 8.31–32; note also Ex 21.6). These two laws (17.2–7,8–13) thus fill the judicial void created by Deuteronomy's prohibition of the local sanctuaries (ch 12). Now, any case that requires recourse to the altar is remanded to the central sanctuary; all other cases, even capital ones, may be tried locally (vv. 2–7). **8:** These cases must be referred to the central sanctuary because, in the absence of witnesses or evidence, local officials cannot make a ruling. *Between one kind of bloodshed and another,* the legal distinction between murder and manslaughter (Ex 21.12–14; Num 35.16–23). In each pair, the distinction is between premeditated or unintentional offenses. **9:** The tribunal at the sanctuary includes both priestly and lay members. The account of Jehoshaphat's setting up tribunals throughout Judah composed of lay and clerical judges reflects this law (2 Chr 19.5–11).

they instruct you. 11You must carry out ful-
ly the law that they interpret for you or the
ruling that they announce to you; do not
turn aside from the decision that they an-
nounce to you, either to the right or to the
left. 12As for anyone who presumes to dis-
obey the priest appointed to minister there
to the LORD your God, or the judge, that
person shall die. So you shall purge the evil
from Israel. 13All the people will hear and
be afraid, and will not act presumptuously
again.

14 When you have come into the land
that the LORD your God is giving you, and
have taken possession of it and settled in it,
and you say, "I will set a king over me, like
all the nations that are around me," 15you
may indeed set over you a king whom the
LORD your God will choose. One of your
own community you may set as king over
you; you are not permitted to put a foreign-
er over you, who is not of your own com-
munity. 16Even so, he must not acquire
many horses for himself, or return the peo-
ple to Egypt in order to acquire more
horses, since the LORD has said to you,
"You must never return that way again."
17And he must not acquire many wives for
himself, or else his heart will turn away;
also silver and gold he must not acquire in
great quantity for himself. 18When he has
taken the throne of his kingdom, he shall
have a copy of this law written for him
in the presence of the levitical priests. 19It
shall remain with him and he shall read in
it all the days of his life, so that he may
learn to fear the LORD his God, diligently
observing all the words of this law and
these statutes, 20neither exalting himself
above other members of the community
nor turning aside from the commandment,
either to the right or to the left, so that he
and his descendants may reign long over his
kingdom in Israel.

18 The levitical priests, the whole tribe
of Levi, shall have no allotment or
inheritance within Israel. They may eat the
sacrifices that are the LORD's portion[a]
2but they shall have no inheritance among
the other members of the community; the
LORD is their inheritance, as he promised
them.

3 This shall be the priests' due from the
people, from those offering a sacrifice,

a Meaning of Heb uncertain

17.14–20: The law of the king. Deuteronomy greatly restricts royal authority. Generally Near Eastern monarchs promulgated law; here the monarch is subject to the law and required to read the Torah daily (v. 19). Deuteronomy even denies the king his typical judicial role as court of last appeal (cf. Ps 72.1–4; 2 Sam 12.1–14; 14.1–24; 1 Kings 3.16–28). This law far more emphasizes what the king cannot do than what he may do. **14:** *Like all the nations,* see 1 Sam 8.10–18. **16–18:** The offenses parallel warnings against royal autocracy outlined at the very founding of the monarchy (1 Sam 8.10–18). They likely presuppose Solomon's trade in horses (1 Kings 10.26–29) and his multiple foreign wives (1 Kings 11.1–8). The Deuteronomistic Historian believed those marriages led to idolatry (1 Kings 11.9–13). *A copy of this law,* the Septuagint reads "this repetition of the law" (Gk "to deuteronomion touto"), the source of the book's name. Like later traditional views, it sees Deuteronomy as a reprise (of Ex, Lev, Num), ignoring the extent to which it revises and challenges earlier law.

18.1–8: The Levitical priesthood. Centralization also affected the Israelite priesthood. A "job description" (vv. 1–5) precedes discussion of this impact (vv. 6–8). **1:** *Levitical priests,* the Deuteronomic conception differs from that of Priestly literature, which speaks of two distinct groups, "the priests" and "the Levites." The Priestly source sees a hierarchy within the tribe of Levi between direct descendants of Aaron and the rest. Only the Aaronide priests officiate at the altar (Num 18.5,7) and receive the priestly share of the offerings (Num 18.8–20). The Levites serve the priests, and are prohibited from officiating (Num 18.3–4,6); they receive tithes and in turn tithe to the priests (Num 18.21–31). Here, in Deuteronomy, all within the tribe are Levitical priests and both serve at the altar and receive sacrifices. **2:** *No inheritance,* see 12.12n. *The LORD is their inheritance,* God grants them a share of the sacrificial offerings, making them dependent upon other Israelites for support. In contrast, the priest-prophet Ezekiel allocates land to the priests and the Levites in his vision of the future restoration of Judah (Ezek 48.10–14). **5:** *Stand*

whether an ox or a sheep: they shall give to
the priest the shoulder, the two jowls, and
the stomach. 4 The first fruits of your grain,
your wine, and your oil, as well as the first
of the fleece of your sheep, you shall give
him. 5 For the LORD your God has chosen
Levi[a] out of all your tribes, to stand and
minister in the name of the LORD, him and
his sons for all time.
6 If a Levite leaves any of your towns,
from wherever he has been residing in Isra-
el, and comes to the place that the LORD
will choose (and he may come whenever he
wishes), 7 then he may minister in the name
of the LORD his God, like all his fellow-
Levites who stand to minister there before
the LORD. 8 They shall have equal portions
to eat, even though they have income from
the sale of family possessions.[b]
9 When you come into the land that the
LORD your God is giving you, you must not
learn to imitate the abhorrent practices of
those nations. 10 No one shall be found
among you who makes a son or daughter
pass through fire, or who practices divina-
tion, or is a soothsayer, or an augur, or a
sorcerer, 11 or one who casts spells, or who
consults ghosts or spirits, or who seeks ora-
cles from the dead. 12 For whoever does
these things is abhorrent to the LORD; it is
because of such abhorrent practices that
the LORD your God is driving them out be-
fore you. 13 You must remain completely
loyal to the LORD your God. 14 Although
these nations that you are about to dispos-
sess do give heed to soothsayers and divin-
ers, as for you, the LORD your God does
not permit you to do so.
15 The LORD your God will raise up for
you a prophet[c] like me from among your
own people; you shall heed such a proph-
et.[d] 16 This is what you requested of the
LORD your God at Horeb on the day of the
assembly when you said: "If I hear the
voice of the LORD my God any more, or
ever again see this great fire, I will die."
17 Then the LORD replied to me: "They are
right in what they have said. 18 I will raise
up for them a prophet[c] like you from

a Heb *him* *b* Meaning of Heb uncertain
c Or *prophets* *d* Or *such prophets*

and minister, officiate at the altar. **6–8:** When the local altars throughout the land are outlawed (12.8–12,13–15), the Levites serving there would be unemployed and, owning no land, would become destitute. Accordingly a Levite who *leaves any of your towns . . . and comes* to the central sanctuary in Jerusalem must be provided for (contrast 2 Kings 23.9). This emphasis underscores that the countryside altars were not entirely Canaanite sanctuaries (as 12.2–4 asserts). **8:** *Equal portions,* the choice meats, grains, and oil assigned the tribe in vv. 3–4.

18.9–22: The Mosaic prophet. 9–14: Just as the legal corpus prohibits sacrificial worship it condemns as Canaanite (12.1–4,29–31; also 7.1–6,25–26; Ex 23.24; 34.11–16), it prohibits forms of divination it brands as foreign and abhorrent. In each case it requires its own alternative: here, prophecy rather than divination. However, divination is not elsewhere typified as foreign (1 Sam 28.3–25; Isa 8.19–22; 28.4). Thus, describing the practice as foreign may actually cloak a condemnation of Israelite popular religion. **10:** *Pass through fire,* child sacrifice (see 12.31n.), joined with divination for condemnation because each is "abhorrent" (v. 9). *Practices divination, or is a soothsayer,* the most comprehensive compilation of such activities in the Bible (Ex 22.18; Lev 19.30–31; 20.6,27; Isa 8.19; Ezek 21.21). **11:** *Who consults ghosts or spirits . . . dead,* necromancy or conjuring the dead (1 Sam 28.7–15; Isa 8.19–20; 29.4). Popular religion in antiquity devoted extensive attention to communicating with the dead, especially with ancestors. **12:** *Abhorrent,* more commonly "abomination," as at Lev 26.26–27,29. There is no claim that divination is ineffective; it is, however, illegitimate (see 1 Sam 28.7–25). **15–22:** Deuteronomy transforms prophecy, viewing the prophet as the spokesperson of Torah (see 13.1–5n.) and defining Moses as the paradigmatic prophet. **15:** *The LORD . . . will raise up,* prophecy by divine election. That God alone appoints the prophet makes the prophet independent of all institutions and able to challenge them. More than one prophet is clearly intended. *Like me,* at Horeb (5.23–33), Moses established the model of prophecy as mediating God's word to the people. Thus the prophet, like the king (17.15), should be *from among your own people.* **16–17:** See 5.23–31; Ex 20.18–21. **18:** The prophet's oracles do not originate

among their own people; I will put my
words in the mouth of the prophet,[a] who
shall speak to them everything that I com-
mand. 19 Anyone who does not heed the
words that the prophet[b] shall speak in my
name, I myself will hold accountable. 20 But
any prophet who speaks in the name of
other gods, or who presumes to speak in
my name a word that I have not command-
ed the prophet to speak—that prophet shall
die." 21 You may say to yourself, "How can
we recognize a word that the LORD has not
spoken?" 22 If a prophet speaks in the name
of the LORD but the thing does not take
place or prove true, it is a word that the
LORD has not spoken. The prophet has
spoken it presumptuously; do not be fright-
ened by it.

19 When the LORD your God has cut
off the nations whose land the
LORD your God is giving you, and you have
dispossessed them and settled in their
towns and in their houses, 2 you shall set
apart three cities in the land that the LORD
your God is giving you to possess. 3 You
shall calculate the distances[c] and divide
into three regions the land that the LORD
your God gives you as a possession, so that
any homicide can flee to one of them.

4 Now this is the case of a homicide who
might flee there and live, that is, someone
who has killed another person unintention-
ally when the two had not been at enmity
before: 5 Suppose someone goes into the
forest with another to cut wood, and when
one of them swings the ax to cut down a
tree, the head slips from the handle and
strikes the other person who then dies; the
killer may flee to one of these cities and
live. 6 But if the distance is too great, the
avenger of blood in hot anger might pursue
and overtake and put the killer to death,
although a death sentence was not de-
served, since the two had not been at enmi-
ty before. 7 Therefore I command you: You
shall set apart three cities.

8 If the LORD your God enlarges your
territory, as he swore to your ancestors—
and he will give you all the land that he
promised your ancestors to give you, 9 pro-
vided you diligently observe this entire
commandment that I command you today,
by loving the LORD your God and walking
always in his ways—then you shall add
three more cities to these three, 10 so that

a Or *mouths of the prophets* b Heb *he*
c Or *prepare roads to them*

from other deities, from dead spirits, from skilled manipulation of objects, or from the prophet's own reflections. **20–23:** Having established an Israelite model of prophecy, the law provides two criteria to distinguish true from false prophecy. The first is that the prophet should speak exclusively on behalf of God, and report only God's words. The second makes the fulfillment of a prophet's oracle the measure of its truth (Jer 28.9). That approach attempts to solve a critical problem: If two prophets each claim to speak on behalf of God yet make mutually exclusive claims (1 Kings 22.6 versus v. 17; Jer 27.8 versus 28.2), how may one decide which speaks the truth? The solution offered is not free of difficulty. If a false prophet is distinguished by the failure of his oracle to come true, then making a decision in the present about which prophet to obey becomes impossible. Nor can this criterion easily be reconciled with 13.2, which concedes that the oracles of false prophets might come true.

19.1–13: Cities of refuge (see 4.41–43n.). Sanctuary for those who killed unintentionally shielded them from revenge killing by the kin of the dead person (vv. 6,12). In light of centralization, Deuteronomy proscribes the previous site of refuge, the local altar (Ex 21.13), and instead designates three "neutral" cities. **1:** For the formulaic introduction, see 12.29. **4:** *Who might flee there,* more literally, "where he might flee (there)," an exact citation of Ex 21.13b, the older law that requires revision. **5:** *May flee to one of these cities,* explicitly amended to include the city reference. **6:** *But if the distance is too great,* Deuteronomy's updating of older law; see 14.24. *In hot anger,* if the kinsman kills the slayer in hot pursuit, the law is powerless. **8:** *Enlarges your territory,* a means for updating older law to address present realities by casting the provision for change as intended from the beginning (see 12.20; Ex 34.20). **10:** *The blood of an innocent person,* killing someone who has unintentionally committed homicide would constitute murder. *Bloodguilt,* the spilling of innocent blood, which defiles the land (see 21.1–9n.). **12:** Revising

the blood of an innocent person may not be
shed in the land that the LORD your God is
giving you as an inheritance, thereby bring-
ing bloodguilt upon you.
11 But if someone at enmity with anoth-
er lies in wait and attacks and takes the life
of that person, and flees into one of these
cities, 12 then the elders of the killer's city
shall send to have the culprit taken from
there and handed over to the avenger of
blood to be put to death. 13 Show no pity;
you shall purge the guilt of innocent blood
from Israel, so that it may go well with you.
14 You must not move your neighbor's
boundary marker, set up by former genera-
tions, on the property that will be allotted
to you in the land that the LORD your God
is giving you to possess.
15 A single witness shall not suffice to
convict a person of any crime or wrongdo-
ing in connection with any offense that may
be committed. Only on the evidence of two
or three witnesses shall a charge be sus-
tained. 16 If a malicious witness comes for-
ward to accuse someone of wrongdoing,
17 then both parties to the dispute shall ap-
pear before the LORD, before the priests
and the judges who are in office in those
days, 18 and the judges shall make a thor-
ough inquiry. If the witness is a false wit-
ness, having testified falsely against anoth-
er, 19 then you shall do to the false witness
just as the false witness had meant to do to
the other. So you shall purge the evil from
your midst. 20 The rest shall hear and be
afraid, and a crime such as this shall never
again be committed among you. 21 Show
no pity: life for life, eye for eye, tooth for
tooth, hand for hand, foot for foot.

20 When you go out to war against
your enemies, and see horses and
chariots, an army larger than your own,

Ex 21.14. *Handed over to the avenger,* the law regulates but does not replace the clan-based system of justice. **14:** A transitional verse. The sacrosanct status of a *boundary marker* was a legal tradition in the ancient Near East (see 27.17; Isa 5.8; Hos 5.10; Job 24.2; Prov 22.28).

19.15–21: The integrity of the judicial system. A law that requires probity on the part of the newly established judges (16.18) and a law that demands corresponding integrity from witnesses (19.21) form an inclusio around this large unit by emphasizing the honesty required of all participants in the judicial system. **15:** *A single witness,* the same Heb phrase as "only one witness" at 17.6. *On the evidence of two or three witnesses shall a charge be sustained,* broadening the focus of 17.6 on capital crimes and prohibiting hearsay or spurious accusation (one person's word against another's). **17:** *Both parties,* the accuser and the accused. *Before the LORD,* testimony before the altar at the central sanctuary (12.7; 14.23; 17.8–13). **19:** *Do to the false witness . . . meant to do to the other,* reciprocal justice, called "talion," the technical term for "an eye for an eye," elsewhere employed for bodily injury or homicide (Ex 21.23–25; Lev 24.17–21). It distinguishes crimes against the person (requiring talion) from property crimes (where alone financial compensation is permitted). By applying it to crimes against the judicial system, the legislators here seek to ensure the integrity of the law by using the highest sanction available to them.

20.1–20: Rules for waging holy war. In contrast to other legal collections, which include only brief sections concerning military engagement (Ex 23.23–33; 34.11–16; Num 35.50–56), Deuteronomy, reflecting a literary setting of Israel about to enter the land, concerns itself extensively with the laws of holy war. God as divine warrior directly confronts the adversary on behalf of the nation, and God's presence in the camp imposes additional purity requirements on the people (23.10–14). The holy war is fought to extirpate iniquity and to create a covenantal community organized by divine law (Lev 18.24–29; 20.22–24). Accordingly, seizing the spoils of war, including human prisoners, is prohibited; all had to be devoted exclusively to God, like the "whole burnt offering" (13.16). Contemporary inscriptions like the Moabite Stone (ca. 850 BCE) establish that similar theologies of holy war were shared by a number of nations. In Deuteronomy, the conception of the conquest as a holy war represents a highly schematized idealization, formulated half a millennium after the settlement, at a time when ethnic Canaanites would already long have assimilated into the Israelite population. **1:** *Horses and chariots,* the adversary is superior both in numbers and in military equipment (see Ex 14.9; 15.4; Josh 11.4). *Army,* lit. "people." **3–4:** See 9.1–3; 31.3–6; cf. Ex 14.14,25; 15.1–4. **5–9:** A reverse muster, designed to thin the ranks by removing conscripts

you shall not be afraid of them; for the
LORD your God is with you, who brought
you up from the land of Egypt. [2]Before you
engage in battle, the priest shall come for-
ward and speak to the troops, [3]and shall
say to them: "Hear, O Israel! Today you
are drawing near to do battle against your
enemies. Do not lose heart, or be afraid, or
panic, or be in dread of them; [4]for it is the
LORD your God who goes with you, to
fight for you against your enemies, to give
you victory." [5]Then the officials shall ad-
dress the troops, saying, "Has anyone built
a new house but not dedicated it? He
should go back to his house, or he might
die in the battle and another dedicate it.
[6]Has anyone planted a vineyard but not yet
enjoyed its fruit? He should go back to his
house, or he might die in the battle and
another be first to enjoy its fruit. [7]Has any-
one become engaged to a woman but not
yet married her? He should go back to his
house, or he might die in the battle and
another marry her." [8]The officials shall
continue to address the troops, saying, "Is
anyone afraid or disheartened? He should
go back to his house, or he might cause the
heart of his comrades to melt like his own."
[9]When the officials have finished address-
ing the troops, then the commanders shall
take charge of them.

10 When you draw near to a town to
fight against it, offer it terms of peace. [11]If
it accepts your terms of peace and surren-
ders to you, then all the people in it shall
serve you at forced labor. [12]If it does not
submit to you peacefully, but makes war
against you, then you shall besiege it; [13]and
when the LORD your God gives it into your
hand, you shall put all its males to the
sword. [14]You may, however, take as your
booty the women, the children, livestock,
and everything else in the town, all its spoil.
You may enjoy the spoil of your enemies,
which the LORD your God has given you.
[15]Thus you shall treat all the towns that are
very far from you, which are not towns of
the nations here. [16]But as for the towns of
these peoples that the LORD your God is
giving you as an inheritance, you must not
let anything that breathes remain alive.
[17]You shall annihilate them—the Hittites
and the Amorites, the Canaanites and the
Perizzites, the Hivites and the Jebusites—
just as the LORD your God has command-
ed, [18]so that they may not teach you to do
all the abhorrent things that they do for
their gods, and you thus sin against the
LORD your God.

19 If you besiege a town for a long time,
making war against it in order to take it,
you must not destroy its trees by wielding
an ax against them. Although you may take
food from them, you must not cut them

who have competing priorities because they are in a transitional state. **5:** *Dedicated* (or "inaugurated"), although Solomon's dedication of the Temple is narrated (1 Kings 8), there are no specific rituals of home dedication recorded in the Bible. The parallel curse employs "live" (28.30). **6:** *Enjoyed its fruit,* priestly law required that newly planted fruit trees could only be harvested in the fifth year (Lev 19.23–25). **7:** *Engaged . . . married,* see 22.13–30n. **8:** *Comrades,* lit. "brothers," to which Deuteronomy frequently, and distinctively, gives the meaning, "fellow citizens" (cf. 24.7); NRSV also translates the same word as "neighbor" (15.7,9,11; 22.1–4; 24.13; 25.3) and "Israelite" (23.19–20; 24.14). **11:** The use of a defeated people for *forced labor* was widespread. Israelites so used the indigenous population of Canaan (Judg 1.27–36). David's cabinet included an official responsible for "forced labor" (2 Sam 20.24). **15–18:** *Thus you shall treat all the towns that are very far from you,* a secondary addition retroactively restricts the preceding rules of engagement (vv. 10–14), which tolerate the taking of captives as "forced labor," so that they apply only to foreign wars. The stipulation that the indigenous population of Canaan should uniformly be exterminated is a literary fiction (see v. 11n.; 7.2n.). **15:** *The nations,* the Canaanites. *Here,* on the anachronism, see 1.1n.; 2.12n. **16:** *But as for the towns of these peoples that the LORD . . . is giving you* refers to the inhabitants of the land (v. 17). **17:** *You shall annihilate them,* the Heb phrase is elsewhere translated as "utterly destroy" (7.2; 13.15). **19–20:** Wars often involved the kind of "scorched earth policy" prohibited here (2 Kings 3.19,25). **20:** *Siegeworks* were regularly built against walled cities (1 Sam 20.15; 2 Kings 25.1).

down. Are trees in the field human beings
that they should come under siege from
you? 20 You may destroy only the trees that
you know do not produce food; you may
cut them down for use in building siege-
works against the town that makes war
with you, until it falls.

21 If, in the land that the LORD your
God is giving you to possess, a body
is found lying in open country, and it is not
known who struck the person down, 2 then
your elders and your judges shall come out
to measure the distances to the towns that
are near the body. 3 The elders of the town
nearest the body shall take a heifer that has
never been worked, one that has not pulled
in the yoke; 4 the elders of that town shall
bring the heifer down to a wadi with run-
ning water, which is neither plowed nor
sown, and shall break the heifer's neck
there in the wadi. 5 Then the priests, the
sons of Levi, shall come forward, for the
LORD your God has chosen them to minis-
ter to him and to pronounce blessings in the
name of the LORD, and by their decision all
cases of dispute and assault shall be settled.
6 All the elders of that town nearest the
body shall wash their hands over the heifer
whose neck was broken in the wadi, 7 and
they shall declare: "Our hands did not shed
this blood, nor were we witnesses to it.
8 Absolve, O LORD, your people Israel,
whom you redeemed; do not let the guilt of
innocent blood remain in the midst of your
people Israel." Then they will be absolved
of bloodguilt. 9 So you shall purge the guilt
of innocent blood from your midst, because
you must do what is right in the sight of the
LORD.

10 When you go out to war against your
enemies, and the LORD your God hands
them over to you and you take them cap-
tive, 11 suppose you see among the captives
a beautiful woman whom you desire and
want to marry, 12 and so you bring her
home to your house: she shall shave her

21.1–9: Atonement for an unsolved murder. Since a murder victim's blood tainted the land (Gen 4.10; Num 35.33–34), it was imperative to "purge the guilt of innocent blood from Israel" (19.13). This law, which has gone through several stages of reworking, addresses how to do so when the perpetrator cannot be identified. There are similar ancient Near Eastern laws for corpses discovered outside cities; these emphasize financial liability rather than atoning for the spilled blood (*Laws of Hammurabi* §§ 23–24; *Hittite Laws* § 6). The original significance of the law's rituals is difficult to recover. **1:** *Open country,* beyond the legal jurisdiction of any particular town (see 22.23,25), and where witnesses are unlikely. **2:** *Elders . . . judges,* see 16.18n. *Measure the distances* to establish legal jurisdiction, as in the similar *Hittite Laws* § 6. **3:** *Never been worked . . . not pulled in the yoke,* symbolizing the human victim's innocence (similarly, Num 19.2). **4:** *Wadi with running water* (Am 5.24), lit. "with reliable water," in contrast to unreliable seasonal streams (Jer 15.18). *Break the heifer's neck,* nonsacrificial killing; sacrifice requires slitting the throat (see Ex 13.13; 34.20). **5:** *Priests,* not mentioned in v. 2, and likely a later addition. *All cases* contrasts with 17.9, where the Levitical priests at the central sanctuary adjudicated only cases that could not be resolved locally. **6:** *Wash their hands over the heifer,* with no laying on of hands, and thus without symbolic transfer of culpability to the animal (contrast Lev 16.21–22). **7:** *Our hands . . . witnesses,* stronger in Heb: "As for our hands, they did not shed this blood nor did our eyes see," covering both direct action and failure to avert or report a crime (cf. Lev 5.1). **8:** *Absolve, O LORD,* the ritual of vv. 3–6 has no intrinsic efficacy; prayer is the means of absolution. *They will be absolved,* better, "that they may be absolved," since absolution ultimately depends upon divine action, not human ritual.

21.10–25.19: Miscellaneous civil and family laws. The following laws are concerned with family, civil, and ethical issues. Laws to extend legal protection to women when they would otherwise be disenfranchised concern female captives (21.10–14), property rights of the less-favored wife (21.15–17), and false charges of infidelity (22.13–19).

21.10–14: Legal obligations toward female captives. This procedure most likely originally applied to the Canaanite population (20.15–18n.). Female war captives routinely became concubines. This law accords such women dignity and protection against enslavement. **12–13:** The rituals provide both captive and captor means to effect a transition from one status to another. **13:** *Full month,* full period of

head, pare her nails, 13 discard her captive's
garb, and shall remain in your house a full
month, mourning for her father and moth-
er; after that you may go in to her and be
her husband, and she shall be your wife.
14 But if you are not satisfied with her, you
shall let her go free and not sell her for
money. You must not treat her as a slave,
since you have dishonored her.
15 If a man has two wives, one of them
loved and the other disliked, and if both the
loved and the disliked have borne him sons,
the firstborn being the son of the one who
is disliked, 16 then on the day when he wills
his possessions to his sons, he is not permit-
ted to treat the son of the loved as the first-
born in preference to the son of the dis-
liked, who is the firstborn. 17 He must
acknowledge as firstborn the son of the one
who is disliked, giving him a double por-
tion[a] of all that he has; since he is the first
issue of his virility, the right of the firstborn
is his.
18 If someone has a stubborn and rebel-
lious son who will not obey his father and
mother, who does not heed them when they
discipline him, 19 then his father and his
mother shall take hold of him and bring
him out to the elders of his town at the gate
of that place. 20 They shall say to the elders
of his town, "This son of ours is stubborn
and rebellious. He will not obey us. He is a
glutton and a drunkard." 21 Then all the
men of the town shall stone him to death.
So you shall purge the evil from your midst;
and all Israel will hear, and be afraid.
22 When someone is convicted of a
crime punishable by death and is executed,
and you hang him on a tree, 23 his corpse
must not remain all night upon the tree;
you shall bury him that same day, for any-
one hung on a tree is under God's curse.
You must not defile the land that the LORD
your God is giving you for possession.
22 You shall not watch your neigh-
bor's ox or sheep straying away and

a Heb *two-thirds*

mourning, as for Aaron and Moses (Num 20.29; Deut 34.8). *Mourning,* it is unclear whether the parents actually died in the war or are lost to her because of her captivity. The time to grieve implies legal respect for the female captive as a person. *Go in to her,* approach her sexually; consummation provides the legal means to become *husband and . . . wife.* **14:** Cf. Ex 21.7–8. *Dishonored,* "violated" sexually (22.24,29; Gen 34.2; Judg 19.24; 2 Sam 13.12).

21.15–17: Legal protection of the less-favored wife. The law uses the norm of primogeniture (Gen 25.29–34; *Laws of Hammurabi* §§ 165–70) to protect the son of the less-favored wife from disinheritance. **17:** *Double portion,* as text note *a* indicates, two-thirds (see Zech 13.8), leaving one-third for the other son. *Right of the firstborn,* ironically, the foundation narratives concerning Isaac, Jacob, and Joseph subvert the legal norm here affirmed (Gen 17.15–22; 21.8–14; 27.1–40; 48.8–22).

21.18–21: The rebellious son. The Decalogue requirement to honor the parents (5.16; Ex 20.12) carries no explicit sanction; here flagrant and sustained disobedience is a capital offense. **19:** *Elders* were judges of family law and held court at the city *gate,* a public forum (22.15; 25.7; Job 29.7; Ruth 4.1–2,11; Lam 5.14). The professionalized judiciary established at the same site (16.18) may have had jurisdiction specifically over religious and criminal law (17.2–7). **21:** Here, mere parental testimony suffices (contrast 13.14; 17.4). *Stone him,* see 13.10n.

21.22–23: Treatment of the executed. Public exposure of the corpse of an executed criminal, which was not the norm, was a form of reproach directed against enemies of the state (Josh 8.29; 10.26; 1 Sam 31.10; Esth 9.6–14). Out of respect for the body, to prevent it from serving as carrion (2 Sam 21.10), this law sets stringent limits to that procedure. **22:** *Hang . . . on a tree,* the Heb word for "tree" is broader; the law could also refer to suspension from "gallows" (Esth 9.13) or a "pole" (Gen 40.19), or possibly, based upon Neo-Assyrian precedent, impalement upon a stake.

22.1–12: Various moral and religious responsibilities of citizenship. The rationale for the sequence and selection of these laws is often unclear.

22.1–4: Moral duties toward the neighbor. Two laws (vv. 1–3,4) that develop two corresponding laws from the earlier Covenant Collection. **1–3:** The earlier law governing the return of wandering animals (Ex

ignore them; you shall take them back to
their owner. 2 If the owner does not reside
near you or you do not know who the own-
er is, you shall bring it to your own house,
and it shall remain with you until the own-
er claims it; then you shall return it. 3 You
shall do the same with a neighbor's donkey;
you shall do the same with a neighbor's
garment; and you shall do the same with
anything else that your neighbor loses and
you find. You may not withhold your help.
4 You shall not see your neighbor's don-
key or ox fallen on the road and ignore it;
you shall help to lift it up.
5 A woman shall not wear a man's ap-
parel, nor shall a man put on a woman's
garment; for whoever does such things is
abhorrent to the LORD your God.
6 If you come on a bird's nest, in any
tree or on the ground, with fledglings or
eggs, with the mother sitting on the fledg-
lings or on the eggs, you shall not take the
mother with the young. 7 Let the mother go,
taking only the young for yourself, in order
that it may go well with you and you may
live long.
8 When you build a new house, you
shall make a parapet for your roof; other-
wise you might have bloodguilt on your
house, if anyone should fall from it.
9 You shall not sow your vineyard with
a second kind of seed, or the whole yield
will have to be forfeited, both the crop that
you have sown and the yield of the vine-
yard itself.
10 You shall not plow with an ox and a
donkey yoked together.
11 You shall not wear clothes made of
wool and linen woven together.
12 You shall make tassels on the four
corners of the cloak with which you cover
yourself.
13 Suppose a man marries a woman, but
after going in to her, he dislikes her 14 and
makes up charges against her, slandering
her by saying, "I married this woman; but
when I lay with her, I did not find evidence
of her virginity." 15 The father of the young
woman and her mother shall then submit
the evidence of the young woman's virgini-
ty to the elders of the city at the gate. 16 The
father of the young woman shall say to the
elders: "I gave my daughter in marriage to
this man but he dislikes her; 17 now he has

21.1–3) is here revised and extended. **1:** *Your neighbor's ox,* in contrast to "your enemy's ox" (Ex 23.4). *Neighbor,* lit. "brother"; see 20.8n. **3:** *Anything else,* the earlier law is universalized to apply to any lost property. **4:** Reworking Ex 23.5 to emphasize the neighbor, as in v. 1.

22.5–12: Miscellaneous laws. 5: The prohibition against cross-dressing seeks to maintain gender boundaries; a similar concern for boundaries is evident in vv. 10–12. **6–7:** Avoiding simultaneous consumption of two generations of the same creature is also evident in other laws (14.21; Ex 23.19; 34.26; Lev 22.28). **8:** The *roof* was used as living space (Josh 2.6; Judg 3.20–25; 2 Sam 11.2). *Bloodguilt,* criminal negligence; a capital offense (see 19.10n.). **9–10:** Corresponding to Lev 19.19, these laws attempt to maintain specific boundaries between categories seen as incompatible (as in v. 5; 14.3–20). **9:** *Forfeited,* not permitted for human consumption. **12:** *Tassels,* this may reflect an application of royal garb, seen, for example, in Neo-Assyrian palace reliefs, to the nation as a whole. Num 15.37–40 gives a theological rationale.

22.13–30: Violations of marriage law. In the ancient Near East, marriage was a contractual relationship. The woman could not act independently: She remained in her father's household until a suitor paid a bride-price (vv. 28–29; Ex 22.16–17) to compensate for the reduction of the household. At that point she became formally "engaged," although still residing with her father (v. 21). Later, at the marriage feast, the union was consummated (Gen 29.22–25) and the woman took up residence in her husband's house.

22.13–21: False accusation of breach of marital contract. 14: *Makes up charges against her,* possibly for mercenary reasons, since nonfulfillment of the marital contract would entail refund of the bride-price and possibly a payment of a penalty for breach of contract. The *evidence,* the blood-stained cloth of v. 17. **15:** *Elders,* see 16.18n.; 21.19n. **17:** *The cloth* upon which husband and wife slept upon consummation of the relationship. It was understood that the cloth should have been bloodstained from the couple's first

made up charges against her, saying, 'I did
not find evidence of your daughter's virgin-
ity.' But here is the evidence of my daugh-
ter's virginity." Then they shall spread out
the cloth before the elders of the town.
18 The elders of that town shall take the
man and punish him; 19 they shall fine him
one hundred shekels of silver (which they
shall give to the young woman's father)
because he has slandered a virgin of Isra-
el. She shall remain his wife; he shall not
be permitted to divorce her as long as he
lives.

20 If, however, this charge is true, that
evidence of the young woman's virginity
was not found, 21 then they shall bring the
young woman out to the entrance of her
father's house and the men of her town
shall stone her to death, because she com-
mitted a disgraceful act in Israel by prosti-
tuting herself in her father's house. So you
shall purge the evil from your midst.

22 If a man is caught lying with the wife
of another man, both of them shall die, the
man who lay with the woman as well as the
woman. So you shall purge the evil from
Israel.

23 If there is a young woman, a virgin
already engaged to be married, and a man
meets her in the town and lies with her,
24 you shall bring both of them to the gate
of that town and stone them to death, the
young woman because she did not cry for
help in the town and the man because he
violated his neighbor's wife. So you shall
purge the evil from your midst.

25 But if the man meets the engaged
woman in the open country, and the man
seizes her and lies with her, then only the
man who lay with her shall die. 26 You shall
do nothing to the young woman; the young
woman has not committed an offense pun-
ishable by death, because this case is like
that of someone who attacks and murders
a neighbor. 27 Since he found her in the
open country, the engaged woman may
have cried for help, but there was no one to
rescue her.

28 If a man meets a virgin who is not
engaged, and seizes her and lies with her,
and they are caught in the act, 29 the man
who lay with her shall give fifty shekels of
silver to the young woman's father, and she
shall become his wife. Because he violated

intercourse; there is scant medical support for this widespread assumption. **19:** *They shall fine him,* the penalty for his slanderous accusation is financial, although the penalty for her infidelity, if proven true, is capital (vv. 20–21); contrast 19.19. *One hundred shekels,* about 1.1 kg (2.5 lb), twice the fine for rape (v. 29). **21:** *Entrance of her father's house,* at the very site of the offense. *Stone her to death,* see 13.10n. *Disgraceful act in Israel,* a violation of basic community sexual and religious norms (Gen 34.7; Josh 7.15; Judg 19.23–34; 20.6,10). *Purge the evil,* see 13.5n.

22.22–30: Adultery and rape. 22: Adultery is a violation of the seventh commandment (5.18) and a capital offense (Lev 18.20; 20.10). *Both of them shall die,* a contrast with ancient Near Eastern norms, which required the male's death but left the wife's fate to her husband. The law removes the wife from her husband's authority and defines her as a legal person accountable for her actions. **23–27:** Two laws to determine culpability (vv. 23–24) or nonculpability (vv. 25–27) in cases of rape. Both laws show detailed points of contact with *Middle Assyrian Laws* (*M.A.L.;* ca. 1076 BCE). **23:** *Engaged to be married,* this legal status permits the transition from adultery to rape: Although the woman still resides with her father, she is contractually bound to her future husband. *In the town,* where there are potential witnesses (*M.A.L.* § A 12). **25:** The assault in *open country,* where there are no likely witnesses, suggests planned malice. **26:** *Like . . . someone who attacks and murders a neighbor,* i.e., premeditated (19.11–13). Rape is a criminal assault rather than a sex crime. **28–29:** These conditions correspond to *M.A.L.* § A 55, which implies forced rape. In contrast, Ex 22.16–17 specifies intercourse with, but not forced rape of, a "virgin who is not engaged." The conflation of these two models in this law leaves it unclear whether or not it refers to consensual intercourse. **28:** *And lies with her,* as in Ex 22.16, placing the woman in a legally ambiguous position, unavailable to others (v. 14). **29:** *Fifty shekels,* presumably the bride-price. In contrast to Ex 22.17, the father's consent is not sought. Postbiblical Jewish law granted both father and daughter the right to refuse. **30:** A transition to the next section. *Father's wife,* i.e., a widowed step-

her he shall not be permitted to divorce her
as long as he lives.
30[a] A man shall not marry his father's
wife, thereby violating his father's rights.[b]
23 No one whose testicles are crushed
or whose penis is cut off shall be
admitted to the assembly of the LORD.
2 Those born of an illicit union shall not
be admitted to the assembly of the LORD.
Even to the tenth generation, none of their
descendants shall be admitted to the assem-
bly of the LORD.
3 No Ammonite or Moabite shall be ad-
mitted to the assembly of the LORD. Even
to the tenth generation, none of their de-
scendants shall be admitted to the assembly
of the LORD, 4 because they did not meet
you with food and water on your journey
out of Egypt, and because they hired
against you Balaam son of Beor, from Pe-
thor of Mesopotamia, to curse you. 5 (Yet
the LORD your God refused to heed Ba-
laam; the LORD your God turned the curse
into a blessing for you, because the LORD
your God loved you.) 6 You shall never pro-
mote their welfare or their prosperity as
long as you live.
7 You shall not abhor any of the Edom-
ites, for they are your kin. You shall not
abhor any of the Egyptians, because you
were an alien residing in their land. 8 The
children of the third generation that are
born to them may be admitted to the as-
sembly of the LORD.
9 When you are encamped against your
enemies you shall guard against any impro-
priety.
10 If one of you becomes unclean be-
cause of a nocturnal emission, then he shall
go outside the camp; he must not come
within the camp. 11 When evening comes,
he shall wash himself with water, and when
the sun has set, he may come back into the
camp.
12 You shall have a designated area out-
side the camp to which you shall go.
13 With your utensils you shall have a trow-
el; when you relieve yourself outside, you
shall dig a hole with it and then cover up
your excrement. 14 Because the LORD your
God travels along with your camp, to save
you and to hand over your enemies to you,
therefore your camp must be holy, so that

a Ch 23.1 in Heb *b* Heb *uncovering his father's skirt*

mother (see Lev 18.7–8). *Violating his father's rights,* lit. "uncovering his father's skirt" (text note *b*); i.e., even indirect sexual contact with him must be avoided (Gen 9.23–24; 49.4; Lev 18.8; 20.11).

23.1–8: Restrictions on access to Israel's assembly. *The assembly of the LORD* (v. 1), the national governing body, or popular legislature, was charged with a broad range of judicial, political, and policy matters (Judg 20.2). **1:** *Testicles . . . penis,* the same physiological qualification that the Holiness Collection requires of the priesthood (Lev 21.17–23), now extended to all Israel (see 14.2n.). **2:** *Illicit union,* incestuous marriages (v. 3; 22.30; Lev 18.6–18). *Tenth generation,* see v. 3n. **3–8:** The restrictions do not entail denial of residence rights, and those named would retain the protection afforded by the legal status of "resident alien" (see 1.16; 5.14; Lev 19.10,33–34; 23.22). **3–6:** These laws were reused in the postexilic context to prohibit intermarriage (Ezra 9–10; Neh 13.1–3). **3:** *Ammonite or Moabite,* perhaps introduced after v. 2 because of an older tradition concerning their incestuous origins (Gen 19.30–38). *Tenth generation,* "forever," as explicitly stated in the Hebrew. **4:** The rationale varies from the earlier report that Israel detoured around Ammon without requesting assistance and received food and water from Moab (2.19,29,37). *Balaam,* see Num 22–24. **7:** *Not abhor . . . Edomites,* an extraordinary inclusion, since the Edomites participated in the destruction of Jerusalem (Ps 137.7; Obadiah). *Kin,* through Esau (Gen 25.24–26; 36.1). *Egyptians,* this injunction remarkably overlooks the enslavement (26.6; 28.60,68; Ex 1–15), going back to the provision of sanctuary (Gen 12; 37–50).

23.9–14: Special rules for the military camp. The theology of holy war assumes God's direct participation in the campaign (7.17–24; 20.4), creating a demand for heightened purity, like that required of the entire people at Sinai (Ex 19.10,14). Sexual abstinence seems also to have been required (1 Sam 21.4–5; 2 Sam 11.8–11; cf. Ex 19.15). **10–11:** Cf. Lev 15.16–18. **12:** *Designated area,* a latrine. **14:** *Travels along,* see 20.4; 31.6. *Anything indecent,* as in 24.1.

he may not see anything indecent among
you and turn away from you.
15 Slaves who have escaped to you from
their owners shall not be given back to
them. 16 They shall reside with you, in your
midst, in any place they choose in any one
of your towns, wherever they please; you
shall not oppress them.
17 None of the daughters of Israel shall
be a temple prostitute; none of the sons of
Israel shall be a temple prostitute. 18 You
shall not bring the fee of a prostitute or the
wages of a male prostitute[a] into the house
of the LORD your God in payment for any
vow, for both of these are abhorrent to the
LORD your God.
19 You shall not charge interest on
loans to another Israelite, interest on mon-
ey, interest on provisions, interest on any-
thing that is lent. 20 On loans to a foreigner
you may charge interest, but on loans to
another Israelite you may not charge inter-
est, so that the LORD your God may bless
you in all your undertakings in the land
that you are about to enter and possess.
21 If you make a vow to the LORD your
God, do not postpone fulfilling it; for the
LORD your God will surely require it of
you, and you would incur guilt. 22 But if
you refrain from vowing, you will not incur
guilt. 23 Whatever your lips utter you must
diligently perform, just as you have freely
vowed to the LORD your God with your
own mouth.
24 If you go into your neighbor's vine-
yard, you may eat your fill of grapes, as
many as you wish, but you shall not put
any in a container.
25 If you go into your neighbor's stand-
ing grain, you may pluck the ears with your
hand, but you shall not put a sickle to your
neighbor's standing grain.
24 Suppose a man enters into marriage
with a woman, but she does not

a Heb *a dog*

23.15–25.19: The heightened moral responsibilities of the covenant community.

23.15–16: Prohibition of the return of escaped slaves. The law rejects the almost universal stipulation within ancient Near Eastern law that escaped slaves must be returned (*Laws of Hammurabi* §§ 16–20; *Hittite Laws* §§ 22–24). **16:** The extraordinary repetition emphasizes that the entire community must be open to them.

23.17–18: Restrictions on prostitution. These verses presuppose the inevitability of prostitution, while proscribing it for Israelites and regulating it in such a way as to preserve the Temple's sanctity. **17:** *Temple prostitute* (Heb "qedesha"), the translation reflects belief in the existence of sacred prostitution in Israel and the ancient Near East, for which there is scant evidence; more likely "qedesha" is a standard euphemism for the coarser term for prostitute (v. 18). The same alternation between the two terms appears in Gen 38.15,21. The word might better be translated as "one set aside." **18:** *Prostitute,* Heb "zonah," closer to "whore" (Hos 1.2). *Male prostitute* (lit. "dog"), in context, the male counterpart to a common female prostitute. To maintain holiness, the law proscribes the donation of income gained from prostitution to the Temple (cf. Hos 4.14; Mic 1.7).

23.19–25: Financial ethics, vows, gathering by the needy. 19–20: This law builds on Ex 22.25, which clarifies that lending served primarily as a means of social support for "the poor among you" (similarly Lev 25.36–37). Charging interest would amount to profiteering from the misfortunes of others. **20:** *A foreigner,* as distinct from the "resident alien," who fully participated in Israel's social welfare system (see 1.16n.); for similar distinctions, see 15.3; Lev 25.44–45. **21–23:** A *vow* (v. 21) promises payment of something to God (usually a sacrifice at a temple) in exchange for receiving something (see 1 Sam 1.11). This cautious reserve about vows, understandable in light of Judg 11.29–40, closely corresponds to wisdom teachings (Eccl 5.4–6). For a more positive view, see Ps 50.14. **24–25:** These rules prohibit exploitation of Deuteronomy's extensive support system for the needy (14.28–29; 24.19–22; 25.4). **25:** *Pluck . . . hand,* to address immediate hunger (Lk 6.1; cf. Mt 12.1; Mk 2.23).

Chs 24–25: Laws promoting social harmony. 24.1–22: The chapter, like the previous one, begins with a restriction on marriage and concludes stipulating care for those in need (note 22.30 = 23.1 Heb). **1–4:** This complex law, theologically applied by two prophets (Isa 50.1; Jer 3.1,8), addresses only remarriage

please him because he finds something ob-
jectionable about her, and so he writes her
a certificate of divorce, puts it in her hand,
and sends her out of his house; she then
leaves his house 2 and goes off to become
another man's wife. 3 Then suppose the sec-
ond man dislikes her, writes her a bill of
divorce, puts it in her hand, and sends her
out of his house (or the second man who
married her dies); 4 her first husband, who
sent her away, is not permitted to take her
again to be his wife after she has been de-
filed; for that would be abhorrent to the
LORD, and you shall not bring guilt on the
land that the LORD your God is giving you
as a possession.
5 When a man is newly married, he shall
not go out with the army or be charged
with any related duty. He shall be free at
home one year, to be happy with the wife
whom he has married.
6 No one shall take a mill or an upper
millstone in pledge, for that would be tak-
ing a life in pledge.
7 If someone is caught kidnaping anoth-
er Israelite, enslaving or selling the Israelite,
then that kidnaper shall die. So you shall
purge the evil from your midst.
8 Guard against an outbreak of a lep-
rous[a] skin disease by being very careful;
you shall carefully observe whatever the le-
vitical priests instruct you, just as I have
commanded them. 9 Remember what the
LORD your God did to Miriam on your
journey out of Egypt.
10 When you make your neighbor a
loan of any kind, you shall not go into the
house to take the pledge. 11 You shall wait
outside, while the person to whom you are
making the loan brings the pledge out to
you. 12 If the person is poor, you shall not
sleep in the garment given you as[b] the
pledge. 13 You shall give the pledge back by
sunset, so that your neighbor may sleep in
the cloak and bless you; and it will be to
your credit before the LORD your God.
14 You shall not withhold the wages of
poor and needy laborers, whether other Is-
raelites or aliens who reside in your land in
one of your towns. 15 You shall pay them
their wages daily before sunset, because
they are poor and their livelihood depends
on them; otherwise they might cry to the
LORD against you, and you would incur
guilt.
16 Parents shall not be put to death for
their children, nor shall children be put to

a A term for several skin diseases; precise meaning uncertain *b* Heb lacks *the garment given you as*

after divorce to a wife who subsequently married another; it does not prohibit remarriage in general. Biblical law includes no general laws of either marriage or divorce, only special cases that raise particular ethical or religious issues. **1:** Male-initiated divorce was the norm, though there is some evidence in the Near East and in the Jewish Elephantine papyri (fifth century BCE) of contracts permitting either party to initiate proceedings. *He finds . . . about her,* formula for disloyal action or betrayal of trust (1 Sam 29.3,6,8; 2 Kings 17.4; cf. 1 Sam 12.5). *Objectionable,* "indecent" (23.14). It is unclear from the term used what valid criteria for divorce were. *Certificate of divorce,* legally freeing her to remarry. **4:** *After she has been defiled,* not in general, since she is permitted to remarry, but specifically as regards relations with her first husband. **5:** Another of the rules for holy war (20.1–20; 21.10–14; 23.9–14). *Newly married,* contrast the premarital deferral from service in 20.7. *Be happy with,* better, "give happiness to," including conjugal joy. **6:** The law prohibits oppression in economic relations (like vv. 10–15). *Take . . . in pledge,* accept as collateral for a loan. *Mill or an upper millstone,* like the "garment" of v. 12, they are essential to survival, and thus may not be taken. **7:** Restricts the application of Ex 21.16 to kidnappers of fellow Israelites; perhaps also an interpretation of Deut 5.19. **8–9:** *Leprous skin disease,* not leprosy but an unidentified inflammation; see Lev 13.1–14.57. *Remember . . . Miriam,* see Num 12.1–15. **10–13:** Expands upon Ex 22.26–27 (cf. Am 2.8; Prov 20.16; 22.27; 27.13; Job 22.6). The Yavneh Yam inscription (late seventh century BCE) deals with a similar case. **14–15:** See Ex 22.21–24; Lev 19.13. Israel's ethics are based upon the conviction that God identifies with and vindicates the oppressed. **14:** The prohibition against economic exploitation is not contingent upon ethnicity or nationality; see 1.16n. **16:** This law restricting punishment to the responsible individual, cited in 2 Kings 14.6, applies to both civil and criminal law. Collective

death for their parents; only for their own
crimes may persons be put to death.
17 You shall not deprive a resident alien
or an orphan of justice; you shall not take
a widow's garment in pledge. 18 Remember
that you were a slave in Egypt and the
LORD your God redeemed you from there;
therefore I command you to do this.
19 When you reap your harvest in your
field and forget a sheaf in the field, you
shall not go back to get it; it shall be left for
the alien, the orphan, and the widow, so
that the LORD your God may bless you in
all your undertakings. 20 When you beat
your olive trees, do not strip what is left; it
shall be for the alien, the orphan, and the
widow.
21 When you gather the grapes of your
vineyard, do not glean what is left; it shall
be for the alien, the orphan, and the wid-
ow. 22 Remember that you were a slave in
the land of Egypt; therefore I am com-
manding you to do this.
25 Suppose two persons have a dispute
and enter into litigation, and the
judges decide between them, declaring one
to be in the right and the other to be in the
wrong. 2 If the one in the wrong deserves to
be flogged, the judge shall make that per-
son lie down and be beaten in his presence
with the number of lashes proportionate to
the offense. 3 Forty lashes may be given but
not more; if more lashes than these are giv-
en, your neighbor will be degraded in your
sight.
4 You shall not muzzle an ox while it is
treading out the grain.
5 When brothers reside together, and
one of them dies and has no son, the wife of
the deceased shall not be married outside
the family to a stranger. Her husband's
brother shall go in to her, taking her in
marriage, and performing the duty of a
husband's brother to her, 6 and the first-
born whom she bears shall succeed to the
name of the deceased brother, so that his
name may not be blotted out of Israel. 7 But
if the man has no desire to marry his broth-
er's widow, then his brother's widow shall
go up to the elders at the gate and say, "My
husband's brother refuses to perpetuate his
brother's name in Israel; he will not per-

responsibility applies to offenses against God (5.9–10; Ex 34.7; Num 16.31–33; Josh 7.24–25; 2 Sam 21.1–9), a theological principle subsequently brought into conformity with the law of individual liability (7.10; Jer 31.29–30; Ezek 18). **17:** *You shall not deprive . . . of justice,* in Hebrew, identical to the comprehensive "You shall not distort justice" (16.19). This law, therefore, ensures protection of the most vulnerable, the *resident alien* or the *orphan. Take . . . in pledge,* better, "seize" to force payment (see Job 24.3). This accords the *widow* special protection; for day laborers, see vv. 10–13. **18:** See 15.15. **19–22:** Lev 19.9–10; 23.22. The story of Ruth, both a widow and an alien, presupposes such laws, which assign harvest gleanings to the needy, allowing them to eat without begging for food. **20:** *Beat,* with poles, so as to harvest the olives (Isa 17.6). **25.1–3:** A double restriction upon judicial flogging, also employed for discipline in nonjudicial contexts (Ex 21.20; Prov 10.13; 26.3; 1 Kings 12.14). **2:** *In his presence,* under the judge's direct supervision, "by [his] count" (the more likely rendering of NRSV *number of lashes*). **3:** *Forty lashes,* a definitive restriction for which there is no parallel in Near Eastern law; the *Middle Assyrian Laws* stipulate floggings of five to one hundred lashes. *Your neighbor,* the criminal, despite his judicial status, retains human dignity. **4:** For similar humane treatment of animals, see 22.6–7; Prov 12.10. **5–10:** Biblical, Near Eastern, and Roman inheritance law assigned special responsibilities to the "husband's brother" (vv. 5–7), for which Hebrew had a special term (cf. Latin "levir," hence "levirate marriage"). See Gen 38.8 and Ruth 4.5–6, which reflect variations of this law. **5:** *Outside the family,* NRSV has added *the family;* more likely, the frame of reference is the larger clan. The widow's marriage outside of the clan would diminish the landholding of her clan and add it to the husband's, affecting the original equitable division of land among the tribes (Josh 13–21). *Her husband's brother shall go in to her,* possibly the brother's death provided an exception to the incest prohibition of marrying a sister-in-law (Lev 18.16; 20.21); alternatively, the Holiness Collection's incest laws might intend to prohibit levirate marriage altogether. **6:** *Firstborn* alone here counts to the brother; cf. Gen 38.8. **9:** Legal title was symbolically claimed by walking over the land (see 11.24n.). Thus, transfer of title

form the duty of a husband's brother to
me." [8]Then the elders of his town shall
summon him and speak to him. If he per-
sists, saying, "I have no desire to marry
her," [9]then his brother's wife shall go up to
him in the presence of the elders, pull his
sandal off his foot, spit in his face, and de-
clare, "This is what is done to the man who
does not build up his brother's house."
[10]Throughout Israel his family shall be
known as "the house of him whose sandal
was pulled off."

11 If men get into a fight with one an-
other, and the wife of one intervenes to res-
cue her husband from the grip of his oppo-
nent by reaching out and seizing his
genitals, [12]you shall cut off her hand; show
no pity.

13 You shall not have in your bag two
kinds of weights, large and small. [14]You
shall not have in your house two kinds of
measures, large and small. [15]You shall have
only a full and honest weight; you shall
have only a full and honest measure, so that
your days may be long in the land that the
LORD your God is giving you. [16]For all
who do such things, all who act dishonest-
ly, are abhorrent to the LORD your God.

17 Remember what Amalek did to you
on your journey out of Egypt, [18]how he
attacked you on the way, when you were
faint and weary, and struck down all who
lagged behind you; he did not fear God.
[19]Therefore when the LORD your God has
given you rest from all your enemies on
every hand, in the land that the LORD your
God is giving you as an inheritance to pos-
sess, you shall blot out the remembrance of
Amalek from under heaven; do not forget.

26 When you have come into the land
that the LORD your God is giving
you as an inheritance to possess, and you
possess it, and settle in it, [2]you shall take
some of the first of all the fruit of the
ground, which you harvest from the land
that the LORD your God is giving you, and
you shall put it in a basket and go to the
place that the LORD your God will choose
as a dwelling for his name. [3]You shall go to
the priest who is in office at that time, and
say to him, "Today I declare to the LORD
your God that I have come into the land
that the LORD swore to our ancestors to
give us." [4]When the priest takes the basket
from your hand and sets it down before the
altar of the LORD your God, [5]you shall

entailed passing the *sandal* (Ruth 4.7), while renunciation of title, as here, was symbolized by removal of the *sandal.* The intent of the ceremony is public shaming, since the dereliction of duty makes the brother's wife a widow, abandoning her to the class of the impoverished: "the resident aliens, the orphans, and the widows" (14.29n.). **10:** *Known as,* lit. "called by the name of," thus explicitly applying a form of retributive justice (19.19n.). For refusing to build up the deceased's "name" (vv. 6–7) and "house" (v. 9), the brother's own *house* is stigmatized by its new name. **11–12:** An additional law dealing with threats to reproduction (cf. Ex 21.22–25). Physical mutilation (characteristic in the *Middle Assyrian Laws*) is nowhere else prescribed in the Bible, except in the general formula for talion (19.21; Ex 21.23–24; Lev 24.19–20). That rationale does not apply here, however, since there is no symmetry between injury and punishment. The issue may rather be the perceived insult to dignity (cf. *Laws of Hammurabi* § 195). **13–16:** Cf. *Laws of Hammurabi* § 108; Lev 19.35–36; Am 8.5. **14:** By fraudulently using two different sets of counterweights—small ones to sell grain but large ones to purchase it—a merchant could turn a tidy profit. **17–19:** The tradition presupposes Ex 17.8–16, in which the Amalekites, a fierce desert tribe, attacked Israel (cf. Ps 83.4–8). **18:** These details are not reflected in Ex 17.8–16; they may have been supplied by the Deuteronomic author in order to justify the extirpation of Amalek (v. 19; cf. Ex 17.14; 1 Sam 15.2–3). **19:** *Rest,* see 3.20; 12.9n.

26.1–15: Concluding liturgies. Two already prescribed laws (14.22–29) are given a historical and theological foundation (similarly, 16.12, for the festival of weeks). **1–11:** The context is the festival of weeks (16.9–12), when the Israelite was to make an annual pilgrimage to the central sanctuary, bringing the first fruits of the harvest, to thank God for the land's bounty. **4:** *When the priest,* contrast v. 10. Vv. 3–4 may be a later addition intended to emphasize the role of priests in the ceremony. Thus, v. 5 may have originally continued v. 2. **5:** *Wandering Aramean* suggests the Jacob tradition (Gen 25.20).

make this response before the LORD your
God: "A wandering Aramean was my an-
cestor; he went down into Egypt and lived
there as an alien, few in number, and there
he became a great nation, mighty and pop-
ulous. 6 When the Egyptians treated us
harshly and afflicted us, by imposing hard
labor on us, 7 we cried to the LORD, the
God of our ancestors; the LORD heard our
voice and saw our affliction, our toil, and
our oppression. 8 The LORD brought us out
of Egypt with a mighty hand and an out-
stretched arm, with a terrifying display of
power, and with signs and wonders; 9 and
he brought us into this place and gave us
this land, a land flowing with milk and
honey. 10 So now I bring the first of the fruit
of the ground that you, O LORD, have giv-
en me." You shall set it down before the
LORD your God and bow down before the
LORD your God. 11 Then you, together with
the Levites and the aliens who reside
among you, shall celebrate with all the
bounty that the LORD your God has given
to you and to your house.

12 When you have finished paying all
the tithe of your produce in the third year
(which is the year of the tithe), giving it to
the Levites, the aliens, the orphans, and the
widows, so that they may eat their fill with-
in your towns, 13 then you shall say before
the LORD your God: "I have removed the
sacred portion from the house, and I have
given it to the Levites, the resident aliens,
the orphans, and the widows, in accor-
dance with your entire commandment that
you commanded me; I have neither trans-
gressed nor forgotten any of your com-
mandments: 14 I have not eaten of it while
in mourning; I have not removed any of it
while I was unclean; and I have not offered
any of it to the dead. I have obeyed the
LORD my God, doing just as you com-
manded me. 15 Look down from your holy
habitation, from heaven, and bless your
people Israel and the ground that you have
given us, as you swore to our ancestors—a
land flowing with milk and honey."

16 This very day the LORD your God is
commanding you to observe these statutes

6: *Afflicted . . . hard labor,* see Ex 1.11–14. **8–9:** It is striking that the giving of the law on Horeb is missing here. Perhaps this ancient liturgy did not know of this event. Alternatively, the giving of the law might not be thematically appropriate to a unit that emphasizes God's role as liberator. **11:** *Celebrate,* or "rejoice" (16.11,14–15), specifically in a festive meal consumed at the central sanctuary (12.7,18), which must include *the Levites and the aliens.* The mention of these marginal groups provides a transition to the following law. **12–15:** Produce was tithed annually and consumed by the farmer and his household at the central sanctuary (14.22–27); every third year that tithe was used locally to support the poor (14.28–29). **12:** *Aliens . . . widows,* see 1.16n.; 14.29; 23.3–8,20n. **14:** The formula, containing a triple confession of the donor's ritual purity, probably originated in donations of produce to God at a sanctuary, where purity would be expected. That formula has now been reused for the donation of food to the poor "within your towns" (v. 12). *Offered any of it to the dead,* the duty of the living to care for dead ancestors through food offerings at their place of burial was widely assumed in the ancient Near East (see the Ugaritic Aqhat epic), and continued to be carried out in Second Temple times (Tob 4.17). This practice is not in itself condemned; it is viewed as improper only in relation to sacred donations, because of the impurity associated with death (Lev 22.2–4). **15:** *From your holy habitation, from heaven,* as in 1 Kings 8.30. The double proposition may point to the correction of an older theology in light of a newer one, following Deuteronomy's normal view that only God's name resides in the Temple (12.11; 16.11; 26.2). For the earlier idea, that God himself inhabits the Temple, see 1 Kings 8.13; cf. Deut 12.5. *Bless your people Israel and the ground,* the farmer prays for the blessing of the community and of the land, not directly for fertility or the abundance of his own crops.

26.16–19: Formal conclusion, which presents the legal corpus as a mutually binding relationship between God and Israel. Having just read the law to the people, Moses presents it to them in a formal ratification ceremony (vv. 17–18; cf. 2 Kings 23.1–3). **16:** *Statutes and ordinances . . . observe . . . diligently* forms an inclusio with 12.1, thus providing the laws of chs 12–26 with an elegant frame to mark their conclusion. **17–18:** *Obtained,* the past tense points to a prior action or speech, no record of which

and ordinances; so observe them diligently
with all your heart and with all your soul.
[17]Today you have obtained the LORD's
agreement: to be your God; and for you to
walk in his ways, to keep his statutes, his
commandments, and his ordinances, and to
obey him. [18]Today the LORD has obtained
your agreement: to be his treasured people,
as he promised you, and to keep his com-
mandments; [19]for him to set you high
above all nations that he has made, in
praise and in fame and in honor; and for
you to be a people holy to the LORD your
God, as he promised.

27 Then Moses and the elders of Israel
charged all the people as follows:
Keep the entire commandment that I am
commanding you today. [2]On the day that
you cross over the Jordan into the land that
the LORD your God is giving you, you shall
set up large stones and cover them with
plaster. [3]You shall write on them all the
words of this law when you have crossed
over, to enter the land that the LORD your
God is giving you, a land flowing with milk
and honey, as the LORD, the God of your
ancestors, promised you. [4]So when you
have crossed over the Jordan, you shall set
up these stones, about which I am com-
manding you today, on Mount Ebal, and
you shall cover them with plaster. [5]And
you shall build an altar there to the LORD

survives, in which each party has proclaimed what is here described. Deuteronomy emphasizes that both Israel and God have explicitly assented to the covenant and have affirmed the mutuality of the obligations that each undertakes. This reciprocal model contrasts with the Sinai covenant, which was unilaterally offered by God (Ex 19.3–6) and unilaterally agreed to by Israel (Ex 19.8; 24.3,7). Deuteronomy invokes the language of the Sinai covenant as a model while revising it in the process. **18:** *His treasured people,* see 7.6n. *In praise . . . fame . . . and . . . honor,* NRSV implies that the accolades will be given to Israel. The Hebrew also allows for the possibility that the honors will go to God because of his action on Israel's behalf (see Jer 13.11; 33.9). *As he promised you,* Ex 19.5–6. **19:** *High above all nations,* see 28.13–14n. *That he has made,* see Ex 19.5b. *A people holy to the LORD* continues the reference to Ex 19.5–6, while substituting *people* for "nation," which Deuteronomy uses for non-Israelites (12.29).

27.1–26: The ceremonies at Shechem. The injunctions of 11.29–32 are here reiterated and detailed. The laws of chs 12–26 are thus framed with ceremonies that connect entry into the land with obedience to Torah. The chapter joins four separate sections that are only loosely connected to one another and to the rest of Deuteronomy. A later editor has aligned the sections with one another, while breaking up the continuity of the Mosaic speech of chs 26 and 28. The resulting digression preserves several competing traditions about how and where the covenant between God and Israel was concluded: at Sinai; or on the plains of Moab; or at Gilgal immediately upon entering the land; or at the important northern shrine of Shechem (see 11.29n.). **1–8:** This section combines two separate requirements: the raising of plastered stones inscribed with the Torah (vv. 1–4,8) and the construction of a stone altar for sacrifice (vv. 5–7). **1:** Moses is here referred to in the third person, interrupting his first-person address (chs 5–26; 28). *And the elders,* nowhere else in Deuteronomy do they join Moses in addressing the people; this plural subject does not easily fit the following singular *I*. **2:** *On the day . . . large stones,* the Deuteronomistic Historian understands this command to have been fulfilled at Gilgal, just across the Jordan and less than a mile from Jericho (see Josh 4). *Cover them with plaster,* to serve as a surface for inscription. Archaeology attests the use of plaster-covered wall or stele inscriptions. **4:** *Mount Ebal,* at over 1,000 m (3,000 ft), the tallest mountain in the region. It lies in central Canaan, adjacent to the city of Shechem. But that site, more than 50 km (30 mi) from the Jordan, is inconsistent with v. 2 and the beginning of this verse, which each anticipate that the ceremony will take place immediately upon crossing the river. It would be impossible to reach Shechem in a day. The most logical explanation is that Josh 4 points to the original form of these verses, with Gilgal as the site where Israel complied with this command. That older tradition was then replaced here by the reference to the mountains around Shechem, the chief town of the northern tribes (Josh 24.1,32). **5–7:** These verses are an insertion that reinterprets the plastered stones on which the Torah is to be inscribed as an altar of *unhewn stones,* following Ex 20.25. Such an altar, outside of Jerusalem, conflicts with the centralization requirement of ch 12, and further suggests the antiquity and

your God, an altar of stones on which you
have not used an iron tool. 6 You must
build the altar of the LORD your God of
unhewn[a] stones. Then offer up burnt
offerings on it to the LORD your God,
7 make sacrifices of well-being, and eat
them there, rejoicing before the LORD your
God. 8 You shall write on the stones all the
words of this law very clearly.
9 Then Moses and the levitical priests
spoke to all Israel, saying: Keep silence and
hear, O Israel! This very day you have be-
come the people of the LORD your God.
10 Therefore obey the LORD your God, ob-
serving his commandments and his statutes
that I am commanding you today.
11 The same day Moses charged the
people as follows: 12 When you have
crossed over the Jordan, these shall stand
on Mount Gerizim for the blessing of the
people: Simeon, Levi, Judah, Issachar, Jo-
seph, and Benjamin. 13 And these shall
stand on Mount Ebal for the curse: Reu-
ben, Gad, Asher, Zebulun, Dan, and Naph-
tali. 14 Then the Levites shall declare in a
loud voice to all the Israelites:
15 "Cursed be anyone who makes an
idol or casts an image, anything abhorrent
to the LORD, the work of an artisan, and
sets it up in secret." All the people shall
respond, saying, "Amen!"
16 "Cursed be anyone who dishonors
father or mother." All the people shall say,
"Amen!"
17 "Cursed be anyone who moves a
neighbor's boundary marker." All the peo-
ple shall say, "Amen!"
18 "Cursed be anyone who misleads a
blind person on the road." All the people
shall say, "Amen!"
19 "Cursed be anyone who deprives the
alien, the orphan, and the widow of jus-
tice." All the people shall say, "Amen!"
20 "Cursed be anyone who lies with his
father's wife, because he has violated his
father's rights."[b] All the people shall say,
"Amen!"
21 "Cursed be anyone who lies with any
animal." All the people shall say, "Amen!"
22 "Cursed be anyone who lies with his
sister, whether the daughter of his father or
the daughter of his mother." All the people
shall say, "Amen!"
23 "Cursed be anyone who lies with his
mother-in-law." All the people shall say,
"Amen!"

a Heb *whole* b Heb *uncovered his father's skirt*

the independence of this tradition from the rest of Deuteronomy. The fulfillment of this law is narrated in Josh 8.30–35. **9–10:** This is a new paragraph, independent of what precedes it. **9:** *And the levitical priests,* see v. 1n.; here too the plural subject is continued by "I" (v. 10). *This very day,* contrast statements that define the bond as previously formed, either at the time of the Exodus (Ex 6.6–7) or at Sinai (4.20; Ex 19.5–6). **11–13:** A fragment that refers to an ancient covenant ceremony at Shechem, instituted at the command of Moses (Josh 8.30–35). The antiquity of the tribal list is seen in the facts that Levi is listed as a tribe (Gen 49.5–7) and that the division of the house of Joseph into Manasseh and Ephraim has not yet occurred (Gen 49.22–26; contrast Deut 33.17). The division of the tribes into two groups of six is attested only here. **11:** *The same day,* lit. "on that day," without further specification. **12–13:** *Mount Gerizim for the blessing . . . Mount Ebal for the curse,* see 11.29n. One group of tribes, on Gerizim, proclaims a set of blessings (see 28.1–14); the other, on Ebal, a set of curses (see 28.15–68). **14–26:** Despite the paragraphing in NRSV, v. 14 more likely begins a new section, with a very different conception of the ceremony: The tribe of Levi alone proclaims a set of prohibited actions and *all the people*—acting in unison and not divided into tribes—respond, *Amen* (see Jer 11.3–5). There is no list of blessings (cf. v. 12). Nor is the "curse" intended by v. 13 (a description of divine punishment for wrongful action, as in 28.15–68) provided. The "cursed be" proclamations here stigmatize a summary list of rejected actions while making no references to the consequences of the transgressions. **14:** *Levites,* Deuteronomy's normal term is "Levitical priests" (v. 9; 18.1). **15–26:** The twelve curses correspond to the twelve tribes, although this section makes no reference to the tribal division and the people function as a single entity (v. 14). The resulting incongruence points to the many editorial revisions that this chapter has undergone.

24 "Cursed be anyone who strikes down
a neighbor in secret." All the people shall
say, "Amen!"
25 "Cursed be anyone who takes a bribe
to shed innocent blood." All the people
shall say, "Amen!"
26 "Cursed be anyone who does not up-
hold the words of this law by observing
them." All the people shall say, "Amen!"

28 If you will only obey the LORD your
God, by diligently observing all his
commandments that I am commanding you
today, the LORD your God will set you high
above all the nations of the earth; 2 all these
blessings shall come upon you and overtake
you, if you obey the LORD your God:
3 Blessed shall you be in the city, and
blessed shall you be in the field.
4 Blessed shall be the fruit of your
womb, the fruit of your ground, and the
fruit of your livestock, both the increase of
your cattle and the issue of your flock.
5 Blessed shall be your basket and your
kneading bowl.
6 Blessed shall you be when you come
in, and blessed shall you be when you go
out.
7 The LORD will cause your enemies
who rise against you to be defeated before
you; they shall come out against you one
way, and flee before you seven ways. 8 The
LORD will command the blessing upon you
in your barns, and in all that you under-
take; he will bless you in the land that the
LORD your God is giving you. 9 The LORD
will establish you as his holy people, as he
has sworn to you, if you keep the com-
mandments of the LORD your God and
walk in his ways. 10 All the peoples of the
earth shall see that you are called by the
name of the LORD, and they shall be afraid
of you. 11 The LORD will make you abound
in prosperity, in the fruit of your womb, in
the fruit of your livestock, and in the fruit
of your ground in the land that the LORD
swore to your ancestors to give you. 12 The
LORD will open for you his rich storehouse,
the heavens, to give the rain of your land in
its season and to bless all your undertak-
ings. You will lend to many nations, but

28.1–68: The consequences of obedience or disobedience: blessing or curse. The covenant specifies a series of blessings and curses that follow upon national obedience or disobedience to the law. These are modeled after ancient Near Eastern state treaties, in which the consequences of breach of the treaty are spelled out at its conclusion; this chapter has several close parallels to the *Vassal Treaty of Esarhaddon* (*VTE*), a Neo-Assyrian treaty dating to 672 BCE. The disproportion between the sections devoted to blessing (vv. 1–14) and to curse (vv. 15–68) may be a reaction to the Babylonian conquest, deportation, and exile of Judah (597 and 586 BCE), here recast as a prophetic warning. Two appendices, vv. 47–57 and 58–68, each seek to make theological sense of that catastrophe. The two other legal collections of the Pentateuch (the Covenant Collection of Ex 21–23; the Holiness Collection of Lev 17–26) similarly end with exhortations to obedience, accompanied by blessings and curses (Ex 23.20–33; Lev 26). Here an inclusio frames and defines the blessings section: *if you . . . obey . . . by diligently observing* (vv. 1,13). **1–2:** The proem emphasizes the conditionality of the exalted status of Israel, perhaps because of the exile. *High above all the nations* (see also v. 13), a metaphor for the nation's election, also applied to the Davidic dynasty (Ps 89.27). (Contrast 26.19, where this affirmation is unconditional, fulfilling God's past promises.) **3–6:** The six benedictions have their malediction counterpart at vv. 16–19. The two antonym pairs (vv. 3,6) provide a frame to the unit. The opposites form a merism to stress totality (like "night and day"); see 6.7n. **3:** *City* and *field,* "everywhere," urban and rural. **4:** *Fruit . . . livestock,* fecundity is contingent upon obedience to God; see 7.12–14n. **7:** Military success is conditional upon covenantal obedience, rather than strength of arms (9.1–3; Josh 1.6–8). **9:** *The LORD will establish . . . if you keep,* holiness is conditional upon obedience, a shift from other passages where Israel's holiness is not future but present, and not conditional but unconditional (7.6; 14.2; cf. 26.19). **10:** *Called by the name of the LORD,* relationship with God includes accountability and corresponding divine oversight. The formula can apply to either the nation (here; 2 Chr 7.14; Isa 63.19; Jer 14.9) or an individual (Ex 33.12; Jer 15.16). **12:** *Storehouse,* in Israelite and Near Eastern cosmology, primordial waters above the dome of the sky were released as rain (Gen 1.7; 7.11). *Lend . . . borrow,* see 15.6.

you will not borrow. 13 The LORD will
make you the head, and not the tail; you
shall be only at the top, and not at the bot-
tom—if you obey the commandments of
the LORD your God, which I am command-
ing you today, by diligently observing
them, 14 and if you do not turn aside from
any of the words that I am commanding
you today, either to the right or to the left,
following other gods to serve them.

15 But if you will not obey the LORD
your God by diligently observing all his
commandments and decrees, which I am
commanding you today, then all these
curses shall come upon you and overtake
you:

16 Cursed shall you be in the city, and
cursed shall you be in the field.

17 Cursed shall be your basket and your
kneading bowl.

18 Cursed shall be the fruit of your
womb, the fruit of your ground, the in-
crease of your cattle and the issue of your
flock.

19 Cursed shall you be when you come
in, and cursed shall you be when you go
out.

20 The LORD will send upon you disas-
ter, panic, and frustration in everything you
attempt to do, until you are destroyed and
perish quickly, on account of the evil of
your deeds, because you have forsaken me.
21 The LORD will make the pestilence cling
to you until it has consumed you off the
land that you are entering to possess. 22 The
LORD will afflict you with consumption,
fever, inflammation, with fiery heat and
drought, and with blight and mildew; they
shall pursue you until you perish. 23 The
sky over your head shall be bronze, and the
earth under you iron. 24 The LORD will
change the rain of your land into powder,
and only dust shall come down upon you
from the sky until you are destroyed.

25 The LORD will cause you to be de-
feated before your enemies; you shall go
out against them one way and flee before
them seven ways. You shall become an ob-
ject of horror to all the kingdoms of the
earth. 26 Your corpses shall be food for ev-
ery bird of the air and animal of the earth,
and there shall be no one to frighten them
away. 27 The LORD will afflict you with the
boils of Egypt, with ulcers, scurvy, and itch,
of which you cannot be healed. 28 The
LORD will afflict you with madness, blind-
ness, and confusion of mind; 29 you shall
grope about at noon as blind people grope

28.15–68: Consequences of disobedience. A broad range of misfortunes, from infertility to military defeat (vv. 15–46), precede a second section (vv. 47–68) on foreign invasion, siege, national defeat, and exile, a reversal of the covenantal promises and of the nation's history of salvation: By disobeying the covenant, the nation undoes its own history. **15–46:** A chiastic inclusio frames the section: the initial sequence AB (*not obey . . . observing, curses . . . overtake,* v. 15) is repeated at the end as B´A´ (*curses . . . overtaking, not obey . . . observing,* v. 45). **15:** A negation of v. 1. **16–19:** Negating vv. 3–6. **20:** Corresponding to the tripartite blessing for obedience (v. 8) stands the triple threat of *disaster* [better, "curse"], *panic, and frustration.* The threats are spelled out in vv. 21–44. *Me,* the first-person reference shifts from Moses to God, as at 7.4; 17.3. **21–44:** This section echoes treaties that the Neo-Assyrian empire imposed on its vassal states, suggesting that the curse section of these state treaties, perhaps in Aramaic translation, provided a model for this chapter. Judah was a vassal to the Assyrian empire (2 Kings 18.13–18) and both Neo-Assyrian and Judean officials spoke Aramaic (2 Kings 18.26–27). **23:** *Bronze . . . iron,* see *VTE* §§ 63–64: "May [the gods] make your ground like iron . . . Just as rain does not fall from a bronze sky . . ." **25:** Negates v. 7. **26:** Even executed criminals must be buried by sundown, lest the corpse become carrion (21.22–23); abrogation of that law underscores the punishment's horror (Jer 7.33). **27–35:** The apparently arbitrary sequence of punishments corresponds to *VTE* §§ 39–43, where each curse is associated with a particular Neo-Assyrian god: the moon god Sin with leprosy; the sun god Shamash, blindness; and Dilipat (the planet Venus), rape, dispossession, and pillage. **27:** *Boils of Egypt,* inversion of 7.15. See Ex 9.9–11. **28–29:** *Blindness,* Shamash, the god of justice, punishes disobedience by withholding light and vision; this punishment entails the breakdown of civil order and legal standards. **30:** *Woman . . . house . . . vineyard,* contrast 20.7, which provides the same conditions for

in darkness, but you shall be unable to find
your way; and you shall be continually
abused and robbed, without anyone to
help. 30 You shall become engaged to a
woman, but another man shall lie with her.
You shall build a house, but not live in it.
You shall plant a vineyard, but not enjoy its
fruit. 31 Your ox shall be butchered before
your eyes, but you shall not eat of it. Your
donkey shall be stolen in front of you, and
shall not be restored to you. Your sheep
shall be given to your enemies, without
anyone to help you. 32 Your sons and
daughters shall be given to another people,
while you look on; you will strain your eyes
looking for them all day but be powerless
to do anything. 33 A people whom you do
not know shall eat up the fruit of your
ground and of all your labors; you shall
be continually abused and crushed, 34 and
driven mad by the sight that your eyes shall
see. 35 The LORD will strike you on the
knees and on the legs with grievous boils of
which you cannot be healed, from the sole
of your foot to the crown of your head.
36 The LORD will bring you, and the king
whom you set over you, to a nation that
neither you nor your ancestors have
known, where you shall serve other gods,
of wood and stone. 37 You shall become an
object of horror, a proverb, and a byword
among all the peoples where the LORD will
lead you.

38 You shall carry much seed into the
field but shall gather little in, for the locust
shall consume it. 39 You shall plant vine-
yards and dress them, but you shall neither
drink the wine nor gather the grapes, for
the worm shall eat them. 40 You shall have
olive trees throughout all your territory,
but you shall not anoint yourself with the
oil, for your olives shall drop off. 41 You
shall have sons and daughters, but they
shall not remain yours, for they shall go
into captivity. 42 All your trees and the fruit
of your ground the cicada shall take over.
43 Aliens residing among you shall ascend
above you higher and higher, while you
shall descend lower and lower. 44 They
shall lend to you but you shall not lend to
them; they shall be the head and you shall
be the tail.

45 All these curses shall come upon you,
pursuing and overtaking you until you are
destroyed, because you did not obey the
LORD your God, by observing the com-
mandments and the decrees that he com-
manded you. 46 They shall be among you
and your descendants as a sign and a por-
tent forever.

47 Because you did not serve the LORD
your God joyfully and with gladness of
heart for the abundance of everything,
48 therefore you shall serve your enemies
whom the LORD will send against you, in
hunger and thirst, in nakedness and lack of
everything. He will put an iron yoke on
your neck until he has destroyed you.

exemption from conscription, in different order. **32:** The sale of the children to foreigners as slaves guarantees their non-return (Gen 37.25–38). **36:** Both the Neo-Assyrian army (2 Kings 17) and the Neo-Babylonian invaders (2 Kings 24–25) practiced deportation. **37:** *Byword,* the opposite idea was central to God's covenant with Abraham, whose people were to become the paradigm of divine providence (Gen 12.3). **38–42:** Futility curses. The frustration of human labor through infertility of the harvest (caused by invasion from insects or other natural enemies) is punishment for infringement of the covenant (Lev 26.20; Am 4.7–12), reversing the blessings of vv. 7–15. **43–44:** Reversing vv. 12b–13. **46:** *A sign and a portent,* the normal phrase for miracles God performed on behalf of Israel at the time of the Exodus, "signs and wonders" (4.34; 6.22; 7.19; 29.3; 34.11; Ex 7.3; 8.23; 10.1–2; 11.9–10), in the singular here designates the divine punishment of Israel.

28.47–57: Scenario of foreign invasion. A later appendix, outside the frame provided by vv. 45–46. **47:** *Because you did not serve,* the future curse is based upon wrongdoing in the past, in contrast to the conditional, future formulation of v. 15, which presents disobedience as a future possibility. *Abundance,* prosperity in the land will cause Israel to forget its source (see 6.11–12; 8.11–20; 33.15,18). **48:** The punishment corresponds precisely to the offense: *Serve* means both sacrificial worship of God (13.5) and labor as a servant or slave (5.13; 13.12). *Iron yoke,* symbolizing vassal status, as in Jer 27–28. **49–57:**

49 The LORD will bring a nation from far
away, from the end of the earth, to swoop
down on you like an eagle, a nation whose
language you do not understand, 50 a grim-
faced nation showing no respect to the old
or favor to the young. 51 It shall consume
the fruit of your livestock and the fruit of
your ground until you are destroyed, leav-
ing you neither grain, wine, and oil, nor the
increase of your cattle and the issue of your
flock, until it has made you perish. 52 It
shall besiege you in all your towns until
your high and fortified walls, in which you
trusted, come down throughout your land;
it shall besiege you in all your towns
throughout the land that the LORD your
God has given you. 53 In the desperate
straits to which the enemy siege reduces
you, you will eat the fruit of your womb,
the flesh of your own sons and daughters
whom the LORD your God has given you.
54 Even the most refined and gentle of men
among you will begrudge food to his own
brother, to the wife whom he embraces,
and to the last of his remaining children,
55 giving to none of them any of the flesh of
his children whom he is eating, because
nothing else remains to him, in the desper-
ate straits to which the enemy siege will
reduce you in all your towns. 56 She who is
the most refined and gentle among you, so
gentle and refined that she does not venture
to set the sole of her foot on the ground,
will begrudge food to the husband whom
she embraces, to her own son, and to her
own daughter, 57 begrudging even the after-
birth that comes out from between her
thighs, and the children that she bears, be-
cause she is eating them in secret for lack of
anything else, in the desperate straits to
which the enemy siege will reduce you in
your towns.

58 If you do not diligently observe all
the words of this law that are written in this
book, fearing this glorious and awesome
name, the LORD your God, 59 then the
LORD will overwhelm both you and your
offspring with severe and lasting afflictions
and grievous and lasting maladies. 60 He
will bring back upon you all the diseases of
Egypt, of which you were in dread, and
they shall cling to you. 61 Every other mala-
dy and affliction, even though not recorded
in the book of this law, the LORD will in-

Systematic presentation of foreign conquest, proceeding from invasion (vv. 48–50), to the invaders' plunder and despoiling of the land (v. 51), to crippling siege (v. 52), and culminating in the horrors of starvation that arise from the siege (vv. 53–57). These descriptions of the invader and of the consequences of the siege are based upon the literary model of the *Vassal Treaty of Esarhaddon.* **49–52:** Closely parallels Jer 5.15–19. **49:** *Like an eagle,* cf. Ezek 17.3,7; Hab 1.8. **51:** Contrast the idealist war laws of 20.19–20, which prohibit occupiers from despoiling the land. **52:** *It shall besiege you . . . until your . . . walls . . . come down,* the Neo-Assyrian (2 Kings 17.5) and Babylonian armies (2 Kings 24.3; 25.1–7) employed advanced engineering to mount a siege campaign involving ramparts, battering rams, and catapults. **53–57:** The starvation resulting from the siege causes a complete breakdown of the normal social order, as parents become predators of their children and family members compete for food. For cannibalism under siege conditions, see Lev 26.29; 2 Kings 6.28–32; Jer 19.9; Lam 4.10; Ezek 5.10; and *VTE* §§ 47,69,71,75.

28.58–68: Undoing the Exodus. This seems to represent a third layer to the chapter. **58:** *This book,* how the commandments have become transformed from oral proclamation to written text is unexplained, since it is not until 31.9,24 that Moses commands that the Torah be put into writing. Moreover, hitherto the required obedience was to the plural "commandments" (vv. 1,9,13,15,45). Here, for the first time in the chapter, Israel must obey a codified, single *law* (better, "Torah" or "teaching"). *This . . . name,* NRSV should have capitalized "Name" to clarify its distinctive use; it stands directly for God (elsewhere in the Pentateuch only Lev 24.11). **59–68:** Consistent with the "book" perspective, the consequences for breach of the written Torah have a different focus: a systematic reversal of the national history, covenantal promises, and theology included in that Torah. The punishment amounts to an anti-Torah that will dissolve the national identity. **59–61:** After the miracle of the Exodus, God had promised, if the people obeyed, "I will not bring upon you any of the diseases that I brought upon the Egyptians" (Ex 15.26).

flict on you until you are destroyed. 62 Al-
though once you were as numerous as the
stars in heaven, you shall be left few in
number, because you did not obey the
LORD your God. 63 And just as the LORD
took delight in making you prosperous and
numerous, so the LORD will take delight in
bringing you to ruin and destruction; you
shall be plucked off the land that you are
entering to possess. 64 The LORD will scat-
ter you among all peoples, from one end of
the earth to the other; and there you shall
serve other gods, of wood and stone, which
neither you nor your ancestors have
known. 65 Among those nations you shall
find no ease, no resting place for the sole of
your foot. There the LORD will give you
a trembling heart, failing eyes, and a lan-
guishing spirit. 66 Your life shall hang in
doubt before you; night and day you shall
be in dread, with no assurance of your life.
67 In the morning you shall say, "If only it
were evening!" and at evening you shall
say, "If only it were morning!"—because
of the dread that your heart shall feel and
the sights that your eyes shall see. 68 The
LORD will bring you back in ships to Egypt,
by a route that I promised you would never
see again; and there you shall offer your-
selves for sale to your enemies as male and
female slaves, but there will be no buyer.

29 [a]These are the words of the cove-
nant that the LORD commanded
Moses to make with the Israelites in the
land of Moab, in addition to the covenant
that he had made with them at Horeb.

2 [b]Moses summoned all Israel and said
to them: You have seen all that the LORD
did before your eyes in the land of Egypt, to
Pharaoh and to all his servants and to all
his land, 3 the great trials that your eyes
saw, the signs, and those great wonders.
4 But to this day the LORD has not given
you a mind to understand, or eyes to see, or
ears to hear. 5 I have led you forty years in
the wilderness. The clothes on your back
have not worn out, and the sandals on your
feet have not worn out; 6 you have not eat-

a Ch 28.69 in Heb *b* Ch 29.1 in Heb

62: *Stars . . . heaven,* God will cancel the promise made to Abraham that his people shall be as numerous as the stars of heaven (Gen 15.5–6). **63:** Dispossession and exile (as in 4.26; Lev 26.33–39) rescind the covenantal promise of the land, contravening even the unconditional divine promises of Gen 12.7; 13.17. **64:** The double loss of Israel's identity: Dispersion of the population dissolves its political identity, and idol worship dissolves its religious identity. **65–67:** In the absence of the national destiny provided by the covenant, historical existence has no meaning. **68:** Forced return to Egypt, where the former taskmasters spurn Israel's desperate bid to sell itself back into slavery and thus to undo their own history. For selling oneself into slavery under financial hardship to pay off debts or gain support ("indenture"), see Lev 25.39. *Route . . . never see again* (cf. 17.16), reverses the unconditional promise at the time of the Exodus: "the Egyptians whom you see today you shall never see again" (Ex 14.13).

29.1–30.20: Third discourse of Moses. The ratification ceremony for the covenant of the Plains of Moab. Israel is formally adjured to enter the covenant: to swear to obey the laws of chs 12–26 under penalty of the sanctions of ch 28. **29.1–29:** A didactic review of Israel's history (vv. 2–9) precedes an imprecation to ensure loyal adherence to the covenant (vv. 10–29). **1: Editorial heading.** The laws, hitherto plural ("statutes and ordinances," 5.1; 12.1; cf. 4.45), are now a coherent, single tradition: *the covenant. In addition to,* presentation of the laws as a supplement to the Decalogue, in contrast to 4.44–45; 12.1, which mention neither the Decalogue nor the laws' supplementary status. This may be an effort to explain addition of the Decalogue to an earlier form of Deuteronomy. **2:** *You have seen,* as at 5.2–4, the present generation is in reality one generation removed from the miraculous events. **3:** *Signs . . . wonders,* see 28.46n. **4:** *But to this day,* more accurately: "The LORD has not given you . . . until today." The admonition creates a tension with the preceding two verses: The addressees who "have seen" the miraculous events (v. 2), which their own "eyes saw" (v. 3), are accused of having lacked *eyes to see.* The castigation reflects the episodes of rebellion (9.7–24). **5–6:** The Mosaic homily reinterprets the wilderness wandering, originally intended as divine punishment of Israel (Num 14.13–35), and presents it positively, in didactic terms. **5:** *I,* see 7.4; 17.3; 28.20,68. *Clothes . . . feet,* see 8.4. **6:** *You have not eaten*

en bread, and you have not drunk wine or
strong drink—so that you may know that I
am the LORD your God. 7When you came
to this place, King Sihon of Heshbon and
King Og of Bashan came out against us for
battle, but we defeated them. 8We took
their land and gave it as an inheritance to
the Reubenites, the Gadites, and the half-
tribe of Manasseh. 9Therefore diligently
observe the words of this covenant, in or-
der that you may succeed[a] in everything
that you do.

10 You stand assembled today, all of
you, before the LORD your God—the lead-
ers of your tribes,[b] your elders, and your
officials, all the men of Israel, 11your chil-
dren, your women, and the aliens who are
in your camp, both those who cut your
wood and those who draw your water—
12to enter into the covenant of the LORD
your God, sworn by an oath, which the
LORD your God is making with you today;
13in order that he may establish you today
as his people, and that he may be your God,
as he promised you and as he swore to your
ancestors, to Abraham, to Isaac, and to Ja-
cob. 14I am making this covenant, sworn
by an oath, not only with you who stand
here with us today before the LORD our
God, 15but also with those who are not
here with us today. 16You know how we
lived in the land of Egypt, and how we
came through the midst of the nations
through which you passed. 17You have
seen their detestable things, the filthy idols
of wood and stone, of silver and gold, that
were among them. 18It may be that there is
among you a man or woman, or a family or
tribe, whose heart is already turning away
from the LORD our God to serve the gods
of those nations. It may be that there is
among you a root sprouting poisonous and
bitter growth. 19All who hear the words of
this oath and bless themselves, thinking in
their hearts, "We are safe even though we
go our own stubborn ways" (thus bringing
disaster on moist and dry alike)[c]— 20the
LORD will be unwilling to pardon them, for
the LORD's anger and passion will smoke
against them. All the curses written in this
book will descend on them, and the LORD
will blot out their names from under heav-
en. 21The LORD will single them out from

a Or *deal wisely* *b* Gk Syr: Heb *your leaders, your tribes* *c* Meaning of Heb uncertain

bread . . . not drunk wine, the sense is, "It was not bread that you ate . . . nor wine that you drank." The manna, quails, and water that Israel consumed were supplied by divine providence (8.2–5; Ex 16; Num 11.4–9,31–33). *Know,* not abstract speculation but the recognition of God's historical actions on behalf of the nation. *I am the LORD your God,* better, "I, Yahweh, am your God" (6.4; Ex 20.2). **7–8:** See 1.4; 2.26–3.22; Num 21.21–35. **10:** *Stand assembled* in formal array for a public legal ceremony (cf. Ps 82.1). *Today,* transition from historical review (vv. 1–8) to present adjuration (similarly, *VTE* § 33). **12:** *Covenant . . . sworn by an oath,* the formula recurs at v. 14, thus framing the central idea, the binding relationship between God and Israel. *Oath,* more accurately, "its imprecation" or "its curse." Neo-Assyrian treaties were validated by means of a concluding imprecation (*VTE* §§ 37–56,58–106). The partner accepts the consequences of noncompliance. The laws of chs 12–26 represent the stipulations; ch 28, the sanctions; and ch 29, the imprecation. **14–15:** The covenant binds even future generations (as in *VTE* §§ 25,33,34,57); consequently, punishment for infraction extends to the third and fourth generation (5.9; Ex 20.5; 34.7). **17–27:** A stark, two-part warning, showing how the attempt of even a single individual secretly to withdraw from the covenant (vv. 17–19) jeopardizes the entire nation (vv. 20–28). **18:** *Turning away,* transferring loyalty to other gods (13.6–11; 17.2–7). *Poisonous and bitter growth,* Hos 10.4; Am 5.7; 6.12. **19:** *Bless themselves,* rather than proclaim the imprecation, hoping to escape the sanctions of the covenant. *Moist and dry,* probably paired antonyms designating totality (see 28.3–6n.). **20:** *Passion,* God's zeal to defend the mutual exclusivity of the covenant relation (5.9; Ex 34.14). *Descend on them,* more literally, "crouch down upon them" (cf. Gen 4.7), an animate image. *Blot out,* the erasure of a tablet or scroll (Num 5.23), given a theological cast: Following Mesopotamian models, the divine decree of human fate is recorded in a heavenly book, with erasure symbolizing punishment (9.14; Gen 6.7; Ex 17.14; 32.32; 2 Kings 14.27; Ps 9.6). **22–28:** The negative instruction. As the wilderness wandering

all the tribes of Israel for calamity, in accor-
dance with all the curses of the covenant
written in this book of the law. 22 The next
generation, your children who rise up after
you, as well as the foreigner who comes
from a distant country, will see the devasta-
tion of that land and the afflictions with
which the LORD has afflicted it— 23 all its
soil burned out by sulfur and salt, nothing
planted, nothing sprouting, unable to sup-
port any vegetation, like the destruction of
Sodom and Gomorrah, Admah and Zeboi-
im, which the LORD destroyed in his fierce
anger— 24 they and indeed all the nations
will wonder, "Why has the LORD done thus
to this land? What caused this great display
of anger?" 25 They will conclude, "It is be-
cause they abandoned the covenant of the
LORD, the God of their ancestors, which he
made with them when he brought them out
of the land of Egypt. 26 They turned and
served other gods, worshiping them, gods
whom they had not known and whom he
had not allotted to them; 27 so the anger of
the LORD was kindled against that land,
bringing on it every curse written in this
book. 28 The LORD uprooted them from
their land in anger, fury, and great wrath,
and cast them into another land, as is now
the case." 29 The secret things belong to the
LORD our God, but the revealed things be-
long to us and to our children forever, to
observe all the words of this law.

30 When all these things have hap-
pened to you, the blessings and the
curses that I have set before you, if you call
them to mind among all the nations where
the LORD your God has driven you, 2 and
return to the LORD your God, and you and
your children obey him with all your heart
and with all your soul, just as I am com-
manding you today, 3 then the LORD your
God will restore your fortunes and have
compassion on you, gathering you again
from all the peoples among whom the
LORD your God has scattered you. 4 Even if
you are exiled to the ends of the world,[a]
from there the LORD your God will gather
you, and from there he will bring you back.
5 The LORD your God will bring you into

a Heb *of heaven*

provided an instructional lesson for the nation (vv. 5–6), so will Israel, transformed into a devastation, provide an object lesson. Vv. 24–28 provide a reversal of the Israelite child's inquiry about God's redemptive acts (4.32–38; Ex 12.25–27; 13.8–10). **23:** *Sulfur and salt* were used in antiquity as chemical defoliants by invading armies. *Sodom . . . Zeboiim,* proverbial wicked cities in the arid area around the Dead Sea (cf. Gen 19.24–25; Isa 1.9–10). **25:** *The covenant,* conflating the covenants of Horeb and Moab (29.1). **26:** *Gods . . . not allotted to them,* as at 32.8–9, each nation is allocated its own god, and the LORD is the God of Israel. As at 5.8–9, the existence of other deities is here conceded. Contrast 4.19, where it is rather only inanimate "stars . . . that God has allotted," which reinterprets the polytheistic image from the later perspective of monotheism. **28:** *As is now the case,* reference to the present implies that the chapter was composed subsequent to the Babylonian exile of 586 BCE. **29:** *Secret,* concealed acts that God will punish (vv. 18–19), or future events. More likely, the antithesis with *revealed* rejects religions of esoteric speculation that restrict access to truth to a learned few. Torah, based upon a public revelation (ch 5) and Mosaic instruction (chs 12–26), is accessible to all.

30.1–10: Reassurance of restoration. This section, with its emphasis on restoration, does not logically follow ch 29, and is most likely an insertion that serves the religious needs of a community different from that of the book's original audience (see v. 5n.). The unit employs the Heb word "shub," translated "return," "repent," or "restore," in seven different ways to establish the close bond between human repentance and divine forgiveness: (v. 1) "If you *call* them to mind . . . (v. 2) and *return* . . . (v. 3) then the LORD will *restore your fortunes* . . . and gathering you *again* . . . (v. 8) Then you shall *again* obey . . . (v. 9) For the LORD will *again* take delight . . . (v. 10) because you *turn.*" **1:** *Call them to mind,* lit. "take [them] to heart." **4:** Cf. Am 9.2–3. **5:** *Bring you into the land that your ancestors possessed,* the "you" explicitly refers to the Judean exiles in Babylon, rather than the desert generation whom Moses addresses on the plains of Transjordan. *More . . . numerous,* the covenantal promise (Gen 17.2; 22.17). For similar claims that the future will repeat the past while also supposing it, see Isa 42.9; 43.6–20; 51.9–11. **6:** *The*

the land that your ancestors possessed, and
you will possess it; he will make you more
prosperous and numerous than your ancestors.

6 Moreover, the LORD your God will
circumcise your heart and the heart of your
descendants, so that you will love the LORD
your God with all your heart and with all
your soul, in order that you may live. [7]The
LORD your God will put all these curses on
your enemies and on the adversaries who
took advantage of you. [8]Then you shall
again obey the LORD, observing all his
commandments that I am commanding you
today, [9]and the LORD your God will make
you abundantly prosperous in all your undertakings,
in the fruit of your body, in the
fruit of your livestock, and in the fruit of
your soil. For the LORD will again take delight
in prospering you, just as he delighted
in prospering your ancestors, [10]when you
obey the LORD your God by observing his
commandments and decrees that are written
in this book of the law, because you
turn to the LORD your God with all your
heart and with all your soul.

11 Surely, this commandment that I am
commanding you today is not too hard for
you, nor is it too far away. [12]It is not in
heaven, that you should say, "Who will go
up to heaven for us, and get it for us so that
we may hear it and observe it?" [13]Neither
is it beyond the sea, that you should say,
"Who will cross to the other side of the sea
for us, and get it for us so that we may hear
it and observe it?" [14]No, the word is very
near to you; it is in your mouth and in your
heart for you to observe.

15 See, I have set before you today life
and prosperity, death and adversity. [16]If
you obey the commandments of the LORD
your God[a] that I am commanding you today,
by loving the LORD your God, walking
in his ways, and observing his commandments,
decrees, and ordinances, then you
shall live and become numerous, and the
LORD your God will bless you in the land
that you are entering to possess. [17]But if
your heart turns away and you do not hear,
but are led astray to bow down to other
gods and serve them, [18]I declare to you today
that you shall perish; you shall not live
long in the land that you are crossing the
Jordan to enter and possess. [19]I call heaven
and earth to witness against you today that
I have set before you life and death, blessings
and curses. Choose life so that you and
your descendants may live, [20]loving the
LORD your God, obeying him, and holding

a Gk: Heb lacks *If you obey the commandments of the LORD your God*

LORD . . . will circumcise your heart, God is the agent; previously Israel itself was to "circumcise . . . the foreskin of your heart" (see 10.16n.). The change suggests skepticism about the people's ability to effect such a change of heart independently (see Jer 31.31–34; Ezek 11.19–20; 36.26–27). **7:** The curses are deflected from Israel to the adversary; contrast 28.47,49, where the foreign nation is God's agent to punish Israel. **9:** *Fruit,* blessings upon return conforming to those promised upon initial entry (28.4). **10:** *Obey the LORD . . . by observing . . . this book of the law,* or, more precisely, "this book of the Teaching" (Torah). The reference is to the text of Deuteronomy itself, which replaces the live speech of Moses (12.28,32) or prophetic speech (18.18–9) as revealer of God's word.

30.11–20: The original continuation of ch 29 is composed of two sections, vv. 11–14,15–20. **11–14:** Turning their own imagery against them, the passage challenges the assumptions of Near Eastern wisdom schools about the inaccessibility of divine wisdom and the limits of human knowledge (cf. Job 28). **11:** *Surely,* better, "because," logically continuing 29.29 and emphasizing the ready accessibility of the Torah. (The NRSV translation is an accommodation to the insertion of vv. 1–10.) *This commandment,* the Torah as a whole (as at 6.1). **12:** See Prov 30.4. *That we may hear it,* lit. "so that he may proclaim it to us." **14:** *In your mouth,* in antiquity, texts were normally read, taught, and recited aloud (6.7; 31.19, 21; Josh 1.8). **15–20:** Life outside the covenant is *death.* **16:** *Loving . . . walking in his ways,* in Near Eastern treaties, "love" means to act loyally and to honor the commitments of the treaty (6.5n.). **19:** *Heaven and earth to witness,* see 4.26n.; 32.1n. *Choose life,* the didactic use of life and death suggests the influence of wisdom teachings upon the authors (Prov 11.19; 14.27; 18.21; cf. Jer 8.3; 21.8).

fast to him; for that means life to you and
length of days, so that you may live in the
land that the LORD swore to give to your
ancestors, to Abraham, to Isaac, and to Ja-
cob.

31 When Moses had finished speaking
all[a] these words to all Israel, 2 he
said to them: "I am now one hundred twen-
ty years old. I am no longer able to get
about, and the LORD has told me, 'You
shall not cross over this Jordan.' 3 The
LORD your God himself will cross over be-
fore you. He will destroy these nations be-
fore you, and you shall dispossess them.
Joshua also will cross over before you, as
the LORD promised. 4 The LORD will do to
them as he did to Sihon and Og, the kings
of the Amorites, and to their land, when he
destroyed them. 5 The LORD will give them
over to you and you shall deal with them in
full accord with the command that I have
given to you. 6 Be strong and bold; have no

a Q Ms Gk: MT *Moses went and spoke*

31.1–34.14: The death of Moses and the formation of the Torah. With the imprecation of ch 30 concluding the treaty between God and Israel, Deuteronomy now returns to Moses, the mediator of the treaty. His life is ending, and the question of succession is given a two-fold answer, since Moses was both political and religious leader of Israel. Joshua will be his political and military successor (31.1–8,14–15,23; 32.44,48–52; 34.9) and "a book . . . of this law" (31.24) will instruct the nation in religion. Deuteronomy thus ends in paradox: Moses, ostensibly the book's narrator, narrates his own death (ch 34), and the book of the Torah, already presupposed (29.27), nevertheless provides an account of its own formation (31.9–13,24–29). The conclusion of Deuteronomy also ends the Pentateuch. In incorporating Deuteronomy into that larger work, editors with the background of the exile added perspectives on the function of the Torah in the people's life. Finally, the Pentateuch's literary precedent of a patriarch's death-bed bequest and blessing (Gen 27; 48–49) led to the incorporation of "The Song of Moses" (32.1–43) and of "The Blessing of Moses" (ch 33), each of which may originally have circulated independently. The resulting text thus blends several viewpoints. Themes like the Mosaic appointment of Joshua begin, then begin again from a different perspective, and then are continued only after an apparent digression, which marks the insertion of new material.

31.1–29: Moses makes arrangements for his death. Publicly announcing his imminent death, Moses invests Joshua with leadership and initiates the writing of the Torah, which is to be taught regularly to the entire people. These two legacies seem independent of each other and suggest that an earlier narrative about leadership has been expanded with an account of the formation of Deuteronomy. Each tradition, furthermore, is doubled; the chapter thus contains many layers of tradition. First is a double announcement of Moses' imminent death: v. 2 (at his own initiative, citing previous divine commandment, in which he appoints Joshua directly) and vv. 14–15 (with no reference to a previous announcement, and with divine appointment of Joshua). Second is a double tradition of transfer of leadership: Although Moses begins a public ceremony in order himself to appoint the new leader (vv. 7–8), a variant tradition has God commission Joshua directly (vv. 14–15,23). Third is a double tradition of Moses' writing: one of "the book . . . of this law" (v. 24) and one of "this song" (v. 19). Each is a "witness" (vv. 21,26). The first tradition, which refers to Deuteronomy, was supplemented by the second in order to integrate the following "Song of Moses" (32.1–43). Fourth, in the "Song" tradition, Israel's future apostasy is already a foregone conclusion (vv. 16–22,28–29); in the covenant-making tradition, there is yet hope that, by taking the law to heart, Israel might avoid catastrophe (vv. 9–13,24–27). **2:** *One hundred twenty years old,* the Hebrew places the age first, thus immediately announcing the key issue: Moses has reached the maximum age for humans (Gen 6.3), making it urgent to assure continuity of leadership. *I am no longer able to get about,* lit. "to go out and come in," i.e., lead the nation in military campaigns (28.6; Num 27.17; 1 Kings 3.7; cf. 2 Sam 11.1). **2–3:** Resumes 1.37–38; 3.27–28. The death of a key leader and the transfer of his authority mark important turning points within the larger context of the Deuteronomistic History and partially follow a common model (cf. Josh 23.2; 1 Sam 12.2; 1 Kings 2.1–2). **4:** The successful military campaigns in Transjordan provide assurance in the conquest of Canaan; Moses aims to counter Israel's intimidation (1.27–28; Num 13–14). **5:** *Command,* the ban (7.1–7; 12.29–31; 20.16–18).

fear or dread of them, because it is the
LORD your God who goes with you; he will
not fail you or forsake you."
7 Then Moses summoned Joshua and
said to him in the sight of all Israel: "Be
strong and bold, for you are the one who
will go with this people into the land that
the LORD has sworn to their ancestors to
give them; and you will put them in posses-
sion of it. 8 It is the LORD who goes before
you. He will be with you; he will not fail
you or forsake you. Do not fear or be dis-
mayed."
9 Then Moses wrote down this law, and
gave it to the priests, the sons of Levi, who
carried the ark of the covenant of the
LORD, and to all the elders of Israel. 10 Mo-
ses commanded them: "Every seventh year,
in the scheduled year of remission, during
the festival of booths,[a] 11 when all Israel
comes to appear before the LORD your God
at the place that he will choose, you shall
read this law before all Israel in their hear-
ing. 12 Assemble the people—men, women,
and children, as well as the aliens residing
in your towns—so that they may hear and
learn to fear the LORD your God and to
observe diligently all the words of this law,
13 and so that their children, who have not
known it, may hear and learn to fear the
LORD your God, as long as you live in the
land that you are crossing over the Jordan
to possess."
14 The LORD said to Moses, "Your time
to die is near; call Joshua and present your-
selves in the tent of meeting, so that I may
commission him." So Moses and Joshua
went and presented themselves in the tent
of meeting, 15 and the LORD appeared at the
tent in a pillar of cloud; the pillar of cloud
stood at the entrance to the tent.
16 The LORD said to Moses, "Soon you
will lie down with your ancestors. Then
this people will begin to prostitute them-
selves to the foreign gods in their midst, the
gods of the land into which they are going;
they will forsake me, breaking my covenant
that I have made with them. 17 My anger
will be kindled against them in that day. I
will forsake them and hide my face from
them; they will become easy prey, and
many terrible troubles will come upon
them. In that day they will say, 'Have not
these troubles come upon us because our
God is not in our midst?' 18 On that day I
will surely hide my face on account of all
the evil they have done by turning to other
gods. 19 Now therefore write this song, and
teach it to the Israelites; put it in their
mouths, in order that this song may be a
witness for me against the Israelites. 20 For
when I have brought them into the land
flowing with milk and honey, which I
promised on oath to their ancestors, and
they have eaten their fill and grown fat,
they will turn to other gods and serve them,
despising me and breaking my covenant.
21 And when many terrible troubles come
upon them, this song will confront them as
a witness, because it will not be lost from
the mouths of their descendants. For I
know what they are inclined to do even
now, before I have brought them into the
land that I promised them on oath." 22 That

a Or *tabernacles*; Heb *succoth*

9–13: The institution of a covenant ceremony to be held in the sabbatical year (15.1–11), during the *festival of booths* (16.13–15). **12:** Stipulating that the Torah is taught to women, minors, and aliens, the law does not restrict the responsibility to observe the covenant to males (contrast Ex 19.15). **14:** *Tent of meeting,* in the Yahwistic source (J), the site outside camp where God speaks to Moses, with Joshua in attendance (Ex 33.7–11); contrast the Priestly literature's tabernacle, located in the center of the Israelite encampment, which houses the ark of the covenant and the altar (Ex 26–27; Num 7.1–3; 18.1–7). *So that I may commission him,* the standard tradition involves direct commission by Moses at God's command (3.27–28; 34.9; Num 27.18–23). **15:** The double reference to the *pillar of cloud,* located both *at* [or, "in"] *the tent* (cf. Ex 30.36; 40.34–35; Lev 16.2) and *at the entrance to the tent* (cf. Ex 33.9–10; Num 12.5) blends the traditions associated with each of the two tents (see v. 14n.). **17–18:** *Our God,* better, "our gods": The people will have strayed so far from the covenant that they attribute the resulting divine punishment to other gods, leading to God's angry response. **22–23:** The sequence of *Moses wrote*

very day Moses wrote this song and taught
it to the Israelites.
23 Then the LORD commissioned Josh-
ua son of Nun and said, "Be strong and
bold, for you shall bring the Israelites into
the land that I promised them; I will be
with you."
24 When Moses had finished writing
down in a book the words of this law to the
very end, 25 Moses commanded the Levites
who carried the ark of the covenant of the
LORD, saying, 26 "Take this book of the law
and put it beside the ark of the covenant of
the LORD your God; let it remain there as a
witness against you. 27 For I know well how
rebellious and stubborn you are. If you al-
ready have been so rebellious toward the
LORD while I am still alive among you, how
much more after my death! 28 Assemble to
me all the elders of your tribes and your
officials, so that I may recite these words in
their hearing and call heaven and earth to
witness against them. 29 For I know that
after my death you will surely act corrupt-
ly, turning aside from the way that I have
commanded you. In time to come trouble
will befall you, because you will do what is
evil in the sight of the LORD, provoking
him to anger through the work of your
hands."
30 Then Moses recited the words of this
song, to the very end, in the hearing of the
whole assembly of Israel:

32 Give ear, O heavens, and I will
speak;
let the earth hear the words of my
mouth.
2 May my teaching drop like the rain,
my speech condense like the dew;
like gentle rain on grass,
like showers on new growth.
3 For I will proclaim the name of the
LORD;
ascribe greatness to our God!

4 The Rock, his work is perfect,
and all his ways are just.
A faithful God, without deceit,
just and upright is he;
5 yet his degenerate children have dealt
falsely with him,[a]
a perverse and crooked generation.
6 Do you thus repay the LORD,
O foolish and senseless people?
Is not he your father, who created
you,
who made you and established
you?
7 Remember the days of old,
consider the years long past;

a Meaning of Heb uncertain

(v. 22) and . . . *commissioned* (v. 23) uses the same key terms as "When Moses finished writing . . . Moses commanded" (vv. 24–25). The repetition of the paired terms provided a means for editors to insert the section on the song (vv. 16–22). **23:** *The LORD commissioned,* lit. "he commanded," with no subject identified. NRSV has added the divine reference to clarify that the verse does not continue v. 22, but directly resumes vv. 14–15.

31.30–32.43: The Song of Moses. The Song is a late insertion that reflects upon Israel's history, probably presupposing the exile. In form it is a revised and expanded prophetic lawsuit (Isa 1; Jer 2; Mic 6; Ps 50) with this structure: introduction and summoning of witnesses (vv. 1–3); accusation (vv. 4–6); recital of God's loving actions (vv. 7–14); indictment (vv. 15–18); declaration of punishment (vv. 19–25). Yet God interrupts his own judicial sentence to recognize a risk to his honor: Other nations might conclude that Israel's God was weak should they see Israel destroyed (vv. 26–27). God reverses himself, cancels the punishment, and decides instead to punish Israel's enemies so as to vindicate Israel (vv. 28–42). The Song concludes with a call for the divine council to praise God for his actions; the call may originate from within the divine council itself (v. 43; similarly Ps 29.1). A prose frame links the Song to Deuteronomy, identifying Moses, otherwise unmentioned, as its speaker (31.30; 32.44). **32.2:** *Teaching,* the original prophetic lawsuit has been combined with wisdom themes (Prov 1.5; 4.2; 17.21). **4:** *Rock,* more accurately, "Mountain," a title applied to the high god of ancient Canaan (see v. 8n.) and to the biblical God (vv. 15,18,30–31,37; Isa 44.8; Ps 78.35). **6:** *Created you,* when God redeemed Israel

ask your father, and he will inform
you;
your elders, and they will tell you.
8 When the Most High[a] apportioned
the nations,
when he divided humankind,
he fixed the boundaries of the peoples
according to the number of the
gods;[b]
9 the LORD's own portion was his
people,
Jacob his allotted share.

10 He sustained[c] him in a desert land,
in a howling wilderness waste;
he shielded him, cared for him,
guarded him as the apple of his eye.
11 As an eagle stirs up its nest,
and hovers over its young;
as it spreads its wings, takes them up,
and bears them aloft on its pinions,
12 the LORD alone guided him;
no foreign god was with him.
13 He set him atop the heights of the
land,
and fed him with[d] produce of the
field;
he nursed him with honey from the
crags,
with oil from flinty rock;
14 curds from the herd, and milk from
the flock,
with fat of lambs and rams;
Bashan bulls and goats,
together with the choicest wheat—
you drank fine wine from the blood
of grapes.
15 Jacob ate his fill;[e]
Jeshurun grew fat, and kicked.
You grew fat, bloated, and gorged!
He abandoned God who made him,
and scoffed at the Rock of his
salvation.
16 They made him jealous with strange
gods,
with abhorrent things they
provoked him.
17 They sacrificed to demons, not God,
to deities they had never known,
to new ones recently arrived,
whom your ancestors had not feared.
18 You were unmindful of the Rock that
bore you;[f]
you forgot the God who gave you
birth.

19 The LORD saw it, and was jealous;[g]
he spurned[h] his sons and
daughters.
20 He said: I will hide my face from
them,
I will see what their end will be;
for they are a perverse generation,

a Traditional rendering of Heb *Elyon* *b* Q Ms Compare Gk Tg: MT *the Israelites* *c* Sam Gk Compare Tg: MT *found* *d* Sam Gk Syr Tg: MT *he ate* *e* Q Mss Sam Gk: MT lacks *Jacob ate his fill* *f* Or *that begot you* *g* Q Mss Gk: MT lacks *was jealous* *h* Cn: Heb *he spurned because of provocation*

from Egypt (Ex 15.16, correcting NRSV "acquired"). **8:** *Most High,* or *Elyon* (text note *a*), is the title of El, the senior god who sat at the head of the divine council in the Ugaritic literature of ancient Canaan. The Bible applies El's title to Israel's God (Gen 14.18–22; Num 24.16; Ps 46.4; 47.2; esp. 78.35, where it is parallel to Rock). *Gods,* the lesser gods who make up the divine council (Ps 82.1; 89.6–7), to each of whom Elyon here assigns a foreign nation. **9:** *The LORD's own portion,* NRSV has added *own* in order to identify Yahweh with Elyon and avoid the impression that Yahweh is merely a member of the pantheon; see also 4.19n. **10:** *Sustained,* more likely "found" (Hos 9.10). Overlooking the Egypt traditions, the Song here traces the beginnings of Israel to the wilderness period, romanticizing its ideal purity (similarly Hos 2.14–15; Jer 2.2–3; contrast Deut 9.6–7,22–27; Ezek 20). *Apple of his eye,* lit. the aperture or pupil of the eye. **11:** Israel as God's fledgling; see Ex 19.4. **13:** *Heights,* see Ex 15.17. **14:** *Curds,* symbolic of extravagant hospitality offered to special guests (Gen 18.8; Judg 5.25). *Bashan,* in northern Transjordan, was famous for its cattle. **15:** *Jeshurun,* probably meaning "upright," is a poetic term for Israel (33.5,26; Isa 44.2). **17:** *Demons,* better, "protective spirits" (also Ps 106.37). *Not God,* the language is sarcastic: "a non-god" (see v. 21). *To deities,* better, "to gods." **18:** God is depicted as a woman; *gave you birth* refers specifically to labor pain (Isa 51.2; cf. Isa 42.14). **21:** *Jealous* refers to the covenant's

children in whom there is no
faithfulness.
21 They made me jealous with what is
no god,
provoked me with their idols.
So I will make them jealous with
what is no people,
provoke them with a foolish nation.
22 For a fire is kindled by my anger,
and burns to the depths of Sheol;
it devours the earth and its increase,
and sets on fire the foundations of
the mountains.
23 I will heap disasters upon them,
spend my arrows against them:
24 wasting hunger,
burning consumption,
bitter pestilence.
The teeth of beasts I will send against
them,
with venom of things crawling in
the dust.
25 In the street the sword shall bereave,
and in the chambers terror,
for young man and woman alike,
nursing child and old gray head.
26 I thought to scatter them[a]
and blot out the memory of them
from humankind;
27 but I feared provocation by the
enemy,
for their adversaries might
misunderstand
and say, "Our hand is triumphant;
it was not the LORD who did all
this."

28 They are a nation void of sense;
there is no understanding in them.
29 If they were wise, they would
understand this;
they would discern what the end
would be.
30 How could one have routed a
thousand,
and two put a myriad to flight,
unless their Rock had sold them,
the LORD had given them up?
31 Indeed their rock is not like our
Rock;
our enemies are fools.[a]
32 Their vine comes from the vinestock
of Sodom,
from the vineyards of Gomorrah;
their grapes are grapes of poison,
their clusters are bitter;
33 their wine is the poison of serpents,
the cruel venom of asps.

34 Is not this laid up in store with me,

a Gk: Meaning of Heb uncertain

demand for exclusive loyalty to God (5.8; 6.15; Num 25.11). Accordingly, the punishment for breach of the covenant metes out precise retributive justice (see 19.19n.). The Hebrew emphasizes the sarcasm: thus, *with what is no god* and *what is no people,* lit. "with a non-god," "with a non-people." *Their idols,* lit. "their vapors" or "their vanities," even "their vapidities" (Jer 8.19; 10.15; 16.19; Eccl 1.2). **22:** *Sheol,* the underworld (Gen 37.35; 1 Sam 2.6; Ps 139.8). The abode of all the dead, not a place of damnation like the later idea of hell. **23:** *Arrows,* divine punishments (v. 42; Ezek 5.16; Ps 7.13; 18.14; 38.2). **24:** *Burning consumption,* the name of the Ugaritic god of pestilence; thus better, "devoured by Plague." **25:** *Woman,* better, "young woman," to emphasize the double merism (28.3–6n.), which symbolizes the totality of the slaughter. **26–27:** The Song here pivots from judgment of Israel to her vindication at the expense of the foreign invaders. **27:** *I feared,* God has feelings and vulnerabilities (as at Gen 6.6). **28–33:** God's soliloquy is interrupted by another voice, who refers to God in the third person and speaks on behalf of Israel (vv. 30–31). **28–29:** The foreign nation, like Israel, has failed in wisdom, justifying God's judgment (see v. 6). **30:** Ironically inverts the holy war idea (3.22; 20.1): The enemy is reproached for failing to understand that it owes its triumph over Israel to God rather than force of arms. God will thus punish Israel's conquerors to preserve his own honor (see 9.25–29; Num 14.13–16). **32:** *Sodom . . . Gomorrah,* here symbolizing moral corruption more than ruinous devastation (cf. 29.23n.). **34:** *This,* the punishment of the foreign nation, which is about to be announced (vv. 35–42). *Laid up . . . sealed up,* the formal legal procedures for rolling and then sealing a witnessed deed or contract with wax, so that the unaltered document can subsequently be introduced into court as evidence (Isa 8.16; Jer 32.9–15). **35:**

sealed up in my treasuries?
35 Vengeance is mine, and recompense,
for the time when their foot shall slip;
because the day of their calamity is at hand,
their doom comes swiftly.
36 Indeed the LORD will vindicate his people,
have compassion on his servants,
when he sees that their power is gone,
neither bond nor free remaining.
37 Then he will say: Where are their gods,
the rock in which they took refuge,
38 who ate the fat of their sacrifices,
and drank the wine of their libations?
Let them rise up and help you,
let them be your protection!
39 See now that I, even I, am he;
there is no god besides me.
I kill and I make alive;
I wound and I heal;
and no one can deliver from my hand.
40 For I lift up my hand to heaven,
and swear: As I live forever,
41 when I whet my flashing sword,
and my hand takes hold on judgment;
I will take vengeance on my adversaries,
and will repay those who hate me.
42 I will make my arrows drunk with blood,
and my sword shall devour flesh—
with the blood of the slain and the captives,
from the long-haired enemy.
43 Praise, O heavens,[a] his people,
worship him, all you gods![b]
For he will avenge the blood of his children,[c]
and take vengeance on his adversaries;
he will repay those who hate him,[b]
and cleanse the land for his people.[d]

44 Moses came and recited all the words of this song in the hearing of the people, he and Joshua[e] son of Nun. 45 When Moses had finished reciting all these words to all Israel, 46 he said to them: "Take to heart all the words that I am giving in witness against you today; give them as a command

a Q Ms Gk: MT *nations* *b* Q Ms Gk: MT lacks this line *c* Q Ms Gk: MT *his servants* *d* Q Ms Sam Gk Vg: MT *his land his people* *e* Sam Gk Syr Vg: MT *Hoshea*

Vengeance, better, "vindication," since the idea is not revenge but justice. **36:** *Their power is gone, neither bond nor free,* God will act when no one survives who can take charge or provide assistance (2 Kings 14.26; cf. 1 Kings 14.10; 21.21; 2 Kings 9.8). **39:** Similar to exilic Second Isaiah (Isa 41.4; 43.10,13; 44.6; 45.6–7,22; 48.12). **41:** *Take,* lit. "return," in retributive justice. Thus, *vengeance* gives the wrong idea (see v. 35n.). *Those who hate me,* treaty language that refers to disloyal action that violates the covenant; thus better translated, "those who reject me" (5.9). **43:** The second, fourth, and fifth lines have been restored in light of the Dead Sea Scrolls. With *heavens* and *land,* the verse forms a frame or inclusio to "heavens . . . earth" (v. 1), thus framing the poem and returning the focus to Israel's impending entry into the promised land. *All you gods,* the divine council (v. 8n.; Ps 29.1), probably removed from the received Heb text because of the conflict with monotheism (see vv. 8–9n.). *Avenge the blood,* God as divine blood avenger (cf. 19.6), who removes the stain of Israel's blood from the land by requiting the aggressor for having spilled it (19.11–13). *Cleanse,* since the moral stain on the land can only be "wiped clean" (the word's literal meaning) with the blood of the murderer (Num 35.33–34; cf. Deut 21.8): here, the foreign nation. God's position is nonetheless morally ambiguous, since it was he who had sanctioned the foreign invasion as punishment for Israel's wrongdoing (vv. 19–26). *His people,* instead, referring to God: "O heavens, rejoice with him!"

32.44–47: Double conclusion. Two originally separate conclusions joined by Deuteronomy's editors. **44:** *All the words . . . ,* an inclusio (see 31.30). **45–47:** A separate section, the original continuation of

to your children, so that they may diligently
observe all the words of this law. 47 This is
no trifling matter for you, but rather your
very life; through it you may live long in the
land that you are crossing over the Jordan
to possess."
48 On that very day the LORD addressed
Moses as follows: 49 "Ascend this mountain
of the Abarim, Mount Nebo, which is in
the land of Moab, across from Jericho, and
view the land of Canaan, which I am giving
to the Israelites for a possession; 50 you
shall die there on the mountain that you
ascend and shall be gathered to your kin, as
your brother Aaron died on Mount Hor
and was gathered to his kin; 51 because
both of you broke faith with me among the
Israelites at the waters of Meribath-kadesh
in the wilderness of Zin, by failing to main-
tain my holiness among the Israelites. 52 Al-
though you may view the land from a dis-
tance, you shall not enter it—the land that
I am giving to the Israelites."

33 This is the blessing with which Mo-
ses, the man of God, blessed the Is-
raelites before his death. 2 He said:

31.29 prior to the insertion of the Song. **46:** *All the words,* the laws of Deuteronomy (31.24); now, following the insertion of the Song, reinterpreted to refer to both.

32.48–52: Moses commanded to die. This section repeats the announcement of Moses' death (Num 27.12–14) and thus joins it to its logical continuation, the narrative of that death (Deut 34). The original connection between these two Priestly sections was broken by Deuteronomy's insertion into the Pentateuch. **49:** *This mountain of the Abarim, Mount Nebo,* as in the Priestly narrative (Num 27.12; 33.47); but, according to the Deuteronomistic tradition, Pisgah (3.27). The two traditions are joined at 34.1. **50:** *You shall die,* lit. "Die . . . !" This unusual imperative establishes that Moses both lives and dies at God's command (34.5n.). *Gathered to your kin,* burial in a family tomb, where the bones of the generations would be gathered together (2 Kings 8.24; 22.20; cf. 1 Kings 13.31); here used metaphorically, since Moses' burial place is unknown (34.6). *Mount Hor,* consistent with the Priestly tradition (Num 20.22–29; 33.37–39); but, in the Deuteronomistic tradition, "Moserah" (10.6). **51:** *You broke faith,* see Num 20.1–13.

33.1–29: The blessing of Moses. In form a father's blessing of his progeny when death is imminent (Gen 27.27–29; 48.15–16; 49.1–28; cf. 1 Kings 2.1–4), Moses' address to the tribes arrayed before him (29.2,10; 31.7,30) treats all Israel as his own progeny, gathered before the deathbed (Gen 48.2; 49.33). Following the model of other blessings, the speaker addresses the tribes in the singular, as if they were individual sons (contrast v. 19). This poem is clearly an insertion, intruding between God's command to Moses to ascend Nebo to prepare for his death (32.49–50) and Moses' compliance (34.1–5). The literary model of the patriarchal blessing of the twelve tribes (vv. 6–25) has been consciously embedded in a framing poem addressed to a united Israel (vv. 1–5,26–29) that imitates victory hymns to the divine warrior (Judg 5; Ps 18.7–15; Hab 3; cf. Ex 15). That older model has been significantly transformed, however. In vv. 1–4, the expected climax of the divine theophany in the military defeat of the enemy has been totally eclipsed (cf. vv. 26–29), although it is the logical precondition for the proclamation of God as king (v. 5). The new climax is instead Moses' proclamation of Torah (v. 4n.). The reference here to Sinai instead of Deuteronomy's usual Horeb (see 1.2n.) is an attempt to integrate Deuteronomy with the other literary sources of the Pentateuch (Ex 19–20; Lev 25.1; Num 10.12). The editors have used an inclusio pattern to embed the blessing (with its focus upon the individual tribes) into the framing hymn to the divine warrior (where united Israel is the focus). Thus the word symmetry LORD:Jacob:Jeshurun::Jeshurun´:Jacob´:LORD´ (A:B:C::C´:B´:A´; vv. 2,4,5,26,28,29) brackets the inserted blessing. Older hymns to the divine warrior sometimes list the tribes' contributions to the battle (Judg 5.14–18), which facilitates the combination of the two models. Although it draws upon older textual traditions, the poem in its present form is almost certainly exilic or postexilic. The combination of two separate literary models and the emphasis on Torah rather than the divine warrior's manifestation in battle suggest the later literary setting. **1:** *Man of God,* a type of prophet (Josh 14.6; 1 Sam 9.6; 1 Kings 13.1–32; 17.18,24; 2 Kings 4.7–41); this term is not used earlier of Moses in Deuteronomy. **2:** *The LORD . . . dawned,* God's departure from his distant mountain stronghold, dramatically coming to the rescue

The LORD came from Sinai,
and dawned from Seir upon us;[a]
he shone forth from Mount Paran.
With him were myriads of holy ones;[b]
at his right, a host of his own.[c]
3 Indeed, O favorite among[d] peoples,
all his holy ones were in your charge;
they marched at your heels,
accepted direction from you.
4 Moses charged us with the law,
as a possession for the assembly of Jacob.
5 There arose a king in Jeshurun,
when the leaders of the people assembled—
the united tribes of Israel.

6 May Reuben live, and not die out,
even though his numbers are few.

7 And this he said of Judah:
O LORD, give heed to Judah,
and bring him to his people;
strengthen his hands for him,[e]
and be a help against his adversaries.

8 And of Levi he said:
Give to Levi[f] your Thummim,
and your Urim to your loyal one,
whom you tested at Massah,
with whom you contended at the waters of Meribah;
9 who said of his father and mother,
"I regard them not";
he ignored his kin,
and did not acknowledge his children.
For they observed your word,
and kept your covenant.
10 They teach Jacob your ordinances,
and Israel your law;
they place incense before you,
and whole burnt offerings on your altar.
11 Bless, O LORD, his substance,
and accept the work of his hands;
crush the loins of his adversaries,
of those that hate him, so that they do not rise again.

12 Of Benjamin he said:
The beloved of the LORD rests in safety—
the High God[g] surrounds him all day long—
the beloved[h] rests between his shoulders.

a Gk Syr Vg Compare Tg: Heb *upon them* *b* Cn Compare Gk Sam Syr Vg: MT *He came from Ribeboth-kodesh,* *c* Cn Compare Gk: meaning of Heb uncertain *d* Or *O lover of the* *e* Cn: Heb *with his hands he contended* *f* Q Ms Gk: MT lacks *Give to Levi* *g* Heb *above him* *h* Heb *he*

of his people, closely follows the model of Judg 5.4; Hab 3.3. *Myriads of holy ones,* the divine council who accompany God into battle (32.8n.; Ps 68.17; 89.7). *Sinai . . . Seir,* the parallelism locates *Sinai* near *Seir,* associated with Edom (Judg 5.4), in southern Transjordan. This tradition diverges from the one placing the mountain in the Sinai Peninsula, far to the southwest. **3:** *His holy ones,* originally, the divine council of v. 2, reinterpreted to refer to Israel (7.6; 14.2, 21; 26.19; 28.9; Lev 19.2; Num 16.3) to provide a transition to v. 4. **4:** *Moses charged us,* since Moses is himself the speaker (v. 1), this verse is an insertion that presents the promulgation of the Torah as the climax of the divine warrior's theophany. **5:** *A king,* almost certainly God as divine king of Israel (Ex 15.18; Num 23.21; Judg 8.22–23; 1 Sam 8.7; Isa 33.22; Ps 29.10). *Jeshurun,* see 32.15n. **6:** *Reuben,* who once had the leadership of the firstborn (see Gen 49.3–4), is apparently threatened with extinction. (Simeon, Jacob's second-born, is entirely missing.) **7:** *Judah,* in sore trouble because of an unnamed adversary, should be helped by other tribes. **8–11:** Levi, once a warlike tribe (Gen 49.5–7), is to receive the prerogatives of the priesthood: to teach *law,* or Torah (v. 10), and to officiate at the altar. **8:** *Thummim* and *Urim,* the priestly divination devices (Ex 28.30; Ezra 2.63). *Massah* and *Meribah,* see Ex 17.1–7; Num 20.2–13. **9:** On Levi's zealous loyalty to the covenant, at the expense of *father and mother . . . kin, and . . . his children,* thus complying with 13.7, see Ex 32.25–29. **13–17:** See Gen 49.25–26. **16–17:** By ascribing primacy of rule and the status of *firstborn* to

13 And of Joseph he said:
Blessed by the LORD be his land,
with the choice gifts of heaven above,
and of the deep that lies beneath;
14 with the choice fruits of the sun,
and the rich yield of the months;
15 with the finest produce of the ancient mountains,
and the abundance of the everlasting hills;
16 with the choice gifts of the earth and its fullness,
and the favor of the one who dwells on Sinai.[a]
Let these come on the head of Joseph,
on the brow of the prince among his brothers.
17 A firstborn[b] bull—majesty is his!
His horns are the horns of a wild ox;
with them he gores the peoples,
driving them to[c] the ends of the earth;
such are the myriads of Ephraim,
such the thousands of Manasseh.

18 And of Zebulun he said:
Rejoice, Zebulun, in your going out;
and Issachar, in your tents.
19 They call peoples to the mountain;
there they offer the right sacrifices;
for they suck the affluence of the seas
and the hidden treasures of the sand.

20 And of Gad he said:
Blessed be the enlargement of Gad!
Gad lives like a lion;
he tears at arm and scalp.
21 He chose the best for himself,
for there a commander's allotment was reserved;
he came at the head of the people,
he executed the justice of the LORD,
and his ordinances for Israel.

22 And of Dan he said:
Dan is a lion's whelp
that leaps forth from Bashan.

23 And of Naphtali he said:
O Naphtali, sated with favor,
full of the blessing of the LORD,
possess the west and the south.

24 And of Asher he said:
Most blessed of sons be Asher;
may he be the favorite of his brothers,
and may he dip his foot in oil.
25 Your bars are iron and bronze;
and as your days, so is your strength.

26 There is none like God, O Jeshurun,
who rides through the heavens to your help,
majestic through the skies.
27 He subdues the ancient gods,[d]

a Cn: Heb *in the bush* *b* Q Ms Gk Syr Vg: MT *His firstborn* *c* Cn: Heb *the peoples, together* *d* Or *The eternal God is a dwelling place*

Joseph, this blessing conflicts with the law affirming the norm of primogeniture (21.15–17). **16:** *Who dwells on Sinai* refers to Ex 3.1–6 (see text note *a*); 19.1–20.21. *Prince,* Joseph (the Northern Kingdom, destroyed in 722 BCE) enjoyed greater prestige than Judah (v. 7). **17:** *Ephraim* and *Manasseh,* the two tribes making up "the house of Joseph" (Gen 48.13–14). **18–19:** *Zebulun* and *Issachar* will enjoy great influence owing to the resources of the Mediterranean and Lake Chinnereth, later known as the Sea of Galilee (Gen 49.13). **20–21:** *Gad* occupied the *best* tableland in Transjordan but aided the other tribes in the occupation of Canaan (Num 32). **22:** *Dan,* vigorous as a *lion's whelp,* must here already have migrated from its original tribal allotment on the coastal plain to the far north at the base of Mount Hermon (Judg 18). *Bashan,* see 32.14n. **23:** *Naphtali,* located in the region of the Sea of Galilee *west* and *south* of Dan. **24–25:** *Asher,* located below Phoenicia, is to be strong and prosperous. **26–29:** The resumption of the hymn to the divine warrior (vv. 2–5), and a return to the focus upon *Jeshurun* (v. 26), meaning all *Israel* (v. 28). **26:** Much like the Canaanite storm god Baal, Israel's divine warrior rides upon the clouds (Ps 18.10; 68.33; Isa 19.1). **27:** NRSV justifiably reinterprets the Hebrew (see text notes *a, b*)

shatters[a] the forces of old;[b]
he drove out the enemy before you,
and said, "Destroy!"
28 So Israel lives in safety,
untroubled is Jacob's abode[c]
in a land of grain and wine,
where the heavens drop down dew.
29 Happy are you, O Israel! Who is like
you,
a people saved by the LORD,
the shield of your help,
and the sword of your triumph!
Your enemies shall come fawning to
you,
and you shall tread on their backs.

34 Then Moses went up from the
plains of Moab to Mount Nebo, to
the top of Pisgah, which is opposite Jericho,
and the LORD showed him the whole land:
Gilead as far as Dan, 2 all Naphtali, the
land of Ephraim and Manasseh, all the land
of Judah as far as the Western Sea, 3 the
Negeb, and the Plain—that is, the valley of
Jericho, the city of palm trees—as far as
Zoar. 4 The LORD said to him, "This is
the land of which I swore to Abraham, to
Isaac, and to Jacob, saying, 'I will give it to
your descendants'; I have let you see it with
your eyes, but you shall not cross over
there." 5 Then Moses, the servant of the
LORD, died there in the land of Moab, at
the LORD's command. 6 He was buried in a
valley in the land of Moab, opposite Beth-
peor, but no one knows his burial place to
this day. 7 Moses was one hundred twenty
years old when he died; his sight was unim-
paired and his vigor had not abated. 8 The
Israelites wept for Moses in the plains of
Moab thirty days; then the period of
mourning for Moses was ended.
9 Joshua son of Nun was full of the spir-

a Cn: Heb *from underneath* *b* Or *the everlasting arms* *c* Or *fountain*

in order to continue the mythic imagery of v. 26. **28:** As in Ugaritic epic, the theophany of the divine warrior and his proclamation as king results in the fertility of the land. **29:** *Tread on their backs,* a standard symbol of military triumph (Josh 10.24; Ps 110.1; also attested in Neo-Assyrian reliefs).

34.1–12: The death of Moses. This chapter, the original continuation of ch 31 and 32.48–52, highlights the absence of access to Moses; since his burial site is unknown, it cannot become a venerated shrine. The Torah alone is his enduring bequest. At another level, however, it also continues Num 27, where God had commanded Moses to "go up this mountain" to survey the promised land before his death, and to "lay your hand" upon Joshua, to transfer the mantle of authority to him (vv. 12,18), bracketing Deuteronomy and suggesting that editors interrupted the narrative in order to include Deuteronomy in the Pentateuch. **1:** *Went up,* responding to the command of 32.49; Num 27.12. The verse joins two different traditions about the site of Moses' death: *Mount Nebo,* which is in Transjordan, east of Jericho; and Mount *Pisgah,* which is slightly to its west, and unmentioned in 32.49. Seeking to preserve both traditions, the editor presents them as if they were the same. **2–3:** The lofty vantage point allows Moses to look northward to the Sea of Galilee (area of the tribal allotment of Dan and *Naphtali*), to the *Western Sea* (the Mediterranean), south to the *Negeb* desert and along the Jordan rift valley as far south as *Zoar* (once located at the southern end of the Dead Sea as one of the "cities of the Plain"; Gen 14.2,8; 19.29). **5:** *At the LORD's command,* see 32.50n. The unusual formulation greatly honors Moses, who, despite advanced age, does not die of old age nor succumb to physical or intellectual infirmity. **6:** *He was buried,* the Heb states, "He buried him," a clear indication that God himself buried Moses, as he himself sealed Noah into the ark (Gen 7.16). Instead of Moses' progeny assuming the responsibility of caring for the dead, God undertook it personally. *Beth-peor,* 3.29; 4.46; Josh 13.20. *No one knows his burial place,* thus precluding pilgrimages to the site as a shrine. **7:** *One hundred twenty,* see 31.2n. **8:** *Thirty days,* so also for Aaron (Num 20.29), the full mourning period stipulated for a parent (21.13). **9:** *Full of the spirit of wisdom,* as at 1.13 and 16.18–20, Deuteronomy revises earlier traditions to stress wisdom as the essential qualification of office, and thus what Joshua receives from Moses. In Num 27.18, Joshua already possessed an undefined "spirit" (often associated with prophecy or possession), while Moses was to transfer his "authority" to him. *Laid his hands on him,* as at Num 27.22–23, a means of transfer of attributes (Lev 16.21; Num 8.10–13), here used for investiture into office. **10–12:** Moses as the apogee

it of wisdom, because Moses had laid his
hands on him; and the Israelites obeyed
him, doing as the LORD had commanded
Moses.
10 Never since has there arisen a proph-
et in Israel like Moses, whom the LORD
knew face to face. 11 He was unequaled for
all the signs and wonders that the LORD
sent him to perform in the land of Egypt,
against Pharaoh and all his servants and his
entire land, 12 and for all the mighty deeds
and all the terrifying displays of power
that Moses performed in the sight of all
Israel.

of prophecy both in direct access to divine revelation and in power to work miracles. The double elevation, which differs from his more human representation elsewhere in the book, suggests an editor's later, idealizing retrospective, with Deuteronomy now worked into the Pentateuch as a whole. **10:** *Never since,* more correctly, "But there never again arose in Israel a prophet like Moses." NRSV obscures the discrepancy between the perspective of this verse and the divine promise to Moses that the line of prophetic succession will continue in the future: "I will raise up for them a prophet like you" (18.18). *Face to face,* rather than through dreams or visions (13.1); similarly, Ex 33.11; Num 12.8–10. Other traditions reject the concept that Moses had such direct access to God (Ex 33.20–23).

INTRODUCTION
to the Historical Books

THE HISTORICAL BOOKS AND HISTORIOGRAPHY

THE CHRISTIAN BISHOP Athanasius, in the fourth century CE, first used the term "histories" for this section of the Bible, which now covers the books Joshua, Judges, Ruth, Samuel, Kings, Chronicles, Ezra-Nehemiah, and Esther. It is a misleading title, since these books cover a wide range of genres and often are not historical in modern senses of the word. Furthermore, there are several books that are similar to some of these Historical Books, yet they are found in different sections of the Bible.

Large sections of Genesis, Exodus, and Numbers, and much of the introduction to Deuteronomy in the Torah, contain narratives about the past. Similarly, there are several psalms that survey the past (e.g., Ps 78, 105, 106, 107). Yet, this material is not incorporated into the Historical Books. Thus, this section does not represent the collection of all works of the same genre, and its development as a canonical division is best understood in relation to the broader development of the biblical canon (see pp. 453–460 ESSAYS). Moreover, in the traditional Jewish arrangement of the books of the Bible, the books of Joshua, Judges, Samuel, and Kings are called the Former Prophets, thus opening the second major division of the Hebrew Bible, the Prophets, which follows the Torah. The books of Ruth, Chronicles, Ezra-Nehemiah, and Esther, however, are found in the third major division, the Writings. For these reasons, the rest of this introduction examines the nature of biblical historical texts, broadly construed, with a focus on the books Joshua through Esther, which now comprise the section of the Bible called Historical Books.

The idea that historical writing should capture the events "as they really were," that historians should attempt to write an objective account of the events of the past, is a relatively recent notion that developed in the European universities several centuries ago. Before that, history was often didactic in nature, teaching the readers how to be good citizens or how to lead proper religious lives. Sometimes histories were produced in the royal court, in which case they were apologetic, showing how the king fulfilled his royal duties. Surviving historical documents from the ancient Near East show similar religious and ideological goals. Thus, it should not be surprising that the biblical writers are not primarily interested in the accurate recording of real events; rather, they use narratives about the past to illustrate various issues of significance to their earliest audience, the ancient Israelite community.

It is easiest to understand the biblical notion of history by first focusing on works that are outside this canonical division. Exodus 13.3 begins: "Moses said to the people, 'Remember this day on which you came out of Egypt, out of the house of slavery.'" This would seem to suggest the importance of history for its own sake. However, this unit continues with a set of commandments that directly result from this event: "no leavened bread shall be eaten" (v. 3); "Seven days you shall eat unleavened bread, and on the seventh day there shall be a festival to the LORD" (v. 6); "no leavened bread shall be seen in your possession, and no leaven shall be seen among you in all your territory" (v. 7); "You shall tell your child on that day . . ." (v. 8); "It shall serve for you as a sign on your hand and as a reminder on your forehead" (v. 9); "you shall set apart to the LORD all that first opens the womb. All the firstborn of your livestock that are males shall be the LORD's" (v. 12). Read in context, it is not important to remember the Exodus as a disembodied historical event, as the beginning of v. 3 might suggest; rather, the Exodus is key because it serves as the basis for the observance of a central set of laws or norms.

The use of historical material in Psalms is even more instructive, since these traditions about the past are typically surrounded by a framework that explicitly highlights their theological significance or purpose. For example, in Psalm 78 a particular set of traditions is chosen and shaped so:

> "that the next generation might know them,
>   the children yet unborn,
> and rise up and tell them to their children,
>   so that they should set their hope in God,
> and not forget the works of God,
>   but keep his commandments;
> and that they should not be like their ancestors,
>   a stubborn and rebellious generation,
> a generation whose heart was not steadfast,
>   whose spirit was not faithful to God" (vv. 6–8).

Psalm 106 tells how God saved Israel time after time, despite their covenant violations. This is used as an argument to God that they should be rescued again:

> "Save us, O LORD our God,
>   and gather us from among the nations,
> that we may give thanks to your holy name
>   and glory in your praise" (v. 47).

Unfortunately, the material collected in the Historical Books is not as straightforward about its purposes as these psalms or Exodus 13; for this reason, the Historical Books need to be subjected to internal analysis, in order to see what motivations and interests best explain their shape.

ORGANIZATION INTO BOOKS AND LARGER UNITS

In pursuing this task, we must be mindful that the division of some biblical writings into separate books is just as arbitrary as the designation of a particular set of books as a single canonical unit, such as Historical Books. The division of Samuel, Kings, and Chronicles into separate books is not original and was first done in the Greek Bible so that each book would have a more reasonable size. In the formation of the canon, Ezra-Nehemiah was originally considered a single work, and it is possible that Joshua and Judges, which blend together well (see especially Josh 24.29–31 and Judg 2.8–10), were also perceived as a single work at an earlier period. Even the divisions between these larger works are not always certain; the first two chapters of Kings, for example, which narrate events at the end of David's life, fit the book of Samuel better than their current place.

In fact, it has been proposed that since the books of Joshua, Judges, Samuel, and Kings, along with the preceding book of Deuteronomy, fit so well together, these five books were edited together as a single work. This work is typically called the Deuteronomistic History, meaning the history written under the influence of ideas found in the book of Deuteronomy. This theory has much to commend it: These five books do read as a unified whole from a chronological perspective, narrating a continuous history from the end of the life of Moses through the Babylonian exile (586 BCE), and they share many phrases and ideological notions, such as an insistence on exclusive worship of God and the tragic consequences of idolatry, a concern with the centrality of Jerusalem, and a belief in the supremacy of the eternal Davidic dynasty. If this theory is correct, the size of the Deuteronomistic History, and the long period that it depicts, is quite remarkable, especially for an ancient historical work.

Many details of this theory remain debated; some scholars suggest that these books are not quite unified enough to represent the product of a single individual, intellectual school, or movement. For example, the book of Samuel shows remarkably few contacts with the language of Deuteronomy, and the book of Kings contains narratives in which the great prophets Elijah and Elisha are legitimately active outside the Jerusalem Temple (see especially 1 Kings 18, concerning Elijah on Mount Carmel). Thus, various theories have been suggested concerning successive editions of the Deuteronomistic History, which many believe was begun in the seventh century under the Judean King Josiah (640–609 BCE), but completed only in the Babylonian exile (586–538 BCE) or beyond. Some suggest that the lack of unity is due to non-Deuteronomistic material that has been added at a late stage to an earlier Deuteronomistic History. There have also been attempts to isolate narratives that might have preceded the Deuteronomistic History and other sources used by the Deuteronomist(s), and to discern their original purposes before these narratives and sources became integrated into the larger literary work. In sum, this collection has a long and complicated history, so it is impossible to speak of a unified purpose or interest in the compilation of the books of Joshua, Judges, Samuel, and Kings. They reflect many different interests and stages of development: pre-Deuteronomic, Deuteronomistic, and later, postexilic concerns. The interests of each individual book of the Deuteronomistic History are discussed in the Introduction to that particular book.

Scholars have also found many similarities between Chronicles and Ezra-Nehemiah and have posited that these works belong to a single large history composed by the Chronicler, which parallels the Deuteronomistic History. A closer look at Chronicles and Ezra-Nehemiah, however, shows that they differ from each other in outlook and vocabulary, and that the general similarities between them are best attributed to the common time in which they were written, most likely the fourth century BCE.

Chronicles is a retelling with significant variations of the books of Genesis through Kings. It is unclear if its author had access to a significant number of external sources not found in our canonical Bibles, but in any case, a close examination of the book illustrates the remarkable way in which its author deals with sources, rewriting them to fit a particular notion of "historical probability," namely, what really could have happened based on notions of how the world worked. For example, in the book of Kings, which does not have a clear retribution theory (a theory concerning punishment and reward), the Judean King Manasseh (698/687–642 BCE) is depicted as the most evil king of Judah, who is ultimately responsible for the destruction of the Temple in 586 (2 Kings 21). However, the same source indicates that Manasseh reigned for fifty-five years.

This "contradiction" between the behavior of Manasseh and his long reign did not bother the Deuteronomist, who did not believe that each individual king needs to be punished or rewarded for his behavior. However, the Chronicler did believe in this type of retribution theology, and the Deuteronomist's depiction of Manasseh in Kings was clearly very troublesome. For this reason, the Chronicler rewrote the life of Manasseh, adding 2 Chronicles 33.10–13: "The LORD spoke to Manasseh and to his people, but they gave no heed. Therefore the LORD brought against them the commanders of the army of the king of Assyria, who took Manasseh captive in manacles, bound him with fetters, and brought him to Babylon. While he was in distress he entreated the favor of the LORD his God and humbled himself greatly before the God of his ancestors. He prayed to him, and God received his entreaty, heard his plea, and restored him again to Jerusalem and to his kingdom. Then Manasseh knew that the LORD indeed was God." Thus, Manasseh fits the paradigms that the author of Chronicles believed to be true: All people need to be warned before they are punished; repentance is extremely efficacious; and individuals may only succeed if their behavior is meritorious. These external beliefs forced a revision of the source's account so that Manasseh's life could be properly illustrative. Other examples of this type of revisionism are found throughout Chronicles and are discussed in the Introduction to that book; since, in the case of Samuel and Kings, we do not have access to the sources on which they are based, we can only wonder if this type of radical reworking characterizes the entire corpus of Historical Texts.

SMALLER WORKS

Ruth and Esther are both short stories, historical fictions, which are quite different in nature from the works discussed above, but very similar to the books of Tobit and Judith in the Apocrypha. They are more literary than these larger works; that is, their authors self-consciously manipulated their prose for esthetic as well as ideological purposes. For example, part of the structuring of Ruth involves symmetry, whereby an "'eshet ḥayil" ("a worthy woman" [3.11]), meets and marries a "gibbor ḥayil" ("a worthy man"; NRSV "a prominent rich man" [2.1]), and they live happily ever after. The book also opens with an ironic statement that is only apparent in the Hebrew: There is a famine in "the house of bread" (Bethlehem). Esther as well is tightly structured, for example, using dinner parties as a major plot device for the book's progress. Despite the literary artistry of these books, however, they are also history in the sense outlined above: They narrate a past in order to convey lessons relevant to the community. The particular characteristics of these two very different books, each from a distinct country and time period, and each reflecting remarkably different ideologies, may be found in the Introduction to each book.

Ezra differs from these other Historical Books in its use of extensive quotations of official Persian documents (e.g., 7.12–26), which many believe to be authentic. Nehemiah lacks these documents but is exceptional in its own way: It is the only book in this collection to narrate history from the first-person perspective, as in 13.15: "In those days I saw in Judah people treading wine presses on the sabbath, and bringing in heaps of grain and loading them on donkeys; and also wine, grapes, figs, and all kinds of burdens, which they brought into Jerusalem on the sabbath day; and I warned them at that time against selling food." In general, Ezra-Nehemiah is closer to the events that it narrates than any other biblical book, and it is thus possible that it may reflect those events with greater accuracy than other biblical works, which are typically removed by centuries from the events being described. Nevertheless, we must also recognize the strong biases of this book, which is interested in fostering the importance of the Torah as the central document for the postexilic community (see esp. Neh 8–9), and in emphasizing the grave dangers of intermarriage (Ezra 9–10, Neh 13). Thus, even Ezra-Nehemiah, which contains archival material and first-person accounts, and is among the latest of the books in this canonical division, should not be seen as straightforward, representative, and accurate history.

THE HISTORICAL BOOKS AND HISTORICITY

The problematic nature of all of these texts as historical documents does not mean that we have no idea of the historical periods that they cover, or that they are entirely useless as historical sources. Each text needs to be weighed individually in terms of its date of composition and its likely goals. Using these criteria, there are reasons to accept the veracity of, for example, the dry notice in 1 Kings 14.25–26 ("In the fifth year of King Rehoboam, King Shishak of Egypt came up against Jerusalem; he took away the treasures of the house of the LORD and the treasures of the king's house; he took everything. He also took away all the shields of gold that Solomon had made"), which might even come from an archival source. In contrast, there are good reasons to be suspicious of the historicity of the long, detailed, and embellished story of David slaying Goliath in 1 Sam 17; this story uses late biblical Hebrew language, comes from a different source than the surrounding material in Samuel, and is structured like a fairy-tale, in that the poor, short, unexpected hero gets to marry the tall king's daughter by killing the giant who had vilified God. Additionally, 2 Sam 21.19 reads: "Then there was another battle with the Philistines at Gob; and Elhanan son of Jaare-oregim, the Bethlehemite, killed Goliath the Gittite, the shaft of whose spear was like a weaver's beam." It is much more likely that a short tradition in which Goliath is killed by a relatively unknown figure (Elhanan) would be the source for the long, elaborate tale attributing the same event to the well-known David, rather than vice versa. Thus, the modern historian must subject each text in these Historical Books to the type of internal analysis used on nonbiblical historical texts when external information bearing on the text is lacking.

There are a number of cases where we do have external, ancient Near Eastern written evidence that deals with events depicted in these Historical Books. For example, the events surrounding the siege of Jerusalem by the Assyrian King Sennacherib in 701 BCE are narrated in several Assyrian sources and are also depicted in the palace reliefs of that king. These sources suggest that part of the terse account in 2 Kings 18.13–16 is quite accurate, while the highly developed continuation of the story in chs 19 and 20, especially the note in 19.35, that the angel of the LORD killed 185,000 Assyrian soldiers in a single night, is most likely imaginative. Similarly, from various Mesopotamian sources, we know of a "house of Omri"; Omri's name is also mentioned on the Moabite Mesha Stele. This confirms the existence of the northern (Israelite) king mentioned in 1 Kings 16.23–28. However, Kings tells little of his achievements during his twelve years as monarch, other than his building of Samaria and the notice that: "Omri did what was evil in the sight of the LORD; he did more evil than all who were before him. For he walked in all the way of Jeroboam son of Nebat, and in the sins that he caused Israel to commit, provoking the LORD, the God of Israel, to anger by their idols" (vv. 25–26). The external sources, however, suggest that Omri was a powerful king who established a significant name for himself through his military activities. This highlights the extreme selectivity of the biblical sources.

Archaeological evidence confirms the picture suggested above: There may be some truth (or kernel of truth) to some of the biblical stories, but in their current form, they lack historical veracity, because that is not their prime concern. Recent decades, for example, have seen a remarkable reevaluation of the evidence concerning the conquest of the land of Canaan by Joshua. As more sites have been excavated, there is a growing consensus that the main story of Joshua, that of a speedy and complete conquest (e.g., Josh 11.23: "So Joshua took the whole land, according to all that the LORD had spoken to Moses"), cannot be upheld by the archaeological record, though there are indications of some destruction and conquest at the appropriate time. Various events and traditions have been reworked very substantially over time and ultimately included in the Bible in order to substantiate a particular picture of God.

In sum, the title Historical Books must not frame the way we read the following texts. Many of these texts do contain the raw materials for a modern historian researching the history of ancient Israel from the time of the conquest through the fourth century BCE, but this material can only be teased out using sophisticated and complex tools. This is because these various biblical historians each wrote accounts, sometimes using sources, to illustrate particular perspectives concerning the relationship between God and Israel. It is these religious and religio-political perspectives that we must try to appreciate as we study these books; if we read them as we read modern historical accounts, we will misunderstand these texts in the most fundamental way.

JOSHUA

The book of Joshua describes the "conquest" of Canaan and its allotment to the Israelite tribes. Through well-known traditional stories (e.g., Rahab and the spies, the crossing of the Jordan River, the capture of Jericho) as well as non-narrative lists and ritual texts, the book portrays the fulfillment of God's covenantal promise to the patriarchs that their descendants would possess the land. Moreover, these stories challenge the book's readers to live in obedience to the Deuteronomic covenant so that they also will receive God's blessings in the land.

The historicity of the book cannot simply be assumed since it telescopes and simplifies what was a long and complex process of occupation of the land by the Israelite tribes. Some details are lacking (e.g., how the Israelites came into possession of Shechem, 8.30–35), while the other events narrated in the book are selectively arranged to heighten the book's message. Thus the book's presentation of reality does not necessarily reflect the actual course of events. Consequently, archaeological excavations, together with sociological and anthropological analyses, must be used to understand the early history of Israel in the land.

The authorship of the book of Joshua is unknown. Some types of sources for the book's composition are identifiable (for example, the border descriptions and city lists in chs 14–19), though their origin and date are often disputed. Scholars commonly perceive the book in its final form to be part of a larger historical work, the Deuteronomistic History, stretching from Deuteronomy through 2 Kings. The book's final date of composition is unknown; it is dependent upon the dating of the various editions of the Deuteronomistic History, of which it is now a part. One major edition of the larger work is generally agreed to date to the late seventh century BCE. The connections between the book of Joshua and Deuteronomy led earlier scholars to posit a Hexateuch, with the book of Joshua completing the Pentateuch. More recently scholars have viewed Deuteronomy as the introduction to the books of Deuteronomy through Kings, the Deuteronomistic History.

The historiographic materials used in the book of Joshua correspond to those found in the ancient Near East as a whole. Thus there are traditional stories, etiologies, boundary and town lists, summary accounts and lists, and accounts patterned after redundant annalistic documents. These have been woven together with ritual and covenantal materials and other matters of priestly interest to communicate the book's ideological message.

Several themes and literary devices characterize the book. First, the structure of the book has two main divisions: the conquests (1.1–12.24) and the allotment of the land (13.1–24.33). Within each main division, there are two subdivisions: *A*: preparations for the conquest (1.1–5.12) and *B*: the conquest's campaigns (5.13–12.24); *B´*: the allotment of the conquered land (13.1–21.45) and *A´*: epilogue to the conquest and allotment (22.1–24.33). The body of the book (5.13–21.45) is bracketed by specially chosen introductory and concluding materials (1.1–5.12; 22.1–24.33). Each subdivision contains a number of units that contribute to the development of the plot and message of the book.

Second, the book follows a logical geographic arrangement. An east-to-west crossing into Canaan (chs 2–5) is followed by military campaigns directed at the center (chs 6–8), south (chs 9–10), and north (ch 11), concluded by a summary list (ch 12). The division of the land first covers the Transjordanian tribes (ch 13), then the south and central tribes (chs 14–17), then the northern and peripheral tribes (chs 18–19), and finally entities of marginal status (chs 20–21). At times, however, the technique of "backtrack and overlap" is imposed upon the narration, as the story backs up and retells the events in a type of flashback. This is especially noticeable in chs 3–4 (the crossing of the Jordan) and 10 (the conquest of the south).

Third, the law (Heb "torah") plays a normative role in the book, and Israel's obedience or disobedience to the law determines success or failure. This law, especially prominent in chs 1 and 23, is further specified as "the law of Moses" and refers to the law or teaching of Moses as contained in some form of the book of Deuteronomy.

Fourth, typology (that is, representing one character or event as an echo or foreshadowing of another) is utilized to portray Joshua as parallel to Moses. A few examples will illustrate: Moses leads the Israelites out of Egypt, Joshua leads the Israelites into Canaan; Moses leads Israel in a miraculous crossing of the Reed Sea, Joshua leads Israel in a miraculous crossing of the Jordan River; Moses sends out spies, Joshua sends out spies; Moses allots land to the tribes east of the Jordan, Joshua allots land to the tribes west of the Jordan.

Fifth, the book utilizes a number of different land ideologies. Some of these may be anchored in concrete reality, while others are purely idealistic or a mixture of the two. In the book's final form, these produce an abstract, idealized concept of the land, create tensions, and set the stage for irony. The dominant land ideology is the territory of the twelve tribes (both west and east of the Jordan) who completely fill up the land (chs 15–19; cf. Deut 4.45–49). In this view, the two and one-half Transjordanian tribes (those settled east of the Jordan) are an integral and vital part of "all Israel." A second, contrasting ideology restricts the true land of inheritance to the territory west of the Jordan (Cisjordan, the land of Canaan) (cf. Deut 12.10). It is this image of the land that lies behind the belief that crossing the Jordan was a step of outstanding significance (chs 3–4). This view also creates ironic tensions in 22.10–34, where the two and one-half tribes set up an altar in Transjordan. A third ideology presents the land as claimed but unconquered, noting "the land that remains" (13.2–6); and a fourth ideology is an expansionistic, utopian "Euphratic Israel," which claims the distant Euphrates as the northern boundary of Israel's inheritance (1.4; cf. Gen 15.18; Deut 1.7; 11.24). These last two notions instill the book with the flavor of unredeemed promise, and again set the stage for irony. The text develops two understandings of Israel's unfulfilled expectations. On the one hand, the incomplete conquest is judged to be the result of Israel's disobedience or military inability (15.63; 16.10; 17.12–13; 19.47). This serves as the basis for future threats to Israel's well-being (7.12; 23.12–13). On the other hand, the last two land ideologies function as hopeful indications of greater future land blessings to Israel (13.6b; 17.18; 23.5).

Sixth, ritual concerns dictate some of the narration. For example, the crossing of the Jordan River (chs 3–4), circumcision and Passover (ch 5), the conquest of Jericho (ch 6), and the implementations of the "ḥerem" (chs 6–8) all reflect ritual concerns that undergird the book's land claims.

Finally, the concept of the "ḥerem" plays a significant role in the book. This noun is usually translated "devoted thing" (7.1) and the related verb "utterly destroy" (10.28). The term is used primarily in contexts of warfare and destruction where the "ḥerem" stories are connected with the notion of obedience/disobedience to the LORD (cf. Deut 7; 20). Its purpose was to "drive out" or "dispossess" the Canaanites in order to carry out divine judgment on them, to protect the Israelites from Canaanite religious influence, and to fulfill the promises concerning the land. This kind of warfare is part of the political ideology that Israel shared with other nations in the ancient Near East, in which wars were dedicated to the glorification of the deity and the extension of the deity's land and reign.

Thus the book of Joshua plays an important role not only in the story of the early history of Israel in the land, but also in the development of the theology of the Hebrew Bible. In many ways, it serves as the prologue for the remainder of the Deuteronomistic History's story of Israel's struggles in the land.

1 After the death of Moses the servant of
the LORD, the LORD spoke to Joshua
son of Nun, Moses' assistant, saying, 2 "My
servant Moses is dead. Now proceed to
cross the Jordan, you and all this people,
into the land that I am giving to them, to
the Israelites. 3 Every place that the sole of
your foot will tread upon I have given to
you, as I promised to Moses. 4 From the
wilderness and the Lebanon as far as the
great river, the river Euphrates, all the land
of the Hittites, to the Great Sea in the west
shall be your territory. 5 No one shall be
able to stand against you all the days of
your life. As I was with Moses, so I will be
with you; I will not fail you or forsake you.
6 Be strong and courageous; for you shall
put this people in possession of the land
that I swore to their ancestors to give them.
7 Only be strong and very courageous, be-
ing careful to act in accordance with all the
law that my servant Moses commanded
you; do not turn from it to the right hand
or to the left, so that you may be successful
wherever you go. 8 This book of the law
shall not depart out of your mouth; you
shall meditate on it day and night, so that
you may be careful to act in accordance
with all that is written in it. For then you
shall make your way prosperous, and then
you shall be successful. 9 I hereby command
you: Be strong and courageous; do not be
frightened or dismayed, for the LORD your
God is with you wherever you go."
10 Then Joshua commanded the officers
of the people, 11 "Pass through the camp,
and command the people: 'Prepare your
provisions; for in three days you are to
cross over the Jordan, to go in to take pos-
session of the land that the LORD your God
gives you to possess.' "
12 To the Reubenites, the Gadites, and
the half-tribe of Manasseh Joshua said,
13 "Remember the word that Moses the ser-
vant of the LORD commanded you, saying,
'The LORD your God is providing you a
place of rest, and will give you this land.'
14 Your wives, your little ones, and your
livestock shall remain in the land that Mo-
ses gave you beyond the Jordan. But all the
warriors among you shall cross over armed
before your kindred and shall help them,
15 until the LORD gives rest to your kindred
as well as to you, and they too take posses-

1.1–5.12: Preparation for the conquest. 1.1–18: The commission. 1: Moses' death (Deut 34) provides the setting for Joshua's commission. God did not allow Moses to enter the land (Deut 32.48–52). **2–18:** The commission itself contains four speeches (vv. 2–9, 10–11, 12–15, 16–18). **2–9:** The LORD's speech outlines the means of success for Joshua and the Israelites: obedience to the book of the law. The LORD's speech also anticipates the main themes of the book: the crossing of the Jordan (1.1–5.12), the conquest (5.13–12.24), the distribution of the land (13.1–22.34), and obedience to the law of Moses (23.1–24.33). **2–5:** The idealized boundaries of the land, given with the assurance of God's presence, were the *Jordan* River to the east, *the wilderness* or semidesert to the south and east, the *Lebanon* mountain range to the northwest, the *river Euphrates* to the north, and the *Great Sea,* the Mediterranean Sea, to the west (cf. Deut 11.24–25). **4:** *All the land of the Hittites* is likely a later gloss, probably referring to northern Syria. **5:** An explicit recognition that Joshua is the new Moses; cf. Ex 3.12. **6–9:** As currently formulated, the text emphasizes that military success comes from the law's internalization, spoken of in 1.8 in terms of meditation with consequent obedience (cf. Deut 31.7–8; Ps 1.2–3). **11:** *In three days* reflects ritual concerns (cf. Ex 3.18; 19.11). **12–15:** Joshua's speech to the Transjordanian tribes is suffused with vocabulary that typifies Deuteronomy. Since the other tribes had helped the Transjordanians conquer their land, the Transjordanians were to help the other Israelites acquire their land west of the Jordan. *The half-tribe of Manasseh,* according to territorial lists (see 13.29–31; 17) part of Manasseh occupied land east of the Jordan

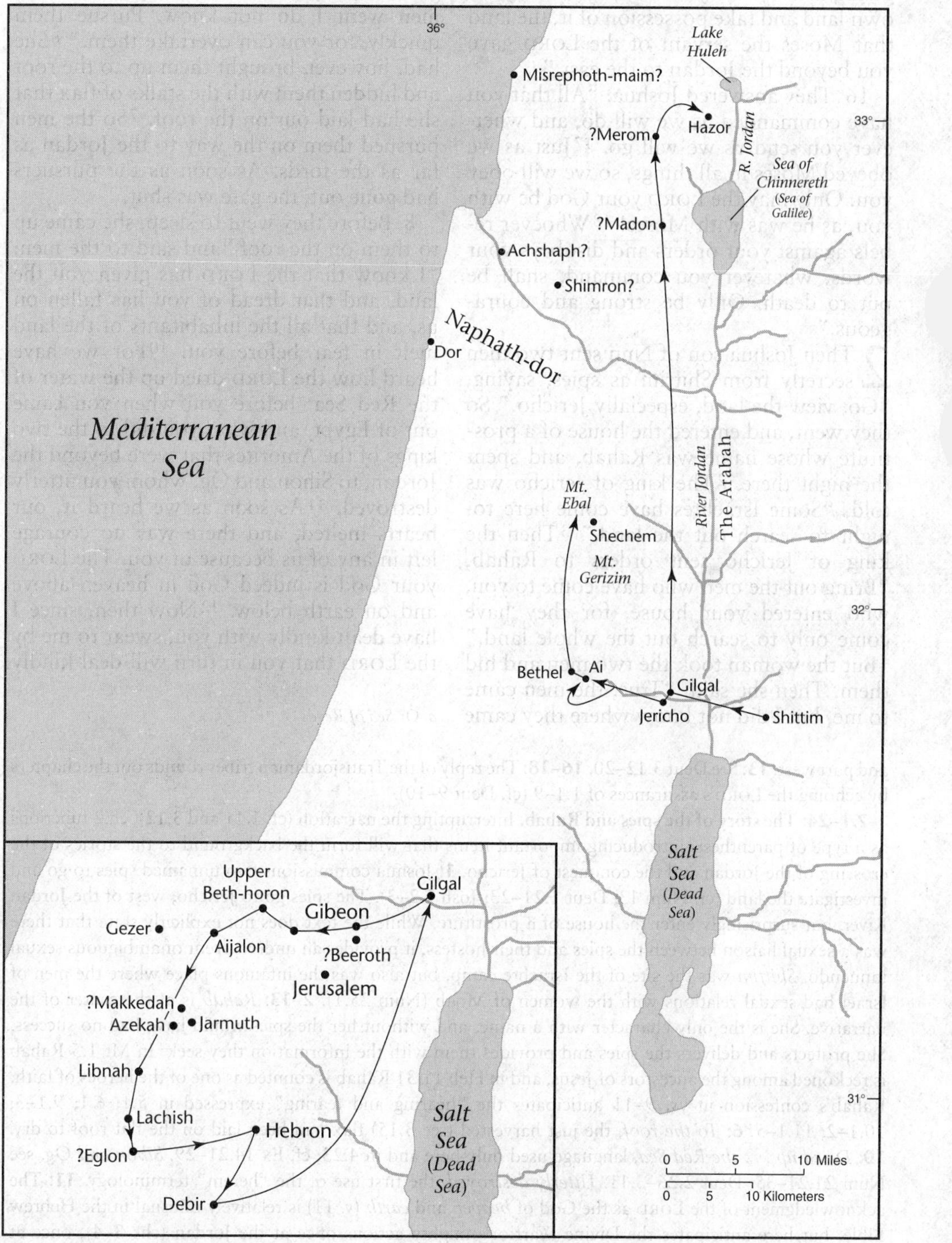

Chs 1–12: The conquest of Canaan.

sion of the land that the LORD your God is
giving them. Then you shall return to your
own land and take possession of it, the land
that Moses the servant of the LORD gave
you beyond the Jordan to the east."

16 They answered Joshua: "All that you
have commanded us we will do, and wher-
ever you send us we will go. 17 Just as we
obeyed Moses in all things, so we will obey
you. Only may the LORD your God be with
you, as he was with Moses! 18 Whoever re-
bels against your orders and disobeys your
words, whatever you command, shall be
put to death. Only be strong and coura-
geous."

2 Then Joshua son of Nun sent two men
secretly from Shittim as spies, saying,
"Go, view the land, especially Jericho." So
they went, and entered the house of a pros-
titute whose name was Rahab, and spent
the night there. 2 The king of Jericho was
told, "Some Israelites have come here to-
night to search out the land." 3 Then the
king of Jericho sent orders to Rahab,
"Bring out the men who have come to you,
who entered your house, for they have
come only to search out the whole land."
4 But the woman took the two men and hid
them. Then she said, "True, the men came
to me, but I did not know where they came
from. 5 And when it was time to close the
gate at dark, the men went out. Where the
men went I do not know. Pursue them
quickly, for you can overtake them." 6 She
had, however, brought them up to the roof
and hidden them with the stalks of flax that
she had laid out on the roof. 7 So the men
pursued them on the way to the Jordan as
far as the fords. As soon as the pursuers
had gone out, the gate was shut.

8 Before they went to sleep, she came up
to them on the roof 9 and said to the men:
"I know that the LORD has given you the
land, and that dread of you has fallen on
us, and that all the inhabitants of the land
melt in fear before you. 10 For we have
heard how the LORD dried up the water of
the Red Sea[a] before you when you came
out of Egypt, and what you did to the two
kings of the Amorites that were beyond the
Jordan, to Sihon and Og, whom you utterly
destroyed. 11 As soon as we heard it, our
hearts melted, and there was no courage
left in any of us because of you. The LORD
your God is indeed God in heaven above
and on earth below. 12 Now then, since I
have dealt kindly with you, swear to me by
the LORD that you in turn will deal kindly

a Or *Sea of Reeds*

and part west. **13:** See Deut 3.12–20. **16–18:** The reply of the Transjordanian tribes rounds out the chapters by echoing the LORD's assurances of 1.1–9 (cf. Deut 9–10).

2.1–24: The story of the spies and Rahab. Interrupting the narration (cf. 1.11 and 3.12), ch 2 functions as a type of parenthesis introducing important items that will form the background to the stories of the crossing of the Jordan and the conquest of Jericho. **1:** Joshua commissions two unnamed spies to go and investigate the land (cf. Num 13; Deut 1.21–23; Josh 7.2–3). The spies go to Jericho, west of the Jordan River, but surprisingly enter the house of a prostitute. While the text does not explicitly state that there was a sexual liaison between the spies and their hostess, it provides an undercurrent of ambiguous sexual innuendo. *Shittim* was the site of the Israelite camp, but also was the infamous place where the men of Israel had sexual relations with the women of Moab (Num 25.1). **2–13:** *Rahab* is at the center of the narrative. She is the only character with a name, and without her the spies would have had no success. She protects and delivers the spies and provides them with the information they seek. In Mt 1.5 Rahab is reckoned among the ancestors of Jesus, and in Heb 11.31 Rahab is counted as one of the heroes of faith. Rahab's confession in vv. 9–11 anticipates the "hearing and fearing" expressed in 5.1; 6.1; 9.1–3; 10.1–2; 11.1–5. **6:** *To the roof,* the just harvested (see 3.15) flax had been laid on the flat roof to dry. **10:** *Dried up . . . the Red Sea,* language used only here and in 4.23; cf. Ex 14.21–29. *Sihon and Og,* see Num 21.21–35; Deut 2.26–3.11. *Utterly destroyed,* the first use of the "ḥerem" terminology. **11:** The acknowledgment of the LORD as the God of *heaven* and *earth* (v. 11) is relatively unusual in the Hebrew Bible, but here anticipates the Divine Warrior's mighty actions once at the Jordan (chs 3–4), once at Jericho (ch 6) and twice in the skies over Gibeon (ch 10). **14–21:** Ironically, Rahab, the Canaanite

with my family. Give me a sign of good
faith 13 that you will spare my father and
mother, my brothers and sisters, and all
who belong to them, and deliver our lives
from death." 14 The men said to her, "Our
life for yours! If you do not tell this busi-
ness of ours, then we will deal kindly and
faithfully with you when the LORD gives us
the land."

15 Then she let them down by a rope
through the window, for her house was on
the outer side of the city wall and she resid-
ed within the wall itself. 16 She said to them,
"Go toward the hill country, so that the
pursuers may not come upon you. Hide
yourselves there three days, until the pursu-
ers have returned; then afterward you may
go your way." 17 The men said to her, "We
will be released from this oath that you
have made us swear to you 18 if we invade
the land and you do not tie this crimson
cord in the window through which you let
us down, and you do not gather into your
house your father and mother, your broth-
ers, and all your family. 19 If any of you go
out of the doors of your house into the
street, they shall be responsible for their
own death, and we shall be innocent; but if
a hand is laid upon any who are with you
in the house, we shall bear the responsibili-
ty for their death. 20 But if you tell this busi-
ness of ours, then we shall be released from
this oath that you made us swear to you."
21 She said, "According to your words, so
be it." She sent them away and they depart-
ed. Then she tied the crimson cord in the
window.

22 They departed and went into the hill
country and stayed there three days, until
the pursuers returned. The pursuers had
searched all along the way and found noth-
ing. 23 Then the two men came down again
from the hill country. They crossed over,
came to Joshua son of Nun, and told him
all that had happened to them. 24 They said
to Joshua, "Truly the LORD has given all
the land into our hands; moreover all the
inhabitants of the land melt in fear be-
fore us."

3 Early in the morning Joshua rose and
set out from Shittim with all the Israel-
ites, and they came to the Jordan. They
camped there before crossing over. 2 At the
end of three days the officers went through
the camp 3 and commanded the people,
"When you see the ark of the covenant of
the LORD your God being carried by the
levitical priests, then you shall set out from
your place. Follow it, 4 so that you may
know the way you should go, for you have

prostitute, shows unconditional loyalty toward the spies, risking everything; but the spies show conditioned loyalty to Rahab, minimizing their risks. **16:** *Toward the hill country,* to the west. **22–24:** The report of the spies to Joshua is based on Rahab's words. In contrast to the spies of Num 13, they did not "view the land" as they were told (v. 1). Without Rahab these men would not have returned to give a report on the Canaanite disposition.

3.1–5.1: The crossing of the Jordan. The crossing of the Jordan is narrated in five units (3.1–17; 4.1–10; 4.11–14; 4.15–18; 4.19–5.1) that backtrack and overlap so that a number of events are recounted more than once. The use of anticipatory statements and resumptive repetitions provides a means of linking the units together (e.g., the anticipatory statement in 3.12 is tied to the resumptive repetition in 4.1). In this way a redactor has attempted to meld together different sources.

3.1–17: The initial story of the crossing. This unit notes that the Jordan is in flood (v. 15) because otherwise it is a relatively narrow river. The Jordan functions primarily as a ritual and ideological symbol representing the boundary between landlessness and settled peoplehood. It anticipates the importance of all boundaries in the book, particularly those of the allotments (chs 13–21) and the tribal dispute of ch 22. The fact that the procession begins and ends at early Israelite religious centers ([Abel]-Shittim and Gilgal) reinforces the ritual significance. **2:** Resumptive of 1.11. **3:** *The ark of the covenant* was the container for the text of the law; see Deut 31.26. It also symbolized God's presence among the tribes; it could be carried only by priests. It could be brought into battle, assuring the deity's presence among the nation (see 1 Sam 4.6–7). **4:** The people were to keep their distance because of the presence of God. *Two thousand cubits,* about 885 m (2,900 ft). **5:** *Sanctify yourselves* reflects the ritual background of the story.

not passed this way before. Yet there shall
be a space between you and it, a distance of
about two thousand cubits; do not come
any nearer to it." 5 Then Joshua said to the
people, "Sanctify yourselves; for tomorrow
the LORD will do wonders among you."
6 To the priests Joshua said, "Take up the
ark of the covenant, and pass on in front of
the people." So they took up the ark of the
covenant and went in front of the people.
7 The LORD said to Joshua, "This day I
will begin to exalt you in the sight of all
Israel, so that they may know that I will be
with you as I was with Moses. 8 You are the
one who shall command the priests who
bear the ark of the covenant, 'When you
come to the edge of the waters of the Jor-
dan, you shall stand still in the Jordan.' "
9 Joshua then said to the Israelites, "Draw
near and hear the words of the LORD your
God." 10 Joshua said, "By this you shall
know that among you is the living God
who without fail will drive out from before
you the Canaanites, Hittites, Hivites, Periz-
zites, Girgashites, Amorites, and Jebusites:
11 the ark of the covenant of the Lord of all
the earth is going to pass before you into
the Jordan. 12 So now select twelve men
from the tribes of Israel, one from each
tribe. 13 When the soles of the feet of the
priests who bear the ark of the LORD, the
Lord of all the earth, rest in the waters of
the Jordan, the waters of the Jordan flow-
ing from above shall be cut off; they shall
stand in a single heap."
14 When the people set out from their
tents to cross over the Jordan, the priests
bearing the ark of the covenant were in
front of the people. 15 Now the Jordan
overflows all its banks throughout the time
of harvest. So when those who bore the ark
had come to the Jordan, and the feet of the
priests bearing the ark were dipped in the
edge of the water, 16 the waters flowing
from above stood still, rising up in a single
heap far off at Adam, the city that is beside
Zarethan, while those flowing toward the
sea of the Arabah, the Dead Sea,[a] were
wholly cut off. Then the people crossed
over opposite Jericho. 17 While all Israel
were crossing over on dry ground, the
priests who bore the ark of the covenant of
the LORD stood on dry ground in the mid-
dle of the Jordan, until the entire nation
finished crossing over the Jordan.

4 When the entire nation had finished
crossing over the Jordan, the LORD said
to Joshua: 2 "Select twelve men from the
people, one from each tribe, 3 and com-
mand them, 'Take twelve stones from here
out of the middle of the Jordan, from the
place where the priests' feet stood, carry
them over with you, and lay them down
in the place where you camp tonight.' "
4 Then Joshua summoned the twelve men
from the Israelites, whom he had appoint-
ed, one from each tribe. 5 Joshua said to
them, "Pass on before the ark of the LORD
your God into the middle of the Jordan,
and each of you take up a stone on his
shoulder, one for each of the tribes of the
Israelites, 6 so that this may be a sign among
you. When your children ask in time to
come, 'What do those stones mean to you?'

a Heb *Salt Sea*

The Israelites were to purify themselves in preparation for the divine presence (cf. Ex 19.10–15). **10:** A stereotypical listing of the pre-Israelite population of Canaan; it is difficult to identify the individual groups specifically. *Hittites,* apparently a group in the land of Canaan (see Gen 23; Judg 3.5; contrast 1.4n.). The *Jebusites* are associated with Jerusalem (see 15.63). If the chronological setting for these events is approximately the thirteenth century BCE, the Canaan that the Israelite tribes entered was in a state of economic, social, and political turmoil, due in large measure to the collapsing Egyptian empire and many Canaanite city-state structures. **12:** Anticipates 4.2. **13:** *Stand,* cf. 10.13, where the moon is commanded to "stand still." *Heap,* a rare word used elsewhere only of the splitting of the Red Sea (Ex 15.8; Ps 78.13). **16:** *Adam,* 18 km (12 mi) north of Jericho, is probably Tell ed-Damiyeh. *Zarethan* is farther north. **17:** The continued presence of the priests with the ark in the midst of the dry riverbed anticipates 4.10.

4.1–10: The erecting of the twelve-stone memorial. This unit is quite repetitive (e.g., cf. vv. 6 and 21), and lightly preserves different traditions. **9:** Another, perhaps later, tradition that locates a

7then you shall tell them that the waters of
the Jordan were cut off in front of the ark
of the covenant of the LORD. When it
crossed over the Jordan, the waters of the
Jordan were cut off. So these stones shall be
to the Israelites a memorial forever."
8 The Israelites did as Joshua command-
ed. They took up twelve stones out of the
middle of the Jordan, according to the
number of the tribes of the Israelites, as the
LORD told Joshua, carried them over with
them to the place where they camped, and
laid them down there. 9(Joshua set up
twelve stones in the middle of the Jordan,
in the place where the feet of the priests
bearing the ark of the covenant had stood;
and they are there to this day.)
10 The priests who bore the ark re-
mained standing in the middle of the Jor-
dan, until everything was finished that the
LORD commanded Joshua to tell the peo-
ple, according to all that Moses had com-
manded Joshua. The people crossed over in
haste. 11As soon as all the people had fin-
ished crossing over, the ark of the LORD,
and the priests, crossed over in front of the
people. 12The Reubenites, the Gadites, and
the half-tribe of Manasseh crossed over
armed before the Israelites, as Moses had
ordered them. 13About forty thousand
armed for war crossed over before the
LORD to the plains of Jericho for battle.
14 On that day the LORD exalted Joshua
in the sight of all Israel; and they stood in
awe of him, as they had stood in awe of
Moses, all the days of his life.
15 The LORD said to Joshua, 16"Com-
mand the priests who bear the ark of the
covenant,[a] to come up out of the Jordan."
17Joshua therefore commanded the priests,
"Come up out of the Jordan." 18When the
priests bearing the ark of the covenant of
the LORD came up from the middle of the
Jordan, and the soles of the priests' feet
touched dry ground, the waters of the Jor-
dan returned to their place and overflowed
all its banks, as before.
19 The people came up out of the Jor-
dan on the tenth day of the first month, and
they camped in Gilgal on the east border of
Jericho. 20Those twelve stones, which they
had taken out of the Jordan, Joshua set up
in Gilgal, 21saying to the Israelites, "When
your children ask their parents in time to
come, 'What do these stones mean?' 22then
you shall let your children know, 'Israel
crossed over the Jordan here on dry
ground.' 23For the LORD your God dried
up the waters of the Jordan for you until
you crossed over, as the LORD your God
did to the Red Sea,[b] which he dried up for
us until we crossed over, 24so that all the
peoples of the earth may know that the
hand of the LORD is mighty, and so that
you may fear the LORD your God forever."

a Or *treaty*, or *testimony*; Heb *eduth* *b* Or *Sea of Reeds*

memorial of twelve stones in the bed of the Jordan itself; v. 8 narrates the removal of stones from the river bed to the shore, where they are part of the sanctuary of Gilgal (see v. 20). **10:** *In haste,* cf. Ex 12.33–34. **11–14:** The unit backtracks and narrates again the crossing, emphasizing the role of the Transjordanians and the exaltation of Joshua. **12–13:** A flashback reports that the eastern tribes have done what Moses commanded and Joshua reiterated (1.14; Deut 3.18). **14:** Resumptive repetition stresses again the fulfillment of the LORD's exaltation of Joshua as with Moses. **15–18:** This unit backtracks and retells the ark's crossing and the unstopping of the river. **18:** An item-by-item reversal of what happened in 3.15–16. In fact, the verse backtracks to *the middle of the Jordan* before reporting that the priests actually leave the water.

4.19–5.1: The final unit emphasizes the instructional value of the memorial through comparison with the Red Sea crossing. **19:** The focus turns from the priests to the people. *The first month* was Abib (March-April), later called Nisan. The preparations for the first Passover began on the tenth day of the first month (Ex 12.3). *Gilgal,* whose precise location is disputed, was an important Israelite shrine; its name means "circle," perhaps referring to the stone configuration. **23:** The connection of this event to the Exodus from Egypt is made explicit. **24:** As with the Exodus, both foreigner and Israelite (v. 22) must learn from this event (Ex 10.1–2). **5.1:** Resuming 2.9–11 and anticipating 9.1; 10.1; 11.1.

5 When all the kings of the Amorites be-
yond the Jordan to the west, and all the
kings of the Canaanites by the sea, heard
that the LORD had dried up the waters of
the Jordan for the Israelites until they had
crossed over, their hearts melted, and there
was no longer any spirit in them, because of
the Israelites.

2 At that time the LORD said to Joshua,
"Make flint knives and circumcise the Isra-
elites a second time." 3 So Joshua made flint
knives, and circumcised the Israelites at
Gibeath-haaraloth.[a] 4 This is the reason
why Joshua circumcised them: all the males
of the people who came out of Egypt, all
the warriors, had died during the journey
through the wilderness after they had come
out of Egypt. 5 Although all the people who
came out had been circumcised, yet all the
people born on the journey through the
wilderness after they had come out of
Egypt had not been circumcised. 6 For the
Israelites traveled forty years in the wilder-
ness, until all the nation, the warriors who
came out of Egypt, perished, not having lis-
tened to the voice of the LORD. To them the
LORD swore that he would not let them see
the land that he had sworn to their ances-
tors to give us, a land flowing with milk
and honey. 7 So it was their children, whom
he raised up in their place, that Joshua cir-
cumcised; for they were uncircumcised, be-
cause they had not been circumcised on the
way.

8 When the circumcising of all the na-
tion was done, they remained in their
places in the camp until they were healed.
9 The LORD said to Joshua, "Today I have
rolled away from you the disgrace of
Egypt." And so that place is called Gilgal[b]
to this day.

10 While the Israelites were camped in
Gilgal they kept the passover in the evening
on the fourteenth day of the month in the
plains of Jericho. 11 On the day after the
passover, on that very day, they ate the pro-
duce of the land, unleavened cakes and
parched grain. 12 The manna ceased on the
day they ate the produce of the land, and
the Israelites no longer had manna; they ate
the crops of the land of Canaan that year.

13 Once when Joshua was by Jericho, he

[a] That is *the Hill of the Foreskins* [b] Related to Heb *galal* to roll

5.2–12: Final preparatory events at Gilgal. Three connected ritual events are recounted: circumcision (vv. 2–9), Passover (v. 10), and the first consumption of the produce of the land at Gilgal (vv. 11–12). **2–9:** The disobedience of the older generation (those of the first circumcision who came out of Egypt and died in the wilderness) is contrasted to the obedience of the new generation (those participating in this circumcision). Circumcision was a ritual required of all males who were to celebrate the Passover (Ex 12.48). **2:** At one time circumcision was a common practice in the ancient Near East; it became a sign of Israel's relationship with God. *A second time,* probably a later addition to mitigate the failure (see v. 5) to observe the obligation of Gen 17.9–14 or to emphasize Joshua as a parallel to Moses. **6:** To *give us,* an unusual authorial inclusion. The description *a land flowing with milk and honey* anticipates the consumption of the land's produce (vv. 10–12). **9:** This is a folk-etymology of *Gilgal,* "the round place." The precise nature of the *disgrace* is unclear; it may refer to Deut 9.28, demonstrating that the crossing and the circumcision are God's graciousness toward Israel in spite of Israel's lack of faithfulness in the wilderness. **10:** The celebration of the Passover reinforces the portrayal of Joshua as parallel to Moses (cf. Ex 12). **11–12:** Land claims are usually presented as a matter of conquests (chs 6–12) and geographic lists (chs 13–21), but here they are set forth in terms of ritual events and diet. The change from manna to the produce of the land signifies Israel's relocation from wilderness to land. Unleavened bread and roasted grain are used in rituals connected to Passover and first fruits (Lev 23.9–14).

5.13–12.24: Conquest of the land. The conquest of the land is recounted as three major campaigns: central (5.13–8.35), southern (9.1–10.43), and northern (11.1–15).

5.13–8.35: Central campaign. The central campaign, which is described in the greatest detail, has three sections: 5.13–6.27; 7.1–8.29; and 8.30–35.

looked up and saw a man standing before
him with a drawn sword in his hand. Josh-
ua went to him and said to him, "Are you
one of us, or one of our adversaries?" [14]He
replied, "Neither; but as commander of the
army of the LORD I have now come." And
Joshua fell on his face to the earth and wor-
shiped, and he said to him, "What do you
command your servant, my lord?" [15]The
commander of the army of the LORD said
to Joshua, "Remove the sandals from your
feet, for the place where you stand is holy."
And Joshua did so.

6 Now Jericho was shut up inside and out
because of the Israelites; no one came
out and no one went in. [2]The LORD said to
Joshua, "See, I have handed Jericho over to
you, along with its king and soldiers. [3]You
shall march around the city, all the war-
riors circling the city once. Thus you shall
do for six days, [4]with seven priests bearing
seven trumpets of rams' horns before the
ark. On the seventh day you shall march
around the city seven times, the priests
blowing the trumpets. [5]When they make a
long blast with the ram's horn, as soon as
you hear the sound of the trumpet, then all
the people shall shout with a great shout;
and the wall of the city will fall down flat,
and all the people shall charge straight
ahead." [6]So Joshua son of Nun summoned
the priests and said to them, "Take up the
ark of the covenant, and have seven priests
carry seven trumpets of rams' horns in
front of the ark of the LORD." [7]To the
people he said, "Go forward and march
around the city; have the armed men pass
on before the ark of the LORD."

8 As Joshua had commanded the people,
the seven priests carrying the seven trum-
pets of rams' horns before the LORD went
forward, blowing the trumpets, with the
ark of the covenant of the LORD following
them. [9]And the armed men went before the
priests who blew the trumpets; the rear
guard came after the ark, while the trum-
pets blew continually. [10]To the people
Joshua gave this command: "You shall not
shout or let your voice be heard, nor shall
you utter a word, until the day I tell you to
shout. Then you shall shout." [11]So the ark
of the LORD went around the city, circling
it once; and they came into the camp, and
spent the night in the camp.

12 Then Joshua rose early in the morn-
ing, and the priests took up the ark of the
LORD. [13]The seven priests carrying the sev-
en trumpets of rams' horns before the ark
of the LORD passed on, blowing the trum-
pets continually. The armed men went be-
fore them, and the rear guard came after
the ark of the LORD, while the trumpets
blew continually. [14]On the second day they
marched around the city once and then re-

5.13–6.27: Jericho: first application of "ḥerem." Jericho's capture is important because it is the first implementation of the "ḥerem" by the Israelites in the conquest. The interpretation of the archaeological evidence from Tell es-Sultan (ancient Jericho) is disputed, but in the thirteenth century BCE there was at best an unfortified village on the site, rather than the walled city depicted here. Like Moses (see Ex 3.1–4.17), Joshua receives a theophany followed by detailed instructions; 6.2–5 thus continues the scene of 5.13–15, with 6.1 being a parenthetical aside. **5.13–15:** The appearance of the *commander of the army of the LORD* is probably a fragment of a fuller tradition. He is not mentioned in the rest of the book. **14:** The commander is neither Israelite nor Canaanite. He is not part of a human army, but rather the commander of the heavenly forces (see Deut 33.2; Judg 5.20; Zech 9.14). **15:** A direct quotation from Ex 3.5, again showing that Joshua was the divinely appointed successor of Moses.

6.6–27: Jericho is captured by following the LORD's instructions. Ritual ceremony plays an important symbolic function, overcoming the walls of Jericho: seven priests, seven trumpets, seven days, seven encirclements on the seventh day, and a seventh-day climactic victory. The preponderance of "sevens" recalls the seven days of creation (Gen 1), implying the creation of a new order in the land and continuing the ritual land claim of 3.1–5.12. This is the first implementation of the "ḥerem," a ritual act. Ironically, the Canaanite prostitute Rahab and her family are exempted from the "ḥerem" (v. 17). The account of the fall of Jericho is more ritually symbolic than military in its significance, though as a victory in the first battle, it prefigures success in the campaigns that will follow. **18:** *Bringing trouble upon it* anticipates the

turned to the camp. They did this for six
days.
15 On the seventh day they rose early, at
dawn, and marched around the city in the
same manner seven times. It was only on
that day that they marched around the city
seven times. 16 And at the seventh time,
when the priests had blown the trumpets,
Joshua said to the people, "Shout! For the
LORD has given you the city. 17 The city and
all that is in it shall be devoted to the LORD
for destruction. Only Rahab the prostitute
and all who are with her in her house shall
live because she hid the messengers we sent.
18 As for you, keep away from the things
devoted to destruction, so as not to covet[a]
and take any of the devoted things and
make the camp of Israel an object for de-
struction, bringing trouble upon it. 19 But
all silver and gold, and vessels of bronze
and iron, are sacred to the LORD; they shall
go into the treasury of the LORD." 20 So the
people shouted, and the trumpets were
blown. As soon as the people heard the
sound of the trumpets, they raised a great
shout, and the wall fell down flat; so the
people charged straight ahead into the city
and captured it. 21 Then they devoted to de-
struction by the edge of the sword all in the
city, both men and women, young and old,
oxen, sheep, and donkeys.
22 Joshua said to the two men who had
spied out the land, "Go into the prostitute's
house, and bring the woman out of it and
all who belong to her, as you swore to her."
23 So the young men who had been spies
went in and brought Rahab out, along with
her father, her mother, her brothers, and all
who belonged to her—they brought all her
kindred out—and set them outside the
camp of Israel. 24 They burned down the
city, and everything in it; only the silver and
gold, and the vessels of bronze and iron,
they put into the treasury of the house of
the LORD. 25 But Rahab the prostitute, with
her family and all who belonged to her,
Joshua spared. Her family[b] has lived in Is-
rael ever since. For she hid the messengers
whom Joshua sent to spy out Jericho.
26 Joshua then pronounced this oath,
saying,

"Cursed before the LORD be anyone
    who tries
  to build this city—this Jericho!
At the cost of his firstborn he shall
    lay its foundation,
  and at the cost of his youngest he
    shall set up its gates!"

27 So the LORD was with Joshua; and
his fame was in all the land.
7 But the Israelites broke faith in regard
to the devoted things: Achan son of
Carmi son of Zabdi son of Zerah, of the
tribe of Judah, took some of the devoted
things; and the anger of the LORD burned
against the Israelites.
2 Joshua sent men from Jericho to Ai,
which is near Beth-aven, east of Bethel, and
said to them, "Go up and spy out the
land." And the men went up and spied out
Ai. 3 Then they returned to Joshua and said

a Gk: Heb *devote to destruction* Compare 7.21
b Heb *She*

next story (7.25). **19–24:** Israel's faithfulness in the implementation of the "ḥerem" is emphasized and Achan's unfaithfulness is anticipated. Jericho represents a paradigm for the entire enterprise of conquest (8.2; 10.1; 24.11). **25:** *Ever since* indicates that the descendants of Rahab (i.e., Canaanites) survived and lived among the Israelites. **26:** The fulfillment of this enigmatic curse is recorded in 1 Kings 16.34. **27:** The climactic conclusion: The LORD was with Joshua (see 1.5) and his fame was in all the land.

7.1–8.29: Achan and Ai. 7.1–5: First battle of Ai and Achan's sin. In contrast to the climactic conclusion in which Joshua is exalted (6.27), Achan's sin is described. Although only one person was unfaithful, all Israel was liable because the state of being devoted ("ḥerem") is contagious, and the booty would contaminate Israel's camp and put it into a state of devotion ("ḥerem"). **2:** The name *Ai* (modern et-Tell) means "the ruin." The site, 3 km (2 mi) east of Bethel, was uninhabited during the Late Bronze Age. **3–5:** The spies believe that Israel is too strong to worry about such a small fortress (contrast Num 13–14). Overconfidence spells a lack of consultation and of dependence on the LORD. The men of Ai thoroughly repulsed the Israelite contingent (cf. Num 14.42–45).

to him, "Not all the people need go up;
about two or three thousand men should
go up and attack Ai. Since they are so few,
do not make the whole people toil up
there." 4So about three thousand of the
people went up there; and they fled before
the men of Ai. 5The men of Ai killed about
thirty-six of them, chasing them from out-
side the gate as far as Shebarim and killing
them on the slope. The hearts of the people
melted and turned to water.
6 Then Joshua tore his clothes, and fell
to the ground on his face before the ark of
the LORD until the evening, he and the el-
ders of Israel; and they put dust on their
heads. 7Joshua said, "Ah, Lord GOD! Why
have you brought this people across the
Jordan at all, to hand us over to the Amo-
rites so as to destroy us? Would that we
had been content to settle beyond the Jor-
dan! 8O Lord, what can I say, now that
Israel has turned their backs to their ene-
mies! 9The Canaanites and all the inhabi-
tants of the land will hear of it, and sur-
round us, and cut off our name from the
earth. Then what will you do for your great
name?"
10 The LORD said to Joshua, "Stand up!
Why have you fallen upon your face? 11Is-
rael has sinned; they have transgressed my
covenant that I imposed on them. They
have taken some of the devoted things; they
have stolen, they have acted deceitfully,
and they have put them among their own
belongings. 12Therefore the Israelites are
unable to stand before their enemies; they
turn their backs to their enemies, because
they have become a thing devoted for de-
struction themselves. I will be with you no
more, unless you destroy the devoted things
from among you. 13Proceed to sanctify the
people, and say, 'Sanctify yourselves for to-
morrow; for thus says the LORD, the God
of Israel, "There are devoted things among
you, O Israel; you will be unable to stand
before your enemies until you take away
the devoted things from among you." 14In
the morning therefore you shall come for-
ward tribe by tribe. The tribe that the LORD
takes shall come near by clans, the clan that
the LORD takes shall come near by house-
holds, and the household that the LORD
takes shall come near one by one. 15And
the one who is taken as having the devoted
things shall be burned with fire, together
with all that he has, for having transgressed
the covenant of the LORD, and for having
done an outrageous thing in Israel.' "
16 So Joshua rose early in the morning,
and brought Israel near tribe by tribe, and
the tribe of Judah was taken. 17He brought
near the clans of Judah, and the clan of the
Zerahites was taken; and he brought near
the clan of the Zerahites, family by fami-
ly,[a] and Zabdi was taken. 18And he
brought near his household one by one,
and Achan son of Carmi son of Zabdi son
of Zerah, of the tribe of Judah, was taken.
19Then Joshua said to Achan, "My son,
give glory to the LORD God of Israel and
make confession to him. Tell me now what
you have done; do not hide it from me."
20And Achan answered Joshua, "It is true;
I am the one who sinned against the LORD
God of Israel. This is what I did: 21when I
saw among the spoil a beautiful mantle

a Mss Syr: MT *man by man*

7.6–26: Second application of "ḥerem": Achan's execution. 6–9: Joshua's prayer of intercession recalls prayers of Moses (e.g., Ex 32.11–13; Num 11.11–15; 14.13–19; Deut 9.26–29). **6:** *Tore his clothes . . . dust on their heads,* traditional expressions of grief. **7:** *Amorites,* here a generic designation of the inhabitants of the land (see 24.15). **10–15:** God's answer to Joshua is a rebuke. **11–13:** There has been a covenant violation: a theft of God's property, the *devoted things* ("ḥerem") from Jericho. Only sanctifying themselves and removing the *devoted things* can prevent Israel from being a *devoted thing.* **14:** *The LORD takes,* by the casting of lots (a device that when thrown yields the proper yes-or-no answer through divine assistance). **16–21:** The process of selection successfully narrows down the guilty group, finding the guilty party. It also reinforces Achan's guilt. **20–21:** The actual "ḥerem" objects are listed in Achan's admission: a beautiful mantle from Shinar (Babylon), two hundred shekels of silver (about 2.7 kg [6 lbs]), and a fifty-shekel bar of gold (about 560 gm [1.25 lbs]). **22–26:** The resolution of the problem is found

from Shinar, and two hundred shekels of
silver, and a bar of gold weighing fifty
shekels, then I coveted them and took
them. They now lie hidden in the ground
inside my tent, with the silver underneath."
22 So Joshua sent messengers, and they
ran to the tent; and there it was, hidden in
his tent with the silver underneath. 23 They
took them out of the tent and brought them
to Joshua and all the Israelites; and they
spread them out before the LORD. 24 Then
Joshua and all Israel with him took Achan
son of Zerah, with the silver, the mantle,
and the bar of gold, with his sons and
daughters, with his oxen, donkeys, and
sheep, and his tent and all that he had; and
they brought them up to the Valley of
Achor. 25 Joshua said, "Why did you bring
trouble on us? The LORD is bringing trou-
ble on you today." And all Israel stoned
him to death; they burned them with fire,
cast stones on them, 26 and raised over him
a great heap of stones that remains to this
day. Then the LORD turned from his burn-
ing anger. Therefore that place to this day
is called the Valley of Achor.[a]

8 Then the LORD said to Joshua, "Do not
fear or be dismayed; take all the fight-
ing men with you, and go up now to Ai.
See, I have handed over to you the king of
Ai with his people, his city, and his land.
2 You shall do to Ai and its king as you did
to Jericho and its king; only its spoil and its
livestock you may take as booty for your-
selves. Set an ambush against the city, be-
hind it."
3 So Joshua and all the fighting men set
out to go up against Ai. Joshua chose thirty
thousand warriors and sent them out by
night 4 with the command, "You shall lie in
ambush against the city, behind it; do not
go very far from the city, but all of you stay
alert. 5 I and all the people who are with me
will approach the city. When they come out
against us, as before, we shall flee from
them. 6 They will come out after us until we
have drawn them away from the city; for
they will say, 'They are fleeing from us,
as before.' While we flee from them, 7 you
shall rise up from the ambush and seize the
city; for the LORD your God will give it into
your hand. 8 And when you have taken the
city, you shall set the city on fire, doing as
the LORD has ordered; see, I have com-
manded you." 9 So Joshua sent them out;
and they went to the place of ambush, and
lay between Bethel and Ai, to the west of
Ai; but Joshua spent that night in the
camp.[b]
10 In the morning Joshua rose early and
mustered the people, and went up, with the
elders of Israel, before the people to Ai.
11 All the fighting men who were with him
went up, and drew near before the city, and
camped on the north side of Ai, with a ra-
vine between them and Ai. 12 Taking about
five thousand men, he set them in ambush
between Bethel and Ai, to the west of the
city. 13 So they stationed the forces, the
main encampment that was north of the
city and its rear guard west of the city.
But Joshua spent that night in the valley.
14 When the king of Ai saw this, he and all
his people, the inhabitants of the city, hur-

a That is *Trouble* *b* Heb *among the people*

in the "ḥerem" of Achan and his family. **25:** This refers to 6.18. *Trouble* (Heb "ʿakar") is removed from Israel and ritually placed on Achan. **26:** *Valley of Achor,* a name derived from a word play on Achan's final state of "trouble" ("ʿakar"). The valley is probably the Buqeiah, just west of the northern end of the Dead Sea; in 15.7 it is on the border between Benjamin and Judah. The text juxtaposes the ironic outcomes for Rahab and her family and Achan and his family.

8.1–29: Third application of "ḥerem": second battle of Ai and Ai's destruction. 1–2: The LORD gives assurance and instructions, making clear that Achan's sin has been removed so that God can once again give Israel the land. Note also the modification of the "ḥerem": They may have the plunder of Ai. **3–8:** Joshua relates the LORD's instructions to the Israelites. The repetitions build suspense. **9–29:** Ai is captured and put under the "ḥerem." **9:** *Bethel,* the modern village of Beitin, is 17 km (11 mi) north of Jerusalem. Later it became one of the principal shrines of the Northern Kingdom (1 Kings 12.28–30; Gen 12.8; 28.11–22). **14–15:** *Facing the Arabah . . . in the direction of the wilderness,* toward the Rift Valley,

ried out early in the morning to the meeting
place facing the Arabah to meet Israel in
battle; but he did not know that there was
an ambush against him behind the city.
15 And Joshua and all Israel made a pre-
tense of being beaten before them, and fled
in the direction of the wilderness. 16 So all
the people who were in the city were called
together to pursue them, and as they pur-
sued Joshua they were drawn away from
the city. 17 There was not a man left in Ai or
Bethel who did not go out after Israel; they
left the city open, and pursued Israel.

18 Then the LORD said to Joshua,
"Stretch out the sword that is in your hand
toward Ai; for I will give it into your
hand." And Joshua stretched out the sword
that was in his hand toward the city. 19 As
soon as he stretched out his hand, the
troops in ambush rose quickly out of their
place and rushed forward. They entered the
city, took it, and at once set the city on fire.
20 So when the men of Ai looked back, the
smoke of the city was rising to the sky.
They had no power to flee this way or that,
for the people who fled to the wilderness
turned back against the pursuers. 21 When
Joshua and all Israel saw that the ambush
had taken the city and that the smoke of the
city was rising, then they turned back and
struck down the men of Ai. 22 And the oth-
ers came out from the city against them; so
they were surrounded by Israelites, some
on one side, and some on the other; and
Israel struck them down until no one was
left who survived or escaped. 23 But the
king of Ai was taken alive and brought to
Joshua.

24 When Israel had finished slaughter-
ing all the inhabitants of Ai in the open
wilderness where they pursued them, and
when all of them to the very last had fallen
by the edge of the sword, all Israel returned
to Ai, and attacked it with the edge of the
sword. 25 The total of those who fell that
day, both men and women, was twelve
thousand—all the people of Ai. 26 For Josh-
ua did not draw back his hand, with which
he stretched out the sword, until he had
utterly destroyed all the inhabitants of Ai.
27 Only the livestock and the spoil of that
city Israel took as their booty, according to
the word of the LORD that he had issued to
Joshua. 28 So Joshua burned Ai, and made
it forever a heap of ruins, as it is to this day.
29 And he hanged the king of Ai on a tree
until evening; and at sunset Joshua com-
manded, and they took his body down
from the tree, threw it down at the entrance
of the gate of the city, and raised over it a
great heap of stones, which stands there to
this day.

30 Then Joshua built on Mount Ebal an
altar to the LORD, the God of Israel, 31 just

to the east. **18–29:** Joshua's stretching out his sword is similar to Moses' actions in Ex 14.15–21,26–27; 17.9–12. The third implementation of the "ḥerem" is the Canaanite city of Ai, which is depicted as a sacrificial burnt offering. Ironically, God allowed the Israelites to take some of the plunder from Ai that was under the "ḥerem" (v. 27), perhaps to avoid a repeat of the action of Achan. **28:** *Forever a heap of ruins,* lit. "an eternal tell, a devastation," cf. 11.13n.; Deut 13.16. **29:** The hanging of the king of Ai and his stone memorial in the gate of the city are common actions in ancient Near Eastern warfare. This also anticipates the execution of the five kings in 10.26–27 and follows the Deuteronomic injunction (Deut 21.22–23). It also offers a contrast to 1 Sam 15, where Saul does not put Agag, the Amalekite king, to death, thereby disqualifying himself from leadership.

8.30–35: Covenant renewal as land grant: Shechem. The events narrated in ch 9 are the natural sequel to the story about the fall of Ai (note that 8.29 flows into 9.3). Hence this account of covenant renewal is parenthetical to the main action and is connected by many scholars with 24.1–28. Traveling to Ebal would have required the tribes to make a trip of about 50 km (30 mi) by road from Ai to Ebal and then to retrace their steps to encamp at Gilgal (9.6). This narrative serves to portray Joshua as carrying out the command given to Moses in Deut 27.4–7 (cf. Deut 11.29–30). Joshua, who obeyed, is the foil to Achan, who did not (cf. 6.27 and 7.1). The connections between this section and Deuteronomy are especially strong. **30:** *Mount Ebal* is one of the two mountains (Gerizim being the other) that flank the pass of Shechem in central Canaan. **31:** Quoting Deut 27.5. **32:** *On the stones,* not the stones of the altar,

as Moses the servant of the LORD had com-
manded the Israelites, as it is written in the
book of the law of Moses, "an altar of un-
hewn[a] stones, on which no iron tool has
been used"; and they offered on it burnt
offerings to the LORD, and sacrificed offer-
ings of well-being. 32 And there, in the pres-
ence of the Israelites, Joshua[b] wrote on the
stones a copy of the law of Moses, which he
had written. 33 All Israel, alien as well as
citizen, with their elders and officers and
their judges, stood on opposite sides of the
ark in front of the levitical priests who car-
ried the ark of the covenant of the LORD,
half of them in front of Mount Gerizim and
half of them in front of Mount Ebal, as
Moses the servant of the LORD had com-
manded at the first, that they should bless
the people of Israel. 34 And afterward he
read all the words of the law, blessings and
curses, according to all that is written in the
book of the law. 35 There was not a word of
all that Moses commanded that Joshua did
not read before all the assembly of Israel,
and the women, and the little ones, and the
aliens who resided among them.

9 Now when all the kings who were be-
yond the Jordan in the hill country and
in the lowland all along the coast of the
Great Sea toward Lebanon—the Hittites,
the Amorites, the Canaanites, the Periz-
zites, the Hivites, and the Jebusites—heard
of this, 2 they gathered together with one
accord to fight Joshua and Israel.

3 But when the inhabitants of Gibeon
heard what Joshua had done to Jericho and
to Ai, 4 they on their part acted with cun-
ning: they went and prepared provisions,[c]
and took worn-out sacks for their donkeys,
and wineskins, worn-out and torn and
mended, 5 with worn-out, patched sandals
on their feet, and worn-out clothes; and all
their provisions were dry and moldy. 6 They
went to Joshua in the camp at Gilgal, and
said to him and to the Israelites, "We have
come from a far country; so now make a
treaty with us." 7 But the Israelites said to
the Hivites, "Perhaps you live among us;
then how can we make a treaty with you?"
8 They said to Joshua, "We are your ser-
vants." And Joshua said to them, "Who
are you? And where do you come from?"
9 They said to him, "Your servants have
come from a very far country, because of
the name of the LORD your God; for we
have heard a report of him, of all that he
did in Egypt, 10 and of all that he did to the
two kings of the Amorites who were be-
yond the Jordan, King Sihon of Heshbon,
and King Og of Bashan who lived in Ashta-
roth. 11 So our elders and all the inhabitants

a Heb *whole* *b* Heb *he* *c* Cn: Meaning of Heb uncertain

but those Moses had commanded to be used; see Deut 27.2–3; cf. Josh 24.26–27. *A copy of the law,* see Deut 17.18. **34:** *Blessings and curses,* see Deut 27.11–13; 28; cf. Lev 26.3–39. **35:** Patterned after the ritual of Deut 31.9–13.

9.1–11.15: The southern and northern campaigns. The conquests of southern and northern Canaan share the same geographic pattern: center to periphery. However, the account of the southern campaign is a much more developed narrative than that of the northern campaign. This augmentation is observable in the basic components of 9.3–10.43 and 11.1–15. Thus the region that became Judah's tribal allotment receives the greater emphasis (a pattern also found in chs 13–19 and Judg 1).

9.1–2: Introductory statement. The section recalls the motif of the inhabitants hearing and fearing (2.10 and 5.1; see also 10.1, 11.1), but in this case the reaction is not fear, but aggressive hostility. The exception is Gibeon, narrated first for contrastive reasons.

9.3–10.43: Southern campaign. 9.3–27: Gibeon. Ironically, Israel has just defeated Ai by means of a ruse; now Israel is the victim of a ruse. The Israelites do not turn to God to discern the Gibeonite strategy. As in the case of the first battle of Ai, the Israelites' overconfidence in their ability to discern the situation leads to a lack of dependence on the LORD. **3–15:** The Gibeonites are apparently Hivites. Fearing Israel, they pretend to be *from a far country* so as to take advantage of the more lenient treatment afforded to such people (Deut 20.15). **3:** *Gibeon* is the modern el-Jib, about 4 km (7 mi) southwest of Ai. **6:** *Treaty,* Heb "berit," also translated "covenant." **10:** See 2.10n. **14:** Although *the leaders* (lit. "the men") of Israel

of our country said to us, 'Take provisions
in your hand for the journey; go to meet
them, and say to them, "We are your ser-
vants; come now, make a treaty with us." '
12 Here is our bread; it was still warm when
we took it from our houses as our food for
the journey, on the day we set out to come
to you, but now, see, it is dry and moldy;
13 these wineskins were new when we filled
them, and see, they are burst; and these gar-
ments and sandals of ours are worn out
from the very long journey." 14 So the lead-
ers[a] partook of their provisions, and did
not ask direction from the LORD. 15 And
Joshua made peace with them, guarantee-
ing their lives by a treaty; and the leaders of
the congregation swore an oath to them.

16 But when three days had passed after
they had made a treaty with them, they
heard that they were their neighbors and
were living among them. 17 So the Israelites
set out and reached their cities on the third
day. Now their cities were Gibeon, Chephi-
rah, Beeroth, and Kiriath-jearim. 18 But the
Israelites did not attack them, because the
leaders of the congregation had sworn to
them by the LORD, the God of Israel. Then
all the congregation murmured against the
leaders. 19 But all the leaders said to all the
congregation, "We have sworn to them by
the LORD, the God of Israel, and now we
must not touch them. 20 This is what we
will do to them: We will let them live, so
that wrath may not come upon us, because
of the oath that we swore to them." 21 The
leaders said to them, "Let them live." So
they became hewers of wood and drawers
of water for all the congregation, as the
leaders had decided concerning them.

22 Joshua summoned them, and said to
them, "Why did you deceive us, saying,
'We are very far from you,' while in fact
you are living among us? 23 Now therefore
you are cursed, and some of you shall al-
ways be slaves, hewers of wood and draw-
ers of water for the house of my God."
24 They answered Joshua, "Because it was
told to your servants for a certainty that the
LORD your God had commanded his ser-
vant Moses to give you all the land, and to
destroy all the inhabitants of the land be-
fore you; so we were in great fear for our
lives because of you, and did this thing.
25 And now we are in your hand: do as it
seems good and right in your sight to do to
us." 26 This is what he did for them: he
saved them from the Israelites; and they did
not kill them. 27 But on that day Joshua
made them hewers of wood and drawers of
water for the congregation and for the altar
of the LORD, to continue to this day, in the
place that he should choose.

10 When King Adoni-zedek of Jerusa-
lem heard how Joshua had taken Ai,

a Gk: Heb *men*

are specifically blamed for not consulting the LORD, Joshua is apparently included. None of Israel's leadership was exempt from blame. **16–27:** Discovery of the ruse and reaction. The Israelites discover the ruse of the Gibeonites, who readily admit their deception (vv. 24–25) because they know that Israel has to honor the pact between them (v. 20). The subservience of the Gibeonites is narrated twice in parallel: The leaders of the people save them and conclude their slave status, and so does Joshua (vv. 18–21 and vv. 22–27). **21:** *Hewers of wood and drawers of water,* according to Deut 29.10–13, the covenant was to erase distinctions between such lower class occupations and others. This designation thus suggests that the Gibeonites are outside the covenantal community. **24:** See Deut 20.16–18. Tensions with the Gibeonites persist into the monarchy (2 Sam 21.1–14). **27:** *The place that he should choose* is Deuteronomy's term for the central place of worship, later identified as Jerusalem (e.g., Deut 12.5–18).

10.1–43: The defeat of the Amorite alliance. This passage contains two scenes (vv. 1–15, vv. 16–43), both of which end with identical statements (vv. 15,43). Both scenes utilize temporal panels that backtrack and overlap: Each subsequent panel takes a part of the previous panel and further develops it.

10.1–15: Scene one contains three panels (vv. 1–10, 11, 12–15). **1–10: The initial circumstances of the battle.** This panel is composed of two parts: the formation of the Amorite alliance headed by Adoni-zedek of Jerusalem (vv. 1–5), and the initial open-field battle between the Israelites and the Amorite alliance with the slaughter and pursuit to Azekah (vv. 6–10). **1–2:** The treaty between Gibeon and Israel incited

and had utterly destroyed it, doing to Ai
and its king as he had done to Jericho and
its king, and how the inhabitants of Gibeon
had made peace with Israel and were
among them, 2he[a] became greatly fright-
ened, because Gibeon was a large city, like
one of the royal cities, and was larger than
Ai, and all its men were warriors. 3So King
Adoni-zedek of Jerusalem sent a message to
King Hoham of Hebron, to King Piram of
Jarmuth, to King Japhia of Lachish, and to
King Debir of Eglon, saying, 4"Come up
and help me, and let us attack Gibeon; for
it has made peace with Joshua and with the
Israelites." 5Then the five kings of the Am-
orites—the king of Jerusalem, the king of
Hebron, the king of Jarmuth, the king of
Lachish, and the king of Eglon—gathered
their forces, and went up with all their ar-
mies and camped against Gibeon, and
made war against it.
6 And the Gibeonites sent to Joshua at
the camp in Gilgal, saying, "Do not aban-
don your servants; come up to us quickly,
and save us, and help us; for all the kings of
the Amorites who live in the hill country
are gathered against us." 7So Joshua went
up from Gilgal, he and all the fighting force
with him, all the mighty warriors. 8The
LORD said to Joshua, "Do not fear them,
for I have handed them over to you; not
one of them shall stand before you." 9So
Joshua came upon them suddenly, having
marched up all night from Gilgal. 10And
the LORD threw them into a panic before
Israel, who inflicted a great slaughter on
them at Gibeon, chased them by the way of
the ascent of Beth-horon, and struck them
down as far as Azekah and Makkedah.
11As they fled before Israel, while they were
going down the slope of Beth-horon, the
LORD threw down huge stones from heav-
en on them as far as Azekah, and they died;
there were more who died because of the
hailstones than the Israelites killed with the
sword.
12 On the day when the LORD gave the
Amorites over to the Israelites, Joshua
spoke to the LORD; and he said in the sight
of Israel,

"Sun, stand still at Gibeon,
  and Moon, in the valley of
    Aijalon."
13 And the sun stood still, and the moon
    stopped,
  until the nation took vengeance on
    their enemies.

Is this not written in the Book of Jashar?
The sun stopped in midheaven, and did not
hurry to set for about a whole day. 14There
has been no day like it before or since,
when the LORD heeded a human voice; for
the LORD fought for Israel.
15 Then Joshua returned, and all Israel
with him, to the camp at Gilgal.

a Heb *they*

the kings of five Amorite city-states to attack Gibeon. Jerusalem, an important Bronze Age city-state, and later the capital of Judah, is the driving force in the alliance. **3:** See Map on p. 317 HB. **10:** The reference to *Azekah* and *Makkedah* anticipates the second panel of scene one as well as the first panel of scene two. *Azekah* is identified with Tell Zakariya; *Makkedah* is perhaps Khirbet el-Qom.

10.11: Divine intervention with hailstones. The second panel of scene one backtracks and overlaps the first panel, describing the enemy flight again to Azekah with the further development of the divine intervention with deadly *hailstones* (lit. "large stones from heaven"). Divine interventions are common motifs in ancient war accounts. These large hailstones (Heb "abanim gedolot") anticipate the large stones (Heb "abanim gedolot") that seal the kings in the caves (10.18,27; cf. 7.26).

10.12–15: Joshua's request to the LORD and the divine intervention. The third panel of scene one also backtracks and overlaps, describing Joshua's request to the LORD at the beginning of the battle with the further development of the divine intervention concerning the sun and moon (cf. Hab 3.11; Judg 5.20). The exact meaning of the divine intervention is difficult to ascertain because it is described only in poetry. **13:** *The Book of Jashar,* no longer extant, appears to have been a collection of poetry that extolled Israel's military victories and heroes (see 2 Sam 1.18). Scene one concludes with Joshua and Israel's return to Gilgal (10.15), which is repeated at the chapter's conclusion (v. 43) and should not be pressed literally.

16 Meanwhile, these five kings fled and
hid themselves in the cave at Makkedah.
17 And it was told Joshua, "The five kings
have been found, hidden in the cave at
Makkedah." 18 Joshua said, "Roll large
stones against the mouth of the cave, and
set men by it to guard them; 19 but do not
stay there yourselves; pursue your enemies,
and attack them from the rear. Do not let
them enter their towns, for the LORD your
God has given them into your hand."
20 When Joshua and the Israelites had fin-
ished inflicting a very great slaughter on
them, until they were wiped out, and when
the survivors had entered into the fortified
towns, 21 all the people returned safe to
Joshua in the camp at Makkedah; no one
dared to speak[a] against any of the Israel-
ites.

22 Then Joshua said, "Open the mouth
of the cave, and bring those five kings out
to me from the cave." 23 They did so, and
brought the five kings out to him from the
cave, the king of Jerusalem, the king of He-
bron, the king of Jarmuth, the king of La-
chish, and the king of Eglon. 24 When they
brought the kings out to Joshua, Joshua
summoned all the Israelites, and said to the
chiefs of the warriors who had gone with
him, "Come near, put your feet on the
necks of these kings." Then they came near
and put their feet on their necks. 25 And
Joshua said to them, "Do not be afraid or
dismayed; be strong and courageous; for
thus the LORD will do to all the enemies
against whom you fight." 26 Afterward
Joshua struck them down and put them to
death, and he hung them on five trees. And
they hung on the trees until evening. 27 At
sunset Joshua commanded, and they took
them down from the trees and threw them
into the cave where they had hidden them-
selves; they set large stones against the
mouth of the cave, which remain to this
very day.

28 Joshua took Makkedah on that day,
and struck it and its king with the edge of
the sword; he utterly destroyed every per-
son in it; he left no one remaining. And he
did to the king of Makkedah as he had
done to the king of Jericho.

29 Then Joshua passed on from Makke-
dah, and all Israel with him, to Libnah, and
fought against Libnah. 30 The LORD gave it
also and its king into the hand of Israel; and
he struck it with the edge of the sword, and
every person in it; he left no one remaining
in it; and he did to its king as he had done
to the king of Jericho.

31 Next Joshua passed on from Libnah,
and all Israel with him, to Lachish, and laid
siege to it, and assaulted it. 32 The LORD
gave Lachish into the hand of Israel, and he
took it on the second day, and struck it
with the edge of the sword, and every per-
son in it, as he had done to Libnah.

33 Then King Horam of Gezer came up
to help Lachish; and Joshua struck him and
his people, leaving him no survivors.

34 From Lachish Joshua passed on with

a Heb *moved his tongue*

10.16–43: Scene two contains two panels (vv. 16–27; 28–39) and a summary (vv. 40–43). **16–27: The capture and execution of the kings.** The first panel backtracks and overlaps the pursuit, developing the capture and execution of the Amorite kings. The mention of *Makkedah* in v. 16 is resumptive (see v. 10). Ironically, the cave that the kings choose as their hiding place becomes first their prison, then their tomb. **24:** *Feet on their necks,* symbolizing subjugation, as in 1 Kings 5.3; Ps 110.1. **26–27:** The public display of corpses after execution was psychological in its effects; see 8.29n.

10.28–39: The capture and "ḥerem" of the cities. The second panel backtracks to the pursuit and develops the capture and "ḥerem" of the cities in a stereotyped and redundant manner. (A verbal form of "ḥerem" is translated "utterly destroyed" in vv. 28,35,37,39,40). This typical ancient Near Eastern war account uses hyperbole to emphasize the success of Israel and its God. The king of Gezer, at the center of the seven short episodes, emphasizes that city's importance. While the city is not captured, the defeat of its king and army in open battle crowns the southern campaign. **31–32:** *Lachish* (Tell ed-Duweir) was one of the more important southern cities. **33:** *Gezer* becomes an Israelite city only in the time of Solomon (see 1 Kings 9.16). The Ephraimites had failed to capture it (16.10; Judg 1.29). **34–35:** *Eglon* may be

all Israel to Eglon; and they laid siege to it,
and assaulted it; 35 and they took it that
day, and struck it with the edge of the
sword; and every person in it he utterly de-
stroyed that day, as he had done to La-
chish.
36 Then Joshua went up with all Israel
from Eglon to Hebron; they assaulted it,
37 and took it, and struck it with the edge of
the sword, and its king and its towns, and
every person in it; he left no one remaining,
just as he had done to Eglon, and utterly
destroyed it with every person in it.
38 Then Joshua, with all Israel, turned
back to Debir and assaulted it, 39 and he
took it with its king and all its towns; they
struck them with the edge of the sword,
and utterly destroyed every person in it; he
left no one remaining; just as he had done
to Hebron, and, as he had done to Libnah
and its king, so he did to Debir and its king.
40 So Joshua defeated the whole land,
the hill country and the Negeb and the low-
land and the slopes, and all their kings; he
left no one remaining, but utterly destroyed
all that breathed, as the LORD God of Israel
commanded. 41 And Joshua defeated them
from Kadesh-barnea to Gaza, and all the
country of Goshen, as far as Gibeon.
42 Joshua took all these kings and their land
at one time, because the LORD God of Isra-
el fought for Israel. 43 Then Joshua re-
turned, and all Israel with him, to the camp
at Gilgal.
11 When King Jabin of Hazor heard of
this, he sent to King Jobab of Ma-
don, to the king of Shimron, to the king of
Achshaph, 2 and to the kings who were in
the northern hill country, and in the Ara-
bah south of Chinneroth, and in the low-
land, and in Naphoth-dor on the west, 3 to
the Canaanites in the east and the west, the
Amorites, the Hittites, the Perizzites, and
the Jebusites in the hill country, and the
Hivites under Hermon in the land of Miz-
pah. 4 They came out, with all their troops,
a great army, in number like the sand on
the seashore, with very many horses and
chariots. 5 All these kings joined their
forces, and came and camped together at
the waters of Merom, to fight with Israel.
6 And the LORD said to Joshua, "Do not
be afraid of them, for tomorrow at this
time I will hand over all of them, slain, to
Israel; you shall hamstring their horses, and
burn their chariots with fire." 7 So Joshua
came suddenly upon them with all his fight-
ing force, by the waters of Merom, and fell

identified with Tell Aitun. **36–39:** *Hebron* and *Debir* (probably Khirbet Rabud) fall to "all" Israel. In 14.6–15 Caleb is credited with victory at Hebron (see 15.13–14), but Judah in general gets credit in Judg 1.10. In 15.15–17 and Judg 1.11–13 Othniel is credited with the capture of Debir. These conflicting accounts highlight the perspective of chs 1–12, a conquest by "all Israel."

10.40–43: Summary of the southern campaign. Overstatement emphasizes the greatness of the Israelite victory. Scene two concludes (like scene one) with Joshua and Israel returning to Gilgal (10.43). **40:** *Negeb*, the semidesert region in the south; see Map on p. 317 HB. **41:** *Kadesh-barnea*, see Deut 1.19; 9.23. *Goshen*, a designation of the region north of the Negeb (see also 11.16); not the region with the same name in the Egyptian Delta (Gen 45.10; etc.).

11.1–15: Northern campaign. A literary mirror of 10.1–43 both in general structure and vocabulary, though less developed.

11.1–11: Defeat of the Canaanite coalition. A large and powerful Canaanite coalition is organized and headed by Jabin, the king of Hazor. The name *Jabin* occurs here and in Judg 4 and Ps 83.10. Scholars generally see Judg 4–5 as the source for this story. **1:** The final occurrence of the "hearing" motif, see 5.1n. The locations of *Madon, Shimron,* and *Achshaph* are not certain. **2:** The *Arabah* is the Jordan Valley; *Chinneroth,* the Sea of Galilee. **3–5:** This enemy is superior to the Israelite army, both numerically and technologically (they have dreaded horses and chariots). This coalition presents the most significant threat to Israel's success in conquering the land. *Hermon,* the high mountain in the extreme north of Israel. *Merom* is a city in Galilee known from extrabiblical sources; its precise location is not certain. **6:** The LORD's oracle of assurance precedes the victory (cf. 8.1; 10.8). *Hamstring their horses* means cutting a tendon of a rear leg to make them useless (see 2 Sam 8.4). **10–11:** Hazor, the most important northern

upon them. 8 And the LORD handed them
over to Israel, who attacked them and
chased them as far as Great Sidon and
Misrephoth-maim, and eastward as far as
the valley of Mizpeh. They struck them
down, until they had left no one remaining.
9 And Joshua did to them as the LORD com-
manded him; he hamstrung their horses,
and burned their chariots with fire.
10 Joshua turned back at that time, and
took Hazor, and struck its king down with
the sword. Before that time Hazor was the
head of all those kingdoms. 11 And they put
to the sword all who were in it, utterly de-
stroying them; there was no one left who
breathed, and he burned Hazor with fire.
12 And all the towns of those kings, and all
their kings, Joshua took, and struck them
with the edge of the sword, utterly destroy-
ing them, as Moses the servant of the LORD
had commanded. 13 But Israel burned none
of the towns that stood on mounds except
Hazor, which Joshua did burn. 14 All the
spoil of these towns, and the livestock, the
Israelites took for their booty; but all the
people they struck down with the edge of
the sword, until they had destroyed them,
and they did not leave any who breathed.
15 As the LORD had commanded his servant
Moses, so Moses commanded Joshua, and
so Joshua did; he left nothing undone of all
that the LORD had commanded Moses.
16 So Joshua took all that land: the hill
country and all the Negeb and all the land
of Goshen and the lowland and the Arabah
and the hill country of Israel and its low-
land, 17 from Mount Halak, which rises to-
ward Seir, as far as Baal-gad in the valley of
Lebanon below Mount Hermon. He took
all their kings, struck them down, and put
them to death. 18 Joshua made war a long
time with all those kings. 19 There was not
a town that made peace with the Israelites,
except the Hivites, the inhabitants of Gibe-
on; all were taken in battle. 20 For it was the
LORD's doing to harden their hearts so that
they would come against Israel in battle, in
order that they might be utterly destroyed,
and might receive no mercy, but be exter-
minated, just as the LORD had commanded
Moses.
21 At that time Joshua came and wiped
out the Anakim from the hill country, from
Hebron, from Debir, from Anab, and from
all the hill country of Judah, and from all
the hill country of Israel; Joshua utterly de-
stroyed them with their towns. 22 None of
the Anakim was left in the land of the Isra-
elites; some remained only in Gaza, in
Gath, and in Ashdod. 23 So Joshua took the
whole land, according to all that the LORD
had spoken to Moses; and Joshua gave it
for an inheritance to Israel according to
their tribal allotments. And the land had
rest from war.

12 Now these are the kings of the land,
whom the Israelites defeated, whose
land they occupied beyond the Jordan to-

city, is totally destroyed by burning just like Jericho and Ai (cf. 6.24; 8.8,19). Jericho and Hazor frame the "conquest" of the land of Canaan.

11.12–15: Summary of northern campaign. The Israelite conquest in the north is summarized by noting several times that "all" was conquered by Joshua, the worthy successor to Moses, who fulfilled the requirements of Deut 20.16–17. **13:** *Mounds,* translating the Hebrew word for "tells," cf. 8.28n.

11.16–23: Summary of total conquest. 16–19: The word *all* characterizes these verses, emphasizing the totality of the conquest. **18–20:** The depiction here somewhat conflicts with the earlier accounts, suggesting that a protracted war was necessary. **20:** *Harden their hearts,* this phrase is elsewhere used of Pharaoh in Egypt (Ex 4.21; etc.), and suggests that, for the LORD and for the author, the inhabitants of the land were enemies comparable to the Egyptians. **21:** *The Anakim,* a term for pre-Israelite inhabitants of Canaan renowned for their size and strength (Deut 9.2). **23:** *And the land had rest from war,* a conclusion formula, moving toward a transition from the conquest to the division of land. This declaration recurs in 14.15, forming a literary link between the defeat of the Anakim by Joshua (ch 11) and their defeat by Caleb (ch 14).

12.1–24: A selective list of defeated cities' kings. An additional conclusion to the first section of the book. **1–6: Moses' exploits in Transjordan.** This summary draws from Deut 2–3. **2:** The story of *King*

ward the east, from the Wadi Arnon to
Mount Hermon, with all the Arabah east-
ward: 2 King Sihon of the Amorites who
lived at Heshbon, and ruled from Aroer,
which is on the edge of the Wadi Arnon,
and from the middle of the valley as far as
the river Jabbok, the boundary of the Am-
monites, that is, half of Gilead, 3 and the
Arabah to the Sea of Chinneroth eastward,
and in the direction of Beth-jeshimoth, to
the sea of the Arabah, the Dead Sea,[a]
southward to the foot of the slopes of Pis-
gah; 4 and King Og[b] of Bashan, one of the
last of the Rephaim, who lived at Ashtaroth
and at Edrei 5 and ruled over Mount Her-
mon and Salecah and all Bashan to the
boundary of the Geshurites and the Maaca-
thites, and over half of Gilead to the
boundary of King Sihon of Heshbon. 6 Mo-
ses, the servant of the LORD, and the Israel-
ites defeated them; and Moses the servant
of the LORD gave their land for a posses-
sion to the Reubenites and the Gadites and
the half-tribe of Manasseh.
7 The following are the kings of the land
whom Joshua and the Israelites defeated on
the west side of the Jordan, from Baal-gad
in the valley of Lebanon to Mount Halak,
that rises toward Seir (and Joshua gave
their land to the tribes of Israel as a posses-
sion according to their allotments, 8 in the
hill country, in the lowland, in the Arabah,
in the slopes, in the wilderness, and in the
Negeb, the land of the Hittites, Amorites,
Canaanites, Perizzites, Hivites, and Jebu-
sites):

9 the king of Jericho one
the king of Ai, which is next to Bethel one
10 the king of Jerusalem one
the king of Hebron one
11 the king of Jarmuth one
the king of Lachish one
12 the king of Eglon one
the king of Gezer one
13 the king of Debir one
the king of Geder one
14 the king of Hormah one
the king of Arad one
15 the king of Libnah one
the king of Adullam one
16 the king of Makkedah one
the king of Bethel one
17 the king of Tappuah one
the king of Hepher one
18 the king of Aphek one
the king of Lasharon one
19 the king of Madon one
the king of Hazor one
20 the king of Shimron-meron one
the king of Achshaph one
21 the king of Taanach one
the king of Megiddo one
22 the king of Kedesh one
the king of Jokneam in Carmel one
23 the king of Dor in Naphath-dor one
the king of Goiim in Galilee,[c] one
24 the king of Tirzah one
thirty-one kings in all.

13 Now Joshua was old and advanced in years; and the LORD said to him,

a Heb *Salt Sea* *b* Gk: Heb *the boundary of King Og*
c Gk: Heb *Gilgal*

Sihon is narrated in Num 21.21–31 and Deut 2.26–37. **4:** The defeat of *Og* is related in Num 21.33–35 and Deut 3.1–17. *Bashan,* northern Transjordan. *Rephaim,* here another term for pre-Israelite inhabitants of Canaan.

12.7–24: Joshua's victories west of the Jordan. Previous narratives mention fewer than half of these cities. Vv. 9–13a follow the order of chs 6–10, but after that there is no clear pattern. This section thus seems to be adapted from a different type of source than the previous chapters. Moreover, the length of this list shows that previous narratives are selective, highlighting particular stories for ideological and theological purposes. For the location of the places, see Map on p. 317 HB.

13.1–21.45: Division of the land. Having completed his first task, the conquest (1.2–5), Joshua turns his attention to his second task (1.6): "Put this people in possession of the land" ("naḥal" cf. Deut 4.21; 15.4; 19.10). The concern over allotment or inheritance ("naḥalah") unifies this section (13.6; 14.3,13; 17.4,6,14; 19.49). The section emphasizes that the division follows the divine will, as mediated by Joshua and Eleazar the priest. It utilizes four types of sources: boundary descriptions; town lists integrated into

"You are old and advanced in years, and
very much of the land still remains to be
possessed. 2 This is the land that still re-
mains: all the regions of the Philistines, and
all those of the Geshurites 3 (from the Shi-
hor, which is east of Egypt, northward to
the boundary of Ekron, it is reckoned as
Canaanite; there are five rulers of the Phil-
istines, those of Gaza, Ashdod, Ashkelon,
Gath, and Ekron), and those of the Avvim
4 in the south; all the land of the Canaan-
ites, and Mearah that belongs to the Sidoni-
ans, to Aphek, to the boundary of the Amo-
rites, 5 and the land of the Gebalites, and all
Lebanon, toward the east, from Baal-gad
below Mount Hermon to Lebo-hamath,
6 all the inhabitants of the hill country from
Lebanon to Misrephoth-maim, even all the
Sidonians. I will myself drive them out
from before the Israelites; only allot the
land to Israel for an inheritance, as I have
commanded you. 7 Now therefore divide
this land for an inheritance to the nine
tribes and the half-tribe of Manasseh."

8 With the other half-tribe of Manas-
seh[a] the Reubenites and the Gadites re-
ceived their inheritance, which Moses gave
them, beyond the Jordan eastward, as Mo-
ses the servant of the LORD gave them:
9 from Aroer, which is on the edge of the
Wadi Arnon, and the town that is in the
middle of the valley, and all the tableland
from[b] Medeba as far as Dibon; 10 and all
the cities of King Sihon of the Amorites,
who reigned in Heshbon, as far as the
boundary of the Ammonites; 11 and Gilead,
and the region of the Geshurites and Maac-
athites, and all Mount Hermon, and all Ba-
shan to Salecah; 12 all the kingdom of Og in
Bashan, who reigned in Ashtaroth and in
Edrei (he alone was left of the survivors of
the Rephaim); these Moses had defeated
and driven out. 13 Yet the Israelites did not
drive out the Geshurites or the Maaca-
thites; but Geshur and Maacath live within
Israel to this day.

14 To the tribe of Levi alone Moses gave
no inheritance; the offerings by fire to the
LORD God of Israel are their inheritance, as
he said to them.

15 Moses gave an inheritance to the
tribe of the Reubenites according to their
clans. 16 Their territory was from Aroer,
which is on the edge of the Wadi Arnon,
and the town that is in the middle of the
valley, and all the tableland by Medeba;

a Cn: Heb *With it* *b* Compare Gk: Heb lacks *from*

boundary descriptions; town lists; and short narratives that relate incidents of importance within the allotments, providing didactic significance to the division of the land. The cities of refuge and Levitical cities are attached at the end of the section since it is necessary for the tribes to receive their inheritance before they can allocate parts of it to others. For this entire section, see Map on p. 346 HB.

13.1–7: Land remaining. The land remaining is defined by those towns and regions inside the borders of Canaan (cf. Num 34.1–12) that are not under Israelite control. This foreshadows other passages in chs 13–21 that contrast with the first half of the book, by documenting Israel's failure to capture all of the land, or by noting that foreigners live among the Israelites. These contrast ironically with the idealistic reports given in the text (cf. 15.63; 16.10; 17.11–13; 18.2; 19.47). The particular areas designated as outside Israelite possession are *the regions of the Philistines* (the southwestern coastal area), *and all those of the Geshurites* (east of the Sea of Galilee) (cf. 13.13), and the land of Phoenicia (northern coastal areas). Philistia and Geshur came under Israelite control during the period of David and Solomon (2 Sam 8.1–2; 3.3).

13.8–33: Transjordanian tribal allotment. Before the allotments west of the Jordan can be described, the Transjordanian allotments that Moses made are recounted: a general description of the extent of the Transjordanian lands (13.8–13), a declaration that the Levites received no inheritance (13.14), a specific description of the Transjordanian territories (13.15–32), and again a declaration that the Levites received no inheritance (13.33). Israel had great difficulties controlling this territory throughout its history, though Deuteronomy considered it part of Israel (see Deut 3.12–17). **12:** *Rephaim,* see 12.4n. **13:** The first of a number of qualifications about Israelite success in possessing the land. **14:** *Offerings by fire,* as the priestly tribe, the Levites were in charge of worship and shared the offerings; cf. Lev 7.29–36; etc. **21:** *Midian,*

17 with Heshbon, and all its towns that are
in the tableland; Dibon, and Bamoth-baal,
and Beth-baal-meon, 18 and Jahaz, and
Kedemoth, and Mephaath, 19 and Kiriatha-
im, and Sibmah, and Zereth-shahar on the
hill of the valley, 20 and Beth-peor, and the
slopes of Pisgah, and Beth-jeshimoth,
21 that is, all the towns of the tableland, and
all the kingdom of King Sihon of the Amo-
rites, who reigned in Heshbon, whom Mo-
ses defeated with the leaders of Midian, Evi
and Rekem and Zur and Hur and Reba, as
princes of Sihon, who lived in the land.
22 Along with the rest of those they put to
death, the Israelites also put to the sword
Balaam son of Beor, who practiced divina-
tion. 23 And the border of the Reubenites
was the Jordan and its banks. This was the
inheritance of the Reubenites according to
their families, with their towns and villages.

24 Moses gave an inheritance also to the
tribe of the Gadites, according to their fam-
ilies. 25 Their territory was Jazer, and all the
towns of Gilead, and half the land of the
Ammonites, to Aroer, which is east of Rab-
bah, 26 and from Heshbon to Ramath-
mizpeh and Betonim, and from Mahanaim
to the territory of Debir,[a] 27 and in the val-
ley Beth-haram, Beth-nimrah, Succoth, and
Zaphon, the rest of the kingdom of King
Sihon of Heshbon, the Jordan and its
banks, as far as the lower end of the Sea of
Chinnereth, eastward beyond the Jordan.
28 This is the inheritance of the Gadites ac-
cording to their clans, with their towns and
villages.

29 Moses gave an inheritance to the
half-tribe of Manasseh; it was allotted to
the half-tribe of the Manassites according
to their families. 30 Their territory extended
from Mahanaim, through all Bashan, the
whole kingdom of King Og of Bashan, and
all the settlements of Jair, which are in Ba-
shan, sixty towns, 31 and half of Gilead,
and Ashtaroth, and Edrei, the towns of the
kingdom of Og in Bashan; these were allot-
ted to the people of Machir son of Manas-
seh according to their clans—for half the
Machirites.

32 These are the inheritances that Moses
distributed in the plains of Moab, beyond
the Jordan east of Jericho. 33 But to the tribe
of Levi Moses gave no inheritance; the
LORD God of Israel is their inheritance, as
he said to them.

14 These are the inheritances that the
Israelites received in the land of Ca-
naan, which the priest Eleazar, and Joshua
son of Nun, and the heads of the families of
the tribes of the Israelites distributed to
them. 2 Their inheritance was by lot, as the
LORD had commanded Moses for the nine
and one-half tribes. 3 For Moses had given
an inheritance to the two and one-half
tribes beyond the Jordan; but to the Levites
he gave no inheritance among them. 4 For
the people of Joseph were two tribes, Ma-
nasseh and Ephraim; and no portion was
given to the Levites in the land, but only
towns to live in, with their pasture lands for
their flocks and herds. 5 The Israelites did as
the LORD commanded Moses; they allotted
the land.

6 Then the people of Judah came to
Joshua at Gilgal; and Caleb son of Jephun-
neh the Kenizzite said to him, "You know

a Gk Syr Vg: Heb *Lidebir*

see Num 31.1–12. **22:** *Balaam,* in contrast to the narrative about him in Num 22–24, here this non-Israelite prophet is presented in a negative light, and only here and in Num 31.8 are the Israelites said to have killed him.

14.1–19.51: Cisjordanian tribal allotment. The story of the allotments to the tribes west of the Jordan is framed by an introduction (14.1–5) and a summary (19.51). The main text is divided into two major sections: the Judah and Joseph allotments (14.6–17.18) and the seven other tribal allotments (18.1–19.51).

14.1–5: Introduction to the process of allotment. Eleazar (the chief priest), Joshua, and the heads of the tribal families oversaw this allotment, which was performed by lot (see 7.14n.). **4–5:** See Num 34.13–15; 35.3. To maintain the number of tribes at twelve, the *people of Joseph* were counted as two tribes, *Manasseh and Ephraim,* to make up for Levi's lack of inheritance.

what the LORD said to Moses the man of
God in Kadesh-barnea concerning you and
me. 7 I was forty years old when Moses the
servant of the LORD sent me from Kadesh-
barnea to spy out the land; and I brought
him an honest report. 8 But my companions
who went up with me made the heart of the
people melt; yet I wholeheartedly followed
the LORD my God. 9 And Moses swore on
that day, saying, 'Surely the land on which
your foot has trodden shall be an inheri-
tance for you and your children forever,
because you have wholeheartedly followed
the LORD my God.' 10 And now, as you see,
the LORD has kept me alive, as he said,
these forty-five years since the time that the
LORD spoke this word to Moses, while Is-
rael was journeying through the wilderness;
and here I am today, eighty-five years old.
11 I am still as strong today as I was on the
day that Moses sent me; my strength now is
as my strength was then, for war, and for
going and coming. 12 So now give me this
hill country of which the LORD spoke on
that day; for you heard on that day how the
Anakim were there, with great fortified cit-
ies; it may be that the LORD will be with
me, and I shall drive them out, as the LORD
said."
13 Then Joshua blessed him, and gave
Hebron to Caleb son of Jephunneh for an
inheritance. 14 So Hebron became the inher-
itance of Caleb son of Jephunneh the Ken-
izzite to this day, because he wholehearted-
ly followed the LORD, the God of Israel.
15 Now the name of Hebron formerly was
Kiriath-arba;[a] this Arba was[b] the greatest
man among the Anakim. And the land had
rest from war.

15 The lot for the tribe of the people of
Judah according to their families
reached southward to the boundary of
Edom, to the wilderness of Zin at the far-
thest south. 2 And their south boundary ran
from the end of the Dead Sea,[c] from the
bay that faces southward; 3 it goes out
southward of the ascent of Akrabbim,
passes along to Zin, and goes up south of
Kadesh-barnea, along by Hezron, up to
Addar, makes a turn to Karka, 4 passes
along to Azmon, goes out by the Wadi of
Egypt, and comes to its end at the sea. This
shall be your south boundary. 5 And the
east boundary is the Dead Sea,[c] to the
mouth of the Jordan. And the boundary on
the north side runs from the bay of the
sea at the mouth of the Jordan; 6 and the
boundary goes up to Beth-hoglah, and
passes along north of Beth-arabah; and the
boundary goes up to the Stone of Bohan,
Reuben's son; 7 and the boundary goes up

a That is *the city of Arba* *b* Heb lacks *this Arba was* *c* Heb *Salt Sea*

14.6–17.18: Judah and Joseph allotments. Parallel structures are used to describe the allotments to these tribes: narrative frames, boundary descriptions, and town lists, with vignettes in the center.

14.6–15.63: Judah. The tribe from which David would arise is first.

14.6–15: Caleb's conquest. The success of Judah is specifically illustrated in the narrative frame story of Caleb's conquest of Hebron. *Caleb* was one of the original twelve spies sent into the land of Canaan (Num 13.30; 14.24). Caleb and his clan conquer Hebron, the home of the Anakim. The repetition in v. 15 of the statement *and the land had rest from war* connects this story to 11.21–23. Ironically, it was the fear of these very Anakim that caused Israel's disobedience and failure at Kadesh-barnea, according to Num 13.28 and Deut 1.28. **10:** According to Deut 2.14, thirty-eight years elapsed from the events at Kadesh to the entry into the land; the events of the preceding chapters thus took seven years. **13:** *Hebron* (Tell Rumeideh) is 31 km (19 mi) south of Jerusalem. **14:** Also ironically, this prime example of Judahite success is accomplished by a non-Israelite: Caleb is a Kenizzite (14.6,14) who is, however, ultimately incorporated into Judah's genealogy (1 Chr 2.9,18).

15.1–12: Judah's boundary description is given in a counterclockwise arrangement: south (vv. 2–4), east (v. 5), north (vv. 6–11), west (v. 12a; cf. 11.21–22; Judg 1.18–19; Josh 15.63), with a concluding boundary description (v. 12b). See Map on p. 346 HB. **1:** *Wilderness of Zin,* the locale of Kadesh-barnea, in the southern Negeb (Deut 32.51). **4:** *Wadi of Egypt,* either the Wadi Besor or the Wadi el-Arish, both south of Gaza. **6:** *Bohan,* means "thumb"; see 18.17. No son of Reuben with this name is mentioned

to Debir from the Valley of Achor, and so
northward, turning toward Gilgal, which is
opposite the ascent of Adummim, which is
on the south side of the valley; and the
boundary passes along to the waters of En-
shemesh, and ends at En-rogel; 8 then the
boundary goes up by the valley of the son
of Hinnom at the southern slope of the Jeb-
usites (that is, Jerusalem); and the bounda-
ry goes up to the top of the mountain that
lies over against the valley of Hinnom, on
the west, at the northern end of the valley
of Rephaim; 9 then the boundary extends
from the top of the mountain to the spring
of the Waters of Nephtoah, and from there
to the towns of Mount Ephron; then the
boundary bends around to Baalah (that is,
Kiriath-jearim); 10 and the boundary circles
west of Baalah to Mount Seir, passes along
to the northern slope of Mount Jearim (that
is, Chesalon), and goes down to Beth-
shemesh, and passes along by Timnah;
11 the boundary goes out to the slope of the
hill north of Ekron, then the boundary
bends around to Shikkeron, and passes
along to Mount Baalah, and goes out to
Jabneel; then the boundary comes to an end
at the sea. 12 And the west boundary was
the Mediterranean with its coast. This is
the boundary surrounding the people of Ju-
dah according to their families.

13 According to the commandment of
the LORD to Joshua, he gave to Caleb son
of Jephunneh a portion among the people
of Judah, Kiriath-arba,[a] that is, Hebron
(Arba was the father of Anak). 14 And Ca-
leb drove out from there the three sons of
Anak: Sheshai, Ahiman, and Talmai, the
descendants of Anak. 15 From there he went
up against the inhabitants of Debir; now
the name of Debir formerly was Kiriath-
sepher. 16 And Caleb said, "Whoever at-
tacks Kiriath-sepher and takes it, to him I
will give my daughter Achsah as wife."
17 Othniel son of Kenaz, the brother of Ca-
leb, took it; and he gave him his daughter
Achsah as wife. 18 When she came to him,
she urged him to ask her father for a field.
As she dismounted from her donkey, Caleb
said to her, "What do you wish?" 19 She
said to him, "Give me a present; since you
have set me in the land of the Negeb, give
me springs of water as well." So Caleb gave
her the upper springs and the lower springs.

20 This is the inheritance of the tribe of
the people of Judah according to their fami-
lies. 21 The towns belonging to the tribe of
the people of Judah in the extreme south,
toward the boundary of Edom, were Kab-
zeel, Eder, Jagur, 22 Kinah, Dimonah, Ada-
dah, 23 Kedesh, Hazor, Ithnan, 24 Ziph, Te-
lem, Bealoth, 25 Hazor-hadattah, Kerioth-
hezron (that is, Hazor), 26 Amam, Shema,
Moladah, 27 Hazar-gaddah, Heshmon,
Beth-pelet, 28 Hazar-shual, Beer-sheba,
Biziothiah, 29 Baalah, Iim, Ezem, 30 Eltolad,
Chesil, Hormah, 31 Ziklag, Madmannah,
Sansannah, 32 Lebaoth, Shilhim, Ain, and
Rimmon: in all, twenty-nine towns, with
their villages.

33 And in the lowland, Eshtaol, Zorah,
Ashnah, 34 Zanoah, En-gannim, Tappuah,
Enam, 35 Jarmuth, Adullam, Socoh, Aze-
kah, 36 Shaaraim, Adithaim, Gederah, Ged-
erothaim: fourteen towns with their vil-
lages.

a That is *the city of Arba*

elsewhere, and the location of part of the tribe of Reuben west of the Jordan is unusual. **7–8:** For the geography of Jerusalem, see Map 9 at the end of this volume.

15.13–19: Vignettes about Judah's heroes (cf. 10.36–39; Judg 1.9–15): male, Caleb and Othniel (15.13–17), and female, Achsah (15.18–19). In the first vignette, Caleb conquers Hebron (cf. 14.6–15) and attacks the city of Debir. After recording Caleb's challenge and offer of his daughter in marriage (cf. 1 Sam 17.25), Othniel steps forward as the conquering hero of Debir (Kiriath-sepher). In the second, Achsah takes the initiative, urging her husband to ask for a field and then requesting her father to give her springs or pools since land without water is land without life. She seeks a sufficient blessing in the land.

15.20–62: A list of Judah's towns according to districts that is generally considered to have originated in the monarchic period. A similar list is found in 1 Kings 4.7–19.

37 Zenan, Hadashah, Migdal-gad,
38 Dilan, Mizpeh, Jokthe-el, 39 Lachish,
Bozkath, Eglon, 40 Cabbon, Lahmam, Chit-
lish, 41 Gederoth, Beth-dagon, Naamah,
and Makkedah: sixteen towns with their
villages.
42 Libnah, Ether, Ashan, 43 Iphtah, Ash-
nah, Nezib, 44 Keilah, Achzib, and Mare-
shah: nine towns with their villages.
45 Ekron, with its dependencies and its
villages; 46 from Ekron to the sea, all that
were near Ashdod, with their villages.
47 Ashdod, its towns and its villages;
Gaza, its towns and its villages; to the Wadi
of Egypt, and the Great Sea with its coast.
48 And in the hill country, Shamir, Jat-
tir, Socoh, 49 Dannah, Kiriath-sannah (that
is, Debir), 50 Anab, Eshtemoh, Anim, 51 Go-
shen, Holon, and Giloh: eleven towns with
their villages.
52 Arab, Dumah, Eshan, 53 Janim, Beth-
tappuah, Aphekah, 54 Humtah, Kiriath-
arba (that is, Hebron), and Zior: nine
towns with their villages.
55 Maon, Carmel, Ziph, Juttah, 56 Jezre-
el, Jokdeam, Zanoah, 57 Kain, Gibeah, and
Timnah: ten towns with their villages.
58 Halhul, Beth-zur, Gedor, 59 Maarath,
Beth-anoth, and Eltekon: six towns with
their villages.
60 Kiriath-baal (that is, Kiriath-jearim)
and Rabbah: two towns with their villages.
61 In the wilderness, Beth-arabah, Mid-
din, Secacah, 62 Nibshan, the City of Salt,
and En-gedi: six towns with their villages.
63 But the people of Judah could not
drive out the Jebusites, the inhabitants of
Jerusalem; so the Jebusites live with the
people of Judah in Jerusalem to this day.

16 The allotment of the Josephites
went from the Jordan by Jericho,
east of the waters of Jericho, into the wil-
derness, going up from Jericho into the hill
country to Bethel; 2 then going from Bethel
to Luz, it passes along to Ataroth, the terri-
tory of the Archites; 3 then it goes down
westward to the territory of the Japhletites,
as far as the territory of Lower Beth-horon,
then to Gezer, and it ends at the sea.
4 The Josephites—Manasseh and Ephra-
im—received their inheritance.
5 The territory of the Ephraimites by
their families was as follows: the boundary
of their inheritance on the east was
Ataroth-addar as far as Upper Beth-horon,
6 and the boundary goes from there to the
sea; on the north is Michmethath; then on
the east the boundary makes a turn toward
Taanath-shiloh, and passes along beyond it
on the east to Janoah, 7 then it goes down
from Janoah to Ataroth and to Naarah,
and touches Jericho, ending at the Jordan.
8 From Tappuah the boundary goes west-
ward to the Wadi Kanah, and ends at the
sea. Such is the inheritance of the tribe of
the Ephraimites by their families, 9 together
with the towns that were set apart for the
Ephraimites within the inheritance of the
Manassites, all those towns with their vil-
lages. 10 They did not, however, drive out

15.63: A narrative postscript noting Judah's failure to conquer Jerusalem. This failure contrasts with Caleb's success in the initial narrative of Judah's allotment (14.6–15). David would later capture this city (2 Sam 5.6–9). *Jebusites,* Jebus was a name by which Jerusalem was known before its conquest by David.

16.1–17.18: Joseph (Ephraim and Half-Manasseh). As the primary power in the Northern Kingdom, Joseph is mentioned next. See Map on p. 346 HB.

16.1–4: A narrative frame that gives the general outline of the southern borders of the Joseph tribes (i.e., the southern boundary of Ephraim). There is ambiguity concerning the people of Joseph. They receive one allotment (16.1), as if they constitute one tribe, yet they are recognized as two distinct tribal units (Manasseh and Ephraim; 14.4a). In addition, one of the tribes, Manasseh, is further divided. Part of the tribe has already received an allotment in Transjordan, while the remainder receives its allotment in Cisjordan.

16.5–10: Ephraim's boundary description is delineated. The fragmentary description here contrasts with that devoted to Judah (15.1–12). **10:** The Ephraimites failed to dispossess the Canaanites, though putting them under forced labor; cf. 15.63; Judg 1.29.

the Canaanites who lived in Gezer: so the
Canaanites have lived within Ephraim to
this day but have been made to do forced
labor.

17 Then allotment was made to the
tribe of Manasseh, for he was the
firstborn of Joseph. To Machir the first-
born of Manasseh, the father of Gilead,
were allotted Gilead and Bashan, because
he was a warrior. 2 And allotments were
made to the rest of the tribe of Manasseh,
by their families, Abiezer, Helek, Asriel,
Shechem, Hepher, and Shemida; these were
the male descendants of Manasseh son of
Joseph, by their families.

3 Now Zelophehad son of Hepher son
of Gilead son of Machir son of Manasseh
had no sons, but only daughters; and these
are the names of his daughters: Mahlah,
Noah, Hoglah, Milcah, and Tirzah. 4 They
came before the priest Eleazar and Joshua
son of Nun and the leaders, and said, "The
LORD commanded Moses to give us an in-
heritance along with our male kin." So ac-
cording to the commandment of the LORD
he gave them an inheritance among the
kinsmen of their father. 5 Thus there fell to
Manasseh ten portions, besides the land of
Gilead and Bashan, which is on the other
side of the Jordan, 6 because the daughters
of Manasseh received an inheritance along
with his sons. The land of Gilead was allot-
ted to the rest of the Manassites.

7 The territory of Manasseh reached
from Asher to Michmethath, which is east
of Shechem; then the boundary goes along
southward to the inhabitants of En-
tappuah. 8 The land of Tappuah belonged
to Manasseh, but the town of Tappuah on
the boundary of Manasseh belonged to the
Ephraimites. 9 Then the boundary went
down to the Wadi Kanah. The towns here,
to the south of the wadi, among the towns
of Manasseh, belong to Ephraim. Then the
boundary of Manasseh goes along the
north side of the wadi and ends at the sea.
10 The land to the south is Ephraim's and
that to the north is Manasseh's, with the
sea forming its boundary; on the north
Asher is reached, and on the east Issachar.
11 Within Issachar and Asher, Manasseh
had Beth-shean and its villages, Ibleam and
its villages, the inhabitants of Dor and its
villages, the inhabitants of En-dor and its
villages, the inhabitants of Taanach and its
villages, and the inhabitants of Megiddo
and its villages (the third is Naphath).[a]
12 Yet the Manassites could not take posses-
sion of those towns; but the Canaanites
continued to live in that land. 13 But when
the Israelites grew strong, they put the Ca-
naanites to forced labor, but did not utterly
drive them out.

14 The tribe of Joseph spoke to Joshua,
saying, "Why have you given me but one
lot and one portion as an inheritance, since

a Meaning of Heb uncertain

17.1–6: Ephraim's heroes. This somewhat disjointed section corresponds to Judah's vignettes of heroes. **1–2:** The mighty *warrior* (parallel to Caleb and Othniel in 15.13–17) is Machir, Manasseh's firstborn (cf. Num 32.39–40). Yet the allotment for *the rest of the tribe of Manasseh* is given in the form of a town list without any connection to the ancestral hero. Although Ephraim's territory was listed first, Manasseh is considered the firstborn, as in Gen 48.13–20. **3–6:** The tribes' heroic women (corresponding to Achsah in 15.18–19) are the daughters of Zelophehad (see Num 27.1–11; 36.1–12).

17.7–13: Manasseh's boundary description is given. It includes a list of towns that the tribe had within the tribal allotments of Issachar and Asher (v. 11). As in the case of Ephraim, the Canaanites were not driven out, but were put to forced labor (vv. 12–13, cf. Judg 1.27–28). While the description of Judah's borders is related with precision and detail, those of Ephraim and Manasseh are fragmentary, take up much less textual space, and present numerous topographical difficulties. The integrity of Judah's territory is thus contrasted with the broken borders of the Joseph tribes.

17.14–18: Joseph's portion. This narrative frame describes the demand of the people of Joseph and the double portion that they receive. This story is an ironic counterbalance to the quest for land by Caleb (14.6–15), and perhaps also by Achsah (15.18–19). The Josephites convey trepidation, contentiousness, and failure.

we are a numerous people, whom all along
the LORD has blessed?" 15 And Joshua said
to them, "If you are a numerous people, go
up to the forest, and clear ground there for
yourselves in the land of the Perizzites and
the Rephaim, since the hill country of
Ephraim is too narrow for you." 16 The
tribe of Joseph said, "The hill country is
not enough for us; yet all the Canaanites
who live in the plain have chariots of iron,
both those in Beth-shean and its villages
and those in the Valley of Jezreel." 17 Then
Joshua said to the house of Joseph, to
Ephraim and Manasseh, "You are indeed a
numerous people, and have great power;
you shall not have one lot only, 18 but the
hill country shall be yours, for though it is
a forest, you shall clear it and possess it to
its farthest borders; for you shall drive out
the Canaanites, though they have chariots
of iron, and though they are strong."

18 Then the whole congregation of the
Israelites assembled at Shiloh, and
set up the tent of meeting there. The land
lay subdued before them.

2 There remained among the Israelites
seven tribes whose inheritance had not yet
been apportioned. 3 So Joshua said to the
Israelites, "How long will you be slack
about going in and taking possession of the
land that the LORD, the God of your ances-
tors, has given you? 4 Provide three men
from each tribe, and I will send them out
that they may begin to go throughout the
land, writing a description of it with a view
to their inheritances. Then come back to
me. 5 They shall divide it into seven por-
tions, Judah continuing in its territory on
the south, and the house of Joseph in their
territory on the north. 6 You shall describe
the land in seven divisions and bring the
description here to me; and I will cast lots
for you here before the LORD our God.
7 The Levites have no portion among you,
for the priesthood of the LORD is their heri-
tage; and Gad and Reuben and the half-
tribe of Manasseh have received their in-
heritance beyond the Jordan eastward,
which Moses the servant of the LORD gave
them."

8 So the men started on their way; and
Joshua charged those who went to write
the description of the land, saying, "Go
throughout the land and write a description
of it, and come back to me; and I will cast
lots for you here before the LORD in Shi-
loh." 9 So the men went and traversed the
land and set down in a book a description
of it by towns in seven divisions; then they
came back to Joshua in the camp at Shiloh,
10 and Joshua cast lots for them in Shiloh
before the LORD; and there Joshua appor-
tioned the land to the Israelites, to each a
portion.

11 The lot of the tribe of Benjamin ac-
cording to its families came up, and the ter-
ritory allotted to it fell between the tribe of
Judah and the tribe of Joseph. 12 On the
north side their boundary began at the
Jordan; then the boundary goes up to the
slope of Jericho on the north, then up
through the hill country westward; and it
ends at the wilderness of Beth-aven. 13 From
there the boundary passes along southward
in the direction of Luz, to the slope of
Luz (that is, Bethel), then the boundary
goes down to Ataroth-addar, on the moun-
tain that lies south of Lower Beth-horon.
14 Then the boundary goes in another direc-
tion, turning on the western side southward
from the mountain that lies to the south,
opposite Beth-horon, and it ends at
Kiriath-baal (that is, Kiriath-jearim), a
town belonging to the tribe of Judah. This

18.1–19.51: Seven other tribal allotments. The narration of the allotments to the remaining seven tribes is recounted.

18.1–10: Assembly of Shiloh. General introduction to the allotment. The geographical shape of Israel in the land is asserted as the result of the LORD's will and of Israel's obedience, not human will or historical contingency. **1:** *Shiloh,* an important Israelite sanctuary in the period before the monarchy (Judg 18.31; 1 Sam 4.3–4). It is 31 km (19 mi) north of Jerusalem.

18.11–28: Benjamin. The territory of Benjamin is immediately north of Judah. **12–20:** A counterclockwise boundary description is given. **21–28:** Benjamin's town list follows. Two districts of towns

forms the western side. 15 The southern side
begins at the outskirts of Kiriath-jearim;
and the boundary goes from there to
Ephron,[a] to the spring of the Waters of
Nephtoah; 16 then the boundary goes down
to the border of the mountain that over-
looks the valley of the son of Hinnom,
which is at the north end of the valley of
Rephaim; and it then goes down the valley
of Hinnom, south of the slope of the Jebu-
sites, and downward to En-rogel; 17 then it
bends in a northerly direction going on to
En-shemesh, and from there goes to Geli-
loth, which is opposite the ascent of Adum-
mim; then it goes down to the Stone of Bo-
han, Reuben's son; 18 and passing on to the
north of the slope of Beth-arabah[b] it goes
down to the Arabah; 19 then the boundary
passes on to the north of the slope of Beth-
hoglah; and the boundary ends at the
northern bay of the Dead Sea,[c] at the
south end of the Jordan: this is the southern
border. 20 The Jordan forms its boundary
on the eastern side. This is the inheritance
of the tribe of Benjamin, according to its
families, boundary by boundary all around.

21 Now the towns of the tribe of Benja-
min according to their families were Jeri-
cho, Beth-hoglah, Emek-keziz, 22 Beth-
arabah, Zemaraim, Bethel, 23 Avvim,
Parah, Ophrah, 24 Chephar-ammoni, Oph-
ni, and Geba—twelve towns with their
villages: 25 Gibeon, Ramah, Beeroth,
26 Mizpeh, Chephirah, Mozah, 27 Rekem,
Irpeel, Taralah, 28 Zela, Haeleph, Jebus[d]
(that is, Jerusalem), Gibeah[e] and Kiriath-
jearim[f]—fourteen towns with their vil-
lages. This is the inheritance of the tribe of
Benjamin according to its families.

19 The second lot came out for Simeon,
for the tribe of Simeon, according to
its families; its inheritance lay within the
inheritance of the tribe of Judah. 2 It had for
its inheritance Beer-sheba, Sheba, Mola-
dah, 3 Hazar-shual, Balah, Ezem, 4 Eltolad,
Bethul, Hormah, 5 Ziklag, Beth-marcaboth,
Hazar-susah, 6 Beth-lebaoth, and Sharu-
hen—thirteen towns with their villages;
7 Ain, Rimmon, Ether, and Ashan—four
towns with their villages; 8 together with all
the villages all around these towns as far as
Baalath-beer, Ramah of the Negeb. This
was the inheritance of the tribe of Simeon
according to its families. 9 The inheritance
of the tribe of Simeon formed part of the
territory of Judah; because the portion of
the tribe of Judah was too large for them,
the tribe of Simeon obtained an inheritance
within their inheritance.

10 The third lot came up for the tribe
of Zebulun, according to its families. The
boundary of its inheritance reached as far
as Sarid; 11 then its boundary goes up west-
ward, and on to Maralah, and touches
Dabbesheth, then the wadi that is east of
Jokneam; 12 from Sarid it goes in the other
direction eastward toward the sunrise to
the boundary of Chisloth-tabor; from there
it goes to Daberath, then up to Japhia;
13 from there it passes along on the east to-
ward the sunrise to Gath-hepher, to Eth-
kazin, and going on to Rimmon it bends
toward Neah; 14 then on the north the
boundary makes a turn to Hannathon, and
it ends at the valley of Iphtah-el; 15 and Kat-
tath, Nahalal, Shimron, Idalah, and Bethle-
hem—twelve towns with their villages.
16 This is the inheritance of the tribe of
Zebulun, according to its families—these
towns with their villages.

a Cn See 15.9. Heb *westward* *b* Gk: Heb *to the slope over against the Arabah* *c* Heb *Salt Sea* *d* Gk Syr Vg: Heb *the Jebusite* *e* Heb *Gibeath* *f* Gk: Heb *Kiriath*

(vv. 21–24 and vv. 25–28) are presented in the same format as those for Judah (many scholars assume from the same source). **28:** *Jerusalem,* assigned to Judah in 15.63.

19.1–9: Simeon. The allotment is described only in terms of a town list (cf. 1 Chr 4.28–33). **9:** A gloss explaining why these do not follow a boundary description. A conjoining of Judah and Simeon is also found in Judg 1.3.

19.10–16: Zebulun. 10–14: Zebulun's boundary description is given. **15:** A town list integrated into a boundary description follows.

17 The fourth lot came out for Issachar,
for the tribe of Issachar, according to its
families. 18 Its territory included Jezreel,
Chesulloth, Shunem, 19 Hapharaim, Shion,
Anaharath, 20 Rabbith, Kishion, Ebez,
21 Remeth, En-gannim, En-haddah, Beth-
pazzez; 22 the boundary also touches Ta-
bor, Shahazumah, and Beth-shemesh, and
its boundary ends at the Jordan—sixteen
towns with their villages. 23 This is the in-
heritance of the tribe of Issachar, according
to its families—the towns with their vil-
lages.

24 The fifth lot came out for the tribe
of Asher according to its families. 25 Its
boundary included Helkath, Hali, Beten,
Achshaph, 26 Allammelech, Amad, and Mi-
shal; on the west it touches Carmel and
Shihor-libnath, 27 then it turns eastward,
goes to Beth-dagon, and touches Zebulun
and the valley of Iphtah-el northward to
Beth-emek and Neiel; then it continues in
the north to Cabul, 28 Ebron, Rehob, Ham-
mon, Kanah, as far as Great Sidon; 29 then
the boundary turns to Ramah, reaching to
the fortified city of Tyre; then the boundary
turns to Hosah, and it ends at the sea; Ma-
halab,[a] Achzib, 30 Ummah, Aphek, and
Rehob—twenty-two towns with their vil-
lages. 31 This is the inheritance of the tribe
of Asher according to its families—these
towns with their villages.

32 The sixth lot came out for the tribe of
Naphtali, for the tribe of Naphtali, accord-
ing to its families. 33 And its boundary ran
from Heleph, from the oak in Zaanannim,
and Adami-nekeb, and Jabneel, as far as
Lakkum; and it ended at the Jordan; 34 then
the boundary turns westward to Aznoth-
tabor, and goes from there to Hukkok,
touching Zebulun at the south, and Asher
on the west, and Judah on the east at the
Jordan. 35 The fortified towns are Ziddim,
Zer, Hammath, Rakkath, Chinnereth,
36 Adamah, Ramah, Hazor, 37 Kedesh, Ed-
rei, En-hazor, 38 Iron, Migdal-el, Horem,
Beth-anath, and Beth-shemesh—nineteen
towns with their villages. 39 This is the in-
heritance of the tribe of Naphtali according
to its families—the towns with their vil-
lages.

40 The seventh lot came out for the tribe
of Dan, according to its families. 41 The ter-
ritory of its inheritance included Zorah,
Eshtaol, Ir-shemesh, 42 Shaalabbin, Aija-
lon, Ithlah, 43 Elon, Timnah, Ekron, 44 Elte-
keh, Gibbethon, Baalath, 45 Jehud, Bene-
berak, Gath-rimmon, 46 Me-jarkon, and
Rakkon at the border opposite Joppa.
47 When the territory of the Danites was
lost to them, the Danites went up and
fought against Leshem, and after capturing
it and putting it to the sword, they took
possession of it and settled in it, calling Le-
shem, Dan, after their ancestor Dan. 48 This
is the inheritance of the tribe of Dan, ac-
cording to their families—these towns with
their villages.

a Cn Compare Gk: Heb *Mehebel*

19.17–23: Issachar. 18–21: Issachar's town list. **22:** A boundary fragment with v. 17 providing a formulaic introduction. Issachar's boundaries correspond to Solomon's tenth district (1 Kings 4.17). Consequently, there may be some relationship between this data and that administrative unit. Issachar is missing in the outline of Judg 1.

19.24–31: Asher. Asher's allotment is fragmentary, with a boundary description (vv. 26–30) and a town list integrated into a boundary description (vv. 25–26,28,30). The list includes some Phoenician cities such as Tyre (v. 29) that were never under Israelite control, suggesting that idealized elements are found in these lists.

19.32–39: Naphtali. Naphtali's allotment has a boundary description (vv. 33–34) and a town list (vv. 35–38). Vv. 32 and 39 provide the framework. The allotment is missing a northern border.

19.40–48: Dan. Like Simeon (vv. 1–9), the allotment is given only in the form of a town list (vv. 41–47), with vv. 40 and 48 providing a formulaic framework. Ancient tradition located Dan in the south (cf. Judg 1.34). **47:** Sometime before the time of the monarchy the Danites migrated to the north (see Judg 18.1–31). Judg 18.27 refers to *Leshem* as Laish.

49 When they had finished distributing
the several territories of the land as inheri-
tances, the Israelites gave an inheritance
among them to Joshua son of Nun. 50 By
command of the LORD they gave him the
town that he asked for, Timnath-serah in
the hill country of Ephraim; he rebuilt the
town, and settled in it.

51 These are the inheritances that the
priest Eleazar and Joshua son of Nun and
the heads of the families of the tribes of the
Israelites distributed by lot at Shiloh before
the LORD, at the entrance of the tent of
meeting. So they finished dividing the land.

20 Then the LORD spoke to Joshua,
saying, 2 "Say to the Israelites, 'Ap-
point the cities of refuge, of which I spoke
to you through Moses, 3 so that anyone
who kills a person without intent or by mis-
take may flee there; they shall be for you a
refuge from the avenger of blood. 4 The
slayer shall flee to one of these cities and
shall stand at the entrance of the gate of the
city, and explain the case to the elders of
that city; then the fugitive shall be taken
into the city, and given a place, and shall
remain with them. 5 And if the avenger of
blood is in pursuit, they shall not give up
the slayer, because the neighbor was killed
by mistake, there having been no enmity
between them before. 6 The slayer shall re-
main in that city until there is a trial before
the congregation, until the death of the one
who is high priest at the time: then the slay-
er may return home, to the town in which
the deed was done.' "

7 So they set apart Kedesh in Galilee in
the hill country of Naphtali, and Shechem
in the hill country of Ephraim, and Kiriath-
arba (that is, Hebron) in the hill country of
Judah. 8 And beyond the Jordan east of Jeri-
cho, they appointed Bezer in the wilderness
on the tableland, from the tribe of Reuben,
and Ramoth in Gilead, from the tribe of
Gad, and Golan in Bashan, from the tribe
of Manasseh. 9 These were the cities desig-
nated for all the Israelites, and for the aliens
residing among them, that anyone who
killed a person without intent could flee
there, so as not to die by the hand of the
avenger of blood, until there was a trial
before the congregation.

21 Then the heads of the families of the
Levites came to the priest Eleazar

19.49–50: Final allotment. The allotments of two former "spies" (Num 13.6,8) frame the larger unit: Joshua's individual allotment concludes the division of the land, just as Caleb's individual allotment began it (14.6–15). Caleb's success and vigor in capturing Hebron is contrasted to Joshua, who requests a city in the Ephraimite hill country that he (re)builds for himself. The city's name, *Timnath-seraḥ* ("portion of excess") (cf. 24.30), is preserved as Timnath-ḥeres ("portion of the sun") in Judg 2.9. The difference is not easily resolved. Joshua appears to prefer the sparsely settled hills to fortified cities of giants.

19.51: Summary of the process of allotment. The verse serves as a closing bracket for the structural segments of both 14.1–19.51 (nine and one-half tribes) and 18.1–19.51 (seven tribes).

20.1–21.42: Allotments to persons of marginal status. This section delineates secondary allotments that form a transition to the practical concerns of how life is to be lived in the land. Neither group is bounded by the tribal borders just enumerated in chs 13–19. The establishment of both the cities of refuge and the Levitical cities was on the basis of Mosaic commandments. Both are supplemental land grants.

20.1–9: Cities of refuge. The towns of asylum provided the right of asylum for someone who committed involuntary manslaughter until the case was adjudicated. The passage shows how Joshua fulfilled what God had commanded Moses (Num 35.9–34) and Moses commanded Israel (Deut 19.1–13). The right of asylum helped to limit the social damage of unrestrained blood vengeance or feuding, especially important in a tribal context (see Judg 12.1–5; 19.1–21.25). Three towns were allotted on each side of the Jordan. All six were also Levitical cities (21.1,11,27,32,36,38). **3:** *The avenger* (Heb "go'el") *of blood* was the deceased's nearest relative (cf. 2 Sam 14.2–17). **4:** *The gate of the city* was where *the elders* of the city met to adjudicate disputes (cf. Ruth 4.1–12). **6:** Probably a later addition, with trial by the *congregation* (rather than the elders of v. 4), and implying that *the death of the . . . high priest* expiated the victim's death. **7–10:** See Map on p. 346 HB.

21.1–42: Levitical cities. Elsewhere the Levites have no inheritance (13.14,33; 18.7; Deut 10.8–9);

and to Joshua son of Nun and to the heads
of the families of the tribes of the Israelites;
2 they said to them at Shiloh in the land of
Canaan, "The LORD commanded through
Moses that we be given towns to live in,
along with their pasture lands for our live-
stock." 3 So by command of the LORD the
Israelites gave to the Levites the following
towns and pasture lands out of their inheri-
tance.

4 The lot came out for the families of the
Kohathites. So those Levites who were de-
scendants of Aaron the priest received by
lot thirteen towns from the tribes of Judah,
Simeon, and Benjamin.

5 The rest of the Kohathites received by
lot ten towns from the families of the tribe
of Ephraim, from the tribe of Dan, and the
half-tribe of Manasseh.

6 The Gershonites received by lot thir-
teen towns from the families of the tribe of
Issachar, from the tribe of Asher, from the
tribe of Naphtali, and from the half-tribe of
Manasseh in Bashan.

7 The Merarites according to their fami-
lies received twelve towns from the tribe of
Reuben, the tribe of Gad, and the tribe of
Zebulun.

8 These towns and their pasture lands
the Israelites gave by lot to the Levites, as
the LORD had commanded through Moses.

9 Out of the tribe of Judah and the tribe
of Simeon they gave the following towns
mentioned by name, 10 which went to the
descendants of Aaron, one of the families
of the Kohathites who belonged to the Le-
vites, since the lot fell to them first. 11 They
gave them Kiriath-arba (Arba being the fa-
ther of Anak), that is Hebron, in the hill
country of Judah, along with the pasture
lands around it. 12 But the fields of the town
and its villages had been given to Caleb son
of Jephunneh as his holding.

13 To the descendants of Aaron the
priest they gave Hebron, the city of refuge
for the slayer, with its pasture lands, Lib-
nah with its pasture lands, 14 Jattir with its
pasture lands, Eshtemoa with its pasture
lands, 15 Holon with its pasture lands, De-
bir with its pasture lands, 16 Ain with its
pasture lands, Juttah with its pasture lands,
and Beth-shemesh with its pasture lands—
nine towns out of these two tribes. 17 Out
of the tribe of Benjamin: Gibeon with its
pasture lands, Geba with its pasture lands,
18 Anathoth with its pasture lands, and Al-
mon with its pasture lands—four towns.
19 The towns of the descendants of Aaron—
the priests—were thirteen in all, with their
pasture lands.

20 As to the rest of the Kohathites be-
longing to the Kohathite families of the Le-
vites, the towns allotted to them were out
of the tribe of Ephraim. 21 To them were
given Shechem, the city of refuge for the
slayer, with its pasture lands in the hill
country of Ephraim, Gezer with its pasture
lands, 22 Kibzaim with its pasture lands,
and Beth-horon with its pasture lands—
four towns. 23 Out of the tribe of Dan: Elte-
ke with its pasture lands, Gibbethon with
its pasture lands, 24 Aijalon with its pasture
lands, Gath-rimmon with its pasture
lands—four towns. 25 Out of the half-tribe
of Manasseh: Taanach with its pasture
lands, and Gath-rimmon with its pasture
lands—two towns. 26 The towns of the
families of the rest of the Kohathites were
ten in all, with their pasture lands.

27 To the Gershonites, one of the fami-
lies of the Levites, were given out of the
half-tribe of Manasseh, Golan in Bashan
with its pasture lands, the city of refuge for
the slayer, and Beeshterah with its pasture
lands—two towns. 28 Out of the tribe of
Issachar: Kishion with its pasture lands,
Daberath with its pasture lands, 29 Jarmuth
with its pasture lands, En-gannim with its
pasture lands—four towns. 30 Out of the
tribe of Asher: Mishal with its pasture

nevertheless, they are integrated into the unity of Israel. As in the delineation of the tribal boundaries, there is a touch of idealization. The total number of Levitical cities (forty-eight) is likely symbolic (being a multiple of twelve). But the towns are not equally divided among the tribes. They are allotted to the three clans of the Levites: the Kohathites, Gershonites, and Merarites. **11–12:** See 14.13–15n.; 15.13–19n. **13–40:** See Map on p. 346 HB.

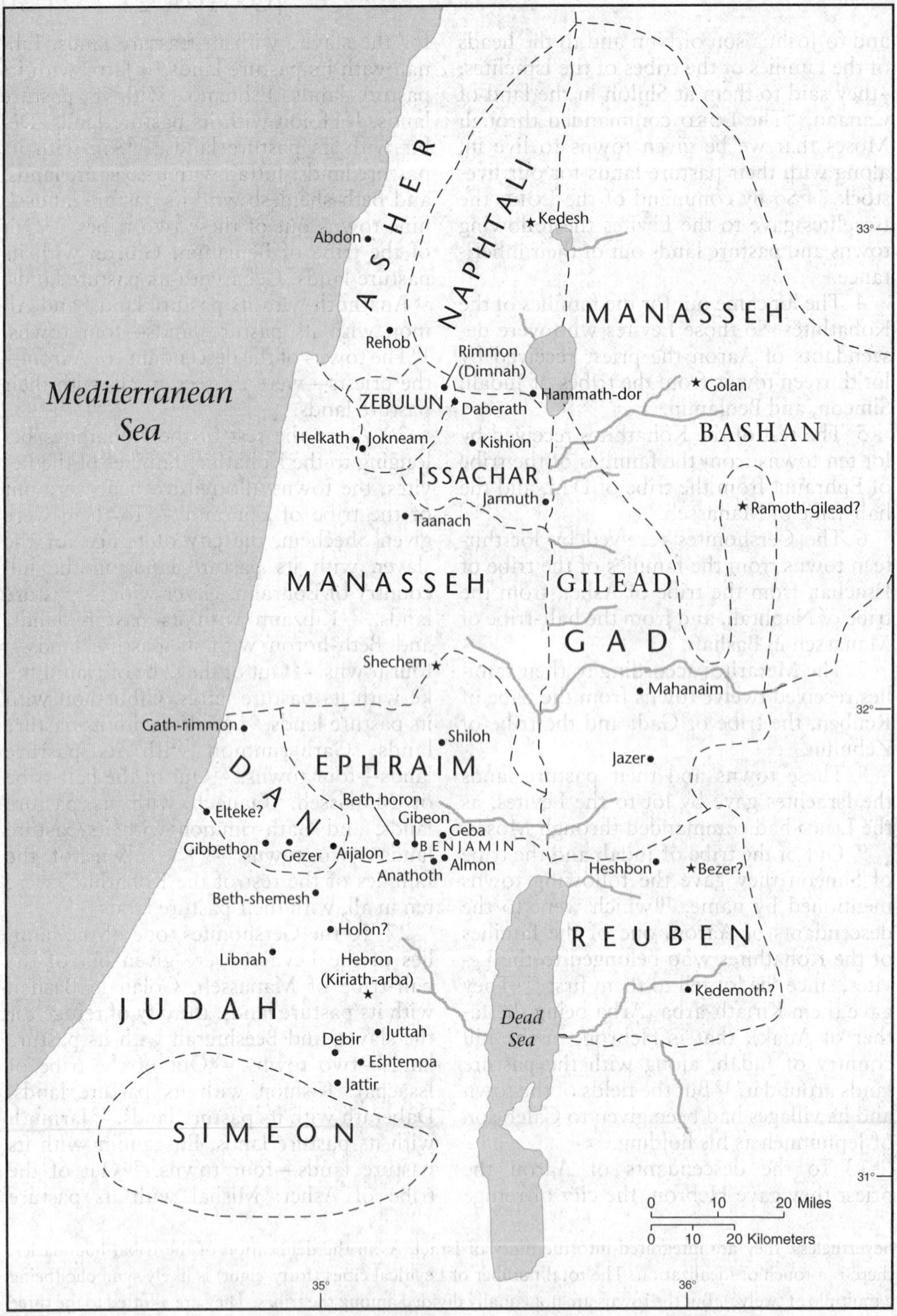

Chs 20–21: The Levitical Cities. Cities of refuge are highlighted with a star. The tribal boundaries are shown by a dashed line.

lands, Abdon with its pasture lands, [31]Hel-
kath with its pasture lands, and Rehob with
its pasture lands—four towns. [32]Out of the
tribe of Naphtali: Kedesh in Galilee with its
pasture lands, the city of refuge for the slay-
er, Hammoth-dor with its pasture lands,
and Kartan with its pasture lands—three
towns. [33]The towns of the several families
of the Gershonites were in all thirteen, with
their pasture lands.
34 To the rest of the Levites—the Mera-
rite families—were given out of the tribe of
Zebulun: Jokneam with its pasture lands,
Kartah with its pasture lands, [35]Dimnah
with its pasture lands, Nahalal with its pas-
ture lands—four towns. [36]Out of the tribe
of Reuben: Bezer with its pasture lands,
Jahzah with its pasture lands, [37]Kedemoth
with its pasture lands, and Mephaath with
its pasture lands—four towns. [38]Out of the
tribe of Gad: Ramoth in Gilead with its
pasture lands, the city of refuge for the
slayer, Mahanaim with its pasture lands,
[39]Heshbon with its pasture lands, Jazer
with its pasture lands—four towns in all.
[40]As for the towns of the several Merarite
families, that is, the remainder of the fami-
lies of the Levites, those allotted to them
were twelve in all.
41 The towns of the Levites within the
holdings of the Israelites were in all forty-
eight towns with their pasture lands.
[42]Each of these towns had its pasture lands
around it; so it was with all these towns.
43 Thus the LORD gave to Israel all the
land that he swore to their ancestors that he
would give them; and having taken posses-
sion of it, they settled there. [44]And the
LORD gave them rest on every side just as
he had sworn to their ancestors; not one of
all their enemies had withstood them, for
the LORD had given all their enemies into
their hands. [45]Not one of all the good
promises that the LORD had made to the
house of Israel had failed; all came to pass.

22 Then Joshua summoned the Reu-
benites, the Gadites, and the half-
tribe of Manasseh, [2]and said to them,
"You have observed all that Moses the ser-
vant of the LORD commanded you, and
have obeyed me in all that I have com-
manded you; [3]you have not forsaken your
kindred these many days, down to this day,
but have been careful to keep the charge of
the LORD your God. [4]And now the LORD
your God has given rest to your kindred, as
he promised them; therefore turn and go to
your tents in the land where your posses-
sion lies, which Moses the servant of the
LORD gave you on the other side of the
Jordan. [5]Take good care to observe the
commandment and instruction that Moses
the servant of the LORD commanded you,
to love the LORD your God, to walk in all
his ways, to keep his commandments, and
to hold fast to him, and to serve him with
all your heart and with all your soul." [6]So
Joshua blessed them and sent them away,
and they went to their tents.
7 Now to the one half of the tribe of

21.43–45: Ironic conclusion. This is an ironic conclusion to the conquest and allotment sections of the book. The overstated claims of unmitigated success (note the use of Heb "kol" ["all" or "every"] six times) in these verses seem incongruent with the subtle statements given throughout 13.1–21.42 asserting that there were failures among the tribes—some quite significant—as each attempted to secure its allotment. Nevertheless, the stress on the LORD's faithfulness contrasts with the squabbling over the Transjordanian altar in the next section (22.10–34).

22.1–24.33: Epilogue to the conquest and allotment. Three concluding sections are used to foster Israel's fidelity in the land. These take the form of a warning narrative (22.1–34) and a pair of exhorting addresses (23.1–16; 24.1–28) in which commitments to the covenant are renewed. Originally disparate materials have been selected and arranged to frame the book. In particular, participants and motifs from 1.1–18 recur in this section.

22.1–34: Misunderstanding with the Transjordanian tribes. The ties binding the tribes together were not firm, and conflicts were a continuing problem. The issue here is the place of legitimate worship, a central concern of Deuteronomy. **1–9: The Transjordanians return to their homes on the east bank. 1–5:** Joshua's farewell to the Transjordanians structurally balances the introduction to them in 1.12–18. **5:** To

Manasseh Moses had given a possession in
Bashan; but to the other half Joshua had
given a possession beside their fellow Isra-
elites in the land west of the Jordan. And
when Joshua sent them away to their tents
and blessed them, 8 he said to them, "Go
back to your tents with much wealth, and
with very much livestock, with silver, gold,
bronze, and iron, and with a great quantity
of clothing; divide the spoil of your enemies
with your kindred." 9 So the Reubenites
and the Gadites and the half-tribe of Ma-
nasseh returned home, parting from the Is-
raelites at Shiloh, which is in the land of
Canaan, to go to the land of Gilead, their
own land of which they had taken posses-
sion by command of the LORD through
Moses.

10 When they came to the region[a] near
the Jordan that lies in the land of Canaan,
the Reubenites and the Gadites and the
half-tribe of Manasseh built there an altar
by the Jordan, an altar of great size. 11 The
Israelites heard that the Reubenites and the
Gadites and the half-tribe of Manasseh had
built an altar at the frontier of the land of
Canaan, in the region[b] near the Jordan, on
the side that belongs to the Israelites. 12 And
when the people of Israel heard of it, the
whole assembly of the Israelites gathered at
Shiloh, to make war against them.

13 Then the Israelites sent the priest
Phinehas son of Eleazar to the Reubenites
and the Gadites and the half-tribe of Ma-
nasseh, in the land of Gilead, 14 and with
him ten chiefs, one from each of the tribal
families of Israel, every one of them the
head of a family among the clans of Israel.
15 They came to the Reubenites, the Gad-
ites, and the half-tribe of Manasseh, in the
land of Gilead, and they said to them,
16 "Thus says the whole congregation of the
LORD, 'What is this treachery that you have
committed against the God of Israel in
turning away today from following the
LORD, by building yourselves an altar to-
day in rebellion against the LORD? 17 Have
we not had enough of the sin at Peor from
which even yet we have not cleansed our-
selves, and for which a plague came upon
the congregation of the LORD, 18 that you
must turn away today from following the
LORD! If you rebel against the LORD today,
he will be angry with the whole congrega-
tion of Israel tomorrow. 19 But now, if your
land is unclean, cross over into the LORD's
land where the LORD's tabernacle now
stands, and take for yourselves a possession
among us; only do not rebel against the
LORD, or rebel against us[c] by building
yourselves an altar other than the altar of
the LORD our God. 20 Did not Achan son of
Zerah break faith in the matter of the de-
voted things, and wrath fell upon all the
congregation of Israel? And he did not per-
ish alone for his iniquity!' "

21 Then the Reubenites, the Gadites,
and the half-tribe of Manasseh said in an-
swer to the heads of the families of Israel,
22 "The LORD, God of gods! The LORD,
God of gods! He knows; and let Israel itself
know! If it was in rebellion or in breach of
faith toward the LORD, do not spare us to-
day 23 for building an altar to turn away
from following the LORD; or if we did so to
offer burnt offerings or grain offerings or
offerings of well-being on it, may the LORD
himself take vengeance. 24 No! We did it

a Or *to Geliloth* *b* Or *at Geliloth* *c* Or *make rebels of us*

love the LORD anticipates 23.11; the language is Deuteronomic (see Deut 6.5; 10.12–13; 30.16; etc.). **7:** See Deut 3.13; Josh 17.

22.10–34: The debate over the altar built by the Transjordanians. The central role of *Phinehas* (see Ex 6.25; Num 25) in dealing with this conflict leads some scholars to conclude that priestly circles edited this story. **12:** Holding strictly to the Deuteronomic law that forbade the offering of sacrifice anywhere except in the one central sanctuary (Deut 12.13–14), the other tribes apparently interpret the building of the altar as an act of disloyalty to Israel and to its God, and therefore prepare *to make war against them.* **17:** *The sin at Peor,* Num 25.3–5. **19:** Highly charged theological language suggests the superiority of the Cisjordanians. **20:** *Achan,* see ch 7. **24–25:** The Transjordanians' motive was honorable; they built the altar as

from fear that in time to come your chil-
dren might say to our children, 'What have
you to do with the LORD, the God of Israel?
25 For the LORD has made the Jordan a
boundary between us and you, you Reu-
benites and Gadites; you have no portion in
the LORD.' So your children might make
our children cease to worship the LORD.
26 Therefore we said, 'Let us now build an
altar, not for burnt offering, nor for sacri-
fice, 27 but to be a witness between us and
you, and between the generations after us,
that we do perform the service of the LORD
in his presence with our burnt offerings and
sacrifices and offerings of well-being; so
that your children may never say to our
children in time to come, "You have no
portion in the LORD." ' 28 And we thought,
If this should be said to us or to our descen-
dants in time to come, we could say, 'Look
at this copy of the altar of the LORD, which
our ancestors made, not for burnt offer-
ings, nor for sacrifice, but to be a witness
between us and you.' 29 Far be it from us
that we should rebel against the LORD, and
turn away this day from following the
LORD by building an altar for burnt offer-
ing, grain offering, or sacrifice, other than
the altar of the LORD our God that stands
before his tabernacle!"
30 When the priest Phinehas and the
chiefs of the congregation, the heads of the
families of Israel who were with him, heard
the words that the Reubenites and the Gad-
ites and the Manassites spoke, they were
satisfied. 31 The priest Phinehas son of Elea-
zar said to the Reubenites and the Gadites
and the Manassites, "Today we know that
the LORD is among us, because you have
not committed this treachery against the
LORD; now you have saved the Israelites
from the hand of the LORD."
32 Then the priest Phinehas son of Elea-
zar and the chiefs returned from the Reu-
benites and the Gadites in the land of Gile-
ad to the land of Canaan, to the Israelites,
and brought back word to them. 33 The re-
port pleased the Israelites; and the Israelites
blessed God and spoke no more of making
war against them, to destroy the land
where the Reubenites and the Gadites were
settled. 34 The Reubenites and the Gadites
called the altar Witness;[a] "For," said they,
"it is a witness between us that the LORD is
God."

23 A long time afterward, when the
LORD had given rest to Israel from
all their enemies all around, and Joshua
was old and well advanced in years, 2 Josh-
ua summoned all Israel, their elders and
heads, their judges and officers, and said to
them, "I am now old and well advanced in
years; 3 and you have seen all that the LORD
your God has done to all these nations for
your sake, for it is the LORD your God who
has fought for you. 4 I have allotted to you
as an inheritance for your tribes those na-
tions that remain, along with all the nations
that I have already cut off, from the Jordan
to the Great Sea in the west. 5 The LORD
your God will push them back before you,
and drive them out of your sight; and you
shall possess their land, as the LORD your
God promised you. 6 Therefore be very
steadfast to observe and do all that is writ-
ten in the book of the law of Moses, turn-
ing aside from it neither to the right nor to
the left, 7 so that you may not be mixed

a Cn Compare Syr: Heb lacks *Witness*

a witness to their loyalty to the LORD. They feared that in the future the Cisjordanians might discriminate against them—a well-founded fear in light of this story (see Judg 12.1–5). **26–27:** It was not a real sacrificial altar, they claimed, but merely a memorial, *a witness* (cf. Gen 31.47–48; Josh 24.27).

23.1–24.33: Concluding charges. There are a number of similarities between Joshua's speech to the leaders (23.1–16) and his charge to the people (24.1–28). Both resemble the testaments of prior Israelite leaders: Jacob (Gen 48–49), Joseph (Gen 50.22–26), and especially Moses (Deut 32–33). Additionally, both have framing links with 1.2–9.

23.1–16: Covenantal charge to the leaders. Joshua's address to the leaders consists almost entirely of Deuteronomistic reflections. **1–5:** God's mighty acts of conquest. **6–11:** An exhortation to remain faithful to the LORD and his covenant so that the remaining land can be conquered. **12–16:** Warnings of judg-

with these nations left here among you, or
make mention of the names of their gods,
or swear by them, or serve them, or bow
yourselves down to them, 8 but hold fast to
the LORD your God, as you have done to
this day. 9 For the LORD has driven out be-
fore you great and strong nations; and as
for you, no one has been able to withstand
you to this day. 10 One of you puts to flight
a thousand, since it is the LORD your God
who fights for you, as he promised you.
11 Be very careful, therefore, to love the
LORD your God. 12 For if you turn back,
and join the survivors of these nations left
here among you, and intermarry with
them, so that you marry their women and
they yours, 13 know assuredly that the
LORD your God will not continue to drive
out these nations before you; but they shall
be a snare and a trap for you, a scourge on
your sides, and thorns in your eyes, until
you perish from this good land that the
LORD your God has given you.
14 "And now I am about to go the way
of all the earth, and you know in your
hearts and souls, all of you, that not one
thing has failed of all the good things that
the LORD your God promised concerning
you; all have come to pass for you, not one
of them has failed. 15 But just as all the good
things that the LORD your God promised
concerning you have been fulfilled for you,
so the LORD will bring upon you all the bad
things, until he has destroyed you from this
good land that the LORD your God has giv-
en you. 16 If you transgress the covenant of
the LORD your God, which he enjoined on
you, and go and serve other gods and bow
down to them, then the anger of the LORD
will be kindled against you, and you shall
perish quickly from the good land that he
has given to you."

24 Then Joshua gathered all the tribes
of Israel to Shechem, and sum-
moned the elders, the heads, the judges,
and the officers of Israel; and they present-
ed themselves before God. 2 And Joshua
said to all the people, "Thus says the LORD,
the God of Israel: Long ago your ances-
tors—Terah and his sons Abraham and
Nahor—lived beyond the Euphrates and
served other gods. 3 Then I took your father
Abraham from beyond the River and led
him through all the land of Canaan and
made his offspring many. I gave him Isaac;
4 and to Isaac I gave Jacob and Esau. I gave
Esau the hill country of Seir to possess, but
Jacob and his children went down to Egypt.
5 Then I sent Moses and Aaron, and I
plagued Egypt with what I did in its midst;
and afterwards I brought you out. 6 When I
brought your ancestors out of Egypt, you
came to the sea; and the Egyptians pursued
your ancestors with chariots and horsemen
to the Red Sea.[a] 7 When they cried out to
the LORD, he put darkness between you
and the Egyptians, and made the sea come
upon them and cover them; and your eyes
saw what I did to Egypt. Afterwards you
lived in the wilderness a long time. 8 Then I
brought you to the land of the Amorites,
who lived on the other side of the Jordan;
they fought with you, and I handed them
over to you, and you took possession of
their land, and I destroyed them before
you. 9 Then King Balak son of Zippor of

a Or *Sea of Reeds*

ments if Israel is unfaithful to the covenant, worshiping foreign gods. **14:** *Way of all the earth,* i.e., to die; see 1 Kings 2.2.

24.1–28: Covenant renewal of the people. Joshua fulfills the commands of Moses in Deut 11; 27; 31. All Israel unites under Joshua's leadership in the service of the LORD. Joshua's final meeting with the people takes place at Shechem (cf. 8.30–35). **1:** *Shechem* (Tell Balata) became an important Israelite religious and political center, and was already important in Genesis. The setting of Shechem thus frames the Hexateuch. **2–13:** A historical summary analogous to the prologues of ancient Near Eastern suzerainty treaties divides into three subdivisions: the ancestral period (vv. 2–4), the Egyptian period (vv. 5–7), and the conquest period (vv. 8–13). **2–4:** A summary of Gen 11.26–46.27. **5–10:** A summary of Exodus and Numbers, omitting any reference to the events at Mount Sinai. **9:** *Balak* and *Balaam,* see Num 22–24; Josh 13.22n. **11:** Perhaps a different tradition about Jericho from that found in ch 6. **12:** *The hornet,* a

Moab, set out to fight against Israel. He
sent and invited Balaam son of Beor to
curse you, 10 but I would not listen to Ba-
laam; therefore he blessed you; so I rescued
you out of his hand. 11 When you went over
the Jordan and came to Jericho, the citizens
of Jericho fought against you, and also the
Amorites, the Perizzites, the Canaanites,
the Hittites, the Girgashites, the Hivites,
and the Jebusites; and I handed them over
to you. 12 I sent the hornet[a] ahead of you,
which drove out before you the two kings
of the Amorites; it was not by your sword
or by your bow. 13 I gave you a land on
which you had not labored, and towns that
you had not built, and you live in them; you
eat the fruit of vineyards and oliveyards
that you did not plant.

14 "Now therefore revere the LORD,
and serve him in sincerity and in faithful-
ness; put away the gods that your ancestors
served beyond the River and in Egypt, and
serve the LORD. 15 Now if you are unwilling
to serve the LORD, choose this day whom
you will serve, whether the gods your an-
cestors served in the region beyond the Riv-
er or the gods of the Amorites in whose
land you are living; but as for me and my
household, we will serve the LORD."

16 Then the people answered, "Far be it
from us that we should forsake the LORD to
serve other gods; 17 for it is the LORD our
God who brought us and our ancestors up
from the land of Egypt, out of the house of
slavery, and who did those great signs in
our sight. He protected us along all the way
that we went, and among all the peoples
through whom we passed; 18 and the LORD
drove out before us all the peoples, the Am-
orites who lived in the land. Therefore we
also will serve the LORD, for he is our
God."

19 But Joshua said to the people, "You
cannot serve the LORD, for he is a holy
God. He is a jealous God; he will not for-
give your transgressions or your sins. 20 If
you forsake the LORD and serve foreign
gods, then he will turn and do you harm,
and consume you, after having done you
good." 21 And the people said to Joshua,
"No, we will serve the LORD!" 22 Then
Joshua said to the people, "You are wit-
nesses against yourselves that you have
chosen the LORD, to serve him." And they
said, "We are witnesses." 23 He said, "Then
put away the foreign gods that are among
you, and incline your hearts to the LORD,
the God of Israel." 24 The people said to
Joshua, "The LORD our God we will serve,
and him we will obey." 25 So Joshua made
a covenant with the people that day, and
made statutes and ordinances for them at
Shechem. 26 Joshua wrote these words in
the book of the law of God; and he took a
large stone, and set it up there under the
oak in the sanctuary of the LORD. 27 Joshua
said to all the people, "See, this stone shall
be a witness against us; for it has heard all
the words of the LORD that he spoke to us;
therefore it shall be a witness against you, if
you deal falsely with your God." 28 So Josh-
ua sent the people away to their inheri-
tances.

29 After these things Joshua son of Nun,
the servant of the LORD, died, being one
hundred ten years old. 30 They buried him
in his own inheritance at Timnath-serah,
which is in the hill country of Ephraim,
north of Mount Gaash.

31 Israel served the LORD all the days of
Joshua, and all the days of the elders who
outlived Joshua and had known all the
work that the LORD did for Israel.

32 The bones of Joseph, which the Isra-

a Meaning of Heb uncertain

vivid but obscure image; see Ex 23.28; Deut 7.20. **13:** See Deut 6.10–11. **14–24:** A dialogue between Joshua and the people in which the issue of serving the LORD, not other gods, is weighed. The Israelites' commitment to the covenant with the LORD is formalized. **14:** *The River,* the Euphrates. *In Egypt,* cf. Ezek 20.5–8; 23.3,8. **23:** See Gen 35.2–4. **26:** *A large stone,* cf. 8.32. *The oak,* see Gen 12.6; 35.4; Deut 11.30; Judg 9.6.

24.29–33: Appendices. Three short notices are given. **29–31:** The death and burial of Joshua, with a comment concerning Israel's faithfulness to the LORD; cf. Judg 2.6–9. **32:** The reburial of the bones of elites had brought up from Egypt, were buried at Shechem, in the portion of ground that Jacob had bought from the children of Hamor, the father of Shechem, for one hundred pieces of money;[a] it became an inheritance of the descendants of Joseph.

33 Eleazar son of Aaron died; and they buried him at Gibeah, the town of his son Phinehas, which had been given him in the hill country of Ephraim.

a Heb *one hundred qesitah*

Joseph in Shechem in the patriarchal plot (see Gen 50.25; Ex 13.19). Here again our attention is returned to Genesis. **33:** The death and burial of the priest Eleazar (see 13.1). This is a surprising ending, but it indicates the strength of the priestly interests in the book.

JUDGES

The book of Judges continues Israel's story from the death of Joshua (1.1; 2.8) to just before the birth of Samuel, who is depicted as Israel's last judge (1 Sam 7.15). After Israel's failure to conquer all the land (described in this book's initial chapters), the nation's life fell into a downward moral and religious spiral that reached its low point under the leadership of the judge Samson. The final portion of the book, in which "judges" are absent, describes Israel's further deterioration into idolatry and civil war. The title "Judges" should not be interpreted in a strictly judicial sense; the "judges" are really rulers in the wider sense (see 2.16–19), often with significant military roles.

It is apparent that the book is a collection of various blocks of material concerning different tribal heroes. Some of the stories may have existed in oral or written form before they became part of the book, but none are attributed to any particular source in the text. Most scholars believe that at one point this collection became part of a larger work, the Deuteronomistic History (see "Introduction to the Historical Books"). The author of that history utilized these stories of local tribal judges, adding introductions and conclusions at various points to underscore his message. The book does not attempt to fully depict this time period; not every oppression that Israel suffered during the judges' era is fully narrated (see 10.11–14). A precise chronology of the period of the judges is unknown since the oppressions and judgeships noted were local or regional, and may at places overlap. The book is not primarily interested in the real history of this period. Rather, the book's selective presentation is clearly designed to instruct the reader, to communicate a coherent, didactic message concerning the consequences of disobedience to God.

The book of Judges has three main parts: a double introduction (1.1–3.6), a double conclusion (17.1–21.25) and a main section, commonly called the "cycles" section (3.7–16.31).

The double introduction is symmetrical to the double conclusion, framing the "cycles." The first introduction (*A*: foreign wars with the "herem" being applied, 1.1–2.5) is balanced by the second conclusion (*A´*: domestic wars with the "ḥerem" being applied, 19.1–21.25). The second introduction (*B*: difficulties in Israel with foreign idols, 2.6–3.6) is balanced by the first conclusion (*B´*: difficulties with domestic idols, 17.1–18.31). For the meaning of "ḥerem" see the Introduction to the book of Joshua.

The double introduction initiates paradigms that create literary expectations for the main "cycles" section. Judges 1.1–2.5 introduces the reader to the pattern of Israel's increasing failure to drive out the Canaanites, which will be mirrored in the degeneration of the "cycles" section. It also reveals the geographic sequence pattern of Judah to Dan reflected in the major judge cycles (Othniel to Samson). Judges 2.6–3.6 introduces the reader to the all-important "cycles" pattern, the very framework of the "cycles" section.

The double conclusion is unified by the four-time repetition of a distinctive refrain: *In those days there was no king in Israel;* twice this is supplemented by *all the people did what was right in their own eyes: A* (17.6), *B* (18.1), *B´* (19.1), *A´* (21.25). Although this refrain serves as a bridge to Samuel, in which the monarchy is introduced, this is more than simply a promonarchic statement; it also has implications in light of the Deuteronomistic, covenantal concerns about the theocracy (see 8.23, the LORD's rule as king over Israel).

The "cycles" section (3.7–16.31) contains six major judge stories built around a basic literary cycle made up of the following components: (1) Israel does evil in the eyes of the LORD; (2) the LORD gives them into the hands of oppressors; (3) Israel serves the oppressor for x years; (4) Israel cries out to the LORD; (5) the LORD raises up a deliverer (i.e., a judge); (6) the spirit of the LORD is upon the deliverer; (7) the oppressor is subdued; (8) the land has "rest" for x years.

It is very important that the six major judge cycles (Othniel, Ehud, Deborah, Gideon, Jephthah, Samson) be read within the larger narrative complex of 3.7–16.31. The components are varied in such a way as to contribute to the book's message. With each major judge, the cycle unravels. In turn, this unraveling enhances the communication of the moral deterioration taking place throughout the period of the judges. In fact, by the time of Samson, the cycle has almost disappeared. The Samson cycle serves as both the literary climax and moral nadir of the "cycles" section.

Moreover, this moral decline can also be seen in the characterization of the women of the book, degenerating from the outspoken Achsah (1.12–15), to Deborah and Jael (4.1–5.31), to the "certain woman" (9.53), to Jephthah's daughter (11.35), to Delilah (16.4–22), and finally to the completely dependent and silent women of 19.1–21.25.

Finally, this section also contains interspersed stories of minor judges (10.1–5; 12.8–15), occurring in a one, two, three sequence. These stories also contribute literarily to the section's message. The exact function of these minor judges, however, remains unclear.

1 After the death of Joshua, the Israelites
inquired of the LORD, "Who shall go
up first for us against the Canaanites, to
fight against them?" 2 The LORD said, "Ju-
dah shall go up. I hereby give the land into
his hand." 3 Judah said to his brother Sime-
on, "Come up with me into the territory
allotted to me, that we may fight against
the Canaanites; then I too will go with you
into the territory allotted to you." So Sime-
on went with him. 4 Then Judah went up
and the LORD gave the Canaanites and the
Perizzites into their hand; and they defeated
ten thousand of them at Bezek. 5 They came
upon Adoni-bezek at Bezek, and fought
against him, and defeated the Canaanites
and the Perizzites. 6 Adoni-bezek fled; but
they pursued him, and caught him, and cut
off his thumbs and big toes. 7 Adoni-bezek
said, "Seventy kings with their thumbs and
big toes cut off used to pick up scraps under
my table; as I have done, so God has paid
me back." They brought him to Jerusalem,
and he died there.

8 Then the people of Judah fought
against Jerusalem and took it. They put it
to the sword and set the city on fire. 9 After-
ward the people of Judah went down to

1.1–3.6: Double introduction. 1.1–2.5: Foreign wars of subjugation with the "ḥerem" being applied. This first introduction, perhaps Deuteronomistic in origin, utilizes materials from the book of Joshua (especially Josh 13–19), along with some expansions. It describes the general success of Judah and the increasing failure of the other Israelite tribes, especially Dan, in the process of dispossessing the Canaanites from the individual tribal allotments. There are four stages in this declining success.

1.1–20: Stage 1: The general success of Judah is narrated through a number of vignettes. The Judahites with their Simeonite allies are able to drive out the Canaanites everywhere except in the plain. No Canaanites live among the Judahites. **3–8:** The defeat of *Adoni-bezek* (lit. "lord of Bezek"). **3:** The tribe of *Judah* in time absorbed *Simeon,* a tribe that played no significant role in the later history of Israel (see Josh 19.9). **4:** The precise location of *Bezek* is uncertain. **5:** *Perizzites,* one of the groups that inhabited the land of Canaan (see Gen 15.20; Deut 7.1; Josh 3.11). **6–7:** Adoni-bezek's capture, mutilation, and death. The humiliation of the Canaanite ruler is dwelt upon with apparent relish since it emphasizes retributive justice. **8:** *Jerusalem* is not yet an Israelite city in its only other appearance in Judges (19.10; see Josh 15.63). It was David who later brought Jerusalem into the Israelite orbit (2 Sam 5.6–9). **9–16:** Three reports of Judahite activities in the south: the capture of Hebron (vv. 9–10), the capture of Debir

fight against the Canaanites who lived in
the hill country, in the Negeb, and in the
lowland. 10 Judah went against the Canaan-
ites who lived in Hebron (the name of He-
bron was formerly Kiriath-arba); and they
defeated Sheshai and Ahiman and Talmai.
11 From there they went against the in-
habitants of Debir (the name of Debir was
formerly Kiriath-sepher). 12 Then Caleb
said, "Whoever attacks Kiriath-sepher and
takes it, I will give him my daughter Achsah
as wife." 13 And Othniel son of Kenaz, Ca-
leb's younger brother, took it; and he gave
him his daughter Achsah as wife. 14 When
she came to him, she urged him to ask her
father for a field. As she dismounted from
her donkey, Caleb said to her, "What do
you wish?" 15 She said to him, "Give me a
present; since you have set me in the land of
the Negeb, give me also Gulloth-mayim."[a]
So Caleb gave her Upper Gulloth and Low-
er Gulloth.
16 The descendants of Hobab[b] the Ke-
nite, Moses' father-in-law, went up with
the people of Judah from the city of palms
into the wilderness of Judah, which lies in
the Negeb near Arad. Then they went and
settled with the Amalekites.[c] 17 Judah
went with his brother Simeon, and they de-
feated the Canaanites who inhabited Ze-
phath, and devoted it to destruction. So
the city was called Hormah. 18 Judah took
Gaza with its territory, Ashkelon with its
territory, and Ekron with its territory.
19 The LORD was with Judah, and he took
possession of the hill country, but could not
drive out the inhabitants of the plain, be-
cause they had chariots of iron. 20 Hebron
was given to Caleb, as Moses had said; and
he drove out from it the three sons of Anak.
21 But the Benjaminites did not drive out the
Jebusites who lived in Jerusalem; so the
Jebusites have lived in Jerusalem among the
Benjaminites to this day.
22 The house of Joseph also went up
against Bethel; and the LORD was with
them. 23 The house of Joseph sent out spies
to Bethel (the name of the city was formerly
Luz). 24 When the spies saw a man coming
out of the city, they said to him, "Show us
the way into the city, and we will deal kind-
ly with you." 25 So he showed them the way
into the city; and they put the city to the
sword, but they let the man and all his fam-
ily go. 26 So the man went to the land of the
Hittites and built a city, and named it Luz;
that is its name to this day.
27 Manasseh did not drive out the in-
habitants of Beth-shean and its villages, or
Taanach and its villages, or the inhabitants
of Dor and its villages, or the inhabitants of

a That is *Basins of Water* *b* Gk: Heb lacks *Hobab*
c See 1 Sam 15.6: Heb *people*

with the Othniel and Achsah story (vv. 11–15) and the movement of the Kenites (v. 16). These narratives are dependent on Josh 15.13–19. **10:** *Hebron,* 32 km (20 mi) south-southeast of Jerusalem. Cf. Gen 23.2; Josh 14.15. **11–15:** Josh 15.13–19. **11:** *Debir* is probably Khirbet Rabud, ca. 16 km (10 mi) southwest of Hebron. **16:** According to this verse, the Kenites were relatives of Moses; contrast Ex 2.18–21; 3.1; Num 10.29. The verse anticipates 4.11,17. *The city of palms* is probably Jericho (as in 3.13). *Arad* is ca. 36 km (22 mi) south of Hebron. **17:** The Simeonites seize Zephath and rename it *Hormah* (whose name is here related to Heb "ḥerem," the total destruction of a city and its inhabitants; see Introduction to Joshua). **18–20:** The last endeavors of the Judahites in the coastal plain. **18:** *Gaza . . . Ashkelon . . . Ekron* were three of the five principal cities of the Philistine confederation (see 14.19). It was David who captured these Philistine cities. The Septuagint asserts that Judah did not capture these cities. **19:** The *chariots of iron* anticipate the chariots of Sisera in Judg 4.3.

1.21–30: Stage 2: Benjamin, Manasseh, Ephraim, and Zebulun do not drive out the Canaanites, and the Canaanites live among them, though some Canaanites are forced laborers. Compare Josh 16–17; 18.11–28. The contrast between Judg 1.21 and Josh 15.63 is especially telling. **22–26:** The capture of *Bethel* ("House of El/God"), formerly called *Luz* ("deception"), 17 km (8 mi) north of Jerusalem. **26:** Nonetheless, a Canaanite city named *Luz* continues to exist in *the land of the Hittites,* probably a reference to north Syria. **27:** *Beth-shean* (also called Beth-shan) is at the eastern end of the Valley of Jezreel; *Taanach, Ibleam,* and *Megiddo* are important sites guarding the valley on its south; and *Dor* is

Ibleam and its villages, or the inhabitants of
Megiddo and its villages; but the Canaan-
ites continued to live in that land. 28 When
Israel grew strong, they put the Canaanites
to forced labor, but did not in fact drive
them out.
29 And Ephraim did not drive out the
Canaanites who lived in Gezer; but the Ca-
naanites lived among them in Gezer.
30 Zebulun did not drive out the inhabi-
tants of Kitron, or the inhabitants of Naha-
lol; but the Canaanites lived among them,
and became subject to forced labor.
31 Asher did not drive out the inhabi-
tants of Acco, or the inhabitants of Sidon,
or of Ahlab, or of Achzib, or of Helbah, or
of Aphik, or of Rehob; 32 but the Asherites
lived among the Canaanites, the inhabi-
tants of the land; for they did not drive
them out.
33 Naphtali did not drive out the inhab-
itants of Beth-shemesh, or the inhabitants
of Beth-anath, but lived among the Ca-
naanites, the inhabitants of the land; never-
theless the inhabitants of Beth-shemesh and
of Beth-anath became subject to forced la-
bor for them.
34 The Amorites pressed the Danites
back into the hill country; they did not al-
low them to come down to the plain. 35 The
Amorites continued to live in Har-heres, in
Aijalon, and in Shaalbim, but the hand of
the house of Joseph rested heavily on them,
and they became subject to forced labor.
36 The border of the Amorites ran from the
ascent of Akrabbim, from Sela and up-
ward.

2 Now the angel of the LORD went up
from Gilgal to Bochim, and said, "I
brought you up from Egypt, and brought
you into the land that I had promised to
your ancestors. I said, 'I will never break
my covenant with you. 2 For your part, do
not make a covenant with the inhabitants
of this land; tear down their altars.' But you
have not obeyed my command. See what
you have done! 3 So now I say, I will not
drive them out before you; but they shall
become adversaries[a] to you, and their gods
shall be a snare to you." 4 When the angel
of the LORD spoke these words to all the
Israelites, the people lifted up their voices
and wept. 5 So they named that place Bo-
chim,[b] and there they sacrificed to the
LORD.
6 When Joshua dismissed the people, the
Israelites all went to their own inheritances
to take possession of the land. 7 The people
worshiped the LORD all the days of Joshua,
and all the days of the elders who outlived
Joshua, who had seen all the great work
that the LORD had done for Israel. 8 Joshua

a OL Vg Compare Gk: Heb *sides* *b* That is *Weepers*

on the Mediterranean coast to the west. On the last three cities, cf. Josh 12.21,23. **29:** *Gezer,* ca. 27 km (17 mi) west of Jerusalem; cf. Josh 10.33.

1.31–33: Stage 3: Asher and Naphtali do not drive out the Canaanites but live among the Canaanites, the inhabitants of the land. A few Canaanites become forced laborers. **31:** The territory of *Asher* is on the northern Mediterranean coast. **33:** The territory of *Naphtali* is in eastern Galilee.

1.34: Stage 4: Dan, in the southwestern hill country, is oppressed or confined by the Amorites, not allowed into the coastal plain. This utter failure of the Danites is the nadir of the chapter, and anticipates their move in ch 18. *The Amorites pressed the Danites,* cf. Ex 3.9, where the Egyptians "oppress" the Israelites. The phrase anticipates 2.18; 4.3; 6.9; 10.12. **35–36:** Conclusion: The Amorites were determined to live in the land. Ironically, theirs is the border described in 1.36.

2.1–5: The angel of the LORD indicts the Israelites who had not done as he commanded. 1: *The angel of the LORD* may be a way of speaking about an appearance of God (cf. Gen 16.7) or could simply refer to a human messenger of God. The precise location of Gilgal (Josh 4.19; 5.8) is uncertain. *Bochim* ("Weepers") occurs nowhere else in the Bible; the Septuagint reads Bethel (cf. Gen 35.8; Judg 21.2).

2.6–3.6: Apostasy and its consequences. The passage introduces the outline of the plot, the all-important cyclic pattern, the very framework of the "cycles" section. **2.6–10:** This passage is apparently dependent on Josh 24.28–31; the faithfulness of Joshua and his era is contrasted with the infidelity of the subsequent generation. **9:** *Timnath-heres,* see Josh 19.50n. **11–19:** The cycle components are introduced.

son of Nun, the servant of the LORD, died
at the age of one hundred ten years. 9 So
they buried him within the bounds of his
inheritance in Timnath-heres, in the hill
country of Ephraim, north of Mount Ga-
ash. 10 Moreover, that whole generation
was gathered to their ancestors, and anoth-
er generation grew up after them, who did
not know the LORD or the work that he
had done for Israel.

11 Then the Israelites did what was evil
in the sight of the LORD and worshiped the
Baals; 12 and they abandoned the LORD, the
God of their ancestors, who had brought
them out of the land of Egypt; they fol-
lowed other gods, from among the gods of
the peoples who were all around them, and
bowed down to them; and they provoked
the LORD to anger. 13 They abandoned the
LORD, and worshiped Baal and the Astar-
tes. 14 So the anger of the LORD was kindled
against Israel, and he gave them over to
plunderers who plundered them, and he
sold them into the power of their enemies
all around, so that they could no longer
withstand their enemies. 15 Whenever they
marched out, the hand of the LORD was
against them to bring misfortune, as the
LORD had warned them and sworn to
them; and they were in great distress.

16 Then the LORD raised up judges, who
delivered them out of the power of those
who plundered them. 17 Yet they did not
listen even to their judges; for they lusted
after other gods and bowed down to them.
They soon turned aside from the way in
which their ancestors had walked, who had
obeyed the commandments of the LORD;
they did not follow their example. 18 When-
ever the LORD raised up judges for them,
the LORD was with the judge, and he deliv-
ered them from the hand of their enemies
all the days of the judge; for the LORD
would be moved to pity by their groaning
because of those who persecuted and op-
pressed them. 19 But whenever the judge
died, they would relapse and behave worse
than their ancestors, following other gods,
worshiping them and bowing down to
them. They would not drop any of their
practices or their stubborn ways. 20 So the
anger of the LORD was kindled against Isra-
el; and he said, "Because this people have
transgressed my covenant that I command-
ed their ancestors, and have not obeyed my
voice, 21 I will no longer drive out before
them any of the nations that Joshua left
when he died." 22 In order to test Israel,
whether or not they would take care to
walk in the way of the LORD as their ances-
tors did, 23 the LORD had left those nations,
not driving them out at once, and had not
handed them over to Joshua.

3 Now these are the nations that the
LORD left to test all those in Israel who
had no experience of any war in Canaan
2 (it was only that successive generations of
Israelites might know war, to teach those
who had no experience of it before): 3 the
five lords of the Philistines, and all the Ca-
naanites, and the Sidonians, and the Hivites
who lived on Mount Lebanon, from Mount
Baal-hermon as far as Lebo-hamath. 4 They
were for the testing of Israel, to know
whether Israel would obey the command-
ments of the LORD, which he commanded

The LORD is the one who gives Israel into the hands of their oppressors and who raises up the deliverers (judges) that save Israel. **13:** *Baal* was the Canaanite storm god with fertility functions (hence important to an agrarian society like ancient Israel), and Astarte was the popular (animal and human) fertility goddess and consort of Baal. She is often pictured in Egyptian iconography as riding on a horse and carrying a bow and arrow or spear and shield (cf. Judg 10.6; 1 Sam 7.4; 12.10). **16:** The traditional title *judges* is misleading. Outside this second introduction, the title "judge" appears only once, and then it refers to the LORD (11.27). According to 2.16, the role of the judges is military, that of "deliverers" or "saviors" of their people from their oppressive enemies. **18:** God raises up saviors because God pities Israel because of *their groaning*. Repentance plays no role here.

2.20–3.4: The resultant conclusion to the cyclical, downward pattern. Due to Israel's disobedience and unfaithfulness and his consequent anger with them, the LORD determines that he will not drive out all the peoples in the land; instead he will use them to test and discipline Israel.

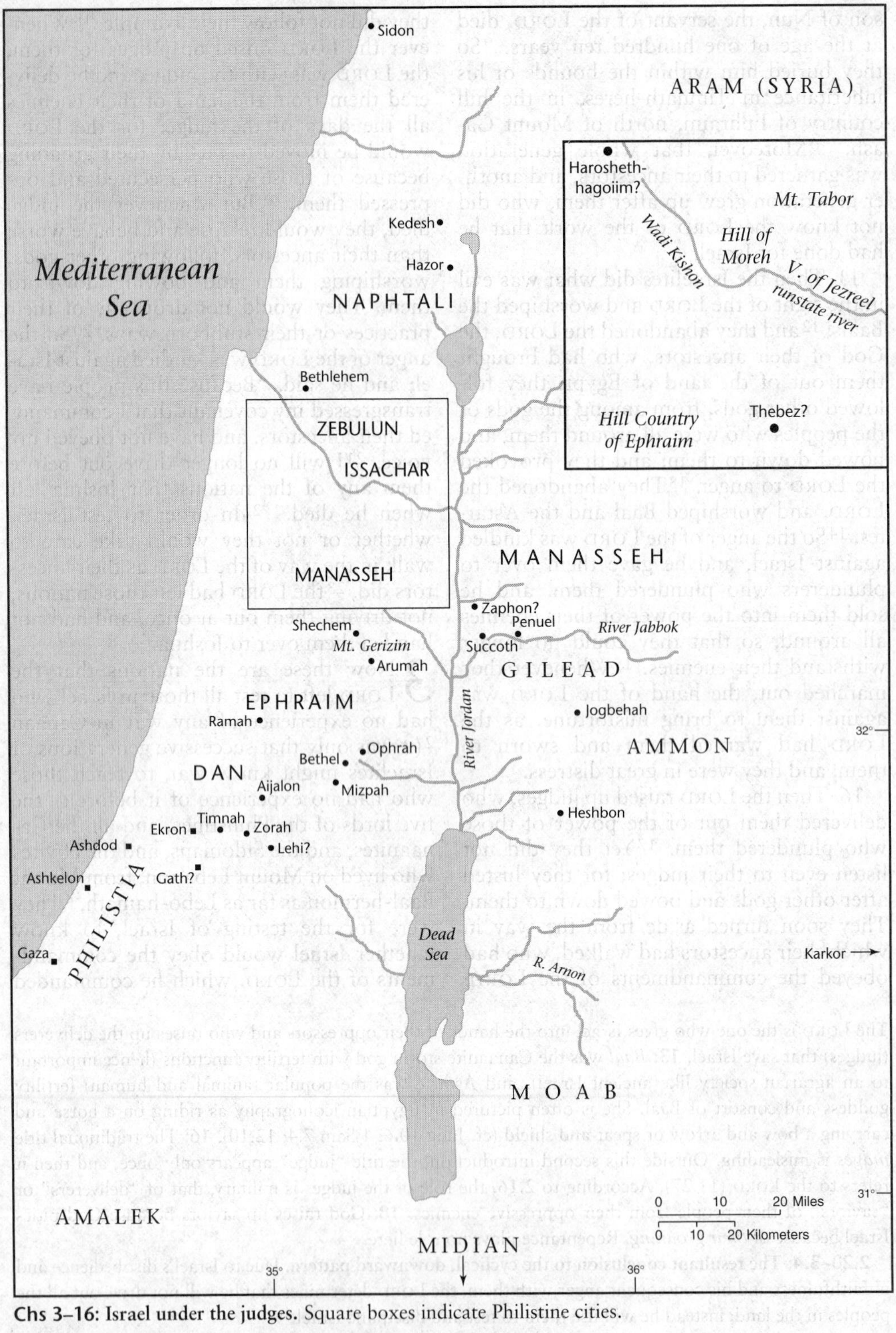

Chs 3–16: Israel under the judges. Square boxes indicate Philistine cities.

their ancestors by Moses. 5 So the Israelites
lived among the Canaanites, the Hittites,
the Amorites, the Perizzites, the Hivites,
and the Jebusites; 6 and they took their
daughters as wives for themselves, and
their own daughters they gave to their sons;
and they worshiped their gods.

7 The Israelites did what was evil in the
sight of the LORD, forgetting the LORD
their God, and worshiping the Baals and
the Asherahs. 8 Therefore the anger of the
LORD was kindled against Israel, and he
sold them into the hand of King Cushan-
rishathaim of Aram-naharaim; and the Is-
raelites served Cushan-rishathaim eight
years. 9 But when the Israelites cried out to
the LORD, the LORD raised up a deliverer
for the Israelites, who delivered them, Oth-
niel son of Kenaz, Caleb's younger brother.
10 The spirit of the LORD came upon him,
and he judged Israel; he went out to war,
and the LORD gave King Cushan-
rishathaim of Aram into his hand; and his
hand prevailed over Cushan-rishathaim.
11 So the land had rest forty years. Then
Othniel son of Kenaz died.

12 The Israelites again did what was evil
in the sight of the LORD; and the LORD
strengthened King Eglon of Moab against
Israel, because they had done what was evil
in the sight of the LORD. 13 In alliance with
the Ammonites and the Amalekites, he
went and defeated Israel; and they took
possession of the city of palms. 14 So the
Israelites served King Eglon of Moab eigh-
teen years.

15 But when the Israelites cried out to
the LORD, the LORD raised up for them a
deliverer, Ehud son of Gera, the Benjamin-
ite, a left-handed man. The Israelites sent
tribute by him to King Eglon of Moab.
16 Ehud made for himself a sword with two
edges, a cubit in length; and he fastened it
on his right thigh under his clothes. 17 Then
he presented the tribute to King Eglon of
Moab. Now Eglon was a very fat man.
18 When Ehud had finished presenting the
tribute, he sent the people who carried the
tribute on their way. 19 But he himself
turned back at the sculptured stones near
Gilgal, and said, "I have a secret message
for you, O king." So the king said,[a] "Si-
lence!" and all his attendants went out
from his presence. 20 Ehud came to him,
while he was sitting alone in his cool roof
chamber, and said, "I have a message from
God for you." So he rose from his seat.
21 Then Ehud reached with his left hand,

a Heb *he said*

3.5–6: A summary conclusion to the whole introduction. Three causally connected things are stressed: the Israelites *lived among* the peoples of the land, they intermarried with the peoples of the land, and they served their gods (cf. Deut 7.1–6). The verses ironically anticipate the Israelites' oath in 21.1–5 concerning marriage with the Benjaminites.

3.7–16.31: Cycles of the judges. 3.7–11: Major judge cycle: Othniel. The hero of 1.12–15 appears here as Israel's first deliverer. With all of the components used in this narration (see Introduction), the story serves as the paragon of the cyclic pattern. The Kenazite (from a southern group eventually assimilated into Judah) Othniel stands as the model judge. *Cushan-rishathaim* (lit. "dark, double wicked") is likely a pejorative created from the real name as a literary device to heighten Othniel's deliverance of Israel. It rhymes with *Aram-naharaim* ("Aram of the Two Rivers"), an area of eastern Syria. **7:** *Asherah* was another female fertility deity associated with Baal. **10:** *The spirit of the LORD* came upon Othniel. Othniel uses this empowerment for positive ends. **11:** The typical conclusion of the cycle (see 3.30; 5.31; 8.28).

3.12–30: Major judge cycle: Ehud. The story is rich in humor, sarcasm and irony. **12:** The Israelites are oppressed by the Moabites, whose king *Eglon* ("young calf") is fat, foreshadowing his sacrificial end. *Moab* was the country immediately east of the Dead Sea. **13:** *The city of palms,* Jericho. **15:** *Ehud* is described as a left-handed Benjaminite ("son of the right hand," Gen 35.18). **16:** *A cubit,* actually a shorter measure. The point of the verse is that the *sword* was short and straight, and could thus be easily concealed. **19:** *The sculptured stones* could be "idols"; in any case these serve as a type of boundary marker (cf. the standing stones at Gilgal in Josh 4.20). A *message,* the Hebrew term also means "thing." **21–22:** The satirical tone presents Eglon as the fattened sacrifice. The *fat* is a sacrificial term used for the

took the sword from his right thigh, and
thrust it into Eglon's[a] belly; 22the hilt also
went in after the blade, and the fat closed
over the blade, for he did not draw the
sword out of his belly; and the dirt came
out.[b] 23Then Ehud went out into the vesti-
bule,[c] and closed the doors of the roof
chamber on him, and locked them.
24 After he had gone, the servants came.
When they saw that the doors of the roof
chamber were locked, they thought, "He
must be relieving himself[d] in the cool
chamber." 25So they waited until they were
embarrassed. When he still did not open
the doors of the roof chamber, they took
the key and opened them. There was their
lord lying dead on the floor.
26 Ehud escaped while they delayed,
and passed beyond the sculptured stones,
and escaped to Seirah. 27When he arrived,
he sounded the trumpet in the hill country
of Ephraim; and the Israelites went down
with him from the hill country, having him
at their head. 28He said to them, "Follow
after me; for the LORD has given your ene-
mies the Moabites into your hand." So they
went down after him, and seized the fords
of the Jordan against the Moabites, and al-
lowed no one to cross over. 29At that time
they killed about ten thousand of the Mo-
abites, all strong, able-bodied men; no one
escaped. 30So Moab was subdued that day
under the hand of Israel. And the land had
rest eighty years.
31 After him came Shamgar son of
Anath, who killed six hundred of the Philis-
tines with an oxgoad. He too delivered Is-
rael.

4 The Israelites again did what was evil in
the sight of the LORD, after Ehud died.
2So the LORD sold them into the hand of
King Jabin of Canaan, who reigned in Ha-
zor; the commander of his army was Sisera,
who lived in Harosheth-ha-goiim. 3Then
the Israelites cried out to the LORD for help;
for he had nine hundred chariots of iron,
and had oppressed the Israelites cruelly
twenty years.
4 At that time Deborah, a prophetess,
wife of Lappidoth, was judging Israel. 5She
used to sit under the palm of Deborah be-
tween Ramah and Bethel in the hill country
of Ephraim; and the Israelites came up to
her for judgment. 6She sent and summoned
Barak son of Abinoam from Kedesh in

a Heb *his* *b* With Tg Vg: Meaning of Heb uncertain
c Meaning of Heb uncertain *d* Heb *covering his feet*

choicest parts, the entrails (cf. Lev 3–6). *And the dirt came out,* Eglon's anal sphincter explodes with the excrement coming out. **24–25:** The scatological satire continues with the comic scene of Eglon's guards waiting to the point of embarrassment for their lord to finish relieving himself, while Ehud escapes. **26–30:** The Moabites, like their monarch, are sacrificially slaughtered so that Israel is delivered.

3.31: Minor judge: Shamgar. This brief account follows the story of Ehud and continues that story's satirical tone. *Shamgar son of Anath,* probably a non-Israelite mercenary, saves Israel with a mighty exploit against the Philistines (cf. 15.14–17; 2 Sam 23.8–23). This verse is likely based on 5.6.

4.1–5.31: Major judge cycle: Deborah and Barak. The prose narrative in ch 4 complements the older poetic account in ch 5, as in Ex 14–15. In both cases, the prose and poetic accounts seem not to tell the same story.

4.1–24: The prose narrative. 1–3: Prologue. The setting of the oppression is narrated. **2:** *Jabin* (see Josh 11.1; cf. Ps 83.9) plays a role only in the prologue and epilogue of the story. *Hazor* was an important city in Galilee because of its proximity to trade routes; it is 15 km (9 mi) north of the Sea of Galilee. *Sisera,* not a Semitic name, is perhaps Anatolian in origin. *Harosheth-ha-goiim,* precise location unknown. **3:** The number of chariots is great and reflects the hopelessness of the situation. Especially difficult for infantry, these *chariots of iron* (cf. 1.19) were a technology that Israel did not possess.

4.4–16: The call of Barak and the defeat of Sisera's army. 4–10: The introduction of Deborah and Barak. **4:** *Deborah* is the only female judge, but women prophets are not infrequent in the Hebrew Bible (Ex 15.20; 2 Kings 22.14; Neh 6.14; Isa 8.3). **5:** *The palm of Deborah,* a location relatively far away from Hazor in contrast to Barak's home in v. 6 (see Map on p. 358 HB). **6–7:** Deborah takes the initiative, "sending for" and "commanding" Barak. *Mount Tabor* is a prominent mountain standing in the northeast corner

Naphtali, and said to him, "The LORD, the
God of Israel, commands you, 'Go, take
position at Mount Tabor, bringing ten
thousand from the tribe of Naphtali and
the tribe of Zebulun. 7 I will draw out Sis-
era, the general of Jabin's army, to meet
you by the Wadi Kishon with his chariots
and his troops; and I will give him into your
hand.' " 8 Barak said to her, "If you will go
with me, I will go; but if you will not go
with me, I will not go." 9 And she said, "I
will surely go with you; nevertheless, the
road on which you are going will not lead
to your glory, for the LORD will sell Sisera
into the hand of a woman." Then Deborah
got up and went with Barak to Kedesh.
10 Barak summoned Zebulun and Naphtali
to Kedesh; and ten thousand warriors went
up behind him; and Deborah went up with
him.

11 Now Heber the Kenite had separated
from the other Kenites,[a] that is, the de-
scendants of Hobab the father-in-law of
Moses, and had encamped as far away as
Elon-bezaanannim, which is near Kedesh.

12 When Sisera was told that Barak son
of Abinoam had gone up to Mount Tabor,
13 Sisera called out all his chariots, nine
hundred chariots of iron, and all the troops
who were with him, from Harosheth-ha-
goiim to the Wadi Kishon. 14 Then Debo-
rah said to Barak, "Up! For this is the day
on which the LORD has given Sisera into
your hand. The LORD is indeed going out
before you." So Barak went down from
Mount Tabor with ten thousand warriors
following him. 15 And the LORD threw Sis-
era and all his chariots and all his army into
a panic[b] before Barak; Sisera got down
from his chariot and fled away on foot,
16 while Barak pursued the chariots and the
army to Harosheth-ha-goiim. All the army
of Sisera fell by the sword; no one was left.

17 Now Sisera had fled away on foot to
the tent of Jael wife of Heber the Kenite; for
there was peace between King Jabin of Ha-
zor and the clan of Heber the Kenite. 18 Jael
came out to meet Sisera, and said to him,
"Turn aside, my lord, turn aside to me;
have no fear." So he turned aside to her
into the tent, and she covered him with a
rug. 19 Then he said to her, "Please give me
a little water to drink; for I am thirsty." So
she opened a skin of milk and gave him a
drink and covered him. 20 He said to her,
"Stand at the entrance of the tent, and if
anybody comes and asks you, 'Is anyone
here?' say, 'No.' " 21 But Jael wife of Heber
took a tent peg, and took a hammer in her
hand, and went softly to him and drove the
peg into his temple, until it went down into
the ground—he was lying fast asleep from
weariness—and he died. 22 Then, as Barak
came in pursuit of Sisera, Jael went out to
meet him, and said to him, "Come, and I
will show you the man whom you are seek-
ing." So he went into her tent; and there
was Sisera lying dead, with the tent peg in
his temple.

a Heb *from the Kain* *b* Heb adds *to the sword;* compare verse 16

of the Jezreel Valley. **7:** The *Wadi Kishon* is a stream that flows northwestward through the Jezreel Valley to the Mediterranean. **8–9:** Barak's insistence that Deborah accompany him diminishes his heroic stature: The honor will go to a woman. **10:** Barak's deployment. *Zebulun and Naphtali,* two tribes from Galilee. **11–16:** The battle. **11:** The *Kenites,* see 1.16n. The mention anticipates 4.17–22. **12–13:** Sisera's deployment. **14:** Deborah, for a second time, commands Barak, giving assurance of victory through the LORD. **15–16:** Sisera is defeated (cf. Ex 14.24; Josh 10.10); Barak expends tremendous effort in pursuing the enemy to Harosheth-ha-goiim, but all for naught.

4.17–22: The murder of Sisera by Jael. 17: Introduction of Jael, the wife of Heber the Kenite. Like Shamgar, Jael is a non-Israelite. **18–20:** Jael demonstrates ancient Near Eastern hospitality, which disarms Sisera. **21:** Jael's murder of Sisera is narrated in the same vivid style as Ehud's murder of Eglon (3.21–22). **22:** Jael has in effect conquered both men: Sisera, by depriving him of his life, and Barak, by depriving him of the honor. Barak is analogous in his role to that of Eglon's courtiers (3.24–25).

23 So on that day God subdued King Jabin of Canaan before the Israelites.
24 Then the hand of the Israelites bore harder and harder on King Jabin of Canaan, until they destroyed King Jabin of Canaan.

5 Then Deborah and Barak son of Abinoam sang on that day, saying:

2 "When locks are long in Israel,
when the people offer themselves
willingly—
bless[a] the LORD!

3 "Hear, O kings; give ear, O princes;
to the LORD I will sing,
I will make melody to the LORD,
the God of Israel.

4 "LORD, when you went out from Seir,
when you marched from the region
of Edom,
the earth trembled,
and the heavens poured,
the clouds indeed poured water.
5 The mountains quaked before the
LORD, the One of Sinai,
before the LORD, the God of Israel.

6 "In the days of Shamgar son of
Anath,
in the days of Jael, caravans ceased
and travelers kept to the byways.
7 The peasantry prospered in Israel,
they grew fat on plunder,
because you arose, Deborah,
arose as a mother in Israel.
8 When new gods were chosen,
then war was in the gates.
Was shield or spear to be seen
among forty thousand in Israel?
9 My heart goes out to the commanders
of Israel
who offered themselves willingly
among the people.
Bless the LORD.

10 "Tell of it, you who ride on white
donkeys,
you who sit on rich carpets[b]
and you who walk by the way.
11 To the sound of musicians[b] at the
watering places,
there they repeat the triumphs of
the LORD,
the triumphs of his peasantry in
Israel.

"Then down to the gates marched the
people of the LORD.

12 "Awake, awake, Deborah!
Awake, awake, utter a song!
Arise, Barak, lead away your captives,
O son of Abinoam.
13 Then down marched the remnant of
the noble;

a Or *You who offer yourselves willingly among the people, bless* *b* Meaning of Heb uncertain

4.23–24: Epilogue. The end of the oppression. The three-fold repetition of King Jabin of Canaan stresses the magnitude of the victory over the oppressor.

5.1–31: The poem: Song of Deborah. The poetic counterpart to the prose of 4.1–24 provides a more emotional celebration of the victory. Many scholars believe that this song is the oldest part of the Bible. It is also one of the most obscure and difficult. It celebrates the LORD's role in the victory over Sisera through a sudden downpour that disabled the chariots in the battle. Its primary attribution to a woman fits the role women have elsewhere in victory celebrations (Ex 15.20–21; Judg 11.34; 1 Sam 18.6–7).

5.2–8: Initial call to praise and report of need. 3: The "lyrical I" is used throughout; the speaker is not meant to be a specific individual, but rather a representative of the group. **4–5:** A cause for praise is the LORD's epiphany upon the earth described in terms of storm and quake. **4:** *From Seir . . . Edom.* The LORD comes from the barren regions of the southeast with an overwhelming storm. **6–8:** The state of affairs before the victory anticipates the LORD's actions. **6:** *Shamgar,* see 3.31n. **8:** Israel's choice of "new" gods was the cause of the military humiliation and servitude (see 2.11–15).

5.9–13: Renewal of call to praise because of the volunteers. 9–10: Invocation to praise the LORD with an exhortation to pay attention. **11:** A cause of praise is the LORD's righteous deeds. **12–13:** Another cause of praise is the leadership of Deborah and Barak.

the people of the LORD marched
down for him[a] against the
mighty.
14 From Ephraim they set out[b] into the
valley,[c]
following you, Benjamin, with your
kin;
from Machir marched down the
commanders,
and from Zebulun those who bear
the marshal's staff;
15 the chiefs of Issachar came with
Deborah,
and Issachar faithful to Barak;
into the valley they rushed out at
his heels.
Among the clans of Reuben
there were great searchings of
heart.
16 Why did you tarry among the
sheepfolds,
to hear the piping for the flocks?
Among the clans of Reuben
there were great searchings of
heart.
17 Gilead stayed beyond the Jordan;
and Dan, why did he abide with
the ships?
Asher sat still at the coast of the sea,
settling down by his landings.
18 Zebulun is a people that scorned
death;
Naphtali too, on the heights of the
field.

19 "The kings came, they fought;
then fought the kings of Canaan,
at Taanach, by the waters of
Megiddo;
they got no spoils of silver.
20 The stars fought from heaven,
from their courses they fought
against Sisera.
21 The torrent Kishon swept them away,
the onrushing torrent, the torrent
Kishon.
March on, my soul, with might!

22 "Then loud beat the horses' hoofs
with the galloping, galloping of his
steeds.

23 "Curse Meroz, says the angel of the
LORD,
curse bitterly its inhabitants,
because they did not come to the help
of the LORD,
to the help of the LORD against the
mighty.

24 "Most blessed of women be Jael,
the wife of Heber the Kenite,
of tent-dwelling women most
blessed.
25 He asked water and she gave him
milk,
she brought him curds in a lordly
bowl.
26 She put her hand to the tent peg
and her right hand to the
workmen's mallet;

a Gk: Heb *me* *b* Cn: Heb *From Ephraim their root*
c Gk: Heb *in Amalek*

5.14–18: Recognition of the tribes who did or did not participate. 14–15a: Praise for the tribes who participated. *Machir,* a subdivision of Manasseh (Gen 50.23; Num 26.29; Josh 13.31) or perhaps a part standing for the whole. **15b–17:** *Reuben, Gilead* (see Num 26.29), *Dan,* and *Asher* do not join the battle. The tribes of Judah, Simeon, and Levi receive no mention in the poem. Perhaps their southern geographical location explains why they were not part of this confederation. **18:** Further praise for participants.

5.19–23: The battle and the curse of Meroz. Vivid, emotional imagery of the defeat of the Canaanite forces. **19:** *Tanaach . . . Megiddo* were cities that guarded two of the passes through the Carmel range into the Valley of Jezreel. **21:** *Kishon,* see 4.13n. **23:** *Meroz* was a nearby Israelite town that did not join in the battle and was cursed (cf. Succoth and Penuel, 8.7,9,16–17).

5.24–31: Jael's deed and Sisera's mother. The climactic conclusion to the poem. **24–27:** Jael, a non-Israelite, delivered the mortal blow to Sisera. The contrast between Jael, who participated, and Meroz in v. 23, which did not, is heightened. The Hebrew "between her legs" (not "at her feet") suggests that Jael used her sexuality to entice Sisera. **28–31:** The final scene is a poignant description of the conflicting

she struck Sisera a blow,
she crushed his head,
she shattered and pierced his temple.
27 He sank, he fell,
he lay still at her feet;
at her feet he sank, he fell;
where he sank, there he fell dead.

28 "Out of the window she peered,
the mother of Sisera gazed[a]
through the lattice:
'Why is his chariot so long in coming?
Why tarry the hoofbeats of his chariots?'
29 Her wisest ladies make answer,
indeed, she answers the question herself:
30 'Are they not finding and dividing the spoil?—
A girl or two for every man;
spoil of dyed stuffs for Sisera,
spoil of dyed stuffs embroidered,
two pieces of dyed work
embroidered for my neck as spoil?'

31 "So perish all your enemies, O LORD!
But may your friends be like the
sun as it rises in its might."

And the land had rest forty years.

6 The Israelites did what was evil in the sight of the LORD, and the LORD gave them into the hand of Midian seven years.
2 The hand of Midian prevailed over Israel;
and because of Midian the Israelites pro-
vided for themselves hiding places in the
mountains, caves and strongholds. 3 For
whenever the Israelites put in seed, the
Midianites and the Amalekites and the peo-
ple of the east would come up against them.
4 They would encamp against them and de-
stroy the produce of the land, as far as the
neighborhood of Gaza, and leave no suste-
nance in Israel, and no sheep or ox or don-
key. 5 For they and their livestock would
come up, and they would even bring their
tents, as thick as locusts; neither they nor
their camels could be counted; so they
wasted the land as they came in. 6 Thus Is-
rael was greatly impoverished because of
Midian; and the Israelites cried out to the
LORD for help.

7 When the Israelites cried to the LORD
on account of the Midianites, 8 the LORD
sent a prophet to the Israelites; and he said
to them, "Thus says the LORD, the God
of Israel: I led you up from Egypt, and
brought you out of the house of slavery;
9 and I delivered you from the hand of the
Egyptians, and from the hand of all who
oppressed you, and drove them out before
you, and gave you their land; 10 and I said
to you, 'I am the LORD your God; you shall
not pay reverence to the gods of the Amo-
rites, in whose land you live.' But you have
not given heed to my voice."

11 Now the angel of the LORD came and

a Gk Compare Tg: Heb *exclaimed*

emotions felt by the women who awaited the return of the Canaanite army. *A girl or two for every man,* highly suggestive sexual connotations. **31:** An appeal for justice over evil and blessing on the righteous; many scholars consider it a later addition to the poem.

6.1–9.57: Major judge cycle: Gideon and Abimelech. The major judge cycle about Gideon extends to the sequel about his aberrant son, Abimelech.

6.1–8.32: Gideon. A hero of the tribe of Manasseh ends the oppression of his tribe by the Midianites, but leads Israel into worship of an idol of his own making before his death.

6.1–10: The setting before Gideon's call. 2: *Midian,* a semi-nomadic group from southern Transjordan that Israel had fought before (Num 25.16–18; 31.1–54). **3:** *The Amalekites,* a semi-nomadic group from the south (Ex 17.8–15; Num 13.19; Judg 1.16). **4–6:** A bitter oppression. **7–10:** This time God answers Israel's cry by sending a prophet who levels a rebuke. God appoints a savior, however, before this rebuke is answered by Israel's repentance.

6.11–32: The call of Gideon. 11–24: A theophanic message from the LORD. Though characterized by extraordinary fearfulness and reluctance, Gideon ("hacker") is the LORD's choice to save Israel. **11:**

sat under the oak at Ophrah, which be-
longed to Joash the Abiezrite, as his son
Gideon was beating out wheat in the wine
press, to hide it from the Midianites. 12 The
angel of the LORD appeared to him and
said to him, "The LORD is with you, you
mighty warrior." 13 Gideon answered him,
"But sir, if the LORD is with us, why then
has all this happened to us? And where are
all his wonderful deeds that our ancestors
recounted to us, saying, 'Did not the LORD
bring us up from Egypt?' But now the
LORD has cast us off, and given us into the
hand of Midian." 14 Then the LORD turned
to him and said, "Go in this might of yours
and deliver Israel from the hand of Midian;
I hereby commission you." 15 He respond-
ed, "But sir, how can I deliver Israel? My
clan is the weakest in Manasseh, and I am
the least in my family." 16 The LORD said to
him, "But I will be with you, and you shall
strike down the Midianites, every one of
them." 17 Then he said to him, "If now I
have found favor with you, then show me a
sign that it is you who speak with me. 18 Do
not depart from here until I come to you,
and bring out my present, and set it before
you." And he said, "I will stay until you
return."
19 So Gideon went into his house and
prepared a kid, and unleavened cakes from
an ephah of flour; the meat he put in a
basket, and the broth he put in a pot, and
brought them to him under the oak and
presented them. 20 The angel of God said to
him, "Take the meat and the unleavened
cakes, and put them on this rock, and pour
out the broth." And he did so. 21 Then the
angel of the LORD reached out the tip of the
staff that was in his hand, and touched the
meat and the unleavened cakes; and fire
sprang up from the rock and consumed the
meat and the unleavened cakes; and the an-
gel of the LORD vanished from his sight.
22 Then Gideon perceived that it was the
angel of the LORD; and Gideon said, "Help
me, Lord GOD! For I have seen the angel of
the LORD face to face." 23 But the LORD
said to him, "Peace be to you; do not fear,
you shall not die." 24 Then Gideon built an
altar there to the LORD, and called it, The
LORD is peace. To this day it still stands at
Ophrah, which belongs to the Abiezrites.
25 That night the LORD said to him,
"Take your father's bull, the second bull
seven years old, and pull down the altar of
Baal that belongs to your father, and cut
down the sacred pole[a] that is beside it;
26 and build an altar to the LORD your God
on the top of the stronghold here, in proper
order; then take the second bull, and offer
it as a burnt offering with the wood of the
sacred pole[a] that you shall cut down."
27 So Gideon took ten of his servants, and
did as the LORD had told him; but because
he was too afraid of his family and the
townspeople to do it by day, he did it by
night.
28 When the townspeople rose early in
the morning, the altar of Baal was broken
down, and the sacred pole[a] beside it was
cut down, and the second bull was offered
on the altar that had been built. 29 So they
said to one another, "Who has done this?"
After searching and inquiring, they were
told, "Gideon son of Joash did it." 30 Then
the townspeople said to Joash, "Bring out
your son, so that he may die, for he has
pulled down the altar of Baal and cut down
the sacred pole[a] beside it." 31 But Joash
said to all who were arrayed against him,
"Will you contend for Baal? Or will you
defend his cause? Whoever contends for
him shall be put to death by morning. If he

a Heb *Asherah*

Abiezrite, Josh 17.2; 1 Chr 7.18. **13:** A dull, cynical question and diatribe about God's treatment of the nation; this introduces, and typifies, Gideon's character. **17:** Gideon is characterized by a need for signs. **21:** *Fire,* a motif that recurs throughout the Gideon and Abimelech cycle (6.26; 7.16,20; 9.15,20,49). **25–32:** Gideon destroys his father's Baal altar and *sacred pole* (i.e., Asherah pole), but only under the cover of darkness. **30–32:** Gideon receives the name *Jerubbaal.* Ironically, judge Gideon ("hacker"), the son of apostate Joash, wears this Baal-name ("Let Baal contend/indict"), a name that occurs with increasing frequency in chs 7 and 8.

is a god, let him contend for himself, be-
cause his altar has been pulled down."
32 Therefore on that day Gideon[a] was
called Jerubbaal, that is to say, "Let Baal
contend against him," because he pulled
down his altar.
33 Then all the Midianites and the Ama-
lekites and the people of the east came to-
gether, and crossing the Jordan they en-
camped in the Valley of Jezreel. 34 But the
spirit of the LORD took possession of Gide-
on; and he sounded the trumpet, and the
Abiezrites were called out to follow him.
35 He sent messengers throughout all Ma-
nasseh, and they too were called out to fol-
low him. He also sent messengers to Asher,
Zebulun, and Naphtali, and they went up
to meet them.
36 Then Gideon said to God, "In order
to see whether you will deliver Israel by my
hand, as you have said, 37 I am going to lay
a fleece of wool on the threshing floor; if
there is dew on the fleece alone, and it is
dry on all the ground, then I shall know
that you will deliver Israel by my hand, as
you have said." 38 And it was so. When he
rose early next morning and squeezed the
fleece, he wrung enough dew from the
fleece to fill a bowl with water. 39 Then
Gideon said to God, "Do not let your anger
burn against me, let me speak one more
time; let me, please, make trial with the
fleece just once more; let it be dry only on
the fleece, and on all the ground let there be
dew." 40 And God did so that night. It was
dry on the fleece only, and on all the
ground there was dew.

7 Then Jerubbaal (that is, Gideon) and all
the troops that were with him rose early
and encamped beside the spring of Harod;
and the camp of Midian was north of them,
below[b] the hill of Moreh, in the valley.
2 The LORD said to Gideon, "The
troops with you are too many for me to
give the Midianites into their hand. Israel
would only take the credit away from me,
saying, 'My own hand has delivered me.'
3 Now therefore proclaim this in the hear-
ing of the troops, 'Whoever is fearful and
trembling, let him return home.' " Thus
Gideon sifted them out;[c] twenty-two
thousand returned, and ten thousand re-
mained.
4 Then the LORD said to Gideon, "The
troops are still too many; take them down
to the water and I will sift them out for you
there. When I say, 'This one shall go with
you,' he shall go with you; and when I say,
'This one shall not go with you,' he shall
not go." 5 So he brought the troops down to
the water; and the LORD said to Gideon,
"All those who lap the water with their
tongues, as a dog laps, you shall put to one
side; all those who kneel down to drink,
putting their hands to their mouths,[d] you
shall put to the other side." 6 The number
of those that lapped was three hundred; but
all the rest of the troops knelt down to
drink water. 7 Then the LORD said to Gide-
on, "With the three hundred that lapped I
will deliver you, and give the Midianites
into your hand. Let all the others go to their
homes." 8 So he took the jars of the troops
from their hands,[e] and their trumpets; and
he sent all the rest of Israel back to their
own tents, but retained the three hundred.
The camp of Midian was below him in the
valley.
9 That same night the LORD said to him,

a Heb *he* *b* Heb *from* *c* Cn: Heb *home, and depart from Mount Gilead' "* *d* Heb places the words *putting their hands to their mouths* after the word *lapped* in verse 6 *e* Cn: Heb *So the people took provisions in their hands*

6.33–7.18: Gideon's struggle with belief in God's promise. 6.33–40: Gideon mobilizes his troops, but he seeks more reassuring signs through the fleece. Gideon's testing of God speaks to his unbelief. The tests with the fleece are God's second sign to Gideon, and they are doubled. No character in the book receives more divine assurance than Gideon, and none displays more doubt. **7.1–8:** Gideon's force is doubly reduced: Fearful Israelites are encouraged to leave (vv. 2–3), and men are selected out arbitrarily according to how they drink water (vv. 4–8). Only three hundred men are left. Hence, it is impossible to ascribe the victory over Midian to human prowess (7.2). **1:** *The spring of Harod* is at the foot of Mount Gilboa. *The hill of Moreh,* a mountain to the north of Mount Gilboa in the Jezreel valley. **9–18:** Gideon overhears

"Get up, attack the camp; for I have given
it into your hand. 10 But if you fear to at-
tack, go down to the camp with your ser-
vant Purah; 11 and you shall hear what they
say, and afterward your hands shall be
strengthened to attack the camp." Then he
went down with his servant Purah to the
outposts of the armed men that were in the
camp. 12 The Midianites and the Amalek-
ites and all the people of the east lay along
the valley as thick as locusts; and their cam-
els were without number, countless as the
sand on the seashore. 13 When Gideon ar-
rived, there was a man telling a dream to
his comrade; and he said, "I had a dream,
and in it a cake of barley bread tumbled
into the camp of Midian, and came to the
tent, and struck it so that it fell; it turned
upside down, and the tent collapsed."
14 And his comrade answered, "This is no
other than the sword of Gideon son of Jo-
ash, a man of Israel; into his hand God has
given Midian and all the army."

15 When Gideon heard the telling of the
dream and its interpretation, he worshiped;
and he returned to the camp of Israel, and
said, "Get up; for the LORD has given the
army of Midian into your hand." 16 After
he divided the three hundred men into three
companies, and put trumpets into the
hands of all of them, and empty jars, with
torches inside the jars, 17 he said to them,
"Look at me, and do the same; when I
come to the outskirts of the camp, do as I
do. 18 When I blow the trumpet, I and all
who are with me, then you also blow the
trumpets around the whole camp, and
shout, 'For the LORD and for Gideon!' "

19 So Gideon and the hundred who
were with him came to the outskirts of the
camp at the beginning of the middle watch,
when they had just set the watch; and they
blew the trumpets and smashed the jars
that were in their hands. 20 So the three
companies blew the trumpets and broke the
jars, holding in their left hands the torches,
and in their right hands the trumpets to
blow; and they cried, "A sword for the
LORD and for Gideon!" 21 Every man stood
in his place all around the camp, and all the
men in camp ran; they cried out and fled.
22 When they blew the three hundred trum-
pets, the LORD set every man's sword
against his fellow and against all the army;
and the army fled as far as Beth-shittah to-
ward Zererah,[a] as far as the border of
Abel-meholah, by Tabbath. 23 And the men
of Israel were called out from Naphtali and
from Asher and from all Manasseh, and
they pursued after the Midianites.

24 Then Gideon sent messengers
throughout all the hill country of Ephraim,
saying, "Come down against the Midian-
ites and seize the waters against them, as
far as Beth-barah, and also the Jordan." So
all the men of Ephraim were called out, and
they seized the waters as far as Beth-barah,
and also the Jordan. 25 They captured the
two captains of Midian, Oreb and Zeeb;
they killed Oreb at the rock of Oreb, and
Zeeb they killed at the wine press of Zeeb,
as they pursued the Midianites. They
brought the heads of Oreb and Zeeb to
Gideon beyond the Jordan.

8 Then the Ephraimites said to him,
"What have you done to us, not to call
us when you went to fight against the Midi-
anites?" And they upbraided him violently.
2 So he said to them, "What have I done
now in comparison with you? Is not the
gleaning of the grapes of Ephraim better
than the vintage of Abiezer? 3 God has giv-
en into your hands the captains of Midian,
Oreb and Zeeb; what have I been able to do
in comparison with you?" When he said
this, their anger against him subsided.

a Another reading is *Zeredah*

a Midianite relate his dream and another interpret it, and mobilizes his force of three hundred for a surprise attack against the Midianites. After this additional sign, he is fully confident in God's promise.

7.19–8.21: God's deliverance from the Midianites. 7.19–8.3: Battle west of Jordan. **19–25:** Gideon's forces surprised the Midianites. The elimination of two of the Midianite leaders, Oreb and Zeeb, consolidated Gideon's victory. **8.1–3:** Gideon diplomatically handles the provocations of the Ephraimites. Contrast Jephthah's lack of diplomacy in 12.1–6. **8.4–21:** Pursuit and battle east of the Jordan. There are

4 Then Gideon came to the Jordan and
crossed over, he and the three hundred who
were with him, exhausted and famished.[a]
5 So he said to the people of Succoth,
"Please give some loaves of bread to my
followers, for they are exhausted, and I am
pursuing Zebah and Zalmunna, the kings
of Midian." 6 But the officials of Succoth
said, "Do you already have in your posses-
sion the hands of Zebah and Zalmunna,
that we should give bread to your army?"
7 Gideon replied, "Well then, when the
LORD has given Zebah and Zalmunna into
my hand, I will trample your flesh on the
thorns of the wilderness and on briers."
8 From there he went up to Penuel, and
made the same request of them; and the
people of Penuel answered him as the peo-
ple of Succoth had answered. 9 So he said to
the people of Penuel, "When I come back
victorious, I will break down this tower."
10 Now Zebah and Zalmunna were in
Karkor with their army, about fifteen thou-
sand men, all who were left of all the army
of the people of the east; for one hundred
twenty thousand men bearing arms had
fallen. 11 So Gideon went up by the caravan
route east of Nobah and Jogbehah, and at-
tacked the army; for the army was off its
guard. 12 Zebah and Zalmunna fled; and he
pursued them and took the two kings of
Midian, Zebah and Zalmunna, and threw
all the army into a panic.
13 When Gideon son of Joash returned
from the battle by the ascent of Heres, 14 he
caught a young man, one of the people of
Succoth, and questioned him; and he listed
for him the officials and elders of Succoth,
seventy-seven people. 15 Then he came to
the people of Succoth, and said, "Here are
Zebah and Zalmunna, about whom you
taunted me, saying, 'Do you already have
in your possession the hands of Zebah and
Zalmunna, that we should give bread to
your troops who are exhausted?' " 16 So he
took the elders of the city and he took
thorns of the wilderness and briers and
with them he trampled[b] the people of Suc-
coth. 17 He also broke down the tower of
Penuel, and killed the men of the city.
18 Then he said to Zebah and Zalmun-
na, "What about the men whom you killed
at Tabor?" They answered, "As you are, so
were they, every one of them; they resem-
bled the sons of a king." 19 And he replied,
"They were my brothers, the sons of my
mother; as the LORD lives, if you had saved
them alive, I would not kill you." 20 So he
said to Jether his firstborn, "Go kill them!"
But the boy did not draw his sword, for
he was afraid, because he was still a boy.
21 Then Zebah and Zalmunna said, "You
come and kill us; for as the man is, so is his
strength." So Gideon proceeded to kill Ze-
bah and Zalmunna; and he took the cres-
cents that were on the necks of their cam-
els.
22 Then the Israelites said to Gideon,
"Rule over us, you and your son and your
grandson also; for you have delivered us
out of the hand of Midian." 23 Gideon said
to them, "I will not rule over you, and my
son will not rule over you; the LORD will
rule over you." 24 Then Gideon said to
them, "Let me make a request of you; each

a Gk: Heb *pursuing* *b* With verse 7, Compare Gk: Heb *he taught*

no indications of the LORD's involvement in this second battle. **4–9:** The cities of Succoth and Penuel refuse to help Gideon, fearing Midianite reprisals. **5:** *Zebah and Zalmunna,* pejoratives or distortions of names (see 3.8n.). *Zebah* means "sacrificial victim"; *Zalmunna* means "protection refused." *Succoth,* a Transjordanian city east of Shechem; see Gen 33.17. **8:** *Penuel,* another Transjordanian city; see Gen 32.30–31; 1 Kings 12.25. **10–12:** The second battle against the Midianites. **13–21:** Gideon takes reprisals against the Israelites in Succoth and Penuel, torturing and killing those who refused to support his army. This anticipates actions of Abimelech (9.46–49) and Jephthah (12.1–6). **18–19:** Gideon's motive is revealed: personal revenge.

8.22–32: Conclusion to Gideon's life after the victory. 22–23: Gideon's refusal reflected the belief that only the LORD was to rule over Israel; cf. 1 Sam 8.7. **24–28:** The precise nature of the *ephod* is unclear; in Ex 28.6–21 and 39.2–7, it is a garment worn by the high priest, though here, as in 17.5, it is an idol

of you give me an earring he has taken as
booty." (For the enemy[a] had golden ear-
rings, because they were Ishmaelites.)
25"We will willingly give them," they an-
swered. So they spread a garment, and each
threw into it an earring he had taken as
booty. 26The weight of the golden earrings
that he requested was one thousand seven
hundred shekels of gold (apart from the
crescents and the pendants and the purple
garments worn by the kings of Midian, and
the collars that were on the necks of their
camels). 27Gideon made an ephod of it and
put it in his town, in Ophrah; and all Israel
prostituted themselves to it there, and it be-
came a snare to Gideon and to his family.
28So Midian was subdued before the Israel-
ites, and they lifted up their heads no more.
So the land had rest forty years in the days
of Gideon.

29 Jerubbaal son of Joash went to live in
his own house. 30Now Gideon had seventy
sons, his own offspring, for he had many
wives. 31His concubine who was in She-
chem also bore him a son, and he named
him Abimelech. 32Then Gideon son of Jo-
ash died at a good old age, and was buried
in the tomb of his father Joash at Ophrah
of the Abiezrites.

33 As soon as Gideon died, the Israelites
relapsed and prostituted themselves with
the Baals, making Baal-berith their god.
34The Israelites did not remember the
LORD their God, who had rescued them
from the hand of all their enemies on every
side; 35and they did not exhibit loyalty to
the house of Jerubbaal (that is, Gideon) in
return for all the good that he had done to
Israel.

9 Now Abimelech son of Jerubbaal went
to Shechem to his mother's kinsfolk
and said to them and to the whole clan of
his mother's family, 2"Say in the hearing of
all the lords of Shechem, 'Which is better
for you, that all seventy of the sons of Jer-
ubbaal rule over you, or that one rule over
you?' Remember also that I am your bone
and your flesh." 3So his mother's kinsfolk
spoke all these words on his behalf in the
hearing of all the lords of Shechem; and
their hearts inclined to follow Abimelech,
for they said, "He is our brother." 4They
gave him seventy pieces of silver out of the
temple of Baal-berith with which Abime-
lech hired worthless and reckless fellows,
who followed him. 5He went to his father's
house at Ophrah, and killed his brothers
the sons of Jerubbaal, seventy men, on one
stone; but Jotham, the youngest son of Jer-
ubbaal, survived, for he hid himself. 6Then
all the lords of Shechem and all Beth-millo
came together, and they went and made

a Heb *they*

of some sort. **26:** The weight of gold was about 20 kg (43 lb). **27:** The ephod was placed in Ophrah, his hometown where his father's Baal altar and sacred ("Asherah") pole had been. *All Israel prostituted themselves,* as they did to the Baals (2.17; 8.33). Israel worships an idol made by its own judge. **30–31:** The accumulation of wives was common among ancient Near Eastern monarchs (cf. Deut 17.17; 1 Kings 11.3). *Abimelech,* a name meaning "my father is king," which could refer either to his parent or to the deity.

8.33–9.57: Abimelech. This complementary sequel resolves numerous issues of the Gideon story. Gideon's disinherited son seizes the kingship that Gideon publicly rejected. The theme of retribution is clearly developed: God causes the evil which Abimelech and the men of Shechem did to redound upon their own heads (9.56–57).

8.33–35: The prologue to the story. 33: *Baal-berith* ("lord" [or "Baal"] of the covenant) was probably an epithet for the god El-berith (9.46). Covenant faithfulness was the problem at the beginning of the cycle (cf. 6.7–10) and is still the problem after the death of Gideon.

9.1–24: Abimelech's rise. 1–6: Abimelech eliminated all potential rivals and took the throne of Shechem, ironically where the Israelite covenant assembly took place (Josh 24.1–27). **4:** *Seventy pieces of silver,* corresponding to Gideon's seventy sons. **5:** The murders take place *on one stone* (cf. 9.53). Only Jotham ("Yahweh is blameless") escapes. **6:** *Beth-millo,* apparently a subdivision of Shechem. *The oak of the pillar,* Gen 35.4; Josh 24.26. **7–21:** Jotham's fable and curse. The four-part plant fable satirizes and

Abimelech king, by the oak of the pillar[a]
at Shechem.
7 When it was told to Jotham, he went
and stood on the top of Mount Gerizim,
and cried aloud and said to them, "Listen
to me, you lords of Shechem, so that God
may listen to you.

8 The trees once went out
to anoint a king over themselves.
So they said to the olive tree,
'Reign over us.'
9 The olive tree answered them,
'Shall I stop producing my rich oil
by which gods and mortals are
honored,
and go to sway over the trees?'
10 Then the trees said to the fig tree,
'You come and reign over us.'
11 But the fig tree answered them,
'Shall I stop producing my
sweetness
and my delicious fruit,
and go to sway over the trees?'
12 Then the trees said to the vine,
'You come and reign over us.'
13 But the vine said to them,
'Shall I stop producing my wine
that cheers gods and mortals,
and go to sway over the trees?'
14 So all the trees said to the bramble,
'You come and reign over us.'
15 And the bramble said to the trees,
'If in good faith you are anointing
me king over you,
then come and take refuge in my
shade;
but if not, let fire come out of the
bramble
and devour the cedars of
Lebanon.'

16 "Now therefore, if you acted in good
faith and honor when you made Abimelech
king, and if you have dealt well with Jerub-
baal and his house, and have done to him
as his actions deserved— 17 for my father
fought for you, and risked his life, and res-
cued you from the hand of Midian; 18 but
you have risen up against my father's house
this day, and have killed his sons, seventy
men on one stone, and have made Abime-
lech, the son of his slave woman, king over
the lords of Shechem, because he is your
kinsman— 19 if, I say, you have acted in
good faith and honor with Jerubbaal and
with his house this day, then rejoice in
Abimelech, and let him also rejoice in you;
20 but if not, let fire come out from Abime-
lech, and devour the lords of Shechem, and
Beth-millo; and let fire come out from the
lords of Shechem, and from Beth-millo,
and devour Abimelech." 21 Then Jotham
ran away and fled, going to Beer, where he
remained for fear of his brother Abimelech.

22 Abimelech ruled over Israel three
years. 23 But God sent an evil spirit between
Abimelech and the lords of Shechem; and
the lords of Shechem dealt treacherously
with Abimelech. 24 This happened so that
the violence done to the seventy sons of
Jerubbaal might be avenged[b] and their
blood be laid on their brother Abimelech,
who killed them, and on the lords of She-
chem, who strengthened his hands to kill
his brothers. 25 So, out of hostility to him,
the lords of Shechem set ambushes on the
mountain tops. They robbed all who
passed by them along that way; and it was
reported to Abimelech.

26 When Gaal son of Ebed moved into
Shechem with his kinsfolk, the lords of She-
chem put confidence in him. 27 They went
out into the field and gathered the grapes
from their vineyards, trod them, and cele-
brated. Then they went into the temple of
their god, ate and drank, and ridiculed
Abimelech. 28 Gaal son of Ebed said, "Who

a Cn: Meaning of Heb uncertain *b* Heb *might come*

rebukes the monarchy of his brother Abimelech. **7:** *Mount Gerizim* is just south of Shechem. **8:** *The olive tree* is the noblest tree, while *the bramble* (9.14) is a useless bush. **21:** The location of *Beer* ("well") is unknown. **22–24:** God takes action against Abimelech to revenge the murder of Jerubbaal's sons. **22:** Abimelech neither "judged" nor "reigned" but ruled.

9.25–57: Abimelech's decline. 25–41: Treachery against Abimelech is narrated. The Shechemites turn their loyalties to Gaal, another raw opportunist. But with Abimelech's military action, Gaal flees. **28:**

is Abimelech, and who are we of Shechem,
that we should serve him? Did not the son
of Jerubbaal and Zebul his officer serve the
men of Hamor father of Shechem? Why
then should we serve him? 29 If only this
people were under my command! Then I
would remove Abimelech; I would say[a] to
him, 'Increase your army, and come out.' "
30 When Zebul the ruler of the city
heard the words of Gaal son of Ebed, his
anger was kindled. 31 He sent messengers to
Abimelech at Arumah,[b] saying, "Look,
Gaal son of Ebed and his kinsfolk have
come to Shechem, and they are stirring up[c]
the city against you. 32 Now therefore, go
by night, you and the troops that are with
you, and lie in wait in the fields. 33 Then
early in the morning, as soon as the sun
rises, get up and rush on the city; and when
he and the troops that are with him come
out against you, you may deal with them as
best you can."
34 So Abimelech and all the troops with
him got up by night and lay in wait against
Shechem in four companies. 35 When Gaal
son of Ebed went out and stood in the en-
trance of the gate of the city, Abimelech
and the troops with him rose from the am-
bush. 36 And when Gaal saw them, he said
to Zebul, "Look, people are coming down
from the mountain tops!" And Zebul said
to him, "The shadows on the mountains
look like people to you." 37 Gaal spoke
again and said, "Look, people are coming
down from Tabbur-erez, and one company
is coming from the direction of Elon-
meonenim."[d] 38 Then Zebul said to him,
"Where is your boast[e] now, you who said,
'Who is Abimelech, that we should serve
him?' Are not these the troops you made
light of? Go out now and fight with them."
39 So Gaal went out at the head of the lords
of Shechem, and fought with Abimelech.
40 Abimelech chased him, and he fled before
him. Many fell wounded, up to the en-
trance of the gate. 41 So Abimelech resided
at Arumah; and Zebul drove out Gaal and
his kinsfolk, so that they could not live on
at Shechem.
42 On the following day the people
went out into the fields. When Abimelech
was told, 43 he took his troops and divided
them into three companies, and lay in wait
in the fields. When he looked and saw the
people coming out of the city, he rose
against them and killed them. 44 Abimelech
and the company that was[f] with him
rushed forward and stood at the entrance
of the gate of the city, while the two com-
panies rushed on all who were in the fields
and killed them. 45 Abimelech fought
against the city all that day; he took the
city, and killed the people that were in it;
and he razed the city and sowed it with salt.
46 When all the lords of the Tower of
Shechem heard of it, they entered the
stronghold of the temple of El-berith.
47 Abimelech was told that all the lords of
the Tower of Shechem were gathered to-
gether. 48 So Abimelech went up to Mount
Zalmon, he and all the troops that were
with him. Abimelech took an ax in his
hand, cut down a bundle of brushwood,
and took it up and laid it on his shoulder.
Then he said to the troops with him, "What
you have seen me do, do quickly, as I have
done." 49 So every one of the troops cut
down a bundle and following Abimelech
put it against the stronghold, and they set
the stronghold on fire over them, so that all
the people of the Tower of Shechem also
died, about a thousand men and women.

a Gk: Heb *and he said* *b* Cn See 9.41. Heb *Tormah* *c* Cn: Heb *are besieging* *d* That is *Diviners' Oak* *e* Heb *mouth* *f* Vg and some Gk Mss: Heb *companies that were*

Hamor, cf. Gen 34.2. **37:** *Tabbur-erez,* a designation of Mount Gerizim (see v. 7n.) probably meaning "the navel of the land" (cf. Ezek 38.12). *Elon-meonenim,* "Diviners' Oak," see v. 6n. **41:** *Arumah,* 8 km (5 mi) southeast of Shechem. **42–55:** Abimelech carries out three acts of repression: slaughter of the Shechemites (vv. 42–45), the destruction of the tower of Shechem (vv. 46–49), and the attack on Thebez (vv. 50–52). He is, however, ignominiously slain by a woman with a single upper millstone, which ends the siege of that city (vv. 53–55, cf. 2 Sam 11.21). **46:** *El-berith,* see 8.33n. **48:** *Mount Zalmon,* probably Mount Ebal, just north of Shechem. **50:** *Thebez,* location uncertain; some scholars identify it as Tirzah,

50 Then Abimelech went to Thebez, and encamped against Thebez, and took it. 51 But there was a strong tower within the city, and all the men and women and all the lords of the city fled to it and shut themselves in; and they went to the roof of the tower. 52 Abimelech came to the tower, and fought against it, and came near to the entrance of the tower to burn it with fire. 53 But a certain woman threw an upper millstone on Abimelech's head, and crushed his skull. 54 Immediately he called to the young man who carried his armor and said to him, "Draw your sword and kill me, so people will not say about me, 'A woman killed him.' " So the young man thrust him through, and he died. 55 When the Israelites saw that Abimelech was dead, they all went home. 56 Thus God repaid Abimelech for the crime he committed against his father in killing his seventy brothers; 57 and God also made all the wickedness of the people of Shechem fall back on their heads, and on them came the curse of Jotham son of Jerubbaal.

10 After Abimelech, Tola son of Puah son of Dodo, a man of Issachar, who lived at Shamir in the hill country of Ephraim, rose to deliver Israel. 2 He judged Israel twenty-three years. Then he died, and was buried at Shamir.

3 After him came Jair the Gileadite, who judged Israel twenty-two years. 4 He had thirty sons who rode on thirty donkeys; and they had thirty towns, which are in the land of Gilead, and are called Havvoth-jair to this day. 5 Jair died, and was buried in Kamon.

6 The Israelites again did what was evil in the sight of the LORD, worshiping the Baals and the Astartes, the gods of Aram, the gods of Sidon, the gods of Moab, the gods of the Ammonites, and the gods of the Philistines. Thus they abandoned the LORD, and did not worship him. 7 So the anger of the LORD was kindled against Israel, and he sold them into the hand of the Philistines and into the hand of the Ammonites, 8 and they crushed and oppressed the Israelites that year. For eighteen years they oppressed all the Israelites that were beyond the Jordan in the land of the Amorites, which is in Gilead. 9 The Ammonites also crossed the Jordan to fight against Judah and against Benjamin and against the house of Ephraim; so that Israel was greatly distressed.

10 So the Israelites cried to the LORD, saying, "We have sinned against you, because we have abandoned our God and have worshiped the Baals." 11 And the LORD said to the Israelites, "Did I not deliver you[a] from the Egyptians and from the Amorites, from the Ammonites and from the Philistines? 12 The Sidonians also, and the Amalekites, and the Maonites, oppressed you; and you cried to me, and I

a Heb lacks *Did I not deliver you*

ca. 10 km (6 mi) north-northeast of Shechem. **56–57:** It was God who brought retribution on Abimelech and the Shechemites.

10.1–2: Minor judge: Tola. Tola *deliver*ed *Israel.* Terminology used only of Othniel, Shamgar, and Deborah, though here there is no mention of an oppressor. The names *Tola* and *Puah* are clan names in 1 Chr 7.1. *Shamir* is identified by some scholars as Samaria (see 1 Kings 16.24).

10.3–5: Minor judge: Jair. 4: Jair was a powerful man. To have *thirty sons* requires a harem, and these sons become rulers over *thirty towns* (cf. Num 32.41; 1 Chr 2.22). Monarchs often rode on donkeys (2 Sam 13.29; 18.9; 1 Kings 1.33; Zech 9.9 [cf. Mt 21.5]; cf. Judg 12.14).

10.6–12.7: Major judge cycle: Jephthah. The Transjordanian setting is unique in Judges. The story unfolds as a series of crises. Though Jephthah saved Israel, he faced a personal tragedy of his own doing because of his victory.

10.6–16: The Deuteronomistic introduction. Israel's problems resulted from its infidelity toward the LORD. **6:** Seven groups of deities are listed. **10:** This act of repentance in 10.16 is the only such act in the book. **11:** Seven oppressors, not all of which the book narrates. **12:** *Amalekites* and *Maonites,* from southern Transjordan. **13:** God's refusal to deliver Israel showed the degree of Israel's failures. This was

delivered you out of their hand. 13 Yet you
have abandoned me and worshiped other
gods; therefore I will deliver you no more.
14 Go and cry to the gods whom you have
chosen; let them deliver you in the time of
your distress." 15 And the Israelites said to
the LORD, "We have sinned; do to us what-
ever seems good to you; but deliver us this
day!" 16 So they put away the foreign gods
from among them and worshiped the
LORD; and he could no longer bear to see
Israel suffer.
17 Then the Ammonites were called to
arms, and they encamped in Gilead; and
the Israelites came together, and they en-
camped at Mizpah. 18 The commanders of
the people of Gilead said to one another,
"Who will begin the fight against the Am-
monites? He shall be head over all the in-
habitants of Gilead."

11 Now Jephthah the Gileadite, the
son of a prostitute, was a mighty
warrior. Gilead was the father of Jephthah.
2 Gilead's wife also bore him sons; and
when his wife's sons grew up, they drove
Jephthah away, saying to him, "You shall
not inherit anything in our father's house;
for you are the son of another woman."
3 Then Jephthah fled from his brothers and
lived in the land of Tob. Outlaws collected
around Jephthah and went raiding with
him.
4 After a time the Ammonites made war
against Israel. 5 And when the Ammonites
made war against Israel, the elders of Gile-
ad went to bring Jephthah from the land of
Tob. 6 They said to Jephthah, "Come and
be our commander, so that we may fight
with the Ammonites." 7 But Jephthah said
to the elders of Gilead, "Are you not the
very ones who rejected me and drove me
out of my father's house? So why do you
come to me now when you are in trouble?"
8 The elders of Gilead said to Jephthah,
"Nevertheless, we have now turned back to
you, so that you may go with us and fight
with the Ammonites, and become head
over us, over all the inhabitants of Gilead."
9 Jephthah said to the elders of Gilead, "If
you bring me home again to fight with the
Ammonites, and the LORD gives them over
to me, I will be your head." 10 And the el-
ders of Gilead said to Jephthah, "The LORD
will be witness between us; we will surely
do as you say." 11 So Jephthah went with
the elders of Gilead, and the people made
him head and commander over them; and
Jephthah spoke all his words before the
LORD at Mizpah.
12 Then Jephthah sent messengers to the
king of the Ammonites and said, "What is
there between you and me, that you have
come to me to fight against my land?"
13 The king of the Ammonites answered the
messengers of Jephthah, "Because Israel,
on coming from Egypt, took away my land
from the Arnon to the Jabbok and to the
Jordan; now therefore restore it peace-
ably." 14 Once again Jephthah sent messen-
gers to the king of the Ammonites 15 and
said to him: "Thus says Jephthah: Israel did
not take away the land of Moab or the land
of the Ammonites, 16 but when they came
up from Egypt, Israel went through the wil-

a harbinger of the tragedy to come, since God was not swayed even by a claim of repentance. Jephthah does, however, save them.

10.17–11.11: The elders' choice of Jephthah. The Israelites considered their problem to be a military one, so they chose an accomplished military leader. Because of Jephthah's previous experience with the Gileadites (having been disinherited and banished), he accepted their commission only on his terms. A ritual at Mizpah sealed the commission. **11.3:** *Tob,* a small town east of Gilead, in the territory of Aram (Syria). **4:** *The Ammonites,* a Transjordanian people traditionally identified as descendants of Lot (Gen 19.38). **5:** *Gilead,* the territory east of the Jordan River, west of the Ammonite border. **11:** *Head and commander,* the title "commander" was apparently a lesser title, probably less permanent than the title "head." While the elders attempted to get Jephthah cheap, he held out for both titles. *Mizpah* (lit. "watchtower") in Gilead (11.29), not in Benjamin (20.1).

11.12–28: Jephthah attempts diplomacy with the Ammonite king. Religious beliefs and historical precedents were the bases of the claims of Israel and the counterclaims of Ammon. **17:** Num 20.14–21.

derness to the Red Sea[a] and came to Ka-
desh. 17 Israel then sent messengers to the
king of Edom, saying, 'Let us pass through
your land'; but the king of Edom would not
listen. They also sent to the king of Moab,
but he would not consent. So Israel re-
mained at Kadesh. 18 Then they journeyed
through the wilderness, went around the
land of Edom and the land of Moab, ar-
rived on the east side of the land of Moab,
and camped on the other side of the Arnon.
They did not enter the territory of Moab,
for the Arnon was the boundary of Moab.
19 Israel then sent messengers to King Sihon
of the Amorites, king of Heshbon; and Isra-
el said to him, 'Let us pass through your
land to our country.' 20 But Sihon did not
trust Israel to pass through his territory; so
Sihon gathered all his people together, and
encamped at Jahaz, and fought with Israel.
21 Then the LORD, the God of Israel, gave
Sihon and all his people into the hand of
Israel, and they defeated them; so Israel oc-
cupied all the land of the Amorites, who
inhabited that country. 22 They occupied all
the territory of the Amorites from the Ar-
non to the Jabbok and from the wilderness
to the Jordan. 23 So now the LORD, the God
of Israel, has conquered the Amorites for
the benefit of his people Israel. Do you in-
tend to take their place? 24 Should you not
possess what your god Chemosh gives you
to possess? And should we not be the ones
to possess everything that the LORD our
God has conquered for our benefit? 25 Now
are you any better than King Balak son of
Zippor of Moab? Did he ever enter into
conflict with Israel, or did he ever go to war
with them? 26 While Israel lived in Heshbon
and its villages, and in Aroer and its vil-
lages, and in all the towns that are along
the Arnon, three hundred years, why did
you not recover them within that time? 27 It
is not I who have sinned against you, but
you are the one who does me wrong by
making war on me. Let the LORD, who is
judge, decide today for the Israelites or for
the Ammonites." 28 But the king of the Am-
monites did not heed the message that
Jephthah sent him.

29 Then the spirit of the LORD came
upon Jephthah, and he passed through Gil-
ead and Manasseh. He passed on to Miz-
pah of Gilead, and from Mizpah of Gilead
he passed on to the Ammonites. 30 And
Jephthah made a vow to the LORD, and
said, "If you will give the Ammonites into
my hand, 31 then whoever comes out of the
doors of my house to meet me, when I re-
turn victorious from the Ammonites, shall
be the LORD's, to be offered up by me as
a burnt offering." 32 So Jephthah crossed
over to the Ammonites to fight against
them; and the LORD gave them into his
hand. 33 He inflicted a massive defeat on
them from Aroer to the neighborhood of
Minnith, twenty towns, and as far as Abel-
keramim. So the Ammonites were subdued
before the people of Israel.

34 Then Jephthah came to his home at
Mizpah; and there was his daughter com-
ing out to meet him with timbrels and with

a Or *Sea of Reeds*

19–23: Num 21.21–32. **24:** *Chemosh* was the national god of the Moabites, while the god of the Ammonites was Milcom or Molech (1 Kings 11.5–7). The reason for the confusion here is unclear. The LORD gave the Ammonites their allotment according to Deut 2.19. **25:** *Balak,* see Num 22–24. **28:** The Ammonites reject the Israelite contention that the fact of conquest determines the legitimacy of a territorial claim.

11.29–40: Jephthath's vow is the centerpiece of this story; the outcome of the battle with Ammon is almost an aside. **29:** The coming of *the spirit of the LORD* upon Jephthah should have been the guarantee of victory. **30–36:** Jephthah promises a burnt offering in exchange for victory. It is unclear if v. 31 should be translated *whoever,* or whatever, *comes out of the doors of my house to meet me.* Given the arrangement of homes with courtyards that housed domesticated animals, Jephthah may have intended that one of these animals would be encountered first upon his return home. Nevertheless, it was a distinct possibility that it would be a human being, especially his daughter, given the prominence of women in military victory rituals (see 5.1–31n.). **33:** The locations of the sites are uncertain. **37–38:** Because a woman could

dancing. She was his only child; he had no
son or daughter except her. 35 When he saw
her, he tore his clothes, and said, "Alas, my
daughter! You have brought me very low;
you have become the cause of great trouble
to me. For I have opened my mouth to the
LORD, and I cannot take back my vow."
36 She said to him, "My father, if you have
opened your mouth to the LORD, do to me
according to what has gone out of your
mouth, now that the LORD has given you
vengeance against your enemies, the Am-
monites." 37 And she said to her father,
"Let this thing be done for me: Grant me
two months, so that I may go and wander[a]
on the mountains, and bewail my virginity,
my companions and I." 38 "Go," he said
and sent her away for two months. So she
departed, she and her companions, and be-
wailed her virginity on the mountains. 39 At
the end of two months, she returned to her
father, who did with her according to the
vow he had made. She had never slept with
a man. So there arose an Israelite custom
that 40 for four days every year the daugh-
ters of Israel would go out to lament the
daughter of Jephthah the Gileadite.

12 The men of Ephraim were called to
arms, and they crossed to Zaphon
and said to Jephthah, "Why did you cross
over to fight against the Ammonites, and
did not call us to go with you? We will burn
your house down over you!" 2 Jephthah
said to them, "My people and I were en-
gaged in conflict with the Ammonites who
oppressed us[b] severely. But when I called
you, you did not deliver me from their
hand. 3 When I saw that you would not de-
liver me, I took my life in my hand, and
crossed over against the Ammonites, and
the LORD gave them into my hand. Why
then have you come up to me this day, to
fight against me?" 4 Then Jephthah gath-
ered all the men of Gilead and fought with
Ephraim; and the men of Gilead defeated
Ephraim, because they said, "You are fugi-
tives from Ephraim, you Gileadites—in the
heart of Ephraim and Manasseh."[c] 5 Then
the Gileadites took the fords of the Jordan
against the Ephraimites. Whenever one of
the fugitives of Ephraim said, "Let me go
over," the men of Gilead would say to him,
"Are you an Ephraimite?" When he said,
"No," 6 they said to him, "Then say Shib-
boleth," and he said, "Sibboleth," for he
could not pronounce it right. Then they
seized him and killed him at the fords of the
Jordan. Forty-two thousand of the Ephra-
imites fell at that time.

7 Jephthah judged Israel six years. Then
Jephthah the Gileadite died, and was bur-
ied in his town in Gilead.[d]

8 After him Ibzan of Bethlehem judged
Israel. 9 He had thirty sons. He gave his
thirty daughters in marriage outside his
clan and brought in thirty young women

a Cn: Heb *go down* *b* Gk OL, Syr H: Heb lacks *who oppressed us* *c* Meaning of Heb uncertain: Gk omits *because . . . Manasseh* *d* Gk: Heb *in the towns of Gilead*

suffer no greater disgrace than to die childless, Jephthah's daughter asks for time to *bewail* her *virginity.* She thus moves from victim to actor. **39–40:** Ironically, Molech was worshiped by child sacrifice (cf. Lev 18.21; 20.2–5). Thus Jephthah delivers the Israelites from the Ammonites, who sacrifice their children to Molech; and then he sacrifices his own daughter.

12.1–7: Objections of the Ephraimites. The Ephraimites are depicted as upstarts who want to be included where they do not belong. Perhaps they are upset that they will miss out on some of the plunder from Jephthah's victory. Note their earlier complaint to Gideon (8.1–3). **4:** *Fugitives from Ephraim,* an insult to the Gileadites' legitimacy as Israelites (cf. Josh 22), a taunt particularly personal to Jephthah (11.1–2). The LORD's noninvolvement shows that this is an intertribal feud that God has not sanctioned. The episode anticipates chs 19–21. **6:** The meaning of the word *Shibboleth* is uncertain, probably "ear of wheat," or possibly "current of water." The word was chosen because it exposed the inability of the Ephraimites to pronounce it.

12.8–10: Minor judge: Ibzan. 8: *Bethlehem* is understood by most scholars to refer to the northern Bethlehem of Josh 19.15, on the Asher-Zebulun border. **9:** After Jephthah's barrenness comes Ibzan's fecundity, which underscores the tragedy of 11.34–40. The number *thirty* recalls Jair (10.4). Ibzan

from outside for his sons. He judged Israel
seven years. 10 Then Ibzan died, and was
buried at Bethlehem.
11 After him Elon the Zebulunite judged
Israel; and he judged Israel ten years.
12 Then Elon the Zebulunite died, and was
buried at Aijalon in the land of Zebulun.
13 After him Abdon son of Hillel the
Pirathonite judged Israel. 14 He had forty
sons and thirty grandsons, who rode on
seventy donkeys; he judged Israel eight
years. 15 Then Abdon son of Hillel the Pira-
thonite died, and was buried at Pirathon in
the land of Ephraim, in the hill country of
the Amalekites.

13 The Israelites again did what was
evil in the sight of the LORD, and the
LORD gave them into the hand of the Philis-
tines forty years.
2 There was a certain man of Zorah, of
the tribe of the Danites, whose name was
Manoah. His wife was barren, having
borne no children. 3 And the angel of the
LORD appeared to the woman and said to
her, "Although you are barren, having
borne no children, you shall conceive and
bear a son. 4 Now be careful not to drink
wine or strong drink, or to eat anything
unclean, 5 for you shall conceive and bear a
son. No razor is to come on his head, for
the boy shall be a nazirite[a] to God from
birth. It is he who shall begin to deliver
Israel from the hand of the Philistines."
6 Then the woman came and told her hus-
band, "A man of God came to me, and his
appearance was like that of an angel[b] of
God, most awe-inspiring; I did not ask him
where he came from, and he did not tell me
his name; 7 but he said to me, 'You shall
conceive and bear a son. So then drink no
wine or strong drink, and eat nothing un-
clean, for the boy shall be a nazirite[a] to
God from birth to the day of his death.'"
8 Then Manoah entreated the LORD,
and said, "O LORD, I pray, let the man of

a That is *one separated* or *one consecrated* *b* Or *the angel*

deliberately arranges marriages for all of his children to individuals outside his clan, securing his power base.

12.11–12: Minor judge: Elon. The name Elon is also that of a clan in the tribe of Zebulun (Gen 46.14; Num 26.26).

12.13–15: Minor judge: Abdon. Like Jair's sons, Abdon's sons ride on donkeys, evidence that their power over the region approaches that of kingship (10.4n.). But Abdon has extended the control to another generation. The *forty* and *thirty* is reminiscent of Gideon's seventy (8.30). Ironically, Abdon is buried not in "Israel," but *in the hill country of the Amalekites.*

13.1–16.31: Major judge cycle: Samson. The final "deliverer" is the moral nadir of the major judges. He broke his nazirite vows, had intercourse with non-Israelite women, never associated with other Israelites in his conflicts with the Philistines, and did not deliver the Israelites from the Philistine oppression.

13.1–25: Samson's birth. Divine appearances to Samson's parents lead to his birth. **1:** *The Philistines* were of Aegean origin, part of the large movements of Sea Peoples at the beginning of the twelfth century BCE. Prophetic tradition identified Caphtor (Crete) as their precise place of origin (see Am 9.7; Jer 47.4). **2:** *Zorah,* a town on the border between Judah and Dan (Josh 15.33; 19.41). Here the *Danites* are a southern tribe. Their migration to the north is described later, in chs 17–18. The Samson stories illustrate some of the reasons for the migration. Commonly in the cycles, the Israelites "cry out to the LORD." But in the Samson cycle, they show no indication of even wanting to be delivered. **3–7:** *The angel of the LORD,* the first theophany of the LORD to Samson's mother (see 2.1–5; 6.11–24). Any Israelite, male or female, could take a nazirite vow (Num 6.1–21), a lifestyle dedicated to the LORD's service. **4:** The requirement that the *nazirite* abstain from wine is extended to prenatal care (13.7). **6–7:** Samson's mother only perceived this to be a divine being, not the angel of the LORD, the LORD himself. The Hebrew allows for the possibility that this angel has fathered Samson (cf. Gen 6.1–4), explaining his supernatural strength. **8–23:** The second theophany of the LORD also comes to Samson's mother, not Manoah. No additional revelation about Samson is communicated in the second visit, which is unnecessary, except to

God whom you sent come to us again and
teach us what we are to do concerning the
boy who will be born." 9 God listened to
Manoah, and the angel of God came again
to the woman as she sat in the field; but her
husband Manoah was not with her. 10 So
the woman ran quickly and told her hus-
band, "The man who came to me the other
day has appeared to me." 11 Manoah got
up and followed his wife, and came to the
man and said to him, "Are you the man
who spoke to this woman?" And he said, "I
am." 12 Then Manoah said, "Now when
your words come true, what is to be the
boy's rule of life; what is he to do?" 13 The
angel of the LORD said to Manoah, "Let
the woman give heed to all that I said to
her. 14 She may not eat of anything that
comes from the vine. She is not to drink
wine or strong drink, or eat any unclean
thing. She is to observe everything that I
commanded her."

15 Manoah said to the angel of the
LORD, "Allow us to detain you, and pre-
pare a kid for you." 16 The angel of the
LORD said to Manoah, "If you detain me, I
will not eat your food; but if you want to
prepare a burnt offering, then offer it to the
LORD." (For Manoah did not know that he
was the angel of the LORD.) 17 Then Mano-
ah said to the angel of the LORD, "What
is your name, so that we may honor you
when your words come true?" 18 But the
angel of the LORD said to him, "Why do
you ask my name? It is too wonderful."

19 So Manoah took the kid with the
grain offering, and offered it on the rock to
the LORD, to him who works[a] wonders.[b]
20 When the flame went up toward heaven
from the altar, the angel of the LORD as-
cended in the flame of the altar while Ma-
noah and his wife looked on; and they fell
on their faces to the ground. 21 The angel of
the LORD did not appear again to Manoah
and his wife. Then Manoah realized that it
was the angel of the LORD. 22 And Manoah
said to his wife, "We shall surely die, for we
have seen God." 23 But his wife said to him,
"If the LORD had meant to kill us, he would
not have accepted a burnt offering and a
grain offering at our hands, or shown us all
these things, or now announced to us such
things as these."

24 The woman bore a son, and named
him Samson. The boy grew, and the LORD
blessed him. 25 The spirit of the LORD be-
gan to stir him in Mahaneh-dan, between
Zorah and Eshtaol.

14 Once Samson went down to Tim-
nah, and at Timnah he saw a Philis-
tine woman. 2 Then he came up, and told
his father and mother, "I saw a Philistine
woman at Timnah; now get her for me as
my wife." 3 But his father and mother said
to him, "Is there not a woman among your
kin, or among all our[c] people, that you
must go to take a wife from the uncircum-
cised Philistines?" But Samson said to his
father, "Get her for me, because she pleases
me." 4 His father and mother did not know
that this was from the LORD; for he was

a Gk Vg: Heb *and working* *b* Heb *wonders, while Manoah and his wife looked on* *c* Cn: Heb *my*

characterize Manoah negatively. **15–23:** Manoah's hospitality parallels that of Gideon (6.11–24), although the reassurance comes from Manoah's wife, who chides him for not comprehending the purpose of the divine visit (13.23). **18:** *Wonderful,* a word used in a similar revelatory context, Gen 18.14. **24:** *Samson,* a name related to the Hebrew word for sun, and perhaps not a Yahwistic name. **25:** *Mahaneh-dan, between Zorah and Eshtaol,* the location of Mahaneh-dan is problematic. Here it is between Zorah and Eshtaol, in western Judah; in 18.12, it is west of Kiriath-jearim, farther north. This latter occurrence may not be a place name, but may simply mean "camp of Dan."

14.1–20: Samson's wedding. The stories about Samson reveal that he was a judge who chased women instead of enemies and who avenged only personal grievances. **1:** *Timnah* may be Tell el-Batashi, 7 km (4 mi) northwest of Beth-shemesh. **2:** Samson is a man dominated by his senses, not logic. **3:** Cf. Gen 24.4; 28.1–2. Samson's marriage to a non-Israelite will cause all of the events of 14.5–15.19. **4:** An editorial comment reflecting the belief that God can use human sin and folly to accomplish his divine purpose. In other words, God used Samson in spite of his wrong motives and actions (cf. Gen 50.20).

seeking a pretext to act against the Philis-
tines. At that time the Philistines had do-
minion over Israel.
5 Then Samson went down with his fa-
ther and mother to Timnah. When he came
to the vineyards of Timnah, suddenly a
young lion roared at him. 6 The spirit of the
LORD rushed on him, and he tore the lion
apart barehanded as one might tear apart a
kid. But he did not tell his father or his
mother what he had done. 7 Then he went
down and talked with the woman, and she
pleased Samson. 8 After a while he returned
to marry her, and he turned aside to see the
carcass of the lion, and there was a swarm
of bees in the body of the lion, and honey.
9 He scraped it out into his hands, and went
on, eating as he went. When he came to his
father and mother, he gave some to them,
and they ate it. But he did not tell them that
he had taken the honey from the carcass of
the lion.
10 His father went down to the woman,
and Samson made a feast there as the
young men were accustomed to do.
11 When the people saw him, they brought
thirty companions to be with him. 12 Sam-
son said to them, "Let me now put a riddle
to you. If you can explain it to me within
the seven days of the feast, and find it out,
then I will give you thirty linen garments
and thirty festal garments. 13 But if you can-
not explain it to me, then you shall give me
thirty linen garments and thirty festal gar-
ments." So they said to him, "Ask your rid-
dle; let us hear it." 14 He said to them,

"Out of the eater came something to
eat.
Out of the strong came something
sweet."

But for three days they could not explain
the riddle.
15 On the fourth[a] day they said to Sam-
son's wife, "Coax your husband to explain
the riddle to us, or we will burn you and
your father's house with fire. Have you in-
vited us here to impoverish us?" 16 So Sam-
son's wife wept before him, saying, "You
hate me; you do not really love me. You
have asked a riddle of my people, but you
have not explained it to me." He said to
her, "Look, I have not told my father or my
mother. Why should I tell you?" 17 She
wept before him the seven days that their
feast lasted; and because she nagged him,
on the seventh day he told her. Then she
explained the riddle to her people. 18 The
men of the town said to him on the seventh
day before the sun went down,

"What is sweeter than honey?
What is stronger than a lion?"

And he said to them,

"If you had not plowed with my
heifer,
you would not have found out my
riddle."

19 Then the spirit of the LORD rushed on
him, and he went down to Ashkelon. He
killed thirty men of the town, took their
spoil, and gave the festal garments to those
who had explained the riddle. In hot anger
he went back to his father's house. 20 And
Samson's wife was given to his companion,
who had been his best man.

15 After a while, at the time of the
wheat harvest, Samson went to visit
his wife, bringing along a kid. He said, "I
want to go into my wife's room." But her

a Gk Syr: Heb *seventh*

6: *He did not tell his father or his mother,* defilement of a nazirite through uncleanness required an eight-day purification ritual (Num 6.9–12), a ritual that Samson did not want to perform. **8–9:** A flagrant violation of his nazirite status and a careless defiling of his parents. **10–18:** The hostility between Samson and the Philistines flared up because of verbal jousting between Samson and his guests; many of these riddles and responses may have sexual overtones. Samson proposed a riddle that could not be solved, or so he thought. Samson's bride betrayed him (anticipatory of Delilah). **19:** *Ashkelon,* a Mediterranean coastal city, one of the five main Philistine cities. Samson murdered thirty men and robbed them of their clothing just to pay his debts to his wedding companions. His unbridled anger sets the stage for his bride being given to another (14.20).

15.1–20: Samson's revenge. Samson's anger after his wife was given to another man led him to destroy

father would not allow him to go in. 2Her
father said, "I was sure that you had reject-
ed her; so I gave her to your companion. Is
not her younger sister prettier than she?
Why not take her instead?" 3Samson said
to them, "This time, when I do mischief to
the Philistines, I will be without blame."
4So Samson went and caught three hun-
dred foxes, and took some torches; and he
turned the foxes[a] tail to tail, and put a
torch between each pair of tails. 5When he
had set fire to the torches, he let the foxes
go into the standing grain of the Philistines,
and burned up the shocks and the standing
grain, as well as the vineyards and[b] olive
groves. 6Then the Philistines asked, "Who
has done this?" And they said, "Samson,
the son-in-law of the Timnite, because he
has taken Samson's wife and given her to
his companion." So the Philistines came up,
and burned her and her father. 7Samson
said to them, "If this is what you do, I
swear I will not stop until I have taken re-
venge on you." 8He struck them down hip
and thigh with great slaughter; and he went
down and stayed in the cleft of the rock of
Etam.

9 Then the Philistines came up and en-
camped in Judah, and made a raid on Lehi.
10The men of Judah said, "Why have you
come up against us?" They said, "We have
come up to bind Samson, to do to him as he
did to us." 11Then three thousand men of
Judah went down to the cleft of the rock of
Etam, and they said to Samson, "Do you
not know that the Philistines are rulers over
us? What then have you done to us?" He
replied, "As they did to me, so I have done
to them." 12They said to him, "We have
come down to bind you, so that we may
give you into the hands of the Philistines."
Samson answered them, "Swear to me that
you yourselves will not attack me." 13They
said to him, "No, we will only bind you
and give you into their hands; we will not
kill you." So they bound him with two new
ropes, and brought him up from the rock.

14 When he came to Lehi, the Philistines
came shouting to meet him; and the spirit
of the LORD rushed on him, and the ropes
that were on his arms became like flax that
has caught fire, and his bonds melted off
his hands. 15Then he found a fresh jaw-
bone of a donkey, reached down and took
it, and with it he killed a thousand men.
16And Samson said,

"With the jawbone of a donkey,
  heaps upon heaps,
with the jawbone of a donkey
  I have slain a thousand men."

17When he had finished speaking, he threw
away the jawbone; and that place was
called Ramath-lehi.[c]

18 By then he was very thirsty, and he
called on the LORD, saying, "You have
granted this great victory by the hand of
your servant. Am I now to die of thirst, and
fall into the hands of the uncircumcised?"
19So God split open the hollow place that is
at Lehi, and water came from it. When he
drank, his spirit returned, and he revived.
Therefore it was named En-hakkore,[d]

a Heb *them* *b* Gk Tg Vg: Heb lacks *and* *c* That is *The Hill of the Jawbone* *d* That is *The Spring of the One who Called*

the Philistines' grain crop. This began a cycle of revenge with escalating violence between Samson and the Philistines. **1:** *A kid,* a substantial gift, reflecting his desire for reconciliation. **4:** A great physical feat, but purely for personal revenge and counter to the law (Ex 22.6). **6:** Samson's arson leads, in the measure-for-measure structure of this unit, to the incineration of his wife and father-in-law by the Philistines. **8:** *Etam* cannot be located with certainty. *Hip and thigh,* a formulaic expression describing complete devastation. **9–13:** The people of Judah refuse to provide Samson with sanctuary and even attempt to apprehend Samson for the Philistines. For the Philistines, the Judahites, and Samson, the only thing that matters is reprisal and counterreprisal. The location of *Lehi* (v. 9) is unknown. **14–17:** Another great feat motivated by personal revenge. **15:** The *fresh jawbone of a donkey,* an improvised weapon (like Shamgar, 3.31); however, it was probably ritually unclean. **16:** The couplet involves a pun, for the same Hebrew word can mean both *donkey* and *heap.* **18–19:** Samson's first prayer, phrased as a demand for water (cf. Israel's

which is at Lehi to this day. 20 And he
judged Israel in the days of the Philistines
twenty years.

16 Once Samson went to Gaza, where
he saw a prostitute and went in to
her. 2 The Gazites were told,[a] "Samson has
come here." So they circled around and lay
in wait for him all night at the city gate.
They kept quiet all night, thinking, "Let us
wait until the light of the morning; then we
will kill him." 3 But Samson lay only until
midnight. Then at midnight he rose up,
took hold of the doors of the city gate and
the two posts, pulled them up, bar and all,
put them on his shoulders, and carried
them to the top of the hill that is in front of
Hebron.

4 After this he fell in love with a woman
in the valley of Sorek, whose name was De-
lilah. 5 The lords of the Philistines came to
her and said to her, "Coax him, and find
out what makes his strength so great, and
how we may overpower him, so that we
may bind him in order to subdue him; and
we will each give you eleven hundred pieces
of silver." 6 So Delilah said to Samson,
"Please tell me what makes your strength
so great, and how you could be bound, so
that one could subdue you." 7 Samson said
to her, "If they bind me with seven fresh
bowstrings that are not dried out, then I
shall become weak, and be like anyone
else." 8 Then the lords of the Philistines
brought her seven fresh bowstrings that
had not dried out, and she bound him with
them. 9 While men were lying in wait in an
inner chamber, she said to him, "The Phil-
istines are upon you, Samson!" But he
snapped the bowstrings, as a strand of fiber
snaps when it touches the fire. So the secret
of his strength was not known.

10 Then Delilah said to Samson, "You
have mocked me and told me lies; please
tell me how you could be bound." 11 He
said to her, "If they bind me with new
ropes that have not been used, then I shall
become weak, and be like anyone else."
12 So Delilah took new ropes and bound
him with them, and said to him, "The Phil-
istines are upon you, Samson!" (The men
lying in wait were in an inner chamber.)
But he snapped the ropes off his arms like
a thread.

13 Then Delilah said to Samson, "Until
now you have mocked me and told me lies;
tell me how you could be bound." He said
to her, "If you weave the seven locks of my
head with the web and make it tight with
the pin, then I shall become weak, and be
like anyone else." 14 So while he slept, Deli-
lah took the seven locks of his head and
wove them into the web,[b] and made them
tight with the pin. Then she said to him,
"The Philistines are upon you, Samson!"
But he awoke from his sleep, and pulled
away the pin, the loom, and the web.

15 Then she said to him, "How can you
say, 'I love you,' when your heart is not
with me? You have mocked me three times
now and have not told me what makes
your strength so great." 16 Finally, after she
had nagged him with her words day after

a Gk: Heb lacks *were told* *b* Compare Gk: in verses 13-14, Heb lacks *and make it tight . . . into the web*

demands in the wilderness, Ex 17.1–7; Num 20.2–13). **20:** An editorial comment to authenticate Samson as a judge. Such comments are typically found at the end of the judge's narrative.

16.1–31: Samson's death. Samson's weakness for women leads to his betrayal and death. **1–3:** The incident with the prostitute of Gaza. **1:** *Gaza,* the southernmost Philistine coastal city. Samson's trek to this city is deliberate, i.e., for his own gratification. **3:** A great feat, again for personal motives. The distance from Gaza to Hebron is 65 km (40 mi) and involves a considerable ascent. Here he escapes from Gaza; in 16.21 he will be enslaved in Gaza. **4–22:** The Delilah incident. **4:** The *valley of Sorek* is the modern Wadi-es-Sarar that begins west of Jerusalem. The name *Delilah* may be related to an Arabic root that means "flirt." While the text does not say that she was a Philistine, Samson has demonstrated a distinct preference for "foreign" Philistine women, not Israelites. **5:** *The lords* (lit. "the tyrants") *of the Philistines* make the most of this opportunity. **6–21:** Four times, Delilah unleashes a verbal attack on Samson in order to subdue him and receive her payment. **13:** *The web* and *the pin* were parts of a loom.

day, and pestered him, he was tired to
death. 17 So he told her his whole secret,
and said to her, "A razor has never come
upon my head; for I have been a nazirite[a]
to God from my mother's womb. If my
head were shaved, then my strength would
leave me; I would become weak, and be like
anyone else."
18 When Delilah realized that he had
told her his whole secret, she sent and
called the lords of the Philistines, saying,
"This time come up, for he has told his
whole secret to me." Then the lords of the
Philistines came up to her, and brought the
money in their hands. 19 She let him fall
asleep on her lap; and she called a man, and
had him shave off the seven locks of his
head. He began to weaken,[b] and his
strength left him. 20 Then she said, "The
Philistines are upon you, Samson!" When
he awoke from his sleep, he thought, "I will
go out as at other times, and shake myself
free." But he did not know that the LORD
had left him. 21 So the Philistines seized him
and gouged out his eyes. They brought him
down to Gaza and bound him with bronze
shackles; and he ground at the mill in the
prison. 22 But the hair of his head began to
grow again after it had been shaved.
23 Now the lords of the Philistines gath-
ered to offer a great sacrifice to their god
Dagon, and to rejoice; for they said, "Our
god has given Samson our enemy into our
hand." 24 When the people saw him, they
praised their god; for they said, "Our god
has given our enemy into our hand, the rav-
ager of our country, who has killed many
of us." 25 And when their hearts were mer-
ry, they said, "Call Samson, and let him
entertain us." So they called Samson out
of the prison, and he performed for them.
They made him stand between the pillars;
26 and Samson said to the attendant who
held him by the hand, "Let me feel the pil-
lars on which the house rests, so that I may
lean against them." 27 Now the house was
full of men and women; all the lords of the
Philistines were there, and on the roof there
were about three thousand men and wom-
en, who looked on while Samson per-
formed.
28 Then Samson called to the LORD and
said, "Lord GOD, remember me and
strengthen me only this once, O God, so
that with this one act of revenge I may pay
back the Philistines for my two eyes."[c]
29 And Samson grasped the two middle pil-
lars on which the house rested, and he
leaned his weight against them, his right
hand on the one and his left hand on the
other. 30 Then Samson said, "Let me die
with the Philistines." He strained with all
his might; and the house fell on the lords
and all the people who were in it. So those
he killed at his death were more than those
he had killed during his life. 31 Then his
brothers and all his family came down and
took him and brought him up and buried
him between Zorah and Eshtaol in the
tomb of his father Manoah. He had judged
Israel twenty years.

17 There was a man in the hill country
of Ephraim whose name was Mi-

a That is *one separated* or *one consecrated*
b Gk: Heb *She began to torment him* *c* Or *so that I may be avenged upon the Philistines for one of my two eyes*

17: As with his Timnite wife (14.15–17), Samson succumbs and reveals the truth (cf. 13.5) to a nagging woman. **18–21:** Samson's humiliation by the Philistines: blinded and set to work grinding grain, usually considered a slave's or woman's occupation. **23–31:** Samson's final act of vengeance. **23:** *Dagon* was a Canaanite grain deity adopted by the Philistines after their migration to Canaan. **28:** Samson's second (see 15.18) and final prayer: a prayer for personal revenge.

17.1–21.25: Double conclusion. The double conclusion is symmetrical to the double introduction (see Introduction). These describe the self-destructiveness of the Israelites during the period of the judges. Judges 17–18, the first conclusion, describes the difficulties with domestic idols as Israel disintegrated religiously, and Judges 19–21, the second conclusion, describes a civil war in which the "ḥerem" was being internally applied. The refrain repeated in 17.6, 18.1, 19.1, and 21.25 (see Introduction) ties both conclusions together. These conclusions also serve as a bridge to the following books of Samuel and Kings.

cah. 2He said to his mother, "The eleven
hundred pieces of silver that were taken
from you, about which you uttered a curse,
and even spoke it in my hearing,—that sil-
ver is in my possession; I took it; but now
I will return it to you."[a] And his mother
said, "May my son be blessed by the
LORD!" 3Then he returned the eleven hun-
dred pieces of silver to his mother; and his
mother said, "I consecrate the silver to the
LORD from my hand for my son, to make
an idol of cast metal." 4So when he re-
turned the money to his mother, his mother
took two hundred pieces of silver, and gave
it to the silversmith, who made it into an
idol of cast metal; and it was in the house
of Micah. 5This man Micah had a shrine,
and he made an ephod and teraphim, and
installed one of his sons, who became his
priest. 6In those days there was no king in
Israel; all the people did what was right in
their own eyes.

7 Now there was a young man of Bethle-
hem in Judah, of the clan of Judah. He was
a Levite residing there. 8This man left the
town of Bethlehem in Judah, to live wher-
ever he could find a place. He came to
the house of Micah in the hill country of
Ephraim to carry on his work.[b] 9Micah
said to him, "From where do you come?"
He replied, "I am a Levite of Bethlehem in
Judah, and I am going to live wherever I
can find a place." 10Then Micah said to
him, "Stay with me, and be to me a father
and a priest, and I will give you ten pieces
of silver a year, a set of clothes, and your
living."[c] 11The Levite agreed to stay with
the man; and the young man became to him
like one of his sons. 12So Micah installed
the Levite, and the young man became his
priest, and was in the house of Micah.
13Then Micah said, "Now I know that the
LORD will prosper me, because the Levite
has become my priest."

18 In those days there was no king in
Israel. And in those days the tribe of
the Danites was seeking for itself a territory
to live in; for until then no territory among
the tribes of Israel had been allotted to
them. 2So the Danites sent five valiant men
from the whole number of their clan, from
Zorah and from Eshtaol, to spy out the
land and to explore it; and they said to
them, "Go, explore the land." When they

a The words *but now I will return it to you* are transposed from the end of verse 3 in Heb
b Or *Ephraim, continuing his journey* *c* Heb *living, and the Levite went*

Chs 19–21 contain several allusions to the kingship of Saul, while 17–18 focus on the illegitimate worship of the Northern Kingdom, a major theme of Kings.

17.1–18.31: Difficulties with domestic idols. The first conclusion should be read in the light of Deut 12.1–13.1, which insists on centralized worship. It is the thematic antithesis of that passage.

17.1–5: The shrine of Micah. 1: *The hill country of Ephraim* was the central highlands north of Bethel and south of Shechem. Shiloh was in this region, and the tabernacle was located there. The story begins with an ironic twist: *Micah* is an abbreviation of a name that means "who is like the LORD?" An Israelite with such a name built a shrine with an image! **2–4:** Theft and return of the silver which is used to make the image, an obvious violation of the second commandment (see Ex 20.4,23; 34.17; Lev 19.4) as well as a specific Deuteronomic curse (Deut 27.15). **5:** *A shrine,* lit. "house of god." An *ephod* was an elaborate priestly vestment (cf. 8.27), though here, used in conjunction with Teraphim, it is more likely some sort of idol. *Teraphim,* some type of household deities used for divinatory purposes (see Gen 31.19; Ezek 21.21; Zech 10.2). The installation of someone other than a Levite as a priest is a violation of priestly legislation (Ex 29.9; Num 16.10). **6:** The first occurrence of the refrain in full (see Introduction).

17.6–13: Micah's priest. An opportunistic Levite becomes Micah's priest. **7:** This *Bethlehem* (see 12.8n.) was in the territory of Judah, just south of Jerusalem. It was not a Levitical town (Josh 21.9–16).

18.1–31: The migration of the tribe of Dan. The story of the Danite migration starts with a partial repetition of the refrain. The ellipsis of the second line forces the reader to supply the thought (see 17.6 for the full refrain). The Danites could not control their allotment in the south (Judg 1.34). They abandoned this and migrated to the far north of Galilee. **1–6:** The Danites seek an oracle from the Levite serving at Micah's shrine; the Levite's oracle to them assures them of divine support. **5:** Here to *inquire*

came to the hill country of Ephraim, to the
house of Micah, they stayed there. 3 While
they were at Micah's house, they recog-
nized the voice of the young Levite; so they
went over and asked him, "Who brought
you here? What are you doing in this place?
What is your business here?" 4 He said to
them, "Micah did such and such for me,
and he hired me, and I have become his
priest." 5 Then they said to him, "Inquire of
God that we may know whether the mis-
sion we are undertaking will succeed."
6 The priest replied, "Go in peace. The mis-
sion you are on is under the eye of the
LORD."
7 The five men went on, and when they
came to Laish, they observed the people
who were there living securely, after the
manner of the Sidonians, quiet and unsus-
pecting, lacking[a] nothing on earth, and
possessing wealth.[b] Furthermore, they
were far from the Sidonians and had no
dealings with Aram.[c] 8 When they came to
their kinsfolk at Zorah and Eshtaol, they
said to them, "What do you report?"
9 They said, "Come, let us go up against
them; for we have seen the land, and it is
very good. Will you do nothing? Do not be
slow to go, but enter in and possess the
land. 10 When you go, you will come to an
unsuspecting people. The land is broad—
God has indeed given it into your hands—a
place where there is no lack of anything on
earth."
11 Six hundred men of the Danite clan,
armed with weapons of war, set out from
Zorah and Eshtaol, 12 and went up and en-
camped at Kiriath-jearim in Judah. On this
account that place is called Mahaneh-dan[d]
to this day; it is west of Kiriath-jearim.
13 From there they passed on to the hill
country of Ephraim, and came to the house
of Micah.
14 Then the five men who had gone to
spy out the land (that is, Laish) said to their
comrades, "Do you know that in these
buildings there are an ephod, teraphim, and
an idol of cast metal? Now therefore con-
sider what you will do." 15 So they turned
in that direction and came to the house of
the young Levite, at the home of Micah,
and greeted him. 16 While the six hundred
men of the Danites, armed with their weap-
ons of war, stood by the entrance of the
gate, 17 the five men who had gone to spy
out the land proceeded to enter and take
the idol of cast metal, the ephod, and the
teraphim.[e] The priest was standing by the
entrance of the gate with the six hundred
men armed with weapons of war. 18 When
the men went into Micah's house and took
the idol of cast metal, the ephod, and the
teraphim, the priest said to them, "What
are you doing?" 19 They said to him, "Keep
quiet! Put your hand over your mouth, and
come with us, and be to us a father and a
priest. Is it better for you to be priest to the
house of one person, or to be priest to a
tribe and clan in Israel?" 20 Then the priest
accepted the offer. He took the ephod, the
teraphim, and the idol, and went along
with the people.
21 So they resumed their journey, put-
ting the little ones, the livestock, and the
goods in front of them. 22 When they were
some distance from the home of Micah, the
men who were in the houses near Micah's

a Cn Compare 18.10: Meaning of Heb uncertain
b Meaning of Heb uncertain *c* Symmachus: Heb *with anyone* *d* That is *Camp of Dan* *e* Compare 17.4, 5; 18.14: Heb *teraphim and the cast metal*

of God refers to divination. **7:** *Laish* (modern Tel Dan) was a city in the upper Jordan valley at the foot of Mount Hermon. *Living securely* means "undefended." Sidon was a Phoenician city along the Mediterranean. It was too far from Laish to offer it effective protection. *Aram* was to the northeast of Laish. Without proper defenses or effective alliances Laish was easy prey. **11–26:** On their way to Laish, the Danites stole Micah's religious objects and induced his priest to join them. *Six hundred men* is reminiscent of the Philistine contingent that Shamgar defeated (Judg 3.31). **15–17:** The Danites, who properly should have destroyed Micah's shrine (according to Deut 12.2–3), instead find it worthy of acquisition, even if by means of theft. This further deprecates northern worship. **18–20:** The Levite joined the Danites, who made him a better offer. **27–31:** The Danites took Laish, renamed it, and installed Micah's images and

house were called out, and they overtook
the Danites. 23 They shouted to the Danites,
who turned around and said to Micah,
"What is the matter that you come with
such a company?" 24 He replied, "You take
my gods that I made, and the priest, and go
away, and what have I left? How then can
you ask me, 'What is the matter?' " 25 And
the Danites said to him, "You had better
not let your voice be heard among us or else
hot-tempered fellows will attack you, and
you will lose your life and the lives of your
household." 26 Then the Danites went their
way. When Micah saw that they were too
strong for him, he turned and went back to
his home.

27 The Danites, having taken what Mi-
cah had made, and the priest who belonged
to him, came to Laish, to a people quiet and
unsuspecting, put them to the sword, and
burned down the city. 28 There was no de-
liverer, because it was far from Sidon and
they had no dealings with Aram.[a] It was in
the valley that belongs to Beth-rehob. They
rebuilt the city, and lived in it. 29 They
named the city Dan, after their ancestor
Dan, who was born to Israel; but the name
of the city was formerly Laish. 30 Then the
Danites set up the idol for themselves. Jon-
athan son of Gershom, son of Moses,[b] and
his sons were priests to the tribe of the Dan-
ites until the time the land went into captiv-
ity. 31 So they maintained as their own Mi-
cah's idol that he had made, as long as the
house of God was at Shiloh.

19 In those days, when there was no
king in Israel, a certain Levite, resid-
ing in the remote parts of the hill country of
Ephraim, took to himself a concubine from
Bethlehem in Judah. 2 But his concubine be-
came angry with[c] him, and she went away
from him to her father's house at Bethle-
hem in Judah, and was there some four
months. 3 Then her husband set out after
her, to speak tenderly to her and bring her
back. He had with him his servant and a
couple of donkeys. When he reached[d] her
father's house, the girl's father saw him and
came with joy to meet him. 4 His father-in-
law, the girl's father, made him stay, and he
remained with him three days; so they ate
and drank, and he[e] stayed there. 5 On the
fourth day they got up early in the morn-
ing, and he prepared to go; but the girl's
father said to his son-in-law, "Fortify your-
self with a bit of food, and after that you
may go." 6 So the two men sat and ate and
drank together; and the girl's father said to
the man, "Why not spend the night and
enjoy yourself?" 7 When the man got up to
go, his father-in-law kept urging him until
he spent the night there again. 8 On the fifth
day he got up early in the morning to leave;
and the girl's father said, "Fortify your-
self." So they lingered[f] until the day de-

a Cn Compare verse 7: Heb *with anyone* *b* Another reading is *son of Manasseh* *c* Gk OL: Heb *prostituted herself against* *d* Gk: Heb *she brought him to* *e* Compare verse 7 and Gk: Heb *they* *f* Cn: Heb *Linger*

the Levite there. **30:** A priesthood descended from Moses is associated with this illegitimate worship at Dan (see Ex 2.22; 1 Chr 23.14–15). If the grandson (rather than descendant) of Moses is intended, this story is clearly out of chronological order. **31:** A Deuteronomistic indictment against the shrine at Dan that became an important center of worship for the Northern Kingdom (1 Kings 12.29). *Shiloh,* see 21.12n.

19.1–21.25: Domestic wars with the "ḥerem" being applied. The second conclusion opens and closes with the refrain: partial (19.1) and full (21.25) (see Introduction). The section has a chiastic structure: *A:* The rape of the concubine (19.1–30); *B:* The "ḥerem" of Benjamin (20.1–48); *C:* The oaths: Benjamin threatened with extinction (21.1–5); *B′*: The "ḥerem" of Jabesh-gilead (21.6–14); and *A′*: The rape of the daughters of Shiloh (21.15–25).

19.1–30: The rape of the concubine. 1–9: This incident set up a conflict that eventually pitted the tribal assembly against Benjamin. **2:** The woman of Bethlehem was not the full legal wife of the Levite, so the text calls her his *concubine*. Much is topsy-turvy in the story. It is the woman who initiates the separation. The Levite went to Bethlehem to recover his concubine. His father-in-law's hospitality borders on the excessive, which serves as a foil to the inhospitality found in Gibeah. **10–30:** The incident at Gibeah.

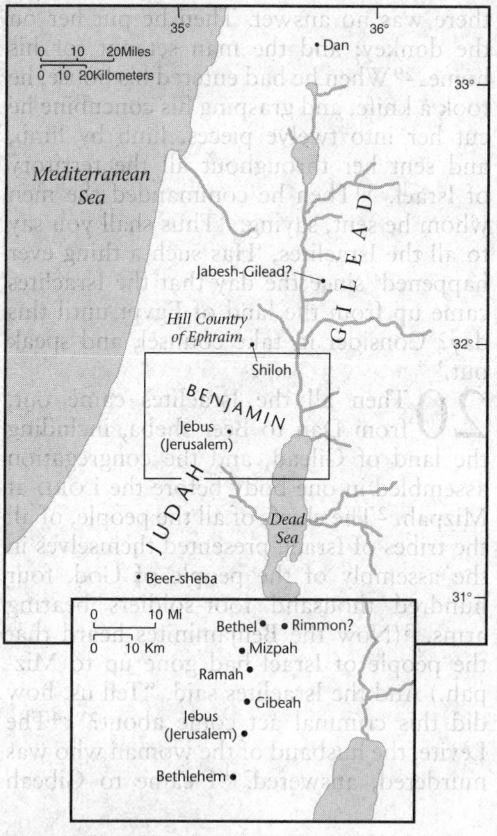

Chs 19–21: The Benjaminite War.

clined, and the two of them ate and
drank.[a] 9When the man with his concu-
bine and his servant got up to leave, his
father-in-law, the girl's father, said to him,
"Look, the day has worn on until it is al-
most evening. Spend the night. See, the day
has drawn to a close. Spend the night here
and enjoy yourself. Tomorrow you can get
up early in the morning for your journey,
and go home."
10 But the man would not spend the
night; he got up and departed, and arrived
opposite Jebus (that is, Jerusalem). He had
with him a couple of saddled donkeys, and
his concubine was with him. 11When they
were near Jebus, the day was far spent, and
the servant said to his master, "Come now,
let us turn aside to this city of the Jebusites,
and spend the night in it." 12But his master
said to him, "We will not turn aside into a
city of foreigners, who do not belong to the
people of Israel; but we will continue on to
Gibeah." 13Then he said to his servant,
"Come, let us try to reach one of these
places, and spend the night at Gibeah or at
Ramah." 14So they passed on and went
their way; and the sun went down on them
near Gibeah, which belongs to Benjamin.
15They turned aside there, to go in and
spend the night at Gibeah. He went in and
sat down in the open square of the city, but
no one took them in to spend the night.
16 Then at evening there was an old
man coming from his work in the field. The
man was from the hill country of Ephraim,
and he was residing in Gibeah. (The people
of the place were Benjaminites.) 17When
the old man looked up and saw the wayfar-
er in the open square of the city, he said,
"Where are you going and where do you
come from?" 18He answered him, "We are
passing from Bethlehem in Judah to the re-
mote parts of the hill country of Ephraim,
from which I come. I went to Bethlehem in
Judah; and I am going to my home.[b] No-
body has offered to take me in. 19We your
servants have straw and fodder for our
donkeys, with bread and wine for me and
the woman and the young man along with
us. We need nothing more." 20The old man
said, "Peace be to you. I will care for all
your wants; only do not spend the night in
the square." 21So he brought him into his
house, and fed the donkeys; they washed
their feet, and ate and drank.

a Gk: Heb lacks *and drank* *b* Gk Compare 19.29. Heb *to the house of the* LORD

10–21: The Levite prefers to spend the night in an Israelite rather than a Canaanite (or more precisely Jebusite) town. Ironically, by seeking to avoid the potential inhospitality of a foreign city, the Levite and his party suffer that very fate in Gibeah, an Israelite city. **11:** *City of the Jebusites,* see 1.21. **12:** *Gibeah* is identified with Tell el-Ful, 6 km (4 mi) north of Jerusalem. It became Saul's royal residence (1 Sam 15.34). **13:** *Ramah* is identified with er-Ram, 7 km (5 mi) north of Jerusalem. **16–21:** An old man from Ephraim finally shows hospitality and at first appears to be the model host. **22–26:** The old man's actions

22 While they were enjoying themselves,
the men of the city, a perverse lot, sur-
rounded the house, and started pounding
on the door. They said to the old man, the
master of the house, "Bring out the man
who came into your house, so that we may
have intercourse with him." 23 And the
man, the master of the house, went out to
them and said to them, "No, my brothers,
do not act so wickedly. Since this man is my
guest, do not do this vile thing. 24 Here are
my virgin daughter and his concubine; let
me bring them out now. Ravish them and
do whatever you want to them; but against
this man do not do such a vile thing." 25 But
the men would not listen to him. So the
man seized his concubine, and put her out
to them. They wantonly raped her, and
abused her all through the night until the
morning. And as the dawn began to break,
they let her go. 26 As morning appeared, the
woman came and fell down at the door of
the man's house where her master was, un-
til it was light.
27 In the morning her master got up,
opened the doors of the house, and when
he went out to go on his way, there was his
concubine lying at the door of the house,
with her hands on the threshold. 28 "Get
up," he said to her, "we are going." But
there was no answer. Then he put her on
the donkey; and the man set out for his
home. 29 When he had entered his house, he
took a knife, and grasping his concubine he
cut her into twelve pieces, limb by limb,
and sent her throughout all the territory
of Israel. 30 Then he commanded the men
whom he sent, saying, "Thus shall you say
to all the Israelites, 'Has such a thing ever
happened[a] since the day that the Israelites
came up from the land of Egypt until this
day? Consider it, take counsel, and speak
out.' "

20 Then all the Israelites came out,
from Dan to Beer-sheba, including
the land of Gilead, and the congregation
assembled in one body before the LORD at
Mizpah. 2 The chiefs of all the people, of all
the tribes of Israel, presented themselves in
the assembly of the people of God, four
hundred thousand foot-soldiers bearing
arms. 3 (Now the Benjaminites heard that
the people of Israel had gone up to Miz-
pah.) And the Israelites said, "Tell us, how
did this criminal act come about?" 4 The
Levite, the husband of the woman who was
murdered, answered, "I came to Gibeah

a Compare Gk: Heb 30 *And all who saw it said, "Such a thing has not happened or been seen*

are reminiscent of Lot's (Gen 19.1–11). The men at the door refuse to listen to the old man, so to forestall his own rape by the men of Gibeah, the Levite himself offers them his concubine. Raped, abused, and discarded, she collapses at the door of the old man's house. **27–30:** The Levite, having slept throughout the night, callously commands her to *Get up . . . we are going*. When he returns home, he takes a knife and cuts her up, limb by limb, in order to obtain his personal revenge—we are not even sure when she has died! **29:** In 1 Sam 11.7, Saul calls up the tribes of Israel in a strikingly similar fashion. This dismembering probably alludes to the ceremony of making (lit. "cutting") a covenant; see Gen 15.10–18; Jer 34.18. The inhabitants of Gibeah had violated the covenant that bound the tribes of Israel to each other.

20.1–48: The "ḥerem" of Benjamin. 1–11: The nameless Levite ironically gets the greatest response from the greatest number of tribes in Israel in all of the book of Judges. The Levite, who calls the tribes to muster by the grotesque mutilation of his concubine, has become a self-appointed judge. He is the sole witness; and he bears false witness, heightening the crime of the men of Gibeah while downplaying his own guilt. Ironically, the Levite sacrificed his concubine to save himself and now is willing to sacrifice the sons of Israel to get his personal revenge on the Gibeahites. Without any additional testimony, the tribal assembly condemns the crime against the Levite's concubine and takes steps to punish the guilty. The Levite now disappears. **1:** *Dan* was the northernmost Israelite city, while *Beer-sheba* was the southernmost. *Gilead* refers to the Transjordanian territories. *Mizpah* was the name of several Israelite towns. The one intended here was probably the Mizpah of Benjamin (Josh 18.26). It is identified with Tell en-Nasbeh, 13 km (8 mi) north of Jerusalem. **6:** *Vile outrage,* cf. 19.23; Gen 34.7; Deut 22.21; Josh 7.15; 2 Sam

that belongs to Benjamin, I and my concu-
bine, to spend the night. 5 The lords of Gib-
eah rose up against me, and surrounded the
house at night. They intended to kill me,
and they raped my concubine until she
died. 6 Then I took my concubine and cut
her into pieces, and sent her throughout the
whole extent of Israel's territory; for they
have committed a vile outrage in Israel. 7 So
now, you Israelites, all of you, give your
advice and counsel here."

8 All the people got up as one, saying,
"We will not any of us go to our tents, nor
will any of us return to our houses. 9 But
now this is what we will do to Gibeah: we
will go up[a] against it by lot. 10 We will take
ten men of a hundred throughout all the
tribes of Israel, and a hundred of a thou-
sand, and a thousand of ten thousand, to
bring provisions for the troops, who are
going to repay[b] Gibeah of Benjamin for all
the disgrace that they have done in Israel."
11 So all the men of Israel gathered against
the city, united as one.

12 The tribes of Israel sent men through
all the tribe of Benjamin, saying, "What
crime is this that has been committed
among you? 13 Now then, hand over those
scoundrels in Gibeah, so that we may put
them to death, and purge the evil from Isra-
el." But the Benjaminites would not listen
to their kinsfolk, the Israelites. 14 The Ben-
jaminites came together out of the towns to
Gibeah, to go out to battle against the Isra-
elites. 15 On that day the Benjaminites mus-
tered twenty-six thousand armed men from
their towns, besides the inhabitants of Gib-
eah. 16 Of all this force, there were seven
hundred picked men who were left-handed;
every one could sling a stone at a hair, and
not miss. 17 And the Israelites, apart from
Benjamin, mustered four hundred thou-
sand armed men, all of them warriors.

18 The Israelites proceeded to go up to
Bethel, where they inquired of God,
"Which of us shall go up first to battle
against the Benjaminites?" And the LORD
answered, "Judah shall go up first."

19 Then the Israelites got up in the
morning, and encamped against Gibeah.
20 The Israelites went out to battle against
Benjamin; and the Israelites drew up the
battle line against them at Gibeah. 21 The
Benjaminites came out of Gibeah, and
struck down on that day twenty-two thou-
sand of the Israelites. 23 [c] The Israelites
went up and wept before the LORD until
the evening; and they inquired of the LORD,
"Shall we again draw near to battle against
our kinsfolk the Benjaminites?" And the
LORD said, "Go up against them." 22 The
Israelites took courage, and again formed
the battle line in the same place where they
had formed it on the first day.

24 So the Israelites advanced against the
Benjaminites the second day. 25 Benjamin
moved out against them from Gibeah the
second day, and struck down eighteen
thousand of the Israelites, all of them
armed men. 26 Then all the Israelites, the
whole army, went back to Bethel and wept,
sitting there before the LORD; they fasted

a Gk: Heb lacks *we will go up* *b* Compare Gk: Meaning of Heb uncertain *c* Verses 22 and 23 are transposed

13.12; Jer 29.23. **10:** *Disgrace,* see v. 6n. **12–17:** The Benjaminites, who would later produce King Saul, refused to subject themselves to the authority of the tribal assembly, and civil war ensued. **16:** The Benjaminite elite contingent of left-handed slingers is reminiscent of Ehud (3.15). **18–48:** Three battles are narrated in which the Israelites attempt to subdue Benjamin. **18–21:** In the first battle, the Israelites attack en masse, but suffer a severe defeat, even though they followed a divine oracle that is reminiscent of 1.2. **18:** *Bethel,* once known as Luz, had associations with both Abraham (Gen 12.8; 13.3) and Jacob (Gen 28.10–22). **22–25:** In the second battle, the Israelites also attack en masse, and again suffer a severe defeat. **26–48:** In the third battle, the Israelites set an ambush and completely destroy ("ḥerem") the Benjaminites—men, women, children, and animals—all except six hundred men. Ironically, the determination and thoroughness surpasses anything evidenced in Israel's wars against the Canaanites elsewhere in Judges. Thematically, it is a return to Joshua, suggesting that these two books might be read together as a thematic unit. **28:** *Phinehas,* see Num 25.7–13; Josh 22. **33:** The precise locations of *Baal-tamar* and

that day until evening. Then they offered
burnt offerings and sacrifices of well-being
before the LORD. 27 And the Israelites in-
quired of the LORD (for the ark of the cove-
nant of God was there in those days, 28 and
Phinehas son of Eleazar, son of Aaron,
ministered before it in those days), saying,
"Shall we go out once more to battle
against our kinsfolk the Benjaminites, or
shall we desist?" The LORD answered, "Go
up, for tomorrow I will give them into your
hand."
29 So Israel stationed men in ambush
around Gibeah. 30 Then the Israelites went
up against the Benjaminites on the third
day, and set themselves in array against
Gibeah, as before. 31 When the Benjamin-
ites went out against the army, they were
drawn away from the city. As before they
began to inflict casualties on the troops,
along the main roads, one of which goes up
to Bethel and the other to Gibeah, as well
as in the open country, killing about thirty
men of Israel. 32 The Benjaminites thought,
"They are being routed before us, as previ-
ously." But the Israelites said, "Let us re-
treat and draw them away from the city
toward the roads." 33 The main body of the
Israelites drew back its battle line to Baal-
tamar, while those Israelites who were in
ambush rushed out of their place west[a] of
Geba. 34 There came against Gibeah ten
thousand picked men out of all Israel, and
the battle was fierce. But the Benjaminites
did not realize that disaster was close upon
them.
35 The LORD defeated Benjamin before
Israel; and the Israelites destroyed twenty-
five thousand one hundred men of Benja-
min that day, all of them armed.
36 Then the Benjaminites saw that they
were defeated.[b]

The Israelites gave ground to Benjamin,
because they trusted to the troops in am-
bush that they had stationed against Gibe-
ah. 37 The troops in ambush rushed quickly
upon Gibeah. Then they put the whole city
to the sword. 38 Now the agreement be-
tween the main body of Israel and the men
in ambush was that when they sent up a
cloud of smoke out of the city 39 the main
body of Israel should turn in battle. But
Benjamin had begun to inflict casualties on
the Israelites, killing about thirty of them;
so they thought, "Surely they are defeated
before us, as in the first battle." 40 But when
the cloud, a column of smoke, began to rise
out of the city, the Benjaminites looked be-
hind them—and there was the whole city
going up in smoke toward the sky! 41 Then
the main body of Israel turned, and the
Benjaminites were dismayed, for they saw
that disaster was close upon them. 42 There-
fore they turned away from the Israelites in
the direction of the wilderness; but the bat-
tle overtook them, and those who came out
of the city[c] were slaughtering them in be-
tween.[d] 43 Cutting down[e] the Benjamin-
ites, they pursued them from Nohah[f] and
trod them down as far as a place east of
Gibeah. 44 Eighteen thousand Benjaminites
fell, all of them courageous fighters.
45 When they turned and fled toward the
wilderness to the rock of Rimmon, five
thousand of them were cut down on the
main roads, and they were pursued as far as
Gidom, and two thousand of them were
slain. 46 So all who fell that day of Benjamin
were twenty-five thousand arms-bearing
men, all of them courageous fighters. 47 But
six hundred turned and fled toward the wil-
derness to the rock of Rimmon, and re-
mained at the rock of Rimmon for four
months. 48 Meanwhile, the Israelites turned
back against the Benjaminites, and put
them to the sword—the city, the people,
the animals, and all that remained. Also the
remaining towns they set on fire.

a Gk Vg: Heb *in the plain* *b* This sentence is continued by verse 45. *c* Compare Vg and some Gk Mss: Heb *cities* *d* Compare Syr: Meaning of Heb uncertain *e* Gk: Heb *Surrounding* *f* Gk: Heb *pursued them at their resting place*

Geba are uncertain; Geba may be the same as Gibeah (cf. v. 43). **43–45:** *Nohah, Rimmon,* and *Gidom* cannot be identified with certainty.

21 Now the Israelites had sworn at
Mizpah, "No one of us shall give his
daughter in marriage to Benjamin." 2 And
the people came to Bethel, and sat there
until evening before God, and they lifted up
their voices and wept bitterly. 3 They said,
"O LORD, the God of Israel, why has it
come to pass that today there should be one
tribe lacking in Israel?" 4 On the next day,
the people got up early, and built an altar
there, and offered burnt offerings and sacri-
fices of well-being. 5 Then the Israelites
said, "Which of all the tribes of Israel did
not come up in the assembly to the LORD?"
For a solemn oath had been taken concern-
ing whoever did not come up to the LORD
to Mizpah, saying, "That one shall be put
to death." 6 But the Israelites had compas-
sion for Benjamin their kin, and said, "One
tribe is cut off from Israel this day. 7 What
shall we do for wives for those who are left,
since we have sworn by the LORD that we
will not give them any of our daughters as
wives?"

8 Then they said, "Is there anyone from
the tribes of Israel who did not come up to
the LORD to Mizpah?" It turned out that
no one from Jabesh-gilead had come to the
camp, to the assembly. 9 For when the roll
was called among the people, not one of the
inhabitants of Jabesh-gilead was there.
10 So the congregation sent twelve thousand
soldiers there and commanded them, "Go,
put the inhabitants of Jabesh-gilead to the
sword, including the women and the little
ones. 11 This is what you shall do; every
male and every woman that has lain with
a male you shall devote to destruction."
12 And they found among the inhabitants of
Jabesh-gilead four hundred young virgins
who had never slept with a man and
brought them to the camp at Shiloh, which
is in the land of Canaan.

13 Then the whole congregation sent
word to the Benjaminites who were at the
rock of Rimmon, and proclaimed peace to
them. 14 Benjamin returned at that time;
and they gave them the women whom
they had saved alive of the women of
Jabesh-gilead; but they did not suffice for
them.

15 The people had compassion on Ben-
jamin because the LORD had made a breach
in the tribes of Israel. 16 So the elders of the
congregation said, "What shall we do for
wives for those who are left, since there are
no women left in Benjamin?" 17 And they
said, "There must be heirs for the survivors
of Benjamin, in order that a tribe may not
be blotted out from Israel. 18 Yet we cannot
give any of our daughters to them as
wives." For the Israelites had sworn,
"Cursed be anyone who gives a wife to
Benjamin." 19 So they said, "Look, the
yearly festival of the LORD is taking place
at Shiloh, which is north of Bethel, on the

21.1–5: The oaths: Benjamin threatened with extinction. The inept handling of the Gibeah incident led to the near extinction of the tribe of Benjamin. **1:** However, the Israelites face a dilemma: They have taken a rash oath not to give their daughters to the Benjaminites (cf. Jephthah's vow in 11.30–31). Ironically, the daughters of Benjamin suffer the same fate as the Levite's concubine. **5:** A second oath is revealed concerning nonparticipation in the war against Benjamin. This oath resolves the problem of the initial oath.

21.6–14: The "ḥerem" of Jabesh-gilead. In order to repopulate the tribe of Benjamin, the Israelites resort to applying the "ḥerem" on Jabesh-gilead, who had not supplied troops for the war against Benjamin. This city later had close ties to King Saul (1 Sam 11; 2 Sam 2.4). **9:** This was not discovered through divine guidance (note the LORD's silence), but through the pragmatics of a roll-call. *Jabesh-gilead,* a town in northern Transjordan; the town that Jephthah rescued from the Ammonites' threat is ironically destroyed by the Israelites (11.4–33). **12:** *Four hundred young virgins* are spared and given to the remaining Benjaminites as wives (21.14). *Shiloh* was about 15 km (9 mi) north of Bethel.

21.15–25: The rape of the daughters of Shiloh. The elders of Israel are the devisers of the second strategy for repopulating Benjamin, which is nothing short of another rape. The Benjaminites are allowed to abduct unprotected dancers among the women of Shiloh without fear of reprisal. The annual festival of the LORD provides the context. **22:** The elders use the Mizpah oath against the girls' fathers. The rape

east of the highway that goes up from Beth-
el to Shechem, and south of Lebonah."
20 And they instructed the Benjaminites,
saying, "Go and lie in wait in the vineyards,
21 and watch; when the young women of
Shiloh come out to dance in the dances,
then come out of the vineyards and each of
you carry off a wife for himself from the
young women of Shiloh, and go to the land
of Benjamin. 22 Then if their fathers or their
brothers come to complain to us, we will
say to them, 'Be generous and allow us to
have them; because we did not capture in
battle a wife for each man. But neither did
you incur guilt by giving your daughters to
them.' " 23 The Benjaminites did so; they
took wives for each of them from the danc-
ers whom they abducted. Then they went
and returned to their territory, and rebuilt
the towns, and lived in them. 24 So the Isra-
elites departed from there at that time by
tribes and families, and they went out from
there to their own territories.

25 In those days there was no king in
Israel; all the people did what was right in
their own eyes.

of the daughters of Shiloh is an ironic counterpoint to the rape of the concubine. **25:** A final verdict on the events of chs 19–21 is given by the refrain that characterizes the double conclusion. The verdict is certainly justified by the actions narrated, and suggests, at the book's conclusion, that the institution of judges is unsatisfactory as a political institution. It clearly points forward to Samuel, the last judge, who will anoint Saul as the first king.

RUTH

Ruth is an exquisite short story that instructs and delights. The three main characters—Naomi, Ruth, and Boaz—and the pastoral landscape in which they move come to life with the deftest of verbal strokes. Four chapters of elegant Hebrew prose transport Ruth and Naomi from sorrow to triumphant joy by means of dramatic dialogues, suspense, extended word play, and intricate compositional symmetries. The book's verbal sophistication suggests that its author was a literate member of the upper classes—a court scribe, perhaps. At the same time, the folktale patterns and motifs provide evidence of the story's origins in the oral tales enjoyed and embellished by ordinary Israelites as they raised their families and worked the fields.

The dilemmas faced by two women left destitute and isolated by the deaths of their husbands and sons are the focus of the plot. The turning point in their fortunes occurs when Ruth takes advantage of an Israelite legal tradition that allowed foreigners, widows, and the poor to gather grain during the harvest (Lev 19.9–10; 23.22; Deut 24.19–22). In the fields of rural Israel, which demanded the labor of men and women alike, the socially mandated boundaries separating the worlds of men and women lost their rigidity. In that context Ruth encounters Boaz, her future husband. The themes of life and fertility evoked so richly by the harvest scenes carry over to the final chapter of the book when Naomi embraces the newborn son of Ruth and Boaz.

The book ends with a genealogy and the delightful revelation that Ruth of Moab is the great-grandmother of King David himself. Early Christian tradition concerning the ancestry of Jesus names only four women (three of them non-Israelite): Mary, Tamar, Rahab, and Ruth (Mt 1.5). Rabbinic tradition celebrates Ruth the Moabite as the model proselyte (convert). Christian Bibles place the book of Ruth between Judges and Samuel, reflecting the historical context of the story. In Jewish tradition, however, Ruth is the liturgical reading for the harvest festival of Shabuot/Weeks, reflecting the book's agricultural setting. Consequently, it is grouped with the other festival scrolls (the Megillot), including Esther, Song of Solomon, Ecclesiastes, and Lamentations.

Although the story is set "in the days when the judges ruled" (ca. 1200–1025 BCE), the date of Ruth's composition remains unresolved. On the one hand, a date during the monarchy is suggested by the book's obvious interest in celebrating the ancestry of King David, whose descendants continued to rule until the Babylonian capture of Jerusalem in 586 BCE. Equally pronounced, however, are the story's frequent reminders that its heroine is not an Israelite. Indeed, the storyteller suggests that Boaz's gracious treatment of Ruth the Moabite is unusual as well as exemplary. This insistence on an inclusive attitude toward foreigners suggests to many scholars a date of composition in the fifth century BCE when the issue of intermarriage between Israelites and non-Israelites had become extremely controversial (see Neh 13.1; Ezra 9.1). Whatever its date, however, Ruth is not a polemical book. The values it proclaims—loyalty, love of family, and generosity toward strangers—are universal and timeless.

1 In the days when the judges ruled, there
was a famine in the land, and a certain
man of Bethlehem in Judah went to live in
the country of Moab, he and his wife and
two sons. 2 The name of the man was Elim-
elech and the name of his wife Naomi, and
the names of his two sons were Mahlon
and Chilion; they were Ephrathites from
Bethlehem in Judah. They went into the
country of Moab and remained there. 3 But
Elimelech, the husband of Naomi, died,
and she was left with her two sons. 4 These
took Moabite wives; the name of the one
was Orpah and the name of the other Ruth.
When they had lived there about ten years,
5 both Mahlon and Chilion also died, so
that the woman was left without her two
sons and her husband.

6 Then she started to return with her
daughters-in-law from the country of
Moab, for she had heard in the country of
Moab that the LORD had considered his
people and given them food. 7 So she set out
from the place where she had been living,
she and her two daughters-in-law, and they
went on their way to go back to the land
of Judah. 8 But Naomi said to her two
daughters-in-law, "Go back each of you to
your mother's house. May the LORD deal
kindly with you, as you have dealt with the
dead and with me. 9 The LORD grant that
you may find security, each of you in the
house of your husband." Then she kissed
them, and they wept aloud. 10 They said to
her, "No, we will return with you to your
people." 11 But Naomi said, "Turn back,
my daughters, why will you go with me?
Do I still have sons in my womb that they
may become your husbands? 12 Turn back,
my daughters, go your way, for I am too
old to have a husband. Even if I thought
there was hope for me, even if I should have
a husband tonight and bear sons, 13 would
you then wait until they were grown?

1.1–22: Naomi and Ruth. 1: *When the judges ruled,* that is, in premonarchic Israel. Although *famine* is often God's mode of punishment (Lev 26.19–20; Deut 28.23–24; 1 Kings 17.1; Jer 24.10; Ezek 6.12), here, reminiscent of Abraham (Gen 12.10), Isaac (Gen. 26.1), and Jacob (Gen 45.6–28), it explains why an Israelite family would abandon its homeland. *In the land* implies a widespread, not merely local, famine. *Bethlehem,* 8 km (5 mi) south of Jerusalem, was the home of David's family (1 Sam 16.1–5). One meaning of the name Bethlehem ("house of bread/food") is ironic in view of the famine of ch 1, but also foreshadows the grain harvest of ch 2, and the parallel human harvest, the birth of an heir, in ch 4. Food and fertility are key themes in Ruth. *Moab* occupied the land east of the Dead Sea. Territorial disputes led to enmity between Israel and Moab (Deut 23.3–6). Israelites claimed the Moabites were related to them through Lot (Gen 19.37), nephew of Abraham, but many references to Moabites in the Bible are hostile or derogatory (Num 22–25; Deut 23.3–5; Isa 15–16; Jer 48). **2:** *Ephrathites,* people of Ephrathah (see 4.11), either another name for Bethlehem or a nearby settlement; it was a place associated with David's family (1 Sam 17.12). Several of the characters' names have thematic significance. Naomi ("Pleasantness") pointedly changes her name in v. 21. Although Elimelech's name ("My God is King") does not seem symbolically charged, the names of his sons, Mahlon ("Sickly") and Chilion ("Frail") foreshadow their early deaths (v. 5). **4:** The etymology of both Orpah and Ruth remains obscure. **6:** Only here and in 4.13 does the LORD actively intervene in the story. *Food* (Heb "leḥem") supplies the impetus for Naomi's return home and is also an example of word play on the name Bethlehem. *Return* (Heb "shub"), although not always evident in English translation, this thematically important word occurs ten times in ch 1. See 4.15. **8–9:** The first of a series of blessings (2.4; 2.12; 2.19–20; 3.10; 4.11–12; 4.14) that punctuate the story at key moments. *Deal kindly* (or do "ḥesed"), an expression (repeated in 2.20 and 3.10) that describes, above all, God's covenant relationship with Israel (Ex 20.5–6; 34.6–7; Deut 5.9–10); both Orpah and Ruth have exemplified this ideal on a human scale. The designation, *mother's house,* rather than the usual "father's house" (Gen 38.11; Lev 22.13; etc.), may have been used in circumstances associated with marriage (Gen 24.28; Song 3.4; 8.2). Only remarriage would ensure a childless young widow's *security.* **12:** In a society that valued women primarily as childbearers, postmenopausal Naomi is *too old* to remarry. She faces destitution. **13:** Naomi's experience of *the hand of the LORD* has been destructive (see Ex 9.15; 1 Sam 5.9), but she will find that the LORD's hand also rescues (Deut 6.21) and

Would you then refrain from marrying?
No, my daughters, it has been far more bit-
ter for me than for you, because the hand of
the LORD has turned against me." 14 Then
they wept aloud again. Orpah kissed her
mother-in-law, but Ruth clung to her.
15 So she said, "See, your sister-in-law
has gone back to her people and to her
gods; return after your sister-in-law."
16 But Ruth said,

"Do not press me to leave you
or to turn back from following
you!
Where you go, I will go;
where you lodge, I will lodge;
your people shall be my people,
and your God my God.
17 Where you die, I will die—
there will I be buried.
May the LORD do thus and so to me,
and more as well,
if even death parts me from you!"

18 When Naomi saw that she was deter-
mined to go with her, she said no more to
her.
19 So the two of them went on until they
came to Bethlehem. When they came to
Bethlehem, the whole town was stirred be-
cause of them; and the women said, "Is this
Naomi?" 20 She said to them,

"Call me no longer Naomi,[a]
call me Mara,[b]
for the Almighty[c] has dealt bitterly
with me.
21 I went away full,
but the LORD has brought me back
empty;
why call me Naomi
when the LORD has dealt harshly
with[d] me,
and the Almighty[c] has brought
calamity upon me?"

22 So Naomi returned together with
Ruth the Moabite, her daughter-in-law,
who came back with her from the country
of Moab. They came to Bethlehem at the
beginning of the barley harvest.

2 Now Naomi had a kinsman on her hus-
band's side, a prominent rich man, of
the family of Elimelech, whose name was
Boaz. 2 And Ruth the Moabite said to Nao-
mi, "Let me go to the field and glean
among the ears of grain, behind someone in
whose sight I may find favor." She said to
her, "Go, my daughter." 3 So she went. She
came and gleaned in the field behind the
reapers. As it happened, she came to the
part of the field belonging to Boaz, who
was of the family of Elimelech. 4 Just then
Boaz came from Bethlehem. He said to the
reapers, "The LORD be with you." They

a That is *Pleasant* *b* That is *Bitter* *c* Traditional rendering of Heb *Shaddai* *d* Or *has testified against*

brings joy (Eccl 2.24). **17:** Swearing by *the LORD,* Ruth makes good her new religious allegiance. She affirms her new kinship ties by her promise to stay with Naomi even in *death,* an allusion to burial according to Israelite custom in Naomi's family tomb. **19:** The *women* of Bethlehem, commenting collectively on the new arrivals (cf. 1 Sam 18.6–7) call attention to Naomi's sad fate; in 4.17 they will celebrate her good fortune. **20:** *Almighty* (Heb "Shaddai") is an ancient name for God (Gen 17.1; 28.3; 35.11; 43.14; 48.3; 49.25; Ex 6.3; Num 24.4; Ps 68.14) that reappeared in the postexilic era (Job 27.2; Ezek 1.24; Joel 1.15; Job 27.2). **22:** Describing Ruth as *the Moabite . . . from the country of Moab,* the narrative emphasizes her outsider status in Bethlehem. Notice of the *barley harvest* (April-May), ironic in view of Ruth and Naomi's poverty, nevertheless hints at a reversal of the motif of emptiness in 1.21 and propels the story into the next chapter.

2.1–23: Ruth and Boaz. With the appearance of Boaz, its third essential character, Ruth and Naomi's story can proceed. **1:** *Boaz,* whose name includes the word "strength" (see also 1 Kings 7.21–22; 2 Chr 3.15–17) belonged to the extended family of Naomi's deceased husband. The Hebrew phrase translated *prominent rich man* ("'ish ḥayil") can have a range of meanings, all connoting admirable and distinguished qualities. In 3.11, Boaz will praise Ruth using the feminine form of the phrase. **2:** On her own initiative, Ruth takes advantage of Israelite law, which required farmers to leave a part of their harvest for gleaning by the poor, the alien, and widows (Lev 19.9–10; 23.22; Deut 24.19–22). Ruth is a poor foreign widow, triply entitled to *glean* after the reapers have finished their work. **8:** Harvesting required

answered, "The LORD bless you." 5Then
Boaz said to his servant who was in charge
of the reapers, "To whom does this young
woman belong?" 6The servant who was in
charge of the reapers answered, "She is the
Moabite who came back with Naomi from
the country of Moab. 7She said, 'Please, let
me glean and gather among the sheaves be-
hind the reapers.' So she came, and she has
been on her feet from early this morning
until now, without resting even for a mo-
ment."[a]

8 Then Boaz said to Ruth, "Now listen,
my daughter, do not go to glean in another
field or leave this one, but keep close to my
young women. 9Keep your eyes on the field
that is being reaped, and follow behind
them. I have ordered the young men not to
bother you. If you get thirsty, go to the
vessels and drink from what the young men
have drawn." 10Then she fell prostrate,
with her face to the ground, and said to
him, "Why have I found favor in your
sight, that you should take notice of me,
when I am a foreigner?" 11But Boaz an-
swered her, "All that you have done for
your mother-in-law since the death of your
husband has been fully told me, and how
you left your father and mother and your
native land and came to a people that you
did not know before. 12May the LORD re-
ward you for your deeds, and may you
have a full reward from the LORD, the God
of Israel, under whose wings you have
come for refuge!" 13Then she said, "May I
continue to find favor in your sight, my
lord, for you have comforted me and spo-
ken kindly to your servant, even though I
am not one of your servants."

14 At mealtime Boaz said to her, "Come
here, and eat some of this bread, and dip
your morsel in the sour wine." So she sat
beside the reapers, and he heaped up for
her some parched grain. She ate until she
was satisfied, and she had some left over.
15When she got up to glean, Boaz instruct-
ed his young men, "Let her glean even
among the standing sheaves, and do not
reproach her. 16You must also pull out
some handfuls for her from the bundles,
and leave them for her to glean, and do not
rebuke her."

17 So she gleaned in the field until eve-
ning. Then she beat out what she had
gleaned, and it was about an ephah of bar-
ley. 18She picked it up and came into the
town, and her mother-in-law saw how
much she had gleaned. Then she took out
and gave her what was left over after she
herself had been satisfied. 19Her mother-
in-law said to her, "Where did you glean
today? And where have you worked?
Blessed be the man who took notice of
you." So she told her mother-in-law with
whom she had worked, and said, "The
name of the man with whom I worked to-
day is Boaz." 20Then Naomi said to her
daughter-in-law, "Blessed be he by the

a Compare Gk Vg: Meaning of Heb uncertain

the labor of both men and *women.* **10:** In taking *notice* of Ruth the *foreigner,* Boaz formally signals that he does not consider Ruth an outsider (against Deut 23.3–6; Neh 13.23–27). The narrative cleverly highlights Boaz's unexpected graciousness with word play on the similar-sounding Hebrew words for *take notice* ("nakar"), *I* ("'anoki"), and *foreigner* ("nokriyah"). **11:** Ruth's willingness to leave her *father, mother,* and *native land* resembles that of Abraham (Gen 12.1). In Jewish tradition, Ruth became the model proselyte (convert). **12:** The reference to God's protective *wings* (Deut 32.11; Ps 17.8; 36.7; 57.1; 61.4; 91.4) is echoed in 3.9 when Ruth asks Boaz to "spread" his cloak (lit. "wing") over her. **14:** In the hot fields, *sour wine* was a refreshing drink (Num 6.3; but see Ps 69.21). *Parched grain* was a staple food (1 Sam 17.17; 25.18). **14–16:** From verse to verse, Boaz's generosity increases, far outstripping his legal obligations to Ruth. **17:** An *ephah* (approximately 22 l, or 2/3 bu) would be an impressive day's work (1 Sam 17.17; Judg 6.19). **19:** Ruth dramatically withholds Boaz's name until the end of her report to Naomi. **20:** Whether the blessing refers to the *kindness* (Heb "ḥesed," see 1.8–9n.) of Boaz or the LORD is ambiguous. As one of Naomi's husband's *nearest kin* (Heb "go'el") Boaz belongs to a kinship group with shared covenantal obligations to protect the honor and property of the family (Lev 25.25; Jer 32.6–15). **21:** By referring here to Ruth as *the Moabite,* the narrator stresses yet again the uniqueness of

LORD, whose kindness has not forsaken the
living or the dead!" Naomi also said to her,
"The man is a relative of ours, one of our
nearest kin."[a] 21 Then Ruth the Moabite
said, "He even said to me, 'Stay close by my
servants, until they have finished all my
harvest.' " 22 Naomi said to Ruth, her
daughter-in-law, "It is better, my daughter,
that you go out with his young women,
otherwise you might be bothered in anoth-
er field." 23 So she stayed close to the young
women of Boaz, gleaning until the end of
the barley and wheat harvests; and she
lived with her mother-in-law.

3 Naomi her mother-in-law said to her,
"My daughter, I need to seek some se-
curity for you, so that it may be well with
you. 2 Now here is our kinsman Boaz, with
whose young women you have been work-
ing. See, he is winnowing barley tonight at
the threshing floor. 3 Now wash and anoint
yourself, and put on your best clothes and
go down to the threshing floor; but do not
make yourself known to the man until he
has finished eating and drinking. 4 When he
lies down, observe the place where he lies;
then, go and uncover his feet and lie down;
and he will tell you what to do." 5 She said
to her, "All that you tell me I will do."

6 So she went down to the threshing
floor and did just as her mother-in-law had
instructed her. 7 When Boaz had eaten and
drunk, and he was in a contented mood, he
went to lie down at the end of the heap of
grain. Then she came stealthily and uncov-
ered his feet, and lay down. 8 At midnight
the man was startled, and turned over, and
there, lying at his feet, was a woman! 9 He
said, "Who are you?" And she answered,
"I am Ruth, your servant; spread your
cloak over your servant, for you are next-
of-kin."[a] 10 He said, "May you be blessed
by the LORD, my daughter; this last in-
stance of your loyalty is better than the
first; you have not gone after young men,
whether poor or rich. 11 And now, my
daughter, do not be afraid, I will do for you
all that you ask, for all the assembly of my
people know that you are a worthy wom-
an. 12 But now, though it is true that I am
a near kinsman, there is another kinsman
more closely related than I. 13 Remain this
night, and in the morning, if he will act as
next-of-kin[a] for you, good; let him do it. If
he is not willing to act as next-of-kin[a] for
you, then, as the LORD lives, I will act as
next-of-kin[a] for you. Lie down until the
morning."

14 So she lay at his feet until morning,
but got up before one person could recog-
nize another; for he said, "It must not be
known that the woman came to the thresh-
ing floor." 15 Then he said, "Bring the cloak
you are wearing and hold it out." So she
held it, and he measured out six measures
of barley, and put it on her back; then he

a Or *one with the right to redeem*

Boaz's inclusive treatment of a foreign outsider. **23:** The end of the *wheat harvest* (early June), closing the chapter that began during the barley harvest, signals a new phase in the progress of Naomi and Ruth.

3.1–18: Naomi instructs, Ruth acts, and Boaz makes a promise. 4: In Hebrew, *feet* (cf. v. 7) can be a euphemism for genitals, thus giving a sexual overtone to Naomi's instructions and Ruth's subsequent actions. **7:** Boaz's *contented mood* could indicate inebriation (1 Sam 25.36; Esth 1.10) or a general sense of well-being (1 Kings 8.66; Prov 15.15). **8:** Death strikes at *midnight* (Ex 12.29; Job 34.20; Ps 91.5), which may partly explain why Boaz is so *startled* (the Heb conveys the idea of trembling with fear; Ex 19.16; 1 Sam 14.15; Isa 66.2); perhaps Boaz at first mistakes Ruth for a "lilitu" or night-demon (Isa 34.14). **9–13:** Ruth's request that Boaz *spread* his *cloak* over her could be interpreted as a request that he marry her (Ezek 16.8), though it might also be a general request for protection and assistance. Her reference to him as *next-of-kin* has caused many to appeal to Deut 25.5–10 for an explanation. But Deut 25.5–10 requires only that a surviving brother marry the widow of his deceased sibling. Since neither Boaz nor the anonymous kinsman (4.1) is Ruth's brother-in-law, the legal requirement would not apply here. More likely, the author is teasing the reader to increase suspense. **11:** *Worthy woman* (Heb "eshet ḥayil"), see 2.1n.; Prov 31.10. **17:** Boaz's care that Ruth not return to Naomi *empty-handed* explicitly reverses Naomi's emptiness in 1.21. These are Ruth's last spoken words in the story.

went into the city. 16 She came to her
mother-in-law, who said, "How did things
go with you,[a] my daughter?" Then she
told her all that the man had done for her,
17 saying, "He gave me these six measures
of barley, for he said, 'Do not go back to
your mother-in-law empty-handed.' "
18 She replied, "Wait, my daughter, until
you learn how the matter turns out, for the
man will not rest, but will settle the matter
today."

4 No sooner had Boaz gone up to the gate
and sat down there than the next-of-
kin,[b] of whom Boaz had spoken, came
passing by. So Boaz said, "Come over,
friend; sit down here." And he went over
and sat down. 2 Then Boaz took ten men of
the elders of the city, and said, "Sit down
here"; so they sat down. 3 He then said to
the next-of-kin,[b] "Naomi, who has come
back from the country of Moab, is selling
the parcel of land that belonged to our
kinsman Elimelech. 4 So I thought I would
tell you of it, and say: Buy it in the presence
of those sitting here, and in the presence of
the elders of my people. If you will redeem
it, redeem it; but if you will not, tell me, so
that I may know; for there is no one prior
to you to redeem it, and I come after you."
So he said, "I will redeem it." 5 Then Boaz
said, "The day you acquire the field from
the hand of Naomi, you are also acquiring
Ruth[c] the Moabite, the widow of the dead
man, to maintain the dead man's name on
his inheritance." 6 At this, the next-of-kin[b]
said, "I cannot redeem it for myself without
damaging my own inheritance. Take my
right of redemption yourself, for I cannot
redeem it."

7 Now this was the custom in former
times in Israel concerning redeeming and
exchanging: to confirm a transaction, the
one took off a sandal and gave it to the
other; this was the manner of attesting in
Israel. 8 So when the next-of-kin[b] said to
Boaz, "Acquire it for yourself," he took off
his sandal. 9 Then Boaz said to the elders
and all the people, "Today you are wit-
nesses that I have acquired from the hand
of Naomi all that belonged to Elimelech
and all that belonged to Chilion and Mah-
lon. 10 I have also acquired Ruth the Moab-
ite, the wife of Mahlon, to be my wife, to
maintain the dead man's name on his inher-
itance, in order that the name of the dead
may not be cut off from his kindred and
from the gate of his native place; today you
are witnesses." 11 Then all the people who

a Or "*Who are you,* *b* Or *one with the right to redeem* *c* OL Vg: Heb *from the hand of Naomi and from Ruth*

4.1–12: Boaz acquires Ruth as wife and redeems the family property. 1–2: In Israel legal matters were settled at the city *gate* (Josh 20.4; Deut 21.19–20; 22.15; 25.7; Isa 29.21; Am 5.15) by *elders* who were leading and influential men of the community (Deut 19.12; 22.15; 25.7; 1 Sam 16.4; Ex 3.16; Josh 24.1). **3–4:** Boaz makes a play on the word for *kinsman* (Heb "go'el") when he says he wants to *tell* (Heb "galah") the kinsman about the land sale. The existence of this property has not been mentioned previously. **3:** A woman could not sell her dead husband's land on her own. Boaz is acting on behalf of Naomi. **5:** No known Israelite law obliges the kinsman to marry Ruth. Instead of the NRSV translation, following an alternative textual tradition one could translate "The day you acquire the field . . . I am acquiring Ruth . . . to maintain the dead man's name." Though under no legal obligation to do so, Boaz states his intention to produce an heir through Ruth for the lineage of Elimelech and Mahlon. **6:** Such an act would have financial consequences for the kinsman if he were to purchase the field, for a child born to Boaz and Ruth would be the legal heir to the property. Thus through his clever strategy Boaz ends up with both Ruth and the property. **7:** The *sandal* ritual and the reference to Tamar and Judah (4.12; Gen 38) recall the law in Deut 25.5–10, but the circumstances and procedure described here do not follow that law's prescriptions. Ceremonies to resolve family inheritance questions presumably involved similar symbolic gestures. **9:** Gen 23.17–20. **10:** *Acquired,* Boaz specifically uses the word for "buy." Boaz may be speaking formally in the context of a legal commercial transaction because Ruth's status is bound up with the question of Elimelech's land. **11–12:** The tripartite form of this blessing closely resembles Canaanite royal marriage blessings found at Ugarit. Mention of prominent forebears and glorification of the family

were at the gate, along with the elders, said,
"We are witnesses. May the LORD make
the woman who is coming into your house
like Rachel and Leah, who together built
up the house of Israel. May you produce
children in Ephrathah and bestow a name
in Bethlehem; 12 and, through the children
that the LORD will give you by this young
woman, may your house be like the house
of Perez, whom Tamar bore to Judah."
13 So Boaz took Ruth and she became
his wife. When they came together, the
LORD made her conceive, and she bore a
son. 14 Then the women said to Naomi,
"Blessed be the LORD, who has not left you
this day without next-of-kin;[a] and may his
name be renowned in Israel! 15 He shall be
to you a restorer of life and a nourisher
of your old age; for your daughter-in-law
who loves you, who is more to you than
seven sons, has borne him." 16 Then Naomi
took the child and laid him in her bosom,
and became his nurse. 17 The women of the
neighborhood gave him a name, saying, "A
son has been born to Naomi." They named
him Obed; he became the father of Jesse,
the father of David.
18 Now these are the descendants of Pe-
rez: Perez became the father of Hezron,
19 Hezron of Ram, Ram of Amminadab,
20 Amminadab of Nahshon, Nahshon of
Salmon, 21 Salmon of Boaz, Boaz of Obed,
22 Obed of Jesse, and Jesse of David.

a Or *one with the right to redeem*

name (2 Sam 7.9; Isa 9.6–7; see Gen 12.2) are motifs related to the theme of royal dynasties. From this point the narrative alludes in various ways to king David's ancestry, and David's name is the climax of the genealogy at the end of the book (4.22). *Rachel and Leah,* the wives of *Israel*/Jacob, had Bethlehem connections. Rachel died and was buried near there (Gen 35.18–20); Leah was the mother of *Judah* (Gen 29.35), David's ancestor, in whose tribal territory Bethlehem was located. *Ephrathah,* see 1.2n. The foreign widow *Tamar,* like Ruth, took matters into her own hands to secure both her own future and the *name* of her Israelite husband's family (Gen 38).

4.13–17: Naomi embraces Ruth's newborn son. Naomi and Ruth the Moabite, whose familial and social barrenness the story emphasized at its beginning (1.19–21), are now encircled and celebrated in the name of the LORD by Bethlehem's community of women. **13:** Following sexual intercourse (lit. "he went in to her"; see Gen 16.2; 30.3) with her husband Boaz, Ruth *conceive*s with the LORD's assistance; see 1.6n. This detail and the subsequent blessing may allude to the birth of Isaac (Gen 21.1–7). **15:** A *restorer of life* (Heb "nephesh") may be human (Lam 1.16; Prov 25.13) or divine (Ps 19.7; 23.3). *Restorer,* using the verbal root meaning to return or turn back, intentionally echoes the key recurring word in ch 1 (see 1.6n.). *Seven* (like ten, cf.1 Sam 1.8) is a conventional number to suggest a happy abundance of sons and, by comparison, Ruth's superior worth. **16:** As the child's *nurse,* Naomi is a guardian, not a wetnurse; she clasps him to her breast in affection (1 Kings 3.20–21). **17:** Seldom would non-family members, especially a group of unrelated women, *name* a newborn son. Uniquely in the Hebrew Bible, Ruth's child is also announced as being *born to* a female (Naomi). *Obed,* "servant," is a short form of a name like Obadiah, "servant of the LORD." Ruth is the great-grandmother of David and, in the New Testament, ancestress of Jesus (Mt 1.4–6; cf. Lk 3.32).

4.18–21: The ancestors of King David. 1 Chr 2.5–15. *These are the descendants,* cf. Gen 5; 11.10–30; 25.12–19; ch 36. It is unclear whether this genealogy belonged originally to the text of Ruth or was appended later.

1 SAMUEL

First Samuel and Second Samuel were originally a single work recounting the beginning of the monarchy and the reigns of its first two kings, Saul and David. They were divided into two books in the Greek translation (the Septuagint) of the Hebrew Bible and were named after Samuel, who plays a prominent role in its beginning section, which was even attributed to his authorship. The name is not entirely appropriate, however, since Samuel dies before 1 Samuel ends (25.1).

First Samuel has three sections built around its principal characters, Samuel (chs 1–7), Saul (chs 8–15), and David (chs 16–31). Samuel is a transitional figure—the last of the judges and the prophet who anoints Saul and then announces his rejection by the LORD and anoints David in his place. Saul is a tragic figure—plucked from obscurity and thrust into a position of power for which he ultimately proves unfit. David is the focal figure of 1 Samuel, for whom both Samuel and Saul pave the way. Like Saul, he is presented as humble and without personal ambition for kingship. But although Saul was initially the divinely designated ruler, in the end he fell out of divine favor and "the LORD was with David"—a major theme in the book.

Most scholars view 1–2 Samuel as part of a larger original composition called the Deuteronomistic History, which encompasses the books of Deuteronomy, Joshua, Judges, 1–2 Samuel, and 1–2 Kings and relates Israel's history from the conquest under Joshua to the end of the kingdoms of Israel and Judah. The Deuteronomistic History is a theological history; it evaluates Israel's past according to the principles of the book of Deuteronomy, with which it begins. It stresses such matters as obedience to the law and God's choice of Jerusalem as the central place of worship for Israel and of David as its king.

The Deuteronomistic History was composed by one or more nameless "Deuteronomists," probably in the exile (after 586 BCE), though some scholars date its initial edition to the reign of Josiah. The Deuteronomist(s), abbreviated Dtr(s), edited various traditions into a single, running historical account. They occasionally inserted speeches or commentary in their own distinctive Deuteronomistic style into the narrative. Examples of Deuteronomistic style are 8.8 (the Exodus), 8.12 (the people crying out), and 12.14–15 (the review of Israel's history and the command to "heed the voice of the LORD").

First and Second Samuel are a literary masterpiece, but they may also contain genuine history. While they were written hundreds of years after the events they describe, they seem to contain older source material. Some scholars have suggested that an old "Ark Narrative" underlies 4.1–7.1, that a cycle of stories about Saul and his reign is behind chs 8–15, and that chs 16–31 are based on a "History of David's Rise." Still, these documents are theoretical reconstructions, and the exact nature of the sources used by the Dtr(s) remains uncertain.

The central character of the Deuteronomistic History is David. The Dtr(s) explained the long duration of the Davidic dynasty theologically as the reward for David's faithfulness to God (see 2 Sam 7). David may also have been viewed as the model for the restoration of the monarchy after the crisis of the exile. The pro-Davidic tone of 1 Samuel is evident. While Saul falters at every step, David can do no wrong. God abandons Saul but is constantly with David. At some stage in its development the section dealing with David's rise seems to have been designed as an "apology" or defense of David and his kingship. The charge that David usurped the throne to which he had no hereditary right and did so through multiple assassinations is subtly and effectively addressed in 1 Samuel and the beginning of 2 Samuel. The reader, who may draw closer to actual history by asking whether Saul was really as bad and David as innocent as their portraits in 1 Samuel indicate, is aided in answering such questions by materials presented in the Deuteronomistic History.

1 There was a certain man of Ramatha-
im, a Zuphite[a] from the hill country of
Ephraim, whose name was Elkanah son of
Jeroham son of Elihu son of Tohu son of
Zuph, an Ephraimite. 2He had two wives;
the name of the one was Hannah, and the
name of the other Peninnah. Peninnah had
children, but Hannah had no children.
3 Now this man used to go up year by
year from his town to worship and to sacri-
fice to the LORD of hosts at Shiloh, where
the two sons of Eli, Hophni and Phinehas,
were priests of the LORD. 4On the day
when Elkanah sacrificed, he would give
portions to his wife Peninnah and to all her
sons and daughters; 5but to Hannah he
gave a double portion,[b] because he loved
her, though the LORD had closed her
womb. 6Her rival used to provoke her se-
verely, to irritate her, because the LORD
had closed her womb. 7So it went on year
by year; as often as she went up to the
house of the LORD, she used to provoke
her. Therefore Hannah wept and would
not eat. 8Her husband Elkanah said to her,
"Hannah, why do you weep? Why do you
not eat? Why is your heart sad? Am I not
more to you than ten sons?"
9 After they had eaten and drunk at Shi-
loh, Hannah rose and presented herself be-
fore the LORD.[c] Now Eli the priest was
sitting on the seat beside the doorpost of
the temple of the LORD. 10She was deeply
distressed and prayed to the LORD, and
wept bitterly. 11She made this vow:
"O LORD of hosts, if only you will look on
the misery of your servant, and remember
me, and not forget your servant, but will
give to your servant a male child, then I will
set him before you as a nazirite[d] until the
day of his death. He shall drink neither
wine nor intoxicants,[e] and no razor shall
touch his head."
12 As she continued praying before the
LORD, Eli observed her mouth. 13Hannah
was praying silently; only her lips moved,

a Compare Gk and 1 Chr 6.35-36: Heb *Ramathaim-zophim* *b* Syr: Meaning of Heb uncertain *c* Gk: Heb lacks *and presented herself before the LORD* *d* That is *one separated* or *one consecrated* *e* Cn Compare Gk Q Ms 1.22: MT *then I will give him to the LORD all the days of his life*

1.1–28: The birth and consecration of Samuel. The story of a barren woman who bears a child as a favor from God appears several other times in the Bible: Sarah (Gen 17.16–19), Rebekah (Gen 25.21–26), Rachel (Gen 29.31; 30.22–24), the mother of Samson (Judg 13.2–5), and Elizabeth (Lk 1.5–17). Such a child is designated by God for a special purpose. **1:** *Ramathaim,* a town in Ephraim, is called Ramah later in this chapter (v. 19). But in later chapters the Ramah that was Samuel's home seems to be located in Benjamin (7.16–17). **2:** *Peninnah* is "the second" (translated *the other* in the NRSV) wife; *Hannah* is obviously the favored one. Elkanah probably married Peninnah because of Hannah's failure to produce an heir (see Gen 16.1–2). Elkanah, therefore, was probably prosperous. **3:** Elkanah's annual pilgrimage to worship in Shiloh shows him to be a righteous man. The *LORD of hosts* or "armies" (Heb "tseba'ot") is a title describing Yahweh's leadership in war on Israel's behalf. *Hophni and Phinehas* are Egyptian names. **7:** The *house of the LORD* usually refers to a temple (Jer 7.12). But Josh 18.1; Ps 78.60 mention a tent of meeting or tabernacle in Shiloh, and 2 Sam 7.6–7 denies that the LORD dwelt in a "house" before Solomon's Temple. See 2.22. **9:** Eli's *seat beside the doorpost of the temple* (or "sanctuary," Heb "hekal") allowed him to see Hannah praying outside of the temple proper (see also 4.18). **11:** *Nazirites* were "devoted" to the LORD for a set period of time and were prohibited from drinking alcohol or eating grapes, cutting their hair or beards, and approaching a dead body (Num 6.1–21). *Intoxicants,* probably distilled wine or beer. **13:** *Eli thought she was drunk* because prayers were not usually silent. **17:** *The*

but her voice was not heard; therefore Eli
thought she was drunk. 14 So Eli said to her,
"How long will you make a drunken spec-
tacle of yourself? Put away your wine."
15 But Hannah answered, "No, my lord, I
am a woman deeply troubled; I have drunk
neither wine nor strong drink, but I have
been pouring out my soul before the LORD.
16 Do not regard your servant as a worth-
less woman, for I have been speaking out
of my great anxiety and vexation all this
time." 17 Then Eli answered, "Go in peace;
the God of Israel grant the petition you
have made to him." 18 And she said, "Let
your servant find favor in your sight."
Then the woman went to her quarters,[a]
ate and drank with her husband,[b] and her
countenance was sad no longer.[c]

19 They rose early in the morning and

a Gk: Heb *went her way* *b* Gk: Heb lacks *and drank with her husband* *c* Gk: Meaning of Heb uncertain

petition you have made, the first of several word plays in this chapter on the name of Saul, which sounds like the Hebrew verb for "ask, petition." **19:** *Elkanah knew his wife,* an idiom for sexual relations. **20:** *I have asked him of the LORD.* "Asked" (Heb "sha'al") is another pun on the name Saul. **22–24:** *Weaned,*

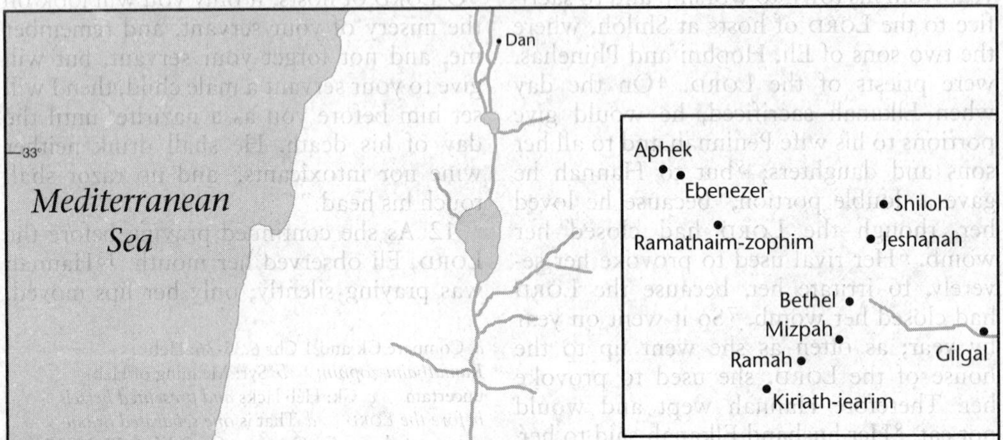

Chs 1–6: The activity of Samuel.

worshiped before the LORD; then they went
back to their house at Ramah. Elkanah
knew his wife Hannah, and the LORD re-
membered her. 20 In due time Hannah con-
ceived and bore a son. She named him Sam-
uel, for she said, "I have asked him of the
LORD."
21 The man Elkanah and all his house-
hold went up to offer to the LORD the year-
ly sacrifice, and to pay his vow. 22 But Han-
nah did not go up, for she said to her
husband, "As soon as the child is weaned,
I will bring him, that he may appear in the
presence of the LORD, and remain there
forever; I will offer him as a nazirite[a] for
all time."[b] 23 Her husband Elkanah said to
her, "Do what seems best to you, wait until
you have weaned him; only—may the
LORD establish his word."[c] So the woman
remained and nursed her son, until she
weaned him. 24 When she had weaned him,
she took him up with her, along with a
three-year-old bull,[d] an ephah of flour,
and a skin of wine. She brought him to the
house of the LORD at Shiloh; and the child
was young. 25 Then they slaughtered the
bull, and they brought the child to Eli.
26 And she said, "Oh, my lord! As you live,
my lord, I am the woman who was stand-
ing here in your presence, praying to the
LORD. 27 For this child I prayed; and the
LORD has granted me the petition that I
made to him. 28 Therefore I have lent him to
the LORD; as long as he lives, he is given to
the LORD."

She left him there for[e] the LORD.

2 Hannah prayed and said,
"My heart exults in the LORD;
  my strength is exalted in my God.[f]
My mouth derides my enemies,
  because I rejoice in my[g] victory.

2 "There is no Holy One like the LORD,
  no one besides you;
  there is no Rock like our God.
3 Talk no more so very proudly,
  let not arrogance come from your
   mouth;
for the LORD is a God of knowledge,
  and by him actions are weighed.
4 The bows of the mighty are broken,
  but the feeble gird on strength.
5 Those who were full have hired
   themselves out for bread,
  but those who were hungry are fat
   with spoil.
The barren has borne seven,
  but she who has many children is
   forlorn.
6 The LORD kills and brings to life;
  he brings down to Sheol and raises
   up.

a That is *one separated* or *one consecrated*
b Cn Compare Q Ms: MT lacks *I will offer him as a nazirite for all time* c MT: Q Ms Gk Compare Syr *that which goes out of your mouth* d Q Ms Gk Syr: MT *three bulls* e Gk (Compare Q Ms) and Gk at 2.11: MT *And he* (that is, Elkanah) *worshiped there before* f Gk: Heb *the LORD* g Q Ms: MT *your*

taken off breast milk. Samuel's age is not given, but he is older than an infant or toddler. *An ephah of flour* (v. 24), about half a bushel. **27:** *The petition that I made,* another pun on Saul's name. **28:** *Given* in both occurrences in this verse is yet another pun on Saul's name. *He is given* is exactly the same as Saul's name in Hebrew ("sha'ul") and could be translated, "he is Saul to the LORD." Some scholars believe, based on these puns, that this story was originally about Saul's birth rather than Samuel's. Or, they may be allusions to Saul as Israel's first king.

2.1–10: The Song of Hannah. Biblical writers sometimes inserted poems into prose books where they seemed appropriate. In this case the poem seems to be considerably later than the surrounding context. It is a psalm of national thanksgiving, but its thankful tone appropriately reflects Hannah's sentiments. It was later used as a model for Lk 1.46–55. **1:** *Strength,* lit. "horn," draws on the image of a proud animal. **2:** *Rock,* a common metaphor for God (2 Sam 22.2–3; Ps 18.2; 28.1; 62.2,6). **3:** The enemies of Israel are addressed. **4:** The reversal of fortune for the downtrodden and oppressed. **5:** *The barren has borne seven,* this line probably suggested the insertion of the poem at this place. *Seven* is symbolic of a sizable family; Hannah had only six children (2.21). **6–7:** *Brings to life* refers to birth, not resurrection from the dead. *Sheol* was the underworld (Isa 14.9–21), where all people were believed to go after death.

7 The LORD makes poor and makes
rich;
he brings low, he also exalts.
8 He raises up the poor from the dust;
he lifts the needy from the ash heap,
to make them sit with princes
and inherit a seat of honor.[a]
For the pillars of the earth are the
LORD's,
and on them he has set the world.

9 "He will guard the feet of his faithful
ones,
but the wicked shall be cut off in
darkness;
for not by might does one prevail.
10 The LORD! His adversaries shall be
shattered;
the Most High[b] will thunder in
heaven.
The LORD will judge the ends of the
earth;
he will give strength to his king,
and exalt the power of his anointed."
11 Then Elkanah went home to Ramah,
while the boy remained to minister to the
LORD, in the presence of the priest Eli.
12 Now the sons of Eli were scoundrels;
they had no regard for the LORD
13 or for
the duties of the priests to the people. When
anyone offered sacrifice, the priest's servant
would come, while the meat was boiling,
with a three-pronged fork in his hand,
14 and he would thrust it into the pan, or
kettle, or caldron, or pot; all that the fork
brought up the priest would take for him-
self.[c] This is what they did at Shiloh to all
the Israelites who came there.
15 Moreover,
before the fat was burned, the priest's ser-
vant would come and say to the one who
was sacrificing, "Give meat for the priest to
roast; for he will not accept boiled meat
from you, but only raw."
16 And if the man
said to him, "Let them burn the fat first,
and then take whatever you wish," he
would say, "No, you must give it now; if
not, I will take it by force."
17 Thus the sin
of the young men was very great in the
sight of the LORD; for they treated the
offerings of the LORD with contempt.
18 Samuel was ministering before the
LORD, a boy wearing a linen ephod.
19 His
mother used to make for him a little robe
and take it to him each year, when she went
up with her husband to offer the yearly sac-
rifice.
20 Then Eli would bless Elkanah and
his wife, and say, "May the LORD repay[d]
you with children by this woman for the
gift that she made to[e] the LORD"; and then
they would return to their home.
21 And[f] the LORD took note of Han-
nah; she conceived and bore three sons and
two daughters. And the boy Samuel grew
up in the presence of the LORD.
22 Now Eli was very old. He heard all

a Gk (Compare Q Ms) adds *He grants the vow of the one who vows, and blesses the years of the just*
b Cn Heb *against him he* *c* Gk Syr Vg: Heb *with it*
d Q Ms Gk: MT *give* *e* Q Ms Gk: MT *for the petition that she asked of* *f* Q Ms Gk: MT *When*

(The idea of heaven and hell does not exist yet in the Bible.) Sheol may be metaphorical for conditions near death (Ps 86.13; 88.3–7), injuries, or serious trouble. **8:** *He raises up the poor . . . he lifts the needy,* God's concern for the poor and oppressed is a common theme in the Bible. *Pillars of the earth,* the earth is conceived of as a platform resting upon great pillars. **10:** *His king* shows that the psalm was written later than Hannah since there was no king of Israel yet in her time. *Anointed* (Heb "mashiaḥ") was a title for the king and the source of the term "messiah."

2.12–26: The wicked sons of Eli. Samuel's faithful service, in contrast to the evil deeds of Eli's sons, hints that he will replace Eli. **12:** *They had no regard for,* lit. "they did not know." **13–17:** Priests made their living by receiving a portion of the sacrifices. The custom in Shiloh (vv. 13–14) was for the priest to get whatever the fork brought up while the meat was boiling, which is different from that prescribed elsewhere (contrast Lev 7.28–36; Deut 18.3). By demanding the fat portion, which properly belonged to God, and taking it before the sacrifice was made, Eli's sons were sinning against the LORD (v. 25) by treating him with contempt (vv. 12,17). They also threatened violence against worshipers who tried to do right (v. 16). **18:** This *linen ephod* was a kind of apron worn by priests. **20:** *The gift that she made,* another pun on Saul's name. **22:** *And how they lay with the women who served at the entrance to the*

that his sons were doing to all Israel, and
how they lay with the women who served
at the entrance to the tent of meeting. 23 He
said to them, "Why do you do such things?
For I hear of your evil dealings from all
these people. 24 No, my sons; it is not a
good report that I hear the people of the
LORD spreading abroad. 25 If one person
sins against another, someone can intercede
for the sinner with the LORD;[a] but if some-
one sins against the LORD, who can make
intercession?" But they would not listen to
the voice of their father; for it was the will
of the LORD to kill them.

26 Now the boy Samuel continued to
grow both in stature and in favor with the
LORD and with the people.

27 A man of God came to Eli and said to
him, "Thus the LORD has said, 'I revealed[b]
myself to the family of your ancestor in
Egypt when they were slaves[c] to the house
of Pharaoh. 28 I chose him out of all the
tribes of Israel to be my priest, to go up to
my altar, to offer incense, to wear an ephod
before me; and I gave to the family of your
ancestor all my offerings by fire from the
people of Israel. 29 Why then look with
greedy eye[d] at my sacrifices and my offer-
ings that I commanded, and honor your
sons more than me by fattening yourselves
on the choicest parts of every offering of
my people Israel?' 30 Therefore the LORD
the God of Israel declares: 'I promised that
your family and the family of your ancestor
should go in and out before me forever';
but now the LORD declares: 'Far be it from
me; for those who honor me I will honor,
and those who despise me shall be treated
with contempt. 31 See, a time is coming
when I will cut off your strength and the
strength of your ancestor's family, so that
no one in your family will live to old age.
32 Then in distress you will look with
greedy eye[e] on all the prosperity that shall
be bestowed upon Israel; and no one in
your family shall ever live to old age. 33 The
only one of you whom I shall not cut off
from my altar shall be spared to weep out
his[f] eyes and grieve his[g] heart; all the
members of your household shall die by
the sword.[h] 34 The fate of your two sons,
Hophni and Phinehas, shall be the sign to
you—both of them shall die on the same
day. 35 I will raise up for myself a faithful
priest, who shall do according to what is in
my heart and in my mind. I will build him
a sure house, and he shall go in and out
before my anointed one forever. 36 Every-

a Gk Compare Q Ms: MT *another, God will mediate for him* *b* Gk Tg Syr: Heb *Did I reveal* *c* Q Ms Gk: MT lacks *slaves* *d* Q Ms Gk: MT *then kick* *e* Q Ms Gk: MT *will kick* *f* Q Ms Gk: MT *your* *g* Q Ms Gk: Heb *your* *h* Q Ms See Gk: MT *die like mortals*

tent of meeting. This line, if original, indicates that the shrine at Shiloh was a portable tent or tabernacle (see 1.7n.). However, this line is not in some of the best witnesses to the text of Samuel and may be borrowed from Ex 38.8. **25:** *It was the will of the LORD to kill them,* compare God's hardening of Pharaoh's heart in Ex 4–12.

2.27–36: The oracle against Eli. This passage was probably written by the Deuteronomistic editor to justify the exclusion of Abiathar and his descendants from the priesthood in favor of Zadok and his descendants (1 Kings 2.27,35), which occurred due to Josiah's centralization of worship in Jerusalem (2 Kings 23.9). **27–28:** *Your ancestor* may refer to Moses, to whom Eli's family traced their ancestry. But the statement that he was chosen *out of all the tribes of Israel* seems to indicate Levi, and Moses was a Levite (Ex 2.1). **28:** *To go up to my altar, to offer incense, to wear an ephod,* three principal duties of priests. Going up to the altar refers to offering sacrifices. **30:** The promise mentioned here is not explicitly found in the Bible but resembles Ex 29.2, which is directed to Aaron. **31–33:** The cutting off of Eli's household probably refers not to the death of Eli and his sons in 4.11,18 but to Saul's annihilation of the priests of Nob in ch 22. *The only one of you* is Abiathar, who alone escaped the slaughter (22.18–23; 1 Kings 2.26–27). The Hebrew of v. 32a is obscure. **35:** The *faithful priest* is Zadok, who came to prominence when Abiathar was banished by Solomon (1 Kings 1–2). The language of this verse is very similar to that of 2 Sam 7.11–16, which promises a dynasty to David. Both were probably written by the Deuteronomistic Historian.

one who is left in your family shall come to implore him for a piece of silver or a loaf of bread, and shall say, Please put me in one of the priest's places, that I may eat a morsel of bread.' "

3 Now the boy Samuel was ministering to the LORD under Eli. The word of the LORD was rare in those days; visions were not widespread.

2 At that time Eli, whose eyesight had begun to grow dim so that he could not see, was lying down in his room; 3 the lamp of God had not yet gone out, and Samuel was lying down in the temple of the LORD, where the ark of God was. 4 Then the LORD called, "Samuel! Samuel!"[a] and he said, "Here I am!" 5 and ran to Eli, and said, "Here I am, for you called me." But he said, "I did not call; lie down again." So he went and lay down. 6 The LORD called again, "Samuel!" Samuel got up and went to Eli, and said, "Here I am, for you called me." But he said, "I did not call, my son; lie down again." 7 Now Samuel did not yet know the LORD, and the word of the LORD had not yet been revealed to him. 8 The LORD called Samuel again, a third time. And he got up and went to Eli, and said, "Here I am, for you called me." Then Eli perceived that the LORD was calling the boy. 9 Therefore Eli said to Samuel, "Go, lie down; and if he calls you, you shall say, 'Speak, LORD, for your servant is listening.' " So Samuel went and lay down in his place.

10 Now the LORD came and stood there, calling as before, "Samuel! Samuel!" And Samuel said, "Speak, for your servant is listening." 11 Then the LORD said to Samuel, "See, I am about to do something in Israel that will make both ears of anyone who hears of it tingle. 12 On that day I will fulfill against Eli all that I have spoken concerning his house, from beginning to end. 13 For I have told him that I am about to punish his house forever, for the iniquity that he knew, because his sons were blaspheming God,[b] and he did not restrain them. 14 Therefore I swear to the house of Eli that the iniquity of Eli's house shall not be expiated by sacrifice or offering forever."

15 Samuel lay there until morning; then he opened the doors of the house of the LORD. Samuel was afraid to tell the vision to Eli. 16 But Eli called Samuel and said, "Samuel, my son." He said, "Here I am." 17 Eli said, "What was it that he told you? Do not hide it from me. May God do so to you and more also, if you hide anything from me of all that he told you." 18 So Samuel told him everything and hid nothing from him. Then he said, "It is the LORD; let him do what seems good to him."

19 As Samuel grew up, the LORD was with him and let none of his words fall to the ground. 20 And all Israel from Dan to Beer-sheba knew that Samuel was a trustworthy prophet of the LORD. 21 The LORD continued to appear at Shiloh, for the LORD revealed himself to Samuel at Shiloh

4 by the word of the LORD. 1 And the word of Samuel came to all Israel.

a Q Ms Gk See 3.10: MT *the LORD called Samuel*
b Another reading is *for themselves*

3.1–4.1a: Samuel's call. 3.1: *Word of the LORD . . . visions* are means of prophetic revelation. **3:** The lamp in the temple burned at night (see Ex 27.21). *The lamp of God had not yet gone out,* hence it was just before dawn. Samuel's bed was inside the temple near the inner sanctuary where the *ark of God* was kept. The ark was a portable shrine or chest representing God's presence; see 4.5n. **7:** *Samuel did not yet know the LORD,* Samuel's role as a prophet had not yet been established since *the word of the LORD had not yet been revealed to him.* In this story Samuel comes to "know" the LORD by learning to recognize God's revelations. **9–10:** *Your servant,* a polite way of referring to oneself. **14:** Eli's sons profaned the sacrifices that might otherwise have *expiated* or atoned for their sins (2.12–17). **17:** *May God do so to you and more also,* a typical oath formula. Eli adjures Samuel, forcing him to reveal his conversation with the LORD. **19:** All of Samuel's prophecies come true (none *fall to the ground*). **20:** *Dan to Beer-sheba,* the traditional northern and southern limits of Israel.

4.1b–22: The capture of the ark. Many scholars believe that 4.1–7.1 and possibly 2 Sam 6 are based

In those days the Philistines mustered for
war against Israel,[a] and Israel went out to
battle against them;[b] they encamped at Eb-
enezer, and the Philistines encamped at
Aphek. 2 The Philistines drew up in line
against Israel, and when the battle was
joined,[c] Israel was defeated by the Philis-
tines, who killed about four thousand men
on the field of battle. 3 When the troops
came to the camp, the elders of Israel said,
"Why has the LORD put us to rout today
before the Philistines? Let us bring the ark
of the covenant of the LORD here from Shi-
loh, so that he may come among us and
save us from the power of our enemies."
4 So the people sent to Shiloh, and brought
from there the ark of the covenant of the
LORD of hosts, who is enthroned on the
cherubim. The two sons of Eli, Hophni and
Phinehas, were there with the ark of the
covenant of God.
5 When the ark of the covenant of the
LORD came into the camp, all Israel gave a
mighty shout, so that the earth resounded.
6 When the Philistines heard the noise of the
shouting, they said, "What does this great
shouting in the camp of the Hebrews
mean?" When they learned that the ark of
the LORD had come to the camp, 7 the Phil-
istines were afraid; for they said, "Gods
have[d] come into the camp." They also
said, "Woe to us! For nothing like this has
happened before. 8 Woe to us! Who can de-
liver us from the power of these mighty

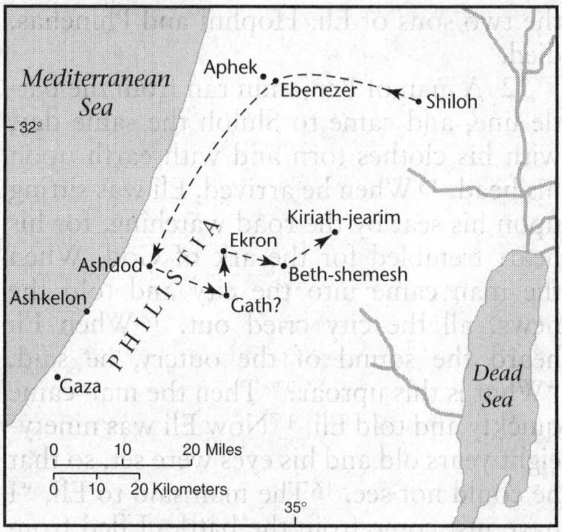

Chs 4–6: Wanderings of the ark of the covenant.

gods? These are the gods who struck the
Egyptians with every sort of plague in the
wilderness. 9 Take courage, and be men,
O Philistines, in order not to become slaves
to the Hebrews as they have been to you; be
men and fight."
10 So the Philistines fought; Israel was
defeated, and they fled, everyone to his
home. There was a very great slaughter, for
there fell of Israel thirty thousand foot sol-
diers. 11 The ark of God was captured; and

a Gk: Heb lacks *In those days the Philistines mustered for war against Israel* *b* Gk: Heb *against the Philistines* *c* Meaning of Heb uncertain *d* Or *A god has*

on an old document called the "Ark Narrative" that described the capture and return of the ark. The ark is the focus of this section rather than Samuel, who is not mentioned. **1b:** The *Philistines* came from the northeastern Mediterranean area (including the island of Crete; see Am 9.7) and entered Palestine (which is derived from "Philistine") in approximately 1200 BCE, about the same time the Israelites were emerging in the central highlands. In this period they were Israel's great enemy. **2:** *Four thousand men,* the numbers throughout this account are exaggerated, or the Hebrew word translated "thousand" refers to a military unit of far fewer than 1000 men. **4:** *Cherubim* were mythical griffin-like creatures with body parts from different creatures, especially human heads, and wings. They were commonly depicted in palaces and temples. As the throne of "the LORD of hosts who sits *enthroned on the cherubim*" (cf. 3.3), the ark represented the LORD's presence in battle. The early form of the ark may have been simple (Deut 10.2–3) and without cherubim, but in later conception it became ornate (Ex 25.10–22; 37.1–9) **6:** *Hebrews* is commonly used to distinguish Israelites ethnically from foreigners (Gen 14.13; Ex 1.15; 2.11,13; 3.18; 1 Sam 14.21; Jon 1.9). Sometimes, however, it seems to designate a broader socioeconomic group (Gen 39.14; 43.32). **8:** *Gods* implies that the Philistines had no conception that the Israelites worshiped only one God (but cf. 5.7–8,10–11). The Philistines also locate the plagues in the *wilderness* rather than in Egypt. In both cases the Israelite writer may be mocking the Philistines. **10:** *Thirty thousand,* see v. 3n.

the two sons of Eli, Hophni and Phinehas,
died.
12 A man of Benjamin ran from the bat-
tle line, and came to Shiloh the same day,
with his clothes torn and with earth upon
his head. 13 When he arrived, Eli was sitting
upon his seat by the road watching, for his
heart trembled for the ark of God. When
the man came into the city and told the
news, all the city cried out. 14 When Eli
heard the sound of the outcry, he said,
"What is this uproar?" Then the man came
quickly and told Eli. 15 Now Eli was ninety-
eight years old and his eyes were set, so that
he could not see. 16 The man said to Eli, "I
have just come from the battle; I fled from
the battle today." He said, "How did it go,
my son?" 17 The messenger replied, "Israel
has fled before the Philistines, and there
has also been a great slaughter among the
troops; your two sons also, Hophni and
Phinehas, are dead, and the ark of God has
been captured." 18 When he mentioned the
ark of God, Eli[a] fell over backward from
his seat by the side of the gate; and his neck
was broken and he died, for he was an old
man, and heavy. He had judged Israel forty
years.
19 Now his daughter-in-law, the wife
of Phinehas, was pregnant, about to give
birth. When she heard the news that the ark
of God was captured, and that her father-
in-law and her husband were dead, she
bowed and gave birth; for her labor pains
overwhelmed her. 20 As she was about to
die, the women attending her said to her,
"Do not be afraid, for you have borne a
son." But she did not answer or give heed.
21 She named the child Ichabod, meaning,
"The glory has departed from Israel," be-
cause the ark of God had been captured
and because of her father-in-law and her
husband. 22 She said, "The glory has de-
parted from Israel, for the ark of God has
been captured."

5 When the Philistines captured the ark
of God, they brought it from Ebenezer
to Ashdod; 2 then the Philistines took the
ark of God and brought it into the house of
Dagon and placed it beside Dagon. 3 When
the people of Ashdod rose early the next
day, there was Dagon, fallen on his face to
the ground before the ark of the LORD. So
they took Dagon and put him back in his
place. 4 But when they rose early on the
next morning, Dagon had fallen on his face
to the ground before the ark of the LORD,
and the head of Dagon and both his hands
were lying cut off upon the threshold; only
the trunk of[b] Dagon was left to him. 5 This
is why the priests of Dagon and all who
enter the house of Dagon do not step on the
threshold of Dagon in Ashdod to this day.
6 The hand of the LORD was heavy upon
the people of Ashdod, and he terrified and
struck them with tumors, both in Ashdod
and in its territory. 7 And when the inhabi-
tants of Ashdod saw how things were, they
said, "The ark of the God of Israel must not
remain with us; for his hand is heavy on us
and on our god Dagon." 8 So they sent and
gathered together all the lords of the Philis-

a Heb *he* *b* Heb lacks *the trunk of*

12: *With his clothes torn and with earth upon his head,* conventional signs of mourning. **18:** Pious *Eli* is moved by the loss of the ark more than the loss of his (wicked) sons. *Forty years,* a round number for a generation. **21–22:** *Ichabod,* "Where is the glory?" or "Alas for the glory." "Glory" alludes to the ark.

5.1–12: The ark troubles the Philistines. In the ancient Near East, wars between nations were interpreted as contests between their respective gods. This story explains that although the Philistines defeated Israel, the LORD was superior to Dagon, a Philistine god. **1:** *Ashdod,* one of five principal Philistine cities along with Ashkelon, Ekron, Gath, and Gaza. **2:** *Beside Dagon* means beside the statue of Dagon in his temple. Dagon was a Canaanite god of grain whom the Philistines adopted as a major deity. **3:** *There was Dagon, fallen on his face to the ground before the ark of the LORD,* bowing prostrate was a sign of subservience. **4–5:** This is an etiology (a story that explains a custom, name, etc.) for the practice of jumping over thresholds in order to avoid offending the spirits of a particular building or space (see Zeph 1.9). **6–12:** The tumors and mice (in the next chapter) suggest that this outbreak was bubonic plague, which was common in coastlands. According to this story, however, the plague is the LORD's doing. **8:**

tines, and said, "What shall we do with the
ark of the God of Israel?" The inhabitants
of Gath replied, "Let the ark of God be
moved on to us."[a] So they moved the ark
of the God of Israel to Gath.[b] 9 But after
they had brought it to Gath,[c] the hand of
the LORD was against the city, causing a
very great panic; he struck the inhabitants
of the city, both young and old, so that
tumors broke out on them. 10 So they sent
the ark of the God of Israel[d] to Ekron. But
when the ark of God came to Ekron, the
people of Ekron cried out, "Why[e] have
they brought around to us[f] the ark of the
God of Israel to kill us[f] and our[g] peo-
ple?" 11 They sent therefore and gathered
together all the lords of the Philistines, and
said, "Send away the ark of the God of
Israel, and let it return to its own place, that
it may not kill us and our people." For
there was a deathly panic[h] throughout the
whole city. The hand of God was very
heavy there; 12 those who did not die were
stricken with tumors, and the cry of the city
went up to heaven.

6 The ark of the LORD was in the country
of the Philistines seven months. 2 Then
the Philistines called for the priests and the
diviners and said, "What shall we do with
the ark of the LORD? Tell us what we
should send with it to its place." 3 They
said, "If you send away the ark of the God
of Israel, do not send it empty, but by all
means return him a guilt offering. Then you
will be healed and will be ransomed;[i] will
not his hand then turn from you?" 4 And
they said, "What is the guilt offering that
we shall return to him?" They answered,
"Five gold tumors and five gold mice, ac-
cording to the number of the lords of the
Philistines; for the same plague was upon
all of you and upon your lords. 5 So you
must make images of your tumors and im-
ages of your mice that ravage the land, and
give glory to the God of Israel; perhaps he
will lighten his hand on you and your gods
and your land. 6 Why should you harden
your hearts as the Egyptians and Pharaoh
hardened their hearts? After he had made
fools of them, did they not let the people
go, and they departed? 7 Now then, get
ready a new cart and two milch cows that
have never borne a yoke, and yoke the
cows to the cart, but take their calves
home, away from them. 8 Take the ark of
the LORD and place it on the cart, and put
in a box at its side the figures of gold,
which you are returning to him as a guilt
offering. Then send it off, and let it go its
way. 9 And watch; if it goes up on the way
to its own land, to Beth-shemesh, then it is
he who has done us this great harm; but if
not, then we shall know that it is not his
hand that struck us; it happened to us by
chance."

10 The men did so; they took two milch
cows and yoked them to the cart, and shut
up their calves at home. 11 They put the ark
of the LORD on the cart, and the box with
the gold mice and the images of their tu-
mors. 12 The cows went straight in the di-

a Gk Compare Q Ms: MT *They answered, "Let the ark of the God of Israel be brought around to Gath."*
b Gk: Heb lacks *to Gath* *c* Q Ms: MT lacks *to Gath* *d* Q Ms Gk: MT lacks *of Israel* *e* Q Ms Gk: MT lacks *Why* *f* Heb *me* *g* Heb *my*
h Q Ms reads *a panic from the LORD* *i* Q Ms Gk: MT *and it will be known to you*

The *lords of the Philistines* are the rulers of the Philistine pentapolis. The word "lord" ("seren") is Philistine and cognate with the Greek word "tyrannos," ("tyrant").

6.1–7.1: The return of the ark. 6.3: *Guilt offering,* not a sacrifice but compensation for taking the ark and appeasement of the LORD in hopes of avoiding further punishment. **4–5:** There is one gold tumor and one gold mouse for each of the five Philistine rulers (vv. 4,17–18). The images serve as substitutes for the rulers and their cities in order to carry the plague away by magic. **6:** Cf. Ex 8.19,32. A creative enhancement by the author, since the Philistines would not have known the story of the Exodus. **7:** A new cart is ritually pure. The two cows have never been yoked and are therefore fit to be sacrificed (cf. Num 19.2; Deut 21.3). *Milch cows* means that they have young calves. **9:** Unaccustomed to pulling a cart, these two cows would be expected to wander aimlessly in search of their calves. If instead they headed for Israelite territory, the Philistines would know that their sufferings had indeed been sent by the LORD. **12:** The cows

rection of Beth-shemesh along one high-
way, lowing as they went; they turned
neither to the right nor to the left, and the
lords of the Philistines went after them as
far as the border of Beth-shemesh.
13 Now the people of Beth-shemesh
were reaping their wheat harvest in the val-
ley. When they looked up and saw the ark,
they went with rejoicing to meet it.[a] 14 The
cart came into the field of Joshua of Beth-
shemesh, and stopped there. A large stone
was there; so they split up the wood of the
cart and offered the cows as a burnt offer-
ing to the LORD. 15 The Levites took down
the ark of the LORD and the box that was
beside it, in which were the gold objects,
and set them upon the large stone. Then
the people of Beth-shemesh offered burnt
offerings and presented sacrifices on that
day to the LORD. 16 When the five lords of
the Philistines saw it, they returned that day
to Ekron.
17 These are the gold tumors, which the
Philistines returned as a guilt offering to the
LORD: one for Ashdod, one for Gaza, one
for Ashkelon, one for Gath, one for Ekron;
18 also the gold mice, according to the num-
ber of all the cities of the Philistines belong-
ing to the five lords, both fortified cities
and unwalled villages. The great stone, be-
side which they set down the ark of the
LORD, is a witness to this day in the field of
Joshua of Beth-shemesh.
19 The descendants of Jeconiah did not
rejoice with the people of Beth-shemesh
when they greeted[b] the ark of the LORD;
and he killed seventy men of them.[c] The
people mourned because the LORD had
made a great slaughter among the people.
20 Then the people of Beth-shemesh said,
"Who is able to stand before the LORD, this
holy God? To whom shall he go so that we
may be rid of him?" 21 So they sent messen-
gers to the inhabitants of Kiriath-jearim,
saying, "The Philistines have returned the
ark of the LORD. Come down and take it
7 up to you." 1 And the people of Kiriath-
jearim came and took up the ark of the
LORD, and brought it to the house of Abin-
adab on the hill. They consecrated his son,
Eleazar, to have charge of the ark of the
LORD.
2 From the day that the ark was lodged
at Kiriath-jearim, a long time passed, some
twenty years, and all the house of Israel
lamented[d] after the LORD.
3 Then Samuel said to all the house of
Israel, "If you are returning to the LORD
with all your heart, then put away the for-
eign gods and the Astartes from among
you. Direct your heart to the LORD, and
serve him only, and he will deliver you out
of the hand of the Philistines." 4 So Israel
put away the Baals and the Astartes, and
they served the LORD only.
5 Then Samuel said, "Gather all Israel at

a Gk: Heb *rejoiced to see it* *b* Gk: Heb *And he killed some of the people of Beth-shemesh, because they looked into* *c* Heb *killed seventy men, fifty thousand men* *d* Meaning of Heb uncertain

take the most direct route into Israelite territory. **15:** This verse is likely a later addition by an editor concerned to have the Levites, the priestly tribe, handle the ark. **19:** It was *seventy* of the people of Beth-shemesh, not seventy of the *descendants of Jeconiah,* who were killed. The reason is uncertain, since nothing else is known about Jeconiah or his family. **20:** *To stand before the LORD* is a technical expression for priestly service, suggesting that the people are asking for a priest to handle the ark. It remains unclear how the absence of a priest relates to Jeconiah. **7.1:** *Abinadab* is the father of several important priests (2 Sam 6.3–4,6–8; 1 Chr 13.7,9–11).

7.2–17: Samuel judges Israel. Samuel is depicted as a transitional figure between the judges and the monarchy. He embodies the roles of priest, prophet, and now judge (cf. Judg 10.6–16). **2:** *Twenty years* is a way of designating half a generation. This notice fits Samuel into the structure of the book of Judges where a period of foreign oppression precedes Israel's repentance. **3–4:** *Returning to the LORD with all your heart* is Deuteronomistic language (cf. Deut 30.10; Josh 22.5; 23.14; 24.23; Judg 10.16; 1 Sam 12.20,24; 1 Kings 8.23,48; 14.8; 2 Kings 10.31; 23.25). *Baal* and *Astarte,* the leading male and female gods of Canaan. **5:** *Mizpah* became the administrative and religious capital of Judah after Jerusalem's destruction in 586 BCE (2 Kings 25.23). Hence, the setting of this story in Mizpah may indicate a date

Mizpah, and I will pray to the LORD for
you." 6 So they gathered at Mizpah, and
drew water and poured it out before the
LORD. They fasted that day, and said, "We
have sinned against the LORD." And Sam-
uel judged the people of Israel at Mizpah.
7 When the Philistines heard that the
people of Israel had gathered at Mizpah,
the lords of the Philistines went up against
Israel. And when the people of Israel heard
of it they were afraid of the Philistines.
8 The people of Israel said to Samuel, "Do
not cease to cry out to the LORD our God
for us, and pray that he may save us from
the hand of the Philistines." 9 So Samuel
took a sucking lamb and offered it as a
whole burnt offering to the LORD; Samuel
cried out to the LORD for Israel, and the
LORD answered him. 10 As Samuel was
offering up the burnt offering, the Philis-
tines drew near to attack Israel; but the
LORD thundered with a mighty voice that
day against the Philistines and threw them
into confusion; and they were routed be-
fore Israel. 11 And the men of Israel went
out of Mizpah and pursued the Philistines,
and struck them down as far as beyond
Beth-car.
12 Then Samuel took a stone and set it
up between Mizpah and Jeshanah,[a] and
named it Ebenezer;[b] for he said, "Thus far
the LORD has helped us." 13 So the Philis-
tines were subdued and did not again enter
the territory of Israel; the hand of the LORD
was against the Philistines all the days of
Samuel. 14 The towns that the Philistines
had taken from Israel were restored to Isra-
el, from Ekron to Gath; and Israel recov-
ered their territory from the hand of the
Philistines. There was peace also between
Israel and the Amorites.
15 Samuel judged Israel all the days of
his life. 16 He went on a circuit year by year
to Bethel, Gilgal, and Mizpah; and he
judged Israel in all these places. 17 Then he
would come back to Ramah, for his home
was there; he administered justice there to
Israel, and built there an altar to the LORD.
8 When Samuel became old, he made his
sons judges over Israel. 2 The name of

a Gk Syr: Heb *Shen* *b* That is *Stone of Help*

of composition after 586 (similarly Judg 19–21). **6:** The elements of this ritual—prayer, libation, fasting, and confession—do not occur together anywhere else in the Bible. Since fasting suggests contrition and pouring out water suggests cleansing, a community purification ritual may be envisioned, perhaps in preparation for war. **8–9:** Samuel is an intercessor for the people in the tradition of Moses and Jeremiah. *A whole burnt offering,* one that is entirely consumed (Ex 29.18; Lev 8.21; Deut 13.16; 33.10). **10:** Thunder is considered the *voice* of God. **12:** An etiology for the name *Ebenezer,* which means "stone of the helper/warrior (God)." **13–14:** The statement that the Philistines *did not again enter the territory of Israel* is contradicted later in 1 Samuel. It may refer only to Samuel's lifetime. It serves the author's effort to cast Samuel as a judge; compare the Deuteronomistic formulas in Judg 3.30; 8.28; 11.33. *Amorites,* in Deuteronomy and Deuteronomistic literature the pre-Israelite inhabitants of Canaan. Contrast, e.g., Gen 14.7; 15.20, where "Amorites" refers to one pre-Israelite group. **15–17:** Scholars often identify two types of judges in the book of Judges: military leaders and legal functionaries. This chapter ascribes both roles to Samuel: His intercession brings victory over the Philistines (vv. 10–11), and he rides a circuit judging Israel (vv. 15–17). *Bethel, Gilgal, Mizpah,* and *Ramah* were all within traditional Benjaminite territory.

Chs 8–12: The beginning of kingship in Israel. These chapters recount the events in five distinct episodes: the people's request for a king and Samuel's response (ch 8); Saul's search for his father's asses and his anointing (9.1–10.16); the designation of Saul by lot (10.17–27a); Saul's victory over the Ammonites (10.27b–11.15); and Samuel's farewell address (ch 12). The stories in 9.1–10.16 and 10.27b–11.15 are generally recognized as older and neutral or positive in their attitude toward monarchy, while the other three episodes view kingship with suspicion and depict the people's request as a sin. The latter three texts are also widely recognized as Deuteronomistic. In the end, God allows a king but also warns the people against letting their king lead them astray.

8.1–22: The people request a king. 2: *Beer-sheba,* the southernmost city in Judah and far outside

his firstborn son was Joel, and the name
of his second, Abijah; they were judges in
Beer-sheba. 3 Yet his sons did not follow in
his ways, but turned aside after gain; they
took bribes and perverted justice.
4 Then all the elders of Israel gathered
together and came to Samuel at Ramah,
5 and said to him, "You are old and your
sons do not follow in your ways; appoint
for us, then, a king to govern us, like other
nations." 6 But the thing displeased Samuel
when they said, "Give us a king to govern
us." Samuel prayed to the LORD, 7 and the
LORD said to Samuel, "Listen to the voice
of the people in all that they say to you; for
they have not rejected you, but they have
rejected me from being king over them.
8 Just as they have done to me,[a] from the
day I brought them up out of Egypt to this
day, forsaking me and serving other gods,
so also they are doing to you. 9 Now then,
listen to their voice; only—you shall sol-
emnly warn them, and show them the ways
of the king who shall reign over them."
10 So Samuel reported all the words of
the LORD to the people who were asking
him for a king. 11 He said, "These will be
the ways of the king who will reign over
you: he will take your sons and appoint
them to his chariots and to be his horse-
men, and to run before his chariots; 12 and
he will appoint for himself commanders of
thousands and commanders of fifties, and
some to plow his ground and to reap his
harvest, and to make his implements of war
and the equipment of his chariots. 13 He
will take your daughters to be perfumers
and cooks and bakers. 14 He will take the
best of your fields and vineyards and olive
orchards and give them to his courtiers.
15 He will take one-tenth of your grain and
of your vineyards and give it to his officers
and his courtiers. 16 He will take your male
and female slaves, and the best of your
cattle[b] and donkeys, and put them to his
work. 17 He will take one-tenth of your
flocks, and you shall be his slaves. 18 And in
that day you will cry out because of your
king, whom you have chosen for your-
selves; but the LORD will not answer you in
that day."
19 But the people refused to listen to the
voice of Samuel; they said, "No! but we are
determined to have a king over us, 20 so that
we also may be like other nations, and that
our king may govern us and go out before
us and fight our battles." 21 When Samuel
had heard all the words of the people, he
repeated them in the ears of the LORD.
22 The LORD said to Samuel, "Listen to
their voice and set a king over them." Sam-

a Gk: Heb lacks *to me* *b* Gk: Heb *young men*

Samuel's jurisdiction in 7.15–17. It became an administrative center during Judah's monarchy. **3:** Samuel's sons, like Eli's, are corrupt (Deut 16.19 denounces taking bribes). Their unfitness to rule impels the elders to ask for a king. **4:** The *elders* were the leading and usually senior citizens. **6–7:** Samuel and the LORD are displeased by the request and consider it a rejection of the LORD. But is kingship regarded as inherently evil? Or does the request demonstrate a lack of faith in the LORD? **8:** The review of Israel's history is in typical Deuteronomistic style (cf. 2 Kings 21.15). **10:** *Asking* is a play on the name "Saul"; see 1.17n. **11–17:** These verses may preserve an older treaty document that described the rights and privileges of the king. *Ways,* the Hebrew word means "custom" or "judgment." The king to whom the people look for justice will follow the typical ancient Near Eastern practices of taxation and conscription. The items in this list appear to be based on Solomon's reign (cf. 1 Kings 4.7; 5.13). **18:** This verse is in characteristic Deuteronomistic language and resembles that of the framework of Judges, in which the people constantly *cry out* for relief from their oppressors. **19:** True to his name ("listen" in Hebrew sounds like "Samuel"), Samuel listens to God, while the people *refused to listen.* **20:** The desire to *be like other nations* is opposed to the LORD's desire that Israel be his special people. *Govern* is elsewhere translated "judge." *Go out before us* is an idiom for military leadership. The people trust in a king instead of God for protection from their enemies. **22:** The LORD will permit Israel to have a king even though he does not approve of their request. *Each of you return home* is editorial and sets the stage for Samuel to call another convocation in 10.17.

uel then said to the people of Israel, "Each
of you return home."

9 There was a man of Benjamin whose
name was Kish son of Abiel son of Ze-
ror son of Becorath son of Aphiah, a Benja-
minite, a man of wealth. 2 He had a son
whose name was Saul, a handsome young
man. There was not a man among the peo-
ple of Israel more handsome than he; he
stood head and shoulders above everyone
else.

3 Now the donkeys of Kish, Saul's fa-
ther, had strayed. So Kish said to his son
Saul, "Take one of the boys with you; go
and look for the donkeys." 4 He passed
through the hill country of Ephraim and
passed through the land of Shalishah, but
they did not find them. And they passed
through the land of Shaalim, but they were
not there. Then he passed through the land
of Benjamin, but they did not find them.

5 When they came to the land of Zuph,
Saul said to the boy who was with him,
"Let us turn back, or my father will stop
worrying about the donkeys and worry
about us." 6 But he said to him, "There is a
man of God in this town; he is a man held
in honor. Whatever he says always comes
true. Let us go there now; perhaps he will
tell us about the journey on which we have
set out." 7 Then Saul replied to the boy,
"But if we go, what can we bring the man?
For the bread in our sacks is gone, and
there is no present to bring to the man of
God. What have we?" 8 The boy answered
Saul again, "Here, I have with me a quarter
shekel of silver; I will give it to the man of
God, to tell us our way." 9 (Formerly in Is-
rael, anyone who went to inquire of God
would say, "Come, let us go to the seer";
for the one who is now called a prophet
was formerly called a seer.) 10 Saul said to
the boy, "Good; come, let us go." So they
went to the town where the man of God
was.

11 As they went up the hill to the town,
they met some girls coming out to draw
water, and said to them, "Is the seer here?"
12 They answered, "Yes, there he is just
ahead of you. Hurry; he has come just now
to the town, because the people have a sac-
rifice today at the shrine. 13 As soon as you
enter the town, you will find him, before he
goes up to the shrine to eat. For the people
will not eat until he comes, since he must
bless the sacrifice; afterward those eat who
are invited. Now go up, for you will meet
him immediately." 14 So they went up to the
town. As they were entering the town, they
saw Samuel coming out toward them on his
way up to the shrine.

15 Now the day before Saul came, the
LORD had revealed to Samuel: 16 "Tomor-
row about this time I will send to you a
man from the land of Benjamin, and you
shall anoint him to be ruler over my people

9.1–10.16: Saul's anointing. This is an old story that has been edited by the Deuteronomist. Samuel appears not as a judge but as a "man of God." Both Saul and kingship are depicted positively. **9.2:** *Handsome* (lit. "good"), a description often attributed to leaders (Joseph, Gen 39.6; baby Moses, Ex 2.2; David, 1 Sam 16.12). Saul's height is also an important theme in 1 Samuel, especially for its contrast with David. **3:** *Boys* (better: "servants") need not have been young. **4:** *Shalishah* and *Shaalim* may both be puns on Saul's name. **6–7:** *What can we bring,* a single word in Hebrew, spelled exactly like the word "prophet." The *man of God,* a title for a prophet, turns out to be Samuel (v. 14). But the identification is secondary, since Saul and his servant do not initially know who Samuel is. In the original tale, Saul's encounter was with an anonymous seer. The *town,* probably Ramah, Samuel's home. The *present* was a payment to the man of God for divining the whereabouts of the donkeys. **8:** A *quarter shekel* was a measure of weight (about one-eighth oz.). **9:** A note by an editor indicating that the word *seer* had gone out of use. **11:** *Drawing water* was done by women, usually in the morning or evening when it was cooler. Hence, it was around sundown. **12:** The *shrine* ("high place") was a hill or raised platform where worship, especially sacrifices, took place. Deuteronomistic literature condemns the high places once the temple is built. **13:** Sacrifices provided occasions for feasting after the portions of the animal designated for God were burned. **16:** *Ruler,* a special term meaning "king designate." *Their outcry has come to me,* cf. Ex 3.9. **18:** *The gate,* a fortified entryway into a walled city. It was the site of commerce and judicial

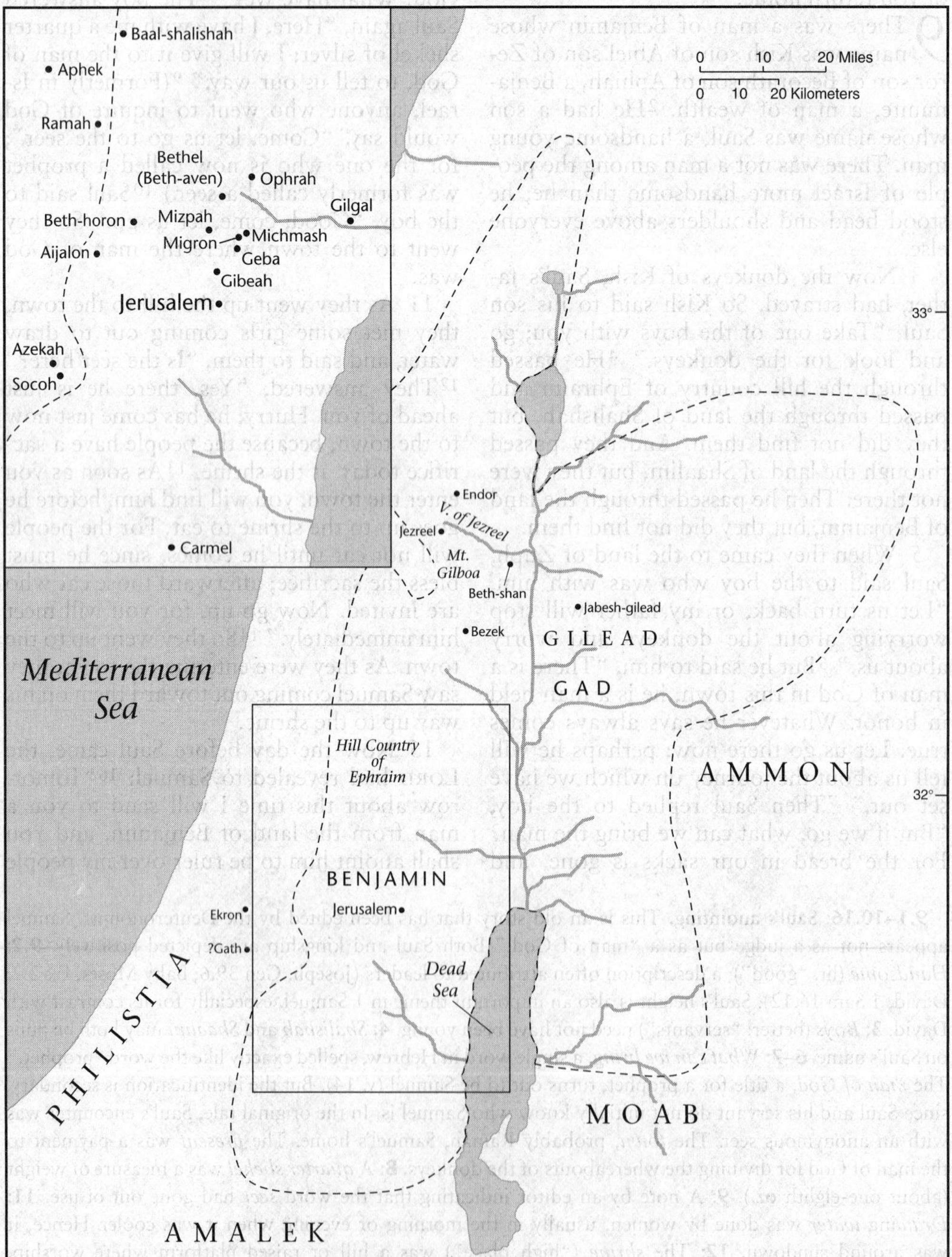

Chs 9–31: The kingdom of Saul. The dashed line shows the approximate outer boundary of his kingdom.

Israel. He shall save my people from the
hand of the Philistines; for I have seen the
suffering of[a] my people, because their out-
cry has come to me." 17When Samuel saw
Saul, the LORD told him, "Here is the man
of whom I spoke to you. He it is who shall
rule over my people." 18Then Saul ap-
proached Samuel inside the gate, and said,
"Tell me, please, where is the house of the
seer?" 19Samuel answered Saul, "I am the
seer; go up before me to the shrine, for to-
day you shall eat with me, and in the morn-
ing I will let you go and will tell you all that
is on your mind. 20As for your donkeys
that were lost three days ago, give no fur-
ther thought to them, for they have been
found. And on whom is all Israel's desire
fixed, if not on you and on all your ances-
tral house?" 21Saul answered, "I am only a
Benjaminite, from the least of the tribes of
Israel, and my family is the humblest of all
the families of the tribe of Benjamin. Why
then have you spoken to me in this way?"
22 Then Samuel took Saul and his
servant-boy and brought them into the
hall, and gave them a place at the head of
those who had been invited, of whom there
were about thirty. 23And Samuel said to the
cook, "Bring the portion I gave you, the
one I asked you to put aside." 24The cook
took up the thigh and what went with it[b]
and set them before Saul. Samuel said,
"See, what was kept is set before you. Eat;
for it is set[c] before you at the appointed
time, so that you might eat with the
guests."[d]
So Saul ate with Samuel that day.
25When they came down from the shrine
into the town, a bed was spread for Saul[e]
on the roof, and he lay down to sleep.[f]
26Then at the break of dawn[g] Samuel
called to Saul upon the roof, "Get up, so
that I may send you on your way." Saul got
up, and both he and Samuel went out into
the street.
27 As they were going down to the out-
skirts of the town, Samuel said to Saul,
"Tell the boy to go on before us, and when
he has passed on, stop here yourself for a
while, that I may make known to you the
10 word of God." 1Samuel took a vial
of oil and poured it on his head, and
kissed him; he said, "The LORD has anoint-
ed you ruler over his people Israel. You
shall reign over the people of the LORD and
you will save them from the hand of their
enemies all around. Now this shall be the
sign to you that the LORD has anointed you
ruler[h] over his heritage: 2When you depart
from me today you will meet two men by
Rachel's tomb in the territory of Benjamin
at Zelzah; they will say to you, 'The don-
keys that you went to seek are found, and
now your father has stopped worrying
about them and is worrying about you, say-
ing: What shall I do about my son?' 3Then
you shall go on from there further and
come to the oak of Tabor; three men going
up to God at Bethel will meet you there,
one carrying three kids, another carrying
three loaves of bread, and another carrying
a skin of wine. 4They will greet you and
give you two loaves of bread, which you

a Gk: Heb lacks *the suffering of* *b* Meaning of Heb uncertain *c* Q Ms Gk: MT *it was kept* *d* Cn: Heb *it was kept for you, saying, I have invited the people* *e* Gk: Heb *and he spoke with Saul* *f* Gk: Heb lacks *and he lay down to sleep* *g* Gk: Heb *and they arose early and at break of dawn* *h* Gk: Heb lacks *over his people Israel. You shall . . . anointed you ruler*

proceedings. **19–20:** In the original tale, the seer consulted God overnight in order to address Saul's need (v. 19). But in the present, edited version, Samuel has been told to expect Saul (vv. 15–17) and now goes ahead and tells him *all that is on* his *mind,* assuring him that the donkeys have been found (v. 20). The next morning is reserved for Saul's anointing. **21:** Like others called by God (Moses, Ex 3–4; Jeremiah, Jer 1), Saul objects that he is unworthy. **22–24:** Saul is the honored guest. *The thigh* is usually reserved for the deity or priests. These verses are likely editorial, since they presuppose Samuel's foreknowledge of Saul's arrival. **10.1:** The LORD's *heritage* is the land of Israel. Every nation is understood as the inheritance of the god it worships. The LORD, creator of the world, is envisioned as having chosen Israel as his people (Deut 10.14–15; 32.8–9). **3:** The *three men going up to God at Bethel* are carrying items for sacrifice. **4:** *Greet* is a pun on Saul's name. The men give *two loaves of bread,* one for Saul and one for his

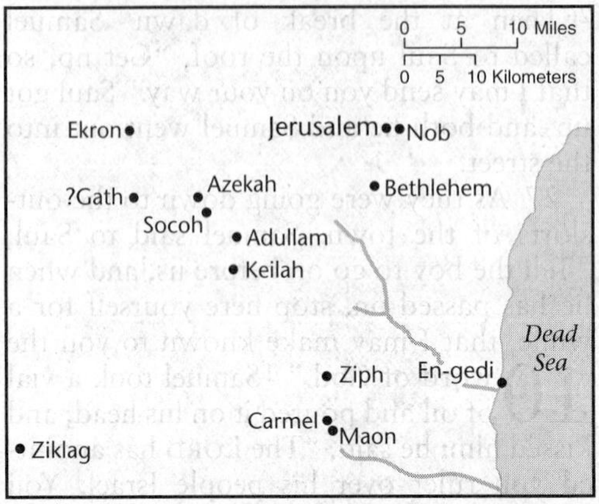

Chs 9–28: David's early career and his flight from Saul.

shall accept from them. 5 After that you
shall come to Gibeath-elohim,[a] at the
place where the Philistine garrison is; there,
as you come to the town, you will meet a
band of prophets coming down from the
shrine with harp, tambourine, flute, and
lyre playing in front of them; they will be in
a prophetic frenzy. 6 Then the spirit of the
LORD will possess you, and you will be in a
prophetic frenzy along with them and be
turned into a different person. 7 Now when
these signs meet you, do whatever you see
fit to do, for God is with you. 8 And you
shall go down to Gilgal ahead of me; then
I will come down to you to present burnt
offerings and offer sacrifices of well-being.
Seven days you shall wait, until I come to
you and show you what you shall do."

9 As he turned away to leave Samuel,
God gave him another heart; and all these
signs were fulfilled that day. 10 When they
were going from there[b] to Gibeah,[c] a
band of prophets met him; and the spirit of
God possessed him, and he fell into a prophetic frenzy along with them. 11 When all
who knew him before saw how he prophesied with the prophets, the people said to
one another, "What has come over the son
of Kish? Is Saul also among the prophets?"
12 A man of the place answered, "And who
is their father?" Therefore it became a
proverb, "Is Saul also among the prophets?" 13 When his prophetic frenzy had ended, he went home.[d]

14 Saul's uncle said to him and to the
boy, "Where did you go?" And he replied,
"To seek the donkeys; and when we saw
they were not to be found, we went to Samuel." 15 Saul's uncle said, "Tell me what
Samuel said to you." 16 Saul said to his uncle, "He told us that the donkeys had been
found." But about the matter of the kingship, of which Samuel had spoken, he did
not tell him anything.

17 Samuel summoned the people to the
LORD at Mizpah 18 and said to them,[e]
"Thus says the LORD, the God of Israel, 'I
brought up Israel out of Egypt, and I rescued you from the hand of the Egyptians
and from the hand of all the kingdoms that

a Or *the Hill of God* *b* Gk: Heb *they came there*
c Or *the hill* *d* Cn: Heb *he came to the shrine*
e Heb *to the people of Israel*

servant. The Greek (LXX) reading, "two offerings of bread," suggests that Saul again receives the portion of a priest. **5–7:** Music was used to induce an ecstatic condition in which prophets uttered their oracles (2 Kings 3.15–16); *frenzy* (vv. 5–6,10,13) is misleadingly pejorative. Like the judges, Saul will be moved to action by the spirit of the LORD. The instruction to *do whatever you see fit to do* is a military commission. **8:** This verse connects this story to 13.7b–15. **10–13:** An etiology for the proverb, *Is Saul also among the prophets?* Here the proverb has a positive sense, showing that the LORD's spirit empowers Saul to prophesy and rule. A different explanation of the proverb occurs in 19.19–24. The *father* of a group of prophets (v. 12) is their leader. **14–16:** It is surprising that Saul's uncle rather than his father questions him, since the uncle has not been mentioned before in the story. These verses prepare for the following story (10.17–27a) by pointing out that since Saul's anointing was private, a public proclamation of his kingship is needed.

10.17–27a: Saul chosen by lot. 17: *Mizpah,* see 7.5n. **18–19:** The language of these verses is Deuteronomistic, especially the references to bringing up *Israel out of Egypt* and the accusation that they have *rejected* their God. **20–21:** Israelite society was structured in a descending hierarchy of tribe, clan,

were oppressing you.' 19 But today you
have rejected your God, who saves you
from all your calamities and your dis-
tresses; and you have said, 'No! but set a
king over us.' Now therefore present your-
selves before the LORD by your tribes and
by your clans."
20 Then Samuel brought all the tribes of
Israel near, and the tribe of Benjamin was
taken by lot. 21 He brought the tribe of Ben-
jamin near by its families, and the family of
the Matrites was taken by lot. Finally he
brought the family of the Matrites near
man by man,[a] and Saul the son of Kish
was taken by lot. But when they sought
him, he could not be found. 22 So they in-
quired again of the LORD, "Did the man
come here?"[b] and the LORD said, "See, he
has hidden himself among the baggage."
23 Then they ran and brought him from
there. When he took his stand among the
people, he was head and shoulders taller
than any of them. 24 Samuel said to all the
people, "Do you see the one whom the
LORD has chosen? There is no one like him
among all the people." And all the people
shouted, "Long live the king!"
25 Samuel told the people the rights and
duties of the kingship; and he wrote them
in a book and laid it up before the LORD.
Then Samuel sent all the people back to
their homes. 26 Saul also went to his home
at Gibeah, and with him went warriors
whose hearts God had touched. 27 But some
worthless fellows said, "How can this man
save us?" They despised him and brought
him no present. But he held his peace.
Now Nahash, king of the Ammonites,
had been grievously oppressing the Gadites
and the Reubenites. He would gouge out
the right eye of each of them and would not
grant Israel a deliverer. No one was left of
the Israelites across the Jordan whose right
eye Nahash, king of the Ammonites, had
not gouged out. But there were seven thou-
sand men who had escaped from the Am-
monites and had entered Jabesh-gilead.[c]
11 About a month later,[d] Nahash the
Ammonite went up and besieged
Jabesh-gilead; and all the men of Jabesh
said to Nahash, "Make a treaty with us,
and we will serve you." 2 But Nahash the
Ammonite said to them, "On this condition
I will make a treaty with you, namely that
I gouge out everyone's right eye, and thus
put disgrace upon all Israel." 3 The elders of
Jabesh said to him, "Give us seven days'

a Gk: Heb lacks *Finally . . . man by man* *b* Gk: Heb *Is there yet a man to come here?* *c* Q Ms Compare Josephus, *Antiquities* VI.v.1 (68-71): MT lacks *Now Nahash . . . entered Jabesh-gilead.* *d* Q Ms Gk: MT lacks *About a month later*

family ("house of the father"), and individual. In the Bible (Josh 7.14; 1 Sam 14.41) the lot is used to find a person guilty of breaking a law or vow. Some scholars believe that two stories are combined at this point, one in which Saul was present and chosen by lot and another in which he was chosen by oracle or because of his height. **22:** *Inquired,* another pun on Saul's name. **25:** *The rights and duties of the kingship* probably set out the responsibilities of king and people to each other. The expression here is nearly identical to "the ways of the king" in 8.9,11, although they may not refer to the same document. **26–27a:** Saul's return to Gibeah and the doubts of the *worthless fellows* prepare for the subsequent story in which Saul proves his ability to save Israel. By bringing him *no present* these people refuse to accept him as king.

10.27b–11.15: Saul proves himself able to lead in battle and is publicly made king. 10.27b: This paragraph was lost from the Hebrew text and has been restored from a Dead Sea Scroll fragment of Samuel, as the translators' note indicates. The paragraph explains the reason for the conflict in ch 11. *The Gadites and the Reubenites* were Israelites living east of the Jordan in territory that the Ammonite king, Nahash, considered his. The city of Jabesh in Gilead was farther north, outside the disputed area, but Nahash threatened it because some of the Israelites from Gad and Reuben had fled there. **2:** As a visible sign of their subjugation and a punishment for encroaching on his land, *Nahash* had been gouging out *everyone's right eye* among the Gadites and Reubenites (10.27b). The *elders of Jabesh* are willing to accept Nahash as their overlord. But he insists on the same measure against them as a punishment for their harboring those who fled from him and as a sign of *disgrace upon all Israel.* **3:** The messengers are not

respite that we may send messengers
through all the territory of Israel. Then, if
there is no one to save us, we will give our-
selves up to you." 4 When the messengers
came to Gibeah of Saul, they reported the
matter in the hearing of the people; and all
the people wept aloud.

5 Now Saul was coming from the field
behind the oxen; and Saul said, "What is
the matter with the people, that they are
weeping?" So they told him the message
from the inhabitants of Jabesh. 6 And the
spirit of God came upon Saul in power
when he heard these words, and his anger
was greatly kindled. 7 He took a yoke of
oxen, and cut them in pieces and sent them
throughout all the territory of Israel by
messengers, saying, "Whoever does not
come out after Saul and Samuel, so shall it
be done to his oxen!" Then the dread of the
LORD fell upon the people, and they came
out as one. 8 When he mustered them at
Bezek, those from Israel were three hun-
dred thousand, and those from Judah sev-
enty[a] thousand. 9 They said to the messen-
gers who had come, "Thus shall you say to
the inhabitants of Jabesh-gilead: 'Tomor-
row, by the time the sun is hot, you shall
have deliverance.'" When the messengers
came and told the inhabitants of Jabesh,
they rejoiced. 10 So the inhabitants of Ja-
besh said, "Tomorrow we will give our-
selves up to you, and you may do to us
whatever seems good to you." 11 The next
day Saul put the people in three companies.
At the morning watch they came into the
camp and cut down the Ammonites until
the heat of the day; and those who survived
were scattered, so that no two of them were
left together.

12 The people said to Samuel, "Who is
it that said, 'Shall Saul reign over us?' Give
them to us so that we may put them to
death." 13 But Saul said, "No one shall be
put to death this day, for today the LORD
has brought deliverance to Israel."

14 Samuel said to the people, "Come, let
us go to Gilgal and there renew the king-
ship." 15 So all the people went to Gilgal,
and there they made Saul king before the
LORD in Gilgal. There they sacrificed offer-
ings of well-being before the LORD, and
there Saul and all the Israelites rejoiced
greatly.

12 Samuel said to all Israel, "I have lis-
tened to you in all that you have
said to me, and have set a king over you.
2 See, it is the king who leads you now; I am

a Q Ms Gk: MT *thirty*

sent directly to Saul but *through all the territory of Israel.* **4–5:** Even in Gibeah the messengers do not seek out Saul; he learns of their mission because of the weeping of the people as he returns from the field. The story, then, does not assume that Saul is king. **6:** The *spirit of God* spurs Saul to military action as in the book of Judges. **7:** Saul's dismembering the oxen represents a threat against those who do not join in the war. Dismemberment was a common curse for breaking a treaty, so that Saul's actions assume a treaty or covenant among the tribes. **8:** The distinction between Israel and Judah either is an anachronism or reflects a differentiation that was always felt if not institutionalized until after Solomon's reign. **10:** *We will give ourselves up to you,* lit. "we will come out to you" as in v. 3, could also be understood as "we will fight against you." **11:** Their day began at sundown, hence *the next day* would be "that evening" in our reckoning. *The morning watch* was in the early hours before sunrise. The Israelites marched all night to attack by surprise before dawn. **12–14:** An editorial addition that links 10.17–27a with 10.27b–11.15. *Samuel* plays no role in the battle account and may reflect a secondary addition. The editor also speaks of *renewing the kingship.* These verses, and the story as a whole, show how Saul succeeded in delivering Israel and thus answering his critics, and thereby present him in a positive light. **15:** The original story did not assume that Saul was already king but explained that the people *made Saul king* as a result of his victory on this occasion.

12.1–25: Samuel's address. This chapter is a Deuteronomistic composition. Ancient historians often placed speeches, which they themselves composed and considered appropriate to the occasion, into the mouths of their characters. See, e.g., Josh 23–24 and 1 Kings 8. Most of Deuteronomy is cast as a speech of Moses. **2:** *My sons are with you,* Samuel is not putting his sons forward as leaders but mentions them

old and gray, but my sons are with you. I
have led you from my youth until this day.
3 Here I am; testify against me before the
LORD and before his anointed. Whose ox
have I taken? Or whose donkey have I tak-
en? Or whom have I defrauded? Whom
have I oppressed? Or from whose hand
have I taken a bribe to blind my eyes with
it? Testify against me[a] and I will restore it
to you." 4 They said, "You have not de-
frauded us or oppressed us or taken any-
thing from the hand of anyone." 5 He said
to them, "The LORD is witness against you,
and his anointed is witness this day, that
you have not found anything in my hand."
And they said, "He is witness."

6 Samuel said to the people, "The LORD
is witness, who[b] appointed Moses and
Aaron and brought your ancestors up out
of the land of Egypt. 7 Now therefore take
your stand, so that I may enter into judg-
ment with you before the LORD, and I will
declare to you[c] all the saving deeds of the
LORD that he performed for you and for
your ancestors. 8 When Jacob went into
Egypt and the Egyptians oppressed them,[d]
then your ancestors cried to the LORD and
the LORD sent Moses and Aaron, who
brought forth your ancestors out of Egypt,
and settled them in this place. 9 But they
forgot the LORD their God; and he sold
them into the hand of Sisera, commander
of the army of King Jabin of[e] Hazor, and
into the hand of the Philistines, and into the
hand of the king of Moab; and they fought
against them. 10 Then they cried to the
LORD, and said, 'We have sinned, because
we have forsaken the LORD, and have
served the Baals and the Astartes; but now
rescue us out of the hand of our enemies,
and we will serve you.' 11 And the LORD
sent Jerubbaal and Barak,[f] and Jephthah,
and Samson,[g] and rescued you out of the
hand of your enemies on every side; and
you lived in safety. 12 But when you saw
that King Nahash of the Ammonites came
against you, you said to me, 'No, but a king
shall reign over us,' though the LORD your
God was your king. 13 See, here is the king
whom you have chosen, for whom you
have asked; see, the LORD has set a king
over you. 14 If you will fear the LORD and
serve him and heed his voice and not rebel
against the commandment of the LORD,
and if both you and the king who reigns
over you will follow the LORD your God, it
will be well; 15 but if you will not heed the
voice of the LORD, but rebel against the
commandment of the LORD, then the hand
of the LORD will be against you and your
king.[h] 16 Now therefore take your stand
and see this great thing that the LORD will
do before your eyes. 17 Is it not the wheat
harvest today? I will call upon the LORD,
that he may send thunder and rain; and you
shall know and see that the wickedness that
you have done in the sight of the LORD is
great in demanding a king for yourselves."
18 So Samuel called upon the LORD, and the
LORD sent thunder and rain that day; and
all the people greatly feared the LORD and
Samuel.

a Gk: Heb lacks *Testify against me* *b* Gk: Heb lacks *is witness, who* *c* Gk: Heb lacks *and I will declare to you* *d* Gk: Heb lacks *and the Egyptians oppressed them* *e* Gk: Heb lacks *King Jabin of* *f* Gk Syr: Heb *Bedan* *g* Gk: Heb *Samuel* *h* Gk: Heb *and your ancestors*

as illustrating his old age; they are fully grown. **3:** Samuel's actions contrast with the "ways of the king" in 8.11–18; cf. Moses' words in Num 16.15. **6–12:** This retrospective on Israel's history is Deuteronomistic in language and orientation. **9:** *Sisera,* see Judg 4.2. *Philistines,* see Judg 13.1. *Moab,* see Judg 3.12. **10:** *Baals and the Astartes,* see 7.4. **11:** *Barak,* see Judg 4.6. The Hebrew text reads "Bedan." There is no story about Bedan in the book of Judges. Some scholars think Bedan reflects a distinct tradition; others think it is another name for Jephthah. If Barak is correct, the order here differs from Judges. *Jephthah,* see Judg 11. *Samson,* see Judg 13–16. The Hebrew has "Samuel"; in either case, the reference is to the last judge. **12:** The mention of *Nahash* differs from ch 8, in which the Philistine threat leads the Israelites to request a king. **13:** *For whom you have asked,* a pun on Saul's name. **16–18:** The *wheat harvest* was in early summer, when rain would be rare and a threat to the crops. Thus, it shows the LORD's response to Samuel and hints at his displeasure with the people. *Demanding* (vv. 17,19) is another pun on "Saul."

19 All the people said to Samuel, "Pray
to the LORD your God for your servants, so
that we may not die; for we have added to
all our sins the evil of demanding a king for
ourselves." 20 And Samuel said to the peo-
ple, "Do not be afraid; you have done all
this evil, yet do not turn aside from follow-
ing the LORD, but serve the LORD with all
your heart; 21 and do not turn aside after
useless things that cannot profit or save, for
they are useless. 22 For the LORD will not
cast away his people, for his great name's
sake, because it has pleased the LORD to
make you a people for himself. 23 Moreover
as for me, far be it from me that I should sin
against the LORD by ceasing to pray for
you; and I will instruct you in the good and
the right way. 24 Only fear the LORD, and
serve him faithfully with all your heart; for
consider what great things he has done for
you. 25 But if you still do wickedly, you
shall be swept away, both you and your
king."

13 Saul was . . .[a] years old when he
began to reign; and he reigned . . .
and two[b] years over Israel.
2 Saul chose three thousand out of Isra-
el; two thousand were with Saul in Mich-
mash and the hill country of Bethel, and a
thousand were with Jonathan in Gibeah of
Benjamin; the rest of the people he sent
home to their tents. 3 Jonathan defeated the
garrison of the Philistines that was at Geba;
and the Philistines heard of it. And Saul
blew the trumpet throughout all the land,
saying, "Let the Hebrews hear!" 4 When all
Israel heard that Saul had defeated the gar-
rison of the Philistines, and also that Israel
had become odious to the Philistines, the
people were called out to join Saul at Gil-
gal.
5 The Philistines mustered to fight with
Israel, thirty thousand chariots, and six
thousand horsemen, and troops like the
sand on the seashore in multitude; they
came up and encamped at Michmash, to
the east of Beth-aven. 6 When the Israelites
saw that they were in distress (for the
troops were hard pressed), the people hid
themselves in caves and in holes and in
rocks and in tombs and in cisterns. 7 Some
Hebrews crossed the Jordan to the land of
Gad and Gilead. Saul was still at Gilgal,
and all the people followed him trembling.
8 He waited seven days, the time ap-
pointed by Samuel; but Samuel did not
come to Gilgal, and the people began to slip
away from Saul.[c] 9 So Saul said, "Bring the
burnt offering here to me, and the offerings
of well-being." And he offered the burnt
offering. 10 As soon as he had finished
offering the burnt offering, Samuel arrived;
and Saul went out to meet him and salute
him. 11 Samuel said, "What have you
done?" Saul replied, "When I saw that the
people were slipping away from me, and
that you did not come within the days ap-
pointed, and that the Philistines were mus-
tering at Michmash, 12 I said, 'Now the
Philistines will come down upon me at Gil-
gal, and I have not entreated the favor of
the LORD'; so I forced myself, and offered
the burnt offering." 13 Samuel said to Saul,
"You have done foolishly; you have not

a The number is lacking in the Heb text (the verse is lacking in the Septuagint). *b* *Two* is not the entire number; something has dropped out. *c* Heb *him*

22: *For his great name's sake,* the LORD's reputation might be damaged if he destroyed them too readily; see Num 14.13–16. **24–25:** The theology of divine reward/retribution is Deuteronomistic.

13.1–7a: Saul begins the war with the Philistines. 1: Saul's age and length of reign are uncertain. The Hebrew literally says that he was a year old when he began to reign and reigned two years; see the translators' notes. **3:** *Jonathan,* Saul's son, appears here for the first time, and as a grown man, indicating that this story is much later than 9.1–10.16, in which Saul is a young man. *Geba* and Gibeah are very similar in Hebrew and may be confused here. **4:** Saul, as king, is apparently given credit for his son's victory. **5:** *Beth-aven,* probably an alternative name for Bethel. **7:** *Gad and Gilead,* east of the Jordan.

13.7b–15a: Saul's sin and rejection by God. 8: *The time appointed by Samuel* was *seven days* (10.8), but the intervening events in chs 10–12 require a much longer time. **13–14:** The nature of Saul's sin is

kept the commandment of the LORD your
God, which he commanded you. The LORD
would have established your kingdom over
Israel forever, 14 but now your kingdom
will not continue; the LORD has sought out
a man after his own heart; and the LORD
has appointed him to be ruler over his peo-
ple, because you have not kept what the
LORD commanded you." 15 And Samuel left
and went on his way from Gilgal.[a] The
rest of the people followed Saul to join the
army; they went up from Gilgal toward
Gibeah of Benjamin.[b]

Saul counted the people who were
present with him, about six hundred men.
16 Saul, his son Jonathan, and the people
who were present with them stayed in Geba
of Benjamin; but the Philistines encamped
at Michmash. 17 And raiders came out of
the camp of the Philistines in three compa-
nies; one company turned toward Ophrah,
to the land of Shual, 18 another company
turned toward Beth-horon, and another
company turned toward the mountain[c]
that looks down upon the valley of Zeboim
toward the wilderness.

19 Now there was no smith to be found
throughout all the land of Israel; for the
Philistines said, "The Hebrews must not
make swords or spears for themselves";
20 so all the Israelites went down to the Phil-
istines to sharpen their plowshares, mat-
tocks, axes, or sickles;[d] 21 The charge was
two-thirds of a shekel[e] for the plowshares
and for the mattocks, and one-third of a
shekel for sharpening the axes and for set-
ting the goads.[f] 22 So on the day of the
battle neither sword nor spear was to be
found in the possession of any of the people
with Saul and Jonathan; but Saul and his
son Jonathan had them.

23 Now a garrison of the Philistines had
gone out to the pass of Michmash.

14
gone out to the pass of Michmash.
1 One day Jonathan son of Saul said
to the young man who carried his armor,
"Come, let us go over to the Philistine gar-
rison on the other side." But he did not tell
his father. 2 Saul was staying in the out-
skirts of Gibeah under the pomegranate
tree that is at Migron; the troops that were
with him were about six hundred men,
3 along with Ahijah son of Ahitub, Icha-
bod's brother, son of Phinehas son of Eli,
the priest of the LORD in Shiloh, carrying
an ephod. Now the people did not know
that Jonathan had gone. 4 In the pass,[g] by
which Jonathan tried to go over to the Phil-
istine garrison, there was a rocky crag on
one side and a rocky crag on the other; the
name of the one was Bozez, and the name

a Gk: Heb *went up from Gilgal to Gibeah of Benjamin* *b* Gk: Heb lacks *The rest . . . of Benjamin*
c Cn Compare Gk: Heb *toward the border*
d Gk: Heb *plowshare* *e* Heb *was a pim*
f Cn: Meaning of Heb uncertain *g* Heb *Between the passes*

not clear; perhaps he tried to usurp Samuel's role of religious leadership. But cf. 14.31–35. *Your kingdom,* like David (2 Sam 7.13–16), Saul had a chance to establish a long-lasting dynasty, but his sin prevented this. Another rejection, perhaps of Saul's individual kingship, occurs in ch 15. The *man after* the LORD's *own heart,* an allusion to David, is a way of saying he is chosen by the LORD.

13.15b–14.52: Continuation of the Philistine war. 13.15b–23: These verses set the stage for the battle account in the next chapter. *Geba* and *Michmash* (v. 16) were across from each other on opposite sides of a valley. The Philistine domination took two forms: *Raiders* customarily went out from Michmash to attack Israelite settlements (vv. 17–18), and the Philistines controlled metalworking and hence the manufacture of weapons (vv. 19–22). The Israelites may eventually have learned iron working from the Philistines. **23:** The battle begins with the Philistines moving to the pass on their side of the valley. **14.1:** *The Philistine garrison on the other side* was the one sent as reinforcements (13.23). The Israelites and Philistines were camped on opposite sides of the ravine at Geba and Michmash, respectively (14.5). Jonathan's plan is to defeat this garrison and then perhaps to rally the Israelites who were hiding (vv. 11,22) into joining in and driving the Philistines back. **3:** *Carrying an ephod,* not the linen ephod of 2.18, but a box whose contents were used to divine the will of God (v. 41; Ex 28.30). It was carried in priestly garments, which may be why the same word was used for both. *The people* often means the army. **6:** *These uncircumcised,* a derogatory term for the Philistines. **11:** *Hebrews,* see 4.6n. **18:** *The ark*

of the other Seneh. 5 One crag rose on the
north in front of Michmash, and the other
on the south in front of Geba.
6 Jonathan said to the young man who
carried his armor, "Come, let us go over to
the garrison of these uncircumcised; it may
be that the LORD will act for us; for nothing
can hinder the LORD from saving by many
or by few." 7 His armor-bearer said to him,
"Do all that your mind inclines to.[a] I am
with you; as your mind is, so is mine."[b]
8 Then Jonathan said, "Now we will cross
over to those men and will show ourselves
to them. 9 If they say to us, 'Wait until we
come to you,' then we will stand still in our
place, and we will not go up to them. 10 But
if they say, 'Come up to us,' then we will go
up; for the LORD has given them into our
hand. That will be the sign for us." 11 So
both of them showed themselves to the gar-
rison of the Philistines; and the Philistines
said, "Look, Hebrews are coming out of
the holes where they have hidden them-
selves." 12 The men of the garrison hailed
Jonathan and his armor-bearer, saying,
"Come up to us, and we will show you
something." Jonathan said to his armor-
bearer, "Come up after me; for the LORD
has given them into the hand of Israel."
13 Then Jonathan climbed up on his hands
and feet, with his armor-bearer following
after him. The Philistines[c] fell before Jona-
than, and his armor-bearer, coming after
him, killed them. 14 In that first slaughter
Jonathan and his armor-bearer killed about
twenty men within an area about half a
furrow long in an acre[d] of land. 15 There
was a panic in the camp, in the field, and
among all the people; the garrison and even
the raiders trembled; the earth quaked; and
it became a very great panic.
16 Saul's lookouts in Gibeah of Benja-
min were watching as the multitude was
surging back and forth.[e] 17 Then Saul said
to the troops that were with him, "Call the
roll and see who has gone from us." When
they had called the roll, Jonathan and his
armor-bearer were not there. 18 Saul said to
Ahijah, "Bring the ark[f] of God here." For
at that time the ark[f] of God went with the
Israelites. 19 While Saul was talking to the
priest, the tumult in the camp of the Philis-
tines increased more and more; and Saul
said to the priest, "Withdraw your hand."
20 Then Saul and all the people who were
with him rallied and went into the battle;
and every sword was against the other, so
that there was very great confusion. 21 Now
the Hebrews who previously had been with
the Philistines and had gone up with them
into the camp turned and joined the Israel-
ites who were with Saul and Jonathan.
22 Likewise, when all the Israelites who had
gone into hiding in the hill country of
Ephraim heard that the Philistines were
fleeing, they too followed closely after them
in the battle. 23 So the LORD gave Israel the
victory that day.
The battle passed beyond Beth-aven, and
the troops with Saul numbered altogether
about ten thousand men. The battle spread
out over the hill country of Ephraim.
24 Now Saul committed a very rash act
on that day.[g] He had laid an oath on the
troops, saying, "Cursed be anyone who
eats food before it is evening and I have
been avenged on my enemies." So none of
the troops tasted food. 25 All the troops[h]
came upon a honeycomb; and there was
honey on the ground. 26 When the troops
came upon the honeycomb, the honey was

a Gk: Heb *Do all that is in your mind. Turn*
b Gk: Heb lacks *so is mine* *c* Heb *They*
d Heb *yoke* *e* Gk: Heb *they went and there*
f Gk *the ephod* *g* Gk: Heb *The Israelites were distressed that day* *h* Heb *land*

of God, the Greek reading, "the ephod," is probably better (see v. 3). **19:** *Withdraw your hand,* Saul had called Ahijah the priest in order to consult the LORD through him, but the growing sound of battle made him decide to attack before finishing his inquiry. **21:** The *Hebrews* here are distinguished from the *Israelites.* They are first allied with the Philistines and then turn against them; they may have been mercenaries (cf. 4.6). **24–30:** Saul's oath was an expression of piety to attract God's aid in the battle. It was foolish because his troops became faint from hunger. Most *honey* was made from dates; Jonathan has found a true delicacy (cf. Prov 25.16). **31–35:** The soldiers commit a ritual offense by slaughtering

dripping out; but they did not put their
hands to their mouths, for they feared the
oath. 27 But Jonathan had not heard his fa-
ther charge the troops with the oath; so he
extended the staff that was in his hand, and
dipped the tip of it in the honeycomb, and
put his hand to his mouth; and his eyes
brightened. 28 Then one of the soldiers said,
"Your father strictly charged the troops
with an oath, saying, 'Cursed be anyone
who eats food this day.' And so the troops
are faint." 29 Then Jonathan said, "My fa-
ther has troubled the land; see how my eyes
have brightened because I tasted a little of
this honey. 30 How much better if today the
troops had eaten freely of the spoil taken
from their enemies; for now the slaughter
among the Philistines has not been great."

31 After they had struck down the Phil-
istines that day from Michmash to Aijalon,
the troops were very faint; 32 so the troops
flew upon the spoil, and took sheep and
oxen and calves, and slaughtered them on
the ground; and the troops ate them with
the blood. 33 Then it was reported to Saul,
"Look, the troops are sinning against the
LORD by eating with the blood." And he
said, "You have dealt treacherously; roll a
large stone before me here."[a] 34 Saul said,
"Disperse yourselves among the troops,
and say to them, 'Let all bring their oxen or
their sheep, and slaughter them here, and
eat; and do not sin against the LORD by
eating with the blood.' " So all of the
troops brought their oxen with them that
night, and slaughtered them there. 35 And
Saul built an altar to the LORD; it was the
first altar that he built to the LORD.

36 Then Saul said, "Let us go down af-
ter the Philistines by night and despoil them
until the morning light; let us not leave one
of them." They said, "Do whatever seems
good to you." But the priest said, "Let us
draw near to God here." 37 So Saul inquired
of God, "Shall I go down after the Philis-
tines? Will you give them into the hand of
Israel?" But he did not answer him that
day. 38 Saul said, "Come here, all you lead-
ers of the people; and let us find out how
this sin has arisen today. 39 For as the LORD
lives who saves Israel, even if it is in my son
Jonathan, he shall surely die!" But there
was no one among all the people who an-
swered him. 40 He said to all Israel, "You
shall be on one side, and I and my son Jona-
than will be on the other side." The people
said to Saul, "Do what seems good to you."
41 Then Saul said, "O LORD God of Israel,
why have you not answered your servant
today? If this guilt is in me or in my son
Jonathan, O LORD God of Israel, give
Urim; but if this guilt is in your people Isra-
el,[b] give Thummim." And Jonathan and
Saul were indicated by the lot, but the peo-
ple were cleared. 42 Then Saul said, "Cast
the lot between me and my son Jonathan."
And Jonathan was taken.

43 Then Saul said to Jonathan, "Tell me
what you have done." Jonathan told him,
"I tasted a little honey with the tip of the
staff that was in my hand; here I am, I will
die." 44 Saul said, "God do so to me and
more also; you shall surely die, Jonathan!"
45 Then the people said to Saul, "Shall Jon-
athan die, who has accomplished this great
victory in Israel? Far from it! As the LORD
lives, not one hair of his head shall fall to
the ground; for he has worked with God
today." So the people ransomed Jonathan,
and he did not die. 46 Then Saul withdrew
from pursuing the Philistines; and the Phil-
istines went to their own place.

47 When Saul had taken the kingship

a Gk: Heb *me this day* *b* Vg Compare Gk: Heb 41*Saul said to the LORD, the God of Israel*

animals *on the ground* so that the blood does not drain out and eating meat cooked *with the blood,* contrary to laws such as Lev 19.26; Deut 12.16. Animals slaughtered on the *large stone* could be propped up to allow their blood to drain before cooking. **37:** *Inquired,* a pun on Saul's name. The lack of response indicates divine disfavor and may hint at God's future displeasure with Saul (see 28.6) **41–42:** The *Urim* and *Thummim* answered yes-or-no questions and decided between two alternatives. **45:** It is not clear exactly how *the people ransomed Jonathan.* Perhaps an animal was substituted (Gen 22.13; Ex 13.13; 34.20). The story may foreshadow Jonathan's death. **47–48:** Saul's military successes contrast with the

over Israel, he fought against all his ene-
mies on every side—against Moab, against
the Ammonites, against Edom, against the
kings of Zobah, and against the Philistines;
wherever he turned he routed them. 48 He
did valiantly, and struck down the Amalek-
ites, and rescued Israel out of the hands of
those who plundered them.

49 Now the sons of Saul were Jonathan,
Ishvi, and Malchishua; and the names of
his two daughters were these: the name of
the firstborn was Merab, and the name of
the younger, Michal. 50 The name of Saul's
wife was Ahinoam daughter of Ahimaaz.
And the name of the commander of his
army was Abner son of Ner, Saul's uncle;
51 Kish was the father of Saul, and Ner the
father of Abner was the son of Abiel.

52 There was hard fighting against the
Philistines all the days of Saul; and when
Saul saw any strong or valiant warrior, he
took him into his service.

15 Samuel said to Saul, "The LORD
sent me to anoint you king over his
people Israel; now therefore listen to the
words of the LORD. 2 Thus says the LORD
of hosts, 'I will punish the Amalekites for
what they did in opposing the Israelites
when they came up out of Egypt. 3 Now go
and attack Amalek, and utterly destroy all
that they have; do not spare them, but kill
both man and woman, child and infant, ox
and sheep, camel and donkey.' "

4 So Saul summoned the people, and
numbered them in Telaim, two hundred
thousand foot soldiers, and ten thousand
soldiers of Judah. 5 Saul came to the city of
the Amalekites and lay in wait in the valley.
6 Saul said to the Kenites, "Go! Leave!
Withdraw from among the Amalekites, or I
will destroy you with them; for you showed
kindness to all the people of Israel when
they came up out of Egypt." So the Kenites
withdrew from the Amalekites. 7 Saul de-
feated the Amalekites, from Havilah as far
as Shur, which is east of Egypt. 8 He took
King Agag of the Amalekites alive, but ut-
terly destroyed all the people with the edge
of the sword. 9 Saul and the people spared
Agag, and the best of the sheep and of the
cattle and of the fatlings, and the lambs,
and all that was valuable, and would not
utterly destroy them; all that was despised
and worthless they utterly destroyed.

10 The word of the LORD came to Sam-
uel: 11 "I regret that I made Saul king, for he
has turned back from following me, and
has not carried out my commands." Sam-
uel was angry; and he cried out to the LORD
all night. 12 Samuel rose early in the morn-
ing to meet Saul, and Samuel was told,
"Saul went to Carmel, where he set up a
monument for himself, and on returning he
passed on down to Gilgal." 13 When Sam-
uel came to Saul, Saul said to him, "May
you be blessed by the LORD; I have carried
out the command of the LORD." 14 But
Samuel said, "What then is this bleating of
sheep in my ears, and the lowing of cattle
that I hear?" 15 Saul said, "They have
brought them from the Amalekites; for the
people spared the best of the sheep and the

surrounding negative portrait of Saul. **49:** *Ishvi,* perhaps another spelling of Ishbaal (2 Sam 2.8). **52:** *Any strong or valiant warrior,* an allusion to David (cf. 16.14–23).

15.1–35: Another story of Saul's rejection. Compare 13.7b–15a. **2:** *Amalekites,* a nomadic people south of Judah. The story mentioned here is recounted in Ex 17.8–16 and Deut 25.17–19. **3:** *Utterly destroy,* the "ban" or "devotion to destruction" (Heb "ḥerem") used by Israel (see Josh 6.17) and other peoples in the ancient Near East. The enemy and their property were exterminated as a kind of sacrifice to the deity. The instructions are given explicitly here in anticipation of Saul's disobedience. **4:** The numbers may be exaggerated or the word "thousand" may refer to a military unit much smaller than a thousand men. **6:** *Kenites,* a clan in southern Judah; this verse indicates that they had settled with the Amalekites. Their name means "metalworkers." Their *kindness* to the Israelites is unknown. **9:** *Spared,* a direct violation of the order in v. 3. **12:** Carmel, not the famous mount, but a town in Judah (Josh 15.55). **15:** Saul says his troops (*the people*) *spared the best of the sheep and the cattle,* though he is implicated in v. 9. His claim that the animals were spared for sacrifice provides the ground for Samuel's rebuke. *Your God* suggests that Saul has abandoned the LORD. **17–19:** The verbs are singulars and directed at

cattle, to sacrifice to the LORD your God;
but the rest we have utterly destroyed."
16 Then Samuel said to Saul, "Stop! I will
tell you what the LORD said to me last
night." He replied, "Speak."
17 Samuel said, "Though you are little
in your own eyes, are you not the head of
the tribes of Israel? The LORD anointed you
king over Israel. 18 And the LORD sent you
on a mission, and said, 'Go, utterly destroy
the sinners, the Amalekites, and fight
against them until they are consumed.'
19 Why then did you not obey the voice of
the LORD? Why did you swoop down on
the spoil, and do what was evil in the sight
of the LORD?" 20 Saul said to Samuel, "I
have obeyed the voice of the LORD, I have
gone on the mission on which the LORD
sent me, I have brought Agag the king of
Amalek, and I have utterly destroyed the
Amalekites. 21 But from the spoil the people
took sheep and cattle, the best of the things
devoted to destruction, to sacrifice to the
LORD your God in Gilgal." 22 And Samuel
said,

"Has the LORD as great delight in
burnt offerings and sacrifices,
as in obedience to the voice of the
LORD?
Surely, to obey is better than sacrifice,
and to heed than the fat of rams.
23 For rebellion is no less a sin than
divination,
and stubbornness is like iniquity
and idolatry.
Because you have rejected the word of
the LORD,
he has also rejected you from being
king."

24 Saul said to Samuel, "I have sinned;
for I have transgressed the commandment
of the LORD and your words, because I
feared the people and obeyed their voice.
25 Now therefore, I pray, pardon my sin,
and return with me, so that I may worship
the LORD." 26 Samuel said to Saul, "I will
not return with you; for you have rejected
the word of the LORD, and the LORD has
rejected you from being king over Israel."
27 As Samuel turned to go away, Saul
caught hold of the hem of his robe, and
it tore. 28 And Samuel said to him, "The
LORD has torn the kingdom of Israel from
you this very day, and has given it to a
neighbor of yours, who is better than you.
29 Moreover the Glory of Israel will not re-
cant[a] or change his mind; for he is not a
mortal, that he should change his mind."
30 Then Saul[b] said, "I have sinned; yet hon-
or me now before the elders of my people
and before Israel, and return with me, so
that I may worship the LORD your God."
31 So Samuel turned back after Saul; and
Saul worshiped the LORD.
32 Then Samuel said, "Bring Agag king
of the Amalekites here to me." And Agag
came to him haltingly.[c] Agag said, "Surely
this is the bitterness of death."[d] 33 But
Samuel said,

"As your sword has made women
childless,

a Q Ms Gk: MT *deceive* *b* Heb *he*
c Cn Compare Gk: Meaning of Heb uncertain
d Q Ms Gk: MT *Surely the bitterness of death is past*

Saul alone as *the head of the tribes of Israel* (v. 17). **22:** *The fat of rams,* the part of the animal burned in sacrifices. The poetic form of this verse and the next recalls the oracles of the "writing" prophets (see Hos 6.6; Am 5.21–24; Mic 6.6–8). **23:** The *divination* condemned here is often related to foreign idolatry (see Deut 18.9–14). *Rebellion* and *stubbornness,* like *divination,* involve turning away from the LORD. **26:** This verse illustrates a narrative technique known to later rabbinic authors as "measure for measure"; Saul's punishment corresponds to his sin (both labeled "rejection"). **27–28:** Grasping the *hem* of a person's garment was a way of submitting or pleading. Samuel uses the torn hem as an object lesson. The *neighbor* is David. Saul's robe is symbolic of his kingdom and becomes a literary motif in 1 Samuel (see ch 24.). **29:** *The Glory of Israel,* an epithet for the LORD. The message of the verse seems to contradict the larger context in which the LORD has changed his mind about Saul being king. Some scholars address this contradiction by positing v. 29 as a late gloss. **33:** Samuel's dismemberment of Agag *before the LORD* was a ritual execution, perhaps for war crimes or violation of a treaty. **35:** *Samuel did not see Saul again until the day of his death,* anticipates ch 28 but stands in tension with 19.18–24.

so your mother shall be childless
among women."
And Samuel hewed Agag in pieces before
the LORD in Gilgal.
34 Then Samuel went to Ramah; and
Saul went up to his house in Gibeah of
Saul. 35 Samuel did not see Saul again until
the day of his death, but Samuel grieved
over Saul. And the LORD was sorry that he
had made Saul king over Israel.

16 The LORD said to Samuel, "How
long will you grieve over Saul? I
have rejected him from being king over Is-
rael. Fill your horn with oil and set out; I
will send you to Jesse the Bethlehemite, for
I have provided for myself a king among his
sons." 2 Samuel said, "How can I go? If
Saul hears of it, he will kill me." And the
LORD said, "Take a heifer with you, and
say, 'I have come to sacrifice to the LORD.'
3 Invite Jesse to the sacrifice, and I will
show you what you shall do; and you shall
anoint for me the one whom I name to
you." 4 Samuel did what the LORD com-
manded, and came to Bethlehem. The el-
ders of the city came to meet him trem-
bling, and said, "Do you come peaceably?"
5 He said, "Peaceably; I have come to sacri-
fice to the LORD; sanctify yourselves and
come with me to the sacrifice." And he
sanctified Jesse and his sons and invited
them to the sacrifice.
6 When they came, he looked on Eliab
and thought, "Surely the LORD's anointed
is now before the LORD."[a] 7 But the LORD
said to Samuel, "Do not look on his ap-
pearance or on the height of his stature,
because I have rejected him; for the LORD
does not see as mortals see; they look on
the outward appearance, but the LORD
looks on the heart." 8 Then Jesse called
Abinadab, and made him pass before Sam-
uel. He said, "Neither has the LORD chosen
this one." 9 Then Jesse made Shammah pass
by. And he said, "Neither has the LORD
chosen this one." 10 Jesse made seven of his
sons pass before Samuel, and Samuel said
to Jesse, "The LORD has not chosen any
of these." 11 Samuel said to Jesse, "Are all
your sons here?" And he said, "There re-
mains yet the youngest, but he is keeping
the sheep." And Samuel said to Jesse,
"Send and bring him; for we will not sit
down until he comes here." 12 He sent and
brought him in. Now he was ruddy, and
had beautiful eyes, and was handsome. The
LORD said, "Rise and anoint him; for this is
the one." 13 Then Samuel took the horn of
oil, and anointed him in the presence of his
brothers; and the spirit of the LORD came
mightily upon David from that day for-
ward. Samuel then set out and went to Ra-
mah.
14 Now the spirit of the LORD departed
from Saul, and an evil spirit from the LORD
tormented him. 15 And Saul's servants said

a Heb *him*

16.1–13: The anointing of David. 1: *Fill your horn with oil,* fine olive oil carried in a ram's horn was used for anointing a new king. **4–5:** Jesse seems to be among the *elders* or civic leaders of Bethlehem. Their *trembling* is perhaps because they suspect the nature of Samuel's mission and fear that his visit will bring consequences from Saul. Or perhaps they are afraid that he has come to condemn them for some wrongdoing. **6–7:** Eliab's height and good looks are reminiscent of Saul, whom the LORD has rejected as king. God is more impressed with inner qualities or the *heart,* which Samuel cannot know. **8–9:** Samuel is likely using some device like the Urim and Thummim to determine whether each of Jesse's sons is the chosen one. **10:** This verse and 17.12 credit Jesse with eight sons, while 1 Chr 2.13–15 mentions only seven. As the seventh son David would have been seen as specially blessed. His description as the eighth son may highlight his humble origins. **11:** *Youngest* may also mean "the smallest" and contrasts David with Saul. *Keeping the sheep,* shepherd was a common metaphor for a king (2 Sam 5.2). **12:** *Ruddy* means "reddish" of hair and complexion (see Gen 25.25). *Handsome,* see 9.2n.

16.14–23: David wins a position at Saul's court. 14: The departure of *the spirit of the LORD* from Saul and its replacement by an *evil spirit from the LORD* further contrasts Saul and David (v. 13). The evil spirit may describe mental illness. The theological point is that the LORD abandoned Saul. **16:** *Lyre,* a hand-held

to him, "See now, an evil spirit from God is
tormenting you. 16 Let our lord now com-
mand the servants who attend you to look
for someone who is skillful in playing the
lyre; and when the evil spirit from God is
upon you, he will play it, and you will feel
better." 17 So Saul said to his servants,
"Provide for me someone who can play
well, and bring him to me." 18 One of the
young men answered, "I have seen a son of
Jesse the Bethlehemite who is skillful in
playing, a man of valor, a warrior, prudent
in speech, and a man of good presence; and
the LORD is with him." 19 So Saul sent mes-
sengers to Jesse, and said, "Send me your
son David who is with the sheep." 20 Jesse
took a donkey loaded with bread, a skin of
wine, and a kid, and sent them by his son
David to Saul. 21 And David came to Saul,
and entered his service. Saul loved him
greatly, and he became his armor-bearer.
22 Saul sent to Jesse, saying, "Let David re-
main in my service, for he has found favor
in my sight." 23 And whenever the evil spirit
from God came upon Saul, David took the
lyre and played it with his hand, and Saul
would be relieved and feel better, and the
evil spirit would depart from him.

17 Now the Philistines gathered their
armies for battle; they were gath-
ered at Socoh, which belongs to Judah, and
encamped between Socoh and Azekah, in
Ephes-dammim. 2 Saul and the Israelites
gathered and encamped in the valley of
Elah, and formed ranks against the Philis-
tines. 3 The Philistines stood on the moun-
tain on the one side, and Israel stood on the
mountain on the other side, with a valley
between them. 4 And there came out from
the camp of the Philistines a champion
named Goliath, of Gath, whose height was
six[a] cubits and a span. 5 He had a helmet
of bronze on his head, and he was armed
with a coat of mail; the weight of the coat
was five thousand shekels of bronze. 6 He
had greaves of bronze on his legs and a
javelin of bronze slung between his shoul-
ders. 7 The shaft of his spear was like a
weaver's beam, and his spear's head
weighed six hundred shekels of iron; and
his shield-bearer went before him. 8 He
stood and shouted to the ranks of Israel,
"Why have you come out to draw up for
battle? Am I not a Philistine, and are you
not servants of Saul? Choose a man for
yourselves, and let him come down to me.
9 If he is able to fight with me and kill me,
then we will be your servants; but if I pre-
vail against him and kill him, then you shall
be our servants and serve us." 10 And the
Philistine said, "Today I defy the ranks of
Israel! Give me a man, that we may fight
together." 11 When Saul and all Israel heard

a MT: Q Ms Gk *four*

stringed instrument. Musicians were thought to ward off evil spirits. **18:** *A man of valor,* a "nobleman" or "man of wealth" (9.1). *Prudent in speech* implies both eloquence and cleverness. *The LORD is with him,* a central theme of the David story. **19:** David's role as a shepherd again hints at his future as king. **21:** *Armor-bearer* indicates David's skill as a warrior and his closeness to Saul.

17.1–58: David defeats the Philistine champion. An initial version of this story in vv. 1–11,32–49, 51–54 has been extensively supplemented in the Hebrew text by vv. 12–31,50,55–58; 18.1–5. The supplementary material is absent from the Greek translation (the Septuagint, or LXX). Its addition has caused inconsistencies relating to David's presence in Saul's army, the way in which the Philistine died, and Saul's acquaintance with David. **4:** *Goliath,* a Philistine name, occurs only here and in v. 23, which is supplemental. Otherwise, David's opponent is called "the Philistine." The name has come into the story because of 2 Sam 21.19, which says that a certain Elhanan killed Goliath. *Six cubits and a span,* about nine and one-half feet. The Greek reading, "four cubits and a span," is more realistic and probably original. David's small stature contrasts with Goliath's as with Saul's. **5–7:** The armor described here reflects items from different armies at different times and is designed to give an imposing picture of the Philistine. **5:** *Five thousand shekels,* almost 126 pounds. **6:** *Javelin,* better: "scimitar." **7:** The spear's description is borrowed from 2 Sam 21.19. *A weaver's beam* may refer to size or to a leather thong attached to some spears to facilitate hurling. *Six hundred shekels of iron,* more than fifteen pounds.

these words of the Philistine, they were dis-
mayed and greatly afraid.
12 Now David was the son of an Eph-
rathite of Bethlehem in Judah, named Jesse,
who had eight sons. In the days of Saul
the man was already old and advanced in
years.[a] 13 The three eldest sons of Jesse had
followed Saul to the battle; the names of his
three sons who went to the battle were Eli-
ab the firstborn, and next to him Abinadab,
and the third Shammah. 14 David was the
youngest; the three eldest followed Saul,
15 but David went back and forth from Saul
to feed his father's sheep at Bethlehem.
16 For forty days the Philistine came for-
ward and took his stand, morning and eve-
ning.
17 Jesse said to his son David, "Take for
your brothers an ephah of this parched
grain and these ten loaves, and carry them
quickly to the camp to your brothers;
18 also take these ten cheeses to the com-
mander of their thousand. See how your
brothers fare, and bring some token from
them."
19 Now Saul, and they, and all the men
of Israel, were in the valley of Elah, fighting
with the Philistines. 20 David rose early in
the morning, left the sheep with a keeper,
took the provisions, and went as Jesse had
commanded him. He came to the encamp-
ment as the army was going forth to the
battle line, shouting the war cry. 21 Israel
and the Philistines drew up for battle, army
against army. 22 David left the things in
charge of the keeper of the baggage, ran to
the ranks, and went and greeted his broth-
ers. 23 As he talked with them, the champi-
on, the Philistine of Gath, Goliath by name,
came up out of the ranks of the Philistines,
and spoke the same words as before. And
David heard him.
24 All the Israelites, when they saw the
man, fled from him and were very much
afraid. 25 The Israelites said, "Have you
seen this man who has come up? Surely he
has come up to defy Israel. The king will
greatly enrich the man who kills him, and
will give him his daughter and make his
family free in Israel." 26 David said to the
men who stood by him, "What shall be
done for the man who kills this Philistine,
and takes away the reproach from Israel?
For who is this uncircumcised Philistine
that he should defy the armies of the living
God?" 27 The people answered him in the
same way, "So shall it be done for the man
who kills him."
28 His eldest brother Eliab heard him
talking to the men; and Eliab's anger was
kindled against David. He said, "Why have
you come down? With whom have you left
those few sheep in the wilderness? I know
your presumption and the evil of your
heart; for you have come down just to see
the battle." 29 David said, "What have I
done now? It was only a question." 30 He
turned away from him toward another and
spoke in the same way; and the people an-
swered him again as before.
31 When the words that David spoke
were heard, they repeated them before
Saul; and he sent for him. 32 David said to
Saul, "Let no one's heart fail because of
him; your servant will go and fight with
this Philistine." 33 Saul said to David, "You
are not able to go against this Philistine to
fight with him; for you are just a boy, and
he has been a warrior from his youth."
34 But David said to Saul, "Your servant
used to keep sheep for his father; and
whenever a lion or a bear came, and took a

a Gk Syr: Heb *among men*

12: *Ephrathites*, a subgroup within the Calebite clan, which was part of the tribe of Judah. The introduction of David suggests the beginning of a once independent version of the story. **14–15:** Here, David is a shepherd boy running errands rather than a warrior as in 16.14–23. **16:** In this supplementary version of the story, the Philistine had been challenging the Israelites *for forty days,* while the initial version had David fight him the first time he comes out. **17:** *An ephah,* about half a bushel. **18:** *Some token,* a personal effect showing that the brothers were well. **25:** *Free in Israel* means exempt from slavery and from taxes and conscription. **31:** *Saul* appears for the first time in the story here. Though king of Israel, he is eclipsed by David. **32:** *Your servant,* a polite term for oneself before a superior. **38–39:** David's inability to move

lamb from the flock, 35I went after it and
struck it down, rescuing the lamb from its
mouth; and if it turned against me, I would
catch it by the jaw, strike it down, and kill
it. 36Your servant has killed both lions and
bears; and this uncircumcised Philistine
shall be like one of them, since he has de-
fied the armies of the living God." 37David
said, "The LORD, who saved me from the
paw of the lion and from the paw of the
bear, will save me from the hand of this
Philistine." So Saul said to David, "Go, and
may the LORD be with you!"

38 Saul clothed David with his armor;
he put a bronze helmet on his head and
clothed him with a coat of mail. 39David
strapped Saul's sword over the armor, and
he tried in vain to walk, for he was not used
to them. Then David said to Saul, "I cannot
walk with these; for I am not used to
them." So David removed them. 40Then he
took his staff in his hand, and chose five
smooth stones from the wadi, and put them
in his shepherd's bag, in the pouch; his sling
was in his hand, and he drew near to the
Philistine.

41 The Philistine came on and drew near
to David, with his shield-bearer in front of
him. 42When the Philistine looked and saw
David, he disdained him, for he was only a
youth, ruddy and handsome in appearance.
43The Philistine said to David, "Am I a
dog, that you come to me with sticks?"
And the Philistine cursed David by his
gods. 44The Philistine said to David,
"Come to me, and I will give your flesh to
the birds of the air and to the wild animals
of the field." 45But David said to the Philis-
tine, "You come to me with sword and
spear and javelin; but I come to you in the
name of the LORD of hosts, the God of the
armies of Israel, whom you have defied.
46This very day the LORD will deliver you
into my hand, and I will strike you down
and cut off your head; and I will give the
dead bodies of the Philistine army this very
day to the birds of the air and to the wild
animals of the earth, so that all the earth
may know that there is a God in Israel,
47and that all this assembly may know that
the LORD does not save by sword and
spear; for the battle is the LORD's and he
will give you into our hand."

48 When the Philistine drew nearer to
meet David, David ran quickly toward the
battle line to meet the Philistine. 49David
put his hand in his bag, took out a stone,
slung it, and struck the Philistine on his
forehead; the stone sank into his forehead,
and he fell face down on the ground.

50 So David prevailed over the Philistine
with a sling and a stone, striking down the
Philistine and killing him; there was no
sword in David's hand. 51Then David ran
and stood over the Philistine; he grasped his
sword, drew it out of its sheath, and killed
him; then he cut off his head with it.

When the Philistines saw that their
champion was dead, they fled. 52The
troops of Israel and Judah rose up with a
shout and pursued the Philistines as far as
Gath[a] and the gates of Ekron, so that the
wounded Philistines fell on the way from

a Gk Syr: Heb *Gai*

in Saul's armor emphasizes his lack of experience as a soldier. It also shows Saul's failure to understand that David's advantage lay in his mobility. **40:** *His staff,* a shepherd's staff, not a weapon. The Philistine sees it as a stick (v. 43). *Wadi,* a dry streambed. The *sling* was not a toy but a standard weapon of ancient warfare. It consisted of two cords attached to a pouch from which a stone could be hurled with great accuracy (Judg 20.16). **41–47:** Ancient warfare included taunting and trying to demoralize one's enemy. David's speech (vv. 45–47) is religious in nature and promises retribution for the Philistine's defiance of the LORD. David says he does not need the Philistine's arms because the LORD fights for him. The Philistine is distracted by David's staff (v. 43) and overlooks his real weapon, the sling. **49:** David's stone strikes the Philistine in the spot where he is vulnerable. David's speech shows that this is understood as God's doing. **50–51:** These verses make it appear as though David killed the Philistine twice, once with the sling stone (v. 50) and once by beheading him with his own sword (v. 51). The repetition results from the combination of two versions of the story, but v. 50 can be read as an overview of the entire episode.

Shaaraim as far as Gath and Ekron. 53The
Israelites came back from chasing the Phil-
istines, and they plundered their camp.
54David took the head of the Philistine and
brought it to Jerusalem; but he put his ar-
mor in his tent.
55 When Saul saw David go out against
the Philistine, he said to Abner, the com-
mander of the army, "Abner, whose son is
this young man?" Abner said, "As your
soul lives, O king, I do not know." 56The
king said, "Inquire whose son the stripling
is." 57On David's return from killing the
Philistine, Abner took him and brought
him before Saul, with the head of the Philis-
tine in his hand. 58Saul said to him,
"Whose son are you, young man?" And
David answered, "I am the son of your ser-
vant Jesse the Bethlehemite."

18 When David[a] had finished speak-
ing to Saul, the soul of Jonathan
was bound to the soul of David, and Jona-
than loved him as his own soul. 2Saul took
him that day and would not let him return
to his father's house. 3Then Jonathan made
a covenant with David, because he loved
him as his own soul. 4Jonathan stripped
himself of the robe that he was wearing,
and gave it to David, and his armor, and
even his sword and his bow and his belt.
5David went out and was successful wher-
ever Saul sent him; as a result, Saul set him
over the army. And all the people, even the
servants of Saul, approved.
6 As they were coming home, when Da-
vid returned from killing the Philistine, the
women came out of all the towns of Israel,
singing and dancing, to meet King Saul,
with tambourines, with songs of joy, and
with musical instruments.[b] 7And the
women sang to one another as they made
merry,

"Saul has killed his thousands,
and David his ten thousands."

8Saul was very angry, for this saying dis-
pleased him. He said, "They have ascribed
to David ten thousands, and to me they
have ascribed thousands; what more can he
have but the kingdom?" 9So Saul eyed Da-
vid from that day on.
10 The next day an evil spirit from God
rushed upon Saul, and he raved within his
house, while David was playing the lyre, as
he did day by day. Saul had his spear in his
hand; 11and Saul threw the spear, for he
thought, "I will pin David to the wall." But
David eluded him twice.
12 Saul was afraid of David, because the
LORD was with him but had departed from
Saul. 13So Saul removed him from his pres-
ence, and made him a commander of a

a Heb *he* *b* Or *triangles,* or *three-stringed instruments*

54: *Jerusalem,* an anachronism, since Jerusalem was conquered after David became king of Israel (2 Sam 5.6–9). *His tent,* perhaps read "the tent (shrine) of Yahweh." Goliath's sword later surfaces with the priests at Nob (21.9). **55:** *Whose son is this young man?,* idiomatic for "Who is this?" It indicates the story's originally independent nature, since according to 16.14–23 Saul and David already had a close relationship.

18.1–30: Saul becomes jealous of David. 1–3: *Loved* implies political loyalty in addition to personal affection. **4:** Jonathan's royal robe and armor represent his status as crown prince. David is thus depicted as Saul's true successor, by the initiative of Jonathan himself. But David does not usurp the throne (see 17.38–39 where he does not wear Saul's armor). **6:** *As they were coming home, when David returned from killing the Philistine,* this is the obvious continuation of ch 17, showing that vv. 1–5 are an interruption of the initial narrative and part of the supplemental material in ch 17. **7:** *David* has slain *his ten thousands,* but David has killed only the single Philistine, Goliath. This is another indication of the interpolation of ch 17's portrait of David as a young shepherd rather than a warrior. **9:** *Saul eyed David* means that Saul was suspicious of David. **10–11:** These verses are also supplemental; initially, Saul's attempt to kill David with his spear (19.8–10) provided the climax to a series of subtle moves against David. *He raved,* elsewhere translated "prophesy." It refers to ecstatic behavior. **13–14:** Saul promotes David because he is afraid to have David nearby and hopes that David will be killed in battle. *Marched out and came in,* an idiom for "went to war." **16:** *All Israel and Judah loved David* expresses political

thousand; and David marched out and
came in, leading the army. 14 David had
success in all his undertakings; for the
LORD was with him. 15 When Saul saw that
he had great success, he stood in awe of
him. 16 But all Israel and Judah loved Da-
vid; for it was he who marched out and
came in leading them.
17 Then Saul said to David, "Here is my
elder daughter Merab; I will give her to you
as a wife; only be valiant for me and fight
the LORD's battles." For Saul thought, "I
will not raise a hand against him; let the
Philistines deal with him." 18 David said to
Saul, "Who am I and who are my kinsfolk,
my father's family in Israel, that I should be
son-in-law to the king?" 19 But at the time
when Saul's daughter Merab should have
been given to David, she was given to Adri-
el the Meholathite as a wife.
20 Now Saul's daughter Michal loved
David. Saul was told, and the thing pleased
him. 21 Saul thought, "Let me give her to
him that she may be a snare for him and
that the hand of the Philistines may be
against him." Therefore Saul said to David
a second time,[a] "You shall now be my
son-in-law." 22 Saul commanded his ser-
vants, "Speak to David in private and say,
'See, the king is delighted with you, and all
his servants love you; now then, become
the king's son-in-law.' " 23 So Saul's ser-
vants reported these words to David in pri-
vate. And David said, "Does it seem to you
a little thing to become the king's son-in-
law, seeing that I am a poor man and of no
repute?" 24 The servants of Saul told him,
"This is what David said." 25 Then Saul
said, "Thus shall you say to David, 'The
king desires no marriage present except a
hundred foreskins of the Philistines, that he
may be avenged on the king's enemies.' "
Now Saul planned to make David fall by
the hand of the Philistines. 26 When his ser-
vants told David these words, David was
well pleased to be the king's son-in-law.
Before the time had expired, 27 David rose
and went, along with his men, and killed
one hundred[b] of the Philistines; and David
brought their foreskins, which were given
in full number to the king, that he might
become the king's son-in-law. Saul gave
him his daughter Michal as a wife. 28 But
when Saul realized that the LORD was with
David, and that Saul's daughter Michal
loved him, 29 Saul was still more afraid of
David. So Saul was David's enemy from
that time forward.
30 Then the commanders of the Philis-
tines came out to battle; and as often as
they came out, David had more success
than all the servants of Saul, so that his
fame became very great.

19 Saul spoke with his son Jonathan
and with all his servants about kill-
ing David. But Saul's son Jonathan took
great delight in David. 2 Jonathan told Da-
vid, "My father Saul is trying to kill you;
therefore be on guard tomorrow morning;

a Heb *by two* *b* Gk Compare 2 Sam 3.14: Heb *two hundred*

loyalty and anticipates David's rule over both North and South (2 Sam 5.5). The army was devoted to David because of his military success. **17–19:** These verses are supplemental as they are lacking in the Greek (the Septuagint, or LXX). If these verses are related to 17.25, Saul has changed the conditions of his promise. David's response in v. 18 shows his humility and lack of ambition to be king. *Son-in-law to the king* was an important political position as a potential heir to the throne. In the end (v. 19), Saul reneges on his promise despite David's heroic deeds. **20:** *Michal,* Saul's younger daughter. **21:** This plan of Saul's is slightly more direct than his hope that David's promotion over the army would lead to his death. *Therefore Saul said to David a second time, "You shall now be my son-in-law,"* an editorial addition accommodating the Merab story in vv. 17–19. **23–25:** The *marriage present* was set by the bride's father and paid by the groom. The use of foreskins as a bride-price plays on the mocking references to the Philistines as uncircumcised (14.6; 31.4). **26:** *David was well pleased to be the king's son-in-law,* despite his claim to lack of ambition. **28:** *Michal loved him,* Michal's affection also entailed political loyalty.

19.1–24: Saul actively seeks David's life. 5: Killing an innocent person could bring God's wrath on an

stay in a secret place and hide yourself. 3 I
will go out and stand beside my father in
the field where you are, and I will speak to
my father about you; if I learn anything I
will tell you." 4 Jonathan spoke well of Da-
vid to his father Saul, saying to him, "The
king should not sin against his servant Da-
vid, because he has not sinned against you,
and because his deeds have been of good
service to you; 5 for he took his life in his
hand when he attacked the Philistine, and
the LORD brought about a great victory for
all Israel. You saw it, and rejoiced; why
then will you sin against an innocent per-
son by killing David without cause?" 6 Saul
heeded the voice of Jonathan; Saul swore,
"As the LORD lives, he shall not be put to
death." 7 So Jonathan called David and re-
lated all these things to him. Jonathan then
brought David to Saul, and he was in his
presence as before.

8 Again there was war, and David went
out to fight the Philistines. He launched a
heavy attack on them, so that they fled
before him. 9 Then an evil spirit from the
LORD came upon Saul, as he sat in his
house with his spear in his hand, while Da-
vid was playing music. 10 Saul sought to pin
David to the wall with the spear; but he
eluded Saul, so that he struck the spear into
the wall. David fled and escaped that night.

11 Saul sent messengers to David's
house to keep watch over him, planning to
kill him in the morning. David's wife Mi-
chal told him, "If you do not save your life
tonight, tomorrow you will be killed." 12 So
Michal let David down through the win-
dow; he fled away and escaped. 13 Michal
took an idol[a] and laid it on the bed; she
put a net[b] of goats' hair on its head, and
covered it with the clothes. 14 When Saul
sent messengers to take David, she said,
"He is sick." 15 Then Saul sent the messen-
gers to see David for themselves. He said,
"Bring him up to me in the bed, that I may
kill him." 16 When the messengers came in,
the idol[c] was in the bed, with the cover-
ing[b] of goats' hair on its head. 17 Saul said
to Michal, "Why have you deceived me like
this, and let my enemy go, so that he has
escaped?" Michal answered Saul, "He said
to me, 'Let me go; why should I kill you?' "

18 Now David fled and escaped; he
came to Samuel at Ramah, and told him all
that Saul had done to him. He and Samuel
went and settled at Naioth. 19 Saul was
told, "David is at Naioth in Ramah."
20 Then Saul sent messengers to take David.
When they saw the company of the proph-
ets in a frenzy, with Samuel standing in
charge of[b] them, the spirit of God came
upon the messengers of Saul, and they also
fell into a prophetic frenzy. 21 When Saul
was told, he sent other messengers, and
they also fell into a frenzy. Saul sent mes-
sengers again the third time, and they also
fell into a frenzy. 22 Then he himself went to
Ramah. He came to the great well that is in
Secu;[d] he asked, "Where are Samuel and
David?" And someone said, "They are at
Naioth in Ramah." 23 He went there, to-
ward Naioth in Ramah; and the spirit of
God came upon him. As he was going, he
fell into a prophetic frenzy, until he came to

a Heb *took the teraphim* *b* Meaning of Heb uncertain *c* Heb *the teraphim* *d* Gk reads *to the well of the threshing floor on the bare height*

entire nation. Jonathan emphasizes that David is *innocent,* and Saul has no cause to kill him. **6:** *Saul swore,* an oath was a serious matter as it often involved the deity. In 1 Samuel, however, Saul consistently breaks his oaths. **11–17:** This incident follows naturally upon the marriage in 18.20–29. **12:** The house was evidently built into the city wall (see Josh 2.15), so that David went *through the window* and escaped from the city. **13:** *An idol* (lit. "teraphim"), household gods (see Gen. 31.33–35n.; Judg 17.5n.). The one used by Michal seems to have been close to life size. **17:** Michal lies to protect herself. A threat from David does not explain her ruse with the bed after his departure. **18:** *Ramah,* Samuel's hometown, was about 3 km (2 mi) north of Gibeah. It seems unlikely that David would have fled there rather than south to his home in Bethlehem. The story is included for literary and theological reasons. *Naioth* may be not a proper name but a word meaning "camps" or "huts" where the prophets lived near Ramah. **23–24:** *Is Saul also among the prophets?* here has a negative explanation (contrast 10.10–12). His loss of self-control and his

Naioth in Ramah. 24 He too stripped off his
clothes, and he too fell into a frenzy before
Samuel. He lay naked all that day and all
that night. Therefore it is said, "Is Saul also
among the prophets?"

20 David fled from Naioth in Ramah.
He came before Jonathan and said,
"What have I done? What is my guilt? And
what is my sin against your father that he is
trying to take my life?" 2 He said to him,
"Far from it! You shall not die. My father
does nothing either great or small without
disclosing it to me; and why should my fa-
ther hide this from me? Never!" 3 But Da-
vid also swore, "Your father knows well
that you like me; and he thinks, 'Do not let
Jonathan know this, or he will be grieved.'
But truly, as the LORD lives and as you
yourself live, there is but a step between me
and death." 4 Then Jonathan said to David,
"Whatever you say, I will do for you."
5 David said to Jonathan, "Tomorrow is the
new moon, and I should not fail to sit with
the king at the meal; but let me go, so that
I may hide in the field until the third eve-
ning. 6 If your father misses me at all, then
say, 'David earnestly asked leave of me to
run to Bethlehem his city; for there is a
yearly sacrifice there for all the family.' 7 If
he says, 'Good!' it will be well with your
servant; but if he is angry, then know that
evil has been determined by him. 8 There-
fore deal kindly with your servant, for you
have brought your servant into a sacred
covenant[a] with you. But if there is guilt in
me, kill me yourself; why should you bring
me to your father?" 9 Jonathan said, "Far
be it from you! If I knew that it was decided
by my father that evil should come upon
you, would I not tell you?" 10 Then David
said to Jonathan, "Who will tell me if your
father answers you harshly?" 11 Jonathan
replied to David, "Come, let us go out into
the field." So they both went out into the
field.

12 Jonathan said to David, "By the
LORD, the God of Israel! When I have
sounded out my father, about this time to-
morrow, or on the third day, if he is well
disposed toward David, shall I not then
send and disclose it to you? 13 But if my
father intends to do you harm, the LORD do
so to Jonathan, and more also, if I do not
disclose it to you, and send you away, so
that you may go in safety. May the LORD
be with you, as he has been with my father.
14 If I am still alive, show me the faithful
love of the LORD; but if I die,[b] 15 never cut
off your faithful love from my house, even
if the LORD were to cut off every one of
the enemies of David from the face of the
earth." 16 Thus Jonathan made a covenant
with the house of David, saying, "May the
LORD seek out the enemies of David."
17 Jonathan made David swear again by his
love for him; for he loved him as he loved
his own life.

18 Jonathan said to him, "Tomorrow is
the new moon; you will be missed, because

a Heb *a covenant of the LORD* b Meaning of Heb uncertain

nakedness are degrading. If Saul is among the prophets it is only because God is using prophecy to prevent him from harming David.

20.1–42: The covenant of David and Jonathan. 2: Jonathan is unaware that Saul has tried to kill David and still believes that his father would not act without first consulting him. **5:** *New moon,* a day of sacrificing and feasting. **8:** David asks Jonathan to *deal kindly* with him. The term implies loyalty to a treaty, and David goes on to mention the covenant between them. **13:** *The LORD do so to Jonathan and more also,* an oath formula. Jonathan swears that he will warn David. Jonathan's wish that the LORD be with David as he was with Saul hints that David will be king. **14–15:** *Faithful love,* "loyalty," the same word as in v. 8. *My house* means Jonathan's descendants. David's oath of loyalty to Jonathan's house furnishes the reason for his treatment of Mephibosheth in 2 Sam 9. **16:** *The enemies of David* include Saul! **17:** *Love* again expresses political loyalty. **18–22:** Jonathan will signal David secretly during his target practice. If Jonathan tells his servant retrieving the arrows that they are back toward Jonathan, it is safe for David to come out of hiding. But if Jonathan tells the servant to go farther, David should flee immediately. **26:** *He is not clean,* ritual uncleanness, which could be caused by a variety of factors,

your place will be empty. 19 On the day
after tomorrow, you shall go a long way
down; go to the place where you hid your-
self earlier, and remain beside the stone
there.[a] 20 I will shoot three arrows to the
side of it, as though I shot at a mark.
21 Then I will send the boy, saying, 'Go,
find the arrows.' If I say to the boy, 'Look,
the arrows are on this side of you, collect
them,' then you are to come, for, as the
LORD lives, it is safe for you and there is no
danger. 22 But if I say to the young man,
'Look, the arrows are beyond you,' then
go; for the LORD has sent you away. 23 As
for the matter about which you and I have
spoken, the LORD is witness[b] between you
and me forever."

24 So David hid himself in the field.
When the new moon came, the king sat at
the feast to eat. 25 The king sat upon his
seat, as at other times, upon the seat by the
wall. Jonathan stood, while Abner sat by
Saul's side; but David's place was empty.

26 Saul did not say anything that day;
for he thought, "Something has befallen
him; he is not clean, surely he is not clean."
27 But on the second day, the day after the
new moon, David's place was empty. And
Saul said to his son Jonathan, "Why has the
son of Jesse not come to the feast, either
yesterday or today?" 28 Jonathan answered
Saul, "David earnestly asked leave of me to
go to Bethlehem; 29 he said, 'Let me go; for
our family is holding a sacrifice in the city,
and my brother has commanded me to be
there. So now, if I have found favor in your
sight, let me get away, and see my broth-
ers.' For this reason he has not come to the
king's table."

30 Then Saul's anger was kindled
against Jonathan. He said to him, "You son
of a perverse, rebellious woman! Do I not
know that you have chosen the son of Jesse
to your own shame, and to the shame of
your mother's nakedness? 31 For as long as
the son of Jesse lives upon the earth, neither
you nor your kingdom shall be established.
Now send and bring him to me, for he shall
surely die." 32 Then Jonathan answered his
father Saul, "Why should he be put to
death? What has he done?" 33 But Saul
threw his spear at him to strike him; so
Jonathan knew that it was the decision of
his father to put David to death. 34 Jona-
than rose from the table in fierce anger
and ate no food on the second day of the
month, for he was grieved for David, and
because his father had disgraced him.

35 In the morning Jonathan went out
into the field to the appointment with Da-
vid, and with him was a little boy. 36 He
said to the boy, "Run and find the arrows
that I shoot." As the boy ran, he shot an
arrow beyond him. 37 When the boy came
to the place where Jonathan's arrow had
fallen, Jonathan called after the boy and
said, "Is the arrow not beyond you?"
38 Jonathan called after the boy, "Hurry, be
quick, do not linger." So Jonathan's boy
gathered up the arrows and came to his
master. 39 But the boy knew nothing; only
Jonathan and David knew the arrange-
ment. 40 Jonathan gave his weapons to the
boy and said to him, "Go and carry them to
the city." 41 As soon as the boy had gone,
David rose from beside the stone heap[c]
and prostrated himself with his face to the
ground. He bowed three times, and they
kissed each other, and wept with each oth-
er; David wept the more.[d] 42 Then Jona-
than said to David, "Go in peace, since
both of us have sworn in the name of the
LORD, saying, 'The LORD shall be between
me and you, and between my descendants
and your descendants, forever.' " He got

a Meaning of Heb uncertain *b* Gk: Heb lacks *witness* *c* Gk: Heb *from beside the south* *d* Vg: Meaning of Heb uncertain

disqualified a person from participation in ritual activity (Lev 11–15). **27:** *The son of Jesse,* a disdainful reference to David. **30:** *Chosen the son of Jesse,* Saul accuses Jonathan of treason. *Nakedness,* a euphemism for the genitals. **33:** Saul tries to kill Jonathan with his spear, exactly as he had tried to kill David (18.10–11; 19.8–10). **41–42a:** An addition reiterating the affection and loyalty between David and Jonathan. If they could have met openly like this, the previous signal would have been unnecessary.

up and left; and Jonathan went into the
city.[a]

21 [b]David came to Nob to the priest
Ahimelech. Ahimelech came trem-
bling to meet David, and said to him, "Why
are you alone, and no one with you?" 2Da-
vid said to the priest Ahimelech, "The king
has charged me with a matter, and said to
me, 'No one must know anything of the
matter about which I send you, and with
which I have charged you.' I have made
an appointment[c] with the young men for
such and such a place. 3Now then, what
have you at hand? Give me five loaves of
bread, or whatever is here." 4The priest an-
swered David, "I have no ordinary bread at
hand, only holy bread—provided that the
young men have kept themselves from
women." 5David answered the priest, "In-
deed women have been kept from us as al-
ways when I go on an expedition; the ves-
sels of the young men are holy even when it
is a common journey; how much more to-
day will their vessels be holy?" 6So the
priest gave him the holy bread; for there
was no bread there except the bread of the
Presence, which is removed from before the
LORD, to be replaced by hot bread on the
day it is taken away.

7 Now a certain man of the servants of
Saul was there that day, detained before the
LORD; his name was Doeg the Edomite, the
chief of Saul's shepherds.

8 David said to Ahimelech, "Is there no
spear or sword here with you? I did not
bring my sword or my weapons with me,
because the king's business required haste."
9The priest said, "The sword of Goliath the
Philistine, whom you killed in the valley of
Elah, is here wrapped in a cloth behind the
ephod; if you will take that, take it, for
there is none here except that one." David
said, "There is none like it; give it to me."

10 David rose and fled that day from
Saul; he went to King Achish of Gath.
11The servants of Achish said to him, "Is
this not David the king of the land? Did
they not sing to one another of him in
dances,

'Saul has killed his thousands,
and David his ten thousands'?"

12David took these words to heart and was
very much afraid of King Achish of Gath.
13So he changed his behavior before them;
he pretended to be mad when in their pres-
ence.[d] He scratched marks on the doors of
the gate, and let his spittle run down his
beard. 14Achish said to his servants,
"Look, you see the man is mad; why then
have you brought him to me? 15Do I lack
madmen, that you have brought this fellow
to play the madman in my presence? Shall
this fellow come into my house?"

22 David left there and escaped to the
cave of Adullam; when his brothers
and all his father's house heard of it, they

a This sentence is 21.1 in Heb *b* Ch 21.2 in Heb
c Q Ms Vg Compare Gk: Meaning of MT uncertain
d Heb *in their hands*

21.1–15: David escapes to Nob. 1: *Nob* was between Gibeah and Jerusalem. *Ahimelech,* the great-grandson of Eli, *came trembling to meet David* apparently because David was alone, suggesting his fugitive status. **4:** *Provided that the young men have kept themselves from women,* those involved in sacred activities, such as worship and preparing for holy war, were prohibited from engaging in sexual relations (see Ex 19.15). **5:** *Vessels,* a euphemism for the sexual organs. **7:** *Detained before the LORD* probably means *Doeg* had a vow to fulfill. The fact that he is an *Edomite* is ominous, because Edomites are often depicted as Israel's hated enemies. **9:** *The sword of Goliath,* see 17.54n. The *ephod* mentioned here seems to be an idol (Judg 8.27) rather than a priestly garment. **10:** *Achish,* a Philistine name. In chs 27–29, David is his trusted vassal. **11:** *The king of the land,* if it is not an anachronism, indicates that the Philistines already recognize David as a ruler. The Philistines quote the song in 18.7. **13–15:** *To be mad* was to be divinely "touched" (see the references to Saul prophesying in 18.10–11; 19.23–24). Thus, the Philistines, fearing divine wrath, leave David alone. The story ridicules the Philistines, who cannot tell madness from sanity and who admit to having plenty of *madmen.*

22.1–23: David at Adullam; massacre of the priests of Nob. 1: *Cave,* possibly an error for stronghold

went down there to him. 2 Everyone who
was in distress, and everyone who was in
debt, and everyone who was discontented
gathered to him; and he became captain
over them. Those who were with him num-
bered about four hundred.
3 David went from there to Mizpeh of
Moab. He said to the king of Moab,
"Please let my father and mother come[a] to
you, until I know what God will do for
me." 4 He left them with the king of Moab,
and they stayed with him all the time that
David was in the stronghold. 5 Then the
prophet Gad said to David, "Do not re-
main in the stronghold; leave, and go into
the land of Judah." So David left, and went
into the forest of Hereth.
6 Saul heard that David and those who
were with him had been located. Saul was
sitting at Gibeah, under the tamarisk tree
on the height, with his spear in his hand,
and all his servants were standing around
him. 7 Saul said to his servants who stood
around him, "Hear now, you Benjaminites;
will the son of Jesse give every one of you
fields and vineyards, will he make you all
commanders of thousands and command-
ers of hundreds? 8 Is that why all of you
have conspired against me? No one dis-
closes to me when my son makes a league
with the son of Jesse, none of you is sorry
for me or discloses to me that my son has
stirred up my servant against me, to lie in
wait, as he is doing today." 9 Doeg the
Edomite, who was in charge of Saul's ser-
vants, answered, "I saw the son of Jesse
coming to Nob, to Ahimelech son of Ahi-
tub; 10 he inquired of the LORD for him,
gave him provisions, and gave him the
sword of Goliath the Philistine."
11 The king sent for the priest Ahime-
lech son of Ahitub and for all his father's
house, the priests who were at Nob; and all
of them came to the king. 12 Saul said, "Lis-
ten now, son of Ahitub." He answered,
"Here I am, my lord." 13 Saul said to him,
"Why have you conspired against me, you
and the son of Jesse, by giving him bread
and a sword, and by inquiring of God for
him, so that he has risen against me, to lie
in wait, as he is doing today?"
14 Then Ahimelech answered the king,
"Who among all your servants is so faithful
as David? He is the king's son-in-law, and
is quick[b] to do your bidding, and is hon-
ored in your house. 15 Is today the first time
that I have inquired of God for him? By no
means! Do not let the king impute anything
to his servant or to any member of my fa-
ther's house; for your servant has known
nothing of all this, much or little." 16 The
king said, "You shall surely die, Ahimelech,
you and all your father's house." 17 The
king said to the guard who stood around
him, "Turn and kill the priests of the LORD,
because their hand also is with David; they
knew that he fled, and did not disclose it to
me." But the servants of the king would not
raise their hand to attack the priests of the
LORD. 18 Then the king said to Doeg, "You,
Doeg, turn and attack the priests." Doeg
the Edomite turned and attacked the
priests; on that day he killed eighty-five
who wore the linen ephod. 19 Nob, the city
of the priests, he put to the sword; men and
women, children and infants, oxen, don-
keys, and sheep, he put to the sword.
20 But one of the sons of Ahimelech son
of Ahitub, named Abiathar, escaped and
fled after David. 21 Abiathar told David

a Syr Vg: Heb *come out* *b* Heb *and turns aside*

(v. 4). *Adullam* served as David's headquarters. **2:** The wilderness of Judah around Adullam had long been a hideout of fugitives. **3–4:** The book of Ruth indicates that David had a Moabite ancestry. *Stronghold,* probably Adullam. **5:** *The prophet Gad,* see 2 Sam 24.11. **7:** *Son of Jesse,* a disparaging reference to David. Kings commonly rewarded their servants with *fields and vineyards* and military appointments. The *Benjaminites* can expect no such rewards if David becomes king because his native tribe is Judah. **10:** Ch 21 does not mention that Ahimelech *inquired of the LORD for* David, but the accusation (whether true or not) plays an important role in the confrontation to follow. **18:** Only *Doeg* (see 21.7) dares to attack the LORD's priests, because he is an *Edomite. Linen ephod,* a garment worn by priests (2.18) **19:** Saul devotes the LORD's priests to destruction. Ironically, this is what he failed to do

that Saul had killed the priests of the LORD.
22 David said to Abiathar, "I knew on that
day, when Doeg the Edomite was there,
that he would surely tell Saul. I am respon-
sible[a] for the lives of all your father's
house. 23 Stay with me, and do not be
afraid; for the one who seeks my life seeks
your life; you will be safe with me."

23 Now they told David, "The Philis-
tines are fighting against Keilah,
and are robbing the threshing floors." 2 Da-
vid inquired of the LORD, "Shall I go and
attack these Philistines?" The LORD said to
David, "Go and attack the Philistines and
save Keilah." 3 But David's men said to
him, "Look, we are afraid here in Judah;
how much more then if we go to Keilah
against the armies of the Philistines?"
4 Then David inquired of the LORD again.
The LORD answered him, "Yes, go down to
Keilah; for I will give the Philistines into
your hand." 5 So David and his men went
to Keilah, fought with the Philistines,
brought away their livestock, and dealt
them a heavy defeat. Thus David rescued
the inhabitants of Keilah.

6 When Abiathar son of Ahimelech fled
to David at Keilah, he came down with an
ephod in his hand. 7 Now it was told Saul
that David had come to Keilah. And Saul
said, "God has given[b] him into my hand;
for he has shut himself in by entering a
town that has gates and bars." 8 Saul sum-
moned all the people to war, to go down
to Keilah, to besiege David and his men.
9 When David learned that Saul was plot-
ting evil against him, he said to the priest
Abiathar, "Bring the ephod here." 10 David
said, "O LORD, the God of Israel, your ser-
vant has heard that Saul seeks to come to
Keilah, to destroy the city on my account.
11 And now, will[c] Saul come down as your
servant has heard? O LORD, the God of Is-
rael, I beseech you, tell your servant." The
LORD said, "He will come down." 12 Then
David said, "Will the men of Keilah surren-
der me and my men into the hand of Saul?"
The LORD said, "They will surrender you."
13 Then David and his men, who were
about six hundred, set out and left Keilah;
they wandered wherever they could go.
When Saul was told that David had es-
caped from Keilah, he gave up the expedi-
tion. 14 David remained in the strongholds
in the wilderness, in the hill country of the
Wilderness of Ziph. Saul sought him every
day, but the LORD[d] did not give him into
his hand.

15 David was in the Wilderness of Ziph
at Horesh when he learned that[e] Saul had
come out to seek his life. 16 Saul's son Jona-
than set out and came to David at Horesh;
there he strengthened his hand through the
LORD.[f] 17 He said to him, "Do not be
afraid; for the hand of my father Saul shall
not find you; you shall be king over Israel,
and I shall be second to you; my father Saul
also knows that this is so." 18 Then the two
of them made a covenant before the LORD;
David remained at Horesh, and Jonathan
went home.

19 Then some Ziphites went up to Saul
at Gibeah and said, "David is hiding
among us in the strongholds of Horesh, on
the hill of Hachilah, which is south of Jeshi-
mon. 20 Now, O king, whenever you wish
to come down, do so; and our part will be

a Gk Vg: Meaning of Heb uncertain *b* Gk Tg: Heb *made a stranger of* *c* Q Ms Compare Gk: MT *Will the men of Keilah surrender me into his hand? Will* *d* Q Ms Gk: MT *God* *e* Or *saw that* *f* Compare Q Ms Gk: MT *God*

against the Amalekites in ch 15 (see vv. 8–9,14,19). **20–23:** The one escapee is Abiathar in fulfillment of the oracle in 2.27–36.

23.1–13: David's relief of Keilah. 1: *Keilah,* an independent city within Philistine territory. *Threshing floors,* open-air surfaces where grain was separated from chaff. **2–5:** This episode illustrates the importance of Abiathar's ability to divine through the ephod. David's inquiries require a yes-or-no answer, which could be determined through the *ephod* (v. 6). **7–13:** David receives forewarning from the ephod, which allows him to escape Saul. Saul, in contrast, has no ephod, and later his efforts to consult the LORD go unanswered (28.6) **17:** It is extraordinary and unbelievable that Jonathan would admit that David would be king in his place. **25–29:** This story illustrates the LORD's protection of David, even though the

to surrender him into the king's hand."
21 Saul said, "May you be blessed by the
LORD for showing me compassion! 22 Go
and make sure once more; find out exactly
where he is, and who has seen him there;
for I am told that he is very cunning.
23 Look around and learn all the hiding
places where he lurks, and come back to me
with sure information. Then I will go with
you; and if he is in the land, I will search
him out among all the thousands of Judah."
24 So they set out and went to Ziph
ahead of Saul.

David and his men were in the wilderness
of Maon, in the Arabah to the south of
Jeshimon. 25 Saul and his men went to
search for him. When David was told, he
went down to the rock and stayed in the
wilderness of Maon. When Saul heard that,
he pursued David into the wilderness of
Maon. 26 Saul went on one side of the
mountain, and David and his men on the
other side of the mountain. David was hurrying
to get away from Saul, while Saul and
his men were closing in on David and his
men to capture them. 27 Then a messenger
came to Saul, saying, "Hurry and come; for
the Philistines have made a raid on the
land." 28 So Saul stopped pursuing David,
and went against the Philistines; therefore
that place was called the Rock of Escape.[a]
29 [b] David then went up from there, and
lived in the strongholds of En-gedi.

24 When Saul returned from following
the Philistines, he was told, "David
is in the wilderness of En-gedi." 2 Then Saul
took three thousand chosen men out of all
Israel, and went to look for David and his
men in the direction of the Rocks of the
Wild Goats. 3 He came to the sheepfolds
beside the road, where there was a cave;
and Saul went in to relieve himself.[c] Now
David and his men were sitting in the innermost
parts of the cave. 4 The men of David
said to him, "Here is the day of which the
LORD said to you, 'I will give your enemy
into your hand, and you shall do to him as
it seems good to you.' " Then David went
and stealthily cut off a corner of Saul's
cloak. 5 Afterward David was stricken to
the heart because he had cut off a corner of
Saul's cloak. 6 He said to his men, "The
LORD forbid that I should do this thing to
my lord, the LORD's anointed, to raise my
hand against him; for he is the LORD's
anointed." 7 So David scolded his men severely
and did not permit them to attack
Saul. Then Saul got up and left the cave,
and went on his way.

8 Afterwards David also rose up and
went out of the cave and called after Saul,
"My lord the king!" When Saul looked behind
him, David bowed with his face to the
ground, and did obeisance. 9 David said to
Saul, "Why do you listen to the words of
those who say, 'David seeks to do you
harm'? 10 This very day your eyes have seen
how the LORD gave you into my hand in
the cave; and some urged me to kill you,
but I spared[d] you. I said, 'I will not raise
my hand against my lord; for he is the
LORD's anointed.' 11 See, my father, see the
corner of your cloak in my hand; for by the
fact that I cut off the corner of your cloak,

a Or *Rock of Division*; meaning of Heb uncertain
b Ch 24.1 in Heb *c* Heb *to cover his feet*
d Gk Syr Tg Vg: Heb *it* (my eye) *spared*

LORD is not mentioned. By "providence" Saul is forced to withdraw just at the moment he has David trapped. The name of this place (v. 28) means either "rock of escape" or "rock of division." Both are appropriate to the story.

24.1–22: David spares Saul's life. 2: *Three thousand,* either an exaggerated number or "thousand" refers to a much smaller military unit. **3:** *To relieve himself,* lit. "to cover his feet." **4a:** The prophecy cited by David's men is not recorded and could be their own invention. **4b–5:** These verses may have originally belonged after v. 7a. David's cutting off Saul's hem is symbolic for emasculation or usurpation of Saul's kingdom, which is why David's conscience bothers him. **6:** To attack the LORD's anointed (Saul) was to attack the LORD. **8:** *David bowed with his face to the ground, and did obeisance,* David thus shows the proper respect toward Saul as the LORD's anointed. **11:** *My father* is a respectful address from the younger David; it may also imply David's right to inherit Saul's kingdom. **14:** *A dead dog? A single flea?* David

and did not kill you, you may know for
certain that there is no wrong or treason in
my hands. I have not sinned against you,
though you are hunting me to take my life.
12 May the LORD judge between me and
you! May the LORD avenge me on you; but
my hand shall not be against you. 13 As the
ancient proverb says, 'Out of the wicked
comes forth wickedness'; but my hand shall
not be against you. 14 Against whom has
the king of Israel come out? Whom do you
pursue? A dead dog? A single flea? 15 May
the LORD therefore be judge, and give sen-
tence between me and you. May he see to
it, and plead my cause, and vindicate me
against you."

16 When David had finished speaking
these words to Saul, Saul said, "Is this your
voice, my son David?" Saul lifted up his
voice and wept. 17 He said to David, "You
are more righteous than I; for you have re-
paid me good, whereas I have repaid you
evil. 18 Today you have explained how you
have dealt well with me, in that you did not
kill me when the LORD put me into your
hands. 19 For who has ever found an ene-
my, and sent the enemy safely away? So
may the LORD reward you with good for
what you have done to me this day. 20 Now
I know that you shall surely be king, and
that the kingdom of Israel shall be estab-
lished in your hand. 21 Swear to me there-
fore by the LORD that you will not cut off
my descendants after me, and that you will
not wipe out my name from my father's
house." 22 So David swore this to Saul.
Then Saul went home; but David and his
men went up to the stronghold.

25 Now Samuel died; and all Israel as-
sembled and mourned for him.
They buried him at his home in Ramah.
Then David got up and went down to the
wilderness of Paran.

2 There was a man in Maon, whose
property was in Carmel. The man was very
rich; he had three thousand sheep and a
thousand goats. He was shearing his sheep
in Carmel. 3 Now the name of the man was
Nabal, and the name of his wife Abigail.
The woman was clever and beautiful, but
the man was surly and mean; he was a Ca-
lebite. 4 David heard in the wilderness that
Nabal was shearing his sheep. 5 So David
sent ten young men; and David said to the
young men, "Go up to Carmel, and go to
Nabal, and greet him in my name. 6 Thus
you shall salute him: 'Peace be to you, and
peace be to your house, and peace be to all
that you have. 7 I hear that you have shear-
ers; now your shepherds have been with us,
and we did them no harm, and they missed
nothing, all the time they were in Carmel.
8 Ask your young men, and they will tell
you. Therefore let my young men find favor
in your sight; for we have come on a feast
day. Please give whatever you have at hand
to your servants and to your son David.' "

9 When David's young men came, they

could be disparaging himself as insignificant, or he could be saying that Saul is mistaken if he thinks David is insignificant. **16:** Saul's reference to David as *my son* recalls their once close relationship and hints that David will be Saul's successor. **20:** Saul recognizes that David will succeed him. **21–22:** A new king commonly killed all the descendants of the previous king in order to be rid of potential rivals. David's oath not to wipe out Saul's descendants anticipates his treatment of Mephibosheth (2 Sam 9).

25.1a: The death of Samuel. An editor's note that prepares for ch 28.

25.1b–43: Nabal and Abigail. In chs 24 and 26 David refuses to kill Saul, but in ch 25 he is almost guilty of killing many innocent people in Nabal's household. **2–3:** Carmel, see 15.12n. Nabal, like Saul, is a rich and powerful man. *Calebite,* a member of the leading clan of Judah. *Nabal,* meaning "fool" (v. 25), is an unlikely name for parents to give to a child. Either the name "Nabal" was invented as appropriate to this man's character, or it originally meant something different (there are several other possible meanings). Nabal's wife, *Abigail,* is his complete opposite. The only other Abigail in the Bible is David's sister (1 Chr 2.16). **4–8:** *Shearing his sheep,* a time of celebration. David hopes that Nabal, in the spirit of the festival, will give a generous gift. This gift is more or less obligatory as payment for not harming or for "protecting" Nabal's shepherds. The *ten young men* give Nabal an idea of the size of gift David is expecting—whatever ten men can carry; they may also be meant to intimidate Nabal.

said all this to Nabal in the name of David;
and then they waited. 10 But Nabal an-
swered David's servants, "Who is David?
Who is the son of Jesse? There are many
servants today who are breaking away
from their masters. 11 Shall I take my bread
and my water and the meat that I have
butchered for my shearers, and give it to
men who come from I do not know
where?" 12 So David's young men turned
away, and came back and told him all this.
13 David said to his men, "Every man strap
on his sword!" And every one of them
strapped on his sword; David also strapped
on his sword; and about four hundred men
went up after David, while two hundred
remained with the baggage.

14 But one of the young men told Abi-
gail, Nabal's wife, "David sent messengers
out of the wilderness to salute our master;
and he shouted insults at them. 15 Yet the
men were very good to us, and we suffered
no harm, and we never missed anything
when we were in the fields, as long as we
were with them; 16 they were a wall to us
both by night and by day, all the while we
were with them keeping the sheep. 17 Now
therefore know this and consider what you
should do; for evil has been decided against
our master and against all his house; he is
so ill-natured that no one can speak to
him."

18 Then Abigail hurried and took two
hundred loaves, two skins of wine, five
sheep ready dressed, five measures of
parched grain, one hundred clusters of rai-
sins, and two hundred cakes of figs. She
loaded them on donkeys 19 and said to her
young men, "Go on ahead of me; I am
coming after you." But she did not tell her
husband Nabal. 20 As she rode on the don-
key and came down under cover of the
mountain, David and his men came down
toward her; and she met them. 21 Now Da-
vid had said, "Surely it was in vain that I
protected all that this fellow has in the wil-
derness, so that nothing was missed of all
that belonged to him; but he has returned
me evil for good. 22 God do so to David[a]
and more also, if by morning I leave so
much as one male of all who belong to
him."

23 When Abigail saw David, she hurried
and alighted from the donkey, and fell be-
fore David on her face, bowing to the
ground. 24 She fell at his feet and said,
"Upon me alone, my lord, be the guilt;
please let your servant speak in your ears,
and hear the words of your servant. 25 My
lord, do not take seriously this ill-natured
fellow, Nabal; for as his name is, so is he;
Nabal[b] is his name, and folly is with him;
but I, your servant, did not see the young
men of my lord, whom you sent.

26 "Now then, my lord, as the LORD
lives, and as you yourself live, since the
LORD has restrained you from bloodguilt
and from taking vengeance with your own
hand, now let your enemies and those who
seek to do evil to my lord be like Nabal.
27 And now let this present that your ser-
vant has brought to my lord be given to the
young men who follow my lord. 28 Please
forgive the trespass of your servant; for the
LORD will certainly make my lord a sure
house, because my lord is fighting the bat-
tles of the LORD; and evil shall not be found
in you so long as you live. 29 If anyone

a Gk Compare Syr: Heb *the enemies of David*
b That is *Fool*

10–11: *Who is David? Who is the son of Jesse?* demean David as insignificant. Nabal goes on to call David a runaway slave and a vagabond. **14:** Nabal's own servants go to Abigail because they recognize him as ill-natured and untrustworthy. **18:** *Five measures* (Heb "se'ah"), about a bushel. *Cakes of figs,* clumps rather than a bakery product. **22:** David vows to annihilate every *male* in Nabal's household. Only the woman, Abigail, can prevent the tragedy. **23:** Abigail bows to David as before a king. **24:** Abigail is eloquent and tactful, calling herself David's *servant* (v. 24). **26:** This verse anticipates the conclusion of the story, according to which Nabal dies but not by David's hand. It may be out of place. **27:** Abigail diplomatically refers to the supplies she brings as a *present* for David's men. **28:** *Sure house* suggests that Abigail knows David will be king. **29:** *If anyone should rise up to pursue you and to seek*

should rise up to pursue you and to seek
your life, the life of my lord shall be bound
in the bundle of the living under the care of
the LORD your God; but the lives of your
enemies he shall sling out as from the hol-
low of a sling. 30 When the LORD has done
to my lord according to all the good that he
has spoken concerning you, and has ap-
pointed you prince over Israel, 31 my lord
shall have no cause of grief, or pangs of
conscience, for having shed blood without
cause or for having saved himself. And
when the LORD has dealt well with my
lord, then remember your servant."
32 David said to Abigail, "Blessed be the
LORD, the God of Israel, who sent you to
meet me today! 33 Blessed be your good
sense, and blessed be you, who have kept
me today from bloodguilt and from aveng-
ing myself by my own hand! 34 For as surely
as the LORD the God of Israel lives, who
has restrained me from hurting you, unless
you had hurried and come to meet me, tru-
ly by morning there would not have been
left to Nabal so much as one male." 35 Then
David received from her hand what she had
brought him; he said to her, "Go up to your
house in peace; see, I have heeded your
voice, and I have granted your petition."
36 Abigail came to Nabal; he was hold-
ing a feast in his house, like the feast of a
king. Nabal's heart was merry within him,
for he was very drunk; so she told him
nothing at all until the morning light. 37 In
the morning, when the wine had gone out
of Nabal, his wife told him these things,
and his heart died within him; he became
like a stone. 38 About ten days later the
LORD struck Nabal, and he died.
39 When David heard that Nabal was
dead, he said, "Blessed be the LORD who
has judged the case of Nabal's insult to me,
and has kept back his servant from evil; the
LORD has returned the evildoing of Nabal
upon his own head." Then David sent and
wooed Abigail, to make her his wife.
40 When David's servants came to Abigail
at Carmel, they said to her, "David has sent
us to you to take you to him as his wife."
41 She rose and bowed down, with her face
to the ground, and said, "Your servant is a
slave to wash the feet of the servants of my
lord." 42 Abigail got up hurriedly and rode
away on a donkey; her five maids attended
her. She went after the messengers of David
and became his wife.
43 David also married Ahinoam of Jez-
reel; both of them became his wives. 44 Saul
had given his daughter Michal, David's
wife, to Palti son of Laish, who was from
Gallim.

26 Then the Ziphites came to Saul at
Gibeah, saying, "David is in hiding
on the hill of Hachilah, which is opposite

your life alludes to Saul. The *bundle of the living,* the list of those who are alive. *Sling out* recalls David's victory in ch 17 and anticipates Nabal's death in 25.37. **30–31:** Abigail points out that shedding innocent blood would be an obstacle to David's kingship. *Prince,* the one designated as king. *When the LORD has dealt well with my lord* may refer to David's becoming king or ironically to Nabal's death. *Remember your servant* is a marriage proposal. **32–33:** David praises *the LORD* for sending Abigail because she saved him from committing murder and thus incurring *bloodguilt.* **35:** *I have granted your petition,* David already speaks as a king. **36:** *Feast,* the etymological meaning of the word is a drinking bout. *Like the feast of a king,* Nabal is again compared to a king. **37:** *When the wine had gone out of Nabal,* the name "Nabal" is similar to the word for wineskin in v. 18. *He became like a stone,* perhaps a coma. **43:** Saul's wife was also named *Ahinoam* (14.50). *Jezreel,* apparently a town near Carmel (Josh 15.56) rather than the northern valley of that name. **44:** *Saul had given his daughter Michal, David's wife, to Palti son of Laish,* this notice illustrates Saul's enmity toward David and prepares for the story of Michal's return in 2 Sam 3.13–16.

26.1–25: David spares Saul's life again. This story is similar to the one in ch 24, and the two may be variants of a single original. In both, Saul is unknowingly defenseless before David, who is urged by his men to kill Saul (24.4,7) but refuses because of Saul's status as the LORD's anointed. David then reveals to Saul that he could have killed him, and Saul expresses remorse for persecuting David and hints or states that David will succeed him as king (24.20; 26.25). **5:** The army sleeps around the king in order to protect

Jeshimon."[a] 2 So Saul rose and went down
to the Wilderness of Ziph, with three thou-
sand chosen men of Israel, to seek David in
the Wilderness of Ziph. 3 Saul encamped on
the hill of Hachilah, which is opposite Je-
shimon[a] beside the road. But David re-
mained in the wilderness. When he learned
that Saul had come after him into the wil-
derness, 4 David sent out spies, and learned
that Saul had indeed arrived. 5 Then David
set out and came to the place where Saul
had encamped; and David saw the place
where Saul lay, with Abner son of Ner, the
commander of his army. Saul was lying
within the encampment, while the army
was encamped around him.

6 Then David said to Ahimelech the Hit-
tite, and to Joab's brother Abishai son of
Zeruiah, "Who will go down with me into
the camp to Saul?" Abishai said, "I will go
down with you." 7 So David and Abishai
went to the army by night; there Saul lay
sleeping within the encampment, with his
spear stuck in the ground at his head; and
Abner and the army lay around him.
8 Abishai said to David, "God has given
your enemy into your hand today; now
therefore let me pin him to the ground with
one stroke of the spear; I will not strike him
twice." 9 But David said to Abishai, "Do
not destroy him; for who can raise his hand
against the LORD's anointed, and be guilt-
less?" 10 David said, "As the LORD lives,
the LORD will strike him down; or his day
will come to die; or he will go down into
battle and perish. 11 The LORD forbid that I
should raise my hand against the LORD's
anointed; but now take the spear that is at
his head, and the water jar, and let us go."
12 So David took the spear that was at
Saul's head and the water jar, and they
went away. No one saw it, or knew it, nor
did anyone awake; for they were all asleep,
because a deep sleep from the LORD had
fallen upon them.

13 Then David went over to the other
side, and stood on top of a hill far away,
with a great distance between them. 14 Da-
vid called to the army and to Abner son
of Ner, saying, "Abner! Will you not an-
swer?" Then Abner replied, "Who are you
that calls to the king?" 15 David said to Ab-
ner, "Are you not a man? Who is like you
in Israel? Why then have you not kept
watch over your lord the king? For one of
the people came in to destroy your lord the
king. 16 This thing that you have done is not
good. As the LORD lives, you deserve to die,
because you have not kept watch over your
lord, the LORD's anointed. See now, where
is the king's spear, or the water jar that was
at his head?"

17 Saul recognized David's voice, and
said, "Is this your voice, my son David?"
David said, "It is my voice, my lord,
O king." 18 And he added, "Why does my
lord pursue his servant? For what have I
done? What guilt is on my hands? 19 Now
therefore let my lord the king hear the
words of his servant. If it is the LORD who
has stirred you up against me, may he ac-
cept an offering; but if it is mortals, may
they be cursed before the LORD, for they
have driven me out today from my share in
the heritage of the LORD, saying, 'Go, serve
other gods.' 20 Now therefore, do not let my
blood fall to the ground, away from the
presence of the LORD; for the king of Israel
has come out to seek a single flea, like one
who hunts a partridge in the mountains."

21 Then Saul said, "I have done wrong;
come back, my son David, for I will never
harm you again, because my life was pre-
cious in your sight today; I have been a

a Or *opposite the wasteland*

him. **6:** *Joab,* David's nephew (1 Chr 2.16), later the commander of his army. **8:** The same *spear* that Saul used to try to kill David is now available for David to use against Saul. **13:** *David went over to the other side,* if Saul pursues him he can lead Saul's army away from his own men. **19:** David curses anyone who caused Saul to pursue him, because this has driven him from the land of Israel, which is the LORD's *heritage.* Each god was believed to have his own nation and each nation its god. *Other gods,* the gods of countries outside Israel where David says he has been driven. **20:** *A partridge,* lit. "the caller." David calls to Saul from a mountain. **25:** Saul's blessing hints that David will be king (cf. 24.20).

fool, and have made a great mistake."
22 David replied, "Here is the spear,
O king! Let one of the young men come
over and get it. 23 The LORD rewards every-
one for his righteousness and his faithful-
ness; for the LORD gave you into my hand
today, but I would not raise my hand
against the LORD's anointed. 24 As your life
was precious today in my sight, so may my
life be precious in the sight of the LORD,
and may he rescue me from all tribulation."
25 Then Saul said to David, "Blessed be
you, my son David! You will do many
things and will succeed in them." So David
went his way, and Saul returned to his
place.

27 David said in his heart, "I shall now
perish one day by the hand of Saul;
there is nothing better for me than to es-
cape to the land of the Philistines; then Saul
will despair of seeking me any longer with-
in the borders of Israel, and I shall escape
out of his hand." 2 So David set out and
went over, he and the six hundred men who
were with him, to King Achish son of Ma-
och of Gath. 3 David stayed with Achish at
Gath, he and his troops, every man with his
household, and David with his two wives,
Ahinoam of Jezreel, and Abigail of Carmel,
Nabal's widow. 4 When Saul was told that
David had fled to Gath, he no longer
sought for him.

5 Then David said to Achish, "If I have
found favor in your sight, let a place be
given me in one of the country towns, so
that I may live there; for why should your
servant live in the royal city with you?" 6 So
that day Achish gave him Ziklag; therefore
Ziklag has belonged to the kings of Judah
to this day. 7 The length of time that David
lived in the country of the Philistines was
one year and four months.

8 Now David and his men went up and
made raids on the Geshurites, the Girzites,
and the Amalekites; for these were the
landed settlements from Telam[a] on the
way to Shur and on to the land of Egypt.
9 David struck the land, leaving neither man
nor woman alive, but took away the sheep,
the oxen, the donkeys, the camels, and the
clothing, and came back to Achish. 10 When
Achish asked, "Against whom[b] have you
made a raid today?" David would say,
"Against the Negeb of Judah," or "Against
the Negeb of the Jerahmeelites," or,
"Against the Negeb of the Kenites." 11 Da-
vid left neither man nor woman alive to
be brought back to Gath, thinking, "They
might tell about us, and say, 'David has
done so and so.' " Such was his practice all
the time he lived in the country of the Phil-
istines. 12 Achish trusted David, thinking,
"He has made himself utterly abhorrent to
his people Israel; therefore he shall always
be my servant."

28 In those days the Philistines gath-
ered their forces for war, to fight
against Israel. Achish said to David, "You
know, of course, that you and your men are
to go out with me in the army." 2 David
said to Achish, "Very well, then you shall
know what your servant can do." Achish
said to David, "Very well, I will make you
my bodyguard for life."

a Compare Gk 15.4: Heb *from of old* *b* Q Ms Gk Vg: MT lacks *whom*

27.1–28.2: David becomes a vassal of the Philistines. This chapter is in tension with 21.10–15, in which David escapes from *Achish* by pretending to be mad. **27.3:** *Gath,* Goliath's home (17.4). **6:** Kings commonly gave land grants to faithful servants. *Ziklag* also guarded the southern frontier of Achish's territory. **8–12:** *The Negeb,* the southern wilderness area of Palestine. David conducts raids against non-Israelite peoples (v. 8). The mention of *Amalekites* is inconsistent with ch 15, in which they are all killed. David fools Achish by claiming to attack clans within Judah such as the "Kennizzites" (a better reading than *Kenites*) and *Jerahmeelites.* Thus, while Achish felt confident of David's loyalty because he thought David had betrayed his own people, the writer asserts that David's loyalty remained with Israel. **28.2:** *Then you shall know what your servant can do,* Achish thinks David is saying that he will show his potential against Israel. The reader knows that David is actually saying that in the heat of battle Achish will find out how David remains loyal to Israel.

3 Now Samuel had died, and all Israel
had mourned for him and buried him in
Ramah, his own city. Saul had expelled the
mediums and the wizards from the land.
4 The Philistines assembled, and came and
encamped at Shunem. Saul gathered all Is-
rael, and they encamped at Gilboa. 5 When
Saul saw the army of the Philistines, he was
afraid, and his heart trembled greatly.
6 When Saul inquired of the LORD, the
LORD did not answer him, not by dreams,
or by Urim, or by prophets. 7 Then Saul
said to his servants, "Seek out for me a
woman who is a medium, so that I may go
to her and inquire of her." His servants said
to him, "There is a medium at Endor."

8 So Saul disguised himself and put on
other clothes and went there, he and two
men with him. They came to the woman by
night. And he said, "Consult a spirit for
me, and bring up for me the one whom I
name to you." 9 The woman said to him,
"Surely you know what Saul has done, how
he has cut off the mediums and the wizards
from the land. Why then are you laying a
snare for my life to bring about my death?"
10 But Saul swore to her by the LORD, "As
the LORD lives, no punishment shall come
upon you for this thing." 11 Then the wom-
an said, "Whom shall I bring up for you?"
He answered, "Bring up Samuel for me."
12 When the woman saw Samuel, she cried
out with a loud voice; and the woman said
to Saul, "Why have you deceived me? You
are Saul!" 13 The king said to her, "Have no
fear; what do you see?" The woman said to
Saul, "I see a divine being[a] coming up out
of the ground." 14 He said to her, "What is
his appearance?" She said, "An old man is
coming up; he is wrapped in a robe." So
Saul knew that it was Samuel, and he
bowed with his face to the ground, and did
obeisance.

15 Then Samuel said to Saul, "Why
have you disturbed me by bringing me up?"
Saul answered, "I am in great distress, for
the Philistines are warring against me, and
God has turned away from me and answers
me no more, either by prophets or by
dreams; so I have summoned you to tell me
what I should do." 16 Samuel said, "Why
then do you ask me, since the LORD has
turned from you and become your enemy?
17 The LORD has done to you just as he
spoke by me; for the LORD has torn the
kingdom out of your hand, and given it to
your neighbor, David. 18 Because you did
not obey the voice of the LORD, and did not
carry out his fierce wrath against Amalek,
therefore the LORD has done this thing to
you today. 19 Moreover the LORD will give
Israel along with you into the hands of the
Philistines; and tomorrow you and your
sons shall be with me; the LORD will also
give the army of Israel into the hands of the
Philistines."

20 Immediately Saul fell full length on
the ground, filled with fear because of the
words of Samuel; and there was no strength
in him, for he had eaten nothing all day and
all night. 21 The woman came to Saul, and
when she saw that he was terrified, she said
to him, "Your servant has listened to you;
I have taken my life in my hand, and have

a Or *a god*; or *gods*

28.3–25: Saul consults a spirit. 3: *Mediums* and *wizards* refer to devices used to communicate with the dead; these are forbidden in Lev 19.31; 20.6,27; Deut 18.10. Ironically, Saul, who *expelled* them, now seeks one out. **4:** *Shunem* and *Gilboa,* near the Jezreel Valley, far north of the Negeb where the previous stories were set. **6:** Three means of divining were *dreams,* or incubation, in which one slept at a holy place anticipating the answer to an inquiry; *Urim* or lots, used earlier in 14.41; and *prophets* like the man of God in 9.1–10.16. **7:** *A woman who is a medium,* lit. "a woman of spirits," using the word translated "medium" in v. 3. **11–12a:** An insertion identifying Samuel as the ghost. Originally, the woman recognized Saul because of his oath not to punish her in v. 10. **13:** *Divine being,* a god or a ghost or spirit. *The ground,* better: "the underworld." **14:** *Robe,* Samuel's characteristic garment by which Saul recognizes him. **15:** *Disturbed me,* the spirits in the underworld were viewed as sleeping. **17–18:** See ch 15. **19:** *Tomorrow you and your sons shall be with me,* they will be dead. **20:** Saul's being *filled with fear* is unbecoming of the king and suggests that he is unfit for the role. **21:** *The woman* who is the medium is

listened to what you have said to me.
22 Now therefore, you also listen to your
servant; let me set a morsel of bread before
you. Eat, that you may have strength when
you go on your way." 23 He refused, and
said, "I will not eat." But his servants, to-
gether with the woman, urged him; and he
listened to their words. So he got up from
the ground and sat on the bed. 24 Now the
woman had a fatted calf in the house. She
quickly slaughtered it, and she took flour,
kneaded it, and baked unleavened cakes.
25 She put them before Saul and his ser-
vants, and they ate. Then they rose and
went away that night.

29 Now the Philistines gathered all
their forces at Aphek, while the Isra-
elites were encamped by the fountain that is
in Jezreel. 2 As the lords of the Philistines
were passing on by hundreds and by thou-
sands, and David and his men were passing
on in the rear with Achish, 3 the command-
ers of the Philistines said, "What are these
Hebrews doing here?" Achish said to the
commanders of the Philistines, "Is this not
David, the servant of King Saul of Israel,
who has been with me now for days and
years? Since he deserted to me I have found
no fault in him to this day." 4 But the com-
manders of the Philistines were angry with
him; and the commanders of the Philistines
said to him, "Send the man back, so that he
may return to the place that you have as-
signed to him; he shall not go down with us
to battle, or else he may become an adver-
sary to us in the battle. For how could this
fellow reconcile himself to his lord? Would
it not be with the heads of the men here? 5 Is
this not David, of whom they sing to one
another in dances,

'Saul has killed his thousands,
and David his ten thousands'?"

6 Then Achish called David and said to
him, "As the LORD lives, you have been
honest, and to me it seems right that you
should march out and in with me in the
campaign; for I have found nothing wrong
in you from the day of your coming to me
until today. Nevertheless the lords do not
approve of you. 7 So go back now; and go
peaceably; do nothing to displease the lords
of the Philistines." 8 David said to Achish,
"But what have I done? What have you
found in your servant from the day I en-
tered your service until now, that I should
not go and fight against the enemies of my
lord the king?" 9 Achish replied to David,
"I know that you are as blameless in my
sight as an angel of God; nevertheless, the
commanders of the Philistines have said,
'He shall not go up with us to the battle.'
10 Now then rise early in the morning, you
and the servants of your lord who came
with you, and go to the place that I ap-
pointed for you. As for the evil report, do
not take it to heart, for you have done well
before me.[a] Start early in the morning, and
leave as soon as you have light." 11 So Da-
vid set out with his men early in the morn-
ing, to return to the land of the Philistines.
But the Philistines went up to Jezreel.

30 Now when David and his men came
to Ziklag on the third day, the Ama-

a Gk: Heb lacks *and go to the place . . . done well before me*

calmer and stronger than the *terrified* Saul. **24:** *A fatted calf in the house,* livestock were kept on the ground floor of houses with sleeping quarters on a second story.

29.1–11: The Philistines reject David. 2: *The lords of the Philistines,* the rulers of the five main Philistine cities. **3:** It is the *commanders* of the Philistine army who will actually be in battle, rather than the Philistine lords, who object to the presence of David and his men. *Hebrews,* see 4.6n. **5:** The same song as in 18.7. **6:** *As the LORD lives,* Achish, the Philistine, swears by Yahweh, the God of Israel! **8:** *The enemies of my lord the king,* Achish takes this as a reference to himself, but David means Saul. **10:** *The place that I appointed for you,* Ziklag. **11:** David and the Philistines separate and go in opposite directions. Thus, the writer shows that David is far away from the battle and had nothing to do with Saul's death.

30.1–31: The burning of Ziklag and David's pursuit of the Amalekites. 1: *On the third day.* Ziklag was about 80 km (50 mi) south of Aphek. Again, the writer emphasizes David's distance from the battle lekites had made a raid on the Negeb and on Ziklag. They had attacked Ziklag, burned it down, 2 and taken captive the women and all[a] who were in it, both small and great; they killed none of them, but carried them off, and went their way. 3 When David and his men came to the city, they found it burned down, and their wives and sons and daughters taken captive. 4 Then David and the people who were with him raised their voices and wept, until they had no more strength to weep. 5 David's two wives also had been taken captive, Ahinoam of Jezreel, and Abigail the widow of Nabal of Carmel. 6 David was in great danger; for the people spoke of stoning him, because all the people were bitter in spirit for their sons and daughters. But David strengthened himself in the LORD his God.

7 David said to the priest Abiathar son of Ahimelech, "Bring me the ephod." So Abiathar brought the ephod to David. 8 David inquired of the LORD, "Shall I pursue this band? Shall I overtake them?" He answered him, "Pursue; for you shall surely overtake and shall surely rescue." 9 So David set out, he and the six hundred men who were with him. They came to the Wadi Besor, where those stayed who were left behind. 10 But David went on with the pursuit, he and four hundred men; two hundred stayed behind, too exhausted to cross the Wadi Besor.

11 In the open country they found an Egyptian, and brought him to David. They gave him bread and he ate; they gave him water to drink; 12 they also gave him a piece of fig cake and two clusters of raisins. When he had eaten, his spirit revived; for he had not eaten bread or drunk water for three days and three nights. 13 Then David said to him, "To whom do you belong? Where are you from?" He said, "I am a young man of Egypt, servant to an Amalekite. My master left me behind because I fell sick three days ago. 14 We had made a raid on the Negeb of the Cherethites and on that which belongs to Judah and on the Negeb of Caleb; and we burned Ziklag down." 15 David said to him, "Will you take me down to this raiding party?" He said, "Swear to me by God that you will not kill me, or hand me over to my master, and I will take you down to them."

16 When he had taken him down, they were spread out all over the ground, eating and drinking and dancing, because of the great amount of spoil they had taken from the land of the Philistines and from the land of Judah. 17 David attacked them from twilight until the evening of the next day. Not one of them escaped, except four hundred young men, who mounted camels and fled. 18 David recovered all that the Amalekites had taken; and David rescued his two wives. 19 Nothing was missing, whether small or great, sons or daughters, spoil or anything that had been taken; David brought back everything. 20 David also captured all the flocks and herds, which were driven ahead of the other cattle; people said, "This is David's spoil."

21 Then David came to the two hundred men who had been too exhausted to follow David, and who had been left at the Wadi Besor. They went out to meet David and to meet the people who were with him. When David drew near to the people he saluted them. 22 Then all the corrupt and worthless

a Gk: Heb lacks *and all*

where Saul was killed. The Amalekite *raid* on Ziklag may have been in retaliation for David's raids against them (27.8). This story is inconsistent with ch 15, in which the Amalekites were supposedly all destroyed. **2:** *Both small and great,* poor and unimportant or wealthy and socially prominent, a figure of speech meaning "everyone." **6:** *Strengthened himself* may mean summoning courage as well as gathering support within the army. David is here depicted as an ideal ruler. **7–8:** *Ephod,* an instrument used by priests to divine the answers to yes-or-no questions. David's access to God through the ephod contrasts with Saul's lack of response from God in 28.6 and highlights the theme: "the LORD was with him (David)." **12:** *Fig cake,* see 25.18n. **14:** *Cherethites,* probably "Cretans," mercenaries from Crete, identical to or associated with the Philistines. **19:** *Small or great,* see v. 2n. **23–25:** An etiology for a custom in the writer's day.

fellows among the men who had gone with
David said, "Because they did not go with
us, we will not give them any of the spoil
that we have recovered, except that each
man may take his wife and children, and
leave." 23 But David said, "You shall not do
so, my brothers, with what the LORD has
given us; he has preserved us and handed
over to us the raiding party that attacked
us. 24 Who would listen to you in this mat-
ter? For the share of the one who goes
down into the battle shall be the same as
the share of the one who stays by the bag-
gage; they shall share alike." 25 From that
day forward he made it a statute and an
ordinance for Israel; it continues to the
present day.

26 When David came to Ziklag, he sent
part of the spoil to his friends, the elders of
Judah, saying, "Here is a present for you
from the spoil of the enemies of the LORD";
27 it was for those in Bethel, in Ramoth of
the Negeb, in Jattir, 28 in Aroer, in Siph-
moth, in Eshtemoa, 29 in Racal, in the
towns of the Jerahmeelites, in the towns of
the Kenites, 30 in Hormah, in Bor-ashan, in
Athach, 31 in Hebron, all the places where
David and his men had roamed.

31 Now the Philistines fought against
Israel; and the men of Israel fled
before the Philistines, and many fell[a] on
Mount Gilboa. 2 The Philistines overtook
Saul and his sons; and the Philistines killed
Jonathan and Abinadab and Malchishua,
the sons of Saul. 3 The battle pressed hard
upon Saul; the archers found him, and he
was badly wounded by them. 4 Then Saul
said to his armor-bearer, "Draw your
sword and thrust me through with it, so
that these uncircumcised may not come and
thrust me through, and make sport of me."
But his armor-bearer was unwilling; for he
was terrified. So Saul took his own sword
and fell upon it. 5 When his armor-bearer
saw that Saul was dead, he also fell upon
his sword and died with him. 6 So Saul and
his three sons and his armor-bearer and all
his men died together on the same day.
7 When the men of Israel who were on the
other side of the valley and those beyond
the Jordan saw that the men of Israel had
fled and that Saul and his sons were dead,
they forsook their towns and fled; and the
Philistines came and occupied them.

8 The next day, when the Philistines
came to strip the dead, they found Saul and
his three sons fallen on Mount Gilboa.
9 They cut off his head, stripped off his ar-
mor, and sent messengers throughout the
land of the Philistines to carry the good
news to the houses of their idols and to the
people. 10 They put his armor in the temple
of Astarte;[b] and they fastened his body to
the wall of Beth-shan. 11 But when the in-
habitants of Jabesh-gilead heard what the
Philistines had done to Saul, 12 all the val-
iant men set out, traveled all night long,
and took the body of Saul and the bodies of
his sons from the wall of Beth-shan. They
came to Jabesh and burned them there.
13 Then they took their bones and buried
them under the tamarisk tree in Jabesh, and
fasted seven days.

a Heb *and they fell slain* b Heb plural

A statute and an ordinance for Israel, an illustration of David's kingly decisiveness and authority. **26–31:** David's gifts to the *elders* of these cities, all in southern Judah, would cause them to look favorably upon him when the time came to choose a king over Judah (2 Sam 2.4).

31.1–13: Saul's death. Compare 1 Chr 10 and 2 Sam 1. **4:** *These uncircumcised,* a deprecating term for the Philistines. **5:** Although not condemned, suicide is rare in the Bible; see 2 Sam 17.23; 1 Kings 16.18; Mt 27.5. **9–10:** The Philistines humiliate Saul's corpse and credit their gods with the victory. *Astarte,* a leading Canaanite goddess. **11–13:** The men of Jabesh are likely moved to rescue Saul's body because of his rescue of their city at the beginning of his reign (10.27b–11.15). Cremation (vv. 12–13) was not practiced by the Israelites. They may have burned the bodies in this case to avoid further desecration of them by the Philistines. They *fasted seven days* apparently in mourning for Saul and his sons.

2 SAMUEL

Second Samuel and First Samuel were originally a single work, so that the information about date and composition in the Introduction to 1 Samuel pertains to 2 Samuel as well. Second Samuel continues the focus on David that began in 1 Sam 16. But David's situation changes radically from what it was in 1 Samuel. He rises quickly to fill the power vacuum left by Saul's death (1.1–5.5), becoming king first over Judah and then over Israel. The pro-Davidic, apologetic character of 1 Samuel continues in these chapters as those who stand in David's way perish, though never by David's hand or order. David then conquers Jerusalem, establishing it as his capital, and moves the ark there (chs 5–6). He proposes building a temple and is rewarded with the promise of an enduring dynasty (ch 7). Further wars, however, delay the temple building until the reign of Solomon (7.13; chs 8 and 10; 1 Kings 5.3).

The annihilation of Saul's line secures David's hold on the throne. (The story in 21.1–14 may once have preceded ch 9.) Only Mephibosheth, Jonathan's crippled son, remains alive, and David keeps a watchful eye on him by bringing him to the royal court (ch 9). The real dangers to David's kingship, however, spring from his own weaknesses and his own family. Chapters 11–12 narrate David's adultery with Bathsheba and the resulting condemnation by Nathan. Chapters 13–19 present Absalom's revolt as punishment for David's sin. Another revolt, led by Sheba, follows in ch 20. The book then ends with a miscellaneous collection of stories and poems in chs 21–24.

The major critical issues in 2 Samuel revolve around chs 9–20. These chapters (or in some views chs 13–20) and 1 Kings 1–2 have been dubbed the "Court History" or "Succession Narrative" (after its perceived intention of dealing with the question of who David's successor would be). Although many scholars have viewed it as almost contemporaneous with the events it narrates, the dimensions and early date of this material have been questioned recently. It is impossible to extract these chapters cleanly from the surrounding narrative and to see them as a separate source; there are, for example, ties between chs 9–20 and chs 2–4, such as the description of Mephibosheth's injury in 4.4 and 9.3 and the importance of the "sons of Zeruiah," Joab and his brothers.

Scholars also disagree about the perspective on David in these chapters. Some point to his adultery and his inability to control his children and argue that the Court History paints both David and the monarchy in a very negative light. Others contend that the pro-Davidic, apologetic flavor of 1 Samuel continues in that Joab and the "sons of Zeruiah" are blamed for the murders of David's enemies—Abner (3.26–30), Absalom (18.1–15), Amasa (20.4–10)—while David is too tender for such deeds (3.39; 16.10; 19.22) and is deeply grieved by these deaths (3.31–37; 18.22–19.8). Even when he commits adultery, it has been argued, David's repentance is exemplary, and is immediately accepted (12.13). Perhaps it is best to say that 2 Samuel in its current form depicts David as a complex, ambiguous character.

1 After the death of Saul, when David
had returned from defeating the Ama-
lekites, David remained two days in Ziklag.
2 On the third day, a man came from Saul's
camp, with his clothes torn and dirt on his
head. When he came to David, he fell to the
ground and did obeisance. 3 David said to
him, "Where have you come from?" He
said to him, "I have escaped from the camp
of Israel." 4 David said to him, "How did
things go? Tell me!" He answered, "The
army fled from the battle, but also many of
the army fell and died; and Saul and his son
Jonathan also died." 5 Then David asked
the young man who was reporting to him,
"How do you know that Saul and his son
Jonathan died?" 6 The young man report-
ing to him said, "I happened to be on
Mount Gilboa; and there was Saul leaning
on his spear, while the chariots and the
horsemen drew close to him. 7 When he
looked behind him, he saw me, and called
to me. I answered, 'Here sir.' 8 And he said
to me, 'Who are you?' I answered him, 'I
am an Amalekite.' 9 He said to me, 'Come,
stand over me and kill me; for convulsions
have seized me, and yet my life still lingers.'
10 So I stood over him, and killed him, for I
knew that he could not live after he had
fallen. I took the crown that was on his
head and the armlet that was on his arm,
and I have brought them here to my lord."

11 Then David took hold of his clothes
and tore them; and all the men who were
with him did the same. 12 They mourned
and wept, and fasted until evening for Saul
and for his son Jonathan, and for the army
of the LORD and for the house of Israel,
because they had fallen by the sword.
13 David said to the young man who had
reported to him, "Where do you come
from?" He answered, "I am the son of a
resident alien, an Amalekite." 14 David said
to him, "Were you not afraid to lift your
hand to destroy the LORD's anointed?"
15 Then David called one of the young men
and said, "Come here and strike him
down." So he struck him down and he
died. 16 David said to him, "Your blood be
on your head; for your own mouth has tes-
tified against you, saying, 'I have killed the
LORD's anointed.' "

17 David intoned this lamentation over
Saul and his son Jonathan. 18 (He ordered
that The Song of the Bow[a] be taught to the
people of Judah; it is written in the Book of
Jashar.) He said:

19 Your glory, O Israel, lies slain upon
your high places!
How the mighty have fallen!
20 Tell it not in Gath,
proclaim it not in the streets of
Ashkelon;
or the daughters of the Philistines will
rejoice,

a Heb *that The Bow*

1.1–16: David learns of the death of Saul and Jonathan. Some scholars believe this is a separate tradition of the account in 1 Sam 31, with which it disagrees. Another possibility is that the man who brings the news to David changes the story for his own benefit. **6:** *The young man*'s claim that he *happened to be on Mount Gilboa* in the heat of battle is probably a lie (see v. 10). **8:** *Amalekite,* David has just come from successfully pursuing Amalekites (1 Sam 30), who are depicted as scavengers. It is ironic that an Amalekite killed Saul, who (according to 1 Sam 15) lost his kingship because he did not kill off the Amalekites. **10:** The Amalekite stripped Saul's corpse and brought the *crown* and *armlet* to David hoping for a reward. **11–12:** Tearing clothes and fasting were signs of mourning. **13–16:** As a *resident alien* (v. 13), the Amalekite was subject to the same laws as an Israelite citizen, and therefore David holds him responsible for killing *the LORD's anointed.*

1.17–27: David's elegy over Saul and Jonathan. Many of the Hebrew verses are "Qinah" (dirge or lament) meter, with the first half longer than the second. Many scholars consider plausible the text's attribution of authorship to David himself. **18:** *Song of the Bow,* the Hebrew has simply "bow." If not a copyist's mistake, this may refer to a type of song or a title. *Book of Jashar,* a lost collection of poems (see Josh 10.13). **20:** *Gath, Ashkelon,* Philistine cities. *Uncircumcised,* a disparaging term for the Philistines. **21:** *Mountains of Gilboa,* the site of the battle where Saul and Jonathan were killed. *Shields* were

the daughters of the uncircumcised
will exult.

21 You mountains of Gilboa,
let there be no dew or rain upon
you,
nor bounteous fields![a]
For there the shield of the mighty was
defiled,
the shield of Saul, anointed with oil
no more.

22 From the blood of the slain,
from the fat of the mighty,
the bow of Jonathan did not turn
back,
nor the sword of Saul return
empty.

23 Saul and Jonathan, beloved and
lovely!
In life and in death they were not
divided;
they were swifter than eagles,
they were stronger than lions.

24 O daughters of Israel, weep over Saul,
who clothed you with crimson, in
luxury,
who put ornaments of gold on your
apparel.

25 How the mighty have fallen
in the midst of the battle!

Jonathan lies slain upon your high
places.

26 I am distressed for you, my brother
Jonathan;
greatly beloved were you to me;
your love to me was wonderful,
passing the love of women.

27 How the mighty have fallen,
and the weapons of war perished!

2 After this David inquired of the LORD,
"Shall I go up into any of the cities of
Judah?" The LORD said to him, "Go up."
David said, "To which shall I go up?" He
said, "To Hebron." 2 So David went up
there, along with his two wives, Ahinoam
of Jezreel, and Abigail the widow of Nabal
of Carmel. 3 David brought up the men
who were with him, every one with his
household; and they settled in the towns of
Hebron. 4 Then the people of Judah came,
and there they anointed David king over
the house of Judah.

When they told David, "It was the peo-
ple of Jabesh-gilead who buried Saul,"
5 David sent messengers to the people of
Jabesh-gilead, and said to them, "May you
be blessed by the LORD, because you
showed this loyalty to Saul your lord, and
buried him! 6 Now may the LORD show
steadfast love and faithfulness to you! And
I too will reward you because you have
done this thing. 7 Therefore let your hands
be strong, and be valiant; for Saul your lord
is dead, and the house of Judah has anoint-
ed me king over them."

8 But Abner son of Ner, commander of

a Meaning of Heb uncertain

made of leather and were *anointed with oil* to keep them battle-ready. **24:** Saul's reign brought prosperity to Israel. **26:** *Passing the love of women* expresses the closeness of David's relationship to Jonathan but does not necessarily imply a sexual relationship.

2.1–11: David becomes king of Judah. 1: *Inquired,* probably by means of the ephod and Urim and Thummim (1 Sam 14.3,41; 28.6; 30.7–8). *Hebron,* principal city of the Calebites (see Josh 14.13; Judg 1.20), the leading clan in Judah and also the traditional site of the tombs of Israel's ancestors (Gen 23.19; 25.9; 49.29–32). **2:** *Ahinoam of Jezreel, Abigail the widow of Nabal of Carmel,* see 1 Sam 25, esp. v. 43. Both women were from the Calebite region. Nabal had been a leading Calebite, and marriage to his wife strengthened David's claims to the throne of Judah. **4:** David's gifts to the elders of Judah (1 Sam 30.26–31) further helped his bid to be their king. *Jabesh-gilead,* see 1 Sam 11; 31.11–13. **5–7:** In wooing Jabesh-gilead, David is seeking to win over the strongest enclave of support for Saul. **8:** *Ishbaal* (Heb "Ish-bosheth"), pious scribes substituted the word "bosheth," meaning "shame," for the name of the Canaanite god Baal. But the Hebrew word "ba'al" can also simply mean "lord" and might have been

Saul's army, had taken Ishbaal[a] son of
Saul, and brought him over to Mahanaim.
9 He made him king over Gilead, the Ashur-
ites, Jezreel, Ephraim, Benjamin, and over
all Israel. 10 Ishbaal,[a] Saul's son, was forty
years old when he began to reign over Isra-
el, and he reigned two years. But the house
of Judah followed David. 11 The time that
David was king in Hebron over the house
of Judah was seven years and six months.

12 Abner son of Ner, and the servants of
Ishbaal[a] son of Saul, went out from Maha-
naim to Gibeon. 13 Joab son of Zeruiah,
and the servants of David, went out and
met them at the pool of Gibeon. One group
sat on one side of the pool, while the other
sat on the other side of the pool. 14 Abner
said to Joab, "Let the young men come for-
ward and have a contest before us." Joab
said, "Let them come forward." 15 So they
came forward and were counted as they
passed by, twelve for Benjamin and Ishba-
al[a] son of Saul, and twelve of the servants
of David. 16 Each grasped his opponent by
the head, and thrust his sword in his oppo-
nent's side; so they fell down together.
Therefore that place was called Helkath-
hazzurim,[b] which is at Gibeon. 17 The bat-
tle was very fierce that day; and Abner and
the men of Israel were beaten by the ser-
vants of David.

18 The three sons of Zeruiah were there,
Joab, Abishai, and Asahel. Now Asahel
was as swift of foot as a wild gazelle. 19 As-
ahel pursued Abner, turning neither to the
right nor to the left as he followed him.
20 Then Abner looked back and said, "Is it
you, Asahel?" He answered, "Yes, it is."
21 Abner said to him, "Turn to your right or
to your left, and seize one of the young
men, and take his spoil." But Asahel would
not turn away from following him. 22 Ab-
ner said again to Asahel, "Turn away from
following me; why should I strike you to
the ground? How then could I show my
face to your brother Joab?" 23 But he re-
fused to turn away. So Abner struck him in
the stomach with the butt of his spear, so
that the spear came out at his back. He fell
there, and died where he lay. And all those
who came to the place where Asahel had
fallen and died, stood still.

24 But Joab and Abishai pursued Abner.
As the sun was going down they came to
the hill of Ammah, which lies before Giah
on the way to the wilderness of Gibeon.
25 The Benjaminites rallied around Abner
and formed a single band; they took their
stand on the top of a hill. 26 Then Abner
called to Joab, "Is the sword to keep de-
vouring forever? Do you not know that the
end will be bitter? How long will it be be-
fore you order your people to turn from the
pursuit of their kinsmen?" 27 Joab said, "As
God lives, if you had not spoken, the peo-
ple would have continued to pursue their
kinsmen, not stopping until morning."
28 Joab sounded the trumpet and all the
people stopped; they no longer pursued Is-
rael or engaged in battle any further.

29 Abner and his men traveled all that
night through the Arabah; they crossed the
Jordan, and, marching the whole fore-
noon,[c] they came to Mahanaim. 30 Joab
returned from the pursuit of Abner; and
when he had gathered all the people togeth-
er, there were missing of David's servants
nineteen men besides Asahel. 31 But the ser-
vants of David had killed of Benjamin three
hundred sixty of Abner's men. 32 They took

a Gk Compare 1 Chr 8.33; 9.39: Heb *Ish-bosheth*, "man of shame" *b* That is *Field of Sword-edges*
c Meaning of Heb uncertain

an epithet for Yahweh. The original form of the name, Ishbaal, is preserved in 1 Chr 8.33; 9.39 and in some early Greek translations. *Mahanaim* was east of the Jordan in Gilead. Abner was forced to go there because the Philistines controlled the territory west of the Jordan. **9:** This list of Ishbaal's domains is idealistic at best considering the Philistine domination.

2.12–32: War between Israel and Judah. 14–17: This contest, the exact nature of which is unclear, quickly turned to war. **18:** *Zeruiah,* David's sister, according to 1 Chr 2.16. **19–23:** Asahel's death provides the motive for Joab's murder of Abner in 3.26–30. **29:** *Arabah,* the rift valley of which the Jordan valley is a part.

up Asahel and buried him in the tomb of
his father, which was at Bethlehem. Joab
and his men marched all night, and the day
broke upon them at Hebron.

3 There was a long war between the
house of Saul and the house of David;
David grew stronger and stronger, while
the house of Saul became weaker and
weaker.

2 Sons were born to David at Hebron:
his firstborn was Amnon, of Ahinoam of
Jezreel; 3 his second, Chileab, of Abigail the
widow of Nabal of Carmel; the third, Ab-
salom son of Maacah, daughter of King
Talmai of Geshur; 4 the fourth, Adonijah
son of Haggith; the fifth, Shephatiah son of
Abital; 5 and the sixth, Ithream, of David's
wife Eglah. These were born to David in
Hebron.

6 While there was war between the
house of Saul and the house of David, Ab-
ner was making himself strong in the house
of Saul. 7 Now Saul had a concubine whose
name was Rizpah daughter of Aiah. And
Ishbaal[a] said to Abner, "Why have you
gone in to my father's concubine?" 8 The
words of Ishbaal[b] made Abner very angry;
he said, "Am I a dog's head for Judah? To-
day I keep showing loyalty to the house of
your father Saul, to his brothers, and to his
friends, and have not given you into the
hand of David; and yet you charge me now
with a crime concerning this woman. 9 So
may God do to Abner and so may he add to
it! For just what the LORD has sworn to
David, that will I accomplish for him, 10 to
transfer the kingdom from the house of
Saul, and set up the throne of David over
Israel and over Judah, from Dan to Beer-
sheba." 11 And Ishbaal[a] could not answer
Abner another word, because he feared
him.

12 Abner sent messengers to David at
Hebron,[c] saying, "To whom does the land
belong? Make your covenant with me, and
I will give you my support to bring all Israel
over to you." 13 He said, "Good; I will
make a covenant with you. But one thing I
require of you: you shall never appear in
my presence unless you bring Saul's daugh-
ter Michal when you come to see me."
14 Then David sent messengers to Saul's son
Ishbaal,[d] saying, "Give me my wife Mi-
chal, to whom I became engaged at the
price of one hundred foreskins of the Philis-
tines." 15 Ishbaal[d] sent and took her from
her husband Paltiel the son of Laish. 16 But
her husband went with her, weeping as he
walked behind her all the way to Bahurim.
Then Abner said to him, "Go back home!"
So he went back.

17 Abner sent word to the elders of Isra-

a Heb *And he* *b* Gk Compare 1 Chr 8.33; 9.39: Heb *Ish-bosheth*, "man of shame" *c* Gk: Heb *where he was* *d* Heb *Ish-bosheth*

3.1–5: David's sons. 1: The suggestion that there was *a long war* indicates that Saul and his family received more popular support than the book of 1 Samuel might imply. **2:** *Amnon,* see ch 13. *Ahinoam,* see 1 Sam 25.43; 2 Sam 2.2. **3:** Nothing more is known of *Chileab,* who apparently died young; in 1 Chr 3.1 he is called Daniel. *Abigail,* see 1 Sam 25. *Absalom,* see chs 13–18. *Geshur,* a small kingdom east of the Sea of Galilee. David's marriage to *Maacah* indicates that he had a political alliance with her father, *King Talmai.* **4–5:** *Adonijah,* see 1 Kings 1. *Shephatiah* and *Ithream* are mentioned only here and in 1 Chr 3.3.

3.6–39: Abner's death. 7: *Concubine,* a woman (usually a slave) acquired for sexual purposes. To sleep with a member of the royal harem was to claim the throne (see 16.21–22; 1 Kings 2.13–25). Hence, Ishbaal's question is tantamount to an accusation of treason. **8:** *Dog's head,* used only here in the Bible, this expression is obviously reproachful, but its origin is unknown, although comparison to a dog or a dead dog is a frequent form of self-deprecation (see 9.8; 2 Kings 18.3). Abner does not deny Ishbaal's accusation but is contemptuous. Although the power is his (2.8–9), he has been loyal to Ishbaal. **10:** *From Dan to Beer-sheba,* the traditional northern and southern limits of Israel. **13:** David demands the return of *Saul's daughter Michal* because it is through her that he claims a right to Saul's kingdom. **14:** See 1 Sam 18.20–29. **15:** It is not clear why *Ishbaal* returns Michal to David. Some scholars have suggested that he was under legal obligation. *Paltiel,* or Palti (1 Sam 25.44). **17:** *The elders of Israel,* the tribal leaders. **18:**

el, saying, "For some time past you have
been seeking David as king over you.
18 Now then bring it about; for the LORD
has promised David: Through my servant
David I will save my people Israel from the
hand of the Philistines, and from all their
enemies." 19 Abner also spoke directly to
the Benjaminites; then Abner went to tell
David at Hebron all that Israel and the
whole house of Benjamin were ready to do.
20 When Abner came with twenty men
to David at Hebron, David made a feast for
Abner and the men who were with him.
21 Abner said to David, "Let me go and ral-
ly all Israel to my lord the king, in order
that they may make a covenant with you,
and that you may reign over all that your
heart desires." So David dismissed Abner,
and he went away in peace.
22 Just then the servants of David ar-
rived with Joab from a raid, bringing much
spoil with them. But Abner was not with
David at Hebron, for David[a] had dis-
missed him, and he had gone away in
peace. 23 When Joab and all the army that
was with him came, it was told Joab, "Ab-
ner son of Ner came to the king, and he has
dismissed him, and he has gone away in
peace." 24 Then Joab went to the king and
said, "What have you done? Abner came to
you; why did you dismiss him, so that he
got away? 25 You know that Abner son of
Ner came to deceive you, and to learn your
comings and goings and to learn all that
you are doing."
26 When Joab came out from David's
presence, he sent messengers after Abner,
and they brought him back from the cistern
of Sirah; but David did not know about it.
27 When Abner returned to Hebron, Joab
took him aside in the gateway to speak
with him privately, and there he stabbed
him in the stomach. So he died for shed-
ding[b] the blood of Asahel, Joab's[c] broth-
er. 28 Afterward, when David heard of it, he
said, "I and my kingdom are forever guilt-
less before the LORD for the blood of Abner
son of Ner. 29 May the guilt[d] fall on the
head of Joab, and on all his father's house;
and may the house of Joab never be with-
out one who has a discharge, or who is
leprous,[e] or who holds a spindle, or who
falls by the sword, or who lacks food!"
30 So Joab and his brother Abishai mur-
dered Abner because he had killed their
brother Asahel in the battle at Gibeon.
31 Then David said to Joab and to all
the people who were with him, "Tear your
clothes, and put on sackcloth, and mourn
over Abner." And King David followed the
bier. 32 They buried Abner at Hebron. The
king lifted up his voice and wept at the
grave of Abner, and all the people wept.
33 The king lamented for Abner, saying,

"Should Abner die as a fool dies?
34 Your hands were not bound,
your feet were not fettered;
as one falls before the wicked
you have fallen."

And all the people wept over him again.
35 Then all the people came to persuade Da-
vid to eat something while it was still day;
but David swore, saying, "So may God do
to me, and more, if I taste bread or any-

a Heb *he* *b* Heb lacks *shedding* *c* Heb *his*
d Heb *May it* *e* A term for several skin diseases; precise meaning uncertain

The Philistines, Israel's principal enemy in 1 Samuel, whose defeat of Saul (1 Sam 31) meant that they were still a problem for David, which he will resolve in 5.17–25; cf. 21.15–22. **19:** *Benjamin,* the tribe of both Saul and Abner; they would be the most reluctant to make David, a non-Benjaminite, king. **21:** *In peace,* the writer emphasizes (perhaps too much) David's noninvolvement in Abner's death. **25:** *Comings and goings,* military maneuvers. Joab accuses Abner of spying. **26–27:** The writer stresses that Joab, seeking to avenge his brother (2.18–23), acted alone. Some have suggested that Joab also feared losing his position as army commander to Abner (see 19.13; 20.8–10). **29:** While David curses Joab, he does not now punish him (but see 1 Kings 2.5–6). *Spindle,* better: "crutch." **30:** *Abishai* is not mentioned in the story but may have helped Joab plan Abner's murder. **31:** *Sackcloth,* material worn by mourners. **33:** *Fool* (Heb "nabal") recalls the story in 1 Sam 25. **35–39:** These verses continue to stress (perhaps too strongly) David's lack of involvement in Abner's death.

thing else before the sun goes down!" 36 All
the people took notice of it, and it pleased
them; just as everything the king did
pleased all the people. 37 So all the people
and all Israel understood that day that the
king had no part in the killing of Abner son
of Ner. 38 And the king said to his servants,
"Do you not know that a prince and a great
man has fallen this day in Israel? 39 Today
I am powerless, even though anointed king;
these men, the sons of Zeruiah, are too vio-
lent for me. The LORD pay back the one
who does wickedly in accordance with his
wickedness!"

4 When Saul's son Ishbaal[a] heard that
Abner had died at Hebron, his courage
failed, and all Israel was dismayed. 2 Saul's
son had two captains of raiding bands; the
name of the one was Baanah, and the name
of the other Rechab. They were sons of
Rimmon a Benjaminite from Beeroth—for
Beeroth is considered to belong to Benja-
min. 3 (Now the people of Beeroth had fled
to Gittaim and are there as resident aliens
to this day).

4 Saul's son Jonathan had a son who
was crippled in his feet. He was five years
old when the news about Saul and Jona-
than came from Jezreel. His nurse picked
him up and fled; and, in her haste to flee, it
happened that he fell and became lame. His
name was Mephibosheth.[b]

5 Now the sons of Rimmon the Beeroth-
ite, Rechab and Baanah, set out, and about
the heat of the day they came to the house
of Ishbaal,[c] while he was taking his noon-
day rest. 6 They came inside the house as
though to take wheat, and they struck him
in the stomach; then Rechab and his broth-
er Baanah escaped.[d] 7 Now they had come
into the house while he was lying on his
couch in his bedchamber; they attacked
him, killed him, and beheaded him. Then
they took his head and traveled by way of
the Arabah all night long. 8 They brought
the head of Ishbaal[c] to David at Hebron
and said to the king, "Here is the head of
Ishbaal,[c] son of Saul, your enemy, who
sought your life; the LORD has avenged my
lord the king this day on Saul and on his
offspring."

9 David answered Rechab and his
brother Baanah, the sons of Rimmon the
Beerothite, "As the LORD lives, who has
redeemed my life out of every adversity,
10 when the one who told me, 'See, Saul is
dead,' thought he was bringing good news,
I seized him and killed him at Ziklag—this
was the reward I gave him for his news.
11 How much more then, when wicked men
have killed a righteous man on his bed in
his own house! And now shall I not require
his blood at your hand, and destroy you
from the earth?" 12 So David commanded
the young men, and they killed them; they
cut off their hands and feet, and hung their
bodies beside the pool at Hebron. But the
head of Ishbaal[c] they took and buried in
the tomb of Abner at Hebron.

5 Then all the tribes of Israel came to Da-
vid at Hebron, and said, "Look, we are
your bone and flesh. 2 For some time, while
Saul was king over us, it was you who led
out Israel and brought it in. The LORD said

a Heb lacks *Ishbaal* *b* In 1 Chr 8.34 and 9.40, *Merib-baal* *c* Heb *Ish-bosheth* *d* Meaning of Heb of verse 6 uncertain

4.1–12: The assassination of Ishbaal. Here, too, the author stresses that David was in no way involved in the death of his enemy. **3:** An explanation of how *Beeroth* came to be considered a Benjaminite city; the event referred to here is otherwise unknown. **4:** *Mephibosheth,* the original form of the name was Merib-baal (1 Chr 8.34; 9.40). **7:** *Arabah,* see 2.29n. **8:** The assassins bring Ishbaal's head to David expecting a reward for killing his enemy. **9–10:** See 1.1–16. **11:** *A righteous man,* David does not recognize Ishbaal's kingship and therefore does not call him the LORD's anointed. **12:** Ritual execution of this nature was reserved for traitors.

5.1–16: David becomes king of all Israel and conquers Jerusalem. **1:** *All the tribes of Israel,* the northern tribes, excluding Judah where David is already king. **2:** *Led out* and *brought . . . in* are idioms for military leadership. *Shepherd,* a common metaphor for kings. *Ruler,* "king designate" (translated "prince" in 7.8). **3:** *Elders,* senior tribal leaders. **4:** *Forty years,* a round number for a generation. The

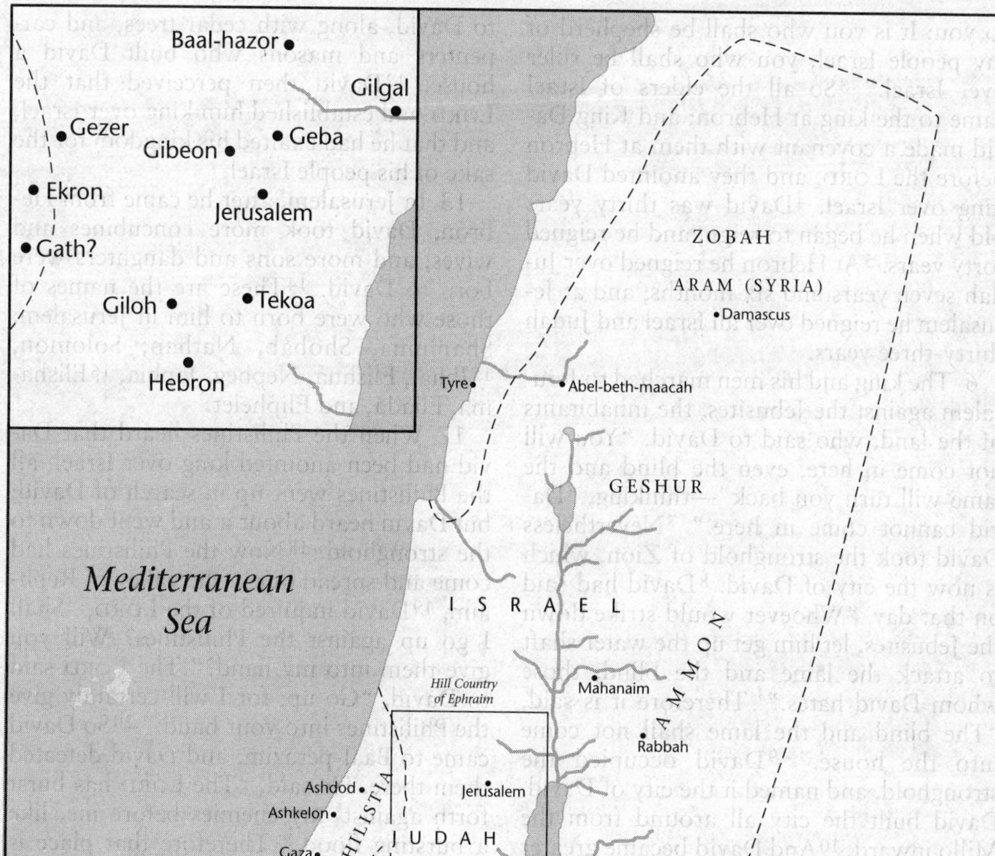

Chs 5–21: The kingdom of David. The dashed line shows the approximate boundary of the kingdom at its greatest extent.

to you: It is you who shall be shepherd of
my people Israel, you who shall be ruler
over Israel." 3 So all the elders of Israel
came to the king at Hebron; and King Da-
vid made a covenant with them at Hebron
before the LORD, and they anointed David
king over Israel. 4 David was thirty years
old when he began to reign, and he reigned
forty years. 5 At Hebron he reigned over Ju-
dah seven years and six months; and at Je-
rusalem he reigned over all Israel and Judah
thirty-three years.

6 The king and his men marched to Jeru-
salem against the Jebusites, the inhabitants
of the land, who said to David, "You will
not come in here, even the blind and the
lame will turn you back"—thinking, "Da-
vid cannot come in here." 7 Nevertheless
David took the stronghold of Zion, which
is now the city of David. 8 David had said
on that day, "Whoever would strike down
the Jebusites, let him get up the water shaft
to attack the lame and the blind, those
whom David hates."[a] Therefore it is said,
"The blind and the lame shall not come
into the house." 9 David occupied the
stronghold, and named it the city of David.
David built the city all around from the
Millo inward. 10 And David became greater
and greater, for the LORD, the God of
hosts, was with him.

11 King Hiram of Tyre sent messengers
to David, along with cedar trees, and car-
penters and masons who built David a
house. 12 David then perceived that the
LORD had established him king over Israel,
and that he had exalted his kingdom for the
sake of his people Israel.

13 In Jerusalem, after he came from He-
bron, David took more concubines and
wives; and more sons and daughters were
born to David. 14 These are the names of
those who were born to him in Jerusalem:
Shammua, Shobab, Nathan, Solomon,
15 Ibhar, Elishua, Nepheg, Japhia, 16 Elisha-
ma, Eliada, and Eliphelet.

17 When the Philistines heard that Da-
vid had been anointed king over Israel, all
the Philistines went up in search of David;
but David heard about it and went down to
the stronghold. 18 Now the Philistines had
come and spread out in the valley of Reph-
aim. 19 David inquired of the LORD, "Shall
I go up against the Philistines? Will you
give them into my hand?" The LORD said
to David, "Go up; for I will certainly give
the Philistines into your hand." 20 So David
came to Baal-perazim, and David defeated
them there. He said, "The LORD has burst
forth against[b] my enemies before me, like
a bursting flood." Therefore that place is

a Another reading is *those who hate David*
b Heb *paraz*

actual length of David's reign is not certain, but scholars have proposed ca. 1005–965 BCE as likely dates. **6–8:** Exactly how David conquered Jerusalem is not clear. The parallel in 1 Chr 11.5–6 leaves out these verses, perhaps indicating that the Chronicler found them confusing. The account may be an etiology for the saying in v. 8. **6:** *Jebusites,* one group of pre-Israelite inhabitants of the land; see Gen 15.21; Ex 3.8; etc. **8:** One scholar has argued that *get up the water shaft* means "strike at the wind pipe" so as to kill the enemy rather than leaving any wounded (blind and lame). The saying may refer to the prohibition in Lev 21.18. **9:** *City of David,* Jerusalem's location between Israel and Judah was ideal for a neutral capital in David's effort to unite the two. *Millo,* meaning "fill," apparently refers to a landfill or artificial platform created near the *stronghold.* **11:** *Tyre,* the capital of Phoenicia, the country north of Israel. *Cedar,* a luxury item for which Lebanon in Phoenician territory was renowned. **13–16:** A large harem was a sign of royal prestige. Marriages were also a way of sealing treaties with foreign powers. *Solomon* is born later; these verses are an anticipatory summary. Alternatively, the mention of Solomon here may suggest that the material has been organized thematically rather than chronologically.

5.17–25: War with the Philistines. 17: David's defeat of the Philistines (see 3.18n.) probably preceded his conquest of Jerusalem, since they stood between Hebron and Jerusalem and would have resisted the unification of Israel and Judah. *The stronghold,* probably Adullam, not Jerusalem. **18:** *The valley of Rephaim,* probably located southwest of Jerusalem. **19:** *David inquired,* see 2.1n. **20:** An etiology explaining the name *Baal-perazim* (see note *b*); Yahweh and Baal are here equated. **21:** A victorious army

called Baal-perazim.[a] 21The Philistines
abandoned their idols there, and David and
his men carried them away.

22 Once again the Philistines came up,
and were spread out in the valley of Repha-
im. 23When David inquired of the LORD,
he said, "You shall not go up; go around to
their rear, and come upon them opposite
the balsam trees. 24When you hear the
sound of marching in the tops of the bal-
sam trees, then be on the alert; for then the
LORD has gone out before you to strike
down the army of the Philistines." 25David
did just as the LORD had commanded him;
and he struck down the Philistines from
Geba all the way to Gezer.

6 David again gathered all the chosen
men of Israel, thirty thousand. 2David
and all the people with him set out and
went from Baale-judah, to bring up from
there the ark of God, which is called by
the name of the LORD of hosts who is en-
throned on the cherubim. 3They carried the
ark of God on a new cart, and brought it
out of the house of Abinadab, which was
on the hill. Uzzah and Ahio,[b] the sons of
Abinadab, were driving the new cart 4with
the ark of God;[c] and Ahio[b] went in front
of the ark. 5David and all the house of Isra-
el were dancing before the LORD with all
their might, with songs[d] and lyres and
harps and tambourines and castanets and
cymbals.

6 When they came to the threshing floor
of Nacon, Uzzah reached out his hand to
the ark of God and took hold of it, for the
oxen shook it. 7The anger of the LORD was
kindled against Uzzah; and God struck him
there because he reached out his hand to
the ark;[e] and he died there beside the ark
of God. 8David was angry because the
LORD had burst forth with an outburst
upon Uzzah; so that place is called Perez-
uzzah,[f] to this day. 9David was afraid of
the LORD that day; he said, "How can the
ark of the LORD come into my care?" 10So
David was unwilling to take the ark of the
LORD into his care in the city of David;
instead David took it to the house of Obed-
edom the Gittite. 11The ark of the LORD
remained in the house of Obed-edom the
Gittite three months; and the LORD blessed
Obed-edom and all his household.

12 It was told King David, "The LORD
has blessed the household of Obed-edom
and all that belongs to him, because of the
ark of God." So David went and brought
up the ark of God from the house of Obed-
edom to the city of David with rejoicing;
13and when those who bore the ark of the
LORD had gone six paces, he sacrificed an
ox and a fatling. 14David danced before the
LORD with all his might; David was girded
with a linen ephod. 15So David and all the
house of Israel brought up the ark of the
LORD with shouting, and with the sound of
the trumpet.

16 As the ark of the LORD came into the

a That is *Lord of Bursting Forth* *b* Or *and his brother* *c* Compare Gk: Heb *and brought it out of the house of Abinadab, which was on the hill with the ark of God* *d* Q Ms Gk 1 Chr 13.8: Heb *fir trees* *e* 1 Chr 13.10 Compare Q Ms: Meaning of Heb uncertain *f* That is *Bursting Out Against Uzzah*

typically captured the religious symbols that its opponent brought to the battlefield to show the superiority of its own gods; this is an ironic reversal of 1 Sam 4.5–11. **25:** *From Geba* near Jerusalem *all the way to Gezer* near the border of Philistine territory.

6.1–23: David brings the ark to Jerusalem. 1: *Thousand* probably designates a military unit of much smaller size. **2:** *Baale-judah,* another name for Kiriath-jearim, according to Josh 15.9, where the ark was left in 1 Sam 7.1. The *ark of God* was viewed as the throne of the LORD. Having it in Jerusalem would make the city the religious as well as the political capital. *Cherubim,* mythical griffins that often guarded temples and palaces (see 1 Sam 4.4n.). **6–8:** *Uzzah*'s death shows the awesome holiness of the ark, which was not to be touched. The story is also an etiology explaining the name Perez-uzzah ("Uzzah's breach"). **10:** *Obed-edom the Gittite* (i.e., from Gath) was apparently among the Philistines who followed David from his days with Achish (1 Sam 27; 29). **13–14:** *He sacrificed,* David officiates as a priest here, which was not unusual for kings in the ancient Near East (8.18; 1 Kings 3.15; 9.25; Gen 14.18). *Linen ephod,* an apron typically worn by priests (1 Sam 2.18). Apparently David is wearing little else (see v. 20).

city of David, Michal daughter of Saul
looked out of the window, and saw King
David leaping and dancing before the
LORD; and she despised him in her heart.
17 They brought in the ark of the LORD,
and set it in its place, inside the tent that
David had pitched for it; and David offered
burnt offerings and offerings of well-being
before the LORD. 18 When David had fin-
ished offering the burnt offerings and the
offerings of well-being, he blessed the peo-
ple in the name of the LORD of hosts, 19 and
distributed food among all the people, the
whole multitude of Israel, both men and
women, to each a cake of bread, a portion
of meat,[a] and a cake of raisins. Then all
the people went back to their homes.
20 David returned to bless his house-
hold. But Michal the daughter of Saul came
out to meet David, and said, "How the
king of Israel honored himself today, un-
covering himself today before the eyes of
his servants' maids, as any vulgar fellow
might shamelessly uncover himself!" 21 Da-
vid said to Michal, "It was before the
LORD, who chose me in place of your fa-
ther and all his household, to appoint me as
prince over Israel, the people of the LORD,
that I have danced before the LORD. 22 I will
make myself yet more contemptible than
this, and I will be abased in my own eyes;
but by the maids of whom you have spo-
ken, by them I shall be held in honor."
23 And Michal the daughter of Saul had no
child to the day of her death.

7 Now when the king was settled in his
house, and the LORD had given him rest
from all his enemies around him, 2 the king
said to the prophet Nathan, "See now, I am
living in a house of cedar, but the ark of
God stays in a tent." 3 Nathan said to the
king, "Go, do all that you have in mind; for
the LORD is with you."
4 But that same night the word of the
LORD came to Nathan: 5 Go and tell my
servant David: Thus says the LORD: Are
you the one to build me a house to live in?
6 I have not lived in a house since the day I
brought up the people of Israel from Egypt
to this day, but I have been moving about
in a tent and a tabernacle. 7 Wherever I
have moved about among all the people of
Israel, did I ever speak a word with any of
the tribal leaders[b] of Israel, whom I com-
manded to shepherd my people Israel, say-
ing, "Why have you not built me a house of
cedar?" 8 Now therefore thus you shall say
to my servant David: Thus says the LORD
of hosts: I took you from the pasture, from

a Vg: Meaning of Heb uncertain *b* Or *any of the tribes*

20: Michal accuses David of fraternizing with the lowest element of society, implying that he is not dignified enough to be king. **21–22:** David replies that the LORD made him king in place of her father, Saul. **23:** *Michal . . . had no child,* probably because David had no relations with her; her children would have been Saul's heirs and a threat to David's rule.

7.1–29: A dynasty for David. This chapter with the LORD's promise to David of an eternal dynasty is a key passage in the Deuteronomistic History. It combines the themes of Jerusalem as the divinely chosen center for worship and the Davidic line as the chosen dynasty in Judah. God's promise of an eternal dynasty (vv. 13–16) explains Judah's survival beyond the destruction of Israel in 722 BCE. The language and style of the chapter are thoroughly Deuteronomistic, although many scholars believe one or more older oracles underlie vv. 1–7. This promise is reflected in various forms in the Deuteronomistic History and in Ps 89 and 132, as well as in Chronicles. Some of these texts temper the unconditional, eternal nature of the promise. **1:** *And the LORD had given him rest from all his enemies around him,* this statement is inconsistent with the accounts of David's wars in chs 8–20 and with 1 Kings 5.3–4, which says that rest came only to Solomon. It is not in the parallel in 1 Chr 17.1. **4–17:** The LORD's promise to David. **5–7:** The *house* ("bayit") David proposes to build is a temple. The LORD says instead (v. 11) that he will build David a house ("bayit"), that is, a dynasty. The claim in vv. 6–7 that the LORD has never had a *house* (i.e., temple) seems to overlook the temple in Shiloh (1 Sam 1–3). **8:** *Following the sheep,* see 1 Sam 17.15, 34. Kings in the ancient Near East were often described as shepherds; see 24.17; 1 Chr 11.2; Ps 78.70; Isa 44.28. *Prince,* "king designate" (translated "ruler" in 5.2). **10:** *Place* in Hebrew may mean a

following the sheep to be prince over my
people Israel; 9and I have been with you
wherever you went, and have cut off all
your enemies from before you; and I will
make for you a great name, like the name
of the great ones of the earth. 10And I will
appoint a place for my people Israel and
will plant them, so that they may live in
their own place, and be disturbed no more;
and evildoers shall afflict them no more, as
formerly, 11from the time that I appointed
judges over my people Israel; and I will give
you rest from all your enemies. Moreover
the LORD declares to you that the LORD
will make you a house. 12When your days
are fulfilled and you lie down with your
ancestors, I will raise up your offspring af-
ter you, who shall come forth from your
body, and I will establish his kingdom.
13He shall build a house for my name, and
I will establish the throne of his kingdom
forever. 14I will be a father to him, and he
shall be a son to me. When he commits
iniquity, I will punish him with a rod such
as mortals use, with blows inflicted by hu-
man beings. 15But I will not take[a] my
steadfast love from him, as I took it from
Saul, whom I put away from before you.
16Your house and your kingdom shall be
made sure forever before me;[b] your throne
shall be established forever. 17In accor-
dance with all these words and with all this
vision, Nathan spoke to David.

18 Then King David went in and sat
before the LORD, and said, "Who am I,
O Lord GOD, and what is my house, that
you have brought me thus far? 19And yet
this was a small thing in your eyes, O Lord
GOD; you have spoken also of your ser-
vant's house for a great while to come. May
this be instruction for the people,[c] O Lord
GOD! 20And what more can David say to
you? For you know your servant, O Lord
GOD! 21Because of your promise, and ac-
cording to your own heart, you have
wrought all this greatness, so that your ser-
vant may know it. 22Therefore you are
great, O LORD God; for there is no one like
you, and there is no God besides you, ac-
cording to all that we have heard with our
ears. 23Who is like your people, like Israel?
Is there another[d] nation on earth whose
God went to redeem it as a people, and to
make a name for himself, doing great and
awesome things for them,[e] by driving
out[f] before his people nations and their
gods?[g] 24And you established your people
Israel for yourself to be your people forev-
er; and you, O LORD, became their God.
25And now, O LORD God, as for the word
that you have spoken concerning your ser-
vant and concerning his house, confirm it
forever; do as you have promised. 26Thus
your name will be magnified forever in the
saying, 'The LORD of hosts is God over Is-
rael'; and the house of your servant David
will be established before you. 27For you,
O LORD of hosts, the God of Israel, have
made this revelation to your servant, say-
ing, 'I will build you a house'; therefore
your servant has found courage to pray this
prayer to you. 28And now, O Lord GOD,
you are God, and your words are true, and
you have promised this good thing to your
servant; 29now therefore may it please you
to bless the house of your servant, so that it
may continue forever before you; for you,
O Lord GOD, have spoken, and with your

a Gk Syr Vg 1 Chr 17.13: Heb *shall not depart* *b* Gk Heb Mss: MT *before you*; Compare 2 Sam 7.26, 29 *c* Meaning of Heb uncertain *d* Gk: Heb *one* *e* Heb *you* *f* Gk 1 Chr 17.21: Heb *for your land* *g* Cn: Heb *before your people, whom you redeemed for yourself from Egypt, nations and its gods*

shrine or place of worship. Here it refers to the Jerusalem temple. **11–12:** See vv. 5–7n. **13:** David's son, Solomon, will build the temple. *Forever* here (and in v. 16) characterizes the dynasty as enduring but does not necessarily mean for all eternity. **14:** *Father . . . son,* a king was often described as the "son" of God; see, e.g., Ps 2.7; 89.26–27. **15:** *Steadfast love,* another form of the promise; see Ps 89.1,24. **18–29:** David's prayer to the LORD. Compare Solomon's prayers in 1 Kings 3.6–9 and 8.22–53. **23:** *Redeem . . . driving out* refer to the Exodus from Egypt and the conquest of Canaan. The language is Deuteronomic. **24:** Cf. Ex 6.7; Deut 29.10–15. **27–29:** *Your servant,* a way of referring to oneself before a superior.

blessing shall the house of your servant be
blessed forever."

8 Some time afterward, David attacked
the Philistines and subdued them; Da-
vid took Metheg-ammah out of the hand of
the Philistines.
2 He also defeated the Moabites and,
making them lie down on the ground, mea-
sured them off with a cord; he measured
two lengths of cord for those who were to
be put to death, and one length[a] for those
who were to be spared. And the Moabites
became servants to David and brought trib-
ute.
3 David also struck down King Hadade-
zer son of Rehob of Zobah, as he went to
restore his monument[b] at the river Eu-
phrates. 4 David took from him one thou-
sand seven hundred horsemen, and twenty
thousand foot soldiers. David hamstrung
all the chariot horses, but left enough for a
hundred chariots. 5 When the Arameans of
Damascus came to help King Hadadezer of
Zobah, David killed twenty-two thousand
men of the Arameans. 6 Then David put
garrisons among the Arameans of Damas-
cus; and the Arameans became servants to
David and brought tribute. The LORD gave
victory to David wherever he went. 7 David
took the gold shields that were carried by
the servants of Hadadezer, and brought
them to Jerusalem. 8 From Betah and from
Berothai, towns of Hadadezer, King David
took a great amount of bronze.
9 When King Toi of Hamath heard that
David had defeated the whole army of
Hadadezer, 10 Toi sent his son Joram to
King David, to greet him and to congratu-
late him because he had fought against
Hadadezer and defeated him. Now Hadad-
ezer had often been at war with Toi. Joram
brought with him articles of silver, gold,
and bronze; 11 these also King David dedi-
cated to the LORD, together with the silver
and gold that he dedicated from all the na-
tions he subdued, 12 from Edom, Moab, the
Ammonites, the Philistines, Amalek, and
from the spoil of King Hadadezer son of
Rehob of Zobah.
13 David won a name for himself. When
he returned, he killed eighteen thousand
Edomites[c] in the Valley of Salt. 14 He put
garrisons in Edom; throughout all Edom he
put garrisons, and all the Edomites became
David's servants. And the LORD gave victo-
ry to David wherever he went.
15 So David reigned over all Israel; and
David administered justice and equity to all
his people. 16 Joab son of Zeruiah was over
the army; Jehoshaphat son of Ahilud was
recorder; 17 Zadok son of Ahitub and
Ahimelech son of Abiathar were priests; Se-
raiah was secretary; 18 Benaiah son of Je-
hoiada was over[d] the Cherethites and the
Pelethites; and David's sons were priests.

9 David asked, "Is there still anyone left
of the house of Saul to whom I may
show kindness for Jonathan's sake?" 2 Now

a Heb *one full length* *b* Compare 1 Sam 15.12 and 2 Sam 18.18 *c* Gk: Heb *returned from striking down eighteen thousand Arameans* *d* Syr Tg Vg 20.23; 1 Chr 18.17: Heb lacks *was over*

8.1–18: David's wars. 1: This verse represents David's decisive defeat of the Philistines, the archenemies of Saul. They never surface again as enemies during his reign. **2:** The *Moabites* lived on the other side of the Dead Sea from Israel. **3:** *Zobah* was an Aramean (Syrian) city-state. *Restore* may also mean "leave," so that David, rather than Hadadezer, was traveling to the Euphrates to erect a monument. **4:** *Hamstrung,* David crippled the hind legs of the horses he could not use to keep someone else from using them against him (see Josh 11.6). Thus the Israelites probably did not yet make extensive use of chariots. **5:** *Twenty-two thousand* probably means twenty-two military units (see 6.1n.). **9:** *Hamath,* an important city-state in central Syria north of Zobah. **10:** *Joram* is an Israelite (Yahwistic) name; 1 Chr 18.18 calls him "Hadoram," an Aramaic name. **12:** *Edom* was the southernmost country east of the Jordan. *Ammonites,* the ancient residents in the vicinity of the modern city of Amman, Jordan. **13:** *Eighteen thousand,* see v. 5n. **16–18:** Cf. the similar list of David's cabinet in 20.23–26. *Cherethites and the Pelethites,* "Cretans" and "Philistines" who composed the royal bodyguard (23.23), probably mercenaries. *David's sons were priests,* the restriction of priesthood to the Levites had apparently not yet arisen.

9.1–13: Jonathan's son. 1: *Is there still anyone left of the house of Saul?* David's execution of Saul's

there was a servant of the house of Saul
whose name was Ziba, and he was summoned to David. The king said to him,
"Are you Ziba?" And he said, "At your
service!" 3 The king said, "Is there anyone
remaining of the house of Saul to whom I
may show the kindness of God?" Ziba said
to the king, "There remains a son of Jonathan; he is crippled in his feet." 4 The king
said to him, "Where is he?" Ziba said to
the king, "He is in the house of Machir son
of Ammiel, at Lo-debar." 5 Then King David sent and brought him from the house of
Machir son of Ammiel, at Lo-debar. 6 Mephibosheth[a] son of Jonathan son of Saul
came to David, and fell on his face and did
obeisance. David said, "Mephibosheth!"[a]
He answered, "I am your servant." 7 David
said to him, "Do not be afraid, for I will
show you kindness for the sake of your father Jonathan; I will restore to you all the
land of your grandfather Saul, and you
yourself shall eat at my table always." 8 He
did obeisance and said, "What is your servant, that you should look upon a dead dog
such as I?"

9 Then the king summoned Saul's servant Ziba, and said to him, "All that belonged to Saul and to all his house I have
given to your master's grandson. 10 You
and your sons and your servants shall till
the land for him, and shall bring in the produce, so that your master's grandson may
have food to eat; but your master's grandson Mephibosheth[a] shall always eat at my
table." Now Ziba had fifteen sons and
twenty servants. 11 Then Ziba said to the
king, "According to all that my lord the
king commands his servant, so your servant
will do." Mephibosheth[a] ate at David's[b]
table, like one of the king's sons. 12 Mephibosheth[a] had a young son whose name
was Mica. And all who lived in Ziba's
house became Mephibosheth's[c] servants.
13 Mephibosheth[a] lived in Jerusalem, for
he always ate at the king's table. Now he
was lame in both his feet.

10 Some time afterward, the king of the
Ammonites died, and his son Hanun succeeded him. 2 David said, "I will
deal loyally with Hanun son of Nahash,
just as his father dealt loyally with me." So
David sent envoys to console him concerning his father. When David's envoys came
into the land of the Ammonites, 3 the
princes of the Ammonites said to their lord
Hanun, "Do you really think that David is
honoring your father just because he has
sent messengers with condolences to you?
Has not David sent his envoys to you to
search the city, to spy it out, and to overthrow it?" 4 So Hanun seized David's envoys, shaved off half the beard of each, cut

a Or *Merib-baal*: See 4.4 note *b* Gk: Heb *my*
c Or *Merib-baal's*: See 4.4 note

sons and grandsons in 21.1–14 provides background to this question, and the story in 21.1–14 may have originally preceded ch 9. *Kindness* is covenant faithfulness. David wants to keep the promise of loyalty he made to Jonathan (1 Sam 18.1–4; 20.14–17). **3:** *Crippled in his feet,* see 4.4. This handicap made Mephibosheth unable to go to war and therefore unsuitable to be king. **4:** *Machir* became a loyal supporter of David (17.27). *Lo-debar,* a northern Israelite city east of the Jordan. **6:** *Fell on his face and did obeisance,* prostrating oneself was a sign of submission to God or the king. *Mephibosheth,* the name was originally Merib-baal; see 4.4n. **7:** Eating at the king's *table* was a sign of favor. In this case it allowed David to keep a close watch on Merib-baal, who was still heir to Saul's kingdom and therefore a potential rival (see 16.1–4; 19.24–30). **8:** *Dead dog,* a term of self-reproach (see 3.8n.). **9–13:** Merib-baal was to receive the income from Saul's lands, which Ziba and his family would work.

10.1–19: David defeats the Ammonites and Arameans. 2: *Nahash,* Saul's enemy in 1 Sam 10.27b–11.15. *Ammonites,* see 8.12n. *Deal loyally . . . dealt loyally,* indicate that David and Nahash had a treaty. *Hanun*'s actions in the following verses indicate that Israel was the superior partner in the treaty or that David was trying to make Israel the superior partner, and Hanun resisted. **4:** *The beard* was a symbol of masculinity, and cutting off half of it was symbolic emasculation. According to the Lachish reliefs, Judean men were typically bearded. Cutting off *their garments* below the waist was symbolic castration. **5:** *Jericho,* the closest Israelite city west of the Jordan opposite Ammon. **6:** *Beth-rehob, Zobah,*

off their garments in the middle at their
hips, and sent them away. 5 When David
was told, he sent to meet them, for the men
were greatly ashamed. The king said, "Re-
main at Jericho until your beards have
grown, and then return."
6 When the Ammonites saw that they
had become odious to David, the Ammon-
ites sent and hired the Arameans of Beth-
rehob and the Arameans of Zobah, twenty
thousand foot soldiers, as well as the king
of Maacah, one thousand men, and the
men of Tob, twelve thousand men. 7 When
David heard of it, he sent Joab and all the
army with the warriors. 8 The Ammonites
came out and drew up in battle array at the
entrance of the gate; but the Arameans of
Zobah and of Rehob, and the men of Tob
and Maacah, were by themselves in the
open country.
9 When Joab saw that the battle was set
against him both in front and in the rear, he
chose some of the picked men of Israel, and
arrayed them against the Arameans; 10 the
rest of his men he put in the charge of his
brother Abishai, and he arrayed them
against the Ammonites. 11 He said, "If the
Arameans are too strong for me, then you
shall help me; but if the Ammonites are too
strong for you, then I will come and help
you. 12 Be strong, and let us be courageous
for the sake of our people, and for the cities
of our God; and may the LORD do what
seems good to him." 13 So Joab and the
people who were with him moved forward
into battle against the Arameans; and they
fled before him. 14 When the Ammonites
saw that the Arameans fled, they likewise
fled before Abishai, and entered the city.
Then Joab returned from fighting against
the Ammonites, and came to Jerusalem.
15 But when the Arameans saw that
they had been defeated by Israel, they gath-
ered themselves together. 16 Hadadezer sent
and brought out the Arameans who were
beyond the Euphrates; and they came to
Helam, with Shobach the commander of
the army of Hadadezer at their head.
17 When it was told David, he gathered all
Israel together, and crossed the Jordan, and
came to Helam. The Arameans arrayed
themselves against David and fought with
him. 18 The Arameans fled before Israel;
and David killed of the Arameans seven
hundred chariot teams, and forty thousand
horsemen,[a] and wounded Shobach the
commander of their army, so that he died
there. 19 When all the kings who were ser-
vants of Hadadezer saw that they had been
defeated by Israel, they made peace with
Israel, and became subject to them. So the
Arameans were afraid to help the Ammon-
ites any more.

11 In the spring of the year, the time
when kings go out to battle, David
sent Joab with his officers and all Israel
with him; they ravaged the Ammonites,
and besieged Rabbah. But David remained
at Jerusalem.
2 It happened, late one afternoon, when
David rose from his couch and was walking
about on the roof of the king's house, that
he saw from the roof a woman bathing; the
woman was very beautiful. 3 David sent

a 1 Chr 19.18 and some Gk Mss read *foot soldiers*

Aramean (Syrian) city-states. *Thousand,* probably used for a military unit of far fewer than 1,000 men. *Maacah, Tob,* small states in northern Transjordan. **8:** *The gate,* the city in question is Rabbah, capital of the Ammonites (see 12.26). *Rehob,* another Aramean city-state. **12:** *The cities of our God* were the cities Israel claimed east of the Jordan. Joab is rousing the army for "holy war." **18:** *Forty thousand,* see v. 6.

11.1–27: David and Bathsheba. 1: *In the spring of the year, the time when kings go out to battle,* an alternate translation is: "A year after the kings had gone out to battle." The story is set a year after the events in ch 10. *David remained at Jerusalem,* perhaps at the insistence of his army to avoid danger to himself (see 21.15–17), although here this may be a possible disparagement of David. **2:** *The roof of the king's house* was breezy and cool in the late afternoon, the ideal place for a nap. From there he was able to look down into the courtyard of surrounding houses, where he saw the *woman bathing.* **3:** *Inquire about the woman,* David wants to know whether she is married; if not, he can add her to his harem.

someone to inquire about the woman. It
was reported, "This is Bathsheba daughter
of Eliam, the wife of Uriah the Hittite." 4 So
David sent messengers to get her, and she
came to him, and he lay with her. (Now she
was purifying herself after her period.)
Then she returned to her house. 5 The wom-
an conceived; and she sent and told David,
"I am pregnant."
6 So David sent word to Joab, "Send me
Uriah the Hittite." And Joab sent Uriah to
David. 7 When Uriah came to him, David
asked how Joab and the people fared, and
how the war was going. 8 Then David said
to Uriah, "Go down to your house, and
wash your feet." Uriah went out of the
king's house, and there followed him a
present from the king. 9 But Uriah slept at
the entrance of the king's house with all the
servants of his lord, and did not go down to
his house. 10 When they told David, "Uriah
did not go down to his house," David said
to Uriah, "You have just come from a jour-
ney. Why did you not go down to your
house?" 11 Uriah said to David, "The ark
and Israel and Judah remain in booths;[a]
and my lord Joab and the servants of my
lord are camping in the open field; shall I
then go to my house, to eat and to drink,
and to lie with my wife? As you live, and as
your soul lives, I will not do such a thing."
12 Then David said to Uriah, "Remain here
today also, and tomorrow I will send you
back." So Uriah remained in Jerusalem that
day. On the next day, 13 David invited him
to eat and drink in his presence and made
him drunk; and in the evening he went out
to lie on his couch with the servants of his
lord, but he did not go down to his house.
14 In the morning David wrote a letter
to Joab, and sent it by the hand of Uriah.
15 In the letter he wrote, "Set Uriah in the
forefront of the hardest fighting, and then
draw back from him, so that he may be
struck down and die." 16 As Joab was be-
sieging the city, he assigned Uriah to the
place where he knew there were valiant
warriors. 17 The men of the city came out
and fought with Joab; and some of the ser-
vants of David among the people fell. Uriah
the Hittite was killed as well. 18 Then Joab
sent and told David all the news about the
fighting; 19 and he instructed the messenger,
"When you have finished telling the king
all the news about the fighting, 20 then, if
the king's anger rises, and if he says to you,
'Why did you go so near the city to fight?
Did you not know that they would shoot
from the wall? 21 Who killed Abimelech son
of Jerubbaal?[b] Did not a woman throw an
upper millstone on him from the wall, so
that he died at Thebez? Why did you go so
near the wall?' then you shall say, 'Your
servant Uriah the Hittite is dead too.' "
22 So the messenger went, and came and

a Or *at Succoth* *b* Gk Syr Judg 7.1: Heb *Jerubbesheth*

Eliam, perhaps the son of Ahithophel, David's advisor (see 23.34; 16.15–17.23). *Uriah,* one of the "thirty" best soldiers of David, according to 23.39. Thus, Bathsheba was well-married and came from a distinguished family. **4:** Bathsheba *was purifying herself after her period;* hence her bath (see Lev 15.19–28). She was at the most fertile time of her cycle when she slept with David. It is clear that David must be her child's father. **6–7:** It was unusual for a soldier to be called back from battle for a personal audience. Since David asked Uriah only the most general questions, Uriah may have thought he was being tested, which in turn motivated him to demonstrate his loyalty to David and the army in the following verses. The *people,* the army. **8:** *Wash your feet,* a euphemism for sexual intercourse. *Feet* can refer to the genitals (see Isa 6.2; 7.20). **9–13:** As a pious soldier consecrated for war (see 1 Sam 21.5), Uriah refuses to have sexual relations with his wife, even when David gets him drunk. **14:** David trusts Uriah's loyalty enough to send his death warrant by his own hand, knowing that Uriah, if he could read, would not open it. **16–17:** Joab places Uriah in a dangerous place but does not have time to implement David's order fully. Uriah is killed because of a tactical error by Joab. **18–21:** Joab uses Uriah's death to cover up his mistake in allowing the troops to come too close to the city wall. The story of *Abimelech son of Jerubbaal* (v. 21) is in Judg 9. *An upper millstone,* a large stone used for grinding grain. **25:** David's attitude toward Joab

told David all that Joab had sent him to
tell. 23 The messenger said to David, "The
men gained an advantage over us, and
came out against us in the field; but we
drove them back to the entrance of the
gate. 24 Then the archers shot at your ser-
vants from the wall; some of the king's ser-
vants are dead; and your servant Uriah the
Hittite is dead also." 25 David said to the
messenger, "Thus you shall say to Joab,
'Do not let this matter trouble you, for the
sword devours now one and now another;
press your attack on the city, and over-
throw it.' And encourage him."

26 When the wife of Uriah heard that
her husband was dead, she made lamenta-
tion for him. 27 When the mourning was
over, David sent and brought her to his
house, and she became his wife, and bore
him a son.

But the thing that David had done dis-
12 pleased the LORD, 1 and the LORD
sent Nathan to David. He came to
him, and said to him, "There were two men
in a certain city, the one rich and the other
poor. 2 The rich man had very many flocks
and herds; 3 but the poor man had nothing
but one little ewe lamb, which he had
bought. He brought it up, and it grew up
with him and with his children; it used to
eat of his meager fare, and drink from his
cup, and lie in his bosom, and it was like a
daughter to him. 4 Now there came a travel-
er to the rich man, and he was loath to take
one of his own flock or herd to prepare for
the wayfarer who had come to him, but he
took the poor man's lamb, and prepared
that for the guest who had come to him."
5 Then David's anger was greatly kindled
against the man. He said to Nathan, "As
the LORD lives, the man who has done this
deserves to die; 6 he shall restore the lamb
fourfold, because he did this thing, and be-
cause he had no pity."

7 Nathan said to David, "You are the
man! Thus says the LORD, the God of Isra-
el: I anointed you king over Israel, and I
rescued you from the hand of Saul; 8 I gave
you your master's house, and your master's
wives into your bosom, and gave you the
house of Israel and of Judah; and if that
had been too little, I would have added as
much more. 9 Why have you despised the
word of the LORD, to do what is evil in his
sight? You have struck down Uriah the Hit-
tite with the sword, and have taken his wife
to be your wife, and have killed him with
the sword of the Ammonites. 10 Now there-
fore the sword shall never depart from your
house, for you have despised me, and have
taken the wife of Uriah the Hittite to be
your wife. 11 Thus says the LORD: I will
raise up trouble against you from within
your own house; and I will take your wives
before your eyes, and give them to your
neighbor, and he shall lie with your wives
in the sight of this very sun. 12 For you did
it secretly; but I will do this thing before all
Israel, and before the sun." 13 David said to
Nathan, "I have sinned against the LORD."
Nathan said to David, "Now the LORD
has put away your sin; you shall not die.

changes when he learns of Uriah's death. **27b:** *David . . . displeased the LORD,* the author's moral condemnation links the account of David's offense in ch 11 with the judgment in ch 12.

12.1–25: David's punishment. 1–6: Nathan couches his parable as a legal case to get David to pronounce judgment on himself. As king he was responsible for protecting the rights of the poor. *Fourfold* (v. 6), as prescribed in Ex 22.1; other textual witnesses have "sevenfold." **8:** There is some textual support for reading "daughter(s)" (Heb "bet") instead of *house* (Heb "bayit") in this verse. "Daughter(s)" would fit the point of the verse better—that David had many women as wives and concubines, but like the rich man in Nathan's parable, he stole what belonged to his poor neighbor. *Your master's wives,* David took over Saul's harem. **10:** *The sword,* a metaphor for violence, alluding to the events in chs 13–20. **11–12:** An allusion to Absalom's revolt, specifically his deed in 16.20–23. **13–18:** David's sin is transferred (not *put away*) to his newborn son, who dies because of it. This is the clearest indication in the Hebrew Bible of the application of intergenerational punishment by God (see Ex 20.5; 34.7; Deut 5.9), where the sin is perceived as property that may be inherited. **20:** *House of the LORD,* an anachronism, since the Temple

14 Nevertheless, because by this deed you
have utterly scorned the LORD,[a] the child
that is born to you shall die." 15 Then Na-
than went to his house.
The LORD struck the child that Uriah's
wife bore to David, and it became very ill.
16 David therefore pleaded with God for the
child; David fasted, and went in and lay all
night on the ground. 17 The elders of his
house stood beside him, urging him to rise
from the ground; but he would not, nor did
he eat food with them. 18 On the seventh
day the child died. And the servants of Da-
vid were afraid to tell him that the child
was dead; for they said, "While the child
was still alive, we spoke to him, and he did
not listen to us; how then can we tell him
the child is dead? He may do himself some
harm." 19 But when David saw that his ser-
vants were whispering together, he per-
ceived that the child was dead; and David
said to his servants, "Is the child dead?"
They said, "He is dead."
20 Then David rose from the ground,
washed, anointed himself, and changed his
clothes. He went into the house of the
LORD, and worshiped; he then went to his
own house; and when he asked, they set
food before him and he ate. 21 Then his ser-
vants said to him, "What is this thing that
you have done? You fasted and wept for
the child while it was alive; but when the
child died, you rose and ate food." 22 He
said, "While the child was still alive, I fast-
ed and wept; for I said, 'Who knows? The
LORD may be gracious to me, and the child
may live.' 23 But now he is dead; why
should I fast? Can I bring him back again?
I shall go to him, but he will not return
to me."
24 Then David consoled his wife Bath-
sheba, and went to her, and lay with her;
and she bore a son, and he named him Sol-
omon. The LORD loved him, 25 and sent a
message by the prophet Nathan; so he
named him Jedidiah,[b] because of the
LORD.
26 Now Joab fought against Rabbah of
the Ammonites, and took the royal city.
27 Joab sent messengers to David, and said,
"I have fought against Rabbah; moreover, I
have taken the water city. 28 Now, then,
gather the rest of the people together, and
encamp against the city, and take it; or I
myself will take the city, and it will be
called by my name." 29 So David gathered
all the people together and went to Rab-
bah, and fought against it and took it. 30 He
took the crown of Milcom[c] from his head;
the weight of it was a talent of gold, and in
it was a precious stone; and it was placed
on David's head. He also brought forth the
spoil of the city, a very great amount. 31 He
brought out the people who were in it, and
set them to work with saws and iron picks
and iron axes, or sent them to the brick-
works. Thus he did to all the cities of the
Ammonites. Then David and all the people
returned to Jerusalem.

13 Some time passed. David's son Ab-
salom had a beautiful sister whose
name was Tamar; and David's son Amnon

a Ancient scribal tradition: Compare 1 Sam 25.22 note: Heb *scorned the enemies of the LORD* *b* That is *Beloved of the LORD* *c* Gk See 1 Kings 11.5, 33: Heb *their kings*

in Jerusalem had not yet been built. **24–25:** *Solomon* means "his replacement"; he was a replacement for the dead child. *Jedidiah* ("beloved of Yahweh"), which does not occur elsewhere for Solomon, hints that he will replace David (whose name means "beloved") as king.

12.26–31: The conclusion of the Ammonite war. 26–29: Joab captured the citadel and the water supply of Rabbah, the Ammonite capital, so that conquering the rest of the city was fairly simple. This Joab left for David, as the king, to complete. **30:** *Milcom,* the national Ammonite god. *A talent,* about 34 kg (75 lb).

13.1–39: The rape of Tamar and the murder of Amnon. In its current context, this and the following chapter reflect a measure-for-measure punishment of David. He appropriated Bathsheba and arranged for Uriah's death, so rape and death are unleashed against his house. **1:** Tamar was Absalom's full *sister,* Amnon's half-sister. *Amnon* was David's oldest son and the crown prince. The next oldest had apparently died (perhaps as a child), leaving Absalom as second in line of succession to the throne (cf. 3.2–3). **2:** *It*

fell in love with her. 2 Amnon was so tor-
mented that he made himself ill because of
his sister Tamar, for she was a virgin and it
seemed impossible to Amnon to do any-
thing to her. 3 But Amnon had a friend
whose name was Jonadab, the son of Da-
vid's brother Shimeah; and Jonadab was a
very crafty man. 4 He said to him, "O son
of the king, why are you so haggard morn-
ing after morning? Will you not tell me?"
Amnon said to him, "I love Tamar, my
brother Absalom's sister." 5 Jonadab said
to him, "Lie down on your bed, and pre-
tend to be ill; and when your father comes
to see you, say to him, 'Let my sister Tamar
come and give me something to eat, and
prepare the food in my sight, so that I may
see it and eat it from her hand.' " 6 So Am-
non lay down, and pretended to be ill; and
when the king came to see him, Amnon
said to the king, "Please let my sister Tamar
come and make a couple of cakes in my
sight, so that I may eat from her hand."

7 Then David sent home to Tamar, say-
ing, "Go to your brother Amnon's house,
and prepare food for him." 8 So Tamar
went to her brother Amnon's house, where
he was lying down. She took dough, knead-
ed it, made cakes in his sight, and baked the
cakes. 9 Then she took the pan and set
them[a] out before him, but he refused to
eat. Amnon said, "Send out everyone from
me." So everyone went out from him.
10 Then Amnon said to Tamar, "Bring the
food into the chamber, so that I may eat
from your hand." So Tamar took the cakes
she had made, and brought them into the
chamber to Amnon her brother. 11 But
when she brought them near him to eat, he
took hold of her, and said to her, "Come,
lie with me, my sister." 12 She answered
him, "No, my brother, do not force me; for
such a thing is not done in Israel; do not do
anything so vile! 13 As for me, where could
I carry my shame? And as for you, you
would be as one of the scoundrels in Israel.
Now therefore, I beg you, speak to the
king; for he will not withhold me from
you." 14 But he would not listen to her; and
being stronger than she, he forced her and
lay with her.

15 Then Amnon was seized with a very
great loathing for her; indeed, his loathing
was even greater than the lust he had felt
for her. Amnon said to her, "Get out!"
16 But she said to him, "No, my brother;[b]
for this wrong in sending me away is great-
er than the other that you did to me." But
he would not listen to her. 17 He called the
young man who served him and said, "Put
this woman out of my presence, and bolt
the door after her." 18 (Now she was wear-
ing a long robe with sleeves; for this is
how the virgin daughters of the king were
clothed in earlier times.[c]) So his servant
put her out, and bolted the door after her.
19 But Tamar put ashes on her head, and
tore the long robe that she was wearing; she
put her hand on her head, and went away,
crying aloud as she went.

20 Her brother Absalom said to her,

a Heb *and poured* *b* Cn Compare Gk Vg: Meaning of Heb uncertain *c* Cn: Heb *were clothed in robes*

seemed impossible to Amnon to do anything to her, as the king's virgin daughter Tamar may have been guarded. **6:** *Cakes,* the Hebrew word is similar to the word for "heart" and may indicate their shape. **10:** *The chamber,* Amnon's bedroom where he is feigning illness. **11:** *My sister* not only reflects the kinship of Amnon to Tamar but is also a term of endearment and sexual desire in ancient love poetry (Song 4.9–10; 5.1). **12:** *Such a thing* may refer to incest or rape or both. **13:** *He will not withhold me from you,* Tamar suggests that David would allow their marriage despite its incestuous nature. Perhaps she is just trying to buy time. **16:** Ex 22.16 and Deut 22.28–29 required marriage in such cases. Tamar may have such laws in mind when she says that in sending her away Amnon is committing a *greater* wrong than the rape itself. **17:** *This woman,* a contemptuous reference. Having robbed Tamar of her virginity, Amnon takes her identity as well. **18:** *A long robe with sleeves,* used also for Joseph's garment in Gen 37.3; the exact nature of this garment is unknown. **19:** Putting ashes on the head and tearing clothes were signs of grief, though Tamar may also have torn *the long robe* worn by the king's virgin daughters because it was no longer appropriate. **20:** *Desolate,* because she is unmarried. **21:** *Because he loved him* may be the

"Has Amnon your brother been with you?
Be quiet for now, my sister; he is your
brother; do not take this to heart." So Ta-
mar remained, a desolate woman, in her
brother Absalom's house. 21 When King
David heard of all these things, he became
very angry, but he would not punish his son
Amnon, because he loved him, for he was
his firstborn.[a] 22 But Absalom spoke to
Amnon neither good nor bad; for Absalom
hated Amnon, because he had raped his sis-
ter Tamar.

23 After two full years Absalom had
sheepshearers at Baal-hazor, which is near
Ephraim, and Absalom invited all the
king's sons. 24 Absalom came to the king,
and said, "Your servant has sheepshearers;
will the king and his servants please go with
your servant?" 25 But the king said to Absa-
lom, "No, my son, let us not all go, or else
we will be burdensome to you." He pressed
him, but he would not go but gave him his
blessing. 26 Then Absalom said, "If not,
please let my brother Amnon go with us."
The king said to him, "Why should he go
with you?" 27 But Absalom pressed him un-
til he let Amnon and all the king's sons
go with him. Absalom made a feast like a
king's feast.[b] 28 Then Absalom command-
ed his servants, "Watch when Amnon's
heart is merry with wine, and when I say to
you, 'Strike Amnon,' then kill him. Do not
be afraid; have I not myself commanded
you? Be courageous and valiant." 29 So the
servants of Absalom did to Amnon as Ab-
salom had commanded. Then all the king's
sons rose, and each mounted his mule and
fled.

30 While they were on the way, the re-
port came to David that Absalom had
killed all the king's sons, and not one of
them was left. 31 The king rose, tore his gar-
ments, and lay on the ground; and all his
servants who were standing by tore their
garments. 32 But Jonadab, the son of Da-
vid's brother Shimeah, said, "Let not my
lord suppose that they have killed all the
young men the king's sons; Amnon alone is
dead. This has been determined by Absa-
lom from the day Amnon[c] raped his sister
Tamar. 33 Now therefore, do not let my
lord the king take it to heart, as if all the
king's sons were dead; for Amnon alone is
dead."

34 But Absalom fled. When the young
man who kept watch looked up, he saw
many people coming from the Horonaim
road[d] by the side of the mountain. 35 Jona-
dab said to the king, "See, the king's sons
have come; as your servant said, so it has
come about." 36 As soon as he had finished
speaking, the king's sons arrived, and
raised their voices and wept; and the king
and all his servants also wept very bitterly.

37 But Absalom fled, and went to Tal-
mai son of Ammihud, king of Geshur. Da-
vid mourned for his son day after day.
38 Absalom, having fled to Geshur, stayed
there three years. 39 And the heart of[e] the
king went out, yearning for Absalom; for

a Q Ms Gk: MT lacks *but he would not punish . . . firstborn* *b* Gk Compare Q Ms: MT lacks *Absalom made a feast like a king's feast* *c* Heb *he*
d Cn Compare Gk: Heb *the road behind him*
e Q Ms Gk: MT *And David*

writer's way of assuring the reader that David had nothing to do with Amnon's death. **22:** *Neither good nor bad* means not at all. **23:** Sheepshearing was a time of celebration. **24–25:** In light of what follows, Absalom's invitation to David makes the reader wonder whether he already intended to kill his father and assume the throne. **27:** The *feast* was a drinking bout, as indicated by the word's etymology and the next verse. **29:** David and his sons rode on *mules* (18.9; 1 Kings 1.33). **30–33:** David initially thought that Absalom had killed all the king's sons, which would make sense if he were attempting a coup. But his intention at this point is purely revenge against Amnon. *Jonadab* appears as a false friend to Amnon. **36:** *The king . . . wept very bitterly,* David's great love for Amnon and his noninvolvement in Amnon's death are stressed. **37:** *Talmai . . . king of Geshur,* Absalom's maternal grandfather (see 3.3n.). **39:** *And the heart of the king went out, yearning for Absalom,* better: "The king's spirit for marching out against Absalom was exhausted." David did not yearn for Absalom but was tired of going out after him; hence David's reluctance in the next chapter to allow Absalom back into his presence.

he was now consoled over the death of Am-
non.

14 Now Joab son of Zeruiah perceived
that the king's mind was on Absa-
lom. 2 Joab sent to Tekoa and brought from
there a wise woman. He said to her, "Pre-
tend to be a mourner; put on mourning gar-
ments, do not anoint yourself with oil, but
behave like a woman who has been mourn-
ing many days for the dead. 3 Go to the king
and speak to him as follows." And Joab put
the words into her mouth.
4 When the woman of Tekoa came to
the king, she fell on her face to the ground
and did obeisance, and said, "Help,
O king!" 5 The king asked her, "What is
your trouble?" She answered, "Alas, I am a
widow; my husband is dead. 6 Your servant
had two sons, and they fought with one
another in the field; there was no one to
part them, and one struck the other and
killed him. 7 Now the whole family has ris-
en against your servant. They say, 'Give up
the man who struck his brother, so that we
may kill him for the life of his brother
whom he murdered, even if we destroy the
heir as well.' Thus they would quench my
one remaining ember, and leave to my hus-
band neither name nor remnant on the face
of the earth."
8 Then the king said to the woman, "Go
to your house, and I will give orders con-
cerning you." 9 The woman of Tekoa said
to the king, "On me be the guilt, my lord
the king, and on my father's house; let the
king and his throne be guiltless." 10 The
king said, "If anyone says anything to you,
bring him to me, and he shall never touch
you again." 11 Then she said, "Please, may
the king keep the LORD your God in mind,
so that the avenger of blood may kill no
more, and my son not be destroyed." He
said, "As the LORD lives, not one hair of
your son shall fall to the ground."
12 Then the woman said, "Please let
your servant speak a word to my lord the
king." He said, "Speak." 13 The woman
said, "Why then have you planned such a
thing against the people of God? For in giv-
ing this decision the king convicts himself,
inasmuch as the king does not bring his
banished one home again. 14 We must all
die; we are like water spilled on the ground,
which cannot be gathered up. But God will
not take away a life; he will devise plans so
as not to keep an outcast banished forever
from his presence.[a] 15 Now I have come to
say this to my lord the king because the
people have made me afraid; your servant
thought, 'I will speak to the king; it may be

a Meaning of Heb uncertain

14.1–33: Absalom's return. 1: *The king's mind was on Absalom* does not mean that David was now favorably inclined toward Absalom, as this story makes clear. **2:** *Tekoa,* a village south of Bethlehem (see Am 1.1). Perhaps David took an interest in this case because the woman was from his home territory. *Wise* in the Hebrew Bible often means skilled (see Ex 28.3). This woman was a skilled actress. **4:** *Fell . . . to the ground and did obeisance,* prostration was the proper way of bowing before a king. **5–7:** As in ch 12, a fictional legal case is presented to David in order to get him to pronounce judgment on a matter concerning himself. *Two sons* (v. 6), one of whom kills the other, like Amnon and Absalom. *Leave to my husband neither name nor remnant* (v. 7). This part of the woman's case is not paralleled in David's family since he has many other sons. But this difference does not figure in the outcome of the story. **8–11:** David grants the woman's request and swears by the LORD that her one remaining son will not be harmed. The woman will urge David to apply this oath to his situation with Absalom. Since David's ruling is contrary to the customary punishment, the woman accepts any guilt that David may incur (v. 9). *Avenger of blood,* one charged with taking vengeance for the death of a relative. **13:** *The woman* now applies David's decree to the situation with Absalom. It is not clear how David's refusal to bring Absalom back is *a thing against the people of God.* **14:** Amnon is dead and cannot be brought to life again, but David can accept Absalom, who is still alive. **15–17:** These verses seem out of place and may originally have gone after v. 7. The woman continues to plead for her son, but David has already rendered his decision. *The man who would cut both me and my son off,* the avenger of blood (see v. 11). *The heritage of God,* the land of Israel and its people. **19:** *Your servant,* a polite form of self-reference. **21–24:** David allows

that the king will perform the request of his
servant. 16 For the king will hear, and deliv-
er his servant from the hand of the man
who would cut both me and my son off
from the heritage of God.' 17 Your servant
thought, 'The word of my lord the king will
set me at rest'; for my lord the king is like
the angel of God, discerning good and evil.
The LORD your God be with you!"

18 Then the king answered the woman,
"Do not withhold from me anything I ask
you." The woman said, "Let my lord the
king speak." 19 The king said, "Is the hand
of Joab with you in all this?" The woman
answered and said, "As surely as you live,
my lord the king, one cannot turn right or
left from anything that my lord the king has
said. For it was your servant Joab who
commanded me; it was he who put all these
words into the mouth of your servant. 20 In
order to change the course of affairs your
servant Joab did this. But my lord has wis-
dom like the wisdom of the angel of God to
know all things that are on the earth."

21 Then the king said to Joab, "Very
well, I grant this; go, bring back the young
man Absalom." 22 Joab prostrated himself
with his face to the ground and did obei-
sance, and blessed the king; and Joab said,
"Today your servant knows that I have
found favor in your sight, my lord the king,
in that the king has granted the request of
his servant." 23 So Joab set off, went to Ge-
shur, and brought Absalom to Jerusalem.
24 The king said, "Let him go to his own
house; he is not to come into my presence."
So Absalom went to his own house, and did
not come into the king's presence.

25 Now in all Israel there was no one to
be praised so much for his beauty as Absa-
lom; from the sole of his foot to the crown
of his head there was no blemish in him.
26 When he cut the hair of his head (for at
the end of every year he used to cut it; when
it was heavy on him, he cut it), he weighed
the hair of his head, two hundred shekels
by the king's weight. 27 There were born
to Absalom three sons, and one daughter
whose name was Tamar; she was a beauti-
ful woman.

28 So Absalom lived two full years in
Jerusalem, without coming into the king's
presence. 29 Then Absalom sent for Joab to
send him to the king; but Joab would not
come to him. He sent a second time, but
Joab would not come. 30 Then he said to
his servants, "Look, Joab's field is next to
mine, and he has barley there; go and set it
on fire." So Absalom's servants set the field
on fire. 31 Then Joab rose and went to Ab-
salom at his house, and said to him, "Why
have your servants set my field on fire?"
32 Absalom answered Joab, "Look, I sent
word to you: Come here, that I may send
you to the king with the question, 'Why
have I come from Geshur? It would be bet-
ter for me to be there still.' Now let me go
into the king's presence; if there is guilt in
me, let him kill me!" 33 Then Joab went to
the king and told him; and he summoned
Absalom. So he came to the king and pros-
trated himself with his face to the ground
before the king; and the king kissed Absa-
lom.

15 After this Absalom got himself a
chariot and horses, and fifty men to
run ahead of him. 2 Absalom used to rise
early and stand beside the road into the
gate; and when anyone brought a suit be-
fore the king for judgment, Absalom would

Absalom to return but refuses to see him personally. **26:** *Two hundred shekels,* ca. 2.3 kg (5 lb), an extraordinary amount of hair. The reference to his hair foreshadows Absalom's mode of death (18.9–15). **27:** Absalom named his daughter after his sister, *Tamar* (ch 13). **28–33:** This episode further shows Absalom's violent nature and suggests that Joab may have held a grudge against him. *The king kissed Absalom,* a gesture of recognition and reconciliation, performed only after Absalom did his obeisance to David. This subservience, however, did not last long.

15.1–12: Absalom revolts. 1: *Chariot and horses, and fifty men to run ahead,* parts of the king's entourage (1 Kings 1.5). The fifty men were probably a royal bodyguard. **2:** *When anyone brought a suit before the king for judgment,* one of the king's roles in the ancient world was to serve as a judge in special cases. David may have been weak in this role, and Absalom took advantage. **5:** *Do obeisance to him,* the

call out and say, "From what city are you?"
When the person said, "Your servant is of
such and such a tribe in Israel," 3 Absalom
would say, "See, your claims are good and
right; but there is no one deputed by the
king to hear you." 4 Absalom said more-
over, "If only I were judge in the land!
Then all who had a suit or cause might
come to me, and I would give them jus-
tice." 5 Whenever people came near to do
obeisance to him, he would put out his
hand and take hold of them, and kiss them.
6 Thus Absalom did to every Israelite who
came to the king for judgment; so Absalom
stole the hearts of the people of Israel.
7 At the end of four[a] years Absalom
said to the king, "Please let me go to He-
bron and pay the vow that I have made to
the LORD. 8 For your servant made a vow
while I lived at Geshur in Aram: If the
LORD will indeed bring me back to Jerusa-
lem, then I will worship the LORD in He-
bron."[b] 9 The king said to him, "Go in
peace." So he got up, and went to Hebron.
10 But Absalom sent secret messengers
throughout all the tribes of Israel, saying,
"As soon as you hear the sound of the
trumpet, then shout: Absalom has become
king at Hebron!" 11 Two hundred men
from Jerusalem went with Absalom; they
were invited guests, and they went in their
innocence, knowing nothing of the matter.
12 While Absalom was offering the sacri-
fices, he sent for[c] Ahithophel the Gilonite,
David's counselor, from his city Giloh. The
conspiracy grew in strength, and the people
with Absalom kept increasing.
13 A messenger came to David, saying,
"The hearts of the Israelites have gone after
Absalom." 14 Then David said to all his of-
ficials who were with him at Jerusalem,
"Get up! Let us flee, or there will be no
escape for us from Absalom. Hurry, or he
will soon overtake us, and bring disaster
down upon us, and attack the city with the
edge of the sword." 15 The king's officials
said to the king, "Your servants are ready
to do whatever our lord the king decides."
16 So the king left, followed by all his
household, except ten concubines whom he
left behind to look after the house. 17 The
king left, followed by all the people; and
they stopped at the last house. 18 All his
officials passed by him; and all the Chereth-
ites, and all the Pelethites, and all the six
hundred Gittites who had followed him
from Gath, passed on before the king.
19 Then the king said to Ittai the Gittite,
"Why are you also coming with us? Go
back, and stay with the king; for you are
a foreigner, and also an exile from your
home. 20 You came only yesterday, and
shall I today make you wander about with
us, while I go wherever I can? Go back, and
take your kinsfolk with you; and may the

a Gk Syr: Heb *forty* *b* Gk Mss: Heb lacks *in Hebron* *c* Or *he sent*

proper attitude before a king, but Absalom presented himself as a "man of the people." **6:** *Stole the hearts* or "deceived" (cf. Gen 31.20). **7–10:** Absalom has made a vow to worship at the local shrine of *the LORD in Hebron* (v. 8) and must go there to fulfill it. But he has ulterior motives for choosing Hebron. He is deliberately recalling his father's rise by declaring himself king in Hebron, the capital of Judah, where David had been made king of both Judah and Israel and had ruled Judah for seven years (5.1–7). Absalom probably found supporters in Hebron among those discontented that David had moved the capital. His revolt, however, spread *throughout all the tribes of Israel* (v. 10). *Geshur in Aram* (v. 8), where Absalom fled after killing Amnon (13.37–39). **12:** *Ahithophel* was renowned as *David's counselor* (see 16.15–23). His presence with Absalom meant that *the conspiracy grew in strength.*

15.13–16.14: David flees Jerusalem. 15.13: *Israelites,* perhaps only the residents of the north. But since Absalom began the revolt in Hebron, it has now spread through the entire country. **16:** *Concubines,* see 3.7n. **17:** *The last house,* on the outskirts of Jerusalem. **18:** *Cherethites* and *Pelethites,* see 8.18n. *Gittites,* Philistines from Gath. All these groups had followed David from his days with the Philistines (1 Sam 27; 29). **19:** *Ittai,* commander of the Gittites. **20:** *Yesterday,* an idiom for "recently." David is amazed that these Philistines who only recently joined him are more loyal than his own people. **23:** *The Wadi Kidron,* the valley between Jerusalem and the Mount of Olives. David heads east toward the Jordan.

LORD show[a] steadfast love and faithful-
ness to you." 21 But Ittai answered the king,
"As the LORD lives, and as my lord the king
lives, wherever my lord the king may be,
whether for death or for life, there also
your servant will be." 22 David said to Ittai,
"Go then, march on." So Ittai the Gittite
marched on, with all his men and all the
little ones who were with him. 23 The whole
country wept aloud as all the people passed
by; the king crossed the Wadi Kidron, and
all the people moved on toward the wilder-
ness.

24 Abiathar came up, and Zadok also,
with all the Levites, carrying the ark of the
covenant of God. They set down the ark of
God, until the people had all passed out of
the city. 25 Then the king said to Zadok,
"Carry the ark of God back into the city. If
I find favor in the eyes of the LORD, he will
bring me back and let me see both it and
the place where it stays. 26 But if he says, 'I
take no pleasure in you,' here I am, let him
do to me what seems good to him." 27 The
king also said to the priest Zadok, "Look,[b]
go back to the city in peace, you and Abia-
thar,[c] with your two sons, Ahimaaz your
son, and Jonathan son of Abiathar. 28 See, I
will wait at the fords of the wilderness until
word comes from you to inform me." 29 So
Zadok and Abiathar carried the ark of God
back to Jerusalem, and they remained
there.

30 But David went up the ascent of the
Mount of Olives, weeping as he went, with
his head covered and walking barefoot; and
all the people who were with him covered
their heads and went up, weeping as they
went. 31 David was told that Ahithophel
was among the conspirators with Absalom.
And David said, "O LORD, I pray you, turn
the counsel of Ahithophel into foolish-
ness."

32 When David came to the summit,
where God was worshiped, Hushai the Ar-
chite came to meet him with his coat torn
and earth on his head. 33 David said to him,
"If you go on with me, you will be a burden
to me. 34 But if you return to the city and
say to Absalom, 'I will be your servant,
O king; as I have been your father's servant
in time past, so now I will be your servant,'
then you will defeat for me the counsel of
Ahithophel. 35 The priests Zadok and Abia-
thar will be with you there. So whatever
you hear from the king's house, tell it to the
priests Zadok and Abiathar. 36 Their two
sons are with them there, Zadok's son
Ahimaaz and Abiathar's son Jonathan; and
by them you shall report to me everything
you hear." 37 So Hushai, David's friend,
came into the city, just as Absalom was en-
tering Jerusalem.

16 When David had passed a little be-
yond the summit, Ziba the servant
of Mephibosheth[d] met him, with a couple
of donkeys saddled, carrying two hundred
loaves of bread, one hundred bunches of
raisins, one hundred of summer fruits, and
one skin of wine. 2 The king said to Ziba,
"Why have you brought these?" Ziba an-
swered, "The donkeys are for the king's
household to ride, the bread and summer
fruit for the young men to eat, and the wine
is for those to drink who faint in the wilder-
ness." 3 The king said, "And where is your

a Gk Compare 2.6: Heb lacks *may the LORD show*
b Gk: Heb *Are you a seer* or *Do you see?*
c Cn: Heb lacks *and Abiathar* *d* Or *Merib-baal*: See 4.4 note

24: *Abiathar* and *Zadok,* David's two priests. **25–29:** Caring for the ark properly would slow David's retreat (see 6.1–11). Besides, the priests could serve as David's spies in Jerusalem. **30:** *His head covered and walking barefoot,* conventional signs of mourning. **31–37:** David was disheartened to learn that his wise adviser, Ahithophel (see 16.23), had joined Absalom. As he walked up the Mount of Olives (v. 31), he prayed for help against Ahithophel. His prayer was answered at the *summit* when he met Hushai, who would help him defeat Ahithophel's advice. *Where God was worshiped* (v. 32), a shrine at the top of the Mount of Olives; such "high places" are outlawed in the Deuteronomistic History once the Temple is built. *David's friend* (v. 37), perhaps a title for an intimate adviser. **16.2:** *Young men,* soldiers. **3–4:** *Your master's son,* Merib-baal (Mephibosheth), Saul's grandson (see ch 9). Ziba claims that Merib-baal is planning

master's son?" Ziba said to the king, "He
remains in Jerusalem; for he said, 'Today
the house of Israel will give me back my
grandfather's kingdom.' " 4 Then the king
said to Ziba, "All that belonged to Mephib-
osheth[a] is now yours." Ziba said, "I do
obeisance; let me find favor in your sight,
my lord the king."
5 When King David came to Bahurim, a
man of the family of the house of Saul came
out whose name was Shimei son of Gera;
he came out cursing. 6 He threw stones at
David and at all the servants of King David;
now all the people and all the warriors
were on his right and on his left. 7 Shimei
shouted while he cursed, "Out! Out! Mur-
derer! Scoundrel! 8 The LORD has avenged
on all of you the blood of the house of Saul,
in whose place you have reigned; and
the LORD has given the kingdom into the
hand of your son Absalom. See, disaster
has overtaken you; for you are a man of
blood."
9 Then Abishai son of Zeruiah said to
the king, "Why should this dead dog curse
my lord the king? Let me go over and take
off his head." 10 But the king said, "What
have I to do with you, you sons of Zeruiah?
If he is cursing because the LORD has said
to him, 'Curse David,' who then shall say,
'Why have you done so?' " 11 David said to
Abishai and to all his servants, "My own
son seeks my life; how much more now
may this Benjaminite! Let him alone, and
let him curse; for the LORD has bidden him.
12 It may be that the LORD will look on my
distress,[b] and the LORD will repay me with
good for this cursing of me today." 13 So
David and his men went on the road, while
Shimei went along on the hillside opposite
him and cursed as he went, throwing stones
and flinging dust at him. 14 The king and all
the people who were with him arrived wea-
ry at the Jordan;[c] and there he refreshed
himself.
15 Now Absalom and all the Israelites[d]
came to Jerusalem; Ahithophel was with
him. 16 When Hushai the Archite, David's
friend, came to Absalom, Hushai said to
Absalom, "Long live the king! Long live the
king!" 17 Absalom said to Hushai, "Is this
your loyalty to your friend? Why did you
not go with your friend?" 18 Hushai said
to Absalom, "No; but the one whom the
LORD and this people and all the Israelites
have chosen, his I will be, and with him I
will remain. 19 Moreover, whom should
I serve? Should it not be his son? Just as
I have served your father, so I will serve
you."
20 Then Absalom said to Ahithophel,
"Give us your counsel; what shall we do?"
21 Ahithophel said to Absalom, "Go in to
your father's concubines, the ones he has
left to look after the house; and all Israel
will hear that you have made yourself odi-

a Or *Merib-baal*: See 4.4 note *b* Gk Vg: Heb *iniquity* *c* Gk: Heb lacks *at the Jordan* *d* Gk: Heb *all the people, the men of Israel*

to take over his grandfather's place as king. But Ziba may be lying (19.24–30). David rewards Ziba by giving him Saul's property. There is some question about whether David has the legal right to do this. **5:** *Shimei* belonged not only to Saul's tribe (Benjamin) but also to his *family* or clan. **6–8:** Shimei accused David of murdering members of Saul's family and usurping the throne. He may have in mind the deaths of Abner and Ishbaal and/or those of Saul's sons and grandsons in 21.1–14. **9–10:** *Abishai,* the brother of Joab and Asahel (see 2.18–23). Called the *sons of Zeruiah* (David's sister) in 2 Samuel and portrayed as violent men. *Dead dog,* see 9.8n.; 3.8n. **11:** *This Benjaminite,* a demeaning reference to Shimei.

16.15–17.29: Overcoming Ahithophel. 16.16: *David's friend,* see 15.37. *Long live the king,* the utterance is ironic; for Hushai, David is still king. **18:** *The one whom the LORD and this people and all the Israelites have chosen,* again, Hushai means David. **19:** Hushai's duplicity continues. *Should it not be his son?* For Hushai, the answer is no. *Just as I have served your father, so I will serve you,* Hushai is saying that by serving Absalom he is actually serving David. In all cases (vv. 16–19), Absalom is unaware of Hushai's true meaning. **20–22:** To sleep with a member of the harem is to claim the throne. Hence, by having relations with David's concubines, Absalom makes his claim to kingship emphatic. He also fulfills

ous to your father, and the hands of all who
are with you will be strengthened." 22 So
they pitched a tent for Absalom upon the
roof; and Absalom went in to his father's
concubines in the sight of all Israel. 23 Now
in those days the counsel that Ahithophel
gave was as if one consulted the oracle[a] of
God; so all the counsel of Ahithophel was
esteemed, both by David and by Absalom.
17 Moreover Ahithophel said to Absa-
lom, "Let me choose twelve thou-
sand men, and I will set out and pursue
David tonight. 2 I will come upon him while
he is weary and discouraged, and throw
him into a panic; and all the people who are
with him will flee. I will strike down only
the king, 3 and I will bring all the people
back to you as a bride comes home to her
husband. You seek the life of only one
man,[b] and all the people will be at peace."
4 The advice pleased Absalom and all the
elders of Israel.
5 Then Absalom said, "Call Hushai the
Archite also, and let us hear too what he
has to say." 6 When Hushai came to Absa-
lom, Absalom said to him, "This is what
Ahithophel has said; shall we do as he ad-
vises? If not, you tell us." 7 Then Hushai
said to Absalom, "This time the counsel
that Ahithophel has given is not good."
8 Hushai continued, "You know that your
father and his men are warriors, and that
they are enraged, like a bear robbed of her
cubs in the field. Besides, your father is ex-
pert in war; he will not spend the night with
the troops. 9 Even now he has hidden him-
self in one of the pits, or in some other
place. And when some of our troops[c] fall
at the first attack, whoever hears it will say,
'There has been a slaughter among the
troops who follow Absalom.' 10 Then even
the valiant warrior, whose heart is like the
heart of a lion, will utterly melt with fear;
for all Israel knows that your father is a
warrior, and that those who are with him
are valiant warriors. 11 But my counsel is
that all Israel be gathered to you, from Dan
to Beer-sheba, like the sand by the sea for
multitude, and that you go to battle in per-
son. 12 So we shall come upon him in what-
ever place he may be found, and we shall
light on him as the dew falls on the ground;
and he will not survive, nor will any of
those with him. 13 If he withdraws into a
city, then all Israel will bring ropes to that
city, and we shall drag it into the valley,
until not even a pebble is to be found
there." 14 Absalom and all the men of Israel
said, "The counsel of Hushai the Archite is
better than the counsel of Ahithophel." For
the LORD had ordained to defeat the good
counsel of Ahithophel, so that the LORD
might bring ruin on Absalom.
15 Then Hushai said to the priests Za-
dok and Abiathar, "Thus and so did Ahith-
ophel counsel Absalom and the elders of
Israel; and thus and so I have counseled.
16 Therefore send quickly and tell David,
'Do not lodge tonight at the fords of the
wilderness, but by all means cross over;
otherwise the king and all the people who
are with him will be swallowed up.' "
17 Jonathan and Ahimaaz were waiting at
En-rogel; a servant-girl used to go and tell

a Heb *word* b Gk: Heb *like the return of the whole (is) the man whom you seek* c Gk Mss: Heb *some of them*

Nathan's prophecy (12.12). **23:** *Ahithophel* may have been Bathsheba's grandfather (cf. 11.3 and 23.34) and may have held a grudge against David for his treatment of Bathsheba and Uriah. **17.1–4:** *Ahithophel*'s sensible advice is to attack while David's forces are weak from fleeing. Once David is dead, he says, all who followed him will turn to Absalom. **5–14:** *Hushai* says that David will not be so easy to find or his troops so easy to defeat (vv. 8–10). He advises Absalom to wait, gather the full force of Israel, then attack (vv. 11–13). Hushai is trying to buy time for David to reorganize his forces. Hushai also plays on Absalom's ego, saying that all the people will follow him, and he can lead them into battle (v. 12). Even though Ahithophel's advice is better than Hushai's, *the LORD had ordained* that Absalom would be persuaded to follow Hushai. **15:** *Hushai* sends word to David through *the priests Zadok and Abiathar* and their sons (see 15.24–29). **16:** Hushai has bought David some time but urges him to cross the Jordan quickly and escape. **17:** *Jonathan and Ahimaaz,* the sons of Zadok and Abiathar. *En-rogel,* "the spring of

them, and they would go and tell King Da-
vid; for they could not risk being seen en-
tering the city. 18 But a boy saw them, and
told Absalom; so both of them went away
quickly, and came to the house of a man at
Bahurim, who had a well in his courtyard;
and they went down into it. 19 The man's
wife took a covering, stretched it over the
well's mouth, and spread out grain on it;
and nothing was known of it. 20 When Ab-
salom's servants came to the woman at the
house, they said, "Where are Ahimaaz and
Jonathan?" The woman said to them,
"They have crossed over the brook[a] of
water." And when they had searched and
could not find them, they returned to Jeru-
salem.

21 After they had gone, the men came
up out of the well, and went and told King
David. They said to David, "Go and cross
the water quickly; for thus and so has
Ahithophel counseled against you." 22 So
David and all the people who were with
him set out and crossed the Jordan; by day-
break not one was left who had not crossed
the Jordan.

23 When Ahithophel saw that his coun-
sel was not followed, he saddled his donkey
and went off home to his own city. He set
his house in order, and hanged himself; he
died and was buried in the tomb of his fa-
ther.

24 Then David came to Mahanaim,
while Absalom crossed the Jordan with all
the men of Israel. 25 Now Absalom had set
Amasa over the army in the place of Joab.
Amasa was the son of a man named Ithra
the Ishmaelite,[b] who had married Abigal
daughter of Nahash, sister of Zeruiah,
Joab's mother. 26 The Israelites and Absa-
lom encamped in the land of Gilead.

27 When David came to Mahanaim,
Shobi son of Nahash from Rabbah of the
Ammonites, and Machir son of Ammiel
from Lo-debar, and Barzillai the Gileadite
from Rogelim, 28 brought beds, basins, and
earthen vessels, wheat, barley, meal,
parched grain, beans and lentils,[c] 29 honey
and curds, sheep, and cheese from the herd,
for David and the people with him to eat;
for they said, "The troops are hungry and
weary and thirsty in the wilderness."

18 Then David mustered the men who
were with him, and set over them
commanders of thousands and command-
ers of hundreds. 2 And David divided the
army into three groups:[d] one third under
the command of Joab, one third under the
command of Abishai son of Zeruiah, Joab's
brother, and one third under the command
of Ittai the Gittite. The king said to the
men, "I myself will also go out with you."
3 But the men said, "You shall not go out.
For if we flee, they will not care about us.
If half of us die, they will not care about us.
But you are worth ten thousand of us;[e]
therefore it is better that you send us help
from the city." 4 The king said to them,
"Whatever seems best to you I will do." So
the king stood at the side of the gate, while
all the army marched out by hundreds and
by thousands. 5 The king ordered Joab and
Abishai and Ittai, saying, "Deal gently for

a Meaning of Heb uncertain *b* 1 Chr 2.17: Heb *Israelite* *c* Heb *and lentils and parched grain* *d* Gk: Heb *sent forth the army* *e* Gk Vg Symmachus: Heb *for now there are ten thousand such as we*

the fuller," in the Kidron Valley south of Jerusalem. **18–19:** *Well,* a simple pit whose opening could be covered with a blanket and *grain* spread over it for camouflage. **23:** *Ahithophel . . . hanged himself,* perhaps because he knew that the end of Absalom's reign was imminent. There is no stigma associated with suicide in the Bible; see 1 Sam 31.5n. **24:** *Mahanaim,* the site east of the Jordan where Abner had conducted Ishbaal after making him king (2.8); it was easily defensible. **25:** *Amasa,* David's nephew, the son of his sister *Zeruiah* (see 1 Chr 2.16). Zeruiah is called the daughter of *Nahash* here rather than the daughter of Jesse. This may be a scribal error (note that Nahash occurs in v. 27), or *Abigal* may have been David's half sister. **27:** *Nahash,* the Ammonite king with whom David had a treaty (10.1–2). His son, *Shobi,* loyal to the treaty, now helps David in exile. *Machir,* see 9.4.

18.1–19.10: The defeat and death of Absalom. 18.3: *You shall not go out,* cf. the story in 21.15–17.

my sake with the young man Absalom."
And all the people heard when the king
gave orders to all the commanders concern-
ing Absalom.

6 So the army went out into the field
against Israel; and the battle was fought in
the forest of Ephraim. 7 The men of Israel
were defeated there by the servants of Da-
vid, and the slaughter there was great on
that day, twenty thousand men. 8 The battle
spread over the face of all the country; and
the forest claimed more victims that day
than the sword.

9 Absalom happened to meet the ser-
vants of David. Absalom was riding on his
mule, and the mule went under the thick
branches of a great oak. His head caught
fast in the oak, and he was left hanging[a]
between heaven and earth, while the mule
that was under him went on. 10 A man saw
it, and told Joab, "I saw Absalom hanging
in an oak." 11 Joab said to the man who
told him, "What, you saw him! Why then
did you not strike him there to the ground?
I would have been glad to give you ten
pieces of silver and a belt." 12 But the man
said to Joab, "Even if I felt in my hand the
weight of a thousand pieces of silver, I
would not raise my hand against the king's
son; for in our hearing the king command-
ed you and Abishai and Ittai, saying: For
my sake protect the young man Absalom!
13 On the other hand, if I had dealt treach-
erously against his life[b] (and there is noth-
ing hidden from the king), then you your-
self would have stood aloof." 14 Joab said,
"I will not waste time like this with you."
He took three spears in his hand, and thrust
them into the heart of Absalom, while he
was still alive in the oak. 15 And ten young
men, Joab's armor-bearers, surrounded
Absalom and struck him, and killed him.

16 Then Joab sounded the trumpet, and
the troops came back from pursuing Israel,
for Joab restrained the troops. 17 They took
Absalom, threw him into a great pit in the
forest, and raised over him a very great
heap of stones. Meanwhile all the Israelites
fled to their homes. 18 Now Absalom in his
lifetime had taken and set up for himself a
pillar that is in the King's Valley, for he
said, "I have no son to keep my name in
remembrance"; he called the pillar by his
own name. It is called Absalom's Monu-
ment to this day.

19 Then Ahimaaz son of Zadok said,
"Let me run, and carry tidings to the king
that the LORD has delivered him from the
power of his enemies." 20 Joab said to him,
"You are not to carry tidings today; you
may carry tidings another day, but today
you shall not do so, because the king's son
is dead." 21 Then Joab said to a Cushite,
"Go, tell the king what you have seen."
The Cushite bowed before Joab, and ran.
22 Then Ahimaaz son of Zadok said again
to Joab, "Come what may, let me also run
after the Cushite." And Joab said, "Why
will you run, my son, seeing that you have
no reward[c] for the tidings?" 23 "Come
what may," he said, "I will run." So he said
to him, "Run." Then Ahimaaz ran by the
way of the Plain, and outran the Cushite.

a Gk Syr Tg: Heb *was put* *b* Another reading is *at the risk of my life* *c* Meaning of Heb uncertain

5: Through David's order concerning Absalom, the writer shows that David was not responsible for Absalom's death. **6–8:** David chooses the rugged *forest of Ephraim* as the battle site, thereby countering the larger numbers of Absalom's army. **9:** *Mule,* the royal mount for King David and his sons (see 13.29; 1 Kings 1.38). Thus, Absalom's unseating from the mule symbolizes his loss of the kingdom. His being caught by the head recalls his glorious hair (14.26) and suggests that his pride was his downfall. **12:** *In our hearing the king commanded,* see v. 5. **14:** *Spears* may also be translated "sticks." Apparently, Joab stabbed or struck Absalom with them in order to dislodge him from the tree and finish him off (v. 15). **15:** *Ten young men,* hence, no individual could be blamed for the actual killing. **17:** *A very great heap of stones,* this kind of burial was reserved for a cursed person (Josh 7.26). **18:** *Absalom's Monument,* later identified with the late Hellenistic or Roman tomb in the Kidron valley. **19–20:** *Ahimaaz* wants to deliver the good news of the victory to David, but Joab refuses because he knows that Absalom's death will not be welcome news to David. *Because the king's son* was *dead* may be the narrator's words rather than Joab's

24 Now David was sitting between the
two gates. The sentinel went up to the roof
of the gate by the wall, and when he looked
up, he saw a man running alone. 25 The sen-
tinel shouted and told the king. The king
said, "If he is alone, there are tidings in his
mouth." He kept coming, and drew near.
26 Then the sentinel saw another man run-
ning; and the sentinel called to the gate-
keeper and said, "See, another man run-
ning alone!" The king said, "He also is
bringing tidings." 27 The sentinel said, "I
think the running of the first one is like the
running of Ahimaaz son of Zadok." The
king said, "He is a good man, and comes
with good tidings."
28 Then Ahimaaz cried out to the king,
"All is well!" He prostrated himself before
the king with his face to the ground, and
said, "Blessed be the LORD your God, who
has delivered up the men who raised their
hand against my lord the king." 29 The king
said, "Is it well with the young man Absa-
lom?" Ahimaaz answered, "When Joab
sent your servant,[a] I saw a great tumult,
but I do not know what it was." 30 The king
said, "Turn aside, and stand here." So he
turned aside, and stood still.
31 Then the Cushite came; and the
Cushite said, "Good tidings for my lord the
king! For the LORD has vindicated you this
day, delivering you from the power of all
who rose up against you." 32 The king said
to the Cushite, "Is it well with the young
man Absalom?" The Cushite answered,
"May the enemies of my lord the king, and
all who rise up to do you harm, be like that
young man."
33[b] The king was deeply moved, and
went up to the chamber over the gate, and
wept; and as he went, he said, "O my son
Absalom, my son, my son Absalom! Would
I had died instead of you, O Absalom, my
son, my son!"

19 It was told Joab, "The king is weep-
ing and mourning for Absalom."
2 So the victory that day was turned into
mourning for all the troops; for the troops
heard that day, "The king is grieving for his
son." 3 The troops stole into the city that
day as soldiers steal in who are ashamed
when they flee in battle. 4 The king covered
his face, and the king cried with a loud
voice, "O my son Absalom, O Absalom,
my son, my son!" 5 Then Joab came into
the house to the king, and said, "Today you
have covered with shame the faces of all
your officers who have saved your life to-
day, and the lives of your sons and your
daughters, and the lives of your wives and
your concubines, 6 for love of those who
hate you and for hatred of those who love
you. You have made it clear today that
commanders and officers are nothing to
you; for I perceive that if Absalom were
alive and all of us were dead today, then
you would be pleased. 7 So go out at once
and speak kindly to your servants; for I
swear by the LORD, if you do not go, not a
man will stay with you this night; and this
will be worse for you than any disaster that
has come upon you from your youth until
now." 8 Then the king got up and took his
seat in the gate. The troops were all told,
"See, the king is sitting in the gate"; and all
the troops came before the king.
Meanwhile, all the Israelites had fled to
their homes. 9 All the people were disputing
throughout all the tribes of Israel, saying,

a Heb *the king's servant, your servant* *b* Ch 19.1 in Heb

(see v. 29). **21:** *Cushite,* an Ethiopian. **27:** *Good tidings,* victory usually constitutes good news. But the writer goes on to depict David as focused on Absalom, whose death will be bad news to David despite the victory. **29:** *Ahimaaz* apparently does not know that Absalom is dead. **32:** The *Cushite* thinks that Absalom's death is also good news. **18.33–19.8:** David is portrayed as distraught at his son's death, despite the political gain it means for him. Compare David's laments over Saul and Jonathan (1.11–27) and Abner (3.31–39), whose deaths also benefited him. **19.6:** *Love* and *hate* can be political terms for loyalty and disloyalty. Joab's point is that David shows love to those who are disloyal to him (Absalom) while failing to show love or appreciation toward his loyal subjects. **9:** *All the tribes of Israel* may refer to the northern tribes, not Judah, which is the focus of the subsequent narrative.

"The king delivered us from the hand of
our enemies, and saved us from the hand of
the Philistines; and now he has fled out of
the land because of Absalom. 10 But Absa-
lom, whom we anointed over us, is dead
in battle. Now therefore why do you say
nothing about bringing the king back?"
11 King David sent this message to the
priests Zadok and Abiathar, "Say to the
elders of Judah, 'Why should you be the
last to bring the king back to his house?
The talk of all Israel has come to the king.[a]
12 You are my kin, you are my bone and my
flesh; why then should you be the last to
bring back the king?' 13 And say to Amasa,
'Are you not my bone and my flesh? So
may God do to me, and more, if you are
not the commander of my army from now
on, in place of Joab.' " 14 Amasa[b] swayed
the hearts of all the people of Judah as one,
and they sent word to the king, "Return,
both you and all your servants." 15 So the
king came back to the Jordan; and Judah
came to Gilgal to meet the king and to
bring him over the Jordan.
16 Shimei son of Gera, the Benjaminite,
from Bahurim, hurried to come down with
the people of Judah to meet King David;
17 with him were a thousand people from
Benjamin. And Ziba, the servant of the
house of Saul, with his fifteen sons and his
twenty servants, rushed down to the Jordan
ahead of the king, 18 while the crossing was
taking place,[c] to bring over the king's
household, and to do his pleasure.
Shimei son of Gera fell down before the
king, as he was about to cross the Jordan,
19 and said to the king, "May my lord not
hold me guilty or remember how your ser-
vant did wrong on the day my lord the king
left Jerusalem; may the king not bear it in
mind. 20 For your servant knows that I have
sinned; therefore, see, I have come this day,
the first of all the house of Joseph to come
down to meet my lord the king." 21 Abishai
son of Zeruiah answered, "Shall not Shimei
be put to death for this, because he cursed
the LORD's anointed?" 22 But David said,
"What have I to do with you, you sons of
Zeruiah, that you should today become an
adversary to me? Shall anyone be put to
death in Israel this day? For do I not know
that I am this day king over Israel?" 23 The
king said to Shimei, "You shall not die."
And the king gave him his oath.
24 Mephibosheth[d] grandson of Saul
came down to meet the king; he had not
taken care of his feet, or trimmed his beard,
or washed his clothes, from the day the
king left until the day he came back in safe-

a Gk: Heb *to the king, to his house* *b* Heb *He*
c Cn: Heb *the ford crossed* *d* Or *Merib-baal*: See 4.4 note

19.11–43: David returns to Jerusalem. 11–12: David contacts the tribal leaders or *elders* of Judah to encourage them to welcome him back as king before *all Israel* (i.e., the northern tribes) does so. **13:** David appoints *Amasa* as his army commander in place of Joab because of Amasa's influence in Judah's army (see 17.25), and perhaps also because David shrewdly calculated that this would gain favor with the troops who had been loyal to Absalom, since Amasa was Absalom's commander-in-chief. It may also be intended to express David's anger at Joab for having disobeyed his instructions regarding Absalom. All of these factors may provide motivation for Joab's murder of Amasa (20.10). *My bone and my flesh,* David was Amasa's uncle (see 17.25). **14:** Amasa, in turn, persuades the *people* (i.e., army) of Judah to return to David. **15:** *Gilgal,* west of the Jordan River, was an ancient Israelite shrine where Saul had been made king (1 Sam 11.15). **16–23:** *Shimei* and those with him were from the tribe of *Benjamin,* Saul's tribe. Shimei had ridiculed David when he fled from Jerusalem (16.5–13). Now that David is victorious, he asks forgiveness. David grants it, perhaps in part because of the *thousand people from Benjamin* with Shimei. *House of Joseph* (v. 20), the northern tribes, Israel as opposed to Judah. *Abishai* still wants to kill Shimei (16.9), but David refuses. This is part of the author's portrayal of David as gentle, in contrast to the violent *sons of Zeruiah* (v. 22). It may also have been customary for a new king to pardon criminals on the day of his coronation (see 1 Sam 11.13). **24:** *Taken care of his feet* may mean trimmed his toenails, since the writer cites it as evidence that Merib-baal (*Mephibosheth*) had been mourning David's exile.

ty. 25 When he came from Jerusalem to
meet the king, the king said to him, "Why
did you not go with me, Mephibosheth?"[a]
26 He answered, "My lord, O king, my ser-
vant deceived me; for your servant said to
him, 'Saddle a donkey for me,[b] so that I
may ride on it and go with the king.' For
your servant is lame. 27 He has slandered
your servant to my lord the king. But my
lord the king is like the angel of God; do
therefore what seems good to you. 28 For all
my father's house were doomed to death
before my lord the king; but you set your
servant among those who eat at your table.
What further right have I, then, to appeal
to the king?" 29 The king said to him, "Why
speak any more of your affairs? I have de-
cided: you and Ziba shall divide the land."
30 Mephibosheth[a] said to the king, "Let
him take it all, since my lord the king has
arrived home safely."

31 Now Barzillai the Gileadite had come
down from Rogelim; he went on with the
king to the Jordan, to escort him over the
Jordan. 32 Barzillai was a very aged man,
eighty years old. He had provided the king
with food while he stayed at Mahanaim,
for he was a very wealthy man. 33 The king
said to Barzillai, "Come over with me, and
I will provide for you in Jerusalem at my
side." 34 But Barzillai said to the king,
"How many years have I still to live, that I
should go up with the king to Jerusalem?
35 Today I am eighty years old; can I discern
what is pleasant and what is not? Can your
servant taste what he eats or what he
drinks? Can I still listen to the voice of sing-
ing men and singing women? Why then
should your servant be an added burden to
my lord the king? 36 Your servant will go a
little way over the Jordan with the king.
Why should the king recompense me with
such a reward? 37 Please let your servant
return, so that I may die in my own town,
near the graves of my father and my moth-
er. But here is your servant Chimham; let
him go over with my lord the king; and
do for him whatever seems good to you."
38 The king answered, "Chimham shall go
over with me, and I will do for him whatev-
er seems good to you; and all that you de-
sire of me I will do for you." 39 Then all the
people crossed over the Jordan, and the
king crossed over; the king kissed Barzillai
and blessed him, and he returned to his
own home. 40 The king went on to Gilgal,
and Chimham went on with him; all the
people of Judah, and also half the people of
Israel, brought the king on his way.

41 Then all the people of Israel came to
the king, and said to him, "Why have our
kindred the people of Judah stolen you
away, and brought the king and his house-
hold over the Jordan, and all David's men
with him?" 42 All the people of Judah an-
swered the people of Israel, "Because the
king is near of kin to us. Why then are you
angry over this matter? Have we eaten at
all at the king's expense? Or has he given us
any gift?" 43 But the people of Israel an-
swered the people of Judah, "We have ten
shares in the king, and in David also we
have more than you. Why then did you de-
spise us? Were we not the first to speak of
bringing back our king?" But the words of
the people of Judah were fiercer than the
words of the people of Israel.

a Or *Merib-baal*: See 4.4 note *b* Gk Syr Vg: Heb *said, 'I will saddle a donkey for myself*

25–30: *Ziba* had accused Merib-baal of plotting to take the throne (16.1–4). Merib-baal here defends himself, saying that Ziba refused to help him to flee with David, and he could not leave on his own accord because of his physical condition. David's decision (v. 29) indicates that he does not know which of them is telling the truth. *All my father's house were doomed to death before my lord the king,* a new king often executed all heirs of his predecessor in order to have no rival for the throne. **31–40:** *Barzillai* had helped to provide for David in exile (17.27). David now invites him to come live in his palace in Jerusalem. Barzillai replies that he is too old to enjoy it, but he arranges for the king to take his son Chimham instead. **35:** *Can I discern . . . ,* lit. "Can I know between good and evil?" Cf. Gen 2.9; Isa 7.15. **41:** The army (*people*) of Judah welcomes David back before the army of Israel. **42:** The army of Judah denies that it has received any special favors or bribes from David. **43:** *Ten shares,* the ten northern tribes of Israel.

20 Now a scoundrel named Sheba son
of Bichri, a Benjaminite, happened
to be there. He sounded the trumpet and
cried out,

"We have no portion in David,
no share in the son of Jesse!
Everyone to your tents, O Israel!"

2 So all the people of Israel withdrew from
David and followed Sheba son of Bichri;
but the people of Judah followed their king
steadfastly from the Jordan to Jerusalem.
3 David came to his house at Jerusalem;
and the king took the ten concubines whom
he had left to look after the house, and put
them in a house under guard, and provided
for them, but did not go in to them. So they
were shut up until the day of their death,
living as if in widowhood.
4 Then the king said to Amasa, "Call the
men of Judah together to me within three
days, and be here yourself." 5 So Amasa
went to summon Judah; but he delayed be-
yond the set time that had been appointed
him. 6 David said to Abishai, "Now Sheba
son of Bichri will do us more harm than
Absalom; take your lord's servants and
pursue him, or he will find fortified cities
for himself, and escape from us." 7 Joab's
men went out after him, along with the
Cherethites, the Pelethites, and all the war-
riors; they went out from Jerusalem to pur-
sue Sheba son of Bichri. 8 When they were
at the large stone that is in Gibeon, Amasa
came to meet them. Now Joab was wearing
a soldier's garment and over it was a belt
with a sword in its sheath fastened at his
waist; as he went forward it fell out. 9 Joab
said to Amasa, "Is it well with you, my
brother?" And Joab took Amasa by the
beard with his right hand to kiss him. 10 But
Amasa did not notice the sword in Joab's
hand; Joab struck him in the belly so that
his entrails poured out on the ground, and
he died. He did not strike a second blow.
Then Joab and his brother Abishai pur-
sued Sheba son of Bichri. 11 And one of
Joab's men took his stand by Amasa, and
said, "Whoever favors Joab, and whoever
is for David, let him follow Joab." 12 Amasa
lay wallowing in his blood on the highway,
and the man saw that all the people were
stopping. Since he saw that all who came
by him were stopping, he carried Amasa
from the highway into a field, and threw a
garment over him. 13 Once he was removed
from the highway, all the people went on
after Joab to pursue Sheba son of Bichri.
14 Sheba[a] passed through all the tribes
of Israel to Abel of Beth-maacah;[b] and all
the Bichrites[c] assembled, and followed
him inside. 15 Joab's forces[d] came and be-
sieged him in Abel of Beth-maacah; they
threw up a siege ramp against the city, and
it stood against the rampart. Joab's forces
were battering the wall to break it down.
16 Then a wise woman called from the city,
"Listen! Listen! Tell Joab, 'Come here, I
want to speak to you.' " 17 He came near
her; and the woman said, "Are you Joab?"
He answered, "I am." Then she said to
him, "Listen to the words of your servant."

a Heb *He* *b* Compare 20.15: Heb *and Beth-maacah*
c Compare Gk Vg: Heb *Berites* *d* Heb *They*

20.1–26: Sheba's revolt. 1: *Happened to be there,* at the scene in Gilgal described in 19.41–43. Ch 20 continues that story. *Everyone to your tents,* an idiom for military demobilization; Sheba is calling for the army of Israel to withdraw from David; cf. 1 Kings 12.16. **2:** *All the people of Israel,* the northern tribes. The phrase exaggerates the extent of the northern disaffection with David (see v. 21). **3:** David no longer had sexual relations with the *ten concubines* he had left behind, because Absalom had slept with them (16.20–22). **7:** *The Cherethites* and *Pelethites,* "Cretans" and "Philistines" who composed the royal bodyguard (8.19). **8–10:** *Joab*'s assassination of *Amasa* is similar to his murder of Abner (3.26–39). His implied motive had to do with the fact that Amasa had taken Joab's place as army commander (19.13). His actual motive was more likely political: to rid David of a powerful rival for the leadership of Judah. **13:** *The people,* the army. **14:** *Abel of Beth-maacah* is in the extreme northern part of Israel. **15:** Ancient Israelite cities were surrounded by thick walls that had to be broken through with battering rams. **16:** *Wise woman* (cf. ch 14) in this case could be a title for a city official. She is certainly intelligent and eloquent and acts on behalf of her city. **18:** *Let them inquire at Abel* implies that Abel was a central city

He answered, "I am listening." 18 Then she
said, "They used to say in the old days, 'Let
them inquire at Abel'; and so they would
settle a matter. 19 I am one of those who are
peaceable and faithful in Israel; you seek to
destroy a city that is a mother in Israel; why
will you swallow up the heritage of the
LORD?" 20 Joab answered, "Far be it from
me, far be it, that I should swallow up or
destroy! 21 That is not the case! But a man
of the hill country of Ephraim, called Sheba
son of Bichri, has lifted up his hand against
King David; give him up alone, and I will
withdraw from the city." The woman said
to Joab, "His head shall be thrown over the
wall to you." 22 Then the woman went to
all the people with her wise plan. And they
cut off the head of Sheba son of Bichri, and
threw it out to Joab. So he blew the trum-
pet, and they dispersed from the city, and
all went to their homes, while Joab re-
turned to Jerusalem to the king.

23 Now Joab was in command of all the
army of Israel;[a] Benaiah son of Jehoiada
was in command of the Cherethites and the
Pelethites; 24 Adoram was in charge of the
forced labor; Jehoshaphat son of Ahilud
was the recorder; 25 Sheva was secretary;
Zadok and Abiathar were priests; 26 and Ira
the Jairite was also David's priest.

21 Now there was a famine in the days
of David for three years, year after
year; and David inquired of the LORD. The
LORD said, "There is bloodguilt on Saul
and on his house, because he put the Gibe-
onites to death." 2 So the king called the
Gibeonites and spoke to them. (Now the
Gibeonites were not of the people of Israel,
but of the remnant of the Amorites; al-
though the people of Israel had sworn to
spare them, Saul had tried to wipe them out
in his zeal for the people of Israel and Ju-
dah.) 3 David said to the Gibeonites, "What
shall I do for you? How shall I make expia-
tion, that you may bless the heritage of the
LORD?" 4 The Gibeonites said to him, "It is
not a matter of silver or gold between us
and Saul or his house; neither is it for us to

a Cn: Heb *Joab to all the army, Israel*

for settling legal disputes or for divination. **19:** *A mother in Israel,* a large city, a metropolis. *The heritage of the LORD,* the land and people of Israel; see 1 Sam 10.1. **21:** The woman does not know about Sheba, indicating that his revolt did not reach to all Israel but included only part of Benjamin and *the hill country of Ephraim.* **23–26:** This cabinet list is similar to the one in 8.16–18. It probably came to this location by attachment to 21.1–14. Alternatively, the two lists are used to frame the section, sometimes called "David under the curse." The two lists are probably variants, although according to some scholars they reflect different periods in David's reign. *The Cherethites and the Pelethites,* see v. 7n. *Forced labor,* conscripted from the northern tribes by David and Solomon. *Adoram* or Adoniram (1 Kings 4.6) was later stoned when the Israelites rebelled against the Davidic dynasty (1 Kings 12.18).

Chs 21–24: An appendix of miscellaneous stories and poems. The final four chapters of 2 Samuel contain six passages arranged in symmetrical (chiastic) order: narrative (21.1–14), list (21.15–22), poem (22.1–51), poem (23.1–7), list (23.8–38), narrative (24.1–25). The accumulation of these passages may have come about as follows. 21.1–14 was moved from its original place before ch 9. The motive was likely to lessen the impression that David had Saul's heirs killed for political reasons. The story in 24.1–25 was added to 21.1–14 (see 24.1) and placed as the final episode in David's life before the account of his death because it anticipated the founding of the Temple under Solomon. The lists may have been added next, separating the two narratives. The two psalms were then inserted. Ch 22 is a song of deliverance and praise for victory. It is appropriate following the list of victories in 21.15–22. Then 23.1–7 provides David's "last words," in the tradition of other leading biblical characters.

21.1–14: The execution of Saul's heirs. 1–2: The *Gibeonites* had a special treaty with Israel (Josh 9). This story assumes that the violation of that treaty brought divine wrath. The Hebrew Bible nowhere recounts Saul's attempted extermination of the Gibeonites. *Amorites,* one of several groups of pre-Israelite residents of the land of Canaan, often used in the Deuteronomistic History for all of them. **3:** *The heritage of the LORD,* the land and people of Israel; see 1 Sam 10.1. **4:** The Gibeonites regard this as a matter for blood vengeance, but as resident aliens in Israel they do not have that right. **5–9:** Typically,

put anyone to death in Israel." He said,
"What do you say that I should do for
you?" 5 They said to the king, "The man
who consumed us and planned to destroy
us, so that we should have no place in all
the territory of Israel— 6 let seven of his
sons be handed over to us, and we will im-
pale them before the LORD at Gibeon on
the mountain of the LORD."[a] The king
said, "I will hand them over."

7 But the king spared Mephibosheth,[b]
the son of Saul's son Jonathan, because of
the oath of the LORD that was between
them, between David and Jonathan son of
Saul. 8 The king took the two sons of Riz-
pah daughter of Aiah, whom she bore to
Saul, Armoni and Mephibosheth;[b] and the
five sons of Merab[c] daughter of Saul,
whom she bore to Adriel son of Barzillai
the Meholathite; 9 he gave them into the
hands of the Gibeonites, and they impaled
them on the mountain before the LORD.
The seven of them perished together. They
were put to death in the first days of har-
vest, at the beginning of barley harvest.

10 Then Rizpah the daughter of Aiah
took sackcloth, and spread it on a rock for
herself, from the beginning of harvest until
rain fell on them from the heavens; she did
not allow the birds of the air to come on the
bodies[d] by day, or the wild animals by
night. 11 When David was told what Rizpah
daughter of Aiah, the concubine of Saul,
had done, 12 David went and took the
bones of Saul and the bones of his son Jon-
athan from the people of Jabesh-gilead,
who had stolen them from the public
square of Beth-shan, where the Philistines
had hung them up, on the day the Philis-
tines killed Saul on Gilboa. 13 He brought
up from there the bones of Saul and the
bones of his son Jonathan; and they gath-
ered the bones of those who had been im-
paled. 14 They buried the bones of Saul and
of his son Jonathan in the land of Benjamin
in Zela, in the tomb of his father Kish; they
did all that the king commanded. After
that, God heeded supplications for the
land.

15 The Philistines went to war again
with Israel, and David went down together
with his servants. They fought against the
Philistines, and David grew weary. 16 Ishbi-
benob, one of the descendants of the giants,
whose spear weighed three hundred shekels
of bronze, and who was fitted out with new
weapons,[e] said he would kill David. 17 But
Abishai son of Zeruiah came to his aid, and
attacked the Philistine and killed him. Then
David's men swore to him, "You shall not
go out with us to battle any longer, so that
you do not quench the lamp of Israel."

18 After this a battle took place with the
Philistines, at Gob; then Sibbecai the Hu-
shathite killed Saph, who was one of the
descendants of the giants. 19 Then there was
another battle with the Philistines at Gob;

a Cn Compare Gk and 21.9: Heb *at Gibeah of Saul, the chosen of the LORD* *b* Or *Merib-baal*: See 4.4 note *c* Two Heb Mss Syr Compare Gk: MT *Michal* *d* Heb *them* *e* Heb *was belted anew*

the founder of a new dynasty annihilated the potential claimants from the previous dynasty as David does here. Saul's alleged offense provides a religious legitimation for this political act. Only Merib-baal is spared (v. 7), probably because he is crippled and therefore cannot be king, though this may also reflect David's relationship with Jonathan (see 1 Sam 18.1–3; 20.17,41–42). This event took place early in David's reign over Israel and originally came before 9.1, where David asks if anyone is left in Saul's house. *Sons* (v. 6) also includes grandsons. *Mephibosheth* (v. 8), not Jonathan's son, Merib-baal, who was spared. The *barley harvest* was in April-May. **10:** *Rizpah* was Saul's concubine (3.7–11). **11–14:** As a result of Rizpah's action, David tries to honor the memory of Saul and Jonathan; see 1 Sam 31.12–13.

21.15–22: Stories from the Philistine wars. The stories recounted here come from the battles with the Philistines earlier in David's reign. **16:** *Three hundred shekels* was about 3.5 kg (8 lb). **17:** The insistence of David's men that he not go to battle may lie behind 11.1; 18.3. **19:** This represents an earlier tradition than 1 Sam 17 concerning the death of Goliath; the otherwise unknown Elhanan, rather than David, slays him. The story in 1 Samuel is an elaboration and reworking of this tradition, attributing the victory to the better-known David, cf. 1 Chr 20.5.

and Elhanan son of Jaare-oregim, the Beth-
lehemite, killed Goliath the Gittite, the
shaft of whose spear was like a weaver's
beam. 20 There was again war at Gath,
where there was a man of great size, who
had six fingers on each hand, and six toes
on each foot, twenty-four in number; he
too was descended from the giants. 21 When
he taunted Israel, Jonathan son of David's
brother Shimei, killed him. 22 These four
were descended from the giants in Gath;
they fell by the hands of David and his ser-
vants.

22 David spoke to the LORD the words
of this song on the day when the
LORD delivered him from the hand of all
his enemies, and from the hand of Saul.
2 He said:

The LORD is my rock, my fortress,
and my deliverer,
3 my God, my rock, in whom I take
refuge,
my shield and the horn of my
salvation,
my stronghold and my refuge,
my savior; you save me from
violence.
4 I call upon the LORD, who is worthy
to be praised,
and I am saved from my enemies.

5 For the waves of death encompassed
me,
the torrents of perdition assailed
me;
6 the cords of Sheol entangled me,
the snares of death confronted me.

7 In my distress I called upon the LORD;
to my God I called.
From his temple he heard my voice,
and my cry came to his ears.

8 Then the earth reeled and rocked;
the foundations of the heavens
trembled
and quaked, because he was angry.
9 Smoke went up from his nostrils,
and devouring fire from his mouth;
glowing coals flamed forth from
him.
10 He bowed the heavens, and came
down;
thick darkness was under his feet.
11 He rode on a cherub, and flew;
he was seen upon the wings of the
wind.
12 He made darkness around him a
canopy,
thick clouds, a gathering of water.
13 Out of the brightness before him
coals of fire flamed forth.
14 The LORD thundered from heaven;
the Most High uttered his voice.
15 He sent out arrows, and scattered
them
—lightning, and routed them.
16 Then the channels of the sea were
seen,
the foundations of the world were
laid bare
at the rebuke of the LORD,
at the blast of the breath of his
nostrils.

17 He reached from on high, he
took me,
he drew me out of mighty waters.
18 He delivered me from my strong
enemy,

22.1–51: A psalm of praise. This psalm, which is essentially the same as Psalm 18, was written long after David's time but is inserted here as appropriate to his sentiments. The psalm praises the LORD for appearing to rescue the psalmist (vv. 1–20) and for continued support of the psalmist's military activities (vv. 21–51). Its placement following the exploits of David's heroes in 21.15–22 and David's own rescue (vv. 15–17) is appropriate. **2–3:** *Rock,* a metaphor for the LORD as protector. **5–6:** *Perdition,* the underworld, the abode of the dead, known in the Bible as *Sheol.* **7:** *Temple* suggests that this psalm was written after David, since the Temple was built by Solomon, although it may refer to God's heavenly abode (see Ps 11.4). **8:** The LORD's appearance is accompanied by earthquake. **9:** The LORD is pictured here as a fire-breathing dragon. **11–16:** The LORD is depicted here as the storm God. *Cherub* (v. 11), a

from those who hated me;
for they were too mighty for me.
19 They came upon me in the day of my calamity,
but the LORD was my stay.
20 He brought me out into a broad place;
he delivered me, because he delighted in me.

21 The LORD rewarded me according to my righteousness;
according to the cleanness of my hands he recompensed me.
22 For I have kept the ways of the LORD,
and have not wickedly departed from my God.
23 For all his ordinances were before me,
and from his statutes I did not turn aside.
24 I was blameless before him,
and I kept myself from guilt.
25 Therefore the LORD has recompensed me according to my righteousness,
according to my cleanness in his sight.

26 With the loyal you show yourself loyal;
with the blameless you show yourself blameless;
27 with the pure you show yourself pure,
and with the crooked you show yourself perverse.
28 You deliver a humble people,
but your eyes are upon the haughty to bring them down.
29 Indeed, you are my lamp, O LORD,
the LORD lightens my darkness.
30 By you I can crush a troop,
and by my God I can leap over a wall.
31 This God—his way is perfect;
the promise of the LORD proves true;
he is a shield for all who take refuge in him.

32 For who is God, but the LORD?
And who is a rock, except our God?
33 The God who has girded me with strength[a]
has opened wide my path.[b]
34 He made my[c] feet like the feet of deer,
and set me secure on the heights.
35 He trains my hands for war,
so that my arms can bend a bow of bronze.
36 You have given me the shield of your salvation,
and your help[d] has made me great.
37 You have made me stride freely,
and my feet do not slip;
38 I pursued my enemies and destroyed them,
and did not turn back until they were consumed.
39 I consumed them; I struck them down, so that they did not rise;
they fell under my feet.
40 For you girded me with strength for the battle;
you made my assailants sink under me.
41 You made my enemies turn their backs to me,
those who hated me, and I destroyed them.
42 They looked, but there was no one to save them;
they cried to the LORD, but he did not answer them.
43 I beat them fine like the dust of the earth,

a Q Ms Gk Syr Vg Compare Ps 18.32: MT *God is my strong refuge* *b* Meaning of Heb uncertain *c* Another reading is *his* *d* Q Ms: MT *your answering*

mythical, griffin-like creature. God's *voice* (v. 14) is thunder (Job 40.9; Ps 29.3), and he throws *lightning* bolts at his enemies (v. 15). The psalmist envisions the world as flat; he is trapped in the underworld beneath *the foundations of the world,* which the LORD's roar uncovers (v. 16). **32:** This is a monotheistic claim; the LORD (Yahweh) alone is God. **33–43:** The LORD equips the psalmist for battle. **47:** *Rock,* see

I crushed them and stamped them
down like the mire of the
streets.

44 You delivered me from strife with the
peoples;[a]
you kept me as the head of the
nations;
people whom I had not known
served me.
45 Foreigners came cringing to me;
as soon as they heard of me, they
obeyed me.
46 Foreigners lost heart,
and came trembling out of their
strongholds.

47 The LORD lives! Blessed be my rock,
and exalted be my God, the rock of
my salvation,
48 the God who gave me vengeance
and brought down peoples under
me,
49 who brought me out from my
enemies;
you exalted me above my
adversaries,
you delivered me from the violent.

50 For this I will extol you, O LORD,
among the nations,
and sing praises to your name.
51 He is a tower of salvation for his
king,
and shows steadfast love to his
anointed,
to David and his descendants
forever.

23 Now these are the last words of David:
The oracle of David, son of Jesse,
the oracle of the man whom God
exalted,[b]
the anointed of the God of Jacob,
the favorite of the Strong One of
Israel:

2 The spirit of the LORD speaks
through me,
his word is upon my tongue.
3 The God of Israel has spoken,
the Rock of Israel has said to me:
One who rules over people justly,
ruling in the fear of God,
4 is like the light of morning,
like the sun rising on a cloudless
morning,
gleaming from the rain on the
grassy land.

5 Is not my house like this with God?
For he has made with me an
everlasting covenant,
ordered in all things and secure.
Will he not cause to prosper
all my help and my desire?
6 But the godless are[c] all like thorns
that are thrown away;
for they cannot be picked up with
the hand;
7 to touch them one uses an iron bar
or the shaft of a spear.

a Gk: Heb *from strife with my people* *b* Q Ms: MT *who was raised on high* *c* Heb *But worthlessness*

vv. 2–3. **51:** *Steadfast love,* loyalty. *Anointed,* Heb "mashiaḥ" ("messiah"), a royal title appropriate for any king. *David and his descendants,* if original, suggests that the psalm comes from royal circles in Judah.

23.1–7: The last words of David. There may have been a literary tradition in the Bible of ascribing poems to leading characters as their "last words." Compare the poems attributed to Jacob in Gen 49 and to Moses in Deut 32–33. David's last words, though, do not consist of a benediction of Israel. Like Moses, however, David is portrayed as a prophet pronouncing an oracle (23.1–2). The actual date of David's "last words" is uncertain. In contrast to ch 22, 23.1–7 has no parallel in Psalms. **1:** *Anointed,* a royal title, here referring to David, echoing the end of ch 22. *Strong One of Israel,* an epithet for the LORD. **3:** *Rock,* see 22.3,47. **4:** The image of the king as the sun was common in the ancient Near East, especially in Egypt, although less so in Israel. **5:** *House,* the king's (David's) dynasty. *Everlasting covenant,* the LORD's promise of a dynasty for David in 7.16; cf. Ps 89.28–29. **6–7:** These verses continue the image of vv. 3–4. The *godless* are like *thorns* consumed by the sun's heat.

And they are entirely consumed in
fire on the spot.[a]

8 These are the names of the warriors
whom David had: Josheb-basshebeth a
Tahchemonite; he was chief of the Three;[b]
he wielded his spear[c] against eight hun-
dred whom he killed at one time.
9 Next to him among the three warriors
was Eleazar son of Dodo son of Ahohi. He
was with David when they defied the Philis-
tines who were gathered there for battle.
The Israelites withdrew, 10 but he stood his
ground. He struck down the Philistines un-
til his arm grew weary, though his hand
clung to the sword. The LORD brought
about a great victory that day. Then the
people came back to him—but only to strip
the dead.
11 Next to him was Shammah son of
Agee, the Hararite. The Philistines gathered
together at Lehi, where there was a plot of
ground full of lentils; and the army fled
from the Philistines. 12 But he took his
stand in the middle of the plot, defended it,
and killed the Philistines; and the LORD
brought about a great victory.
13 Towards the beginning of harvest
three of the thirty[d] chiefs went down to
join David at the cave of Adullam, while a
band of Philistines was encamped in the
valley of Rephaim. 14 David was then in the
stronghold; and the garrison of the Philis-
tines was then at Bethlehem. 15 David said
longingly, "O that someone would give me
water to drink from the well of Bethlehem
that is by the gate!" 16 Then the three war-
riors broke through the camp of the Philis-
tines, drew water from the well of Bethle-
hem that was by the gate, and brought it to
David. But he would not drink of it; he
poured it out to the LORD, 17 for he said,
"The LORD forbid that I should do this.
Can I drink the blood of the men who went
at the risk of their lives?" Therefore he
would not drink it. The three warriors did
these things.
18 Now Abishai son of Zeruiah, the
brother of Joab, was chief of the Thirty.[e]
With his spear he fought against three hun-
dred men and killed them, and won a name
beside the Three. 19 He was the most re-
nowned of the Thirty,[f] and became their
commander; but he did not attain to the
Three.
20 Benaiah son of Jehoiada was a val-
iant warrior[g] from Kabzeel, a doer of great
deeds; he struck down two sons of Ariel[h]
of Moab. He also went down and killed a
lion in a pit on a day when snow had fallen.
21 And he killed an Egyptian, a handsome
man. The Egyptian had a spear in his hand;
but Benaiah went against him with a staff,
snatched the spear out of the Egyptian's
hand, and killed him with his own spear.
22 Such were the things Benaiah son of Je-
hoiada did, and won a name beside the
three warriors. 23 He was renowned among
the Thirty, but he did not attain to the
Three. And David put him in charge of his
bodyguard.
24 Among the Thirty were Asahel
brother of Joab; Elhanan son of Dodo of

a Heb *in sitting* *b* Gk Vg Compare 1 Chr 11.11: Meaning of Heb uncertain *c* 1 Chr 11.11: Meaning of Heb uncertain *d* Heb adds *head* *e* Two Heb Mss Syr: MT *Three* *f* Syr Compare 1 Chr 11.25: Heb *Was he the most renowned of the Three?* *g* Another reading is *the son of Ish-hai* *h* Gk: Heb lacks *sons of*

23.8–39: David's heroes. 8–12: Nothing more is known about *the Three* greatest warriors in David's army. **13–17:** This story is not about the three warriors just listed but about three anonymous members of the honor guard of *the thirty.* **13:** *The beginning of harvest,* the weather was hot and dry, which is why David became thirsty. *The cave of Adullam,* "cave" may be an error for "stronghold"; the two words are similar in Hebrew. *Adullam* was David's headquarters and hideout when he fled from Saul (cf. 1 Sam 22.1–4). **14:** *Stronghold,* the fortress at Adullam. Since a *garrison of the Philistines was then at Bethlehem,* this must have been early in David's reign or even before he became king. *Bethlehem,* David's hometown, hence his fond remembrance of the water there. **16–17:** *He poured it out to the LORD,* a libation or sacrifice to God, a great honor to the three men. **20–23:** *Benaiah,* the commander of David's bodyguard and later of the army under Solomon. **24:** *Asahel* seems to be a young warrior aspiring to

Bethlehem; 25 Shammah of Harod; Elika of
Harod; 26 Helez the Paltite; Ira son of Ik-
kesh of Tekoa; 27 Abiezer of Anathoth; Me-
bunnai the Hushathite; 28 Zalmon the Aho-
hite; Maharai of Netophah; 29 Heleb son of
Baanah of Netophah; Ittai son of Ribai of
Gibeah of the Benjaminites; 30 Benaiah of
Pirathon; Hiddai of the torrents of Gaash;
31 Abi-albon the Arbathite; Azmaveth of
Bahurim; 32 Eliahba of Shaalbon; the sons
of Jashen: Jonathan 33 son of[a] Shammah
the Hararite; Ahiam son of Sharar the
Hararite; 34 Eliphelet son of Ahasbai of
Maacah; Eliam son of Ahithophel the Gilo-
nite; 35 Hezro[b] of Carmel; Paarai the
Arbite; 36 Igal son of Nathan of Zobah;
Bani the Gadite; 37 Zelek the Ammonite; Na-
harai of Beeroth, the armor-bearer of Joab
son of Zeruiah; 38 Ira the Ithrite; Gareb
the Ithrite; 39 Uriah the Hittite—thirty-seven
in all.

24 Again the anger of the LORD was
kindled against Israel, and he incit-
ed David against them, saying, "Go, count
the people of Israel and Judah." 2 So the
king said to Joab and the commanders of
the army,[c] who were with him, "Go
through all the tribes of Israel, from Dan to
Beer-sheba, and take a census of the peo-
ple, so that I may know how many there
are." 3 But Joab said to the king, "May the
LORD your God increase the number of the
people a hundredfold, while the eyes of my
lord the king can still see it! But why does
my lord the king want to do this?" 4 But the
king's word prevailed against Joab and the
commanders of the army. So Joab and the
commanders of the army went out from
the presence of the king to take a census of
the people of Israel. 5 They crossed the Jor-
dan, and began from[d] Aroer and from the
city that is in the middle of the valley, to-
ward Gad and on to Jazer. 6 Then they
came to Gilead, and to Kadesh in the land
of the Hittites;[e] and they came to Dan, and
from Dan[f] they went around to Sidon,
7 and came to the fortress of Tyre and to all
the cities of the Hivites and Canaanites;
and they went out to the Negeb of Judah

a Gk: Heb lacks *son of*   *b* Another reading is *Hezrai*
c 1 Chr 21.2 Gk: Heb *to Joab the commander of the army*   *d* Gk Mss: Heb *encamped in Aroer south of*
e Gk: Heb *to the land of Tahtim-hodshi*
f Cn Compare Gk: Heb *they came to Dan-jaan and*

greatness in the story of his death (2.18–23). *Elhanan* killed Goliath (21.19). **30:** *Benaiah,* a different man from the Benaiah in vv. 20–23. **39:** *Uriah,* Bathsheba's husband (ch 11). It is uncertain how the count of *thirty-seven* is achieved. The list in vv. 24–39 has thirty names in it. The addition of the "Three" plus Abishai and Benaiah brings the number to thirty-five. Joab may have been counted as a member of this elite group, though his name is not specifically mentioned. There are textual variations in vv. 24–39 where an additional name may have been read.

24.1–25: David's census. The final story in 2 Samuel. It must be remembered that 2 Samuel and 1 Kings were originally part of a larger work and not separate books. This story, then, was not written as a conclusion to 2 Samuel. Rather, it anticipates the building of the Temple under Solomon (vv. 18–25; see 1 Kings chs 5–6; 8) and thus looks forward to the important results of David's reign. **1:** *Again* implies that this story is the sequel to an earlier one, perhaps 21.1–14. This same story is found in 1 Chr 21, which says that Satan rather than the anger of the LORD *incited* David. It is only in postexilic texts that (the) Satan becomes important in biblical Israel. Both reflect the typical biblical belief that natural calamity is the result of human sin. It is not clear why taking a census was sinful. Some scholars suggest it was a sign of David's inordinate pride or that the census was meant to bring about unacceptable changes in Israelite society. (A census usually provided the basis for conscription and taxation.) Another possibility is that all men enrolled in the census were required to be ritually pure as when they went to battle, and this requirement was easily broken. **2:** *From Dan to Beer-sheba,* the traditional northern and southern limits of Israel. **5–7:** The census takers began at *Aroer* east of the Dead Sea and moved north as far as *Dan,* then crossed over the Jordan and went south through traditional Israel until they reached *Beer-sheba.* **9:** The count is limited to men of military age. *Thousand* may refer to a much smaller military unit. Israel and

at Beer-sheba. 8 So when they had gone
through all the land, they came back to
Jerusalem at the end of nine months and
twenty days. 9 Joab reported to the king the
number of those who had been recorded: in
Israel there were eight hundred thousand
soldiers able to draw the sword, and those
of Judah were five hundred thousand.
10 But afterward, David was stricken
to the heart because he had numbered the
people. David said to the LORD, "I have
sinned greatly in what I have done. But
now, O LORD, I pray you, take away the
guilt of your servant; for I have done very
foolishly." 11 When David rose in the
morning, the word of the LORD came to the
prophet Gad, David's seer, saying, 12 "Go
and say to David: Thus says the LORD:
Three things I offer[a] you; choose one of
them, and I will do it to you." 13 So Gad
came to David and told him; he asked him,
"Shall three[b] years of famine come to you
on your land? Or will you flee three months
before your foes while they pursue you? Or
shall there be three days' pestilence in your
land? Now consider, and decide what an-
swer I shall return to the one who sent me."
14 Then David said to Gad, "I am in great
distress; let us fall into the hand of the
LORD, for his mercy is great; but let me not
fall into human hands."
15 So the LORD sent a pestilence on Isra-
el from that morning until the appointed
time; and seventy thousand of the people
died, from Dan to Beer-sheba. 16 But when
the angel stretched out his hand toward Je-
rusalem to destroy it, the LORD relented
concerning the evil, and said to the angel
who was bringing destruction among the
people, "It is enough; now stay your
hand." The angel of the LORD was then by
the threshing floor of Araunah the Jebusite.
17 When David saw the angel who was de-
stroying the people, he said to the LORD, "I
alone have sinned, and I alone have done
wickedly; but these sheep, what have they
done? Let your hand, I pray, be against me
and against my father's house."
18 That day Gad came to David and
said to him, "Go up and erect an altar to
the LORD on the threshing floor of Arau-
nah the Jebusite." 19 Following Gad's in-
structions, David went up, as the LORD had
commanded. 20 When Araunah looked
down, he saw the king and his servants
coming toward him; and Araunah went out
and prostrated himself before the king with
his face to the ground. 21 Araunah said,
"Why has my lord the king come to his
servant?" David said, "To buy the thresh-
ing floor from you in order to build an altar
to the LORD, so that the plague may be
averted from the people." 22 Then Araunah
said to David, "Let my lord the king take
and offer up what seems good to him; here
are the oxen for the burnt offering, and the
threshing sledges and the yokes of the oxen
for the wood. 23 All this, O king, Araunah

a Or *hold over* *b* 1 Chr 21.12 Gk: Heb *seven*

Judah are numbered separately because Judah, as David's native tribe, was exempted from taxation. **10–14:** *Stricken to the heart,* conscience-stricken; the language David uses is similar to 2 Sam 12.13. David is given a choice of three punishments. He chooses *the hand of the LORD,* an idiom for plague, trusting in the LORD's mercy. **15–16:** David's strategy works. The plague is stopped after only one day and Jerusalem is spared. *The appointed time* (v. 15) may be the time of the evening meal. *Thousand* may be a military unit of much fewer than 1,000. *Evil* (v. 16), not moral evil but destruction. *Araunah,* called Ornan in 1 Chr 21. *Jebusite,* a pre-Israelite native of Jerusalem (5.6–10). *Threshing floor,* a flat, high area where grain was separated from the chaff. God also appears to people at threshing floors elsewhere in the Bible (Judg 6.11–12). **17:** *Sheep,* the people of Jerusalem with David, as king, imagined as their shepherd; see 7.8n. **18–25:** These verses indicate that the plague was stopped after David built his altar and made his offerings rather than by the LORD's free will as in v. 16. The site of David's altar is the location of the later altar of burnt offering of Solomon's Temple. *Fifty shekels* was about .57 kg (1.25 lb).

gives to the king." And Araunah said to the
king, "May the LORD your God respond
favorably to you."
24 But the king said to Araunah, "No,
but I will buy them from you for a price; I
will not offer burnt offerings to the LORD
my God that cost me nothing." So David
bought the threshing floor and the oxen for
fifty shekels of silver. 25 David built there
an altar to the LORD, and offered burnt
offerings and offerings of well-being. So the
LORD answered his supplication for the
land, and the plague was averted from Is-
rael.

1 KINGS

First Kings continues the story of Israel begun in the early chapters of Genesis, carrying forward in particular the account of the period of the monarchy already begun in 1–2 Samuel. It opens with the transition of power from David to Solomon (chs 1–2) and proceeds to recount the reign of Solomon over a united Israel (chs 3–11) and the subsequent history of the divided kingdoms of (northern) Israel and (southern) Judah through to the reigns of Ahaziah of Israel and Jehoshaphat of Judah (chs 12–22). The artificial break between First and Second Kings right in the middle of the account of Ahaziah's reign (1 Kings 22.51–2 Kings 1.18) is evidence that they originally formed one book, relating Israel's story under kingly rule from the death of David until the exile. The division into two books was originally made in the ancient Greek translation, the Septuagint (LXX), of the Hebrew Bible.

The books of Kings probably resulted from a long process of collecting, writing, editing, and revising diverse materials that themselves were based upon written documents or oral traditions. Among the written documents we must no doubt include temple and palace annals (for instance, the Book of the Acts of Solomon, 11.41; the Book of the Annals of the Kings of Israel, 14.19; and the Book of the Annals of the Kings of Judah, 14.29). Some scholars have thought that the opening two chapters of 1 Kings belonged originally to an extended narrative about David's reign known as the Succession or Court Narrative. Among the oral traditions, we should think primarily of the stories of Elijah and Elisha in 1 Kings 17–19,21 and 2 Kings 1–8, although other prophetical cycles of stories may also have existed. Decisive moments in this process of composition may have occurred as early as the reigns of the reforming kings Hezekiah and Josiah (eighth-seventh centuries BCE), with revisions taking place after 586 BCE in light of the Judean exile. Those involved in the process seem to have been particularly influenced by the book of Deuteronomy, whose language and theological themes are prominent (for instance, in the long review of the history of Israel in 2 Kings 17). For this reason 1–2 Kings are often thought of as comprising part of a "Deuteronomistic History" that includes Joshua, Judges, and Samuel. The close connection between Deuteronomy and Kings should not, however, distract attention from the many ways in which 1–2 Kings also invite reflection in the light of Pentateuchal writings (especially the book of Exodus) and of the latter prophets. The process of composition was also a process by which different biblical books were progressively viewed more and more as one scripture.

In summarizing the character of the books of Kings, we should emphasize three distinct but interrelated features. First of all, these books tell us a story, bound together by multiple verbal and thematic links between its parts—they are *narrative* literature. The main characters in this story are the LORD God of Israel, various Israelite kings and prophets, and a number of significant foreigners. The plot concerns the attempt Israel makes (or more often, fails to make) under its monarchy to live as the people of God in the promised land, and how God deals with his people in their success and failure. It is a plot worked out in an ordered way, as the reign of each king finds its particular place in the framework (the so-called "regnal formulae") around which the books are constructed. This framework (e.g., 22.41–43,45,50) characteristically tells us when, in relation to another king, a certain monarch came to the throne; how long he reigned; and the name of his capital city. It gives us information about his death/burial and his successor, and tells us where to look for further information about him. It offers an evaluation of him in terms of his religious policy. In the case of Judean (rather than northern Israelite) kings, it tells us the name of his mother and his age at his accession to the throne. These formulae, with their general regularity of expression throughout Kings, contribute much to the books' sense of coherence. The narrative more generally also gives every impression of the care and artistry exercised by the authors as they composed them.

The story told in Kings is, secondly, a story about the past. We are dealing here with *historiographical* literature. For all the narrative artistry involved in the telling, there is a concern to write about a real past that is shared by other peoples in the ancient Near East (whose own records frequently shed light on this period of Israel's history). The concern is best evidenced in the frequent reference to royal annals that may otherwise be consulted by the original reader (e.g., 14.29; 15.31). The portrait painted of the past is naturally only one among the many that it might have been possible to paint. It is clear on any reading of Kings that the authors do not tell us everything that happened in the region of Palestine during that part of the Iron Age about which they are writing, nor do they claim to do so. Theirs is a highly selective account, in which fairly long periods can be passed over very briefly, and periods of a year or less can occupy considerable space. They present a particular view of the past, with its own highlights and its own persuasive appeal. All historiographers must inevitably do this—a point whose force has not always been grasped by those who in recent years have expressed skepticism about the idea that literature like Kings should be regarded as historiographical literature. The political history of Israel, for our biblical authors, is important not so much in itself as for what it reveals about the moral and religious failure that eventually led to the loss of national identity and autonomy. This failure is rooted especially in the apostasy of Solomon (ch 11), which precedes the long and troubled story of the divided kingdoms, and of Jeroboam who, as the first king of the North, fell away from God's (and David's) ways and paved the way in this respect for his successors (chs 11–14).

Finally, the books of Kings are *didactic literature*. They seek to teach their readers something about the God of Israel and his ways. Several themes are prominent in the story when viewed from this perspective. The first is that the LORD is indeed God, and must not be confused with the various gods worshiped within Israel and outside, which are simply human creations (see 12.25–30; 2 Kings 19.14–19). The LORD is the incomparable creator of heaven and earth, distinct from the world that he has created, yet powerfully active within it. It is he, and not any god, who controls nature (e.g., chs 17–19). It is he, and neither god, nor king, nor prophet, who controls history (see 22.1–38; 2 Kings 5.1–18). This latter point is perhaps illustrated most clearly in the way that prophets generally function within Kings, describing the future before God brings it about (e.g., 11.29–39; 2 Kings 17.13). A second theme is that as the only God there is, the LORD demands exclusive worship. Much of 1–2 Kings is therefore concerned to describe what is illegitimate in terms of worship. The main interest is in the *content* of this worship, which must not involve idols or images, nor reflect any aspect of the fertility and other rituals of "the nations" (see 11.1–40; 12.25–13.34). There is an accompanying concern about the *place* of worship, which is ideally the Jerusalem Temple, and not the local "high places" (see 3.2; 15.14). The books also elaborate the moral wrongs that inevitably accompany false worship (see ch 21; 2 Kings 16.1–4). Third, as the giver of the law that defines true worship, right thinking, and overall behavior, the LORD is also one who executes judgment upon wrongdoers. The world of Kings is a moral world, in which wrongdoing is punished, whether the sinner be king (11.9–13), prophet (13.7–25), or ordinary Israelite (2 Kings 7.17–20). There is, on the other hand, no neat correlation between sin and judgment in Kings, largely because of the compassionate character of the Judge who accepts the repentant sinner, who does not desire final judgment to fall upon his creatures (see 2 Kings 13.23; 14.27), and who is always ready to find cause why such judgment should be delayed or mitigated (as in 21.25–28; 2 Kings 22.15–20). Yet sin can, nevertheless, accumulate to such an extent that judgment falls not only upon individuals but upon whole cultures, sweeping the relatively innocent away with the guilty (see 2 Kings 23.29–25.26). A final prominent theme in Kings is divine promise, especially the repeated promise to David that he should have an eternal dynasty (11.36; 15.4); note also the reference to the promise to Israel's ancestors in 2 Kings 13.23. These promises each in their own way hold out hope for Israel that, even after the exile, there may be forgiveness in place of judgment (see 8.22–53) and a future for the Davidic line through the descendants of King Jehoiachin (see 2 Kings 25.27–30).

1 King David was old and advanced in
years; and although they covered him
with clothes, he could not get warm. 2 So
his servants said to him, "Let a young vir-
gin be sought for my lord the king, and let
her wait on the king, and be his attendant;
let her lie in your bosom, so that my lord
the king may be warm." 3 So they searched
for a beautiful girl throughout all the terri-
tory of Israel, and found Abishag the Shu-
nammite, and brought her to the king.
4 The girl was very beautiful. She became
the king's attendant and served him, but
the king did not know her sexually.
5 Now Adonijah son of Haggith exalted
himself, saying, "I will be king"; he pre-
pared for himself chariots and horsemen,
and fifty men to run before him. 6 His fa-
ther had never at any time displeased him
by asking, "Why have you done thus and
so?" He was also a very handsome man,
and he was born next after Absalom. 7 He
conferred with Joab son of Zeruiah and
with the priest Abiathar, and they support-
ed Adonijah. 8 But the priest Zadok, and
Benaiah son of Jehoiada, and the prophet
Nathan, and Shimei, and Rei, and David's
own warriors did not side with Adonijah.
9 Adonijah sacrificed sheep, oxen, and
fatted cattle by the stone Zoheleth, which
is beside En-rogel, and he invited all his
brothers, the king's sons, and all the royal
officials of Judah, 10 but he did not invite
the prophet Nathan or Benaiah or the war-
riors or his brother Solomon.
11 Then Nathan said to Bathsheba, Sol-
omon's mother, "Have you not heard that
Adonijah son of Haggith has become king

1.1–53: Solomon becomes king. The opening chapters of 1 Kings are the last chapter of the story of David as much as the first of the story of Solomon (see Introduction to 2 Samuel). They resolve the question of how God's promise to raise up one of David's sons and establish his kingdom forever (2 Sam 7.12–13) is to be fulfilled. **1–4:** The *Abishag* incident suggests to the watching court that the aging David has lost his virility (see v. 4b), and thus his ability to govern (contrast the David of 2 Sam 11). **3:** *Shunammite,* from the town of Shunem in northern Israel. **5–6:** *Adonijah* was the fourth of David's sons born in Hebron (2 Sam 3.2–5) and apparently the eldest surviving. Amnon and Absalom had died (2 Sam 14; 18), and Chileab is absent from the narrative after 2 Sam 3. It is not clear to what extent the eldest son was normally expected in Israel to succeed his father to the throne (e.g., see 2 Kings 23.31–37), but Adonijah appears to have been regarded by at least some (and by himself) as having a particular claim. He is presented as similar in several ways to *Absalom* (see 2 Sam 14.25–26; 15.1), perhaps with the hint that similar disaster awaits him. **7–10:** Support divides between Adonijah and Solomon partly in terms of how long the parties named have been associated with David. *Joab* and *Abiathar* have deep roots in David's Judean past (see 1 Sam 22.20–23; 2 Sam 2–3). The opposing group contains some such men (e.g., *Benaiah* and *David's own warriors,* see 2 Sam 23.8–39), but also others who either do not appear in the narrative before David's move from his Hebron stronghold to Jerusalem in 2 Sam 5.6–10 (*Nathan* and *Zadok*) or who are previous antagonists of David's from the house of Saul (*Shimei,* 2 Sam 16.5–14). These support the Jerusalem-born Solomon. **9:** *En-rogel,* "the fuller's spring," just south of Jerusalem. **11–27:** Whether David ever really had sworn an (otherwise unrecorded) oath to *Bathsheba* (v. 13), or whether she and Nathan are trying to manipulate the ailing king, is unclear. Their approach to him is cleverly designed to avoid the impression of collusion. **33:** *Gihon,* the main spring of Jerusalem, on the

and our lord David does not know it?
12 Now therefore come, let me give you ad-
vice, so that you may save your own life
and the life of your son Solomon. 13 Go in
at once to King David, and say to him, 'Did
you not, my lord the king, swear to your
servant, saying: Your son Solomon shall
succeed me as king, and he shall sit on
my throne? Why then is Adonijah king?'
14 Then while you are still there speaking
with the king, I will come in after you and
confirm your words."
15 So Bathsheba went to the king in his
room. The king was very old; Abishag the
Shunammite was attending the king.
16 Bathsheba bowed and did obeisance to
the king, and the king said, "What do you
wish?" 17 She said to him, "My lord, you
swore to your servant by the LORD your
God, saying: Your son Solomon shall suc-
ceed me as king, and he shall sit on my
throne. 18 But now suddenly Adonijah has
become king, though you, my lord the king,
do not know it. 19 He has sacrificed oxen,
fatted cattle, and sheep in abundance, and
has invited all the children of the king, the
priest Abiathar, and Joab the commander
of the army; but your servant Solomon he
has not invited. 20 But you, my lord the
king—the eyes of all Israel are on you to
tell them who shall sit on the throne of my
lord the king after him. 21 Otherwise it will
come to pass, when my lord the king sleeps
with his ancestors, that my son Solomon
and I will be counted offenders."
22 While she was still speaking with the
king, the prophet Nathan came in. 23 The
king was told, "Here is the prophet Na-
than." When he came in before the king, he
did obeisance to the king, with his face to
the ground. 24 Nathan said, "My lord the
king, have you said, 'Adonijah shall suc-
ceed me as king, and he shall sit on my
throne'? 25 For today he has gone down and
has sacrificed oxen, fatted cattle, and sheep
in abundance, and has invited all the king's
children, Joab the commander[a] of the
army, and the priest Abiathar, who are
now eating and drinking before him, and
saying, 'Long live King Adonijah!' 26 But he
did not invite me, your servant, and the
priest Zadok, and Benaiah son of Jehoiada,
and your servant Solomon. 27 Has this
thing been brought about by my lord the
king and you have not let your servants
know who should sit on the throne of my
lord the king after him?"
28 King David answered, "Summon
Bathsheba to me." So she came into the
king's presence, and stood before the king.
29 The king swore, saying, "As the LORD
lives, who has saved my life from every ad-
versity, 30 as I swore to you by the LORD,
the God of Israel, 'Your son Solomon shall
succeed me as king, and he shall sit on my
throne in my place,' so will I do this day."
31 Then Bathsheba bowed with her face to
the ground, and did obeisance to the king,
and said, "May my lord King David live
forever!"
32 King David said, "Summon to me the
priest Zadok, the prophet Nathan, and Be-
naiah son of Jehoiada." When they came
before the king, 33 the king said to them,
"Take with you the servants of your lord,
and have my son Solomon ride on my own
mule, and bring him down to Gihon.
34 There let the priest Zadok and the proph-
et Nathan anoint him king over Israel; then
blow the trumpet, and say, 'Long live King
Solomon!' 35 You shall go up following
him. Let him enter and sit on my throne; he
shall be king in my place; for I have ap-
pointed him to be ruler over Israel and over
Judah." 36 Benaiah son of Jehoiada an-
swered the king, "Amen! May the LORD,
the God of my lord the king, so ordain.
37 As the LORD has been with my lord the
king, so may he be with Solomon, and
make his throne greater than the throne of
my lord King David."
38 So the priest Zadok, the prophet Na-

a Gk: Heb *the commanders*

city's east side (see 2 Chr 32.30). **34:** The precise significance of the anointing of kings in ancient Israel (cf. 1 Sam 9.16; 10.1) is unclear, but at least two elements are involved. It signifies both the consecration of the king and his authorization to rule. **38:** The *Cherethites* and *Pelethites* are probably the servants of

than, and Benaiah son of Jehoiada, and the
Cherethites and the Pelethites, went down
and had Solomon ride on King David's
mule, and led him to Gihon. 39 There the
priest Zadok took the horn of oil from the
tent and anointed Solomon. Then they
blew the trumpet, and all the people said,
"Long live King Solomon!" 40 And all the
people went up following him, playing on
pipes and rejoicing with great joy, so that
the earth quaked at their noise.
41 Adonijah and all the guests who were
with him heard it as they finished feasting.
When Joab heard the sound of the trumpet,
he said, "Why is the city in an uproar?"
42 While he was still speaking, Jonathan son
of the priest Abiathar arrived. Adonijah
said, "Come in, for you are a worthy man
and surely you bring good news." 43 Jona-
than answered Adonijah, "No, for our lord
King David has made Solomon king; 44 the
king has sent with him the priest Zadok,
the prophet Nathan, and Benaiah son of
Jehoiada, and the Cherethites and the Pele-
thites; and they had him ride on the king's
mule; 45 the priest Zadok and the prophet
Nathan have anointed him king at Gihon;
and they have gone up from there rejoicing,
so that the city is in an uproar. This is the
noise that you heard. 46 Solomon now sits
on the royal throne. 47 Moreover the king's
servants came to congratulate our lord
King David, saying, 'May God make the
name of Solomon more famous than yours,
and make his throne greater than your
throne.' The king bowed in worship on the
bed 48 and went on to pray thus, 'Blessed be
the LORD, the God of Israel, who today has
granted one of my offspring[a] to sit on my
throne and permitted me to witness it.' "
49 Then all the guests of Adonijah got
up trembling and went their own ways.
50 Adonijah, fearing Solomon, got up and
went to grasp the horns of the altar. 51 Solo-
mon was informed, "Adonijah is afraid of
King Solomon; see, he has laid hold of the
horns of the altar, saying, 'Let King Solo-
mon swear to me first that he will not kill
his servant with the sword.' " 52 So Solo-
mon responded, "If he proves to be a wor-
thy man, not one of his hairs shall fall to
the ground; but if wickedness is found in
him, he shall die." 53 Then King Solomon
sent to have him brought down from the
altar. He came to do obeisance to King
Solomon; and Solomon said to him, "Go
home."

2 When David's time to die drew near, he
charged his son Solomon, saying: 2 "I
am about to go the way of all the earth.
Be strong, be courageous, 3 and keep the
charge of the LORD your God, walking in
his ways and keeping his statutes, his com-
mandments, his ordinances, and his testi-
monies, as it is written in the law of Moses,
so that you may prosper in all that you do
and wherever you turn. 4 Then the LORD
will establish his word that he spoke con-
cerning me: 'If your heirs take heed to their
way, to walk before me in faithfulness with

a Gk: Heb *one*

v. 33—David's own personal troops, most likely of Cretan and Philistine origin. **39:** *Horn of oil,* see 1 Sam 16.1n. *Tent,* where the ark of the covenant was kept; see 2 Sam 6.17; 7.2. **40:** *Pipes,* elsewhere the NRSV translates as "flutes." **50:** Adonijah seeks refuge in the tent of the LORD, grasping *the horns of the altar* (projections at the four corners of the altar, see Ex 29.12; 30.10; Lev 4.7; Ps 118.27), because sacred areas were often places of asylum and refuge (but see Ex 21.12–14). He is confident that Solomon will not inflict violence upon him there (but see 2.29–30).

2.1–46: David's last instructions and Solomon's consolidation of his position. 1–4: David's parting words to Solomon are similar to God's words to Joshua upon his succession to the leadership of Israel after Moses' death (Josh 1.6–9). The exercise of royal power must not be arbitrary, for the king is not a law unto himself. It must be in accordance with *the law of Moses;* vv. 3–4 point in particular to the book of Deuteronomy (see Deut 4.29; 6.2; 8.6; 9.5; 11.1; 29.9). The continuance of the dynasty apparently depends upon obedience to this law code, as in the law of the king in Deut 17.18–20 (see Ps 132.12, but cf. 2 Sam 7.14–16). This last text is itself reflected in some passages in Kings (e.g., 15.4), resulting in some tension in the book between conditional and unconditional divine promises to the dynasty. **5–11:** In singling

all their heart and with all their soul, there
shall not fail you a successor on the throne
of Israel.'
5 "Moreover you know also what Joab
son of Zeruiah did to me, how he dealt
with the two commanders of the armies of
Israel, Abner son of Ner, and Amasa son of
Jether, whom he murdered, retaliating in
time of peace for blood that had been shed
in war, and putting the blood of war on the
belt around his waist, and on the sandals
on his feet. 6 Act therefore according to
your wisdom, but do not let his gray head
go down to Sheol in peace. 7 Deal loyally,
however, with the sons of Barzillai the Gile-
adite, and let them be among those who eat
at your table; for with such loyalty they met
me when I fled from your brother Absalom.
8 There is also with you Shimei son of Gera,
the Benjaminite from Bahurim, who cursed
me with a terrible curse on the day when
I went to Mahanaim; but when he came
down to meet me at the Jordan, I swore to
him by the LORD, 'I will not put you to
death with the sword.' 9 Therefore do not
hold him guiltless, for you are a wise man;
you will know what you ought to do to
him, and you must bring his gray head
down with blood to Sheol."
10 Then David slept with his ancestors,
and was buried in the city of David. 11 The
time that David reigned over Israel was for-
ty years; he reigned seven years in Hebron,
and thirty-three years in Jerusalem. 12 So
Solomon sat on the throne of his father
David; and his kingdom was firmly estab-
lished.
13 Then Adonijah son of Haggith came
to Bathsheba, Solomon's mother. She
asked, "Do you come peaceably?" He said,
"Peaceably." 14 Then he said, "May I have
a word with you?" She said, "Go on."
15 He said, "You know that the kingdom
was mine, and that all Israel expected me to
reign; however, the kingdom has turned
about and become my brother's, for it was
his from the LORD. 16 And now I have one
request to make of you; do not refuse me."
She said to him, "Go on." 17 He said,
"Please ask King Solomon—he will not re-
fuse you—to give me Abishag the Shunam-
mite as my wife." 18 Bathsheba said, "Very
well; I will speak to the king on your be-
half."
19 So Bathsheba went to King Solomon,
to speak to him on behalf of Adonijah. The
king rose to meet her, and bowed down to
her; then he sat on his throne, and had a
throne brought for the king's mother, and
she sat on his right. 20 Then she said, "I
have one small request to make of you; do
not refuse me." And the king said to her,
"Make your request, my mother; for I will
not refuse you." 21 She said, "Let Abishag
the Shunammite be given to your brother
Adonijah as his wife." 22 King Solomon an-
swered his mother, "And why do you ask
Abishag the Shunammite for Adonijah?
Ask for him the kingdom as well! For he is
my elder brother; ask not only for him but

out *Joab, Barzillai,* and *Shimei* for attention, David suggests to Solomon which kinds of people are to be rewarded and removed if he is to rule in peace over a united Israel. *Barzillai* is a model of dutiful service to his king, rewarded in peaceful fellowship around the king's table (2 Sam 17.27–29; 19.31–39). *Shimei* is a partisan of northern Israel (2 Sam 16.5–14; 19.16–23), and *Joab* is a stalwart of David's Judean past who had previously undermined his attempts at reconciliation between two warring factions within Israel (2 Sam 3.22–30; 20.4–10). David's ruthlessness toward a loyal supporter and his evasion of an earlier oath (2 Sam 19.23) do not reflect well upon him. **11–12:** David died in about 965 BCE. Since Solomon was anointed before his father's death (1.39), Solomon's reign can be dated to about 968–928. **12–35:** The political wisdom that David had urged Solomon to use in ridding himself of Joab and Shimei (vv. 6,9) is now deployed. 2 Sam 16.20–22 suggests that sexual liaison with the king's concubines legitimated a claim to the throne. Adonijah's request of Bathsheba gives Solomon the opportunity to remove from the scene not only his half-brother, but also (vv. 26–27) the priest *Abiathar* (banished from the royal court in fulfillment of 1 Sam 2.27–36) and Joab (struck down at the sacred altar, v. 34; cf. 1.49–53). Solomon is as ruthless as his father. **36–46:** Shimei's house arrest seems designed to prevent him from operating within his own

also for the priest Abiathar and for Joab
son of Zeruiah!" 23 Then King Solomon
swore by the LORD, "So may God do to
me, and more also, for Adonijah has de-
vised this scheme at the risk of his life!
24 Now therefore as the LORD lives, who
has established me and placed me on the
throne of my father David, and who has
made me a house as he promised, today
Adonijah shall be put to death." 25 So King
Solomon sent Benaiah son of Jehoiada; he
struck him down, and he died.

26 The king said to the priest Abiathar,
"Go to Anathoth, to your estate; for you
deserve death. But I will not at this time put
you to death, because you carried the ark of
the Lord GOD before my father David, and
because you shared in all the hardships my
father endured." 27 So Solomon banished
Abiathar from being priest to the LORD,
thus fulfilling the word of the LORD that he
had spoken concerning the house of Eli in
Shiloh.

28 When the news came to Joab—for
Joab had supported Adonijah though he
had not supported Absalom—Joab fled to
the tent of the LORD and grasped the horns
of the altar. 29 When it was told King Solo-
mon, "Joab has fled to the tent of the LORD
and now is beside the altar," Solomon sent
Benaiah son of Jehoiada, saying, "Go,
strike him down." 30 So Benaiah came to
the tent of the LORD and said to him, "The
king commands, 'Come out.'" But he said,
"No, I will die here." Then Benaiah
brought the king word again, saying,
"Thus said Joab, and thus he answered
me." 31 The king replied to him, "Do as he
has said, strike him down and bury him;
and thus take away from me and from my
father's house the guilt for the blood that
Joab shed without cause. 32 The LORD will
bring back his bloody deeds on his own
head, because, without the knowledge of
my father David, he attacked and killed
with the sword two men more righteous
and better than himself, Abner son of Ner,
commander of the army of Israel, and Am-
asa son of Jether, commander of the army
of Judah. 33 So shall their blood come back
on the head of Joab and on the head of his
descendants forever; but to David, and to
his descendants, and to his house, and to
his throne, there shall be peace from the
LORD forevermore." 34 Then Benaiah son
of Jehoiada went up and struck him down
and killed him; and he was buried at his
own house near the wilderness. 35 The king
put Benaiah son of Jehoiada over the army
in his place, and the king put the priest Za-
dok in the place of Abiathar.

36 Then the king sent and summoned
Shimei, and said to him, "Build yourself a
house in Jerusalem, and live there, and do
not go out from there to any place whatev-
er. 37 For on the day you go out, and cross
the Wadi Kidron, know for certain that you
shall die; your blood shall be on your own
head." 38 And Shimei said to the king, "The
sentence is fair; as my lord the king has
said, so will your servant do." So Shimei
lived in Jerusalem many days.

39 But it happened at the end of three
years that two of Shimei's slaves ran away
to King Achish son of Maacah of Gath.
When it was told Shimei, "Your slaves are
in Gath," 40 Shimei arose and saddled a
donkey, and went to Achish in Gath, to
search for his slaves; Shimei went and
brought his slaves from Gath. 41 When Sol-
omon was told that Shimei had gone from
Jerusalem to Gath and returned, 42 the king
sent and summoned Shimei, and said to
him, "Did I not make you swear by the
LORD, and solemnly adjure you, saying,
'Know for certain that on the day you go
out and go to any place whatever, you shall
die'? And you said to me, 'The sentence is
fair; I accept.' 43 Why then have you not
kept your oath to the LORD and the com-
mandment with which I charged you?"
44 The king also said to Shimei, "You know

power-base in Benjamin; he would naturally cross the *Wadi Kidron* (v. 37), on the east side of Jerusalem, if heading there. When he eventually leaves Jerusalem, he heads westward to *Gath* without crossing the Kidron (v. 40), but Solomon takes the opportunity to have him executed anyway (v. 46).

in your own heart all the evil that you did
to my father David; so the LORD will bring
back your evil on your own head. 45 But
King Solomon shall be blessed, and the
throne of David shall be established before
the LORD forever." 46 Then the king com-
manded Benaiah son of Jehoiada; and he
went out and struck him down, and he
died.

So the kingdom was established in the
hand of Solomon.

3 Solomon made a marriage alliance with
Pharaoh king of Egypt; he took Phar-
aoh's daughter and brought her into the
city of David, until he had finished building
his own house and the house of the LORD
and the wall around Jerusalem. 2 The peo-
ple were sacrificing at the high places, how-
ever, because no house had yet been built
for the name of the LORD.

3 Solomon loved the LORD, walking in
the statutes of his father David; only, he
sacrificed and offered incense at the high
places. 4 The king went to Gibeon to sacri-
fice there, for that was the principal high
place; Solomon used to offer a thousand
burnt offerings on that altar. ⑤ At Gibeon
the LORD appeared to Solomon in a dream
by night; and God said, "Ask what I should
give you." 6 And Solomon said, "You have
shown great and steadfast love to your ser-
vant my father David, because he walked
before you in faithfulness, in righteousness,
and in uprightness of heart toward you;
and you have kept for him this great and
steadfast love, and have given him a son
to sit on his throne today. 7 And now,
O LORD my God, you have made your ser-
vant king in place of my father David, al-
though I am only a little child; I do not
know how to go out or come in. 8 And your
servant is in the midst of the people whom
you have chosen, a great people, so numer-
ous they cannot be numbered or counted.
9 Give your servant therefore an under-
standing mind to govern your people, able
to discern between good and evil; for who
can govern this your great people?"

10 It pleased the Lord that Solomon had
asked this. 11 God said to him, "Because
you have asked this, and have not asked for
yourself long life or riches, or for the life of
your enemies, but have asked for yourself
understanding to discern what is right, 12 I
now do according to your word. Indeed I
give you a wise and discerning mind; no
one like you has been before you and no
one like you shall arise after you. 13 I give
you also what you have not asked, both
riches and honor all your life; no other king
shall compare with you. 14 If you will walk
in my ways, keeping my statutes and my
commandments, as your father David
walked, then I will lengthen your life."

15 Then Solomon awoke; it had been
a dream. He came to Jerusalem where he
stood before the ark of the covenant of the
LORD. He offered up burnt offerings and
offerings of well-being, and provided a
feast for all his servants.

3.1–28: More on Solomon and wisdom. 1–3: The "wisdom" that has guided Solomon in ch 2 has led him to actions that are questionable from a moral point of view. Ch 3 opens with another. Deuteronomy warns against too-close relations with *Egypt* (Deut 17.16) and explicitly forbids intermarriage with foreigners, lest Israelites be led into apostasy (Deut 7.3). Solomon, although he *loved the LORD* (v. 3), starts out here on a path that will lead to his downfall (ch 11). He and his people are already in contravention of Deuteronomic law in that they worship at *the high places* (vv. 2–3), local places of worship (as opposed to the one place of worship described in Deut 12) that are frequently condemned as idolatrous. In this respect Solomon's own life sets the pattern for what happens in the life of Israel later (cf. 11.7–8; 2 Kings 21.3–9). **1:** *Pharaoh's daughter,* see 9.16. **4–15:** *Gibeon,* see Josh 9; 2 Sam 21.2. Confronted by God in a dream, Solomon implicitly admits that his royal rule thus far has been flawed. The self-serving wisdom of ch 2 must be replaced with a higher wisdom (3.12) so that the king may rule justly and well over his subjects (vv. 9,11). Without it Solomon is like *a little child,* who does not know how *to go out or to come in* (v. 7; the phrase probably implies a lack of military experience). **12–13:** Both Solomon's wisdom and his wealth are themes developed in the following account of his reign. **16–28:** Solomon's newly

16 Later, two women who were prosti-
tutes came to the king and stood before
him. 17 The one woman said, "Please, my
lord, this woman and I live in the same
house; and I gave birth while she was in the
house. 18 Then on the third day after I gave
birth, this woman also gave birth. We were
together; there was no one else with us in
the house, only the two of us were in the
house. 19 Then this woman's son died in the
night, because she lay on him. 20 She got up
in the middle of the night and took my son
from beside me while your servant slept.
She laid him at her breast, and laid her dead
son at my breast. 21 When I rose in the
morning to nurse my son, I saw that he was
dead; but when I looked at him closely in
the morning, clearly it was not the son I
had borne." 22 But the other woman said,
"No, the living son is mine, and the dead
son is yours." The first said, "No, the dead
son is yours, and the living son is mine." So
they argued before the king.

23 Then the king said, "The one says,
'This is my son that is alive, and your son
is dead'; while the other says, 'Not so! Your
son is dead, and my son is the living one.' "
24 So the king said, "Bring me a sword,"
and they brought a sword before the king.
25 The king said, "Divide the living boy in
two; then give half to the one, and half to
the other." 26 But the woman whose son
was alive said to the king—because com-
passion for her son burned within her—
"Please, my lord, give her the living boy;
certainly do not kill him!" The other said,
"It shall be neither mine nor yours; divide
it." 27 Then the king responded: "Give the
first woman the living boy; do not kill him.
She is his mother." 28 All Israel heard of the
judgment that the king had rendered; and
they stood in awe of the king, because they
perceived that the wisdom of God was in
him, to execute justice.

4 King Solomon was king over all Israel,
2 and these were his high officials: Aza-
riah son of Zadok was the priest; 3 Eliho-
reph and Ahijah sons of Shisha were secre-
taries; Jehoshaphat son of Ahilud was
recorder; 4 Benaiah son of Jehoiada was in
command of the army; Zadok and Abia-
thar were priests; 5 Azariah son of Nathan
was over the officials; Zabud son of Na-
than was priest and king's friend; 6 Ahishar
was in charge of the palace; and Adoniram
son of Abda was in charge of the forced
labor.

7 Solomon had twelve officials over all
Israel, who provided food for the king and
his household; each one had to make provi-
sion for one month in the year. 8 These were
their names: Ben-hur, in the hill country of
Ephraim; 9 Ben-deker, in Makaz, Shaalbim,
Beth-shemesh, and Elon-beth-hanan;

acquired wisdom is evident in his administration of justice, an important royal function (see 2 Sam 8.15; 15.2–6). His old "wisdom" had led to the use of the *sword* only for arguably unjust executions. His new wisdom leads to a more positive use of his weapon (v. 24), threatening execution in order to achieve justice.

4.1–20: Solomon's rule over Israel. The kingdom that results from Solomon's gift of wisdom is well ordered, a key quality of ancient wisdom, (vv. 1–19), happy and prosperous (v. 20, in fulfillment of the Abrahamic promise in Gen 22.17). **1–6:** *High officials,* differences from the lists of David's officials (2 Sam 8.16–18; 20.23–26) probably indicate changes in the administrative structure of the kingdom, especially in an era of relative peace (see v. 20). **4:** *Abiathar,* apparently reinstated since 2.27. **5:** *King's friend,* a royal official. **6:** *Adoniram,* see 5.14; 12.18 (where he is called Adoram). *Forced labor,* provided by non-Israelites (9.20–22), including foreign captives (2 Sam 12.31). This cadre of *forced labor* is not to be confused with another Israelite labor force mentioned alongside it in 5.13; also in 11.28; 12.3–4. **7–20:** Solomon's representatives in the various regions of northern Israel (only partially based on traditional tribal areas) organized provisions for the king and his household on an annual rotation, each being responsible for one month a year. The NRSV reference to *Judah* in v. 19 is found in some Greek manuscripts but not in the Hebrew, which says only that there was "one governor over the land," i.e., a governor (the "Azariah" of 4.5?) over the whole land of Israel, to whom the *twelve officials* were responsible.

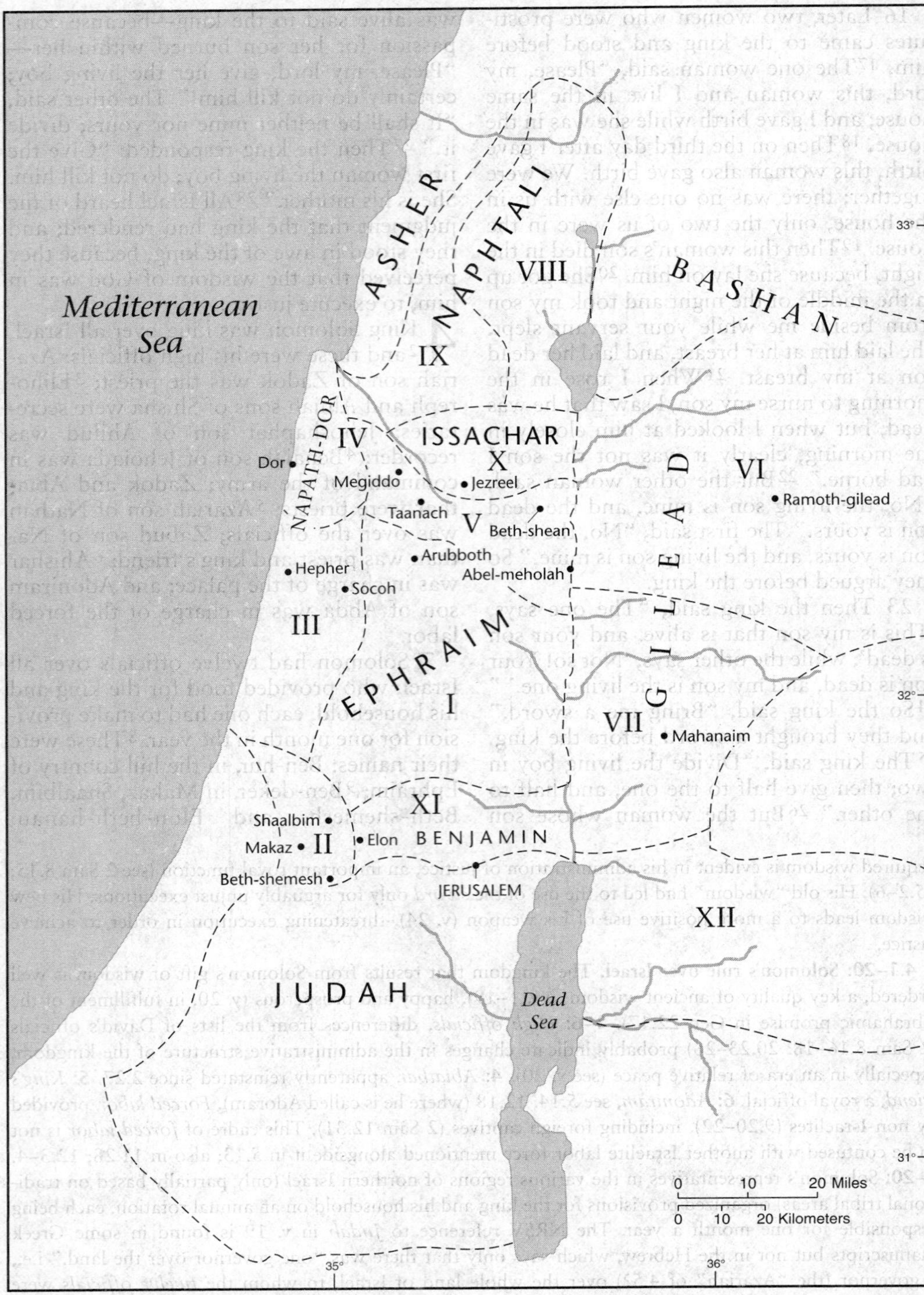

4.7–19: Solomon's twelve administrative districts.

10 Ben-hesed, in Arubboth (to him belonged
Socoh and all the land of Hepher); 11 Ben-
abinadab, in all Naphath-dor (he had Ta-
phath, Solomon's daughter, as his wife);
12 Baana son of Ahilud, in Taanach, Megid-
do, and all Beth-shean, which is beside Zar-
ethan below Jezreel, and from Beth-shean
to Abel-meholah, as far as the other side of
Jokmeam; 13 Ben-geber, in Ramoth-gilead
(he had the villages of Jair son of Manas-
seh, which are in Gilead, and he had the
region of Argob, which is in Bashan, sixty
great cities with walls and bronze bars);
14 Ahinadab son of Iddo, in Mahanaim;
15 Ahimaaz, in Naphtali (he had taken Bas-
emath, Solomon's daughter, as his wife);
16 Baana son of Hushai, in Asher and Bea-
loth; 17 Jehoshaphat son of Paruah, in Issa-
char; 18 Shimei son of Ela, in Benjamin;
19 Geber son of Uri, in the land of Gilead,
the country of King Sihon of the Amorites
and of King Og of Bashan. And there was
one official in the land of Judah.

20 Judah and Israel were as numerous as
the sand by the sea; they ate and drank and
were happy. 21[a] Solomon was sovereign
over all the kingdoms from the Euphrates
to the land of the Philistines, even to the
border of Egypt; they brought tribute and
served Solomon all the days of his life.

22 Solomon's provision for one day was
thirty cors of choice flour, and sixty cors of
meal, 23 ten fat oxen, and twenty pasture-
fed cattle, one hundred sheep, besides deer,
gazelles, roebucks, and fatted fowl. 24 For
he had dominion over all the region west of
the Euphrates from Tiphsah to Gaza, over
all the kings west of the Euphrates; and he
had peace on all sides. 25 During Solomon's
lifetime Judah and Israel lived in safety,
from Dan even to Beer-sheba, all of them
under their vines and fig trees. 26 Solomon
also had forty thousand stalls of horses for
his chariots, and twelve thousand horse-
men. 27 Those officials supplied provisions
for King Solomon and for all who came
to King Solomon's table, each one in his
month; they let nothing be lacking. 28 They
also brought to the required place barley
and straw for the horses and swift steeds,
each according to his charge.

29 God gave Solomon very great wis-
dom, discernment, and breadth of under-
standing as vast as the sand on the sea-
shore, 30 so that Solomon's wisdom
surpassed the wisdom of all the people of
the east, and all the wisdom of Egypt. 31 He
was wiser than anyone else, wiser than
Ethan the Ezrahite, and Heman, Calcol,
and Darda, children of Mahol; his fame
spread throughout all the surrounding na-
tions. 32 He composed three thousand prov-
erbs, and his songs numbered a thousand
and five. 33 He would speak of trees, from
the cedar that is in the Lebanon to the hys-
sop that grows in the wall; he would speak
of animals, and birds, and reptiles, and fish.
34 People came from all the nations to hear
the wisdom of Solomon; they came from all
the kings of the earth who had heard of his
wisdom.

a Ch 5.1 in Heb

4.21–34: Solomon and the nations. Solomon and Israel are set in the broader international context. Solomon is described (v. 24) as the dominant ruler of the area stretching from *Tiphsah* (on the Euphrates, east of Aleppo in Syria) to *Gaza* (on the western coast, in the far south of Philistia)—a large area corresponding to the ideal extent of Israel's dominion as promised to Abraham (Gen 15.18). Because of this, all Israel *from Dan . . . to Beer-sheba* (the traditional northern and southern limits of the land) lived under God's blessing with a degree of economic independence (*under their vines and fig trees,* v. 25). **29–34:** Solomon was wiser than those proverbial for their wisdom (*the people of the east* and from *Egypt*) or famed for it (*Ethan, Heman, Calcol,* and *Darda;* see 1 Chr 2.6; 6.33–48; Ps 88.1; 89.1), and he attracted visitors to Israel to listen to what he had to say (see 10.1–13). The gift of ch 3 has truly produced the glory of ch 4. **32:** On Solomon's reputation as a maker of *proverbs,* see Prov 1.1; 10.1; 25.1. For the attribution of *songs* to Solomon, see Ps 72; 127; and Song 1.1. **33:** One type of ancient Near Eastern wisdom literature was lists of flora and fauna.

5 [a]Now King Hiram of Tyre sent his ser-
vants to Solomon, when he heard that
they had anointed him king in place of his
father; for Hiram had always been a friend
to David. 2 Solomon sent word to Hiram,
saying, 3 "You know that my father David
could not build a house for the name of the
LORD his God because of the warfare with
which his enemies surrounded him, until
the LORD put them under the soles of his
feet.[b] 4 But now the LORD my God has giv-
en me rest on every side; there is neither
adversary nor misfortune. 5 So I intend to
build a house for the name of the LORD my
God, as the LORD said to my father David,
'Your son, whom I will set on your throne
in your place, shall build the house for my
name.' 6 Therefore command that cedars
from the Lebanon be cut for me. My ser-
vants will join your servants, and I will give
you whatever wages you set for your ser-
vants; for you know that there is no one
among us who knows how to cut timber
like the Sidonians."
7 When Hiram heard the words of Solo-
mon, he rejoiced greatly, and said, "Blessed
be the LORD today, who has given to David
a wise son to be over this great people."
8 Hiram sent word to Solomon, "I have
heard the message that you have sent to me;
I will fulfill all your needs in the matter of
cedar and cypress timber. 9 My servants
shall bring it down to the sea from the Leb-
anon; I will make it into rafts to go by sea
to the place you indicate. I will have them
broken up there for you to take away. And
you shall meet my needs by providing food
for my household." 10 So Hiram supplied
Solomon's every need for timber of cedar
and cypress. 11 Solomon in turn gave Hiram
twenty thousand cors of wheat as food for
his household, and twenty cors of fine oil.
Solomon gave this to Hiram year by year.
12 So the LORD gave Solomon wisdom, as
he promised him. There was peace between
Hiram and Solomon; and the two of them
made a treaty.
13 King Solomon conscripted forced la-
bor out of all Israel; the levy numbered thir-
ty thousand men. 14 He sent them to the
Lebanon, ten thousand a month in shifts;
they would be a month in the Lebanon and
two months at home; Adoniram was in
charge of the forced labor. 15 Solomon also
had seventy thousand laborers and eighty
thousand stonecutters in the hill country,
16 besides Solomon's three thousand three
hundred supervisors who were over the
work, having charge of the people who did
the work. 17 At the king's command, they
quarried out great, costly stones in order
to lay the foundation of the house with
dressed stones. 18 So Solomon's builders
and Hiram's builders and the Gebalites did
the stonecutting and prepared the timber
and the stone to build the house.
6 In the four hundred eightieth year after
the Israelites came out of the land of
Egypt, in the fourth year of Solomon's

a Ch 5.15 in Heb *b* Gk Tg Vg: Heb *my feet* or *his feet*

5.1–18: Preparations for building the Temple. *King Hiram of Tyre* was an ally of David (2 Sam 5.11), sending him materials and men to help build his palace. Now that Solomon has achieved the *rest* that eluded his father (but see 2 Sam 7.1), and the time is right for the Temple to be built (2 Sam 7.10–13), it is to Hiram that he turns for the same kind of help. **1:** *A friend to David,* literally "loved David," a term used of formal treaty relationships (see v. 12). **6:** *Sidonians,* a general term for Phoenicians; Sidon, like Tyre, was a city on the Phoenician coast, south of Beirut. From these two cities, the Phoenicians carried on a vast maritime enterprise, two of their chief articles of commerce being cedar wood and purple dye (see Ezek 27). About a century after the time of Solomon they established their most famous colony, Carthage in North Africa. **13–18:** The task force sent to Lebanon consists of conscripted workers from the Canaanite population of Israel and of 150,000 Israelites; see 4.6n. **18:** The preparation of materials involves not only the craftsmen of Solomon and Hiram, but also the *Gebalites,* the men of Byblos on the coast to the north of Tyre.

6.1–38: Solomon builds the Temple. The Temple that Solomon built was similar in design, not only reign over Israel, in the month of Ziv, which is the second month, he began to build the house of the LORD. 2 The house that King Solomon built for the LORD was sixty cubits long, twenty cubits wide, and thirty cubits high. 3 The vestibule in front of the nave of the house was twenty cubits wide, across the width of the house. Its depth was ten cubits in front of the house. 4 For the house he made windows with recessed frames.[a] 5 He also built a structure against the wall of the house, running around the walls of the house, both the nave and the inner sanctuary; and he made side chambers all around. 6 The lowest story[b] was five cubits wide, the middle one was six cubits wide, and the third was seven cubits wide; for around the outside of the house he made offsets on the wall in

a Gk: Meaning of Heb uncertain *b* Gk: Heb *structure*

to the tabernacle of the Exodus traditions (cf. Ex 26–31), but also to other temples found in Egypt, Assyria, Syria, and Palestine itself. The parallels in Syro-Phoenicia are especially interesting in view of the fact that Phoenician craftsmen are mentioned in our biblical text as contributing to the Solomonic project. **1:** *The fourth year of Solomon's reign,* about 965 BCE. *The four hundred eightieth year* before this would date the Exodus earlier than most scholars propose; the number may be symbolic rather than real. **2–5:** The description begins with the external structure of the Temple: its overall proportions (the *cubit* is approximately 45 cm [18 in] long); its basic form (a tripartite arrangement, comprising the *vestibule* or entrance hall, the *nave* or main hall, and the *inner sanctuary* or "most holy place" [v. 16]); and the structure around it with its *side chambers.* **7:** The work was carried out with reverence, avoiding the use of

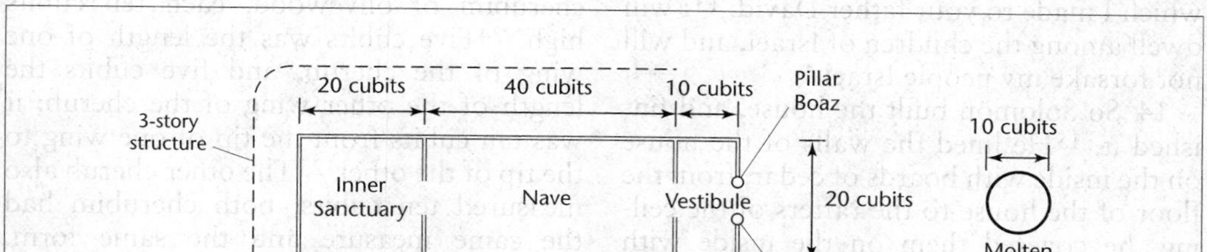

Chs 6–7: The Temple and palace of Solomon.

order that the supporting beams should not
be inserted into the walls of the house.

7 The house was built with stone fin-
ished at the quarry, so that neither hammer
nor ax nor any tool of iron was heard in the
temple while it was being built.

8 The entrance for the middle story was
on the south side of the house: one went up
by winding stairs to the middle story, and
from the middle story to the third. 9 So he
built the house, and finished it; he roofed
the house with beams and planks of cedar.
10 He built the structure against the whole
house, each story[a] five cubits high, and it
was joined to the house with timbers of
cedar.

11 Now the word of the LORD came to
Solomon, 12 "Concerning this house that
you are building, if you will walk in my
statutes, obey my ordinances, and keep all
my commandments by walking in them,
then I will establish my promise with you,
which I made to your father David. 13 I will
dwell among the children of Israel, and will
not forsake my people Israel."

14 So Solomon built the house, and fin-
ished it. 15 He lined the walls of the house
on the inside with boards of cedar; from the
floor of the house to the rafters of the ceil-
ing, he covered them on the inside with
wood; and he covered the floor of the
house with boards of cypress. 16 He built
twenty cubits of the rear of the house with
boards of cedar from the floor to the raf-
ters, and he built this within as an inner
sanctuary, as the most holy place. 17 The
house, that is, the nave in front of the inner
sanctuary, was forty cubits long. 18 The ce-
dar within the house had carvings of
gourds and open flowers; all was cedar, no
stone was seen. 19 The inner sanctuary he
prepared in the innermost part of the
house, to set there the ark of the covenant
of the LORD. 20 The interior of the inner
sanctuary was twenty cubits long, twenty
cubits wide, and twenty cubits high; he
overlaid it with pure gold. He also overlaid
the altar with cedar.[b] 21 Solomon overlaid
the inside of the house with pure gold, then
he drew chains of gold across, in front of
the inner sanctuary, and overlaid it with
gold. 22 Next he overlaid the whole house
with gold, in order that the whole house
might be perfect; even the whole altar that
belonged to the inner sanctuary he overlaid
with gold.

23 In the inner sanctuary he made two
cherubim of olivewood, each ten cubits
high. 24 Five cubits was the length of one
wing of the cherub, and five cubits the
length of the other wing of the cherub; it
was ten cubits from the tip of one wing to
the tip of the other. 25 The other cherub also
measured ten cubits; both cherubim had
the same measure and the same form.
26 The height of one cherub was ten cubits,
and so was that of the other cherub. 27 He
put the cherubim in the innermost part of

a Heb lacks *each story* *b* Meaning of Heb uncertain

iron tools at the Temple site; cf. Ex 20.25; Deut 27.5–6. **11–13:** The Temple itself, for all its splendor, does not change the essential terms of the divine-human relationship. The phrasing is Deuteronomistic. **14–35:** The inside of the Temple is described. Most attention is paid to the *inner sanctuary* or *most holy place* (vv. 16,19–32), where the *ark of the covenant* was to be placed—according to some conceptions, the very dwelling place of God himself (e.g., chs 8–13). Here we find the *cherubim* (vv. 23–28): large, winged creatures that dominated the sanctuary, reaching half-way up to its ceiling and all the way across from wall to wall (cf. 1 Sam 4.4; Ps 80.1; 99.1). As with the overall design of the Temple and some of the other ritual objects found within it, parallels to the cherubim are found elsewhere in the ancient Near East. Phoenicia, in particular, provides pictorial examples of winged sphinxes supporting royal thrones, which is interesting in view of biblical ideas about the cherubim supporting God's throne and about the ark of the covenant as God's footstool (e.g., Ps 80.1; 99.1; 2 Kings 19.15; 1 Chr 28.2; Ps 132.7; cf. 1 Kings 8.6–7). The authors show considerable interest in the splendor of the decoration in general; note the *gold* (vv. 20–22,28,30,32,35), and the carvings of further *cherubim* (vv. 29,32,35), *gourds* (v. 18, a wild fruit), *open flowers* (vv. 18,29,32,35) and *palm trees* (vv. 29,32,35)—symbols of God's gift of fertility. **36–38:** The building took seven years to complete, or more precisely, seven years and six

the house; the wings of the cherubim were
spread out so that a wing of one was touch-
ing the one wall, and a wing of the other
cherub was touching the other wall; their
other wings toward the center of the house
were touching wing to wing. 28 He also
overlaid the cherubim with gold.
29 He carved the walls of the house all
around about with carved engravings of
cherubim, palm trees, and open flowers, in
the inner and outer rooms. 30 The floor of
the house he overlaid with gold, in the in-
ner and outer rooms.
31 For the entrance to the inner sanctu-
ary he made doors of olivewood; the lintel
and the doorposts were five-sided.[a] 32 He
covered the two doors of olivewood with
carvings of cherubim, palm trees, and open
flowers; he overlaid them with gold, and
spread gold on the cherubim and on the
palm trees.
33 So also he made for the entrance to
the nave doorposts of olivewood, four-
sided each, 34 and two doors of cypress
wood; the two leaves of the one door were
folding, and the two leaves of the other
door were folding. 35 He carved cherubim,
palm trees, and open flowers, overlaying
them with gold evenly applied upon the
carved work. 36 He built the inner court
with three courses of dressed stone to one
course of cedar beams.
37 In the fourth year the foundation of
the house of the LORD was laid, in the
month of Ziv. 38 In the eleventh year, in the
month of Bul, which is the eighth month,
the house was finished in all its parts, and
according to all its specifications. He was
seven years in building it.

7 Solomon was building his own house
thirteen years, and he finished his entire
house.
2 He built the House of the Forest of the
Lebanon one hundred cubits long, fifty cu-
bits wide, and thirty cubits high, built on
four rows of cedar pillars, with cedar
beams on the pillars. 3 It was roofed with
cedar on the forty-five rafters, fifteen in
each row, which were on the pillars. 4 There
were window frames in the three rows, fac-
ing each other in the three rows. 5 All the
doorways and doorposts had four-sided
frames, opposite, facing each other in the
three rows.
6 He made the Hall of Pillars fifty cubits
long and thirty cubits wide. There was a
porch in front with pillars, and a canopy in
front of them.
7 He made the Hall of the Throne where
he was to pronounce judgment, the Hall of
Justice, covered with cedar from floor to
floor.
8 His own house where he would reside,
in the other court back of the hall, was of
the same construction. Solomon also made
a house like this hall for Pharaoh's daugh-
ter, whom he had taken in marriage.
9 All these were made of costly stones,
cut according to measure, sawed with saws,
back and front, from the foundation to the
coping, and from outside to the great court.
10 The foundation was of costly stones,
huge stones, stones of eight and ten cubits.
11 There were costly stones above, cut to
measure, and cedarwood. 12 The great
court had three courses of dressed stone to

a Meaning of Heb uncertain

months, given that *Ziv* is the second month (April-May) and *Bul* the eighth month (October-November) of the Israelite year.

7.1–12: Solomon builds his palace. The description of the Temple is now interrupted by an account of the building of the royal palace complex, perhaps suggesting criticism of Solomon's priorities. He spent almost twice as long on his own *house* as he did on the house of the LORD (v. 1). Just the first of its several buildings (*the house of the Forest of the Lebanon,* so named because of its rows of cedar pillars) was indeed much bigger than the Temple (v. 2; cf. 6.2). **6–12:** The remaining buildings that formed part of the palace complex were a colonnade (*Hall of Pillars,* v. 6), almost as large as the Temple, but of uncertain use; a throne hall, also called *Hall of Justice,* for the dispensing of justice; and two palaces, one for Solomon and one for his Egyptian wife (see 3.1). The precise relationship of all these buildings to each other in terms of their geography is obscure.

one layer of cedar beams all around; so had
the inner court of the house of the LORD,
and the vestibule of the house.
13 Now King Solomon invited and re-
ceived Hiram from Tyre. 14 He was the son
of a widow of the tribe of Naphtali, whose
father, a man of Tyre, had been an artisan
in bronze; he was full of skill, intelligence,
and knowledge in working bronze. He
came to King Solomon, and did all his
work.
15 He cast two pillars of bronze. Eigh-
teen cubits was the height of the one, and a
cord of twelve cubits would encircle it; the
second pillar was the same.[a] 16 He also
made two capitals of molten bronze, to set
on the tops of the pillars; the height of the
one capital was five cubits, and the height
of the other capital was five cubits. 17 There
were nets of checker work with wreaths of
chain work for the capitals on the tops of
the pillars; seven[b] for the one capital, and
seven[b] for the other capital. 18 He made
the columns with two rows around each
latticework to cover the capitals that were
above the pomegranates; he did the same
with the other capital. 19 Now the capitals
that were on the tops of the pillars in the
vestibule were of lily-work, four cubits
high. 20 The capitals were on the two pillars
and also above the rounded projection that
was beside the latticework; there were two
hundred pomegranates in rows all around;
and so with the other capital. 21 He set up
the pillars at the vestibule of the temple; he
set up the pillar on the south and called it
Jachin; and he set up the pillar on the north
and called it Boaz. 22 On the tops of the
pillars was lily-work. Thus the work of the
pillars was finished.
23 Then he made the molten sea; it was
round, ten cubits from brim to brim, and
five cubits high. A line of thirty cubits
would encircle it completely. 24 Under its
brim were panels all around it, each of ten
cubits, surrounding the sea; there were two
rows of panels, cast when it was cast. 25 It
stood on twelve oxen, three facing north,
three facing west, three facing south, and
three facing east; the sea was set on them.
The hindquarters of each were toward the
inside. 26 Its thickness was a handbreadth;
its brim was made like the brim of a cup,
like the flower of a lily; it held two thou-
sand baths.[c]
27 He also made the ten stands of
bronze; each stand was four cubits long,
four cubits wide, and three cubits high.
28 This was the construction of the stands:
they had borders; the borders were within
the frames; 29 on the borders that were set
in the frames were lions, oxen, and cheru-
bim. On the frames, both above and below
the lions and oxen, there were wreaths of
beveled work. 30 Each stand had four
bronze wheels and axles of bronze; at the
four corners were supports for a basin. The
supports were cast with wreaths at the

a Cn: Heb *and a cord of twelve cubits encircled the second pillar*; Compare Jer 52.21 *b* Heb: Gk *a net*
c A Heb measure of volume

7.13–51: The Temple's furnishings. The *Hiram* (called Huram-abi in 2 Chr 2.13) now introduced as the creator of the Temple furnishings fashioned from bronze is not to be confused with the king of ch 5. The detail about his mother has probably been provided to reassure us that he was not simply a Gentile with no Israelite roots (cf. Ezra 4.1–3 for similar sensitivity to the question of involvement in Temple building). He reminds us of Bezaleel son of Uri, the chief craftsman involved in the construction of the tabernacle (Ex 31.1–11; 35.30–35). **15–22:** *Jachin* and *Boaz* were two massive *pillars,* perhaps free-standing, positioned at the Temple entrance (see 2 Kings 11.14; 22.3), which along with their *capitals* stood almost as high as the Temple itself. *Jachin* means "he will establish," referring to God's will to establish the throne of the Temple builder (see 2 Sam 7.13). *Boaz* probably embodies the hope that God would act in divine strength on behalf of the king (cf. Ps 21.1,13). **23–47:** The *molten sea* was a large, metal basin representing the forces of primeval watery chaos subdued and brought to order by the LORD who is creator of the world (cf. Gen 1.1–23) and used for priestly washing (2 Chr 4.6; cf. Ex 30.18–21). The other utensils mentioned also had a practical function. **26:** *Bath,* a liquid measure equal to about 23 l (6 gal). **46:** *Succoth and Zarethan,* located in the central Jordan valley. **48–51:** Bezaleel son of Uri side of each. 31 Its opening was within the crown whose height was one cubit; its opening was round, as a pedestal is made; it was a cubit and a half wide. At its opening there were carvings; its borders were four-sided, not round. 32 The four wheels were underneath the borders; the axles of the wheels were in the stands; and the height of a wheel was a cubit and a half. 33 The wheels were made like a chariot wheel; their axles, their rims, their spokes, and their hubs were all cast. 34 There were four supports at the four corners of each stand; the supports were of one piece with the stands. 35 On the top of the stand there was a round band half a cubit high; on the top of the stand, its stays and its borders were of one piece with it. 36 On the surfaces of its stays and on its borders he carved cherubim, lions, and palm trees, where each had space, with wreaths all around. 37 In this way he made the ten stands; all of them were cast alike, with the same size and the same form.

38 He made ten basins of bronze; each basin held forty baths,[a] each basin measured four cubits; there was a basin for each of the ten stands. 39 He set five of the stands on the south side of the house, and five on the north side of the house; he set the sea on the southeast corner of the house.

40 Hiram also made the pots, the shovels, and the basins. So Hiram finished all the work that he did for King Solomon on the house of the LORD: 41 the two pillars, the two bowls of the capitals that were on the tops of the pillars, the two latticeworks to cover the two bowls of the capitals that were on the tops of the pillars; 42 the four hundred pomegranates for the two latticeworks, two rows of pomegranates for each latticework, to cover the two bowls of the capitals that were on the pillars; 43 the ten stands, the ten basins on the stands; 44 the one sea, and the twelve oxen underneath the sea.

45 The pots, the shovels, and the basins, all these vessels that Hiram made for King Solomon for the house of the LORD were of burnished bronze. 46 In the plain of the Jordan the king cast them, in the clay ground between Succoth and Zarethan. 47 Solomon left all the vessels unweighed, because there were so many of them; the weight of the bronze was not determined.

48 So Solomon made all the vessels that were in the house of the LORD: the golden altar, the golden table for the bread of the Presence, 49 the lampstands of pure gold, five on the south side and five on the north, in front of the inner sanctuary; the flowers, the lamps, and the tongs, of gold; 50 the cups, snuffers, basins, dishes for incense, and firepans, of pure gold; the sockets for the doors of the innermost part of the house, the most holy place, and for the doors of the nave of the temple, of gold.

51 Thus all the work that King Solomon did on the house of the LORD was finished. Solomon brought in the things that his father David had dedicated, the silver, the gold, and the vessels, and stored them in the treasuries of the house of the LORD.

8 Then Solomon assembled the elders of Israel and all the heads of the tribes, the leaders of the ancestral houses of the Israelites, before King Solomon in Jerusalem, to bring up the ark of the covenant of the LORD out of the city of David, which is Zion. 2 All the people of Israel assembled to King Solomon at the festival in the month Ethanim, which is the seventh month. 3 And all the elders of Israel came, and the priests

a A Heb measure of volume

was sufficiently wise that he could work in gold, silver, and bronze (Ex 31.3–4), but Hiram is apparently not so gifted. The manufacture of ritual objects made of *gold* is thus attributed to wise Solomon himself, rather than to Hiram. **48:** *Bread of the Presence,* see Ex 25.30; Lev 24.5–9. **51:** *David had dedicated,* see 2 Sam 8.9–12.

8.1–21: The ark of the covenant brought to the Temple. The ark had been in a tent-sanctuary somewhere in the old city of David (2 Sam 6.16–17; 7.2; 1 Kings 3.15). **1–2:** The *festival* is Tabernacles (see vv. 65–66; Lev 23.33–43), which in some places functions as a new year festival (Ex 34.22). **3:** *The* carried the ark. 4 So they brought up the ark of the LORD, the tent of meeting, and all the holy vessels that were in the tent; the priests and the Levites brought them up. 5 King Solomon and all the congregation of Israel, who had assembled before him, were with him before the ark, sacrificing so many sheep and oxen that they could not be counted or numbered. 6 Then the priests brought the ark of the covenant of the LORD to its place, in the inner sanctuary of the house, in the most holy place, underneath the wings of the cherubim. 7 For the cherubim spread out their wings over the place of the ark, so that the cherubim made a covering above the ark and its poles. 8 The poles were so long that the ends of the poles were seen from the holy place in front of the inner sanctuary; but they could not be seen from outside; they are there to this day. 9 There was nothing in the ark except the two tablets of stone that Moses had placed there at Horeb, where the LORD made a covenant with the Israelites, when they came out of the land of Egypt. 10 And when the priests came out of the holy place, a cloud filled the house of the LORD, 11 so that the priests could not stand to minister because of the cloud; for the glory of the LORD filled the house of the LORD.

12 Then Solomon said,

"The LORD has said that he would
dwell in thick darkness.
13 I have built you an exalted house,
a place for you to dwell in
forever."

14 Then the king turned around and blessed all the assembly of Israel, while all the assembly of Israel stood. 15 He said, "Blessed be the LORD, the God of Israel, who with his hand has fulfilled what he promised with his mouth to my father David, saying, 16 'Since the day that I brought my people Israel out of Egypt, I have not chosen a city from any of the tribes of Israel in which to build a house, that my name might be there; but I chose David to be over my people Israel.' 17 My father David had it in mind to build a house for the name of the LORD, the God of Israel. 18 But the LORD said to my father David, 'You did well to consider building a house for my name; 19 nevertheless you shall not build the house, but your son who shall be born to you shall build the house for my name.' 20 Now the LORD has upheld the promise that he made; for I have risen in the place of my father David; I sit on the throne of Israel, as the LORD promised, and have built the house for the name of the LORD, the God of Israel. 21 There I have provided a place for the ark, in which is the covenant of the LORD that he made with our ancestors when he brought them out of the land of Egypt."

22 Then Solomon stood before the altar of the LORD in the presence of all the assembly of Israel, and spread out his hands to heaven. 23 He said, "O LORD, God of Israel, there is no God like you in heaven above or on earth beneath, keeping covenant and steadfast love for your servants who walk before you with all their heart, 24 the covenant that you kept for your servant my father David as you declared to him; you promised with your mouth and have this day fulfilled with your hand. 25 Therefore, O LORD, God of Israel, keep for your servant my father David that which you promised him, saying, 'There

priests carry the ark, for not even the *elders* are safe in its immediate proximity (cf. Josh 3.3–4; 2 Sam 6.1–7). **9:** *Two tablets,* see Deut 10.1–5. *Horeb,* the name used in Deuteronomy for Mount Sinai. **10–11:** A *cloud* is often associated with divine appearances (e.g., Ex 13.21–22; 16.10; 19.9) and covers the tabernacle upon its completion in Ex 40.34–38. Like Moses, the priests could not perform their service because of the *glory of the LORD* (Ex 40.35)—a sure sign that the new arrangements for worship have the divine blessing. **15–21:** See 2 Sam 7.5–16; 1 Kings 5.3; 1 Chr 28.2–7.

8.22–9.9: Solomon's prayer and vision. The language is characteristically Deuteronomistic. The main concern of the first part of the prayer (vv. 22–26) is to pick up the divine promise of 2 Sam 7 to David already alluded to in 8.15–21: the promise of an eternal dynasty. Throughout this section the significance of the Temple is interpreted in terms of this promise. **8.27–53:** The Temple's broader significance was as

shall never fail you a successor before me to
sit on the throne of Israel, if only your chil-
dren look to their way, to walk before me
as you have walked before me.' 26 There-
fore, O God of Israel, let your word be con-
firmed, which you promised to your ser-
vant my father David.
27 "But will God indeed dwell on the
earth? Even heaven and the highest heaven
cannot contain you, much less this house
that I have built! 28 Regard your servant's
prayer and his plea, O LORD my God,
heeding the cry and the prayer that your
servant prays to you today; 29 that your
eyes may be open night and day toward this
house, the place of which you said, 'My
name shall be there,' that you may heed the
prayer that your servant prays toward this
place. 30 Hear the plea of your servant and
of your people Israel when they pray to-
ward this place; O hear in heaven your
dwelling place; heed and forgive.
31 "If someone sins against a neighbor
and is given an oath to swear, and comes
and swears before your altar in this house,
32 then hear in heaven, and act, and judge
your servants, condemning the guilty by
bringing their conduct on their own head,
and vindicating the righteous by rewarding
them according to their righteousness.
33 "When your people Israel, having
sinned against you, are defeated before an
enemy but turn again to you, confess your
name, pray and plead with you in this
house, 34 then hear in heaven, forgive the
sin of your people Israel, and bring them
again to the land that you gave to their
ancestors.
35 "When heaven is shut up and there is
no rain because they have sinned against
you, and then they pray toward this place,
confess your name, and turn from their sin,
because you punish[a] them, 36 then hear in
heaven, and forgive the sin of your ser-
vants, your people Israel, when you teach
them the good way in which they should
walk; and grant rain on your land, which
you have given to your people as an inheri-
tance.
37 "If there is famine in the land, if there
is plague, blight, mildew, locust, or cater-
pillar; if their enemy besieges them in any[b]
of their cities; whatever plague, whatever
sickness there is; 38 whatever prayer, what-
ever plea there is from any individual or
from all your people Israel, all knowing the
afflictions of their own hearts so that they
stretch out their hands toward this house;
39 then hear in heaven your dwelling place,
forgive, act, and render to all whose hearts
you know—according to all their ways, for
only you know what is in every human
heart— 40 so that they may fear you all the
days that they live in the land that you gave
to our ancestors.
41 "Likewise when a foreigner, who is
not of your people Israel, comes from a dis-
tant land because of your name 42—for
they shall hear of your great name, your
mighty hand, and your outstretched arm—
when a foreigner comes and prays toward
this house, 43 then hear in heaven your
dwelling place, and do according to all that
the foreigner calls to you, so that all the
peoples of the earth may know your name
and fear you, as do your people Israel, and
so that they may know that your name has
been invoked on this house that I have
built.
44 "If your people go out to battle

a Or *when you answer* b Gk Syr: Heb *in the land*

a focal point for prayer. Although God cannot literally *dwell* on earth (v. 27), he hears in heaven (vv. 32,34,36,39,43,45,49) when people pray toward the Temple. Seven specific petitions are described. **31–32:** The first petition concerns a legal case in which difficulties over evidence or witnesses make resolution of the case in any normal way impossible. God is invoked as judge to condemn the *guilty* and clear the innocent (*righteous*). **33–40:** The next three petitions concern disasters that might befall the people of Israel more generally: defeat in battle and subsequent exile from the land; drought; and assorted perils such as *famine, plague,* and siege (vv. 37–40). In each case the cause of the problem is sin, and the main requirement of the situation is forgiveness. **41–43:** The *foreigner* should also know answered prayer. **44–45:** The people of God should know victory in God's cause. **46–51:** If exile should take place and the

against their enemy, by whatever way you
shall send them, and they pray to the LORD
toward the city that you have chosen and
the house that I have built for your name,
45 then hear in heaven their prayer and their
plea, and maintain their cause.

46 "If they sin against you—for there is
no one who does not sin—and you are an-
gry with them and give them to an enemy,
so that they are carried away captive to the
land of the enemy, far off or near; 47 yet if
they come to their senses in the land to
which they have been taken captive, and
repent, and plead with you in the land of
their captors, saying, 'We have sinned, and
have done wrong; we have acted wickedly';
48 if they repent with all their heart and soul
in the land of their enemies, who took them
captive, and pray to you toward their land,
which you gave to their ancestors, the city
that you have chosen, and the house that I
have built for your name; 49 then hear in
heaven your dwelling place their prayer
and their plea, maintain their cause 50 and
forgive your people who have sinned
against you, and all their transgressions
that they have committed against you; and
grant them compassion in the sight of their
captors, so that they may have compassion
on them 51 (for they are your people and
heritage, which you brought out of Egypt,
from the midst of the iron-smelter). 52 Let
your eyes be open to the plea of your ser-
vant, and to the plea of your people Israel,
listening to them whenever they call to you.
53 For you have separated them from
among all the peoples of the earth, to be
your heritage, just as you promised through
Moses, your servant, when you brought
our ancestors out of Egypt, O Lord GOD."

54 Now when Solomon finished offer-
ing all this prayer and this plea to the
LORD, he arose from facing the altar of the
LORD, where he had knelt with hands out-
stretched toward heaven; 55 he stood and
blessed all the assembly of Israel with a
loud voice:

56 "Blessed be the LORD, who has given
rest to his people Israel according to all that
he promised; not one word has failed of all
his good promise, which he spoke through
his servant Moses. 57 The LORD our God be
with us, as he was with our ancestors; may
he not leave us or abandon us, 58 but incline
our hearts to him, to walk in all his ways,
and to keep his commandments, his stat-
utes, and his ordinances, which he com-
manded our ancestors. 59 Let these words
of mine, with which I pleaded before the
LORD, be near to the LORD our God day
and night, and may he maintain the cause
of his servant and the cause of his people
Israel, as each day requires; 60 so that all the
peoples of the earth may know that the
LORD is God; there is no other. 61 Therefore
devote yourselves completely to the LORD
our God, walking in his statutes and keep-
ing his commandments, as at this day."

62 Then the king, and all Israel with
him, offered sacrifice before the LORD.
63 Solomon offered as sacrifices of well-
being to the LORD twenty-two thousand
oxen and one hundred twenty thousand
sheep. So the king and all the people of
Israel dedicated the house of the LORD.
64 The same day the king consecrated the
middle of the court that was in front of the
house of the LORD; for there he offered the
burnt offerings and the grain offerings and
the fat pieces of the sacrifices of well-being,
because the bronze altar that was before
the LORD was too small to receive the burnt

people should repent and pray, then God should uphold their cause. This last petition is remarkable for its pun on Heb "shub" ("to repent") and Heb "shabah" ("carry away" or "captive"), used a total of seven times. **51:** *Iron-smelter,* see Deut 4.20. **8.54–9.9:** God's first appearance to Solomon (3.4–15) marked the beginning of his rise to greatness; the second points ahead to disaster. The future of Temple and dynasty, as well as possession of the land of Israel itself, is made dependent upon the obedience of Solomon and future generations of Israelites (9.6–9). Idolatry will conversely make Israel into a nation that is a *proverb* and a *taunt* (object of ridicule) among the nations (v. 7; cf. Deut 28:37). Given that Solomon's prayer presupposes the inevitability of sin, Solomon's vision cannot provide much hope. **8.65:** *From Lebo-hamath*

offerings and the grain offerings and the fat
pieces of the sacrifices of well-being.
65 So Solomon held the festival at that
time, and all Israel with him—a great as-
sembly, people from Lebo-hamath to the
Wadi of Egypt—before the LORD our God,
seven days.[a] 66 On the eighth day he sent
the people away; and they blessed the king,
and went to their tents, joyful and in good
spirits because of all the goodness that the
LORD had shown to his servant David and
to his people Israel.

9 When Solomon had finished building
the house of the LORD and the king's
house and all that Solomon desired to
build, 2 the LORD appeared to Solomon a
second time, as he had appeared to him at
Gibeon. 3 The LORD said to him, "I have
heard your prayer and your plea, which
you made before me; I have consecrated
this house that you have built, and put my
name there forever; my eyes and my heart
will be there for all time. 4 As for you, if you
will walk before me, as David your father
walked, with integrity of heart and upright-
ness, doing according to all that I have
commanded you, and keeping my statutes
and my ordinances, 5 then I will establish
your royal throne over Israel forever, as I
promised your father David, saying, 'There
shall not fail you a successor on the throne
of Israel.'
6 "If you turn aside from following me,
you or your children, and do not keep my
commandments and my statutes that I have
set before you, but go and serve other gods
and worship them, 7 then I will cut Israel off
from the land that I have given them; and
the house that I have consecrated for my
name I will cast out of my sight; and Israel
will become a proverb and a taunt among
all peoples. 8 This house will become a heap
of ruins;[b] everyone passing by it will be
astonished, and will hiss; and they will say,
'Why has the LORD done such a thing to
this land and to this house?' 9 Then they
will say, 'Because they have forsaken the
LORD their God, who brought their ances-
tors out of the land of Egypt, and embraced
other gods, worshiping them and serving
them; therefore the LORD has brought this
disaster upon them.' "
10 At the end of twenty years, in which
Solomon had built the two houses, the
house of the LORD and the king's house,
11 King Hiram of Tyre having supplied Sol-
omon with cedar and cypress timber and
gold, as much as he desired, King Solomon
gave to Hiram twenty cities in the land of
Galilee. 12 But when Hiram came from Tyre
to see the cities that Solomon had given
him, they did not please him. 13 Therefore
he said, "What kind of cities are these that
you have given me, my brother?" So they
are called the land of Cabul[c] to this day.
14 But Hiram had sent to the king one hun-
dred twenty talents of gold.
15 This is the account of the forced la-
bor that King Solomon conscripted to build
the house of the LORD and his own house,
the Millo and the wall of Jerusalem, Hazor,
Megiddo, Gezer 16 (Pharaoh king of Egypt

a Compare Gk: Heb *seven days and seven days, fourteen days* *b* Syr Old Latin: Heb *will become high* *c* Perhaps meaning *a land good for nothing*

to the Wadi of Egypt, the northern and southern limits of Solomon's rule (less extensive than those given in 4.21,24). *Lebo-hamath* is probably in the southern Orontes valley in Lebanon. *The Wadi of Egypt,* either the Wadi Besor or the Wadi el-Arish, both south of Gaza.

9.10–10.29: The glory of Solomon reviewed. Themes from chs 4–5 are revisited in ways that hint of Solomon's downfall. **9.10–14:** Solomon in 9.10–10.29 is a king who accumulates *gold* in extraordinarily large amounts, which increase as we read (120 talents in 9.14; 420 in 9.28; 666 in 10.14; a *talent* weighed about 34 kg [75 lb]). Deut 17.17 prohibits excessive royal wealth, associating it with apostasy. The emphasis in chs 9–10 is on the luxury of the royal court, rather than the prosperity of the people as a whole (contrast 4.20,25).

9.15–28: Miscellaneous notices. 15: *Millo,* probably the terraces supporting the walls and public buildings of Jerusalem. The cities in vv. 15–18 were strategically located throughout the kingdom. **16:** Pharaoh's daughter, see 3.1; 9.24; 11.1. **20:** *Amorites,* etc., some of the traditional inhabitants of the land

had gone up and captured Gezer and
burned it down, had killed the Canaanites
who lived in the city, and had given it as
dowry to his daughter, Solomon's wife;
17 so Solomon rebuilt Gezer), Lower Beth-
horon, 18 Baalath, Tamar in the wilderness,
within the land, 19 as well as all of Solo-
mon's storage cities, the cities for his chari-
ots, the cities for his cavalry, and whatever
Solomon desired to build, in Jerusalem, in
Lebanon, and in all the land of his domin-
ion. 20 All the people who were left of the
Amorites, the Hittites, the Perizzites, the
Hivites, and the Jebusites, who were not of
the people of Israel— 21 their descendants
who were still left in the land, whom the
Israelites were unable to destroy complete-
ly—these Solomon conscripted for slave la-
bor, and so they are to this day. 22 But of
the Israelites Solomon made no slaves; they
were the soldiers, they were his officials, his
commanders, his captains, and the com-
manders of his chariotry and cavalry.

23 These were the chief officers who
were over Solomon's work: five hundred
fifty, who had charge of the people who
carried on the work.

24 But Pharaoh's daughter went up
from the city of David to her own house
that Solomon had built for her; then he
built the Millo.

25 Three times a year Solomon used to
offer up burnt offerings and sacrifices of
well-being on the altar that he built for the
LORD, offering incense[a] before the LORD.
So he completed the house.

26 King Solomon built a fleet of ships at
Ezion-geber, which is near Eloth on the
shore of the Red Sea,[b] in the land of Edom.
27 Hiram sent his servants with the fleet,
sailors who were familiar with the sea, to-
gether with the servants of Solomon.
28 They went to Ophir, and imported from
there four hundred twenty talents of gold,
which they delivered to King Solomon.

10 When the queen of Sheba heard of
the fame of Solomon (fame due to[c]
the name of the LORD), she came to test
him with hard questions. 2 She came to Je-
rusalem with a very great retinue, with
camels bearing spices, and very much gold,
and precious stones; and when she came to
Solomon, she told him all that was on her
mind. 3 Solomon answered all her ques-
tions; there was nothing hidden from the
king that he could not explain to her.
4 When the queen of Sheba had observed all
the wisdom of Solomon, the house that he
had built, 5 the food of his table, the seating
of his officials, and the attendance of his
servants, their clothing, his valets, and his
burnt offerings that he offered at the house
of the LORD, there was no more spirit in
her.

6 So she said to the king, "The report
was true that I heard in my own land of
your accomplishments and of your wis-
dom, 7 but I did not believe the reports until
I came and my own eyes had seen it. Not
even half had been told me; your wisdom
and prosperity far surpass the report that I
had heard. 8 Happy are your wives![d] Hap-
py are these your servants, who continually
attend you and hear your wisdom! 9 Blessed
be the LORD your God, who has delighted
in you and set you on the throne of Israel!
Because the LORD loved Israel forever, he
has made you king to execute justice and
righteousness." 10 Then she gave the king
one hundred twenty talents of gold, a great
quantity of spices, and precious stones;
never again did spices come in such quanti-

a Gk: Heb *offering incense with it that was*
b Or *Sea of Reeds* *c* Meaning of Heb uncertain
d Gk Syr: Heb *men*

of Canaan; see Gen 15.20; Deut 20.17. **26:** *Eloth,* elsewhere often spelled Elath. **28:** *Ophir* is in Arabia (Gen 10.29; cf. Ps 45.9; Isa 13.12 for its fame), whence the queen of Sheba also comes (Gen 10.28).

10.1–13: The visit of the queen of Sheba. The worldwide fame of Solomon, which attracted foreigners to his court (4.34), also brought the *queen of Sheba* (see 9.28n.), who was left breathless (*there was no more spirit in her,* v. 5) by Solomon's magnificence. The focus is again on the benefits royal wisdom brings to the royal court, and particularly to Solomon himself, rather than on any benefit to the people (vv. 7–8). **12:** *Almug,* a wood of uncertain species.

ty as that which the queen of Sheba gave to
King Solomon.
11 Moreover, the fleet of Hiram, which
carried gold from Ophir, brought from
Ophir a great quantity of almug wood and
precious stones. 12 From the almug wood
the king made supports for the house of the
LORD, and for the king's house, lyres also
and harps for the singers; no such almug
wood has come or been seen to this day.
13 Meanwhile King Solomon gave to
the queen of Sheba every desire that she
expressed, as well as what he gave her out
of Solomon's royal bounty. Then she re-
turned to her own land, with her servants.
14 The weight of gold that came to Solo-
mon in one year was six hundred sixty-six
talents of gold, 15 besides that which came
from the traders and from the business of
the merchants, and from all the kings of
Arabia and the governors of the land.
16 King Solomon made two hundred large
shields of beaten gold; six hundred shekels
of gold went into each large shield. 17 He
made three hundred shields of beaten gold;
three minas of gold went into each shield;
and the king put them in the House of the
Forest of Lebanon. 18 The king also made a
great ivory throne, and overlaid it with the
finest gold. 19 The throne had six steps. The
top of the throne was rounded in the back,
and on each side of the seat were arm rests
and two lions standing beside the arm rests,
20 while twelve lions were standing, one on
each end of a step on the six steps. Nothing
like it was ever made in any kingdom. 21 All
King Solomon's drinking vessels were of
gold, and all the vessels of the House of the
Forest of Lebanon were of pure gold; none
were of silver—it was not considered as
anything in the days of Solomon. 22 For the
king had a fleet of ships of Tarshish at sea
with the fleet of Hiram. Once every three
years the fleet of ships of Tarshish used to
come bringing gold, silver, ivory, apes, and
peacocks.[a]
23 Thus King Solomon excelled all the
kings of the earth in riches and in wisdom.
24 The whole earth sought the presence of
Solomon to hear his wisdom, which God
had put into his mind. 25 Every one of them
brought a present, objects of silver and
gold, garments, weaponry, spices, horses,
and mules, so much year by year.
26 Solomon gathered together chariots
and horses; he had fourteen hundred chari-
ots and twelve thousand horses, which he
stationed in the chariot cities and with the
king in Jerusalem. 27 The king made silver
as common in Jerusalem as stones, and he
made cedars as numerous as the sycamores
of the Shephelah. 28 Solomon's import of
horses was from Egypt and Kue, and the
king's traders received them from Kue at a
price. 29 A chariot could be imported from
Egypt for six hundred shekels of silver, and
a horse for one hundred fifty; so through
the king's traders they were exported to all
the kings of the Hittites and the kings of
Aram.

11 King Solomon loved many foreign
women along with the daughter of

a Or *baboons*

10.14–29: Royal wealth. *Gold* is mentioned eleven times in these verses (vv. 14,16–18,21–22,25). A *mina* weighed about 570 gr (20 oz). Solomon decorates his palace with it, makes household items with it, and overlays the finest *throne* ever seen with it. There are ancient Near Eastern parallels to the throne's design. **22:** *Tarshish,* probably the city of Tarsus on the southern coast of Turkey, or Tartessus in southern Spain. **26:** He also accumulates *chariots and horses* (see the prohibition of Deut 17.16). All but one of the instructions about kingship in Deut 17.16–17 have now been abrogated by Solomon; the remaining one ("he must not take many wives") is treated in ch 11. **27:** *The Shephelah,* the foothills between the coastal plain and the Judean hills. **28:** *Kue* was Cilicia, in southern Asia Minor. **29:** The *kings of the Hittites* ruled over what is now northern Syria; *Aram* was southern Syria. A *shekel* weighed about 11.5 g (.4 oz).

11.1–40: Solomon's apostasy and its consequences. Solomon loved the LORD (3.3), yet he also loved *the daughter of Pharaoh* (see 3.1; 9.16,24) and many other women besides, clinging to them (vv. 1–2). "Loving" and "clinging," in Deuteronomy, however, speak of unswerving human loyalty to God (Deut

Pharaoh: Moabite, Ammonite, Edomite, Si-
donian, and Hittite women, 2from the na-
tions concerning which the LORD had said
to the Israelites, "You shall not enter into
marriage with them, neither shall they with
you; for they will surely incline your heart
to follow their gods"; Solomon clung to
these in love. 3Among his wives were seven
hundred princesses and three hundred con-
cubines; and his wives turned away his
heart. 4For when Solomon was old, his
wives turned away his heart after other
gods; and his heart was not true to the
LORD his God, as was the heart of his fa-
ther David. 5For Solomon followed Astarte
the goddess of the Sidonians, and Milcom
the abomination of the Ammonites. 6So
Solomon did what was evil in the sight of
the LORD, and did not completely follow
the LORD, as his father David had done.
7Then Solomon built a high place for Che-
mosh the abomination of Moab, and for
Molech the abomination of the Ammon-
ites, on the mountain east of Jerusalem.
8He did the same for all his foreign wives,
who offered incense and sacrificed to their
gods.

9 Then the LORD was angry with Solo-
mon, because his heart had turned away
from the LORD, the God of Israel, who had
appeared to him twice, 10and had com-
manded him concerning this matter, that he
should not follow other gods; but he did
not observe what the LORD commanded.
11Therefore the LORD said to Solomon,
"Since this has been your mind and you
have not kept my covenant and my statutes
that I have commanded you, I will surely
tear the kingdom from you and give it to
your servant. 12Yet for the sake of your
father David I will not do it in your life-
time; I will tear it out of the hand of your
son. 13I will not, however, tear away the
entire kingdom; I will give one tribe to your
son, for the sake of my servant David and
for the sake of Jerusalem, which I have
chosen."

14 Then the LORD raised up an adver-
sary against Solomon, Hadad the Edomite;
he was of the royal house in Edom. 15For
when David was in Edom, and Joab the
commander of the army went up to bury
the dead, he killed every male in Edom
16(for Joab and all Israel remained there six
months, until he had eliminated every male
in Edom); 17but Hadad fled to Egypt with
some Edomites who were servants of his
father. He was a young boy at that time.
18They set out from Midian and came to
Paran; they took people with them from
Paran and came to Egypt, to Pharaoh king
of Egypt, who gave him a house, assigned
him an allowance of food, and gave him
land. 19Hadad found great favor in the
sight of Pharaoh, so that he gave him his
sister-in-law for a wife, the sister of Queen
Tahpenes. 20The sister of Tahpenes gave
birth by him to his son Genubath, whom
Tahpenes weaned in Pharaoh's house; Ge-
nubath was in Pharaoh's house among the
children of Pharaoh. 21When Hadad heard
in Egypt that David slept with his ancestors
and that Joab the commander of the army
was dead, Hadad said to Pharaoh, "Let me
depart, that I may go to my own country."
22But Pharaoh said to him, "What do you

6.5; 10.12,20; 11.1,22; 13.4; 30.20)—the God who had forbidden intermarriage with foreign women (Deut 7.3–4, generalized here beyond its original focus on intermarriage with the inhabitants of Canaan). The language is carefully chosen to suggest Solomon's apostasy. **4–7:** A divided heart led Solomon in the end *after other gods,* including (v. 5) *Astarte,* a leading Canaanite goddess, and *Milcom,* the national God of the Ammonites. Solomon built sanctuaries for them on the Mount of Olives (*the mountain east of Jerusalem,* v. 7) and elsewhere, rivaling the Temple. **9–13:** Because of David, the punishment will be delayed, and Solomon's successor will be left with a kingdom, albeit a smaller one. **14–25:** Two enemies who had hitherto not caused Solomon significant problems are *raised up* by God to oppose the apostate king. **14–22:** *Hadad* was a victim of David's wars (2 Sam 8.13–14), previously resident in *Egypt.* Solomon's first adversary is thus set upon him by an old enemy of Israel whom he had unwisely treated as a friend (3.1). **23–25:** *Rezon son of Eliada* apparently either escaped from the battle described

lack with me that you now seek to go to
your own country?" And he said, "No, do
let me go."
23 God raised up another adversary
against Solomon,[a] Rezon son of Eliada,
who had fled from his master, King Hadad-
ezer of Zobah. 24 He gathered followers
around him and became leader of a ma-
rauding band, after the slaughter by David;
they went to Damascus, settled there, and
made him king in Damascus. 25 He was an
adversary of Israel all the days of Solomon,
making trouble as Hadad did; he despised
Israel and reigned over Aram.
26 Jeroboam son of Nebat, an Ephraim-
ite of Zeredah, a servant of Solomon,
whose mother's name was Zeruah, a wid-
ow, rebelled against the king. 27 The fol-
lowing was the reason he rebelled against
the king. Solomon built the Millo, and
closed up the gap in the wall[b] of the city of
his father David. 28 The man Jeroboam was
very able, and when Solomon saw that the
young man was industrious he gave him
charge over all the forced labor of the
house of Joseph. 29 About that time, when
Jeroboam was leaving Jerusalem, the
prophet Ahijah the Shilonite found him on
the road. Ahijah had clothed himself with a
new garment. The two of them were alone
in the open country 30 when Ahijah laid
hold of the new garment he was wearing
and tore it into twelve pieces. 31 He then
said to Jeroboam: Take for yourself ten
pieces; for thus says the LORD, the God of
Israel, "See, I am about to tear the kingdom
from the hand of Solomon, and will give
you ten tribes. 32 One tribe will remain his,
for the sake of my servant David and for
the sake of Jerusalem, the city that I have
chosen out of all the tribes of Israel. 33 This
is because he has[c] forsaken me, worshiped
Astarte the goddess of the Sidonians, Che-
mosh the god of Moab, and Milcom the
god of the Ammonites, and has[c] not
walked in my ways, doing what is right in
my sight and keeping my statutes and my
ordinances, as his father David did. 34 Nev-
ertheless I will not take the whole kingdom
away from him but will make him ruler all
the days of his life, for the sake of my ser-
vant David whom I chose and who did
keep my commandments and my statutes;
35 but I will take the kingdom away from
his son and give it to you—that is, the ten
tribes. 36 Yet to his son I will give one tribe,
so that my servant David may always have
a lamp before me in Jerusalem, the city
where I have chosen to put my name. 37 I
will take you, and you shall reign over all
that your soul desires; you shall be king
over Israel. 38 If you will listen to all that I
command you, walk in my ways, and do
what is right in my sight by keeping my
statutes and my commandments, as David
my servant did, I will be with you, and will
build you an enduring house, as I built for
David, and I will give Israel to you. 39 For
this reason I will punish the descendants of
David, but not forever." 40 Solomon sought
therefore to kill Jeroboam; but Jeroboam

a Heb *him* *b* Heb lacks *in the wall* *c* Gk Syr Vg: Heb *they have*

in 2 Sam 8.3–4 or fled from Hadadezer later. His bandit group at some unspecified point in Solomon's reign took control of *Damascus,* the capital of the southern Syrian state of *Aram.* **26–40:** Solomon's most important enemy was *Jeroboam son of Nebat,* who had been superintendent of the labor force of *the house of Joseph,* which had been helping with the construction work in Jerusalem (vv. 27–28). *Millo,* see 9.15n. In a scene reminiscent of the rejection of Saul in 1 Sam 15.27–28, *the prophet Ahijah* (v. 29) tore an outer garment as a symbol of the loss of the northern part of the kingdom. He was from Shiloh, a principal sanctuary of the premonarchic period (see 1 Sam 1.3; 2.21; 4.4). **32:** If ten tribes are given to Jeroboam (vv. 30–31), it is strange that only *one tribe* (Judah) is to remain for the sake of *David* and *Jerusalem.* Benjamin, for some reason, is not highlighted in 11.30–39 (cf. 12.21), perhaps because Benjamin was regarded simply as Jerusalem's own territory as city-state. **39:** Even such punishment as has been meted out to the Davidic dynasty because of Solomon's sin is *not forever,* because of the eternal promise to David in 2 Sam 7.11–16. **40:** *Shishak* (Shoshenq I) ruled Egypt 945–924 BCE; he is the first Pharaoh named in the Bible.

promptly fled to Egypt, to King Shishak
of Egypt, and remained in Egypt until the
death of Solomon.
41 Now the rest of the acts of Solomon,
all that he did as well as his wisdom, are
they not written in the Book of the Acts of
Solomon? 42 The time that Solomon reigned
in Jerusalem over all Israel was forty years.
43 Solomon slept with his ancestors and was
buried in the city of his father David; and
his son Rehoboam succeeded him.

12 Rehoboam went to Shechem, for all
Israel had come to Shechem to make
him king. 2 When Jeroboam son of Nebat
heard of it (for he was still in Egypt, where
he had fled from King Solomon), then Jero-

11.41–43: Conclusion of Solomon's reign. *The book of the Acts of Solomon,* presumably royal annals, was one of the sources used by Deuteronomistic historians. *Rehoboam* ruled ca. 928–911 BCE.

12.1–33: The kingdom torn away; Jeroboam's sin. 2: *Shechem* was a site of covenant renewal (Josh 24.1–27) and the place where kingship first briefly intruded itself into the tribal life of Israel (Judg 8.22–23; 9)—an ideal place to which to invite a prospective king (*Rehoboam*) if the desire is to ask him

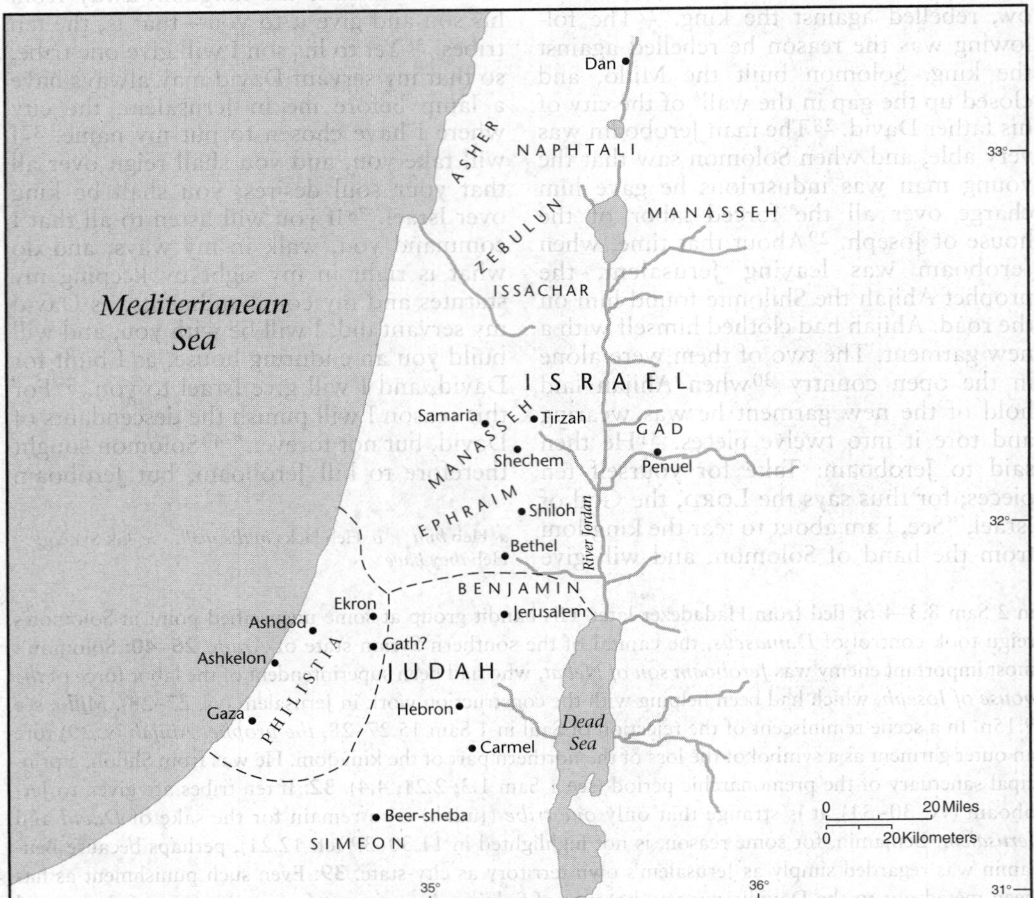

Chs 12–14: The divided monarchy. The dashed line shows the approximate boundaries between Israel, Judah, and Philistia.

boam returned from[a] Egypt. 3And they
sent and called him; and Jeroboam and all
the assembly of Israel came and said to
Rehoboam, 4"Your father made our yoke
heavy. Now therefore lighten the hard ser-
vice of your father and his heavy yoke that
he placed on us, and we will serve you."
5He said to them, "Go away for three days,
then come again to me." So the people
went away.
6 Then King Rehoboam took counsel
with the older men who had attended his
father Solomon while he was still alive, say-
ing, "How do you advise me to answer this
people?" 7They answered him, "If you will
be a servant to this people today and serve
them, and speak good words to them when
you answer them, then they will be your
servants forever." 8But he disregarded the
advice that the older men gave him, and
consulted with the young men who had
grown up with him and now attended him.
9He said to them, "What do you advise
that we answer this people who have said
to me, 'Lighten the yoke that your father
put on us'?" 10The young men who had
grown up with him said to him, "Thus you
should say to this people who spoke to you,
'Your father made our yoke heavy, but you
must lighten it for us'; thus you should say
to them, 'My little finger is thicker than my
father's loins. 11Now, whereas my father
laid on you a heavy yoke, I will add to your
yoke. My father disciplined you with
whips, but I will discipline you with scorpi-
ons.' "
12 So Jeroboam and all the people came
to Rehoboam the third day, as the king had
said, "Come to me again the third day."
13The king answered the people harshly.
He disregarded the advice that the older
men had given him 14and spoke to them
according to the advice of the young men,
"My father made your yoke heavy, but I
will add to your yoke; my father disciplined
you with whips, but I will discipline you
with scorpions." 15So the king did not lis-
ten to the people, because it was a turn of
affairs brought about by the LORD that he
might fulfill his word, which the LORD had
spoken by Ahijah the Shilonite to Jeroboam
son of Nebat.
16 When all Israel saw that the king
would not listen to them, the people an-
swered the king,

"What share do we have in David?
We have no inheritance in the son
of Jesse.
To your tents, O Israel!
Look now to your own house,
O David."

So Israel went away to their tents. 17But
Rehoboam reigned over the Israelites who
were living in the towns of Judah. 18When
King Rehoboam sent Adoram, who was
taskmaster over the forced labor, all Israel
stoned him to death. King Rehoboam then
hurriedly mounted his chariot to flee to Je-
rusalem. 19So Israel has been in rebellion
against the house of David to this day.
20 When all Israel heard that Jeroboam
had returned, they sent and called him to
the assembly and made him king over all
Israel. There was no one who followed the
house of David, except the tribe of Judah
alone.

a Gk Vg Compare 2 Chr 10.2: Heb *lived in*

how his kingship is going to be exercised so that it fits the nature of the covenant people of God. **3–4:** The Israelites have become once more a people under *hard service,* as they were in Egypt (Ex 1.14; 2.23). *Jeroboam* appears as a second Moses who will liberate them. **5–15:** *Rehoboam* plays the part of Pharaoh, increasing oppression in response to complaint (v. 14; see Ex 5.1–21) and hardening his heart (v. 15; see Ex 7.13). Using a vulgarity, he claims to be stronger than his father Solomon, and he substitutes *scorpions* (vv. 11,14, perhaps a particularly vicious form of whip) for mere *whips.* **16–24:** *All Israel* (with the exception of Judah, as it turns out) reacts by making it clear that kingship cannot be imposed upon the people, but must have their consent. They take upon their lips a cry (v. 16) similar to that of Sheba son of Bichri in 2 Sam 20.1, and they leave for their *tents.* Their choice of *Jeroboam* as king is preordained (11.31,35,37–38), and *Rehoboam* is eventually persuaded by the prophet *Shemaiah* to accept this. **18:** *Adoram,* see 4.6n. **20:** Jeroboam I ruled 928–907 BCE. **25–33:** It is not long before the new "exodus"

21 When Rehoboam came to Jerusalem,
he assembled all the house of Judah and
the tribe of Benjamin, one hundred eighty
thousand chosen troops to fight against the
house of Israel, to restore the kingdom to
Rehoboam son of Solomon. 22 But the
word of God came to Shemaiah the man of
God: 23 Say to King Rehoboam of Judah,
son of Solomon, and to all the house of
Judah and Benjamin, and to the rest of the
people, 24 "Thus says the LORD, You shall
not go up or fight against your kindred the
people of Israel. Let everyone go home, for
this thing is from me." So they heeded the
word of the LORD and went home again,
according to the word of the LORD.

25 Then Jeroboam built Shechem in the
hill country of Ephraim, and resided there;
he went out from there and built Penuel.
26 Then Jeroboam said to himself, "Now
the kingdom may well revert to the house
of David. 27 If this people continues to go
up to offer sacrifices in the house of the
LORD at Jerusalem, the heart of this people
will turn again to their master, King Reho-
boam of Judah; they will kill me and return
to King Rehoboam of Judah." 28 So the
king took counsel, and made two calves of
gold. He said to the people,[a] "You have
gone up to Jerusalem long enough. Here
are your gods, O Israel, who brought you
up out of the land of Egypt." 29 He set one
in Bethel, and the other he put in Dan.
30 And this thing became a sin, for the peo-
ple went to worship before the one at Beth-
el and before the other as far as Dan.[b]
31 He also made houses[c] on high places,
and appointed priests from among all the
people, who were not Levites. 32 Jeroboam
appointed a festival on the fifteenth day of
the eighth month like the festival that was
in Judah, and he offered sacrifices on the
altar; so he did in Bethel, sacrificing to the
calves that he had made. And he placed in
Bethel the priests of the high places that he
had made. 33 He went up to the altar that he
had made in Bethel on the fifteenth day in
the eighth month, in the month that he
alone had devised; he appointed a festival
for the people of Israel, and he went up to
the altar to offer incense.

13 While Jeroboam was standing by
the altar to offer incense, a man of
God came out of Judah by the word of the
LORD to Bethel 2 and proclaimed against
the altar by the word of the LORD, and
said, "O altar, altar, thus says the LORD: 'A
son shall be born to the house of David,
Josiah by name; and he shall sacrifice on
you the priests of the high places who offer
incense on you, and human bones shall be
burned on you.' " 3 He gave a sign the same

a Gk: Heb *to them* *b* Compare Gk: Heb *went to the one as far as Dan* *c* Gk Vg Compare 13.32: Heb *a house*

out of Rehoboam's "Egypt" leads, as a result of lack of trust in God, to the worship of golden calves (as in the case of the first Exodus). It is Jeroboam's action in leading the people to such worship that is constantly mentioned in the subsequent narrative about the Northern Kingdom, as Israel's characteristic sin that leads them eventually to exile in a foreign land (e.g., 15.26; 2 Kings 17.20–23). **25:** *Penuel,* see Gen 32.30–31. **28:** Jeroboam's words are almost exactly those with which the people greet the construction of the first golden calf (Ex 32.4). **29:** The centers of worship that Jeroboam builds within his own territory to compete with the Jerusalem Temple are in the far north (*Dan*) and the far south (*Bethel*) of northern Israel. **31–33:** *Bethel* is the more important: It is here that the king builds his own temple ("house of high places," cf. NRSV footnote) with its own *altar* and—from this Judean author's perspective—illegitimate priesthood, creating his own version of the *festival* of Tabernacles (which was celebrated in Jerusalem in the seventh month; cf. 8.2; Lev 23.33–43).

13.1–34: The man of God from Judah. Prophetic opposition now confronts Jeroboam at his new *altar.* The anonymous prophet assumes the end of Jeroboam's dynasty even before it has begun, for his words point forward to a time when all northern dynasties have come to an end, and only the *house of David* remains to take action against *Bethel* (cf. the description of the reign of *Josiah* in 2 Kings 22.1–23.30). The *sign* of the broken altar indicates that the prophecy is true, and what happened to Jeroboam's *hand* demonstrates his impotence with respect to the prophetic word. **7–34:** The point of the story is that

day, saying, "This is the sign that the LORD
has spoken: 'The altar shall be torn down,
and the ashes that are on it shall be poured
out.' " 4 When the king heard what the man
of God cried out against the altar at Bethel,
Jeroboam stretched out his hand from the
altar, saying, "Seize him!" But the hand
that he stretched out against him withered
so that he could not draw it back to him-
self. 5 The altar also was torn down, and the
ashes poured out from the altar, according
to the sign that the man of God had given
by the word of the LORD. 6 The king said to
the man of God, "Entreat now the favor of
the LORD your God, and pray for me, so
that my hand may be restored to me." So
the man of God entreated the LORD; and
the king's hand was restored to him, and
became as it was before. 7 Then the king
said to the man of God, "Come home with
me and dine, and I will give you a gift."
8 But the man of God said to the king, "If
you give me half your kingdom, I will not
go in with you; nor will I eat food or drink
water in this place. 9 For thus I was com-
manded by the word of the LORD: You
shall not eat food, or drink water, or return
by the way that you came." 10 So he went
another way, and did not return by the way
that he had come to Bethel.

11 Now there lived an old prophet in
Bethel. One of his sons came and told him
all that the man of God had done that day
in Bethel; the words also that he had spo-
ken to the king, they told to their father.
12 Their father said to them, "Which way
did he go?" And his sons showed him the
way that the man of God who came from
Judah had gone. 13 Then he said to his sons,
"Saddle a donkey for me." So they saddled
a donkey for him, and he mounted it. 14 He
went after the man of God, and found him
sitting under an oak tree. He said to him,
"Are you the man of God who came from
Judah?" He answered, "I am." 15 Then he
said to him, "Come home with me and eat
some food." 16 But he said, "I cannot return
with you, or go in with you; nor will I eat
food or drink water with you in this place;
17 for it was said to me by the word of the
LORD: You shall not eat food or drink wa-
ter there, or return by the way that you
came." 18 Then the other[a] said to him, "I
also am a prophet as you are, and an angel
spoke to me by the word of the LORD:
Bring him back with you into your house so
that he may eat food and drink water." But
he was deceiving him. 19 Then the man of
God[a] went back with him, and ate food
and drank water in his house.

20 As they were sitting at the table, the
word of the LORD came to the prophet who
had brought him back; 21 and he pro-
claimed to the man of God who came from
Judah, "Thus says the LORD: Because you
have disobeyed the word of the LORD, and
have not kept the commandment that the
LORD your God commanded you, 22 but
have come back and have eaten food and
drunk water in the place of which he said to
you, 'Eat no food, and drink no water,'
your body shall not come to your ancestral
tomb." 23 After the man of God[a] had eaten
food and had drunk, they saddled for him
a donkey belonging to the prophet who had
brought him back. 24 Then as he went
away, a lion met him on the road and killed
him. His body was thrown in the road, and
the donkey stood beside it; the lion also
stood beside the body. 25 People passed by
and saw the body thrown in the road, with
the lion standing by the body. And they
came and told it in the town where the old
prophet lived.

26 When the prophet who had brought
him back from the way heard of it, he said,
"It is the man of God who disobeyed the
word of the LORD; therefore the LORD has
given him to the lion, which has torn him
and killed him according to the word that

a Heb *he*

complete and radical obedience is required by God to what he has commanded. The *man of God* ought to have followed through the word of the LORD he had received, rather than being led off his path by another's claim that God had spoken to him (v. 18). Even the prophets who deliver God's word must themselves obey it. **28:** Lions would not normally be expected to kill a man and then simply stand over

the LORD spoke to him." 27 Then he said to
his sons, "Saddle a donkey for me." So they
saddled one, 28 and he went and found the
body thrown in the road, with the donkey
and the lion standing beside the body. The
lion had not eaten the body or attacked the
donkey. 29 The prophet took up the body of
the man of God, laid it on the donkey, and
brought it back to the city,[a] to mourn and
to bury him. 30 He laid the body in his own
grave; and they mourned over him, saying,
"Alas, my brother!" 31 After he had buried
him, he said to his sons, "When I die, bury
me in the grave in which the man of God
is buried; lay my bones beside his bones.
32 For the saying that he proclaimed by the
word of the LORD against the altar in Beth-
el, and against all the houses of the high
places that are in the cities of Samaria, shall
surely come to pass."

33 Even after this event Jeroboam did
not turn from his evil way, but made priests
for the high places again from among all
the people; any who wanted to be priests he
consecrated for the high places. 34 This mat-
ter became sin to the house of Jeroboam, so
as to cut it off and to destroy it from the
face of the earth.

14 At that time Abijah son of Jeroboam
fell sick. 2 Jeroboam said to his wife,
"Go, disguise yourself, so that it will not be
known that you are the wife of Jeroboam,
and go to Shiloh; for the prophet Ahijah is
there, who said of me that I should be
king over this people. 3 Take with you ten
loaves, some cakes, and a jar of honey, and
go to him; he will tell you what shall hap-
pen to the child."

4 Jeroboam's wife did so; she set out and
went to Shiloh, and came to the house of
Ahijah. Now Ahijah could not see, for his
eyes were dim because of his age. 5 But the
LORD said to Ahijah, "The wife of Jerobo-
am is coming to inquire of you concerning
her son; for he is sick. Thus and thus you
shall say to her."

When she came, she pretended to be an-
other woman. 6 But when Ahijah heard the
sound of her feet, as she came in at the
door, he said, "Come in, wife of Jeroboam;
why do you pretend to be another? For I
am charged with heavy tidings for you.
7 Go, tell Jeroboam, 'Thus says the LORD,
the God of Israel: Because I exalted you
from among the people, made you leader
over my people Israel, 8 and tore the king-
dom away from the house of David to give
it to you; yet you have not been like my
servant David, who kept my command-
ments and followed me with all his heart,
doing only that which was right in my
sight, 9 but you have done evil above all
those who were before you and have gone
and made for yourself other gods, and cast
images, provoking me to anger, and have
thrust me behind your back; 10 therefore, I
will bring evil upon the house of Jeroboam.
I will cut off from Jeroboam every male,
both bond and free in Israel, and will con-
sume the house of Jeroboam, just as one
burns up dung until it is all gone. 11 Anyone
belonging to Jeroboam who dies in the city,
the dogs shall eat; and anyone who dies in
the open country, the birds of the air shall
eat; for the LORD has spoken.' 12 Therefore
set out, go to your house. When your feet
enter the city, the child shall die. 13 All Isra-
el shall mourn for him and bury him; for he

a Gk: Heb *he came to the town of the old prophet*

the body with an uneaten donkey for company. The point is thus to stress the miraculous, divinely initiated nature of what has happened. **32:** As a city, *Samaria* became the capital of the Northern Kingdom under Omri (16.24). The name is used here by extension for the whole territory of which Samaria was the capital.

14.1–31: The end of Jeroboam and Rehoboam. Jeroboam's *wife* goes to the prophet Ahijah (see 11.29–30) to find out about her sick *child.* She discovers when she arrives at Ahijah's house, however, that in fact he has been given a message for her about the kingship (v. 6). Jeroboam's failure to be like David will result in the end of his dynasty for want of male descendants (v. 10), and it will be a dishonorable end since the bodies will not be buried but will be eaten by *dogs* and *birds* (v. 11; see 1 Sam 31.8–13 for the importance of proper burial). **15:** In the absence of a strong dynasty to rule Israel, the

alone of Jeroboam's family shall come to
the grave, because in him there is found
something pleasing to the LORD, the God
of Israel, in the house of Jeroboam.
14 Moreover the LORD will raise up for
himself a king over Israel, who shall cut off
the house of Jeroboam today, even right
now![a]
15 "The LORD will strike Israel, as a
reed is shaken in the water; he will root up
Israel out of this good land that he gave to
their ancestors, and scatter them beyond
the Euphrates, because they have made
their sacred poles,[b] provoking the LORD to
anger. 16 He will give Israel up because of
the sins of Jeroboam, which he sinned and
which he caused Israel to commit."
17 Then Jeroboam's wife got up and
went away, and she came to Tirzah. As she
came to the threshold of the house, the
child died. 18 All Israel buried him and
mourned for him, according to the word of
the LORD, which he spoke by his servant
the prophet Ahijah.
19 Now the rest of the acts of Jeroboam,
how he warred and how he reigned, are
written in the Book of the Annals of the
Kings of Israel. 20 The time that Jeroboam
reigned was twenty-two years; then he slept
with his ancestors, and his son Nadab succeeded him.
21 Now Rehoboam son of Solomon
reigned in Judah. Rehoboam was forty-one
years old when he began to reign, and he
reigned seventeen years in Jerusalem, the
city that the LORD had chosen out of all the
tribes of Israel, to put his name there. His
mother's name was Naamah the Ammonite.
22 Judah did what was evil in the sight
of the LORD; they provoked him to jealousy
with their sins that they committed, more
than all that their ancestors had done.
23 For they also built for themselves high
places, pillars, and sacred poles[b] on every
high hill and under every green tree; 24 there
were also male temple prostitutes in the
land. They committed all the abominations
of the nations that the LORD drove out before the people of Israel.
25 In the fifth year of King Rehoboam,
King Shishak of Egypt came up against Jerusalem;
26 he took away the treasures of
the house of the LORD and the treasures of
the king's house; he took everything. He
also took away all the shields of gold that
Solomon had made; 27 so King Rehoboam
made shields of bronze instead, and committed them to the hands of the officers of
the guard, who kept the door of the king's
house. 28 As often as the king went into the
house of the LORD, the guard carried them
and brought them back to the guardroom.
29 Now the rest of the acts of Rehoboam, and all that he did, are they not written
in the Book of the Annals of the Kings of
Judah? 30 There was war between Rehoboam and Jeroboam continually.
31 Rehoboam slept with his ancestors and was buried
with his ancestors in the city of David. His
mother's name was Naamah the Ammonite. His son Abijam succeeded him.

a Meaning of Heb uncertain *b* Heb *Asherim*

Northern Kingdom is destined to know only the instability of the *reed* that is *shaken* (blown by the wind) *in the water,* and eventually exile to a land *beyond the Euphrates* River (Assyria). The political instability of which Ahijah speaks is well described in the account of the Northern Kingdom that follows. The goddess Asherah was the consort of Baal, the Canaanite god of fertility, and *sacred poles* were wooden objects used in her worship, prohibited in Deut 17.21. The golden calves are thus being associated already with the worship of foreign deities, which will intensify in Israel during the reign of Ahab (see 18.18–19). **17:** Jeroboam has by this point moved his court from Shechem to *Tirzah.* **21–24:** *Judah* also became involved in setting up *high places* at which idolatrous worship could take place, engaging in the *abominations* current in the land before God *drove out* its previous inhabitants. The implicit threat is that Judah will be driven out of the land as well. Both North and South are equally sinful and heading for the same fate. **24:** *Temple prostitutes* are also associated with the fertility cult in Hos 4.14, although there they are female. **25:** *Shishak,* see 11.40n. His invasion of Israel is documented in Egyptian sources and in the archaeological record, the first event in the Bible to have such independent witnesses.

15 Now in the eighteenth year of King
Jeroboam son of Nebat, Abijam be-
gan to reign over Judah. 2 He reigned for
three years in Jerusalem. His mother's
name was Maacah daughter of Abishalom.
3 He committed all the sins that his father
did before him; his heart was not true to the
LORD his God, like the heart of his father
David. 4 Nevertheless for David's sake the
LORD his God gave him a lamp in Jerusa-
lem, setting up his son after him, and estab-
lishing Jerusalem; 5 because David did what
was right in the sight of the LORD, and did
not turn aside from anything that he com-
manded him all the days of his life, except
in the matter of Uriah the Hittite. 6 The war
begun between Rehoboam and Jeroboam
continued all the days of his life. 7 The rest
of the acts of Abijam, and all that he did,
are they not written in the Book of the An-
nals of the Kings of Judah? There was war
between Abijam and Jeroboam. 8 Abijam
slept with his ancestors, and they buried
him in the city of David. Then his son Asa
succeeded him.
9 In the twentieth year of King Jerobo-
am of Israel, Asa began to reign over Judah;
10 he reigned forty-one years in Jerusalem.
His mother's name was Maacah daughter
of Abishalom. 11 Asa did what was right in
the sight of the LORD, as his father David
had done. 12 He put away the male temple
prostitutes out of the land, and removed all
the idols that his ancestors had made. 13 He
also removed his mother Maacah from be-
ing queen mother, because she had made an
abominable image for Asherah; Asa cut
down her image and burned it at the Wadi
Kidron. 14 But the high places were not tak-
en away. Nevertheless the heart of Asa was
true to the LORD all his days. 15 He brought
into the house of the LORD the votive gifts
of his father and his own votive gifts—sil-
ver, gold, and utensils.
16 There was war between Asa and
King Baasha of Israel all their days. 17 King
Baasha of Israel went up against Judah, and
built Ramah, to prevent anyone from going
out or coming in to King Asa of Judah.
18 Then Asa took all the silver and the gold
that were left in the treasures of the house
of the LORD and the treasures of the king's
house, and gave them into the hands of his
servants. King Asa sent them to King Ben-
hadad son of Tabrimmon son of Hezion of
Aram, who resided in Damascus, saying,
19 "Let there be an alliance between me and
you, like that between my father and your
father: I am sending you a present of silver
and gold; go, break your alliance with King
Baasha of Israel, so that he may withdraw
from me." 20 Ben-hadad listened to King
Asa, and sent the commanders of his armies
against the cities of Israel. He conquered
Ijon, Dan, Abel-beth-maacah, and all
Chinneroth, with all the land of Naphtali.
21 When Baasha heard of it, he stopped
building Ramah and lived in Tirzah.

15.1–24: Abijam and Asa. Abijam is the characteristically bad Judean king, indulging in the idolatry of the later Solomon and of Rehoboam. Asa, on the other hand, is the characteristically good Judean king, behaving relatively faithfully like David and the earlier Solomon. These two set the pattern for all the Judean kings who follow, who are measured in terms of whether they have been "like David" or not. **1–8:** *Abijam* (911–908 BCE) is called Abijah in Chronicles; his mother was the daughter of David's son Absalom (*Abishalom;* see 2 Chr 11.20). He was just as bad as his father Rehoboam, yet *for David's sake the LORD his God gave him a lamp in Jerusalem* (v. 4; see 11.36). David's dynasty, unlike Jeroboam's, is secure; sin cannot affect its fortunes in any ultimate sense (2 Sam 7.12–16). **9–15:** *Asa* (908–867 BCE) followed the Davidic pattern and eschewed idolatry, taking action against the *temple prostitutes* mentioned in 14.24 and removing both the *idols* made in previous reigns (on *Asherah* see 4.5n.) and his own idolatrous *mother* (who is called Micaiah in 2 Chr 13.2). He unwisely failed to intervene, however, to end worship of the LORD at the local sanctuaries, called "high places" in Kings (v. 14). **16–24:** Asa's reign in Judah was a long one, and he saw five Israelite kings rise and fall before Ahab began his rule. *Baasha* was the second of these (see 15.33–16.7). He pushed into Benjamin and *built* (fortified) *Ramah,* only a few miles north of Jerusalem, forcing Asa to try to buy a new ally (vv. 18–19).

22 Then King Asa made a proclamation to
all Judah, none was exempt: they carried
away the stones of Ramah and its timber,
with which Baasha had been building; with
them King Asa built Geba of Benjamin and
Mizpah. 23 Now the rest of all the acts of
Asa, all his power, all that he did, and the
cities that he built, are they not written in
the Book of the Annals of the Kings of Ju-
dah? But in his old age he was diseased in
his feet. 24 Then Asa slept with his ances-
tors, and was buried with his ancestors in
the city of his father David; his son Jehosh-
aphat succeeded him.
25 Nadab son of Jeroboam began to
reign over Israel in the second year of King
Asa of Judah; he reigned over Israel two
years. 26 He did what was evil in the sight of
the LORD, walking in the way of his ances-
tor and in the sin that he caused Israel to
commit.
27 Baasha son of Ahijah, of the house of
Issachar, conspired against him; and Baa-
sha struck him down at Gibbethon, which
belonged to the Philistines; for Nadab and
all Israel were laying siege to Gibbethon.
28 So Baasha killed Nadab[a] in the third
year of King Asa of Judah, and succeeded
him. 29 As soon as he was king, he killed all
the house of Jeroboam; he left to the house
of Jeroboam not one that breathed, until he
had destroyed it, according to the word of
the LORD that he spoke by his servant Ahi-
jah the Shilonite— 30 because of the sins of
Jeroboam that he committed and that he
caused Israel to commit, and because of the
anger to which he provoked the LORD, the
God of Israel.
31 Now the rest of the acts of Nadab,
and all that he did, are they not written in
the Book of the Annals of the Kings of Isra-
el? 32 There was war between Asa and King
Baasha of Israel all their days.
33 In the third year of King Asa of Ju-
dah, Baasha son of Ahijah began to reign
over all Israel at Tirzah; he reigned twenty-
four years. 34 He did what was evil in the
sight of the LORD, walking in the way of
Jeroboam and in the sin that he caused Isra-
el to commit.

16 The word of the LORD came to Jehu
son of Hanani against Baasha, say-
ing, 2 "Since I exalted you out of the dust
and made you leader over my people Israel,
and you have walked in the way of Jerobo-
am, and have caused my people Israel to
sin, provoking me to anger with their sins,
3 therefore, I will consume Baasha and his
house, and I will make your house like the
house of Jeroboam son of Nebat. 4 Anyone
belonging to Baasha who dies in the city the
dogs shall eat; and anyone of his who dies
in the field the birds of the air shall eat."
5 Now the rest of the acts of Baasha,
what he did, and his power, are they not
written in the Book of the Annals of the
Kings of Israel? 6 Baasha slept with his an-
cestors, and was buried at Tirzah; and his
son Elah succeeded him. 7 Moreover the
word of the LORD came by the prophet
Jehu son of Hanani against Baasha and his
house, both because of all the evil that he
did in the sight of the LORD, provoking him
to anger with the work of his hands, in
being like the house of Jeroboam, and also
because he destroyed it.
8 In the twenty-sixth year of King Asa of
Judah, Elah son of Baasha began to reign

a Heb *him*

15.25–16.34: From Nadab to Ahab. The fulfillment of the prophecy against the house of Jeroboam has been delayed until it has been made clear how different is God's treatment of the house of David. Now king succeeds king in this fast-moving tale of northern intrigue and violence. **15.25–32:** The reign of *Nadab* (907–906 BCE) is short-lived, as he follows Jeroboam's example (doing *evil in the sight of the LORD*) and is murdered by *Baasha,* who in turn kills all the other members of Jeroboam's family. **29–30:** See 14.7–16. **15.33–16.7:** Baasha (906–883 BCE), too, walks *in the way of Jeroboam* and is confronted like him by a prophet who announces the end of his dynasty. **8–14:** *Elah* (883–882 BCE) lasts no longer than Nadab. He, too, is the subject of a conspiracy, though he is murdered, not in battle, but at home in *Tirzah* (v. 9). The assassin is *Zimri,* whose butchery is not restricted only to the family of Baasha, but also extends to

over Israel in Tirzah; he reigned two years.
9 But his servant Zimri, commander of half
his chariots, conspired against him. When
he was at Tirzah, drinking himself drunk in
the house of Arza, who was in charge of
the palace at Tirzah, 10 Zimri came in and
struck him down and killed him, in the
twenty-seventh year of King Asa of Judah,
and succeeded him.

11 When he began to reign, as soon as
he had seated himself on his throne, he
killed all the house of Baasha; he did not
leave him a single male of his kindred or his
friends. 12 Thus Zimri destroyed all the
house of Baasha, according to the word of
the LORD, which he spoke against Baasha
by the prophet Jehu— 13 because of all the
sins of Baasha and the sins of his son Elah
that they committed, and that they caused
Israel to commit, provoking the LORD God
of Israel to anger with their idols. 14 Now
the rest of the acts of Elah, and all that he
did, are they not written in the Book of the
Annals of the Kings of Israel?

15 In the twenty-seventh year of King
Asa of Judah, Zimri reigned seven days in
Tirzah. Now the troops were encamped
against Gibbethon, which belonged to the
Philistines, 16 and the troops who were en-
camped heard it said, "Zimri has con-
spired, and he has killed the king"; there-
fore all Israel made Omri, the commander
of the army, king over Israel that day in the
camp. 17 So Omri went up from Gibbethon,
and all Israel with him, and they besieged
Tirzah. 18 When Zimri saw that the city was
taken, he went into the citadel of the king's
house; he burned down the king's house
over himself with fire, and died— 19 be-
cause of the sins that he committed, doing
evil in the sight of the LORD, walking in the
way of Jeroboam, and for the sin that he
committed, causing Israel to sin. 20 Now the
rest of the acts of Zimri, and the conspiracy
that he made, are they not written in the
Book of the Annals of the Kings of Israel?

21 Then the people of Israel were divid-
ed into two parts; half of the people fol-
lowed Tibni son of Ginath, to make him
king, and half followed Omri. 22 But the
people who followed Omri overcame the
people who followed Tibni son of Ginath;
so Tibni died, and Omri became king. 23 In
the thirty-first year of King Asa of Judah,
Omri began to reign over Israel; he reigned
for twelve years, six of them in Tirzah.

24 He bought the hill of Samaria from
Shemer for two talents of silver; he fortified
the hill, and called the city that he built,
Samaria, after the name of Shemer, the
owner of the hill.

25 Omri did what was evil in the sight of
the LORD; he did more evil than all who
were before him. 26 For he walked in all the
way of Jeroboam son of Nebat, and in the
sins that he caused Israel to commit, pro-
voking the LORD, the God of Israel, to an-
ger by their idols. 27 Now the rest of the acts
of Omri that he did, and the power that he
showed, are they not written in the Book of
the Annals of the Kings of Israel? 28 Omri
slept with his ancestors, and was buried in
Samaria; his son Ahab succeeded him.

29 In the thirty-eighth year of King Asa

family friends (v. 11). **15–22:** Zimri is the most spectacularly unsuccessful king of all. His suicide brings his seven-day "reign" (in 882 BCE) to its end. After a lengthy power struggle (cf. 16.15,23), *Omri* fights off the challenge of *Tibni* to his kingship and rules over Israel unopposed. **23–28:** *Omri* (882–871 BCE) was regarded as an able and important king by other observers of Israel in this period. The Moabite Stone tells us that he subjugated Moab, and the Assyrian records refer to Israel as "the land of the house of Omri" long after Omri's descendants had ceased to rule. Yet the only event of Omri's reign described to us by the authors of Kings is his purchase of *the hill of Samaria* and his building of the new northern capital there. His life as king is simply subsumed under the heading "idolater" (vv. 25–26): He took the throne, he sinned, he died. This is what the writer views as most important about his life. **29–34:** The last (and, in the view of the writer, the worst) Israelite king to gain the throne during the reign of Asa in Judah is *Ahab son of Omri* (873–852). He adds to the *sins of Jeroboam* a marriage to a foreign woman, *Jezebel,* who inevitably leads him into the worship of *Baal,* the Canaanite fertility god. To the temple and altar for

of Judah, Ahab son of Omri began to reign
over Israel; Ahab son of Omri reigned over
Israel in Samaria twenty-two years. 30 Ahab
son of Omri did evil in the sight of the
LORD more than all who were before him.
31 And as if it had been a light thing for
him to walk in the sins of Jeroboam son of
Nebat, he took as his wife Jezebel daughter
of King Ethbaal of the Sidonians, and went
and served Baal, and worshiped him. 32 He
erected an altar for Baal in the house of
Baal, which he built in Samaria. 33 Ahab
also made a sacred pole.[a] Ahab did more
to provoke the anger of the LORD, the God
of Israel, than had all the kings of Israel
who were before him. 34 In his days Hiel of
Bethel built Jericho; he laid its foundation
at the cost of Abiram his firstborn, and set
up its gates at the cost of his youngest son
Segub, according to the word of the LORD,
which he spoke by Joshua son of Nun.

17 Now Elijah the Tishbite, of Tishbe[b]
in Gilead, said to Ahab, "As the
LORD the God of Israel lives, before whom
I stand, there shall be neither dew nor rain
these years, except by my word." 2 The
word of the LORD came to him, saying,
3 "Go from here and turn eastward, and
hide yourself by the Wadi Cherith, which is
east of the Jordan. 4 You shall drink from
the wadi, and I have commanded the ra-
vens to feed you there." 5 So he went and
did according to the word of the LORD; he
went and lived by the Wadi Cherith, which
is east of the Jordan. 6 The ravens brought
him bread and meat in the morning, and
bread and meat in the evening; and he
drank from the wadi. 7 But after a while the
wadi dried up, because there was no rain in
the land.
8 Then the word of the LORD came to
him, saying, 9 "Go now to Zarephath,
which belongs to Sidon, and live there; for
I have commanded a widow there to feed
you." 10 So he set out and went to Zare-
phath. When he came to the gate of the
town, a widow was there gathering sticks;
he called to her and said, "Bring me a little
water in a vessel, so that I may drink." 11 As
she was going to bring it, he called to her
and said, "Bring me a morsel of bread in
your hand." 12 But she said, "As the LORD
your God lives, I have nothing baked, only
a handful of meal in a jar, and a little oil
in a jug; I am now gathering a couple of
sticks, so that I may go home and prepare
it for myself and my son, that we may eat it,
and die." 13 Elijah said to her, "Do not be
afraid; go and do as you have said; but first
make me a little cake of it and bring it to
me, and afterwards make something for
yourself and your son. 14 For thus says the
LORD the God of Israel: The jar of meal
will not be emptied and the jug of oil will
not fail until the day that the LORD sends
rain on the earth." 15 She went and did as

a Heb *Asherah* b Gk: Heb *of the settlers*

the calf at Bethel is added now an *altar for Baal* in a temple of Baal in *Samaria.* **34:** Joshua had pronounced a curse on the man who rebuilt Jericho (Josh 6.26), who turns out to be *Hiel of Bethel* (reminding us that Bethel has now become a thoroughly impious city, whose residents treat Joshua's "prophecy" with contempt).

17.1–24: Elijah and the drought. The major theme of chs 12–16 has been that God is in control of history, rather than kings or the other gods whom the kings worship. Everything comes to pass just as the prophets say. The Elijah and Elisha cycles, placed at the center of 1–2 Kings, further establish this perspective. In chs 17–18 in particular, the most sinful of Israel's kings, Ahab, is forced to reckon with the most powerful of prophetic interventions, in the person of Elijah. These chapters make clear that Baal is no more a god in any real sense than Jeroboam's calves are. The divinely ordained drought (17.1) provides the context for showing that it is the LORD, and not Baal, who controls both life and death, both fertility and infertility. **1–3:** *Gilead* is the territory *east of the Jordan* River, often under Israelite control. The exact location of *Tishbe* and the *Wadi Cherith* (v. 2) is not known. **4–6:** God is able to provide for Elijah, for he controls not just the rain but the whole natural order, including the *ravens.* As the Israelites had once been the beneficiaries of God's provision of *bread and meat* in the wilderness (Ex 16, esp. vv.

Elijah said, so that she as well as he and her
household ate for many days. 16 The jar of
meal was not emptied, neither did the jug
of oil fail, according to the word of the
LORD that he spoke by Elijah.
17 After this the son of the woman, the
mistress of the house, became ill; his illness
was so severe that there was no breath left
in him. 18 She then said to Elijah, "What
have you against me, O man of God? You
have come to me to bring my sin to remem-
brance, and to cause the death of my son!"
19 But he said to her, "Give me your son."
He took him from her bosom, carried him
up into the upper chamber where he was
lodging, and laid him on his own bed. 20 He
cried out to the LORD, "O LORD my God,
have you brought calamity even upon the

8,12–13), now Elijah also eats this food, but even more liberally than they had, since he receives each sort of food twice daily. **7–16:** The region of *Sidon* on the coast of Phoenicia (modern Lebanon) is the very heartland of Baal-worship (cf. 16.31), yet here too the LORD can bring drought and provide sustenance.

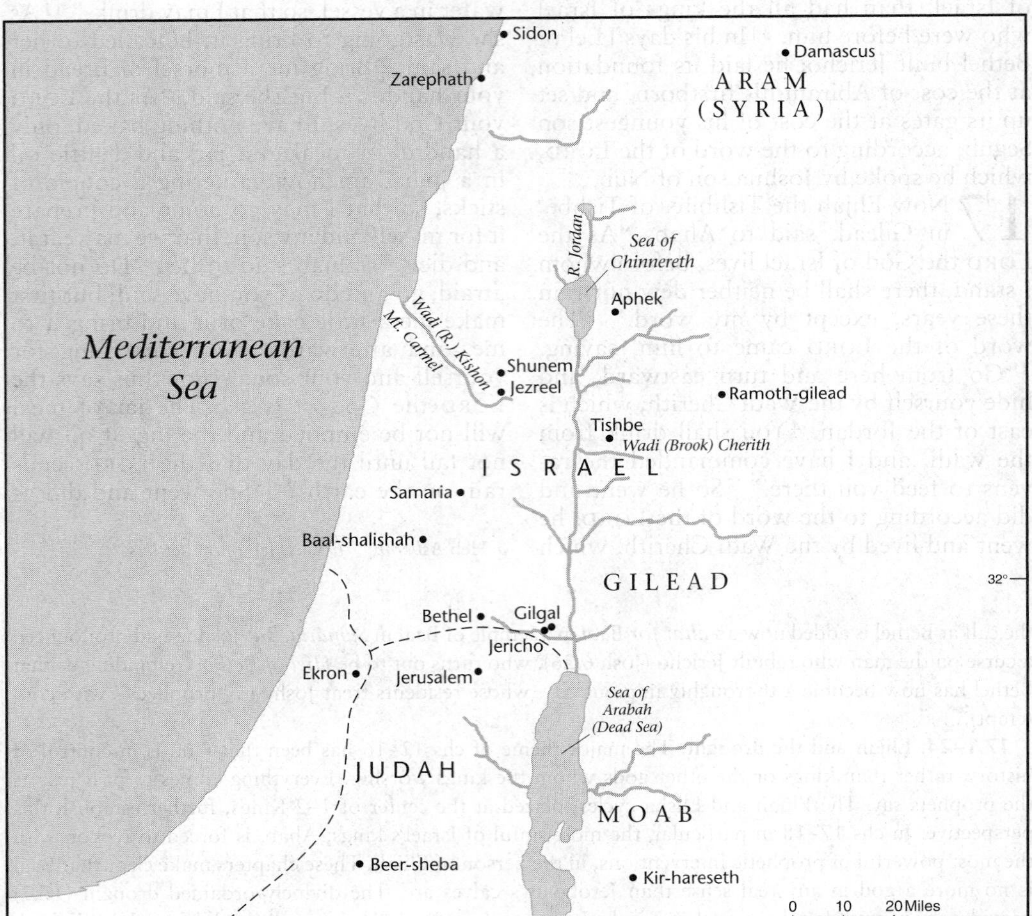

Chs 17–22: The Elijah narratives. The dashed line shows the approximate boundaries between Israel, Judah, and Philistia.

widow with whom I am staying, by killing
her son?” 21Then he stretched himself upon
the child three times, and cried out to the
LORD, “O LORD my God, let this child’s
life come into him again.” 22The LORD lis-
tened to the voice of Elijah; the life of the
child came into him again, and he revived.
23Elijah took the child, brought him down
from the upper chamber into the house,
and gave him to his mother; then Elijah
said, “See, your son is alive.” 24So the
woman said to Elijah, “Now I know that
you are a man of God, and that the word of
the LORD in your mouth is truth.”

18 After many days the word of the
LORD came to Elijah, in the third
year of the drought,[a] saying, “Go, present
yourself to Ahab; I will send rain on the
earth.” 2So Elijah went to present himself
to Ahab. The famine was severe in Samaria.
3Ahab summoned Obadiah, who was in
charge of the palace. (Now Obadiah re-
vered the LORD greatly; 4when Jezebel was
killing off the prophets of the LORD, Oba-
diah took a hundred prophets, hid them
fifty to a cave, and provided them with
bread and water.) 5Then Ahab said to Oba-
diah, “Go through the land to all the
springs of water and to all the wadis; per-
haps we may find grass to keep the horses
and mules alive, and not lose some of the
animals.” 6So they divided the land be-
tween them to pass through it; Ahab went
in one direction by himself, and Obadiah
went in another direction by himself.

7 As Obadiah was on the way, Elijah
met him; Obadiah recognized him, fell on
his face, and said, “Is it you, my lord Eli-
jah?” 8He answered him, “It is I. Go, tell
your lord that Elijah is here.” 9And he said,
“How have I sinned, that you would hand
your servant over to Ahab, to kill me? 10As
the LORD your God lives, there is no nation
or kingdom to which my lord has not sent
to seek you; and when they would say, ‘He
is not here,’ he would require an oath of the
kingdom or nation, that they had not found
you. 11But now you say, ‘Go, tell your lord
that Elijah is here.’ 12As soon as I have
gone from you, the spirit of the LORD will
carry you I know not where; so, when I
come and tell Ahab and he cannot find you,
he will kill me, although I your servant
have revered the LORD from my youth.
13Has it not been told my lord what I did
when Jezebel killed the prophets of the
LORD, how I hid a hundred of the LORD’s
prophets fifty to a cave, and provided them
with bread and water? 14Yet now you say,
‘Go, tell your lord that Elijah is here’; he
will surely kill me.” 15Elijah said, “As the
LORD of hosts lives, before whom I stand,
I will surely show myself to him today.”
16So Obadiah went to meet Ahab, and told
him; and Ahab went to meet Elijah.

17 When Ahab saw Elijah, Ahab said to
him, “Is it you, you troubler of Israel?”
18He answered, “I have not troubled Israel;
but you have, and your father’s house, be-
cause you have forsaken the command-
ments of the LORD and followed the Baals.
19Now therefore have all Israel assemble
for me at Mount Carmel, with the four
hundred fifty prophets of Baal and the four

a Heb lacks *of the drought*

17–24: The death of the widow’s son provides the ultimate test of the LORD’s authority over life and death. **21:** The purpose of Elijah’s stretching action is not made clear. The prayer is in any case the crucial element in the scene (v. 22).

18.1–46: Elijah and the prophets of Baal. Ahab, like Baal, is powerless: He can find neither Elijah (v. 10) nor grass to keep his animals alive (v. 5). All the initiative must come from God and his prophet. The drought is soon to end, but it must be clear before then to all Israel (not only to the widow of Zarephath) who is truly God. There must be a public test of strength. **12:** Similar transport of prophets is found in Ezek 3.14; 11.1; Bel 1.34–36; cf. 2 Kings 2.11. **17–24:** Ahab holds Elijah responsible for what has happened: He is the *troubler of Israel* (v. 17; cf. Josh 6.18; 7.25, where Achan’s sin brings God’s judgment on Israel). Elijah holds that it is Ahab’s apostasy (the worship of the *Baals,* the various local manifestations of Baal) that has brought the “trouble.” **19:** As the identity of the true troubler of Israel in Josh 7 was settled in public before “all Israel,” so also here *all Israel* is gathered on *Mount Carmel* (on the

hundred prophets of Asherah, who eat at
Jezebel's table."
20 So Ahab sent to all the Israelites, and
assembled the prophets at Mount Carmel.
21 Elijah then came near to all the people,
and said, "How long will you go limping
with two different opinions? If the LORD is
God, follow him; but if Baal, then follow
him." The people did not answer him a
word. 22 Then Elijah said to the people, "I,
even I only, am left a prophet of the LORD;
but Baal's prophets number four hundred
fifty. 23 Let two bulls be given to us; let
them choose one bull for themselves, cut it
in pieces, and lay it on the wood, but put no
fire to it; I will prepare the other bull and
lay it on the wood, but put no fire to it.
24 Then you call on the name of your god
and I will call on the name of the LORD; the
god who answers by fire is indeed God."
All the people answered, "Well spoken!"
25 Then Elijah said to the prophets of Baal,
"Choose for yourselves one bull and pre-
pare it first, for you are many; then call on
the name of your god, but put no fire to it."
26 So they took the bull that was given
them, prepared it, and called on the name
of Baal from morning until noon, crying,
"O Baal, answer us!" But there was no
voice, and no answer. They limped about
the altar that they had made. 27 At noon
Elijah mocked them, saying, "Cry aloud!
Surely he is a god; either he is meditating,
or he has wandered away, or he is on a
journey, or perhaps he is asleep and must
be awakened." 28 Then they cried aloud
and, as was their custom, they cut them-
selves with swords and lances until the
blood gushed out over them. 29 As midday
passed, they raved on until the time of the
offering of the oblation, but there was no
voice, no answer, and no response.
30 Then Elijah said to all the people,
"Come closer to me"; and all the people
came closer to him. First he repaired the
altar of the LORD that had been thrown
down; 31 Elijah took twelve stones, accord-
ing to the number of the tribes of the sons
of Jacob, to whom the word of the LORD
came, saying, "Israel shall be your name";
32 with the stones he built an altar in the
name of the LORD. Then he made a trench
around the altar, large enough to contain
two measures of seed. 33 Next he put the
wood in order, cut the bull in pieces, and
laid it on the wood. He said, "Fill four jars
with water and pour it on the burnt offer-
ing and on the wood." 34 Then he said, "Do
it a second time"; and they did it a second
time. Again he said, "Do it a third time";
and they did it a third time, 35 so that the
water ran all around the altar, and filled the
trench also with water.
36 At the time of the offering of the
oblation, the prophet Elijah came near and
said, "O LORD, God of Abraham, Isaac,
and Israel, let it be known this day that you
are God in Israel, that I am your servant,
and that I have done all these things at your
bidding. 37 Answer me, O LORD, answer
me, so that this people may know that you,
O LORD, are God, and that you have
turned their hearts back." 38 Then the fire
of the LORD fell and consumed the burnt

coast, about 35 km [22 mi] northwest of Jezreel) to resolve the matter. *Asherah,* see 14.5n. **21:** Cf. Josh 24.15. **22:** Elijah apparently exaggerates for effect (cf. 18.4,13; 20.35–43; 22.1–28). **24:** The LORD's association with *fire* (perhaps lightning) is well attested in the Bible (see Lev 9.24; 10.2; Num 16.35), and Baal was also thought of as a god who controls fire and lightning. **25–29:** The prophets of Baal fail to get a god to answer them, and Elijah taunts them with some disrespectful suggestions for that failure (including the idea that he had *wandered away*—probably a euphemism for attending to bodily functions, relieving himself). They respond by slashing themselves with *swords and lances* (spears)—the kind of violent, prophetic frenzy also attested by the Egyptian traveler Wen-Amon (around 1100 BCE) in Byblos, a city on the Phoenician coast to the north of Jezebel's hometown of Sidon. **29:** *They raved,* lit. "they prophesied." *The time . . . of the oblation* was sunset. **30–40:** The *twelve stones* remind the people of their true identity as the LORD's people (vv. 30–31; cf. Gen 35.10); the pouring of *water* is designed to dispel any suggestion of spontaneous combustion here. Elijah's simple prayer stands in stark contrast to the dancing, shouting, and self-mutilation of the prophets of Baal. **39:** The words of the people, not of the prophet, are

offering, the wood, the stones, and the
dust, and even licked up the water that was
in the trench. 39 When all the people saw it,
they fell on their faces and said, "The LORD
indeed is God; the LORD indeed is God."
40 Elijah said to them, "Seize the prophets
of Baal; do not let one of them escape."
Then they seized them; and Elijah brought
them down to the Wadi Kishon, and killed
them there.
41 Elijah said to Ahab, "Go up, eat and
drink; for there is a sound of rushing rain."
42 So Ahab went up to eat and to drink.
Elijah went up to the top of Carmel; there
he bowed himself down upon the earth and
put his face between his knees. 43 He said to
his servant, "Go up now, look toward the
sea." He went up and looked, and said,
"There is nothing." Then he said, "Go
again seven times." 44 At the seventh time
he said, "Look, a little cloud no bigger than
a person's hand is rising out of the sea."
Then he said, "Go say to Ahab, 'Harness
your chariot and go down before the rain
stops you.' " 45 In a little while the heavens
grew black with clouds and wind; there
was a heavy rain. Ahab rode off and went
to Jezreel. 46 But the hand of the LORD was
on Elijah; he girded up his loins and ran in
front of Ahab to the entrance of Jezreel.

19 Ahab told Jezebel all that Elijah had
done, and how he had killed all the
prophets with the sword. 2 Then Jezebel
sent a messenger to Elijah, saying, "So may
the gods do to me, and more also, if I do
not make your life like the life of one of
them by this time tomorrow." 3 Then he
was afraid; he got up and fled for his life,
and came to Beer-sheba, which belongs to
Judah; he left his servant there.
4 But he himself went a day's journey
into the wilderness, and came and sat down
under a solitary broom tree. He asked that
he might die: "It is enough; now, O LORD,
take away my life, for I am no better than
my ancestors." 5 Then he lay down under
the broom tree and fell asleep. Suddenly an
angel touched him and said to him, "Get up
and eat." 6 He looked, and there at his head
was a cake baked on hot stones, and a jar
of water. He ate and drank, and lay down
again. 7 The angel of the LORD came a sec-
ond time, touched him, and said, "Get up
and eat, otherwise the journey will be too
much for you." 8 He got up, and ate and
drank; then he went in the strength of that
food forty days and forty nights to Horeb
the mount of God. 9 At that place he came
to a cave, and spent the night there.
Then the word of the LORD came to him,

the climactic utterance. **40:** *Wadi Kishon,* at the eastern base of Mount Carmel. **41–46:** Ahab survives, for the moment, to join in the postsacrificial meal (v. 41). **42:** The significance of Elijah's action is unclear; he may be exhausted, or praying for rain. **44:** The *cloud,* although *no bigger than a person's hand,* is enough to assure Elijah that the drought is over. **45–46:** He leaves for *Jezreel,* in the valley to the southeast, where Ahab and Jezebel had a palace (21.1)—presumably because he thinks that the war is over.

19.1–21: Elijah and the LORD. The realization that Jezebel will not be so easily cowed as her husband sends Elijah into retreat, both physical and mental. His fear takes him to *Beer-sheba* in the very south of the promised land (v. 3)—as far away from Jezebel as he can travel. Having reached Beer-sheba, he heads alone for the *wilderness,* seeking a lonely place in which to *die;* he has had *enough* (v. 4); cf. Jon 1.3; 4.3. **5–9:** Unexpected divine provision enables Elijah, against his expectation, to reach *Horeb the mount of God* (v. 8; cf. Ex 3.1). The *forty days and forty nights* of his travels recall Israel's own wandering in the wilderness (Num 14.33–34) and Moses' first sojourn on the mountain (Ex 24.18). **8:** *Horeb* is the name used for Sinai in Deuteronomy. **9:** *A cave,* lit. "the cave"; cf. Ex 33.21–23. Elijah returns to the site of the theophany that Moses had experienced. **9–18:** The emphasis at Carmel had been on God's spectacular ways, and particularly on his use of *fire.* The emphasis here is upon God's quiet ways. He is not to be found on this occasion in the spectacular elements of the storm outside the cave (*wind . . . earthquake . . . fire*), elements accompanying the divine manifestation at Sinai/Horeb (see Ex 19.18; Deut 4.12), but in the *sheer silence* (v. 12; lit. "a voice, a barely audible whisper"). This is not unconnected to God's new instructions to Elijah to *anoint Hazael . . . Jehu . . . Elisha* (vv. 15–16). A new order is to succeed the old,

saying, "What are you doing here, Elijah?"
10 He answered, "I have been very zealous
for the LORD, the God of hosts; for the
Israelites have forsaken your covenant,
thrown down your altars, and killed your
prophets with the sword. I alone am left,
and they are seeking my life, to take it
away."
11 He said, "Go out and stand on the
mountain before the LORD, for the LORD is
about to pass by." Now there was a great
wind, so strong that it was splitting moun-
tains and breaking rocks in pieces before
the LORD, but the LORD was not in the
wind; and after the wind an earthquake,
but the LORD was not in the earthquake;
12 and after the earthquake a fire, but the
LORD was not in the fire; and after the fire
a sound of sheer silence. 13 When Elijah
heard it, he wrapped his face in his mantle
and went out and stood at the entrance of
the cave. Then there came a voice to him
that said, "What are you doing here, Eli-
jah?" 14 He answered, "I have been very
zealous for the LORD, the God of hosts; for
the Israelites have forsaken your covenant,
thrown down your altars, and killed your
prophets with the sword. I alone am left,
and they are seeking my life, to take it
away." 15 Then the LORD said to him, "Go,
return on your way to the wilderness of
Damascus; when you arrive, you shall
anoint Hazael as king over Aram. 16 Also
you shall anoint Jehu son of Nimshi as king
over Israel; and you shall anoint Elisha son
of Shaphat of Abel-meholah as prophet in
your place. 17 Whoever escapes from the
sword of Hazael, Jehu shall kill; and who-
ever escapes from the sword of Jehu, Elisha
shall kill. 18 Yet I will leave seven thousand
in Israel, all the knees that have not bowed
to Baal, and every mouth that has not
kissed him."
19 So he set out from there, and found
Elisha son of Shaphat, who was plowing.
There were twelve yoke of oxen ahead of
him, and he was with the twelfth. Elijah
passed by him and threw his mantle over
him. 20 He left the oxen, ran after Elijah,
and said, "Let me kiss my father and my
mother, and then I will follow you." Then
Elijah[a] said to him, "Go back again; for
what have I done to you?" 21 He returned
from following him, took the yoke of oxen,
and slaughtered them; using the equipment
from the oxen, he boiled their flesh, and
gave it to the people, and they ate. Then he
set out and followed Elijah, and became his
servant.

20 King Ben-hadad of Aram gathered
all his army together; thirty-two
kings were with him, along with horses and
chariots. He marched against Samaria, laid
siege to it, and attacked it. 2 Then he sent
messengers into the city to King Ahab of
Israel, and said to him: "Thus says Ben-
hadad: 3 Your silver and gold are mine;
your fairest wives and children also are
mine." 4 The king of Israel answered, "As
you say, my lord, O king, I am yours, and
all that I have." 5 The messengers came
again and said: "Thus says Ben-hadad: I
sent to you, saying, 'Deliver to me your
silver and gold, your wives and children';

a Heb *he*

and it is that order which will bring about the final victory over Baal worship, not through obviously spectacular demonstrations of divine power as in ch 18, but through the (quieter) political process, as God removes certain kings and sets up others. **19–21:** *Elisha* is found and enlisted as Elijah's *servant* (v. 21; the word is also used of Joshua's relationship with Moses, cf. Ex 24.13; 33.11; Num 11.28). He decisively turns his back on his old way of life by destroying his previous means of sustenance (cf. 1 Sam 11.5–7). It is Elisha who will anoint Hazael (2 Kings 8.7–15) and Jehu (2 Kings 9.1–13).

20.1–43: Ahab's war against Aram. Elijah is not the only servant of God left, despite his claim (19.10,14); the narrative here continues without him. **1–12:** Asa, king of Judah, had first involved *Aram* (see 10.29n.) in the affairs of Israel, inviting a previous *Ben-hadad* to attack Baasha, king of Israel (15.16–22). As this part of the story opens, the current king of Aram, at the head of a powerful alliance, has now moved in strength to put pressure on Ahab's capital, *Samaria* itself. **11:** That is, it is unwise to

6 nevertheless I will send my servants to you
tomorrow about this time, and they shall
search your house and the houses of your
servants, and lay hands on whatever
pleases them,[a] and take it away."
7 Then the king of Israel called all the
elders of the land, and said, "Look now!
See how this man is seeking trouble; for he
sent to me for my wives, my children, my
silver, and my gold; and I did not refuse
him." 8 Then all the elders and all the peo-
ple said to him, "Do not listen or consent."
9 So he said to the messengers of Ben-
hadad, "Tell my lord the king: All that you
first demanded of your servant I will do;
but this thing I cannot do." The messengers
left and brought him word again. 10 Ben-
hadad sent to him and said, "The gods do
so to me, and more also, if the dust of Sa-
maria will provide a handful for each of the
people who follow me." 11 The king of Isra-
el answered, "Tell him: One who puts on
armor should not brag like one who takes
it off." 12 When Ben-hadad heard this mes-
sage—now he had been drinking with the
kings in the booths—he said to his men,
"Take your positions!" And they took their
positions against the city.
13 Then a certain prophet came up to
King Ahab of Israel and said, "Thus says
the LORD, Have you seen all this great mul-
titude? Look, I will give it into your hand
today; and you shall know that I am the
LORD." 14 Ahab said, "By whom?" He
said, "Thus says the LORD, By the young
men who serve the district governors."
Then he said, "Who shall begin the battle?"
He answered, "You." 15 Then he mustered
the young men who served the district gov-
ernors, two hundred thirty-two; after them
he mustered all the people of Israel, seven
thousand.
16 They went out at noon, while Ben-
hadad was drinking himself drunk in the
booths, he and the thirty-two kings allied
with him. 17 The young men who served
the district governors went out first. Ben-
hadad had sent out scouts,[b] and they re-
ported to him, "Men have come out from
Samaria." 18 He said, "If they have come
out for peace, take them alive; if they have
come out for war, take them alive."
19 But these had already come out of the
city: the young men who served the district
governors, and the army that followed
them. 20 Each killed his man; the Arameans
fled and Israel pursued them, but King Ben-
hadad of Aram escaped on a horse with the
cavalry. 21 The king of Israel went out, at-
tacked the horses and chariots, and defeat-
ed the Arameans with a great slaughter.
22 Then the prophet approached the
king of Israel and said to him, "Come,
strengthen yourself, and consider well what
you have to do; for in the spring the king of
Aram will come up against you."
23 The servants of the king of Aram said
to him, "Their gods are gods of the hills,
and so they were stronger than we; but let
us fight against them in the plain, and sure-
ly we shall be stronger than they. 24 Also do
this: remove the kings, each from his post,
and put commanders in place of them;
25 and muster an army like the army that

a Gk Syr Vg: Heb *you* *b* Heb lacks *scouts*

boast about one's exploits before the battle has even begun. There is time enough for boasting when it is over. **13–21:** Thus far in the story Ahab has known only prophetic opposition, but now he receives from a prophet, for the first time, good news. The LORD is still the same God as previously, and Israel is still the same people; reality has not changed, simply because Israel has sought to define it differently by worshiping other gods. The prophetic plan benefits from the fact that Ben-hadad is the worse for drink (vv. 12,16), and seemingly incapable of uttering coherent or sensible instructions (v. 18). **22–34:** The Aramean preparations for the continuation of warfare in the following *spring* (v. 22; cf. 2 Sam 11.1) involve a reorganization of the empire (the replacement of vassal kings with officials directly accountable to Ben-hadad, v. 24) and the raising of a new army to replace the one previously destroyed. **23:** On open ground the larger of two armies, particularly if it has numerous horses and chariots, has an advantage all too easily lost in the *hills* (cf. Judg 1.19). **26:** The Israelites, better prepared, meet the hostile force

you have lost, horse for horse, and chariot
for chariot; then we will fight against them
in the plain, and surely we shall be stronger
than they." He heeded their voice, and
did so.
26 In the spring Ben-hadad mustered the
Arameans and went up to Aphek to fight
against Israel. 27 After the Israelites had
been mustered and provisioned, they went
out to engage them; the people of Israel
encamped opposite them like two little
flocks of goats, while the Arameans filled
the country. 28 A man of God approached
and said to the king of Israel, "Thus says
the LORD: Because the Arameans have said,
'The LORD is a god of the hills but he is not
a god of the valleys,' therefore I will give all
this great multitude into your hand, and
you shall know that I am the LORD."
29 They encamped opposite one another
seven days. Then on the seventh day the
battle began; the Israelites killed one hun-
dred thousand Aramean foot soldiers in
one day. 30 The rest fled into the city of
Aphek; and the wall fell on twenty-seven
thousand men that were left.
Ben-hadad also fled, and entered the city
to hide. 31 His servants said to him, "Look,
we have heard that the kings of the house
of Israel are merciful kings; let us put sack-
cloth around our waists and ropes on our
heads, and go out to the king of Israel; per-
haps he will spare your life." 32 So they tied
sackcloth around their waists, put ropes on
their heads, went to the king of Israel, and
said, "Your servant Ben-hadad says,
'Please let me live.' " And he said, "Is he
still alive? He is my brother." 33 Now the
men were watching for an omen; they
quickly took it up from him and said, "Yes,
Ben-hadad is your brother." Then he said,
"Go and bring him." So Ben-hadad came
out to him; and he had him come up into
the chariot. 34 Ben-hadad[a] said to him, "I
will restore the towns that my father took
from your father; and you may establish
bazaars for yourself in Damascus, as my
father did in Samaria." The king of Israel
responded,[b] "I will let you go on those
terms." So he made a treaty with him and
let him go.
35 At the command of the LORD a cer-
tain member of a company of prophets[c]
said to another, "Strike me!" But the man
refused to strike him. 36 Then he said to
him, "Because you have not obeyed the
voice of the LORD, as soon as you have left
me, a lion will kill you." And when he had
left him, a lion met him and killed him.
37 Then he found another man and said,
"Strike me!" So the man hit him, striking
and wounding him. 38 Then the prophet de-
parted, and waited for the king along the
road, disguising himself with a bandage
over his eyes. 39 As the king passed by, he
cried to the king and said, "Your servant
went out into the thick of the battle; then a
soldier turned and brought a man to me,
and said, 'Guard this man; if he is missing,
your life shall be given for his life, or else
you shall pay a talent of silver.' 40 While
your servant was busy here and there, he
was gone." The king of Israel said to him,
"So shall your judgment be; you yourself
have decided it." 41 Then he quickly took
the bandage away from his eyes. The king
of Israel recognized him as one of the
prophets. 42 Then he said to him, "Thus
says the LORD, 'Because you have let the
man go whom I had devoted to destruction,
therefore your life shall be for his life, and

a Heb *He* b Heb lacks *The king of Israel responded*
c Heb *of the sons of the prophets*

farther north at *Aphek*, probably east of the Sea of Chinnereth (Galilee), whose wall falls, Jericho-like, on those who have sought refuge in the city (cf. Josh 6). **33:** *Brother* here connotes an equal treaty partner. **35–43:** Prophetic encouragement turns once again to prophetic opposition. Like Saul, Ahab had released an enemy king whom God had *devoted to destruction* (see 1 Sam 15). Ahab's life is therefore forfeit, as the life of the hypothetical guard of vv. 39–40 would have been. On *a company of prophets* (v. 35), see note *c* and 2 Kings 4.1–7n. **39:** It is taken for granted that *a talent of silver* (about 34 kg [75 lb]) is an impossible amount to raise; death is the only option that can realistically be considered.

your people for his people.' " 43 The king of
Israel set out toward home, resentful and
sullen, and came to Samaria.

21 Later the following events took
place: Naboth the Jezreelite had a
vineyard in Jezreel, beside the palace of
King Ahab of Samaria. 2 And Ahab said to
Naboth, "Give me your vineyard, so that I
may have it for a vegetable garden, because
it is near my house; I will give you a better
vineyard for it; or, if it seems good to you,
I will give you its value in money." 3 But
Naboth said to Ahab, "The LORD forbid
that I should give you my ancestral inheri-
tance." 4 Ahab went home resentful and
sullen because of what Naboth the Jezreel-
ite had said to him; for he had said, "I will
not give you my ancestral inheritance." He
lay down on his bed, turned away his face,
and would not eat.

5 His wife Jezebel came to him and said,
"Why are you so depressed that you will
not eat?" 6 He said to her, "Because I spoke
to Naboth the Jezreelite and said to him,
'Give me your vineyard for money; or else,
if you prefer, I will give you another vine-
yard for it'; but he answered, 'I will not give
you my vineyard.' " 7 His wife Jezebel said
to him, "Do you now govern Israel? Get
up, eat some food, and be cheerful; I will
give you the vineyard of Naboth the Jezre-
elite."

8 So she wrote letters in Ahab's name
and sealed them with his seal; she sent the
letters to the elders and the nobles who
lived with Naboth in his city. 9 She wrote in
the letters, "Proclaim a fast, and seat Na-
both at the head of the assembly; 10 seat
two scoundrels opposite him, and have
them bring a charge against him, saying,
'You have cursed God and the king.' Then
take him out, and stone him to death."
11 The men of his city, the elders and the
nobles who lived in his city, did as Jezebel
had sent word to them. Just as it was writ-
ten in the letters that she had sent to them,
12 they proclaimed a fast and seated Naboth
at the head of the assembly. 13 The two
scoundrels came in and sat opposite him;
and the scoundrels brought a charge
against Naboth, in the presence of the peo-
ple, saying, "Naboth cursed God and the
king." So they took him outside the city,
and stoned him to death. 14 Then they sent
to Jezebel, saying, "Naboth has been
stoned; he is dead."

15 As soon as Jezebel heard that Naboth
had been stoned and was dead, Jezebel said
to Ahab, "Go, take possession of the vine-
yard of Naboth the Jezreelite, which he re-
fused to give you for money; for Naboth is
not alive, but dead." 16 As soon as Ahab
heard that Naboth was dead, Ahab set out
to go down to the vineyard of Naboth the
Jezreelite, to take possession of it.

17 Then the word of the LORD came to

21.1–29: Naboth's vineyard. An apparently reinvigorated Elijah appears again in Jezreel (see 18.45–46n.) to denounce a new and heinous crime, and finally to foretell the destruction of Ahab's family for all its sins. **3:** Naboth's refusal must be understood in the light of laws about the possession and use of land in Israel which were designed to inhibit the alienation of family property (e.g., Lev 25.8–34; Num 27.9–11). **5–7:** Throughout the Elijah cycle Jezebel is represented as the real driving force in the kingdom of Israel (e.g., see 18.4; 19.1–2)—the power behind a rather passive Ahab. It is consistent with that picture that Jezebel, contemptuous of her husband's unwillingness to be a proper king, should be the one to take decisive action in respect to Naboth (cf. 21.15). **8:** *The elders and the nobles* of Jezreel should be the guardians of justice (cf. Deut 19.11–14; 21.1–9,18–21). With judges such as these, and *scoundrels* as the two witnesses required by biblical law (v. 10; cf. Deut 19.15), Naboth has no chance. **13:** Cf. Ex 22.28; Lev 24.14–16. **15–29:** As in 18.16–19, Ahab is confronted in his travels by Elijah, who brings a word from the LORD both about the immediate crime Ahab has committed and about the general religious context in which the vile deed has been done. Ahab's house is to suffer the same fate as the houses of *Jeroboam* and *Baasha* (v. 22; cf. 14.10–11; 16.3–4) because Ahab has, like them, *provoked* the LORD to *anger* and *caused Israel to sin.* Yet his penitence delays, though it cannot prevent, the disaster which Elijah has foretold (vv. 27–29). **19:** *In the place where dogs licked up* is better rendered (in light of 22.38)

Elijah the Tishbite, saying: 18 Go down to
meet King Ahab of Israel, who rules[a] in
Samaria; he is now in the vineyard of Na-
both, where he has gone to take possession.
19 You shall say to him, “Thus says the
LORD: Have you killed, and also taken pos-
session?” You shall say to him, “Thus says
the LORD: In the place where dogs licked
up the blood of Naboth, dogs will also lick
up your blood.”
20 Ahab said to Elijah, “Have you
found me, O my enemy?” He answered, “I
have found you. Because you have sold
yourself to do what is evil in the sight of the
LORD, 21 I will bring disaster on you; I will
consume you, and will cut off from Ahab
every male, bond or free, in Israel; 22 and I
will make your house like the house of Jer-
oboam son of Nebat, and like the house of
Baasha son of Ahijah, because you have
provoked me to anger and have caused Is-
rael to sin. 23 Also concerning Jezebel the
LORD said, ‘The dogs shall eat Jezebel with-
in the bounds of Jezreel.’ 24 Anyone belong-
ing to Ahab who dies in the city the dogs
shall eat; and anyone of his who dies in the
open country the birds of the air shall eat.”
25 (Indeed, there was no one like Ahab,
who sold himself to do what was evil in the
sight of the LORD, urged on by his wife
Jezebel. 26 He acted most abominably in go-
ing after idols, as the Amorites had done,
whom the LORD drove out before the Isra-
elites.)
27 When Ahab heard those words, he
tore his clothes and put sackcloth over his
bare flesh; he fasted, lay in the sackcloth,
and went about dejectedly. 28 Then the
word of the LORD came to Elijah the Tish-
bite: 29 “Have you seen how Ahab has
humbled himself before me? Because he has
humbled himself before me, I will not bring
the disaster in his days; but in his son’s days
I will bring the disaster on his house.”

22 For three years Aram and Israel con-
tinued without war. 2 But in the
third year King Jehoshaphat of Judah came
down to the king of Israel. 3 The king of
Israel said to his servants, “Do you know
that Ramoth-gilead belongs to us, yet we
are doing nothing to take it out of the hand
of the king of Aram?” 4 He said to Jehosha-
phat, “Will you go with me to battle at
Ramoth-gilead?” Jehoshaphat replied to
the king of Israel, “I am as you are; my
people are your people, my horses are your
horses.”
5 But Jehoshaphat also said to the king
of Israel, “Inquire first for the word of the
LORD.” 6 Then the king of Israel gathered
the prophets together, about four hundred
of them, and said to them, “Shall I go to
battle against Ramoth-gilead, or shall I re-
frain?” They said, “Go up; for the LORD
will give it into the hand of the king.” 7 But
Jehoshaphat said, “Is there no other proph-
et of the LORD here of whom we may in-
quire?” 8 The king of Israel said to Jehosha-
phat, “There is still one other by whom we
may inquire of the LORD, Micaiah son of
Imlah; but I hate him, for he never proph-
esies anything favorable about me, but only
disaster.” Jehoshaphat said, “Let the king
not say such a thing.” 9 Then the king of
Israel summoned an officer and said,
“Bring quickly Micaiah son of Imlah.”
10 Now the king of Israel and King Jehosha-
phat of Judah were sitting on their thrones,
arrayed in their robes, at the threshing floor
at the entrance of the gate of Samaria; and
all the prophets were prophesying before
them. 11 Zedekiah son of Chenaanah made

a Heb *who is*

“Instead of dogs licking up.” **23–24:** Failure to receive proper burial is a frequent curse; see Deut 28.26; Jer 34.20.

22.1–53: Ahab, Jehoshaphat, and Ahaziah. The peace that followed the battle of Aphek (20.26–34) lasted *three years* (v. 1). Even after such a crushing defeat, the *king of Aram* was still able to hold on to the strategically important city of *Ramoth-gilead* in Transjordan (v. 2). Ahab seeks help in recovering it from *Jehoshaphat . . . of . . . Judah* (see v. 41), who first demands prophetic counsel. **9–25:** The antics of the prophets at the *threshing floor* (an open space created for agricultural purposes, see Ruth 3) recalls the scene on Mount Carmel (ch 18) and suggests that these are not trustworthy advisers. **11:** The prophet’s

for himself horns of iron, and he said,
"Thus says the LORD: With these you shall
gore the Arameans until they are de-
stroyed." 12 All the prophets were proph-
esying the same and saying, "Go up to
Ramoth-gilead and triumph; the LORD will
give it into the hand of the king."
13 The messenger who had gone to sum-
mon Micaiah said to him, "Look, the
words of the prophets with one accord are
favorable to the king; let your word be like
the word of one of them, and speak favor-
ably." 14 But Micaiah said, "As the LORD
lives, whatever the LORD says to me, that I
will speak."
15 When he had come to the king, the
king said to him, "Micaiah, shall we go to
Ramoth-gilead to battle, or shall we re-
frain?" He answered him, "Go up and tri-
umph; the LORD will give it into the hand
of the king." 16 But the king said to him,
"How many times must I make you swear
to tell me nothing but the truth in the name
of the LORD?" 17 Then Micaiah[a] said, "I
saw all Israel scattered on the mountains,
like sheep that have no shepherd; and the
LORD said, 'These have no master; let each
one go home in peace.' " 18 The king of Is-
rael said to Jehoshaphat, "Did I not tell you
that he would not prophesy anything favor-
able about me, but only disaster?"
19 Then Micaiah[a] said, "Therefore
hear the word of the LORD: I saw the LORD
sitting on his throne, with all the host of
heaven standing beside him to the right and
to the left of him. 20 And the LORD said,
'Who will entice Ahab, so that he may go
up and fall at Ramoth-gilead?' Then one
said one thing, and another said another,
21 until a spirit came forward and stood be-
fore the LORD, saying, 'I will entice him.'
22 'How?' the LORD asked him. He replied,
'I will go out and be a lying spirit in the
mouth of all his prophets.' Then the
LORD[a] said, 'You are to entice him, and
you shall succeed; go out and do it.' 23 So
you see, the LORD has put a lying spirit in
the mouth of all these your prophets; the
LORD has decreed disaster for you."
24 Then Zedekiah son of Chenaanah
came up to Micaiah, slapped him on the
cheek, and said, "Which way did the spirit
of the LORD pass from me to speak to
you?" 25 Micaiah replied, "You will find
out on that day when you go in to hide in
an inner chamber." 26 The king of Israel
then ordered, "Take Micaiah, and return
him to Amon the governor of the city and
to Joash the king's son, 27 and say, 'Thus
says the king: Put this fellow in prison, and
feed him on reduced rations of bread and
water until I come in peace.' " 28 Micaiah
said, "If you return in peace, the LORD has
not spoken by me." And he said, "Hear,
you peoples, all of you!"
29 So the king of Israel and King Jehosh-
aphat of Judah went up to Ramoth-gilead.
30 The king of Israel said to Jehoshaphat, "I
will disguise myself and go into battle, but
you wear your robes." So the king of Israel
disguised himself and went into battle.
31 Now the king of Aram had commanded
the thirty-two captains of his chariots,
"Fight with no one small or great, but only
with the king of Israel." 32 When the cap-
tains of the chariots saw Jehoshaphat, they
said, "It is surely the king of Israel." So
they turned to fight against him; and Je-
hoshaphat cried out. 33 When the captains
of the chariots saw that it was not the king

a Heb *he*

action is symbolic; cf. Jer 13; 27–28; Ezek 4. **21–23:** The imagery is that of a council of war, with the heavenly king sitting on his throne surrounded by his army, making plans to defeat Ahab in battle (cf. v. 10). A similar council provides the background for Job 1–2. The image of these verses is quite remarkable: The prophets are true prophets who, at God's initiative, prophesy misleadingly, as in Deut 13.2–6. **26–40:** The majority view prevails, yet Ahab is so lacking in confidence that he enters the battle in *disguise* (v. 30). This is a harbinger of disaster, for it recalls the actions of Jeroboam (cf. 14.1–18) and before him Saul (1 Sam 28) just before their own deaths. **26:** It is not clear whether the *king's son,* responsible for the confinement of prisoners (Jer 36.26; 38.6), need literally be the son of the king. **31–33:** Jehoshaphat's Judean shout reveals that he is not the man Ben-hadad is determined to kill. **34:** An arrow shot at random flies

of Israel, they turned back from pursuing
him. 34 But a certain man drew his bow and
unknowingly struck the king of Israel be-
tween the scale armor and the breastplate;
so he said to the driver of his chariot,
"Turn around, and carry me out of the bat-
tle, for I am wounded." 35 The battle grew
hot that day, and the king was propped up
in his chariot facing the Arameans, until at
evening he died; the blood from the wound
had flowed into the bottom of the chariot.
36 Then about sunset a shout went through
the army, "Every man to his city, and every
man to his country!"
37 So the king died, and was brought to
Samaria; they buried the king in Samaria.
38 They washed the chariot by the pool of
Samaria; the dogs licked up his blood, and
the prostitutes washed themselves in it,[a]
according to the word of the LORD that he
had spoken. 39 Now the rest of the acts of
Ahab, and all that he did, and the ivory
house that he built, and all the cities that he
built, are they not written in the Book of
the Annals of the Kings of Israel? 40 So
Ahab slept with his ancestors; and his son
Ahaziah succeeded him.
41 Jehoshaphat son of Asa began to
reign over Judah in the fourth year of King
Ahab of Israel. 42 Jehoshaphat was thirty-
five years old when he began to reign, and
he reigned twenty-five years in Jerusalem.
His mother's name was Azubah daughter
of Shilhi. 43 He walked in all the way of his
father Asa; he did not turn aside from it,
doing what was right in the sight of the
LORD; yet the high places were not taken
away, and the people still sacrificed and of-
fered incense on the high places. 44 Jehosha-
phat also made peace with the king of Is-
rael.
45 Now the rest of the acts of Jehosha-
phat, and his power that he showed, and
how he waged war, are they not written in
the Book of the Annals of the Kings of Ju-
dah? 46 The remnant of the male temple
prostitutes who were still in the land in the
days of his father Asa, he exterminated.
47 There was no king in Edom; a deputy
was king. 48 Jehoshaphat made ships of the
Tarshish type to go to Ophir for gold; but
they did not go, for the ships were wrecked
at Ezion-geber. 49 Then Ahaziah son of
Ahab said to Jehoshaphat, "Let my ser-
vants go with your servants in the ships,"
but Jehoshaphat was not willing. 50 Jehosh-
aphat slept with his ancestors and was bur-
ied with his ancestors in the city of his fa-
ther David; his son Jehoram succeeded him.
51 Ahaziah son of Ahab began to reign
over Israel in Samaria in the seventeenth
year of King Jehoshaphat of Judah; he
reigned two years over Israel. 52 He did
what was evil in the sight of the LORD, and
walked in the way of his father and mother,
and in the way of Jeroboam son of Nebat,
who caused Israel to sin. 53 He served Baal
and worshiped him; he provoked the
LORD, the God of Israel, to anger, just as
his father had done.

[a] Heb lacks *in it*

unerringly to one of the few undefended spots on Ahab's body. This is one of many cases where the Bible implies that God is behind such apparently random events. **38:** Deut 23.17–18 enjoins the Israelite never to bring into the Temple the earnings of a female *prostitute* or a male prostitute (lit. *dogs*). We are thus reminded by both words here of the whole idolatrous career that has brought Ahab to this ignominious end (cf. the association of prostitutes with the fertility cult in 14.24; 15.12). He has fed the people idolatry and is now consumed by it. **41–50:** Revolution, war, apostasy, and prophetic intervention have passed the Southern Kingdom by. *Jehoshaphat* (ruled 870–846 BCE), like his father Asa, is a good king, who nevertheless takes no action against the *high places.* **47–48:** Because Jehoshaphat rules over *Edom,* he is able to build a fleet of ships at *Ezion-geber* (near Elath in Edom; cf. 9.26–28). They are *ships of the Tarshish type* (capable of making long voyages), recalling the Solomonic expeditions to Ophir that brought back gold (10.22). Jehoshaphat is, however, no Solomon: These ships were *wrecked* as they lay in port. **51–53:** The religious commitments of *Ahaziah* (ruled 852–851 BCE) are those of his father *Ahab.*

2 KINGS

Second Kings, originally joined with 1 Kings as a single work, continues the story of Israel under its monarchy, which was begun in 1–2 Samuel and carried forward in 1 Kings. The book opens during the short reign of Ahaziah king of Israel (mid-ninth century BCE) with the conclusion of Elijah's mission (chs 1–2). The ministry of Elijah's successor Elisha occupies the bulk of the subsequent seven chapters (chs 3–9), woven together with an account of the reign of King Jehoram of Israel, who was ultimately overthrown by his army commander Jehu (chs 9–10). This continues a pattern first seen in 1 Kings: Prophets oppose the apostate northern kings walking in Jeroboam's sins (1 Kings 12.25–13.34), and their dynasties come to an end, sometimes with great speed, as the judgment of God falls upon them. The prophets Elijah and Elisha in some respects go beyond this judgmental role: They are presented as mitigating the full force of God's wrath, offering the opportunity of repentance leading to reprieve in the midst of judgment. God's promises and his compassion are also presented as reasons for the divine forbearance (e.g., 10.30; 13.23). Eventually, however, description of the reigns of Israel's kings gives way to description of severe divine judgment, and the Northern Kingdom is exiled by the Assyrians (ch 17). Description of Judah also coheres with what we have previously read in 1 Kings, in which the religious situation is by no means described as a tale of continuous apostasy. Relatively good kings did rule in the gaps between the wicked kings (1 Kings 15.9–22.50). This pattern is continued in 2 Kings (e.g., see 8.16–19,25–27; 12.1–15.38). Toward the end of Judah's story, indeed, we are presented with two of the most righteous kings there ever were. Hezekiah and Josiah reformed Israelite worship and obeyed and trusted in God (18.1–20.21; 22.1–23.30). Yet in the end Judah's sins, and especially the sins of Manasseh (ch 21), which are presented as breaking the divine patience, were also punished. Jerusalem was captured and destroyed by Nebuchadnezzar in 586 BCE, and many inhabitants of Judah were exiled to Babylon (chs 24–25). The book ends with the future of the Davidic line hanging by the slender thread of a displaced Judean ruler sitting at the table of the king of Babylon (25.27–30).

For a discussion of the composition and character of 1–2 Kings overall, see the Introduction to 1 Kings.

1 After the death of Ahab, Moab rebelled
against Israel.
2 Ahaziah had fallen through the lattice
in his upper chamber in Samaria, and lay
injured; so he sent messengers, telling them,
"Go, inquire of Baal-zebub, the god of Ekron,
whether I shall recover from this injury."
3 But the angel of the LORD said to
Elijah the Tishbite, "Get up, go to meet the
messengers of the king of Samaria, and say
to them, 'Is it because there is no God in
Israel that you are going to inquire of Baal-

1.1–17: Ahaziah and Elijah. King *Ahaziah's* decision upon falling out of a window (the probable meaning of *lattice,* v. 2) to send *messengers* to consult one of the many local manifestations of Baal in *Ekron* (a Philistine city about 40 km [25 mi] west of Jerusalem) leads to a confrontation with the prophet *Elijah.* **2:** *Baal-zebub* is literally "Baal/lord of the flies," perhaps a deliberate Heb corruption of "Baal-zebul" ("Baal the exalted"; see Mk 3.22), intended to express the authors' scorn of or hostility toward

zebub, the god of Ekron?' 4 Now therefore
thus says the LORD, 'You shall not leave the
bed to which you have gone, but you shall
surely die.' " So Elijah went.
5 The messengers returned to the king,
who said to them, "Why have you re-
turned?" 6 They answered him, "There
came a man to meet us, who said to us, 'Go
back to the king who sent you, and say
to him: Thus says the LORD: Is it because
there is no God in Israel that you are send-
ing to inquire of Baal-zebub, the god of
Ekron? Therefore you shall not leave the
bed to which you have gone, but shall sure-
ly die.' " 7 He said to them, "What sort of
man was he who came to meet you and told
you these things?" 8 They answered him,
"A hairy man, with a leather belt around
his waist." He said, "It is Elijah the Tish-
bite."
9 Then the king sent to him a captain of
fifty with his fifty men. He went up to Eli-
jah, who was sitting on the top of a hill,
and said to him, "O man of God, the king
says, 'Come down.' " 10 But Elijah an-
swered the captain of fifty, "If I am a man
of God, let fire come down from heaven
and consume you and your fifty." Then fire
came down from heaven, and consumed
him and his fifty.
11 Again the king sent to him another
captain of fifty with his fifty. He went up[a]
and said to him, "O man of God, this is the
king's order: Come down quickly!" 12 But
Elijah answered them, "If I am a man of
God, let fire come down from heaven and
consume you and your fifty." Then the fire
of God came down from heaven and con-
sumed him and his fifty.
13 Again the king sent the captain of a
third fifty with his fifty. So the third captain
of fifty went up, and came and fell on his
knees before Elijah, and entreated him,
"O man of God, please let my life, and the
life of these fifty servants of yours, be pre-
cious in your sight. 14 Look, fire came down
from heaven and consumed the two former
captains of fifty men with their fifties; but
now let my life be precious in your sight."
15 Then the angel of the LORD said to Eli-
jah, "Go down with him; do not be afraid
of him." So he set out and went down with
him to the king, 16 and said to him, "Thus
says the LORD: Because you have sent mes-
sengers to inquire of Baal-zebub, the god of
Ekron,—is it because there is no God in
Israel to inquire of his word?—therefore
you shall not leave the bed to which you
have gone, but you shall surely die."
17 So he died according to the word of
the LORD that Elijah had spoken. His
brother,[b] Jehoram succeeded him as king
in the second year of King Jehoram son
of Jehoshaphat of Judah, because Ahaziah
had no son. 18 Now the rest of the acts of
Ahaziah that he did, are they not written in
the Book of the Annals of the Kings of Is-
rael?

2 Now when the LORD was about to take
Elijah up to heaven by a whirlwind, Eli-
jah and Elisha were on their way from Gil-

a Gk Compare verses 9, 13: Heb *He answered*
b Gk Syr: Heb lacks *His brother*

this deity. **8:** *Hairy man,* lit. "a man who was a lord/owner of hair," possibly a play on words with "lord of the flies" in v. 2. **9–14:** This entire section plays on the Heb words "'ish 'elohim," *man of God,* and "'esh 'elohim," *fire of God.* When the officer speaks rudely to Elijah, asking the "'ish 'elohim" to descend, Elijah sends down the "'esh 'elohim" instead. Only when the third officer speaks to Elijah properly, treating him with respect, does he accede. **10:** Fire is a well-known vehicle of God's judgment in the Bible (e.g., Gen 19.24; Ex 9.23–24; cf. 1 Kings 18.38). The prophetic word cannot be brought under human control (cf. 1 Kings 13.1–7). **17:** If *Jehoram* of Israel did indeed succeed Ahaziah only after *Jehoram son of Jehoshaphat* had properly succeeded his father (cf. 1 Kings 22.50), then ch 3 (in which Jehoshaphat goes to war along with Jehoram of Israel) presents a difficulty. We must assume either that there is some textual or historical confusion here or that there was a co-regency between Jehoshaphat and his son toward the end of the former's reign.

2.1–25: Elijah gives way to Elisha. The prophetic mantle passes from Elijah to Elisha, who is authen-

gal. 2 Elijah said to Elisha, "Stay here; for
the LORD has sent me as far as Bethel." But
Elisha said, "As the LORD lives, and as you
yourself live, I will not leave you." So they
went down to Bethel. 3 The company of
prophets[a] who were in Bethel came out to
Elisha, and said to him, "Do you know that
today the LORD will take your master away
from you?" And he said, "Yes, I know;
keep silent."

4 Elijah said to him, "Elisha, stay here;
for the LORD has sent me to Jericho." But
he said, "As the LORD lives, and as you
yourself live, I will not leave you." So they
came to Jericho. 5 The company of proph-
ets[a] who were at Jericho drew near to Eli-
sha, and said to him, "Do you know that
today the LORD will take your master away

a Heb *sons of the prophets*

ticated as one who stands in true succession to him as a prophet of the LORD. **1–6:** That Elijah wishes Elisha to remain behind, when it is clear that Elisha is to succeed Elijah *today* (vv. 3,5; for Elijah's

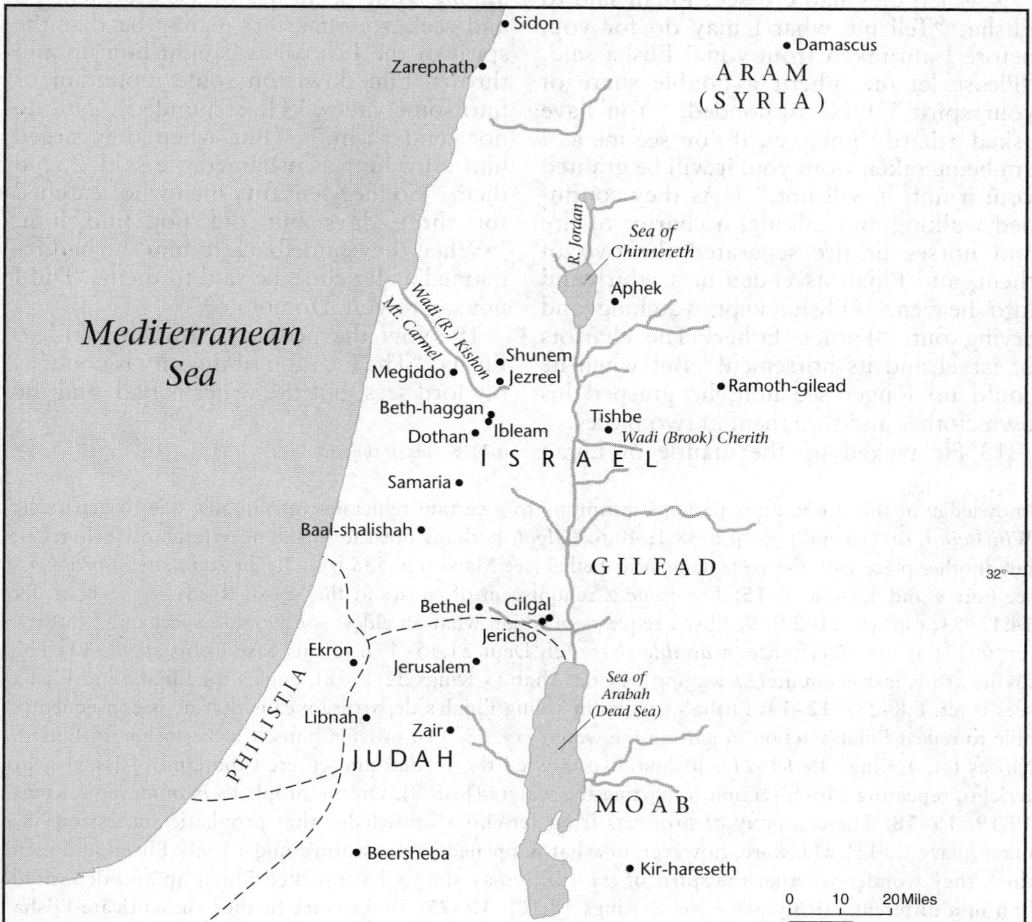

Chs 2–13: The Eligha narratives. The dashed line shows the approximate boundaries between Israel, Judah, and Philistia.

from you?" And he answered, "Yes, I
know; be silent."
6 Then Elijah said to him, "Stay here;
for the LORD has sent me to the Jordan."
But he said, "As the LORD lives, and as you
yourself live, I will not leave you." So the
two of them went on. 7 Fifty men of the
company of prophets[a] also went, and
stood at some distance from them, as they
both were standing by the Jordan. 8 Then
Elijah took his mantle and rolled it up, and
struck the water; the water was parted to
the one side and to the other, until the two
of them crossed on dry ground.
9 When they had crossed, Elijah said to
Elisha, "Tell me what I may do for you,
before I am taken from you." Elisha said,
"Please let me inherit a double share of
your spirit." 10 He responded, "You have
asked a hard thing; yet, if you see me as I
am being taken from you, it will be granted
you; if not, it will not." 11 As they contin-
ued walking and talking, a chariot of fire
and horses of fire separated the two of
them, and Elijah ascended in a whirlwind
into heaven. 12 Elisha kept watching and
crying out, "Father, father! The chariots
of Israel and its horsemen!" But when he
could no longer see him, he grasped his
own clothes and tore them in two pieces.
13 He picked up the mantle of Elijah
that had fallen from him, and went back
and stood on the bank of the Jordan. 14 He
took the mantle of Elijah that had fallen
from him, and struck the water, saying,
"Where is the LORD, the God of Elijah?"
When he had struck the water, the water
was parted to the one side and to the other,
and Elisha went over.
15 When the company of prophets[a]
who were at Jericho saw him at a distance,
they declared, "The spirit of Elijah rests on
Elisha." They came to meet him and bowed
to the ground before him. 16 They said to
him, "See now, we have fifty strong men
among your servants; please let them go
and seek your master; it may be that the
spirit of the LORD has caught him up and
thrown him down on some mountain or
into some valley." He responded, "No, do
not send them." 17 But when they urged
him until he was ashamed, he said, "Send
them." So they sent fifty men who searched
for three days but did not find him.
18 When they came back to him (he had re-
mained at Jericho), he said to them, "Did I
not say to you, Do not go?"
19 Now the people of the city said to
Elisha, "The location of this city is good, as
my lord sees; but the water is bad, and the

a Heb *sons of the prophets*

knowledge of this see v. 9), is perhaps testimony to a certain reluctance on Elijah's side to depart. **1:** *Whirlwind,* or "storm"; see Job 38.1; 40.6. *Gilgal,* perhaps not the shrine near Jericho (Josh 4.19), but another place with the same name near Bethel (see Map on p. 535 HB). **3:** *The company of prophets,* see note *a* and 4.1–7n. **7–15:** The scene is reminiscent of Moses at the Sea of Reeds (vv. 7–8; cf. Ex 14.15–31, esp. vv. 21–22). **9:** Elisha requests of Elijah what an eldest son would expect of a "father" (cf. v. 12) as his inheritance: a *double share* (cf. Deut 21.15–17), in this case of his *spirit.* **11:** The divine army, last encountered waging war on Ahab (1 Kings 22.1–38), comes for Elijah, and Elisha sees it (cf. 6.8–23). **12–14:** Elisha's success in seeing Elijah's departure means that he is consequently able to repeat Elijah's action in parting the waters (vv. 13–14), proving himself to be Joshua to Elijah's Moses (cf. 1 Kings 19.19–21). Joshua also crossed the *Jordan* and entered the land of Israel near Jericho, repeating Moses' action in parting the waters (Josh 3). On the prophet's *mantle,* see 1 Kings 19.19. **15–18:** The *company of prophets* from Jericho acknowledge that prophetic succession has taken place (v. 15). Unaware, however, of what happened in the storm's midst (only Elisha had seen this), they wonder whether the *spirit of the LORD* may simply have picked Elijah up and deposited him in a different earthly place (see 1 Kings 18.12). **19–25:** Two stories further authenticate Elisha as Elijah's prophetic successor, showing that he is a man able both to bless and to curse in the LORD's name. The succession narrative ends with Elisha's trips to *Mount Carmel* (v. 25)—the scene of Elijah's great victory over the priests of Baal (1 Kings 18.20–46)—and then to *Samaria,* to take up the war against Baal.

land is unfruitful." 20 He said, "Bring me
a new bowl, and put salt in it." So they
brought it to him. 21 Then he went to the
spring of water and threw the salt into it,
and said, "Thus says the LORD, I have
made this water wholesome; from now on
neither death nor miscarriage shall come
from it." 22 So the water has been whole-
some to this day, according to the word
that Elisha spoke.
23 He went up from there to Bethel; and
while he was going up on the way, some
small boys came out of the city and jeered
at him, saying, "Go away, baldhead! Go
away, baldhead!" 24 When he turned
around and saw them, he cursed them in
the name of the LORD. Then two she-bears
came out of the woods and mauled forty-
two of the boys. 25 From there he went on
to Mount Carmel, and then returned to Sa-
maria.

3 In the eighteenth year of King Jehosha-
phat of Judah, Jehoram son of Ahab
became king over Israel in Samaria; he
reigned twelve years. 2 He did what was evil
in the sight of the LORD, though not like his
father and mother, for he removed the pil-
lar of Baal that his father had made. 3 Nev-
ertheless he clung to the sin of Jeroboam
son of Nebat, which he caused Israel to
commit; he did not depart from it.
4 Now King Mesha of Moab was a
sheep breeder, who used to deliver to the
king of Israel one hundred thousand lambs,
and the wool of one hundred thousand
rams. 5 But when Ahab died, the king of
Moab rebelled against the king of Israel.
6 So King Jehoram marched out of Samaria
at that time and mustered all Israel. 7 As he
went he sent word to King Jehoshaphat of
Judah, "The king of Moab has rebelled
against me; will you go with me to battle
against Moab?" He answered, "I will; I am
with you, my people are your people, my
horses are your horses." 8 Then he asked,
"By which way shall we march?" Jehoram
answered, "By the way of the wilderness of
Edom."
9 So the king of Israel, the king of Judah,
and the king of Edom set out; and when
they had made a roundabout march of sev-
en days, there was no water for the army
or for the animals that were with them.
10 Then the king of Israel said, "Alas! The
LORD has summoned us, three kings, only
to be handed over to Moab." 11 But Jehosh-
aphat said, "Is there no prophet of the
LORD here, through whom we may inquire
of the LORD?" Then one of the servants of
the king of Israel answered, "Elisha son of
Shaphat, who used to pour water on the
hands of Elijah, is here." 12 Jehoshaphat
said, "The word of the LORD is with him."
So the king of Israel and Jehoshaphat and
the king of Edom went down to him.
13 Elisha said to the king of Israel,

3.1–27: Elisha and the conquest of Moab. Echoes of 1 Kings 22.1–28 are everywhere to be heard, as Jehoshaphat, previously found in alliance with Ahab, is now found in alliance with Ahab's son. **1–3:** Jehoram, though a *son of Ahab,* is distanced from the rest of his family by the way in which his reign (851–842 BCE) is described. He is indeed never explicitly accused of Baal-worship in the succeeding narratives. His own sins are of the rather less spectacular sort committed by the sons of Jeroboam and Baasha (1 Kings 15.25–26; 16.13). **4–12:** Jehoshaphat's initial response to Jehoram (v. 7) we recognize from 1 Kings 22.4, yet here he makes no attempt to discover the counsel of the LORD before going off to war (contrast 22.5). It is not unexpected that a military venture undertaken without prophetic advice should face disaster in the desert without a blow being struck. **4:** *Mesha* is also known from the Moabite Stone, an inscribed stela celebrating a victory over Israel. **8:** The idea is to attack Moab from the south, rather than from the north. This is possible because Edom is under Judean rule (1 Kings 22.47). **11:** Jehoshaphat remedies his oversight (cf. 1 Kings 22.7). Elisha's pouring of *water on the hands of Elijah* may allude to an earlier water-miracle of Elisha (unrecorded in Kings), known to those at the time. **13–27:** Elisha's prophecy, given under the influence of music (v. 15; cf. 1 Sam 10.5–6), is positive. The immediate crisis ("no water," v. 9) is to be dealt with by a miracle, as the *wadi* is filled with water from an unspecified and unexpected source (vv. 16–17). God will also grant the alliance a comprehensive

"What have I to do with you? Go to your
father's prophets or to your mother's." But
the king of Israel said to him, "No; it is the
LORD who has summoned us, three kings,
only to be handed over to Moab." 14 Elisha
said, "As the LORD of hosts lives, whom I
serve, were it not that I have regard for
King Jehoshaphat of Judah, I would give
you neither a look nor a glance. 15 But get
me a musician." And then, while the musi-
cian was playing, the power of the LORD
came on him. 16 And he said, "Thus says
the LORD, 'I will make this wadi full of
pools.' 17 For thus says the LORD, 'You
shall see neither wind nor rain, but the
wadi shall be filled with water, so that you
shall drink, you, your cattle, and your ani-
mals.' 18 This is only a trifle in the sight of
the LORD, for he will also hand Moab over
to you. 19 You shall conquer every fortified
city and every choice city; every good tree
you shall fell, all springs of water you shall
stop up, and every good piece of land you
shall ruin with stones." 20 The next day,
about the time of the morning offering,
suddenly water began to flow from the di-
rection of Edom, until the country was
filled with water.

21 When all the Moabites heard that the
kings had come up to fight against them, all
who were able to put on armor, from the
youngest to the oldest, were called out and
were drawn up at the frontier. 22 When they
rose early in the morning, and the sun
shone upon the water, the Moabites saw
the water opposite them as red as blood.
23 They said, "This is blood; the kings must
have fought together, and killed one anoth-
er. Now then, Moab, to the spoil!" 24 But
when they came to the camp of Israel, the
Israelites rose up and attacked the Moab-
ites, who fled before them; as they entered
Moab they continued the attack.[a] 25 The
cities they overturned, and on every good
piece of land everyone threw a stone, until
it was covered; every spring of water they
stopped up, and every good tree they felled.
Only at Kir-hareseth did the stone walls
remain, until the slingers surrounded and
attacked it. 26 When the king of Moab saw
that the battle was going against him, he
took with him seven hundred swordsmen
to break through, opposite the king of
Edom; but they could not. 27 Then he took
his firstborn son who was to succeed him,
and offered him as a burnt offering on the
wall. And great wrath came upon Israel, so
they withdrew from him and returned to
their own land.

4 Now the wife of a member of the com-
pany of prophets[b] cried to Elisha,
"Your servant my husband is dead; and
you know that your servant feared the
LORD, but a creditor has come to take my
two children as slaves." 2 Elisha said to her,
"What shall I do for you? Tell me, what do
you have in the house?" She answered,
"Your servant has nothing in the house,
except a jar of oil." 3 He said, "Go outside,
borrow vessels from all your neighbors,
empty vessels and not just a few. 4 Then go

a Compare Gk Syr: Meaning of Heb uncertain
b Heb *the sons of the prophets*

victory over Moab. **20:** Water duly appears. **22–23:** Because the water appears *red* (see Gen 25.25n.), the Moabites are tempted into a reckless advance on the Israelite camp, which is met with force. **27:** On the verge of the total victory Elisha had apparently prophesied, the Israelites encounter unexpected difficulty. Child sacrifice upon the city *wall* of "Kir-haresheth" (modern Kerak) saves this city from the fate of all the others, as *wrath* comes upon Israel and they withdraw from Moab. The nature of the *wrath* is left unspecified, although in this context it most likely refers to a superhuman fury that impels Mesha's troops to victory.

4.1–44: Elisha's miracles. The Moabite affair has established Elisha's credentials as a prophet in the line of Elijah. A number of further miracles, both of provision and healing, now remind us of Elijah in the same way. **1–7:** A widow of a man from one of the prophetic groups over which Elisha apparently exercises leadership (cf. 2.3,15; 4.38–41; 6.1–7; 9.1) has sons who are to be taken as *slaves* in payment of debt (cf. Isa 50.1; Neh 5.4–5). She still possesses a small amount of *oil,* however, (cf. 1 Kings 17.7–16),

in, and shut the door behind you and your
children, and start pouring into all these
vessels; when each is full, set it aside." 5 So
she left him and shut the door behind her
and her children; they kept bringing vessels
to her, and she kept pouring. 6 When the
vessels were full, she said to her son, "Bring
me another vessel." But he said to her,
"There are no more." Then the oil stopped
flowing. 7 She came and told the man of
God, and he said, "Go sell the oil and pay
your debts, and you and your children can
live on the rest."
8 One day Elisha was passing through
Shunem, where a wealthy woman lived,
who urged him to have a meal. So whenev-
er he passed that way, he would stop there
for a meal. 9 She said to her husband,
"Look, I am sure that this man who regu-
larly passes our way is a holy man of God.
10 Let us make a small roof chamber with
walls, and put there for him a bed, a table,
a chair, and a lamp, so that he can stay
there whenever he comes to us."
11 One day when he came there, he
went up to the chamber and lay down
there. 12 He said to his servant Gehazi,
"Call the Shunammite woman." When he
had called her, she stood before him. 13 He
said to him, "Say to her, Since you have
taken all this trouble for us, what may be
done for you? Would you have a word spo-
ken on your behalf to the king or to the
commander of the army?" She answered,
"I live among my own people." 14 He said,
"What then may be done for her?" Gehazi
answered, "Well, she has no son, and her
husband is old." 15 He said, "Call her."
When he had called her, she stood at the
door. 16 He said, "At this season, in due
time, you shall embrace a son." She replied,
"No, my lord, O man of God; do not de-
ceive your servant."
17 The woman conceived and bore a
son at that season, in due time, as Elisha
had declared to her.
18 When the child was older, he went
out one day to his father among the reap-
ers. 19 He complained to his father, "Oh,
my head, my head!" The father said to his
servant, "Carry him to his mother." 20 He
carried him and brought him to his mother;
the child sat on her lap until noon, and he
died. 21 She went up and laid him on the
bed of the man of God, closed the door on
him, and left. 22 Then she called to her hus-
band, and said, "Send me one of the ser-
vants and one of the donkeys, so that I may
quickly go to the man of God and come
back again." 23 He said, "Why go to him
today? It is neither new moon nor sab-
bath." She said, "It will be all right."
24 Then she saddled the donkey and said to
her servant, "Urge the animal on; do not
hold back for me unless I tell you." 25 So
she set out, and came to the man of God at
Mount Carmel.
When the man of God saw her coming,
he said to Gehazi his servant, "Look, there
is the Shunammite woman; 26 run at once to
meet her, and say to her, Are you all right?
Is your husband all right? Is the child all
right?" She answered, "It is all right."
27 When she came to the man of God at the
mountain, she caught hold of his feet. Ge-
hazi approached to push her away. But the
man of God said, "Let her alone, for she is
in bitter distress; the LORD has hidden it
from me and has not told me." 28 Then she
said, "Did I ask my lord for a son? Did I
not say, Do not mislead me?" 29 He said to
Gehazi, "Gird up your loins, and take my
staff in your hand, and go. If you meet any-
one, give no greeting, and if anyone greets
you, do not answer; and lay my staff on the
face of the child." 30 Then the mother of the

which becomes an abundance and enables self-sufficiency. **8–37:** This story is reminiscent of 1 Kings 17.17–24. The son in this instance was conceived when the *husband* of Elisha's *Shunammite* hostess was considered too old to father a child in any natural way (vv. 8–17). Unexpected life later gives way to unforeseen death (vv. 18–21). **8:** *Shunem,* a town in the Jezreel Valley (see Map on p. 535 HB). **16:** Cf. Gen 18.10. **23:** This verse suggests that it was the custom to consult prophets on rest days. **30–31:** The woman is not willing to accept Elisha's plan to resurrect the boy from a distance by means of his *staff* (cf. the power of Moses' staff in Ex 14.16; 17.19). She wishes his personal attention, which proves crucial

child said, "As the LORD lives, and as you
yourself live, I will not leave without you."
So he rose up and followed her. 31 Gehazi
went on ahead and laid the staff on the face
of the child, but there was no sound or sign
of life. He came back to meet him and told
him, "The child has not awakened."
32 When Elisha came into the house, he
saw the child lying dead on his bed. 33 So he
went in and closed the door on the two of
them, and prayed to the LORD. 34 Then he
got up on the bed[a] and lay upon the child,
putting his mouth upon his mouth, his eyes
upon his eyes, and his hands upon his
hands; and while he lay bent over him, the
flesh of the child became warm. 35 He got
down, walked once to and fro in the room,
then got up again and bent over him; the
child sneezed seven times, and the child
opened his eyes. 36 Elisha[b] summoned Ge-
hazi and said, "Call the Shunammite wom-
an." So he called her. When she came to
him, he said, "Take your son." 37 She came
and fell at his feet, bowing to the ground;
then she took her son and left.
38 When Elisha returned to Gilgal, there
was a famine in the land. As the company
of prophets was[c] sitting before him, he
said to his servant, "Put the large pot on,
and make some stew for the company of
prophets."[d] 39 One of them went out into
the field to gather herbs; he found a wild
vine and gathered from it a lapful of wild
gourds, and came and cut them up into the
pot of stew, not knowing what they were.
40 They served some for the men to eat. But
while they were eating the stew, they cried
out, "O man of God, there is death in the
pot!" They could not eat it. 41 He said,
"Then bring some flour." He threw it into
the pot, and said, "Serve the people and let
them eat." And there was nothing harmful
in the pot.
42 A man came from Baal-shalishah,
bringing food from the first fruits to the
man of God: twenty loaves of barley and
fresh ears of grain in his sack. Elisha said,
"Give it to the people and let them eat."
43 But his servant said, "How can I set this
before a hundred people?" So he repeated,
"Give it to the people and let them eat, for
thus says the LORD, 'They shall eat and
have some left.' " 44 He set it before them,
they ate, and had some left, according to
the word of the LORD.

5 Naaman, commander of the army of
the king of Aram, was a great man and
in high favor with his master, because by
him the LORD had given victory to Aram.
The man, though a mighty warrior, suf-
fered from leprosy.[e] 2 Now the Arameans
on one of their raids had taken a young girl
captive from the land of Israel, and she
served Naaman's wife. 3 She said to her
mistress, "If only my lord were with the
prophet who is in Samaria! He would cure
him of his leprosy."[e] 4 So Naaman[b] went
in and told his lord just what the girl from
the land of Israel had said. 5 And the king of

a Heb lacks *on the bed* b Heb *he* c Heb *sons of the prophets were* d Heb *sons of the prophets*
e A term for several skin diseases; precise meaning uncertain

as *Gehazi* fails to evoke any response from the corpse. **33–35:** It is only Elisha's own *prayer* and mysterious actions that succeed in bringing the boy back to life (cf. 1 Kings 17.19–23). **38–44:** Elisha has the remarkable ability to use a common ingredient like flour to miraculously make a pot of stew edible after harmful gourds were accidentally mixed into it. **42–44:** A limited amount of food is once again multiplied (cf. 4.1–7), in face of the *servant*'s incomprehension (v. 43), so that it not only provides people with their immediate needs, but also produces a surplus (cf. 4.7).

5.1–27: An Aramean is healed. Again a narrative picks up themes from the Elijah story, as the LORD is seen to be God, not only of Israelites (1 Kings 17.17–24), but also of foreigners, and is, indeed, acknowledged as the only real God there is (1 Kings 18.20–40). Additionally, this chapter exemplifies the sacredness of the land of Israel. **1:** The sovereignty of Israel's God over the whole world is announced right at the beginning of the story: Naaman's success in life (see 1 Kings 22.29–36 for an account of Aram's *victory*) comes as the LORD's gift. *Aram* refers to Aram-Damascus; see 1 Kings 19.15. **3:** *Samaria* was the capital of the Northern Kingdom of Israel. **5:** *Ten talents,* about 343 kg (756 lb); *six thousand shekels,*

Aram said, "Go then, and I will send along
a letter to the king of Israel."
He went, taking with him ten talents of
silver, six thousand shekels of gold, and ten
sets of garments. 6 He brought the letter to
the king of Israel, which read, "When this
letter reaches you, know that I have sent
to you my servant Naaman, that you may
cure him of his leprosy."[a] 7 When the king
of Israel read the letter, he tore his clothes
and said, "Am I God, to give death or life,
that this man sends word to me to cure a
man of his leprosy?[a] Just look and see how
he is trying to pick a quarrel with me."
8 But when Elisha the man of God heard
that the king of Israel had torn his clothes,
he sent a message to the king, "Why have
you torn your clothes? Let him come to me,
that he may learn that there is a prophet in
Israel." 9 So Naaman came with his horses
and chariots, and halted at the entrance of
Elisha's house. 10 Elisha sent a messenger to
him, saying, "Go, wash in the Jordan seven
times, and your flesh shall be restored and
you shall be clean." 11 But Naaman became
angry and went away, saying, "I thought
that for me he would surely come out, and
stand and call on the name of the LORD his
God, and would wave his hand over the
spot, and cure the leprosy![a] 12 Are not Ab-
ana[b] and Pharpar, the rivers of Damascus,
better than all the waters of Israel? Could
I not wash in them, and be clean?" He
turned and went away in a rage. 13 But his
servants approached and said to him, "Fa-
ther, if the prophet had commanded you to
do something difficult, would you not have
done it? How much more, when all he said
to you was, 'Wash, and be clean'?" 14 So he
went down and immersed himself seven
times in the Jordan, according to the word
of the man of God; his flesh was restored
like the flesh of a young boy, and he was
clean.
15 Then he returned to the man of God,
he and all his company; he came and stood
before him and said, "Now I know that
there is no God in all the earth except in
Israel; please accept a present from your
servant." 16 But he said, "As the LORD
lives, whom I serve, I will accept nothing!"
He urged him to accept, but he refused.
17 Then Naaman said, "If not, please let
two mule-loads of earth be given to your
servant; for your servant will no longer of-
fer burnt offering or sacrifice to any god
except the LORD. 18 But may the LORD par-
don your servant on one count: when my
master goes into the house of Rimmon to
worship there, leaning on my arm, and I
bow down in the house of Rimmon, when
I do bow down in the house of Rimmon,
may the LORD pardon your servant on this
one count." 19 He said to him, "Go in
peace."

But when Naaman had gone from him a

a A term for several skin diseases; precise meaning uncertain *b* Another reading is *Amana*

about 69 kg (151 lb). **7:** Only God can *give death or life* (cf. 4.8–37; Deut 32.39; 1 Sam 2.6; Hos 6.1–2). **9–19:** Like other characters in Kings, Naaman thinks that prophets are in control of their prophetic gift, able to say and do as they choose, and with a responsibility to please their superiors (e.g., 1 Kings 22.13). He expects personal and immediate attention (v. 11). **12:** He seems to have heard Elisha as speaking, not about healing, but only about ritual cleansing, which he could have obtained at home; his words evoke the cleansing ritual of Lev 13–14. **13:** Fortunately for Naaman, his servants are more attentive and persuade him to reconsider his hasty interpretation of Elisha's words; the last part of their speech here is better rendered "Has he really said to you, 'Wash and be clean'?" **15–18:** The result of his experience is religious conversion: His worship henceforth will be focused upon an altar made of *earth* taken from God's special land, whose waters had such remarkable healing powers. His "worship" of the Syrian god *Rimmon* (another name for Hadad, the god of storm and thunder and principal deity of Aram), now clearly understood to be merely an idol, will be restricted to those unavoidable occasions when he is found in Rimmon's temple in the course of his official duties. For these occasions he asks the LORD's *pardon,* in language reminiscent of Solomon's prayer (1 Kings 8.30,34,36,39,50; cf. esp.

short distance, 20 Gehazi, the servant of Eli-
sha the man of God, thought, "My master
has let that Aramean Naaman off too light-
ly by not accepting from him what he of-
fered. As the LORD lives, I will run after
him and get something out of him." 21 So
Gehazi went after Naaman. When Naaman
saw someone running after him, he jumped
down from the chariot to meet him and
said, "Is everything all right?" 22 He re-
plied, "Yes, but my master has sent me to
say, 'Two members of a company of proph-
ets[a] have just come to me from the hill
country of Ephraim; please give them a tal-
ent of silver and two changes of clothing.' "
23 Naaman said, "Please accept two tal-
ents." He urged him, and tied up two tal-
ents of silver in two bags, with two changes
of clothing, and gave them to two of his
servants, who carried them in front of Ge-
hazi.[b] 24 When he came to the citadel, he
took the bags[c] from them, and stored
them inside; he dismissed the men, and they
left.

25 He went in and stood before his mas-
ter; and Elisha said to him, "Where have
you been, Gehazi?" He answered, "Your
servant has not gone anywhere at all."
26 But he said to him, "Did I not go with
you in spirit when someone left his chariot
to meet you? Is this a time to accept money
and to accept clothing, olive orchards and
vineyards, sheep and oxen, and male and
female slaves? 27 Therefore the leprosy[d] of
Naaman shall cling to you, and to your de-
scendants forever." So he left his presence
leprous,[d] as white as snow.

6 Now the company of prophets[a] said to
Elisha, "As you see, the place where we
live under your charge is too small for us.
2 Let us go to the Jordan, and let us collect
logs there, one for each of us, and build a
place there for us to live." He answered,
"Do so." 3 Then one of them said, "Please
come with your servants." And he an-
swered, "I will." 4 So he went with them.
When they came to the Jordan, they cut
down trees. 5 But as one was felling a log,
his ax head fell into the water; he cried out,
"Alas, master! It was borrowed." 6 Then
the man of God said, "Where did it fall?"
When he showed him the place, he cut off
a stick, and threw it in there, and made the
iron float. 7 He said, "Pick it up." So he
reached out his hand and took it.

8 Once when the king of Aram was at
war with Israel, he took counsel with his
officers. He said, "At such and such a place
shall be my camp." 9 But the man of God
sent word to the king of Israel, "Take care
not to pass this place, because the Arame-
ans are going down there." 10 The king of
Israel sent word to the place of which the
man of God spoke. More than once or
twice he warned such a place[e] so that it
was on the alert.

11 The mind of the king of Aram was
greatly perturbed because of this; he called
his officers and said to them, "Now tell me
who among us sides with the king of Isra-
el?" 12 Then one of his officers said, "No
one, my lord king. It is Elisha, the prophet
in Israel, who tells the king of Israel the
words that you speak in your bedcham-
ber." 13 He said, "Go and find where he is;
I will send and seize him." He was told,

a Heb *sons of the prophets* *b* Heb *him*
c Heb lacks *the bags* *d* A term for several skin diseases; precise meaning uncertain *e* Heb *warned it*

8.41–43, where Solomon considers the case of the foreigner who prays toward the Temple). **20–27:** Elisha had not wished the miracle to be misunderstood and had refused payment (v. 16). He is no professional prophet, working miracles for pay (see 1 Sam 9.6–7), but a true "man of God." *Gehazi,* on the other hand, pursues profit, with the result that Naaman's disease becomes his own. A *talent* (v. 22) weighed about 34 kg (76 lb).

6.1–23: More miracles. God looks after individual Israelites as well as Israel through the medium of Elisha's prophetic ministry. **1–7:** Elisha has past experience of manipulating the waters of the Jordan (2.14; cf. 5.10), and he is able, miraculously, to make *the iron float* like the piece of wood he has thrown in beside it. **8–23:** Relations between *Aram* and Israel have deteriorated since ch 5. In the midst of *war,* Elisha's prophetic gift allows Jehoram access to information about Aramean troop movements.

"He is in Dothan." 14 So he sent horses and
chariots there and a great army; they came
by night, and surrounded the city.
15 When an attendant of the man of
God rose early in the morning and went
out, an army with horses and chariots was
all around the city. His servant said, "Alas,
master! What shall we do?" 16 He replied,
"Do not be afraid, for there are more with
us than there are with them." 17 Then Eli-
sha prayed: "O LORD, please open his eyes
that he may see." So the LORD opened the
eyes of the servant, and he saw; the moun-
tain was full of horses and chariots of fire
all around Elisha. 18 When the Arameans[a]
came down against him, Elisha prayed to
the LORD, and said, "Strike this people,
please, with blindness." So he struck them
with blindness as Elisha had asked. 19 Eli-
sha said to them, "This is not the way, and
this is not the city; follow me, and I will
bring you to the man whom you seek."
And he led them to Samaria.
20 As soon as they entered Samaria, Eli-
sha said, "O LORD, open the eyes of these
men so that they may see." The LORD
opened their eyes, and they saw that they
were inside Samaria. 21 When the king of
Israel saw them he said to Elisha, "Father,
shall I kill them? Shall I kill them?" 22 He
answered, "No! Did you capture with your
sword and your bow those whom you want
to kill? Set food and water before them so
that they may eat and drink; and let them
go to their master." 23 So he prepared for
them a great feast; after they ate and drank,
he sent them on their way, and they went to
their master. And the Arameans no longer
came raiding into the land of Israel.
24 Some time later King Ben-hadad of
Aram mustered his entire army; he
marched against Samaria and laid siege to
it. 25 As the siege continued, famine in Sa-
maria became so great that a donkey's head
was sold for eighty shekels of silver, and
one-fourth of a kab of dove's dung for five
shekels of silver. 26 Now as the king of Isra-
el was walking on the city wall, a woman
cried out to him, "Help, my lord king!"
27 He said, "No! Let the LORD help you.
How can I help you? From the threshing
floor or from the wine press?" 28 But then
the king asked her, "What is your com-
plaint?" She answered, "This woman said
to me, 'Give up your son; we will eat him
today, and we will eat my son tomorrow.'
29 So we cooked my son and ate him. The
next day I said to her, 'Give up your son
and we will eat him.' But she has hidden
her son." 30 When the king heard the words
of the woman he tore his clothes—now
since he was walking on the city wall, the
people could see that he had sackcloth on
his body underneath— 31 and he said, "So
may God do to me, and more, if the head of
Elisha son of Shaphat stays on his shoul-

a Heb *they*

13: *Dothan* was about 18 km (11 mi) north of Samaria. **15–17:** Aramean troops may surround the city, but Elisha himself is surrounded by the army of the LORD (see 2.11n.). **18–20:** The Arameans' blindness to the odds is quickly compounded by a *blindness* to their surroundings, which puts them entirely at the mercy of the seer they had come to capture. Dependent upon Elisha for guidance, they are led to the Israelite capital, where they too (like the "servant" in v. 17) move from blindness to sight and discover they have been captured.

6.24–7.20: The siege of Samaria. The second siege of Samaria by *Ben-hadad of Aram* is significantly more serious than the first (cf. 1 Kings 20.1) and inflicts much greater hardship on the population of the city. **6.25:** The point is that there is no food worth speaking of. *Eighty shekels* would have been about 900 gr (2 lb), *a kab* about 1.3 l (1.3 qt), and *five shekels* about 57 gr (2 oz). **28–29:** The famine is so severe that one woman has been driven to the unthinkable. Cannibalism is hinted at or explicitly described as a consequence of siege elsewhere in the Hebrew Bible (Deut 28.53–57; Lam 2.20; 4.10; Ezek 5.10) and in nonbiblical texts. **30–31:** Jehoram has been wearing *sackcloth,* humbling himself before the LORD because of the disaster (cf. 1 Kings 21.27). Faced with the horror about which he has just been told, he is unwilling to wait for God any longer, but seeks vengeance on his prophet. **6.32–7.2:** Elisha's prophetic

ders today." 32 So he dispatched a man
from his presence.
Now Elisha was sitting in his house, and
the elders were sitting with him. Before the
messenger arrived, Elisha said to the elders,
"Are you aware that this murderer has sent
someone to take off my head? When the
messenger comes, see that you shut the
door and hold it closed against him. Is not
the sound of his master's feet behind him?"
33 While he was still speaking with them,
the king[a] came down to him and said,
"This trouble is from the LORD! Why
should I hope in the LORD any longer?"
7 1 But Elisha said, "Hear the word of the
LORD: thus says the LORD, Tomorrow
about this time a measure of choice meal
shall be sold for a shekel, and two measures
of barley for a shekel, at the gate of Samar-
ia." 2 Then the captain on whose hand the
king leaned said to the man of God, "Even
if the LORD were to make windows in the
sky, could such a thing happen?" But he
said, "You shall see it with your own eyes,
but you shall not eat from it."
3 Now there were four leprous[b] men
outside the city gate, who said to one an-
other, "Why should we sit here until we
die? 4 If we say, 'Let us enter the city,' the
famine is in the city, and we shall die there;
but if we sit here, we shall also die. There-
fore, let us desert to the Aramean camp; if
they spare our lives, we shall live; and if
they kill us, we shall but die." 5 So they
arose at twilight to go to the Aramean
camp; but when they came to the edge of
the Aramean camp, there was no one there
at all. 6 For the Lord had caused the Arame-
an army to hear the sound of chariots, and
of horses, the sound of a great army, so that
they said to one another, "The king of Isra-
el has hired the kings of the Hittites and the
kings of Egypt to fight against us." 7 So they
fled away in the twilight and abandoned
their tents, their horses, and their donkeys
leaving the camp just as it was, and fled for
their lives. 8 When these leprous[b] men had
come to the edge of the camp, they went
into a tent, ate and drank, carried off silver,
gold, and clothing, and went and hid them.
Then they came back, entered another tent,
carried off things from it, and went and hid
them.
9 Then they said to one another, "What
we are doing is wrong. This is a day of
good news; if we are silent and wait until
the morning light, we will be found guilty;
therefore let us go and tell the king's house-
hold." 10 So they came and called to the
gatekeepers of the city, and told them, "We
went to the Aramean camp, but there was
no one to be seen or heard there, nothing
but the horses tied, the donkeys tied, and
the tents as they were." 11 Then the gate-
keepers called out and proclaimed it to the
king's household. 12 The king got up in the
night, and said to his servants, "I will tell
you what the Arameans have prepared
against us. They know that we are starving;
so they have left the camp to hide them-
selves in the open country, thinking, 'When
they come out of the city, we shall take
them alive and get into the city.' " 13 One of
his servants said, "Let some men take five
of the remaining horses, since those left
here will suffer the fate of the whole multi-
tude of Israel that have perished already;[c]

a See 7.2: Heb *messenger* *b* A term for several skin diseases; precise meaning uncertain *c* Compare Gk Syr Vg: Meaning of Heb uncertain

sight forewarns him. He is able to promise that normal business *at the gate of Samaria* will shortly be resumed: Produce worth eating will change hands once again at much lower prices (7.1). Jehoram's officer's unbelief will result in his exclusion from this blessing. **3–20:** A leper had first brought the Arameans to Samaria during Jehoram's reign (5.1–7), and *four leprous men* now drive them away. Lepers were considered impure and thus had to reside outside the city (Lev 13.46). Faced with certain death if they go into the city or stay where they are, these men instead choose possible death in the *Aramean camp*. **5–7:** But the camp is empty, because once again Samaria is delivered by the appearance of the divine army (see 6.15–17n.), misinterpreted by the Arameans as the Egyptians and the Hittites, frequent rivals for control of the Levant in the late second millennium BCE. **14:** *Two mounted men*, a better translation is

let us send and find out." 14 So they took
two mounted men, and the king sent them
after the Aramean army, saying, "Go and
find out." 15 So they went after them as far
as the Jordan; the whole way was littered
with garments and equipment that the Ara-
means had thrown away in their haste. So
the messengers returned, and told the king.
16 Then the people went out, and plun-
dered the camp of the Arameans. So a mea-
sure of choice meal was sold for a shekel,
and two measures of barley for a shekel,
according to the word of the LORD. 17 Now
the king had appointed the captain on
whose hand he leaned to have charge of the
gate; the people trampled him to death in
the gate, just as the man of God had said
when the king came down to him. 18 For
when the man of God had said to the king,
"Two measures of barley shall be sold for a
shekel, and a measure of choice meal for a
shekel, about this time tomorrow in the
gate of Samaria," 19 the captain had an-
swered the man of God, "Even if the LORD
were to make windows in the sky, could
such a thing happen?" And he had an-
swered, "You shall see it with your own
eyes, but you shall not eat from it." 20 It did
indeed happen to him; the people trampled
him to death in the gate.

8 Now Elisha had said to the woman
whose son he had restored to life, "Get
up and go with your household, and settle
wherever you can; for the LORD has called
for a famine, and it will come on the land
for seven years." 2 So the woman got up
and did according to the word of the man
of God; she went with her household and
settled in the land of the Philistines seven
years. 3 At the end of the seven years, when
the woman returned from the land of the
Philistines, she set out to appeal to the king
for her house and her land. 4 Now the king
was talking with Gehazi the servant of the
man of God, saying, "Tell me all the great
things that Elisha has done." 5 While he
was telling the king how Elisha had re-
stored a dead person to life, the woman
whose son he had restored to life appealed
to the king for her house and her land. Ge-
hazi said, "My lord king, here is the wom-
an, and here is her son whom Elisha re-
stored to life." 6 When the king questioned
the woman, she told him. So the king ap-
pointed an official for her, saying, "Restore
all that was hers, together with all the reve-
nue of the fields from the day that she left
the land until now."
7 Elisha went to Damascus while King
Ben-hadad of Aram was ill. When it was
told him, "The man of God has come
here," 8 the king said to Hazael, "Take a
present with you and go to meet the man of
God. Inquire of the LORD through him,
whether I shall recover from this illness."
9 So Hazael went to meet him, taking a
present with him, all kinds of goods of Da-
mascus, forty camel loads. When he en-
tered and stood before him, he said, "Your
son King Ben-hadad of Aram has sent me
to you, saying, 'Shall I recover from this
illness?' " 10 Elisha said to him, "Go, say to

"two chariot teams." **17:** The skeptical officer, ironically stationed at the very *gate* at which he had anticipated seeing no trade (v. 2), is *trampled* in the scramble to acquire goods.

8.1–6: Elisha and the Shunammite. The woman no longer has a home and now needs the help that Elisha had previously offered her (cf. 4.13), for she has followed Elisha's advice and avoided the general state of *famine* by sojourning in Philistia. While she has been away, the story implies, someone has taken her land. Providentially, just at the moment she arrives at the royal court to *appeal . . . for her house and her land, Gehazi* is telling the king all about her. His words serve as the advocacy on her behalf that Elisha earlier had in mind. God looks after those who look after his prophets.

8.7–15: Elisha and Hazael. As Elijah's successor, Elisha carries out the divine commission to anoint Hazael as king of Aram-Damascus (see 1 Kings 19.15). *Hazael* is sent to *inquire of the LORD* about Ben-hadad's illness, with an extravagant gift to smooth his way. Ben-hadad will *die* (v. 10); but Elisha also sees beyond his death into Aram's future, in which Hazael will be king and will inflict great suffering on Israel (vv. 12–13) as he ravages the land and brutalizes the people (cf. Am 1.13; Hos 13.16; 2 Kings

him, 'You shall certainly recover'; but the
LORD has shown me that he shall certainly
die." 11 He fixed his gaze and stared at him,
until he was ashamed. Then the man of
God wept. 12 Hazael asked, "Why does my
lord weep?" He answered, "Because I
know the evil that you will do to the people
of Israel; you will set their fortresses on fire,
you will kill their young men with the
sword, dash in pieces their little ones, and
rip up their pregnant women." 13 Hazael
said, "What is your servant, who is a mere
dog, that he should do this great thing?"
Elisha answered, "The LORD has shown me
that you are to be king over Aram." 14 Then
he left Elisha, and went to his master Ben-
hadad,[a] who said to him, "What did Eli-
sha say to you?" And he answered, "He
told me that you would certainly recover."
15 But the next day he took the bed-cover
and dipped it in water and spread it over
the king's face, until he died. And Hazael
succeeded him.

16 In the fifth year of King Joram son of
Ahab of Israel,[b] Jehoram son of King Je-
hoshaphat of Judah began to reign. 17 He
was thirty-two years old when he became
king, and he reigned eight years in Jerusa-
lem. 18 He walked in the way of the kings of
Israel, as the house of Ahab had done, for
the daughter of Ahab was his wife. He did
what was evil in the sight of the LORD.
19 Yet the LORD would not destroy Judah,
for the sake of his servant David, since he
had promised to give a lamp to him and to
his descendants forever.

20 In his days Edom revolted against the
rule of Judah, and set up a king of their
own. 21 Then Joram crossed over to Zair
with all his chariots. He set out by night
and attacked the Edomites and their chari-
ot commanders who had surrounded
him;[c] but his army fled home. 22 So Edom
has been in revolt against the rule of Judah
to this day. Libnah also revolted at the
same time. 23 Now the rest of the acts of
Joram, and all that he did, are they not
written in the Book of the Annals of the
Kings of Judah? 24 So Joram slept with his
ancestors, and was buried with them in the
city of David; his son Ahaziah succeeded
him.

25 In the twelfth year of King Joram son
of Ahab of Israel, Ahaziah son of King Je-
horam of Judah began to reign. 26 Ahaziah
was twenty-two years old when he began
to reign; he reigned one year in Jerusalem.
His mother's name was Athaliah, a grand-
daughter of King Omri of Israel. 27 He also
walked in the way of the house of Ahab,
doing what was evil in the sight of the
LORD, as the house of Ahab had done, for
he was son-in-law to the house of Ahab.

28 He went with Joram son of Ahab to
wage war against King Hazael of Aram
at Ramoth-gilead, where the Arameans
wounded Joram. 29 King Joram returned to
be healed in Jezreel of the wounds that the
Arameans had inflicted on him at Ramah,
when he fought against King Hazael of
Aram. King Ahaziah son of Jehoram of Ju-
dah went down to see Joram son of Ahab in
Jezreel, because he was wounded.

9 Then the prophet Elisha called a mem-
ber of the company of prophets[d] and
said to him, "Gird up your loins; take this

a Heb lacks *Ben-hadad* *b* Gk Syr: Heb adds *Jehoshaphat being king of Judah,* *c* Meaning of Heb uncertain *d* Heb *sons of the prophets*

15.16). **13:** Hazael's obscure origins are well captured in his own self-description: *a mere dog.* He was the "son of nobody," according to an Assyrian source.

8.16–29: Jehoram (also Joram; 851–843 BCE) and Ahaziah (843–842) of Judah. Both these Judean kings followed Ahab and his successors into idolatry and the worship of Baal, being related to the northern dynasty through intermarriage. Yet God had promised David an everlasting *lamp* (v. 19; cf. 1 Kings 11.36; 15.4), so *the LORD would not destroy Judah* because of these sins. **21:** *Zair,* probably Zoar, at the southern end of the Dead Sea. **22:** *Libnah . . . revolted,* the rebellion of a city in the kingdom was unusual, but no details are given. Libnah was about 40 km (25 mi) southwest of Jerusalem. **28–29:** *Ramoth-gilead,* the site of an earlier encounter between Israel and Aram; see 1 Kings 22.29–36.

9.1–37: The end of Omri's dynasty. Elisha now fulfills the command to Elijah to anoint *Jehu* king over

flask of oil in your hand, and go to
Ramoth-gilead. 2 When you arrive, look
there for Jehu son of Jehoshaphat, son of
Nimshi; go in and get him to leave his com-
panions, and take him into an inner cham-
ber. 3 Then take the flask of oil, pour it on
his head, and say, 'Thus says the LORD: I
anoint you king over Israel.' Then open the
door and flee; do not linger."

4 So the young man, the young prophet,
went to Ramoth-gilead. 5 He arrived while
the commanders of the army were in coun-
cil, and he announced, "I have a message
for you, commander." "For which one of
us?" asked Jehu. "For you, commander."
6 So Jehu[a] got up and went inside; the
young man poured the oil on his head, say-
ing to him, "Thus says the LORD the God
of Israel: I anoint you king over the people
of the LORD, over Israel. 7 You shall strike
down the house of your master Ahab, so
that I may avenge on Jezebel the blood of
my servants the prophets, and the blood
of all the servants of the LORD. 8 For the
whole house of Ahab shall perish; I will cut
off from Ahab every male, bond or free, in
Israel. 9 I will make the house of Ahab like
the house of Jeroboam son of Nebat, and
like the house of Baasha son of Ahijah.
10 The dogs shall eat Jezebel in the territory
of Jezreel, and no one shall bury her." Then
he opened the door and fled.

11 When Jehu came back to his master's
officers, they said to him, "Is everything
all right? Why did that madman come to
you?" He answered them, "You know the
sort and how they babble." 12 They said,
"Liar! Come on, tell us!" So he said, "This
is just what he said to me: 'Thus says the
LORD, I anoint you king over Israel.' "
13 Then hurriedly they all took their cloaks
and spread them for him on the bare[b]
steps; and they blew the trumpet, and pro-
claimed, "Jehu is king."

14 Thus Jehu son of Jehoshaphat son of
Nimshi conspired against Joram. Joram
with all Israel had been on guard at
Ramoth-gilead against King Hazael of
Aram; 15 but King Joram had returned to
be healed in Jezreel of the wounds that
the Arameans had inflicted on him, when
he fought against King Hazael of Aram. So
Jehu said, "If this is your wish, then let no
one slip out of the city to go and tell the
news in Jezreel." 16 Then Jehu mounted his
chariot and went to Jezreel, where Joram
was lying ill. King Ahaziah of Judah had
come down to visit Joram.

17 In Jezreel, the sentinel standing on
the tower spied the company of Jehu arriv-
ing, and said, "I see a company." Joram
said, "Take a horseman; send him to meet
them, and let him say, 'Is it peace?' " 18 So
the horseman went to meet him; he said,
"Thus says the king, 'Is it peace?' " Jehu
responded, "What have you to do with
peace? Fall in behind me." The sentinel
reported, saying, "The messenger reached
them, but he is not coming back." 19 Then
he sent out a second horseman, who came
to them and said, "Thus says the king, 'Is it
peace?' " Jehu answered, "What have you
to do with peace? Fall in behind me."
20 Again the sentinel reported, "He reached
them, but he is not coming back. It looks
like the driving of Jehu son of Nimshi; for
he drives like a maniac."

21 Joram said, "Get ready." And they
got his chariot ready. Then King Joram of
Israel and King Ahaziah of Judah set out,

[a] Heb *he* [b] Meaning of Heb uncertain

Israel (1 Kings 19.16). **2:** The anointing is secret, and reminiscent of Samuel's anointing of Saul (1 Sam 9.27–10.1). **7:** *Jezebel,* see 1 Kings 16.31n. **11–13:** Jehu's reaction to his anointing is also similar to Saul's: He does not wish to respond to questions about what has happened (1 Sam 10.15–16). His reluctance is overcome by the persistence of his companions, who prove eager to proclaim him king; perhaps there was already unrest in the army due to Jehoram's lack of success in his military ventures. **21:** The two kings meet Jehu outside the city at *property* that had belonged to *Naboth the Jezreelite.* The name has fateful connotations, for it was an incident involving a piece of ground belonging to Naboth that elicited Elijah's oracle against Ahab in the first place (1 Kings 21, esp. vv. 1–2,16–24) and precipitated that king's death (1 Kings 22, esp. v. 38). **29:** Contrast 8.25. **30–31:** Jezebel is discovered sitting

each in his chariot, and went to meet Jehu;
they met him at the property of Naboth the
Jezreelite. 22 When Joram saw Jehu, he said,
"Is it peace, Jehu?" He answered, "What
peace can there be, so long as the many
whoredoms and sorceries of your mother
Jezebel continue?" 23 Then Joram reined
about and fled, saying to Ahaziah, "Trea-
son, Ahaziah!" 24 Jehu drew his bow with
all his strength, and shot Joram between
the shoulders, so that the arrow pierced his
heart; and he sank in his chariot. 25 Jehu
said to his aide Bidkar, "Lift him out, and
throw him on the plot of ground belonging
to Naboth the Jezreelite; for remember,
when you and I rode side by side behind his
father Ahab how the LORD uttered this ora-
cle against him: 26 'For the blood of Naboth
and for the blood of his children that I saw
yesterday, says the LORD, I swear I will re-
pay you on this very plot of ground.' Now
therefore lift him out and throw him on the
plot of ground, in accordance with the
word of the LORD."
27 When King Ahaziah of Judah saw
this, he fled in the direction of Beth-
haggan. Jehu pursued him, saying, "Shoot
him also!" And they shot him[a] in the char-
iot at the ascent to Gur, which is by Ibleam.
Then he fled to Megiddo, and died there.
28 His officers carried him in a chariot to
Jerusalem, and buried him in his tomb with
his ancestors in the city of David.
29 In the eleventh year of Joram son of
Ahab, Ahaziah began to reign over Judah.
30 When Jehu came to Jezreel, Jezebel
heard of it; she painted her eyes, and
adorned her head, and looked out of the
window. 31 As Jehu entered the gate, she
said, "Is it peace, Zimri, murderer of your
master?" 32 He looked up to the window
and said, "Who is on my side? Who?" Two
or three eunuchs looked out at him. 33 He
said, "Throw her down." So they threw her
down; some of her blood spattered on the
wall and on the horses, which trampled on
her. 34 Then he went in and ate and drank;
he said, "See to that cursed woman and
bury her; for she is a king's daughter."
35 But when they went to bury her, they
found no more of her than the skull and the
feet and the palms of her hands. 36 When
they came back and told him, he said,
"This is the word of the LORD, which he
spoke by his servant Elijah the Tishbite, 'In
the territory of Jezreel the dogs shall eat the
flesh of Jezebel; 37 the corpse of Jezebel
shall be like dung on the field in the territo-
ry of Jezreel, so that no one can say, This is
Jezebel.'"

10 Now Ahab had seventy sons in Sa-
maria. So Jehu wrote letters and
sent them to Samaria, to the rulers of Jezre-
el,[b] to the elders, and to the guardians of
the sons of[c] Ahab, saying, 2 "Since your
master's sons are with you and you have at
your disposal chariots and horses, a forti-
fied city, and weapons, 3 select the son of
your master who is the best qualified, set
him on his father's throne, and fight for
your master's house." 4 But they were utter-
ly terrified and said, "Look, two kings
could not withstand him; how then can we
stand?" 5 So the steward of the palace, and
the governor of the city, along with the el-
ders and the guardians, sent word to Jehu:
"We are your servants; we will do anything
you say. We will not make anyone king; do
whatever you think right." 6 Then he wrote
them a second letter, saying, "If you are on
my side, and if you are ready to obey me,
take the heads of your master's sons and

a Syr Vg Compare Gk: Heb lacks *and they shot him*
b Or *of the city*; Vg Compare Gk c Gk: Heb lacks *of the sons of*

at a window, fully adorned as a prostitute (cf. Jer 4.30; Ezek 23.40). She taunts Jehu as one unlikely to survive his own revolution: His reign will be as short as the seven-day reign of *Zimri* (1 Kings 16.8–20). **32:** Officials of royal courts in the ancient Near East, especially those in charge of the women's quarters, were often *eunuchs*. **36–37:** See 1 Kings 21.23.

10.1–36: The destruction continues. Jehu turns his attention to the wider family (cf. Elijah's prophecy in 1 Kings 21.21). **1:** The *seventy sons* (cf. Judg 8.30) were the people from among whom a successor to

come to me at Jezreel tomorrow at this
time." Now the king's sons, seventy per-
sons, were with the leaders of the city, who
were charged with their upbringing. 7 When
the letter reached them, they took the
king's sons and killed them, seventy per-
sons; they put their heads in baskets and
sent them to him at Jezreel. 8 When the mes-
senger came and told him, "They have
brought the heads of the king's sons," he
said, "Lay them in two heaps at the en-
trance of the gate until the morning."
9 Then in the morning when he went out, he
stood and said to all the people, "You are
innocent. It was I who conspired against
my master and killed him; but who struck
down all these? 10 Know then that there
shall fall to the earth nothing of the word of
the LORD, which the LORD spoke concern-
ing the house of Ahab; for the LORD has
done what he said through his servant Eli-
jah." 11 So Jehu killed all who were left of
the house of Ahab in Jezreel, all his leaders,
close friends, and priests, until he left him
no survivor.

12 Then he set out and went to Samaria.
On the way, when he was at Beth-eked of
the Shepherds, 13 Jehu met relatives of King
Ahaziah of Judah and said, "Who are
you?" They answered, "We are kin of Aha-
ziah; we have come down to visit the royal
princes and the sons of the queen mother."
14 He said, "Take them alive." They took
them alive, and slaughtered them at the pit
of Beth-eked, forty-two in all; he spared
none of them.

15 When he left there, he met Jehonadab
son of Rechab coming to meet him; he
greeted him, and said to him, "Is your heart
as true to mine as mine is to yours?"[a] Je-
honadab answered, "It is." Jehu said,[b] "If
it is, give me your hand." So he gave him
his hand. Jehu took him up with him into
the chariot. 16 He said, "Come with me,
and see my zeal for the LORD." So he[c] had
him ride in his chariot. 17 When he came to
Samaria, he killed all who were left to Ahab
in Samaria, until he had wiped them out,
according to the word of the LORD that he
spoke to Elijah.

18 Then Jehu assembled all the people
and said to them, "Ahab offered Baal small
service; but Jehu will offer much more.
19 Now therefore summon to me all the
prophets of Baal, all his worshipers, and all
his priests; let none be missing, for I have a
great sacrifice to offer to Baal; whoever is
missing shall not live." But Jehu was acting
with cunning in order to destroy the wor-
shipers of Baal. 20 Jehu decreed, "Sanctify a
solemn assembly for Baal." So they pro-
claimed it. 21 Jehu sent word throughout all
Israel; all the worshipers of Baal came, so
that there was no one left who did not
come. They entered the temple of Baal, un-
til the temple of Baal was filled from wall to
wall. 22 He said to the keeper of the ward-
robe, "Bring out the vestments for all the
worshipers of Baal." So he brought out the
vestments for them. 23 Then Jehu entered
the temple of Baal with Jehonadab son of
Rechab; he said to the worshipers of Baal,
"Search and see that there is no worshiper
of the LORD here among you, but only wor-

a Gk: Heb *Is it right with your heart, as my heart is with your heart?* *b* Gk: Heb lacks *Jehu said* *c* Gk Syr Tg: Heb *they*

Jehoram would normally be chosen. **9:** Jehu knows who killed the princes, but the people, asleep when the heads arrive, do not. The aim is to convince them that it is the LORD who is at work in overthrowing the house of Ahab. **12–17:** *Jehonadab son of Rechab* appears in Jer 35 as the founder of a purist religious group committed to Israel's older ways. He becomes a witness to events in Samaria, as all who are left there of the house of the innovator Ahab are destroyed (v. 17; see 1 Kings 21.21). **18–31:** Samaria had been a focal point for the worship of Baal (see 1 Kings 16.32–33). Jehu's strategy in removing it is to pretend to enthusiasm while preparing for slaughter. His efforts result in a dynastic promise, although this promise is weaker than the eternal promise to David: His descendants will sit on the throne of Israel to the *fourth generation* (v. 30). What Jehu has done that is *right* (v. 30) far outweighs what he continues to do that is wrong—retaining the *golden calves* at Bethel and Dan (vv. 29,31; see 1 Kings 12.25–33n.).

shipers of Baal." 24 Then they proceeded to
offer sacrifices and burnt offerings.
Now Jehu had stationed eighty men out-
side, saying, "Whoever allows any of those
to escape whom I deliver into your hands
shall forfeit his life." 25 As soon as he had
finished presenting the burnt offering, Jehu
said to the guards and to the officers,
"Come in and kill them; let no one escape."
So they put them to the sword. The guards
and the officers threw them out, and then
went into the citadel of the temple of Baal.
26 They brought out the pillar[a] that was in
the temple of Baal, and burned it. 27 Then
they demolished the pillar of Baal, and de-
stroyed the temple of Baal, and made it a
latrine to this day.
28 Thus Jehu wiped out Baal from Isra-
el. 29 But Jehu did not turn aside from the
sins of Jeroboam son of Nebat, which he
caused Israel to commit—the golden calves
that were in Bethel and in Dan. 30 The
LORD said to Jehu, "Because you have done
well in carrying out what I consider right,
and in accordance with all that was in my
heart have dealt with the house of Ahab,
your sons of the fourth generation shall sit
on the throne of Israel." 31 But Jehu was
not careful to follow the law of the LORD
the God of Israel with all his heart; he did
not turn from the sins of Jeroboam, which
he caused Israel to commit.
32 In those days the LORD began to trim
off parts of Israel. Hazael defeated them
throughout the territory of Israel: 33 from
the Jordan eastward, all the land of Gilead,
the Gadites, the Reubenites, and the Ma-
nassites, from Aroer, which is by the Wadi
Arnon, that is, Gilead and Bashan. 34 Now
the rest of the acts of Jehu, all that he did,
and all his power, are they not written in
the Book of the Annals of the Kings of Isra-
el? 35 So Jehu slept with his ancestors, and
they buried him in Samaria. His son Jehoa-
haz succeeded him. 36 The time that Jehu
reigned over Israel in Samaria was twenty-
eight years.

11 Now when Athaliah, Ahaziah's
mother, saw that her son was dead,
she set about to destroy all the royal family.
2 But Jehosheba, King Joram's daughter,
Ahaziah's sister, took Joash son of Ahazi-
ah, and stole him away from among the
king's children who were about to be
killed; she put[b] him and his nurse in a bed-
room. Thus she[c] hid him from Athaliah,
so that he was not killed; 3 he remained
with her six years, hidden in the house of
the LORD, while Athaliah reigned over the
land.
4 But in the seventh year Jehoiada sum-
moned the captains of the Carites and of
the guards and had them come to him in
the house of the LORD. He made a cove-
nant with them and put them under oath in
the house of the LORD; then he showed
them the king's son. 5 He commanded
them, "This is what you are to do: one-

a Gk Vg Syr Tg: Heb *pillars* *b* With 2 Chr 22.11: Heb lacks *she put* *c* Gk Syr Vg Compare 2 Chr 22.11: Heb *they*

32–36: 1 Kings 19.15–18 anticipated a time when God's judgment would fall upon Israel because of Baal-worship: Jehu would deal with those who escaped Hazael, and Elisha with those who escaped Jehu. This order implies that Hazael would turn out to be the greatest destroyer of the three. It is no surprise, therefore, to find that toward the end of the account of Jehu's reign, when *his* slaughter has ceased, we are first told of Hazael's aggression against Israel. **33:** The *Wadi Arnon* was the southern limit of Israelite territory in Transjordan (Josh 12.2), all of which Hazael captured. **36:** Jehu reigned ca. 842–814 BCE.

11.1–21: The reign of Athaliah, 842–836 BCE. *Athaliah, Ahaziah's mother* could well have been a daughter of Jezebel (cf. 8.26). She certainly displays the same ruthless streak. Her reign lacks the typical introductory and concluding formulae. **4:** It is not immediately clear who *Jehoiada* is, but it becomes so in the course of the narrative (vv. 9,15). The *Carites* appear in the consonantal Heb text of 2 Sam 20.23 as part of the elite royal bodyguard. They may well be the same as the Cherethites (cf. 1 Kings 1.38). **5–8:** The details of the arrangements are obscure, largely due to our ignorance as to how the troops involved were organized and subdivided. Clearly sufficient security is provided for the ceremony to take place

third of you, those who go off duty on the
sabbath and guard the king's house 6 (an-
other third being at the gate Sur and a third
at the gate behind the guards), shall guard
the palace; 7 and your two divisions that
come on duty in force on the sabbath and
guard the house of the LORD[a] 8 shall sur-
round the king, each with weapons in
hand; and whoever approaches the ranks is
to be killed. Be with the king in his comings
and goings."

9 The captains did according to all that
the priest Jehoiada commanded; each
brought his men who were to go off duty
on the sabbath, with those who were to
come on duty on the sabbath, and came to
the priest Jehoiada. 10 The priest delivered
to the captains the spears and shields that
had been King David's, which were in the
house of the LORD; 11 the guards stood, ev-
ery man with his weapons in his hand, from
the south side of the house to the north side
of the house, around the altar and the
house, to guard the king on every side.
12 Then he brought out the king's son, put
the crown on him, and gave him the cove-
nant;[b] they proclaimed him king, and
anointed him; they clapped their hands and
shouted, "Long live the king!"

13 When Athaliah heard the noise of the
guard and of the people, she went into the
house of the LORD to the people; 14 when
she looked, there was the king standing by
the pillar, according to custom, with the
captains and the trumpeters beside the
king, and all the people of the land rejoic-
ing and blowing trumpets. Athaliah tore
her clothes and cried, "Treason! Treason!"
15 Then the priest Jehoiada commanded the
captains who were set over the army,
"Bring her out between the ranks, and kill
with the sword anyone who follows her."
For the priest said, "Let her not be killed in
the house of the LORD." 16 So they laid
hands on her; she went through the horses'
entrance to the king's house, and there she
was put to death.

17 Jehoiada made a covenant between
the LORD and the king and people, that
they should be the LORD's people; also be-
tween the king and the people. 18 Then all
the people of the land went to the house of
Baal, and tore it down; his altars and his
images they broke in pieces, and they killed
Mattan, the priest of Baal, before the altars.
The priest posted guards over the house of
the LORD. 19 He took the captains, the Car-
ites, the guards, and all the people of the
land; then they brought the king down
from the house of the LORD, marching
through the gate of the guards to the king's
house. He took his seat on the throne of the
kings. 20 So all the people of the land re-

a Heb *the LORD to the king* *b* Or *treaty* or *testimony*; Heb *eduth*

within the Temple precincts. **10:** The soldiers probably did not need to be armed by the priest; the weapons were symbols of the Davidic dynasty. **12:** Joash is crowned and presented with *the covenant* (probably a list of divinely ordained laws; see Deut 17.18–20), or perhaps "the jewels"; in either case, some symbol of royal office. **13–16:** Athaliah, rushing from her unguarded palace to the Temple precincts to find out what is happening, discovers the conspiracy much too late, and, unwisely drawing attention to herself, is taken away from holy ground to be executed. **14:** The *pillar* is most likely either Jachin or Boaz (cf. 2 Chr 23.13; see 1 Kings 7.21). The emphasis on *custom* is significant, reflecting the authors' interest in stressing the legitimacy of Joash's claim to the throne. The *people of the land* have been variously interpreted as simple provincial people (the proletariat), property owners, those faithful to the Yahwistic tradition, and the voting citizenry of Judah. It is difficult in the absence of further data to know which, if any, of these suggestions is correct. **17–21:** An unusual three-way covenant-renewal ceremony follows the coronation: *The king and people* once more identify themselves, in the aftermath of the idolatrous interlude represented by the reigns of Jehoram and Ahaziah, as *the LORD's people* (cf. Josh 24.1–27; 2 Kings 23.1–3). At the same time, a *covenant* is made between the *king* and the *people* (cf. 2 Sam 5.1–3). It is important to redefine kingship in distinctively Israelite terms. The worship of Baal is then removed from the city.

joiced; and the city was quiet after Athaliah
had been killed with the sword at the king's
house.
21[a]Jehoash[b] was seven years old when
he began to reign.

12 In the seventh year of Jehu, Jehoash
began to reign; he reigned forty
years in Jerusalem. His mother's name was
Zibiah of Beer-sheba. 2 Jehoash did what
was right in the sight of the LORD all his
days, because the priest Jehoiada instructed
him. 3 Nevertheless the high places were not
taken away; the people continued to sacri-
fice and make offerings on the high places.
4 Jehoash said to the priests, "All the
money offered as sacred donations that is
brought into the house of the LORD, the
money for which each person is assessed—
the money from the assessment of per-
sons—and the money from the voluntary
offerings brought into the house of the
LORD, 5 let the priests receive from each of
the donors; and let them repair the house
wherever any need of repairs is discov-
ered." 6 But by the twenty-third year of
King Jehoash the priests had made no re-
pairs on the house. 7 Therefore King Jeho-
ash summoned the priest Jehoiada with the
other priests and said to them, "Why are
you not repairing the house? Now there-
fore do not accept any more money from
your donors but hand it over for the repair
of the house." 8 So the priests agreed that
they would neither accept more money
from the people nor repair the house.
9 Then the priest Jehoiada took a chest,
made a hole in its lid, and set it beside the
altar on the right side as one entered the
house of the LORD; the priests who guarded
the threshold put in it all the money that
was brought into the house of the LORD.
10 Whenever they saw that there was a great
deal of money in the chest, the king's secre-
tary and the high priest went up, counted
the money that was found in the house of
the LORD, and tied it up in bags. 11 They
would give the money that was weighed
out into the hands of the workers who had
the oversight of the house of the LORD;
then they paid it out to the carpenters and
the builders who worked on the house of
the LORD, 12 to the masons and the stone-
cutters, as well as to buy timber and quar-
ried stone for making repairs on the house
of the LORD, as well as for any outlay for
repairs of the house. 13 But for the house
of the LORD no basins of silver, snuffers,
bowls, trumpets, or any vessels of gold, or
of silver, were made from the money that
was brought into the house of the LORD,
14 for that was given to the workers who
were repairing the house of the LORD with
it. 15 They did not ask an accounting from
those into whose hand they delivered the
money to pay out to the workers, for they
dealt honestly. 16 The money from the guilt
offerings and the money from the sin offer-
ings was not brought into the house of the
LORD; it belonged to the priests.
17 At that time King Hazael of Aram
went up, fought against Gath, and took
it. But when Hazael set his face to go up
against Jerusalem, 18 King Jehoash of Judah
took all the votive gifts that Jehoshaphat,
Jehoram, and Ahaziah, his ancestors, the
kings of Judah, had dedicated, as well as
his own votive gifts, all the gold that was

a Ch 12.1 in Heb *b* Another spelling is *Joash*; see verse 19

12.1–21: The reign of Joash (also Jehoash; 836–798 BCE). *Joash* was a relatively good Judean king, eschewing idolatry, but failing to centralize the worship of the LORD (vv. 2–3). His main project was the repair of the Temple (cf. 22.3–7), which would have suffered some neglect during the years in which the worship of Baal was encouraged. **4:** See Ex 30.11–16; Lev 27.1–8. **6–8:** His initial plan to leave the restoration to the priests themselves failed because (it is implied) the priests were not anxious to spend good money on mere buildings. Joash himself therefore took control of the project. **13:** Only a very humble restoration took place: The Temple was a pale reflection of its former glory (cf. 1 Kings 7.50). **16:** *Guilt offerings . . . sin offerings,* see Lev 4–5. **17–18:** Judah, too, was oppressed by *Hazael of Aram* in this period (see 10.32–33 for his assault on Israel) as he turned east from the Philistine city of *Gath* to

found in the treasuries of the house of the
LORD and of the king's house, and sent
these to King Hazael of Aram. Then Hazael
withdrew from Jerusalem.
19 Now the rest of the acts of Joash, and
all that he did, are they not written in the
Book of the Annals of the Kings of Judah?
20 His servants arose, devised a conspiracy,
and killed Joash in the house of Millo, on
the way that goes down to Silla. 21 It was
Jozacar son of Shimeath and Jehozabad son
of Shomer, his servants, who struck him
down, so that he died. He was buried with
his ancestors in the city of David; then his
son Amaziah succeeded him.

13 In the twenty-third year of King Jo-
ash son of Ahaziah of Judah, Jehoa-
haz son of Jehu began to reign over Israel in
Samaria; he reigned seventeen years. 2 He
did what was evil in the sight of the LORD,
and followed the sins of Jeroboam son of
Nebat, which he caused Israel to sin; he did
not depart from them. 3 The anger of the
LORD was kindled against Israel, so that he
gave them repeatedly into the hand of King
Hazael of Aram, then into the hand of Ben-
hadad son of Hazael. 4 But Jehoahaz en-
treated the LORD, and the LORD heeded
him; for he saw the oppression of Israel,
how the king of Aram oppressed them.
5 Therefore the LORD gave Israel a savior,
so that they escaped from the hand of the
Arameans; and the people of Israel lived in
their homes as formerly. 6 Nevertheless they
did not depart from the sins of the house of
Jeroboam, which he caused Israel to sin,
but walked[a] in them; the sacred pole[b]
also remained in Samaria. 7 So Jehoahaz
was left with an army of not more than fifty
horsemen, ten chariots and ten thousand
footmen; for the king of Aram had de-
stroyed them and made them like the dust
at threshing. 8 Now the rest of the acts of
Jehoahaz and all that he did, including his
might, are they not written in the Book of
the Annals of the Kings of Israel? 9 So Jeho-
ahaz slept with his ancestors, and they bur-
ied him in Samaria; then his son Joash suc-
ceeded him.
10 In the thirty-seventh year of King Jo-
ash of Judah, Jehoash son of Jehoahaz be-
gan to reign over Israel in Samaria; he
reigned sixteen years. 11 He also did what
was evil in the sight of the LORD; he did not
depart from all the sins of Jeroboam son of
Nebat, which he caused Israel to sin, but he
walked in them. 12 Now the rest of the acts
of Joash, and all that he did, as well as the
might with which he fought against King
Amaziah of Judah, are they not written in
the Book of the Annals of the Kings of Isra-
el? 13 So Joash slept with his ancestors, and
Jeroboam sat upon his throne; Joash was
buried in Samaria with the kings of Israel.
14 Now when Elisha had fallen sick
with the illness of which he was to die, King

a Gk Syr Tg Vg: Heb *he walked* *b* Heb *Asherah*

attack Jerusalem. **19–21:** Aside from the wicked Ahaziah (9.27), Joash is the only Judean king to suffer violent death so far in Kings. There is a suggestion here that Joash turned to wickedness later in his reign (cf. 2 Chr 24.15–25). **20:** *Millo*, see 1 Kings 9.15n.

13.1–25: Jehoahaz (817–800 BCE) and Jehoash (also Joash; 800–784). We are now updated on what has been happening in Israel during the reigns of those two kings whose accessions took place within Joash's lifetime. Both kings hold on to their thrones all their days, and both survive (if only just) the Aramean onslaught. **1–9:** *Jehoahaz* is depicted as a wicked king, indulging as his predecessors had done in *the sins of Jeroboam.* Yet the divine promise to Jehu (10.30) is functioning at this point like the earlier promise to David (2 Sam 7.1–17), and the Israelite royal house is thus, for the moment, being treated like the Judean. Divine punishment is severe, making the royal forces as insubstantial as the *dust at threshing* time which is caught by the wind and blown away (v. 7); but there is no rejection of Jehu's dynasty. God responds to Jehoahaz's pleas, in fact, and Israel is saved (v. 5). **5:** The *savior* (cf. Judg 2.18; 3.9,15) is not identified, and may be Elisha, a gifted Israelite general, or perhaps a foreign king, distracting Aram from its war with Israel. **10–19:** The importance of the reign of *Jehoash* lies mainly in the fact that it provides the context for the death of Elisha. **14:** Joash addresses the prophet with the same words that he himself had used at the ascension of Elijah (2.12). **15–19:** Using symbolic gestures, Elisha is able

Joash of Israel went down to him, and wept
before him, crying, "My father, my father!
The chariots of Israel and its horsemen!"
15 Elisha said to him, "Take a bow and
arrows"; so he took a bow and arrows.
16 Then he said to the king of Israel, "Draw
the bow"; and he drew it. Elisha laid his
hands on the king's hands. 17 Then he said,
"Open the window eastward"; and he
opened it. Elisha said, "Shoot"; and he
shot. Then he said, "The LORD's arrow of
victory, the arrow of victory over Aram!
For you shall fight the Arameans in Aphek
until you have made an end of them." 18 He
continued, "Take the arrows"; and he took
them. He said to the king of Israel, "Strike
the ground with them"; he struck three
times, and stopped. 19 Then the man of God
was angry with him, and said, "You should
have struck five or six times; then you
would have struck down Aram until you
had made an end of it, but now you will
strike down Aram only three times."
20 So Elisha died, and they buried him.
Now bands of Moabites used to invade the
land in the spring of the year. 21 As a man
was being buried, a marauding band was
seen and the man was thrown into the
grave of Elisha; as soon as the man touched
the bones of Elisha, he came to life and
stood on his feet.
22 Now King Hazael of Aram oppressed
Israel all the days of Jehoahaz. 23 But the
LORD was gracious to them and had com-
passion on them; he turned toward them,
because of his covenant with Abraham,
Isaac, and Jacob, and would not destroy
them; nor has he banished them from his
presence until now.
24 When King Hazael of Aram died, his
son Ben-hadad succeeded him. 25 Then Je-
hoash son of Jehoahaz took again from
Ben-hadad son of Hazael the towns that he
had taken from his father Jehoahaz in war.
Three times Joash defeated him and recov-
ered the towns of Israel.

14 In the second year of King Joash son
of Joahaz of Israel, King Amaziah
son of Joash of Judah, began to reign. 2 He
was twenty-five years old when he began to
reign, and he reigned twenty-nine years in
Jerusalem. His mother's name was Jehoad-
din of Jerusalem. 3 He did what was right in
the sight of the LORD, yet not like his ances-
tor David; in all things he did as his father
Joash had done. 4 But the high places were
not removed; the people still sacrificed and
made offerings on the high places. 5 As soon
as the royal power was firmly in his hand
he killed his servants who had murdered his
father the king. 6 But he did not put to
death the children of the murderers; ac-
cording to what is written in the book of
the law of Moses, where the LORD com-
manded, "The parents shall not be put to
death for the children, or the children be
put to death for the parents; but all shall be
put to death for their own sins."
7 He killed ten thousand Edomites in the
Valley of Salt and took Sela by storm; he

to offer Jehoash words of some comfort (vv. 15–19), although they are not unqualified, since the king's response to the prophetic commands is not unreserved. **17:** *Aphek,* see 1 Kings 20.26n. **20–25:** The two episodes may be more related than at first appears. The second (vv. 22–25) provides a deeper reason for Israel's survival during Jehoahaz's reign than the one given in 10.30. Long before he made promises to Jehu about kingship, God was dealing with Israel's ancestors (Gen 15.1–21; 17.1–27), committing himself to Israel as a people and promising them a land. This *covenant* is now mentioned as the reason for God's help in the face of foreign oppression. The evidence that Elisha's powers of resurrection survive his death (vv. 20–21; cf. 4.8–37) provides hope that the "death" of Israel in exile (note *until now,* v. 23) may yet be followed by unexpected resurrection (cf. Ezek 37.1–14).

14.1–15.7: Amaziah, Jeroboam, and Azariah. Ch 13 ended with the description of a modest upturn in Israel's fortunes. The impetus of that recovery continues into ch 14, as the house of Jehu brings Israel relief, not only from Aram but also from a foolishly hostile Judah.

14.1–22: The reign of Amaziah (798–769 BCE). **6:** See Deut 24.16. **7–14:** Amaziah's military exploits included a successful campaign against the *Edomites* in northern Edom (v. 7; cf. the *Valley of Salt* in

called it Jokthe-el, which is its name to this
day.
8 Then Amaziah sent messengers to
King Jehoash son of Jehoahaz, son of Jehu,
of Israel, saying, "Come, let us look one
another in the face." 9 King Jehoash of Isra-
el sent word to King Amaziah of Judah, "A
thornbush on Lebanon sent to a cedar on
Lebanon, saying, 'Give your daughter to
my son for a wife'; but a wild animal of
Lebanon passed by and trampled down the
thornbush. 10 You have indeed defeated
Edom, and your heart has lifted you up. Be
content with your glory, and stay at home;
for why should you provoke trouble so that
you fall, you and Judah with you?"
11 But Amaziah would not listen. So
King Jehoash of Israel went up; he and
King Amaziah of Judah faced one another
in battle at Beth-shemesh, which belongs to
Judah. 12 Judah was defeated by Israel; ev-
eryone fled home. 13 King Jehoash of Israel
captured King Amaziah of Judah son of Je-
hoash, son of Ahaziah, at Beth-shemesh; he
came to Jerusalem, and broke down the
wall of Jerusalem from the Ephraim Gate
to the Corner Gate, a distance of four hun-
dred cubits. 14 He seized all the gold and
silver, and all the vessels that were found in
the house of the LORD and in the treasuries
of the king's house, as well as hostages;
then he returned to Samaria.
15 Now the rest of the acts that Jehoash
did, his might, and how he fought with
King Amaziah of Judah, are they not writ-
ten in the Book of the Annals of the Kings
of Israel? 16 Jehoash slept with his ances-
tors, and was buried in Samaria with the
kings of Israel; then his son Jeroboam suc-
ceeded him.
17 King Amaziah son of Joash of Judah
lived fifteen years after the death of King
Jehoash son of Jehoahaz of Israel. 18 Now
the rest of the deeds of Amaziah, are they
not written in the Book of the Annals of the
Kings of Judah? 19 They made a conspiracy
against him in Jerusalem, and he fled to
Lachish. But they sent after him to Lachish,
and killed him there. 20 They brought him
on horses; he was buried in Jerusalem with
his ancestors in the city of David. 21 All the
people of Judah took Azariah, who was
sixteen years old, and made him king to
succeed his father Amaziah. 22 He rebuilt
Elath and restored it to Judah, after King
Amaziah[a] slept with his ancestors.
23 In the fifteenth year of King Amaziah
son of Joash of Judah, King Jeroboam son
of Joash of Israel began to reign in Samaria;
he reigned forty-one years. 24 He did what
was evil in the sight of the LORD; he did not
depart from all the sins of Jeroboam son of
Nebat, which he caused Israel to sin. 25 He
restored the border of Israel from Lebo-

a Heb *the king*

2 Sam 8.13—probably the depression south of the Dead Sea) and a disastrous one against Israel (vv. 8–14). **9:** A puny *thornbush* (i.e., Amaziah), easily trampled upon by any *wild animal,* should not think more highly of itself than it ought in relation to the mighty and immovable *cedar* of *Lebanon* (Jehoash). **13:** *Four hundred cubits,* ca. 182 m (200 yd). The *Ephraim Gate* was in the north wall, and the *Corner Gate* was probably near the northwest angle of the wall (cf. Jer 31.38; Neh 8.16). **15–20:** The concluding regnal formulae for *Jehoash* are perhaps repeated (vv. 15–16; cf. 13.12–13) just before the information about Amaziah's demise because of the contrast that exists between the two kings in death as in life: The innocent party dies in peace, while the aggressor is murdered at Lachish, an important Judean city ca. 45 km (28 mi) southwest of Jerusalem. **21–22:** *Azariah* (see 15.1–7n.) was later able to consolidate Amaziah's gains in Edom by claiming the port of *Elath* (see 1 Kings 9.26).

14.23–29: The reign of Jeroboam. The Israelite recovery continues with *Jeroboam* II (788–747 BCE), who is able to restore the border of Israel from *Lebo-hamath* (see 1 Kings 8.65n.) to the *Sea of the Arabah* (the Dead Sea; see Josh 3.16; 12.3), incorporating Aram into his kingdom (cf. *Damascus and Hamath* in v. 28) as well as recovering all the territory in Transjordan captured by Hazael in 10.32–33. The ideal borders of northern Israel as they had existed under Solomon are thus reestablished (see 1 Kings 8.65). Much is known about Jeroboam from other sources, both biblical and nonbiblical. The prophets Amos (1.1; 7.9–11) and Hosea (1.1) were active during his reign, although neither is mentioned in 2 Kings. The

hamath as far as the Sea of the Arabah,
according to the word of the LORD, the
God of Israel, which he spoke by his ser-
vant Jonah son of Amittai, the prophet,
who was from Gath-hepher. 26 For the
LORD saw that the distress of Israel was
very bitter; there was no one left, bond or
free, and no one to help Israel. 27 But the
LORD had not said that he would blot out
the name of Israel from under heaven, so he
saved them by the hand of Jeroboam son of
Joash.
28 Now the rest of the acts of Jeroboam,
and all that he did, and his might, how he
fought, and how he recovered for Israel Da-
mascus and Hamath, which had belonged
to Judah, are they not written in the Book
of the Annals of the Kings of Israel? 29 Jero-
boam slept with his ancestors, the kings of
Israel; his son Zechariah succeeded him.
15 In the twenty-seventh year of King
Jeroboam of Israel King Azariah
son of Amaziah of Judah began to reign.
2 He was sixteen years old when he began
to reign, and he reigned fifty-two years in
Jerusalem. His mother's name was Jecoliah
of Jerusalem. 3 He did what was right in the
sight of the LORD, just as his father Amazi-
ah had done. 4 Nevertheless the high places
were not taken away; the people still sacri-
ficed and made offerings on the high places.
5 The LORD struck the king, so that he was
leprous[a] to the day of his death, and lived
in a separate house. Jotham the king's son
was in charge of the palace, governing the
people of the land. 6 Now the rest of the
acts of Azariah, and all that he did, are they
not written in the Book of the Annals of the
Kings of Judah? 7 Azariah slept with his an-
cestors; they buried him with his ancestors
in the city of David; his son Jotham suc-
ceeded him.
8 In the thirty-eighth year of King Azari-
ah of Judah, Zechariah son of Jeroboam
reigned over Israel in Samaria six months.
9 He did what was evil in the sight of the
LORD, as his ancestors had done. He did
not depart from the sins of Jeroboam son
of Nebat, which he caused Israel to sin.
10 Shallum son of Jabesh conspired against
him, and struck him down in public and
killed him, and reigned in place of him.
11 Now the rest of the deeds of Zechariah
are written in the Book of the Annals of the
Kings of Israel. 12 This was the promise of
the LORD that he gave to Jehu, "Your sons
shall sit on the throne of Israel to the fourth
generation." And so it happened.
13 Shallum son of Jabesh began to reign
in the thirty-ninth year of King Uzziah of
Judah; he reigned one month in Samaria.
14 Then Menahem son of Gadi came up
from Tirzah and came to Samaria; he
struck down Shallum son of Jabesh in Sa-
maria and killed him; he reigned in place of
him. 15 Now the rest of the deeds of Shal-
lum, including the conspiracy that he made,
are written in the Book of the Annals of the
Kings of Israel. 16 At that time Menahem

a A term for several skin diseases; precise meaning uncertain

authors' treatment of Jeroboam is cursory because their interests lie elsewhere. **25:** *Jonah son of Amittai,* the hero of the book of Jonah (see Jon 1.1 and Introduction to the book of Jonah).

15.1–7: The reign of Azariah. *Azariah* (also called Uzziah; cf. 15.13,30,32,34; 785–733 BCE) was a faithful king, but he was at some point afflicted with leprosy and found himself unable to govern. The authors of Kings do not explain why he was so afflicted, (cf. 12.19–21n.) while the Chronicler offers a reason (2 Chr 26.16–21). **5:** The *separate house* is lit. "house of freedom," either a euphemism or a metaphor for being relieved of responsibility in government. *The people of the land,* see 11.14n.

15.8–31: Israel's last days. With the death of Jeroboam II, we reach the "fourth generation" of the divine promise to Jehu (10.30) and return to the unstable government of the Northern Kingdom implied by 1 Kings 14.15. **8–12:** *Zechariah* (747 BCE) repeats the evil of his fathers and is assassinated by *Shallum.* **13–16:** *Shallum* (747 BCE) holds on to power for a mere *month* before losing both crown and life to *Menahem* (747–737), whose power base is apparently in the old Israelite capital of *Tirzah* (1 Kings 15.33; 16.8,15,23). In what will be the last action of an Israelite king claiming control of a Solomon-like empire, Menahem attacks *Tiphsah* on the Euphrates River (cf. 1 Kings 4.24). **17–22:** In a flash the

sacked Tiphsah, all who were in it and its
territory from Tirzah on; because they did
not open it to him, he sacked it. He ripped
open all the pregnant women in it.
17 In the thirty-ninth year of King Aza-
riah of Judah, Menahem son of Gadi began
to reign over Israel; he reigned ten years in
Samaria. 18 He did what was evil in the
sight of the LORD; he did not depart all his
days from any of the sins of Jeroboam son
of Nebat, which he caused Israel to sin.
19 King Pul of Assyria came against the
land; Menahem gave Pul a thousand talents
of silver, so that he might help him confirm
his hold on the royal power. 20 Menahem
exacted the money from Israel, that is, from
all the wealthy, fifty shekels of silver from
each one, to give to the king of Assyria. So
the king of Assyria turned back, and did
not stay there in the land. 21 Now the rest of
the deeds of Menahem, and all that he did,
are they not written in the Book of the An-
nals of the Kings of Israel? 22 Menahem
slept with his ancestors, and his son Pekahi-
ah succeeded him.
23 In the fiftieth year of King Azariah of
Judah, Pekahiah son of Menahem began to
reign over Israel in Samaria; he reigned two
years. 24 He did what was evil in the sight of
the LORD; he did not turn away from the
sins of Jeroboam son of Nebat, which he
caused Israel to sin. 25 Pekah son of Remali-
ah, his captain, conspired against him with
fifty of the Gileadites, and attacked him in
Samaria, in the citadel of the palace along
with Argob and Arieh; he killed him, and
reigned in place of him. 26 Now the rest of
the deeds of Pekahiah, and all that he did,
are written in the Book of the Annals of the
Kings of Israel.
27 In the fifty-second year of King Aza-
riah of Judah, Pekah son of Remaliah be-
gan to reign over Israel in Samaria; he
reigned twenty years. 28 He did what was
evil in the sight of the LORD; he did not
depart from the sins of Jeroboam son of
Nebat, which he caused Israel to sin.
29 In the days of King Pekah of Israel,
King Tiglath-pileser of Assyria came and
captured Ijon, Abel-beth-maacah, Janoah,
Kedesh, Hazor, Gilead, and Galilee, all the
land of Naphtali; and he carried the people
captive to Assyria. 30 Then Hoshea son of
Elah made a conspiracy against Pekah son
of Remaliah, attacked him, and killed him;
he reigned in place of him, in the twentieth
year of Jotham son of Uzziah. 31 Now the
rest of the acts of Pekah, and all that he did,
are written in the Book of the Annals of the
Kings of Israel.
32 In the second year of King Pekah son
of Remaliah of Israel, King Jotham son of
Uzziah of Judah began to reign. 33 He was
twenty-five years old when he began to
reign and reigned sixteen years in Jerusa-
lem. His mother's name was Jerusha
daughter of Zadok. 34 He did what was
right in the sight of the LORD, just as his
father Uzziah had done. 35 Nevertheless the
high places were not removed; the people

recently reconstituted empire of Jeroboam disappears, as *King Pul of Assyria* (Tiglath-pileser III, cf. v. 29) invades the land. Menahem pays to turn an enemy into a friend, as Asa had once bought Ben-hadad's support against his enemy Baasha (1 Kings 15.16–19). **19:** *A thousand talents,* about 34,000 kg (75,000 lb). **20:** *Fifty shekels,* about 570 gr (1.25 lb). **23–26:** *Pekahiah* (737–735 BCE), too, is the victim of conspiracy, as *Pekah* launches an attack on the royal palace. *Argob and Arieh* ("the lion," a nickname perhaps) were perhaps the king's sons. **27–31:** The figure of *twenty years* for the reign of *Pekah* is inconsistent with other dates in the Hebrew Bible and with evidence in Assyrian records, and cannot refer to the period of his sole reign; he probably ruled for a much shorter time, ca. 735–732. *Pekah* lives to see *Tiglath-pileser* (ruled 745–727) replace the Arameans as Israel's great foe. In his campaigns of 734–732 he annexed much of Israel's northern and eastern territory, and he deported to Assyria a significant percentage of the population. He also captured and destroyed Damascus, extending Assyrian control over the coast as far south as Gaza (see Map on p. 558 HB).

15.32–16.20: Jotham and Ahaz of Judah. *Jotham* had already been exercising power in Judah because of his father's illness (15.5); he ruled ca. 759–743 BCE. **15.35:** The *upper gate* of the Temple was presumably

still sacrificed and made offerings on the
high places. He built the upper gate of the
house of the LORD. 36 Now the rest of the
acts of Jotham, and all that he did, are they
not written in the Book of the Annals of the
Kings of Judah? 37 In those days the LORD
began to send King Rezin of Aram and Pe-
kah son of Remaliah against Judah. 38 Jo-
tham slept with his ancestors, and was bur-
ied with his ancestors in the city of David,
his ancestor; his son Ahaz succeeded him.

16 In the seventeenth year of Pekah son
of Remaliah, King Ahaz son of Jo-
tham of Judah began to reign. 2 Ahaz was

damaged in the course of Jehoash's incursion into Jerusalem in 14.13–14. **37:** This is the beginning of the so-called Syro-Ephraimite war, which features so prominently in Isa 7–9; see 16.5–9n. **16.1–4:** With Jotham's son *Ahaz* (743/735–727/715 BCE; the data are unclear) we return to a period of officially sanctioned idolatry in Judah. The language is largely that of 1 Kings 14.23–24, in which Judah's adherence to the fertility cult was first described (compare v. 3b with 14.24b; and v. 4b with 14.23b). A new element here is the sacrifice of the son in the *fire* (v. 3a), which is an allusion to participation in the

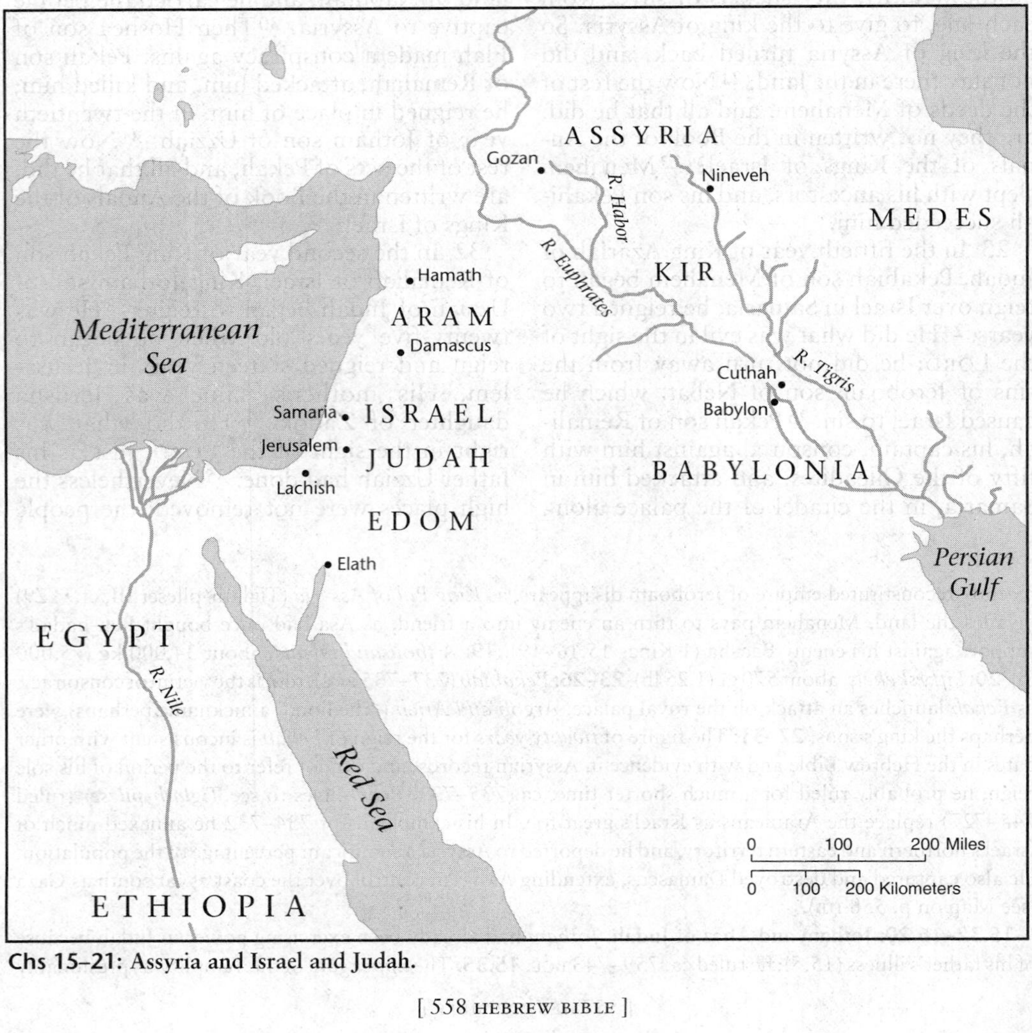

Chs 15–21: Assyria and Israel and Judah.

twenty years old when he began to reign; he
reigned sixteen years in Jerusalem. He did
not do what was right in the sight of the
LORD his God, as his ancestor David had
done, 3 but he walked in the way of the
kings of Israel. He even made his son pass
through fire, according to the abominable
practices of the nations whom the LORD
drove out before the people of Israel. 4 He
sacrificed and made offerings on the high
places, on the hills, and under every green
tree.

5 Then King Rezin of Aram and King
Pekah son of Remaliah of Israel came up to
wage war on Jerusalem; they besieged Ahaz
but could not conquer him. 6 At that time
the king of Edom[a] recovered Elath for
Edom,[b] and drove the Judeans from Elath;
and the Edomites came to Elath, where
they live to this day. 7 Ahaz sent messengers
to King Tiglath-pileser of Assyria, saying,
"I am your servant and your son. Come up,
and rescue me from the hand of the king of
Aram and from the hand of the king of
Israel, who are attacking me." 8 Ahaz also
took the silver and gold found in the house
of the LORD and in the treasures of the
king's house, and sent a present to the king
of Assyria. 9 The king of Assyria listened
to him; the king of Assyria marched up
against Damascus, and took it, carrying its
people captive to Kir; then he killed Rezin.

10 When King Ahaz went to Damascus
to meet King Tiglath-pileser of Assyria, he
saw the altar that was at Damascus. King
Ahaz sent to the priest Uriah a model of the
altar, and its pattern, exact in all its details.
11 The priest Uriah built the altar; in accor-
dance with all that King Ahaz had sent
from Damascus, just so did the priest Uriah
build it, before King Ahaz arrived from Da-
mascus. 12 When the king came from Da-
mascus, the king viewed the altar. Then the
king drew near to the altar, went up on it,
13 and offered his burnt offering and his
grain offering, poured his drink offering,
and dashed the blood of his offerings of
well-being against the altar. 14 The bronze
altar that was before the LORD he removed
from the front of the house, from the place
between his altar and the house of the
LORD, and put it on the north side of his
altar. 15 King Ahaz commanded the priest
Uriah, saying, "Upon the great altar offer
the morning burnt offering, and the eve-
ning grain offering, and the king's burnt
offering, and his grain offering, with the
burnt offering of all the people of the land,
their grain offering, and their drink offer-
ing; then dash against it all the blood of the
burnt offering, and all the blood of the sac-
rifice; but the bronze altar shall be for me
to inquire by." 16 The priest Uriah did ev-
erything that King Ahaz commanded.

17 Then King Ahaz cut off the frames
of the stands, and removed the laver from
them; he removed the sea from the bronze
oxen that were under it, and put it on a
pediment of stone. 18 The covered portal for
use on the sabbath that had been built in-
side the palace, and the outer entrance for
the king he removed from[c] the house of
the LORD. He did this because of the king
of Assyria. 19 Now the rest of the acts of
Ahaz that he did, are they not written in the
Book of the Annals of the Kings of Judah?
20 Ahaz slept with his ancestors, and was

a Cn: Heb *King Rezin of Aram* *b* Cn: Heb *Aram*
c Cn: Heb lacks *from*

worship of Molech mentioned in 1 Kings 11.7 (see Ezek 16.20–21; 20.26–31; Lev 18.21; Jer 32.35). **5–9:** The reason for the attack was apparently to force Judah to join a coalition to block the Assyrian advance. The Syro-Ephraimite alliance besieges Ahaz in Jerusalem and *Rezin* (NRSV footnote) deprives him of *Elath* (only recently won back for Judah by Azariah, 14.22). In response Ahaz becomes a vassal of the king of *Assyria* and requests his help. The Arameans are deported to *Kir,* the original Aramean homeland, according to Am 9.7 (cf. Am 1.5). **10–20:** The intervention of Assyria into Judean affairs is fateful in its consequences not simply in terms of politics, but also in terms of religion. A new *altar* for the Temple displaces the old (see 1 Kings 8.64), now to be used only for inquiry (v. 15)—perhaps for sacrifice in relation to divination (the reading of entrails). **17–18:** Other innovations follow (cf. 1 Kings 7.23–36), the motivation for which is unclear; *because of the king of Assyria* is vague and its interpretation is disputed.

buried with his ancestors in the city of Da-
vid; his son Hezekiah succeeded him.
17 In the twelfth year of King Ahaz of
Judah, Hoshea son of Elah began to
reign in Samaria over Israel; he reigned nine
years. 2 He did what was evil in the sight of
the LORD, yet not like the kings of Israel
who were before him. 3 King Shalmaneser
of Assyria came up against him; Hoshea
became his vassal, and paid him tribute.
4 But the king of Assyria found treachery in
Hoshea; for he had sent messengers to King
So of Egypt, and offered no tribute to the
king of Assyria, as he had done year by
year; therefore the king of Assyria confined
him and imprisoned him.
5 Then the king of Assyria invaded all
the land and came to Samaria; for three
years he besieged it. 6 In the ninth year of
Hoshea the king of Assyria captured Sa-
maria; he carried the Israelites away to As-
syria. He placed them in Halah, on the Ha-
bor, the river of Gozan, and in the cities of
the Medes.
7 This occurred because the people of
Israel had sinned against the LORD their
God, who had brought them up out of the
land of Egypt from under the hand of Phar-
aoh king of Egypt. They had worshiped
other gods 8 and walked in the customs of
the nations whom the LORD drove out be-
fore the people of Israel, and in the customs
that the kings of Israel had introduced.[a]
9 The people of Israel secretly did things
that were not right against the LORD their
God. They built for themselves high places
at all their towns, from watchtower to for-
tified city; 10 they set up for themselves pil-
lars and sacred poles[b] on every high hill
and under every green tree; 11 there they
made offerings on all the high places, as the
nations did whom the LORD carried away
before them. They did wicked things, pro-
voking the LORD to anger; 12 they served
idols, of which the LORD had said to them,
"You shall not do this." 13 Yet the LORD
warned Israel and Judah by every prophet
and every seer, saying, "Turn from your
evil ways and keep my commandments and
my statutes, in accordance with all the law
that I commanded your ancestors and that
I sent to you by my servants the prophets."
14 They would not listen but were stubborn,
as their ancestors had been, who did not
believe in the LORD their God. 15 They de-
spised his statutes, and his covenant that he
made with their ancestors, and the warn-
ings that he gave them. They went after
false idols and became false; they followed
the nations that were around them, con-
cerning whom the LORD had commanded
them that they should not do as they did.
16 They rejected all the commandments of
the LORD their God and made for them-
selves cast images of two calves; they made
a sacred pole,[c] worshiped all the host of
heaven, and served Baal. 17 They made their
sons and their daughters pass through fire;
they used divination and augury; and they

a Meaning of Heb uncertain *b* Heb *Asherim*
c Heb *Asherah*

17.1–41: The end of Israel. The political maneuvering of *Hoshea* (732–722 BCE) between *Assyria* and *Egypt* (see Hos 7.11) brought down the full wrath of the Assyrian *Shalmaneser* V (ruled 727–722 BCE). Hoshea was imprisoned; Samaria was captured; and in 722 the *Israelites* were carried off to Assyria and dispersed in various places throughout the empire. **4:** *King So,* no Egyptian ruler with this name is known, and it may be a scribal error or an otherwise unknown epithet for someone better known by another name. **6:** See Map on p. 558 HB. **7–18:** Of the possible explanations for the end of the Northern Kingdom, the authors of Kings give only one, which for them is fundamental: Israel had sinned against *the LORD their God,* worshiping other gods. The passage is an extended exposition of Deuteronomistic theology. **9:** *From watchtower to fortified city,* i.e., across the whole land. **10:** See 1 Kings 14.15n. **14:** They sinned with the stubbornness and pride of those who had first come out of Egypt (cf. Deut 9–10, esp. 9.6,13; 10.16). **16:** *Two calves,* see 1 Kings 12.28–30. **16–17:** Neither worship of the *host of heaven* (the planets and stars) nor the sin of *augury* have been introduced to us so far in the narrative. The passage already embraces the later sins of Judah (cf. 21.3–6). *Pass through fire,* see 16.3n. **19–20:** The way

sold themselves to do evil in the sight of the
LORD, provoking him to anger. 18 There-
fore the LORD was very angry with Israel
and removed them out of his sight; none
was left but the tribe of Judah alone.
19 Judah also did not keep the com-
mandments of the LORD their God but
walked in the customs that Israel had intro-
duced. 20 The LORD rejected all the descen-
dants of Israel; he punished them and gave
them into the hand of plunderers, until he
had banished them from his presence.
21 When he had torn Israel from the
house of David, they made Jeroboam son
of Nebat king. Jeroboam drove Israel from
following the LORD and made them com-
mit great sin. 22 The people of Israel contin-
ued in all the sins that Jeroboam commit-
ted; they did not depart from them 23 until
the LORD removed Israel out of his sight, as
he had foretold through all his servants the
prophets. So Israel was exiled from their
own land to Assyria until this day.
24 The king of Assyria brought people
from Babylon, Cuthah, Avva, Hamath, and
Sepharvaim, and placed them in the cities
of Samaria in place of the people of Israel;
they took possession of Samaria, and set-
tled in its cities. 25 When they first settled
there, they did not worship the LORD;
therefore the LORD sent lions among them,
which killed some of them. 26 So the king of
Assyria was told, "The nations that you
have carried away and placed in the cities
of Samaria do not know the law of the god
of the land; therefore he has sent lions
among them; they are killing them, because
they do not know the law of the god of the
land." 27 Then the king of Assyria com-
manded, "Send there one of the priests
whom you carried away from there; let
him[a] go and live there, and teach them the
law of the god of the land." 28 So one of the
priests whom they had carried away from
Samaria came and lived in Bethel; he taught
them how they should worship the LORD.
29 But every nation still made gods of its
own and put them in the shrines of the high
places that the people of Samaria had
made, every nation in the cities in which
they lived; 30 the people of Babylon made
Succoth-benoth, the people of Cuth made
Nergal, the people of Hamath made Ashi-
ma; 31 the Avvites made Nibhaz and Tar-
tak; the Sepharvites burned their children
in the fire to Adrammelech and Anamme-
lech, the gods of Sepharvaim. 32 They also
worshiped the LORD and appointed from
among themselves all sorts of people as
priests of the high places, who sacrificed for
them in the shrines of the high places. 33 So
they worshiped the LORD but also served
their own gods, after the manner of the na-
tions from among whom they had been car-
ried away. 34 To this day they continue to
practice their former customs.

They do not worship the LORD and they
do not follow the statutes or the ordinances
or the law or the commandment that the
LORD commanded the children of Jacob,

a Syr Vg: Heb *them*

Judah followed Israel's example is highlighted, raising the specter of future doom for Judah as well. *Plunderers,* see Judg 2.14. **21–23:** A summary of the history of the Northern Kingdom of Israel from the Deuteronomistic perspective. **24–41:** The land of Israel is not left empty. The first part of the passage (vv. 25–33) seems at first sight to suggest that the new peoples (see Map on p. 558 HB) truly worship the LORD alongside other gods—a claim at variance with the authors' presentation of the story of Kings thus far. It is most unlikely that the authors of Kings are only now telling us that a broad pantheon of gods is acceptable. They are, rather, setting up a particular point of view in order to demolish it, as they go on to do in vv. 34–41. The "worship" of these people is not truly worship at all. The exile of Israel for her sins has evidently not led to any improvement in the religion of the people dwelling in the land. It is still syncretistic. **24:** *The king of Assyria,* according to Assyrian records, would probably have been Sargon II (722–705 BCE). The former Northern Kingdom of Israel is called *Samaria,* its designation in the Assyrian provincial system and later (see also 1 Kings 21.1; 2 Kings 1.3), and in v. 29 its inhabitants are called "the people of Samaria," lit. "the Samarians." (Identification of these polytheistic inhabitants of Samaria as the ancestors of the Samaritans of the postexilic periods is a later polemic). **30–31:** *Nergal* was a Mesopotamian god

whom he named Israel. 35The LORD had
made a covenant with them and command-
ed them, "You shall not worship other
gods or bow yourselves to them or serve
them or sacrifice to them, 36but you shall
worship the LORD, who brought you out of
the land of Egypt with great power and
with an outstretched arm; you shall bow
yourselves to him, and to him you shall sac-
rifice. 37The statutes and the ordinances
and the law and the commandment that he
wrote for you, you shall always be careful
to observe. You shall not worship other
gods; 38you shall not forget the covenant
that I have made with you. You shall not
worship other gods, 39but you shall wor-
ship the LORD your God; he will deliver
you out of the hand of all your enemies."
40They would not listen, however, but they
continued to practice their former custom.
41 So these nations worshiped the
LORD, but also served their carved images;
to this day their children and their chil-
dren's children continue to do as their an-
cestors did.

18 In the third year of King Hoshea son
of Elah of Israel, Hezekiah son of
King Ahaz of Judah began to reign. 2He
was twenty-five years old when he began to
reign; he reigned twenty-nine years in Jeru-
salem. His mother's name was Abi daugh-
ter of Zechariah. 3He did what was right in
the sight of the LORD just as his ancestor
David had done. 4He removed the high
places, broke down the pillars, and cut
down the sacred pole.[a] He broke in pieces
the bronze serpent that Moses had made,
for until those days the people of Israel had
made offerings to it; it was called Nehush-
tan. 5He trusted in the LORD the God of
Israel; so that there was no one like him
among all the kings of Judah after him, or
among those who were before him. 6For he
held fast to the LORD; he did not depart
from following him but kept the command-
ments that the LORD commanded Moses.
7The LORD was with him; wherever he
went, he prospered. He rebelled against the
king of Assyria and would not serve him.
8He attacked the Philistines as far as Gaza
and its territory, from watchtower to forti-
fied city.
9 In the fourth year of King Hezekiah,
which was the seventh year of King Hoshea
son of Elah of Israel, King Shalmaneser of
Assyria came up against Samaria, besieged
it, 10and at the end of three years, took it.
In the sixth year of Hezekiah, which was
the ninth year of King Hoshea of Israel,
Samaria was taken. 11The king of Assyria
carried the Israelites away to Assyria, set-
tled them in Halah, on the Habor, the river
of Gozan, and in the cities of the Medes,
12because they did not obey the voice of the
LORD their God but transgressed his cove-
nant—all that Moses the servant of the
LORD had commanded; they neither lis-
tened nor obeyed.
13 In the fourteenth year of King Heze-
kiah, King Sennacherib of Assyria came up

a Heb *Asherah*

of the underworld. None of the other deities can be identified with certainty. **35–39:** A collage of Deuteronomic ideas rather than direct quotations.

18.1–12: Hezekiah (727/715–698/687 BCE; the data are unclear). *Hezekiah* is one of the kings for whom the authors have unqualified praise—a second David, who did what is *right in the sight of the LORD* and reformed Judean worship. He at last removed the *high places* (v. 4; cf. 1 Kings 15.14; 22.43; 2 Kings 12.3; 14.4; 15.4,35), taking action even against ancient relics like Moses' *bronze serpent* (Num 21.4–9) that had become focal points for idolatry. **5–6:** Hezekiah was incomparable not least in his trust in the LORD, which evidenced itself in the way that he *held fast* to God throughout his life, keeping the law of *Moses* (in contrast to Solomon, who in his old age "held fast" to foreign wives, 1 Kings 11.2, and broke this law). **7:** Similar as he was to David, he was utterly dissimilar to Ahaz, for he would not continue to *serve* the king of Assyria. **9–12:** The reiteration of 17.1–6 reminds us of the context in which Hezekiah pursued this bold policy.

18.13–19.37: The Assyrian assault on Judah (see Map on p. 564 HB). Many commentators have suspected that this section is a combination of two originally separate versions of the Assyrian siege of Jerusalem,

against all the fortified cities of Judah and
captured them. 14 King Hezekiah of Judah
sent to the king of Assyria at Lachish, say-
ing, "I have done wrong; withdraw from
me; whatever you impose on me I will
bear." The king of Assyria demanded of
King Hezekiah of Judah three hundred tal-
ents of silver and thirty talents of gold.
15 Hezekiah gave him all the silver that was
found in the house of the LORD and in the
treasuries of the king's house. 16 At that
time Hezekiah stripped the gold from the
doors of the temple of the LORD, and from
the doorposts that King Hezekiah of Judah
had overlaid and gave it to the king of As-
syria. 17 The king of Assyria sent the Tar-
tan, the Rabsaris, and the Rabshakeh with
a great army from Lachish to King Hezeki-
ah at Jerusalem. They went up and came to
Jerusalem. When they arrived, they came
and stood by the conduit of the upper pool,
which is on the highway to the Fuller's
Field. 18 When they called for the king,
there came out to them Eliakim son of Hil-
kiah, who was in charge of the palace, and
Shebnah the secretary, and Joah son of
Asaph, the recorder.

19 The Rabshakeh said to them, "Say to
Hezekiah: Thus says the great king, the
king of Assyria: On what do you base this
confidence of yours? 20 Do you think that
mere words are strategy and power for
war? On whom do you now rely, that you
have rebelled against me? 21 See, you are
relying now on Egypt, that broken reed of
a staff, which will pierce the hand of any-
one who leans on it. Such is Pharaoh king
of Egypt to all who rely on him. 22 But if
you say to me, 'We rely on the LORD our
God,' is it not he whose high places and
altars Hezekiah has removed, saying to Ju-
dah and to Jerusalem, 'You shall worship
before this altar in Jerusalem'? 23 Come
now, make a wager with my master the
king of Assyria: I will give you two thou-
sand horses, if you are able on your part to
set riders on them. 24 How then can you
repulse a single captain among the least of
my master's servants, when you rely on
Egypt for chariots and for horsemen?
25 Moreover, is it without the LORD that I
have come up against this place to destroy
it? The LORD said to me, Go up against this
land, and destroy it."

26 Then Eliakim son of Hilkiah, and
Shebnah, and Joah said to the Rabshakeh,
"Please speak to your servants in the Ara-
maic language, for we understand it; do not
speak to us in the language of Judah within
the hearing of the people who are on the

now forming a unified narrative. **18.13–16:** In 701 the Assyrian king Sennacherib (705–681 BCE) invaded Judah. 18.13–20.19 is repeated in Isa 36.39 with some additions and deletions; see Isa 36–39n. Hezekiah's first response to the crisis is to raid *the house of the LORD* (cf. 1 Kings 14.25; 15.18; 2 Kings 12.18; 16.8). This apparently regrettable lapse in trust is a disappointing prologue to what will turn out to be Hezekiah's finest hour. Sennacherib's own account of the invasion reports that forty-six of the *fortified cities* of Judah and countless small villages were taken, while Hezekiah was shut up in Jerusalem "like a bird in a cage." **14:** Lachish (see 14.15–20n.), which had been captured, was the location of the Assyrian headquarters. A *talent* weighed about 34 kg (75 lb). **17:** *The king of Assyria* attempts to punish Judah, as he had punished Israel, for lack of payment of tribute, and decides (for reasons undisclosed in the narrative) that payment is not enough. While Jerusalem's gates remain closed to him, he continues to regard Hezekiah as a rebel. *The Tartan, the Rabsaris, and the Rabshakeh* were high Assyrian officials. *The upper pool,* see Isa 7.3n. **19–25:** The issue at the heart of the speech is "trust" (cf. 18.5, the verbal idea being repeated in vv. 19–22,24), whether in Pharaoh or the LORD. Hezekiah had attempted to form an alliance with Egypt (v. 21; see Isa 30.1–7n.; 31.1–3), but Pharaoh is weak, unable to offer any genuine support (v. 21). Since it is the LORD's *high places and altars* that have been removed (v. 22), he is also unlikely to help. The *Rabshakeh* knows of Hezekiah's reform (v. 22) and claims that the LORD is on the Assyrian side (v. 25; cf. Isa 10.5–11). **26–27:** Hezekiah's officials are anxious that the *people who are on the wall* should not hear these powerful arguments, and they ask the Assyrian to speak in *Aramaic,* the language of international diplomacy, rather than in Hebrew, called here *the language of Judah*

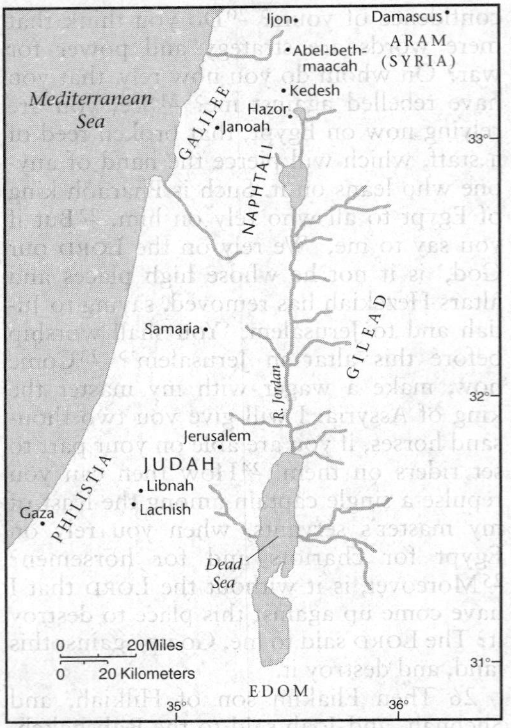

Chs 18–20: Sennacherib's invasion of Judah.

wall." 27 But the Rabshakeh said to them,
"Has my master sent me to speak these
words to your master and to you, and not
to the people sitting on the wall, who are
doomed with you to eat their own dung
and to drink their own urine?"
28 Then the Rabshakeh stood and called
out in a loud voice in the language of Ju-
dah, "Hear the word of the great king, the
king of Assyria! 29 Thus says the king: 'Do
not let Hezekiah deceive you, for he will
not be able to deliver you out of my hand.
30 Do not let Hezekiah make you rely on the
LORD by saying, The LORD will surely de-
liver us, and this city will not be given into
the hand of the king of Assyria.' 31 Do not
listen to Hezekiah; for thus says the king of
Assyria: 'Make your peace with me and
come out to me; then every one of you will
eat from your own vine and your own fig
tree, and drink water from your own cis-
tern, 32 until I come and take you away to a
land like your own land, a land of grain
and wine, a land of bread and vineyards, a
land of olive oil and honey, that you may
live and not die. Do not listen to Hezekiah
when he misleads you by saying, The LORD
will deliver us. 33 Has any of the gods of the
nations ever delivered its land out of the
hand of the king of Assyria? 34 Where are
the gods of Hamath and Arpad? Where are
the gods of Sepharvaim, Hena, and Ivvah?
Have they delivered Samaria out of my
hand? 35 Who among all the gods of the
countries have delivered their countries out
of my hand, that the LORD should deliver
Jerusalem out of my hand?'"
36 But the people were silent and an-
swered him not a word, for the king's com-
mand was, "Do not answer him." 37 Then
Eliakim son of Hilkiah, who was in charge
of the palace, and Shebna the secretary, and
Joah son of Asaph, the recorder, came to
Hezekiah with their clothes torn and told
him the words of the Rabshakeh.

19 When King Hezekiah heard it, he
tore his clothes, covered himself
with sackcloth, and went into the house of
the LORD. 2 And he sent Eliakim, who was
in charge of the palace, and Shebna the sec-
retary, and the senior priests, covered with
sackcloth, to the prophet Isaiah son of
Amoz. 3 They said to him, "Thus says Hez-
ekiah, This day is a day of distress, of re-
buke, and of disgrace; children have come
to the birth, and there is no strength to
bring them forth. 4 It may be that the LORD
your God heard all the words of the Rab-
shakeh, whom his master the king of Assyr-
ia has sent to mock the living God, and will

(cf. Isa 19.18). **31–32:** Surrender will mean escape from the horrors of a long siege (cf. v. 27). Although the people will be taken into exile, they will find themselves in a new "promised land" like their own (cf. Deut 8.7–9). **34:** Other cities conquered by the Assyrians are listed; see Map above. *Hena* and *Ivvah* are textually suspect (cf. Isa 36.19). **19.1–13:** Hezekiah consults the prophet *Isaiah* on this day of great humiliation and powerlessness (v. 3) and receives comfort. **2:** *Sackcloth,* see 6.30–31n. **8:** *Libnah,* see 8.22n.

rebuke the words that the LORD your God
has heard; therefore lift up your prayer for
the remnant that is left.” 5 When the ser-
vants of King Hezekiah came to Isaiah,
6 Isaiah said to them, “Say to your master,
‘Thus says the LORD: Do not be afraid be-
cause of the words that you have heard,
with which the servants of the king of As-
syria have reviled me. 7 I myself will put a
spirit in him, so that he shall hear a rumor
and return to his own land; I will cause him
to fall by the sword in his own land.’ ”
8 The Rabshakeh returned, and found
the king of Assyria fighting against Libnah;
for he had heard that the king had left La-
chish. 9 When the king[a] heard concerning
King Tirhakah of Ethiopia,[b] “See, he has
set out to fight against you,” he sent mes-
sengers again to Hezekiah, saying, 10 “Thus
shall you speak to King Hezekiah of Judah:
Do not let your God on whom you rely
deceive you by promising that Jerusalem
will not be given into the hand of the king
of Assyria. 11 See, you have heard what the
kings of Assyria have done to all lands, de-
stroying them utterly. Shall you be deliv-
ered? 12 Have the gods of the nations deliv-
ered them, the nations that my predecessors
destroyed, Gozan, Haran, Rezeph, and the
people of Eden who were in Telassar?
13 Where is the king of Hamath, the king of
Arpad, the king of the city of Sepharvaim,
the king of Hena, or the king of Ivvah?”
14 Hezekiah received the letter from the
hand of the messengers and read it; then
Hezekiah went up to the house of the LORD
and spread it before the LORD. 15 And Hez-
ekiah prayed before the LORD, and said:
“O LORD the God of Israel, who are en-
throned above the cherubim, you are God,
you alone, of all the kingdoms of the earth;
you have made heaven and earth. 16 Incline
your ear, O LORD, and hear; open your
eyes, O LORD, and see; hear the words of
Sennacherib, which he has sent to mock the
living God. 17 Truly, O LORD, the kings of
Assyria have laid waste the nations and
their lands, 18 and have hurled their gods
into the fire, though they were no gods but
the work of human hands—wood and
stone—and so they were destroyed. 19 So
now, O LORD our God, save us, I pray you,
from his hand, so that all the kingdoms of
the earth may know that you, O LORD, are
God alone.”
20 Then Isaiah son of Amoz sent to Hez-
ekiah, saying, “Thus says the LORD, the
God of Israel: I have heard your prayer
to me about King Sennacherib of Assyria.
21 This is the word that the LORD has spo-
ken concerning him:

She despises you, she scorns you—
virgin daughter Zion;
she tosses her head—behind your
back,
daughter Jerusalem.

22 “Whom have you mocked and
reviled?

a Heb *he* *b* Or *Nubia*; Heb *Cush*

9: *Tirhakah of Ethiopia* was not Pharaoh of Egypt until ca. 690 BCE, but was old enough in 701 to command the Egyptian forces. **10–13:** Sennacherib compounds his sin of blasphemy by committing it a second time. The argument is subtly different on this occasion. Now it is not Hezekiah who is deceiving the people (18.29), but Hezekiah who is deceived by the God in whom he trusts (19.10). **12–13:** More cities conquered by the Assyrians; see 18.34n. and Map on p. 564 HB. *The city* may also be read as a place name, “Lair.” **14–19:** Hezekiah prays and reaffirms that the LORD, *enthroned above the cherubim* in the Temple (see 1 Kings 6.23–28n.), is God *alone,* creator of *heaven and earth*. That all the *kingdoms of the earth* should know the difference between God and the gods, Hezekiah now asks that Jerusalem be delivered. **20–37:** A second prophecy from Isaiah brings God’s response to Hezekiah’s prayer. **21:** *Virgin daughter Zion,* see Isa 37.22n. The judgment of the all-knowing God will come upon Assyria. Sennacherib will withdraw from Jerusalem before the army encamped outside the city can take any military action against it (v. 32). Recovery in Judah will be slow, but certain: The people will be able to survive (v. 29) because of the crops that spring up from what is already in the ground; and “in the third year” it will be possible to

Against whom have you raised your
voice
and haughtily lifted your eyes?
Against the Holy One of Israel!
23 By your messengers you have mocked
the Lord,
and you have said, 'With my many
chariots
I have gone up the heights of the
mountains,
to the far recesses of Lebanon;
I felled its tallest cedars,
its choicest cypresses;
I entered its farthest retreat,
its densest forest.
24 I dug wells
and drank foreign waters,
I dried up with the sole of my foot
all the streams of Egypt.'

25 "Have you not heard
that I determined it long ago?
I planned from days of old
what now I bring to pass,
that you should make fortified cities
crash into heaps of ruins,
26 while their inhabitants, shorn of
strength,
are dismayed and confounded;
they have become like plants of the
field
and like tender grass,
like grass on the housetops,
blighted before it is grown.

27 "But I know your rising[a] and your
sitting,
your going out and coming in,
and your raging against me.
28 Because you have raged against me
and your arrogance has come to my
ears,
I will put my hook in your nose
and my bit in your mouth;
I will turn you back on the way
by which you came.

29 "And this shall be the sign for you:
This year you shall eat what grows of itself,
and in the second year what springs from
that; then in the third year sow, reap, plant
vineyards, and eat their fruit.
30 The surviving remnant of the house of Judah shall
again take root downward, and bear fruit
upward;
31 for from Jerusalem a remnant
shall go out, and from Mount Zion a band
of survivors. The zeal of the LORD of hosts
will do this.
32 "Therefore thus says the LORD concerning the king of Assyria: He shall not
come into this city, shoot an arrow there,
come before it with a shield, or cast up a
siege ramp against it.
33 By the way that he
came, by the same he shall return; he shall
not come into this city, says the LORD.
34 For I will defend this city to save it, for
my own sake and for the sake of my servant
David."
35 That very night the angel of the
LORD set out and struck down one hundred
eighty-five thousand in the camp of the Assyrians; when morning dawned, they were
all dead bodies.
36 Then King Sennacherib
of Assyria left, went home, and lived at
Nineveh.
37 As he was worshiping in the
house of his god Nisroch, his sons Adrammelech and Sharezer killed him with the
sword, and they escaped into the land of
Ararat. His son Esar-haddon succeeded
him.

a Gk Compare Isa 37.27 Q Ms: MT lacks *rising*

resume normal agricultural practice. **35–36:** Sennacherib's own records are silent about the circumstances under which the assault upon Jerusalem concluded, leaving the city unscathed, in contrast to the details these records provide about the capitulation of other kings in the region. The biblical text relates a mysterious reversal suffered by the Assyrians while Jerusalem lay at their mercy. Some commentators suggest that natural causes, such as plague, may lie behind the reference to the action of the *angel of the LORD*. **37:** The names of Sennacherib's assassins are not found in Mesopotamian records, which are sketchy and not entirely consistent with each other. *Nisroch,* either a scribal error or an otherwise unknown Assyrian deity. *Ararat,* a region in Armenia.

20 In those days Hezekiah became sick
and was at the point of death. The
prophet Isaiah son of Amoz came to him,
and said to him, "Thus says the LORD: Set
your house in order, for you shall die; you
shall not recover." 2 Then Hezekiah turned
his face to the wall and prayed to the LORD:
3 "Remember now, O LORD, I implore you,
how I have walked before you in faithful-
ness with a whole heart, and have done
what is good in your sight." Hezekiah wept
bitterly. 4 Before Isaiah had gone out of the
middle court, the word of the LORD came
to him: 5 "Turn back, and say to Hezekiah
prince of my people, Thus says the LORD,
the God of your ancestor David: I have
heard your prayer, I have seen your tears;
indeed, I will heal you; on the third day you
shall go up to the house of the LORD. 6 I will
add fifteen years to your life. I will deliver
you and this city out of the hand of the king
of Assyria; I will defend this city for my
own sake and for my servant David's
sake." 7 Then Isaiah said, "Bring a lump of
figs. Let them take it and apply it to the
boil, so that he may recover."

8 Hezekiah said to Isaiah, "What shall
be the sign that the LORD will heal me, and
that I shall go up to the house of the LORD
on the third day?" 9 Isaiah said, "This is the
sign to you from the LORD, that the LORD
will do the thing that he has promised: the
shadow has now advanced ten intervals;
shall it retreat ten intervals?" 10 Hezekiah
answered, "It is normal for the shadow to
lengthen ten intervals; rather let the shad-
ow retreat ten intervals." 11 The prophet
Isaiah cried to the LORD; and he brought
the shadow back the ten intervals, by which
the sun[a] had declined on the dial of Ahaz.

12 At that time King Merodach-baladan
son of Baladan of Babylon sent envoys with
letters and a present to Hezekiah, for he
had heard that Hezekiah had been sick.
13 Hezekiah welcomed them;[b] he showed
them all his treasure house, the silver, the
gold, the spices, the precious oil, his armo-
ry, all that was found in his storehouses;
there was nothing in his house or in all his
realm that Hezekiah did not show them.
14 Then the prophet Isaiah came to King
Hezekiah, and said to him, "What did these
men say? From where did they come to
you?" Hezekiah answered, "They have
come from a far country, from Babylon."
15 He said, "What have they seen in your
house?" Hezekiah answered, "They have
seen all that is in my house; there is nothing
in my storehouses that I did not show
them."

16 Then Isaiah said to Hezekiah, "Hear
the word of the LORD: 17 Days are coming
when all that is in your house, and that
which your ancestors have stored up until
this day, shall be carried to Babylon; noth-
ing shall be left, says the LORD. 18 Some of
your own sons who are born to you shall be
taken away; they shall be eunuchs in the
palace of the king of Babylon." 19 Then
Hezekiah said to Isaiah, "The word of the
LORD that you have spoken is good." For
he thought, "Why not, if there will be peace
and security in my days?"

a Syr See Isa 38.8 and Tg: Heb *it* *b* Gk Vg Syr: Heb *When Hezekiah heard about them*

20.1–21: Hezekiah's illness and recovery. The chapter opens with an account of a life-threatening illness that leads Hezekiah to prayer (cf. 19.4, 15–19). The prayer receives a positive response, both in terms of prophecy and medical treatment (the fig-poultice of v. 7). **8–11:** The king appears unwilling to believe that temporary remission will indeed lead to a recovery of complete health and asks for a further *sign.* The movement of a *shadow* as it miraculously recovers ground in defiance of normal rules signifies that God has likewise intervened in the normal processes of the world in the case of Hezekiah. **11:** *The dial of Ahaz,* lit. "the steps of Ahaz," an otherwise unknown structure. **12–21:** The promise of 20.6 implies no more than that the LORD would protect Jerusalem from the king of Assyria for another fifteen years. This passage addresses the question, what then? What Hezekiah's Babylonian visitors see, Isaiah tells the king, they will one day take away to Babylon, along with some of the king's descendants (cf. chs 24–25). The precise purpose of the Babylonian embassy is not given. **12:** *Merodach-baladan,* see Isa 39.1n.

20 The rest of the deeds of Hezekiah, all
his power, how he made the pool and the
conduit and brought water into the city, are
they not written in the Book of the Annals
of the Kings of Judah? 21 Hezekiah slept
with his ancestors; and his son Manasseh
succeeded him.

21 Manasseh was twelve years old
when he began to reign; he reigned
fifty-five years in Jerusalem. His mother's
name was Hephzibah. 2 He did what was
evil in the sight of the LORD, following the
abominable practices of the nations that
the LORD drove out before the people of
Israel. 3 For he rebuilt the high places that
his father Hezekiah had destroyed; he
erected altars for Baal, made a sacred
pole,[a] as King Ahab of Israel had done,
worshiped all the host of heaven, and
served them. 4 He built altars in the house
of the LORD, of which the LORD had said,
"In Jerusalem I will put my name." 5 He
built altars for all the host of heaven in the
two courts of the house of the LORD. 6 He
made his son pass through fire; he practiced
soothsaying and augury, and dealt with
mediums and with wizards. He did much
evil in the sight of the LORD, provoking
him to anger. 7 The carved image of Ashe-
rah that he had made he set in the house of
which the LORD said to David and to his
son Solomon, "In this house, and in Jerusa-
lem, which I have chosen out of all the
tribes of Israel, I will put my name forever;
8 I will not cause the feet of Israel to wander
any more out of the land that I gave to their
ancestors, if only they will be careful to do
according to all that I have commanded
them, and according to all the law that my
servant Moses commanded them." 9 But
they did not listen; Manasseh misled them
to do more evil than the nations had done
that the LORD destroyed before the people
of Israel.

10 The LORD said by his servants the
prophets, 11 "Because King Manasseh of
Judah has committed these abominations,
has done things more wicked than all that
the Amorites did, who were before him,
and has caused Judah also to sin with his
idols; 12 therefore thus says the LORD, the
God of Israel, I am bringing upon Jerusa-
lem and Judah such evil that the ears of
everyone who hears of it will tingle. 13 I will
stretch over Jerusalem the measuring line
for Samaria, and the plummet for the house
of Ahab; I will wipe Jerusalem as one wipes
a dish, wiping it and turning it upside
down. 14 I will cast off the remnant of my
heritage, and give them into the hand of
their enemies; they shall become a prey and
a spoil to all their enemies, 15 because they
have done what is evil in my sight and have
provoked me to anger, since the day their
ancestors came out of Egypt, even to this
day."

16 Moreover Manasseh shed very much
innocent blood, until he had filled Jerusa-
lem from one end to another, besides the
sin that he caused Judah to sin so that

a Heb *Asherah*

21.1–26: Manasseh and Amon. *Manasseh* (698/687–642 BCE; the data are unclear) is the very worst of the Judean kings, indulging in all that has been most reprehensible in the religion of Israel in the preceding chapters of Kings and adding to it. He makes his son *pass through fire* (see 16.1–4n.), practices *augury,* and consults *mediums* and *wizards* (v. 6; cf. Deut 18.9–13); and he takes it upon himself to install *the host of heaven* (sun, moon, stars) as fit objects for worship alongside the LORD in the Temple (vv. 4–5,7). The LORD of hosts (1 Kings 18.15; 19.10) has thus become merely a god among hosts, with a consort goddess for company (*Asherah,* v. 7), open to manipulation by occult means. **7–8:** Another collage of Deuteronomistic phrases (cf. 17.35–39n.). **11:** *Amorites,* see 1 Kings 21.6. **13:** Jerusalem will therefore be assessed by the divine architect (cf. the use of the *measuring line* in Isa 34.11; Lam 2.8; Am 7.7–9) and, like a dangerous building, condemned. It will be emptied of all that is in it, wiped clean like a *dish* after a meal is finished. The divine judgment will be analogous to the judgment that earlier fell upon *Samaria* (ch 17; Am 7.7–9), and similar also to what happened to the *house of Ahab:* judgment that completely destroyed the royal house (1 Kings 21.21–22; 2 Kings 9–10). The judgment is presented as

they did what was evil in the sight of the
LORD.
17 Now the rest of the acts of Manas-
seh, all that he did, and the sin that he com-
mitted, are they not written in the Book of
the Annals of the Kings of Judah? 18 Ma-
nasseh slept with his ancestors, and was
buried in the garden of his house, in the
garden of Uzza. His son Amon succeeded
him.
19 Amon was twenty-two years old
when he began to reign; he reigned two
years in Jerusalem. His mother's name was
Meshullemeth daughter of Haruz of Jot-
bah. 20 He did what was evil in the sight
of the LORD, as his father Manasseh had
done. 21 He walked in all the way in which
his father walked, served the idols that his
father served, and worshiped them; 22 he
abandoned the LORD, the God of his ances-
tors, and did not walk in the way of the
LORD. 23 The servants of Amon conspired
against him, and killed the king in his
house. 24 But the people of the land killed
all those who had conspired against King
Amon, and the people of the land made his
son Josiah king in place of him. 25 Now the
rest of the acts of Amon that he did, are
they not written in the Book of the Annals
of the Kings of Judah? 26 He was buried in
his tomb in the garden of Uzza; then his son
Josiah succeeded him.
22 Josiah was eight years old when he
began to reign; he reigned thirty-
one years in Jerusalem. His mother's name
was Jedidah daughter of Adaiah of Boz-
kath. 2 He did what was right in the sight of
the LORD, and walked in all the way of his
father David; he did not turn aside to the
right or to the left.
3 In the eighteenth year of King Josiah,
the king sent Shaphan son of Azaliah, son
of Meshullam, the secretary, to the house
of the LORD, saying, 4 "Go up to the high
priest Hilkiah, and have him count the en-
tire sum of the money that has been
brought into the house of the LORD, which
the keepers of the threshold have collected
from the people; 5 let it be given into the
hand of the workers who have the over-
sight of the house of the LORD; let them
give it to the workers who are at the house
of the LORD, repairing the house, 6 that is,
to the carpenters, to the builders, to the
masons; and let them use it to buy timber
and quarried stone to repair the house.
7 But no accounting shall be asked from
them for the money that is delivered into
their hand, for they deal honestly."
8 The high priest Hilkiah said to Sha-
phan the secretary, "I have found the book
of the law in the house of the LORD." When
Hilkiah gave the book to Shaphan, he read
it. 9 Then Shaphan the secretary came to the
king, and reported to the king, "Your ser-
vants have emptied out the money that was
found in the house, and have delivered it
into the hand of the workers who have
oversight of the house of the LORD."
10 Shaphan the secretary informed the king,
"The priest Hilkiah has given me a book."
Shaphan then read it aloud to the king.
11 When the king heard the words of
the book of the law, he tore his clothes.
12 Then the king commanded the priest Hil-
kiah, Ahikam son of Shaphan, Achbor son
of Micaiah, Shaphan the secretary, and the
king's servant Asaiah, saying, 13 "Go, in-
quire of the LORD for me, for the people,
and for all Judah, concerning the words of

absolute, though not immediate. **19–26:** In the shadow of such spectacular apostasy, the reign of Manasseh's son *Amon* (641–640 BCE) has the appearance of an unimportant footnote. **24:** *The people of the land,* see 11.14n.

22.1–23.30: Josiah (640–609 BCE). At this crucial juncture in Judean history, when judgment has been announced and disaster is imminent, Judah acquires yet another righteous king—*Josiah,* a second Moses or Joshua to match the second David (Hezekiah). Here is a king who does not *turn aside to the right or to the left* (22.2; cf. Deut 5.32; 17.20; Josh 1.7; etc.) from the law of Moses (23.25; cf. Josh 8.31–32; 23.6). **22.3–13:** Josiah's initial concern is simply to repair the Temple (cf. 12.1–16). It is not until *Shaphan* returns with *the book of the law* that Josiah becomes worried about the state of worship in Judah (v. 11). The *book of the law* is some form of Deuteronomy (see Deut 28.61; 29.21; 30.10). **14–20:** The prophet

this book that has been found; for great
is the wrath of the LORD that is kindled
against us, because our ancestors did not
obey the words of this book, to do accord-
ing to all that is written concerning us."
14 So the priest Hilkiah, Ahikam, Ach-
bor, Shaphan, and Asaiah went to the
prophetess Huldah the wife of Shallum son
of Tikvah, son of Harhas, keeper of the
wardrobe; she resided in Jerusalem in the
Second Quarter, where they consulted her.
15 She declared to them, "Thus says the
LORD, the God of Israel: Tell the man who
sent you to me, 16 Thus says the LORD, I
will indeed bring disaster on this place and
on its inhabitants—all the words of the
book that the king of Judah has read. 17 Be-
cause they have abandoned me and have
made offerings to other gods, so that they
have provoked me to anger with all the
work of their hands, therefore my wrath
will be kindled against this place, and it will
not be quenched. 18 But as to the king of
Judah, who sent you to inquire of the
LORD, thus shall you say to him, Thus says
the LORD, the God of Israel: Regarding the
words that you have heard, 19 because your
heart was penitent, and you humbled your-
self before the LORD, when you heard how
I spoke against this place, and against its
inhabitants, that they should become a des-
olation and a curse, and because you have
torn your clothes and wept before me, I
also have heard you, says the LORD.
20 Therefore, I will gather you to your an-
cestors, and you shall be gathered to your
grave in peace; your eyes shall not see all
the disaster that I will bring on this place."
They took the message back to the king.

23 Then the king directed that all the
elders of Judah and Jerusalem
should be gathered to him. 2 The king went
up to the house of the LORD, and with him
went all the people of Judah, all the inhabi-
tants of Jerusalem, the priests, the proph-
ets, and all the people, both small and
great; he read in their hearing all the words
of the book of the covenant that had been
found in the house of the LORD. 3 The king
stood by the pillar and made a covenant
before the LORD, to follow the LORD, keep-
ing his commandments, his decrees, and his
statutes, with all his heart and all his soul,
to perform the words of this covenant that
were written in this book. All the people
joined in the covenant.
4 The king commanded the high priest
Hilkiah, the priests of the second order,
and the guardians of the threshold, to bring
out of the temple of the LORD all the vessels
made for Baal, for Asherah, and for all the
host of heaven; he burned them outside Je-
rusalem in the fields of the Kidron, and car-
ried their ashes to Bethel. 5 He deposed the
idolatrous priests whom the kings of Judah
had ordained to make offerings in the high
places at the cities of Judah and around
Jerusalem; those also who made offerings
to Baal, to the sun, the moon, the constella-
tions, and all the host of the heavens. 6 He
brought out the image of[a] Asherah from
the house of the LORD, outside Jerusalem,

a Heb lacks *image of*

chosen by Josiah's officials for consultation was not Jeremiah, whose ministry had begun five years earlier (according to Jer 1.2), nor Zephaniah (Zeph 1.1), but *Huldah,* the wife of a Temple official (v. 14; cf. 10.22). Her words confirm those of the unnamed prophets of 21.10–15: *Disaster* is imminent. Because Josiah has *humbled* himself before the LORD, however, he will not personally see this disaster (v. 20); he will die while Judah and Jerusalem still know *peace,* rather than the sword. **23.1–3:** Josiah is a pious king, and Huldah's dire oracle about the future does not deflect him from the path of religious reform. The book of the law here becomes the *book of the covenant,* for the purpose of its public reading is to prepare the way for a renewal of the covenant between the LORD and his people, to which Deuteronomy is the supreme witness (see Deut 5.2–3; 29.1–28; cf. another covenant-renewal ceremony in 2 Kings 11.12–14, when the king also *stood by the pillar*). **4–25:** Josiah now proceeds to remove all trace of apostasy from Jerusalem (cf. the aftermath of Joash's renewal of the covenant in 11.17–18) and Judah, and indeed from *Bethel* (vv. 15–20; cf. the prophecy of the *man of God* in 1 Kings 13.2). **7:** The verse probably refers

to the Wadi Kidron, burned it at the Wadi
Kidron, beat it to dust and threw the dust
of it upon the graves of the common peo-
ple. 7 He broke down the houses of the male
temple prostitutes that were in the house of
the LORD, where the women did weaving
for Asherah. 8 He brought all the priests out
of the towns of Judah, and defiled the high
places where the priests had made offer-
ings, from Geba to Beer-sheba; he broke
down the high places of the gates that were
at the entrance of the gate of Joshua the
governor of the city, which were on the left
at the gate of the city. 9 The priests of the
high places, however, did not come up to
the altar of the LORD in Jerusalem, but ate
unleavened bread among their kindred.
10 He defiled Topheth, which is in the valley
of Ben-hinnom, so that no one would make
a son or a daughter pass through fire as
an offering to Molech. 11 He removed the
horses that the kings of Judah had dedicat-
ed to the sun, at the entrance to the house
of the LORD, by the chamber of the eunuch
Nathan-melech, which was in the pre-
cincts;[a] then he burned the chariots of the
sun with fire. 12 The altars on the roof of
the upper chamber of Ahaz, which the
kings of Judah had made, and the altars
that Manasseh had made in the two courts
of the house of the LORD, he pulled down
from there and broke in pieces, and threw
the rubble into the Wadi Kidron. 13 The
king defiled the high places that were east
of Jerusalem, to the south of the Mount of
Destruction, which King Solomon of Israel
had built for Astarte the abomination of
the Sidonians, for Chemosh the abomina-
tion of Moab, and for Milcom the abomi-
nation of the Ammonites. 14 He broke the
pillars in pieces, cut down the sacred
poles,[b] and covered the sites with human
bones.

15 Moreover, the altar at Bethel, the
high place erected by Jeroboam son of Ne-
bat, who caused Israel to sin—he pulled
down that altar along with the high place.
He burned the high place, crushing it to
dust; he also burned the sacred pole.[c] 16 As
Josiah turned, he saw the tombs there on
the mount; and he sent and took the bones
out of the tombs, and burned them on the
altar, and defiled it, according to the word
of the LORD that the man of God pro-
claimed,[d] when Jeroboam stood by the al-
tar at the festival; he turned and looked up
at the tomb of the man of God who had
predicted these things. 17 Then he said,
"What is that monument that I see?" The
people of the city told him, "It is the tomb
of the man of God who came from Judah
and predicted these things that you have
done against the altar at Bethel." 18 He
said, "Let him rest; let no one move his
bones." So they let his bones alone, with
the bones of the prophet who came out of
Samaria. 19 Moreover, Josiah removed all
the shrines of the high places that were in
the towns of Samaria, which kings of Israel
had made, provoking the LORD to anger;
he did to them just as he had done at Beth-
el. 20 He slaughtered on the altars all the
priests of the high places who were there,
and burned human bones on them. Then he
returned to Jerusalem.

21 The king commanded all the people,
"Keep the passover to the LORD your God
as prescribed in this book of the covenant."
22 No such passover had been kept since the
days of the judges who judged Israel, even
during all the days of the kings of Israel and
of the kings of Judah; 23 but in the eigh-

a Meaning of Heb uncertain b Heb *Asherim*
c Heb *Asherah* d Gk: Heb *proclaimed, who had predicted these things*

to the manufacture of ritual garments for worship of the goddess (cf. 10.22). **11:** Nonbiblical evidence suggests a particularly close connection between *horses* and *chariots* and worship of the sun. **13:** The *Mount of Destruction* is the Mount of Olives, referred to in this manner to express the authors' distaste for the worship that was practiced there; cf. 1 Kings 11.7. **14:** *With human bones,* to defile the sanctuaries; cf. v. 16. **21–22:** In celebrating *the passover* according to the stipulations of Deuteronomy (Deut 16.1–8, noting esp. v. 6), Josiah not only outstrips Hezekiah in faithfulness to God, but even David

teenth year of King Josiah this passover
was kept to the LORD in Jerusalem.
24 Moreover Josiah put away the mediums, wizards, teraphim,[a] idols, and all the abominations that were seen in the land of Judah and in Jerusalem, so that he established the words of the law that were written in the book that the priest Hilkiah had
found in the house of the LORD. 25 Before
him there was no king like him, who turned to the LORD with all his heart, with all his soul, and with all his might, according to all the law of Moses; nor did any like him arise after him.
26 Still the LORD did not turn from the fierceness of his great wrath, by which his anger was kindled against Judah, because of all the provocations with which Manasseh had provoked him. 27 The LORD said,
"I will remove Judah also out of my sight, as I have removed Israel; and I will reject this city that I have chosen, Jerusalem, and the house of which I said, My name shall be there."
28 Now the rest of the acts of Josiah, and all that he did, are they not written in the Book of the Annals of the Kings of Ju-
dah? 29 In his days Pharaoh Neco king of
Egypt went up to the king of Assyria to the river Euphrates. King Josiah went to meet him; but when Pharaoh Neco met him at
Megiddo, he killed him. 30 His servants car-
ried him dead in a chariot from Megiddo, brought him to Jerusalem, and buried him in his own tomb. The people of the land took Jehoahaz son of Josiah, anointed him, and made him king in place of his father.
31 Jehoahaz was twenty-three years old when he began to reign; he reigned three months in Jerusalem. His mother's name was Hamutal daughter of Jeremiah of Lib-
nah. 32 He did what was evil in the sight of
the LORD, just as his ancestors had done.
33 Pharaoh Neco confined him at Riblah in
the land of Hamath, so that he might not reign in Jerusalem, and imposed tribute on the land of one hundred talents of silver
and a talent of gold. 34 Pharaoh Neco made
Eliakim son of Josiah king in place of his father Josiah, and changed his name to Jehoiakim. But he took Jehoahaz away; he
came to Egypt, and died there. 35 Jehoiakim
gave the silver and the gold to Pharaoh, but he taxed the land in order to meet Pharaoh's demand for money. He exacted the silver and the gold from the people of the land, from all according to their assessment, to give it to Pharaoh Neco.
36 Jehoiakim was twenty-five years old when he began to reign; he reigned eleven years in Jerusalem. His mother's name was Zebidah daughter of Pedaiah of Rumah.
37 He did what was evil in the sight of the
LORD, just as all his ancestors had done.

a Or *household gods*

himself, for a Passover like this had not been observed since *the days of the judges who judged Israel* (cf. Josh 5.10–12). **26–30:** Judah's fate was already settled, and Josiah's reforms changed nothing. Even Josiah himself did not come to a happy end. Unwisely attempting to prevent *Egypt* from going to *Assyria*'s aid in its struggle with Babylon, he was killed at *Megiddo,* suffering the same ignominious exit from the stage as his apostate ancestor Ahaziah (cf. 9.27–28). A fuller account of Josiah's death is found in 2 Chr 35.20–24.

23.31–25.30: The end of Judah. Gradually the glory of Solomon is dismantled, as imperial power passes from Assyria to Babylon; Temple and palace are destroyed, and Jerusalem's treasures are carried off to a foreign land. **23.31–35:** *Jehoahaz* (609 BCE) is not a ruler acceptable to the Pharaoh of Egypt; and Pharaoh is (temporarily) Judah's new overlord, in the aftermath of Josiah's death at Megiddo. He is therefore replaced with his brother *Jehoiakim* (608–598). **33:** *A talent* weighed about 34 kg (75 lb). **35:** *The people of the land,* see 11.14n. The succession was probably irregular (cf. 1 Chr 3.15; Jer 22.11). **23.36–24.7:** The Babylonians (here called *Chaldeans)* are the ultimate agent of divine judgment upon Judah (cf. 20.16–18). *Nebuchadnezzar* (also called Nebuchadrezzar) ruled Babylon 605–562 BCE. He subdues *Egypt* and comes into possession of the whole Solomonic empire, *from the Wadi of Egypt to the River Euphrates* (cf. 1 Kings 4.21,24; 8.65; see Map on p. 573 HB). *Jehoiakim* first becomes his vassal

24 In his days King Nebuchadnezzar of
Babylon came up; Jehoiakim be-
came his servant for three years; then he
turned and rebelled against him. 2 The
LORD sent against him bands of the Chal-
deans, bands of the Arameans, bands of the
Moabites, and bands of the Ammonites; he
sent them against Judah to destroy it, ac-
cording to the word of the LORD that he
spoke by his servants the prophets. 3 Surely
this came upon Judah at the command of
the LORD, to remove them out of his sight,
for the sins of Manasseh, for all that he had
committed, 4 and also for the innocent
blood that he had shed; for he filled Jerusa-
lem with innocent blood, and the LORD
was not willing to pardon. 5 Now the rest of
the deeds of Jehoiakim, and all that he did,
are they not written in the Book of the An-
nals of the Kings of Judah? 6 So Jehoiakim
slept with his ancestors; then his son Jehoi-
achin succeeded him. 7 The king of Egypt
did not come again out of his land, for the
king of Babylon had taken over all that be-
longed to the king of Egypt from the Wadi
of Egypt to the River Euphrates.

8 Jehoiachin was eighteen years old
when he began to reign; he reigned three
months in Jerusalem. His mother's name
was Nehushta daughter of Elnathan of Je-
rusalem. 9 He did what was evil in the sight
of the LORD, just as his father had done.

10 At that time the servants of King
Nebuchadnezzar of Babylon came up to Je-
rusalem, and the city was besieged. 11 King
Nebuchadnezzar of Babylon came to the
city, while his servants were besieging it;
12 King Jehoiachin of Judah gave himself up
to the king of Babylon, himself, his mother,
his servants, his officers, and his palace of-
ficials. The king of Babylon took him pris-
oner in the eighth year of his reign.

13 He carried off all the treasures of the
house of the LORD, and the treasures of the
king's house; he cut in pieces all the vessels
of gold in the temple of the LORD, which
King Solomon of Israel had made, all this
as the LORD had foretold. 14 He carried

(24.1), but then rebels. **8–17:** His son *Jehoiachin* succeeds him and has to pay the price for his father's rebellion, a siege of Jerusalem and his own exile to Babylon, both in 597 BCE. He is replaced by an uncle,

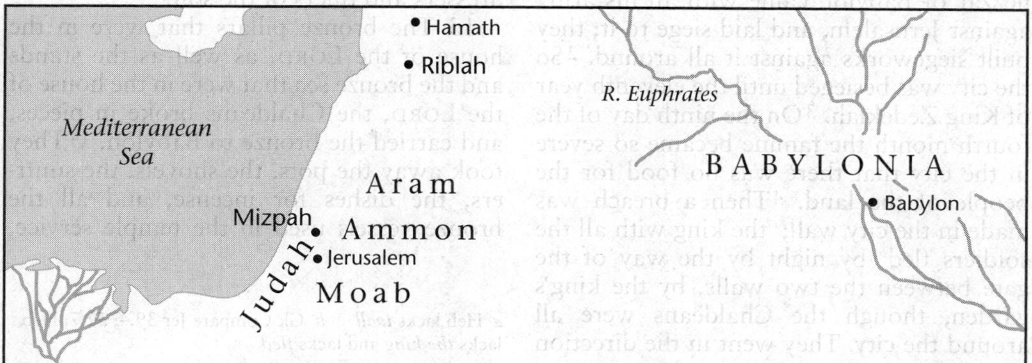

Chs 24–25: Babylon and Judah.

away all Jerusalem, all the officials, all the
warriors, ten thousand captives, all the arti-
sans and the smiths; no one remained, ex-
cept the poorest people of the land. 15 He
carried away Jehoiachin to Babylon; the
king's mother, the king's wives, his offi-
cials, and the elite of the land, he took into
captivity from Jerusalem to Babylon. 16 The
king of Babylon brought captive to Bab-
ylon all the men of valor, seven thousand,
the artisans and the smiths, one thousand,
all of them strong and fit for war. 17 The
king of Babylon made Mattaniah, Jehoia-
chin's uncle, king in his place, and changed
his name to Zedekiah.

18 Zedekiah was twenty-one years old
when he began to reign; he reigned eleven
years in Jerusalem. His mother's name was
Hamutal daughter of Jeremiah of Libnah.
19 He did what was evil in the sight of the
LORD, just as Jehoiakim had done. 20 In-
deed, Jerusalem and Judah so angered the
LORD that he expelled them from his pres-
ence.

Zedekiah rebelled against the king of
25 Babylon. 1 And in the ninth year of
his reign, in the tenth month, on the
tenth day of the month, King Nebuchad-
nezzar of Babylon came with all his army
against Jerusalem, and laid siege to it; they
built siegeworks against it all around. 2 So
the city was besieged until the eleventh year
of King Zedekiah. 3 On the ninth day of the
fourth month the famine became so severe
in the city that there was no food for the
people of the land. 4 Then a breach was
made in the city wall;[a] the king with all the
soldiers fled[b] by night by the way of the
gate between the two walls, by the king's
garden, though the Chaldeans were all
around the city. They went in the direction
of the Arabah. 5 But the army of the Chal-
deans pursued the king, and overtook him
in the plains of Jericho; all his army was
scattered, deserting him. 6 Then they cap-
tured the king and brought him up to the
king of Babylon at Riblah, who passed sen-
tence on him. 7 They slaughtered the sons of
Zedekiah before his eyes, then put out the
eyes of Zedekiah; they bound him in fetters
and took him to Babylon.

8 In the fifth month, on the seventh day
of the month—which was the nineteenth
year of King Nebuchadnezzar, king of Bab-
ylon—Nebuzaradan, the captain of the
bodyguard, a servant of the king of Bab-
ylon, came to Jerusalem. 9 He burned the
house of the LORD, the king's house, and
all the houses of Jerusalem; every great
house he burned down. 10 All the army of
the Chaldeans who were with the captain
of the guard broke down the walls around
Jerusalem. 11 Nebuzaradan the captain of
the guard carried into exile the rest of the
people who were left in the city and the
deserters who had defected to the king of
Babylon—all the rest of the population.
12 But the captain of the guard left some of
the poorest people of the land to be vine-
dressers and tillers of the soil.

13 The bronze pillars that were in the
house of the LORD, as well as the stands
and the bronze sea that were in the house of
the LORD, the Chaldeans broke in pieces,
and carried the bronze to Babylon. 14 They
took away the pots, the shovels, the snuff-
ers, the dishes for incense, and all the
bronze vessels used in the temple service,

a Heb lacks *wall* *b* Gk Compare Jer 39.4; 52.7: Heb lacks *the king* and lacks *fled*

Mattaniah. **24.18–25.21:** Most of ch 25 is repeated in Jer 52 with some variations. Mattaniah, like *Zedekiah* (597–586 BCE) is at first a loyal vassal, but eventually also rebels against *the king of Babylon* (24.20). The result is another *siege* of Jerusalem, lasting about a year and a half (25.1–2). Zedekiah's army flees when faced with a breach in the city wall, and the king flees with them, only to be overtaken near *Jericho* (25.4–5). The site of Israel's first military victory in their new land (Josh 6) thus becomes a place associated with their final defeat in it. Zedekiah is taken to Nebuchadnezzar's headquarters at Riblah in Syria, and his sons are executed, apparently to thwart dynastic hopes (25.6–7). A few weeks after the fall of Jerusalem (see 25.3,8), the full vengeance of the Babylonian king is visited upon the city and the Temple is plundered. The threats of 1 Kings 9.6–9 have become reality. **25.13–17:** A detailed description of the

15 as well as the firepans and the basins.
What was made of gold the captain of the
guard took away for the gold, and what
was made of silver, for the silver. 16 As for
the two pillars, the one sea, and the stands,
which Solomon had made for the house of
the LORD, the bronze of all these vessels
was beyond weighing. 17 The height of the
one pillar was eighteen cubits, and on it
was a bronze capital; the height of the capi-
tal was three cubits; latticework and pome-
granates, all of bronze, were on the capital
all around. The second pillar had the same,
with the latticework.

18 The captain of the guard took the
chief priest Seraiah, the second priest Zeph-
aniah, and the three guardians of the
threshold; 19 from the city he took an offi-
cer who had been in command of the sol-
diers, and five men of the king's council
who were found in the city; the secretary
who was the commander of the army who
mustered the people of the land; and sixty
men of the people of the land who were
found in the city. 20 Nebuzaradan the cap-
tain of the guard took them, and brought
them to the king of Babylon at Riblah.
21 The king of Babylon struck them down
and put them to death at Riblah in the land
of Hamath. So Judah went into exile out of
its land.

22 He appointed Gedaliah son of Ahi-
kam son of Shaphan as governor over the
people who remained in the land of Judah,
whom King Nebuchadnezzar of Babylon
had left. 23 Now when all the captains of
the forces and their men heard that the king
of Babylon had appointed Gedaliah as gov-
ernor, they came with their men to Gedali-
ah at Mizpah, namely, Ishmael son of
Nethaniah, Johanan son of Kareah, Seraiah
son of Tanhumeth the Netophathite, and
Jaazaniah son of the Maacathite. 24 Gedali-
ah swore to them and their men, saying,
"Do not be afraid because of the Chaldean
officials; live in the land, serve the king of
Babylon, and it shall be well with you."
25 But in the seventh month, Ishmael son of
Nethaniah son of Elishama, of the royal
family, came with ten men; they struck
down Gedaliah so that he died, along with
the Judeans and Chaldeans who were with
him at Mizpah. 26 Then all the people, high
and low,[a] and the captains of the forces set
out and went to Egypt; for they were afraid
of the Chaldeans.

27 In the thirty-seventh year of the exile
of King Jehoiachin of Judah, in the twelfth
month, on the twenty-seventh day of the
month, King Evil-merodach of Babylon, in
the year that he began to reign, released
King Jehoiachin of Judah from prison; 28 he
spoke kindly to him, and gave him a seat
above the other seats of the kings who were
with him in Babylon. 29 So Jehoiachin put
aside his prison clothes. Every day of his
life he dined regularly in the king's pres-
ence. 30 For his allowance, a regular allow-
ance was given him by the king, a portion
every day, as long as he lived.

a Or *young and old*

looted furnishings of the Temple; cf. 1 Kings 7.15–51. **18–21:** Execution of leading Judean officials. On *the people of the land,* see 11.14n. **22–26:** A fuller version of these events is found in Jer 40–43. *Gedaliah,* the grandson of Josiah's secretary Shaphan (23.12), is appointed to govern what is left, and the remnants of the scattered army (v. 5) gather to him at the new administrative center of *Mizpah,* just 12 km (7 mi) north of the ruined capital (v. 23). *Ishmael* apparently has ambitions to be the next king (he is *of the royal family,* v. 25), however, and takes it upon himself to slaughter everyone at Mizpah. The final exile of the book of Kings is a voluntary one, as the remaining people flee to *Egypt* (v. 26; cf. Jer 40.7–43.7). **27–30:** An epilogue holds out the faint hope that the Davidic promise (see esp. 2 Sam 7.15–16) may even yet, after awful judgment has fallen, remain in force—that God's wrath having been poured out upon good Josiah's sons, his (admittedly wicked) grandson Jehoiachin might still produce a further "lamp in Jerusalem" (1 Kings 11.36; 15.4; 2 Kings 8.19). *Evil-merodach* (Amel-marduk) ruled Babylon ca. 562–560 BCE.

1 CHRONICLES

Like many books in the Bible, Chronicles was originally anonymous and untitled. The title ascribed to it by the early rabbis, "the book of the events of the days" ("seper dibre hayyamim") suggests that this is the book referred to often in Kings (e.g., 1 Kings 14.19), where one may find additional material about individual kings. The name Chronicles in the Septuagint, *Paralipomena*, "the things left out," similarly testifies that Chronicles records the events left out of earlier biblical history. This understanding of Chronicles is not accepted by most modern scholars. It was St. Jerome's description of the book as a "chronicle," a summary of divine history, that has proved to be most influential in the history of modern interpretation.

There is little doubt that the author lived in Jerusalem and had great familiarity with the Temple and its assorted traditions. Many scholars have suggested that the anonymous author of Chronicles also composed Ezra-Nehemiah. Since Ezra begins where Chronicles ends, with Cyrus's decree allowing the exiled Jews to return home and rebuild the Temple, some scholars assume that these books are a unity, the work of a single author or editor. Other scholars think that the linguistic, thematic, and historiographical differences between Chronicles and Ezra-Nehemiah are too great to warrant positing a common authorship for Chronicles, Ezra, and Nehemiah. Seen in this latter perspective, the Chronicler's History, which begins with the first person (Adam) and ends with the Babylonian exile and Cyrus the Great's summons to the exiled Jews to return home (2 Chr 36.21–23), must be separated from the postexilic history of Ezra-Nehemiah. This latter approach makes the most sense. Although there are significant similarities between the Chronicles, Ezra, and Nehemiah, the differences outweigh the similarities, and one individual is unlikely to have written all three works. Hence, in the following annotation, "the Chronicler" designates the author of Chronicles.

The Chronicler wrote during the Persian period (539–332 BCE), after much of the literature of the Hebrew Bible had already been written, and he draws extensively upon this rich literary tradition. The dependence of Chronicles upon Genesis is evident in the genealogies (1 Chr 1–9); the dependence upon Samuel is clear in the narration of Saul's demise and David's reign (1 Chr 10–29); and the dependence upon Kings is unmistakable in the narration of Solomon and the Judahite kingdom (2 Chr 1–36). The Chronicler's work is also informed by a variety of earlier biblical texts. Citations from or allusions to the Torah, Joshua, Isaiah, Jeremiah, Ezekiel, the Psalms, and Ruth all appear in Chronicles. In fact, one of the significant issues that the Chronicler must deal with is how all of these authoritative sources may be reconciled. Scholars generally agree that the Chronicler also had access to some nonbiblical sources, but the nature and extent of these sources are disputed.

It is difficult to date Chronicles precisely, beyond noting that it is postexilic. A range of over three hundred and fifty years, from the late sixth to the mid-second century BCE, has been suggested for its date of composition. Of the possibilities, a date in the fourth century seems most plausible, because it would account for both the author's studious references to a variety of other biblical writings and those literary features within the work that anticipate some familiar features of Jewish Hellenistic writings. But there are no specific references, no absolute synchronisms, and no extrabiblical citations that could definitively situate the book within a given decade or quarter-century.

Chronicles has three major sections: the genealogies (1 Chr 1–9), the history of the United Monarchy (1 Chr 10–2 Chr 9), and the history of the Judahite monarchy (2 Chr 10–36). The first section, which forms the introduction to the work, begins with Adam (1 Chr 1), but focuses upon the identity, interrelationships, and location of Israel's twelve tribes (1 Chr 2–9). Such genealogies, which are found in traditional societies, explain and justify the place and function of various individuals, people, and institutions. In the case of 1 Chr 1–8, the Chronicler stresses the ties between Israel and the land. The very scope and structure of the Chronicler's genealogical system underscore the indivisibility of Israel. Within this larger structure, Judah, Levi, and Benjamin receive by far the most extensive genealogies. In the Chronicler's work, these three tribes are deemed critical to preserving Israel's distinctive legacy. The list of those Jews who returned from exile (1 Chr 9) concludes these chapters by highlighting the continuity between postexilic Judah (the Persian province of Yehud) and earlier Israel.

The Chronicler's coverage of the monarchy proceeds according to a fundamentally historical outline. After briefly addressing and condemning the reign of Saul (1 Chr 10), the Chronicler devotes most of his attention to the highly successful reigns of David (1 Chr 11–29) and Solomon (2 Chr 1–9), which clearly represent a high point of the history. The rest of the book engages the emergence, continuation, and fall of the kingdom of Judah (2 Chr 10–36). By placing David and Solomon's achievements at the center of Israelite history, the author underscores the prominence of those Israelite institutions he believed developed, were consolidated, or were transformed during this period—the Aaronic priesthood; the Levites in all their responsibilities as singers, teachers, administrators, and ancillaries to the priests; the Davidic dynasty; and, last but not least, the Temple itself. Having portrayed the establishment of Israel's normative political and cultic institutions in the time of David and Solomon, the Chronicler never reneges on their pertinence to the lives of all Israelites in later centuries.

Following the death of Solomon and the ascension of his son Rehoboam, the ten northern tribes secede from southern rule (2 Chr 11.1–17). Whereas the author of Kings follows synchronistically the course of both the Northern and Southern Kingdoms, the Chronicler concentrates his attention upon the tribes of Judah, Benjamin, and Levi, who make up the Southern Kingdom of Judah (2 Chr 11.5–6,12,13–17,23). In Chronicles the course of the Judahite monarchy is characterized by both defeats and successes. The Chronicler consistently documents the achievements of Judah's best kings—Abijah (2 Chr 13.2–21), Asa (2 Chr 14.1–6; 15.8–15), Jehoshaphat (2 Chr 17.1–9; 19.4–11), Hezekiah (2 Chr 29–31), and Josiah (2 Chr 34.1–7)—to institute reforms, reunite the people, and recover lost territories. Major regressions occur in the reigns of Ahaz (2 Chr 28), Manasseh (2 Chr 33.1–11), and the final kings of Judah (2 Chr 36.1–13). In depicting their history, the Chronicler is largely dependent on Kings, but as the episode concerning Manasseh's repentance and restoration (2 Chr 33.12–19; cf. 2 Kings 21.1–16) demonstrates, he may revise these sources so they fit his theology. Throughout the work, God sends prophets to warn monarchs, leaders, and people alike about the consequences of their actions, imploring them to repent. This is seen especially in his commentary on the defeat and exile of Judah, in which the Chronicler states that Judah was exiled only after the LORD sent a steady supply of prophets to stir the people and priestly leaders to reform, but their warnings went unheeded (2 Chr 36.14–16).

Both Kings and Chronicles end by describing events from the sixth century BCE, but Cyrus's decree, commending the return of the Babylonian exiles to Judah (2 Chr 36.22–23), offers a clearer hope for the future than the conclusion of Kings. In this manner, Chronicles contains and relativizes the tremendous tragedy of the Babylonian deportations soberly depicted in 2 Kings 24–25. Thus Chronicles, with its positive ending and emphasis on the power of repentance, may be seen as more optimistic than the history of Samuel-Kings, which it has rewritten.

1 Adam, Seth, Enosh; 2 Kenan, Mahala-
lel, Jared; 3 Enoch, Methuselah, La-
mech; 4 Noah, Shem, Ham, and Japheth.
5 The descendants of Japheth: Gomer,
Magog, Madai, Javan, Tubal, Meshech,
and Tiras. 6 The descendants of Gomer:
Ashkenaz, Diphath,[a] and Togarmah. 7 The
descendants of Javan: Elishah, Tarshish,
Kittim, and Rodanim.[b]
8 The descendants of Ham: Cush,
Egypt, Put, and Canaan. 9 The descendants
of Cush: Seba, Havilah, Sabta, Raama, and
Sabteca. The descendants of Raamah: She-
ba and Dedan. 10 Cush became the father of
Nimrod; he was the first to be a mighty one
on the earth.
11 Egypt became the father of Ludim,
Anamim, Lehabim, Naphtuhim, 12 Pathru-
sim, Casluhim, and Caphtorim, from
whom the Philistines come.[c]
13 Canaan became the father of Sidon
his firstborn, and Heth, 14 and the Jebu-
sites, the Amorites, the Girgashites, 15 the
Hivites, the Arkites, the Sinites, 16 the Ar-
vadites, the Zemarites, and the Hamathites.
17 The descendants of Shem: Elam, As-
shur, Arpachshad, Lud, Aram, Uz, Hul,
Gether, and Meshech.[d] 18 Arpachshad be-
came the father of Shelah; and Shelah be-
came the father of Eber. 19 To Eber were
born two sons: the name of the one was
Peleg (for in his days the earth was divid-
ed), and the name of his brother Joktan.
20 Joktan became the father of Almodad,
Sheleph, Hazarmaveth, Jerah, 21 Hadoram,
Uzal, Diklah, 22 Ebal, Abimael, Sheba,
23 Ophir, Havilah, and Jobab; all these
were the descendants of Joktan.
24 Shem, Arpachshad, Shelah; 25 Eber,
Peleg, Reu; 26 Serug, Nahor, Terah;
27 Abram, that is, Abraham.
28 The sons of Abraham: Isaac and Ish-

a Gen 10.3 *Ripath*; See Gk Vg *b* Gen 10.4 *Dodanim*; See Syr Vg *c* Heb *Casluhim, from which the Philistines come, Caphtorim*; See Am 9.7, Jer 47.4 *d* *Mash* in Gen 10.23

1.1–22. From the first person to Israel: a universal genealogy. Drawing upon numerous lineages in Genesis, the author traces the development of and interrelationships among a variety of nations, ending with Israel—the focal point of his interest. **1–4:** The ten names represent ten generations, beginning with Adam and ending with Noah. The Chronicler's tally is a marvel of condensation, having been culled from the much longer and more detailed narrative lineage of Adam in Gen 5.1–32. **4:** Each of Noah's three sons can be associated with a relatively large geographic area: Shem (peoples to the east of ancient Israel); Ham (peoples to the south and southwest); Japheth (peoples to the north and west). Although most modern scholars believe that Canaan was ethnically and linguistically Semitic, and thus should be descended from Shem, in the Hebrew Bible Canaan is descended from Ham, perhaps because of Canaan's long political relationship to Egypt.

1.5–23: Descendants of Noah. These verses are largely drawn from Gen 10.1–29, the "Table of Nations," which enumerates some seventy descendants of Noah's sons, symbolizing seventy peoples of the world. This creates both a genealogical tree and map by which all the world's nations are related to each other through a common ancestor, Noah. **5–7:** The sons of Japheth include Anatolia (e.g., Togarmah, Tubal, Meshech), Asia Minor including Greek settlements (Javan), and islands in the Mediterranean Sea, such as Elishah (Cyprus), Kittim (Caphtor and other isles), and Rodanim (Rhodes). **5:** Ham's children represent peoples and areas in the Egyptian political sphere: Cush to the south of Egypt (Sudan or Ethiopia), Egypt, Put to the west (Libya), and Canaan to the north. **11–16:** These lists of Egypt's and Canaan's descendants closely follow Gen 10.13–18. **11:** *Philistines,* see Jer 47.4; Am 9.7. **13–15:** The sons of Canaan inhabit Sidon (the Phoenician coast) and include the traditional inhabitants of the land of Canaan (*Heth* [the Hittites] and those in v. 14), and those of coastal (*Arkites, Sinites, Arvadites, Zemarites*) and inland (*Hamathites*) Syria. **17:** Located in Mesopotamia (*Elam, Asshur, Arpachshad*), Asia Minor (*Lud* and *Meshech*), Syria (*Aram*); others cannot be identified. **17–18:** Although in v. 8 Canaan is descended from Ham, Eber, after whom the Hebrews (gentilic "'ibri") are named, is a descendant of Shem, indicating Israelite feelings of kinship to the Semitic peoples of the east. **19:** *The earth was divided,* the Hebrew puns on Peleg's name, which is derived from a verb meaning "to divide, split." **20:** *Joktan*'s descendants inhabit the Arabian peninsula.

mael. 29 These are their genealogies: the
firstborn of Ishmael, Nebaioth; and Kedar,
Adbeel, Mibsam, 30 Mishma, Dumah, Mas-
sa, Hadad, Tema, 31 Jetur, Naphish, and
Kedemah. These are the sons of Ishmael.
32 The sons of Keturah, Abraham's concu-
bine: she bore Zimran, Jokshan, Medan,
Midian, Ishbak, and Shuah. The sons of
Jokshan: Sheba and Dedan. 33 The sons of
Midian: Ephah, Epher, Hanoch, Abida,
and Eldaah. All these were the descendants
of Keturah.

34 Abraham became the father of Isaac.
The sons of Isaac: Esau and Israel. 35 The
sons of Esau: Eliphaz, Reuel, Jeush, Jalam,
and Korah. 36 The sons of Eliphaz: Teman,
Omar, Zephi, Gatam, Kenaz, Timna, and
Amalek. 37 The sons of Reuel: Nahath, Ze-
rah, Shammah, and Mizzah.

38 The sons of Seir: Lotan, Shobal, Zib-
eon, Anah, Dishon, Ezer, and Dishan.
39 The sons of Lotan: Hori and Homam;
and Lotan's sister was Timna. 40 The sons
of Shobal: Alian, Manahath, Ebal, Shephi,
and Onam. The sons of Zibeon: Aiah and
Anah. 41 The sons of Anah: Dishon. The
sons of Dishon: Hamran, Eshban, Ithran,
and Cheran. 42 The sons of Ezer: Bilhan,
Zaavan, and Jaakan.[a] The sons of Di-
shan:[b] Uz and Aran.

43 These are the kings who reigned in
the land of Edom before any king reigned
over the Israelites: Bela son of Beor, whose
city was called Dinhabah. 44 When Bela
died, Jobab son of Zerah of Bozrah suc-
ceeded him. 45 When Jobab died, Husham
of the land of the Temanites succeeded him.
46 When Husham died, Hadad son of Be-
dad, who defeated Midian in the country of
Moab, succeeded him; and the name of his
city was Avith. 47 When Hadad died, Sam-
lah of Masrekah succeeded him. 48 When
Samlah died, Shaul[c] of Rehoboth on the
Euphrates succeeded him. 49 When Shaul[c]
died, Baal-hanan son of Achbor succeeded
him. 50 When Baal-hanan died, Hadad suc-
ceeded him; the name of his city was Pai,
and his wife's name Mehetabel daughter of
Matred, daughter of Me-zahab. 51 And Ha-
dad died.

The clans[d] of Edom were: clans[d] Tim-
na, Aliah,[e] Jetheth, 52 Oholibamah, Elah,
Pinon, 53 Kenaz, Teman, Mibzar, 54 Magdi-
el, and Iram; these are the clans[d] of Edom.

2 These are the sons of Israel: Reuben,
Simeon, Levi, Judah, Issachar, Zebu-
lun, 2 Dan, Joseph, Benjamin, Naphtali,
Gad, and Asher. 3 The sons of Judah: Er,
Onan, and Shelah; these three the Canaan-
ite woman Bath-shua bore to him. Now Er,
Judah's firstborn, was wicked in the sight
of the LORD, and he put him to death. 4 His

a Or *and Akan*; See Gen 36.27 *b* See 1.38: Heb *Dishon* *c* Or *Saul* *d* Or *chiefs* *e* Or *Alvah*; See Gen 36.40

1.24–27: Shem's genealogy is extracted from Gen 11.10–26. **27:** *Abram,* this begins the second major unit in the Chronicler's universal genealogy; the first was dominated by the descendants of Noah (1 Chr 1.4b–23). **28:** For *Isaac and Ishmael,* the Chronicler fashions a very brief genealogy from narrative materials in Genesis (16.11; 17.18–19; 25.9). Ishmael is associated with the northern part of the Sinai peninsula and northwestern Arabia (Gen 16.10–12; 17.20; 21.13), as are the descendants of Keturah (vv. 32–33). **29–31:** Drawn from the Ishmaelite genealogy in Gen 25.12–18. **32–33:** In the source text (Gen 25.1–13), *Keturah* appears as Abraham's second wife, taken sometime after the death of Sarah (Gen 25.1–3). The Chronicler's reference to her as a concubine may be based on his reading of Gen 25.1–2 in light of Gen 25.5–6. **34–37:** The genealogy of Sarah and Abraham draws upon Gen 25.19–26 and Gen 36.2–14. The Chronicler always refers to Jacob as *Israel* (see Gen 32.22–32). **38–42:** *The sons of Seir,* abridged and adapted from Gen 36.20–28. **43–54:** The lists of Edomite monarchs (1.43–51a) and Edomite chieftains (1.51b–54) are adapted and slightly abridged from Gen 36.31–39 and Gen 36.40–43, respectively. The Chronicler presents the history of Edom in capsule form up to the time of the inception of the Israelite monarchy, the beginning of his own narrative history (ch 10). **2.1–2:** This list of Israel's descendants is the natural continuation of the progeny of Abraham (1.28–33) and Isaac (1.34–37) and serves as the introduction to the lineages of Israel's twelve sons, which follows in 2.3–9.1.

2.3–4.23: The descendants of Judah. The Chronicler first offers a long genealogy of Judah, demonstrat-

daughter-in-law Tamar also bore him Pe-
rez and Zerah. Judah had five sons in all.
5 The sons of Perez: Hezron and Hamul.
6 The sons of Zerah: Zimri, Ethan, Heman,
Calcol, and Dara,[a] five in all. 7 The sons of
Carmi: Achar, the troubler of Israel, who
transgressed in the matter of the devoted
thing; 8 and Ethan's son was Azariah.
9 The sons of Hezron, who were born
to him: Jerahmeel, Ram, and Chelubai.
10 Ram became the father of Amminadab,
and Amminadab became the father of Nah-
shon, prince of the sons of Judah. 11 Nah-
shon became the father of Salma, Salma
of Boaz, 12 Boaz of Obed, Obed of Jesse.
13 Jesse became the father of Eliab his first-
born, Abinadab the second, Shimea the
third, 14 Nethanel the fourth, Raddai the
fifth, 15 Ozem the sixth, David the seventh;
16 and their sisters were Zeruiah and Abi-
gail. The sons of Zeruiah: Abishai, Joab,
and Asahel, three. 17 Abigail bore Amasa,
and the father of Amasa was Jether the Ish-
maelite.
18 Caleb son of Hezron had children by
his wife Azubah, and by Jerioth; these were
her sons: Jesher, Shobab, and Ardon.
19 When Azubah died, Caleb married Eph-
rath, who bore him Hur. 20 Hur became the
father of Uri, and Uri became the father of
Bezalel.
21 Afterward Hezron went in to the
daughter of Machir father of Gilead, whom
he married when he was sixty years old;
and she bore him Segub; 22 and Segub be-
came the father of Jair, who had twenty-
three towns in the land of Gilead. 23 But
Geshur and Aram took from them
Havvoth-jair, Kenath and its villages, sixty
towns. All these were descendants of Ma-
chir, father of Gilead. 24 After the death of
Hezron, in Caleb-ephrathah, Abijah wife
of Hezron bore him Ashhur, father of Te-
koa.
25 The sons of Jerahmeel, the firstborn
of Hezron: Ram his firstborn, Bunah,
Oren, Ozem, and Ahijah. 26 Jerahmeel also
had another wife, whose name was Atarah;
she was the mother of Onam. 27 The sons of
Ram, the firstborn of Jerahmeel: Maaz, Ja-
min, and Eker. 28 The sons of Onam: Sham-
mai and Jada. The sons of Shammai: Na-
dab and Abishur. 29 The name of Abishur's
wife was Abihail, and she bore him Ahban
and Molid. 30 The sons of Nadab: Seled and
Appaim; and Seled died childless. 31 The
son[b] of Appaim: Ishi. The son[b] of Ishi:
Sheshan. The son[b] of Sheshan: Ahlai.
32 The sons of Jada, Shammai's brother: Je-
ther and Jonathan; and Jether died child-
less. 33 The sons of Jonathan: Peleth and
Zaza. These were the descendants of Jerah-
meel. 34 Now Sheshan had no sons, only
daughters; but Sheshan had an Egyptian
slave, whose name was Jarha. 35 So Sheshan

a Or *Darda*; Compare Syr Tg some Gk Mss; See 1 Kings 4.31 *b* Heb *sons*

ing Judah's importance to the Chronicler's History. **2.4:** *Daughter-in-law,* an allusion to the sexual relationship between Judah and Tamar (Gen 38.12–26). Having earlier referred to the Canaanite status of Bath-shua (v. 3; cf. Gen 38.1–5), the Chronicler presents another unusual feature of Judah's lineage, which did not disqualify it from preeminence. **6–8:** Drawn from two sources: Josh 7.1 (2.6a,7) and 1 Kings 5.11 (2.6b). **7:** *Achar,* called Achan in Josh 7, but cf. Josh 7.24–25. **10:** *Amminadab,* as the father of Nahshon, see Num 2.3. **11:** Taken from Ruth 4.20–21. **13–17:** The lineages of Jesse's sons and daughters have been drawn, in part, from 1 Sam 16.1–23; 17.1–51; 2 Sam 2.18. **18–20:** The descendants of Caleb are a major interest of the Chronicler, taking up a sizable portion of Judah's lineages (2.18–20,42–50a,50b–55; 4.1–7). This may be because some earlier sources suggest that he was a Kenizzite (e.g., Num 32.12), and thus not part of Israel. **21:** *Machir* is sometimes associated with Manasseh, most often as Manasseh's son (Gen 50.23; Num 32.39–40; Deut 3.14–15; cf. Judg 5.14). The connection with Manasseh is affirmed in 7.14–17. **22–23:** The subject shifts back to Hezron, last mentioned in v. 9. **22:** *Jair* is a son of Manasseh in Num 32.41 and Deut 3.14, but he appears here as the grandson of Hezron. **24:** *Father of Tekoa,* Tekoa in earlier books is the name of a Judean city, but in genealogies, ethnic and geographic dimensions of names can clearly overlap. **25–41:** Both the genealogy of Jerahmeel (vv. 25–33), the first-born of Hezron (vv. 9,25) and the genealogy of Sheshan (vv. 34–41) are unique to Chronicles.

gave his daughter in marriage to his slave
Jarha; and she bore him Attai. 36 Attai be-
came the father of Nathan, and Nathan of
Zabad. 37 Zabad became the father of Eph-
lal, and Ephlal of Obed. 38 Obed became
the father of Jehu, and Jehu of Azariah.
39 Azariah became the father of Helez, and
Helez of Eleasah. 40 Eleasah became the fa-
ther of Sismai, and Sismai of Shallum.
41 Shallum became the father of Jekamiah,
and Jekamiah of Elishama.
42 The sons of Caleb brother of Jerah-
meel: Mesha[a] his firstborn, who was fa-
ther of Ziph. The sons of Mareshah father
of Hebron. 43 The sons of Hebron: Korah,
Tappuah, Rekem, and Shema. 44 Shema be-
came father of Raham, father of Jorkeam;
and Rekem became the father of Shammai.
45 The son of Shammai: Maon; and Maon
was the father of Beth-zur. 46 Ephah also,
Caleb's concubine, bore Haran, Moza, and
Gazez; and Haran became the father of Ga-
zez. 47 The sons of Jahdai: Regem, Jotham,
Geshan, Pelet, Ephah, and Shaaph. 48 Maa-
cah, Caleb's concubine, bore Sheber and
Tirhanah. 49 She also bore Shaaph father of
Madmannah, Sheva father of Machbenah
and father of Gibea; and the daughter of
Caleb was Achsah. 50 These were the de-
scendants of Caleb.
The sons[b] of Hur the firstborn of Ephra-
thah: Shobal father of Kiriath-jearim,
51 Salma father of Bethlehem, and Hareph
father of Beth-gader. 52 Shobal father of
Kiriath-jearim had other sons: Haroeh, half
of the Menuhoth. 53 And the families of
Kiriath-jearim: the Ithrites, the Puthites,
the Shumathites, and the Mishraites; from
these came the Zorathites and the Eshtao-
lites. 54 The sons of Salma: Bethlehem, the
Netophathites, Atroth-beth-joab, and half
of the Manahathites, the Zorites. 55 The
families also of the scribes that lived at Ja-
bez: the Tirathites, the Shimeathites, and
the Sucathites. These are the Kenites who
came from Hammath, father of the house
of Rechab.

3 These are the sons of David who were
born to him in Hebron: the firstborn
Amnon, by Ahinoam the Jezreelite; the sec-
ond Daniel, by Abigail the Carmelite; 2 the
third Absalom, son of Maacah, daughter of
King Talmai of Geshur; the fourth Adoni-
jah, son of Haggith; 3 the fifth Shephatiah,
by Abital; the sixth Ithream, by his wife
Eglah; 4 six were born to him in Hebron,
where he reigned for seven years and six
months. And he reigned thirty-three years
in Jerusalem. 5 These were born to him in
Jerusalem: Shimea, Shobab, Nathan, and
Solomon, four by Bath-shua, daughter of
Ammiel; 6 then Ibhar, Elishama, Eliphelet,
7 Nogah, Nepheg, Japhia, 8 Elishama, Elia-
da, and Eliphelet, nine. 9 All these were Da-
vid's sons, besides the sons of the concu-
bines; and Tamar was their sister.
10 The descendants of Solomon: Reho-
boam, Abijah his son, Asa his son, Jehosha-
phat his son, 11 Joram his son, Ahaziah his
son, Joash his son, 12 Amaziah his son, Aza-
riah his son, Jotham his son, 13 Ahaz his
son, Hezekiah his son, Manasseh his son,
14 Amon his son, Josiah his son. 15 The sons
of Josiah: Johanan the firstborn, the second

a Gk reads *Mareshah* *b* Gk Vg: Heb *son*

42–50: The second of the genealogies for Caleb's descendants (cf. vv. 18–20n.). Many of the sites listed also occur in the Judahite town list of Josh 15. **50b–55:** Largely without parallel, this genealogy reverts to the line of Hur (v. 19). Each of Hur's three sons is depicted as a founder (lit. "father") of a town. The *Kenites* (Num 24.20–22; Judg 4.11,17–21; 5.24–27; 1 Sam 15.6; 30.29) ultimately descend from their eponymous ancestor, Cain (Gen 4.1–25).

3.1–24: The descendants of David. 1–9: Some names of David's sons, and their order, are different in the present text of 2 Samuel. **1–3:** These verses are based on 2 Sam 3.2–4. David's lineage follows naturally 2.9–17, which enumerates the descendants of Ram, including David and the children of David's two sisters Zeruiah and Abigail. **4:** This verse draws upon and reworks 2 Sam 5.5. Consistent with David's rule over all Israel in chs 11–29, the writer avoids the distinction between Israel and Judah found in his source. **5–9:** These verses are largely dependent upon 2 Sam 5.13–16. **10–14:** A fifteen-generation genealogy from Solomon to Josiah, noting only the Davidic king in each generation. **15–18:** A largely

Jehoiakim, the third Zedekiah, the fourth
Shallum. 16 The descendants of Jehoiakim:
Jeconiah his son, Zedekiah his son; 17 and
the sons of Jeconiah, the captive: Shealtiel
his son, 18 Malchiram, Pedaiah, Shenazzar,
Jekamiah, Hoshama, and Nedabiah; 19 The
sons of Pedaiah: Zerubbabel and Shimei;
and the sons of Zerubbabel: Meshullam
and Hananiah, and Shelomith was their sis-
ter; 20 and Hashubah, Ohel, Berechiah,
Hasadiah, and Jushab-hesed, five. 21 The
sons of Hananiah: Pelatiah and Jeshaiah,
his son[a] Rephaiah, his son[a] Arnan, his
son[a] Obadiah, his son[a] Shecaniah. 22 The
son[b] of Shecaniah: Shemaiah. And the
sons of Shemaiah: Hattush, Igal, Bariah,
Neariah, and Shaphat, six. 23 The sons of
Neariah: Elioenai, Hizkiah, and Azrikam,
three. 24 The sons of Elioenai: Hodaviah,
Eliashib, Pelaiah, Akkub, Johanan, Dela-
iah, and Anani, seven.

4 The sons of Judah: Perez, Hezron, Car-
mi, Hur, and Shobal. 2 Reaiah son of
Shobal became the father of Jahath, and
Jahath became the father of Ahumai and
Lahad. These were the families of the Zo-
rathites. 3 These were the sons[c] of Etam:
Jezreel, Ishma, and Idbash; and the name of
their sister was Hazzelelponi, 4 and Penuel
was the father of Gedor, and Ezer the fa-
ther of Hushah. These were the sons of
Hur, the firstborn of Ephrathah, the father
of Bethlehem. 5 Ashhur father of Tekoa had
two wives, Helah and Naarah; 6 Naarah
bore him Ahuzzam, Hepher, Temeni, and
Haahashtari.[d] These were the sons of Naa-
rah. 7 The sons of Helah: Zereth, Izhar,[e]
and Ethnan. 8 Koz became the father of
Anub, Zobebah, and the families of Ahar-
hel son of Harum. 9 Jabez was honored
more than his brothers; and his mother
named him Jabez, saying, "Because I bore
him in pain." 10 Jabez called on the God of
Israel, saying, "Oh that you would bless me
and enlarge my border, and that your hand
might be with me, and that you would keep
me from hurt and harm!" And God granted
what he asked. 11 Chelub the brother of
Shuhah became the father of Mehir, who
was the father of Eshton. 12 Eshton became
the father of Beth-rapha, Paseah, and Te-
hinnah the father of Ir-nahash. These are
the men of Recah. 13 The sons of Kenaz:
Othniel and Seraiah; and the sons of Othni-
el: Hathath and Meonothai.[f] 14 Meono-
thai became the father of Ophrah; and Se-
raiah became the father of Joab father of
Ge-harashim,[g] so-called because they
were artisans. 15 The sons of Caleb son of
Jephunneh: Iru, Elah, and Naam; and the
son[b] of Elah: Kenaz. 16 The sons of Jehalle-
lel: Ziph, Ziphah, Tiria, and Asarel. 17 The
sons of Ezrah: Jether, Mered, Epher, and
Jalon. These are the sons of Bithiah, daugh-
ter of Pharaoh, whom Mered married;[h]
and she conceived and bore[i] Miriam,
Shammai, and Ishbah father of Eshtemoa.
18 And his Judean wife bore Jered father of
Gedor, Heber father of Soco, and Jekuthiel
father of Zanoah. 19 The sons of the wife of
Hodiah, the sister of Naham, were the fa-
thers of Keilah the Garmite and Eshtemoa

a Gk Compare Syr Vg: Heb *sons of* *b* Heb *sons* *c* Gk Compare Vg: Heb *the father* *d* Or *Ahashtari* *e* Another reading is *Zohar* *f* Gk Vg: Heb lacks *and Meonothai* *g* That is *Valley of artisans* *h* The clause: *These are . . . married* is transposed from verse 18 *i* Heb lacks *and bore*

unparalleled genealogy from Josiah to Pediah. The second half of ch 3 gives special attention to Josiah and his various offspring. **18:** *Shenazzar,* some identify him with Sheshbazzar of Ezra 1.8, who led a group of early returnees from exile. **19–24:** The list of Davidic descendants from *Pedaiah* to *the sons of Elioenai* is unique to the Chronicler and likely reflects aspirations for a renewed Davidic monarchy in the postexilic period. **19:** *Zerubbabel* was a leader of the postexilic Judean community in the late sixth century BCE; see Ezra 3.2; Hag 1.1. **22:** *Hattush* returned from exile in Babylon (Ezra 8.2).

4.1–23: Descendants of Judah. *The sons of Judah,* in contrast to the largely linear genealogy of David (ch 3), this chapter describes several unconnected branches of Judeans. It also narrates several short anecdotes about individual Judeans (e.g., vv. 9–10,23). As in other genealogies, names of individuals here occur as place names elsewhere. **1:** The sequence *Perez . . . Shobal* signifies a line of descent; these persons are not brothers. **4b–7:** Return to the genealogy of Caleb; see 2.18–20n. **21:** In referring to Shelah, the text

the Maacathite. 20 The sons of Shimon:
Amnon, Rinnah, Ben-hanan, and Tilon.
The sons of Ishi: Zoheth and Ben-zoheth.
21 The sons of Shelah son of Judah: Er fa-
ther of Lecah, Laadah father of Mareshah,
and the families of the guild of linen work-
ers at Beth-ashbea; 22 and Jokim, and the
men of Cozeba, and Joash, and Saraph,
who married into Moab but returned to
Lehem[a] (now the records[b] are ancient).
23 These were the potters and inhabitants of
Netaim and Gederah; they lived there with
the king in his service.

24 The sons of Simeon: Nemuel, Jamin,
Jarib, Zerah, Shaul;[c] 25 Shallum was his
son, Mibsam his son, Mishma his son.
26 The sons of Mishma: Hammuel his son,
Zaccur his son, Shimei his son. 27 Shimei
had sixteen sons and six daughters; but his
brothers did not have many children, nor
did all their family multiply like the Ju-
deans. 28 They lived in Beer-sheba, Mola-
dah, Hazar-shual, 29 Bilhah, Ezem, Tolad,
30 Bethuel, Hormah, Ziklag, 31 Beth-
marcaboth, Hazar-susim, Beth-biri, and
Shaaraim. These were their towns until Da-
vid became king. 32 And their villages were
Etam, Ain, Rimmon, Tochen, and Ashan,
five towns, 33 along with all their villages
that were around these towns as far as
Baal. These were their settlements. And
they kept a genealogical record.

34 Meshobab, Jamlech, Joshah son of
Amaziah, 35 Joel, Jehu son of Joshibiah son
of Seraiah son of Asiel, 36 Elioenai, Jaako-
bah, Jeshohaiah, Asaiah, Adiel, Jesimiel,
Benaiah, 37 Ziza son of Shiphi son of Allon
son of Jedaiah son of Shimri son of Shema-
iah— 38 these mentioned by name were
leaders in their families, and their clans in-
creased greatly. 39 They journeyed to the
entrance of Gedor, to the east side of the
valley, to seek pasture for their flocks,
40 where they found rich, good pasture, and
the land was very broad, quiet, and peace-
ful; for the former inhabitants there be-
longed to Ham. 41 These, registered by
name, came in the days of King Hezekiah
of Judah, and attacked their tents and the
Meunim who were found there, and exter-
minated them to this day, and settled in
their place, because there was pasture there
for their flocks. 42 And some of them, five
hundred men of the Simeonites, went to
Mount Seir, having as their leaders Pelati-
ah, Neariah, Rephaiah, and Uzziel, sons of
Ishi; 43 they destroyed the remnant of the
Amalekites that had escaped, and they have
lived there to this day.

5 The sons of Reuben the firstborn of Is-
rael. (He was the firstborn, but because
he defiled his father's bed his birthright was
given to the sons of Joseph son of Israel, so

a Vg Compare Gk: Heb *and Jashubi-lahem*
b Or *matters* *c* Or *Saul*

reverts to discussing the original sons of Judah (2.3–4). **22:** *Married into Moab,* the Chronicler again posits some close links between Judah and its neighbors. Possible links may be hinted at in Ezra 2.6; 8.4; 10.30. Intermarriage with Moabites in the postexilic period is also attested (Ezra 9.1; Neh 13.23; Ruth), but in the case of Ezra and Nehemiah these are construed as illegitimate.

4.24–43: The descendants of Simeon. Here too, the Chronicler punctuates his genealogical prologue with anecdotes about geography, migrations, and wars (vv. 27–33,38–43). The genealogy of Simeon immediately follows that of its neighbor, Judah. **24–27:** The lineage of Simeon is traced through his son Saul. The names listed in v. 25 (Nemuel, Jamin, Jarib, Zerah, and Saul) are derived from Gen 46.10; Ex 6.15; and esp. Num 26.12–14. The rest of the genealogy (vv. 26–27) is unique to the Chronicler. **28–33:** Taken, with some changes, from Josh 19.2–8. **33–43:** A list of Simeonite leaders (v. 38) is followed by a description of the expansion of the tribe demographically and geographically. The ruthlessness displayed by the Simeonites recalls the intemperate behavior of their eponymous ancestor (Gen 34.25–29; 49.5–7). **41:** *Hezekiah,* see 2 Chr 29–32.

5.1–10: The descendants of Reuben. Reuben was firstborn (Gen 29.31–30.21; 35.23–26; 46.8–9; Ex 1.2; 6.14; Num 26.5; Ezek 48.31–35), but he does not appear first in the Chronicler's genealogies. **1:** Joseph, firstborn of Rachel, rather than Reuben, firstborn of Leah, attained to the birthright because Reuben had sexual relations with Jacob's concubine Bilhah (Gen 35.22; 49.4). **2:** *A ruler came from him,* that he is not enrolled in the genealogy according to the birthright; 2 though Judah became prominent among his brothers and a ruler came from him, yet the birthright belonged to Joseph.) 3 The sons of Reuben, the firstborn of Israel: Hanoch, Pallu, Hezron, and Carmi. 4 The sons of Joel: Shemaiah his son, Gog his son, Shimei his son, 5 Micah his son, Reaiah his son, Baal his son, 6 Beerah his son, whom King Tilgath-pilneser of Assyria carried away into exile; he was a chieftain of the Reubenites. 7 And his kindred by their families, when the genealogy of their generations was reckoned: the chief, Jeiel, and Zechariah, 8 and Bela son of Azaz, son of Shema, son of Joel, who lived in Aroer, as far as Nebo and Baal-meon. 9 He also lived to the east as far as the beginning of the desert this side of the Euphrates, because their cattle had multiplied in the land of Gilead. 10 And in the days of Saul they made war on the Hagrites, who fell by their hand; and they lived in their tents throughout all the region east of Gilead.

11 The sons of Gad lived beside them in the land of Bashan as far as Salecah: 12 Joel the chief, Shapham the second, Janai, and Shaphat in Bashan. 13 And their kindred according to their clans: Michael, Meshullam, Sheba, Jorai, Jacan, Zia, and Eber, seven. 14 These were the sons of Abihail son of Huri, son of Jaroah, son of Gilead, son of Michael, son of Jeshishai, son of Jahdo, son of Buz; 15 Ahi son of Abdiel, son of Guni, was chief in their clan; 16 and they lived in Gilead, in Bashan and in its towns, and in all the pasture lands of Sharon to their limits. 17 All of these were enrolled by genealogies in the days of King Jotham of Judah, and in the days of King Jeroboam of Israel.

18 The Reubenites, the Gadites, and the half-tribe of Manasseh had valiant warriors, who carried shield and sword, and drew the bow, expert in war, forty-four thousand seven hundred sixty, ready for service. 19 They made war on the Hagrites, Jetur, Naphish, and Nodab; 20 and when they received help against them, the Hagrites and all who were with them were given into their hands, for they cried to God in the battle, and he granted their entreaty because they trusted in him. 21 They captured their livestock: fifty thousand of their camels, two hundred fifty thousand sheep, two thousand donkeys, and one hundred thousand captives. 22 Many fell slain, because the war was of God. And they lived in their territory until the exile.

the writer alludes to David's kingship, which eventually encompassed all twelve tribes (28.4; 1 Sam 13.14; 25.30; Mic 5.2). **3:** The Chronicler derives this list from Num 26.5–6. *Carmi* is one of the Reubenite clans with possible ties to Judah (Gen 46.9; Ex 6.14; Num 26.6; Josh 7.1,18,24,26; 1 Chr 2.7; 4.1). **6:** In contrast to Kings, which largely loses its concentration upon individual tribes in its coverage of the dual monarchies, the Chronicler's history maintains a continuous interest in the fate of individual tribes. *Tilgath-pilneser,* the Chronicler's spelling (5.26; 2 Chr 28.20) of Tiglath-pileser (III), King of Assyria (745–727 BCE); cf. 2 Kings 15.29. **9:** In this case, *Gilead* refers to the territory east of the Jordan, which is south of the Jabbok and north of the Arnon. There is some overlap with Gad's territorial holdings in Josh 13. **10:** *The days of Saul,* who was the first king of Israel, in the late eleventh century BCE.

5.11–17: The descendants of Gad. Like the Reubenites, the Gadites were located east of the Jordan River. **16:** Rather than signifying a *pasture land,* Heb "migrash" means the belt of land or open space outside a town or a sanctuary. *Sharon* refers here not to the (coastal) Sharon plain, the common designation of Sharon in the Bible, but to the town of Sharon in Transjordan, a place also mentioned in the Moabite Mesha inscription (line 13). **17:** *King Jotham of Judah* (759–743 BCE) and *King Jeroboam* (II) *of Israel* (788–747 BCE).

5.18–22: The wars of the Transjordan tribes. In some traditions (Num 32.1–42; Deut 3.12–16; 29.6–7; Josh 13.8–31) and once elsewhere in Chronicles (1 Chr 12.38), Reuben, Gad, and East Manasseh are treated as a larger entity. These two and a half tribes join forces, share a common muster, partake in the spoils gained by fighting a collective enemy, and experience a common fate (vv. 22,25–26). The number *forty-four thousand seven hundred sixty* (v. 18) is notable for its specificity, not for its magnitude.

23 The members of the half-tribe of Ma-
nasseh lived in the land; they were very nu-
merous from Bashan to Baal-hermon, Se-
nir, and Mount Hermon. 24 These were the
heads of their clans: Epher,[a] Ishi, Eliel,
Azriel, Jeremiah, Hodaviah, and Jahdiel,
mighty warriors, famous men, heads of
their clans. 25 But they transgressed against
the God of their ancestors, and prostituted
themselves to the gods of the peoples of the
land, whom God had destroyed before
them. 26 So the God of Israel stirred up the
spirit of King Pul of Assyria, the spirit of
King Tilgath-pilneser of Assyria, and he
carried them away, namely, the Reubenites,
the Gadites, and the half-tribe of Manas-
seh, and brought them to Halah, Habor,
Hara, and the river Gozan, to this day.

6 [b]The sons of Levi: Gershom,[c] Kohath,
and Merari. 2 The sons of Kohath: Am-
ram, Izhar, Hebron, and Uzziel. 3 The chil-
dren of Amram: Aaron, Moses, and Miri-
am. The sons of Aaron: Nadab, Abihu,
Eleazar, and Ithamar. 4 Eleazar became the
father of Phinehas, Phinehas of Abishua,
5 Abishua of Bukki, Bukki of Uzzi, 6 Uzzi of
Zerahiah, Zerahiah of Meraioth, 7 Mera-
ioth of Amariah, Amariah of Ahitub, 8 Ahi-
tub of Zadok, Zadok of Ahimaaz, 9 Ahima-
az of Azariah, Azariah of Johanan, 10 and
Johanan of Azariah (it was he who served
as priest in the house that Solomon built in
Jerusalem). 11 Azariah became the father of
Amariah, Amariah of Ahitub, 12 Ahitub of
Zadok, Zadok of Shallum, 13 Shallum of
Hilkiah, Hilkiah of Azariah, 14 Azariah
of Seraiah, Seraiah of Jehozadak; 15 and Je-
hozadak went into exile when the LORD
sent Judah and Jerusalem into exile by the
hand of Nebuchadnezzar.

16 [d]The sons of Levi: Gershom, Kohath,
and Merari. 17 These are the names of the
sons of Gershom: Libni and Shimei. 18 The
sons of Kohath: Amram, Izhar, Hebron,
and Uzziel. 19 The sons of Merari: Mahli
and Mushi. These are the clans of the Le-
vites according to their ancestry. 20 Of Ger-
shom: Libni his son, Jahath his son, Zim-
mah his son, 21 Joah his son, Iddo his son,
Zerah his son, Jeatherai his son. 22 The sons
of Kohath: Amminadab his son, Korah his
son, Assir his son, 23 Elkanah his son, Ebia-

a Gk Vg: Heb *and Epher* *b* Ch 5.27 in Heb
c Heb *Gershon*, variant of *Gershom*; See 6.16
d Ch 6.1 in Heb

5.23–24: The descendants of Half-Manasseh. This part of the tribe of Manasseh was located east of the Jordan River, to the north of Gad.

5.25–26: The exile of the Transjordanian tribes. The campaigns of 733–732 BCE by *Tiglath-pilneser* III (whose nickname was *Pul*), were primarily directed against King Rezin of Damascus, but also resulted in the capture of Gilead and Galilee (2 Kings 15.29). The list of sites in v. 26 is borrowed, however, from 2 Kings 17.6 (parallel 2 Kings 18.11), which details the destinations of the later Samarian deportees in the Assyrian exile of 722 BCE.

6.1–81: The descendants of Levi take center stage in the genealogies of Chronicles. For the Chronicler, the Levites are second in importance only to the Judeans, so their genealogy is especially long and detailed. As with other tribes, attention is paid to issues of identity and location: who the Levites are (vv. 1–53) and where they live (vv. 54–81). **1–15:** A priestly line is traced from Levi in the ancestral period (cf. Gen 46.11; Ex 6.16–25; Num 3.17–20) all the way to Jehozadak (v. 15), who was taken to Babylon in the exile of 586 BCE. **8:** Scholars debate the origin of David's main priest Zadok; this genealogy in Chronicles is the first source to explicitly connect him to the line of Aaron and Levi. Twelve generations of priests precede Zadok and twelve generation of priests succeed him, hence the era of Zadok, which coincides with the construction of the Temple, marks the halfway point between the ancestral era and the exile. **10:** *Azariah,* cf. 1 Kings 4.2. **14:** *Seraiah,* see 2 Kings 25.18. **16–48:** Lineages for three major groups within the Levites—the Gershonites, the Kohathites, and the Merarites (vv. 16–30)—preface lineages of Levitical singers from the same three groups (vv. 31–48). Levitical choirs are an intrinsic component of the Chronicler's system of worship, appearing some thirty times in his history. The genealogies thus are not purely antiquarian, but in places justify the institutions of postexilic Judah. **28:** *Samuel,* cf. 1 Sam 1.1; 8.2.

saph his son, Assir his son, 24 Tahath his
son, Uriel his son, Uzziah his son, and Sha-
ul his son. 25 The sons of Elkanah: Amasai
and Ahimoth, 26 Elkanah his son, Zophai
his son, Nahath his son, 27 Eliab his son,
Jeroham his son, Elkanah his son. 28 The
sons of Samuel: Joel[a] his firstborn, the sec-
ond Abijah.[b] 29 The sons of Merari: Mahli,
Libni his son, Shimei his son, Uzzah his
son, 30 Shimea his son, Haggiah his son,
and Asaiah his son.

31 These are the men whom David put
in charge of the service of song in the house
of the LORD, after the ark came to rest
there. 32 They ministered with song before
the tabernacle of the tent of meeting, until
Solomon had built the house of the LORD
in Jerusalem; and they performed their ser-
vice in due order. 33 These are the men who
served; and their sons were: Of the Kohath-
ites: Heman, the singer, son of Joel, son of
Samuel, 34 son of Elkanah, son of Jeroham,
son of Eliel, son of Toah, 35 son of Zuph,
son of Elkanah, son of Mahath, son of
Amasai, 36 son of Elkanah, son of Joel, son
of Azariah, son of Zephaniah, 37 son of Ta-
hath, son of Assir, son of Ebiasaph, son of
Korah, 38 son of Izhar, son of Kohath, son
of Levi, son of Israel; 39 and his brother
Asaph, who stood on his right, namely,
Asaph son of Berechiah, son of Shimea,
40 son of Michael, son of Baaseiah, son of
Malchijah, 41 son of Ethni, son of Zerah,
son of Adaiah, 42 son of Ethan, son of Zim-
mah, son of Shimei, 43 son of Jahath, son of
Gershom, son of Levi. 44 On the left were
their kindred the sons of Merari: Ethan son
of Kishi, son of Abdi, son of Malluch,
45 son of Hashabiah, son of Amaziah, son
of Hilkiah, 46 son of Amzi, son of Bani, son
of Shemer, 47 son of Mahli, son of Mushi,
son of Merari, son of Levi; 48 and their kin-
dred the Levites were appointed for all the
service of the tabernacle of the house of
God.

49 But Aaron and his sons made offer-
ings on the altar of burnt offering and on
the altar of incense, doing all the work of
the most holy place, to make atonement for
Israel, according to all that Moses the ser-
vant of God had commanded. 50 These are
the sons of Aaron: Eleazar his son, Phine-
has his son, Abishua his son, 51 Bukki his
son, Uzzi his son, Zerahiah his son, 52 Me-
raioth his son, Amariah his son, Ahitub his
son, 53 Zadok his son, Ahimaaz his son.

54 These are their dwelling places ac-
cording to their settlements within their
borders: to the sons of Aaron of the fami-
lies of Kohathites—for the lot fell to them
first— 55 to them they gave Hebron in the
land of Judah and its surrounding pasture

a Gk Syr Compare verse 33 and 1 Sam 8.2: Heb lacks *Joel* *b* Heb reads *Vashni, and Abijah* for *the second Abijah*, taking *the second* as a proper name

31–32: Referring back to the three Levitical clans, the writer summarizes the duties of the Gershonites, Kohathites, and Merarites adopted during the United Monarchy of David and Solomon, the time in which the Temple was built. Three specific descendants—Asaph from Gershon (vv. 24–27), Heman from Qohath (vv. 18–23), and Ethan from Merari (vv. 29–32)—took on official roles in the state religion. **33:** *Heman*, "Asaph" (v. 39), and "Ethan" (v. 42) represent three classes or guilds of singers. Because David's reign is definitive for the Levitical singers, the patronyms Asaph, Heman, and Ethan serve as organizing principles for them (2 Chr 5.12; 29.14; 35.15). **44:** *Ethan* represents the Merarites (6.18,29; 15.17), but in many other instances Jeduthun serves this role (16.41; 25.1,3,6; 2 Chr 5.12; 29.14; 35.15). **49–53:** The Aaronic priests officiate within the sanctuary and make offerings (23.30–32; Ex 38–42; 30.1–10; Lev 8.1–9.24; 18.8–20; Ezek 44.13). **49:** *The most holy place* (lit. "holy of holies") is the exclusive domain of the priests (Ex 26.33–34; Num 18.1–5; Ezek 44.15–16; 2 Chr 5.11; 29.7). Other members of the tribe of Levi may serve as Temple staff, but the priests alone officiate at the inner sanctuary. *To make atonement for Israel* refers to the Day of Atonement ritual of Lev 16. This festival probably became especially significant during the time of the Chronicler. **54–81:** The list of Levitical towns is drawn from an earlier version of Josh 21.3–42. **55–60:** The location of Aaronide settlements is limited to the traditional domains of three tribes: Judah, Simeon, and Benjamin. On *pasture lands*, see 5.16n. **57:** The creation of *cities of refuge* was de-

6.54–81: **The Levitical cities.** The dashed lines show the approximate boundaries of the tribes.

lands, 56 but the fields of the city and its
villages they gave to Caleb son of Jephun-
neh. 57 To the sons of Aaron they gave the
cities of refuge: Hebron, Libnah with its
pasture lands, Jattir, Eshtemoa with its pas-
ture lands, 58 Hilen[a] with its pasture lands,
Debir with its pasture lands, 59 Ashan with
its pasture lands, and Beth-shemesh with its
pasture lands. 60 From the tribe of Benja-
min, Geba with its pasture lands, Alemeth
with its pasture lands, and Anathoth with
its pasture lands. All their towns through-
out their families were thirteen.

61 To the rest of the Kohathites were
given by lot out of the family of the tribe,
out of the half-tribe, the half of Manasseh,
ten towns. 62 To the Gershomites according
to their families were allotted thirteen
towns out of the tribes of Issachar, Asher,
Naphtali, and Manasseh in Bashan. 63 To
the Merarites according to their families
were allotted twelve towns out of the tribes
of Reuben, Gad, and Zebulun. 64 So the
people of Israel gave the Levites the towns
with their pasture lands. 65 They also gave
them by lot out of the tribes of Judah, Sime-
on, and Benjamin these towns that are
mentioned by name.

66 And some of the families of the sons
of Kohath had towns of their territory out
of the tribe of Ephraim. 67 They were given
the cities of refuge: Shechem with its pas-
ture lands in the hill country of Ephraim,
Gezer with its pasture lands, 68 Jokmeam
with its pasture lands, Beth-horon with its
pasture lands, 69 Aijalon with its pasture
lands, Gath-rimmon with its pasture lands;
70 and out of the half-tribe of Manasseh,
Aner with its pasture lands, and Bileam
with its pasture lands, for the rest of the
families of the Kohathites.

71 To the Gershomites: out of the half-
tribe of Manasseh: Golan in Bashan with
its pasture lands and Ashtaroth with its
pasture lands; 72 and out of the tribe of Issa-
char: Kedesh with its pasture lands, Dabe-
rath[b] with its pasture lands, 73 Ramoth
with its pasture lands, and Anem with its
pasture lands; 74 out of the tribe of Asher:
Mashal with its pasture lands, Abdon with
its pasture lands, 75 Hukok with its pasture
lands, and Rehob with its pasture lands;
76 and out of the tribe of Naphtali: Kedesh
in Galilee with its pasture lands, Hammon
with its pasture lands, and Kiriathaim with
its pasture lands. 77 To the rest of the Mera-
rites out of the tribe of Zebulun: Rimmono
with its pasture lands, Tabor with its pas-
ture lands, 78 and across the Jordan from
Jericho, on the east side of the Jordan, out
of the tribe of Reuben: Bezer in the steppe
with its pasture lands, Jahzah with its pas-
ture lands, 79 Kedemoth with its pasture
lands, and Mephaath with its pasture
lands; 80 and out of the tribe of Gad: Ra-
moth in Gilead with its pasture lands, Ma-
hanaim with its pasture lands, 81 Heshbon
with its pasture lands, and Jazer with its
pasture lands.

7 The sons[c] of Issachar: Tola, Puah, Ja-
shub, and Shimron, four. 2 The sons of
Tola: Uzzi, Rephaiah, Jeriel, Jahmai, Ib-
sam, and Shemuel, heads of their ancestral
houses, namely of Tola, mighty warriors of
their generations, their number in the days
of David being twenty-two thousand six
hundred. 3 The son[d] of Uzzi: Izrahiah. And
the sons of Izrahiah: Michael, Obadiah,
Joel, and Isshiah, five, all of them chiefs;
4 and along with them, by their generations,
according to their ancestral houses, were
units of the fighting force, thirty-six thou-
sand, for they had many wives and sons.
5 Their kindred belonging to all the families
of Issachar were in all eighty-seven thou-

a Other readings *Hilez, Holon*; See Josh 21.15
b Or *Dobrath* *c* Syr Compare Vg: Heb *And to the sons* *d* Heb *sons*

manded in Deuteronomic (Deut 4.41–43; 19.1–13) and Priestly law (Num 35.6–15,25–28,32). Most, if not all, of the towns designated for asylum (Josh 20.7–8) doubled as Levitical settlements.

7.1–5: The descendants of Issachar. Issachar's progeny are traced through his eldest son Tola (Gen 46.13; Num 26.23–25; Judg 5.15). As in some other genealogies (4.42–43; 5.7–10,18–22; 7.9–12,40), large numbers, growth, and military prowess are stressed.

sand mighty warriors, enrolled by geneal-
ogy.
6 The sons of Benjamin: Bela, Becher,
and Jediael, three. 7 The sons of Bela: Ez-
bon, Uzzi, Uzziel, Jerimoth, and Iri, five,
heads of ancestral houses, mighty warriors;
and their enrollment by genealogies was
twenty-two thousand thirty-four. 8 The
sons of Becher: Zemirah, Joash, Eliezer,
Elioenai, Omri, Jeremoth, Abijah, Ana-
thoth, and Alemeth. All these were the sons
of Becher; 9 and their enrollment by geneal-
ogies, according to their generations, as
heads of their ancestral houses, mighty
warriors, was twenty thousand two hun-
dred. 10 The sons of Jediael: Bilhan. And the
sons of Bilhan: Jeush, Benjamin, Ehud,
Chenaanah, Zethan, Tarshish, and Ahisha-
har. 11 All these were the sons of Jediael
according to the heads of their ancestral
houses, mighty warriors, seventeen thou-
sand two hundred, ready for service in war.
12 And Shuppim and Huppim were the sons
of Ir, Hushim the son[a] of Aher.
13 The descendants of Naphtali: Jahziel,
Guni, Jezer, and Shallum, the descendants
of Bilhah.
14 The sons of Manasseh: Asriel, whom
his Aramean concubine bore; she bore Ma-
chir the father of Gilead. 15 And Machir
took a wife for Huppim and for Shuppim.
The name of his sister was Maacah. And
the name of the second was Zelophehad;
and Zelophehad had daughters. 16 Maacah
the wife of Machir bore a son, and she
named him Peresh; the name of his brother
was Sheresh; and his sons were Ulam and
Rekem. 17 The son[a] of Ulam: Bedan. These
were the sons of Gilead son of Machir, son
of Manasseh. 18 And his sister Hammole-
cheth bore Ishhod, Abiezer, and Mahlah.
19 The sons of Shemida were Ahian, She-
chem, Likhi, and Aniam.
20 The sons of Ephraim: Shuthelah, and
Bered his son, Tahath his son, Eleadah his
son, Tahath his son, 21 Zabad his son, Shu-
thelah his son, and Ezer and Elead. Now
the people of Gath, who were born in the
land, killed them, because they came down
to raid their cattle. 22 And their father
Ephraim mourned many days, and his
brothers came to comfort him. 23 Ephra-
im[b] went in to his wife, and she conceived
and bore a son; and he named him Beriah,
because disaster[c] had befallen his house.
24 His daughter was Sheerah, who built
both Lower and Upper Beth-horon, and
Uzzen-sheerah. 25 Rephah was his son, Re-
sheph his son, Telah his son, Tahan his son,
26 Ladan his son, Ammihud his son, Elisha-
ma his son, 27 Nun[d] his son, Joshua his
son. 28 Their possessions and settlements
were Bethel and its towns, and eastward
Naaran, and westward Gezer and its
towns, Shechem and its towns, as far as
Ayyah and its towns; 29 also along the bor-
ders of the Manassites, Beth-shean and its
towns, Taanach and its towns, Megiddo
and its towns, Dor and its towns. In these
lived the sons of Joseph son of Israel.

a Heb *sons* *b* Heb *He* *c* Heb *beraah* *d* Here spelled *Non*; see Ex 33.11

7.6–12: The descendants of Benjamin. A genealogy of Zebulun may be missing here (Gen 46.17–27; Num 26.23–50), as another genealogy of Benjamin is found in 8.1–40. **12:** Some commentators emend *sons of Ir* to "sons of Dan" on the supposition that this verse retains a fragment of the apparently missing genealogy of Dan (Gen 46.13; Num 26.42; Judg 5.17).

7.13: The descendants of Naphtali. In accordance with Gen 46.23–25, *Bilhah* appears as the mother of *Naphtali* (where she is also the mother of Dan).

7.14–19: The descendants of Manasseh (cf. Num 26.29–34). For the progeny of Manasseh east of the Jordan, see 5.23–24. **15:** On the daughters of *Zelophehad,* see Num 27.1–11; 36.1–12; Josh 17.3.

7.20–29: The descendants of Ephraim. Tradition (Gen 48.8–22; Deut 33.17) posits a close relationship between the two sons of Joseph—Manasseh and Ephraim. This is why the Chronicler treats them sequentially and considers their settlements (vv. 28–29; cf. Josh 16–18) together. **27:** *Joshua,* the hero of the book of Joshua; see Josh 1.1; 24.29–30.

30 The sons of Asher: Imnah, Ishvah,
Ishvi, Beriah, and their sister Serah. 31 The
sons of Beriah: Heber and Malchiel, who
was the father of Birzaith. 32 Heber became
the father of Japhlet, Shomer, Hotham, and
their sister Shua. 33 The sons of Japhlet: Pa-
sach, Bimhal, and Ashvath. These are the
sons of Japhlet. 34 The sons of Shemer: Ahi,
Rohgah, Hubbah, and Aram. 35 The sons of
Helem[a] his brother: Zophah, Imna, She-
lesh, and Amal. 36 The sons of Zophah:
Suah, Harnepher, Shual, Beri, Imrah, 37 Be-
zer, Hod, Shamma, Shilshah, Ithran, and
Beera. 38 The sons of Jether: Jephunneh,
Pispa, and Ara. 39 The sons of Ulla: Arah,
Hanniel, and Rizia. 40 All of these were men
of Asher, heads of ancestral houses, select
mighty warriors, chief of the princes. Their
number enrolled by genealogies, for service
in war, was twenty-six thousand men.

8 Benjamin became the father of Bela his
firstborn, Ashbel the second, Aharah
the third, 2 Nohah the fourth, and Rapha
the fifth. 3 And Bela had sons: Addar, Gera,
Abihud,[b] 4 Abishua, Naaman, Ahoah,
5 Gera, Shephuphan, and Huram. 6 These
are the sons of Ehud (they were heads of
ancestral houses of the inhabitants of Geba,
and they were carried into exile to Mana-
hath): 7 Naaman,[c] Ahijah, and Gera, that
is, Heglam,[d] who became the father of
Uzza and Ahihud. 8 And Shaharaim had
sons in the country of Moab after he had
sent away his wives Hushim and Baara.
9 He had sons by his wife Hodesh: Jobab,
Zibia, Mesha, Malcam, 10 Jeuz, Sachia, and
Mirmah. These were his sons, heads of an-
cestral houses. 11 He also had sons by Hu-
shim: Abitub and Elpaal. 12 The sons of
Elpaal: Eber, Misham, and Shemed, who
built Ono and Lod with its towns, 13 and
Beriah and Shema (they were heads of an-
cestral houses of the inhabitants of Aijalon,
who put to flight the inhabitants of Gath);
14 and Ahio, Shashak, and Jeremoth.
15 Zebadiah, Arad, Eder, 16 Michael, Ish-
pah, and Joha were sons of Beriah. 17 Zeba-
diah, Meshullam, Hizki, Heber, 18 Ishme-
rai, Izliah, and Jobab were the sons of
Elpaal. 19 Jakim, Zichri, Zabdi, 20 Elienai,
Zillethai, Eliel, 21 Adaiah, Beraiah, and
Shimrath were the sons of Shimei. 22 Ish-
pan, Eber, Eliel, 23 Abdon, Zichri, Hanan,
24 Hananiah, Elam, Anthothijah, 25 Iphde-
iah, and Penuel were the sons of Shashak.
26 Shamsherai, Shehariah, Athaliah, 27 Jaa-
reshiah, Elijah, and Zichri were the sons of
Jeroham. 28 These were the heads of ances-
tral houses, according to their generations,
chiefs. These lived in Jerusalem.

29 Jeiel[e] the father of Gibeon lived in
Gibeon, and the name of his wife was Maa-
cah. 30 His firstborn son: Abdon, then Zur,
Kish, Baal,[f] Nadab, 31 Gedor, Ahio, Ze-
cher, 32 and Mikloth, who became the fa-
ther of Shimeah. Now these also lived op-
posite their kindred in Jerusalem, with their
kindred. 33 Ner became the father of Kish,
Kish of Saul,[g] Saul[g] of Jonathan, Malchi-
shua, Abinadab, and Esh-baal; 34 and the
son of Jonathan was Merib-baal; and
Merib-baal became the father of Micah.
35 The sons of Micah: Pithon, Melech, Ta-
rea, and Ahaz. 36 Ahaz became the father of
Jehoaddah; and Jehoaddah became the fa-
ther of Alemeth, Azmaveth, and Zimri;
Zimri became the father of Moza. 37 Moza
became the father of Binea; Raphah was his
son, Eleasah his son, Azel his son. 38 Azel
had six sons, and these are their names:

a Or *Hotham*; see 7.32 *b* Or *father of Ehud*; see 8.6
c Heb *and Naaman* *d* Or *he carried them into exile*
e Compare 9.35: Heb lacks *Jeiel* *f* Gk Ms adds *Ner*;
Compare 8.33 and 9.36 *g* Or *Shaul*

7.30–40: The descendants of Asher. The genealogy may be compared with Gen 46.17 and Num 26.44–47, but much of its information is unparalleled in the Hebrew Bible.

8.1–9.1: The descendants of Benjamin. Another genealogy, fuller than that in 8.6–12. Along with Judah and Levi, Benjamin receives substantial attention from the Chronicler. The great coverage these three tribes receive reflects both the author's interests and circumstances in postexilic Judah, into which sections of Benjamin were incorporated. The author's interest in Benjamin is also reflected in the narrative portions of the Chronicler's work (2 Chr 11.1,3,12,23). **8.33–40:** Saul's genealogy is followed for eleven generations (cf. 10.1–14). **33–34:** *Esh-baal* and *Meri-baal* are variants (and probably earlier forms) of

Azrikam, Bocheru, Ishmael, Sheariah, Oba-
diah, and Hanan; all these were the sons
of Azel. 39 The sons of his brother Eshek:
Ulam his firstborn, Jeush the second, and
Eliphelet the third. 40 The sons of Ulam
were mighty warriors, archers, having
many children and grandchildren, one hun-
dred fifty. All these were Benjaminites.

9 So all Israel was enrolled by genealo-
gies; and these are written in the Book
of the Kings of Israel. And Judah was taken
into exile in Babylon because of their un-
faithfulness. 2 Now the first to live again in
their possessions in their towns were Israel-
ites, priests, Levites, and temple servants.
3 And some of the people of Judah, Ben-
jamin, Ephraim, and Manasseh lived in Je-
rusalem: 4 Uthai son of Ammihud, son of
Omri, son of Imri, son of Bani, from the
sons of Perez son of Judah. 5 And of the
Shilonites: Asaiah the firstborn, and his
sons. 6 Of the sons of Zerah: Jeuel and their
kin, six hundred ninety. 7 Of the Benjamin-
ites: Sallu son of Meshullam, son of Hoda-
viah, son of Hassenuah, 8 Ibneiah son of
Jeroham, Elah son of Uzzi, son of Michri,
and Meshullam son of Shephatiah, son of
Reuel, son of Ibnijah; 9 and their kindred
according to their generations, nine hun-
dred fifty-six. All these were heads of fami-
lies according to their ancestral houses.
10 Of the priests: Jedaiah, Jehoiarib, Ja-
chin, 11 and Azariah son of Hilkiah, son of
Meshullam, son of Zadok, son of Mera-
ioth, son of Ahitub, the chief officer of the
house of God; 12 and Adaiah son of Jero-
ham, son of Pashhur, son of Malchijah, and
Maasai son of Adiel, son of Jahzerah, son
of Meshullam, son of Meshillemith, son of
Immer; 13 besides their kindred, heads of
their ancestral houses, one thousand seven
hundred sixty, qualified for the work of the
service of the house of God.
14 Of the Levites: Shemaiah son of Has-
shub, son of Azrikam, son of Hashabiah, of
the sons of Merari; 15 and Bakbakkar, He-
resh, Galal, and Mattaniah son of Mica,
son of Zichri, son of Asaph; 16 and Obadi-
ah son of Shemaiah, son of Galal, son of
Jeduthun, and Berechiah son of Asa, son of
Elkanah, who lived in the villages of the
Netophathites.
17 The gatekeepers were: Shallum, Ak-
kub, Talmon, Ahiman; and their kindred
Shallum was the chief, 18 stationed previ-
ously in the king's gate on the east side.
These were the gatekeepers of the camp of
the Levites. 19 Shallum son of Kore, son of
Ebiasaph, son of Korah, and his kindred of
his ancestral house, the Korahites, were in
charge of the work of the service, guardians
of the thresholds of the tent, as their ances-
tors had been in charge of the camp of the
LORD, guardians of the entrance. 20 And
Phinehas son of Eleazar was chief over
them in former times; the LORD was with
him. 21 Zechariah son of Meshelemiah was
gatekeeper at the entrance of the tent of

"Ishbosheth" (2 Sam 2.8) and "Mephibosheth" (2 Sam 4.4). **9.1:** The reference to genealogical registrations concludes the Chronicler's introductions to Israel's twelve tribes, begun in 2.1–2. In the Chronicler's theology, the exile marks an important dividing line between monarchic Israel and Judah in the Persian period. *Unfaithfulness* is a Priestly term. Its use here, as the cause for exile, reflects the significance of Priestly material to this author.

9.2–34: The genealogies of Jerusalem families in postexilic Judah. This first section of this passage (vv. 2–18) is partially paralleled in Neh 11.3–19. By mentioning these families, officials, and their interrelationships, the author establishes links between the Israel of old (outlined in chs 2–8) and the Jerusalem community of his own time. **3:** The detail of people of *Ephraim and Manasseh* living in Jerusalem is not found in Nehemiah, and reflects the Chronicler's interest in all of Israel. **10–11:** The list of priests should be read in light of the preexilic succession of priests found in 6.1–15. **17–34:** The list of Levitical gatekeepers and singers, as well as the description of their duties, is unparalleled in the list of Neh 11. The passage illustrates the Chronicler's interest in continuity by insisting that the arrangements David (and here Samuel, v. 22) made on their behalf (chs 15–17; 26) were followed when the Jewish exiles returned from Babylon. The gatekeepers perform multiple functions: not only guard duty, but also administration and meeting. 22 All these, who were chosen as gatekeepers at the thresholds, were two hundred twelve. They were enrolled by genealogies in their villages. David and the seer Samuel established them in their office of trust. 23 So they and their descendants were in charge of the gates of the house of the LORD, that is, the house of the tent, as guards. 24 The gatekeepers were on the four sides, east, west, north, and south; 25 and their kindred who were in their villages were obliged to come in every seven days, in turn, to be with them; 26 for the four chief gatekeepers, who were Levites, were in charge of the chambers and the treasures of the house of God. 27 And they would spend the night near the house of God; for on them lay the duty of watching, and they had charge of opening it every morning.

28 Some of them had charge of the utensils of service, for they were required to count them when they were brought in and taken out. 29 Others of them were appointed over the furniture, and over all the holy utensils, also over the choice flour, the wine, the oil, the incense, and the spices. 30 Others, of the sons of the priests, prepared the mixing of the spices, 31 and Mattithiah, one of the Levites, the firstborn of Shallum the Korahite, was in charge of making the flat cakes. 32 Also some of their kindred of the Kohathites had charge of the rows of bread, to prepare them for each sabbath.

33 Now these are the singers, the heads of ancestral houses of the Levites, living in the chambers of the temple free from other service, for they were on duty day and night. 34 These were heads of ancestral houses of the Levites, according to their generations; these leaders lived in Jerusalem.

35 In Gibeon lived the father of Gibeon, Jeiel, and the name of his wife was Maacah. 36 His firstborn son was Abdon, then Zur, Kish, Baal, Ner, Nadab, 37 Gedor, Ahio, Zechariah, and Mikloth; 38 and Mikloth became the father of Shimeam; and these also lived opposite their kindred in Jerusalem, with their kindred. 39 Ner became the father of Kish, Kish of Saul, Saul of Jonathan, Malchishua, Abinadab, and Eshbaal; 40 and the son of Jonathan was Merib-baal; and Merib-baal became the father of Micah. 41 The sons of Micah: Pithon, Melech, Tahrea, and Ahaz;[a] 42 and Ahaz became the father of Jarah, and Jarah of Alemeth, Azmaveth, and Zimri; and Zimri became the father of Moza. 43 Moza became the father of Binea; and Rephaiah was his son, Eleasah his son, Azel his son. 44 Azel had six sons, and these are their names: Azrikam, Bocheru, Ishmael, Sheariah, Obadiah, and Hanan; these were the sons of Azel.

10 Now the Philistines fought against Israel; and the men of Israel fled before the Philistines, and fell slain on Mount Gilboa. 2 The Philistines overtook Saul and his sons; and the Philistines killed Jonathan and Abinadab and Malchishua, sons of Saul. 3 The battle pressed hard on Saul; and the archers found him, and he was wounded by the archers. 4 Then Saul said to his

a Compare 8.35: Heb lacks *and Ahaz*

even baking. **20:** *Phinehas,* cf. 25.11–13. **32:** *Rows of bread,* cf. Lev 24.5–9. **35–44:** A segue, repeating the genealogy of Saul from 8.29–38 to introduce the first king of the United Monarchy (10.1–14).

10.1–14: The demise of Saul. Verses 1–12 are parallel to 1 Sam 31.1–13. Of the many incidents in Saul's career, the Chronicler presents only the last—the story of Saul's death, assuming that the reader is generally familiar with the earlier part of the story from 1 Samuel. The evaluation of Saul's reign—the Chronicler's own addition—plays on both the Heb roots "mʿl" ("to be unfaithful, disobedient"; see 1.9) and "drš" ("to seek out, consult"), which are key terms in Chronicles. Saul dies because of his infidelity, even consulting a necromancer (1 Sam 28.3,7–25). Consultation with mediums to obtain contact with the dead is forbidden in legal texts (Lev 19.31; 20.6,27; Deut 18.11) and condemned in at least one prophetic text (Isa 8.18–19). This addition typifies the Chronicler, who must find in his sources a clear theological cause for each disaster. **4–5:** *Uncircumcised,* unlike most of their contemporaries in the Near East, the Philistines did not practice circumcision. *Fell on his sword,* suicide is infrequent in the Bible; see 2 Sam

armor-bearer, "Draw your sword, and
thrust me through with it, so that these un-
circumcised may not come and make sport
of me." But his armor-bearer was unwill-
ing, for he was terrified. So Saul took his
own sword and fell on it. 5 When his
armor-bearer saw that Saul was dead, he
also fell on his sword and died. 6 Thus Saul
died; he and his three sons and all his house
died together. 7 When all the men of Israel
who were in the valley saw that the army[a]
had fled and that Saul and his sons were
dead, they abandoned their towns and fled;
and the Philistines came and occupied
them.

8 The next day when the Philistines
came to strip the dead, they found Saul and
his sons fallen on Mount Gilboa. 9 They
stripped him and took his head and his ar-
mor, and sent messengers throughout the
land of the Philistines to carry the good
news to their idols and to the people.
10 They put his armor in the temple of their
gods, and fastened his head in the temple of
Dagon. 11 But when all Jabesh-gilead heard
everything that the Philistines had done to
Saul, 12 all the valiant warriors got up and
took away the body of Saul and the bodies
of his sons, and brought them to Jabesh.
Then they buried their bones under the oak
in Jabesh, and fasted seven days.

13 So Saul died for his unfaithfulness; he
was unfaithful to the LORD in that he did
not keep the command of the LORD; more-
over, he had consulted a medium, seeking
guidance, 14 and did not seek guidance
from the LORD. Therefore the LORD[b] put
him to death and turned the kingdom over
to David son of Jesse.

11 Then all Israel gathered together to
David at Hebron and said, "See, we
are your bone and flesh. 2 For some time
now, even while Saul was king, it was you
who commanded the army of Israel. The
LORD your God said to you: It is you who
shall be shepherd of my people Israel, you
who shall be ruler over my people Israel."
3 So all the elders of Israel came to the king
at Hebron, and David made a covenant
with them at Hebron before the LORD. And
they anointed David king over Israel, ac-
cording to the word of the LORD by Sam-
uel.

4 David and all Israel marched to Jeru-
salem, that is Jebus, where the Jebusites
were, the inhabitants of the land. 5 The in-
habitants of Jebus said to David, "You will
not come in here." Nevertheless David
took the stronghold of Zion, now the city
of David. 6 David had said, "Whoever at-
tacks the Jebusites first shall be chief and
commander." And Joab son of Zeruiah
went up first, so he became chief. 7 David
resided in the stronghold; therefore it was
called the city of David. 8 He built the city
all around, from the Millo in complete cir-

a Heb *they* *b* Heb *he*

17.23; 1 Kings 16.18; and, in the New Testament, Mt 27.5. **6:** *All his house died,* a generalization, ignoring the continuing genealogy of Saul (cf. 8.33–40; 9.35–44). **10:** *Dagon,* a Canaanite god of grain, adopted by the Philistines as one of their principal deities. **11–12:** *Jabesh-gilead,* in 1 Sam 11, Saul is acclaimed king after his rescue of this city east of the Jordan from Ammonite oppression. **14:** As elsewhere in Chronicles, the choice of kings belongs to God (e.g., 28.2–5; 29.10–12).

11.1–47: The impressive beginnings of David's reign. David does not seek out the kingship; the Israelites *gathered together to David* to make him king (v. 1). Pan-Israelite assemblies are regular occurrences in Chronicles (13.2; 2 Chr 15.9; 20.4; 23.2; 24.5; 25.5; 32.4,6). In this case, the consequences are clear. David immediately becomes king over all twelve tribes. In Samuel David first becomes king over two tribes and only after considerable struggle becomes king over the northern tribes as well (2 Sam 2–5), but this information, which casts doubt on the greatness of David, is omitted by the Chronicler. **4–9:** David, leading *all Israel* (v. 4; cf. 2 Sam 5.6), captures Jerusalem as his first public act upon being made king. By situating the capture of Jerusalem (borrowed from 2 Sam 5.6–10) at this point in the narrative, the author underscores the primacy of Jerusalem. **6:** *Joab* became the head of the army (see 18.15); his role in the capture of Jerusalem is not reported in 2 Sam 5 (cf. v. 8, another mention of Joab not in 2 Sam). **8:** David's building projects consisted essentially of a palace and fortifications in Jerusalem. The

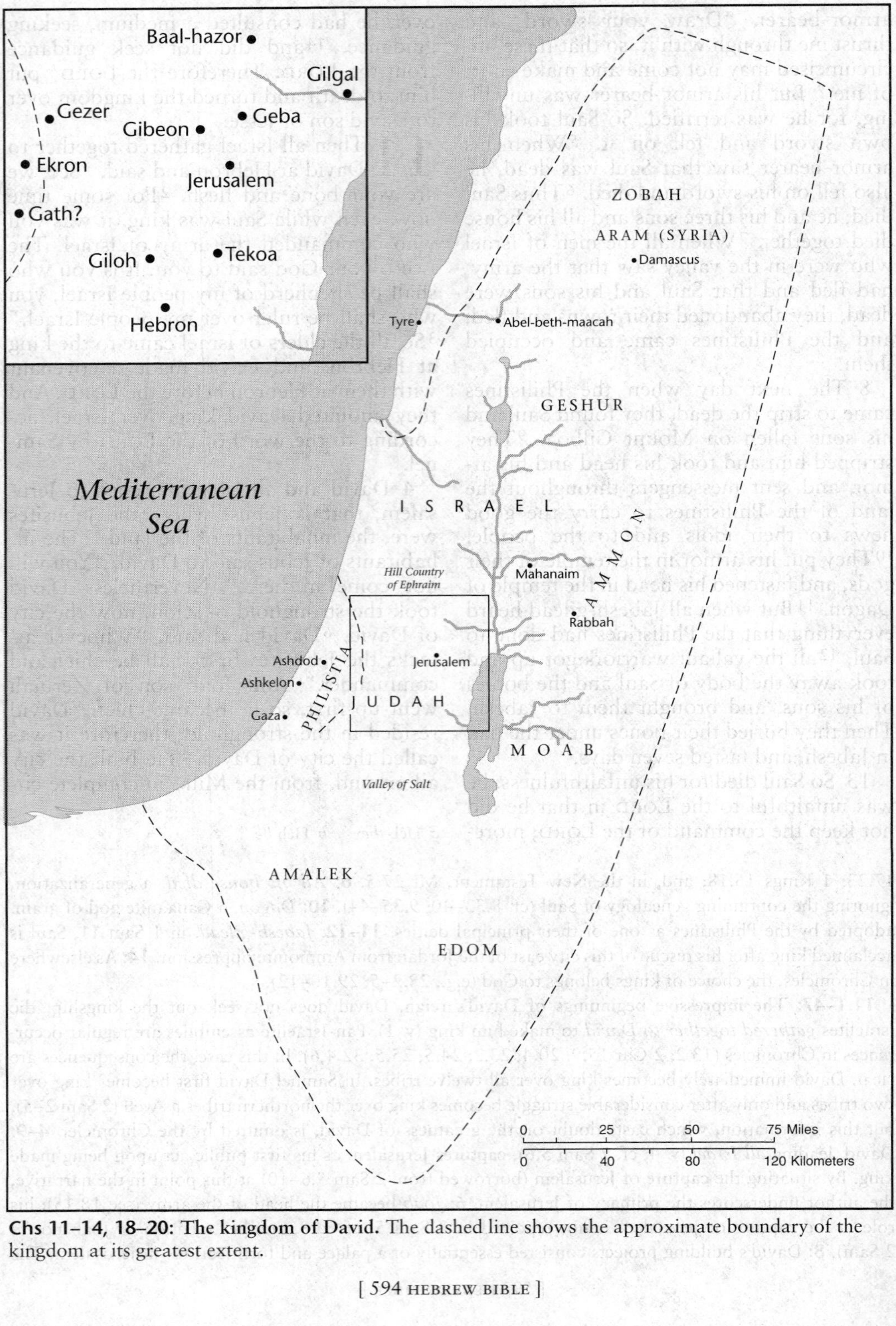

Chs 11–14, 18–20: The kingdom of David. The dashed line shows the approximate boundary of the kingdom at its greatest extent.

cuit; and Joab repaired the rest of the city.
9 And David became greater and greater,
for the LORD of hosts was with him.
10 Now these are the chiefs of David's
warriors, who gave him strong support in
his kingdom, together with all Israel, to
make him king, according to the word of
the LORD concerning Israel. 11 This is an
account of David's mighty warriors: Jasho-
beam, son of Hachmoni,[a] was chief of the
Three;[b] he wielded his spear against three
hundred whom he killed at one time.
12 And next to him among the three
warriors was Eleazar son of Dodo, the
Ahohite. 13 He was with David at Pas-
dammim when the Philistines were gath-
ered there for battle. There was a plot of
ground full of barley. Now the people had
fled from the Philistines, 14 but he and Da-
vid took their stand in the middle of the
plot, defended it, and killed the Philistines;
and the LORD saved them by a great vic-
tory.
15 Three of the thirty chiefs went down
to the rock to David at the cave of Adul-
lam, while the army of Philistines was en-
camped in the valley of Rephaim. 16 David
was then in the stronghold; and the garri-
son of the Philistines was then at Bethle-
hem. 17 David said longingly, "O that
someone would give me water to drink
from the well of Bethlehem that is by the
gate!" 18 Then the Three broke through the
camp of the Philistines, and drew water
from the well of Bethlehem that was by the
gate, and they brought it to David. But Da-
vid would not drink of it; he poured it out
to the LORD, 19 and said, "My God forbid
that I should do this. Can I drink the blood
of these men? For at the risk of their lives
they brought it." Therefore he would not
drink it. The three warriors did these
things.
20 Now Abishai,[c] the brother of Joab,
was chief of the Thirty.[d] With his spear he
fought against three hundred and killed
them, and won a name beside the Three.
21 He was the most renowned[e] of the Thir-
ty,[d] and became their commander; but he
did not attain to the Three.
22 Benaiah son of Jehoiada was a val-
iant man[f] of Kabzeel, a doer of great
deeds; he struck down two sons of[g] Ariel
of Moab. He also went down and killed a
lion in a pit on a day when snow had fallen.
23 And he killed an Egyptian, a man of great
stature, five cubits tall. The Egyptian had in
his hand a spear like a weaver's beam; but
Benaiah went against him with a staff,
snatched the spear out of the Egyptian's
hand, and killed him with his own spear.
24 Such were the things Benaiah son of Je-
hoiada did, and he won a name beside the
three warriors. 25 He was renowned among
the Thirty, but he did not attain to the
Three. And David put him in charge of his
bodyguard.
26 The warriors of the armies were Asa-
hel brother of Joab, Elhanan son of Dodo
of Bethlehem, 27 Shammoth of Harod,[h]
Helez the Pelonite, 28 Ira son of Ikkesh of
Tekoa, Abiezer of Anathoth, 29 Sibbecai the
Hushathite, Ilai the Ahohite, 30 Maharai of
Netophah, Heled son of Baanah of Neto-
phah, 31 Ithai son of Ribai of Gibeah of the

a Or *a Hachmonite* *b* Compare 2 Sam 23.8: Heb *Thirty* or *captains* *c* Gk Vg Tg Compare 2 Sam 23.18: Heb *Abshai* *d* Syr: Heb *Three* *e* Compare 2 Sam 23.19: Heb *more renowned among the two* *f* Syr: Heb *the son of a valiant man* *g* See 2 Sam 23.20: Heb lacks *sons of* *h* Compare 2 Sam 23.25: Heb *the Harorite*

Chronicler attributes more building activity to David than do the authors of Samuel (2 Sam 5.9,11; 7.2; 1 Chr 17.1; 2 Chr 2.2). *Millo,* probably "fill" for artificial terraces. **10–47:** The list of *the chiefs of David's warriors* largely follows in the appendix to 2 Samuel (23.8–39). It is moved here, early in David's reign, to illustrate the consolidation of David's kingship. Israel's call to David to serve as king is followed by a visible demonstration of military support from various commanders, *together with all Israel* (v. 10). Little is otherwise known about these heroes. **18:** *He poured it out to the LORD* as a libation (1 Sam 7.6; Jer 44.16–18); such water libations became especially important in the later Second Temple period, especially in connection with the festival of booths (Sukkot). See 5.14. **41a:** *Uriah,* the only reference in Chroni-

Benjaminites, Benaiah of Pirathon, 32 Hurai
of the wadis of Gaash, Abiel the Arbathite,
33 Azmaveth of Baharum, Eliahba of Shaal-
bon, 34 Hashem[a] the Gizonite, Jonathan
son of Shagee the Hararite, 35 Ahiam son
of Sachar the Hararite, Eliphal son of Ur,
36 Hepher the Mecherathite, Ahijah the Pel-
onite, 37 Hezro of Carmel, Naarai son of
Ezbai, 38 Joel the brother of Nathan, Mib-
har son of Hagri, 39 Zelek the Ammonite,
Naharai of Beeroth, the armor-bearer of
Joab son of Zeruiah, 40 Ira the Ithrite, Ga-
reb the Ithrite, 41 Uriah the Hittite, Zabad
son of Ahlai, 42 Adina son of Shiza the Reu-
benite, a leader of the Reubenites, and thir-
ty with him, 43 Hanan son of Maacah, and
Joshaphat the Mithnite, 44 Uzzia the Ashte-
rathite, Shama and Jeiel sons of Hotham
the Aroerite, 45 Jediael son of Shimri, and
his brother Joha the Tizite, 46 Eliel the Ma-
havite, and Jeribai and Joshaviah sons of
Elnaam, and Ithmah the Moabite, 47 Eliel,
and Obed, and Jaasiel the Mezobaite.

12 The following are those who came
to David at Ziklag, while he could
not move about freely because of Saul son
of Kish; they were among the mighty war-
riors who helped him in war. 2 They were
archers, and could shoot arrows and sling
stones with either the right hand or the left;
they were Benjaminites, Saul's kindred.
3 The chief was Ahiezer, then Joash, both
sons of Shemaah of Gibeah; also Jeziel and
Pelet sons of Azmaveth; Beracah, Jehu of
Anathoth, 4 Ishmaiah of Gibeon, a warrior
among the Thirty and a leader over the
Thirty; Jeremiah,[b] Jahaziel, Johanan, Joza-
bad of Gederah, 5 Eluzai,[c] Jerimoth, Beali-
ah, Shemariah, Shephatiah the Haruphite;
6 Elkanah, Isshiah, Azarel, Joezer, and Ja-
shobeam, the Korahites; 7 and Joelah and
Zebadiah, sons of Jeroham of Gedor.

8 From the Gadites there went over to
David at the stronghold in the wilderness
mighty and experienced warriors, expert
with shield and spear, whose faces were
like the faces of lions, and who were swift
as gazelles on the mountains: 9 Ezer the
chief, Obadiah second, Eliab third, 10 Mish-
mannah fourth, Jeremiah fifth, 11 Attai
sixth, Eliel seventh, 12 Johanan eighth, Elza-
bad ninth, 13 Jeremiah tenth, Machbannai
eleventh. 14 These Gadites were officers of
the army, the least equal to a hundred and
the greatest to a thousand. 15 These are the
men who crossed the Jordan in the first
month, when it was overflowing all its
banks, and put to flight all those in the val-
leys, to the east and to the west.

16 Some Benjaminites and Judahites
came to the stronghold to David. 17 David
went out to meet them and said to them, "If
you have come to me in friendship, to help
me, then my heart will be knit to you; but
if you have come to betray me to my adver-
saries, though my hands have done no
wrong, then may the God of our ancestors
see and give judgment." 18 Then the spirit
came upon Amasai, chief of the Thirty, and
he said,

"We are yours, O David;
  and with you, O son of Jesse!
Peace, peace to you,
  and peace to the one who helps
    you!

a Compare Gk and 2 Sam 23.32: Heb *the sons of Hashem* *b* Heb verse 5 *c* Heb verse 6

cles to the man known in 2 Sam 11–12 as the husband of Bathsheba before David. **41b–47:** These verses are unparalleled in 2 Sam 23.8–39.

12.1–40: David's national prestige and power grow. Warriors from Benjamin (vv. 1–8), Gad (vv. 9–16), Benjamin and Judah (vv. 17–19), and Manasseh (vv. 20–23) rally to David, consolidating his rule. This is set during an early stage of David's career (v. 1), suggesting that the Benjaminites defected to David while Saul was still alive (cf. 2 Sam 2.12–32). This material has few parallels in Samuel, and scholars debate whether it is based on other sources or is an imaginative composition of the Chronicler. **1:** *Ziklag,* see 1 Sam 27.6; 30. **2:** Cf. Judg 20.16. **8:** *Like . . . lions,* cf. Deut 33.20. **15:** *The first month,* in the spring. **18:** *The spirit came upon,* lit. "a spirit clothed"; cf. Judg 6.34; 2 Chr 24.20. The acclamation of Amasai, *peace, peace to you,* contrasts with the anti-David sentiment sometimes found in Samuel

For your God is the one who helps
you."

Then David received them, and made them
officers of his troops.

19 Some of the Manassites deserted to
David when he came with the Philistines
for the battle against Saul. (Yet he did not
help them, for the rulers of the Philistines
took counsel and sent him away, saying,
"He will desert to his master Saul at the
cost of our heads.") 20 As he went to Ziklag
these Manassites deserted to him: Adnah,
Jozabad, Jediael, Michael, Jozabad, Elihu,
and Zillethai, chiefs of the thousands in
Manasseh. 21 They helped David against
the band of raiders,[a] for they were all war-
riors and commanders in the army. 22 In-
deed from day to day people kept coming
to David to help him, until there was a
great army, like an army of God.

23 These are the numbers of the divi-
sions of the armed troops who came to Da-
vid in Hebron to turn the kingdom of Saul
over to him, according to the word of the
LORD. 24 The people of Judah bearing
shield and spear numbered six thousand
eight hundred armed troops. 25 Of the Sim-
eonites, mighty warriors, seven thousand
one hundred. 26 Of the Levites four thou-
sand six hundred. 27 Jehoiada, leader of the
house of Aaron, and with him three thou-
sand seven hundred. 28 Zadok, a young
warrior, and twenty-two commanders
from his own ancestral house. 29 Of the
Benjaminites, the kindred of Saul, three
thousand, of whom the majority had con-
tinued to keep their allegiance to the house
of Saul. 30 Of the Ephraimites, twenty thou-
sand eight hundred, mighty warriors, nota-
bles in their ancestral houses. 31 Of the half-
tribe of Manasseh, eighteen thousand, who
were expressly named to come and make
David king. 32 Of Issachar, those who had
understanding of the times, to know what
Israel ought to do, two hundred chiefs, and
all their kindred under their command.
33 Of Zebulun, fifty thousand seasoned
troops, equipped for battle with all the
weapons of war, to help David[b] with sin-
gleness of purpose. 34 Of Naphtali, a thou-
sand commanders, with whom there were
thirty-seven thousand armed with shield
and spear. 35 Of the Danites, twenty-eight
thousand six hundred equipped for battle.
36 Of Asher, forty thousand seasoned
troops ready for battle. 37 Of the Reuben-
ites and Gadites and the half-tribe of Ma-
nasseh from beyond the Jordan, one hun-
dred twenty thousand armed with all the
weapons of war.

38 All these, warriors arrayed in battle
order, came to Hebron with full intent to
make David king over all Israel; likewise all
the rest of Israel were of a single mind to
make David king. 39 They were there with
David for three days, eating and drinking,

a Or *as officers of his troops* *b* Gk: Heb lacks *David*

(e.g., 2 Sam 20.1). Because of the divine support for David, those who support David may also be blessed. **19–20:** *The battle against Saul,* this is the battle referred to in ch 10. The Chronicler here summarizes 1 Sam 29.1–30.1. **22:** *An army* (lit. "camp") *of God,* either expressing the superlative, or referring to the heavenly armies (e.g., see Deut 33.2; Josh 5.14). **23:** *In Hebron,* see 11.1. **23–39a:** The beginning of v. 23, *these are the numbers,* introduces a long stylized list (vv. 25–38) of David's armed forces. The tribal muster, totaling thirteen, is the fullest tally of the Israelite tribes in the Hebrew Bible. The active allegiance shown by Israelite military officials to David accords with divine will and results in a smooth transfer of power (10.14; 11.3,10). The heroic portrayal of intertribal solidarity (v. 38) contrasts with the tribal disorganization and civil strife found in Judges. **28:** *Zadok, a young warrior,* probably to be identified as the priest who served with Abiathar at the court of David (15.11; 2 Sam 8.17) and who subsequently enjoyed Solomon's exclusive patronage following Solomon's purge of Abiathar (1 Kings 2.35; cf. 29.22). **39–40:** Elaborate feasts, like the one celebrated by David and representatives from the various Israelite tribes, punctuate high points in Israelite and Judean history (15.25–16.3; 29.20–22; 2 Chr 7.8–10; 20.27–28; 29.30–36; 30.21–27) and also play a crucial role in Esther, also from the Persian period. The nationwide celebration concludes the initial phase of David's reign.

for their kindred had provided for them.
40 And also their neighbors, from as far
away as Issachar and Zebulun and Naphta-
li, came bringing food on donkeys, camels,
mules, and oxen—abundant provisions of
meal, cakes of figs, clusters of raisins, wine,
oil, oxen, and sheep, for there was joy in
Israel.

13 David consulted with the com-
manders of the thousands and of the
hundreds, with every leader. 2 David said to
the whole assembly of Israel, "If it seems
good to you, and if it is the will of the LORD
our God, let us send abroad to our kindred
who remain in all the land of Israel, includ-
ing the priests and Levites in the cities that
have pasture lands, that they may come to-
gether to us. 3 Then let us bring again the
ark of our God to us; for we did not turn to
it in the days of Saul." 4 The whole assem-
bly agreed to do so, for the thing pleased all
the people.

5 So David assembled all Israel from the
Shihor of Egypt to Lebo-hamath, to bring
the ark of God from Kiriath-jearim. 6 And
David and all Israel went up to Baalah, that
is, to Kiriath-jearim, which belongs to Ju-
dah, to bring up from there the ark of God,
the LORD, who is enthroned on the cheru-
bim, which is called by his[a] name. 7 They
carried the ark of God on a new cart, from
the house of Abinadab, and Uzzah and
Ahio[b] were driving the cart. 8 David and
all Israel were dancing before God with all
their might, with song and lyres and harps
and tambourines and cymbals and trum-
pets.

9 When they came to the threshing floor
of Chidon, Uzzah put out his hand to hold
the ark, for the oxen shook it. 10 The anger
of the LORD was kindled against Uzzah; he
struck him down because he put out his
hand to the ark; and he died there before
God. 11 David was angry because the LORD
had burst out against Uzzah; so that place
is called Perez-uzzah[c] to this day. 12 David
was afraid of God that day; he said, "How
can I bring the ark of God into my care?"
13 So David did not take the ark into his
care into the city of David; he took it in-
stead to the house of Obed-edom the Git-
tite. 14 The ark of God remained with the
household of Obed-edom in his house three
months, and the LORD blessed the house-
hold of Obed-edom and all that he had.

14 King Hiram of Tyre sent messengers
to David, along with cedar logs, and
masons and carpenters to build a house for

a Heb lacks *his* *b* Or *and his brother* *c* That is *Bursting Out Against Uzzah*

13.1–14: David and the ark, Part 1. Having been firmly and unanimously established as king, David leads all Israel in the attempt to retrieve a national symbol of Israel's religion and bring it to the new capital. **2:** The Chronicler's Levites live at various sites within Israel's tribal territories (6.54–81). Because this priestly tribe is an essential component of Israel and Israel's most sacred symbol to Jerusalem must be transferred properly to Jerusalem, the Chronicler adds to his source participation of the priests and Levites, along with an emphasis on all Israel. **3:** No reference is made to the capture of the ark by the Philistines (cf. 1 Sam 4.11–7.1); here its neglect is implicitly another example of Saul's unfaithfulness (see 10.13–14). **5:** *From the Shihor of Egypt* (probably the easternmost branch of the Nile) *to Lebo-hamath* (in Syria), the northern and southern limits of Israel (cf. 2 Chr 7.8). **6–14:** This material is largely drawn from 2 Sam 6.2–11. **6:** *The ark,* a portable box, was a unifying religious symbol in the premonarchic period (Josh 3.1–17; 4.1–18; 1 Sam 4.1–7.1). According to Ex 25.10–21; 37.1–9, its construction was ordained by God and implemented by Moses. *Enthroned on the cherubim,* see 1 Sam 4.4n. **11:** *Burst out,* see note *c.* **13:** The *city of David* refers to Mount Zion, the section of Jerusalem fortified by David and renamed in his honor (11.7). In Chronicles *Obed-edom* is a Levite, who functions as a gatekeeper (15.18,24) and a musician (15.21; 16.5; 26.4–8). **14:** The blessing on Obed-edom's house hints that the setback suffered by David is only temporary.

14.1–7: David's success in Jerusalem (cf. 2 Sam 5.11–16). According to 1 Kings 5.15–26 (cf. 2 Chr 2.2–15), Hiram (Huram in Chronicles) had very good relations with David. The tie between blessings for David and blessings for Israel anticipates Nathan's dynastic oracle (17.1–17). **3:** Accumulating wives and

him. 2David then perceived that the LORD
had established him as king over Israel, and
that his kingdom was highly exalted for the
sake of his people Israel.
3 David took more wives in Jerusalem,
and David became the father of more sons
and daughters. 4These are the names of the
children whom he had in Jerusalem: Sham-
mua, Shobab, and Nathan; Solomon, 5Ib-
har, Elishua, and Elpelet; 6Nogah, Nepheg,
and Japhia; 7Elishama, Beeliada, and
Eliphelet.
8 When the Philistines heard that David
had been anointed king over all Israel, all
the Philistines went up in search of David;
and David heard of it and went out against
them. 9Now the Philistines had come and
made a raid in the valley of Rephaim. 10Da-
vid inquired of God, "Shall I go up against
the Philistines? Will you give them into my
hand?" The LORD said to him, "Go up, and
I will give them into your hand." 11So he
went up to Baal-perazim, and David de-
feated them there. David said, "God has
burst out[a] against my enemies by my
hand, like a bursting flood." Therefore that
place is called Baal-perazim.[b] 12They
abandoned their gods there, and at David's
command they were burned.
13 Once again the Philistines made a
raid in the valley. 14When David again in-
quired of God, God said to him, "You shall
not go up after them; go around and come
on them opposite the balsam trees. 15When
you hear the sound of marching in the tops
of the balsam trees, then go out to battle;
for God has gone out before you to strike
down the army of the Philistines." 16David
did as God had commanded him, and they
struck down the Philistine army from Gibe-
on to Gezer. 17The fame of David went out
into all lands, and the LORD brought the
fear of him on all nations.
15 David[c] built houses for himself in
the city of David, and he prepared a
place for the ark of God and pitched a tent
for it. 2Then David commanded that no
one but the Levites were to carry the ark of
God, for the LORD had chosen them to car-
ry the ark of the LORD and to minister to
him forever. 3David assembled all Israel in

a Heb *paraz* *b* That is *Lord of Bursting Out*
c Heb *He*

progeny is consistently a positive sign of stature in Chronicles (25.5; 26.4–5; 2 Chr 11.18–23; 13.21; 14.3–7). For David's sons, see 3.1–9.

14.8–17: Philistine attacks (cf. 2 Sam 5.17–25). If the mishandling of the ark (13.9–11) represented an internal challenge to the establishment of Jerusalem's worship, the Philistine aggressions were an external threat to the viability of David's rule. The two narratives detailing David's exploits against the Philistines are replete with holy-war phraseology, reflecting the notion that the LORD fights on behalf of his people and secures victory for them (Ex 14.4,18; Josh 11.2,24; Judg 3.28; 4.7,17; 18.10; 20.28; 1 Sam 14.12,23; 23.4). **12:** In 2 Sam 5.21, David carries these images home. In having the images consigned to fire, the Chronicler has David act in accordance with Deuteronomic law (Deut 7.25; 12.3). **16:** *From Gibeon to Gezer,* about 28 km (18 mi), a limited area. **17:** International respect denotes divine blessing (2 Chr 9.5–8,23; 17.10; 26.8,15; 32.23).

15.1–16.3: David and the ark, Part 2. Having been successful in war and blessed by God, David turns his attention again to the matter of the ark. In the ancient Near East successful kings were expected to honor the deities who led them by supporting and endowing places of worship. Much of chs 15–16, which supplements material from 2 Sam 6 with original material concerning the Levites, elaborates on this very point. **15.1:** The houses David builds for himself most likely refer to domiciles in addition to the palace built by Huram of Tyre (14.1). David's construction activity establishes a positive pattern for other kings to follow (2 Chr 11.5–12; 14.6; 26.2; 32.27–30). **2:** David's command that *no one but the Levites* carry the ark responds to Uzzah's unfortunate death (13.10) through the lens of the Priestly material (Num 4.4–15; 7.9), the implication being that the proper personnel had not been involved in the first attempt to bring the ark into the City of David (v. 13). The following verses detail what personnel and actions David deems necessary to install the ark successfully. **3:** The reference to *a place* for the ark of God bears connotations of a sacred precinct or sanctuary (Deut 12.5,11; 14.23–25; 15.20; Josh 9.27; 1 Chr 21.22,25; 2 Chr 3.1).

Jerusalem to bring up the ark of the LORD
to its place, which he had prepared for it.
4 Then David gathered together the descen-
dants of Aaron and the Levites: 5 of the sons
of Kohath, Uriel the chief, with one hun-
dred twenty of his kindred; 6 of the sons of
Merari, Asaiah the chief, with two hundred
twenty of his kindred; 7 of the sons of Ger-
shom, Joel the chief, with one hundred thir-
ty of his kindred; 8 of the sons of Elizaphan,
Shemaiah the chief, with two hundred of
his kindred; 9 of the sons of Hebron, Eliel
the chief, with eighty of his kindred; 10 of
the sons of Uzziel, Amminadab the chief,
with one hundred twelve of his kindred.
11 David summoned the priests Zadok
and Abiathar, and the Levites Uriel, Asa-
iah, Joel, Shemaiah, Eliel, and Amminadab.
12 He said to them, "You are the heads of
families of the Levites; sanctify yourselves,
you and your kindred, so that you may
bring up the ark of the LORD, the God of
Israel, to the place that I have prepared for
it. 13 Because you did not carry it the first
time,[a] the LORD our God burst out against
us, because we did not give it proper care."
14 So the priests and the Levites sanctified
themselves to bring up the ark of the LORD,
the God of Israel. 15 And the Levites carried
the ark of God on their shoulders with the
poles, as Moses had commanded according
to the word of the LORD.
16 David also commanded the chiefs of
the Levites to appoint their kindred as the
singers to play on musical instruments, on
harps and lyres and cymbals, to raise loud
sounds of joy. 17 So the Levites appointed
Heman son of Joel; and of his kindred
Asaph son of Berechiah; and of the sons of
Merari, their kindred, Ethan son of Kusha-
iah; 18 and with them their kindred of the
second order, Zechariah, Jaaziel, Shemira-
moth, Jehiel, Unni, Eliab, Benaiah, Maase-
iah, Mattithiah, Eliphelehu, and Mikneiah,
and the gatekeepers Obed-edom and Jeiel.
19 The singers Heman, Asaph, and Ethan
were to sound bronze cymbals; 20 Zechari-
ah, Aziel, Shemiramoth, Jehiel, Unni, Eliab,
Maaseiah, and Benaiah were to play harps
according to Alamoth; 21 but Mattithiah,
Eliphelehu, Mikneiah, Obed-edom, Jeiel,
and Azaziah were to lead with lyres accord-
ing to the Sheminith. 22 Chenaniah, leader
of the Levites in music, was to direct the
music, for he understood it. 23 Berechiah
and Elkanah were to be gatekeepers for the
ark. 24 Shebaniah, Joshaphat, Nethanel,
Amasai, Zechariah, Benaiah, and Eliezer,
the priests, were to blow the trumpets be-
fore the ark of God. Obed-edom and Jehi-
ah also were to be gatekeepers for the ark.
25 So David and the elders of Israel, and

a Meaning of Heb uncertain

11: The two priests *Zadok and Abiathar* appear together during the first part of the reign of David (15.29,35; 18.16; 19.11; 20.25). Each of these priests headed or represented major priestly houses. **13:** The Chronicler plays on Hebrew roots "prṣ," "to break out" (13.3,11; 14.11; 15.13) and "drš," "to seek." The earlier attempt to redress neglect of the ark—"for we did not seek (drš) it in the days of Saul" (13.3)—was brought to a swift end by the divine outbreak ("prṣ"; 13.10–11) against Uzza. As later events made clear, the problem was not Israel's communal decision "to seek" the ark, but the manner in which the people involved handled the arrangements. In the new attempt David insists on the intimate involvement of the priests and Levites to rectify the deficiency. **15:** *On their shoulders with the poles,* the Chronicler asserts that Mosaic law was followed (Num 7.9). **16:** *Musical instruments* figure prominently in the Chronicler's ritual liturgies (16.42; 2 Chr 5.13; 7.6; 23.13; 34.12). In some texts the instruments are associated with David himself (2 Chr 29.24,26–27; Neh 12.36; cf. Am 6.5). Though David could not build the Temple (ch 17, 2 Sam 7), the Chronicler emphasizes here and elsewhere that David initiated the project, in their case by establishing the guilds of Levitical Temple singers. **18:** Many of these singers are mentioned again in vv. 20–21 and 16.5–6. **20–21:** *Alamoth* and *Sheminith* are obscure musical terms (see Ps 6.1; 12.1; 46.1). **25–28:** The Chronicler rewrites 2 Sam 6.12–15 to underscore the broad support for David in his campaign to complete the transfer of the ark. The elaborate apparel worn by the Levites in Chronicles contrasts markedly with that depicted in Samuel (see Ex 28.6–14,39–43; Sir 45.8).

the commanders of the thousands, went to
bring up the ark of the covenant of the
LORD from the house of Obed-edom with
rejoicing. 26 And because God helped the
Levites who were carrying the ark of the
covenant of the LORD, they sacrificed seven
bulls and seven rams. 27 David was clothed
with a robe of fine linen, as also were all the
Levites who were carrying the ark, and the
singers, and Chenaniah the leader of the
music of the singers; and David wore a lin-
en ephod. 28 So all Israel brought up the ark
of the covenant of the LORD with shouting,
to the sound of the horn, trumpets, and
cymbals, and made loud music on harps
and lyres.

29 As the ark of the covenant of the
LORD came to the city of David, Michal
daughter of Saul looked out of the window,
and saw King David leaping and dancing;
and she despised him in her heart.

16 They brought in the ark of God, and
set it inside the tent that David had
pitched for it; and they offered burnt offer-
ings and offerings of well-being before
God. 2 When David had finished offering
the burnt offerings and the offerings of
well-being, he blessed the people in the
name of the LORD; 3 and he distributed to
every person in Israel—man and woman
alike—to each a loaf of bread, a portion of
meat,[a] and a cake of raisins.

4 He appointed certain of the Levites as
ministers before the ark of the LORD, to
invoke, to thank, and to praise the LORD,
the God of Israel. 5 Asaph was the chief,
and second to him Zechariah, Jeiel, Shemir-
amoth, Jehiel, Mattithiah, Eliab, Benaiah,
Obed-edom, and Jeiel, with harps and
lyres; Asaph was to sound the cymbals,
6 and the priests Benaiah and Jahaziel were
to blow trumpets regularly, before the ark
of the covenant of God.

7 Then on that day David first appoint-
ed the singing of praises to the LORD by
Asaph and his kindred.

8 O give thanks to the LORD, call on
his name,
make known his deeds among the
peoples.
9 Sing to him, sing praises to him,
tell of all his wonderful works.
10 Glory in his holy name;
let the hearts of those who seek the
LORD rejoice.
11 Seek the LORD and his strength,
seek his presence continually.
12 Remember the wonderful works he
has done,
his miracles, and the judgments he
uttered,
13 O offspring of his servant Israel,[b]
children of Jacob, his chosen ones.

14 He is the LORD our God;
his judgments are in all the earth.
15 Remember his covenant forever,
the word that he commanded, for a
thousand generations,
16 the covenant that he made with
Abraham,
his sworn promise to Isaac,
17 which he confirmed to Jacob as a
statute,
to Israel as an everlasting covenant,
18 saying, "To you I will give the land
of Canaan
as your portion for an inheritance."

a Compare Gk Syr Vg: Meaning of Heb uncertain
b Another reading is *Abraham* (compare Ps 105.6)

15.29–16.3: Michal and all Israel. A significant abridgment of 2 Sam 6.16–23, omitting the details of how Michal mocked David.

16.4–43: Staffing the national sanctuaries. With the ark successfully elevated to the place David prepared for it, David designates certain Levites and priests to officiate there. He also staffs the tabernacle at the *high place* in Gibeon (vv. 39–42). **7–36:** The *praises* David instructs the Levites to sing are a medley of extracts, with some variations, from the Psalms: vv. 8–22, cf. Ps 105.1–15; vv. 23–33, cf. Ps 96; vv. 34–36, cf. Ps 106.1,47–48. By the period of the Chronicler, some form of the book of Psalms probably already existed as a liturgical collection, and possibly was already attributed to David.

19 When they were few in number,
of little account, and strangers in
the land,[a]
20 wandering from nation to nation,
from one kingdom to another
people,
21 he allowed no one to oppress them;
he rebuked kings on their account,
22 saying, "Do not touch my anointed
ones;
do my prophets no harm."

23 Sing to the LORD, all the earth.
Tell of his salvation from day to
day.
24 Declare his glory among the nations,
his marvelous works among all the
peoples.
25 For great is the LORD, and greatly to
be praised;
he is to be revered above all gods.
26 For all the gods of the peoples are
idols,
but the LORD made the heavens.
27 Honor and majesty are before him;
strength and joy are in his place.

28 Ascribe to the LORD, O families of
the peoples,
ascribe to the LORD glory and
strength.
29 Ascribe to the LORD the glory due his
name;
bring an offering, and come before
him.
Worship the LORD in holy splendor;
30 tremble before him, all the earth.
The world is firmly established; it
shall never be moved.
31 Let the heavens be glad, and let the
earth rejoice,
and let them say among the
nations, "The LORD is king!"
32 Let the sea roar, and all that fills it;
let the field exult, and everything in
it.
33 Then shall the trees of the forest sing
for joy
before the LORD, for he comes to
judge the earth.
34 O give thanks to the LORD, for he is
good;
for his steadfast love endures
forever.

35 Say also:
"Save us, O God of our salvation,
and gather and rescue us from
among the nations,
that we may give thanks to your holy
name,
and glory in your praise.
36 Blessed be the LORD, the God of
Israel,
from everlasting to everlasting."
Then all the people said "Amen!" and
praised the LORD.

37 David left Asaph and his kinsfolk
there before the ark of the covenant of the
LORD to minister regularly before the ark
as each day required, 38 and also Obed-
edom and his[b] sixty-eight kinsfolk; while
Obed-edom son of Jeduthun and Hosah
were to be gatekeepers. 39 And he left the
priest Zadok and his kindred the priests be-
fore the tabernacle of the LORD in the high
place that was at Gibeon, 40 to offer burnt
offerings to the LORD on the altar of burnt
offering regularly, morning and evening,
according to all that is written in the law
of the LORD that he commanded Israel.
41 With them were Heman and Jeduthun,
and the rest of those chosen and expressly
named to render thanks to the LORD, for
his steadfast love endures forever. 42 He-
man and Jeduthun had with them trumpets

a Heb *in it* *b* Gk Syr Vg: Heb *their*

37–43: David provides for both the ark in Jerusalem and the tabernacle at Gibeon. The Chronicler does not deem the Gibeon shrine to be inherently illicit. The sacrifices performed there by Zadok and his priests accorded with *all that is written in the law of the LORD* (v. 40). Like the newly dedicated ministry of praise associated with the ark in Jerusalem, the Gibeon precinct has its own singers and musicians, authorized to praise God (v. 42). Two guilds of singers, represented by Heman and Jeduthun, serve at Gibeon, while the third guild of singers, represented by Asaph (v. 37) serves in Jerusalem. Only after the

and cymbals for the music, and instruments
for sacred song. The sons of Jeduthun were
appointed to the gate.
43 Then all the people departed to their
homes, and David went home to bless his
household.

17 Now when David settled in his
house, David said to the prophet
Nathan, "I am living in a house of cedar,
but the ark of the covenant of the LORD is
under a tent." 2 Nathan said to David, "Do
all that you have in mind, for God is with
you."
3 But that same night the word of the
LORD came to Nathan, saying: 4 Go and tell
my servant David: Thus says the LORD:
You shall not build me a house to live in.
5 For I have not lived in a house since the
day I brought out Israel to this very day,
but I have lived in a tent and a tabernacle.[a]
6 Wherever I have moved about among all
Israel, did I ever speak a word with any of
the judges of Israel, whom I commanded to
shepherd my people, saying, Why have you
not built me a house of cedar? 7 Now there-
fore thus you shall say to my servant David:
Thus says the LORD of hosts: I took you
from the pasture, from following the sheep,
to be ruler over my people Israel; 8 and I
have been with you wherever you went,
and have cut off all your enemies before
you; and I will make for you a name, like
the name of the great ones of the earth. 9 I
will appoint a place for my people Israel,
and will plant them, so that they may live in
their own place, and be disturbed no more;
and evildoers shall wear them down no
more, as they did formerly, 10 from the time
that I appointed judges over my people Is-
rael; and I will subdue all your enemies.
Moreover I declare to you that the LORD
will build you a house. 11 When your days
are fulfilled to go to be with your ancestors,
I will raise up your offspring after you, one
of your own sons, and I will establish his
kingdom. 12 He shall build a house for me,
and I will establish his throne forever. 13 I
will be a father to him, and he shall be a son
to me. I will not take my steadfast love
from him, as I took it from him who was
before you, 14 but I will confirm him in my
house and in my kingdom forever, and his
throne shall be established forever. 15 In ac-
cordance with all these words and all this
vision, Nathan spoke to David.
16 Then King David went in and sat
before the LORD, and said, "Who am I,
O LORD God, and what is my house, that
you have brought me thus far? 17 And even

a Gk 2 Sam 7.6: Heb *but I have been from tent to tent and from tabernacle*

construction of the long awaited Temple will worship outside Jerusalem be prohibited (2 Chr 1.3–6; 5.5). **43:** Taken from 2 Sam 6.19–20, a continuation of v. 3.

17.1–15: The promises to David. The narration largely follows 2 Sam 7.1–16. *Under a tent,* see Ex 26.1–2,7; Num 4.21–28. **2:** Nathan here is offering his personal opinion, which is corrected by God in the prophecy that follows. David's lack of suitability for this project is explained later in 22.7–10. **5:** After the Exodus, Israel's system of worship was mobile. The roving nature of God's presence with Israel was consistent with the mobility of Israel itself. **8–9:** The Chronicler, like the Deuteronomist (1 Kings 5.17–18), associates national stability and peace with the establishment of a permanent sanctuary in the land. In this manner, Nathan's oracle points forward to the reign of Solomon, an unprecedented age of peace, prosperity, and international prestige (1 Kings 4.20; 5.4; 8.66; 1 Chr 22.9,18; 2 Chr 1.7–18; 8.1–9,31). **10:** In speaking of the LORD building a house for David, the prophet develops a wordplay on the different connotations of Hebrew "bayit" ("house," "temple," "dynasty"). **13:** *I will be a father to him,* a formula of adoption (2 Sam 7.14; Ps 2.7–8; Isa 9.6; cf. Ps 89.26). *I will not take my steadfast love from him,* the guarantee of succession is not predicated upon the loyalty of the sons. In fact, the second part of 2 Sam 7.14, which stresses that the individual Davidic king may be punished, is lacking here, further highlighting the Chronicler's positive vision of Davidic kingship. **14:** *In my kingdom forever,* God manifests his kingship through the kingdom of David and his heirs (17.14; 28.5; 29.11; 2 Chr 13.8; cf. 2 Sam 7.16).

17.16–27: David's prayer. The narration largely follows 2 Sam 7.17–29. **21:** God's incomparability

this was a small thing in your sight, O God;
you have also spoken of your servant's
house for a great while to come. You re-
gard me as someone of high rank,[a]
O LORD God! 18 And what more can David
say to you for honoring your servant? You
know your servant. 19 For your servant's
sake, O LORD, and according to your own
heart, you have done all these great deeds,
making known all these great things.
20 There is no one like you, O LORD, and
there is no God besides you, according to
all that we have heard with our ears.
21 Who is like your people Israel, one na-
tion on the earth whom God went to re-
deem to be his people, making for yourself
a name for great and terrible things, in driv-
ing out nations before your people whom
you redeemed from Egypt? 22 And you
made your people Israel to be your people
forever; and you, O LORD, became their
God.

23 "And now, O LORD, as for the word
that you have spoken concerning your ser-
vant and concerning his house, let it be
established forever, and do as you have
promised. 24 Thus your name will be estab-
lished and magnified forever in the saying,
'The LORD of hosts, the God of Israel, is
Israel's God'; and the house of your servant
David will be established in your presence.
25 For you, my God, have revealed to your
servant that you will build a house for him;
therefore your servant has found it possible
to pray before you. 26 And now, O LORD,
you are God, and you have promised this
good thing to your servant; 27 therefore
may it please you to bless the house of your
servant, that it may continue forever before
you. For you, O LORD, have blessed and
are blessed[b] forever."

18 Some time afterward, David at-
tacked the Philistines and subdued
them; he took Gath and its villages from
the Philistines.

2 He defeated Moab, and the Moabites
became subject to David and brought trib-
ute.

3 David also struck down King Hadade-
zer of Zobah, toward Hamath,[a] as he
went to set up a monument at the river
Euphrates. 4 David took from him one
thousand chariots, seven thousand cavalry,
and twenty thousand foot soldiers. David
hamstrung all the chariot horses, but left
one hundred of them. 5 When the Arameans
of Damascus came to help King Hadadezer
of Zobah, David killed twenty-two thou-
sand Arameans. 6 Then David put garri-
sons[c] in Aram of Damascus; and the Ara-
means became subject to David, and
brought tribute. The LORD gave victory to
David wherever he went. 7 David took the
gold shields that were carried by the ser-
vants of Hadadezer, and brought them to
Jerusalem. 8 From Tibhath and from Cun,
cities of Hadadezer, David took a vast

a Meaning of Heb uncertain *b* Or *and it is blessed*
c Gk Vg 2 Sam 8.6 Compare Syr: Heb lacks *garrisons*

and unique status are linked to Israel's unique status. **23–24:** David's only petitions focus on the promises directed toward his dynasty (cf. vv. 8b–14).

18.1–20.8: The kingdom expanded. A new phase in David's reign begins, one dominated by foreign military campaigns. David's success in war is evident in all directions: to the west against the Philistines (18.1; 20.4–8), to the southeast against Edom (18.12–13), to the east against Moab (18.2) and Ammon (19.1–19; 20.1–3), and to the northeast against a variety of Aramean states (18.3–8; 19.6–19). In this way, David uses the fulfillment of one of Nathan's promises—the subjugation of all his enemies—to lay the foundations for the fulfillment of another—the construction of a temple by David's son. The juxtaposition suggests that David's hands were bloodied by war, so he could not build the Temple (22.7–10). **18.1–13:** Drawn from 2 Sam 8.1–14. **5:** *The Arameans of Damascus,* the defeat of one state by an invading power may upset the balance of power in the entire region, especially affecting neighboring states of the defeated kingdom. **7–11:** It was customary for pious kings in the ancient world to dedicate war spoils to the temples of the deities who granted them victory. In this instance, David's plunder, which according to 2 Sam 8.7 was merely brought to Jerusalem, is incorporated into the Temple built by Solomon (1 Kings 7.13–47; 2 Chr 3.15–4.22; Josephus, *Ant.* 7.106). **8:** *Tibhath* and *Cun* occur only

quantity of bronze; with it Solomon made
the bronze sea and the pillars and the ves-
sels of bronze.
9 When King Tou of Hamath heard that
David had defeated the whole army of King
Hadadezer of Zobah, 10 he sent his son Ha-
doram to King David, to greet him and to
congratulate him, because he had fought
against Hadadezer and defeated him. Now
Hadadezer had often been at war with Tou.
He sent all sorts of articles of gold, of silver,
and of bronze; 11 these also King David
dedicated to the LORD, together with the
silver and gold that he had carried off from
all the nations, from Edom, Moab, the Am-
monites, the Philistines, and Amalek.
12 Abishai son of Zeruiah killed eigh-
teen thousand Edomites in the Valley of
Salt. 13 He put garrisons in Edom; and all
the Edomites became subject to David. And
the LORD gave victory to David wherever
he went.
14 So David reigned over all Israel; and
he administered justice and equity to all his
people. 15 Joab son of Zeruiah was over the
army; Jehoshaphat son of Ahilud was re-
corder; 16 Zadok son of Ahitub and Ahime-
lech son of Abiathar were priests; Shavsha
was secretary; 17 Benaiah son of Jehoiada
was over the Cherethites and the Pelethites;
and David's sons were the chief officials in
the service of the king.

19 Some time afterward, King Nahash
of the Ammonites died, and his son
succeeded him. 2 David said, "I will deal
loyally with Hanun son of Nahash, for his
father dealt loyally with me." So David sent
messengers to console him concerning his
father. When David's servants came to Ha-
nun in the land of the Ammonites, to con-
sole him, 3 the officials of the Ammonites
said to Hanun, "Do you think, because Da-
vid has sent consolers to you, that he is
honoring your father? Have not his ser-
vants come to you to search and to over-
throw and to spy out the land?" 4 So Hanun
seized David's servants, shaved them, cut
off their garments in the middle at their
hips, and sent them away; 5 and they de-
parted. When David was told about the
men, he sent messengers to them, for they
felt greatly humiliated. The king said, "Re-
main at Jericho until your beards have
grown, and then return."
6 When the Ammonites saw that they
had made themselves odious to David, Ha-
nun and the Ammonites sent a thousand
talents of silver to hire chariots and cavalry
from Mesopotamia, from Aram-maacah
and from Zobah. 7 They hired thirty-two
thousand chariots and the king of Maacah
with his army, who came and camped be-
fore Medeba. And the Ammonites were
mustered from their cities and came to bat-
tle. 8 When David heard of it, he sent Joab
and all the army of the warriors. 9 The Am-
monites came out and drew up in battle
array at the entrance of the city, and the
kings who had come were by themselves in
the open country.
10 When Joab saw that the line of battle
was set against him both in front and in the

here in the Bible. **9:** *Tou,* Toi in 2 Sam 8.9. **12:** In 2 Sam 8.13 this victory is attributed to David himself. **14–17:** Taken from 2 Sam 8.15–18, the list of officials reflects the growth of the bureaucracy as the kingdom expanded. **16:** *Ahimelech* probably became one of David's priests as the replacement for his father Abiathar (15.11). **17:** David employs his sons as high-ranking officials in his cabinet instead of as priests (2 Sam 8.18); two other kings make use of princes in managing state affairs (2 Chr 11.22–23; 21.3). **19.1:** The death of a king could usher in a period of instability and uncertainty for his people. Given that international arrangements were made between the leaders of nations, and not between the nations themselves, the death of a leader could signal the end of such agreements. **3:** *To spy out the land,* to Hanun's counselors, David's string of victories against the Philistines, Moabites, Edomites, and Arameans establish an imperialistic pattern that they could ignore only at their own peril. **5:** The quarantine furnishes David's aides with the requisite time to recover and regain their dignity. **7:** *Medeba,* ca. 30 km (20 mi) south-southwest of the Ammonite capital of Rabbah; not mentioned in 2 Sam 10, the source for this chapter. **16:** *The Euphrates,* lit. "the river." In biblical narratives, "the river" usually designates the Euphrates (e.g., Gen 2.14; 15.18; Deut 1.7; 2 Kings 23.29; 24.7; 1 Chr 5.9), but the Jordan and the Yarmuk

rear, he chose some of the picked men of
Israel and arrayed them against the Arame-
ans; 11 the rest of his troops he put in the
charge of his brother Abishai, and they
were arrayed against the Ammonites. 12 He
said, "If the Arameans are too strong for
me, then you shall help me; but if the Am-
monites are too strong for you, then I will
help you. 13 Be strong, and let us be coura-
geous for our people and for the cities of
our God; and may the LORD do what seems
good to him." 14 So Joab and the troops
who were with him advanced toward the
Arameans for battle; and they fled before
him. 15 When the Ammonites saw that the
Arameans fled, they likewise fled before
Abishai, Joab's brother, and entered the
city. Then Joab came to Jerusalem.
16 But when the Arameans saw that
they had been defeated by Israel, they sent
messengers and brought out the Arameans
who were beyond the Euphrates, with Sho-
phach the commander of the army of Had-
adezer at their head. 17 When David was
informed, he gathered all Israel together,
crossed the Jordan, came to them, and
drew up his forces against them. When Da-
vid set the battle in array against the Ara-
means, they fought with him. 18 The Ara-
means fled before Israel; and David killed
seven thousand Aramean charioteers and
forty thousand foot soldiers, and also killed
Shophach the commander of their army.
19 When the servants of Hadadezer saw that
they had been defeated by Israel, they made
peace with David, and became subject to
him. So the Arameans were not willing to
help the Ammonites any more.

20 In the spring of the year, the time
when kings go out to battle, Joab
led out the army, ravaged the country of
the Ammonites, and came and besieged
Rabbah. But David remained at Jerusalem.
Joab attacked Rabbah, and overthrew it.
2 David took the crown of Milcom[a] from
his head; he found that it weighed a talent
of gold, and in it was a precious stone; and
it was placed on David's head. He also
brought out the booty of the city, a very
great amount. 3 He brought out the people
who were in it, and set them to work[b] with
saws and iron picks and axes.[c] Thus David
did to all the cities of the Ammonites. Then
David and all the people returned to Jerusa-
lem.
4 After this, war broke out with the Phil-
istines at Gezer; then Sibbecai the Hushath-
ite killed Sippai, who was one of the de-
scendants of the giants; and the Philistines
were subdued. 5 Again there was war with
the Philistines; and Elhanan son of Jair
killed Lahmi the brother of Goliath the Git-
tite, the shaft of whose spear was like a
weaver's beam. 6 Again there was war at

a Gk Vg See 1 Kings 11.5, 33: MT *of their king*
b Compare 2 Sam 12.31: Heb *and he sawed*
c Compare 2 Sam 12.31: Heb *saws*

are also possibilities. **19:** The new balance of power in the region, tilted in Israel's favor, leaves the Ammonites isolated from their former allies. The victories of Joab and David succeed in disrupting the traditional military ties between the Ammonites and the Arameans. **20.1–3:** Verse 1 is taken from 2 Sam 11.1, while vv. 2–3 are taken from 2 Sam 12.26a,30–31. In Samuel the reference to David's staying in Jerusalem provides the background to the troubling story of David's affair with Bathsheba. But in Chronicles, the same notice is incidental, providing the reader an explanation as to David's whereabouts. The Chronicler omits completely the story of David's liaison with Bathsheba (2 Sam 11.2–12.25), which casts David in a negative light. *Milkom* was the national deity of the Ammonites (1 Kings 11.5,7,33; 2 Kings 23.13). **4–8:** The final exploits of David and his soldiers are taken from 2 Sam 21.18–22. The stories in 2 Samuel about the rape of Tamar, Absalom's rebellion, the execution of Saul's descendants, and the disaffection of the northern tribes, which cast David in a negative light, do not appear in Chronicles. **5:** The text may harmonize two different claims found in Samuel: In 1 Sam 17.50 David kills the Philistine giant, identified earlier as Goliath of Gath (1 Sam 17.4), but in 2 Sam 21.19 Elhanan kills Goliath the Gittite. By having Elhanan kill the brother of Goliath the Gittite, and not Goliath himself, the Chronicler accommodates both claims.

Gath, where there was a man of great size,
who had six fingers on each hand, and six
toes on each foot, twenty-four in number;
he also was descended from the giants.
7When he taunted Israel, Jonathan son of
Shimea, David's brother, killed him.
8These were descended from the giants in
Gath; they fell by the hand of David and his
servants.

21 Satan stood up against Israel, and
incited David to count the people of
Israel. 2So David said to Joab and the com-
manders of the army, "Go, number Israel,
from Beer-sheba to Dan, and bring me a
report, so that I may know their number."
3But Joab said, "May the LORD increase
the number of his people a hundredfold!
Are they not, my lord the king, all of them
my lord's servants? Why then should my
lord require this? Why should he bring guilt
on Israel?" 4But the king's word prevailed
against Joab. So Joab departed and went
throughout all Israel, and came back to Je-
rusalem. 5Joab gave the total count of the
people to David. In all Israel there were one
million one hundred thousand men who
drew the sword, and in Judah four hundred
seventy thousand who drew the sword.
6But he did not include Levi and Benjamin
in the numbering, for the king's command
was abhorrent to Joab.

7 But God was displeased with this
thing, and he struck Israel. 8David said to
God, "I have sinned greatly in that I have
done this thing. But now, I pray you, take
away the guilt of your servant; for I have
done very foolishly." 9The LORD spoke to
Gad, David's seer, saying, 10"Go and say
to David, 'Thus says the LORD: Three
things I offer you; choose one of them, so
that I may do it to you.' " 11So Gad came
to David and said to him, "Thus says the
LORD, 'Take your choice: 12either three
years of famine; or three months of devas-
tation by your foes, while the sword of
your enemies overtakes you; or three days
of the sword of the LORD, pestilence on the
land, and the angel of the LORD destroying
throughout all the territory of Israel.' Now
decide what answer I shall return to the one
who sent me." 13Then David said to Gad,
"I am in great distress; let me fall into the
hand of the LORD, for his mercy is very
great; but let me not fall into human
hands."

14 So the LORD sent a pestilence on Isra-
el; and seventy thousand persons fell in Is-
rael. 15And God sent an angel to Jerusalem
to destroy it; but when he was about to
destroy it, the LORD took note and relented
concerning the calamity; he said to the de-
stroying angel, "Enough! Stay your hand."
The angel of the LORD was then standing
by the threshing floor of Ornan the Jebu-
site. 16David looked up and saw the angel
of the LORD standing between earth and
heaven, and in his hand a drawn sword
stretched out over Jerusalem. Then David
and the elders, clothed in sackcloth, fell on
their faces. 17And David said to God, "Was
it not I who gave the command to count the
people? It is I who have sinned and done

21.1–22.1: David the repentant sinner. The Chronicler recasts and supplements a story also found in 2 Sam 24. The guilt of David is pronounced in Chronicles (vv. 1–7), in which Joab warns David that it is sinful to count Israel in a casual fashion (cf. Ex 31.11–16); but so are his repentance and his efforts to intercede on behalf of Israel (vv. 8–17). David is thus forewarned before he is punished, reflecting a major tendency of the Chronicler. **21.1:** *Satan,* Heb "satan" should be translated as "an adversary" rather than "Satan" (cf. 2 Sam 24.1; see Job 1.6n.; Zech 3.1n.). Significantly, it replaces "the anger of the LORD" of 2 Sam 24.1. Having just experienced a string of impressive military victories against the Ammonites, Syrians, and Philistines (chs 18–20), David uncritically falls prey to the designs of one of his opponents. **2:** *From Beer-sheba to Dan,* the southern and northern limits of Israel proper. **5:** The total is lower in 2 Sam 24.9, but the number for Judah is higher there. In both cases the figures are improbable. **8:** *Take away,* better "transfer," as in 2 Sam 12.13. In both cases, the sin of David is transferred elsewhere. **15:** *Ornan,* called Araunah in 2 Sam 24. **17:** Along with the authors of Deut 7.9–10; 24.16; Jer 31.28–30; Ezek 18; 33.12–20, David argues for limiting the scope of divinely administered punishment of humans to the

very wickedly. But these sheep, what have
they done? Let your hand, I pray, O LORD
my God, be against me and against my fa-
ther's house; but do not let your people be
plagued!"
18 Then the angel of the LORD com-
manded Gad to tell David that he should go
up and erect an altar to the LORD on the
threshing floor of Ornan the Jebusite. 19 So
David went up following Gad's instruc-
tions, which he had spoken in the name of
the LORD. 20 Ornan turned and saw the an-
gel; and while his four sons who were with
him hid themselves, Ornan continued to
thresh wheat. 21 As David came to Ornan,
Ornan looked and saw David; he went out
from the threshing floor, and did obeisance
to David with his face to the ground. 22 Da-
vid said to Ornan, "Give me the site of the
threshing floor that I may build on it an
altar to the LORD—give it to me at its full
price—so that the plague may be averted
from the people." 23 Then Ornan said to
David, "Take it; and let my lord the king
do what seems good to him; see, I present
the oxen for burnt offerings, and the
threshing sledges for the wood, and the
wheat for a grain offering. I give it all."
24 But King David said to Ornan, "No; I
will buy them for the full price. I will not
take for the LORD what is yours, nor offer
burnt offerings that cost me nothing." 25 So
David paid Ornan six hundred shekels of
gold by weight for the site. 26 David built
there an altar to the LORD and presented
burnt offerings and offerings of well-being.
He called upon the LORD, and he answered
him with fire from heaven on the altar of
burnt offering. 27 Then the LORD com-
manded the angel, and he put his sword
back into its sheath.
28 At that time, when David saw that
the LORD had answered him at the thresh-
ing floor of Ornan the Jebusite, he made his
sacrifices there. 29 For the tabernacle of the
LORD, which Moses had made in the wil-
derness, and the altar of burnt offering
were at that time in the high place at Gibe-
on; 30 but David could not go before it to
inquire of God, for he was afraid of the
22 sword of the angel of the LORD.
1 Then David said, "Here shall be
the house of the LORD God and here the
altar of burnt offering for Israel."
2 David gave orders to gather together
the aliens who were residing in the land of
Israel, and he set stonecutters to prepare
dressed stones for building the house of
God. 3 David also provided great stores of
iron for nails for the doors of the gates and
for clamps, as well as bronze in quantities
beyond weighing, 4 and cedar logs without
number—for the Sidonians and Tyrians
brought great quantities of cedar to David.
5 For David said, "My son Solomon is
young and inexperienced, and the house
that is to be built for the LORD must be
exceedingly magnificent, famous and glori-
fied throughout all lands; I will therefore
make preparation for it." So David provid-
ed materials in great quantity before his
death.
6 Then he called for his son Solomon
and charged him to build a house for the
LORD, the God of Israel. 7 David said to
Solomon, "My son, I had planned to build

guilty parties themselves. **26:** The addition of a divine confirmation of David's sacrifices by fire, following the pattern of Lev 9.24 and 1 Kings 18.36–39, establishes David's altar as an enduring fixture in Israelite worship. **22.1:** David then declares the site to be the home of the future Temple. Here and elsewhere (2 Chr 3.1), the Chronicler shows unusual interest in offering explanations why the Temple was built on its current site.

22.2–19: David prepares for the construction of the Temple. David wants the future Temple to be *famous and glorified throughout all the lands,* because palace-temple complexes communicated the power of a god and his king to the god(s), populace, vassals, and foreign emissaries. But Solomon is *young and inexperienced,* so David undertakes the preparations himself. Of David's many sons (see 3.1–4; 14.3–7), Solomon was one of the youngest (1 Sam 20.31; 2 Sam 13.21b; 1 Kings 1.12,17; 2.22). **7–16:** This learned passage, which quotes from the dynastic promise (ch 17; cf. 2 Sam 7) and other texts, explains David's inability to build the Temple, suggesting that only Solomon (Heb "shelomoh"), understood as a man of peace ("shalom"), may build it. David, however, both here and in the following chapters, does much

a house to the name of the LORD my God.
8 But the word of the LORD came to me,
saying, 'You have shed much blood and
have waged great wars; you shall not build
a house to my name, because you have shed
so much blood in my sight on the earth.
9 See, a son shall be born to you; he shall be
a man of peace. I will give him peace from
all his enemies on every side; for his name
shall be Solomon,[a] and I will give peace[b]
and quiet to Israel in his days. 10 He shall
build a house for my name. He shall be a
son to me, and I will be a father to him, and
I will establish his royal throne in Israel
forever.' 11 Now, my son, the LORD be with
you, so that you may succeed in building
the house of the LORD your God, as he has
spoken concerning you. 12 Only, may the
LORD grant you discretion and understand-
ing, so that when he gives you charge over
Israel you may keep the law of the LORD
your God. 13 Then you will prosper if you
are careful to observe the statutes and the
ordinances that the LORD commanded Mo-
ses for Israel. Be strong and of good cour-
age. Do not be afraid or dismayed. 14 With
great pains I have provided for the house of
the LORD one hundred thousand talents
of gold, one million talents of silver, and
bronze and iron beyond weighing, for there
is so much of it; timber and stone too I have
provided. To these you must add more.
15 You have an abundance of workers:
stonecutters, masons, carpenters, and all
kinds of artisans without number, skilled in
working 16 gold, silver, bronze, and iron.
Now begin the work, and the LORD be with
you."

17 David also commanded all the lead-
ers of Israel to help his son Solomon, say-
ing, 18 "Is not the LORD your God with
you? Has he not given you peace on every
side? For he has delivered the inhabitants of
the land into my hand; and the land is
subdued before the LORD and his people.
19 Now set your mind and heart to seek the
LORD your God. Go and build the sanctu-
ary of the LORD God so that the ark of the
covenant of the LORD and the holy vessels
of God may be brought into a house built
for the name of the LORD."

23 When David was old and full of
days, he made his son Solomon king
over Israel.

2 David assembled all the leaders of Is-
rael and the priests and the Levites. 3 The
Levites, thirty years old and upward, were
counted, and the total was thirty-eight
thousand. 4 "Twenty-four thousand of
these," David said, "shall have charge of the
work in the house of the LORD, six thou-
sand shall be officers and judges, 5 four
thousand gatekeepers, and four thousand
shall offer praises to the LORD with the
instruments that I have made for praise."
6 And David organized them in divisions

a Heb *Shelomoh* *b* Heb *shalom*

groundwork for the project. **14:** *One hundred thousand talents of gold* and *one million talents of silver,* the point is not realism but extravagance; a talent weighed ca. 34 kg (75 lb). David's gifts are deliberately excessive. **17–19:** Following the norms of Deut 12.8–14, only once peace is established may the Temple be built.

23.1–32: Establishing a national administration. David attains a venerable stage in his life (v. 1), *full of days,* much like Abraham (Gen 25.8), Isaac (Gen 35.29), and Job (42.17) before him. He begins preparing for his death and the reign of his son by convening his administrative leadership. This transition is smooth, in contrast to 2 Sam 15–1 Kings 2, which are omitted. The Chronicler will eventually return to the issue of Solomon's accession, but his first priority is to detail David's appointment of and instructions to *the leaders of Israel, the priests, and the Levites* (v. 2), who will help Solomon to succeed in his various tasks, especially completing the Temple. The summit of select leaders forms the background of David's major administrative initiatives, outlined in the narratives and the lists of 23.3–27.34. **5:** The divisions and responsibilities of the gatekeepers are outlined in ch 26. **6:** The tripartite segmentation of the Levites in vv. 6–23 resembles that of earlier Priestly sources (Ex 6.16–19; Num 3.17–39; 1 Chr

corresponding to the sons of Levi: Ger-
shon,[a] Kohath, and Merari.
7 The sons of Gershon[b] were Ladan
and Shimei. 8 The sons of Ladan: Jehiel the
chief, Zetham, and Joel, three. 9 The sons
of Shimei: Shelomoth, Haziel, and Haran,
three. These were the heads of families of
Ladan. 10 And the sons of Shimei: Jahath,
Zina, Jeush, and Beriah. These four were
the sons of Shimei. 11 Jahath was the chief,
and Zizah the second; but Jeush and Beriah
did not have many sons, so they were en-
rolled as a single family.
12 The sons of Kohath: Amram, Izhar,
Hebron, and Uzziel, four. 13 The sons of
Amram: Aaron and Moses. Aaron was set
apart to consecrate the most holy things, so
that he and his sons forever should make
offerings before the LORD, and minister to
him and pronounce blessings in his name
forever; 14 but as for Moses the man of
God, his sons were to be reckoned among
the tribe of Levi. 15 The sons of Moses: Ger-
shom and Eliezer. 16 The sons of Gershom:
Shebuel the chief. 17 The sons of Eliezer: Re-
habiah the chief; Eliezer had no other sons,
but the sons of Rehabiah were very numer-
ous. 18 The sons of Izhar: Shelomith the
chief. 19 The sons of Hebron: Jeriah the
chief, Amariah the second, Jahaziel the
third, and Jekameam the fourth. 20 The
sons of Uzziel: Micah the chief and Isshiah
the second.
21 The sons of Merari: Mahli and Mu-
shi. The sons of Mahli: Eleazar and Kish.
22 Eleazar died having no sons, but only
daughters; their kindred, the sons of Kish,
married them. 23 The sons of Mushi: Mahli,
Eder, and Jeremoth, three.
24 These were the sons of Levi by their
ancestral houses, the heads of families as
they were enrolled according to the number
of the names of the individuals from twenty
years old and upward who were to do the
work for the service of the house of the
LORD. 25 For David said, "The LORD, the
God of Israel, has given rest to his people;
and he resides in Jerusalem forever. 26 And
so the Levites no longer need to carry the
tabernacle or any of the things for its ser-
vice"— 27 for according to the last words of
David these were the number of the Levites
from twenty years old and upward—
28 "but their duty shall be to assist the de-
scendants of Aaron for the service of the
house of the LORD, having the care of the
courts and the chambers, the cleansing of
all that is holy, and any work for the service
of the house of God; 29 to assist also with
the rows of bread, the choice flour for the
grain offering, the wafers of unleavened
bread, the baked offering, the offering
mixed with oil, and all measures of quanti-
ty or size. 30 And they shall stand every
morning, thanking and praising the LORD,
and likewise at evening, 31 and whenever
burnt offerings are offered to the LORD on

a Or *Gershom*; See 1 Chr 6.1, note, and 23.15
b Vg Compare Gk Syr: Heb *to the Gershonite*

6.1,16–47). **7–23:** The advent of the Temple, and the centralized worship that it represents, leads to the establishment of a system of divisions or courses among the Levites and priests. Each division was to work its appointed turn in rotation until a round was completed and a new round was begun. Although ascribed to David's initiative, this development, unattested in preexilic texts, is only attested in the Second Temple period. It persists to the Roman period (see Lk 1.5). Thus, here the Chronicler is legitimating worship as he knew it by attributing it to David. **13:** The mandate for the sons of Aaron to *make offerings before the LORD* is detailed in a number of contexts (Ex 29.38–42; 30.1–10; Lev 8.1–9.24; 18.8–20). **18:** Although included in the earlier genealogy (6.37), the line of Korah is not mentioned here; this is probably connected with the tradition of Korah's rebellion narrated in Num 16. **25–32:** The Levitical job description is revised in light of the move toward one permanent, stationary sanctuary. **28:** The Heb means "stand at the side of," rather than *to assist* the descendants of Aaron. In Chronicles the Levites and the priests have different but complimentary responsibilities (see also Neh 12.45). **29:** *Rows of bread,* cf. Lev 25.4–9. **30–31:** The Levites are to praise the LORD *whenever burnt offerings are offered* by the priests (16.4,7–38; 23.5). This contrasts with other descriptions of Temple worship, which depict a sanctuary of silence.

sabbaths, new moons, and appointed festi-
vals, according to the number required of
them, regularly before the LORD. 32 Thus
they shall keep charge of the tent of meet-
ing and the sanctuary, and shall attend the
descendants of Aaron, their kindred, for
the service of the house of the LORD."

24 The divisions of the descendants of
Aaron were these. The sons of Aar-
on: Nadab, Abihu, Eleazar, and Ithamar.
2 But Nadab and Abihu died before their
father, and had no sons; so Eleazar and Ith-
amar became the priests. 3 Along with Za-
dok of the sons of Eleazar, and Ahimelech
of the sons of Ithamar, David organized
them according to the appointed duties in
their service. 4 Since more chief men were
found among the sons of Eleazar than
among the sons of Ithamar, they organized
them under sixteen heads of ancestral
houses of the sons of Eleazar, and eight of
the sons of Ithamar. 5 They organized them
by lot, all alike, for there were officers of
the sanctuary and officers of God among
both the sons of Eleazar and the sons of
Ithamar. 6 The scribe Shemaiah son of Ne-
thanel, a Levite, recorded them in the pres-
ence of the king, and the officers, and Za-
dok the priest, and Ahimelech son of
Abiathar, and the heads of ancestral houses
of the priests and of the Levites; one ances-
tral house being chosen for Eleazar and one
chosen for Ithamar.

7 The first lot fell to Jehoiarib, the sec-
ond to Jedaiah, 8 the third to Harim, the
fourth to Seorim, 9 the fifth to Malchijah,
the sixth to Mijamin, 10 the seventh to Hak-
koz, the eighth to Abijah, 11 the ninth to
Jeshua, the tenth to Shecaniah, 12 the elev-
enth to Eliashib, the twelfth to Jakim, 13 the
thirteenth to Huppah, the fourteenth to Je-
shebeab, 14 the fifteenth to Bilgah, the six-
teenth to Immer, 15 the seventeenth to He-
zir, the eighteenth to Happizzez, 16 the
nineteenth to Pethahiah, the twentieth to
Jehezkel, 17 the twenty-first to Jachin, the
twenty-second to Gamul, 18 the twenty-
third to Delaiah, the twenty-fourth to Maa-
ziah. 19 These had as their appointed duty
in their service to enter the house of the
LORD according to the procedure estab-
lished for them by their ancestor Aaron, as
the LORD God of Israel had commanded
him.

20 And of the rest of the sons of Levi: of
the sons of Amram, Shubael; of the sons of
Shubael, Jehdeiah. 21 Of Rehabiah: of the
sons of Rehabiah, Isshiah the chief. 22 Of
the Izharites, Shelomoth; of the sons of She-
lomoth, Jahath. 23 The sons of Hebron:[a]
Jeriah the chief,[b] Amariah the second, Ja-
haziel the third, Jekameam the fourth.
24 The sons of Uzziel, Micah; of the sons of
Micah, Shamir. 25 The brother of Micah,
Isshiah; of the sons of Isshiah, Zechariah.
26 The sons of Merari: Mahli and Mushi.
The sons of Jaaziah: Beno.[c] 27 The sons of
Merari: of Jaaziah, Beno,[c] Shoham, Zac-
cur, and Ibri. 28 Of Mahli: Eleazar, who
had no sons. 29 Of Kish, the sons of Kish:
Jerahmeel. 30 The sons of Mushi: Mahli,
Eder, and Jerimoth. These were the sons
of the Levites according to their ancestral
houses. 31 These also cast lots correspond-
ing to their kindred, the descendants of
Aaron, in the presence of King David, Za-
dok, Ahimelech, and the heads of ancestral
houses of the priests and of the Levites, the
chief as well as the youngest brother.

25 David and the officers of the army
also set apart for the service the sons
of Asaph, and of Heman, and of Jeduthun,

a See 23.19: Heb lacks *Hebron* *b* See 23.19: Heb lacks *the chief* *c* Or *his son*: Meaning of Heb uncertain

24.1–19: David's priestly appointments. David organizes the priests into twenty-four divisions, which cast lots for places. **3:** *The sons of . . . Eleazar and Ithamar* represent the two major priestly families (15.11; 18.16–17; 25.1; cf. 2 Sam 8.16–18). **20–31:** This list of Levites overlaps with that of 23.7–23. **31:** The Levites rotate by courses just as the priests do.

25.1–31: The singers. Speaking of the singers as being *set apart* (v. 1) establishes a parallelism between David's choice and investiture of the singers, the Levites, and the priests (cf. 23.13; Num 8.14; 16.9,21; Deut 10.8; Ezra 10.8,16). On *the sons of Asaph, Heman,* and *Jeduthun,* see 6.33,44n. The allusion to

who should prophesy with lyres, harps, and
cymbals. The list of those who did the work
and of their duties was: 2 Of the sons of
Asaph: Zaccur, Joseph, Nethaniah, and As-
arelah, sons of Asaph, under the direction
of Asaph, who prophesied under the direc-
tion of the king. 3 Of Jeduthun, the sons of
Jeduthun: Gedaliah, Zeri, Jeshaiah, Shim-
ei,[a] Hashabiah, and Mattithiah, six, under
the direction of their father Jeduthun, who
prophesied with the lyre in thanksgiving
and praise to the LORD. 4 Of Heman, the
sons of Heman: Bukkiah, Mattaniah, Uzzi-
el, Shebuel, and Jerimoth, Hananiah, Ha-
nani, Eliathah, Giddalti, and Romamti-
ezer, Joshbekashah, Mallothi, Hothir,
Mahazioth. 5 All these were the sons of He-
man the king's seer, according to the prom-
ise of God to exalt him; for God had given
Heman fourteen sons and three daughters.
6 They were all under the direction of their
father for the music in the house of the
LORD with cymbals, harps, and lyres for
the service of the house of God. Asaph, Je-
duthun, and Heman were under the order
of the king. 7 They and their kindred, who
were trained in singing to the LORD, all of
whom were skillful, numbered two hun-
dred eighty-eight. 8 And they cast lots for
their duties, small and great, teacher and
pupil alike.
9 The first lot fell for Asaph to Joseph;
the second to Gedaliah, to him and his
brothers and his sons, twelve; 10 the third to
Zaccur, his sons and his brothers, twelve;
11 the fourth to Izri, his sons and his broth-
ers, twelve; 12 the fifth to Nethaniah, his
sons and his brothers, twelve; 13 the sixth to
Bukkiah, his sons and his brothers, twelve;
14 the seventh to Jesarelah,[b] his sons and
his brothers, twelve; 15 the eighth to Jesha-
iah, his sons and his brothers, twelve; 16 the
ninth to Mattaniah, his sons and his broth-
ers, twelve; 17 the tenth to Shimei, his sons
and his brothers, twelve; 18 the eleventh to
Azarel, his sons and his brothers, twelve;
19 the twelfth to Hashabiah, his sons and
his brothers, twelve; 20 to the thirteenth,
Shubael, his sons and his brothers, twelve;
21 to the fourteenth, Mattithiah, his sons
and his brothers, twelve; 22 to the fifteenth,
to Jeremoth, his sons and his brothers,
twelve; 23 to the sixteenth, to Hananiah, his
sons and his brothers, twelve; 24 to the sev-
enteenth, to Joshbekashah, his sons and his
brothers, twelve; 25 to the eighteenth, to
Hanani, his sons and his brothers, twelve;
26 to the nineteenth, to Mallothi, his sons
and his brothers, twelve; 27 to the twenti-
eth, to Eliathah, his sons and his brothers,
twelve; 28 to the twenty-first, to Hothir, his
sons and his brothers, twelve; 29 to the
twenty-second, to Giddalti, his sons and his
brothers, twelve; 30 to the twenty-third, to
Mahazioth, his sons and his brothers,
twelve; 31 to the twenty-fourth, to
Romamti-ezer, his sons and his brothers,
twelve.

26 As for the divisions of the gatekeep-
ers: of the Korahites, Meshelemiah
son of Kore, of the sons of Asaph. 2 Meshel-
emiah had sons: Zechariah the firstborn,
Jediael the second, Zebadiah the third,
Jathniel the fourth, 3 Elam the fifth, Jehoha-
nan the sixth, Eliehoenai the seventh.

a One Ms: Gk: MT lacks *Shimei* *b* Or *Asarelah*; see 25.2

music and song as a kind of prophecy (vv. 1–3; cf. 2 Chr 24.19–22) is striking and may be connected to the later tradition of David as a prophet who composed the psalms through divine inspiration; cf. 2 Kings 3.15. **1:** The *officers of the army,* as part of David's governmental apparatus, have a say in the establishment of courses for the singers. **8:** As with the priests (24.5) and other Levites (24.31), a lottery is held to determine the twenty-four courses for the singers.

26.1–19: The gatekeepers. Part of David's administrative organization involves the gatekeepers, whom the Chronicler counts as Levites (cf. Ezra 2.42,70; Neh 11.19). Sanctuary guards were active in David's earlier reign when David transported the ark (15.18,23–24; 16.38,42; 23.5). Along with performing guard duty, the gatekeepers open the Temple in the morning; administer the use of the vessels, including the holy utensils; take charge of the flour, wine, spices, and oil (9.17–32); and perform administrative service on behalf of the king (2 Chr 31.14; 34.13). **13:** Because the lottery was held to determine which family was

4 Obed-edom had sons: Shemaiah the first-
born, Jehozabad the second, Joah the third,
Sachar the fourth, Nethanel the fifth, 5 Am-
miel the sixth, Issachar the seventh, Peulle-
thai the eighth; for God blessed him. 6 Also
to his son Shemaiah sons were born who
exercised authority in their ancestral
houses, for they were men of great ability.
7 The sons of Shemaiah: Othni, Rephael,
Obed, and Elzabad, whose brothers were
able men, Elihu and Semachiah. 8 All these,
sons of Obed-edom with their sons and
brothers, were able men qualified for the
service; sixty-two of Obed-edom. 9 Meshel-
emiah had sons and brothers, able men,
eighteen. 10 Hosah, of the sons of Merari,
had sons: Shimri the chief (for though he
was not the firstborn, his father made him
chief), 11 Hilkiah the second, Tebaliah the
third, Zechariah the fourth: all the sons and
brothers of Hosah totaled thirteen.

12 These divisions of the gatekeepers,
corresponding to their leaders, had duties,
just as their kindred did, ministering in the
house of the LORD; 13 and they cast lots by
ancestral houses, small and great alike, for
their gates. 14 The lot for the east fell to
Shelemiah. They cast lots also for his son
Zechariah, a prudent counselor, and his lot
came out for the north. 15 Obed-edom's
came out for the south, and to his sons was
allotted the storehouse. 16 For Shuppim and
Hosah it came out for the west, at the gate
of Shallecheth on the ascending road.
Guard corresponded to guard. 17 On the
east there were six Levites each day,[a] on
the north four each day, on the south four
each day, as well as two and two at the
storehouse; 18 and for the colonnade[b] on
the west there were four at the road and
two at the colonnade.[b] 19 These were the
divisions of the gatekeepers among the Ko-
rahites and the sons of Merari.

20 And of the Levites, Ahijah had
charge of the treasuries of the house of God
and the treasuries of the dedicated gifts.
21 The sons of Ladan, the sons of the Ger-
shonites belonging to Ladan, the heads of
families belonging to Ladan the Gershon-
ite: Jehieli.[c]

22 The sons of Jehieli, Zetham and his
brother Joel, were in charge of the treasur-
ies of the house of the LORD. 23 Of the Am-
ramites, the Izharites, the Hebronites, and
the Uzzielites: 24 Shebuel son of Gershom,
son of Moses, was chief officer in charge of
the treasuries. 25 His brothers: from Eliezer
were his son Rehabiah, his son Jeshaiah, his
son Joram, his son Zichri, and his son She-
lomoth. 26 This Shelomoth and his brothers
were in charge of all the treasuries of the
dedicated gifts that King David, and the
heads of families, and the officers of the
thousands and the hundreds, and the com-
manders of the army, had dedicated.
27 From booty won in battles they dedicat-
ed gifts for the maintenance of the house of
the LORD. 28 Also all that Samuel the seer,
and Saul son of Kish, and Abner son of
Ner, and Joab son of Zeruiah had dedicat-
ed—all dedicated gifts were in the care of
Shelomoth[d] and his brothers.

29 Of the Izharites, Chenaniah and his
sons were appointed to outside duties for
Israel, as officers and judges. 30 Of the He-
bronites, Hashabiah and his brothers, one
thousand seven hundred men of ability,
had the oversight of Israel west of the Jor-
dan for all the work of the LORD and for
the service of the king. 31 Of the Hebron-
ites, Jerijah was chief of the Hebronites. (In
the fortieth year of David's reign search

a Gk: Heb lacks *each day* *b* Heb *parbar*: meaning uncertain *c* The Hebrew text of verse 21 is confused *d* Gk Compare 26.28: Heb *Shelomith*

to serve at which gate, the number of members within a particular family did not determine or affect the process of selection. **16:** *Shuppim,* perhaps a scribal error, repeating the previous word. *Gate of Shallecheth,* the name occurs only here, and may also be a scribal error.

26.20–32: Treasurers, regional officials, and judges. Israel's leadership makes the task of Solomon easier by endowing the Temple and organizing its finances. The Levites also take on broad responsibilities, such as *oversight of Israel west of the Jordan* as *officers and judges* (vv. 29–30; cf. 23.3–5; 2 Chr 17.2; 19.5). **31:** *Fortieth year,* i.e., David's last; see 29.27. **32:** The (Persian period) distinction between matters

was made, of whatever genealogy or fami-
ly, and men of great ability among them
were found at Jazer in Gilead.) 32 King Da-
vid appointed him and his brothers, two
thousand seven hundred men of ability,
heads of families, to have the oversight of
the Reubenites, the Gadites, and the half-
tribe of the Manassites for everything per-
taining to God and for the affairs of the
king.

27 This is the list of the people of Isra-
el, the heads of families, the com-
manders of the thousands and the hun-
dreds, and their officers who served the
king in all matters concerning the divisions
that came and went, month after month
throughout the year, each division number-
ing twenty-four thousand:
2 Jashobeam son of Zabdiel was in
charge of the first division in the first
month; in his division were twenty-four
thousand. 3 He was a descendant of Perez,
and was chief of all the commanders of the
army for the first month. 4 Dodai the Aho-
hite was in charge of the division of the
second month; Mikloth was the chief offi-
cer of his division. In his division were
twenty-four thousand. 5 The third com-
mander, for the third month, was Benaiah
son of the priest Jehoiada, as chief; in his
division were twenty-four thousand. 6 This
is the Benaiah who was a mighty man of
the Thirty and in command of the Thirty;
his son Ammizabad was in charge of his
division.[a] 7 Asahel brother of Joab was
fourth, for the fourth month, and his son
Zebadiah after him; in his division were
twenty-four thousand. 8 The fifth com-
mander, for the fifth month, was Sham-
huth, the Izrahite; in his division were
twenty-four thousand. 9 Sixth, for the sixth
month, was Ira son of Ikkesh the Tekoite;
in his division were twenty-four thousand.
10 Seventh, for the seventh month, was He-
lez the Pelonite, of the Ephraimites; in his
division were twenty-four thousand.
11 Eighth, for the eighth month, was Sibbe-
cai the Hushathite, of the Zerahites; in his
division were twenty-four thousand.
12 Ninth, for the ninth month, was Abiezer
of Anathoth, a Benjaminite; in his division
were twenty-four thousand. 13 Tenth, for
the tenth month, was Maharai of Neto-
phah, of the Zerahites; in his division were
twenty-four thousand. 14 Eleventh, for the
eleventh month, was Benaiah of Pirathon,
of the Ephraimites; in his division were
twenty-four thousand. 15 Twelfth, for the
twelfth month, was Heldai the Netopha-
thite, of Othniel; in his division were
twenty-four thousand.
16 Over the tribes of Israel, for the Reu-
benites, Eliezer son of Zichri was chief offi-
cer; for the Simeonites, Shephatiah son of
Maacah; 17 for Levi, Hashabiah son of
Kemuel; for Aaron, Zadok; 18 for Judah,
Elihu, one of David's brothers; for Issachar,
Omri son of Michael; 19 for Zebulun, Ish-
maiah son of Obadiah; for Naphtali, Jeri-
moth son of Azriel; 20 for the Ephraimites,
Hoshea son of Azaziah; for the half-tribe of
Manasseh, Joel son of Pedaiah; 21 for the
half-tribe of Manasseh in Gilead, Iddo son
of Zechariah; for Benjamin, Jaasiel son of
Abner; 22 for Dan, Azarel son of Jeroham.
These were the leaders of the tribes of Isra-
el. 23 David did not count those below
twenty years of age, for the LORD had

a Gk Vg: Heb *Ammizabad was his division*

pertaining to the king and matters pertaining to God is found only in Chronicles (26.30,32; 2 Chr 19.11) and Ezra (7.26).

27.1–24: Military leaders. The orderly organization of the military, no less than the organization of the priests and the Levites, is part of the Davidic legacy in Chronicles. The system established—twelve monthly relays of 24,000, each headed by a divisional leader (vv. 2–16)—reflect David's standard administrative procedure (23.6–23; 24.1–19; 25.8–31; 26.1–12). **1:** The noun "mispar" may be translated as "census" (rather than as *list*) both here and in vv. 23–24 (cf. 23.3). **2–15:** Many of the names in this list are also found in 11.11–47; 2 Sam 23.8–39. **16–22:** Each of the tribes has its own "chief officer" participate in the national government. See 5.6n. **23:** The enumeration of twelve military divisions (288,000) leads the writer to explain why no general census of Israel is included (cf. Num 1.3,45). By count-

promised to make Israel as numerous as the
stars of heaven. 24 Joab son of Zeruiah be-
gan to count them, but did not finish; yet
wrath came upon Israel for this, and the
number was not entered into the account of
the Annals of King David.
25 Over the king's treasuries was Azma-
veth son of Adiel. Over the treasuries in the
country, in the cities, in the villages and in
the towers, was Jonathan son of Uzziah.
26 Over those who did the work of the field,
tilling the soil, was Ezri son of Chelub.
27 Over the vineyards was Shimei the Ra-
mathite. Over the produce of the vineyards
for the wine cellars was Zabdi the Shiph-
mite. 28 Over the olive and sycamore trees
in the Shephelah was Baal-hanan the Gede-
rite. Over the stores of oil was Joash.
29 Over the herds that pastured in Sharon
was Shitrai the Sharonite. Over the herds
in the valleys was Shaphat son of Adlai.
30 Over the camels was Obil the Ishmaelite.
Over the donkeys was Jehdeiah the Meron-
othite. Over the flocks was Jaziz the Hag-
rite. 31 All these were stewards of King Da-
vid's property.
32 Jonathan, David's uncle, was a coun-
selor, being a man of understanding and a
scribe; Jehiel son of Hachmoni attended the
king's sons. 33 Ahithophel was the king's
counselor, and Hushai the Archite was the
king's friend. 34 After Ahithophel came Je-
hoiada son of Benaiah, and Abiathar. Joab
was commander of the king's army.

28 David assembled at Jerusalem all
the officials of Israel, the officials of
the tribes, the officers of the divisions that
served the king, the commanders of the
thousands, the commanders of the hun-
dreds, the stewards of all the property and
cattle of the king and his sons, together
with the palace officials, the mighty war-
riors, and all the warriors. 2 Then King Da-
vid rose to his feet and said: "Hear me, my
brothers and my people. I had planned to
build a house of rest for the ark of the cove-
nant of the LORD, for the footstool of our
God; and I made preparations for building.
3 But God said to me, 'You shall not build
a house for my name, for you are a warrior
and have shed blood.' 4 Yet the LORD God
of Israel chose me from all my ancestral
house to be king over Israel forever; for he
chose Judah as leader, and in the house of
Judah my father's house, and among my
father's sons he took delight in making me
king over all Israel. 5 And of all my sons, for
the LORD has given me many, he has cho-
sen my son Solomon to sit upon the throne
of the kingdom of the LORD over Israel.
6 He said to me, 'It is your son Solomon
who shall build my house and my courts,

ing Israelite males who were less than twenty years of age, David would be casting aspersions on the validity of one of God's solemn promises to Abraham (Gen 22.17). **24:** See ch 21.

27.25–32: Other administrators. The Davidic state is multifaceted. The king owns agricultural estates (v. 27), operates storehouses in both urban and rural areas for agricultural produce (vv. 27–28), and has an investment in, if not some control over, trade (v. 30). The king employs a variety of high officials who supervise his estates, fieldworkers, and storage facilities. The king also has a coterie of advisors and officers (vv. 32–34) at his disposal. Some aspects of this complicated system may be anachronistic. **30:** The *camels* and *donkeys* (or she-asses) are related directly not to agriculture, but to trade. Because the major trade routes of the ancient Near East passed through the region, trade was an important sector of the Israelite economy. **33:** On *Ahithophel* and *Hushai,* see 2 Sam 15.12,23–37.

28.1–10: All Israel ratifies accession. Having concluded his administrative organization, David assembles a large national convocation to prepare the way for Solomon's rule. **1:** Assemblies are common in the Chronicler's history (13.5; 15.3; 2 Chr 5.2–3; 11.1; 20.26). In this case, David convokes all of his nation's dignitaries to Jerusalem to witness his charge to Solomon and to enlist their support for Solomon. **2:** On the ark as God's footstool, cf. Ps 99.5; 132.7. **3:** See 22.6–8. **4:** *Chose* ("bḥr") *me.* In Chronicles the Levites (15.2; 2 Chr 29.11), the tribe of Judah, and more specifically David and Solomon are all elect of God. Emphasis on Solomon's election contrasts sharply with 1 Kings 1–2. **6–7:** Cf. 17.11–14; 22.9–10. **7:** The perdurability of Davidic kingship is contingent on Solomon's obedience (cf. 17.11;

for I have chosen him to be a son to me,
and I will be a father to him. 7 I will estab-
lish his kingdom forever if he continues res-
olute in keeping my commandments and
my ordinances, as he is today.' 8 Now there-
fore in the sight of all Israel, the assembly
of the LORD, and in the hearing of our God,
observe and search out all the command-
ments of the LORD your God; that you may
possess this good land, and leave it for an
inheritance to your children after you for-
ever.

9 "And you, my son Solomon, know the
God of your father, and serve him with sin-
gle mind and willing heart; for the LORD
searches every mind, and understands every
plan and thought. If you seek him, he will
be found by you; but if you forsake him,
he will abandon you forever. 10 Take heed
now, for the LORD has chosen you to build
a house as the sanctuary; be strong, and
act."

11 Then David gave his son Solomon
the plan of the vestibule of the temple, and
of its houses, its treasuries, its upper rooms,
and its inner chambers, and of the room for
the mercy seat;[a] 12 and the plan of all that
he had in mind: for the courts of the house
of the LORD, all the surrounding chambers,
the treasuries of the house of God, and the
treasuries for dedicated gifts; 13 for the divi-
sions of the priests and of the Levites, and
all the work of the service in the house of
the LORD; for all the vessels for the service
in the house of the LORD, 14 the weight of
gold for all golden vessels for each service,
the weight of silver vessels for each service,
15 the weight of the golden lampstands and
their lamps, the weight of gold for each
lampstand and its lamps, the weight of sil-
ver for a lampstand and its lamps, accord-
ing to the use of each in the service, 16 the
weight of gold for each table for the rows
of bread, the silver for the silver tables,
17 and pure gold for the forks, the basins,
and the cups; for the golden bowls and the
weight of each; for the silver bowls and the
weight of each; 18 for the altar of incense
made of refined gold, and its weight; also
his plan for the golden chariot of the cheru-
bim that spread their wings and covered the
ark of the covenant of the LORD.

19 "All this, in writing at the LORD's di-
rection, he made clear to me—the plan of
all the works."

20 David said further to his son Solo-
mon, "Be strong and of good courage, and
act. Do not be afraid or dismayed; for the
LORD God, my God, is with you. He will
not fail you or forsake you, until all the
work for the service of the house of the
LORD is finished. 21 Here are the divisions
of the priests and the Levites for all the
service of the house of God; and with you
in all the work will be every volunteer who
has skill for any kind of service; also the
officers and all the people will be wholly at
your command."

29 King David said to the whole assem-
bly, "My son Solomon, whom alone
God has chosen, is young and inexperi-
enced, and the work is great; for the tem-
ple[b] will not be for mortals but for the
LORD God. 2 So I have provided for the
house of my God, so far as I was able, the
gold for the things of gold, the silver for

a Or *the cover* b Heb *fortress*

1 Kings 3.14; 8.61; 9.4), which the duty to build the Temple exemplifies (v. 10). **8:** The addressee is Israel. Much like the authors of Deuteronomy (4.23–28; 28.58–64; 30.18), the Chronicler conditions Israel's possession of the land upon its obedience to God.

28.11–21: A plan for the Temple. Much as Moses received plans for the tabernacle (Ex 25.9), David has a divinely composed Temple blueprint (v. 19), which he presents to Solomon. **20:** The transition from David to Solomon is patterned after Moses and Joshua; note especially the use of "Be strong and of good courage" (Deut 31.7; 31.23; Josh 1.6–18).

29.1–9: Endowments for the Temple. To account for his own copious preparations, David contrasts young Solomon's youthful vulnerability with the tremendous task that lies ahead (cf. 22.5). David's generosity sets the stage for Israel's leadership to show similar benevolence (vv. 6–9). There are parallels with Israel's gifts to the tabernacle (Ex 25.1–7; 35.4–9,20–29). **4:** *Ophir,* probably in southern Arabia,

the things of silver, and the bronze for the
things of bronze, the iron for the things of
iron, and wood for the things of wood, be-
sides great quantities of onyx and stones
for setting, antimony, colored stones, all
sorts of precious stones, and marble in
abundance. 3 Moreover, in addition to all
that I have provided for the holy house, I
have a treasure of my own of gold and sil-
ver, and because of my devotion to the
house of my God I give it to the house of
my God: 4 three thousand talents of gold, of
the gold of Ophir, and seven thousand tal-
ents of refined silver, for overlaying the
walls of the house, 5 and for all the work to
be done by artisans, gold for the things of
gold and silver for the things of silver. Who
then will offer willingly, consecrating them-
selves today to the LORD?"

6 Then the leaders of ancestral houses
made their freewill offerings, as did also the
leaders of the tribes, the commanders of the
thousands and of the hundreds, and the of-
ficers over the king's work. 7 They gave for
the service of the house of God five thou-
sand talents and ten thousand darics of
gold, ten thousand talents of silver, eigh-
teen thousand talents of bronze, and one
hundred thousand talents of iron. 8 Whoev-
er had precious stones gave them to the
treasury of the house of the LORD, into the
care of Jehiel the Gershonite. 9 Then the
people rejoiced because these had given
willingly, for with single mind they had of-
fered freely to the LORD; King David also
rejoiced greatly.

10 Then David blessed the LORD in the
presence of all the assembly; David said:
"Blessed are you, O LORD, the God of our
ancestor Israel, forever and ever. 11 Yours,
O LORD, are the greatness, the power, the
glory, the victory, and the majesty; for all
that is in the heavens and on the earth is
yours; yours is the kingdom, O LORD, and
you are exalted as head above all. 12 Riches
and honor come from you, and you rule
over all. In your hand are power and might;
and it is in your hand to make great and to
give strength to all. 13 And now, our God,
we give thanks to you and praise your glo-
rious name.

14 "But who am I, and what is my peo-
ple, that we should be able to make this
freewill offering? For all things come from
you, and of your own have we given you.
15 For we are aliens and transients before
you, as were all our ancestors; our days on
the earth are like a shadow, and there is no
hope. 16 O LORD our God, all this abun-
dance that we have provided for building
you a house for your holy name comes
from your hand and is all your own. 17 I
know, my God, that you search the heart,
and take pleasure in uprightness; in the up-
rightness of my heart I have freely offered
all these things, and now I have seen your
people, who are present here, offering free-
ly and joyously to you. 18 O LORD, the God
of Abraham, Isaac, and Israel, our ances-
tors, keep forever such purposes and
thoughts in the hearts of your people, and
direct their hearts toward you. 19 Grant to
my son Solomon that with single mind he
may keep your commandments, your de-
crees, and your statutes, performing all of
them, and that he may build the temple[a]
for which I have made provision."

20 Then David said to the whole assem-

a Heb *fortress*

was famous for its gold; see Isa 13.12. On the quantities, see 22.14n. **7:** The *daric* was a Persian coin, generally thought to be 8.4 gr, minted sometime after 515 BCE (cf. Ezra 8.27).

29.10–19: David's farewell prayer. The Chronicler follows a paradigm in which final addresses are made by great leaders—Jacob (Gen 49.1–28), Moses (Deut 32.1–44,45–47; 33.1–29), Joshua (23.1–16; 24.1–28), Samuel (1 Sam 12.1–25), and David (2 Sam 23.1–7; 1 Kings 2.1–10). David's acclamation of the LORD's sovereignty (vv. 10–13) resonates with sentiments expressed earlier in the Psalm anthology (16.24–26) and with the prayer, which he offered following Nathan's dynastic oracle (17.16–27). From David's point of view, all that he and the people donate to God ultimately stems from God himself (v. 14). Thus, following earlier biblical norms, these gifts serve as acknowledgments of God's sovereignty.

29.20–30: David's death and the transition to Solomon. David's final blessing of Israel is coupled with

bly, "Bless the LORD your God." And all
the assembly blessed the LORD, the God of
their ancestors, and bowed their heads and
prostrated themselves before the LORD and
the king. 21 On the next day they offered
sacrifices and burnt offerings to the LORD,
a thousand bulls, a thousand rams, and a
thousand lambs, with their libations, and
sacrifices in abundance for all Israel; 22 and
they ate and drank before the LORD on that
day with great joy.

They made David's son Solomon king
a second time; they anointed him as the
LORD's prince, and Zadok as priest.
23 Then Solomon sat on the throne of the
LORD, succeeding his father David as king;
he prospered, and all Israel obeyed him.
24 All the leaders and the mighty warriors,
and also all the sons of King David, pledged
their allegiance to King Solomon. 25 The
LORD highly exalted Solomon in the sight
of all Israel, and bestowed upon him such
royal majesty as had not been on any king
before him in Israel.

26 Thus David son of Jesse reigned over
all Israel. 27 The period that he reigned over
Israel was forty years; he reigned seven
years in Hebron, and thirty-three years in
Jerusalem. 28 He died in a good old age, full
of days, riches, and honor; and his son Sol-
omon succeeded him. 29 Now the acts of
King David, from first to last, are written in
the records of the seer Samuel, and in the
records of the prophet Nathan, and in the
records of the seer Gad, 30 with accounts of
all his rule and his might and of the events
that befell him and Israel and all the king-
doms of the earth.

the anointing of Solomon as his chosen successor. The transition is smooth and without incident. **22:** Another all-Israelite feast (see 12.39n.). *A second time,* whereas David earlier designated Solomon king over Israel (23.1), all of Israel's leaders now publicly endorse Solomon's enthronement. **24:** Even *all the sons of King David* acclaim Solomon, a clear polemic against the account in Samuel-Kings (2 Sam 15.1–16.14; 1 Kings 1.9–10,25–26; 2.15). **25:** In *royal majesty* ("hod malkut") Solomon's reign is unparalleled. **27:** David's reign is dated to ca. 1005–965 BCE. **28:** David enjoys a long, productive, and respected life. Security and longevity are marks of divine blessing (2 Chr 24.15; Deut 4.40; 5.16; Isa 52.10; 65.17–19). *Full of days,* see 23.1n.

2 CHRONICLES

The organization of 2 Chronicles falls into two major parts: the reign of Solomon (chs 1–9) and the kingdom of Judah (chs 10–36). In Chronicles the tenure of Solomon represents the apex of Israelite history, a time of unprecedented glory, prosperity, and peace. If David's reign was highly successful because David consolidated Israel's international position and prepared for the long-awaited Temple, Solomon's reign was highly successful because he brought these plans to fruition. Accordingly, much space is devoted in chs 2–7 to the construction, furnishings, and dedication of this national edifice. As the home of the ark and the tabernacle, the Temple represents the continuation and fulfillment of earlier Israelite religious institutions. For the Chronicler, the Temple is the divinely sanctioned place for both sacrifice and prayer (6.1–7.22).

The Chronicler's account of the divided monarchy differs in many respects from that found in 1 and 2 Kings, even though he draws heavily from Kings to write his own work. The writer excludes the independent history of the Northern Kingdom because he regards both the kingship and the sanctuaries of this new state as an affront to God (13.4–12). The choice not to recount the record of northern Israel also means that the stories of the northern prophets (e.g., Elijah and Elisha) are not found in Chronicles. The author does add, however, much coverage to the Judahite kingdom, some of which reflects well on the reigns of major Judahite monarchs, such as Asa (chs 14–16), Jehoshaphat (chs 17–20), and Hezekiah (chs 29–32). Throughout his presentation, the Chronicler exhibits a concern for all Israelite tribes. The Chronicler criticizes the Northern Kingdom and its monarchs, but he still considers the northern tribes as Israelite and shows a sustained interest in the contacts with Judah. In the latter part of its history, Judah lost ground to its enemies and was exiled from its land to Babylon (586 BCE). A major concern of Chronicles is not only to trace this decline, but also to commend the reforms aimed at reversing it. On the whole, he presents a more balanced and optimistic presentation of this period than do the authors of Kings (see the Introduction to 1 Chronicles).

1 Solomon son of David established him-
self in his kingdom; the LORD his God
was with him and made him exceedingly
great.
2 Solomon summoned all Israel, the
commanders of the thousands and of the
hundreds, the judges, and all the leaders of
all Israel, the heads of families. 3Then Solo-

1.1–17: Solomon takes charge, journeys to Gibeon, and prospers. The Israel Solomon encounters is unified and unhampered by internal factions or strife. Solomon's legitimacy is stressed by repeated references to him as David's rightful successor and king by divine choice (1 Chr 17.11; 23.1; 28.6; 29.23–25; 2 Chr 1.1; 6.10; 7.17–18). The Chronicler presents the United Monarchy as the time when Israel's authoritative institutions took shape. The idealized presentation of David and Solomon effectively establishes a model by which later periods are judged. **1:** Solomon ruled ca. 968–928 BCE. When Solomon took office, he immediately *established himself in his kingdom* and enjoyed the LORD's blessings (v. 1). There was no need to pacify, eliminate, or exile his domestic foes (1 Kings 1–2) because David had already consolidated domestic support for Solomon (1 Chr 23–29). **2–13:** Along with the support of

mon, and the whole assembly with him,
went to the high place that was at Gibeon;
for God's tent of meeting, which Moses the
servant of the LORD had made in the wil-
derness, was there. 4(But David had
brought the ark of God up from Kiriath-
jearim to the place that David had prepared
for it; for he had pitched a tent for it in
Jerusalem.) 5Moreover the bronze altar
that Bezalel son of Uri, son of Hur, had
made, was there in front of the tabernacle
of the LORD. And Solomon and the assem-
bly inquired at it. 6Solomon went up there
to the bronze altar before the LORD, which
was at the tent of meeting, and offered a
thousand burnt offerings on it.
7 That night God appeared to Solomon,
and said to him, "Ask what I should give
you." 8Solomon said to God, "You have
shown great and steadfast love to my father
David, and have made me succeed him as
king. 9O LORD God, let your promise to
my father David now be fulfilled, for you
have made me king over a people as numer-
ous as the dust of the earth. 10Give me now
wisdom and knowledge to go out and come
in before this people, for who can rule this
great people of yours?" 11God answered
Solomon, "Because this was in your heart,
and you have not asked for possessions,
wealth, honor, or the life of those who hate
you, and have not even asked for long life,
but have asked for wisdom and knowledge
for yourself that you may rule my people
over whom I have made you king, 12wis-
dom and knowledge are granted to you. I
will also give you riches, possessions, and
honor, such as none of the kings had who
were before you, and none after you shall
have the like." 13So Solomon came from[a]
the high place at Gibeon, from the tent of
meeting, to Jerusalem. And he reigned over
Israel.
14 Solomon gathered together chariots
and horses; he had fourteen hundred chari-
ots and twelve thousand horses, which he
stationed in the chariot cities and with the
king in Jerusalem. 15The king made silver
and gold as common in Jerusalem as stone,
and he made cedar as plentiful as the syca-
more of the Shephelah. 16Solomon's horses
were imported from Egypt and Kue; the
king's traders received them from Kue at
the prevailing price. 17They imported from
Egypt, and then exported, a chariot for six
hundred shekels of silver, and a horse for
one hundred fifty; so through them these
were exported to all the kings of the Hit-
tites and the kings of Aram.
2 [b]Solomon decided to build a temple for
the name of the LORD, and a royal pal-

[a] Gk Vg: Heb *to* [b] Ch 1.18 in Heb

David and Solomon, the support of military, local, and civil officials enables the nation to embark on major new initiatives in a harmonious fashion (1 Chr 11.1–3; 13.1–4; 23.1–2; 28.1; 29.1–25). In this case, the author transforms a story about Solomon's private pilgrimage to the high place at Gibeon (1 Kings 3.3–15) into a national pilgrimage, adding that the tent of meeting (see Ex 38–39) was located at Gibeon (1 Chr 16.39–42). This type of addition, which explains away problematic aspects of an earlier text, typifies Chronicles. **4:** See 1 Chr 13; 15. **5:** On *Bezalel* and the *bronze altar,* cf. Ex 27.1–2; 31.1; 1 Chr 2.20. The emphasis here is on continuity. **11–12:** The divine gifts of unprecedented *wisdom and knowledge,* as well as *riches, possessions, and honor* set the tone and tenor of Solomon's reign. **14–17:** These verses, drawn from 1 Kings 10.26–29, illustrate that God's promises to Solomon at Gibeon are being realized. The rearrangement of earlier sources is typical of the Chronicler. **15:** *The Shephelah,* the foothills between the coastal plain and the Judean hill country. **16:** *Kue,* in Cilicia, in southern Asia Minor. **17:** A *shekel* weighed about 11.5 gr (.4 oz). The *kings of the Hittites* ruled over northern Syria; *Aram* was southern Syria.

2.1–18: Solomon prepares to build the Temple. As David's appointed successor, Solomon brings his father's hopes and designs to fruition by focusing much of his energy on constructing, equipping, and staffing the Temple. Like David, Solomon is a devoted patron of his nation's worship. **1–10:** These verses, largely drawn from 1 Kings 5.1–6,11, provide external confirmation of both Solomon's gifts and the plan to build a temple. Vv. 4–5, however, have no source in Kings, and reflect later theological notions. **3:**

ace for himself. 2[a] Solomon conscripted
seventy thousand laborers and eighty thou-
sand stonecutters in the hill country, with
three thousand six hundred to oversee
them.
3 Solomon sent word to King Huram of
Tyre: "Once you dealt with my father Da-
vid and sent him cedar to build himself a
house to live in. 4 I am now about to build
a house for the name of the LORD my God
and dedicate it to him for offering fragrant
incense before him, and for the regular
offering of the rows of bread, and for burnt
offerings morning and evening, on the sab-
baths and the new moons and the appoint-
ed festivals of the LORD our God, as or-
dained forever for Israel. 5 The house that I
am about to build will be great, for our
God is greater than other gods. 6 But who is
able to build him a house, since heaven,
even highest heaven, cannot contain him?
Who am I to build a house for him, except
as a place to make offerings before him?
7 So now send me an artisan skilled to work
in gold, silver, bronze, and iron, and in pur-
ple, crimson, and blue fabrics, trained also
in engraving, to join the skilled workers
who are with me in Judah and Jerusalem,
whom my father David provided. 8 Send me
also cedar, cypress, and algum timber from
Lebanon, for I know that your servants are
skilled in cutting Lebanon timber. My ser-
vants will work with your servants 9 to pre-
pare timber for me in abundance, for the
house I am about to build will be great and
wonderful. 10 I will provide for your ser-
vants, those who cut the timber, twenty
thousand cors of crushed wheat, twenty
thousand cors of barley, twenty thousand
baths[b] of wine, and twenty thousand baths
of oil."

11 Then King Huram of Tyre answered
in a letter that he sent to Solomon, "Be-
cause the LORD loves his people he has
made you king over them." 12 Huram also
said, "Blessed be the LORD God of Israel,
who made heaven and earth, who has given
King David a wise son, endowed with dis-
cretion and understanding, who will build
a temple for the LORD, and a royal palace
for himself.
13 "I have dispatched Huram-abi, a
skilled artisan, endowed with understand-
ing, 14 the son of one of the Danite women,
his father a Tyrian. He is trained to work in
gold, silver, bronze, iron, stone, and wood,
and in purple, blue, and crimson fabrics
and fine linen, and to do all sorts of engrav-
ing and execute any design that may be as-
signed him, with your artisans, the artisans
of my lord, your father David. 15 Now, as
for the wheat, barley, oil, and wine, of
which my lord has spoken, let him send
them to his servants. 16 We will cut whatev-
er timber you need from Lebanon, and
bring it to you as rafts by sea to Joppa; you
will take it up to Jerusalem."
17 Then Solomon took a census of all
the aliens who were residing in the land of
Israel, after the census that his father David
had taken; and there were found to be one
hundred fifty-three thousand six hundred.
18 Seventy thousand of them he assigned as
laborers, eighty thousand as stonecutters in
the hill country, and three thousand six
hundred as overseers to make the people
work.

3 Solomon began to build the house of
the LORD in Jerusalem on Mount Mori-
ah, where the LORD had appeared to his

a Ch 2.1 in Heb *b* A Hebrew measure of volume

Huram (called Hiram in 1 Kings) had been an ally of David (see 2 Sam 5.11), sending him materials to build his palace. **4:** *Rows of bread,* see 1 Chr 9.32; Lev 24.5–9. *Burnt offerings,* see 1 Chr 16.40; Ex 29.38–42; Lev 6.20. **8:** *Algum* ("almug" in 1 Kings), an unidentified species of tree. **10:** A *cor* was about 230 l (6.5 bu); a *bath* about 23 l (6 gal). **11–12:** An elaborate version of 1 Kings 5.7. **13–16:** Cf. 1 Kings 7.13–14. There *Huram-abi* is called Hiram and hails from Naphtali. **17–18:** The census of *aliens* is a prelude to conscription for the Temple's construction (1 Kings 9.22; cf. 5.13–18; 12.4).

3.1–17: Temple construction (see Map on p. 622 HB). A condensed and rewritten version of 1 Kings 6; 7.15–22 (see also the notes there). **1:** Only here is *Mount Moriah,* the site of the binding of Isaac (Gen 22.2),

father David, at the place that David had
designated, on the threshing floor of Ornan
the Jebusite. 2 He began to build on the sec-
ond day of the second month of the fourth
year of his reign. 3 These are Solomon's
measurements[a] for building the house of
God: the length, in cubits of the old stand-
ard, was sixty cubits, and the width twenty
cubits. 4 The vestibule in front of the nave
of the house was twenty cubits long, across
the width of the house;[b] and its height was
one hundred twenty cubits. He overlaid it
on the inside with pure gold. 5 The nave
he lined with cypress, covered it with fine
gold, and made palms and chains on it. 6 He
adorned the house with settings of precious
stones. The gold was gold from Parvaim.
7 So he lined the house with gold—its
beams, its thresholds, its walls, and its
doors; and he carved cherubim on the
walls.

8 He made the most holy place; its
length, corresponding to the width of the
house, was twenty cubits, and its width was
twenty cubits; he overlaid it with six hun-
dred talents of fine gold. 9 The weight of the
nails was fifty shekels of gold. He overlaid
the upper chambers with gold.

10 In the most holy place he made two

a Syr: Heb *foundations* *b* Compare 1 Kings 6.3: Meaning of Heb uncertain

explicitly identified with the Temple site. According to the Chronicler, it is also the location in which David was instructed to build an altar to God (1 Chr 21.15–22.1) following his calamitous census (1 Chr 21.1–14). **3:** *House of God:* Solomon's Temple had three major sections: a "vestibule" (v. 4), a "nave" (vv. 4–5), and a "most holy place" (v. 8). Of these "the most holy place" was the most exclusive and sacred, but the "nave" (or sanctuary) was the largest and contained an incense altar, the "ten golden lampstands" (v. 7), and the "ten tables" (v. 8). Archaeology has revealed a variety of ancient Near Eastern parallels to the tripartite design depicted here. A *cubit* was about 45 cm (18 in); the cubit of *the old standard* may have been slightly longer. **4:** The measurement of *one hundred twenty cubits* for the height of the main part of the building dwarfs the thirty cubits measurement of Solomon's Temple in 1 Kings 6.2. **6:** The location of *Parvaim* is unknown. **8–9:** The Chronicler portrays Solomon, like David (1 Chr 29.1–5), as deliberately excessive in providing for the Temple. The *six hundred talents of fine gold* is the equivalent of over 20,000 kg (45,000 lbs). 1 Kings 6.19–22 simply speaks of "pure gold." **10–14:** Largely abridged from 1 Kings 6.23–28. **10:** *Cherubim* were winged, sphinxlike creatures with human faces (cf. Gen 3.24; 1 Kings 6.23; Ezek 41.18–19). In the ancient Near East, kings were sometimes repre-

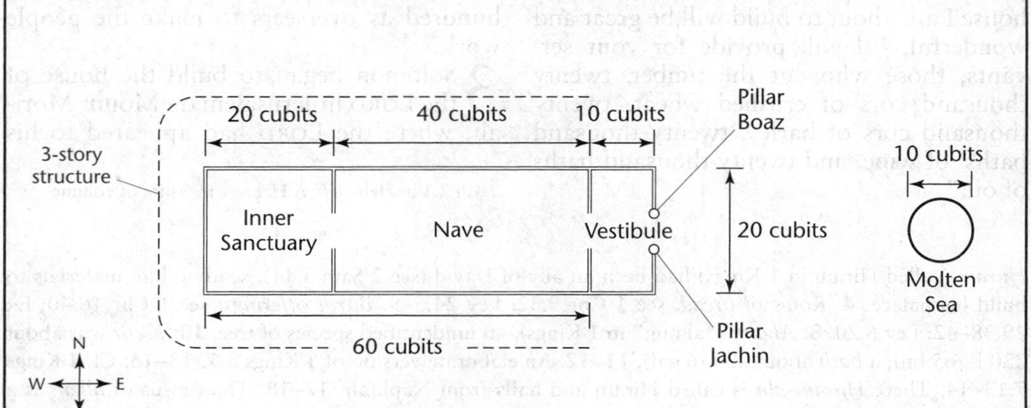

Chs 3–5: The Temple of Solomon.

carved cherubim and overlaid[a] them with
gold. 11 The wings of the cherubim together
extended twenty cubits: one wing of the
one, five cubits long, touched the wall of
the house, and its other wing, five cubits
long, touched the wing of the other cherub;
12 and of this cherub, one wing, five cubits
long, touched the wall of the house, and the
other wing, also five cubits long, was joined
to the wing of the first cherub. 13 The wings
of these cherubim extended twenty cubits;
the cherubim[b] stood on their feet, facing
the nave. 14 And Solomon[c] made the cur-
tain of blue and purple and crimson fabrics
and fine linen, and worked cherubim
into it.
15 In front of the house he made two
pillars thirty-five cubits high, with a capital
of five cubits on the top of each. 16 He made
encircling[d] chains and put them on the
tops of the pillars; and he made one hun-
dred pomegranates, and put them on the
chains. 17 He set up the pillars in front of
the temple, one on the right, the other on
the left; the one on the right he called Ja-
chin, and the one on the left, Boaz.

4 He made an altar of bronze, twenty cu-
bits long, twenty cubits wide, and ten
cubits high. 2 Then he made the molten sea;
it was round, ten cubits from rim to rim,
and five cubits high. A line of thirty cubits
would encircle it completely. 3 Under it
were panels all around, each of ten cubits,
surrounding the sea; there were two rows
of panels, cast when it was cast. 4 It stood
on twelve oxen, three facing north, three
facing west, three facing south, and three
facing east; the sea was set on them. The
hindquarters of each were toward the in-
side. 5 Its thickness was a handbreadth; its
rim was made like the rim of a cup, like
the flower of a lily; it held three thousand
baths.[e] 6 He also made ten basins in which
to wash, and set five on the right side, and
five on the left. In these they were to rinse
what was used for the burnt offering. The
sea was for the priests to wash in.
7 He made ten golden lampstands as
prescribed, and set them in the temple, five
on the south side and five on the north. 8 He
also made ten tables and placed them in the
temple, five on the right side and five on the

a Heb *they overlaid* *b* Heb *they* *c* Heb *he* *d* Cn: Heb *in the inner sanctuary* *e* A Hebrew measure of volume

sented as sitting on a throne supported by such cherubim. In this case, the "cherubim" symbolized the invisible LORD's enthronement in *the most holy place.* **14:** The reference to the *curtain* draws a parallel between the tabernacle (Ex 26.31) and the Temple. 1 Kings 6.31 instead mentions doors. The Chronicler often buttresses the antiquity of the Jerusalem Temple by stressing the continuity between it and older religious institutions such as the tabernacle. **15–17:** On *Jachin* and *Boaz,* see 1 Kings 7.15–22n. **15:** *Pillars,* one pillar stood on each side of the Temple's entrance. Their height of *thirty-five cubits* is nearly double that registered in 1 Kings 7.15.

4.1–22: The Temple furnishings. Largely taken from 1 Kings 7.23–51 (excepting vv. 27–37). **1:** The reference to the *altar of bronze* may have been drawn from 1 Kings 8.64 (cf. 2 Kings 16.14). See also 2 Chr 1.5 and Ezek 43.13–17. This formidable object, made from cast bronze, rested upon a foundation of twelve oxen or bulls, which were traditionally associated with strength and fertility in ancient Canaan. Given that one bath measured approximately 23 l (6 gal), this Temple furnishing was of monumental size. **2–6:** 1 Kings 7.23–26 also describes the *molten sea,* but does not mention that it was used for priestly ablutions. **4:** The *twelve oxen* supporting the molten sea are grouped in threes and face outward in each of the four directions of the compass. **6:** *Ten basins,* see 1 Kings 7.38–39. The tabernacle had only one basin (Ex 30.17). *To wash,* the explanation is not found in Kings. It has been drawn from the description of the tent of meeting (Ex 30.17–21). **7:** *Ten golden lampstands,* Chronicles, in conformity with Kings, mentions multiple lampstands in the Temple (1 Chr 28.15; 2 Chr 4.20 ‖ 1 Kings 7.49). In contrast, the tabernacle has one lampstand (Ex 25.31–40; 31.8; Lev 24.1–4; Num 8.2–4). As "a statute forever throughout your generations" (Lev 24.3), the candelabrum's lamps were to burn every evening (Ex 25.37; 30.7–8; Lev 24.3; Num 8.2; 2 Chr 13.11). **8:** *Ten tables,* in contrast with the one table in the tabernacle (Ex 25.23–30; 26.35; Lev 24.5–9; 2 Chr 13.11) and the one table in the Temple described by 1 Kings 7.48,

left. And he made one hundred basins of
gold. 9He made the court of the priests, and
the great court, and doors for the court; he
overlaid their doors with bronze. 10He
set the sea at the southeast corner of the
house.
11 And Huram made the pots, the shov-
els, and the basins. Thus Huram finished
the work that he did for King Solomon on
the house of God: 12the two pillars, the
bowls, and the two capitals on the top of
the pillars; and the two latticeworks to cov-
er the two bowls of the capitals that were
on the top of the pillars; 13the four hundred
pomegranates for the two latticeworks,
two rows of pomegranates for each lattice-
work, to cover the two bowls of the capi-
tals that were on the pillars. 14He made the
stands, the basins on the stands, 15the one
sea, and the twelve oxen underneath it.
16The pots, the shovels, the forks, and all
the equipment for these Huram-abi made
of burnished bronze for King Solomon for
the house of the LORD. 17In the plain of
the Jordan the king cast them, in the clay
ground between Succoth and Zeredah.
18Solomon made all these things in great
quantities, so that the weight of the bronze
was not determined.
19 So Solomon made all the things that
were in the house of God: the golden altar,
the tables for the bread of the Presence,
20the lampstands and their lamps of pure
gold to burn before the inner sanctuary, as
prescribed; 21the flowers, the lamps, and
the tongs, of purest gold; 22the snuffers,
basins, ladles, and firepans, of pure gold.
As for the entrance to the temple: the inner
doors to the most holy place and the doors
of the nave of the temple were of gold.

5 Thus all the work that Solomon did for
the house of the LORD was finished.
Solomon brought in the things that his fa-
ther David had dedicated, and stored the
silver, the gold, and all the vessels in the
treasuries of the house of God.
2 Then Solomon assembled the elders of
Israel and all the heads of the tribes, the
leaders of the ancestral houses of the people
of Israel, in Jerusalem, to bring up the ark
of the covenant of the LORD out of the city
of David, which is Zion. 3And all the Isra-
elites assembled before the king at the festi-
val that is in the seventh month. 4And all
the elders of Israel came, and the Levites
carried the ark. 5So they brought up the
ark, the tent of meeting, and all the holy
vessels that were in the tent; the priests and
the Levites brought them up. 6King Solo-
mon and all the congregation of Israel, who
had assembled before him, were before the
ark, sacrificing so many sheep and oxen
that they could not be numbered or count-
ed. 7Then the priests brought the ark of the
covenant of the LORD to its place, in the
inner sanctuary of the house, in the most
holy place, underneath the wings of the
cherubim. 8For the cherubim spread out

the Chronicler's Temple had ten. On these tables the "bread of the Presence" would be laid. **9:** The reference to the *court of the priests* likely reflects the Temple of the Chronicler's own day in which the inner court (1 Kings 6.36; 7.12) was reserved for priests and the outer court was for laity, at least on some occasions (1 Chr 28.12; 2 Chr 7.7; 29.16; Neh 8.16). See also Ezekiel's restored temple (Ezek 41.15; 42.7–14; 44.19; 45.19; 46.1). **11:** *Huram,* see 2.13–16n. The *pots, the shovels, and the basins* were employed in sacrificial rituals (Ex 27.3; 1 Kings 7.40). **17:** *Succoth and Zeredah* (Zarethan in 1 Kings 7.46) were towns situated east of the Jordan River. **19:** *Bread of the Presence,* see Ex 25.30; Lev 24.5–9.

5.1–14: The ark and the tent of meeting ascend into the Temple. These verses, excepting vv. 11b–13a, are largely drawn from 1 Kings 8.1–13. The incorporation of both the tabernacle and the ark into the Temple means that both of these older religious institutions find their fulfillment in the Jerusalem sanctuary. Like the authors of Deuteronomy (ch 12) and the Deuteronomistic History (Joshua–2 Kings), the Chronicler commends the centralization of Yahwistic worship and the abolition of all other sanctuaries. Sacrifices are to be carried out only at the Jerusalem Temple and prayers are to be offered at or toward this site (5.5–6.42). In this way, the Temple is to become a focal point of national life. **2:** On the importance of assemblies in Chronicles, see 1.2–13n. **4:** That the Levites carry the ark conforms to David's instructions (1 Chr 15.2) and Deuteronomic law (Deut 10.8). In 1 Kings 8.3, the "priests" do so.

their wings over the place of the ark, so that
the cherubim made a covering above the
ark and its poles. 9 The poles were so long
that the ends of the poles were seen from
the holy place in front of the inner sanctu-
ary; but they could not be seen from out-
side; they are there to this day. 10 There was
nothing in the ark except the two tablets
that Moses put there at Horeb, where the
LORD made a covenant[a] with the people of
Israel after they came out of Egypt.
11 Now when the priests came out of
the holy place (for all the priests who were
present had sanctified themselves, without
regard to their divisions), 12 all the levitical
singers, Asaph, Heman, and Jeduthun,
their sons and kindred, arrayed in fine lin-
en, with cymbals, harps, and lyres, stood
east of the altar with one hundred twenty
priests who were trumpeters. 13 It was the
duty of the trumpeters and singers to make
themselves heard in unison in praise and
thanksgiving to the LORD, and when the
song was raised, with trumpets and cym-
bals and other musical instruments, in
praise to the LORD,

"For he is good,
for his steadfast love endures
forever,"

the house, the house of the LORD, was filled
with a cloud, 14 so that the priests could not
stand to minister because of the cloud; for
the glory of the LORD filled the house of
God.

6 Then Solomon said, "The LORD has
said that he would reside in thick dark-
ness. 2 I have built you an exalted house, a
place for you to reside in forever."
3 Then the king turned around and
blessed all the assembly of Israel, while all
the assembly of Israel stood. 4 And he said,
"Blessed be the LORD, the God of Israel,
who with his hand has fulfilled what he
promised with his mouth to my father Da-
vid, saying, 5 'Since the day that I brought
my people out of the land of Egypt, I have
not chosen a city from any of the tribes of
Israel in which to build a house, so that my
name might be there, and I chose no one as
ruler over my people Israel; 6 but I have
chosen Jerusalem in order that my name
may be there, and I have chosen David to
be over my people Israel.' 7 My father Da-
vid had it in mind to build a house for the
name of the LORD, the God of Israel. 8 But
the LORD said to my father David, 'You did
well to consider building a house for my
name; 9 nevertheless you shall not build the
house, but your son who shall be born to
you shall build the house for my name.'
10 Now the LORD has fulfilled his promise
that he made; for I have succeeded my fa-
ther David, and sit on the throne of Israel,
as the LORD promised, and have built the
house for the name of the LORD, the God of
Israel. 11 There I have set the ark, in which
is the covenant of the LORD that he made
with the people of Israel."
12 Then Solomon[b] stood before the al-
tar of the LORD in the presence of the

a Heb lacks *a covenant* *b* Heb *he*

10: *Two tablets,* see Deut 10.1–5. *Horeb* is another name for Sinai. **11–13:** The Chronicler's addition to the Kings narrative points out that David's Levitical and priestly arrangements (1 Chr 15–16; 25–26) were broadly implemented. *Asaph, Heman, and Jeduthun,* see 1 Chr 6.33n.,44n. *Cloud,* see 1 Kings 8.10–11n.

6.1–42: Solomon's blessing and Temple dedication prayer. With the exception of vv. 13 and 41–42, this entire chapter is reproduced, with some significant modifications, from the author's version of 1 Kings 8.12–52. Solomon's public speeches situate the Temple's construction in Israel's national life—past, present, and future. **4–11:** In his blessing, Solomon praises God that a number of the Davidic promises (1 Chr 17.1–15) have been fulfilled. **12–40:** The pattern of divine fidelity recounted in Solomon's blessing becomes the occasion for Solomon to request that other divine promises be realized (vv. 14–17). The heart of the prayer of dedication (vv. 22–40) consists of seven petitions detailing a variety of predicaments in which the nation may find herself, including defeat by the enemy (vv. 24–25), drought (vv. 26–27), open pitched battles (vv. 34–35), and even exile (vv. 36–39). In each case Solomon prays that God might listen from his heavenly dwelling and be attentive to the prayers of his people.

whole assembly of Israel, and spread out
his hands. 13 Solomon had made a bronze
platform five cubits long, five cubits wide,
and three cubits high, and had set it in the
court; and he stood on it. Then he knelt on
his knees in the presence of the whole as-
sembly of Israel, and spread out his hands
toward heaven. 14 He said, "O LORD, God
of Israel, there is no God like you, in heav-
en or on earth, keeping covenant in stead-
fast love with your servants who walk be-
fore you with all their heart— 15 you who
have kept for your servant, my father Da-
vid, what you promised to him. Indeed, you
promised with your mouth and this day
have fulfilled with your hand. 16 Therefore,
O LORD, God of Israel, keep for your ser-
vant, my father David, that which you
promised him, saying, 'There shall never
fail you a successor before me to sit on the
throne of Israel, if only your children keep
to their way, to walk in my law as you have
walked before me.' 17 Therefore, O LORD,
God of Israel, let your word be confirmed,
which you promised to your servant David.

18 "But will God indeed reside with
mortals on earth? Even heaven and the
highest heaven cannot contain you, how
much less this house that I have built! 19 Re-
gard your servant's prayer and his plea,
O LORD my God, heeding the cry and the
prayer that your servant prays to you.
20 May your eyes be open day and night
toward this house, the place where you
promised to set your name, and may you
heed the prayer that your servant prays to-
ward this place. 21 And hear the plea of
your servant and of your people Israel,
when they pray toward this place; may you
hear from heaven your dwelling place; hear
and forgive.

22 "If someone sins against another and
is required to take an oath and comes and
swears before your altar in this house,
23 may you hear from heaven, and act, and
judge your servants, repaying the guilty by
bringing their conduct on their own head,
and vindicating those who are in the right
by rewarding them in accordance with their
righteousness.

24 "When your people Israel, having
sinned against you, are defeated before an
enemy but turn again to you, confess your
name, pray and plead with you in this
house, 25 may you hear from heaven, and
forgive the sin of your people Israel, and
bring them again to the land that you gave
to them and to their ancestors.

26 "When heaven is shut up and there is
no rain because they have sinned against
you, and then they pray toward this place,
confess your name, and turn from their sin,
because you punish them, 27 may you hear
in heaven, forgive the sin of your servants,
your people Israel, when you teach them
the good way in which they should walk;
and send down rain upon your land, which
you have given to your people as an inheri-
tance.

28 "If there is famine in the land, if there
is plague, blight, mildew, locust, or cater-
pillar; if their enemies besiege them in any
of the settlements of the lands; whatever
suffering, whatever sickness there is;
29 whatever prayer, whatever plea from any
individual or from all your people Israel, all
knowing their own suffering and their own
sorrows so that they stretch out their hands
toward this house; 30 may you hear from
heaven, your dwelling place, forgive, and
render to all whose heart you know, ac-
cording to all their ways, for only you
know the human heart. 31 Thus may they
fear you and walk in your ways all the days
that they live in the land that you gave to
our ancestors.

32 "Likewise when foreigners, who are
not of your people Israel, come from a dis-
tant land because of your great name, and
your mighty hand, and your outstretched
arm, when they come and pray toward this
house, 33 may you hear from heaven your

13: The *bronze platform* is found only here. **16:** *My law* (Heb "torah"), replacing "before me" of 1 Kings 8.25. This small change likely reflects the new importance of the Torah-book in the postexilic community. **41–42:** Solomon's prayer of 1 Kings 8 is given a new conclusion from Ps 132.8–10.

7.1–22: Divine consecration, national thanksgiving, and a warning. Both the Deuteronomist (1 Kings

dwelling place, and do whatever the for-
eigners ask of you, in order that all the peo-
ples of the earth may know your name and
fear you, as do your people Israel, and that
they may know that your name has been
invoked on this house that I have built.
34 "If your people go out to battle
against their enemies, by whatever way you
shall send them, and they pray to you to-
ward this city that you have chosen and
the house that I have built for your name,
35 then hear from heaven their prayer and
their plea, and maintain their cause.
36 "If they sin against you—for there is
no one who does not sin—and you are an-
gry with them and give them to an enemy,
so that they are carried away captive to a
land far or near; 37 then if they come to
their senses in the land to which they have
been taken captive, and repent, and plead
with you in the land of their captivity, say-
ing, 'We have sinned, and have done
wrong; we have acted wickedly'; 38 if they
repent with all their heart and soul in the
land of their captivity, to which they were
taken captive, and pray toward their land,
which you gave to their ancestors, the city
that you have chosen, and the house that I
have built for your name, 39 then hear from
heaven your dwelling place their prayer
and their pleas, maintain their cause and
forgive your people who have sinned
against you. 40 Now, O my God, let your
eyes be open and your ears attentive to
prayer from this place.
41 "Now rise up, O LORD God, and go
to your resting place,
you and the ark of your might.
Let your priests, O LORD God, be
clothed with salvation,
and let your faithful rejoice in your
goodness.
42 O LORD God, do not reject your
anointed one.
Remember your steadfast love for
your servant David."

7 When Solomon had ended his prayer,
fire came down from heaven and con-
sumed the burnt offering and the sacrifices;
and the glory of the LORD filled the temple.
2 The priests could not enter the house of
the LORD, because the glory of the LORD
filled the LORD's house. 3 When all the peo-
ple of Israel saw the fire come down and
the glory of the LORD on the temple, they
bowed down on the pavement with their
faces to the ground, and worshiped and
gave thanks to the LORD, saying,
"For he is good,
for his steadfast love endures
forever."
4 Then the king and all the people of-
fered sacrifice before the LORD. 5 King Sol-
omon offered as a sacrifice twenty-two
thousand oxen and one hundred twenty
thousand sheep. So the king and all the
people dedicated the house of God. 6 The
priests stood at their posts; the Levites also,
with the instruments for music to the LORD
that King David had made for giving
thanks to the LORD—for his steadfast love
endures forever—whenever David offered
praises by their ministry. Opposite them
the priests sounded trumpets; and all Israel
stood.
7 Solomon consecrated the middle of the
court that was in front of the house of the
LORD; for there he offered the burnt offer-
ings and the fat of the offerings of well-
being because the bronze altar Solomon

9.1–9) and the Chronicler mention a divine response to Solomon's prayer (vv. 16–22), but the Chronicler also includes other material affirming both the Temple (vv. 1–3,11) and King Solomon's petitions (vv. 13–15). **1:** The divine consecration of *the burnt offering and the sacrifices* by *fire,* not found in 1 Kings 8–9, dramatically legitimates the Jerusalem Temple as an enduring fixture of Israelite life (Lev 9.24; 1 Kings 18.36–39; 1 Chr 21.26). **3:** The people's liturgical refrain—*"For he is good, for his steadfast love endures forever"*—also found in Ps 136 (2 Chr 5.13; 7.6; 20.21; Ezra 3.11), was likely a significant element of the postexilic Temple liturgy. **7–8:** Taken in part from 1 Kings 8.65–66. *From Lebo-hamath to the Wadi of Egypt,* the northern and southern limits of Solomon's rule. *Lebo-hamath* is probably in the southern Orontes valley in Lebanon. *The Wadi of Egypt,* either the Wadi Besor or the Wadi el-Arish, both south of Gaza. See Map on p. 629 HB. **9–10:** The festivities last far longer than in

had made could not hold the burnt offering
and the grain offering and the fat parts.
8 At that time Solomon held the festival
for seven days, and all Israel with him, a
very great congregation, from Lebo-
hamath to the Wadi of Egypt. 9 On the
eighth day they held a solemn assembly; for
they had observed the dedication of the al-
tar seven days and the festival seven days.
10 On the twenty-third day of the seventh
month he sent the people away to their
homes, joyful and in good spirits because of
the goodness that the LORD had shown to
David and to Solomon and to his people
Israel.
11 Thus Solomon finished the house of
the LORD and the king's house; all that Sol-
omon had planned to do in the house of the
LORD and in his own house he successfully
accomplished.
12 Then the LORD appeared to Solomon
in the night and said to him: "I have heard
your prayer, and have chosen this place for
myself as a house of sacrifice. 13 When I
shut up the heavens so that there is no rain,
or command the locust to devour the land,
or send pestilence among my people, 14 if
my people who are called by my name
humble themselves, pray, seek my face, and
turn from their wicked ways, then I will
hear from heaven, and will forgive their sin
and heal their land. 15 Now my eyes will be
open and my ears attentive to the prayer
that is made in this place. 16 For now I have
chosen and consecrated this house so that
my name may be there forever; my eyes and
my heart will be there for all time. 17 As for
you, if you walk before me, as your father
David walked, doing according to all that I
have commanded you and keeping my stat-
utes and my ordinances, 18 then I will estab-
lish your royal throne, as I made covenant
with your father David saying, 'You shall
never lack a successor to rule over Israel.'
19 "But if you[a] turn aside and forsake
my statutes and my commandments that I
have set before you, and go and serve other
gods and worship them, 20 then I will pluck
you[b] up from the land that I have given
you;[b] and this house, which I have conse-
crated for my name, I will cast out of my
sight, and will make it a proverb and a by-
word among all peoples. 21 And regarding
this house, now exalted, everyone passing
by will be astonished, and say, 'Why has
the LORD done such a thing to this land and
to this house?' 22 Then they will say, 'Be-
cause they abandoned the LORD the God of
their ancestors who brought them out of
the land of Egypt, and they adopted other
gods, and worshiped them and served
them; therefore he has brought all this ca-
lamity upon them.' "

8 At the end of twenty years, during
which Solomon had built the house of
the LORD and his own house, 2 Solomon
rebuilt the cities that Huram had given to
him, and settled the people of Israel in
them.
3 Solomon went to Hamath-zobah, and
captured it. 4 He built Tadmor in the wil-
derness and all the storage towns that he

a The word *you* in this verse is plural *b* Heb *them*

1 Kings 8.66, in which the Priestly legislation is not a consideration (cf. Lev 23.36; Num 29.35–38; Neh 8.18). **13–14:** The Temple is approved as an appropriate means of divine-human communications. Should king or people find themselves in duress, they may respond in four ways: *humble themselves, pray, seek my face, and turn from their wicked ways.* For his part, the LORD will *hear from heaven, and will forgive their sin and heal their land* (v. 14). **19–22:** Israel's possession of the land, as well as the longevity of the Temple itself, are keyed to national obedience (cf. 1 Chr 28.7).

8.1–18: Solomon the successful king. Following the Temple's dedication, Solomon advances his program of public works (vv. 3–6,11), continues his patronage of the nation's worship (vv. 12–15), employs the tribute from a foreign king to good advantage (v. 2; cf. 1 Kings 9.10–14), and engages in international trade (vv. 17–18). **2:** This reflects a remarkable reversal of the tradition recorded in 1 Kings 9.11–13. **3:** An otherwise unattested campaign. No place named *Hamath-zobah* is known; elsewhere Hamath and Zobah are separate kingdoms in Syria. **4:** Solomon's control reaches to Syria (see Map on p. 629 HB). *Tadmor* is later Palmyra, an important oasis in the desert ca. 225 km (140 mi) northeast of

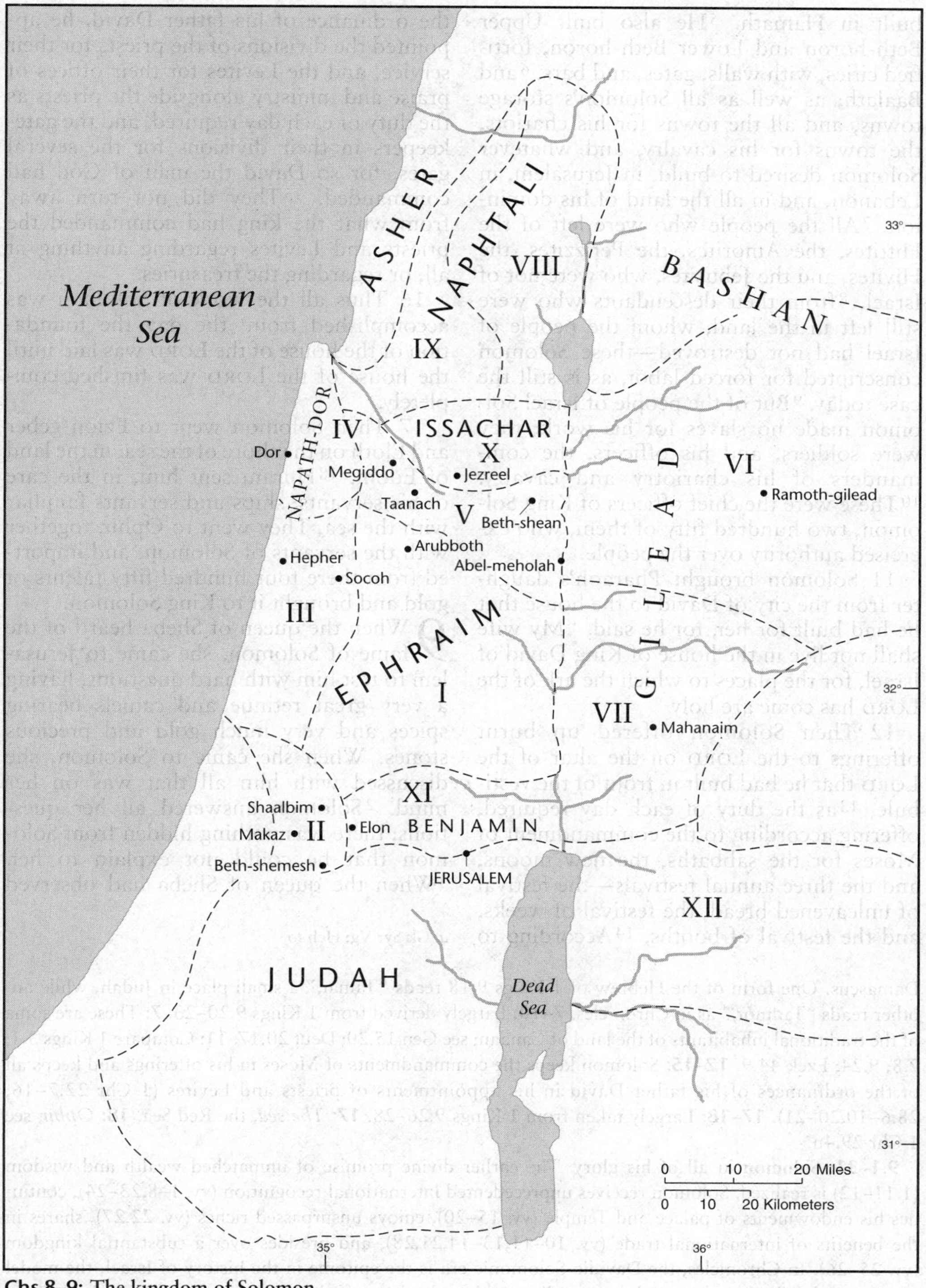

Chs 8–9: The kingdom of Solomon.

built in Hamath. 5He also built Upper
Beth-horon and Lower Beth-horon, forti-
fied cities, with walls, gates, and bars, 6and
Baalath, as well as all Solomon's storage
towns, and all the towns for his chariots,
the towns for his cavalry, and whatever
Solomon desired to build, in Jerusalem, in
Lebanon, and in all the land of his domin-
ion. 7All the people who were left of the
Hittites, the Amorites, the Perizzites, the
Hivites, and the Jebusites, who were not of
Israel, 8from their descendants who were
still left in the land, whom the people of
Israel had not destroyed—these Solomon
conscripted for forced labor, as is still the
case today. 9But of the people of Israel Sol-
omon made no slaves for his work; they
were soldiers, and his officers, the com-
manders of his chariotry and cavalry.
10These were the chief officers of King Sol-
omon, two hundred fifty of them, who ex-
ercised authority over the people.

11 Solomon brought Pharaoh's daugh-
ter from the city of David to the house that
he had built for her, for he said, "My wife
shall not live in the house of King David of
Israel, for the places to which the ark of the
LORD has come are holy."

12 Then Solomon offered up burnt
offerings to the LORD on the altar of the
LORD that he had built in front of the vesti-
bule, 13as the duty of each day required,
offering according to the commandment of
Moses for the sabbaths, the new moons,
and the three annual festivals—the festival
of unleavened bread, the festival of weeks,
and the festival of booths. 14According to
the ordinance of his father David, he ap-
pointed the divisions of the priests for their
service, and the Levites for their offices of
praise and ministry alongside the priests as
the duty of each day required, and the gate-
keepers in their divisions for the several
gates; for so David the man of God had
commanded. 15They did not turn away
from what the king had commanded the
priests and Levites regarding anything at
all, or regarding the treasuries.

16 Thus all the work of Solomon was
accomplished from[a] the day the founda-
tion of the house of the LORD was laid until
the house of the LORD was finished com-
pletely.

17 Then Solomon went to Ezion-geber
and Eloth on the shore of the sea, in the land
of Edom. 18Huram sent him, in the care
of his servants, ships and servants familiar
with the sea. They went to Ophir, together
with the servants of Solomon, and import-
ed from there four hundred fifty talents of
gold and brought it to King Solomon.

9 When the queen of Sheba heard of the
fame of Solomon, she came to Jerusa-
lem to test him with hard questions, having
a very great retinue and camels bearing
spices and very much gold and precious
stones. When she came to Solomon, she
discussed with him all that was on her
mind. 2Solomon answered all her ques-
tions; there was nothing hidden from Solo-
mon that he could not explain to her.
3When the queen of Sheba had observed

a Gk Syr Vg: Heb *to*

Damascus. One form of the Hebrew of 1 Kings 9.18 reads "Tamar," a small place in Judah, while another reads "Tadmor," as in Chronicles. **7–10:** Largely derived from 1 Kings 9.20–23. **7:** These are some of the traditional inhabitants of the land of Canaan; see Gen 15.20; Deut 20.17. **11:** Compare 1 Kings 3.1; 7.8; 9.24; Ezek 44.9. **12–15:** Solomon keeps the commandments of Moses in his offerings and keeps all of the ordinances of his father David in his appointments of priests and Levites (1 Chr 22.7–16; 28.6–10,20–21). **17–18:** Largely taken from 1 Kings 9.26–28. **17:** *The sea,* the Red Sea. **18:** *Ophir,* see 1 Chr 29.4n.

9.1–31: Solomon in all of his glory. The earlier divine promise of unmatched wealth and wisdom (1.11–12) is realized. Solomon receives unprecedented international recognition (vv. 1–8,23–24), continues his endowments of palace and Temple (vv. 15–20), enjoys unsurpassed riches (vv. 22,27), shares in the benefits of international trade (vv. 10–11,13–14,21,28), and presides over a substantial kingdom (vv. 25–26). In Chronicles, the Davidic-Solomonic era is the epitome in the history of Israel, the model of unity and orthodoxy by which both earlier and later leaders, officials, and people will be judged (7.10;

the wisdom of Solomon, the house that he
had built, 4 the food of his table, the seating
of his officials, and the attendance of his
servants, and their clothing, his valets, and
their clothing, and his burnt offerings[a]
that he offered at the house of the LORD,
there was no more spirit left in her.
5 So she said to the king, "The report
was true that I heard in my own land of
your accomplishments and of your wis-
dom, 6 but I did not believe the[b] reports
until I came and my own eyes saw it. Not
even half of the greatness of your wisdom
had been told to me; you far surpass the
report that I had heard. 7 Happy are your
people! Happy are these your servants,
who continually attend you and hear your
wisdom! 8 Blessed be the LORD your God,
who has delighted in you and set you on his
throne as king for the LORD your God. Be-
cause your God loved Israel and would es-
tablish them forever, he has made you king
over them, that you may execute justice
and righteousness." 9 Then she gave the
king one hundred twenty talents of gold, a
very great quantity of spices, and precious
stones: there were no spices such as those
that the queen of Sheba gave to King Solo-
mon.
10 Moreover the servants of Huram and
the servants of Solomon who brought gold
from Ophir brought algum wood and pre-
cious stones. 11 From the algum wood, the
king made steps[c] for the house of the
LORD and for the king's house, lyres also
and harps for the singers; there never was
seen the like of them before in the land of
Judah.

12 Meanwhile King Solomon granted
the queen of Sheba every desire that she
expressed, well beyond what she had
brought to the king. Then she returned to
her own land, with her servants.
13 The weight of gold that came to Solo-
mon in one year was six hundred sixty-six
talents of gold, 14 besides that which the
traders and merchants brought; and all the
kings of Arabia and the governors of the
land brought gold and silver to Solomon.
15 King Solomon made two hundred large
shields of beaten gold; six hundred shekels
of beaten gold went into each large shield.
16 He made three hundred shields of beaten
gold; three hundred shekels of gold went
into each shield; and the king put them in
the House of the Forest of Lebanon. 17 The
king also made a great ivory throne, and
overlaid it with pure gold. 18 The throne
had six steps and a footstool of gold, which
were attached to the throne, and on each
side of the seat were arm rests and two li-
ons standing beside the arm rests, 19 while
twelve lions were standing, one on each end
of a step on the six steps. The like of it was
never made in any kingdom. 20 All King
Solomon's drinking vessels were of gold,
and all the vessels of the House of the For-
est of Lebanon were of pure gold; silver
was not considered as anything in the days
of Solomon. 21 For the king's ships went to
Tarshish with the servants of Huram; once
every three years the ships of Tarshish used

a Gk Syr Vg 1 Kings 10.5: Heb *ascent* *b* Heb *their*
c Gk Vg: Meaning of Heb uncertain

11.17; 30.26; 35.3–4). **1–12:** Taken from 1 Kings 10.1–13. **1:** *Sheba* is in Arabia. **4:** *No more spirit left,* that is, she was breathless. **9:** A *talent* weighed about 34 kg (75 lb). **11:** *Algum,* see 2.8n. **13–28:** Largely drawn from 1 Kings 10.14–28a. **15:** *Large shields*, these ornamental objects of great value were later taken by King Shishak of Egypt during his campaign through parts of Canaan (12.9–11). **16:** *The House of the Forest of Lebanon,* perhaps named because of the extensive use of Lebanon cedar inside. This complex, which was probably located south of the Temple, actually contained five buildings. Being most interested in the Temple, the Chronicler does not pursue the description and functions of this "house" (cf. 1 Kings 7.1–12). **17:** *Great ivory throne,* both Solomon's official seat and a symbol of his prestige, wealth, and power (cf. Ex 11.5; 2 Sam 3.10). **18:** *Footstool,* another royal symbol (cf. 1 Kings 10.18–20). The term is also used to represent defeated enemies (Ps 110.1), the ark (1 Chr 28.2), Zion (Lam 2.1), and the earth itself (Isa 66.1). **21:** *Tarshish,* probably the city of Tarsus on the southern coast of Turkey, or perhaps Tartessus in southern Spain. **25–29:** Cf. 1.14–16n. V. 26 is drawn from 1 Kings 4.21; Solomon is the dominant

to come bringing gold, silver, ivory, apes,
and peacocks.[a]
22 Thus King Solomon excelled all the
kings of the earth in riches and in wisdom.
23 All the kings of the earth sought the pres-
ence of Solomon to hear his wisdom, which
God had put into his mind. 24 Every one of
them brought a present, objects of silver
and gold, garments, weaponry, spices,
horses, and mules, so much year by year.
25 Solomon had four thousand stalls for
horses and chariots, and twelve thousand
horses, which he stationed in the chariot
cities and with the king in Jerusalem. 26 He
ruled over all the kings from the Euphrates
to the land of the Philistines, and to the
border of Egypt. 27 The king made silver as
common in Jerusalem as stone, and cedar
as plentiful as the sycamore of the Shephe-
lah. 28 Horses were imported for Solomon
from Egypt and from all lands.
29 Now the rest of the acts of Solomon,
from first to last, are they not written in the
history of the prophet Nathan, and in the
prophecy of Ahijah the Shilonite, and in the
visions of the seer Iddo concerning Jerobo-
am son of Nebat? 30 Solomon reigned in
Jerusalem over all Israel forty years. 31 Solo-
mon slept with his ancestors and was bur-
ied in the city of his father David; and his
son Rehoboam succeeded him.

10 Rehoboam went to Shechem, for all
Israel had come to Shechem to make
him king. 2 When Jeroboam son of Nebat
heard of it (for he was in Egypt, where he
had fled from King Solomon), then Jerobo-
am returned from Egypt. 3 They sent and
called him; and Jeroboam and all Israel
came and said to Rehoboam, 4 "Your fa-
ther made our yoke heavy. Now therefore
lighten the hard service of your father and
his heavy yoke that he placed on us, and we
will serve you." 5 He said to them, "Come
to me again in three days." So the people
went away.
6 Then King Rehoboam took counsel
with the older men who had attended his
father Solomon while he was still alive, say-
ing, "How do you advise me to answer this
people?" 7 They answered him, "If you will

a Or *baboons*

ruler of the region from northern Syria to the border of Egypt (cf. 7.8). **29:** *Nathan,* see 1 Chr 17.1–15; *Ahijah,* see 1 Kings 11.29–39; *Iddo* is not known apart from notices such as this (see 12.15; 13.22). **29–31:** Solomon's reign ends as it began with a unified nation under an exemplary king. Israel is unhampered by internal factions or strife. The nation enjoys unparalleled glory. Solomon's tenure is untainted by sin or misadventure. Any information that would potentially tarnish Solomon's reputation has been omitted (1 Kings 9.11–16; 11.1–38). Solomon is not blamed for the later division of the kingdom (cf. 1 Kings 11.1–13,31–38). Because the Chronicler heightens the great benefit of Davidic-Solomonic leadership for the people, those who might deviate from this norm (10.3) will be suspect. It is unclear if the sources mentioned in v. 29 and elsewhere are nonbiblical sources, refer to the sections of the Bible, or never existed, and are cited here as a way of justifying the Chronicler's history, which differs in such significant ways from Kings.

10.1–18: The difficult beginning to Rehoboam's reign (928–911 BCE). Compared with 1 Kings 12.1–24; 14.21–31, Chronicles almost doubles the amount of coverage devoted to *Rehoboam* and presents a much more complex narration of his reign (10.1–12.16). Rehoboam's accession is not characterized by the unanimity that both David (1 Chr 11) and Solomon (2 Chr 1) enjoyed. **1:** Rehoboam ascends to the throne and immediately finds himself thrust into a national assembly at *Shechem* bargaining for the future of his nation with disaffected representatives of the northern tribes (cf. 1 Kings 12.1–24). *Shechem* was located in the hill country of Ephraim between Mounts Ebal and Gerizim. The national convocation was likely held here, because Shechem was an important and historic town in ancient Israel (Josh 8.30–35; 20.7; 17.7; 21.21; 24.1–28; 1 Kings 12.1–17; 1 Chr 6.52; 7.28). **2–3:** Jeroboam, the head of the northern tribes (1 Kings 11.26–43), is both present and an active protagonist in the proceedings (also v. 12). In Chronicles Jeroboam and Rehoboam each become more personally responsible for the events of the secession (13.4–12). **15:** *His word . . . by Ahijah,* see 1 Kings 11.29–39. Ultimately, the division is a *turn of affairs* that could not have occurred without divine assent. This verse

be kind to this people and please them, and
speak good words to them, then they will
be your servants forever." 8But he rejected
the advice that the older men gave him, and
consulted the young men who had grown
up with him and now attended him. 9He
said to them, "What do you advise that we
answer this people who have said to me,
'Lighten the yoke that your father put on
us'?" 10The young men who had grown up
with him said to him, "Thus should you
speak to the people who said to you, 'Your
father made our yoke heavy, but you must
lighten it for us'; tell them, 'My little finger
is thicker than my father's loins. 11Now,
whereas my father laid on you a heavy
yoke, I will add to your yoke. My father
disciplined you with whips, but I will disci-
pline you with scorpions.' "
12 So Jeroboam and all the people came
to Rehoboam the third day, as the king had
said, "Come to me again the third day."
13The king answered them harshly. King
Rehoboam rejected the advice of the older
men; 14he spoke to them in accordance
with the advice of the young men, "My fa-
ther made your yoke heavy, but I will add
to it; my father disciplined you with whips,
but I will discipline you with scorpions."
15So the king did not listen to the people,

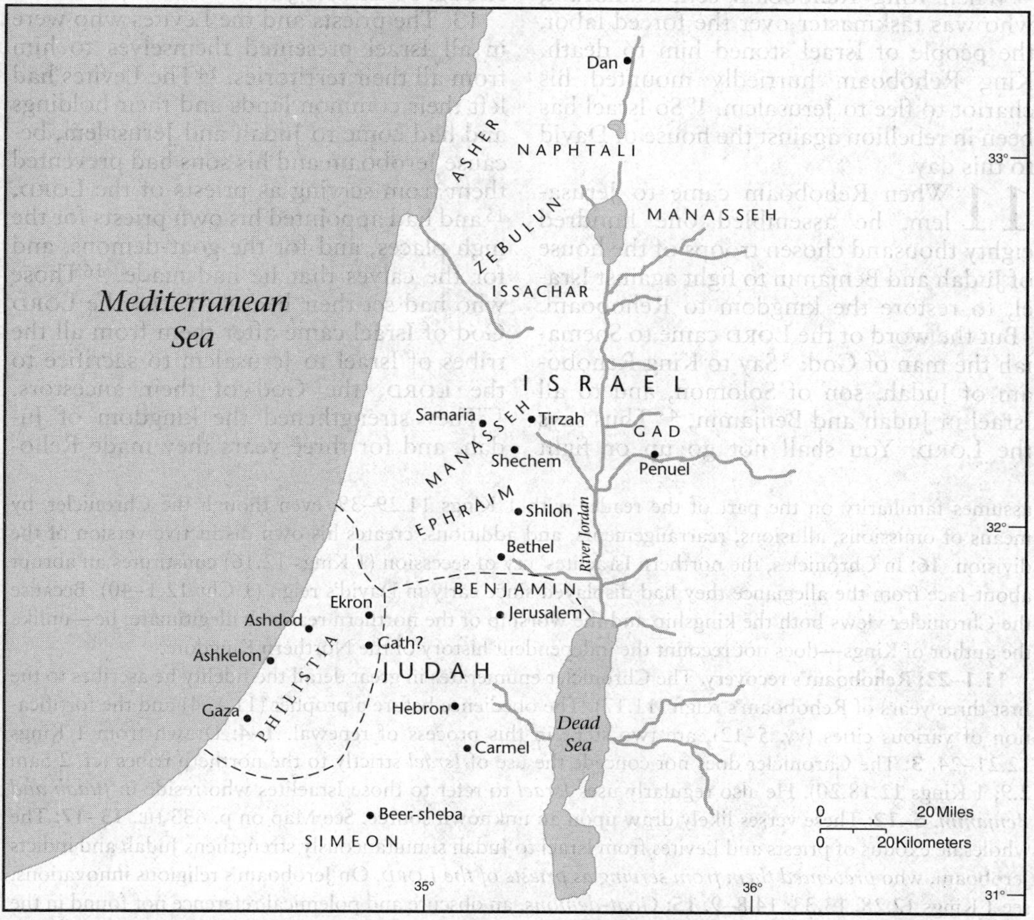

Chs 10–12: The divided monarchy. The dashed line shows the approximate boundaries between Israel, Judah, and Philistia.

because it was a turn of affairs brought
about by God so that the LORD might fulfill
his word, which he had spoken by Ahijah
the Shilonite to Jeroboam son of Nebat.
16 When all Israel saw that the king
would not listen to them, the people an-
swered the king,

"What share do we have in David?
We have no inheritance in the son
of Jesse.
Each of you to your tents, O Israel!
Look now to your own house,
O David."

So all Israel departed to their tents. 17 But
Rehoboam reigned over the people of Israel
who were living in the cities of Judah.
18 When King Rehoboam sent Hadoram,
who was taskmaster over the forced labor,
the people of Israel stoned him to death.
King Rehoboam hurriedly mounted his
chariot to flee to Jerusalem. 19 So Israel has
been in rebellion against the house of David
to this day.

11 When Rehoboam came to Jerusa-
lem, he assembled one hundred
eighty thousand chosen troops of the house
of Judah and Benjamin to fight against Isra-
el, to restore the kingdom to Rehoboam.
2 But the word of the LORD came to Shema-
iah the man of God: 3 Say to King Rehobo-
am of Judah, son of Solomon, and to all
Israel in Judah and Benjamin, 4 "Thus says
the LORD: You shall not go up or fight
against your kindred. Let everyone return
home, for this thing is from me." So they
heeded the word of the LORD and turned
back from the expedition against Jero-
boam.
5 Rehoboam resided in Jerusalem, and
he built cities for defense in Judah. 6 He
built up Bethlehem, Etam, Tekoa, 7 Beth-
zur, Soco, Adullam, 8 Gath, Mareshah,
Ziph, 9 Adoraim, Lachish, Azekah, 10 Zo-
rah, Aijalon, and Hebron, fortified cities
that are in Judah and in Benjamin. 11 He
made the fortresses strong, and put com-
manders in them, and stores of food, oil,
and wine. 12 He also put large shields and
spears in all the cities, and made them very
strong. So he held Judah and Benjamin.
13 The priests and the Levites who were
in all Israel presented themselves to him
from all their territories. 14 The Levites had
left their common lands and their holdings
and had come to Judah and Jerusalem, be-
cause Jeroboam and his sons had prevented
them from serving as priests of the LORD,
15 and had appointed his own priests for the
high places, and for the goat-demons, and
for the calves that he had made. 16 Those
who had set their hearts to seek the LORD
God of Israel came after them from all the
tribes of Israel to Jerusalem to sacrifice to
the LORD, the God of their ancestors.
17 They strengthened the kingdom of Ju-
dah, and for three years they made Reho-

assumes familiarity on the part of the reader with 1 Kings 11.29–39, even though the Chronicler, by means of omissions, allusions, rearrangements, and additions, creates his own distinctive version of the division. **16:** In Chronicles, the northern Israelites' cry of secession (1 Kings 12.16) constitutes an abrupt about-face from the allegiance they had displayed since early in David's reign (1 Chr 12.1–40). Because the Chronicler views both the kingship and the worship of the northern realm as illegitimate, he—unlike the author of Kings—does not recount the independent history of the Northern Kingdom.

11.1–23: Rehoboam's recovery. The Chronicler enumerates in great detail the fidelity he ascribes to the first three years of Rehoboam's reign (11.17). The obedience before a prophet (11.1–4) and the fortification of various cities (vv. 5–12), are two steps in this process of renewal. **1–4:** Drawn from 1 Kings 12.21–24. **3:** The Chronicler does not concede the use of *Israel* strictly to the northern tribes (cf. 2 Sam 2.9; 1 Kings 12.18,20). He also regularly uses *Israel* to refer to those Israelites who reside in *Judah and Benjamin*. **5–12:** These verses likely draw upon an unknown source. See Map on p. 633 HB. **13–17:** The wholesale exodus of priests and Levites from Israel to Judah simultaneously strengthens Judah and indicts Jeroboam, who *prevented them from serving as priests of the LORD*. On Jeroboam's religious innovations, see 1 Kings 12.28; 13.33; 14.8–9. **15:** *Goat-demons,* an obscure and polemical reference not found in the source text depicting Jeroboam's religious innovations (1 Kings 12.28). Worship of goat-demons is outlawed in Priestly legislation (Lev 17.7). **18–21:** Large families signify stature in Chronicles (1 Chr 14.3;

boam son of Solomon secure, for they
walked for three years in the way of David
and Solomon.
18 Rehoboam took as his wife Maha-
lath daughter of Jerimoth son of David,
and of Abihail daughter of Eliab son of Jes-
se. 19 She bore him sons: Jeush, Shemariah,
and Zaham. 20 After her he took Maacah
daughter of Absalom, who bore him Abi-
jah, Attai, Ziza, and Shelomith. 21 Rehobo-
am loved Maacah daughter of Absalom
more than all his other wives and concu-
bines (he took eighteen wives and sixty
concubines, and became the father of
twenty-eight sons and sixty daughters).
22 Rehoboam appointed Abijah son of Ma-
acah as chief prince among his brothers, for
he intended to make him king. 23 He dealt
wisely, and distributed some of his sons
through all the districts of Judah and Benja-
min, in all the fortified cities; he gave them
abundant provisions, and found many
wives for them.

12 When the rule of Rehoboam was
established and he grew strong, he
abandoned the law of the LORD, he and all
Israel with him. 2 In the fifth year of King
Rehoboam, because they had been unfaith-
ful to the LORD, King Shishak of Egypt
came up against Jerusalem 3 with twelve
hundred chariots and sixty thousand caval-
ry. A countless army came with him from
Egypt—Libyans, Sukkiim, and Ethiopi-
ans.[a] 4 He took the fortified cities of Judah
and came as far as Jerusalem. 5 Then the
prophet Shemaiah came to Rehoboam and
to the officers of Judah, who had gathered
at Jerusalem because of Shishak, and said
to them, "Thus says the LORD: You aban-
doned me, so I have abandoned you to the
hand of Shishak." 6 Then the officers of Is-
rael and the king humbled themselves and
said, "The LORD is in the right." 7 When
the LORD saw that they humbled them-
selves, the word of the LORD came to She-
maiah, saying: "They have humbled them-
selves; I will not destroy them, but I will
grant them some deliverance, and my
wrath shall not be poured out on Jerusalem
by the hand of Shishak. 8 Nevertheless they
shall be his servants, so that they may know
the difference between serving me and serv-
ing the kingdoms of other lands."
9 So King Shishak of Egypt came up
against Jerusalem; he took away the trea-
sures of the house of the LORD and the trea-
sures of the king's house; he took every-
thing. He also took away the shields of gold
that Solomon had made; 10 but King Reho-
boam made in place of them shields of
bronze, and committed them to the hands
of the officers of the guard, who kept the
door of the king's house. 11 Whenever the
king went into the house of the LORD, the
guard would come along bearing them, and
would then bring them back to the guard-
room. 12 Because he humbled himself the
wrath of the LORD turned from him, so as
not to destroy them completely; moreover,
conditions were good in Judah.
13 So King Rehoboam established him-
self in Jerusalem and reigned. Rehoboam
was forty-one years old when he began to
reign; he reigned seventeen years in Jerusa-
lem, the city that the LORD had chosen out
of all the tribes of Israel to put his name

a Or *Nubians*; Heb *Cushites*

2 Chr 11.18–23; 13.21; 14.3–7; cf. Gen 1.28). **22–23:** Like his grandfather, Rehoboam gainfully employs his sons in administration (1 Chr 18.17).

12.1–16: National decline and a reprieve. After a short recovery (11.1–23), Rehoboam and Judah abandon *the law of the LORD* and Egypt invades (cf. 1 Kings 14.25). The outlines of the Egyptian invasion are found in 1 Kings 14.25–28, but the Chronicler has elaborated them significantly, especially in his addition of v. 1, which suggests that the invasion was punishment for apostasy. **2:** *Shishak* (Shoshenq I) ruled Egypt 945–924 BCE. **3:** *Sukkiim,* unknown. **5:** The prophet's speech, like many other biblical texts, invokes the principle of measure for measure: Those who abandon God will be abandoned by God. **6–8:** Because of their repentance (cf. 11.1–4), Rehoboam and the people stave off complete disaster. Hence, Rehoboam is the first of many kings to benefit from God's promises in response to Solomon's Temple prayer (7.12–15). **13–16:** Cf. 1 Kings 14.21–24,29–31. **15:** *Iddo,* see 9.29n.

there. His mother's name was Naamah the
Ammonite. 14 He did evil, for he did not set
his heart to seek the LORD.

15 Now the acts of Rehoboam, from
first to last, are they not written in the
records of the prophet Shemaiah and of the
seer Iddo, recorded by genealogy? There
were continual wars between Rehoboam
and Jeroboam. 16 Rehoboam slept with his
ancestors and was buried in the city of Da-
vid; and his son Abijah succeeded him.

13 In the eighteenth year of King Jero-
boam, Abijah began to reign over
Judah. 2 He reigned for three years in Jeru-
salem. His mother's name was Micaiah
daughter of Uriel of Gibeah.

Now there was war between Abijah and
Jeroboam. 3 Abijah engaged in battle, hav-
ing an army of valiant warriors, four hun-
dred thousand picked men; and Jeroboam
drew up his line of battle against him with
eight hundred thousand picked mighty
warriors. 4 Then Abijah stood on the slope
of Mount Zemaraim that is in the hill coun-
try of Ephraim, and said, "Listen to me,
Jeroboam and all Israel! 5 Do you not know
that the LORD God of Israel gave the king-
ship over Israel forever to David and his
sons by a covenant of salt? 6 Yet Jeroboam
son of Nebat, a servant of Solomon son
of David, rose up and rebelled against his
lord; 7 and certain worthless scoundrels
gathered around him and defied Rehoboam
son of Solomon, when Rehoboam was
young and irresolute and could not with-
stand them.

8 "And now you think that you can
withstand the kingdom of the LORD in the
hand of the sons of David, because you are
a great multitude and have with you the
golden calves that Jeroboam made as gods
for you. 9 Have you not driven out the
priests of the LORD, the descendants of
Aaron, and the Levites, and made priests
for yourselves like the peoples of other
lands? Whoever comes to be consecrated

13.1–22: The successful reign of Abijah (911–908 BCE). In Chronicles, as opposed to 1 Kings 15.1–8, Abijah (called Abijam in 1 Kings) is one of Judah's better monarchs. In a war against *Jeroboam and all Israel,* he defends the standards established by David and Solomon as normative for all Israelites. Much of the chapter is an original composition of the Chronicler, elaborating on 1 Kings 15.6. The fundamental principle illustrated through this narrative is "the people of Judah prevailed, because they relied on the LORD, the God of their ancestors" (v. 8). **2:** *Micaiah,* there is a text-critical issue here. The Hebrew gives Abijah's mother a Yahwistic name ("who is like the LORD"), whereas the ancient versions name her "Maacah" in conformity with 1 Kings 15.2 and 2 Chr 11.20. **3:** Developing a theme of earlier sacral war narratives (Judg 7.2–8; 1 Sam 14.6; 17.45–47), the Chronicler here and elsewhere stresses that great numbers do not guarantee victory (14.7–14; 20.1–30; 24.24; cf. Zech 4.6). *Eight hundred thousand,* the Chronicler's numbers here and elsewhere are sometimes stupendous (e.g., 1 Chr 5.18; 23.3–5; 27.1–15; 2 Chr 14.8–9; 17.14–18; 25.5–6; 26.12–13; 28.6–8). Some have thought that the Hebrew word for "thousand" refers simply to one unit, meaning that the actual numbers involved would be far less. But it is more likely that the incredible numbers are a literary convention or scribal embellishment to mark off (what is for the Chronicler) Israel's classical past. The use of large, round numbers is also sometimes found in earlier biblical sources (e.g., 1 Kings 8.5,62–64). **5:** In speaking to *Jeroboam and all Israel* (v. 4) of *the kingship over Israel* as belonging to the Davidic dynasty, Abijah plays on the different connotations of Israel. *Covenant of salt,* the reference to "salt" indicates that the kingship that has been covenanted to David will be enduring (Lev 2.13; Num 18.19). In v. 8, the kingdom of the LORD is itself said to be in the hands of David and his descendants (cf. 1 Chr 17.14; 28.5). **6–7:** Disunion occurred when Jeroboam and *worthless scoundrels* exploited a young and inexperienced Rehoboam. This polemicizes against 1 Kings 11.11–13,29–38. **8–11:** Abijah's enumeration of Judean orthopraxis is heavily indebted to the descriptions of Temple worship during the United Monarchy (1 Chr 15–16; 23–29; 2 Chr 2–4) and the descriptions of tabernacle worship during the era of Moses (Ex 25.30–40; 29.1–9,38–42; 30.7–10; Lev 24.3–9; Num 8.2–4; 28.3–8). **19:** Judah recaptures some of the territory it presumably lost in the secession. The Chronicler commends Judean kings who exercise influence in the northern realm (15.8–9; 17.2; 30.5–12;

with a young bull or seven rams becomes a
priest of what are no gods. 10 But as for us,
the LORD is our God, and we have not
abandoned him. We have priests minister-
ing to the LORD who are descendants of
Aaron, and Levites for their service. 11 They
offer to the LORD every morning and every
evening burnt offerings and fragrant in-
cense, set out the rows of bread on the table
of pure gold, and care for the golden lamp-
stand so that its lamps may burn every eve-
ning; for we keep the charge of the LORD
our God, but you have abandoned him.
12 See, God is with us at our head, and his
priests have their battle trumpets to sound
the call to battle against you. O Israelites,
do not fight against the LORD, the God of
your ancestors; for you cannot succeed."
13 Jeroboam had sent an ambush
around to come on them from behind; thus
his troops[a] were in front of Judah, and the
ambush was behind them. 14 When Judah
turned, the battle was in front of them and
behind them. They cried out to the LORD,
and the priests blew the trumpets. 15 Then
the people of Judah raised the battle shout.
And when the people of Judah shouted,
God defeated Jeroboam and all Israel be-
fore Abijah and Judah. 16 The Israelites fled
before Judah, and God gave them into their
hands. 17 Abijah and his army defeated
them with great slaughter; five hundred
thousand picked men of Israel fell slain.
18 Thus the Israelites were subdued at that
time, and the people of Judah prevailed,
because they relied on the LORD, the God
of their ancestors. 19 Abijah pursued Jero-
boam, and took cities from him: Bethel
with its villages and Jeshanah with its vil-
lages and Ephron[b] with its villages. 20 Jero-
boam did not recover his power in the days
of Abijah; the LORD struck him down, and
he died. 21 But Abijah grew strong. He took
fourteen wives, and became the father of
twenty-two sons and sixteen daughters.
22 The rest of the acts of Abijah, his behav-
ior and his deeds, are written in the story of
the prophet Iddo.

14 [c]So Abijah slept with his ancestors,
and they buried him in the city of
David. His son Asa succeeded him. In his
days the land had rest for ten years. 2 [d] Asa
did what was good and right in the sight of
the LORD his God. 3 He took away the for-
eign altars and the high places, broke down
the pillars, hewed down the sacred poles,[e]
4 and commanded Judah to seek the LORD,
the God of their ancestors, and to keep the
law and the commandment. 5 He also re-
moved from all the cities of Judah the high
places and the incense altars. And the king-
dom had rest under him. 6 He built fortified
cities in Judah while the land had rest. He
had no war in those years, for the LORD
gave him peace. 7 He said to Judah, "Let us
build these cities, and surround them with

a Heb *they* *b* Another reading is *Ephrain*
c Ch 13.23 in Heb *d* Ch 14.1 in Heb
e Heb *Asherim*

34.6–7,33). **20:** Here God himself struck Jeroboam *and he died;* cf. 1 Kings 14.19–20. **21:** See 11.18–21n. **22:** The Hebrew word for *story* ("midrash") can also be translated as exposition, study, or "commentary" (24.27; cf. Sir 51.23). The reference thus designates a writing or commentary of *Iddo* (rather than an annalistic account) on the early monarchy. See also 9.29n. and 12.15n.

14.1–15.19: Reforms, victory, and expansion: the first period of Asa's reign (908–867 BCE). The Chronicler's treatment of Asa (14.1–16.14), almost three times longer than that of 1 Kings 15.9–24, presents two distinct phases in Asa's reign: a long 34-year period of fidelity and a short 7-year period of infidelity (16.1–12). The shorter text of Kings is supplemented significantly. Kings has a pattern of piety followed by lack of trust in God. The Chronicler subsumes this to his retribution theology, creating a pattern of piety and its reward, then impiety and its punishment. Prophetic figures play a significant role in these elaborations. **14.1:** In Chronicles *rest* from war is a sign of divine blessing (1 Chr 17.8–9; 22.9; 2 Chr 14.6; 32.22). **2–8:** At the beginning of his reign Asa takes advantage of peaceful conditions to institute religious reforms (cf. 1 Kings 15.12–15) and embark on a series of public works. **8–9:** On the incredible numbers, see 13.3n. **9–15:** Another sacral war narrative (cf. 13.2–20) in which an outnumbered

walls and towers, gates and bars; the land is
still ours because we have sought the LORD
our God; we have sought him, and he has
given us peace on every side." So they built
and prospered. 8 Asa had an army of three
hundred thousand from Judah, armed with
large shields and spears, and two hundred
eighty thousand troops from Benjamin who
carried shields and drew bows; all these
were mighty warriors.
9 Zerah the Ethiopian[a] came out
against them with an army of a million men
and three hundred chariots, and came as
far as Mareshah. 10 Asa went out to meet
him, and they drew up their lines of battle
in the valley of Zephathah at Mareshah.
11 Asa cried to the LORD his God,
"O LORD, there is no difference for you be-
tween helping the mighty and the weak.
Help us, O LORD our God, for we rely
on you, and in your name we have come
against this multitude. O LORD, you are
our God; let no mortal prevail against
you." 12 So the LORD defeated the Ethiopi-
ans[b] before Asa and before Judah, and the
Ethiopians[b] fled. 13 Asa and the army with
him pursued them as far as Gerar, and the
Ethiopians[b] fell until no one remained
alive; for they were broken before the
LORD and his army. The people of Judah[c]
carried away a great quantity of booty.
14 They defeated all the cities around Gerar,
for the fear of the LORD was on them. They
plundered all the cities; for there was much
plunder in them. 15 They also attacked the
tents of those who had livestock,[d] and car-
ried away sheep and goats in abundance,
and camels. Then they returned to Jerusa-
lem.

15 The spirit of God came upon Azari-
ah son of Oded. 2 He went out to
meet Asa and said to him, "Hear me, Asa,
and all Judah and Benjamin: The LORD is
with you, while you are with him. If you
seek him, he will be found by you, but if
you abandon him, he will abandon you.
3 For a long time Israel was without the true
God, and without a teaching priest, and
without law; 4 but when in their distress
they turned to the LORD, the God of Israel,
and sought him, he was found by them. 5 In
those times it was not safe for anyone to go
or come, for great disturbances afflicted all
the inhabitants of the lands. 6 They were
broken in pieces, nation against nation and
city against city, for God troubled them
with every sort of distress. 7 But you, take
courage! Do not let your hands be weak,
for your work shall be rewarded."
8 When Asa heard these words, the
prophecy of Azariah son of Oded,[e] he
took courage, and put away the abomina-
ble idols from all the land of Judah and
Benjamin and from the towns that he had
taken in the hill country of Ephraim. He
repaired the altar of the LORD that was in
front of the vestibule of the house of the
LORD.[f] 9 He gathered all Judah and Benja-
min, and those from Ephraim, Manasseh,
and Simeon who were residing as aliens

a Or *Nubian*; Heb *Cushite* b Or *Nubians*; Heb *Cushites* c Heb *They* d Meaning of Heb uncertain e Compare Syr Vg: Heb *the prophecy, the prophet Obed* f Heb *the vestibule of the LORD*

Judah confronts a much more powerful foe (Zerah, who is otherwise unknown). In the midst of battle, Asa calls out to the LORD for deliverance in accordance with the petitions of Solomon's prayer (6.34–35). When king and people rely on God, they are able to achieve a major victory and take enormous booty (vv. 12–15). **9:** *Ethiopian,* the Hebrew literally speaks of a Cushite. Cush was an area to the south of Egypt. Sudan, Nubia, and Ethiopia are all possibilities. **10:** *Mareshah,* ca. 40 km (25 mi) southwest of Jerusalem, one of the southern cities fortified by Rehoboam (see 11.5–10). See Map on p. 633 HB. **15.1–7:** The prophet Azariah appears only in this chapter. His oracle speaks of the benefits of reciprocity in divine-human relations. *The LORD is with you, while you are with him* (15.2), the corollary of the measure-for-measure principle articulated earlier by Shemaiah (12.5). Pointing to the chaos of the distant past, the prophet warns Asa about the perils of abandoning God. **8–19:** In response to Azariah's admonitions, Asa initiates a covenant renewal (vv. 8–15; cf. Ex 19.3–8) and institutes further religious reforms (vv. 16–18; cf. 1 Kings 15.13–15).

with them, for great numbers had deserted
to him from Israel when they saw that the
LORD his God was with him. 10 They were
gathered at Jerusalem in the third month
of the fifteenth year of the reign of Asa.
11 They sacrificed to the LORD on that day,
from the booty that they had brought, sev-
en hundred oxen and seven thousand
sheep. 12 They entered into a covenant to
seek the LORD, the God of their ancestors,
with all their heart and with all their soul.
13 Whoever would not seek the LORD, the
God of Israel, should be put to death,
whether young or old, man or woman.
14 They took an oath to the LORD with a
loud voice, and with shouting, and with
trumpets, and with horns. 15 All Judah re-
joiced over the oath; for they had sworn
with all their heart, and had sought him
with their whole desire, and he was found
by them, and the LORD gave them rest all
around.

16 King Asa even removed his mother
Maacah from being queen mother because
she had made an abominable image for
Asherah. Asa cut down her image, crushed
it, and burned it at the Wadi Kidron. 17 But
the high places were not taken out of Israel.
Nevertheless the heart of Asa was true all
his days. 18 He brought into the house of
God the votive gifts of his father and his
own votive gifts—silver, gold, and utensils.
19 And there was no more war until the
thirty-fifth year of the reign of Asa.

16 In the thirty-sixth year of the reign
of Asa, King Baasha of Israel went
up against Judah, and built Ramah, to pre-
vent anyone from going out or coming into
the territory of[a] King Asa of Judah. 2 Then
Asa took silver and gold from the treasures
of the house of the LORD and the king's
house, and sent them to King Ben-hadad of
Aram, who resided in Damascus, saying,
3 "Let there be an alliance between me and
you, like that between my father and your
father; I am sending to you silver and gold;
go, break your alliance with King Baasha of
Israel, so that he may withdraw from me."
4 Ben-hadad listened to King Asa, and sent
the commanders of his armies against the
cities of Israel. They conquered Ijon, Dan,
Abel-maim, and all the store-cities of
Naphtali. 5 When Baasha heard of it, he
stopped building Ramah, and let his work
cease. 6 Then King Asa brought all Judah,
and they carried away the stones of Ramah
and its timber, with which Baasha had been
building, and with them he built up Geba
and Mizpah.

7 At that time the seer Hanani came to
King Asa of Judah, and said to him, "Be-
cause you relied on the king of Aram, and
did not rely on the LORD your God, the
army of the king of Aram has escaped you.
8 Were not the Ethiopians[b] and the Liby-
ans a huge army with exceedingly many
chariots and cavalry? Yet because you re-
lied on the LORD, he gave them into your
hand. 9 For the eyes of the LORD range
throughout the entire earth, to strengthen
those whose heart is true to him. You have
done foolishly in this; for from now on you
will have wars." 10 Then Asa was angry
with the seer, and put him in the stocks, in
prison, for he was in a rage with him be-
cause of this. And Asa inflicted cruelties on
some of the people at the same time.

a Heb lacks *the territory of* *b* Or *Nubians*; Heb *Cushites*

16.1–14: Asa's decline. The war with Baasha (cf. 1 Kings 15.16–22) marks a turning point in Asa's tenure because he enters an alliance with *Ben-hadad of Aram* to counter an invasion by *Baasha of Israel.* Even though Asa enters this treaty in self-defense, the Chronicler considers such alliances as compromising Judah's commitment to the deity, who can defend the powerless from the mighty. Opposition to pacts with foreign powers is also found in earlier biblical literature (Deut 7.2; Hos 7.10–13; 8.9–10; Isa 20; 28.14–28; 30.1–5; Jer 2.14–19,33–37). **1:** *Ramah* was located just 9 km (6 mi) north of Jerusalem. **7–9:** The judgment oracle of *the seer Hanani* (apparently the father of the prophet Jehu; 19.2) heightens the disparity between the two terms in Asa's rule. Whereas Asa formerly relied on God and was able to defeat the vast armies of *Ethiopia* and *Libya* (14.7–14; 15.8), Asa's reliance on Ben-hadad is tantamount to nonreliance on the LORD (16.7). Ironically, Asa will now always be plagued by *wars* (cf. 1 Kings 15.16).

11 The acts of Asa, from first to last, are
written in the Book of the Kings of Judah
and Israel. 12 In the thirty-ninth year of his
reign Asa was diseased in his feet, and his
disease became severe; yet even in his dis-
ease he did not seek the LORD, but sought
help from physicians. 13 Then Asa slept
with his ancestors, dying in the forty-first
year of his reign. 14 They buried him in the
tomb that he had hewn out for himself in
the city of David. They laid him on a bier
that had been filled with various kinds of
spices prepared by the perfumer's art; and
they made a very great fire in his honor.

17 His son Jehoshaphat succeeded him,
and strengthened himself against Is-
rael. 2 He placed forces in all the fortified
cities of Judah, and set garrisons in the land
of Judah, and in the cities of Ephraim that
his father Asa had taken. 3 The LORD was
with Jehoshaphat, because he walked in the
earlier ways of his father;[a] he did not seek
the Baals, 4 but sought the God of his father
and walked in his commandments, and not
according to the ways of Israel. 5 Therefore
the LORD established the kingdom in his
hand. All Judah brought tribute to Jehosha-
phat, and he had great riches and honor.
6 His heart was courageous in the ways of
the LORD; and furthermore he removed the
high places and the sacred poles[b] from Ju-
dah.

7 In the third year of his reign he sent his
officials, Ben-hail, Obadiah, Zechariah,
Nethanel, and Micaiah, to teach in the cit-
ies of Judah. 8 With them were the Levites,
Shemaiah, Nethaniah, Zebadiah, Asahel,
Shemiramoth, Jehonathan, Adonijah, To-
bijah, and Tob-adonijah; and with these
Levites, the priests Elishama and Jehoram.
9 They taught in Judah, having the book of
the law of the LORD with them; they went
around through all the cities of Judah and
taught among the people.

10 The fear of the LORD fell on all the
kingdoms of the lands around Judah, and
they did not make war against Jehosha-
phat. 11 Some of the Philistines brought Je-
hoshaphat presents, and silver for tribute;
and the Arabs also brought him seven thou-
sand seven hundred rams and seven thou-
sand seven hundred male goats. 12 Jehosha-
phat grew steadily greater. He built
fortresses and storage cities in Judah. 13 He
carried out great works in the cities of Ju-
dah. He had soldiers, mighty warriors, in
Jerusalem. 14 This was the muster of them
by ancestral houses: Of Judah, the com-
manders of the thousands: Adnah the com-
mander, with three hundred thousand
mighty warriors, 15 and next to him Jeho-

a Another reading is *his father David*
b Heb *Asherim*

12: The infirmity in Asa's feet (1 Kings 15.23) becomes another indication of Asa's unfaithfulness, because *in his disease he did not seek the LORD.* His reliance on physicians reflects a folk-etymology of Asa's name, which may be another word for "healer" or "physician."

17.1–19: The promising beginning to the reign of Jehoshaphat (870–846 BCE). Both Kings and Chronicles commend Jehoshaphat (1 Kings 22.43–44; 2 Chr 17.3–4; 20.32–33), but the Chronicler's depiction of Jehoshaphat's reign is much more extensive and includes major events not recorded in Kings. Scholars continue to debate whether these events were based on the additional sources that the Chronicler had, or were freely composed. Most of the new material, such as Jehoshaphat's civil, military, and judicial reforms (17.1–19; 19.4–11) and his war against the eastern coalition (20.1–30), reflects well on Jehoshaphat. Upon taking office, Jehoshaphat immediately takes charge of his kingdom. As he institutes reforms, deploys troops, and fortifies cities Jehoshaphat only grows stronger and more widely respected. Prophetic material concerning the northern prophet Elijah, which is embedded in Jehoshaphat's reign in Kings, is absent here. **2:** *Cities of Ephraim,* probably referring to 13.19. **7–9:** Jehoshaphat initiates a campaign to educate the Judean people in *the book of the law of the LORD* (cf. Deut 17.18–20; 2 Kings 22.8–13) by sending officers, Levites, and priests throughout the cities of Judah. This addition reflects the growing importance in the postexilic era of the Torah-book, and of the Levites as teachers (see esp. Neh 8). **11:** Tribute from the nations is a sign of divine favor (1 Chr 18.6; 2 Chr 8.2; 9.1–9; 26.8). **14–18:** On the large numbers, see 13.3n.

hanan the commander, with two hundred
eighty thousand, 16 and next to him Amasi-
ah son of Zichri, a volunteer for the service
of the LORD, with two hundred thousand
mighty warriors. 17 Of Benjamin: Eliada, a
mighty warrior, with two hundred thou-
sand armed with bow and shield, 18 and
next to him Jehozabad with one hundred
eighty thousand armed for war. 19 These
were in the service of the king, besides
those whom the king had placed in the for-
tified cities throughout all Judah.

18 Now Jehoshaphat had great riches
and honor; and he made a marriage
alliance with Ahab. 2 After some years he
went down to Ahab in Samaria. Ahab
slaughtered an abundance of sheep and
oxen for him and for the people who were
with him, and induced him to go up against
Ramoth-gilead. 3 King Ahab of Israel said
to King Jehoshaphat of Judah, "Will you
go with me to Ramoth-gilead?" He an-
swered him, "I am with you, my people are
your people. We will be with you in the
war."

4 But Jehoshaphat also said to the king
of Israel, "Inquire first for the word of the
LORD." 5 Then the king of Israel gathered
the prophets together, four hundred of
them, and said to them, "Shall we go to
battle against Ramoth-gilead, or shall I re-
frain?" They said, "Go up; for God will
give it into the hand of the king." 6 But Je-
hoshaphat said, "Is there no other prophet
of the LORD here of whom we may in-
quire?" 7 The king of Israel said to Jehosha-
phat, "There is still one other by whom we
may inquire of the LORD, Micaiah son of
Imlah; but I hate him, for he never proph-
esies anything favorable about me, but only
disaster." Jehoshaphat said, "Let the king
not say such a thing." 8 Then the king of
Israel summoned an officer and said,
"Bring quickly Micaiah son of Imlah."
9 Now the king of Israel and King Jehosha-
phat of Judah were sitting on their thrones,
arrayed in their robes; and they were sitting
at the threshing floor at the entrance of the
gate of Samaria; and all the prophets were
prophesying before them. 10 Zedekiah son
of Chenaanah made for himself horns of
iron, and he said, "Thus says the LORD:
With these you shall gore the Arameans un-
til they are destroyed." 11 All the prophets
were prophesying the same and saying,
"Go up to Ramoth-gilead and triumph; the
LORD will give it into the hand of the
king."

12 The messenger who had gone to sum-
mon Micaiah said to him, "Look, the
words of the prophets with one accord are
favorable to the king; let your word be like
the word of one of them, and speak favor-
ably." 13 But Micaiah said, "As the LORD
lives, whatever my God says, that I will
speak."

14 When he had come to the king, the
king said to him, "Micaiah, shall we go to
Ramoth-gilead to battle, or shall I refrain?"
He answered, "Go up and triumph; they
will be given into your hand." 15 But the
king said to him, "How many times must I
make you swear to tell me nothing but the
truth in the name of the LORD?" 16 Then
Micaiah[a] said, "I saw all Israel scattered
on the mountains, like sheep without a
shepherd; and the LORD said, 'These have
no master; let each one go home in
peace.' " 17 The king of Israel said to Je-
hoshaphat, "Did I not tell you that he

a Heb *he*

18.1–19.3: Jehoshaphat's first misstep. The Chronicler relates two shortcomings of Jehoshaphat, and both of these involve his relations with northern Israel. The first involves Jehoshaphat's ill-fated treaty with Ahab in 1 Kings 22.1–40, which is reproduced with very few changes. **18.1:** Presumably this *marriage alliance* involved Jehoshaphat's son, Jehoram, and Ahab's daughter, Athaliah (21.6; 22.2; cf. 2 Kings 8.18). In the reign of Jehoshaphat's successors, the relationship with Ahab's dynasty becomes the conduit for Judah's royalty to adopt ill-advised and iniquitous policies (21.6; 22.3–5). **2:** The lavish feast, during which Ahab incites his Judean counterpart, does not appear in 1 Kings 22. **2–3:** *Ramoth-gilead* was an Israelite city in northern Jordan that had apparently been captured by the Arameans. **10:** A symbolic action, as elsewhere in the prophetic repertoire. **18:** The LORD is meeting with his heavenly council (see

would not prophesy anything favorable
about me, but only disaster?"
18 Then Micaiah[a] said, "Therefore
hear the word of the LORD: I saw the LORD
sitting on his throne, with all the host of
heaven standing to the right and to the left
of him. 19 And the LORD said, 'Who will
entice King Ahab of Israel, so that he may
go up and fall at Ramoth-gilead?' Then one
said one thing, and another said another,
20 until a spirit came forward and stood be-
fore the LORD, saying, 'I will entice him.'
The LORD asked him, 'How?' 21 He replied,
'I will go out and be a lying spirit in the
mouth of all his prophets.' Then the
LORD[a] said, 'You are to entice him, and
you shall succeed; go out and do it.' 22 So
you see, the LORD has put a lying spirit
in the mouth of these your prophets; the
LORD has decreed disaster for you."
23 Then Zedekiah son of Chenaanah
came up to Micaiah, slapped him on the
cheek, and said, "Which way did the spirit
of the LORD pass from me to speak to
you?" 24 Micaiah replied, "You will find
out on that day when you go in to hide in
an inner chamber." 25 The king of Israel
then ordered, "Take Micaiah, and return
him to Amon the governor of the city and
to Joash the king's son; 26 and say, 'Thus
says the king: Put this fellow in prison, and
feed him on reduced rations of bread and
water until I return in peace.' " 27 Micaiah
said, "If you return in peace, the LORD has
not spoken by me." And he said, "Hear,
you peoples, all of you!"
28 So the king of Israel and King Jehosh-
aphat of Judah went up to Ramoth-gilead.
29 The king of Israel said to Jehoshaphat, "I
will disguise myself and go into battle, but
you wear your robes." So the king of Israel
disguised himself, and they went into bat-
tle. 30 Now the king of Aram had com-
manded the captains of his chariots, "Fight
with no one small or great, but only with
the king of Israel." 31 When the captains of
the chariots saw Jehoshaphat, they said, "It
is the king of Israel." So they turned to fight
against him; and Jehoshaphat cried out,
and the LORD helped him. God drew them
away from him, 32 for when the captains of
the chariots saw that it was not the king of
Israel, they turned back from pursuing him.
33 But a certain man drew his bow and un-
knowingly struck the king of Israel between
the scale armor and the breastplate; so he
said to the driver of his chariot, "Turn
around, and carry me out of the battle, for
I am wounded." 34 The battle grew hot that
day, and the king of Israel propped himself
up in his chariot facing the Arameans until
evening; then at sunset he died.

19 King Jehoshaphat of Judah returned
in safety to his house in Jerusalem.
2 Jehu son of Hanani the seer went out to
meet him and said to King Jehoshaphat,
"Should you help the wicked and love
those who hate the LORD? Because of this,
wrath has gone out against you from the
LORD. 3 Nevertheless, some good is found
in you, for you destroyed the sacred poles[b]
out of the land, and have set your heart to
seek God."
4 Jehoshaphat resided at Jerusalem; then

a Heb *he* *b* Heb *Asheroth*

Job 1.6; 2.1; Ps 82.1), and the prophet is a witness to the proceedings (see Jer 23.18,22). **21–22:** The revelation that the prophets have received is itself false; cf. Deut 13.3. **31:** *The LORD helped him,* this phrase, which does not appear in 1 Kings 22, resonates with the divine promises of 7.12–15. The Chronicler adds this phrase to reinforce his theology: God, who is fair, is in total control of events. **19.1–20.30:** In contrast to the previous Jehoshaphat material, this has no parallel in Kings. **19.1–3:** This rebuke by the prophet *Jehu son of Hanani* (see 16.7–9n.) chastises Jehoshaphat for entering into a coalition with Ahab of Israel (see 16.1–6n.). Jehoshaphat was disloyal to God in that he proposed to *help the wicked* and was loyal to *those who hate the LORD*. Fidelity to one precludes fidelity to the other.

19.4–11: Recovery and further reforms. Jehoshaphat returns to and develops policies he instituted at the beginning of his reign (17.1–19). The geographic scope of the restoration (v. 4) is extensive, reclaiming Jehoshaphat's entire realm, including sections of the Northern Kingdom over which he held sway (17.1–2). Other texts depict the juridical responsibilities of monarchs (e.g., 2 Sam 8.15–18; 1 Kings

he went out again among the people, from
Beer-sheba to the hill country of Ephraim,
and brought them back to the LORD, the
God of their ancestors. 5He appointed
judges in the land in all the fortified cities of
Judah, city by city, 6and said to the judges,
"Consider what you are doing, for you
judge not on behalf of human beings but on
the LORD's behalf; he is with you in giving
judgment. 7Now, let the fear of the LORD
be upon you; take care what you do, for
there is no perversion of justice with the
LORD our God, or partiality, or taking of
bribes."
8 Moreover in Jerusalem Jehoshaphat
appointed certain Levites and priests and
heads of families of Israel, to give judgment
for the LORD and to decide disputed cases.
They had their seat at Jerusalem. 9He
charged them: "This is how you shall act:
in the fear of the LORD, in faithfulness, and
with your whole heart; 10whenever a case
comes to you from your kindred who live
in their cities, concerning bloodshed, law
or commandment, statutes or ordinances,
then you shall instruct them, so that they
may not incur guilt before the LORD and
wrath may not come on you and your kin-
dred. Do so, and you will not incur guilt.
11See, Amariah the chief priest is over you
in all matters of the LORD; and Zebadiah
son of Ishmael, the governor of the house
of Judah, in all the king's matters; and the
Levites will serve you as officers. Deal cou-
rageously, and may the LORD be with the
good!"

20 After this the Moabites and Am-
monites, and with them some of the
Meunites,[a] came against Jehoshaphat for
battle. 2Messengers[b] came and told Je-
hoshaphat, "A great multitude is coming
against you from Edom,[c] from beyond the
sea; already they are at Hazazon-tamar"
(that is, En-gedi). 3Jehoshaphat was afraid;
he set himself to seek the LORD, and pro-
claimed a fast throughout all Judah. 4Judah
assembled to seek help from the LORD;
from all the towns of Judah they came to
seek the LORD.
5 Jehoshaphat stood in the assembly of
Judah and Jerusalem, in the house of the
LORD, before the new court, 6and said,
"O LORD, God of our ancestors, are you
not God in heaven? Do you not rule over
all the kingdoms of the nations? In your
hand are power and might, so that no one
is able to withstand you. 7Did you not,
O our God, drive out the inhabitants of

a Compare 26.7: Heb *Ammonites* *b* Heb *They*
c One Ms: MT *Aram*

3.16–28), but only with Jehoshaphat in Chronicles do we find a full-blown judicial reform. Some see this as reflecting the creativity of the Chronicler, who derived this reform from the element "shaphat," "to judge," in the king's name (cf. 16.12n.). **11:** The distinction between matters of the LORD and the king's matters is only found in Chronicles (1 Chr 26.30,32; 2 Chr 19.11) and Ezra (7.26), suggesting that this reform may be the creation of the Chronicler.

20.1–30: Dramatic triumph in sacral war. Sometime after his judicial reformation, Jehoshaphat is confronted with an international crisis that threatens to overwhelm his people, the invasion of Judah (see v. 2) by a southeastern coalition of powers. **1:** *Meunites,* a textually difficult term. The Meunites are a group of disputed origin, who are mentioned only in late biblical texts (1 Chr 4.41; 2 Chr 20.2; 26.7). In one theory the Meunites were a Transjordanian or Arabian group, while in another the Meunites were from one of several sites or areas called Maon—most likely either Maon 20 km (12 mi) south of Gaza or the Maon region of southwestern Edom. Given the existence of another Maon in Judah (e.g., 1 Chr 2.45), more than one entity with the name "Meunites" may be meant (see Ezra 2.50 ‖ Neh 7.52). **3–4:** Afraid, Jehoshaphat *set himself to seek the LORD* and proclaimed a national *fast* (cf. Judg 20.26 and 1 Sam 7.6; Jer 36.6,9; Zech 8.19; Joel 2.12; 2 Chr 1.5; 25.20). In resorting to Jerusalem, the people honor the divine directive given at Solomon's Temple dedication to seek the LORD in times of need (7.14). **6–12:** Jehoshaphat's prayer, which laments Judah's plight and solicits a divine response, recalls specific features of previous royal prayers (1 Chr 14.9,14; 29.10–19; 2 Chr 14.10–11). By contrasting divine omnipotence with human helplessness, the king lays the foundation for the petition that follows (v. 12).

this land before your people Israel, and give
it forever to the descendants of your friend
Abraham? 8 They have lived in it, and in it
have built you a sanctuary for your name,
saying, 9 'If disaster comes upon us, the
sword, judgment,[a] or pestilence, or fam-
ine, we will stand before this house, and
before you, for your name is in this house,
and cry to you in our distress, and you will
hear and save.' 10 See now, the people of
Ammon, Moab, and Mount Seir, whom
you would not let Israel invade when they
came from the land of Egypt, and whom
they avoided and did not destroy— 11 they
reward us by coming to drive us out of your
possession that you have given us to inher-
it. 12 O our God, will you not execute judg-
ment upon them? For we are powerless
against this great multitude that is coming
against us. We do not know what to do,
but our eyes are on you."
13 Meanwhile all Judah stood before
the LORD, with their little ones, their wives,
and their children. 14 Then the spirit of the
LORD came upon Jahaziel son of Zechari-
ah, son of Benaiah, son of Jeiel, son of Mat-
taniah, a Levite of the sons of Asaph, in the
middle of the assembly. 15 He said, "Listen,
all Judah and inhabitants of Jerusalem, and
King Jehoshaphat: Thus says the LORD to
you: 'Do not fear or be dismayed at this
great multitude; for the battle is not yours
but God's. 16 Tomorrow go down against
them; they will come up by the ascent of
Ziz; you will find them at the end of the
valley, before the wilderness of Jeruel.
17 This battle is not for you to fight; take
your position, stand still, and see the victo-
ry of the LORD on your behalf, O Judah
and Jerusalem.' Do not fear or be dis-
mayed; tomorrow go out against them, and
the LORD will be with you."
18 Then Jehoshaphat bowed down with
his face to the ground, and all Judah and
the inhabitants of Jerusalem fell down be-
fore the LORD, worshiping the LORD.
19 And the Levites, of the Kohathites and
the Korahites, stood up to praise the LORD,
the God of Israel, with a very loud voice.
20 They rose early in the morning and
went out into the wilderness of Tekoa; and
as they went out, Jehoshaphat stood and
said, "Listen to me, O Judah and inhabi-
tants of Jerusalem! Believe in the LORD
your God and you will be established; be-
lieve his prophets." 21 When he had taken
counsel with the people, he appointed those
who were to sing to the LORD and praise
him in holy splendor, as they went before
the army, saying,

"Give thanks to the LORD,
for his steadfast love endures
forever."

22 As they began to sing and praise, the
LORD set an ambush against the Ammon-
ites, Moab, and Mount Seir, who had come
against Judah, so that they were routed.
23 For the Ammonites and Moab attacked
the inhabitants of Mount Seir, destroying
them utterly; and when they had made an
end of the inhabitants of Seir, they all
helped to destroy one another.
24 When Judah came to the watchtower
of the wilderness, they looked toward the
multitude; they were corpses lying on the
ground; no one had escaped. 25 When Je-
hoshaphat and his people came to take the

a Or *the sword of judgment*

8–9: Echoing Solomon's prayer (see 6.28,34), Jehoshaphat's appeal is based on the existence of the Temple, because this sanctuary was accepted by God as the place where efficacious prayers could be offered (7.1–2,14). **11–12:** The very nations spared when the Israelites entered the land (Deut 2.1–22) are now threatening Judah's existence within it. **14–15:** The Levitical singer *Jahaziel* serves as the designate priest, as in other sacral wars (cf. Deut 20.2–4; 1 Chr 25.1–8). His assurance of victory, evoked as elsewhere by faith in God, quotes both Moses (Ex 14.13–14) and David (1 Sam 17.47). **16:** *Ziz . . . Jeruel,* occurring only here and precise location unknown. **17:** The residents of Jerusalem and Judah are to play the role of onlookers. **20:** Cf. Isa 7.9. **22–23:** The divine warrior throws Israel's enemies into a panic (cf. Judg 7.22; 1 Sam 14.20) so that they attack each other. **29:** As in other holy wars, *the fear of God* descends

booty from them, they found livestock[a] in
great numbers, goods, clothing, and pre-
cious things, which they took for them-
selves until they could carry no more. They
spent three days taking the booty, because
of its abundance. 26 On the fourth day they
assembled in the Valley of Beracah, for
there they blessed the LORD; therefore that
place has been called the Valley of Bera-
cah[b] to this day. 27 Then all the people of
Judah and Jerusalem, with Jehoshaphat at
their head, returned to Jerusalem with joy,
for the LORD had enabled them to rejoice
over their enemies. 28 They came to Jerusa-
lem, with harps and lyres and trumpets, to
the house of the LORD. 29 The fear of God
came on all the kingdoms of the countries
when they heard that the LORD had fought
against the enemies of Israel. 30 And the
realm of Jehoshaphat was quiet, for his
God gave him rest all around.

31 So Jehoshaphat reigned over Judah.
He was thirty-five years old when he began
to reign; he reigned twenty-five years in Je-
rusalem. His mother's name was Azubah
daughter of Shilhi. 32 He walked in the way
of his father Asa and did not turn aside
from it, doing what was right in the sight of
the LORD. 33 Yet the high places were not
removed; the people had not yet set their
hearts upon the God of their ancestors.

34 Now the rest of the acts of Jehosha-
phat, from first to last, are written in the
Annals of Jehu son of Hanani, which are
recorded in the Book of the Kings of Israel.

35 After this King Jehoshaphat of Judah
joined with King Ahaziah of Israel, who did
wickedly. 36 He joined him in building ships
to go to Tarshish; they built the ships in
Ezion-geber. 37 Then Eliezer son of Doda-
vahu of Mareshah prophesied against Je-
hoshaphat, saying, "Because you have
joined with Ahaziah, the LORD will destroy
what you have made." And the ships were
wrecked and were not able to go to Tar-
shish.

21 Jehoshaphat slept with his ancestors
and was buried with his ancestors in
the city of David; his son Jehoram succeed-
ed him. 2 He had brothers, the sons of Je-
hoshaphat: Azariah, Jehiel, Zechariah, Az-
ariah, Michael, and Shephatiah; all these
were the sons of King Jehoshaphat of Ju-
dah.[c] 3 Their father gave them many gifts,
of silver, gold, and valuable possessions, to-
gether with fortified cities in Judah; but he
gave the kingdom to Jehoram, because he
was the firstborn. 4 When Jehoram had as-
cended the throne of his father and was
established, he put all his brothers to the
sword, and also some of the officials of
Israel. 5 Jehoram was thirty-two years old
when he began to reign; he reigned eight
years in Jerusalem. 6 He walked in the way
of the kings of Israel, as the house of Ahab
had done; for the daughter of Ahab was his
wife. He did what was evil in the sight of
the LORD. 7 Yet the LORD would not de-
stroy the house of David because of the

a Gk: Heb *among them* b That is *Blessing*
c Gk Syr: Heb *Israel*

upon *all the kingdoms of the countries* (Ex 15.14–16; Deut 2.25; 11.25; Josh 2.9,11,24; 5.1; 10.1–2; 1 Sam 4.7–8; 14.15; 1 Chr 14.7; 2 Chr 14.13).

20.31–37: Jehoshaphat's second misstep. Following the concluding notices to Jehoshaphat's reign (vv. 31–34; on *Jehu* see 16.7n.; cf. 1 Kings 22.41–45), the author narrates a failure. Again (18.1–19.3), a pact with Israel (vv. 35–37) marks a regression in Jehoshaphat's rule. Here, after the covenant is ridiculed by a prophetic figure, *the ships were wrecked* (cf. 1 Kings 22.48–49). **36:** *Tarshish,* see 9.21n. *Ezion-geber* was a port city on the Red Sea.

21.1–20: Decline under Jehoram (851–843 BCE). Like the Elijah material, the Elisha material, found in Kings as part of the account of Jehoram's reign, is lacking in Chronicles. Jehoram appears as a more wicked king in Chronicles than in the briefer, but also negative, account of 2 Kings 8.16–24. Jehoram intensifies the pattern of close cooperation with the Northern Kingdom begun by his father (21.6; cf. 18.1–34; 20.35–37). **2–4:** Jehoram's *brothers,* who had possessions and administrative responsibilities in their own right (see 11.22–23n.), are eliminated by the new king. **5–7:** The Davidic promises (1 Chr 17.1–15) restrain the exercise of divine wrath against *the house of David* (cf. 2 Kings 8.17–19). **7:** *Lamp,*

covenant that he had made with David, and
since he had promised to give a lamp to him
and to his descendants forever.
8 In his days Edom revolted against the
rule of Judah and set up a king of their
own. 9 Then Jehoram crossed over with his
commanders and all his chariots. He set out
by night and attacked the Edomites, who
had surrounded him and his chariot com-
manders. 10 So Edom has been in revolt
against the rule of Judah to this day. At that
time Libnah also revolted against his rule,
because he had forsaken the LORD, the God
of his ancestors.
11 Moreover he made high places in the
hill country of Judah, and led the inhabi-
tants of Jerusalem into unfaithfulness, and
made Judah go astray. 12 A letter came to
him from the prophet Elijah, saying: "Thus
says the LORD, the God of your father Da-
vid: Because you have not walked in the
ways of your father Jehoshaphat or in the
ways of King Asa of Judah, 13 but have
walked in the way of the kings of Israel,
and have led Judah and the inhabitants of
Jerusalem into unfaithfulness, as the house
of Ahab led Israel into unfaithfulness, and
because you also have killed your brothers,
members of your father's house, who were
better than yourself, 14 see, the LORD will
bring a great plague on your people, your
children, your wives, and all your posses-
sions, 15 and you yourself will have a severe
sickness with a disease of your bowels, un-
til your bowels come out, day after day,
because of the disease."
16 The LORD aroused against Jehoram
the anger of the Philistines and of the Arabs
who are near the Ethiopians.[a] 17 They
came up against Judah, invaded it, and car-
ried away all the possessions they found
that belonged to the king's house, along
with his sons and his wives, so that no son
was left to him except Jehoahaz, his youn-
gest son.
18 After all this the LORD struck him in
his bowels with an incurable disease. 19 In
course of time, at the end of two years, his
bowels came out because of the disease,
and he died in great agony. His people
made no fire in his honor, like the fires
made for his ancestors. 20 He was thirty-
two years old when he began to reign; he
reigned eight years in Jerusalem. He depart-
ed with no one's regret. They buried him in
the city of David, but not in the tombs of
the kings.

22 The inhabitants of Jerusalem made
his youngest son Ahaziah king as his
successor; for the troops who came with
the Arabs to the camp had killed all the

a Or *Nubians*; Heb *Cushites*

fief or territorial dominion might be a better translation of the Hebrew. The Davidic promises (1 Chr 17.3–15 ‖ 2 Sam 7.4–16) are interpreted as involving continued rule for David's descendants in Jerusalem and not necessarily sovereignty over all of the territory inhabited by Israel's twelve tribes (1 Kings 11.36; 15.4; 2 Kings 8.19). **8–10:** Largely taken from 2 Kings 8.20–22. **10:** The revolt of Libnah (see 2 Kings 8.22) is explained by the Chronicler as another divine punishment. **12–15:** Elijah's letter, unparalleled in Kings, is remarkable. Elijah has not previously been mentioned in Chronicles and, according to the chronology in Kings, may have already ascended at this point. Furthermore, early prophecy was primarily oral. The letter might be used as a way for a northern prophet to communicate with a southern king, but it also reflects the increasing significance of a written book-culture in the Chronicler's time. **16–17:** A foreign invasion plunders Judah and leaves Jehoram with only his youngest son still living in Jerusalem (cf. v. 14). On the *Ethiopians,* see 14.9n. **18–19:** A fulfillment of Elijah's prediction (v. 15). *Fire,* see 16.14. **20:** Cf. 2 Kings 8.23–24.

22.1–9: The brief and ill-fated reign of Ahaziah (Jehoahaz; 843–842 BCE). Following the premature death of Jehoram (21.18–20), the inhabitants of Jerusalem install young Ahaziah as king (v. 1), but this effort at restoration soon comes to nought. The effects of Ahaziah's collaboration with the Northern Kingdom and emulation of northern practices threaten to topple both the Davidic dynasty and the traditional pattern of Temple worship in Jerusalem (23.18; 24.7). **2:** *Forty-two years,* there is a text-

older sons. So Ahaziah son of Jehoram
reigned as king of Judah. 2 Ahaziah was
forty-two years old when he began to reign;
he reigned one year in Jerusalem. His moth-
er's name was Athaliah, a granddaughter of
Omri. 3 He also walked in the ways of the
house of Ahab, for his mother was his
counselor in doing wickedly. 4 He did what
was evil in the sight of the LORD, as the
house of Ahab had done; for after the death
of his father they were his counselors, to his
ruin. 5 He even followed their advice, and
went with Jehoram son of King Ahab of
Israel to make war against King Hazael of
Aram at Ramoth-gilead. The Arameans
wounded Joram, 6 and he returned to be
healed in Jezreel of the wounds that he had
received at Ramah, when he fought King
Hazael of Aram. And Ahaziah son of King
Jehoram of Judah went down to see Joram
son of Ahab in Jezreel, because he was sick.
7 But it was ordained by God that the
downfall of Ahaziah should come about
through his going to visit Joram. For when
he came there he went out with Jehoram to
meet Jehu son of Nimshi, whom the LORD
had anointed to destroy the house of Ahab.
8 When Jehu was executing judgment on
the house of Ahab, he met the officials of
Judah and the sons of Ahaziah's brothers,
who attended Ahaziah, and he killed them.
9 He searched for Ahaziah, who was cap-
tured while hiding in Samaria and was
brought to Jehu, and put to death. They
buried him, for they said, "He is the grand-
son of Jehoshaphat, who sought the LORD
with all his heart." And the house of Ahazi-
ah had no one able to rule the kingdom.
10 Now when Athaliah, Ahaziah's
mother, saw that her son was dead, she set
about to destroy all the royal family of the
house of Judah. 11 But Jehoshabeath, the
king's daughter, took Joash son of Ahazi-
ah, and stole him away from among the
king's children who were about to be
killed; she put him and his nurse in a bed-
room. Thus Jehoshabeath, daughter of
King Jehoram and wife of the priest Jehoia-
da—because she was a sister of Ahaziah—
hid him from Athaliah, so that she did not
kill him; 12 he remained with them six
years, hidden in the house of God, while
Athaliah reigned over the land.
23 But in the seventh year Jehoiada
took courage, and entered into a
compact with the commanders of the hun-
dreds, Azariah son of Jeroham, Ishmael son
of Jehohanan, Azariah son of Obed, Maa-
seiah son of Adaiah, and Elishaphat son of
Zichri. 2 They went around through Judah
and gathered the Levites from all the towns
of Judah, and the heads of families of Isra-
el, and they came to Jerusalem. 3 Then the
whole assembly made a covenant with the

critical issue here. The more likely figure is "twenty-two years," as in 2 Kings 8.26. Ahaziah's father died at age forty (21.20). **3–4:** The supplementation of Ahaziah's evaluation in 2 Kings 8.27 draws attention to the intimate involvement of *the house of Ahab* from the Northern Kingdom in Judean royal affairs. Here too the Chronicler assumes familiarity with the book of Kings. **5–9:** The failure of the alliance with Joram (2 Kings 8.28–29), the death of Ahaziah's kinsmen (2 Kings 10.12–14), and the death of Ahaziah himself (2 Kings 9.27) leaves a vacuum in Davidic leadership (v. 9). In Chronicles Ahaziah's demise is attributed to divine purpose (v. 7a). On the anointing of Jehu and the assassination of Joram, see 2 Kings 9.1–26.

22.10–23.15: The tenure and fall of Athaliah. Athaliah's reign (842–836 BCE; cf. 2 Kings 11.1–16) marks the point of gravest threat in a long sequence of repeated blows to the Davidic dynasty. Her plan to eliminate all potential heirs is thwarted, however, by *Jehoshabeath, daughter of King Jehoram* (vv. 11–12; called Jehosheba in Kings). **23.1–7:** The first steps in the plot against Athaliah (2 Kings 11.4–8) are rewritten according to the Chronicler's characteristic interests in the Levites, priests, gatekeepers, *the heads of* the *families of Israel,* and the people at large (cf. 1 Chr 15–16; 23–27). From the outset, the coup is the work of all the people, not just select military officers. **1:** *Compact,* Heb "berith," elsewhere translated "covenant." **3:** The restoration honors the enduring political standards bequeathed to Israel during the United Monarchy. A return to normalcy after a period of apostasy or upheaval includes the restoration of the Davidic dynasty (22.1; 23.20–21; 26.1; 33.25; 36.1). **7:** On the military

king in the house of God. Jehoiada[a] said
to them, "Here is the king's son! Let him
reign, as the LORD promised concerning the
sons of David. 4 This is what you are to do:
one-third of you, priests and Levites, who
come on duty on the sabbath, shall be gate-
keepers, 5 one-third shall be at the king's
house, and one-third at the Gate of the
Foundation; and all the people shall be in
the courts of the house of the LORD. 6 Do
not let anyone enter the house of the LORD
except the priests and ministering Levites;
they may enter, for they are holy, but all the
other[b] people shall observe the instruc-
tions of the LORD. 7 The Levites shall sur-
round the king, each with his weapons in
his hand; and whoever enters the house
shall be killed. Stay with the king in his
comings and goings."

8 The Levites and all Judah did accord-
ing to all that the priest Jehoiada com-
manded; each brought his men, who were
to come on duty on the sabbath, with those
who were to go off duty on the sabbath; for
the priest Jehoiada did not dismiss the divi-
sions. 9 The priest Jehoiada delivered to the
captains the spears and the large and small
shields that had been King David's, which
were in the house of God; 10 and he set all
the people as a guard for the king, everyone
with weapon in hand, from the south side
of the house to the north side of the house,
around the altar and the house. 11 Then he
brought out the king's son, put the crown
on him, and gave him the covenant;[c] they
proclaimed him king, and Jehoiada and his
sons anointed him; and they shouted,
"Long live the king!"

12 When Athaliah heard the noise of the
people running and praising the king, she
went into the house of the LORD to the
people; 13 and when she looked, there was
the king standing by his pillar at the en-
trance, and the captains and the trumpeters
beside the king, and all the people of the
land rejoicing and blowing trumpets, and
the singers with their musical instruments
leading in the celebration. Athaliah tore her
clothes, and cried, "Treason! Treason!"
14 Then the priest Jehoiada brought out the
captains who were set over the army, say-
ing to them, "Bring her out between the
ranks; anyone who follows her is to be put
to the sword." For the priest said, "Do not
put her to death in the house of the LORD."
15 So they laid hands on her; she went into
the entrance of the Horse Gate of the king's
house, and there they put her to death.

16 Jehoiada made a covenant between
himself and all the people and the king that
they should be the LORD's people. 17 Then
all the people went to the house of Baal,
and tore it down; his altars and his images
they broke in pieces, and they killed Mat-
tan, the priest of Baal, in front of the altars.
18 Jehoiada assigned the care of the house
of the LORD to the levitical priests whom
David had organized to be in charge of the
house of the LORD, to offer burnt offerings
to the LORD, as it is written in the law of
Moses, with rejoicing and with singing, ac-
cording to the order of David. 19 He sta-
tioned the gatekeepers at the gates of the
house of the LORD so that no one should
enter who was in any way unclean. 20 And
he took the captains, the nobles, the gover-
nors of the people, and all the people of the
land, and they brought the king down from
the house of the LORD, marching through
the upper gate to the king's house. They set
the king on the royal throne. 21 So all the

a Heb *He* b Heb lacks *other* c Or *treaty*, or *testimony*; Heb *eduth*

dimension of Levitical duties, see 1 Chr 26.1–19n. **11:** *The covenant,* see 2 Kings 11.12n. **13:** The *pillar,* probably Jachin or Boaz; see 3.15–17. On *the people of the land* see 2 Kings 11.14n.

23.16–21: The reformation of Jehoiada. This priest leads *the people* in undoing the damage inflicted by Athaliah and her predecessors (cf. 2 Kings 11.17–20). His efforts result in the destruction of the temple of Baal, the reinstitution of proper personnel at the Temple, and the enthronement of young Joah. **16:** As in Asa's reign, a national covenant is made or renewed (15.8–19). **18–19:** These verses are an addition by the Chronicler in the middle of a narrative that otherwise largely follows Kings. They emphasize two issues that are key to the Chronicler: the role of *the law of Moses* and the role of *David* in organizing the

people of the land rejoiced, and the city was
quiet after Athaliah had been killed with
the sword.

24 Joash was seven years old when he
began to reign; he reigned forty
years in Jerusalem; his mother's name was
Zibiah of Beer-sheba. 2 Joash did what was
right in the sight of the LORD all the days
of the priest Jehoiada. 3 Jehoiada got two
wives for him, and he became the father of
sons and daughters.

4 Some time afterward Joash decided to
restore the house of the LORD. 5 He assem-
bled the priests and the Levites and said to
them, "Go out to the cities of Judah and
gather money from all Israel to repair the
house of your God, year by year; and see
that you act quickly." But the Levites did
not act quickly. 6 So the king summoned
Jehoiada the chief, and said to him, "Why
have you not required the Levites to bring
in from Judah and Jerusalem the tax levied
by Moses, the servant of the LORD, on[a] the
congregation of Israel for the tent of the
covenant?"[b] 7 For the children of Athaliah,
that wicked woman, had broken into the
house of God, and had even used all the
dedicated things of the house of the LORD
for the Baals.

8 So the king gave command, and they
made a chest, and set it outside the gate of
the house of the LORD. 9 A proclamation
was made throughout Judah and Jerusalem
to bring in for the LORD the tax that Moses
the servant of God laid on Israel in the wil-
derness. 10 All the leaders and all the people
rejoiced and brought their tax and dropped
it into the chest until it was full. 11 Whenev-
er the chest was brought to the king's offi-
cers by the Levites, when they saw that
there was a large amount of money in it,
the king's secretary and the officer of the
chief priest would come and empty the
chest and take it and return it to its place.
So they did day after day, and collected
money in abundance. 12 The king and Je-
hoiada gave it to those who had charge of
the work of the house of the LORD, and
they hired masons and carpenters to restore
the house of the LORD, and also workers in
iron and bronze to repair the house of the
LORD. 13 So those who were engaged in the
work labored, and the repairing went for-
ward at their hands, and they restored the
house of God to its proper condition and
strengthened it. 14 When they had finished,
they brought the rest of the money to the
king and Jehoiada, and with it were made
utensils for the house of the LORD, utensils
for the service and for the burnt offerings,
and ladles, and vessels of gold and silver.
They offered burnt offerings in the house of
the LORD regularly all the days of Jehoiada.

15 But Jehoiada grew old and full of
days, and died; he was one hundred thirty
years old at his death. 16 And they buried
him in the city of David among the kings,

a Compare Vg: Heb *and* *b* Or *treaty*, or *testimony*; Heb *eduth*

Temple service. **21:** The *quiet* that descends on Jerusalem is a sign of divine blessing (1 Chr 4.40; 22.9; 2 Chr 14.1,6; 20.30).

24.1–27: The Temple restoration of Joash (836–798 BCE) **and his later regression.** Following Kings, where the king's name is Jehoash, the Chronicler devotes considerable attention to Joash's good deed on behalf of the Temple, but in contrast to his source, limits them to the life of Jehoiada (cf. 2 Kings 12). After the good priest dies (vv. 15–16), Joash falls under the influence of his officers and backslides (vv. 17–22). He subsequently confronts a disastrous foreign invasion (vv. 23–24) and a successful conspiracy (vv. 25–26). **3:** On large families, see 11.18–21n. **4–14:** Joash expends great effort to rebuild the neglected Temple. He displays strong leadership in ensuring that the renovations proceed apace (vv. 5–6). The Chronicler, in an attempt to bolster the significance of the Temple, adds to his source, insisting that all donated funds were given with great enthusiasm (v. 10). **6:** *The tax levied by Moses,* see Ex 30.11–16; Lev 27.1–8. **13–14:** The collections for Temple renovation are so successful that funds are left to fashion new *utensils, ladles,* and *vessels.* **15–16:** The highly positive evaluation of Jehoiada's tenure resembles those written about Judah's better kings. **17–22:** These episodes, not found in Kings, detail the extent of

because he had done good in Israel, and for
God and his house.
17 Now after the death of Jehoiada the
officials of Judah came and did obeisance
to the king; then the king listened to them.
18 They abandoned the house of the LORD,
the God of their ancestors, and served the
sacred poles[a] and the idols. And wrath
came upon Judah and Jerusalem for this
guilt of theirs. 19 Yet he sent prophets
among them to bring them back to the
LORD; they testified against them, but they
would not listen.
20 Then the spirit of God took posses-
sion of[b] Zechariah son of the priest Jehoia-
da; he stood above the people and said to
them, "Thus says God: Why do you trans-
gress the commandments of the LORD, so
that you cannot prosper? Because you have
forsaken the LORD, he has also forsaken
you." 21 But they conspired against him,
and by command of the king they stoned
him to death in the court of the house of the
LORD. 22 King Joash did not remember the
kindness that Jehoiada, Zechariah's father,
had shown him, but killed his son. As he
was dying, he said, "May the LORD see and
avenge!"
23 At the end of the year the army of
Aram came up against Joash. They came to
Judah and Jerusalem, and destroyed all the
officials of the people from among them,
and sent all the booty they took to the king
of Damascus. 24 Although the army of
Aram had come with few men, the LORD
delivered into their hand a very great army,
because they had abandoned the LORD, the
God of their ancestors. Thus they executed
judgment on Joash.
25 When they had withdrawn, leaving
him severely wounded, his servants con-
spired against him because of the blood of
the son[c] of the priest Jehoiada, and they
killed him on his bed. So he died; and they
buried him in the city of David, but they
did not bury him in the tombs of the kings.
26 Those who conspired against him were
Zabad son of Shimeath the Ammonite, and
Jehozabad son of Shimrith the Moabite.
27 Accounts of his sons, and of the many
oracles against him, and of the rebuilding[d]
of the house of God are written in the Com-
mentary on the Book of the Kings. And his
son Amaziah succeeded him.
25 Amaziah was twenty-five years old
when he began to reign, and he
reigned twenty-nine years in Jerusalem. His
mother's name was Jehoaddan of Jerusa-
lem. 2 He did what was right in the sight of
the LORD, yet not with a true heart. 3 As
soon as the royal power was firmly in his
hand he killed his servants who had mur-
dered his father the king. 4 But he did not
put their children to death, according to
what is written in the law, in the book of
Moses, where the LORD commanded, "The
parents shall not be put to death for the
children, or the children be put to death for
the parents; but all shall be put to death for
their own sins."
5 Amaziah assembled the people of Ju-

a Heb *Asherim* *b* Heb *clothed itself with*
c Gk Vg: Heb *sons* *d* Heb *founding*

Joash's regression. They follow typical patterns of the Chronicler: apostasy, prophet's warning, lack of repentance, (a second warning), and punishment. **20–21:** The assassination of the prophet *Zechariah* is the work of both Joash and his officials. **25–26:** Joash himself falls victim to assassination (cf. 2 Kings 12.19–21). **27:** *Commentary,* see 13.22n.

25.1–28: The mixed record of Amaziah (789–769 BCE). The Chronicler expands the coverage devoted to Amaziah (2 Kings 14.2–14,17–20) through the addition of two sections (vv. 5–10 and vv. 12–16), each of which contains a prophetic figure. His reign is divided into two periods: In the first half of his tenure (vv. 1–13) Amaziah proves obedient to the prophetic word and enjoys success, while in the second half of his reign Amaziah engages in idolatry and suffers defeat (vv. 14–28). **3–4:** Amaziah avenges his father's death, but manages not to violate Deut 24.16. **5–10:** The king's attempt to supplement his country's muster by hiring Israelite mercenaries encounters a prophetic reprimand. **5–6:** On the large numbers, see 13.3n. A *hundred talents* weighed about 3,400 kg (7,000 lb). The Chronicler regards any alliance, whether with foreign powers or with northern Israel, as illicit (see 16.1–14n.). **11–13:** The

dah, and set them by ancestral houses un-
der commanders of the thousands and of
the hundreds for all Judah and Benjamin.
He mustered those twenty years old and
upward, and found that they were three
hundred thousand picked troops fit for
war, able to handle spear and shield. 6He
also hired one hundred thousand mighty
warriors from Israel for one hundred tal-
ents of silver. 7But a man of God came to
him and said, "O king, do not let the army
of Israel go with you, for the LORD is not
with Israel—all these Ephraimites. 8Rath-
er, go by yourself and act; be strong in bat-
tle, or God will fling you down before the
enemy; for God has power to help or to
overthrow." 9Amaziah said to the man of
God, "But what shall we do about the hun-
dred talents that I have given to the army of
Israel?" The man of God answered, "The
LORD is able to give you much more than
this." 10Then Amaziah discharged the
army that had come to him from Ephraim,
letting them go home again. But they be-
came very angry with Judah, and returned
home in fierce anger.

11 Amaziah took courage, and led out
his people; he went to the Valley of Salt,
and struck down ten thousand men of Seir.
12The people of Judah captured another
ten thousand alive, took them to the top of
Sela, and threw them down from the top of
Sela, so that all of them were dashed to
pieces. 13But the men of the army whom
Amaziah sent back, not letting them go
with him to battle, fell on the cities of Ju-
dah from Samaria to Beth-horon; they
killed three thousand people in them, and
took much booty.

14 Now after Amaziah came from the
slaughter of the Edomites, he brought the
gods of the people of Seir, set them up as
his gods, and worshiped them, making
offerings to them. 15The LORD was angry
with Amaziah and sent to him a prophet,
who said to him, "Why have you resorted
to a people's gods who could not deliver
their own people from your hand?" 16But
as he was speaking the king[a] said to him,
"Have we made you a royal counselor?
Stop! Why should you be put to death?" So
the prophet stopped, but said, "I know that
God has determined to destroy you, be-
cause you have done this and have not lis-
tened to my advice."

17 Then King Amaziah of Judah took
counsel and sent to King Joash son of Jeho-
ahaz son of Jehu of Israel, saying, "Come,
let us look one another in the face." 18King
Joash of Israel sent word to King Amaziah
of Judah, "A thornbush on Lebanon sent to
a cedar on Lebanon, saying, 'Give your
daughter to my son for a wife'; but a wild
animal of Lebanon passed by and trampled
down the thornbush. 19You say, 'See, I
have defeated Edom,' and your heart has
lifted you up in boastfulness. Now stay at
home; why should you provoke trouble so
that you fall, you and Judah with you?"

20 But Amaziah would not listen—it
was God's doing, in order to hand them
over, because they had sought the gods of
Edom. 21So King Joash of Israel went up;
he and King Amaziah of Judah faced one
another in battle at Beth-shemesh, which
belongs to Judah. 22Judah was defeated by
Israel; everyone fled home. 23King Joash of
Israel captured King Amaziah of Judah, son
of Joash, son of Ahaziah, at Beth-shemesh;
he brought him to Jerusalem, and broke
down the wall of Jerusalem from the
Ephraim Gate to the Corner Gate, a dis-
tance of four hundred cubits. 24He seized
all the gold and silver, and all the vessels
that were found in the house of God, and
Obed-edom with them; he seized also the
treasuries of the king's house, also hos-
tages; then he returned to Samaria.

25 King Amaziah son of Joash of Judah,
lived fifteen years after the death of King

a Heb *he*

prophet's counsel of complete reliance on God results in Judah's victory (cf. 13.13–21; 14.7–14; 20.1–30), but the alienated mercenaries wreak some havoc in Judah and Samaria. **20**: The second part of the verse is an expansion of the Chronicler's source (2 Kings 14.11), emphasizing that this was not a whim, but the fair punishment of God.

Joash son of Jehoahaz of Israel. 26 Now the
rest of the deeds of Amaziah, from first to
last, are they not written in the Book of the
Kings of Judah and Israel? 27 From the time
that Amaziah turned away from the LORD
they made a conspiracy against him in Jeru-
salem, and he fled to Lachish. But they sent
after him to Lachish, and killed him there.
28 They brought him back on horses; he
was buried with his ancestors in the city of
David.

26 Then all the people of Judah took
Uzziah, who was sixteen years old,
and made him king to succeed his father
Amaziah. 2 He rebuilt Eloth and restored it
to Judah, after the king slept with his ances-
tors. 3 Uzziah was sixteen years old when he
began to reign, and he reigned fifty-two
years in Jerusalem. His mother's name was
Jecoliah of Jerusalem. 4 He did what was
right in the sight of the LORD, just as his
father Amaziah had done. 5 He set himself
to seek God in the days of Zechariah, who
instructed him in the fear of God; and as
long as he sought the LORD, God made him
prosper.

6 He went out and made war against the
Philistines, and broke down the wall of
Gath and the wall of Jabneh and the wall of
Ashdod; he built cities in the territory of
Ashdod and elsewhere among the Philis-
tines. 7 God helped him against the Philis-
tines, against the Arabs who lived in Gur-
baal, and against the Meunites. 8 The
Ammonites paid tribute to Uzziah, and his
fame spread even to the border of Egypt,
for he became very strong. 9 Moreover Uz-
ziah built towers in Jerusalem at the Corner
Gate, at the Valley Gate, and at the Angle,
and fortified them. 10 He built towers in the
wilderness and hewed out many cisterns,
for he had large herds, both in the Shephe-
lah and in the plain, and he had farmers
and vinedressers in the hills and in the fer-
tile lands, for he loved the soil. 11 Moreover
Uzziah had an army of soldiers, fit for war,
in divisions according to the numbers in the
muster made by the secretary Jeiel and the
officer Maaseiah, under the direction of
Hananiah, one of the king's commanders.
12 The whole number of the heads of ances-
tral houses of mighty warriors was two
thousand six hundred. 13 Under their com-
mand was an army of three hundred seven
thousand five hundred, who could make
war with mighty power, to help the king
against the enemy. 14 Uzziah provided for
all the army the shields, spears, helmets,
coats of mail, bows, and stones for slinging.
15 In Jerusalem he set up machines, invented
by skilled workers, on the towers and the
corners for shooting arrows and large
stones. And his fame spread far, for he was
marvelously helped until he became strong.

16 But when he had become strong he
grew proud, to his destruction. For he was
false to the LORD his God, and entered the
temple of the LORD to make offering on the
altar of incense. 17 But the priest Azariah
went in after him, with eighty priests of the
LORD who were men of valor; 18 they with-
stood King Uzziah, and said to him, "It is
not for you, Uzziah, to make offering to the
LORD, but for the priests the descendants of

26.1–15: The builder and reformer, Uzziah (785–733 BCE). Kings presents Uzziah (Azariah) as a minor figure (2 Kings 14.21–22; 15.1–7), but Chronicles presents this monarch as a major reformer whose fame extended all the way to Egypt (26.8). The additional material is of various types; some may be based on sources, while other pieces are likely composed by the Chronicler. **1–4:** Cf. 2 Kings 14.21–22; 15.2–3. **5:** The Chronicler links Uzziah's good conduct to the influence of Zechariah, an otherwise unattested prophet; cf. 24.2. **6–15:** Uzziah's achievements include territorial expansion, victory in war, rebuilding towns, and amassing a large, well-equipped army. Like David (1 Chr 27.25–31), Uzziah also enhances the condition of his royal estates. **7:** *Meunites,* see 20.2n. **12–13:** On the large numbers, see 13.3n.

26.16–23: Uzziah's hubris. Having consolidated his rule and realm (1.1; 11.12; 17.1), Uzziah overreaches by turning against God and encroaching on the sacrificial duties of the priests. Most of this material is lacking in Kings, and it is likely a clever composition of the Chronicler, who imagined that the leprosy resulted from assuming Priestly prerogatives and entering the sanctuary with incense. Leprosy caused serious impurity (Lev 13–14), and thus Uzziah could never enter the Temple again. **21–23:** Except for the

Aaron, who are consecrated to make offer-
ing. Go out of the sanctuary; for you have
done wrong, and it will bring you no honor
from the LORD God." 19 Then Uzziah was
angry. Now he had a censer in his hand to
make offering, and when he became angry
with the priests a leprous[a] disease broke
out on his forehead, in the presence of the
priests in the house of the LORD, by the
altar of incense. 20 When the chief priest Az-
ariah, and all the priests, looked at him, he
was leprous[a] in his forehead. They hurried
him out, and he himself hurried to get out,
because the LORD had struck him. 21 King
Uzziah was leprous[a] to the day of his
death, and being leprous[a] lived in a sepa-
rate house, for he was excluded from the
house of the LORD. His son Jotham was in
charge of the palace of the king, governing
the people of the land.

22 Now the rest of the acts of Uzziah,
from first to last, the prophet Isaiah son of
Amoz wrote. 23 Uzziah slept with his ances-
tors; they buried him near his ancestors in
the burial field that belonged to the kings,
for they said, "He is leprous."[a] His son
Jotham succeeded him.

27 Jotham was twenty-five years old
when he began to reign; he reigned
sixteen years in Jerusalem. His mother's
name was Jerushah daughter of Zadok.
2 He did what was right in the sight of the
LORD just as his father Uzziah had done—
only he did not invade the temple of the
LORD. But the people still followed corrupt
practices. 3 He built the upper gate of the
house of the LORD, and did extensive build-
ing on the wall of Ophel. 4 Moreover he
built cities in the hill country of Judah, and
forts and towers on the wooded hills. 5 He
fought with the king of the Ammonites and
prevailed against them. The Ammonites
gave him that year one hundred talents of
silver, ten thousand cors of wheat and ten
thousand of barley. The Ammonites paid
him the same amount in the second and the
third years. 6 So Jotham became strong be-
cause he ordered his ways before the LORD
his God. 7 Now the rest of the acts of Jo-
tham, and all his wars and his ways, are
written in the Book of the Kings of Israel
and Judah. 8 He was twenty-five years old
when he began to reign; he reigned sixteen
years in Jerusalem. 9 Jotham slept with his
ancestors, and they buried him in the city of
David; and his son Ahaz succeeded him.

28 Ahaz was twenty years old when he
began to reign; he reigned sixteen
years in Jerusalem. He did not do what was
right in the sight of the LORD, as his ances-
tor David had done, 2 but he walked in the
ways of the kings of Israel. He even made
cast images for the Baals; 3 and he made
offerings in the valley of the son of Hin-
nom, and made his sons pass through fire,
according to the abominable practices of
the nations whom the LORD drove out be-
fore the people of Israel. 4 He sacrificed and
made offerings on the high places, on the
hills, and under every green tree.

5 Therefore the LORD his God gave him

a A term for several skin diseases; precise meaning uncertain

reference to Isaiah, this material is taken from 2 Kings 15.5–7. The attribution to Isaiah means that the Chronicler can lay claim to prophetic authority for at least some of the material in his narration of Uzziah's reign (cf. 1 Chr 29.29; 2 Chr 9.29; 13.22).

27.1–9: The accomplishments of Jotham (759–743 BCE). As in Kings, Jotham is rated positively (2 Kings 15.32–38), but the Chronicler adds more material about his reign, especially about his public works and military might. **4:** Like Uzziah (26.6–10), Jotham does not confine his building initiatives to Jerusalem. He establishes towns in the hill country of Judah, and he builds fortresses and towers in the wooded areas. **5:** A *talent* weighed about 34 kg (75 lb), and a *cor* was about 230 l (6.5 bu).

28.1–27: Unending failure under Ahaz (743/753–727/715 BCE; the data are inconsistent). Unlike the reigns of almost all monarchs in Chronicles, the reign of Ahaz is one of unmitigated decline. The author draws on 2 Kings 16, but his own presentation is substantially longer and different. Ahaz's refusal to turn from his wicked ways affords him the dubious distinction of being Judah's worst king (cf. 33.12–17). **3:** *Pass through fire,* see 2 Kings 16.1–4n. **5–7:** The Chronicler directly attributes the onslaughts by Assyria

into the hand of the king of Aram, who
defeated him and took captive a great num-
ber of his people and brought them to Da-
mascus. He was also given into the hand of
the king of Israel, who defeated him with
great slaughter. 6 Pekah son of Remaliah
killed one hundred twenty thousand in Ju-
dah in one day, all of them valiant war-
riors, because they had abandoned the
LORD, the God of their ancestors. 7 And
Zichri, a mighty warrior of Ephraim, killed
the king's son Maaseiah, Azrikam the com-
mander of the palace, and Elkanah the next
in authority to the king.
8 The people of Israel took captive two
hundred thousand of their kin, women,
sons, and daughters; they also took much
booty from them and brought the booty to
Samaria. 9 But a prophet of the LORD was
there, whose name was Oded; he went out
to meet the army that came to Samaria, and
said to them, "Because the LORD, the God

and Israel (2 Kings 16.5) to divine retribution for Ahaz's religious improprieties (2 Kings 16.2–4; 2 Chr 28.2–4). Chronicles depicts two separate and distinct invasions, whereas Kings presents Syria and Israel as acting in consort (2 Kings 16.5–6). **8–15:** The people of Israel seize a vast number of captives, but this

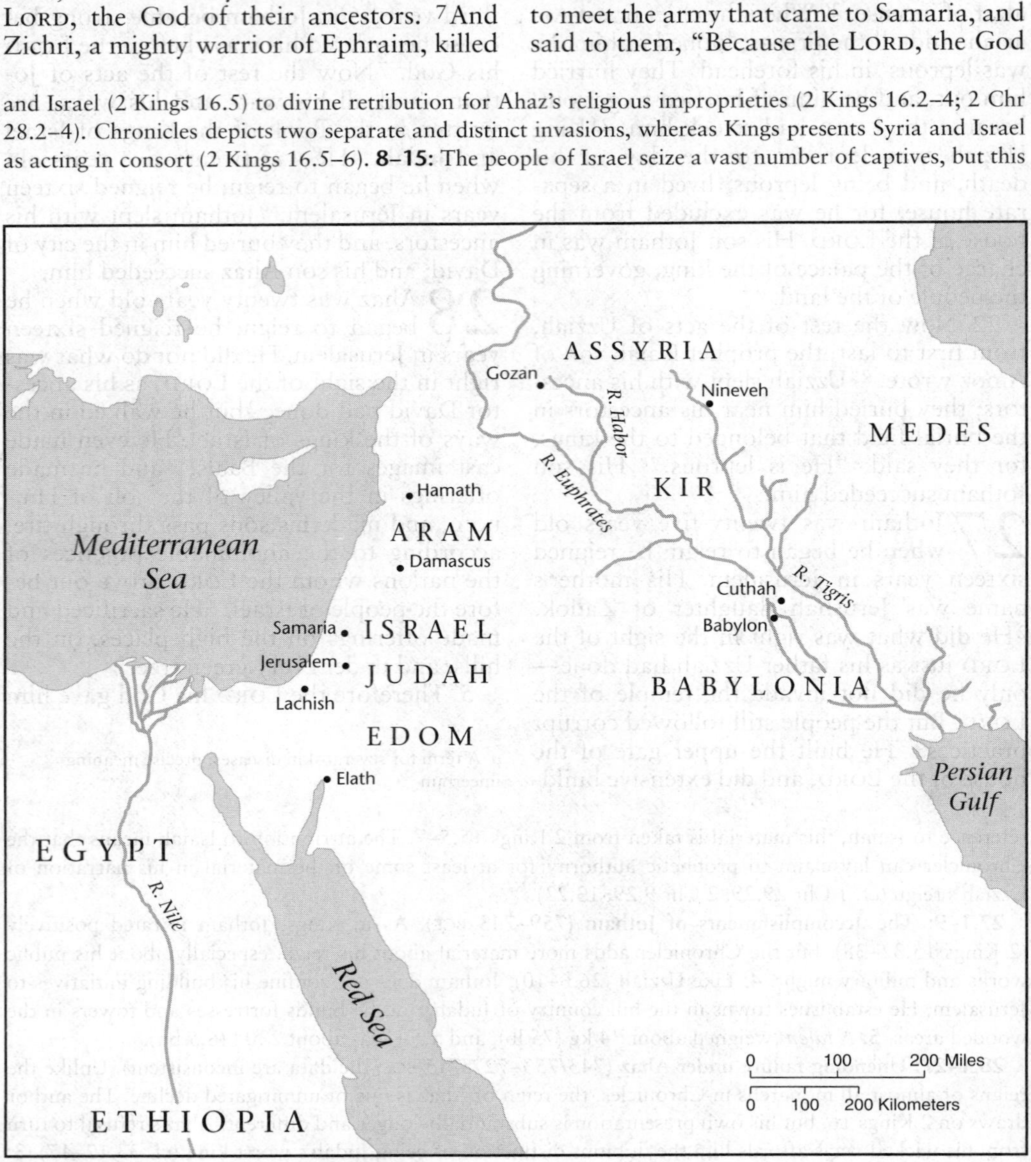

Chs 28–33: Assyria and Israel and Judah.

of your ancestors, was angry with Judah,
he gave them into your hand, but you have
killed them in a rage that has reached up to
heaven. 10 Now you intend to subjugate the
people of Judah and Jerusalem, male and
female, as your slaves. But what have you
except sins against the LORD your God?
11 Now hear me, and send back the captives
whom you have taken from your kindred,
for the fierce wrath of the LORD is upon
you." 12 Moreover, certain chiefs of the
Ephraimites, Azariah son of Johanan, Bere-
chiah son of Meshillemoth, Jehizkiah son
of Shallum, and Amasa son of Hadlai,
stood up against those who were coming
from the war, 13 and said to them, "You
shall not bring the captives in here, for you
propose to bring on us guilt against the
LORD in addition to our present sins and
guilt. For our guilt is already great, and
there is fierce wrath against Israel." 14 So
the warriors left the captives and the booty
before the officials and all the assembly.
15 Then those who were mentioned by
name got up and took the captives, and
with the booty they clothed all that were
naked among them; they clothed them,
gave them sandals, provided them with
food and drink, and anointed them; and
carrying all the feeble among them on don-
keys, they brought them to their kindred at
Jericho, the city of palm trees. Then they
returned to Samaria.

16 At that time King Ahaz sent to the
king[a] of Assyria for help. 17 For the Edom-
ites had again invaded and defeated Judah,
and carried away captives. 18 And the Phil-
istines had made raids on the cities in the
Shephelah and the Negeb of Judah, and
had taken Beth-shemesh, Aijalon, Gede-
roth, Soco with its villages, Timnah with its
villages, and Gimzo with its villages; and
they settled there. 19 For the LORD brought
Judah low because of King Ahaz of Israel,
for he had behaved without restraint in Ju-
dah and had been faithless to the LORD.
20 So King Tilgath-pilneser of Assyria came
against him, and oppressed him instead of
strengthening him. 21 For Ahaz plundered
the house of the LORD and the houses of
the king and of the officials, and gave trib-
ute to the king of Assyria; but it did not
help him.

22 In the time of his distress he became
yet more faithless to the LORD—this same
King Ahaz. 23 For he sacrificed to the gods
of Damascus, which had defeated him, and
said, "Because the gods of the kings of
Aram helped them, I will sacrifice to them
so that they may help me." But they were
the ruin of him, and of all Israel. 24 Ahaz
gathered together the utensils of the house
of God, and cut in pieces the utensils of the
house of God. He shut up the doors of the
house of the LORD and made himself altars
in every corner of Jerusalem. 25 In every city
of Judah he made high places to make
offerings to other gods, provoking to anger
the LORD, the God of his ancestors. 26 Now
the rest of his acts and all his ways, from
first to last, are written in the Book of the
Kings of Judah and Israel. 27 Ahaz slept
with his ancestors, and they buried him
in the city, in Jerusalem; but they did not
bring him into the tombs of the kings of
Israel. His son Hezekiah succeeded him.

29 Hezekiah began to reign when he
was twenty-five years old; he

a Gk Syr Vg Compare 2 Kings 16.7: Heb *kings*

act brings a strong prophetic censure and the prisoners are compassionately released. This section, most likely a free composition of the Chronicler, illustrates his basic concerns, including the need for prophetic warning before punishment, and the complete efficacy of repentance. **16–20:** Invasions by the Edomites and the Philistines prompted Ahaz to send Temple tribute to the king of Assyria (Tiglath-pileser III, 745–727 BCE; here called *Tilgath-pilneser*) for *help* (cf. 2 Kings 16.7–8), but the Assyrian king *oppressed him* instead. On the opposition to alliances, see 16.1–14n. **22–25:** Ahaz's foreign policy disasters lead him to abandon his own religious institutions and worship the gods of the lands who defeated him. In Chronicles this is but one more indication of the ignominy that characterizes Ahaz's rule.

29.1–36: Restoring the Temple: the beginning of Hezekiah's rule. The Chronicler devotes more attention to Hezekiah (ruled 727/715–698/687 BCE; the data are inconsistent) than to any other king except

reigned twenty-nine years in Jerusalem. His
mother's name was Abijah daughter of
Zechariah. 2 He did what was right in the
sight of the LORD, just as his ancestor Da-
vid had done.
3 In the first year of his reign, in the first
month, he opened the doors of the house of
the LORD and repaired them. 4 He brought
in the priests and the Levites and assembled
them in the square on the east. 5 He said to
them, "Listen to me, Levites! Sanctify your-
selves, and sanctify the house of the LORD,
the God of your ancestors, and carry out
the filth from the holy place. 6 For our an-
cestors have been unfaithful and have done
what was evil in the sight of the LORD our
God; they have forsaken him, and have
turned away their faces from the dwelling
of the LORD, and turned their backs. 7 They
also shut the doors of the vestibule and put
out the lamps, and have not offered incense
or made burnt offerings in the holy place to
the God of Israel. 8 Therefore the wrath of
the LORD came upon Judah and Jerusalem,
and he has made them an object of horror,
of astonishment, and of hissing, as you see
with your own eyes. 9 Our fathers have fall-
en by the sword and our sons and our
daughters and our wives are in captivity for
this. 10 Now it is in my heart to make a
covenant with the LORD, the God of Israel,
so that his fierce anger may turn away from
us. 11 My sons, do not now be negligent, for
the LORD has chosen you to stand in his
presence to minister to him, and to be his
ministers and make offerings to him."
12 Then the Levites arose, Mahath son
of Amasai, and Joel son of Azariah, of the
sons of the Kohathites; and of the sons of
Merari, Kish son of Abdi, and Azariah son
of Jehallelel; and of the Gershonites, Joah
son of Zimmah, and Eden son of Joah;
13 and of the sons of Elizaphan, Shimri and
Jeuel; and of the sons of Asaph, Zechariah
and Mattaniah; 14 and of the sons of He-
man, Jehuel and Shimei; and of the sons of
Jeduthun, Shemaiah and Uzziel. 15 They
gathered their brothers, sanctified them-
selves, and went in as the king had com-
manded, by the words of the LORD, to
cleanse the house of the LORD. 16 The
priests went into the inner part of the house
of the LORD to cleanse it, and they brought
out all the unclean things that they found in
the temple of the LORD into the court of the
house of the LORD; and the Levites took
them and carried them out to the Wadi
Kidron. 17 They began to sanctify on the
first day of the first month, and on the
eighth day of the month they came to the
vestibule of the LORD; then for eight days
they sanctified the house of the LORD, and
on the sixteenth day of the first month they
finished. 18 Then they went inside to King
Hezekiah and said, "We have cleansed all
the house of the LORD, the altar of burnt
offering and all its utensils, and the table
for the rows of bread and all its utensils.
19 All the utensils that King Ahaz repudiat-
ed during his reign when he was faithless,
we have made ready and sanctified; see,
they are in front of the altar of the LORD."
20 Then King Hezekiah rose early, as-
sembled the officials of the city, and went

David and Solomon (29.1–32.33); the Chronicler views Hezekiah as an "ideal" king of the post Davidic-Solomonic era. Sennacherib's invasion, which dominates the coverage of Hezekiah in 2 Kings 18.9–19.37, thus appears in condensed form (32.1–23). Instead, the Chronicler focuses on Hezekiah's reforms and restoration of the Temple, which are described in much greater detail than in his sources (29.1–31.21; cf. 2 Kings 18.4,16,22). **3–11:** Hezekiah begins by engaging a domestic policy crisis—the sorry legacy left by his predecessor (28.24). He oversees the repair of the Temple (vv. 3–4) and encourages the Levites to resume their traditional tasks (vv. 5–11). He makes a covenant with the LORD (v. 10; cf. 15.8–19) to move the nation from a state of wrath (v. 8) to one of blessing. He does this immediately upon assuming the throne (v. 3), reflecting his great righteousness. **12–19:** The priests and Levites complete the Temple purification (cf. 13.10–11). **18:** *Rows of bread,* see 2.4n. **20–36:** As in the time of Solomon's Temple dedication (5.2–7.6), the praises of the Levites follow the offering of sacrifices. The swift (re)establishment of *the service of the house of the LORD* (vv. 35–36) effectively reverses the neglect of the Temple in Ahaz's reign. The restoration of the proper Temple service results in great joy up to the house of the LORD. 21 They brought seven bulls, seven rams, seven lambs, and seven male goats for a sin offering for the kingdom and for the sanctuary and for Judah. He commanded the priests the descendants of Aaron to offer them on the altar of the LORD. 22 So they slaughtered the bulls, and the priests received the blood and dashed it against the altar; they slaughtered the rams and their blood was dashed against the altar; they also slaughtered the lambs and their blood was dashed against the altar. 23 Then the male goats for the sin offering were brought to the king and the assembly; they laid their hands on them, 24 and the priests slaughtered them and made a sin offering with their blood at the altar, to make atonement for all Israel. For the king commanded that the burnt offering and the sin offering should be made for all Israel.

25 He stationed the Levites in the house of the LORD with cymbals, harps, and lyres, according to the commandment of David and of Gad the king's seer and of the prophet Nathan, for the commandment was from the LORD through his prophets. 26 The Levites stood with the instruments of David, and the priests with the trumpets. 27 Then Hezekiah commanded that the burnt offering be offered on the altar. When the burnt offering began, the song to the LORD began also, and the trumpets, accompanied by the instruments of King David of Israel. 28 The whole assembly worshiped, the singers sang, and the trumpeters sounded; all this continued until the burnt offering was finished. 29 When the offering was finished, the king and all who were present with him bowed down and worshiped. 30 King Hezekiah and the officials commanded the Levites to sing praises to the LORD with the words of David and of the seer Asaph. They sang praises with gladness, and they bowed down and worshiped.

31 Then Hezekiah said, "You have now consecrated yourselves to the LORD; come near, bring sacrifices and thank offerings to the house of the LORD." The assembly brought sacrifices and thank offerings; and all who were of a willing heart brought burnt offerings. 32 The number of the burnt offerings that the assembly brought was seventy bulls, one hundred rams, and two hundred lambs; all these were for a burnt offering to the LORD. 33 The consecrated offerings were six hundred bulls and three thousand sheep. 34 But the priests were too few and could not skin all the burnt offerings, so, until other priests had sanctified themselves, their kindred, the Levites, helped them until the work was finished—for the Levites were more conscientious[a] than the priests in sanctifying themselves. 35 Besides the great number of burnt offerings there was the fat of the offerings of well-being, and there were the drink offerings for the burnt offerings. Thus the service of the house of the LORD was restored. 36 And Hezekiah and all the people rejoiced because of what God had done for the people; for the thing had come about suddenly.

30 Hezekiah sent word to all Israel and Judah, and wrote letters also to Ephraim and Manasseh, that they should

a Heb *upright in heart*

(cf. 30.25–26). **22:** Cf. Num 18.17; Lev 17.6. **34:** *Levites,* the Chronicler has a special sympathy for the plight of the Levites, even though he normally maintains a distinction between their roles and responsibilities and those of the priests. The Chronicler stresses cooperation and complimentarity between the priests and Levites, not competition and hierarchy (1 Chr 23.28–32; 28.12–13,21; 2 Chr 5.4–14; 13.9–12; 23.1–11; 35.3). In Chronicles, the priests and Levites share a common genealogy (1 Chr 6.1–81).

30.1–31.1: National Passover and further religious reforms. The consecration and rededication of the Temple complete, Hezekiah leads the people in celebrating a national Passover. The reclamation of true worship moves from the Passover offering, to destroying illicit altars in Jerusalem (vv. 13–14), to celebrating the Festival of Unleavened Bread (vv. 13,21; cf. Ex 23.14–17; Deut 16.16–17), to shattering *the pillars,* hacking apart *the sacred poles,* and tearing down *the high places and the altars throughout all Judah and*

come to the house of the LORD at Jerusa-
lem, to keep the passover to the LORD the
God of Israel. 2 For the king and his offi-
cials and all the assembly in Jerusalem had
taken counsel to keep the passover in the
second month 3 (for they could not keep it
at its proper time because the priests had
not sanctified themselves in sufficient num-
ber, nor had the people assembled in Jeru-
salem). 4 The plan seemed right to the king
and all the assembly. 5 So they decreed to
make a proclamation throughout all Israel,
from Beer-sheba to Dan, that the people
should come and keep the passover to the
LORD the God of Israel, at Jerusalem; for
they had not kept it in great numbers as
prescribed. 6 So couriers went throughout
all Israel and Judah with letters from the
king and his officials, as the king had com-
manded, saying, "O people of Israel, return
to the LORD, the God of Abraham, Isaac,
and Israel, so that he may turn again to the
remnant of you who have escaped from the
hand of the kings of Assyria. 7 Do not be
like your ancestors and your kindred, who
were faithless to the LORD God of their an-
cestors, so that he made them a desolation,
as you see. 8 Do not now be stiff-necked as
your ancestors were, but yield yourselves to
the LORD and come to his sanctuary, which
he has sanctified forever, and serve the
LORD your God, so that his fierce anger
may turn away from you. 9 For as you re-
turn to the LORD, your kindred and your
children will find compassion with their
captors, and return to this land. For the
LORD your God is gracious and merciful,
and will not turn away his face from you, if
you return to him."

10 So the couriers went from city to city
through the country of Ephraim and Ma-
nasseh, and as far as Zebulun; but they
laughed them to scorn, and mocked them.
11 Only a few from Asher, Manasseh, and
Zebulun humbled themselves and came to
Jerusalem. 12 The hand of God was also on
Judah to give them one heart to do what
the king and the officials commanded by
the word of the LORD.

13 Many people came together in Jeru-
salem to keep the festival of unleavened
bread in the second month, a very large
assembly. 14 They set to work and removed
the altars that were in Jerusalem, and all
the altars for offering incense they took
away and threw into the Wadi Kidron.
15 They slaughtered the passover lamb on
the fourteenth day of the second month.
The priests and the Levites were ashamed,
and they sanctified themselves and brought
burnt offerings into the house of the LORD.
16 They took their accustomed posts ac-
cording to the law of Moses the man of
God; the priests dashed the blood that they
received[a] from the hands of the Levites.
17 For there were many in the assembly who
had not sanctified themselves; therefore the
Levites had to slaughter the passover lamb
for everyone who was not clean, to make it
holy to the LORD. 18 For a multitude of the
people, many of them from Ephraim, Ma-
nasseh, Issachar, and Zebulun, had not
cleansed themselves, yet they ate the pass-
over otherwise than as prescribed. But Hez-
ekiah prayed for them, saying, "The good
LORD pardon all 19 who set their hearts to

a Heb lacks *that they received*

Benjamin, and in Ephraim and Manasseh (31.1). The alternation in Hezekiah's reforms is significant—from reestablishing ritual purity at the Temple to enforcing ritual unity in both Judah and the former Northern Kingdom. **30.2:** A similar delay in observing the Passover is legislated in Num 9.9–13. **5–9:** Hezekiah appeals to the remnant of the northern tribes and invites them to participate in the Passover. In spite of the Assyrian exile (v. 6; cf. 2 Kings 18.9–12), the northerners are still Israelites, and their positive response may elicit compassion for their relatives in exile (v. 9). **5:** *From Beer-sheba to Dan,* the traditional southern and northern limits of Israel; see 1 Chr 21.2. **10–14:** Hezekiah's offer meets with an enthusiastic response from Judah and a mixed response from the northern tribes. **15–27:** The national celebration is reminiscent of the heady days of the United Monarchy. **18–20:** These verses suggest that the stereotypical view of postexilic Judaism as legalistic and inflexible is incorrect.

seek God, the LORD the God of their ances-
tors, even though not in accordance with
the sanctuary's rules of cleanness." 20 The
LORD heard Hezekiah, and healed the peo-
ple. 21 The people of Israel who were
present at Jerusalem kept the festival of un-
leavened bread seven days with great glad-
ness; and the Levites and the priests praised
the LORD day by day, accompanied by loud
instruments for the LORD. 22 Hezekiah
spoke encouragingly to all the Levites who
showed good skill in the service of the
LORD. So the people ate the food of the
festival for seven days, sacrificing offerings
of well-being and giving thanks to the
LORD the God of their ancestors.
23 Then the whole assembly agreed to-
gether to keep the festival for another seven
days; so they kept it for another seven days
with gladness. 24 For King Hezekiah of Ju-
dah gave the assembly a thousand bulls and
seven thousand sheep for offerings, and the
officials gave the assembly a thousand bulls
and ten thousand sheep. The priests sancti-
fied themselves in great numbers. 25 The
whole assembly of Judah, the priests and
the Levites, and the whole assembly that
came out of Israel, and the resident aliens
who came out of the land of Israel, and the
resident aliens who lived in Judah, rejoiced.
26 There was great joy in Jerusalem, for
since the time of Solomon son of King Da-
vid of Israel there had been nothing like this
in Jerusalem. 27 Then the priests and the Le-
vites stood up and blessed the people, and
their voice was heard; their prayer came to
his holy dwelling in heaven.

31 Now when all this was finished, all
Israel who were present went out to
the cities of Judah and broke down the pil-
lars, hewed down the sacred poles,[a] and
pulled down the high places and the altars
throughout all Judah and Benjamin, and in
Ephraim and Manasseh, until they had de-
stroyed them all. Then all the people of Is-
rael returned to their cities, all to their indi-
vidual properties.
2 Hezekiah appointed the divisions of
the priests and of the Levites, division by
division, everyone according to his service,
the priests and the Levites, for burnt offer-
ings and offerings of well-being, to minister
in the gates of the camp of the LORD and to
give thanks and praise. 3 The contribution
of the king from his own possessions was
for the burnt offerings: the burnt offerings
of morning and evening, and the burnt
offerings for the sabbaths, the new moons,
and the appointed festivals, as it is written
in the law of the LORD. 4 He commanded
the people who lived in Jerusalem to give
the portion due to the priests and the Le-
vites, so that they might devote themselves
to the law of the LORD. 5 As soon as the
word spread, the people of Israel gave in
abundance the first fruits of grain, wine,
oil, honey, and of all the produce of the
field; and they brought in abundantly the
tithe of everything. 6 The people of Israel
and Judah who lived in the cities of Judah
also brought in the tithe of cattle and sheep,
and the tithe of the dedicated things that
had been consecrated to the LORD their
God, and laid them in heaps. 7 In the third
month they began to pile up the heaps, and
finished them in the seventh month. 8 When
Hezekiah and the officials came and saw
the heaps, they blessed the LORD and his
people Israel. 9 Hezekiah questioned the
priests and the Levites about the heaps.
10 The chief priest Azariah, who was of the
house of Zadok, answered him, "Since they
began to bring the contributions into the
house of the LORD, we have had enough to
eat and have plenty to spare; for the LORD
has blessed his people, so that we have this
great supply left over."
11 Then Hezekiah commanded them to

[a] Heb *Asherim*

31.2–19: The priestly and Levitical courses reestablished. Hezekiah continues his reforms by reinstituting the priestly and Levitical divisions first set out by David (1 Chr 23–26; 28.13,21) and implemented by Solomon (2 Chr 8.14). **4–10:** Like David (1 Chr 22.14–16; 29.2–5), the king contributes toward the support of the Temple and its staff. As in David's time (1 Chr 29.6–9), the people respond with their own generous gifts. **11–20:** Hezekiah ensures that the contributions and tithes will be properly cared for and

prepare store-chambers in the house of the
LORD; and they prepared them. 12 Faithful-
ly they brought in the contributions, the
tithes and the dedicated things. The chief
officer in charge of them was Conaniah the
Levite, with his brother Shimei as second;
13 while Jehiel, Azaziah, Nahath, Asahel,
Jerimoth, Jozabad, Eliel, Ismachiah, Ma-
hath, and Benaiah were overseers assisting
Conaniah and his brother Shimei, by the
appointment of King Hezekiah and of Aza-
riah the chief officer of the house of God.
14 Kore son of Imnah the Levite, keeper of
the east gate, was in charge of the freewill
offerings to God, to apportion the contri-
bution reserved for the LORD and the most
holy offerings. 15 Eden, Miniamin, Jeshua,
Shemaiah, Amariah, and Shecaniah were
faithfully assisting him in the cities of the
priests, to distribute the portions to their
kindred, old and young alike, by divisions,
16 except those enrolled by genealogy,
males from three years old and upwards, all
who entered the house of the LORD as the
duty of each day required, for their service
according to their offices, by their divi-
sions. 17 The enrollment of the priests was
according to their ancestral houses; that of
the Levites from twenty years old and up-
wards was according to their offices, by
their divisions. 18 The priests were enrolled
with all their little children, their wives,
their sons, and their daughters, the whole
multitude; for they were faithful in keep-
ing themselves holy. 19 And for the descen-
dants of Aaron, the priests, who were in the
fields of common land belonging to their
towns, town by town, the people desig-
nated by name were to distribute portions
to every male among the priests and to
everyone among the Levites who was en-
rolled.

20 Hezekiah did this throughout all Ju-
dah; he did what was good and right and
faithful before the LORD his God. 21 And
every work that he undertook in the service
of the house of God, and in accordance
with the law and the commandments, to
seek his God, he did with all his heart; and
he prospered.

32 After these things and these acts of
faithfulness, King Sennacherib of
Assyria came and invaded Judah and en-
camped against the fortified cities, thinking
to win them for himself. 2 When Hezekiah
saw that Sennacherib had come and intend-
ed to fight against Jerusalem, 3 he planned
with his officers and his warriors to stop
the flow of the springs that were outside the
city; and they helped him. 4 A great many
people were gathered, and they stopped all
the springs and the wadi that flowed
through the land, saying, "Why should the
Assyrian kings come and find water in
abundance?" 5 Hezekiah[a] set to work res-
olutely and built up the entire wall that was
broken down, and raised towers on it,[b]
and outside it he built another wall; he also
strengthened the Millo in the city of David,
and made weapons and shields in abun-
dance. 6 He appointed combat commanders
over the people, and gathered them togeth-
er to him in the square at the gate of the city
and spoke encouragingly to them, saying,
7 "Be strong and of good courage. Do not
be afraid or dismayed before the king of
Assyria and all the horde that is with him;
for there is one greater with us than with

a Heb *He* *b* Vg: Heb *and raised on the towers*

stored. **20–21:** A summation and commendation of Hezekiah's reforms, which emphasize that anyone who serves God *in accordance with the law and the commandments . . . with all his heart* will *prosper.*

32.1–23: Sennacherib's invasion of Judah and threat to Jerusalem (see Map on p. 661 HB). The Chronicler borrows from and abbreviates 2 Kings 18.13–19.13, omitting Hezekiah's stripping of the Temple and his tribute to Sennacherib (2 Kings 18.13–16), which might reflect negatively on Hezekiah. The complex account of Kings is simplified, and some parallel texts from the source have been conflated to create a smoother depiction of the events. **2–8:** Sennacherib's campaign took place in 701 BCE. Repairs to Jerusalem's infrastructure, including the construction of the Siloam water tunnel (see 32.30), are made to prepare for the eventuality of an attack by Sennacherib. To this end, Hezekiah also initiates a program of urban mobilization. **5:** *Millo,* see 1 Chr 11.8n. **9–19:** As in Kings, the Assyrians try to convince the Jerusalemites

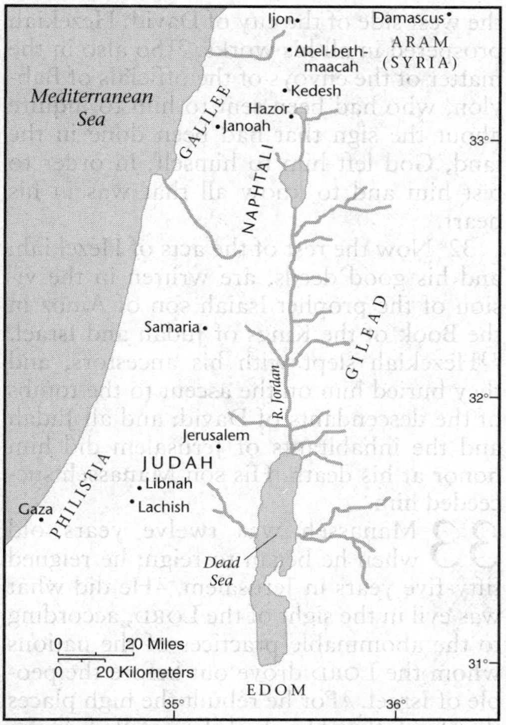

Chs 32: Sennacherib's invasion of Judah.

him. 8With him is an arm of flesh; but with
us is the LORD our God, to help us and to
fight our battles." The people were encour-
aged by the words of King Hezekiah of Ju-
dah.
9 After this, while King Sennacherib of
Assyria was at Lachish with all his forces,
he sent his servants to Jerusalem to King
Hezekiah of Judah and to all the people
of Judah that were in Jerusalem, saying,
10"Thus says King Sennacherib of Assyria:
On what are you relying, that you undergo
the siege of Jerusalem? 11Is not Hezekiah
misleading you, handing you over to die by
famine and by thirst, when he tells you,
'The LORD our God will save us from the
hand of the king of Assyria'? 12Was it not
this same Hezekiah who took away his
high places and his altars and commanded
Judah and Jerusalem, saying, 'Before one
altar you shall worship, and upon it you
shall make your offerings'? 13Do you not
know what I and my ancestors have done
to all the peoples of other lands? Were the
gods of the nations of those lands at all able
to save their lands out of my hand? 14Who
among all the gods of those nations that my
ancestors utterly destroyed was able to save
his people from my hand, that your God
should be able to save you from my hand?
15Now therefore do not let Hezekiah de-
ceive you or mislead you in this fashion,
and do not believe him, for no god of any
nation or kingdom has been able to save his
people from my hand or from the hand of
my ancestors. How much less will your
God save you out of my hand!"
16 His servants said still more against
the Lord GOD and against his servant Hez-
ekiah. 17He also wrote letters to throw
contempt on the LORD the God of Israel
and to speak against him, saying, "Just as
the gods of the nations in other lands did
not rescue their people from my hands, so
the God of Hezekiah will not rescue his
people from my hand." 18They shouted it
with a loud voice in the language of Judah
to the people of Jerusalem who were on the
wall, to frighten and terrify them, in order
that they might take the city. 19They spoke
of the God of Jerusalem as if he were like
the gods of the peoples of the earth, which
are the work of human hands.
20 Then King Hezekiah and the prophet
Isaiah son of Amoz prayed because of this
and cried to heaven. 21And the LORD sent
an angel who cut off all the mighty war-
riors and commanders and officers in the

that their God is no different from the defeated deities of other peoples. From the perspective of the Chronicler, this is blasphemy because the deities of other nations are *the work of human hands* (cf. 2 Kings 18.17–35). **18:** *The language of Judah* was Hebrew. **20:** Like other pious kings before him, Hezekiah appeals to God in conformity with the precedent established by David (1 Chr 17.16–27; 29.10–19) and Solomon (2 Chr 5.13–6.42); cf. 2 Kings 19.1–34. **21:** The LORD's dramatic deliverance of Hezekiah and Jerusalem responds directly to the prayer uttered by Hezekiah and Isaiah (v. 20; cf. 2 Kings 19.1–14) and

camp of the king of Assyria. So he returned
in disgrace to his own land. When he came
into the house of his god, some of his own
sons struck him down there with the
sword. 22 So the LORD saved Hezekiah and
the inhabitants of Jerusalem from the hand
of King Sennacherib of Assyria and from
the hand of all his enemies; he gave them
rest[a] on every side. 23 Many brought gifts
to the LORD in Jerusalem and precious
things to King Hezekiah of Judah, so that
he was exalted in the sight of all nations
from that time onward.
24 In those days Hezekiah became sick
and was at the point of death. He prayed to
the LORD, and he answered him and gave
him a sign. 25 But Hezekiah did not respond
according to the benefit done to him, for
his heart was proud. Therefore wrath came
upon him and upon Judah and Jerusalem.
26 Then Hezekiah humbled himself for the
pride of his heart, both he and the inhabi-
tants of Jerusalem, so that the wrath of the
LORD did not come upon them in the days
of Hezekiah.
27 Hezekiah had very great riches and
honor; and he made for himself treasuries
for silver, for gold, for precious stones, for
spices, for shields, and for all kinds of cost-
ly objects; 28 storehouses also for the yield
of grain, wine, and oil; and stalls for all
kinds of cattle, and sheepfolds.[b] 29 He like-
wise provided cities for himself, and flocks
and herds in abundance; for God had given
him very great possessions. 30 This same
Hezekiah closed the upper outlet of the wa-
ters of Gihon and directed them down to
the west side of the city of David. Hezekiah
prospered in all his works. 31 So also in the
matter of the envoys of the officials of Bab-
ylon, who had been sent to him to inquire
about the sign that had been done in the
land, God left him to himself, in order to
test him and to know all that was in his
heart.
32 Now the rest of the acts of Hezekiah,
and his good deeds, are written in the vi-
sion of the prophet Isaiah son of Amoz in
the Book of the Kings of Judah and Israel.
33 Hezekiah slept with his ancestors, and
they buried him on the ascent to the tombs
of the descendants of David; and all Judah
and the inhabitants of Jerusalem did him
honor at his death. His son Manasseh suc-
ceeded him.

33 Manasseh was twelve years old
when he began to reign; he reigned
fifty-five years in Jerusalem. 2 He did what
was evil in the sight of the LORD, according
to the abominable practices of the nations
whom the LORD drove out before the peo-
ple of Israel. 3 For he rebuilt the high places
that his father Hezekiah had pulled down,
and erected altars to the Baals, made sacred
poles,[c] worshiped all the host of heaven,
and served them. 4 He built altars in the
house of the LORD, of which the LORD had
said, "In Jerusalem shall my name be forev-
er." 5 He built altars for all the host of heav-
en in the two courts of the house of the
LORD. 6 He made his son pass through fire

a Gk Vg: Heb *guided them* *b* Gk Vg: Heb *flocks for folds* *c* Heb *Asheroth*

accords with the LORD's earlier promises to Solomon (7.12–15; cf. 6.28–30). **22–23:** *Rest on every side* is a sign of divine favor (14.1n.), as is tribute from the nations (1 Chr 18.6; 2 Chr 8.2; 17.5,11).

32.24–33: Hezekiah's sickness, recovery, and wealth. Even this pious king was not without his faults (32.24–26; cf. 2 Kings 20.1–19; Isa 38–39), after all "there is no one who does not sin" (2 Chr 6.36 ‖ 1 Kings 8.46). But like David (1 Chr 21.8,17) and Rehoboam (2 Chr 12.7) before him, Hezekiah *humbled himself* before God (see 7.14). **27–30:** Most of these economic and political initiatives are focused outside Jerusalem (cf. vv. 2–8). **27:** Royal wealth indicates divine blessing in Chronicles, and Hezekiah's assets rival those of Solomon (1.11–12,14–17; 9.1–8,23–24). **31:** Cf. 2 Kings 20.12–19.

33.1–20: Manasseh: regression and repentance. Like the Manasseh of Kings (2 Kings 21.1–18), Manasseh (ruled 698/687–642 BCE; the data are inconsistent) is a wicked king (vv. 2–9). Nevertheless, after Manasseh suffers divine punishment in the form of exile (v. 11), he repents, changes course, and is forgiven (vv. 12–19). These elements have no source in Kings. **2–9:** Drawn from 2 Kings 21.2–9. **3:** *Pass through fire,* see 2 Kings 16.3n. **10:** The long-range prophecy of terrible disaster in 2 Kings 21.10–15 be-

in the valley of the son of Hinnom, prac-
ticed soothsaying and augury and sorcery,
and dealt with mediums and with wizards.
He did much evil in the sight of the LORD,
provoking him to anger. 7 The carved image
of the idol that he had made he set in the
house of God, of which God said to David
and to his son Solomon, "In this house, and
in Jerusalem, which I have chosen out of all
the tribes of Israel, I will put my name for-
ever; 8 I will never again remove the feet of
Israel from the land that I appointed for
your ancestors, if only they will be careful
to do all that I have commanded them, all
the law, the statutes, and the ordinances
given through Moses." 9 Manasseh misled
Judah and the inhabitants of Jerusalem, so
that they did more evil than the nations
whom the LORD had destroyed before the
people of Israel.
10 The LORD spoke to Manasseh and to
his people, but they gave no heed. 11 There-
fore the LORD brought against them the
commanders of the army of the king of As-
syria, who took Manasseh captive in mana-
cles, bound him with fetters, and brought
him to Babylon. 12 While he was in distress
he entreated the favor of the LORD his God
and humbled himself greatly before the
God of his ancestors. 13 He prayed to him,
and God received his entreaty, heard his
plea, and restored him again to Jerusalem
and to his kingdom. Then Manasseh knew
that the LORD indeed was God.
14 Afterward he built an outer wall for
the city of David west of Gihon, in the val-
ley, reaching the entrance at the Fish Gate;
he carried it around Ophel, and raised it to
a very great height. He also put command-
ers of the army in all the fortified cities in
Judah. 15 He took away the foreign gods
and the idol from the house of the LORD,
and all the altars that he had built on the
mountain of the house of the LORD and in
Jerusalem, and he threw them out of the
city. 16 He also restored the altar of the
LORD and offered on it sacrifices of well-
being and of thanksgiving; and he com-
manded Judah to serve the LORD the God
of Israel. 17 The people, however, still sacri-
ficed at the high places, but only to the
LORD their God.
18 Now the rest of the acts of Manas-
seh, his prayer to his God, and the words of
the seers who spoke to him in the name of
the LORD God of Israel, these are in the
Annals of the Kings of Israel. 19 His prayer,
and how God received his entreaty, all his
sin and his faithlessness, the sites on which
he built high places and set up the sacred
poles[a] and the images, before he humbled
himself, these are written in the records of
the seers.[b] 20 So Manasseh slept with his
ancestors, and they buried him in his house.
His son Amon succeeded him.
21 Amon was twenty-two years old
when he began to reign; he reigned two
years in Jerusalem. 22 He did what was evil

a Heb *Asherim* *b* One Ms Gk: MT *of Hozai*

comes a summons to repent, which temporarily goes unheeded. **11–13:** The exile of Manasseh, which does not appear in Kings, leads the Judean king to entreat the favor of the LORD and humble himself. **11:** *Babylon,* the reference is not impossible, because the Assyrians maintained a major presence in Babylon at this time. Nevertheless, Assyrian records mention that Manasseh was a loyal vassal. Whatever its origins, the story demonstrates how even one of Judah's worst kings, with God's help, could reverse course in exile, be brought back to his land, institute reforms, and make a new beginning. In this respect, the entire episode offered hope and confirmation to members of the Judean postexilic community, some of whom had ancestors who returned from the Babylonian exile. **13:** Going beyond his earlier pledge to Solomon (7.14), God restores Manasseh to his land. Manasseh becomes a model of how to deal with self-made adversity (6.36–39). **14–17:** Like other reformer kings (11.5–12; 14.3–7; 17.1–19; 32.27–30), Manasseh constructs fortifications and enforces religious centralization. **18–20:** Cf. 2 Kings 21.17–18. **18–19:** *His prayer,* this is the basis for the later composition "The Prayer of Manasseh," now a book of the Apocrypha.

33.21–25: Degeneracy under Amon (641–640 BCE). This monarch follows the model of the earlier, rather than the later, Manasseh, who *humbled himself* (33.2–9). The account is adapted from 2 Kings

in the sight of the LORD, as his father Ma-
nasseh had done. Amon sacrificed to all the
images that his father Manasseh had made,
and served them. 23 He did not humble him-
self before the LORD, as his father Manas-
seh had humbled himself, but this Amon
incurred more and more guilt. 24 His ser-
vants conspired against him and killed him
in his house. 25 But the people of the land
killed all those who had conspired against
King Amon; and the people of the land
made his son Josiah king to succeed him.

34 Josiah was eight years old when he
began to reign; he reigned thirty-
one years in Jerusalem. 2 He did what was
right in the sight of the LORD, and walked
in the ways of his ancestor David; he did
not turn aside to the right or to the left.
3 For in the eighth year of his reign, while he
was still a boy, he began to seek the God of
his ancestor David, and in the twelfth year
he began to purge Judah and Jerusalem of
the high places, the sacred poles,[a] and the
carved and the cast images. 4 In his presence
they pulled down the altars of the Baals; he
demolished the incense altars that stood
above them. He broke down the sacred
poles[a] and the carved and the cast images;
he made dust of them and scattered it over
the graves of those who had sacrificed to
them. 5 He also burned the bones of the
priests on their altars, and purged Judah
and Jerusalem. 6 In the towns of Manasseh,
Ephraim, and Simeon, and as far as Naph-
tali, in their ruins[b] all around, 7 he broke
down the altars, beat the sacred poles[a] and
the images into powder, and demolished all
the incense altars throughout all the land of
Israel. Then he returned to Jerusalem.

8 In the eighteenth year of his reign,
when he had purged the land and the
house, he sent Shaphan son of Azaliah, Ma-
aseiah the governor of the city, and Joah
son of Joahaz, the recorder, to repair the
house of the LORD his God. 9 They came to
the high priest Hilkiah and delivered the
money that had been brought into the
house of God, which the Levites, the keep-
ers of the threshold, had collected from
Manasseh and Ephraim and from all the
remnant of Israel and from all Judah and
Benjamin and from the inhabitants of Jeru-
salem. 10 They delivered it to the workers
who had the oversight of the house of the
LORD, and the workers who were working
in the house of the LORD gave it for repair-
ing and restoring the house. 11 They gave it
to the carpenters and the builders to buy
quarried stone, and timber for binders, and
beams for the buildings that the kings of
Judah had let go to ruin. 12 The people did
the work faithfully. Over them were ap-
pointed the Levites Jahath and Obadiah, of
the sons of Merari, along with Zechariah
and Meshullam, of the sons of the Kohath-
ites, to have oversight. Other Levites, all
skillful with instruments of music, 13 were
over the burden bearers and directed all

a Heb *Asherim* *b* Meaning of Heb uncertain

21.19–26. **23–25:** In refusing to correct his policies, Amon follows the obstinate course set by Ahaz (28.1–27), worsens Judah's plight, and is punished. **25:** *People of the land,* see 2 Kings 11.14n.

34.1–33: Josiah (640–609 BCE): the champion of centralization. Both Kings (2 Kings 22.1–23.30) and Chronicles (34.1–35.27) acclaim Josiah's many reforms throughout Jerusalem and the land of Israel and Judah, but the Chronicler makes these reforms the work of all the people and not simply Josiah himself. **3–7:** The Chronicler likely restructures the account of the reform found in Kings in several ways, including the idea that Josiah began to see the LORD in the eighth year of his reign, rather than later, as in Kings (2 Kings 22.3). In the twelfth year he initiates a number of national expeditions, which *purge Judah and Jerusalem* of all rival religious shrines to the Temple. **6:** The geographic extent of Josiah's interventions, from Simeon to Naphtali, are an addition to the Kings source material. Josiah is interested in all Israel and restores the kingdom to almost Davidic-Solomonic proportions. **8–21:** Adapted in part from 2 Kings 22.3–13. The discovery of *the book of the law of the LORD,* while Temple repairs are underway (vv. 8–14), becomes a matter of grave concern to Josiah because its contents bode ill for Judah. **9:** Since Josiah has already implemented reforms in North and South, it is no great surprise that funds for the Temple restoration project do not merely stem from the people in Judah (2 Kings 22.4), but also from *Manasseh and*

who did work in every kind of service; and
some of the Levites were scribes, and offi-
cials, and gatekeepers.
14 While they were bringing out the
money that had been brought into the
house of the LORD, the priest Hilkiah
found the book of the law of the LORD
given through Moses. 15 Hilkiah said to the
secretary Shaphan, "I have found the book
of the law in the house of the LORD"; and
Hilkiah gave the book to Shaphan. 16 Sha-
phan brought the book to the king, and
further reported to the king, "All that was
committed to your servants they are doing.
17 They have emptied out the money that
was found in the house of the LORD and
have delivered it into the hand of the over-
seers and the workers." 18 The secretary
Shaphan informed the king, "The priest
Hilkiah has given me a book." Shaphan
then read it aloud to the king.
19 When the king heard the words of
the law he tore his clothes. 20 Then the king
commanded Hilkiah, Ahikam son of Sha-
phan, Abdon son of Micah, the secretary
Shaphan, and the king's servant Asaiah:
21 "Go, inquire of the LORD for me and for
those who are left in Israel and in Judah,
concerning the words of the book that has
been found; for the wrath of the LORD that
is poured out on us is great, because our
ancestors did not keep the word of the
LORD, to act in accordance with all that is
written in this book."
22 So Hilkiah and those whom the king
had sent went to the prophet Huldah, the
wife of Shallum son of Tokhath son of Has-
rah, keeper of the wardrobe (who lived in
Jerusalem in the Second Quarter) and
spoke to her to that effect. 23 She declared
to them, "Thus says the LORD, the God of
Israel: Tell the man who sent you to me,
24 Thus says the LORD: I will indeed bring
disaster upon this place and upon its inhab-
itants, all the curses that are written in the
book that was read before the king of Ju-
dah. 25 Because they have forsaken me and
have made offerings to other gods, so that
they have provoked me to anger with all
the works of their hands, my wrath will be
poured out on this place and will not be
quenched. 26 But as to the king of Judah,
who sent you to inquire of the LORD, thus
shall you say to him: Thus says the LORD,
the God of Israel: Regarding the words that
you have heard, 27 because your heart was
penitent and you humbled yourself before
God when you heard his words against this
place and its inhabitants, and you have
humbled yourself before me, and have torn
your clothes and wept before me, I also
have heard you, says the LORD. 28 I will
gather you to your ancestors and you shall
be gathered to your grave in peace; your
eyes shall not see all the disaster that I will
bring on this place and its inhabitants."
They took the message back to the king.
29 Then the king sent word and gath-
ered together all the elders of Judah and
Jerusalem. 30 The king went up to the house
of the LORD, with all the people of Judah,
the inhabitants of Jerusalem, the priests
and the Levites, all the people both great
and small; he read in their hearing all the
words of the book of the covenant that had
been found in the house of the LORD.
31 The king stood in his place and made a
covenant before the LORD, to follow the
LORD, keeping his commandments, his de-
crees, and his statutes, with all his heart
and all his soul, to perform the words of the
covenant that were written in this book.
32 Then he made all who were present in
Jerusalem and in Benjamin pledge them-
selves to it. And the inhabitants of Jerusa-
lem acted according to the covenant of

Ephraim and from all the remnant of Israel. **14:** *The book of the law of the LORD* is generally thought to be some form of the book of Deuteronomy. **22–28:** Huldah's oracle, drawn from 2 Kings 22.14–20, portrays a bleak future for Judah. **29–33:** Like some other noted Judean leaders who wish to avoid or counter a period of decline (15.8–19; 23.16; 29.10), Josiah leads the nation in covenant renewal (cf. 2 Kings 23.1–3). The ratification of the covenant leads to the implementation of reforms throughout his land (cf. 2 Kings 23.4–10). The result is religious unity for the nation *all his days.*

God, the God of their ancestors. 33 Josiah
took away all the abominations from all
the territory that belonged to the people of
Israel, and made all who were in Israel wor-
ship the LORD their God. All his days they
did not turn away from following the LORD
the God of their ancestors.

35 Josiah kept a passover to the LORD
in Jerusalem; they slaughtered the
passover lamb on the fourteenth day of the
first month. 2 He appointed the priests to
their offices and encouraged them in the
service of the house of the LORD. 3 He said
to the Levites who taught all Israel and who
were holy to the LORD, "Put the holy ark in
the house that Solomon son of David, king
of Israel, built; you need no longer carry it
on your shoulders. Now serve the LORD
your God and his people Israel. 4 Make
preparations by your ancestral houses by
your divisions, following the written direc-
tions of King David of Israel and the writ-
ten directions of his son Solomon. 5 Take
position in the holy place according to the
groupings of the ancestral houses of your
kindred the people, and let there be Levites
for each division of an ancestral house.[a]
6 Slaughter the passover lamb, sanctify
yourselves, and on behalf of your kindred
make preparations, acting according to the
word of the LORD by Moses."

7 Then Josiah contributed to the people,
as passover offerings for all that were
present, lambs and kids from the flock to
the number of thirty thousand, and three
thousand bulls; these were from the king's
possessions. 8 His officials contributed will-
ingly to the people, to the priests, and to the
Levites. Hilkiah, Zechariah, and Jehiel, the
chief officers of the house of God, gave to
the priests for the passover offerings two
thousand six hundred lambs and kids and
three hundred bulls. 9 Conaniah also, and
his brothers Shemaiah and Nethanel, and
Hashabiah and Jeiel and Jozabad, the
chiefs of the Levites, gave to the Levites for
the passover offerings five thousand lambs
and kids and five hundred bulls.

10 When the service had been prepared
for, the priests stood in their place, and the
Levites in their divisions according to the
king's command. 11 They slaughtered the
passover lamb, and the priests dashed
the blood that they received[b] from them,
while the Levites did the skinning. 12 They
set aside the burnt offerings so that they
might distribute them according to the
groupings of the ancestral houses of the
people, to offer to the LORD, as it is written
in the book of Moses. And they did the
same with the bulls. 13 They roasted the
passover lamb with fire according to the
ordinance; and they boiled the holy offer-
ings in pots, in caldrons, and in pans, and
carried them quickly to all the people. 14 Af-
terward they made preparations for them-
selves and for the priests, because the
priests the descendants of Aaron were oc-
cupied in offering the burnt offerings and
the fat parts until night; so the Levites made
preparations for themselves and for the

a Meaning of Heb uncertain *b* Heb lacks *that they received*

35.1–19: Passover celebration. As in 2 Kings (23.4–20), national reforms (34.33) lead to a national Passover (2 Kings 23.21–23). Josiah's Passover offering is described in much more detail than in Kings. **3:** The only reference to the ark during the Judahite monarchy (chs 10–36). The pedagogical responsibility of the Levites, who *taught all Israel,* is found elsewhere (Deut 33.8–11) but is most patent in postexilic texts (17.7–9; Neh 8.7–8). **4–6:** The provisions made during the United Monarchy are the model for the Levitical and priestly divisions (31.2–19n.). **7–9:** The contributions of king, officials, and Levites (cf. 34.9) help make the Passover a civic event. **13:** The preparations of the Passover lamb are said to accord with the ordinance (cf. vv. 6,12). The beginning of the verse, properly translated, reads, "They boiled the Passover lamb with fire." This difficult idea reflects a combination of Ex 12.8, which prescribes that the lamb must be broiled on a fire, and Deut 16.7, which prescribes that it must be boiled. These reflect different customs, which ultimately came into contact when the Torah was canonized. Chronicles and later rabbinic texts often dealt with such problems through harmonization, thus "boiling with fire." **18:** The national Passover is unparalleled since the days of Samuel (cf. 2 Kings 23.22). Chronicles, like 2 Kings

priests, the descendants of Aaron. 15The
singers, the descendants of Asaph, were in
their place according to the command of
David, and Asaph, and Heman, and the
king's seer Jeduthun. The gatekeepers were
at each gate; they did not need to interrupt
their service, for their kindred the Levites
made preparations for them.
16 So all the service of the LORD was
prepared that day, to keep the passover and
to offer burnt offerings on the altar of the
LORD, according to the command of King
Josiah. 17The people of Israel who were
present kept the passover at that time, and
the festival of unleavened bread seven days.
18No passover like it had been kept in Isra-
el since the days of the prophet Samuel;
none of the kings of Israel had kept such
a passover as was kept by Josiah, by the
priests and the Levites, by all Judah and
Israel who were present, and by the inhabi-
tants of Jerusalem. 19In the eighteenth year
of the reign of Josiah this passover was
kept.
20 After all this, when Josiah had set the
temple in order, King Neco of Egypt went
up to fight at Carchemish on the Euphrates,
and Josiah went out against him. 21But
Neco[a] sent envoys to him, saying, "What
have I to do with you, king of Judah? I am
not coming against you today, but against
the house with which I am at war; and God
has commanded me to hurry. Cease oppos-
ing God, who is with me, so that he will not
destroy you." 22But Josiah would not turn
away from him, but disguised himself in
order to fight with him. He did not listen to
the words of Neco from the mouth of God,
but joined battle in the plain of Megiddo.
23The archers shot King Josiah; and the
king said to his servants, "Take me away,
for I am badly wounded." 24So his servants
took him out of the chariot and carried him
in his second chariot[b] and brought him to
Jerusalem. There he died, and was buried in
the tombs of his ancestors. All Judah and
Jerusalem mourned for Josiah. 25Jeremiah
also uttered a lament for Josiah, and all the
singing men and singing women have spo-
ken of Josiah in their laments to this day.
They made these a custom in Israel; they
are recorded in the Laments. 26Now the
rest of the acts of Josiah and his faithful
deeds in accordance with what is written in
the law of the LORD, 27and his acts, first
and last, are written in the Book of the
Kings of Israel and Judah.

36 The people of the land took Jehoa-
haz son of Josiah and made him
king to succeed his father in Jerusalem. 2Je-
hoahaz was twenty-three years old when he
began to reign; he reigned three months
in Jerusalem. 3Then the king of Egypt de-
posed him in Jerusalem and laid on the land
a tribute of one hundred talents of silver
and one talent of gold. 4The king of Egypt

a Heb *he* *b* Or *the chariot of his deputy*

23.21–22, attributes to Josiah an incomparably successful Passover celebration. The Passover of Hezekiah (30.1–22) was also important, but enjoyed more limited participation than Josiah's Passover, which was attended by the *priests and the Levites, by all Judah and Israel,* and *the inhabitants of Jerusalem* (cf. 30.10–11).

35.20–27: Josiah's defeat and death by Pharaoh Neco. In Chronicles Neco acts explicitly as a messenger and agent of God; the text of 2 Kings 23.29–30 is much more ambiguous. The addition justifies the death of the otherwise righteous Josiah; he did not heed the prophetic voice. **20:** *Neco,* it is unclear why Josiah intervened against one of the superpowers of his day. Josiah may have been in an alliance with Neco's enemies (cf. 2 Kings 23.29). **23:** *Archers shot,* in conformity with Huldah's prophecy (34.24–28), Josiah is gathered to his fathers (v. 24) and does not see great calamity come to Jerusalem (36.17–21). But Josiah suffers an unpeaceful death (cf. 34.28).

36.1–14: Judah's last four kings. The Chronicler's history of Judah's final decades is much briefer and less gruesome than that of 2 Kings 24–25. Either the Chronicler had a shorter version of our book of Kings, or living in the postexilic restoration community, he felt no need to dwell on the details of the disaster of the exile. **1–4:** The account of the reign of Jehoahaz (609 BCE) is largely taken from 2 Kings 23.30–34. In Chronicles Jehoahaz receives no evaluation. **5–8:** The reign of Jehoiakim (608–598) is

made his brother Eliakim king over Judah and Jerusalem, and changed his name to Jehoiakim; but Neco took his brother Jehoahaz and carried him to Egypt.
5 Jehoiakim was twenty-five years old when he began to reign; he reigned eleven years in Jerusalem. He did what was evil in the sight of the LORD his God.
6 Against him King Nebuchadnezzar of Babylon came up, and bound him with fetters to take him to Babylon.
7 Nebuchadnezzar also carried some of the vessels of the house of the LORD to Babylon and put them in his palace in Babylon.
8 Now the rest of the acts of Jehoiakim, and the abominations that he did, and what was found against him, are written in the Book of the Kings of Israel and Judah; and his son Jehoiachin succeeded him.
9 Jehoiachin was eight years old when he began to reign; he reigned three months and ten days in Jerusalem. He did what was evil in the sight of the LORD.
10 In the spring of the year King Nebuchadnezzar sent and brought him to Babylon, along with the precious vessels of the house of the LORD, and made his brother Zedekiah king over Judah and Jerusalem.

much abridged and adapted from 2 Kings 23.36–24.6. See also Dan 1.1–2. **6:** *Nebuchadnezzar* II who ruled Babylon from 605 to 562 BCE, was one of its most powerful and successful kings. Among his foreign policy accomplishments were the conquest of Tyre (Ezek 27.12) and the invasion of Egypt (Ezek 29.19–21). Both Chronicles and 2 Kings 24.1–17 mention a Babylonian invasion, which affected both Jehoiakim and his son Jehoiachin (598/7 BCE). But only Chronicles claims that the Babylonian king came to Jerusalem to bring both *Jehoiakim* and later his son Jehoiachin, along with various precious Temple *vessels,* to Babylon (v. 10). **9–10:** Jehoiachin (597) suffers a personal exile, along with *the precious vessels of the house of the LORD,* but in 2 Kings 24.8–17 the exile of 597 BCE is a more widespread deportation. **11–14:** Taken in part from 2 Kings 25.18–20. Like Ahaz (ch 28) and Amon (33.23), Zedekiah (597–586) refused to *humble himself.* The Chronicler criticizes Zedekiah, *the leading priests,* and *the people* for being *exceedingly unfaithful.* Thus, the Chronicler, unlike the author of Kings, offers a specific reason for

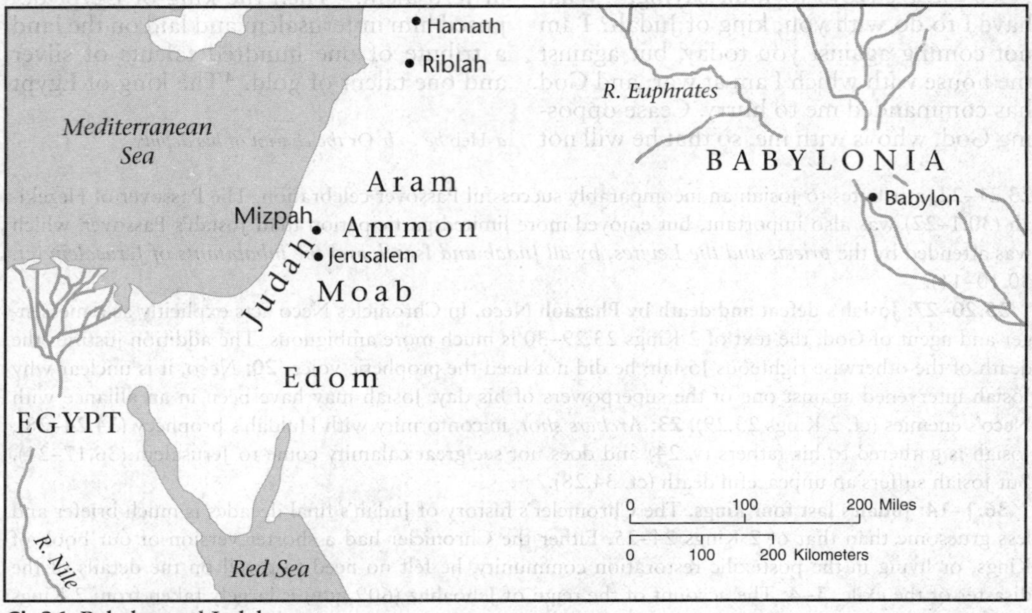

Ch 36: Babylon and Judah.

11 Zedekiah was twenty-one years old
when he began to reign; he reigned eleven
years in Jerusalem. 12 He did what was evil
in the sight of the LORD his God. He did
not humble himself before the prophet Jere-
miah who spoke from the mouth of the
LORD. 13 He also rebelled against King
Nebuchadnezzar, who had made him
swear by God; he stiffened his neck and
hardened his heart against turning to the
LORD, the God of Israel. 14 All the leading
priests and the people also were exceeding-
ly unfaithful, following all the abomina-
tions of the nations; and they polluted the
house of the LORD that he had consecrated
in Jerusalem.

15 The LORD, the God of their ances-
tors, sent persistently to them by his mes-
sengers, because he had compassion on his
people and on his dwelling place; 16 but
they kept mocking the messengers of God,
despising his words, and scoffing at his
prophets, until the wrath of the LORD
against his people became so great that
there was no remedy.

17 Therefore he brought up against
them the king of the Chaldeans, who killed
their youths with the sword in the house
of their sanctuary, and had no compassion
on young man or young woman, the aged
or the feeble; he gave them all into his hand.
18 All the vessels of the house of God,
large and small, and the treasures of the
house of the LORD, and the treasures of
the king and of his officials, all these he
brought to Babylon. 19 They burned the
house of God, broke down the wall of
Jerusalem, burned all its palaces with fire,
and destroyed all its precious vessels. 20 He
took into exile in Babylon those who had
escaped from the sword, and they became
servants to him and to his sons until the
establishment of the kingdom of Persia,
21 to fulfill the word of the LORD by the
mouth of Jeremiah, until the land had
made up for its sabbaths. All the days that
it lay desolate it kept sabbath, to fulfill
seventy years.

22 In the first year of King Cyrus of Per-
sia, in fulfillment of the word of the LORD
spoken by Jeremiah, the LORD stirred up

why the exile transpired under Zedekiah. **13:** *Rebelled,* the Babylonians under *Nebuchadnezzar* II did not take kindly to vassals who chose to revolt. In this case, the Chronicler finds fault with Zedekiah himself for violating his oath to God and refusing to reverse his course. The fall of Jerusalem took place in 586 BCE.

36.15–23: Exile and the call to return. The Deuteronomist places a great deal of blame for Judah's fall on the sins of Manasseh (2 Kings 21.10–15; 23.26–27; 24.3–4), but this is impossible for the Chronicler, who narrated Manasseh's repentance (33.12–13). Instead, the references to the gradual rise in divine wrath, the repeated lack of repentance, and the succession of unheeded messengers and prophets (cf. 15.1–8; 21.12–15; 25.15–17) suggest that the Chronicler attributes the exile to a preponderance of unrequited sins during the last generations of Judah's independence. **17–21:** The record of Judah's exile in 586 BCE is partially drawn from 2 Kings 25.1–21. This author does not depict an Egyptian exile of 582 BCE (2 Kings 25.22–26). **17:** *The Chaldeans,* the Babylonians. **20:** The *kingdom of Persia,* under Cyrus the Great (v. 22), defeated the kingdoms of Media, Lydia, and Babylon, thus becoming one of the ancient world's great empires. At the height of its power, Persia ruled a vast territory stretching from Greece in the west to India in the east. **21:** On the prophecies of Jeremiah, see Jer 25.11–12; 29.10, which is here conflated with Lev 26.34–35,43. **22–23:** Kings ends with the mercies shown to Jehoiachin in exile (2 Kings 25.27–30), but Chronicles offers a clearer hope for the future: King Cyrus's decree in 538 BCE of an end to exile. As Chronicles repeatedly demonstrates, exile need not be a final conclusion, but a condition from which it is possible to return (6.36–39; 7.12–15; 33.12–13). Indeed, from the perspective of the books of Ezra-Nehemiah, Cyrus's decree marks the beginning of Persian-period Judah (Ezra 1.1–3). The return is *in fulfillment of the word of the LORD spoken by Jeremiah,* emphasizing one last time, at the book's conclusion, the power of the prophetic word. Some versions of the Hebrew Bible end with Chronicles, in which case the scriptures conclude with an optimistic note of anticipation.

the spirit of King Cyrus of Persia so that he
sent a herald throughout all his kingdom
and also declared in a written edict:
23 "Thus says King Cyrus of Persia: The
LORD, the God of heaven, has given me
all the kingdoms of the earth, and he has
charged me to build him a house at Jerusalem, which is in Judah. Whoever is among
you of all his people, may the LORD his
God be with him! Let him go up."

EZRA

Ezra-Nehemiah forms a single book in the Hebrew Bible, though its two parts are separated in Christian tradition. It begins where Chronicles ends (2 Chr 36.22–23 || Ezra 1.1–3), with an account of the return from exile (538 BCE). The return, authorized by the edict of the Persian king Cyrus, marks the beginning of a lengthy process of rebuilding of the Temple and Jerusalem. During this period, under Persian control, Israel reconstitutes itself as the "people of the Book," with scripture, specifically the first five books of the Bible (the Torah, also known as the Law of Moses, or the Pentateuch), becoming authoritative for communal and personal life. These developments take place in the period of Ezra and Nehemiah. While the Temple and its clergy gain unprecedented powers, so does the community itself, as new criteria for identity and membership develop.

Cyrus's edict permitting the return sets the agenda for the entire book. For Ezra-Nehemiah, it launches a national and religious rebirth and reconstruction that includes a rebuilding of the Temple, of the community, and of Jerusalem. The edict also establishes Persian legitimation of Jewish life in the Persian province of Yehud (or Judah), claiming harmony between Persian imperial policies and the will of Israel's God, a position that pervades Ezra-Nehemiah.

It is difficult to reconstruct the actual history of this period. Most likely, the return and rebuilding took place in three or four stages. First, the initial returnees, led by Sheshbazzar in 538, began to rebuild the Temple but were forced to abandon the project. Second, a further group of exiles, under the leadership of Zerubbabel and Jeshua, returned during the reign of the Persian king Darius I (522–486) and completed the Temple reconstruction in 515. Third, a group led by Ezra in 458 during the reign of Artaxerxes I (465–424) reestablished the Torah, i.e., Law of Moses, as the authority for Jews in Judah. Finally, a group led by Nehemiah beginning in 445, also during the time of Artaxerxes I, restored Jerusalem's walls and repopulated Jerusalem. Some scholars have suggested that Ezra's return took place after Nehemiah's. The majority of scholars, however, favor the reconstruction noted above, which will be used in the annotations.

The returned exiles were concerned not only with restoring preexilic institutions, such as the altar, Temple, and city, but with establishing religious practice that conformed to their understanding of the book of the Torah, which likely reached its final form in the late exilic or early postexilic period. To the author, the returned exiles were a godly remnant with a renewed commitment to perpetuate the covenantal teachings that kept them distinct. The author was especially worried that the community might repeat the mistakes that caused the exile, and a new destruction would follow.

The returned exiles were a minority within the vast, polytheistic and multi-cultural Persian Empire. Consequently, they sought to protect their ethnic and religious identity by establishing rigorous religious boundaries between themselves and their neighbors through the observance of the Torah. For Ezra-Nehemiah, mixed marriages posed a serious threat to maintaining distinctiveness, hence its objection to exogamous marriages.

Ezra-Nehemiah utilizes contemporary sources in composing its account: memoirs of Ezra, memoirs of Nehemiah (two first-person reports), Aramaic letters, and assorted lists. These are organized theologically rather than merely historically into a three-stage fulfillment of God's promise and Cyrus's exhortation to build the house of God in Judah. Each stage begins in exile and ends in

Jerusalem; each expands the scope of the house of God—from Temple (Ezra 3–6), to community (Ezra 7–9), to Jerusalem as a whole (Neh 1–7), reconstituted finally as a holy city (Neh 11.1). Two lists of returnees (Ezra 2 and Neh 7) frame the activities of the returned exiles, melding the stages into a continuous development. Completion is celebrated with extensive ceremonies of rededication (Neh 8–13).

Ezra-Nehemiah was probably composed in Judah shortly after 400 BCE. It shares some themes and vocabulary with Chronicles, another Persian-period book, but is not by that author (see Introduction to 1 Chronicles). It also shares elements with several later books under the name of Ezra that circulated in antiquity and are preserved in the Apocrypha and Pseudepigrapha, especially 1 Esdras.

The structure of the book is as follows: Ezra-Nehemiah opens with God's promise and Cyrus's decree (Ezra 1.1–4), and continues with exiled Israel's response (Ezra 1.5–Neh 7.73), culminating in celebration of reconstruction (Neh 8–13). After an anticipatory summary of enthusiastic response (Ezra 1.5–11) and a framing section of the list of returnees (Ezra 2.1–70), the response takes place in three stages: the first stage of reconstruction, building the Temple in 538–516 BCE (Ezra 3.1–6.22); the second stage, the mission of Ezra and the formation of the community according to Torah in 458 (Ezra 7.1–10.44); and the third stage, rebuilding Jerusalem under Nehemiah's leadership in 445–444 (Neh 1.1–7.5). These stages close with another framing section, the repeated list of returnees (Neh 7.6–73). Then follows a celebration of renewal and reconstruction (Neh 8–13), consisting of the reading and implementation of the Torah (Neh 8); the confession and commitment of the people (Neh 9–10); the repopulation of the city and review of the people (Neh 11.1–12.26); and a service of dedication, including celebration, purification, procession, and separation (Neh 12.27–13.3). The work as a whole closes with a coda (Neh 13.4–31) in which Nehemiah recounts some of his reforms and invokes God's remembrance.

1 In the first year of King Cyrus of Persia,
in order that the word of the LORD by
the mouth of Jeremiah might be accom-
plished, the LORD stirred up the spirit of
King Cyrus of Persia so that he sent a her-
ald throughout all his kingdom, and also in
a written edict declared:
2 "Thus says King Cyrus of Persia: The
LORD, the God of heaven, has given me
all the kingdoms of the earth, and he has
charged me to build him a house at Jerusa-
lem in Judah. 3 Any of those among you
who are of his people—may their God be
with them!—are now permitted to go up to
Jerusalem in Judah, and rebuild the house
of the LORD, the God of Israel—he is the
God who is in Jerusalem; 4 and let all survi-
vors, in whatever place they reside, be as-
sisted by the people of their place with sil-
ver and gold, with goods and with animals,
besides freewill offerings for the house of
God in Jerusalem."
5 The heads of the families of Judah and
Benjamin, and the priests and the Levites—

1.1–4: God's promise and Cyrus's decree. 1: *King Cyrus,* a Persian king who conquered Babylon in 539 BCE and issued this decree in 538. The decree is in line with Persian religious policy: Cyrus's inscriptions depict him as restorer of several temples. *Jeremiah,* see Jer 29.10. **2–4:** The decree is also found in 2 Chr 36.22–23, and in a different form in Ezra 6.2–5. **3:** *His people,* i.e., worshipers of the LORD, Israel's God. *Are now permitted,* better translated as a command to go up (see 2 Chr 36.23; 1 Esd 2.5). *Rebuild the house of the LORD,* the Temple had been destroyed by the Babylonians in 586 BCE (see 2 Chr 36.19). **4:** *Survivors,* Jews still in exile.

1.5–Neh 7.73: Exiled Israel responds: three stages of return and reconstruction.

1.5–11: Anticipatory summary. 5–6: These two verses form the heading for the three stages of return from exile, depicted in Ezra 2–Neh 7. The end of Nehemiah celebrates the completion of the return. **5:** *Judah* and *Benjamin* formerly constituted the kingdom of Judah (destroyed by Babylon); the "ten tribes"

everyone whose spirit God had stirred—
got ready to go up and rebuild the house of
the LORD in Jerusalem. 6 All their neighbors
aided them with silver vessels, with gold,
with goods, with animals, and with valu-
able gifts, besides all that was freely of-
fered. 7 King Cyrus himself brought out the
vessels of the house of the LORD that Nebu-
chadnezzar had carried away from Jerusa-
lem and placed in the house of his gods.
8 King Cyrus of Persia had them released
into the charge of Mithredath the treasurer,
who counted them out to Sheshbazzar the
prince of Judah. 9 And this was the invento-
ry: gold basins, thirty; silver basins, one
thousand; knives,[a] twenty-nine; 10 gold
bowls, thirty; other silver bowls, four hun-
dred ten; other vessels, one thousand; 11 the
total of the gold and silver vessels was five
thousand four hundred. All these Sheshbaz-
zar brought up, when the exiles were
brought up from Babylonia to Jerusalem.

2 Now these were the people of the prov-
ince who came from those captive ex-
iles whom King Nebuchadnezzar of Bab-
ylon had carried captive to Babylonia; they
returned to Jerusalem and Judah, all to
their own towns. 2 They came with Zerub-
babel, Jeshua, Nehemiah, Seraiah, Reela-
iah, Mordecai, Bilshan, Mispar, Bigvai, Re-
hum, and Baanah.

The number of the Israelite people: 3 the
descendants of Parosh, two thousand one
hundred seventy-two. 4 Of Shephatiah,
three hundred seventy-two. 5 Of Arah, sev-
en hundred seventy-five. 6 Of Pahath-
moab, namely the descendants of Jeshua
and Joab, two thousand eight hundred
twelve. 7 Of Elam, one thousand two hun-
dred fifty-four. 8 Of Zattu, nine hundred
forty-five. 9 Of Zaccai, seven hundred sixty.
10 Of Bani, six hundred forty-two. 11 Of Be-
bai, six hundred twenty-three. 12 Of Azgad,
one thousand two hundred twenty-two.
13 Of Adonikam, six hundred sixty-six.
14 Of Bigvai, two thousand fifty-six. 15 Of
Adin, four hundred fifty-four. 16 Of Ater,
namely of Hezekiah, ninety-eight. 17 Of Be-
zai, three hundred twenty-three. 18 Of Jo-
rah, one hundred twelve. 19 Of Hashum,
two hundred twenty-three. 20 Of Gibbar,
ninety-five. 21 Of Bethlehem, one hundred
twenty-three. 22 The people of Netophah,
fifty-six. 23 Of Anathoth, one hundred
twenty-eight. 24 The descendants of Azma-
veth, forty-two. 25 Of Kiriatharim, Chephi-
rah, and Beeroth, seven hundred forty-
three. 26 Of Ramah and Geba, six hundred
twenty-one. 27 The people of Michmas, one
hundred twenty-two. 28 Of Bethel and Ai,
two hundred twenty-three. 29 The descen-
dants of Nebo, fifty-two. 30 Of Magbish,
one hundred fifty-six. 31 Of the other Elam,
one thousand two hundred fifty-four. 32 Of
Harim, three hundred twenty. 33 Of Lod,
Hadid, and Ono, seven hundred twenty-
five. 34 Of Jericho, three hundred forty-five.
35 Of Senaah, three thousand six hundred
thirty.

36 The priests: the descendants of Jeda-

a Vg: Meaning of Heb uncertain

of the Northern Kingdom (destroyed and exiled by Assyria in 722 BCE according to 2 Kings 17) had assimilated, and did not return. *The Levites* were religious functionaries; *the priests* were a more exclusive subgroup of Levites who claimed descent from Aaron, the first priest (see Ex 28.1). **7–11:** Restoration of Temple vessels, symbols of continuity. **7:** *Nebuchadnezzar,* the Babylonian king who destroyed the first Temple in 586 BCE (see 2 Kings 25). **8:** *Sheshbazzar,* possibly a Davidic descendant.

2.1–70: Frame: initial list of returnees (|| in Neh 7.6–73a). With its repetition in Neh 7.6–73a, the list frames three separate stages of return and reflects combined waves of immigration between 538 and 444 BCE. It identifies three groups that become normative in Judaism: Israelites (laity), Levites, and priests. **1–2:** *Zerubbabel, Jeshua, Nehemiah,* only these three (if this Nehemiah is the governor of Neh 1.1) will play a role in Ezra-Nehemiah. *Zerubbabel* is among the last known Davidic descendants in the Hebrew Bible (see 1 Chr 3.19) and is elsewhere called "governor" (e.g., Hag 1.1). *Jeshua* the priest is elsewhere called "high priest" (e.g., Hag 1.1). **2b–35:** Lay Israelites listed by family ancestral names (vv. 2b–20) and towns of origin (vv. 21–35). **36–39:** *Priests* include only four families (cf. 1 Chr 24).

iah, of the house of Jeshua, nine hundred
seventy-three. 37 Of Immer, one thousand
fifty-two. 38 Of Pashhur, one thousand two
hundred forty-seven. 39 Of Harim, one
thousand seventeen.
40 The Levites: the descendants of Jesh-
ua and Kadmiel, of the descendants of
Hodaviah, seventy-four. 41 The singers: the
descendants of Asaph, one hundred
twenty-eight. 42 The descendants of the
gatekeepers: of Shallum, of Ater, of Tal-
mon, of Akkub, of Hatita, and of Shobai,
in all one hundred thirty-nine.
43 The temple servants: the descendants
of Ziha, Hasupha, Tabbaoth, 44 Keros, Sia-
ha, Padon, 45 Lebanah, Hagabah, Akkub,
46 Hagab, Shamlai, Hanan, 47 Giddel, Ga-
har, Reaiah, 48 Rezin, Nekoda, Gazzam,
49 Uzza, Paseah, Besai, 50 Asnah, Meunim,
Nephisim, 51 Bakbuk, Hakupha, Harhur,
52 Bazluth, Mehida, Harsha, 53 Barkos, Sis-
era, Temah, 54 Neziah, and Hatipha.
55 The descendants of Solomon's ser-
vants: Sotai, Hassophereth, Peruda, 56 Jaa-
lah, Darkon, Giddel, 57 Shephatiah, Hattil,
Pochereth-hazzebaim, and Ami.
58 All the temple servants and the de-
scendants of Solomon's servants were three
hundred ninety-two.
59 The following were those who came
up from Tel-melah, Tel-harsha, Cherub,
Addan, and Immer, though they could not
prove their families or their descent, wheth-
er they belonged to Israel: 60 the descen-
dants of Delaiah, Tobiah, and Nekoda, six
hundred fifty-two. 61 Also, of the descen-
dants of the priests: the descendants of Ha-
baiah, Hakkoz, and Barzillai (who had
married one of the daughters of Barzillai
the Gileadite, and was called by their
name). 62 These looked for their entries in
the genealogical records, but they were not
found there, and so they were excluded
from the priesthood as unclean; 63 the gov-
ernor told them that they were not to par-
take of the most holy food, until there
should be a priest to consult Urim and
Thummim.
64 The whole assembly together was
forty-two thousand three hundred sixty,
65 besides their male and female servants,
of whom there were seven thousand three
hundred thirty-seven; and they had two
hundred male and female singers. 66 They
had seven hundred thirty-six horses, two
hundred forty-five mules, 67 four hundred
thirty-five camels, and six thousand seven
hundred twenty donkeys.
68 As soon as they came to the house of
the LORD in Jerusalem, some of the heads
of families made freewill offerings for the
house of God, to erect it on its site. 69 Ac-
cording to their resources they gave to the
building fund sixty-one thousand darics of
gold, five thousand minas of silver, and one
hundred priestly robes.
70 The priests, the Levites, and some of
the people lived in Jerusalem and its vicini-

40–42: *Levites* are recorded according to their Temple function in the postexilic period. **43–58:** Other Temple functionaries and miscellaneous groups. **59–63:** As a result of the book's concern with religious purity, uncertain genealogies jeopardize membership in the community. Several of these names are incorporated into the community later, however. **61–63:** Priestly legitimacy depends on descent from Aaron. **61:** *Barzillai the Gileadite,* see 2 Sam 17.27; 19.31. The practice of taking on the name of the father-in-law suggests that Barzillai did not have a male heir. **63:** *Urim and Thummim* are the sacred lots, a device used by priests to ascertain divine guidance in certain situations (Ex 28.30, Lev 8.8; Deut 33.8). **64:** The total here exceeds the sum of the enumerated groups. **65–67:** *Servants,* the number of servants, singers, and livestock suggests modest, though not impoverished, economic means. **69:** The precise monetary value of this contribution to the Temple is uncertain because the value of the *daric* and the *mina* fluctuated. Nevertheless, the passage suggests that the community invested a great deal in restoring its Temple. The *priestly robes* are singled out as expensive, specialized garments for official service. **70:** *All Israel in their towns,* Ezra-Nehemiah emphasizes continuity, suggesting a return to preexilic settlements. In reality, however, the Persian province of Yehud is considerably smaller than the earlier kingdom of Judah.

ty;[a] and the singers, the gatekeepers, and
the temple servants lived in their towns,
and all Israel in their towns.

3 When the seventh month came, and the
Israelites were in the towns, the peo-
ple gathered together in Jerusalem. 2 Then
Jeshua son of Jozadak, with his fellow
priests, and Zerubbabel son of Shealtiel
with his kin set out to build the altar of
the God of Israel, to offer burnt offer-
ings on it, as prescribed in the law of Moses
the man of God. 3 They set up the altar on
its foundation, because they were in dread
of the neighboring peoples, and they offered
burnt offerings upon it to the LORD, morn-
ing and evening. 4 And they kept the festi-
val of booths,[b] as prescribed, and offered
the daily burnt offerings by number ac-
cording to the ordinance, as required for
each day, 5 and after that the regular burnt
offerings, the offerings at the new moon
and at all the sacred festivals of the LORD,
and the offerings of everyone who made a
freewill offering to the LORD. 6 From the
first day of the seventh month they began to
offer burnt offerings to the LORD. But the
foundation of the temple of the LORD was
not yet laid. 7 So they gave money to the
masons and the carpenters, and food,
drink, and oil to the Sidonians and the
Tyrians to bring cedar trees from Leba-
non to the sea, to Joppa, according to the
grant that they had from King Cyrus of
Persia.
8 In the second year after their arrival at
the house of God at Jerusalem, in the sec-
ond month, Zerubbabel son of Shealtiel
and Jeshua son of Jozadak made a begin-
ning, together with the rest of their people,
the priests and the Levites and all who had
come to Jerusalem from the captivity. They
appointed the Levites, from twenty years
old and upward, to have the oversight of
the work on the house of the LORD. 9 And
Jeshua with his sons and his kin, and Kad-
miel and his sons, Binnui and Hodaviah[c]
along with the sons of Henadad, the Le-
vites, their sons and kin, together took
charge of the workers in the house of God.
10 When the builders laid the founda-
tion of the temple of the LORD, the priests
in their vestments were stationed to praise
the LORD with trumpets, and the Levites,
the sons of Asaph, with cymbals, according
to the directions of King David of Israel;
11 and they sang responsively, praising and
giving thanks to the LORD,

"For he is good,
for his steadfast love endures forever
toward Israel."

a 1 Esdras 5.46: Heb lacks *lived in Jerusalem and its vicinity* *b* Or *tabernacles*; Heb *succoth*
c Compare 2.40; Neh 7.43; 1 Esdras 5.58: Heb *sons of Judah*

3.1–6.22: First stage of reconstruction: building the Temple.

3.1–7: First step: rebuilding the altar. The restoration of the altar and a functioning priesthood allows a return of sacrificial worship, a central means of religious expression in the preexilic period. **1:** *The seventh month,* September-October. **2:** *Jeshua . . . and Zerubbabel,* Ezra-Nehemiah assumes a pattern of dual leadership. *The law of Moses,* most likely the Torah, more or less as we now have it (see notes to Neh 8). **3–6:** The detailed catalogue of sacrifices underscores the official, institutional nature of the resumption of worship according to "the law of Moses." **3:** *Dread of the neighboring peoples,* introducing a major theme of the book. Tension with local inhabitants emerges because renewed Jewish cultic life is perceived by neighbors as intrusion and competition. Additionally, some of these tensions reflect a debate over the nature and composition of "Israel." *The festival of booths,* see Lev 23.34. *Offerings at the new moon,* see Num 29.6. **7:** Sidon and Tyre helped build Solomon's Temple (1 Kings 5–6).

3.8–13: Second step: founding the Second Temple. **8:** *Second year,* implicitly 537 or 536. Hag 2.18 dates the founding differently, to 520 BCE. Ezra 5.16 credits Sheshbazzar, not Zerubbabel and Jeshua, with laying foundations. Ezra-Nehemiah idealizes and compresses various events. **10–13:** Celebration of temple foundings is a common ancient Near Eastern practice. **10:** *Vestments,* formally dressed to underscore continuity with earlier practice. *David*'s crowning achievement for Ezra-Nehemiah (as for Chronicles) is the development and organization of liturgy. **11:** *For he is good,* a frequent phrase in the Psalms (Ps 100.5; 106.1; 118.2,3,4,29; 136.1–26). **12:** *Old people . . . wept,* postexilic sources consistently

And all the people responded with a great
shout when they praised the LORD, because
the foundation of the house of the LORD
was laid. 12 But many of the priests and Le-
vites and heads of families, old people who
had seen the first house on its foundations,
wept with a loud voice when they saw this
house, though many shouted aloud for joy,
13 so that the people could not distinguish
the sound of the joyful shout from the
sound of the people's weeping, for the peo-
ple shouted so loudly that the sound was
heard far away.

4 When the adversaries of Judah and
Benjamin heard that the returned exiles
were building a temple to the LORD, the
God of Israel, 2 they approached Zerubba-
bel and the heads of families and said to
them, "Let us build with you, for we wor-
ship your God as you do, and we have been
sacrificing to him ever since the days of
King Esar-haddon of Assyria who brought
us here." 3 But Zerubbabel, Jeshua, and the
rest of the heads of families in Israel said to
them, "You shall have no part with us in
building a house to our God; but we alone
will build to the LORD, the God of Israel, as
King Cyrus of Persia has commanded us."
4 Then the people of the land discour-
aged the people of Judah, and made them
afraid to build, 5 and they bribed officials to
frustrate their plan throughout the reign of
King Cyrus of Persia and until the reign of
King Darius of Persia.
6 In the reign of Ahasuerus, in his acces-
sion year, they wrote an accusation against
the inhabitants of Judah and Jerusalem.
7 And in the days of Artaxerxes, Bish-
lam and Mithredath and Tabeel and the
rest of their associates wrote to King Arta-
xerxes of Persia; the letter was written in
Aramaic and translated.[a] 8 Rehum the roy-
al deputy and Shimshai the scribe wrote a
letter against Jerusalem to King Artaxerxes
as follows 9 (then Rehum the royal deputy,
Shimshai the scribe, and the rest of their
associates, the judges, the envoys, the offi-
cials, the Persians, the people of Erech, the
Babylonians, the people of Susa, that is,
the Elamites, 10 and the rest of the nations

a Heb adds *in Aramaic,* indicating that 4.8-6.18 is in Aramaic. Another interpretation is *The letter was written in the Aramaic script and set forth in the Aramaic language*

contrast the splendor of Solomon's Temple with the less glorious, postexilic Second Temple. Only in the first century BCE would Herod renovate extensively the Second Temple. **13:** *Sound was heard far away,* the rejoicing alerts the neighbors and triggers the opposition of the following chapter.

4.1–6.22: Opposition and support (including Aramaic documents).

4.1–24: Opposition from neighbors halts rebuilding. 1–6: Initial opposition. 2: *We worship your God,* i.e., we worship the LORD. According to 2 Kings 17, Assyria forcibly repopulated Samaria after deporting the Israelites, and these foreigners developed a syncretistic religion (2 Kings 17.41). Their history and practice may account for their rejection. *Esar-haddon,* king of Assyria (681–669). According to 2 Kings 17.3; 18.9, the king was Shalmaneser (727–722); see 2 Kings 17.24. **3:** *We alone will build . . . as King Cyrus . . . commanded us,* the returnees claim that Cyrus's decree applies only to them. They consider themselves the sole legitimate remnant of Judah, the heir of the Israel called by God out of Egypt. They seek to preserve ethnic and religious boundaries in the multicultural milieu of the Persian Empire. At a later period, Ezra-Nehemiah shows some readiness to include outsiders (see 6.21). **4:** *The people of the land,* local inhabitants who did not share the experience and ideology of the returning exiles. **5:** *King Darius of Persia,* ruled 522–486. The Temple was rebuilt in his time (see 6.15). **6:** *Ahasuerus,* Xerxes I (486–465 BCE), prominent in the book of Esther. This letter is not preserved.

4.7–24: Further opposition during the reign of Artaxerxes. This correspondence (mostly in Aramaic) is out of chronological order. Here, it serves thematic functions, documenting how adversaries successfully sabotaged Jewish activities, and identifying the opponents as foreigners who displaced the legitimate inhabitants (4.10). **7a:** *Artaxerxes* I, king of Persia (465–424 BCE). **7b–11:** The senders include Persian officials and local inhabitants. **7b:** *Aramaic,* the lingua franca of the Persian period. **8–10:** Various explanatory material. The letter begins only in v. 11. **10:** *Osnappar,* Ashurbanipal, king of Assyria (669–627). *Samaria,* the name used for the northern Israelite kingdom, named after its capital. In the

whom the great and noble Osnappar de-
ported and settled in the cities of Samaria
and in the rest of the province Beyond the
River wrote—and now 11 this is a copy of
the letter that they sent):
"To King Artaxerxes: Your servants, the
people of the province Beyond the River,
send greeting. And now 12 may it be known
to the king that the Jews who came up from
you to us have gone to Jerusalem. They are
rebuilding that rebellious and wicked city;
they are finishing the walls and repairing
the foundations. 13 Now may it be known
to the king that, if this city is rebuilt and the
walls finished, they will not pay tribute,
custom, or toll, and the royal revenue will
be reduced. 14 Now because we share the
salt of the palace and it is not fitting for us
to witness the king's dishonor, therefore
we send and inform the king, 15 so that a
search may be made in the annals of your
ancestors. You will discover in the annals
that this is a rebellious city, hurtful to kings
and provinces, and that sedition was stirred
up in it from long ago. On that account this
city was laid waste. 16 We make known to
the king that, if this city is rebuilt and its
walls finished, you will then have no pos-
session in the province Beyond the River."
17 The king sent an answer: "To Rehum
the royal deputy and Shimshai the scribe
and the rest of their associates who live in
Samaria and in the rest of the province Be-
yond the River, greeting. And now 18 the
letter that you sent to us has been read in
translation before me. 19 So I made a de-
cree, and someone searched and discovered
that this city has risen against kings from
long ago, and that rebellion and sedition
have been made in it. 20 Jerusalem has had
mighty kings who ruled over the whole
province Beyond the River, to whom trib-
ute, custom, and toll were paid. 21 There-
fore issue an order that these people be
made to cease, and that this city not be
rebuilt, until I make a decree. 22 Moreover,
take care not to be slack in this matter; why
should damage grow to the hurt of the
king?"
23 Then when the copy of King Arta-
xerxes' letter was read before Rehum and
the scribe Shimshai and their associates,
they hurried to the Jews in Jerusalem and
by force and power made them cease. 24 At
that time the work on the house of God in
Jerusalem stopped and was discontinued
until the second year of the reign of King
Darius of Persia.

5 Now the prophets, Haggai[a] and Zech-
ariah son of Iddo, prophesied to the
Jews who were in Judah and Jerusalem, in
the name of the God of Israel who was over

a Aram adds *the prophet*

Persian period Samaria emerged as a center of provincial administration as well. *Province Beyond the River,* the Persian satrapy west of the Euphrates River, including Yehud (Judah) and Samaria. By the fifth century BCE Samaria and Yehud were separate provinces, each with its own governor.

4.11–16: The opponents' letter. 12: *Rebuilding that . . . city,* Neh 1–7 records the rebuilding of the city in the twentieth year of Artaxerxes. **13–14:** The opponents warn that sedition and loss of income will result. Inadvertently, however, their letter proves the antiquity of the city and of Jewish claims to it. *Share the salt of the palace,* an idiomatic expression of loyalty to the palace as well as mutual vested interests. **15:** *Annals of your ancestors,* Assyrians and Babylonians kept careful records. Persia inherited and enlarged their bureaucracy. **16:** *No possession,* revolt in Jerusalem will endanger Persian rule throughout the western region of the empire.

4.17–24: Royal response, prohibiting building. 19: *Rebellion and sedition,* presumably the earlier rebellions against Assyria and Babylonia. **21:** *Until I make a decree,* this loophole will enable Nehemiah to secure a new decree. **24:** *At that time* returns to 4.5 and restores the story to its chronological sequence. *The second year of . . . Darius,* i.e., 520 BCE, when rebuilding resumes.

5.1–6.12: Third step: resumption of rebuilding of the Temple.

5.1–2: Resumption of building. 1: *Haggai and Zechariah,* In the prophetic books Haggai and Zechariah, these prophets exhort leaders and community to build, starting in the second year of Darius (520 BCE). **2:** *Then Zerubbabel . . . and Jeshua,* see 2.1–2n.

them. 2 Then Zerubbabel son of Shealtiel
and Jeshua son of Jozadak set out to re-
build the house of God in Jerusalem; and
with them were the prophets of God, help-
ing them.
3 At the same time Tattenai the gover-
nor of the province Beyond the River and
Shethar-bozenai and their associates came
to them and spoke to them thus, "Who
gave you a decree to build this house and to
finish this structure?" 4 They[a] also asked
them this, "What are the names of the men
who are building this building?" 5 But the
eye of their God was upon the elders of the
Jews, and they did not stop them until a
report reached Darius and then answer was
returned by letter in reply to it.
6 The copy of the letter that Tattenai the
governor of the province Beyond the River
and Shethar-bozenai and his associates the
envoys who were in the province Beyond
the River sent to King Darius; 7 they sent
him a report, in which was written as fol-
lows: "To Darius the king, all peace! 8 May
it be known to the king that we went to the
province of Judah, to the house of the great
God. It is being built of hewn stone, and
timber is laid in the walls; this work is be-
ing done diligently and prospers in their
hands. 9 Then we spoke to those elders and
asked them, 'Who gave you a decree to
build this house and to finish this struc-
ture?' 10 We also asked them their names,
for your information, so that we might
write down the names of the men at their
head. 11 This was their reply to us: 'We
are the servants of the God of heaven and
earth, and we are rebuilding the house that
was built many years ago, which a great
king of Israel built and finished. 12 But be-
cause our ancestors had angered the God of
heaven, he gave them into the hand of King
Nebuchadnezzar of Babylon, the Chaldean,
who destroyed this house and carried away
the people to Babylonia. 13 However, King
Cyrus of Babylon, in the first year of his
reign, made a decree that this house of God
should be rebuilt. 14 Moreover, the gold
and silver vessels of the house of God,
which Nebuchadnezzar had taken out of
the temple in Jerusalem and had brought
into the temple of Babylon, these King Cy-
rus took out of the temple of Babylon, and
they were delivered to a man named Shesh-
bazzar, whom he had made governor. 15 He
said to him, "Take these vessels; go and put
them in the temple in Jerusalem, and let the
house of God be rebuilt on its site." 16 Then
this Sheshbazzar came and laid the founda-
tions of the house of God in Jerusalem; and
from that time until now it has been under
construction, and it is not yet finished.'
17 And now, if it seems good to the king,
have a search made in the royal archives
there in Babylon, to see whether a decree
was issued by King Cyrus for the rebuilding
of this house of God in Jerusalem. Let the
king send us his pleasure in this matter."

6 Then King Darius made a decree, and
they searched the archives where the
documents were stored in Babylon. 2 But it
was in Ecbatana, the capital in the province
of Media, that a scroll was found on which
this was written: "A record. 3 In the first

a Gk Syr: Aram *We*

5.3–17: New inquiry. New official Persian inquiry and correspondence lead to renewal of building permit. **3:** *Tattenai,* a Persian official mentioned in nonbiblical sources as governor of the entire *province Beyond the River,* of which Yehud is a subunit. *Beyond the River,* see 4.10.

5.6–17: Tattenai's letter. New correspondence from sympathetic officials reverses the letters of 4.7–16. **8:** *Judah,* Yehud in the Aramaic text. The report indicates building activities well in progress. **11–16:** This report generally parallels Ezra 1, but emphasizes Sheshbazzar's role as governor and does not mention Zerubbabel. **11:** *A great king,* Solomon; see 2 Chr 3–4. **12:** *Nebuchadnezzar,* see 1.7n. *Chaldeans,* a biblical term for the Babylonians. **13:** *King Cyrus of Babylon,* the Persian king who controlled Babylon, where the Temple treasures were stored. **14:** *Sheshbazzar,* see 1.7n. **17:** Tattenai seeks to ascertain both whether Cyrus authorized building, and if Darius wishes it to continue.

6.1–12: Darius's edict in support of the Temple. 2: *Ecbatana,* the summer residence of Persian kings, now Hamadan in Iran. **3–5:** This archival version of Cyrus's decree emphasizes building size and funding

year of his reign, King Cyrus issued a decree: Concerning the house of God at Jerusalem, let the house be rebuilt, the place where sacrifices are offered and burnt offerings are brought;[a] its height shall be sixty cubits and its width sixty cubits,
4 with three courses of hewn stones and one course of timber; let the cost be paid from
the royal treasury. 5 Moreover, let the gold and silver vessels of the house of God, which Nebuchadnezzar took out of the temple in Jerusalem and brought to Babylon, be restored and brought back to the temple in Jerusalem, each to its place; you shall put them in the house of God."

6 "Now you, Tattenai, governor of the province Beyond the River, Shethar-bozenai, and you, their associates, the envoys in the province Beyond the River, keep
away; 7 let the work on this house of God alone; let the governor of the Jews and the elders of the Jews rebuild this house of God
on its site. 8 Moreover I make a decree regarding what you shall do for these elders of the Jews for the rebuilding of this house of God: the cost is to be paid to these people, in full and without delay, from the royal revenue, the tribute of the prov-
ince Beyond the River. 9 Whatever is needed—young bulls, rams, or sheep for burnt offerings to the God of heaven, wheat, salt, wine, or oil, as the priests in Jerusalem require—let that be given to
them day by day without fail, 10 so that they may offer pleasing sacrifices to the God of heaven, and pray for the life of the king and
his children. 11 Furthermore I decree that if anyone alters this edict, a beam shall be pulled out of the house of the perpetrator, who then shall be impaled on it. The house
shall be made a dunghill. 12 May the God who has established his name there overthrow any king or people that shall put forth a hand to alter this, or to destroy this house of God in Jerusalem. I, Darius, make a decree; let it be done with all diligence."

13 Then, according to the word sent by King Darius, Tattenai, the governor of the province Beyond the River, Shethar-bozenai, and their associates did with all diligence what King Darius had ordered.
14 So the elders of the Jews built and prospered, through the prophesying of the prophet Haggai and Zechariah son of Iddo. They finished their building by command of the God of Israel and by decree of Cyrus, Darius, and King Artaxerxes of Persia;
15 and this house was finished on the third day of the month of Adar, in the sixth year of the reign of King Darius.

16 The people of Israel, the priests and the Levites, and the rest of the returned exiles, celebrated the dedication of this house
of God with joy. 17 They offered at the dedi-

a Meaning of Aram uncertain

and is more generous than the public version (Ezra 1.1–4), explicitly offering royal financial support (v. 4). **3:** *Sixty cubits,* a cubit is 45 cm (18 in). The measurements are incomplete. **6–12:** Darius's support of the Temple is extremely generous, perhaps in an attempt to stabilize Persia's hold in the Mediterranean area by securing the goodwill of the people of Yehud. Nonbiblical sources show that Darius also supported Egypt's religious institutions. **7:** *Governor,* Tattenai does not name a contemporary governor of Yehud itself (presumably Zerubbabel). **8:** *The cost,* Darius designates provincial revenue for the Temple, though this may antagonize other local, taxpaying districts.

6.13–15: Fourth step: completion of the Temple. 14: The conclusion highlights the elders and prophetic inspiration. *Cyrus, Darius and King Artaxerxes,* the Temple itself was rebuilt during Cyrus's and Darius's reigns. But the fuller restoration of the house of God, which will include both people and city, will culminate in Neh 7 under Artaxerxes. Ezra 6.14 thus suggests the unity of Ezra-Nehemiah. The joint authorization, first by God and then by kings, is crucial to Ezra-Nehemiah's historical understanding. **15:** Completion on the *third day . . . of Adar . . . sixth year,* March 12, 516/5 BCE.

6.16–22: Concluding celebrations of the first stage. 16–18: The dedication of the Temple. **16:** *People of Israel,* that is, *returned exiles* (lit. "children of exile") who now constitute the fullness of Israel. **17:** *Sin offering,* see Num 7. *Twelve male goats . . . the number of the tribes,* the remnant that includes only Judah, Benjamin, and the Levites nevertheless worships on behalf of the full house of Israel, which it now

cation of this house of God one hundred
bulls, two hundred rams, four hundred
lambs, and as a sin offering for all Israel,
twelve male goats, according to the number
of the tribes of Israel. 18 Then they set the
priests in their divisions and the Levites in
their courses for the service of God at Jeru-
salem, as it is written in the book of Moses.
19 On the fourteenth day of the first
month the returned exiles kept the pass-
over. 20 For both the priests and the Levites
had purified themselves; all of them were
clean. So they killed the passover lamb for
all the returned exiles, for their fellow
priests, and for themselves. 21 It was eaten
by the people of Israel who had returned
from exile, and also by all who had joined
them and separated themselves from the
pollutions of the nations of the land to wor-
ship the LORD, the God of Israel. 22 With
joy they celebrated the festival of unleav-
ened bread seven days; for the LORD had
made them joyful, and had turned the heart
of the king of Assyria to them, so that he
aided them in the work on the house of
God, the God of Israel.
7 After this, in the reign of King Arta-
xerxes of Persia, Ezra son of Seraiah,
son of Azariah, son of Hilkiah, 2 son of
Shallum, son of Zadok, son of Ahitub, 3 son
of Amariah, son of Azariah, son of Mera-
ioth, 4 son of Zerahiah, son of Uzzi, son of
Bukki, 5 son of Abishua, son of Phinehas,
son of Eleazar, son of the chief priest Aar-
on— 6 this Ezra went up from Babylonia.
He was a scribe skilled in the law of Moses
that the LORD the God of Israel had given;
and the king granted him all that he asked,
for the hand of the LORD his God was upon
him.
7 Some of the people of Israel, and some
of the priests and Levites, the singers and
gatekeepers, and the temple servants also
went up to Jerusalem, in the seventh year of
King Artaxerxes. 8 They came to Jerusalem
in the fifth month, which was in the seventh
year of the king. 9 On the first day of the
first month the journey up from Babylon
was begun, and on the first day of the fifth
month he came to Jerusalem, for the gra-
cious hand of his God was upon him. 10 For
Ezra had set his heart to study the law of
the LORD, and to do it, and to teach the
statutes and ordinances in Israel.
11 This is a copy of the letter that King
Artaxerxes gave to the priest Ezra, the

represents. **18:** *Written in the book of Moses,* Ex 29, Lev 8, Num 3, 4, and 8 designate priestly and Levitical tasks. Ezra-Nehemiah stresses the religious, Jewish legitimacy of the Temple, which complements the political, imperial legitimacy granted by Cyrus and Darius. **19–22:** Celebrating Passover and the Feast of Unleavened Bread. The priestly laws of Lev 23.4–6 are followed here. **19:** *Passover* has special significance for the returned exiles since the return from exile was viewed by some as a second Exodus (cf. Isa 52.11–12). **21:** *All who had joined them,* according to Ex 12.48, circumcised non-Israelites may participate in the Passover offering. **22:** *King of Assyria,* an anachronistic reference to the Persian king, alluding to the earliest exile by Assyria, which is now reversed.

7.1–10.44: Second stage of reconstruction: the mission of Ezra and the formation of community according to the Torah in 458 BCE.

7.1–10: The narrator's introduction of Ezra. 1–6: Ezra's long pedigree establishes his impeccable credentials as priest of the most distinguished line and scribe—the two roles that will account for his stature and acceptance within the Jewish community. **1:** Probably *Artaxerxes* I (465–424 BCE); see Introduction. **5:** *Chief priest* may refer to Ezra as well. **6:** *Scribe,* a highly educated person, often in an important advisory position to kings. *Skilled in the law of Moses,* knowledgeable about the Torah. **7:** *Israel . . . priests . . . Levites,* Ezra's caravan includes the same basic groups as Ezra 2. *The seventh year of king Artaxerxes,* 458 BCE. **8:** *The fifth month,* August. **9:** *The first day of the first month,* April. Although the dates may be symbolic, reflecting the Exodus from Egypt in the first month and the destruction of the Temple in the fifth, five months would be a reasonable time for a journey of about 1,600 km (1,000 mi). **10:** Ezra's goals of studying, teaching, and implementing the Torah account for his subsequent actions.

7.11–26: Royal introduction of Ezra and his mission (in Aramaic). This final Aramaic royal letter

scribe, a scholar of the text of the com-
mandments of the LORD and his statutes
for Israel: 12 "Artaxerxes, king of kings, to
the priest Ezra, the scribe of the law of the
God of heaven: Peace.[a] And now 13 I de-
cree that any of the people of Israel or their
priests or Levites in my kingdom who freely
offers to go to Jerusalem may go with you.
14 For you are sent by the king and his seven
counselors to make inquiries about Judah
and Jerusalem according to the law of your
God, which is in your hand, 15 and also to
convey the silver and gold that the king and
his counselors have freely offered to the
God of Israel, whose dwelling is in Jerusa-
lem, 16 with all the silver and gold that you
shall find in the whole province of Babylo-
nia, and with the freewill offerings of the
people and the priests, given willingly for
the house of their God in Jerusalem.
17 With this money, then, you shall with all
diligence buy bulls, rams, and lambs, and
their grain offerings and their drink offer-
ings, and you shall offer them on the altar
of the house of your God in Jerusalem.
18 Whatever seems good to you and your
colleagues to do with the rest of the silver
and gold, you may do, according to the will
of your God. 19 The vessels that have been
given you for the service of the house of
your God, you shall deliver before the God
of Jerusalem. 20 And whatever else is re-
quired for the house of your God, which
you are responsible for providing, you may
provide out of the king's treasury.

21 "I, King Artaxerxes, decree to all the
treasurers in the province Beyond the Riv-
er: Whatever the priest Ezra, the scribe of
the law of the God of heaven, requires of
you, let it be done with all diligence, 22 up
to one hundred talents of silver, one hun-
dred cors of wheat, one hundred baths[b] of
wine, one hundred baths[b] of oil, and un-
limited salt. 23 Whatever is commanded by
the God of heaven, let it be done with zeal
for the house of the God of heaven, or
wrath will come upon the realm of the king
and his heirs. 24 We also notify you that it
shall not be lawful to impose tribute, cus-
tom, or toll on any of the priests, the Le-
vites, the singers, the doorkeepers, the tem-
ple servants, or other servants of this house
of God.

25 "And you, Ezra, according to the
God-given wisdom you possess, appoint
magistrates and judges who may judge all
the people in the province Beyond the River
who know the laws of your God; and you
shall teach those who do not know them.
26 All who will not obey the law of your
God and the law of the king, let judgment
be strictly executed on them, whether for
death or for banishment or for confiscation
of their goods or for imprisonment."

27 Blessed be the LORD, the God of our
ancestors, who put such a thing as this into
the heart of the king to glorify the house of
the LORD in Jerusalem, 28 and who extend-
ed to me steadfast love before the king and
his counselors, and before all the king's

a Syr Vg 1 Esdras 8.9: Aram *Perfect* *b* A Heb measure of volume

establishes Ezra's credentials within the Persian bureaucratic structures. It reauthorizes immigration to Judah (v. 13) and royal subsidy for the Temple (vv. 14–24). It refers to the Torah but does not overly emphasize it; in fact, in v. 26 it is mentioned alongside royal law. **14:** *Seven counselors,* Persian royal advisers (see Esth 1.14 and Herodotus *Histories* 3.84). *The law of your God,* the book of the Torah. **15–19:** The royal privileges include financial support for the Temple by the king himself, voluntary contributions from Babylonian Jews for the Temple, and a free hand to use the surplus. **20:** Virtually a blank check, showing the king's great trust in Ezra. **21–24:** A generous year's supply of provisions for the Temple. **21:** Additional support from local officials. **22:** For the equivalents of the *talent, cor,* and *bath,* see Weights and Measures, p. 534 ES. **24:** Tax exemption for Temple personnel. **25:** *All the people,* probably means Jews in the province. **26:** Ezra's comprehensive authority affirmed. The crucial phrase, *the law of your God and the law of the king,* sets the Torah as legally authoritative for the Jewish community in Yehud. Something akin to religious autonomy and self-rule in matters of religion is implied.

7.27–9.15: Ezra's memoirs. The text resumes in Hebrew. **7.27–8.36: Ezra's journey and arrival.**

mighty officers. I took courage, for the
hand of the LORD my God was upon me,
and I gathered leaders from Israel to go up
with me.

8 These are their family heads, and this is
the genealogy of those who went up
with me from Babylonia, in the reign of
King Artaxerxes: 2 Of the descendants of
Phinehas, Gershom. Of Ithamar, Daniel.
Of David, Hattush, 3 of the descendants of
Shecaniah. Of Parosh, Zechariah, with
whom were registered one hundred fifty
males. 4 Of the descendants of Pahath-
moab, Eliehoenai son of Zerahiah, and
with him two hundred males. 5 Of the de-
scendants of Zattu,[a] Shecaniah son of Ja-
haziel, and with him three hundred males.
6 Of the descendants of Adin, Ebed son of
Jonathan, and with him fifty males. 7 Of the
descendants of Elam, Jeshaiah son of Atha-
liah, and with him seventy males. 8 Of the
descendants of Shephatiah, Zebadiah son
of Michael, and with him eighty males. 9 Of
the descendants of Joab, Obadiah son of
Jehiel, and with him two hundred eighteen
males. 10 Of the descendants of Bani,[b] She-
lomith son of Josiphiah, and with him one
hundred sixty males. 11 Of the descendants
of Bebai, Zechariah son of Bebai, and with
him twenty-eight males. 12 Of the descen-
dants of Azgad, Johanan son of Hakkatan,
and with him one hundred ten males. 13 Of
the descendants of Adonikam, those who
came later, their names being Eliphelet, Je-
uel, and Shemaiah, and with them sixty
males. 14 Of the descendants of Bigvai,
Uthai and Zaccur, and with them seventy
males.

15 I gathered them by the river that runs
to Ahava, and there we camped three days.
As I reviewed the people and the priests, I
found there none of the descendants of
Levi. 16 Then I sent for Eliezer, Ariel, She-
maiah, Elnathan, Jarib, Elnathan, Nathan,
Zechariah, and Meshullam, who were lead-
ers, and for Joiarib and Elnathan, who
were wise, 17 and sent them to Iddo, the
leader at the place called Casiphia, telling
them what to say to Iddo and his colleagues
the temple servants at Casiphia, namely, to
send us ministers for the house of our God.
18 Since the gracious hand of our God was
upon us, they brought us a man of discre-
tion, of the descendants of Mahli son of
Levi son of Israel, namely Sherebiah, with
his sons and kin, eighteen; 19 also Hashabi-
ah and with him Jeshaiah of the descen-
dants of Merari, with his kin and their
sons, twenty; 20 besides two hundred twen-
ty of the temple servants, whom David and
his officials had set apart to attend the Le-
vites. These were all mentioned by name.

21 Then I proclaimed a fast there, at
the river Ahava, that we might deny our-
selves[c] before our God, to seek from him
a safe journey for ourselves, our children,
and all our possessions. 22 For I was
ashamed to ask the king for a band of sol-
diers and cavalry to protect us against the

a Gk 1 Esdras 8.32: Heb lacks *of Zattu*
b Gk 1 Esdras 8.36: Heb lacks *Bani* *c* Or *might fast*

27–28: An expression of gratitude to God, rather than to the king. **8.1–20:** Ezra's caravan numbers almost 1,500 men (women are not mentioned); like Ezra 2, the list mingles clan names and place names, though some individuals are also singled out. The twelve groups symbolize the twelve tribes. **2:** A listing of the most important individuals of priestly and Davidic descent. *Hattush,* 1 Chr 3.22 mentions a descendant of David with this name, though nothing further is reported about him. Davidic descendants remained in Babylonia after the return to Judah had begun; at this point, the leadership of Ezra, and later that of Nehemiah, replaces aspirations for a restored Davidic monarchy.

8.4–20: Additional members and clans in Ezra's caravan. Some names already appeared in Ezra 2 (e.g., Pahath-moab in Ezra 2.6 and 8.4). **15:** *Ahava,* an unknown location along one of the canals of the *river* Euphrates. *None of . . . Levi,* Ezra demonstrates concern for the proper maintenance of the Temple and broadens the scope of its personnel.

8.21–30: Preparations. 21–23: Spiritual preparations. **21:** *Fast,* a common preparation for beseeching God. *All our possessions,* a long journey was hazardous, especially when transporting gold and silver.

enemy on our way, since we had told the
king that the hand of our God is gracious to
all who seek him, but his power and his
wrath are against all who forsake him. 23 So
we fasted and petitioned our God for this,
and he listened to our entreaty.

24 Then I set apart twelve of the leading
priests: Sherebiah, Hashabiah, and ten of
their kin with them. 25 And I weighed out to
them the silver and the gold and the vessels,
the offering for the house of our God that
the king, his counselors, his lords, and all
Israel there present had offered; 26 I
weighed out into their hand six hundred
fifty talents of silver, and one hundred sil-
ver vessels worth . . . talents,[a] and one
hundred talents of gold, 27 twenty gold
bowls worth a thousand darics, and two
vessels of fine polished bronze as precious
as gold. 28 And I said to them, "You are
holy to the LORD, and the vessels are holy;
and the silver and the gold are a freewill
offering to the LORD, the God of your an-
cestors. 29 Guard them and keep them until
you weigh them before the chief priests and
the Levites and the heads of families in Isra-
el at Jerusalem, within the chambers of the
house of the LORD." 30 So the priests and
the Levites took over the silver, the gold,
and the vessels as they were weighed out, to
bring them to Jerusalem, to the house of
our God.

31 Then we left the river Ahava on the
twelfth day of the first month, to go to Je-
rusalem; the hand of our God was upon us,
and he delivered us from the hand of the
enemy and from ambushes along the way.
32 We came to Jerusalem and remained
there three days. 33 On the fourth day, with-
in the house of our God, the silver, the
gold, and the vessels were weighed into the
hands of the priest Meremoth son of Uriah,
and with him was Eleazar son of Phinehas,
and with them were the Levites, Jozabad
son of Jeshua and Noadiah son of Binnui.
34 The total was counted and weighed, and
the weight of everything was recorded.

35 At that time those who had come
from captivity, the returned exiles, offered
burnt offerings to the God of Israel, twelve
bulls for all Israel, ninety-six rams, seventy-
seven lambs, and as a sin offering twelve
male goats; all this was a burnt offering to
the LORD. 36 They also delivered the king's
commissions to the king's satraps and to
the governors of the province Beyond the
River; and they supported the people and
the house of God.

9 After these things had been done, the
officials approached me and said, "The
people of Israel, the priests, and the Levites
have not separated themselves from the

a The number of talents is lacking

22: *I was ashamed . . .*, expressing Ezra's timidity and trust that God's power is ultimately greater than that of the Persian king's army.

8.24–30: Further preparations: empowering clergy. 24: *Leading priests: Sherebiah, Hashabiah,* better "leading priests with Sherebiah, Hashabiah . . ." since these are Levites, not priests (see 8.18–19). **26:** *Talents* weigh about 34 kg (75 lbs) each. **27:** *Darics,* see 2.69n. **28:** *You are holy,* for Ezra, Levites, not only priests, are holy. *The vessels are holy,* holiness derives from their dedication to God.

8.31–36: Arrival and celebration. 31: *Twelfth day of the first month* means April, two days before the Passover commemorating the Exodus. A new Exodus may be implicit; however, spring was the season for expeditions (see 2 Sam 11.1). **33:** Ezra credits an equal number of priests and Levites. **35:** *Returned exiles,* the restored community. **36:** *Satraps,* high officials in the Persian government.

9.1–15: The crisis of mixed marriages. The crisis in the second stage of reconstruction comes when men, including Jewish leaders, marry foreign women. To ensure survival as a small (see Ezra 9.8) minority in the midst of surrounding cultures, Ezra-Nehemiah advocates separatist policies. **1:** *Have not separated,* Deut 7.1–5 prohibits any relation with the people of Canaan and demands their destruction on the ground that they lead to religious defection. Ezra-Nehemiah substitutes separatism for destruction. *Their abominations, from the Canaanites . . .*, more accurately, "their abominations like the Canaanites . . ." The informants equate the religious practices of the present inhabitants with those of the earlier nations at the time of Joshua. *Canaanites . . . Amorites,* Deut 7 specifically prohibits relations with Canaanites, Periz-

peoples of the lands with their abomina-
tions, from the Canaanites, the Hittites, the
Perizzites, the Jebusites, the Ammonites,
the Moabites, the Egyptians, and the Amo-
rites. 2For they have taken some of their
daughters as wives for themselves and for
their sons. Thus the holy seed has mixed
itself with the peoples of the lands, and in
this faithlessness the officials and leaders
have led the way." 3When I heard this, I
tore my garment and my mantle, and
pulled hair from my head and beard, and
sat appalled. 4Then all who trembled at the
words of the God of Israel, because of the
faithlessness of the returned exiles, gath-
ered around me while I sat appalled until
the evening sacrifice.
5 At the evening sacrifice I got up from
my fasting, with my garments and my man-
tle torn, and fell on my knees, spread out
my hands to the LORD my God, 6and said,
"O my God, I am too ashamed and em-
barrassed to lift my face to you, my God,
for our iniquities have risen higher than our
heads, and our guilt has mounted up to the
heavens. 7From the days of our ancestors
to this day we have been deep in guilt, and
for our iniquities we, our kings, and our
priests have been handed over to the kings
of the lands, to the sword, to captivity, to
plundering, and to utter shame, as is now
the case. 8But now for a brief moment fa-
vor has been shown by the LORD our God,
who has left us a remnant, and given us a
stake in his holy place, in order that he[a]
may brighten our eyes and grant us a little
sustenance in our slavery. 9For we are
slaves; yet our God has not forsaken us
in our slavery, but has extended to us his
steadfast love before the kings of Persia, to
give us new life to set up the house of our
God, to repair its ruins, and to give us a
wall in Judea and Jerusalem.
10 "And now, our God, what shall we
say after this? For we have forsaken your
commandments, 11which you commanded
by your servants the prophets, saying, 'The
land that you are entering to possess is a
land unclean with the pollutions of the peo-
ples of the lands, with their abominations.
They have filled it from end to end with
their uncleanness. 12Therefore do not give
your daughters to their sons, neither take
their daughters for your sons, and never
seek their peace or prosperity, so that you
may be strong and eat the good of the land
and leave it for an inheritance to your chil-
dren forever.' 13After all that has come
upon us for our evil deeds and for our great
guilt, seeing that you, our God, have pun-
ished us less than our iniquities deserved
and have given us such a remnant as this,
14shall we break your commandments
again and intermarry with the peoples who
practice these abominations? Would you
not be angry with us until you destroy us
without remnant or survivor? 15O LORD,
God of Israel, you are just, but we have

a Heb *our God*

zites, Hittites, Jebusites and Amorites. Deut 23.3–8 specifically excludes Ammonites and Moabites from the congregation, but permits the incorporation of Egyptians at some point. This verse has thus extended the range of the earlier prohibition. **2:** *Holy seed* is progeny dedicated to the LORD. The term is also found in Isa 6.13, in reference to the purified remnant.

9.3–4: Ezra reacts with mourning and prayer. His self-punishment produces remorse and generates support.

9.5–15: Ezra's prayer. More a sermon than a confession, the prayer teaches values and history in order to alter community behavior. Like the prophets and the Deuteronomistic History, Ezra interprets Israel's political devastation as the consequence of religious and moral failings by Israel, and uses the fear of a recurrence to motivate the community. **7:** *As is now the case,* the end of exile is understood as a result of divine forgiveness, not Israel's changed behavior. **8:** *Little sustenance,* Ezra's confession expresses the vulnerability of a small remnant. **9:** *For we are slaves,* i.e., a colonized people under Persian control. *Repair its ruins,* i.e., physical and spiritual reconstruction. *A wall,* actually "a fence," a metaphor for a weak protective barrier. **11–12:** A paraphrase of Lev 18.24–30 and Deut 7.3–4. Such blending of Priestly and Deuteronomic material characterizes this new period, when the Torah as a book is authoritative.

escaped as a remnant, as is now the case.
Here we are before you in our guilt, though
no one can face you because of this."

10 While Ezra prayed and made con-
fession, weeping and throwing him-
self down before the house of God, a very
great assembly of men, women, and chil-
dren gathered to him out of Israel; the peo-
ple also wept bitterly. 2 Shecaniah son of
Jehiel, of the descendants of Elam, ad-
dressed Ezra, saying, "We have broken
faith with our God and have married for-
eign women from the peoples of the land,
but even now there is hope for Israel in
spite of this. 3 So now let us make a cove-
nant with our God to send away all these
wives and their children, according to the
counsel of my lord and of those who trem-
ble at the commandment of our God; and
let it be done according to the law. 4 Take
action, for it is your duty, and we are with
you; be strong, and do it." 5 Then Ezra
stood up and made the leading priests, the
Levites, and all Israel swear that they
would do as had been said. So they swore.
6 Then Ezra withdrew from before the
house of God, and went to the chamber of
Jehohanan son of Eliashib, where he spent
the night.[a] He did not eat bread or drink
water, for he was mourning over the faith-
lessness of the exiles. 7 They made a procla-
mation throughout Judah and Jerusalem to
all the returned exiles that they should as-
semble at Jerusalem, 8 and that if any did
not come within three days, by order of the
officials and the elders all their property
should be forfeited, and they themselves
banned from the congregation of the exiles.
9 Then all the people of Judah and Ben-
jamin assembled at Jerusalem within the
three days; it was the ninth month, on the
twentieth day of the month. All the people
sat in the open square before the house of
God, trembling because of this matter and
because of the heavy rain. 10 Then Ezra the
priest stood up and said to them, "You
have trespassed and married foreign wom-
en, and so increased the guilt of Israel.
11 Now make confession to the LORD the
God of your ancestors, and do his will; sep-
arate yourselves from the peoples of the
land and from the foreign wives." 12 Then
all the assembly answered with a loud
voice, "It is so; we must do as you have

a 1 Esdras 9.2: Heb *where he went*

10.1–44: Resolution of crisis. The crisis is resolved through communal consensus to apply earlier laws to present circumstances, and therefore to oppose mixed marriages within the covenant community.

10.1–6: The impact of Ezra's prayer. Ezra's confession attracts a crowd and inspires remorse and repentance. **2:** *Have married* (lit. "have been settled"), i.e., established on the land. Inheritance of land is a concern (see Ezra 9.12; Deut 7). The proposal to exclude foreign wives comes from *Shecaniah,* a community member (his father's name, *Jehiel,* appears in 10.26 among the transgressors). The resolution will be determined by consensus. **3:** Remarkably, the children of such marriages are to be sent away as well. **4:** The people authorize Ezra to act. **5:** Only after he has been invited to do so does Ezra assume leadership. **6:** *The chamber,* an office within the Temple complex which, as a priest, Ezra may use. *Jehohanan son of Eliashib* appears in the priestly lists (Neh 12.23), though both names are common in the postexilic period.

10.7–8: Steps toward resolution. 8: *Their property should be forfeited,* this statement suggests communal control over members' property. Although Artaxerxes's letter authorizes Ezra to issue decrees, Ezra resorts to a communal process instead (see 10.5,16). The assembly is for the purpose of communal decision. Threats of confiscation apply to those who refuse to participate in the general assembly, not those who offer a different opinion as to what should be done. This distinction is essential to the civic processes initiated by Ezra (see 10.15 for opposing community members).

10.9–17: A communal process for resolution. The report focuses on the process in which the entire community participates in deciding and enforcing criteria for membership. **9:** *Heavy rains* are typical of the cold *ninth month* (November-December). **10–11:** *Married* (lit. "settled"), see 10.2n. This is Ezra's first directive; he commands only at the invitation of the community. **12–14:** The community assents and offers the mechanism for resolution. **14:** *Have taken* (lit. "have settled"), see 10.2n. Again, the community

said. 13 But the people are many, and it is a
time of heavy rain; we cannot stand in the
open. Nor is this a task for one day or for
two, for many of us have transgressed in
this matter. 14 Let our officials represent the
whole assembly, and let all in our towns
who have taken foreign wives come at ap-
pointed times, and with them the elders and
judges of every town, until the fierce wrath
of our God on this account is averted from
us." 15 Only Jonathan son of Asahel and
Jahzeiah son of Tikvah opposed this, and
Meshullam and Shabbethai the Levites sup-
ported them.

16 Then the returned exiles did so. Ezra
the priest selected men,[a] heads of families,
according to their families, each of them
designated by name. On the first day of the
tenth month they sat down to examine the
matter. 17 By the first day of the first month
they had come to the end of all the men
who had married foreign women.

18 There were found of the descendants
of the priests who had married foreign
women, of the descendants of Jeshua son of
Jozadak and his brothers: Maaseiah, Elie-
zer, Jarib, and Gedaliah. 19 They pledged
themselves to send away their wives, and
their guilt offering was a ram of the flock
for their guilt. 20 Of the descendants of Im-
mer: Hanani and Zebadiah. 21 Of the de-
scendants of Harim: Maaseiah, Elijah, She-
maiah, Jehiel, and Uzziah. 22 Of the
descendants of Pashhur: Elioenai, Maase-
iah, Ishmael, Nethanel, Jozabad, and Ela-
sah.

23 Of the Levites: Jozabad, Shimei, Ke-
laiah (that is, Kelita), Pethahiah, Judah,
and Eliezer. 24 Of the singers: Eliashib.
Of the gatekeepers: Shallum, Telem, and
Uri.

25 And of Israel: of the descendants of
Parosh: Ramiah, Izziah, Malchijah, Mija-
min, Eleazar, Hashabiah,[b] and Benaiah.
26 Of the descendants of Elam: Mattaniah,
Zechariah, Jehiel, Abdi, Jeremoth, and Eli-
jah. 27 Of the descendants of Zattu: Elioe-
nai, Eliashib, Mattaniah, Jeremoth, Zabad,
and Aziza. 28 Of the descendants of Bebai:
Jehohanan, Hananiah, Zabbai, and Athlai.
29 Of the descendants of Bani: Meshullam,
Malluch, Adaiah, Jashub, Sheal, and Jere-
moth. 30 Of the descendants of Pahath-
moab: Adna, Chelal, Benaiah, Maaseiah,
Mattaniah, Bezalel, Binnui, and Manasseh.
31 Of the descendants of Harim: Eliezer, Is-
shijah, Malchijah, Shemaiah, Shimeon,
32 Benjamin, Malluch, and Shemariah. 33 Of
the descendants of Hashum: Mattenai,
Mattattah, Zabad, Eliphelet, Jeremai, Ma-
nasseh, and Shimei. 34 Of the descendants
of Bani: Maadai, Amram, Uel, 35 Benaiah,
Bedeiah, Cheluhi, 36 Vaniah, Meremoth,
Eliashib, 37 Mattaniah, Mattenai, and Jaa-
su. 38 Of the descendants of Binnui:[c] Shim-
ei, 39 Shelemiah, Nathan, Adaiah, 40 Mach-
nadebai, Shashai, Sharai, 41 Azarel,

a 1 Esdras 9.16: Syr: Heb *And there were selected Ezra,* *b* 1 Esdras 9.26 Gk: Heb *Malchijah*
c Gk: Heb *Bani, Binnui*

is responsible for action, devising a representative form (*our officials*) of governing for itself. **15:** A minority opposition is registered, establishing that majority decision carries even without unanimity. *Meshullam* could be Ezra's companion in 8.16.

10.16–44: Results: compliance with communal decision. The issue of mixed marriages constitutes the first test of the new, legal status of the Torah, illustrating how an ancient book may shape the present and future through communal interpretive process. **16:** *The returned exiles did so* on the basis of a democratic process. *Ezra . . . selected men,* the Hebrew text states that the community selects the committee, with Ezra serving as a member. This is more consistent with the rest of Ezra-Nehemiah. **17:** *By the first day of the first month,* the commission's deliberations began in December 458 (v. 16) and concluded three months later in March 457 BCE, about one year after Ezra's caravan first set out for Jerusalem (7.9). **18:** *Had married* (lit. "had settled"), see 10.2n. *Jeshua son of Jozadak,* the high priest in the early return. See 2.1–2n. **18–19:** An explicit report that the high priest's most powerful family fully complied with the communal decision. Given the power they exercise over the community, their cooperation and compliance signal a crucial victory for this process. **20–44:** List of other offenders. **44:** *They sent them away with their*

Shelemiah, Shemariah, 42 Shallum, Amari-
ah, and Joseph. 43 Of the descendants of
Nebo: Jeiel, Mattithiah, Zabad, Zebina,
Jaddai, Joel, and Benaiah. 44 All these had
married foreign women, and they sent them
away with their children.[a]

a 1 Esdras 9.36; meaning of Heb uncertain

children, this sentence is from the later 1 Esdras, while the Hebrew here states: "Some had wives with whom they had sons." Ezra 10.44 thus does not say that the women and children were expelled. The fate of these families is not recorded in the Hebrew text. The conclusion of the second stage (Ezra 7–10) focuses on establishing communally determined boundaries based on the Torah without resorting to military force. It offers a counterexample to the destruction in the book of Joshua (e.g., Josh 6.21), although with its own casualties.

NEHEMIAH

The introductory material for Nehemiah is found in the Introduction to Ezra-Nehemiah. The section known as the book of Nehemiah depicts the third stage of reconstruction under Nehemiah, focusing on building Jerusalem's walls (1.1–7.5), followed by the repetition of the list of returnees (7.6–73) that frames the three stages, and concluding with the celebration of the achievements of the return and reconstruction by the rededicated Jewish community (chs 8–13).

1 The words of Nehemiah son of Hacali-
ah. In the month of Chislev, in the
twentieth year, while I was in Susa the capi-
tal, 2 one of my brothers, Hanani, came
with certain men from Judah; and I asked
them about the Jews that survived, those
who had escaped the captivity, and about
Jerusalem. 3 They replied, "The survivors
there in the province who escaped captivity
are in great trouble and shame; the wall of
Jerusalem is broken down, and its gates
have been destroyed by fire."
4 When I heard these words I sat down
and wept, and mourned for days, fasting
and praying before the God of heaven. 5 I
said, "O LORD God of heaven, the great
and awesome God who keeps covenant and
steadfast love with those who love him and
keep his commandments; 6 let your ear be
attentive and your eyes open to hear the
prayer of your servant that I now pray be-
fore you day and night for your servants,
the people of Israel, confessing the sins of
the people of Israel, which we have sinned
against you. Both I and my family have
sinned. 7 We have offended you deeply, fail-
ing to keep the commandments, the stat-
utes, and the ordinances that you com-
manded your servant Moses. 8 Remember
the word that you commanded your ser-
vant Moses, 'If you are unfaithful, I will
scatter you among the peoples; 9 but if you
return to me and keep my commandments
and do them, though your outcasts are un-
der the farthest skies, I will gather them
from there and bring them to the place at
which I have chosen to establish my name.'
10 They are your servants and your people,
whom you redeemed by your great power
and your strong hand. 11 O Lord, let your
ear be attentive to the prayer of your ser-
vant, and to the prayer of your servants
who delight in revering your name. Give
success to your servant today, and grant
him mercy in the sight of this man!"
At the time, I was cupbearer to the king.

1.1–7.5: Third stage of reconstruction: rebuilding Jerusalem under Nehemiah's leadership. These chapters come from Nehemiah's memoirs, first-person material that is also found in chs 12–13.

1.1–2.10: The commission of Nehemiah. **1.1:** *Nehemiah,* a cupbearer (v. 11) to King Artaxerxes I (464–424 BCE), who, as governor of the Persian province of Yehud (Judah), will lead the rebuilding of Jerusalem's walls. *Chislev* (November-December) *in the twentieth year* of Artaxerxes I (2.1), namely 445/444 BCE. *Susa,* the winter residence of Persian kings. **2–3:** *Jews that survived,* those who remained in the land after exile in 586, as well as those who had returned since (see Ezra 1.1–4). *The wall of Jerusalem,* broken by the Babylonians in 586 BCE.

1.4–11: Nehemiah's prayer. **5:** *God of heaven,* a typical postexilic designation, also found in Ezra 7.12. **8–9:** A paraphrase of themes in Deuteronomy (e.g., Deut 30.1–5). **11:** *This man,* Artaxerxes I. *Cupbearer,* a high royal courtier who sampled wine for quality and safety (see 2.1).

2 In the month of Nisan, in the twentieth
year of King Artaxerxes, when wine
was served him, I carried the wine and gave
it to the king. Now, I had never been sad in
his presence before. 2 So the king said to
me, "Why is your face sad, since you are
not sick? This can only be sadness of the
heart." Then I was very much afraid. 3 I
said to the king, "May the king live forever!
Why should my face not be sad, when the
city, the place of my ancestors' graves, lies
waste, and its gates have been destroyed by
fire?" 4 Then the king said to me, "What do
you request?" So I prayed to the God of
heaven. 5 Then I said to the king, "If it
pleases the king, and if your servant has
found favor with you, I ask that you send
me to Judah, to the city of my ancestors'
graves, so that I may rebuild it." 6 The king
said to me (the queen also was sitting be-
side him), "How long will you be gone, and
when will you return?" So it pleased the
king to send me, and I set him a date.
7 Then I said to the king, "If it pleases the
king, let letters be given me to the gover-
nors of the province Beyond the River, that
they may grant me passage until I arrive in
Judah; 8 and a letter to Asaph, the keeper of
the king's forest, directing him to give me
timber to make beams for the gates of the
temple fortress, and for the wall of the city,
and for the house that I shall occupy." And
the king granted me what I asked, for the
gracious hand of my God was upon me.
9 Then I came to the governors of the
province Beyond the River, and gave them
the king's letters. Now the king had sent
officers of the army and cavalry with me.
10 When Sanballat the Horonite and Tobi-
ah the Ammonite official heard this, it dis-
pleased them greatly that someone had
come to seek the welfare of the people of
Israel.
11 So I came to Jerusalem and was there
for three days. 12 Then I got up during the
night, I and a few men with me; I told no
one what my God had put into my heart to
do for Jerusalem. The only animal I took
was the animal I rode. 13 I went out by night
by the Valley Gate past the Dragon's Spring
and to the Dung Gate, and I inspected the
walls of Jerusalem that had been broken
down and its gates that had been destroyed
by fire. 14 Then I went on to the Fountain

2.1–8: Nehemiah's commission. 1: *Nisan,* March-April, the month of the Exodus from Egypt. The chronology of 1.1 (November-December) and 2.1 (March-April), both in the twentieth year, makes sense if Nehemiah's reckoning begins the year in the fall, as in subsequent Judaism, rather than with the spring month of Nisan as in Ex 12.2. **2:** *I was . . . afraid,* because his request could suggest divided loyalties, even treason. **3:** *My ancestors' graves,* depicting Jerusalem as graveyard dramatizes the importance of honoring ancestors and minimizes the threat that rebuilding Jerusalem might otherwise suggest. Ezra 4.21 suggests that this king had prohibited rebuilding of Jerusalem's walls until further notice. **6:** The presence of the *queen* indicates the intimate setting of the conversation. *I set him a date,* 5.14 and 13.6 indicate that Nehemiah's mission as governor lasted twelve years. **8:** *Temple fortress,* explicit plans for the Temple's gates and fortifications, including the city's walls, appear only now.

2.9–10: Nehemiah's journey. Nehemiah's military escort visibly testifies to royal support for his mission, and contrasts with Ezra 8.22. **10:** *Sanballat* is mentioned in the fifth-century BCE Elephantine papyri from Egypt as a governor of Samaria, Judah's northern neighbor; see Ezra 4.10. *Tobiah,* a high official, probably Jewish (his name means, "the LORD is good"; see also 6.18), is in the service of the Ammonites, Judah's eastern neighbor. *Displeased,* as in Ezra 4, Jewish renewal meets with local opposition. Threatened with diminished political and economic control in the region, Samaria seeks to sabotage rebuilding.

2.11–18: Nehemiah's initial work in Jerusalem. 11–16: Nighttime inspection of the walls. **12:** *I told no one* (see v. 16), he seeks to camouflage his activities from local opponents. **13–15:** Nehemiah's circuit of the walls confirms their dilapidated condition. **13:** The *Valley Gate* is in the western wall, the *Dragon's Spring* is unknown, and the *Dung Gate* is at the southern end of the wall (in a different location from the present Dung Gate in Jerusalem). **14:** The location of the *Fountain Gate* is uncertain; the *King's Pool* is probably the Pool of Siloam (3.15). *No place . . . to continue,* earlier structures and pathways of the eastern slope have collapsed beyond speedy repair. As a result, rebuilt Jerusalem will be smaller.

Gate and to the King's Pool; but there was
no place for the animal I was riding to con-
tinue. 15 So I went up by way of the valley
by night and inspected the wall. Then I
turned back and entered by the Valley
Gate, and so returned. 16 The officials did
not know where I had gone or what I was
doing; I had not yet told the Jews, the
priests, the nobles, the officials, and the rest
that were to do the work.
17 Then I said to them, "You see the
trouble we are in, how Jerusalem lies in
ruins with its gates burned. Come, let us
rebuild the wall of Jerusalem, so that we
may no longer suffer disgrace." 18 I told
them that the hand of my God had been
gracious upon me, and also the words that
the king had spoken to me. Then they said,
"Let us start building!" So they committed
themselves to the common good. 19 But
when Sanballat the Horonite and Tobiah
the Ammonite official, and Geshem the
Arab heard of it, they mocked and ridiculed
us, saying, "What is this that you are do-
ing? Are you rebelling against the king?"
20 Then I replied to them, "The God of
heaven is the one who will give us success,
and we his servants are going to start build-
ing; but you have no share or claim or his-
toric right in Jerusalem."

3 Then the high priest Eliashib set to
work with his fellow priests and rebuilt
the Sheep Gate. They consecrated it and set
up its doors; they consecrated it as far as
the Tower of the Hundred and as far as the
Tower of Hananel. 2 And the men of Jeri-
cho built next to him. And next to them[a]
Zaccur son of Imri built.
3 The sons of Hassenaah built the Fish
Gate; they laid its beams and set up its
doors, its bolts, and its bars. 4 Next to them
Meremoth son of Uriah son of Hakkoz
made repairs. Next to them Meshullam son
of Berechiah son of Meshezabel made re-
pairs. Next to them Zadok son of Baana
made repairs. 5 Next to them the Tekoites
made repairs; but their nobles would not
put their shoulders to the work of their
Lord.[b]
6 Joiada son of Paseah and Meshullam
son of Besodeiah repaired the Old Gate;
they laid its beams and set up its doors, its
bolts, and its bars. 7 Next to them repairs
were made by Melatiah the Gibeonite and

a Heb *him* b Or *lords*

2.17–18: Decision to build. Nehemiah now galvanizes the Jews of Yehud to rebuild by appealing to communal pride and disclosing divine and royal support.

2.19–20: Opposition. 19: *Sanballat . . . and Tobiah,* see 2.10n. *Geshem,* king of Qedar in Arabia, controlled territory south-southeast of Yehud. *Rebelling,* a trumped-up charge to antagonize Persian authorities; cf. Ezra 4. **20:** *You have no share . . . in Jerusalem,* independence from neighbors' control explains Nehemiah's achievement and the opposition it meets. Like Zerubbabel earlier (Ezra 4), Nehemiah limits participation in rebuilding, insisting on the superiority of God to any human power.

3.1–32: Building the walls despite opposition. Rebuilding Jerusalem's walls reinforces the religious, political, and commercial power of Jerusalem. The list of participants offers important information for discerning the territory of Jerusalem and the province of Yehud in Nehemiah's time, which is limited to portions of Judah and Benjamin. Persian-period seals and seal impressions from Yehud corroborate this picture. Jerusalem's new circumference is considerably reduced.

3.1–5: Restoring Jerusalem's northern boundary. 1: *The high priest Eliashib,* grandson of the priest Jeshua (12.10; Ezra 3.2). *They consecrated it,* this marks the project as a holy task: The city as a whole is by extension holy as a house of God. *The Tower of Hananel,* a boundary in Zech 14.10 for a newly sanctified Jerusalem. Most of the gates and other places named in the chapter cannot be located with certainty; see 2.13–14n. **2:** *Men of Jericho,* here and in vv. 9–11, volunteers from various districts of Yehud take responsibility for specific segments of the wall. **4:** *Hakkoz,* one of the families whose genealogy had been suspect initially (Ezra 2.61), but which has now been integrated. **5:** *The Tekoites,* residents of Tekoa, 16 km (10 mi) south of Jerusalem. Their efforts, despite abstention by leaders, underscore the popular nature of rebuilding.

3.6–14: Restoring Jerusalem's western boundary. The individuals named here are otherwise unknown.

Jadon the Meronothite—the men of Gibe-
on and of Mizpah—who were under the
jurisdiction of[a] the governor of the prov-
ince Beyond the River. 8 Next to them Uzzi-
el son of Harhaiah, one of the goldsmiths,
made repairs. Next to him Hananiah, one
of the perfumers, made repairs; and they
restored Jerusalem as far as the Broad Wall.
9 Next to them Rephaiah son of Hur, ruler
of half the district of[b] Jerusalem, made re-
pairs. 10 Next to them Jedaiah son of Haru-
maph made repairs opposite his house; and
next to him Hattush son of Hashabneiah
made repairs. 11 Malchijah son of Harim
and Hasshub son of Pahath-moab repaired
another section and the Tower of the Ov-
ens. 12 Next to him Shallum son of Hallo-
hesh, ruler of half the district of[b] Jerusa-
lem, made repairs, he and his daughters.

13 Hanun and the inhabitants of Zano-
ah repaired the Valley Gate; they rebuilt it
and set up its doors, its bolts, and its bars,
and repaired a thousand cubits of the wall,
as far as the Dung Gate.

14 Malchijah son of Rechab, ruler of the
district of[c] Beth-haccherem, repaired the
Dung Gate; he rebuilt it and set up its
doors, its bolts, and its bars.

15 And Shallum son of Col-hozeh, ruler
of the district of[c] Mizpah, repaired the
Fountain Gate; he rebuilt it and covered it
and set up its doors, its bolts, and its bars;
and he built the wall of the Pool of Shelah
of the king's garden, as far as the stairs that
go down from the City of David. 16 After
him Nehemiah son of Azbuk, ruler of half
the district of[b] Beth-zur, repaired from a
point opposite the graves of David, as far as
the artificial pool and the house of the war-
riors. 17 After him the Levites made repairs:
Rehum son of Bani; next to him Hashabi-
ah, ruler of half the district of[b] Keilah,
made repairs for his district. 18 After him
their kin made repairs: Binnui,[d] son of
Henadad, ruler of half the district of[b] Kei-
lah; 19 next to him Ezer son of Jeshua, rul-
er[e] of Mizpah, repaired another section
opposite the ascent to the armory at the
Angle. 20 After him Baruch son of Zabbai
repaired another section from the Angle to
the door of the house of the high priest
Eliashib. 21 After him Meremoth son of Uri-
ah son of Hakkoz repaired another section
from the door of the house of Eliashib to
the end of the house of Eliashib. 22 After
him the priests, the men of the surrounding
area, made repairs. 23 After them Benjamin
and Hasshub made repairs opposite their
house. After them Azariah son of Maaseiah
son of Ananiah made repairs beside his
own house. 24 After him Binnui son of Hen-
adad repaired another section, from the
house of Azariah to the Angle and to the
corner. 25 Palal son of Uzai repaired oppo-
site the Angle and the tower projecting
from the upper house of the king at the
court of the guard. After him Pedaiah son
of Parosh 26 and the temple servants liv-
ing[f] on Ophel made repairs up to a point
opposite the Water Gate on the east and the
projecting tower. 27 After him the Tekoites
repaired another section opposite the great
projecting tower as far as the wall of
Ophel.

28 Above the Horse Gate the priests
made repairs, each one opposite his own
house. 29 After them Zadok son of Immer
made repairs opposite his own house. After
him Shemaiah son of Shecaniah, the keeper

a Meaning of Heb uncertain *b* Or *supervisor of half the portion assigned to* *c* Or *supervisor of the portion assigned to* *d* Gk Syr Compare verse 24, 10.9: Heb *Bavvai* *e* Or *supervisor* *f* Cn: Heb *were living*

8: *Goldsmiths . . . perfumers,* further evidence of growing commerce and urbanization. *They restored,* more accurately "they left out," suggesting that the rebuilt city was smaller than earlier Jerusalem. *The Broad Wall,* originally built by Hezekiah (late eighth century BCE; see 2 Chr 32.5) to enlarge the defensible scope of Jerusalem. **9–12:** The task is divided among leaders of five districts, some outside Jerusalem. **12:** *His daughters,* the daughters' role, like the men's, may have entailed physical participation and/or financial sponsorship.

3.15–32: Restoring Jerusalem's southern and eastern boundaries. **16:** *Graves of David,* see 2 Chr 23.33. **23–24:** Jerusalemites take charge of areas adjacent to their dwellings.

of the East Gate, made repairs. 30 After him
Hananiah son of Shelemiah and Hanun
sixth son of Zalaph repaired another sec-
tion. After him Meshullam son of Berechi-
ah made repairs opposite his living quar-
ters. 31 After him Malchijah, one of the
goldsmiths, made repairs as far as the
house of the temple servants and of the
merchants, opposite the Muster Gate,[a]
and to the upper room of the corner. 32 And
between the upper room of the corner and
the Sheep Gate the goldsmiths and the mer-
chants made repairs.

4 [b]Now when Sanballat heard that we
were building the wall, he was angry
and greatly enraged, and he mocked the
Jews. 2 He said in the presence of his associ-
ates and of the army of Samaria, "What are
these feeble Jews doing? Will they restore
things? Will they sacrifice? Will they finish
it in a day? Will they revive the stones out
of the heaps of rubbish—and burned ones
at that?" 3 Tobiah the Ammonite was be-
side him, and he said, "That stone wall they
are building—any fox going up on it would
break it down!" 4 Hear, O our God, for we
are despised; turn their taunt back on their
own heads, and give them over as plunder
in a land of captivity. 5 Do not cover their
guilt, and do not let their sin be blotted out
from your sight; for they have hurled in-
sults in the face of the builders.

6 So we rebuilt the wall, and all the wall
was joined together to half its height; for
the people had a mind to work.

7[c]But when Sanballat and Tobiah and
the Arabs and the Ammonites and the Ash-
dodites heard that the repairing of the walls
of Jerusalem was going forward and the
gaps were beginning to be closed, they were
very angry, 8 and all plotted together to
come and fight against Jerusalem and to
cause confusion in it. 9 So we prayed to
our God, and set a guard as a protection
against them day and night.

10 But Judah said, "The strength of the
burden bearers is failing, and there is too
much rubbish so that we are unable to
work on the wall." 11 And our enemies
said, "They will not know or see anything
before we come upon them and kill them
and stop the work." 12 When the Jews who
lived near them came, they said to us ten
times, "From all the places where they
live[d] they will come up against us."[e] 13 So
in the lowest parts of the space behind the
wall, in open places, I stationed the people
according to their families,[f] with their
swords, their spears, and their bows. 14 Af-
ter I looked these things over, I stood up
and said to the nobles and the officials and
the rest of the people, "Do not be afraid of
them. Remember the LORD, who is great
and awesome, and fight for your kin, your
sons, your daughters, your wives, and your
homes."

15 When our enemies heard that their
plot was known to us, and that God had
frustrated it, we all returned to the wall,
each to his work. 16 From that day on, half
of my servants worked on construction,
and half held the spears, shields, bows, and
body-armor; and the leaders posted them-
selves behind the whole house of Judah,

a Or *Hammiphkad Gate* *b* Ch 3.33 in Heb
c Ch 4.1 in Heb *d* Cn: Heb *you return*
e Compare Gk Syr: Meaning of Heb uncertain
f Meaning of Heb uncertain

4.1–6.14: Obstacles to reconstruction. Nehemiah's memoirs about Sanballat's opposition (2.19) resume. Nehemiah, like the earlier returnees (Ezra 3–6 and Ezra 7–10), encounters obstacles that hamper progress. Three forms of threats to building activities are mentioned: intimidation by outsiders (4.1–23), economic hardships (5.1–19), and plots against Nehemiah (6.1–14).

4.1–23: First obstacle: intimidation. 1: The neighboring people under Sanballat (see 2.10n.) use taunts and threats. **2:** The opposition from Samaria reproduces ancient competition between the two preexilic capitals. **4–5:** Nehemiah punctuates his report with several invocations of God, often with a formulaic "remember me" (see 5.19). **10–12:** The builders temporarily succumb to the difficulties of the work and their opponents' intimidation. **10:** *Judah,* the Jewish community. *Rubbish,* debris. **13–14:** Nehemiah demonstrates readiness for physical combat, confident in God's help. **15–23:** Successful rallying of the Judean builders due to improved security measures.

17 who were building the wall. The burden
bearers carried their loads in such a way
that each labored on the work with one
hand and with the other held a weapon.
18 And each of the builders had his sword
strapped at his side while he built. The man
who sounded the trumpet was beside me.
19 And I said to the nobles, the officials, and
the rest of the people, "The work is great
and widely spread out, and we are separat-
ed far from one another on the wall. 20 Ral-
ly to us wherever you hear the sound of the
trumpet. Our God will fight for us."
21 So we labored at the work, and half
of them held the spears from break of dawn
until the stars came out. 22 I also said to the
people at that time, "Let every man and his
servant pass the night inside Jerusalem, so
that they may be a guard for us by night
and may labor by day." 23 So neither I nor
my brothers nor my servants nor the men
of the guard who followed me ever took off
our clothes; each kept his weapon in his
right hand.[a]

5 Now there was a great outcry of the
people and of their wives against their
Jewish kin. 2 For there were those who said,
"With our sons and our daughters, we are
many; we must get grain, so that we may
eat and stay alive." 3 There were also those
who said, "We are having to pledge our
fields, our vineyards, and our houses in or-
der to get grain during the famine." 4 And
there were those who said, "We are having
to borrow money on our fields and vine-
yards to pay the king's tax. 5 Now our flesh
is the same as that of our kindred; our chil-
dren are the same as their children; and yet
we are forcing our sons and daughters to be
slaves, and some of our daughters have
been ravished; we are powerless, and our
fields and vineyards now belong to others."
6 I was very angry when I heard their
outcry and these complaints. 7 After think-
ing it over, I brought charges against the
nobles and the officials; I said to them,
"You are all taking interest from your own
people." And I called a great assembly to
deal with them, 8 and said to them, "As far
as we were able, we have bought back our
Jewish kindred who had been sold to other
nations; but now you are selling your own
kin, who must then be bought back by us!"
They were silent, and could not find a word
to say. 9 So I said, "The thing that you are
doing is not good. Should you not walk in
the fear of our God, to prevent the taunts of
the nations our enemies? 10 Moreover I and
my brothers and my servants are lending
them money and grain. Let us stop this tak-
ing of interest. 11 Restore to them, this very
day, their fields, their vineyards, their olive
orchards, and their houses, and the interest
on money, grain, wine, and oil that you

a Cn: Heb *each his weapon the water*

5.1–19: Second obstacle: economic hardships. Economic hardships, including heavy taxes to the Persian king (5.4), are aggravated by the wealthier Jews who exploit the situation to their own profit. To redress the balance, Nehemiah initiates economic reforms. Inconsistent laws about slavery incorporated into the Torah may have compounded this problem (compare Ex 21.2–6 and Deut 15.12–18 with Lev 25.35–43). **2:** *We are many,* alternately, as "pledge" (see v. 3), suggesting that sons and daughters are pledged as security for loans and become slaves when loans are defaulted. **3:** The problem is the default on loans during famine and the consequent loss of property and family. **4:** *The king's tax,* the heavy levy from the provinces extracted by the Persian government. **5:** Results: indentured slavery and loss of land and home to wealthier compatriots. *Ravished,* daughters were particularly vulnerable at times of economic hardship.

5.6–19: Nehemiah's response. Nehemiah combats economic hardships by reforming practices of the wealthy and contributing personally to the economy from his own funds. **7:** *The nobles and the officials,* upper-class members exploiting the economic instability. *Taking interest,* more accurately, "taking pledges," i.e., keeping items used as pledges (family members, fields, and houses); this is prohibited in Ex 22.24–26; Deut 24.10. **8:** *We have bought back,* following Lev 25.47–48. **10:** Nehemiah helps the nobles save face by admitting a measure of responsibility. Nehemiah's measures resemble the remission of debts in the jubilee year (Lev 25). **12:** Like Ezra (see Ezra 10), but in a different manner, Nehemiah extracts a public have been exacting from them." 12 Then they said, "We will restore everything and demand nothing more from them. We will do as you say." And I called the priests, and made them take an oath to do as they had promised. 13 I also shook out the fold of my garment and said, "So may God shake out everyone from house and from property who does not perform this promise. Thus may they be shaken out and emptied." And all the assembly said, "Amen," and praised the LORD. And the people did as they had promised.

14 Moreover from the time that I was appointed to be their governor in the land of Judah, from the twentieth year to the thirty-second year of King Artaxerxes, twelve years, neither I nor my brothers ate the food allowance of the governor. 15 The former governors who were before me laid heavy burdens on the people, and took food and wine from them, besides forty shekels of silver. Even their servants lorded it over the people. But I did not do so, because of the fear of God. 16 Indeed, I devoted myself to the work on this wall, and acquired no land; and all my servants were gathered there for the work. 17 Moreover there were at my table one hundred fifty people, Jews and officials, besides those who came to us from the nations around us. 18 Now that which was prepared for one day was one ox and six choice sheep; also fowls were prepared for me, and every ten days skins of wine in abundance; yet with all this I did not demand the food allowance of the governor, because of the heavy burden of labor on the people. 19 Remember for my good, O my God, all that I have done for this people.

6 Now when it was reported to Sanballat and Tobiah and to Geshem the Arab and to the rest of our enemies that I had built the wall and that there was no gap left in it (though up to that time I had not set up the doors in the gates), 2 Sanballat and Geshem sent to me, saying, "Come and let us meet together in one of the villages in the plain of Ono." But they intended to do me harm. 3 So I sent messengers to them, saying, "I am doing a great work and I cannot come down. Why should the work stop while I leave it to come down to you?" 4 They sent to me four times in this way, and I answered them in the same manner. 5 In the same way Sanballat for the fifth time sent his servant to me with an open letter in his hand. 6 In it was written, "It is reported among the nations—and Geshem[a] also says it—that you and the Jews intend to rebel; that is why you are building the wall; and according to this report you wish to become their king. 7 You have also set up prophets to proclaim in Jerusalem concerning you, 'There is a king in Judah!' And now it will be reported to the king according to these words. So come, therefore, and let us confer together." 8 Then I sent to him, saying, "No such things as you say have been done; you are inventing them

a Heb *Gashmu*

oath from leaders. *The priests* administer a religiously binding oath to ensure the efficacy of the appended curses. **13:** Symbolic actions could accompany curses in the ancient Near East. *Fold,* the equivalent of a pocket. The gesture connotes removing all excessive matter (including wealth). **14–19:** The Persian government expected local populations to support the governors. Nehemiah forgoes such privileges and subsidizes the office with his own personal funds. **14:** *Governor* was a title for several different ranks of officials. *Twentieth year,* see 1.1n. **15:** The Bible does not preserve names of other governors after Zerubbabel, though archaeology has uncovered some names, possibly from the intervening period. *Forty shekels,* about 456 gr (1 lb). **17:** *Those who to us came from the nations,* officials and guests from the rest of the empire. **19:** *Remember for my good,* such conclusions typify Nehemiah (see 4.4–5; 13.31).

6.1–14: Third obstacle: plots against Nehemiah. 1–4: Attempts to harm Nehemiah in an unprotected place. **1:** *Sanballat and Tobiah and . . . Geshem.* See 2.10n.,19n. The opposition comes from different directions. **2:** *Plain of Ono,* in the northwest of the province of Yehud, far from the safety of Jerusalem. **5–7:** Attempts to frighten Nehemiah by threatening to report his alleged rebellion to the king. **7:** *Prophets,* in Israel, prophets anointed kings (e.g., 1 Kings 1.34; 19.15–16). **10–13:** Attempts to entice Nehemiah out of your own mind" 9—for they all wanted to frighten us, thinking, "Their hands will drop from the work, and it will not be done." But now, O God, strengthen my hands.

10 One day when I went into the house of Shemaiah son of Delaiah son of Mehetabel, who was confined to his house, he said, "Let us meet together in the house of God, within the temple, and let us close the doors of the temple, for they are coming to kill you; indeed, tonight they are coming to kill you." 11 But I said, "Should a man like me run away? Would a man like me go into the temple to save his life? I will not go in!" 12 Then I perceived and saw that God had not sent him at all, but he had pronounced the prophecy against me because Tobiah and Sanballat had hired him. 13 He was hired for this purpose, to intimidate me and make me sin by acting in this way, and so they could give me a bad name, in order to taunt me. 14 Remember Tobiah and Sanballat, O my God, according to these things that they did, and also the prophetess Noadiah and the rest of the prophets who wanted to make me afraid.

15 So the wall was finished on the twenty-fifth day of the month Elul, in fifty-two days. 16 And when all our enemies heard of it, all the nations around us were afraid[a] and fell greatly in their own esteem; for they perceived that this work had been accomplished with the help of our God. 17 Moreover in those days the nobles of Judah sent many letters to Tobiah, and Tobiah's letters came to them. 18 For many in Judah were bound by oath to him, because he was the son-in-law of Shecaniah son of Arah: and his son Jehohanan had married the daughter of Meshullam son of Berechiah. 19 Also they spoke of his good deeds in my presence, and reported my words to him. And Tobiah sent letters to intimidate me.

7 Now when the wall had been built and I had set up the doors, and the gatekeepers, the singers, and the Levites had been appointed, 2 I gave my brother Hanani charge over Jerusalem, along with Hananiah the commander of the citadel—for he was a faithful man and feared God more than many. 3 And I said to them, "The gates of Jerusalem are not to be opened until the sun is hot; while the gatekeepers[b] are still standing guard, let them shut and bar the doors. Appoint guards from among the inhabitants of Jerusalem, some at their watch posts, and others before their own houses." 4 The city was wide and large, but the people within it were few and no houses had been built.

5 Then my God put it into my mind to assemble the nobles and the officials and the people to be enrolled by genealogy. And I found the book of the genealogy of those

a Another reading is *saw* *b* Heb *while they*

to discredit himself with religious authorities by entering the inner part of the Temple. **10:** *Shemaiah* is a suspected enemy within the community. **13:** Entering sections of the Temple reserved for clergy would cast Nehemiah as a sinful usurper violating the priestly domain and the Temple's sanctity. **14:** Nehemiah's repeated plea for divine remembrance (cf. 5.19). *The prophetess Noadiah* is one of four named prophetesses in the Hebrew Bible (the others are Miriam, Deborah, and Huldah).

6.15–19: The completion of the walls. 15: *Elul,* August-September. *Fifty-two days,* illustrating the zeal and dedication of the volunteers under Nehemiah. Excavated remnants of Nehemiah's wall reflect the haste of the builders. **17–19:** The opposition did not fall silent, but only changed its tactics. However, these attempts to create internal discord failed. *Tobiah,* see 2.10n.

7.1–5: Setting up guards. 1: *Gatekeepers . . . singers . . . Levites,* these people ordinarily officiated at the Temple. As guards of the city's gates, they symbolize the new sanctity of the city as a whole (see 11.1). **2:** *Hanani,* see 1.2. *Citadel,* fortress (see 2.8). **3:** For reasons of safety, *the gates* are to be open only during broad daylight. **4:** *The people within it were few,* most returnees had resumed a largely agrarian life in the surrounding countryside. Nehemiah's measures allow greater urbanization, which is facilitated in ch 11. **5:** The sparse population of Jerusalem is used as an editorial device to repeat this list from Ezra 2.

who were the first to come back, and I
found the following written in it:
6 These are the people of the province
who came up out of the captivity of those
exiles whom King Nebuchadnezzar of Bab-
ylon had carried into exile; they returned
to Jerusalem and Judah, each to his town.
7 They came with Zerubbabel, Jeshua, Ne-
hemiah, Azariah, Raamiah, Nahamani,
Mordecai, Bilshan, Mispereth, Bigvai, Ne-
hum, Baanah.
The number of the Israelite people: 8 the
descendants of Parosh, two thousand one
hundred seventy-two. 9 Of Shephatiah,
three hundred seventy-two. 10 Of Arah, six
hundred fifty-two. 11 Of Pahath-moab,
namely the descendants of Jeshua and Joab,
two thousand eight hundred eighteen. 12 Of
Elam, one thousand two hundred fifty-
four. 13 Of Zattu, eight hundred forty-five.
14 Of Zaccai, seven hundred sixty. 15 Of
Binnui, six hundred forty-eight. 16 Of Be-
bai, six hundred twenty-eight. 17 Of Azgad,
two thousand three hundred twenty-two.
18 Of Adonikam, six hundred sixty-
seven. 19 Of Bigvai, two thousand sixty-
seven. 20 Of Adin, six hundred fifty-five.
21 Of Ater, namely of Hezekiah, ninety-
eight. 22 Of Hashum, three hundred twenty-
eight. 23 Of Bezai, three hundred twenty-
four. 24 Of Hariph, one hundred twelve.
25 Of Gibeon, ninety-five. 26 The people
of Bethlehem and Netophah, one hundred
eighty-eight. 27 Of Anathoth, one hundred
twenty-eight. 28 Of Beth-azmaveth, forty-
two. 29 Of Kiriath-jearim, Chephirah, and
Beeroth, seven hundred forty-three. 30 Of
Ramah and Geba, six hundred twenty-one.
31 Of Michmas, one hundred twenty-two.
32 Of Bethel and Ai, one hundred twenty-
three. 33 Of the other Nebo, fifty-two.
34 The descendants of the other Elam, one
thousand two hundred fifty-four. 35 Of Ha-
rim, three hundred twenty. 36 Of Jericho,
three hundred forty-five. 37 Of Lod, Hadid,
and Ono, seven hundred twenty-one. 38 Of
Senaah, three thousand nine hundred
thirty.
39 The priests: the descendants of Jeda-
iah, namely the house of Jeshua, nine
hundred seventy-three. 40 Of Immer, one
thousand fifty-two. 41 Of Pashhur, one
thousand two hundred forty-seven. 42 Of
Harim, one thousand seventeen.
43 The Levites: the descendants of Jesh-
ua, namely of Kadmiel of the descendants
of Hodevah, seventy-four. 44 The singers:
the descendants of Asaph, one hundred
forty-eight. 45 The gatekeepers: the descen-
dants of Shallum, of Ater, of Talmon, of
Akkub, of Hatita, of Shobai, one hundred
thirty-eight.
46 The temple servants: the descendants
of Ziha, of Hasupha, of Tabbaoth, 47 of Ke-
ros, of Sia, of Padon, 48 of Lebana, of Haga-
ba, of Shalmai, 49 of Hanan, of Giddel, of
Gahar, 50 of Reaiah, of Rezin, of Nekoda,
51 of Gazzam, of Uzza, of Paseah, 52 of Be-
sai, of Meunim, of Nephushesim, 53 of Bak-
buk, of Hakupha, of Harhur, 54 of Bazlith,
of Mehida, of Harsha, 55 of Barkos, of Sis-
era, of Temah, 56 of Neziah, of Hatipha.
57 The descendants of Solomon's ser-
vants: of Sotai, of Sophereth, of Perida,
58 of Jaala, of Darkon, of Giddel, 59 of
Shephatiah, of Hattil, of Pochereth-
hazzebaim, of Amon.
60 All the temple servants and the de-
scendants of Solomon's servants were three
hundred ninety-two.
61 The following were those who came
up from Tel-melah, Tel-harsha, Cherub,
Addon, and Immer, but they could not
prove their ancestral houses or their de-

7.6–73: Frame: repeated list of returnees. Essentially reproducing Ezra 2.1–70, with insignificant variations, the list serves a twofold purpose here. First, it connects the last stage of reconstruction with the successful efforts of the previous generations, as a continuous response to Cyrus's original decree (Ezra 1). By repeating the list from Ezra 2, Ezra-Nehemiah frames and melds the three stages of return and reconstruction (Temple, community, city) into a single, unified event, spanning nearly a century (538–444 BCE). Second, it identifies who now legitimately belongs to the community and is subject to the legal and religious practices, privileges, and responsibilities that follow. On the list itself, see the notes to Ezra 2. **66:** *Forty-two thousand three hundred sixty,* same total for the population as Ezra 2.64, though

scent, whether they belonged to Israel:
62 the descendants of Delaiah, of Tobiah, of
Nekoda, six hundred forty-two. 63 Also, of
the priests: the descendants of Hobaiah, of
Hakkoz, of Barzillai (who had married one
of the daughters of Barzillai the Gileadite
and was called by their name). 64 These
sought their registration among those en-
rolled in the genealogies, but it was not
found there, so they were excluded from
the priesthood as unclean; 65 the governor
told them that they were not to partake of
the most holy food, until a priest with Urim
and Thummim should come.
66 The whole assembly together was
forty-two thousand three hundred sixty,
67 besides their male and female slaves, of
whom there were seven thousand three
hundred thirty-seven; and they had two
hundred forty-five singers, male and fe-
male. 68 They had seven hundred thirty-six
horses, two hundred forty-five mules,[a]
69 four hundred thirty-five camels, and six
thousand seven hundred twenty donkeys.
70 Now some of the heads of ancestral
houses contributed to the work. The gover-
nor gave to the treasury one thousand dar-
ics of gold, fifty basins, and five hundred
thirty priestly robes. 71 And some of the
heads of ancestral houses gave into the
building fund twenty thousand darics of
gold and two thousand two hundred minas
of silver. 72 And what the rest of the people
gave was twenty thousand darics of gold,
two thousand minas of silver, and sixty-
seven priestly robes.
73 So the priests, the Levites, the gate-
keepers, the singers, some of the people, the
temple servants, and all Israel settled in
their towns.
When the seventh month came—the peo-
ple of Israel being settled in their towns—
8 1 all the people gathered together into
the square before the Water Gate. They
told the scribe Ezra to bring the book of the
law of Moses, which the LORD had given
to Israel. 2 Accordingly, the priest Ezra
brought the law before the assembly, both
men and women and all who could hear
with understanding. This was on the first
day of the seventh month. 3 He read from it
facing the square before the Water Gate
from early morning until midday, in the
presence of the men and the women and
those who could understand; and the ears
of all the people were attentive to the book
of the law. 4 The scribe Ezra stood on a
wooden platform that had been made for
the purpose; and beside him stood Matti-

a Ezra 2.66 and the margins of some Hebrew Mss: MT lacks *They had . . . forty-five mules*

some numbers within the two lists do not match. **70–72:** The parallel in Ezra 2.68–69 differs. For the value of such contributions, see note there. **73:** *The seventh month,* September-October (see Ezra 3.1), designated as a beginning of the new year in later Judaism. Lev 23.23–24 and Num 29.1–6 specify practices for this date without mention of reading the Torah (see ch 8).

8.1–13.31: Celebration of renewal and reconstruction. The great celebration that inaugurates the reconstructed community extends over several weeks, at least from the first day of the seventh month (8.2) to the twenty-fourth (9.1), longer than any other celebration in the Bible. The narrative depicts four steps and a coda.

8.1–18: First step: reading and implementing the Torah. The reconstruction culminates in this momentous event, as the community summons Ezra to bring *the book of the law of Moses* (8.1), i.e., the Torah. Ch 8 signals the historical moment when the Pentateuch is publicly (re)introduced and receives communal sanction. Thus ch 8 parallels Sinai in its impact as the receiving of God's teachings by the entire people, transforming them into "the people of the Book." The account is no longer Nehemiah's memoirs but an anonymous, third-person report.

8.1–12: First reading of the book of Torah. 1: *They told the scribe Ezra,* the people, not Ezra, initiate the ceremony. **2:** *Both men and women* participate in this ceremony of hearing and receiving the Torah (see Deut 31.12). The date for the reading is September 444 or 443 (see 6.15). **3–8:** The reading. **4:** *Beside him stood . . . ,* Ezra's assistants include laity, as well as Levites, who are elsewhere connected to the study of the law. **5:** *When he opened it,* i.e., unrolled the scroll, *all the people stood up* in veneration for God's

thiah, Shema, Anaiah, Uriah, Hilkiah, and
Maaseiah on his right hand; and Pedaiah,
Mishael, Malchijah, Hashum, Hash-
baddanah, Zechariah, and Meshullam on
his left hand. 5 And Ezra opened the book
in the sight of all the people, for he was
standing above all the people; and when he
opened it, all the people stood up. 6 Then
Ezra blessed the LORD, the great God, and
all the people answered, "Amen, Amen,"
lifting up their hands. Then they bowed
their heads and worshiped the LORD with
their faces to the ground. 7 Also Jeshua,
Bani, Sherebiah, Jamin, Akkub, Shabbe-
thai, Hodiah, Maaseiah, Kelita, Azariah,
Jozabad, Hanan, Pelaiah, the Levites,[a]
helped the people to understand the law,
while the people remained in their places.
8 So they read from the book, from the law
of God, with interpretation. They gave the
sense, so that the people understood the
reading.

9 And Nehemiah, who was the gover-
nor, and Ezra the priest and scribe, and the
Levites who taught the people said to all
the people, "This day is holy to the LORD
your God; do not mourn or weep." For all
the people wept when they heard the words
of the law. 10 Then he said to them, "Go
your way, eat the fat and drink sweet wine
and send portions of them to those for
whom nothing is prepared, for this day is
holy to our LORD; and do not be grieved,
for the joy of the LORD is your strength."
11 So the Levites stilled all the people, say-
ing, "Be quiet, for this day is holy; do not
be grieved." 12 And all the people went their
way to eat and drink and to send portions
and to make great rejoicing, because they
had understood the words that were de-
clared to them.

13 On the second day the heads of an-
cestral houses of all the people, with the
priests and the Levites, came together to the
scribe Ezra in order to study the words of
the law. 14 And they found it written in the
law, which the LORD had commanded by
Moses, that the people of Israel should live
in booths[b] during the festival of the sev-
enth month, 15 and that they should publish
and proclaim in all their towns and in Jeru-
salem as follows, "Go out to the hills and
bring branches of olive, wild olive, myrtle,
palm, and other leafy trees to make
booths,[b] as it is written." 16 So the people
went out and brought them, and made
booths[b] for themselves, each on the roofs
of their houses, and in their courts and in
the courts of the house of God, and in the
square at the Water Gate and in the square
at the Gate of Ephraim. 17 And all the as-
sembly of those who had returned from the
captivity made booths[b] and lived in them;
for from the days of Jeshua son of Nun to
that day the people of Israel had not done
so. And there was very great rejoicing.
18 And day by day, from the first day to the

a 1 Esdras 9.48 Vg: Heb *and the Levites*
b Or *tabernacles*; Heb *succoth*

presence reflected in the book. **7:** *Helped the people to understand,* either the Hebrew was translated into the more familiar Aramaic or the content was expounded for greater clarity. **9:** *Nehemiah . . . and Ezra* together represent political and religious leadership. *The people wept,* either because of the warnings in the Torah or because they were overwhelmed by the moment. Ezra and Nehemiah emphasize that the Torah is ultimately a source of joy.

8.13–18: Implementing Torah: the festival of booths. 13: The people take initiative to study and implement the Torah. **14:** *They found it written,* reading the Torah made them aware of the regulations for the festival. *They . . . should live in booths* (Heb "sukkot"), see Lev 23.42–43. The fast of the Day of Atonement (set for the tenth of the month in Lev 23.26–32) is not mentioned. **15:** Lev 23.40 specifies types of tree branches, though it is not clear that these were to be used for building booths. **17:** Ezra-Nehemiah identifies the community as *those who had returned from the captivity* and links it with the first settlement of the land, and *Jeshua* (Joshua), *son of Nun.* As in the opening of Joshua (1.7–8), it is ultimately Torah study that will assure survival. **18:** Deut 31.10–13 demands public readings of the Torah on Sukkot only every seventh year. As a result of chs 8–9, public reading became a weekly feature of Jewish worship. *The ordinance,* in Lev 23.36.

last day, he read from the book of the law
of God. They kept the festival seven days;
and on the eighth day there was a solemn
assembly, according to the ordinance.
9 Now on the twenty-fourth day of this
month the people of Israel were assem-
bled with fasting and in sackcloth, and with
earth on their heads.[a] 2 Then those of Isra-
elite descent separated themselves from all
foreigners, and stood and confessed their
sins and the iniquities of their ancestors.
3 They stood up in their place and read
from the book of the law of the LORD their
God for a fourth part of the day, and for
another fourth they made confession and
worshiped the LORD their God. 4 Then
Jeshua, Bani, Kadmiel, Shebaniah, Bunni,
Sherebiah, Bani, and Chenani stood on the
stairs of the Levites and cried out with a
loud voice to the LORD their God. 5 Then
the Levites, Jeshua, Kadmiel, Bani, Hash-
abneiah, Sherebiah, Hodiah, Shebaniah,
and Pethahiah, said, "Stand up and bless
the LORD your God from everlasting to ev-
erlasting. Blessed be your glorious name,
which is exalted above all blessing and
praise."
6 And Ezra said:[b] "You are the LORD,
you alone; you have made heaven, the
heaven of heavens, with all their host, the
earth and all that is on it, the seas and all
that is in them. To all of them you give life,
and the host of heaven worships you. 7 You
are the LORD, the God who chose Abram
and brought him out of Ur of the Chalde-
ans and gave him the name Abraham; 8 and
you found his heart faithful before you, and
made with him a covenant to give to his
descendants the land of the Canaanite, the
Hittite, the Amorite, the Perizzite, the Jebu-
site, and the Girgashite; and you have ful-
filled your promise, for you are righteous.
9 "And you saw the distress of our an-
cestors in Egypt and heard their cry at the
Red Sea.[c] 10 You performed signs and
wonders against Pharaoh and all his ser-
vants and all the people of his land, for you
knew that they acted insolently against our
ancestors. You made a name for yourself,
which remains to this day. 11 And you di-
vided the sea before them, so that they
passed through the sea on dry land, but you
threw their pursuers into the depths, like a
stone into mighty waters. 12 Moreover, you
led them by day with a pillar of cloud, and
by night with a pillar of fire, to give them
light on the way in which they should go.
13 You came down also upon Mount Sinai,
and spoke with them from heaven, and
gave them right ordinances and true laws,
good statutes and commandments, 14 and

a Heb *on them* *b* Gk: Heb lacks *And Ezra said*
c Or *Sea of Reeds*

9.1–10.39: Second step: confession and commitment.

9.1–37: The great communal confession rehearses Israel's history. 1–5: The preparations for prayer. **1:** Fasting as spiritual preparation is undertaken on *the twenty-fourth,* a date not marked elsewhere for special worship. **2:** The recitation of shared history and confession of ancestral sins apply only to the Israelites. **3:** The combination of prayer and Torah reading would characterize later synagogue worship. **4–5:** Some of the Levites who shared the platform with Ezra earlier (8.4,7) now lead the congregation without him.

9.6–37: The communal prayer. This communal profession of faith articulates shared history and leads to renewed formal commitment to God's teaching (in ch 10). The community recalls the cycles of God's forbearance despite Israel's earlier infidelities (vv. 6–31) and hopes to be worthy of it in the present dire circumstances (vv. 32–37). As in the "historical psalms," history is not invoked for its own sake (e.g., Ps 105–106). **6:** *And Ezra said.* Not in the Hebrew version. Although Greek versions insert Ezra's name, in the Hebrew Ezra's role concluded when he placed the Torah into the care of the community (8.13) and trained others to guide the community accordingly. The great prayer in the Hebrew Bible is thus assigned to the community and its representatives.

9.7–31: Recitation of historical experience. A summary of traditions preserved in Genesis–2 Kings. **7–8:** See Gen 12–26. **9–23:** Highlights of events in Exodus–Deuteronomy. **13:** Unlike some of the earlier historical summaries (e.g., Deut 26.5–9; Josh 24.2–13), this one mentions the revelation at Sinai.

you made known your holy sabbath to
them and gave them commandments and
statutes and a law through your servant
Moses. 15 For their hunger you gave them
bread from heaven, and for their thirst you
brought water for them out of the rock,
and you told them to go in to possess the
land that you swore to give them.
16 "But they and our ancestors acted
presumptuously and stiffened their necks
and did not obey your commandments;
17 they refused to obey, and were not mind-
ful of the wonders that you performed
among them; but they stiffened their necks
and determined to return to their slavery in
Egypt. But you are a God ready to forgive,
gracious and merciful, slow to anger and
abounding in steadfast love, and you did
not forsake them. 18 Even when they had
cast an image of a calf for themselves and
said, 'This is your God who brought you up
out of Egypt,' and had committed great
blasphemies, 19 you in your great mercies
did not forsake them in the wilderness; the
pillar of cloud that led them in the way did
not leave them by day, nor the pillar of fire
by night that gave them light on the way by
which they should go. 20 You gave your
good spirit to instruct them, and did not
withhold your manna from their mouths,
and gave them water for their thirst. 21 For-
ty years you sustained them in the wilder-
ness so that they lacked nothing; their
clothes did not wear out and their feet did
not swell. 22 And you gave them kingdoms
and peoples, and allotted to them every
corner,[a] so they took possession of the
land of King Sihon of Heshbon and the
land of King Og of Bashan. 23 You multi-
plied their descendants like the stars of
heaven, and brought them into the land
that you had told their ancestors to enter
and possess. 24 So the descendants went in
and possessed the land, and you subdued
before them the inhabitants of the land,
the Canaanites, and gave them into their
hands, with their kings and the peoples of
the land, to do with them as they pleased.
25 And they captured fortress cities and a
rich land, and took possession of houses
filled with all sorts of goods, hewn cisterns,
vineyards, olive orchards, and fruit trees in
abundance; so they ate, and were filled and
became fat, and delighted themselves in
your great goodness.
26 "Nevertheless they were disobedient
and rebelled against you and cast your law
behind their backs and killed your proph-
ets, who had warned them in order to turn
them back to you, and they committed
great blasphemies. 27 Therefore you gave
them into the hands of their enemies, who
made them suffer. Then in the time of their
suffering they cried out to you and you
heard them from heaven, and according to
your great mercies you gave them saviors
who saved them from the hands of their
enemies. 28 But after they had rest, they
again did evil before you, and you aban-
doned them to the hands of their enemies,
so that they had dominion over them; yet
when they turned and cried to you, you
heard from heaven, and many times you
rescued them according to your mercies.
29 And you warned them in order to turn
them back to your law. Yet they acted pre-
sumptuously and did not obey your com-
mandments, but sinned against your ordi-
nances, by the observance of which a
person shall live. They turned a stubborn
shoulder and stiffened their neck and
would not obey. 30 Many years you were
patient with them, and warned them by
your spirit through your prophets; yet they
would not listen. Therefore you handed
them over to the peoples of the lands.
31 Nevertheless, in your great mercies you
did not make an end of them or forsake

a Meaning of Heb uncertain

19: *Pillar,* see Ex 13.21. **20:** *Good spirit,* perhaps a reference to the appointment of elders (Num 11.17–29). **22:** *Sihon . . . Og,* kings defeated in the battles for the land of Canaan (Num 21.21–35). **24–25:** The events described in Joshua. **26–31:** A summary interpretation of the period from Joshua to the destruction of Jerusalem (see Judges–2 Kings). **27:** *Saviors,* the same Heb word is translated "deliverer" in Judg 3.9,15.

them, for you are a gracious and merciful
God.
32 "Now therefore, our God—the great
and mighty and awesome God, keeping
covenant and steadfast love—do not treat
lightly all the hardship that has come upon
us, upon our kings, our officials, our
priests, our prophets, our ancestors, and all
your people, since the time of the kings of
Assyria until today. 33 You have been just
in all that has come upon us, for you have
dealt faithfully and we have acted wicked-
ly; 34 our kings, our officials, our priests,
and our ancestors have not kept your law
or heeded the commandments and the
warnings that you gave them. 35 Even in
their own kingdom, and in the great good-
ness you bestowed on them, and in the
large and rich land that you set before
them, they did not serve you and did not
turn from their wicked works. 36 Here we
are, slaves to this day—slaves in the land
that you gave to our ancestors to enjoy its
fruit and its good gifts. 37 Its rich yield goes
to the kings whom you have set over us
because of our sins; they have power also
over our bodies and over our livestock at
their pleasure, and we are in great distress."
38[a] Because of all this we make a firm
agreement in writing, and on that sealed
document are inscribed the names of our
officials, our Levites, and our priests.
10 [b] Upon the sealed document are the
names of Nehemiah the governor,
son of Hacaliah, and Zedekiah; 2 Seraiah,
Azariah, Jeremiah, 3 Pashhur, Amariah,
Malchijah, 4 Hattush, Shebaniah, Malluch,
5 Harim, Meremoth, Obadiah, 6 Daniel,
Ginnethon, Baruch, 7 Meshullam, Abijah,
Mijamin, 8 Maaziah, Bilgai, Shemaiah;
these are the priests. 9 And the Levites: Jesh-
ua son of Azaniah, Binnui of the sons of
Henadad, Kadmiel; 10 and their associates,
Shebaniah, Hodiah, Kelita, Pelaiah, Ha-
nan, 11 Mica, Rehob, Hashabiah, 12 Zaccur,
Sherebiah, Shebaniah, 13 Hodiah, Bani, Be-
ninu. 14 The leaders of the people: Parosh,
Pahath-moab, Elam, Zattu, Bani, 15 Bunni,
Azgad, Bebai, 16 Adonijah, Bigvai, Adin,
17 Ater, Hezekiah, Azzur, 18 Hodiah, Ha-
shum, Bezai, 19 Hariph, Anathoth, Nebai,
20 Magpiash, Meshullam, Hezir, 21 Meshez-
abel, Zadok, Jaddua, 22 Pelatiah, Hanan,
Anaiah, 23 Hoshea, Hananiah, Hasshub,
24 Hallohesh, Pilha, Shobek, 25 Rehum, Ha-
shabnah, Maaseiah, 26 Ahiah, Hanan,
Anan, 27 Malluch, Harim, and Baanah.
28 The rest of the people, the priests, the
Levites, the gatekeepers, the singers, the
temple servants, and all who have separat-
ed themselves from the peoples of the lands
to adhere to the law of God, their wives,
their sons, their daughters, all who have
knowledge and understanding, 29 join with
their kin, their nobles, and enter into a
curse and an oath to walk in God's law,
which was given by Moses the servant of
God, and to observe and do all the com-
mandments of the LORD our Lord and his
ordinances and his statutes. 30 We will not
give our daughters to the peoples of the
land or take their daughters for our sons;

a Ch 10.1 in Heb *b* Ch 10.2 in Heb

9.32–37: The present distress. 32: *Now therefore,* after reciting a history of God's loyalty and Israel's disobedience, the community affirms God's righteousness. *The time of the kings of Assyria,* the mid-eighth to the late seventh centuries BCE. **36:** *Here we are, slaves,* still subject to Persian rulers.

9.38–10.39: Commitment: the communal pledge. 38: *Because of all this,* because of this history the community commits itself unilaterally by a binding pledge to obedience.

10.1–27: Signatories on behalf of the entire community. These signatories include persons and clan names from several previous lists (Ezra 2 || Neh 7; Ezra 8), but also reflects a broader religious and social participation. **28:** *The rest of the people,* the entire people affirm their voluntary commitment to the pledge. *Separated themselves,* see 9.2; 13.3.

10.30–39: Voluntarily assumed obligations. The obligations reflect practices important for Jewish identity in the fifth century BCE. They combine legislation from various Torah sources as well as obligations not reflected in the Torah as it now exists.

10.30–31: Protecting religious and ethnic boundaries. 30: *We will not give our daughters,* see Ezra

31 and if the peoples of the land bring in
merchandise or any grain on the sabbath
day to sell, we will not buy it from them on
the sabbath or on a holy day; and we will
forego the crops of the seventh year and the
exaction of every debt.
32 We also lay on ourselves the obliga-
tion to charge ourselves yearly one-third of
a shekel for the service of the house of our
God: 33 for the rows of bread, the regular
grain offering, the regular burnt offering,
the sabbaths, the new moons, the appoint-
ed festivals, the sacred donations, and the
sin offerings to make atonement for Israel,
and for all the work of the house of our
God. 34 We have also cast lots among the
priests, the Levites, and the people, for the
wood offering, to bring it into the house of
our God, by ancestral houses, at appointed
times, year by year, to burn on the altar of
the LORD our God, as it is written in the
law. 35 We obligate ourselves to bring the
first fruits of our soil and the first fruits of
all fruit of every tree, year by year, to the
house of the LORD; 36 also to bring to the
house of our God, to the priests who minis-
ter in the house of our God, the firstborn of
our sons and of our livestock, as it is writ-
ten in the law, and the firstlings of our
herds and of our flocks; 37 and to bring the
first of our dough, and our contributions,
the fruit of every tree, the wine and the oil,
to the priests, to the chambers of the house
of our God; and to bring to the Levites the
tithes from our soil, for it is the Levites who
collect the tithes in all our rural towns.
38 And the priest, the descendant of Aaron,
shall be with the Levites when the Levites
receive the tithes; and the Levites shall
bring up a tithe of the tithes to the house
of our God, to the chambers of the store-
house. 39 For the people of Israel and the
sons of Levi shall bring the contribution
of grain, wine, and oil to the storerooms
where the vessels of the sanctuary are, and
where the priests that minister, and the
gatekeepers and the singers are. We will not
neglect the house of our God.

11 Now the leaders of the people lived
in Jerusalem; and the rest of the
people cast lots to bring one out of ten to
live in the holy city Jerusalem, while nine-
tenths remained in the other towns. 2 And
the people blessed all those who willingly
offered to live in Jerusalem.
3 These are the leaders of the province
who lived in Jerusalem; but in the towns of
Judah all lived on their property in their
towns: Israel, the priests, the Levites, the
temple servants, and the descendants of
Solomon's servants. 4 And in Jerusalem
lived some of the Judahites and of the Ben-

9–10. **31:** *Buy . . . on the sabbath,* sabbath laws prohibit work on this day (e.g., Ex 31.12–17). *Forego the crops,* see Ex 23.11. *Debt,* see Deut 15.1–3 (though the vocabulary differs).

10.32–39: Securing religious and social institutions. 32: *We also lay on ourselves the obligation,* the voluntary Temple tax reflects the utmost seriousness with which the renewed community assumes responsibility for implementing the Torah's commandments. *One-third of a shekel,* no annual Temple tax is required in the Torah (Ex 30.13 is a one-time requirement). This pledge innovates by making it mandatory—a practice that endures throughout the Second Temple period (see Mt 17.24). **33–38:** Provisions for regular Temple sacrifices and worship. **33:** *Rows of bread* are placed on a special table at the sanctuary on the sabbath (Ex 25.29; Lev 24.5–9). *Sin offerings,* a regular sacrifice in the Temple for public or personal transgression (Lev 4.13–21). **34:** *Wood* for the altar's fires. This obligation is also not prescribed by the Torah. **35:** *First fruits,* see Ex 22.29; 23.19; Num 18.15–18. **36:** *Firstborn,* see Ex 22.29. **37–38:** *Tithes,* see Lev 27.30; Num 18.25–32. *The chambers* were the Temple storerooms (13.13; Ezra 8.29; 10.6). **38:** The Levites and priests depended on contributions.

11.1–12.26: Third step: repopulation and review.

11.1–36: Repopulation. The restored community repopulates the rebuilt city. The lists of chs 11–12 are compiled from different sources. **1:** *Holy city,* for Ezra-Nehemiah, the entire city, not only the Temple, is holy (see Ezek 48.35). *Nine-tenths remained,* if the total of Jerusalem's population, about 3,000 according to this chapter, is one-tenth of the entire province, then the province contained 30,000 Jews.

11.3–24: Census of repopulated Jerusalem. 4–6: Judahites are traced back to their ancestor Judah

jaminites. Of the Judahites: Athaiah son of
Uzziah son of Zechariah son of Amariah
son of Shephatiah son of Mahalalel, of the
descendants of Perez; 5 and Maaseiah son
of Baruch son of Col-hozeh son of Hazaiah
son of Adaiah son of Joiarib son of Zecha-
riah son of the Shilonite. 6 All the descen-
dants of Perez who lived in Jerusalem were
four hundred sixty-eight valiant warriors.
7 And these are the Benjaminites: Sallu
son of Meshullam son of Joed son of Peda-
iah son of Kolaiah son of Maaseiah son of
Ithiel son of Jeshaiah. 8 And his brothers[a]
Gabbai, Sallai: nine hundred twenty-eight.
9 Joel son of Zichri was their overseer; and
Judah son of Hassenuah was second in
charge of the city.
10 Of the priests: Jedaiah son of Joiarib,
Jachin, 11 Seraiah son of Hilkiah son of Me-
shullam son of Zadok son of Meraioth son
of Ahitub, officer of the house of God,
12 and their associates who did the work of
the house, eight hundred twenty-two; and
Adaiah son of Jeroham son of Pelaliah son
of Amzi son of Zechariah son of Pashhur
son of Malchijah, 13 and his associates,
heads of ancestral houses, two hundred
forty-two; and Amashsai son of Azarel son
of Ahzai son of Meshillemoth son of Im-
mer, 14 and their associates, valiant war-
riors, one hundred twenty-eight; their over-
seer was Zabdiel son of Haggedolim.
15 And of the Levites: Shemaiah son of
Hasshub son of Azrikam son of Hashabiah
son of Bunni; 16 and Shabbethai and Joza-
bad, of the leaders of the Levites, who were
over the outside work of the house of God;
17 and Mattaniah son of Mica son of Zabdi
son of Asaph, who was the leader to begin
the thanksgiving in prayer, and Bakbukiah,
the second among his associates; and Abda
son of Shammua son of Galal son of Jedu-
thun. 18 All the Levites in the holy city were
two hundred eighty-four.
19 The gatekeepers, Akkub, Talmon
and their associates, who kept watch at
the gates, were one hundred seventy-two.
20 And the rest of Israel, and of the priests
and the Levites, were in all the towns of
Judah, all of them in their inheritance.
21 But the temple servants lived on Ophel;
and Ziha and Gishpa were over the temple
servants.
22 The overseer of the Levites in Jerusa-
lem was Uzzi son of Bani son of Hashabiah
son of Mattaniah son of Mica, of the de-
scendants of Asaph, the singers, in charge
of the work of the house of God. 23 For
there was a command from the king con-
cerning them, and a settled provision for
the singers, as was required every day.
24 And Pethahiah son of Meshezabel, of the
descendants of Zerah son of Judah, was at
the king's hand in all matters concerning
the people.
25 And as for the villages, with their
fields, some of the people of Judah lived in
Kiriath-arba and its villages, and in Dibon
and its villages, and in Jekabzeel and its
villages, 26 and in Jeshua and in Moladah
and Beth-pelet, 27 in Hazar-shual, in Beer-
sheba and its villages, 28 in Ziklag, in Meco-
nah and its villages, 29 in En-rimmon, in
Zorah, in Jarmuth, 30 Zanoah, Adullam,
and their villages, Lachish and its fields,
and Azekah and its villages. So they
camped from Beer-sheba to the valley of
Hinnom. 31 The people of Benjamin also
lived from Geba onward, at Michmash,
Aija, Bethel and its villages, 32 Anathoth,
Nob, Ananiah, 33 Hazor, Ramah, Gittaim,
34 Hadid, Zeboim, Neballat, 35 Lod, and
Ono, the valley of artisans. 36 And certain
divisions of the Levites in Judah were
joined to Benjamin.

a Gk Mss: Heb *And after him*

through his three sons: *Perez* (11.4; cf. Gen 38.29); the *Shilonite* (11.5), probably Shelah (Gen 38.4); and Zerah (11.24; Gen 38.30). **7–9:** *Benjaminites,* the individual names are otherwise unknown. **10–14:** *Priests,* three families. Some of these names appear also in Ezra's pedigree (Ezra 7.1–5). **19:** *Gatekeepers,* see Ezra 2.42 || Neh 7.45. **24:** *At the king's hand,* i.e., directly accountable to the king.

11.25–36: Census of other Jewish settlements. *The villages,* this list is either an ideal echoing Josh 15, envisioning a greater province, or (more likely) a register of Jews in towns outside Yehud proper.

12 These are the priests and the Levites
who came up with Zerubbabel son
of Shealtiel, and Jeshua: Seraiah, Jeremiah,
Ezra, 2 Amariah, Malluch, Hattush, 3 Shec-
aniah, Rehum, Meremoth, 4 Iddo, Ginne-
thoi, Abijah, 5 Mijamin, Maadiah, Bilgah,
6 Shemaiah, Joiarib, Jedaiah, 7 Sallu, Amok,
Hilkiah, Jedaiah. These were the leaders of
the priests and of their associates in the
days of Jeshua.
8 And the Levites: Jeshua, Binnui, Kad-
miel, Sherebiah, Judah, and Mattaniah,
who with his associates was in charge of
the songs of thanksgiving. 9 And Bakbukiah
and Unno their associates stood opposite
them in the service. 10 Jeshua was the father
of Joiakim, Joiakim the father of Eliashib,
Eliashib the father of Joiada, 11 Joiada the
father of Jonathan, and Jonathan the father
of Jaddua.
12 In the days of Joiakim the priests,
heads of ancestral houses, were: of Seraiah,
Meraiah; of Jeremiah, Hananiah; 13 of
Ezra, Meshullam; of Amariah, Jehohanan;
14 of Malluchi, Jonathan; of Shebaniah, Jo-
seph; 15 of Harim, Adna; of Meraioth, Hel-
kai; 16 of Iddo, Zechariah; of Ginnethon,
Meshullam; 17 of Abijah, Zichri; of Minia-
min, of Moadiah, Piltai; 18 of Bilgah, Sham-
mua; of Shemaiah, Jehonathan; 19 of Joia-
rib, Mattenai; of Jedaiah, Uzzi; 20 of Sallai,
Kallai; of Amok, Eber; 21 of Hilkiah, Hash-
abiah; of Jedaiah, Nethanel.
22 As for the Levites, in the days of Elia-
shib, Joiada, Johanan, and Jaddua, there
were recorded the heads of ancestral
houses; also the priests until the reign of
Darius the Persian. 23 The Levites, heads
of ancestral houses, were recorded in the
Book of the Annals until the days of Joha-
nan son of Eliashib. 24 And the leaders of
the Levites: Hashabiah, Sherebiah, and
Jeshua son of Kadmiel, with their associ-
ates over against them, to praise and to give
thanks, according to the commandment of
David the man of God, section opposite to
section. 25 Mattaniah, Bakbukiah, Obadi-
ah, Meshullam, Talmon, and Akkub were
gatekeepers standing guard at the store-
houses of the gates. 26 These were in the
days of Joiakim son of Jeshua son of Joza-
dak, and in the days of the governor Nehe-
miah and of the priest Ezra, the scribe.
27 Now at the dedication of the wall of
Jerusalem they sought out the Levites in all
their places, to bring them to Jerusalem
to celebrate the dedication with rejoicing,
with thanksgivings and with singing, with
cymbals, harps, and lyres. 28 The companies
of the singers gathered together from the
circuit around Jerusalem and from the vil-
lages of the Netophathites; 29 also from
Beth-gilgal and from the region of Geba
and Azmaveth; for the singers had built
for themselves villages around Jerusalem.
30 And the priests and the Levites purified
themselves; and they purified the people
and the gates and the wall.
31 Then I brought the leaders of Judah
up onto the wall, and appointed two great

12.1–26: Review of priestly and Levitical genealogies. The reconstituted community articulates again (cf. ch 7) its relation to past generations, this time through a web of Temple personnel spanning the entire era of reconstruction (520–444 BCE). The list is artificial and problematic, but its existence reflects the importance of priests and Levites in this period, a concern also reflected in Chronicles. Although many names are familiar from other lists, the information resists clear chronological schematization. **1:** *Came up with Zerubbabel . . . and Jeshua,* i.e., the governor and priest leading the first stage of the return (see Ezra 2.1–2n.). **22:** *Until the days of Darius the Persian,* Darius I (522–486). **24:** *David,* see Ezra 3.10n. **26:** *Joiakim . . . Nehemiah . . . Ezra,* the officiating priest, the governor, and the priest Ezra in his capacity as scribe mark the period of completion of the task. Now all is ready for the grand finale.

12.27–13.3: Fourth step: a service of dedication: celebration, purification, procession, and separation. 12.27: The initiative for the grand finale again comes from the community (cf. 8.1). **30:** Unique in the Hebrew Bible, the purification signals that Israel is holy and Jerusalem a "holy city" (11.1).

12.31–42: The procession. Two groups circled the city on the wall and alongside it. On the gates named, see 2.13–14n.; 3.1n. **31:** *Then I,* Nehemiah. *Two great companies,* two processions marched in opposite directions and met at the Temple. **36:** *The scribe Ezra,* this final appearance by Ezra is striking;

companies that gave thanks and went in
procession. One went to the right on the
wall to the Dung Gate; 32 and after them
went Hoshaiah and half the officials of Ju-
dah, 33 and Azariah, Ezra, Meshullam,
34 Judah, Benjamin, Shemaiah, and Jeremi-
ah, 35 and some of the young priests with
trumpets: Zechariah son of Jonathan son of
Shemaiah son of Mattaniah son of Micaiah
son of Zaccur son of Asaph; 36 and his kin-
dred, Shemaiah, Azarel, Milalai, Gilalai,
Maai, Nethanel, Judah, and Hanani, with
the musical instruments of David the man
of God; and the scribe Ezra went in front of
them. 37 At the Fountain Gate, in front of
them, they went straight up by the stairs of
the city of David, at the ascent of the wall,
above the house of David, to the Water
Gate on the east.
38 The other company of those who
gave thanks went to the left,[a] and I fol-
lowed them with half of the people on the
wall, above the Tower of the Ovens, to
the Broad Wall, 39 and above the Gate of
Ephraim, and by the Old Gate, and by the
Fish Gate and the Tower of Hananel and
the Tower of the Hundred, to the Sheep
Gate; and they came to a halt at the Gate of
the Guard. 40 So both companies of those
who gave thanks stood in the house of
God, and I and half of the officials with me;
41 and the priests Eliakim, Maaseiah, Min-
iamin, Micaiah, Elioenai, Zechariah, and
Hananiah, with trumpets; 42 and Maaseiah,
Shemaiah, Eleazar, Uzzi, Jehohanan, Mal-
chijah, Elam, and Ezer. And the singers
sang with Jezrahiah as their leader. 43 They
offered great sacrifices that day and re-
joiced, for God had made them rejoice with
great joy; the women and children also re-
joiced. The joy of Jerusalem was heard far
away.
44 On that day men were appointed
over the chambers for the stores, the contri-
butions, the first fruits, and the tithes, to
gather into them the portions required by
the law for the priests and for the Levites
from the fields belonging to the towns; for
Judah rejoiced over the priests and the Le-
vites who ministered. 45 They performed
the service of their God and the service of
purification, as did the singers and the gate-
keepers, according to the command of Da-
vid and his son Solomon. 46 For in the days
of David and Asaph long ago there was a
leader of the singers, and there were songs
of praise and thanksgiving to God. 47 In the
days of Zerubbabel and in the days of Ne-
hemiah all Israel gave the daily portions for
the singers and the gatekeepers. They set
apart that which was for the Levites; and
the Levites set apart that which was for the
descendants of Aaron.
13 On that day they read from the
book of Moses in the hearing of the
people; and in it was found written that no
Ammonite or Moabite should ever enter
the assembly of God, 2 because they did not
meet the Israelites with bread and water,
but hired Balaam against them to curse
them—yet our God turned the curse into a
blessing. 3 When the people heard the law,
they separated from Israel all those of for-
eign descent.
4 Now before this, the priest Eliashib,
who was appointed over the chambers of

a Cn: Heb *opposite*

as a priest (Ezra 7.1–5), he leads the priests. **42:** Antiphonal singing by the professional liturgical singers.

12.43–13.3: Three additional communal actions on the day of dedication (12.43–44; 13.1). **12.47:** *The days of Zerubbabel and . . . Nehemiah,* from the beginning of the return (Ezra 2) to Nehemiah. **13.1–3:** In the climactic third action *on that day,* the community implements the Torah by separating from foreigners. *No Ammonite or Moabite should ever enter,* see Deut 23.3. **2:** *Balaam,* see Num 22–24.

13.4–31: Coda. Nehemiah's memoirs resume with a retrospective from a time after 433/2 BCE, after completing his twelve years as governor (13.6; 5.14). At some point after returning to King Artaxerxes, Nehemiah came back to Jerusalem, discovered violations of the communal pledge of ch 10, and took steps to restore order. **4–9:** Nehemiah purifies the desecrated Temple precinct. **4:** *The priest Eliashib,* possibly, but not necessarily (the name was common in this era), the high priest (of 3.1 and 13.28). *Appointed over the chambers,* hence controlling the storage and distribution of Temple resources. *Tobiah,* Nehemiah

the house of our God, and who was related
to Tobiah, 5 prepared for Tobiah a large
room where they had previously put the
grain offering, the frankincense, the vessels,
and the tithes of grain, wine, and oil, which
were given by commandment to the Le-
vites, singers, and gatekeepers, and the con-
tributions for the priests. 6 While this was
taking place I was not in Jerusalem, for in
the thirty-second year of King Artaxerxes
of Babylon I went to the king. After some
time I asked leave of the king 7 and returned
to Jerusalem. I then discovered the wrong
that Eliashib had done on behalf of Tobiah,
preparing a room for him in the courts of
the house of God. 8 And I was very angry,
and I threw all the household furniture of
Tobiah out of the room. 9 Then I gave or-
ders and they cleansed the chambers, and I
brought back the vessels of the house of
God, with the grain offering and the frank-
incense.

10 I also found out that the portions of
the Levites had not been given to them; so
that the Levites and the singers, who had
conducted the service, had gone back to
their fields. 11 So I remonstrated with the
officials and said, "Why is the house of
God forsaken?" And I gathered them to-
gether and set them in their stations.
12 Then all Judah brought the tithe of the
grain, wine, and oil into the storehouses.
13 And I appointed as treasurers over the
storehouses the priest Shelemiah, the scribe
Zadok, and Pedaiah of the Levites, and as
their assistant Hanan son of Zaccur son of
Mattaniah, for they were considered faith-
ful; and their duty was to distribute to their
associates. 14 Remember me, O my God,
concerning this, and do not wipe out my
good deeds that I have done for the house
of my God and for his service.

15 In those days I saw in Judah people
treading wine presses on the sabbath, and
bringing in heaps of grain and loading them
on donkeys; and also wine, grapes, figs,
and all kinds of burdens, which they
brought into Jerusalem on the sabbath day;
and I warned them at that time against sell-
ing food. 16 Tyrians also, who lived in the
city, brought in fish and all kinds of mer-
chandise and sold them on the sabbath to
the people of Judah, and in Jerusalem.
17 Then I remonstrated with the nobles of
Judah and said to them, "What is this evil
thing that you are doing, profaning the sab-
bath day? 18 Did not your ancestors act in
this way, and did not our God bring all this
disaster on us and on this city? Yet you
bring more wrath on Israel by profaning
the sabbath."

19 When it began to be dark at the gates
of Jerusalem before the sabbath, I com-
manded that the doors should be shut and
gave orders that they should not be opened
until after the sabbath. And I set some of
my servants over the gates, to prevent any
burden from being brought in on the sab-
bath day. 20 Then the merchants and sellers
of all kinds of merchandise spent the night
outside Jerusalem once or twice. 21 But I
warned them and said to them, "Why do
you spend the night in front of the wall?
If you do so again, I will lay hands on

evicts his old enemy (see 2.10n.). On Tobiah's priestly relations, see 6.18. Note that 13.2 emphasizes the Deuteronomic exclusion of Ammonites. **6:** Artaxerxes's *thirty-second year,* 433 BCE. **9:** *Cleansed,* Tobiah's illegitimate presence contaminated the room.

13.10–13: Nehemiah rectifies violations regarding Levites and singers (cf. 10.37–39). **10:** *Levites . . . had gone,* Tobiah's presence likely hastened the departure of Levites. **11:** *Gathered them,* i.e., the dispersed Levites. **12:** Should be read as "all Judah *had* brought." Nehemiah alleges that the desertion of Levites resulted less from lack of contributions than from mismanagement, probably by Tobiah. **13:** *And I appointed,* Nehemiah's new supervisors are representative of the groups involved. *Considered faithful,* an important trait because of previous corruption under Tobiah and Eliashib. **14:** Conclusion: Nehemiah's plea for remembrance for these restoration efforts.

13.15–22: Nehemiah rectifies sabbath violations (cf. 10.31). **15:** *In those days,* when Nehemiah returned to Jerusalem. **16:** *Tyrians,* merchants from Tyre. **19–22:** Shutting the gates during the sabbath prevented foreign trading in the city during the sabbath. **22:** *They should purify themselves,* purified

you." From that time on they did not come
on the sabbath. 22 And I commanded the
Levites that they should purify themselves
and come and guard the gates, to keep
the sabbath day holy. Remember this also
in my favor, O my God, and spare me ac-
cording to the greatness of your steadfast
love.

23 In those days also I saw Jews who
had married women of Ashdod, Ammon,
and Moab; 24 and half of their children
spoke the language of Ashdod, and they
could not speak the language of Judah, but
spoke the language of various peoples.
25 And I contended with them and cursed
them and beat some of them and pulled out
their hair; and I made them take an oath in
the name of God, saying, "You shall not
give your daughters to their sons, or take
their daughters for your sons or for your-
selves. 26 Did not King Solomon of Israel
sin on account of such women? Among the
many nations there was no king like him,
and he was beloved by his God, and God
made him king over all Israel; nevertheless,
foreign women made even him to sin.
27 Shall we then listen to you and do all this
great evil and act treacherously against our
God by marrying foreign women?"

28 And one of the sons of Jehoiada, son
of the high priest Eliashib, was the son-in-
law of Sanballat the Horonite; I chased him
away from me. 29 Remember them, O my
God, because they have defiled the priest-
hood, the covenant of the priests and the
Levites.

30 Thus I cleansed them from every-
thing foreign, and I established the duties of
the priests and Levites, each in his work;
31 and I provided for the wood offering, at
appointed times, and for the first fruits. Re-
member me, O my God, for good.

Levites guard the gates (7.1–3; 11.1) to secure sanctity, especially on the holy sabbath. Such measures are unique to the book of Ezra-Nehemiah, underscoring the holiness of the entire city.

13.23–29: Intermarriage problems (cf. 10.30). On marriage with foreigners in Ezra-Nehemiah, see Ezra 9–10, especially Ezra 9.1–15n. **23:** *Ashdod,* a Philistine-Phoenician city on the southeast coast of the Mediterranean. **26:** *Solomon,* Solomon's marriages corrupted his relations with God (1 Kings 11.1–8). **28:** *Son-in-law of Sanballat,* Sanballat (see 2.10n.) from Samaria, a member of a group who considered themselves Israelite (but not Jewish, i.e., from Judah). According to nonbiblical sources, Sanballat's sons had Hebrew names, and apparently some Jews accepted intermarriage with the Samarians. Like Ezra, Nehemiah vehemently objects.

13.29–31: Conclusion: Nehemiah's final calls for remembrance. The purification of the priesthood and Temple administration was the most difficult and consequential task because of the status of the opposing priests. Therefore, Nehemiah presents restoring order and sanctity to the worship system as the crown of his achievement. **31:** *I provided for the wood offering . . . and for the first fruits,* see 10.34–35, in which the community pledges to provide these. *For good,* with "good" as the last word, Nehemiah invokes a final blessing.

ESTHER

The book of Esther tells the story of how two wise and courageous Jews, Mordecai and Queen Esther, aided by the providential hand of fate, foil the genocidal schemes of Haman, the "enemy of the Jews." The ensuing victory celebration on the fourteenth and fifteenth of the month of Adar (February-March) becomes the occasion for inaugurating a new Jewish festival, Purim. On both the evening and morning of Purim, Jews have traditionally read aloud the entire book of Esther, the last of the five festal scrolls (Megillot) in the Hebrew Bible.

The story of Esther (or Hadassah, her Jewish name) unfolds in the royal court at Susa, the Persian capital, during the reign of Xerxes I ("Ahasuerus," 486–465 BCE), king of the Achaemenid Persian Empire. Esther and Mordecai belong to the Jewish Diaspora community in Persia where the story originated and whose concerns are the focus of the book.

Despite the setting and the author's familiarity with Persian customs, vocabulary, and names, Esther is not a work of history but a historical novella, that is, a fictional story within a historical framework. Its purpose is to entertain, but also to demonstrate the inevitability of retributive justice and, paradoxically, the need for the oppressed to act shrewdly and boldly for that justice to prevail. The seemingly historical presentation also serves to legitimate the festival of Purim, which was probably a Babylonian or Persian holiday adopted by Diaspora Jews, and which was not authorized by the law of Moses.

The version of Esther found in the Hebrew Bible was probably composed in the early Hellenistic period (late fourth-third century BCE) before Jewish antagonism toward Gentiles was exacerbated by the struggles of the Maccabean period (167–135 BCE). Later in the Hellenistic period the translation of Esther made for Greek-speaking Jews lengthened the book by the addition of 107 verses and extra phrases intended to make it a more conventionally religious book. The King James Version (1611) included these Greek "Additions to the Book of Esther" (which are not accepted as canonical by Jews or Protestant Christians) among the books of the Apocrypha. A translation of the full Greek text of Esther, including these additions, is included among the Apocryphal and Deuterocanonical Books in this translation.

No other book of the Hebrew Bible has received such mixed reviews from Jews and Christians alike. Not until the third century CE was Esther fully accepted into the Jewish canon of scripture, and the Protestant reformer Martin Luther (1483–1546) wished it had never been written. Some have criticized the book for what it contains; others, for what it lacks. The Persian king, for instance, is mentioned 190 times, but the God of Israel not once; nor are such basic Jewish practices and concerns as the Law, covenant, prayer, dietary regulations, or Jerusalem. Because fate is an acknowledged factor in the story, some readers suggest that God, though hidden, is arranging the events. Others see fate as impersonal and the heroes' triumph as a measure of their individual resolve and quick-wittedness.

Jews and Christians have also been deeply troubled by the story's uncritically enthusiastic account of the violence of the Jewish community's response to their enemies, which involves not only self-defense but also the slaughter of women and children, including the sons of Haman (8.11–12; 9.9–10). The bloodthirsty language, however, derives from the story's symmetric pattern of reversals, not from any historical reality. Furthermore, the Hebrew version of Esther, in contrast to the Greek version, does not view Gentiles as a whole in a negative light.

The author-editor of Hebrew Esther may have been a Persian Jew determined to live a full Jewish life within the Diaspora. This perspective could account for the story's neglect of Jewish themes as it focuses instead on an innovative Diaspora tradition, Purim. Esther herself, as a woman, represents the marginal and sometimes precarious status of Diaspora Jews who were obliged to accommodate their lives to an alien environment. The point of view, therefore, differs markedly from the outlook of Diaspora Jews like Ezra and Nehemiah.

Having acknowledged what makes Esther unusual in the Jewish canon of scripture, it should be noted that the book is steeped in the literary traditions of ancient Israel. In this way Esther resembles such later Jewish compositions as Daniel and Judith. Most notable are the allusions to the Joseph story (Gen 37–50), but either obliquely or directly, the author also alludes to the Exodus story (Ex 1–15), to the conquest of Canaan (Josh 1–12) by the principles of holy war as found in Deuteronomy (Deut 20), to the career of King Saul (1 Sam 15), and to the story of Naboth's vineyard (1 Kings 21). Esther contains quotations from the prophets Jeremiah, Zephaniah, Third Isaiah, and Zechariah. Moreover, Esther contains vivid practical demonstrations of maxims found in Israel's wisdom tradition; Proverbs, for example, cautions against anger and boastfulness, distinguishes between true and false joy, and advises the proper treatment of superiors, especially kings.

In Esther one encounters a surprisingly modern tension between comedy (satire, irony, farce) and tragedy. These the author has adroitly bound together and balanced within the narrative by complex patterns of symmetries, reversals, foreshadowing, and recurring motifs. For example, the story begins and ends with feasts, while additional banquets punctuate the narrative at key moments. Royal edicts similarly mark the course of the action, but they are also highly ironic, particularly in relation to each other. At different points in the story, the leading characters variously resemble each other directly or in reverse; the disobedient queen Vashti is deposed, but Esther, the new queen who replaces her, triumphantly defies the law. Esther successfully begs the king for the lives of her people whom Haman has doomed; Haman in vain supplicates Esther for his own life. The most cleverly constructed moment of the story occurs in ch 6 when Haman suddenly finds himself in the humiliating position of presenting the royal reward he expected himself to his hated nemesis, Mordecai, instead.

While the main characters in Esther are essentially familiar stereotypes without distinctive personalities, one character does change over the course of the story. Esther begins as a passive figure notable only for the beauty that gains her entry into the royal citadel and for her obedient nature. Once in the royal harem, Esther's charm wins her special advantages. After Mordecai's challenge to Esther in 4.13–14, Esther seems to embrace her Jewishness anew; with this self-recognition, Esther becomes the decisive actor in the story, risking her life, issuing orders to Mordecai and, later, to the king himself. Ultimately it is on Esther's authority, albeit in concert with Mordecai, that Purim is established, making Esther the only woman to authorize a Jewish religious tradition.

1 This happened in the days of Ahasue-
rus, the same Ahasuerus who ruled over
one hundred twenty-seven provinces from
India to Ethiopia.[a] 2 In those days when
King Ahasuerus sat on his royal throne in
the citadel of Susa, 3 in the third year of his
reign, he gave a banquet for all his officials
and ministers. The army of Persia and
Media and the nobles and governors of
the provinces were present, 4 while he dis-
played the great wealth of his kingdom
and the splendor and pomp of his majesty
for many days, one hundred eighty days in
all.
5 When these days were completed, the
king gave for all the people present in the
citadel of Susa, both great and small, a ban-
quet lasting for seven days, in the court
of the garden of the king's palace. 6 There
were white cotton curtains and blue hang-
ings tied with cords of fine linen and purple
to silver rings[b] and marble pillars. There
were couches of gold and silver on a mosaic
pavement of porphyry, marble, mother-of-
pearl, and colored stones. 7 Drinks were
served in golden goblets, goblets of differ-
ent kinds, and the royal wine was lavished
according to the bounty of the king.
8 Drinking was by flagons, without re-
straint; for the king had given orders to all
the officials of his palace to do as each one
desired. 9 Furthermore, Queen Vashti gave
a banquet for the women in the palace of
King Ahasuerus.
10 On the seventh day, when the king
was merry with wine, he commanded Me-
human, Biztha, Harbona, Bigtha and Abag-
tha, Zethar and Carkas, the seven eunuchs
who attended him, 11 to bring Queen Vash-
ti before the king, wearing the royal crown,
in order to show the peoples and the offi-
cials her beauty; for she was fair to behold.
12 But Queen Vashti refused to come at the
king's command conveyed by the eunuchs.
At this the king was enraged, and his anger
burned within him.
13 Then the king consulted the sages
who knew the laws[c] (for this was the
king's procedure toward all who were
versed in law and custom, 14 and those next
to him were Carshena, Shethar, Admatha,
Tarshish, Meres, Marsena, and Memucan,
the seven officials of Persia and Media,
who had access to the king, and sat first in
the kingdom): 15 "According to the law,
what is to be done to Queen Vashti because
she has not performed the command of
King Ahasuerus conveyed by the eunuchs?"
16 Then Memucan said in the presence of
the king and the officials, "Not only has
Queen Vashti done wrong to the king, but

a Or *Nubia*; Heb *Cush* *b* Or *rods* *c* Cn: Heb *times*

1.1–9: King Ahasuerus holds a feast. 1: *Ahasuerus* (Ezra 4.6; not the same as in Dan 9.1 or Tob 14.15) is probably Xerxes I (486–465 BCE) whose Persian Empire from *India* (i.e., the Indus Valley) to *Ethiopia* (Heb "Cush," modern Sudan and modern Ethiopia) included some twenty satrapies (Herodotus 3.89) subdivided into *provinces.* **2:** *Susa,* Ahasuerus's winter capital in north-western Iran, 400 km (180 mi) east of ancient Babylon. The *citadel* or acropolis was a fortified section of the palace. **3–4:** *The third year,* 484 BCE. Greek writers mention fabulous feasts given by Persian kings. The *banquet,* with its exaggerated length of *one hundred and eighty days* (see Jdt 1.16) is the first of several banquets at key points (1.5,9; 2.18; 3.15; 5.7; 7.1; 9.17,19,22,31). **5–6:** *Garden . . . curtains . . . couches,* the extravagance emphasizes power and wealth. **9:** *Vashti,* a Persian name, means "beloved." There are no ancient references to a *Queen Vashti;* Xerxes I's queen was Amestris (Herodotus 7.61). Vashti's *banquet for the women* emphasizes the separate worlds of king and queen, a factor in Esther's later bravery, and sets the scene for a quasi-comic contest of the sexes.

1.10–22: Queen Vashti's downfall. 10: A person *merry with wine,* especially a king (Prov 15.15), may meet with disaster (see 5.9; 1 Sam 25.36; 2 Sam 13.28; Dan 5.2). **12:** An inversion of this event occurs when Esther, Vashti's replacement, violates the king's law by coming unbidden into his presence (4.11; 5.2). **13–18:** The narrative turns satirical as the king's *sages who knew the laws* legalistically inflate a domestic dispute between husband and wife into a national crisis. **14:** Only the Persian king's most trusted advisers had free *access to the king* (see 4.11). The names here are Persian. **19:** There is no evidence that

also to all the officials and all the peoples
who are in all the provinces of King Ahasu-
erus. 17 For this deed of the queen will be
made known to all women, causing them
to look with contempt on their husbands,
since they will say, 'King Ahasuerus com-
manded Queen Vashti to be brought before
him, and she did not come.' 18 This very day
the noble ladies of Persia and Media who
have heard of the queen's behavior will re-
bel against[a] the king's officials, and there
will be no end of contempt and wrath! 19 If
it pleases the king, let a royal order go out
from him, and let it be written among the
laws of the Persians and the Medes so that
it may not be altered, that Vashti is never
again to come before King Ahasuerus; and
let the king give her royal position to an-
other who is better than she. 20 So when the
decree made by the king is proclaimed
throughout all his kingdom, vast as it is, all
women will give honor to their husbands,
high and low alike."
21 This advice pleased the king and the
officials, and the king did as Memucan pro-
posed; 22 he sent letters to all the royal
provinces, to every province in its own
script and to every people in its own lan-
guage, declaring that every man should be
master in his own house.[b]

2 After these things, when the anger of
King Ahasuerus had abated, he remem-
bered Vashti and what she had done and
what had been decreed against her. 2 Then
the king's servants who attended him said,
"Let beautiful young virgins be sought out
for the king. 3 And let the king appoint
commissioners in all the provinces of his
kingdom to gather all the beautiful young
virgins to the harem in the citadel of Susa
under custody of Hegai, the king's eunuch,
who is in charge of the women; let their
cosmetic treatments be given them. 4 And
let the girl who pleases the king be queen
instead of Vashti." This pleased the king,
and he did so.
5 Now there was a Jew in the citadel of
Susa whose name was Mordecai son of Jair
son of Shimei son of Kish, a Benjaminite.
6 Kish[c] had been carried away from Jeru-

a Cn: Heb *will tell* b Heb adds *and speak according to the language of his people* c Heb *a Benjaminite* ⁶*who*

the *law of the Medes and the Persians* was unalterable (8.8; Dan 6.9,13), but this narrative device provides tension between rigid legalism and true justice. The *royal order* is the first in a series of formal edicts (see 2.8; 3.12; 8.9–11; 9.20–22,29–32). **20:** By decreeing that *all women* must *give honor to their husbands,* the king ironically succeeds in drawing attention to his own inability to rule his wife. In further irony, his next wife, Esther, will ultimately rule him. **22:** Aramaic was the official language of Persian diplomacy, but pronouncements were also issued in the *languages* of subject peoples (see Ezra 6.3–5). *Letters,* the Persian postal system was renowned (Herodotus 8.98).

2.1–18: Esther becomes queen. 1–4: The king agrees to seek a new queen. 1: *Remembered,* i.e., positively (Gen 40.14); the king may be regretting his treatment of Vashti or missing her companionship. **2:** Perhaps custom required the king to marry a *virgin* (see 1 Kings 1.1–14; Lev 21.13). Persian kings in fact could only marry women from certain noble Persian families. **3:** *Let the king appoint commissioners,* the phrasing echoes Gen 41.34–35. *Eunuch,* an infertile castrated man, and therefore acceptable as overseer of the king's *harem* (lit. "house of women"). The *cosmetic treatment* (see vv. 9,12) was an extended program of massage.

2.5–11: Introducing two Jewish heroes: Mordecai and Esther. 5: *Mordecai,* a name derived from the Babylonian god Marduk. Mordecai's affiliation with the tribe of Benjamin and his ancestry recall King Saul (1 Sam 9.1; 2 Sam 16.5–18), while Haman's genealogy (3.1) will connect him to Saul's enemy, King Agag (1 Sam 15). *Jew* (Heb "yehudi"), originally meaning someone from the kingdom of Judah (2 Kings 16.6), is used here in its usual later sense of an adherent to Judaism. Mordecai's presence *in the citadel* may indicate he was a minor court official (see 2.19). **6:** The Hebrew implies it was Mordecai who was exiled with *Judah*'s last king, Jehoiachin (here called *Jeconiah*), when the Babylonian king *Nebuchadnezzar* conquered Judah in 597 BCE (2 Kings 24), 114 years before. Because Mordecai would therefore be a centenarian when the book begins, translators emend the text to make Mordecai's grandfather Kish the

salem among the captives carried away
with King Jeconiah of Judah, whom King
Nebuchadnezzar of Babylon had carried
away. 7 Mordecai[a] had brought up Hadas-
sah, that is Esther, his cousin, for she had
neither father nor mother; the girl was fair
and beautiful, and when her father and her
mother died, Mordecai adopted her as his
own daughter. 8 So when the king's order
and his edict were proclaimed, and when
many young women were gathered in the
citadel of Susa in custody of Hegai, Esther
also was taken into the king's palace and
put in custody of Hegai, who had charge of
the women. 9 The girl pleased him and won
his favor, and he quickly provided her with
her cosmetic treatments and her portion of
food, and with seven chosen maids from
the king's palace, and advanced her and her
maids to the best place in the harem. 10 Es-
ther did not reveal her people or kindred,
for Mordecai had charged her not to tell.
11 Every day Mordecai would walk around
in front of the court of the harem, to learn
how Esther was and how she fared.

12 The turn came for each girl to go in
to King Ahasuerus, after being twelve
months under the regulations for the wom-
en, since this was the regular period of their
cosmetic treatment, six months with oil of
myrrh and six months with perfumes and
cosmetics for women. 13 When the girl went
in to the king she was given whatever she
asked for to take with her from the harem
to the king's palace. 14 In the evening she
went in; then in the morning she came back
to the second harem in custody of Shaash-
gaz, the king's eunuch, who was in charge
of the concubines; she did not go in to the
king again, unless the king delighted in her
and she was summoned by name.

15 When the turn came for Esther
daughter of Abihail the uncle of Mordecai,
who had adopted her as his own daughter,
to go in to the king, she asked for nothing
except what Hegai the king's eunuch, who
had charge of the women, advised. Now
Esther was admired by all who saw her.
16 When Esther was taken to King Ahasue-
rus in his royal palace in the tenth month,
which is the month of Tebeth, in the sev-
enth year of his reign, 17 the king loved Es-
ther more than all the other women; of all
the virgins she won his favor and devotion,
so that he set the royal crown on her head
and made her queen instead of Vashti.
18 Then the king gave a great banquet to all
his officials and ministers—"Esther's ban-
quet." He also granted a holiday[b] to the
provinces, and gave gifts with royal liberal-
ity.

19 When the virgins were being gath-

a Heb *He* *b* Or *an amnesty*

exile. **7:** Esther's Hebrew name, *Hadassah,* means "myrtle." Her Gentile name, *Esther,* derives from Ishtar, the Babylonian goddess of love and war, or from the Persian word for "star," or both. Likewise, Daniel and his friends have two names, one Jewish, one Babylonian (Dan 1.6–7). **9:** In winning the *favor* of Hegai (foreshadowing v. 17 and 5.2), Esther resembles Joseph in the house of Potiphar (Gen 39.2–6) and Daniel at the Babylonian court (Dan 1.9). Unlike Daniel (Dan 1.8), Esther eats the palace *food,* untroubled by the requirements of Jewish dietary laws. The *seven . . . maids* recall the seven eunuchs (1.10) and seven sages (1.14).

2.12–18: Esther becomes queen. 14: The impossibility of seeing the king again unless *summoned by name* foreshadows Esther's dilemma in 4.11–16 when she must violate this law to save her people (1.12,19n.). **15:** *Abihail,* only as Esther takes her fateful step toward queenship is her father's name supplied (see 9.29), perhaps by analogy with those provided for the queen mothers of Judahite kings. In asking only for what Hegai *advised,* Esther demonstrates prudence (see 5.4; 7.2; 9.12). **16:** *Tebeth,* December-January. **17:** Gen. 37.3. Esther is given the *royal crown* that Vashti refused to wear for Ahasuerus's guests (1.11). **18:** *Esther's banquet,* probably a wedding feast, foreshadows the two she gives later (5.5; 6.14–7.1) and the feast of Purim (9.22). A *holiday,* declared by the king on special occasions, was primarily economic (see Jer 34.8–11) and could involve forgiveness of tribute obligations and taxes, freedom from debt-slavery, and release from military service (see Lev 25.10–11). *Gifts* foreshadows 9.22.

2.19–23: Mordecai and Esther save the king's life. 20: As in v. 10, Esther's silence demonstrates

ered together,[a] Mordecai was sitting at the
king's gate. 20 Now Esther had not revealed
her kindred or her people, as Mordecai had
charged her; for Esther obeyed Mordecai
just as when she was brought up by him.
21 In those days, while Mordecai was sitting
at the king's gate, Bigthan and Teresh, two
of the king's eunuchs, who guarded the
threshold, became angry and conspired to
assassinate[b] King Ahasuerus. 22 But the
matter came to the knowledge of Morde-
cai, and he told it to Queen Esther, and
Esther told the king in the name of Morde-
cai. 23 When the affair was investigated and
found to be so, both the men were hanged
on the gallows. It was recorded in the book
of the annals in the presence of the king.

3 After these things King Ahasuerus pro-
moted Haman son of Hammedatha the
Agagite, and advanced him and set his seat
above all the officials who were with him.
2 And all the king's servants who were at
the king's gate bowed down and did obei-
sance to Haman; for the king had so com-
manded concerning him. But Mordecai did
not bow down or do obeisance. 3 Then the
king's servants who were at the king's gate
said to Mordecai, "Why do you disobey the
king's command?" 4 When they spoke to
him day after day and he would not listen
to them, they told Haman, in order to see
whether Mordecai's words would avail; for
he had told them that he was a Jew. 5 When
Haman saw that Mordecai did not bow
down or do obeisance to him, Haman was
infuriated. 6 But he thought it beneath him
to lay hands on Mordecai alone. So, having
been told who Mordecai's people were,
Haman plotted to destroy all the Jews, the
people of Mordecai, throughout the whole
kingdom of Ahasuerus.

7 In the first month, which is the month
of Nisan, in the twelfth year of King Ahasu-
erus, they cast Pur—which means "the
lot"—before Haman for the day and for
the month, and the lot fell on the thirteenth
day[c] of the twelfth month, which is the
month of Adar. 8 Then Haman said to King
Ahasuerus, "There is a certain people scat-
tered and separated among the peoples in
all the provinces of your kingdom; their
laws are different from those of every other
people, and they do not keep the king's
laws, so that it is not appropriate for the
king to tolerate them. 9 If it pleases the king,
let a decree be issued for their destruction,
and I will pay ten thousand talents of silver
into the hands of those who have charge of

a Heb adds *a second time* *b* Heb *to lay hands on*
c Cn Compare Gk and verse 13 below: Heb *the twelfth month*

obedience. **21:** Mysterious coincidences (see 4.14; 6.1–3) suggest divine intervention. The verse may echo Gen 40.2–3. **23:** *On the gallows* (lit. "on a tree"), i.e., by impalement, a disgraceful death, not by strangulation with a rope; it foreshadows the gallows Haman prepares for Mordecai (5.14) only to die upon it himself (7.9–10; also 9.13–14).

3.1–15: Wicked Haman plots to annihilate the Jews. 1: *Agagite,* descended from Agag, the Amalekite king and vanquished foe of King Saul (1 Sam 15.8; 2.5n.). **4:** *Day after day,* a parallel to Gen 39.10, where Joseph resists Potiphar's wife (see Dan 6.14). Both Mordecai and Joseph are falsely accused, then vindicated and promoted. Mordecai's motives for refusing to bow are not clearly stated, but as with Vashti's similarly enigmatic refusal, what might have been a private matter becomes a crisis involving the entire empire. **6:** *To destroy,* translated "to assassinate" in 2.21; *plotted,* translated "conspired" in 2.21. Similar wording implies a parallel between Haman and the conspirators of 2.21–23. **7:** This garbled verse with its reference to *pur,* a Babylonian loan-word for *"lot,"* may have been inserted by a later editor to connect the plot of Esther more closely with the Purim festival (see 9.20–32n.). Haman resorts to the lot to determine the date. Passover (Ex 12) occurs in *Nisan* (March-April), the first month of the Babylonian and Jewish year. Traditional Jewish interpretation drew elaborate parallels between the story of Esther and that of Passover. *Adar,* February-March. **8:** Haman begins with the truth: The Jews were indeed *scattered and separated* (Zech 7.14) and, like other subject peoples, their statutes (Deut 4.5–6) were different; but he slides into falsehood with his assertion that Jews *do not keep the king's laws.* **9:** *Ten thousand talents of silver,* an astronomical sum, the equivalent of hundreds of millions of U.S. dollars.

the king's business, so that they may put it
into the king's treasuries." 10 So the king
took his signet ring from his hand and gave
it to Haman son of Hammedatha the Agag-
ite, the enemy of the Jews. 11 The king said
to Haman, "The money is given to you,
and the people as well, to do with them as
it seems good to you."

12 Then the king's secretaries were sum-
moned on the thirteenth day of the first
month, and an edict, according to all that
Haman commanded, was written to the
king's satraps and to the governors over all
the provinces and to the officials of all the
peoples, to every province in its own script
and every people in its own language; it
was written in the name of King Ahasuerus
and sealed with the king's ring. 13 Letters
were sent by couriers to all the king's prov-
inces, giving orders to destroy, to kill, and
to annihilate all Jews, young and old, wom-
en and children, in one day, the thirteenth
day of the twelfth month, which is the
month of Adar, and to plunder their goods.
14 A copy of the document was to be issued
as a decree in every province by proclama-
tion, calling on all the peoples to be ready
for that day. 15 The couriers went quickly
by order of the king, and the decree was
issued in the citadel of Susa. The king and
Haman sat down to drink; but the city of
Susa was thrown into confusion.

4 When Mordecai learned all that had
been done, Mordecai tore his clothes
and put on sackcloth and ashes, and went
through the city, wailing with a loud and
bitter cry; 2 he went up to the entrance of
the king's gate, for no one might enter the
king's gate clothed with sackcloth. 3 In ev-
ery province, wherever the king's command
and his decree came, there was great
mourning among the Jews, with fasting and
weeping and lamenting, and most of them
lay in sackcloth and ashes.

4 When Esther's maids and her eunuchs
came and told her, the queen was deeply
distressed; she sent garments to clothe
Mordecai, so that he might take off his
sackcloth; but he would not accept them.
5 Then Esther called for Hathach, one of the
king's eunuchs, who had been appointed to
attend her, and ordered him to go to Mor-
decai to learn what was happening and
why. 6 Hathach went out to Mordecai in
the open square of the city in front of the
king's gate, 7 and Mordecai told him all
that had happened to him, and the exact
sum of money that Haman had promised to
pay into the king's treasuries for the de-
struction of the Jews. 8 Mordecai also gave
him a copy of the written decree issued in
Susa for their destruction, that he might
show it to Esther, explain it to her, and
charge her to go to the king to make suppli-
cation to him and entreat him for her peo-
ple.

9 Hathach went and told Esther what
Mordecai had said. 10 Then Esther spoke to
Hathach and gave him a message for Mor-
decai, saying, 11 "All the king's servants
and the people of the king's provinces
know that if any man or woman goes to the
king inside the inner court without being
called, there is but one law—all alike are to
be put to death. Only if the king holds out
the golden scepter to someone, may that

10: The *signet ring* gave Haman unlimited power to sign documents in the king's name (3.12; 8.2,8; Gen 41.41–42). The circumstances are reminiscent of the Gentile Queen Jezebel's plot against Naboth (1 Kings 21.8–9). After a reminder of Haman's wicked ancestry, Haman's epithet *enemy of the Jews* (8.1; 9.10,24) makes its first appearance. **12:** Another ironic touch, the *edict* (see 1.19–22; ch 8; 9.20,29–32) is sent out on the day before Passover (Ex 12.6; Lev 23.5; v. 7n.). **13:** *Couriers,* see 1.22n.

4.1–17: Mordecai persuades Esther to risk her life to save her people. 1: *Sackcloth and ashes* and torn clothing were traditional signs of mourning and repentance (2 Sam 3.31; Job 42.6; Dan 9.3; Jon 3.6). **3:** *Fasting* was believed to influence the deity (Lev 16.29–31; Judg 20.26; 2 Sam 12.16; 1 Kings 21.27; Jon 3.5,8; Ezra 8.21–23; Joel 1.14; 2.12,15; 1 Macc 3.47). **4–10:** Esther, whose Jewish identity is still a secret, is unaware of the edict. **6:** The city *square* is a traditional place of mourning (Amos 5.16; Isa 15.3; Jer 48.38). **11:** Like others called to save the people (Ex 3.11; 4.10; 10.28; Judg 6.15; Jer 1.6), Esther initially objects. **14:** *From another quarter,* Gen 28.11; Deut 12.11, perhaps a reference to divine providence (see

person live. I myself have not been called
to come in to the king for thirty days."
12When they told Mordecai what Esther
had said, 13Mordecai told them to reply to
Esther, "Do not think that in the king's pal-
ace you will escape any more than all the
other Jews. 14For if you keep silence at
such a time as this, relief and deliverance
will rise for the Jews from another quarter,
but you and your father's family will per-
ish. Who knows? Perhaps you have come
to royal dignity for just such a time as this."
15Then Esther said in reply to Mordecai,
16"Go, gather all the Jews to be found in
Susa, and hold a fast on my behalf, and
neither eat nor drink for three days, night
or day. I and my maids will also fast as you
do. After that I will go to the king, though
it is against the law; and if I perish, I per-
ish." 17Mordecai then went away and did
everything as Esther had ordered him.

5 On the third day Esther put on her roy-
al robes and stood in the inner court of
the king's palace, opposite the king's hall.
The king was sitting on his royal throne
inside the palace opposite the entrance to
the palace. 2As soon as the king saw Queen
Esther standing in the court, she won his
favor and he held out to her the golden
scepter that was in his hand. Then Esther
approached and touched the top of the
scepter. 3The king said to her, "What is it,
Queen Esther? What is your request? It
shall be given you, even to the half of my
kingdom." 4Then Esther said, "If it pleases
the king, let the king and Haman come to-
day to a banquet that I have prepared for
the king." 5Then the king said, "Bring Ha-
man quickly, so that we may do as Esther
desires." So the king and Haman came to
the banquet that Esther had prepared.
6While they were drinking wine, the king
said to Esther, "What is your petition? It
shall be granted you. And what is your re-
quest? Even to the half of my kingdom, it
shall be fulfilled." 7Then Esther said, "This
is my petition and request: 8If I have won
the king's favor, and if it pleases the king to
grant my petition and fulfill my request, let
the king and Haman come tomorrow to the
banquet that I will prepare for them, and
then I will do as the king has said."

9 Haman went out that day happy and
in good spirits. But when Haman saw Mor-
decai in the king's gate, and observed that
he neither rose nor trembled before him, he
was infuriated with Mordecai; 10neverthe-
less Haman restrained himself and went
home. Then he sent and called for his
friends and his wife Zeresh, 11and Haman
recounted to them the splendor of his
riches, the number of his sons, all the pro-
motions with which the king had honored
him, and how he had advanced him above
the officials and the ministers of the king.
12Haman added, "Even Queen Esther let
no one but myself come with the king to the
banquet that she prepared. Tomorrow also
I am invited by her, together with the king.
13Yet all this does me no good so long as I
see the Jew Mordecai sitting at the king's
gate." 14Then his wife Zeresh and all his
friends said to him, "Let a gallows fifty cu-
bits high be made, and in the morning tell

2.10n.). *Who knows?* often precedes an expression of hope for divine mercy (2 Sam 12.22; Joel 2.14; Jon 3.9). **16–17:** Esther's request for a community fast foreshadows her authority in 9.29. *If . . . perish,* resignation or selfless dedication (see Gen 43.14).

5.1–5: Esther before the king. 2: Esther resembles women who plead on another's behalf (1 Sam 25.24–31; 2 Sam 14.4–17). *Favor,* see 2.9,17 (Ex 12.36). **3:** Three times the king will offer *half of my kingdom* (5.6; 7.2), exaggerated for emphasis. As in folktales, the third offer (7.2) succeeds. **4:** *Banquet,* see 1.3–4n. Food, reassuring and nurturing, is a common motif in stories of women confronting powerful men; Esther works indirectly before moving on to her task of salvation (Judg 5.25; see Jdt 10.5; 12.1,17–20).

5.9–14: Haman's happiness is spoiled. 9: *Good spirits,* the same term is used of Ahasuerus ("merry") in 1.10. **10–14:** *Zeresh* is an exemplary son-bearing wife (5.11; 9.7–10) and Esther's negative counterpart, whose loyal advice her husband follows. *Gallows,* see 2.23n. *Fifty cubits,* ca. 22 m (72 ft), an exaggerated height. Only *the king* can order an execution.

the king to have Mordecai hanged on it;
then go with the king to the banquet in
good spirits." This advice pleased Haman,
and he had the gallows made.
6 On that night the king could not sleep,
and he gave orders to bring the book of
records, the annals, and they were read to
the king. 2 It was found written how Mor-
decai had told about Bigthana and Teresh,
two of the king's eunuchs, who guarded the
threshold, and who had conspired to assas-
sinate[a] King Ahasuerus. 3 Then the king
said, "What honor or distinction has been
bestowed on Mordecai for this?" The
king's servants who attended him said,
"Nothing has been done for him." 4 The
king said, "Who is in the court?" Now Ha-
man had just entered the outer court of the
king's palace to speak to the king about
having Mordecai hanged on the gallows
that he had prepared for him. 5 So the
king's servants told him, "Haman is there,
standing in the court." The king said, "Let
him come in." 6 So Haman came in, and the
king said to him, "What shall be done for
the man whom the king wishes to honor?"
Haman said to himself, "Whom would the
king wish to honor more than me?" 7 So
Haman said to the king, "For the man
whom the king wishes to honor, 8 let royal
robes be brought, which the king has worn,
and a horse that the king has ridden, with
a royal crown on its head. 9 Let the robes
and the horse be handed over to one of the
king's most noble officials; let him[b] robe
the man whom the king wishes to honor,
and let him[b] conduct the man on horse-
back through the open square of the city,
proclaiming before him: 'Thus shall it be
done for the man whom the king wishes to
honor.' " 10 Then the king said to Haman,
"Quickly, take the robes and the horse, as
you have said, and do so to the Jew Morde-
cai who sits at the king's gate. Leave out
nothing that you have mentioned." 11 So
Haman took the robes and the horse and
robed Mordecai and led him riding through
the open square of the city, proclaiming,
"Thus shall it be done for the man whom
the king wishes to honor."
12 Then Mordecai returned to the king's
gate, but Haman hurried to his house,
mourning and with his head covered.
13 When Haman told his wife Zeresh and
all his friends everything that had happened
to him, his advisers and his wife Zeresh
said to him, "If Mordecai, before whom
your downfall has begun, is of the Jewish
people, you will not prevail against him,
but will surely fall before him."
14 While they were still talking with
him, the king's eunuchs arrived and hurried
Haman off to the banquet that Esther had
7 prepared. 1 So the king and Haman
went in to feast with Queen Esther.
2 On the second day, as they were drinking
wine, the king again said to Esther, "What
is your petition, Queen Esther? It shall be
granted you. And what is your request?
Even to the half of my kingdom, it shall be
fulfilled." 3 Then Queen Esther answered,
"If I have won your favor, O king, and if it
pleases the king, let my life be given me—
that is my petition—and the lives of my
people—that is my request. 4 For we have
been sold, I and my people, to be destroyed,

[a] Heb *to lay hands on* [b] Heb *them*

6.1–13: Mordecai's triumph. This masterpiece of ironic narrative uses alliteration, repetition, understatement, and reversal. **1:** The king's insomnia, a traditional folktale motif (Dan 6.18, 1 Esdras 3.3), is not explained and is another instance of opportune fate in Esther (see 2.9,15,17,21; 3.7; 4.14; 5.2; 6.13). **6:** *Whom the king wishes to honor,* the phrase is repeated six times between vv. 6 and 11. The king's omission of the name parallels Haman's concealment of the identity of those he intended to annihilate (3.8). **8:** *Robe,* a gesture of favor (Gen 37.3; 41.42; 1 Sam 18.4; 1 Kings 1.33). *Crown,* an ornament for the horse's head often pictured on Mesopotamian and Persian reliefs. **12:** *Head covered,* a sign of grief (2 Sam 15.30; 19.4; Jer 14.4; Ezek 24.17).

6.14–7.10: Esther's second banquet and Haman's fall. 7.2: *Half my kingdom,* see 5.3n. **3:** No longer self-effacing (see 5.4n.) Esther seizes the right moment to speak directly of herself and of her people. **4:** *Sold,* probably a reference to Haman's bribe in 3.11 (see 4.7; but note the metaphorical use of the

to be killed, and to be annihilated. If we
had been sold merely as slaves, men and
women, I would have held my peace; but
no enemy can compensate for this damage
to the king."[a] 5 Then King Ahasuerus said
to Queen Esther, "Who is he, and where is
he, who has presumed to do this?" 6 Esther
said, "A foe and enemy, this wicked Ha-
man!" Then Haman was terrified before
the king and the queen. 7 The king rose
from the feast in wrath and went into the
palace garden, but Haman stayed to beg his
life from Queen Esther, for he saw that
the king had determined to destroy him.
8 When the king returned from the palace
garden to the banquet hall, Haman had
thrown himself on the couch where Esther
was reclining; and the king said, "Will he
even assault the queen in my presence, in
my own house?" As the words left the
mouth of the king, they covered Haman's
face. 9 Then Harbona, one of the eunuchs in
attendance on the king, said, "Look, the
very gallows that Haman has prepared for
Mordecai, whose word saved the king,
stands at Haman's house, fifty cubits
high." And the king said, "Hang him on
that." 10 So they hanged Haman on the gal-
lows that he had prepared for Mordecai.
Then the anger of the king abated.

8 On that day King Ahasuerus gave to
Queen Esther the house of Haman, the
enemy of the Jews; and Mordecai came be-
fore the king, for Esther had told what he
was to her. 2 Then the king took off his
signet ring, which he had taken from Ha-
man, and gave it to Mordecai. So Esther set
Mordecai over the house of Haman.

3 Then Esther spoke again to the king;
she fell at his feet, weeping and pleading
with him to avert the evil design of Haman
the Agagite and the plot that he had devised
against the Jews. 4 The king held out the
golden scepter to Esther, 5 and Esther rose
and stood before the king. She said, "If it
pleases the king, and if I have won his fa-
vor, and if the thing seems right before the
king, and I have his approval, let an order
be written to revoke the letters devised by
Haman son of Hammedatha the Agagite,
which he wrote giving orders to destroy the
Jews who are in all the provinces of the
king. 6 For how can I bear to see the calami-
ty that is coming on my people? Or how
can I bear to see the destruction of my
kindred?" 7 Then King Ahasuerus said to
Queen Esther and to the Jew Mordecai,
"See, I have given Esther the house of Ha-
man, and they have hanged him on the gal-
lows, because he plotted to lay hands on
the Jews. 8 You may write as you please
with regard to the Jews, in the name of the
king, and seal it with the king's ring; for an
edict written in the name of the king and
sealed with the king's ring cannot be re-
voked."

9 The king's secretaries were summoned
at that time, in the third month, which is
the month of Sivan, on the twenty-third
day; and an edict was written, according to

a Meaning of Heb uncertain

verb in Deut 32.30; Judg 2.14; 3.6; 4.2,9; 10.7). *To be destroyed,* etc., Esther quotes from the king's edict (3.13). *Damage to the king,* perhaps the king would be shamed if his queen were dishonored. **8:** Following common custom (8.3; 1 Sam 25.23–24; 2 Kings 4.27; Mk 7.25), Haman tries to supplicate the queen by falling at her feet. His gesture contrasts with Mordecai's in 3.2. *Assault the queen,* Ahasuerus mistakes Haman's gesture as a sexual assault, an unpardonable affront to both male and royal honor and as such, a capital offense (see 2 Sam 16.20–22; 1 Kings 2.13–25). **9–10:** *Gallows,* see 2.23n. Poetic justice prevails (cf. Prov 26.27).

8.1–17: The rise of Mordecai and the revocation of the anti-Jewish edict. The chapter overflows with reversals (see 1 Sam 2.1–10). **1:** In 3.9 Haman offered the king money. Now the king gives Haman's wealth to Esther. **2:** Haman's exalted position becomes Mordecai's with the transfer of the king's signet ring (see 3.10). **3:** The edict against the Jews still stands. **5:** *Devised by Haman,* Esther diplomatically dissociates the king from the royal edict. **8:** The king's earlier edict *cannot be revoked* (see 1.19n.), but a new edict can neutralize the former's intent. **9:** The verse follows the same general structure as 3.12–13 (see 2.19–21) while reversing the effect. *Sivan,* May-June. **11:** *Allowed,* not commanded. The bloodthirsty all that Mordecai commanded, to the Jews and to the satraps and the governors and the officials of the provinces from India to Ethiopia,[a] one hundred twenty-seven provinces, to every province in its own script and to every people in its own language, and also to the Jews in their script and their language. 10 He wrote letters in the name of King Ahasuerus, sealed them with the king's ring, and sent them by mounted couriers riding on fast steeds bred from the royal herd.[b] 11 By these letters the king allowed the Jews who were in every city to assemble and defend their lives, to destroy, to kill, and to annihilate any armed force of any people or province that might attack them, with their children and women, and to plunder their goods 12 on a single day throughout all the provinces of King Ahasuerus, on the thirteenth day of the twelfth month, which is the month of Adar. 13 A copy of the writ was to be issued as a decree in every province and published to all peoples, and the Jews were to be ready on that day to take revenge on their enemies. 14 So the couriers, mounted on their swift royal steeds, hurried out, urged by the king's command. The decree was issued in the citadel of Susa.

15 Then Mordecai went out from the presence of the king, wearing royal robes of blue and white, with a great golden crown and a mantle of fine linen and purple, while the city of Susa shouted and rejoiced. 16 For the Jews there was light and gladness, joy and honor. 17 In every province and in every city, wherever the king's command and his edict came, there was gladness and joy among the Jews, a festival and a holiday. Furthermore, many of the peoples of the country professed to be Jews, because the fear of the Jews had fallen upon them.

9 Now in the twelfth month, which is the month of Adar, on the thirteenth day, when the king's command and edict were about to be executed, on the very day when the enemies of the Jews hoped to gain power over them, but which had been changed to a day when the Jews would gain power over their foes, 2 the Jews gathered in their cities throughout all the provinces of King Ahasuerus to lay hands on those who had sought their ruin; and no one could withstand them, because the fear of them had fallen upon all peoples. 3 All the officials of the provinces, the satraps and the governors, and the royal officials were supporting the Jews, because the fear of Mordecai had fallen upon them. 4 For Mordecai was powerful in the king's house, and his fame spread throughout all the provinces as the man Mordecai grew more and more powerful. 5 So the Jews struck down all their enemies with the sword, slaughtering, and destroying them, and did as they pleased to those who hated them. 6 In the citadel of Susa the Jews killed and destroyed five hundred people. 7 They killed Parshandatha, Dalphon, Aspatha, 8 Poratha, Adalia, Arid-

a Or *Nubia*; Heb *Cush* *b* Meaning of Heb uncertain

language derives from the story's structure of reversals and retribution, not from historical reality. **12:** The date of the intended extermination (3.7,13) becomes a day of triumph. It is carefully stressed since it relates to the Purim festival. **14:** See 1.22n. **15–17:** Mordecai's attire contrasts with 4.1, as the Jews' mourning in 4.1–4 turns to joy. **16:** *Light and gladness, joy and honor* contrast with 4.3. **17:** *Professed to be Jews,* this translation is likely, but the Heb may simply mean that Gentiles took the Jews' part in their resistance. An earlier version of the book may have ended here with no mention of the festival.

9.1–10.3: The origins of Purim. 9.1–19: The Jews triumph over their enemies. 1: A reminder that the king's edict against the Jews still stands; the terms of the second edict allow the Jews to defend themselves. **2–4:** The Jews' victory is described in language reminiscent of holy war, the Exodus, and the conquest of Canaan. Opposition to the Jews is implied by *no one could withstand them* (Josh 23.9). *The fear of them,* a supernatural terror (Ex 15.14–16; Josh 2.8–11; Ps 105.38). **4:** Mordecai's power resembles that of Moses (Ex 11.3). **7–10:** Haman boasted unwisely about his many sons (5.11). Hebrew manuscripts arrange the names of Haman's ten sons in unusual formations. The names are recited in a single breath during Purim synagogue services. **10:** The emphasis (as in vv. 10,15) that the Jews did not *plunder* is a

atha, [9]Parmashta, Arisai, Aridai, Vaizatha,
[10]the ten sons of Haman son of Hammeda-
tha, the enemy of the Jews; but they did not
touch the plunder.
11 That very day the number of those
killed in the citadel of Susa was reported to
the king. [12]The king said to Queen Esther,
"In the citadel of Susa the Jews have killed
five hundred people and also the ten sons of
Haman. What have they done in the rest of
the king's provinces? Now what is your pe-
tition? It shall be granted you. And what
further is your request? It shall be ful-
filled." [13]Esther said, "If it pleases the king,
let the Jews who are in Susa be allowed
tomorrow also to do according to this day's
edict, and let the ten sons of Haman be
hanged on the gallows." [14]So the king
commanded this to be done; a decree was
issued in Susa, and the ten sons of Haman
were hanged. [15]The Jews who were in Susa
gathered also on the fourteenth day of the
month of Adar and they killed three hun-
dred persons in Susa; but they did not
touch the plunder.
16 Now the other Jews who were in the
king's provinces also gathered to defend
their lives, and gained relief from their ene-
mies, and killed seventy-five thousand of
those who hated them; but they laid no
hands on the plunder. [17]This was on the
thirteenth day of the month of Adar, and
on the fourteenth day they rested and made
that a day of feasting and gladness.
18 But the Jews who were in Susa gath-
ered on the thirteenth day and on the four-
teenth, and rested on the fifteenth day,
making that a day of feasting and gladness.
[19]Therefore the Jews of the villages, who
live in the open towns, hold the fourteenth
day of the month of Adar as a day for glad-
ness and feasting, a holiday on which they
send gifts of food to one another.
20 Mordecai recorded these things, and
sent letters to all the Jews who were in all
the provinces of King Ahasuerus, both near
and far, [21]enjoining them that they should
keep the fourteenth day of the month Adar
and also the fifteenth day of the same
month, year by year, [22]as the days on
which the Jews gained relief from their ene-
mies, and as the month that had been
turned for them from sorrow into gladness
and from mourning into a holiday; that
they should make them days of feasting and
gladness, days for sending gifts of food to
one another and presents to the poor. [23]So
the Jews adopted as a custom what they
had begun to do, as Mordecai had written
to them.
24 Haman son of Hammedatha the Ag-
agite, the enemy of all the Jews, had plotted
against the Jews to destroy them, and had
cast Pur—that is "the lot"—to crush and
destroy them; [25]but when Esther came be-
fore the king, he gave orders in writing that
the wicked plot that he had devised against
the Jews should come upon his own head,
and that he and his sons should be hanged
on the gallows. [26]Therefore these days are

reminder of the Agag story (see 2.5; 3.1), where the Israelites plundered to their own hurt (1 Sam 15.9). **12–15:** At Esther's *request* (5.3,6; 7.2) the king allows the Jews of Susa (as distinct from the Jews in the *citadel of Susa*) to continue their self-defense for a second day and to further dishonor Haman by hanging (i.e., impaling, see 2.23n.) the corpses of his sons in public (Josh 8.29; 10.26; 1 Sam 17.54; 31.10). Notice of the extra day for observing the king's edict is probably a device to explain why city Jews celebrated Purim for two days and country Jews only one (see vv. 18–19). **18–19:** Jews today observe Purim with *feasting* and *gifts of food* (see 2.9, "portion of food"; Neh 8.10).

9.20–32: The inauguration of the feast of Purim. The emphasis upon the written word, a particular concern in postexilic Judaism, is probably intended to legitimize a festival not mentioned in the Torah (cf. the origin of Hanukkah: 1 Macc 4.56–59; 2 Macc 1.1–2.28; 10.1–8). **20:** *Near and far,* Isa 57.19. **22:** Purim occurs not on the day of the Jews' military triumph but on the day they obtained their *relief. Sorrow into gladness,* Isa 61.3; Jer 31.13. **23:** Ex 24.3; see 3.7n. **24–26:** A plot summary that differs slightly from the book. Esther's name does not appear in the Heb text of v. 25 and has been added by the translator. The festival came to be called Purim for the lot, *pur* (plural, *purim*), which Haman cast (see 3.7n.). **24:** *Crush,* (Heb "hummam") ironic word play on Haman's name. **28:** *Remembered; com-*

called Purim, from the word Pur. Thus because of all that was written in this letter, and of what they had faced in this matter, and of what had happened to them, 27 the Jews established and accepted as a custom for themselves and their descendants and all who joined them, that without fail they would continue to observe these two days every year, as it was written and at the time appointed. 28 These days should be remembered and kept throughout every generation, in every family, province, and city; and these days of Purim should never fall into disuse among the Jews, nor should the commemoration of these days cease among their descendants.

29 Queen Esther daughter of Abihail, along with the Jew Mordecai, gave full written authority, confirming this second letter about Purim. 30 Letters were sent wishing peace and security to all the Jews, to the one hundred twenty-seven provinces of the kingdom of Ahasuerus, 31 and giving orders that these days of Purim should be observed at their appointed seasons, as the Jew Mordecai and Queen Esther enjoined on the Jews, just as they had laid down for themselves and for their descendants regulations concerning their fasts and their lamentations. 32 The command of Queen Esther fixed these practices of Purim, and it was recorded in writing.

10 King Ahasuerus laid tribute on the land and on the islands of the sea. 2 All the acts of his power and might, and the full account of the high honor of Mordecai, to which the king advanced him, are they not written in the annals of the kings of Media and Persia? 3 For Mordecai the Jew was next in rank to King Ahasuerus, and he was powerful among the Jews and popular with his many kindred, for he sought the good of his people and interceded for the welfare of all his descendants.

memoration, see Ex 13.3; 20.8. **29–32:** Probably added later. The Heb text is extremely corrupt and the verses do not appear in some ancient versions. **30:** *Peace and security,* the wording suggests Purim fulfills the prophecy of Zech 8.19 (see Isa 39.8; Jer 33.6) and therefore the humanly inaugurated festival is legitimate. **31:** *Fasts,* not the Jewish Fast of Esther, which came to be universally observed on the thirteenth of Adar only by the ninth century CE. **32:** Queen Esther is the only woman in the Bible credited with authorizing a religious observance.

10.1–3: Postscript: the greatness of Ahasuerus and Mordecai. 1: This unrelated comment may mean that the king prospered with Mordecai's assistance (see Gen 47.1–26). **2:** A standard formula for historical reports in Kings and Chronicles (1 Kings 14.19,29; 2 Chr 25.26; 32.32). **3:** Mordecai is the ideal portrait of a successful Diaspora Jew and of Jews living harmoniously in the Gentile world.

INTRODUCTION
to the Poetical and Wisdom Books

CONTENTS AND PLACEMENT

THE POETICAL AND WISDOM BOOKS—Job, Psalms, Proverbs, Ecclesiastes, and the Song of Solomon—do not form a totally coherent unit, especially when compared to other canonical divisions, such as the Historical Books or the Prophetic Books. These five books were written or collected at widely different times and consist of a number of literary types: love poetry (the Song of Solomon), Temple liturgy (Psalms), and wisdom literature (Job, Proverbs, and Ecclesiastes). It is also likely that they entered the canon for quite different reasons: Psalms was used for prayers; the Song of Solomon was probably first canonized as an ancient erotic poem used in wedding ceremonies; while Job, Proverbs, and Ecclesiastes may have been placed together in the canon because all three belong to a category of writings known as wisdom literature.

"Wisdom literature" describes works that do not focus on the nation Israel, on its great formative historical memories, such as Exodus and conquest, on the Temple and Jerusalem, and on covenant as the central theological notion binding together God, the people Israel, and the land of Israel. Wisdom books are thus in some ways a departure from the concerns of other biblical books. They share, rather, as their focus, reflection on universal human concerns, especially the understanding of individual experiences and the maintenance of ordered relationships that lead both to success on the human plane and to divine approval. In more recent scholarship, the concept of "wisdom" has been criticized as too elastic and amorphous. Indeed, the three wisdom books in this collection are remarkably different from one another and do not form a clear unit: Proverbs, in contrast to Job, suggests that the righteous are rewarded and do not suffer, while Ecclesiastes, in contrast to both Job and Proverbs, is deeply skeptical of the utility of wisdom. In addition, "wisdom" is a modern category, deriving from the beginning of the twentieth century, and thus Job, Proverbs, and Ecclesiastes were not originally grouped together on generic grounds. They nevertheless share a thematic interdependence. Proverbs provides a normative version of a type of ancient Near Eastern thought that looked for pattern and repetition in nature and in the moral life. In this tradition, the regular recurrence of natural phenomena could provide an analogy to guide human beings in their social interactions:

> As charcoal is to hot embers and wood to fire,
> so is a quarrelsome person for kindling strife (26.21).

The inevitability of the natural occurrence is mirrored in the inevitability of the social one. This kind of thinking then was extended to moral behavior, with the argument that good behavior, like good farming practice, will be rewarded:

> Anyone who tends a fig tree will eat its fruit,
> and anyone who takes care of a master will be honored (27.18).

Job and Ecclesiastes relate to this normative tradition in different ways. Job denies the inevitability of rewards for living an upright life and decisively refutes the idea that human suffering is always deserved. Ecclesiastes treats the idea of inevitability in a different way: The natural repetitions of seasons, tasks, and occupations become the image of futility. Each therefore, depends on the reader's acquaintance with the normative tradition. It should be noted that the themes of the wisdom tradition are continued in the Apocryphal/Deuterocanonical books of the Wisdom of Solomon and

Sirach (Ecclesiasticus), both of which combine didactic themes and style familiar especially from the book of Proverbs with retrospective summaries of Israel's history.

Though these five books are loosely described as Poetical Books, they are not all poetry, nor are all biblical poetic works found in this canonical section. Although Ecclesiastes contains some poetical sections, such as the poem of 3.1–8 ("For everything there is season . . ."), or quoted poetic proverbs (e.g., 7.1–6), the book is predominantly prose. Additionally, the nature of the poetry in these books is very different, ranging from the highly structured, largely static poetry of Proverbs, to the intensely erotic, more free-flowing poetry of Song of Solomon.

The creation of a canonical division called the "Poetical Books" is a relatively late development. In Jewish tradition these five books are included in the Writings, the third division of the canon; their order varies in different sources. The earliest evidence for seeing these five books as a unit comes from the second century CE, though it took many centuries for these five books, in the order found here, to be recognized as the third section of the Bible. The order of these books was variable, and some traditions placed them at the end of the Christian Old Testament, while others put them as the second part of that book immediately following the Pentateuch. Its current placement in English Bibles follows some manuscript traditions which most likely sought to organize the first section of the Bible by placing the Torah, the most authoritative section, first, followed by works about the past (the Historical Books), books about the present (the Poetical Books), and books about the future (the Prophetic Books). This arrangement, which places the prophets last, would be especially significant once the Hebrew Bible became the Old Testament and was seen as a kind of introduction to the New Testament. The Prophetic Books would then immediately precede the Gospels as prophecy followed by fulfillment.

AUTHORSHIP

At least four of the five Poetical Books cohere in terms of traditionally ascribed authorship. Many of the Psalms contain superscriptions or titles incorporating "of David," and many early Jewish and Christian traditions ascribe the Psalter as a whole to David. Proverbs 1.1 ("The proverbs of Solomon son of David, king of Israel"), 10.1, and 25.1 explicitly ascribe (sections of) that book to Solomon. Ecclesiastes, in its opening chapter, presents itself as the work of "the Teacher, when king over Israel in Jerusalem" (1.12; cf. 1.1); Jewish and Christian tradition understands this royal teacher to be Solomon, who is described in 1 Kings as being exceedingly rich, just like the protagonist of Ecclesiastes. Finally, the Song of Solomon opens with an explicit (but secondary) ascription of authorship: "the Song of Songs, which is Solomon's." Given the clear connection of Psalms, Proverbs, Ecclesiastes, and Song of Solomon to David and Solomon, it is noteworthy that some early Christian interpreters connected Job as well to the period of Solomon. It is thus likely that this canonical division of five books came into being as the compilations connected to David and Solomon, and was only secondarily labeled the "Poetical Books." The traditional attributions of authorship, however, have for the most part been rejected by modern scholarship; see the Introduction to each book for a detailed discussion.

THE CHARACTERISTICS OF BIBLICAL POETRY

These books do, as noted above, incorporate a large amount of poetry, so it is appropriate to here examine the basic structures of biblical poetry. Poetry is a cross-cultural phenomenon: Most cultures distinguish between an everyday type of discourse (prose), and heightened discourse (poetry). This heightening may be accomplished in a number of different ways, which include the use of figuration (e.g., metaphor, simile), meter, and certain types of sound patterning, such as alliteration and rhyme. Yet there is no cross-cultural pattern for poetry. Thus Hebrew poetry, unlike its classical English counterpart, has neither (true) rhythm nor rhyme; nevertheless, it is poetic in that it uses certain devices in significant enough concentration to distinguish it from everyday speech, or prose. Obviously, the prose-poetry distinction is relative rather than absolute; as in English, we may speak of poetic prose and prosaic poetry. Thus, "pure prose" and "pure poetry" should be seen as opposites on a continuum, within which a large variety of possibilities evince themselves in the Bible as in other literary traditions.

The main shared characteristic between typical English poetry and biblical poetry is the use of figuration. This may be seen, for example, in Ps 23. The central image of this psalm is introduced by the metaphor, "The LORD is my shepherd" (v. 1). The following verses unpack or clarify the meaning of this metaphor, noting in vv. 2–3 how God, the ideal shepherd, tends his people/sheep:

> He makes me lie down in green pastures;
> he leads me beside still waters;
> he restores my soul.
> He leads me in right paths
> for his name's sake.

Psalm 1 is characterized by a set of two contrasting similes: the righteous

> . . . are like trees
> planted by streams of water,
> which yield their fruit in its season,
> and their leaves do not wither (v. 3),

while the wicked "are like chaff that the wind drives away" (v. 4). The Song of Solomon is especially rich in similes and metaphors, as in the beginning of ch 2:

> I am a rose of Sharon,
> a lily of the valleys.
> As a lily among brambles,
> so is my love among maidens.
> As an apple tree among the trees of the wood,
> so is my beloved among young men.
> With great delight I sat in his shadow,
> and his fruit was sweet to my taste.

The main characteristic of biblical poetry, nevertheless, is not figuration, but parallelism, in which most poetic lines may be divided into two (or sometimes three) parts; the second part of the line is intimately connected to the first part, and typically seconds it in some way. For example, Ps 6.2 reads:

> Be gracious to me, O LORD, for I am languishing;
> O LORD, heal me, for my bones are shaking with terror.

The verse clearly divides into two more or less equal sections, and each element in the first part is mirrored, seconded, or paralleled in the second: Be gracious to me || heal me; O LORD || O LORD; for I am languishing || for my bones are shaking with terror. This parallelism, which is not typical of biblical prose, serves as the backbone of biblical poetry.

Since the eighteenth century, it has been customary to see three main types of parallelism in the Bible: synonymous, antithetical, and synthetic. The quotation above from Ps 6.2 is an example of synonymous parallelism. Antithetical parallelism can be seen in Prov 10.1:

A wise child makes a glad father,
 but a foolish child is a mother's grief.

In this balanced, two-part line, "a wise child" is antithetical, or opposite, to "a foolish child," and "makes a glad father" is antithetical to "is a mother's grief." In synthetic parallelism, the second part of the line completes the thought of the first part, and is neither the same nor the opposite. For example, Song 1.9 reads:

I compare you, my love,
 to a mare among Pharaoh's chariots.

Here the second part concludes the thought of the first.

The appropriateness of the three labels—synonymous, antithetical, and synthetic—which were accepted in biblical scholarship for two centuries, has now been called into question on several grounds. First, some have noted that languages have no true synonyms; thus "synonymous parallelism" is a misleading term. Furthermore, very often two parallel words can be similar, but are not truly synonymous, as may be seen in the example from Ps 6.2: "I am languishing" ‖ "my bones are shaking with terror." The term antithetical parallelism has been questioned because not all elements of part B are the antithesis of part A. This may be seen in the example from Prov 10.1, where "child" is used in both parts A and B; a true antithesis might contrast a "wise child" with a "foolish parent." Finally, "synthetic" has been criticized as too vague a term. These criticisms should not be underestimated. Nevertheless, the three terms, if understood as ideal types from which actual lines may deviate to a greater or lesser extent, remain useful.

A much more serious criticism of the classical model emerged in the middle 1980s when several scholars began to question the notion that parallelism is formulaic in that the second half of the poetic line typically adds little to the line, but merely seconds it. Several scholars have suggested just the opposite, that the second part heightens or extends the first. Thus, the typical biblical verse should be read "A, and even more so, B." According to this model, which has gained substantial support in the last two decades, we would not read Ps 6.2b, "O LORD, heal me, for my bones are shaking with terror" as a type of filler that merely restates "Be gracious to me, O LORD, for I am languishing." Rather we would understand the verse as a whole as: "Be gracious to me, O LORD, for I am languishing," and moreover, "O LORD, heal me, for my bones are shaking with terror," where the claim "for my bones are shaking with terror" is a more vivid description that intensifies the verse's opening "for I am languishing."

Sometimes it is quite clear that the second part of the verse does not merely parallel the first but does go beyond it in some significant fashion, and thus justifies this newer model. Yet, there are a substantial number of cases in which the second part actually does seem to function as a mere filler, carrying little if any semantic weight, let alone intensifying the first. For example, the major image of Ps 121 is the ability of God to protect the individual. This is expressed at the psalm's center, where God is imagined metaphorically as a "shade" (v. 5) from the intense Mediterranean heat. The psalm continues (v. 6): "The sun shall not strike you by day, nor the moon by night." Clearly, the second part, "nor the moon by night" is not an intensification; in fact, it makes no sense, since no one in ancient Israel was afflicted with moonburn or moonstroke. The second part here is probably a(n antithetical) filler and carries no semantic weight. It should be seen as part of an ancient Near Eastern and biblical pattern of word pairs, where a particular word (e.g., "sun" or "father") automatically evokes a related ("synonymous" or "antithetical") word (e.g., "moon" or "mother").

Thus, parallelism is much more complicated than would appear on the surface. Clearly it is characterized by sets of lines, each of which may be divided into two parts, typically of the same length and mirroring each other on the semantic, syntactic, and phonological levels. It is unclear if the second should typically be read as an intensification of the first, or as a filler that carries little or no semantic value. This uncertainty is extremely frustrating, not only because it leaves us unsure how to read much of biblical poetry, especially the extent to which we do or do not need to pay close attention to the second half of the line, but also because our understanding of biblical poetry will affect our reconstruction of many Israelite institutions. To return to Prov 10.1—"A wise child makes a glad father, but a foolish child is a mother's grief"—if we follow the older understanding of parallelism, the second half is largely a filler, indicating that the father had the major role in the child's upbringing in ancient Israel, while if we follow the newer understanding, where the second intensifies the first, the mother was primarily responsible for the child.

Another area that has engendered significant controversy over the last few decades concerns the extent to which meter or rhythm existed in biblical poetry. Much of this debate concerns the definition of meter. In English and other modern Western languages, meter is generally understood as a pattern of stressed and unstressed syllables; if this is how we should understand it in biblical poetic texts, these texts in their current form lack meter or rhythm. Metrical patterns can only be found in biblical texts if they are emended or reconstructed extensively. There is, however, a tendency for the parts of each line, in most poetic genres, to be approximately the same length. There is some possibility that this reflects the remnant of some metrical system, and that at an earlier time, each part had not only the same length, but the same meter, but this pattern of stressed and unstressed syllables has been lost as a result of changes in the pronunciation of ancient Hebrew. More likely, the similarity of length is part of the larger system of parallelism, which encouraged each part to mirror its counterpart in length, as well as in semantic, syntactic, and phonological structure.

Scholars have until recently been primarily concerned with the line as the main unit of biblical poetry. This is not really surprising, given how foreign biblical parallelism is to the modern Western (but not the ancient Near Eastern) ear. This interest in the line has obscured the significance of the strophe or stanza and of the poem as a whole. But the last few decades have seen a legitimate return to these larger units. For example, it had become a habit when studying passages like Job 3 to concentrate solely on the parallelism of lines like v. 5:

Let gloom and deep darkness claim it.
　　Let clouds settle upon it;
　　let the blackness of the day terrify it.

Now, in addition to this type of analysis, scholars study how the poet uses images of day and night, light and darkness, throughout the chapter, in order to create this exquisite poem. This is not, however, an either-or proposition: By studying how the individual line functions as poetry and how these lines join together into stanzas, which combine into complete poems, we gain a much fuller appreciation and understanding of these Poetical Books.

JOB

The book of Job is named after its protagonist, an innocent man who suffered loss and endured pain through no fault of his own. For many, the man Job is most well-known through the cliché about "the patience of Job," derived from the traditional translation of Jas 5.11. The Greek term that is translated as "patience," however, means not so much patience as "endurance," "persistence," or "steadfastness." And, indeed, the Job that one encounters in the book that bears his name is not patient, but he is persistent in his claim that he has suffered undeservedly.

The provenance of the book is unknown. Its author is anonymous, while its date and place of origin are matters of debate. Most scholars place the bulk of the book, if not its final form, somewhere between the seventh and the fourth centuries BCE, although also recognizing that the final form is the result of a complex history of transmission. The prose framework, what are now the book's prologue (1.1–2.13) and epilogue (42.7–17), consists of a narrative that is likely based on an ancient folktale about the undeserved suffering and final restoration of the protagonist. The rest of the book consists of dialogues (written in poetic style) between Job and the friends who had ostensibly come to comfort him (3.1–31.40), and between Job and God (38.1–42.6). Intruding into this material are a poetic interlude on the inaccessibility of Wisdom (28.1–28) and the speeches of Elihu (32.1–37.24) that appear to have been added at a later time. Interpreters have called attention to certain linguistic and stylistic shifts, as well as occasional inconsistencies in the story line. Such discrepancies have been explained in terms of multiple authors, a single author with multiple sources, a primary work that has been redacted two or three times, or a single author who has worked with the materials over a long period of time. Whatever the truth, the book in its present form must be read as a whole.

Although the book of Job in its entirety is unique in ancient literature, it draws on a variety of traditions and genres that were known throughout the ancient Near East. The character of Job himself is presented as a non-Israelite from the land of Uz (perhaps northern Arabia), and it is likely that versions of the story of Job were told by many of the peoples of the region. In the sixth century the prophet Ezekiel mentions Job, along with Noah and Dan'el, as heroes of antiquity who saved others by their righteousness (Ezek 14.14,20). This Dan'el is not the Daniel from the biblical book of that name but an ancient Canaanite king whose story is known from the tablets found in the ruins of the second millennium BCE city of Ugarit. Similar to Ezekiel's setting of Job among the legendary figures of antiquity is the way in which the prose tale presents Job as someone who apparently lived in the remote ancestral period.

The influence of ancient Near Eastern literary forms and traditions are also evident in the poetic dialogues. The problem of enigmatic suffering was one that was explored in Mesopotamian literature in poetic compositions in which a righteous or emblematic sufferer described his sufferings, his confusion about the cause of his misery, and his passionate desire for restoration (e.g., "I will Praise the Lord of Wisdom" and the "Sumerian Job"). The most striking similarity, however, exists between the dialogue sections of Job and "The Babylonian Theodicy." In this composition an unnamed sufferer and his friend speak alternately in a cycle of twenty-seven speeches. The sufferer protests his misery, describing the injustice of the world and the unfairness of the gods. His friend attempts to defend the rationality of the world and urges his friend to seek the mercy of the gods. In contrast to Job, however, "The Babylonian Theodicy" ends without any appearance of the deity or narrative resolution.

Finally, the book of Job contains many allusions to mythological traditions known throughout the ancient Near East. Repeated reference is made to the cosmogonic struggle between God and the sea, especially as represented by the dragon of chaos, Rahab or Leviathan (3.8; 7.12; 10.13; 26.12; 38.8–11; 41.1–34). It is often suggested that the long descriptions of Behemoth and Leviathan in chs 40–41 draw on Egyptian imagery from the myths of Horus and Seth. The descriptions of creation and of cosmic geography in chs 26 and 38 also evoke the mythic traditions common to Israel and the other cultures of the Near East.

Like other wisdom literature in the Hebrew Bible, the book of Job does not make reference to specific Israelite legal or historical traditions. It does, however, make a rich use of psalmic and other wisdom traditions. In the dialogues the characters often make use of proverbs (e.g., 5.10,17; 8.11; 12.11) or hymns (e.g., 5.8–16). Job is particularly adept at evoking a hymn or psalm only to parody it. Although the clearest example is his parody of Psalm 8 in 7.17–19, he uses this technique often (e.g., 9.5–12; 12.13–25).

The enigma of the suffering of the righteous and the good fortune of the wicked was one addressed by Israelite literature, both in the psalms and in other wisdom texts. Although not prominent in the book of Proverbs, it emerges more strongly in the later wisdom books of Ecclesiastes and Sirach. Several Psalms also address aspects of these issues (Ps 37; 39; 49; 73), but they do not exhibit the radical protest and questioning that one finds in the book of Job.

Distinctive to the book of Job is the way it situates these issues. The book is neither a treatise on innocent suffering, as often supposed, nor an apology for God's justice in the face of inexplicable human suffering. Rather, the principal theological issue that the book raises is, ironically, the question posed by the adversary in the divine council (see 1.9): Will mortals be religious ("fear God") apart from rewards and punishment? As the dialogue develops, however, the questions of divine justice that torture Job's mind are not satisfactorily met by the arguments of the friends. Job himself seeks to imagine a way in which he might go to trial with God for a vindication of his righteousness and perhaps an acknowledgment from God of God's mistreatment of Job (9.2–35; 13.13–28; 16.18–22; 19.23–27; 23.1–7; 31.35–37). Yet when God answers Job, it is neither as the friends have imagined God would speak nor as Job had hoped God would answer him. The meaning and significance of the divine speeches continue to be among the most debated issues in the book. Some interpret the speeches as a repudiation of a human's right to question God. Others understand them as a necessary correction to Job's too limited understanding of the nature of the cosmos as a place where all suffering can be reduced to legal categories of guilt or innocence. All agree that the extraordinary beauty of the poetry is part of its meaning. Perhaps the very elusiveness of the divine speeches implies that no answer from God to Job's questions can satisfy the human intellect. Yet the ending suggests that there is a resolution to be found in the depths of a pious life lived before a mysterious God.

1 There was once a man in the land of Uz
whose name was Job. That man was
blameless and upright, one who feared God
and turned away from evil. 2 There were
born to him seven sons and three daugh-
ters. 3 He had seven thousand sheep, three
thousand camels, five hundred yoke of
oxen, five hundred donkeys, and very many
servants; so that this man was the greatest
of all the people of the east. 4 His sons used
to go and hold feasts in one another's
houses in turn; and they would send and
invite their three sisters to eat and drink
with them. 5 And when the feast days had
run their course, Job would send and sanc-
tify them, and he would rise early in the
morning and offer burnt offerings accord-
ing to the number of them all; for Job said,
"It may be that my children have sinned,
and cursed God in their hearts." This is
what Job always did.
6 One day the heavenly beings[a] came to
present themselves before the LORD, and
Satan[b] also came among them. 7 The LORD
said to Satan,[b] "Where have you come
from?" Satan[b] answered the LORD, "From
going to and fro on the earth, and from
walking up and down on it." 8 The LORD
said to Satan,[b] "Have you considered my
servant Job? There is no one like him on the
earth, a blameless and upright man who
fears God and turns away from evil."
9 Then Satan[b] answered the LORD, "Does
Job fear God for nothing? 10 Have you not
put a fence around him and his house and
all that he has, on every side? You have
blessed the work of his hands, and his pos-
sessions have increased in the land. 11 But
stretch out your hand now, and touch all
that he has, and he will curse you to your
face." 12 The LORD said to Satan,[b] "Very
well, all that he has is in your power; only
do not stretch out your hand against him!"
So Satan[b] went out from the presence of
the LORD.
13 One day when his sons and daugh-
ters were eating and drinking wine in the
eldest brother's house, 14 a messenger came
to Job and said, "The oxen were plowing
and the donkeys were feeding beside them,
15 and the Sabeans fell on them and carried
them off, and killed the servants with the
edge of the sword; I alone have escaped to
tell you." 16 While he was still speaking, an-
other came and said, "The fire of God fell
from heaven and burned up the sheep and
the servants, and consumed them; I alone
have escaped to tell you." 17 While he was
still speaking, another came and said, "The
Chaldeans formed three columns, made a
raid on the camels and carried them off,
and killed the servants with the edge of the
sword; I alone have escaped to tell you."
18 While he was still speaking, another

a Heb *sons of God*   *b* Or *the Accuser*; Heb *ha-satan*

1.1–2.13: The prologue. The opening narrative is structured according to a series of five scenes (1.1–5, 6–12, 13–22; 2.1–6, 7–13), which alternate between earth and heaven. **1.1–5:** The style with its evocation of a setting long ago and far away, its idealized hero, and its fondness for round numbers that add up to multiples of ten, gives the story the air of a folk or fairy tale. **1:** *The land of Uz* is probably just south of Edom, in northern Arabia (see Gen 36.28; Jer 25.20; Lam 4.21; 1 Chr 2.42; and the Greek text of Job 42.17). Job's personal name, attested in various texts from the second millennium BCE, etymologically means "Where is the Father?" (a reference to God). The form in Hebrew may, however, be taken to mean "one who is treated as an enemy" (see 13.24). **5:** *Cursed*, the Heb text actually has the word "blessed" here, apparently as a euphemism or pious scribal correction (so also in 1.11; 2.5,9). The same euphemism occurs in 1 Kings 21.13. **6–12:** The scene is a meeting of the council of *heavenly beings* presided over by the LORD (cf. 1 Kings 22.19–22; Job 15.8; Ps 82.1; 89.7; Jer 23.18). In the book of Job, *Satan* is not yet the personal name of the devil, as in later Jewish and Christian literature. Rather, the Hebrew (with the definite article) simply means "the adversary" or "the accuser" (see textual note *b*), a reference to one of the members of the divine council who served as a sort of independent prosecutor (cf. Zech 3.1). The accuser suggests that Job's piety may have been bought with divine protection and provision. **15:** *Sabeans,* Arabian nomads. **16:** *Fire of God,* cf. Gen 19.24; Num 11.1; 16.35; 2 Kings 1.10–12. **17:** *Chaldeans,* Neo-Babylonians from southern Mesopotamia. **19:** *Wind,* cf. 27.20–23. **20:** The traditional acts of

came and said, "Your sons and daughters
were eating and drinking wine in their el-
dest brother's house, 19 and suddenly a
great wind came across the desert, struck
the four corners of the house, and it fell
on the young people, and they are dead; I
alone have escaped to tell you."
20 Then Job arose, tore his robe, shaved
his head, and fell on the ground and wor-
shiped. 21 He said, "Naked I came from my
mother's womb, and naked shall I return
there; the LORD gave, and the LORD has
taken away; blessed be the name of the
LORD."
22 In all this Job did not sin or charge
God with wrongdoing.

2 One day the heavenly beings[a] came to
present themselves before the LORD,
and Satan[b] also came among them to
present himself before the LORD. 2 The
LORD said to Satan,[b] "Where have you
come from?" Satan[c] answered the LORD,
"From going to and fro on the earth, and
from walking up and down on it." 3 The
LORD said to Satan,[b] "Have you consid-
ered my servant Job? There is no one like
him on the earth, a blameless and upright
man who fears God and turns away from
evil. He still persists in his integrity, al-
though you incited me against him, to de-
stroy him for no reason." 4 Then Satan[b]
answered the LORD, "Skin for skin! All that
people have they will give to save their
lives.[d] 5 But stretch out your hand now and
touch his bone and his flesh, and he will
curse you to your face." 6 The LORD said to
Satan,[b] "Very well, he is in your power;
only spare his life."
7 So Satan[b] went out from the presence
of the LORD, and inflicted loathsome sores
on Job from the sole of his foot to the
crown of his head. 8 Job[e] took a potsherd
with which to scrape himself, and sat
among the ashes.
9 Then his wife said to him, "Do you
still persist in your integrity? Curse[f] God,
and die." 10 But he said to her, "You speak
as any foolish woman would speak. Shall
we receive the good at the hand of God,
and not receive the bad?" In all this Job did
not sin with his lips.
11 Now when Job's three friends heard
of all these troubles that had come upon
him, each of them set out from his home—
Eliphaz the Temanite, Bildad the Shuhite,
and Zophar the Naamathite. They met to-
gether to go and console and comfort him.
12 When they saw him from a distance, they
did not recognize him, and they raised their
voices and wept aloud; they tore their robes
and threw dust in the air upon their heads.
13 They sat with him on the ground seven
days and seven nights, and no one spoke a

a Heb *sons of God* b Or *the Accuser*; Heb *ha-satan* c Or *The Accuser*; Heb *ha-satan* d Or *All that the man has he will give for his life* e Heb *He* f Heb *Bless*

mourning; see 2.12; Gen 37.34; 2 Sam 13.31; Jer 16.6. **22:** In this traditional saying (see also Eccl 5.15; Sir 40.1), the *womb* from which one comes is one's mother; that to which one returns is probably a metaphor for the earth (cf. Gen 3.19). **2.1–6:** These verses describe a second gathering of the divine council in heaven, including a second encounter between the heavenly prosecutor and the LORD. **4:** *Skin for skin,* an idiom perhaps derived from barter trade, expressing willingness to trade up to an equivalent value; anything offered beyond that maximum value would be a loss. The prosecutor's argument is that Job is willing to remain faithful up to a point, indeed, to leave the world "naked" just as he came (1.21). If Job's own body were harmed, however, he would respond differently. **7:** Job is afflicted with a painful skin affliction, which could have been viewed as evidence of divine judgment (see Deut 28.35). **8:** *Sat among the ashes,* another expression of grief; see Ezek 27.30; Jon 3.6. **10:** The term *foolish woman* perhaps implies that her talk is like that of an unbeliever (see Ps 14.1 ‖ 53.2; 39.8; 74.22). Despite Job's refusal to curse God directly, the narrator notes only that *Job did not sin with his lips,* a provocative statement in light of the simpler conclusion in 1.21 that he *did not sin.* **11:** *Eliphaz the Temanite,* Teman is probably somewhere in Edom or north Arabia, as is the home of *Bildad the Shuhite* (see Gen 25.1–2). *Zophar the Naamathite* is possibly a Sabean (see 1.15n.). **12:** See 1.20n.; 2.8n. *Dust . . . upon their heads,* another act of mourning; see Josh 7.6; Lam 2.10. **13:** *Seven days,* see Gen 50.10; Sir 22.12.

word to him, for they saw that his suffering was very great.

3 After this Job opened his mouth and cursed the day of his birth. 2 Job said:

3 "Let the day perish in which I was born,
and the night that said,
'A man-child is conceived.'
4 Let that day be darkness!
May God above not seek it,
or light shine on it.
5 Let gloom and deep darkness claim it.
Let clouds settle upon it;
let the blackness of the day terrify it.
6 That night—let thick darkness seize it!
let it not rejoice among the days of the year;
let it not come into the number of the months.
7 Yes, let that night be barren;
let no joyful cry be heard[a] in it.
8 Let those curse it who curse the Sea,[b]
those who are skilled to rouse up Leviathan.
9 Let the stars of its dawn be dark;
let it hope for light, but have none;
may it not see the eyelids of the morning—
10 because it did not shut the doors of my mother's womb,
and hide trouble from my eyes.

11 "Why did I not die at birth,
come forth from the womb and expire?
12 Why were there knees to receive me,
or breasts for me to suck?
13 Now I would be lying down and quiet;
I would be asleep; then I would be at rest
14 with kings and counselors of the earth
who rebuild ruins for themselves,
15 or with princes who have gold,
who fill their houses with silver.
16 Or why was I not buried like a stillborn child,
like an infant that never sees the light?
17 There the wicked cease from troubling,
and there the weary are at rest.
18 There the prisoners are at ease together;
they do not hear the voice of the taskmaster.
19 The small and the great are there,
and the slaves are free from their masters.

20 "Why is light given to one in misery,
and life to the bitter in soul,
21 who long for death, but it does not come,
and dig for it more than for hidden treasures;
22 who rejoice exceedingly,
and are glad when they find the grave?
23 Why is light given to one who cannot see the way,
whom God has fenced in?
24 For my sighing comes like[c] my bread,
and my groanings are poured out like water.
25 Truly the thing that I fear comes upon me,
and what I dread befalls me.

a Heb *come* *b* Cn: Heb *day* *c* Heb *before*

3.1–26: Job's curse of the day of his birth consists of the curse proper (vv. 3–10) and a long lament (vv. 11–26). Cf. Jer 20.14–18. **8:** *Those who are skilled to rouse up Leviathan* are professional diviners, experts in rendering effective curses. *Leviathan,* both in the Bible (Job 41; Ps 74.14; Isa 27.1; see also Job 7.12; Isa 51.9; Hab 3.8) and in other ancient Near Eastern literature, is a sea monster representing cosmic chaos. The threat to the cosmos is evident, too, in the darkening of the skies (vv. 4–6,9). **13–19:** In death there is *rest* (vv. 13,17); cf. 14.13; Eccl 6.3–5; Sir 30.17. **14:** Cf. Isa 14.9. **23:** *Fenced in,* an ironic reprise of 1.10.

26 I am not at ease, nor am I quiet;
I have no rest; but trouble comes."

4 Then Eliphaz the Temanite answered:
2 "If one ventures a word with you,
will you be offended?
But who can keep from speaking?
3 See, you have instructed many;
you have strengthened the weak
hands.
4 Your words have supported those
who were stumbling,
and you have made firm the feeble
knees.
5 But now it has come to you, and you
are impatient;
it touches you, and you are
dismayed.
6 Is not your fear of God your
confidence,
and the integrity of your ways your
hope?

7 "Think now, who that was innocent
ever perished?
Or where were the upright cut
off?
8 As I have seen, those who plow
iniquity
and sow trouble reap the same.
9 By the breath of God they perish,
and by the blast of his anger they
are consumed.
10 The roar of the lion, the voice of the
fierce lion,
and the teeth of the young lions are
broken.
11 The strong lion perishes for lack of
prey,
and the whelps of the lioness are
scattered.

12 "Now a word came stealing to me,
my ear received the whisper of it.
13 Amid thoughts from visions of the
night,
when deep sleep falls on mortals,
14 dread came upon me, and trembling,
which made all my bones shake.
15 A spirit glided past my face;
the hair of my flesh bristled.
16 It stood still,
but I could not discern its
appearance.
A form was before my eyes;
there was silence, then I heard a
voice:
17 'Can mortals be righteous before[a]
God?
Can human beings be pure before[a]
their Maker?
18 Even in his servants he puts no trust,
and his angels he charges with
error;
19 how much more those who live in
houses of clay,
whose foundation is in the dust,
who are crushed like a moth.
20 Between morning and evening they
are destroyed;
they perish forever without any
regarding it.
21 Their tent-cord is plucked up within
them,
and they die devoid of wisdom.'

5 "Call now; is there anyone who will
answer you?
To which of the holy ones will you
turn?
2 Surely vexation kills the fool,

a Or *more than*

4.1–5.25: Eliphaz's first discourse. 4.1–6: Eliphaz begins by expressing understanding and concern for Job, suggesting that Job has lost perspective because of his pain and urging him to take a longer view. **7–11:** Eliphaz assumes Job's acceptance of the widespread view of just retribution (Prov 22.8; Eccl 8.12–13; Hos 10.13). **10:** Cf. Ps 58.6. **12–16:** Appeal to revelatory experience is unusual in wisdom books (see 33.15–18), but dreams and night visions are recognized as means of divine communication (Gen 15.12–17; 28.10–15; 1 Sam 3.1–14; 1 Kings 3.5). **17–21:** The message from the vision is that mortals are inevitably imperfect, a view also attested in the "Babylonian Theodicy" (*ANET,* 601–604); cf. 25.4–6. **5.1:** The *holy ones* are members of the divine council (see 1.6). **2–5:** Rage has dangerous consequences

and jealousy slays the simple.
3 I have seen fools taking root,
but suddenly I cursed their
dwelling.
4 Their children are far from safety,
they are crushed in the gate,
and there is no one to deliver them.
5 The hungry eat their harvest,
and they take it even out of the
thorns;[a]
and the thirsty[b] pant after their
wealth.
6 For misery does not come from the
earth,
nor does trouble sprout from the
ground;
7 but human beings are born to trouble
just as sparks[c] fly upward.

8 "As for me, I would seek God,
and to God I would commit my
cause.
9 He does great things and
unsearchable,
marvelous things without number.
10 He gives rain on the earth
and sends waters on the fields;
11 he sets on high those who are lowly,
and those who mourn are lifted to
safety.
12 He frustrates the devices of the crafty,
so that their hands achieve no
success.
13 He takes the wise in their own
craftiness;
and the schemes of the wily are
brought to a quick end.
14 They meet with darkness in the
daytime,
and grope at noonday as in the
night.
15 But he saves the needy from the
sword of their mouth,
from the hand of the mighty.
16 So the poor have hope,
and injustice shuts its mouth.

17 "How happy is the one whom God
reproves;
therefore do not despise the
discipline of the Almighty.[d]
18 For he wounds, but he binds up;
he strikes, but his hands heal.
19 He will deliver you from six troubles;
in seven no harm shall touch you.
20 In famine he will redeem you from
death,
and in war from the power of the
sword.
21 You shall be hidden from the scourge
of the tongue,
and shall not fear destruction when
it comes.
22 At destruction and famine you shall
laugh,
and shall not fear the wild animals
of the earth.
23 For you shall be in league with the
stones of the field,
and the wild animals shall be at
peace with you.
24 You shall know that your tent is safe,
you shall inspect your fold and miss
nothing.
25 You shall know that your descendants
will be many,
and your offspring like the grass of
the earth.
26 You shall come to your grave in ripe
old age,
as a shock of grain comes up to the
threshing floor in its season.
27 See, we have searched this out; it is
true.
Hear, and know it for yourself."

a Meaning of Heb uncertain *b* Aquila Symmachus Syr Vg: Heb *snare* *c* Or *birds*; Heb *sons of Resheph* *d* Traditional rendering of Heb *Shaddai*

(Prov 12.16; 14.30; Sir 30.24). The reference to the threat to one's children (v. 4) is horribly insensitive, for Job had lost all of his. **6–7:** Word play here echoes Gen 3.17–19: Trouble does not originate from the ground (Heb "'adamah"), but mortals ("'adam") inevitably get into trouble. **8–16:** Eliphaz uses a hymnic style (cf. Ps 147) to argue that hope for mortals lies in the greatness of God. **17–27:** Eliphaz suggests that suffering may be divine discipline (cf. Deut 32.39; Ps 94.12; Prov 3.11–12; Hos 6.1). **17:** *Almighty*, "Shaddai"; see Introduction.

6 Then Job answered:
2 "O that my vexation were weighed,
and all my calamity laid in the balances!
3 For then it would be heavier than the sand of the sea;
therefore my words have been rash.
4 For the arrows of the Almighty[a] are in me;
my spirit drinks their poison;
the terrors of God are arrayed against me.
5 Does the wild ass bray over its grass,
or the ox low over its fodder?
6 Can that which is tasteless be eaten without salt,
or is there any flavor in the juice of mallows?[b]
7 My appetite refuses to touch them;
they are like food that is loathsome to me.[b]

8 "O that I might have my request,
and that God would grant my desire;
9 that it would please God to crush me,
that he would let loose his hand and cut me off!
10 This would be my consolation;
I would even exult[b] in unrelenting pain;
for I have not denied the words of the Holy One.
11 What is my strength, that I should wait?
And what is my end, that I should be patient?
12 Is my strength the strength of stones,
or is my flesh bronze?
13 In truth I have no help in me,
and any resource is driven from me.

14 "Those who withhold[c] kindness from a friend
forsake the fear of the Almighty.[a]
15 My companions are treacherous like a torrent-bed,
like freshets that pass away,
16 that run dark with ice,
turbid with melting snow.
17 In time of heat they disappear;
when it is hot, they vanish from their place.
18 The caravans turn aside from their course;
they go up into the waste, and perish.
19 The caravans of Tema look,
the travelers of Sheba hope.
20 They are disappointed because they were confident;
they come there and are confounded.
21 Such you have now become to me;[d]
you see my calamity, and are afraid.
22 Have I said, 'Make me a gift'?
Or, 'From your wealth offer a bribe for me'?
23 Or, 'Save me from an opponent's hand'?
Or, 'Ransom me from the hand of oppressors'?

24 "Teach me, and I will be silent;
make me understand how I have gone wrong.

a Traditional rendering of Heb *Shaddai* *b* Meaning of Heb uncertain *c* Syr Vg Compare Tg: Meaning of Heb uncertain *d* Cn Compare Gk Syr: Meaning of Heb uncertain

6.1–7.21: Job's response. The traditional explanations given by Eliphaz are inadequate, for even if he were basically right, Job's suffering far outweighs any offenses he might have committed. **6.4:** *Arrows of the Almighty,* see Deut 32.23; Lam 2.4. **6:** *The juice of mallows,* the precise meaning of the Hebrew is uncertain. Context suggests something repulsive to consume, slimy but tasteless. **10:** *Denied* would be more properly translated as "concealed." Job is consoled to know that even under extreme duress he has not concealed that it was God who had decided against him. **11–13:** Contrast Ps 40.1. **15–17:** The *torrent-bed* and *freshets* are the wadis (gulches or arroyos) that sometimes bring flash floods during the rainy seasons but are dry during the summer when water is needed (Jer 15.18). **18–20:** *Tema* and *Sheba,* areas in northern and southwestern parts of Arabia, respectively. **27:** The hollow words of Eliphaz are

25 How forceful are honest words!
But your reproof, what does it reprove?
26 Do you think that you can reprove words,
as if the speech of the desperate were wind?
27 You would even cast lots over the orphan,
and bargain over your friend.

28 "But now, be pleased to look at me;
for I will not lie to your face.
29 Turn, I pray, let no wrong be done.
Turn now, my vindication is at stake.
30 Is there any wrong on my tongue?
Cannot my taste discern calamity?

7 "Do not human beings have a hard service on earth,
and are not their days like the days of a laborer?
2 Like a slave who longs for the shadow,
and like laborers who look for their wages,
3 so I am allotted months of emptiness,
and nights of misery are apportioned to me.
4 When I lie down I say, 'When shall I rise?'
But the night is long,
and I am full of tossing until dawn.
5 My flesh is clothed with worms and dirt;
my skin hardens, then breaks out again.
6 My days are swifter than a weaver's shuttle,
and come to their end without hope.[a]

7 "Remember that my life is a breath;
my eye will never again see good.
8 The eye that beholds me will see me no more;
while your eyes are upon me, I shall be gone.
9 As the cloud fades and vanishes,
so those who go down to Sheol do not come up;
10 they return no more to their houses,
nor do their places know them any more.

11 "Therefore I will not restrain my mouth;
I will speak in the anguish of my spirit;
I will complain in the bitterness of my soul.
12 Am I the Sea, or the Dragon,
that you set a guard over me?
13 When I say, 'My bed will comfort me,
my couch will ease my complaint,'
14 then you scare me with dreams
and terrify me with visions,
15 so that I would choose strangling
and death rather than this body.
16 I loathe my life; I would not live forever.
Let me alone, for my days are a breath.
17 What are human beings, that you make so much of them,
that you set your mind on them,
18 visit them every morning,

a Or *as the thread runs out*

tantamount to moral betrayal. **7.1–6:** Eliphaz had urged patience and focused on hope for the future, but Job states why he cannot be patient: the misery that makes his life like that of a *slave* or day-*laborer.* **6:** Job compares his life to a weaver's shuttle that moves at great speed until the "tiqwah" (the Heb word meaning both *thread* and *hope*) runs out. **7–21:** Job now addresses God directly, reminding the deity that life is all too brief. The implication is that God should intervene before it is too late. **9:** *Sheol,* the abode of the dead. **12:** Reflecting wider ancient Near Eastern mythology, *Sea* and *Dragon* appear in the Bible as symbols of cosmic chaos (see 3.8n.; Ps 74.13). Job implies that God is treating him as that cosmic evil force. **17–18:** A parody of Ps 8. Acknowledging the insignificance of humanity, the psalmist praises God for giving humanity a particularly prominent place in creation. Job, however, ironically points to God's undue focus on him despite his insignificance.

test them every moment?
19 Will you not look away from me for a while,
let me alone until I swallow my spittle?
20 If I sin, what do I do to you, you watcher of humanity?
Why have you made me your target?
Why have I become a burden to you?
21 Why do you not pardon my transgression
and take away my iniquity?
For now I shall lie in the earth;
you will seek me, but I shall not be."

8 Then Bildad the Shuhite answered:
2 "How long will you say these things,
and the words of your mouth be a great wind?
3 Does God pervert justice?
Or does the Almighty[a] pervert the right?
4 If your children sinned against him,
he delivered them into the power of their transgression.
5 If you will seek God
and make supplication to the Almighty,[a]
6 if you are pure and upright,
surely then he will rouse himself for you
and restore to you your rightful place.
7 Though your beginning was small,
your latter days will be very great.
8 "For inquire now of bygone generations,
and consider what their ancestors have found;
9 for we are but of yesterday, and we know nothing,
for our days on earth are but a shadow.
10 Will they not teach you and tell you
and utter words out of their understanding?

11 "Can papyrus grow where there is no marsh?
Can reeds flourish where there is no water?
12 While yet in flower and not cut down,
they wither before any other plant.
13 Such are the paths of all who forget God;
the hope of the godless shall perish.
14 Their confidence is gossamer,
a spider's house their trust.
15 If one leans against its house, it will not stand;
if one lays hold of it, it will not endure.
16 The wicked thrive[b] before the sun,
and their shoots spread over the garden.
17 Their roots twine around the stoneheap;
they live among the rocks.[c]
18 If they are destroyed from their place,

a Traditional rendering of Heb *Shaddai* *b* Heb *He thrives* *c* Gk Vg: Meaning of Heb uncertain

8.1–22: Bildad's first discourse. 2: From this point forward many of the speeches will begin with a criticism of the previous speaker's words (see 11.2–3; 12.2–3; 15.2–6; 16.2–3; 18.2–3; 19.2–3; 20.2–3; 21.2–3; 26.2–4), an expected element in a wisdom dialogue (cf. the "Babylonian Theodicy" [*ANET*, 601–604], a poem whose theme is similar to that of the book of Job). **3–4:** Bildad holds to the orthodox axiom that God does not distort justice (e.g., Ps 33.5; 97.2) and raises the possibility, already considered by Job (1.5), that his children had offended God. **5–7:** See 5.8 (Eliphaz) and 11.13–14 (Zophar). **8–10:** Bildad's trust in the wisdom of *bygone generations* instead of *we* [who] *know nothing* is contrasted with Job's reliance on his own experience (6.4–7,30). **11:** Traditional sayings that illustrate cause and effect are a common feature of wisdom tradition's rhetoric (e.g., Prov 17.14; 26.21). **12–19:** Plant metaphors contrasting the condition of the righteous and the wicked are also common (see Ps 1.3–4; 92.12–14; Jer 17.7–8).

then it will deny them, saying, 'I
have never seen you.'
19 See, these are their happy ways,[a]
and out of the earth still others will
spring.
20 "See, God will not reject a blameless
person,
nor take the hand of evildoers.
21 He will yet fill your mouth with
laughter,
and your lips with shouts of joy.
22 Those who hate you will be clothed
with shame,
and the tent of the wicked will be
no more."

9 Then Job answered:
2 "Indeed I know that this is so;
but how can a mortal be just before
God?
3 If one wished to contend with him,
one could not answer him once in a
thousand.
4 He is wise in heart, and mighty in
strength
—who has resisted him, and
succeeded?—
5 he who removes mountains, and they
do not know it,
when he overturns them in his
anger;
6 who shakes the earth out of its place,
and its pillars tremble;
7 who commands the sun, and it does
not rise;
who seals up the stars;
8 who alone stretched out the heavens
and trampled the waves of the
Sea;[b]
9 who made the Bear and Orion,
the Pleiades and the chambers of
the south;
10 who does great things beyond
understanding,
and marvelous things without
number.
11 Look, he passes by me, and I do not
see him;
he moves on, but I do not perceive
him.
12 He snatches away; who can stop him?
Who will say to him, 'What are
you doing?'

13 "God will not turn back his anger;
the helpers of Rahab bowed
beneath him.
14 How then can I answer him,
choosing my words with him?
15 Though I am innocent, I cannot
answer him;
I must appeal for mercy to my
accuser.[c]
16 If I summoned him and he answered
me,
I do not believe that he would
listen to my voice.
17 For he crushes me with a tempest,
and multiplies my wounds without
cause;
18 he will not let me get my breath,
but fills me with bitterness.

a Meaning of Heb uncertain *b* Or *trampled the back of the sea dragon* *c* Or *for my right*

9.1–10.22: Job's response. Job complains that it is impossible to be vindicated in a lawsuit with God because the deity holds every advantage. **9.1–3:** Eliphaz had cited the axiom that no human can "be righteous" (Heb "yitsdaq") before God (4.17). Job seems to agree, except that he uses the term in a legal sense. No one can *be just* ("yitsdaq"), that is, declared innocent before God because the deity holds every advantage. **4–11:** Idioms used elsewhere to praise God's power (cf. 5.9; Ps 29; Am 5.8–9) are used here to suggest the impossibility of true justice in the face of such overwhelming disparity of power. **9:** *Bear, Orion, Pleiades,* in the translation the familiar names of the constellations derived from Greek tradition are substituted for the Heb terms; cf. 38.31–33; Am 5.8. **11:** Contrast Ex 33.18–23; 34.6; 1 Kings 19.11–13. **12:** Cf. Isa 43.13; 45.9. **13:** *Rahab* is a mythological sea monster symbolizing cosmic chaos (Job 26.12; Isa 51.9; Ps 89.10). **15:** Bildad had called upon Job to plead for mercy with God (8.5), but it is a perverted justice when an innocent victim has to plead for mercy with the accuser. **22:** The moral

19 If it is a contest of strength, he is the
strong one!
If it is a matter of justice, who can
summon him?[a]
20 Though I am innocent, my own
mouth would condemn me;
though I am blameless, he would
prove me perverse.
21 I am blameless; I do not know myself;
I loathe my life.
22 It is all one; therefore I say,
he destroys both the blameless and
the wicked.
23 When disaster brings sudden death,
he mocks at the calamity[b] of the
innocent.
24 The earth is given into the hand of
the wicked;
he covers the eyes of its judges—
if it is not he, who then is it?

25 "My days are swifter than a runner;
they flee away, they see no good.
26 They go by like skiffs of reed,
like an eagle swooping on the prey.
27 If I say, 'I will forget my complaint;
I will put off my sad countenance
and be of good cheer,'
28 I become afraid of all my suffering,
for I know you will not hold me
innocent.
29 I shall be condemned;
why then do I labor in vain?
30 If I wash myself with soap
and cleanse my hands with lye,
31 yet you will plunge me into filth,
and my own clothes will abhor me.
32 For he is not a mortal, as I am, that I
might answer him,
that we should come to trial
together.
33 There is no umpire[c] between us,
who might lay his hand on us both.
34 If he would take his rod away from
me,
and not let dread of him terrify me,
35 then I would speak without fear of
him,
for I know I am not what I am
thought to be.[d]

10 "I loathe my life;
I will give free utterance to my
complaint;
I will speak in the bitterness of my
soul.
2 I will say to God, Do not condemn
me;
let me know why you contend
against me.
3 Does it seem good to you to oppress,
to despise the work of your hands
and favor the schemes of the
wicked?
4 Do you have eyes of flesh?
Do you see as humans see?
5 Are your days like the days of
mortals,
or your years like human years,
6 that you seek out my iniquity
and search for my sin,
7 although you know that I am not
guilty,
and there is no one to deliver out
of your hand?
8 Your hands fashioned and made me;
and now you turn and destroy
me.[e]
9 Remember that you fashioned me like
clay;
and will you turn me to dust again?

a Compare Gk: Heb *me* *b* Meaning of Heb uncertain *c* Another reading is *Would that there were an umpire* *d* Cn: Heb *for I am not so in myself* *e* Cn Compare Gk Syr: Heb *made me together all around, and you destroy me*

distinction between the righteous and the wicked was fundamental to ancient Israelite thought (Ps 1.6; 7.8–9; 9.4–5). To claim that God destroys both is to deny that a moral order exists. **26:** *Eagle*, probably "vulture." **33–35:** The *umpire* or arbitrator (Heb "mokhiaḥ") was a figure in Israelite dispute resolution who apparently functioned "in the gate" (Isa 29.21; Am 5.10), i.e., where much of a town's public business was conducted. Independency and impartiality were essential if the "mokhiaḥ" was to function properly. **10.4–7:** Elsewhere (e.g., 1 Sam 16.7; Ps 139.2–6) God is assumed to have effortless and complete knowledge of persons. **9:** Cf. 33.6; Isa 64.8; Gen 2.7; 3.19. **10:** The cheese-making imagery here

10 Did you not pour me out like milk
and curdle me like cheese?
11 You clothed me with skin and flesh,
and knit me together with bones
and sinews.
12 You have granted me life and
steadfast love,
and your care has preserved my
spirit.
13 Yet these things you hid in your
heart;
I know that this was your purpose.
14 If I sin, you watch me,
and do not acquit me of my
iniquity.
15 If I am wicked, woe to me!
If I am righteous, I cannot lift up
my head,
for I am filled with disgrace
and look upon my affliction.
16 Bold as a lion you hunt me;
you repeat your exploits against
me.
17 You renew your witnesses against me,
and increase your vexation toward
me;
you bring fresh troops against me.[a]

18 "Why did you bring me forth from
the womb?
Would that I had died before any
eye had seen me,
19 and were as though I had not been,
carried from the womb to the
grave.
20 Are not the days of my life few?[b]
Let me alone, that I may find a
little comfort[c]
21 before I go, never to return,
to the land of gloom and deep
darkness,
22 the land of gloom[d] and chaos,
where light is like darkness."

11 Then Zophar the Naamathite answered:
2 "Should a multitude of words go
unanswered,
and should one full of talk be
vindicated?
3 Should your babble put others to
silence,
and when you mock, shall no one
shame you?
4 For you say, 'My conduct[e] is pure,
and I am clean in God's[f] sight.'
5 But O that God would speak,
and open his lips to you,
6 and that he would tell you the secrets
of wisdom!
For wisdom is many-sided.[g]
Know then that God exacts of you
less than your guilt deserves.

7 "Can you find out the deep things of
God?
Can you find out the limit of the
Almighty?[h]
8 It is higher than heaven[i]—what can
you do?

a Cn Compare Gk: Heb *toward me; changes and a troop are with me* *b* Cn Compare Gk Syr: Heb *Are not my days few? Let him cease!* *c* Heb *that I may brighten up a little* *d* Heb *gloom as darkness, deep darkness* *e* Gk: Heb *teaching* *f* Heb *your* *g* Meaning of Heb uncertain *h* Traditional rendering of Heb *Shaddai* *i* Heb *The heights of heaven*

is possibly a metaphor for the formation of the embryo, pictured as a congealing of seminal fluids (cf. Ps 139.13–16; Wis 7.2). **18–22:** Job again expresses preference for death or nonexistence (cf. 3.11–22; 7.16,21). Here, however, he describes death in negative terms.

11.1–20: Zophar's first discourse. 2: Picking up on Job's complaint that he cannot "be in the right" ("yitsdaq," see 9.2), Zophar argues that one who is as full of talk as Job cannot *be vindicated* ("yitsdaq"). Whereas Job uses the term in the legal sense, Zophar uses it in the broader sense employed in the wisdom tradition, which emphasizes prudence and restraint in speaking. **4:** As NRSV has it (emending on the basis of the Greek), Job had been claiming purity of *conduct.* The Heb text suggests, however, that what is at issue to Zophar is the purity of doctrine (Heb "leqaḥ"). Zophar is focused not on the reality of Job's experience but on the incorrectness of Job's doctrine. **6:** Since God is unquestionably wise, Job must be suffering because he is guilty. **10:** God is portrayed as an itinerant judge who freely imprisons and

Deeper than Sheol—what can you
know?
9 Its measure is longer than the earth,
and broader than the sea.
10 If he passes through, and imprisons,
and assembles for judgment, who
can hinder him?
11 For he knows those who are
worthless;
when he sees iniquity, will he not
consider it?
12 But a stupid person will get
understanding,
when a wild ass is born human.[a]

13 "If you direct your heart rightly,
you will stretch out your hands
toward him.
14 If iniquity is in your hand, put it far
away,
and do not let wickedness reside in
your tents.
15 Surely then you will lift up your face
without blemish;
you will be secure, and will not
fear.
16 You will forget your misery;
you will remember it as waters that
have passed away.
17 And your life will be brighter than the
noonday;
its darkness will be like the
morning.
18 And you will have confidence,
because there is hope;
you will be protected[b] and take
your rest in safety.
19 You will lie down, and no one will
make you afraid;
many will entreat your favor.
20 But the eyes of the wicked will fail;
all way of escape will be lost to
them,
and their hope is to breathe their
last."

12 Then Job answered:
2 "No doubt you are the people,
and wisdom will die with you.
3 But I have understanding as well as
you;
I am not inferior to you.
Who does not know such things as
these?
4 I am a laughingstock to my friends;
I, who called upon God and he
answered me,
a just and blameless man, I am a
laughingstock.
5 Those at ease have contempt for
misfortune,[a]
but it is ready for those whose feet
are unstable.
6 The tents of robbers are at peace,
and those who provoke God are
secure,
who bring their god in their hands.[c]

7 "But ask the animals, and they will
teach you;

a Meaning of Heb uncertain *b* Or *you will look around* *c* Or *whom God brought forth by his hand;* Meaning of Heb uncertain

assembles the court for judgment. **13–20:** To "direct the heart" is the idiom that Rabbinic Judaism used to describe the meditative preparation for prayer (cf. 5.8; 8.5–6a).

12.1–14.22: Job's response. Job addresses first his friends (12.1–13.19), then God (13.20–14.22). **12.2:** In this bitter sarcasm, Job implies that his friends are effectively killing wisdom. **4:** The Heb text is difficult and may be misleadingly translated. Apart from the first *I am,* all the other first-person references in this verse are either third-person in the Hebrew or completely absent. The passage lists the names that Job's mockers use of him: "a laughing stock to his friends," "one who calls on God and he answered him," "a just and blameless man," "a laughing stock." **6:** The last phrase, *who bring their god in their hands,* may be better translated as "those whom God brings by his hand." The point is that the wicked seem to be favored by God. The *hand* of God here anticipates the mention of the deity's hand in vv. 9–10. **7–9:** Zophar wishes for the mysteries of wisdom to be revealed to Job (11.6), but Job points out that nature already reveals that God is the one responsible for what is happening (cf. Isa 41.20). Here

the birds of the air, and they will
tell you;
8 ask the plants of the earth,[a] and they
will teach you;
and the fish of the sea will declare
to you.
9 Who among all these does not know
that the hand of the LORD has done
this?
10 In his hand is the life of every living
thing
and the breath of every human
being.
11 Does not the ear test words
as the palate tastes food?
12 Is wisdom with the aged,
and understanding in length of
days?

13 "With God[b] are wisdom and
strength;
he has counsel and understanding.
14 If he tears down, no one can rebuild;
if he shuts someone in, no one can
open up.
15 If he withholds the waters, they dry
up;
if he sends them out, they
overwhelm the land.
16 With him are strength and wisdom;
the deceived and the deceiver are
his.
17 He leads counselors away stripped,
and makes fools of judges.
18 He looses the sash of kings,
and binds a waistcloth on their
loins.
19 He leads priests away stripped,
and overthrows the mighty.
20 He deprives of speech those who are
trusted,
and takes away the discernment of
the elders.
21 He pours contempt on princes,
and looses the belt of the strong.
22 He uncovers the deeps out of
darkness,
and brings deep darkness to light.
23 He makes nations great, then destroys
them;
he enlarges nations, then leads them
away.
24 He strips understanding from the
leaders[c] of the earth,
and makes them wander in a
pathless waste.
25 They grope in the dark without light;
he makes them stagger like a
drunkard.

13 "Look, my eye has seen all this,
my ear has heard and understood
it.
2 What you know, I also know;
I am not inferior to you.
3 But I would speak to the Almighty,[d]
and I desire to argue my case with
God.
4 As for you, you whitewash with lies;
all of you are worthless physicians.
5 If you would only keep silent,
that would be your wisdom!
6 Hear now my reasoning,
and listen to the pleadings of my
lips.
7 Will you speak falsely for God,
and speak deceitfully for him?
8 Will you show partiality toward him,
will you plead the case for God?
9 Will it be well with you when he
searches you out?
Or can you deceive him, as one
person deceives another?
10 He will surely rebuke you
if in secret you show partiality.
11 Will not his majesty terrify you,

a Or *speak to the earth* *b* Heb *him* *c* Heb adds *of the people* *d* Traditional rendering of Heb *Shaddai*

is the only place in the poetic dialogues where the deity is called by the name *the LORD*. **14–25:** A parody of a hymn. Compare 21a and 24b with Ps 107.40. See also Isa 44.24–28; Dan 2.20–23. **13.1–12:** Job wants to bring his case directly to God. Several expressions in vv. 6–8 suggest legal terminology (e.g., *pleadings, speak falsely, plead the case*). **13–19:** In contrast to his friends, Job would risk his life in

and the dread of him fall upon
you?
12 Your maxims are proverbs of ashes,
your defenses are defenses of
clay.

13 "Let me have silence, and I will
speak,
and let come on me what may.
14 I will take my flesh in my teeth,
and put my life in my hand.[a]
15 See, he will kill me; I have no hope;[b]
but I will defend my ways to his
face.
16 This will be my salvation,
that the godless shall not come
before him.
17 Listen carefully to my words,
and let my declaration be in your
ears.
18 I have indeed prepared my case;
I know that I shall be vindicated.
19 Who is there that will contend with
me?
For then I would be silent and die.
20 Only grant two things to me,
then I will not hide myself from
your face:
21 withdraw your hand far from me,
and do not let dread of you terrify
me.
22 Then call, and I will answer;
or let me speak, and you reply to
me.
23 How many are my iniquities and my
sins?
Make me know my transgression
and my sin.
24 Why do you hide your face,
and count me as your enemy?
25 Will you frighten a windblown leaf
and pursue dry chaff?
26 For you write bitter things against
me,
and make me reap[c] the iniquities
of my youth.
27 You put my feet in the stocks,
and watch all my paths;
you set a bound to the soles of my
feet.
28 One wastes away like a rotten thing,
like a garment that is moth-eaten.

14 "A mortal, born of woman, few of
days and full of trouble,
2 comes up like a flower and withers,
flees like a shadow and does not
last.
3 Do you fix your eyes on such a one?
Do you bring me into judgment
with you?
4 Who can bring a clean thing out of
an unclean?
No one can.
5 Since their days are determined,
and the number of their months is
known to you,
and you have appointed the bounds
that they cannot pass,
6 look away from them, and desist,[d]
that they may enjoy, like laborers,
their days.

7 "For there is hope for a tree,
if it is cut down, that it will sprout
again,
and that its shoots will not cease.
8 Though its root grows old in the
earth,
and its stump dies in the ground,

a Gk: Heb *Why should I take . . . in my hand?*
b Or *Though he kill me, yet I will trust in him*
c Heb *inherit* *d* Cn: Heb *that they may desist*

speaking honestly about God. Here, too, his language contains legal expressions (vv. 17–19). **15:** The traditional translation of the verse (see note *b*) is based on an alternate reading of the Hebrew. **20:** Job begins to address God, appealing to God to let him make his case without intimidation. **24:** *Enemy,* see 1.1n. **26:** The *bitter things* written against Job perhaps refer to aspects of his sentence, which he deduces to have been written on account of offenses he committed as a *youth* (cf. Ps 25.7). **14.1:** The expression *born of woman* is simply a synonym for any human being (see 15.14). Nothing is implied about the weakness or impurity of womanhood. **2:** Cf. Ps 103.15–16; Isa 40.6–8. **7–10:** Job contests the traditional analogy between the regenerative power of plants and human beings (cf. Ps 1.3; 92.12–15; Jer 17.7–8).

9 yet at the scent of water it will bud
and put forth branches like a young plant.
10 But mortals die, and are laid low;
humans expire, and where are they?
11 As waters fail from a lake,
and a river wastes away and dries up,
12 so mortals lie down and do not rise again;
until the heavens are no more, they will not awake
or be roused out of their sleep.
13 O that you would hide me in Sheol,
that you would conceal me until your wrath is past,
that you would appoint me a set time, and remember me!
14 If mortals die, will they live again?
All the days of my service I would wait
until my release should come.
15 You would call, and I would answer you;
you would long for the work of your hands.
16 For then you would not[a] number my steps,
you would not keep watch over my sin;
17 my transgression would be sealed up in a bag,
and you would cover over my iniquity.
18 "But the mountain falls and crumbles away,
and the rock is removed from its place;
19 the waters wear away the stones;
the torrents wash away the soil of the earth;
so you destroy the hope of mortals.
20 You prevail forever against them, and they pass away;
you change their countenance, and send them away.
21 Their children come to honor, and they do not know it;
they are brought low, and it goes unnoticed.
22 They feel only the pain of their own bodies,
and mourn only for themselves."

15 Then Eliphaz the Temanite answered:
2 "Should the wise answer with windy knowledge,
and fill themselves with the east wind?
3 Should they argue in unprofitable talk,
or in words with which they can do no good?
4 But you are doing away with the fear of God,
and hindering meditation before God.
5 For your iniquity teaches your mouth,
and you choose the tongue of the crafty.
6 Your own mouth condemns you, and not I;
your own lips testify against you.

7 "Are you the firstborn of the human race?

a Syr: Heb lacks *not*

11: When lakes and rivers "die" as a result of geological disturbances, they remain dry forever. **13:** Since "those who go down to Sheol [the abode of the dead] do not come up" (7.9), Job is here apparently imagining that God could somehow hide him alive in Sheol until God's anger subsided. **16:** Instead of *you would not number my steps,* one should read with the Heb text, "you number my steps." God would pay close attention to Job's steps, but not observe Job's sins. **18–20:** Hope is likened to a mountain that has been eroded by none other than God.

15.1–35: Eliphaz's second discourse. 2–3: Eliphaz had begun diplomatically in his first discourse (4.1–4), but now he is blunt, comparing Job's arguments to the *east wind,* the oppressively hot wind from the desert. **4:** *Fear of God,* a Heb idiom for the respect and awe due to the deity (see Prov 1.7). Thus Job is accused of being utterly irreligious and undermining religion. **7–8:** Job had argued on the basis of his

Were you brought forth before the
hills?
8 Have you listened in the council of
God?
And do you limit wisdom to
yourself?
9 What do you know that we do not
know?
What do you understand that is not
clear to us?
10 The gray-haired and the aged are on
our side,
those older than your father.
11 Are the consolations of God too small
for you,
or the word that deals gently with
you?
12 Why does your heart carry you
away,
and why do your eyes flash,[a]
13 so that you turn your spirit against
God,
and let such words go out of your
mouth?
14 What are mortals, that they can be
clean?
Or those born of woman, that they
can be righteous?
15 God puts no trust even in his holy
ones,
and the heavens are not clean in his
sight;
16 how much less one who is
abominable and corrupt,
one who drinks iniquity like water!

17 "I will show you; listen to me;
what I have seen I will declare—
18 what sages have told,
and their ancestors have not
hidden,
19 to whom alone the land was given,
and no stranger passed among
them.
20 The wicked writhe in pain all their
days,
through all the years that are laid
up for the ruthless.
21 Terrifying sounds are in their ears;
in prosperity the destroyer will
come upon them.
22 They despair of returning from
darkness,
and they are destined for the
sword.
23 They wander abroad for bread,
saying, 'Where is it?'
They know that a day of darkness
is ready at hand;
24 distress and anguish terrify them;
they prevail against them, like a
king prepared for battle.
25 Because they stretched out their hands
against God,
and bid defiance to the Almighty,[b]
26 running stubbornly against him
with a thick-bossed shield;
27 because they have covered their faces
with their fat,
and gathered fat upon their loins,
28 they will live in desolate cities,
in houses that no one should
inhabit,
houses destined to become heaps of
ruins;

a Meaning of Heb uncertain *b* Traditional rendering of Heb *Shaddai*

personal experience, but Eliphaz now asks if Job considers himself the archetypal mortal, or if he has been privy to the deliberations in the divine council (cf. 1 Kings 22.19–22; Jer 23.18,21–22; Am 3.7). **10:** Instead of relying on an individual's experience, Eliphaz would prefer to turn to the traditions passed down through the generations (cf. Ps 78.1–4). **14–16:** No mortal can claim to be perfectly pure, nor can the heavenly beings (see 4.17–19; 25.4–6). **17–19:** It is not clear to what tradition Eliphaz refers when he appeals to the ancestors at a time when no stranger was present, though clearly his claim is that the tradition in which he stands is authentic and orthodox. **20–35:** Eliphaz's speech is the first of three in which the friends argue that the wicked necessarily come to a bad end because evil is ultimately subject to divine punishment and hence necessarily self-destructive (see 18.5–21; 20.5–29). **27:** The meaning of the verse is clearer if one takes the Heb particle at the beginning to mean "although" (rather than *because*) and reads the verse with what follows. Despite their surfeit, the rich will end up impoverished.

29 they will not be rich, and their wealth
will not endure,
nor will they strike root in the
earth;[a]
30 they will not escape from darkness;
the flame will dry up their shoots,
and their blossom[b] will be swept
away[c] by the wind.
31 Let them not trust in emptiness,
deceiving themselves;
for emptiness will be their
recompense.
32 It will be paid in full before their
time,
and their branch will not be green.
33 They will shake off their unripe
grape, like the vine,
and cast off their blossoms, like the
olive tree.
34 For the company of the godless is
barren,
and fire consumes the tents of
bribery.
35 They conceive mischief and bring
forth evil
and their heart prepares deceit."

16 Then Job answered:
2 "I have heard many such
things;
miserable comforters are you all.
3 Have windy words no limit?
Or what provokes you that you
keep on talking?
4 I also could talk as you do,
if you were in my place;
I could join words together against
you,
and shake my head at you.
5 I could encourage you with my
mouth,
and the solace of my lips would
assuage your pain.

6 "If I speak, my pain is not assuaged,
and if I forbear, how much of it
leaves me?
7 Surely now God has worn me out;
he has[d] made desolate all my
company.
8 And he has[d] shriveled me up,
which is a witness against me;
my leanness has risen up against me,
and it testifies to my face.
9 He has torn me in his wrath, and
hated me;
he has gnashed his teeth at me;
my adversary sharpens his eyes
against me.
10 They have gaped at me with their
mouths;
they have struck me insolently on
the cheek;
they mass themselves together
against me.
11 God gives me up to the ungodly,
and casts me into the hands of the
wicked.
12 I was at ease, and he broke me in
two;
he seized me by the neck and
dashed me to pieces;
he set me up as his target;
13 his archers surround me.
He slashes open my kidneys, and
shows no mercy;
he pours out my gall on the
ground.
14 He bursts upon me again and again;
he rushes at me like a warrior.
15 I have sewed sackcloth upon my skin,
and have laid my strength in the
dust.
16 My face is red with weeping,

a Vg: Meaning of Heb uncertain *b* Gk: Heb *mouth*
c Cn: Heb *will depart* *d* Heb *you have*

16.1–17.16: Job's response. 16.1–5: Job regards the words and gestures of his friends as nothing more than rote responses to pain. As one familiar with the tradition, he could offer the same tokens of consolation to them if he were in their place and they in his. **9–17:** Descriptions of divine violence occur in psalms of lament (e.g., Ps 38.1–8), but the intensity of Job's account is unusual (cf. Lam 3.1–20). **10–11:** In traditional laments the victim prays for rescue from the *wicked* (e.g., Ps 3.7; 17.9–13; 71.4); here God has joined them in their attacks on Job. **18:** Job portrays himself as a murder victim whose innocent blood has been shed and now demands vindication (cf. Gen 4.10; 9.5–6). **19:** Job seeks a

and deep darkness is on my eyelids,
17 though there is no violence in my hands,
and my prayer is pure.

18 "O earth, do not cover my blood;
let my outcry find no resting place.
19 Even now, in fact, my witness is in heaven,
and he that vouches for me is on high.
20 My friends scorn me;
my eye pours out tears to God,
21 that he would maintain the right of a mortal with God,
as[a] one does for a neighbor.
22 For when a few years have come,
I shall go the way from which I shall not return.

17 My spirit is broken, my days are extinct,
the grave is ready for me.
2 Surely there are mockers around me,
and my eye dwells on their provocation.

3 "Lay down a pledge for me with yourself;
who is there that will give surety for me?
4 Since you have closed their minds to understanding,
therefore you will not let them triumph.
5 Those who denounce friends for reward—
the eyes of their children will fail.

6 "He has made me a byword of the peoples,
and I am one before whom people spit.
7 My eye has grown dim from grief,
and all my members are like a shadow.
8 The upright are appalled at this,
and the innocent stir themselves up against the godless.
9 Yet the righteous hold to their way,
and they that have clean hands grow stronger and stronger.
10 But you, come back now, all of you,
and I shall not find a sensible person among you.
11 My days are past, my plans are broken off,
the desires of my heart.
12 They make night into day;
'The light,' they say, 'is near to the darkness.'[b]
13 If I look for Sheol as my house,
if I spread my couch in darkness,
14 if I say to the Pit, 'You are my father,'
and to the worm, 'My mother,' or 'My sister,'
15 where then is my hope?
Who will see my hope?
16 Will it go down to the bars of Sheol?
Shall we descend together into the dust?"

18 Then Bildad the Shuhite answered:
2 "How long will you hunt for words?
Consider, and then we shall speak.
3 Why are we counted as cattle?
Why are we stupid in your sight?
4 You who tear yourself in your anger—
shall the earth be forsaken because of you,

a Syr Vg Tg: Heb *and* *b* Meaning of Heb uncertain

heavenly witness to vouch for him in this case with God (cf. 33.22–26, where Elihu describes an angelic witness/intercessor). **17.3:** NRSV's rendering suggests that Job is asking God to stand surety for him. The Hebrew may, however, be translated more literally, "Set my pledge beside you!" Finding no one else who is willing to stand surety for him, Job offers his own life as a pledge in order to establish his innocence (cf. 13.13–16). **10–16:** Job calls his friends back to face his conditions again and explain how there could really be hope for him. Death is inevitable, and final. **13–14:** *Sheol* and *the Pit* are terms for the abode of the dead.

18.1–21: Bildad's second discourse. 3: Cf. Ps 73.22. **4:** Bildad speaks of Job's action in terms used to

or the rock be removed out of its
place?

5 "Surely the light of the wicked is put
out,
and the flame of their fire does not
shine.
6 The light is dark in their tent,
and the lamp above them is put
out.
7 Their strong steps are shortened,
and their own schemes throw them
down.
8 For they are thrust into a net by their
own feet,
and they walk into a pitfall.
9 A trap seizes them by the heel;
a snare lays hold of them.
10 A rope is hid for them in the ground,
a trap for them in the path.
11 Terrors frighten them on every side,
and chase them at their heels.
12 Their strength is consumed by
hunger,[a]
and calamity is ready for their
stumbling.
13 By disease their skin is consumed,[b]
the firstborn of Death consumes
their limbs.
14 They are torn from the tent in which
they trusted,
and are brought to the king of
terrors.
15 In their tents nothing remains;
sulfur is scattered upon their
habitations.
16 Their roots dry up beneath,
and their branches wither above.
17 Their memory perishes from the
earth,
and they have no name in the
street.
18 They are thrust from light into
darkness,
and driven out of the world.
19 They have no offspring or descendant
among their people,
and no survivor where they used to
live.
20 They of the west are appalled at their
fate,
and horror seizes those of the east.
21 Surely such are the dwellings of the
ungodly,
such is the place of those who do
not know God."

19 Then Job answered:
2 "How long will you torment
me,
and break me in pieces with words?
3 These ten times you have cast
reproach upon me;
are you not ashamed to wrong me?
4 And even if it is true that I have
erred,
my error remains with me.
5 If indeed you magnify yourselves
against me,
and make my humiliation an
argument against me,
6 know then that God has put me in
the wrong,

a Or *Disaster is hungry for them* *b* Cn: Heb *It consumes the limbs of his skin*

describe mauling animals, except that he suggests that the attack is stupidly self-directed: *You . . . tear yourself in . . . anger.* **5–21:** The second of the three poems in which the friends describe the dismal fate of the wicked (see 15.20–35n.; 20.5–29). Bildad's images evoke common wisdom convictions that evil lacks true substance (vv. 5–6) and is ultimately self-defeating (vv. 7–8). See Ps 1.4–6; Prov 26.27. **13:** *The firstborn of Death,* plague. **14:** *The king of terrors,* Death himself. **15:** For *sulfur* as characteristic of divine judgment, see Gen 19.24; Ps 11.6; Isa 34.9; Ezek 38.22. **20:** *They of the west . . . those of the east,* i.e., all peoples.

19.1–29: Job's response. 3: Ten times, not to be taken literally. The expression simply means numerous times (cf. Gen 31.7; Num 14.22). **4:** *My error remains with me* is better translated "my error will lodge with me." Job is saying that the error would no doubt bring its consequences. He is confident, however, that the error is not his but God's. **6:** Bildad suggested that God does not deal crookedly (8.3), but Job insists that God had *put* [him] *in the wrong,* literally dealt crookedly with him. **7–19:** See 16.9–17n.

and closed his net around me.
7 Even when I cry out, 'Violence!' I am not answered;
I call aloud, but there is no justice.
8 He has walled up my way so that I cannot pass,
and he has set darkness upon my paths.
9 He has stripped my glory from me,
and taken the crown from my head.
10 He breaks me down on every side, and I am gone,
he has uprooted my hope like a tree.
11 He has kindled his wrath against me,
and counts me as his adversary.
12 His troops come on together;
they have thrown up siegeworks[a] against me,
and encamp around my tent.

13 "He has put my family far from me,
and my acquaintances are wholly estranged from me.
14 My relatives and my close friends have failed me;
15 the guests in my house have forgotten me;
my serving girls count me as a stranger;
I have become an alien in their eyes.
16 I call to my servant, but he gives me no answer;
I must myself plead with him.
17 My breath is repulsive to my wife;
I am loathsome to my own family.
18 Even young children despise me;
when I rise, they talk against me.
19 All my intimate friends abhor me,
and those whom I loved have turned against me.
20 My bones cling to my skin and to my flesh,
and I have escaped by the skin of my teeth.
21 Have pity on me, have pity on me,
O you my friends,
for the hand of God has touched me!
22 Why do you, like God, pursue me,
never satisfied with my flesh?

23 "O that my words were written down!
O that they were inscribed in a book!
24 O that with an iron pen and with lead
they were engraved on a rock forever!
25 For I know that my Redeemer[b] lives,
and that at the last he[c] will stand upon the earth;[d]
26 and after my skin has been thus destroyed,
then in[e] my flesh I shall see God,[f]
27 whom I shall see on my side,[g]
and my eyes shall behold, and not another.
My heart faints within me!
28 If you say, 'How we will persecute him!'

a Cn: Heb *their way* *b* Or *Vindicator* *c* Or *that he the Last* *d* Heb *dust* *e* Or *without* *f* Meaning of Heb of this verse uncertain *g* Or *for myself*

7: Cf. Jer 20.8; Hab 1.2. **10:** Cf. 14.7–9. **13–20:** The motif of the alienation of the sufferer from friends and family occurs often in laments (see Ps 31.11–13; 38.11; 55.12–14). **20:** Job is so emaciated that he might as well not have escaped. Since teeth have no skin, to escape with the skin of one's teeth is to escape with nothing at all. **23–24:** Job wishes that his complaint could be permanently recorded—on leather (*book*), on metal, and on a rock. **25:** The *Redeemer* or *Vindicator* (see note *b*) is usually the next-of-kin and heir (Lev 25.25; Deut. 25.5–10; Ruth 2.20). Although God is sometimes called "Redeemer" (Ex 6.6; Ps 103.4), Job is not referring here to the deity. He has already called for a mediator to come between him and God (9.33–35) and for a witness who will defend him before God (16.19–21); now he hopes to obtain through a vindicator a direct audience with God. **26–27:** Job insists that even after his *skin* has been *destroyed,* he will *see God* for himself (see note *g*)—from his own *flesh* and with his own *eyes.* **28–29:** Job expects judgment against his accusers.

and, 'The root of the matter is
found in him';
29 be afraid of the sword,
for wrath brings the punishment of
the sword,
so that you may know there is a
judgment."

20 Then Zophar the Naamathite answered:
2 "Pay attention! My thoughts urge me
to answer,
because of the agitation within me.
3 I hear censure that insults me,
and a spirit beyond my
understanding answers me.
4 Do you not know this from of old,
ever since mortals were placed on
earth,
5 that the exulting of the wicked is
short,
and the joy of the godless is but for
a moment?
6 Even though they mount up high as
the heavens,
and their head reaches to the
clouds,
7 they will perish forever like their own
dung;
those who have seen them will say,
'Where are they?'
8 They will fly away like a dream, and
not be found;
they will be chased away like a
vision of the night.
9 The eye that saw them will see them
no more,
nor will their place behold them
any longer.
10 Their children will seek the favor of
the poor,
and their hands will give back their
wealth.
11 Their bodies, once full of youth,
will lie down in the dust with
them.

12 "Though wickedness is sweet in their
mouth,
though they hide it under their
tongues,
13 though they are loath to let it go,
and hold it in their mouths,
14 yet their food is turned in their
stomachs;
it is the venom of asps within them.
15 They swallow down riches and vomit
them up again;
God casts them out of their bellies.
16 They will suck the poison of asps;
the tongue of a viper will kill them.
17 They will not look on the rivers,
the streams flowing with honey and
curds.
18 They will give back the fruit of their
toil,
and will not swallow it down;
from the profit of their trading
they will get no enjoyment.
19 For they have crushed and abandoned
the poor,
they have seized a house that they
did not build.

20 "They knew no quiet in their bellies;
in their greed they let nothing
escape.
21 There was nothing left after they had
eaten;
therefore their prosperity will not
endure.
22 In full sufficiency they will be in
distress;
all the force of misery will come
upon them.
23 To fill their belly to the full

20.1–29: Zophar's second discourse, the third of the poems concerning the fate of the wicked (see 15.15–35n.; 18.5–21). **4:** Zophar, too, appeals to the authority of tradition (see 8.8–10; 15.7–11). **6:** *Their head reaches to the clouds* is reminiscent of the arrogance of those who built the Tower of Babel (Gen 11.1–19; see also Isa 14.13–14; Ezek 31.3; Dan 4.11). **8:** Cf. Ps 73.20. **12:** *Wickedness* is likened to delicious food; cf. Prov 9.17; 20.17; 26.22. **14:** The delicious food will turn out to be putrid, even poisonous. **23:** God, who provided manna from heaven for the hungry (Ex 16.4) *will send his fierce anger* into the bellies of the wicked.

God[a] will send his fierce anger
into them,
and rain it upon them as their
food.[b]
24 They will flee from an iron weapon;
a bronze arrow will strike them
through.
25 It is drawn forth and comes out of
their body,
and the glittering point comes out
of their gall;
terrors come upon them.
26 Utter darkness is laid up for their
treasures;
a fire fanned by no one will devour
them;
what is left in their tent will be
consumed.
27 The heavens will reveal their iniquity,
and the earth will rise up against
them.
28 The possessions of their house will be
carried away,
dragged off in the day of God's[c]
wrath.
29 This is the portion of the wicked from
God,
the heritage decreed for them by
God."

21 Then Job answered:
2 "Listen carefully to my words,
and let this be your consolation.
3 Bear with me, and I will speak;
then after I have spoken, mock on.
4 As for me, is my complaint addressed
to mortals?
Why should I not be impatient?
5 Look at me, and be appalled,
and lay your hand upon your
mouth.
6 When I think of it I am dismayed,
and shuddering seizes my flesh.
7 Why do the wicked live on,
reach old age, and grow mighty in
power?
8 Their children are established in their
presence,
and their offspring before their
eyes.
9 Their houses are safe from fear,
and no rod of God is upon them.
10 Their bull breeds without fail;
their cow calves and never
miscarries.
11 They send out their little ones like a
flock,
and their children dance around.
12 They sing to the tambourine and the
lyre,
and rejoice to the sound of the
pipe.
13 They spend their days in prosperity,
and in peace they go down to
Sheol.
14 They say to God, 'Leave us alone!
We do not desire to know your
ways.
15 What is the Almighty,[d] that we
should serve him?
And what profit do we get if we
pray to him?'
16 Is not their prosperity indeed their
own achievement?[e]
The plans of the wicked are
repugnant to me.
17 "How often is the lamp of the wicked
put out?
How often does calamity come
upon them?
How often does God[a] distribute
pains in his anger?
18 How often are they like straw before
the wind,

a Heb *he* *b* Cn: Meaning of Heb uncertain
c Heb *his* *d* Traditional rendering of Heb *Shaddai*
e Heb *in their hand*

21.1–34: Job's response. Challenging the friends' portrayal of the fate of the wicked (chs 15; 18; 20), Job contends that the wicked do, in fact, escape unscathed. **2:** The noun *consolation* here and the related verb in v. 34 frame the chapter. What the friends offer is not true consolation. **5:** *Lay your hand upon your mouth,* that is, be silent (29.9; Judg 18.19; Prov 30.32; Mic 7.16). **9:** Cf. 9.34. **13:** *Sheol,* the abode of the dead. **17:** Job challenges the notion that the wicked do not live long (cf. 18.5; Prov 13.9; 24.20).

and like chaff that the storm carries
away?
19 You say, 'God stores up their iniquity
for their children.'
Let it be paid back to them, so that
they may know it.
20 Let their own eyes see their
destruction,
and let them drink of the wrath of
the Almighty.[a]
21 For what do they care for their
household after them,
when the number of their months is
cut off?
22 Will any teach God knowledge,
seeing that he judges those that are
on high?
23 One dies in full prosperity,
being wholly at ease and secure,
24 his loins full of milk
and the marrow of his bones moist.
25 Another dies in bitterness of soul,
never having tasted of good.
26 They lie down alike in the dust,
and the worms cover them.

27 "Oh, I know your thoughts,
and your schemes to wrong me.
28 For you say, 'Where is the house of
the prince?
Where is the tent in which the
wicked lived?'
29 Have you not asked those who travel
the roads,
and do you not accept their
testimony,
30 that the wicked are spared in the day
of calamity,
and are rescued in the day of
wrath?
31 Who declares their way to their face,
and who repays them for what they
have done?
32 When they are carried to the grave,
a watch is kept over their tomb.
33 The clods of the valley are sweet to
them;
everyone will follow after,
and those who went before are
innumerable.
34 How then will you comfort me with
empty nothings?
There is nothing left of your
answers but falsehood."

22 Then Eliphaz the Temanite answered:
2 "Can a mortal be of use to God?
Can even the wisest be of service to
him?
3 Is it any pleasure to the Almighty[a] if
you are righteous,
or is it gain to him if you make
your ways blameless?
4 Is it for your piety that he reproves
you,
and enters into judgment with you?
5 Is not your wickedness great?
There is no end to your iniquities.
6 For you have exacted pledges from
your family for no reason,
and stripped the naked of their
clothing.

a Traditional rendering of Heb *Shaddai*

18: Job disputes the axiom that the wicked are *straw before the wind* or *like chaff that the storm carries away* (Ps 1.4; 35.5). **19:** *You say* is not in the Hebrew; Job is quoting his accusers or citing a hypothetical argument that they might use (see v. 28). **22:** Job cites the axiom that knowledge is not lacking for God (cf. Isa 40.13–14), who even *judges those that are on high,* perhaps a reference to celestial beings (cf. Ps 82). **23–26:** Despite God's complete knowledge (v. 22), people are subjected to completely different fates. **28:** These words encapsulate the argument one finds in 8.14–15; 15.34; 18.15–21; 20.26–28. **32:** The wicked are, ironically, honorably interred (cf. Eccl 8.10).

22.1–30: Eliphaz's third discourse. Specific accusations are now leveled at Job. **2–3:** Job had suggested that the wicked had dismissed piety as an unprofitable enterprise (21.5). Eliphaz now defends God, maintaining that the deity has no need of any mortal and does not profit from anyone's piety. **6–9:** The specific charges leveled against Job are crimes perpetrated by the rich: avarice and callousness to the needs of the poor. **12–14:** The claim that God is too far removed to know what is happening on earth is

7 You have given no water to the weary
to drink,
and you have withheld bread from
the hungry.
8 The powerful possess the land,
and the favored live in it.
9 You have sent widows away
empty-handed,
and the arms of the orphans you
have crushed.[a]
10 Therefore snares are around you,
and sudden terror overwhelms
you,
11 or darkness so that you cannot see;
a flood of water covers you.

12 "Is not God high in the heavens?
See the highest stars, how lofty they
are!
13 Therefore you say, 'What does God
know?
Can he judge through the deep
darkness?
14 Thick clouds enwrap him, so that he
does not see,
and he walks on the dome of
heaven.'
15 Will you keep to the old way
that the wicked have trod?
16 They were snatched away before their
time;
their foundation was washed away
by a flood.
17 They said to God, 'Leave us alone,'
and 'What can the Almighty[b] do
to us?'[c]
18 Yet he filled their houses with good
things—
but the plans of the wicked are
repugnant to me.
19 The righteous see it and are glad;
the innocent laugh them to scorn,
20 saying, 'Surely our adversaries are cut
off,
and what they left, the fire has
consumed.'

21 "Agree with God,[d] and be at peace;
in this way good will come to you.
22 Receive instruction from his mouth,
and lay up his words in your heart.
23 If you return to the Almighty,[b] you
will be restored,
if you remove unrighteousness from
your tents,
24 if you treat gold like dust,
and gold of Ophir like the stones of
the torrent-bed,
25 and if the Almighty[b] is your gold
and your precious silver,
26 then you will delight yourself in the
Almighty,[b]
and lift up your face to God.
27 You will pray to him, and he will
hear you,
and you will pay your vows.
28 You will decide on a matter, and it
will be established for you,
and light will shine on your ways.
29 When others are humiliated, you say
it is pride;
for he saves the humble.
30 He will deliver even those who are
guilty;
they will escape because of the
cleanness of your hands."[e]

23 Then Job answered:
2 "Today also my complaint is
bitter;[f]

a Gk Syr Tg Vg: Heb *were crushed* *b* Traditional rendering of Heb *Shaddai* *c* Gk Syr: Heb *them* *d* Heb *him* *e* Meaning of Heb uncertain *f* Syr Vg Tg: Heb *rebellious*

elsewhere attributed to the wicked (Ps 10.4,11,13; Ezek 8.12). Here Eliphaz appears to be distorting the arguments of Job, who had in fact only affirmed God's ability to see and to know what is on earth (cf. 7.19–20; 14.3; 16.9). **17–18:** Job's characterization of the attitude of the wicked (21.14–16) is taken out of context and represented as Job's own perspective. **24:** There is a pun at play here involving the words for *gold* ("batser") and *like the stones* ("betsur") on the one hand, and *dust* ("ʿapar") and *Ophir* ("ʾopir") on the other. Job is expected to treat his wealth as valueless and to replace it with piety.

23.1–24.17: Job's response. Job seems to ignore all that Eliphaz has said and delves, instead, into his own thoughts. **23.2:** *My complaint is bitter* reflects the reading of some ancient textual witnesses (cf. also

his[a] hand is heavy despite my
groaning.
3 Oh, that I knew where I might find
him,
that I might come even to his
dwelling!
4 I would lay my case before him,
and fill my mouth with arguments.
5 I would learn what he would answer
me,
and understand what he would say
to me.
6 Would he contend with me in the
greatness of his power?
No; but he would give heed to me.
7 There an upright person could reason
with him,
and I should be acquitted forever
by my judge.

8 "If I go forward, he is not there;
or backward, I cannot perceive
him;
9 on the left he hides, and I cannot
behold him;
I turn[b] to the right, but I cannot
see him.
10 But he knows the way that I take;
when he has tested me, I shall come
out like gold.
11 My foot has held fast to his steps;
I have kept his way and have not
turned aside.
12 I have not departed from the
commandment of his lips;
I have treasured in[c] my bosom the
words of his mouth.
13 But he stands alone and who can
dissuade him?
What he desires, that he does.
14 For he will complete what he
appoints for me;
and many such things are in his
mind.
15 Therefore I am terrified at his
presence;
when I consider, I am in dread of
him.
16 God has made my heart faint;
the Almighty[d] has terrified me;
17 If only I could vanish in darkness,
and thick darkness would cover my
face![e]

24 "Why are times not kept by the
Almighty,[d]
and why do those who know him
never see his days?
2 The wicked[f] remove landmarks;
they seize flocks and pasture them.
3 They drive away the donkey of the
orphan;
they take the widow's ox for a
pledge.
4 They thrust the needy off the road;
the poor of the earth all hide
themselves.
5 Like wild asses in the desert
they go out to their toil,
scavenging in the wasteland
food for their young.
6 They reap in a field not their own
and they glean in the vineyard of
the wicked.

a Gk Syr: Heb *my* *b* Syr Vg: Heb *he turns* *c* Gk Vg: Heb *from* *d* Traditional rendering of Heb *Shaddai* *e* Or *But I am not destroyed by the darkness; he has concealed the thick darkness from me* *f* Gk: Heb *they*

7.11). The Heb text, however, suggests that Job's complaint is "contentious" or, perhaps, "defiant." The latter reading is probably correct, although the choice of the word here may reflect both defiance and bitterness. **8:** *Forward, backward, left,* and *right* designate the four cardinal directions: east, west, south, and north, respectively. **17:** *If only I could vanish in darkness* is based on a slight emendation of the Hebrew. The text should, however, be taken at face value to mean: "Nevertheless, I have not been silent because of darkness or because of the gloom that has covered my face." **24.1:** God knows the right times (presumably the times for judgment) but does not seem to abide by them. **2:** *Remove landmarks,* illegally disregard the markers of property boundaries (see Deut 9.14; 27.17; Prov 22.28; 23.10; Hos 5.10). **3:** The *donkey* and the *ox* are essential for the economic well-being of the poor (cf. 1 Sam 12.3). **5:** *Wild asses* inhabited particularly desolate land (39.5–9; Jer 14.6). **10:** The hungry are employed as gatherers at the

7 They lie all night naked, without
clothing,
and have no covering in the cold.
8 They are wet with the rain of the
mountains,
and cling to the rock for want of
shelter.

9 "There are those who snatch the
orphan child from the breast,
and take as a pledge the infant of
the poor.
10 They go about naked, without
clothing;
though hungry, they carry the
sheaves;
11 between their terraces[a] they press out
oil;
they tread the wine presses, but
suffer thirst.
12 From the city the dying groan,
and the throat of the wounded cries
for help;
yet God pays no attention to their
prayer.

13 "There are those who rebel against
the light,
who are not acquainted with its
ways,
and do not stay in its paths.
14 The murderer rises at dusk
to kill the poor and needy,
and in the night is like a thief.
15 The eye of the adulterer also waits for
the twilight,
saying, 'No eye will see me';
and he disguises his face.
16 In the dark they dig through houses;
by day they shut themselves up;
they do not know the light.
17 For deep darkness is morning to all of
them;
for they are friends with the terrors
of deep darkness.

18 "Swift are they on the face of the
waters;
their portion in the land is cursed;
no treader turns toward their
vineyards.
19 Drought and heat snatch away the
snow waters;
so does Sheol those who have
sinned.
20 The womb forgets them;
the worm finds them sweet;
they are no longer remembered;
so wickedness is broken like a tree.

21 "They harm[b] the childless woman,
and do no good to the widow.
22 Yet God[c] prolongs the life of the
mighty by his power;
they rise up when they despair of
life.
23 He gives them security, and they are
supported;
his eyes are upon their ways.
24 They are exalted a little while, and
then are gone;
they wither and fade like the
mallow;[d]
they are cut off like the heads of
grain.
25 If it is not so, who will prove me a
liar,
and show that there is nothing in
what I say?"

25 Then Bildad the Shuhite answered:
2 "Dominion and fear are with
God;[e]

a Meaning of Heb uncertain *b* Gk Tg: Heb *feed on* or *associate with* *c* Heb *he* *d* Gk: Heb *like all others* *e* Heb *him*

plentiful harvest of the wicked. **11:** The thirsty are employed in the production of wine and oil. **18–25:** These verses seem out of place, for they contradict Job's views elsewhere. If Job were the speaker, one should view these sentences as quotations of Job's opponents, or follow some of the ancient versions in interpreting them as expressions of Job's wishes about how things should turn out.

25.1–6: Bildad speaks. The pattern of alternating speeches by Job and his friends is not continued. The conversation has, to some extent at least, broken down. Bildad's speech is uncommonly short (or else

he makes peace in his high heaven.
3 Is there any number to his armies?
Upon whom does his light not arise?
4 How then can a mortal be righteous before God?
How can one born of woman be pure?
5 If even the moon is not bright
and the stars are not pure in his sight,
6 how much less a mortal, who is a maggot,
and a human being, who is a worm!"

26 Then Job answered:
2 "How you have helped one who has no power!
How you have assisted the arm that has no strength!
3 How you have counseled one who has no wisdom,
and given much good advice!
4 With whose help have you uttered words,
and whose spirit has come forth from you?
5 The shades below tremble,
the waters and their inhabitants.
6 Sheol is naked before God,
and Abaddon has no covering.
7 He stretches out Zaphon[a] over the void,
and hangs the earth upon nothing.
8 He binds up the waters in his thick clouds,
and the cloud is not torn open by them.
9 He covers the face of the full moon,
and spreads over it his cloud.
10 He has described a circle on the face of the waters,
at the boundary between light and darkness.
11 The pillars of heaven tremble,
and are astounded at his rebuke.
12 By his power he stilled the Sea;
by his understanding he struck down Rahab.
13 By his wind the heavens were made fair;
his hand pierced the fleeing serpent.
14 These are indeed but the outskirts of his ways;
and how small a whisper do we hear of him!
But the thunder of his power who can understand?"

27 Job again took up his discourse and said:

a Or *the North*

interrupted) and Zophar does not speak again. **2–3:** *He makes peace in his high heaven,* the text is alluding, perhaps, to the deity's establishment of order in heaven with the assistance of the celestial hosts (see Judg 5.20; Ps 68.17–18). The notion of conflict in heaven occurs in many ancient Near Eastern myths and appears in apocalyptic writings (Dan 10.13–14,20–21). **4–6:** See 4.17–21; 15.14–16.

26.1–4: Job interrupts. Job does not address all the friends together, as he has done so far, but speaks directly to Bildad. His words are sarcastic. **4:** Job questions the source of Bildad's advice.

26.5–14: Bildad continues. The ideas in this section do not fit Job's preceding words (vv. 1–4) or his response beginning in 27.2. They are, however, consonant with Bildad's perspective in 25.2–6. **5:** *The shades* are the dead who are now in the netherworld (Ps 88.10; Prov 2.18; 9.18; 21.16; Isa 26.14–19), which is thought to be located beneath the waters (2 Sam 22.5–6; Jon 2.5–6; Ps 88.6–7). **6:** *Sheol* and *Abaddon* are synonymous designations for the abode of the dead (cf. Prov 15.11; 27.20). Here, as elsewhere, both are personified and associated with Death (see Job 28.22; Prov 27.20). **7:** *Zaphon* ("North") is known in mythology as a mountain where the divine council convenes (see Isa 14.13). **8:** The clouds are described as waterskins. **10:** Cf. Prov 8.27. **12–13:** A reference to the divine warrior's defeat of the sea monsters—*Sea, Rahab* (9.13; Ps 89.10; Isa 51.9), *the fleeing serpent* (see Isa 27.1)—that symbolize the forces of cosmic chaos (see also 3.8n.).

27.1–12: Job continues. 1: The introductory formula here and in 29.1 differs from previous notices. Instead of the expected "then Job answered" (6.1; 9.1; 12.1; 16.1; 19.1; 21.1; 23.1; 26.1), the text has

2 "As God lives, who has taken away
my right,
and the Almighty,[a] who has made
my soul bitter,
3 as long as my breath is in me
and the spirit of God is in my
nostrils,
4 my lips will not speak falsehood,
and my tongue will not utter deceit.
5 Far be it from me to say that you are
right;
until I die I will not put away my
integrity from me.
6 I hold fast my righteousness, and will
not let it go;
my heart does not reproach me for
any of my days.

7 "May my enemy be like the wicked,
and may my opponent be like the
unrighteous.
8 For what is the hope of the godless
when God cuts them off,
when God takes away their lives?
9 Will God hear their cry
when trouble comes upon them?
10 Will they take delight in the
Almighty?[a]
Will they call upon God at all
times?
11 I will teach you concerning the hand
of God;
that which is with the Almighty[a] I
will not conceal.
12 All of you have seen it yourselves;
why then have you become
altogether vain?

13 "This is the portion of the wicked
with God,
and the heritage that oppressors
receive from the Almighty:[a]
14 If their children are multiplied, it is
for the sword;
and their offspring have not enough
to eat.
15 Those who survive them the
pestilence buries,
and their widows make no
lamentation.
16 Though they heap up silver like dust,
and pile up clothing like clay—
17 they may pile it up, but the just will
wear it,
and the innocent will divide the
silver.
18 They build their houses like nests,
like booths made by sentinels of the
vineyard.
19 They go to bed with wealth, but will
do so no more;
they open their eyes, and it is gone.
20 Terrors overtake them like a flood;
in the night a whirlwind carries
them off.
21 The east wind lifts them up and they
are gone;
it sweeps them out of their place.
22 It[b] hurls at them without pity;
they flee from its[c] power in
headlong flight.
23 It[b] claps its[c] hands at them,
and hisses at them from its[c] place.

28 "Surely there is a mine for silver,
and a place for gold to be refined.
2 Iron is taken out of the earth,

a Traditional rendering of Heb *Shaddai* *b* Or *He* (that is God) *c* Or *his*

Job again took up his discourse and said (v. 1), suggesting that he is returning to where he had left off (26.1–4). **2:** There is bitter irony in the fact that Job swears by the God who has denied him justice and embittered him. **7–12:** The oath is followed by a curse. **7–23:** The perspective in these verses is a traditional one and much more like what the friends would say rather than what Job would say. Many scholars conjecture, therefore, that this portion is the lost third discourse of Zophar. Alternatively, one may assume that Job is quoting his friends or mimicking their pat answers and hollow declarations. **7:** *My enemy* is a generic reference to any adversary. **11:** *I will teach you,* the Hebrew for *you* is plural here, suggesting that Job is addressing his friends.

28.1–28: A poem on Wisdom. This elegant meditation on Wisdom is not introduced as a speech by Job

and copper is smelted from ore.
3 Miners put[a] an end to darkness,
and search out to the farthest bound
the ore in gloom and deep darkness.
4 They open shafts in a valley away from human habitation;
they are forgotten by travelers,
they sway suspended, remote from people.
5 As for the earth, out of it comes bread;
but underneath it is turned up as by fire.
6 Its stones are the place of sapphires,[b]
and its dust contains gold.

7 "That path no bird of prey knows,
and the falcon's eye has not seen it.
8 The proud wild animals have not trodden it;
the lion has not passed over it.

9 "They put their hand to the flinty rock,
and overturn mountains by the roots.
10 They cut out channels in the rocks,
and their eyes see every precious thing.
11 The sources of the rivers they probe;[c]
hidden things they bring to light.

12 "But where shall wisdom be found?
And where is the place of understanding?
13 Mortals do not know the way to it,[d]
and it is not found in the land of the living.
14 The deep says, 'It is not in me,'
and the sea says, 'It is not with me.'
15 It cannot be gotten for gold,
and silver cannot be weighed out as its price.
16 It cannot be valued in the gold of Ophir,
in precious onyx or sapphire.[b]
17 Gold and glass cannot equal it,
nor can it be exchanged for jewels of fine gold.
18 No mention shall be made of coral or of crystal;
the price of wisdom is above pearls.
19 The chrysolite of Ethiopia[e] cannot compare with it,
nor can it be valued in pure gold.

20 "Where then does wisdom come from?
And where is the place of understanding?
21 It is hidden from the eyes of all living,

a Heb *He puts* *b* Or *lapis lazuli* *c* Gk Vg: Heb *bind* *d* Gk: Heb *its price* *e* Or *Nubia*; Heb *Cush*

or any of the other characters in the book. Since it immediately follows the speech of Job, one might conceivably read it as the continuation of what Job said. Yet, 29.1 has it that Job is returning to his discourse, suggesting that this poem is from a different source. It is best to treat it as an interlude, perhaps a later addition to the book. **1–11:** Human ingenuity makes it possible to find precious minerals and locate their hidden sources, even where the keen eyesight of birds and the free wanderings of wild beasts fail. **9:** *They,* i.e., the human miners (v. 3). **12:** Unlike minerals, which are located in a mine (v. 1 "motsa'", lit. "a coming out place") or some other *place* ("maqom"), Wisdom cannot be *found* ("mts'") in any *place* ("maqom"). **13–24:** The pronouns used of Wisdom may be translated either "it" or "she/her." A personified Wisdom is described as God's companion and partner in creation elsewhere (Prov 8.22–30; Wis 9.9; Sir 24.1–21; Bar 3.9–4.4), and may also be referred to here. **13–14:** *The deep,* the primordial waters that exist under the earth and above the firmament of the sky (Gen 1.1,6–7). *The sea,* the waters that surround dry land (Gen 1.9). Together, they represent the uttermost reaches of the cosmos. See 7.12n.; 26.12n. **15–19:** Wisdom is more precious than metals or jewels (Prov 3.13–15). The negative particle appears seven times in the Heb text, suggesting that Wisdom is absolutely without price. **20–22:** *Abaddon and Death,* see 26.6n. The realm of the dead is often invoked to suggest a most distant and inaccessible place (Ps 139.7–9; Am 9.2–3). In Near Eastern mythology, Death, like the Sea, is a deity

and concealed from the birds of the
air.
22 Abaddon and Death say,
'We have heard a rumor of it with
our ears.'

23 "God understands the way to it,
and he knows its place.
24 For he looks to the ends of the earth,
and sees everything under the
heavens.
25 When he gave to the wind its weight,
and apportioned out the waters by
measure;
26 when he made a decree for the rain,
and a way for the thunderbolt;
27 then he saw it and declared it;
he established it, and searched it
out.
28 And he said to humankind,
'Truly, the fear of the Lord, that is
wisdom;
and to depart from evil is
understanding.'"

29 Job again took up his discourse and
said:
2 "O that I were as in the months of
old,
as in the days when God watched
over me;
3 when his lamp shone over my head,
and by his light I walked through
darkness;
4 when I was in my prime,
when the friendship of God was
upon my tent;
5 when the Almighty[a] was still with
me,
when my children were around me;
6 when my steps were washed with
milk,
and the rock poured out for me
streams of oil!
7 When I went out to the gate of the
city,
when I took my seat in the square,
8 the young men saw me and withdrew,
and the aged rose up and stood;
9 the nobles refrained from talking,
and laid their hands on their
mouths;
10 the voices of princes were hushed,
and their tongues stuck to the roof
of their mouths.
11 When the ear heard, it commended
me,
and when the eye saw, it approved;
12 because I delivered the poor who
cried,
and the orphan who had no helper.
13 The blessing of the wretched came
upon me,
and I caused the widow's heart to
sing for joy.
14 I put on righteousness, and it clothed
me;
my justice was like a robe and a
turban.
15 I was eyes to the blind,
and feet to the lame.
16 I was a father to the needy,
and I championed the cause of the
stranger.
17 I broke the fangs of the unrighteous,
and made them drop their prey
from their teeth.

a Traditional rendering of Heb *Shaddai*

who threatens the cosmic order. **25–27:** As in Prov 8.22–31; Wis 9.9, Wisdom was present at the creation. **26:** Cf. 38.25. **28:** This verse, although perhaps a secondary addition (cf. Ps 111.10; Prov 1.7; 9.10), provides an interpretive key to the entire poem. It makes the point that Wisdom, which is not discoverable by mortals, is about a way of being. The One who knows where Wisdom is to be found instructs mortals that piety, clarified as departure from evil, is Wisdom; cf. 1.1.

29.1–31.40: Job's speech. In this long speech, he longs for the good life he once had (ch 29), laments his present condition (ch 30), and passionately asserts his innocence (ch 31). **29.6:** *My steps were washed with milk . . . streams of oil,* images of abundant blessings (Deut 32.13–14; 33.24; Ps 133). **8:** *The young men saw me and withdrew,* a mark of their deference. **12–17:** A catalogue of the virtuous actions expected of a leader (see Ps 72.12–14). **18:** *Like the phoenix,* a mythical bird thought to rise to a new life from

18 Then I thought, 'I shall die in my
nest,
and I shall multiply my days like
the phoenix;[a]
19 my roots spread out to the waters,
with the dew all night on my
branches;
20 my glory was fresh with me,
and my bow ever new in my hand.'

21 "They listened to me, and waited,
and kept silence for my counsel.
22 After I spoke they did not speak
again,
and my word dropped upon them
like dew.[b]
23 They waited for me as for the rain;
they opened their mouths as for the
spring rain.
24 I smiled on them when they had no
confidence;
and the light of my countenance
they did not extinguish.[c]
25 I chose their way, and sat as chief,
and I lived like a king among his
troops,
like one who comforts mourners.

30 "But now they make sport of me,
those who are younger than I,
whose fathers I would have disdained
to set with the dogs of my flock.
2 What could I gain from the strength
of their hands?
All their vigor is gone.
3 Through want and hard hunger
they gnaw the dry and desolate
ground,
4 they pick mallow and the leaves of
bushes,
and to warm themselves the roots
of broom.
5 They are driven out from society;
people shout after them as after a
thief.
6 In the gullies of wadis they must live,
in holes in the ground, and in the
rocks.
7 Among the bushes they bray;
under the nettles they huddle
together.
8 A senseless, disreputable brood,
they have been whipped out of the
land.

9 "And now they mock me in song;
I am a byword to them.
10 They abhor me, they keep aloof from
me;
they do not hesitate to spit at the
sight of me.
11 Because God has loosed my bowstring
and humbled me,
they have cast off restraint in my
presence.
12 On my right hand the rabble rise up;
they send me sprawling,
and build roads for my ruin.
13 They break up my path,
they promote my calamity;
no one restrains[d] them.
14 As through a wide breach they come;
amid the crash they roll on.
15 Terrors are turned upon me;
my honor is pursued as by the
wind,
and my prosperity has passed away
like a cloud.

16 "And now my soul is poured out
within me;
days of affliction have taken hold
of me.
17 The night racks my bones,
and the pain that gnaws me takes
no rest.

a Or *like sand* *b* Heb lacks *like dew* *c* Meaning of Heb uncertain *d* Cn: Heb *helps*

its ashes. **20:** *Glory* may also be interpreted as "power." *Bow* is a metaphor throughout the ancient Near East for virility. **22:** The words *like dew* are not in the Hebrew, which simply suggests that Job's *word* falls upon them like rain (see v. 23; cf. Judg 5.4; Joel 3.18). **30.1–10:** Contrast Job's words in 24.1–12. Even the outcasts of society now scorn Job. **11:** *Loosed my bowstring,* God has rendered Job defenseless (cf. Ps 18.34). **19:** *Dust and ashes,* here an image of humiliation, elsewhere an image of self-deprecating humility

18 With violence he seizes my garment;[a]
he grasps me by[b] the collar of my tunic.
19 He has cast me into the mire,
and I have become like dust and ashes.
20 I cry to you and you do not answer me;
I stand, and you merely look at me.
21 You have turned cruel to me;
with the might of your hand you persecute me.
22 You lift me up on the wind, you make me ride on it,
and you toss me about in the roar of the storm.
23 I know that you will bring me to death,
and to the house appointed for all living.

24 "Surely one does not turn against the needy,[c]
when in disaster they cry for help.[d]
25 Did I not weep for those whose day was hard?
Was not my soul grieved for the poor?
26 But when I looked for good, evil came;
and when I waited for light, darkness came.
27 My inward parts are in turmoil, and are never still;
days of affliction come to meet me.
28 I go about in sunless gloom;
I stand up in the assembly and cry for help.
29 I am a brother of jackals,
and a companion of ostriches.
30 My skin turns black and falls from me,
and my bones burn with heat.
31 My lyre is turned to mourning,
and my pipe to the voice of those who weep.

31 "I have made a covenant with my eyes;
how then could I look upon a virgin?
2 What would be my portion from God above,
and my heritage from the Almighty[e] on high?
3 Does not calamity befall the unrighteous,
and disaster the workers of iniquity?
4 Does he not see my ways,
and number all my steps?

5 "If I have walked with falsehood,
and my foot has hurried to deceit—
6 let me be weighed in a just balance,
and let God know my integrity!—
7 if my step has turned aside from the way,
and my heart has followed my eyes,
and if any spot has clung to my hands;
8 then let me sow, and another eat;
and let what grows for me be rooted out.

9 "If my heart has been enticed by a woman,
and I have lain in wait at my neighbor's door;
10 then let my wife grind for another,
and let other men kneel over her.
11 For that would be a heinous crime;

a Gk: Heb *my garment is disfigured* *b* Heb *like*
c Heb *ruin* *d* Cn: Meaning of Heb uncertain
e Traditional rendering of Heb *Shaddai*

(Gen 18.27). See Job 42.6. **29:** *Jackals* and *ostriches* are creatures that inhabit desolate places (cf. Isa 34.13; 35.7; Jer 9.11; 10.22; Ps 44.19). **31.1–34:** Job provides a kind of detailed affidavit listing every possible offense that he might be accused of committing and vigorously insisting on his innocence. He is prepared to be judged by the highest legal and ethical standards. **1:** *A covenant with my eyes,* Job is so virtuous that he pledges not to even look at a virgin (cf. Mt 5.28). **8:** *Let me sow . . . another eat,* cf. Lev 26.16; Deut 28.30–31,38–40; Hos 4.10; Mic 6.15). **9:** *Lain in wait at my neighbor's door,* i.e., for the neighbor's wife (cf. Prov 5.8). **10:** The verbs *grind* and *kneel* have sexual overtones. **12:** *Abaddon,* the

that would be a criminal offense;
12 for that would be a fire consuming
down to Abaddon,
and it would burn to the root all
my harvest.

13 "If I have rejected the cause of my
male or female slaves,
when they brought a complaint
against me;
14 what then shall I do when God rises
up?
When he makes inquiry, what shall
I answer him?
15 Did not he who made me in the
womb make them?
And did not one fashion us in the
womb?

16 "If I have withheld anything that the
poor desired,
or have caused the eyes of the
widow to fail,
17 or have eaten my morsel alone,
and the orphan has not eaten from
it—
18 for from my youth I reared the
orphan[a] like a father,
and from my mother's womb I
guided the widow[b]—
19 if I have seen anyone perish for lack
of clothing,
or a poor person without covering,
20 whose loins have not blessed me,
and who was not warmed with the
fleece of my sheep;
21 if I have raised my hand against the
orphan,
because I saw I had supporters at
the gate;
22 then let my shoulder blade fall from
my shoulder,
and let my arm be broken from its
socket.
23 For I was in terror of calamity from
God,
and I could not have faced his
majesty.

24 "If I have made gold my trust,
or called fine gold my confidence;
25 if I have rejoiced because my wealth
was great,
or because my hand had gotten
much;
26 if I have looked at the sun[c] when it
shone,
or the moon moving in splendor,
27 and my heart has been secretly
enticed,
and my mouth has kissed my hand;
28 this also would be an iniquity to be
punished by the judges,
for I should have been false to God
above.

29 "If I have rejoiced at the ruin of those
who hated me,
or exulted when evil overtook
them—
30 I have not let my mouth sin
by asking for their lives with a
curse—
31 if those of my tent ever said,
'O that we might be sated with his
flesh!'[d]—
32 the stranger has not lodged in the
street;
I have opened my doors to the
traveler—
33 if I have concealed my transgressions
as others do,[e]
by hiding my iniquity in my bosom,
34 because I stood in great fear of the
multitude,
and the contempt of families
terrified me,
so that I kept silence, and did not
go out of doors—

a Heb *him* *b* Heb *her* *c* Heb *the light*
d Meaning of Heb uncertain *e* Or *as Adam did*

abode of the dead (see 26.6n.). **26**: *Looked at the sun . . . or the moon,* probably in worship (cf. Deut 4.19; 17.2–3; 2 Kings 21.3–5; 23.5; Jer 8.1–2). **27**: Another reference to illicit worship. **31**: *Sated with his flesh,* in the context of Job's claims to have been hospitable to strangers, may refer to feeding guests; the Hebrew, however, is obscure (see note *d*). **35**: *Here is my signature* or "here is my mark," a reference to

35 O that I had one to hear me!
(Here is my signature! Let the Almighty[a] answer me!)
O, that I had the indictment written by my adversary!
36 Surely I would carry it on my shoulder;
I would bind it on me like a crown;
37 I would give him an account of all my steps;
like a prince I would approach him.

38 "If my land has cried out against me,
and its furrows have wept together;
39 if I have eaten its yield without payment,
and caused the death of its owners;
40 let thorns grow instead of wheat,
and foul weeds instead of barley."

The words of Job are ended.

32 So these three men ceased to answer
Job, because he was righteous in his
own eyes. 2 Then Elihu son of Barachel the
Buzite, of the family of Ram, became an-
gry. He was angry at Job because he justi-
fied himself rather than God; 3 he was an-
gry also at Job's three friends because they
had found no answer, though they had de-
clared Job to be in the wrong.[b] 4 Now Eli-
hu had waited to speak to Job, because they
were older than he. 5 But when Elihu saw
that there was no answer in the mouths of
these three men, he became angry.
6 Elihu son of Barachel the Buzite an-
swered:
"I am young in years,
and you are aged;
therefore I was timid and afraid
to declare my opinion to you.
7 I said, 'Let days speak,
and many years teach wisdom.'
8 But truly it is the spirit in a mortal,
the breath of the Almighty,[a] that makes for understanding.
9 It is not the old[c] that are wise,
nor the aged that understand what is right.

a Traditional rendering of Heb *Shaddai* *b* Another ancient tradition reads *answer, and had put God in the wrong* *c* Gk Syr Vg: Heb *many*

the X-shaped symbol that was the last letter of the Heb alphabet in antiquity. That symbol was used as a mark of exemption from judgment (Ezek 9.4,6). So confident is Job in his own innocence that he asks for a written *indictment* from the one who would bring the charge against him. **40:** The observation that *the words of Job are ended* may be a play on words. The Hebrew for *ended* is built on the same root as the Hebrew for "integrity" and "blameless."

32.1–37.24: Elihu's disputations. Most commentators maintain that these chapters, with their distinctive vocabulary, compositional, and stylistic features, are a later addition to the book. Elihu, the only human character in the book with an Israelite name, is not mentioned in the prologue or epilogue. Job's concluding words in the preceding chapter call for a divine response, which does not come until ch 38, after these intrusive chapters. This secondary addition probably came from someone who was dissatisfied with the conclusion of the book. It is interesting to note the number of times the text speaks of answers. Impatient with the failure of Job's friends to provide compelling answers to Job, Elihu proceeds to engage Job's ideas directly. His arguments, however, are often similar to those of the three friends.

32.1–33.7: Prose and poetic introduction. 32.2: The prose introduction (vv. 1–6) provides details of the speaker's name, patronym, place of origin, and clan affiliation. *Elihu* ("He is God") is a good Israelite name (1 Sam 1.1; 1 Chr 12.20; 26.7; 27.18). *Buzite,* one from Buz, identified as the brother of Uz (see Job 1.1) in Gen 22.21. Buz is also located in northern Arabia (Jer 25.23). *Barachel* ("God has blessed") is attested as a Jewish name in documents from the fifth century BCE. *Ram* is also the name of one of David's ancestors (Ruth 4.19; 1 Chr 2.9–10, 25,27). **3:** There is some evidence that the statement that Job's friends *had declared Job to be in the wrong* originally read "they had put God in the wrong" (see note *b*), but the scribes changed the text for theological reasons. If this is correct, Elihu's view is that Job's friends had, in fact, done God a disservice. **4:** *Elihu had waited to speak* out of respect for elders (cf. 15.10; 29.8; 30.1). **8:** Elihu justifies speaking in spite of his youth. It is *the spirit* that

10 Therefore I say, 'Listen to me;
let me also declare my opinion.'
11 "See, I waited for your words,
I listened for your wise sayings,
while you searched out what to
say.
12 I gave you my attention,
but there was in fact no one that
confuted Job,
no one among you that answered
his words.
13 Yet do not say, 'We have found
wisdom;
God may vanquish him, not a
human.'
14 He has not directed his words against
me,
and I will not answer him with
your speeches.

15 "They are dismayed, they answer no
more;
they have not a word to say.
16 And am I to wait, because they do
not speak,
because they stand there, and
answer no more?
17 I also will give my answer;
I also will declare my opinion.
18 For I am full of words;
the spirit within me constrains me.
19 My heart is indeed like wine that has
no vent;
like new wineskins, it is ready to
burst.
20 I must speak, so that I may find
relief;
I must open my lips and answer.
21 I will not show partiality to any
person
or use flattery toward anyone.
22 For I do not know how to flatter—
or my Maker would soon put an
end to me!

33 "But now, hear my speech, O Job,
and listen to all my words.
2 See, I open my mouth;
the tongue in my mouth speaks.
3 My words declare the uprightness of
my heart,
and what my lips know they speak
sincerely.
4 The spirit of God has made me,
and the breath of the Almighty[a]
gives me life.
5 Answer me, if you can;
set your words in order before me;
take your stand.
6 See, before God I am as you are;
I too was formed from a piece of
clay.
7 No fear of me need terrify you;
my pressure will not be heavy on
you.

8 "Surely, you have spoken in my
hearing,
and I have heard the sound of your
words.
9 You say, 'I am clean, without
transgression;
I am pure, and there is no iniquity
in me.
10 Look, he finds occasions against me,
he counts me as his enemy;
11 he puts my feet in the stocks,
and watches all my paths.'
12 "But in this you are not right. I will
answer you:
God is greater than any mortal.
13 Why do you contend against him,

a Traditional rendering of Heb *Shaddai*

gives wisdom, not age. **33.4–7:** Job had asserted that God's overwhelming power had made dialogue impossible (13.17–28). Elihu argues that Job should be able to face him, a mortal and a peer. **6:** Cf. 10.9; Gen 2.7; Isa 64.8.

33.8–33: Elihu's first disputation. 9: Elihu refers to Job's claim of innocence (9.20–21; 27.4–6; 31.1–40). **10–11:** Quotations of Job's words (13.24b,27a). **13:** A reference to Job's words in 9.3, although Job's words there probably meant that one could not answer God, not that God would not answer. **15–16:** For warnings communicated through dreams, see Gen 20.3–7; Dan 4.10–17. **18:** *Pit,*

saying, 'He will answer none of
my[a] words'?
14 For God speaks in one way,
and in two, though people do not
perceive it.
15 In a dream, in a vision of the night,
when deep sleep falls on mortals,
while they slumber on their beds,
16 then he opens their ears,
and terrifies them with warnings,
17 that he may turn them aside from
their deeds,
and keep them from pride,
18 to spare their souls from the Pit,
their lives from traversing the
River.
19 They are also chastened with pain
upon their beds,
and with continual strife in their
bones,
20 so that their lives loathe bread,
and their appetites dainty food.
21 Their flesh is so wasted away that it
cannot be seen;
and their bones, once invisible, now
stick out.
22 Their souls draw near the Pit,
and their lives to those who bring
death.
23 Then, if there should be for one of
them an angel,
a mediator, one of a thousand,
one who declares a person upright,
24 and he is gracious to that person, and
says,
'Deliver him from going down into
the Pit;
I have found a ransom;
25 let his flesh become fresh with youth;
let him return to the days of his
youthful vigor';
26 then he prays to God, and is accepted
by him,
he comes into his presence with joy,
and God[b] repays him for his
righteousness.
27 That person sings to others and
says,
'I sinned, and perverted what was
right,
and it was not paid back to me.
28 He has redeemed my soul from going
down to the Pit,
and my life shall see the light.'

29 "God indeed does all these things,
twice, three times, with mortals,
30 to bring back their souls from the Pit,
so that they may see the light of
life.[c]
31 Pay heed, Job, listen to me;
be silent, and I will speak.
32 If you have anything to say, answer
me;
speak, for I desire to justify you.
33 If not, listen to me;
be silent, and I will teach you
wisdom."

34 Then Elihu continued and said:
2 "Hear my words, you wise
men,
and give ear to me, you who know;
3 for the ear tests words
as the palate tastes food.
4 Let us choose what is right;
let us determine among ourselves
what is good.
5 For Job has said, 'I am innocent,
and God has taken away my right;
6 in spite of being right I am counted a
liar;

a Compare Gk: Heb *his* *b* Heb *he* *c* Syr: Heb *to be lighted with the light of life*

River, images of death (Ps 88.6). In Mesopotamian mythology the dead cross the river Hubur; in Greek myths, the Styx. **19–22:** See 5.17–18; Prov 3.11–12. **23:** *One who declares a person upright* should probably be translated "to tell mortals what is right for them," namely, how they might be redeemed and restored (vv. 24–28). **29:** The persistence of God is indicated by the increase from "one way . . . two" (v. 14) to *twice, three times.*

34.1–37: Elihu's second disputation. 3: Job had cited this proverb before (12.11). **5–6:** A reference to the gist of Job's arguments in 9.20 and 27.2. **7:** *Who drinks up scoffing,* see 15.16. **9:** The quote is from

my wound is incurable, though I
am without transgression.'
7 Who is there like Job,
who drinks up scoffing like water,
8 who goes in company with evildoers
and walks with the wicked?
9 For he has said, 'It profits one
nothing
to take delight in God.'

10 "Therefore, hear me, you who have
sense,
far be it from God that he should
do wickedness,
and from the Almighty[a] that he
should do wrong.
11 For according to their deeds he will
repay them,
and according to their ways he will
make it befall them.
12 Of a truth, God will not do wickedly,
and the Almighty[a] will not pervert
justice.
13 Who gave him charge over the earth
and who laid on him[b] the whole
world?
14 If he should take back his spirit[c] to
himself,
and gather to himself his breath,
15 all flesh would perish together,
and all mortals return to dust.

16 "If you have understanding, hear this;
listen to what I say.
17 Shall one who hates justice govern?
Will you condemn one who is
righteous and mighty,
18 who says to a king, 'You scoundrel!'
and to princes, 'You wicked men!';
19 who shows no partiality to nobles,
nor regards the rich more than the
poor,
for they are all the work of his
hands?
20 In a moment they die;
at midnight the people are shaken
and pass away,
and the mighty are taken away by
no human hand.

21 "For his eyes are upon the ways of
mortals,
and he sees all their steps.
22 There is no gloom or deep darkness
where evildoers may hide
themselves.
23 For he has not appointed a time[d] for
anyone
to go before God in judgment.
24 He shatters the mighty without
investigation,
and sets others in their place.
25 Thus, knowing their works,
he overturns them in the night, and
they are crushed.
26 He strikes them for their wickedness
while others look on,
27 because they turned aside from
following him,
and had no regard for any of his
ways,
28 so that they caused the cry of the
poor to come to him,
and he heard the cry of the
afflicted—
29 When he is quiet, who can condemn?
When he hides his face, who can
behold him,
whether it be a nation or an
individual?—
30 so that the godless should not reign,
or those who ensnare the people.

31 "For has anyone said to God,
'I have endured punishment; I will
not offend any more;
32 teach me what I do not see;

a Traditional rendering of Heb *Shaddai* *b* Heb lacks *on him* *c* Heb *his heart his spirit* *d* Cn: Heb *yet*

Job's speech (21.15), although in that context, Job was quoting the wicked. The implication is that Job's complaints (like those in 9.22; 21.7–12; 30.26) reflect the same attitude. **12:** Cf. 8.3n. **14–15:** See Gen 1.30; 2.7; 3.19. **17:** The same is assumed of human rulers; see Prov 16.12. **21–22:** A response to Job's charge that God is oblivious to wickedness (24.13–17). **23:** Cf. Job's complaint in 24.1. **28:** Cf. Deut 24.15. **37:** Job's guilt is not just in the past, but also in the present, in his blasphemous challenges to God.

if I have done iniquity, I will do it
no more'?
33 Will he then pay back to suit you,
because you reject it?
For you must choose, and not I;
therefore declare what you know.[a]
34 Those who have sense will say to me,
and the wise who hear me will say,
35 'Job speaks without knowledge,
his words are without insight.'
36 Would that Job were tried to the
limit,
because his answers are those of the
wicked.
37 For he adds rebellion to his sin;
he claps his hands among us,
and multiplies his words against
God."

35 Elihu continued and said:
2 "Do you think this to be just?
You say, 'I am in the right before
God.'
3 If you ask, 'What advantage have I?
How am I better off than if I had
sinned?'
4 I will answer you
and your friends with you.
5 Look at the heavens and see;
observe the clouds, which are
higher than you.
6 If you have sinned, what do you
accomplish against him?
And if your transgressions are
multiplied, what do you do to
him?
7 If you are righteous, what do you give
to him;
or what does he receive from your
hand?
8 Your wickedness affects others like
you,
and your righteousness, other
human beings.
9 "Because of the multitude of
oppressions people cry out;
they call for help because of the
arm of the mighty.
10 But no one says, 'Where is God my
Maker,
who gives strength in the night,
11 who teaches us more than the animals
of the earth,
and makes us wiser than the birds
of the air?'
12 There they cry out, but he does not
answer,
because of the pride of evildoers.
13 Surely God does not hear an empty
cry,
nor does the Almighty[b] regard it.
14 How much less when you say that
you do not see him,
that the case is before him, and you
are waiting for him!
15 And now, because his anger does not
punish,
and he does not greatly heed
transgression,[c]
16 Job opens his mouth in empty talk,
he multiplies words without
knowledge."

36 Elihu continued and said:
2 "Bear with me a little, and I
will show you,
for I have yet something to say on
God's behalf.

a Meaning of Heb of verses 29-33 uncertain
b Traditional rendering of Heb *Shaddai*
c Theodotion Symmachus Compare Vg: Meaning of Heb uncertain

35.1–16: Elihu's third disputation. *I am in the right before God,* translate, "I am more in the right than God," a distortion of Job's view that no mortal can be in the right before God (9.2; cf. the words of Eliphaz in 4.17). **3:** Cf. 34.9, also alleged to be the words of Job. These words more accurately reflect Eliphaz's view (22.2–4). **6–7:** Cf. 22.2–3. **9–13:** Job had complained about the silence of God despite human cries for help (24.12). Elihu now explains divine silence. People may cry for help, and yet not seek divine presence through prayer (vv. 10–11). Or there may be no response because of human pride (v. 12). Or the prayers may be hollow (v. 13). **14:** Allusions to Job's words in 23.8–9.

36.1–37.24: Elihu's fourth disputation. 36.5–12: Cf. the account of King Manasseh in 2 Chr 33.1–13

3 I will bring my knowledge from far
away,
and ascribe righteousness to my
Maker.
4 For truly my words are not false;
one who is perfect in knowledge is
with you.

5 "Surely God is mighty and does not
despise any;
he is mighty in strength of
understanding.
6 He does not keep the wicked alive,
but gives the afflicted their right.
7 He does not withdraw his eyes from
the righteous,
but with kings on the throne
he sets them forever, and they are
exalted.
8 And if they are bound in fetters
and caught in the cords of
affliction,
9 then he declares to them their work
and their transgressions, that they
are behaving arrogantly.
10 He opens their ears to instruction,
and commands that they return
from iniquity.
11 If they listen, and serve him,
they complete their days in
prosperity,
and their years in pleasantness.
12 But if they do not listen, they shall
perish by the sword,
and die without knowledge.

13 "The godless in heart cherish anger;
they do not cry for help when he
binds them.
14 They die in their youth,
and their life ends in shame.[a]
15 He delivers the afflicted by their
affliction,
and opens their ear by adversity.
16 He also allured you out of distress
into a broad place where there was
no constraint,
and what was set on your table was
full of fatness.

17 "But you are obsessed with the case
of the wicked;
judgment and justice seize you.
18 Beware that wrath does not entice
you into scoffing,
and do not let the greatness of the
ransom turn you aside.
19 Will your cry avail to keep you from
distress,
or will all the force of your
strength?
20 Do not long for the night,
when peoples are cut off in their
place.
21 Beware! Do not turn to iniquity;
because of that you have been tried
by affliction.
22 See, God is exalted in his power;
who is a teacher like him?
23 Who has prescribed for him his way,
or who can say, 'You have done
wrong'?

24 "Remember to extol his work,
of which mortals have sung.
25 All people have looked on it;
everyone watches it from far away.
26 Surely God is great, and we do not
know him;
the number of his years is
unsearchable.
27 For he draws up the drops of water;
he distills[b] his mist in rain,

a Heb *ends among the temple prostitutes* *b* Cn: Heb *they distill*

and Nebuchadnezzar in Dan 4. **17–21:** Elihu warns Job to respond properly to adversity. Job's obsession with his pain may cause him to turn to sin. **22:** The God who afflicts is praised as an incomparable *teacher.* It was believed in the ancient Near East that learning necessarily entailed discipline and, hence, a good teacher or parent would not hesitate to administer painful lessons. **36.24–37.24:** Elihu's poem in praise of the wonders of God is organized according to the seasons: autumn (36.27–33, *rain* and *clouds*), winter (37.1–13, *snow* and *ice*), and summer (37.14–22, *hot* and *south wind*). Cf. 38.1–38; Sir 43.1–33. **36.31:** Through the rains, God *governs* (lit. "judges") people and, at the same time,

28 which the skies pour down
and drop upon mortals abundantly.
29 Can anyone understand the spreading of the clouds,
the thunderings of his pavilion?
30 See, he scatters his lightning around him
and covers the roots of the sea.
31 For by these he governs peoples;
he gives food in abundance.
32 He covers his hands with the lightning,
and commands it to strike the mark.
33 Its crashing[a] tells about him;
he is jealous[a] with anger against iniquity.

37 "At this also my heart trembles,
and leaps out of its place.
2 Listen, listen to the thunder of his voice
and the rumbling that comes from his mouth.
3 Under the whole heaven he lets it loose,
and his lightning to the corners of the earth.
4 After it his voice roars;
he thunders with his majestic voice
and he does not restrain the lightnings[b] when his voice is heard.
5 God thunders wondrously with his voice;
he does great things that we cannot comprehend.
6 For to the snow he says, 'Fall on the earth';
and the shower of rain, his heavy shower of rain,
7 serves as a sign on everyone's hand,
so that all whom he has made may know it.[c]
8 Then the animals go into their lairs
and remain in their dens.
9 From its chamber comes the whirlwind,
and cold from the scattering winds.
10 By the breath of God ice is given,
and the broad waters are frozen fast.
11 He loads the thick cloud with moisture;
the clouds scatter his lightning.
12 They turn round and round by his guidance,
to accomplish all that he commands them
on the face of the habitable world.
13 Whether for correction, or for his land,
or for love, he causes it to happen.

14 "Hear this, O Job;
stop and consider the wondrous works of God.
15 Do you know how God lays his command upon them,
and causes the lightning of his cloud to shine?
16 Do you know the balancings of the clouds,
the wondrous works of the one whose knowledge is perfect,
17 you whose garments are hot
when the earth is still because of the south wind?
18 Can you, like him, spread out the skies,
hard as a molten mirror?
19 Teach us what we shall say to him;
we cannot draw up our case because of darkness.
20 Should he be told that I want to speak?

a Meaning of Heb uncertain *b* Heb *them*
c Meaning of Heb of verse 7 uncertain

provides them with plenty. **37.2:** The call to pay attention to the thunder is, in effect, a call to heed the lessons that the storm brings. **12–13:** A reiteration of the pedagogical function of the storm: It provides guidance to the purposes of the divine teacher, and it may be for correction or for love. **18:** In summer, there is no rain, and the sky was considered hard (cf. Lev 26.19; Deut 28.23). **20:** *To be swallowed up,* that is, by personified Death.

Did anyone ever wish to be
swallowed up?
21 Now, no one can look on the light
when it is bright in the skies,
when the wind has passed and
cleared them.
22 Out of the north comes golden
splendor;
around God is awesome majesty.
23 The Almighty[a]—we cannot find him;
he is great in power and justice,
and abundant righteousness he will
not violate.
24 Therefore mortals fear him;
he does not regard any who are
wise in their own conceit."

38 Then the LORD answered Job out of the whirlwind:
2 "Who is this that darkens counsel by
words without knowledge?
3 Gird up your loins like a man,
I will question you, and you shall
declare to me.

4 "Where were you when I laid the
foundation of the earth?
Tell me, if you have understanding.
5 Who determined its measurements—
surely you know!
Or who stretched the line upon it?
6 On what were its bases sunk,
or who laid its cornerstone
7 when the morning stars sang together
and all the heavenly beings[b]
shouted for joy?

8 "Or who shut in the sea with doors
when it burst out from the
womb?—
9 when I made the clouds its garment,
and thick darkness its swaddling
band,
10 and prescribed bounds for it,
and set bars and doors,
11 and said, 'Thus far shall you come,
and no farther,
and here shall your proud waves be
stopped'?

12 "Have you commanded the morning
since your days began,
and caused the dawn to know its
place,
13 so that it might take hold of the skirts
of the earth,
and the wicked be shaken out of it?
14 It is changed like clay under the seal,
and it is dyed[c] like a garment.
15 Light is withheld from the wicked,
and their uplifted arm is broken.

16 "Have you entered into the springs of
the sea,
or walked in the recesses of the
deep?
17 Have the gates of death been revealed
to you,
or have you seen the gates of deep
darkness?
18 Have you comprehended the expanse
of the earth?
Declare, if you know all this.

a Traditional rendering of Heb *Shaddai* *b* Heb *sons of God* *c* Cn: Heb *and they stand forth*

38.1–42.6: God speaks from the whirlwind. God finally responds to Job and does so in a series of speeches that show humanity's limited knowledge and power. **38.1–39.30:** God's first speech is structured as a series of rhetorical questions concerning creation. **38.1:** *The whirlwind,* cf. 9.17; 40.6. In the biblical worldview, storms typically accompanied a theophany (cf. Ps 18.7–15; 50.3; 58.3; Ezek 1.4; Nah 1.3; Zech 9.14; Hab 3). *The LORD* (Heb "yhwh"), otherwise found only in the prose prologue (1.1–2.13) and epilogue (42.7–17). **3:** *Gird up your loins like a man,* an image of preparation for combat. **4–11:** For the creator as architect, see Prov 8.27–30. The earth was built on foundations (vv. 4–6; see Ps 78.69; 102.25; 104.5; Isa 48.13), and strict limits were set for the primeval waters of chaos (vv. 8–11; 26.10; Ps 104.9; 148.6). **7:** *Heavenly beings,* lit. "sons of God"; see 1.6–12n. On the *stars* as members of the divine council, see 25.5; Judg 5.20. **12–15:** Daylight both transforms the earth and cleanses it of the wicked. **21:** Here God sarcastically answers his own questions. **22–30:** Meteorological phenomena are

19 "Where is the way to the dwelling of
light,
and where is the place of darkness,
20 that you may take it to its territory
and that you may discern the paths
to its home?
21 Surely you know, for you were born
then,
and the number of your days is
great!

22 "Have you entered the storehouses of
the snow,
or have you seen the storehouses of
the hail,
23 which I have reserved for the time of
trouble,
for the day of battle and war?
24 What is the way to the place where
the light is distributed,
or where the east wind is scattered
upon the earth?

25 "Who has cut a channel for the
torrents of rain,
and a way for the thunderbolt,
26 to bring rain on a land where no one
lives,
on the desert, which is empty of
human life,
27 to satisfy the waste and desolate land,
and to make the ground put forth
grass?

28 "Has the rain a father,
or who has begotten the drops of
dew?
29 From whose womb did the ice come
forth,
and who has given birth to the
hoarfrost of heaven?
30 The waters become hard like
stone,
and the face of the deep is
frozen.

31 "Can you bind the chains of the
Pleiades,
or loose the cords of Orion?
32 Can you lead forth the Mazzaroth in
their season,
or can you guide the Bear with its
children?
33 Do you know the ordinances of the
heavens?
Can you establish their rule on the
earth?

34 "Can you lift up your voice to the
clouds,
so that a flood of waters may cover
you?
35 Can you send forth lightnings, so that
they may go
and say to you, 'Here we are'?
36 Who has put wisdom in the inward
parts,[a]
or given understanding to the
mind?[a]
37 Who has the wisdom to number the
clouds?
Or who can tilt the waterskins of
the heavens,
38 when the dust runs into a mass
and the clods cling together?

39 "Can you hunt the prey for the lion,
or satisfy the appetite of the young
lions,
40 when they crouch in their dens,
or lie in wait in their covert?
41 Who provides for the raven its prey,
when its young ones cry to God,
and wander about for lack of food?

39 "Do you know when the
mountain goats give birth?
Do you observe the calving of the
deer?

a Meaning of Heb uncertain

carefully, if extravagantly, dispensed by God; cf. vv. 34–38; 28.26; 37.6–13; Ps 135.7. **31–33:** On the constellations, see 9.9n. **38.39–39.30:** God, not Job, knows the design of the animal world: the lions and ravens with their appetites, mountain goats and deer with their reproductive activities, the wild ass and wild ox with their freedom, the ostrich, both foolish and swift, the fearless battle-stallion, and the hawk and the vulture with the ability to soar up high. **38.39:** *Lion,* more precisely "lioness," as in 4.11.

2 Can you number the months that they fulfill,
and do you know the time when they give birth,
3 when they crouch to give birth to their offspring,
and are delivered of their young?
4 Their young ones become strong, they grow up in the open;
they go forth, and do not return to them.

5 "Who has let the wild ass go free?
Who has loosed the bonds of the swift ass,
6 to which I have given the steppe for its home,
the salt land for its dwelling place?
7 It scorns the tumult of the city;
it does not hear the shouts of the driver.
8 It ranges the mountains as its pasture,
and it searches after every green thing.

9 "Is the wild ox willing to serve you?
Will it spend the night at your crib?
10 Can you tie it in the furrow with ropes,
or will it harrow the valleys after you?
11 Will you depend on it because its strength is great,
and will you hand over your labor to it?
12 Do you have faith in it that it will return,
and bring your grain to your threshing floor?[a]

13 "The ostrich's wings flap wildly,
though its pinions lack plumage.[b]
14 For it leaves its eggs to the earth,
and lets them be warmed on the ground,
15 forgetting that a foot may crush them,
and that a wild animal may trample them.
16 It deals cruelly with its young, as if they were not its own;
though its labor should be in vain, yet it has no fear;
17 because God has made it forget wisdom,
and given it no share in understanding.
18 When it spreads its plumes aloft,[b]
it laughs at the horse and its rider.

19 "Do you give the horse its might?
Do you clothe its neck with mane?
20 Do you make it leap like the locust?
Its majestic snorting is terrible.
21 It paws[c] violently, exults mightily;
it goes out to meet the weapons.
22 It laughs at fear, and is not dismayed;
it does not turn back from the sword.
23 Upon it rattle the quiver,
the flashing spear, and the javelin.
24 With fierceness and rage it swallows the ground;
it cannot stand still at the sound of the trumpet.
25 When the trumpet sounds, it says 'Aha!'
From a distance it smells the battle,
the thunder of the captains, and the shouting.

26 "Is it by your wisdom that the hawk soars,
and spreads its wings toward the south?
27 Is it at your command that the eagle mounts up
and makes its nest on high?
28 It lives on the rock and makes its home
in the fastness of the rocky crag.
29 From there it spies the prey;
its eyes see it from far away.

a Heb *your grain and your threshing floor*
b Meaning of Heb uncertain *c* Gk Syr Vg: Heb *they dig*

41: Cf. Ps 147.9. **39.16:** On the ostrich's cruelty, see Lam 4.3. **26:** *Toward the south,* when it migrates. **27:** *Eagle,* probably "vulture."

30 Its young ones suck up blood;
and where the slain are, there it is."

40 And the LORD said to Job:
2 "Shall a faultfinder contend
with the Almighty?[a]
Anyone who argues with God must
respond."

3 Then Job answered the LORD:
4 "See, I am of small account; what
shall I answer you?
I lay my hand on my mouth.
5 I have spoken once, and I will not
answer;
twice, but will proceed no further."

6 Then the LORD answered Job out of
the whirlwind:
7 "Gird up your loins like a man;
I will question you, and you declare
to me.
8 Will you even put me in the wrong?
Will you condemn me that you may
be justified?
9 Have you an arm like God,
and can you thunder with a voice
like his?

10 "Deck yourself with majesty and
dignity;
clothe yourself with glory and
splendor.
11 Pour out the overflowings of your
anger,
and look on all who are proud, and
abase them.
12 Look on all who are proud, and bring
them low;
tread down the wicked where they
stand.
13 Hide them all in the dust together;
bind their faces in the world
below.[b]
14 Then I will also acknowledge to you
that your own right hand can give
you victory.

15 "Look at Behemoth,
which I made just as I made you;
it eats grass like an ox.
16 Its strength is in its loins,
and its power in the muscles of its
belly.
17 It makes its tail stiff like a cedar;
the sinews of its thighs are knit
together.
18 Its bones are tubes of bronze,
its limbs like bars of iron.

19 "It is the first of the great acts of
God—
only its Maker can approach it
with the sword.
20 For the mountains yield food for it
where all the wild animals play.
21 Under the lotus plants it lies,
in the covert of the reeds and in the
marsh.
22 The lotus trees cover it for shade;
the willows of the wadi surround it.
23 Even if the river is turbulent, it is not
frightened;
it is confident though Jordan rushes
against its mouth.
24 Can one take it with hooks[c]
or pierce its nose with a snare?

41 [d]"Can you draw out Leviathan[e]
with a fishhook,

a Traditional rendering of Heb *Shaddai* *b* Heb *the hidden place* *c* Cn: Heb *in his eyes* *d* Ch 40.25 in Heb *e* Or *the crocodile*

40.1–5: Question and response. 1–2: Job had insisted on the legal disputation (13.22; 23.1–7; 31.35–37). Now Job is challenged to respond. **3–5:** Job acknowledges his relatively insignificant position and is willing to be silent.

40.6–41.34: God's second speech. 40.6–7: Cf. 38.1,3. **8–14:** The deity relates the design of the cosmos to the design of governance. Job had defined the issue of his suffering in legal terms; God defines it in terms of power: As long as Job is unable to govern as God does, he has no standing to challenge divine justice. **15–24:** *Behemoth* ("animal"), a primeval monster (v. 19) and a mythical symbol of chaos and evil, is a creature of God, just as Job is, and therefore subject to God's will. **19:** Cf. Prov 8.22. Even God must

or press down its tongue with a cord?
2 Can you put a rope in its nose,
or pierce its jaw with a hook?
3 Will it make many supplications to you?
Will it speak soft words to you?
4 Will it make a covenant with you
to be taken as your servant forever?
5 Will you play with it as with a bird,
or will you put it on leash for your girls?
6 Will traders bargain over it?
Will they divide it up among the merchants?
7 Can you fill its skin with harpoons,
or its head with fishing spears?
8 Lay hands on it;
think of the battle; you will not do it again!
9[a] Any hope of capturing it[b] will be disappointed;
were not even the gods[c] overwhelmed at the sight of it?
10 No one is so fierce as to dare to stir it up.
Who can stand before it?[d]
11 Who can confront it[d] and be safe?[e]
—under the whole heaven, who?[f]
12 "I will not keep silence concerning its limbs,
or its mighty strength, or its splendid frame.
13 Who can strip off its outer garment?
Who can penetrate its double coat of mail?[g]
14 Who can open the doors of its face?
There is terror all around its teeth.
15 Its back[h] is made of shields in rows,
shut up closely as with a seal.
16 One is so near to another
that no air can come between them.
17 They are joined one to another;
they clasp each other and cannot be separated.
18 Its sneezes flash forth light,
and its eyes are like the eyelids of the dawn.
19 From its mouth go flaming torches;
sparks of fire leap out.
20 Out of its nostrils comes smoke,
as from a boiling pot and burning rushes.
21 Its breath kindles coals,
and a flame comes out of its mouth.
22 In its neck abides strength,
and terror dances before it.
23 The folds of its flesh cling together;
it is firmly cast and immovable.
24 Its heart is as hard as stone,
as hard as the lower millstone.
25 When it raises itself up the gods are afraid;
at the crashing they are beside themselves.
26 Though the sword reaches it, it does not avail,
nor does the spear, the dart, or the javelin.
27 It counts iron as straw,
and bronze as rotten wood.
28 The arrow cannot make it flee;
slingstones, for it, are turned to chaff.
29 Clubs are counted as chaff;
it laughs at the rattle of javelins.
30 Its underparts are like sharp potsherds;
it spreads itself like a threshing sledge on the mire.
31 It makes the deep boil like a pot;
it makes the sea like a pot of ointment.
32 It leaves a shining wake behind it;
one would think the deep to be white-haired.
33 On earth it has no equal,
a creature without fear.
34 It surveys everything that is lofty;
it is king over all that are proud."

42 Then Job answered the LORD:
2 "I know that you can do all things,
and that no purpose of yours can be thwarted.

a Ch 41.1 in Heb *b* Heb *of it* *c* Cn Compare Symmachus Syr: Heb *one is* *d* Heb *me* *e* Gk: Heb *that I shall repay* *f* Heb *to me* *g* Gk: Heb *bridle* *h* Cn Compare Gk Vg: Heb *pride*

3 'Who is this that hides counsel
without knowledge?'
Therefore I have uttered what I did
not understand,
things too wonderful for me, which
I did not know.
4 'Hear, and I will speak;
I will question you, and you declare
to me.'
5 I had heard of you by the hearing of
the ear,
but now my eye sees you;
6 therefore I despise myself,
and repent in dust and ashes."

7 After the LORD had spoken these
words to Job, the LORD said to Eliphaz the
Temanite: "My wrath is kindled against
you and against your two friends; for you
have not spoken of me what is right, as my
servant Job has. 8 Now therefore take seven
bulls and seven rams, and go to my servant
Job, and offer up for yourselves a burnt
offering; and my servant Job shall pray for
you, for I will accept his prayer not to deal
with you according to your folly; for you
have not spoken of me what is right, as my
servant Job has done." 9 So Eliphaz the Te-
manite and Bildad the Shuhite and Zophar
the Naamathite went and did what the
LORD had told them; and the LORD accept-
ed Job's prayer.

10 And the LORD restored the fortunes
of Job when he had prayed for his friends;
and the LORD gave Job twice as much as he
had before. 11 Then there came to him all
his brothers and sisters and all who had
known him before, and they ate bread with
him in his house; they showed him sympa-
thy and comforted him for all the evil that
the LORD had brought upon him; and each
of them gave him a piece of money[a] and a
gold ring. 12 The LORD blessed the latter
days of Job more than his beginning; and
he had fourteen thousand sheep, six thou-

a Heb *a qesitah*

approach this primeval beast with caution, and no one can tame it (v. 24). **41.1–34:** *Leviathan,* a sea monster symbolizing cosmic chaos (see 3.8n.). Though Leviathan reigns supreme on earth, he is but a creature, a plaything to God (cf. Ps 104.26). **42.1–6: Job's second response.** Job acknowledges the power of God and accepts God's judgment in 38.2 that he has spoken without knowledge and understanding (v. 3). **4–5:** Job has indeed heard God, as God had charged him to do (40.7), and now he *sees* God, an idiom for an exceptional and profound individual experience of deity's presence (cf. Gen 16.13; Ex 24.9–11; 33.20–23; Isa 6.1). **6:** The concluding words of Job are ambiguous or, perhaps, multivalent. The Heb word rendered by the NRSV *I despise myself* should probably be translated as "I relent" or "I recant"; the word for *repent* may also mean "regret" or "console"; the preposition *in* is either literally "upon" or "concerning"/"about." Thus, Job may be understood to say that he recants and regrets mournfully (upon *dust and ashes;* see 30.19n.), or that he relents and is consoled about the limitations of humanity (i.e., about being dust and ashes; see Gen 18.27).

42.7–17: Epilogue. This prose epilogue has the same style, language, and perspective as the prologue (1.1–2.13). **7–9:** Job is judged in 38.2 to have spoken ignorantly about God, yet he is judged here to have spoken correctly about God; Job was right about his innocence and the fact that his suffering came from God. The friends who were quick to defend God, on the other hand, were wrong. Moreover, the friends are regarded as fools, just like Job's wife, who had encouraged Job to curse God and die (2.10). Still, there is hope for them through sacrifice and through intercession by Job, a veritable testimony to his acceptance by God. **10:** Job's fortune is restored, but no mention is made of the healing of his disease. **11–12:** Job is given back the blessing of having family and friends, each of whom brought him a gold ring and *a piece of money,* apparently a significant sum (cf. Gen 33.19; Josh 24.32). **13–15:** Whereas Job had previously lost all his children, he now has a new brood of them, including the daughters, *Jemimah* ("Dove"), *Keziah* ("Cinnamon"), and *Keren-happuch* ("Horn of Eyeshadow"). Along with his sons, his daughters are given an inheritance, an unusual but attested practice (see Num 27.1–11). **16:** Job had an exceptionally long life, witnessing four generations of his descendants. **17:** Cf. Gen 25.8; 35.9.

sand camels, a thousand yoke of oxen, and
a thousand donkeys. 13 He also had seven
sons and three daughters. 14 He named the
first Jemimah, the second Keziah, and the
third Keren-happuch. 15 In all the land
there were no women so beautiful as Job's
daughters; and their father gave them an
inheritance along with their brothers. 16 Af-
ter this Job lived one hundred and forty
years, and saw his children, and his chil-
dren's children, four generations. 17 And
Job died, old and full of days.

PSALMS

The book of Psalms is a collection of sung poetic prayers (see Introduction to the Poetical and Wisdom Books) associated with divine worship in Israel. The word "psalm" is derived from the Greek "psalmos," which translates the Hebrew "mizmor"; these all mean a song recited to the accompaniment of a stringed instrument. The times of composition for the psalms range across at least five centuries; the earliest psalm is probably Ps 29, which is adapted from early Canaanite worship, while several psalms contain contextual (e.g., Ps 126), linguistic, or other evidence that they are from the postexilic period (Ps 51; 114; 137). While most psalms are Judean in origin, the language or internal references in several psalms suggest that they originated in the Northern Kingdom (e.g., Ps 80 and 81, which contain references to Joseph); these most likely were brought to Judah after the destruction of the Northern Kingdom in 722 BCE. The majority of the psalms, however, originated in the preexilic, monarchic period, and are associated with the Jerusalem Temple.

These psalms likely functioned as a musical libretto for sections of the Temple worship, though exactly when and how they were used is unclear. Psalm 118.27, "The LORD is God, and he has given us light. Bind the festal procession with branches, up to the horns of the altar" suggests that some psalms were used in connection to the sacrifices, while Ps 141.2, "Let my prayer be counted as incense before you, and the lifting up of my hands as an evening sacrifice" might indicate that some were recited when the incense was offered. Several psalms contain allusions to musical performance (e.g., 13.6; 26.7; 30.4; 33.2–3), and many of the superscriptions (headings) contain detailed, technical references to how the performance should be completed. Unfortunately, many of the technical terms that are ubiquitous in the psalms, including the frequent "Selah," are imperfectly understood, and it is thus very difficult to reconstruct with any certainty exactly how these poems were performed.

From the beginning of this century, many attempts have been made, especially by biblical scholars interested in form criticism (see "Form Criticism" in the essay on p. 493 ES), to follow clues in the psalms, in order to reconstruct the original "Sitz im Leben," or setting in life, of the psalms. This scholarship has suggested that the psalms are to be divided into several genres. The two main types are laments, forming approximately a third of the Psalter, and hymns. Laments can be either individual (e.g., Ps 3) or communal (e.g., Ps 44). The lament's component parts include the invocation of the name of God, the complaint wherein the psalmist describes the distress experienced, and appeals for divine intervention. Many of these laments include expressions of trust, couched in the past (e.g., Ps 6.9, "The LORD has heard my supplication; the LORD accepts my prayer"). It is unclear if this is a reflection of the psalmist's great faith, which is furthered through the recitation of the psalms, or if part of the recitation of the psalm might have included a response to the lament by a cultic official, and the psalmist might have expressed trust only after this divine reassurance, which does not usually appear in the psalm. The hymns typically focus on the role of God as creator (e.g., Ps 8; 19; 104) or redeemer (Ps 66; 98). These hymns are not connected to specific requests; they are reflective of the religious individual, who wants to have a close connection with God, in the belief that "It is good to give thanks to the LORD, to sing praises to your name, O Most High" (Ps 92.1).

The Hebrew title of Psalms, "tehillim" ("praises"), reflects the significance of the genre of hymns to the book.

Still other types of psalms may be isolated in Psalms. For example, Ps 15, which recounts the ideal qualities of the individual who "may abide in your tent" and "may dwell on your holy hill" (v. 1) is likely an entrance liturgy, recited by the worshiper while approaching the Temple. There are several royal psalms (e.g., Ps 2), which focus on the king. The number of these psalms, and by extension, the extent to which the Psalter should be viewed as a work with specifically royal focus, is debated, with some scholars contending that the "I" of the Psalter is typically the king. A handful of psalms (e.g., 37; 119) contain the vocabulary of the wisdom books—Job, Proverbs, and Ecclesiastes—and focus on issues that characterize those books, such as righteousness in contrast to evil; for this reason, they are often called wisdom psalms. Several psalms, especially 93–99, focus on the kingship of God; it is unclear how these might have been used ritually, and especially if they might reflect a Judean New Year festival, which had significant parallels to a Babylonian festival, in which the deity was ritually reinstated as king. Form critics continue to debate the genres of specific psalms, the number of different genres contained in the Psalter, and the psalms' Sitz im Leben, namely the ways in which they were connected to ancient Israelite worship.

The book of Psalms came together over a long period of time. This is clear from the final verse of Ps 72, "The prayers of David son of Jesse are ended." This is further reflected through the existence of several collections or anthologies within the Psalter; the clearest of these is composed of Ps 120–134, each of which begins "A song of ascents." Ps 42–83 are also a collection ("the elohistic Psalter"); these typically call the deity "elohim" (translated "God"), rather than "yhwh" (translated "LORD"), which typifies the rest of the Psalter. A comparison of Ps 14 to the parallel Ps 53 (from the elohistic Psalter) is especially enlightening as an illustration of the anthological nature of the Psalter. Clusters of psalms also begin or end with the words "halelu-yah," "Praise the LORD" (Ps 105–106; 111–113; 115–117; 146–150).

This brief reconstruction of the history of the Psalter indicates that the early Jewish and Christian tradition, reflected among the Dead Sea community as well, that David composed the entirety of the book of Psalms, is secondary. The tradition arose from an interpretation of the many psalms that do begin "of David," a phrase understood to mean of Davidic authorship, as well as the traditions in other books that David was a poet and musician (1 Sam 16.16–17; 2 Sam 1.17–27) and the patron of the Jerusalem Temple (1 Chr 29.1–5), constructed by his son, Solomon. The historical headings of several psalms (e.g., Ps 3; 18; 34; 51) reflect early exegetical attempts to link the psalms with incidents in the life of David in 1–2 Samuel. This desire to connect the psalms directly to the life of David is further reflected in additional historical headings found in the Septuagint, the second-century BCE translation of the Bible, as well as in later Jewish exegesis. These reflect a movement away from understanding Psalms as a loose collection of liturgical works, to viewing it as a thematic book.

This attempt to understand Psalms as a book is also reflected in the manner in which the book is subdivided into five parts or books, through the secondary insertion of doxologies (detailed praises of God), at the end of Ps 41; 72; 89; 106, and through the functioning of the last psalm(s) of the Psalter (Ps 146–150 or Ps 150 alone) as a doxology. Thus the book in its final form is structured as a Pentateuch (five books), just like the Torah. The reference to "the Torah (NRSV "law") of the LORD" in the introductory psalm (v. 2) suggests that, at some level, the book of Psalms as a whole is to be read as Torah and is to be studied as Torah. This may reflect the period after the destruction of the Second Temple (70 CE), when study of psalms replaced their liturgical recitation.

There are thus many ways that the individual psalms might be read. In their earliest stages, they reflect individual compositions, recited for particular occasions at a variety of sacred sites. Later, some of these were anthologized, and might be understood within the anthology that they are in;

e.g., Ps 123 might be understood within the Songs of Ascent. Finally, individual psalms might be understood within the Psalter as a book, either narrating a biography of David, or a book of teaching like the Torah. The main function of psalms within later Jewish and Christian tradition, however, has been as a type of inspirational literature, where later worshipers may find proper words in tradition to express the depths of their religious feelings.

BOOK ONE

PSALM 1

1 Happy are those
who do not follow the advice of the wicked,
or take the path that sinners tread,
or sit in the seat of scoffers;
2 but their delight is in the law of the LORD,
and on his law they meditate day and night.
3 They are like trees
planted by streams of water,
which yield their fruit in its season,
and their leaves do not wither.
In all that they do, they prosper.

4 The wicked are not so,
but are like chaff that the wind drives away.
5 Therefore the wicked will not stand in the judgment,
nor sinners in the congregation of the righteous;
6 for the LORD watches over the way of the righteous,
but the way of the wicked will perish.

PSALM 2

1 Why do the nations conspire,
and the peoples plot in vain?
2 The kings of the earth set themselves,
and the rulers take counsel together,
against the LORD and his anointed, saying,
3 "Let us burst their bonds asunder,
and cast their cords from us."

4 He who sits in the heavens laughs;
the LORD has them in derision.
5 Then he will speak to them in his wrath,
and terrify them in his fury, saying,
6 "I have set my king on Zion, my holy hill."

7 I will tell of the decree of the LORD:
He said to me, "You are my son;
today I have begotten you.
8 Ask of me, and I will make the
nations your heritage,

Ps 1: The two ways. A wisdom psalm, used as a preface to the Psalter, intended as a guide to the Psalter as a repository of divine instruction. Wisdom characteristics include the introductory assertion that the virtuous are *happy* (e.g., Prov 3.13); it continues with the language of *the way,* and the sharp contrast between the *righteous* and the *wicked.* **1–3:** The psalmist's nonassociation with the wicked and devotion to the Torah. **4–5:** The wicked are like worthless, insubstantial chaff; this contrasts with the righteous, who are like flourishing trees (v. 3; cf. Jer 17.7–8). **6:** The final verse brings the *righteous* and *wicked* together for a sharper contrast.

Ps 2: God's royal son. A royal psalm, announcing one of the Psalter's major themes, the Davidic monarchy; perhaps a coronation ode. **1–3:** The revolt of the *kings* and *rulers . . . against the LORD* and the Israelite monarch, perhaps vassal kings of the Israelite empire (2 Sam 8; 1 Kings 4.24). **2:** *Anointed,* Heb "mashiah" (messiah), always used in the Hebrew Bible of the actual ruler, rather than of a future king. **4–6:** The LORD addresses the nations, confirming his choice of the monarch. *Zion,* Jerusalem. **7:** The king speaks, responding to the words of a court poet or prophet, in which he is identified as the adopted *son* of God (see 2 Sam 7.14; Ps 89.26–27). **10–11:** The homage of the defeated kings to the

and the ends of the earth your
possession.
9 You shall break them with a rod of
iron,
and dash them in pieces like a
potter's vessel."

10 Now therefore, O kings, be wise;
be warned, O rulers of the earth.
11 Serve the LORD with fear,
with trembling 12 kiss his feet,[a]
or he will be angry, and you will
perish in the way;
for his wrath is quickly kindled.

Happy are all who take refuge in
him.

PSALM 3

A Psalm of David, when he fled from his son Absalom.

1 O LORD, how many are my foes!
Many are rising against me;
2 many are saying to me,
"There is no help for you[b] in
God." *Selah*

3 But you, O LORD, are a shield around
me,
my glory, and the one who lifts up
my head.
4 I cry aloud to the LORD,
and he answers me from his
holy hill. *Selah*

5 I lie down and sleep;
I wake again, for the LORD sustains
me.
6 I am not afraid of ten thousands of
people
who have set themselves against me
all around.

7 Rise up, O LORD!
Deliver me, O my God!
For you strike all my enemies on the
cheek;
you break the teeth of the wicked.

8 Deliverance belongs to the LORD;
may your blessing be on your
people! *Selah*

PSALM 4

To the leader: with stringed instruments. A Psalm of David.

1 Answer me when I call, O God of my
right!
You gave me room when I was in
distress.
Be gracious to me, and hear my
prayer.

2 How long, you people, shall my
honor suffer shame?

a Cn: Meaning of Heb of verses 11b and 12a is uncertain *b* Syr: Heb *him*

LORD, concluding with the statement that those who trust in the LORD are *happy.* This returns to the introduction of Ps 1, and helps to explain why some early traditions saw Ps 1–2 as a unit.

Ps 3: Prayer for deliverance from enemies. An individual lament, with a superscription that relates the psalm to 2 Sam 15–16, the story of Absalom's revolt and David's flight from Jerusalem. The introductory "A Psalm of David" may reflect the (secondary) attribution of Davidic authorship, or may mean a psalm after the style of David, like a Miltonic ode. **1–6:** Beset by many enemies, the psalmist is nevertheless confident of divine support and protection. **2:** *Selah* (also vv. 4,8), a Hebrew term, of unknown meaning, appearing only in Psalms (and the psalmic Hab 3). It often separates subunits of psalms, and is most likely a musicological technical term. **4:** *His holy hill,* the Temple mount. **7:** The psalmist's foes have spoken against the psalmist (v. 2); by the law of talion or equivalent retribution (see Ex 21.23–25; Deut 19.21), their organs of speech are destroyed. **8:** The appeal to God to bless the people may point to the king as speaker.

Ps 4: Prayer for deliverance from enemies. A psalm of trust in which the psalmist expresses confidence in the *God of my right.* **2:** The people's pursuit of vanity and *lies* may involve the worship of other gods. *Selah* (also v. 4), see Ps 3.2n. **3:** It is unclear if *faithful* is a generic term, or refers to a specific group in

How long will you love vain words,
and seek after lies? *Selah*
3 But know that the LORD has set apart
the faithful for himself;
the LORD hears when I call to him.

4 When you are disturbed,[a] do not sin;
ponder it on your beds, and be
silent. *Selah*
5 Offer right sacrifices,
and put your trust in the LORD.

6 There are many who say, "O that we
might see some good!
Let the light of your face shine on
us, O LORD!"
7 You have put gladness in my heart
more than when their grain and
wine abound.

8 I will both lie down and sleep in
peace;
for you alone, O LORD, make me
lie down in safety.

PSALM 5

To the leader: for the flutes. A Psalm of David.

1 Give ear to my words, O LORD;
give heed to my sighing.
2 Listen to the sound of my cry,
my King and my God,
for to you I pray.
3 O LORD, in the morning you hear my
voice;
in the morning I plead my case to
you, and watch.

4 For you are not a God who delights
in wickedness;
evil will not sojourn with you.
5 The boastful will not stand before
your eyes;
you hate all evildoers.
6 You destroy those who speak lies;
the LORD abhors the bloodthirsty
and deceitful.

7 But I, through the abundance of your
steadfast love,
will enter your house,
I will bow down toward your holy
temple
in awe of you.
8 Lead me, O LORD, in your
righteousness
because of my enemies;
make your way straight before me.

9 For there is no truth in their mouths;
their hearts are destruction;
their throats are open graves;
they flatter with their tongues.
10 Make them bear their guilt, O God;
let them fall by their own counsels;
because of their many transgressions
cast them out,
for they have rebelled against you.

11 But let all who take refuge in you
rejoice;
let them ever sing for joy.
Spread your protection over them,
so that those who love your name
may exult in you.
12 For you bless the righteous, O LORD;
you cover them with favor as with
a shield.

a Or *are angry*

Israel. **4–5:** The people are called to penitence and *right sacrifices* (to the LORD, not to other gods). **6–7:** The *good* is agricultural bounty. The shining face of God is the visible expression of divine benevolence (Num 6.24–26).

Ps 5: Prayer for access to the Temple. An individual lament, associated with the "entrance liturgies" (Ps 15; 24.3–6), instruction about the moral qualities required of one seeking access to the Temple. **3:** The morning is the time for divine assistance, after the perils of the night (Ps 90.14; 143.8). **4–8:** The wicked are denied access to the Temple; the psalmist is admitted. **9–10:** The evildoers' sins of speech (perhaps slander or false testimony), as in vv. 5–6. **11–12:** Divine protection for the psalmist in the Temple.

PSALM 6

To the leader: with stringed instruments; according to The Sheminith. A Psalm of David.

1 O LORD, do not rebuke me in your anger,
or discipline me in your wrath.
2 Be gracious to me, O LORD, for I am languishing;
O LORD, heal me, for my bones are shaking with terror.
3 My soul also is struck with terror,
while you, O LORD—how long?

4 Turn, O LORD, save my life;
deliver me for the sake of your steadfast love.
5 For in death there is no remembrance of you;
in Sheol who can give you praise?

6 I am weary with my moaning;
every night I flood my bed with tears;
I drench my couch with my weeping.
7 My eyes waste away because of grief;
they grow weak because of all my foes.

8 Depart from me, all you workers of evil,
for the LORD has heard the sound of my weeping.
9 The LORD has heard my supplication;
the LORD accepts my prayer.
10 All my enemies shall be ashamed and struck with terror;
they shall turn back, and in a moment be put to shame.

PSALM 7

A Shiggaion of David, which he sang to the LORD concerning Cush, a Benjaminite.

1 O LORD my God, in you I take refuge;
save me from all my pursuers, and deliver me,
2 or like a lion they will tear me apart;
they will drag me away, with no one to rescue.

3 O LORD my God, if I have done this,
if there is wrong in my hands,
4 if I have repaid my ally with harm
or plundered my foe without cause,
5 then let the enemy pursue and overtake me,
trample my life to the ground,
and lay my soul in the dust. *Selah*

6 Rise up, O LORD, in your anger;
lift yourself up against the fury of my enemies;
awake, O my God;[a] you have appointed a judgment.
7 Let the assembly of the peoples be gathered around you,

a Or *awake for me*

Ps 6: Prayer for healing. An individual lament, which in later Christian tradition forms the first of the seven penitential psalms (6; 32; 38; 51; 102; 130; 143). *Sheminith,* "the eighth" (cf. "octave"), a musical term of uncertain significance. **1–3:** The complaint of the psalmist (also in vv. 6–7) is apparently life-threatening sickness, though v. 7 mentions "foes." **4–5:** *Save my life,* the psalmist's death will diminish the praise due to God, and so reduce the divine status and glory, a typical appeal (Ps 30.9; 88.10–12; 115.17). **5:** *Sheol,* the abode of the dead. **8–10:** The shift from complaint to praise is a feature of many of the psalms of lament; see Introduction.

Ps 7: Prayer for deliverance from enemies. An individual lament in which the psalmist complains of assaults by foes and petitions God to take up arms against them. The superscription *concerning Cush* refers to an otherwise unknown incident; cf. Ps 3n. *Shiggaion,* a musical term occurring only here, of unknown meaning. **1–2:** The psalmist's enemy, described as a fierce subhuman predator (*a lion,* Ps 10.9; 22.13,21; 57.4). **3–5:** A strong self-imprecation (see Job 31); such vows were viewed with great seriousness in ancient Israel. **5:** *Ground . . . dust,* synonyms for Sheol, the abode of the dead. *Selah,* see Ps 3.2n. **6–11:** God convenes his court, for *judgment* of the enemies and salvation for the psalmist. **12–14:** God

and over it take your seat[a] on
high.
8 The LORD judges the peoples;
judge me, O LORD, according to
my righteousness
and according to the integrity that
is in me.

9 O let the evil of the wicked come to
an end,
but establish the righteous,
you who test the minds and hearts,
O righteous God.
10 God is my shield,
who saves the upright in heart.
11 God is a righteous judge,
and a God who has indignation
every day.

12 If one does not repent, God[b] will
whet his sword;
he has bent and strung his
bow;
13 he has prepared his deadly weapons,
making his arrows fiery shafts.
14 See how they conceive evil,
and are pregnant with mischief,
and bring forth lies.
15 They make a pit, digging it out,
and fall into the hole that they have
made.
16 Their mischief returns upon their own
heads,
and on their own heads their
violence descends.

17 I will give to the LORD the thanks
due to his righteousness,
and sing praise to the name of the
LORD, the Most High.

PSALM 8

To the leader: according to The Gittith.
A Psalm of David.

1 O LORD, our Sovereign,
how majestic is your name in all
the earth!

You have set your glory above the
heavens.
2 Out of the mouths of babes and
infants
you have founded a bulwark because
of your foes,
to silence the enemy and the
avenger.

3 When I look at your heavens, the
work of your fingers,
the moon and the stars that you
have established;
4 what are human beings that you are
mindful of them,
mortals[c] that you care for them?

5 Yet you have made them a little lower
than God,[d]
and crowned them with glory and
honor.
6 You have given them dominion over
the works of your hands;
you have put all things under their
feet,
7 all sheep and oxen,
and also the beasts of the field,

a Cn: Heb *return* *b* Heb *he* *c* Heb *ben adam*, lit. *son of man* *d* Or *than the divine beings* or *angels*: Heb *elohim*

arms himself for battle against the enemies (Ps 35.2–3; 38.2). **14:** See Isa 59.4. **15–16:** The law of talion or equivalent retribution (see 3.7n.): The enemies fall into the pit dug to trap others (Ps 9.15–16; 35.7–8). **17:** The psalmist's praise of the divine *name*, the theme of the psalm that follows.

Ps 8: Praise of the creator. A hymn that echoes the creation account in Gen 1; the identical vv. 1 and 9 form a frame around the hymn. (*The Gittith*, an unknown musical term, also in Ps 81; 84.) **2:** Meaning unclear, perhaps referring to lost mythological traditions. **4–8:** The royal status of human beings, with dominion over subhuman creation (Gen 1.26). **4:** Contrast Ps 144.3 and Job 7.17 for negative understandings. **5:** Humans are endowed with divine *glory and honor*, perhaps the psalm's equivalent to the human being as "image of God" (Gen 1.27). **6–8:** Humanity's *dominion* over the animals is similarly recounted in Gen 1.28.

8 the birds of the air, and the fish of the sea,
whatever passes along the paths of the seas.

9 O LORD, our Sovereign,
how majestic is your name in all the earth!

PSALM 9

To the leader: according to Muth-labben. A Psalm of David.

1 I will give thanks to the LORD with my whole heart;
I will tell of all your wonderful deeds.
2 I will be glad and exult in you;
I will sing praise to your name, O Most High.

3 When my enemies turned back,
they stumbled and perished before you.
4 For you have maintained my just cause;
you have sat on the throne giving righteous judgment.

5 You have rebuked the nations, you have destroyed the wicked;
you have blotted out their name forever and ever.
6 The enemies have vanished in everlasting ruins;
their cities you have rooted out;
the very memory of them has perished.

7 But the LORD sits enthroned forever,
he has established his throne for judgment.
8 He judges the world with righteousness;
he judges the peoples with equity.
9 The LORD is a stronghold for the oppressed,
a stronghold in times of trouble.
10 And those who know your name put their trust in you,
for you, O LORD, have not forsaken those who seek you.

11 Sing praises to the LORD, who dwells in Zion.
Declare his deeds among the peoples.
12 For he who avenges blood is mindful of them;
he does not forget the cry of the afflicted.

13 Be gracious to me, O LORD.
See what I suffer from those who hate me;
you are the one who lifts me up from the gates of death,
14 so that I may recount all your praises,
and, in the gates of daughter Zion,
rejoice in your deliverance.

15 The nations have sunk in the pit that they made;
in the net that they hid has their own foot been caught.
16 The LORD has made himself known,
he has executed judgment;

Ps 9–10: Victory over enemies and petition for justice. Although these are separate psalms in the Heb text, the Gk Septuagint correctly understands them as a single psalm, a thanksgiving (Ps 9) linked to a lament (Ps 10). It is an acrostic poem: The initial letters of the stanzas are the Hebrew alphabet in order, although some are missing. Acrostics are used in the Psalter (Ps 25; 34; 37; 111; 112; 119; 145), as well as elsewhere (e.g., Lam 1–4; Prov 31.10–31). *Muth-labben,* a musical term of unknown meaning. Like Ps 8, it begins with praise of the divine name (v. 2). **1–6:** Thanksgiving to God for the annihilation of the psalmist's enemies. **5–6:** *Their name . . . the very memory of them,* the children of the evildoers, destroyed along with them (Ps 37.38). **7–10:** The LORD as righteous judge and defender of the oppressed, a common theme in Psalms (e.g., 98.9). **11–14:** Praise of God for his salvation of the psalmist. *Zion,* Jerusalem. **15–16:** See Ps 7.15–16n. **16:** *Higgaion,* a technical musicological term, like *selah* (also v. 20); see Ps 3.2n.

the wicked are snared in the work
of their own hands. *Higgaion.*
Selah

17 The wicked shall depart to Sheol,
all the nations that forget God.

18 For the needy shall not always be
forgotten,
nor the hope of the poor perish
forever.

19 Rise up, O LORD! Do not let mortals
prevail;
let the nations be judged before
you.
20 Put them in fear, O LORD;
let the nations know that they are
only human. *Selah*

PSALM 10

1 Why, O LORD, do you stand far off?
Why do you hide yourself in times
of trouble?
2 In arrogance the wicked persecute the
poor—
let them be caught in the schemes
they have devised.

3 For the wicked boast of the desires of
their heart,
those greedy for gain curse and
renounce the LORD.
4 In the pride of their countenance the
wicked say, "God will not seek
it out";
all their thoughts are, "There is no
God."

5 Their ways prosper at all times;
your judgments are on high, out of
their sight;
as for their foes, they scoff at them.
6 They think in their heart, "We shall
not be moved;
throughout all generations we shall
not meet adversity."

7 Their mouths are filled with cursing
and deceit and oppression;
under their tongues are mischief
and iniquity.
8 They sit in ambush in the villages;
in hiding places they murder the
innocent.

Their eyes stealthily watch for the
helpless;
9 they lurk in secret like a lion in its
covert;
they lurk that they may seize the
poor;
they seize the poor and drag them
off in their net.

10 They stoop, they crouch,
and the helpless fall by their might.
11 They think in their heart, "God has
forgotten,
he has hidden his face, he will
never see it."

12 Rise up, O LORD; O God, lift up
your hand;
do not forget the oppressed.
13 Why do the wicked renounce God,
and say in their hearts, "You will
not call us to account"?

14 But you do see! Indeed you note
trouble and grief,
that you may take it into your
hands;
the helpless commit themselves
to you;

17: *Sheol,* the abode of the dead. **19–20:** The reference to hostile *nations* (also in vv. 15,17; 10.16) may suggest that this is a royal psalm. **10.1:** God's hiddenness and distance. The motif of a hidden or quiet deity is often used in Psalms (e.g., Ps 13) to explain how evil triumphs in the presence of a good, powerful God. **4:** The indifference of *the wicked* to God (cf. Ps 14.1) and the divine law (v. 13). **5–6:** The prosperity of the wicked (Job 21.7–15). **7–11:** Their ambush and assault against the helpless. **12–14:** *The wicked* claim that God does not care about human affairs (vv. 4,6); on the contrary, God is attentive to the helpless. **15–18:** Destruction of the wicked and support of the oppressed by the divine king (Ps 9.5–8).

you have been the helper of the
orphan.

15 Break the arm of the wicked and
evildoers;
seek out their wickedness until you
find none.
16 The LORD is king forever and ever;
the nations shall perish from his
land.

17 O LORD, you will hear the desire of
the meek;
you will strengthen their heart, you
will incline your ear
18 to do justice for the orphan and the
oppressed,
so that those from earth may strike
terror no more.[a]

PSALM 11

To the leader. Of David.

1 In the LORD I take refuge; how can
you say to me,
"Flee like a bird to the
mountains;[b]
2 for look, the wicked bend the bow,
they have fitted their arrow to the
string,
to shoot in the dark at the upright
in heart.
3 If the foundations are destroyed,
what can the righteous do?"

4 The LORD is in his holy temple;
the LORD's throne is in heaven.
His eyes behold, his gaze examines
humankind.
5 The LORD tests the righteous and the
wicked,
and his soul hates the lover of
violence.
6 On the wicked he will rain coals of
fire and sulfur;
a scorching wind shall be the
portion of their cup.
7 For the LORD is righteous;
he loves righteous deeds;
the upright shall behold his face.

PSALM 12

*To the leader: according to The Sheminith.
A Psalm of David.*

1 Help, O LORD, for there is no longer
anyone who is godly;
the faithful have disappeared from
humankind.
2 They utter lies to each other;
with flattering lips and a double
heart they speak.

3 May the LORD cut off all flattering
lips,
the tongue that makes great boasts,
4 those who say, "With our tongues we
will prevail;
our lips are our own—who is our
master?"

5 "Because the poor are despoiled,
because the needy groan,

a Meaning of Heb uncertain *b* Gk Syr Jerome Tg: Heb *flee to your mountain, O bird*

Ps 11: The LORD, just protector of the upright. A psalm of trust in God as refuge. **1:** The psalmist flees for safety to an inaccessible place (Isa 16.2; Ezek 7.16). **2–3:** The collapse of the moral order (the assault on the upright by the wicked) threatens the stability of the physical order (Gen 6–8; Ps 82.5; Jer 4.23–26). **4–5:** The LORD, enthroned in heaven, has the ideal place from which to view and examine humankind, distinguishing between the righteous and the wicked (Ps 14.2; 102.19). **6:** The wicked are punished by God's weapons: a *rain . . . of fire* and searing *wind* (Gen 19.24; Am 7.4). **7:** The upright see the LORD's face (experience the divine presence in the Temple; see Ps 27.8–9; 42.2).

Ps 12: Prayer for deliverance and divine response. An individual lament. (*Sheminith,* see Ps 6n.) **2:** The psalmist complains about his enemies' damaging speech. **3–4:** The law of talion, or equivalent retribution (see 3.7n.); the lips and tongues of the psalmist's foes are destroyed (cf. Ps 3.7). **5:** A salvation oracle, whereby a temple official assures the petitioner of God's coming intervention. The presence of such

I will now rise up," says the LORD;
"I will place them in the safety for
which they long."
6 The promises of the LORD are
promises that are pure,
silver refined in a furnace on the
ground,
purified seven times.

7 You, O LORD, will protect us;
you will guard us from this
generation forever.
8 On every side the wicked prowl,
as vileness is exalted among
humankind.

PSALM 13

To the leader. A Psalm of David.

1 How long, O LORD? Will you forget
me forever?
How long will you hide your face
from me?
2 How long must I bear pain[a] in my
soul,
and have sorrow in my heart all
day long?
How long shall my enemy be exalted
over me?

3 Consider and answer me, O LORD my
God!
Give light to my eyes, or I will
sleep the sleep of death,
4 and my enemy will say, "I have
prevailed";
my foes will rejoice because I am
shaken.
5 But I trusted in your steadfast love;
my heart shall rejoice in your
salvation.
6 I will sing to the LORD,
because he has dealt bountifully
with me.

PSALM 14

To the leader. Of David.

1 Fools say in their hearts, "There is no
God."
They are corrupt, they do
abominable deeds;
there is no one who does good.

2 The LORD looks down from heaven
on humankind
to see if there are any who are
wise,
who seek after God.

3 They have all gone astray, they are all
alike perverse;
there is no one who does good,
no, not one.

4 Have they no knowledge, all the
evildoers
who eat up my people as they eat
bread,
and do not call upon the LORD?

5 There they shall be in great terror,
for God is with the company of the
righteous.

a Syr: Heb *hold counsels*

oracles in psalms suggests that they were recited in a temple, where a functionary, sometimes called a cultic prophet, could speak for God, offering assurance that a prayer has been heeded. **6–8:** A statement of trust in the LORD's promises of protection from the wicked.

Ps 13: Prayer for deliverance from enemies. An individual lament. **1–2:** The psalmist prays that God not forget the psalmist, nor hide his benevolent face. *How long?* Typical lament language (Ps 6.3; 62.3; 90.13). **3:** Enlightening the eyes is a metaphor for vitality and joy (Ps 38.10; 1 Sam 14.27,29). **5–6:** The lament ends with expressions of trust and thanksgiving, which offer God a reason to heed the complaint.

Ps 14: Condemnation of foolish evildoers. An individual lament, with wisdom language, which reappears with minor variants as Ps 53. **1:** *Fool,* a moral category, not an intellectual one. The fool denies not God's existence, but divine governance of the world and attention to humankind (Ps 10.4,11). **2:** See Ps 11.4–5n. **3:** The universality of evil (Jer 5.1). **4:** The evildoers' oppression of God's people. **5–6:** God's protection of the righteous and the poor, proving the fool (v. 1) to be wrong. **7:** A late (exilic)

6 You would confound the plans of the poor,
but the LORD is their refuge.

7 O that deliverance for Israel would come from Zion!
When the LORD restores the fortunes of his people,
Jacob will rejoice; Israel will be glad.

PSALM 15

A Psalm of David.

1 O LORD, who may abide in your tent?
Who may dwell on your holy hill?

2 Those who walk blamelessly, and do what is right,
and speak the truth from their heart;
3 who do not slander with their tongue,
and do no evil to their friends,
nor take up a reproach against their neighbors;
4 in whose eyes the wicked are despised,
but who honor those who fear the LORD;
who stand by their oath even to their hurt;
5 who do not lend money at interest,
and do not take a bribe against the innocent.

Those who do these things shall never be moved.

PSALM 16

A Miktam of David.

1 Protect me, O God, for in you I take refuge.
2 I say to the LORD, "You are my Lord;
I have no good apart from you."[a]

3 As for the holy ones in the land, they are the noble,
in whom is all my delight.

4 Those who choose another god multiply their sorrows;[b]
their drink offerings of blood I will not pour out
or take their names upon my lips.

5 The LORD is my chosen portion and my cup;
you hold my lot.
6 The boundary lines have fallen for me in pleasant places;
I have a goodly heritage.

7 I bless the LORD who gives me counsel;
in the night also my heart instructs me.
8 I keep the LORD always before me;
because he is at my right hand, I shall not be moved.

a Jerome Tg: Meaning of Heb uncertain
b Cn: Meaning of Heb uncertain

addition concluding the psalm, extending the psalm's meaning to the national level. *Zion,* Jerusalem.

Ps 15: Ritual for admission to the Temple. An entrance liturgy (see Ps 5). Admittance to the Temple is a concern of Ps 15–17. **1:** *Tent,* traditional language for the Temple (Ps 26.8; 27.5). **2–5:** The moral qualities enjoined are right action and truthful speech, specifically refraining from *slander* (Lev 19.16), nonassociation with the wicked (Ps 1.1), keeping one's *oath,* and honesty in business and legal matters. As in some prophets (e.g., Am 5.21–24; Isa 1.10–17), religion is defined in terms of moral behavior rather than ritual activities. **5b:** For a *bribe* meant to pervert or deny justice, see Ex 23.6–8; Prov 17.23. **5c:** Prov 10.30.

Ps 16: A prayer for admission to the Temple. A psalm of trust. **2–4:** The psalmist's faith, contrasted with idolaters who put their trust in false gods. **3:** *Holy ones,* unclear; perhaps gods or deified ancestors. **4:** The psalmist refuses to pour out libations of blood (of sacrificed animals) to other gods, or to invoke them in prayer. **5–6:** The psalmist may be a priest (Num 18.20; Josh 18.7). **10–11:** *Sheol,* the abode of

9 Therefore my heart is glad, and my
soul rejoices;
my body also rests secure.
10 For you do not give me up to Sheol,
or let your faithful one see the Pit.

11 You show me the path of life.
In your presence there is fullness of
joy;
in your right hand are pleasures
forevermore.

PSALM 17

A Prayer of David.

1 Hear a just cause, O LORD; attend to
my cry;
give ear to my prayer from lips free
of deceit.
2 From you let my vindication come;
let your eyes see the right.

3 If you try my heart, if you visit me by
night,
if you test me, you will find no
wickedness in me;
my mouth does not transgress.
4 As for what others do, by the word
of your lips
I have avoided the ways of the
violent.
5 My steps have held fast to your
paths;
my feet have not slipped.

6 I call upon you, for you will answer
me, O God;
incline your ear to me, hear my
words.
7 Wondrously show your steadfast love,
O savior of those who seek refuge
from their adversaries at your right
hand.

8 Guard me as the apple of the eye;
hide me in the shadow of your
wings,
9 from the wicked who despoil me,
my deadly enemies who
surround me.
10 They close their hearts to pity;
with their mouths they speak
arrogantly.
11 They track me down;[a] now they
surround me;
they set their eyes to cast me to the
ground.
12 They are like a lion eager to tear,
like a young lion lurking in
ambush.

13 Rise up, O LORD, confront them,
overthrow them!
By your sword deliver my life from
the wicked,
14 from mortals—by your hand,
O LORD—
from mortals whose portion in life
is in this world.
May their bellies be filled with what
you have stored up for them;
may their children have more than
enough;
may they leave something over to
their little ones.

15 As for me, I shall behold your face in
righteousness;
when I awake I shall be satisfied,
beholding your likeness.

a One Ms Compare Syr: MT *Our steps*

the dead, also called *the Pit,* is contrasted with the Temple, *the path of life,* where the psalmist can experience the divine presence (Ps 11.7).

Ps 17: Prayer for deliverance from enemies. An individual lament. **1–5:** Appealing to a just God, the psalmist protests his innocence (Ps 26.4–5; 101.3–4). **8–9:** Shelter in the shadow of God's *wings* may refer to safety in the Temple (Ps 36.7–8; 57.1; 61.4). *The apple of the eye,* the pupil. **11–12:** The enemies are described as predators (Ps 7.2). **13:** The *LORD* as divine warrior arms himself with a sword (Ps 7.12–13). **14:** The psalmist's enemies and their progeny will get their fill of punishment (2 Kings 9.26; Ps 37.38; Job 21.19). **15:** Safe from the assaults of the enemy, the psalmist is sated with the presence (*face*) of God in the Temple, as in the conclusion of the previous psalm.

PSALM 18

To the leader. A Psalm of David the servant of the LORD, who addressed the words of this song to the LORD on the day when the LORD delivered him from the hand of all his enemies, and from the hand of Saul. He said:

1 I love you, O LORD, my strength.
2 The LORD is my rock, my fortress, and my deliverer,
my God, my rock in whom I take refuge,
my shield, and the horn of my salvation, my stronghold.
3 I call upon the LORD, who is worthy to be praised,
so I shall be saved from my enemies.

4 The cords of death encompassed me;
the torrents of perdition assailed me;
5 the cords of Sheol entangled me;
the snares of death confronted me.
6 In my distress I called upon the LORD;
to my God I cried for help.
From his temple he heard my voice,
and my cry to him reached his ears.

7 Then the earth reeled and rocked;
the foundations also of the mountains trembled
and quaked, because he was angry.
8 Smoke went up from his nostrils,
and devouring fire from his mouth;
glowing coals flamed forth from him.
9 He bowed the heavens, and came down;
thick darkness was under his feet.
10 He rode on a cherub, and flew;
he came swiftly upon the wings of the wind.
11 He made darkness his covering around him,
his canopy thick clouds dark with water.
12 Out of the brightness before him
there broke through his clouds
hailstones and coals of fire.
13 The LORD also thundered in the heavens,
and the Most High uttered his voice.[a]
14 And he sent out his arrows, and scattered them;
he flashed forth lightnings, and routed them.
15 Then the channels of the sea were seen,
and the foundations of the world were laid bare
at your rebuke, O LORD,
at the blast of the breath of your nostrils.

16 He reached down from on high, he took me;
he drew me out of mighty waters.
17 He delivered me from my strong enemy,
and from those who hated me;
for they were too mighty for me.
18 They confronted me in the day of my calamity;

a Gk See 2 Sam 22.14: Heb adds *hailstones and coals of fire*

Ps 18: A royal thanksgiving hymn. This hymn is also found in 2 Sam 22, and there are borrowings from it in Ps 144. **2:** The longest string of divine epithets in the Bible. **3:** The main theme of the poem: God is praised for saving David from his enemies (see superscription and cf. Ps 3n.). **4–5:** The enemies are cosmic, both the chaotic waters engulfing the royal psalmist and the powers of the abode of the dead, *Sheol.* **6–15:** Answering the appeal of the psalmist, a theophany (manifestation of God) of the Divine Warrior, portrayed as a storm god (Ex 19.16–19; 20.18; 24.15–18; see also Ps 29; 97.2–5; Isa 30.27; Hab 3.3–12). **10:** *Cherub,* one of the bearers of God's throne (Ex 25.18–20) and mythological creatures who assisted divine mobility (Ezek 1; 10). **16–19:** The deliverance of the psalmist from a tight spot (v. 6) into a *broad,* unconfined space (v. 36; Ps 4.1), a metaphor for salvation. **20–24:** The psalmist's obedience to

but the LORD was my support.
19 He brought me out into a broad place;
he delivered me, because he delighted in me.

20 The LORD rewarded me according to my righteousness;
according to the cleanness of my hands he recompensed me.
21 For I have kept the ways of the LORD,
and have not wickedly departed from my God.
22 For all his ordinances were before me,
and his statutes I did not put away from me.
23 I was blameless before him,
and I kept myself from guilt.
24 Therefore the LORD has recompensed me according to my righteousness,
according to the cleanness of my hands in his sight.

25 With the loyal you show yourself loyal;
with the blameless you show yourself blameless;
26 with the pure you show yourself pure;
and with the crooked you show yourself perverse.
27 For you deliver a humble people,
but the haughty eyes you bring down.
28 It is you who light my lamp;
the LORD, my God, lights up my darkness.
29 By you I can crush a troop,
and by my God I can leap over a wall.
30 This God—his way is perfect;
the promise of the LORD proves true;
he is a shield for all who take refuge in him.

31 For who is God except the LORD?
And who is a rock besides our God?—
32 the God who girded me with strength,
and made my way safe.
33 He made my feet like the feet of a deer,
and set me secure on the heights.
34 He trains my hands for war,
so that my arms can bend a bow of bronze.
35 You have given me the shield of your salvation,
and your right hand has supported me;
your help[a] has made me great.
36 You gave me a wide place for my steps under me,
and my feet did not slip.
37 I pursued my enemies and overtook them;
and did not turn back until they were consumed.
38 I struck them down, so that they were not able to rise;
they fell under my feet.
39 For you girded me with strength for the battle;
you made my assailants sink under me.
40 You made my enemies turn their backs to me,
and those who hated me I destroyed.
41 They cried for help, but there was no one to save them;
they cried to the LORD, but he did not answer them.
42 I beat them fine, like dust before the wind;
I cast them out like the mire of the streets.

43 You delivered me from strife with the peoples;[b]

a Or *gentleness* *b* Gk Tg: Heb *people*

the divine will, a justification for his salvation. **25–30:** A description of a fair, powerful God, who assists the faithful. **31–45:** The royal psalmist's victory over historical enemies. **38–39:** See Judg 5.26–27. **41:** Unlike the psalmist's successful appeal to God, the enemies' cries for help go unanswered. **45:** See Mic

you made me head of the nations;
people whom I had not known
served me.
44 As soon as they heard of me they
obeyed me;
foreigners came cringing to me.
45 Foreigners lost heart,
and came trembling out of their
strongholds.

46 The LORD lives! Blessed be my rock,
and exalted be the God of my
salvation,
47 the God who gave me vengeance
and subdued peoples under me;
48 who delivered me from my enemies;
indeed, you exalted me above my
adversaries;
you delivered me from the violent.

49 For this I will extol you, O LORD,
among the nations,
and sing praises to your name.
50 Great triumphs he gives to his king,
and shows steadfast love to his
anointed,
to David and his descendants
forever.

PSALM 19

To the leader. A Psalm of David.

1 The heavens are telling the glory of
God;
and the firmament[a] proclaims his
handiwork.
2 Day to day pours forth speech,
and night to night declares
knowledge.
3 There is no speech, nor are there
words;
their voice is not heard;
4 yet their voice[b] goes out through all
the earth,
and their words to the end of the
world.

In the heavens[c] he has set a tent for
the sun,
5 which comes out like a bridegroom
from his wedding canopy,
and like a strong man runs its
course with joy.
6 Its rising is from the end of the
heavens,
and its circuit to the end of them;
and nothing is hid from its heat.

7 The law of the LORD is perfect,
reviving the soul;
the decrees of the LORD are sure,
making wise the simple;
8 the precepts of the LORD are right,
rejoicing the heart;
the commandment of the LORD is
clear,
enlightening the eyes;
9 the fear of the LORD is pure,
enduring forever;
the ordinances of the LORD are true
and righteous altogether.
10 More to be desired are they than
gold,
even much fine gold;
sweeter also than honey,
and drippings of the honeycomb.

11 Moreover by them is your servant
warned;
in keeping them there is great
reward.

a Or *dome* *b* Gk Jerome Compare Syr: Heb *line*
c Heb *In them*

7.17. **46–48:** The LORD is praised for the king's victory and the submission of his foes. **50:** God's eternal commitment to the Davidic dynasty (cf. 2 Sam 7.13).

Ps 19: Hymn to God the creator and lawgiver. A hymn, combining the two themes of the creation of heaven and sun (vv. 1–6) and the giving of the law (vv. 7–14). These two sections, which might have originally been separate compositions, are linked by the recognition of the sun as god of law and justice in the ancient Near East (Mal 4.2). **1–4:** The revelation of God by the natural world. **3–4a:** A riddle: How can one speak without words? **7–10:** These verses have particular affinity with wisdom literature, and Ps 119. **7,10:** The metaphor of divine instruction as food (Deut 8.3) reviving the life-force (Ps 23.3). **11–14:**

12 But who can detect their errors?
Clear me from hidden faults.
13 Keep back your servant also from the insolent;[a]
do not let them have dominion over me.
Then I shall be blameless,
and innocent of great transgression.

14 Let the words of my mouth and the meditation of my heart
be acceptable to you,
O LORD, my rock and my redeemer.

PSALM 20

To the leader. A Psalm of David.

1 The LORD answer you in the day of trouble!
The name of the God of Jacob protect you!
2 May he send you help from the sanctuary,
and give you support from Zion.
3 May he remember all your offerings,
and regard with favor your burnt sacrifices. *Selah*

4 May he grant you your heart's desire,
and fulfill all your plans.
5 May we shout for joy over your victory,
and in the name of our God set up our banners.
May the LORD fulfill all your petitions.

6 Now I know that the LORD will help his anointed;
he will answer him from his holy heaven
with mighty victories by his right hand.
7 Some take pride in chariots, and some in horses,
but our pride is in the name of the LORD our God.
8 They will collapse and fall,
but we shall rise and stand upright.

9 Give victory to the king, O LORD;
answer us when we call.[b]

PSALM 21

To the leader. A Psalm of David.

1 In your strength the king rejoices, O LORD,
and in your help how greatly he exults!
2 You have given him his heart's desire,
and have not withheld the request of his lips. *Selah*
3 For you meet him with rich blessings;
you set a crown of fine gold on his head.
4 He asked you for life; you gave it to him—
length of days forever and ever.
5 His glory is great through your help;
splendor and majesty you bestow on him.

a Or *from proud thoughts* *b* Gk: Heb *give victory, O LORD; let the King answer us when we call*

A prayer for forgiveness for disobedience to the divine law, and for divine acceptance of the psalmist's words in this psalm.

Ps 20: Prayer for the king's victory in battle. A communal prayer of petition for the king's success in military ventures, linked with the royal thanksgiving in Ps 21. **2:** *Help from the sanctuary,* perhaps angelic forces from the heavenly sanctuary (represented in the Temple in *Zion* [Jerusalem]), battling on the side of the king (v. 6; Ps 57.3). **3:** *Selah,* see Ps 3.2n. **6:** *His anointed,* i.e., the king; see Ps 2.2n. **7:** See Josh 24.12; Ps 44.3; 147.10. **8:** The collapse of defeated enemies (cf. 2 Kings 9.24; Ps 18.39). **9:** As the textual note indicates, it is uncertain if the king is the human monarch (the Gk reading), or is an epithet for God (the Heb).

Ps 21: Royal thanksgiving for victory. A hymn sharing vocabulary and theme with Ps 20 (cf. 20.4 and 21.2; 20.6–7 and 21.9,13). **2:** *Selah,* see Ps 3.2n. **4:** Prayer for long life of the king (1 Kings 3.14; Ps 61.6). **5:** *Glory . . . splendor and majesty,* the nimbus of light surrounding gods and kings (Ps 8.5). **7:** This

6 You bestow on him blessings forever;
you make him glad with the joy of your presence.
7 For the king trusts in the LORD,
and through the steadfast love of the Most High he shall not be moved.

8 Your hand will find out all your enemies;
your right hand will find out those who hate you.
9 You will make them like a fiery furnace
when you appear.
The LORD will swallow them up in his wrath,
and fire will consume them.
10 You will destroy their offspring from the earth,
and their children from among humankind.
11 If they plan evil against you,
if they devise mischief, they will not succeed.
12 For you will put them to flight;
you will aim at their faces with your bows.

13 Be exalted, O LORD, in your strength!
We will sing and praise your power.

PSALM 22

To the leader: according to The Deer of the Dawn. A Psalm of David.

1 My God, my God, why have you forsaken me?
Why are you so far from helping me, from the words of my groaning?
2 O my God, I cry by day, but you do not answer;
and by night, but find no rest.

3 Yet you are holy,
enthroned on the praises of Israel.
4 In you our ancestors trusted;
they trusted, and you delivered them.
5 To you they cried, and were saved;
in you they trusted, and were not put to shame.

6 But I am a worm, and not human;
scorned by others, and despised by the people.
7 All who see me mock at me;
they make mouths at me, they shake their heads;
8 "Commit your cause to the LORD; let him deliver—
let him rescue the one in whom he delights!"

9 Yet it was you who took me from the womb;
you kept me safe on my mother's breast.
10 On you I was cast from my birth,
and since my mother bore me you have been my God.
11 Do not be far from me,
for trouble is near
and there is no one to help.

12 Many bulls encircle me,

abundant royal blessing is here predicated on royal obedience. **9:** For the fiery wrath of God, see Isa 29.6; 66.15–16. **10:** See Ps 37.38.

Ps 22: Prayer of a person abandoned by God. An individual lament. There is a refrainlike repetition in vv. 1,11,19. The plight of the psalmist may be mortal illness. *According to the Deer of the Dawn,* a musical term, perhaps indicating the melody to which the words were sung. **1–11:** Why does God, who cared for the ancestors (vv. 4–5) and the psalmist (vv. 9–10) in the past, not do so now? **1:** Divine abandonment is a major theme of the psalter; see Ps 10.1n. The opening words are quoted by Jesus at his death, according to Mt 27.46; Mk 15.34. **6–7:** The dehumanized psalmist is mocked by his enemies. **8–9:** The enemies open their mouths to mock and to devour (v. 15). **12–21:** The psalmist's enemies as animal predators (Ps 17.12). **12:** *Bashan,* a region in northern Transjordan famous for its cattle. **23–24:** See Ps

strong bulls of Bashan surround
me;
13 they open wide their mouths at me,
like a ravening and roaring lion.

14 I am poured out like water,
and all my bones are out of joint;
my heart is like wax;
it is melted within my breast;
15 my mouth[a] is dried up like a
potsherd,
and my tongue sticks to my jaws;
you lay me in the dust of death.

16 For dogs are all around me;
a company of evildoers
encircles me.
My hands and feet have shriveled;[b]
17 I can count all my bones.
They stare and gloat over me;
18 they divide my clothes among
themselves,
and for my clothing they cast lots.

19 But you, O LORD, do not be far
away!
O my help, come quickly to
my aid!
20 Deliver my soul from the sword,
my life[c] from the power of the
dog!
21 Save me from the mouth of the
lion!

From the horns of the wild oxen you
have rescued[d] me.
22 I will tell of your name to my
brothers and sisters;[e]
in the midst of the congregation I
will praise you:
23 You who fear the LORD, praise him!
All you offspring of Jacob, glorify
him;
stand in awe of him, all you
offspring of Israel!

24 For he did not despise or abhor
the affliction of the afflicted;
he did not hide his face from me,[f]
but heard when I[g] cried to him.

25 From you comes my praise in the
great congregation;
my vows I will pay before those
who fear him.
26 The poor[h] shall eat and be satisfied;
those who seek him shall praise the
LORD.
May your hearts live forever!

27 All the ends of the earth shall
remember
and turn to the LORD;
and all the families of the nations
shall worship before him.[i]
28 For dominion belongs to the LORD,
and he rules over the nations.

29 To him,[j] indeed, shall all who sleep
in[k] the earth bow down;
before him shall bow all who go
down to the dust,
and I shall live for him.[l]
30 Posterity will serve him;
future generations will be told
about the Lord,
31 and[m] proclaim his deliverance to a
people yet unborn,
saying that he has done it.

a Cn: Heb *strength* *b* Meaning of Heb uncertain *c* Heb *my only one* *d* Heb *answered* *e* Or *kindred* *f* Heb *him* *g* Heb *he* *h* Or *afflicted* *i* Gk Syr Jerome: Heb *you* *j* Cn: Heb *They have eaten and* *k* Cn: Heb *all the fat ones* *l* Compare Gk Syr Vg: Heb *and he who cannot keep himself alive* *m* Compare Gk: Heb *it will be told about the Lord to the generation, 31they will come and*

35.18–19. As elsewhere in Psalms (e.g., Ps 6.5), a major motivating factor used by the psalmist for salvation is the idea that God enjoys praise. **25–26:** The psalmist's recovery and reintegration into the community; all Israel is invited to join him in praise. **27:** On praise of God by the nations, see Ps 67.2–4; 86.9; 117.1. **29–31:** Past (the dead), present (the psalmist), and future (people yet unborn) revere the LORD. On worship by the dead, contrast Ps 6.5; 30.9; 88.10–12; 115.17.

PSALM 23

A Psalm of David.

1 The LORD is my shepherd, I shall not
want.
2 He makes me lie down in green
pastures;
he leads me beside still waters;[a]
3 he restores my soul.[b]
He leads me in right paths[c]
for his name's sake.

4 Even though I walk through the
darkest valley,[d]
I fear no evil;
for you are with me;
your rod and your staff—
they comfort me.

5 You prepare a table before me
in the presence of my enemies;
you anoint my head with oil;
my cup overflows.
6 Surely[e] goodness and mercy[f] shall
follow me
all the days of my life,
and I shall dwell in the house of the
LORD
my whole life long.[g]

PSALM 24

Of David. A Psalm.

1 The earth is the LORD's and all that is
in it,
the world, and those who live in it;
2 for he has founded it on the seas,
and established it on the rivers.

3 Who shall ascend the hill of the LORD?
And who shall stand in his holy
place?
4 Those who have clean hands and pure
hearts,
who do not lift up their souls to
what is false,
and do not swear deceitfully.
5 They will receive blessing from the
LORD,
and vindication from the God of
their salvation.
6 Such is the company of those who
seek him,
who seek the face of the God of
Jacob.[h] *Selah*

a Heb *waters of rest* b Or *life* c Or *paths of righteousness* d Or *the valley of the shadow of death* e Or *Only* f Or *kindness* g Heb *for length of days* h Gk Syr: Heb *your face, O Jacob*

Ps 23: The LORD as shepherd-king and host. A psalm of trust in the divine shepherd, who leads his people in a new Exodus (Isa 40.3–5; 49.8–13) through danger (vv. 1–4) to security (vv. 5–6). In both parts, God provides the people with food and drink. **1:** *Shepherd* is a frequent biblical and ancient Near Eastern metaphor for royalty (Isa 40.11; Ezek 34; Ps 80). **3:** See Ps 31.3. **4:** The divine king leads the people safely through dangerous terrain, using a shepherd's *rod* (Lev 27.32) and *staff.* **5:** For the preparation of *a table* in the wilderness for the first Exodus generation, see Ps 78.19. **6a:** *Goodness and mercy,* covenant blessings, rather than curses, pursue the psalmist (Deut 28.3,15,45). **6b:** Exiled Israel is led back into the *house of the LORD* (the land; see Jer 12.7–8). People did not *dwell* in the temple for their *whole life long;* this favors the allegorical interpretation for *the house of the LORD* as the land of Israel.

Ps 24: A liturgy on entering the sanctuary. A hymn celebrating God, creator and victor, with an "entrance liturgy" (vv. 3–6; Ps 5; 15). The connections between the creation of the world and the construction of the sanctuary (Gen 2.1–3; Ex 39.32,42–43) and the double entrance into the sanctuary, by the worshipers (v. 6) and the LORD (vv. 7–10) join these two parts. **2:** The chaotic primeval waters are defeated and pacified by God the creator. **3–6:** The requirements for participation in temple worship are predominantly moral; see Ps 15.2–5n. **6:** *Selah* (also v. 10), see Ps 3.2n. **7–10:** The return of God, victorious over the forces of chaos, to his sanctuary. It is unclear what role these verses might have had in an actual ceremony. **7:** Confronted by the chaotic waters (v. 2), the (personified) city *gates* and towers were despondent and fearful (Ps 46.1–3); now they are invited to "lift their heads," a sign of joy.

7 Lift up your heads, O gates!
and be lifted up, O ancient doors!
that the King of glory may come in.
8 Who is the King of glory?
The LORD, strong and mighty,
the LORD, mighty in battle.
9 Lift up your heads, O gates!
and be lifted up, O ancient doors!
that the King of glory may come in.
10 Who is this King of glory?
The LORD of hosts,
he is the King of glory. *Selah*

PSALM 25

Of David.

1 To you, O LORD, I lift up my soul.
2 O my God, in you I trust;
do not let me be put to shame;
do not let my enemies exult over me.
3 Do not let those who wait for you be put to shame;
let them be ashamed who are wantonly treacherous.

4 Make me to know your ways, O LORD;
teach me your paths.
5 Lead me in your truth, and teach me,
for you are the God of my salvation;
for you I wait all day long.

6 Be mindful of your mercy, O LORD,
and of your steadfast love,
for they have been from of old.
7 Do not remember the sins of my youth or my transgressions;
according to your steadfast love remember me,
for your goodness' sake, O LORD!

8 Good and upright is the LORD;
therefore he instructs sinners in the way.
9 He leads the humble in what is right,
and teaches the humble his way.
10 All the paths of the LORD are steadfast love and faithfulness,
for those who keep his covenant and his decrees.

11 For your name's sake, O LORD,
pardon my guilt, for it is great.
12 Who are they that fear the LORD?
He will teach them the way that they should choose.

13 They will abide in prosperity,
and their children shall possess the land.
14 The friendship of the LORD is for those who fear him,
and he makes his covenant known to them.
15 My eyes are ever toward the LORD,
for he will pluck my feet out of the net.

16 Turn to me and be gracious to me,
for I am lonely and afflicted.
17 Relieve the troubles of my heart,
and bring me[a] out of my distress.
18 Consider my affliction and my trouble,
and forgive all my sins.

19 Consider how many are my foes,
and with what violent hatred they hate me.

a Or *The troubles of my heart are enlarged; bring me*

Ps 25: Prayer for deliverance from enemies. An individual lament in acrostic form: The first line begins with the first letter of the Hebrew alphabet, the first word of the second line with the second letter of the alphabet, and so on to the final letter (see Ps 9–10n.). The psalm is made up of alternating petitions and expressions of trust. **2–3:** The plea for the "shaming" of one's enemies is frequent in laments (Ps 6.10; 35.4,26; 40.14–15). **4–5:** Prayer for (moral) guidance, with a wisdom cast; cf. vv. 8–10,12. **6–7:** Prayer for divine mercy and forgiveness of sins. **11:** The request for forgiveness of sins closes the first half of the lament; *name* here means essence. **12–13:** Those who fear the LORD and their children shall be blessed (Ps 37.28–29). Possession of *the land* is a major theme of Ps 37. **16:** The singular, *lonely* petitioner is introduced to highlight the many foes (v. 19). **17–18:** Prayer for relief from *distress* and for forgiveness.

20 O guard my life, and deliver me;
do not let me be put to shame, for
I take refuge in you.
21 May integrity and uprightness
preserve me,
for I wait for you.

22 Redeem Israel, O God,
out of all its troubles.

PSALM 26

Of David.

1 Vindicate me, O LORD,
for I have walked in my integrity,
and I have trusted in the LORD
without wavering.
2 Prove me, O LORD, and try me;
test my heart and mind.
3 For your steadfast love is before my
eyes,
and I walk in faithfulness to you.[a]

4 I do not sit with the worthless,
nor do I consort with hypocrites;
5 I hate the company of evildoers,
and will not sit with the wicked.

6 I wash my hands in innocence,
and go around your altar, O LORD,
7 singing aloud a song of thanksgiving,
and telling all your wondrous
deeds.

8 O LORD, I love the house in which
you dwell,
and the place where your glory
abides.
9 Do not sweep me away with sinners,
nor my life with the bloodthirsty,
10 those in whose hands are evil devices,
and whose right hands are full of
bribes.

11 But as for me, I walk in my integrity;
redeem me, and be gracious to me.
12 My foot stands on level ground;
in the great congregation I will
bless the LORD.

PSALM 27

Of David.

1 The LORD is my light and my
salvation;
whom shall I fear?
The LORD is the stronghold[b] of my
life;
of whom shall I be afraid?

2 When evildoers assail me
to devour my flesh—
my adversaries and foes—
they shall stumble and fall.

a Or *in your faithfulness* *b* Or *refuge*

21: *Integrity and uprightness,* personified (angelic) guardians protecting the psalmist (cf. Ps 43.3). **22:** A possibly secondary plea, moving from the individual to the community; see Ps 130.8.

Ps 26: Prayer for divine justice. An individual lament, in which the psalmist, perhaps a priest (vv. 6–7) claims that the conduct of his life has been according to divine law and hopes to commune with God in the Temple (vv. 6–8). The psalm is based on one biblical retribution theology, that proper behavior is rewarded by God; yet it shows that this expectation was not always fulfilled. **1–3:** The psalmist prays that God try him and find him righteous (Ps 17.3–5). **4–5:** The psalmist's protestation of innocence and his nonassociation with the wicked (Ps 1.1–2). **6–7:** Access to the *altar* suggests that the psalmist is a priest. **8:** *Glory,* the light streaming from the deity (Ps 36.9; 63.2). **9–10:** Evildoers, hated by the psalmist (v. 5), will be denied access to the Temple, which the psalmist loves (v. 8). **12:** *Level ground* recalls the psalmist's walking in *integrity* (vv. 1,11) and *faithfulness* (v. 3). As in other psalms, the petitioner here assumes that God wants to be praised (see Ps 22.22).

Ps 27: Protection in the Temple of the trustworthy God. A psalm of trust; the psalmist has no fear of enemies in the protective refuge of the Temple. **1:** *My light,* see Mic 7.8; Job 33.30. As in other psalms, various metaphors, here *light* and *stronghold,* are combined to reflect different aspects of God's great power. **2:** *Devour my flesh,* an idiom for harmful, malicious speech (cf. English "backbite"); it can also refer to enemies as predators. **4:** *Live in the house of the LORD,* the psalmist hopes to visit the Temple on

3 Though an army encamp against me,
my heart shall not fear;
though war rise up against me,
yet I will be confident.

4 One thing I asked of the LORD,
that will I seek after:
to live in the house of the LORD
all the days of my life,
to behold the beauty of the LORD,
and to inquire in his temple.

5 For he will hide me in his shelter
in the day of trouble;
he will conceal me under the cover of
his tent;
he will set me high on a rock.

6 Now my head is lifted up
above my enemies all around me,
and I will offer in his tent
sacrifices with shouts of joy;
I will sing and make melody to the
LORD.

7 Hear, O LORD, when I cry aloud,
be gracious to me and answer
me!
8 "Come," my heart says, "seek his
face!"
Your face, LORD, do I seek.
9 Do not hide your face from me.

Do not turn your servant away in
anger,
you who have been my help.
Do not cast me off, do not
forsake me,
O God of my salvation!
10 If my father and mother forsake me,
the LORD will take me up.
11 Teach me your way, O LORD,
and lead me on a level path
because of my enemies.
12 Do not give me up to the will of
my adversaries,
for false witnesses have risen
against me,
and they are breathing out violence.

13 I believe that I shall see the goodness
of the LORD
in the land of the living.
14 Wait for the LORD;
be strong, and let your heart take
courage;
wait for the LORD!

PSALM 28

Of David.

1 To you, O LORD, I call;
my rock, do not refuse to hear me,
for if you are silent to me,
I shall be like those who go down
to the Pit.
2 Hear the voice of my supplication,
as I cry to you for help,
as I lift up my hands
toward your most holy sanctuary.[a]

3 Do not drag me away with the
wicked,
with those who are workers of evil,
who speak peace with their neighbors,

a Heb *your innermost sanctuary*

a pilgrimage (Ps 84.5). **5–9:** The Temple as a place of refuge, where the psalmist can experience the divine presence, the LORD's *face.* This contrasts sharply, for example, with Deuteronomy's assertion that only God's name resides in the Temple (e.g., Deut 12.11), and God's face is never seen (e.g., Deut 4.12,15). **10:** Abandonment by one's parents probably means that they have died; God is thus asked to serve as an adoptive parent. **12:** *Will* (lit. "throat"), the enemies pictured as predators (v. 2; Ps 17.9–12); the foes are also judicial, lying witnesses testifying against the psalmist. **13:** *The land of the living,* a metaphor for the Temple. **14:** Possibly a response to the psalmist's prayer.

Ps 28: Royal plea for deliverance from enemies. An individual lament, perhaps a royal lament, given the military language and the reference to the LORD's anointed (vv. 7–8). **1:** *The Pit,* a synonym for Sheol, the abode of the dead. **2:** *Lifting up . . . hands* was the typical position of biblical prayer (see, e.g., 1 Kings 8.22). **3:** The deceitful, untrustworthy speech of the wicked may refer to conspiracy against the king.

while mischief is in their hearts.
4 Repay them according to their work,
and according to the evil of their deeds;
repay them according to the work of their hands;
render them their due reward.
5 Because they do not regard the works of the LORD,
or the work of his hands,
he will break them down and build them up no more.

6 Blessed be the LORD,
for he has heard the sound of my pleadings.
7 The LORD is my strength and my shield;
in him my heart trusts;
so I am helped, and my heart exults,
and with my song I give thanks to him.

8 The LORD is the strength of his people;
he is the saving refuge of his anointed.
9 O save your people, and bless your heritage;
be their shepherd, and carry them forever.

PSALM 29

A Psalm of David.

1 Ascribe to the LORD, O heavenly beings,[a]
ascribe to the LORD glory and strength.
2 Ascribe to the LORD the glory of his name;
worship the LORD in holy splendor.

3 The voice of the LORD is over the waters;
the God of glory thunders,
the LORD, over mighty waters.
4 The voice of the LORD is powerful;
the voice of the LORD is full of majesty.

5 The voice of the LORD breaks the cedars;
the LORD breaks the cedars of Lebanon.
6 He makes Lebanon skip like a calf,
and Sirion like a young wild ox.

7 The voice of the LORD flashes forth flames of fire.
8 The voice of the LORD shakes the wilderness;
the LORD shakes the wilderness of Kadesh.

9 The voice of the LORD causes the oaks to whirl,[b]
and strips the forest bare;
and in his temple all say, "Glory!"

10 The LORD sits enthroned over the flood;

a Heb *sons of gods* b Or *causes the deer to calve*

4: Prayer for retribution (Ps 94.2). **6–7:** The characteristic move of the lament from complaint and petition to praise, with expressions of trust. **9:** The king's prayer for the people (Ps 3.8), addressed to the divine shepherd-king.

Ps 29: Hymn to the God of the storm. Perhaps originally a Canaanite hymn of praise, appropriated by Israel as a prayer for rain for the fall feast of Tabernacles. The geographical placement in Lebanon and Sirion (v. 6) suggests a non-Israelite origin of this psalm. **1:** *Heavenly beings,* lit. "sons of God," or "sons of gods," subordinate deities in the heavenly assembly (Ex 15.11; Ps 82.1; 89.5–7). **2:** *In holy splendor* could also be translated as "when the Holy One appears." **3–9:** *The voice of the LORD* (thunder), occurring seven times in these verses. **3:** The LORD battles the *mighty waters,* the primeval forces of chaos. **6–8:** Earthquake is a traditional accompaniment of a theophany or divine manifestation (Ps 18.7; 114.7). **6:** *Sirion,* Mount Hermon (see Deut 3.9), at the southern border of *Lebanon.* **8:** *The wilderness of Kadesh,* in western Syria. **9:** The wind and rain of the storm defoliate the forest. *In his temple,* praise from the subordinate deities in the heavenly temple. **10:** The LORD's enthronement as king over *the flood* (defeated

the LORD sits enthroned as king
forever.
11 May the LORD give strength to his
people!
May the LORD bless his people
with peace!

PSALM 30

A Psalm. A Song at the dedication of the temple. Of David.

1 I will extol you, O LORD, for you
have drawn me up,
and did not let my foes rejoice over
me.
2 O LORD my God, I cried to you for
help,
and you have healed me.
3 O LORD, you brought up my soul
from Sheol,
restored me to life from among
those gone down to the Pit.[a]
4 Sing praises to the LORD, O you his
faithful ones,
and give thanks to his holy name.
5 For his anger is but for a moment;
his favor is for a lifetime.
Weeping may linger for the night,
but joy comes with the morning.

6 As for me, I said in my prosperity,
"I shall never be moved."
7 By your favor, O LORD,
you had established me as a strong
mountain;
you hid your face;
I was dismayed.

8 To you, O LORD, I cried,
and to the LORD I made
supplication:
9 "What profit is there in my death,
if I go down to the Pit?
Will the dust praise you?
Will it tell of your faithfulness?
10 Hear, O LORD, and be gracious to
me!
O LORD, be my helper!"

11 You have turned my mourning into
dancing;
you have taken off my sackcloth
and clothed me with joy,
12 so that my soul[b] may praise you and
not be silent.
O LORD my God, I will give thanks
to you forever.

PSALM 31

To the leader. A Psalm of David.

1 In you, O LORD, I seek refuge;
do not let me ever be put to shame;
in your righteousness deliver me.

a Or *that I should not go down to the Pit*
b Heb *that glory*

forces of chaos); a double entendre is likely intended, with the LORD reigning since the flood, and forever. **11:** Perhaps an Israelite blessing added to the Canaanite original. Only a deity with the great strength described above has the power also to bestow peace.

Ps 30: Thanksgiving after recovery from illness. A thanksgiving psalm. *The dedication of the temple* occurred under Solomon (1 Kings 8; 2 Chr 5–7), which makes the ascription to David anachronistic; see Ps 3n. **2–3:** The psalmist, seriously ill, was preserved from imminent death; here, as in Mesopotamian literature, the image of being brought up from death (*Sheol* and *the Pit;* Ps 28.1n.) reflects recovery from grave illness, and not resurrection from death. **4–5:** The ritual of thanksgiving in the Temple, involving family and friends celebrating the psalmist's reintegration into the community. **6–7:** The psalmist's former prosperous and secure state. **8–10:** The psalmist's appeals for divine help. **9:** No praise of God from the dead (Ps 6.5). **11:** The psalmist replaces *mourning* with *dancing,* the soiled, torn garments of penitence with a festal robe (Gen 41.42).

Ps 31: Prayer for deliverance from enemies. An individual lament, with strong affirmations of trust (vv. 1–5,6,8,14–15,19–20,25–26). **1–5:** God the source of stability and protection (*refuge, rock, fortress*). **5:** *Spirit,* better, "life"; the Bible does not view people as composed of a body and a separate *spirit*

2 Incline your ear to me;
rescue me speedily.
Be a rock of refuge for me,
a strong fortress to save me.

3 You are indeed my rock and my fortress;
for your name's sake lead me and guide me,
4 take me out of the net that is hidden for me,
for you are my refuge.
5 Into your hand I commit my spirit;
you have redeemed me, O LORD, faithful God.

6 You hate[a] those who pay regard to worthless idols,
but I trust in the LORD.
7 I will exult and rejoice in your steadfast love,
because you have seen my affliction;
you have taken heed of my adversities,
8 and have not delivered me into the hand of the enemy;
you have set my feet in a broad place.

9 Be gracious to me, O LORD, for I am in distress;
my eye wastes away from grief,
my soul and body also.
10 For my life is spent with sorrow,
and my years with sighing;
my strength fails because of my misery,[b]
and my bones waste away.

11 I am the scorn of all my adversaries,
a horror[c] to my neighbors,
an object of dread to my acquaintances;
those who see me in the street flee from me.
12 I have passed out of mind like one who is dead;
I have become like a broken vessel.
13 For I hear the whispering of many—
terror all around!—
as they scheme together against me,
as they plot to take my life.

14 But I trust in you, O LORD;
I say, "You are my God."
15 My times are in your hand;
deliver me from the hand of my enemies and persecutors.
16 Let your face shine upon your servant;
save me in your steadfast love.
17 Do not let me be put to shame, O LORD,
for I call on you;
let the wicked be put to shame;
let them go dumbfounded to Sheol.
18 Let the lying lips be stilled
that speak insolently against the righteous
with pride and contempt.

19 O how abundant is your goodness
that you have laid up for those who fear you,
and accomplished for those who take refuge in you,
in the sight of everyone!
20 In the shelter of your presence you hide them
from human plots;
you hold them safe under your shelter
from contentious tongues.

21 Blessed be the LORD,

a One Heb Ms Gk Syr Jerome: MT *I hate*
b Gk Syr: Heb *my iniquity* *c* Cn: Heb *exceedingly*

or soul. **6–8:** The psalmist's life is not entrapped in an enemy's "net" (v. 4), but in the care of God (Ps 9.15; 10.9; 25.15). **9–13:** Because of illness the psalmist is shunned by all (Ps 38.11; 88.8). **11:** The *scorn* or shame felt by the petitioner is a major theme of Psalms (e.g., Ps 22.6), and of the Bible as a whole (e.g., Job 19.19; Jer 23.40), reflecting the fact that ancient Israel was a shame culture. **12:** Cf. Eccl 9.5. **13:** Cf. Jer 20.10. **16:** See Ps 4.6n. **17–20:** Counterpoised to Sheol, the abode of the silent dead, is the Temple, residence of the living God. **22:** *Driven far from your sight,* separated from the presence of God in the

for he has wondrously shown his
steadfast love to me
when I was beset as a city under
siege.
22 I had said in my alarm,
"I am driven far[a] from your
sight."
But you heard my supplications
when I cried out to you for help.

23 Love the LORD, all you his saints.
The LORD preserves the faithful,
but abundantly repays the one who
acts haughtily.
24 Be strong, and let your heart take
courage,
all you who wait for the LORD.

PSALM 32

Of David. A Maskil.

1 Happy are those whose transgression
is forgiven,
whose sin is covered.
2 Happy are those to whom the LORD
imputes no iniquity,
and in whose spirit there is no
deceit.

3 While I kept silence, my body wasted
away
through my groaning all day long.
4 For day and night your hand was
heavy upon me;
my strength was dried up[b] as by
the heat of summer. *Selah*

5 Then I acknowledged my sin to you,
and I did not hide my iniquity;
I said, "I will confess my
transgressions to the LORD,"
and you forgave the guilt of my sin. *Selah*

6 Therefore let all who are faithful
offer prayer to you;
at a time of distress,[c] the rush of
mighty waters
shall not reach them.
7 You are a hiding place for me;
you preserve me from trouble;
you surround me with glad cries of
deliverance. *Selah*

8 I will instruct you and teach you the
way you should go;
I will counsel you with my eye
upon you.
9 Do not be like a horse or a mule,
without understanding,
whose temper must be curbed with
bit and bridle,
else it will not stay near you.

10 Many are the torments of the wicked,
but steadfast love surrounds those
who trust in the LORD.
11 Be glad in the LORD and rejoice,
O righteous,
and shout for joy, all you upright
in heart.

a Another reading is *cut off* *b* Meaning of Heb uncertain *c* Cn: Heb *at a time of finding only*

Temple (2 Chr 26.21; Hos 9.15; Jon 2.5). **23–24:** A ritual of thanksgiving with the psalmist's community (Ps 30.11–12).

Ps 32: The happiness of the penitent and forgiven. A thanksgiving psalm (one of the penitential psalms; see Ps 6n.), with wisdom characteristics; it assumes that human affliction is the punishment of a just God, and along with "confession" (v. 5), transforms the individual. **1:** *Forgiven . . . covered,* divine passives; it is God who forgives and "covers" (puts out of sight) sin. **3–5:** The psalmist's silence (not confessing his sin) brought on illness; acknowledgment of sin brought healing and forgiveness. **4:** *Selah* (also vv. 5,7), see Ps 3.2n. **7:** *Glad cries* of the psalmist's family and friends (v. 11). **8–9:** A wisdom teacher's instruction (or a divine oracle), promising guidance for the psalmist's life. **10–11:** The varying fates of the wicked and the upright (Ps 1.6).

PSALM 33

1 Rejoice in the LORD, O you righteous.
Praise befits the upright.
2 Praise the LORD with the lyre;
make melody to him with the harp of ten strings.
3 Sing to him a new song;
play skillfully on the strings, with loud shouts.

4 For the word of the LORD is upright,
and all his work is done in faithfulness.
5 He loves righteousness and justice;
the earth is full of the steadfast love of the LORD.

6 By the word of the LORD the heavens were made,
and all their host by the breath of his mouth.
7 He gathered the waters of the sea as in a bottle;
he put the deeps in storehouses.

8 Let all the earth fear the LORD;
let all the inhabitants of the world stand in awe of him.
9 For he spoke, and it came to be;
he commanded, and it stood firm.

10 The LORD brings the counsel of the nations to nothing;
he frustrates the plans of the peoples.
11 The counsel of the LORD stands forever,
the thoughts of his heart to all generations.
12 Happy is the nation whose God is the LORD,
the people whom he has chosen as his heritage.

13 The LORD looks down from heaven;
he sees all humankind.
14 From where he sits enthroned he watches
all the inhabitants of the earth—
15 he who fashions the hearts of them all,
and observes all their deeds.
16 A king is not saved by his great army;
a warrior is not delivered by his great strength.
17 The war horse is a vain hope for victory,
and by its great might it cannot save.

18 Truly the eye of the LORD is on those who fear him,
on those who hope in his steadfast love,
19 to deliver their soul from death,
and to keep them alive in famine.

20 Our soul waits for the LORD;
he is our help and shield.
21 Our heart is glad in him,
because we trust in his holy name.
22 Let your steadfast love, O LORD, be upon us,
even as we hope in you.

PSALM 34

Of David, when he feigned madness before Abimelech, so that he drove him out, and he went away.

1 I will bless the LORD at all times;
his praise shall continually be in my mouth.

Ps 33: Praise of God, creator and redeemer. A hymn of praise with wisdom characteristics. **1–3:** For music in worship, see Ps 81.1–3; 92.1–3; 150.3–5. **6–9:** As in Gen 1, creation is by the divine *word:* the making of the *heavens,* the confinement of the chaotic *waters,* and the peopling of the earth (Gen 1.6–10). **10–13:** Creation and wisdom are connected in Prov 3.19–20; 8.22–31. **16–17:** Human weapons are ineffective against such a powerful creator deity; see Ps 20.7; 44.3.

Ps 34: Praise of God for deliverance from trouble. An acrostic thanksgiving psalm (see Ps 9–10n.), divided into two sections, vv. 1–10 and 11–22; the second half in particular has wisdom affinities. (For the superscription, see 1 Sam 21.12–15 [where the king Abimelech is called Achish]; see also Ps 3n.) **2:**

2 My soul makes its boast in the LORD;
let the humble hear and be glad.
3 O magnify the LORD with me,
and let us exalt his name together.

4 I sought the LORD, and he answered me,
and delivered me from all my fears.
5 Look to him, and be radiant;
so your[a] faces shall never be ashamed.
6 This poor soul cried, and was heard by the LORD,
and was saved from every trouble.
7 The angel of the LORD encamps around those who fear him, and delivers them.
8 O taste and see that the LORD is good;
happy are those who take refuge in him.
9 O fear the LORD, you his holy ones,
for those who fear him have no want.
10 The young lions suffer want and hunger,
but those who seek the LORD lack no good thing.

11 Come, O children, listen to me;
I will teach you the fear of the LORD.
12 Which of you desires life,
and covets many days to enjoy good?
13 Keep your tongue from evil,
and your lips from speaking deceit.
14 Depart from evil, and do good;
seek peace, and pursue it.

15 The eyes of the LORD are on the righteous,
and his ears are open to their cry.
16 The face of the LORD is against evildoers,
to cut off the remembrance of them from the earth.
17 When the righteous cry for help, the LORD hears,
and rescues them from all their troubles.
18 The LORD is near to the brokenhearted,
and saves the crushed in spirit.

19 Many are the afflictions of the righteous,
but the LORD rescues them from them all.
20 He keeps all their bones;
not one of them will be broken.
21 Evil brings death to the wicked,
and those who hate the righteous will be condemned.
22 The LORD redeems the life of his servants;
none of those who take refuge in him will be condemned.

PSALM 35

Of David.

1 Contend, O LORD, with those who contend with me;
fight against those who fight against me!
2 Take hold of shield and buckler,
and rise up to help me!
3 Draw the spear and javelin

a Gk Syr Jerome: Heb *their*

Humble, completely dependent on God. **5:** *Be radiant,* the external manifestation of happiness, a bright, smiling face (Jer 31.12). **7:** Protection by a guardian angel (Ps 43.3). **9–10:** Predatory carnivores (the proud and arrogant) suffer want, while the humble are sustained by God. **11–14:** A sage's address to students, teaching fear of the LORD (Job 28.28; Prov 1.7). **15–17:** The LORD's benevolent gaze on the righteous, and his angry face, glaring at evildoers. The correct order of these verses is probably 15, 17, 16, following the order of the acrostics in Lam 2–4. **18:** *Brokenhearted . . . crushed in spirit,* the depressed and despondent (mourners and penitents). **19–22:** The varying fates of *the righteous* and *the wicked.*

Ps 35: Royal prayer for deliverance. A lament uttered by a king. **1–3:** Prayer that the Divine Warrior arm himself for battle against the psalmist's foes. **4–6:** Traditional invective against enemies; punishment

against my pursuers;
say to my soul,
"I am your salvation."

4 Let them be put to shame and
dishonor
who seek after my life.
Let them be turned back and
confounded
who devise evil against me.
5 Let them be like chaff before the
wind,
with the angel of the LORD driving
them on.
6 Let their way be dark and slippery,
with the angel of the LORD
pursuing them.

7 For without cause they hid their net[a]
for me;
without cause they dug a pit[b] for
my life.
8 Let ruin come on them unawares.
And let the net that they hid ensnare
them;
let them fall in it—to their ruin.

9 Then my soul shall rejoice in the
LORD,
exulting in his deliverance.
10 All my bones shall say,
"O LORD, who is like you?
You deliver the weak
from those too strong for them,
the weak and needy from those
who despoil them."

11 Malicious witnesses rise up;
they ask me about things I do not
know.
12 They repay me evil for good;
my soul is forlorn.
13 But as for me, when they were sick,
I wore sackcloth;
I afflicted myself with fasting.
I prayed with head bowed[c] on my
bosom,
14 as though I grieved for a friend or
a brother;
I went about as one who laments for
a mother,
bowed down and in mourning.

15 But at my stumbling they gathered in
glee,
they gathered together against me;
ruffians whom I did not know
tore at me without ceasing;
16 they impiously mocked more and
more,[d]
gnashing at me with their teeth.

17 How long, O LORD, will you look
on?
Rescue me from their ravages,
my life from the lions!
18 Then I will thank you in the great
congregation;
in the mighty throng I will
praise you.

19 Do not let my treacherous enemies
rejoice over me,
or those who hate me without
cause wink the eye.
20 For they do not speak peace,
but they conceive deceitful words
against those who are quiet in the
land.
21 They open wide their mouths against
me;
they say, "Aha, Aha,
our eyes have seen it."

22 You have seen, O LORD; do not be
silent!

a Heb *a pit, their net* *b* The word *pit* is transposed from the preceding line *c* Or *My prayer turned back* *d* Cn Compare Gk: Heb *like the profanest of mockers of a cake*

by God's angelic forces (Jer 23.12; Ezek 9.9; Ps 40.15). **5:** As in the previous psalm (v. 7), the focus moves to *the angel of the LORD,* a manifestation of God. This commonality may explain the adjacent placement of these two psalms. **7–8:** By the law of talion or equivalent retribution (see 3.7n.), net and pit entrap those who used them to ensnare. **10:** Hyperbolic poetic language. **13–18:** The king is betrayed by those he prayed for (former allies). **19–21:** The language of conspiracy. **22–25:** Appeal to God to intervene; the

O Lord, do not be far from me!
23 Wake up! Bestir yourself for my
defense,
for my cause, my God and my
Lord!
24 Vindicate me, O LORD, my God,
according to your righteousness,
and do not let them rejoice
over me.
25 Do not let them say to themselves,
"Aha, we have our heart's
desire."
Do not let them say, "We have
swallowed you[a] up."

26 Let all those who rejoice at my
calamity
be put to shame and confusion;
let those who exalt themselves against
me
be clothed with shame and
dishonor.

27 Let those who desire my vindication
shout for joy and be glad,
and say evermore,
"Great is the LORD,
who delights in the welfare of his
servant."
28 Then my tongue shall tell of your
righteousness
and of your praise all day long.

PSALM 36

To the leader. Of David, the servant of the LORD.

1 Transgression speaks to the wicked
deep in their hearts;
there is no fear of God
before their eyes.
2 For they flatter themselves in their
own eyes
that their iniquity cannot be found
out and hated.
3 The words of their mouths are
mischief and deceit;
they have ceased to act wisely and
do good.
4 They plot mischief while on their
beds;
they are set on a way that is
not good;
they do not reject evil.

5 Your steadfast love, O LORD, extends
to the heavens,
your faithfulness to the clouds.
6 Your righteousness is like the mighty
mountains,
your judgments are like the great
deep;
you save humans and animals alike,
O LORD.

7 How precious is your steadfast love,
O God!
All people may take refuge in the
shadow of your wings.
8 They feast on the abundance of your
house,
and you give them drink from the
river of your delights.
9 For with you is the fountain of life;
in your light we see light.

10 O continue your steadfast love to
those who know you,
and your salvation to the upright of
heart!

a Heb *him*

psalmist assumes that God has *seen* (v. 22), but for unknown reasons, has not acted. **27–28:** In place of the enemies' damaging speech (vv. 11–12,20–21), the psalmist's tongue tells of the LORD's victory.

Ps 36: Hymn of rejoicing in the Temple. The poem consists of a wisdom instruction on the wicked (vv. 1–4), a hymn lauding the Temple (vv. 5–9), and a prayer for the righteous with an imprecation against the wicked (vv. 10–12); the psalm coheres very loosely. **1:** *Transgression speaks,* lit. "An oracle of transgression to the wicked" (cf. Ps 110.1). **2–4:** Those addressed by an "oracle of transgression" engage in sinful speech, privately (*on their beds*) and publicly (*on* the *way*). **7–8:** Feasting and celebrating divine love in the Temple; *river of your delights,* cf. Ezek 47.1–2; Joel 3.18; Zech 14.8; Ps 46.4. **9–12:** As a result of God's benevolent gaze, we live out our lives. **12:** Evildoers are consigned to the abode of the dead.

11 Do not let the foot of the arrogant
tread on me,
or the hand of the wicked drive me
away.
12 There the evildoers lie prostrate;
they are thrust down, unable
to rise.

PSALM 37

Of David.

1 Do not fret because of the wicked;
do not be envious of wrongdoers,
2 for they will soon fade like the grass,
and wither like the green herb.

3 Trust in the LORD, and do good;
so you will live in the land, and
enjoy security.
4 Take delight in the LORD,
and he will give you the desires of
your heart.

5 Commit your way to the LORD;
trust in him, and he will act.
6 He will make your vindication shine
like the light,
and the justice of your cause like
the noonday.

7 Be still before the LORD, and wait
patiently for him;
do not fret over those who prosper
in their way,
over those who carry out evil
devices.

8 Refrain from anger, and forsake
wrath.
Do not fret—it leads only to evil.

9 For the wicked shall be cut off,
but those who wait for the LORD
shall inherit the land.

10 Yet a little while, and the wicked will
be no more;
though you look diligently for their
place, they will not be there.
11 But the meek shall inherit the land,
and delight themselves in abundant
prosperity.

12 The wicked plot against the righteous,
and gnash their teeth at them;
13 but the LORD laughs at the wicked,
for he sees that their day is coming.

14 The wicked draw the sword and bend
their bows
to bring down the poor and needy,
to kill those who walk uprightly;
15 their sword shall enter their own
heart,
and their bows shall be broken.

16 Better is a little that the righteous
person has
than the abundance of many
wicked.
17 For the arms of the wicked shall be
broken,
but the LORD upholds the
righteous.

18 The LORD knows the days of the
blameless,
and their heritage will abide
forever;
19 they are not put to shame in evil
times,

Ps 37: The certainty of retribution. An acrostic (see Ps 9–10n.; Ps 25n.) wisdom psalm, in which the righteous are promised possession of the land. The themes, structure, and vocabulary of the psalm are characteristic of Proverbs, and "wisdom" is mentioned explicitly in v. 30. **1–2:** Repeated in vv. 7–8; see Prov 23.17–18; 24.1,19–20. **2:** *Like the grass,* the evanescence of the wicked (Ps 102.4,11; Job 8.12–13). **3:** The first occurrence of the refrainlike promise of possessing the land (vv. 9,11,22,29,34). **9–10:** *Cut off,* separated from the land (Prov 2.21–22). **13:** God's derisory laughter at the pretensions of the wicked (Ps 2.4; 59.8). **14–15:** The weapons of the wicked "backfire" and are broken, as are their arms (v. 17). **16–17:** *Better . . . than,* characteristic wording of wisdom literature (e.g., Prov 15.16–17). **18–20:** The varying fates of the righteous and the wicked. **27:** See v. 3; Ps 34.14; Prov 13.19; Job 28.28. **35–38:** The

in the days of famine they have
abundance.

20 But the wicked perish,
and the enemies of the LORD are
like the glory of the pastures;
they vanish—like smoke they
vanish away.

21 The wicked borrow, and do not pay
back,
but the righteous are generous and
keep giving;
22 for those blessed by the LORD shall
inherit the land,
but those cursed by him shall be
cut off.

23 Our steps[a] are made firm by the
LORD,
when he delights in our[b] way;
24 though we stumble,[c] we[d] shall not
fall headlong,
for the LORD holds us[e] by the
hand.

25 I have been young, and now am
old,
yet I have not seen the righteous
forsaken
or their children begging bread.
26 They are ever giving liberally and
lending,
and their children become a
blessing.

27 Depart from evil, and do good;
so you shall abide forever.
28 For the LORD loves justice;
he will not forsake his faithful ones.

The righteous shall be kept safe
forever,
but the children of the wicked shall
be cut off.
29 The righteous shall inherit the land,
and live in it forever.

30 The mouths of the righteous utter
wisdom,
and their tongues speak justice.
31 The law of their God is in their
hearts;
their steps do not slip.

32 The wicked watch for the righteous,
and seek to kill them.
33 The LORD will not abandon them to
their power,
or let them be condemned when
they are brought to trial.

34 Wait for the LORD, and keep to his
way,
and he will exalt you to inherit the
land;
you will look on the destruction of
the wicked.

35 I have seen the wicked oppressing,
and towering like a cedar of
Lebanon.[f]
36 Again I[g] passed by, and they were no
more;
though I sought them, they could
not be found.

37 Mark the blameless, and behold the
upright,
for there is posterity for the
peaceable.
38 But transgressors shall be altogether
destroyed;
the posterity of the wicked shall be
cut off.

39 The salvation of the righteous is from
the LORD;
he is their refuge in the time of
trouble.
40 The LORD helps them and rescues
them;

a Heb *A man's steps* *b* Heb *his* *c* Heb *he stumbles* *d* Heb *he* *e* Heb *him* *f* Gk: Meaning of Heb uncertain *g* Gk Syr Jerome: Heb *he*

varying fates of the children of the righteous (v. 25) and of the transgressors; this type of contrast also typifies wisdom literature.

he rescues them from the wicked,
and saves them,
because they take refuge in him.

PSALM 38

A Psalm of David, for the memorial offering.

1 O LORD, do not rebuke me in your anger,
or discipline me in your wrath.
2 For your arrows have sunk into me,
and your hand has come down on me.

3 There is no soundness in my flesh
because of your indignation;
there is no health in my bones
because of my sin.
4 For my iniquities have gone over my head;
they weigh like a burden too heavy for me.

5 My wounds grow foul and fester
because of my foolishness;
6 I am utterly bowed down and prostrate;
all day long I go around mourning.
7 For my loins are filled with burning,
and there is no soundness in my flesh.
8 I am utterly spent and crushed;
I groan because of the tumult of my heart.

9 O Lord, all my longing is known to you;
my sighing is not hidden from you.
10 My heart throbs, my strength fails me;
as for the light of my eyes—it also has gone from me.
11 My friends and companions stand aloof from my affliction,
and my neighbors stand far off.

12 Those who seek my life lay their snares;
those who seek to hurt me speak of ruin,
and meditate treachery all day long.

13 But I am like the deaf, I do not hear;
like the mute, who cannot speak.
14 Truly, I am like one who does not hear,
and in whose mouth is no retort.

15 But it is for you, O LORD, that I wait;
it is you, O Lord my God, who will answer.
16 For I pray, "Only do not let them rejoice over me,
those who boast against me when my foot slips."

17 For I am ready to fall,
and my pain is ever with me.
18 I confess my iniquity;
I am sorry for my sin.
19 Those who are my foes without cause[a] are mighty,
and many are those who hate me wrongfully.
20 Those who render me evil for good
are my adversaries because I follow after good.

21 Do not forsake me, O LORD;
O my God, do not be far from me;
22 make haste to help me,
O Lord, my salvation.

a Q Ms: MT *my living foes*

Ps 38: Prayer for healing. An individual lament over a serious illness afflicting the psalmist; it is one of the penitential psalms (see Ps 6n.). **1:** Cf. Ps 6.1; the similarity suggests that either some psalmists copied from each other, or that psalmists used various stock phrases or verses. **2:** The punishing illness is described as arrows sent by God (Job 6.4; 16.12–13). **3–5:** Sin as the cause of the psalmist's malady (Isa 1.5–6). Most individual psalms of lament lack confessions. **11:** The psalmist is isolated from friends and family (see Ps 31.9–13n.). **13–14:** *Deaf*, i.e., ignorant of the plotting of his foes in v. 12 (Jer 11.19). **18:** Confession of sin (Ps 32.5). **21–22:** Ps 22.11,19; 40.13.

PSALM 39

To the leader: to Jeduthun. A Psalm of David.

1 I said, "I will guard my ways
that I may not sin with my tongue;
I will keep a muzzle on my mouth
as long as the wicked are in my presence."
2 I was silent and still;
I held my peace to no avail;
my distress grew worse,
3 my heart became hot within me.
While I mused, the fire burned;
then I spoke with my tongue:

4 "LORD, let me know my end,
and what is the measure of my days;
let me know how fleeting my life is.
5 You have made my days a few handbreadths,
and my lifetime is as nothing in your sight.
Surely everyone stands as a mere breath. *Selah*
6 Surely everyone goes about like a shadow.
Surely for nothing they are in turmoil;
they heap up, and do not know who will gather.

7 "And now, O Lord, what do I wait for?
My hope is in you.
8 Deliver me from all my transgressions.
Do not make me the scorn of the fool.
9 I am silent; I do not open my mouth,
for it is you who have done it.
10 Remove your stroke from me;
I am worn down by the blows[a] of your hand.

11 "You chastise mortals
in punishment for sin,
consuming like a moth what is dear to them;
surely everyone is a mere breath. *Selah*

12 "Hear my prayer, O LORD,
and give ear to my cry;
do not hold your peace at my tears.
For I am your passing guest,
an alien, like all my forebears.
13 Turn your gaze away from me, that I may smile again,
before I depart and am no more."

PSALM 40

To the leader. Of David. A Psalm.

1 I waited patiently for the LORD;
he inclined to me and heard my cry.
2 He drew me up from the desolate pit,[b]
out of the miry bog,
and set my feet upon a rock,
making my steps secure.
3 He put a new song in my mouth,
a song of praise to our God.
Many will see and fear,
and put their trust in the LORD.

a Heb *hostility* *b* Cn: Heb *pit of tumult*

Ps 39: The brevity of human life. An individual lament (cf. Ps 90; 102) with a refrain in vv. 5 and 11. *Jeduthun* was a famous Temple musician; 1 Chr 16.42; 25.6; Ps 62; 77. **1–3:** A vow to avoid sins of speech, a common concern of laments. Such sins could evoke serious punishment (see Num 12). **2:** *Silent and still,* not only uncomplaining, but on the point of entering the silent world of the dead (Ps 30.12). **4:** How long will my suffering go on? **5:** *Selah* (also v. 11), see Ps 3.2n. **6:** For the theme of one's wealth left for others, see Ps 49.16–17; Sir 11.19. **7–11:** Prayer for forgiveness and for relief of the suffering brought on by sin. **12:** Lev 25.23; 1 Chr 29.15.

Ps 40: Thanksgiving for deliverance and prayer for help. A thanksgiving psalm (vv. 1–12) followed by a lament (vv. 13–17). The lament reappears, with slight variations, as Ps 70. **2:** *Pit . . . bog,* synonyms for the abode of the dead; as in 30.3, death is used to refer to grave illness. **4:** Ps 34.9; Prov 16.20. **6–8:**

4 Happy are those who make
the LORD their trust,
who do not turn to the proud,
to those who go astray after false
gods.
5 You have multiplied, O LORD my
God,
your wondrous deeds and your
thoughts toward us;
none can compare with you.
Were I to proclaim and tell of them,
they would be more than can be
counted.

6 Sacrifice and offering you do not
desire,
but you have given me an open
ear.[a]
Burnt offering and sin offering
you have not required.
7 Then I said, "Here I am;
in the scroll of the book it is
written of me.[b]
8 I delight to do your will, O my God;
your law is within my heart."

9 I have told the glad news of
deliverance
in the great congregation;
see, I have not restrained my lips,
as you know, O LORD.
10 I have not hidden your saving help
within my heart,
I have spoken of your faithfulness
and your salvation;
I have not concealed your steadfast
love and your faithfulness
from the great congregation.

11 Do not, O LORD, withhold
your mercy from me;
let your steadfast love and your
faithfulness
keep me safe forever.
12 For evils have encompassed me
without number;
my iniquities have overtaken me,
until I cannot see;
they are more than the hairs of my
head,
and my heart fails me.

13 Be pleased, O LORD, to deliver me;
O LORD, make haste to help me.
14 Let all those be put to shame and
confusion
who seek to snatch away my life;
let those be turned back and brought
to dishonor
who desire my hurt.
15 Let those be appalled because of their
shame
who say to me, "Aha, Aha!"

16 But may all who seek you
rejoice and be glad in you;
may those who love your salvation
say continually, "Great is the
LORD!"
17 As for me, I am poor and needy,
but the Lord takes thought for me.
You are my help and my deliverer;
do not delay, O my God.

PSALM 41

To the leader. A Psalm of David.

1 Happy are those who consider the
poor;[c]

a Heb *ears you have dug for me* *b* Meaning of Heb uncertain *c* Or *weak*

For obedience as better than *sacrifice,* see 1 Sam 15.22; Ps 50.8–9; Mic 6.6–7. This may point to the time of the exile and the destruction of the Temple. **7:** *The scroll of the book* reflects the Mesopotamian notion of a book of life, which appears elsewhere in the Bible (e.g., Ex 32.32; Ps 69.28; 139.16; Dan 12.1; cf. Rev 20.12–15); this idea is further developed in later Judaism, especially in the New Year liturgy. **9:** *The great congregation,* the psalmist's community, participants in the thanksgiving ritual. **14–16:** The psalmist prays that the enemy be repulsed and shamed, and that the community of Godseekers join the psalmist in praise, a typical reason why God should save the petitioner—so that God may enjoy greater praise (see 22.21–22n.).

Ps 41: Prayer for healing. An individual lament of someone mortally ill (vv. 4–10). **1–3:** The LORD's

the LORD delivers them in the day
of trouble.
2 The LORD protects them and keeps
them alive;
they are called happy in the land.
You do not give them up to the
will of their enemies.
3 The LORD sustains them on their
sickbed;
in their illness you heal all their
infirmities.[a]

4 As for me, I said, "O LORD, be
gracious to me;
heal me, for I have sinned against
you."
5 My enemies wonder in malice
when I will die, and my name
perish.
6 And when they come to see me, they
utter empty words,
while their hearts gather mischief;
when they go out, they tell it
abroad.
7 All who hate me whisper together
about me;
they imagine the worst for me.

8 They think that a deadly thing has
fastened on me,
that I will not rise again from
where I lie.
9 Even my bosom friend in whom I
trusted,
who ate of my bread, has lifted the
heel against me.
10 But you, O LORD, be gracious to me,
and raise me up, that I may repay
them.

11 By this I know that you are pleased
with me;
because my enemy has not
triumphed over me.
12 But you have upheld me because of
my integrity,
and set me in your presence
forever.

13 Blessed be the LORD, the God of
Israel,
from everlasting to everlasting.
Amen and Amen.

BOOK TWO

PSALM 42

To the leader. A Maskil of the Korahites.

1 As a deer longs for flowing streams,
so my soul longs for you, O God.
2 My soul thirsts for God,
for the living God.
When shall I come and behold
the face of God?
3 My tears have been my food

a Heb *you change all his bed*

protection of the oppressed and ill. **4:** The petitioner believes that sin is the cause of the illness (Ps 39.11). **5–7:** The psalmist's enemies are guilty of insincere and damaging speech. **8:** *Not rise again,* from the sickbed and from the abode of the dead. **11–12:** Once excluded from the Temple by illness (2 Chr 26.21), the psalmist is confident that he will be healed and readmitted to God's presence. **12:** *Integrity* and being in God's *presence forever* are found elsewhere at the close of a psalm (e.g., Ps 23; 26). **13:** The doxology or blessing that closes Book I of the Psalter is not original to the psalm, but reflects the structuring of the psalter into five books (see Introduction).

Ps 42–43: Thirst for the living God. Ps 42–43 form a single psalm, an individual lament in which each section ends with a refrain (42.5,11; 43.5) and with refrainlike repetitions (42.3,10; 42.9; 43.2). It is unclear why this single psalm became separated into two psalms, as it is often unknown why two or more poems sometimes coalesce into a single psalm (e.g., Ps 40). This psalm is the first of a Korahite collection of psalms, which concludes in Ps 49; another group is Ps 84–85 and 87–88. Korah, a Levite, was understood to be a head of a guild of psalm-writers (cf. 1 Chr 9.19; 2 Chr 20.19). The central unifying image is water: thirst-quenching streams of water, the tears of the psalmist, and the threatening primeval waters of chaos. **2:** *Behold the face of God,* by participating in Temple worship, though the strong longing to see God borders on the mystical. **3:** *Tears . . . my food,* see Ps 80.5; 102.9. **6:** *The land of Jordan,* the

day and night,
while people say to me continually,
"Where is your God?"

4 These things I remember,
as I pour out my soul:
how I went with the throng,[a]
and led them in procession to the house of God,
with glad shouts and songs of thanksgiving,
a multitude keeping festival.
5 Why are you cast down, O my soul,
and why are you disquieted within me?
Hope in God; for I shall again praise him,
my help 6 and my God.

My soul is cast down within me;
therefore I remember you
from the land of Jordan and of Hermon,
from Mount Mizar.
7 Deep calls to deep
at the thunder of your cataracts;
all your waves and your billows
have gone over me.
8 By day the LORD commands his steadfast love,
and at night his song is with me,
a prayer to the God of my life.

9 I say to God, my rock,
"Why have you forgotten me?
Why must I walk about mournfully
because the enemy oppresses me?"
10 As with a deadly wound in my body,
my adversaries taunt me,
while they say to me continually,
"Where is your God?"

11 Why are you cast down, O my soul,
and why are you disquieted within me?
Hope in God; for I shall again praise him,
my help and my God.

PSALM 43

1 Vindicate me, O God, and defend my cause
against an ungodly people;
from those who are deceitful and unjust
deliver me!
2 For you are the God in whom I take refuge;
why have you cast me off?
Why must I walk about mournfully
because of the oppression of the enemy?

3 O send out your light and your truth;
let them lead me;
let them bring me to your holy hill
and to your dwelling.
4 Then I will go to the altar of God,
to God my exceeding joy;
and I will praise you with the harp,
O God, my God.

5 Why are you cast down, O my soul,
and why are you disquieted within me?
Hope in God; for I shall again praise him,
my help and my God.

PSALM 44

To the leader. Of the Korahites. A Maskil.

1 We have heard with our ears, O God,
our ancestors have told us,

a Meaning of Heb uncertain

sources of the Jordan River, on the slopes of Mount *Hermon* in northern Israel; *Mount Mizar* is presumably in the same area. **7:** The waters of chaos, about to engulf the psalmist. **43.3–4:** *Your light and your truth,* personified guardians sent by God to lead the psalmist to the Temple (cf. Ps 25.21; 57.3; 61.7; 91.11).

Ps 44: Prayer for divine help after a national defeat. A communal lament, in view of an unknown national military disaster involving the loss of the land. **1:** *Days of old,* the settlement era, when God's

what deeds you performed in their
days,
in the days of old:
2 you with your own hand drove out
the nations,
but them you planted;
you afflicted the peoples,
but them you set free;
3 for not by their own sword did they
win the land,
nor did their own arm give them
victory;
but your right hand, and your arm,
and the light of your countenance,
for you delighted in them.

4 You are my King and my God;
you command[a] victories for Jacob.
5 Through you we push down our foes;
through your name we tread down
our assailants.
6 For not in my bow do I trust,
nor can my sword save me.
7 But you have saved us from our foes,
and have put to confusion those
who hate us.
8 In God we have boasted continually,
and we will give thanks to your
name forever. *Selah*

9 Yet you have rejected us and abased
us,
and have not gone out with our
armies.
10 You made us turn back from the foe,
and our enemies have gotten spoil.
11 You have made us like sheep for
slaughter,
and have scattered us among
the nations.
12 You have sold your people for a
trifle,
demanding no high price for
them.
13 You have made us the taunt of our
neighbors,
the derision and scorn of those
around us.
14 You have made us a byword among
the nations,
a laughingstock[b] among the
peoples.
15 All day long my disgrace is before me,
and shame has covered my face
16 at the words of the taunters and
revilers,
at the sight of the enemy and the
avenger.

17 All this has come upon us,
yet we have not forgotten you,
or been false to your covenant.
18 Our heart has not turned back,
nor have our steps departed from
your way,
19 yet you have broken us in the haunt
of jackals,
and covered us with deep darkness.

20 If we had forgotten the name of our
God,
or spread out our hands to a
strange god,
21 would not God discover this?
For he knows the secrets of the
heart.
22 Because of you we are being killed all
day long,
and accounted as sheep for the
slaughter.

23 Rouse yourself! Why do you sleep,
O Lord?
Awake, do not cast us off forever!
24 Why do you hide your face?

a Gk Syr: Heb *You are my King, O God; command*
b Heb *a shaking of the head*

power was understood to be especially visible (see Judg 6.13). **3:** Victory is not by might of arms, but by the luminous appearance of the Divine Warrior (v. 6; Ex 14.24). **8:** *Selah,* see Ps 3.2n. **9–12:** Defeat is followed by exile. **13–16:** Derision by victorious foes and the shame of the defeated (Ps 22.7; 79.4; 80.6). **20:** Breach of the first commandment of the Sinai covenant (v. 17; Ex 20.3). **22:** *Because of you* might suggest that members of the community have been killed as martyrs, though this is a rare and late biblical idea. **23–26:** God's inattention to the plight of the community (sleeping, hiding the divine luminous face).

Why do you forget our affliction
and oppression?
25 For we sink down to the dust;
our bodies cling to the ground.
26 Rise up, come to our help.
Redeem us for the sake of your
steadfast love.

PSALM 45

To the leader: according to Lilies.
Of the Korahites. A Maskil. A love song.

1 My heart overflows with a goodly
theme;
I address my verses to the king;
my tongue is like the pen of a
ready scribe.

2 You are the most handsome of men;
grace is poured upon your lips;
therefore God has blessed you
forever.
3 Gird your sword on your thigh,
O mighty one,
in your glory and majesty.

4 In your majesty ride on victoriously
for the cause of truth and to
defend[a] the right;
let your right hand teach you dread
deeds.
5 Your arrows are sharp
in the heart of the king's enemies;
the peoples fall under you.

6 Your throne, O God,[b] endures
forever and ever.
Your royal scepter is a scepter of
equity;
7 you love righteousness and hate
wickedness.
Therefore God, your God, has
anointed you
with the oil of gladness beyond
your companions;
8 your robes are all fragrant with
myrrh and aloes and cassia.
From ivory palaces stringed
instruments make you glad;
9 daughters of kings are among your
ladies of honor;
at your right hand stands the queen
in gold of Ophir.

10 Hear, O daughter, consider and
incline your ear;
forget your people and your
father's house,
11 and the king will desire your
beauty.
Since he is your lord, bow to him;
12 the people[c] of Tyre will seek your
favor with gifts,
the richest of the people 13 with all
kinds of wealth.

The princess is decked in her chamber
with gold-woven robes;[d]
14 in many-colored robes she is led to
the king;

a Cn: Heb *and the meekness of* b Or *Your throne is a throne of God, it* c Heb *daughter* d Or *people.* 13*All glorious is the princess within, gold embroidery is her clothing*

25: The vanquished, prostrate before the victors (Josh 10.24). **26:** God owes Israel *steadfast love* as a result of the covenant; this, along with the desire of God to be praised, is invoked elsewhere, especially in psalms (e.g., Ps 6.4; 69.13; 85.7; cf. Num 14.19) to convince God to relent.

Ps 45: A royal wedding song. The psalm is ancient and difficult, and its meaning in several places is not clear. Its presence highlights the diversity of genres in the Psalter, and the psalm is an important source for reconstructing the ideologies of Israelite kingship. *Korahites,* see Ps 42–43n. *According to Lilies,* probably refers to a melody (cf. Ps 22n.); also in Ps 69; 80. **2–3:** Like David, the king is an ideal figure, possessing both physical beauty and military valor (1 Sam 16.12). **4:** The king is the promoter of justice, especially for the powerless (Ps 72.1–4). **6:** The most debated verse in the psalm, often emended, which seems to attribute divinity to the king (Ps 2.7; 89.25–27). **7:** The anointing of the king was the central act of the coronation ritual. **9:** *Ophir,* see 1 Kings 9.28; 10.11. **10–12:** The queen is to leave the authority of her father for that of her husband; on the marriage of an Israelite king to a Canaanite princess, see 1 Kings 16.29–31. **16:** The dynasty (children to be born of the royal couple). **17:** A remarkable

behind her the virgins, her
companions, follow.
15 With joy and gladness they are
led along
as they enter the palace of the king.

16 In the place of ancestors you,
O king,[a] shall have sons;
you will make them princes in all
the earth.
17 I will cause your name to be
celebrated in all generations;
therefore the peoples will praise
you forever and ever.

PSALM 46

To the leader. Of the Korahites.
According to Alamoth. A Song.

1 God is our refuge and strength,
a very present[b] help in trouble.
2 Therefore we will not fear, though the
earth should change,
though the mountains shake in the
heart of the sea;
3 though its waters roar and foam,
though the mountains tremble with
its tumult. *Selah*

4 There is a river whose streams make
glad the city of God,
the holy habitation of the
Most High.
5 God is in the midst of the city;[c] it
shall not be moved;
God will help it when the morning
dawns.
6 The nations are in an uproar, the
kingdoms totter;
he utters his voice, the earth melts.
7 The LORD of hosts is with us;
the God of Jacob is our refuge.[d]
Selah

8 Come, behold the works of the LORD;
see what desolations he has brought
on the earth.
9 He makes wars cease to the end of
the earth;
he breaks the bow, and shatters the
spear;
he burns the shields with fire.
10 "Be still, and know that I am God!
I am exalted among the nations,
I am exalted in the earth."
11 The LORD of hosts is with us;
the God of Jacob is our refuge.[d]
Selah

PSALM 47

To the leader. Of the Korahites. A Psalm.

1 Clap your hands, all you peoples;
shout to God with loud songs
of joy.
2 For the LORD, the Most High, is
awesome,
a great king over all the earth.
3 He subdued peoples under us,
and nations under our feet.

a Heb lacks *O king* *b* Or *well proved* *c* Heb *of it*
d Or *fortress*

verse, attributing to the human king the type of praise elsewhere associated with God (e.g., Ps 145.21).

Ps 46: Praise of Zion and its victorious king. A Zion hymn (praise of Jerusalem and the Temple, with a refrain in vv. 7,11). *Korahites,* see Ps 42–43n. *Alamoth,* probably a melody; see 1 Chr 15.20. **1–3:** The primeval waters of chaos rise against the created order, challenging the LORD's supremacy (Ps 93.3–4). **3:** *Selah* (also vv. 7,11), see Ps 3.2n. **4:** *River,* see Ps 36.8n. **6:** God is opposed by historical as well as by cosmic foes. **8–10:** The LORD brings destruction on the kingdoms rising against Jerusalem (Ps 48.4–7), bringing ultimate peace; this proves God's great power (v. 10). **10:** The nations' weapons are sacrificed to the exalted divine victor (Josh 7). **11:** The psalm, although it narrates the nations' defeat, is not universalistic; their defeat illustrates the great power of the God of Israel, as illustrated in the refrain in vv. 7 and 11.

Ps 47: God's enthronement. A psalm lauding the kingship of the LORD, like Ps 93; 95–99; *Korahites,* see Ps 42–43n. **1–2:** In contrast to the previous psalm, all nations are invited to praise the God of Israel, the *great king,* the supreme imperial ruler. **4:** The LORD is also the divine king of chosen and beloved Israel

4 He chose our heritage for us,
the pride of Jacob whom he loves.
Selah

5 God has gone up with a shout,
the LORD with the sound of a trumpet.
6 Sing praises to God, sing praises;
sing praises to our King, sing praises.
7 For God is the king of all the earth;
sing praises with a psalm.[a]

8 God is king over the nations;
God sits on his holy throne.
9 The princes of the peoples gather
as the people of the God of Abraham.
For the shields of the earth belong to God;
he is highly exalted.

PSALM 48

A Song. A Psalm of the Korahites.

1 Great is the LORD and greatly to be praised
in the city of our God.
His holy mountain, 2 beautiful in elevation,
is the joy of all the earth,
Mount Zion, in the far north,
the city of the great King.
3 Within its citadels God
has shown himself a sure defense.
4 Then the kings assembled,
they came on together.
5 As soon as they saw it, they were astounded;
they were in panic, they took to flight;
6 trembling took hold of them there,
pains as of a woman in labor,
7 as when an east wind shatters
the ships of Tarshish.
8 As we have heard, so have we seen
in the city of the LORD of hosts,
in the city of our God,
which God establishes forever.
Selah

9 We ponder your steadfast love, O God,
in the midst of your temple.
10 Your name, O God, like your praise,
reaches to the ends of the earth.
Your right hand is filled with victory.
11 Let Mount Zion be glad,
let the towns[b] of Judah rejoice
because of your judgments.

12 Walk about Zion, go all around it,
count its towers,
13 consider well its ramparts;
go through its citadels,
that you may tell the next generation
14 that this is God,

a Heb *Maskil* b Heb *daughters*

(Deut 32.8), chosen and beloved. *Selah,* see Ps 3.2n. **5–7:** God's enthronement; the shouting, the sounding of the trumpet, and the singing reflect the coronation ritual (e.g., 1 Kings 1.39–40). **8–9:** The imperial sway of the LORD, to whom the nations bring tribute. The psalm may be Davidic in origin, and the nations his vassals (Ps 2.1–2).

Ps 48: Praise of Zion. Like Ps 46, a hymn of praise of Jerusalem as the city of God. *Korahites,* see Ps 42–43n. **1–2:** The hymn begins with seven epithets describing the holy city; the description of the city is highly idealized. **2:** *In the far north,* the mountain called Zaphon (which means "north") in Syria, was home of the Canaanite gods, especially Baal; cf. Isa 14.13. **4–7:** At the sight of the LORD's invincible city, its attackers panic and flee. **6:** A common expression for fear and anguish (Isa 26.17; Jer 4.31). **7:** *Tarshish,* see 1 Kings 10.22n. **8:** Having heard from their forebears about the magnificence of the city, the pilgrims now see it for themselves. *Selah,* see Ps 3.2n. **12–14:** This likely reflects a ritual procession through the city (Ps 84.7). **14:** The pilgrims relate to the next generation that "this is God," i.e., that the mighty city is a symbol of the mighty God who dwells there. The final word, here rendered "forever," is actually "over death." It is out of place here, and likely belongs with the superscription (title) of the following psalm (cf. Ps 9.1; 46.1).

our God forever and ever.
He will be our guide forever.

PSALM 49

To the leader. Of the Korahites. A Psalm.

1 Hear this, all you peoples;
give ear, all inhabitants of the world,
2 both low and high,
rich and poor together.
3 My mouth shall speak wisdom;
the meditation of my heart shall be understanding.
4 I will incline my ear to a proverb;
I will solve my riddle to the music of the harp.

5 Why should I fear in times of trouble,
when the iniquity of my persecutors surrounds me,
6 those who trust in their wealth
and boast of the abundance of their riches?
7 Truly, no ransom avails for one's life,[a]
there is no price one can give to God for it.
8 For the ransom of life is costly,
and can never suffice,
9 that one should live on forever
and never see the grave.[b]

10 When we look at the wise, they die;
fool and dolt perish together
and leave their wealth to others.
11 Their graves[c] are their homes forever,
their dwelling places to all generations,
though they named lands their own.
12 Mortals cannot abide in their pomp;
they are like the animals that perish.

13 Such is the fate of the foolhardy,
the end of those[d] who are pleased with their lot. *Selah*
14 Like sheep they are appointed for Sheol;
Death shall be their shepherd;
straight to the grave they descend,[e]
and their form shall waste away;
Sheol shall be their home.[f]
15 But God will ransom my soul from the power of Sheol,
for he will receive me. *Selah*

16 Do not be afraid when some become rich,
when the wealth of their houses increases.
17 For when they die they will carry nothing away;
their wealth will not go down after them.
18 Though in their lifetime they count themselves happy
—for you are praised when you do well for yourself—
19 they[g] will go to the company of their ancestors,
who will never again see the light.
20 Mortals cannot abide in their pomp;
they are like the animals that perish.

a Another reading is *no one can ransom a brother*
b Heb *the pit* *c* Gk Syr Compare Tg: Heb *their inward* (thought) *d* Tg: Heb *after them*
e Cn: Heb *the upright shall have dominion over them in the morning* *f* Meaning of Heb uncertain
g Cn: Heb *you*

Ps 49: Transience of life and wealth. A wisdom psalm (vv. 3–4), in places obscure and difficult, as the textual notes in the NRSV attest. A meditation on death as the common fate of humankind (v. 10), it shares a particular affinity with Ecclesiastes. Vv. 12 and 20 are a refrain. **1–4:** The wisdom teacher addresses all people, not Israel alone; like Ps 47, it is universalistic. **5–9:** The grave is the end of those who trust in their wealth, a theme repeated in vv. 16–19 (Prov 13.8; 22.2). **13:** *Selah* (also v. 15), see Ps 3.2n. **14:** *Sheol,* the abode of the dead. *Death . . . their shepherd,* contrast Ps 23.1. **15:** Incipient hope for life with God after death. *Receive me,* an idiom for divine deliverance from death (Gen 5.24; 2 Kings 2.10). **16–17:** Cf. Eccl 5.15. **20:** People are similarly compared to *animals* in Eccl 3.18–19.

PSALM 50

A Psalm of Asaph.

1 The mighty one, God the LORD,
speaks and summons the earth
from the rising of the sun to its setting.
2 Out of Zion, the perfection of beauty,
God shines forth.

3 Our God comes and does not keep silence,
before him is a devouring fire,
and a mighty tempest all around him.
4 He calls to the heavens above
and to the earth, that he may judge his people:
5 "Gather to me my faithful ones,
who made a covenant with me by sacrifice!"
6 The heavens declare his righteousness,
for God himself is judge. *Selah*

7 "Hear, O my people, and I will speak,
O Israel, I will testify against you.
I am God, your God.
8 Not for your sacrifices do I rebuke you;
your burnt offerings are continually before me.
9 I will not accept a bull from your house,
or goats from your folds.
10 For every wild animal of the forest is mine,
the cattle on a thousand hills.
11 I know all the birds of the air,[a]
and all that moves in the field is mine.
12 "If I were hungry, I would not tell you,
for the world and all that is in it is mine.
13 Do I eat the flesh of bulls,
or drink the blood of goats?
14 Offer to God a sacrifice of thanksgiving,[b]
and pay your vows to the Most High.
15 Call on me in the day of trouble;
I will deliver you, and you shall glorify me."

16 But to the wicked God says:
"What right have you to recite my statutes,
or take my covenant on your lips?
17 For you hate discipline,
and you cast my words behind you.
18 You make friends with a thief when you see one,
and you keep company with adulterers.

19 "You give your mouth free rein for evil,
and your tongue frames deceit.
20 You sit and speak against your kin;
you slander your own mother's child.
21 These things you have done and I have been silent;
you thought that I was one just like yourself.
But now I rebuke you, and lay the charge before you.

a Gk Syr Tg: Heb *mountains* *b* Or *make thanksgiving your sacrifice to God*

Ps 50: Theophany of the divine judge. A prophetic psalm; in a long divine speech (vv. 8–23), God lays out his case against the people (v. 21; Ps 82; Mic 6.1–8). *Asaph,* a Levite who was ancestor of a guild of Temple singers (1 Chr 16.7); Ps 73–83 have the same title. **1–3:** Theophany of the storm God, who appears on the Temple mount in Jerusalem (*Zion*) to judge his people; cf. Ex 19.16–18; Isa 29.6. **4–6:** The convening of the court. **6:** *Selah,* see Ps 3.2n. **7–13:** Prophetic critique of insincere worship, and on reliance on sacrifice (see Ps 40.6–8n.). **14–15:** Thanksgiving sacrifices (v. 23), from which the worshiper eats, and prayer are pleasing to God; this seems to be a rejection of other types of sacrifices, which might be perceived as feeding a God who owns all (vv. 10–11). **17:** *Cast my words behind you,* disregard them,

22 "Mark this, then, you who forget
God,
or I will tear you apart, and there
will be no one to deliver.
23 Those who bring thanksgiving as their
sacrifice honor me;
to those who go the right way[a]
I will show the salvation of God."

PSALM 51

To the leader. A Psalm of David, when the prophet Nathan came to him, after he had gone in to Bathsheba.

1 Have mercy on me, O God,
according to your steadfast love;
according to your abundant mercy
blot out my transgressions.
2 Wash me thoroughly from my
iniquity,
and cleanse me from my sin.

3 For I know my transgressions,
and my sin is ever before me.
4 Against you, you alone, have I sinned,
and done what is evil in your sight,
so that you are justified in your
sentence
and blameless when you pass
judgment.
5 Indeed, I was born guilty,
a sinner when my mother conceived
me.

6 You desire truth in the inward
being;[b]
therefore teach me wisdom in my
secret heart.
7 Purge me with hyssop, and I shall be
clean;
wash me, and I shall be whiter than
snow.
8 Let me hear joy and gladness;
let the bones that you have crushed
rejoice.
9 Hide your face from my sins,
and blot out all my iniquities.

10 Create in me a clean heart, O God,
and put a new and right[c] spirit
within me.
11 Do not cast me away from your
presence,
and do not take your holy spirit
from me.
12 Restore to me the joy of your
salvation,
and sustain in me a willing[d] spirit.

13 Then I will teach transgressors your
ways,
and sinners will return to you.
14 Deliver me from bloodshed, O God,
O God of my salvation,
and my tongue will sing aloud of
your deliverance.

15 O Lord, open my lips,

a Heb *who set a way* *b* Meaning of Heb uncertain
c Or *steadfast* *d* Or *generous*

put them out of sight (1 Kings 14.9; Ezek 23.35; Neh 9.26). **19–20:** Sins of speech (see 39.1–3n.). **22–23:** Varying fates of the wicked and the righteous, as in the conclusion to Ps 1.

Ps 51: Prayer for forgiveness. An exilic individual lament (one of the penitential psalms; see Ps 6n.), divided into two parts (vv. 1–9,10–19). Each part begins with a vocative appeal to God and ends with a reference to the Temple. (For the superscription, see 2 Sam 12 and cf. Ps 3n.) **3–4:** Conscious of sin, the remorseful psalmist confesses his sin, a precondition for forgiveness (Ps 32.5). Verse 4 echoes 2 Sam 12.9,13; this is why the tradition reflected in the superscription (title) connects the psalm with David's adultery with Bathsheba. **5:** An expression of the guilt-prone nature of humanity (see Job 7.17–21). **7:** See Lev 14.6–9 for an example of cleansing involving hyssop, a wild bush whose branches were used for sprinkling liquids. **8:** *Hear joy and gladness,* the prayers and songs the psalmist hopes to hear in the (rebuilt) Temple. **11:** *Your presence . . . your holy spirit,* expressions indicating God's presence ("face") and power (Isa 63.10–11). **13:** *Teach transgressors,* warning them to return to God (Ezek 3.18–21; 33.7–9). **15–17:** With the Temple destroyed, the psalmist can only offer hymns of praise and a penitent heart in place of sacrifice. The anti-sacrificial sentiment of these verses, though tempered in the following

and my mouth will declare your
praise.
16 For you have no delight in sacrifice;
if I were to give a burnt offering,
you would not be pleased.
17 The sacrifice acceptable to God[a] is a
broken spirit;
a broken and contrite heart,
O God, you will not despise.

18 Do good to Zion in your good
pleasure;
rebuild the walls of Jerusalem,
19 then you will delight in right
sacrifices,
in burnt offerings and whole burnt
offerings;
then bulls will be offered on your
altar.

PSALM 52

To the leader. A Maskil of David, when Doeg the Edomite came to Saul and said to him, "David has come to the house of Ahimelech."

1 Why do you boast, O mighty one,
of mischief done against the
godly?[b]
All day long 2 you are plotting
destruction.
Your tongue is like a sharp razor,
you worker of treachery.
3 You love evil more than good,
and lying more than speaking the
truth. *Selah*
4 You love all words that devour,
O deceitful tongue.
5 But God will break you down forever;
he will snatch and tear you from
your tent;
he will uproot you from the land of
the living. *Selah*
6 The righteous will see, and fear,
and will laugh at the evildoer,[c]
saying,
7 "See the one who would not take
refuge in God,
but trusted in abundant riches,
and sought refuge in wealth!"[d]

8 But I am like a green olive tree
in the house of God.
I trust in the steadfast love of God
forever and ever.
9 I will thank you forever,
because of what you have done.
In the presence of the faithful
I will proclaim[e] your name, for it
is good.

PSALM 53

To the leader: according to Mahalath. A Maskil of David.

1 Fools say in their hearts, "There is no
God."
They are corrupt, they commit
abominable acts;
there is no one who does good.

2 God looks down from heaven on
humankind

a Or *My sacrifice, O God,* b Cn Compare Syr: Heb *the kindness of God* c Heb *him* d Syr Tg: Heb *in his destruction* e Cn: Heb *wait for*

verses, may explain this psalm's juxtaposition to Ps 50 (see esp. vv. 8–13). **18–19:** The psalmist looks forward in hope to the rebuilding of the Temple and its reinstituted sacrificial worship.

Ps 52: Divine judgment against an oppressor. Ps 52 does not fit into any typical form-critical category. The addressee's identity ("O mighty one," v. 1) is unclear, but whoever he is, in the psalm he is the enemy of the godly. (For the superscription, see 1 Sam 22.9–19 and cf. Ps 3n.) **2–4:** His weapons are treacherous, deceitful speech. **3:** *Selah* (also v. 5), see Ps 3.2n. **5:** *Your tent* [lit. "the tent"] . . . *land of the living,* idioms for the Temple. **8:** Unlike his uprooted adversary, denied admittance to the Temple, (v. 5), the psalmist is planted in the Temple precincts, where he thanks God for his rescue. This notion of being planted in the Temple is a final stereotypical image (see Ps 92.13).

Ps 53: Condemnation of foolish evildoers. A doublet of Ps 14, with major divergence from Ps 14 only in v. 5, whose meaning remains unclear. In vv. 2, 4, and 6, "God" replaces Ps 14's "LORD"; see Introduction. *Mahalath,* see Ps 88n.

to see if there are any who are
wise,
who seek after God.

3 They have all fallen away, they are all
alike perverse;
there is no one who does good,
no, not one.

4 Have they no knowledge, those
evildoers,
who eat up my people as they eat
bread,
and do not call upon God?

5 There they shall be in great terror,
in terror such as has not been.
For God will scatter the bones of the
ungodly;[a]
they will be put to shame,[b] for
God has rejected them.

6 O that deliverance for Israel would
come from Zion!
When God restores the fortunes of
his people,
Jacob will rejoice; Israel will be
glad.

PSALM 54

To the leader: with stringed instruments. A Maskil of David, when the Ziphites went and told Saul, "David is in hiding among us."

1 Save me, O God, by your name,
and vindicate me by your might.
2 Hear my prayer, O God;
give ear to the words of my mouth.

3 For the insolent have risen
against me,
the ruthless seek my life;
they do not set God before them.
Selah

4 But surely, God is my helper;
the Lord is the upholder of[c] my
life.
5 He will repay my enemies for their
evil.
In your faithfulness, put an end to
them.

6 With a freewill offering I will sacrifice
to you;
I will give thanks to your name,
O LORD, for it is good.
7 For he has delivered me from every
trouble,
and my eye has looked in triumph
on my enemies.

PSALM 55

To the leader: with stringed instruments. A Maskil of David.

1 Give ear to my prayer, O God;
do not hide yourself from my
supplication.
2 Attend to me, and answer me;
I am troubled in my complaint.
I am distraught 3 by the noise of the
enemy,
because of the clamor of the
wicked.
For they bring[d] trouble upon me,
and in anger they cherish enmity
against me.

a Cn Compare Gk Syr: Heb *him who encamps against you* *b* Gk: Heb *you have put (them) to shame* *c* Gk Syr Jerome: Heb *is of those who uphold* or *is with those who uphold* *d* Cn Compare Gk: Heb *they cause to totter*

Ps 54: Prayer for deliverance from enemies. A lament, perhaps prayed by the king, attacked by savage enemies. (For the superscription, see 1 Sam 23.19, and cf. Ps 3n.) **1–2:** Appeal to God for intervention against the psalmist's enemies with his powerful presence (*name;* see v. 6). **3:** *The insolent* (see Ps 86.14), or better, the Heb text's "foreigners," appropriate in a royal lament. *Selah,* see Ps 3.2n. **4–5:** Prayer for retribution, contrasting the psalmist to the godless enemies of the previous verse.

Ps 55: Prayer for deliverance from enemies. An individual lament, in two parts (vv. 1–15,16–23). **1–3:** Appeal for divine help against wicked enemies. **6–8:** The fearful psalmist's longing for a place of safety

4 My heart is in anguish within me,
the terrors of death have fallen upon me.
5 Fear and trembling come upon me,
and horror overwhelms me.
6 And I say, "O that I had wings like a dove!
I would fly away and be at rest;
7 truly, I would flee far away;
I would lodge in the wilderness; *Selah*
8 I would hurry to find a shelter for myself
from the raging wind and tempest."

9 Confuse, O Lord, confound their speech;
for I see violence and strife in the city.
10 Day and night they go around it
on its walls,
and iniquity and trouble are within it;
11 ruin is in its midst;
oppression and fraud
do not depart from its marketplace.

12 It is not enemies who taunt me—
I could bear that;
it is not adversaries who deal insolently with me—
I could hide from them.
13 But it is you, my equal,
my companion, my familiar friend,
14 with whom I kept pleasant company;
we walked in the house of God with the throng.
15 Let death come upon them;
let them go down alive to Sheol;
for evil is in their homes and in their hearts.

16 But I call upon God,
and the LORD will save me.
17 Evening and morning and at noon
I utter my complaint and moan,
and he will hear my voice.
18 He will redeem me unharmed
from the battle that I wage,
for many are arrayed against me.
19 God, who is enthroned from of old, *Selah*
will hear, and will humble them—
because they do not change,
and do not fear God.

20 My companion laid hands on a friend
and violated a covenant with me[a]
21 with speech smoother than butter,
but with a heart set on war;
with words that were softer than oil,
but in fact were drawn swords.

22 Cast your burden[b] on the LORD,
and he will sustain you;
he will never permit
the righteous to be moved.

23 But you, O God, will cast them down
into the lowest pit;
the bloodthirsty and treacherous
shall not live out half their days.
But I will trust in you.

a Heb lacks *with me* *b* Or *Cast what he has given you*

from his enemies (Jer 9.1,9). **7:** *Selah* (also v. 19), see Ps 3.2n. **9–11:** The place of safety in the wilderness is contrasted with the violent city, the location of the psalmist's enemies (cf. Jer 6.6–7; Ezek 7.23; 12.19). **12–14:** The psalmist inveighs against the false friend, the deceitful ally (v. 21; Ps 41.9). **15–19:** An effective contrast: The false friend descends into Sheol, the abode of the dead, while God is enthroned in his heavenly palace. **15:** *Alive,* in the prime of life (Num 16.30; Ps 124.3). **22–23:** The psalmist is assured, perhaps by a cultic prophet, that he will never *be moved* ("be unsteady, totter") and fall into Sheol, the abode of the dead (*the lowest pit*), like the violent. **23:** *Not live out half their days,* premature death (v. 15).

PSALM 56

To the leader: according to The Dove on Far-off Terebinths. Of David. A Miktam, when the Philistines seized him in Gath.

1 Be gracious to me, O God, for people
trample on me;
all day long foes oppress me;
2 my enemies trample on me all day
long,
for many fight against me.
O Most High, 3 when I am afraid,
I put my trust in you.
4 In God, whose word I praise,
in God I trust; I am not afraid;
what can flesh do to me?

5 All day long they seek to injure my
cause;
all their thoughts are against me for
evil.
6 They stir up strife, they lurk,
they watch my steps.
As they hoped to have my life,
7 so repay[a] them for their crime;
in wrath cast down the peoples,
O God!

8 You have kept count of my tossings;
put my tears in your bottle.
Are they not in your record?
9 Then my enemies will retreat
in the day when I call.
This I know, that[b] God is for me.
10 In God, whose word I praise,
in the LORD, whose word I praise,
11 in God I trust; I am not afraid.
What can a mere mortal do to me?

12 My vows to you I must perform,
O God;
I will render thank offerings to
you.
13 For you have delivered my soul from
death,
and my feet from falling,
so that I may walk before God
in the light of life.

PSALM 57

To the leader: Do Not Destroy. Of David. A Miktam, when he fled from Saul, in the cave.

1 Be merciful to me, O God, be
merciful to me,
for in you my soul takes refuge;
in the shadow of your wings I will
take refuge,
until the destroying storms pass by.
2 I cry to God Most High,
to God who fulfills his purpose for
me.
3 He will send from heaven and
save me,

a Cn: Heb *rescue* b Or *because*

Ps 56: Prayer for deliverance from enemies. An individual lament, with a refrain in vv. 4,10–11. If the language of battle and victory (vv. 1–2,5–7,9) is not simply metaphorical, the speaker may be the king. The language of the psalm is highly repetitious; see, for example, "trample" in vv. 1–2. *According to the Dove . . .*, probably a melody. For the reference in David's life, see 1 Sam 21.11–15, and cf. Ps 3n. **1–3:** Appeal for help against enemies. **5–6:** For evil plotting and warfare, see Ps 140.2. **7:** *Cast down,* in defeat, to Sheol, the abode of the dead (Ps 55.23). **8:** *Record,* lit. "book"; see Ps 40.7n. **11:** A common sentiment in Psalms; see esp. 118.6. **12:** A thanksgiving ritual (Ps 50.14; 66.13). **13:** God preserves the psalmist's life by keeping him from falling into dark Sheol (Ps 116.8–9; Job 33.28), *walk*ing instead in light.

Ps 57: Prayer for deliverance from enemies. An individual lament of someone unjustly accused; vv. 7–11 reappear in Ps 108.1–5. There is a refrain in vv. 5 and 11. With its theme and vocabulary, it is easy to see how it might be (secondarily) applied to *David . . . when he fled from Saul, in the cave* (see 1 Sam 22.1; cf. Ps 3n.). *Do Not Destroy,* probably a melody. **1:** *Refuge . . . shadow of your wings,* asylum and protection in the Temple. **2–3:** Answering the appeal of the psalmist, God will send aid from his heavenly court, personified *love* and *faithfulness* (Ps 25.21; 43.3; 61.7). **3:** *Selah* (also v. 6), see Ps 3.2n.

he will put to shame those who
trample on me. *Selah*
God will send forth his steadfast love
and his faithfulness.

4 I lie down among lions
that greedily devour[a] human prey;
their teeth are spears and arrows,
their tongues sharp swords.

5 Be exalted, O God, above the
heavens.
Let your glory be over all the earth.

6 They set a net for my steps;
my soul was bowed down.
They dug a pit in my path,
but they have fallen into it
themselves. *Selah*
7 My heart is steadfast, O God,
my heart is steadfast.
I will sing and make melody.
8 Awake, my soul!
Awake, O harp and lyre!
I will awake the dawn.
9 I will give thanks to you, O Lord,
among the peoples;
I will sing praises to you among the
nations.
10 For your steadfast love is as high as
the heavens;
your faithfulness extends to the
clouds.

11 Be exalted, O God, above the
heavens.
Let your glory be over all the earth.

PSALM 58

To the leader: Do Not Destroy. Of David.
A Miktam.

1 Do you indeed decree what is right,
you gods?[b]
Do you judge people fairly?
2 No, in your hearts you devise wrongs;
your hands deal out violence on
earth.

3 The wicked go astray from the womb;
they err from their birth, speaking
lies.
4 They have venom like the venom of a
serpent,
like the deaf adder that stops
its ear,
5 so that it does not hear the voice of
charmers
or of the cunning enchanter.

6 O God, break the teeth in their
mouths;
tear out the fangs of the young
lions, O LORD!
7 Let them vanish like water that runs
away;
like grass let them be trodden
down[c] and wither.
8 Let them be like the snail that
dissolves into slime;
like the untimely birth that never
sees the sun.

a Cn: Heb *are aflame for* *b* Or *mighty lords*
c Cn: Meaning of Heb uncertain

4: The psalmist's foes are likened to predatory beasts (Ps 7.2; 10.9; 22.12–13,16). **6:** The law of talion or equivalent retribution (see 3.7n.): The enemies fall into the pit they dug for the psalmist (Ps 7.15); this idea was especially attractive to wisdom authors (Prov 26.27; Eccl 10.8). **7:** The lament shifts to a hymn of praise. **8:** The motif of God's help coming in the morning (Ps 5.3; 59.16; 90.14). **9–10:** The universal audience of the psalmist is matched by the universal extent of divine love and faithfulness.

Ps 58: A curse upon enemies. A psalm of petition difficult to classify; the initial questions to the gods (v. 1) about their failures in justice and cosmic governance recall Ps 82; and both psalms end with an appeal to God to judge the earth. The poetic language of the psalm is especially difficult. *Do Not Destroy,* see Ps 57n. **1:** God's impassioned questions to subordinate heavenly beings for their misgovernance (Ps 82.2). **3:** The refusal of the gods to decree what is right is taken up by human beings who speak *lies* (Ps 5.6; 63.11; 101.7). **4:** A metaphor for slander by the psalmist's stealthy enemies. **6:** As in Ps 57.6, the law of equivalent retribution (see 3.7n.): God destroys the organs of speech of liars and slanderers. **7–9:** Extremely difficult; there seem to be seven curses here (Ps 35.4–8). **10:** The gory image expresses the

9 Sooner than your pots can feel the heat of thorns,
whether green or ablaze, may he sweep them away!

10 The righteous will rejoice when they see vengeance done;
they will bathe their feet in the blood of the wicked.
11 People will say, "Surely there is a reward for the righteous;
surely there is a God who judges on earth."

PSALM 59

To the leader: Do Not Destroy. Of David. A Miktam, when Saul ordered his house to be watched in order to kill him.

1 Deliver me from my enemies, O my God;
protect me from those who rise up against me.
2 Deliver me from those who work evil;
from the bloodthirsty save me.

3 Even now they lie in wait for my life;
the mighty stir up strife against me.
For no transgression or sin of mine, O LORD,
4 for no fault of mine, they run and make ready.

Rouse yourself, come to my help and see!
5 You, LORD God of hosts, are God of Israel.
Awake to punish all the nations;
spare none of those who treacherously plot evil. *Selah*

6 Each evening they come back, howling like dogs
and prowling about the city.
7 There they are, bellowing with their mouths,
with sharp words[a] on their lips—
for "Who," they think,[b] "will hear us?"

8 But you laugh at them, O LORD;
you hold all the nations in derision.
9 O my strength, I will watch for you;
for you, O God, are my fortress.
10 My God in his steadfast love will meet me;
my God will let me look in triumph on my enemies.

11 Do not kill them, or my people may forget;
make them totter by your power, and bring them down,
O Lord, our shield.
12 For the sin of their mouths, the words of their lips,
let them be trapped in their pride.
For the cursing and lies that they utter,
13 consume them in wrath;
consume them until they are no more.
Then it will be known to the ends of the earth
that God rules over Jacob. *Selah*

14 Each evening they come back, howling like dogs
and prowling about the city.

a Heb *with swords* b Heb lacks *they think*

totality of God's victory; the righteous will wade through the blood of the defeated (cf. 68.23; Isa 63.1–6).

Ps 59: Prayer for deliverance from enemies. An individual lament with two refrains (vv. 6,14; 9,17). *Do Not Destroy,* see Ps 57n. (For the superscription, see 1 Sam 19.11, and cf. Ps 3n.) **1–4:** Fourfold appeal to God, followed by four actions of the enemies. The psalmist protests his innocence of disloyalty and rebellion. **4–5:** *Rouse yourself . . . awake,* for judgment (Ps 35.23) or warfare (Ps 44.23). *All the nations* may imply that the speaker is the king. **5:** *Selah* (also v. 13), see Ps 3.2n. **6:** The enemies are described as predatory dogs (Ps 22.16,20), whose weapons are damaging, abusive speech (v. 12; see Ps 52.2–3; 55.21; 57.4). **8:** God derides the psalmist's disloyal betrayers (Ps 2.4; 37.13; Wis 4.18). **10:** See Ps 54.7. **11:** A very odd request; perhaps greatly weakened enemies are a better witness to God's greatness than dead enemies.

15 They roam about for food,
and growl if they do not get
their fill.
16 But I will sing of your might;
I will sing aloud of your steadfast
love in the morning.
For you have been a fortress for me
and a refuge in the day of my
distress.
17 O my strength, I will sing praises to
you,
for you, O God, are my fortress,
the God who shows me steadfast
love.

PSALM 60

To the leader: according to the Lily of the Covenant. A Miktam of David; for instruction; when he struggled with Aram-naharaim and with Aram-zobah, and when Joab on his return killed twelve thousand Edomites in the Valley of Salt.

1 O God, you have rejected us, broken
our defenses;
you have been angry; now
restore us!
2 You have caused the land to quake;
you have torn it open;
repair the cracks in it, for it is
tottering.
3 You have made your people suffer
hard things;
you have given us wine to drink
that made us reel.
4 You have set up a banner for those
who fear you,
to rally to it out of bowshot.[a]
Selah
5 Give victory with your right hand,
and answer us,[b]
so that those whom you love may
be rescued.
6 God has promised in his sanctuary:[c]
"With exultation I will divide up
Shechem,
and portion out the Vale of Succoth.
7 Gilead is mine, and Manasseh is
mine;
Ephraim is my helmet;
Judah is my scepter.
8 Moab is my washbasin;
on Edom I hurl my shoe;
over Philistia I shout in triumph."
9 Who will bring me to the fortified
city?
Who will lead me to Edom?
10 Have you not rejected us, O God?
You do not go out, O God, with
our armies.
11 O grant us help against the foe,
for human help is worthless.

a Gk Syr Jerome: Heb *because of the truth*
b Another reading is *me* *c* Or *by his holiness*

Ps 60: Prayer for deliverance from enemies. An exilic communal lament; the lament proper (vv. 1–3) is followed by a prayer for divine help (vv. 4–5), a salvation oracle (vv. 6–8), and a prayer for victory over Edom (vv. 9–12); like Ps 137 it combines laments over the fall of Judah with a message of doom and defeat for Edom. Verses 5–12 reappear in Ps 108.6–13. *The Lily,* see Ps 45n., cf. Ps 80; for the reference to David, see 2 Sam 8.3–8,13–14; cf. Ps 3n. **1–3:** A complaint of some national defeat, brought about because of God's anger. According to ancient Near Eastern theology, the people rejected or abandoned by their god are open to enemy conquest (see Ezek 8–11). **1:** *Rejected us,* occurs in several communal laments (Ps 44.9,23–24; 74.1; 89.38). **3:** *Wine . . . that made us reel,* a symbol of divine punishment (Isa 51.17,22; Zech 12.2). **4:** *Selah,* see Ps 3.2n. **6–8:** An oracle of victory. God will regain control of and redistribute Israelite territory that had been taken over by others: *Shechem,* a major city in central Israel (*Ephraim*); *the Vale of Succoth,* in the east Jordan Valley; *Gilead* and *Manasseh,* in Transjordan; *Judah.* Moreover, the Davidic empire, with its vassal states (*Moab, Edom, Philistia;* see 2 Sam 8.11–12), will be restored. *Washbasin . . . hurl my shoe,* the precise meaning of the metaphors is unclear. **9–12:** The psalmist's reaction to the oracle. **9:** *Fortified city,* Bozrah, capital of Edom. **10:** See Ps 44.9. **12:** See Ps 44.5; Isa 63.6.

12 With God we shall do valiantly;
it is he who will tread down our foes.

PSALM 61

To the leader: with stringed instruments. Of David.

1 Hear my cry, O God;
listen to my prayer.
2 From the end of the earth I call to you,
when my heart is faint.

Lead me to the rock
that is higher than I;
3 for you are my refuge,
a strong tower against the enemy.

4 Let me abide in your tent forever,
find refuge under the shelter of your wings. *Selah*
5 For you, O God, have heard my vows;
you have given me the heritage of those who fear your name.

6 Prolong the life of the king;
may his years endure to all generations!
7 May he be enthroned forever before God;
appoint steadfast love and faithfulness to watch over him!

8 So I will always sing praises to your name,
as I pay my vows day after day.

PSALM 62

To the leader: according to Jeduthun. A Psalm of David.

1 For God alone my soul waits in silence;
from him comes my salvation.
2 He alone is my rock and my salvation,
my fortress; I shall never be shaken.

3 How long will you assail a person,
will you batter your victim, all of you,
as you would a leaning wall, a tottering fence?
4 Their only plan is to bring down a person of prominence.
They take pleasure in falsehood;
they bless with their mouths,
but inwardly they curse. *Selah*

5 For God alone my soul waits in silence,
for my hope is from him.
6 He alone is my rock and my salvation,
my fortress; I shall not be shaken.
7 On God rests my deliverance and my honor;
my mighty rock, my refuge is in God.

8 Trust in him at all times, O people;
pour out your heart before him;
God is a refuge for us. *Selah*

9 Those of low estate are but a breath,

Ps 61: Protection in the Temple. A royal lament (vv. 6–7). **1–2:** Prayer of the king, gravely ill (cf. Isa 38.9–20) and on the brink of death (*end of the earth*). **3–4:** *Refuge . . . tower . . . tent . . . shelter of your wings,* synonyms for the Temple. **4:** *Selah,* see Ps 3.2n. **6–7:** Prayer of the people for the king's recovery and long life. **7:** *Steadfast love and faithfulness,* personified guardians of the king (Ps 57.3). **8:** Typical motivations for God to heed a prayer (see Ps 9.2; 22.25).

Ps 62: Trust in God. A psalm of trust, with refrain (vv. 1–2,5–6). Unlike most psalms, which use a variety of imagery to depict God, this psalm is thematically unified through the image of God's strength and power. **2:** Language suggestive of the Temple. **3–4:** The enemy's attacks on the psalmist (physical violence and false testimony). **4:** *Selah* (also v. 8), see Ps 3.2n. **5–7:** A highly poetic interlude, resuming the psalm's theme of God's strength. **8:** *Pour out your heart,* in a lament (1 Sam 1.15; Lam 2.19). **9:** All human beings are as insubstantial as a puff of air (Ps 39.5; 144.4; Prov 21.6) in contrast to God's great

those of high estate are a delusion;
in the balances they go up;
they are together lighter than a breath.
10 Put no confidence in extortion,
and set no vain hopes on robbery;
if riches increase, do not set your heart on them.

11 Once God has spoken;
twice have I heard this:
that power belongs to God,
12 and steadfast love belongs to you, O Lord.
For you repay to all
according to their work.

PSALM 63

A Psalm of David, when he was in the Wilderness of Judah.

1 O God, you are my God, I seek you,
my soul thirsts for you;
my flesh faints for you,
as in a dry and weary land where there is no water.
2 So I have looked upon you in the sanctuary,
beholding your power and glory.
3 Because your steadfast love is better than life,
my lips will praise you.
4 So I will bless you as long as I live;
I will lift up my hands and call on your name.
5 My soul is satisfied as with a rich feast,[a]
and my mouth praises you with joyful lips
6 when I think of you on my bed,
and meditate on you in the watches of the night;
7 for you have been my help,
and in the shadow of your wings I sing for joy.
8 My soul clings to you;
your right hand upholds me.

9 But those who seek to destroy my life
shall go down into the depths of the earth;
10 they shall be given over to the power of the sword,
they shall be prey for jackals.
11 But the king shall rejoice in God;
all who swear by him shall exult,
for the mouths of liars will be stopped.

PSALM 64

To the leader. A Psalm of David.

1 Hear my voice, O God, in my complaint;
preserve my life from the dread enemy.
2 Hide me from the secret plots of the wicked,
from the scheming of evildoers,

a Heb *with fat and fatness*

power. The image of weighing deeds *in the balances* is common in Egypt, and is also found in Isa 40.15. **10**: Trust in God, not in ill-gotten wealth (Ps 49.6,16–17). **11–12**: Oracle of salvation by the mighty and loving God, who uses strength to *repay* all fairly.

Ps 63: Thirsting for God. A psalm of trust describing an encounter with God in the Temple (vv. 2,7). The strong desire to see God (see 27.4) borders on the mystical (see Ps 42). (For the superscription, see 1 Sam 23.14,15; 24.1; cf. Ps 3n.) **1**: See Ps 42.1–2; 143.6. **2**: *Your power and glory,* a poetic description of the ark. **3**: A highly unusual hyperbole, for Israelites for whom life is the highest good. **5**: Appropriately for a psalm about the desire to reach the Temple, sacrifice (Ps 36.8–9) and prayer are used in its similes. **6**: *On my bed,* in private (Ps 36.4; 149.5). **8–11**: The psalmist, upheld by God, will not be consigned to Sheol, the domain of the silent dead, as the wicked will be. **11**: A reflection of the significance of the king (Ps 45.6).

Ps 64: Prayer for deliverance from enemies. An individual lament. **1–6**: The complaint of the psalmist against his enemies. The description of these activities is unusually long and detailed. For the metaphor of tongues as swords (damaging speech) in v. 3, cf. Ps 57.4; 59.7. **5**: *"Who can see us?"*, the confidence

3 who whet their tongues like swords,
who aim bitter words like arrows,
4 shooting from ambush at the blameless;
they shoot suddenly and without fear.
5 They hold fast to their evil purpose;
they talk of laying snares secretly,
thinking, "Who can see us?[a]
6 Who can search out our crimes?[b]
We have thought out a cunningly conceived plot."
For the human heart and mind are deep.

7 But God will shoot his arrow at them;
they will be wounded suddenly.
8 Because of their tongue he will bring them to ruin;[c]
all who see them will shake with horror.
9 Then everyone will fear;
they will tell what God has brought about,
and ponder what he has done.

10 Let the righteous rejoice in the LORD
and take refuge in him.
Let all the upright in heart glory.

PSALM 65

To the leader. A Psalm of David. A Song.

1 Praise is due to you,
O God, in Zion;
and to you shall vows be performed,
2 O you who answer prayer!
To you all flesh shall come.
3 When deeds of iniquity overwhelm us,
you forgive our transgressions.
4 Happy are those whom you choose
and bring near
to live in your courts.
We shall be satisfied with the goodness of your house,
your holy temple.

5 By awesome deeds you answer us
with deliverance,
O God of our salvation;
you are the hope of all the ends of the earth
and of the farthest seas.
6 By your[d] strength you established the mountains;
you are girded with might.
7 You silence the roaring of the seas,
the roaring of their waves,
the tumult of the peoples.
8 Those who live at earth's farthest bounds are awed by your signs;
you make the gateways of the morning and the evening shout for joy.

9 You visit the earth and water it,
you greatly enrich it;
the river of God is full of water;
you provide the people with grain,
for so you have prepared it.
10 You water its furrows abundantly,
settling its ridges,
softening it with showers,

a Syr: Heb *them* *b* Cn: Heb *They search out crimes* *c* Cn: Heb *They will bring him to ruin, their tongue being against them* *d* Gk Jerome: Heb *his*

of the evildoers that their activity goes unnoticed (Ps 10.11; 59.7). **7–8:** The law of equivalent retribution (see 3.7n.): God's arrows directed at those who attacked the innocent with (metaphorical) arrows (Ps 7.12–13; 38.2). The description of God's activities is short; minimal actions by God are sufficient to overturn complex evil activity. **9–10:** Vengeance is not presented as a motive; rather the defeat of the wicked causes *everyone* to *fear* and *ponder* God, and causes the *righteous* to *rejoice.*

Ps 65: Thanksgiving for agricultural bounty. A hymn thanking God for a good harvest. **1:** *Zion,* Jerusalem. **2:** *All flesh,* a universalistic note that may locate this hymn in the postexilic era (cf. Isa 66.23). **3:** Divine forgiveness of sin, the precondition for winter rains and an abundant harvest (Deut 11.13–17). **5–7:** *Awesome deeds,* God's acts of creation by his victory over the forces of primeval chaos (*the seas;* Ps 29; 93) and his provision of rain. **9:** *The river of God,* the conduit that brings rain to the earth (Job 38.25–26), perhaps associated with the Temple (see Ps 36.8n.). **11:** *Your wagon tracks,* God's rain-cloud

and blessing its growth.
11 You crown the year with your bounty;
your wagon tracks overflow with richness.
12 The pastures of the wilderness overflow,
the hills gird themselves with joy,
13 the meadows clothe themselves with flocks,
the valleys deck themselves with grain,
they shout and sing together for joy.

PSALM 66

To the leader. A Song. A Psalm.

1 Make a joyful noise to God, all the earth;
2 sing the glory of his name;
give to him glorious praise.
3 Say to God, "How awesome are your deeds!
Because of your great power, your enemies cringe before you.
4 All the earth worships you;
they sing praises to you,
sing praises to your name." *Selah*

5 Come and see what God has done:
he is awesome in his deeds among mortals.
6 He turned the sea into dry land;
they passed through the river on foot.
There we rejoiced in him,
7 who rules by his might forever,
whose eyes keep watch on the nations—
let the rebellious not exalt themselves. *Selah*

8 Bless our God, O peoples,
let the sound of his praise be heard,
9 who has kept us among the living,
and has not let our feet slip.
10 For you, O God, have tested us;
you have tried us as silver is tried.
11 You brought us into the net;
you laid burdens on our backs;
12 you let people ride over our heads;
we went through fire and through water;
yet you have brought us out to a spacious place.[a]

13 I will come into your house with burnt offerings;
I will pay you my vows,
14 those that my lips uttered
and my mouth promised when I was in trouble.
15 I will offer to you burnt offerings of fatlings,
with the smoke of the sacrifice of rams;
I will make an offering of bulls and goats. *Selah*

16 Come and hear, all you who fear God,
and I will tell what he has done for me.
17 I cried aloud to him,
and he was extolled with my tongue.

a Cn Compare Gk Syr Jerome Tg: Heb *to a saturation*

chariot. **12–13:** The natural world joins humankind in the praise of the beneficent God (Ps 69.39; 96.11–12; 98.7–8). The abundance of the harvest is almost mythological; cf. Joel 3.18; Am 9.13.

Ps 66: Praise of God the savior. A composite psalm, consisting of a hymn of praise (vv. 1–7), a communal thanksgiving (vv. 5–12), and an individual thanksgiving (vv. 13–20). **1–4:** Praise of God for the *awesome . . . deeds,* his acts of liberation, which are so great that *all the earth worships* him (Josh 2.9–11). **4:** *Selah* (also vv. 7,15), see Ps 3.2n. **5–7:** The passage of Israel through the sea (Ex 14.21–22; Josh 4.23). **8–9:** Invitation to Gentiles to praise Israel's God, who has not let his people perish. **10–12:** Probably a reference to the escape from slavery in Egypt, the arduous trek through the wilderness (*fire*), and the crossing of the Jordan (*water*), as well as to Israel's subsequent history; cf. Isa 43.2. **13–15:**

18 If I had cherished iniquity in my
heart,
the Lord would not have listened.
19 But truly God has listened;
he has given heed to the words of
my prayer.

20 Blessed be God,
because he has not rejected my
prayer
or removed his steadfast love from
me.

PSALM 67

To the leader: with stringed instruments.
A Psalm. A Song.

1 May God be gracious to us and bless
us
and make his face to shine upon us,
Selah
2 that your way may be known upon
earth,
your saving power among all
nations.
3 Let the peoples praise you, O God;
let all the peoples praise you.

4 Let the nations be glad and sing
for joy,
for you judge the peoples with
equity
and guide the nations upon earth.
Selah
5 Let the peoples praise you,
O God;
let all the peoples praise you.

6 The earth has yielded its increase;
God, our God, has blessed us.
7 May God continue to bless us;
let all the ends of the earth revere
him.

PSALM 68

To the leader. Of David. A Psalm. A Song.

1 Let God rise up, let his enemies be
scattered;
let those who hate him flee before
him.
2 As smoke is driven away, so drive
them away;
as wax melts before the fire,
let the wicked perish before God.
3 But let the righteous be joyful;
let them exult before God;
let them be jubilant with joy.

4 Sing to God, sing praises to his name;
lift up a song to him who rides
upon the clouds[a]—
his name is the LORD—
be exultant before him.

5 Father of orphans and protector of
widows
is God in his holy habitation.
6 God gives the desolate a home to live
in;
he leads out the prisoners to
prosperity,

a Or *cast up a highway for him who rides through the deserts*

Abundant thanksgiving sacrifices in the Temple. **18:** The psalmist's protestation of innocence. **20:** Final benediction (2 Sam 7.15).

Ps 67: Thanksgiving for agricultural bounty. A prayer that good harvests continue, with a refrain in vv. 3 and 5. It continues the theme of blessing found in the conclusion of the previous psalm. **1:** An echo of the Aaronic blessing (Num 6.24–26; Ps 4.6). The shining *face* of God is the visible expression of his benevolence. In general, this psalm is derivative, using many stock phrases from elsewhere in Psalms and other sources. *Selah* (also vv. 4,7), see Ps 3.2n. **4:** See Ps 96.10–13; 98.7–9. **6:** *God . . . has blessed us,* with copious winter rain (Lev 26.4; Deut 11.17; Ezek 34.27). The hymn may be associated with the fall festival of Tabernacles.

Ps 68: A victory hymn. An ancient hymn of praise describing God's victory over his foes and his choice of Jerusalem as the place of his dominion. At several points the psalm is very disjointed and difficult. At several places it appears to echo Judg 5. **1–2:** God manifests himself as Divine Warrior (Num 10.35). **4:** *Who rides upon the clouds,* God's storm-cloud chariot (v. 33; Ps 65.11). **7–10:** God's march through the

but the rebellious live in a parched
land.
7 O God, when you went out before
your people,
when you marched through the
wilderness, *Selah*
8 the earth quaked, the heavens poured
down rain
at the presence of God, the God of
Sinai,
at the presence of God, the God of
Israel.
9 Rain in abundance, O God, you
showered abroad;
you restored your heritage when it
languished;
10 your flock found a dwelling in it;
in your goodness, O God, you
provided for the needy.

11 The Lord gives the command;
great is the company of those[a]
who bore the tidings:
12 "The kings of the armies, they flee,
they flee!"
The women at home divide the spoil,
13 though they stay among the
sheepfolds—
the wings of a dove covered with silver,
its pinions with green gold.
14 When the Almighty[b] scattered kings
there,
snow fell on Zalmon.

15 O mighty mountain, mountain of
Bashan;
O many-peaked mountain,
mountain of Bashan!
16 Why do you look with envy,
O many-peaked mountain,
at the mount that God desired for
his abode,
where the LORD will reside forever?
17 With mighty chariotry, twice ten
thousand,
thousands upon thousands,
the Lord came from Sinai into the
holy place.[c]
18 You ascended the high mount,
leading captives in your train
and receiving gifts from people,
even from those who rebel against the
LORD God's abiding there.
19 Blessed be the Lord,
who daily bears us up;
God is our salvation. *Selah*
20 Our God is a God of salvation,
and to GOD, the Lord, belongs
escape from death.

21 But God will shatter the heads of his
enemies,
the hairy crown of those who walk
in their guilty ways.
22 The Lord said,
"I will bring them back from
Bashan,
I will bring them back from the
depths of the sea,
23 so that you may bathe[d] your feet in
blood,
so that the tongues of your dogs
may have their share from the
foe."

a Or *company of the women* *b* Traditional rendering of Heb *Shaddai* *c* Cn: Heb *The Lord among them Sinai in the holy* (place) *d* Gk Syr Tg: Heb *shatter*

wilderness to the land where the divine shepherd provides for his flock (Ps 23.1). **7:** *Selah* (also vv. 19,32), see Ps 3.2n. **8:** One of the few references to *Sinai* outside of the Pentateuch; cf. Judg 5.4–5. **11–14:** God gives the command for war; women announce the good news of God's victory (Ex 15.20; 1 Sam 18.6–7). **12:** *Divide the spoil,* Judg 5.30. **13:** *Among the sheepfolds,* Judg 5.16. *The wings of a dove . . . ,* presumably some treasure found among the spoil. **14:** The specific incident referred to cannot be identified. *Zalmon* may be the same mountain mentioned in Judg 9.48. **15–23:** The divine victor's move from Sinai (v. 8) to Zion, God's choice for his royal residence (Isa 2.3). **15:** *Bashan,* a region in northern Transjordan. The specific mountain referred to is unknown. **16:** *The mount . . . his abode,* cf. Ex 15.17; Ps 132.13–14. **17:** Cf. Deut 33.2. **23:** *Feet in blood,* see 58.10n. *Dogs,* cf. 1 Kings 21.19; 22.38. **24–27:**

24 Your solemn processions are seen,[a]
O God,
the processions of my God, my
King, into the sanctuary—
25 the singers in front, the musicians
last,
between them girls playing
tambourines:
26 "Bless God in the great congregation,
the LORD, O you who are of
Israel's fountain!"
27 There is Benjamin, the least of them,
in the lead,
the princes of Judah in a body,
the princes of Zebulun, the princes
of Naphtali.

28 Summon your might, O God;
show your strength, O God, as you
have done for us before.
29 Because of your temple at Jerusalem
kings bear gifts to you.
30 Rebuke the wild animals that live
among the reeds,
the herd of bulls with the calves of
the peoples.
Trample[b] under foot those who lust
after tribute;
scatter the peoples who delight in
war.[c]
31 Let bronze be brought from Egypt;
let Ethiopia[d] hasten to stretch out
its hands to God.

32 Sing to God, O kingdoms of the
earth;
sing praises to the Lord, *Selah*
33 O rider in the heavens, the ancient
heavens;
listen, he sends out his voice, his
mighty voice.
34 Ascribe power to God,
whose majesty is over Israel;
and whose power is in the skies.
35 Awesome is God in his[e] sanctuary,
the God of Israel;
he gives power and strength to his
people.

Blessed be God!

PSALM 69

To the leader: according to Lilies.
Of David.

1 Save me, O God,
for the waters have come up to my
neck.
2 I sink in deep mire,
where there is no foothold;
I have come into deep waters,
and the flood sweeps over me.
3 I am weary with my crying;
my throat is parched.
My eyes grow dim
with waiting for my God.

4 More in number than the hairs of my
head
are those who hate me without
cause;
many are those who would destroy
me,
my enemies who accuse me falsely.
What I did not steal
must I now restore?
5 O God, you know my folly;
the wrongs I have done are not
hidden from you.

6 Do not let those who hope in you be
put to shame because of me,

a Or *have been seen* *b* Cn: Heb *Trampling*
c Meaning of Heb of verse 30 is uncertain
d Or *Nubia*; Heb *Cush* *e* Gk: Heb *from your*

Procession of the Divine Warrior into the temple, accompanied by Israel's praise (Ps 24.7–10). **27:** Cf. Judg 5.14–18. **28–35:** International praise of God and tribute from defeated enemies. **33–35:** Cf. 29.1–3,11.

Ps 69: Prayer for deliverance from enemies. A lament that moves from an individual to a communal complaint. *According to Lilies,* see Ps 45n. **1–2:** Almost overcome by the chaotic waters, the psalmist cries out to God (Ps 130.1). **4–5:** Attacked by legal or judicial opponents, who are accused of false testimony, the psalmist protests his innocence. **8:** See Ps 38.11; Job 19.13–15. **9:** If this psalm is a royal

O Lord GOD of hosts;
do not let those who seek you be
dishonored because of me,
O God of Israel.
7 It is for your sake that I have borne
reproach,
that shame has covered my face.
8 I have become a stranger to my
kindred,
an alien to my mother's children.

9 It is zeal for your house that has
consumed me;
the insults of those who insult you
have fallen on me.
10 When I humbled my soul with
fasting,[a]
they insulted me for doing so.
11 When I made sackcloth my clothing,
I became a byword to them.
12 I am the subject of gossip for those
who sit in the gate,
and the drunkards make songs
about me.

13 But as for me, my prayer is to you,
O LORD.
At an acceptable time, O God,
in the abundance of your steadfast
love, answer me.
With your faithful help 14 rescue me
from sinking in the mire;
let me be delivered from my enemies
and from the deep waters.
15 Do not let the flood sweep over me,
or the deep swallow me up,
or the Pit close its mouth over me.

16 Answer me, O LORD, for your
steadfast love is good;
according to your abundant mercy,
turn to me.
17 Do not hide your face from your
servant,
for I am in distress—make haste to
answer me.
18 Draw near to me, redeem me,
set me free because of my enemies.

19 You know the insults I receive,
and my shame and dishonor;
my foes are all known to you.
20 Insults have broken my heart,
so that I am in despair.
I looked for pity, but there was none;
and for comforters, but I found
none.
21 They gave me poison for food,
and for my thirst they gave me
vinegar to drink.

22 Let their table be a trap for them,
a snare for their allies.
23 Let their eyes be darkened so that
they cannot see,
and make their loins tremble
continually.
24 Pour out your indignation upon them,
and let your burning anger overtake
them.
25 May their camp be a desolation;
let no one live in their tents.
26 For they persecute those whom you
have struck down,
and those whom you have
wounded, they attack still
more.[b]
27 Add guilt to their guilt;
may they have no acquittal from
you.
28 Let them be blotted out of the book
of the living;
let them not be enrolled among the
righteous.

a Gk Syr: Heb *I wept, with fasting my soul,* or *I made my soul mourn with fasting* *b* Gk Syr: Heb *recount the pain of*

lament, *zeal for your house* could refer to the king's responsibility for the construction and provisioning of the Temple. If in its final form it dates from the exile (see vv. 30–36n.) the *zeal* would be directed toward rebuilding the Temple. **10–11:** Penitential or mourning practices. **13:** *At an acceptable time,* perhaps connected to the common notion that God sometimes "sleeps" (44.23) or hides his face (13.1); see vv. 16–18. **16–18:** The psalmist prays that God will not *hide* his *face* (be inattentive to the psalmist's prayers). **23–26:** The psalmist curses his enemies, praying for their defeat by sickness, exile, and death.

29 But I am lowly and in pain;
let your salvation, O God, protect me.

30 I will praise the name of God with a song;
I will magnify him with thanksgiving.
31 This will please the LORD more than an ox
or a bull with horns and hoofs.
32 Let the oppressed see it and be glad;
you who seek God, let your hearts revive.
33 For the LORD hears the needy,
and does not despise his own that are in bonds.

34 Let heaven and earth praise him,
the seas and everything that moves in them.
35 For God will save Zion
and rebuild the cities of Judah;
and his servants shall live[a] there and possess it;
36 the children of his servants shall inherit it,
and those who love his name shall live in it.

PSALM 70

To the leader. Of David, for the memorial offering.

1 Be pleased, O God, to deliver me.
O LORD, make haste to help me!
2 Let those be put to shame and confusion
who seek my life.
Let those be turned back and brought to dishonor
who desire to hurt me.
3 Let those who say, "Aha, Aha!"
turn back because of their shame.

4 Let all who seek you
rejoice and be glad in you.
Let those who love your salvation
say evermore, "God is great!"
5 But I am poor and needy;
hasten to me, O God!
You are my help and my deliverer;
O LORD, do not delay!

PSALM 71

1 In you, O LORD, I take refuge;
let me never be put to shame.
2 In your righteousness deliver me and rescue me;
incline your ear to me and save me.
3 Be to me a rock of refuge,
a strong fortress,[b] to save me,
for you are my rock and my fortress.

4 Rescue me, O my God, from the hand of the wicked,
from the grasp of the unjust and cruel.
5 For you, O Lord, are my hope,
my trust, O LORD, from my youth.
6 Upon you I have leaned from my birth;
it was you who took me from my mother's womb.
My praise is continually of you.

7 I have been like a portent to many,

a Syr: Heb *and they shall live* *b* Gk Compare 31.3: Heb *to come continually you have commanded*

28: *The book of the living,* see Ex 32.32–33; Dan 12.1,4. **30–36:** The replacement of animal sacrifice with prayer locates this lament in the exile (Ps 51.16–17); this is also reflected in the wish that all nature will *praise* God, who will *save Zion* (Jerusalem) and *rebuild . . . Judah.*

Ps 70: Prayer for deliverance from enemies. An individual lament, which repeats with minor variations Ps 40.13–17. "The LORD" in Ps 40.13,16 is replaced here by *God* (vv. 1,4).

Ps 71: Prayer in old age. An individual lament by someone aged and infirm (vv. 9,18), with a high degree of refrainlike repetitions (vv. 9,18; 8,15,24). **1–3:** Initial petition; *refuge* and *fortress* perhaps indicate the Temple, where the psalmist prays for healing. **5–9:** Divine care for the psalmist, from birth to old age (Ps 22.9–10). **7:** *Portent,* something evil and dangerous (perhaps sickness), shunned by others.

but you are my strong refuge.
8 My mouth is filled with your praise,
and with your glory all day long.
9 Do not cast me off in the time of old age;
do not forsake me when my strength is spent.
10 For my enemies speak concerning me,
and those who watch for my life consult together.
11 They say, "Pursue and seize that person
whom God has forsaken,
for there is no one to deliver."

12 O God, do not be far from me;
O my God, make haste to help me!
13 Let my accusers be put to shame and consumed;
let those who seek to hurt me
be covered with scorn and disgrace.
14 But I will hope continually,
and will praise you yet more and more.
15 My mouth will tell of your righteous acts,
of your deeds of salvation all day long,
though their number is past my knowledge.
16 I will come praising the mighty deeds of the Lord GOD,
I will praise your righteousness, yours alone.

17 O God, from my youth you have taught me,
and I still proclaim your wondrous deeds.
18 So even to old age and gray hairs,
O God, do not forsake me,
until I proclaim your might
to all the generations to come.[a]
Your power 19 and your righteousness, O God,
reach the high heavens.

You who have done great things,
O God, who is like you?
20 You who have made me see many troubles and calamities
will revive me again;
from the depths of the earth
you will bring me up again.
21 You will increase my honor,
and comfort me once again.

22 I will also praise you with the harp
for your faithfulness, O my God;
I will sing praises to you with the lyre,
O Holy One of Israel.
23 My lips will shout for joy
when I sing praises to you;
my soul also, which you have rescued.
24 All day long my tongue will talk of your righteous help,
for those who tried to do me harm
have been put to shame, and disgraced.

PSALM 72
Of Solomon.

1 Give the king your justice, O God,
and your righteousness to a king's son.

a Gk Compare Syr: Heb *to a generation, to all that come*

9: On abandonment of aged parents, cf. Prov 19.26; 20.20–21. **12:** See Ps 22.1,11,19. **14–16:** The psalmist looks forward to praising God in the Temple. **20:** *Depths of the earth,* Sheol, the abode of the dead. The psalmist prays that God will *revive* him (cure his malady). **22:** His illness cured, the psalmist performs a thanksgiving ritual in the Temple (Ps 50.14; 56.12); alternatively, the verses serve as a motivation for God, narrating the activities that the psalmist vows to perform in the future, if saved (cf. Ps 6.5n.).

Ps 72: The Davidic king and the dynasty. A royal psalm, perhaps a coronation ode. Only Ps 72 and 127 are headed by *Of Solomon.* **1–2:** The king's responsibility to uphold and administer justice (2 Sam 8.15; Jer 22.15–16), with divine assistance. **3–4:** Moral order (justice for the poor and oppressed) in the

2 May he judge your people with righteousness,
and your poor with justice.
3 May the mountains yield prosperity for the people,
and the hills, in righteousness.
4 May he defend the cause of the poor of the people,
give deliverance to the needy,
and crush the oppressor.

5 May he live[a] while the sun endures,
and as long as the moon,
throughout all generations.
6 May he be like rain that falls on the mown grass,
like showers that water the earth.
7 In his days may righteousness flourish
and peace abound, until the moon is no more.

8 May he have dominion from sea to sea,
and from the River to the ends of the earth.
9 May his foes[b] bow down before him,
and his enemies lick the dust.
10 May the kings of Tarshish and of the isles
render him tribute,
may the kings of Sheba and Seba bring gifts.
11 May all kings fall down before him,
all nations give him service.

12 For he delivers the needy when they call,
the poor and those who have no helper.
13 He has pity on the weak and the needy,
and saves the lives of the needy.
14 From oppression and violence he redeems their life;
and precious is their blood in his sight.

15 Long may he live!
May gold of Sheba be given to him.
May prayer be made for him continually,
and blessings invoked for him all day long.
16 May there be abundance of grain in the land;
may it wave on the tops of the mountains;
may its fruit be like Lebanon;
and may people blossom in the cities
like the grass of the field.
17 May his name endure forever,
his fame continue as long as the sun.
May all nations be blessed in him;[c]
may they pronounce him happy.

18 Blessed be the LORD, the God of Israel,
who alone does wondrous things.
19 Blessed be his glorious name forever;
may his glory fill the whole earth.
Amen and Amen.

20 The prayers of David son of Jesse are ended.

a Gk: Heb *may they fear you* *b* Cn: Heb *those who live in the wilderness* *c* Or *bless themselves by him*

world brings about cosmic order (fertility and bounty). **5:** Prayer for king's long life and reign (Ps 61.6; cf. 89.36–37). **8:** The extent of the king's dominion from the Mediterranean Sea to the Persian Gulf (hyperbolic court style). **10–11:** Homage to the Israelite monarch by distant kings (1 Kings 4.21); a reflection of the king's great power. *Tarshish,* see 1 Kings 10.22n. *The isles,* the islands of the eastern Aegean Sea. *Sheba,* in southwestern Arabia; cf. 1 Kings 10.1. *Seba,* probably also southwestern Arabia, or perhaps Ethiopia; cf. Isa 43.3. **16:** Extremely difficult; it apparently deals with agricultural bounty, as in v. 3. **17:** The king's *name* means both his fame (1 Kings 3.14) and his progeny. *All nations . . . blessed,* the promises to the ancestors (Gen 12.3) fulfilled in the Davidic realm and dynasty. **18–19:** Not a part of the psalm, but the concluding doxology of Book II of the Psalter (see Introduction). **20:** Important evidence for the gradual editing of the psalter; contrast the "Davidic" psalms found later, e.g., Ps 86; 101; 103.

BOOK THREE

PSALM 73

A Psalm of Asaph.

1 Truly God is good to the upright,[a]
to those who are pure in heart.
2 But as for me, my feet had almost stumbled;
my steps had nearly slipped.
3 For I was envious of the arrogant;
I saw the prosperity of the wicked.

4 For they have no pain;
their bodies are sound and sleek.
5 They are not in trouble as others are;
they are not plagued like other people.
6 Therefore pride is their necklace;
violence covers them like a garment.
7 Their eyes swell out with fatness;
their hearts overflow with follies.
8 They scoff and speak with malice;
loftily they threaten oppression.
9 They set their mouths against heaven,
and their tongues range over the earth.

10 Therefore the people turn and praise them,[b]
and find no fault in them.[c]
11 And they say, "How can God know?
Is there knowledge in the Most High?"
12 Such are the wicked;
always at ease, they increase in riches.
13 All in vain I have kept my heart clean
and washed my hands in innocence.
14 For all day long I have been plagued,
and am punished every morning.

15 If I had said, "I will talk on in this way,"
I would have been untrue to the circle of your children.
16 But when I thought how to understand this,
it seemed to me a wearisome task,
17 until I went into the sanctuary of God;
then I perceived their end.
18 Truly you set them in slippery places;
you make them fall to ruin.
19 How they are destroyed in a moment,
swept away utterly by terrors!
20 They are[d] like a dream when one awakes;
on awaking you despise their phantoms.

21 When my soul was embittered,
when I was pricked in heart,
22 I was stupid and ignorant;
I was like a brute beast toward you.
23 Nevertheless I am continually with you;
you hold my right hand.
24 You guide me with your counsel,
and afterward you will receive me with honor.[e]
25 Whom have I in heaven but you?
And there is nothing on earth that I desire other than you.

a Or *good to Israel* b Cn: Heb *his people return here* c Cn: Heb *abundant waters are drained by them* d Cn: Heb *Lord* e Or *to glory*

Ps 73: A meditation on the justice of God. A wisdom psalm (typical wisdom themes include the two ways, retribution, and theodicy or God's justice in an unjust world). This psalm begins a collection attributed to Asaph (Ps 72–83), a Levite who established a guild of Temple singers (1 Chr 25); see also Ps 50n. **1–2:** The psalmist doubts God's goodness to the upright, given the good fortune of the wicked. **4–10:** The prosperity and contentment of the wicked. **11:** See Ps 10.11; 64.6; 94.7. **15–20:** Tempted to throw in his lot with the wicked, the psalmist, after an experience in the Temple, is dissuaded by considering their fate, falling into the world of the dead. This emphasis on receiving a revelation at the *sanctuary of God* is uncharacteristic of wisdom literature, which tends to be more universal and emphasizes that the laws of nature are evident in nature, rather than revealed. **23–26:** Incipient belief in life with

26 My flesh and my heart may fail,
but God is the strength[a] of my
heart and my portion forever.
27 Indeed, those who are far from you
will perish;
you put an end to those who are
false to you.
28 But for me it is good to be near God;
I have made the Lord GOD my
refuge,
to tell of all your works.

PSALM 74

A Maskil of Asaph.

1 O God, why do you cast us off
forever?
Why does your anger smoke
against the sheep of your
pasture?
2 Remember your congregation, which
you acquired long ago,
which you redeemed to be the tribe
of your heritage.
Remember Mount Zion, where you
came to dwell.
3 Direct your steps to the perpetual ruins;
the enemy has destroyed everything
in the sanctuary.

4 Your foes have roared within your
holy place;
they set up their emblems there.
5 At the upper entrance they hacked
the wooden trellis with axes.[b]
6 And then, with hatchets and
hammers,
they smashed all its carved work.
7 They set your sanctuary on fire;
they desecrated the dwelling place
of your name,
bringing it to the ground.
8 They said to themselves, "We will
utterly subdue them";
they burned all the meeting places
of God in the land.

9 We do not see our emblems;
there is no longer any prophet,
and there is no one among us who
knows how long.
10 How long, O God, is the foe to
scoff?
Is the enemy to revile your name
forever?
11 Why do you hold back your hand;
why do you keep your hand in[c]
your bosom?

12 Yet God my King is from of old,
working salvation in the earth.
13 You divided the sea by your might;
you broke the heads of the dragons
in the waters.
14 You crushed the heads of Leviathan;
you gave him as food[d] for the
creatures of the wilderness.
15 You cut openings for springs and
torrents;
you dried up ever-flowing streams.
16 Yours is the day, yours also the night;
you established the luminaries[e]
and the sun.

a Heb *rock* *b* Cn Compare Gk Syr: Meaning of Heb uncertain *c* Cn: Heb *do you consume your right hand from* *d* Heb *food for the people* *e* Or *moon;* Heb *light*

God after death; for *receive* in this context, see Gen 5.24; Ps 49.15. **26:** *My portion,* see Num 18.20; Ps 16.5. Perhaps the author is a priest.

Ps 74: Zion attacked, the Temple destroyed. An exilic communal lament, on the destruction of the Jerusalem Temple (vv. 3–8). *Asaph,* see Ps 73n. **1–2:** Experiencing disaster and exile, the psalmist recalls the creation and salvation of Israel, *the sheep of your pasture,* in the Exodus (Ex 15.13,16–17). **5:** For the Babylonians coming as woodcutters *with axes,* see Jer 46.22–23. **9–10:** There is no reliable prophet to tell them the extent of their affliction; perhaps prophecy was understood to be connected to the Temple, or the people are in exile and understood prophecy as connected to the land of Israel. **12–17:** The creator God's victory over the forces of chaos. These verses reflect an alternative creation story to Gen 1–3; this story is known, however, in Canaanite literature; cf. also Ps 89.9–14. **14:** *Leviathan,* the forces of chaos represented as a marine monster (Job 3.8; 26.12–13; 41.1; Isa 27.1). **19:** *Your dove,* sacrificial animal of

17 You have fixed all the bounds of the earth;
you made summer and winter.

18 Remember this, O LORD, how the enemy scoffs,
and an impious people reviles your name.
19 Do not deliver the soul of your dove to the wild animals;
do not forget the life of your poor forever.

20 Have regard for your[a] covenant,
for the dark places of the land are full of the haunts of violence.
21 Do not let the downtrodden be put to shame;
let the poor and needy praise your name.
22 Rise up, O God, plead your cause;
remember how the impious scoff at you all day long.
23 Do not forget the clamor of your foes,
the uproar of your adversaries that goes up continually.

PSALM 75

To the leader: Do Not Destroy. A Psalm of Asaph. A Song.

1 We give thanks to you, O God;
we give thanks; your name is near.
People tell of your wondrous deeds.

2 At the set time that I appoint
I will judge with equity.
3 When the earth totters, with all its inhabitants,
it is I who keep its pillars steady. *Selah*
4 I say to the boastful, "Do not boast,"
and to the wicked, "Do not lift up your horn;
5 do not lift up your horn on high,
or speak with insolent neck."

6 For not from the east or from the west
and not from the wilderness comes lifting up;
7 but it is God who executes judgment,
putting down one and lifting up another.
8 For in the hand of the LORD there is a cup
with foaming wine, well mixed;
he will pour a draught from it,
and all the wicked of the earth
shall drain it down to the dregs.
9 But I will rejoice[b] forever;
I will sing praises to the God of Jacob.

10 All the horns of the wicked I will cut off,
but the horns of the righteous shall be exalted.

PSALM 76

To the leader: with stringed instruments. A Psalm of Asaph. A Song.

1 In Judah God is known,
his name is great in Israel.

a Gk Syr: Heb *the*   *b* Gk: Heb *declare*

the poor; used here of those slaughtered by Babylon like sacrificed animals (Isa 34.6–7). **23:** Here the *foes* and *adversaries* are both the Babylonians and the forces of chaos (vv. 12–17). This conflation makes the Babylonians look more dangerous, so God will destroy them.

Ps 75: Thanksgiving for divine victory over evil. A prophetic psalm, like Ps 50. God appears to judge the arrogant. *Do Not Destroy,* see Ps 57n. *Asaph,* see Ps 73n. **1:** *Your name is near,* expressing divine presence and accessibility. **3:** *Pillars,* see 1 Sam 2.8. *Selah,* see Ps 3.2n. **4,10:** *Lift up your horn,* an image of pride and arrogance; *cut off* the *horns,* to humiliate and deprive of power and status. **8:** The *cup* (of the LORD's wrath in Isa 51.17; Jer 25.15) is a metaphor for punishment.

Ps 76: Praise of Zion. A Zion hymn praising Jerusalem and the Temple where the LORD resides. *Asaph,* see Ps 73n. **2:** *Salem,* variant name for Jerusalem (Gen 14.18). **3:** For the breaking of the (enemies')

2 His abode has been established in
Salem,
his dwelling place in Zion.
3 There he broke the flashing arrows,
the shield, the sword, and the
weapons of war. *Selah*

4 Glorious are you, more majestic
than the everlasting mountains.[a]
5 The stouthearted were stripped of
their spoil;
they sank into sleep;
none of the troops
was able to lift a hand.
6 At your rebuke, O God of Jacob,
both rider and horse lay stunned.

7 But you indeed are awesome!
Who can stand before you
when once your anger is roused?
8 From the heavens you uttered
judgment;
the earth feared and was still
9 when God rose up to establish
judgment,
to save all the oppressed of the
earth. *Selah*

10 Human wrath serves only to
praise you,
when you bind the last bit of
your[b] wrath around you.
11 Make vows to the LORD your God,
and perform them;
let all who are around him bring
gifts
to the one who is awesome,
12 who cuts off the spirit of princes,
who inspires fear in the kings of the
earth.

PSALM 77

To the leader: according to Jeduthun. Of Asaph. A Psalm.

1 I cry aloud to God,
aloud to God, that he may hear me.
2 In the day of my trouble I seek
the Lord;
in the night my hand is stretched
out without wearying;
my soul refuses to be comforted.
3 I think of God, and I moan;
I meditate, and my spirit faints.
Selah

4 You keep my eyelids from closing;
I am so troubled that I cannot
speak.
5 I consider the days of old,
and remember the years of long
ago.
6 I commune[c] with my heart in the
night;
I meditate and search my spirit:[d]
7 "Will the Lord spurn forever,
and never again be favorable?
8 Has his steadfast love ceased forever?
Are his promises at an end for all
time?
9 Has God forgotten to be gracious?
Has he in anger shut up his
compassion?" *Selah*
10 And I say, "It is my grief
that the right hand of the Most
High has changed."

a Gk: Heb *the mountains of prey* *b* Heb lacks *your* *c* Gk Syr: Heb *My music* *d* Syr Jerome: Heb *my spirit searches*

weapons in another Zion hymn, see Ps 46.9. *Selah* (also v. 9), see Ps 3.2n. **6:** *At your rebuke* ("roar"), God's war cry. **8–9:** God intervenes on behalf of those who seek justice and the end of oppression. **10:** Very difficult; *human wrath* may be a metaphor for Israel's enemies. **11:** Tribute is brought to the Davidic monarch and his God by the kings of the earth (Ps 72.10–11).

Ps 77: Prayer for deliverance from enemies. An individual lament (vv. 1–10), in which the petitioner asks for God's attention, but admits no guilt. This is followed by a hymn (vv. 11–20), meant to remind God of his ability to act powerfully. *Jeduthun,* see Ps 39n. *Asaph,* see Ps 73n. **1–3:** Initial appeal for divine help (Ps 142.1–3). **3:** *Selah* (also vv. 9,15), see Ps 3.2n. **5–7:** *The days of old,* the time of the Exodus, the paradigmatic act of divine liberation (vv. 19–20). **8–9:** The psalmist remembers and questions the creed of Ex 34.6. **11–15:** The wonder-working redeemer of the Exodus; *Jacob and Joseph,* perhaps an indica-

11 I will call to mind the deeds of the
LORD;
I will remember your wonders of old.
12 I will meditate on all your work,
and muse on your mighty deeds.
13 Your way, O God, is holy.
What god is so great as our God?
14 You are the God who works
wonders;
you have displayed your might
among the peoples.
15 With your strong arm you redeemed
your people,
the descendants of Jacob and
Joseph. *Selah*

16 When the waters saw you, O God,
when the waters saw you, they
were afraid;
the very deep trembled.
17 The clouds poured out water;
the skies thundered;
your arrows flashed on every side.
18 The crash of your thunder was in the
whirlwind;
your lightnings lit up the world;
the earth trembled and shook.
19 Your way was through the sea,
your path, through the mighty
waters;
yet your footprints were unseen.
20 You led your people like a flock
by the hand of Moses and Aaron.

PSALM 78

A Maskil of Asaph.

1 Give ear, O my people, to my
teaching;
incline your ears to the words of
my mouth.
2 I will open my mouth in a parable;
I will utter dark sayings from
of old,
3 things that we have heard and
known,
that our ancestors have told us.
4 We will not hide them from their
children;
we will tell to the coming
generation
the glorious deeds of the LORD, and
his might,
and the wonders that he has
done.

5 He established a decree in Jacob,
and appointed a law in Israel,
which he commanded our
ancestors
to teach to their children;
6 that the next generation might know
them,
the children yet unborn,
and rise up and tell them to their
children,
7 so that they should set their hope in
God,
and not forget the works of God,
but keep his commandments;
8 and that they should not be like their
ancestors,
a stubborn and rebellious
generation,
a generation whose heart was not
steadfast,
whose spirit was not faithful
to God.

tion that this psalm comes from the Northern Kingdom. **16–20:** The *waters* of chaos, defeated by God, are identified with the vanquished sea of the Exodus (Isa 51.9–10; cf. Ps 18.7–15; 114.3–6).

Ps 78: Israel's rebellion in the wilderness. Ps 78 is a lengthy review of Israel's history, focusing on the wilderness period; see generally the narratives in the books of Exodus and Numbers. There is a double recital of Israel's rebellion in the wilderness (vv. 12–32; 40–64), both followed by a divine merciful response (vv. 33–39; 65–72). As the final verses make clear, it is primarily interested in justifying God's choice of Judah and David. Its narrative of history largely reflects the Yahwistic source (J) of the Pentateuch. *Asaph,* see Ps 73n. **1–6:** The poem is didactic, communicating to generations to come the lessons learned from Israel's past. **7–10:** The Northern Kingdom (v. 9, *The Ephraimites*) is accused of disregarding the redemptive works of God. It is uncertain what specific incident, if any, is referred to. **12:** *Zoan,*

9 The Ephraimites, armed with[a] the bow,
turned back on the day of battle.
10 They did not keep God's covenant,
but refused to walk according to his law.
11 They forgot what he had done,
and the miracles that he had shown them.
12 In the sight of their ancestors he worked marvels
in the land of Egypt, in the fields of Zoan.
13 He divided the sea and let them pass through it,
and made the waters stand like a heap.
14 In the daytime he led them with a cloud,
and all night long with a fiery light.
15 He split rocks open in the wilderness,
and gave them drink abundantly as from the deep.
16 He made streams come out of the rock,
and caused waters to flow down like rivers.

17 Yet they sinned still more against him,
rebelling against the Most High in the desert.
18 They tested God in their heart
by demanding the food they craved.
19 They spoke against God, saying,
"Can God spread a table in the wilderness?
20 Even though he struck the rock so that water gushed out
and torrents overflowed,
can he also give bread,
or provide meat for his people?"
21 Therefore, when the LORD heard, he was full of rage;
a fire was kindled against Jacob,
his anger mounted against Israel,
22 because they had no faith in God,
and did not trust his saving power.
23 Yet he commanded the skies above,
and opened the doors of heaven;
24 he rained down on them manna to eat,
and gave them the grain of heaven.
25 Mortals ate of the bread of angels;
he sent them food in abundance.
26 He caused the east wind to blow in the heavens,
and by his power he led out the south wind;
27 he rained flesh upon them like dust,
winged birds like the sand of the seas;
28 he let them fall within their camp,
all around their dwellings.
29 And they ate and were well filled,
for he gave them what they craved.
30 But before they had satisfied their craving,
while the food was still in their mouths,
31 the anger of God rose against them
and he killed the strongest of them,
and laid low the flower of Israel.

32 In spite of all this they still sinned;
they did not believe in his wonders.
33 So he made their days vanish like a breath,
and their years in terror.
34 When he killed them, they sought for him;
they repented and sought God earnestly.

a Heb *armed with shooting*

a city in northern Egypt. **13:** Ex 14.21,29; 15.8. **14:** Ex 13.21–22; 14.19–20. **15–16:** Ex 17.6; Num 20.11; Isa 48.21. *The deep,* the chaotic waters vanquished by God, which serve Israel's need for water (Ps 104.5–13). **17:** A type of refrain (vv. 32,40,56), stressing the psalm's theme: Northern Israel as an ingrate. **18–31:** The provisioning of the people with food in the desert is drawn from Ex 16 and Num 11. **33–35:** *Like a breath,* the evanescence of human life, contrasted with divine stability (*God was their rock*). See Ps 39.5,11. **45–51:** The plagues (Ex 7–11; Ps 105.26–36). Only seven plagues are mentioned,

35 They remembered that God was their
rock,
the Most High God their redeemer.
36 But they flattered him with their
mouths;
they lied to him with their tongues.
37 Their heart was not steadfast toward
him;
they were not true to his covenant.
38 Yet he, being compassionate,
forgave their iniquity,
and did not destroy them;
often he restrained his anger,
and did not stir up all his wrath.
39 He remembered that they were but
flesh,
a wind that passes and does not
come again.
40 How often they rebelled against him
in the wilderness
and grieved him in the desert!
41 They tested God again and again,
and provoked the Holy One of
Israel.
42 They did not keep in mind his power,
or the day when he redeemed them
from the foe;
43 when he displayed his signs in Egypt,
and his miracles in the fields of
Zoan.
44 He turned their rivers to blood,
so that they could not drink of
their streams.
45 He sent among them swarms of flies,
which devoured them,
and frogs, which destroyed them.
46 He gave their crops to the caterpillar,
and the fruit of their labor to the
locust.
47 He destroyed their vines with hail,
and their sycamores with frost.
48 He gave over their cattle to the hail,
and their flocks to thunderbolts.
49 He let loose on them his fierce anger,
wrath, indignation, and distress,
a company of destroying angels.
50 He made a path for his anger;
he did not spare them from death,
but gave their lives over to the
plague.
51 He struck all the firstborn in Egypt,
the first issue of their strength in
the tents of Ham.
52 Then he led out his people like sheep,
and guided them in the wilderness
like a flock.
53 He led them in safety, so that they
were not afraid;
but the sea overwhelmed their
enemies.
54 And he brought them to his holy hill,
to the mountain that his right hand
had won.
55 He drove out nations before them;
he apportioned them for a
possession
and settled the tribes of Israel in
their tents.

56 Yet they tested the Most High God,
and rebelled against him.
They did not observe his decrees,
57 but turned away and were faithless
like their ancestors;
they twisted like a treacherous bow.
58 For they provoked him to anger with
their high places;
they moved him to jealousy with
their idols.
59 When God heard, he was full of
wrath,
and he utterly rejected Israel.
60 He abandoned his dwelling at Shiloh,
the tent where he dwelt among
mortals,
61 and delivered his power to captivity,
his glory to the hand of the foe.
62 He gave his people to the sword,

in distinction to the ten plagues of the final, edited form of the Exodus narrative; these seven plagues agree with the Yahwistic narrative (J) incorporated into Exodus. **51:** *Ham,* a poetic synonym for Egypt; cf. Gen 10.6. **52–55:** The Exodus, guided by the divine shepherd (Ex 15.13; Ps 77.20). **59–68:** The continuing rebellion of the Northern Kingdom leads to its rejection. **60:** The destruction of the temple at *Shiloh* is mentioned elsewhere only in Jer 7.12–14; 26.6; the period was apparently that of the events described in 1 Sam 4.1–7.2. **61:** *His power . . . his glory,* the ark; see 1 Sam 4.21; Ps 63.2. **67–72:** In place of the

and vented his wrath on his
heritage.
63 Fire devoured their young men,
and their girls had no marriage
song.
64 Their priests fell by the sword,
and their widows made no
lamentation.
65 Then the Lord awoke as from sleep,
like a warrior shouting because of
wine.
66 He put his adversaries to rout;
he put them to everlasting disgrace.

67 He rejected the tent of Joseph,
he did not choose the tribe of
Ephraim;
68 but he chose the tribe of Judah,
Mount Zion, which he loves.
69 He built his sanctuary like the high
heavens,
like the earth, which he has
founded forever.
70 He chose his servant David,
and took him from the sheepfolds;
71 from tending the nursing ewes he
brought him
to be the shepherd of his people
Jacob,
of Israel, his inheritance.
72 With upright heart he tended them,
and guided them with skillful hand.

PSALM 79

A Psalm of Asaph.

1 O God, the nations have come into
your inheritance;
they have defiled your holy temple;
they have laid Jerusalem in ruins.
2 They have given the bodies of your
servants
to the birds of the air for food,
the flesh of your faithful to the wild
animals of the earth.
3 They have poured out their blood like
water
all around Jerusalem,
and there was no one to bury
them.
4 We have become a taunt to our
neighbors,
mocked and derided by those
around us.

5 How long, O LORD? Will you be
angry forever?
Will your jealous wrath burn like
fire?
6 Pour out your anger on the nations
that do not know you,
and on the kingdoms
that do not call on your name.
7 For they have devoured Jacob
and laid waste his habitation.

8 Do not remember against us the
iniquities of our ancestors;
let your compassion come speedily
to meet us,
for we are brought very low.
9 Help us, O God of our salvation,
for the glory of your name;
deliver us, and forgive our sins,
for your name's sake.
10 Why should the nations say,
"Where is their God?"
Let the avenging of the outpoured
blood of your servants
be known among the nations before
our eyes.

11 Let the groans of the prisoners come
before you;

Northern Kingdom, God chooses *Zion* (Jerusalem), *Judah*, and the Davidic dynasty (Ps 132.11–14). **70–71:** 1 Sam 17.15; 2 Sam 7.8.

Ps 79: The Temple destroyed. An exilic communal lament, mourning like Ps 74 the fall of Judah to Babylon and the destruction of the Temple. Rather than emphasizing Israel's repentance, the psalm demands pity and vengeance, as God must take care of his people (v. 13) for the sake of his name (v. 9). *Asaph,* see Ps 73n. **1:** *The nations,* Babylon and its allies (Ps 137.7). **2:** To be left unburied and exposed to scavengers is in the ancient Near East a terrible fate (Josh 10.27; 2 Kings 9.25–26). **5:** The question about the duration of divine wrath is typical of laments (Ps 74.9–10). **12:** The psalmist appeals for

according to your great power
preserve those doomed to die.
12 Return sevenfold into the bosom of our neighbors
the taunts with which they taunted you, O Lord!
13 Then we your people, the flock of your pasture,
will give thanks to you forever;
from generation to generation we will recount your praise.

PSALM 80

To the leader: on Lilies, a Covenant. Of Asaph. A Psalm.

1 Give ear, O Shepherd of Israel,
you who lead Joseph like a flock!
You who are enthroned upon the cherubim, shine forth
2 before Ephraim and Benjamin and Manasseh.
Stir up your might,
and come to save us!

3 Restore us, O God;
let your face shine, that we may be saved.

4 O LORD God of hosts,
how long will you be angry with your people's prayers?
5 You have fed them with the bread of tears,
and given them tears to drink in full measure.
6 You make us the scorn[a] of our neighbors;
our enemies laugh among themselves.

7 Restore us, O God of hosts;
let your face shine, that we may be saved.

8 You brought a vine out of Egypt;
you drove out the nations and planted it.
9 You cleared the ground for it;
it took deep root and filled the land.
10 The mountains were covered with its shade,
the mighty cedars with its branches;
11 it sent out its branches to the sea,
and its shoots to the River.
12 Why then have you broken down its walls,
so that all who pass along the way pluck its fruit?
13 The boar from the forest ravages it,
and all that move in the field feed on it.

14 Turn again, O God of hosts;
look down from heaven, and see;
have regard for this vine,
15 the stock that your right hand planted.[b]
16 They have burned it with fire, they have cut it down;[c]
may they perish at the rebuke of your countenance.

a Syr: Heb *strife* *b* Heb adds from verse 17 *and upon the one whom you made strong for yourself* *c* Cn: Heb *it is cut down*

sevenfold retribution on Babylon's allies. **13:** Like Ps 77 and 78, Ps 79 ends with, and Ps 80 begins with the image of the divine shepherd, joining together this cluster of Asaphite psalms.

Ps 80: Prayer for deliverance from national enemies. A communal lament on the fall of the Northern Kingdom (722 BCE), with a refrain in vv. 3,7,14. In attitude toward the North, it contrasts sharply with Ps 78, and much of Kings. *On Lilies,* see Ps 45n.; cf. Ps 60.1. *Asaph,* see Ps 73n. **1–2:** *Israel . . . Joseph . . . Ephraim and Benjamin and Manasseh,* the Northern Kingdom. **1:** The psalm calls upon God as *Shepherd of Israel; shine forth,* theophany (divine manifestation) language (Ps 50.2; 94.1). **3:** The shining *face* of God is a face brightened with a smile, expressing God's benevolence; see Ps 4.6n. **4–6:** The lament: how long will your anger last? (Ps 79.5). **5:** See Ps 42.3; 102.9. **8–11:** The imagery shifts from pastoral to agricultural, a *vine* brought *out of Egypt,* filling the land (Isa 5.1–7; Ezek 17.1–10). **11:** *The River,* the Euphrates. **16:** See Ps 74.5–7. **17:** *The one at your right hand,* a reference to the king (Ps 110.1). The final

17 But let your hand be upon the one at
your right hand,
the one whom you made strong for
yourself.
18 Then we will never turn back from
you;
give us life, and we will call on
your name.

19 Restore us, O LORD God of hosts;
let your face shine, that we may be
saved.

PSALM 81

To the leader: according to The Gittith.
Of Asaph.

1 Sing aloud to God our strength;
shout for joy to the God of Jacob.
2 Raise a song, sound the tambourine,
the sweet lyre with the harp.
3 Blow the trumpet at the new moon,
at the full moon, on our festal day.
4 For it is a statute for Israel,
an ordinance of the God of Jacob.
5 He made it a decree in Joseph,
when he went out over[a] the land
of Egypt.

I hear a voice I had not known:
6 "I relieved your[b] shoulder of the
burden;
your[b] hands were freed from the
basket.
7 In distress you called, and I rescued
you;
I answered you in the secret place
of thunder;
I tested you at the waters of
Meribah. *Selah*
8 Hear, O my people, while I admonish
you;
O Israel, if you would but listen to
me!
9 There shall be no strange god among
you;
you shall not bow down to a
foreign god.
10 I am the LORD your God,
who brought you up out of the
land of Egypt.
Open your mouth wide and I will
fill it.

11 "But my people did not listen to my
voice;
Israel would not submit to me.
12 So I gave them over to their stubborn
hearts,
to follow their own counsels.
13 O that my people would listen to me,
that Israel would walk in my ways!
14 Then I would quickly subdue their
enemies,
and turn my hand against their
foes.
15 Those who hate the LORD would
cringe before him,

a Or *against* *b* Heb *his*

verses clarify that the psalmist's main concern is not the North but Judah, which he fears might also be defeated through Assyrian imperialism.

Ps 81: A hymn for the feast of booths (Deut 16.13–15). The psalm is composed of a hymn of praise (vv. 1–5a) and a divine oracle (vv. 5b–16). *The Gittith,* see Ps 8n. *Asaph,* see Ps 73n. **1:** *The God of Jacob,* repeated in v. 4; this epithet, along with "Israel" (vv. 4,8,11,13) and "Joseph" (v. 5) indicate northern provenance (seven uses in all). **3:** *Our festal day,* the festival of booths, when the law would be proclaimed (vv. 9–10) and the covenant ("ordinance" in v. 4) renewed. According to Lev 23.24, the festival began *at the full moon.* **6:** Salvation from slavery and oppression in Egypt (Ex 6.6–7). **7:** *Meribah,* Ex 17.7; Num 20.13. *Selah,* see Ps 3.2n. **9–10:** The first commandment (Ex 20.1–2) quoted in reverse order (*There shall be no strange God . . . I am the LORD your God*). *Foreign god,* see Deut 32.12. **10:** God fills the mouths of the people with food (v. 16). **11–12:** The infidelity of the wilderness generation (Ps 78.17,40), a warning to the psalmist's contemporaries. **13–16:** Israel's obedience would mean victory over foes and agricultural bounty. *Finest of the wheat,* Deut 32.14; Ps 147.14. *Honey from the rock,* see Deut 32.13.

and their doom would last forever.
16 I would feed you[a] with the finest of the wheat,
and with honey from the rock I would satisfy you."

PSALM 82

A Psalm of Asaph.

1 God has taken his place in the divine council;
in the midst of the gods he holds judgment:
2 "How long will you judge unjustly
and show partiality to the wicked? *Selah*
3 Give justice to the weak and the orphan;
maintain the right of the lowly and the destitute.
4 Rescue the weak and the needy;
deliver them from the hand of the wicked."

5 They have neither knowledge nor understanding,
they walk around in darkness;
all the foundations of the earth are shaken.

6 I say, "You are gods,
children of the Most High, all of you;
7 nevertheless, you shall die like mortals,
and fall like any prince."[b]

8 Rise up, O God, judge the earth;
for all the nations belong to you!

PSALM 83

A Song. A Psalm of Asaph.

1 O God, do not keep silence;
do not hold your peace or be still, O God!
2 Even now your enemies are in tumult;
those who hate you have raised their heads.
3 They lay crafty plans against your people;
they consult together against those you protect.
4 They say, "Come, let us wipe them out as a nation;
let the name of Israel be remembered no more."
5 They conspire with one accord;
against you they make a covenant—
6 the tents of Edom and the Ishmaelites,
Moab and the Hagrites,
7 Gebal and Ammon and Amalek,
Philistia with the inhabitants of Tyre;
8 Assyria also has joined them;
they are the strong arm of the children of Lot. *Selah*

9 Do to them as you did to Midian,

a Cn Compare verse 16b: Heb *he would feed him*
b Or *fall as one man, O princes*

Ps 82: A vision of the divine judge. A prophetic vision report (1 Kings 22; Isa 6). In a heavenly trial, God sentences the subordinate deities to death because of their judicial improprieties. *Asaph,* see Ps 73n. **1:** Ps 76.9; Isa 3.13–14. **2–4:** The subordinate deities have failed to ensure justice to the needy and oppressed (Ps 58.1–2). **2:** *Selah,* see Ps 3.2n. **5:** Failures in the moral realm have effects in the physical world (Jer 4.23–26). **6–7:** The gods, condemned to death, descend to Sheol, the abode of the dead (Ezek 28.8–9). **8:** The prophet prays that God, now acting as sole judge, will provide justice among the nations.

Ps 83: Prayer for deliverance from national enemies. A communal lament appealing for divine action against a coalition of hostile nations (vv. 6–8) and rulers (vv. 9–11). This coalition matches no events known elsewhere in the Bible. *Asaph,* see Ps 73n. **1–5:** The silence of God is contrasted with the *tumult* and speech of the enemies against Israel and its God. **2:** Israel's enemies are, according to this psalmist, by definition *your* (God's) *enemies.* **6–8:** Traditional enemies of Israel. *Hagrites,* a tribe of pastoralists in northern Transjordan (1 Chr 5.10,18–22). *Gebal,* later Byblos, north of Beirut on the coast of Lebanon. *The children of Lot,* Moab and Edom (Gen 19.36–38). *Selah,* see Ps 3.2n. **9–12:** See Judg 4–8. **13–15:**

as to Sisera and Jabin at the Wadi Kishon,
10 who were destroyed at En-dor,
who became dung for the ground.
11 Make their nobles like Oreb and Zeeb,
all their princes like Zebah and Zalmunna,
12 who said, "Let us take the pastures of God
for our own possession."

13 O my God, make them like whirling dust,[a]
like chaff before the wind.
14 As fire consumes the forest,
as the flame sets the mountains ablaze,
15 so pursue them with your tempest
and terrify them with your hurricane.
16 Fill their faces with shame,
so that they may seek your name, O LORD.
17 Let them be put to shame and dismayed forever;
let them perish in disgrace.
18 Let them know that you alone,
whose name is the LORD,
are the Most High over all the earth.

PSALM 84

To the leader: according to The Gittith. Of the Korahites. A Psalm.

1 How lovely is your dwelling place,
O LORD of hosts!
2 My soul longs, indeed it faints
for the courts of the LORD;
my heart and my flesh sing for joy
to the living God.

3 Even the sparrow finds a home,
and the swallow a nest for herself,
where she may lay her young,
at your altars, O LORD of hosts,
my King and my God.
4 Happy are those who live in your house,
ever singing your praise. *Selah*

5 Happy are those whose strength is in you,
in whose heart are the highways to Zion.[b]
6 As they go through the valley of Baca
they make it a place of springs;
the early rain also covers it with pools.
7 They go from strength to strength;
the God of gods will be seen in Zion.

8 O LORD God of hosts, hear my prayer;
give ear, O God of Jacob! *Selah*
9 Behold our shield, O God;
look on the face of your anointed.

10 For a day in your courts is better
than a thousand elsewhere.
I would rather be a doorkeeper in the house of my God
than live in the tents of wickedness.
11 For the LORD God is a sun and shield;
he bestows favor and honor.

a Or *a tumbleweed* *b* Heb lacks *to Zion*

See Isa 17.13–14. **16:** The defiant heads of the enemies (v. 2) become *faces* filled with *shame.* **18:** The ultimate desired result is not military victory, but exaltation of God as "Most High" by all (Ps 47.2; 97.9).

Ps 84: Pilgrimage to Zion. A pilgrimage hymn expressing the joy of the pilgrim traveling to Jerusalem, perhaps for the festival of booths (cf. Ps 81). Like Ps 42 and 63, it borders on the mystical as the worshiper describes the great longing to reside in the Temple, in the proximity of God. *The Gittith,* see Ps 8n. *Korahites,* see Ps 42–43n. **1–2:** Longing for the beauty of the Temple (Ps 42.1–2; 63.1–2). **4:** *Selah* (also v. 8), see Ps 3.2n. **5–6:** The pilgrimage and the coming of the winter rains. *The valley of Baca* is unknown. **8–9:** *Our shield,* the Davidic king as the people's defender; the king and Zion are intimately connected (78.67–72). **11:** The good not withheld by God is the winter rain (v. 6) and the bounty it produces (Hag 1.10).

No good thing does the LORD
withhold
from those who walk uprightly.
12 O LORD of hosts,
happy is everyone who trusts
in you.

PSALM 85

To the leader. Of the Korahites. A Psalm.

1 LORD, you were favorable to your
land;
you restored the fortunes of
Jacob.
2 You forgave the iniquity of your
people;
you pardoned all their sin. *Selah*
3 You withdrew all your wrath;
you turned from your hot anger.

4 Restore us again, O God of our
salvation,
and put away your indignation
toward us.
5 Will you be angry with us forever?
Will you prolong your anger to all
generations?
6 Will you not revive us again,
so that your people may rejoice
in you?
7 Show us your steadfast love, O LORD,
and grant us your salvation.

8 Let me hear what God the LORD will
speak,
for he will speak peace to his
people,
to his faithful, to those who turn to
him in their hearts.[a]
9 Surely his salvation is at hand for
those who fear him,
that his glory may dwell in our
land.

10 Steadfast love and faithfulness
will meet;
righteousness and peace will kiss
each other.
11 Faithfulness will spring up from the
ground,
and righteousness will look down
from the sky.
12 The LORD will give what is good,
and our land will yield its increase.
13 Righteousness will go before him,
and will make a path for his steps.

PSALM 86

A Prayer of David.

1 Incline your ear, O LORD, and answer
me,
for I am poor and needy.
2 Preserve my life, for I am devoted to
you;
save your servant who trusts
in you.
You are my God; 3 be gracious to me,
O Lord,
for to you do I cry all day long.
4 Gladden the soul of your servant,
for to you, O Lord, I lift up my
soul.
5 For you, O Lord, are good and
forgiving,

a Gk: Heb *but let them not turn back to folly*

Ps 85: Prayer for divine favor and blessing. A communal lament, to which God responds with an oracle of salvation. *Korahites,* see Ps 42–43n. **1–3:** God's past favor to the land, making it fertile and productive. Unrepented and unforgiven sin can hold back the winter rains (Deut 11.17; Jer 5.24–25). **2:** *Selah,* see Ps 3.2n. **4–7:** God's desire to be praised and his *steadfast love* are invoked in a petition that God cease being angry and act favorably again, restoring and reviving the people. **8–13:** An oracle promising peace and salvation to Israel. **12:** *Good,* rain (Lev 26.1–6; Ps 67.6).

Ps 86: Prayer for deliverance from enemies. An individual lament (vv. 1–7,14–17) interrupted by a thanksgiving hymn (vv. 8–13). The psalm is anthological, reusing language and motifs occurring elsewhere in the Hebrew Bible. **1–3:** Typical lament language (Ps 17.6; 31.2; 40.8). **5:** The first of two references to Ex 34.6–7 (v. 15). **8:** Divine incomparability is an expression of Israel's monotheism (Ps

abounding in steadfast love to all
who call on you.
6 Give ear, O LORD, to my prayer;
listen to my cry of supplication.
7 In the day of my trouble I call
on you,
for you will answer me.

8 There is none like you among the
gods, O Lord,
nor are there any works like yours.
9 All the nations you have made shall
come
and bow down before you, O Lord,
and shall glorify your name.
10 For you are great and do wondrous
things;
you alone are God.
11 Teach me your way, O LORD,
that I may walk in your truth;
give me an undivided heart to
revere your name.
12 I give thanks to you, O Lord my
God, with my whole heart,
and I will glorify your name
forever.
13 For great is your steadfast love
toward me;
you have delivered my soul from
the depths of Sheol.

14 O God, the insolent rise up against
me;
a band of ruffians seeks my life,
and they do not set you before
them.
15 But you, O Lord, are a God merciful
and gracious,
slow to anger and abounding in
steadfast love and faithfulness.
16 Turn to me and be gracious to me;
give your strength to your servant;
save the child of your serving girl.
17 Show me a sign of your favor,
so that those who hate me may see
it and be put to shame,
because you, LORD, have helped me
and comforted me.

PSALM 87

Of the Korahites. A Psalm. A Song.

1 On the holy mount stands the city he
founded;
2 the LORD loves the gates of Zion
more than all the dwellings of
Jacob.
3 Glorious things are spoken of you,
O city of God. *Selah*

4 Among those who know me I
mention Rahab and Babylon;
Philistia too, and Tyre, with
Ethiopia[a]—
"This one was born there," they
say.

5 And of Zion it shall be said,
"This one and that one were born
in it";
for the Most High himself will
establish it.
6 The LORD records, as he registers the
peoples,
"This one was born there." *Selah*
7 Singers and dancers alike say,
"All my springs are in you."

a Or *Nubia*; Heb *Cush*

40.4; 71.19; cf. Ex 15.11). **9:** See 22.27n. **13:** *Sheol,* the abode of the dead. **14:** See Ps 54.3. **16:** *Turn to me and be gracious to me,* a paraphrase of the middle of the Priestly blessing (Num 6.25). *Child of your serving girl,* synonymous with *your servant* but expressing even more humility.

Ps 87: Praise of Zion. A hymn celebrating the coming of other nations to Jerusalem (Isa 2.2–4). *Korahites,* see Ps 42–43n. **2:** *All the dwellings of Jacob,* the northern temples (Bethel, Dan) replaced by Zion (Ps 78.67–69). **3:** *Selah* (also v. 6), see Ps 3.2n. **4–6:** The LORD records the names of the converts and proselytes from the Gentiles, now part of God's people (Isa 44.5). **4:** *Rahab,* a designation of Egypt; see Isa 30.7. **7:** *Springs,* of water, the source of life. See Ps 36.8; 46.4; Ezek 47.1–12.

PSALM 88

A Song. A Psalm of the Korahites.
To the leader: according to Mahalath
Leannoth. A Maskil of Heman the Ezrahite.

1 O LORD, God of my salvation,
when, at night, I cry out in your
presence,
2 let my prayer come before you;
incline your ear to my cry.

3 For my soul is full of troubles,
and my life draws near to Sheol.
4 I am counted among those who go
down to the Pit;
I am like those who have no help,
5 like those forsaken among the dead,
like the slain that lie in the grave,
like those whom you remember
no more,
for they are cut off from your
hand.
6 You have put me in the depths of the
Pit,
in the regions dark and deep.
7 Your wrath lies heavy upon me,
and you overwhelm me with all
your waves. *Selah*

8 You have caused my companions to
shun me;
you have made me a thing of
horror to them.
I am shut in so that I cannot escape;
9 my eye grows dim through sorrow.
Every day I call on you, O LORD;
I spread out my hands to you.
10 Do you work wonders for the dead?
Do the shades rise up to praise
you? *Selah*
11 Is your steadfast love declared in the
grave,
or your faithfulness in Abaddon?
12 Are your wonders known in the
darkness,
or your saving help in the land of
forgetfulness?

13 But I, O LORD, cry out to you;
in the morning my prayer comes
before you.
14 O LORD, why do you cast me off?
Why do you hide your face from
me?
15 Wretched and close to death from my
youth up,
I suffer your terrors; I am
desperate.[a]
16 Your wrath has swept over me;
your dread assaults destroy me.
17 They surround me like a flood all day
long;
from all sides they close in on me.
18 You have caused friend and neighbor
to shun me;
my companions are in darkness.

PSALM 89

A Maskil of Ethan the Ezrahite.

1 I will sing of your steadfast love,
O LORD,[b] forever;

a Meaning of Heb uncertain *b* Gk: Heb *the steadfast love of the LORD*

Ps 88: A Job-like lament. The most dismal of the laments, by a person mortally ill. It contains neither expressions of trust nor a concluding thanksgiving. The author of Job likely drew upon such traditional laments in composing Job's speeches. *Korahites,* see Ps 42–43n. *Mahalath Leannoth,* probably a melody. *Heman,* a famous Temple musician (1 Chr 25.5–6). **3–5:** The psalmist is on the brink of *Sheol,* the abode of the dead, separated from and forgotten by God. *The Pit,* another designation for Sheol. **6–8:** As with Job, the psalmist's troubles come from God. **7:** The threatening chaotic waters (Ps 42.7; 69.1–2). *Selah* (also v. 10), see Ps 3.2n. **8:** See v. 18; 31.9–13n.; Job 19.13; 30.10. **10–12:** The world of the dead, with no praise of God and no remembrance of his saving acts (Ps 6.5; 30.9). The psalmist perceives himself to be a victim of God's wrath rather than experiencing justified punishment. **11:** *Abaddon,* "destruction," another name for the abode of the dead. **18:** Shunned by his community (v. 8), the psalmist's only companions are other residents of Sheol.

Ps 89: The king defeated, the dynasty at an end. A royal lament, consisting of a hymn of praise

with my mouth I will proclaim
your faithfulness to all
generations.
2 I declare that your steadfast love is
established forever;
your faithfulness is as firm as the
heavens.

3 You said, "I have made a covenant
with my chosen one,
I have sworn to my servant David:
4 'I will establish your descendants
forever,
and build your throne for all
generations.' " *Selah*

5 Let the heavens praise your wonders,
O LORD,
your faithfulness in the assembly of
the holy ones.
6 For who in the skies can be compared
to the LORD?
Who among the heavenly beings is
like the LORD,
7 a God feared in the council of the
holy ones,
great and awesome[a] above all that
are around him?
8 O LORD God of hosts,
who is as mighty as you, O LORD?
Your faithfulness surrounds you.
9 You rule the raging of the sea;
when its waves rise, you still them.
10 You crushed Rahab like a carcass;
you scattered your enemies with
your mighty arm.
11 The heavens are yours, the earth also
is yours;
the world and all that is in it—you
have founded them.
12 The north and the south[b]—you
created them;
Tabor and Hermon joyously praise
your name.
13 You have a mighty arm;
strong is your hand, high your right
hand.
14 Righteousness and justice are the
foundation of your throne;
steadfast love and faithfulness go
before you.
15 Happy are the people who know the
festal shout,
who walk, O LORD, in the light of
your countenance;
16 they exult in your name all day long,
and extol[c] your righteousness.
17 For you are the glory of their
strength;
by your favor our horn is exalted.
18 For our shield belongs to the LORD,
our king to the Holy One of Israel.

19 Then you spoke in a vision to your
faithful one, and said:
"I have set the crown[d] on one who
is mighty,
I have exalted one chosen from the
people.
20 I have found my servant David;
with my holy oil I have anointed
him;

a Gk Syr: Heb *greatly awesome* *b* Or *Zaphon and Yamin* *c* Cn: Heb *are exalted in* *d* Cn: Heb *help*

(vv. 1–18), a poetic version of the covenant with David in 2 Sam 7.11–17 (vv. 19–37), and a lament (vv. 38–51), provoked by some major defeat. *Ethan,* a famous Temple musician; 1 Chr 15.17,19. **1–4:** The psalmist's praise of the LORD, for choosing David, concluding with a paraphrase of the conclusion to the dynastic oracle (2 Sam 7.16). **4:** *Selah* (also vv. 37,45,48), see Ps 3.2n. **5–8:** The heavenly council praises the incomparable and awesome LORD; cf. Ps 29.1n.; 82.1; Ex 15.11. **9–13:** Having defeated the chaotic waters, the LORD is victorious creator (see 74.12–17). **10:** *Rahab,* a name for the primeval chaos monster; Job 26.12; Isa 51.9. **12:** *Tabor and Hermon,* two prominent mountains, in southern Galilee and northern Transjordan, respectively. **14–18:** Celebration of God's kingship by earthly Israel. **17:** *Horn,* a metaphor for *strength* (also v. 24). **18:** A transition verse, moving from God, to David as king. **19–37:** The covenant with David and his descendants, which will be eternal (vv. 28–29,35–37) and unalterable by human sin (vv. 30–34). As noted, this is a poetic reformulation of 2 Sam 7.11–17, which like that text assumes an eternal, unbreakable Davidic covenant; contrast Ps 132.11–12; 1 Kings 9.4–9. **23:** Cf. Ps

21 my hand shall always remain with
him;
my arm also shall strengthen him.
22 The enemy shall not outwit him,
the wicked shall not humble him.
23 I will crush his foes before him
and strike down those who hate
him.
24 My faithfulness and steadfast love
shall be with him;
and in my name his horn shall be
exalted.
25 I will set his hand on the sea
and his right hand on the rivers.
26 He shall cry to me, 'You are my
Father,
my God, and the Rock of my
salvation!'
27 I will make him the firstborn,
the highest of the kings of the
earth.
28 Forever I will keep my steadfast love
for him,
and my covenant with him will
stand firm.
29 I will establish his line forever,
and his throne as long as the
heavens endure.
30 If his children forsake my law
and do not walk according to my
ordinances,
31 if they violate my statutes
and do not keep my
commandments,
32 then I will punish their transgression
with the rod
and their iniquity with scourges;
33 but I will not remove from him my
steadfast love,
or be false to my faithfulness.
34 I will not violate my covenant,
or alter the word that went forth
from my lips.
35 Once and for all I have sworn by my
holiness;
I will not lie to David.
36 His line shall continue forever,
and his throne endure before me
like the sun.
37 It shall be established forever like the
moon,
an enduring witness in the skies."
Selah

38 But now you have spurned and
rejected him;
you are full of wrath against your
anointed.
39 You have renounced the covenant
with your servant;
you have defiled his crown in
the dust.
40 You have broken through all
his walls;
you have laid his strongholds
in ruins.
41 All who pass by plunder him;
he has become the scorn of his
neighbors.
42 You have exalted the right hand of
his foes;
you have made all his enemies
rejoice.
43 Moreover, you have turned back the
edge of his sword,
and you have not supported him in
battle.
44 You have removed the scepter from
his hand,[a]
and hurled his throne to the
ground.
45 You have cut short the days of his
youth;
you have covered him with shame.
Selah

46 How long, O LORD? Will you hide
yourself forever?
How long will your wrath burn like
fire?
47 Remember how short my time is—[b]

a Cn: Heb *removed his cleanness* *b* Meaning of Heb uncertain

2.8–9. **25:** The king shares the divine task of controlling the primeval forces of watery chaos. **38–51:** The lament: In light of the glorious promises of vv. 19–37, how is the collapse of the eternal dynasty and the destruction of Jerusalem to be explained? **45:** The premature death of the king (Ps 102.23; Job 14.1). **48:**

for what vanity you have created
all mortals!
48 Who can live and never see death?
Who can escape the power of
Sheol? *Selah*

49 Lord, where is your steadfast love of
old,
which by your faithfulness you
swore to David?
50 Remember, O Lord, how your servant
is taunted;
how I bear in my bosom the insults
of the peoples,[a]
51 with which your enemies taunt,
O LORD,
with which they taunted the
footsteps of your anointed.

52 Blessed be the LORD forever.
Amen and Amen.

BOOK FOUR

PSALM 90

A Prayer of Moses, the man of God.

1 Lord, you have been our dwelling
place[b]
in all generations.
2 Before the mountains were brought
forth,
or ever you had formed the earth
and the world,
from everlasting to everlasting you
are God.

3 You turn us[c] back to dust,
and say, "Turn back, you mortals."
4 For a thousand years in your sight
are like yesterday when it is past,
or like a watch in the night.

5 You sweep them away; they are like a
dream,
like grass that is renewed in the
morning;
6 in the morning it flourishes and is
renewed;
in the evening it fades and withers.

7 For we are consumed by your anger;
by your wrath we are
overwhelmed.
8 You have set our iniquities
before you,
our secret sins in the light of your
countenance.

9 For all our days pass away under
your wrath;
our years come to an end[d] like
a sigh.
10 The days of our life are seventy years,
or perhaps eighty, if we are strong;
even then their span[e] is only toil and
trouble;
they are soon gone, and we fly
away.

11 Who considers the power of your
anger?
Your wrath is as great as the fear
that is due you.
12 So teach us to count our days
that we may gain a wise heart.

13 Turn, O LORD! How long?
Have compassion on your servants!
14 Satisfy us in the morning with your
steadfast love,

a Cn: Heb *bosom all of many peoples* *b* Another reading is *our refuge* *c* Heb *humankind*
d Syr: Heb *we bring our years to an end*
e Cn Compare Gk Syr Jerome Tg: Heb *pride*

Sheol, the abode of the dead. **49–51:** Perhaps a crisis of royal succession is alluded to. **52:** A doxology closing Book III of the Psalter, see Introduction.

Ps 90: The eternity of God and the brevity of human life. A communal lament with wisdom associations (v. 12). This psalm alone is associated with Moses, perhaps because he died prematurely, before entering the land. **1–2:** Hymnic affirmation of the eternity of God, creator of the world. **3:** *Back to dust,* see Gen 2.7; 3.19. **3–6:** The fragility of humankind, as evanescent as *grass* (Ps 102.25–28; Isa 40.6–8). **7–9:** God's wrath directed at human sinfulness. **12–15:** The psalmist prays for parity between days of joy and days

so that we may rejoice and be glad
all our days.
15 Make us glad as many days as you
have afflicted us,
and as many years as we have seen
evil.
16 Let your work be manifest to your
servants,
and your glorious power to their
children.
17 Let the favor of the Lord our God be
upon us,
and prosper for us the work of our
hands—
O prosper the work of our hands!

PSALM 91

1 You who live in the shelter of the
Most High,
who abide in the shadow of the
Almighty,[a]
2 will say to the LORD, "My refuge and
my fortress;
my God, in whom I trust."
3 For he will deliver you from the snare
of the fowler
and from the deadly pestilence;
4 he will cover you with his pinions,
and under his wings you will find
refuge;
his faithfulness is a shield and
buckler.
5 You will not fear the terror of the
night,
or the arrow that flies by day,
6 or the pestilence that stalks in
darkness,
or the destruction that wastes at
noonday.
7 A thousand may fall at your side,
ten thousand at your right hand,
but it will not come near you.
8 You will only look with your eyes
and see the punishment of the
wicked.

9 Because you have made the LORD
your refuge,[b]
the Most High your dwelling
place,
10 no evil shall befall you,
no scourge come near your tent.

11 For he will command his angels
concerning you
to guard you in all your ways.
12 On their hands they will bear you
up,
so that you will not dash your foot
against a stone.
13 You will tread on the lion and the
adder,
the young lion and the serpent you
will trample under foot.

14 Those who love me, I will deliver;
I will protect those who know my
name.
15 When they call to me, I will answer
them;
I will be with them in trouble,
I will rescue them and honor
them.
16 With long life I will satisfy them,
and show them my salvation.

a Traditional rendering of Heb *Shaddai* *b* Cn: Heb *Because you, LORD, are my refuge; you have made*

of evil and affliction. **16–17:** The limited "immortality" of human beings in their children and their achievements, *the work of our hands.*

Ps 91: God the protector from demonic foes. A psalm of trust (v. 2), in which the psalmist looks to God for protection against enemies superhuman (vv. 3–6) and subhuman (v. 13). The theology of the psalm, with various demons and a guardian angel, likely reflects Israelite popular religion. **1–2:** *Shelter . . . shadow . . . refuge and . . . fortress,* the Temple as a place of protection (v. 9; Ps 27.5; 31.20). **3–4:** A metaphor for divine protection, the outspread wings of a bird (Ps 17.8; 36.7). **5–8:** Attacked by demonic forces, the psalmist is protected by God. **11–12:** The psalmist's "guardian angels" (Ex 23.20; Ps 43.3n.). **14–16:** God responds to the psalmist with a salvation oracle, with seven first-person singular verbs.

PSALM 92

A Psalm. A Song for the Sabbath Day.

1 It is good to give thanks to the
LORD,
to sing praises to your name,
O Most High;
2 to declare your steadfast love in the
morning,
and your faithfulness by night,
3 to the music of the lute and the harp,
to the melody of the lyre.
4 For you, O LORD, have made me glad
by your work;
at the works of your hands I sing
for joy.

5 How great are your works, O LORD!
Your thoughts are very deep!
6 The dullard cannot know,
the stupid cannot understand this:
7 though the wicked sprout like grass
and all evildoers flourish,
they are doomed to destruction
forever,
8 but you, O LORD, are on high
forever.
9 For your enemies, O LORD,
for your enemies shall perish;
all evildoers shall be scattered.

10 But you have exalted my horn like
that of the wild ox;
you have poured over me[a]
fresh oil.
11 My eyes have seen the downfall of my
enemies;
my ears have heard the doom of
my evil assailants.

12 The righteous flourish like the palm
tree,
and grow like a cedar in Lebanon.
13 They are planted in the house of the
LORD;
they flourish in the courts of our
God.
14 In old age they still produce fruit;
they are always green and full
of sap,
15 showing that the LORD is upright;
he is my rock, and there is no
unrighteousness in him.

PSALM 93

1 The LORD is king, he is robed in
majesty;
the LORD is robed, he is girded
with strength.
He has established the world; it shall
never be moved;
2 your throne is established from
of old;
you are from everlasting.

3 The floods have lifted up, O LORD,
the floods have lifted up their voice;

a Syr: Meaning of Heb uncertain

Ps 92: Thanksgiving for deliverance from enemies. A thanksgiving psalm, with wisdom characteristics (vv. 5–7,12–15). Its reflective references to creation make it suitable *for the Sabbath Day.* This is the only reference to the sabbath in the book of Psalms. **1–4:** The joy and goodness of thanksgiving; praise of God for his *work,* his creation and governance of the world. **5–9:** Destruction is the ultimate fate of the wicked. **5:** The morally obtuse do not recognize God's *works.* **7:** *Grass,* evanescent life (see 90.3–6n.). **10–15:** If the wicked are as impermanent as grass (v. 7), the righteous are like a stable, productive tree (Ps 1.3; 52.8), specifically the gracious *palm,* yielding dates, and the strong, fragrant *cedar.* **10:** *Horn,* a metaphor for strength.

Ps 93: The LORD's enthronement. An enthronement psalm, praising the LORD as king. It begins a series of similar psalms (Ps 95; 96; 97; 99) characterized by the assertion, "The LORD is king!" Others translate "The LORD has become king," and connect these psalms to the fall new year festival, in which God was symbolically (re-)enthroned. These psalms reflect many of the rituals connected to the enthronement of the human king. **1–2:** God's kingship revealed in his creating and stabilizing the world (Ps 96.10). **3–4:** The LORD wins kingship by defeating the chaotic, world-destroying waters; this assertion has its origin

the floods lift up their roaring.
4 More majestic than the thunders of mighty waters,
more majestic than the waves[a] of the sea,
majestic on high is the LORD!

5 Your decrees are very sure;
holiness befits your house,
O LORD, forevermore.

PSALM 94

1 O LORD, you God of vengeance,
you God of vengeance, shine forth!
2 Rise up, O judge of the earth;
give to the proud what they deserve!
3 O LORD, how long shall the wicked,
how long shall the wicked exult?

4 They pour out their arrogant words;
all the evildoers boast.
5 They crush your people, O LORD,
and afflict your heritage.
6 They kill the widow and the stranger,
they murder the orphan,
7 and they say, "The LORD does not see;
the God of Jacob does not perceive."

8 Understand, O dullest of the people;
fools, when will you be wise?
9 He who planted the ear, does he not hear?
He who formed the eye, does he not see?
10 He who disciplines the nations,
he who teaches knowledge to humankind,
does he not chastise?
11 The LORD knows our thoughts,[b]
that they are but an empty breath.

12 Happy are those whom you discipline, O LORD,
and whom you teach out of your law,
13 giving them respite from days of trouble,
until a pit is dug for the wicked.
14 For the LORD will not forsake his people;
he will not abandon his heritage;
15 for justice will return to the righteous,
and all the upright in heart will follow it.

16 Who rises up for me against the wicked?
Who stands up for me against evildoers?
17 If the LORD had not been my help,
my soul would soon have lived in the land of silence.
18 When I thought, "My foot is slipping,"
your steadfast love, O LORD, held me up.
19 When the cares of my heart are many,
your consolations cheer my soul.
20 Can wicked rulers be allied with you,
those who contrive mischief by statute?
21 They band together against the life of the righteous,
and condemn the innocent to death.

a Cn: Heb *majestic are the waves* *b* Heb *the thoughts of humankind*

in the Canaanite myth of the storm god Baal's defeat of Sea; cf. Ps 29; 76.12–14; 89.9–10; 104.6–9. **5:** The Temple, the residence of the victorious God.

Ps 94: Prayer for deliverance from evildoers. A communal lament, with wisdom motifs (vv. 8–13), framed by themes of divine vengeance and retribution. **1–2:** The vengeance of God is his commitment to overcome and punish evil (Ps 99.8). *Shine forth,* the language of theophany (Ps 50.2; 80.1). *Judge of the earth,* Gen 18.25. **3–7:** The psalmist is troubled by the good fortune of the wicked, who believe that God is inactive (Ps 73.3–12). **8–11:** The psalmist addresses the morally obtuse (*fools*), assuring them that God is attentive. **12:** *Discipline* is a typical biblical form of instruction, especially in Proverbs (e.g., Prov 13.24). **17–18:** On the brink of death, the psalmist is sustained by divine love (Ps 21.7; 66.9). **21:** The wicked

22 But the LORD has become my stronghold,
and my God the rock of my refuge.
23 He will repay them for their iniquity
and wipe them out for their wickedness;
the LORD our God will wipe them out.

PSALM 95

1 O come, let us sing to the LORD;
let us make a joyful noise to the rock of our salvation!
2 Let us come into his presence with thanksgiving;
let us make a joyful noise to him with songs of praise!
3 For the LORD is a great God,
and a great King above all gods.
4 In his hand are the depths of the earth;
the heights of the mountains are his also.
5 The sea is his, for he made it,
and the dry land, which his hands have formed.

6 O come, let us worship and bow down,
let us kneel before the LORD, our Maker!
7 For he is our God,
and we are the people of his pasture,
and the sheep of his hand.
O that today you would listen to his voice!
8 Do not harden your hearts, as at Meribah,
as on the day at Massah in the wilderness,
9 when your ancestors tested me,
and put me to the proof, though they had seen my work.
10 For forty years I loathed that generation
and said, "They are a people whose hearts go astray,
and they do not regard my ways."
11 Therefore in my anger I swore,
"They shall not enter my rest."

PSALM 96

1 O sing to the LORD a new song;
sing to the LORD, all the earth.
2 Sing to the LORD, bless his name;
tell of his salvation from day to day.
3 Declare his glory among the nations,
his marvelous works among all the peoples.
4 For great is the LORD, and greatly to be praised;
he is to be revered above all gods.
5 For all the gods of the peoples are idols,
but the LORD made the heavens.
6 Honor and majesty are before him;
strength and beauty are in his sanctuary.

are guilty of judicial murder, the condemnation of the innocent (e.g., 1 Kings 21.8–14). **23:** Retribution: The wicked will be destroyed.

Ps 95: God's kingship. A hymn celebrating God's rule (see Ps 93n.). **1–2:** Invitation to participate in Temple worship. **3–5:** God's supremacy over all other gods, revealed in his power to create (Ps 89.6–12; 96.5). **6–7a:** God is the divine shepherd (a royal metaphor; Ps 23.1; 78.52,71; 79.13; 80.1; 100.3; Ex 15.13). **7b–11:** A warning not to rebel, like the ancestors in the wilderness (Ex 17.1–7; Num 20.1–13; Ps 81.7; 106.32), lest they not be admitted to *my rest* (the land; Deut 12.9). *Forty years,* Num 14.33; 32.13; Josh 5.6.

Ps 96: The LORD's enthronement. An enthronement psalm (see Ps 93n.) of anthological character, quoting Ps 29.1–3 (vv. 7–9); 93.1–2 (v. 10); 98.7–9 (vv. 11–13). In contrast to the previous psalm, all nations are called upon to enthrone God as the sole, universal God. **1:** See Ps 33.3; 98.1. **6:** *Honor and majesty,* the light enveloping and streaming from God; *strength and beauty,* the ark in the Temple (Ps 63.2). **7–9:** In the quotation of Ps 29, the Gentile nations replace the divine beings. **11–13:** The natural

7 Ascribe to the LORD, O families of
the peoples,
ascribe to the LORD glory and
strength.
8 Ascribe to the LORD the glory due his
name;
bring an offering, and come into his
courts.
9 Worship the LORD in holy splendor;
tremble before him, all the earth.

10 Say among the nations, "The LORD is
king!
The world is firmly established; it
shall never be moved.
He will judge the peoples with
equity."
11 Let the heavens be glad, and let the
earth rejoice;
let the sea roar, and all that fills it;
12 let the field exult, and everything in
it.
Then shall all the trees of the forest
sing for joy
13 before the LORD; for he is coming,
for he is coming to judge the earth.
He will judge the world with
righteousness,
and the peoples with his truth.

PSALM 97

1 The LORD is king! Let the earth
rejoice;
let the many coastlands be glad!
2 Clouds and thick darkness are all
around him;
righteousness and justice are the
foundation of his throne.
3 Fire goes before him,
and consumes his adversaries on
every side.
4 His lightnings light up the world;
the earth sees and trembles.
5 The mountains melt like wax before
the LORD,
before the Lord of all the earth.

6 The heavens proclaim his
righteousness;
and all the peoples behold his
glory.
7 All worshipers of images are put
to shame,
those who make their boast in
worthless idols;
all gods bow down before him.
8 Zion hears and is glad,
and the towns[a] of Judah rejoice,
because of your judgments, O God.
9 For you, O LORD, are most high over
all the earth;
you are exalted far above all gods.

10 The LORD loves those who hate[b]
evil;
he guards the lives of his faithful;
he rescues them from the hand of
the wicked.
11 Light dawns[c] for the righteous,
and joy for the upright in heart.
12 Rejoice in the LORD, O you righteous,
and give thanks to his holy name!

a Heb *daughters* *b* Cn: Heb *You who love the LORD hate* *c* Gk Syr Jerome: Heb *is sown*

world rejoices at the coming of the winter rains, the evidence of God's just governance of his creation. This joy also reflects the joy of human coronations (2 Kings 11.20); it is emphasized here because God is an ideal *judge*, judging *with righteousness*.

Ps 97: The LORD's enthronement. An enthronement hymn (see Ps 93n.). **1–5:** The language of theophany (Ps 18.7–15). *Many coastlands,* even those at a great distance. *Clouds,* a frequent symbol of the divine presence, bring the winter rains (Ps 68.4,7–9). **6:** *The heavens,* perhaps the other gods (vv. 7,9). This replaces and extends the notion of the previous psalms, where people *proclaim* God's greatness. **7–9:** The impotence of idols and the homage of the other gods to the LORD. Cf. Ps 89.5–8. **8:** *Zion,* Jerusalem. **10–12:** The implication of the depiction of this powerfully enthroned God is that one should be righteous.

PSALM 98

A Psalm.

1 O sing to the LORD a new song,
for he has done marvelous things.
His right hand and his holy arm
have gotten him victory.
2 The LORD has made known his
victory;
he has revealed his vindication in
the sight of the nations.
3 He has remembered his steadfast love
and faithfulness
to the house of Israel.
All the ends of the earth have seen
the victory of our God.

4 Make a joyful noise to the LORD, all
the earth;
break forth into joyous song and
sing praises.
5 Sing praises to the LORD with the
lyre,
with the lyre and the sound of
melody.
6 With trumpets and the sound of the
horn
make a joyful noise before the
King, the LORD.

7 Let the sea roar, and all that fills it;
the world and those who live in it.
8 Let the floods clap their hands;
let the hills sing together for joy
9 at the presence of the LORD, for he is
coming
to judge the earth.
He will judge the world with
righteousness,
and the peoples with equity.

PSALM 99

1 The LORD is king; let the peoples
tremble!
He sits enthroned upon the
cherubim; let the earth quake!
2 The LORD is great in Zion;
he is exalted over all the peoples.
3 Let them praise your great and
awesome name.
Holy is he!
4 Mighty King,[a] lover of justice,
you have established equity;
you have executed justice
and righteousness in Jacob.
5 Extol the LORD our God;
worship at his footstool.
Holy is he!

6 Moses and Aaron were among his
priests,
Samuel also was among those who
called on his name.
They cried to the LORD, and he
answered them.
7 He spoke to them in the pillar of
cloud;
they kept his decrees,
and the statutes that he gave them.

8 O LORD our God, you answered
them;
you were a forgiving God to them,
but an avenger of their
wrongdoings.
9 Extol the LORD our God,
and worship at his holy mountain;
for the LORD our God is holy.

a Cn: Heb *And a king's strength*

Ps 98: God's kingship. A hymn celebrating God's rule. It is highly universalistic: *All the . . . earth* (v. 4) as well as the natural world (vv. 7–8), must acknowledge his just kingship. **1:** See Ps 96.1; for the LORD's saving right hand and arm, cf. Ex 15.6,12,16; Ps 89.13. **2–3:** God proclaimed as victor to Israel and the nations (Ps 96.3; 97.6). **4–6:** Worship of the LORD in the Temple. **7–9:** See Ps 96.11–13.

Ps 99: The LORD's enthronement. An enthronement hymn (see Ps 93n.) with a refrain in vv. 3,5,9, reminiscent of Isa 6.3. **1:** *Enthroned upon the cherubim,* an epithet associated with the ark (1 Sam 4.4); the LORD rules from Jerusalem (*Zion*). **4:** Ancient Near Eastern kings, human and divine, were responsible for promoting *justice* (Ps 9.7; 72.1–3); for this psalmist, God's justice rather than military power expresses his strength. **5:** *His footstool,* the ark. **6–7:** The psalmist recalls Moses and Aaron, from the wilderness

PSALM 100

A Psalm of thanksgiving.

1 Make a joyful noise to the LORD, all
the earth.
2 Worship the LORD with gladness;
come into his presence with singing.

3 Know that the LORD is God.
It is he that made us, and we are
his;[a]
we are his people, and the sheep of
his pasture.

4 Enter his gates with thanksgiving,
and his courts with praise.
Give thanks to him, bless his
name.

5 For the LORD is good;
his steadfast love endures forever,
and his faithfulness to all
generations.

PSALM 101

Of David. A Psalm.

1 I will sing of loyalty and of justice;
to you, O LORD, I will sing.
2 I will study the way that is blameless.
When shall I attain it?

I will walk with integrity of heart
within my house;
3 I will not set before my eyes
anything that is base.
I hate the work of those who
fall away;
it shall not cling to me.
4 Perverseness of heart shall be far from
me;
I will know nothing of evil.

5 One who secretly slanders a
neighbor
I will destroy.
A haughty look and an arrogant
heart
I will not tolerate.

6 I will look with favor on the faithful
in the land,
so that they may live with me;
whoever walks in the way that is
blameless
shall minister to me.

7 No one who practices deceit
shall remain in my house;
no one who utters lies
shall continue in my presence.

8 Morning by morning I will destroy
all the wicked in the land,
cutting off all evildoers
from the city of the LORD.

a Another reading is *and not we ourselves*

era, and Samuel, inaugurator of the monarchy. *Pillar of cloud,* Ex 13.21; 33.9; Deut 31.15. **8:** See Ps 94.1. **9:** *His holy mountain,* Mount Zion, the site of the Temple.

Ps 100: Praise of God from the nations. This hymn of praise forms a suitable conclusion to the enthronement psalms, with their theme of the revelation of the divine glory to the nations (Ps 96.3; 97.6; 98.2–3). **1–2:** All the earth is invited to worship God joyously in the Temple (v. 4). **3:** For the LORD as creator and shepherd, see Ps 95.6–7n. **5:** The eternity of divine love (Ps 117.2, and the refrain in Ps 136). *For the LORD is good; his steadfast love endures forever* became a key liturgical element in the postexilic period (Ezra 3.11; 1 Chr 16.41).

Ps 101: The king as wise ruler. A royal lament, including a negative confession by the king (vv. 3–5) and a responding divine oracle (vv. 6–7). **1:** The psalmist sings of the LORD's loyalty to the Davidic monarchy. **2:** *I will study,* see Deut 17.19. **3–5:** The king's protestation of innocence (Ps 18.21–23); for nonassociation with evildoers, see Ps 1.1; 26.4–5. **6–7:** The oracle, promising divine favor to a righteous king. **8:** The king's response, promising to purge the land of evildoers.

PSALM 102

A prayer of one afflicted, when faint and pleading before the LORD.

1 Hear my prayer, O LORD;
let my cry come to you.
2 Do not hide your face from me
in the day of my distress.
Incline your ear to me;
answer me speedily in the day when I call.

3 For my days pass away like smoke,
and my bones burn like a furnace.
4 My heart is stricken and withered like grass;
I am too wasted to eat my bread.
5 Because of my loud groaning
my bones cling to my skin.
6 I am like an owl of the wilderness,
like a little owl of the waste places.
7 I lie awake;
I am like a lonely bird on the housetop.
8 All day long my enemies taunt me;
those who deride me use my name for a curse.
9 For I eat ashes like bread,
and mingle tears with my drink,
10 because of your indignation and anger;
for you have lifted me up and thrown me aside.
11 My days are like an evening shadow;
I wither away like grass.

12 But you, O LORD, are enthroned forever;
your name endures to all generations.
13 You will rise up and have compassion on Zion,
for it is time to favor it;
the appointed time has come.
14 For your servants hold its stones dear,
and have pity on its dust.
15 The nations will fear the name of the LORD,
and all the kings of the earth your glory.
16 For the LORD will build up Zion;
he will appear in his glory.
17 He will regard the prayer of the destitute,
and will not despise their prayer.

18 Let this be recorded for a generation to come,
so that a people yet unborn may praise the LORD:
19 that he looked down from his holy height,
from heaven the LORD looked at the earth,
20 to hear the groans of the prisoners,
to set free those who were doomed to die;
21 so that the name of the LORD may be declared in Zion,
and his praise in Jerusalem,
22 when peoples gather together,
and kingdoms, to worship the LORD.

23 He has broken my strength in midcourse;
he has shortened my days.
24 "O my God," I say, "do not take me away
at the midpoint of my life,

Ps 102: Prayer for personal and national restoration. One of the penitential psalms (see Ps 6n.). An individual lament (vv. 1–11,23–28) framing a hymn about the hoped-for rebuilding of Zion (Jerusalem) after the exile (vv. 12–22). **1–2:** The psalmist's initial appeal in typical lament language. **3–8:** The psalmist is beset with bodily disease, isolation, and abusive enemies. **9:** Fasting and weeping are characteristic activities of lament; cf. Ps 42.3; 80.5. **11–12:** The transitory character of humankind (*grass*), contrasted with the eternity of God (see Ps 90.1–6n.). **13–16:** The psalmist prays that God will rebuild Zion and that the divine glory will again appear there (Ezek 43.1–5); foreign kings will come to acknowledge the LORD's supremacy (Isa 60.1–3; Jer 30.18). **19–20:** God hears the groaning of the exiles (Ps 79.11), as he looks down from heaven (Ps 11.4–5; 14.2). **23–24:** The psalmist prays that he not suffer premature death (Ps 55.23; 89.45). **25:** Job 38.4; Ps 104.5; Prov 8.29; Isa 48.13. **26–28:** The

you whose years endure
throughout all generations."

25 Long ago you laid the foundation of the earth,
and the heavens are the work of your hands.
26 They will perish, but you endure;
they will all wear out like a garment.
You change them like clothing, and they pass away;
27 but you are the same, and your years have no end.
28 The children of your servants shall live secure;
their offspring shall be established in your presence.

PSALM 103

Of David.

1 Bless the LORD, O my soul,
and all that is within me,
bless his holy name.
2 Bless the LORD, O my soul,
and do not forget all his benefits—
3 who forgives all your iniquity,
who heals all your diseases,
4 who redeems your life from the Pit,
who crowns you with steadfast love and mercy,
5 who satisfies you with good as long as you live[a]
so that your youth is renewed like the eagle's.

6 The LORD works vindication
and justice for all who are oppressed.
7 He made known his ways to Moses,
his acts to the people of Israel.
8 The LORD is merciful and gracious,
slow to anger and abounding in steadfast love.
9 He will not always accuse,
nor will he keep his anger forever.
10 He does not deal with us according to our sins,
nor repay us according to our iniquities.
11 For as the heavens are high above the earth,
so great is his steadfast love toward those who fear him;
12 as far as the east is from the west,
so far he removes our transgressions from us.
13 As a father has compassion for his children,
so the LORD has compassion for those who fear him.
14 For he knows how we were made;
he remembers that we are dust.

15 As for mortals, their days are like grass;
they flourish like a flower of the field;
16 for the wind passes over it, and it is gone,
and its place knows it no more.
17 But the steadfast love of the LORD is from everlasting to everlasting
on those who fear him,
and his righteousness to children's children,
18 to those who keep his covenant
and remember to do his commandments.

a Meaning of Heb uncertain

eternity of God is contrasted with a human being's limited "immortality" through *children* (Ps 90.16).

Ps 103: Praise of the savior God. A hymn of praise for God's salvation of Israel; it contains quotations and allusions to the book of Exodus. **1–2:** A double self-invitation to praise God. *Bless the LORD, O my soul* was likely a stock introduction to a psalm (104.1). **3–4:** Among God's blessings are the forgiveness of sin and the healing of mortal illness (Ps 32.1–5). **3:** *Who forgives all your iniquity,* see Ex 34.7. **4:** *The Pit,* a poetic term for the abode of the dead. **7–8:** See Ex 33.13; 34.6. **9–13:** An exegesis of Ex 34.6, quoted in v. 8. **13:** *Compassion* is here associated with a *father* rather than mother, probably because the psalmist did not want to envision God as a woman. **14–17:** The creaturely and ephemeral status of humanity (Gen 2.7; Ps 90.3–6n.), and the reliability of divine love for God-fearers and their descendants. **19–22:** God's

19 The LORD has established his throne
in the heavens,
and his kingdom rules over all.
20 Bless the LORD, O you his angels,
you mighty ones who do his
bidding,
obedient to his spoken word.
21 Bless the LORD, all his hosts,
his ministers that do his will.
22 Bless the LORD, all his works,
in all places of his dominion.
Bless the LORD, O my soul.

PSALM 104

1 Bless the LORD, O my soul.
O LORD my God, you are very
great.
You are clothed with honor and
majesty,
2 wrapped in light as with a
garment.
You stretch out the heavens like
a tent,
3 you set the beams of your[a]
chambers on the waters,
you make the clouds your[a] chariot,
you ride on the wings of the wind,
4 you make the winds your[a]
messengers,
fire and flame your[a] ministers.

5 You set the earth on its foundations,
so that it shall never be shaken.
6 You cover it with the deep as with a
garment;
the waters stood above the
mountains.
7 At your rebuke they flee;
at the sound of your thunder they
take to flight.
8 They rose up to the mountains, ran
down to the valleys
to the place that you appointed for
them.
9 You set a boundary that they may not
pass,
so that they might not again cover
the earth.

10 You make springs gush forth in the
valleys;
they flow between the hills,
11 giving drink to every wild animal;
the wild asses quench their thirst.
12 By the streams[b] the birds of the air
have their habitation;
they sing among the branches.
13 From your lofty abode you water the
mountains;
the earth is satisfied with the fruit
of your work.

14 You cause the grass to grow for the
cattle,
and plants for people to use,[c]
to bring forth food from the earth,
15 and wine to gladden the human
heart,
oil to make the face shine,

a Heb *his* *b* Heb *By them* *c* Or *to cultivate*

kingship is lauded by his heavenly council, which is to be emulated by people. The psalm ends as it began, forming an inclusio.

Ps 104: God the creator and sustainer. A hymn describing the cycle of the Palestinian agricultural year, celebrating both the initial act of creation and God's continuing providential care. Its depiction differs in many details from Gen 1–3, and is more mythological in its language. It resembles both the divine catalogue of creation in Job 38–39 and the Egyptian *Hymn to Aten* (*ANET* 369–371). **1–2a:** The LORD surrounded by radiant *light* (Ps 94.1). **2b–9:** The initial act of creation, involving the construction of God's heavenly dwelling, the founding of the earth, and the retreat of the chaotic waters. **2:** *Stretch out the heavens,* Job 9.8; Isa 40.22; 42.5; Zech 12.2. **3:** *Ride on . . . the wind,* Ps 18.10; 68.4. **4:** Ps 148.8. **5:** See Ps 102.25n. **6–9:** Job 38.8–10; Prov 8.29; Jer 5.22. **7:** *At your rebuke,* God's war cry, putting the chaotic waters to flight (Ps 18.15). **10–18:** The emergence of the ordered, habitable world, where God provides water and food to his subhuman and human creatures. **13:** See Ps 36.8n.; 65.9. **14:** Ps 147.8. **15:** The three main crops of the agricultural year: grain (for *bread,* May-June), grapes (for *wine,* August-September), and olives (for *oil,* October). **19–24:** Predators seek their food at night, and people labor

and bread to strengthen the human
heart.
16 The trees of the LORD are watered
abundantly,
the cedars of Lebanon that he
planted.
17 In them the birds build their nests;
the stork has its home in the fir
trees.
18 The high mountains are for the wild
goats;
the rocks are a refuge for the
coneys.
19 You have made the moon to mark the
seasons;
the sun knows its time for setting.
20 You make darkness, and it is night,
when all the animals of the forest
come creeping out.
21 The young lions roar for their prey,
seeking their food from God.
22 When the sun rises, they withdraw
and lie down in their dens.
23 People go out to their work
and to their labor until the evening.

24 O LORD, how manifold are your
works!
In wisdom you have made them all;
the earth is full of your creatures.
25 Yonder is the sea, great and wide,
creeping things innumerable are
there,
living things both small and great.
26 There go the ships,
and Leviathan that you formed
to sport in it.

27 These all look to you
to give them their food in due
season;
28 when you give to them, they gather it
up;
when you open your hand, they are
filled with good things.
29 When you hide your face, they are
dismayed;
when you take away their breath,
they die
and return to their dust.
30 When you send forth your spirit,[a]
they are created;
and you renew the face of the
ground.

31 May the glory of the LORD endure
forever;
may the LORD rejoice in his
works—
32 who looks on the earth and it
trembles,
who touches the mountains and
they smoke.
33 I will sing to the LORD as long as
I live;
I will sing praise to my God while I
have being.
34 May my meditation be pleasing
to him,
for I rejoice in the LORD.
35 Let sinners be consumed from the
earth,
and let the wicked be no more.
Bless the LORD, O my soul.
Praise the LORD!

PSALM 105

1 O give thanks to the LORD, call on
his name,

a Or *your breath*

through the day. **21:** Job 38.39. **25–26:** *Leviathan,* the great marine chaos monster (Ps 74.14n.) is simply a plaything for the creator; contrast Job 41. **27–30:** The LORD maintains his providential governance of the world by providing the rain needed for food production. **31–32:** A theophany of the divine glory, accompanied by convulsions of the earth (Ps 114.7) and the mountains surrounded with smoke (Ps 144.5). **35:** The presence of sinners could prevent the coming of the winter rains (Jer 5.23–26). As in the previous psalm, this concludes as it began. *Praise the LORD,* Heb "halelu-yah." These words occur at the end and sometimes at the beginning of a number of psalms from this point on (see Ps 105; 106; 111–113; 115–117; 135; 146–150), which may have been part of one or more subcollections.

Ps 105: Recital of God's saving acts for Israel. Like Ps 78, a didactic hymn recounting Israel's history.

make known his deeds among the
peoples.
2 Sing to him, sing praises to him;
tell of all his wonderful works.
3 Glory in his holy name;
let the hearts of those who seek the
LORD rejoice.
4 Seek the LORD and his strength;
seek his presence continually.
5 Remember the wonderful works he
has done,
his miracles, and the judgments he
has uttered,
6 O offspring of his servant Abraham,[a]
children of Jacob, his chosen ones.

7 He is the LORD our God;
his judgments are in all the earth.
8 He is mindful of his covenant forever,
of the word that he commanded,
for a thousand generations,
9 the covenant that he made with
Abraham,
his sworn promise to Isaac,
10 which he confirmed to Jacob as a
statute,
to Israel as an everlasting covenant,
11 saying, "To you I will give the land
of Canaan
as your portion for an inheritance."

12 When they were few in number,
of little account, and strangers
in it,
13 wandering from nation to nation,
from one kingdom to another
people,
14 he allowed no one to oppress them;
he rebuked kings on their account,
15 saying, "Do not touch my anointed
ones;
do my prophets no harm."
16 When he summoned famine against
the land,
and broke every staff of bread,
17 he had sent a man ahead of them,
Joseph, who was sold as a slave.
18 His feet were hurt with fetters,
his neck was put in a collar of iron;
19 until what he had said came to pass,
the word of the LORD kept testing
him.
20 The king sent and released him;
the ruler of the peoples set
him free.
21 He made him lord of his house,
and ruler of all his possessions,
22 to instruct[b] his officials at his
pleasure,
and to teach his elders wisdom.

23 Then Israel came to Egypt;
Jacob lived as an alien in the land
of Ham.
24 And the LORD made his people very
fruitful,
and made them stronger than their
foes,
25 whose hearts he then turned to hate
his people,
to deal craftily with his servants.

26 He sent his servant Moses,
and Aaron whom he had chosen.

a Another reading is *Israel* (compare 1 Chr 16.13)
b Gk Syr Jerome: Heb *to bind*

After reviewing Israel's past (vv. 12–44), the psalmist appeals for Israel's obedience (v. 45). Vv. 1–15 are quoted in 1 Chr 16.8–22. This psalm's historical review includes details not known from the Torah, including putting Joseph in fetters (v. 18), and darkness as a plague preceding blood (vv. 28–29). **1–6:** The descendants of the ancestors of Israel are invited to praise the LORD, to *seek his presence* (in the Temple), and to recall his redemptive acts. **7–11:** The LORD, whose acts of governance (*judgments*) are in all the earth, keeps the covenant with the ancestors (Gen 15; 28.13–14) to give Israel the land. **12–15:** The ancestors in Canaan, before possessing the land. The verses recall Gen 20, where God *rebuked* King Abimelech, and where Abraham is called a *prophet.* Cf. also Gen 12.10–20; 26.1–2. **16–22:** The *Joseph* story (Gen 37–50) retold with significant variants, ending with Joseph as a wisdom teacher (Gen 41.39). **23–25:** Israel in *Egypt,* oppressed yet fruitful (Ex 1). *Ham,* see 78.51n. **26–36:** The plagues (Ex 7–12; Ps 78.42–51). The number and order of plagues differs from the Exodus account.

27 They performed his signs among them,
and miracles in the land of Ham.
28 He sent darkness, and made the land dark;
they rebelled[a] against his words.
29 He turned their waters into blood,
and caused their fish to die.
30 Their land swarmed with frogs,
even in the chambers of their kings.
31 He spoke, and there came swarms of flies,
and gnats throughout their country.
32 He gave them hail for rain,
and lightning that flashed through their land.
33 He struck their vines and fig trees,
and shattered the trees of their country.
34 He spoke, and the locusts came,
and young locusts without number;
35 they devoured all the vegetation in their land,
and ate up the fruit of their ground.
36 He struck down all the firstborn in their land,
the first issue of all their strength.

37 Then he brought Israel[b] out with silver and gold,
and there was no one among their tribes who stumbled.
38 Egypt was glad when they departed,
for dread of them had fallen upon it.
39 He spread a cloud for a covering,
and fire to give light by night.
40 They asked, and he brought quails,
and gave them food from heaven in abundance.
41 He opened the rock, and water gushed out;
it flowed through the desert like a river.
42 For he remembered his holy promise,
and Abraham, his servant.

43 So he brought his people out with joy,
his chosen ones with singing.
44 He gave them the lands of the nations,
and they took possession of the wealth of the peoples,
45 that they might keep his statutes
and observe his laws.
Praise the LORD!

PSALM 106

1 Praise the LORD!
O give thanks to the LORD, for he is good;
for his steadfast love endures forever.
2 Who can utter the mighty doings of the LORD,
or declare all his praise?
3 Happy are those who observe justice,
who do righteousness at all times.

4 Remember me, O LORD, when you show favor to your people;
help me when you deliver them;
5 that I may see the prosperity of your chosen ones,
that I may rejoice in the gladness of your nation,
that I may glory in your heritage.

a Cn Compare Gk Syr: Heb *they did not rebel*
b Heb *them*

37–44: The Exodus from Egypt (Ex 12.35); divine guidance in the wilderness and the provision of Israel with food (Ex 13.21–22; 16.1–17.7). **45:** The purpose of the psalm is instruction, on obedience as the proper response of the community.

Ps 106: Confession of national sin. A penitential companion piece to Ps 105, which reviewed the history of Israel's redemption from Egypt. Ps 106 is concerned with Israel's history of rebellion, of their disregarding ("forgetting") divine love expressed in acts of salvation (vv. 7,13,21). The final appeal for an end to exile (v. 47) locates the psalm in the exilic era (sixth century BCE). **1:** *Give thanks,* see Ps 105.1; 107.1; 136.1. **4–5:** Prayer for divine favor and deliverance. **6:** This verse likely reflects a confession recited in the

6 Both we and our ancestors have sinned;
we have committed iniquity, have done wickedly.
7 Our ancestors, when they were in Egypt,
did not consider your wonderful works;
they did not remember the abundance of your steadfast love,
but rebelled against the Most High[a] at the Red Sea.[b]
8 Yet he saved them for his name's sake,
so that he might make known his mighty power.
9 He rebuked the Red Sea,[b] and it became dry;
he led them through the deep as through a desert.
10 So he saved them from the hand of the foe,
and delivered them from the hand of the enemy.
11 The waters covered their adversaries;
not one of them was left.
12 Then they believed his words;
they sang his praise.

13 But they soon forgot his works;
they did not wait for his counsel.
14 But they had a wanton craving in the wilderness,
and put God to the test in the desert;
15 he gave them what they asked,
but sent a wasting disease among them.

16 They were jealous of Moses in the camp,
and of Aaron, the holy one of the LORD.
17 The earth opened and swallowed up Dathan,
and covered the faction of Abiram.
18 Fire also broke out in their company;
the flame burned up the wicked.

19 They made a calf at Horeb
and worshiped a cast image.
20 They exchanged the glory of God[c]
for the image of an ox that eats grass.
21 They forgot God, their Savior,
who had done great things in Egypt,
22 wondrous works in the land of Ham,
and awesome deeds by the Red Sea.[b]
23 Therefore he said he would destroy them—
had not Moses, his chosen one,
stood in the breach before him,
to turn away his wrath from destroying them.

24 Then they despised the pleasant land,
having no faith in his promise.
25 They grumbled in their tents,
and did not obey the voice of the LORD.
26 Therefore he raised his hand and swore to them
that he would make them fall in the wilderness,
27 and would disperse[d] their descendants among the nations,
scattering them over the lands.

a Cn Compare 78.17, 56: Heb *rebelled at the sea* *b* Or *Sea of Reeds* *c* Compare Gk Mss: Heb *exchanged their glory* *d* Syr Compare Ezek 20.23: Heb *cause to fall*

exilic period (1 Kings 8.47; Dan 9.5). **8–12:** God's salvation of Israel at the sea (Ex 14.26–28), and Israel's initial obedience. **13–33:** Rebellion in the wilderness: vv. 13–15, the feeding of Israel and their testing of God (Ex 16–17); vv. 16–18, the rebellion of Dathan and Abiram (Num 16; the rebellion of Korah, from a different source, is not mentioned); vv. 19–20, the making of the golden calf (Ex 32.1–10); vv. 24–27, the refusal to enter Canaan (Num 14.1–35); vv. 28–29, the worship of Baal of Peor (Num 25); vv. 32–33, *the waters of Meribah,* Num 20.2–13 (cf. Ex 17.1–7). **19:** *Horeb,* an alternate name for Sinai. **22:** *Ham,* see 78.51n. **23:** The intercession of Moses (Ex 32.11–13). **30–31:** The Zadokite priests, who

28 Then they attached themselves to the
Baal of Peor,
and ate sacrifices offered to
the dead;
29 they provoked the LORD to anger
with their deeds,
and a plague broke out among
them.
30 Then Phinehas stood up and
interceded,
and the plague was stopped.
31 And that has been reckoned to him as
righteousness
from generation to generation
forever.

32 They angered the LORD[a] at the
waters of Meribah,
and it went ill with Moses on their
account;
33 for they made his spirit bitter,
and he spoke words that were
rash.

34 They did not destroy the peoples,
as the LORD commanded them,
35 but they mingled with the nations
and learned to do as they did.
36 They served their idols,
which became a snare to them.
37 They sacrificed their sons
and their daughters to the demons;
38 they poured out innocent blood,
the blood of their sons and
daughters,
whom they sacrificed to the idols of
Canaan;
and the land was polluted with
blood.
39 Thus they became unclean by their
acts,
and prostituted themselves in their
doings.

40 Then the anger of the LORD was
kindled against his people,
and he abhorred his heritage;
41 he gave them into the hand of the
nations,
so that those who hated them ruled
over them.
42 Their enemies oppressed them,
and they were brought into
subjection under their power.
43 Many times he delivered them,
but they were rebellious in their
purposes,
and were brought low through their
iniquity.
44 Nevertheless he regarded their distress
when he heard their cry.
45 For their sake he remembered his
covenant,
and showed compassion according
to the abundance of his
steadfast love.
46 He caused them to be pitied
by all who held them captive.

47 Save us, O LORD our God,
and gather us from among the
nations,
that we may give thanks to your holy
name
and glory in your praise.

48 Blessed be the LORD, the God of
Israel,
from everlasting to everlasting.
And let all the people say, "Amen."
Praise the LORD!

a Heb *him*

ministered during the Judean monarchy, traced themselves to Phinehas (1 Chr 5.30–41). **34–36:** Because they left the holy war (extermination of their enemies) incomplete, the Israelites learned their practices (Deut 20.18), and the land was polluted with idolatry. **37–39:** The sacrifice of children to foreign gods (2 Kings 16.3; 21.6; Jer 19.5; Ezek 20.31; 23.37). **44–47:** As God saved the people in the past, the exiles ask for a new act of salvation, the regathering of the people from their captivity (v. 27; 1 Chr 16.35–36). **48:** The doxology ending Book IV of the Psalter; see Introduction.

BOOK FIVE

PSALM 107

1 O give thanks to the LORD, for he is good;
for his steadfast love endures forever.
2 Let the redeemed of the LORD say so,
those he redeemed from trouble
3 and gathered in from the lands,
from the east and from the west,
from the north and from the south.[a]

4 Some wandered in desert wastes,
finding no way to an inhabited town;
5 hungry and thirsty,
their soul fainted within them.
6 Then they cried to the LORD in their trouble,
and he delivered them from their distress;
7 he led them by a straight way,
until they reached an inhabited town.
8 Let them thank the LORD for his steadfast love,
for his wonderful works to humankind.
9 For he satisfies the thirsty,
and the hungry he fills with good things.

10 Some sat in darkness and in gloom,
prisoners in misery and in irons,
11 for they had rebelled against the words of God,
and spurned the counsel of the Most High.
12 Their hearts were bowed down with hard labor;
they fell down, with no one to help.
13 Then they cried to the LORD in their trouble,
and he saved them from their distress;
14 he brought them out of darkness and gloom,
and broke their bonds asunder.
15 Let them thank the LORD for his steadfast love,
for his wonderful works to humankind.
16 For he shatters the doors of bronze,
and cuts in two the bars of iron.

17 Some were sick[b] through their sinful ways,
and because of their iniquities endured affliction;
18 they loathed any kind of food,
and they drew near to the gates of death.
19 Then they cried to the LORD in their trouble,
and he saved them from their distress;
20 he sent out his word and healed them,
and delivered them from destruction.
21 Let them thank the LORD for his steadfast love,
for his wonderful works to humankind.
22 And let them offer thanksgiving sacrifices,
and tell of his deeds with songs of joy.

23 Some went down to the sea in ships,
doing business on the mighty waters;

a Cn: Heb *sea* *b* Cn: Heb *fools*

Ps 107: Thanksgiving for return from exile. A thanksgiving hymn, in which the returned exiles (vv. 2–3) praise God who delivered them from the trackless desert (vv. 4–9), imprisonment (vv. 10–16), sickness (vv. 17–22), and the stormy sea (vv. 23–32). The hymn includes two refrains, the first in vv. 6,13,19,25, and the second in vv. 8,15,21,31. **1:** Ps 136.1; quoted in 1 Chr 16.34. **4–9:** The danger of the great eastern desert, where travelers, low on provisions, can lose their way. God delivers them by leading them to an inhabited city. **17–22:** God heals mortal illness. **23–32:** God stills the chaotic waters of *the sea*, here a threat to seafaring merchants. **33–38:** God has the power to reverse the natural order

24 they saw the deeds of the LORD,
his wondrous works in the deep.
25 For he commanded and raised the stormy wind,
which lifted up the waves of the sea.
26 They mounted up to heaven, they went down to the depths;
their courage melted away in their calamity;
27 they reeled and staggered like drunkards,
and were at their wits' end.
28 Then they cried to the LORD in their trouble,
and he brought them out from their distress;
29 he made the storm be still,
and the waves of the sea were hushed.
30 Then they were glad because they had quiet,
and he brought them to their desired haven.
31 Let them thank the LORD for his steadfast love,
for his wonderful works to humankind.
32 Let them extol him in the congregation of the people,
and praise him in the assembly of the elders.

33 He turns rivers into a desert,
springs of water into thirsty ground,
34 a fruitful land into a salty waste,
because of the wickedness of its inhabitants.
35 He turns a desert into pools of water,
a parched land into springs of water.
36 And there he lets the hungry live,
and they establish a town to live in;
37 they sow fields, and plant vineyards,
and get a fruitful yield.
38 By his blessing they multiply greatly,
and he does not let their cattle decrease.

39 When they are diminished and brought low
through oppression, trouble, and sorrow,
40 he pours contempt on princes
and makes them wander in trackless wastes;
41 but he raises up the needy out of distress,
and makes their families like flocks.
42 The upright see it and are glad;
and all wickedness stops its mouth.
43 Let those who are wise give heed to these things,
and consider the steadfast love of the LORD.

PSALM 108

A Song. A Psalm of David.

1 My heart is steadfast, O God, my heart is steadfast;[a]
I will sing and make melody.
Awake, my soul![b]
2 Awake, O harp and lyre!
I will awake the dawn.
3 I will give thanks to you, O LORD, among the peoples,
and I will sing praises to you among the nations.
4 For your steadfast love is higher than the heavens,
and your faithfulness reaches to the clouds.

5 Be exalted, O God, above the heavens,

a Heb Mss Gk Syr: MT lacks *my heart is steadfast*
b Compare 57.8: Heb *also my soul*

(cf. Isa 50.2), and the return from exile is described as a new Exodus (Isa 41.18; 43.19) and resettlement in the land (cf. Josh 24.13). **40:** Job 12.21,24. **43:** Possibly a gloss, a wisdom addition concluding the psalm (cf. Job 5.16; 22.19; Hos 14.9).

Ps 108: Request for victory over national enemies. A composite psalm, made up of Ps 57.7–11 (vv. 1–5) and Ps 60.5–12 (vv. 6–13).

and let your glory be over all the
earth.
6 Give victory with your right hand,
and answer me,
so that those whom you love may
be rescued.

7 God has promised in his sanctuary:[a]
"With exultation I will divide up
Shechem,
and portion out the Vale of
Succoth.
8 Gilead is mine; Manasseh is mine;
Ephraim is my helmet;
Judah is my scepter.
9 Moab is my washbasin;
on Edom I hurl my shoe;
over Philistia I shout in triumph."

10 Who will bring me to the fortified
city?
Who will lead me to Edom?
11 Have you not rejected us, O God?
You do not go out, O God, with
our armies.
12 O grant us help against the foe,
for human help is worthless.
13 With God we shall do valiantly;
it is he who will tread down
our foes.

PSALM 109

To the leader. Of David. A Psalm.

1 Do not be silent, O God of my praise.
2 For wicked and deceitful mouths are
opened against me,
speaking against me with lying
tongues.
3 They beset me with words of hate,
and attack me without cause.
4 In return for my love they accuse me,
even while I make prayer for
them.[b]
5 So they reward me evil for good,
and hatred for my love.

6 They say,[c] "Appoint a wicked man
against him;
let an accuser stand on his right.
7 When he is tried, let him be found
guilty;
let his prayer be counted as sin.
8 May his days be few;
may another seize his position.
9 May his children be orphans,
and his wife a widow.
10 May his children wander about
and beg;
may they be driven out of[d] the
ruins they inhabit.
11 May the creditor seize all that he has;
may strangers plunder the fruits of
his toil.
12 May there be no one to do him a
kindness,
nor anyone to pity his orphaned
children.
13 May his posterity be cut off;
may his name be blotted out in the
second generation.
14 May the iniquity of his father[e] be
remembered before the LORD,
and do not let the sin of his mother
be blotted out.
15 Let them be before the LORD
continually,

a Or *by his holiness* *b* Syr: Heb *I prayer*
c Heb lacks *They say* *d* Gk: Heb *and seek*
e Cn: Heb *fathers*

Ps 109: Prayer for deliverance from enemies. An imprecatory psalm, in which the psalmist, beset by lying enemies, hurls a terrible curse at them (vv. 6–19); alternatively, these verses have been understood as the words of the psalmist's foes (the NRSV adds *They say* in v. 6, but without textual support). **1–3:** The psalmist appeals for active intervention by God against deceitful enemies, probably judicial adversaries in a trial. **4:** Out of love for his accusers, the psalmist prayed for them (Ps 35.11–14). **6–7:** The law of talion or equivalent retribution: Let those who falsely accuse the psalmist be themselves tried and sentenced to death. **8–14:** The psalmist's curse extends through three generations: the lying accusers (v. 8), their *children* (vv. 9–13), and their parents (v. 14); see Ex 20.5; 34.7. **15:** *Memory* (like "name" in v. 13) may refer to the enemies' offspring (Ps 9.5–6). **17–18:** The same metaphor (curse as a coat)

and may his[a] memory be cut off
from the earth.
16 For he did not remember to show
kindness,
but pursued the poor and needy
and the brokenhearted to their
death.
17 He loved to curse; let curses come on
him.
He did not like blessing; may it be
far from him.
18 He clothed himself with cursing as his
coat,
may it soak into his body like
water,
like oil into his bones.
19 May it be like a garment that he
wraps around himself,
like a belt that he wears every
day."
20 May that be the reward of my
accusers from the LORD,
of those who speak evil against my
life.
21 But you, O LORD my Lord,
act on my behalf for your name's
sake;
because your steadfast love is good,
deliver me.
22 For I am poor and needy,
and my heart is pierced within me.
23 I am gone like a shadow at evening;
I am shaken off like a locust.
24 My knees are weak through fasting;
my body has become gaunt.
25 I am an object of scorn to my
accusers;
when they see me, they shake their
heads.
26 Help me, O LORD my God!
Save me according to your steadfast
love.
27 Let them know that this is your hand;
you, O LORD, have done it.
28 Let them curse, but you will bless.
Let my assailants be put to
shame;[b] may your servant be
glad.
29 May my accusers be clothed with
dishonor;
may they be wrapped in their own
shame as in a mantle.
30 With my mouth I will give great
thanks to the LORD;
I will praise him in the midst of the
throng.
31 For he stands at the right hand of the
needy,
to save them from those who
would condemn them to death.

PSALM 110

Of David. A Psalm.

1 The LORD says to my lord,
"Sit at my right hand
until I make your enemies your
footstool."

2 The LORD sends out from Zion
your mighty scepter.
Rule in the midst of your foes.
3 Your people will offer themselves
willingly
on the day you lead your forces

a Gk: Heb *their* *b* Gk: Heb *They have risen up and have been put to shame*

occurs in v. 29. **21–23:** The psalmist, in his misery, appeals for divine aid. **24:** *Through fasting,* characteristic of mourning (for the psalmist's imminent death). **30–31:** The deceitful mouths of the wicked are replaced by the *mouth* of the psalmist, praising God for saving *the needy* (i.e., the psalmist; see v. 22). **31:** The final verse, where God *stands at the right hand of the needy,* links this psalm with the following, where the Davidic king is to God's right.

Ps 110: The Davidic king. A royal oracle proclaimed to the Davidic monarch, perhaps at his coronation. The psalm is frequently used in the New Testament of Jesus' resurrection (Acts 2.34–35; 1 Cor 15.25; Eph 1.20; Heb 1.13). **1–2:** God promises the Davidic monarch in Jerusalem (*Zion*) victory over his enemies, prostrate before him (Josh 10.24). **3:** The Heb text is extremely difficult; it may refer to the king's warrior exploits and his "birth" into royal status (Ps 2.7n.). **4:** The king as *priest;* David and

on the holy mountains.[a]
From the womb of the morning,
like dew, your youth[b] will come to you.
4 The LORD has sworn and will not change his mind,
"You are a priest forever according to the order of Melchizedek."[c]

5 The Lord is at your right hand;
he will shatter kings on the day of his wrath.
6 He will execute judgment among the nations,
filling them with corpses;
he will shatter heads
over the wide earth.
7 He will drink from the stream by the path;
therefore he will lift up his head.

PSALM 111

1 Praise the LORD!
I will give thanks to the LORD with my whole heart,
in the company of the upright, in the congregation.
2 Great are the works of the LORD,
studied by all who delight in them.
3 Full of honor and majesty is his work,
and his righteousness endures forever.
4 He has gained renown by his wonderful deeds;
the LORD is gracious and merciful.
5 He provides food for those who fear him;
he is ever mindful of his covenant.
6 He has shown his people the power of his works,
in giving them the heritage of the nations.
7 The works of his hands are faithful and just;
all his precepts are trustworthy.
8 They are established forever and ever,
to be performed with faithfulness and uprightness.
9 He sent redemption to his people;
he has commanded his covenant forever.
Holy and awesome is his name.
10 The fear of the LORD is the beginning of wisdom;
all those who practice it[d] have a good understanding.
His praise endures forever.

PSALM 112

1 Praise the LORD!
Happy are those who fear the LORD,
who greatly delight in his commandments.
2 Their descendants will be mighty in the land;

a Another reading is *in holy splendor* *b* Cn: Heb *the dew of your youth* *c* Or *forever, a rightful king by my edict* *d* Gk Syr: Heb *them*

Solomon frequently served in priestly roles (see 2 Sam 6.13,17; 8.18; 1 Kings 3.4). For *Melchizedek,* see Gen 14.17–24. **5–6:** With divine help, the king will destroy rulers of the nations, perhaps rebellious vassals of the Davidic empire (Ps 2.2,10–11). **7:** Refreshment for the king after battle, or a ritual of coronation (1 Kings 1.9,39).

Ps 111: Praise of God for his wondrous deeds. An acrostic (see Ps 9–10n.) thanksgiving psalm, paired with Ps 112, also an acrostic of similar length, with similar language and themes (cf. Ps 111.3; 112.3,9). It is largely a description of God and his attributes. **1–6:** The wondrous deeds for which the psalmist praises the LORD include the Exodus, the covenant, food in the wilderness, and the gift of the land. **4:** Cf. Ex 34.6. **7–8:** Israel's response to God's *works:* obedience to his commandments. **10:** The psalm concludes on a wisdom note (Prov 9.10; Job 28.28).

Ps 112: The contrasting fates of the righteous and the wicked. An acrostic (see Ps 9–10n.) wisdom psalm, like Ps 1 and 37; it forms a pair with Ps 111. **1:** An assertion that the virtuous are *happy,* continuing the theme of Ps 111.10, the *fear of the LORD.* In contrast to the previous psalm, its focus is on the people rather than God. **2–3:** The blessings conferred on the God-fearer: children and prosperity.

the generation of the upright will
be blessed.
3 Wealth and riches are in their
houses,
and their righteousness endures
forever.
4 They rise in the darkness as a light
for the upright;
they are gracious, merciful, and
righteous.
5 It is well with those who deal
generously and lend,
who conduct their affairs with
justice.
6 For the righteous will never
be moved;
they will be remembered forever.
7 They are not afraid of evil tidings;
their hearts are firm, secure in the
LORD.
8 Their hearts are steady, they will not
be afraid;
in the end they will look in triumph
on their foes.
9 They have distributed freely, they
have given to the poor;
their righteousness endures
forever;
their horn is exalted in honor.
10 The wicked see it and are angry;
they gnash their teeth and melt
away;
the desire of the wicked comes
to nothing.

PSALM 113

1 Praise the LORD!
Praise, O servants of the LORD;
praise the name of the LORD.

2 Blessed be the name of the LORD
from this time on and forevermore.
3 From the rising of the sun to its
setting
the name of the LORD is to be
praised.
4 The LORD is high above all nations,
and his glory above the heavens.

5 Who is like the LORD our God,
who is seated on high,
6 who looks far down
on the heavens and the earth?
7 He raises the poor from the dust,
and lifts the needy from the ash
heap,
8 to make them sit with princes,
with the princes of his people.
9 He gives the barren woman a home,
making her the joyous mother of
children.
Praise the LORD!

PSALM 114

1 When Israel went out from Egypt,
the house of Jacob from a people of
strange language,

4: The psalmist alludes to the divine attributes in Ex 34.6–7 (cf. Ps 111.4) and applies them here to the righteous. **5:** The righteous are characterized by their generosity and justice (Ps 37.21,26; Prov 19.17). **6–9:** The reward of the righteous, an increase of dignity and power. **9:** *Horn,* a metaphor for strength. **10:** A wisdom saying: As the righteous see the downfall of the wicked, so the wicked will see the reward of the righteous (Prov 10.27–28; 11.7; Job 8.13).

Ps 113: Praise of the divine name. A hymn echoing in vv. 6–9 the song of Hannah (1 Sam 2.5,8). **1–3:** Praise of the LORD's name by the assembled worshipers. **3:** *From the rising of the sun to its setting,* from east to west, i.e., universally. **4–9:** The psalm moves from the LORD's name to the LORD, whose incomparability (a monotheistic confession) is manifest in his reversal of the situation of the *poor* and *barren* (Ps 35.10).

Ps 114: Praise of the God of the Exodus. A hymn, in which the passage through the sea (Ex 14.29) is paralleled by the crossing of the Jordan (Josh 3.14–17), the beginning and end of the Exodus. The psalm may reflect a ritual reenactment of the events. *Sea* and the *Jordan* River have mythic referents as well as historical, describing the chaotic waters. **1–2:** In v. 1, *Israel* is the entire nation, *the house of Jacob;* in v. 2, *Judah* and *Israel* refer to the Southern and Northern Kingdoms. For the whole land as a shrine, see

2 Judah became God's[a] sanctuary,
Israel his dominion.

3 The sea looked and fled;
Jordan turned back.
4 The mountains skipped like rams,
the hills like lambs.

5 Why is it, O sea, that you flee?
O Jordan, that you turn back?
6 O mountains, that you skip like
rams?
O hills, like lambs?

7 Tremble, O earth, at the presence of
the LORD,
at the presence of the God of
Jacob,
8 who turns the rock into a pool of
water,
the flint into a spring of water.

PSALM 115

1 Not to us, O LORD, not to us, but to
your name give glory,
for the sake of your steadfast love
and your faithfulness.
2 Why should the nations say,
"Where is their God?"

3 Our God is in the heavens;
he does whatever he pleases.
4 Their idols are silver and gold,
the work of human hands.
5 They have mouths, but do not speak;
eyes, but do not see.
6 They have ears, but do not hear;
noses, but do not smell.
7 They have hands, but do not feel;
feet, but do not walk;
they make no sound in their
throats.
8 Those who make them are like them;
so are all who trust in them.

9 O Israel, trust in the LORD!
He is their help and their shield.
10 O house of Aaron, trust in the LORD!
He is their help and their shield.
11 You who fear the LORD, trust in
the LORD!
He is their help and their shield.

12 The LORD has been mindful of us; he
will bless us;
he will bless the house of Israel;
he will bless the house of Aaron;
13 he will bless those who fear the
LORD,
both small and great.

14 May the LORD give you increase,
both you and your children.
15 May you be blessed by the LORD,
who made heaven and earth.

16 The heavens are the LORD's heavens,
but the earth he has given to
human beings.
17 The dead do not praise the LORD,
nor do any that go down into
silence.
18 But we will bless the LORD
from this time on and forevermore.
Praise the LORD!

a Heb *his*

Ex 15.17. **4–6:** A theophany: The sea flees in terror from the Divine Warrior (Ps 104.7), and the earth quakes (Ps 68.8) with fear. **8:** Water in the desert (Ex 17.6; Num 20.11).

Ps 115: The LORD's supremacy over the gods. This psalm, probably postexilic, does not fit any standard category. **2:** *Where is their God?* While Israel glorifies the divine name, the nations question God's effective presence (Ps 42.3; Ezek 36.22–32). **3:** Israel's answer to the mocking question of v. 2. **4–8:** The other gods are unreal, their worshipers as powerless as their idols (Deut 4.28; 2 Kings 17.15); cf. Ps 135.15–18. **10:** *House of Aaron,* the priestly leaders of the postexilic community. **11:** *You who fear the LORD,* possibly proselytes in the community (Ezra 6.21; Neh 10.28). **12–16:** The creator gives the earth and its goods to all human beings, not to Israel alone. **17–18:** The unconverted of the nations who do not acknowledge the LORD descend into the *silence* of the abode of the dead, Sheol (Ps 94.17), while Israel continues its vocal praise of the LORD (Ps 30.12).

PSALM 116

1 I love the LORD, because he has heard
my voice and my supplications.
2 Because he inclined his ear to me,
therefore I will call on him as long
as I live.
3 The snares of death encompassed me;
the pangs of Sheol laid hold on me;
I suffered distress and anguish.
4 Then I called on the name of
the LORD:
"O LORD, I pray, save my life!"

5 Gracious is the LORD, and righteous;
our God is merciful.
6 The LORD protects the simple;
when I was brought low, he saved
me.
7 Return, O my soul, to your rest,
for the LORD has dealt bountifully
with you.

8 For you have delivered my soul from
death,
my eyes from tears,
my feet from stumbling.
9 I walk before the LORD
in the land of the living.
10 I kept my faith, even when I said,
"I am greatly afflicted";
11 I said in my consternation,
"Everyone is a liar."

12 What shall I return to the LORD
for all his bounty to me?
13 I will lift up the cup of salvation
and call on the name of the
LORD,
14 I will pay my vows to the LORD
in the presence of all his people.
15 Precious in the sight of the LORD
is the death of his faithful ones.
16 O LORD, I am your servant;
I am your servant, the child of your
serving girl.
You have loosed my bonds.
17 I will offer to you a thanksgiving
sacrifice
and call on the name of the LORD.
18 I will pay my vows to the LORD
in the presence of all his people,
19 in the courts of the house of
the LORD,
in your midst, O Jerusalem.
Praise the LORD!

PSALM 117

1 Praise the LORD, all you nations!
Extol him, all you peoples!
2 For great is his steadfast love toward
us,
and the faithfulness of the LORD
endures forever.
Praise the LORD!

PSALM 118

1 O give thanks to the LORD, for he is
good;
his steadfast love endures forever!

Ps 116: Thanksgiving for healing. A thanksgiving psalm of anthological character, quoting from other psalms. **1–4:** See Ps 18.1–6. The psalmist's love for the LORD is based on a past experience of salvation (Ps 18.4–6); seriously ill, the psalmist appeals to God to save him again. **3:** *Sheol,* the abode of the dead. **5:** An echo of the creedal statement of Ex 34.6. **6–7:** Expressions of trust, characteristic of laments and thanksgivings. **8–9:** See Ps 56.13. **15:** The idea expressed in this rendering is alien to Israelite faith. With a slight emendation, *death* can be read as "fidelity," yielding a sense more in keeping with the rest of the psalm (e.g., vv. 10,14,18). **16:** *Child . . . serving girl,* see 86.16n. **17–19:** The *thanksgiving sacrifice* in the Temple after the psalmist's rescue from mortal illness, accompanied by libation and prayer (v. 13).

Ps 117: Praise of God from the nations. The shortest hymn in the Psalter, calling on all the nations to praise the LORD (Ps 67; 100). **2:** The reason for this praise is unexpected—God's *steadfast love* bestowed specifically on Israel!

Ps 118: Thanksgiving for victory in battle. An anthological thanksgiving hymn (like Ps 116; 135) with numerous allusions to other texts; v. 1 is quoted in 1 Chr 16.34. **1–4:** Praise from Israel, the Aaronic priesthood, and the God-fearers (proselytes?); see Ps 115.9–11. **5:** *Distress,* literally, a narrow, constricted

2 Let Israel say,
"His steadfast love endures forever."
3 Let the house of Aaron say,
"His steadfast love endures forever."
4 Let those who fear the LORD say,
"His steadfast love endures forever."

5 Out of my distress I called on the LORD;
the LORD answered me and set me in a broad place.
6 With the LORD on my side I do not fear.
What can mortals do to me?
7 The LORD is on my side to help me;
I shall look in triumph on those who hate me.
8 It is better to take refuge in the LORD
than to put confidence in mortals.
9 It is better to take refuge in the LORD
than to put confidence in princes.

10 All nations surrounded me;
in the name of the LORD I cut them off!
11 They surrounded me, surrounded me on every side;
in the name of the LORD I cut them off!
12 They surrounded me like bees;
they blazed[a] like a fire of thorns;
in the name of the LORD I cut them off!
13 I was pushed hard,[b] so that I was falling,
but the LORD helped me.
14 The LORD is my strength and my might;
he has become my salvation.

15 There are glad songs of victory in the tents of the righteous:
"The right hand of the LORD does valiantly;
16 the right hand of the LORD is exalted;
the right hand of the LORD does valiantly."
17 I shall not die, but I shall live,
and recount the deeds of the LORD.
18 The LORD has punished me severely,
but he did not give me over to death.

19 Open to me the gates of righteousness,
that I may enter through them
and give thanks to the LORD.

20 This is the gate of the LORD;
the righteous shall enter through it.

21 I thank you that you have answered me
and have become my salvation.
22 The stone that the builders rejected
has become the chief cornerstone.
23 This is the LORD's doing;
it is marvelous in our eyes.
24 This is the day that the LORD has made;
let us rejoice and be glad in it.[c]
25 Save us, we beseech you, O LORD!
O LORD, we beseech you, give us success!

26 Blessed is the one who comes in the name of the LORD.[d]
We bless you from the house of the LORD.

a Gk: Heb *were extinguished* *b* Gk Syr Jerome: Heb *You pushed me hard* *c* Or *in him* *d* Or *Blessed in the name of the LORD is the one who comes*

space; correspondingly, a "broad space" connotes salvation, release (Ps 4.1; 18.19). **6:** See Ps 56.4,11. **8–9:** See Ps 146.3. *Better . . . than,* a form of expression characteristic of wisdom literature (Ps 37.16; Prov 15.16–17). **10–13:** The attack of the nations; the one praying is perhaps the king. **14–16:** See Ex 15.2,6; Isa 12.2. **19–20:** An allusion to entrance rituals whereby the righteous gain admittance to the Temple (Ps 15; 24.3–6). **22:** A metaphor of reversal of expectations (cf. Ps 113.7–9). **23–28:** A thanksgiving ritual in the Temple amid the psalmist's friends and family (*we* in vv. 23–26). **27:** *Bind the festal . . .*, likely

27 The LORD is God,
and he has given us light.
Bind the festal procession with branches,
up to the horns of the altar.[a]

28 You are my God, and I will give thanks to you;
you are my God, I will extol you.

29 O give thanks to the LORD, for he is good,
for his steadfast love endures forever.

PSALM 119

1 Happy are those whose way is blameless,
who walk in the law of the LORD.
2 Happy are those who keep his decrees,
who seek him with their whole heart,
3 who also do no wrong,
but walk in his ways.
4 You have commanded your precepts
to be kept diligently.
5 O that my ways may be steadfast
in keeping your statutes!
6 Then I shall not be put to shame,
having my eyes fixed on all your commandments.
7 I will praise you with an upright heart,
when I learn your righteous ordinances.
8 I will observe your statutes;
do not utterly forsake me.

9 How can young people keep their way pure?
By guarding it according to your word.
10 With my whole heart I seek you;
do not let me stray from your commandments.
11 I treasure your word in my heart,
so that I may not sin against you.
12 Blessed are you, O LORD;
teach me your statutes.
13 With my lips I declare
all the ordinances of your mouth.
14 I delight in the way of your decrees
as much as in all riches.
15 I will meditate on your precepts,
and fix my eyes on your ways.
16 I will delight in your statutes;
I will not forget your word.

17 Deal bountifully with your servant,
so that I may live and observe your word.
18 Open my eyes, so that I may behold
wondrous things out of your law.
19 I live as an alien in the land;
do not hide your commandments from me.
20 My soul is consumed with longing

a Meaning of Heb uncertain

a liturgical direction or rubric which entered the text of the psalm. This suggests that other psalms may have been the ritual words accompanying ritual actions such as sacrifices.

Ps 119: Meditation on God's law. The longest psalm in the Psalter, Ps 119 is an elaborate acrostic (see Ps 9–10n.) wisdom psalm, divided into twenty-two eight-line stanzas. The first word of each line of vv. 1–8 begins with the first letter of the Hebrew alphabet ("aleph"), the first word of each line of vv. 9–16 begins with "beth," and so on to "taw," the last letter of the alphabet (vv. 169–176). The theme of the poem is the law, described by an array of synonyms, such as "decrees," "precepts," "commandments," "statutes," and "word(s)." The psalmist is enjoined throughout to keep and to teach the law, not to forget it, to rejoice in it, and thereby to possess life. The psalmist's opponents are the insolent who depart from the way of the law (vv. 21,51,69,78,85,122). In this postexilic poem, the psalmist desires the same close relationship to the law that previous psalmists sought with God in the Temple (Ps 63). Both proximity to God, and to God's law, may be characterized by great joy. **1–2:** *Happy are those,* a double assertion of the relation between virtue and happiness. **9:** A wisdom saying urging the young to follow the right *way* (Ps 34.11–14). **19:** *An alien in the land,* probably a reference to the exile. **25:** *Dust,* a

for your ordinances at all times.
21 You rebuke the insolent, accursed ones,
who wander from your commandments;
22 take away from me their scorn and contempt,
for I have kept your decrees.
23 Even though princes sit plotting against me,
your servant will meditate on your statutes.
24 Your decrees are my delight,
they are my counselors.

25 My soul clings to the dust;
revive me according to your word.
26 When I told of my ways, you answered me;
teach me your statutes.
27 Make me understand the way of your precepts,
and I will meditate on your wondrous works.
28 My soul melts away for sorrow;
strengthen me according to your word.
29 Put false ways far from me;
and graciously teach me your law.
30 I have chosen the way of faithfulness;
I set your ordinances before me.
31 I cling to your decrees, O LORD;
let me not be put to shame.
32 I run the way of your commandments,
for you enlarge my understanding.

33 Teach me, O LORD, the way of your statutes,
and I will observe it to the end.
34 Give me understanding, that I may keep your law
and observe it with my whole heart.
35 Lead me in the path of your commandments,
for I delight in it.
36 Turn my heart to your decrees,
and not to selfish gain.
37 Turn my eyes from looking at vanities;
give me life in your ways.
38 Confirm to your servant your promise,
which is for those who fear you.
39 Turn away the disgrace that I dread,
for your ordinances are good.
40 See, I have longed for your precepts;
in your righteousness give me life.

41 Let your steadfast love come to me, O LORD,
your salvation according to your promise.
42 Then I shall have an answer for those who taunt me,
for I trust in your word.
43 Do not take the word of truth utterly out of my mouth,
for my hope is in your ordinances.
44 I will keep your law continually,
forever and ever.
45 I shall walk at liberty,
for I have sought your precepts.
46 I will also speak of your decrees before kings,
and shall not be put to shame;
47 I find my delight in your commandments,
because I love them.
48 I revere your commandments, which I love,
and I will meditate on your statutes.

49 Remember your word to your servant,
in which you have made me hope.
50 This is my comfort in my distress,
that your promise gives me life.
51 The arrogant utterly deride me,
but I do not turn away from your law.
52 When I think of your ordinances from of old,
I take comfort, O LORD.

metaphor for Sheol, the abode of the dead (Ps 22.15); the psalmist prays for life (v. 50). **41–47**: Despite the taunters, the psalmist loves and delights in God's commandments. **54**: Another reference to exile (see

53 Hot indignation seizes me because of
the wicked,
those who forsake your law.
54 Your statutes have been my songs
wherever I make my home.
55 I remember your name in the night,
O LORD,
and keep your law.
56 This blessing has fallen to me,
for I have kept your precepts.

57 The LORD is my portion;
I promise to keep your words.
58 I implore your favor with all my
heart;
be gracious to me according to
your promise.
59 When I think of your ways,
I turn my feet to your decrees;
60 I hurry and do not delay
to keep your commandments.
61 Though the cords of the wicked
ensnare me,
I do not forget your law.
62 At midnight I rise to praise you,
because of your righteous
ordinances.
63 I am a companion of all who fear
you,
of those who keep your precepts.
64 The earth, O LORD, is full of your
steadfast love;
teach me your statutes.

65 You have dealt well with your
servant,
O LORD, according to your word.
66 Teach me good judgment and
knowledge,
for I believe in your
commandments.
67 Before I was humbled I went astray,
but now I keep your word.
68 You are good and do good;
teach me your statutes.
69 The arrogant smear me with
lies,
but with my whole heart I keep
your precepts.
70 Their hearts are fat and gross,
but I delight in your law.
71 It is good for me that I was humbled,
so that I might learn your statutes.
72 The law of your mouth is better
to me
than thousands of gold and silver
pieces.

73 Your hands have made and fashioned
me;
give me understanding that I may
learn your commandments.
74 Those who fear you shall see me and
rejoice,
because I have hoped in your word.
75 I know, O LORD, that your judgments
are right,
and that in faithfulness you have
humbled me.
76 Let your steadfast love become my
comfort
according to your promise to your
servant.
77 Let your mercy come to me, that I
may live;
for your law is my delight.
78 Let the arrogant be put to shame,
because they have subverted me
with guile;
as for me, I will meditate on your
precepts.
79 Let those who fear you turn to me,
so that they may know your
decrees.
80 May my heart be blameless in your
statutes,
so that I may not be put to shame.

81 My soul languishes for your salvation;
I hope in your word.

v. 19). **55:** For praise through the night, see v. 62 (Ps 42.8; 77.6). **57:** *My portion,* see Ps 16.5; perhaps the author is a priest. **64:** See Ps 33.5. **65–72:** The disciplinary value of suffering. **73:** Creation theology is common in wisdom (vv. 90–91; Prov 3.19–20). **77:** God's mercy is life-giving (v. 156). **81–88:** The "kaph" stanza, the end of the first half of the alphabet and of the psalm, wherein the psalmist, weeping (v. 82), pleads for deliverance from persecution for his obedience. In the following "lamed" stanza

82 My eyes fail with watching for your
promise;
I ask, "When will you comfort
me?"
83 For I have become like a wineskin in
the smoke,
yet I have not forgotten your
statutes.
84 How long must your servant endure?
When will you judge those who
persecute me?
85 The arrogant have dug pitfalls for me;
they flout your law.
86 All your commandments are enduring;
I am persecuted without cause; help
me!
87 They have almost made an end of me
on earth;
but I have not forsaken your
precepts.
88 In your steadfast love spare my life,
so that I may keep the decrees of
your mouth.

89 The LORD exists forever;
your word is firmly fixed in heaven.
90 Your faithfulness endures to all
generations;
you have established the earth, and
it stands fast.
91 By your appointment they stand
today,
for all things are your servants.
92 If your law had not been my delight,
I would have perished in my
misery.
93 I will never forget your precepts,
for by them you have given me life.
94 I am yours; save me,
for I have sought your precepts.
95 The wicked lie in wait to destroy me,
but I consider your decrees.
96 I have seen a limit to all perfection,
but your commandment is
exceedingly broad.

97 Oh, how I love your law!
It is my meditation all day long.
98 Your commandment makes me wiser
than my enemies,
for it is always with me.
99 I have more understanding than all
my teachers,
for your decrees are my meditation.
100 I understand more than the aged,
for I keep your precepts.
101 I hold back my feet from every evil
way,
in order to keep your word.
102 I do not turn away from your
ordinances,
for you have taught me.
103 How sweet are your words to my
taste,
sweeter than honey to my mouth!
104 Through your precepts I get
understanding;
therefore I hate every false way.

105 Your word is a lamp to my feet
and a light to my path.
106 I have sworn an oath and
confirmed it,
to observe your righteous
ordinances.
107 I am severely afflicted;
give me life, O LORD, according to
your word.
108 Accept my offerings of praise,
O LORD,
and teach me your ordinances.
109 I hold my life in my hand continually,
but I do not forget your law.
110 The wicked have laid a snare for me,
but I do not stray from your
precepts.
111 Your decrees are my heritage forever;
they are the joy of my heart.
112 I incline my heart to perform your
statutes
forever, to the end.

113 I hate the double-minded,
but I love your law.

(vv. 89–96), the mood changes from grief and fear to security and life in obedience to divine law. **96:** A *broad* commandment connotes safety and security (Ps 118.5). **97:** Ps 1.2. **103:** For God's words as food, cf. Deut 8.3; Ps 19.10; Ezek 3.3. **121:** *What is just and right,* social justice. **135:** God's shining face is the

114 You are my hiding place and my shield;
I hope in your word.
115 Go away from me, you evildoers,
that I may keep the commandments of my God.
116 Uphold me according to your promise, that I may live,
and let me not be put to shame in my hope.
117 Hold me up, that I may be safe
and have regard for your statutes continually.
118 You spurn all who go astray from your statutes;
for their cunning is in vain.
119 All the wicked of the earth you count as dross;
therefore I love your decrees.
120 My flesh trembles for fear of you,
and I am afraid of your judgments.

121 I have done what is just and right;
do not leave me to my oppressors.
122 Guarantee your servant's well-being;
do not let the godless oppress me.
123 My eyes fail from watching for your salvation,
and for the fulfillment of your righteous promise.
124 Deal with your servant according to your steadfast love,
and teach me your statutes.
125 I am your servant; give me understanding,
so that I may know your decrees.
126 It is time for the LORD to act,
for your law has been broken.
127 Truly I love your commandments
more than gold, more than fine gold.
128 Truly I direct my steps by all your precepts;[a]
I hate every false way.

129 Your decrees are wonderful;
therefore my soul keeps them.
130 The unfolding of your words gives light;
it imparts understanding to the simple.
131 With open mouth I pant,
because I long for your commandments.
132 Turn to me and be gracious to me,
as is your custom toward those who love your name.
133 Keep my steps steady according to your promise,
and never let iniquity have dominion over me.
134 Redeem me from human oppression,
that I may keep your precepts.
135 Make your face shine upon your servant,
and teach me your statutes.
136 My eyes shed streams of tears
because your law is not kept.

137 You are righteous, O LORD,
and your judgments are right.
138 You have appointed your decrees in righteousness
and in all faithfulness.
139 My zeal consumes me
because my foes forget your words.
140 Your promise is well tried,
and your servant loves it.
141 I am small and despised,
yet I do not forget your precepts.
142 Your righteousness is an everlasting righteousness,
and your law is the truth.
143 Trouble and anguish have come upon me,
but your commandments are my delight.
144 Your decrees are righteous forever;
give me understanding that I may live.

a Gk Jerome: Meaning of Heb uncertain

visible expression of divine joy and benevolence; see Ps 4.6; Num 6.24–26. **137:** The parallelism between *LORD* and *judgments* typifies this psalm: God's law is the major vehicle of divine revelation. **175:** Only

145 With my whole heart I cry; answer
me, O LORD.
I will keep your statutes.
146 I cry to you; save me,
that I may observe your decrees.
147 I rise before dawn and cry for help;
I put my hope in your words.
148 My eyes are awake before each watch
of the night,
that I may meditate on your
promise.
149 In your steadfast love hear my voice;
O LORD, in your justice preserve
my life.
150 Those who persecute me with evil
purpose draw near;
they are far from your law.
151 Yet you are near, O LORD,
and all your commandments
are true.
152 Long ago I learned from your decrees
that you have established them
forever.

153 Look on my misery and rescue me,
for I do not forget your law.
154 Plead my cause and redeem me;
give me life according to your
promise.
155 Salvation is far from the wicked,
for they do not seek your statutes.
156 Great is your mercy, O LORD;
give me life according to your
justice.
157 Many are my persecutors and my
adversaries,
yet I do not swerve from your
decrees.
158 I look at the faithless with disgust,
because they do not keep your
commands.
159 Consider how I love your precepts;
preserve my life according to your
steadfast love.
160 The sum of your word is truth;
and every one of your righteous
ordinances endures forever.

161 Princes persecute me without cause,
but my heart stands in awe of your
words.
162 I rejoice at your word
like one who finds great spoil.
163 I hate and abhor falsehood,
but I love your law.
164 Seven times a day I praise you
for your righteous ordinances.
165 Great peace have those who love
your law;
nothing can make them stumble.
166 I hope for your salvation, O LORD,
and I fulfill your commandments.
167 My soul keeps your decrees;
I love them exceedingly.
168 I keep your precepts and decrees,
for all my ways are before you.

169 Let my cry come before you,
O LORD;
give me understanding according to
your word.
170 Let my supplication come before you;
deliver me according to your
promise.
171 My lips will pour forth praise,
because you teach me your statutes.
172 My tongue will sing of your promise,
for all your commandments are
right.
173 Let your hand be ready to help me,
for I have chosen your precepts.
174 I long for your salvation, O LORD,
and your law is my delight.
175 Let me live that I may praise you,
and let your ordinances help me.
176 I have gone astray like a lost sheep;
seek out your servant,
for I do not forget your
commandments.

PSALM 120

A Song of Ascents.

1 In my distress I cry to the LORD,
that he may answer me:

the living can praise God (Isa 38.18–19; Ps 114.17–18); Sheol, the abode of the dead, is a place of silence (Ps 94.17). **176:** For the exiles like *lost sheep* searched for by God, see Jer 50.6; Ezek 34.2–5,15–16.

Ps 120: Prayer for deliverance from enemies. Ps 120–134 form a collection within the Psalter, the

2 "Deliver me, O LORD,
from lying lips,
from a deceitful tongue."

3 What shall be given to you?
And what more shall be done
to you,
you deceitful tongue?
4 A warrior's sharp arrows,
with glowing coals of the broom
tree!

5 Woe is me, that I am an alien in
Meshech,
that I must live among the tents of
Kedar.
6 Too long have I had my dwelling
among those who hate peace.
7 I am for peace;
but when I speak,
they are for war.

PSALM 121

A Song of Ascents.

1 I lift up my eyes to the hills—
from where will my help come?
2 My help comes from the LORD,
who made heaven and earth.

3 He will not let your foot be moved;
he who keeps you will not slumber.
4 He who keeps Israel
will neither slumber nor sleep.

5 The LORD is your keeper;
the LORD is your shade at your
right hand.
6 The sun shall not strike you by day,
nor the moon by night.

7 The LORD will keep you from all
evil;
he will keep your life.
8 The LORD will keep
your going out and your coming in
from this time on and forevermore.

PSALM 122

A Song of Ascents. Of David.

1 I was glad when they said to me,
"Let us go to the house of the
LORD!"
2 Our feet are standing
within your gates, O Jerusalem.

3 Jerusalem—built as a city
that is bound firmly together.
4 To it the tribes go up,
the tribes of the LORD,
as was decreed for Israel,

"ascent psalms," so designated from their common heading, "A Song of Ascents" (perhaps songs for those going up to Jerusalem on pilgrimage). Ps 120 is the lament of a Diaspora Jew; note how vv. 2–7 end with terms of distress and adversity. **2–4:** The comparison of harmful speech with weapons is common (Ps 52.2–4; 55.21; 57.4). **5:** *Meshech* in the far north (Ezek 38.2) and *Kedar* in the far south (Isa 21.13–17) represent the totality of the hostile, bellicose nations of the Diaspora and its geographical limits. **6–7:** *Peace* is a recurring theme in this collection (Ps 122.6–8; 125.5; 128.6), and the psalmist's enemies are haters of peace. There may be a purposeful double meaning here, since the text could also be read as "those who hate Salem (i.e., Jerusalem)"; cf. "all who hate Zion" in Ps 129.5.

Ps 121: On pilgrimage to Jerusalem. *Ascents,* see Ps 120n. A psalm of trust, a dialogue between a pilgrim to Jerusalem (vv. 1–2) and a responding priest (vv. 3–8). Cf. Ps 15; 24.3–4. **1–2:** The LORD is the psalmist's savior (*my help*) and the creator (Ps 124.8; 134.3). **3–8:** The pilgrimage replicates the Exodus journey (Isa 49.8–11). The verb "to guard," or *keep* (six times in Ps 121), is used of the Exodus in Ex 23.20; Josh 24.17. **5–6:** God offers *shade* in the Middle Eastern *sun; moon* is used as a formal poetic parallel to sun, although according to some ancient views, exposure to the moon was also harmful (cf. Mt 17.15, Gk). **8:** An expression for constant protection; perhaps also an allusion to the Exodus (*going out* from Egypt, *coming in* to the land.).

Ps 122: Praise of Zion. *Ascents,* see Ps 120n. A psalm celebrating Jerusalem, the goal of the pilgrimage. **1:** *The house of the LORD*, the Jerusalem Temple (v. 9). For the invitation (*Let us go*) to the pilgrimage, see Isa 2.3; Jer 31.6. **3:** The impressive appearance of Jerusalem (Ps 48.3,12–14). **5:** For royal acts of

to give thanks to the name of
the LORD.
5 For there the thrones for judgment
were set up,
the thrones of the house of David.

6 Pray for the peace of Jerusalem:
"May they prosper who love you.
7 Peace be within your walls,
and security within your towers."
8 For the sake of my relatives and
friends
I will say, "Peace be within you."
9 For the sake of the house of the
LORD our God,
I will seek your good.

PSALM 123

A Song of Ascents.

1 To you I lift up my eyes,
O you who are enthroned in the
heavens!
2 As the eyes of servants
look to the hand of their master,
as the eyes of a maid
to the hand of her mistress,
so our eyes look to the LORD
our God,
until he has mercy upon us.

3 Have mercy upon us, O LORD, have
mercy upon us,
for we have had more than enough
of contempt.
4 Our soul has had more than its fill
of the scorn of those who are
at ease,
of the contempt of the proud.

PSALM 124

A Song of Ascents. Of David.

1 If it had not been the LORD who was
on our side
—let Israel now say—
2 if it had not been the LORD who was
on our side,
when our enemies attacked us,
3 then they would have swallowed us
up alive,
when their anger was kindled
against us;
4 then the flood would have swept us
away,
the torrent would have gone
over us;
5 then over us would have gone
the raging waters.

6 Blessed be the LORD,
who has not given us
as prey to their teeth.
7 We have escaped like a bird
from the snare of the fowlers;
the snare is broken,
and we have escaped.

8 Our help is in the name of the LORD,
who made heaven and earth.

judgment in Jerusalem, see 1 Kings 7.7; Isa 16.5; Jer 21.12; 22.16; cf. Isa 2.4. **6–9:** Prayer for Jerusalem and its peace; the theme of the destruction of weapons of enemies occurs in Ps 46.9; 76.3 (Zion hymns). **6:** *Jerusalem . . . who love you,* the antonym of "all who hate Zion" (129.5). **9:** Closing as it opens (an inclusio), with reference to the Temple (*the house of the* LORD).

Ps 123: Prayer for deliverance from enemies. *Ascents,* see Ps 120n. A lament, composed of an invocation to the divine king (v. 1), a threefold appeal for mercy (vv. 2–3), and the psalmist's oppression by enemies (v. 4). **1–2:** As servant of the divine king (Ps 5.2; 44.4; 86.16n.), the psalmist prays for rescue from oppression. **3–4:** The psalmist's opponents are the wealthy (*at ease*) and the arrogant.

Ps 124: Thanksgiving for national deliverance. *Ascents,* see Ps 120n. A highly structured ("If it had not been . . . then") communal thanksgiving, hymning Israel's escape from the engulfing cosmic waters. **2–5:** The attacking enemy can be metaphorically described as chaotic *waters* (Isa 8.7–8). For being *swallowed . . . alive* and descending into Sheol, the abode of the dead, see Num 16.31–34; Ps 69.15; Prov 1.11. **6–7:** The created order includes in ascending order the subterranean waters, the earth (habitat for predatory land animals), and the heavens (for birds). **8:** The LORD is creator, victorious over the chaotic waters (Ps 89.9–11; 93.1–4).

PSALM 125

A Song of Ascents.

1 Those who trust in the LORD are like
Mount Zion,
which cannot be moved, but abides
forever.
2 As the mountains surround Jerusalem,
so the LORD surrounds his people,
from this time on and forevermore.
3 For the scepter of wickedness shall
not rest
on the land allotted to the
righteous,
so that the righteous might not stretch
out
their hands to do wrong.
4 Do good, O LORD, to those who are
good,
and to those who are upright in
their hearts.
5 But those who turn aside to their own
crooked ways
the LORD will lead away with
evildoers.
Peace be upon Israel!

PSALM 126

A Song of Ascents.

1 When the LORD restored the fortunes
of Zion,[a]
we were like those who dream.
2 Then our mouth was filled with
laughter,
and our tongue with shouts of joy;
then it was said among the nations,
"The LORD has done great things
for them."
3 The LORD has done great things
for us,
and we rejoiced.

4 Restore our fortunes, O LORD,
like the watercourses in the Negeb.
5 May those who sow in tears
reap with shouts of joy.
6 Those who go out weeping,
bearing the seed for sowing,
shall come home with shouts of joy,
carrying their sheaves.

PSALM 127

A Song of Ascents. Of Solomon.

1 Unless the LORD builds the house,
those who build it labor in vain.
Unless the LORD guards the city,
the guard keeps watch in vain.
2 It is in vain that you rise up early
and go late to rest,

a Or *brought back those who returned to Zion*

Ps 125: A psalm of trust. *Ascents,* see Ps 120n. Ps 125 eludes exact categorization, having connections with psalms of trust and the Zion hymns (vv. 1–2). **1–2:** The LORD protects those who trust in him as he protects Jerusalem (*Zion*) with its topography. **3:** *The scepter of wickedness,* perhaps referring to the harsh foreign domination of Israel in the exilic or postexilic period. The psalmist prays that the righteous, deprived of land and resources, not be forced into wrongdoing for survival. **5:** Appropriate retribution for the upright and the evildoers.

Ps 126: Thanksgiving from returning exiles. *Ascents,* see Ps 120n. A thanksgiving psalm and a petition that may reflect the sixth-century BCE return from exile, imaged as a new Exodus. **1–3:** The joy of the return to Jerusalem (*Zion*) from exile, the LORD's redemptive act witnessed by the nations (Ps 96.10), who acknowledge God as Israel's savior (117.1–2). **4–6:** Petition for abundant winter rains, even in the relatively arid *Negeb* in the south, and a good harvest after the return to the land (Ps 67.6), also used here as a metaphor for national restoration.

Ps 127: The blessings of family life. *Ascents,* see Ps 120n. Ps 127–128 form a pair of poems with wisdom characteristics and shared themes (human labor and family life). Ps 127 also has royal and dynastic concerns, as the heading *Of Solomon* (cf. Ps 72) indicates. **1–2:** The futility of human labor apart from the LORD. *House,* referring both to the family's dwelling place and to the Davidic dynasty upheld by God (2 Sam 7.13–16). **2:** *Beloved,* recalling Solomon's birth name, Jedidiah ("Beloved of the LORD"; 2 Sam

eating the bread of anxious toil;
for he gives sleep to his beloved.[a]

3 Sons are indeed a heritage from the LORD,
the fruit of the womb a reward.
4 Like arrows in the hand of a warrior
are the sons of one's youth.
5 Happy is the man who has
his quiver full of them.
He shall not be put to shame
when he speaks with his enemies in the gate.

PSALM 128

A Song of Ascents.

1 Happy is everyone who fears the LORD,
who walks in his ways.
2 You shall eat the fruit of the labor of your hands;
you shall be happy, and it shall go well with you.

3 Your wife will be like a fruitful vine
within your house;
your children will be like olive shoots
around your table.
4 Thus shall the man be blessed
who fears the LORD.

5 The LORD bless you from Zion.
May you see the prosperity of Jerusalem
all the days of your life.
6 May you see your children's children.
Peace be upon Israel!

PSALM 129

A Song of Ascents.

1 "Often have they attacked me from my youth"
—let Israel now say—
2 "often have they attacked me from my youth,
yet they have not prevailed against me.
3 The plowers plowed on my back;
they made their furrows long."
4 The LORD is righteous;
he has cut the cords of the wicked.
5 May all who hate Zion
be put to shame and turned backward.
6 Let them be like the grass on the housetops
that withers before it grows up,
7 with which reapers do not fill their hands
or binders of sheaves their arms,
8 while those who pass by do not say,
"The blessing of the LORD be upon you!
We bless you in the name of the LORD!"

PSALM 130

A Song of Ascents.

1 Out of the depths I cry to you,
O LORD.
2 Lord, hear my voice!

a Or *for he provides for his beloved during sleep*

12.25). **3–6:** The happiness of a father blessed with a large family. **5:** *In the gate,* in public or civic affairs. *The gate* also recalls the architectural imagery of the psalm's opening.

Ps 128: The blessings of family life. *Ascents,* see Ps 120n. **1:** *Happy,* Ps 128 begins as Ps 127 ends. Fear of the LORD and right conduct are wisdom themes (v. 4). **2–3:** A picture of ideal family life from a man's perspective (abundant food, wife, and children). **5–6:** A petition for the divine blessings of prosperity, progeny, and long life. The psalm ends like Ps 122; 125, with a prayer for Jerusalem's peace.

Ps 129: Prayer for deliverance from enemies. *Ascents,* see Ps 120n. A communal psalm of trust with a closing petition. The psalmist sees the haters of Zion to be as ephemeral as withering grass. In general, agricultural imagery unifies this psalm. **1:** See Ps 124.1. **2:** *From my youth,* the nation's oppressive slavery in Egypt (Jer 2.3; Hos 11.1). **5:** Prayer that national foes (*all who hate Zion*) be defeated. **6:** See 2 Kings 19.26; Isa 37.27.

Ps 130: A cry from the depths. *Ascents,* see Ps 120n. An individual lament, one of the penitential psalms (see Ps 6n.), in which the psalmist invokes God as a fundamentally forgiving deity. **1–3:** About to be

Let your ears be attentive
to the voice of my supplications!

3 If you, O LORD, should mark
iniquities,
Lord, who could stand?
4 But there is forgiveness with you,
so that you may be revered.

5 I wait for the LORD, my soul waits,
and in his word I hope;
6 my soul waits for the Lord
more than those who watch for the
morning,
more than those who watch for the
morning.

7 O Israel, hope in the LORD!
For with the LORD there is
steadfast love,
and with him is great power to
redeem.
8 It is he who will redeem Israel
from all its iniquities.

PSALM 131

A Song of Ascents. Of David.

1 O LORD, my heart is not lifted up,
my eyes are not raised too high;
I do not occupy myself with things
too great and too marvelous
for me.
2 But I have calmed and quieted
my soul,
like a weaned child with its mother;
my soul is like the weaned child
that is with me.[a]

3 O Israel, hope in the LORD
from this time on and forevermore.

PSALM 132

A Song of Ascents.

1 O LORD, remember in David's favor
all the hardships he endured;
2 how he swore to the LORD
and vowed to the Mighty One of
Jacob,
3 "I will not enter my house
or get into my bed;
4 I will not give sleep to my eyes
or slumber to my eyelids,
5 until I find a place for the LORD,
a dwelling place for the Mighty
One of Jacob."

6 We heard of it in Ephrathah;
we found it in the fields of Jaar.
7 "Let us go to his dwelling place;
let us worship at his footstool."

8 Rise up, O LORD, and go to your
resting place,
you and the ark of your might.

a Or *my soul within me is like a weaned child*

overwhelmed by the chaotic waters (*the depths*) and without a secure foothold, the psalmist cries out to the LORD (Ps 69.1–3). **4:** 1 Kings 8.39–40 similarly links forgiveness and fear of God. **5–6:** The psalmist prays through the night for divine help in the morning (Ps 59.16; 90.14). **7–8:** The psalmist moves outside himself, to a prayer for the community's redemption.

Ps 131: A prayer of humble trust. *Ascents,* see Ps 120n. A psalm of trust, perhaps composed by a woman. **1:** A negative confession (Ps 15.3). **2:** A rare feminine image in the Psalter. **3:** As in the previous psalm, the conclusion moves from the individual to the community.

Ps 132: The LORD's choice of David and Zion. *Ascents,* see Ps 120n. A royal psalm, recalling the divine choice of the Davidic dynasty (vv. 11–12,17–18) and of Jerusalem as God's residence (vv. 13–16); vv. 8–10 are quoted in 1 Chr 6.41–42. **1–5:** A prayer for David, recalling in a lengthy poetic form his oath to provide a suitable dwelling place for the LORD (2 Sam 7.2), *the Mighty One of Jacob* (vv. 2,5; Gen 49.24; Isa 1.24; 49.26). **6–8:** Allusion to the ark narrative (1 Sam 7; 2 Sam 6), in a ritual reenactment of David's transport to Jerusalem of the ark of the covenant, sign of divine presence and *footstool* of the invisible enthroned deity (2 Sam 6.2). **6:** *Ephrathah,* near Bethlehem, in Judah (1 Chr 4.4; Mic 5.2). *Jaar,* an alternate name for Kiriath-jearim (1 Sam 7.1–2; 2 Chr 1.4). **8:** Cf. Num 10.35–36. **11–12:** The

9 Let your priests be clothed with
righteousness,
and let your faithful shout for
joy.
10 For your servant David's sake
do not turn away the face of your
anointed one.

11 The LORD swore to David a sure
oath
from which he will not turn back:
"One of the sons of your body
I will set on your throne.
12 If your sons keep my covenant
and my decrees that I shall teach
them,
their sons also, forevermore,
shall sit on your throne."

13 For the LORD has chosen Zion;
he has desired it for his habitation:
14 "This is my resting place forever;
here I will reside, for I have desired
it.
15 I will abundantly bless its provisions;
I will satisfy its poor with bread.
16 Its priests I will clothe with salvation,
and its faithful will shout for joy.
17 There I will cause a horn to sprout up
for David;
I have prepared a lamp for my
anointed one.
18 His enemies I will clothe with
disgrace,
but on him, his crown will gleam."

PSALM 133

A Song of Ascents.

1 How very good and pleasant it is
when kindred live together in unity!
2 It is like the precious oil on the head,
running down upon the beard,
on the beard of Aaron,
running down over the collar of his
robes.
3 It is like the dew of Hermon,
which falls on the mountains of
Zion.
For there the LORD ordained his
blessing,
life forevermore.

PSALM 134

A Song of Ascents.

1 Come, bless the LORD, all you
servants of the LORD,
who stand by night in the house of
the LORD!
2 Lift up your hands to the holy place,
and bless the LORD.

3 May the LORD, maker of heaven and
earth,
bless you from Zion.

PSALM 135

1 Praise the LORD!
Praise the name of the LORD;

LORD's oath to David, a promise of a dynasty conditional upon the obedience of David's descendants (1 Kings 8.25; 9.4; cf. 2 Sam 7.13–16; Ps 89.28–37). **15:** The ritual concludes with a festal meal (1 Kings 8.62–65). **17–18:** David's might (*horn*) defeats his enemies. *Lamp,* cf. 2 Sam 21.17.

Ps 133: Prayer for national unity. *Ascents,* see Ps 120n. A psalm expressing hope for the reunification of the Northern and Southern Kingdoms, with Jerusalem as capital and a descendant of David as king. **2:** The allusion to royal anointing (1 Sam 16.3) and to Aaron as priest of a reunified worship brings together the two themes of Ps 132, the divine choice of king and Temple. **3:** The hoped-for reunification is symbolized by the linkage of Mount *Hermon* in the far North and *Zion* (Jerusalem) in the South.

Ps 134: A doxology. *Ascents,* see Ps 120n. The doxological conclusion to the ascent psalms. **1–2:** Servants in the house of the LORD are priests (Ps 132.9,16; 133.2). **2:** *Lift up your hands,* a gesture of prayer (1 Kings 8.38; Ps 28.2) **3:** Possibly the text of this priestly blessing (see Ps 124.8; 128.5). *Zion,* Jerusalem.

Ps 135: A hymn of praise. An anthological psalm of praise made up of quotations and paraphrases of other biblical texts. Like Ps 136, Ps 135 moves from creation to Exodus to landtaking. Despite its anthological nature, it is tightly structured, opening with calls to "Praise the LORD" and closing with calls

give praise, O servants of
the LORD,
2 you that stand in the house of
the LORD,
in the courts of the house of
our God.
3 Praise the LORD, for the LORD
is good;
sing to his name, for he is gracious.
4 For the LORD has chosen Jacob for
himself,
Israel as his own possession.

5 For I know that the LORD is great;
our Lord is above all gods.
6 Whatever the LORD pleases he does,
in heaven and on earth,
in the seas and all deeps.
7 He it is who makes the clouds rise at
the end of the earth;
he makes lightnings for the rain
and brings out the wind from his
storehouses.

8 He it was who struck down the
firstborn of Egypt,
both human beings and animals;
9 he sent signs and wonders
into your midst, O Egypt,
against Pharaoh and all his
servants.
10 He struck down many nations
and killed mighty kings—
11 Sihon, king of the Amorites,
and Og, king of Bashan,
and all the kingdoms of
Canaan—
12 and gave their land as a heritage,
a heritage to his people Israel.

13 Your name, O LORD, endures forever,
your renown, O LORD, throughout
all ages.
14 For the LORD will vindicate his
people,
and have compassion on his
servants.

15 The idols of the nations are silver and
gold,
the work of human hands.
16 They have mouths, but they do not
speak;
they have eyes, but they do not see;
17 they have ears, but they do not hear,
and there is no breath in their
mouths.
18 Those who make them
and all who trust them
shall become like them.

19 O house of Israel, bless the LORD!
O house of Aaron, bless the LORD!
20 O house of Levi, bless the LORD!
You that fear the LORD, bless
the LORD!
21 Blessed be the LORD from Zion,
he who resides in Jerusalem.
Praise the LORD!

PSALM 136

1 O give thanks to the LORD, for he is
good,
for his steadfast love endures
forever.
2 O give thanks to the God of gods,
for his steadfast love endures
forever.
3 O give thanks to the Lord of lords,
for his steadfast love endures
forever;

to "Bless the LORD." **1–2:** See Ps 113.1; 134.1–2. **5:** The LORD's supremacy over other gods (Ps 29.1; 96.11). **6–7:** Creation (Ps 115.3; Jer 10.13). **8–12:** From the Exodus to the entrance into the land, an abbreviated paraphrase of Ps 136.10–22. **15–20:** Repeats Ps 115.4–11 with slight alterations. **21:** Cf. Ps 128.5; 134.3.

Ps 136: Praise of God, creator and redeemer. A hymn of praise recounting the acts of God, from creation (vv. 5–9) to the Exodus (vv. 10–16) to the battles for the possession of the land (vv. 17–22). As in some other summaries (Deut 26.5–9; Josh 24.2–13), there is no mention of revelation on Sinai. There is a repeated refrain (Ps 118.1–4). **5:** For the connection of wisdom and creation, see Prov 3.19–20. **7–9:**

4 who alone does great wonders,
for his steadfast love endures
forever;
5 who by understanding made the
heavens,
for his steadfast love endures
forever;
6 who spread out the earth on the
waters,
for his steadfast love endures
forever;
7 who made the great lights,
for his steadfast love endures
forever;
8 the sun to rule over the day,
for his steadfast love endures
forever;
9 the moon and stars to rule over
the night,
for his steadfast love endures
forever;

10 who struck Egypt through their
firstborn,
for his steadfast love endures
forever;
11 and brought Israel out from among
them,
for his steadfast love endures
forever;
12 with a strong hand and an
outstretched arm,
for his steadfast love endures
forever;
13 who divided the Red Sea[a] in two,
for his steadfast love endures
forever;
14 and made Israel pass through the
midst of it,
for his steadfast love endures
forever;
15 but overthrew Pharaoh and his army
in the Red Sea,[a]
for his steadfast love endures
forever;
16 who led his people through the
wilderness,
for his steadfast love endures
forever;
17 who struck down great kings,
for his steadfast love endures
forever;
18 and killed famous kings,
for his steadfast love endures
forever;
19 Sihon, king of the Amorites,
for his steadfast love endures
forever;
20 and Og, king of Bashan,
for his steadfast love endures
forever;
21 and gave their land as a heritage,
for his steadfast love endures
forever;
22 a heritage to his servant Israel,
for his steadfast love endures
forever.

23 It is he who remembered us in our
low estate,
for his steadfast love endures
forever;
24 and rescued us from our foes,
for his steadfast love endures
forever;
25 who gives food to all flesh,
for his steadfast love endures
forever.

26 O give thanks to the God of heaven,
for his steadfast love endures
forever.

a Or *Sea of Reeds*

See Gen 1.16. **12:** A Deuteronomic expression, used especially of the Exodus (Deut 4.34; 5.15; 7.19). **19–20:** *Sihon . . . and Og,* Num 21.21–35. **23–25:** A summary of the Exodus theme: God *remembered* the people (Ex 2.24), delivered them (Ex 14–15), and fed them with heavenly bread (Ex 16.4,15). **26:** Returning to the psalm's beginning: The implication of these divine activities is to *give thanks to . . . God.*

PSALM 137

1 By the rivers of Babylon—
there we sat down and there we wept
when we remembered Zion.
2 On the willows[a] there
we hung up our harps.
3 For there our captors
asked us for songs,
and our tormentors asked for mirth, saying,
"Sing us one of the songs of Zion!"

4 How could we sing the LORD's song
in a foreign land?
5 If I forget you, O Jerusalem,
let my right hand wither!
6 Let my tongue cling to the roof of my mouth,
if I do not remember you,
if I do not set Jerusalem
above my highest joy.

7 Remember, O LORD, against the Edomites
the day of Jerusalem's fall,
how they said, "Tear it down! Tear it down!
Down to its foundations!"
8 O daughter Babylon, you devastator![b]
Happy shall they be who pay you back
what you have done to us!
9 Happy shall they be who take your little ones
and dash them against the rock!

PSALM 138

Of David.

1 I give you thanks, O LORD, with my whole heart;
before the gods I sing your praise;
2 I bow down toward your holy temple
and give thanks to your name for your steadfast love and your faithfulness;
for you have exalted your name and your word
above everything.[c]
3 On the day I called, you answered me,
you increased my strength of soul.[d]

4 All the kings of the earth shall praise you, O LORD,
for they have heard the words of your mouth.
5 They shall sing of the ways of the LORD,
for great is the glory of the LORD.
6 For though the LORD is high, he regards the lowly;
but the haughty he perceives from far away.

7 Though I walk in the midst of trouble,
you preserve me against the wrath of my enemies;

a Or *poplars* *b* Or *you who are devastated*
c Cn: Heb *you have exalted your word above all your name* *d* Syr Compare Gk Tg: Heb *you made me arrogant in my soul with strength*

Ps 137: Remembering Zion. A lament from the exilic or postexilic era, as the references to the Babylonian captivity attest (vv. 1,2,4,8). Two compositions (1–6,7–9) may be combined here. **2–4:** Exile is equivalent to descent into the world of the dead; like the dead, the exiles are unable to praise God (Ps 30.9; 88.11–13). Alternatively, God can only be praised at a Temple in Israel. **3:** *Songs of Zion,* possibly the Zion hymns (Ps 46; 48) or the pilgrimage psalms (Ps 84; 120–134). **5–6:** The paralysis of the *right hand* and *tongue* make it impossible to play the lyre and sing. **7:** The Edomites, who joined Babylon in the attack on Jerusalem (Obad 11–14) are cursed. **8–9:** Though anti-Babylonian sentiments are found elsewhere (e.g., Jer 50–51; Lam 4.21), none are as vividly compact as this.

Ps 138: Thanksgiving in the Temple. Ps 138 is the first of a collection of hymns (Ps 138–145) that concludes the Psalter. **1:** The LORD, supreme in the divine council (Ps 82; 89.6–7; 95.2). **2:** In Deuteronomic theology, the name of the LORD resides in the Temple (Deut 12.11). **4–5:** Like the gods, human kings praise the LORD; cf. Ps 67.3–5; 126.2. **7–8:** See Ps 23.4; *the work of your hands,* creation and deliverance (*your hand . . . your right hand* in v. 7).

you stretch out your hand,
and your right hand delivers me.
8 The LORD will fulfill his purpose
for me;
your steadfast love, O LORD,
endures forever.
Do not forsake the work of your
hands.

PSALM 139

To the leader. Of David. A Psalm.

1 O LORD, you have searched me and
known me.
2 You know when I sit down and when
I rise up;
you discern my thoughts from
far away.
3 You search out my path and my lying
down,
and are acquainted with all my ways.
4 Even before a word is on my tongue,
O LORD, you know it completely.
5 You hem me in, behind and before,
and lay your hand upon me.
6 Such knowledge is too wonderful for
me;
it is so high that I cannot attain it.

7 Where can I go from your spirit?
Or where can I flee from your
presence?
8 If I ascend to heaven, you are there;
if I make my bed in Sheol, you are
there.
9 If I take the wings of the morning
and settle at the farthest limits of
the sea,
10 even there your hand shall lead me,
and your right hand shall hold me
fast.
11 If I say, "Surely the darkness shall
cover me,
and the light around me become
night,"
12 even the darkness is not dark to you;
the night is as bright as the day,
for darkness is as light to you.

13 For it was you who formed my
inward parts;
you knit me together in my
mother's womb.
14 I praise you, for I am fearfully and
wonderfully made.
Wonderful are your works;
that I know very well.
15 My frame was not hidden from
you,
when I was being made in secret,
intricately woven in the depths of
the earth.
16 Your eyes beheld my unformed
substance.
In your book were written
all the days that were formed
for me,
when none of them as yet existed.
17 How weighty to me are your
thoughts, O God!
How vast is the sum of them!
18 I try to count them—they are more
than the sand;
I come to the end[a]—I am still with
you.

19 O that you would kill the wicked,
O God,
and that the bloodthirsty would
depart from me—

a Or *I awake*

Ps 139: Prayer for deliverance from enemies. An individual lament, with connections to wisdom. The text is difficult in vv. 6,14–15,18. The psalm has two parts: vv. 1–18 (praise of God's wonders) and vv. 19–24 (prayer for the destruction of the wicked). The first part serves as an invocation of God and his attributes, calling God to action in vv. 19–24. **1–18:** The most detailed and poetic description of divine omniscience in the Bible. **2:** *Sit down . . . rise up,* an expression comprising the whole of one's life and activity (Deut 6.7). **5:** The hand of the LORD is an expression for divine control and assistance (v. 10). **8:** *Sheol,* the abode of the dead. **11–12:** *Darkness,* characteristic of Sheol, is overcome by God. **13–16:** The mysterious process of creation. **16:** Cf. Job 14.5; Jer 1.5. **17–18:** The unknowable thoughts of God (Isa 55.8–9; cf. Rom 11.33). **21–22:** An oath confirming the psalmist's solidarity with God. **23–24:** A

20 those who speak of you maliciously,
and lift themselves up against you
for evil![a]
21 Do I not hate those who hate you,
O LORD?
And do I not loathe those who rise
up against you?
22 I hate them with perfect hatred;
I count them my enemies.
23 Search me, O God, and know my
heart;
test me and know my thoughts.
24 See if there is any wicked[b] way
in me,
and lead me in the way
everlasting.[c]

PSALM 140

To the leader. A Psalm of David.

1 Deliver me, O LORD, from
evildoers;
protect me from those who
are violent,
2 who plan evil things in their minds
and stir up wars continually.
3 They make their tongue sharp as a
snake's,
and under their lips is the venom of
vipers. *Selah*
4 Guard me, O LORD, from the hands
of the wicked;
protect me from the violent
who have planned my downfall.
5 The arrogant have hidden a trap for
me,
and with cords they have spread a
net,[d]
along the road they have set snares
for me. *Selah*
6 I say to the LORD, "You are my
God;
give ear, O LORD, to the voice
of my supplications."
7 O LORD, my Lord, my strong
deliverer,
you have covered my head in
the day of battle.
8 Do not grant, O LORD, the desires of
the wicked;
do not further their evil plot.[e]
Selah
9 Those who surround me lift up their
heads;[f]
let the mischief of their lips
overwhelm them!
10 Let burning coals fall on them!
Let them be flung into pits, no
more to rise!
11 Do not let the slanderer be established
in the land;
let evil speedily hunt down the
violent!
12 I know that the LORD maintains the
cause of the needy,
and executes justice for the poor.
13 Surely the righteous shall give thanks
to your name;
the upright shall live in your
presence.

a Cn: Meaning of Heb uncertain *b* Heb *hurtful* *c* Or *the ancient way.* Compare Jer 6.16 *d* Or *they have spread cords as a net* *e* Heb adds *they are exalted* *f* Cn Compare Gk: Heb *those who surround me are uplifted in head;* Heb divides verses 8 and 9 differently

return to the theme of omniscience: An omniscient God surely knows the psalmist's righteousness, and should thus save him from his enemies.

Ps 140: Prayer for deliverance from enemies. An individual lament. **3:** Sins of speech of the psalmist's foes (v. 11). For the metaphor of *tongue* and *venom* used of damaging speech, see Ps 57.4; 58.4–6. *Selah* (also vv. 5,8), see Ps 3.2n. **4–5:** The psalmist is hunted down by his foes, who mean to send him to Sheol (*downfall*), the abode of the dead. **9–11:** Three instances of the law of equivalent retribution: Evildoers are overcome by their own venom (v. 3), are cast into Sheol (v. 4), and are themselves hunted down (v. 5). **12–13:** The psalmist's assurance of divine justice.

PSALM 141

A Psalm of David.

1 I call upon you, O LORD; come
quickly to me;
give ear to my voice when I call to
you.
2 Let my prayer be counted as incense
before you,
and the lifting up of my hands as
an evening sacrifice.

3 Set a guard over my mouth, O LORD;
keep watch over the door of
my lips.
4 Do not turn my heart to any evil,
to busy myself with wicked deeds
in company with those who work
iniquity;
do not let me eat of their delicacies.

5 Let the righteous strike me;
let the faithful correct me.
Never let the oil of the wicked anoint
my head,[a]
for my prayer is continually[b]
against their wicked deeds.
6 When they are given over to those
who shall condemn them,
then they shall learn that my words
were pleasant.
7 Like a rock that one breaks apart and
shatters on the land,
so shall their bones be strewn at the
mouth of Sheol.[c]

8 But my eyes are turned toward you,
O GOD, my Lord;
in you I seek refuge; do not leave
me defenseless.
9 Keep me from the trap that they have
laid for me,
and from the snares of evildoers.
10 Let the wicked fall into their
own nets,
while I alone escape.

PSALM 142

A Maskil of David. When he was in the cave. A Prayer.

1 With my voice I cry to the LORD;
with my voice I make supplication
to the LORD.
2 I pour out my complaint before him;
I tell my trouble before him.
3 When my spirit is faint,
you know my way.

In the path where I walk
they have hidden a trap for me.
4 Look on my right hand and see—
there is no one who takes notice of
me;
no refuge remains to me;
no one cares for me.

5 I cry to you, O LORD;
I say, "You are my refuge,
my portion in the land of the
living."
6 Give heed to my cry,
for I am brought very low.

Save me from my persecutors,
for they are too strong for me.
7 Bring me out of prison,
so that I may give thanks to your
name.

a Gk: Meaning of Heb uncertain *b* Cn: Heb *for continually and my prayer* *c* Meaning of Heb of verses 5-7 is uncertain

Ps 141: Prayer for deliverance from enemies. An individual lament; the text of vv. 5–7 is difficult. **2:** See Ps 134.1–2. **3–4:** Prayer that God will save the psalmist from sinful speech and from association with the wicked (Ps 1.1; 26.4). **7:** *Sheol,* the abode of the dead. **9–10:** Retribution: Planning to entrap the psalmist, the evildoers are themselves entrapped (Ps 35.7–8; 140.5).

Ps 142: Prayer for deliverance from enemies. An individual lament. *In the cave,* see Ps 57n. **3:** Ps 140.5; 141.9–10. **7:** *Prison,* a metaphor for Sheol, the abode of the dead, to which the psalmist's illness brought him near; healed and released from silent Sheol, the psalmist can once again praise God (Ps 30.3–4; 115.17–18).

The righteous will surround me,
for you will deal bountifully
with me.

PSALM 143

A Psalm of David.

1 Hear my prayer, O LORD;
give ear to my supplications in your
faithfulness;
answer me in your righteousness.
2 Do not enter into judgment with your
servant,
for no one living is righteous before
you.

3 For the enemy has pursued me,
crushing my life to the ground,
making me sit in darkness like
those long dead.
4 Therefore my spirit faints within me;
my heart within me is appalled.

5 I remember the days of old,
I think about all your deeds,
I meditate on the works of your
hands.
6 I stretch out my hands to you;
my soul thirsts for you like a
parched land. *Selah*

7 Answer me quickly, O LORD;
my spirit fails.
Do not hide your face from me,
or I shall be like those who go
down to the Pit.
8 Let me hear of your steadfast love in
the morning,
for in you I put my trust.
Teach me the way I should go,
for to you I lift up my soul.

9 Save me, O LORD, from my enemies;
I have fled to you for refuge.[a]
10 Teach me to do your will,
for you are my God.
Let your good spirit lead me
on a level path.

11 For your name's sake, O LORD,
preserve my life.
In your righteousness bring me out
of trouble.
12 In your steadfast love cut off my
enemies,
and destroy all my adversaries,
for I am your servant.

PSALM 144

Of David.

1 Blessed be the LORD, my rock,
who trains my hands for war, and
my fingers for battle;
2 my rock[b] and my fortress,
my stronghold and my deliverer,
my shield, in whom I take refuge,
who subdues the peoples[c]
under me.

3 O LORD, what are human beings that
you regard them,
or mortals that you think of them?
4 They are like a breath;

a One Heb Ms Gk: MT *to you I have hidden*
b With 18.2 and 2 Sam 22.2: Heb *my steadfast love*
c Heb Mss Syr Aquila Jerome: MT *my people*

Ps 143: Prayer for deliverance from enemies. A lament, the last of the penitential psalms (see Ps 6n.). **2–4:** Prayer for healing from mortal illness brought on by the psalmist's sin (Ps 32.3–5). **2:** *For no one living is righteous before you* is a typical biblical idea, also expressed by Job's friends (Job 4.17–21). **5–6:** See Ps 63.1; 77.11–12. **6:** *Selah,* see Ps 3.2n. **7:** *The Pit,* a poetic term for Sheol, the abode of the dead. **10:** *Your good spirit,* an expression for divine power, contrasted with the weakness of the psalmist (vv. 4,7). **11–12:** Since this psalmist believes in humanity's basic culpability (v. 2), he cannot protest his innocence or claim that God is angry or unfair; instead, he depends on God's care for his *name,* and on his *steadfast love.*

Ps 144: Royal prayer for deliverance. A royal lament (vv. 1–11) and a prayer for blessings on the people (vv. 12–15). **1–2:** The king as warrior (Ps 18.1–2). **3:** See Ps 8.4; Job 7.7,17. **4:** The transience of human life (Ps 39.5,7; 109.23). **5–7:** The king prays that the Divine Warrior will vanquish both cosmic (*mighty*

their days are like a passing
shadow.

5 Bow your heavens, O LORD, and
come down;
touch the mountains so that they
smoke.
6 Make the lightning flash and scatter
them;
send out your arrows and rout
them.
7 Stretch out your hand from on high;
set me free and rescue me from the
mighty waters,
from the hand of aliens,
8 whose mouths speak lies,
and whose right hands are false.

9 I will sing a new song to you, O God;
upon a ten-stringed harp I will play
to you,
10 the one who gives victory to kings,
who rescues his servant David.
11 Rescue me from the cruel sword,
and deliver me from the hand of
aliens,
whose mouths speak lies,
and whose right hands are false.

12 May our sons in their youth
be like plants full grown,
our daughters like corner pillars,
cut for the building of a palace.
13 May our barns be filled,
with produce of every kind;
may our sheep increase by thousands,
by tens of thousands in our fields,
14 and may our cattle be heavy with
young.
May there be no breach in the
walls,[a] no exile,
and no cry of distress in our streets.

15 Happy are the people to whom such
blessings fall;
happy are the people whose God is
the LORD.

PSALM 145

Praise. Of David.

1 I will extol you, my God and King,
and bless your name forever
and ever.
2 Every day I will bless you,
and praise your name forever
and ever.
3 Great is the LORD, and greatly to be
praised;
his greatness is unsearchable.

4 One generation shall laud your works
to another,
and shall declare your mighty acts.
5 On the glorious splendor of your
majesty,
and on your wondrous works, I
will meditate.
6 The might of your awesome deeds
shall be proclaimed,
and I will declare your greatness.
7 They shall celebrate the fame of your
abundant goodness,
and shall sing aloud of your
righteousness.

8 The LORD is gracious and merciful,
slow to anger and abounding in
steadfast love.
9 The LORD is good to all,
and his compassion is over all that
he has made.

10 All your works shall give thanks to
you, O LORD,

a Heb lacks *in the walls*

waters) and historical (*aliens*) foes. **9–10:** *David* is a poet and a musician, as well as a warrior (1 Sam 16.18; Ps 149.6). **12–14:** For the connection of the king and fertility, see Ps 72.6–7,17.

Ps 145: Praise of the divine king. A hymn in acrostic form (see Ps 9–10n.), focusing on the kingship of God. **1–2:** Eternal blessing of the divine name recurs in v. 21. **3:** See Ps 147.5. **5:** See Ps 77.12; 105.2; 119.27. **8:** The creed of Ex 34.6 (Ps 86.5). **11–13:** God's glorious and everlasting kingdom; Dan 4.3.

and all your faithful shall bless
you.
11 They shall speak of the glory of your
kingdom,
and tell of your power,
12 to make known to all people your[a]
mighty deeds,
and the glorious splendor of your[b]
kingdom.
13 Your kingdom is an everlasting
kingdom,
and your dominion endures
throughout all generations.

The LORD is faithful in all his words,
and gracious in all his deeds.[c]
14 The LORD upholds all who are
falling,
and raises up all who are bowed
down.
15 The eyes of all look to you,
and you give them their food in due
season.
16 You open your hand,
satisfying the desire of every living
thing.
17 The LORD is just in all his ways,
and kind in all his doings.
18 The LORD is near to all who call
on him,
to all who call on him in truth.
19 He fulfills the desire of all who
fear him;
he also hears their cry, and saves
them.
20 The LORD watches over all who
love him,
but all the wicked he will destroy.

21 My mouth will speak the praise of the
LORD,
and all flesh will bless his holy
name forever and ever.

PSALM 146

1 Praise the LORD!
Praise the LORD, O my soul!
2 I will praise the LORD as long as
I live;
I will sing praises to my God all my
life long.

3 Do not put your trust in princes,
in mortals, in whom there is no
help.
4 When their breath departs, they
return to the earth;
on that very day their plans perish.

5 Happy are those whose help is the
God of Jacob,
whose hope is in the LORD their
God,
6 who made heaven and earth,
the sea, and all that is in them;
who keeps faith forever;
7 who executes justice for the
oppressed;
who gives food to the hungry.

The LORD sets the prisoners free;
8 the LORD opens the eyes of
the blind.
The LORD lifts up those who are
bowed down;
the LORD loves the righteous.
9 The LORD watches over the strangers;
he upholds the orphan and the
widow,
but the way of the wicked he brings
to ruin.

10 The LORD will reign forever,

a Gk Jerome Syr: Heb *his* *b* Heb *his* *c* These two lines supplied by Q Ms Gk Syr

14–16: As the ideal king, God sustains the oppressed and starving (Ps 104.27–28; 146.7–8). An epitome of the efficacy of prayer. **21:** David's praise (v. 1) is joined by *all flesh.*

Ps 146: Praise of God, creator and savior. Ps 146–150 form the concluding doxology of the Psalter. Ps 146 is a hymn praising God as creator (v. 6) and redeemer (vv. 7–9). **3–4:** *Mortals,* even *princes,* serve as a foil to the all-powerful God. **4:** An allusion to the creation story (Gen 3.19; Ps 104.29). **6–8:** God relieves oppression and hunger, as he did in the wilderness (Ex 14–16; Isa 49.9) **9:** See Jer 7.5–6; Zech 7.10. **10:** The conclusion recalls and supplements Ex 15.18. *Zion,* Jerusalem.

your God, O Zion, for all
generations.
Praise the LORD!

PSALM 147

1 Praise the LORD!
How good it is to sing praises to our
God;
for he is gracious, and a song of
praise is fitting.
2 The LORD builds up Jerusalem;
he gathers the outcasts of Israel.
3 He heals the brokenhearted,
and binds up their wounds.
4 He determines the number of
the stars;
he gives to all of them their names.
5 Great is our Lord, and abundant
in power;
his understanding is beyond
measure.
6 The LORD lifts up the downtrodden;
he casts the wicked to the ground.

7 Sing to the LORD with thanksgiving;
make melody to our God on
the lyre.
8 He covers the heavens with clouds,
prepares rain for the earth,
makes grass grow on the hills.
9 He gives to the animals their food,
and to the young ravens when they
cry.
10 His delight is not in the strength of
the horse,
nor his pleasure in the speed of
a runner;[a]
11 but the LORD takes pleasure in those
who fear him,
in those who hope in his steadfast
love.

12 Praise the LORD, O Jerusalem!
Praise your God, O Zion!
13 For he strengthens the bars of
your gates;
he blesses your children within you.
14 He grants peace[b] within your
borders;
he fills you with the finest of
wheat.
15 He sends out his command to the
earth;
his word runs swiftly.
16 He gives snow like wool;
he scatters frost like ashes.
17 He hurls down hail like crumbs—
who can stand before his cold?
18 He sends out his word, and melts
them;
he makes his wind blow, and the
waters flow.
19 He declares his word to Jacob,
his statutes and ordinances to
Israel.
20 He has not dealt thus with any other
nation;
they do not know his ordinances.
Praise the LORD!

PSALM 148

1 Praise the LORD!
Praise the LORD from the heavens;
praise him in the heights!
2 Praise him, all his angels;
praise him, all his host!

a Heb *legs of a person* *b* Or *prosperity*

Ps 147: Praise of God, creator and savior. A postexilic hymn celebrating God's acts of creation and redemption; the reference to the rebuilding of Jerusalem (vv. 2–3) reflects the postexilic situation. In the Septuagint, vv. 12–20 are a separate psalm. **3:** *Brokenhearted,* penitent (Ps 51.17). **7–9:** God, the creator and sustainer, provides abundant rain; cf. Ps 104.10–16. **13:** See Ps 127.5 for the image of a secure city and sons. **15–19:** God's creative word (vv. 15,18) becomes in v. 19 his word to Israel, in their laws (Ps 33.4–6). **20:** God's *ordinances* are ultimately viewed as Israel's special gift (Ps 119).

Ps 148: Praise of God from heaven and earth. A hymn of praise from heavenly beings (vv. 1–6) and from the earth's subhuman (vv. 7–10) and human creatures (vv. 11–14). Human prayer thus mirrors heavenly prayer. **1–3:** Where the praise is to be uttered (in *the heavens*) and by whom (heavenly *host, sun, moon, stars*). **6:** Prov 8.29; Jer 5.22. **7–10:** Where the praise is to be uttered (on the *earth*) and by whom

3 Praise him, sun and moon;
praise him, all you shining stars!
4 Praise him, you highest heavens,
and you waters above the heavens!

5 Let them praise the name of
the LORD,
for he commanded and they
were created.
6 He established them forever and
ever;
he fixed their bounds, which cannot
be passed.[a]

7 Praise the LORD from the earth,
you sea monsters and all deeps,
8 fire and hail, snow and frost,
stormy wind fulfilling his
command!

9 Mountains and all hills,
fruit trees and all cedars!
10 Wild animals and all cattle,
creeping things and flying birds!

11 Kings of the earth and all peoples,
princes and all rulers of the earth!
12 Young men and women alike,
old and young together!

13 Let them praise the name of
the LORD,
for his name alone is exalted;
his glory is above earth and
heaven.
14 He has raised up a horn for his
people,
praise for all his faithful,
for the people of Israel who are
close to him.
Praise the LORD!

PSALM 149

1 Praise the LORD!
Sing to the LORD a new song,
his praise in the assembly of the
faithful.
2 Let Israel be glad in its Maker;
let the children of Zion rejoice in
their King.
3 Let them praise his name with
dancing,
making melody to him with
tambourine and lyre.
4 For the LORD takes pleasure in
his people;
he adorns the humble with victory.
5 Let the faithful exult in glory;
let them sing for joy on their
couches.
6 Let the high praises of God be in
their throats
and two-edged swords in their
hands,
7 to execute vengeance on the nations
and punishment on the peoples,
8 to bind their kings with fetters
and their nobles with chains
of iron,
9 to execute on them the judgment
decreed.
This is glory for all his faithful
ones.
Praise the LORD!

PSALM 150

1 Praise the LORD!
Praise God in his sanctuary;

a Or *he set a law that cannot pass away*

(*mountains, trees, animals*). **11–14:** Praise from the human world, especially from Israel, the people close to him.

Ps 149: Praise to Israel's creator and king. A hymn praising God for his deliverance of the lowly. **2:** *Zion,* Jerusalem. **3:** See Ex 15.20; 2 Sam 6.5. **5:** *On their couches,* in private (Ps 36.4), coordinated with the public praise of vv. 1–3,6. **7–9:** Israel's victory over her Gentile enemies, reflecting an overturning of the expected outcome, through God's help. **9:** *The judgment decreed,* what God has decreed as the fate of the enemy (like the divine setting of fates in Mesopotamian theology).

Ps 150: Praise of God in the Temple. A hymn, concluding the doxological series of hymns that closes Book V and the whole Psalter. **2:** *His mighty deeds,* the saving events Israel remembered and celebrated.

praise him in his mighty
firmament![a]
2 Praise him for his mighty deeds;
praise him according to his
surpassing greatness!

3 Praise him with trumpet sound;
praise him with lute and harp!
4 Praise him with tambourine and
dance;
praise him with strings and pipe!
5 Praise him with clanging cymbals;
praise him with loud clashing
cymbals!
6 Let everything that breathes praise the
LORD!
Praise the LORD!

a Or *dome*

3–5: See Ps 149.3. A loud cacophony of praise is described; each verse is slightly longer than the previous one, indicating increasing praise. **6:** *Everything that breathes,* recalling "all flesh" of Ps 145.21. In conclusion, *everything that breathes praise*s *the* LORD everywhere (v. 1) using all possible means (vv. 3–5), for his great acts (v. 2).

PROVERBS

The purpose of the book of Proverbs is to transmit insights whereby one might learn to cope with life (1.2–6). Its emphasis is on teachings gathered from tradition of the elders (e.g., 4.1–4) and from experience (e.g., 6.6–11). In contrast to many other books of the Hebrew Bible, major themes such as the Mosaic and Davidic covenants are absent; Temple worship and sacrifice are rarely mentioned.

Although some sayings are neutral observations, on the whole a moral ideal is inculcated. Guided by the principle that "the fear of the Lord is the beginning of wisdom" (9.10; 1.7; 15.33), the sages emphasize values such as honesty, diligence, trustworthiness, self-restraint, and appropriate attitudes toward wealth and poverty. Proverbs acknowledges the limitations of human wisdom (16.1–2,9; 21.30), yet the book offers a clear view of divine reward and punishment: Wisdom (generally equated with righteousness) brings success; folly (or wickedness) leads to destruction. The books of Job and Ecclesiastes, however, show that this schematic account of divine justice remained a problem for the sages.

The authorship of this composite work is multiple and essentially anonymous. Some of the material appears to be preexilic, but the book was completed in the post-exilic period. The attribution to Solomon (1.1; 10.1; 25.1) derives from traditional accounts of his legendary wisdom (1 Kings 4.29–34) and lends authority to the collection. The book is typical of the wisdom literature of the Hebrew Bible and also of the ancient Near East, especially Egypt. In fact, most scholars agree that 22.17–23.11 is in some way dependent upon the "Instruction" of the Egyptian sage, Amen-em-ope (ca. 1100 BCE). Royal scribes are responsible for much of the material in Proverbs; hence the sayings sometimes reflect an elite point of view. But the learned editors of the book also preserve the folk wisdom of ancient Israelite villages and extended families.

The original audience of Proverbs was primarily young men preparing for adult responsibilities; a male-centered perspective prevails in the book. There is intense interest in finding a "good wife" (e.g., 12.4) and in governing a household successfully. In chs 1–9, presented as the instruction of a father to his son, the center of attention is a vibrant feminine personification of divine Wisdom. She is opposed to the foolish woman (ch 9) and to the complex, threatening figure of the "strange woman" (chs 2,5,7).

Proverbs contains several sub-collections of short proverbial sayings framed by sets of longer wisdom poems in chs 1–9 and 30–31. The book opens (1.1–7) with a title (1.1) followed by a programmatic statement of purpose and theme (1.2–7). Then comes a lengthy instruction in Wisdom (1.8–9.18), consisting of extended poems in second-person address, with commands and admonitions usually completed by motive clauses. Personified Wisdom and her opposites, the "strange woman" and the foolish woman, are prominent. A collection of proverbial sayings follows (10.1–22.16), each of which is typically two lines in parallel thought, as is characteristic of Hebrew poetry. Antithetical parallelism predominates in chs 10–15; synonymous or synthetic parallelism (in which the second line repeats or extends the thought of the first) in 16.1–22.16. Another collection is "the words of the wise" (22.17–24.34), which are teachings, chiefly brief admonitions, patterned after the Egyptian "Instruction of Amen-em-ope" (esp. 22.17–23.11), with an appendix of additional "sayings of the wise" in 24.23–34. Another collection of sayings (25.1–29.27), credited to the "officials of King Hezekiah" (25.1), comprises two main sub-units, chs 25–27 and 28–29. The words of Agur and other sayings (30.1–33) are a wisdom dialogue and a prayer (vv. 1–9) followed by admonitions and numerical sayings (vv. 10–33). The words of Lemuel (31.1–9) consist of teachings on sobriety and responsibility attributed to King Lemuel's mother. Ending the collection, and expressing both closure and completeness by its acrostic form, is the section in praise of the woman of worth (31.10–31), a poem on the ideal wife, the embodiment of Wisdom.

The reader should begin with chs 1–9, which form an extended invitation to the pursuit of Wisdom. Especially noteworthy are the programmatic statements of 1.1–7 and 8–19 and the speeches of divine Wisdom in 1.20–33 and 8.1–36. The sayings collections of chs 10–29 may be approached as exercises in judicious reading. The artful arrangement of discrete proverbs creates a certain coherence in the Hebrew by means of catchwords, plays on words, alliteration and assonance, and thematic associations. Some sayings have been repeated in other collections (e.g., 21.9 = 25.24); others are meaningfully paired (e.g., 17.27–28; 26.4–5), or gathered in thematic groups (e.g., 25.1–7). Although these verbal characteristics and thematic arrangements may have been an aid to memorization, the care given to these groupings indicates that the interpretation of the sayings is meant to be an exacting discipline (cf. 26.7,9). Individual proverbs are not simply to be mechanically applied; rather they should be read in creative tension with one another. Proverbs invites the reader to intellectual discipline as a life-giving synthesis of keen observation and reflection, ethical concern, and piety.

1 The proverbs of Solomon son of David,
king of Israel:

2 For learning about wisdom and
instruction,
for understanding words of insight,
3 for gaining instruction in wise
dealing,
righteousness, justice, and equity;
4 to teach shrewdness to the simple,
knowledge and prudence to the
young—
5 let the wise also hear and gain in
learning,
and the discerning acquire skill,
6 to understand a proverb and a figure,
the words of the wise and their
riddles.

7 The fear of the LORD is the beginning
of knowledge;
fools despise wisdom and
instruction.

8 Hear, my child, your father's
instruction,
and do not reject your mother's
teaching;

1.1–7: Introduction. 1: *Proverbs of Solomon,* see the Introduction (10.1; 25.1). **2–6: The purpose of the book.** Addressed to the *simple* and the *young,* as well as the *wise,* Proverbs teaches discernment and ethical responsibility. A highly practical discipline, wisdom entails living in accord with *righteousness, justice, and equity.* **6:** *Figure,* an allusive saying or an extended metaphor, as in 1.20–33. *Riddle,* a comparison or analogy that provokes reflection and requires readers to decide the meaning (e.g., 30.15–16,18–19). **7: A basic wisdom theme.** Reverence toward God is the prerequisite to knowledge (9.10; 15.33; 31.30b; Job 28.28; Ps 111.10; Sir 1.14). *Fools* are not simply unintelligent, but unethical in their conduct.

1.8–9.18: Instruction in Wisdom. These chapters contain mostly long poems, in contrast to the short proverbial sayings of chs 10–29.

1.8–19: Instruction as a moral safeguard against the temptations of the wicked. **8:** *My child* (lit. "my son"), a typical usage of the sages when referring to the teacher-student relationship (vv. 10,15; 2.1; 4.10; Sir 2.1; 3.12,17). The pairing of the *father's instruction* and the *mother's teaching* alludes to the family as the place where wisdom instruction first takes place (see 6.20; 23.22; 31.1). The term *teaching* (Heb

9 for they are a fair garland for your head,
and pendants for your neck.
10 My child, if sinners entice you,
do not consent.
11 If they say, "Come with us, let us lie in wait for blood;
let us wantonly ambush the innocent;
12 like Sheol let us swallow them alive
and whole, like those who go down to the Pit.
13 We shall find all kinds of costly things;
we shall fill our houses with booty.
14 Throw in your lot among us;
we will all have one purse"—
15 my child, do not walk in their way,
keep your foot from their paths;
16 for their feet run to evil,
and they hurry to shed blood.
17 For in vain is the net baited
while the bird is looking on;
18 yet they lie in wait—to kill themselves!
and set an ambush—for their own lives!
19 Such is the end[a] of all who are greedy for gain;
it takes away the life of its possessors.

20 Wisdom cries out in the street;
in the squares she raises her voice.
21 At the busiest corner she cries out;
at the entrance of the city gates she speaks:
22 "How long, O simple ones, will you love being simple?
How long will scoffers delight in their scoffing
and fools hate knowledge?
23 Give heed to my reproof;
I will pour out my thoughts to you;
I will make my words known to you.
24 Because I have called and you refused,
have stretched out my hand and no one heeded,
25 and because you have ignored all my counsel
and would have none of my reproof,
26 I also will laugh at your calamity;
I will mock when panic strikes you,
27 when panic strikes you like a storm,
and your calamity comes like a whirlwind,
when distress and anguish come upon you.
28 Then they will call upon me, but I will not answer;
they will seek me diligently, but will not find me.
29 Because they hated knowledge
and did not choose the fear of the LORD,
30 would have none of my counsel,
and despised all my reproof,
31 therefore they shall eat the fruit of their way
and be sated with their own devices.
32 For waywardness kills the simple,
and the complacency of fools destroys them;
33 but those who listen to me will be secure
and will live at ease, without dread of disaster."

a Gk: Heb *are the ways*

"torah") is used elsewhere in the Bible as a term for covenant law. In Proverbs, however, it refers primarily to wisdom instruction. But see Sir 24, which identifies the two. **12:** *Sheol . . . the Pit,* common expressions for death and the place and state of the dead. **16:** An editorial quotation of Isa 59.7. **17:** The sage cites a popular proverb to affirm that the consequences of crime ought to be obvious.

1.20–33: Wisdom personified as a prophet. She speaks publicly in the city streets and gates. In language that echoes the prophets (for v. 22 see Jer 4.14,21; v. 24 see Isa 65.2,12; 66.4; Jer 7.13,24–27), Wisdom pronounces dire threats against those who will not listen to her (vv. 26–32). **22:** The *simple* (see 1.4) are considered teachable, but *scoffers* and *fools* are generally represented as (fatally) resistant to instruction (see 1.7; 15.12; 26.3).

2 My child, if you accept my words
and treasure up my commandments
within you,
2 making your ear attentive to wisdom
and inclining your heart to
understanding;
3 if you indeed cry out for insight,
and raise your voice for
understanding;
4 if you seek it like silver,
and search for it as for hidden
treasures—
5 then you will understand the fear of
the LORD
and find the knowledge of God.
6 For the LORD gives wisdom;
from his mouth come knowledge
and understanding;
7 he stores up sound wisdom for the
upright;
he is a shield to those who walk
blamelessly,
8 guarding the paths of justice
and preserving the way of his
faithful ones.
9 Then you will understand
righteousness and justice
and equity, every good path;
10 for wisdom will come into your heart,
and knowledge will be pleasant to
your soul;
11 prudence will watch over you;
and understanding will guard
you.
12 It will save you from the way of evil,
from those who speak perversely,
13 who forsake the paths of uprightness
to walk in the ways of darkness,
14 who rejoice in doing evil
and delight in the perverseness
of evil;
15 those whose paths are crooked,
and who are devious in their ways.

16 You will be saved from the loose[a]
woman,
from the adulteress with her
smooth words,
17 who forsakes the partner of her youth
and forgets her sacred covenant;
18 for her way[b] leads down to death,
and her paths to the shades;
19 those who go to her never come back,
nor do they regain the paths of life.

20 Therefore walk in the way of the
good,
and keep to the paths of the just.
21 For the upright will abide in the land,
and the innocent will remain in it;
22 but the wicked will be cut off from
the land,
and the treacherous will be rooted
out of it.

3 My child, do not forget my teaching,
but let your heart keep my
commandments;
2 for length of days and years of life
and abundant welfare they will give
you.

3 Do not let loyalty and faithfulness
forsake you;
bind them around your neck,
write them on the tablet of your
heart.

a Heb *strange* b Cn: Heb *house*

2.1–22: The fruits of the search for wisdom are summarized in this carefully fashioned poem of 22 lines (the number of letters in the Hebrew alphabet; cf. the acrostic pattern of 31.10–31). **4:** Wisdom is frequently compared to a *treasure* or wealth (see 3.14–16; 8.18–19; Job 28.15–19). **5:** 1.7n. **10:** *Heart,* not only the seat of affections, but the center of the whole person, including will and thought (4.23). **16:** *Loose woman,* lit. "strange woman" (Heb "zarah," see 5.3,20; 7.5; 22.14); *adulteress,* lit. "alien" or "foreign woman" (Heb "nokriyyah," see 5.20; 6.24; 7.5; 23.27; Ezra 10.2,10–11,14,17–18,44; Neh 13.26–27). **17:** *Her sacred covenant,* here as in Mal 2.10–16, imagery of unfaithfulness in marriage is associated with breaking a religious covenant. **19:** See 7.26–27.

3.1–12: Instruction in fear of the LORD. 3: Wisdom teachings and values are often described in imagery that suggests protective amulets worn on the body (see 6.21; 7.3) or ornaments (see 1.9; 3.22). Cf. Deut 6.8–9. **7:** See 1.7n. **9:** *First fruits,* see Ex 23.19; Deut 26.1–11. This is the only direct instruction

4 So you will find favor and good
repute
in the sight of God and of people.
5 Trust in the LORD with all your heart,
and do not rely on your own
insight.
6 In all your ways acknowledge him,
and he will make straight your
paths.
7 Do not be wise in your own eyes;
fear the LORD, and turn away from
evil.
8 It will be a healing for your flesh
and a refreshment for your body.

9 Honor the LORD with your substance
and with the first fruits of all your
produce;
10 then your barns will be filled with
plenty,
and your vats will be bursting with
wine.

11 My child, do not despise the LORD's
discipline
or be weary of his reproof,
12 for the LORD reproves the one he
loves,
as a father the son in whom he
delights.

13 Happy are those who find wisdom,
and those who get understanding,
14 for her income is better than silver,
and her revenue better than gold.
15 She is more precious than jewels,
and nothing you desire can
compare with her.
16 Long life is in her right hand;
in her left hand are riches and
honor.
17 Her ways are ways of pleasantness,
and all her paths are peace.
18 She is a tree of life to those who lay
hold of her;
those who hold her fast are called
happy.

19 The LORD by wisdom founded the
earth;
by understanding he established the
heavens;
20 by his knowledge the deeps broke
open,
and the clouds drop down the dew.
21 My child, do not let these escape
from your sight:
keep sound wisdom and prudence,
22 and they will be life for your soul
and adornment for your neck.
23 Then you will walk on your way
securely
and your foot will not stumble.
24 If you sit down,[a] you will not be
afraid;
when you lie down, your sleep will
be sweet.
25 Do not be afraid of sudden panic,
or of the storm that strikes the
wicked;
26 for the LORD will be your confidence

a Gk: Heb *lie down*

concerning Temple worship in Proverbs (cf. 15.8; 21.3; 28.13). **11–12:** Suffering can be a sign of beneficent divine *discipline* (Deut 8.5; Job 5.17; Ps 94.12–13; Sir 6.18–37).

3.13–20: In praise of Wisdom. 13: *Happy are those,* a characteristic formula in wisdom rhetoric (8.34; 20.7; 28.14; 29.18; 31.28). In the New Testament the Beatitudes ("Blessed are"; Mt 5.3–11; Lk 6.20–23) reflect the equivalent formula in Greek. **14–15:** Cf. Job 28.15–19. **16:** The Egyptian goddess of truth and justice, Maat, was portrayed with the symbol of *life* in one hand, wealth and dignity in the other. **18:** *Tree of life,* a widespread ancient Near Eastern symbol of longevity and well-being (Gen 2.9; 3.22; Sir 1.20; 14.26; 24.12–17; Rev 2.7; 22.2). **19–20:** Wisdom's role in creation (8.22–31). The *deeps* and the *dew* represent the waters below and above, at the perimeter of God's well-ordered creation (8.29; Gen 1.6–9; 7.11; Job 38.8–11; Ps 104.5–9).

3.21–35: An admonition followed by six prohibitions, and a statement about the fate of the righteous and wicked. **27:** The language suggests that the issue concerns loans and their repayment; see 6.1–5; 11.24. **29:** Cf. 26.24–26.

and will keep your foot from being
caught.
27 Do not withhold good from those to
whom it is due,[a]
when it is in your power to do it.
28 Do not say to your neighbor, "Go,
and come again,
tomorrow I will give it"—when
you have it with you.
29 Do not plan harm against your
neighbor
who lives trustingly beside you.
30 Do not quarrel with anyone without
cause,
when no harm has been done
to you.
31 Do not envy the violent
and do not choose any of their
ways;
32 for the perverse are an abomination
to the LORD,
but the upright are in his
confidence.
33 The LORD's curse is on the house of
the wicked,
but he blesses the abode of the
righteous.
34 Toward the scorners he is scornful,
but to the humble he shows favor.
35 The wise will inherit honor,
but stubborn fools, disgrace.

4 Listen, children, to a father's
instruction,
and be attentive, that you may
gain[b] insight;
2 for I give you good precepts:
do not forsake my teaching.
3 When I was a son with my father,
tender, and my mother's favorite,
4 he taught me, and said to me,
"Let your heart hold fast my words;
keep my commandments, and live.
5 Get wisdom; get insight: do not
forget, nor turn away
from the words of my mouth.
6 Do not forsake her, and she will keep
you;
love her, and she will guard you.
7 The beginning of wisdom is this: Get
wisdom,
and whatever else you get, get
insight.
8 Prize her highly, and she will
exalt you;
she will honor you if you
embrace her.
9 She will place on your head a fair
garland;
she will bestow on you a beautiful
crown."
10 Hear, my child, and accept my words,
that the years of your life may
be many.
11 I have taught you the way of wisdom;
I have led you in the paths of
uprightness.
12 When you walk, your step will not be
hampered;
and if you run, you will not
stumble.
13 Keep hold of instruction; do not
let go;
guard her, for she is your life.
14 Do not enter the path of the wicked,
and do not walk in the way of
evildoers.
15 Avoid it; do not go on it;
turn away from it and pass on.
16 For they cannot sleep unless they have
done wrong;
they are robbed of sleep unless they
have made someone stumble.
17 For they eat the bread of wickedness

a Heb *from its owners* *b* Heb *know*

4.1–9: Get Wisdom. The sage urges ardent loyalty toward Wisdom. The student will *love her* and *embrace her* as if she were a beloved wife (5.15–20; 7.4). **10–27:** The two ways: wisdom's *way* or *path* (vv. 11,18) is contrasted with the *path* or *way of the wicked* (vv. 14,19). The image of *way* or *path* for conduct of life occurs frequently in the book (1.15–16; 2.7–20; 3.6,17,23; 5.5–8,21; 6.23; 7.25; 8.13,20,32; 9.6; 10.9; 11.5; 16.17; 28.6).

and drink the wine of violence.
18 But the path of the righteous is like
the light of dawn,
which shines brighter and brighter
until full day.
19 The way of the wicked is like deep
darkness;
they do not know what they
stumble over.
20 My child, be attentive to my words;
incline your ear to my sayings.
21 Do not let them escape from
your sight;
keep them within your heart.
22 For they are life to those who
find them,
and healing to all their flesh.
23 Keep your heart with all vigilance,
for from it flow the springs of life.
24 Put away from you crooked speech,
and put devious talk far from you.
25 Let your eyes look directly forward,
and your gaze be straight
before you.
26 Keep straight the path of your feet,
and all your ways will be sure.
27 Do not swerve to the right or to
the left;
turn your foot away from evil.

5 My child, be attentive to my wisdom;
incline your ear to my
understanding,
2 so that you may hold on to prudence,
and your lips may guard
knowledge.
3 For the lips of a loose[a] woman drip
honey,
and her speech is smoother
than oil;
4 but in the end she is bitter as
wormwood,
sharp as a two-edged sword.
5 Her feet go down to death;
her steps follow the path to Sheol.
6 She does not keep straight to the path
of life;
her ways wander, and she does not
know it.

7 And now, my child,[b] listen to me,
and do not depart from the words
of my mouth.
8 Keep your way far from her,
and do not go near the door of her
house;
9 or you will give your honor to others,
and your years to the merciless,
10 and strangers will take their fill of
your wealth,
and your labors will go to the
house of an alien;
11 and at the end of your life you will
groan,
when your flesh and body are
consumed,
12 and you say, "Oh, how I hated
discipline,
and my heart despised reproof!
13 I did not listen to the voice of my
teachers
or incline my ear to my instructors.
14 Now I am at the point of utter ruin
in the public assembly."

15 Drink water from your own cistern,
flowing water from your own well.
16 Should your springs be scattered
abroad,
streams of water in the streets?
17 Let them be for yourself alone,
and not for sharing with strangers.

a Heb *strange* *b* Gk Vg: Heb *children*

5.1–23: The dangers of the "strange woman." The identity of the forbidden woman is unclear. Elsewhere she is compared to a prostitute and is implicated in adultery (7.10,19). Here the focus on her alien status as a "strange woman" (Heb "zarah," vv. 3,20a) and "foreign woman" (Heb "nokriyyah," v. 20b; cf. vv. 8–10) might reflect in part the postexilic prohibition of marriage to foreign women (Ezra 9–10, Neh 13.23–30). **5:** *Sheol,* the abode of the dead. **14:** *Ruin in the public assembly,* cf. Ezra 10.8. Shame was a strong social sanction in ancient Israelite society, just as honor was a powerful reward (3.35; 5.9; 6.33; 25.7c–10; etc.). **15–20:** The wise man will *rejoice* in exclusive intimacy with his lawful *wife. Cistern, well,* and *fountain* are metaphors for the woman (Song 4.12,15). **19:** Cf. Song 4.5.

18 Let your fountain be blessed,
and rejoice in the wife of your youth,
19 a lovely deer, a graceful doe.
May her breasts satisfy you at all times;
may you be intoxicated always by her love.
20 Why should you be intoxicated, my son, by another woman
and embrace the bosom of an adulteress?
21 For human ways are under the eyes of the LORD,
and he examines all their paths.
22 The iniquities of the wicked ensnare them,
and they are caught in the toils of their sin.
23 They die for lack of discipline,
and because of their great folly they are lost.

6 My child, if you have given your pledge to your neighbor,
if you have bound yourself to another,[a]
2 you are snared by the utterance of your lips,[b]
caught by the words of your mouth.
3 So do this, my child, and save yourself,
for you have come into your neighbor's power:
go, hurry,[c] and plead with your neighbor.
4 Give your eyes no sleep
and your eyelids no slumber;
5 save yourself like a gazelle from the hunter,[d]
like a bird from the hand of the fowler.

6 Go to the ant, you lazybones;
consider its ways, and be wise.
7 Without having any chief
or officer or ruler,
8 it prepares its food in summer,
and gathers its sustenance in harvest.
9 How long will you lie there,
O lazybones?
When will you rise from your sleep?
10 A little sleep, a little slumber,
a little folding of the hands to rest,
11 and poverty will come upon you like a robber,
and want, like an armed warrior.

12 A scoundrel and a villain
goes around with crooked speech,
13 winking the eyes, shuffling the feet,
pointing the fingers,
14 with perverted mind devising evil,
continually sowing discord;
15 on such a one calamity will descend suddenly;
in a moment, damage beyond repair.

16 There are six things that the LORD hates,
seven that are an abomination to him:
17 haughty eyes, a lying tongue,
and hands that shed innocent blood,
18 a heart that devises wicked plans,
feet that hurry to run to evil,
19 a lying witness who testifies falsely,
and one who sows discord in a family.

a Or *a stranger* b Cn Compare Gk Syr: Heb *the words of your mouth* c Or *humble yourself* d Cn: Heb *from the hand*

6.1–19: Warning. 1–5: Do not offer your property as collateral for your neighbor's debts (11.15; 17.18; 20.16; 22.26–27; Sir 8.12–13; 29.1–7,14–20). **6–11:** Avoid laziness (20.4,13; 22.13; 24.30–34; 26.13–16). Didactic comparisons between human behavior and the characteristics of plants and animals are a recognized form of wisdom speech (Prov 30.15–19,24–31; see also Judg 9.8–15; 1 Kings 4.33–34). **12–15:** Beware of disreputable characters. For *winking the eyes* as a sign of duplicity, see 10.10; 16.30; Sir 27.22. **16–19:** A numerical saying (see 30.18–31; Am 1.3–2.8) about seven vices.

20 My child, keep your father's
commandment,
and do not forsake your mother's
teaching.
21 Bind them upon your heart always;
tie them around your neck.
22 When you walk, they[a] will lead you;
when you lie down, they[a] will
watch over you;
and when you awake, they[a] will
talk with you.
23 For the commandment is a lamp and
the teaching a light,
and the reproofs of discipline are
the way of life,
24 to preserve you from the wife of
another,[b]
from the smooth tongue of the
adulteress.
25 Do not desire her beauty in your
heart,
and do not let her capture you with
her eyelashes;
26 for a prostitute's fee is only a loaf of
bread,[c]
but the wife of another stalks a
man's very life.
27 Can fire be carried in the bosom
without burning one's clothes?
28 Or can one walk on hot coals
without scorching the feet?
29 So is he who sleeps with his
neighbor's wife;
no one who touches her will go
unpunished.
30 Thieves are not despised who
steal only
to satisfy their appetite when they
are hungry.
31 Yet if they are caught, they will pay
sevenfold;
they will forfeit all the goods of
their house.
32 But he who commits adultery has no
sense;
he who does it destroys himself.
33 He will get wounds and dishonor,
and his disgrace will not be wiped
away.
34 For jealousy arouses a husband's fury,
and he shows no restraint when he
takes revenge.
35 He will accept no compensation,
and refuses a bribe no matter how
great.

7 My child, keep my words
and store up my commandments
with you;
2 keep my commandments and live,
keep my teachings as the apple of
your eye;
3 bind them on your fingers,
write them on the tablet of your
heart.
4 Say to wisdom, "You are my sister,"
and call insight your intimate
friend,
5 that they may keep you from the
loose[d] woman,

a Heb *it* *b* Gk: MT *the evil woman*
c Cn Compare Gk Syr Vg Tg: Heb *for because of a harlot to a piece of bread* *d* Heb *strange*

6.20–35: The perils of adultery. The man who *sleeps with his neighbor's wife* (v. 29) suffers dire consequences, including the implacable *husband's fury* (v. 34). As is typical in chs 1–9, the focus here is on advice to men. Women are not addressed directly; they appear as dangerous temptations (vv. 24–25) or as exemplary wives and mothers (v. 20). **20–22:** See 3.3n.; Deut 6.6–8. **26:** The contrast between the "cost" of the *prostitute* and the *wife of another* suggests that the issue was not simply one of sexual conduct itself but the danger posed to the social system, including the system of inheritance, by adultery, which could result in uncertainty about paternity.

7.1–27: Another warning against the "strange woman." 1–5: The young man is advised to cling to Wisdom as *sister* and *friend* (as if she were a beloved; see Song 4.9–12; 5.1). She will keep him safe from the *loose woman* (lit. "strange woman") or the *adulteress* (lit. "alien" or "foreign woman"; see 2.16; 5.1–23). **2–3:** See 3.3n. *Apple of your eye,* i.e., pupil. **4:** *Sister,* in poetry, a term of endearment for the beloved, not implying kinship (see Song 4.9). **6–27:** The teacher vividly describes a seduction leading to

from the adulteress with her
smooth words.

6 For at the window of my house
I looked out through my lattice,
7 and I saw among the simple ones,
I observed among the youths,
a young man without sense,
8 passing along the street near her
corner,
taking the road to her house
9 in the twilight, in the evening,
at the time of night and darkness.

10 Then a woman comes toward him,
decked out like a prostitute, wily of
heart.[a]
11 She is loud and wayward;
her feet do not stay at home;
12 now in the street, now in the squares,
and at every corner she lies in
wait.
13 She seizes him and kisses him,
and with impudent face she says to
him:
14 "I had to offer sacrifices,
and today I have paid my vows;
15 so now I have come out to meet you,
to seek you eagerly, and I have
found you!
16 I have decked my couch with
coverings,
colored spreads of Egyptian linen;
17 I have perfumed my bed with myrrh,
aloes, and cinnamon.
18 Come, let us take our fill of love until
morning;
let us delight ourselves with love.
19 For my husband is not at home;
he has gone on a long journey.
20 He took a bag of money with him;
he will not come home until full
moon."
21 With much seductive speech she
persuades him;
with her smooth talk she
compels him.
22 Right away he follows her,
and goes like an ox to the
slaughter,
or bounds like a stag toward
the trap[b]
23 until an arrow pierces its entrails.
He is like a bird rushing into a snare,
not knowing that it will cost him
his life.

24 And now, my children, listen to me,
and be attentive to the words of my
mouth.
25 Do not let your hearts turn aside to
her ways;
do not stray into her paths.
26 For many are those she has laid low,
and numerous are her victims.
27 Her house is the way to Sheol,
going down to the chambers of
death.

8 Does not wisdom call,
and does not understanding raise
her voice?
2 On the heights, beside the way,
at the crossroads she takes her
stand;
3 beside the gates in front of the town,
at the entrance of the portals she
cries out:
4 "To you, O people, I call,
and my cry is to all that live.
5 O simple ones, learn prudence;
acquire intelligence, you who lack
it.

a Meaning of Heb uncertain *b* Cn Compare Gk: Meaning of Heb uncertain

death. **10:** It is not clear whether the woman is a *prostitute,* or simply dressed like one. Since she is married (vv. 19–20), a liason with her would constitute adultery (see 6.24–35). **17:** *Myrrh,* an aromatic resin; *aloes and cinnamon,* aromatic spices from India. **22–27:** The emphasis on the "strange woman's" inexorable pull toward death heightens her stark opposition to Wisdom, personified as a woman who offers life (3.16; 8.35–36). *Sheol,* 1.12n.

8.1–36: Wisdom speaks (cf. Sir 24.1–34). **1–5:** Wisdom publicly addresses all *people,* but especially the *simple* in need of instruction (1.20–22). **6–11:** Wisdom's value is incomparable (see 2.4n.; cf. Job

6 Hear, for I will speak noble things,
and from my lips will come what is right;
7 for my mouth will utter truth;
wickedness is an abomination to my lips.
8 All the words of my mouth are righteous;
there is nothing twisted or crooked in them.
9 They are all straight to one who understands
and right to those who find knowledge.
10 Take my instruction instead of silver,
and knowledge rather than choice gold;
11 for wisdom is better than jewels,
and all that you may desire cannot compare with her.
12 I, wisdom, live with prudence,[a]
and I attain knowledge and discretion.
13 The fear of the LORD is hatred of evil.
Pride and arrogance and the way of evil
and perverted speech I hate.
14 I have good advice and sound wisdom;
I have insight, I have strength.
15 By me kings reign,
and rulers decree what is just;
16 by me rulers rule,
and nobles, all who govern rightly.
17 I love those who love me,
and those who seek me diligently find me.
18 Riches and honor are with me,
enduring wealth and prosperity.
19 My fruit is better than gold, even fine gold,
and my yield than choice silver.
20 I walk in the way of righteousness,
along the paths of justice,
21 endowing with wealth those who love me,
and filling their treasuries.
22 The LORD created me at the beginning[b] of his work,[c]
the first of his acts of long ago.
23 Ages ago I was set up,
at the first, before the beginning of the earth.
24 When there were no depths I was brought forth,
when there were no springs abounding with water.
25 Before the mountains had been shaped,
before the hills, I was brought forth—
26 when he had not yet made earth and fields,[a]
or the world's first bits of soil.
27 When he established the heavens, I was there,
when he drew a circle on the face of the deep,
28 when he made firm the skies above,
when he established the fountains of the deep,
29 when he assigned to the sea its limit,
so that the waters might not transgress his command,
when he marked out the foundations of the earth,
30 then I was beside him, like a master worker;[d]
and I was daily his[e] delight,
rejoicing before him always,

a Meaning of Heb uncertain *b* Or *me as the beginning* *c* Heb *way* *d* Another reading is *little child* *e* Gk: Heb lacks *his*

28.15–19). **12–16:** Her authority is that by which *kings reign* (Sir 4.15). **17–21:** Wisdom's blessings begin with returning the *love* of *those who love* her (v. 17; Sir 4.14; Wis 6.12–13). **22–31:** Wisdom recounts her divine origin, before anything was created (Sir 1.4; 24.9). She was with God as a *master worker* (v. 30), and thus had a role in creation (Sir 1.9–10; Wis 7.22; 9.9). Wisdom is seen *delighting in* God's human creatures (v. 31; Sir 1.15; 24.7–12). **22:** *Created,* the proper translation of the Heb word ("qanah") is debated, but "acquired" (see 4.5,7) or even "engendered, conceived" (see Gen 4.1) are also

31 rejoicing in his inhabited world
and delighting in the human race.

32 "And now, my children, listen to me:
happy are those who keep
my ways.
33 Hear instruction and be wise,
and do not neglect it.
34 Happy is the one who listens to me,
watching daily at my gates,
waiting beside my doors.
35 For whoever finds me finds life
and obtains favor from the LORD;
36 but those who miss me injure
themselves;
all who hate me love death."

9 Wisdom has built her house,
she has hewn her seven pillars.
2 She has slaughtered her animals, she
has mixed her wine,
she has also set her table.
3 She has sent out her servant-girls, she
calls
from the highest places in the town,
4 "You that are simple, turn in here!"
To those without sense she says,
5 "Come, eat of my bread
and drink of the wine I have mixed.
6 Lay aside immaturity,[a] and live,
and walk in the way of insight."

7 Whoever corrects a scoffer wins
abuse;
whoever rebukes the wicked
gets hurt.
8 A scoffer who is rebuked will only
hate you;
the wise, when rebuked, will
love you.
9 Give instruction[b] to the wise, and
they will become wiser still;
teach the righteous and they will
gain in learning.
10 The fear of the LORD is the beginning
of wisdom,
and the knowledge of the Holy One
is insight.
11 For by me your days will be
multiplied,
and years will be added to your life.
12 If you are wise, you are wise for
yourself;
if you scoff, you alone will bear it.

13 The foolish woman is loud;
she is ignorant and knows nothing.
14 She sits at the door of her house,
on a seat at the high places of the
town,
15 calling to those who pass by,
who are going straight on their
way,
16 "You who are simple, turn in here!"
And to those without sense she
says,
17 "Stolen water is sweet,
and bread eaten in secret is
pleasant."
18 But they do not know that the dead[c]
are there,
that her guests are in the depths of
Sheol.

10 The proverbs of Solomon.

A wise child makes a glad father,

a Or *simpleness* *b* Heb lacks *instruction*
c Heb *shades*

possible. **24–29:** See Gen 1; Job 38.4–11; Ps 104.5–9. **32–36:** The speech concludes with an offer of *life* in place of *death*.

9.1–18: Wisdom invites the unwise, or *simple,* to her banquet (vv. 1–6), but the foolish woman also seeks their attention (vv. 13–18). Between the invitations are aphorisms about *scoffers* and the *wise* (vv. 7–12). **1:** The *seven pillars* of *her house* may allude to the pillars on which the earth was founded (Job 9.6; 26.11; Ps 75.3; cf. 8.29–30). **2:** *Wine* was sometimes *mixed* with spices. **5:** Cf. Sir 24.19; 51.23–30. **10:** Cf. 1.7. **17:** *Stolen water . . . bread,* probably veiled references to illicit sex (see 5.15–17; Sir 23.17). **18:** Like the "strange woman" of ch 7, the foolish woman is associated with death. *Sheol,* 1.12n.

10.1–22.16: Proverbial sayings. The originally separate sayings in this collection are often bound

but a foolish child is a mother's
grief.
2 Treasures gained by wickedness do
not profit,
but righteousness delivers from
death.
3 The LORD does not let the righteous
go hungry,
but he thwarts the craving of the
wicked.
4 A slack hand causes poverty,
but the hand of the diligent makes
rich.
5 A child who gathers in summer is
prudent,
but a child who sleeps in harvest
brings shame.
6 Blessings are on the head of the
righteous,
but the mouth of the wicked
conceals violence.
7 The memory of the righteous is a
blessing,
but the name of the wicked
will rot.
8 The wise of heart will heed
commandments,
but a babbling fool will come
to ruin.
9 Whoever walks in integrity walks
securely,
but whoever follows perverse ways
will be found out.
10 Whoever winks the eye causes
trouble,
but the one who rebukes boldly
makes peace.[a]
11 The mouth of the righteous is a
fountain of life,
but the mouth of the wicked
conceals violence.
12 Hatred stirs up strife,
but love covers all offenses.
13 On the lips of one who has
understanding wisdom
is found,
but a rod is for the back of one
who lacks sense.
14 The wise lay up knowledge,
but the babbling of a fool brings
ruin near.
15 The wealth of the rich is their
fortress;
the poverty of the poor is their
ruin.
16 The wage of the righteous leads
to life,
the gain of the wicked to sin.
17 Whoever heeds instruction is on the
path to life,
but one who rejects a rebuke goes
astray.
18 Lying lips conceal hatred,
and whoever utters slander is
a fool.
19 When words are many, transgression
is not lacking,
but the prudent are restrained in
speech.
20 The tongue of the righteous is choice
silver;

a Gk: Heb *but a babbling fool will come to ruin*

together by catchwords and thematic associations. There is a general equation between wise and righteous on the one hand, fool and wicked on the other. Antithetical parallelism is characteristic of chs 10–15; chs 16–22 favor synonymous or synthetic parallelism in which the second line repeats or extends the thought of the first. **10.1:** *Proverbs of Solomon,* see Introduction. This opening proverb takes up the motif of father-son instruction from chs 1–9 (15.20; Sir 3.1–16). **2–3:** These two sayings assume that divine retribution occurs in the present life. Misfortune, including an early or unhappy *death,* is punishment for sin, while righteousness is rewarded with long and prosperous life (cf. 3.2,16; 9.11; 10.27; 13.21). Other proverbs complicate this doctrine of divine reward and punishment (e.g., 15.16; 16.8), and the books of Job and Ecclesiastes challenge it profoundly. **4–5:** See 6.6–11. **10:** *Winks the eye,* cf. 6.13; Sir 27.22. **11:** *Fountain of life,* an image repeatedly associated with the wise and wisdom (see 13.14; 14.27; 16.22). **15–16:** V. 15 is a neutral observation about the reality of *wealth* and *poverty;* v. 16 adds ethical comment on the *gain of the wicked.* Cf. 11.28 and 18.11, where the protection of wealth is declared to be illusory. **18–21:** Proper speech is a frequent topic in wisdom literature (e.g., 2.12; 12.13–14,17–19,22–23; 13.3;

the mind of the wicked is of
little worth.
21 The lips of the righteous feed many,
but fools die for lack of sense.
22 The blessing of the LORD makes
rich,
and he adds no sorrow with it.[a]
23 Doing wrong is like sport to a fool,
but wise conduct is pleasure to a
person of understanding.
24 What the wicked dread will come
upon them,
but the desire of the righteous will
be granted.
25 When the tempest passes, the wicked
are no more,
but the righteous are established
forever.
26 Like vinegar to the teeth, and smoke
to the eyes,
so are the lazy to their employers.
27 The fear of the LORD prolongs life,
but the years of the wicked will be
short.
28 The hope of the righteous ends in
gladness,
but the expectation of the wicked
comes to nothing.
29 The way of the LORD is a stronghold
for the upright,
but destruction for evildoers.
30 The righteous will never be removed,
but the wicked will not remain in
the land.
31 The mouth of the righteous brings
forth wisdom,
but the perverse tongue will be cut
off.
32 The lips of the righteous know what
is acceptable,
but the mouth of the wicked what
is perverse.

11 A false balance is an abomination
to the LORD,
but an accurate weight is his
delight.
2 When pride comes, then comes
disgrace;
but wisdom is with the humble.
3 The integrity of the upright guides
them,
but the crookedness of the
treacherous destroys them.
4 Riches do not profit in the day
of wrath,
but righteousness delivers from
death.
5 The righteousness of the blameless
keeps their ways straight,
but the wicked fall by their own
wickedness.
6 The righteousness of the upright saves
them,
but the treacherous are taken
captive by their schemes.
7 When the wicked die, their hope
perishes,
and the expectation of the godless
comes to nothing.
8 The righteous are delivered from
trouble,
and the wicked get into it instead.
9 With their mouths the godless would
destroy their neighbors,
but by knowledge the righteous are
delivered.
10 When it goes well with the righteous,
the city rejoices;
and when the wicked perish, there
is jubilation.
11 By the blessing of the upright a city is
exalted,
but it is overthrown by the mouth
of the wicked.
12 Whoever belittles another lacks sense,
but an intelligent person remains
silent.
13 A gossip goes about telling secrets,
but one who is trustworthy in spirit
keeps a confidence.

a Or *and toil adds nothing to it*

Sir 19.4–12; 23.7–11). **25:** *Tempest,* a divine manifestation; see Job 27.20; Hos 8.7. **11.1:** On dishonest trade, cf. 16.11; 20.10,23; Lev 19.35–37; Deut 25.13–16. **2:** The *humble* are closely associated with the wise (15.33; 18.12; 22.4; Sir 3.17–24). **12–13:** A pair of proverbs contrasting indiscreet speech with the virtue of the *silent* and the *trustworthy* (20.19; 25.9; Sir 27.16–17). **15:** Cf. 6.1–5. **22:** This saying,

14 Where there is no guidance, a
nation[a] falls,
but in an abundance of counselors
there is safety.
15 To guarantee loans for a stranger
brings trouble,
but there is safety in refusing
to do so.
16 A gracious woman gets honor,
but she who hates virtue is covered
with shame.[b]
The timid become destitute,[c]
but the aggressive gain riches.
17 Those who are kind reward
themselves,
but the cruel do themselves
harm.
18 The wicked earn no real gain,
but those who sow righteousness
get a true reward.
19 Whoever is steadfast in righteousness
will live,
but whoever pursues evil will die.
20 Crooked minds are an abomination to
the LORD,
but those of blameless ways are his
delight.
21 Be assured, the wicked will not go
unpunished,
but those who are righteous will
escape.
22 Like a gold ring in a pig's snout
is a beautiful woman without good
sense.
23 The desire of the righteous ends only
in good;
the expectation of the wicked in
wrath.
24 Some give freely, yet grow all the
richer;
others withhold what is due, and
only suffer want.
25 A generous person will be enriched,
and one who gives water will
get water.
26 The people curse those who hold
back grain,
but a blessing is on the head of
those who sell it.
27 Whoever diligently seeks good seeks
favor,
but evil comes to the one who
searches for it.
28 Those who trust in their riches will
wither,[d]
but the righteous will flourish like
green leaves.
29 Those who trouble their households
will inherit wind,
and the fool will be servant to the
wise.
30 The fruit of the righteous is a tree of
life,
but violence[e] takes lives away.
31 If the righteous are repaid on earth,
how much more the wicked and the
sinner!

12 Whoever loves discipline loves
knowledge,
but those who hate to be rebuked
are stupid.
2 The good obtain favor from the
LORD,
but those who devise evil he
condemns.
3 No one finds security by wickedness,
but the root of the righteous will
never be moved.
4 A good wife is the crown of her
husband,
but she who brings shame is like
rottenness in his bones.

a Or *an army* *b* Compare Gk Syr: Heb lacks *but she . . . shame* *c* Gk: Heb lacks *The timid . . . destitute* *d* Cn: Heb *fall* *e* Cn Compare Gk Syr: Heb *a wise man*

arresting for its imagery and its male-centered point of view, is best taken as criticism of superficial esteem for beauty (see 31.30). **24–26:** The paradox of v. 24 is explained by v. 25: A *generous person* inspires others to reciprocate (cf. v. 17). In contrast, *those who hold back grain* (especially in time of scarcity, to maximize personal gain), receive a *curse.* **27:** Divine *favor* is chiefly meant here (cf. 8.35; 12.2; 18.22). **28,30:** Cf. Ps 1.3; 92.12–14. **12.1:** The wise cultivate *discipline,* and listen to criticism (13.1). **4:** The original addressees of the book were principally young men, for whom the choice of a *good wife* was an acute interest (cf. 18.22; 19.13–14; 31.10–31; Sir 26.1–3,13–18). **9:** The "better" saying, a favorite form

5 The thoughts of the righteous are just;
the advice of the wicked is treacherous.
6 The words of the wicked are a deadly ambush,
but the speech of the upright delivers them.
7 The wicked are overthrown and are no more,
but the house of the righteous will stand.
8 One is commended for good sense,
but a perverse mind is despised.
9 Better to be despised and have a servant,
than to be self-important and lack food.
10 The righteous know the needs of their animals,
but the mercy of the wicked is cruel.
11 Those who till their land will have plenty of food,
but those who follow worthless pursuits have no sense.
12 The wicked covet the proceeds of wickedness,[a]
but the root of the righteous bears fruit.
13 The evil are ensnared by the transgression of their lips,
but the righteous escape from trouble.
14 From the fruit of the mouth one is filled with good things,
and manual labor has its reward.
15 Fools think their own way is right,
but the wise listen to advice.
16 Fools show their anger at once,
but the prudent ignore an insult.
17 Whoever speaks the truth gives honest evidence,
but a false witness speaks deceitfully.
18 Rash words are like sword thrusts,
but the tongue of the wise brings healing.
19 Truthful lips endure forever,
but a lying tongue lasts only a moment.
20 Deceit is in the mind of those who plan evil,
but those who counsel peace have joy.
21 No harm happens to the righteous,
but the wicked are filled with trouble.
22 Lying lips are an abomination to the LORD,
but those who act faithfully are his delight.
23 One who is clever conceals knowledge,
but the mind of a fool[b] broadcasts folly.
24 The hand of the diligent will rule,
while the lazy will be put to forced labor.
25 Anxiety weighs down the human heart,
but a good word cheers it up.
26 The righteous gives good advice to friends,[c]
but the way of the wicked leads astray.
27 The lazy do not roast[d] their game,
but the diligent obtain precious wealth.[d]
28 In the path of righteousness there is life,
in walking its path there is no death.

13 A wise child loves discipline,[e]
but a scoffer does not listen to rebuke.

a Or *covet the catch of the wicked* b Heb *the heart of fools* c Syr: Meaning of Heb uncertain d Meaning of Heb uncertain e Cn: Heb *A wise child the discipline of his father*

of speech of the sages, conveys insight through paradox (15.16–17; 16.8,19,32; 17.1,12; 19.1,22; 21.9,19; 22.1; 25.24; 27.5,10c; 28.6; Eccl 4.6,13; 7.1–3; 9.4). On this saying, cf. Sir 10.27. **10:** Cf. 27.23. The second line is an oxymoron; what passes for *mercy* with the *wicked* is *cruel.* **11:** Cf. 28.19. **13–23:** See 10.18–21n. **17:** The setting is the law court (cf. 14.25; 25.18). **25:** Cf. 15.13; 17.22. **27:** Some

2 From the fruit of their words good
persons eat good things,
but the desire of the treacherous is
for wrongdoing.
3 Those who guard their mouths
preserve their lives;
those who open wide their lips
come to ruin.
4 The appetite of the lazy craves, and
gets nothing,
while the appetite of the diligent is
richly supplied.
5 The righteous hate falsehood,
but the wicked act shamefully and
disgracefully.
6 Righteousness guards one whose way
is upright,
but sin overthrows the wicked.
7 Some pretend to be rich, yet have
nothing;
others pretend to be poor, yet have
great wealth.
8 Wealth is a ransom for a person's life,
but the poor get no threats.
9 The light of the righteous rejoices,
but the lamp of the wicked
goes out.
10 By insolence the heedless make strife,
but wisdom is with those who take
advice.
11 Wealth hastily gotten[a] will dwindle,
but those who gather little by little
will increase it.
12 Hope deferred makes the heart sick,
but a desire fulfilled is a tree of life.
13 Those who despise the word bring
destruction on themselves,
but those who respect the
commandment will be
rewarded.
14 The teaching of the wise is a fountain
of life,
so that one may avoid the snares of
death.
15 Good sense wins favor,
but the way of the faithless is their
ruin.[b]
16 The clever do all things intelligently,
but the fool displays folly.
17 A bad messenger brings trouble,
but a faithful envoy, healing.
18 Poverty and disgrace are for the one
who ignores instruction,
but one who heeds reproof is
honored.
19 A desire realized is sweet to the soul,
but to turn away from evil is an
abomination to fools.
20 Whoever walks with the wise
becomes wise,
but the companion of fools suffers
harm.
21 Misfortune pursues sinners,
but prosperity rewards the
righteous.
22 The good leave an inheritance to their
children's children,
but the sinner's wealth is laid up
for the righteous.
23 The field of the poor may yield much
food,
but it is swept away through
injustice.
24 Those who spare the rod hate their
children,
but those who love them are
diligent to discipline them.

a Gk Vg: Heb *from vanity* *b* Cn Compare Gk Syr Vg Tg: Heb *is enduring*

are too *lazy* to cook their own food, or even to hunt for *game* in the first place (cf. 13.4; 19.24). **13.2:** Good words bring good results (12.14). **7–8:** A pair of proverbs that plays on ambiguities of the *rich* and *poor.* V. 8b suggests that the *poor* are not subject to criminal *threats* such as robbery and blackmail. **9:** *Light* and *lamp* are symbols of life (20.20; 24.20; Job 3.20; Ps 97.11). **12:** *Tree of life,* as in 3.18; 11.30; a symbol of the fullness of life. **13:** *Word* and *commandment* here originally referred to the teaching of the sages, but soon came to be understood also as references to the Torah (Deut 30.11,14; Sir 24.23; Bar 4.1). **14:** See 10.11n. **17:** The *messenger* played a vital role in the ancient world (cf. 22.21; 25.13,25; 26.6). **21–22:** A proverb pair teaching that prosperity as a reward for righteousness carries over from one generation to the next. **24:** *Spare the rod,* the sages oppose cruelty (even against animals, cf. 12.10), but they take physical punishment for granted as a necessary means of discipline (cf. 22.15; 23.13–14; 26.3;

25 The righteous have enough to satisfy
their appetite,
but the belly of the wicked is
empty.

14 The wise woman[a] builds her
house,
but the foolish tears it down with
her own hands.
2 Those who walk uprightly fear the
LORD,
but one who is devious in conduct
despises him.
3 The talk of fools is a rod for their
backs,[b]
but the lips of the wise preserve
them.
4 Where there are no oxen, there is no
grain;
abundant crops come by the
strength of the ox.
5 A faithful witness does not lie,
but a false witness breathes out lies.
6 A scoffer seeks wisdom in vain,
but knowledge is easy for one who
understands.
7 Leave the presence of a fool,
for there you do not find words of
knowledge.
8 It is the wisdom of the clever to
understand where they go,
but the folly of fools misleads.
9 Fools mock at the guilt offering,[c]
but the upright enjoy God's favor.
10 The heart knows its own bitterness,
and no stranger shares its joy.
11 The house of the wicked is destroyed,
but the tent of the upright
flourishes.
12 There is a way that seems right to a
person,
but its end is the way to death.[d]
13 Even in laughter the heart is sad,
and the end of joy is grief.
14 The perverse get what their ways
deserve,
and the good, what their deeds
deserve.[e]
15 The simple believe everything,
but the clever consider their steps.
16 The wise are cautious and turn away
from evil,
but the fool throws off restraint
and is careless.
17 One who is quick-tempered acts
foolishly,
and the schemer is hated.
18 The simple are adorned with[f] folly,
but the clever are crowned with
knowledge.
19 The evil bow down before the good,
the wicked at the gates of the
righteous.
20 The poor are disliked even by their
neighbors,
but the rich have many friends.
21 Those who despise their neighbors are
sinners,
but happy are those who are kind
to the poor.
22 Do they not err that plan evil?
Those who plan good find loyalty
and faithfulness.
23 In all toil there is profit,
but mere talk leads only to poverty.
24 The crown of the wise is their
wisdom,[g]
but folly is the garland[h] of fools.
25 A truthful witness saves lives,
but one who utters lies is a
betrayer.
26 In the fear of the LORD one has
strong confidence,
and one's children will have a
refuge.

a Heb *Wisdom of women* *b* Cn: Heb *a rod of pride*
c Meaning of Heb uncertain *d* Heb *ways of death*
e Cn: Heb *from upon him* *f* Or *inherit*
g Cn Compare Gk: Heb *riches* *h* Cn: Heb *is the folly*

29.15; Sir 22.6; 30.1–13). **14.1:** *Builds her house* might refer to personified Wisdom (9.1; cf. 24.3–4). **2:** Beginning with ch 14, proverbs that mention the *LORD* appear with increasing frequency. **6–12:** Several proverbs in this section concern discernment, which can be a matter of life and *death* (cf. 12.15; 16.25). **13:** Cf. Eccl 7.2–4. **20–21:** A proverb pair: V. 20 observes a social reality (cf. 19.4–7; Sir 6.8–12); v. 21 applies to it a moral evaluation (cf. v. 31; 17.5). **27:** See 10.11n. **29–30:** Self-control is a primary virtue

27 The fear of the LORD is a fountain of
life,
so that one may avoid the snares of
death.
28 The glory of a king is a multitude of
people;
without people a prince is ruined.
29 Whoever is slow to anger has great
understanding,
but one who has a hasty temper
exalts folly.
30 A tranquil mind gives life to the flesh,
but passion makes the bones rot.
31 Those who oppress the poor insult
their Maker,
but those who are kind to the
needy honor him.
32 The wicked are overthrown by their
evildoing,
but the righteous find a refuge in
their integrity.[a]
33 Wisdom is at home in the mind of
one who has understanding,
but it is not[b] known in the heart
of fools.
34 Righteousness exalts a nation,
but sin is a reproach to any people.
35 A servant who deals wisely has the
king's favor,
but his wrath falls on one who acts
shamefully.

15 A soft answer turns away wrath,
but a harsh word stirs up anger.
2 The tongue of the wise dispenses
knowledge,[c]
but the mouths of fools pour
out folly.
3 The eyes of the LORD are in every
place,
keeping watch on the evil and the
good.
4 A gentle tongue is a tree of life,
but perverseness in it breaks the
spirit.
5 A fool despises a parent's instruction,
but the one who heeds admonition
is prudent.
6 In the house of the righteous there is
much treasure,
but trouble befalls the income of
the wicked.
7 The lips of the wise spread
knowledge;
not so the minds of fools.
8 The sacrifice of the wicked is an
abomination to the LORD,
but the prayer of the upright is his
delight.
9 The way of the wicked is an
abomination to the LORD,
but he loves the one who pursues
righteousness.
10 There is severe discipline for one who
forsakes the way,
but one who hates a rebuke
will die.
11 Sheol and Abaddon lie open before
the LORD,
how much more human hearts!
12 Scoffers do not like to be rebuked;
they will not go to the wise.
13 A glad heart makes a cheerful
countenance,
but by sorrow of heart the spirit is
broken.
14 The mind of one who has
understanding seeks
knowledge,
but the mouths of fools feed
on folly.
15 All the days of the poor are hard,
but a cheerful heart has a continual
feast.
16 Better is a little with the fear of the
LORD

a Gk Syr: Heb *in their death* *b* Gk Syr: Heb lacks *not* *c* Cn: Heb *makes knowledge good*

in wisdom thought (e.g., 12.16; 15.18; 19.19; 20.3; 25.28; Sir 28.8,11–12). Here "passion" refers not to sexual passion but to strong, unregulated emotions of any sort. **31:** Cf. 22.16; 28.3. The same view is often found in the prophets (e.g., Ezek 22.29; Am 4.1; Zech 7.10). **35:** Cf. 16.14; 19.12. **15.8:** Sincerity in worship is essential (v. 29; 21.3,27). **11:** *Sheol,* the underworld, and *Abaddon* (lit. "Destruction") are the place and state of the dead (cf. 1.12; for v. 11b, cf. 20.27; Sir 42.18). **16–17:** A proverb pair that puts into question the value of prosperity (cf. 16.8; 17.1). *Dinner of vegetables,* simple fare in contrast to the

than great treasure and trouble
with it.
17 Better is a dinner of vegetables where
love is
than a fatted ox and hatred with it.
18 Those who are hot-tempered stir up
strife,
but those who are slow to anger
calm contention.
19 The way of the lazy is overgrown
with thorns,
but the path of the upright is a
level highway.
20 A wise child makes a glad father,
but the foolish despise their
mothers.
21 Folly is a joy to one who has no
sense,
but a person of understanding
walks straight ahead.
22 Without counsel, plans go wrong,
but with many advisers they
succeed.
23 To make an apt answer is a joy to
anyone,
and a word in season, how good it
is!
24 For the wise the path of life leads
upward,
in order to avoid Sheol below.
25 The LORD tears down the house of
the proud,
but maintains the widow's
boundaries.
26 Evil plans are an abomination to the
LORD,
but gracious words are pure.
27 Those who are greedy for unjust gain
make trouble for their
households,
but those who hate bribes will
live.
28 The mind of the righteous ponders
how to answer,
but the mouth of the wicked pours
out evil.
29 The LORD is far from the wicked,
but he hears the prayer of the
righteous.
30 The light of the eyes rejoices the
heart,
and good news refreshes the body.
31 The ear that heeds wholesome
admonition
will lodge among the wise.
32 Those who ignore instruction despise
themselves,
but those who heed admonition
gain understanding.
33 The fear of the LORD is instruction in
wisdom,
and humility goes before honor.

16 The plans of the mind belong to
mortals,
but the answer of the tongue is
from the LORD.
2 All one's ways may be pure in one's
own eyes,
but the LORD weighs the spirit.
3 Commit your work to the LORD,
and your plans will be established.
4 The LORD has made everything for its
purpose,
even the wicked for the day of
trouble.
5 All those who are arrogant are an
abomination to the LORD;
be assured, they will not go
unpunished.
6 By loyalty and faithfulness iniquity is
atoned for,
and by the fear of the LORD one
avoids evil.
7 When the ways of people please
the LORD,
he causes even their enemies to be
at peace with them.

luxury of a *fatted ox*. **23:** A prized goal of the sages (cf. 25.11). **25:** *Boundaries,* the markers that indicate the extent of a field (see 22.28; Deut 19.4). Since the powerful might attempt to encroach on the land of *widows* and orphans (Job 24.2–3), these persons were held to be under special divine protection (see 23.10–11). **27:** Cf. 17.23; Sir 20.29. **16.1:** No human activity escapes divine providence (vv. 9,33; 19.21; 20.24; 21.30–31). **2:** See 17.3; 21.2; 24.12. **4:** Everything belongs to the LORD's purposes (see Sir 33.7–15; 39.16–35). **6:** *Loyalty and faithfulness* might refer to human or divine actions (see 3.3; 14.22).

8 Better is a little with righteousness
than large income with injustice.
9 The human mind plans the way,
but the LORD directs the steps.
10 Inspired decisions are on the lips of a king;
his mouth does not sin in judgment.
11 Honest balances and scales are the LORD's;
all the weights in the bag are his work.
12 It is an abomination to kings to do evil,
for the throne is established by righteousness.
13 Righteous lips are the delight of a king,
and he loves those who speak what is right.
14 A king's wrath is a messenger of death,
and whoever is wise will appease it.
15 In the light of a king's face there is life,
and his favor is like the clouds that bring the spring rain.
16 How much better to get wisdom than gold!
To get understanding is to be chosen rather than silver.
17 The highway of the upright avoids evil;
those who guard their way preserve their lives.
18 Pride goes before destruction,
and a haughty spirit before a fall.
19 It is better to be of a lowly spirit among the poor
than to divide the spoil with the proud.
20 Those who are attentive to a matter will prosper,
and happy are those who trust in the LORD.
21 The wise of heart is called perceptive,
and pleasant speech increases persuasiveness.
22 Wisdom is a fountain of life to one who has it,
but folly is the punishment of fools.
23 The mind of the wise makes their speech judicious,
and adds persuasiveness to their lips.
24 Pleasant words are like a honeycomb,
sweetness to the soul and health to the body.
25 Sometimes there is a way that seems to be right,
but in the end it is the way to death.
26 The appetite of workers works for them;
their hunger urges them on.
27 Scoundrels concoct evil,
and their speech is like a scorching fire.
28 A perverse person spreads strife,
and a whisperer separates close friends.
29 The violent entice their neighbors,
and lead them in a way that is not good.
30 One who winks the eyes plans[a] perverse things;
one who compresses the lips brings evil to pass.
31 Gray hair is a crown of glory;
it is gained in a righteous life.
32 One who is slow to anger is better than the mighty,
and one whose temper is controlled than one who captures a city.
33 The lot is cast into the lap,
but the decision is the LORD's alone.

a Gk Syr Vg Tg: Heb *to plan*

10–15: A small collection of sayings concerning the *king*. **10:** *Inspired decisions,* the king speaks with indisputable authority (20.8). **11:** See 11.1n. **14:** *King's wrath,* cf. 19.12; 20.2. **15:** Royal favor is compared to life-giving sunshine (Num 6.25; Hos 6.3). **18:** See 11.2. **22:** See 10.11n. **25:** Also 14.12. **29:** Cf. 1.10–19. **30:** See 6.12–15; 10.10. **31:** *Gray hair* is prized as evidence of a long life, the reward of the wise and virtuous (20.29; Sir 25.3–6). **33:** Nothing happens by chance; even the fall of *the lot* (18.18) is

17 Better is a dry morsel with quiet
than a house full of feasting
with strife.
2 A slave who deals wisely will rule
over a child who acts
shamefully,
and will share the inheritance as
one of the family.
3 The crucible is for silver, and the
furnace is for gold,
but the LORD tests the heart.
4 An evildoer listens to wicked lips;
and a liar gives heed to a
mischievous tongue.
5 Those who mock the poor insult their
Maker;
those who are glad at calamity will
not go unpunished.
6 Grandchildren are the crown of
the aged,
and the glory of children is their
parents.
7 Fine speech is not becoming to a fool;
still less is false speech to a ruler.[a]
8 A bribe is like a magic stone in the
eyes of those who give it;
wherever they turn they prosper.
9 One who forgives an affront fosters
friendship,
but one who dwells on disputes will
alienate a friend.
10 A rebuke strikes deeper into a
discerning person
than a hundred blows into a fool.
11 Evil people seek only rebellion,
but a cruel messenger will be sent
against them.
12 Better to meet a she-bear robbed of
its cubs
than to confront a fool immersed in
folly.
13 Evil will not depart from the house
of one who returns evil for good.
14 The beginning of strife is like letting
out water;
so stop before the quarrel
breaks out.
15 One who justifies the wicked and one
who condemns the righteous
are both alike an abomination to
the LORD.
16 Why should fools have a price
in hand
to buy wisdom, when they have no
mind to learn?
17 A friend loves at all times,
and kinsfolk are born to share
adversity.
18 It is senseless to give a pledge,
to become surety for a neighbor.
19 One who loves transgression
loves strife;
one who builds a high threshold
invites broken bones.
20 The crooked of mind do not prosper,
and the perverse of tongue fall into
calamity.
21 The one who begets a fool gets
trouble;
the parent of a fool has no joy.
22 A cheerful heart is a good medicine,
but a downcast spirit dries up
the bones.
23 The wicked accept a concealed bribe
to pervert the ways of justice.
24 The discerning person looks to
wisdom,
but the eyes of a fool to the ends of
the earth.
25 Foolish children are a grief to their
father
and bitterness to her who
bore them.

a Or *a noble person*

determined by God. **17.1:** Cf. 15.16–17. **3:** Cf. 27.21; Sir 2.5. **5:** Cf. 14.31. **8:** *A bribe* works (see 18.16; 21.14); elsewhere bribery is condemned (cf. v. 23). **10:** *A hundred blows,* the law limits corporal punishment to forty blows (Deut 25.3). **12:** *She-bear,* cf. 2 Sam 17.8; Hos 13.8. **14:** *Letting out water,* as when a dam is breached, the torrent is unstoppable. **16:** *Price in hand,* perhaps a reference to tuition paid to wisdom teachers. **18:** Cf. 6.1–5; 11.15; 20.16. **19:** *Builds a high threshold,* a "cause and effect" proverb. Just as a badly built (and perhaps ostentatious) *threshold invites* problems, so does transgression serve as an invitation to conflict. **23:** Cf. v. 8; 15.27; Sir 20.29. **24:** *The eyes of a fool* seek unattainable goals.

26 To impose a fine on the innocent is
not right,
or to flog the noble for their
integrity.
27 One who spares words is
knowledgeable;
one who is cool in spirit has
understanding.
28 Even fools who keep silent are
considered wise;
when they close their lips, they are
deemed intelligent.

18 The one who lives alone is
self-indulgent,
showing contempt for all who have
sound judgment.[a]
2 A fool takes no pleasure in
understanding,
but only in expressing personal
opinion.
3 When wickedness comes, contempt
comes also;
and with dishonor comes disgrace.
4 The words of the mouth are deep
waters;
the fountain of wisdom is a gushing
stream.
5 It is not right to be partial to
the guilty,
or to subvert the innocent in
judgment.
6 A fool's lips bring strife,
and a fool's mouth invites a
flogging.
7 The mouths of fools are their ruin,
and their lips a snare to themselves.
8 The words of a whisperer are like
delicious morsels;
they go down into the inner parts
of the body.
9 One who is slack in work
is close kin to a vandal.
10 The name of the LORD is a strong
tower;
the righteous run into it and
are safe.
11 The wealth of the rich is their strong
city;
in their imagination it is like a high
wall.
12 Before destruction one's heart is
haughty,
but humility goes before honor.
13 If one gives answer before hearing,
it is folly and shame.
14 The human spirit will endure sickness;
but a broken spirit—who can bear?
15 An intelligent mind acquires
knowledge,
and the ear of the wise seeks
knowledge.
16 A gift opens doors;
it gives access to the great.
17 The one who first states a case seems
right,
until the other comes and
cross-examines.
18 Casting the lot puts an end to
disputes
and decides between powerful
contenders.
19 An ally offended is stronger than
a city;[b]
such quarreling is like the bars of a
castle.
20 From the fruit of the mouth one's
stomach is satisfied;
the yield of the lips brings
satisfaction.
21 Death and life are in the power of the
tongue,

a Meaning of Heb uncertain *b* Gk Syr Vg Tg: Meaning of Heb uncertain

27–28: A proverb pair on the ambiguity of silence (cf. 10.19; Sir 20.5–6). **18.4:** *Deep waters,* an ambiguous metaphor: Speech can be profound and life-giving, or it can be dangerous (v. 21; 10.11). By the first alternative, the two lines would be synonymous, otherwise antithetical. **8:** Some people take in slander with relish; it affects them deeply (also 26.22). **10–11:** A proverb pair: The *name of the LORD* is reliable (Ps 61.3; 124.8); the protection of *wealth* may prove to be imaginary (10.15–16; 11.4). **13:** Cf. v. 2; Sir 11.8. **17–18:** Both sides of a case must be heard; intractable *disputes* are settled by *casting the lot* (i.e., seeking the LORD's decision, see 16.33). **19:** The Heb text is poorly preserved, but the point is that

and those who love it will eat
its fruits.
22 He who finds a wife finds a
good thing,
and obtains favor from the LORD.
23 The poor use entreaties,
but the rich answer roughly.
24 Some[a] friends play at friendship[b]
but a true friend sticks closer than
one's nearest kin.

19 Better the poor walking in
integrity
than one perverse of speech who is
a fool.
2 Desire without knowledge is
not good,
and one who moves too hurriedly
misses the way.
3 One's own folly leads to ruin,
yet the heart rages against
the LORD.
4 Wealth brings many friends,
but the poor are left friendless.
5 A false witness will not go
unpunished,
and a liar will not escape.
6 Many seek the favor of the generous,
and everyone is a friend to a giver
of gifts.
7 If the poor are hated even by their
kin,
how much more are they shunned
by their friends!
When they call after them, they are
not there.[c]
8 To get wisdom is to love oneself;
to keep understanding is to prosper.
9 A false witness will not go
unpunished,
and the liar will perish.
10 It is not fitting for a fool to live
in luxury,
much less for a slave to rule over
princes.
11 Those with good sense are slow
to anger,
and it is their glory to overlook an
offense.
12 A king's anger is like the growling of
a lion,
but his favor is like dew on
the grass.
13 A stupid child is ruin to a father,
and a wife's quarreling is a
continual dripping of rain.
14 House and wealth are inherited from
parents,
but a prudent wife is from
the LORD.
15 Laziness brings on deep sleep;
an idle person will suffer hunger.
16 Those who keep the commandment
will live;
those who are heedless of their
ways will die.
17 Whoever is kind to the poor lends to
the LORD,
and will be repaid in full.
18 Discipline your children while there is
hope;
do not set your heart on their
destruction.
19 A violent tempered person will pay
the penalty;
if you effect a rescue, you will only
have to do it again.[c]
20 Listen to advice and accept
instruction,
that you may gain wisdom for the
future.

a Syr Tg: Heb *A man of* *b* Cn Compare Syr Vg Tg: Meaning of Heb uncertain *c* Meaning of Heb uncertain

quarreling prevents reconciliation, *like the bars of a castle.* **23:** Cf. Sir 13.3. **19.1:** *Better the poor,* see 15.16–17; 16.8; 17.1; 28.6. **4:** *The poor are left friendless,* see vv. 6–7; 14.20; Eccl 9.16; Sir 6.8–12; 13.21. **5:** The *false witness* is a frequent topic (see v. 9; 6.19; 12.17; 14.5,25; 21.28; 25.7c–10,18; Ex 20.16; 23.1–3,7). **10:** The sages sometimes reflect the perspective of the upper classes (30.22; Eccl 10.6–7). **13–14:** This teaching patently occupies the viewpoint of the male head of household (18.22; 21.9,19; 25.24; 27.15). **16:** *The commandment,* of the parent or sage, but ultimately also of the LORD (see 13.13). **17:** See 14.31; 17.5; 28.27. **18:** *While there is hope,* during childhood, when lasting formation can occur (22.6). **21:** See 16.1,9,33; 21.30–31. **24:** One can be too lazy even to eat (v. 15; 12.27; 13.4;

21 The human mind may devise
many plans,
but it is the purpose of the LORD
that will be established.
22 What is desirable in a person
is loyalty,
and it is better to be poor than
a liar.
23 The fear of the LORD is life indeed;
filled with it one rests secure
and suffers no harm.
24 The lazy person buries a hand in the
dish,
and will not even bring it back to
the mouth.
25 Strike a scoffer, and the simple will
learn prudence;
reprove the intelligent, and they
will gain knowledge.
26 Those who do violence to their father
and chase away their mother
are children who cause shame and
bring reproach.
27 Cease straying, my child, from the
words of knowledge,
in order that you may hear
instruction.
28 A worthless witness mocks at justice,
and the mouth of the wicked
devours iniquity.
29 Condemnation is ready for scoffers,
and flogging for the backs of fools.

20 Wine is a mocker, strong drink a
brawler,
and whoever is led astray by it is
not wise.
2 The dread anger of a king is like the
growling of a lion;
anyone who provokes him to anger
forfeits life itself.
3 It is honorable to refrain from strife,
but every fool is quick to quarrel.
4 The lazy person does not plow
in season;
harvest comes, and there is nothing
to be found.
5 The purposes in the human mind are
like deep water,
but the intelligent will draw them
out.
6 Many proclaim themselves loyal,
but who can find one worthy
of trust?
7 The righteous walk in integrity—
happy are the children who follow
them!
8 A king who sits on the throne of
judgment
winnows all evil with his eyes.
9 Who can say, "I have made my heart
clean;
I am pure from my sin"?
10 Diverse weights and diverse measures
are both alike an abomination to
the LORD.
11 Even children make themselves known
by their acts,
by whether what they do is pure
and right.
12 The hearing ear and the seeing eye—
the LORD has made them both.
13 Do not love sleep, or else you will
come to poverty;
open your eyes, and you will have
plenty of bread.
14 "Bad, bad," says the buyer,
then goes away and boasts.
15 There is gold, and abundance of
costly stones;
but the lips informed by knowledge
are a precious jewel.
16 Take the garment of one who has
given surety for a stranger;
seize the pledge given as surety for
foreigners.
17 Bread gained by deceit is sweet,
but afterward the mouth will be
full of gravel.

26.15). **20.1:** Caution concerning *wine* and *strong drink* (23.19–21,29–35; 31.4–5; Sir 19.2; 31.25–26,29–30). **2:** Royal *anger* is a threat to the king's subjects (16.14–15; 19.12). **4:** See 6.6–11. **5:** *Like deep water,* see 18.4. **8:** *Winnows,* by his sharp judgment (v. 26). **10:** See v. 23; 11.1n. **14:** In the bargaining process, the *buyer* claims to be losing, even when the deal is a good one. **16:** See 6.1–5; 27.13. The *stranger* or *foreigner,* with no ties of kinship in the community, makes a poor security risk. **17:** *Full of gravel,* see Lam 3.16. **20:** *Lamp will go out,* see 13.9. **21:** *Estate quickly acquired,* not properly

18 Plans are established by taking advice;
wage war by following wise guidance.
19 A gossip reveals secrets;
therefore do not associate with a babbler.
20 If you curse father or mother,
your lamp will go out in utter darkness.
21 An estate quickly acquired in the beginning
will not be blessed in the end.
22 Do not say, "I will repay evil";
wait for the LORD, and he will help you.
23 Differing weights are an abomination to the LORD,
and false scales are not good.
24 All our steps are ordered by the LORD;
how then can we understand our own ways?
25 It is a snare for one to say rashly, "It is holy,"
and begin to reflect only after making a vow.
26 A wise king winnows the wicked,
and drives the wheel over them.
27 The human spirit is the lamp of the LORD,
searching every inmost part.
28 Loyalty and faithfulness preserve the king,
and his throne is upheld by righteousness.[a]
29 The glory of youths is their strength,
but the beauty of the aged is their gray hair.
30 Blows that wound cleanse away evil;
beatings make clean the innermost parts.

21 The king's heart is a stream of water in the hand of the LORD;
he turns it wherever he will.
2 All deeds are right in the sight of the doer,
but the LORD weighs the heart.
3 To do righteousness and justice
is more acceptable to the LORD than sacrifice.
4 Haughty eyes and a proud heart—
the lamp of the wicked—are sin.
5 The plans of the diligent lead surely to abundance,
but everyone who is hasty comes only to want.
6 The getting of treasures by a lying tongue
is a fleeting vapor and a snare[b] of death.
7 The violence of the wicked will sweep them away,
because they refuse to do what is just.
8 The way of the guilty is crooked,
but the conduct of the pure is right.
9 It is better to live in a corner of the housetop
than in a house shared with a contentious wife.
10 The souls of the wicked desire evil;
their neighbors find no mercy in their eyes.
11 When a scoffer is punished, the simple become wiser;
when the wise are instructed, they increase in knowledge.
12 The Righteous One observes the house of the wicked;
he casts the wicked down to ruin.
13 If you close your ear to the cry of the poor,
you will cry out and not be heard.
14 A gift in secret averts anger;
and a concealed bribe in the bosom, strong wrath.
15 When justice is done, it is a joy to the righteous,
but dismay to evildoers.

a Gk: Heb *loyalty*   *b* Gk: Heb *seekers*

inherited. **25:** A sacred *vow* (see Lev 27.1–25) should not be made casually (Eccl 5.1–6). **26:** *The wheel,* a threshing implement (v. 8; Isa 28.27). **29:** See 16.31n. **21.1:** Even the mind of a *king* is controlled by God (vv. 30–31). **2:** See 16.2. **3:** See 15.8,29; 28.9,13; 1 Sam 15.22; Hos 6.6; Mic 6.6–8. **9:** *In a corner of the housetop,* i.e., in a small room constructed there (cf. 2 Kings 4.10); see 19.13–14n. **14:** See 17.8n.

16 Whoever wanders from the way of
understanding
will rest in the assembly of
the dead.
17 Whoever loves pleasure will suffer
want;
whoever loves wine and oil will not
be rich.
18 The wicked is a ransom for the
righteous,
and the faithless for the upright.
19 It is better to live in a desert land
than with a contentious and fretful
wife.
20 Precious treasure remains[a] in the
house of the wise,
but the fool devours it.
21 Whoever pursues righteousness and
kindness
will find life[b] and honor.
22 One wise person went up against a
city of warriors
and brought down the stronghold
in which they trusted.
23 To watch over mouth and tongue
is to keep out of trouble.
24 The proud, haughty person, named
"Scoffer,"
acts with arrogant pride.
25 The craving of the lazy person
is fatal,
for lazy hands refuse to labor.
26 All day long the wicked covet,[c]
but the righteous give and do not
hold back.
27 The sacrifice of the wicked is an
abomination;
how much more when brought
with evil intent.
28 A false witness will perish,
but a good listener will testify
successfully.
29 The wicked put on a bold face,
but the upright give thought to[d]
their ways.
30 No wisdom, no understanding, no
counsel,
can avail against the LORD.
31 The horse is made ready for the day
of battle,
but the victory belongs to
the LORD.

22 A good name is to be chosen
rather than great riches,
and favor is better than silver
or gold.
2 The rich and the poor have this in
common:
the LORD is the maker of them all.
3 The clever see danger and hide;
but the simple go on, and suffer for
it.
4 The reward for humility and fear of
the LORD
is riches and honor and life.
5 Thorns and snares are in the way of
the perverse;
the cautious will keep far from
them.
6 Train children in the right way,
and when old, they will not stray.
7 The rich rule over the poor,
and the borrower is the slave of the
lender.
8 Whoever sows injustice will reap
calamity,
and the rod of anger will fail.
9 Those who are generous are blessed,
for they share their bread with the
poor.
10 Drive out a scoffer, and strife
goes out;
quarreling and abuse will cease.

a Gk: Heb *and oil* *b* Gk: Heb *life and righteousness*
c Gk: Heb *all day long one covets covetously*
d Another reading is *establish*

18: The meaning of *ransom* here is obscure; perhaps it means that trouble befalls the *wicked* instead of the *righteous,* as in 11.8. **19:** See 19.13–14n. **22:** *One wise person,* see Eccl 9.14–15. **28:** See 19.5n. **30–31:** Such sayings indicate that the sages recognized the limitations of human wisdom, in view of the LORD's greater wisdom and providence (cf. 16.1,9,33; 19.21; 20.18,24). **22.1:** On the value of a *good name,* see Eccl 7.1; Sir 41.12–13. **2:** See 29.13; Job 31.15. **7:** *The borrower is the slave,* not only a figurative expression; debt slavery was a reality in ancient Israel (Ex 21.2–7; 2 Kings 4.1; Neh 5.5). **13:** See 26.13. **14:** See 2.16–19; 7.10–27. **15:** See 13.24n.

11 Those who love a pure heart and are
gracious in speech
will have the king as a friend.
12 The eyes of the LORD keep watch
over knowledge,
but he overthrows the words of the
faithless.
13 The lazy person says, "There is a lion
outside!
I shall be killed in the streets!"
14 The mouth of a loose[a] woman is a
deep pit;
he with whom the LORD is angry
falls into it.
15 Folly is bound up in the heart of
a boy,
but the rod of discipline drives it
far away.
16 Oppressing the poor in order to
enrich oneself,
and giving to the rich, will lead
only to loss.

17 The words of the wise:

Incline your ear and hear my words,[b]
and apply your mind to my
teaching;
18 for it will be pleasant if you keep
them within you,
if all of them are ready on
your lips.
19 So that your trust may be in
the LORD,
I have made them known to you
today—yes, to you.
20 Have I not written for you thirty
sayings
of admonition and knowledge,
21 to show you what is right and true,
so that you may give a true answer
to those who sent you?

22 Do not rob the poor because they are
poor,
or crush the afflicted at the gate;
23 for the LORD pleads their cause
and despoils of life those who
despoil them.
24 Make no friends with those given to
anger,
and do not associate with hotheads,
25 or you may learn their ways
and entangle yourself in a snare.
26 Do not be one of those who give
pledges,
who become surety for debts.
27 If you have nothing with which
to pay,
why should your bed be taken from
under you?
28 Do not remove the ancient landmark
that your ancestors set up.
29 Do you see those who are skillful in
their work?
They will serve kings;
they will not serve common people.

23 When you sit down to eat with
a ruler,
observe carefully what[c] is
before you,
2 and put a knife to your throat

a Heb *strange* *b* Cn Compare Gk: Heb *Incline your ear, and hear the words of the wise* *c* Or *who*

22.17–24.34: The words of the wise. This collection is closely related to the Egyptian "Instruction of Amen-em-ope" (ca. 1100 BCE). In contrast to the short, discrete sayings of chs 10–21, the form here changes to longer units of second-person address, like the Egyptian "Instruction" (cf. chs 1–9). Several sayings, especially in 22.17–23.11, appear to be Hebrew adaptations of Amen-em-ope's teaching. **22.17–21:** A prologue, patterned after the introduction to the "Instruction of Amen-em-ope." **20:** *Thirty sayings,* Amen-em-ope is composed of thirty sections. It is not clear how there are thirty units in this collection. **21:** *Those who sent you,* instruction equips students to serve as reliable delegates for important people (cf. v. 29; 13.17; 25.13; 26.6). **22:** Priority is given here, as in Amen-em-ope, to concern for *the poor.* **28:** *Ancient landmark,* not a memorial stone but a marker indicating property boundaries; see Deut 19.14; 27.17. **23.1–3:** Etiquette at the table of the powerful is an important topic in Amen-em-ope and other Egyptian instruction texts; see also Sir 31.12–18. **4–5:** *Like an eagle,* this passage is very close to

if you have a big appetite.
3 Do not desire the ruler's[a] delicacies,
for they are deceptive food.
4 Do not wear yourself out to get rich;
be wise enough to desist.
5 When your eyes light upon it,
it is gone;
for suddenly it takes wings to itself,
flying like an eagle toward heaven.
6 Do not eat the bread of the stingy;
do not desire their delicacies;
7 for like a hair in the throat, so
are they.[b]
"Eat and drink!" they say to you;
but they do not mean it.
8 You will vomit up the little you have
eaten,
and you will waste your pleasant
words.
9 Do not speak in the hearing of a fool,
who will only despise the wisdom
of your words.
10 Do not remove an ancient landmark
or encroach on the fields of
orphans,
11 for their redeemer is strong;
he will plead their cause
against you.
12 Apply your mind to instruction
and your ear to words of
knowledge.
13 Do not withhold discipline from your
children;
if you beat them with a rod, they
will not die.
14 If you beat them with the rod,
you will save their lives from Sheol.
15 My child, if your heart is wise,
my heart too will be glad.
16 My soul will rejoice
when your lips speak what is right.
17 Do not let your heart envy sinners,
but always continue in the fear of
the LORD.
18 Surely there is a future,
and your hope will not be cut
off.

19 Hear, my child, and be wise,
and direct your mind in the way.
20 Do not be among winebibbers,
or among gluttonous eaters
of meat;
21 for the drunkard and the glutton will
come to poverty,
and drowsiness will clothe them
with rags.

22 Listen to your father who begot you,
and do not despise your mother
when she is old.
23 Buy truth, and do not sell it;
buy wisdom, instruction, and
understanding.
24 The father of the righteous will
greatly rejoice;
he who begets a wise son will be
glad in him.
25 Let your father and mother be glad;
let her who bore you rejoice.

26 My child, give me your heart,
and let your eyes observe[c] my
ways.
27 For a prostitute is a deep pit;
an adulteress[d] is a narrow well.
28 She lies in wait like a robber
and increases the number of the
faithless.

29 Who has woe? Who has sorrow?
Who has strife? Who has
complaining?
Who has wounds without cause?
Who has redness of eyes?
30 Those who linger late over wine,
those who keep trying mixed wines.
31 Do not look at wine when it is red,
when it sparkles in the cup
and goes down smoothly.

a Heb *his* *b* Meaning of Heb uncertain
c Another reading is *delight in* *d* Heb *an alien woman*

Amen-em-ope, in which the flight of geese symbolizes fleeting wealth. **10–11**: See 15.25n.; 22.28n. **13–14**: See 13.24n.; Sir 22.6; 30.1–13. *Sheol,* the abode of the dead. **27**: See 2.16n.; 6.26; 7.10. **29–35**: A vivid description of the ill effects of drunkenness (cf. vv. 20–21; 20.1; 31.4–5). **34**: The text is difficult,

32 At the last it bites like a serpent,
and stings like an adder.
33 Your eyes will see strange things,
and your mind utter perverse
things.
34 You will be like one who lies down in
the midst of the sea,
like one who lies on the top of
a mast.[a]
35 "They struck me," you will say,[b]
"but I was not hurt;
they beat me, but I did not feel it.
When shall I awake?
I will seek another drink."

24 Do not envy the wicked,
nor desire to be with them;
2 for their minds devise violence,
and their lips talk of mischief.

3 By wisdom a house is built,
and by understanding it is
established;
4 by knowledge the rooms are filled
with all precious and pleasant
riches.
5 Wise warriors are mightier than
strong ones,[c]
and those who have knowledge
than those who have strength;
6 for by wise guidance you can wage
your war,
and in abundance of counselors
there is victory.
7 Wisdom is too high for fools;
in the gate they do not open
their mouths.

8 Whoever plans to do evil
will be called a mischief-maker.
9 The devising of folly is sin,
and the scoffer is an abomination
to all.

10 If you faint in the day of adversity,
your strength being small;
11 if you hold back from rescuing those
taken away to death,
those who go staggering to the
slaughter;
12 if you say, "Look, we did not
know this"—
does not he who weighs the heart
perceive it?
Does not he who keeps watch over
your soul know it?
And will he not repay all according
to their deeds?

13 My child, eat honey, for it is good,
and the drippings of the
honeycomb are sweet to
your taste.
14 Know that wisdom is such to
your soul;
if you find it, you will find a
future,
and your hope will not be cut off.

15 Do not lie in wait like an outlaw
against the home of the
righteous;
do no violence to the place where
the righteous live;
16 for though they fall seven times, they
will rise again;
but the wicked are overthrown by
calamity.

17 Do not rejoice when your enemies
fall,
and do not let your heart be glad
when they stumble,
18 or else the LORD will see it and be
displeased,
and turn away his anger
from them.

a Meaning of Heb uncertain *b* Gk Syr Vg Tg: Heb lacks *you will say* *c* Gk Compare Syr Tg: Heb *A wise man is strength*

but the comparison is evidently to the dizziness and nausea of seasickness (cf. Ps 107.26–27). **24.3:** *A house is built,* cf. v. 27; 9.1; 14.1. **5–6:** Strategy can outdo might (21.22; but contrast 21.30–31). **10–12:** A good person should intervene on behalf of victims of violence. The one *who weighs the heart* is the LORD (16.2; 21.2). **13:** *Eat honey,* a figure for acquiring wisdom (v. 14; cf. 16.24; Ps 19.10). **16:** *Seven times,* i.e., any number of times; the righteous will *rise again,* in contrast to *the wicked.* **17:** See Job 31.29.

19 Do not fret because of evildoers.
Do not envy the wicked;
20 for the evil have no future;
the lamp of the wicked will go out.

21 My child, fear the LORD and the king,
and do not disobey either of them;[a]
22 for disaster comes from them suddenly,
and who knows the ruin that both can bring?

23 These also are sayings of the wise:

Partiality in judging is not good.
24 Whoever says to the wicked, "You are innocent,"
will be cursed by peoples, abhorred by nations;
25 but those who rebuke the wicked will have delight,
and a good blessing will come upon them.
26 One who gives an honest answer
gives a kiss on the lips.
27 Prepare your work outside,
get everything ready for you in the field;
and after that build your house.

28 Do not be a witness against your neighbor without cause,
and do not deceive with your lips.
29 Do not say, "I will do to others as they have done to me;
I will pay them back for what they have done."

30 I passed by the field of one who was lazy,
by the vineyard of a stupid person;
31 and see, it was all overgrown with thorns;
the ground was covered with nettles,
and its stone wall was broken down.
32 Then I saw and considered it;
I looked and received instruction.
33 A little sleep, a little slumber,
a little folding of the hands to rest,
34 and poverty will come upon you like a robber,
and want, like an armed warrior.

25 These are other proverbs of Solomon that the officials of King Hezekiah of Judah copied.

2 It is the glory of God to conceal things,
but the glory of kings is to search things out.
3 Like the heavens for height, like the earth for depth,
so the mind of kings is unsearchable.
4 Take away the dross from the silver,
and the smith has material for a vessel;
5 take away the wicked from the presence of the king,
and his throne will be established in righteousness.
6 Do not put yourself forward in the king's presence
or stand in the place of the great;

a Gk: Heb *do not associate with those who change*

20: Job 18.5–6; 21.17. **23:** A title for another short collection (vv. 23–34). **23b–25:** 28.21; Lev 19.15; Deut 16.19. **26:** *Kiss on the lips,* obscure; the gesture would seem to demonstrate friendship or trustworthiness. **27:** Literally, food comes before shelter; figuratively, any major undertaking requires proper preparation. **29:** Cf. vv. 17–18. **30–34:** See 6.6–11.

25.1–29.27: Another sayings collection. 25.1: *Officials of King Hezekiah* are scribes of this famous king of Judah in the late eighth to early seventh century BCE; *copied* probably refers to the editing and arranging of sayings. **2–3:** Like God, the king questions but cannot be questioned. **4–5:** For the metaphor of refining metals, see also 27.21–22. **6–7:** See Sir 7.4; 13.10. **7c–10:** A caution against rash accusations. *Shame,* see 5.14n. **11:** A goal of the sages: right and timely expressions (cf. 15.23). **15b:** A "fitly

7 for it is better to be told, "Come
up here,"
than to be put lower in the
presence of a noble.

What your eyes have seen
8 do not hastily bring into court;
for[a] what will you do in the end,
when your neighbor puts you to
shame?
9 Argue your case with your neighbor
directly,
and do not disclose another's
secret;
10 or else someone who hears you will
bring shame upon you,
and your ill repute will have
no end.

11 A word fitly spoken
is like apples of gold in a setting of
silver.
12 Like a gold ring or an ornament
of gold
is a wise rebuke to a listening ear.
13 Like the cold of snow in the time
of harvest
are faithful messengers to those
who send them;
they refresh the spirit of their
masters.
14 Like clouds and wind without rain
is one who boasts of a gift never
given.
15 With patience a ruler may be
persuaded,
and a soft tongue can break bones.
16 If you have found honey, eat only
enough for you,
or else, having too much, you will
vomit it.
17 Let your foot be seldom in your
neighbor's house,
otherwise the neighbor will become
weary of you and hate you.
18 Like a war club, a sword, or a sharp
arrow
is one who bears false witness
against a neighbor.
19 Like a bad tooth or a lame foot
is trust in a faithless person in time
of trouble.
20 Like vinegar on a wound[b]
is one who sings songs to a heavy
heart.
Like a moth in clothing or a worm in
wood,
sorrow gnaws at the human
heart.[c]
21 If your enemies are hungry, give them
bread to eat;
and if they are thirsty, give them
water to drink;
22 for you will heap coals of fire on
their heads,
and the LORD will reward you.
23 The north wind produces rain,
and a backbiting tongue, angry
looks.
24 It is better to live in a corner of the
housetop
than in a house shared with a
contentious wife.
25 Like cold water to a thirsty soul,
so is good news from a far country.
26 Like a muddied spring or a polluted
fountain
are the righteous who give way
before the wicked.
27 It is not good to eat much honey,
or to seek honor on top of honor.
28 Like a city breached, without walls,
is one who lacks self-control.

26 Like snow in summer or rain in
harvest,
so honor is not fitting for a fool.

a Cn: Heb *or else* b Gk: Heb *Like one who takes off a garment on a cold day, like vinegar on lye* c Gk Syr Tg: Heb lacks *Like a moth . . . human heart*

spoken" paradox (cf. 15.4; Sir 28.17–18). **18:** See 19.5n. **21–22:** *Coals of fire,* in an Egyptian ritual perhaps known to the biblical sages, submitting to coals on the head demonstrated contrition. The sense here seems to be that undeserved kindness awakens the remorse and hence conversion of the *enemies;* cf. 24.17–18. **24:** See 21.9n. **26:** *Muddied spring,* the comparison is to livestock trampling and otherwise fouling the clear water. **26.1–12: Concerning fools and their folly. 4–5:** Juxtaposing the two sayings

2 Like a sparrow in its flitting, like a swallow in its flying,
an undeserved curse goes nowhere.
3 A whip for the horse, a bridle for the donkey,
and a rod for the back of fools.
4 Do not answer fools according to their folly,
or you will be a fool yourself.
5 Answer fools according to their folly,
or they will be wise in their own eyes.
6 It is like cutting off one's foot and drinking down violence,
to send a message by a fool.
7 The legs of a disabled person hang limp;
so does a proverb in the mouth of a fool.
8 It is like binding a stone in a sling
to give honor to a fool.
9 Like a thornbush brandished by the hand of a drunkard
is a proverb in the mouth of a fool.
10 Like an archer who wounds everybody
is one who hires a passing fool or drunkard.[a]
11 Like a dog that returns to its vomit
is a fool who reverts to his folly.
12 Do you see persons wise in their own eyes?
There is more hope for fools than for them.
13 The lazy person says, "There is a lion in the road!
There is a lion in the streets!"
14 As a door turns on its hinges,
so does a lazy person in bed.
15 The lazy person buries a hand in the dish,
and is too tired to bring it back to the mouth.
16 The lazy person is wiser in self-esteem
than seven who can answer discreetly.
17 Like somebody who takes a passing dog by the ears
is one who meddles in the quarrel of another.
18 Like a maniac who shoots deadly firebrands and arrows,
19 so is one who deceives a neighbor
and says, "I am only joking!"
20 For lack of wood the fire goes out,
and where there is no whisperer, quarreling ceases.
21 As charcoal is to hot embers and wood to fire,
so is a quarrelsome person for kindling strife.
22 The words of a whisperer are like delicious morsels;
they go down into the inner parts of the body.
23 Like the glaze[b] covering an earthen vessel
are smooth[c] lips with an evil heart.
24 An enemy dissembles in speaking
while harboring deceit within;
25 when an enemy speaks graciously, do not believe it,
for there are seven abominations concealed within;
26 though hatred is covered with guile,
the enemy's wickedness will be exposed in the assembly.
27 Whoever digs a pit will fall into it,
and a stone will come back on the one who starts it rolling.
28 A lying tongue hates its victims,
and a flattering mouth works ruin.

a Meaning of Heb uncertain *b* Cn: Heb *silver of dross* *c* Gk: Heb *burning*

provokes reflection on their competing claims. Depending on the circumstances, one might interpret *according to their folly* to mean "in fools' terms" (v. 4) or "as fools deserve" (v. 5). **7:** *A fool* is by definition unable to benefit from *a proverb.* **8:** The *sling* is used to hurl objects; to fasten *a stone* defeats the purpose. **9:** The expression may indicate uselessness (cf. vv. 7–8), or the use of a proverb in a hurtful way. **13–16:** The lazy person. **13:** A ridiculous excuse; *a lion* is not likely to appear in the city *streets* and squares (cf. 22.13). **15:** See 19.24n. **17–28:** A loose collection on the consequences of various forms of antisocial speech and behavior. **22:** See 18.8n. **27:** A kind of "poetic justice" (cf. Ps 7.15; Eccl 10.8;

27 Do not boast about tomorrow,
for you do not know what a day
may bring.
2 Let another praise you, and not your
own mouth—
a stranger, and not your own lips.
3 A stone is heavy, and sand is weighty,
but a fool's provocation is heavier
than both.
4 Wrath is cruel, anger is
overwhelming,
but who is able to stand before
jealousy?
5 Better is open rebuke
than hidden love.
6 Well meant are the wounds a friend
inflicts,
but profuse are the kisses of an
enemy.
7 The sated appetite spurns honey,
but to a ravenous appetite even the
bitter is sweet.
8 Like a bird that strays from its nest
is one who strays from home.
9 Perfume and incense make the heart
glad,
but the soul is torn by trouble.[a]
10 Do not forsake your friend or the
friend of your parent;
do not go to the house of your
kindred in the day of your
calamity.
Better is a neighbor who is nearby
than kindred who are far away.
11 Be wise, my child, and make my heart
glad,
so that I may answer whoever
reproaches me.
12 The clever see danger and hide;
but the simple go on, and suffer for
it.
13 Take the garment of one who has
given surety for a stranger;
seize the pledge given as surety for
foreigners.[b]
14 Whoever blesses a neighbor with a
loud voice,
rising early in the morning,
will be counted as cursing.
15 A continual dripping on a rainy day
and a contentious wife are alike;
16 to restrain her is to restrain the wind
or to grasp oil in the right hand.[c]
17 Iron sharpens iron,
and one person sharpens the wits[d]
of another.
18 Anyone who tends a fig tree will eat
its fruit,
and anyone who takes care of a
master will be honored.
19 Just as water reflects the face,
so one human heart reflects
another.
20 Sheol and Abaddon are never
satisfied,
and human eyes are never satisfied.
21 The crucible is for silver, and the
furnace is for gold,
so a person is tested[e] by being
praised.
22 Crush a fool in a mortar with a pestle
along with crushed grain,
but the folly will not be driven out.

23 Know well the condition of
your flocks,
and give attention to your herds;
24 for riches do not last forever,
nor a crown for all generations.
25 When the grass is gone, and new
growth appears,

a Gk: Heb *the sweetness of a friend is better than one's own counsel* *b* Vg and 20.16: Heb *for a foreign woman* *c* Meaning of Heb uncertain *d* Heb *face* *e* Heb lacks *is tested*

Sir 27.25–27). **27.4:** *Who is able?* A rhetorical question, implying the answer, "no one" (cf. 18.14). **6:** *Profuse,* false, in contrast to *well meant* discipline imposed by *a friend.* **7b:** A paradox, as in 25.15b. **10:** Line b is explained by lines c–d. **13:** See 6.1–5. **14:** The proper or improper timing of an act significantly determines its nature; see Eccl 3.1–8. **15–16:** See 19.13–14n. **20:** For *Sheol and Abaddon,* see 15.11n. **21:** Cf. 17.3, where it is the LORD who tests. **23–27:** This short poem can be read as practical advice on tending *flocks* and *herds* (see 12.10; Sir 7.22). In light, however, of the *crown* mentioned in v. 24 and the widespread ancient image of the king as shepherd (e.g., 1 Kings 22.17; Ps 23.1; Isa 44.28),

and the herbage of the mountains is
gathered,
26 the lambs will provide your clothing,
and the goats the price of a field;
27 there will be enough goats' milk for
your food,
for the food of your household
and nourishment for your
servant-girls.

28 The wicked flee when no one
pursues,
but the righteous are as bold as
a lion.
2 When a land rebels
it has many rulers;
but with an intelligent ruler
there is lasting order.[a]
3 A ruler[b] who oppresses the poor
is a beating rain that leaves
no food.
4 Those who forsake the law praise the
wicked,
but those who keep the law
struggle against them.
5 The evil do not understand justice,
but those who seek the LORD
understand it completely.
6 Better to be poor and walk in
integrity
than to be crooked in one's ways
even though rich.
7 Those who keep the law are wise
children,
but companions of gluttons shame
their parents.
8 One who augments wealth by
exorbitant interest
gathers it for another who is kind
to the poor.
9 When one will not listen to the
law,
even one's prayers are an
abomination.
10 Those who mislead the upright into
evil ways
will fall into pits of their own
making,
but the blameless will have a
goodly inheritance.
11 The rich is wise in self-esteem,
but an intelligent poor person sees
through the pose.
12 When the righteous triumph, there is
great glory,
but when the wicked prevail,
people go into hiding.
13 No one who conceals transgressions
will prosper,
but one who confesses and forsakes
them will obtain mercy.
14 Happy is the one who is never
without fear,
but one who is hard-hearted will
fall into calamity.
15 Like a roaring lion or a charging bear
is a wicked ruler over a poor
people.
16 A ruler who lacks understanding is a
cruel oppressor;
but one who hates unjust gain will
enjoy a long life.
17 If someone is burdened with the
blood of another,
let that killer be a fugitive
until death;
let no one offer assistance.
18 One who walks in integrity will
be safe,
but whoever follows crooked ways
will fall into the Pit.[c]
19 Anyone who tills the land will have
plenty of bread,
but one who follows worthless
pursuits will have plenty
of poverty.
20 The faithful will abound with
blessings,

a Meaning of Heb uncertain *b* Cn: Heb *A poor person* *c* Syr: Heb *fall all at once*

it may also contain implicit royal advice. **28.3:** *Rain that leaves no food,* when grain is ripe for harvest, a hard rain can ruin the crop (cf. 26.1). **4:** *The law,* Heb "torah" (cf. vv. 7,9; 29.18), the term can designate both the sage's teaching (e.g., 3.1), and the LORD's revealed law, or Torah. **5:** See 29.7n. **8:** By the principle of retribution, the oppressor should not be allowed to profit (cf. 13.22; 14.31; 19.17; Ex 22.25). **14:** For the form of the saying, see 3.13n. **21:** *For a piece of bread,* bribery is at issue here (cf. 18.5;

but one who is in a hurry to be
rich will not go unpunished.
21 To show partiality is not good—
yet for a piece of bread a person
may do wrong.
22 The miser is in a hurry to get rich
and does not know that loss is sure
to come.
23 Whoever rebukes a person will
afterward find more favor
than one who flatters with
the tongue.
24 Anyone who robs father or mother
and says, "That is no crime,"
is partner to a thug.
25 The greedy person stirs up strife,
but whoever trusts in the LORD will
be enriched.
26 Those who trust in their own wits are
fools;
but those who walk in wisdom
come through safely.
27 Whoever gives to the poor will lack
nothing,
but one who turns a blind eye will
get many a curse.
28 When the wicked prevail, people go
into hiding;
but when they perish, the righteous
increase.

29 One who is often reproved, yet
remains stubborn,
will suddenly be broken beyond
healing.
2 When the righteous are in authority,
the people rejoice;
but when the wicked rule, the
people groan.
3 A child who loves wisdom makes a
parent glad,
but to keep company with
prostitutes is to squander one's
substance.
4 By justice a king gives stability to the
land,
but one who makes heavy exactions
ruins it.
5 Whoever flatters a neighbor
is spreading a net for the neighbor's
feet.
6 In the transgression of the evil there is
a snare,
but the righteous sing and rejoice.
7 The righteous know the rights of the
poor;
the wicked have no such
understanding.
8 Scoffers set a city aflame,
but the wise turn away wrath.
9 If the wise go to law with fools,
there is ranting and ridicule without
relief.
10 The bloodthirsty hate the blameless,
and they seek the life of the
upright.
11 A fool gives full vent to anger,
but the wise quietly holds it back.
12 If a ruler listens to falsehood,
all his officials will be wicked.
13 The poor and the oppressor have this
in common:
the LORD gives light to the eyes of
both.
14 If a king judges the poor with equity,
his throne will be established
forever.
15 The rod and reproof give wisdom,
but a mother is disgraced by a
neglected child.
16 When the wicked are in authority,
transgression increases,
but the righteous will look upon
their downfall.
17 Discipline your children, and they will
give you rest;
they will give delight to your heart.
18 Where there is no prophecy, the
people cast off restraint,
but happy are those who keep
the law.
19 By mere words servants are not
disciplined,
for though they understand, they
will not give heed.

24.23b). **29.7:** See 28.5. Wisdom literature often associates evil with a failure to perceive the true nature of things. **9:** *With fools,* it is impossible to conduct a reasonable dispute (see 26.4). **13:** Cf. 22.2. **18:**

20 Do you see someone who is hasty
in speech?
There is more hope for a fool than
for anyone like that.
21 A slave pampered from childhood
will come to a bad end.[a]
22 One given to anger stirs up strife,
and the hothead causes much
transgression.
23 A person's pride will bring
humiliation,
but one who is lowly in spirit will
obtain honor.
24 To be a partner of a thief is to hate
one's own life;
one hears the victim's curse, but
discloses nothing.[b]
25 The fear of others[c] lays a snare,
but one who trusts in the LORD
is secure.
26 Many seek the favor of a ruler,
but it is from the LORD that one
gets justice.
27 The unjust are an abomination to the
righteous,
but the upright are an abomination
to the wicked.

30 The words of Agur son of Jakeh. An oracle.

Thus says the man: I am weary,
O God,
I am weary, O God. How can I
prevail?[d]
2 Surely I am too stupid to be human;
I do not have human
understanding.
3 I have not learned wisdom,
nor have I knowledge of the
holy ones.[e]
4 Who has ascended to heaven and
come down?
Who has gathered the wind in the
hollow of the hand?
Who has wrapped up the waters in a
garment?
Who has established all the ends of
the earth?
What is the person's name?
And what is the name of the
person's child?
Surely you know!

5 Every word of God proves true;
he is a shield to those who take
refuge in him.
6 Do not add to his words,
or else he will rebuke you, and you
will be found a liar.

7 Two things I ask of you;
do not deny them to me before
I die:
8 Remove far from me falsehood and
lying;
give me neither poverty nor riches;
feed me with the food that I need,
9 or I shall be full, and deny you,
and say, "Who is the LORD?"
or I shall be poor, and steal,
and profane the name of my God.

10 Do not slander a servant to a master,

a Vg: Meaning of Heb uncertain *b* Meaning of Heb uncertain *c* Or *human fear* *d* Or *I am spent.* Meaning of Heb uncertain *e* Or *Holy One*

Prophecy, lit. vision (see 1 Sam 3.1); law, see 28.4n. **24:** *Partner of a thief,* not an actual accomplice, but someone with knowledge of the crime who *discloses nothing* (see Lev 5.1).

30.1–33: The words of Agur and other sayings. V. 1a is a title, but the extent of Agur's sayings (perhaps as far as v. 9) is uncertain. **1:** *Oracle,* others understand the Heb to mean "from Massa," a region of northern Arabia (Gen 25.14; 1 Chr 1.30). If so, Agur is a non-Israelite. The rest of v. 1 is all but untranslatable. **2–3:** The writer acknowledges *human* limitations. **4:** Rhetorical questions implying the answer "God"; cf. Job 38.4–41. **5–6:** A pious response to vv. 1–4 (see Ps 18.30; 2 Sam 22.31; Deut 4.2; 12.32). **7–9:** A prayer to be kept from *falsehood,* and to be given *neither poverty nor riches* (see Sir 31.1–4).

30.10–33: Admonitions and numerical sayings. Several of these sayings may have originated as riddles

or the servant will curse you, and
you will be held guilty.

11 There are those who curse their
fathers
and do not bless their mothers.
12 There are those who are pure in their
own eyes
yet are not cleansed of their
filthiness.
13 There are those—how lofty are their
eyes,
how high their eyelids lift!—
14 there are those whose teeth are
swords,
whose teeth are knives,
to devour the poor from off the
earth,
the needy from among mortals.

15 The leech[a] has two daughters;
"Give, give," they cry.
Three things are never satisfied;
four never say, "Enough":
16 Sheol, the barren womb,
the earth ever thirsty for water,
and the fire that never says,
"Enough."[a]

17 The eye that mocks a father
and scorns to obey a mother
will be pecked out by the ravens of
the valley
and eaten by the vultures.

18 Three things are too wonderful
for me;
four I do not understand:
19 the way of an eagle in the sky,
the way of a snake on a rock,
the way of a ship on the high seas,
and the way of a man with a girl.

20 This is the way of an adulteress:
she eats, and wipes her mouth,
and says, "I have done no wrong."

21 Under three things the earth trembles;
under four it cannot bear up:
22 a slave when he becomes king,
and a fool when glutted with food;
23 an unloved woman when she gets
a husband,
and a maid when she succeeds her
mistress.

24 Four things on earth are small,
yet they are exceedingly wise:
25 the ants are a people without
strength,
yet they provide their food in
the summer;
26 the badgers are a people without
power,
yet they make their homes in
the rocks;
27 the locusts have no king,
yet all of them march in rank;
28 the lizard[b] can be grasped in
the hand,
yet it is found in kings' palaces.

29 Three things are stately in their stride;
four are stately in their gait:
30 the lion, which is mightiest among
wild animals
and does not turn back before any;
31 the strutting rooster,[c] the he-goat,
and a king striding before[a]
his people.

a Meaning of Heb uncertain *b* Or *spider*
c Gk Syr Tg Compare Vg: Meaning of Heb uncertain

(e.g., vv. 15–16,18–19). **11–14:** Four types of sinners: the unfilial, self-satisfied, arrogant, and avaricious. **15–16:** Two sayings on the insatiable. *Sheol,* the abode of the dead. *Barren womb,* see Gen 30.1. *Fire,* see Am 7.4. **18–19:** Four wonders, comparable as regards a mysterious and irrecoverable *way* (Wis 5.10–11). **20:** A moralizing comment on v. 19d; *eats,* engages in illicit sex (5.15; 9.17; Sir 23.17; 26.12). **21–23:** Four intolerable situations. *Maid . . . mistress,* see Gen 16.3–4. **24–28:** Four small yet instructive creatures. **29–31:** Four examples of grandeur, or perhaps pomposity (the comparison with *a king* might be ironic; cf. vv. 27–28).

32 If you have been foolish, exalting
yourself,
or if you have been devising evil,
put your hand on your mouth.
33 For as pressing milk produces curds,
and pressing the nose produces
blood,
so pressing anger produces strife.

31

The words of King Lemuel. An oracle that his mother taught him:

2 No, my son! No, son of my womb!
No, son of my vows!
3 Do not give your strength to women,
your ways to those who destroy
kings.
4 It is not for kings, O Lemuel,
it is not for kings to drink wine,
or for rulers to desire[a] strong
drink;
5 or else they will drink and forget
what has been decreed,
and will pervert the rights of all
the afflicted.
6 Give strong drink to one who is
perishing,
and wine to those in bitter
distress;
7 let them drink and forget their
poverty,
and remember their misery
no more.
8 Speak out for those who cannot
speak,
for the rights of all the destitute.[b]
9 Speak out, judge righteously,
defend the rights of the poor
and needy.

10 A capable wife who can find?
She is far more precious than
jewels.
11 The heart of her husband trusts
in her,
and he will have no lack of gain.
12 She does him good, and not harm,
all the days of her life.
13 She seeks wool and flax,
and works with willing hands.
14 She is like the ships of the merchant,
she brings her food from far away.
15 She rises while it is still night
and provides food for her
household
and tasks for her servant-girls.
16 She considers a field and buys it;
with the fruit of her hands she
plants a vineyard.
17 She girds herself with strength,
and makes her arms strong.
18 She perceives that her merchandise is
profitable.
Her lamp does not go out at night.
19 She puts her hands to the distaff,
and her hands hold the spindle.
20 She opens her hand to the poor,
and reaches out her hands to
the needy.
21 She is not afraid for her household
when it snows,
for all her household are clothed in
crimson.
22 She makes herself coverings;

a Cn: Heb *where* b Heb *all children of passing away*

31.1–9: The words of Lemuel. 1: *King Lemuel,* otherwise unknown; like Agur (30.1), he may be non-Israelite. *Oracle,* see 30.1n. **2–9:** The king's mother warns him against *women* and *wine* (viewed here as weakening distractions), lest he neglect his duty to care for the powerless.

31.10–31: The woman of worth. An acrostic poem (one in which each successive verse begins with the successive letter of the Heb alphabet) from the point of view of the *husband* (vv. 11,23,28), about the ideal *wife* (v. 10). The woman exemplifies strength, independence, courage, kindness, wisdom, and piety. **10:** *Capable,* variously rendered as "good," "perfect," "virtuous," "noble," "worthy," or "valiant" (see 12.4; Ruth 3.11). *More precious than jewels,* like personified Wisdom herself (3.15; 8.11). **21–22:** Both she and her family are warmly, and luxuriously, dressed. **23:** See v. 31; 22.22; 24.7; Job 29.7–10; 31.21; the city gate was the locale of commercial and legal transactions (see Deut 22.15; Ruth 4.1–12). **27:** *She*

her clothing is fine linen and
purple.
23 Her husband is known in the
city gates,
taking his seat among the elders of
the land.
24 She makes linen garments and sells
them;
she supplies the merchant with
sashes.
25 Strength and dignity are her clothing,
and she laughs at the time to come.
26 She opens her mouth with wisdom,
and the teaching of kindness is on
her tongue.
27 She looks well to the ways of her
household,
and does not eat the bread of
idleness.
28 Her children rise up and call her
happy;
her husband too, and he
praises her:
29 "Many women have done
excellently,
but you surpass them all."
30 Charm is deceitful, and beauty
is vain,
but a woman who fears the LORD
is to be praised.
31 Give her a share in the fruit of her
hands,
and let her works praise her in the
city gates.

looks well to (Heb "tsopiyyah"), perhaps a play on "sophia" (Gk "wisdom"). **31:** *Give her a share in,* here the husband would appear to hold ultimate authority over the household and its resources; another possible translation is "praise for her."

ECCLESIASTES

Ecclesiastes is the Latin transliteration of the Greek rendering of the pen-name of the author, known in Hebrew as Qohelet ("Gatherer," traditionally "the Teacher" or "the Preacher"). The superscription of the book (1.2) presents Qohelet as "the son of David" who ruled in Jerusalem, evoking the memory of Solomon, king of Israel (968–928 BCE), the consummate sage and gatherer of wealth and wisdom (see 1 Kings 3–4; 10). Apart from the superscription and 1.12–2.11, however, the author never speaks as king. The epilogue portrays the author as a teacher, rather than as king (12.9–14). Moreover, the perspective in most of the book is that of an outsider to the royal court (3.16; 4.13–16; 8.1–6; 10.16–20).

The date of the book is a matter of dispute, although most scholars argue on linguistic grounds that it should be dated to the postexilic period. The presence of two indisputable Persian loan words ("parks" in 2.5; "sentence" in 8.11) point to a date some time after 450 BCE, for there are no Persian loan words or Persian names in the Hebrew Bible that can be dated earlier. The abundance of Aramaisms (Aramaic loan words, forms, and constructions) also points to the postexilic period, when Aramaic became the *lingua franca* in Palestine. A number of specific idioms regarding inheritance, grants, prisons, social abuses, judicial problems, and socioeconomic classes are attested in documents from the Persian period; in no other periods in history do we find such a coincidence of terminology. These features, together with the fact that there are no Greek loan words (or indisputable Greek ideas), suggests that the book should be dated sometime between 450 and 330 BCE, although many scholars date it a century or two later.

The period in question was one of tremendous economic growth, spurred on in no small part by the introduction of standardized coinage by the Persian central government. Money quickly became a commodity, desired for its own sake (cf. 5.10; 7.12; 10.19). Standardized currency helped to democratize economic opportunities, so that it became possible for even the poorest people in society to become wealthy. As in any era of tremendous economic innovation, the Persian period brought both opportunities and risks to the average person in the empire.

The context that Ecclesiastes addresses, however, goes beyond the economic one. The sense of the individual as a small part of a large scene is evident in the political allusions (4.1; 5.7), which should be read against the background of empire. Even descriptions of life and death reinforce the idea of the powerless individual (8.8). The inevitability of one's fate (3.15; 6.10), the unavoidability of death (3.19), and the repetitions of life (3.1–8) all work together to create a vision of the remoteness, the inscrutability, and ultimately the indifference of the world to the individual. In a vision of bleak grandeur the author faces this indifference, acknowledges it, and admits an inability to transcend it, but nevertheless derives from it a hard-won wisdom: This is how the world is.

The author appears to have drawn lessons from the wider wisdom tradition. Yet he approached the issues through the socioeconomic idioms current in his generation to address the preoccupations and obsessions of his audience. Despite the newness of their environment, the fundamental problems they face about the possibility of coping with life in a world that is inconsistent, if not contradictory, are not new after all (see 1.10). Every generation must deal with the fact that mortals inevitably live in a world in which they do not have control ("all is vanity") and life can only be lived before a sovereign God who alone determines all that happens on earth.

1 The words of the Teacher,[a] the son of David, king in Jerusalem.
2 Vanity of vanities, says the Teacher,[a]
vanity of vanities! All is vanity.
3 What do people gain from all the toil
at which they toil under the sun?
4 A generation goes, and a generation comes,
but the earth remains forever.
5 The sun rises and the sun goes down,
and hurries to the place where it rises.
6 The wind blows to the south,
and goes around to the north;
round and round goes the wind,
and on its circuits the wind returns.
7 All streams run to the sea,
but the sea is not full;
to the place where the streams flow,
there they continue to flow.
8 All things[b] are wearisome;
more than one can express;
the eye is not satisfied with seeing,
or the ear filled with hearing.
9 What has been is what will be,
and what has been done is what will be done;
there is nothing new under the sun.
10 Is there a thing of which it is said,
"See, this is new"?
It has already been,
in the ages before us.
11 The people of long ago are not remembered,
nor will there be any remembrance
of people yet to come
by those who come after them.
12 I, the Teacher,[a] when king over Isra-

a Heb *Qoheleth*, traditionally rendered *Preacher*
b Or *words*

1.1: Superscription. The author is identified by his pen-name, *Teacher* (Heb "Qohelet"), probably, "Gatherer"—one who is supposed to have accumulated plenty of everything, including wisdom, wealth, and pleasure. The description of the author as *the son of David, king in Jerusalem* evokes images of Solomon, the consummate gatherer of wealth, wisdom, and pleasure (see also 1.2–2.11; 1 Kings 3–4; 10). *Teacher* understands the word to mean one who speaks in the public assembly (Heb "qahal").

1.2–11: Preface. Despite constant activity, the world always remains the same. **2:** *Vanity* (Heb "hebel") translates the Heb word that literally means "breath" or "vapor" (Isa 57.13; Ps 62.9). In Ecclesiastes, it is used repeatedly as a metaphor for things that cannot be grasped either physically or intellectually, things that are ephemeral, insubstantial, enigmatic, or absurd. Elsewhere in the Bible, the human life-span and human beings themselves are said to be "hebel" (see Ps 39.4–11; 62.9; 78.33; Job 7.16). *Vanity of vanities* is a way of expressing the superlative in Hebrew, hence, the phrase means "utter vanity." Virtually identical words are found in 12.8, the last of the book before the epilogue (12.9–14). **3:** The term *gain* does not mean just "benefit," but "excess," "advantage," or "surplus." The Heb phrase translated as *from all* their *toil* may also be translated as "in exchange for all their toil." Here, as elsewhere in the book, *toil* refers not only to the process of work, but to the fruit of one's work (see 2.10). The phrase *under the sun* occurs in the Bible only in Ecclesiastes, but it is attested elsewhere in the ancient Near East. It is a near synonym of "under the heavens" (1.13; 2.3; 3.1). Whereas "under the heavens" is a spatial designation (referring to what is happening "everywhere in the world"), *under the sun* refers to the realm of the living as opposed to the realm of the dead (cf. 4.15; 9.6,9). **4:** The Heb phrase rendered as "the earth remains forever" may be translated as "the world always stays the same." Despite human toiling and the coming and going of human generations, the world remains as it was. **5–7:** The elements of nature—light, air, and water—are also engaged in daily activities, with no new results. The *sun . . . hurries* (lit. "stomps" or "pants") to its destination, only to have to recommence its routine. **8–11:** As with nature, so with knowledge; human speculations and endless instructions produce nothing new. **11:** Cf. 2.16; 9.5.

1.12–2.11: The author's experiences and accomplishments. The style of this passage is similar to that

el in Jerusalem, 13 applied my mind to seek
and to search out by wisdom all that is
done under heaven; it is an unhappy busi-
ness that God has given to human beings to
be busy with. 14 I saw all the deeds that are
done under the sun; and see, all is vanity
and a chasing after wind.[a]

15 What is crooked cannot be made
straight,
and what is lacking cannot
be counted.

16 I said to myself, "I have acquired
great wisdom, surpassing all who were over
Jerusalem before me; and my mind has had
great experience of wisdom and knowl-
edge." 17 And I applied my mind to know
wisdom and to know madness and folly. I
perceived that this also is but a chasing af-
ter wind.[a]

18 For in much wisdom is much
vexation,
and those who increase knowledge
increase sorrow.

2 I said to myself, "Come now, I will
make a test of pleasure; enjoy your-
self." But again, this also was vanity. 2 I
said of laughter, "It is mad," and of plea-
sure, "What use is it?" 3 I searched with my
mind how to cheer my body with wine—
my mind still guiding me with wisdom—
and how to lay hold on folly, until I might
see what was good for mortals to do under
heaven during the few days of their life. 4 I
made great works; I built houses and plant-
ed vineyards for myself; 5 I made myself
gardens and parks, and planted in them all
kinds of fruit trees. 6 I made myself pools
from which to water the forest of growing
trees. 7 I bought male and female slaves,
and had slaves who were born in my house;
I also had great possessions of herds and
flocks, more than any who had been before
me in Jerusalem. 8 I also gathered for myself
silver and gold and the treasure of kings
and of the provinces; I got singers, both
men and women, and delights of the flesh,
and many concubines.[b]

9 So I became great and surpassed all
who were before me in Jerusalem; also my
wisdom remained with me. 10 Whatever my
eyes desired I did not keep from them; I
kept my heart from no pleasure, for my
heart found pleasure in all my toil, and this
was my reward for all my toil. 11 Then I
considered all that my hands had done and
the toil I had spent in doing it, and again,
all was vanity and a chasing after wind,[a]
and there was nothing to be gained under
the sun.

12 So I turned to consider wisdom and
madness and folly; for what can the one do
who comes after the king? Only what has
already been done. 13 Then I saw that wis-
dom excels folly as light excels darkness.

14 The wise have eyes in their head,
but fools walk in darkness.

Yet I perceived that the same fate befalls
all of them. 15 Then I said to myself, "What
happens to the fool will happen to me also;
why then have I been so very wise?" And I
said to myself that this also is vanity. 16 For
there is no enduring remembrance of the
wise or of fools, seeing that in the days
to come all will have been long forgotten.
How can the wise die just like fools? 17 So

a Or *a feeding on wind.* See Hos 12.1 *b* Meaning of Heb uncertain

in many royal inscriptions in the ancient Near East. The author, in his assumed role as king, has experienced all and done all, but even he has to admit that nothing is ultimately reliable. **1.12:** The author takes on the persona of Solomon (1.1n.; 2.9). **13:** *Unhappy business* or "terrible preoccupation" may refer to human anxiety over all that is happening in the world. **14:** *Chasing after wind,* that is, pursuit of futility (Hos 12.2; Prov 15.14; Sir 34.1–2). **15:** A proverb about humanly impossible tasks (see also 7.13). **2.4–11:** A summary of accomplishments like those found in royal inscriptions. Despite his worldly successes, the author concludes that everything is but vanity.

2.12–26: The leveling effect of death. Whatever advantage anyone might have in life is negated by death. **12–17:** Wisdom is obviously better than folly (*as light excels darkness,* v. 13), yet the wise and fools face *the same fate* of death (v. 14; cf. 3.19–20; 9.2–3), and they are all forgotten after their death.

I hated life, because what is done under the
sun was grievous to me; for all is vanity and
a chasing after wind.[a]
18 I hated all my toil in which I had
toiled under the sun, seeing that I must
leave it to those who come after me
19 —and who knows whether they will be
wise or foolish? Yet they will be master of
all for which I toiled and used my wisdom
under the sun. This also is vanity. 20 So I
turned and gave my heart up to despair
concerning all the toil of my labors under
the sun, 21 because sometimes one who has
toiled with wisdom and knowledge and
skill must leave all to be enjoyed by another
who did not toil for it. This also is vanity
and a great evil. 22 What do mortals get
from all the toil and strain with which they
toil under the sun? 23 For all their days are
full of pain, and their work is a vexation;
even at night their minds do not rest. This
also is vanity.
24 There is nothing better for mortals
than to eat and drink, and find enjoyment
in their toil. This also, I saw, is from the
hand of God; 25 for apart from him[b] who
can eat or who can have enjoyment? 26 For
to the one who pleases him God gives wis-
dom and knowledge and joy; but to the
sinner he gives the work of gathering and
heaping, only to give to one who pleases
God. This also is vanity and a chasing after
wind.[a]

3 For everything there is a season, and a
time for every matter under heaven:
2 a time to be born, and a time to die;
a time to plant, and a time to pluck
up what is planted;
3 a time to kill, and a time to heal;
a time to break down, and a time to
build up;
4 a time to weep, and a time to laugh;
a time to mourn, and a time to dance;
5 a time to throw away stones, and a
time to gather stones together;
a time to embrace, and a time to
refrain from embracing;
6 a time to seek, and a time to lose;
a time to keep, and a time to
throw away;
7 a time to tear, and a time to sew;
a time to keep silence, and a time to
speak;
8 a time to love, and a time to hate;
a time for war, and a time for peace.
9 What gain have the workers from their
toil? 10 I have seen the business that God
has given to everyone to be busy with. 11 He
has made everything suitable for its time;
moreover he has put a sense of past and
future into their minds, yet they cannot find
out what God has done from the beginning
to the end. 12 I know that there is nothing

a Or *a feeding on wind.* See Hos 12.1 *b* Gk Syr: Heb *apart from me*

18–23: Toil does not give one any advantage in the face of death. People cannot take the fruit of their toil with them when they die. Even the possibility of passing one's inheritance to one's heirs does not give one assurance, for one's heirs may not be deserving of the inheritance. **24–26:** People do not have control over their future; the only good is to partake of life fully in the present, for enjoyment is *from the hand of God* (v. 24). The sovereign God arbitrarily gives the possibility of enjoyment to those who are somehow favored, but not to *the sinner,* a term that may simply mean "the one who misses out" (cf. 7.26; 9.2,18; Prov 8.36; 13.22; 14.21; 19.2; 20.2).

3.1–15: The determination of events. God is the one who determines time and timing. **1–8:** A rhythmic series of antithetical pairs that together (seven sets, each with two pairs of opposites) represent the totality and variety of the times and seasons encountered by human beings. These events include those that simply happen to people (like being born and dying) and occasions to which they must respond (like planting and plucking up what is planted). **9:** The rhetorical question is essentially the same as in 1.3; 2.22; 6.11, except that human beings are called *the workers* (lit. "the one who acts"), but it becomes clear in the verses that follow that God is the one who acts effectively. **10:** *Business,* see 1.13n. **11:** The same God who *made everything suitable for its time* is the one who puts *a sense of past and future* (lit. "eternity") into human consciousness. Human beings must live with this paradox of knowing the reality that transcends the moment ("eternity"), but being able to cope only with the moment. **12–13:** In view of human

better for them than to be happy and enjoy
themselves as long as they live; 13 moreover,
it is God's gift that all should eat and drink
and take pleasure in all their toil. 14 I know
that whatever God does endures forever;
nothing can be added to it, nor anything
taken from it; God has done this, so that all
should stand in awe before him. 15 That
which is, already has been; that which is to
be, already is; and God seeks out what has
gone by.[a]

16 Moreover I saw under the sun that in
the place of justice, wickedness was there,
and in the place of righteousness, wicked-
ness was there as well. 17 I said in my heart,
God will judge the righteous and the wick-
ed, for he has appointed a time for every
matter, and for every work. 18 I said in my
heart with regard to human beings that
God is testing them to show that they are
but animals. 19 For the fate of humans and
the fate of animals is the same; as one dies,
so dies the other. They all have the same
breath, and humans have no advantage
over the animals; for all is vanity. 20 All go
to one place; all are from the dust, and all
turn to dust again. 21 Who knows whether
the human spirit goes upward and the spirit
of animals goes downward to the earth?
22 So I saw that there is nothing better than
that all should enjoy their work, for that is
their lot; who can bring them to see what
will be after them?

4 Again I saw all the oppressions that are
practiced under the sun. Look, the tears
of the oppressed—with no one to comfort
them! On the side of their oppressors there
was power—with no one to comfort them.
2 And I thought the dead, who have already
died, more fortunate than the living, who
are still alive; 3 but better than both is the
one who has not yet been, and has not seen
the evil deeds that are done under the sun.

4 Then I saw that all toil and all skill in
work come from one person's envy of an-
other. This also is vanity and a chasing af-
ter wind.[b]

5 Fools fold their hands
and consume their own flesh.
6 Better is a handful with quiet
than two handfuls with toil,
and a chasing after wind.[b]

7 Again, I saw vanity under the sun: 8 the
case of solitary individuals, without sons or
brothers; yet there is no end to all their toil,
and their eyes are never satisfied with
riches. "For whom am I toiling," they ask,
"and depriving myself of pleasure?" This
also is vanity and an unhappy business.

a Heb *what is pursued* *b* Or *a feeding on wind.* See Hos 12.1

limitations, one should partake of good, for it is God's gift that one should do so. **14:** *Whatever God does endures forever,* the Hebrew should be taken to mean that God's deeds are "eternal," i.e., not bound by time. The timeless, eternal character of God's doing stands in stark contrast to the "eternity" that exists only in human hearts (v. 1). Human activity is always only "in its time" (v. 11), whereas God's activity is not bound by time. The language of adding and subtracting is used elsewhere for matters that are decisive, authoritative, and invariable (Deut 4.2; 12.32; cf. Jer 26.2; Prov 30.6). **15:** *What has gone by* is a free rendering of the Hebrew which is, properly, "what is pursued." God will take care of what human beings pursue in vain.

3.16–22: The determination of humanity's fate. There are injustices in the world, even in places where one might expect justice. God will, however, adjudicate the situation in God's own time. **19:** As far as mortality is concerned, human beings have no advantage over animals: All must die. **20:** *One place,* Sheol, the abode of the dead (9.10). *Dust,* 12.7; Gen 3.19.

4.1–16: Relative good. In light of the author's insistence that there is nothing better for humanity than to enjoy (3.22), these verses make plain that everything thought by mortals to be goods are only relatively so. **1–3:** The living still have to witness the injustices of life, whereas the dead no longer have to do so, and those who have never been born never have to do so. **4–6:** On the one hand, human toil and strivings are driven by envy. On the other hand, the idleness of fools is self-destructive. The better, if only relatively good, alternative is to have little (material goods, enjoyments, or both), but to have it with peace. **6:** Sayings of the form "*better . . . than*" are common in Proverbs (Prov 12.9; 15.16–17; 16.8). **9–12:** There

9 Two are better than one, because they
have a good reward for their toil. 10 For if
they fall, one will lift up the other; but woe
to one who is alone and falls and does not
have another to help. 11 Again, if two lie
together, they keep warm; but how can one
keep warm alone? 12 And though one might
prevail against another, two will withstand
one. A threefold cord is not quickly broken.

13 Better is a poor but wise youth than
an old but foolish king, who will no longer
take advice. 14 One can indeed come out of
prison to reign, even though born poor in
the kingdom. 15 I saw all the living who,
moving about under the sun, follow that[a]
youth who replaced the king;[b] 16 there was
no end to all those people whom he led. Yet
those who come later will not rejoice in
him. Surely this also is vanity and a chasing
after wind.[c]

5 [d]Guard your steps when you go to the
house of God; to draw near to listen is
better than the sacrifice offered by fools;
for they do not know how to keep from
doing evil.[e] 2 [f]Never be rash with your
mouth, nor let your heart be quick to utter
a word before God, for God is in heaven,
and you upon earth; therefore let your
words be few.

3 For dreams come with many cares,
and a fool's voice with many words.

4 When you make a vow to God, do not
delay fulfilling it; for he has no pleasure in
fools. Fulfill what you vow. 5 It is better
that you should not vow than that you
should vow and not fulfill it. 6 Do not let
your mouth lead you into sin, and do not
say before the messenger that it was a mis-
take; why should God be angry at your
words, and destroy the work of your
hands?

7 With many dreams come vanities and
a multitude of words;[g] but fear God.

8 If you see in a province the oppression
of the poor and the violation of justice and
right, do not be amazed at the matter; for
the high official is watched by a higher, and
there are yet higher ones over them. 9 But
all things considered, this is an advantage
for a land: a king for a plowed field.[g]

a Heb *the second* *b* Heb *him* *c* Or *a feeding on wind.* See Hos 12.1 *d* Ch 4.17 in Heb *e* Cn: Heb *they do not know how to do evil* *f* Ch 5.1 in Heb *g* Meaning of Heb uncertain

is relative advantage in numbers, but no guarantee. A three-ply cord may still snap, although not as easily as a cord with only two strands or one. **13–16:** Every generation will have its new underdog-turned-hero, who will seem to have limitless support from the populace, until the next hero comes along. **16:** *Vanity,* 1.2n. *Chasing after wind,* 1.14n.

5.1–7: Attitude before God. God and human beings do not belong to the same realm. It is necessary, therefore, to have a right attitude before God. **1:** It is more acceptable to obey God than to show off one's religiosity, as fools sometimes do (cf. Prov 21.3; 1 Sam 15.22; Am 5.22–24; Hos 6.6). *They do not know how to keep from doing evil,* fools do not even know that they are doing wrong when they approach God frivolously. **3:** In the ancient Near East, *dreams* are regarded as fleeting, illusory, and sometimes deceptive (cf. Job 20.8; Isa 29.7–8; Sir 34.1–3). As dreams are illusory and unreliable, so are the words of loquacious fools (Prov 10.8). **4–7:** Vows must be taken seriously. Cf. Deut 23.21–22; Sir 18.2. The text warns against the lack of restraint in speech, for the mouth may bring condemnation to the entire person (cf. Lev 5.4; Prov 10.19). It is unclear who *the messenger* in v. 6 refers to; perhaps the author has in mind the Temple priest to whom people went to confess that they have erred (see Num 15.22–31; Lev 4.2,22,27–30). The confession would be useless, however, because God would still be angry at the foolish utterances. **7:** *Fear God,* respect and awe before God are central values in wisdom literature (Job 28.28; Prov 1.7).

5.8–6.9: Enjoy, but do not be greedy. The passage is arranged in such a way that the outer sections lead inwards toward its center in 5.20, with its call for enjoyment. **5.8:** *High official*s (lit. "high ones"), a term elsewhere used of arrogant people (Job 41.34; Ps 138.6; Isa 10.33; Ezek 21.26) and never of officials of any sort. This text does not refer to a government bureaucracy, but to ambitious people who strive to get ahead of one another. No matter how high they get, however, there will always be people higher than they who look down upon them. **9:** The meaning of this verse is obscure. **10:** Wealth itself is not the problem

10 The lover of money will not be satis-
fied with money; nor the lover of wealth,
with gain. This also is vanity.
11 When goods increase, those who eat
them increase; and what gain has their
owner but to see them with his eyes?
12 Sweet is the sleep of laborers, wheth-
er they eat little or much; but the surfeit of
the rich will not let them sleep.
13 There is a grievous ill that I have seen
under the sun: riches were kept by their
owners to their hurt, 14 and those riches
were lost in a bad venture; though they are
parents of children, they have nothing in
their hands. 15 As they came from their
mother's womb, so they shall go again, na-
ked as they came; they shall take nothing
for their toil, which they may carry away
with their hands. 16 This also is a grievous
ill: just as they came, so shall they go; and
what gain do they have from toiling for the
wind? 17 Besides, all their days they eat in
darkness, in much vexation and sickness
and resentment.
18 This is what I have seen to be good:
it is fitting to eat and drink and find enjoy-
ment in all the toil with which one toils
under the sun the few days of the life God
gives us; for this is our lot. 19 Likewise all to
whom God gives wealth and possessions
and whom he enables to enjoy them, and to
accept their lot and find enjoyment in their
toil—this is the gift of God. 20 For they will
scarcely brood over the days of their lives,
because God keeps them occupied with the
joy of their hearts.

6 There is an evil that I have seen under
the sun, and it lies heavy upon human-
kind: 2 those to whom God gives wealth,
possessions, and honor, so that they lack
nothing of all that they desire, yet God does
not enable them to enjoy these things, but a
stranger enjoys them. This is vanity; it is a
grievous ill. 3 A man may beget a hundred
children, and live many years; but however
many are the days of his years, if he does
not enjoy life's good things, or has no buri-
al, I say that a stillborn child is better off
than he. 4 For it comes into vanity and goes
into darkness, and in darkness its name is
covered; 5 moreover it has not seen the sun
or known anything; yet it finds rest rather
than he. 6 Even though he should live a
thousand years twice over, yet enjoy no
good—do not all go to one place?
7 All human toil is for the mouth, yet the

here, but the insatiability of the rich (see Sir 31.5–7). **11:** The rhetorical question presupposes a negative answer. Wealth is good only if it is enjoyed in the present. **12:** The contrast is not between one who works and one who is a sluggard, but between poor *laborers* (or "employees") and the rich who cannot stop worrying despite the plenty that they already possess (Sir 31.1). The surfeit refers perhaps to overindulgence both in food and in economic enterprises. **15–16:** The saying about coming and going *naked* to the *mother's womb* is a proverbial commonplace that echoes Job 1.21 (cf. Sir 40.1; 1 Tim 6.7). The mother's womb is here a metaphor for the earth. **17:** There are people who go through life always anticipating death. Despite their wealth and other possessions, they live in utter misery. **20:** *They will scarcely brood over the days of their lives,* the Hebrew may be injunctive: "They should not much call to mind the days of their lives." The problem for the author is that people do brood over their lives all too frequently, worrying constantly about the day ahead. He calls, instead, for people not to think too much ahead but to enjoy the present because God has given them joy as the antidote to their obsessions. **6.1–2:** There are exceptions to the divinely given right to enjoy (5.18–19)—cases where people are, for whatever reasons, unable to do so. **3:** *But however many are the days of his years,* this translation glosses over a number of syntactical problems in the Hebrew. With a slight change of one word in the Hebrew, one may read, "and yet he complains that the days of his years will come to pass." Even though this person has everything that anyone might desire, including abundant wealth, progeny, and long life, he complains about the days ahead of him, dissatisfied with all that he has and worried about proper burial when he dies. In that case, he is no better off than *a stillborn child* (cf. Job 3.16–18). **7:** *The appetite is not satisfied,* the language alludes to the insatiability of Death in Canaanite mythology (in the Hebrew Bible, Sheol, the realm of the dead, is portrayed in this way; cf. Isa 5.14; Hab 2.5; Prov 27.20; 30.16). As Death swallows all that come its way, so greed endangers the world (cf. Ps 73.8). **8–9:** If even the wise have no

appetite is not satisfied. 8 For what advan-
tage have the wise over fools? And what do
the poor have who know how to conduct
themselves before the living? 9 Better is the
sight of the eyes than the wandering of de-
sire; this also is vanity and a chasing after
wind.[a]
10 Whatever has come to be has already
been named, and it is known what human
beings are, and that they are not able to
dispute with those who are stronger. 11 The
more words, the more vanity, so how is one
the better? 12 For who knows what is good
for mortals while they live the few days of
their vain life, which they pass like a shad-
ow? For who can tell them what will be
after them under the sun?

7 A good name is better than precious
ointment,
and the day of death, than the day
of birth.
2 It is better to go to the house of
mourning
than to go to the house of feasting;
for this is the end of everyone,
and the living will lay it to heart.
3 Sorrow is better than laughter,
for by sadness of countenance the
heart is made glad.
4 The heart of the wise is in the house
of mourning;
but the heart of fools is in the
house of mirth.
5 It is better to hear the rebuke of the
wise
than to hear the song of fools.
6 For like the crackling of thorns under
a pot,
so is the laughter of fools;
this also is vanity.
7 Surely oppression makes the wise
foolish,
and a bribe corrupts the heart.
8 Better is the end of a thing than its
beginning;
the patient in spirit are better than
the proud in spirit.
9 Do not be quick to anger,
for anger lodges in the bosom
of fools.
10 Do not say, "Why were the former
days better than these?"

a Or *a feeding on wind.* See Hos 12.1

advantage over fools, why should the poor learn how to cope with life? The answer lies in the enjoyment of what one has, i.e., in contentment. **9:** For the form of the saying see 4.6n. *Vanity . . . chasing after wind,* 1.2n.; 1.14n.

6.10–7.14: No one knows what is good. The passage begins (6.10–12) and ends (7.13–14) with the author's insistence that no one knows what is good for humanity. The introduction and conclusion emphasize human ignorance and impotence, over against divine determination and the deity's incomprehensible activity. The "better . . . than" sayings in between (7.1–12) are, therefore, quoted in mockery: They illustrate the sort of sayings proffered by those who believe that mortals know what is really good. **6.10–12:** Despite the passive verbs (v. 10), it is clear that the author means that God is the one who has designated and known. There is a possible allusion to Job (cf. Job 9.1–4). Job had disputed with God, engaged in empty talk, and "multiplied words without knowledge" (Job 35.14–16; cf. Job 13.22–28). At the same time, however, the reference to abundant and empty words anticipates the sayings to follow (7.1–12). By using a rhetorical question (v. 11), the author suggests that humans have no advantage, because no one *knows what is good for mortals* (v. 12). Neither the foolish nor the wise can give others advice on what is universally good. **7.1–12:** A series of "better . . . than" sayings that imitate the style of traditional proverbs (see 4.6n.), with their tendency to present issues in dialectical pairs: fame and luxury (v. 1a), birth and death (v. 1b), funeral and wedding (v. 2), merriment and sadness (v. 3), mourning and pleasure (v. 4), rebuke and praise (v. 5), the wise and the fool (vv. 6–7), beginning and end (v. 8), patience and arrogance (v. 8). The sayings are all subverted and relativized, however. The effect of the overall presentation is to show that no one knows what is universally good. Each saying may contain an element of truth, but the sum total of these many words is *vanity*—just so much empty talk (v. 6; cf. 6.11). **13–14:** People should accept good when it is accessible and face adversity when that is a reality; see 1.5; 3.14.

For it is not from wisdom that you
ask this.
11 Wisdom is as good as an inheritance,
an advantage to those who see the
sun.
12 For the protection of wisdom is like
the protection of money,
and the advantage of knowledge is
that wisdom gives life to the
one who possesses it.
13 Consider the work of God;
who can make straight what he has
made crooked?

14 In the day of prosperity be joyful,
and in the day of adversity consider; God
has made the one as well as the other, so
that mortals may not find out anything that
will come after them.

15 In my vain life I have seen everything;
there are righteous people who perish in
their righteousness, and there are wicked
people who prolong their life in their evil-
doing. 16 Do not be too righteous, and do
not act too wise; why should you destroy
yourself? 17 Do not be too wicked, and do
not be a fool; why should you die before
your time? 18 It is good that you should take
hold of the one, without letting go of the
other; for the one who fears God shall suc-
ceed with both.

19 Wisdom gives strength to the wise
more than ten rulers that are in a city.

20 Surely there is no one on earth so
righteous as to do good without ever sin-
ning.

21 Do not give heed to everything that
people say, or you may hear your servant
cursing you; 22 your heart knows that many
times you have yourself cursed others.

23 All this I have tested by wisdom; I
said, "I will be wise," but it was far from
me. 24 That which is, is far off, and deep,
very deep; who can find it out? 25 I turned
my mind to know and to search out and to
seek wisdom and the sum of things, and to
know that wickedness is folly and that fool-
ishness is madness. 26 I found more bitter
than death the woman who is a trap, whose
heart is snares and nets, whose hands are
fetters; one who pleases God escapes her,
but the sinner is taken by her. 27 See, this is
what I found, says the Teacher,[a] adding
one thing to another to find the sum,
28 which my mind has sought repeatedly,
but I have not found. One man among a
thousand I found, but a woman among all
these I have not found. 29 See, this alone I
found, that God made human beings
straightforward, but they have devised
many schemes.

[a] *Qoheleth*, traditionally rendered *Preacher*

7.15–29: Righteousness and wisdom are elusive. This passage consists of two parts: The first concerns the inadvisability of extreme righteousness and wisdom (vv. 15–22); the second concerns the threat of folly and the elusiveness of wisdom (vv. 23–29). **15:** The traditional doctrine of retribution (e.g., Prov 11.3–11) is often contradicted. **16:** Those who aspire to extreme righteousness (also meaning "rightness") may destroy themselves. **17:** Those who are too wicked and foolish will suffer the consequences. In general, the wisdom tradition advocates moderation as the proper mode of conduct (see Sir 7.4–5). **18:** *The one . . . the other* refers to the two ideas in vv. 16–17. The one who is religious (*fears God*) goes forth with both precepts. **19:** Perhaps a proverbial illustration of the value people place on wisdom and power, although neither will avert death. **20:** Perfect righteousness ("rightness") is impossible, for every mortal misses the mark (cf. 1 Kings 8.46; 2 Chr 6.26; Ps 14.1–3; 53.1–3; 143.2; Prov 20.9; Job 4.17). **26:** This is not a polemic against women but echoes in allegorical fashion the warnings in other wisdom writings against Folly, personified as an evilly seductive woman (Prov 2.16–19; 5.20; 6.24–35; 7.5–27; 23.27–28). Wisdom is elusive (vv. 23–25), but Folly is on a hunt to catch people unawares. **27:** *Teacher,* see 1.1n. *Adding one thing to another,* like an accountant or merchant working on a ledger (cf. v. 25). **28:** *One man among a thousand . . . a woman among all of these,* this notoriously difficult sentence may be a gloss prompted by misinterpretation of v. 26 as referring to women in general. The first part of the verse refers to the elusiveness of wisdom (cf. Prov 1.28; 3.13–15; 31.10).

8 Who is like the wise man?
And who knows the interpretation
of a thing?
Wisdom makes one's face shine,
and the hardness of one's
countenance is changed.
2 Keep[a] the king's command because of
your sacred oath. 3 Do not be terrified; go
from his presence, do not delay when the
matter is unpleasant, for he does whatever
he pleases. 4 For the word of the king is
powerful, and who can say to him, "What
are you doing?" 5 Whoever obeys a com-
mand will meet no harm, and the wise
mind will know the time and way. 6 For
every matter has its time and way, although
the troubles of mortals lie heavy upon
them. 7 Indeed, they do not know what is to
be, for who can tell them how it will be?
8 No one has power over the wind[b] to re-
strain the wind,[b] or power over the day of
death; there is no discharge from the battle,
nor does wickedness deliver those who
practice it. 9 All this I observed, applying
my mind to all that is done under the sun,
while one person exercises authority over
another to the other's hurt.
10 Then I saw the wicked buried; they
used to go in and out of the holy place, and
were praised in the city where they had
done such things.[c] This also is vanity.
11 Because sentence against an evil deed is
not executed speedily, the human heart is
fully set to do evil. 12 Though sinners do
evil a hundred times and prolong their
lives, yet I know that it will be well with
those who fear God, because they stand in
fear before him, 13 but it will not be well
with the wicked, neither will they prolong
their days like a shadow, because they do
not stand in fear before God.
14 There is a vanity that takes place on
earth, that there are righteous people who
are treated according to the conduct of the
wicked, and there are wicked people who
are treated according to the conduct of the
righteous. I said that this also is vanity.
15 So I commend enjoyment, for there is
nothing better for people under the sun
than to eat, and drink, and enjoy them-
selves, for this will go with them in their
toil through the days of life that God gives
them under the sun.
16 When I applied my mind to know
wisdom, and to see the business that is
done on earth, how one's eyes see sleep nei-
ther day nor night, 17 then I saw all the
work of God, that no one can find out what
is happening under the sun. However much
they may toil in seeking, they will not find
it out; even though those who are wise
claim to know, they cannot find it out.

9 All this I laid to heart, examining it all,
how the righteous and the wise and
their deeds are in the hand of God; whether

a Heb *I keep* *b* Or *breath* *c* Meaning of Heb uncertain

8.1–17: Reflections on the limits of human power. 1–5: Traditional advice on how to react to arbitrary power only shows the limits of wisdom. **1:** *Makes one's face shine,* elsewhere in the Hebrew Bible (e.g., Num 6.25) this idiom is used of God. **2:** *Because of,* perhaps meaning "in the manner of"; treat a *king's command* like a solemn religious *oath* (Ex 22.11; 1 Kings 2.43). **5b–7:** *Time and way,* lit. "time and judgment" (cf. 3.1,16–17). There are a proper time and a proper judgment, although no one knows when and how. **8:** *Power over the wind to restrain the wind,* or "power over the life-breath . . . to hold back the life-breath." No one has the power to avert death. *There is no discharge from battle,* translate, "no substitution in battle." No one can send a substitute to take his or her place in the final battle that is death. **10:** The wicked are properly interred and honored upon their death (Job 21.32–33). **11:** The slow process of judgment encourages the wicked to do even more evil (Job 21.19–21). **12–13:** The wicked may live long, but the human life-span is finally limited: They will not *prolong their days like a shadow,* itself a transient and unreliable thing (cf. 6.12; Ps 102.11; 109.23; 144.4; Job 8.9; 14.2; 17.7). **15:** *To eat, and drink, and enjoy,* traditionally, "to eat, and to drink, and to be merry"; cf. 2.24; 3.13; 5.18; 9.7. **16–17:** *One's eyes see sleep neither day nor night,* an idiom of earnest fervor. Even those who are so dedicated to understanding God's mysterious activity cannot find what they yearn to know.

9.1–10: Enjoy life. All people face the common fate of death, regardless of their character. Yet life is

it is love or hate one does not know. Every-
thing that confronts them 2 is vanity,[a]
since the same fate comes to all, to the righ-
teous and the wicked, to the good and the
evil,[b] to the clean and the unclean, to those
who sacrifice and those who do not sacri-
fice. As are the good, so are the sinners;
those who swear are like those who shun
an oath. 3 This is an evil in all that happens
under the sun, that the same fate comes to
everyone. Moreover, the hearts of all are
full of evil; madness is in their hearts while
they live, and after that they go to the dead.
4 But whoever is joined with all the living
has hope, for a living dog is better than a
dead lion. 5 The living know that they will
die, but the dead know nothing; they have
no more reward, and even the memory of
them is lost. 6 Their love and their hate and
their envy have already perished; never
again will they have any share in all that
happens under the sun.

7 Go, eat your bread with enjoyment,
and drink your wine with a merry heart; for
God has long ago approved what you do.
8 Let your garments always be white; do not
let oil be lacking on your head. 9 Enjoy life
with the wife whom you love, all the days
of your vain life that are given you under
the sun, because that is your portion in life
and in your toil at which you toil under the
sun. 10 Whatever your hand finds to do, do
with your might; for there is no work or
thought or knowledge or wisdom in Sheol,
to which you are going.

11 Again I saw that under the sun the
race is not to the swift, nor the battle to the
strong, nor bread to the wise, nor riches to
the intelligent, nor favor to the skillful; but
time and chance happen to them all. 12 For
no one can anticipate the time of disaster.
Like fish taken in a cruel net, and like birds
caught in a snare, so mortals are snared at
a time of calamity, when it suddenly falls
upon them.

13 I have also seen this example of wis-
dom under the sun, and it seemed great to
me. 14 There was a little city with few peo-
ple in it. A great king came against it and
besieged it, building great siegeworks
against it. 15 Now there was found in it a
poor wise man, and he by his wisdom deliv-
ered the city. Yet no one remembered that
poor man. 16 So I said, "Wisdom is better
than might; yet the poor man's wisdom is
despised, and his words are not heeded."

17 The quiet words of the wise are more
to be heeded
than the shouting of a ruler among
fools.
18 Wisdom is better than weapons
of war,
but one bungler destroys much
good.

10 Dead flies make the perfumer's
ointment give off a foul odor;

a Syr Compare Gk: Heb *Everything that confronts them* 2*is everything* *b* Gk Syr Vg: Heb lacks *and the evil*

better than death, and one should enjoy life whenever one is able to do so. **1:** *Love* and *hate* are attitudes that generate actions (cf. Ps 25.19; 109.3–5; 139.21–22; Prov 10.12; 26.26). **2:** Death comes to all alike (cf. 2.14–15; 3.19). **4–6:** For all its limitations, life is still better than death, for the dead do not have whatever life has to offer. For the living, there are still possibilities, however uncertain and ephemeral those may be. **7–10:** Enjoy life while you can, for God has already *approved what you do.* There will no longer be this possibility when one dies. A similar passage from the ancient Babylonian epic of Gilgamesh suggests that the advice to enjoy life in the full knowledge of certain death was a piece of folk wisdom (see *ANET,* 90). **8:** *Oil . . . on your head,* cf. Ps 235. **9:** *Vain life,* lit. "days of vanity"; see 1.2n. **10:** *Sheol,* the abode of the dead.

9.11–10.15: The world is full of risks. 9.11–12: There are no guarantees in life and death may come without warning to one and all. **13–16:** An illustration that wisdom provides no guarantee. Wisdom may be *better than might,* but wisdom may not be heeded because of issues of social class; in v. 15, *delivered* should probably be translated "could have delivered." **17:** A proverb that can only be heard ironically in light of v. 16. **18:** The relative virtue of wisdom is readily negated by a single fool. **10.1:** With a slight emendation of the text, we read "a dead fly" instead of *dead flies.* Just as a single fool might negate the

so a little folly outweighs wisdom
and honor.
2 The heart of the wise inclines to the
right,
but the heart of a fool to the
left.
3 Even when fools walk on the road,
they lack sense,
and show to everyone that they are
fools.
4 If the anger of the ruler rises against
you, do not leave your post,
for calmness will undo great
offenses.
5 There is an evil that I have seen under
the sun, as great an error as if it proceeded
from the ruler: 6 folly is set in many high
places, and the rich sit in a low place. 7 I
have seen slaves on horseback, and princes
walking on foot like slaves.
8 Whoever digs a pit will fall into it;
and whoever breaks through a wall
will be bitten by a snake.
9 Whoever quarries stones will be hurt
by them;
and whoever splits logs will be
endangered by them.
10 If the iron is blunt, and one does not
whet the edge,
then more strength must be exerted;
but wisdom helps one to succeed.
11 If the snake bites before it is charmed,
there is no advantage in a charmer.
12 Words spoken by the wise bring them
favor,
but the lips of fools consume them.
13 The words of their mouths begin in
foolishness,
and their talk ends in wicked
madness;
14 yet fools talk on and on.
No one knows what is to happen,
and who can tell anyone what the
future holds?
15 The toil of fools wears them out,
for they do not even know the way
to town.

16 Alas for you, O land, when your king
is a servant,[a]
and your princes feast in the
morning!
17 Happy are you, O land, when your
king is a nobleman,
and your princes feast at the proper
time—
for strength, and not for
drunkenness!
18 Through sloth the roof sinks in,
and through indolence the house
leaks.
19 Feasts are made for laughter;
wine gladdens life,
and money meets every need.

a Or *a child*

value of wisdom, so a single dead fly could ruin a pot of precious ointment. **5–7:** A world turned topsy-turvy (see Prov 26.1; 30.21–23; Isa 3.4–5). **8:** The hunter who *digs a pit* to trap animals is most vulnerable to his own trap. A farmer who *breaks* down old walls to build new ones is susceptible to dangers that come with that task (Prov 26.27). **9:** One who *quarries stones* and one who *splits logs* are vulnerable to certain occupational hazards. **10–11:** Just as precautionary measures might help avert accidents, so wisdom is desirable. Yet, sometimes the precautionary measure may come too late or where there may be no advantage in taking the measure at all (as with snakes that cannot be charmed).

10.16–11.6: Living with risks. Two sections are discernible: The first (10.16–20) deals with political risks, while the second concerns economic risks (11.1–6). **10.16–17:** *Your king is a servant,* or "your king is a boy." The point is that incompetent people have gained ascendancy (cf. 9.17–18; 10.5–6) and other leaders, too, have proven themselves unqualified. **18–19:** *The house leaks,* or, "the house collapses": Subversive political commentary in the guise of an innocuous proverb. The saying appears to be about the ruin of a house because of the owner's laziness, but *the house* may have political overtones, suggesting the incompetence and indiscretion of the leaders. Similarly, v. 19 may be read positively as a proverb affirming life's pleasures and rewards, or it may be read as an oblique reference to the irresponsible lifestyle of the elite who are obsessed with revelry and preoccupied with money. **20:** The Heb verb for

20 Do not curse the king, even in your thoughts,
or curse the rich, even in your bedroom;
for a bird of the air may carry your voice,
or some winged creature tell the matter.

11 Send out your bread upon the waters,
for after many days you will get it back.
2 Divide your means seven ways, or even eight,
for you do not know what disaster may happen on earth.
3 When clouds are full,
they empty rain on the earth;
whether a tree falls to the south or to the north,
in the place where the tree falls, there it will lie.
4 Whoever observes the wind will not sow;
and whoever regards the clouds will not reap.

5 Just as you do not know how the breath comes to the bones in the mother's womb, so you do not know the work of God, who makes everything.

6 In the morning sow your seed, and at evening do not let your hands be idle; for you do not know which will prosper, this or that, or whether both alike will be good.

7 Light is sweet, and it is pleasant for the eyes to see the sun.

8 Even those who live many years should rejoice in them all; yet let them remember that the days of darkness will be many. All that comes is vanity.

9 Rejoice, young man, while you are young, and let your heart cheer you in the days of your youth. Follow the inclination of your heart and the desire of your eyes, but know that for all these things God will bring you into judgment.

10 Banish anxiety from your mind, and put away pain from your body; for youth and the dawn of life are vanity.

12 Remember your creator in the days of your youth, before the days of trouble come, and the years draw near

curse used here simply means "to denigrate" or "to vilify." The author warns against the kinds of subversive activity suggested by the "inside jokes" of vv. 18–19. Even cryptic and private criticisms will become known to those in power. **11.1:** *Send out your bread upon the waters,* a parallel from an Egyptian wisdom text suggests that this saying is about spontaneous good deeds. Liberality is expressed through the figure of bread that is voluntarily given up, released upon the waters, where it will either float downstream or sink. One may do something without thinking much about it, yet all may not be lost in that spontaneous act. **2:** *Divide your means seven ways, or even eight,* the Hebrew reads, simply, "Give to seven or even to eight." This is a numerical saying (Prov 6.16; 30.15–33; Am 1–2); *seven* and *eight* together signify a large, though indefinite, amount (cf. Mic 5.5). The point is that one should be generous "although" (instead of *for*) one does not know what the future may bring. **3–4:** *Clouds* and *wind* are mysterious things that mortals do not control. People are powerless to bring about these natural phenomena, and they do not have the power to prevent them from happening. The farmer who waits for the perfect weather conditions to *sow* or to *reap* will never do so. **5:** The Heb word for *breath* is the same word used for "wind" in v. 4. The word used for *mother* (lit. "full one") echoes the reference to the clouds being "full" (v. 3). Just as the movement of the wind is a mystery, so too the way the life-breath enters a body is a mystery. Likewise, the activity of God is a mystery that is beyond human control. **6:** Instead of waiting for the perfect timing, one should be willing to work at any time—*in the morning* or *at evening.*

11.7–12.8: The conclusion before the epilogue calls on one to enjoy life while there is still time to do so. **11.8:** One should remember that there will be many gloomy days ahead, and so should enjoy life while there is a chance. *All that comes is vanity,* i.e., nothing is permanent. **9:** *But know . . . God will bring you into judgment,* the translation implies that enjoyment is contrary to the will of God. For the author, however, enjoyment is a divine gift (2.24–26; 3.10–15; 5.18–20; 9.7,9). Hence, one should read: "Follow your inclination . . . and know that God will bring you into judgment." God calls people to account for failure to accept the gift of enjoyment. **12.1:** The mention of the *creator* anticipates the reference to

when you will say, "I have no pleasure in
them"; 2 before the sun and the light and
the moon and the stars are darkened and
the clouds return with[a] the rain; 3 in the
day when the guards of the house tremble,
and the strong men are bent, and the wom-
en who grind cease working because they
are few, and those who look through the
windows see dimly; 4 when the doors on the
street are shut, and the sound of the grind-
ing is low, and one rises up at the sound of
a bird, and all the daughters of song are
brought low; 5 when one is afraid of
heights, and terrors are in the road; the al-
mond tree blossoms, the grasshopper drags
itself along[b] and desire fails; because all
must go to their eternal home, and the
mourners will go about the streets; 6 before
the silver cord is snapped,[c] and the golden
bowl is broken, and the pitcher is broken at
the fountain, and the wheel broken at the
cistern, 7 and the dust returns to the earth as
it was, and the breath[d] returns to God who
gave it. 8 Vanity of vanities, says the Teach-
er;[e] all is vanity.

9 Besides being wise, the Teacher[e] also
taught the people knowledge, weighing and
studying and arranging many proverbs.
10 The Teacher[e] sought to find pleasing
words, and he wrote words of truth plainly.

11 The sayings of the wise are like
goads, and like nails firmly fixed are the
collected sayings that are given by one
shepherd.[f] 12 Of anything beyond these,
my child, beware. Of making many books

a Or *after*; Heb *'ahar* *b* Or *is a burden* *c* Syr Vg Compare Gk: Heb *is removed* *d* Or *the spirit* *e* *Qoheleth*, traditionally rendered *Preacher* *f* Meaning of Heb uncertain

creation in v. 7. The call to *remember* points back to the call to enjoy while one is able (11.7–10), but it also points forward to the scene of death at the end of the passage and to the creator who gave and will receive the human life-breath. **2–7:** In a poem couched in eschatological language, the author argues that mortals should take pleasure while they still have a chance, for a time may come when no one can. With poetic exaggeration, the author depicts the end of human life in terms of the end of the world. **2:** The language of the darkening sky is reminiscent of prophetic eschatology (cf. Isa 5.30; 13.10; Ezek 32.7–8; Am 5.8; 8.9; Mic 3.6). The Heb text says that rain clouds return "after" (not *with*) the rain, a sign of disaster, perhaps with the implication of the return of the deluge (Gen 7.11–12; 8.2). **3:** *In the day when,* an allusion to the day of judgment (Mal 3.1–3). Even the strong and valiant are terrified of what is happening. The women who work the mills suddenly stop work (a motif also found in apocalyptic passages in the New Testament; Mt 24.40–41; Lk 17.34–35). Women look out the windows in despair (cf. Judg 5.28). The domestic routines are interrupted. **4:** *The doors* of the street-bazaar *are shut;* the mills that produce meals are silenced. Instead of *rises up at the sound of a bird,* one should translate, "the sound of the birds rises," a reference to the cacophony of birds of prey descending. Thus, while the salutary sound of the mill drops, the unsavory sound of the birds rises. Moreover, the birds (*daughters of song*) actually descend when, from on high, they see the terror on the ground (v. 5). **5:** The translation of the text depends on one's interpretation of the scenario. The consonantal text of the Hebrew suggests not the blossoming of the *almond tree* but the tree becoming hideous. The "locust" tree, too, "droops" (NRSV: *the grasshopper drags itself along*), while the caper-berry tree defoliates (NRSV: *desire fails*). In short, nature languishes (Am 1.2; Joel 2.12; Hab 3.17), as humanity marches toward the grave, *their eternal home,* and an imaginary funeral takes place. **6:** Symbols of the permanent end of life. **7:** See Gen 2.7; 3.19. **8:** *Vanity of vanities,* the words echo 1.2, which, together with 12.8, frame the body of the book.

12.9–14: Epilogue. The epilogue offers an assessment and apology for the author and the book. **9:** The author is a typical sage: He teaches, gathers wisdom sayings, and works with them. **11:** The words of the wise are hard to hear but, like goads and pricks, they have been deliberately applied by a shepherd to his flock. **12:** A formulaic conclusion to establish the authority of the text. Everything intended by the author has been laid out. **13:** *The end of the matter,* these words originally ended the epilogue and, hence, the

there is no end, and much study is a weariness of the flesh.
13 The end of the matter; all has been heard. Fear God, and keep his commandments; for that is the whole duty of everyone.
14 For God will bring every deed into judgment, including[a] every secret thing, whether good or evil.

a Or *into the judgment on*

book. The words beyond this point are secondary. The call to *fear God* is found elsewhere in the book (3.14; 5.7; 8.12–13), but the call to obey God's commandments is not.

THE SONG OF SOLOMON

The Song of Solomon, also known as "Song of Songs" and "Canticles," is a sequence of lyric poems celebrating human love. The poetry is graceful, sensuous, and replete with erotic imagery and allusions. It is unclear whether the composition should be read as a single, unified poem or as a collection of several shorter pieces written in a common style and idiom. Nevertheless, the sequence is coherent and exhibits a lyrical structure that derives its unity from repetitions and juxtapositions rather than from narrative devices such as plot or character development. The poem features the voices of two lovers, one male and one female, and their professions of love for one another. At times the two voices join in dialogue (e.g., 1.9–2.7; 4.1–5.1), but at others they speak separately, addressing each other or the woman's companions, the "daughters of Jerusalem" (3.1–5, 6–11; 7.1–9).

Given its style and theme, it is not surprising that there are no specific allusions that would tie it to a specific historical setting. Although the superscription in 1.1 associates the poem with Solomon, king of Israel (968–928 BCE), he is not the author. The nature of the Hebrew used in the songs, with its Aramaisms and possibly even Persian and Greek loan words, suggests a postexilic date (perhaps sometime in the fourth or third centuries BCE). The connection with Solomon may stem from his reputation as a composer of songs (1 Kings 4.32).

Despite its late date, the Song of Songs is part of an ancient tradition of Near Eastern love poetry. Some of the images and motifs echo those of Mesopotamian sacred marriage poems from the late third and early second millennium BCE. A closer parallel, however, is to be found in Egyptian love songs from the thirteenth and twelfth centuries BCE. These highly erotic compositions use many of the same genres found in the Song of Solomon: poems describing the lover's physical attractions, poems of yearning, poems of admiration and boasting. Also common to both is the use of sensuous imagery, which invokes not only sight but also touch, hearing, and the smell of aromatic fragrances. The Egyptian poems were likely sung at banquets by professional male and female entertainers, and it is possible that the same holds true for the Song of Songs. Although he disapproved of the practice, Rabbi Aqiba (d. 135 CE) attests that the Song of Songs was sung in banquet halls (*Tos. Sanh.* 12.10). By Aqiba's time the Song had already come to be interpreted as a sacred text; hence its continuing profane use was disturbing. At roughly the same time Rabbi Simeon ben Gamaliel associated the Song of Songs with harvest festivals in which the young women of Jerusalem would go out to dance and sing in the vineyards, appealing to the young men to notice them as potential brides (*m. Ta'anit* 4.8).

From a relatively early date (perhaps before the turn of the era) the Song of Songs began to be interpreted symbolically as an account of the love between God and Israel. This interpretation is reflected both in the Targum (Aramaic translation) and in Midrash Rabbah, an early commentary. In the Jewish liturgy Song of Songs is read during the celebration of Passover. The traditional symbolic understanding remained dominant in Jewish interpretation until the modern period. A return to a literal understanding is perhaps first reflected in the translation of the Song by Moses Mendelssohn in 1788. Christian tradition also developed a symbolic or allegorical interpretation, reading the Song as an account of Christ's love for the church and later as an expression of the soul's spiritual union with God. Over the centuries many commentators and homilists, from Origen (third century CE) to Bernard of Clairvaux (twelfth century) to St. John of the Cross (sixteenth century) have developed this allegorical interpretation. Even among the Protestant reformers some form of allegorical interpretation remained dominant until the rise of historical criticism in the eighteenth century.

1 The Song of Songs, which is Solomon's.

2 Let him kiss me with the kisses of his
mouth!
For your love is better than wine,
3 your anointing oils are fragrant,
your name is perfume poured out;
therefore the maidens love you.
4 Draw me after you, let us make haste.
The king has brought me into his
chambers.
We will exult and rejoice in you;
we will extol your love more
than wine;
rightly do they love you.

5 I am black and beautiful,
O daughters of Jerusalem,
like the tents of Kedar,
like the curtains of Solomon.
6 Do not gaze at me because I am dark,
because the sun has gazed on me.
My mother's sons were angry
with me;
they made me keeper of the
vineyards,
but my own vineyard I have
not kept!
7 Tell me, you whom my soul loves,
where you pasture your flock,
where you make it lie down
at noon;
for why should I be like one who
is veiled
beside the flocks of your
companions?
8 If you do not know,

1.1: Title. *Song of Songs,* a superlative, "the best song," like "king of kings" (Dan 2.37). *Which is Solomon's,* i.e., either "about Solomon" (he is named in 3.9,11), or more likely, "by Solomon" (as in Tg); it was common practice in antiquity to attribute authorship to a well-known figure, e.g., David (Ps 3.1; 4.1), Solomon (Prov 1.1), Jeremiah (Gk of Lamentations). The Song, though, because of its relatively late date, was clearly not written by Solomon.

1.2–8: Opening poem. 2: *Wine* is often associated with lovemaking (1.2,4; 2.4; 4.10; 5.1; 7.10; 8.2). *Love,* a plural form that likely refers to physical lovemaking (1.4; 4.10; 5.1; 7.13; cf. Ezek 16.8; 23.17; Prov 7.18). **3:** The repetition of the Hebrew word "shemen" (*oils/perfume*) plays on the term for *name* ("shem"). **4:** The *king,* i.e., the lover (also 1.12 and 7.6), perhaps a pet name or an erotic fantasy, though the royal motif is thematically significant throughout the sequence of poems. The antecedent of *we* is intentionally ambiguous, possibly signifying the woman and her companions (the "maidens" of v. 3 and the "daughters of Jerusalem" in v. 5) and/or the woman and her lover. **5:** Though somewhat ambiguous, the Hebrew word order in the first line suggests that the *and* in *I am black and beautiful* is better rendered disjunctively, "Black am I, but beautiful" (as in Vg). The assertion, however, is affirmative, not apologetic. The woman extols the beauty of her own sun-darkened skin even though a light complexion was apparently prized as a sign of health and beauty (cf. 5.10; Lam 4.7). *Kedar,* a north Arabian tribe whose name means "dark." *Solomon,* or perhaps "Salmah," another north Arabian tribe. **6:** *Mother's sons,* a synonym for "brother" (Gen 27.29; Ps 50.20). *Vineyard,* both literally a garden place (cf. 7.12), and metaphorically a symbol of female sexuality (cf. 8.12). **7:** *Noon* in warm climates is a time for rest and repose, and thus convenient for an amorous tryst. Presumably, the woman is *veiled* as a disguise, though an allusion to prostitution may also be teasingly intended (Gen 38.14–15). **8:** *Kids* contributes to the image of the woman as a shepherdess, symbolizes love (Gen 38.17; Judg 15.1), and may be a figurative reference to the woman's breasts (see "gazelles/fawns," 4.5; 7.3). As with the "gazelles/fawns" in 4.5, the *kids* here are imagined as "grazing"; *pasture* (Heb "reʿi") occurs frequently in wordplays alluding to lovemaking (1.9, "my love," Heb "raʿyati").

O fairest among women,
follow the tracks of the flock,
and pasture your kids
beside the shepherds' tents.

9 I compare you, my love,
to a mare among Pharaoh's
chariots.
10 Your cheeks are comely with
ornaments,
your neck with strings of jewels.
11 We will make you ornaments of gold,
studded with silver.

12 While the king was on his couch,
my nard gave forth its fragrance.
13 My beloved is to me a bag of myrrh
that lies between my breasts.
14 My beloved is to me a cluster of
henna blossoms
in the vineyards of En-gedi.

15 Ah, you are beautiful, my love;
ah, you are beautiful;
your eyes are doves.
16 Ah, you are beautiful, my beloved,
truly lovely.
Our couch is green;
17 the beams of our house are cedar,
our rafters[a] are pine.

2 I am a rose[b] of Sharon,
a lily of the valleys.

2 As a lily among brambles,
so is my love among maidens.

3 As an apple tree among the trees of
the wood,
so is my beloved among young
men.
With great delight I sat in his shadow,
and his fruit was sweet to my taste.
4 He brought me to the banqueting
house,
and his intention toward me
was love.
5 Sustain me with raisins,
refresh me with apples;
for I am faint with love.
6 O that his left hand were under my
head,
and that his right hand embraced
me!
7 I adjure you, O daughters of
Jerusalem,
by the gazelles or the wild does:
do not stir up or awaken love
until it is ready!

8 The voice of my beloved!
Look, he comes,
leaping upon the mountains,
bounding over the hills.
9 My beloved is like a gazelle

a Meaning of Heb uncertain *b* Heb *crocus*

1.9–2.7: A dialogue of mutual admiration. 1.9–11: The man speaks. **9:** *My love,* the man's name for the woman (1.9,15; 2.2,10,13; 4.1,7; 5.2; 6.4). *Mare among Pharaoh's chariots,* the focus is on the woman's beauty and her sexual allure, since the chariotry is only stallions. **10–11:** The Hebrew terms for the ornaments are rare or unique. *We,* i.e., the two lovers. **12–14:** The woman is speaking. *Nard,* an aromatic oil imported from the Himalayan mountains; *myrrh,* an aromatic resin; *henna,* the aromatic flower of the cypress. *My beloved,* the woman's designation for the man (occurring many times). *En-gedi,* an oasis on the western shore of the Dead Sea. Its literal rendering, "spring of the kid," puns on the earlier erotic use of "kids" (1.5). The Song shows a special fondness for exotic place names. **15–17:** The man's (v. 15) and the woman's (v. 16) professions of admiration mirror each other. **2.1:** The woman's self-appraisal, boastful or humble, is unclear because the words translated (*rose* and *lily*) are unknown. *Lily* elsewhere is charged with eroticism (4.5; 6.2–3; 7.3). *Sharon,* either a generic term for "plain" or a reference to the fertile coastal plain. **2–3:** The alternating compliments mirror one another, as in 1.15–16. The *apple* (also 2.5; 7.9; 8.5), not so far identified, is a fragrant fruit and carries erotic overtones (2.5; 7.9). **4:** *Banqueting house,* lit. "house of wine," the couple's trysting place (as in 1.17). *Intention,* the act of lovemaking (2.7; cf. Jer 2.33; Prov 5.19). **6:** Either a wish or a statement of fact, see 8.3. **7:** See 3.5; 8.4.

2.8–17: Springtime of love. The beloved's coming and going as a gazelle frames this poem. **8:** *The voice of my beloved,* better, "Listen, my beloved!" **9:** The word for *gazelle* in Hebrew has a homonym meaning

or a young stag.
Look, there he stands
behind our wall,
gazing in at the windows,
looking through the lattice.
10 My beloved speaks and says to me:
"Arise, my love, my fair one,
and come away;
11 for now the winter is past,
the rain is over and gone.
12 The flowers appear on the earth;
the time of singing has come,
and the voice of the turtledove
is heard in our land.
13 The fig tree puts forth its figs,
and the vines are in blossom;
they give forth fragrance.
Arise, my love, my fair one,
and come away.
14 O my dove, in the clefts of the
rock,
in the covert of the cliff,
let me see your face,
let me hear your voice;
for your voice is sweet,
and your face is lovely.
15 Catch us the foxes,
the little foxes,
that ruin the vineyards—
for our vineyards are in blossom."

16 My beloved is mine and I am his;
he pastures his flock among the
lilies.
17 Until the day breathes
and the shadows flee,
turn, my beloved, be like a gazelle
or a young stag on the cleft
mountains.[a]

3 Upon my bed at night
I sought him whom my soul loves;
I sought him, but found him not;
I called him, but he gave no
answer.[b]
2 "I will rise now and go about
the city,
in the streets and in the squares;
I will seek him whom my soul loves."
I sought him, but found him not.
3 The sentinels found me,
as they went about in the city.
"Have you seen him whom my soul
loves?"
4 Scarcely had I passed them,
when I found him whom my soul
loves.
I held him, and would not let him go
until I brought him into my
mother's house,
and into the chamber of her that
conceived me.
5 I adjure you, O daughters of
Jerusalem,
by the gazelles or the wild does:
do not stir up or awaken love
until it is ready!

6 What is that coming up from the
wilderness,
like a column of smoke,

a Or *on the mountains of Bether*; meaning of Heb uncertain *b* Gk: Heb lacks this line

"beauty" (Isa 13.19; 23.9); a play on these words is likely intended. **11–13:** *Winter,* the rainy season. *Time of singing* may also be read as the "time of pruning," which an ancient Hebrew calendar from Gezer places between the month of harvesting and the month of summer fruit. **14:** *Dove* (cf. 5.2; 6.9), a metaphor for inaccessibility. **15:** Although the Hebrew is obscure, the woman appears to answer teasingly that, far from being inaccessible, her sexuality (*our vineyards*) is in full bloom and in danger of being raided by others (*foxes*). **16:** The mutual pledge of love echoes marriage and adoption formularies.

3.1–5: Nighttime search for the beloved. 1: *Upon my bed at night,* i.e., "Nightly, night after night." **2:** Likely not quoted speech, but contemporaneous narration: "I rise up . . . and search." **5:** See 2.7; 8.4.

3.6–10: Solomon's wedding procession. The significance and exact meaning of this poem is debated. The beloved is imagined as King Solomon on his wedding day. **6:** *Coming up,* commonly used for travel to Jerusalem up in the hill country. It is a homonym of the common Hebrew noun for "whole burnt offering." Thus the procession, viewed from afar, appears as a column of smoke winding its way to

perfumed with myrrh and
frankincense,
with all the fragrant powders of the
merchant?
7 Look, it is the litter of Solomon!
Around it are sixty mighty men
of the mighty men of Israel,
8 all equipped with swords
and expert in war,
each with his sword at his thigh
because of alarms by night.
9 King Solomon made himself a
palanquin
from the wood of Lebanon.
10 He made its posts of silver,
its back of gold, its seat of purple;
its interior was inlaid with love.[a]
Daughters of Jerusalem,
11 come out.
Look, O daughters of Zion,
at King Solomon,
at the crown with which his mother
crowned him
on the day of his wedding,
on the day of the gladness of
his heart.

4 How beautiful you are, my love,
how very beautiful!
Your eyes are doves
behind your veil.
Your hair is like a flock of goats,
moving down the slopes of Gilead.
2 Your teeth are like a flock of
shorn ewes
that have come up from the
washing,
all of which bear twins,
and not one among them is
bereaved.
3 Your lips are like a crimson thread,
and your mouth is lovely.
Your cheeks are like halves of a
pomegranate
behind your veil.
4 Your neck is like the tower of David,
built in courses;
on it hang a thousand bucklers,
all of them shields of warriors.
5 Your two breasts are like two fawns,
twins of a gazelle,
that feed among the lilies.
6 Until the day breathes
and the shadows flee,
I will hasten to the mountain of
myrrh
and the hill of frankincense.
7 You are altogether beautiful, my love;
there is no flaw in you.
8 Come with me from Lebanon,
my bride;
come with me from Lebanon.
Depart[b] from the peak of Amana,
from the peak of Senir and
Hermon,
from the dens of lions,
from the mountains of leopards.

a Meaning of Heb uncertain *b* Or *Look*

Jerusalem. *Myrrh,* see 1.12–14n.; *frankincense,* an aromatic resin from Arabia. **7:** *Litter,* lit. "bed." **10:** *Love,* some emend to "ebony" or "stones."

4.1–5.1: Praise of the woman's beauty. 1: *Doves,* i.e., bashful and full of desire. *Flock of goats,* the woman's hair flows over her shoulders and down her back. *Gilead,* a hilly area of the Transjordan. **2:** Her teeth are white, all present and in good order. **3:** The comparison of *cheeks* with the half of a *pomegranate* evokes rosy cheeks viewed through the *veil.* **4:** An actual *tower of David* is unknown. The image of *bucklers* and *shields* suggests a necklace around the woman's neck (cf. 1.10; 4.9). The architectural imagery applied here and elsewhere in the Song (6.4; 7.4–5) to the woman may draw on the biblical tradition of personifying cities as women (e.g., Isa 47.1–15; 54.1–17; Jer 31.15–17; Am 5.1–3; Lam 1–2). **6:** See 2.17. *Mountain of myrrh, hill of frankincense,* the woman's breasts (cf. 1.13); see 1.12–14n.; 3.6n. **4.8–5.1:** The poem is filled with puns, wordplay, and multiple repetitions. **4.8:** The references to the *Lebanon* and the Anti-Lebanon mountain ranges, which are located north of Israel in modern-day Lebanon and Syria, symbolize danger and the woman's inaccessibility (cf. 2.14). *Amana, Senir,* and *Hermon* are the names of individual peaks in the Anti-Lebanon range. *Bride* (4.9–10,12; 5.1) and "sister" (4.9–10,12; 5.1) are terms of affection. **9:** *Ravish,* either "you take my heart away" or with more specific

9 You have ravished my heart, my
sister, my bride,
you have ravished my heart with a
glance of your eyes,
with one jewel of your necklace.
10 How sweet is your love, my sister, my
bride!
how much better is your love than
wine,
and the fragrance of your oils than
any spice!
11 Your lips distill nectar, my bride;
honey and milk are under your
tongue;
the scent of your garments is like
the scent of Lebanon.
12 A garden locked is my sister,
my bride,
a garden locked, a fountain sealed.
13 Your channel[a] is an orchard of
pomegranates
with all choicest fruits,
henna with nard,
14 nard and saffron, calamus and
cinnamon,
with all trees of frankincense,
myrrh and aloes,
with all chief spices—
15 a garden fountain, a well of living
water,
and flowing streams from Lebanon.

16 Awake, O north wind,
and come, O south wind!
Blow upon my garden
that its fragrance may be wafted
abroad.
Let my beloved come to his garden,
and eat its choicest fruits.

5 I come to my garden, my sister,
my bride;
I gather my myrrh with my spice,
I eat my honeycomb with my
honey,
I drink my wine with my milk.

Eat, friends, drink,
and be drunk with love.

2 I slept, but my heart was awake.
Listen! my beloved is knocking.
"Open to me, my sister, my love,
my dove, my perfect one;
for my head is wet with dew,
my locks with the drops of the
night."
3 I had put off my garment;
how could I put it on again?
I had bathed my feet;
how could I soil them?
4 My beloved thrust his hand into the
opening,
and my inmost being yearned
for him.
5 I arose to open to my beloved,
and my hands dripped with myrrh,
my fingers with liquid myrrh,
upon the handles of the bolt.
6 I opened to my beloved,
but my beloved had turned and was
gone.

a Meaning of Heb uncertain

connotations of sexual arousal. **11:** *The scent of Lebanon,* i.e., the fragrant cedars. **12:** *Garden* and *fountain* are images of female sexuality (cf. Prov 5.15–17), here as inaccessible. **13:** *Channels,* i.e., irrigation channels, or perhaps the area so irrigated. *Henna, nard,* see 1.12–14n. **14:** *Saffron, calamus, cinnamon, aloes* are all spices from India. *Chief spices,* better, "best spices." **16:** The man summons the winds of love using the same word (*awake*) that the woman used earlier to warn about not arousing love prematurely (3.5; cf. 2.7; 8.4). The second couplet is spoken by the woman. **5.1:** As elsewhere, eating and drinking have erotic overtones.

5.2–6.3: The woman's search. This is the longest poem in the collection, unified by the dialogic frame set up between the woman and the "daughters of Jerusalem." **5.2–8:** A sequence like 3.1–4. The verses are freighted with allusions to sexual intercourse. **2:** The juxtaposition of verbs for "sleep" and "wakefulness" suggests a dreamy state. *My,* the repetition enacts the beloved's *knocking.* **3:** The woman's response is probably meant teasingly. **5:** *I arose to open,* better, "I started to open." *Myrrh,* both the woman's toiletry (she has perfumed herself) and the palpable sign of her lover, who in 1.13 was likened to a "bag of myrrh."

My soul failed me when he spoke.
I sought him, but did not find him;
I called him, but he gave
no answer.
7 Making their rounds in the city
the sentinels found me;
they beat me, they wounded me,
they took away my mantle,
those sentinels of the walls.
8 I adjure you, O daughters of
Jerusalem,
if you find my beloved,
tell him this:
I am faint with love.

9 What is your beloved more than
another beloved,
O fairest among women?
What is your beloved more than
another beloved,
that you thus adjure us?

10 My beloved is all radiant and ruddy,
distinguished among ten thousand.
11 His head is the finest gold;
his locks are wavy,
black as a raven.
12 His eyes are like doves
beside springs of water,
bathed in milk,
fitly set.[a]
13 His cheeks are like beds of spices,
yielding fragrance.
His lips are lilies,
distilling liquid myrrh.
14 His arms are rounded gold,
set with jewels.
His body is ivory work,[a]
encrusted with sapphires.[b]
15 His legs are alabaster columns,
set upon bases of gold.
His appearance is like Lebanon,
choice as the cedars.
16 His speech is most sweet,
and he is altogether desirable.
This is my beloved and this is
my friend,
O daughters of Jerusalem.

6 Where has your beloved gone,
O fairest among women?
Which way has your beloved turned,
that we may seek him with you?

2 My beloved has gone down to his
garden,
to the beds of spices,
to pasture his flock in the gardens,
and to gather lilies.
3 I am my beloved's and my beloved is
mine;
he pastures his flock among the
lilies.

4 You are beautiful as Tirzah, my love,
comely as Jerusalem,
terrible as an army with banners.
5 Turn away your eyes from me,
for they overwhelm me!
Your hair is like a flock of goats,

a Meaning of Heb uncertain *b* Heb *lapis lazuli*

6: *My soul failed me* (lit. "went out"), the woman's deep emotional distress at missing her lover, akin to "she nearly dies" (Gen 35.18; Ps 146.4). *When he spoke* is surely not right. Either "because of him" or "when he left." **7:** The brutal treatment the woman receives at the hands of the *sentinels* is abrupt and shocking. **8:** *Tell him this* is ambiguous. It may also be taken as a negative request: "Do not tell him." **5.9–6.3:** The woman's praise of her beloved frequently uses images derived from sculpture and the plastic arts, as does the man's praise song (4.1–7). **5.10:** *Radiant and ruddy,* a sign of vigor and health (Ps 104.15; 1 Sam 16.12; 17.4; Lam 4.7). **12:** *Milk,* associated elsewhere with the idyllic (Ex 3.8,17; Deut 6.3; Isa 55.1; Job 29.6; Song 4.12; 5.1; Lam 4.7). *Fitly set* assumes the practice of making statues with jeweled inlays for eyes (as in 5.14; cf. Ex 25.7; 1 Chr 29.2). **14–15:** The imagery in these verses suggests a statue, the great value and surpassing beauty of which is uppermost in mind. **16:** *His speech* (lit. "his palate"), meaning kisses as well as language (cf. 1.2; 7.10). *Sweet* in Neh 8.10 refers to a drink (cf. 7.10). *My friend* intentionally echoes one of the man's pet names for the woman (cf. 1.9).

6.4–10: In praise of the woman's beauty (cf. 4.1–7; 5.9–6.3; 6.13–7.6). **4:** *Tirzah* (likely Tell el-Farah North), the capital of the Northern Kingdom in the late tenth and early ninth centuries. **5b–7:** Cf. 4.1b–3.

moving down the slopes of Gilead.
6 Your teeth are like a flock of ewes,
that have come up from the washing;
all of them bear twins,
and not one among them is bereaved.
7 Your cheeks are like halves of a pomegranate
behind your veil.
8 There are sixty queens and eighty concubines,
and maidens without number.
9 My dove, my perfect one, is the only one,
the darling of her mother,
flawless to her that bore her.
The maidens saw her and called her happy;
the queens and concubines also,
and they praised her.
10 "Who is this that looks forth like the dawn,
fair as the moon, bright as the sun,
terrible as an army with banners?"

11 I went down to the nut orchard,
to look at the blossoms of the valley,
to see whether the vines had budded,
whether the pomegranates were in bloom.
12 Before I was aware, my fancy set me
in a chariot beside my prince.[a]

13[b] Return, return, O Shulammite!
Return, return, that we may look upon you.

Why should you look upon the Shulammite,
as upon a dance before two armies?[c]

7 How graceful are your feet in sandals,
O queenly maiden!
Your rounded thighs are like jewels,
the work of a master hand.
2 Your navel is a rounded bowl
that never lacks mixed wine.
Your belly is a heap of wheat,
encircled with lilies.
3 Your two breasts are like two fawns,
twins of a gazelle.
4 Your neck is like an ivory tower.

a Cn: Meaning of Heb uncertain *b* Ch 7.1 in Heb
c Or *dance of Mahanaim*

10: *Moon/sun,* not the common terms but poetic metonyms, "whiteness" and "heat" (cf. Isa 24.23; 30.26), which more eloquently evoke dawn imagery.

6.11–12: The exact connection of these stanzas to the surrounding material is unclear. **11:** The identity of the speaker is ambiguous. The garden imagery, usually associated with the woman (e.g., 4.12), may suggest that the man is speaking. If not, the woman at last responds positively to the man's invitation in 2.10 to accompany him (and it echoes the man's entrance into the garden in 4.16–5.1).

6.13–7.13: Praise of the woman and her response. 6.13: The exact significance of *Shulammite* is unclear. *A dance before two armies,* if correct, is also obscure. **7.1:** *Queenly maiden* (Heb "bat nadab"), plays on the reference to "prince" ("nadab") in 6.12. *Your rounded thighs,* better, "the curves of your thighs." **2:** *Navel,* perhaps also a euphemism or double entendre for "vulva," supported structurally by the couplet's placement between couplets describing the woman's *thighs* and *belly. Your belly is a heap of wheat.* The term for *belly* frequently designates "womb" (e.g., Gen 30.2; Judg 16.17; Isa 13.18). When combined with the image of *a heap of wheat* the associations with fertility and nourishment are palpable, and thus eroticism and fertility imagery are closely linked. At another level, the image of heaped wheat suggests the softness and gentle curve of the woman's stomach, as well, perhaps, as its golden and tawny hue. **4:** *Ivory,* meant to convey a notion of splendor and opulence (cf. 1 Kings 10.18; Am 3.15; Ps 45.8). The association of eyes and pools puns on the Heb word "ayin," which means both "eye" and "spring." *Heshbon* is a city located in the central Transjordanian plateau ca. 20 km (12 mi) southwest of Amman. Excavations at Heshbon have revealed a large water reservoir from the ninth and eighth centuries BCE. *Bath-rabbim,* "daughter of noblemen" or the like, as an epithet for the city of Heshbon, alludes to "O queenly maiden" in 7.1; as well as to epithets of personified cities elsewhere (Lam 1.6; 2.13; Isa 23.12).

Your eyes are pools in Heshbon,
by the gate of Bath-rabbim.
Your nose is like a tower of Lebanon,
overlooking Damascus.
5 Your head crowns you like Carmel,
and your flowing locks are like
purple;
a king is held captive in the
tresses.[a]

6 How fair and pleasant you are,
O loved one, delectable maiden![b]
7 You are stately[c] as a palm tree,
and your breasts are like its
clusters.
8 I say I will climb the palm tree
and lay hold of its branches.
O may your breasts be like clusters of
the vine,
and the scent of your breath like
apples,
9 and your kisses[d] like the best wine
that goes down[e] smoothly,
gliding over lips and teeth.[f]

10 I am my beloved's,
and his desire is for me.
11 Come, my beloved,
let us go forth into the fields,
and lodge in the villages;
12 let us go out early to the vineyards,
and see whether the vines have
budded,
whether the grape blossoms have
opened
and the pomegranates are in bloom.
There I will give you my love.
13 The mandrakes give forth fragrance,
and over our doors are all choice
fruits,
new as well as old,
which I have laid up for you, O my
beloved.

8 O that you were like a brother to me,
who nursed at my mother's breast!
If I met you outside, I would
kiss you,
and no one would despise me.
2 I would lead you and bring you
into the house of my mother,
and into the chamber of the one
who bore me.[g]
I would give you spiced wine
to drink,
the juice of my pomegranates.
3 O that his left hand were under
my head,
and that his right hand embraced
me!
4 I adjure you, O daughters of
Jerusalem,
do not stir up or awaken love
until it is ready!

5 Who is that coming up from the
wilderness,
leaning upon her beloved?

a Meaning of Heb uncertain *b* Syr: Heb *in delights* *c* Heb *This your stature is* *d* Heb *palate* *e* Heb *down for my lover* *f* Gk Syr Vg: Heb *lips of sleepers* *g* Gk Syr: Heb *my mother; she* (or *you*) *will teach me*

A *tower of Lebanon* is unknown. Lebanon in association with nose is suggestive of fragrance. **5:** *Carmel* is the mountain range that runs southeast of modern Haifa. As a common noun, "karmel" means "garden, orchard." *Purple,* a dye derived from murex shells, was commonly associated with royalty. **6:** *How fair* echoes the opening of 7.1 ("How graceful"). **7–8:** *Palm tree* denotes inaccessibility; *vine* and wine denote eroticism and sensuality, through the repetition of the term *clusters. Breath* (lit. "nose"), perhaps referring to the custom of nose kissing. *Apples,* see 2.3n. **9:** *Kisses* (lit. "palate"), also a reference to wine. **10:** The woman responds. **11:** The word for *villages* is a homonym, also meaning "henna bushes." **13:** *Mandrakes,* considered an aphrodisiac (Gen 30.14–19). *New as well as old,* i.e., "all kinds of."

8.1–4: A poem of yearning. 1–2: The woman wishes her lover were *like a brother* so that they could express their love freely and publicly without rebuke. **3–4:** Cf. 2.6–7.

8.5–14: Lyrical ending. The song closes with a number of brief poems or poetic fragments. **5:** *Who is that coming up from the wilderness* is a reprise of 3.6, only it is the woman who is envisioned, not the man. *In labor* can also refer to "conception," which is the more likely image here. **6:** Seals were made of

Under the apple tree I awakened you.
There your mother was in labor with
you;
there she who bore you was in
labor.

6 Set me as a seal upon your heart,
as a seal upon your arm;
for love is strong as death,
passion fierce as the grave.
Its flashes are flashes of fire,
a raging flame.
7 Many waters cannot quench love,
neither can floods drown it.
If one offered for love
all the wealth of one's house,
it would be utterly scorned.

8 We have a little sister,
and she has no breasts.
What shall we do for our sister,
on the day when she is spoken for?
9 If she is a wall,
we will build upon her a battlement
of silver;
but if she is a door,
we will enclose her with boards of
cedar.
10 I was a wall,
and my breasts were like towers;
then I was in his eyes
as one who brings[a] peace.
11 Solomon had a vineyard at
Baal-hamon;
he entrusted the vineyard to
keepers;
each one was to bring for its fruit a
thousand pieces of silver.
12 My vineyard, my very own, is
for myself;
you, O Solomon, may have the
thousand,
and the keepers of the fruit two
hundred!

13 O you who dwell in the gardens,
my companions are listening for
your voice;
let me hear it.

14 Make haste, my beloved,
and be like a gazelle
or a young stag
upon the mountains of spices!

a Or *finds*

precious and semiprecious metals and stones and were used to seal documents and to indicate ownership, functioning much like a signature. They were worn on a cord around the neck (Gen 38.18) or as a ring (Gen 41.42; Jer 22.24; Sir 49.11) and were considered a valuable possession. The woman desires to be bound closely and always to her lover. *Love is as strong as death* stresses the inevitability, the utter givenness of the woman's love in all of its manifestations. *Passion,* or "jealousy," which better conveys the image's violence. **7:** *Many waters* are associated with the powers of chaos, which the LORD dominates (Gen 1.2; Isa 51.9–10; Ps 29.3; 76.12–14). **8–10:** Perhaps playful banter between the woman (8.10) and her brothers (cf. 1.6). *Spoken for,* as in marriage (1 Sam 25.39). **11–12:** Here Solomon is addressed literally. The speaker is unclear, though it is likely the man. If so, he is extolling the unparalleled value of his own vineyard—the woman. *Baal-hamon* is an unidentified place. *My vineyard, my very own* is the language used by the woman earlier (1.6). **13–14:** The concluding poem of the sequence, fittingly, ends on a note of expectation and anticipation.

INTRODUCTION
to the Prophetic Books

THE NATURE AND COMPOSITION OF THE PROPHETIC BOOKS

THE PROPHETIC BOOKS are unusual and complex compositions. With the exception of Jonah, which is a story about a prophet, these books all contain extended sayings and speeches that purport to come from the prophet whose name the book bears. While the books undoubtedly do preserve authentic words of the prophets in question, we should not think of the prophetic books simply as transcriptions of the words of prophets. Although much remains unknown about the composition of the prophetic books, it is possible to reconstruct a general picture. Scholars generally agree that the poetic materials in the prophetic books originated as oral pronouncements by the prophet to a public audience. These oral sayings were subsequently written down, perhaps by the prophet or an associate. The circumstances that led to these original written collections were undoubtedly various. A reference in Isaiah suggests that oracles might be written down as a form of authentication (Isa 30.8). The book of Jeremiah describes a situation in which Jeremiah, having been banned from speaking publicly in the Temple, had his assistant Baruch write down a selection of his prophetic words so that they could be taken into the Temple and read to the people (Jer 36.5–6). When King Jehoiakim destroyed the scroll, Jeremiah had Baruch write out another copy, to which they added additional material (Jer 36.27–32). This collection may have formed the nucleus of the book of Jeremiah. (Unlike most of the other prophetic books, Ezekiel may have been composed as a written document from the beginning.) Elsewhere in the Bible there is further evidence of prophetic collections; see 1 Chr 29.29; 2 Chr 9.29.

Once small collections of prophetic oracles and pronouncements were made, they were subject to further editing, rearranging, annotating, and expansion. In some cases narratives about the prophet were added; these are both autobiographical (e.g., Isa 6; 8; Jer 1.4–19; 13.1–11; Hos 1–2; Am 7.1–7) and biographical (e.g., Isa 7; 36–39; Jer 26; 36–44; Hos 3; Am 7.10–17). The occasions for such editorial activity will have differed, but national crises may have prompted some of this process. Most likely, written collections of the oracles of Amos and Hosea, which were originally addressed to the Northern Kingdom (Israel), were brought to Judah after the fall of the Northern Kingdom in 721 BCE, and edited and circulated there. Isaiah of Jerusalem seems to have knowledge of Amos's oracles, and Jeremiah is unquestionably influenced by Hosea. Many of the prophetic books originating before the fall of Judah to the Babylonians in 586 BCE show evidence of editorial additions and reorganizations that reflect the circumstances of exilic and postexilic times. The book of Amos, for example, now includes material that presupposes the fall of Judah (9.11–15). The most dramatic example of the expansion and reworking of prophetic materials is the book of Isaiah. Although it contains extensive material from the eighth-century prophet, chs 40–55 clearly reflect the situation of the Babylonian exile, and chs 56–66 the period of the restoration of the Judean community after the exile. Yet even though the book contains materials dating from several centuries, it is unified by a number of motifs, themes, and topics that recur throughout the work.

The complex activity of preserving and developing the prophetic oracle collections reflects a conviction that the prophet's words were not only significant for the circumstance in which they were originally pronounced but potentially relevant for later ones as well. At the same time, the freedom with which later generations could rework the prophetic oracles indicates that the prophets' words did not at first possess the kind of fixed authority that is later associated with "scripture." Although the processes by which the prophetic books came to assume a relatively final form and canonical status are difficult to trace, this probably occurred during the Persian and early Hellenistic periods (the fifth through the third centuries BCE). Most likely, during this time scribal editors added the superscriptions that introduce most of the books, indicating the identity of the prophet (name, father's name, and occasionally other information) and often the kings of Israel or Judah during whose reigns the prophets were active (e.g., Isa 1.1; Jer 1.1–3; Hos 1.1). In addition to editorial additions to the individual prophetic books, the smaller prophetic books (Hosea–Malachi) were arranged and edited to form a group known as "the book of the Twelve," which was copied on a single scroll. By the beginning of the second century BCE Ben Sira refers to these prophets as "the twelve" (Sir 49.10). The number twelve is symbolic of the twelve sons of Jacob and the twelve tribes of Israel, and considerable editorial work was required to organize these prophetic materials into a grouping of twelve. In fact, the book of Zechariah consists of three separate collections (chs 1–8, 9–11, 12–14) grouped together editorially. Only the first of these comes from the prophet Zechariah, whereas the other two are anonymous. The final book in the collection, Malachi, is also an anonymous piece, since "Malachi" is not a personal name but a phrase meaning "my messenger," picked up from 3.1 to serve as the name of the prophet in the superscription.

THE PHENOMENON OF PROPHECY

The phenomenon of prophecy was widespread in the ancient Near East, and many important themes and genres familiar from biblical prophecy have parallels there. Moreover, many more prophets were active in ancient Israel and Judah than those whose work is represented in the prophetic books of the Bible, and their activities were more varied than these writings suggest. The books of Samuel and Kings provide important additional information. Since our sources are limited, it is difficult to reconstruct the history of prophecy. Some of the features are clear, however. The prophet was essentially an intermediary between God and the people, and one of the major functions was that of messenger. Often prophets introduced their communications with a version of the formula typically used by messengers, "thus says the LORD." But prophets might also carry inquiries from the people to God or make intercession on behalf of the people. In contrast to priesthood, which was exclusively male, both women and men could be prophets. Women prophets included Deborah (Judg 4.4) and Huldah (2 Kings 22.14); see also Joel 2.28. Additional aspects of the prophetic role are suggested by the various terms used to identify them. In addition to "prophet" (Heb *nabi'*, perhaps meaning "one who is called"), the prophets are identified as seers (Heb *ro'eh*), visionaries (Heb *ḥozeh*), and holy men (Heb *'ish'elohim*, lit. "man of God").

The religious phenomenon of Israelite prophecy can be traced for more than a thousand years, from the premonarchical period to the turn of the era. As one would expect, over such a long period of time the nature and function of prophecy altered in response to changing historical, social, and religious circumstances. Four periods define the major epochs of prophecy: the early monarchical period (eleventh through ninth centuries), the Assyrian crisis (eighth century), the Babylonian crisis (late seventh through early-sixth centuries), and the postexilic restoration (mid-sixth through mid-fifth centuries).

In the earliest period prophets may have been local or itinerant holy men and women who were revered for their special religious powers and who might be consulted for a variety of private inquiries, from locating lost property (1 Sam 9.1–10) to learning whether a sick child would live or die (1 Kings 14.1–18). Some lived in prophetic communities that cultivated ecstatic forms of religious experience (1 Sam 19.18–24; 2 Kings 6.1–7). Prophets also had the public function of declaring God's will concerning whether the people should go to war (Judg 4.4–10). The emergence of monarchy in ancient Israel may have changed aspects of the prophets' role. Prophets appear as king-makers and king-breakers, as they announce that God has designated an individual to become king or has rejected a reigning king (1 Sam 10.1; 15.23; 1 Kings 11.29–39; 14.1–18). Though prophets continued their role in advising about matters of war (1 Kings 22), they also served as critics of the king in religious and social affairs. The consolidation of royal power and the foreign religious practices introduced through royal marriages often threatened older tribal institutions and values. The conflict between Elijah, the prophet, and Ahab and Jezebel, the king and queen, illustrates these tensions between prophet and king (1 Kings 18–21).

Prophecy appears to have undergone a dramatic change during the eighth century, although this impression may be affected by the change in the nature of the sources of information. From the eighth century onward, collections of prophetic oracles are preserved, yet, with the exception of Jeremiah, few extended narratives about prophets exist. However, it does appear that in this period prophets began to function less as private counselors and critics of kings and more as public figures who influenced opinion through their pronouncements in the Temple courts and in other public places. Prophets of the eighth century (Amos, Hosea, Isaiah, Micah) interpreted international affairs, critiqued complacent religious practices, and condemned the abuses of social justice that accompanied the increasing urbanization and centralization of state power characteristic of the eighth century. The prophetic careers of Hosea, Micah, and Isaiah took place in the shadow of the expansionist Assyrian Empire, which eventually put an end to the Northern Kingdom of Israel and subjected Judah to the condition of vassalage. They interpreted these events, however, in terms of the judgment of the LORD, not simply as the success of a powerful Assyrian Empire. This perspective allowed Isaiah, for example, to anticipate the ultimate downfall of Assyria because of its overweening arrogance.

The third major period of prophecy occurred during the Babylonian crisis. The prophet Nahum celebrated the defeat of Assyria (612–609 BCE), but the excitement he expressed was soon turned to confusion as Babylon succeeded Assyria as the dominant empire (see Habakkuk). Jeremiah's prophetic career (ca. 627–586) spanned the time from the decline of Assyria through the Babylonian overlordship of Judah, to the revolt and destruction of Judah and the exile of a portion of its population. Although it is difficult to correlate many of his poetic oracles with specific events in this period, the narratives about Jeremiah give a vivid picture of a nation and its leadership deeply conflicted about what political course to follow and the religious significance of the choices that were forced upon it. Even the prophetic community was bitterly divided and gave contradictory advice to the king concerning the will of the LORD (Jer 26–29; 36–44). Overlapping the career of Jeremiah, the prophet Ezekiel (active 593–ca. 571 BCE) was among the Judeans exiled to Babylon after the revolt of 597 BCE, a decade before the final revolt and the destruction of Jerusalem. Ezekiel's prophetic work was first to persuade the exiled Judeans of the inevitability of Jerusalem's destruction, and, following the fall of the city, to begin to articulate the theological grounds for conceiving a possible future, including a return of the exiles and a rebuilding of the destroyed Temple. In contrast to the prophets who preceded him, Ezekiel drew strongly on priestly traditions for his categories of thought, forms of speech, and evocative symbols.

The defeat of the Babylonian Empire by the Persian king Cyrus altered political conditions dramatically. Although Judah did not regain its independence but became a part of the Persian Empire, Cyrus and his successors authorized the rebuilding of the Temple and of Jerusalem, allowing members of the exiled community in Babylon who so desired to return to Judah. Thus the prophetic task during this period largely concerned issues of the restoration of the community and its institutions in a context significantly different from that which prevailed during the Israelite and Judean monarchy. The anonymous prophet whose work is found in Isa 40–55 (often called "Second Isaiah") addressed the Babylonian exiles just at the time that Cyrus was engaged in the conquest of Babylon.

Second Isaiah had to persuade the exilic community that unfolding events represented God's action in history, to interpret the significance of Cyrus (God's "anointed" who would rebuild Jerusalem), and to encourage the exiles to return to Jerusalem. The process of rebuilding the Temple (520–515 BCE) provides the context for the prophets Haggai and Zechariah. Zechariah's work in particular suggests this was a time of expectation that perhaps the monarchy might be restored, an event that did not occur. Issues concerning reorganization of the Judean community and tensions regarding economic justice, institutional corruption, and the boundaries of the community are variously reflected in Zechariah, Isa 56–66, and Malachi, prophets who were active in roughly the period 525–475 BCE.

Although prophets in all periods might speak of the dramatic intervention of God in historical events and the consequent transformation of the conditions of life, this type of language seems to have become more common and more vivid in the postexilic prophets (e.g., Isa 56–66, Zechariah, Malachi, Joel, and postexilic additions to earlier prophetic books, such as Isa 24–27). Some of the passages anticipate a war or other cataclysmic event of cosmic proportions that will precede a time of deliverance, peace, and virtual re-creation of the world. Such imagery and the expectations it expresses suggest to some scholars that apocalypticism emerges out of postexilic prophecy. Though it is true that apocalyptic literature is influenced by these prophetic writings and their imagery, apocalyptic writing cannot simply be understood as an outgrowth of the phenomenon of prophecy.

The book of Daniel, the only book in the Hebrew Bible that could be called an apocalypse, illustrates the complexity of the matter. Although Christian tradition groups Daniel with the prophetic books, Jewish tradition places it in the Writings (see below). The first part of the book consists of a cycle of narratives in which Daniel and his friends are portrayed as sages trained in the technical skills of Babylonian scribal wisdom. Like Joseph, Daniel is able to interpret dreams sent by God. He is not presented as a prophet. In the latter part of the book, however, Daniel is the recipient of visions that disclose the future. These vision reports do bear significant similarities to those found in Ezekiel and especially in Zechariah, though their almost allegorical style is quite different. Similarly, although general claims about God's foreknowledge of historical events can be found in Second Isaiah, Daniel's representation of history as predetermined both with respect to its epochal structure and its specific events is strikingly different from the representation of history by the prophets. A clue to the relationship of apocalyptic writing to prophecy may be found in Dan 9, where Daniel is presented as studying the book of Jeremiah and receiving an angelic interpretation of its significance. As suggested by the representation of Daniel as a technically trained sage, the authors of apocalyptic books were perhaps themselves learned scribes who studied and appropriated aspects of the prophetic tradition and combined them with other influences in their attempts to understand the nature of the cosmos and the course of history.

CANONICAL PLACEMENT AND CONTENTS

In both the Jewish and the Christian canons the prophetic books form a distinct section of the Bible. The two traditions differ, however, with respect to the number, sequence, and placement of the prophetic books. Jewish tradition divides the canon into three parts: the Torah (i.e., Genesis–Deuteronomy), the Prophets, and the Writings. The term "former prophets" is used to designate the historical books Joshua–2 Kings (perhaps reflecting a tradition that these books were written by prophets), and the term "latter prophets" is used for those books that bear the name of a particular prophet (i.e., Isaiah, Jeremiah, Ezekiel, and the twelve minor prophets). In Christian Bibles the prophetic books form the last section of the Old Testament canon, following the Pentateuch, the

Historical Books, and the Poetical Books. Christian tradition includes Daniel among the prophetic books, in contrast to Judaism, which groups Daniel with the Writings. Also, Christian Bibles place Lamentations, which is not a book of prophecy, immediately after the book of Jeremiah, reflecting the tradition of the Septuagint (the ancient Greek translation of the Hebrew Bible) that Jeremiah was the author of Lamentations. Likewise, in some Christian canons, the Apocryphal/Deuterocanonical book of Baruch comes after Lamentations, because of the connection between the prophet Jeremiah and his scribe, Baruch.

ISAIAH

The book of Isaiah in its current form was written and assembled over the course of several centuries. This process began in the eighth century BCE, with the collection of the prophecies of Isaiah son of Amoz, who was active in the Southern Kingdom of Judah during the reigns of Uzziah, Jotham, Ahaz, and Hezekiah (1.1). It was completed no later than the second century BCE, since a complete Isaiah scroll dating from that time has been found among the Dead Sea Scrolls at Qumran (1QIsa[a]), and the Septuagint (LXX), the ancient Greek translation of the Hebrew Scriptures from around the same time, contains the complete book as we know it. The author of Sirach, who wrote in the early second century BCE as well, was familiar with chs 36–39 and 40–55 (Sir 48.22–25), showing that a version of Isaiah containing at least these sections was in general circulation by then.

There is no record of the editing and compiling process that the book of Isaiah went through, but there are explanations for the characteristics of the text as it now stands. The most obvious of these characteristics, and the first one to be noticed, is the division after chs 1–39, which refer mostly to events of the eighth century BCE. Chs 40–66 cannot be earlier than the sixth century, since they clearly address a situation reflecting the fall of Jerusalem and the deportations of large parts of the population of Judah to Babylon. Within chs 40–66, moreover, chs 56–66 (or possibly 55–66) may date from an even later period, after the return of some of the people from the Babylonian exile. These three divisions of the book are usually labeled First, Second, and Third Isaiah. In addition, chs 1–39 are also composed of smaller units dating from a variety of times (see below and the commentary). But it is important to look beyond these divisions of the book for structural and thematic interconnection between different parts, such as its first and last chapters. These interconnections make clear that Isaiah reached its present form not as the result of a haphazard accumulation of different kinds of material, but as the outcome of a cumulative series of interpretations that reapplied and expanded older parts of Isaiah to meet the needs of later periods and situations.

THE BACKGROUND TO ISAIAH

Four pivotal moments in the history of the Israelite people form the background to the various parts of Isaiah.

1. *The Syro-Ephraimite War and its aftermath*. After a period of relative peace between Israel (the Northern Kingdom, often called "Ephraim" in Isaiah after its most important tribe) and Judah (the Southern Kingdom), international tensions rose after Tiglath-pileser III became king of the Assyrian Empire in 745 BCE and began an effort to conquer the lands to the west of Assyria, including Syria, Israel, and Judah. Uzziah, the king of Judah whose reign began during the peaceful era, died in 733 (6.1), and was succeeded first by Jotham (759) and then by Ahaz (743/735; the chronology is disputed). Pekah, king of Israel, and Rezin, king of Syria (Damascus or Aram) tried, beginning in 735, to enlist Ahaz in an alliance against Assyria, and when that effort failed, they attacked Judah to replace Ahaz with a king more amenable to their policies (ch 7). This conflict is known as the Syro-Ephraimite war, since it was a war of Syria and Ephraim against Judah. Ahaz successfully turned to Assyria for help in fending off Israel and Syria. The price he paid was steep: Judah became a vassal of Assyria.

2. *The Assyrian invasion.* During the decades following the Syro-Ephraimite war, the Assyrians expanded their influence in the area, taking over Syria and then attacking the Northern Kingdom, which fell in 722 BCE. When the Assyrian ruler of the time, Sargon II, died in 705, Hezekiah, the king of Judah and son of Ahaz, rebelled against Assyria. Hezekiah had thought to take advantage of the confusion at the change of rulers, and in addition sought support from Egypt that was not forthcoming (36.6). The new Assyrian king, Sennacherib, retaliated and conquered the cities surrounding Jerusalem in 701 BCE. Hezekiah was able to avert the conquest of Jerusalem itself only by paying tribute.

3. *The conquest of Jerusalem and the exile.* During the century following these events, the Assyrian empire gradually weakened. In 612 BCE, the rising Babylonian Empire conquered the Assyrian capital, Nineveh, and the international power struggle became one between Babylon and Egypt, with Judah caught between. In 605 the Babylonian king, Nebuchadnezzar, defeated the Egyptian Pharaoh, Neco, at the battle of Carchemish, and Babylon became the leading empire of the day. Judah came under Babylon's control, and when the last king of Judah, Zedekiah, rebelled against Babylon, the result was an invasion by Nebuchadnezzar. In 586, he destroyed Jerusalem and its Temple and deported a good deal of the population to Babylon, an event referred to as the exile.

4. *The return.* During the sixth century BCE, the Babylonians were increasingly challenged by the rise of another great empire, the Persians. In 539 Cyrus, the Persian king, defeated the Babylonians at the battle of Opis. Cyrus, who was tolerant and (by the standards of the time) benevolent, allowed the Jews to return to Judah, and many (though not all) eventually did so. The returning exiles rebuilt Jerusalem and the Temple.

THE RELATION OF ISAIAH AND HIS SUCCESSORS TO THE HISTORICAL BACKGROUND

Isaiah of Jerusalem, the eighth-century prophet whose work forms the basis of the book, was involved with the first two of these four moments: the Syro-Ephraimite war and the Assyrian invasion. In the first, he counseled against reliance on Assyria (7.7–9); in the second, he counseled against reliance on Egypt (31.1). In each case, the warnings against participating in the international power politics of the day were part of Isaiah's clear teaching that only by relying on the LORD would Judah ultimately prevail.

Two themes dominate the book of Isaiah as it now exists. The first is the proclamation that God is behind all historical events, including the actions of the great empires of the day (10.5; 41.25). The second is the importance and centrality of Jerusalem for Israel, which includes an emphasis on both the kingship and the right worship of God centered in Jerusalem (2.1–4).

These themes reappear in one form or another, adapted to fit the changing historical circumstances, but refashioned with the aim of making earlier pronouncements relevant to a different, later situation. The proclamation that God is behind the events of current history, that God is in control even of the actions of the hated empires of Assyria and Babylon, meant that the prophet's words at the time of the Assyrian threat could be reapplied to the time of the Babylonian invasion. The importance of Jerusalem, and along with it the monarchy and the Temple, attained tremendous resonance at the time of exile and return, when the vision of a restored city carried with it an idealized portrait of the "anointed," the restored king who in later tradition became the paradigm of the messiah. The restoration of Temple worship is set in the context of the worship that includes all people, even those formerly excluded (56.3–5).

CHAPTERS 1–39: CONTENT AND ARRANGEMENT

The first part of the book of Isaiah can be divided into sections, in part guided by headings that have been inserted in the text and by brief passages (usually prose) that mark their endings. Ch 1 may stand by itself as a general introduction; chs 2–4 consist of judgment on and promise to Jerusalem; chs 5–12 contain further warnings, including some to the kings of Judah; chs 13–23 consist largely of judgment on Babylon and other foreign peoples; chs 24–27 contrast the two cities, the city under judgment and the future Jerusalem; chs 28–33 once again warn Judah, and especially condemn Hezekiah's reliance on Egypt; chs 34–35 particularly condemn Edom, which took advantage of the Judean troubles to expand its territory; chs 36–39 form an appendix of historical materials (excerpted from the book of Kings) from the time of Hezekiah.

The title (1.1) describes the book as a vision that came to Isaiah, who was active during the reigns of four Judean kings, thus assigning him a prophetic career of about forty years. The second title (2.1) suggests that the first chapter was intended as an introduction to the message of judgment which takes up so much of the book. In addition, the last stanza of this first poem (1.27–31) has linguistic and thematic links with the last chapter of the book. Chs 2–4 pronounce judgment on Israel and on Jerusalem in ways reminiscent of Amos, but these sayings are bracketed by the prospect of a future restored and purified land and city (2.2–5; 4.2–6). Judgment, therefore, is not the last word.

The vineyard love song (5.1–7) serves as a transition to the account of Isaiah's involvement in the crisis of the Syro–Ephraimite war (734 BCE). This account begins with a vision narrated in the first person (6.1–13), continues with a third-person narrative (7.1–25), and concludes by returning to first-person narration (8.1–22). It is filled out with poems threatening divine judgment (5.8–25; 9.8–10.19) balanced by two poems about the future kingdom of peace and justice (9.1–7; 11.1–9), and it concludes with a psalm of thanksgiving which plays on the names of the principal protagonists, Isaiah and the Holy One of Israel (12.1–6).

Collections of sayings directed against hostile foreign nations form a significant component of several prophetic books. This is a type of saying particularly liable to be "recycled" to fit different historical situations; hence it is not surprising that much of chs 13–23—the nucleus of which is a series of nine oracles against foreign nations—dates from long after the lifetime of Isaiah. Beginning with 13.1–14.27, the focus shifts from the Assyrians to the Babylonians as the dominant world power. The prophet's engagement with events at the time of Ahaz and Assyrian ascendancy provides the key for those who came later to the theological understanding of events in the following centuries, when the Babylonians and after them the Persians succeeded the Assyrians as the major international powers.

The next section of the book, chs 24–27, is often referred to as "the Isaiah apocalypse" though much of it has little in common with apocalyptic. Of uncertain date, its principal theme is the contrast between an unnamed city, condemned to destruction (24.10–13; 25.2; 26.5–6; 27.10–11), and Jerusalem, destined for a glorious future (26.1–4). The connection with the previous section may be that the unnamed city is understood as a symbolic Babylon or a composite image of the cities placed under judgment in chs 13–23.

Chapters 28–33, much of which derive from eighth-century materials, take up once again the theme of judgment on the civil and religious leadership of the two kingdoms, with a special condemnation for Judean overtures to Egypt during the troubled reign of Hezekiah.

With chs 34–35 the focus shifts to the post-disaster period, with Edom taking the place of Babylon as the enemy. The contrast between the devastated land of Edom and the restored and fertile land of Judah in these chapters is clearly intentional, and it makes a fitting conclusion to the alternation of judgment and salvation throughout the book up to this point. The final paragraph or stanza (35.8–10), referring to a way through the wilderness, provides a smooth transition to chs 40–48.

This transition has been interrupted by the historical account of events in Hezekiah's reign in chs 36–39, drawn from the Deuteronomistic History (2 Kings 18.13,17–20.19) and inserted at this point. The insertion does, however, provide the structure of a contrast between Hezekiah's reaction to political crisis (chs 36–39) and that of Ahaz a generation earlier (chs 1–12).

CHAPTERS 40–66: CONTENT AND ARRANGEMENT

The background of chs 40–55 (or for some scholars 40–54) is the international situation during the reign of the last Babylonian ruler, Nabonidus (556–539 BCE). It is most likely that the prophetic author was among those deported to Babylon, though a Judean location is also possible.

The centerpiece of chs 40–48 is a prophetic oracle designating the Persian Cyrus II (the Great) as the instrument for the repatriation of dispersed Israelites and their reestablishment in the Judean homeland in the hands of the God of Israel, the one, true God and creator of the world. The author confidently predicts the imminent fall of Babylon and polemicizes against the Babylonian religious and intellectual tradition.

The note of consolation and hope continues in chs 49–55, though there are also signs of dissatisfaction, anxiety, and internal tension in the community on whose behalf the prophet is speaking and writing (e.g., in the third and fourth of the "Servant Songs," 50.4–11 and 52.13–53.12).

While the third major segment of the book (chs 56–66) has connections with chs 40–55, and also with chs 1–39 by virtue of its concern with the destiny of Jerusalem, the situation is in several important respects quite different. These texts seem to focus exclusively on the internal affairs of the community in the early Persian period (late sixth century BCE). The disappointment of expectations aroused by the conquests of Cyrus has led to a resurgence of non-Yahwistic religious practices (57.1–13; 65.1–7; 66.3–4) and deep religious, social, and economic divisions within the Judean community (e.g., 56.1–8; 58.1–12; 59.1–8). Attention is directed increasingly away from an unsatisfactory present to the projection of a future intervention of God in judgment and salvation, an apocalyptic vision of a purified people and Jerusalem as the religious capital of the world.

THE OVERALL UNITY OF ISAIAH

An understanding of the lengthy process that resulted in the book of Isaiah should not leave the impression that it is simply a collection of fragments or an anthology whose parts have no organic relation to each other. The unity of the book comes in large part from the development and deepening of major themes: the centrality of Jerusalem; the importance of the "anointed" ruler; and the contrast between God's people and the political and military machinations of the great world empires. The image of Jerusalem in later books of the Bible, particularly in the book of Revelation in the New Testament, cannot be fully understood without grasping the development of the idea of Jerusalem in Isaiah. The image of a new ruler who will usher in a new age of justice, righteousness, and peace, and its development into the concept of a "messiah" in early Jewish and early Christian writings, also cannot be fully appreciated without an understanding of how Isaiah developed the concept of the anointed ruler from its historical reality as the Davidic line of Judean rulers to the hoped-for restoration of an idealized king for a purified nation. And the notion of God's people surviving and triumphing even when all of the world's great powers are arrayed against them echoes through the later writings of the Hebrew Scriptures, the Jewish writings of the Diaspora contained in the Apocryphal/Deuterocanonical Books, and the New Testament.

1 The vision of Isaiah son of Amoz,
which he saw concerning Judah and Je-
rusalem in the days of Uzziah, Jotham,
Ahaz, and Hezekiah, kings of Judah.

2 Hear, O heavens, and listen, O earth;
for the LORD has spoken:
I reared children and brought
them up,
but they have rebelled against me.
3 The ox knows its owner,
and the donkey its master's crib;
but Israel does not know,
my people do not understand.

4 Ah, sinful nation,
people laden with iniquity,
offspring who do evil,
children who deal corruptly,
who have forsaken the LORD,
who have despised the Holy One of
Israel,
who are utterly estranged!

5 Why do you seek further beatings?
Why do you continue to rebel?
The whole head is sick,
and the whole heart faint.
6 From the sole of the foot even to the
head,
there is no soundness in it,
but bruises and sores
and bleeding wounds;
they have not been drained, or bound
up,
or softened with oil.

7 Your country lies desolate,
your cities are burned with fire;
in your very presence
aliens devour your land;
it is desolate, as overthrown by
foreigners.
8 And daughter Zion is left
like a booth in a vineyard,
like a shelter in a cucumber field,
like a besieged city.
9 If the LORD of hosts
had not left us a few survivors,
we would have been like Sodom,
and become like Gomorrah.

10 Hear the word of the LORD,

1.1: Superscription. This first title introduces the entire book as a vision (see 2 Chr 32.32; Ob 1; Nah 1.1; cf. Am 1.1; Mic 1.1; Hab 1.1), which in late biblical usage has the broad sense of divine revelation. The name Isaiah means "Yahweh has saved" or "may Yahweh save." Chs 1–39 record the prophet's activity from the death of King Uzziah (785–733 BCE) to the fourteenth year of Hezekiah (727/715–698/687; the chronology is disputed).

1.2–31: An introductory poem. The prophet indicts Israel for religious infidelity. **2–3:** The rhetorical call for attention (cf. 1.10; 28.23; 32.9; 48.1; 51.4; 64.3) appeals to heaven and earth to witness the LORD's grievance against his people in the context of a lawsuit concerning Israel's violation of the covenant (see Deut 32.1; Mic 6.1–8; Ps 50). The idea of rebellious children recalls the penalty of death imposed on the rebellious son (Deut 21.18–21). The appeal to animal behavior is the first of many examples of Isaiah's appropriation of the didactic tradition of Israel's sages (e.g., Prov 6.6–8). **4–6:** This direct address to Israel reminds them that a history of obduracy and sin is responsible for the condition of the land devastated by enemy invasion and occupation, presented under the figure of a bruised and battered body. Several commentators refer this description to the results of the Assyrian king Sennacherib's invasion of Judah in 701 BCE. The title "Holy One of Israel," perhaps originating in the Jerusalem Temple worship, occurs frequently in the book (5.19,24; 10.20; 12.6; 17.7; 29.19; 30.11–12,15; 31.1; 37.23; 41.14,16,20; 43.3,14; 45.11; 47.4; 48.17; 54.5; 55.5; 60.9,14). **7–9:** This more direct description of Judah devastated and Jerusalem barely surviving fits the invasion of Sennacherib, who claimed to have shut Hezekiah up "like a bird in a cage." *Daughter Zion* (also 10.32; 16.1; 37.22; 52.2; 62.11) follows the common practice of presenting cities as female. **10–17:** A very strong statement of the prophetic protest against worship divorced from social justice (cf. Am 5.21–24; Mic 6.6–8; Jer 6.20–21; 7.1–15). **10:** In the prophets, *Sodom* and *Gomorrah* (see Gen 18.16–19.28) became bywords for spectacular divine judgment on immoral conduct (3.9; 13.19; Am 4.11; Jer 23.14; 49.18; 50.40; Ezek 16.46–56; Zeph 2.9), though no mention of sexual immorality occurs before the Hellenistic period. **11–15:** Animal sacrifice is

you rulers of Sodom!
Listen to the teaching of our God,
you people of Gomorrah!
11 What to me is the multitude of your sacrifices?
says the LORD;
I have had enough of burnt offerings of rams
and the fat of fed beasts;
I do not delight in the blood of bulls,
or of lambs, or of goats.

12 When you come to appear before me,[a]
who asked this from your hand?
Trample my courts no more;
13 bringing offerings is futile;
incense is an abomination to me.
New moon and sabbath and calling of convocation—
I cannot endure solemn assemblies with iniquity.
14 Your new moons and your appointed festivals
my soul hates;
they have become a burden to me,
I am weary of bearing them.
15 When you stretch out your hands,
I will hide my eyes from you;
even though you make many prayers,
I will not listen;
your hands are full of blood.
16 Wash yourselves; make yourselves clean;
remove the evil of your doings
from before my eyes;
cease to do evil,
17 learn to do good;
seek justice,
rescue the oppressed,
defend the orphan,
plead for the widow.

18 Come now, let us argue it out,
says the LORD:
though your sins are like scarlet,
they shall be like snow;
though they are red like crimson,
they shall become like wool.
19 If you are willing and obedient,
you shall eat the good of the land;
20 but if you refuse and rebel,
you shall be devoured by the sword;
for the mouth of the LORD has spoken.

21 How the faithful city
has become a whore!
She that was full of justice,
righteousness lodged in her—
but now murderers!
22 Your silver has become dross,
your wine is mixed with water.
23 Your princes are rebels
and companions of thieves.
Everyone loves a bribe
and runs after gifts.
They do not defend the orphan,

a Or *see my face*

also criticized in 1 Sam 15.22; Ps 50.7–15; Hos 6.6. Such sacrifices were also to be offered on the occasion of *sabbath* (weekly) and *new moon* (monthly) festivals. **16–17:** Ritual purification, signified by washing blood from the hands, must be not a substitute for but a sign of moral purification, signified by concern for the marginal classes of society, especially widows and the fatherless (*orphan*), for whom provision is made in the law (Ex 22.22; Deut 24.17–21; 27.19). **18–20:** The tone is one of legal argument but the precise meaning is unclear, depending on whether v. 18b contains two statements or, as it may also be translated, two rhetorical questions. *Crimson* and *scarlet* connote blood and therefore allude to the imagery of vv. 15–16. *Wool,* white, as in Ps 147.16; Dan 7.9. **21–26:** The object of the prophet's polemic is the capital city, Jerusalem (the condition of which is described with a mix of metaphors), and especially the ruling class (cf. 3.1–5; 5.18–23; 30.1–5). The principal accusation, as elsewhere in prophetic diatribe, is the corruption of the judicial process (cf. 5.23; 33.15; Am 5.10,12; Mic 3.9,11). *Dross,* (vv. 22,25), the waste product of metal refining. The prophet foresees a future in which Jerusalem will be restored and will receive a new name and designation (cf. 62.4,12); *righteousness* (Heb "tsedeq") recalls the names of Melchizedek (Gen 14.18) and Zadok (1 Kings 2.35). **27–31:** This final stanza is taken by many to be a

and the widow's cause does not
come before them.

24 Therefore says the Sovereign, the
LORD of hosts, the Mighty
One of Israel:
Ah, I will pour out my wrath on my
enemies,
and avenge myself on my foes!
25 I will turn my hand against you;
I will smelt away your dross as
with lye
and remove all your alloy.
26 And I will restore your judges as at
the first,
and your counselors as at the
beginning.
Afterward you shall be called the city
of righteousness,
the faithful city.

27 Zion shall be redeemed by justice,
and those in her who repent, by
righteousness.
28 But rebels and sinners shall be
destroyed together,
and those who forsake the LORD
shall be consumed.
29 For you shall be ashamed of the oaks
in which you delighted;
and you shall blush for the gardens
that you have chosen.
30 For you shall be like an oak
whose leaf withers,
and like a garden without water.
31 The strong shall become like tinder,
and their work[a] like a spark;
they and their work shall burn
together,
with no one to quench them.

2 The word that Isaiah son of Amoz saw
concerning Judah and Jerusalem.

2 In days to come
the mountain of the LORD's house
shall be established as the highest of
the mountains,
and shall be raised above the hills;
all the nations shall stream to it.
3 Many peoples shall come and say,
"Come, let us go up to the mountain
of the LORD,
to the house of the God of Jacob;
that he may teach us his ways
and that we may walk in his
paths."
For out of Zion shall go forth
instruction,
and the word of the LORD from
Jerusalem.
4 He shall judge between the nations,
and shall arbitrate for many
peoples;
they shall beat their swords into
plowshares,

a Or *its makers*

later, apocalyptic addition to the poem. *Justice* here has more the sense of judgment (see 3.14; 4.4; 28.6; 34.5; 41.1) and *righteousness* of ultimate vindication (see 51.6,8; 56.1; 59.9,16–17; 61.10–11; 63.1); the criterion according to which people are judged is addiction to illicit worship (e.g., in *garden* shrines, as in 65.3 and 66.17) rather than social injustice, as in the last chapters of the book (57.1–13; 65.1–16; 66.17,24); the nation is now divided between those who repent and turn away from evil and the rebels and sinners. For the latter, the end is judgment represented under the image of fire (cf. 66.15–16,24).
2.1: A second superscription. This may introduce either ch 2, or chs 2–4 or chs 2–12. Both here and at 1.1 the Hebrew word translated *saw* means, literally, "saw in vision." **2–5:** This passage occurs also in Mic 4.1–5 with some slight variations, esp. in the last verse. Together with 4.2–6 it brackets the pronouncement of judgment with the prospect of a purified and triumphant Jerusalem. **2:** *The mountain of the LORD, to the house.* Throughout the ancient Near East, temples were described as the houses in which gods dwelt. In common with an ancient motif, Jerusalem is often represented as the cosmic mountain (10.12,32; 11.9; 16.1; 25.6; 29.8; 30.29; 40.9; 57.13; 65.26; Ps 48.1–2; Ezek 20.40; 40.2). It will be the goal of pilgrimage for peoples of all lands (see 45.14–23; 60.1–18) who will come there for instruction (Heb "torah") (perhaps an allusion to proselytes). Disputes between nations will be arbitrated and settled there, and there will be universal disarmament and the end of warfare (9.5; 11.6–9; 60.18; 65.25). **5:**

and their spears into pruning
hooks;
nation shall not lift up sword against
nation,
neither shall they learn war
any more.

5 O house of Jacob,
come, let us walk
in the light of the LORD!
6 For you have forsaken the ways of[a]
your people,
O house of Jacob.
Indeed they are full of diviners[b] from
the east
and of soothsayers like the
Philistines,
and they clasp hands with
foreigners.
7 Their land is filled with silver
and gold,
and there is no end to their
treasures;
their land is filled with horses,
and there is no end to their
chariots.
8 Their land is filled with idols;
they bow down to the work of
their hands,
to what their own fingers
have made.
9 And so people are humbled,
and everyone is brought low—
do not forgive them!
10 Enter into the rock,
and hide in the dust
from the terror of the LORD,
and from the glory of his majesty.
11 The haughty eyes of people shall be
brought low,
and the pride of everyone shall be
humbled;
and the LORD alone will be exalted
on that day.
12 For the LORD of hosts has a day
against all that is proud and lofty,
against all that is lifted up
and high;[c]
13 against all the cedars of Lebanon,
lofty and lifted up;
and against all the oaks of Bashan;
14 against all the high mountains,
and against all the lofty hills;
15 against every high tower,
and against every fortified wall;
16 against all the ships of Tarshish,
and against all the beautiful craft.[d]
17 The haughtiness of people shall be
humbled,

a Heb lacks *the ways of* *b* Cn: Heb lacks *of diviners* *c* Cn Compare Gk: Heb *low* *d* Compare Gk: Meaning of Heb uncertain

House of Jacob, a common designation for the entire nation of Israel; see Gen 32.28; Ex 19.3; Ps 114.1; Isa 46.3.

2.6–22: Indictment of Israel. Beneath the many editorial additions to this textually difficult poem we can detect the outline of a typical prophetic judgment speech: indictment (vv. 6–8) followed by verdict (vv. 12–16). **6:** *Diviners and soothsayers* were proscribed (Deut 18.9–14), but such practices were part of popular religion in Israel at all times (1 Sam 28.8–15; Ezek 13.9). *Clasp hands with foreigners,* in commercial transactions. **7:** The sequence is from silver and gold to horses and chariots—extremely expensive items (see 1 Kings 10.29)—and climactically to idols. The mention of idolatry has triggered a number of prose additions to the poem (vv. 18,20). **9b:** *Do not forgive them!* Together with the final verse 22, this exclamation reflects the apocalyptic mindset and worldview. It is absent from the Qumran Isaiah scroll (1QIsa[a]) and from the parallel 5.15. **10:** The exhortation to take cover from the coming judgment (also at vv. 19,21; cf. 26.20–21) is also characteristic of apocalyptic writers (e.g., Zech 14.5). **12:** The verdict is couched in terms of the traditional theme of the "Day of the LORD" (cf. Am 5.18–20; Ob 15; Joel 1.15). **13:** *Lebanon,* the mountainous area north of Israel famous for its cedars; *Bashan,* the high plateau in northern Transjordan known for its timber (Ezek 27.6). **16:** *Ships of Tarshish,* Tarshish is a location somewhere in the western Mediterranean region or in Turkey (later Tarsus) (Jer 10.9; Ezek 27.12; 38.13; Jon 1.3; 4.2), but it also stands for a type of vessel designed to carry ore (1 Kings 10.22). **20:** The idols will be polluted by association with ritually unclean animals.

and the pride of everyone shall be
brought low;
and the LORD alone will be exalted
on that day.
18 The idols shall utterly pass away.
19 Enter the caves of the rocks
and the holes of the ground,
from the terror of the LORD,
and from the glory of his majesty,
when he rises to terrify the earth.
20 On that day people will throw away
to the moles and to the bats
their idols of silver and their idols of
gold,
which they made for themselves to
worship,
21 to enter the caverns of the rocks
and the clefts in the crags,
from the terror of the LORD,
and from the glory of his majesty,
when he rises to terrify the earth.
22 Turn away from mortals,
who have only breath in their
nostrils,
for of what account are they?

3 For now the Sovereign, the LORD
of hosts,
is taking away from Jerusalem and
from Judah
support and staff—
all support of bread,
and all support of water—
2 warrior and soldier,
judge and prophet,
diviner and elder,
3 captain of fifty
and dignitary,
counselor and skillful magician
and expert enchanter.
4 And I will make boys their princes,
and babes shall rule over them.
5 The people will be oppressed,
everyone by another
and everyone by a neighbor;
the youth will be insolent to the elder,
and the base to the honorable.

6 Someone will even seize a relative,
a member of the clan, saying,
"You have a cloak;
you shall be our leader,
and this heap of ruins
shall be under your rule."
7 But the other will cry out on that
day, saying,
"I will not be a healer;
in my house there is neither bread
nor cloak;
you shall not make me
leader of the people."
8 For Jerusalem has stumbled
and Judah has fallen,
because their speech and their deeds
are against the LORD,
defying his glorious presence.

9 The look on their faces bears witness
against them;
they proclaim their sin like Sodom,
they do not hide it.
Woe to them!
For they have brought evil on
themselves.
10 Tell the innocent how fortunate they
are,
for they shall eat the fruit of their
labors.
11 Woe to the guilty! How unfortunate
they are,
for what their hands have done
shall be done to them.
12 My people—children are their
oppressors,
and women rule over them.
O my people, your leaders mislead
you,

3.1–15: Social and moral chaos. 1–5: The infrastructure of Judean society has collapsed, perhaps during the critical period of Sennacherib's invasion and its aftermath (701 BCE). Military protection has been withdrawn and civic and religious leadership, including prophetic intermediaries, is no longer in place. The social order is subverted. **6–7:** A brief cameo (cf. Am 3.12; 6.9–10) providing a narrative illustration of social disorder (cf. Mic 7.5–6). People will be so concerned with their own survival that no one will want to take charge. **8–12:** Social chaos is traced to moral disorder, especially evident in the Jerusalem leadership. The passage incorporates wisdom teaching (vv. 10–11). *Sodom,* 1.10–17n. **13–15:**

and confuse the course of your
paths.

13 The LORD rises to argue his case;
he stands to judge the peoples.
14 The LORD enters into judgment
with the elders and princes of his
people:
It is you who have devoured the
vineyard;
the spoil of the poor is in your
houses.
15 What do you mean by crushing my
people,
by grinding the face of the poor?
says the Lord GOD of hosts.

16 The LORD said:
Because the daughters of Zion are
haughty
and walk with outstretched necks,
glancing wantonly with their eyes,
mincing along as they go,
tinkling with their feet;
17 the Lord will afflict with scabs
the heads of the daughters of Zion,
and the LORD will lay bare their
secret parts.

18 In that day the Lord will take away
the finery of the anklets, the headbands,
and the crescents; 19 the pendants, the
bracelets, and the scarfs; 20 the headdresses,
the armlets, the sashes, the perfume boxes,
and the amulets; 21 the signet rings and nose
rings; 22 the festal robes, the mantles, the
cloaks, and the handbags; 23 the garments
of gauze, the linen garments, the turbans,
and the veils.

24 Instead of perfume there will be a
stench;
and instead of a sash, a rope;
and instead of well-set hair, baldness;
and instead of a rich robe, a
binding of sackcloth;
instead of beauty, shame.[a]
25 Your men shall fall by the sword
and your warriors in battle.
26 And her gates shall lament and
mourn;
ravaged, she shall sit upon the
ground.

4 Seven women shall take hold of one
man in that day, saying,
"We will eat our own bread and wear
our own clothes;
just let us be called by your name;
take away our disgrace."

2 On that day the branch of the LORD
shall be beautiful and glorious, and the
fruit of the land shall be the pride and glory

a Q Ms: MT lacks *shame*

Indictment of the state leadership. The language is forensic, presupposing location in a court of law; hence the LORD *rises* to deliver the indictment (cf. Mic 6.1–5; Ps.50; 82). Exploitation of the poor (by enclosure and confiscation of lands, indentured service, etc.) is a principal target of eighth-century BCE prophetic polemic (Am 2.6–8; 3.9–11; 6.4–7; 8.4–6; Mic 2.1–3; 3.1–4,9–12).

3.16–4.1: The fate of the court ladies of Jerusalem. A denunciation of the conduct of the Jerusalemite court ladies and a prediction of their brutal treatment at the hands of the enemy (vv. 16–17,24–26), following the example of Amos (4.1–3), has been expanded by a catalogue of female attire and ornament (many items of which are obscure) from a well-informed but obsessive interpolator (vv. 18–23), and rounded off with a narrative cameo similar to 3.6–7. While the conduct of the ladies as described does not represent a serious infraction of the moral order, it constitutes an example of ostentatious wealth condemned by prophet and sage alike (Am 6.4–7; Prov 23.4–5). The situation envisaged in 4.1 results from the decimation of the male population in battle. The seven women, probably acting in concert rather than in competition with each other, are willing to forgo the support mandated by law (Ex 21.10) to avoid the stigma of childlessness (cf. Gen 30.23, Rachel; 1 Sam 1.4–8, Hannah).

4.2–6: Jerusalem renewed. 2: *On that day,* introducing passages with an orientation to a future event of judgment or salvation. *The branch of the LORD,* usually with reference to the Davidic ruler (Jer 23.5; 33.15–16; Ezek 29.21), and specifically to Zerubbabel, grandson of Jehoiachin (Zech 3.8; 6.12), but here referring to the restored community (cf. 61.11). **3:** *Recorded for life in Jerusalem,* inscribed in God's book

of the survivors of Israel. 3 Whoever is left
in Zion and remains in Jerusalem will be
called holy, everyone who has been record-
ed for life in Jerusalem, 4 once the Lord has
washed away the filth of the daughters of
Zion and cleansed the bloodstains of Jeru-
salem from its midst by a spirit of judgment
and by a spirit of burning. 5 Then the LORD
will create over the whole site of Mount
Zion and over its places of assembly a
cloud by day and smoke and the shining of
a flaming fire by night. Indeed over all the
glory there will be a canopy. 6 It will serve
as a pavilion, a shade by day from the heat,
and a refuge and a shelter from the storm
and rain.

5 Let me sing for my beloved
my love-song concerning his
vineyard:
My beloved had a vineyard
on a very fertile hill.
2 He dug it and cleared it of stones,
and planted it with choice vines;
he built a watchtower in the midst of
it,
and hewed out a wine vat in it;
he expected it to yield grapes,
but it yielded wild grapes.

3 And now, inhabitants of Jerusalem
and people of Judah,
judge between me
and my vineyard.
4 What more was there to do for my
vineyard
that I have not done in it?
When I expected it to yield grapes,
why did it yield wild grapes?

5 And now I will tell you
what I will do to my vineyard.
I will remove its hedge,
and it shall be devoured;
I will break down its wall,
and it shall be trampled down.
6 I will make it a waste;
it shall not be pruned or hoed,
and it shall be overgrown with
briers and thorns;
I will also command the clouds
that they rain no rain upon it.

7 For the vineyard of the LORD of hosts
is the house of Israel,
and the people of Judah
are his pleasant planting;
he expected justice,
but saw bloodshed;
righteousness,
but heard a cry!

8 Ah, you who join house to house,

of life (Ex 32.32; Ps 69.28; Mal 3.16; Rev 20.12,15); perhaps also reflecting Nehemiah's repopulation of Jerusalem (Neh 11.1–24). **4:** *The filth of the daughters of Zion,* rather than linking with the previous passage, the allusion is to menstrual blood as symbolic of ritual impurity. **5:** *Places of assembly,* ceremonies, liturgies (cf. 1.13) rather than locations, synagogues. *Cloud by day* and *fire by night,* God's protection of Jerusalem is symbolized by imagery from the Exodus and wilderness traditions (Ex 13.21–22; 40.34–38).

5.1–7: The love song about the vineyard. The prophet composes and sings the song for his friend, identified in v. 7 as the LORD. The genre of the love song is used as a parable with an explanation (cf. 2 Sam 12.1–14) and also a poeticized form of judgment saying with indictment (vv. 1–4) and verdict (vv. 5–6). Vineyard can serve as a metaphor for lover in Ugaritic and biblical poetry (Song 1.6,14; 2.15; 4.12,16; 8.11–12). The vineyard is identified in v. 7 as Israel (cf. 1.8; 3.14; 27.2–6); a closely related metaphor is Israel as the vine (Ps 80.8–16; Jer 2.21; Hos 10.1). **5–6:** The verdict reflects a type of treaty and covenant curse (see also 5.10; 65.21; cf. Deut 28.30,39; Am 5.11). The curse on the vineyard will be reversed in 27.2–6. **6:** *Briers and thorns,* a frequently occurring motif in Isaiah, connoting infertility of the land, ecological degradation, with a moral dimension (7.23–25; 9.18; 10.17; 27.2–5; 32.12–13). **7:** In Hebrew there is a double word play: "mishpat" (*justice*) and "mishpah" (*bloodshed*), and "tsedaqah" (*righteousness*) and "tse'aqah" (*a cry*).

5.8–24: Seven woes. A series of seven short poems (5.8–10, 11–17, 18–19, 20, 21, 22–24; 10.1–4), each beginning with "Woe" (here translated *Ah*). Some commentators hold that 10.1–4 has fallen out of

who add field to field,
until there is room for no one
but you,
and you are left to live alone
in the midst of the land!
9 The LORD of hosts has sworn in my
hearing:
Surely many houses shall be desolate,
large and beautiful houses, without
inhabitant.
10 For ten acres of vineyard shall yield
but one bath,
and a homer of seed shall yield a
mere ephah.[a]

11 Ah, you who rise early in the morning
in pursuit of strong drink,
who linger in the evening
to be inflamed by wine,
12 whose feasts consist of lyre and
harp,
tambourine and flute and wine,
but who do not regard the deeds of
the LORD,
or see the work of his hands!
13 Therefore my people go into exile
without knowledge;
their nobles are dying of hunger,
and their multitude is parched with
thirst.
14 Therefore Sheol has enlarged its
appetite
and opened its mouth beyond
measure;
the nobility of Jerusalem[b] and her
multitude go down,
her throng and all who exult in her.
15 People are bowed down, everyone is
brought low,
and the eyes of the haughty are
humbled.
16 But the LORD of hosts is exalted
by justice,
and the Holy God shows himself
holy by righteousness.
17 Then the lambs shall graze as in their
pasture,
fatlings and kids[c] shall feed among
the ruins.

18 Ah, you who drag iniquity along with
cords of falsehood,
who drag sin along as with cart
ropes,
19 who say, "Let him make haste,
let him speed his work
that we may see it;
let the plan of the Holy One of Israel
hasten to fulfillment,
that we may know it!"
20 Ah, you who call evil good

a The Heb *bath, homer,* and *ephah* are measures of quantity *b* Heb *her nobility* *c* Cn Compare Gk: Heb *aliens*

the lead position in the series and has been attached to the poem on divine anger. "Woe" sayings are often presented in a series (e.g., Am 5.18–6.8; Hab 2.6–19). **8–10:** The first saying targets the ruling class, whose policies undermine the livelihood of the subsistence farmer by enclosing or confiscating patrimonial land, leading to the formation of large estates. This is a frequent concern of eighth-century BCE prophecy (e.g., Mic 2.1–2; cf. 1 Kings 21). **10:** *Bath,* a liquid measure of approximately 6 gal; *homer,* a donkey-load, about 6.5 bu; *ephah,* one tenth of a *homer* (Ezek 45.11). **11–17:** This second poem has been greatly expanded. **11:** Addiction to strong drink is frequently denounced in the prophets (Isa 28.7–8; Hos 4.11; 7.5; Am 4.1; Mic 2.11) and wisdom literature (Prov 21.17; 23.19–21,29–35). **12:** While not in itself reprehensible, musical entertainment is denounced as an aspect of effete urban living (cf. Am 6.1,4–7). *The deeds, work* or plan and agenda of God is a central motif in Isaiah (5.19; 10.12; 14.24–27; 19.12,17; 23.9; 28.21; 30.1). **14–17:** An addition to the "Woe" saying, perhaps a fragment of a judgment saying against Jerusalem. **14:** A fuller description of Sheol, the underworld, will appear in 14.4–20. **15–16:** Cf. 2.9,11,17. **17:** A common motif in Isaiah: The city goes back to nature (13.19–22; 34.8–17). **18–19:** Bearing the burden of sin is represented vividly as dragging along a large and recalcitrant animal; cf. the opposite image in Hos 11.4. **19:** In Isaiah the opposition is often quoted. The sarcastic rejoinder of those addressed by the prophet appears to quote the prophet's own terms back to him. **20:** This fourth saying condemns the moral sophistry of the opposition. **21:** Their wisdom, based on education in the wisdom

and good evil,
who put darkness for light
and light for darkness,
who put bitter for sweet
and sweet for bitter!
21 Ah, you who are wise in your own eyes,
and shrewd in your own sight!
22 Ah, you who are heroes in drinking wine
and valiant at mixing drink,
23 who acquit the guilty for a bribe,
and deprive the innocent of their rights!
24 Therefore, as the tongue of fire devours the stubble,
and as dry grass sinks down in the flame,
so their root will become rotten,
and their blossom go up like dust;
for they have rejected the instruction of the LORD of hosts,
and have despised the word of the Holy One of Israel.

25 Therefore the anger of the LORD was kindled against his people,
and he stretched out his hand against them and struck them;
the mountains quaked,
and their corpses were like refuse in the streets.
For all this his anger has not turned away,
and his hand is stretched out still.

26 He will raise a signal for a nation far away,
and whistle for a people at the ends of the earth;
Here they come, swiftly, speedily!
27 None of them is weary, none stumbles,
none slumbers or sleeps,
not a loincloth is loose,
not a sandal-thong broken;
28 their arrows are sharp,
all their bows bent,
their horses' hoofs seem like flint,
and their wheels like the whirlwind.
29 Their roaring is like a lion,
like young lions they roar;
they growl and seize their prey,
they carry it off, and no one can rescue.
30 They will roar over it on that day,
like the roaring of the sea.
And if one look to the land—
only darkness and distress;
and the light grows dark with clouds.

6 In the year that King Uzziah died, I saw
the Lord sitting on a throne, high and
lofty; and the hem of his robe filled the

tradition of Israel, is counterfeit (cf. Jer 8.8–9). **22–24:** The self-indulgent leadership is guilty of the worst crime, perverting the judicial system by accepting bribes (1.23; Mic 3.11; cf. Ex 23.8; Deut 16.19). Judgment, under the metaphor of fire, will follow rejection of the moral guidance provided by divine *instruction* (Heb "torah") and the prophetic word.

5.25: A displaced stanza. This stanza of the poem about divine anger, identified by the refrain *for all this his anger has not turned away* . . . , should probably follow 9.8–10.4. It provides the clearest allusion to earthquake, perhaps the earthquake mentioned in Am 1.2 and Zech 14.5 during the reigns of Uzziah and Jeroboam II, also attested in the archaeological record at Hazor and elsewhere. Assyrian records attest to a major earthquake on June 15, 763 BCE.

5.26–30: The threat of a double blow: earthquake followed by military assault; cf. 9.18–10.4 and Am 9.1–4. **26:** The God of Israel summons Assyria to punish Israel; cf. 7.18–20; 8.7; 10.5–6. A precise itinerary is given in 10.27b–32, probably referring to the campaign of Sennacherib in 701 BCE. *A signal,* for assembling troops (Jer 6.1). **29:** *Their roaring is like a lion,* references to lions are common in Isaiah, perhaps dependent in part on Amos (Am 1.2; 3.4,8; 5.19). Palestine continued to be a habitat for lions down to the Middle Ages.

6.1–13: The vision of the heavenly throneroom. For the scenario, see 1 Kings 22.19–23; Ezek 1.4–2.1; Job 1–2. This passage is often referred to as the call of Isaiah, but its location suggests it was intended as an introduction to the account in chs 7–8 of Isaiah's intervention in Judean politics at the time of the

temple. 2 Seraphs were in attendance above
him; each had six wings: with two they cov-
ered their faces, and with two they covered
their feet, and with two they flew. 3 And
one called to another and said:

"Holy, holy, holy is the LORD of
hosts;
the whole earth is full of his glory."
4 The pivots[a] on the thresholds shook at
the voices of those who called, and the
house filled with smoke. 5 And I said: "Woe
is me! I am lost, for I am a man of unclean
lips, and I live among a people of unclean
lips; yet my eyes have seen the King, the
LORD of hosts!"
6 Then one of the seraphs flew to me,
holding a live coal that had been taken
from the altar with a pair of tongs. 7 The
seraph[b] touched my mouth with it and
said: "Now that this has touched your lips,
your guilt has departed and your sin is blot-
ted out." 8 Then I heard the voice of the
Lord saying, "Whom shall I send, and who
will go for us?" And I said, "Here am I;
send me!" 9 And he said, "Go and say to
this people:

'Keep listening, but do not
comprehend;
keep looking, but do not understand.'
10 Make the mind of this people dull,
and stop their ears,
and shut their eyes,
so that they may not look with their
eyes,
and listen with their ears,
and comprehend with their minds,
and turn and be healed."
11 Then I said, "How long, O Lord?"
And he said:
"Until cities lie waste
without inhabitant,
and houses without people,
and the land is utterly desolate;
12 until the LORD sends everyone
far away,
and vast is the emptiness in the
midst of the land.
13 Even if a tenth part remain in it,
it will be burned again,
like a terebinth or an oak
whose stump remains standing
when it is felled."[a]
The holy seed is its stump.

7 In the days of Ahaz son of Jotham son
of Uzziah, king of Judah, King Rezin of

a Meaning of Heb uncertain *b* Heb *He*

Syro-Ephraimite war (734 BCE), serving also to explain his failure to influence Ahaz, king of Judah. **1:** *The year,* the chronology of the kings of Israel and Judah is uncertain at this juncture, perhaps 742 (or 733) BCE. *Uzziah,* also known as Azariah (2 Kings 15.1–7). **1–4:** The scene is the throneroom of the celestial court, but there are also suggestions of a liturgy in progress. *The hem of his robe filled the temple,* a hyperbolic expression, perhaps is suggested by Assyrian representations of rulers on a gigantic scale compared to other figures. **2:** *Seraphs* (lit. "burning ones"), perhaps serpentine in form (14.29; 30.6; Num 21.6,8; Deut 8.15). *Feet,* genitals. One pair of wings covered their faces, so as not to look on God; a second pair covered their bodies; and with the third pair they maintained their position around the throne. **3:** *Holy, holy, holy,* an acclamation indicating the otherness, the transcendence of the Enthroned One; the origin of the Jewish Kedusha and the Christian Sanctus (the Trisagion in Orthodox liturgy). **4:** *Smoke,* accompanies the divine presence; 4.5; 30.27; Ex 19.18; Ps 18.8. In this case also from the fire on the altar (v. 6). **5:** Before the holy God, a sinful person cannot stand (Ex 33.18–20). **6–7:** The purification of the lips prepared Isaiah for his prophetic mission, which he accepted eagerly, unlike Moses (Ex 3.11), Jeremiah (Jer 1.6), and Jonah (Jon 1.3). **8:** *Us,* the plural refers to the entire divine assembly. **9–10:** The "hardening of hearts" has given rise to a great deal of theological discussion. In its context in the book, it serves to account for the failure of Isaiah's intervention in Judean politics; cf. 63.17. **11:** *How long, O Lord?,* a question often asked in the psalms of lament; see Ps 74.10; 79.5; 94.3. **12–13:** Perhaps anticipating the devastation of Judah during the Assyrian campaign of 701 BCE. *The holy seed is its stump,* a postexilic gloss identifying the remnant as the Judean community under Persian rule; cf. Ezra 9.2.

7.1–17: Isaiah's intervention in the Syro-Ephraimite war (734 BCE). (2 Kings 15.29–16.20.) This much expanded account of Isaiah's intervention in Judean politics written in the third person is bracketed by

Aram and King Pekah son of Remaliah of
Israel went up to attack Jerusalem, but
could not mount an attack against it.
2 When the house of David heard that Aram
had allied itself with Ephraim, the heart of
Ahaz[a] and the heart of his people shook
as the trees of the forest shake before the
wind.

3 Then the LORD said to Isaiah, Go out
to meet Ahaz, you and your son Shear-
jashub,[b] at the end of the conduit of the
upper pool on the highway to the Fuller's
Field, 4 and say to him, Take heed, be quiet,
do not fear, and do not let your heart be
faint because of these two smoldering
stumps of firebrands, because of the fierce
anger of Rezin and Aram and the son of
Remaliah. 5 Because Aram—with Ephraim
and the son of Remaliah—has plotted evil
against you, saying, 6 Let us go up against
Judah and cut off Jerusalem[c] and conquer
it for ourselves and make the son of Tabeel
king in it; 7 therefore thus says the Lord
GOD:

It shall not stand,
and it shall not come to pass.
8 For the head of Aram is Damascus,
and the head of Damascus is
Rezin.

(Within sixty-five years Ephraim will be
shattered, no longer a people.)
9 The head of Ephraim is Samaria,
and the head of Samaria is the son
of Remaliah.

If you do not stand firm in faith,
you shall not stand at all.

10 Again the LORD spoke to Ahaz, say-
ing, 11 Ask a sign of the LORD your God; let
it be deep as Sheol or high as heaven. 12 But
Ahaz said, I will not ask, and I will not put
the LORD to the test. 13 Then Isaiah[d] said:
"Hear then, O house of David! Is it too
little for you to weary mortals, that you
weary my God also? 14 Therefore the Lord
himself will give you a sign. Look, the
young woman[e] is with child and shall bear
a son, and shall name him Immanuel.[f]
15 He shall eat curds and honey by the time
he knows how to refuse the evil and choose
the good. 16 For before the child knows
how to refuse the evil and choose the good,
the land before whose two kings you are in
dread will be deserted. 17 The LORD will
bring on you and on your people and on

a Heb *his heart* *b* That is *A remnant shall return*
c Heb *cut it off* *d* Heb *he* *e* Gk *the virgin*
f That is *God is with us*

first-person accounts in 6.1–13 and 8.1–22. **1–2:** 2 Kings 16.5. Rezin of Damascus (ca. 750–732) and Pekah of Israel (735–732) attempted to form an anti-Assyrian alliance; when Ahaz of Judah (743/735–727/715) refused to join them, they put a puppet ruler, Tabeel, on the throne. Against Isaiah's advice, Ahaz sought help from Tiglath-pileser III (745–727) and in consequence became an Assyrian vassal. *Ephraim,* the Northern Kingdom of Israel. **3:** *Shear-jashub* ("a remnant will return") was intended to serve as a good omen for Ahaz. Like his predecessor Hosea (see Hos 1.4–8), Isaiah gave his children symbolic names (see also 8.3). *Upper pool,* reservoir south of the Gihon Spring (36.2). **4:** The message is to avoid alliances and, in particular, avoid calling in the Assyrians against the northern allies. **7–8a:** The kings of Aram (Syria) and Israel with their capital cities cannot be compared with the Davidic dynasty and Jerusalem under the protection of the LORD. **8b:** A gloss, perhaps referring to further deportations from Ephraimite (central and northern) territory about the time of the accession of the Assyrian king Ashurbanipal (Ezra 4.9–10). **9b:** The quintessence of Isaiah's political message (30.15). **10–14:** Ahaz is offered some extraordinary indication, not necessarily miraculous (in contrast to 38.7–8), to persuade him of the truth of the prophet's prediction. **11:** *Sheol,* the underworld. **14:** *The young woman,* the mother of the child to be born has been identified as either the wife of Isaiah or the mother of Hezekiah. While the biblical chronology for Hezekiah is confused (2 Kings 15.30; cf. 16.5; 2 Kings 16.2; cf. 18.2; 2 Kings 18.10; cf. 18.13), the latter is strongly suggested by the reference to Immanuel's land, 8.8,10. Following the LXX translation "parthenos" (virgin), early Christian tradition understood the woman to be the mother of Jesus (Mt 1.23). *Immanuel* ("God with us"), symbolizing the saving presence of God; 8.9–10. **15–17:** *Curds and honey,* choice fare, difficult to obtain during a siege; by the time the child is weaned (two to three years) the northern allies will have been totally defeated and the land (of milk and honey)

your ancestral house such days as have not
come since the day that Ephraim departed
from Judah—the king of Assyria."
18 On that day the LORD will whistle
for the fly that is at the sources of the
streams of Egypt, and for the bee that is in
the land of Assyria. 19 And they will all
come and settle in the steep ravines, and in
the clefts of the rocks, and on all the thorn-
bushes, and on all the pastures.
20 On that day the Lord will shave with
a razor hired beyond the River—with the
king of Assyria—the head and the hair of
the feet, and it will take off the beard as
well.
21 On that day one will keep alive a
young cow and two sheep, 22 and will eat
curds because of the abundance of milk
that they give; for everyone that is left in
the land shall eat curds and honey.
23 On that day every place where there
used to be a thousand vines, worth a thou-
sand shekels of silver, will become briers
and thorns. 24 With bow and arrows one
will go there, for all the land will be briers
and thorns; 25 and as for all the hills that
used to be hoed with a hoe, you will not go
there for fear of briers and thorns; but they
will become a place where cattle are let
loose and where sheep tread.

8 Then the LORD said to me, Take a large
tablet and write on it in common char-
acters, "Belonging to Maher-shalal-hash-
baz,"[a] 2 and have it attested[b] for me by
reliable witnesses, the priest Uriah and
Zechariah son of Jeberechiah. 3 And I went
to the prophetess, and she conceived and
bore a son. Then the LORD said to me,
Name him Maher-shalal-hash-baz; 4 for
before the child knows how to call "My
father" or "My mother," the wealth of Da-
mascus and the spoil of Samaria will be
carried away by the king of Assyria.
5 The LORD spoke to me again: 6 Be-
cause this people has refused the waters of
Shiloah that flow gently, and melt in fear
before[c] Rezin and the son of Remaliah;
7 therefore, the Lord is bringing up against
it the mighty flood waters of the River, the
king of Assyria and all his glory; it will rise
above all its channels and overflow all its
banks; 8 it will sweep on into Judah as a

a That is *The spoil speeds, the prey hastens* *b* Q Ms Gk Syr: MT *and I caused to be attested* *c* Cn: Meaning of Heb uncertain

will return to the prosperity it enjoyed under David and Solomon. **17:** The final words are perhaps a gloss, imparting a threatening sense to the rest of the verse, which may originally have been positive.

7.18–25: Four additions. Introduced by the formula "on that day," they deal with the results of an Assyrian invasion, referring either to the conquest of the Northern Kingdom in 722 BCE or the invasion of Judah by Sennacherib in 701. **18–19:** The Assyrians are represented as killer bees (cf. Deut 1.44; Ps 118.12) and the Egyptians as a swarm of flies; perhaps referring to the period of 716–702 when Egypt was pro-Assyrian. **20:** Referring to the shaming of prisoners by the removal of facial and body hair, see 2 Sam 10.1–5. *Feet,* genitals. **21–22:** A reuse of the curds-and-honey motif signifying that the land will go back to pasture as a result of invasion. **23–25:** Reuse of the motif of the reversion of the vineyards to briers and thorns, as in 5.6. **23:** *Shekel,* a half ounce.

8.1–4: The sign of Maher-shalal-hash-baz. The first of three speeches of the LORD to Isaiah (vv. 1–4, 5–10, 11–15), rounded off with a comment (vv. 16–22). The text written on the stone or wood tablet in *common characters,* i.e., in an easily legible form (cf. Hab 2.2), probably contained a prediction of the complete defeat of the northern allies. *Maher-shalal-hash-baz,* something like "hasten for spoil, hurry for plunder." **2:** *Uriah and Zechariah,* the former may be the chief priest of the Jerusalem Temple (2 Kings 16.10–16) and the latter the father-in-law of Ahaz (2 Kings 18.2). **3:** *The prophetess,* Isaiah's wife, perhaps in the service of the Temple or court. **5–10:** Perhaps addressed to the anti-Assyrian faction in Judah. **5:** *The waters of Shiloah,* a gentle stream flowing from the Gihon spring to the pool of Siloam. **6:** *Melt in fear* may also be translated "rejoice in," i.e., favoring the Syro-Ephraimite alliance. **7:** *The River,* the Euphrates. **8:** Invasion is often represented as an inundation or deluge (Ps 124.4–5; Jer 47.2). Here the *Immanuel* ("God is with us") theme may have an ominous connotation. **9–10:** A brief hymn expands on the Immanuel theme with reference to the victorious Jerusalem of the future.

flood, and, pouring over, it will reach up to
the neck; and its outspread wings will fill
the breadth of your land, O Immanuel.

9 Band together, you peoples, and be
dismayed;
listen, all you far countries;
gird yourselves and be dismayed;
gird yourselves and be dismayed!
10 Take counsel together, but it shall be
brought to naught;
speak a word, but it will not stand,
for God is with us.[a]

11 For the LORD spoke thus to me while
his hand was strong upon me, and warned
me not to walk in the way of this people,
saying: 12 Do not call conspiracy all that
this people calls conspiracy, and do not fear
what it fears, or be in dread. 13 But the
LORD of hosts, him you shall regard as
holy; let him be your fear, and let him be
your dread. 14 He will become a sanctuary,
a stone one strikes against; for both houses
of Israel he will become a rock one stum-
bles over—a trap and a snare for the inhab-
itants of Jerusalem. 15 And many among
them shall stumble; they shall fall and be
broken; they shall be snared and taken.

16 Bind up the testimony, seal the teach-
ing among my disciples. 17 I will wait for
the LORD, who is hiding his face from the
house of Jacob, and I will hope in him.
18 See, I and the children whom the LORD
has given me are signs and portents in Israel
from the LORD of hosts, who dwells on
Mount Zion. 19 Now if people say to you,
"Consult the ghosts and the familiar spirits
that chirp and mutter; should not a people
consult their gods, the dead on behalf of the
living, 20 for teaching and for instruction?"
surely, those who speak like this will have
no dawn! 21 They will pass through the
land,[b] greatly distressed and hungry; when
they are hungry, they will be enraged and
will curse[c] their king and their gods. They
will turn their faces upward, 22 or they will
look to the earth, but will see only distress
and darkness, the gloom of anguish; and
they will be thrust into thick darkness.[d]

9 [e]But there will be no gloom for those
who were in anguish. In the former
time he brought into contempt the land of
Zebulun and the land of Naphtali, but in
the latter time he will make glorious the
way of the sea, the land beyond the Jordan,
Galilee of the nations.

a Heb *immanu el* *b* Heb *it* *c* Or *curse by*
d Meaning of Heb uncertain *e* Ch 8.23 in Heb

8.11–15: Isaiah and his co-conspirators. The *hand* of *the LORD* signifies possession by the spirit of God, resulting in transformed prophetic consciousness (1 Kings 18.46; 2 Kings 3.15; Ezek 1.3; 3.22; 8.1; 33.22, etc.). Isaiah's opposition to Ahaz and his circle has apparently led to accusations of conspiracy directed against him and his followers.

8.16–22: Preserving the record. Isaiah's prophecies addressed to Ahaz are committed to writing and confided to his disciples in expectation of a future fulfillment. For the writing and sealing of documents, see 29.11–12; 30.8–11. **18:** *I and the children,* Shear-jashub and Maher-shalal-hash-baz are portents for the future; the name Isaiah (see 1.1n.) connotes the hope of salvation. **19:** *Ghosts and the familiar spirits,* it is uncertain whether recourse to necromancy and contact with ancestors (referred to as *gods* and *the dead*) is being recommended to Isaiah and his followers or to Ahaz. Such practices are well attested in the Hebrew Bible (19.3; Lev 19.31; Deut 18.10–11). The final threat is that those who supported the policies of Ahaz will end up cursing him in the underworld.

9.1–7: New age, new ruler. While the date and circumstances of composition of this poem are disputed, it appears to celebrate the birth or the accession of the heir to the throne. In view of the references to Immanuel and the context in general, Hezekiah is the best candidate. **1–2:** The transition from the dark and gloomy scenario of the previous passage to the bright light of a new age. The Assyrian provinces of Dur (Dor, *the way of the sea*), Gal'azu (Gilead, *the land beyond the Jordan*), and Magidu (Megiddo, *Galilee of the nations*), areas just south and west of Zebulon and Naphtali, were also carved out of Israel in 733 BCE. The birth of the heir to the throne will reverse this situation. **4–5:** Military oppression is

2[a]The people who walked in darkness
have seen a great light;
those who lived in a land of deep
darkness—
on them light has shined.
3 You have multiplied the nation,
you have increased its joy;
they rejoice before you
as with joy at the harvest,
as people exult when dividing
plunder.
4 For the yoke of their burden,
and the bar across their shoulders,
the rod of their oppressor,
you have broken as on the day of
Midian.
5 For all the boots of the tramping
warriors
and all the garments rolled in blood
shall be burned as fuel for the fire.
6 For a child has been born for us,
a son given to us;
authority rests upon his shoulders;
and he is named
Wonderful Counselor, Mighty God,
Everlasting Father, Prince of Peace.
7 His authority shall grow continually,
and there shall be endless peace
for the throne of David and his
kingdom.
He will establish and uphold it
with justice and with righteousness
from this time onward and
forevermore.
The zeal of the LORD of hosts will do
this.

8 The Lord sent a word against Jacob,
and it fell on Israel;
9 and all the people knew it—
Ephraim and the inhabitants of
Samaria—
but in pride and arrogance of heart
they said:
10 "The bricks have fallen,
but we will build with dressed
stones;
the sycamores have been cut down,
but we will put cedars in their
place."
11 So the LORD raised adversaries[b]
against them,
and stirred up their enemies,
12 the Arameans on the east and the
Philistines on the west,
and they devoured Israel with open
mouth.
For all this his anger has not turned
away;
his hand is stretched out still.

13 The people did not turn to him who
struck them,
or seek the LORD of hosts.
14 So the LORD cut off from Israel head
and tail,
palm branch and reed in one day—
15 elders and dignitaries are the head,
and prophets who teach lies are the
tail;

a Ch 9.1 in Heb *b* Cn: Heb *the adversaries of Rezin*

symbolized by the yoke (10.27; 14.25), the bar (10.24), the rod (10.24; 14.5; Gen 49.10), and the trampling boot. **4:** *The day of Midian,* Judg 7.15–25. **6:** Cf. Ps 2.7. *For us,* see 6.8n. The conferring of throne names is reminiscent of Egyptian practice. As in many Israelite personal names, the deity, not the person named, is being described. *Wonderful Counselor,* see 5.19; 25.1; *Mighty God,* see 10.21; *Everlasting Father,* i.e., God as the eternal creator, see 40.28; *Prince of Peace,* a messianic title in Judaism and early Christianity. **7:** *Justice and . . . righteousness,* the maintenance of which is preeminently the task of the ruler (11.3b–5; Ps 72.1–2).

9.8–12: Judgment on Israel. Together with 5.25 and 9.13–10.4, these verses form a judgment poem in five stanzas recognized by the refrain *for all this his anger . . . stretched out still.* **8:** *A word against Jacob,* prophetic condemnation of the Northern Kingdom (Ephraim) and its capital (Samaria), perhaps referring to Amos or Hosea. **10–12:** Judgment through earthquake followed by military disaster from Arameans (Syrians) in the northeast and Philistines in the west.

9.13–17: A further stage in judgment on Israel (Northern Kingdom) with the Assyrian conquests of 733 BCE. **15:** Perhaps a gloss, giving a later twist to the phrase *head* and *tail.*

16 for those who led this people led
them astray,
and those who were led by them
were left in confusion.
17 That is why the Lord did not have
pity on[a] their young people,
or compassion on their orphans
and widows;
for everyone was godless and an
evildoer,
and every mouth spoke folly.
For all this his anger has not turned
away;
his hand is stretched out still.

18 For wickedness burned like a
fire,
consuming briers and thorns;
it kindled the thickets of the forest,
and they swirled upward in a
column of smoke.
19 Through the wrath of the LORD of
hosts
the land was burned,
and the people became like fuel for
the fire;
no one spared another.
20 They gorged on the right, but still
were hungry,
and they devoured on the left, but
were not satisfied;
they devoured the flesh of their own
kindred;[b]
21 Manasseh devoured Ephraim, and
Ephraim Manasseh,
and together they were against
Judah.
For all this his anger has not turned
away;
his hand is stretched out still.

10 Ah, you who make iniquitous
decrees,
who write oppressive statutes,
2 to turn aside the needy from justice
and to rob the poor of my people
of their right,
that widows may be your spoil,
and that you may make the
orphans your prey!
3 What will you do on the day of
punishment,
in the calamity that will come from
far away?
To whom will you flee for help,
and where will you leave your
wealth,
4 so as not to crouch among the
prisoners
or fall among the slain?
For all this his anger has not turned
away;
his hand is stretched out still.

5 Ah, Assyria, the rod of my anger—
the club in their hands is my fury!
6 Against a godless nation I send him,
and against the people of my wrath
I command him,
to take spoil and seize plunder,
and to tread them down like the
mire of the streets.

a Q Ms: MT *rejoice over* *b* Or *arm*

9.18–21: Social breakdown. This stanza describes the Northern Kingdom's descent into chaos from the end of the dynasty of Jehu (ca. 747) to the reign of the last king Hoshea (732–722); see 2 Kings 15.8–31; Hos 4.2; 6.8–10; 7.1–3; 8.4; 13.10. **18:** *Briers and thorns,* 5.6; 7.25. **20–21:** A situation of social chaos reflecting the language of the treaty curses, e.g., the threat of cannibalism (cf. Lev 26.28; Deut 28.53–57), and referring to internecine strife within Israel and between Israel and Judah at that time.

10.1–4: Judgment against aggressors. Judgment, in the form of military defeat and captivity, is pronounced on those who oppress the poor and disadvantaged, including widows and orphans, by manipulating the judicial system (see 31.3–15n.). 5.25 may have followed as the last stanza in the poem (see 5.25n.).

10.5–19: Woe to Assyria. A poem in the form of a woe-saying about Assyria as the instrument of punishment inflicted by the God of Israel on his own people. Assyria goes beyond its commission and will be punished in its turn. **5–7:** Military defeat as the expression of the native deity's anger is a common ancient Near Eastern theme (e.g., Jer 25.8–14). **6b:** An echo of Maher-shalal-hash-baz; 8.1–4.

7 But this is not what he intends,
nor does he have this in mind;
but it is in his heart to destroy,
and to cut off nations not a few.
8 For he says:
"Are not my commanders all kings?
9 Is not Calno like Carchemish?
Is not Hamath like Arpad?
Is not Samaria like Damascus?
10 As my hand has reached to the kingdoms of the idols
whose images were greater than those of Jerusalem and Samaria,
11 shall I not do to Jerusalem and her idols
what I have done to Samaria and her images?"

12 When the Lord has finished all his
work on Mount Zion and on Jerusalem,
he[a] will punish the arrogant boasting of
the king of Assyria and his haughty pride.
13 For he says:
"By the strength of my hand I have done it,
and by my wisdom, for I have understanding;
I have removed the boundaries of peoples,
and have plundered their treasures;
like a bull I have brought down
those who sat on thrones.
14 My hand has found, like a nest,
the wealth of the peoples;
and as one gathers eggs that have been forsaken,
so I have gathered all the earth;
and there was none that moved a wing,
or opened its mouth, or chirped."
15 Shall the ax vaunt itself over the one who wields it,
or the saw magnify itself against the one who handles it?
As if a rod should raise the one who lifts it up,
or as if a staff should lift the one who is not wood!
16 Therefore the Sovereign, the LORD of hosts,
will send wasting sickness among his stout warriors,
and under his glory a burning will be kindled,
like the burning of fire.
17 The light of Israel will become a fire,
and his Holy One a flame;
and it will burn and devour
his thorns and briers in one day.
18 The glory of his forest and his fruitful land
the LORD will destroy, both soul and body,
and it will be as when an invalid wastes away.
19 The remnant of the trees of his forest will be so few
that a child can write them down.

20 On that day the remnant of Israel

a Heb *I*

8–11,13–14: A boasting monologue attributed to an Assyrian ruler, composed mostly of rhetorical questions; cf. the Rabshakeh's monologue, 36.4–20; 37.24–25, and Am 6.2. The six cities mentioned, all except Samaria in Syria, have fallen to the Assyrians; therefore the reference is to a time after the fall of the Northern Kingdom: Calno (Calneh, Am 6.2) in 738, Carchemish 717, Hamath 738 and 720, Arpad 740, Damascus 732. The resident deity of a country or city is involved in the fate of his or her territory. **11:** To Assyria, the LORD was another idol. **12:** A prose insertion that breaks into the monologue, perhaps with application to a later "king of Assyria," i.e., Seleucid ruler. **13–14:** Conclusion of the monologue. The speaker boasts of his easy conquests. **15–19:** The LORD's response, also in the form of rhetorical questions. The punishment may refer to the failure of Sennacherib's siege of Jerusalem; cf. Josephus's reference to bubonic plague (*Ant.* 10.21–23).

10.20–27a: A prose comment introduced with the eschatological formula "on that day," using many Isaian motifs, and holding out the possibility of salvation at a much later time. **20:** *The remnant of Israel,* cf. Shear-yashub. *The Holy One of Israel,* cf. 1.4; 5.19,24; 12.6; 17.7; etc. **21:** *The mighty God,* cf. 9.6.

and the survivors of the house of Jacob will
no more lean on the one who struck them,
but will lean on the LORD, the Holy One of
Israel, in truth. 21 A remnant will return,
the remnant of Jacob, to the mighty God.
22 For though your people Israel were like
the sand of the sea, only a remnant of them
will return. Destruction is decreed, over-
flowing with righteousness. 23 For the Lord
GOD of hosts will make a full end, as de-
creed, in all the earth.[a]
24 Therefore thus says the Lord GOD of
hosts: O my people, who live in Zion, do
not be afraid of the Assyrians when they
beat you with a rod and lift up their staff
against you as the Egyptians did. 25 For in a
very little while my indignation will come
to an end, and my anger will be directed to
their destruction. 26 The LORD of hosts will
wield a whip against them, as when he
struck Midian at the rock of Oreb; his staff
will be over the sea, and he will lift it as he
did in Egypt. 27 On that day his burden will
be removed from your shoulder, and his
yoke will be destroyed from your neck.

He has gone up from Rimmon,[b]
28 he has come to Aiath;
he has passed through Migron,
at Michmash he stores his baggage;
29 they have crossed over the pass,
at Geba they lodge for the night;
Ramah trembles,
Gibeah of Saul has fled.
30 Cry aloud, O daughter Gallim!
Listen, O Laishah!
Answer her, O Anathoth!
31 Madmenah is in flight,
the inhabitants of Gebim flee
for safety.
32 This very day he will halt at Nob,
he will shake his fist
at the mount of daughter Zion,
the hill of Jerusalem.

33 Look, the Sovereign, the LORD
of hosts,
will lop the boughs with terrifying
power;
the tallest trees will be cut down,
and the lofty will be brought low.
34 He will hack down the thickets of the
forest with an ax,
and Lebanon with its majestic
trees[c] will fall.

11 A shoot shall come out from the
stump of Jesse,

a Or *land* *b* Cn: Heb *and his yoke from your neck, and a yoke will be destroyed because of fatness* *c* Cn Compare Gk Vg: Heb *with a majestic one*

22–23: *Sand of the sea,* see Gen 22.17. Judgment is here extended to the entire world, a typical apocalyptic theme. *Righteousness,* see 1.27n. **26–27:** *Midian at the rock of Oreb,* see Judg 7.25. *His yoke,* one of several echoes of the poem about the future ruler; 9.2–7.

10.27b–32: An invasion. The order of the place names suggests the route taken by an invading army approaching Jerusalem from the north. The enemy is not identified, but the context strongly suggests the Assyrians. Sennacherib's attack on Jerusalem is excluded since he approached from the southwest (Mic 1.10–16). The reference may be to one of Sargon II's campaigns against the Philistine cities in 720 and 713–711. **27b:** *Rimmon,* not in the Heb text; Samaria would be the logical point of departure. *Aiath,* a variant of Ai near Bethel. **28:** *Migron,* unidentified, presumably near Gibeah. *Michmash,* unidentified, but in proximity to the village of Muhmas. **29:** *They have crossed over the pass,* crossing the Wadi es-Suwenit to avoid the fortified town of Mizpah (Tell en-Nasbeh). *Geba,* near the village of Jeba. *Ramah,* er-Ram. *Gibeah of Saul,* previous scholarly identification with Tell el-Ful is now considered uncertain. **30–32:** Place names in the last stage of the itinerary, ending on Mount Scopus east of Jerusalem, are unidentified, with the possible exception of Anathoth as Ras el-Kharrube near the modern village of Anata.

10.33–34: Further judgments. Perhaps the original conclusion to 10.15–19, pursuing the theme of deforestation and humbled pride.

11.1–9: The future peaceful kingdom. The date of this splendid poem is disputed. Some commentators attribute it to Isaiah himself, others date it to the reign of Josiah (late seventh century), others again place it in the context of messianic expectations in the postexilic period (cf. Jer 23.5–6; 33.14–22; Ezek

and a branch shall grow out of his
roots.
2 The spirit of the LORD shall rest
on him,
the spirit of wisdom and
understanding,
the spirit of counsel and might,
the spirit of knowledge and the fear
of the LORD.
3 His delight shall be in the fear of the
LORD.

He shall not judge by what his
eyes see,
or decide by what his ears hear;
4 but with righteousness he shall judge
the poor,
and decide with equity for the meek
of the earth;
he shall strike the earth with the rod
of his mouth,
and with the breath of his lips he
shall kill the wicked.
5 Righteousness shall be the belt around
his waist,
and faithfulness the belt around his
loins.

6 The wolf shall live with the lamb,
the leopard shall lie down with the
kid,
the calf and the lion and the fatling
together,
and a little child shall lead them.
7 The cow and the bear shall graze,
their young shall lie down together;
and the lion shall eat straw like the
ox.
8 The nursing child shall play over the
hole of the asp,
and the weaned child shall put its
hand on the adder's den.
9 They will not hurt or destroy
on all my holy mountain;
for the earth will be full of the
knowledge of the LORD
as the waters cover the sea.

10 On that day the root of Jesse shall
stand as a signal to the peoples; the nations
shall inquire of him, and his dwelling shall
be glorious.
11 On that day the Lord will extend his
hand yet a second time to recover the rem-
nant that is left of his people, from Assyria,
from Egypt, from Pathros, from Ethiopia,[a]
from Elam, from Shinar, from Hamath,
and from the coastlands of the sea.
12 He will raise a signal for the nations,
and will assemble the outcasts of
Israel,
and gather the dispersed of Judah
from the four corners of the earth.
13 The jealousy of Ephraim shall depart,
the hostility of Judah shall be
cut off;
Ephraim shall not be jealous of
Judah,
and Judah shall not be hostile
towards Ephraim.

a Or *Nubia*; Heb *Cush*

37.24–28) when there was great emphasis on spirit-endowment (42.1; 44.3; 48.16; 59.21; 61.1). **1:** *Jesse,* father of David, 1 Sam 16.1–20. **2:** *The spirit of the LORD,* the charismatic endowment of the future ruler is expressed in three pairs of attributes; LXX adds "the spirit of piety," providing the basis for the seven gifts of the Holy Spirit in Christian theology. **3–5:** The main attribute of the ruler is the firm and equitable administration of justice (9.7; Ps 7.2; 101). **9a:** *My holy mountain* (see 2.2n.; the exact phrasing recurs in 56.7; 57.13; 65.11,25; 66.20). The entire statement occurs also at 65.25. **9b:** Cf. Hab 2.14.

11.10–16: Three appendices to 11.1–9, the first two in prose introduced with the "on that day" formula, the third in verse. **10:** Cf. 55.3, the Davidic ruler as a witness to the peoples, perhaps implying the unrealistic idea of the reestablishment of a Davidic empire. **11:** The hope of repatriation and the reintegration of dispersed Israelites. *Pathros,* Upper Egypt; *Ethiopia,* Heb "Cush," Nubia; *Elam,* the land east of Babylonia, north of the Persian Gulf; *Shinar,* southern Mesopotamia; *Hamath,* in northern Syria; *the coastlands of the sea,* either the Phoenician littoral or the islands of the eastern Aegean. **12–16:** *A signal,* for an assembly point for those preparing to return to Judah; see 49.22. If this section is postexilic, the allusion would be to enmity between Judah and Samaria, attested in Ezra-Nehemiah. **15:** *The tongue*

14 But they shall swoop down on the
backs of the Philistines in the
west,
together they shall plunder the
people of the east.
They shall put forth their hand
against Edom and Moab,
and the Ammonites shall
obey them.
15 And the LORD will utterly destroy
the tongue of the sea of Egypt;
and will wave his hand over the
River
with his scorching wind;
and will split it into seven channels,
and make a way to cross on foot;
16 so there shall be a highway from
Assyria
for the remnant that is left of
his people,
as there was for Israel
when they came up from the land
of Egypt.

12 You will say in that day:
I will give thanks to you, O LORD,
for though you were angry
with me,
your anger turned away,
and you comforted me.

2 Surely God is my salvation;
I will trust, and will not be afraid,
for the LORD GOD[a] is my strength
and my might;
he has become my salvation.

3 With joy you will draw water from the
wells of salvation. 4 And you will say in that
day:
Give thanks to the LORD,
call on his name;
make known his deeds among the
nations;
proclaim that his name is exalted.

5 Sing praises to the LORD, for he has
done gloriously;
let this be known[b] in all the earth.
6 Shout aloud and sing for joy,
O royal[c] Zion,
for great in your midst is the Holy
One of Israel.

13 The oracle concerning Babylon that
Isaiah son of Amoz saw.

2 On a bare hill raise a signal,
cry aloud to them;
wave the hand for them to enter
the gates of the nobles.
3 I myself have commanded my
consecrated ones,
have summoned my warriors, my
proudly exulting ones,
to execute my anger.

4 Listen, a tumult on the mountains
as of a great multitude!
Listen, an uproar of kingdoms,

a Heb *for Yah, the LORD* b Or *this is made known*
c Or *O inhabitant of*

of the sea of Egypt, the tongue-shaped Red Sea. Echoes of the crossing of the Red Sea at the Exodus from Egypt (Ex 14). On the highway theme, see 35.8–10; 40.3.

12.1–6: Two short hymns of praise and thanksgiving, each introduced with *you will say in that day.* They recapitulate chs 1–11 by playing on the name Isaiah (related to "salvation"; see 1.1n.) and the title *the Holy One of Israel.* The hymns are composed out of a patchwork of phrases from various psalms, e.g., Ps 12.2b; cf. Ps 118.14; Ex 15.2.

Chs 13–23: Oracles against foreign nations. The core of this section is a series of nine oracles against foreign peoples (13.1; 14.28; 15.1; 17.1; 19.1; 21.1,11; 22.1; 23.1), with many expansions and interspersed with the assurance of better times for Israel/Judah. The break with the eighth-century context of chs 1–12 is not complete (see 14.24–27; 17.1–6), but the historical horizon extends far into the future.

13.1–22: An oracle concerning Babylon. Here, as throughout this section, judgment on individual nations is linked with scenes of universal and cosmic doom. The historical situation is unclear, but mention of the Medes (v. 17) points to the years immediately prior to the fall of Babylon in 539 BCE. **1–5:** The scenario is of cosmic proportions, affecting even the heavenly bodies (23.10,13). **6:** The poet makes

of nations gathering together!
The LORD of hosts is mustering
an army for battle.
5 They come from a distant land,
from the end of the heavens,
the LORD and the weapons of his
indignation,
to destroy the whole earth.

6 Wail, for the day of the LORD is near;
it will come like destruction from
the Almighty![a]
7 Therefore all hands will be feeble,
and every human heart will melt,
8 and they will be dismayed.
Pangs and agony will seize them;
they will be in anguish like a
woman in labor.
They will look aghast at one another;
their faces will be aflame.

9 See, the day of the LORD comes,
cruel, with wrath and fierce anger,
to make the earth a desolation,
and to destroy its sinners from it.
10 For the stars of the heavens and their
constellations
will not give their light;
the sun will be dark at its rising,
and the moon will not shed
its light.
11 I will punish the world for its evil,
and the wicked for their iniquity;
I will put an end to the pride of
the arrogant,
and lay low the insolence of
tyrants.
12 I will make mortals more rare than
fine gold,
and humans than the gold of
Ophir.
13 Therefore I will make the heavens
tremble,
and the earth will be shaken out of
its place,

a Traditional rendering of Heb *Shaddai*

use of the ancient motif of the "Day of the LORD," see 2.12n. **12:** *Ophir,* famous for gold, perhaps in the south of the Arabian peninsula (1 Kings 9.26–28; Job 22.24; 28.16; Ps 45.9). **17:** *Medes,* a people

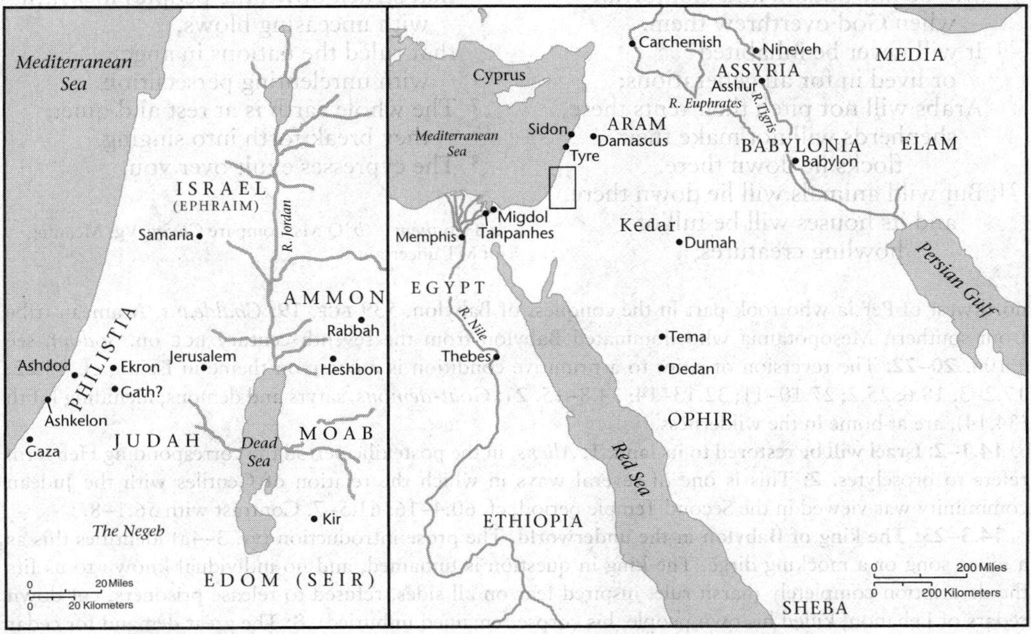

Chs 13–23: The oracles against the nations.

at the wrath of the LORD of hosts
in the day of his fierce anger.
14 Like a hunted gazelle,
or like sheep with no one to gather them,
all will turn to their own people,
and all will flee to their own lands.
15 Whoever is found will be thrust through,
and whoever is caught will fall by the sword.
16 Their infants will be dashed to pieces before their eyes;
their houses will be plundered,
and their wives ravished.
17 See, I am stirring up the Medes against them,
who have no regard for silver
and do not delight in gold.
18 Their bows will slaughter the young men;
they will have no mercy on the fruit of the womb;
their eyes will not pity children.
19 And Babylon, the glory of kingdoms,
the splendor and pride of the Chaldeans,
will be like Sodom and Gomorrah
when God overthrew them.
20 It will never be inhabited
or lived in for all generations;
Arabs will not pitch their tents there,
shepherds will not make their flocks lie down there.
21 But wild animals will lie down there,
and its houses will be full of howling creatures;
there ostriches will live,
and there goat-demons will dance.
22 Hyenas will cry in its towers,
and jackals in the pleasant palaces;
its time is close at hand,
and its days will not be prolonged.

14 But the LORD will have compassion
on Jacob and will again choose Isra-
el, and will set them in their own land; and
aliens will join them and attach themselves
to the house of Jacob. 2 And the nations will
take them and bring them to their place,
and the house of Israel will possess the na-
tions[a] as male and female slaves in the
LORD's land; they will take captive those
who were their captors, and rule over those
who oppressed them.

3 When the LORD has given you rest
from your pain and turmoil and the hard
service with which you were made to serve,
4 you will take up this taunt against the king
of Babylon:
How the oppressor has ceased!
How his insolence[b] has ceased!
5 The LORD has broken the staff of the wicked,
the scepter of rulers,
6 that struck down the peoples in wrath
with unceasing blows,
that ruled the nations in anger
with unrelenting persecution.
7 The whole earth is at rest and quiet;
they break forth into singing.
8 The cypresses exult over you,

a Heb *them* *b* Q Ms Compare Gk Syr Vg: Meaning of MT uncertain

northwest of Persia who took part in the conquest of Babylon, 539 BCE. **19:** *Chaldeans,* Aramean tribe from southern Mesopotamia who dominated Babylon from the seventh century BCE on. *Sodom,* see 1.10n. **20–22:** The reversion of cities to a primitive condition is a common theme in Isaiah, cf. 14.22; 17.2–3; 18.6; 25.2; 27.10–11; 32.13–14; 34.8–15. **21:** *Goat-demons,* satyrs and demons, including Lilith (34.14), are at home in the wilderness.

14.1–2: Israel will be restored to its land. 1: *Aliens,* in the postexilic period the corresponding Heb term refers to proselytes. **2:** This is one of several ways in which the relation of Gentiles with the Judean community was viewed in the Second Temple period, cf. 60.4–16; 61.5–7. Contrast with 56.1–8.

14.3–23: The king of Babylon in the underworld. The prose introduction (vv. 3–4a) identifies this as a taunt song or a mocking dirge. The king in question is unnamed, and no individual known to us fits the description completely (harsh rule, inspired fear on all sides, refused to release prisoners, cut down cedars of Lebanon, killed his own people, his corpse remained unburied). **8:** The great demand for cedar wood led to depletion of the cedar forests of Lebanon, see 37.24. **9–11:** Reaction to the appearance of

the cedars of Lebanon, saying,
"Since you were laid low,
no one comes to cut us down."
9 Sheol beneath is stirred up
to meet you when you come;
it rouses the shades to greet you,
all who were leaders of the earth;
it raises from their thrones
all who were kings of the nations.
10 All of them will speak
and say to you:
"You too have become as weak
as we!
You have become like us!"
11 Your pomp is brought down to Sheol,
and the sound of your harps;
maggots are the bed beneath you,
and worms are your covering.

12 How you are fallen from heaven,
O Day Star, son of Dawn!
How you are cut down to the ground,
you who laid the nations low!
13 You said in your heart,
"I will ascend to heaven;
I will raise my throne
above the stars of God;
I will sit on the mount of assembly
on the heights of Zaphon;[a]
14 I will ascend to the tops of the
clouds,
I will make myself like the
Most High."
15 But you are brought down to Sheol,
to the depths of the Pit.
16 Those who see you will stare at you,
and ponder over you:
"Is this the man who made the earth
tremble,
who shook kingdoms,
17 who made the world like a desert
and overthrew its cities,
who would not let his prisoners go
home?"
18 All the kings of the nations lie
in glory,
each in his own tomb;
19 but you are cast out, away from your
grave,
like loathsome carrion,[b]
clothed with the dead, those pierced
by the sword,
who go down to the stones of
the Pit,
like a corpse trampled underfoot.
20 You will not be joined with them
in burial,
because you have destroyed
your land,
you have killed your people.

May the descendants of evildoers
nevermore be named!
21 Prepare slaughter for his sons
because of the guilt of their
father.[c]
Let them never rise to possess
the earth
or cover the face of the world with
cities.

22 I will rise up against them, says the
LORD of hosts, and will cut off from Bab-
ylon name and remnant, offspring and pos-
terity, says the LORD.
23 And I will make it
a possession of the hedgehog, and pools of

a Or *assembly in the far north* b Cn Compare Gk: Heb *like a loathed branch* c Syr Compare Gk: Heb *fathers*

the tyrant in *Sheol,* the underworld, (cf. Ezek 32.17–32). The dead survive, but in a weakened and diminished state; no distinction is made among the dead on moral grounds. **12–14:** Draws on a Canaanite myth of the gods Helel and Shahar (Morning Star and Dawn), who fall from heaven as a result of rebellion. In Christianity the myth reemerges as the fall of Lucifer and his attendant angels (cf. Lk 10.18). *Mount of assembly,* the mountain on which, according to Canaanite mythology, the gods assembled, identified with Jebel el-Aqra near the mouth of the Orontes in Syria; also called *Zaphon,* the north, cf. Ps 48.2; Israelites transferred the imagery of the cosmic mountain to Mount Zion. **14:** *The Most High,* Heb "Elyon," an archaic title for the head of the pantheon, see Deut 32.8–9; Ps 82.6. **15:** *The Pit,* the underworld. **20b–21:** A curse on the king's descendants. **22–23:** A prose conclusion repeating the motif of reversion to primitive conditions (see 13.20–22n.).

water, and I will sweep it with the broom of destruction, says the LORD of hosts.

24 The LORD of hosts has sworn:
As I have designed,
so shall it be;
and as I have planned,
so shall it come to pass:
25 I will break the Assyrian in my land,
and on my mountains trample him
under foot;
his yoke shall be removed from them,
and his burden from their
shoulders.
26 This is the plan that is planned
concerning the whole earth;
and this is the hand that is stretched
out
over all the nations.
27 For the LORD of hosts has planned,
and who will annul it?
His hand is stretched out,
and who will turn it back?

28 In the year that King Ahaz died this oracle came:

29 Do not rejoice, all you Philistines,
that the rod that struck you
is broken,
for from the root of the snake will
come forth an adder,
and its fruit will be a flying
fiery serpent.
30 The firstborn of the poor will graze,
and the needy lie down in safety;
but I will make your root die
of famine,
and your remnant I[a] will kill.
31 Wail, O gate; cry, O city;
melt in fear, O Philistia, all of you!
For smoke comes out of the north,
and there is no straggler in
its ranks.

32 What will one answer the messengers
of the nation?
"The LORD has founded Zion,
and the needy among his people
will find refuge in her."

15 An oracle concerning Moab.

Because Ar is laid waste in a night,
Moab is undone;
because Kir is laid waste in a night,
Moab is undone.
2 Dibon[b] has gone up to the temple,
to the high places to weep;
over Nebo and over Medeba
Moab wails.

a Q Ms Vg: MT *he* *b* Cn: Heb *the house and Dibon*

14.24–27: Judgment on the Assyrians. This passage may have been isolated from the Assyrian material in chs 1–12 by the insertion of 13.1–14.23. The destruction of the Assyrians in the LORD's land (v. 25) points to the outcome of Sennacherib's campaign, 701 BCE. Cf. 29.1–8; 30.27–33; 31.8–9; 37.36. **27b:** Echoes the refrain in 9.12b, etc.

14.28–32: The revolt of Ashdod. The notice about the death of Ahaz (727/715) introduces the saying that follows, but also indicates, with 6.1 (the death of Uzziah), important turning points in Isaiah's career. The historical reference is to the Philistine, Ashdodite revolt of 714–711, but it is not clear whether the reversal suffered by their enemy refers to Assyria or Judah. **32:** The answer is delivered to envoys from Ashdod attempting to draw Judah into the anti-Assyrian alliance.

15.1–16.14: Judgment on Moab. This long mostly poetic saying concerns Moab, situated east of the Dead Sea between Edom to the south and Ammon to the north, usually on unfriendly terms with Israel and Judah (cf. Gen 19.30–37). Moab has suffered a combination of natural disaster and hostile invasion, perhaps Bedouin raids. **15.1:** *Ar,* on the south bank of the Arnon, near Moab's northern border (Num 21.15,28). *Kir,* probably Kir-hareseth (16.7), perhaps modern Kerak. **2:** *Dibon,* Dhiban, three miles north of the Arnon. *Nebo,* a Moabite city near Heshbon, mentioned on the Moabite stele of king Mesha (Num 32.3,38). *Medeba,* Madaba, six miles south of Heshbon, site of the famous Madaba map, a Byzantine mosaic depicting the Holy Land (see *ANET,* 320). **2b–3:** Mourning ritual included shaving the head and facial hair, wearing sackcloth, and lamenting loudly. **4:** *Heshbon,* Hesban in Moab, fifty miles east of

On every head is baldness,
every beard is shorn;
3 in the streets they bind on sackcloth;
on the housetops and in the squares
everyone wails and melts in tears.
4 Heshbon and Elealeh cry out,
their voices are heard as far
as Jahaz;
therefore the loins of Moab quiver;[a]
his soul trembles.
5 My heart cries out for Moab;
his fugitives flee to Zoar,
to Eglath-shelishiyah.
For at the ascent of Luhith
they go up weeping;
on the road to Horonaim
they raise a cry of destruction;
6 the waters of Nimrim
are a desolation;
the grass is withered, the new growth
fails,
the verdure is no more.
7 Therefore the abundance they
have gained
and what they have laid up
they carry away
over the Wadi of the Willows.
8 For a cry has gone
around the land of Moab;
the wailing reaches to Eglaim,
the wailing reaches to Beer-elim.
9 For the waters of Dibon[b] are full
of blood;
yet I will bring upon Dibon[b] even
more—
a lion for those of Moab who escape,
for the remnant of the land.

16 Send lambs
to the ruler of the land,
from Sela, by way of the desert,
to the mount of daughter Zion.
2 Like fluttering birds,
like scattered nestlings,
so are the daughters of Moab
at the fords of the Arnon.
3 "Give counsel,
grant justice;
make your shade like night
at the height of noon;
hide the outcasts,
do not betray the fugitive;
4 let the outcasts of Moab
settle among you;
be a refuge to them
from the destroyer."

When the oppressor is no more,
and destruction has ceased,
and marauders have vanished from
the land,
5 then a throne shall be established in
steadfast love
in the tent of David,
and on it shall sit in faithfulness
a ruler who seeks justice
and is swift to do what is right.
6 We have heard of the pride of Moab
—how proud he is!—
of his arrogance, his pride, and his
insolence;
his boasts are false.
7 Therefore let Moab wail,
let everyone wail for Moab.
Mourn, utterly stricken,
for the raisin cakes of Kir-hareseth.

8 For the fields of Heshbon languish,
and the vines of Sibmah,

a Cn Compare Gk Syr: Heb *the armed men of Moab cry aloud* *b* Q Ms Vg Compare Syr: MT *Dimon*

Jerusalem. *Elealeh,* near Heshbon. **5–9:** The flight of refugees in the direction of Judah has left much of the land deserted. None of the places named here has been identified. **16.1–4a:** Refugees bring gifts of lambs (the tribute offered by King Mesha, 2 Kings 3.4) to induce Judah to allow them to settle. **1:** *Sela,* unidentified, perhaps Petra. **2:** *Arnon,* the Wadi el-Mujib that flows into the Dead Sea. **3–4:** Addressed to the people of Judah. **4b–5:** A prediction, suggested by the preceding request, that the benefits of Davidic rule will once again be conferred on Moab. **6–7:** Denunciation of Moabite pride and an ironic call to lament the loss of the raisin cakes of Kir-hareseth (15.1n.), connected with a goddess ritual (see Hos 3.1; Jer 7.18; 44.19). **8–11:** Lament for the destruction of the vineyards of Sibmah, apparently the chief wine-producing region of Moab. *Jazer,* near the Ammonite border (Num 21.24, LXX). **12:** A

whose clusters once made drunk
the lords of the nations,
reached to Jazer
and strayed to the desert;
their shoots once spread abroad
and crossed over the sea.
9 Therefore I weep with the weeping of
Jazer
for the vines of Sibmah;
I drench you with my tears,
O Heshbon and Elealeh;
for the shout over your fruit harvest
and your grain harvest has ceased.
10 Joy and gladness are taken away
from the fruitful field;
and in the vineyards no songs
are sung,
no shouts are raised;
no treader treads out wine in
the presses;
the vintage-shout is hushed.[a]
11 Therefore my heart throbs like a harp
for Moab,
and my very soul for Kir-heres.

12 When Moab presents himself, when
he wearies himself upon the high place,
when he comes to his sanctuary to pray, he
will not prevail.

13 This was the word that the LORD
spoke concerning Moab in the past. 14 But
now the LORD says, In three years, like the
years of a hired worker, the glory of Moab
will be brought into contempt, in spite of
all its great multitude; and those who survive will be very few and feeble.

17 An oracle concerning Damascus.

See, Damascus will cease to be a city,
and will become a heap of ruins.
2 Her towns will be deserted forever;[b]
they will be places for flocks,
which will lie down, and no one
will make them afraid.
3 The fortress will disappear from
Ephraim,
and the kingdom from Damascus;
and the remnant of Aram will be
like the glory of the children
of Israel,
says the LORD of hosts.

4 On that day
the glory of Jacob will be
brought low,
and the fat of his flesh will
grow lean.
5 And it shall be as when reapers gather
standing grain
and their arms harvest the ears,
and as when one gleans the ears
of grain
in the Valley of Rephaim.
6 Gleanings will be left in it,
as when an olive tree is beaten—
two or three berries
in the top of the highest bough,
four or five
on the branches of a fruit tree,
says the LORD God of Israel.

7 On that day people will regard their
Maker, and their eyes will look to the Holy
One of Israel; 8 they will not have regard for
the altars, the work of their hands, and they

a Gk: Heb *I have hushed* *b* Cn Compare Gk: Heb *the cities of Aroer are deserted*

separate anti-Moabite saying added as a comment to the preceding poem. **13–14:** A later prophetic oracle of uncertain date attached to the poem predicting the devastation of Moab within three years. An example of literary development in the prophetic literature, new prophecy formed on the basis of old.

17.1–11: The fate of Syria and Israel. The third oracle in the series (17.1–3) deals with the final defeat of the allies in the Syro-Ephraimite war (734–732 BCE; see 7.1–8.4; 2 Kings 16.1–20). **3:** *Ephraim,* the Northern Kingdom of Israel. **4–6:** An "on that day" addition which plays on the Heb word "kabod," meaning "glory" or "weight." Israel (the Northern Kingdom) will be emaciated, i.e., it will be reduced greatly in size, as happened in 732 BCE. **5:** *Rephaim,* a valley near Jerusalem (2 Sam 5.18). **6:** Long sticks were used to knock the fruit from the branches of the *olive tree.* **7–8:** A second expansion. Illicit worship and ritual objects, including *sacred poles,* i.e., tree trunks or monoliths dedicated to the goddess Asherah (2 Kings 17.7–18; 10.16), will come to an end (cf. 27.9). **9:** *Hivites and Amorites,* pre-Israelite inhabi-

will not look to what their own fingers
have made, either the sacred poles[a] or the
altars of incense.
9 On that day their strong cities will be
like the deserted places of the Hivites and
the Amorites,[b] which they deserted be-
cause of the children of Israel, and there
will be desolation.

10 For you have forgotten the God of
your salvation,
and have not remembered the Rock
of your refuge;
therefore, though you plant pleasant
plants
and set out slips of an alien god,
11 though you make them grow on the
day that you plant them,
and make them blossom in the
morning that you sow;
yet the harvest will flee away
in a day of grief and incurable pain.

12 Ah, the thunder of many peoples,
they thunder like the thundering of
the sea!
Ah, the roar of nations,
they roar like the roaring of mighty
waters!
13 The nations roar like the roaring of
many waters,
but he will rebuke them, and they
will flee far away,
chased like chaff on the mountains
before the wind
and whirling dust before the storm.
14 At evening time, lo, terror!
Before morning, they are no more.
This is the fate of those who
despoil us,
and the lot of those who
plunder us.

18 Ah, land of whirring wings
beyond the rivers of Ethiopia,[c]
2 sending ambassadors by the Nile
in vessels of papyrus on the waters!
Go, you swift messengers,
to a nation tall and smooth,
to a people feared near and far,
a nation mighty and conquering,
whose land the rivers divide.

3 All you inhabitants of the world,
you who live on the earth,
when a signal is raised on the
mountains, look!
When a trumpet is blown, listen!
4 For thus the LORD said to me:
I will quietly look from my dwelling
like clear heat in sunshine,
like a cloud of dew in the heat
of harvest.
5 For before the harvest, when the
blossom is over
and the flower becomes a ripening
grape,
he will cut off the shoots with
pruning hooks,
and the spreading branches he will
hew away.
6 They shall all be left

a Heb *Asherim* *b* Cn Compare Gk: Heb *places of the wood and the highest bough* *c* Or *Nubia*; Heb *Cush*

tants of Palestine (Deut 7.1). **10–11:** A much later note pronouncing judgment on the veneration of a vegetation deity, probably Tammuz (see Ezek 8.14–18), also known as Adonis.

17.12–14: An end to political oppression. The roar of the sea's waves (cf. Ps 46.1–3; 93.3–4) and the noise of battle (5.26–30; 13.4–5; 29.5–8) represent the violence of oppression, perhaps with undertones of the myth of cosmogonic warfare leading to the creation of the world.

18.1–7: Against Egypt and Nubia. A saying directed against an Egyptian (Nubian) alliance juxtaposed with the scenario of universal judgment (see 13.2,11–12; 17.12–14; 24.1–6; 26.6,18). It refers either to Egyptian attempts to persuade Judah to join Ashdod in an anti-Assyrian alliance (714–711 BCE) or to negotiations between Judah and the Nubian kingdom of Napata under Shebitku (702–701). **1:** *Land of whirring wings*, Nubia/Ethiopia (Heb "Cush") as an insect-infested land, see Herodotus 2.95. **2:** The poet refers to the extraordinary height and lack of facial hair but not the color of Nubians. *Land the rivers*

to the birds of prey of the
mountains
and to the animals of the earth.
And the birds of prey will summer on
them,
and all the animals of the earth will
winter on them.

7 At that time gifts will be brought to
the LORD of hosts from[a] a people tall and
smooth, from a people feared near and far,
a nation mighty and conquering, whose
land the rivers divide, to Mount Zion, the
place of the name of the LORD of hosts.

19 An oracle concerning Egypt.

See, the LORD is riding on a
swift cloud
and comes to Egypt;
the idols of Egypt will tremble at his
presence,
and the heart of the Egyptians will
melt within them.
2 I will stir up Egyptians against
Egyptians,
and they will fight, one against the
other,
neighbor against neighbor,
city against city, kingdom against
kingdom;
3 the spirit of the Egyptians within
them will be emptied out,
and I will confound their plans;
they will consult the idols and the
spirits of the dead
and the ghosts and the familiar
spirits;
4 I will deliver the Egyptians
into the hand of a hard master;
a fierce king will rule over them,
says the Sovereign, the LORD
of hosts.

5 The waters of the Nile will be
dried up,
and the river will be parched
and dry;
6 its canals will become foul,
and the branches of Egypt's Nile
will diminish and dry up,
reeds and rushes will rot away.
7 There will be bare places by the Nile,
on the brink of the Nile;
and all that is sown by the Nile will
dry up,
be driven away, and be no more.
8 Those who fish will mourn;
all who cast hooks in the Nile will
lament,
and those who spread nets on the
water will languish.
9 The workers in flax will be in despair,
and the carders and those at the
loom will grow pale.
10 Its weavers will be dismayed,
and all who work for wages will be
grieved.

11 The princes of Zoan are utterly
foolish;
the wise counselors of Pharaoh give
stupid counsel.
How can you say to Pharaoh,
"I am one of the sages,
a descendant of ancient kings"?
12 Where now are your sages?
Let them tell you and make known
what the LORD of hosts has
planned against Egypt.

a Q Ms Gk Vg: MT *of*

divide, the Hebrew is obscure; probably refers to the Nile. **7:** An additional note: In the future Nubians will come not to negotiate but to bring votive gifts for the Jerusalem Temple.

19.1–15: Judgment on Egypt. The fourth oracle in the series; cf. Jer 46; Ezek 29–32. **1–4:** The LORD represented as a charioteer comes in judgment (cf. Ps 18.10; 68.5; Deut 33.26). The historical reference is probably to internecine strife at the beginning of the Nubian dynasty in the late eighth century between Upper Egypt (the southern area farther up the Nile) and the princes in the Nile delta. **4:** *A hard master, a fierce king,* identification uncertain; either the Assyrian king Sargon II or the pharaoh Piankhi, founder of the Nubian dynasty, but the description could fit later conquerors of Egypt, especially Esarhaddon, Cambyses, Alexander. **5–10:** Ecological disaster is linked with military defeat, as often in Isaiah. **11:**

13 The princes of Zoan have become fools,
and the princes of Memphis
are deluded;
those who are the cornerstones of its
tribes
have led Egypt astray.
14 The LORD has poured into them[a]
a spirit of confusion;
and they have made Egypt stagger in
all its doings
as a drunkard staggers around
in vomit.
15 Neither head nor tail, palm branch or
reed,
will be able to do anything for
Egypt.

16 On that day the Egyptians will be like
women, and tremble with fear before the
hand that the LORD of hosts raises against
them. 17 And the land of Judah will become
a terror to the Egyptians; everyone to
whom it is mentioned will fear because of
the plan that the LORD of hosts is planning
against them.

18 On that day there will be five cities in
the land of Egypt that speak the language
of Canaan and swear allegiance to the
LORD of hosts. One of these will be called
the City of the Sun.

19 On that day there will be an altar to
the LORD in the center of the land of Egypt,
and a pillar to the LORD at its border. 20 It
will be a sign and a witness to the LORD of
hosts in the land of Egypt; when they cry to
the LORD because of oppressors, he will
send them a savior, and will defend and
deliver them. 21 The LORD will make him-
self known to the Egyptians; and the Egyp-
tians will know the LORD on that day, and
will worship with sacrifice and burnt offer-
ing, and they will make vows to the LORD
and perform them. 22 The LORD will strike
Egypt, striking and healing; they will return
to the LORD, and he will listen to their sup-
plications and heal them.

23 On that day there will be a highway
from Egypt to Assyria, and the Assyrian
will come into Egypt, and the Egyptian into
Assyria, and the Egyptians will worship
with the Assyrians.

24 On that day Israel will be the third
with Egypt and Assyria, a blessing in the
midst of the earth, 25 whom the LORD of
hosts has blessed, saying, "Blessed be Egypt
my people, and Assyria the work of my
hands, and Israel my heritage."

20 In the year that the commander-in-
chief, who was sent by King Sargon
of Assyria, came to Ashdod and fought
against it and took it— 2 at that time the
LORD had spoken to Isaiah son of Amoz,
saying, "Go, and loose the sackcloth from

a Gk Compare Tg: Heb *it*

Zoan, also Tanis, in the northeast delta region. **13:** *Memphis,* also Noph, ancient capital of Lower Egypt. Sarcastic allusion to the Egyptian reputation for wisdom is common in prophetic polemic.

19.16–25: Five addenda, all much later with the possible exception of the first. **16–17:** Egypt will fear the God of Judah whose hand is raised to strike (cf. 11.15). **18:** The Judean Diaspora in Egypt. *The language of Canaan,* Hebrew, perhaps referring to liturgical usage. Five cities in which Judeans were settled are mentioned in Jer 2.16; 43.7; 44.1. *The City of the Sun,* Heliopolis (Jer 43.13). The Jewish high priest Onias IV built a temple in 170 BCE at Leontopolis (Tell el-Yahudyeh) in the Egyptian province of Heliopolis. **19–22:** The LORD will be worshiped in Egypt. *A pillar to the LORD at its border* may refer to the Jewish military colony established at Elephantine in Upper Egypt before the Persian conquest (525 BCE). **23:** Cf. 35.8; 40.3. There will be communication between the main centers of the Diaspora. **24–25:** A remarkably open and universalistic statement, perhaps from the Hellenistic period.

20.1–6: A sign. A rare instance of narrative describing an acted-out prophetic sign, generally assigned to the time of Sargon II's campaign against the Philistine city of Ashdod in 711; but since Egypt did not take part in this revolt, the sign was either meant as a warning about what might happen or the author has conflated this episode with Egyptian involvement in the rebellion against Sennacherib a decade later. **1:** *Commander-in-chief,* Heb "tartan"; cf. 2 Kings 18.17. **3:** Cf. Mic 1.8–9. The demonstration was presumably carried out at intervals over a three-year period, perhaps accompanied with disciples.

your loins and take your sandals off your
feet," and he had done so, walking naked
and barefoot. 3 Then the LORD said, "Just
as my servant Isaiah has walked naked and
barefoot for three years as a sign and a portent against Egypt and Ethiopia,[a] 4 so shall
the king of Assyria lead away the Egyptians as captives and the Ethiopians[b] as exiles, both the young and the old, naked and barefoot, with buttocks uncovered, to the shame of Egypt. 5 And they shall be dis-
mayed and confounded because of Ethiopia[a] their hope and of Egypt their boast.
6 In that day the inhabitants of this coastland will say, 'See, this is what has happened to those in whom we hoped and to whom we fled for help and deliverance from the king of Assyria! And we, how shall we escape?' "

21 The oracle concerning the wilderness of the sea.

As whirlwinds in the Negeb
sweep on,
it comes from the desert,
from a terrible land.
2 A stern vision is told to me;
the betrayer betrays,
and the destroyer destroys.
Go up, O Elam,
lay siege, O Media;
all the sighing she has caused
I bring to an end.
3 Therefore my loins are filled
with anguish;
pangs have seized me,
like the pangs of a woman in labor;
I am bowed down so that I
cannot hear,
I am dismayed so that I cannot see.
4 My mind reels, horror has
appalled me;
the twilight I longed for
has been turned for me into
trembling.
5 They prepare the table,
they spread the rugs,
they eat, they drink.
Rise up, commanders,
oil the shield!
6 For thus the Lord said to me:
"Go, post a lookout,
let him announce what he sees.
7 When he sees riders, horsemen
in pairs,
riders on donkeys, riders on camels,
let him listen diligently,
very diligently."
8 Then the watcher[c] called out:
"Upon a watchtower I stand, O Lord,
continually by day,
and at my post I am stationed
throughout the night.
9 Look, there they come, riders,
horsemen in pairs!"
Then he responded,
"Fallen, fallen is Babylon;
and all the images of her gods
lie shattered on the ground."
10 O my threshed and winnowed one,
what I have heard from the LORD
of hosts,
the God of Israel, I announce
to you.

11 The oracle concerning Dumah.

a Or *Nubia*; Heb *Cush* *b* Or *Nubians*; Heb *Cushites*
c Q Ms: MT *a lion*

21.1–10: Judgment on Babylon. The historical setting of this fifth oracle is uncertain; perhaps shortly before or after the fall of Babylon in 539; cf. Isa 47; Jer 50.2; 51.8,11,28,50–51. **1:** *The wilderness of the sea,* lower Mesopotamia contiguous with the Persian Gulf, known as the Sealand. The *Negeb* is the desert region of southern Palestine. **1b–4:** The onset of prophetic ecstasy, cf. Jer 4.19; Hab 3.16. *Elam,* the nation east of Babylon; see Jer 49.34–39. *Media* aided Persia against Babylon (13.17–19). **5:** *Oil the shield,* to protect the leather, cf. 2 Sam 1.21. **6–9:** The lookout or watcher is the seer preparing for a visionary revelation, cf. Ezek 3.16–21; 33.1–9; Hab 2.1. The fall of Babylon is announced in the vision. **10:** The seer addresses his own people who have suffered so much from the Babylonians.

21.11–17: Two oracular sayings about Arabian peoples. 11–12: The reference is uncertain, but *Seir* is Edom, and *Dumah* is therefore probably a code name for Edom rather than a place with a similar name

One is calling to me from Seir,
"Sentinel, what of the night?
Sentinel, what of the night?"
12 The sentinel says:
"Morning comes, and also the night.
If you will inquire, inquire;
come back again."

13 The oracle concerning the desert
plain.

In the scrub of the desert plain you
will lodge,
O caravans of Dedanites.
14 Bring water to the thirsty,
meet the fugitive with bread,
O inhabitants of the land of Tema.
15 For they have fled from the swords,
from the drawn sword,
from the bent bow,
and from the stress of battle.

16 For thus the Lord said to me: Within
a year, according to the years of a hired
worker, all the glory of Kedar will come to
an end; 17 and the remaining bows of Ke-
dar's warriors will be few; for the LORD,
the God of Israel, has spoken.

22 The oracle concerning the valley of
vision.

What do you mean that you have
gone up,
all of you, to the housetops,
2 you that are full of shoutings,
tumultuous city, exultant town?
Your slain are not slain by the sword,
nor are they dead in battle.
3 Your rulers have all fled together;
they were captured without the use
of a bow.[a]
All of you who were found were
captured,
though they had fled far away.[b]
4 Therefore I said:
Look away from me,
let me weep bitter tears;
do not try to comfort me
for the destruction of my
beloved people.

5 For the Lord GOD of hosts has a day
of tumult and trampling and
confusion
in the valley of vision,
a battering down of walls
and a cry for help to the
mountains.
6 Elam bore the quiver
with chariots and cavalry,[c]
and Kir uncovered the shield.
7 Your choicest valleys were full of
chariots,
and the cavalry took their stand at
the gates.
8 He has taken away the covering
of Judah.

On that day you looked to the weapons
of the House of the Forest, 9 and you saw
that there were many breaches in the city of

a Or *without their bows* *b* Gk Syr Vg: Heb *fled from far away* *c* Meaning of Heb uncertain

in the north-central region of the Arabian peninsula. There is as yet no prophetic answer to the question of how long the night, i.e., the time of distress, will last. **13–15:** An appeal to Arabian tribes to support Arab or Edomite refugees. **13:** *Dedanites,* inhabitants of the oasis of Dedan in the Hijaz on a major trade route. *Tema,* an oasis north of Dedan on the incense route. **16–17:** An appendix similar to 16.13–14. *Kedar,* a north Arabian people who came into hostile contact with Judah at the time of Nehemiah. They were expert archers (Gen 21.20).

22.1–14: The eighth oracle in the series. 1a: The title is taken from v. 5, perhaps referring to the Valley of Jehoshaphat (Joel 3.2,12). **1b–3:** Misplaced rejoicing in Jerusalem, perhaps after the withdrawal of Sennacherib's army in 701. **6:** *Elam,* ally of Babylon against Assyria; see 11.11n. *Kir,* probably in southern Mesopotamia (Am 1.5; 9.7; 2 Kings 16.9). **8b–11:** Prose expansion describing preparations for the siege. **8b:** *The House of the Forest,* the armory; 1 Kings 7.2–5; 10.17. **9:** *City of David,* the oldest section of Jerusalem; see 2 Sam 5.7. *The waters of the lower pool,* hydraulic works including excavating the Siloam Tunnel, 2 Kings 20.20. **12–14:** Bitter, fatalistic rejoicing in a time of disaster, perhaps after 586 BCE.

David, and you collected the waters of the
lower pool. 10 You counted the houses of
Jerusalem, and you broke down the houses
to fortify the wall. 11 You made a reservoir
between the two walls for the water of the
old pool. But you did not look to him who
did it, or have regard for him who planned
it long ago.

12 In that day the Lord GOD of hosts
called to weeping and mourning,
to baldness and putting on
sackcloth;
13 but instead there was joy and
festivity,
killing oxen and slaughtering sheep,
eating meat and drinking wine.
"Let us eat and drink,
for tomorrow we die."
14 The LORD of hosts has revealed
himself in my ears:
Surely this iniquity will not be
forgiven you until you die,
says the Lord GOD of hosts.

15 Thus says the Lord GOD of hosts:
Come, go to this steward, to Shebna, who
is master of the household, and say to him:
16 What right do you have here? Who are
your relatives here, that you have cut out a
tomb here for yourself, cutting a tomb on
the height, and carving a habitation for
yourself in the rock? 17 The LORD is about
to hurl you away violently, my fellow. He
will seize firm hold on you, 18 whirl you
round and round, and throw you like a ball
into a wide land; there you shall die, and
there your splendid chariots shall lie,
O you disgrace to your master's house! 19 I
will thrust you from your office, and you
will be pulled down from your post.
20 On that day I will call my servant
Eliakim son of Hilkiah, 21 and will clothe
him with your robe and bind your sash on
him. I will commit your authority to his
hand, and he shall be a father to the inhabi-
tants of Jerusalem and to the house of Ju-
dah. 22 I will place on his shoulder the key
of the house of David; he shall open, and
no one shall shut; he shall shut, and no one
shall open. 23 I will fasten him like a peg in
a secure place, and he will become a throne
of honor to his ancestral house. 24 And they
will hang on him the whole weight of his
ancestral house, the offspring and issue, ev-
ery small vessel, from the cups to all the
flagons. 25 On that day, says the LORD of
hosts, the peg that was fastened in a secure
place will give way; it will be cut down and
fall, and the load that was on it will perish,
for the LORD has spoken.

23 The oracle concerning Tyre.

Wail, O ships of Tarshish,
for your fortress is destroyed.[a]
When they came in from Cyprus
they learned of it.
2 Be still, O inhabitants of the coast,
O merchants of Sidon,
your messengers crossed over
the sea[b]
3 and were on the mighty waters;
your revenue was the grain of Shihor,
the harvest of the Nile;
you were the merchant of the
nations.
4 Be ashamed, O Sidon, for the sea has
spoken,

a Cn Compare verse 14: Heb *for it is destroyed, without houses* *b* Q Ms: MT *crossing over the sea, they replenished you*

22.15–25: Shebna and Eliakim. Shebna, majordomo of the palace (for the title see 1 Kings 4.6; 16.9; 18.3), is condemned for building a splendid tomb for himself, possibly the rock-hewn tomb excavated in the village of Silwan near Jerusalem bearing the inscription, "This [the tomb of Sheban] yahu who is over the house." **20–23:** Eliakim is invested with the office in place of Shebna; 36.3 and 2 Kings 18.18 suggest that Eliakim replaced Shebna before 701. **24–25:** Eliakim's nepotism will lead to his downfall.

23.1–18: The last of the oracles deals with the fate of the Phoenician coastal cities, especially Tyre. It begins with the Assyrian campaigns (705–701, 678, 671 BCE) but also reflects later events, e.g., the siege of Tyre by Nebuchadnezzar II (585–573; see Ezek 26–28) and Alexander (332). **1:** *Ships of Tarshish,* see 2.16n. **3:** *Shihor,* Lower Egypt. **9:** The disaster inflicted on Tyre falls within the agenda or plan of Israel's

the fortress of the sea, saying:
"I have neither labored nor given
birth,
I have neither reared young men
nor brought up young women."
5 When the report comes to Egypt,
they will be in anguish over the
report about Tyre.
6 Cross over to Tarshish—
wail, O inhabitants of the coast!
7 Is this your exultant city
whose origin is from days of old,
whose feet carried her
to settle far away?
8 Who has planned this
against Tyre, the bestower
of crowns,
whose merchants were princes,
whose traders were the honored of
the earth?
9 The LORD of hosts has planned it—
to defile the pride of all glory,
to shame all the honored of the
earth.
10 Cross over to your own land,
O ships of[a] Tarshish;
this is a harbor[b] no more.
11 He has stretched out his hand over
the sea,
he has shaken the kingdoms;
the LORD has given command
concerning Canaan
to destroy its fortresses.
12 He said:
You will exult no longer,
O oppressed virgin daughter Sidon;
rise, cross over to Cyprus—
even there you will have no rest.

13 Look at the land of the Chaldeans!
This is the people; it was not Assyria. They
destined Tyre for wild animals. They erect-
ed their siege towers, they tore down her
palaces, they made her a ruin.[c]
14 Wail, O ships of Tarshish,
for your fortress is destroyed.
15 From that day Tyre will be forgotten for
seventy years, the lifetime of one king. At
the end of seventy years, it will happen to
Tyre as in the song about the prostitute:
16 Take a harp,
go about the city,
you forgotten prostitute!
Make sweet melody,
sing many songs,
that you may be remembered.
17 At the end of seventy years, the LORD
will visit Tyre, and she will return to her
trade, and will prostitute herself with all
the kingdoms of the world on the face of
the earth. 18 Her merchandise and her
wages will be dedicated to the LORD; her
profits[d] will not be stored or hoarded, but
her merchandise will supply abundant food
and fine clothing for those who live in the
presence of the LORD.

24 Now the LORD is about to lay
waste the earth and make
it desolate,
and he will twist its surface and
scatter its inhabitants.
2 And it shall be, as with the people, so
with the priest;
as with the slave, so with his
master;
as with the maid, so with her
mistress;
as with the buyer, so with the seller;

a Cn Compare Gk: Heb *like the Nile, daughter*
b Cn: Heb *restraint* *c* Meaning of Heb uncertain
d Heb *it*

God; cf. 14.24,26–27; 19.12,17; 22.11. **13:** *Chaldeans,* Babylonians. The Hebrew of the verse is obscure textually, perhaps referring to Nebuchadnezzar's siege of Tyre. **15:** *Seventy years,* a period of tribulation; cf. Jer 25.11–12. **16:** The prostitute's song. From the author's point of view, trade and prostitution are closely connected; see v.17. **17–18:** A later prophetic mitigation of the judgment on Tyre.

Chs 24–27: Judgment on enemies. This loose collection of passages, many beginning "on that day," some in psalm form (25.1–5; 26.7–19), presents a picture of general doom. These chapters are sometimes called the "Isaiah apocalypse" because of the frequent use of eschatological motifs.

24.1–13: Impending judgment on the earth. 2: All social distinctions disappear; cf. Hos 4.9. **4–6:** There

as with the lender, so with the
borrower;
as with the creditor, so with
the debtor.
3 The earth shall be utterly laid waste
and utterly despoiled;
for the LORD has spoken this word.

4 The earth dries up and withers,
the world languishes and withers;
the heavens languish together with
the earth.
5 The earth lies polluted
under its inhabitants;
for they have transgressed laws,
violated the statutes,
broken the everlasting covenant.
6 Therefore a curse devours the earth,
and its inhabitants suffer for their
guilt;
therefore the inhabitants of the earth
dwindled,
and few people are left.
7 The wine dries up,
the vine languishes,
all the merry-hearted sigh.
8 The mirth of the timbrels is stilled,
the noise of the jubilant has ceased,
the mirth of the lyre is stilled.
9 No longer do they drink wine with
singing;
strong drink is bitter to those who
drink it.
10 The city of chaos is broken down,
every house is shut up so that no
one can enter.
11 There is an outcry in the streets for
lack of wine;
all joy has reached its eventide;
the gladness of the earth is
banished.
12 Desolation is left in the city,
the gates are battered into ruins.
13 For thus it shall be on the earth
and among the nations,
as when an olive tree is beaten,
as at the gleaning when the grape
harvest is ended.

14 They lift up their voices, they sing for
joy;
they shout from the west over the
majesty of the LORD.
15 Therefore in the east give glory to the
LORD;
in the coastlands of the sea glorify
the name of the LORD, the
God of Israel.
16 From the ends of the earth we hear
songs of praise,
of glory to the Righteous One.
But I say, I pine away,
I pine away. Woe is me!
For the treacherous deal
treacherously,
the treacherous deal very
treacherously.

17 Terror, and the pit, and the snare
are upon you, O inhabitant of the
earth!
18 Whoever flees at the sound of
the terror
shall fall into the pit;
and whoever climbs out of the pit
shall be caught in the snare.
For the windows of heaven are
opened,
and the foundations of the earth
tremble.
19 The earth is utterly broken,
the earth is torn asunder,

is a connection between social morality and the condition of the physical environment. **5:** *Everlasting covenant,* made by God with the damaged world after the deluge, forbidding bloodshed which pollutes the earth (Gen 9.1–17). **10–13:** *The city of chaos* becomes a ghost town. The city is not identified. It is probably a composite based on the cities mentioned in chs 13–23, or a symbolic Babylon contrasted with Jerusalem, the "city of God," 26.1–2. **13:** *Olive tree . . . beaten,* see 17.6.

24.14–23: Joy and condemnation. An abrupt transition to a joyful liturgy in which the western and eastern Diasporas join; cf. 59.15b–20. **15:** *Coastlands of the sea,* i.e., the west. **16:** *I pine away* or "I have my secret": The seer has a revelation that contradicts the current euphoria. **17–18:** Windows of heaven, see Gen 7.11. Cf. Jer 48.43–44; Am 5.18–19. **21–23:** *The host of heaven,* rebellious astral deities destined

the earth is violently shaken.
20 The earth staggers like a drunkard,
it sways like a hut;
its transgression lies heavy upon it,
and it falls, and will not rise again.

21 On that day the LORD will punish
the host of heaven in heaven,
and on earth the kings of the earth.
22 They will be gathered together
like prisoners in a pit;
they will be shut up in a prison,
and after many days they will be
punished.
23 Then the moon will be abashed,
and the sun ashamed;
for the LORD of hosts will reign
on Mount Zion and in Jerusalem,
and before his elders he will manifest
his glory.

25 O LORD, you are my God;
I will exalt you, I will praise your
name;
for you have done wonderful things,
plans formed of old, faithful
and sure.
2 For you have made the city a heap,
the fortified city a ruin;
the palace of aliens is a city no more,
it will never be rebuilt.
3 Therefore strong peoples will glorify
you;
cities of ruthless nations will
fear you.
4 For you have been a refuge to
the poor,
a refuge to the needy in their
distress,
a shelter from the rainstorm and a
shade from the heat.
When the blast of the ruthless was
like a winter rainstorm,
5 the noise of aliens like heat in a dry
place,
you subdued the heat with the shade
of clouds;
the song of the ruthless was
stilled.

6 On this mountain the LORD of hosts
will make for all peoples
a feast of rich food, a feast of
well-aged wines,
of rich food filled with marrow, of
well-aged wines strained clear.
7 And he will destroy on this mountain
the shroud that is cast over all
peoples,
the sheet that is spread over all
nations;
8 he will swallow up death forever.
Then the Lord GOD will wipe away
the tears from all faces,
and the disgrace of his people he
will take away from all
the earth,
for the LORD has spoken.
9 It will be said on that day,
Lo, this is our God; we have waited
for him, so that he might save
us.
This is the LORD for whom we
have waited;

to be overthrown and bound in the Pit; 14.12–14; cf. 1 Enoch 18.11–19; Jude 13; 2 Pet 2.4; Rev 9.2,11. **23b**: Cf. Ex 24.9–11.

25.1–5: The first of three psalms of praise (with 25.9–12; 26.1–6), cf. Ps 31.15; 86.2; 118.28. In God's wise plan (cf. 9.5; 10.5–19; 14.24–27) the (unnamed) city, symbol of oppression, has been destroyed and the poor and needy vindicated.

25.6–10a: The banquet. The description of the eschatological banquet is closely linked with 24.21–23, referring to the banquet on Mount Sinai (Ex 24.11). The motif of the eschatological (or messianic) banquet is frequent in early Jewish (e.g., the Rule of the Community at Qumran; 1 Enoch 60.24) and in early Christian (Mt 8.11–12; 22.1–14) literatures. **7:** *Shroud, sheet,* garments worn in time of mourning. **8:** *He will swallow up death,* reversing the mythic image of death swallowing up everything; cf. 1 Cor 15.54–55. *The LORD God will wipe away the tears,* cf. Rev 7.17; 21.4. **9–10a:** A second, brief psalm of praise celebrating the day on which the hope and trust placed in God will be vindicated. For this basic attitude, see 30.18. *This mountain,* Zion.

let us be glad and rejoice in his
salvation.
10 For the hand of the LORD will rest on
this mountain.

The Moabites shall be trodden down
in their place
as straw is trodden down in a
dung-pit.
11 Though they spread out their hands
in the midst of it,
as swimmers spread out their hands
to swim,
their pride will be laid low despite
the struggle[a] of their hands.
12 The high fortifications of his walls
will be brought down,
laid low, cast to the ground, even
to the dust.

26 On that day this song will be sung in the land of Judah:
We have a strong city;
he sets up victory
like walls and bulwarks.
2 Open the gates,
so that the righteous nation that
keeps faith
may enter in.
3 Those of steadfast mind you keep
in peace—
in peace because they trust in you.
4 Trust in the LORD forever,
for in the LORD GOD[b]
you have an everlasting rock.
5 For he has brought low
the inhabitants of the height;
the lofty city he lays low.
He lays it low to the ground,
casts it to the dust.
6 The foot tramples it,
the feet of the poor,
the steps of the needy.

7 The way of the righteous is level;
O Just One, you make smooth the
path of the righteous.
8 In the path of your judgments,
O LORD, we wait for you;
your name and your renown
are the soul's desire.
9 My soul yearns for you in the night,
my spirit within me earnestly seeks
you.
For when your judgments are in the
earth,
the inhabitants of the world learn
righteousness.
10 If favor is shown to the wicked,
they do not learn righteousness;
in the land of uprightness they deal
perversely
and do not see the majesty of
the LORD.
11 O LORD, your hand is lifted up,
but they do not see it.
Let them see your zeal for your
people, and be ashamed.
Let the fire for your adversaries
consume them.
12 O LORD, you will ordain peace
for us,
for indeed, all that we have done,
you have done for us.
13 O LORD our God,
other lords besides you have ruled
over us,
but we acknowledge your
name alone.

a Meaning of Heb uncertain *b* Heb *in Yah, the LORD*

25.10b–12: Doom of Moab. Moab, or its capital Dibon, represented as a man being deliberately drowned in a cesspool. Perhaps intended as explanatory of the unnamed city of 25.2.

26.1–6: A psalm in praise of Zion (cf. Ps 48; 76; 84; 87; 122) in contrast to the alien city now destroyed (24.10–13; 25.2), which will be trampled by the poor and needy. *Open the gates,* an element of processional psalms, e.g., 24.7–10; 100.4; 118.19–20.

26.7–27.1: An apocalyptic psalm with attached commentary. The psalm is in the form of a lament introduced by expressions of confidence in God the *Just One* and God's approval of the righteous. **12–15:** The lament proper, on account of foreign domination, with a brief glance at the national history. **14:** *The*

14 The dead do not live;
shades do not rise—
because you have punished and
destroyed them,
and wiped out all memory of them.
15 But you have increased the nation,
O LORD,
you have increased the nation; you
are glorified;
you have enlarged all the borders of
the land.

16 O LORD, in distress they sought you,
they poured out a prayer[a]
when your chastening was on them.
17 Like a woman with child,
who writhes and cries out in
her pangs
when she is near her time,
so were we because of you, O LORD;
18 we were with child, we writhed,
but we gave birth only to wind.
We have won no victories on earth,
and no one is born to inhabit
the world.
19 Your dead shall live, their corpses[b]
shall rise.
O dwellers in the dust, awake and
sing for joy!
For your dew is a radiant dew,
and the earth will give birth to
those long dead.[c]

20 Come, my people, enter your
chambers,
and shut your doors behind you;
hide yourselves for a little while
until the wrath is past.
21 For the LORD comes out from
his place
to punish the inhabitants of the
earth for their iniquity;
the earth will disclose the blood shed
on it,
and will no longer cover its slain.

27 On that day the LORD with his cruel
and great and strong sword will
punish Leviathan the fleeing serpent, Levia-
than the twisting serpent, and he will kill
the dragon that is in the sea.

2 On that day:
A pleasant vineyard, sing about it!
3 I, the LORD, am its keeper;
every moment I water it.
I guard it night and day
so that no one can harm it;
4 I have no wrath.
If it gives me thorns and briers,
I will march to battle against it.
I will burn it up.
5 Or else let it cling to me for
protection,
let it make peace with me,
let it make peace with me.

6 In days to come[d] Jacob shall
take root,
Israel shall blossom and put
forth shoots,
and fill the whole world with fruit.

7 Has he struck them down as he
struck down those who struck
them?

a Meaning of Heb uncertain *b* Cn Compare Syr Tg: Heb *my corpse* *c* Heb *to the shades* *d* Heb *Those to come*

dead do not live, a common theme in the psalms; only the living can praise God (Ps 6.5; 30.9; 49.10–20); see 39.18–19. **15:** Cf. 9.3. **19:** *Your dead shall live,* the response to v. 14, expressing an intuition of a meaningful survival of death; cf. Ezek 37.1–14; Dan 12.2. **20–21:** An injunction to take cover in view of the coming judgment; the devout must wait a little longer for salvation, cf. 2.10,19,21. **27.1:** The coming judgment is restated in mythic terms. *Leviathan,* a monstrous sea creature representing chaos, is described with the same two epithets in the Ugaritic poems; see Job 3.8; 41.4; Ps 74.13–14. *The dragon* (Heb "tannin"), either a distinct embodiment of chaos or another term for Leviathan.

27.2–6: The vineyard, Israel, will be restored (cf. 5.1–7). A good example of exegetical development in the book. **4:** *Thorns and briers,* see 5.24; 7.23–24; 9.18; 10.17; 32.12–13. **6:** Cf. Hos 14.5–7.

27.7–13: Idolatry denounced. Israel will be released from guilt when articles of false worship are

Or have they been killed as their
killers were killed?
8 By expulsion,[a] by exile you struggled
against them;
with his fierce blast he removed
them in the day of the
east wind.
9 Therefore by this the guilt of Jacob
will be expiated,
and this will be the full fruit of the
removal of his sin:
when he makes all the stones of the
altars
like chalkstones crushed to pieces,
no sacred poles[b] or incense altars
will remain standing.
10 For the fortified city is solitary,
a habitation deserted and forsaken,
like the wilderness;
the calves graze there,
there they lie down, and strip its
branches.
11 When its boughs are dry, they
are broken;
women come and make a fire
of them.
For this is a people without
understanding;
therefore he that made them will
not have compassion on them,
he that formed them will show
them no favor.

12 On that day the LORD will thresh
from the channel of the Euphrates to the
Wadi of Egypt, and you will be gathered
one by one, O people of Israel. 13 And on
that day a great trumpet will be blown, and
those who were lost in the land of Assyria
and those who were driven out to the land
of Egypt will come and worship the LORD
on the holy mountain at Jerusalem.

28 Ah, the proud garland of the
drunkards of Ephraim,
and the fading flower of its glorious
beauty,
which is on the head of those
bloated with rich food, of
those overcome with wine!
2 See, the Lord has one who is mighty
and strong;
like a storm of hail, a destroying
tempest,
like a storm of mighty, overflowing
waters;
with his hand he will hurl them
down to the earth.
3 Trampled under foot will be
the proud garland of the drunkards
of Ephraim.
4 And the fading flower of its glorious
beauty,
which is on the head of those
bloated with rich food,
will be like a first-ripe fig before the
summer;
whoever sees it, eats it up
as soon as it comes to hand.

5 In that day the LORD of hosts will be
a garland of glory,
and a diadem of beauty, to the
remnant of his people;
6 and a spirit of justice to the one who
sits in judgment,
and strength to those who turn
back the battle at the gate.

a Meaning of Heb uncertain *b* Heb *Asherim*

removed; cf. 17.7–8. **10:** *The fortified city,* referring to the unnamed city of 24.10; 25.2; 26.5. It will go back to nature, cf. 5.17; 7.24–25; 13.20–22; 17.2; 32.14. **12–13:** An appendix, anticipating the ingathering of dispersed Israelites from the Euphrates to the River of Egypt (Wadi el-Arish).

Chs 28–33: Judgment on Israel and Judah. These chapters return to the situation envisaged by 1–12, implying that the prophetic view of Israel's relations with Assyria provides the key to understanding the future.

28.1–29: Oracles against Israel (Ephraim) and Judah. An oracle against the Northern Kingdom (vv. 1–4) introduces a longer one against Judah (vv. 7–29). **1–4:** The Northern Kingdom (Ephraim) will be overwhelmed by the floodwaters of the Assyrian invasion, cf. 8.7–8. For the drunkenness theme prominent here, see 5.11–13; Am 6.4–7. **5–6:** The survival of the remnant. **7–8:** See 5.11n. **9–10:** The

7 These also reel with wine
and stagger with strong drink;
the priest and the prophet reel with strong drink,
they are confused with wine,
they stagger with strong drink;
they err in vision,
they stumble in giving judgment.
8 All tables are covered with filthy vomit;
no place is clean.

9 "Whom will he teach knowledge,
and to whom will he explain the message?
Those who are weaned from milk,
those taken from the breast?
10 For it is precept upon precept, precept upon precept,
line upon line, line upon line,
here a little, there a little."[a]

11 Truly, with stammering lip
and with alien tongue
he will speak to this people,
12 to whom he has said,
"This is rest;
give rest to the weary;
and this is repose";
yet they would not hear.
13 Therefore the word of the LORD will be to them,
"Precept upon precept, precept upon precept,
line upon line, line upon line,
here a little, there a little;"[a]
in order that they may go, and fall backward,
and be broken, and snared, and taken.

14 Therefore hear the word of the LORD, you scoffers
who rule this people in Jerusalem.
15 Because you have said, "We have made a covenant with death,
and with Sheol we have an agreement;
when the overwhelming scourge passes through
it will not come to us;
for we have made lies our refuge,
and in falsehood we have taken shelter";
16 therefore thus says the Lord GOD,
See, I am laying in Zion a foundation stone,
a tested stone,
a precious cornerstone, a sure foundation:
"One who trusts will not panic."
17 And I will make justice the line,
and righteousness the plummet;
hail will sweep away the refuge of lies,
and waters will overwhelm the shelter.
18 Then your covenant with death will be annulled,
and your agreement with Sheol will not stand;
when the overwhelming scourge passes through
you will be beaten down by it.
19 As often as it passes through, it will take you;
for morning by morning it will pass through,
by day and by night;
and it will be sheer terror to understand the message.
20 For the bed is too short to stretch oneself on it,
and the covering too narrow to wrap oneself in it.
21 For the LORD will rise up as on Mount Perazim,

a Meaning of Heb of this verse uncertain

opposition takes the prophet to task for offering simplistic solutions. The Hebrew behind *precept* and *line* is a kind of singsong mocking the prophet's preaching. **11–13:** The reply: God will speak to them in the harsh and unintelligible language of the Assyrians; see Jer 5.15. **14–15:** The *covenant with death* may refer to an Egyptian alliance in addition to necromantic practices. The situation is the revolt against Assyria in 705–701. *Sheol,* the underworld. **16–22:** The *covenant with death* will be canceled. **21:** As the

he will rage as in the valley of
Gibeon
to do his deed—strange is his deed!—
and to work his work—alien is his
work!
22 Now therefore do not scoff,
or your bonds will be made
stronger;
for I have heard a decree of
destruction
from the Lord GOD of hosts upon
the whole land.

23 Listen, and hear my voice;
Pay attention, and hear my speech.
24 Do those who plow for sowing plow
continually?
Do they continually open and
harrow their ground?
25 When they have leveled its surface,
do they not scatter dill, sow
cummin,
and plant wheat in rows
and barley in its proper place,
and spelt as the border?
26 For they are well instructed;
their God teaches them.

27 Dill is not threshed with a threshing
sledge,
nor is a cart wheel rolled over
cummin;
but dill is beaten out with a stick,
and cummin with a rod.
28 Grain is crushed for bread,
but one does not thresh it forever;
one drives the cart wheel and horses
over it,
but does not pulverize it.
29 This also comes from the LORD
of hosts;
he is wonderful in counsel,
and excellent in wisdom.

29 Ah, Ariel, Ariel,
the city where David encamped!
Add year to year;
let the festivals run their round.
2 Yet I will distress Ariel,
and there shall be moaning and
lamentation,
and Jerusalem[a] shall be to me like
an Ariel.[b]
3 And like David[c] I will encamp
against you;
I will besiege you with towers
and raise siegeworks against you.
4 Then deep from the earth you
shall speak,
from low in the dust your words
shall come;
your voice shall come from the
ground like the voice of
a ghost,
and your speech shall whisper out
of the dust.

5 But the multitude of your foes[d] shall
be like small dust,
and the multitude of tyrants like
flying chaff.
And in an instant, suddenly,
6 you will be visited by the LORD
of hosts
with thunder and earthquake and
great noise,
with whirlwind and tempest, and
the flame of a devouring fire.
7 And the multitude of all the nations
that fight against Ariel,
all that fight against her and her
stronghold, and who
distress her,

a Heb *she* *b* Probable meaning, *altar hearth*; compare Ezek 43.15 *c* Gk: Meaning of Heb uncertain *d* Cn: Heb *strangers*

God of Israel once fought on *Mount Perazim* (2 Sam 5.17–21) and at *Gibeon* (Josh 10.10) for Israel, now he will fight against it; hence the strange character of his work. **25–29:** The parable of the good farmer. A defense of the mysterious work of God, who knows when and how to administer punishment.

29.1–8: Siege of Jerusalem. God will allow Jerusalem to be besieged as David once besieged it (2 Sam 5.6–9). The experience will be like a descent into the underworld (cf. 5.14–15; 8.19), but there will be a sudden deliverance—as happened when Sennacherib withdrew from Jerusalem in 701. **1:** *Ariel,* variously explained; perhaps an altar-hearth (Ezek 43.15), alluding to Jerusalem. **6:** Cf. 30.30.

shall be like a dream, a vision
of the night.
8 Just as when a hungry person dreams
of eating
and wakes up still hungry,
or a thirsty person dreams of drinking
and wakes up faint, still thirsty,
so shall the multitude of all the
nations be
that fight against Mount Zion.

9 Stupefy yourselves and be in a stupor,
blind yourselves and be blind!
Be drunk, but not from wine;
stagger, but not from strong drink!
10 For the LORD has poured out
upon you
a spirit of deep sleep;
he has closed your eyes, you prophets,
and covered your heads, you seers.
11 The vision of all this has become for
you like the words of a sealed document. If
it is given to those who can read, with the
command, "Read this," they say, "We can-
not, for it is sealed." 12 And if it is given
to those who cannot read, saying, "Read
this," they say, "We cannot read."

13 The Lord said:
Because these people draw near with
their mouths
and honor me with their lips,
while their hearts are far from
me,
and their worship of me is a human
commandment learned by rote;
14 so I will again do
amazing things with this people,
shocking and amazing.
The wisdom of their wise shall perish,
and the discernment of the
discerning shall be hidden.

15 Ha! You who hide a plan too deep
for the LORD,
whose deeds are in the dark,
and who say, "Who sees us? Who
knows us?"
16 You turn things upside down!
Shall the potter be regarded as the
clay?
Shall the thing made say of its maker,
"He did not make me";
or the thing formed say of the one
who formed it,
"He has no understanding"?

17 Shall not Lebanon in a very little
while
become a fruitful field,
and the fruitful field be regarded as
a forest?
18 On that day the deaf shall hear
the words of a scroll,
and out of their gloom and darkness
the eyes of the blind shall see.
19 The meek shall obtain fresh joy in the
LORD,
and the neediest people shall exult
in the Holy One of Israel.
20 For the tyrant shall be no more,
and the scoffer shall cease to be;
all those alert to do evil shall be cut
off—
21 those who cause a person to lose a
lawsuit,
who set a trap for the arbiter in the
gate,
and without grounds deny justice to
the one in the right.

22 Therefore thus says the LORD, who
redeemed Abraham, concerning the house
of Jacob:
No longer shall Jacob be ashamed,

29.9–16: Failure of the warning. Blindness, which also affects prophets, is a common metaphor for religious insensitivity in Isaiah; cf. 6.9–10. **11–12:** A later comment applying the idea of literacy to the reception or nonreception of the prophet's message in written form. **13–14:** Against conventional worship carried out without conviction; cf. 1.10–17. **15–16:** Against the professional purveyors of wisdom, especially in the political sphere. For the image of potter and clay, see 45.9; Jer 18.1–6.

29.17–24: A later assurance of a hopeful future. 22: *Abraham,* cf. 41.8; 51.2. Abraham, redeemed by God's call to journey into the promised land, becomes the model for those who returned to Judah in the post-disaster period.

no longer shall his face grow pale.
23 For when he sees his children,
the work of my hands, in his midst,
they will sanctify my name;
they will sanctify the Holy One of Jacob,
and will stand in awe of the God of Israel.
24 And those who err in spirit will come to understanding,
and those who grumble will accept instruction.

30 Oh, rebellious children, says the LORD,
who carry out a plan, but not mine;
who make an alliance, but against my will,
adding sin to sin;
2 who set out to go down to Egypt
without asking for my counsel,
to take refuge in the protection of Pharaoh,
and to seek shelter in the shadow of Egypt;
3 Therefore the protection of Pharaoh
shall become your shame,
and the shelter in the shadow of Egypt your humiliation.
4 For though his officials are at Zoan
and his envoys reach Hanes,
5 everyone comes to shame
through a people that cannot profit them,
that brings neither help nor profit,
but shame and disgrace.

6 An oracle concerning the animals of the Negeb.
Through a land of trouble and distress,
of lioness and roaring[a] lion,
of viper and flying serpent,
they carry their riches on the backs of donkeys,
and their treasures on the humps of camels,
to a people that cannot profit them.
7 For Egypt's help is worthless and empty,
therefore I have called her,
"Rahab who sits still."[b]

8 Go now, write it before them on a tablet,
and inscribe it in a book,
so that it may be for the time to come
as a witness forever.
9 For they are a rebellious people,
faithless children,
children who will not hear
the instruction of the LORD;
10 who say to the seers, "Do not see";
and to the prophets, "Do not prophesy to us what is right;
speak to us smooth things,
prophesy illusions,
11 leave the way, turn aside from the path,
let us hear no more about the Holy One of Israel."
12 Therefore thus says the Holy One of Israel:
Because you reject this word,
and put your trust in oppression and deceit,
and rely on them;
13 therefore this iniquity shall become for you
like a break in a high wall, bulging out, and about to collapse,

a Cn: Heb *from them* *b* Meaning of Heb uncertain

30.1–7: Negotiations with Egypt are condemned (703–701). **1:** *Rebellious children,* cf. 1.2,4 and 30.9. **4:** *Zoan,* see 19.11n.; *Hanes,* in Upper Egypt. The Nubian dynasty held court in both Lower (Zoan) and Upper Egypt (Napata). **6–7:** Judean envoys toil through the dangerous *Negeb* and Sinai on their way to Egypt; a satirical contrast between the difficulty of the journey and its futility. **7:** *Rahab who sits still,* a mythological sea monster occasionally used as a nickname for Egypt (51.9–10; Ps 89.9; Job 9.13).

30.8–17: The record of rejection. The prophet is told to record his sayings against their fulfillment, a reaction to nonacceptance of the oral message; cf. 8.16–18 and Jer 36.1–8. **17:** *A thousand shall flee,* see Lev 26.36–37; Deut 32.30.

whose crash comes suddenly, in an
instant;
14 its breaking is like that of a potter's
vessel
that is smashed so ruthlessly
that among its fragments not a sherd
is found
for taking fire from the hearth,
or dipping water out of the cistern.

15 For thus said the Lord GOD, the Holy
One of Israel:
In returning and rest you shall
be saved;
in quietness and in trust shall be
your strength.
But you refused 16 and said,
"No! We will flee upon horses"—
therefore you shall flee!
and, "We will ride upon swift
steeds"—
therefore your pursuers shall be
swift!
17 A thousand shall flee at the threat of
one,
at the threat of five you shall flee,
until you are left
like a flagstaff on the top of
a mountain,
like a signal on a hill.

18 Therefore the LORD waits to be
gracious to you;
therefore he will rise up to show
mercy to you.
For the LORD is a God of justice;
blessed are all those who wait for
him.

19 Truly, O people in Zion, inhabitants
of Jerusalem, you shall weep no more. He
will surely be gracious to you at the sound
of your cry; when he hears it, he will an-
swer you. 20 Though the Lord may give you
the bread of adversity and the water of af-
fliction, yet your Teacher will not hide him-
self any more, but your eyes shall see your
Teacher. 21 And when you turn to the right
or when you turn to the left, your ears shall
hear a word behind you, saying, "This is
the way; walk in it." 22 Then you will defile
your silver-covered idols and your gold-
plated images. You will scatter them like
filthy rags; you will say to them, "Away
with you!"

23 He will give rain for the seed with
which you sow the ground, and grain, the
produce of the ground, which will be rich
and plenteous. On that day your cattle will
graze in broad pastures; 24 and the oxen
and donkeys that till the ground will eat
silage, which has been winnowed with
shovel and fork. 25 On every lofty mountain
and every high hill there will be brooks run-
ning with water—on a day of the great
slaughter, when the towers fall. 26 More-
over the light of the moon will be like the
light of the sun, and the light of the sun will
be sevenfold, like the light of seven days, on
the day when the LORD binds up the inju-
ries of his people, and heals the wounds
inflicted by his blow.

27 See, the name of the LORD comes
from far away,
burning with his anger, and in thick
rising smoke;[a]
his lips are full of indignation,
and his tongue is like a devouring
fire;
28 his breath is like an overflowing
stream
that reaches up to the neck—

a Meaning of Heb uncertain

30.18–26: An oracle of promise followed by two prose comments. 18: Waiting on the God who waits is a recurrent theme in Isaiah. **19–22:** The consolation of Zion. **20:** The *Teacher,* either God who hides his face (cf. 8.17) or a prophetic teacher whose message guides his followers. **23–26:** Abundant fertility will characterize the transformed land and cosmos.

30.27–33: The destruction of Assyria. For judgment under the image of fire, see 10.16–17; 33.10–14. **28:** Cf. 8.8. **33:** *Burning place,* a "tophet" where children were sacrificed in the fire (2 Kings 23.10; Jer 7.31; 19.4–9). *For the king,* i.e., Molech (see Lev 18.21).

to sift the nations with the sieve of
destruction,
and to place on the jaws of the
peoples a bridle that leads
them astray.

29 You shall have a song as in the night
when a holy festival is kept; and gladness of
heart, as when one sets out to the sound
of the flute to go to the mountain of the
LORD, to the Rock of Israel. 30 And the
LORD will cause his majestic voice to be
heard and the descending blow of his arm
to be seen, in furious anger and a flame of
devouring fire, with a cloudburst and tem-
pest and hailstones. 31 The Assyrian will be
terror-stricken at the voice of the LORD,
when he strikes with his rod. 32 And every
stroke of the staff of punishment that the
LORD lays upon him will be to the sound of
timbrels and lyres; battling with brandished
arm he will fight with him. 33 For his burn-
ing place[a] has long been prepared; truly it
is made ready for the king,[b] its pyre made
deep and wide, with fire and wood in abun-
dance; the breath of the LORD, like a
stream of sulfur, kindles it.

31 Alas for those who go down to
Egypt for help
and who rely on horses,
who trust in chariots because they are
many
and in horsemen because they are
very strong,
but do not look to the Holy One
of Israel
or consult the LORD!
2 Yet he too is wise and brings disaster;
he does not call back his words,
but will rise against the house of the
evildoers,
and against the helpers of those
who work iniquity.
3 The Egyptians are human, and
not God;
their horses are flesh, and not spirit.
When the LORD stretches out
his hand,
the helper will stumble, and the one
helped will fall,
and they will all perish together.

4 For thus the LORD said to me,
As a lion or a young lion growls over
its prey,
and—when a band of shepherds is
called out against it—
is not terrified by their shouting
or daunted at their noise,
so the LORD of hosts will come down
to fight upon Mount Zion and
upon its hill.
5 Like birds hovering overhead, so the
LORD of hosts
will protect Jerusalem;
he will protect and deliver it,
he will spare and rescue it.

6 Turn back to him whom you[c] have
deeply betrayed, O people of Israel. 7 For
on that day all of you shall throw away
your idols of silver and idols of gold, which
your hands have sinfully made for you.
8 "Then the Assyrian shall fall by a
sword, not of mortals;
and a sword, not of humans, shall
devour him;
he shall flee from the sword,
and his young men shall be put to
forced labor.
9 His rock shall pass away in terror,
and his officers desert the standard
in panic,"
says the LORD, whose fire is in Zion,
and whose furnace is in Jerusalem.

a Or *Topheth* *b* Or *Molech* *c* Heb *they*

31.1–3: Another denunciation of the Egyptian alliance, from the same period as 30.1–7. **1:** Cf. Ps 20.7. **2:** *Yet he too is wise and brings disaster,* cf. the strange and alien work of God, 28.29.

31.4–9: God's deliverance of Jerusalem from Assyria. 4–5: God will protect Jerusalem as a lion protects its prey and a bird its young. **6–7:** A prose addition; cf. 2.20. **8–9:** The complete and final annihilation of Assyria; the last time the name occurs in chs 1–35. *Fire, furnace,* a reference to the temple altar.

32 See, a king will reign in
righteousness,
and princes will rule with justice.
2 Each will be like a hiding place from
the wind,
a covert from the tempest,
like streams of water in a dry place,
like the shade of a great rock in a
weary land.
3 Then the eyes of those who have sight
will not be closed,
and the ears of those who have
hearing will listen.
4 The minds of the rash will have good
judgment,
and the tongues of stammerers will
speak readily and distinctly.
5 A fool will no longer be called noble,
nor a villain said to be honorable.
6 For fools speak folly,
and their minds plot iniquity:
to practice ungodliness,
to utter error concerning the LORD,
to leave the craving of the hungry
unsatisfied,
and to deprive the thirsty of drink.
7 The villainies of villains are evil;
they devise wicked devices
to ruin the poor with lying words,
even when the plea of the needy is
right.
8 But those who are noble plan noble
things,
and by noble things they stand.

9 Rise up, you women who are at ease,
hear my voice;
you complacent daughters, listen to
my speech.
10 In little more than a year
you will shudder, you complacent
ones;
for the vintage will fail,
the fruit harvest will not come.
11 Tremble, you women who are at ease,
shudder, you complacent ones;
strip, and make yourselves bare,
and put sackcloth on your loins.
12 Beat your breasts for the pleasant
fields,
for the fruitful vine,
13 for the soil of my people
growing up in thorns and briers;
yes, for all the joyous houses
in the jubilant city.
14 For the palace will be forsaken,
the populous city deserted;
the hill and the watchtower
will become dens forever,
the joy of wild asses,
a pasture for flocks;
15 until a spirit from on high is poured
out on us,
and the wilderness becomes a
fruitful field,
and the fruitful field is deemed
a forest.
16 Then justice will dwell in the
wilderness,
and righteousness abide in the
fruitful field.
17 The effect of righteousness will
be peace,
and the result of righteousness,
quietness and trust forever.
18 My people will abide in a peaceful
habitation,
in secure dwellings, and in quiet
resting places.
19 The forest will disappear
completely,[a]
and the city will be utterly laid low.

a Cn: Heb *And it will hail when the forest comes down*

32.1–8: The ideal commonwealth of the future under a Davidic ruler is a major theme of chs 32–33 (32.1; 33.17). **2–8:** The present unsatisfactory situation will be reversed: The weak will be protected (v. 2), people will be responsive to prophecy and no longer blind and deaf (vv. 3–4; cf. 6.9–10; 30.9–10), and fools and villains will be recognized for what they are (vv. 5–8; cf. 5.20).

32.9–20: Failure of the harvest and restoration of nature. Lamenting, considered as a gender-specific occupation (vv. 9–14), will be followed by a transformation of the natural and moral environment through the spirit of God (vv. 15–20). **13:** *Thorns and briers,* see 5.6n.

20 Happy will you be who sow beside
every stream,
who let the ox and the donkey
range freely.

33 Ah, you destroyer,
who yourself have not been
destroyed;
you treacherous one,
with whom no one has dealt
treacherously!
When you have ceased to destroy,
you will be destroyed;
and when you have stopped dealing
treacherously,
you will be dealt with
treacherously.

2 O LORD, be gracious to us; we wait
for you.
Be our arm every morning,
our salvation in the time of trouble.
3 At the sound of tumult, peoples fled;
before your majesty, nations
scattered.
4 Spoil was gathered as the caterpillar
gathers;
as locusts leap, they leaped[a] upon
it.
5 The LORD is exalted, he dwells
on high;
he filled Zion with justice and
righteousness;
6 he will be the stability of your times,
abundance of salvation, wisdom,
and knowledge;
the fear of the LORD is Zion's
treasure.[b]

7 Listen! the valiant[a] cry in the streets;
the envoys of peace weep bitterly.
8 The highways are deserted,
travelers have quit the road.
The treaty is broken,
its oaths[c] are despised,
its obligation[d] is disregarded.
9 The land mourns and languishes;
Lebanon is confounded and withers
away;
Sharon is like a desert;
and Bashan and Carmel shake off
their leaves.

10 "Now I will arise," says the LORD,
"now I will lift myself up;
now I will be exalted.
11 You conceive chaff, you bring
forth stubble;
your breath is a fire that will
consume you.
12 And the peoples will be as if burned
to lime,
like thorns cut down, that are
burned in the fire."

13 Hear, you who are far away, what I
have done;
and you who are near,
acknowledge my might.
14 The sinners in Zion are afraid;
trembling has seized the godless:
"Who among us can live with the
devouring fire?
Who among us can live with
everlasting flames?"
15 Those who walk righteously and
speak uprightly,
who despise the gain of oppression,
who wave away a bribe instead of
accepting it,

a Meaning of Heb uncertain *b* Heb *his treasure*; meaning of Heb uncertain *c* Q Ms: MT *cities* *d* Or *everyone*

33.1–24: A prophetic liturgy, consisting of entreaties and oracles. 1: The tyrant is not identified; perhaps a composite image in contrast to the ideal Davidic ruler (32.1; 33.17). **2–6:** A brief psalm expressing confidence in deliverance from hostile attack. **2:** *Every morning,* in the hymns the morning is the time of salvation and divine intervention, e.g., Ps 46.5. **7–9:** Describing a period of social unrest following military disaster, perhaps during the siege of 701 BCE. **9:** Regions with abundant vegetation will be defoliated: *Lebanon* and *Bashan,* see 2.13n. *Sharon,* the coastal plain south of Mount Carmel, both of proverbial fertility (see Song 2.1; 7.5). Contrast 35.2. **10–12:** A response in which the God of Israel threatens to arise and burn the enemy like thorns; cf. 10.16–17; 30.27–33. **17–22:** The same theme as

who stop their ears from hearing of
bloodshed
and shut their eyes from looking on
evil,
16 they will live on the heights;
their refuge will be the fortresses of
rocks;
their food will be supplied, their
water assured.

17 Your eyes will see the king in his
beauty;
they will behold a land that
stretches far away.
18 Your mind will muse on the terror:
"Where is the one who counted?
Where is the one who weighed the
tribute?
Where is the one who counted the
towers?"
19 No longer will you see the insolent
people,
the people of an obscure speech
that you cannot comprehend,
stammering in a language that you
cannot understand.
20 Look on Zion, the city of our
appointed festivals!
Your eyes will see Jerusalem,
a quiet habitation, an immovable
tent,
whose stakes will never be pulled
up,
and none of whose ropes will
be broken.
21 But there the LORD in majesty will be
for us
a place of broad rivers and streams,
where no galley with oars can go,
nor stately ship can pass.
22 For the LORD is our judge, the LORD
is our ruler,
the LORD is our king; he will
save us.

23 Your rigging hangs loose;
it cannot hold the mast firm in its
place,
or keep the sail spread out.

Then prey and spoil in abundance
will be divided;
even the lame will fall to
plundering.
24 And no inhabitant will say, "I am
sick";
the people who live there will be
forgiven their iniquity.

34 Draw near, O nations, to hear;
O peoples, give heed!
Let the earth hear, and all that fills it;
the world, and all that comes from
it.
2 For the LORD is enraged against all
the nations,
and furious against all their hordes;
he has doomed them, has given
them over for slaughter.
3 Their slain shall be cast out,
and the stench of their corpses shall
rise;
the mountains shall flow with their
blood.
4 All the host of heaven shall rot away,
and the skies roll up like a scroll.
All their host shall wither
like a leaf withering on a vine,
or fruit withering on a fig tree.

5 When my sword has drunk its fill in
the heavens,
lo, it will descend upon Edom,
upon the people I have doomed to
judgment.

32.1–8, forming an inclusion: the future golden age of Jerusalem. **19:** See 28.11n. **21:** A strange image, since Jerusalem has no broad rivers and is not accessible to attack from the sea; the imaging therefore must be mythological; cf. Ezek 47.1–12. **23–24:** Later editorial additions introducing a more realistic note.

34.1–17: Oracle against Edom. A combination of judgment on Edom with the threat of universal upheaval, like 13.1–22 with Edom taking the place of Babylon. Edom profited by the Babylonian conquest of the sixth century BCE, infiltrating Judean territory; cf. 63.1–6; Ob 8–14. **3:** Cf. 66.24. **4:** *The host of heaven shall rot away,* cf. 13.10; 24.21n. **5–7:** Sacrifice and slaughter are closely connected; cf. Jer 46.10; Ezek 39.17–20. **6:** *Bozrah* (Buseirah), the ancient capital of Edom. **8–15:** Reversion of cultivated

6 The LORD has a sword; it is sated
with blood,
it is gorged with fat,
with the blood of lambs and goats,
with the fat of the kidneys of rams.
For the LORD has a sacrifice in
Bozrah,
a great slaughter in the land
of Edom.
7 Wild oxen shall fall with them,
and young steers with the
mighty bulls.
Their land shall be soaked with
blood,
and their soil made rich with fat.

8 For the LORD has a day of vengeance,
a year of vindication by Zion's
cause.[a]
9 And the streams of Edom[b] shall be
turned into pitch,
and her soil into sulfur;
her land shall become burning
pitch.
10 Night and day it shall not be
quenched;
its smoke shall go up forever.
From generation to generation it shall
lie waste;
no one shall pass through it forever
and ever.
11 But the hawk[c] and the hedgehog[c]
shall possess it;
the owl[c] and the raven shall live in
it.
He shall stretch the line of confusion
over it,
and the plummet of chaos over[d] its
nobles.
12 They shall name it No Kingdom
There,
and all its princes shall be nothing.
13 Thorns shall grow over its
strongholds,
nettles and thistles in its fortresses.
It shall be the haunt of jackals,
an abode for ostriches.
14 Wildcats shall meet with hyenas,
goat-demons shall call to
each other;
there too Lilith shall repose,
and find a place to rest.
15 There shall the owl nest
and lay and hatch and brood in its
shadow;
there too the buzzards shall gather,
each one with its mate.
16 Seek and read from the book of
the LORD:
Not one of these shall be missing;
none shall be without its mate.
For the mouth of the LORD has
commanded,
and his spirit has gathered them.
17 He has cast the lot for them,
his hand has portioned it out to
them with the line;
they shall possess it forever,
from generation to generation they
shall live in it.

35 The wilderness and the dry land
shall be glad,
the desert shall rejoice and blossom;
like the crocus 2 it shall blossom
abundantly,
and rejoice with joy and singing.

a Or *of recompense by Zion's defender* *b* Heb *her streams* *c* Identification uncertain *d* Heb lacks *over*

land to wilderness. Edom will be rendered unfit for human habitation and ecologically devastated. **9–10:** Pitch, sulfur, and smoke recall the devastation of Sodom and Gomorrah (Gen 19.24,28). **11–15:** Cf. 13.19–22. **14:** *Lilith,* a malevolent winged female demon, at home in that devastated environment, in later Jewish tradition identified as Adam's first wife. **16–17:** Perhaps referring to other passages (e.g., 13.1–22) in the Isaiah scroll as it then existed.

35.1–10: A link-chapter that stands in contrast to the description of Edom in 34.1–17 and connects with the theme of return from exile in chs 40–48 (35.8–10; cf. 40.1–5). The insertion of chs 36–39 broke the connection but created a new link (see 39.5–8n.). **1–2:** In contrast to Edom, the barren areas of the land will bloom and all shall see the glory of God (cf. 33.9; 40.5). **3–4:** Perhaps addressed to prophets;

The glory of Lebanon shall be given
to it,
the majesty of Carmel and Sharon.
They shall see the glory of the LORD,
the majesty of our God.

3 Strengthen the weak hands,
and make firm the feeble knees.
4 Say to those who are of a fearful
heart,
"Be strong, do not fear!
Here is your God.
He will come with vengeance,
with terrible recompense.
He will come and save you."

5 Then the eyes of the blind shall
be opened,
and the ears of the deaf unstopped;
6 then the lame shall leap like a deer,
and the tongue of the speechless
sing for joy.
For waters shall break forth in the
wilderness,
and streams in the desert;
7 the burning sand shall become a pool,
and the thirsty ground springs
of water;
the haunt of jackals shall become
a swamp,[a]
the grass shall become reeds and
rushes.

8 A highway shall be there,
and it shall be called the Holy Way;
the unclean shall not travel on it,[b]
but it shall be for God's people;[c]
no traveler, not even fools, shall go
astray.
9 No lion shall be there,
nor shall any ravenous beast come
up on it;
they shall not be found there,
but the redeemed shall walk there.
10 And the ransomed of the LORD shall
return,
and come to Zion with singing;
everlasting joy shall be upon their
heads;
they shall obtain joy and gladness,
and sorrow and sighing shall
flee away.

36 In the fourteenth year of King Heze-
kiah, King Sennacherib of Assyria
came up against all the fortified cities of
Judah and captured them. 2 The king of As-
syria sent the Rabshakeh from Lachish to
King Hezekiah at Jerusalem, with a great
army. He stood by the conduit of the upper
pool on the highway to the Fuller's Field.
3 And there came out to him Eliakim son of
Hilkiah, who was in charge of the palace,
and Shebna the secretary, and Joah son of
Asaph, the recorder.
4 The Rabshakeh said to them, "Say to
Hezekiah: Thus says the great king, the
king of Assyria: On what do you base this
confidence of yours? 5 Do you think that

a Cn: Heb *in the haunt of jackals is her resting place*
b Or *pass it by* *c* Cn: Heb *for them*

cf. 40.1–2. **5–7:** Disabilities will be removed; there will be water in the wilderness (see 41.18–19 and n.) and, in contrast to Edom, ecological renewal. **8–10:** The motif of the *highway* in the wilderness connects with 40.3–4 and 42.16.

Chs 36–39: Historical appendix. Except for 38.9–20, these chapters parallel 2 Kings 18.13,17–20.19, omitting the account of Hezekiah's surrender to Sennacherib (2 Kings 18.14–16). These chapters seem to conflate two accounts: two boastful Assyrian speeches (36.4–20; 37.10–13), two visits of Hezekiah to the Temple (37.1,14–20), two oracular utterances of Isaiah (37.5–7,21–35).

36.1–22: The Assyrian army before Jerusalem. 1: *The fourteenth year,* since according to Assyrian annals Sennacherib's campaign against Judah took place in 701, Hezekiah may have come to the throne in 715, not 729 as inferred from 2 Kings 18.1,9. *All the fortified cities,* 46 according to the Annals of Sennacherib, *ANET,* 287–288. **2:** *Rabshakeh,* chief steward. *Lachish,* the second city of Judah, southwest of Jerusalem in the Shephelah. Its siege and capture are vividly portrayed in bas-reliefs from Sennacherib's palace in Nineveh and in the archaeological record. **3:** *Eliakim, Shebna,* see 22.15–25. **4–10:** The Rabshakeh's boastful speech may have represented Assyrian views but has drawn on 10.8–11,13–14. **6:** Cf. the

mere words are strategy and power for
war? On whom do you now rely, that you
have rebelled against me? 6See, you are re-
lying on Egypt, that broken reed of a staff,
which will pierce the hand of anyone who
leans on it. Such is Pharaoh king of Egypt
to all who rely on him. 7But if you say to
me, 'We rely on the LORD our God,' is it
not he whose high places and altars Hezeki-
ah has removed, saying to Judah and to
Jerusalem, 'You shall worship before this
altar'? 8Come now, make a wager with my
master the king of Assyria: I will give you
two thousand horses, if you are able on
your part to set riders on them. 9How then
can you repulse a single captain among the
least of my master's servants, when you
rely on Egypt for chariots and for horse-
men? 10Moreover, is it without the LORD
that I have come up against this land to
destroy it? The LORD said to me, Go up
against this land, and destroy it."
11 Then Eliakim, Shebna, and Joah said
to the Rabshakeh, "Please speak to your
servants in Aramaic, for we understand it;
do not speak to us in the language of Judah
within the hearing of the people who are on
the wall." 12But the Rabshakeh said, "Has
my master sent me to speak these words to
your master and to you, and not to the peo-
ple sitting on the wall, who are doomed
with you to eat their own dung and drink
their own urine?"
13 Then the Rabshakeh stood and called
out in a loud voice in the language of Ju-
dah, "Hear the words of the great king, the
king of Assyria! 14Thus says the king: 'Do
not let Hezekiah deceive you, for he will
not be able to deliver you. 15Do not let
Hezekiah make you rely on the LORD by
saying, The LORD will surely deliver us; this
city will not be given into the hand of the
king of Assyria.' 16Do not listen to Hezeki-
ah; for thus says the king of Assyria: 'Make
your peace with me and come out to me;

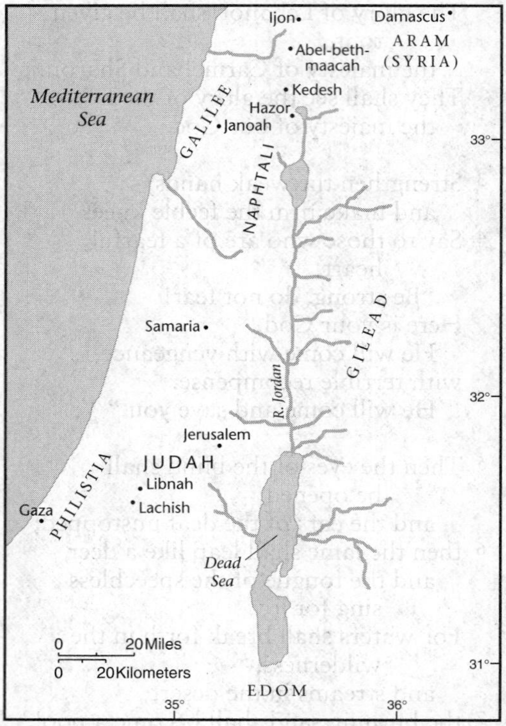

Chs 36–39: Sennacherib's invasion of Judah.

then everyone of you will eat from your
own vine and your own fig tree and drink
water from your own cistern, 17until I
come and take you away to a land like your
own land, a land of grain and wine, a land
of bread and vineyards. 18Do not let Heze-
kiah mislead you by saying, The LORD will
save us. Has any of the gods of the nations
saved their land out of the hand of the king
of Assyria? 19Where are the gods of Ha-
math and Arpad? Where are the gods of
Sepharvaim? Have they delivered Samaria
out of my hand? 20Who among all the gods
of these countries have saved their coun-
tries out of my hand, that the LORD should
save Jerusalem out of my hand?'"
21 But they were silent and answered

sayings on the Egyptian alliance (18.1–19.15; 30.1–7; 31.1–3). **7:** On Hezekiah's removal of the high places, see 2 Kings 18.3–6. **10:** Appeal to the anger of the national deity reflects Isaiah's sayings about Assyria as the LORD's agent for the punishment of Israel. **11:** Aramaic was the language of diplomacy from the late Neo-Assyrian period onward. *The language of Judah* is Hebrew. **13–20:** The Rabshakeh's address to the populace. **18–20:** Cf. 10.8–9 and note. *Sepharvaim,* location uncertain.

him not a word, for the king's command
was, "Do not answer him." 22 Then Elia-
kim son of Hilkiah, who was in charge of
the palace, and Shebna the secretary, and
Joah son of Asaph, the recorder, came to
Hezekiah with their clothes torn, and told
him the words of the Rabshakeh.

37 When King Hezekiah heard it, he
tore his clothes, covered himself
with sackcloth, and went into the house of
the LORD. 2 And he sent Eliakim, who was
in charge of the palace, and Shebna the sec-
retary, and the senior priests, covered with
sackcloth, to the prophet Isaiah son of
Amoz. 3 They said to him, "Thus says Hez-
ekiah, This day is a day of distress, of re-
buke, and of disgrace; children have come
to the birth, and there is no strength to
bring them forth. 4 It may be that the LORD
your God heard the words of the Rabsha-
keh, whom his master the king of Assyria
has sent to mock the living God, and will
rebuke the words that the LORD your God
has heard; therefore lift up your prayer for
the remnant that is left."

5 When the servants of King Hezekiah
came to Isaiah, 6 Isaiah said to them, "Say
to your master, 'Thus says the LORD: Do
not be afraid because of the words that you
have heard, with which the servants of the
king of Assyria have reviled me. 7 I myself
will put a spirit in him, so that he shall hear
a rumor, and return to his own land; I will
cause him to fall by the sword in his own
land.'"

8 The Rabshakeh returned, and found
the king of Assyria fighting against Libnah;
for he had heard that the king had left La-
chish. 9 Now the king[a] heard concerning
King Tirhakah of Ethiopia,[b] "He has set
out to fight against you." When he heard it,
he sent messengers to Hezekiah, saying,
10 "Thus shall you speak to King Hezekiah
of Judah: Do not let your God on whom
you rely deceive you by promising that Je-
rusalem will not be given into the hand of
the king of Assyria. 11 See, you have heard
what the kings of Assyria have done to all
lands, destroying them utterly. Shall you be
delivered? 12 Have the gods of the nations
delivered them, the nations that my prede-
cessors destroyed, Gozan, Haran, Rezeph,
and the people of Eden who were in Telas-
sar? 13 Where is the king of Hamath, the
king of Arpad, the king of the city of Seph-
arvaim, the king of Hena, or the king of
Ivvah?"

14 Hezekiah received the letter from the
hand of the messengers and read it; then
Hezekiah went up to the house of the LORD
and spread it before the LORD. 15 And Hez-
ekiah prayed to the LORD, saying:
16 "O LORD of hosts, God of Israel, who
are enthroned above the cherubim, you are
God, you alone, of all the kingdoms of the
earth; you have made heaven and earth.
17 Incline your ear, O LORD, and hear;
open your eyes, O LORD, and see; hear all
the words of Sennacherib, which he has
sent to mock the living God. 18 Truly,
O LORD, the kings of Assyria have laid
waste all the nations and their lands, 19 and
have hurled their gods into the fire, though
they were no gods, but the work of human
hands—wood and stone—and so they were
destroyed. 20 So now, O LORD our God,
save us from his hand, so that all the king-
doms of the earth may know that you alone
are the LORD."

21 Then Isaiah son of Amoz sent to Hez-
ekiah, saying: "Thus says the LORD, the
God of Israel: Because you have prayed to
me concerning King Sennacherib of Assyr-
ia, 22 this is the word that the LORD has
spoken concerning him:

a Heb *he* *b* Or *Nubia*; Heb *Cush*

37.1–38: The failure of the siege (cf. 2 Kings 19). **1–7:** The delegation to Isaiah recalls the consultation of prophets by earlier and later kings (1 Kings 22.5–28; 2 Kings 1.9–17; 3.11–17; 22.11–14; Jer 21.1–4). **8–13:** A boastful message from Sennacherib. **9:** *King Tirhakah of Ethiopia* may have been a general in the army since he came to the throne of Egypt only in 690. **12–13:** Cf. 36.19–20. The places mentioned are in northern Mesopotamia. **13:** Cf. 10.9; 36.19. **14–20:** Hezekiah's prayer for deliverance. **21–35:** Isaiah, who arrives in answer to Hezekiah's prayer, assures the king of the failure of the siege. **22:** *Virgin*

She despises you, she scorns you—
virgin daughter Zion;
she tosses her head—behind
your back,
daughter Jerusalem.

23 "Whom have you mocked and
reviled?
Against whom have you raised your
voice
and haughtily lifted your eyes?
Against the Holy One of Israel!
24 By your servants you have mocked
the Lord,
and you have said, 'With my many
chariots
I have gone up the heights of the
mountains,
to the far recesses of Lebanon;
I felled its tallest cedars,
its choicest cypresses;
I came to its remotest height,
its densest forest.
25 I dug wells
and drank waters,
I dried up with the sole of my foot
all the streams of Egypt.'

26 "Have you not heard
that I determined it long ago?
I planned from days of old
what now I bring to pass,
that you should make fortified cities
crash into heaps of ruins,
27 while their inhabitants, shorn of
strength,
are dismayed and confounded;
they have become like plants of
the field
and like tender grass,
like grass on the housetops,
blighted[a] before it is grown.
28 "I know your rising up[b] and your
sitting down,
your going out and coming in,
and your raging against me.
29 Because you have raged against me
and your arrogance has come to my
ears,
I will put my hook in your nose
and my bit in your mouth;
I will turn you back on the way
by which you came.

30 "And this shall be the sign for you:
This year eat what grows of itself, and in
the second year what springs from that;
then in the third year sow, reap, plant vine-
yards, and eat their fruit. 31 The surviving
remnant of the house of Judah shall again
take root downward, and bear fruit up-
ward; 32 for from Jerusalem a remnant shall
go out, and from Mount Zion a band of
survivors. The zeal of the LORD of hosts
will do this.

33 "Therefore thus says the LORD con-
cerning the king of Assyria: He shall not
come into this city, shoot an arrow there,
come before it with a shield, or cast up a
siege ramp against it. 34 By the way that he
came, by the same he shall return; he shall
not come into this city, says the LORD.
35 For I will defend this city to save it, for
my own sake and for the sake of my servant
David."

36 Then the angel of the LORD set out
and struck down one hundred eighty-five
thousand in the camp of the Assyrians;
when morning dawned, they were all dead
bodies. 37 Then King Sennacherib of Assyr-

a With 2 Kings 19.26: Heb *field* *b* Q Ms Gk: MT lacks *your rising up*

daughter Zion, cities, Israelite and foreign, are routinely represented as female (e.g., 47.1; Jer 46.11; Lam 1.1–2). **24–25:** Boastful words are put in the mouth of the Assyrian king—a common Isaian rhetorical device. **26–29:** All of these achievements have been in accord with the LORD's plan for Israel; cf. 10.5–6. **30–31:** The sign (cf. 7.10–17; 38.7–8) means that within three years the agrarian life of the country will have returned to normal. **33–35:** This is in essence the "word" announced in v. 22a. For the concept of divine protection of the Davidic dynasty and its capitol, see 38.6; Ps 132.11,13–18. **36–38:** Sennacherib's army is decimated by the destroying angel, cf. 2 Sam 24.15–17, perhaps indicating plague. **38:** Sennacherib was assassinated in 681 BCE. The name Nisroch has so far defied explanation.

ia left, went home, and lived at Nineveh.
38 As he was worshiping in the house of his
god Nisroch, his sons Adrammelech and
Sharezer killed him with the sword, and
they escaped into the land of Ararat. His
son Esar-haddon succeeded him.

38 In those days Hezekiah became sick
and was at the point of death. The
prophet Isaiah son of Amoz came to him,
and said to him, "Thus says the LORD: Set
your house in order, for you shall die; you
shall not recover." 2 Then Hezekiah turned
his face to the wall, and prayed to the
LORD: 3 "Remember now, O LORD, I im-
plore you, how I have walked before you in
faithfulness with a whole heart, and have
done what is good in your sight." And Hez-
ekiah wept bitterly.

4 Then the word of the LORD came to
Isaiah: 5 "Go and say to Hezekiah, Thus
says the LORD, the God of your ancestor
David: I have heard your prayer, I have
seen your tears; I will add fifteen years to
your life. 6 I will deliver you and this city
out of the hand of the king of Assyria, and
defend this city.

7 "This is the sign to you from the
LORD, that the LORD will do this thing that
he has promised: 8 See, I will make the
shadow cast by the declining sun on the
dial of Ahaz turn back ten steps." So the
sun turned back on the dial the ten steps by
which it had declined.[a]

9 A writing of King Hezekiah of Judah, after he had been sick and had recovered from his sickness:

10 I said: In the noontide of my days
I must depart;
I am consigned to the gates of Sheol
for the rest of my years.
11 I said, I shall not see the LORD
in the land of the living;
I shall look upon mortals no more
among the inhabitants of the world.
12 My dwelling is plucked up and
removed from me
like a shepherd's tent;
like a weaver I have rolled up my life;
he cuts me off from the loom;
from day to night you bring me to an
end;[a]
13 I cry for help[b] until morning;
like a lion he breaks all my bones;
from day to night you bring me to
an end.[a]

14 Like a swallow or a crane[a] I clamor,
I moan like a dove.
My eyes are weary with looking
upward.
O Lord, I am oppressed; be my
security!
15 But what can I say? For he has
spoken to me,
and he himself has done it.
All my sleep has fled[c]
because of the bitterness of
my soul.

16 O Lord, by these things people live,
and in all these is the life of
my spirit.[a]
Oh, restore me to health and make
me live!
17 Surely it was for my welfare
that I had great bitterness;

a Meaning of Heb uncertain *b* Cn: Meaning of Heb uncertain *c* Cn Compare Syr: Heb *I will walk slowly all my years*

38.1–22: Hezekiah's sickness and recovery (cf. 2 Kings 20.1–11). **1:** *In those days,* the event precedes the arrival of the Babylonian delegation (39.1) and the siege of Jerusalem (38.6). **3:** For the form of this petition, see Ps 26. The narrative reflects the structure of psalms of thanksgiving, but without a confession of having sins (but see 2 Chr 32.24–26). **5:** *Fifteen years,* calculated on the basis of 2 Kings 18.2,13. **6:** See 37.25n. **8–11:** *Dial* (lit. "stairs" or "steps") is uncertain; the reference may be to the reversal of the natural direction of the shadow on a staircase as the sun was setting. Isaiah is here presented as holy man and miracle-worker, similar to Elijah and Elisha. **9–20:** A thanksgiving psalm attributed to Hezekiah, cf. Ps 30; 107. **10–16:** Lament and petition. **10:** *Sheol,* the underworld. **17–20:** Announcement of deliverance and promise of liturgical thanksgiving. **18:** See 26.14n. *The Pit,* the underworld. **21–22:** These verses

but you have held back[a] my life
from the pit of destruction,
for you have cast all my sins
behind your back.
18 For Sheol cannot thank you,
death cannot praise you;
those who go down to the Pit cannot hope
for your faithfulness.
19 The living, the living, they thank you,
as I do this day;
fathers make known to children
your faithfulness.

20 The LORD will save me,
and we will sing to stringed instruments[b]
all the days of our lives,
at the house of the LORD.

21 Now Isaiah had said, "Let them take a lump of figs, and apply it to the boil, so that he may recover." 22 Hezekiah also had said, "What is the sign that I shall go up to the house of the LORD?"

39 At that time King Merodach-baladan son of Baladan of Babylon sent envoys with letters and a present to Hezekiah, for he heard that he had been sick and had recovered.
2 Hezekiah welcomed them; he showed them his treasure house, the silver, the gold, the spices, the precious oil, his whole armory, all that was found in his storehouses. There was nothing in his house or in all his realm that Hezekiah did not show them.
3 Then the prophet Isaiah came to King Hezekiah and said to him, "What did these men say? From where did they come to you?" Hezekiah answered, "They have come to me from a far country, from Babylon."
4 He said, "What have they seen in your house?" Hezekiah answered, "They have seen all that is in my house; there is nothing in my storehouses that I did not show them."
5 Then Isaiah said to Hezekiah, "Hear the word of the LORD of hosts:
6 Days are coming when all that is in your house, and that which your ancestors have stored up until this day, shall be carried to Babylon; nothing shall be left, says the LORD.
7 Some of your own sons who are born to you shall be taken away; they shall be eunuchs in the palace of the king of Babylon."
8 Then Hezekiah said to Isaiah, "The word of the LORD that you have spoken is good." For he thought, "There will be peace and security in my days."

40 Comfort, O comfort my people,
says your God.
2 Speak tenderly to Jerusalem,
and cry to her
that she has served her term,
that her penalty is paid,

a Cn Compare Gk Vg: Heb *loved* *b* Heb *my stringed instruments*

would fit better between vv. 6 and 7. **21:** Figs were believed to have a curative as well as aphrodisiac capacity.

39.1–8: The Babylonian delegation (cf. 2 Kings 20.12–19). **1:** *Merodach-baladan,* Marduk-apal-iddina, ruler of Babylon 721–710 BCE and again in 703 when his revolt, supported by Judah and passively by Egypt, was crushed by the Assyrians. He continued to plot against Assyria from exile. **2:** Since the purpose of the visit was to form an anti-Assyrian alliance, Hezekiah wished to demonstrate his potential as an ally. Note, however, that earlier he had to empty his treasury to buy off the Assyrians (2 Kings 18.14–16). **5–8:** The prediction of exile in Babylon creates a link with chs 40–48, replacing 35.8–10 after the insertion of chs 36–39.

Chs 40–55: Book of the Consolation of Israel ("Second Isaiah"). Chs 40–48: This first section is centered on the providential role of Cyrus II (559–530 BCE), founder of the Persian Empire, and the expectation of return from exile in Babylonia.

40.1–11: A new epoch is announced. 1–2: The members of the divine council are told to announce the imminent end of Jerusalem's suffering. Repetition of the imperative is a common rhetorical device in this second major section of the book (51.9,17; 52.1; 57.14). Exile is represented as penal servitude, more than long enough to satisfy for past infidelity. *My people . . . your God,* covenant words (Ex 19.4–6; Jer 11.5).

that she has received from the LORD's
hand
double for all her sins.

3 A voice cries out:
"In the wilderness prepare the way of
the LORD,
make straight in the desert a
highway for our God.
4 Every valley shall be lifted up,
and every mountain and hill be
made low;
the uneven ground shall become level,
and the rough places a plain.
5 Then the glory of the LORD shall
be revealed,
and all people shall see it together,
for the mouth of the LORD has
spoken."

6 A voice says, "Cry out!"
And I said, "What shall I cry?"
All people are grass,
their constancy is like the flower of
the field.
7 The grass withers, the flower fades,
when the breath of the LORD blows
upon it;
surely the people are grass.
8 The grass withers, the flower fades;
but the word of our God will stand
forever.
9 Get you up to a high mountain,
O Zion, herald of good tidings;[a]
lift up your voice with strength,
O Jerusalem, herald of good
tidings,[b]
lift it up, do not fear;
say to the cities of Judah,
"Here is your God!"
10 See, the Lord GOD comes with might,
and his arm rules for him;
his reward is with him,
and his recompense before him.
11 He will feed his flock like a shepherd;
he will gather the lambs in
his arms,
and carry them in his bosom,
and gently lead the mother sheep.

12 Who has measured the waters in the
hollow of his hand
and marked off the heavens with a
span,
enclosed the dust of the earth in
a measure,
and weighed the mountains
in scales
and the hills in a balance?
13 Who has directed the spirit of
the LORD,
or as his counselor has instructed
him?
14 Whom did he consult for his
enlightenment,
and who taught him the path of
justice?
Who taught him knowledge,
and showed him the way of
understanding?
15 Even the nations are like a drop from
a bucket,

a Or *O herald of good tidings to Zion*
b Or *O herald of good tidings to Jerusalem*

3–5: An oracle commanding that the way be prepared for return from exile, and therefore for the return of the glory of the LORD, i.e., the visible expression of the LORD's presence, to the land of Israel (cf. Ezek 43.1–5). *The way of the LORD,* a common figure in Second Isaiah (42.16; 43.16,19; 48.17; 51.10). In Mk 1.3 and parallels, v. 3 is rephrased to apply to John the Baptizer. **6–8:** An individual member of the divine council, perhaps identical with the one crying out in vv. 3–5, proclaims the permanent validity of the divine word. The withered vegetation may refer especially to the imminent end of the Babylonian Empire. **9–11:** Announcement to the cities of Judah that the LORD will once more rule over them as a compassionate shepherd, i.e., king (cf. Ezek 34).

40.12–31: The incomparability of the LORD as creator deity. 12–14: The LORD is presented as creator of the subterranean waters, the earth, and the sky, i.e., of the cosmos as the prophet's contemporaries imagined it; cf. Job 38.4–11. **15–17:** In spite of appearances to the contrary, nations and empires like Babylon are of no great account in the eyes of the creator. *Isles,* or coastlands, see 11.11n. **18–20:** The

and are accounted as dust on
the scales;
see, he takes up the isles like fine
dust.
16 Lebanon would not provide fuel
enough,
nor are its animals enough for a
burnt offering.
17 All the nations are as nothing before
him;
they are accounted by him as less
than nothing and emptiness.

18 To whom then will you liken God,
or what likeness compare
with him?
19 An idol?—A workman casts it,
and a goldsmith overlays it
with gold,
and casts for it silver chains.
20 As a gift one chooses mulberry
wood[a]
—wood that will not rot—
then seeks out a skilled artisan
to set up an image that will
not topple.

21 Have you not known? Have you
not heard?
Has it not been told you from the
beginning?
Have you not understood from the
foundations of the earth?
22 It is he who sits above the circle of
the earth,
and its inhabitants are like
grasshoppers;
who stretches out the heavens like a
curtain,
and spreads them like a tent to live
in;
23 who brings princes to naught,
and makes the rulers of the earth as
nothing.

24 Scarcely are they planted, scarcely
sown,
scarcely has their stem taken root
in the earth,
when he blows upon them, and they
wither,
and the tempest carries them off
like stubble.

25 To whom then will you compare me,
or who is my equal? says the Holy
One.
26 Lift up your eyes on high and see:
Who created these?
He who brings out their host and
numbers them,
calling them all by name;
because he is great in strength,
mighty in power,
not one is missing.

27 Why do you say, O Jacob,
and speak, O Israel,
"My way is hidden from the LORD,
and my right is disregarded by my
God"?
28 Have you not known? Have you
not heard?
The LORD is the everlasting God,
the Creator of the ends of
the earth.
He does not faint or grow weary;
his understanding is unsearchable.
29 He gives power to the faint,
and strengthens the powerless.

a Meaning of Heb uncertain

beginning of this prophet's polemic against idolatry, which also targets aspects of the religious and intellectual tradition of the Babylonians (also 41.6–7,29; 42.17; 43.10; 44.9–20; 45.16,20; 46.1–7; Jer 10.1–10). **21–24:** A rhetorical recapitulation of vv. 12–20. The language in which the cosmos is here described should be compared with Gen 1.1–31. **22:** *Grasshoppers,* cf. Num 13.33. **25–26:** The prophet invites the audience to contemplate the heavenly bodies as objects created by the LORD and not as divine beings. The Heb verb "bara" (create) is for the most part restricted to Gen 1 and these chapters (40.28; 41.20; 42.5; 43.7,15; 45.7,8,12,18; 54.16). **27–31:** An attempt to answer the crisis of faith provoked by political disaster by presenting the LORD as a cosmic rather than a purely national deity. Waiting for God, implying trust, is frequently advocated in the book (8.17; 30.18; 49.23; 64.4).

30 Even youths will faint and be weary,
and the young will fall exhausted;
31 but those who wait for the LORD
shall renew their strength,
they shall mount up with wings like
eagles,
they shall run and not be weary,
they shall walk and not faint.

41 Listen to me in silence,
O coastlands;
let the peoples renew their strength;
let them approach, then let
them speak;
let us together draw near for
judgment.

2 Who has roused a victor from
the east,
summoned him to his service?
He delivers up nations to him,
and tramples kings under foot;
he makes them like dust with
his sword,
like driven stubble with his bow.
3 He pursues them and passes on safely,
scarcely touching the path with his
feet.
4 Who has performed and done this,
calling the generations from the
beginning?
I, the LORD, am first,
and will be with the last.
5 The coastlands have seen and
are afraid,
the ends of the earth tremble;
they have drawn near and come.
6 Each one helps the other,
saying to one another, "Take
courage!"
7 The artisan encourages the goldsmith,
and the one who smooths with the
hammer encourages the one
who strikes the anvil,
saying of the soldering, "It is good";
and they fasten it with nails so that
it cannot be moved.
8 But you, Israel, my servant,
Jacob, whom I have chosen,
the offspring of Abraham,
my friend;
9 you whom I took from the ends of
the earth,
and called from its farthest corners,
saying to you, "You are my servant,
I have chosen you and not cast you
off";
10 do not fear, for I am with you,
do not be afraid, for I am your
God;
I will strengthen you, I will help you,
I will uphold you with my
victorious right hand.

11 Yes, all who are incensed against you
shall be ashamed and disgraced;
those who strive against you
shall be as nothing and shall perish.
12 You shall seek those who contend
with you,
but you shall not find them;

41.1–10: A challenge issued to the nations. The rhetoric of the law courts is much in evidence in chs 40–48, with the nations challenged to identify the LORD as responsible for the great changes taking place on the international scene. **1–3:** After the customary call for attention, the seer draws attention to Cyrus II, who by 545 BCE had conquered Media, Lydia, and the Greek-speaking cities on the western seaboard of Asia Minor (the *coastlands*). The seer draws attention to the amazing rapidity of these conquests. **4–7:** The God of Israel is behind these events. He is the first and the last (also 44.6; 48.12; cf. 43.10). *The artisan,* see 40.18–20n. **8–10:** A word of encouragement is addressed to Israel-Jacob, the LORD's servant. Servanthood is a basic motif in chs 40–66, and is used with different meanings and different emphases. In chs 40–48 it refers to the people as a whole, with the possible exception of 42.1–4. **8:** *Abraham, my friend,* see 2 Chr 20.7.

41.11–20: Israel is assured of God's help. 11–16: Though politically insignificant, Israel will survive by the power of its God. In exilic texts the people of Israel are often referred to as Jacob, whose exile in Mesopotamia and return to the homeland mirrors the experience of the deportees and later Judeo-Babylonians who came back to Judah (cf. Gen 28.13–16). The LORD as redeemer (43.14; 44.6; 47.4; see Ex 6.6; 15.13) is the first of many echoes of the Exodus tradition in these chapters. **17–20:** The provision

those who war against you
shall be as nothing at all.
13 For I, the LORD your God,
hold your right hand;
it is I who say to you, "Do not fear,
I will help you."

14 Do not fear, you worm Jacob,
you insect[a] Israel!
I will help you, says the LORD;
your Redeemer is the Holy One of Israel.
15 Now, I will make of you a threshing sledge,
sharp, new, and having teeth;
you shall thresh the mountains and crush them,
and you shall make the hills like chaff.
16 You shall winnow them and the wind shall carry them away,
and the tempest shall scatter them.
Then you shall rejoice in the LORD;
in the Holy One of Israel you shall glory.

17 When the poor and needy seek water,
and there is none,
and their tongue is parched with thirst,
I the LORD will answer them,
I the God of Israel will not forsake them.
18 I will open rivers on the bare heights,[b]
and fountains in the midst of the valleys;
I will make the wilderness a pool of water,
and the dry land springs of water.
19 I will put in the wilderness the cedar,
the acacia, the myrtle, and the olive;
I will set in the desert the cypress,
the plane and the pine together,
20 so that all may see and know,
all may consider and understand,
that the hand of the LORD has done this,
the Holy One of Israel has created it.

21 Set forth your case, says the LORD;
bring your proofs, says the King of Jacob.
22 Let them bring them, and tell us
what is to happen.
Tell us the former things, what they are,
so that we may consider them,
and that we may know their outcome;
or declare to us the things to come.
23 Tell us what is to come hereafter,
that we may know that you are gods;
do good, or do harm,
that we may be afraid and terrified.
24 You, indeed, are nothing
and your work is nothing at all;
whoever chooses you is an abomination.

25 I stirred up one from the north, and he has come,
from the rising of the sun he was summoned by name.[c]
He shall trample[d] on rulers as on mortar,
as the potter treads clay.

a Syr: Heb *men of* *b* Or *trails* *c* Cn Compare Q Ms Gk: MT *and he shall call on my name*
d Cn: Heb *come*

of water in the wilderness recalls the narrative tradition about national origins (Ex 15.22–25; 17.1–7; Num 20.2–13; cf. 49.10). The LORD will facilitate their return from foreign lands.

41.21–29: A challenge addressed to the gods of other lands. 21–24: The LORD proves his power to effect what he proclaims by citing "the former things," earlier prophecies now seen to be fulfilled (42.9; 43.18; 46.9; 48.3). Other deities fail this test and thus demonstrate their ineffectiveness and unreality (vv. 28–29; see 40.18–20n.). **25–29:** Cyrus is represented as coming from the north as well as from the east (as 42.2), since the north traditionally symbolizes danger (Jer 1.13–14; 4.6; etc), because north was the direction from which invading armies from Mesopotamia came. **27:** Cf. 40.9.

26 Who declared it from the beginning,
so that we might know,
and beforehand, so that we might
say, "He is right"?
There was no one who declared it,
none who proclaimed,
none who heard your words.
27 I first have declared it to Zion,[a]
and I give to Jerusalem a herald of
good tidings.
28 But when I look there is no one;
among these there is no counselor
who, when I ask, gives an answer.
29 No, they are all a delusion;
their works are nothing;
their images are empty wind.

42 Here is my servant, whom I
uphold,
my chosen, in whom my soul
delights;
I have put my spirit upon him;
he will bring forth justice to the
nations.
2 He will not cry or lift up his voice,
or make it heard in the street;
3 a bruised reed he will not break,
and a dimly burning wick he will
not quench;
he will faithfully bring forth justice.
4 He will not grow faint or be crushed
until he has established justice in
the earth;
and the coastlands wait for his
teaching.

5 Thus says God, the LORD,
who created the heavens and
stretched them out,
who spread out the earth and what
comes from it,
who gives breath to the people upon
it
and spirit to those who walk in it:
6 I am the LORD, I have called you in
righteousness,
I have taken you by the hand and
kept you;
I have given you as a covenant to the
people,[b]
a light to the nations,
7 to open the eyes that are blind,
to bring out the prisoners from the
dungeon,
from the prison those who sit in
darkness.
8 I am the LORD, that is my name;
my glory I give to no other,
nor my praise to idols.
9 See, the former things have come
to pass,
and new things I now declare;
before they spring forth,
I tell you of them.

10 Sing to the LORD a new song,
his praise from the end of the
earth!

a Cn: Heb *First to Zion—Behold, behold them*
b Meaning of Heb uncertain

42.1–9: The LORD's servant. 1–4: Throughout chs 40–48 Israel is called the LORD's servant (41.8–9; 44.1–2,21; 45.4; 48.20) and the chosen one (41.8–9; 43.10,20; 44.1–2; 45.4); it is the one supported by the LORD (41.10), and it is destined for a nonviolent mission of mercy (42.7). The allusion in 42.1–4 is therefore to an ideal Israel rather than to Cyrus, elsewhere described as engaged in the violent subjugation of nations (41.2–3,25; 45.1–3; 46.11). Not all scholars agree that the so-called "Servant Songs" (42.1–4; 49.1–6; 50.4–11; 52.13–53.12) are distinct compositions inserted into the book. Early Christian tradition applied this passage to Jesus (Mt 12.18–21). **5–9:** A comment on vv. 1–4. The LORD, creator of the world and source of all life (41.22), called Israel for a mission to alleviate ignorance and suffering among the peoples of the world. The mission is confirmed by the "argument from prophecy" (41.21–24 n.). Some commentators prefer the view that the mission is confided either to an individual prophetic figure who stands for Israel (v. 6; cf. 49.6) or to Cyrus.

42.10–17: A psalm of praise. The psalm invites all peoples, from the *Kedar*ite Arabs in the Arabian peninsula and the inhabitants of *Sela* (see 16.1n.) in Edom, to the Mediterranean coastlands (see 11.11n.), to rejoice as the LORD goes out to do battle—a common motif in traditional Israelite poetry (Judg 5.4–5; Deut 33.2; Ps 68.7–8; Hab 3.3–6). The LORD will intervene to prepare the way for the return from exile

Let the sea roar[a] and all that fills it,
the coastlands and their inhabitants.
11 Let the desert and its towns lift up their voice,
the villages that Kedar inhabits;
let the inhabitants of Sela sing for joy,
let them shout from the tops of the mountains.
12 Let them give glory to the LORD,
and declare his praise in the coastlands.
13 The LORD goes forth like a soldier,
like a warrior he stirs up his fury;
he cries out, he shouts aloud,
he shows himself mighty against his foes.

14 For a long time I have held my peace,
I have kept still and restrained myself;
now I will cry out like a woman in labor,
I will gasp and pant.
15 I will lay waste mountains and hills,
and dry up all their herbage;
I will turn the rivers into islands,
and dry up the pools.
16 I will lead the blind
by a road they do not know,
by paths they have not known
I will guide them.
I will turn the darkness before them into light,
the rough places into level ground.
These are the things I will do,
and I will not forsake them.
17 They shall be turned back and utterly put to shame—
those who trust in carved images,
who say to cast images,
"You are our gods."

18 Listen, you that are deaf;
and you that are blind, look up and see!
19 Who is blind but my servant,
or deaf like my messenger whom I send?
Who is blind like my dedicated one,
or blind like the servant of the LORD?
20 He sees many things, but does[b] not observe them;
his ears are open, but he does not hear.
21 The LORD was pleased, for the sake of his righteousness,
to magnify his teaching and make it glorious.
22 But this is a people robbed and plundered,
all of them are trapped in holes
and hidden in prisons;
they have become a prey with no one to rescue,
a spoil with no one to say,
"Restore!"
23 Who among you will give heed to this,
who will attend and listen for the time to come?
24 Who gave up Jacob to the spoiler,
and Israel to the robbers?
Was it not the LORD, against whom we have sinned,
in whose ways they would not walk,
and whose law they would not obey?
25 So he poured upon him the heat of his anger
and the fury of war;
it set him on fire all around, but he did not understand;

a Cn Compare Ps 96.11; 98.7: Heb *Those who go down to the sea* *b* Heb *You see many things but do*

and guide the people once more through the wilderness; cf. 41.17–20. **10:** See 40.18–20n. *Sing to the LORD,* Ps 96.98.

42.18–25: Spiritual imperception and obtuseness, represented as being blind and deaf, is a recurrent theme in Isaiah (6.9–10; 29.9,18; 32.3; 35.5; 42.16; 43.8). In this passage "the servant of the LORD" may refer to an individual prophet; cf. 44.26. The present unsatisfactory condition of the people is the result of a history of infidelity. The rhetorical questions are a prominent stylistic feature of these chapters.

it burned him, but he did not take
it to heart.

43 But now thus says the LORD,
he who created you, O Jacob,
he who formed you, O Israel:
Do not fear, for I have redeemed you;
I have called you by name, you are mine.
2 When you pass through the waters, I will be with you;
and through the rivers, they shall not overwhelm you;
when you walk through fire you shall not be burned,
and the flame shall not consume you.
3 For I am the LORD your God,
the Holy One of Israel, your Savior.
I give Egypt as your ransom,
Ethiopia[a] and Seba in exchange for you.
4 Because you are precious in my sight,
and honored, and I love you,
I give people in return for you,
nations in exchange for your life.
5 Do not fear, for I am with you;
I will bring your offspring from the east,
and from the west I will gather you;
6 I will say to the north, "Give them up,"
and to the south, "Do not withhold;
bring my sons from far away
and my daughters from the end of the earth—
7 everyone who is called by my name,
whom I created for my glory,
whom I formed and made."
8 Bring forth the people who are blind,
yet have eyes,
who are deaf, yet have ears!
9 Let all the nations gather together,
and let the peoples assemble.
Who among them declared this,
and foretold to us the former things?
Let them bring their witnesses to justify them,
and let them hear and say, "It is true."
10 You are my witnesses, says the LORD,
and my servant whom I have chosen,
so that you may know and believe me
and understand that I am he.
Before me no god was formed,
nor shall there be any after me.
11 I, I am the LORD,
and besides me there is no savior.
12 I declared and saved and proclaimed,
when there was no strange god among you;
and you are my witnesses, says the LORD.
13 I am God, and also henceforth I am He;
there is no one who can deliver from my hand;
I work and who can hinder it?

a Or *Nubia*; Heb *Cush*

43.1–7: Israel's redemption is at hand. An oracle of salvation ("do not fear") assuring the hearers that judgment is in the past. The dangers that they foresee will be survived and the deportees or their descendants will return to the homeland. **2:** *Through fire,* cf. Ps 66.12. **3:** Egypt, Ethiopia, and Arabia (Seba), all of which Cyrus was expected to conquer, will be handed over as ransom for the liberation of Judah (cf. 45.11). **6–7:** Cf. vv. 11–12; 49.22; 60.90.

43.8–21: The LORD restores and redeems Israel. 8–15: A judicial process is set up (as in 41.1–5,21–29) in which deities of other lands, and in the first place Babylon, are challenged by the LORD to demonstrate divine status by their ability to predict the future and bring it about. Both sides are invited to call witnesses. Even though blind and deaf, the people of Israel can witness to the LORD's claim. All other gods fail the test; they are impotent and, in effect, nonexistent (see 40.18–20n.). The contest ends with an announcement of release from Babylonian captivity by the LORD, Israel's *Redeemer* (54.5; 59.20) and *Holy One* (41.14; 48.17; 49.7). **16–21:** The allusion is to the Exodus from Egypt (Ex 14–15), prefiguring

14 Thus says the LORD,
your Redeemer, the Holy One
of Israel:
For your sake I will send to Babylon
and break down all the bars,
and the shouting of the Chaldeans
will be turned to
lamentation.[a]
15 I am the LORD, your Holy One,
the Creator of Israel, your King.
16 Thus says the LORD,
who makes a way in the sea,
a path in the mighty waters,
17 who brings out chariot and horse,
army and warrior;
they lie down, they cannot rise,
they are extinguished, quenched like
a wick:
18 Do not remember the former things,
or consider the things of old.
19 I am about to do a new thing;
now it springs forth, do you not
perceive it?
I will make a way in the wilderness
and rivers in the desert.
20 The wild animals will honor me,
the jackals and the ostriches;
for I give water in the wilderness,
rivers in the desert,
to give drink to my chosen people,
21 the people whom I formed
for myself
so that they might declare my praise.

22 Yet you did not call upon me,
O Jacob;
but you have been weary of me,
O Israel!
23 You have not brought me your sheep
for burnt offerings,
or honored me with your sacrifices.
I have not burdened you with
offerings,
or wearied you with frankincense.
24 You have not bought me sweet cane
with money,
or satisfied me with the fat of your
sacrifices.
But you have burdened me with your
sins;
you have wearied me with your
iniquities.

25 I, I am He
who blots out your transgressions
for my own sake,
and I will not remember your sins.
26 Accuse me, let us go to trial;
set forth your case, so that you may
be proved right.
27 Your first ancestor sinned,
and your interpreters transgressed
against me.
28 Therefore I profaned the princes of
the sanctuary,
I delivered Jacob to utter
destruction,
and Israel to reviling.

44 But now hear, O Jacob
my servant,
Israel whom I have chosen!
2 Thus says the LORD who made you,
who formed you in the womb and
will help you:
Do not fear, O Jacob my servant,
Jeshurun whom I have chosen.
3 For I will pour water on the
thirsty land,
and streams on the dry ground;

a Meaning of Heb uncertain

an anticipated exodus from Babylon, the *new thing* announced by the prophet. For the theme of water in the wilderness, see 41.17–20n.

43.22–28: Ritual acts rendered ineffectual by a sinful way of life (cf. 1.10–17). **24:** *Sweet cane,* see Ex 30.25. **25–28:** Israel is invited to convict the LORD of injustice in bringing about the destruction of both kingdoms. The attempt will fail because Israel has a history of infidelity beginning with the first *ancestor,* Jacob (cf. Hos 12.2–4). **27:** *Interpreters transgressed,* translation and meaning are uncertain; perhaps it is a denunciation of optimistic prophets during the time of the monarchy who led the people astray.

44.1–8: A word of assurance and salvation addressed to the people as the LORD's servant. **2:** *Jeshurun,* poetic name for Israel (Deut 32.15; 33.5,26). **3–5:** For the theme of *water* in the wilderness, see

I will pour my spirit upon your
descendants,
and my blessing on your offspring.
4 They shall spring up like a green
tamarisk,
like willows by flowing streams.
5 This one will say, "I am the LORD's,"
another will be called by the name
of Jacob,
yet another will write on the hand,
"The LORD's,"
and adopt the name of Israel.

6 Thus says the LORD, the King
of Israel,
and his Redeemer, the LORD
of hosts:
I am the first and I am the last;
besides me there is no god.
7 Who is like me? Let them proclaim it,
let them declare and set it forth
before me.
Who has announced from of old the
things to come?[a]
Let them tell us[b] what is yet to be.
8 Do not fear, or be afraid;
have I not told you from of old and
declared it?
You are my witnesses!
Is there any god besides me?
There is no other rock; I know not
one.

9 All who make idols are nothing, and
the things they delight in do not profit;
their witnesses neither see nor know. And
so they will be put to shame. 10 Who would
fashion a god or cast an image that can do
no good? 11 Look, all its devotees shall be
put to shame; the artisans too are merely
human. Let them all assemble, let them
stand up; they shall be terrified, they shall
all be put to shame.
12 The ironsmith fashions it[c] and
works it over the coals, shaping it with
hammers, and forging it with his strong
arm; he becomes hungry and his strength
fails, he drinks no water and is faint. 13 The
carpenter stretches a line, marks it out with
a stylus, fashions it with planes, and marks
it with a compass; he makes it in human
form, with human beauty, to be set up in a
shrine. 14 He cuts down cedars or chooses a
holm tree or an oak and lets it grow strong
among the trees of the forest. He plants a
cedar and the rain nourishes it. 15 Then it
can be used as fuel. Part of it he takes and
warms himself; he kindles a fire and bakes
bread. Then he makes a god and worships
it, makes it a carved image and bows down
before it. 16 Half of it he burns in the fire;
over this half he roasts meat, eats it and is
satisfied. He also warms himself and says,
"Ah, I am warm, I can feel the fire!" 17 The
rest of it he makes into a god, his idol, bows
down to it and worships it; he prays to it
and says, "Save me, for you are my god!"
18 They do not know, nor do they com-
prehend; for their eyes are shut, so that they
cannot see, and their minds as well, so that
they cannot understand. 19 No one consid-
ers, nor is there knowledge or discernment
to say, "Half of it I burned in the fire; I also
baked bread on its coals, I roasted meat
and have eaten. Now shall I make the rest
of it an abomination? Shall I fall down
before a block of wood?" 20 He feeds on
ashes; a deluded mind has led him astray,

a Cn: Heb *from my placing an eternal people and things to come* *b* Tg: Heb *them* *c* Cn: Heb *an ax*

41.17–20n. The assurance of blessing on future generations echoes the Abrahamic blessing (Gen 12.1–3). The future Israel will include proselytes, i.e., those who accept the LORD. **5:** *Write on the hand,* cf. Deut 6.8. **6–8:** A restatement of the "argument from prophecy" (see 41.21–24n.) in support of the preeminence and incomparability of the LORD. *First . . . last,* see 41.4n. **8:** *Rock,* traditional metaphor for the God of Israel (17.10; Deut 32.4,18; Ps 18.2).

44.9–20: Polemic against idols. The longest statement about idolatry in these chapters (see 40.18–20n.) has been spliced into the verse oracle vv. 6–8,21–23. Idolatry is subjected to satire by a detailed review of the manufacture of idolatrous objects, consistent with the Israelite prohibition of making religious images (Ex 20.4–6). For a more sophisticated polemic, see Wis 13–15; Let Jer. **21–23: The continuation**

and he cannot save himself or say, "Is not this thing in my right hand a fraud?"

21 Remember these things, O Jacob,
and Israel, for you are my servant;
I formed you, you are my servant;
O Israel, you will not be forgotten
by me.
22 I have swept away your transgressions
like a cloud,
and your sins like mist;
return to me, for I have redeemed
you.

23 Sing, O heavens, for the LORD has
done it;
shout, O depths of the earth;
break forth into singing,
O mountains,
O forest, and every tree in it!
For the LORD has redeemed Jacob,
and will be glorified in Israel.

24 Thus says the LORD, your Redeemer,
who formed you in the womb:
I am the LORD, who made all things,
who alone stretched out the
heavens,
who by myself spread out the earth;
25 who frustrates the omens of liars,
and makes fools of diviners;
who turns back the wise,
and makes their knowledge foolish;
26 who confirms the word of his servant,
and fulfills the prediction of his
messengers;
who says of Jerusalem, "It shall be
inhabited,"
and of the cities of Judah, "They
shall be rebuilt,
and I will raise up their ruins";
27 who says to the deep, "Be dry—
I will dry up your rivers";
28 who says of Cyrus, "He is my
shepherd,
and he shall carry out all my
purpose";
and who says of Jerusalem, "It shall
be rebuilt,"
and of the temple, "Your
foundation shall be laid."

45 Thus says the LORD to his
anointed, to Cyrus,
whose right hand I have grasped
to subdue nations before him
and strip kings of their robes,
to open doors before him—
and the gates shall not be closed:
2 I will go before you
and level the mountains,[a]
I will break in pieces the doors
of bronze
and cut through the bars of iron,
3 I will give you the treasures of
darkness
and riches hidden in secret places,
so that you may know that it is I, the
LORD,
the God of Israel, who call you by
your name.
4 For the sake of my servant Jacob,
and Israel my chosen,
I call you by your name,

a Q Ms Gk: MT *the swellings*

of vv. 6–8. Israel is forgiven and redeemed, and all creation is invited to join in praising God, who has brought this about.

44.24–45.8: The Cyrus oracle. 44.24–28: The God of Israel who has commissioned Cyrus presents himself as the creator of the world and the one who stands behind the predictions of his prophets (see 41.21–24n.) while confounding those of the Babylonian priests and sages. **26:** *His servant,* a prophetic figure, perhaps the author of prophecies contained in chs 40–48. **28:** *Shepherd,* a common metaphor for ruler (56.11; Jer 23.4). **45.1–8:** Cyrus II (558–530 BCE), founder of the Persian Empire, is designated as the LORD's *anointed* or messiah and commissioned to conquer Babylon and other nations, and to do this on behalf of the people of Israel. **1:** The only biblical passage in which "messiah", i.e., anointed ruler, refers to a non-Israelite. **4:** *I surname you,* the translation is anachronistic; the sense is rather that Cyrus is designated as the LORD's shepherd or anointed one (44.5b). **5–7:** The LORD alone dictates the course of history (44.6–8). On his famous cylinder inscription published in 538 BCE, Cyrus attributes his

I surname you, though you do not
know me.
5 I am the LORD, and there is no other;
besides me there is no god.
I arm you, though you do not
know me,
6 so that they may know, from the
rising of the sun
and from the west, that there is no
one besides me;
I am the LORD, and there is
no other.
7 I form light and create darkness,
I make weal and create woe;
I the LORD do all these things.

8 Shower, O heavens, from above,
and let the skies rain down
righteousness;
let the earth open, that salvation may
spring up,[a]
and let it cause righteousness to
sprout up also;
I the LORD have created it.

9 Woe to you who strive with your
Maker,
earthen vessels with the potter![b]
Does the clay say to the one who
fashions it, "What are you
making"?
or "Your work has no handles"?
10 Woe to anyone who says to a father,
"What are you begetting?"
or to a woman, "With what are
you in labor?"
11 Thus says the LORD,
the Holy One of Israel, and its
Maker:
Will you question me[c] about my
children,
or command me concerning the
work of my hands?
12 I made the earth,
and created humankind upon it;
it was my hands that stretched out
the heavens,
and I commanded all their host.
13 I have aroused Cyrus[d] in
righteousness,
and I will make all his paths
straight;
he shall build my city
and set my exiles free,
not for price or reward,
says the LORD of hosts.
14 Thus says the LORD:
The wealth of Egypt and the
merchandise of Ethiopia,[e]
and the Sabeans, tall of stature,
shall come over to you and be yours,
they shall follow you;
they shall come over in chains and
bow down to you.
They will make supplication to you,
saying,
"God is with you alone, and there
is no other;
there is no god besides him."
15 Truly, you are a God who hides
himself,
O God of Israel, the Savior.
16 All of them are put to shame and
confounded,

a Q Ms: MT *that they may bring forth salvation*
b Cn: Heb *with the potsherds*, or *with the potters*
c Cn: Heb *Ask me of things to come* *d* Heb *him*
e Or *Nubia*; Heb *Cush*

success to Marduk, the god of Babylon. **8:** The Cyrus oracle is rounded off with a short and joyful psalm in anticipation of imminent salvation.

45.9–19: A refutation of those who question Cyrus's mission. For the metaphor of the potter and the clay, see 29.16; Jer 18.1–6. **11:** Addressed to the gods of other lands and their devotees who bring up against the LORD his hostile acts recently directed against his own people. **13:** Cyrus's victorious achievements will include the release of exiled Israelites and the restoration of Jerusalem; cf. 2 Chr 36.22–23; Ezra 1.1–4. That these expectations were far from being fulfilled is abundantly in evidence in chs 56–66. **14–17:** Foreign nations will acknowledge the God of Israel as the one, true God. They will be subject to Israel and bring their wealth in tribute (cf. 14.1–2; 60.4–16; 61.5–7). History provides many examples of oppression generating such fantasies of a complete reversal of fortune in the future. **14:** *Sabeans*, from Seba in southwest Arabia (see 43.3). **18–19:** The LORD replies to the charge of abusing his own

the makers of idols go in confusion
together.
17 But Israel is saved by the LORD
with everlasting salvation;
you shall not be put to shame or
confounded
to all eternity.

18 For thus says the LORD,
who created the heavens
(he is God!),
who formed the earth and made it
(he established it;
he did not create it a chaos,
he formed it to be inhabited!):
I am the LORD, and there is no other.
19 I did not speak in secret,
in a land of darkness;
I did not say to the offspring
of Jacob,
"Seek me in chaos."
I the LORD speak the truth,
I declare what is right.

20 Assemble yourselves and come
together,
draw near, you survivors of the
nations!
They have no knowledge—
those who carry about their
wooden idols,
and keep on praying to a god
that cannot save.
21 Declare and present your case;
let them take counsel together!
Who told this long ago?
Who declared it of old?
Was it not I, the LORD?
There is no other god besides me,
a righteous God and a Savior;
there is no one besides me.

22 Turn to me and be saved,
all the ends of the earth!
For I am God, and there is
no other.
23 By myself I have sworn,
from my mouth has gone forth in
righteousness
a word that shall not return:
"To me every knee shall bow,
every tongue shall swear."

24 Only in the LORD, it shall be said
of me,
are righteousness and strength;
all who were incensed against him
shall come to him and be ashamed.
25 In the LORD all the offspring of Israel
shall triumph and glory.

46 Bel bows down, Nebo stoops,
their idols are on beasts and cattle;
these things you carry are loaded
as burdens on weary animals.
2 They stoop, they bow down together;
they cannot save the burden,
but themselves go into captivity.

3 Listen to me, O house of Jacob,
all the remnant of the house of
Israel,
who have been borne by me from
your birth,
carried from the womb;
4 even to your old age I am he,
even when you turn gray I will
carry you.

people: As creator of order out of chaos (cf. Gen 1.1–2), he has always dealt openly with his people.

45.20–25: An offer of salvation addressed to the nations. 20–23: After one more challenge to the foreign gods to match the LORD's ability to predict the future and bring it about (see 40.18–20n.), the nations are invited to seek salvation in the worship of the one, true God and in submission to his will. **24:** *Righteousness,* more correctly, "salvation" or "the power to save," as in 45.8; 56.1b.

46.1–13: A contrast between the ineffectual Babylonian deities and the God of Israel, who announces his intentions and then brings them about. **1–2:** The statues of Bel-Marduk, principal Babylonian deity (Jer 50.2), and his son Nebo (Nabu), patrons of the Neo-Babylonian dynasty, are represented as being carried to safety from the threatened city of Babylon. **3–4:** The LORD, who carries Israel in his arms, is contrasted with Bel and Nebo who have to be carried by their devotees whom, in contrast, they cannot save. **5–7:** See 40.18–20n. The prophet may be referring to the New Year festival procession in Babylon,

I have made, and I will bear;
I will carry and will save.

5 To whom will you liken me and make me equal,
and compare me, as though we were alike?
6 Those who lavish gold from the purse,
and weigh out silver in the scales—
they hire a goldsmith, who makes it into a god;
then they fall down and worship!
7 They lift it to their shoulders, they carry it,
they set it in its place, and it stands there;
it cannot move from its place.
If one cries out to it, it does not answer
or save anyone from trouble.

8 Remember this and consider,[a]
recall it to mind, you transgressors,
9 remember the former things of old;
for I am God, and there is no other;
I am God, and there is no one like me,
10 declaring the end from the beginning
and from ancient times things not yet done,
saying, "My purpose shall stand,
and I will fulfill my intention,"
11 calling a bird of prey from the east,
the man for my purpose from a far country.
I have spoken, and I will bring it to pass;
I have planned, and I will do it.

12 Listen to me, you stubborn of heart,
you who are far from deliverance:
13 I bring near my deliverance, it is not far off,
and my salvation will not tarry;
I will put salvation in Zion,
for Israel my glory.

47 Come down and sit in the dust,
virgin daughter Babylon!
Sit on the ground without a throne,
daughter Chaldea!
For you shall no more be called
tender and delicate.
2 Take the millstones and grind meal,
remove your veil,
strip off your robe, uncover your legs,
pass through the rivers.
3 Your nakedness shall be uncovered,
and your shame shall be seen.
I will take vengeance,
and I will spare no one.
4 Our Redeemer—the LORD of hosts is his name—
is the Holy One of Israel.

5 Sit in silence, and go into darkness,
daughter Chaldea!
For you shall no more be called
the mistress of kingdoms.
6 I was angry with my people,
I profaned my heritage;
I gave them into your hand,
you showed them no mercy;
on the aged you made your yoke
exceedingly heavy.
7 You said, "I shall be mistress forever,"
so that you did not lay these things to heart
or remember their end.

a Meaning of Heb uncertain

cf. 45.20b. **8–11:** Another reminder of the ability of the God of Israel to predict events and bring them about with reference to the career of Cyrus, here represented as a bird of prey. Cf. 41.2; 45.1–2. **12–13:** The skeptical are assured that the vindication and salvation of Jerusalem are close at hand, cf. 56.1.

47.1–15: The end of Babylon. 1–4: Babylon's fate is analogous to that of a female prisoner of war; see 37.22n. In this and similar passages (e.g., Hos 2.10; Ezek 16.15–52; 23.5–31) the language will sound offensive to many modern readers. **5–7:** Babylon will be punished for cruelties inflicted on conquered Judah. **8–11:** Babylon's boast of uniqueness is countered by the claim of the God of Israel's incomparabil-

8 Now therefore hear this, you lover of pleasures,
who sit securely,
who say in your heart,
"I am, and there is no one besides me;
I shall not sit as a widow
or know the loss of children"—
9 both these things shall come upon you
in a moment, in one day:
the loss of children and widowhood
shall come upon you in full measure,
in spite of your many sorceries
and the great power of your enchantments.

10 You felt secure in your wickedness;
you said, "No one sees me."
Your wisdom and your knowledge
led you astray,
and you said in your heart,
"I am, and there is no one besides me."
11 But evil shall come upon you,
which you cannot charm away;
disaster shall fall upon you,
which you will not be able to ward off;
and ruin shall come on you suddenly,
of which you know nothing.

12 Stand fast in your enchantments
and your many sorceries,
with which you have labored from your youth;
perhaps you may be able to succeed,
perhaps you may inspire terror.
13 You are wearied with your many consultations;
let those who study[a] the heavens
stand up and save you,
those who gaze at the stars,
and at each new moon predict
what[b] shall befall you.

14 See, they are like stubble,
the fire consumes them;
they cannot deliver themselves
from the power of the flame.
No coal for warming oneself is this,
no fire to sit before!
15 Such to you are those with whom you have labored,
who have trafficked with you from your youth;
they all wander about in their own paths;
there is no one to save you.

48 Hear this, O house of Jacob,
who are called by the name of Israel,
and who came forth from the loins[c] of Judah;
who swear by the name of the LORD,
and invoke the God of Israel,
but not in truth or right.
2 For they call themselves after the holy city,
and lean on the God of Israel;
the LORD of hosts is his name.

3 The former things I declared long ago,
they went out from my mouth and I made them known;
then suddenly I did them and they came to pass.
4 Because I know that you are obstinate,

a Meaning of Heb uncertain *b* Gk Syr Compare Vg: Heb *from what* *c* Cn: Heb *waters*

ity (41.4b; 43.10–11; 44.6–8; 45.5–6,21–22; 46.9). Magical practices, the consultation of omens, and astronomy were important aspects of the Babylonian religious and intellectual tradition (see 44.24–25; Jer 50.35–36). **12–15:** The Babylonians employed astronomy to establish the religious calendar and to predict good or bad fortune. All of this is rejected as futile by the prophet.

48.1–13: An address to the Israelite community. The fulfillment of prophecy should have persuaded them that the God whom they worshiped, not the gods of other peoples, was in control of events. **3:** *The former things,* cf. 41.22; 43.9; 46.9. **6:** The *new things* are the conquests of Cyrus which are destined to

and your neck is an iron sinew
and your forehead brass,
5 I declared them to you from long ago,
before they came to pass I announced them to you,
so that you would not say, "My idol did them,
my carved image and my cast image commanded them."

6 You have heard; now see all this;
and will you not declare it?
From this time forward I make you hear new things,
hidden things that you have not known.
7 They are created now, not long ago;
before today you have never heard of them,
so that you could not say, "I already knew them."
8 You have never heard, you have never known,
from of old your ear has not been opened.
For I knew that you would deal very treacherously,
and that from birth you were called a rebel.

9 For my name's sake I defer my anger,
for the sake of my praise I restrain it for you,
so that I may not cut you off.
10 See, I have refined you, but not like[a] silver;
I have tested you in the furnace of adversity.
11 For my own sake, for my own sake, I do it,
for why should my name[b] be profaned?
My glory I will not give to another.

12 Listen to me, O Jacob,
and Israel, whom I called:
I am He; I am the first,
and I am the last.
13 My hand laid the foundation of the earth,
and my right hand spread out the heavens;
when I summon them,
they stand at attention.

14 Assemble, all of you, and hear!
Who among them has declared these things?
The LORD loves him;
he shall perform his purpose on Babylon,
and his arm shall be against the Chaldeans.
15 I, even I, have spoken and called him,
I have brought him, and he will prosper in his way.
16 Draw near to me, hear this!
From the beginning I have not spoken in secret,
from the time it came to be I have been there.
And now the Lord GOD has sent me and his spirit.

17 Thus says the LORD,
your Redeemer, the Holy One of Israel:
I am the LORD your God,

a Cn: Heb *with* *b* Gk Old Latin: Heb *for why should it*

lead to a change of fortune for Judah, cf. 43.18–19. Proof is necessary on account of Israel's history of religious infidelity. **10:** *Furnace,* used elsewhere with reference to the sojourn in Egypt (Deut 4.20; Jer 11.4), here refers to exile in Babylon. **12–13:** The God of Israel is *the first* and *the last,* i.e., all-encompassing in reality and power, and the creator. See also 41.4; 43.10; 44.6.

48.14–22: Another statement of the divine purpose. 14–16: A call by the LORD to the gods of the nations to acknowledge that he has commissioned Cyrus to bring the Babylonian Empire to an end. **16b:** A rare instance in which we hear the voice of a prophetic author speaking of himself; see also 61.1–3,17–19. **17–19:** As in Deuteronomy and elsewhere, national prosperity and well-being are contingent on observance of the laws. **20–22:** The return from exile in Babylon is a repeat of the Exodus from

who teaches you for your
own good,
who leads you in the way you
should go.
18 O that you had paid attention to my
commandments!
Then your prosperity would have
been like a river,
and your success like the waves of
the sea;
19 your offspring would have been like
the sand,
and your descendants like its
grains;
their name would never be cut off
or destroyed from before me.

20 Go out from Babylon, flee from
Chaldea,
declare this with a shout of joy,
proclaim it,
send it forth to the end of the earth;
say, "The LORD has redeemed his
servant Jacob!"
21 They did not thirst when he led them
through the deserts;
he made water flow for them from
the rock;
he split open the rock and the
water gushed out.

22 "There is no peace," says the LORD,
"for the wicked."

49 Listen to me, O coastlands,
pay attention, you peoples from
far away!
The LORD called me before I
was born,
while I was in my mother's womb
he named me.
2 He made my mouth like a sharp
sword,
in the shadow of his hand he
hid me;
he made me a polished arrow,
in his quiver he hid me away.
3 And he said to me, "You are my
servant,
Israel, in whom I will be glorified."
4 But I said, "I have labored in vain,
I have spent my strength for
nothing and vanity;
yet surely my cause is with the LORD,
and my reward with my God."

5 And now the LORD says,
who formed me in the womb to be
his servant,
to bring Jacob back to him,
and that Israel might be gathered to
him,
for I am honored in the sight of
the LORD,
and my God has become my
strength—
6 he says,
"It is too light a thing that you
should be my servant
to raise up the tribes of Jacob
and to restore the survivors of
Israel;
I will give you as a light to the
nations,
that my salvation may reach to the
end of the earth."

7 Thus says the LORD,

Egypt, the paradigm of redemption (cf. Ex 17.1–7). This passage forms an inclusion with 40.1–5 and thus rounds off chs 40–48. **22:** See also 57.21.

49.1–6: The LORD's servant presents himself to foreign peoples. This passage is generally identified as the second of the "Servant songs" (see 42.1n.). Predestined to service before birth (cf. Jer 1.5), the servant will fulfill his mission by the spoken word (cf. Jer 1.9). The servant has therefore received a prophetic call, and though conscious of failure is confident of final vindication. **3:** *Israel,* the word, absent from some Heb manuscripts, is probably a gloss. Since the servant's mission is on behalf of Israel, its reunification and restoration, the reference must be to an individual or group within Israel. **6:** *A light to the nations,* see 42.6.

49.7–13: Return and restoration. 7: No matter how the author of vv. 1–6 understood the identity of the servant, this verse promises that the situation of Israel, now subservient to a foreign power, will be

the Redeemer of Israel and his Holy
One,
to one deeply despised, abhorred by
the nations,
the slave of rulers,
"Kings shall see and stand up,
princes, and they shall prostrate
themselves,
because of the LORD, who is faithful,
the Holy One of Israel, who has
chosen you."

8 Thus says the LORD:
In a time of favor I have answered
you,
on a day of salvation I have helped
you;
I have kept you and given you
as a covenant to the people,[a]
to establish the land,
to apportion the desolate heritages;
9 saying to the prisoners, "Come out,"
to those who are in darkness,
"Show yourselves."
They shall feed along the ways,
on all the bare heights[b] shall be
their pasture;
10 they shall not hunger or thirst,
neither scorching wind nor sun
shall strike them down,
for he who has pity on them will lead
them,
and by springs of water will guide
them.
11 And I will turn all my mountains into
a road,
and my highways shall be
raised up.
12 Lo, these shall come from far away,
and lo, these from the north and
from the west,
and these from the land of Syene.[c]

13 Sing for joy, O heavens, and exult,
O earth;
break forth, O mountains, into
singing!
For the LORD has comforted his
people,
and will have compassion on his
suffering ones.

14 But Zion said, "The LORD has
forsaken me,
my Lord has forgotten me."
15 Can a woman forget her nursing
child,
or show no compassion for the
child of her womb?
Even these may forget,
yet I will not forget you.
16 See, I have inscribed you on the palms
of my hands;
your walls are continually
before me.
17 Your builders outdo your
destroyers,[d]
and those who laid you waste go
away from you.
18 Lift up your eyes all around and see;
they all gather, they come to you.
As I live, says the LORD,
you shall put all of them on like an
ornament,

a Meaning of Heb uncertain *b* Or *the trails*
c Q Ms: MT *Sinim* *d* Or *Your children come swiftly; your destroyers*

reversed. **8–12:** An unnamed individual, perhaps Cyrus (see 42.5–9n.), is commissioned to facilitate the return of Judean exiles and their settlement in the homeland. On the "way through the wilderness" theme, see also 40.3–5; 41.17–20; 43.19; 48.20–22. **12:** *Syene,* Aswan in Upper Egypt at the first cataract of the Nile, where a Jewish settlement existed prior to the Persian conquest of Egypt in 525 BCE. **13:** A brief hymn in praise of the God who comforts his people (cf. 40.1; 44.23).

49.14–26: God has not abandoned Israel. 14: Zion is personified as a woman. See also 37.22n.; 50.1; 51.17–52.2; 54.1–14. **15:** God represented metaphorically as mother, cf. 66.13. **16:** Writing (e.g., a name) on the hand was perhaps a way of identifying and remembering a person. It could also serve as indicating close association, cf. the devotee who writes the name of Israel's God on the hand (44.5). **16–19:** Jerusalem, destroyed during the Babylonian conquest, and the other cities of Judah will be rebuilt and repopulated. **18:** This verse is echoed and developed in Bar 5.5–9. **20–21:** Descendants of the

and like a bride you shall bind
them on.

19 Surely your waste and your desolate
places
and your devastated land—
surely now you will be too crowded
for your inhabitants,
and those who swallowed you up
will be far away.

20 The children born in the time of your
bereavement
will yet say in your hearing:
"The place is too crowded for me;
make room for me to settle."

21 Then you will say in your heart,
"Who has borne me these?
I was bereaved and barren,
exiled and put away—
so who has reared these?
I was left all alone—
where then have these come from?"

22 Thus says the Lord GOD:
I will soon lift up my hand to the
nations,
and raise my signal to the peoples;
and they shall bring your sons in their
bosom,
and your daughters shall be carried
on their shoulders.

23 Kings shall be your foster fathers,
and their queens your nursing
mothers.
With their faces to the ground they
shall bow down to you,
and lick the dust of your feet.
Then you will know that I am the
LORD;
those who wait for me shall not be
put to shame.

24 Can the prey be taken from the
mighty,
or the captives of a tyrant[a] be
rescued?

25 But thus says the LORD:
Even the captives of the mighty shall
be taken,
and the prey of the tyrant be
rescued;
for I will contend with those who
contend with you,
and I will save your children.

26 I will make your oppressors eat their
own flesh,
and they shall be drunk with their
own blood as with wine.
Then all flesh shall know
that I am the LORD your Savior,
and your Redeemer, the Mighty
One of Jacob.

50 Thus says the LORD:
Where is your mother's bill of
divorce
with which I put her away?
Or which of my creditors is it
to whom I have sold you?
No, because of your sins you
were sold,
and for your transgressions your
mother was put away.

2 Why was no one there when I came?
Why did no one answer when I
called?

a Q Ms Syr Vg: MT *of a righteous person*

deportees will return to a land already repopulated. See also Jer 31.15–17. **22–26:** The upraised hand and signal will identify an assembly point for the repatriation of dispersed Israelites by Gentiles (cf. 11.11–12; 43.6–7; 60.9; 66.20). These Gentiles will be subject to Israel (cf. 60.12,14). **26:** Eating flesh and drinking blood is to be understood metaphorically (cf. Eccl 4.5) rather than as an allusion to cannibalism during a siege.

50.1–3: God is not responsible for the loss of statehood and exile. The argument is presented by a series of rhetorical questions. The LORD was not responsible for divorcing your mother, i.e., the land of Israel (Deut 24.1–4; Hos 1–3), or for selling you into indentured service, i.e., exile for non-payment of debts (cf. 52.3). Your sin brought it about. This idea is further developed in 59.1–15. **2–3:** The motif of address and response is taken up in the last section of the book (58.9; 65.1,12,24; 66.4). The hand or arm of God is not *shortened,* i.e., his power to destroy or save is not limited by human intentions or actions (cf. 59.1).

Is my hand shortened, that it cannot
redeem?
Or have I no power to deliver?
By my rebuke I dry up the sea,
I make the rivers a desert;
their fish stink for lack of water,
and die of thirst.[a]
3 I clothe the heavens with blackness,
and make sackcloth their covering.

4 The Lord GOD has given me
the tongue of a teacher,[b]
that I may know how to sustain
the weary with a word.
Morning by morning he wakens—
wakens my ear
to listen as those who are taught.
5 The Lord GOD has opened my ear,
and I was not rebellious,
I did not turn backward.
6 I gave my back to those who
struck me,
and my cheeks to those who pulled
out the beard;
I did not hide my face
from insult and spitting.

7 The Lord GOD helps me;
therefore I have not been disgraced;
therefore I have set my face like flint,
and I know that I shall not be put
to shame;
8 he who vindicates me is near.
Who will contend with me?
Let us stand up together.
Who are my adversaries?
Let them confront me.
9 It is the Lord GOD who helps me;
who will declare me guilty?
All of them will wear out like a
garment;
the moth will eat them up.

10 Who among you fears the LORD
and obeys the voice of his servant,
who walks in darkness
and has no light,
yet trusts in the name of the LORD
and relies upon his God?
11 But all of you are kindlers of fire,
lighters of firebrands.[c]
Walk in the flame of your fire,
and among the brands that you
have kindled!
This is what you shall have from my
hand:
you shall lie down in torment.

51 Listen to me, you that pursue
righteousness,
you that seek the LORD.
Look to the rock from which you
were hewn,
and to the quarry from which
you were dug.
2 Look to Abraham your father
and to Sarah who bore you;
for he was but one when I called him,
but I blessed him and made
him many.
3 For the LORD will comfort Zion;
he will comfort all her waste places,

a Or *die on the thirsty ground* b Cn: Heb *of those who are taught* c Syr: Heb *you gird yourselves with firebrands*

50.4–9: The obedience of the prophet. The prophetic individual who is speaking here is identified as "servant" only in the following comment (vv. 10–11). Many take this to be the third of the "Servant Songs" (see 42.1–4n.). **4:** *Taught* by God, cf. Jer 1.4–10. **6:** Like Jeremiah this individual was also persecuted (Jer 11.9; 20.1–2; 26.7–24).

50.10–11: A comment on vv. 4–9, apparently by a follower or disciple, addressed to the unreceptive audience of the prophet, now identified as the servant of the LORD. Their decision to follow their own lights rather than the prophet's teaching will lead them to reprobation and ruin.

51.1–8: An announcement of future salvation. 1–3: Salvation is expressed as the fulfillment of the promise to Abraham, with special reference to land and descendents (Gen 12.1–3). The call to attention—to listen, take heed—is a prominent feature of the rhetoric of these chapters (41.1; 42.18; 44.7; 46.3,12; 48.1,12; 49.1). **3:** *Eden,* allusions to the garden of Eden and what happened in it occur no earlier than the exilic period (Ezek 28.13; 36.35). **4–6:** The enlightening of the nations by means of true teaching (Heb

and will make her wilderness
like Eden,
her desert like the garden of
the LORD;
joy and gladness will be found in
her,
thanksgiving and the voice of song.

4 Listen to me, my people,
and give heed to me, my nation;
for a teaching will go out from me,
and my justice for a light to
the peoples.
5 I will bring near my deliverance
swiftly,
my salvation has gone out
and my arms will rule the peoples;
the coastlands wait for me,
and for my arm they hope.
6 Lift up your eyes to the heavens,
and look at the earth beneath;
for the heavens will vanish like
smoke,
the earth will wear out like a
garment,
and those who live on it will die
like gnats;[a]
but my salvation will be forever,
and my deliverance will never
be ended.

7 Listen to me, you who know
righteousness,
you people who have my teaching
in your hearts;
do not fear the reproach of others,
and do not be dismayed when they
revile you.
8 For the moth will eat them up like a
garment,
and the worm will eat them
like wool;
but my deliverance will be forever,
and my salvation to all generations.

9 Awake, awake, put on strength,
O arm of the LORD!
Awake, as in days of old,
the generations of long ago!
Was it not you who cut Rahab in
pieces,
who pierced the dragon?
10 Was it not you who dried up the sea,
the waters of the great deep;
who made the depths of the sea
a way
for the redeemed to cross over?
11 So the ransomed of the LORD shall
return,
and come to Zion with singing;
everlasting joy shall be upon their
heads;
they shall obtain joy and gladness,
and sorrow and sighing shall
flee away.

12 I, I am he who comforts you;
why then are you afraid of a mere
mortal who must die,
a human being who fades like
grass?
13 You have forgotten the LORD, your
Maker,
who stretched out the heavens

a Or *in like manner*

"torah"), especially ethical teaching, is a prominent theme in these chapters (42.3–4,6; 49.6; cf. 2.3). **6b:** God's promise of salvation is firmer than the created order; cf. 54.10. **7–8:** A reminder that the promises and assurances are addressed only to those in the community who seek righteousness and remain faithful to the teaching (cf. 41.11–13; 42.18; 43.22–24; 46.12–13; 48.1–5; 50.10–11).

51.9–11: A plea for God's intervention using the Israelite version of the combat between a deity and monsters representing chaos and disorder—a contest ending with the creation of the world and humanity. The opponent is variously named Rahab, Tannin (Dragon), Yamm (Sea), Tehom Rabbah (Great Deep), Leviathan (27.1; 30.7; Ezek 29.3; Ps 74.12–17; 87.4; 89.10; Job 3.8; 26.12; 38.8; 41.1–34). As Rahab is elsewhere identified with Egypt (30.7; Ezek 29.3), so here the primordial victory is associated with the rescue of Israel from Egypt at the Red (Reed) Sea (Ex 14–15).

51.12–16: A further word of assurance. If the LORD, creator of the world, is with them, if they are the

and laid the foundations of
the earth.
You fear continually all day long
because of the fury of the
oppressor,
who is bent on destruction.
But where is the fury of the
oppressor?
14 The oppressed shall speedily be
released;
they shall not die and go down to
the Pit,
nor shall they lack bread.
15 For I am the LORD your God,
who stirs up the sea so that its
waves roar—
the LORD of hosts is his name.
16 I have put my words in your mouth,
and hidden you in the shadow of
my hand,
stretching out[a] the heavens
and laying the foundations of
the earth,
and saying to Zion, "You are my
people."

17 Rouse yourself, rouse yourself!
Stand up, O Jerusalem,
you who have drunk at the hand of
the LORD
the cup of his wrath,
who have drunk to the dregs
the bowl of staggering.
18 There is no one to guide her
among all the children she
has borne;
there is no one to take her by
the hand
among all the children she has
brought up.
19 These two things have befallen you
—who will grieve with you?—
devastation and destruction, famine
and sword—
who will comfort you?[b]
20 Your children have fainted,
they lie at the head of every street
like an antelope in a net;
they are full of the wrath of
the LORD,
the rebuke of your God.

21 Therefore hear this, you who are
wounded,[c]
who are drunk, but not with wine:
22 Thus says your Sovereign, the LORD,
your God who pleads the cause of
his people:
See, I have taken from your hand the
cup of staggering;
you shall drink no more
from the bowl of my wrath.
23 And I will put it into the hand of
your tormentors,
who have said to you,
"Bow down, that we may walk
on you";
and you have made your back like the
ground
and like the street for them to walk
on.

52 Awake, awake,
put on your strength, O Zion!
Put on your beautiful garments,
O Jerusalem, the holy city;
for the uncircumcised and the unclean
shall enter you no more.
2 Shake yourself from the dust, rise up,
O captive[d] Jerusalem;
loose the bonds from your neck,
O captive daughter Zion!

3 For thus says the LORD: You were sold

a Syr: Heb *planting* *b* Q Ms Gk Syr Vg: MT *how may I comfort you?* *c* Or *humbled* *d* Cn: Heb *rise up, sit*

LORD's people, no oppressor need be feared. This is a common Isaian theme (cf. 31.3). **14:** *The Pit,* Sheol, the underworld, Hades (cf. 14.9–11).

51.17–23: The anger and mercy of God. Jerusalem has been forced to drink from the bitter cup of God's anger (cf. Jer 25.15–29), resulting in devastation and spiritual disorientation (cf. 29.9–10; Lam 4.21), but now it is the turn of her tormentors to experience the divine anger (cf. 41.1–16).

52.1–6: Jerusalem restored. Repetition of the imperative is a common rhetorical device in chs 40–55

for nothing, and you shall be redeemed
without money. 4 For thus says the Lord
GOD: Long ago, my people went down into
Egypt to reside there as aliens; the Assyrian,
too, has oppressed them without cause.
5 Now therefore what am I doing here, says
the LORD, seeing that my people are taken
away without cause? Their rulers howl,
says the LORD, and continually, all day
long, my name is despised. 6 Therefore my
people shall know my name; therefore in
that day they shall know that it is I who
speak; here am I.

7 How beautiful upon the mountains
are the feet of the messenger who
announces peace,
who brings good news,
who announces salvation,
who says to Zion, "Your God
reigns."
8 Listen! Your sentinels lift up
their voices,
together they sing for joy;
for in plain sight they see
the return of the LORD to Zion.
9 Break forth together into singing,
you ruins of Jerusalem;
for the LORD has comforted his
people,
he has redeemed Jerusalem.
10 The LORD has bared his holy arm
before the eyes of all the nations;
and all the ends of the earth shall see
the salvation of our God.

11 Depart, depart, go out from there!
Touch no unclean thing;
go out from the midst of it, purify
yourselves,
you who carry the vessels of
the LORD.
12 For you shall not go out in haste,
and you shall not go in flight;
for the LORD will go before you,
and the God of Israel will be your
rear guard.

13 See, my servant shall prosper;
he shall be exalted and lifted up,
and shall be very high.
14 Just as there were many who were
astonished at him[a]
—so marred was his appearance,
beyond human semblance,
and his form beyond that of
mortals—
15 so he shall startle[b] many nations;
kings shall shut their mouths
because of him;
for that which had not been told
them they shall see,
and that which they had not heard
they shall contemplate.

a Syr Tg: Heb *you* *b* Meaning of Heb uncertain

(40.1; 51.9,17; 52.11). **3–6:** An additional note in prose referring to the tradition of oppression in Egypt (Ex 1–15) and the Assyrian domination in the eighth century. When the LORD releases his people from Babylon, they will know his name, i.e, his presence and power, as formerly he revealed his name in Egypt (Ex 2.25; 6.28). *Here am I,* the LORD's readiness to be present and to save, cf. 58.9; 65.1.

52.7–12: The approach of the ruler. The basic metaphor is of the triumphant approach of a king to a subject kingdom. His coming is announced by lookouts on mountains along the route and eventually by sentinels on the walls of Jerusalem (cf. 2 Sam 18.25–27; Nah 1.15). **8:** *Sentinels,* also a metaphor for prophet, seer (56.10; 62.6–7; Ezek 3.17; 33.2,6–7). **11–12:** The surviving sacred vessels from the Temple are brought back to Jerusalem (see Ezra 1.7–11). Complete ritual purity was unattainable in a land like Babylon, where foreign cults were practiced. The exodus from Babylon will be different from the first Exodus; cf. Ex 12.11; 13.21–22.

52.13–53.12: The mission and violent death of a servant of the LORD. The fourth of the "Servant Songs" (see 42.1–4n.) consists of an extended comment by an adherent of this unnamed individual (53.1–11a), placed between an opening and closing address of the LORD (52.13–15; 53.11b–12). The passage has been and continues to be the object of an enormous volume of commentary and is beset by problems of interpretation, several still unsolved. **52.13–15:** The LORD proclaims the ultimate vindication and exaltation of his servant, now cruelly disfigured and the object of numbed astonishment to foreign

53 Who has believed what we have
heard?
And to whom has the arm of the
LORD been revealed?
2 For he grew up before him like a
young plant,
and like a root out of dry ground;
he had no form or majesty that we
should look at him,
nothing in his appearance that we
should desire him.
3 He was despised and rejected
by others;
a man of suffering[a] and acquainted
with infirmity;
and as one from whom others hide
their faces[b]
he was despised, and we held him
of no account.

4 Surely he has borne our infirmities
and carried our diseases;
yet we accounted him stricken,
struck down by God, and afflicted.
5 But he was wounded for our
transgressions,
crushed for our iniquities;
upon him was the punishment that
made us whole,
and by his bruises we are healed.
6 All we like sheep have gone astray;
we have all turned to our own way,
and the LORD has laid on him
the iniquity of us all.

7 He was oppressed, and he was
afflicted,
yet he did not open his mouth;
like a lamb that is led to the
slaughter,
and like a sheep that before its
shearers is silent,
so he did not open his mouth.
8 By a perversion of justice he was
taken away.
Who could have imagined his
future?
For he was cut off from the land of
the living,
stricken for the transgression of my
people.
9 They made his grave with the wicked
and his tomb[c] with the rich,[d]
although he had done no violence,
and there was no deceit in
his mouth.

10 Yet it was the will of the LORD to
crush him with pain.[e]
When you make his life an offering
for sin,[f]
he shall see his offspring, and shall
prolong his days;
through him the will of the LORD
shall prosper.
11 Out of his anguish he shall
see light;[g]
he shall find satisfaction through his
knowledge.
The righteous one,[h] my servant,
shall make many righteous,
and he shall bear their iniquities.
12 Therefore I will allot him a portion
with the great,
and he shall divide the spoil with
the strong;

a Or *a man of sorrows* *b* Or *as one who hides his face from us* *c* Q Ms: MT *and in his death* *d* Cn: Heb *with a rich person* *e* Or *by disease*; meaning of Heb uncertain *f* Meaning of Heb uncertain *g* Q Mss: MT lacks *light* *h* Or *and he shall find satisfaction. Through his knowledge, the righteous one*

peoples and their rulers (49.7,23). **53.1–3:** The comment opens by referring to the unprepossessing origins of the servant. Like a leper, he suffers painful loneliness and rejection by the community (Job 19.13–19). **4–6:** The commentator makes the extraordinary statement that the servant's sufferings and the violence inflicted on him were caused by the sins of others and make atonement for sin (cf. Lev 16). **7–9:** Unlike Jeremiah (Jer 11.18–12.6) and Job, the servant suffered in silence. Early Christian interpretation applied Isa 53.4–9 to Jesus (Mt 8.17; Acts 32.33; 1 Pet 2.22–25). **10:** The servant's *offspring* refer to those who follow his example and teaching after his death rather than indicating that he survived and was rehabilitated.

because he poured out himself
to death,
and was numbered with the
transgressors;
yet he bore the sin of many,
and made intercession for the
transgressors.

54 Sing, O barren one who did
not bear;
burst into song and shout,
you who have not been in labor!
For the children of the desolate
woman will be more
than the children of her that is
married, says the LORD.
2 Enlarge the site of your tent,
and let the curtains of your
habitations be stretched out;
do not hold back; lengthen your cords
and strengthen your stakes.
3 For you will spread out to the right
and to the left,
and your descendants will possess
the nations
and will settle the desolate towns.

4 Do not fear, for you will not be
ashamed;
do not be discouraged, for you will
not suffer disgrace;
for you will forget the shame of your
youth,
and the disgrace of your
widowhood you will remember
no more.
5 For your Maker is your husband,
the LORD of hosts is his name;
the Holy One of Israel is your
Redeemer,
the God of the whole earth he
is called.
6 For the LORD has called you
like a wife forsaken and grieved in
spirit,
like the wife of a man's youth when
she is cast off,
says your God.
7 For a brief moment I abandoned you,
but with great compassion I will
gather you.
8 In overflowing wrath for a moment
I hid my face from you,
but with everlasting love I will have
compassion on you,
says the LORD, your Redeemer.

9 This is like the days of Noah to me:
Just as I swore that the waters
of Noah
would never again go over
the earth,
so I have sworn that I will not be
angry with you
and will not rebuke you.
10 For the mountains may depart
and the hills be removed,
but my steadfast love shall not depart
from you,
and my covenant of peace shall not
be removed,
says the LORD, who has
compassion on you.

11 O afflicted one, storm-tossed, and not
comforted,

54.1–17: Apostrophe to Zion. 1–3: A major motif in chs 40–66 is Jerusalem/Zion as mother of a dispersed and depressed family, and as a woman destined no longer to be forsaken, bereaved, or infertile (49.14–21,22,25; 51.17–20; 52.1–2,7–10; 60.1–22; 62.1–12; 66.7–11). Jerusalem, represented as a tent, reminiscent of the tent in the wilderness, will be repopulated together with the other Judean cities. **4–8:** After the separation of the exile, there will be a spousal reconciliation between the LORD and Jerusalem (cf. Hos 1–3). **9–10:** Exile in Babylon is compared with the great flood (Gen 6–9) and the new order envisaged by the prophet with the promise made to all humanity, a promise confirmed by oath, after the water subsided (Gen 8.21–22; 9.8–11). The *covenant of peace* (cf. 55.3; Ezek 34.25) signifies God's commitment to his people's well-being. **11–13a:** The new Jerusalem is adorned with precious stones and gems by builders supernaturally instructed; cf. Ezek 28.13–19. Christian apocalyptic literature draws on this imagery to describe the new Jerusalem (Rev 21.18–21). **17b:** The future Jerusalem will be confided

I am about to set your stones in
antimony,
and lay your foundations with
sapphires.[a]
12 I will make your pinnacles of rubies,
your gates of jewels,
and all your wall of precious
stones.
13 All your children shall be taught by
the LORD,
and great shall be the prosperity of
your children.
14 In righteousness you shall be
established;
you shall be far from oppression,
for you shall not fear;
and from terror, for it shall not
come near you.
15 If anyone stirs up strife,
it is not from me;
whoever stirs up strife with you
shall fall because of you.
16 See it is I who have created the smith
who blows the fire of coals,
and produces a weapon fit for
its purpose;
I have also created the ravager
to destroy.
17 No weapon that is fashioned
against you shall prosper,
and you shall confute every tongue
that rises against you in
judgment.
This is the heritage of the servants of
the LORD
and their vindication from me, says
the LORD.

55 Ho, everyone who thirsts,
come to the waters;
and you that have no money,
come, buy and eat!
Come, buy wine and milk
without money and without price.
2 Why do you spend your money for
that which is not bread,
and your labor for that which does
not satisfy?
Listen carefully to me, and eat what is
good,
and delight yourselves in rich food.
3 Incline your ear, and come to me;
listen, so that you may live.
I will make with you an everlasting
covenant,
my steadfast, sure love for David.
4 See, I made him a witness to
the peoples,
a leader and commander for
the peoples.
5 See, you shall call nations that you do
not know,
and nations that do not know you
shall run to you,
because of the LORD your God, the
Holy One of Israel,
for he has glorified you.

6 Seek the LORD while he may
be found,
call upon him while he is near;
7 let the wicked forsake their way,

a Or *lapis lazuli*

to the servants of the LORD. The mention of this faithful segment of the people serves as a point of transition to the last section of the book (cf. 56.6; 63.17; 65.8–9,13–16; 66.14). Opinions are divided as to whether the second part of the book (Second Isaiah) ends with ch 54 or ch 55.

55.1–5: An appeal to the prophet's audience to participate in the restoration. The metaphor for this new era is life's essential bread and water, and enhancing wine and milk. Compare the invitation to participate in Wisdom's banquet (Prov 9.5). **3–5:** God's promises to David (2 Sam 7.11–17) are now "democratized" and extended to the people as a whole (cf. 54.9–10).

55.6–11: A call to repentance, to seek and call upon God—a common prophetic theme (e.g., Am 5.6; Jer 29.12), frequent in the last section of Isaiah (58.2,9; 65.1,10,12,24; 66.4). The height of the heavens as an image of the contrast between the divine and the human also occurs in Ps 57.10; 103.11. The theme of the effectiveness of God's word echoes the opening passage of Second Isaiah (40.8) and may indicate the end of a major unit in the work.

and the unrighteous their thoughts;
let them return to the LORD, that he
may have mercy on them,
and to our God, for he will
abundantly pardon.
8 For my thoughts are not your
thoughts,
nor are your ways my ways, says
the LORD.
9 For as the heavens are higher than the
earth,
so are my ways higher than
your ways
and my thoughts than your
thoughts.

10 For as the rain and the snow come
down from heaven,
and do not return there until they
have watered the earth,
making it bring forth and sprout,
giving seed to the sower and bread
to the eater,
11 so shall my word be that goes out
from my mouth;
it shall not return to me empty,
but it shall accomplish that which I
purpose,
and succeed in the thing for which I
sent it.

12 For you shall go out in joy,
and be led back in peace;
the mountains and the hills
before you
shall burst into song,
and all the trees of the field shall
clap their hands.
13 Instead of the thorn shall come up the
cypress;
instead of the brier shall come up
the myrtle;
and it shall be to the LORD for a
memorial,
for an everlasting sign that shall not
be cut off.

56 Thus says the LORD:
Maintain justice, and do what is
right,
for soon my salvation will come,
and my deliverance be revealed.

2 Happy is the mortal who does this,
the one who holds it fast,
who keeps the sabbath, not profaning
it,
and refrains from doing any evil.

3 Do not let the foreigner joined to the
LORD say,

55.12–13: Nature will rejoice at the return of the dispersed Israelites, and the land will enjoy unparalleled fertility (cf. 41.17–20; 44.1–4; 51.3). This passage recapitulates the theme of glorious return in 40.3–5 and 48.20–22, the beginning and end of Isaiah 40–48. It therefore indicates a point of closure at a stage in the formation of the book. **13:** *Memorial,* lit. "name," cf. 56.5.

Chs 56–66: Third Isaiah. Despite the common reference to this final section of the book as Third Isaiah, it is not certain that it is a distinct, self-contained unit. These chapters reflect a divisive struggle over the identity and destiny of the Judean community in the postexilic period (primarily 538–515 BCE) with little direct concern for international affairs. Their tone shifts back and forth between a somber assessment of present realities and the envisioning of a glorious future. In them we hear the community attempting, through its prophetic representatives, to come to terms with the fact that reality has fallen short of the expectations, expressed in the previous sections, that had been raised by the fall of the Babylonian Empire and the conquests of Cyrus.

56.1–8: All are worthy to join the community. Foreigners and eunuchs are assured of their good standing in the community. This oracle enjoins observance of right moral order in view of an imminent divine intervention in human affairs (see 46.13). Sabbath observance is the distinguishing mark of the covenant (58.13–14; Neh 10.31; 13.15–22, cf. Ex 31.16–17 where sabbath is described as a perpetual covenant). **3:** *Foreigner,* in the religious sense of proselyte (see v. 6) rather than resident alien; *eunuch,* the sexually mutilated, e.g., for service in a foreign court or harem. The status of both parties is threatened by application of the law in Deut 23.1–8 excluding the sexually mutilated and certain ethnic categories from membership in the community. **6–7:** Proselytes may participate fully and joyfully in Temple wor-

"The LORD will surely separate me
from his people";
and do not let the eunuch say,
"I am just a dry tree."
4 For thus says the LORD:
To the eunuchs who keep my
sabbaths,
who choose the things that
please me
and hold fast my covenant,
5 I will give, in my house and within
my walls,
a monument and a name
better than sons and daughters;
I will give them an everlasting name
that shall not be cut off.

6 And the foreigners who join
themselves to the LORD,
to minister to him, to love the
name of the LORD,
and to be his servants,
all who keep the sabbath, and do not
profane it,
and hold fast my covenant—
7 these I will bring to my holy
mountain,
and make them joyful in my house
of prayer;
their burnt offerings and their
sacrifices
will be accepted on my altar;
for my house shall be called a house
of prayer
for all peoples.
8 Thus says the Lord GOD,
who gathers the outcasts of
Israel,
I will gather others to them
besides those already gathered.[a]

9 All you wild animals,
all you wild animals in the forest,
come to devour!
10 Israel's[b] sentinels are blind,
they are all without knowledge;
they are all silent dogs
that cannot bark;
dreaming, lying down,
loving to slumber.
11 The dogs have a mighty appetite;
they never have enough.
The shepherds also have no
understanding;
they have all turned to their
own way,
to their own gain, one and all.
12 "Come," they say, "let us[c] get wine;
let us fill ourselves with
strong drink.
And tomorrow will be like today,
great beyond measure."

57 The righteous perish,
and no one takes it to heart;
the devout are taken away,
while no one understands.
For the righteous are taken away
from calamity,
2 and they enter into peace;
those who walk uprightly
will rest on their couches.
3 But as for you, come here,

a Heb *besides his gathered ones* b Heb *His*
c Q Ms Syr Vg Tg: MT *me*

ship, including sacrifice and prayer. **8:** A distinct saying that takes up the promise of the return of dispersed Israelites (11.12), adding to it the ingathering of Gentiles (cf. 66.18–21).

56.9–12: An invitation to wild animals (foreigners) **to come and devour the flock** (the Judean community) since the guardians of the community are neglecting their responsibilities (cf. Jer 12.8–9; Ezek 39.17). **10:** *Sentinels,* prophets (21.6–9,11–12, 62.6; Ezek 3.17; 33.2,6–7; cf. Hab 2.1–3). **11:** *Shepherds,* a common metaphor for rulers and community leaders (Ezek 34.1; Zech 11.4–17).

57.1–2: The death of the righteous. A complaint that the (probably violent) death of the righteous goes unnoticed and unlamented, cf. Ps 12.2; Mic 7.2. Placed here as a contrast with the polemic that follows. **2:** *Couches,* graves.

57.3–13: Denunciation of the sorceress and her children. This attack on the practitioners of non-Yahwistic and sexually oriented forms of worship testifies to deep divisions within the Judean community of the early Persian period. **3–5:** Addressed to the *children* of Jerusalem or the land of Judah personified

you children of a sorceress,
you offspring of an adulterer and a whore.[a]
4 Whom are you mocking?
Against whom do you open your mouth wide
and stick out your tongue?
Are you not children of transgression,
the offspring of deceit—
5 you that burn with lust among the oaks,
under every green tree;
you that slaughter your children in the valleys,
under the clefts of the rocks?
6 Among the smooth stones of the valley is your portion;
they, they, are your lot;
to them you have poured out a drink offering,
you have brought a grain offering.
Shall I be appeased for these things?
7 Upon a high and lofty mountain
you have set your bed,
and there you went up to offer sacrifice.
8 Behind the door and the doorpost
you have set up your symbol;
for, in deserting me,[b] you have uncovered your bed,
you have gone up to it,
you have made it wide;
and you have made a bargain for yourself with them,
you have loved their bed,
you have gazed on their nakedness.[c]
9 You journeyed to Molech[d] with oil,
and multiplied your perfumes;
you sent your envoys far away,
and sent down even to Sheol.
10 You grew weary from your many wanderings,
but you did not say, "It is useless."
You found your desire rekindled,
and so you did not weaken.

11 Whom did you dread and fear
so that you lied,
and did not remember me
or give me a thought?
Have I not kept silent and closed my eyes,[e]
and so you do not fear me?
12 I will concede your righteousness and your works,
but they will not help you.
13 When you cry out, let your collection of idols deliver you!
The wind will carry them off,
a breath will take them away.
But whoever takes refuge in me shall possess the land
and inherit my holy mountain.

14 It shall be said,
"Build up, build up, prepare the way,
remove every obstruction from my people's way."
15 For thus says the high and lofty one

a Heb *an adulterer and she plays the whore*
b Meaning of Heb uncertain *c* Or *their phallus*; Heb *the hand* *d* Or *the king* *e* Gk Vg: Heb *silent even for a long time*

as *sorceress* and prostitute (cf. Jer 3.6–14) and the "outsider woman" in Prov 1–9, perhaps from about the same time. These reprobate members of the community engage in sexual rites and sacrifice children to Molech (v. 9). **6–13:** Addressed to the sorceress herself; one of the most violently polemic passages in the prophetic literature, containing much sexual innuendo. The woman is accused of practicing mortuary rites, necromancy, and commerce with the gods of the underworld (cf. 8.19–20; 14.9–11). *Molech,* a Canaanite deity to whom children were apparently sacrificed (Lev 18.21; 20.2–5; 2 Kings 23.10; Jer 7.31; 32.35). *Sheol,* see 28.15. **12:** Probably sarcastic, referring to the "conquests" of the sorceress. **13:** The polemic ends with a typically Isaian promise addressed to those who entrust themselves to the LORD (cf. 30.18). They will gain title to land and control of the Jerusalem Temple, crucial issues in the early Persian period.

57.14–21: A poem of consolation. 14: Cf. 40.3–4, here interpreted metaphorically. **15:** The transcendence of the God seen in Isaiah's vision (6.1–5) is here associated with God's presence with the downtrod-

who inhabits eternity, whose name
is Holy:
I dwell in the high and holy place,
and also with those who are
contrite and humble in spirit,
to revive the spirit of the humble,
and to revive the heart of the
contrite.
16 For I will not continually accuse,
nor will I always be angry;
for then the spirits would grow faint
before me,
even the souls that I have made.
17 Because of their wicked covetousness
I was angry;
I struck them, I hid and was angry;
but they kept turning back to their
own ways.
18 I have seen their ways, but I will heal
them;
I will lead them and repay them
with comfort,
creating for their mourners the fruit
of the lips.[a]
19 Peace, peace, to the far and the near,
says the LORD;
and I will heal them.
20 But the wicked are like the tossing sea
that cannot keep still;
its waters toss up mire and mud.
21 There is no peace, says my God, for
the wicked.

58 Shout out, do not hold back!
Lift up your voice like a trumpet!
Announce to my people their
rebellion,
to the house of Jacob their sins.
2 Yet day after day they seek me
and delight to know my ways,
as if they were a nation that practiced
righteousness
and did not forsake the ordinance
of their God;
they ask of me righteous judgments,
they delight to draw near to God.
3 "Why do we fast, but you do not see?
Why humble ourselves, but you do
not notice?"
Look, you serve your own interest on
your fast day,
and oppress all your workers.
4 Look, you fast only to quarrel and to
fight
and to strike with a wicked fist.
Such fasting as you do today
will not make your voice heard on
high.
5 Is such the fast that I choose,
a day to humble oneself?
Is it to bow down the head like a
bulrush,
and to lie in sackcloth and ashes?
Will you call this a fast,
a day acceptable to the LORD?
6 Is not this the fast that I choose:
to loose the bonds of injustice,
to undo the thongs of the yoke,
to let the oppressed go free,
and to break every yoke?
7 Is it not to share your bread with the
hungry,

a Meaning of Heb uncertain

den and marginalized (66.1–2). **18:** *The fruit of the lips,* praise and joyful prayer in place of mourning, as a concomitant of or substitute for sacrifice (cf. Hos 14.2). **21:** Added to make the point that the reprobate in the community are excluded from the peace and ultimate well-being promised to the far and near (48.22).

58.1–14: On genuine fasting. 1–2: The prophet is told to reveal to the people their immoral way of life, which coexists with traditional religious practices including sacrifice ("drawing near to God") and consulting priests and prophets (cf. Hag 2.10–13; Zech 7.1–14). **3–5:** The complaint is that neither prayer nor fasting has induced God to intervene in their favor. The reply is that fasting, a regular feature of Second Temple piety (cf. Zech 7.1–14; 8.18–19; Joel 1.14; 2.15), is unacceptable to God unless unaccompanied by serious moral reformation. **6–9a:** A definition of genuine fasting. For the language of petition and response see also 65.1,12,24; 66.4. **9b–12:** Another statement of the conditions necessary for the

and bring the homeless poor into
your house;
when you see the naked, to
cover them,
and not to hide yourself from your
own kin?
8 Then your light shall break forth like
the dawn,
and your healing shall spring
up quickly;
your vindicator[a] shall go before you,
the glory of the LORD shall be your
rear guard.
9 Then you shall call, and the LORD
will answer;
you shall cry for help, and he will
say, Here I am.

If you remove the yoke from
among you,
the pointing of the finger, the
speaking of evil,
10 if you offer your food to the hungry
and satisfy the needs of the
afflicted,
then your light shall rise in
the darkness
and your gloom be like the
noonday.
11 The LORD will guide you continually,
and satisfy your needs in parched
places,
and make your bones strong;
and you shall be like a watered
garden,
like a spring of water,
whose waters never fail.
12 Your ancient ruins shall be rebuilt;
you shall raise up the foundations
of many generations;
you shall be called the repairer of the
breach,
the restorer of streets to live in.

13 If you refrain from trampling the
sabbath,
from pursuing your own interests
on my holy day;
if you call the sabbath a delight
and the holy day of the LORD
honorable;
if you honor it, not going your
own ways,
serving your own interests, or
pursuing your own affairs;[b]
14 then you shall take delight in
the LORD,
and I will make you ride upon the
heights of the earth;
I will feed you with the heritage of
your ancestor Jacob,
for the mouth of the LORD has
spoken.

59 See, the LORD's hand is not too
short to save,
nor his ear too dull to hear.
2 Rather, your iniquities have been
barriers
between you and your God,
and your sins have hidden his face
from you
so that he does not hear.
3 For your hands are defiled
with blood,
and your fingers with iniquity;
your lips have spoken lies,
your tongue mutters wickedness.
4 No one brings suit justly,
no one goes to law honestly;
they rely on empty pleas, they speak
lies,
conceiving mischief and begetting
iniquity.
5 They hatch adders' eggs,

a Or *vindication* *b* Heb *or speaking words*

LORD to intervene and give the people strength to continue, adequate resources, and the means to recover from the effects of the Babylonian conquest. *Pointing of the finger,* a gesture of contempt (Prov 6.13). *Ruins . . . foundations,* a reinterpretation of earlier promises of restoration (44.26–28). **13–14:** An addendum on sabbath observance (56.1–8n.). For the final formula, see 40.5.

59.1–8: Why prayers and fasting remain without effect. The reason is to be sought not in the limitation of divine power (50.1–2), or the LORD's unwillingness to listen, but in the people's crimes of violence, social injustice, and perversion of the judicial system.

and weave the spider's web;
whoever eats their eggs dies,
and the crushed egg hatches out a viper.
6 Their webs cannot serve as clothing;
they cannot cover themselves with what they make.
Their works are works of iniquity,
and deeds of violence are in their hands.
7 Their feet run to evil,
and they rush to shed innocent blood;
their thoughts are thoughts of iniquity,
desolation and destruction are in their highways.
8 The way of peace they do not know,
and there is no justice in their paths.
Their roads they have made crooked;
no one who walks in them knows peace.

9 Therefore justice is far from us,
and righteousness does not reach us;
we wait for light, and lo! there is darkness;
and for brightness, but we walk in gloom.
10 We grope like the blind along a wall,
groping like those who have no eyes;
we stumble at noon as in the twilight,
among the vigorous[a] as though we were dead.
11 We all growl like bears;
like doves we moan mournfully.
We wait for justice, but there is none;
for salvation, but it is far from us.
12 For our transgressions before you are many,
and our sins testify against us.
Our transgressions indeed are with us,
and we know our iniquities:
13 transgressing, and denying the LORD,
and turning away from following our God,
talking oppression and revolt,
conceiving lying words and uttering them from the heart.
14 Justice is turned back,
and righteousness stands at a distance;
for truth stumbles in the public square,
and uprightness cannot enter.
15 Truth is lacking,
and whoever turns from evil is despoiled.

The LORD saw it, and it displeased him
that there was no justice.
16 He saw that there was no one,
and was appalled that there was no one to intervene;
so his own arm brought him victory,
and his righteousness upheld him.
17 He put on righteousness like a breastplate,
and a helmet of salvation on his head;
he put on garments of vengeance for clothing,
and wrapped himself in fury as in a mantle.
18 According to their deeds, so will he repay;
wrath to his adversaries, requital to his enemies;
to the coastlands he will render requital.
19 So those in the west shall fear the name of the LORD,

a Meaning of Heb uncertain

59.9–15a: A communal confession of sin, though only v. 12 is addressed to God (cf. Ps 51.5; 90.8). **9:** The key terms "mishpat" and "tsedaqah," here translated *justice* and *righteousness*, respectively, signify rather "vindication" and "salvation"; also in vv. 11,15,16,17.

59.15b–21: The LORD will punish and redeem. As often in psalms of lamentation, the response of the LORD follows confession of sin, especially when no human recourse is available. **17:** The description of military equipment draws on the old motif of the LORD as a warrior deity (see Hab 3.3–15). **18–20:** The

and those in the east, his glory;
for he will come like a pent-up stream
that the wind of the LORD
drives on.

20 And he will come to Zion as
Redeemer,
to those in Jacob who turn from
transgression, says the LORD.
21 And as for me, this is my covenant with
them, says the LORD: my spirit that is upon
you, and my words that I have put in your
mouth, shall not depart out of your mouth,
or out of the mouths of your children, or
out of the mouths of your children's chil-
dren, says the LORD, from now on and for-
ever.

60 Arise, shine; for your light
has come,
and the glory of the LORD has risen
upon you.
2 For darkness shall cover the earth,
and thick darkness the peoples;
but the LORD will arise upon you,
and his glory will appear over you.
3 Nations shall come to your light,
and kings to the brightness of your
dawn.

4 Lift up your eyes and look around;
they all gather together, they come
to you;
your sons shall come from far away,
and your daughters shall be carried
on their nurses' arms.
5 Then you shall see and be radiant;
your heart shall thrill and rejoice,[a]
because the abundance of the sea
shall be brought to you,
the wealth of the nations shall
come to you.
6 A multitude of camels shall
cover you,
the young camels of Midian and
Ephah;
all those from Sheba shall come.
They shall bring gold and
frankincense,
and shall proclaim the praise of the
LORD.
7 All the flocks of Kedar shall be
gathered to you,
the rams of Nebaioth shall minister
to you;
they shall be acceptable on my altar,
and I will glorify my glorious
house.

8 Who are these that fly like a cloud,
and like doves to their windows?
9 For the coastlands shall wait for me,
the ships of Tarshish first,
to bring your children from far away,
their silver and gold with them,
for the name of the LORD your God,
and for the Holy One of Israel,
because he has glorified you.
10 Foreigners shall build up your walls,

a Heb *be enlarged*

final manifestation of God in judgment on the reprobates, both Judeans and Gentiles, and bringing salvation to those who turn from evil. *Coastlands,* see 11.11n. **21:** A prose addendum promising that prophetic guidance will be available to the community through the disciples (*children*) of the anonymous seer (cf. 53.10; 61.1–4). *Covenant,* see Jer 31.31–34; Ezek 36.26–27.

Chs 60–62: The glory and destiny of Zion. This section is generally considered to be the nucleus of chs 56–66, having much in common with chs 40–55.

60.1–22: Jerusalem restored. An address to Zion imagined as a woman (cf. 52.1–2,7–12; 54.1–17); from the first decades of Persian rule (ca. 538–515 BCE). **3–4:** Gentiles will be attracted to Jerusalem as to a zone of light in the surrounding darkness. Dispersed Judeans will return, assisted by Gentiles (also 49.12; 51.9–11; 60.8–9; 66.20). **5–7:** Foreigners will bring tribute and sacrificial animals for Temple worship (45.14,22–23; 60.11,16; cf. Mt 2.11). *Midian,* see Ex 2.15n.; *Ephah,* location of Arab tribes east of the Gulf of Aqaba (Gen 25.4); *Sheba,* a location in southwest Arabia or Ethiopia (Gen 10.7); *Kedar,* 21.16n.; *Nebaioth,* an Arab tribe (Gen 25.13). **8–9:** Some Diaspora Israelites will return by sea. *Coastlands,* 11.11n. *Tarshish,* 2.16n. **10–14:** In the future Judah envisaged by the seer, Gentiles will bring

and their kings shall minister
to you;
for in my wrath I struck you down,
but in my favor I have had mercy
on you.
11 Your gates shall always be open;
day and night they shall not
be shut,
so that nations shall bring you their
wealth,
with their kings led in procession.
12 For the nation and kingdom
that will not serve you shall perish;
those nations shall be utterly
laid waste.
13 The glory of Lebanon shall come
to you,
the cypress, the plane, and the pine,
to beautify the place of my sanctuary;
and I will glorify where my
feet rest.
14 The descendants of those who
oppressed you
shall come bending low to you,
and all who despised you
shall bow down at your feet;
they shall call you the City of
the LORD,
the Zion of the Holy One of Israel.
15 Whereas you have been forsaken and
hated,
with no one passing through,
I will make you majestic forever,
a joy from age to age.
16 You shall suck the milk of nations,
you shall suck the breasts of kings;
and you shall know that I, the LORD,
am your Savior
and your Redeemer, the Mighty
One of Jacob.

17 Instead of bronze I will bring gold,
instead of iron I will bring silver;
instead of wood, bronze,
instead of stones, iron.
I will appoint Peace as your overseer
and Righteousness as your
taskmaster.
18 Violence shall no more be heard in
your land,
devastation or destruction within
your borders;
you shall call your walls Salvation,
and your gates Praise.
19 The sun shall no longer be
your light by day,
nor for brightness shall the moon
give light to you by night;[a]
but the LORD will be your everlasting
light,
and your God will be your glory.
20 Your sun shall no more go down,
or your moon withdraw itself;
for the LORD will be your everlasting
light,
and your days of mourning shall be
ended.
21 Your people shall all be righteous;
they shall possess the land forever.
They are the shoot that I planted, the
work of my hands,
so that I might be glorified.
22 The least of them shall become a clan,
and the smallest one a mighty
nation;
I am the LORD;
in its time I will accomplish
it quickly.

61 The spirit of the Lord GOD is
upon me,
because the LORD has anointed me;

a Q Ms Gk Old Latin Tg: MT lacks *by night*

materials for rebuilding the Temple and serve as manual workers subordinate to the inhabitants (14.2; 45.22–23; 61.5–6). **15–16:** Zion is represented as a woman formerly abandoned but now sought after (54.6–7; 62.12). **17–18:** The new Jerusalem will surpass Solomon's city in splendor (1 Kings 5–7). **19–20:** In the future Jerusalem the light of the sun and moon will be greatly enhanced (cf. 30.26), or no longer be necessary. Perpetual light becomes a feature of apocalyptic descriptions of the heavenly Jerusalem (Rev 22.5). **21–22:** In the future age the Abrahamic promise will be fulfilled (Gen 12.1–3; 15.6; 18.18).

61.1–4: The mission of the prophet. This declaration of an anonymous prophetic figure recalls other

he has sent me to bring good news to
the oppressed,
to bind up the brokenhearted,
to proclaim liberty to the captives,
and release to the prisoners;
2 to proclaim the year of the
LORD's favor,
and the day of vengeance of
our God;
to comfort all who mourn;
3 to provide for those who mourn in
Zion—
to give them a garland instead
of ashes,
the oil of gladness instead of
mourning,
the mantle of praise instead of a
faint spirit.
They will be called oaks of
righteousness,
the planting of the LORD, to display
his glory.
4 They shall build up the ancient ruins,
they shall raise up the former
devastations;
they shall repair the ruined cities,
the devastations of many
generations.

5 Strangers shall stand and feed
your flocks,
foreigners shall till your land and
dress your vines;
6 but you shall be called priests of the
LORD,
you shall be named ministers of our
God;
you shall enjoy the wealth of
the nations,
and in their riches you shall glory.
7 Because their[a] shame was double,
and dishonor was proclaimed as
their lot,
therefore they shall possess a double
portion;
everlasting joy shall be theirs.

8 For I the LORD love justice,
I hate robbery and wrongdoing;[b]
I will faithfully give them their
recompense,
and I will make an everlasting
covenant with them.
9 Their descendants shall be known
among the nations,
and their offspring among the
peoples;
all who see them shall acknowledge
that they are a people whom the
LORD has blessed.
10 I will greatly rejoice in the LORD,
my whole being shall exult in
my God;
for he has clothed me with the
garments of salvation,
he has covered me with the robe of
righteousness,
as a bridegroom decks himself with a
garland,
and as a bride adorns herself with
her jewels.
11 For as the earth brings forth its
shoots,
and as a garden causes what is
sown in it to spring up,

a Heb *your* *b* Or *robbery with a burnt offering*

passages in chs 40–66 spoken by or addressed to individual seers (40.6–9; 49.1–6; 50.4–11; 59.21). The speaker is endowed with the spirit of God (42.1; 48.16b; 59.21) and is anointed (see 1 Kings 19.16). The mission is to proclaim good news to the poor and downtrodden and to proclaim the jubilee year of release from slavery (Lev 25; see Isa 49.8–9). **4:** Judah was still suffering from the effects of the Babylonian conquest (44.26–28).

61.5–11: Announcement of good news. 5–7: Judeans will be to Gentiles as priests to laity (Ex 19.6): They will enjoy ample support and will receive a double share for double punishment (40.2). **8–9:** The refounded community will be the beneficiary of the promise to Abraham in a perpetual covenant: divine blessing including land and descendants (Gen 12.1–3; 17.7; cf. Isa 60.21–22n.). **10–11:** A concluding psalm, spoken by Zion representing the people of Judah, in response to the preceding assurance of blessing. *Garments of salvation,* 52.1–2.

so the Lord God will cause
righteousness and praise
to spring up before all the nations.

62 For Zion's sake I will not keep
silent,
and for Jerusalem's sake I will not
rest,
until her vindication shines out like
the dawn,
and her salvation like a burning
torch.
2 The nations shall see your
vindication,
and all the kings your glory;
and you shall be called by a
new name
that the mouth of the Lord
will give.
3 You shall be a crown of beauty in the
hand of the Lord,
and a royal diadem in the hand of
your God.
4 You shall no more be termed
Forsaken,[a]
and your land shall no more be
termed Desolate;[b]
but you shall be called My Delight Is
in Her,[c]
and your land Married;[d]
for the Lord delights in you,
and your land shall be married.
5 For as a young man marries a young
woman,
so shall your builder[e] marry you,
and as the bridegroom rejoices over
the bride,
so shall your God rejoice over you.
6 Upon your walls, O Jerusalem,
I have posted sentinels;
all day and all night
they shall never be silent.
You who remind the Lord,
take no rest,
7 and give him no rest
until he establishes Jerusalem
and makes it renowned throughout
the earth.
8 The Lord has sworn by his
right hand
and by his mighty arm:
I will not again give your grain
to be food for your enemies,
and foreigners shall not drink
the wine
for which you have labored;
9 but those who garner it shall eat it
and praise the Lord,
and those who gather it shall drink it
in my holy courts.

10 Go through, go through the gates,
prepare the way for the people;
build up, build up the highway,
clear it of stones,
lift up an ensign over the peoples.
11 The Lord has proclaimed
to the end of the earth:
Say to daughter Zion,
"See, your salvation comes;
his reward is with him,
and his recompense before him."
12 They shall be called, "The
Holy People,
The Redeemed of the Lord";
and you shall be called, "Sought Out,
A City Not Forsaken."

a Heb *Azubah* *b* Heb *Shemamah* *c* Heb *Hephzibah* *d* Heb *Beulah* *e* Cn: Heb *your sons*

62.1–12: Zion's destiny. **1–5:** The seer whose voice is heard in 61.1–4 will continue the mission until Jerusalem is vindicated and restored. The bestowal of a new name signifies a change of fortune, a new dispensation (1.26; 62.12; 65.15–16). Marriage symbolism (54.5–6) owes a debt to Hosea (Hos 1–3). **6–9:** On prophets as sentinels, see 56.10n. Here the prophetic function of intercession is emphasized. The response of the Lord is that Judah will no longer be plundered by foreign powers, the reversal of a familiar treaty and covenant curse (cf. Deut 28.30,39; Am 5.11). **10–12:** A summary of the aspirations expressed in chs 60–62, modeled on 40.1–3 interpreted in the light of a new situation (57.14n.). **10b:** The ensign is a signal for dispersed Israelites to assemble in preparation for returning to Judah (11.10–12; 49.22; 66.19).

63 "Who is this that comes from
Edom,
from Bozrah in garments stained
crimson?
Who is this so splendidly robed,
marching in his great might?"

"It is I, announcing vindication,
mighty to save."

2 "Why are your robes red,
and your garments like theirs who
tread the wine press?"

3 "I have trodden the wine press
alone,
and from the peoples no one
was with me;
I trod them in my anger
and trampled them in my wrath;
their juice spattered on my garments,
and stained all my robes.
4 For the day of vengeance was in my
heart,
and the year for my redeeming
work had come.
5 I looked, but there was no helper;
I stared, but there was no one to
sustain me;
so my own arm brought me victory,
and my wrath sustained me.
6 I trampled down peoples in my anger,
I crushed them in my wrath,
and I poured out their lifeblood on
the earth."

7 I will recount the gracious deeds of
the LORD,
the praiseworthy acts of the LORD,
because of all that the LORD has done
for us,
and the great favor to the house of
Israel
that he has shown them according to
his mercy,
according to the abundance of his
steadfast love.
8 For he said, "Surely they are
my people,
children who will not deal falsely";
and he became their savior
9 in all their distress.
It was no messenger[a] or angel
but his presence that saved them;[b]
in his love and in his pity he
redeemed them;
he lifted them up and carried them
all the days of old.

10 But they rebelled
and grieved his holy spirit;
therefore he became their enemy;
he himself fought against them.
11 Then they[c] remembered the days of
old,
of Moses his servant.[d]
Where is the one who brought them
up out of the sea

a Gk: Heb *anguish* *b* Or *savior. ⁹In all their distress he was distressed; the angel of his presence saved them;* *c* Heb *he* *d* Cn: Heb *his people*

63.1–6: Vengeance on Edom. 1–2: The lookout (cf. 62.6) questions the one approaching Jerusalem from Edom and its principal city *Bozrah* about his identity and appearance. Edom, lying to the south and east of Judah, profited by the Babylonian conquest to encroach on Judean territory (34.5–17; Ob 13–14; Jer 49.7–22; Ezek 25.12–14; 35.1–15; Ps 137.7), a situation confirmed by the archaeological record; hence the violence of the metaphoric language in this passage. At a later time "Edom" served as a code name for the oppressive Roman Empire. **3:** Cf. Lam 1.15; Joel 3.13. This imagery influences descriptions of eschatological judgment (Rev 14.19). **4:** *Day of vengeance,* 34.8; 61.2. **5:** A variant of 59.16.

63.7–64.12: A psalm of communal lamentation, composed not long after the Babylonian conquest (see 63.18; 64.10–11) and reflecting the religious disorientation of that time (cf. Ps 44; 74; 79; 89; and Lamentations). **7–9:** Israel's deliverance from Egypt is recalled. For the role of the angel-messenger and the divine presence, see Ex 23.20,23; 32.34; 33.2,14–15. **10–14:** The story of national origins in Egypt and the trek through the wilderness is retold in the manner of the Deuteronomists (e.g., Deut 9.6–21; cf. Ps 78), recounting the LORD's benevolence and Israel's inadequate response, but with emphasis on the spirit of God characteristic of the postexilic period (vv. 10,11,14). **15–16:** The contrast between God as

with the shepherds of his flock?
Where is the one who put
within them
his holy spirit,
12 who caused his glorious arm
to march at the right hand
of Moses,
who divided the waters before them
to make for himself an everlasting
name,
13 who led them through the depths?
Like a horse in the desert,
they did not stumble.
14 Like cattle that go down into
the valley,
the spirit of the LORD gave
them rest.
Thus you led your people,
to make for yourself a glorious
name.
15 Look down from heaven and see,
from your holy and glorious
habitation.
Where are your zeal and your might?
The yearning of your heart and
your compassion?
They are withheld from me.
16 For you are our father,
though Abraham does not know us
and Israel does not acknowledge us;
you, O LORD, are our father;
our Redeemer from of old is
your name.
17 Why, O LORD, do you make us stray
from your ways
and harden our heart, so that we
do not fear you?
Turn back for the sake of your
servants,
for the sake of the tribes that are
your heritage.
18 Your holy people took possession for
a little while;
but now our adversaries have
trampled down your sanctuary.
19 We have long been like those whom
you do not rule,
like those not called by your name.

64 O that you would tear open the
heavens and come down,
so that the mountains would quake
at your presence—
2[a] as when fire kindles brushwood
and the fire causes water to boil—
to make your name known to your
adversaries,
so that the nations might tremble at
your presence!
3 When you did awesome deeds that we
did not expect,
you came down, the mountains
quaked at your presence.
4 From ages past no one has heard,
no ear has perceived,
no eye has seen any God besides you,
who works for those who wait
for him.
5 You meet those who gladly do right,
those who remember you in
your ways.
But you were angry, and we sinned;
because you hid yourself we
transgressed.[b]
6 We have all become like one who is
unclean,
and all our righteous deeds are like
a filthy cloth.
We all fade like a leaf,

a Ch 64.1 in Heb *b* Meaning of Heb uncertain

father (63.16; 64.8; cf. Deut 32.6) and the ancestors reflects the crisis of continuity and tradition in the aftermath of the Babylonian conquest. **17–19:** The loss of independent possession of the land and the destruction of the Temple induced a deep sense of failure, sin, and alienation (cf. Ps 79). **64.1–3:** A direct appeal to God, characteristic of the lament psalms, to intervene, to appear in power as in the days of old (cf. Ex 19.16–18; Judg 5.4–5; Ps 68.7–8; Hab 3.3–15). **4–5a:** While the incomparability of Israel's God is an idea characteristic of the exilic Isaiah (40.18,25; 43.10; 44.6–8; 45.5–6,21; 46.5,9), the call to wait for God in faith and trust is heard throughout the book (8.17; 30.18; 40.31; cf. Hab 2.3; Zeph 3.8). **5b–7:** One of the strongest and most poignant expressions in the Bible of a sense of alienation and distance from God expressed in terms of God's anger, silence, and hiddenness. **8–12:** A final appeal to God as father

and our iniquities, like the wind,
take us away.
7 There is no one who calls on
your name,
or attempts to take hold of you;
for you have hidden your face
from us,
and have delivered[a] us into the
hand of our iniquity.
8 Yet, O LORD, you are our Father;
we are the clay, and you are
our potter;
we are all the work of your hand.
9 Do not be exceedingly angry,
O LORD,
and do not remember iniquity
forever.
Now consider, we are all your
people.
10 Your holy cities have become a
wilderness,
Zion has become a wilderness,
Jerusalem a desolation.
11 Our holy and beautiful house,
where our ancestors praised you,
has been burned by fire,
and all our pleasant places have
become ruins.
12 After all this, will you restrain
yourself, O LORD?
Will you keep silent, and punish us
so severely?

65 I was ready to be sought out by
those who did not ask,
to be found by those who did not
seek me.
I said, "Here I am, here I am,"
to a nation that did not call on my
name.
2 I held out my hands all day long
to a rebellious people,
who walk in a way that is not good,
following their own devices;
3 a people who provoke me
to my face continually,
sacrificing in gardens
and offering incense on bricks;
4 who sit inside tombs,
and spend the night in secret places;
who eat swine's flesh,
with broth of abominable things in
their vessels;
5 who say, "Keep to yourself,
do not come near me, for I am too
holy for you."
These are a smoke in my nostrils,
a fire that burns all day long.
6 See, it is written before me:
I will not keep silent, but I will
repay;
I will indeed repay into their laps
7 their[b] iniquities and their[b]
ancestors' iniquities together,
says the LORD;
because they offered incense on the
mountains

a Gk Syr Old Latin Tg: Heb *melted* *b* Gk Syr: Heb *your*

(cf. 63.16) and creator (cf. 29.16; 45.9) to turn away from anger and observe what has become of God's people as a result of conquest and foreign occupation of God's own land (Lev 25.23): cities destroyed and depopulated, the Temple burnt to the ground. **12:** *Will you keep silent?* Cf. Ps 28.1; 79.5; 85.5–7.

65.1–7: The answer. Since the preceding psalm of communal lament lacks the element of response from God, normal in this type of psalm (e.g., Ps 20; 56; 60), a saying now follows explaining why God has not intervened. God was ready to be approached, but the people looked elsewhere for help. **2:** *A rebellious people,* cf. 1.2; 30.1, with an echo of the law concerning the rebellious son in Deut 21.18. **3:** *Sacrificing in gardens,* see 1.29–30; 66.17. Such rituals carried out in open-air sanctuaries involved the invocation of nature deities, often with overt sexual content (cf. 57.3–13); *offering incense on bricks,* incense was used in Yahwistic and non-Yahwistic rituals. The Qumran Isaiah scroll from Cave 1 (1QIsa[a]) has at this point preserved an alternative reading, which may be original, referring to a sexual ritual. **4:** The accusation extends to mortuary rituals (as in 29.4; 57.6,9), dubious nocturnal ceremonies, eating pork (66.17), perhaps in connection with a pig sacrifice (66.3), and consuming other ritually unclean foods (Lev 11.7; Deut 14.8). **5:** *Keep to yourself,* an insolent response to the LORD's invitation to them to approach (57.3; 65.1), perhaps with reference to their ritual segregation (cf. 66.17).

and reviled me on the hills,
I will measure into their laps
full payment for their actions.
8 Thus says the LORD:
As the wine is found in the cluster,
and they say, "Do not destroy it,
for there is a blessing in it,"
so I will do for my servants' sake,
and not destroy them all.
9 I will bring forth descendants[a] from
Jacob,
and from Judah inheritors[b] of my
mountains;
my chosen shall inherit it,
and my servants shall settle there.
10 Sharon shall become a pasture
for flocks,
and the Valley of Achor a place for
herds to lie down,
for my people who have sought me.
11 But you who forsake the LORD,
who forget my holy mountain,
who set a table for Fortune
and fill cups of mixed wine for
Destiny;
12 I will destine you to the sword,
and all of you shall bow down to
the slaughter;
because, when I called, you did
not answer,
when I spoke, you did not listen,
but you did what was evil in
my sight,
and chose what I did not delight in.
13 Therefore thus says the Lord GOD:
My servants shall eat,
but you shall be hungry;
my servants shall drink,
but you shall be thirsty;
my servants shall rejoice,
but you shall be put to shame;
14 my servants shall sing for gladness of
heart,
but you shall cry out for pain
of heart,
and shall wail for anguish of spirit.
15 You shall leave your name to my
chosen to use as a curse,
and the Lord GOD will put you
to death;
but to his servants he will give a
different name.
16 Then whoever invokes a blessing in
the land
shall bless by the God of
faithfulness,
and whoever takes an oath in
the land
shall swear by the God of
faithfulness;
because the former troubles are
forgotten
and are hidden from my sight.

17 For I am about to create new heavens
and a new earth;

a Or *a descendant* *b* Or *an inheritor*

65.8–12: Division in the Judean community, seen from the writer's point of view as division between the reprobate and the servants of the LORD. From these servants, God's elect, God will raise up a people who will possess the land from Sharon, the northern coastal plain (33.9), to Achor, the desolate region west of the Dead Sea (Josh 7.24; Hos 2.15n.). **11:** In the Heb text *Fortune* and *Destiny* are Gad and Meni, respectively, deities of fate and good luck venerated among Syrians, Arabs, and Nabateans. **12:** Rounds off the polemic by returning to the initial statement (v. 1); cf. Jer 7.13.

65.13–16: Contrast between the destiny of God's servants and that of the reprobate. 13–14: Their situation will be reversed. This theme of eschatological reversal is developed in the New Testament (Mt 5.3–12; 25.31–46; Lk 6.20–26). **15–16:** The name of the reprobate will serve as a curse, like the names of the prophets Ahab and Zedekiah executed by the Babylonians (Jer 29.22). The giving of a new name signifies a new status (43.1,7; 44.1–5; 62.2). **16:** *The God of faithfulness,* the Heb text has "the God Amen," the Heb word "amen" (surely) used here as an epithet for God. This is the God who confirms oaths made in his name and is trustworthy. There is an echo here of the Abrahamic blessing (Gen 12.1–3).

65.17–25: An apocalyptic interpolation. Perhaps added by a later apocalyptic writer. **17–18:** Jerusalem will flourish in a renewed cosmos (66.2), a familiar apocalyptic theme. The emphasis is on Israel's God as a creator deity. *Former things,* 43.18. **19:** This scenario is further developed in 25.6–10. **20:** The

the former things shall not be
remembered
or come to mind.
18 But be glad and rejoice forever
in what I am creating;
for I am about to create Jerusalem as
a joy,
and its people as a delight.
19 I will rejoice in Jerusalem,
and delight in my people;
no more shall the sound of weeping
be heard in it,
or the cry of distress.
20 No more shall there be in it
an infant that lives but a few days,
or an old person who does not live
out a lifetime;
for one who dies at a hundred years
will be considered a youth,
and one who falls short of a
hundred will be considered
accursed.
21 They shall build houses and inhabit
them;
they shall plant vineyards and eat
their fruit.
22 They shall not build and another
inhabit;
they shall not plant and
another eat;
for like the days of a tree shall the
days of my people be,
and my chosen shall long enjoy the
work of their hands.
23 They shall not labor in vain,
or bear children for calamity;[a]
for they shall be offspring blessed by
the LORD—
and their descendants as well.
24 Before they call I will answer,
while they are yet speaking I
will hear.
25 The wolf and the lamb shall feed
together,
the lion shall eat straw like the ox;
but the serpent—its food shall
be dust!
They shall not hurt or destroy
on all my holy mountain,
says the LORD.

66 Thus says the LORD:
Heaven is my throne
and the earth is my footstool;
what is the house that you would
build for me,
and what is my resting place?
2 All these things my hand has made,
and so all these things are mine,[b]
says the LORD.
But this is the one to whom I will
look,
to the humble and contrite in spirit,
who trembles at my word.

3 Whoever slaughters an ox is like one
who kills a human being;
whoever sacrifices a lamb, like one
who breaks a dog's neck;

a Or *sudden terror* b Gk Syr: Heb *these things came to be*

prediction of vastly increased life expectancy connotes a return to the original creation (cf. Gen 5). **21–23:** The future Israel will witness the reversal of familiar curses attached to treaties and covenants; see 62.8–9n. *Days of a tree,* Job 14.7–9; Ps 92.12–15; Jer 17.8. **24:** Rounds off the second, more optimistic section of the chapter, cf. vv. 1,12. **25:** Taken from 11.6–9 to complete the picture of the new Jerusalem: a return to the first creation, a peaceful kingdom in which no creatures, human or animal, kill for food (Gen 1.29–30; cf. 9.1–7).

66.1–6: A community divided. 1–2: A saying directed against false understandings and expectations associated with the Jerusalem Temple and its sacrificial worship (see 1 Kings 8.27) rather than directed against the Temple as such or the project of rebuilding. On the contrast between God's heavenly and earthly abodes and his presence with the lowly and afflicted, see 57.15; 60.13; 63.15. **3–4:** *Like* is not in the Hebrew. The point is that the individuals who perform legitimate cultic acts (sacrificing oxen and sheep, making cereal and memorial offerings) are also engaged in illegitimate acts involving human (probably infant) sacrifice (cf. 57.5) and sacrificing dogs and pigs (cf. 65.4; 66.17). On the failure to respond to God's invitation, see 65.1,12. **5:** An oracle addressed by an anonymous seer to those who

whoever presents a grain offering, like
one who offers swine's
blood;[a]
whoever makes a memorial offering
of frankincense, like one who
blesses an idol.
These have chosen their own ways,
and in their abominations they take
delight;
4 I also will choose to mock[b] them,
and bring upon them what
they fear;
because, when I called, no one
answered,
when I spoke, they did not listen;
but they did what was evil in
my sight,
and chose what did not please me.
5 Hear the word of the LORD,
you who tremble at his word:
Your own people who hate you
and reject you for my name's sake
have said, "Let the LORD be glorified,
so that we may see your joy";
but it is they who shall be put
to shame.

6 Listen, an uproar from the city!
A voice from the temple!
The voice of the LORD,
dealing retribution to his enemies!

7 Before she was in labor
she gave birth;
before her pain came upon her
she delivered a son.
8 Who has heard of such a thing?
Who has seen such things?
Shall a land be born in one day?
Shall a nation be delivered in one
moment?
Yet as soon as Zion was in labor
she delivered her children.
9 Shall I open the womb and not
deliver?
says the LORD;
shall I, the one who delivers, shut the
womb?
says your God.

10 Rejoice with Jerusalem, and be glad
for her,
all you who love her;
rejoice with her in joy,
all you who mourn over her—
11 that you may nurse and be satisfied
from her consoling breast;
that you may drink deeply with
delight
from her glorious bosom.

12 For thus says the LORD:
I will extend prosperity to her like a
river,
and the wealth of the nations like
an overflowing stream;
and you shall nurse and be carried on
her arm,
and dandled on her knees.
13 As a mother comforts her child,
so I will comfort you;
you shall be comforted in
Jerusalem.
14 You shall see, and your heart shall
rejoice;
your bodies[c] shall flourish like the
grass;
and it shall be known that the hand
of the LORD is with his
servants,

a Meaning of Heb uncertain *b* Or *to punish*
c Heb *bones*

tremble at the word of God, meaning either God's law or the prophetic word, cf. 66.1; Ezra 9.4; 10.3. These have been expelled from the Judean Temple community because of their eschatological beliefs; compare the prospect for the "servants" in 65.13–14. **6:** The judgment to come has its source in the Temple; cf. Joel 3.16; Am 1.2.

66.7–14: The destiny of Jerusalem. 7–9: The rebirth of Jerusalem and of a new commonwealth will happen with miraculous speed. **10–11:** Jerusalem will be a mother to those who now mourn (cf. 60.20; 61.2–3). **12–14:** Compare the address to Zion in 54.1–17, which also ends with the vindication of the LORD's servants. For the metaphor of the LORD as a mother, see 49.15.

and his indignation is against
his enemies.
15 For the LORD will come in fire,
and his chariots like the whirlwind,
to pay back his anger in fury,
and his rebuke in flames of fire.
16 For by fire will the LORD execute
judgment,
and by his sword, on all flesh;
and those slain by the LORD shall
be many.

17 Those who sanctify and purify themselves to go into the gardens, following the one in the center, eating the flesh of pigs, vermin, and rodents, shall come to an end together, says the LORD.

18 For I know[a] their works and their thoughts, and I am[b] coming to gather all nations and tongues; and they shall come and shall see my glory,
19 and I will set a sign among them. From them I will send survivors to the nations, to Tarshish, Put,[c] and Lud—which draw the bow—to Tubal and Javan, to the coastlands far away that have not heard of my fame or seen my glory; and they shall declare my glory among the nations.
20 They shall bring all your kindred from all the nations as an offering to the LORD, on horses, and in chariots, and in litters, and on mules, and on dromedaries, to my holy mountain Jerusalem, says the LORD, just as the Israelites bring a grain offering in a clean vessel to the house of the LORD.
21 And I will also take some of them as priests and as Levites, says the LORD.

22 For as the new heavens and the new
earth,
which I will make,
shall remain before me, says
the LORD;
so shall your descendants and your
name remain.
23 From new moon to new moon,
and from sabbath to sabbath,
all flesh shall come to worship before
me,
says the LORD.

24 And they shall go out and look at the dead bodies of the people who have rebelled against me; for their worm shall not die, their fire shall not be quenched, and they shall be an abhorrence to all flesh.

a Gk Syr: Heb lacks *know* *b* Gk Syr Vg Tg: Heb *it is* *c* Gk: Heb *Pul*

66.15–24: Homecoming, vindication, and final judgment. 15–16: Theophanies and scenarios of judgment often feature fire (26.11; 29.5–6; 30.27,33; 31.9; 33.12,14; 34.10) and the LORD's sword (27.1; 31.8; 34.5–7). **17:** A note which may have been appended originally to 65.3. *Gardens,* see 65.3n. *The one in the center,* a female according to the Heb text and the Qumran scroll; perhaps a reference to the leading liturgist of this non-Yahwistic cult. **18–21:** There will be an announcement of God's glory before the final judgment (cf. 56.8), and some Gentiles will even serve as personnel in the Jerusalem Temple. **19:** *Tarshish,* see 2.16n.; *Put,* part of Libya (Ezek 30.5); *Lud,* Lydia, on the western coast of Asia Minor (Ezek 27.10); *Tubal,* in eastern Asia Minor (Ezek 27.13); *Javan,* on the western coast of Asia Minor (Ezek 27.13). **20:** Some commentators take this to be a later attempt to restrict the role of Gentiles to that of repatriating Diaspora Judeans. **22–23:** Within a renewed cosmos (cf. 65.15–16) Jerusalem will be the center of worship from one new moon and sabbath to the next (cf. Zech 14.16). **24:** An apocalyptic addition recalling the fate of the reprobate (cf. 34.3; Dan 12.2). The location may be the Valley of Hinnom or Gehenna south of Jerusalem; cf. Jer 7.31–33.

JEREMIAH

Jeremiah was the son of Hilkiah, a priest at Anathoth (1.1); he may have been a descendant of the priest Abiathar, who was banished by Solomon to Anathoth (1 Kings 2.26,27). The chronology of Jeremiah's life suggested by the superscription (1.2–3) raises a number of problems. If Jeremiah's ministry began in 627 BCE (1.2), he would have been active for over four decades. Despite the efforts of some scholars to interpret chs 2–6 and perhaps portions of chs 30–31 as the prophet's early preaching during Josiah's reign, no material in the book can be unequivocally assigned to that time. Even more enigmatically, although the prose sermons and biographical narratives in the book bear strong linguistic resemblance to Deuteronomy and the so-called Deuteronomistic History (Joshua–2 Kings), Jeremiah is inexplicably silent regarding Josiah's religious reform inspired by the discovery in the Temple of the "book of the law" in 622 BCE (2 Kings 22–23). These difficulties lead some scholars to regard 627 BCE as the date of Jeremiah's birth (1.5) rather than as the beginning of his public career. He died sometime after 586, presumably in Egypt.

No matter which date is chosen, the important events that form the backdrop of Jeremiah's preaching are clear. Jeremiah spoke in the context of the last years of the existence of Judah as an independent political entity: the final years of the seventh century BCE (approximately 610–600) and the first decades of the sixth century (until sometime after 586). These were the years during which the growing power of the Babylonian Empire became more and more threatening to Judah, culminating with the siege of Jerusalem in 598–597 (during which the king, Jehoiakim, died and his son Jehoiachin [Jeconiah or Coniah] assumed the throne). Jehoiachin was deposed and replaced by his uncle, Zedekiah, and the deposed king and a portion of the ruling classes (including the priest-prophet Ezekiel; see Introduction to Ezekiel) were exiled to Babylon. The ensuing decade saw increasingly desperate attempts on the part of Judah to free itself from the Babylonian overlordship, but a final revolt by Zedekiah (based partly on promises of help from Egypt that were unfulfilled) brought about the Babylonian invasion of Jerusalem and the destruction of the city and the Temple in 586, at which point the rest of the rulers were exiled as well. Though Jeremiah wished to remain in Judah with Gedaliah, the governor appointed by the Babylonians, Gedaliah was assassinated, along with a contingent of Babylonian soldiers. Fearing indiscriminate reprisals by the Babylonians, many of the remaining Judean leaders fled to Egypt, taking the protesting Jeremiah with them (chs 40–44).

Understanding the history behind the book of Jeremiah, and how the prophet's statements relate to that history, is made more difficult by the complexity of the organization of the book itself. Alongside the typical prophetic oracles, which are in poetical form, Jeremiah also contains a good deal of prose—often written in the third person, influenced by the language and theology of Deuteronomy and the Deuteronomistic History, and including the historical appendix (ch 52) borrowed from 2 Kings 24.28–25.30. There are many doublets (7.1–15 ‖ 26.4–6; 7.32 ‖ 19.6; 16.14–15 ‖ 23.7–8). The relationship between the standard Hebrew text and other ancient versions of the book is confusing. An apparently artificial system of superscriptions and chronological notes may have been inserted to make the book conform to the Deuteronomistic History. All these qualities suggest that the book represents the product of a long period of editorial activity lasting well into the Hellenistic period (see 33.14–26). According to the structure imposed on the book by the prose superscriptions, it consists essentially of a collection of oracles against Judah and Jerusalem, which Jeremiah dictated to his aide Baruch (1.4–20.18, from the time of Josiah and Jehoiakim; 21.1–25.14, from the time of Zedekiah); narratives about Jeremiah's prophetic activity (chs 26–35; 36–45); and a group of oracles against the foreign nations (25.15–38; chs 46–51), together with an introduction (1.1–3) and the historical appendix (ch 52).

Scholars offer various models to explain the formation of the book. Some point to what they consider to be signs that the book was compiled over a period of time from smaller collections of oracles. One clue to such smaller collections may be the first two scrolls of judgment oracles that Jeremiah is said to have dictated to Baruch (ch 36). The second scroll (36.32) could have formed the nucleus for the material now found in 2.1–20.18. Another small collection may have been the scroll of consolation (30.1–3), which in its original form probably contained much of what is now in chs 30–31. Against this view, however, others point out that the narrative concerning Baruch's scrolls may not be reliable as a guide to the history of the formation of the book because it occurs in the prose narratives of chs 36–44, which are slanted in favor of Babylonian exiles. Also, the narrative clearly contrasts the behavior of the king (ch 36) with the account of Josiah's reaction to the discovery of the scroll of the law (2 Kings 22–23) and may therefore have been written with this aim in mind. If the book of Jeremiah cannot be traced to Baruch's two scrolls, it presumably grew by means of successive additions and redactions of some now unidentifiable core of Jeremiah's preaching.

Perhaps the strongest evidence for this redactional model is that the present Hebrew text differs substantially from the Greek version (the Septuagint) in both content and order. Thus the Septuagint does not contain several passages (for example, 33.14–26) and combines the oracles against the foreign nations into a single section following 25.14, though in a different order. In addition, there are many smaller differences from verse to verse. Remarkably, among the portions of the text of Jeremiah in Hebrew that were found among the Dead Sea Scrolls are not only those that reflect the standard Hebrew text but also those that reflect the text tradition represented by the Septuagint. It is likely, then, that these two text traditions represent the contrasting editorial work on the book of Jeremiah that took place in Egypt (the Septuagint tradition) and in Palestine or Babylon (the traditional Hebrew text).

Much of Jeremiah's prophetic preaching is based on the theme of the covenant relationship between God and the people of Israel and Judah. Drawing on traditions at home in northern Israel, Jeremiah considered the covenant to be a conditional one, which could be broken by the people's persistent apostasy. Influenced by Hosea, Jeremiah used imagery of the people as an unfaithful wife and as rebellious children (chs 2–3). Such infidelity made judgment virtually inevitable. In his vivid poetic oracles Jeremiah dramatizes the grief experienced by God, prophet, and people (e.g., chs 4–6). Interspersed with the words of judgment and anguish, however, are a number of references to repentance and the renewal of the covenant relationship. Because of the complex ways in which the book has been edited, it is difficult to determine whether Jeremiah considered it possible that the people's repentance might forestall judgment or whether he considered repentance and a new beginning possible only after judgment had fallen. In the prose narratives about Jeremiah during the siege and fall of Jerusalem, Jeremiah is represented as insisting that there would be a future for the people in the land of Judah even after the Babylonian conquest (chs 32, 42). The theme of restoration is strongest in chs 30–31, where a future is envisioned in which a new covenant will be made with Israel and Judah, one that will not be broken (31.33).

1

1 The words of Jeremiah son of Hilkiah,
of the priests who were in Anathoth in
the land of Benjamin, 2 to whom the word
of the LORD came in the days of King Josi-
ah son of Amon of Judah, in the thirteenth
year of his reign. 3 It came also in the days
of King Jehoiakim son of Josiah of Judah,
and until the end of the eleventh year of
King Zedekiah son of Josiah of Judah, until
the captivity of Jerusalem in the fifth
month.

4 Now the word of the LORD came to
me saying,

5 "Before I formed you in the womb I
knew you,
and before you were born I
consecrated you;
I appointed you a prophet to the
nations."

6 Then I said, "Ah, Lord GOD! Truly I do
not know how to speak, for I am only a
boy." 7 But the LORD said to me,

"Do not say, 'I am only a boy';
for you shall go to all to whom I send
you,
and you shall speak whatever I
command you.
8 Do not be afraid of them,
for I am with you to deliver you,
says the LORD."

9 Then the LORD put out his hand and
touched my mouth; and the LORD said
to me,

"Now I have put my words in your
mouth.
10 See, today I appoint you over nations
and over kingdoms,
to pluck up and to pull down,
to destroy and to overthrow,
to build and to plant."

11 The word of the LORD came to me,
saying, "Jeremiah, what do you see?" And
I said, "I see a branch of an almond tree."[a]
12 Then the LORD said to me, "You have
seen well, for I am watching[b] over my
word to perform it." 13 The word of the

a Heb *shaqed* *b* Heb *shoqed*

1.1–3: Superscription. The superscription conforms to the superscriptions of several of the prophetic books (Hos 1.1; Am 1.1; Mic 1.1; Zeph 1.1) and seems, therefore, to represent a stage in the gathering and editing of the larger prophetic corpus as a whole. **1**: *Words,* the Heb term may also mean "thing" or "matter." It need not be understood as a claim that all the words contained in the book stem from Jeremiah himself, especially since significant portions are written in the third person. The name *Jeremiah* may mean "the LORD [Yahweh] exalts." *Priests . . . in Anathoth,* see Introduction. Anathoth is located at modern Ras el-Kharrubeh about 4.5 km (2.8 mi) northeast of Jerusalem. **2**: *Thirteenth year of his reign,* 627 BCE. (See Introduction.) **3**: *Eleventh year of King Zedekiah,* 587 BCE. *Captivity . . . fifth month,* 2 Kings 25.8–12.

1.4–19: Jeremiah's call and related visions. The narrative of Jeremiah's call follows a typical pattern (see Ex 3–6; Judg 6.11–18; Isa 6) involving God's identification of a task and commission of the called one to be God's agent (v. 5), the excuses of the commissioned one (v. 6), God's promise to be with the commissioned one (vv. 7–8), and God's giving a sign (vv. 9–10). **4**: *Word of the LORD,* characteristic expression in Jeremiah, emphasizing that his message is God's word. **5**: *Knew,* connotes a profound and intimate knowledge. *To the nations,* the call narrative introduces and presumes the entire book of Jeremiah, including the oracles against the nations. It portrays Jeremiah's ministry as a critical moment in world history (cf. Jer 25). **6–8**: The call narrative invites comparison between Jeremiah and Moses (cf. Ex 4.10–12), suggesting that the editors of the book understood Jeremiah as the "prophet like Moses" predicted in Deut 18.15–19. **7–8**: Cf. Ex 4.11–12. **9**: 15.16; cf. Ex 4.12; Deut 18.18. **10**: *To pluck up and to pull down . . . to build and to plant* anticipates the themes of both judgment and restoration. The phrases are echoed throughout the book in various prose passages (18.7; 24.6; 31.28,40; 42.10; 45.4; cf. 18.14). **11–12**: It is unclear whether vv. 11–19 are to be understood as elements of the call or as subsequent visionary experiences. *Almond tree,* play on words (see textual notes *a* and *b*). Cf. similar vision/puns in Amos (7.7–9; 8.1–3). **13–14**: *Tilted away from the north,* this translation implies that the pot was spilling its hot contents toward the south. Invaders into Palestine often came from *the north,* and

LORD came to me a second time, saying,
"What do you see?" And I said, "I see a
boiling pot, tilted away from the north."
14 Then the LORD said to me: Out of the
north disaster shall break out on all the in-
habitants of the land. 15 For now I am call-
ing all the tribes of the kingdoms of the
north, says the LORD; and they shall come
and all of them shall set their thrones at the
entrance of the gates of Jerusalem, against
all its surrounding walls and against all the
cities of Judah. 16 And I will utter my judg-
ments against them, for all their wickedness
in forsaking me; they have made offerings
to other gods, and worshiped the works of
their own hands. 17 But you, gird up your
loins; stand up and tell them everything
that I command you. Do not break down
before them, or I will break you before
them. 18 And I for my part have made you
today a fortified city, an iron pillar, and a
bronze wall, against the whole land—
against the kings of Judah, its princes, its
priests, and the people of the land. 19 They
will fight against you; but they shall not
prevail against you, for I am with you, says
the LORD, to deliver you.

2 The word of the LORD came to me, say-
ing: 2 Go and proclaim in the hearing of
Jerusalem, Thus says the LORD:

I remember the devotion of your
youth,
your love as a bride,
how you followed me in the
wilderness,
in a land not sown.
3 Israel was holy to the LORD,
the first fruits of his harvest.
All who ate of it were held guilty;
disaster came upon them,
says the LORD.

4 Hear the word of the LORD, O house
of Jacob, and all the families of the house of
Israel. 5 Thus says the LORD:

What wrong did your ancestors find
in me
that they went far from me,
and went after worthless things, and
became worthless themselves?
6 They did not say, "Where is
the LORD
who brought us up from the land
of Egypt,

"the foe from the north" comes to be a stereotype of the invading enemy, even of chaos (6.22; Ezek 38.15). **15–19:** An expansion, perhaps secondary, of the thought in vv. 4–8. The phraseology is characteristic of other prose sections of the book. **15:** *Set their thrones,* 43.10; 49.38. **16:** *Offerings to other gods,* 7.9; 11.12,13,17; 19.4,13; 32.29; 44.3,5,8, etc. **17:** *Gird up your loins,* in preparation for action or combat. **18:** *Fortified city,* 6.27. *Iron pillar, bronze wall,* 15.12,20; cf. 28.13,14.

2.1–4.2: Introduction to Jeremiah's message. The frequent shift of addressee and the carefully arranged progression of thought from consideration of Israel's earliest period (2.1–3), to its abandonment of the LORD (2.4–37), to the possibility and conditions of repentance and restoration (3.1–4.2) indicate the compositional nature of this unit. This retrospective account and assessment of Israel's sinful history and Israel's possible future serve as a theological introduction to the book.

2.1–37: The apostasy of Israel. 1–3: The imagery here intermingles feminine metaphor (2.2b), probably intended originally to refer to Jerusalem, and masculine forms of address denoting Israel as a collective. **2:** *Bride,* for marriage as a metaphor of the relation between God and people, see Hos 2; Isa 54. *Wilderness,* an allusion to the time following the Exodus, when Israel entered into covenant with the LORD (Ex 19–24; see Hos 2.14–15). **3:** *First fruits* were offered to the LORD (Ex 23.19; Deut 26.2). *Guilty,* the guilt associated with improper contact with the holy (Lev 5.2–4,14–16; etc.). **4–8:** Address shifts here to the third-person masculine plural. The LORD develops a "covenant lawsuit" (Heb "rib"; cf. v. 29) against his people, beginning with a declaration of his own innocence in the relationship. While the LORD has been free of fault, the people have been unfaithful without cause. Their failures involved three errors: They failed to remember that only the LORD had delivered them from Egypt (v. 6); their idolatry polluted the good land the LORD had given them (v. 7); their priests, experts in the covenant law, had no knowledge of God (Hos 4.4–6,9), their rulers disregarded the covenant, and their prophets preached in the name of other gods (v. 8). **9–13:** Now the indictment turns from a statement of the

who led us in the wilderness,
in a land of deserts and pits,
in a land of drought and deep darkness,
in a land that no one passes through,
where no one lives?"
7 I brought you into a plentiful land
to eat its fruits and its good things.
But when you entered you defiled my land,
and made my heritage an abomination.
8 The priests did not say, "Where is the LORD?"
Those who handle the law did not know me;
the rulers[a] transgressed against me;
the prophets prophesied by Baal,
and went after things that do not profit.

9 Therefore once more I accuse you,
says the LORD,
and I accuse your children's children.
10 Cross to the coasts of Cyprus and look,
send to Kedar and examine with care;
see if there has ever been such a thing.
11 Has a nation changed its gods,
even though they are no gods?
But my people have changed their glory
for something that does not profit.
12 Be appalled, O heavens, at this,
be shocked, be utterly desolate,
says the LORD,
13 for my people have committed two evils:
they have forsaken me,
the fountain of living water,
and dug out cisterns for themselves,
cracked cisterns
that can hold no water.

14 Is Israel a slave? Is he a homeborn servant?
Why then has he become plunder?
15 The lions have roared against him,
they have roared loudly.
They have made his land a waste;
his cities are in ruins, without inhabitant.
16 Moreover, the people of Memphis and Tahpanhes
have broken the crown of your head.
17 Have you not brought this upon yourself
by forsaking the LORD your God,
while he led you in the way?
18 What then do you gain by going to Egypt,
to drink the waters of the Nile?
Or what do you gain by going to Assyria,

a Heb *shepherds*

LORD's irreproachability (vv. 5–8)—itself an indirect accusation against the people—to an explicit statement of Israel's sin. In it, the LORD calls (upon the heavenly assembly; cf. Isa 1.2; Mic 6.1) to witness the folly unprecedented (8.4) in both west (*Cyprus*) and east (*Kedar,* in northern Arabia) of a people who change gods. **9:** The accusation against the ancestral generation (v. 5) includes their descendants, in reality the readers (see vv. 29–31). **11:** *No gods . . . something that does not profit,* a reference to idols. **13:** Israel's unparalleled sin is twofold: It has abandoned *the fountain of living water,* and it has made for itself cracked cisterns that *can hold no water.* Not so subtly, the cistern image emphasizes both that idols are manufactured by human hands and that they ultimately fail. **14–19:** Now the lawsuit turns to a description of Israel's current state of distress. Israel's subjugation to the powers in Egypt and Mesopotamia is not the result of the LORD's inability but of its own stubborn rebellion (vv. 17–19). Israel has forsaken its covenant birthright of responsible freedom to become a slave of Assyria or Babylonia (*the lions*) and Egypt (*Memphis,* the capital of northern Egypt, 23 km [14 mi] south of Cairo) bringing disgrace (compare v. 16b with Isa 3.17; 7.20) upon itself. *Tahpanhes,* Egyptian border fortress in the eastern delta, also known as Baal-Zaphon, Greek Daphne, modern Tell Defenneh. **16,18:** Cf. v. 36n. **20–25:** Feminine

to drink the waters of the
Euphrates?
19 Your wickedness will punish you,
and your apostasies will
convict you.
Know and see that it is evil and bitter
for you to forsake the LORD
your God;
the fear of me is not in you,
says the Lord GOD of hosts.

20 For long ago you broke your yoke
and burst your bonds,
and you said, "I will not serve!"
On every high hill
and under every green tree
you sprawled and played
the whore.
21 Yet I planted you as a choice vine,
from the purest stock.
How then did you turn degenerate
and become a wild vine?
22 Though you wash yourself with lye
and use much soap,
the stain of your guilt is still before
me,
says the Lord GOD.
23 How can you say, "I am not defiled,
I have not gone after the Baals"?
Look at your way in the valley;
know what you have done—
a restive young camel interlacing her
tracks,
24 a wild ass at home in the wilderness,
in her heat sniffing the wind!
Who can restrain her lust?
None who seek her need weary
themselves;
in her month they will find her.
25 Keep your feet from going unshod
and your throat from thirst.
But you said, "It is hopeless,
for I have loved strangers,
and after them I will go."

26 As a thief is shamed when caught,
so the house of Israel shall be
shamed—
they, their kings, their officials,
their priests, and their prophets,
27 who say to a tree, "You are
my father,"
and to a stone, "You gave
me birth."
For they have turned their backs
to me,
and not their faces.
But in the time of their trouble they
say,
"Come and save us!"
28 But where are your gods
that you made for yourself?
Let them come, if they can save you,
in your time of trouble;
for you have as many gods
as you have towns, O Judah.

29 Why do you complain against me?

forms of address characterize vv. 20–25 and reappear in vv. 33–37. Originally, these feminine passages may have been addressed to Jerusalem personified (2.2b). This material and the masculine plural material addressed to Israel's ancestors were edited together into this lengthy covenant lawsuit/historical retrospective at a relatively late date in the process of the formation of the book. The feminine material exhibits a clear structure. Four times the LORD cites her words of rebellion and objections of innocence (vv. 20,23,25b,35); four times the LORD introduces evidence to the contrary (vv. 20b–22,23b–25a,33–34,35b–37). The unfaithful addressee is compared to a stubborn ox, to a wild vine (Isa 5.1–7; Hos 10.1) germinating from good seed but now inexplicably and irremediably worthless, and to an animal in heat, that is, a nymphomaniacal prostitute (Hos 4.13) who yet denies her guilt in spite of evidence (such as human sacrifice *in the valley;* see 7.31). **26–32:** Features characteristic of vv. 5–19 reappear here: masculine plural forms of address, the cross-generational rhetorical schema (vv. 30–31), a focus on the leadership (v. 26), polemic against idols (vv. 27–28,32), the LORD's protestations of his own faithfulness (vv. 27,29,31), and the claim that Israel's misfortunes result from its own sin (vv. 28,30, such as the *tree* or Asherah and the *stone* or sacred pillar, both ritual objects criticized as having too strong an association with Canaanite practices [Ex 23.24; Deut 12.3; 1 Kings 16.33]). **28:** 10.1–16; 11.13. **29:**

You have all rebelled against me,
says the LORD.
30 In vain I have struck down
your children;
they accepted no correction.
Your own sword devoured your
prophets
like a ravening lion.
31 And you, O generation, behold the
word of the LORD![a]
Have I been a wilderness to Israel,
or a land of thick darkness?
Why then do my people say, "We are
free,
we will come to you no more"?
32 Can a girl forget her ornaments,
or a bride her attire?
Yet my people have forgotten me,
days without number.
33 How well you direct your course
to seek lovers!
So that even to wicked women
you have taught your ways.
34 Also on your skirts is found
the lifeblood of the innocent poor,
though you did not catch them
breaking in.
Yet in spite of all these things[a]
35 you say, "I am innocent;
surely his anger has turned
from me."
Now I am bringing you to judgment
for saying, "I have not sinned."
36 How lightly you gad about,
changing your ways!
You shall be put to shame by Egypt
as you were put to shame
by Assyria.
37 From there also you will come away
with your hands on your head;
for the LORD has rejected those in
whom you trust,
and you will not prosper through
them.

3 If[b] a man divorces his wife
and she goes from him
and becomes another man's wife,
will he return to her?
Would not such a land be greatly
polluted?
You have played the whore with
many lovers;
and would you return to me?
says the LORD.
2 Look up to the bare heights,[c]
and see!
Where have you not been
lain with?
By the waysides you have sat waiting
for lovers,
like a nomad in the wilderness.
You have polluted the land
with your whoring and wickedness.
3 Therefore the showers have been
withheld,
and the spring rain has not come;
yet you have the forehead of a whore,
you refuse to be ashamed.
4 Have you not just now called to me,
"My Father, you are the friend of
my youth—
5 will he be angry forever,
will he be indignant to the end?"

a Meaning of Heb uncertain *b* Q Ms Gk Syr: MT *Saying, If* *c* Or *the trails*

Complain, Heb "rib." **30:** Killing the prophets, see 1 Kings 19.10; 2 Kings 21.16. **32:** See vv. 2–3. **33–37:** The conclusion of the feminine material. **36:** *Put to shame by Egypt . . . by Assyria,* just as Judah's attempt to rely on Assyria for aid in the Syro-Ephraimite war (734–732 BCE) led to Assyrian domination, so reliance on Egypt will result in shame (cf. vv. 15–18).

3.1–4.2: The possibility of repentance and the conditions for restoration. 1–5: The feminine personification characteristic of much of ch 2 continues in parts of ch 3. According to Deut 24.1–4, a man who has divorced his wife cannot remarry her if she has subsequently remarried, even if she should be widowed or divorced by the second husband. The consequence of such an illegitimate reunion would be "guilt on the land" (Deut 24.4). Although the analogy would exclude the possibility of repentance and reconciliation between people and God, later passages in the chapter envision such restoration of the covenant relationship. **3:** *Showers . . . withheld,* Am 4.7–8. **4:** *My Father,* contrast 2.27; cf. 3.19. **6–11:** A

This is how you have spoken,
but you have done all the evil that
you could.

6 The LORD said to me in the days of
King Josiah: Have you seen what she did,
that faithless one, Israel, how she went up
on every high hill and under every green
tree, and played the whore there? 7 And I
thought, "After she has done all this she
will return to me"; but she did not return,
and her false sister Judah saw it. 8 She[a] saw
that for all the adulteries of that faithless
one, Israel, I had sent her away with a de-
cree of divorce; yet her false sister Judah
did not fear, but she too went and played
the whore. 9 Because she took her whore-
dom so lightly, she polluted the land, com-
mitting adultery with stone and tree. 10 Yet
for all this her false sister Judah did not
return to me with her whole heart, but only
in pretense, says the LORD.
11 Then the LORD said to me: Faithless
Israel has shown herself less guilty than
false Judah. 12 Go, and proclaim these
words toward the north, and say:

Return, faithless Israel,
says the LORD.
I will not look on you in anger,
for I am merciful,
says the LORD;
I will not be angry forever.
13 Only acknowledge your guilt,
that you have rebelled against the
LORD your God,
and scattered your favors among
strangers under every
green tree,
and have not obeyed my voice,
says the LORD.
14 Return, O faithless children,
says the LORD,
for I am your master;
I will take you, one from a city and
two from a family,
and I will bring you to Zion.

15 I will give you shepherds after my
own heart, who will feed you with knowl-
edge and understanding. 16 And when you
have multiplied and increased in the land,
in those days, says the LORD, they shall no
longer say, "The ark of the covenant of the
LORD." It shall not come to mind, or be
remembered, or missed; nor shall another
one be made. 17 At that time Jerusalem shall
be called the throne of the LORD, and all
nations shall gather to it, to the presence of
the LORD in Jerusalem, and they shall no
longer stubbornly follow their own evil
will. 18 In those days the house of Judah
shall join the house of Israel, and together

a Q Ms Gk Mss Syr: MT *I*

Deuteronomistic prose commentary that interrupts the sequence of poems. Cf. 2 Kings 17; Ezek 23. **6:** *Days of King Josiah,* 640–609 BCE. **8–10:** *Adulteries . . . decree of divorce,* the faithlessness of the Northern Kingdom, culminating in the defeat and exile by Assyria (2 Kings 18.9–12), should have been a warning to the Southern Kingdom of Judah. Even the reforms under Josiah (2 Kings 22–23) are judged to be *pretense. Stone and tree,* 2.27n. **12–13:** *Faithless Israel,* here still personified as an adulterous wife, is invited to repent and return. The invitation turns on a word play in Hebrew involving the noun "meshubah" ("turned aside = faithless") and "shub" ("to return, repent"). **14–17:** The metaphor shifts from marriage to paternity. The LORD addresses this invitation to sons. Marriages may be dissolved, but parental relationships endure. In light of the problem raised in 3.1, this shift in governing metaphor offers Israel new hope: return from exile and the reunion of Israel and Judah under faithful rulers. This oracle is later than the rest of the section. It may be compared to other late texts in the book that employ eschatological formulas, such as "In those days" or "Behold the days are coming" (5.18; 7.32 = 19.6; 9.25–26; 16.14–15; 23.5–6; 30.3; 31.27–28,29–30,31–34; 33.14,15–16; 50.20). **15:** *Shepherds,* rulers. **16b–17:** For the late penchant for renaming Jerusalem, cf. Isa 58.7,12; 60.18; 61.6; 62.2,4,12; 65.15; Ezek 48.35. Jerusalem will replace the *ark* (Ex 25.10–15; 1 Kings 8.4–7) as the symbol of the *throne of the LORD* (14.21; 17.12). The ark was presumably either captured or destroyed in the Babylonian conquest of Jerusalem in 586 BCE (but see 2 Macc 2.4–8). **19–20:** These verses continue vv. 13–15 and they shall come from the land of the north to the land that I gave your ancestors for a heritage.

19 I thought
how I would set you among
my children,
and give you a pleasant land,
the most beautiful heritage of all
the nations.
And I thought you would call me, My
Father,
and would not turn from following
me.
20 Instead, as a faithless wife leaves her
husband,
so you have been faithless to me,
O house of Israel,
says the LORD.

21 A voice on the bare heights[a]
is heard,
the plaintive weeping of Israel's
children,
because they have perverted
their way,
they have forgotten the LORD their
God:
22 Return, O faithless children,
I will heal your faithlessness.

"Here we come to you;
for you are the LORD our God.
23 Truly the hills are[b] a delusion,
the orgies on the mountains.
Truly in the LORD our God
is the salvation of Israel.

24 "But from our youth the shameful
thing has devoured all for which our ances-
tors had labored, their flocks and their
herds, their sons and their daughters. 25 Let
us lie down in our shame, and let our dis-
honor cover us; for we have sinned against
the LORD our God, we and our ancestors,
from our youth even to this day; and we
have not obeyed the voice of the LORD our
God."

4 If you return, O Israel,
says the LORD,
if you return to me,
if you remove your abominations
from my presence,
and do not waver,
2 and if you swear, "As the LORD
lives!"
in truth, in justice, and in
uprightness,
then nations shall be blessed[c]
by him,
and by him they shall boast.

3 For thus says the LORD to the people
of Judah and to the inhabitants of Jerusa-
lem:
Break up your fallow ground,
and do not sow among thorns.
4 Circumcise yourselves to the LORD,

a Or *the trails* *b* Gk Syr Vg: Heb *Truly from the hills is* *c* Or *shall bless themselves*

allude to v. 4. The tension between parental and marital metaphors continues. **3.21–4.2:** The historical retrospective of ch 2 and the theological discussions of ch 3 culminate in an invitation to return, a model confession of sin, and the LORD's concluding pronouncement on repentance and restoration. **21:** The people weep because of the guilt described in ch 2 (see 2.32). **23:** *Delusion,* see 2.5,8,11,13,27–28, the worship of other gods, often situated on high places (Hos 4.13). **24:** *Shameful thing,* likely a reference to Baal. Scribes often substituted the Heb word "boshet" ("shame") for an original "Baal" (cf. "Ishbaal" and "Ishbosheth," 2 Sam 2.8 and textual note *c*). **4.1–2:** Conditions for true repentance (4.1–2a) are the removal of shrines to other gods and recognition of God's exclusive claim by taking solemn oaths in his name only. Such repentance leads to the fulfillment of the promise to Abraham (Gen 12.1–3).

4.3–6.30: The foe from the north. The tone and substance of historical retrospective and theological deliberation gives way to the frantic pace and motion of the testimony of a witness to the invasion of the northern foe. Even this unit, however, includes theological assessments of the significance of the invasion and has been edited with a view to later generations of readers.

4.3–4: A warning that Judah and Jerusalem (in contrast to "all the families of Israel," 2.4) face the LORD's wrath. **3:** Cf. Hos 10.12. **4:** Circumcision indicated incorporation into the covenant (Gen

remove the foreskin of your hearts,
O people of Judah and inhabitants
of Jerusalem,
or else my wrath will go forth
like fire,
and burn with no one to quench it,
because of the evil of your doings.

5 Declare in Judah, and proclaim in Je-
rusalem, and say:
Blow the trumpet through the land;
shout aloud[a] and say,
"Gather together, and let us go
into the fortified cities!"
6 Raise a standard toward Zion,
flee for safety, do not delay,
for I am bringing evil from the north,
and a great destruction.
7 A lion has gone up from its thicket,
a destroyer of nations has set
out;
he has gone out from his place
to make your land a waste;
your cities will be ruins
without inhabitant.
8 Because of this put on sackcloth,
lament and wail:
"The fierce anger of the LORD
has not turned away from us."

9 On that day, says the LORD, courage shall
fail the king and the officials; the priests
shall be appalled and the prophets astound-
ed. 10 Then I said, "Ah, Lord GOD, how
utterly you have deceived this people and
Jerusalem, saying, 'It shall be well with
you,' even while the sword is at the
throat!"

11 At that time it will be said to this
people and to Jerusalem: A hot wind comes
from me out of the bare heights[b] in the
desert toward my poor people, not to win-
now or cleanse— 12 a wind too strong for
that. Now it is I who speak in judgment
against them.
13 Look! He comes up like clouds,
his chariots like the whirlwind;
his horses are swifter than eagles—
woe to us, for we are ruined!
14 O Jerusalem, wash your heart clean
of wickedness
so that you may be saved.
How long shall your evil schemes
lodge within you?
15 For a voice declares from Dan
and proclaims disaster from Mount
Ephraim.
16 Tell the nations, "Here they are!"
Proclaim against Jerusalem,
"Besiegers come from a distant land;
they shout against the cities of
Judah.
17 They have closed in around her like
watchers of a field,
because she has rebelled against me,
says the LORD.
18 Your ways and your doings
have brought this upon you.

a Or *shout, take your weapons*: Heb *shout, fill* (your hand) *b* Or *the trails*

17.9–27; Lev 12.3). Since the *heart* was considered to be the seat of the will and understanding, circumcision of the heart became an idiom for sincere and willing obedience to God (Deut 10.16).

4.5–31: The invading foe from the north, a recurring theme of Jeremiah (1.13–14; 5.15–17; 6.1–5; etc.). The material gathered here incorporates descriptions of the enemy's advance, the terrified reactions of Lady Zion herself, last-minute calls to repentance, and reflection on false prophecy and guilt. **5–6:** *Blow the trumpet,* Ezek 33.2–3. **7:** *Lion,* a common image for military aggression (Isa 31.4; Mic 5.8; Nah 2.11–12). **8:** Lam 2.9–10. **9–12:** Jeremiah holds the leadership, especially the prophets, responsible for Judah's fate. Prophets like Hananiah (ch 28) offer assurance of the LORD's favor despite conditions Jeremiah considers unambiguously threatening. For God's use of a deceptive word to bring about false complacency, see 1 Kings 22. In contrast to the consolation of these prophets, the LORD (the "I" of v. 12) now declares that his judgment will sweep over the land like the *hot wind* (the sirocco), desiccating everything before it (18.17). **13–18:** Another oracle addressed chiefly (vv. 14–18) to Lady Jerusalem. As the imagery of the sentinel (v. 5) is resumed, communiqués trace the enemy's advance from *Dan* (8.16) in the north, through *Mount Ephraim* (central Palestine), and into Judah's heartland (cf. 6.1–2). **19–22:**

This is your doom; how bitter it is!
It has reached your very heart."

19 My anguish, my anguish! I writhe in pain!
Oh, the walls of my heart!
My heart is beating wildly;
I cannot keep silent;
for I[a] hear the sound of the trumpet,
the alarm of war.
20 Disaster overtakes disaster,
the whole land is laid waste.
Suddenly my tents are destroyed,
my curtains in a moment.
21 How long must I see the standard,
and hear the sound of the trumpet?
22 "For my people are foolish,
they do not know me;
they are stupid children,
they have no understanding.
They are skilled in doing evil,
but do not know how to do good."

23 I looked on the earth, and lo, it was waste and void;
and to the heavens, and they had no light.
24 I looked on the mountains, and lo, they were quaking,
and all the hills moved to and fro.
25 I looked, and lo, there was no one at all,
and all the birds of the air had fled.
26 I looked, and lo, the fruitful land was a desert,
and all its cities were laid in ruins
before the LORD, before his fierce anger.

27 For thus says the LORD: The whole
land shall be a desolation; yet I will not
make a full end.
28 Because of this the earth shall mourn,
and the heavens above grow black;
for I have spoken, I have purposed;
I have not relented nor will I turn back.

29 At the noise of horseman and archer
every town takes to flight;
they enter thickets; they climb among rocks;
all the towns are forsaken,
and no one lives in them.
30 And you, O desolate one,
what do you mean that you dress in crimson,
that you deck yourself with ornaments of gold,
that you enlarge your eyes with paint?
In vain you beautify yourself.
Your lovers despise you;
they seek your life.
31 For I heard a cry as of a woman in labor,
anguish as of one bringing forth her first child,
the cry of daughter Zion gasping for breath,
stretching out her hands,
"Woe is me! I am fainting before killers!"

5 Run to and fro through the streets of Jerusalem,
look around and take note!
Search its squares and see

a Another reading is *for you, O my soul,*

The first-person speech in vv. 19–22 represents the personified city; v. 22 gives God's comment (cf. Isa 1.2–4). **23–28:** In a vision, the prophet sees the terrifying results of God's irrevocable judgment (7.16; 15.1–4). The imagery echoes Gen 1.1–2.4a and describes the destruction in terms of a reversal of primeval creation. **27:** A later prose comment, limiting the totality of the destruction. **29–31:** Like a rejected prostitute (3.2–3), like a woman in the anguish of childbirth, like a victim helpless before her murderer, Jerusalem, the daughter Zion, stretches out her hands in futile appeal and suffers her death throes—alone.

5.1–31: The corruptions that bring judgment. This section illustrates that, although the LORD stands ready to pardon (3.21–4.2), Judah's behavior does not warrant mercy. **1–9:** Jeremiah is commanded to search carefully for someone faithful (6.9–10). If one could be found, the LORD would pardon (cf. Gen 18.23–33). **4–5:** *Poor . . . rich,* the pairing of complementary categories (e.g., great and small, east and

if you can find one person
who acts justly
and seeks truth—
so that I may pardon Jerusalem.[a]
2 Although they say, "As the LORD lives,"
yet they swear falsely.
3 O LORD, do your eyes not look for truth?
You have struck them,
but they felt no anguish;
you have consumed them,
but they refused to take correction.
They have made their faces harder than rock;
they have refused to turn back.

4 Then I said, "These are only the poor,
they have no sense;
for they do not know the way of the LORD,
the law of their God.
5 Let me go to the rich[b]
and speak to them;
surely they know the way of the LORD,
the law of their God."
But they all alike had broken the yoke,
they had burst the bonds.

6 Therefore a lion from the forest shall kill them,
a wolf from the desert shall destroy them.
A leopard is watching against their cities;
everyone who goes out of them shall be torn in pieces—
because their transgressions are many,
their apostasies are great.

7 How can I pardon you?
Your children have forsaken me,
and have sworn by those who are no gods.
When I fed them to the full,
they committed adultery
and trooped to the houses of prostitutes.
8 They were well-fed lusty stallions,
each neighing for his neighbor's wife.
9 Shall I not punish them for these things?
says the LORD;
and shall I not bring retribution
on a nation such as this?

10 Go up through her vine-rows and destroy,
but do not make a full end;
strip away her branches,
for they are not the LORD's.
11 For the house of Israel and the house of Judah
have been utterly faithless to me,
says the LORD.
12 They have spoken falsely of the LORD,
and have said, "He will do nothing.
No evil will come upon us,
and we shall not see sword or famine."
13 The prophets are nothing but wind,
for the word is not in them.
Thus shall it be done to them!

14 Therefore thus says the LORD, the God of hosts:
Because they[c] have spoken this word,

a Heb *it* b Or *the great* c Heb *you*

west) is a merismus, a figure of speech indicating completeness. **7–9:** As often, idolatry and adultery are symbolically associated. *Shall I not punish?* the thematic refrain of ch 5 (v. 29). **10–17:** Following the first instance of the refrain in v. 9, the command sounds once again to go, this time to destroy. The LORD's choice vineyard has grown wild (2.21; Isa 5.1–7). **12–17:** The judgment. Several images unite this section. The empty words of the prophets which are *nothing but wind* are replaced by the divine *words* through Jeremiah which will be a *fire* that *devours*, lit. "eats." Because the people failed to heed the word of God, they will be punished by a foreign nation whose *language* they cannot understand. As an enactment of God's devouring word of judgment, this nation will devour everything. **18–19:** A recurring comment

I am now making my words in your
mouth a fire,
and this people wood, and the fire
shall devour them.
15 I am going to bring upon you
a nation from far away, O house of
Israel,
says the LORD.
It is an enduring nation,
it is an ancient nation,
a nation whose language you do
not know,
nor can you understand what they
say.
16 Their quiver is like an open tomb;
all of them are mighty warriors.
17 They shall eat up your harvest and
your food;
they shall eat up your sons and
your daughters;
they shall eat up your flocks and your
herds;
they shall eat up your vines and
your fig trees;
they shall destroy with the sword
your fortified cities in which
you trust.

18 But even in those days, says the
LORD, I will not make a full end of you.
19 And when your people say, "Why has the
LORD our God done all these things to us?"
you shall say to them, "As you have forsak-
en me and served foreign gods in your land,
so you shall serve strangers in a land that is
not yours."

20 Declare this in the house of Jacob,
proclaim it in Judah:
21 Hear this, O foolish and senseless
people,
who have eyes, but do not see,
who have ears, but do not hear.
22 Do you not fear me? says the LORD;
Do you not tremble before me?
I placed the sand as a boundary for
the sea,
a perpetual barrier that it cannot
pass;
though the waves toss, they cannot
prevail,
though they roar, they cannot pass
over it.
23 But this people has a stubborn and
rebellious heart;
they have turned aside and
gone away.
24 They do not say in their hearts,
"Let us fear the LORD our God,
who gives the rain in its season,
the autumn rain and the
spring rain,
and keeps for us
the weeks appointed for the
harvest."
25 Your iniquities have turned
these away,
and your sins have deprived you of
good.
26 For scoundrels are found among
my people;
they take over the goods of others.
Like fowlers they set a trap;[a]
they catch human beings.
27 Like a cage full of birds,
their houses are full of treachery;
therefore they have become great and
rich,
28 they have grown fat and sleek.
They know no limits in deeds of
wickedness;
they do not judge with justice
the cause of the orphan, to make
it prosper,
and they do not defend the rights
of the needy.

a Meaning of Heb uncertain

in prose (9.12–14; 16.10–13; 22.8–9), modifying Jeremiah's customary warning of total destruction (vv. 16–17; 13.13–14). **20:** Both Israel (house of Jacob) and Judah are addressed. **21:** Isa 6.9–10. **22:** Perhaps a reflection of the ancient myth of a deity's conquest of the mighty monster, the primordial sea (Job 38.8–11; Ps 104.6–9). **24b:** The seven weeks from Passover to Pentecost (Deut 16.9–10) when rain could ruin the harvest (1 Sam 12.16–18). **26–29:** The abuse of the *orphan* and the *needy* by the powerful is a common theme in the prophets (Isa 1.17; Am 2.6–7; Mic 3.1–3; Zech 7.10) and in the legal codes

29 Shall I not punish them for these
things?
says the LORD,
and shall I not bring retribution
on a nation such as this?

30 An appalling and horrible thing
has happened in the land:
31 the prophets prophesy falsely,
and the priests rule as the prophets
direct;[a]
my people love to have it so,
but what will you do when the end
comes?

6 Flee for safety, O children of
Benjamin,
from the midst of Jerusalem!
Blow the trumpet in Tekoa,
and raise a signal on
Beth-haccherem;
for evil looms out of the north,
and great destruction.
2 I have likened daughter Zion
to the loveliest pasture.[b]
3 Shepherds with their flocks shall come
against her.
They shall pitch their tents around
her;
they shall pasture, all in
their places.
4 "Prepare war against her;
up, and let us attack at noon!"
"Woe to us, for the day declines,
the shadows of evening lengthen!"
5 "Up, and let us attack by night,
and destroy her palaces!"
6 For thus says the LORD of hosts:
Cut down her trees;
cast up a siege ramp against
Jerusalem.
This is the city that must be
punished;[c]
there is nothing but oppression
within her.
7 As a well keeps its water fresh,
so she keeps fresh her wickedness;
violence and destruction are heard
within her;
sickness and wounds are ever
before me.
8 Take warning, O Jerusalem,
or I shall turn from you in disgust,
and make you a desolation,
an uninhabited land.

9 Thus says the LORD of hosts:
Glean[d] thoroughly as a vine
the remnant of Israel;
like a grape-gatherer, pass your hand
again
over its branches.

10 To whom shall I speak and give
warning,
that they may hear?
See, their ears are closed,[e]
they cannot listen.
The word of the LORD is to them an
object of scorn;
they take no pleasure in it.
11 But I am full of the wrath of
the LORD;
I am weary of holding it in.

a Or *rule by their own authority* *b* Or *I will destroy daughter Zion, the loveliest pasture* *c* Or *the city of license* *d* Cn: Heb *They shall glean* *e* Heb *are uncircumcised*

(Ex 22.21–24; Deut 24.17–18). **29:** See v. 9n. **30–31:** The people heartily approve of the perversity of priest and prophet (6.13–15; 23.9–22; Mic 3.5–8).

6.1–8: The description of the approach of the foe from the north resumes. 1: *Benjamin,* the territory just north of Jerusalem. *Tekoa,* 18 km (11 mi) south of Jerusalem; *Beth-haccherem,* modern Ramat Rahel, 4 km (2 mi) south of Jerusalem. **3:** *Shepherds with their flocks,* kings with their armies (cf. 1.15; 12.10). **4:** *Prepare,* more literally, "sanctify" (see Joel 3.9 textual note *b*). *Woe to us,* the Jerusalemites express their dread. **6:** The Assyrians and Babylonians employed such techniques for breaching the walls of enemy cities.

6.9–15: Jerusalem's obduracy (5.1,10–17). Jeremiah is to search meticulously for a god-fearing person (5.1), but he finds none (20.7–18; Mic 7.1–2). **10:** *Closed,* lit. "uncircumcised" *ears,* see 4.4n. **11:** In a common metaphor *wrath* is depicted as a liquid that fills the prophet, then overflows in destructive

Pour it out on the children in
the street,
and on the gatherings of young
men as well;
both husband and wife shall be taken,
the old folk and the very aged.
12 Their houses shall be turned over to
others,
their fields and wives together;
for I will stretch out my hand
against the inhabitants of the land,
says the LORD.
13 For from the least to the greatest
of them,
everyone is greedy for unjust gain;
and from prophet to priest,
everyone deals falsely.
14 They have treated the wound of my
people carelessly,
saying, "Peace, peace,"
when there is no peace.
15 They acted shamefully, they
committed abomination;
yet they were not ashamed,
they did not know how to blush.
Therefore they shall fall among those
who fall;
at the time that I punish them, they
shall be overthrown,
says the LORD.
16 Thus says the LORD:
Stand at the crossroads, and look,
and ask for the ancient paths,
where the good way lies; and walk in
it,
and find rest for your souls.
But they said, "We will not walk
in it."
17 Also I raised up sentinels for you:
"Give heed to the sound of the
trumpet!"
But they said, "We will not give
heed."
18 Therefore hear, O nations,
and know, O congregation, what
will happen to them.
19 Hear, O earth; I am going to bring
disaster on this people,
the fruit of their schemes,
because they have not given heed to
my words;
and as for my teaching, they have
rejected it.
20 Of what use to me is frankincense
that comes from Sheba,
or sweet cane from a distant
land?
Your burnt offerings are not
acceptable,
nor are your sacrifices pleasing
to me.
21 Therefore thus says the LORD:
See, I am laying before this people
stumbling blocks against which they
shall stumble;
parents and children together,
neighbor and friend shall perish.
22 Thus says the LORD:
See, a people is coming from the land
of the north,
a great nation is stirring from the
farthest parts of the earth.
23 They grasp the bow and the javelin,
they are cruel and have no mercy,
their sound is like the roaring sea;
they ride on horses,
equipped like a warrior for battle,
against you, O daughter Zion!

judgment on the people (10.25; Ps 69.24; Lam 4.11; Hos 5.10; Zeph 3.8). **14:** Here, as elsewhere, Jeremiah condemns the leaders who promised material and spiritual well-being (*peace*) when none was to be had (8.10–12; Ezek 13.10–11).

6.16–21: Jerusalem is without excuse. 16: *Crossroads, way,* metaphors for habitual modes of conduct (Ps 1.1,6; Prov 2.9–22). **17:** *Sentinels,* prophets (Ezek 3.17; Hos 9.8). **20:** *Frankincense,* an imported gum resin used as incense (Ex 30.34–38; Isa 60.6). *Sheba,* southwest Arabia. *Sweet cane,* producing oil used in anointing (Ex 30.23). The rejection of sacrifice apart from righteous behavior is announced also in Isa 1.10–17 and Am 5.21–24; cf. 1 Sam 15.22; Hos 6.6; Mic 6.6–8.

6.22–23: The foe from the north (4.5–8) strikes terror into the hearts of the people of the invaded land (Am 8.10; Zech 12.10).

24 "We have heard news of them,
our hands fall helpless;
anguish has taken hold of us,
pain as of a woman in labor.
25 Do not go out into the field,
or walk on the road;
for the enemy has a sword,
terror is on every side."

26 O my poor people, put on sackcloth,
and roll in ashes;
make mourning as for an only
child,
most bitter lamentation:
for suddenly the destroyer
will come upon us.

27 I have made you a tester and a
refiner[a] among my people
so that you may know and test
their ways.
28 They are all stubbornly rebellious,
going about with slanders;
they are bronze and iron,
all of them act corruptly.
29 The bellows blow fiercely,
the lead is consumed by the fire;
in vain the refining goes on,
for the wicked are not removed.
30 They are called "rejected silver,"
for the LORD has rejected them.

7 The word that came to Jeremiah from
the LORD: 2 Stand in the gate of the
LORD's house, and proclaim there this
word, and say, Hear the word of the LORD,
all you people of Judah, you that enter
these gates to worship the LORD. 3 Thus
says the LORD of hosts, the God of Israel:
Amend your ways and your doings, and let
me dwell with you[b] in this place. 4 Do not
trust in these deceptive words: "This is[c]
the temple of the LORD, the temple of the
LORD, the temple of the LORD."
5 For if you truly amend your ways and
your doings, if you truly act justly one with
another, 6 if you do not oppress the alien,
the orphan, and the widow, or shed inno-
cent blood in this place, and if you do not
go after other gods to your own hurt, 7 then
I will dwell with you in this place, in the
land that I gave of old to your ancestors
forever and ever.
8 Here you are, trusting in deceptive
words to no avail. 9 Will you steal, murder,

a Or *a fortress* b Or *and I will let you dwell*
c Heb *They are*

6.24–26: The people's lament at the enemy's approach. They make no acknowledgement of their sin. **25:** *Terror is on every side,* a characteristic expression of Jeremiah to describe all-encompassing danger (20.3,10; 46.5; 49.29; Lam 2.22). **26:** *The destroyer will come upon us,* since Heb verbs do not express tense, this verb could also be translated "has come upon us" or, perhaps best, "is coming."

6.27–30: Jeremiah, the assayer. One function of the prophetic office was to assay (test) the faithfulness (*silver*) of the people (cf. Isa 48.10; Zech 13.9; Mal 3.2–4). This section concludes the case against Jerusalem and Judah. The destroyer comes because Jeremiah has proven the people's sin.

7.1–9.26: Judah's fate is sealed. Although ch 7 includes the content of the so-called Temple sermon (vv. 2b–15), the structure of the section focuses attention on the LORD's revelation directly to Jeremiah (cf. 7.1–2,16,27; 8.4). For the account of the delivery of the sermon and reaction to it, see ch 26. The contrast between the message of repentance Jeremiah is instructed to deliver publicly, on the one hand, and the private injunction against intercession (v. 16) and the people's indifference to the message (v. 27), on the other, represent the retrospective insights of the editors of the final form of the book. They know, as the reader does, that despite Jeremiah's call to repent, Judah's stubborn rebelliousness had already sealed its fate (cf. 15.1–4).

7.1–15: The Temple sermon (cf. 26.4–6). **4:** Although liturgical tradition stressed God's protection of Zion and the Temple (Ps 46; 48; 76; see also Isa 31.4) it is *deceptive* (lit. "a lie") to interpret this tradition as necessarily assuring God's protection. The threefold repetition implies that the phrase has become a cliché. **5–7:** The requirements for true sincerity are congruent with the values expressed in Deuteronomy (5.7; 10.18–19; 24.17–22; 27.19) and in the other prophets (Isa 10.2; 59.7; Hos 3.1). **9:** Five of the ten commandments (Ex 20.1–17; Deut 5.6–21). **12:** *Shiloh* (32 km [20 mi] north of Jerusalem), the earlier

commit adultery, swear falsely, make offer-
ings to Baal, and go after other gods that
you have not known, 10 and then come and
stand before me in this house, which is
called by my name, and say, "We are
safe!"—only to go on doing all these abom-
inations? 11 Has this house, which is called
by my name, become a den of robbers in
your sight? You know, I too am watching,
says the LORD. 12 Go now to my place that
was in Shiloh, where I made my name dwell
at first, and see what I did to it for the
wickedness of my people Israel. 13 And
now, because you have done all these
things, says the LORD, and when I spoke to
you persistently, you did not listen, and
when I called you, you did not answer,
14 therefore I will do to the house that is
called by my name, in which you trust, and
to the place that I gave to you and to your
ancestors, just what I did to Shiloh. 15 And
I will cast you out of my sight, just as I cast
out all your kinsfolk, all the offspring of
Ephraim.

16 As for you, do not pray for this peo-
ple, do not raise a cry or prayer on their
behalf, and do not intercede with me, for I
will not hear you. 17 Do you not see what
they are doing in the towns of Judah and in
the streets of Jerusalem? 18 The children
gather wood, the fathers kindle fire, and
the women knead dough, to make cakes for
the queen of heaven; and they pour out
drink offerings to other gods, to provoke
me to anger. 19 Is it I whom they provoke?
says the LORD. Is it not themselves, to their
own hurt? 20 Therefore thus says the Lord
GOD: My anger and my wrath shall be
poured out on this place, on human beings
and animals, on the trees of the field and
the fruit of the ground; it will burn and not
be quenched.

21 Thus says the LORD of hosts, the God
of Israel: Add your burnt offerings to your
sacrifices, and eat the flesh. 22 For in the
day that I brought your ancestors out of the
land of Egypt, I did not speak to them or
command them concerning burnt offerings
and sacrifices. 23 But this command I gave
them, "Obey my voice, and I will be your
God, and you shall be my people; and walk
only in the way that I command you, so
that it may be well with you." 24 Yet they
did not obey or incline their ear, but, in the
stubbornness of their evil will, they walked
in their own counsels, and looked back-
ward rather than forward. 25 From the day
that your ancestors came out of the land of
Egypt until this day, I have persistently sent
all my servants the prophets to them, day
after day; 26 yet they did not listen to me,
or pay attention, but they stiffened their
necks. They did worse than their ancestors
did.

27 So you shall speak all these words to
them, but they will not listen to you. You
shall call to them, but they will not answer
you. 28 You shall say to them: This is the
nation that did not obey the voice of the
LORD their God, and did not accept disci-
pline; truth has perished; it is cut off from
their lips.

central shrine, was destroyed around 1050 BCE in the days of Samuel (1 Sam 4–6; Ps 78.56–72). So also *this house,* desecrated by worshipers, profaned by idolatry and social injustice, will be destroyed (vv. 10–11). **15:** Judah's punishment will be exile, as was that of the Northern Kingdom (*Ephraim*). Immediately following this sermon, Jeremiah was arrested (see 26.8).

7.16–26: Intercession is futile: Judah has gone too far in idolatry. 16–20: Because of Judah's general apostasy, God forbids Jeremiah to exercise one of the functions of the prophetic office: intercession (7.16; 11.14; 15.1; cf. Am 7.2, 5). *Queen of heaven,* the title of a goddess; see 44.15–28n. **21–26:** Faithfulness, not sacrifice, is required; see 6.20n. **21:** Worshipers may as well eat the flesh of the *burnt offerings,* customarily incinerated (Lev 1), as well as the other offerings (Lev 3; 7.11–18). **22:** Cf. Am 5.25. This is inconsistent with other biblical traditions. **25:** *I have persistently sent all my servants the prophets,* the motif of a succession of prophets calling the people to repent is characteristic of the Deuteronomistic tradition (see 2 Kings 17.13).

7.27–8.3: Preaching is futile: Judah will not listen. Like Isaiah (6.9–13), Jeremiah will preach to a people unable or unwilling to hear. **29:** *Cut off your hair,* a sign of mourning (16.6; Mic 1.16), the only

29 Cut off your hair and throw it away;
raise a lamentation on the bare
heights,[a]
for the LORD has rejected and
forsaken
the generation that provoked
his wrath.

30 For the people of Judah have done
evil in my sight, says the LORD; they have
set their abominations in the house that is
called by my name, defiling it. 31 And they
go on building the high place[b] of Topheth,
which is in the valley of the son of Hinnom,
to burn their sons and their daughters in
the fire—which I did not command, nor
did it come into my mind. 32 Therefore, the
days are surely coming, says the LORD,
when it will no more be called Topheth, or
the valley of the son of Hinnom, but the
valley of Slaughter: for they will bury in
Topheth until there is no more room. 33 The
corpses of this people will be food for the
birds of the air, and for the animals of the
earth; and no one will frighten them away.
34 And I will bring to an end the sound of
mirth and gladness, the voice of the bride
and bridegroom in the cities of Judah and
in the streets of Jerusalem; for the land shall
become a waste.

8 At that time, says the LORD, the bones
of the kings of Judah, the bones of its
officials, the bones of the priests, the bones
of the prophets, and the bones of the inhab-
itants of Jerusalem shall be brought out of
their tombs; 2 and they shall be spread be-
fore the sun and the moon and all the host
of heaven, which they have loved and
served, which they have followed, and
which they have inquired of and wor-
shiped; and they shall not be gathered or
buried; they shall be like dung on the sur-
face of the ground. 3 Death shall be pre-
ferred to life by all the remnant that re-
mains of this evil family in all the places
where I have driven them, says the LORD of
hosts.

4 You shall say to them, Thus says the
LORD:
When people fall, do they not get up
again?
If they go astray, do they not turn
back?
5 Why then has this people[c] turned
away
in perpetual backsliding?
They have held fast to deceit,
they have refused to return.
6 I have given heed and listened,
but they do not speak honestly;
no one repents of wickedness,
saying, "What have I done!"
All of them turn to their own course,
like a horse plunging headlong into
battle.
7 Even the stork in the heavens
knows its times;
and the turtledove, swallow, and
crane[d]
observe the time of their coming;
but my people do not know
the ordinance of the LORD.

a Or *the trails* *b* Gk Tg: Heb *high places* *c* One Ms Gk: MT *this people, Jerusalem,* *d* Meaning of Heb uncertain

option under the circumstances. **31:** The sacrifice of children (19.5; 32.35) on the burning platform (*Topheth,* 2 Kings 23.10) is denounced. The original extent of this practice is unclear. Some Israelites and Judeans may have understood child sacrifice as a means of fulfilling the law requiring the giving of the firstborn to God (Ex 22.29–30), although Lev 18.21 expressly forbids the practice. *Valley of the son of Hinnom* (Gehenna), southwest of the city adjoining the Kidron valley (2 Chr 28.3; 33.6). **33:** Corpses as carrion are among the covenant curses (Deut 28.26). **34:** 16.9. **8.1–3:** The desecration of tombs and exposure of bones was an act of humiliation (2 Kings 23.16). **2:** *All the host of heaven,* the astral deities whose worship was forbidden (Deut 4.19; 17.3; 2 Kings 23.4–5; cf. 7.17–18). **3:** *The places where I have driven them,* an indication of the exilic origins of this layer of prose material.

8.4–10.25: Miscellaneous oracles continuing the theme of Judah's sealed fate. 8.4–7: Israel's incredible indifference (18.13–17). Anyone who falls naturally gets up; the birds follow their migratory instincts; but Israel, God's people, forgets God's law. **8–9:** The people's failure to repent is linked with the arrogance and

8 How can you say, "We are wise,
and the law of the LORD is
with us,"
when, in fact, the false pen of
the scribes
has made it into a lie?
9 The wise shall be put to shame,
they shall be dismayed and taken;
since they have rejected the word
of the LORD,
what wisdom is in them?
10 Therefore I will give their wives
to others
and their fields to conquerors,
because from the least to the greatest
everyone is greedy for unjust gain;
from prophet to priest
everyone deals falsely.
11 They have treated the wound of my
people carelessly,
saying, "Peace, peace,"
when there is no peace.
12 They acted shamefully, they
committed abomination;
yet they were not at all ashamed,
they did not know how to blush.
Therefore they shall fall among those
who fall;
at the time when I punish them,
they shall be overthrown,
says the LORD.
13 When I wanted to gather them, says
the LORD,
there are[a] no grapes on the vine,
nor figs on the fig tree;
even the leaves are withered,
and what I gave them has passed
away from them.[b]

14 Why do we sit still?
Gather together, let us go into the
fortified cities
and perish there;
for the LORD our God has doomed us
to perish,
and has given us poisoned water to
drink,
because we have sinned against the
LORD.
15 We look for peace, but find no good,
for a time of healing, but there is
terror instead.

16 The snorting of their horses is heard
from Dan;
at the sound of the neighing of
their stallions
the whole land quakes.
They come and devour the land and
all that fills it,
the city and those who live in it.
17 See, I am letting snakes loose among
you,
adders that cannot be charmed,
and they shall bite you,
says the LORD.

18 My joy is gone, grief is upon me,
my heart is sick.

a Or *I will make an end of them, says the* LORD. *There are* *b* Meaning of Heb uncertain

fraudulence of their leader's failure (2.8; 5.13). *Scribes* were administrators and experts in the royal court and Temple whose responsibilities included preservation and interpretation of the "law of the LORD." Here Jeremiah may be challenging their claim to authority, which was based on literacy and textual interpretation (*wise . . . false pen of the scribes*), and championing the prophetic claim to announce orally the *word of the* LORD. **10c–12:** A doublet of 6.13–15. **14–17:** Jeremiah speaks first in the persona of the people of Judah, panic-stricken before the invader. **14:** *Poisoned water* (9.15; 23.15) was sometimes used as part of a trial by ordeal. Here, however, since *snakes* and *adders* (v. 17) are also mentioned, the allusion may be to the disasters associated with punishment for covenant violation (see, generally, Lev 26.14–33; Deut 28.15–57). **16:** *Dan,* northernmost point in Israel.

8.18–9.1: Jerusalem's lament over Judah. The identification of speakers in this unit is crucial to its interpretation, but exceedingly difficult. The individual who begins speaking may well be Lady Jerusalem, the only other individual lamenter in the book of Jeremiah to this point (compare 4.19–22 and 10.19–21). She quotes her people in vv. 19,20. The LORD's parenthetical comment emphasizes the disingenuous

19 Hark, the cry of my poor people
from far and wide in the land:
"Is the LORD not in Zion?
Is her King not in her?"
("Why have they provoked me to
anger with their images,
with their foreign idols?")
20 "The harvest is past, the summer
is ended,
and we are not saved."
21 For the hurt of my poor people I am
hurt,
I mourn, and dismay has taken
hold of me.

22 Is there no balm in Gilead?
Is there no physician there?
Why then has the health of my poor
people
not been restored?

9 [a]O that my head were a spring of
water,
and my eyes a fountain of tears,
so that I might weep day and night
for the slain of my poor people!
2 [b]O that I had in the desert
a traveler's lodging place,
that I might leave my people
and go away from them!
For they are all adulterers,
a band of traitors.
3 They bend their tongues like bows;
they have grown strong in the land
for falsehood, and not for
truth;
for they proceed from evil to evil,
and they do not know me, says the
LORD.

4 Beware of your neighbors,
and put no trust in any of
your kin;[c]
for all your kin[d] are supplanters,
and every neighbor goes around
like a slanderer.
5 They all deceive their neighbors,
and no one speaks the truth;
they have taught their tongues to
speak lies;
they commit iniquity and are too
weary to repent.[e]
6 Oppression upon oppression, deceit[f]
upon deceit!
They refuse to know me, says
the LORD.

7 Therefore thus says the LORD of
hosts:
I will now refine and test them,
for what else can I do with my
sinful people?[g]
8 Their tongue is a deadly arrow;
it speaks deceit through the mouth.
They all speak friendly words to their
neighbors,
but inwardly are planning to lay an
ambush.
9 Shall I not punish them for these
things? says the LORD;
and shall I not bring retribution
on a nation such as this?

a Ch 8.23 in Heb *b* Ch 9.1 in Heb *c* Heb *in a brother* *d* Heb *for every brother* *e* Cn Compare Gk: Heb *they weary themselves with iniquity.* [6]*Your dwelling* *f* Cn: Heb *Your dwelling in the midst of deceit* *g* Or *my poor people*

character of the people's complaint. **20:** This statement may allude to 8.13. **21:** *My poor people,* literally, Judah (4.11). **22:** *Balm in Gilead,* resin from the storax tree, produced especially in the north Transjordan region of Gilead, widely used for medicinal purposes (46.11; Gen 37.25). **9.1:** *The slain of my poor people,* this statement either anticipates the coming destruction or reflects a post-catastrophe perspective.

9.2–9: The LORD's response. The first-person speech in 9.1, expressing sympathy for the people (cf. 8.19,21), is answered by God's first-person speech in vv. 2–3, expressing contempt. The last clause of v. 3 becomes a minor refrain in ch 9 (see v. 6). The complete corruption of the people is the basis for this accusation. God has no sympathy for the deceitful, untrustworthy nation. **4:** *Supplanters,* Heb "ʿaqob ya ʿqob," a play on the name of Jacob (see Gen 25.26 textual note *a;* 27.36; Hos 12.3). **7:** 6.27–30. **9:** 5.9,29.

10 Take up[a] weeping and wailing for
the mountains,
and a lamentation for the pastures
of the wilderness,
because they are laid waste so that no
one passes through,
and the lowing of cattle is not
heard;
both the birds of the air and the
animals
have fled and are gone.
11 I will make Jerusalem a heap of ruins,
a lair of jackals;
and I will make the towns of Judah a
desolation,
without inhabitant.

12 Who is wise enough to understand
this? To whom has the mouth of the LORD
spoken, so that they may declare it? Why is
the land ruined and laid waste like a wilder-
ness, so that no one passes through? 13 And
the LORD says: Because they have forsaken
my law that I set before them, and have not
obeyed my voice, or walked in accordance
with it, 14 but have stubbornly followed
their own hearts and have gone after the
Baals, as their ancestors taught them.
15 Therefore thus says the LORD of hosts,
the God of Israel: I am feeding this people
with wormwood, and giving them poison-
ous water to drink. 16 I will scatter them
among nations that neither they nor their
ancestors have known; and I will send the
sword after them, until I have consumed
them.

17 Thus says the LORD of hosts:
Consider, and call for the mourning
women to come;
send for the skilled women
to come;
18 let them quickly raise a dirge over us,
so that our eyes may run down
with tears,
and our eyelids flow with water.
19 For a sound of wailing is heard from
Zion:
"How we are ruined!
We are utterly shamed,
because we have left the land,
because they have cast down our
dwellings."

20 Hear, O women, the word of
the LORD,
and let your ears receive the word
of his mouth;
teach to your daughters a dirge,
and each to her neighbor a lament.
21 "Death has come up into our
windows,
it has entered our palaces,
to cut off the children from the streets
and the young men from
the squares."
22 Speak! Thus says the LORD:
"Human corpses shall fall
like dung upon the open field,
like sheaves behind the reaper,
and no one shall gather them."

23 Thus says the LORD: Do not let the
wise boast in their wisdom, do not let the
mighty boast in their might, do not let
the wealthy boast in their wealth; 24 but
let those who boast boast in this, that
they understand and know me, that I am
the LORD; I act with steadfast love, justice,
and righteousness in the earth, for in these
things I delight, says the LORD.
25 The days are surely coming, says the

a Gk Syr: Heb *I will take up*

9.10–22: Lamentation over Zion. 10–11: The displacement of domestic animals by wild animals is a conventional way of representing the destruction of a city or a land (Isa 13.20–22; 34.10–15). **11:** Cf. Mic 3.12. **12–16:** A later prose commentary on Jeremiah's oracle in vv. 10–11,17–22 (cf. 5.18–19). **14:** *Baals* (lit. "lords"), Canaanite gods. **15:** *Wormwood,* a desert shrub with bitter leaves. *Poisonous water,* 8.14; 23.15. **17:** As customary in the ancient world, professional *mourning women* (2 Chr 35.25) are hired to bewail the fate of Zion. **19:** Cf. 4.13; 6.26; 10.20; 25.36; etc. **21:** The personification alludes to Mot, the god of death in Canaanite mythology.

9.23–24: True glory vs. false religious behavior. 25–26: *The days are surely coming,* a phrase fre-

LORD, when I will attend to all those who
are circumcised only in the foreskin:
26 Egypt, Judah, Edom, the Ammonites,
Moab, and all those with shaven temples
who live in the desert. For all these nations
are uncircumcised, and all the house of Israel is uncircumcised in heart.

10 Hear the word that the LORD speaks to you, O house of Israel.
2 Thus says the LORD:
Do not learn the way of the nations,
or be dismayed at the signs of the heavens;
for the nations are dismayed at them.
3 For the customs of the peoples are false:
a tree from the forest is cut down,
and worked with an ax by the hands of an artisan;
4 people deck it with silver and gold;
they fasten it with hammer and nails
so that it cannot move.
5 Their idols[a] are like scarecrows in a cucumber field,
and they cannot speak;
they have to be carried,
for they cannot walk.
Do not be afraid of them,
for they cannot do evil,
nor is it in them to do good.

6 There is none like you, O LORD;
you are great, and your name is great in might.
7 Who would not fear you, O King of the nations?
For that is your due;
among all the wise ones of the nations
and in all their kingdoms
there is no one like you.
8 They are both stupid and foolish;
the instruction given by idols
is no better than wood![b]
9 Beaten silver is brought from Tarshish,
and gold from Uphaz.
They are the work of the artisan and of the hands of the goldsmith;
their clothing is blue and purple;
they are all the product of skilled workers.
10 But the LORD is the true God;
he is the living God and the everlasting King.
At his wrath the earth quakes,
and the nations cannot endure his indignation.

11 Thus shall you say to them: The gods
who did not make the heavens and the
earth shall perish from the earth and from
under the heavens.[c]

12 It is he who made the earth by his power,
who established the world by his wisdom,

a Heb *They* *b* Meaning of Heb uncertain *c* This verse is in Aramaic

quently used in the prose additions to Jeremiah's oracles; 7.32; 16.14; 19.6; 23.5,7; 30.3; 31.27,31; 33.14; 48.12; 51.52. The physical marks of religious devotion, circumcision (practiced not only in Judah but in other neighboring nations) and *shaven temples* (practiced by Arab tribes, 25.23; 49.32) are insufficient without an obedient will (4.4n.; Deut 10.16).

10.1–16: God and the idols (cf. Isa 44.9–20; Ps 115.3–8; Let Jer). This composition probably expresses the concerns of the exilic community. They should not be tempted to *learn the ways of the nations* among whom they now live. **2:** *Signs of the heavens,* eclipses, comets, astrological observations. **4:** *People deck it with silver and gold,* compare the description of making an idol in Isa 40.18–20; 41.6–7. **5:** *They have to be carried,* Isa 46.1–7. *Cucumber field,* Isa 1.8. **6–8:** Isa 40.18–20. **9:** *Tarshish,* a famous seaport, most likely Tarsus in Turkey or Tartessus in southern Spain. *Uphaz,* unknown (Dan 10.5), perhaps an error for Ophir, a land famous for gold (1 Kings 9.28) probably in southern Arabia. **11:** A gloss in Aramaic. **12–16:** He alone is worthy of worship (51.15–19). **12:** *Established the world by his wisdom,* cf. Prov 8.22–31. **13:** See Ps 135.7; cf. Deut 28.12; Job 38.22; Ps 33.7. **16:** *The portion of Jacob;* Lam 3.24.

and by his understanding stretched
out the heavens.
13 When he utters his voice, there is a
tumult of waters in the
heavens,
and he makes the mist rise from the
ends of the earth.
He makes lightnings for the rain,
and he brings out the wind from
his storehouses.
14 Everyone is stupid and without
knowledge;
goldsmiths are all put to shame by
their idols;
for their images are false,
and there is no breath in them.
15 They are worthless, a work of
delusion;
at the time of their punishment they
shall perish.
16 Not like these is the LORD,[a] the
portion of Jacob,
for he is the one who formed
all things,
and Israel is the tribe of his
inheritance;
the LORD of hosts is his name.

17 Gather up your bundle from the
ground,
O you who live under siege!
18 For thus says the LORD:
I am going to sling out the
inhabitants of the land
at this time,
and I will bring distress on them,
so that they shall feel it.

19 Woe is me because of my hurt!
My wound is severe.
But I said, "Truly this is my
punishment,
and I must bear it."
20 My tent is destroyed,
and all my cords are broken;
my children have gone from me,
and they are no more;
there is no one to spread my tent
again,
and to set up my curtains.
21 For the shepherds are stupid,
and do not inquire of the LORD;
therefore they have not prospered,
and all their flock is scattered.
22 Hear, a noise! Listen, it is coming—
a great commotion from the land of
the north
to make the cities of Judah a
desolation,
a lair of jackals.

23 I know, O LORD, that the way of
human beings is not in
their control,
that mortals as they walk cannot
direct their steps.
24 Correct me, O LORD, but in
just measure;
not in your anger, or you will bring
me to nothing.

25 Pour out your wrath on the nations
that do not know you,
and on the peoples that do not call
on your name;
for they have devoured Jacob;
they have devoured him and
consumed him,
and have laid waste his habitation.

a Heb lacks *the LORD*

10.17–22: Prepare to leave! This passage describes a siege (perhaps in 597 BCE) that will not be lifted (cf. 9.10–22). **19–21:** Zion, personified as a mother, speaks of the loss of her children in exile (Isa 49.14–23; 54.1–3) because of the stupidity of Judah's rulers (shepherds). **22b:** 9.11.

10.23–25: A prayer. The one who prays cites Prov 20.24 (v. 23) and Ps 79.6–7 (v. 25) to direct God's attention away from Judah and to neighboring nations instead. This passage is a post-catastrophe editorial addition to the book. Its tone resembles laments that express the people's pain and dismay following the Babylonian crisis (Ps 44; 74; 79).

11 The word that came to Jeremiah
from the LORD: 2 Hear the words of
this covenant, and speak to the people of
Judah and the inhabitants of Jerusalem.
3 You shall say to them, Thus says the
LORD, the God of Israel: Cursed be anyone
who does not heed the words of this cove-
nant, 4 which I commanded your ancestors
when I brought them out of the land of
Egypt, from the iron-smelter, saying, Listen
to my voice, and do all that I command
you. So shall you be my people, and I
will be your God, 5 that I may perform the
oath that I swore to your ancestors, to give
them a land flowing with milk and honey,
as at this day. Then I answered, "So be it,
LORD."
6 And the LORD said to me: Proclaim all
these words in the cities of Judah, and in
the streets of Jerusalem: Hear the words of
this covenant and do them. 7 For I solemnly
warned your ancestors when I brought
them up out of the land of Egypt, warning
them persistently, even to this day, saying,
Obey my voice. 8 Yet they did not obey or
incline their ear, but everyone walked in the
stubbornness of an evil will. So I brought
upon them all the words of this covenant,
which I commanded them to do, but they
did not.
9 And the LORD said to me: Conspiracy
exists among the people of Judah and the
inhabitants of Jerusalem. 10 They have
turned back to the iniquities of their ances-
tors of old, who refused to heed my words;
they have gone after other gods to serve
them; the house of Israel and the house
of Judah have broken the covenant that I
made with their ancestors. 11 Therefore,
thus says the LORD, assuredly I am going to
bring disaster upon them that they cannot
escape; though they cry out to me, I will not
listen to them. 12 Then the cities of Judah
and the inhabitants of Jerusalem will go
and cry out to the gods to whom they make
offerings, but they will never save them in
the time of their trouble. 13 For your gods
have become as many as your towns,
O Judah; and as many as the streets of Je-
rusalem are the altars to shame you have
set up, altars to make offerings to Baal.
14 As for you, do not pray for this peo-
ple, or lift up a cry or prayer on their be-
half, for I will not listen when they call to
me in the time of their trouble. 15 What
right has my beloved in my house, when
she has done vile deeds? Can vows[a] and
sacrificial flesh avert your doom? Can you
then exult? 16 The LORD once called you,
"A green olive tree, fair with goodly fruit";
but with the roar of a great tempest he will
set fire to it, and its branches will be con-
sumed. 17 The LORD of hosts, who planted
you, has pronounced evil against you, be-
cause of the evil that the house of Israel and
the house of Judah have done, provoking
me to anger by making offerings to Baal.

18 It was the LORD who made it known
to me, and I knew;

a Gk: Heb *Can many*

11.1–20.18: Judah's fate is sealed, part 2: An extended section of alternating poetry and prose further demonstrating that Judah's sin has reached such an advanced state that punishment is inevitable; cf. 7.1–9.26. **11.1–14:** This prose sermon, like that of ch 7, is a postexilic interpretation of Jeremiah's preaching. Thus it is not actually addressed to a sixth-century Judean audience, attempting to convince them to repent and obey the covenant. Rather, using the form of a speech by Jeremiah, the editors explain to an audience that has already experienced catastrophe why it came upon them. Since the Lord has already *pronounced evil* (v. 17; cf. v. 11) upon the land, the prophet's intercession would have been futile (v. 14). Much of the language of the sermon echoes the book of Deuteronomy (v. 3, Deut 27.26; v. 4, Deut 4.20; v. 5, *oath . . . ancestors,* Deut 7.8,12–13; *a land flowing with milk and honey,* Deut 6.3; 11.9; *as at this day,* Deut 6.24; 10.15). **13:** *Baal,* the Canaanite storm god associated with fertility.

11.15–17: A fragmentary Lady Zion poem. "She" and "you" (fem. sing.) probably refer to Jerusalem.

11.18–12.6: Jeremiah's first personal lament. A plot against the life of Jeremiah. The first of Jeremiah's six personal laments; the others are 15.10–21; 17.14–18; 18.18–23; 20.7–13; 20.14–18. Typically, the

then you showed me their
evil deeds.
19 But I was like a gentle lamb
led to the slaughter.
And I did not know it was against
me
that they devised schemes, saying,
"Let us destroy the tree with its
fruit,
let us cut him off from the land of
the living,
so that his name will no longer be
remembered!"
20 But you, O LORD of hosts, who judge
righteously,
who try the heart and the mind,
let me see your retribution upon
them,
for to you I have committed
my cause.

21 Therefore thus says the LORD con-
cerning the people of Anathoth, who seek
your life, and say, "You shall not prophesy
in the name of the LORD, or you will die
by our hand"— 22 therefore thus says the
LORD of hosts: I am going to punish them;
the young men shall die by the sword; their
sons and their daughters shall die by fam-
ine; 23 and not even a remnant shall be left
of them. For I will bring disaster upon the
people of Anathoth, the year of their pun-
ishment.

12 You will be in the right, O LORD,
when I lay charges against you;
but let me put my case to you.
Why does the way of the guilty
prosper?
Why do all who are treacherous
thrive?
2 You plant them, and they take root;
they grow and bring forth fruit;
you are near in their mouths
yet far from their hearts.
3 But you, O LORD, know me;
You see me and test me—my heart
is with you.
Pull them out like sheep for the
slaughter,
and set them apart for the day
of slaughter.
4 How long will the land mourn,
and the grass of every field wither?
For the wickedness of those who live
in it
the animals and the birds are swept
away,
and because people said, "He is
blind to our ways."[a]

5 If you have raced with foot-runners
and they have wearied you,
how will you compete with horses?

a Gk: Heb *to our future*

laments consist of the prophet's complaint and a response by God. Uniquely in the prophetic corpus, these laments appear to offer readers an account of the inner life of the prophet, and are often called his "confessions." Modern critical scholarship, however, noting the high incidence of generic language and the complicated relationship between the laments and their context in the book of Jeremiah, has tended to view the laments as editorial constructs reflecting later assessments of the prophet's career, especially the people's opposition to the prophet. Whether the laments originated with the prophet himself or with later editors, attempts to analyze Jeremiah's psyche or reconstruct his biography on the basis of the confessions are risky. **11.18–20:** He learns that he is the object (*gentle lamb;* cf. Isa 53.7) of an assassination plot, and prays for protection (17.10; Ps 26) and for the punishment of his enemies (Ps 3.7; 7.6). **21–23:** The origin of the grievance against Jeremiah may be his identification of certain fellow citizens as false prophets and priests. In his characteristic phraseology (5.12; 18.21; 19.15; 23.12) their end is foretold. Ironically, the priests of Anathoth descended from Abiathar, sole survivor of Saul's attempt to exterminate the priests at Nob who had aided David as he fled Saul. Now, because of their response to Jeremiah, they will be left without remnant. **12.1–6:** Using language evocative of legal proceedings (v. 1), Jeremiah questions divine justice. The wicked, ostensibly faithful, prosper (Job 21; Ps 73). After Jeremiah's assertion of integrity (v. 3; Ps 139.23–24), God cites two proverbs (v. 5), informing Jeremiah that the present is but a preparation for a more demanding future. **5:** *Thickets of the Jordan,* the Jordan valley was a semitropical jungle where lions were found (49.19).

And if in a safe land you fall down,
how will you fare in the thickets of the Jordan?
6 For even your kinsfolk and your own family,
even they have dealt treacherously with you;
they are in full cry after you;
do not believe them,
though they speak friendly words to you.

7 I have forsaken my house,
I have abandoned my heritage;
I have given the beloved of my heart
into the hands of her enemies.
8 My heritage has become to me
like a lion in the forest;
she has lifted up her voice against me—
therefore I hate her.
9 Is the hyena greedy[a] for my heritage at my command?
Are the birds of prey all around her?
Go, assemble all the wild animals;
bring them to devour her.
10 Many shepherds have destroyed my vineyard,
they have trampled down my portion,
they have made my pleasant portion
a desolate wilderness.
11 They have made it a desolation;
desolate, it mourns to me.
The whole land is made desolate,
but no one lays it to heart.
12 Upon all the bare heights[b] in the desert
spoilers have come;
for the sword of the LORD devours
from one end of the land to the other;
no one shall be safe.
13 They have sown wheat and have reaped thorns,
they have tired themselves out but profit nothing.
They shall be ashamed of their[c] harvests
because of the fierce anger of the LORD.

14 Thus says the LORD concerning all
my evil neighbors who touch the heritage
that I have given my people Israel to inher-
it: I am about to pluck them up from their
land, and I will pluck up the house of Judah
from among them. 15 And after I have
plucked them up, I will again have compas-
sion on them, and I will bring them again to
their heritage and to their land, everyone of
them. 16 And then, if they will diligently
learn the ways of my people, to swear by
my name, "As the LORD lives," as they
taught my people to swear by Baal, then
they shall be built up in the midst of my
people. 17 But if any nation will not listen,
then I will completely uproot it and destroy
it, says the LORD.

13 Thus said the LORD to me, "Go and buy yourself a linen loincloth, and put it on your loins, but do not dip it in water." 2 So I bought a loincloth according

a Cn: Heb *Is the hyena, the bird of prey* *b* Or *the trails* *c* Heb *your*

12.7–13: God's lament over Jerusalem. Using several figures (*beloved of my heart,* 11.15; *lion, birds of prey, vineyard,* 5.10; Isa 5.1–7), God laments the necessary ravaging of Jerusalem (*my house,* Hos 9.15; *heritage,* 1 Sam 10.1; note the fem. sing. pronouns; cf. 2.2n.; Mic 1.6–9; 3.12).

12.14–17: Judah's neighbors. If Judah's enemies are converted (16.19–21; Isa 2.1–4 = Mic 4.1–4; Ps 87), God will spare them when Judah is restored; otherwise they will be destroyed (25.12–38). **14:** *Pluck up,* 1.10. **16:** *They,* a reference to the enemies. *Learn the ways of my people,* cf. 10.2. *Swear by my name,* 4.1–2. *Built up,* 1.10. **17:** *Uproot . . . destroy,* 1.10.

13.1–11: The symbolic act involving the loincloth. This is the first of several "symbolic acts" Jeremiah undertakes on the LORD's instruction (cf. chs 16; 18; 19; 32). Like the Temple (ch 7) and covenant (ch 11) sermons, these acts are narrated, for the most part, as though they were private experiences, and signify that Judah's fate is already determined by its sin. In their current forms, these accounts function

to the word of the LORD, and put it on my
loins. 3 And the word of the LORD came to
me a second time, saying, 4 "Take the loin-
cloth that you bought and are wearing, and
go now to the Euphrates,[a] and hide it there
in a cleft of the rock." 5 So I went, and hid
it by the Euphrates,[b] as the LORD com-
manded me. 6 And after many days the
LORD said to me, "Go now to the Euphra-
tes,[a] and take from there the loincloth that
I commanded you to hide there." 7 Then
I went to the Euphrates,[a] and dug, and I
took the loincloth from the place where
I had hidden it. But now the loincloth was
ruined; it was good for nothing.

8 Then the word of the LORD came to
me: 9 Thus says the LORD: Just so I will ruin
the pride of Judah and the great pride of
Jerusalem. 10 This evil people, who refuse
to hear my words, who stubbornly follow
their own will and have gone after other
gods to serve them and worship them, shall
be like this loincloth, which is good for
nothing. 11 For as the loincloth clings to
one's loins, so I made the whole house of
Israel and the whole house of Judah cling to
me, says the LORD, in order that they might
be for me a people, a name, a praise, and a
glory. But they would not listen.

12 You shall speak to them this word:
Thus says the LORD, the God of Israel: Ev-
ery wine-jar should be filled with wine.
And they will say to you, "Do you think we
do not know that every wine-jar should be
filled with wine?" 13 Then you shall say to
them: Thus says the LORD: I am about to
fill all the inhabitants of this land—the
kings who sit on David's throne, the
priests, the prophets, and all the inhabi-
tants of Jerusalem—with drunkenness.
14 And I will dash them one against anoth-
er, parents and children together, says the
LORD. I will not pity or spare or have com-
passion when I destroy them.

15 Hear and give ear; do not be haughty,
for the LORD has spoken.
16 Give glory to the LORD your God
before he brings darkness,
and before your feet stumble
on the mountains at twilight;
while you look for light,
he turns it into gloom
and makes it deep darkness.
17 But if you will not listen,
my soul will weep in secret for your pride;
my eyes will weep bitterly and run down with tears,
because the LORD's flock has been taken captive.

18 Say to the king and the queen mother:
"Take a lowly seat,
for your beautiful crown
has come down from your head."[c]
19 The towns of the Negeb are shut up
with no one to open them;
all Judah is taken into exile,
wholly taken into exile.

a Or *to Parah*; Heb *perath* *b* Or *by Parah*; Heb *perath* *c* Gk Syr Vg: Meaning of Heb uncertain

only in the literary context of the book. They are addressed first and foremost to post-catastrophe readers. Jeremiah evidently associated the name of a village near his home town of Anathoth, Parah (Josh 18.23), where there are rocky cliffs (v. 4), with the Hebrew name of the *Euphrates* (Perath). He buried a linen loincloth only to reclaim it—ruined—later. **8–11:** The LORD explains to Jeremiah that, like the loincloth, Judah *is* ruined by its sin and, therefore, *will* be ruined by the coming destruction.

13.12–14: The allegory of the wine jar. Jeremiah uses a proverb (v. 12a) and the figure of drunkenness (v. 13; cf. 25.15–16; Ezek 23.31) to describe the divine judgment.

13.15–17: The last opportunity for repentance is offered to Judah; her captivity is imminent (v. 17). The language here reflects the "Day of the LORD" tradition and recalls Am 5.18–20.

13.18–19: Exile! Almost resignedly, Jeremiah notes the fall of Jerusalem, the occupation of Judah, and the deportation of Jews to Babylon. It is impossible to date precisely the events alluded to here (the first deportation was in 597; the second, in 586). *Queen mother,* the mother of the ruling king. *Negeb,* the southern territory of Judah.

20 Lift up your eyes and see
those who come from the north.
Where is the flock that was given you,
your beautiful flock?
21 What will you say when they set as head over you
those whom you have trained to be your allies?
Will not pangs take hold of you,
like those of a woman in labor?
22 And if you say in your heart,
"Why have these things come upon me?"
it is for the greatness of your iniquity
that your skirts are lifted up,
and you are violated.
23 Can Ethiopians[a] change their skin
or leopards their spots?
Then also you can do good
who are accustomed to do evil.
24 I will scatter you[b] like chaff
driven by the wind from the desert.
25 This is your lot,
the portion I have measured out to you, says the LORD,
because you have forgotten me
and trusted in lies.
26 I myself will lift up your skirts over your face,
and your shame will be seen.
27 I have seen your abominations,
your adulteries and neighings, your shameless prostitutions
on the hills of the countryside.
Woe to you, O Jerusalem!
How long will it be
before you are made clean?

14 The word of the LORD that came to Jeremiah concerning the drought:
2 Judah mourns
and her gates languish;
they lie in gloom on the ground,
and the cry of Jerusalem goes up.
3 Her nobles send their servants for water;
they come to the cisterns,
they find no water,
they return with their vessels empty.
They are ashamed and dismayed
and cover their heads,
4 because the ground is cracked.
Because there has been no rain on the land
the farmers are dismayed;
they cover their heads.
5 Even the doe in the field forsakes her newborn fawn
because there is no grass.
6 The wild asses stand on the bare heights,[c]
they pant for air like jackals;
their eyes fail
because there is no herbage.

7 Although our iniquities testify against us,
act, O LORD, for your name's sake;
our apostasies indeed are many,
and we have sinned against you.
8 O hope of Israel,
its savior in time of trouble,
why should you be like a stranger in the land,

a Or *Nubians*; Heb *Cushites* *b* Heb *them* *c* Or *the trails*

13.20–27: Jerusalem's shame. Using a common biblical simile for judgment, the exposure of a woman (Isa 47.2; here the untrustworthy shepherdess), Jeremiah describes the approaching rape (vv. 22,26) of Jerusalem by Babylon. **20:** *North,* see 1.13–14n.; 4.6. **23:** *Ethiopians,* the inhabitants of Cush, the land south of Egypt. In her present state, Jerusalem cannot change herself (Hos 5.4; Jn 8.34; cf. 3.22).

14.1–15.9: Lament over catastrophic drought and the coming military defeat of Jerusalem. 14.2–6: By examples drawn from city and country, forest and wilderness, Jeremiah describes the drought. **7–9:** Prostrate on the ground (v. 2), in the words of a prayer for a day of repentance, the people confess their sins and, as they are his covenant people, plead with God to remember them. **7:** Cf. 3.21–25. *For your name's sake,* Ps 25.11; 31.3; 79.9; 109.21; 143.11. **8:** *Savior in times of trouble,* cf. 2.27–28. *A traveler turning aside for the night,* 9.2. **10–12:** No intercession or ritual acts will avert the divine punishment.

like a traveler turning aside for the night?
9 Why should you be like someone confused,
like a mighty warrior who cannot give help?
Yet you, O LORD, are in the midst of us,
and we are called by your name;
do not forsake us!

10 Thus says the LORD concerning this people:
Truly they have loved to wander,
they have not restrained their feet;
therefore the LORD does not accept them,
now he will remember their iniquity
and punish their sins.

11 The LORD said to me: Do not pray
for the welfare of this people. 12 Although
they fast, I do not hear their cry, and al-
though they offer burnt offering and grain
offering, I do not accept them; but by the
sword, by famine, and by pestilence I con-
sume them.
13 Then I said: "Ah, Lord GOD! Here
are the prophets saying to them, 'You shall
not see the sword, nor shall you have fam-
ine, but I will give you true peace in this
place.' " 14 And the LORD said to me: The
prophets are prophesying lies in my name;
I did not send them, nor did I command
them or speak to them. They are prophesy-
ing to you a lying vision, worthless divina-
tion, and the deceit of their own minds.
15 Therefore thus says the LORD concerning
the prophets who prophesy in my name
though I did not send them, and who say,
"Sword and famine shall not come on this
land": By sword and famine those prophets
shall be consumed. 16 And the people to
whom they prophesy shall be thrown out
into the streets of Jerusalem, victims of
famine and sword. There shall be no one to
bury them—themselves, their wives, their
sons, and their daughters. For I will pour
out their wickedness upon them.

17 You shall say to them this word:
Let my eyes run down with tears night and day,
and let them not cease,
for the virgin daughter—my people—
is struck down with a crushing blow,
with a very grievous wound.
18 If I go out into the field,
look—those killed by the sword!
And if I enter the city,
look—those sick with[a] famine!
For both prophet and priest ply their trade throughout the land,
and have no knowledge.

19 Have you completely rejected Judah?
Does your heart loathe Zion?
Why have you struck us down

a Heb *look—the sicknesses of*

10: *Loved to wander,* see 2.23–25. **11–12:** This third and final prohibition against prophetic intercession (see 7.16; 11.14), set here in context with an almost exemplary confession of sin (vv. 7–9), forcefully underscores the fact that Judah's sin has sealed its fate. **13–16:** *In this place,* in the Temple. Jeremiah's effort to excuse the people's heedlessness because they rely on the false prophets' beguiling message is rejected. *Deceit of their own minds,* the false prophets rely on their own reason rather than awaiting the divine commission. For the criterion of false prophecy, see Deut 18.20–22. **17–18:** Jeremiah's lament closely resembles communal laments from the period immediately after the Babylonian conquest of Jerusalem. It describes the calamity, using figures of war, drought, unburied dead, hunger, and confused spiritual leaders (Lam 2.11–14,18–22). **17:** *Virgin daughter—my people,* alternately, "the virgin daughter of my people," Jerusalem. *Grievous wound,* 10.19. **18:** *Have no knowledge,* see 2.8n. **19–22:** The people's lament. The people plead their case, acknowledging their sin (v. 20), calling upon the LORD to think of his own reputation (v. 21), and expressing confidence in the LORD's ability to deliver (v. 22). **19:** Cf. Lam 5.22; Ps 74.1; 79.5. *Healing,* 3.22; 8.22. **20:** Cf. 3.25; Ps 79.8. **21:** Ps 74.2,20–23. **22:** 10.12–16. *Hope,* 14.8.

so that there is no healing for us?
We look for peace, but find no good;
for a time of healing, but there is terror instead.
20 We acknowledge our wickedness, O LORD,
the iniquity of our ancestors,
for we have sinned against you.
21 Do not spurn us, for your name's sake;
do not dishonor your glorious throne;
remember and do not break your covenant with us.
22 Can any idols of the nations bring rain?
Or can the heavens give showers?
Is it not you, O LORD our God?
We set our hope on you,
for it is you who do all this.

15 Then the LORD said to me: Though
Moses and Samuel stood before me,
yet my heart would not turn toward this
people. Send them out of my sight, and
let them go! 2 And when they say to you,
"Where shall we go?" you shall say to
them: Thus says the LORD:
Those destined for pestilence, to pestilence,
and those destined for the sword, to the sword;
those destined for famine, to famine,
and those destined for captivity, to captivity.
3 And I will appoint over them four kinds of
destroyers, says the LORD: the sword to
kill, the dogs to drag away, and the birds of
the air and the wild animals of the earth to
devour and destroy. 4 I will make them a
horror to all the kingdoms of the earth because of what King Manasseh son of Hezekiah of Judah did in Jerusalem.

5 Who will have pity on you, O Jerusalem,
or who will bemoan you?
Who will turn aside
to ask about your welfare?
6 You have rejected me, says the LORD,
you are going backward;
so I have stretched out my hand against you and destroyed you—
I am weary of relenting.
7 I have winnowed them with a winnowing fork
in the gates of the land;
I have bereaved them, I have destroyed my people;
they did not turn from their ways.
8 Their widows became more numerous than the sand of the seas;
I have brought against the mothers of youths
a destroyer at noonday;
I have made anguish and terror
fall upon her suddenly.
9 She who bore seven has languished;
she has swooned away;
her sun went down while it was yet day;
she has been shamed and disgraced.
And the rest of them I will give to the sword
before their enemies,
says the LORD.

10 Woe is me, my mother, that you ever

15.1–16.13: An extended composition on the certainty of Judah's fate. 15.1–4: *Moses* (Ex 32.11–14; Num 14.13–19) and *Samuel* (1 Sam 12.17–18), were Israel's greatest intercessors. V. 1 is one of four references to Moses in prophetic literature (the others are Mic 6.4; Isa 63.11; Mal 4.4). **2:** *Pestilence, the sword,* and *famine* are a common grouping of disasters (21.7; Ezek 7.15). The addition of *captivity* suggests an exilic perspective. **4:** The Deuteronomistic history blamed *King Manasseh* for the eventual fall of Jerusalem (2 Kings 21).

15.5–9: Jerusalem's end. 6: *Weary of relenting,* cf. Am 7.1–9. **7:** *Winnowed them,* a common threshing metaphor (see Isa 21.10; 27.12; Jer 51.2). **8:** *Widows . . . more numerous than the sand of the seas,* contrast the promise to the ancestors (Gen 22.17; 32.13; 41.49). **9:** *She who bore seven,* a sign of favor (Ruth 4.15; 1 Sam 2.5). Jerusalem will be bereaved (cf. Hos 9.12).

15.10–21: Jeremiah's second personal lament, see 11.18–12.6n. The lament consists of two dialogues,

bore me, a man of strife and contention to
the whole land! I have not lent, nor have I
borrowed, yet all of them curse me. 11 The
LORD said: Surely I have intervened in your
life[a] for good, surely I have imposed ene-
mies on you in a time of trouble and in a
time of distress.[b] 12 Can iron and bronze
break iron from the north?
13 Your wealth and your treasures I will
give as plunder, without price, for all your
sins, throughout all your territory. 14 I will
make you serve your enemies in a land that
you do not know, for in my anger a fire is
kindled that shall burn forever.

15 O LORD, you know;
remember me and visit me,
and bring down retribution for me
on my persecutors.
In your forbearance do not take
me away;
know that on your account I suffer
insult.
16 Your words were found, and I
ate them,
and your words became to me
a joy
and the delight of my heart;
for I am called by your name,
O LORD, God of hosts.
17 I did not sit in the company of
merrymakers,
nor did I rejoice;
under the weight of your hand I
sat alone,
for you had filled me with
indignation.
18 Why is my pain unceasing,
my wound incurable,
refusing to be healed?
Truly, you are to me like a deceitful
brook,
like waters that fail.

19 Therefore thus says the LORD:
If you turn back, I will take
you back,
and you shall stand before me.
If you utter what is precious, and not
what is worthless,
you shall serve as my mouth.
It is they who will turn to you,
not you who will turn to them.
20 And I will make you to this people
a fortified wall of bronze;
they will fight against you,
but they shall not prevail over you,
for I am with you
to save you and deliver you,
says the LORD.
21 I will deliver you out of the hand of
the wicked,
and redeem you from the grasp of
the ruthless.

16 The word of the LORD came to me:
2 You shall not take a wife, nor shall

a Heb *intervened with you* b Meaning of Heb uncertain

vv. 10–14 (in prose, apparently composed by an exilic or postexilic editor) and vv. 15–18 (in poetry). **10:** Cf. 20.14–18. The placement of v. 10 suggests that Jeremiah is portrayed here as a son of Jerusalem (the mother in vv. 5–9). The motif of opposition to and persecution of Jeremiah is prominent in the prose narratives of the book (26; 36; 37–38). **12:** A muddled allusion to 1.14–19. **13:** A doublet for 17.3–4, where the idea is better suited. **15:** With the familiar phrase *you know* (Ps 40.9; 139.1), Jeremiah prays to God for retribution against his persecutors. **16:** *Your words . . . I ate them,* see 1.9; Ezek 2.8–3.3. **17:** The *hand* of God, often the symbol of inspiration (Isa 8.11; Ezek 3.14,22), is here a symbol of burden. **18:** The image of the *incurable wound,* elsewhere applied to Jerusalem or Judah, here refers to the prophet. *Deceitful brook,* cf. 2.13; Job 6.15–20. **19–21:** Jeremiah's complaint is interpreted as an abandonment of his prophetic commission. The imagery in God's speech (*stand before me,* cf. 23.18; *my mouth,* cf. 1.9; Ex 4.16; *wall of bronze,* cf. 1.18; *I am with you to . . . deliver you,* cf. 1.8,19) evokes a recommissioning of the prophet.

16.1–9: Jeremiah's remaining unmarried and without children serves as a prophetic sign-act, a symbolic enactment of God's word (Hos 1.2–9; Isa 8.3–4). **1–9:** An illustration of 15.17. Continuing the maternal motif (15.8–10) and heightening the prohibition against intercession (7.16; 11.14; 14.11), Jeremiah is forbidden to marry (vv. 1–4) or even mourn the dead (vv. 5–9). **1–4:** Any children born to

you have sons or daughters in this place.
3 For thus says the LORD concerning the
sons and daughters who are born in this
place, and concerning the mothers who
bear them and the fathers who beget them
in this land: 4 They shall die of deadly dis-
eases. They shall not be lamented, nor shall
they be buried; they shall become like dung
on the surface of the ground. They shall
perish by the sword and by famine, and
their dead bodies shall become food for the
birds of the air and for the wild animals of
the earth.

5 For thus says the LORD: Do not enter
the house of mourning, or go to lament, or
bemoan them; for I have taken away my
peace from this people, says the LORD, my
steadfast love and mercy. 6 Both great and
small shall die in this land; they shall not be
buried, and no one shall lament for them;
there shall be no gashing, no shaving of the
head for them. 7 No one shall break bread[a]
for the mourner, to offer comfort for the
dead; nor shall anyone give them the cup of
consolation to drink for their fathers or
their mothers. 8 You shall not go into the
house of feasting to sit with them, to eat
and drink. 9 For thus says the LORD of
hosts, the God of Israel: I am going to ban-
ish from this place, in your days and before
your eyes, the voice of mirth and the voice
of gladness, the voice of the bridegroom
and the voice of the bride.

10 And when you tell this people all
these words, and they say to you, "Why has
the LORD pronounced all this great evil
against us? What is our iniquity? What is
the sin that we have committed against the
LORD our God?" 11 then you shall say to
them: It is because your ancestors have for-
saken me, says the LORD, and have gone
after other gods and have served and wor-
shiped them, and have forsaken me and
have not kept my law; 12 and because you
have behaved worse than your ancestors,
for here you are, every one of you, follow-
ing your stubborn evil will, refusing to lis-
ten to me. 13 Therefore I will hurl you out of
this land into a land that neither you nor
your ancestors have known, and there you
shall serve other gods day and night, for I
will show you no favor.

14 Therefore, the days are surely com-
ing, says the LORD, when it shall no longer
be said, "As the LORD lives who brought
the people of Israel up out of the land of
Egypt," 15 but "As the LORD lives who
brought the people of Israel up out of the
land of the north and out of all the lands
where he had driven them." For I will bring
them back to their own land that I gave to
their ancestors.

16 I am now sending for many fisher-
men, says the LORD, and they shall catch
them; and afterward I will send for many
hunters, and they shall hunt them from ev-
ery mountain and every hill, and out of the
clefts of the rocks. 17 For my eyes are on all
their ways; they are not hidden from my
presence, nor is their iniquity concealed
from my sight. 18 And[b] I will doubly repay
their iniquity and their sin, because they
have polluted my land with the carcasses of
their detestable idols, and have filled my
inheritance with their abominations.

a Two Mss Gk: MT *break for them* *b* Gk: Heb *And first*

him would be subject to the common fate. *Perish by the sword and by famine,* 15.2–4. **5–7:** All symbols of mourning (*gashing,* 41.5; cf. Lev 19.28; *shaving of the head,* Am 8.10; Isa 22.12; cf. Deut 14.1) are as futile as death is comfortless. *Both great and small,* 5.4–5. **8–9:** 7.34; 25.10; 33.11.

16.10–13: Judah's fate. For the style see 13.12–14n. The reasons given are characteristic of the Deuteronomistic theology that permeates the prose discourses (see Deut 4.25–28; 29.24–29).

16.14–15: Israel's homecoming. Their return, accomplished by God's actions, will be celebrated as a new Exodus. The passage duplicates 23.7–8; both are editorial insertions.

16.16–18: No refuge for Judah. After the editorial insertion of a word of eschatological hope, treatment of the original topic of Judah's fate resumes. Judah cannot escape either Egypt or Babylonia (*fishermen* and *hunters;* Hab 1.14–15). The diction of this passage has affinities with several passages in the book of Isaiah (7.18–19; 40.2; 66.3).

19 O LORD, my strength and my
stronghold,
my refuge in the day of trouble,
to you shall the nations come
from the ends of the earth and say:
Our ancestors have inherited nothing
but lies,
worthless things in which there is
no profit.
20 Can mortals make for themselves
gods?
Such are no gods!

21 "Therefore I am surely going to teach
them, this time I am going to teach them
my power and my might, and they shall
know that my name is the LORD."

17 The sin of Judah is written with an
iron pen; with a diamond point it is
engraved on the tablet of their hearts, and
on the horns of their altars, 2 while their
children remember their altars and their sa-
cred poles,[a] beside every green tree, and on
the high hills, 3 on the mountains in the
open country. Your wealth and all your
treasures I will give for spoil as the price of
your sin[b] throughout all your territory.
4 By your own act you shall lose the heri-
tage that I gave you, and I will make you
serve your enemies in a land that you do
not know, for in my anger a fire is kin-
dled[c] that shall burn forever.

5 Thus says the LORD:
Cursed are those who trust in
mere mortals
and make mere flesh their strength,
whose hearts turn away from
the LORD.
6 They shall be like a shrub in
the desert,
and shall not see when relief comes.
They shall live in the parched places
of the wilderness,
in an uninhabited salt land.

7 Blessed are those who trust in
the LORD,
whose trust is the LORD.
8 They shall be like a tree planted
by water,
sending out its roots by the stream.
It shall not fear when heat comes,
and its leaves shall stay green;
in the year of drought it is
not anxious,
and it does not cease to bear fruit.

9 The heart is devious above all else;
it is perverse—
who can understand it?
10 I the LORD test the mind
and search the heart,

a Heb *Asherim* b Cn: Heb *spoil your high places for sin* c Two Mss Theodotion: *you kindled*

16.19–21: Conversion of the nations (Isa 2.2–4 = Mic 4.1–4; Isa 45.20–24). This unexpected doxology is one of several "liturgical" texts spaced throughout chs 10–20 (10.23–25; 17.12–13; 20.13). They allude to one another and seem to appear at major junctures. In contrast to the focus of the prose material on the inevitability of Judah's fate, these texts look beyond the exile and even beyond Judah to consider human history on a universal scale. Recognizing the vanity of their idol-worship, all nations will join in worshiping Israel's omnipotent God.

17.1–18: The human heart and the justice of God. Several of the passages in this unit are characterized by wisdom forms or motifs.

17.1–4: Judah's sin is engraved in their hearts. This unit succinctly and forcefully states the argument of the prose material that began in ch 7. It is a litany of expressions characteristic of the prose sections of the book (*every green tree, in a land that you do not know,* etc.). **1:** *Iron pen,* a diamond-tipped stylus (Job 19.24). *Horns of their altars,* Ex 29.12.

17.5–8: The human heart and trust in God. These verses share theme and imagery with Ps 1. Godless people, *whose hearts turn away from the LORD,* are like fruitless desert plants; godly people, *who trust in him,* are like fruitful, well-watered trees (Ps 1.3; 92.12–15; Prov 3.18).

17.9–10: The heart is devious. The preceding wisdom psalm evokes confidence that right and blessing, wrong and curse stand in an automatic relationship in the world. Experience teaches otherwise. Vv. 9–10

to give to all according to their ways,
according to the fruit of
their doings.

11 Like the partridge hatching what
it did not lay,
so are all who amass wealth
unjustly;
in mid-life it will leave them,
and at their end they will prove to
be fools.

12 O glorious throne, exalted from the
beginning,
shrine of our sanctuary!
13 O hope of Israel! O LORD!
All who forsake you shall be put to
shame;
those who turn away from you[a] shall
be recorded in the
underworld,[b]
for they have forsaken the fountain
of living water, the LORD.

14 Heal me, O LORD, and I shall
be healed;
save me, and I shall be saved;
for you are my praise.
15 See how they say to me,
"Where is the word of the LORD?
Let it come!"
16 But I have not run away from being a
shepherd[c] in your service,
nor have I desired the fatal day.
You know what came from my lips;
it was before your face.
17 Do not become a terror to me;
you are my refuge in the day
of disaster;
18 Let my persecutors be shamed,
but do not let me be shamed;
let them be dismayed,
but do not let me be dismayed;
bring on them the day of disaster;
destroy them with double
destruction!

19 Thus said the LORD to me: Go and
stand in the People's Gate, by which the
kings of Judah enter and by which they go
out, and in all the gates of Jerusalem, 20 and
say to them: Hear the word of the LORD,
you kings of Judah, and all Judah, and all
the inhabitants of Jerusalem, who enter by
these gates. 21 Thus says the LORD: For the
sake of your lives, take care that you do not
bear a burden on the sabbath day or bring
it in by the gates of Jerusalem. 22 And do
not carry a burden out of your houses on
the sabbath or do any work, but keep the
sabbath day holy, as I commanded your
ancestors. 23 Yet they did not listen or in-
cline their ear; they stiffened their necks
and would not hear or receive instruction.
24 But if you listen to me, says the

a Heb *me* *b* Or *in the earth* *c* Meaning of Heb uncertain

attempt to account for the discrepancy in terms of appearance and reality. V. 9, a proverbial saying in the form of a rhetorical question, is answered by a divine assertion (1 Sam 16.7; Ps 62.12).

17.11: A proverb, addressing the problem of the prosperity of the wicked.

17.12–13: God's ways are high. Another doxology, which echoes themes from the immediate context (*those who turn away from you,* v. 5), the other doxologies (*O hope of Israel,* cf. 16.19), and the book as a whole (*fountain,* 2.13). *Throne,* the ark in the Temple (Isa 6.1). The discussion shifts from confidence in justice, generally, to the judgment of individuals.

17.14–18: Jeremiah's third personal lament (see 11.18–12.6n.). The appeal for help (vv. 14,17–18), the description of his opponents' behavior (v. 15), and his self-justification are standard elements in Jeremiah's laments. Unlike the previous laments, however, this one contains no answer from God. Jeremiah does not want to see God's day of judgment (Am 5.18; Isa 2.11); but if this be the only means of vindication, let it descend in all its fury.

17.19–27: Judah and the sabbath. A postexilic prose discourse (cf. Neh 13.15–22) dealing with the violation of the sabbath (Ex 16.23; 20.8–11; 23.12; 31.12–17; Deut 5.12–15) as symptomatic of the people's general alienation from God (11.1–8; Am 8.5). Keeping the sabbath is linked to the restoration

LORD, and bring in no burden by the gates
of this city on the sabbath day, but keep the
sabbath day holy and do no work on it,
25 then there shall enter by the gates of this
city kings[a] who sit on the throne of David,
riding in chariots and on horses, they and
their officials, the people of Judah and the
inhabitants of Jerusalem; and this city shall
be inhabited forever. 26 And people shall
come from the towns of Judah and the
places around Jerusalem, from the land of
Benjamin, from the Shephelah, from the
hill country, and from the Negeb, bringing
burnt offerings and sacrifices, grain offer-
ings and frankincense, and bringing thank
offerings to the house of the LORD. 27 But if
you do not listen to me, to keep the sabbath
day holy, and to carry in no burden
through the gates of Jerusalem on the sab-
bath day, then I will kindle a fire in its
gates; it shall devour the palaces of Jerusa-
lem and shall not be quenched.

18 The word that came to Jeremiah
from the LORD: 2 "Come, go down
to the potter's house, and there I will let
you hear my words." 3 So I went down to
the potter's house, and there he was work-
ing at his wheel. 4 The vessel he was making
of clay was spoiled in the potter's hand,
and he reworked it into another vessel, as
seemed good to him.
5 Then the word of the LORD came to
me: 6 Can I not do with you, O house of
Israel, just as this potter has done? says the
LORD. Just like the clay in the potter's
hand, so are you in my hand, O house of
Israel. 7 At one moment I may declare con-
cerning a nation or a kingdom, that I will
pluck up and break down and destroy it,
8 but if that nation, concerning which I have
spoken, turns from its evil, I will change my
mind about the disaster that I intended to
bring on it. 9 And at another moment I may
declare concerning a nation or a kingdom
that I will build and plant it, 10 but if it does
evil in my sight, not listening to my voice,
then I will change my mind about the good
that I had intended to do to it. 11 Now,
therefore, say to the people of Judah and
the inhabitants of Jerusalem: Thus says the
LORD: Look, I am a potter shaping evil
against you and devising a plan against
you. Turn now, all of you from your evil
way, and amend your ways and your do-
ings.
12 But they say, "It is no use! We will
follow our own plans, and each of us will
act according to the stubbornness of our
evil will."

13 Therefore thus says the LORD:
Ask among the nations:
  Who has heard the like of this?
The virgin Israel has done
  a most horrible thing.
14 Does the snow of Lebanon leave
  the crags of Sirion?[b]

a Cn: Heb *kings and officials* *b* Cn: Heb *of the field*

of the Davidic dynasty (v. 25). **26:** *Benjamin . . . the Shephelah . . . the hill country . . . the Negeb,* the regions surrounding Jerusalem to the north, the west, and the south.

18.1–12: The symbolic act involving the potter. On the private nature of this experience and the literary function of the account, see 13.1n. The comparison between God and Israel and the potter and the clay (cf. Isa 29.16; 45.9) underscores God's complete control. The examples given in vv. 7–10 concerning the fate of any *nation* or *kingdom* (cf. 1.10) shows that God's decision is not capricious but is responsive to repentance. Again (see chs 7 and 11), the contrast between the possible (repentance, v. 11b) and the actual (the people's obduracy, v. 12) drives home the point that Judah has sealed its own fate.

18.13–17: Faithless Judah is condemned to endless walking. This unit reprises the argument made in ch 2. Jerusalem (*the virgin* [of] *Israel*) has committed the nearly incredible folly of forsaking her God (2.10,32). God will ignore her children (2.27–28) and will scatter them as before the east wind (4.11; 13.24; 23.19). **14:** *Lebanon,* the mountain range north of Israel that parallels the coast of the Mediterranean Sea. The name Lebanon is related to the word for "white," alluding to the snowy peaks. *Sirion,* Mount Hermon, the highest peak in the Anti-Lebanon range, which runs parallel to the Lebanon on the east. *Mountain waters,* perhaps from the Anti-Lebanon Mountains or from Mount Hermon itself, such

Do the mountain[a] waters run dry,[b]
the cold flowing streams?
15 But my people have forgotten me,
they burn offerings to a delusion;
they have stumbled[c] in their ways,
in the ancient roads,
and have gone into bypaths,
not the highway,
16 making their land a horror,
a thing to be hissed at forever.
All who pass by it are horrified
and shake their heads.
17 Like the wind from the east,
I will scatter them before
the enemy.
I will show them my back, not
my face,
in the day of their calamity.

18 Then they said, "Come, let us make plots against Jeremiah—for instruction shall not perish from the priest, nor counsel from the wise, nor the word from the prophet. Come, let us bring charges against him,[d] and let us not heed any of his words."

19 Give heed to me, O LORD,
and listen to what my adversaries
say!
20 Is evil a recompense for good?
Yet they have dug a pit for my life.
Remember how I stood before you
to speak good for them,
to turn away your wrath
from them.
21 Therefore give their children over to
famine;
hurl them out to the power of
the sword,
let their wives become childless and
widowed.
May their men meet death by
pestilence,
their youths be slain by the sword
in battle.
22 May a cry be heard from their
houses,
when you bring the marauder
suddenly upon them!
For they have dug a pit to catch me,
and laid snares for my feet.
23 Yet you, O LORD, know
all their plotting to kill me.
Do not forgive their iniquity,
do not blot out their sin from your
sight.
Let them be tripped up before you;
deal with them while you are
angry.

19 Thus said the LORD: Go and buy a potter's earthenware jug. Take with you[e] some of the elders of the people and some of the senior priests, 2 and go out to the valley of the son of Hinnom at the entry of the Potsherd Gate, and proclaim there the words that I tell you. 3 You shall say: Hear the word of the LORD, O kings of

a Cn: Heb *foreign* *b* Cn: Heb *Are . . . plucked up?*
c Gk Syr Vg: Heb *they made them stumble*
d Heb *strike him with the tongue* *e* Syr Tg Compare Gk: Heb lacks *take with you*

as the Pharpar and Abanah rivers or the sources of the Jordan. **16:** *A thing to be hissed at,* to ward off a similar fate (Zeph 2.15).

18.18–23: Jeremiah's fourth personal lament (see 11.18–12.6n.). *They* (identity unknown) plot against Jeremiah because of his attacks against the leaders (2.8; 8.8). Jeremiah defends his innocence and prays to God for the merciless, total destruction of his enemies and their families. Note the assignment of instruction (Heb "torah") to the priests (v. 18).

19.1–20.6: The public persecution of Jeremiah. In contrast to the prose discourses of chs 7 and 11, which did not describe Jeremiah actually delivering the word he was given to speak, v. 14 reports the public pronouncement. Notably, the invitation to repent that is an element of the prose preaching earlier in the book is absent here. Significant, too, is the reaction to Jeremiah's preaching (20.1–6). **19.1–2:** *Valley of the Son of Hinnom,* see 7.31n. The Potsherd Gate (probably the later Dung Gate, Neh 2.13) in the south wall of the city, apparently the exit through which garbage was removed. **3–9:** Condemnation of the people for forsaking the LORD and for worshiping idols, and worst of all, for the offering of children to Baal (7.30–32). With a play on the Heb words for *jug* ("baqbuq," v. 10) and *make void* ("baqaq,"

Judah and inhabitants of Jerusalem. Thus
says the LORD of hosts, the God of Israel: I
am going to bring such disaster upon this
place that the ears of everyone who hears of
it will tingle. 4 Because the people have for-
saken me, and have profaned this place by
making offerings in it to other gods whom
neither they nor their ancestors nor the
kings of Judah have known, and because
they have filled this place with the blood of
the innocent, 5 and gone on building the
high places of Baal to burn their children in
the fire as burnt offerings to Baal, which I
did not command or decree, nor did it enter
my mind; 6 therefore the days are surely
coming, says the LORD, when this place
shall no more be called Topheth, or the val-
ley of the son of Hinnom, but the valley of
Slaughter. 7 And in this place I will make
void the plans of Judah and Jerusalem, and
will make them fall by the sword before
their enemies, and by the hand of those
who seek their life. I will give their dead
bodies for food to the birds of the air and
to the wild animals of the earth. 8 And I will
make this city a horror, a thing to be hissed
at; everyone who passes by it will be horri-
fied and will hiss because of all its disasters.
9 And I will make them eat the flesh of their
sons and the flesh of their daughters, and
all shall eat the flesh of their neighbors in
the siege, and in the distress with which
their enemies and those who seek their life
afflict them.

10 Then you shall break the jug in the
sight of those who go with you, 11 and shall
say to them: Thus says the LORD of hosts:
So will I break this people and this city, as
one breaks a potter's vessel, so that it can
never be mended. In Topheth they shall
bury until there is no more room to bury.
12 Thus will I do to this place, says the
LORD, and to its inhabitants, making this
city like Topheth. 13 And the houses of Jeru-
salem and the houses of the kings of Judah
shall be defiled like the place of Topheth—
all the houses upon whose roofs offerings
have been made to the whole host of heav-
en, and libations have been poured out to
other gods.

14 When Jeremiah came from Topheth,
where the LORD had sent him to prophesy,
he stood in the court of the LORD's house
and said to all the people: 15 Thus says the
LORD of hosts, the God of Israel: I am now
bringing upon this city and upon all its
towns all the disaster that I have pro-
nounced against it, because they have stiff-
ened their necks, refusing to hear my
words.

20 Now the priest Pashhur son of Im-
mer, who was chief officer in the
house of the LORD, heard Jeremiah proph-
esying these things. 2 Then Pashhur struck
the prophet Jeremiah, and put him in the
stocks that were in the upper Benjamin
Gate of the house of the LORD. 3 The next
morning when Pashhur released Jeremiah
from the stocks, Jeremiah said to him, The
LORD has named you not Pashhur but
"Terror-all-around." 4 For thus says the
LORD: I am making you a terror to yourself
and to all your friends; and they shall fall
by the sword of their enemies while you
look on. And I will give all Judah into the
hand of the king of Babylon; he shall carry
them captive to Babylon, and shall kill
them with the sword. 5 I will give all the
wealth of this city, all its gains, all its prized
belongings, and all the treasures of the
kings of Judah into the hand of their ene-
mies, who shall plunder them, and seize

v. 7), Jeremiah announces the people's horrible fate, which will make them resort to cannibalism, one of the curses for covenant violation (Lev 26.29; Deut 28.53). **6–9:** Cf. 7.30–34. **6:** *Topheth,* see 2 Kings 23.10. **8:** *A thing to be hissed at,* see 18.6n. **10–15:** The breaking of pottery is a conventional image of destruction (Ps 29). *Host of heaven,* 7.18; 8.2n.; 2 Kings 21.3–5. **14–15:** Jeremiah goes to the Temple to proclaim publicly that the LORD has reached his decision (*I have pronounced,* v. 15). This is not the preaching of repentance; it is the proclamation of a verdict. **20.1–6:** To forestall a repetition of this frightful pronouncement, *Pashhur* of the Temple police publicly punishes Jeremiah. On his release (v. 3) he tells Pashhur that *Terror-all-around* (6.25; Ps 31.13) will be his name, for he and his family will share the fate of the doomed city (25.8–11).

them, and carry them to Babylon.
6 And you, Pashhur, and all who live in your house, shall go into captivity, and to Babylon you shall go; there you shall die, and there you shall be buried, you and all your friends, to whom you have prophesied falsely.

7 O LORD, you have enticed me,
and I was enticed;
you have overpowered me,
and you have prevailed.
I have become a laughingstock all day long;
everyone mocks me.
8 For whenever I speak, I must cry out,
I must shout, "Violence and destruction!"
For the word of the LORD has become for me
a reproach and derision all day long.
9 If I say, "I will not mention him,
or speak any more in his name,"
then within me there is something like a burning fire
shut up in my bones;
I am weary with holding it in,
and I cannot.
10 For I hear many whispering:
"Terror is all around!
Denounce him! Let us denounce him!"
All my close friends
are watching for me to stumble.
"Perhaps he can be enticed,
and we can prevail against him,
and take our revenge on him."
11 But the LORD is with me like a dread warrior;
therefore my persecutors will stumble,
and they will not prevail.
They will be greatly shamed,
for they will not succeed.
Their eternal dishonor
will never be forgotten.
12 O LORD of hosts, you test the righteous,
you see the heart and the mind;
let me see your retribution upon them,
for to you I have committed my cause.

13 Sing to the LORD;
praise the LORD!
For he has delivered the life of the needy
from the hands of evildoers.

14 Cursed be the day
on which I was born!
The day when my mother bore me,
let it not be blessed!
15 Cursed be the man
who brought the news to my father, saying,
"A child is born to you, a son,"
making him very glad.
16 Let that man be like the cities
that the LORD overthrew without pity;
let him hear a cry in the morning
and an alarm at noon,
17 because he did not kill me in the womb;
so my mother would have been my grave,

20.7–13, 14–18: Jeremiah's fifth and sixth personal laments (see 11.18–12.6n.). **7–9:** Jeremiah accuses God of deceiving him and of exerting irresistible power over him. The same terms are used to describe the plots of Jeremiah's enemies in v. 10. Regardless of its effect, Jeremiah cannot refrain from his proclamation (Am 3.8). **10–13:** Though his opponents plot his fall, Jeremiah expresses confidence in God's invincible protection of those who rely on him (*the needy*); he uses excerpts from liturgical hymns (cf. Ps 6.9–10; 31.13; 109.30; 140.12–13). The expression of confidence is a common element in psalmic laments (Ps 6.8–10; 12.6–7). **10:** *Terror is all around,* v. 3. **13:** The final liturgical fragment in chs 10–20. See 16.19–21n. A call to praise often concludes a psalm of lament (Ps 7.17; 13.6). **14–18:** In this independent section, the speaker (generally understood to be Jeremiah, but perhaps the editor/narrator) curses not God but his own existence (15.10; Job 3). **16:** *The cities,* Sodom and Gomorrah, 23.14; Gen 19.

and her womb forever great.
18 Why did I come forth from the womb
to see toil and sorrow,
and spend my days in shame?

21 This is the word that came to Jeremiah from the LORD, when King Zedekiah sent to him Pashhur son of Malchiah and the priest Zephaniah son of Maaseiah, saying,
2 "Please inquire of the LORD on our behalf, for King Nebuchadrezzar of Babylon is making war against us; perhaps the LORD will perform a wonderful deed for us, as he has often done, and will make him withdraw from us."
3 Then Jeremiah said to them:
4 Thus you shall say to Zedekiah: Thus says the LORD, the God of Israel: I am going to turn back the weapons of war that are in your hands and with which you are fighting against the king of Babylon and against the Chaldeans who are besieging you outside the walls; and I will bring them together into the center of this city.
5 I myself will fight against you with outstretched hand and mighty arm, in anger, in fury, and in great wrath.
6 And I will strike down the inhabitants of this city, both human beings and animals; they shall die of a great pestilence.
7 Afterward, says the LORD, I will give King Zedekiah of Judah, and his servants, and the people in this city—those who survive the pestilence, sword, and famine—into the hands of King Nebuchadrezzar of Babylon, into the hands of their enemies, into the hands of those who seek their lives. He shall strike them down with the edge of the sword; he shall not pity them, or spare them, or have compassion.
8 And to this people you shall say: Thus says the LORD: See, I am setting before you the way of life and the way of death.
9 Those who stay in this city shall die by the sword, by famine, and by pestilence; but those who go out and surrender to the Chaldeans who are besieging you shall live and shall have their lives as a prize of war.
10 For I have set my face against this city for evil and not for good, says the LORD: it shall be given into the hands of the king of Babylon, and he shall burn it with fire.
11 To the house of the king of Judah say: Hear the word of the LORD,
12 O house of David! Thus says the LORD:
Execute justice in the morning,
and deliver from the hand of the oppressor
anyone who has been robbed,
or else my wrath will go forth
like fire,

21.1–24.10: Oracles from the time of Zedekiah. Zedekiah, a son of Josiah, was appointed king (or regent) over Judah after the Babylonian king Nebuchadrezzar deported the reigning king Jehoiachin to Babylon in 597 BCE after a failed rebellion.

21.1–10: Oracle against Zedekiah and Jerusalem. 1–7: Cf. 37.1–10. Although the accounts are similar, they evidently describe separate events. The historical setting for both passages is apparently 588 BCE, after Zedekiah had committed himself to a rebellion against Babylon. *Pashhur,* the *son of Malchiah,* appears also in ch 38. *Zephaniah* the priest (see 29.29) was later executed at Riblah by Nebuchadrezzar (52.24–27). Pashhur and Zephaniah base their request (v. 2) on the idea that Jerusalem/Zion is God's chosen city/dwelling-place and probably refer specifically to incidents such as those surrounding the invasion of Sennacherib (2 Kings 18.13–19.37). Jeremiah reasserts, however, the claims of the covenant, namely that the LORD requires obedience and will not permit Judah to presume upon election (see 7.1–15). Again, Jeremiah offers no hope that repentance can avert the coming tragedy. **4:** *Chaldeans,* i.e., Babylonians. **5a:** Deut 4.34; 5.15. **5b:** Deut 29.28. **8–10:** *The way of life and the way of death,* cf. Deut 11.26; 30.15. Ironically, Jeremiah offers the people the opportunity to choose, but their choices do not include the option of avoiding the Babylonian onslaught. The only possibility for life is surrender to the enemy besieging the city; Jerusalem, however, will be destroyed (38.17).

21.11–23.8: Oracles concerning the royal house. 21.11–12: The king is to administer justice (1 Kings 3.9; Ps 72.1–4); if he does evil, he will incur the wrath of God. In contrast to texts like 2 Sam 7.11–16 and Ps 89, which speak of disciplinary punishment if kings are disobedient to God, v. 12b suggests a more definitive judgment. **13–14:** The house of David falsely trusts in Jerusalem's invulnerability

and burn, with no one to quench it,
because of your evil doings.

13 See, I am against you, O inhabitant of
the valley,
O rock of the plain,
says the LORD;
you who say, "Who can come down
against us,
or who can enter our places
of refuge?"
14 I will punish you according to the
fruit of your doings,
says the LORD;
I will kindle a fire in its forest,
and it shall devour all that is
around it.

22 Thus says the LORD: Go down to
the house of the king of Judah, and
speak there this word, 2 and say: Hear the
word of the LORD, O King of Judah sitting
on the throne of David—you, and your
servants, and your people who enter these
gates. 3 Thus says the LORD: Act with jus-
tice and righteousness, and deliver from the
hand of the oppressor anyone who has
been robbed. And do no wrong or violence
to the alien, the orphan, and the widow, or
shed innocent blood in this place. 4 For if
you will indeed obey this word, then
through the gates of this house shall enter
kings who sit on the throne of David, riding
in chariots and on horses, they, and their
servants, and their people. 5 But if you will
not heed these words, I swear by myself,
says the LORD, that this house shall become
a desolation. 6 For thus says the LORD con-
cerning the house of the king of Judah:
You are like Gilead to me,
like the summit of Lebanon;
but I swear that I will make you
a desert,
an uninhabited city.[a]
7 I will prepare destroyers against you,
all with their weapons;
they shall cut down your choicest
cedars
and cast them into the fire.
8 And many nations will pass by this
city, and all of them will say one to anoth-
er, "Why has the LORD dealt in this way
with that great city?" 9 And they will an-
swer, "Because they abandoned the cove-
nant of the LORD their God, and worshiped
other gods and served them."
10 Do not weep for him who is dead,
nor bemoan him;
weep rather for him who goes away,
for he shall return no more
to see his native land.
11 For thus says the LORD concerning
Shallum son of King Josiah of Judah, who
succeeded his father Josiah, and who went
away from this place: He shall return here
no more, 12 but in the place where they have
carried him captive he shall die, and he
shall never see this land again.

13 Woe to him who builds his house by
unrighteousness,

a Cn: Heb *uninhabited cities*

to attack. Forest is perhaps a metaphor for the royal palace, which is elsewhere called the "House of the Forest," because of its extensive woodwork (1 Kings 7.2). **22.1–5:** Expansion of 21.11–12 (compare 22.3 with 21.12). If the people repent, their destruction will be averted and the Davidic dynasty (*house*) preserved. The criteria of justice recall Deuteronomy (Deut 16.11,14; 24.19–21); cf. Jer 7.5–7. **6–7:** Parallel to 21.13–14. The mountains of *Gilead,* in northern Transjordan, were thickly forested, as were those of *Lebanon.* Foresters (*destroyers*) with axes and saws (*weapons*) will burn the "forest" (cedar-wood palace), reducing its once beautiful site to wasteland. **8–9:** A later comment (5.19; Deut 29.23–28; 1 Kings 9.8–9) referring to Jerusalem, not the palace.

22.10–30: Oracles concerning Jehoahaz, Jehoiakim, and Jehoiachin, kings of Judah. 10–12: The dead Josiah was better off than Shallum (personal name of Jehoahaz; 1 Chr 3.15), who in 609 BCE was banished (went away) to Egypt by Pharaoh Neco (2 Kings 23.33–34; 2 Chr 36.1–4; Ezek 19.4). **13–19:** Jeremiah censures Jehoiakim (608–598 BCE) for lavishly expanding his palace (*house*) by exploiting his subjects (v. 14). An administration that will *do justice and righteousness,* not one housed in *cedar* (v. 15),

and his upper rooms by injustice;
who makes his neighbors work for
nothing,
and does not give them their wages;
14 who says, "I will build myself a
spacious house
with large upper rooms,"
and who cuts out windows for it,
paneling it with cedar,
and painting it with vermilion.
15 Are you a king
because you compete in cedar?
Did not your father eat and drink
and do justice and righteousness?
Then it was well with him.
16 He judged the cause of the poor
and needy;
then it was well.
Is not this to know me?
says the LORD.
17 But your eyes and heart
are only on your dishonest gain,
for shedding innocent blood,
and for practicing oppression and
violence.

18 Therefore thus says the LORD con-
cerning King Jehoiakim son of Josiah of Ju-
dah:
They shall not lament for him, saying,
"Alas, my brother!" or "Alas,
sister!"
They shall not lament for him, saying,
"Alas, lord!" or "Alas, his
majesty!"
19 With the burial of a donkey he shall
be buried—
dragged off and thrown out beyond
the gates of Jerusalem.
20 Go up to Lebanon, and cry out,
and lift up your voice in Bashan;
cry out from Abarim,
for all your lovers are crushed.
21 I spoke to you in your prosperity,
but you said, "I will not listen."
This has been your way from
your youth,
for you have not obeyed my voice.
22 The wind shall shepherd all your
shepherds,
and your lovers shall go into
captivity;
then you will be ashamed and
dismayed
because of all your wickedness.
23 O inhabitant of Lebanon,
nested among the cedars,
how you will groan[a] when pangs
come upon you,
pain as of a woman in labor!

24 As I live, says the LORD, even if King
Coniah son of Jehoiakim of Judah were the
signet ring on my right hand, even from
there I would tear you off 25 and give you
into the hands of those who seek your life,
into the hands of those of whom you are
afraid, even into the hands of King Nebu-
chadrezzar of Babylon and into the hands
of the Chaldeans. 26 I will hurl you and the
mother who bore you into another country,
where you were not born, and there you
shall die. 27 But they shall not return to the
land to which they long to return.

a Gk Vg Syr: Heb *will be pitied*

is what makes the king (21.11–12; Mic 3.9–10). References to elaborate building projects completed by means of uncompensated labor suggest that Jehoiakim was perceived as imitating Solomon's grandeur and autocratic power (1 Kings 5.13–18). Jehoiakim should rather emulate his father Josiah (vv. 15–16), whose death was mourned. His own death will be accompanied by indignities because of his misdeeds (36.30; 2 Kings 24.1–5). **20–23:** The addressee is an individual feminine figure, presumably Jerusalem; cf. 2.20–25,33–37. From the highest peaks (Lebanon, Bashan in northern Transjordan, Abarim east of the Dead Sea) lamentations will rise over the desertion of Jerusalem by her allies (*lovers;* 3.1), the exile of her leaders (*shepherds;* 23.1), and her own terror (*inhabitant of Lebanon;* cf. 21.13–14). **21:** *But you said,* cf. 2.20,23,25,35. **24–30:** The symbol of authority (signet ring; Hag 2.23) and a broken pot (cf. 19.11) describe the inexorable punishment of Jehoiachin (597 BCE; *King Coniah*) and his mother (13.18). The threefold address (v. 29a; Isa 6.3; Ezek 21.27) emphasizes the following oracle announcing that no descendant of Jehoiachin shall rule Judah.

28 Is this man Coniah a despised broken
pot,
a vessel no one wants?
Why are he and his offspring hurled
out
and cast away in a land that they
do not know?
29 O land, land, land,
hear the word of the LORD!
30 Thus says the LORD:
Record this man as childless,
a man who shall not succeed in his
days;
for none of his offspring shall succeed
in sitting on the throne of David,
and ruling again in Judah.

23 Woe to the shepherds who destroy
and scatter the sheep of my pasture!
says the LORD. 2 Therefore thus says the
LORD, the God of Israel, concerning the
shepherds who shepherd my people: It is
you who have scattered my flock, and have
driven them away, and you have not at-
tended to them. So I will attend to you for
your evil doings, says the LORD. 3 Then I
myself will gather the remnant of my flock
out of all the lands where I have driven
them, and I will bring them back to their
fold, and they shall be fruitful and multiply.
4 I will raise up shepherds over them who
will shepherd them, and they shall not fear
any longer, or be dismayed, nor shall any
be missing, says the LORD.
5 The days are surely coming, says the
LORD, when I will raise up for David a
righteous Branch, and he shall reign as king
and deal wisely, and shall execute justice
and righteousness in the land. 6 In his days
Judah will be saved and Israel will live in
safety. And this is the name by which he
will be called: "The LORD is our righteous-
ness."
7 Therefore, the days are surely coming,
says the LORD, when it shall no longer be
said, "As the LORD lives who brought the
people of Israel up out of the land of
Egypt," 8 but "As the LORD lives who
brought out and led the offspring of the
house of Israel out of the land of the north
and out of all the lands where he[a] had
driven them." Then they shall live in their
own land.

9 Concerning the prophets:
My heart is crushed within me,
all my bones shake;
I have become like a drunkard,
like one overcome by wine,
because of the LORD
and because of his holy words.
10 For the land is full of adulterers;
because of the curse the land
mourns,
and the pastures of the wilderness
are dried up.
Their course has been evil,
and their might is not right.

a Gk: Heb *I*

23.1–8: An oracle of restoration. After reproaching Judah's rulers (*shepherds;* 22.22; Ezek 34) for scattering Judah (his *flock*), God promises to establish a righteous member (*branch;* Zech 3.8; 6.12; cf. Isa 11.1, which uses a different Heb word for *branch*) of David's line over a restored Israel (30.9). He will rule responsibly before God as a king (Isa 9.2–7). **5–6:** Terms for righteous and righteousness (Heb "tsedeq," "tsedeqah") probably allude, in ironic contrast, to Zedekiah, the last king of Judah (597–586 BCE), appointed to the throne by Nebuchadrezzar (2 Kings 24.17). **7–8:** Anticipates a day in which the old Exodus tradition will be superseded by a new redemptive intervention of the LORD (16.14–15; cf. Isa 51.9–11; 52.11–12).

23.9–40: Oracles concerning the prophets. Jeremiah was not the only active prophet claiming divine authority (see chs 26–29). Others proclaimed messages affirming the status quo. Here, following the similar collection devoted to condemnations of Judah's unrighteous kings, a series of oracles dealing with false prophets has been gathered together (see also 4.9–10; chs 27–29). **9–12:** As elsewhere, Jeremiah reports his own anguish (v. 9; cf. 4.19–21), which is then explained by words of divine judgment (vv. 10–12; cf. 4.22; 9.10–11). *Prophet* and *priest,* who should provide leadership, are linked in judgment (6.13–15; 8.10–12). **13:** *Prophets* of the Canaanite god *Baal* in *Samaria,* see 1 Kings 18.20–29. **14:**

11 Both prophet and priest are ungodly;
even in my house I have found their
wickedness,
says the LORD.
12 Therefore their way shall be to them
like slippery paths in the darkness,
into which they shall be driven and
fall;
for I will bring disaster upon them
in the year of their punishment,
says the LORD.
13 In the prophets of Samaria
I saw a disgusting thing:
they prophesied by Baal
and led my people Israel astray.
14 But in the prophets of Jerusalem
I have seen a more shocking thing:
they commit adultery and walk
in lies;
they strengthen the hands of
evildoers,
so that no one turns from
wickedness;
all of them have become like Sodom
to me,
and its inhabitants like Gomorrah.
15 Therefore thus says the LORD of hosts
concerning the prophets:
"I am going to make them eat
wormwood,
and give them poisoned water
to drink;
for from the prophets of Jerusalem
ungodliness has spread throughout
the land."

16 Thus says the LORD of hosts: Do not
listen to the words of the prophets who
prophesy to you; they are deluding you.
They speak visions of their own minds, not
from the mouth of the LORD. 17 They keep
saying to those who despise the word of the
LORD, "It shall be well with you"; and to
all who stubbornly follow their own stub-
born hearts, they say, "No calamity shall
come upon you."

18 For who has stood in the council of
the LORD
so as to see and to hear his word?
Who has given heed to his word so
as to proclaim it?
19 Look, the storm of the LORD!
Wrath has gone forth,
a whirling tempest;
it will burst upon the head of
the wicked.
20 The anger of the LORD will not
turn back
until he has executed and
accomplished
the intents of his mind.
In the latter days you will understand
it clearly.

21 I did not send the prophets,
yet they ran;
I did not speak to them,
yet they prophesied.
22 But if they had stood in my council,
then they would have proclaimed
my words to my people,
and they would have turned them
from their evil way,
and from the evil of their doings.

23 Am I a God near by, says the LORD,
and not a God far off? 24 Who can hide in
secret places so that I cannot see them? says
the LORD. Do I not fill heaven and earth?

Sodom and *Gomorrah,* see Gen 18–19. **15:** *Wormwood,* see 9.15n. **16–22:** The chief distinction between Jeremiah, the true prophet, and his false colleagues, according to this and following units, is between truly acting on divine commission and merely claiming divine authority for one's own words. Jeremiah reproves the prophets for their assurance of well-being to those who flout God's word. Obviously they cannot be sent by God or speak for him. (For the role of the prophet in the divine *council,* see 1 Kings 22.19–23; Isa 6.1–7). *Visions of their own minds,* 14.14. **19–20:** See 30.23–24. The *storm* is imagery frequently used to represent the coming of the LORD as a warrior (Ps 29; Hab 3). **23–32:** God's omnipresence precludes his being unaware of the prophets' misleading his people by their claims of divine revelation through *dreams* (27.9; 29.8). Although dreams could be a legitimate means of divine communication (Gen 41; Dan 2; Joel 2.28), they were also viewed with suspicion (Deut 13.2–6). **26:** *Deceit of their own hearts,*

says the LORD. 25 I have heard what the
prophets have said who prophesy lies in my
name, saying, "I have dreamed, I have
dreamed!" 26 How long? Will the hearts of
the prophets ever turn back—those who
prophesy lies, and who prophesy the deceit
of their own heart? 27 They plan to make
my people forget my name by their dreams
that they tell one another, just as their an-
cestors forgot my name for Baal. 28 Let the
prophet who has a dream tell the dream,
but let the one who has my word speak my
word faithfully. What has straw in com-
mon with wheat? says the LORD. 29 Is not
my word like fire, says the LORD, and like
a hammer that breaks a rock in pieces?
30 See, therefore, I am against the prophets,
says the LORD, who steal my words from
one another. 31 See, I am against the proph-
ets, says the LORD, who use their own
tongues and say, "Says the LORD." 32 See,
I am against those who prophesy lying
dreams, says the LORD, and who tell them,
and who lead my people astray by their lies
and their recklessness, when I did not send
them or appoint them; so they do not profit
this people at all, says the LORD.

33 When this people, or a prophet, or a
priest asks you, "What is the burden of the
LORD?" you shall say to them, "You are
the burden,[a] and I will cast you off, says
the LORD." 34 And as for the prophet,
priest, or the people who say, "The burden
of the LORD," I will punish them and their
households. 35 Thus shall you say to one
another, among yourselves, "What has the
LORD answered?" or "What has the LORD
spoken?" 36 But "the burden of the LORD"
you shall mention no more, for the burden
is everyone's own word, and so you pervert
the words of the living God, the LORD of
hosts, our God. 37 Thus you shall ask the
prophet, "What has the LORD answered
you?" or "What has the LORD spoken?"
38 But if you say, "the burden of the
LORD," thus says the LORD: Because you
have said these words, "the burden of the
LORD," when I sent to you, saying, You
shall not say, "the burden of the LORD,"
39 therefore, I will surely lift you up[b] and
cast you away from my presence, you and
the city that I gave to you and your ances-
tors. 40 And I will bring upon you everlast-
ing disgrace and perpetual shame, which
shall not be forgotten.

24 The LORD showed me two baskets
of figs placed before the temple of
the LORD. This was after King Nebuchad-
rezzar of Babylon had taken into exile from
Jerusalem King Jeconiah son of Jehoiakim
of Judah, together with the officials of Ju-
dah, the artisans, and the smiths, and had
brought them to Babylon. 2 One basket had
very good figs, like first-ripe figs, but the
other basket had very bad figs, so bad that
they could not be eaten. 3 And the LORD
said to me, "What do you see, Jeremiah?"
I said, "Figs, the good figs very good, and
the bad figs very bad, so bad that they can-
not be eaten."

a Gk Vg: Heb *What burden* *b* Heb Mss Gk Vg: MT *forget you*

cf. v. 16. **29:** With biting sarcasm (*tell the dream,* v. 28; *steal my words,* v. 30) and threefold emphasis (vv. 30,31,32), Jeremiah proclaims God's condemnation of their pretensions. **33:** Bitter irony: The Heb word "mass'a" can mean both *burden* (e.g., Ex 23.5) and prophetic "oracle" (e.g., Isa 14.28). **34–40:** This section is a later commentary on v. 33, which it misunderstood, concentrating on the phrase "the burden of the LORD."

24.1–10: The vision of the baskets of figs. A prophetic vision report; see 1.1–16; Am 7.1–9.10. Those remaining in Palestine (and Egypt) after 597 BCE (*the bad figs*) smugly assumed that they were favored over those deported (*the good figs*), who were considered the objects of God's wrath (29.15–19; Ezek 11.14–15). But the exiles will return (29.10–14) and will become a faithful nation, while the others will be destroyed. This passage probably reflects the power struggles between the three principal centers of Judaism in the postexilic period: Mesopotamia, Palestine, and Egypt. Portions of the latter half of the book of Jeremiah adopt a stance that decidedly favors the Babylonian exiles. **1:** *Jeconiah,* i.e., Jehoiachin (Coniah). **5:** *Chaldeans,* Babylonians. **6:** See 1.10.

4 Then the word of the LORD came to
me: 5 Thus says the LORD, the God of Isra-
el: Like these good figs, so I will regard as
good the exiles from Judah, whom I have
sent away from this place to the land of the
Chaldeans. 6 I will set my eyes upon them
for good, and I will bring them back to this
land. I will build them up, and not tear
them down; I will plant them, and not
pluck them up. 7 I will give them a heart to
know that I am the LORD; and they shall be
my people and I will be their God, for they
shall return to me with their whole heart.
8 But thus says the LORD: Like the bad
figs that are so bad they cannot be eaten, so
will I treat King Zedekiah of Judah, his of-
ficials, the remnant of Jerusalem who re-
main in this land, and those who live in the
land of Egypt. 9 I will make them a horror,
an evil thing, to all the kingdoms of the
earth—a disgrace, a byword, a taunt, and a
curse in all the places where I shall drive
them. 10 And I will send sword, famine, and
pestilence upon them, until they are utterly
destroyed from the land that I gave to them
and their ancestors.

25 The word that came to Jeremiah
concerning all the people of Judah,
in the fourth year of King Jehoiakim son of
Josiah of Judah (that was the first year of
King Nebuchadrezzar of Babylon), 2 which
the prophet Jeremiah spoke to all the peo-
ple of Judah and all the inhabitants of Jeru-
salem: 3 For twenty-three years, from the
thirteenth year of King Josiah son of Amon
of Judah, to this day, the word of the LORD
has come to me, and I have spoken persis-
tently to you, but you have not listened.
4 And though the LORD persistently sent
you all his servants the prophets, you have
neither listened nor inclined your ears to
hear 5 when they said, "Turn now, every-
one of you, from your evil way and wicked
doings, and you will remain upon the land
that the LORD has given to you and your
ancestors from of old and forever; 6 do not
go after other gods to serve and worship
them, and do not provoke me to anger with
the work of your hands. Then I will do you
no harm." 7 Yet you did not listen to me,
says the LORD, and so you have provoked
me to anger with the work of your hands to
your own harm.
8 Therefore thus says the LORD of hosts:
Because you have not obeyed my words, 9 I
am going to send for all the tribes of the
north, says the LORD, even for King Nebu-
chadrezzar of Babylon, my servant, and I
will bring them against this land and its
inhabitants, and against all these nations
around; I will utterly destroy them, and
make them an object of horror and of hiss-
ing, and an everlasting disgrace.[a] 10 And I
will banish from them the sound of mirth
and the sound of gladness, the voice of the
bridegroom and the voice of the bride, the
sound of the millstones and the light of the
lamp. 11 This whole land shall become a
ruin and a waste, and these nations shall
serve the king of Babylon seventy years.
12 Then after seventy years are completed, I
will punish the king of Babylon and that
nation, the land of the Chaldeans, for their
iniquity, says the LORD, making the land an
everlasting waste. 13 I will bring upon that
land all the words that I have uttered
against it, everything written in this book,
which Jeremiah prophesied against all the

a Gk Compare Syr: Heb *and everlasting desolations*

25.1–14: Babylon, God's instrument for punishment. *The fourth year of King Jehoiachim* (605 BCE), the year Nebuchadrezzar defeated Neco of Egypt at Carchemish and became king of Babylon. *Thirteenth year of King Josiah* (627 BCE). The language of this section is a compendium of phraseology from the prose sermons and narratives in the book (cf. esp. ch 7) and was probably composed during the exile, if not later. **9:** *Tribes of the north,* a reinterpretation of 6.1. *Hissing,* see 18.16n. **11–12:** *Seventy years* (cf. 29.10). The period from 605 BCE until the defeat of Babylon by Cyrus the Persian in 539 BCE is sixty-six years. *Seventy,* however, is likely a symbolic number, representing the length of a lifetime (Ps 90.10). The prophecy of seventy years was reinterpreted several times in later centuries (see Zech 1.12; 2 Chr 36.21; Dan 9.2,24–27). **13:** What has the book said with respect to the punishment of Babylon to this point? In the Septuagint (LXX) order, in which ch 25 introduces the oracles against the nations, this

nations. [14]For many nations and great
kings shall make slaves of them also; and I
will repay them according to their deeds
and the work of their hands.
15 For thus the LORD, the God of Israel,
said to me: Take from my hand this cup of
the wine of wrath, and make all the nations
to whom I send you drink it. [16]They shall
drink and stagger and go out of their minds
because of the sword that I am sending
among them.
17 So I took the cup from the LORD's
hand, and made all the nations to whom
the LORD sent me drink it: [18]Jerusalem and
the towns of Judah, its kings and officials,
to make them a desolation and a waste, an
object of hissing and of cursing, as they are
today; [19]Pharaoh king of Egypt, his ser-
vants, his officials, and all his people; [20]all
the mixed people;[a] all the kings of the land
of Uz; all the kings of the land of the Philis-
tines—Ashkelon, Gaza, Ekron, and the
remnant of Ashdod; [21]Edom, Moab, and
the Ammonites; [22]all the kings of Tyre, all
the kings of Sidon, and the kings of the
coastland across the sea; [23]Dedan, Tema,
Buz, and all who have shaven temples; [24]all
the kings of Arabia and all the kings of the
mixed peoples[a] that live in the desert; [25]all
the kings of Zimri, all the kings of Elam,
and all the kings of Media; [26]all the kings
of the north, far and near, one after anoth-
er, and all the kingdoms of the world that
are on the face of the earth. And after them
the king of Sheshach[b] shall drink.

27 Then you shall say to them, Thus
says the LORD of hosts, the God of Israel:
Drink, get drunk and vomit, fall and rise no
more, because of the sword that I am send-
ing among you.
28 And if they refuse to accept the cup
from your hand to drink, then you shall say
to them: Thus says the LORD of hosts: You
must drink! [29]See, I am beginning to bring
disaster on the city that is called by my
name, and how can you possibly avoid
punishment? You shall not go unpunished,
for I am summoning a sword against all the
inhabitants of the earth, says the LORD of
hosts.
30 You, therefore, shall prophesy
against them all these words, and say to
them:

The LORD will roar from on high,
and from his holy habitation utter
his voice;
he will roar mightily against his fold,
and shout, like those who tread
grapes,
against all the inhabitants of
the earth.
31 The clamor will resound to the ends
of the earth,
for the LORD has an indictment
against the nations;
he is entering into judgment with all
flesh,

a Meaning of Heb uncertain *b* *Sheshach* is a cryptogram for *Babel*, Babylon

verse would refer to the oracles immediately following. In the Hebrew book of Jeremiah, this verse is, at best, enigmatic.

25.15–38: The cup of wrath. 15–29: The vision may have originally introduced the now separated section of oracles against the nations (chs 46–51; cf. Isa 13–23; Ezek 25–32; Am 1.3–2.3). **15:** The *cup* is a common symbol of God's judgment (note its equation with *sword,* v. 29; 49.12; 51.7; Isa 51.17; Hab 2.15–16; Ps 11.6). **20:** *The land of Uz,* perhaps a location in Edom (Gen 36.28; Job 1.1; Lam 4.21). *Ashkelon, Gaza, Ekron . . . Ashdod,* Philistine cities on the coastal plain, west of Judah. **21:** *Edom, Moab, and the Ammonites,* nations in Transjordan east of Israel and Judah. **23:** *Dedan, Tema, Buz,* cities in Arabia. *Shaven temples,* see 9.26n. **25:** *Zimri,* location unknown. *Elam* and *Media,* nations east of Babylon, in modern Iran. **26:** Babylon is written in the Heb text as Sheshach; in this kind of cipher, called "atbash," letters are substituted for each other according to the following patterns: The last letter of the alphabet is substituted for the first; the next-to-last letter is substituted for the second; and so on through the alphabet, ending with the substitution of the second letter for the next-to-last, and the first letter for the last (see also 51.1,41n.). **30–31:** The judgment is described in conventional figures: roaring (Am 1.2; Ps 46.6); vintage (Isa 16.9–10; 63.1–3); courtroom (12.1); sword (12.12). **32–33:** Distant foe (6.22) and

and the guilty he will put to
the sword,
says the LORD.

32 Thus says the LORD of hosts:
See, disaster is spreading
from nation to nation,
and a great tempest is stirring
from the farthest parts of the earth!
33 Those slain by the LORD on that day
shall extend from one end of the earth to
the other. They shall not be lamented, or
gathered, or buried; they shall become
dung on the surface of the ground.
34 Wail, you shepherds, and cry out;
roll in ashes, you lords of the
flock,
for the days of your slaughter have
come—and your dispersions,[a]
and you shall fall like a
choice vessel.
35 Flight shall fail the shepherds,
and there shall be no escape for the
lords of the flock.
36 Hark! the cry of the shepherds,
and the wail of the lords of
the flock!
For the LORD is despoiling their
pasture,
37 and the peaceful folds are
devastated,
because of the fierce anger of
the LORD.
38 Like a lion he has left his covert;
for their land has become a waste
because of the cruel sword,
and because of his fierce anger.

26 At the beginning of the reign of
King Jehoiakim son of Josiah of Ju-
dah, this word came from the LORD: 2 Thus
says the LORD: Stand in the court of the
LORD's house, and speak to all the cities of
Judah that come to worship in the house of
the LORD; speak to them all the words that
I command you; do not hold back a word.
3 It may be that they will listen, all of them,
and will turn from their evil way, that I
may change my mind about the disaster
that I intend to bring on them because of
their evil doings. 4 You shall say to them:
Thus says the LORD: If you will not listen to
me, to walk in my law that I have set before
you, 5 and to heed the words of my servants
the prophets whom I send to you urgent-
ly—though you have not heeded— 6 then I
will make this house like Shiloh, and I will
make this city a curse for all the nations of
the earth.
7 The priests and the prophets and all

a Meaning of Heb uncertain

heavy casualties (8.2; 16.4). *Tempest,* see 23.19n. **34–38:** The rulers of the nations (*shepherds, lords of the flock*) are confused and desperate.

26.1–29.32: The problem of distinguishing true and false prophecy.

26.1–24: The Temple sermon. The second version of the sermon (cf. 7.1–15) constitutes an episode in the collection of "biographical" accounts of events in Jeremiah's life. These accounts represent an early interpretation of the significance of the life and message of the prophet, likely from a postexilic perspective. The focus is not on the content of the sermon, but on the controversy it engendered. Beginning here and continuing through ch 29, the incidents reported deal with the common theme of true and false prophecy. How does one recognize a prophet sent from the LORD? **1–6:** This version of the sermon contains elements of 7.1–15 and other sayings of Jeremiah (4.1–2; 18.7–11; 36.3). *The beginning of the reign of King Jehoiakim* (609–598 BCE). **3:** Contrast 7.27. **6:** *Like Shiloh,* see 7.12n.

26.7–19: Jeremiah's arrest and release. Jeremiah's message effectively brings two authentic biblical traditions into conflict. The people hear his message as an attack on their belief in the LORD's election of Jerusalem and the Temple. Although this continues to be significant even after the Babylonian crisis (e.g., Isa 40.1–2,9–10), Jeremiah juxtaposes it with the obedience demanded by the Sinai covenant (cf. 7.8–11). The royal officials assemble to hear the case. The people and their leaders regarded Jeremiah's message as near blasphemy (v. 11). Jeremiah's defense reiterates the basic position articulated in his criticism of the false prophets who speak comforting words—namely, that his message must be honored because *the LORD . . . sent me to prophesy against this house and this city* (v. 12). The judges

the people heard Jeremiah speaking these
words in the house of the LORD. 8 And
when Jeremiah had finished speaking all
that the LORD had commanded him to
speak to all the people, then the priests and
the prophets and all the people laid hold of
him, saying, "You shall die! 9 Why have
you prophesied in the name of the LORD,
saying, 'This house shall be like Shiloh, and
this city shall be desolate, without inhabi-
tant'?" And all the people gathered around
Jeremiah in the house of the LORD.
10 When the officials of Judah heard
these things, they came up from the king's
house to the house of the LORD and took
their seat in the entry of the New Gate of
the house of the LORD. 11 Then the priests
and the prophets said to the officials and to
all the people, "This man deserves the sen-
tence of death because he has prophesied
against this city, as you have heard with
your own ears."
12 Then Jeremiah spoke to all the offi-
cials and all the people, saying, "It is the
LORD who sent me to prophesy against this
house and this city all the words you have
heard. 13 Now therefore amend your ways
and your doings, and obey the voice of the
LORD your God, and the LORD will change
his mind about the disaster that he has pro-
nounced against you. 14 But as for me, here
I am in your hands. Do with me as seems
good and right to you. 15 Only know for
certain that if you put me to death, you will
be bringing innocent blood upon your-
selves and upon this city and its inhabi-
tants, for in truth the LORD sent me to you
to speak all these words in your ears."
16 Then the officials and all the people
said to the priests and the prophets, "This
man does not deserve the sentence of death,
for he has spoken to us in the name of the
LORD our God." 17 And some of the elders
of the land arose and said to all the assem-
bled people, 18 "Micah of Moresheth, who
prophesied during the days of King Hezeki-
ah of Judah, said to all the people of Judah:
'Thus says the LORD of hosts,

Zion shall be plowed as a field;
Jerusalem shall become a heap
of ruins,
and the mountain of the house a
wooded height.'

19 Did King Hezekiah of Judah and all Ju-
dah actually put him to death? Did he not
fear the LORD and entreat the favor of the
LORD, and did not the LORD change his
mind about the disaster that he had pro-
nounced against them? But we are about to
bring great disaster on ourselves!"
20 There was another man prophesying
in the name of the LORD, Uriah son of She-
maiah from Kiriath-jearim. He prophesied
against this city and against this land in
words exactly like those of Jeremiah.
21 And when King Jehoiakim, with all his
warriors and all the officials, heard his
words, the king sought to put him to death;
but when Uriah heard of it, he was afraid
and fled and escaped to Egypt. 22 Then

acknowledge Jeremiah's claim (v. 16) and add another criterion: A true prophet warns and admonishes repentance. They base their decision on a precedent set by King Hezekiah in the late eighth century regarding the prophet Micah (Mic 3.12). This precedent calls attention to a paradox regarding the problem of true and false prophecy. According to Deuteronomy (18.22) a prophet's authenticity can be gauged by whether his message comes true. Micah's message (and Jeremiah's) was intended as a warning to motivate repentance. Micah succeeded in bringing Hezekiah to repentance, in the judges' view, and as a consequence his prediction failed to come to pass—as yet. **10:** *New Gate,* perhaps the Benjamin Gate, north of the Temple (20.2; 2 Kings 15.35). **15:** Avenging of *innocent blood,* Gen 4.10; 2 Sam 21.1–14; 1 Kings 21.

26.20–24: Martyrdom of Uriah. This story illustrates Jeremiah's personal danger and fortunate official support. As Egypt's vassal (2 Kings 23.34–35), Jehoiakim had no difficulty arresting Uriah. *Elnathan,* see 36.12,25. Uriah's execution is unusual in the history of Israelite prophecy (2 Chr 24.20–22). *Ahikam son of Shaphan,* the family of royal officials that included Shaphan (2 Kings 22.12–13) seems not only to have been sympathetic with Jeremiah, but also to have been associated with the early transmission of the Jeremiah tradition.

King Jehoiakim sent[a] Elnathan son of
Achbor and men with him to Egypt, 23 and
they took Uriah from Egypt and brought
him to King Jehoiakim, who struck him
down with the sword and threw his dead
body into the burial place of the common
people.
24 But the hand of Ahikam son of Sha-
phan was with Jeremiah so that he was not
given over into the hands of the people to
be put to death.

27 In the beginning of the reign of King
Zedekiah[b] son of Josiah of Judah,
this word came to Jeremiah from the LORD.
2 Thus the LORD said to me: Make yourself
a yoke of straps and bars, and put them on
your neck. 3 Send word[c] to the king of
Edom, the king of Moab, the king of the
Ammonites, the king of Tyre, and the king
of Sidon by the hand of the envoys who
have come to Jerusalem to King Zedekiah
of Judah. 4 Give them this charge for their
masters: Thus says the LORD of hosts, the
God of Israel: This is what you shall say to
your masters: 5 It is I who by my great pow-
er and my outstretched arm have made the
earth, with the people and animals that are
on the earth, and I give it to whomever I
please. 6 Now I have given all these lands
into the hand of King Nebuchadnezzar of
Babylon, my servant, and I have given him
even the wild animals of the field to serve
him. 7 All the nations shall serve him and
his son and his grandson, until the time of
his own land comes; then many nations and
great kings shall make him their slave.
8 But if any nation or kingdom will not
serve this king, Nebuchadnezzar of Bab-
ylon, and put its neck under the yoke of the
king of Babylon, then I will punish that na-
tion with the sword, with famine, and with
pestilence, says the LORD, until I have com-
pleted its[d] destruction by his hand. 9 You,
therefore, must not listen to your prophets,
your diviners, your dreamers,[e] your sooth-
sayers, or your sorcerers, who are saying to
you, "You shall not serve the king of Bab-
ylon." 10 For they are prophesying a lie to
you, with the result that you will be re-
moved far from your land; I will drive you
out, and you will perish. 11 But any nation
that will bring its neck under the yoke of
the king of Babylon and serve him, I will
leave on its own land, says the LORD, to till
it and live there.
12 I spoke to King Zedekiah of Judah in
the same way: Bring your necks under the

a Heb adds *men to Egypt* *b* Another reading is *Jehoiakim* *c* Cn: Heb *send them* *d* Heb *their* *e* Gk Syr Vg: Heb *dreams*

27.1–28.17: The yoke of the king of Babylon. 27.1–11: Another of Jeremiah's symbolic acts (cf. chs 13; 18; 19). The yoke of Babylon was imposed by God upon Judah and her neighbors (21.1–10; 32.3–5); thus their plans for rebellion are against God's will. The occasion for the conspiracy lay in a revolt within Nebuchadrezzar's army (December 595–January 594 BCE) and the accession in Egypt of Psammetichus II (595). Perhaps responding to Jeremiah's warning, Zedekiah did not carry out the rebellion, and so Judah was spared during Nebuchadrezzar's punitive campaign later that year. The form "Nebuchadnezzar" occurs in Jer 27.6–29.3; elsewhere in Jeremiah the name is spelled "Nebuchadrezzar." The Babylonian form is Nabu-kudurri-usur. **1:** *The beginning of the reign of King Zedekiah* would be 597 BCE, but the events described pertain to 595–594 BCE (see 28.1). **3:** The nations planning the revolt include those east of Judah (*Edom, Moab*), as well as the Phoenician coastal cities (*Tyre, Sidon*). **5–6:** The book of Daniel develops Jeremiah's references to wild animals in a series of legends concerning Nebuchadrezzar (Dan 1.36–45; 4.13–37). *Nebuchadnezzar . . . my servant,* a striking designation (cf. Isa 44.28–45.1). He is God's servant because he is the instrument of punishment against Judah and her neighbors. **7:** A prophecy after the fact describing the brief duration of Babylonian rule as an element of the LORD's original plan. **8–14:** Jeremiah offers a choice and limited hope: willing submission to vassalage or destruction. **9:** Associating the prophets who preach rebellion with *diviners, dreamers, soothsayers,* and *sorcerers* is a means of discrediting them (Deut 18.9–12). **12–15:** The warning sent previously to the kings of the conspiring nations (vv. 3–11) is sent also to Zedekiah. **16–22:** He cautions the priests and the people against believing the assurances of these prophets that the Temple equipment taken as booty in 597 BCE would be shortly

yoke of the king of Babylon, and serve him
and his people, and live. 13 Why should you
and your people die by the sword, by fam-
ine, and by pestilence, as the LORD has spo-
ken concerning any nation that will not
serve the king of Babylon? 14 Do not listen
to the words of the prophets who are telling
you not to serve the king of Babylon, for
they are prophesying a lie to you. 15 I have
not sent them, says the LORD, but they are
prophesying falsely in my name, with the
result that I will drive you out and you
will perish, you and the prophets who are
prophesying to you.

16 Then I spoke to the priests and to all
this people, saying, Thus says the LORD:
Do not listen to the words of your prophets
who are prophesying to you, saying, "The
vessels of the LORD's house will soon be
brought back from Babylon," for they are
prophesying a lie to you. 17 Do not listen to
them; serve the king of Babylon and live.
Why should this city become a desolation?
18 If indeed they are prophets, and if the
word of the LORD is with them, then let
them intercede with the LORD of hosts, that
the vessels left in the house of the LORD, in
the house of the king of Judah, and in Jeru-
salem may not go to Babylon. 19 For thus
says the LORD of hosts concerning the pil-
lars, the sea, the stands, and the rest of the
vessels that are left in this city, 20 which
King Nebuchadnezzar of Babylon did not
take away when he took into exile from
Jerusalem to Babylon King Jeconiah son of
Jehoiakim of Judah, and all the nobles of
Judah and Jerusalem— 21 thus says the
LORD of hosts, the God of Israel, concern-
ing the vessels left in the house of the LORD,
in the house of the king of Judah, and in
Jerusalem: 22 They shall be carried to Bab-
ylon, and there they shall stay, until the day
when I give attention to them, says the
LORD. Then I will bring them up and re-
store them to this place.

28 In that same year, at the beginning
of the reign of King Zedekiah of Ju-
dah, in the fifth month of the fourth year,
the prophet Hananiah son of Azzur, from
Gibeon, spoke to me in the house of the
LORD, in the presence of the priests and all
the people, saying, 2 "Thus says the LORD
of hosts, the God of Israel: I have broken
the yoke of the king of Babylon. 3 Within
two years I will bring back to this place all
the vessels of the LORD's house, which King
Nebuchadnezzar of Babylon took away
from this place and carried to Babylon. 4 I
will also bring back to this place King Jeco-
niah son of Jehoiakim of Judah, and all the
exiles from Judah who went to Babylon,
says the LORD, for I will break the yoke of
the king of Babylon."

5 Then the prophet Jeremiah spoke to
the prophet Hananiah in the presence of
the priests and all the people who were
standing in the house of the LORD; 6 and the
prophet Jeremiah said, "Amen! May the
LORD do so; may the LORD fulfill the
words that you have prophesied, and bring
back to this place from Babylon the vessels
of the house of the LORD, and all the exiles.
7 But listen now to this word that I speak in
your hearing and in the hearing of all the

returned. Instead of preaching false messages of hope, they should undertake one task of true prophets—intercession. The *pillars* Jachin and Boaz (1 Kings 7.15–22), the large basin known as the *sea* (1 Kings 7.23–26), and the *stands* and *vessels* (1 Kings 7.27–39) were objects of the Solomonic Temple taken to Babylon in 586 BCE (2 Kings 25.13–17). The vessels, which were not broken up, were later returned by Cyrus in 538 BCE (Ezra 1.7–11).

28.1–17: Jeremiah and Hananiah. The dates in v. 1 are contradictory. *The beginning of the reign of King Zedekiah* would be 597 BCE, whereas *the fourth year* is 594–593 BCE. In August 594, Hananiah faced Jeremiah in the Temple and predicted total restoration within two years, breaking Jeremiah's yoke to emphasize his point. Amplifying the criterion employed by the judges who decided to spare him after the Temple sermon (26.16–19), Jeremiah recalled that earlier prophets had predicted chastisement (Deut 18.20–22; Mic 3.5–12). Because the situation was unchanged (Judah had not repented its sin; Babylon was still building an empire), Hananiah's promises, though attractive, were doubtful. **4:** *Jeconiah,* Jehoia-

people. 8 The prophets who preceded you
and me from ancient times prophesied war,
famine, and pestilence against many coun-
tries and great kingdoms. 9 As for the
prophet who prophesies peace, when the
word of that prophet comes true, then it
will be known that the LORD has truly sent
the prophet."

10 Then the prophet Hananiah took the
yoke from the neck of the prophet Jeremi-
ah, and broke it. 11 And Hananiah spoke
in the presence of all the people, saying,
"Thus says the LORD: This is how I will
break the yoke of King Nebuchadnezzar of
Babylon from the neck of all the nations
within two years." At this, the prophet Jer-
emiah went his way.

12 Sometime after the prophet Hanani-
ah had broken the yoke from the neck of
the prophet Jeremiah, the word of the
LORD came to Jeremiah: 13 Go, tell Hanani-
ah, Thus says the LORD: You have broken
wooden bars only to forge iron bars in
place of them! 14 For thus says the LORD of
hosts, the God of Israel: I have put an iron
yoke on the neck of all these nations so that
they may serve King Nebuchadnezzar of
Babylon, and they shall indeed serve him;
I have even given him the wild animals.
15 And the prophet Jeremiah said to the
prophet Hananiah, "Listen, Hananiah, the
LORD has not sent you, and you made this
people trust in a lie. 16 Therefore thus says
the LORD: I am going to send you off the
face of the earth. Within this year you will
be dead, because you have spoken rebellion
against the LORD."

17 In that same year, in the seventh
month, the prophet Hananiah died.

29 These are the words of the letter
that the prophet Jeremiah sent from
Jerusalem to the remaining elders among
the exiles, and to the priests, the prophets,
and all the people, whom Nebuchadnezzar
had taken into exile from Jerusalem to Bab-
ylon. 2 This was after King Jeconiah, and
the queen mother, the court officials, the
leaders of Judah and Jerusalem, the arti-
sans, and the smiths had departed from Je-
rusalem. 3 The letter was sent by the hand
of Elasah son of Shaphan and Gemariah
son of Hilkiah, whom King Zedekiah of
Judah sent to Babylon to King Nebuchad-
nezzar of Babylon. It said: 4 Thus says the
LORD of hosts, the God of Israel, to all the
exiles whom I have sent into exile from Je-
rusalem to Babylon: 5 Build houses and live
in them; plant gardens and eat what they
produce. 6 Take wives and have sons and
daughters; take wives for your sons, and
give your daughters in marriage, that they
may bear sons and daughters; multiply
there, and do not decrease. 7 But seek the
welfare of the city where I have sent you
into exile, and pray to the LORD on its be-
half, for in its welfare you will find your
welfare. 8 For thus says the LORD of hosts,
the God of Israel: Do not let the prophets
and the diviners who are among you de-
ceive you, and do not listen to the dreams
that they dream,[a] 9 for it is a lie that they
are prophesying to you in my name; I did
not send them, says the LORD.

10 For thus says the LORD: Only when
Babylon's seventy years are completed will
I visit you, and I will fulfill to you my
promise and bring you back to this place.
11 For surely I know the plans I have for
you, says the LORD, plans for your welfare
and not for harm, to give you a future with

a Cn: Heb *your dreams that you cause to dream*

kin. **12–17:** Jeremiah denies that Hananiah has a divine commission, and uses the symbolism of an iron yoke to emphasize that the exile would continue (27.7).

29.1–32: Jeremiah's letters to Babylon. 1–23: Letter to the exiles. 2: *Jeconiah,* i.e., Jehoiachin (2 Kings 24.8–12). **3:** The exiles of the first deportation (597 BCE) were being misled by the same baseless assurances of speedy return as those in Palestine (ch 27). To counter this, Jeremiah sent a letter by *Elasah son of Shaphan* (perhaps the brother of Ahikam, 26.24) and *Gemariah* (36.10), *Son of Hilkiah* (2 Kings 22–23) to the elders of the people (Ezek 8.1; 14.1). **5–7:** Jeremiah's advice was revolutionary. The exiles were to establish homes in Babylonia and even to pray for the welfare of the state. **7:** Contrast Ps 122.6. **8–10:** In contrast to the early return from exile predicted by the other prophets, Jeremiah says the exile

hope. 12 Then when you call upon me and
come and pray to me, I will hear you.
13 When you search for me, you will find
me; if you seek me with all your heart, 14 I
will let you find me, says the LORD, and I
will restore your fortunes and gather you
from all the nations and all the places
where I have driven you, says the LORD,
and I will bring you back to the place from
which I sent you into exile.
15 Because you have said, "The LORD
has raised up prophets for us in Bab-
ylon,"— 16 Thus says the LORD concerning
the king who sits on the throne of David,
and concerning all the people who live in
this city, your kinsfolk who did not go out
with you into exile: 17 Thus says the LORD
of hosts, I am going to let loose on them
sword, famine, and pestilence, and I will
make them like rotten figs that are so bad
they cannot be eaten. 18 I will pursue them
with the sword, with famine, and with pes-
tilence, and will make them a horror to all
the kingdoms of the earth, to be an object
of cursing, and horror, and hissing, and a
derision among all the nations where I have
driven them, 19 because they did not heed
my words, says the LORD, when I persis-
tently sent to you my servants the prophets,
but they[a] would not listen, says the LORD.
20 But now, all you exiles whom I sent away
from Jerusalem to Babylon, hear the word
of the LORD: 21 Thus says the LORD of
hosts, the God of Israel, concerning Ahab
son of Kolaiah and Zedekiah son of Maase-
iah, who are prophesying a lie to you in my
name: I am going to deliver them into the
hand of King Nebuchadrezzar of Babylon,
and he shall kill them before your eyes.
22 And on account of them this curse shall
be used by all the exiles from Judah in Bab-
ylon: "The LORD make you like Zedekiah
and Ahab, whom the king of Babylon
roasted in the fire," 23 because they have
perpetrated outrage in Israel and have com-
mitted adultery with their neighbors' wives,
and have spoken in my name lying words
that I did not command them; I am the one
who knows and bears witness, says the
LORD.
24 To Shemaiah of Nehelam you shall
say: 25 Thus says the LORD of hosts, the
God of Israel: In your own name you sent
a letter to all the people who are in Jerusa-
lem, and to the priest Zephaniah son of
Maaseiah, and to all the priests, saying,
26 The LORD himself has made you priest
instead of the priest Jehoiada, so that there
may be officers in the house of the LORD to
control any madman who plays the proph-
et, to put him in the stocks and the collar.
27 So now why have you not rebuked Jere-
miah of Anathoth who plays the prophet
for you? 28 For he has actually sent to us in
Babylon, saying, "It will be a long time;
build houses and live in them, and plant
gardens and eat what they produce."
29 The priest Zephaniah read this letter
in the hearing of the prophet Jeremiah.
30 Then the word of the LORD came to Jere-
miah: 31 Send to all the exiles, saying, Thus
says the LORD concerning Shemaiah of Ne-
helam: Because Shemaiah has prophesied
to you, though I did not send him, and has

a Syr: Heb *you*

will last an entire lifetime (*seventy years,* 25.11; 27.7). **12–14:** See 23.3; 31.7–10. **16–20:** An editorial comment on Jeremiah's letter written in the spirit of ch 24. These verses intend to make clear that, although the exiles are recipients of a letter of warning, they remain the favored remnant (24.4–7). **18:** *Hissing,* see 18.16n. **21:** Jeremiah (cf. Ezek 13) condemned two of Hananiah's colleagues, Ahab and Zedekiah. He predicted their execution; from the Babylonian point of view their words would be for political subversion.

29.24–32: Jeremiah and Shemaiah. Another prophet, Shemaiah, wrote from Babylon a scathing letter to the new Temple overseer (cf. 20.1), Zephaniah, charging him with dereliction of duty in not arresting Jeremiah for his letter (above). Instead Zephaniah (21.1; 37.3) read the letter to his friend Jeremiah. The latter sent another letter to the exiles, condemning Shemaiah for writing *in your own name* (i.e., *though I* [the LORD] *did not send him*) and predicting that neither he nor his descendants would see the day of restoration (20.6).

led you to trust in a lie, 32 therefore thus
says the LORD: I am going to punish She-
maiah of Nehelam and his descendants; he
shall not have anyone living among this
people to see[a] the good that I am going to
do to my people, says the LORD, for he has
spoken rebellion against the LORD.

30 The word that came to Jeremiah
from the LORD: 2 Thus says the
LORD, the God of Israel: Write in a book all
the words that I have spoken to you. 3 For
the days are surely coming, says the LORD,
when I will restore the fortunes of my peo-
ple, Israel and Judah, says the LORD, and I
will bring them back to the land that I gave
to their ancestors and they shall take pos-
session of it.

4 These are the words that the LORD
spoke concerning Israel and Judah:

5 Thus says the LORD:
We have heard a cry of panic,
of terror, and no peace.
6 Ask now, and see,
can a man bear a child?
Why then do I see every man
with his hands on his loins like a
woman in labor?
Why has every face turned pale?
7 Alas! that day is so great
there is none like it;
it is a time of distress for Jacob;
yet he shall be rescued from it.

8 On that day, says the LORD of hosts, I
will break the yoke from off his[b] neck, and
I will burst his[b] bonds, and strangers shall
no more make a servant of him. 9 But they
shall serve the LORD their God and David
their king, whom I will raise up for them.

10 But as for you, have no fear, my
servant Jacob, says the LORD,
and do not be dismayed, O Israel;
for I am going to save you from
far away,
and your offspring from the land of
their captivity.
Jacob shall return and have quiet and
ease,
and no one shall make him afraid.
11 For I am with you, says the LORD, to
save you;
I will make an end of all the nations
among which I scattered you,
but of you I will not make an end.
I will chastise you in just measure,
and I will by no means leave you
unpunished.

12 For thus says the LORD:
Your hurt is incurable,
your wound is grievous.
13 There is no one to uphold your cause,

a Gk: Heb *and he shall not see* *b* Cn: Heb *your*

30.1–31.37: The book of consolation. This collection includes many themes that suggest a long process of growth. The core of the collection probably concerns the Jacob/Zion poem (30.4,5–7,12–17,18–21; 31.4–5,15,16–17,18–20,21–22,26). A second theme (30.12–17; 31.4–5) is the restoration of all Israel in the land, reversing judgments against Judah and Samaria proclaimed by Jeremiah and Amos, respectively. Another sequence of texts exhibiting marked similarities to Deutero-Isaiah (30.10–11; 31.7–9; 31.35–37) identifies restoration with the return of the Babylonian exiles. Editorial frameworks link restoration to the reestablishment of Jerusalem, and understand the salvation of Israel in terms of a requisite judgment against all the nations of the world.

30.1–4: Introduction. *Write in a book,* see also 36.2,32; 51.60; cf. Isa 30.8; Hab 2.2–3.

30.5–11: Oracles concerning Jacob. After the travail (6.24) of God's judgment (that day [of the LORD], Am 5.18–20), God will break the yoke and a Davidic king will again rule Israel (23.5–6; Hos 3.5). **8:** Cf. 2.14,20. **10–11:** *Have no fear,* common phrase in an oracle of salvation, Gen 15.1; Isa 35.4; 43.1. *Not make an end,* a remnant will be left (see 4.27; 5.10,18; cf. 46.27–28). *I will chastise you in just measure:* The prayer voiced in 10.24 answered.

30.12–17: Oracles concerning Zion. Though ostensibly incurably wounded (8.22; 14.17) and deserted (4.30; 13.21) because of her sinfulness, Zion will be healed (Hos 14.4; cf. Jer 3.22) and her oppressors despoiled (9.25–26; 25.13–14). **14:** *Lovers,* a conventional metaphor for political allies. The reference

no medicine for your wound,
no healing for you.
14 All your lovers have forgotten you;
they care nothing for you;
for I have dealt you the blow of
an enemy,
the punishment of a merciless foe,
because your guilt is great,
because your sins are so numerous.
15 Why do you cry out over your hurt?
Your pain is incurable.
Because your guilt is great,
because your sins are so numerous,
I have done these things to you.
16 Therefore all who devour you shall be
devoured,
and all your foes, everyone of them,
shall go into captivity;
those who plunder you shall be
plundered,
and all who prey on you I will
make a prey.
17 For I will restore health to you,
and your wounds I will heal,
says the LORD,
because they have called you
an outcast:
"It is Zion; no one cares for her!"

18 Thus says the LORD:
I am going to restore the fortunes of
the tents of Jacob,
and have compassion on his
dwellings;
the city shall be rebuilt upon its
mound,
and the citadel set on its
rightful site.
19 Out of them shall come thanksgiving,
and the sound of merrymakers.
I will make them many, and they
shall not be few;
I will make them honored, and they
shall not be disdained.
20 Their children shall be as of old,
their congregation shall be
established before me;
and I will punish all who oppress
them.
21 Their prince shall be one of
their own,
their ruler shall come from their
midst;
I will bring him near, and he shall
approach me,
for who would otherwise dare to
approach me?
says the LORD.
22 And you shall be my people,
and I will be your God.

23 Look, the storm of the LORD!
Wrath has gone forth,
a whirling[a] tempest;
it will burst upon the head of
the wicked.
24 The fierce anger of the LORD will not
turn back
until he has executed and
accomplished
the intents of his mind.
In the latter days you will understand
this.

31 At that time, says the LORD, I will
be the God of all the families of Isra-
el, and they shall be my people.
2 Thus says the LORD:
The people who survived the sword

a One Ms: Meaning of MT uncertain

here is perhaps to Egypt (37.5). **16:** *All who devour you shall be devoured,* once again, as in her earliest days (2.3b). **18–22: Restoration.** *The city* (Samaria or Jerusalem) will be *rebuilt upon its mound;* it was customary in antiquity to rebuild on the leveled rubble of the preceding city, producing the present flat-topped hills, called "tells" (see Josh 11.13). **21:** *I will bring him near* reassures the one who approaches God (Ex 19.21; 33.20; Num 8.19). **22:** The covenant formula; see 7.23; 11.4; 24.7; cf. Ex 6.7. **30.23–31.1:** The storm of the LORD. 30.23–24 = 23.19–20. **31.1–6: Redemption of Israel.** This version of the covenant formula emphasizes the inclusiveness of the term *Israel;* cf. 30.22. **2–6:** Cf. 2.2–3. With a formula taken from the Exodus narrative (*found grace* [favor], Ex 33.12–17; cf. Jer 23.7–8), God promises the joyful restoration of all Israel, including the renewal of pilgrimages to the Jerusalem Temple (*Zion;* 41.5). **6:** Contrast 6.1.

found grace in the wilderness;
when Israel sought for rest,
3 the LORD appeared to him[a] from far away.[b]
I have loved you with an everlasting love;
therefore I have continued my faithfulness to you.
4 Again I will build you, and you shall be built,
O virgin Israel!
Again you shall take[c] your tambourines,
and go forth in the dance of the merrymakers.
5 Again you shall plant vineyards
on the mountains of Samaria;
the planters shall plant,
and shall enjoy the fruit.
6 For there shall be a day when sentinels will call
in the hill country of Ephraim:
"Come, let us go up to Zion,
to the LORD our God."

7 For thus says the LORD:
Sing aloud with gladness for Jacob,
and raise shouts for the chief of the nations;
proclaim, give praise, and say,
"Save, O LORD, your people,
the remnant of Israel."
8 See, I am going to bring them from the land of the north,
and gather them from the farthest parts of the earth,
among them the blind and the lame,
those with child and those in labor, together;
a great company, they shall return here.
9 With weeping they shall come,
and with consolations[d] I will lead them back,
I will let them walk by brooks of water,
in a straight path in which they shall not stumble;
for I have become a father to Israel,
and Ephraim is my firstborn.

10 Hear the word of the LORD, O nations,
and declare it in the coastlands far away;
say, "He who scattered Israel will gather him,
and will keep him as a shepherd a flock."
11 For the LORD has ransomed Jacob,
and has redeemed him from hands too strong for him.
12 They shall come and sing aloud on the height of Zion,
and they shall be radiant over the goodness of the LORD,
over the grain, the wine, and the oil,
and over the young of the flock and the herd;
their life shall become like a watered garden,
and they shall never languish again.
13 Then shall the young women rejoice in the dance,
and the young men and the old shall be merry.
I will turn their mourning into joy,
I will comfort them, and give them gladness for sorrow.
14 I will give the priests their fill of fatness,
and my people shall be satisfied with my bounty,
says the LORD.

a Gk: Heb *me* *b* Or *to him long ago* *c* Or *adorn yourself with* *d* Gk Compare Vg Tg: Heb *supplications*

31.7–14: Homecoming. God will assemble the dispersed in their homeland (Isa 35.5–10). *Israel . . . Ephraim is my firstborn* (Ex 4.22), as Ephraim is restored, so is all Israel (including Judah; 2.3; 3.19). **8:** Isa 35.5–7; 42.16. **9:** Ps 23.2–3. **10–11:** Praises to God will be raised far (*coastlands,* Ps 72.10–11; Isa 41.1,5) and near for deliverance (*shepherd,* Isa 40.11; *redeemed,* Isa 48.20). **12–14:** Bountiful produce will mark the new age (Isa 58.11).

15 Thus says the LORD:
A voice is heard in Ramah,
lamentation and bitter weeping.
Rachel is weeping for her children;
she refuses to be comforted for her children,
because they are no more.
16 Thus says the LORD:
Keep your voice from weeping,
and your eyes from tears;
for there is a reward for your work,
says the LORD:
they shall come back from the land of the enemy;
17 there is hope for your future,
says the LORD:
your children shall come back to their own country.

18 Indeed I heard Ephraim pleading:
"You disciplined me, and I took the discipline;
I was like a calf untrained.
Bring me back, let me come back,
for you are the LORD my God.
19 For after I had turned away I repented;
and after I was discovered, I struck my thigh;
I was ashamed, and I was dismayed
because I bore the disgrace of my youth."
20 Is Ephraim my dear son?
Is he the child I delight in?
As often as I speak against him,
I still remember him.
Therefore I am deeply moved for him;
I will surely have mercy on him,
says the LORD.

21 Set up road markers for yourself,
make yourself signposts;
consider well the highway,
the road by which you went.
Return, O virgin Israel,
return to these your cities.
22 How long will you waver,
O faithless daughter?
For the LORD has created a new thing on the earth:
a woman encompasses[a] a man.

23 Thus says the LORD of hosts, the God of Israel: Once more they shall use these words in the land of Judah and in its towns when I restore their fortunes:
"The LORD bless you, O abode of righteousness,
O holy hill!"
24 And Judah and all its towns shall live there together, and the farmers and those who wander[b] with their flocks.
25 I will satisfy the weary,
and all who are faint I will replenish.
26 Thereupon I awoke and looked, and my sleep was pleasant to me.

a Meaning of Heb uncertain *b* Cn Compare Syr Vg Tg: Heb *and they shall wander*

31.15–20: Lament of the exiles is heard. *Rachel,* mother of Joseph and Benjamin (Gen 30.22; 35.16–20; 1 Sam 10.2), laments their (the northern tribes') exile (Ramah, 1 Sam 8.4). Although this verse reflects the tradition that Rachel's tomb was located in the territory of Benjamin, north of Jerusalem (1 Sam 10.2), another tradition locates it near Bethlehem, south of Jerusalem (Gen 35.16–20; see Mt 2.18). Ramah was the staging area from which the exiles were deported to Babylon (40.1). **18:** *Ephraim* (Joseph's son, Gen 41.50–52; the name was used as a synonym for the northern kingdom, Israel) repents (3.22–25; Hos 6.1–3). *Calf untrained,* cf. Hos 10.11. **20:** Hos 11.3.

31.21–26: The return. 21–22: Israel is instructed to note the *road markers* on her way to exile so that she can find her way home again. *A new thing,* cf. Isa 43.19. *A woman encompasses a man,* a difficult phrase, which may mean that she does not have to be protected by a man; cf. Isa 11.6–9 for the reversal of the usual in the new age. **23–37:** Restoration and the new covenant. **23–26:** As God depopulated and depleted Judah (1.10), he will also restore it (Ezek 36.8–11). **26:** A puzzling comment. Some scholars have understood it to be a scribal note that found its way into the text, characterizing the preceding promises as idealistic dreams. Alternatively, since much of chs 30–31 describes the fulfillment of hopes or the reversal of judgments detailed in earlier portions of the book of Jeremiah, it may call attention to the

27 The days are surely coming, says the
LORD, when I will sow the house of Israel
and the house of Judah with the seed of
humans and the seed of animals. 28 And just
as I have watched over them to pluck up
and break down, to overthrow, destroy,
and bring evil, so I will watch over them to
build and to plant, says the LORD. 29 In
those days they shall no longer say:

"The parents have eaten sour grapes,
and the children's teeth are set on
edge."

30 But all shall die for their own sins; the
teeth of everyone who eats sour grapes
shall be set on edge.

31 The days are surely coming, says the
LORD, when I will make a new covenant
with the house of Israel and the house of
Judah. 32 It will not be like the covenant
that I made with their ancestors when I
took them by the hand to bring them out of
the land of Egypt—a covenant that they
broke, though I was their husband,[a] says
the LORD. 33 But this is the covenant that I
will make with the house of Israel after
those days, says the LORD: I will put my
law within them, and I will write it on their
hearts; and I will be their God, and they
shall be my people. 34 No longer shall they
teach one another, or say to each other,
"Know the LORD," for they shall all know
me, from the least of them to the greatest,
says the LORD; for I will forgive their iniq-
uity, and remember their sin no more.

35 Thus says the LORD,
who gives the sun for light by day
and the fixed order of the moon
and the stars for light by night,
who stirs up the sea so that its waves
roar—
the LORD of hosts is his name:
36 If this fixed order were ever to cease
from my presence, says the LORD,
then also the offspring of Israel would
cease
to be a nation before me forever.

37 Thus says the LORD:
If the heavens above can be measured,
and the foundations of the earth
below can be explored,
then I will reject all the offspring
of Israel
because of all they have done,
says the LORD.

38 The days are surely coming, says the
LORD, when the city shall be rebuilt for the
LORD from the tower of Hananel to the

a Or *master*

recreation of order from the chaos described in the similarly visionary statement in 4.23–26. This understanding is confirmed by the eschatological reversal proclaimed in vv. 27–28.

31.27–38: A chain of eschatological promises. 27–28: Contrast 1.10. Similar imagery of restoration appears in Ezek 36.8–11. **29–30:** This may reflect the contemporary problem concerning the responsibility of each generation for its own deeds (Deut 24.16), discussed in some detail by Ezekiel (ch 18). **31–34:** This unit, like the others in this chain of eschatological texts with their characteristic introductory formulae (see 3.14–17n.), stems from a late stage in the growth of the book. It presumes and interweaves the language of ancestral apostasy (31.32; cf. 2.5; 3.24–25; 7.22,25–26; etc.), an allusion to Judah's hardened heart (31.33; cf. 4.3; 17.1), and references to the failure of the knowledge of God in all strata of society (31.34; cf. 5.1–3; 6.13 = 8.10; 16.6) into a promise of restored relationship. Opposing what was an increasingly limited concept of the Sinai covenant, the eschatologist affirms that God will *make a new covenant* (32.38–40) inscribed in the hearts of his people. **35–37:** In this passage, composed even later than 31.31–34 (cf. 33.14–26), the eternal cycle of nature (5.22) is used to emphasize God's assurance of Israel's continued existence (Isa 44.24; 54.9–10).

31.38–33.26: Appendix to the book of consolation: The future of Jerusalem. 38–40: This passage, composed well into the postexilic period (cf. Zech 14.10–11), and its counterpart in 33.14–26 (cf. esp. vv. 20–21,25), form a framework around chs 32–33, which are devoted to the restoration of Jerusalem to its former glory. Vv. 38–40 describe Jerusalem's four corners: northeast (*Hananel*, Neh 3.1), northwest (*Corner Gate*, 2 Kings 14.13), southeast and southwest (*Gareb*, *Goah*, both unidentified); and southern

Corner Gate. 39 And the measuring line
shall go out farther, straight to the hill Ga-
reb, and shall then turn to Goah. 40 The
whole valley of the dead bodies and the
ashes, and all the fields as far as the Wadi
Kidron, to the corner of the Horse Gate
toward the east, shall be sacred to the
LORD. It shall never again be uprooted or
overthrown.

32 The word that came to Jeremiah
from the LORD in the tenth year of
King Zedekiah of Judah, which was the
eighteenth year of Nebuchadrezzar. 2 At
that time the army of the king of Babylon
was besieging Jerusalem, and the prophet
Jeremiah was confined in the court of the
guard that was in the palace of the king of
Judah, 3 where King Zedekiah of Judah had
confined him. Zedekiah had said, "Why do
you prophesy and say: Thus says the LORD:
I am going to give this city into the hand of
the king of Babylon, and he shall take it;
4 King Zedekiah of Judah shall not escape
out of the hands of the Chaldeans, but shall
surely be given into the hands of the king of
Babylon, and shall speak with him face to
face and see him eye to eye; 5 and he shall
take Zedekiah to Babylon, and there he
shall remain until I attend to him, says the
LORD; though you fight against the Chalde-
ans, you shall not succeed?"
6 Jeremiah said, The word of the LORD
came to me: 7 Hanamel son of your uncle
Shallum is going to come to you and say,
"Buy my field that is at Anathoth, for the
right of redemption by purchase is yours."
8 Then my cousin Hanamel came to me in
the court of the guard, in accordance with
the word of the LORD, and said to me,
"Buy my field that is at Anathoth in the
land of Benjamin, for the right of posses-
sion and redemption is yours; buy it for
yourself." Then I knew that this was the
word of the LORD.
9 And I bought the field at Anathoth
from my cousin Hanamel, and weighed out
the money to him, seventeen shekels of sil-
ver. 10 I signed the deed, sealed it, got wit-
nesses, and weighed the money on scales.
11 Then I took the sealed deed of purchase,
containing the terms and conditions, and
the open copy; 12 and I gave the deed of
purchase to Baruch son of Neriah son of
Mahseiah, in the presence of my cousin
Hanamel, in the presence of the witnesses
who signed the deed of purchase, and in the
presence of all the Judeans who were sitting
in the court of the guard. 13 In their pres-
ence I charged Baruch, saying, 14 Thus says
the LORD of hosts, the God of Israel: Take
these deeds, both this sealed deed of pur-
chase and this open deed, and put them in
an earthenware jar, in order that they may
last for a long time. 15 For thus says the
LORD of hosts, the God of Israel: Houses
and fields and vineyards shall again be
bought in this land.
16 After I had given the deed of pur-
chase to Baruch son of Neriah, I prayed to

(Hinnom, 7.31–32) and eastern (*Wadi Kidron,* 2 Kings 23.4,6) boundaries. *Horse Gate* (southeast corner), Neh 3.28.

32.1–44: Jeremiah purchases land in Anathoth. 1–5: *The tenth year of King Zedekiah,* 588 BCE. For background, see ch 37. Chronologically the account should follow ch 37. Its placement here emphasizes the centrality of the restoration of Jerusalem in postexilic expectations for the future. **4:** *Chaldeans,* Babylonians. **6–15:** To prevent the alienation of family property, Jeremiah's cousin, *Hanamel,* offered to sell his land to Jeremiah (Lev 25.25–28). This is the most detailed account of a business transaction in the Bible (cf. Gen 23.1–6). *Seventeen shekels,* about 194 gr (7 oz). The official copy of the deed, written on papyrus, was rolled up and sealed; *the open copy* was for easy reference. Similar storage of deeds in earthen jars is known from Elephantine in Egypt. *Baruch,* Jeremiah's secretary, see ch 36. Jeremiah's purchase illustrates his confidence in the future of Judah. **16–44:** This section deals with the theme of the future of Jerusalem (*the city,* vv. 24,25,28–29,31,36). Much of it represents editorial expansion. First is a formal prayer (vv. 16–25) in the style of postexilic prayers such as those in Dan 9.4–19; Neh 9.6–37; Ezra 9.6–15. After praising God's power (10.16; 27.5), his justice (10.23–24), and his wondrous deeds in Israel's behalf (11.5), Jeremiah questions the wisdom of his purchase in view of the circumstances

the LORD, saying: 17 Ah Lord GOD! It is
you who made the heavens and the earth by
your great power and by your outstretched
arm! Nothing is too hard for you. 18 You
show steadfast love to the thousandth gen-
eration,[a] but repay the guilt of parents
into the laps of their children after them,
O great and mighty God whose name is
the LORD of hosts, 19 great in counsel and
mighty in deed; whose eyes are open to all
the ways of mortals, rewarding all accord-
ing to their ways and according to the fruit
of their doings. 20 You showed signs and
wonders in the land of Egypt, and to this
day in Israel and among all humankind,
and have made yourself a name that contin-
ues to this very day. 21 You brought your
people Israel out of the land of Egypt with
signs and wonders, with a strong hand and
outstretched arm, and with great terror;
22 and you gave them this land, which you
swore to their ancestors to give them, a
land flowing with milk and honey; 23 and
they entered and took possession of it. But
they did not obey your voice or follow your
law; of all you commanded them to do,
they did nothing. Therefore you have made
all these disasters come upon them. 24 See,
the siege ramps have been cast up against
the city to take it, and the city, faced with
sword, famine, and pestilence, has been
given into the hands of the Chaldeans who
are fighting against it. What you spoke has
happened, as you yourself can see. 25 Yet
you, O Lord GOD, have said to me, "Buy
the field for money and get witnesses"—
though the city has been given into the
hands of the Chaldeans.

26 The word of the LORD came to Jere-
miah: 27 See, I am the LORD, the God of all
flesh; is anything too hard for me? 28 There-
fore, thus says the LORD: I am going to give
this city into the hands of the Chaldeans
and into the hand of King Nebuchadrezzar
of Babylon, and he shall take it. 29 The
Chaldeans who are fighting against this city
shall come, set it on fire, and burn it, with
the houses on whose roofs offerings have
been made to Baal and libations have been
poured out to other gods, to provoke me to
anger. 30 For the people of Israel and the
people of Judah have done nothing but evil
in my sight from their youth; the people of
Israel have done nothing but provoke me to
anger by the work of their hands, says the
LORD. 31 This city has aroused my anger
and wrath, from the day it was built until
this day, so that I will remove it from my
sight 32 because of all the evil of the people
of Israel and the people of Judah that they
did to provoke me to anger—they, their
kings and their officials, their priests and
their prophets, the citizens of Judah and
the inhabitants of Jerusalem. 33 They have
turned their backs to me, not their faces;
though I have taught them persistently,
they would not listen and accept correc-
tion. 34 They set up their abominations in
the house that bears my name, and defiled
it. 35 They built the high places of Baal in
the valley of the son of Hinnom, to offer up
their sons and daughters to Molech, though
I did not command them, nor did it enter
my mind that they should do this abomina-
tion, causing Judah to sin.

36 Now therefore thus says the LORD,
the God of Israel, concerning this city of
which you say, "It is being given into the
hand of the king of Babylon by the sword,
by famine, and by pestilence": 37 See, I am
going to gather them from all the lands to
which I drove them in my anger and my

a Or *to thousands*

(vv. 24–25). God's answer (vv. 26–44) summarizes Jeremiah's (and the Deuteronomistic) interpretation of the contemporary critical events. After a résumé of Jerusalem's idolatry (incense, wine and oil offered on the rooftops, 19.13; comparative sinfulness of Israel and Judah, 3.6–11; human sacrifices, 7.30–32) and her stubborn indifference to God's warnings (17.21–23), her imminent destruction (in conventional terms: sword, pestilence, and famine, 14.11–12; 21.7) is affirmed. The section concludes with assurances of restoration, first with reference to the new covenant (31.31–34) and then the exchange and holding of property (vv. 42–44; cf. 17.26n.). **24:** *Chaldeans,* Babylonians. **35:** *Molech,* a Canaanite deity associated with child sacrifice (2 Kings 23.10; Lev 20.2).

wrath and in great indignation; I will bring
them back to this place, and I will settle
them in safety. 38 They shall be my people,
and I will be their God. 39 I will give them
one heart and one way, that they may fear
me for all time, for their own good and the
good of their children after them. 40 I will
make an everlasting covenant with them,
never to draw back from doing good to
them; and I will put the fear of me in their
hearts, so that they may not turn from me.
41 I will rejoice in doing good to them, and
I will plant them in this land in faithfulness,
with all my heart and all my soul.

42 For thus says the LORD: Just as I have
brought all this great disaster upon this
people, so I will bring upon them all the
good fortune that I now promise them.
43 Fields shall be bought in this land of
which you are saying, It is a desolation,
without human beings or animals; it has
been given into the hands of the Chaldeans.
44 Fields shall be bought for money, and
deeds shall be signed and sealed and wit-
nessed, in the land of Benjamin, in the
places around Jerusalem, and in the cities
of Judah, of the hill country, of the Shephe-
lah, and of the Negeb; for I will restore
their fortunes, says the LORD.

33 The word of the LORD came to Jere-
miah a second time, while he was
still confined in the court of the guard:
2 Thus says the LORD who made the
earth,[a] the LORD who formed it to estab-
lish it—the LORD is his name: 3 Call to me
and I will answer you, and will tell you
great and hidden things that you have not
known. 4 For thus says the LORD, the God
of Israel, concerning the houses of this city
and the houses of the kings of Judah that
were torn down to make a defense against
the siege ramps and before the sword:[b]
5 The Chaldeans are coming in to fight[c]
and to fill them with the dead bodies of
those whom I shall strike down in my anger
and my wrath, for I have hidden my face
from this city because of all their wicked-
ness. 6 I am going to bring it recovery and
healing; I will heal them and reveal to them
abundance[b] of prosperity and security. 7 I
will restore the fortunes of Judah and the
fortunes of Israel, and rebuild them as they
were at first. 8 I will cleanse them from all
the guilt of their sin against me, and I will
forgive all the guilt of their sin and rebel-
lion against me. 9 And this city[d] shall be to
me a name of joy, a praise and a glory be-
fore all the nations of the earth who shall
hear of all the good that I do for them; they
shall fear and tremble because of all the
good and all the prosperity I provide for it.

10 Thus says the LORD: In this place of
which you say, "It is a waste without hu-
man beings or animals," in the towns of
Judah and the streets of Jerusalem that are
desolate, without inhabitants, human or
animal, there shall once more be heard
11 the voice of mirth and the voice of glad-
ness, the voice of the bridegroom and the
voice of the bride, the voices of those who
sing, as they bring thank offerings to the
house of the LORD:

"Give thanks to the LORD of hosts,
for the LORD is good,
for his steadfast love endures
forever!"

For I will restore the fortunes of the land as
at first, says the LORD.

12 Thus says the LORD of hosts: In this
place that is waste, without human beings
or animals, and in all its towns there shall
again be pasture for shepherds resting their

a Gk: Heb *it* *b* Meaning of Heb uncertain
c Cn: Heb *They are coming in to fight against the Chaldeans* *d* Heb *And it*

33.1–13: God will rebuild the walls of Jerusalem. 1: Editorial connection with preceding chapter. **4:** In siege defense measures, there was demolition of houses built in the city wall to allow for the military needs of defenders (Isa 22.10). **5:** *Chaldeans,* Babylonians. **6–8a:** After punishment will come rebuilding and restoration. **8b–9:** Generalizing expansion.

33.10–13: Two proclamations of salvation. Vv. 10–11 reverse 7.34. *For the LORD is good, for his steadfast love endures forever,* Ps 100.5; 106.1; 107.1; 118.1–4,25; 136.1–26; Ezra 3.11; 1 Chr 16.34,41; 2 Chr 7.3,6; 20.21. **12–13:** Cf. 32.44; 17.26n.

flocks. 13In the towns of the hill country, of
the Shephelah, and of the Negeb, in the
land of Benjamin, the places around Jerusa-
lem, and in the towns of Judah, flocks shall
again pass under the hands of the one who
counts them, says the LORD.
14 The days are surely coming, says the
LORD, when I will fulfill the promise I
made to the house of Israel and the house
of Judah. 15In those days and at that time
I will cause a righteous Branch to spring up
for David; and he shall execute justice and
righteousness in the land. 16In those days
Judah will be saved and Jerusalem will live
in safety. And this is the name by which it
will be called: "The LORD is our righteous-
ness."
17 For thus says the LORD: David shall
never lack a man to sit on the throne of the
house of Israel, 18and the levitical priests
shall never lack a man in my presence to
offer burnt offerings, to make grain offer-
ings, and to make sacrifices for all time.
19 The word of the LORD came to Jere-
miah: 20Thus says the LORD: If any of you
could break my covenant with the day and
my covenant with the night, so that day
and night would not come at their appoint-
ed time, 21only then could my covenant
with my servant David be broken, so that
he would not have a son to reign on his
throne, and my covenant with my ministers
the Levites. 22Just as the host of heaven
cannot be numbered and the sands of the
sea cannot be measured, so I will increase
the offspring of my servant David, and the
Levites who minister to me.
23 The word of the LORD came to Jere-
miah: 24Have you not observed how these
people say, "The two families that the
LORD chose have been rejected by him,"
and how they hold my people in such con-
tempt that they no longer regard them as a
nation? 25Thus says the LORD: Only if I
had not established my covenant with day
and night and the ordinances of heaven and
earth, 26would I reject the offspring of Ja-
cob and of my servant David and not
choose any of his descendants as rulers over
the offspring of Abraham, Isaac, and Jacob.
For I will restore their fortunes, and will
have mercy upon them.

34 The word that came to Jeremiah
from the LORD, when King Nebu-
chadrezzar of Babylon and all his army and
all the kingdoms of the earth and all the
peoples under his dominion were fighting
against Jerusalem and all its cities: 2Thus
says the LORD, the God of Israel: Go and
speak to King Zedekiah of Judah and say to
him: Thus says the LORD: I am going to
give this city into the hand of the king of
Babylon, and he shall burn it with fire.
3And you yourself shall not escape from
his hand, but shall surely be captured and
handed over to him; you shall see the king
of Babylon eye to eye and speak with him
face to face; and you shall go to Babylon.
4Yet hear the word of the LORD, O King
Zedekiah of Judah! Thus says the LORD
concerning you: You shall not die by the
sword; 5you shall die in peace. And as
spices were burned[a] for your ancestors,

a Heb *as there was burning*

33.14–26: A variation of 23.5–6. This passage is lacking in the Septuagint, and is probably to be dated to 450–400 BCE. It is modeled on the concluding section of the framework to the "book of consolation" (31.31–37): an eschatological unit ("days are coming"; 31.31–34 par. 33.14–18) followed by an appeal to the fixed order of creation as an assurance of the LORD's faithfulness to his promises (31.35–37 par. 33.19–26). **16:** The new *name* of Jerusalem (see Isa 1.26), in 23.6 the king's name. **17–18:** The reference to David in vv. 14–16 inspires a reaffirmation of the promise to David: There will be not one but a succession of Davidic rulers (2 Sam 7.16; 1 Kings 9.5). The reference to *levitical priests* is unique in Jeremiah (Deut 18.1–5). **22:** A reinterpretation of Gen 22.17–18. **23–26:** As night follows day (31.35–37; Gen 1.5; 8.22), God's promise to the ancestors of Israel and to David will be kept.

34.1–7: Warning to Zedekiah. The siege of Jerusalem (January 587 BCE) was but weeks away; only *Lachish* (45 km [23 mi] southwest of Jerusalem) and *Azekah* (18 km [11 mi] north-northwest of Lachish) held out. Warning Zedekiah of Jerusalem's imminent destruction and his own captivity, Jeremiah

the earlier kings who preceded you, so they
shall burn spices[a] for you and lament for
you, saying, "Alas, lord!" For I have spo-
ken the word, says the LORD.
6 Then the prophet Jeremiah spoke all
these words to Zedekiah king of Judah, in
Jerusalem, 7 when the army of the king of
Babylon was fighting against Jerusalem and
against all the cities of Judah that were left,
Lachish and Azekah; for these were the
only fortified cities of Judah that remained.
8 The word that came to Jeremiah from
the LORD, after King Zedekiah had made a
covenant with all the people in Jerusalem to
make a proclamation of liberty to them—
9 that all should set free their Hebrew
slaves, male and female, so that no one
should hold another Judean in slavery.
10 And they obeyed, all the officials and all
the people who had entered into the cove-
nant that all would set free their slaves,
male or female, so that they would not be
enslaved again; they obeyed and set them
free. 11 But afterward they turned around
and took back the male and female slaves
they had set free, and brought them again
into subjection as slaves. 12 The word of the
LORD came to Jeremiah from the LORD:
13 Thus says the LORD, the God of Israel: I
myself made a covenant with your ances-
tors when I brought them out of the land of
Egypt, out of the house of slavery, saying,
14 "Every seventh year each of you must set
free any Hebrews who have been sold to
you and have served you six years; you
must set them free from your service." But
your ancestors did not listen to me or in-
cline their ears to me. 15 You yourselves re-
cently repented and did what was right in
my sight by proclaiming liberty to one an-
other, and you made a covenant before me
in the house that is called by my name;
16 but then you turned around and pro-
faned my name when each of you took
back your male and female slaves, whom
you had set free according to their desire,
and you brought them again into subjec-
tion to be your slaves. 17 Therefore, thus
says the LORD: You have not obeyed me by
granting a release to your neighbors and
friends; I am going to grant a release to
you, says the LORD—a release to the
sword, to pestilence, and to famine. I will
make you a horror to all the kingdoms of
the earth. 18 And those who transgressed
my covenant and did not keep the terms of
the covenant that they made before me, I
will make like[b] the calf when they cut it in
two and passed between its parts: 19 the of-
ficials of Judah, the officials of Jerusalem,
the eunuchs, the priests, and all the people
of the land who passed between the parts of
the calf 20 shall be handed over to their
enemies and to those who seek their lives.
Their corpses shall become food for the
birds of the air and the wild animals of the
earth. 21 And as for King Zedekiah of Judah
and his officials, I will hand them over to
their enemies and to those who seek their
lives, to the army of the king of Babylon,
which has withdrawn from you. 22 I am go-
ing to command, says the LORD, and will
bring them back to this city; and they will

a Heb *shall burn* *b* Cn: Heb lacks *like*

assured Zedekiah of a peaceful death and appropriate funeral rites (but cf. 52.8–11). **5:** *Burn spices,* an element of a royal funeral (2 Chr 16.14).

34.8–22: Manumission of slaves and perfidy of the Jerusalemites. Probably to simplify the problem of the domestic food supply, to make more people available for Jerusalem's defense, and to propitiate the LORD, Zedekiah proclaimed the manumission of all slaves. But when the Egyptian army approached (37.6–15), causing the Babylonians temporarily to lift the siege, the manumission was rescinded. **13–22:** Making reference to Ex 21.2 and Deut 15.12, Jeremiah condemned this as one more example of notorious faithlessness. He assured the people of punishment like that implied in their covenant ritual (v. 18; Gen 15.9–17); the transgressor should suffer the same fate as the slaughtered animal, a practice known from nonbiblical sources also. The formula "cut a covenant" is clarified here (in vv. 8,13,15, etc., *made* is literally "cut"); cf. Gen 15.7–21.

fight against it, and take it, and burn it with
fire. The towns of Judah I will make a deso-
lation without inhabitant.

35 The word that came to Jeremiah
from the LORD in the days of King
Jehoiakim son of Josiah of Judah: 2 Go to
the house of the Rechabites, and speak with
them, and bring them to the house of the
LORD, into one of the chambers; then offer
them wine to drink. 3 So I took Jaazaniah
son of Jeremiah son of Habazziniah, and
his brothers, and all his sons, and the whole
house of the Rechabites. 4 I brought them to
the house of the LORD into the chamber of
the sons of Hanan son of Igdaliah, the man
of God, which was near the chamber of the
officials, above the chamber of Maaseiah
son of Shallum, keeper of the threshold.
5 Then I set before the Rechabites pitchers
full of wine, and cups; and I said to them,
"Have some wine." 6 But they answered,
"We will drink no wine, for our ancestor
Jonadab son of Rechab commanded us,
'You shall never drink wine, neither you
nor your children; 7 nor shall you ever build
a house, or sow seed; nor shall you plant a
vineyard, or even own one; but you shall
live in tents all your days, that you may live
many days in the land where you reside.'
8 We have obeyed the charge of our ances-
tor Jonadab son of Rechab in all that he
commanded us, to drink no wine all our
days, ourselves, our wives, our sons, or our
daughters, 9 and not to build houses to live
in. We have no vineyard or field or seed;
10 but we have lived in tents, and have
obeyed and done all that our ancestor Jona-
dab commanded us. 11 But when King Neb-
uchadrezzar of Babylon came up against
the land, we said, 'Come, and let us go to
Jerusalem for fear of the army of the Chal-
deans and the army of the Arameans.' That
is why we are living in Jerusalem."

12 Then the word of the LORD came to
Jeremiah: 13 Thus says the LORD of hosts,
the God of Israel: Go and say to the people
of Judah and the inhabitants of Jerusalem,
Can you not learn a lesson and obey my
words? says the LORD. 14 The command
has been carried out that Jonadab son of
Rechab gave to his descendants to drink no
wine; and they drink none to this day, for
they have obeyed their ancestor's com-
mand. But I myself have spoken to you per-
sistently, and you have not obeyed me. 15 I
have sent to you all my servants the proph-
ets, sending them persistently, saying,
"Turn now everyone of you from your evil
way, and amend your doings, and do not
go after other gods to serve them, and then
you shall live in the land that I gave to you
and your ancestors." But you did not in-
cline your ear or obey me. 16 The descen-
dants of Jonadab son of Rechab have car-
ried out the command that their ancestor
gave them, but this people has not obeyed
me. 17 Therefore, thus says the LORD, the
God of hosts, the God of Israel: I am going
to bring on Judah and on all the inhabitants
of Jerusalem every disaster that I have pro-
nounced against them; because I have spo-
ken to them and they have not listened, I
have called to them and they have not an-
swered.

18 But to the house of the Rechabites
Jeremiah said: Thus says the LORD of hosts,
the God of Israel: Because you have obeyed
the command of your ancestor Jonadab,
and kept all his precepts, and done all that
he commanded you, 19 therefore thus says
the LORD of hosts, the God of Israel: Jona-
dab son of Rechab shall not lack a descen-
dant to stand before me for all time.

35.1–19: The symbol of the Rechabites. This episode takes place *in the days of King Jehoiakim* (608–598 BCE). The Rechabites were a religious community, similar to nazirites (Num 6.1–21), founded by Jonadab, son of Rechab, during the reign of Jehu (842–814 BCE). They assisted Jehu in the purge accompanying the revolt against the dynasty of Omri (2 Kings 10.15–28). Jeremiah approves of their faithfulness to their principles, whose origin is unclear, but which contrasts with faithlessness. **4:** *Chamber,* prominent families had open rooms in the Temple complex where they gathered, shared sacrificial meals, and conducted other business (36.10; 2 Kings 23.11). *Maaseiah,* perhaps the father of Zephaniah (cf. 21.1).

36 In the fourth year of King Jehoiakim
son of Josiah of Judah, this word
came to Jeremiah from the LORD: 2 Take a
scroll and write on it all the words that I
have spoken to you against Israel and Ju-
dah and all the nations, from the day I
spoke to you, from the days of Josiah until
today. 3 It may be that when the house of
Judah hears of all the disasters that I intend
to do to them, all of them may turn from
their evil ways, so that I may forgive their
iniquity and their sin.
4 Then Jeremiah called Baruch son of
Neriah, and Baruch wrote on a scroll at
Jeremiah's dictation all the words of the
LORD that he had spoken to him. 5 And Jer-
emiah ordered Baruch, saying, "I am pre-
vented from entering the house of the
LORD; 6 so you go yourself, and on a fast
day in the hearing of the people in the
LORD's house you shall read the words of
the LORD from the scroll that you have
written at my dictation. You shall read
them also in the hearing of all the people of
Judah who come up from their towns. 7 It
may be that their plea will come before the
LORD, and that all of them will turn from
their evil ways, for great is the anger and
wrath that the LORD has pronounced
against this people." 8 And Baruch son of
Neriah did all that the prophet Jeremi-
ah ordered him about reading from the
scroll the words of the LORD in the LORD's
house.
9 In the fifth year of King Jehoiakim son
of Josiah of Judah, in the ninth month, all
the people in Jerusalem and all the people
who came from the towns of Judah to Jeru-
salem proclaimed a fast before the LORD.
10 Then, in the hearing of all the people,
Baruch read the words of Jeremiah from
the scroll, in the house of the LORD, in the
chamber of Gemariah son of Shaphan the
secretary, which was in the upper court, at
the entry of the New Gate of the LORD's
house.
11 When Micaiah son of Gemariah son
of Shaphan heard all the words of the
LORD from the scroll, 12 he went down to
the king's house, into the secretary's cham-
ber; and all the officials were sitting there:
Elishama the secretary, Delaiah son of She-
maiah, Elnathan son of Achbor, Gemariah
son of Shaphan, Zedekiah son of Hanani-
ah, and all the officials. 13 And Micaiah
told them all the words that he had heard,
when Baruch read the scroll in the hearing
of the people. 14 Then all the officials sent
Jehudi son of Nethaniah son of Shelemiah
son of Cushi to say to Baruch, "Bring the
scroll that you read in the hearing of the
people, and come." So Baruch son of Neri-
ah took the scroll in his hand and came to
them. 15 And they said to him, "Sit down
and read it to us." So Baruch read it to
them. 16 When they heard all the words,
they turned to one another in alarm, and
said to Baruch, "We certainly must report

36.1–32: Jehoiakim burns a scroll of Jeremiah, and Jeremiah dictates another. The account preserved here mirrors 2 Kings 22, suggesting to some scholars that it functions as a literary device contrasting the reactions of Josiah (who tore his clothing upon hearing the reading of the scroll containing God's word) with those of Jehoiakim (who tears the *scroll,* itself, in an act of defiance). Therefore, the value of ch 36 as a source for historical reconstruction is in dispute. Efforts to identify some portion of the current book of Jeremiah with Baruch's scroll have proven especially disappointing. **1–4:** *The fourth year of King Jehoiakim* (605 BCE). In light of portentous contemporary events (25.1–14), Jeremiah commissioned *Baruch son of Neriah* and brother of Seraiah, one of King Zedekiah's ministers (32.12; 51.59), to transcribe his oracles (*words of the LORD*) on a papyrus scroll. Seals belonging to Baruch and Seraiah have been discovered. **5–10:** For an unstated reason, Jeremiah was barred from the Temple; so, on the occasion of a fast proclaimed by Jehoiakim because of Nebuchadrezzar's advance against Ashkelon (probably in November, 604 BCE), he instructed Baruch to read the scroll in his stead. *Gemariah son of Shaphan,* a friend of Jeremiah (26.24; see 40.1–6n.). **11–19:** Baruch was asked to re-read the scroll before an assembly of royal officials. Although most cannot be identified, *Elnathan son of Achbor* was perhaps the king's father-in-law (2 Kings 24.8) and was head of the mission that brought the prophet Uriah back from Egypt for execution (26.22–23). **20–26:** Jehoiakim ordered the scroll brought from the court scribe's

all these words to the king." 17 Then they
questioned Baruch, "Tell us now, how did
you write all these words? Was it at his
dictation?" 18 Baruch answered them, "He
dictated all these words to me, and I wrote
them with ink on the scroll." 19 Then the
officials said to Baruch, "Go and hide, you
and Jeremiah, and let no one know where
you are."

20 Leaving the scroll in the chamber of
Elishama the secretary, they went to the
court of the king; and they reported all the
words to the king. 21 Then the king sent
Jehudi to get the scroll, and he took it from
the chamber of Elishama the secretary; and
Jehudi read it to the king and all the offi-
cials who stood beside the king. 22 Now the
king was sitting in his winter apartment (it
was the ninth month), and there was a fire
burning in the brazier before him. 23 As Je-
hudi read three or four columns, the king[a]
would cut them off with a penknife and
throw them into the fire in the brazier, until
the entire scroll was consumed in the fire
that was in the brazier. 24 Yet neither the
king, nor any of his servants who heard all
these words, was alarmed, nor did they tear
their garments. 25 Even when Elnathan and
Delaiah and Gemariah urged the king not
to burn the scroll, he would not listen to
them. 26 And the king commanded Jerah-
meel the king's son and Seraiah son of Azri-
el and Shelemiah son of Abdeel to arrest the
secretary Baruch and the prophet Jeremiah.
But the LORD hid them.

27 Now, after the king had burned the
scroll with the words that Baruch wrote at
Jeremiah's dictation, the word of the LORD
came to Jeremiah: 28 Take another scroll
and write on it all the former words that
were in the first scroll, which King Jehoia-
kim of Judah has burned. 29 And concern-
ing King Jehoiakim of Judah you shall say:
Thus says the LORD, You have dared to
burn this scroll, saying, Why have you writ-
ten in it that the king of Babylon will cer-
tainly come and destroy this land, and will
cut off from it human beings and animals?
30 Therefore thus says the LORD concerning
King Jehoiakim of Judah: He shall have no
one to sit upon the throne of David, and his
dead body shall be cast out to the heat by
day and the frost by night. 31 And I will
punish him and his offspring and his ser-
vants for their iniquity; I will bring on
them, and on the inhabitants of Jerusalem,
and on the people of Judah, all the disasters
with which I have threatened them—but
they would not listen.

32 Then Jeremiah took another scroll
and gave it to the secretary Baruch son of
Neriah, who wrote on it at Jeremiah's dic-
tation all the words of the scroll that King
Jehoiakim of Judah had burned in the fire;
and many similar words were added to
them.

37 Zedekiah son of Josiah, whom King
Nebuchadrezzar of Babylon made
king in the land of Judah, succeeded Coni-
ah son of Jehoiakim. 2 But neither he nor
his servants nor the people of the land lis-
tened to the words of the LORD that he
spoke through the prophet Jeremiah.

3 King Zedekiah sent Jehucal son of
Shelemiah and the priest Zephaniah son of

[a] Heb *he*

office. Despite protests from some officials, he burned it as it was read, three or four columns at a time, and ordered the arrest of Jeremiah and Baruch. *Penknife,* a knife used to sharpen the point of the scribes' reed pens. **24–25:** The explicit statement that Jehoiakim did not tear his garments highlights the contrast between him and King Josiah (2 Kings 22.11). **27–32:** Using the destruction of the scroll as a symbol, Jeremiah announced the ignominious death of Jehoiakim (22.18–19; 2 Kings 24.6–15) and dictated an expanded copy of the scroll.

37.1–44.30: The sufferings of Jeremiah before, during, and after the fall of Jerusalem.

37.1–38.28: Jeremiah, Zedekiah, and the siege. 37.1–2: Editorial transition from ch 36 to 37. *Coniah,* Jehoiachin. **3–10:** Shortly after his accession (spring, 587 BCE), an army of Pharaoh Hophra (Apries) came up from Egypt to relieve besieged Jerusalem (34.21). The inhabitants concluded that a deliverance as in the days of Hezekiah (2 Kings 19.32–37) had occurred, but Jeremiah warned them that such

Maaseiah to the prophet Jeremiah saying,
"Please pray for us to the LORD our God."
4 Now Jeremiah was still going in and out
among the people, for he had not yet been
put in prison. 5 Meanwhile, the army of
Pharaoh had come out of Egypt; and when
the Chaldeans who were besieging Jerusa-
lem heard news of them, they withdrew
from Jerusalem.

6 Then the word of the LORD came to
the prophet Jeremiah: 7 Thus says the
LORD, God of Israel: This is what the two
of you shall say to the king of Judah, who
sent you to me to inquire of me: Pharaoh's
army, which set out to help you, is going to
return to its own land, to Egypt. 8 And the
Chaldeans shall return and fight against
this city; they shall take it and burn it with
fire. 9 Thus says the LORD: Do not deceive
yourselves, saying, "The Chaldeans will
surely go away from us," for they will not
go away. 10 Even if you defeated the whole
army of Chaldeans who are fighting against
you, and there remained of them only
wounded men in their tents, they would
rise up and burn this city with fire.

11 Now when the Chaldean army had
withdrawn from Jerusalem at the approach
of Pharaoh's army, 12 Jeremiah set out from
Jerusalem to go to the land of Benjamin to
receive his share of property[a] among the
people there. 13 When he reached the Benja-
min Gate, a sentinel there named Irijah son
of Shelemiah son of Hananiah arrested the
prophet Jeremiah saying, "You are desert-
ing to the Chaldeans." 14 And Jeremiah
said, "That is a lie; I am not deserting to the
Chaldeans." But Irijah would not listen to
him, and arrested Jeremiah and brought
him to the officials. 15 The officials were en-
raged at Jeremiah, and they beat him and
imprisoned him in the house of the secre-
tary Jonathan, for it had been made a pris-
on. 16 Thus Jeremiah was put in the cistern
house, in the cells, and remained there
many days.

17 Then King Zedekiah sent for him,
and received him. The king questioned him
secretly in his house, and said, "Is there any
word from the LORD?" Jeremiah said,
"There is!" Then he said, "You shall be
handed over to the king of Babylon." 18 Jer-
emiah also said to King Zedekiah, "What
wrong have I done to you or your servants
or this people, that you have put me in
prison? 19 Where are your prophets who
prophesied to you, saying, 'The king of
Babylon will not come against you and
against this land'? 20 Now please hear me,
my lord king: be good enough to listen to
my plea, and do not send me back to the
house of the secretary Jonathan to die
there." 21 So King Zedekiah gave orders,
and they committed Jeremiah to the court
of the guard; and a loaf of bread was given
him daily from the bakers' street, until all
the bread of the city was gone. So Jeremiah
remained in the court of the guard.

38 Now Shephatiah son of Mattan,
Gedaliah son of Pashhur, Jucal son
of Shelemiah, and Pashhur son of Malchiah
heard the words that Jeremiah was saying
to all the people, 2 Thus says the LORD,
Those who stay in this city shall die by the
sword, by famine, and by pestilence; but
those who go out to the Chaldeans shall

a Meaning of Heb uncertain

optimism was wholly unwarranted. *Zephaniah,* 21.1–10; 29.24–32. **5:** *Chaldeans,* Babylonians. **11–15:** Leaving the city by the Benjamin Gate (20.2), Jeremiah was arrested on suspicion of desertion (38.18–19), perhaps based on oracles such as 21.1–10. **12:** *To receive his share,* see 32.6–15, which may suggest the occasion. **16–21:** In a secret interview, Zedekiah sought reassurance for his ill-advised revolt, but in vain (21.2). He modified Jeremiah's imprisonment to house arrest, and guaranteed him a minimum food ration as long as there were supplies. **38.1–13:** The relationship between chs 37 and 38 is unclear; they may be alternate accounts of the same event. Jeremiah's continued insistence on surrender to Nebuchadrezzar was dangerous for Zedekiah's pro-Egyptian counselors (*Gedaliah son of Pashhur,* 20.1; *Jucal* [Jehucal], 37.3; *Pashhur,* 21.1). They persuaded the vacillating Zedekiah that Jeremiah was subverting the war effort (there is similar phraseology in a letter written eighteen months earlier, found in the excavations at Lachish). **6:** The cistern was nearly dry, indicating a time shortly before Nebuchadrezzar's final assault,

live; they shall have their lives as a prize of
war, and live. 3Thus says the LORD, This
city shall surely be handed over to the army
of the king of Babylon and be taken. 4Then
the officials said to the king, "This man
ought to be put to death, because he is dis-
couraging the soldiers who are left in this
city, and all the people, by speaking such
words to them. For this man is not seeking
the welfare of this people, but their harm."
5King Zedekiah said, "Here he is; he is in
your hands; for the king is powerless
against you." 6So they took Jeremiah and
threw him into the cistern of Malchiah, the
king's son, which was in the court of the
guard, letting Jeremiah down by ropes.
Now there was no water in the cistern, but
only mud, and Jeremiah sank in the mud.
7 Ebed-melech the Ethiopian,[a] a eu-
nuch in the king's house, heard that they
had put Jeremiah into the cistern. The king
happened to be sitting at the Benjamin
Gate, 8So Ebed-melech left the king's house
and spoke to the king, 9"My lord king,
these men have acted wickedly in all they
did to the prophet Jeremiah by throwing
him into the cistern to die there of hunger,
for there is no bread left in the city."
10Then the king commanded Ebed-melech
the Ethiopian,[a] "Take three men with you
from here, and pull the prophet Jeremiah
up from the cistern before he dies." 11So
Ebed-melech took the men with him and
went to the house of the king, to a ward-
robe of[b] the storehouse, and took from
there old rags and worn-out clothes, which
he let down to Jeremiah in the cistern by
ropes. 12Then Ebed-melech the Ethiopian[a]
said to Jeremiah, "Just put the rags and
clothes between your armpits and the
ropes." Jeremiah did so. 13Then they drew
Jeremiah up by the ropes and pulled him
out of the cistern. And Jeremiah remained
in the court of the guard.
14 King Zedekiah sent for the prophet
Jeremiah and received him at the third en-
trance of the temple of the LORD. The king
said to Jeremiah, "I have something to ask
you; do not hide anything from me." 15Jer-
emiah said to Zedekiah, "If I tell you, you
will put me to death, will you not? And if
I give you advice, you will not listen to
me." 16So King Zedekiah swore an oath in
secret to Jeremiah, "As the LORD lives, who
gave us our lives, I will not put you to death
or hand you over to these men who seek
your life."
17 Then Jeremiah said to Zedekiah,
"Thus says the LORD, the God of hosts, the
God of Israel, If you will only surrender to
the officials of the king of Babylon, then
your life shall be spared, and this city shall
not be burned with fire, and you and your
house shall live. 18But if you do not surren-
der to the officials of the king of Babylon,
then this city shall be handed over to the
Chaldeans, and they shall burn it with fire,
and you yourself shall not escape from their
hand." 19King Zedekiah said to Jeremiah,
"I am afraid of the Judeans who have de-
serted to the Chaldeans, for I might be
handed over to them and they would abuse
me." 20Jeremiah said, "That will not hap-
pen. Just obey the voice of the LORD in
what I say to you, and it shall go well with
you, and your life shall be spared. 21But if
you are determined not to surrender, this is
what the LORD has shown me— 22a vision

a Or *Nubian*; Heb *Cushite* *b* Cn: Heb *to under*

August 586 BCE (52.5–7). **7:** Ironically, Jeremiah was delivered from murder at the hands of his countrymen by an Ethiopian court official (Heb "saris" does not necessarily refer to a physical *eunuch;* see 39.15–18). **14–28:** Uncertain and fearful, Zedekiah again (37.17–20) summoned Jeremiah for a private interview (location of *the third entrance* is unknown). Justifiably suspicious, Jeremiah exacted an oath from Zedekiah for his safety. He repeated his counsel of "surrender and live" (20.1–16; 21.4–10; 27.1–11) and emphasized it by relating a vision depicting the capture of the royal household and the burning of Jerusalem (*in the mud* recalls Jeremiah's own recent experience, 38.6). Jeremiah assured Zedekiah of safety from Judean deserters (39.9) if he surrendered. Zedekiah characteristically hesitated, exacted a promise of secrecy from Jeremiah, and returned him to house arrest (37.21).

of all the women remaining in the house of
the king of Judah being led out to the offi-
cials of the king of Babylon and saying,

'Your trusted friends have
seduced you
and have overcome you;
Now that your feet are stuck in
the mud,
they desert you.'

23 All your wives and your children shall be
led out to the Chaldeans, and you yourself
shall not escape from their hand, but shall
be seized by the king of Babylon; and this
city shall be burned with fire."
24 Then Zedekiah said to Jeremiah,
"Do not let anyone else know of this con-
versation, or you will die. 25 If the officials
should hear that I have spoken with you,
and they should come and say to you, 'Just
tell us what you said to the king; do not
conceal it from us, or we will put you to
death. What did the king say to you?'
26 then you shall say to them, 'I was pre-
senting my plea to the king not to send
me back to the house of Jonathan to die
there.' " 27 All the officials did come to Jere-
miah and questioned him; and he answered
them in the very words the king had com-
manded. So they stopped questioning him,
for the conversation had not been over-
heard. 28 And Jeremiah remained in the
court of the guard until the day that Jerusa-
lem was taken.

39 In the ninth year of King Zedekiah
of Judah, in the tenth month, King
Nebuchadrezzar of Babylon and all his
army came against Jerusalem and besieged
it; 2 in the eleventh year of Zedekiah, in
the fourth month, on the ninth day of the
month, a breach was made in the city.
3 When Jerusalem was taken,[a] all the offi-
cials of the king of Babylon came and sat in

a This clause has been transposed from 38.28

39.1–40.6: Jeremiah and the fall of Jerusalem. 39.1–14: Vv. 1–10 summarize 52.4–16 (2 Kings 25.1–12), adding the names of Babylonian officials (v. 3). **1–2:** *The ninth . . . eleventh year,* the siege of Jerusalem began in January 587 and lasted until July 586 BCE when the walls were breached. **3:** Alternative reading of v. 3: ". . . Nergal-sharezer the Simmagir, Nebushazban the chief court official, Nergal-sharzer the Rabmag . . ." Simmagir and Rabmag are titles of Babylonian officials. Cf. v. 13.

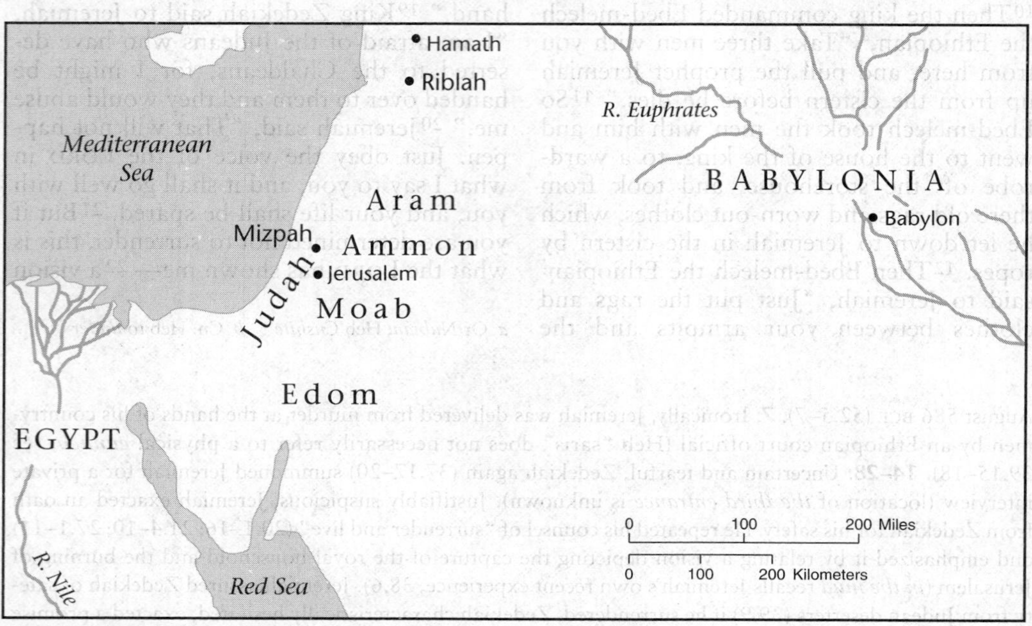

Chs 39, 52: Babylon and Judah.

the middle gate: Nergal-sharezer, Samgar-
nebo, Sarsechim the Rabsaris, Nergal-
sharezer the Rabmag, with all the rest of
the officials of the king of Babylon. 4 When
King Zedekiah of Judah and all the soldiers
saw them, they fled, going out of the city at
night by way of the king's garden through
the gate between the two walls; and they
went toward the Arabah. 5 But the army of
the Chaldeans pursued them, and overtook
Zedekiah in the plains of Jericho; and when
they had taken him, they brought him up to
King Nebuchadrezzar of Babylon, at Rib-
lah, in the land of Hamath; and he passed
sentence on him. 6 The king of Babylon
slaughtered the sons of Zedekiah at Riblah
before his eyes; also the king of Babylon
slaughtered all the nobles of Judah. 7 He
put out the eyes of Zedekiah, and bound
him in fetters to take him to Babylon. 8 The
Chaldeans burned the king's house and the
houses of the people, and broke down the
walls of Jerusalem. 9 Then Nebuzaradan
the captain of the guard exiled to Babylon
the rest of the people who were left in the
city, those who had deserted to him, and
the people who remained. 10 Nebuzaradan
the captain of the guard left in the land of
Judah some of the poor people who owned
nothing, and gave them vineyards and
fields at the same time.
11 King Nebuchadrezzar of Babylon
gave command concerning Jeremiah
through Nebuzaradan, the captain of the
guard, saying, 12 "Take him, look after him
well and do him no harm, but deal with
him as he may ask you." 13 So Nebuzara-
dan the captain of the guard, Nebushazban
the Rabsaris, Nergal-sharezer the Rabmag,
and all the chief officers of the king of Bab-
ylon sent 14 and took Jeremiah from the
court of the guard. They entrusted him to
Gedaliah son of Ahikam son of Shaphan to
be brought home. So he stayed with his
own people.
15 The word of the LORD came to Jere-
miah while he was confined in the court of
the guard: 16 Go and say to Ebed-melech
the Ethiopian:[a] Thus says the LORD of
hosts, the God of Israel: I am going to fulfill
my words against this city for evil and not
for good, and they shall be accomplished in
your presence on that day. 17 But I will save
you on that day, says the LORD, and you
shall not be handed over to those whom
you dread. 18 For I will surely save you, and
you shall not fall by the sword; but you
shall have your life as a prize of war, be-
cause you have trusted in me, says the
LORD.

40 The word that came to Jeremiah
from the LORD after Nebuzaradan
the captain of the guard had let him go
from Ramah, when he took him bound in
fetters along with all the captives of Jerusa-

a Or *Nubian;* Heb *Cushite*

4–5: *Arabah,* the dry wilderness east of Jerusalem in the Jordan valley. *Chaldeans,* Babylonians. *Riblah, in the land of Hamath,* a city on the Orontes River in the Lebanese Beqaa Valley. Riblah was strategically important in controlling movement between Egypt, northern Syria, and Mesopotamia. **8:** According to 52.6–14, the sack of Jerusalem occurred a month after its capture. **11–14:** Cf. 40.1–6. **15–18:** A continuation of 38.27. **40.1–6:** *Ramah* (31.15) was a transit point for deportees. Jeremiah was allowed to choose exile or residence in Judah. Choosing the latter, he was placed in the custody of Gedaliah, the newly appointed governor of Judah with whose family Jeremiah had long been friendly (26.24; 36.10). In fact, Gedaliah's family figures prominently, not only in the life of Jeremiah, but also at the Judean court and in relation to the Deuteronomic reform. Gedaliah's grandfather, Shaphan, delivered the newly discovered law scroll to King Josiah (2 Kings 22.3–13). Gedaliah's father, Ahikam, a member of the delegation sent to the prophetess Huldah (2 Kings 22.12–14), was Jeremiah's champion as well (26.24). Gedaliah's uncle Gemariah (36.25) and first cousin Micaiah (36.25) play similar, though unsuccessful, roles with regard to Jeremiah's scroll that was read to king Jehoiakim. Another of Gedaliah's uncles, Elasah, delivered Jeremiah's letter to the exiles (29.3). The close connection between this aristocratic family, the Deuteronomic/Deuteronomistic movement, and the prose of the book of Jeremiah is intriguing.

lem and Judah who were being exiled to Babylon. 2The captain of the guard took Jeremiah and said to him, "The LORD your God threatened this place with this disaster; 3and now the LORD has brought it about, and has done as he said, because all of you sinned against the LORD and did not obey his voice. Therefore this thing has come upon you. 4Now look, I have just released you today from the fetters on your hands. If you wish to come with me to Babylon, come, and I will take good care of you; but if you do not wish to come with me to Babylon, you need not come. See, the whole land is before you; go wherever you think it good and right to go. 5If you remain,[a] then return to Gedaliah son of Ahikam son of Shaphan, whom the king of Babylon appointed governor of the towns of Judah, and stay with him among the people; or go wherever you think it right to go." So the captain of the guard gave him an allowance of food and a present, and let him go. 6Then Jeremiah went to Gedaliah son of Ahikam at Mizpah, and stayed with him among the people who were left in the land.

7 When all the leaders of the forces in the open country and their troops heard that the king of Babylon had appointed Gedaliah son of Ahikam governor in the land, and had committed to him men, women, and children, those of the poorest of the land who had not been taken into exile to Babylon, 8they went to Gedaliah at Mizpah—Ishmael son of Nethaniah, Johanan son of Kareah, Seraiah son of Tanhumeth, the sons of Ephai the Netophathite, Jezaniah son of the Maacathite, they and their troops. 9Gedaliah son of Ahikam son of Shaphan swore to them and their troops, saying, "Do not be afraid to serve the Chaldeans. Stay in the land and serve the king of Babylon, and it shall go well with you. 10As for me, I am staying at Mizpah to represent you before the Chaldeans who come to us; but as for you, gather wine and summer fruits and oil, and store them in your vessels, and live in the towns that you have taken over." 11Likewise, when all the Judeans who were in Moab and among the Ammonites and in Edom and in other lands heard that the king of Babylon had left a remnant in Judah and had appointed Gedaliah son of Ahikam son of Shaphan as governor over them, 12then all the Judeans returned from all the places to which they had been scattered and came to the land of Judah, to Gedaliah at Mizpah; and they gathered wine and summer fruits in great abundance.

13 Now Johanan son of Kareah and all the leaders of the forces in the open country came to Gedaliah at Mizpah 14and said to him, "Are you at all aware that Baalis king of the Ammonites has sent Ishmael son of Nethaniah to take your life?" But Gedaliah son of Ahikam would not believe them. 15Then Johanan son of Kareah spoke secretly to Gedaliah at Mizpah, "Please let me go and kill Ishmael son of Nethaniah, and no one else will know. Why should he

a Syr: Meaning of Heb uncertain

40.7–44.30: Hope for the future of God's people lies only with the Babylonian exiles. This section, like ch 24 and 29.16–20, demonstrates that those who were not taken into exile in Babylon, and especially those idolatrous Jews who fled to Egypt, continue to be disobedient to the covenant and, therefore, are subject to judgment. The elect remnant, the seed for God's people in the future, has gone into exile in Babylon.

40.7–41.18: The third revolt. 40.7–12: Gedaliah assured his countrymen that he would represent them before the Babylonians (*Chaldeans*) and urged them to return to their fields and cities. Benjamin seems to have been largely spared (32.1–8), and *Mizpah* (probably Tell on-Nasbeh, 12 km [7 mi] north of Jerusalem) became the provincial capital. *They gathered wine and summer fruits in great abundance,* at first, Jeremiah's (and Gedaliah's) assurance that life in the land could and would go on seemed confirmed. **40.13–41.3:** After an unspecified time (some scholars regard Gedaliah's assassination as the motivation for the punitive third deportation in 582 BCE mentioned in 52.30) and with encouragement from Baalis of Ammon (for political reasons), Ishmael, a member of the royal family (as Gedaliah was not), plotted

take your life, so that all the Judeans who
are gathered around you would be scat-
tered, and the remnant of Judah would per-
ish?" 16 But Gedaliah son of Ahikam said to
Johanan son of Kareah, "Do not do such a
thing, for you are telling a lie about Ish-
mael."

41 In the seventh month, Ishmael son
of Nethaniah son of Elishama, of
the royal family, one of the chief officers of
the king, came with ten men to Gedaliah
son of Ahikam, at Mizpah. As they ate
bread together there at Mizpah, 2 Ishmael
son of Nethaniah and the ten men with him
got up and struck down Gedaliah son of
Ahikam son of Shaphan with the sword
and killed him, because the king of Babylon
had appointed him governor in the land.
3 Ishmael also killed all the Judeans who
were with Gedaliah at Mizpah, and the
Chaldean soldiers who happened to be
there.

4 On the day after the murder of Gedali-
ah, before anyone knew of it, 5 eighty men
arrived from Shechem and Shiloh and Sa-
maria, with their beards shaved and their
clothes torn, and their bodies gashed,
bringing grain offerings and incense to
present at the temple of the LORD. 6 And
Ishmael son of Nethaniah came out from
Mizpah to meet them, weeping as he came.
As he met them, he said to them, "Come
to Gedaliah son of Ahikam." 7 When they
reached the middle of the city, Ishmael son
of Nethaniah and the men with him slaugh-
tered them, and threw them[a] into a cistern.
8 But there were ten men among them who
said to Ishmael, "Do not kill us, for we
have stores of wheat, barley, oil, and honey
hidden in the fields." So he refrained, and
did not kill them along with their compan-
ions.

9 Now the cistern into which Ishmael
had thrown all the bodies of the men whom
he had struck down was the large cistern[b]
that King Asa had made for defense against
King Baasha of Israel; Ishmael son of Neth-
aniah filled that cistern with those whom
he had killed. 10 Then Ishmael took captive
all the rest of the people who were in Miz-
pah, the king's daughters and all the people
who were left at Mizpah, whom Nebuzara-
dan, the captain of the guard, had commit-
ted to Gedaliah son of Ahikam. Ishmael
son of Nethaniah took them captive and set
out to cross over to the Ammonites.

11 But when Johanan son of Kareah and
all the leaders of the forces with him heard
of all the crimes that Ishmael son of Netha-
niah had done, 12 they took all their men
and went to fight against Ishmael son of
Nethaniah. They came upon him at the
great pool that is in Gibeon. 13 And when
all the people who were with Ishmael saw
Johanan son of Kareah and all the leaders
of the forces with him, they were glad. 14 So
all the people whom Ishmael had carried
away captive from Mizpah turned around
and came back, and went to Johanan son of
Kareah. 15 But Ishmael son of Nethaniah
escaped from Johanan with eight men, and
went to the Ammonites. 16 Then Johanan

a Syr: Heb lacks *and threw them*; compare verse 9
b Gk: Heb *whom he had killed by the hand of Gedaliah*

Gedaliah's assassination. **41.1:** *As they ate bread,* ancient rules of hospitality and table fellowship bound host and guest to faithfulness toward one another. Ishmael's act was therefore particularly heinous. **3:** *Chaldean,* Babylonian. **4–10:** The next day Ishmael intercepted a group from the North on a pilgrimage to Jerusalem. Significantly, worship continued in the Temple in accordance with Deuteronomy's law of cult centralization (Deut 12.5–6) even after the Babylonians pillaged it. Ishmael slaughtered all but ten, who bought their lives with *stores* of food. After casting the bodies into an old cistern (1 Kings 15.22), the assassins took the remaining people in Mizpah and headed for Ammon. **11–18:** An avenging group under Johanan overtook Ishmael at Gibeon (5 km [3 mi] southwest of Mizpah; 2 Sam 2.13); Ishmael and eight conspirators escaped to Ammon (40.14), but their captives were freed. Fearing Babylonian (*Chaldean*) reprisals, Johanan's group turned toward Egypt, encamping en route at *Geruth Chimham* (perhaps "Chimham's Inn") near Bethlehem, south of Jerusalem.

son of Kareah and all the leaders of the
forces with him took all the rest of the peo-
ple whom Ishmael son of Nethaniah had
carried away captive[a] from Mizpah after
he had slain Gedaliah son of Ahikam—sol-
diers, women, children, and eunuchs,
whom Johanan brought back from Gibe-
on.[b] 17 And they set out, and stopped at
Geruth Chimham near Bethlehem, intend-
ing to go to Egypt 18 because of the Chalde-
ans; for they were afraid of them, because
Ishmael son of Nethaniah had killed Geda-
liah son of Ahikam, whom the king of Bab-
ylon had made governor over the land.

42 Then all the commanders of the
forces, and Johanan son of Kareah
and Azariah[c] son of Hoshaiah, and all the
people from the least to the greatest, ap-
proached 2 the prophet Jeremiah and said,
"Be good enough to listen to our plea, and
pray to the LORD your God for us—for all
this remnant. For there are only a few of us
left out of many, as your eyes can see. 3 Let
the LORD your God show us where we
should go and what we should do." 4 The
prophet Jeremiah said to them, "Very well:
I am going to pray to the LORD your God
as you request, and whatever the LORD an-
swers you I will tell you; I will keep nothing
back from you." 5 They in their turn said to
Jeremiah, "May the LORD be a true and
faithful witness against us if we do not act
according to everything that the LORD your
God sends us through you. 6 Whether it is
good or bad, we will obey the voice of the
LORD our God to whom we are sending
you, in order that it may go well with us
when we obey the voice of the LORD our
God."

7 At the end of ten days the word of the
LORD came to Jeremiah. 8 Then he sum-
moned Johanan son of Kareah and all the
commanders of the forces who were with
him, and all the people from the least to the
greatest, 9 and said to them, "Thus says the
LORD, the God of Israel, to whom you sent
me to present your plea before him: 10 If
you will only remain in this land, then I will
build you up and not pull you down; I will
plant you, and not pluck you up; for I am
sorry for the disaster that I have brought
upon you. 11 Do not be afraid of the king of
Babylon, as you have been; do not be afraid
of him, says the LORD, for I am with you,
to save you and to rescue you from his
hand. 12 I will grant you mercy, and he will
have mercy on you and restore you to your
native soil. 13 But if you continue to say,
'We will not stay in this land,' thus disobey-
ing the voice of the LORD your God 14 and
saying, 'No, we will go to the land of
Egypt, where we shall not see war, or hear
the sound of the trumpet, or be hungry for
bread, and there we will stay,' 15 then hear
the word of the LORD, O remnant of Ju-
dah. Thus says the LORD of hosts, the God
of Israel: If you are determined to enter
Egypt and go to settle there, 16 then the
sword that you fear shall overtake you
there, in the land of Egypt; and the famine
that you dread shall follow close after you
into Egypt; and there you shall die. 17 All
the people who have determined to go to
Egypt to settle there shall die by the sword,
by famine, and by pestilence; they shall
have no remnant or survivor from the di-
saster that I am bringing upon them.

18 "For thus says the LORD of hosts, the
God of Israel: Just as my anger and my
wrath were poured out on the inhabitants
of Jerusalem, so my wrath will be poured
out on you when you go to Egypt. You

a Cn: Heb *whom he recovered from Ishmael son of Nethaniah* *b* Meaning of Heb uncertain
c Gk: Heb *Jezaniah*

42.1–43.7: Flight to Egypt. 42.1–6: Jeremiah was evidently one of the captives freed by Johanan (41.16). He was asked to intercede for the group, who were uncertain what to do. **7–22:** Jeremiah did not speak on the LORD's behalf until given a message to deliver: To remain was God's will and they would receive God's blessing; to flee would only bring suffering. **10:** See 1.10, etc. Jeremiah offered this *remnant of Judah* (vv. 15,19) the same chance for restoration offered to the Babylonian exiles (29.14). **18–22:** Jeremiah's message anticipates the people's disobedience. Despite their protestations to the contrary (vv. 1–6), they have already decided to go to Egypt. **18:** See 44.12. **43.1–7:** Jeremiah was accused

shall become an object of execration and
horror, of cursing and ridicule. You shall
see this place no more. 19 The LORD has
said to you, O remnant of Judah, Do not
go to Egypt. Be well aware that I have
warned you today 20 that you have made a
fatal mistake. For you yourselves sent me to
the LORD your God, saying, 'Pray for us to
the LORD our God, and whatever the LORD
our God says, tell us and we will do it.'
21 So I have told you today, but you have
not obeyed the voice of the LORD your God
in anything that he sent me to tell you. 22 Be
well aware, then, that you shall die by the
sword, by famine, and by pestilence in the
place where you desire to go and settle."

43 When Jeremiah finished speaking to
all the people all these words of the
LORD their God, with which the LORD
their God had sent him to them, 2 Azariah
son of Hoshaiah and Johanan son of Kare-
ah and all the other insolent men said to
Jeremiah, "You are telling a lie. The LORD
our God did not send you to say, 'Do not
go to Egypt to settle there'; 3 but Baruch son
of Neriah is inciting you against us, to hand
us over to the Chaldeans, in order that they
may kill us or take us into exile in Bab-
ylon." 4 So Johanan son of Kareah and all
the commanders of the forces and all the
people did not obey the voice of the LORD,
to stay in the land of Judah. 5 But Johanan
son of Kareah and all the commanders of
the forces took all the remnant of Judah
who had returned to settle in the land of
Judah from all the nations to which they
had been driven— 6 the men, the women,
the children, the princesses, and everyone
whom Nebuzaradan the captain of the
guard had left with Gedaliah son of Ahi-
kam son of Shaphan; also the prophet Jere-
miah and Baruch son of Neriah. 7 And they
came into the land of Egypt, for they did
not obey the voice of the LORD. And they
arrived at Tahpanhes.

8 Then the word of the LORD came to
Jeremiah in Tahpanhes: 9 Take some large
stones in your hands, and bury them in the
clay pavement[a] that is at the entrance to
Pharaoh's palace in Tahpanhes. Let the Ju-
deans see you do it, 10 and say to them,
Thus says the LORD of hosts, the God of
Israel: I am going to send and take my ser-
vant King Nebuchadrezzar of Babylon, and
he[b] will set his throne above these stones
that I have buried, and he will spread his
royal canopy over them. 11 He shall come
and ravage the land of Egypt, giving

those who are destined for pestilence,
to pestilence,
and those who are destined for
captivity, to captivity,
and those who are destined for the
sword, to the sword.

12 He[c] shall kindle a fire in the temples of
the gods of Egypt; and he shall burn them
and carry them away captive; and he shall
pick clean the land of Egypt, as a shepherd
picks his cloak clean of vermin; and he shall
depart from there safely. 13 He shall break
the obelisks of Heliopolis, which is in the
land of Egypt; and the temples of the gods
of Egypt he shall burn with fire.

a Meaning of Heb uncertain *b* Gk Syr: Heb *I*
c Gk Syr Vg: Heb *I*

of being unduly influenced by Baruch, and his oracle was not regarded as God's word. The people decide to go to Egypt, taking Jeremiah and Baruch with them. **5–6:** These verses give the impression that all Judeans not taken into exile in Babylon fled with Johanan to Egypt, and Judah was left unpopulated. Other traditions also make this false assumption to emphasize the degree of the disaster that befell Judah. **7:** *Tahpanhes*, see 2.14–19n.

43.8–44.30: Jeremiah in Egypt. 43.8–13: This symbolic act and accompanying oracle is intended to show that Egypt is no safe refuge from Nebuchadrezzar ("my servant," 25.9; 27.6), who led a successful raid against Amasis (Ahmosis II) in 568/567 BCE, some years later than this oracle (46.13–26). **11:** 15.2. **13:** *Heliopolis* (also called On; Gen 41.45), 10 km (6 mi) northeast of Cairo; ancient center of the worship of sun-god Re (see Isa 19.18). *Obelisks*, monuments, slightly tapered square granite shafts, capped by

44 The word that came to Jeremiah for
all the Judeans living in the land of
Egypt, at Migdol, at Tahpanhes, at Mem-
phis, and in the land of Pathros, 2 Thus says
the LORD of hosts, the God of Israel: You
yourselves have seen all the disaster that I
have brought on Jerusalem and on all the
towns of Judah. Look at them; today they
are a desolation, without an inhabitant in
them, 3 because of the wickedness that they
committed, provoking me to anger, in that
they went to make offerings and serve other
gods that they had not known, neither they,
nor you, nor your ancestors. 4 Yet I persis-
tently sent to you all my servants the
prophets, saying, "I beg you not to do this
abominable thing that I hate!" 5 But they
did not listen or incline their ear, to turn
from their wickedness and make no offer-
ings to other gods. 6 So my wrath and my
anger were poured out and kindled in the
towns of Judah and in the streets of Jerusa-
lem; and they became a waste and a desola-
tion, as they still are today. 7 And now thus
says the LORD God of hosts, the God of
Israel: Why are you doing such great harm
to yourselves, to cut off man and woman,
child and infant, from the midst of Judah,
leaving yourselves without a remnant?
8 Why do you provoke me to anger with the
works of your hands, making offerings to
other gods in the land of Egypt where you
have come to settle? Will you be cut off and
become an object of cursing and ridicule
among all the nations of the earth? 9 Have
you forgotten the crimes of your ancestors,
of the kings of Judah, of their[a] wives, your
own crimes and those of your wives, which
they committed in the land of Judah and
in the streets of Jerusalem? 10 They have
shown no contrition or fear to this day, nor
have they walked in my law and my stat-
utes that I set before you and before your
ancestors.

11 Therefore thus says the LORD of
hosts, the God of Israel: I am determined to
bring disaster on you, to bring all Judah to
an end. 12 I will take the remnant of Judah
who are determined to come to the land of
Egypt to settle, and they shall perish, every-
one; in the land of Egypt they shall fall; by
the sword and by famine they shall perish;
from the least to the greatest, they shall die
by the sword and by famine; and they shall
become an object of execration and horror,
of cursing and ridicule. 13 I will punish
those who live in the land of Egypt, as I
have punished Jerusalem, with the sword,
with famine, and with pestilence, 14 so that
none of the remnant of Judah who have
come to settle in the land of Egypt shall
escape or survive or return to the land of
Judah. Although they long to go back to
live there, they shall not go back, except
some fugitives.

15 Then all the men who were aware

a Heb *his*

a pyramidon. **44.1–14:** This oracle, addressed to the Jewish Diaspora in Egypt, is Jeremiah's warning against repeating the mistakes of their fathers in Judah and suffering the consequences (cf. 42.14–18). It has three parts: vv. 2–6, the example of Judah's recent destruction, described in stereotypical Jeremianic prose (cf. 7.8–34; 11.6–13; etc.); vv. 7–10, the charge that the remnant in Egypt continues the practices that led to the Babylonian catastrophe, again stereotypical (cf. 7; 11; 17.19–27; 25.18; 34.8–22; etc.); and vv. 11–14, the verdict, destruction for the Egyptian remnant (cf. 5.12; 11.22; 14.12–18; 15.2; 16.4; 18.21; 21.7–9; 24.10, etc.). **1:** *Migdol,* just north of present day Tell el-Heir, east of *Tahpanhes* (43.7); *Memphis,* 2.14–16n. *Pathros,* "Land of the South," upper (i.e., southern) Egypt, where perhaps there was already a Jewish colony at Elephantine, known from discoveries of Aramaic papyri dating from the fifth century BCE. **13–14:** In keeping with the stance of the prose in the latter portions of the book (24.8) which favors the Babylonian exile community, the text announces the destruction of the Jews who went into voluntary exile in Egypt. They are lost to Judah's future. **15–28:** The refugees return to the worship of the *queen of heaven* (see 7.16–20n.). First introduced, presumably, by Manasseh (2 Kings 21.1–18), suppressed by Josiah (2 Kings 23.4–14), and restored by Jehoiakim (2 Kings 23.36–24.7), the ritual was especially popular among women. Offerings included wine and star-shaped or crescent-shaped cakes or figurines bearing the *image* of the goddess. As evidenced by fifth-century BCE documents from Elephantine (v. 1n.), at least

that their wives had been making offerings
to other gods, and all the women who
stood by, a great assembly, all the people
who lived in Pathros in the land of Egypt,
answered Jeremiah: 16 “As for the word
that you have spoken to us in the name of
the LORD, we are not going to listen to you.
17 Instead, we will do everything that we
have vowed, make offerings to the queen of
heaven and pour out libations to her, just
as we and our ancestors, our kings and our
officials, used to do in the towns of Judah
and in the streets of Jerusalem. We used to
have plenty of food, and prospered, and
saw no misfortune. 18 But from the time we
stopped making offerings to the queen of
heaven and pouring out libations to her, we
have lacked everything and have perished
by the sword and by famine.” 19 And the
women said,[a] “Indeed we will go on mak-
ing offerings to the queen of heaven and
pouring out libations to her; do you think
that we made cakes for her, marked with
her image, and poured out libations to her
without our husbands' being involved?”

20 Then Jeremiah said to all the people,
men and women, all the people who were
giving him this answer: 21 “As for the offer-
ings that you made in the towns of Judah
and in the streets of Jerusalem, you and
your ancestors, your kings and your offi-
cials, and the people of the land, did not the
LORD remember them? Did it not come
into his mind? 22 The LORD could no longer
bear the sight of your evil doings, the
abominations that you committed; there-
fore your land became a desolation and a
waste and a curse, without inhabitant, as it
is to this day. 23 It is because you burned
offerings, and because you sinned against
the LORD and did not obey the voice of the
LORD or walk in his law and in his statutes
and in his decrees, that this disaster has be-
fallen you, as is still evident today.”

24 Jeremiah said to all the people and all
the women, “Hear the word of the LORD,
all you Judeans who are in the land of
Egypt, 25 Thus says the LORD of hosts, the
God of Israel: You and your wives have
accomplished in deeds what you declared
in words, saying, ‘We are determined to
perform the vows that we have made, to
make offerings to the queen of heaven and
to pour out libations to her.’ By all means,
keep your vows and make your libations!
26 Therefore hear the word of the LORD, all
you Judeans who live in the land of Egypt:
Lo, I swear by my great name, says the
LORD, that my name shall no longer be
pronounced on the lips of any of the people
of Judah in all the land of Egypt, saying,
‘As the Lord GOD lives.’ 27 I am going to
watch over them for harm and not for
good; all the people of Judah who are in the
land of Egypt shall perish by the sword and
by famine, until not one is left. 28 And those
who escape the sword shall return from the
land of Egypt to the land of Judah, few in
number; and all the remnant of Judah, who
have come to the land of Egypt to settle,
shall know whose words will stand, mine
or theirs! 29 This shall be the sign to you,
says the LORD, that I am going to punish
you in this place, in order that you may
know that my words against you will surely
be carried out: 30 Thus says the LORD, I am
going to give Pharaoh Hophra, king of
Egypt, into the hands of his enemies, those
who seek his life, just as I gave King Zede-
kiah of Judah into the hand of King Nebu-
chadrezzar of Babylon, his enemy who
sought his life.”

45 The word that the prophet Jeremiah
spoke to Baruch son of Neriah,

a Compare Syr: Heb lacks *And the women said*

some Jews in Egypt practiced a form of Yahwism that included worship of the goddess Anat-Yahu (“Anat of the LORD”). **27:** *Watch over,* 1.12; 31.28. **29–30:** *Pharaoh Hophra* (Apries, 589–570; 37.5) was assassinated by Ahmosis II (Amasis, 570–526 BCE), a former court official, co-regent for three years, and founder of the Twenty-seventh (Libyan) Dynasty.

45.1–5: God's word to Baruch. *Baruch* recalls God's assurance to him of physical deliverance, given

when he wrote these words in a scroll at the
dictation of Jeremiah, in the fourth year
of King Jehoiakim son of Josiah of Judah:
2 Thus says the LORD, the God of Israel, to
you, O Baruch: 3 You said, "Woe is me!
The LORD has added sorrow to my pain; I
am weary with my groaning, and I find no
rest." 4 Thus you shall say to him, "Thus
says the LORD: I am going to break down
what I have built, and pluck up what I have
planted—that is, the whole land. 5 And
you, do you seek great things for yourself?
Do not seek them; for I am going to bring
disaster upon all flesh, says the LORD; but
I will give you your life as a prize of war in
every place to which you may go."

46 The word of the LORD that came to
the prophet Jeremiah concerning
the nations.
2 Concerning Egypt, about the army of
Pharaoh Neco, king of Egypt, which was
by the river Euphrates at Carchemish and
which King Nebuchadrezzar of Babylon

in the fourth year of Jehoiakim (605 BCE; cf. 36.1). *These words in a scroll,* a superficial reading of 45.1 would suggest that the material falling between chs 36 and 45 constituted the second scroll Baruch wrote at Jeremiah's dictation. The events narrated, however, took place after Jehoiakim's reign. This anachronism suggests the fictive character of the Baruch scroll or scrolls. **4:** See 1.10, etc. For *your life as a prize of war,* see 21.9; 38.2; 39.18.

46.1–51.64: Oracles against foreign nations (cf. Isa 13–23; Ezek 25–32). There are no widely accepted criteria for determining if these oracles are by Jeremiah. Comparison of the Hebrew and the Greek texts of the book (see Introduction and 25.13n.) indicates that the oracles once comprised an independent unit with its own composition history and that, in both versions of the book, these oracles play a significant theological role in relation to the theme of Jeremiah's ministry to the nations. The God who brought Babylon against his people in judgment for their sins also judges Egypt and Babylon. The headings (46.2,13; 47.1; 48.1; etc.) were added after the events detailed in the oracles. Like the book of Jeremiah

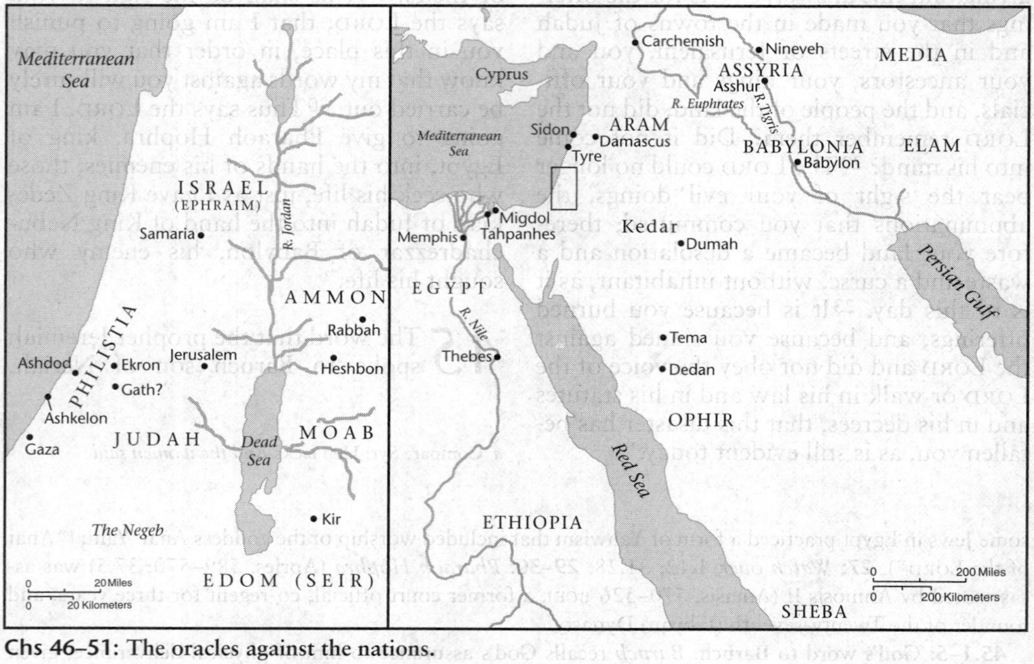

Chs 46–51: The oracles against the nations.

defeated in the fourth year of King Jehoia-
kim son of Josiah of Judah:
3 Prepare buckler and shield,
and advance for battle!
4 Harness the horses;
mount the steeds!
Take your stations with your helmets,
whet your lances,
put on your coats of mail!
5 Why do I see them terrified?
They have fallen back;
their warriors are beaten down,
and have fled in haste.
They do not look back—
terror is all around!
says the LORD.
6 The swift cannot flee away,
nor can the warrior escape;
in the north by the river Euphrates
they have stumbled and fallen.

7 Who is this, rising like the Nile,
like rivers whose waters surge?
8 Egypt rises like the Nile,
like rivers whose waters surge.
It said, Let me rise, let me cover the
earth,
let me destroy cities and their
inhabitants.
9 Advance, O horses,
and dash madly, O chariots!
Let the warriors go forth:
Ethiopia[a] and Put who carry
the shield,
the Ludim, who draw[b] the bow.
10 That day is the day of the Lord GOD
of hosts,
a day of retribution,
to gain vindication from his foes.
The sword shall devour and be sated,
and drink its fill of their blood.
For the Lord GOD of hosts holds
a sacrifice
in the land of the north by the river
Euphrates.
11 Go up to Gilead, and take balm,
O virgin daughter Egypt!
In vain you have used many
medicines;
there is no healing for you.
12 The nations have heard of
your shame,
and the earth is full of your cry;
for warrior has stumbled against
warrior;
both have fallen together.

13 The word that the LORD spoke to the
prophet Jeremiah about the coming of King
Nebuchadrezzar of Babylon to attack the
land of Egypt:
14 Declare in Egypt, and proclaim
in Migdol;
proclaim in Memphis and
Tahpanhes;
Say, "Take your stations and
be ready,

a Or *Nubia*; Heb *Cush* *b* Cn: Heb *who grasp, who draw*

as a whole, these prophecies function not as predictions of the future, but as theological interpretations of history.

46.1: Introduction (1.2; 14.1); see 25.15–38.

46.2–28: Against Egypt. 2–12: In May or June 605 BCE crown Prince Nebuchadrezzar of Babylon defeated Neco II of Egypt at Carchemish, on the northern Euphrates 95 km (60 mi) west of Haran (Gen 11.31), the last capital of Assyria, and pursued him to the borders of Egypt. Like the Nile (vv. 7–8), Egypt was preparing to inundate the lands to the north. Instead she was grievously wounded, driven back, and humiliated before the nations. **5:** *Terror is all around,* 6.25; 20.3,10. **8:** Typically, the oracles against the nations in Jeremiah fault the nations for their arrogance. **9:** *Put,* Cyrene in Libya. *The Ludim,* probably a people from north Africa; Gen 10.13. **11:** *O virgin daughter Egypt,* the prophets, in keeping with ancient Near Eastern literary practice, often address a nation or its capital personified as a woman (cf. 46.19,24; 48.2,4,9,18, etc.). *Gilead . . . balm,* see 8.22n. **13–26:** This oracle may refer to events of 604 BCE, when Babylon captured Ashkelon, or of 587 BCE, when Egypt attempted to relieve the siege of Jerusalem (37.7). The poetic section refers to lower (northern) Egypt (*Memphis*); the prose to upper (southern) Egypt (*Thebes*). *Migdal . . . Memphis . . . Tahpanhes,* see 2.14–19n.; 44.1n. **15:** *Apis,* bull-god

for the sword shall devour those
around you."
15 Why has Apis fled?[a]
Why did your bull not stand?
—because the LORD thrust
him down.
16 Your multitude stumbled[b] and fell,
and one said to another,[c]
"Come, let us go back to our
own people
and to the land of our birth,
because of the destroying sword."
17 Give Pharaoh, king of Egypt,
the name
"Braggart who missed his chance."

18 As I live, says the King,
whose name is the LORD of hosts,
one is coming
like Tabor among the mountains,
and like Carmel by the sea.
19 Pack your bags for exile,
sheltered daughter Egypt!
For Memphis shall become a waste,
a ruin, without inhabitant.

20 A beautiful heifer is Egypt—
a gadfly from the north lights upon
her.
21 Even her mercenaries in her midst
are like fatted calves;
they too have turned and fled
together,
they did not stand;
for the day of their calamity has come
upon them,
the time of their punishment.

22 She makes a sound like a snake
gliding away;
for her enemies march in force,
and come against her with axes,
like those who fell trees.
23 They shall cut down her forest,
says the LORD,
though it is impenetrable,
because they are more numerous
than locusts;
they are without number.
24 Daughter Egypt shall be put
to shame;
she shall be handed over to a
people from the north.

25 The LORD of hosts, the God of Israel, said: See, I am bringing punishment upon Amon of Thebes, and Pharaoh, and Egypt and her gods and her kings, upon Pharaoh and those who trust in him.
26 I will hand them over to those who seek their life, to King Nebuchadrezzar of Babylon and his officers. Afterward Egypt shall be inhabited as in the days of old, says the LORD.

27 But as for you, have no fear, my
servant Jacob,
and do not be dismayed, O Israel;
for I am going to save you from
far away,
and your offspring from the land of
their captivity.
Jacob shall return and have quiet and
ease,
and no one shall make him afraid.
28 As for you, have no fear, my servant
Jacob,
says the LORD,
for I am with you.
I will make an end of all the nations
among which I have banished you,
but I will not make an end of you!
I will chastise you in just measure,
and I will by no means leave you
unpunished.

a Gk: Heb *Why was it swept away* *b* Gk: Meaning of Heb uncertain *c* Gk: Heb *and fell one to another and they said*

of (southern) Egypt. *Tabor,* mountain rising above the plain of Jezreel (Esdraelon; Josh 19.22). **17:** The name given Pharaoh may be a play on words on the name of Pharaoh Apries. **18:** *Carmel,* mountain at the end of the plain of Jezreel, projecting into the Mediterranean (Josh 19.26). **25:** *Amon of Thebes,* Egyptian sun god. **27–28:** A doublet of 30.10–11, which here contrasts the destruction of Egypt (except 28b) and the reconstruction of all Israel.

47 The word of the LORD that came to the prophet Jeremiah concerning the Philistines, before Pharaoh attacked Gaza:

2 Thus says the LORD:
See, waters are rising out of the north
and shall become an overflowing torrent;
they shall overflow the land and all that fills it,
the city and those who live in it.
People shall cry out,
and all the inhabitants of the land shall wail.
3 At the noise of the stamping of the hoofs of his stallions,
at the clatter of his chariots, at the rumbling of their wheels,
parents do not turn back for children,
so feeble are their hands,
4 because of the day that is coming
to destroy all the Philistines,
to cut off from Tyre and Sidon
every helper that remains.
For the LORD is destroying the Philistines,
the remnant of the coastland of Caphtor.
5 Baldness has come upon Gaza,
Ashkelon is silenced.
O remnant of their power![a]
How long will you gash yourselves?
6 Ah, sword of the LORD!
How long until you are quiet?
Put yourself into your scabbard,
rest and be still!
7 How can it[b] be quiet,
when the LORD has given it an order?
Against Ashkelon and against the seashore—
there he has appointed it.

48 Concerning Moab.

Thus says the LORD of hosts, the God of Israel:
Alas for Nebo, it is laid waste!
Kiriathaim is put to shame, it is taken;
the fortress is put to shame and broken down;
2 the renown of Moab is no more.
In Heshbon they planned evil against her:
"Come, let us cut her off from being a nation!"
You also, O Madmen, shall be brought to silence;[c]
the sword shall pursue you.

3 Hark! a cry from Horonaim,
"Desolation and great destruction!"
4 "Moab is destroyed!"
her little ones cry out.
5 For at the ascent of Luhith
they go[d] up weeping bitterly;

a Gk: Heb *their valley* *b* Gk Vg: Heb *you*
c The place-name *Madmen* sounds like the Hebrew verb *to be silent* *d* Cn: Heb *he goes*

47.1–7: Against the Philistines. Dissimilar from other oracles against the Philistines (Isa 14.29–31; Ezek 25.15–17), this oracle may be associated with Nebuchadrezzar's sack of Ashkelon in 604 BCE (vv. 5,7; 36.9). The heading refers to an Egyptian attack on Gaza (v. 1)—a reminder that editors have shaped this collection of oracles. The Phoenician cities, Tyre and Sidon, were perhaps allied also with the Philistines (v. 4; 27.3). The Philistines were related to the Indo-European inhabitants of Crete (*Caphtor;* see Am 9.7; 2 Sam 8.18). **5:** For similar signs of lamentation, cf. 16.6; 41.5. **6–7:** *Sword of the LORD,* 12.1; 25.31; Isa 34.6.

48.1–47: Against Moab. This long chapter appears to be a sequence of three oracles, vv. 1–13, 14–38, and 39–45. Later editors have expanded each of them, especially vv. 14–38, which has been expanded by material from Isa 15–16. **1–10:** The advance of the enemy (perhaps Nebuchadrezzar), against which Moab is defenseless. **1:** *Nebo,* probably modern Khirbet Mekhayyet, 8 km (5 mi) southwest of Heshbon. The location of Kiriathiam is uncertain. **2:** *Heshbon,* a northern Moabite city, modern Hesban. *Madmen,* unknown; perhaps a corruption of "Dibon" (Isa 15.9). **3–5:** The locations of *Horonaim* and *Luhith* are unknown, but were probably in southern Moabite territory. **7:** *Chemosh,* chief god of Moab (Num

for at the descent of Horonaim
they have heard the distressing cry of anguish.
6 Flee! Save yourselves!
Be like a wild ass[a] in the desert!

7 Surely, because you trusted in your strongholds[b] and your treasures,
you also shall be taken;
Chemosh shall go out into exile,
with his priests and his attendants.
8 The destroyer shall come upon every town,
and no town shall escape;
the valley shall perish,
and the plain shall be destroyed,
as the LORD has spoken.

9 Set aside salt for Moab,
for she will surely fall;
her towns shall become a desolation,
with no inhabitant in them.

10 Accursed is the one who is slack in doing the work of the LORD; and accursed is the one who keeps back the sword from bloodshed.

11 Moab has been at ease from his youth,
settled like wine[c] on its dregs;
he has not been emptied from vessel to vessel,
nor has he gone into exile;
therefore his flavor has remained
and his aroma is unspoiled.
12 Therefore, the time is surely coming, says the LORD, when I shall send to him decanters to decant him, and empty his vessels, and break his[d] jars in pieces. 13 Then Moab shall be ashamed of Chemosh, as the house of Israel was ashamed of Bethel, their confidence.

14 How can you say, "We are heroes
and mighty warriors"?
15 The destroyer of Moab and his towns has come up,
and the choicest of his young men
have gone down to slaughter,
says the King, whose name is the LORD of hosts.
16 The calamity of Moab is near at hand
and his doom approaches swiftly.
17 Mourn over him, all you his neighbors,
and all who know his name;
say, "How the mighty scepter is broken,
the glorious staff!"
18 Come down from glory,
and sit on the parched ground,
enthroned daughter Dibon!
For the destroyer of Moab has come up against you;
he has destroyed your strongholds.
19 Stand by the road and watch,
you inhabitant of Aroer!
Ask the man fleeing and the woman escaping;
say, "What has happened?"
20 Moab is put to shame, for it is broken down;
wail and cry!
Tell it by the Arnon,
that Moab is laid waste.

21 Judgment has come upon the table-
land, upon Holon, and Jahzah, and Meph-
aath, 22 and Dibon, and Nebo, and
Beth-diblathaim, 23 and Kiriathaim, and
Beth-gamul, and Beth-meon, 24 and Keri-
oth, and Bozrah, and all the towns of the
land of Moab, far and near. 25 The horn of

a Gk Aquila: Heb *like Aroer* *b* Gk: Heb *works*
c Heb lacks *like wine* *d* Gk Aquila: Heb *their*

21.29). **9:** On salting cities as a sign of destruction, see Judg 9.45. **10:** An editorial comment. **13:** Perhaps here *Bethel* is the name of a god of Aramaic origin, not the city. **18:** In conventional imagery the Moabite city "daughter Dibon," modern Dibhan, is invited to vacate her queenly throne and sit in the dust in debasement (cf. Isa 47.2–7). **19:** *Aroer,* just southeast of Dibon. **20:** *Arnon,* the major wadi bisecting Moab. **21–24:** Only some of these *towns of the land of Moab* can be located. **25:** *Horn,* a metaphor for strength. **26–27:** Cf. 25.15–29. **28:** *Dove,* Ezek 7.16. **29–38:** Moab, once so proud, is humiliated before

Moab is cut off, and his arm is broken, says
the LORD.
26 Make him drunk, because he magni-
fied himself against the LORD; let Moab
wallow in his vomit; he too shall become
a laughingstock. 27 Israel was a laughing-
stock for you, though he was not caught
among thieves; but whenever you spoke of
him you shook your head!

28 Leave the towns, and live on the rock,
O inhabitants of Moab!
Be like the dove that nests
on the sides of the mouth of
a gorge.
29 We have heard of the pride of
Moab—
he is very proud—
of his loftiness, his pride, and his
arrogance,
and the haughtiness of his heart.
30 I myself know his insolence, says the
LORD;
his boasts are false,
his deeds are false.
31 Therefore I wail for Moab;
I cry out for all Moab;
for the people of Kir-heres I mourn.
32 More than for Jazer I weep for you,
O vine of Sibmah!
Your branches crossed over the sea,
reached as far as Jazer;[a]
upon your summer fruits and
your vintage
the destroyer has fallen.
33 Gladness and joy have been
taken away
from the fruitful land of Moab;
I have stopped the wine from the
wine presses;
no one treads them with shouts of
joy;
the shouting is not the shout of joy.

34 Heshbon and Elealeh cry out;[b] as far
as Jahaz they utter their voice, from Zoar
to Horonaim and Eglath-shelishiyah. For
even the waters of Nimrim have become
desolate. 35 And I will bring to an end in
Moab, says the LORD, those who offer sac-
rifice at a high place and make offerings to
their gods. 36 Therefore my heart moans for
Moab like a flute, and my heart moans like
a flute for the people of Kir-heres; for the
riches they gained have perished.
37 For every head is shaved and every
beard cut off; on all the hands there are
gashes, and on the loins sackcloth. 38 On all
the housetops of Moab and in the squares
there is nothing but lamentation; for I have
broken Moab like a vessel that no one
wants, says the LORD. 39 How it is broken!
How they wail! How Moab has turned his
back in shame! So Moab has become a de-
rision and a horror to all his neighbors.

40 For thus says the LORD:
Look, he shall swoop down like
an eagle,
and spread his wings against Moab;
41 the towns[c] shall be taken
and the strongholds seized.
The hearts of the warriors of Moab,
on that day,
shall be like the heart of a woman
in labor.
42 Moab shall be destroyed as a people,
because he magnified himself
against the LORD.
43 Terror, pit, and trap
are before you, O inhabitants
of Moab!
says the LORD.
44 Everyone who flees from the terror

a Two Mss and Isa 16.8: MT *the sea of Jazer*
b Cn: Heb *From the cry of Heshbon to Elealeh*
c Or *Kerioth*

the conqueror. As a broken pot is discarded, so smitten Moab is accounted worthless. **29–30:** Cf. 46.8n. **31:** *Kir-heres,* modern el-Kerak, the imposing and easily defended Moabite city 18 km (11 mi) east of the Dead Sea. **32–33:** Cf. Isa 16.8–10. *Sibmah,* perhaps modern Qurn el-Kibsh, 8 km (5 mi) southwest of Hesban. *Jazer,* a city of the Moabite plateau, located to the west of modern Amman. **34:** Cf. Isa 15.4–6. **36:** Cf. Isa 16.11. **37:** Cf. Isa 15.2–3. **38:** Cf. Isa 15.3. **39–45:** God's judgment against Moab. This oracle quotes and alludes to several other Moab oracles and songs and may be an editorial composition. **40–42:** Cf. 49.22. **43–44:** Cf. Isa 24.17–18. **45–46:** *Sihon,* the Amorite king of Heshbon, see Num 21.21–30;

shall fall into the pit,
and everyone who climbs out of
the pit
shall be caught in the trap.
For I will bring these things[a]
upon Moab
in the year of their punishment,
says the LORD.

45 In the shadow of Heshbon
fugitives stop exhausted;
for a fire has gone out from Heshbon,
a flame from the house of Sihon;
it has destroyed the forehead
of Moab,
the scalp of the people of tumult.[b]
46 Woe to you, O Moab!
The people of Chemosh have
perished,
for your sons have been taken
captive,
and your daughters into captivity.
47 Yet I will restore the fortunes
of Moab
in the latter days, says the LORD.
Thus far is the judgment on Moab.

49 Concerning the Ammonites.

Thus says the LORD:
Has Israel no sons?
Has he no heir?
Why then has Milcom dispossessed
Gad,
and his people settled in its towns?
2 Therefore, the time is surely coming,
says the LORD,
when I will sound the battle alarm
against Rabbah of the Ammonites;
it shall become a desolate mound,
and its villages shall be burned with
fire;
then Israel shall dispossess those who
dispossessed him,
says the LORD.

3 Wail, O Heshbon, for Ai is laid
waste!
Cry out, O daughters[c] of Rabbah!
Put on sackcloth,
lament, and slash yourselves with
whips![d]
For Milcom shall go into exile,
with his priests and his attendants.
4 Why do you boast in your strength?
Your strength is ebbing,
O faithless daughter.
You trusted in your treasures,
saying,
"Who will attack me?"
5 I am going to bring terror upon you,
says the Lord GOD of hosts,
from all your neighbors,
and you will be scattered, each
headlong,
with no one to gather the fugitives.
6 But afterward I will restore the for-
tunes of the Ammonites, says the LORD.

a Gk Syr: Heb *bring upon it* *b* Or *of Shaon*
c Or *villages* *d* Cn: Meaning of Heb uncertain

Deut 2.24–27; Judg 11.18–22. **47:** After thoroughgoing devastation (23.13; Isa 24.17–18) Moab will be restored.

49.1–6: Against Ammon. The circumstances reflected here, namely territorial disputes over Gilead in the north, go back to the time of Amos and before. This oracle may well be traditional material adapted and incorporated here by an editor. Ammon, the northern "brother" of Moab (Gen 19.30–38), had previously occupied Transjordanian territory that was claimed by Israel (Judg 10.6–12.6; 2 Kings 15.29) and became Israelite territory under David (2 Sam 12.26–31; Am 1.13–14 perhaps reflects their war for independence). **1:** *Milcom,* Ammonite national god (1 Kings 11.5,33); alternatively, "their king" (Heb "milkam"), cf. Am 1.15. *Gad,* an Israelite tribe that settled in the area between the Jabbok and Arnon rivers. For conflict with Ammon, see Judg 10.6–12.6; 1 Sam 10.27. **2:** *Rabbah,* capital of Ammon, modern Amman. **3:** *Heshbon,* see 48.2n. *Ai* here probably does not refer to the ancient city of Ai near Bethel. The word is also the Heb term for "ruin," and may be used here in reference to Rabbah. **6:** Cf. 46.26; 48.47.

7 Concerning Edom.

Thus says the LORD of hosts:
Is there no longer wisdom in Teman?
Has counsel perished from the prudent?
Has their wisdom vanished?
8 Flee, turn back, get down low,
inhabitants of Dedan!
For I will bring the calamity of Esau upon him,
the time when I punish him.
9 If grape-gatherers came to you,
would they not leave gleanings?
If thieves came by night,
even they would pillage only what they wanted.
10 But as for me, I have stripped Esau bare,
I have uncovered his hiding places,
and he is not able to conceal himself.
His offspring are destroyed,
his kinsfolk
and his neighbors; and he is no more.
11 Leave your orphans, I will keep them alive;
and let your widows trust in me.

12 For thus says the LORD: If those who
do not deserve to drink the cup still have to
drink it, shall you be the one to go unpun-
ished? You shall not go unpunished; you
must drink it. 13 For by myself I have
sworn, says the LORD, that Bozrah shall
become an object of horror and ridicule, a
waste, and an object of cursing; and all her
towns shall be perpetual wastes.
14 I have heard tidings from the LORD,
and a messenger has been sent among the nations:
"Gather yourselves together and come against her,
and rise up for battle!"
15 For I will make you least among the nations,
despised by humankind.
16 The terror you inspire
and the pride of your heart have deceived you,
you who live in the clefts of the rock,[a]
who hold the height of the hill.
Although you make your nest as high as the eagle's,
from there I will bring you down,
says the LORD.

17 Edom shall become an object of hor-
ror; everyone who passes by it will be horri-
fied and will hiss because of all its disasters.
18 As when Sodom and Gomorrah and their
neighbors were overthrown, says the
LORD, no one shall live there, nor shall any-
one settle in it. 19 Like a lion coming up
from the thickets of the Jordan against a
perennial pasture, I will suddenly chase
Edom[b] away from it; and I will appoint
over it whomever I choose.[c] For who is
like me? Who can summon me? Who is
the shepherd who can stand before me?
20 Therefore hear the plan that the LORD
has made against Edom and the purposes
that he has formed against the inhabitants
of Teman: Surely the little ones of the flock
shall be dragged away; surely their fold
shall be appalled at their fate. 21 At the

a Or *of Sela* b Heb *him* c Or *and I will single out the choicest of his rams*: Meaning of Heb uncertain

49.7–22: Against Edom. After 587 BCE the relationship between Israel and "brother" Edom (Deut 23.7–8) deteriorated to consistent vengefulness because of Edom's occupation of southern Judah (Ps 137.7; Lam 4.21–22; Ezek 25.12–14), an occupation caused by pressure from Arab tribes. Vv. 7–8,10–11,18–22 appear to be original to the book of Jeremiah. V. 9 is a variation of Ob 5; vv. 14–16 are a variation of Ob 1–4. **7:** *Teman,* renowned as a center of wisdom, modern Tawilan, about 5 km (3 mi) east of Sela (Petra). **8:** *Dedan,* a region in northwest Arabia associated with trade (Ezek 27.20). *Esau,* the traditional ancestor of the Edomites (Gen 25.19–28; ch 36). **9–10:** Ob 5–6. **12:** 25.15–29. **13:** *Bozrah,* modern Baseirah, a great fortress city in northern Edom. **14–16:** Ob 4; contrast Isa 40.9. **17:** *Hiss,* see 18.6n. **18:** See Gen 19. **19–21:** Editorial revision of 50.44–46. *Thickets of the Jordan,* see 12.5n.; 50.44. **22:** Cf. 48.40–41.

sound of their fall the earth shall tremble;
the sound of their cry shall be heard at the
Red Sea.[a] 22 Look, he shall mount up and
swoop down like an eagle, and spread his
wings against Bozrah, and the heart of the
warriors of Edom in that day shall be like
the heart of a woman in labor.

23 Concerning Damascus.

Hamath and Arpad are confounded,
for they have heard bad news;
they melt in fear, they are troubled
like the sea[b]
that cannot be quiet.
24 Damascus has become feeble, she
turned to flee,
and panic seized her;
anguish and sorrows have taken hold
of her,
as of a woman in labor.
25 How the famous city is forsaken,[c]
the joyful town![d]
26 Therefore her young men shall fall in
her squares,
and all her soldiers shall be
destroyed in that day,
says the LORD of hosts.
27 And I will kindle a fire at the wall of
Damascus,
and it shall devour the strongholds
of Ben-hadad.

28 Concerning Kedar and the kingdoms of Hazor that King Nebuchadrezzar of Babylon defeated.

Thus says the LORD:

Rise up, advance against Kedar!
Destroy the people of the east!
29 Take their tents and their flocks,
their curtains and all their goods;
carry off their camels for yourselves,
and a cry shall go up: "Terror is all
around!"
30 Flee, wander far away, hide in
deep places,
O inhabitants of Hazor!
says the LORD.
For King Nebuchadrezzar of Babylon
has made a plan against you
and formed a purpose against you.
31 Rise up, advance against a nation at
ease,
that lives secure,
says the LORD,
that has no gates or bars,
that lives alone.
32 Their camels shall become booty,
their herds of cattle a spoil.
I will scatter to every wind
those who have shaven temples,
and I will bring calamity
against them from every side,
says the LORD.
33 Hazor shall become a lair of jackals,
an everlasting waste;
no one shall live there,
nor shall anyone settle in it.

34 The word of the LORD that came to

a Or *Sea of Reeds* b Cn: Heb *there is trouble in the sea* c Vg: Heb *is not forsaken* d Syr Vg Tg: Heb *the town of my joy*

49.23–27: Against Damascus. This composite oracle (cf. v. 27; Am 1.4) also reflects the circumstances of a period prior to Jeremiah's day and was likely included here by an editor interested in creating a complete set of oracles against the nations, omitting none of Israel's traditional enemies. The kingdom of Aram-Damascus lost its independence with the capture of *Arpad* by Tiglath-pileser III in 740 BCE, *Hamath* in 738, and Damascus in 732 (Isa 10.9; 37.13). *Ben-hadad,* 1 Kings 15.18,20. *She turned to flee,* feminine personification of a capital city.

49.28–33: Against Kedar and Hazor. In mid-winter 599–598 BCE Nebuchadrezzar led a successful expedition against the Arab tribes in the desert east of Syria-Palestine, which may have been the occasion for this oracle (9.26; 25.23–24). *Kedar* is a collective term for nomadic or semi-nomadic Arabs (2.10); *Hazor* is not the city in Galilee (Josh 11.1) but apparently an Arab town. Neither would escape attack from the wide-ranging Nebuchadrezzar. **32:** *Shaven temples,* 9.26n.; 25.23.

49.34–39: Against Elam. There is some evidence that Nebuchadrezzar attacked Elam, east of Babylo-

the prophet Jeremiah concerning Elam, at
the beginning of the reign of King Zedekiah
of Judah.
35 Thus says the LORD of hosts: I am
going to break the bow of Elam, the main-
stay of their might; 36 and I will bring upon
Elam the four winds from the four quarters
of heaven; and I will scatter them to all
these winds, and there shall be no nation to
which the exiles from Elam shall not come.
37 I will terrify Elam before their enemies,
and before those who seek their life; I will
bring disaster upon them, my fierce anger,
says the LORD. I will send the sword after
them, until I have consumed them; 38 and I
will set my throne in Elam, and destroy
their king and officials, says the LORD.
39 But in the latter days I will restore the
fortunes of Elam, says the LORD.

50 The word that the LORD spoke con-
cerning Babylon, concerning the
land of the Chaldeans, by the prophet Jere-
miah:

2 Declare among the nations
    and proclaim,
  set up a banner and proclaim,
    do not conceal it, say:
  Babylon is taken,
    Bel is put to shame,
    Merodach is dismayed.
  Her images are put to shame,
    her idols are dismayed.

3 For out of the north a nation has come
up against her; it shall make her land a des-
olation, and no one shall live in it; both
human beings and animals shall flee away.
4 In those days and in that time, says the
LORD, the people of Israel shall come, they
and the people of Judah together; they shall
come weeping as they seek the LORD their
God. 5 They shall ask the way to Zion, with
faces turned toward it, and they shall come
and join[a] themselves to the LORD by an
everlasting covenant that will never be for-
gotten.

6 My people have been lost sheep; their
shepherds have led them astray, turning
them away on the mountains; from moun-
tain to hill they have gone, they have for-
gotten their fold. 7 All who found them
have devoured them, and their enemies
have said, "We are not guilty, because they
have sinned against the LORD, the true pas-
ture, the LORD, the hope of their ances-
tors."

8 Flee from Babylon, and go out of the
land of the Chaldeans, and be like male
goats leading the flock. 9 For I am going to
stir up and bring against Babylon a compa-
ny of great nations from the land of the
north; and they shall array themselves
against her; from there she shall be tak-
en. Their arrows are like the arrows of a

a Gk: Heb *toward it. Come! They shall join*

nia, in the winter of 596 BCE; if so, that attack might have been an occasion for this oracle. *Zedekiah* became king in March 597, when Jehoiachin was deposed. *Bow of Elam* reflects the prowess of Elamite archers (Isa 22.6). **39:** This verse (like 46.26; 48.47; 49.6) is probably an editorial addition.

50.1–51.64: Against Babylon. This collection of oracles contains two main themes: the fall of Babylon (sometimes represented as accomplished, sometimes represented as still in the future) and the return of the exiles (cf. 24.6; 29.10). The attitude toward Babylon is harsher (50.14,24) than elsewhere in the book (27.6; 43.10), but is not unprecedented (e.g., 25.12–14). The oracles concerning Judah (Israel) are marked in the following comments with the letters (*a*) to (*f*). **50.1:** *By the prophet Jeremiah,* lit. "by the hand of Jeremiah the prophet," an idiom found also in Hag 1.1; Mal 1.1; contrast Jer 46.1; 49.34. **2–3:** The downfall of Babylon. The nation *out of the north,* patterned on Jeremiah's expression (4.6), may or may not refer to Cyrus and Persia, before whom Babylon fell in October 539 BCE. *Bel,* 51.44; Isa 46.1, originally chief god of Nippur, later identified in Babylon with the great cosmic god Marduk (*Merodach*). **4–5,6–7:** (*a*) An apostrophe on Israel's homecoming (31.7–9) and guilt (2.20; 23.1–2). Contrast v. 7 with 2.3. **8–16:** The residents are urged to flee before Babylon's approaching doom (13.14) and desolation (18.16). **12:** *Your mother,* the city of Babylon is personified here as the mother of her people. **13:** *Hiss,*

skilled warrior who does not return empty-
handed. 10 Chaldea shall be plundered; all
who plunder her shall be sated, says the
LORD.

11 Though you rejoice, though
you exult,
O plunderers of my heritage,
though you frisk about like a heifer
on the grass,
and neigh like stallions,
12 your mother shall be utterly shamed,
and she who bore you shall
be disgraced.
Lo, she shall be the last of the
nations,
a wilderness, dry land, and a desert.
13 Because of the wrath of the LORD she
shall not be inhabited,
but shall be an utter desolation;
everyone who passes by Babylon shall
be appalled
and hiss because of all her wounds.
14 Take up your positions around
Babylon,
all you that bend the bow;
shoot at her, spare no arrows,
for she has sinned against
the LORD.
15 Raise a shout against her from
all sides,
"She has surrendered;
her bulwarks have fallen,
her walls are thrown down."
For this is the vengeance of the LORD:
take vengeance on her,
do to her as she has done.
16 Cut off from Babylon the sower,
and the wielder of the sickle in time
of harvest;
because of the destroying sword
all of them shall return to their
own people,
and all of them shall flee to their
own land.

17 Israel is a hunted sheep driven away
by lions. First the king of Assyria devoured
it, and now at the end King Nebuchadrez-
zar of Babylon has gnawed its bones.
18 Therefore, thus says the LORD of hosts,
the God of Israel: I am going to punish the
king of Babylon and his land, as I punished
the king of Assyria. 19 I will restore Israel to
its pasture, and it shall feed on Carmel and
in Bashan, and on the hills of Ephraim and
in Gilead its hunger shall be satisfied. 20 In
those days and at that time, says the LORD,
the iniquity of Israel shall be sought, and
there shall be none; and the sins of Judah,
and none shall be found; for I will pardon
the remnant that I have spared.

21 Go up to the land of Merathaim;[a]
go up against her,
and attack the inhabitants of Pekod[b]
and utterly destroy the last
of them,[c]
says the LORD;
do all that I have commanded you.
22 The noise of battle is in the land,
and great destruction!
23 How the hammer of the whole earth
is cut down and broken!
How Babylon has become
a horror among the nations!
24 You set a snare for yourself and you
were caught, O Babylon,
but you did not know it;
you were discovered and seized,
because you challenged the LORD.
25 The LORD has opened his armory,

a Or *of Double Rebellion* *b* Or *of Punishment*
c Tg: Heb *destroy after them*

see 18.6n. **17–20:** *(b)* Though successively subject to Assyria and Babylonia, Israel will be restored (31.4–5; 33.8) and Babylon, as Assyria was earlier, will be destroyed (25.12). *Carmel . . . Bashan,* agriculturally rich areas in Israel (Isa 33.9; Am 4.1). **21–32:** God's judgment against Babylon. *Merathaim,* "double rebellion" is a play on the name of southern Babylonia, "mât marrâti," "land of the lagoons." *Pekod,* "visitation," is a play on the name "Puqûdu," an east Babylonian tribe (Ezek 23.23). The writer derides Babylon as a smashed hammer and a captured bird (cf. 5.26–27). He sees the destruction of the Temple as an affront to God which must and will be avenged (21.14; Am 2.2). **33–34:** *(c)* While Israel

and brought out the weapons of his
wrath,
for the Lord God of hosts has a task
to do
in the land of the Chaldeans.
26 Come against her from every quarter;
open her granaries;
pile her up like heaps of grain, and
destroy her utterly;
let nothing be left of her.
27 Kill all her bulls,
let them go down to the slaughter.
Alas for them, their day has come,
the time of their punishment!

28 Listen! Fugitives and refugees from the land of Babylon are coming to declare in Zion the vengeance of the LORD our God, vengeance for his temple.

29 Summon archers against Babylon, all
who bend the bow. Encamp all around her;
let no one escape. Repay her according to
her deeds; just as she has done, do to her—
for she has arrogantly defied the LORD, the
Holy One of Israel. 30 Therefore her young
men shall fall in her squares, and all her
soldiers shall be destroyed on that day, says
the LORD.

31 I am against you, O arrogant one,
says the Lord God of hosts;
for your day has come,
the time when I will punish you.
32 The arrogant one shall stumble
and fall,
with no one to raise him up,
and I will kindle a fire in his cities,
and it will devour everything
around him.

33 Thus says the LORD of hosts: The
people of Israel are oppressed, and so too
are the people of Judah; all their captors
have held them fast and refuse to let them
go. 34 Their Redeemer is strong; the LORD
of hosts is his name. He will surely plead
their cause, that he may give rest to the
earth, but unrest to the inhabitants of Babylon.

35 A sword against the Chaldeans, says
the LORD,
and against the inhabitants of
Babylon,
and against her officials and
her sages!
36 A sword against the diviners,
so that they may become fools!
A sword against her warriors,
so that they may be destroyed!
37 A sword against her[a] horses and
against her[a] chariots,
and against all the foreign troops in
her midst,
so that they may become women!
A sword against all her treasures,
that they may be plundered!
38 A drought[b] against her waters,
that they may be dried up!
For it is a land of images,
and they go mad over idols.

39 Therefore wild animals shall live
with hyenas in Babylon,[c] and ostriches
shall inhabit her; she shall never again be
peopled, or inhabited for all generations.
40 As when God overthrew Sodom and Gomorrah and their neighbors, says the LORD,
so no one shall live there, nor shall anyone
settle in her.

41 Look, a people is coming from
the north;
a mighty nation and many kings
are stirring from the farthest parts
of the earth.

a Cn: Heb *his* *b* Another reading is *A sword*
c Heb lacks *in Babylon*

is helpless, God, her *Redeemer* (Isa 47.4), will deliver her and discomfit her oppressors. **35–37:** The oracle of the sword. **38–40:** Babylon will lie as a desert, unproductive, and inhabited only by wild animals (Isa 34.13–14). *Sodom and Gomorrah,* see Gen 18–19; cf. Jer 49.18. **41–46:** This oracle reuses and reapplies material from elsewhere in the book of Jeremiah. Babylon, once the foe from the north (6.22–24), now stands in dread anticipation of a foe from the north. As Edom could not escape her punishment

42 They wield bow and spear,
they are cruel and have no mercy.
The sound of them is like the roaring
sea;
they ride upon horses,
set in array as a warrior for battle,
against you, O daughter Babylon!

43 The king of Babylon heard news
of them,
and his hands fell helpless;
anguish seized him,
pain like that of a woman in labor.

44 Like a lion coming up from the thick-
ets of the Jordan against a perennial pas-
ture, I will suddenly chase them away from
her; and I will appoint over her whomever
I choose.[a] For who is like me? Who can
summon me? Who is the shepherd who can
stand before me? 45 Therefore hear the plan
that the LORD has made against Babylon,
and the purposes that he has formed
against the land of the Chaldeans: Surely
the little ones of the flock shall be dragged
away; surely their[b] fold shall be appalled
at their fate. 46 At the sound of the capture
of Babylon the earth shall tremble, and her
cry shall be heard among the nations.

51 Thus says the LORD:
I am going to stir up a destructive
wind[c]
against Babylon
and against the inhabitants of
Leb-qamai;[d]
2 and I will send winnowers to
Babylon,
and they shall winnow her.
They shall empty her land
when they come against her from
every side
on the day of trouble.
3 Let not the archer bend his bow,
and let him not array himself in his
coat of mail.
Do not spare her young men;
utterly destroy her entire army.
4 They shall fall down slain in the land
of the Chaldeans,
and wounded in her streets.
5 Israel and Judah have not been
forsaken
by their God, the LORD of hosts,
though their land is full of guilt
before the Holy One of Israel.

6 Flee from the midst of Babylon,
save your lives, each of you!
Do not perish because of her guilt,
for this is the time of the LORD's
vengeance;
he is repaying her what is due.
7 Babylon was a golden cup in the
LORD's hand,
making all the earth drunken;
the nations drank of her wine,
and so the nations went mad.
8 Suddenly Babylon has fallen and
is shattered;
wail for her!
Bring balm for her wound;
perhaps she may be healed.
9 We tried to heal Babylon,
but she could not be healed.
Forsake her, and let each of us go
to our own country;
for her judgment has reached up
to heaven
and has been lifted up even to the
skies.

a Or *and I will single out the choicest of her rams*: Meaning of Heb uncertain *b* Syr Gk Tg Compare 49.20: Heb lacks *their* *c* Or *stir up the spirit of a destroyer* *d* *Leb-qamai* is a cryptogram for *Kasdim*, Chaldea

(49.19–21), neither can Babylon. There is no king (*shepherd*) who can successfully defy God. **44:** *Thickets of the Jordan,* see 12.5n.; 49.19.

51.1–64: God's judgment against Babylon. 1–4: As grain is winnowed, so will Babylon be cut down and winnowed (see 15.7n.). *Leb-qamai* is an atbash cipher (see 25.26n.) for "Chaldea," i.e., Babylonia. **5–10:** (*d*) A note reminding Israel that while they have hope, Babylon's case is hopeless (50.33–34). Babylon was the golden cup from which the nations would drink of God's wrath (see 25.15–29n.), but now that cup is smashed; she stands desolate (46.11; Ezek 27.27) as God delivers his people. **11–19:** Terse

10 The LORD has brought forth our
vindication;
come, let us declare in Zion
the work of the LORD our God.

11 Sharpen the arrows!
Fill the quivers!
The LORD has stirred up the spirit of the kings of the Medes, because his purpose concerning Babylon is to destroy it, for that is the vengeance of the LORD, vengeance for his temple.
12 Raise a standard against the walls of
Babylon;
make the watch strong;
post sentinels;
prepare the ambushes;
for the LORD has both planned
and done
what he spoke concerning the
inhabitants of Babylon.
13 You who live by mighty waters,
rich in treasures,
your end has come,
the thread of your life is cut.
14 The LORD of hosts has sworn
by himself:
Surely I will fill you with troops like
a swarm of locusts,
and they shall raise a shout of
victory over you.

15 It is he who made the earth by
his power,
who established the world by
his wisdom,
and by his understanding stretched
out the heavens.
16 When he utters his voice there is a
tumult of waters in the
heavens,
and he makes the mist rise from the
ends of the earth.
He makes lightnings for the rain,
and he brings out the wind from
his storehouses.
17 Everyone is stupid and without
knowledge;
goldsmiths are all put to shame by
their idols;
for their images are false,
and there is no breath in them.
18 They are worthless, a work of
delusion;
at the time of their punishment they
shall perish.
19 Not like these is the LORD,[a] the
portion of Jacob,
for he is the one who formed
all things,
and Israel is the tribe of his
inheritance;
the LORD of hosts is his name.

20 You are my war club, my weapon of
battle:
with you I smash nations;
with you I destroy kingdoms;
21 with you I smash the horse and
its rider;
with you I smash the chariot and
the charioteer;
22 with you I smash man and woman;
with you I smash the old man and
the boy;
with you I smash the young man and
the girl;
23 with you I smash shepherds and
their flocks;
with you I smash farmers and
their teams;
with you I smash governors and
deputies.

24 I will repay Babylon and all the in-
habitants of Chaldea before your very eyes

a Heb lacks *the LORD*

military commands precede the attack by the *Medes;* either a reference to Media, northeast of Babylonia, which participated in the overthrow of Assyria and was a threat to Babylonia during this period, or an oblique reference to Persia. Media became a Persian province in 549 BCE. The phrase *mighty waters* refers to the Euphrates and the network of canals around Babylon. **15–19:** In connection with God's judgment on Babylon, the writer appends the oracle against the idols from 10.12–16 (see 50.38). **20–23:** This oracle of the hammer (see 50.23) addresses the destroying enemy of Babylon. **24–26:** *Destroying mountain* may

for all the wrong that they have done in
Zion, says the LORD.

25 I am against you, O destroying
mountain,
says the LORD,
that destroys the whole earth;
I will stretch out my hand
against you,
and roll you down from the crags,
and make you a burned-out
mountain.
26 No stone shall be taken from you for
a corner
and no stone for a foundation,
but you shall be a perpetual waste,
says the LORD.

27 Raise a standard in the land,
blow the trumpet among the
nations;
prepare the nations for war
against her,
summon against her the kingdoms,
Ararat, Minni, and Ashkenaz;
appoint a marshal against her,
bring up horses like bristling
locusts.
28 Prepare the nations for war
against her,
the kings of the Medes, with their
governors and deputies,
and every land under their
dominion.
29 The land trembles and writhes,
for the LORD's purposes against
Babylon stand,
to make the land of Babylon a
desolation,
without inhabitant.
30 The warriors of Babylon have given
up fighting,
they remain in their strongholds;
their strength has failed,
they have become women;
her buildings are set on fire,
her bars are broken.
31 One runner runs to meet another,
and one messenger to meet another,
to tell the king of Babylon
that his city is taken from end
to end:
32 the fords have been seized,
the marshes have been burned with
fire,
and the soldiers are in panic.
33 For thus says the LORD of hosts, the
God of Israel:
Daughter Babylon is like a threshing
floor
at the time when it is trodden;
yet a little while
and the time of her harvest
will come.

34 "King Nebuchadrezzar of Babylon has
devoured me,
he has crushed me;
he has made me an empty vessel,
he has swallowed me like
a monster;
he has filled his belly with my
delicacies,
he has spewed me out.
35 May my torn flesh be avenged on
Babylon,"
the inhabitants of Zion shall say.
"May my blood be avenged on the
inhabitants of Chaldea,"
Jerusalem shall say.
36 Therefore thus says the LORD:
I am going to defend your cause
and take vengeance for you.
I will dry up her sea

reflect the great ziggurat or temple tower of Babylon. *Burned-out mountain,* perhaps "mountain of burnt bricks" (Gen 11.3). **27–33:** As Babylon subdued the nations (25.15–26), so the nations will gather against Babylon. *Ararat,* ancient Urartu, modern Armenia, north of Lake Van. *Minni,* Mannaeans living south of Lake Urmia. *Ashkenaz,* the Scythians. All were defeated by the Medes in the early sixth century BCE. **34–40:** (*e*) Again Jerusalem's deliverance is viewed as a mighty act of God (50.34); he will make Babylonia a desert (9.10); the once mighty lion will become drunk (25.15–16) and fall into a helpless, permanent sleep. **35:** Note the poetic pattern: Babylon/inhabitants of Zion//inhabitants of Chaldea/Jerusalem or city/people//people/city. **37:** *Hissing,* see 18.6n. **41–43:** Babylon (written *Sheshach,* an atbash cipher; see

and make her fountain dry;
37 and Babylon shall become a heap
of ruins,
a den of jackals,
an object of horror and of hissing,
without inhabitant.

38 Like lions they shall roar together;
they shall growl like lions' whelps.
39 When they are inflamed, I will set out
their drink
and make them drunk, until they
become merry
and then sleep a perpetual sleep
and never wake, says the LORD.
40 I will bring them down like lambs to
the slaughter,
like rams and goats.

41 How Sheshach[a] is taken,
the pride of the whole earth seized!
How Babylon has become
an object of horror among the
nations!
42 The sea has risen over Babylon;
she has been covered by its
tumultuous waves.
43 Her cities have become an object
of horror,
a land of drought and a desert,
a land in which no one lives,
and through which no mortal
passes.
44 I will punish Bel in Babylon,
and make him disgorge what he has
swallowed.
The nations shall no longer stream to
him;
the wall of Babylon has fallen.

45 Come out of her, my people!
Save your lives, each of you,
from the fierce anger of the LORD!
46 Do not be fainthearted or fearful
at the rumors heard in the land—
one year one rumor comes,
the next year another,
rumors of violence in the land
and of ruler against ruler.

47 Assuredly, the days are coming
when I will punish the images
of Babylon;
her whole land shall be put to shame,
and all her slain shall fall in
her midst.
48 Then the heavens and the earth,
and all that is in them,
shall shout for joy over Babylon;
for the destroyers shall come
against them out of the north,
says the LORD.
49 Babylon must fall for the slain of
Israel,
as the slain of all the earth have
fallen because of Babylon.

50 You survivors of the sword,
go, do not linger!
Remember the LORD in a distant
land,
and let Jerusalem come into your
mind:
51 We are put to shame, for we have
heard insults;
dishonor has covered our face,
for aliens have come
into the holy places of the
LORD's house.

52 Therefore the time is surely coming,
says the LORD,
when I will punish her idols,
and through all her land
the wounded shall groan.
53 Though Babylon should mount up to
heaven,
and though she should fortify her
strong height,

a Sheshach is a cryptogram for *Babel*, Babylon

25.26n.), will be inundated by the waves of her attackers (46.7–8; Isa 8.7–8); when the flood recedes, she will be a trackless wasteland. **44–49**: In antiquity, the fall of a land was viewed as the defeat of its god(s) (Isa 37.12). **44**: *Bel,* see 50.2–3n. **50–58**: (*f*) The doubts raised by the destruction of the Temple should be allayed by God's assurance of certain punishment for Babylon, which desecrated the holy places.

from me destroyers would come upon
her,
says the LORD.

54 Listen!—a cry from Babylon!
A great crashing from the land of
the Chaldeans!
55 For the LORD is laying Babylon
waste,
and stilling her loud clamor.
Their waves roar like mighty waters,
the sound of their clamor resounds;
56 for a destroyer has come against
her,
against Babylon;
her warriors are taken,
their bows are broken;
for the LORD is a God of recompense,
he will repay in full.
57 I will make her officials and her sages
drunk,
also her governors, her deputies,
and her warriors;
they shall sleep a perpetual sleep and
never wake,
says the King, whose name is the
LORD of hosts.

58 Thus says the LORD of hosts:
The broad wall of Babylon
shall be leveled to the ground,
and her high gates
shall be burned with fire.
The peoples exhaust themselves for
nothing,
and the nations weary themselves
only for fire.[a]

59 The word that the prophet Jeremiah
commanded Seraiah son of Neriah son of
Mahseiah, when he went with King Zede-
kiah of Judah to Babylon, in the fourth year
of his reign. Seraiah was the quartermaster.
60 Jeremiah wrote in a[b] scroll all the disas-
ters that would come on Babylon, all these
words that are written concerning Babylon.
61 And Jeremiah said to Seraiah: "When
you come to Babylon, see that you read
all these words, 62 and say, 'O LORD, you
yourself threatened to destroy this place
so that neither human beings nor animals
shall live in it, and it shall be desolate forev-
er.' 63 When you finish reading this scroll,
tie a stone to it, and throw it into the mid-
dle of the Euphrates, 64 and say, 'Thus shall
Babylon sink, to rise no more, because of
the disasters that I am bringing on her.' "[c]
Thus far are the words of Jeremiah.

52 Zedekiah was twenty-one years old
when he began to reign; he reigned
eleven years in Jerusalem. His mother's
name was Hamutal daughter of Jeremiah
of Libnah. 2 He did what was evil in the
sight of the LORD, just as Jehoiakim had
done. 3 Indeed, Jerusalem and Judah so an-
gered the LORD that he expelled them from
his presence.
Zedekiah rebelled against the king of
Babylon. 4 And in the ninth year of his
reign, in the tenth month, on the tenth day

a Gk Syr Compare Hab 2.13: Heb *and the nations for fire, and they are weary* *b* Or *one* *c* Gk: Heb *on her. And they shall weary themselves*

59–64: The oracles are written in a book and taken to Babylon. Though we know of no journey of Zedekiah, he may have gone to renew his fealty after the abortive plot of 593 BCE (chs 27–28) became known to Nebuchadrezzar. *Seraiah,* brother of Baruch (32.12). **60:** This is the fourth reference to a distinct scroll authored by Jeremiah (30.1; 36.1; 45.2; 51.60). As the book itself acknowledges, the history of the book's growth was complicated indeed. **63:** By a symbolic act the oracle against Babylon is emphasized; this oracle may have been the causative factor for the composition of 50.1–51.58. *Thus far are the words of Jeremiah,* an additional comment calling attention to the supplementary character of the historical appendix in ch 52.

52.1–34: Historical appendix. Though largely a duplicate of 2 Kings 24.18–25.30, this historical section, together with 39.1–10 and 40.7–43.7, provides much important complementary information (for similar historical additions, cf. Isa 36–39). **1–3:** Reign of Zedekiah (2 Kings 24.18–20; 597–587 BCE). For details on the contemporary religious situation, see Ezek 8. **4–27:** Siege and fall of Jerusalem (39.1–10; 2 Kings 24.20b–25.26). **4–11:** January 587 BCE to August 586; see 39.4–5n. **7–9:** *Chaldeans,*

of the month, King Nebuchadrezzar of
Babylon came with all his army against Je-
rusalem, and they laid siege to it; they built
siegeworks against it all around. 5 So the
city was besieged until the eleventh year of
King Zedekiah. 6 On the ninth day of the
fourth month the famine became so severe
in the city that there was no food for the
people of the land. 7 Then a breach was
made in the city wall;[a] and all the soldiers
fled and went out from the city by night by
the way of the gate between the two walls,
by the king's garden, though the Chaldeans
were all around the city. They went in the
direction of the Arabah. 8 But the army of
the Chaldeans pursued the king, and over-
took Zedekiah in the plains of Jericho; and
all his army was scattered, deserting him.
9 Then they captured the king, and brought
him up to the king of Babylon at Riblah in
the land of Hamath, and he passed sentence
on him. 10 The king of Babylon killed the
sons of Zedekiah before his eyes, and also
killed all the officers of Judah at Riblah.
11 He put out the eyes of Zedekiah, and
bound him in fetters, and the king of Bab-
ylon took him to Babylon, and put him in
prison until the day of his death.

12 In the fifth month, on the tenth day
of the month—which was the nineteenth
year of King Nebuchadrezzar, king of Bab-
ylon—Nebuzaradan the captain of the
bodyguard who served the king of Babylon,
entered Jerusalem. 13 He burned the house
of the LORD, the king's house, and all the
houses of Jerusalem; every great house he
burned down. 14 All the army of the Chal-
deans, who were with the captain of the
guard, broke down all the walls around Je-
rusalem. 15 Nebuzaradan the captain of the
guard carried into exile some of the poorest
of the people and the rest of the people who
were left in the city and the deserters who
had defected to the king of Babylon, to-
gether with the rest of the artisans. 16 But
Nebuzaradan the captain of the guard left
some of the poorest people of the land to be
vinedressers and tillers of the soil.

17 The pillars of bronze that were in the
house of the LORD, and the stands and the
bronze sea that were in the house of the
LORD, the Chaldeans broke in pieces, and
carried all the bronze to Babylon. 18 They
took away the pots, the shovels, the snuff-
ers, the basins, the ladles, and all the vessels
of bronze used in the temple service. 19 The
captain of the guard took away the small
bowls also, the firepans, the basins, the
pots, the lampstands, the ladles, and the
bowls for libation, both those of gold and
those of silver. 20 As for the two pillars, the
one sea, the twelve bronze bulls that were
under the sea, and the stands,[b] which King
Solomon had made for the house of the
LORD, the bronze of all these vessels was
beyond weighing. 21 As for the pillars, the
height of the one pillar was eighteen cubits,
its circumference was twelve cubits; it was
hollow and its thickness was four fingers.
22 Upon it was a capital of bronze; the
height of the capital was five cubits; lattice-
work and pomegranates, all of bronze,
encircled the top of the capital. And
the second pillar had the same, with
pomegranates. 23 There were ninety-six
pomegranates on the sides; all the pome-
granates encircling the latticework num-
bered one hundred.

24 The captain of the guard took the
chief priest Seraiah, the second priest Zeph-
aniah, and the three guardians of the
threshold; 25 and from the city he took an
officer who had been in command of the
soldiers, and seven men of the king's coun-
cil who were found in the city; the secretary

a Heb lacks *wall* *b* Cn: Heb *that were under the stands*

Babylonians. The last scene enacted before Zedekiah, the rebellious vassal (37.1; Ezek 17.18–21), at Nebuchadrezzar's headquarters at *Riblah* (see 39.4–5n.) was the slaughter of his sons and court officials. Then he was blinded and taken to Babylon to die in prison. **12–16:** August 586 BCE. The reasons for the actions of Nebuzaradan, Nebuchadrezzar's field general, are unknown. **17–23:** A detailed description of the booty taken from the Temple (cf. 1 Kings 7.15–50). **24–27:** 2 Kings 25.18–21. *Seraiah,* perhaps the same as in 36.26; otherwise unknown. *Zephaniah,* 21.1; 29.29. **28–30:** The first two deportations listed

of the commander of the army who mustered the people of the land; and sixty men of the people of the land who were found inside the city.
26 Then Nebuzaradan the captain of the guard took them, and brought them to the king of Babylon at Riblah.
27 And the king of Babylon struck them down, and put them to death at Riblah in the land of Hamath. So Judah went into exile out of its land.

28 This is the number of the people whom Nebuchadrezzar took into exile: in the seventh year, three thousand twenty-three Judeans;
29 in the eighteenth year of Nebuchadrezzar he took into exile from Jerusalem eight hundred thirty-two persons;
30 in the twenty-third year of Nebuchadrezzar, Nebuzaradan the captain of the guard took into exile of the Judeans seven hundred forty-five persons; all the persons were four thousand six hundred.

31 In the thirty-seventh year of the exile of King Jehoiachin of Judah, in the twelfth month, on the twenty-fifth day of the month, King Evil-merodach of Babylon, in the year he began to reign, showed favor to King Jehoiachin of Judah and brought him out of prison;
32 he spoke kindly to him, and gave him a seat above the seats of the other kings who were with him in Babylon.
33 So Jehoiachin put aside his prison clothes, and every day of his life he dined regularly at the king's table.
34 For his allowance, a regular daily allowance was given him by the king of Babylon, as long as he lived, up to the day of his death.

here coincide with the surrender of Jehoiachin (597 BCE; 2 Kings 24.12–16) and the suppression of Zedekiah's revolt (586). The occasion for the third deportation (582) is not known, although it may have been a police action in response to Ishmael's assassination of Gedaliah (ch 41). **31–34:** 2 Kings 25.27–30. The presence of this material proves that the editing of Jeremiah's material was later than 560 BCE. Jehoiachin's restoration may have been viewed by his contemporaries as the beginning of Judah's restoration (23.5–6).

LAMENTATIONS

Lamentations is a sequence of five lyric poems that lament the destruction of Jerusalem by the Babylonians in 586 BCE (see 2 Kings 25.8–21). The dense and highly charged poetry constitutes some of the Bible's most violent and brutal pieces of writing. Though mostly lacking traditional statements of hope, the poems do manifest a stubborn and tenacious hold on life.

Several of the ancient versions (the Greek, Latin, and Aramaic translations) attribute the authorship of these poems to Jeremiah, which accounts for their placement after the book of Jeremiah in the Christian canon. Although Jeremiah was active during the last days of the kingdom of Judah and spoke in moving and emotional terms of the coming destruction of Jerusalem and the nation (Jer 8.18–9.1; 9.17–22), it is unlikely that he is the author of the poems found in the book of Lamentations. The language, forms of expression, and religious perspectives do not seem to be quite like those expressed in Jeremiah's own prophetic poetry. Moreover, the oldest Hebrew manuscripts of Lamentations do not mention Jeremiah or associate him with the book. In the Jewish canon Lamentations is not placed with the prophets, but in the third division of the canon, the Writings. Thus it is more likely that the tradition connecting Jeremiah with Lamentations is a reflection of the common practice in antiquity of ascribing authorship of anonymous materials to well-known figures, for example, David and the Psalms or Solomon and the books of Proverbs and Song of Songs. The poems of Lamentations may be dated to the sixth century, probably between 586 and 520 BCE, when the Temple was rebuilt. They were likely composed in Palestine for the community that remained in the land after the catastrophe.

In later Jewish tradition Lamentations was counted as one of the five festival scrolls (Megillot), together with Song of Songs, Ruth, Ecclesiastes, and Esther. Lamentations is read as part of the liturgy of the "Ninth of Ab," the day that commemorates the destruction of the Second Temple by the Romans in 70 CE. In Christian tradition readings from Lamentations are part of the liturgies of Holy Week.

Lamentations draws on a variety of literary genres, including communal and individual laments, the funeral dirge, and wisdom traditions, but gets its overarching shape and much of its imagery and subject matter from the city lament, a genre best known from ancient Mesopotamia (e.g., the "Lamentation over the Destruction of Ur," the "Lamentation over the Destruction of Sumer and Ur," and the "Nippur Lament"). Lamentations, however, differs from most of the Mesopotamian city laments, which end happily in celebration of restoration and the return of the gods. It ends tragically: The LORD remains absent and silent throughout, and there is no suggestion of the restoration of Jerusalem or its Temple.

The imagery of Lamentations evokes a sense of fragmentation and discontinuity, reflecting the suffering of the past. There is no narrative structure to give shape to the raw emotions expressed, nor even a clear rhetorical movement from grief to hope, such as one often finds in laments in Psalms. Although the poetic meter varies throughout the book, much of the poetry is composed in "qinah" meter in which the lines are unbalanced, giving a sense of language broken off in grief. In counterpoint to such a sense of fragmentation, however, the formal structures of the poetic form itself produce a strong sense of coherence. The first four chapters of Lamentations are each composed as an alphabetic acrostic, a formal scheme in which the initial word of each stanza begins with successive letters of the Hebrew alphabet, twenty-two in all (ch 5, though not an acrostic, also contains twenty-two verses). In ch 3 all three verses of each stanza begin with the same letter (vv. 1–3 with "'alep," vv. 4–6 with "bet," etc.). The alphabetic acrostic functions as the material, physical container of this poetry, literally holding each poem's component verses together and conveying a strong sense of closure through its clear structure and fixed length. Yet the acrostic conveys meaning symbolically as well. The poet's whole attempt to render the chaos of his world into language, to contain his fragmented lyrics within the frame of the alphabetic acrostic, thus becomes an attempt to control and contain, and ultimately transform, the suffering and hurt that engulfed Jerusalem and its inhabitants.

1 How lonely sits the city
that once was full of people!
How like a widow she has become,
she that was great among the nations!
She that was a princess among the provinces
has become a vassal.

2 She weeps bitterly in the night,
with tears on her cheeks;
among all her lovers
she has no one to comfort her;
all her friends have dealt treacherously with her,
they have become her enemies.

3 Judah has gone into exile with suffering
and hard servitude;
she lives now among the nations,
and finds no resting place;
her pursuers have all overtaken her
in the midst of her distress.

4 The roads to Zion mourn,
for no one comes to the festivals;
all her gates are desolate,
her priests groan;
her young girls grieve,[a]
and her lot is bitter.

5 Her foes have become the masters,
her enemies prosper,
because the LORD has made her suffer
for the multitude of her transgressions;
her children have gone away,
captives before the foe.

6 From daughter Zion has departed
all her majesty.
Her princes have become like stags
that find no pasture;
they fled without strength
before the pursuer.

7 Jerusalem remembers,
in the days of her affliction and wandering,
all the precious things
that were hers in days of old.
When her people fell into the hand of the foe,

a Meaning of Heb uncertain

1.1–11: Lament over Zion. Suffering is refracted through personified Jerusalem. **1:** *How* or "Ah," commonly found in dirges (Isa 1.21; Jer 48.17; cf. Lam 2.1a; 4.1a). *Great among the nations* and *princess among the provinces,* may be titles of Jerusalem (cf. Isa 47.5). **2:** *Lovers,* literally Judah's political allies, but metaphorically her loved ones who have neglected their obligation of compassion. For the metaphor of allies as lovers, see Ezek 16.26–28. **3:** *Suffering* (Ex 3.7,17; 4.31) and *hard servitude* (Ex 1.14; 2.23; 5.11; 6.6), allusions to the Egyptian captivity. **5:** *Transgressions,* although 2 Kings attributes Judah's destruction to specific transgressions (2 Kings 21.10–15), here the sins are not specified. **6:** *Daughter Zion* (lit. "Daughter of Zion"), the personified city's most common epithet (1.6,15; 2.1–2,4–5,8,10,13,15,18; 4.21–22; cf. 3.48; 4.3,6,10; Isa 1.8; 52.2; Jer 4.31; Mic 4.8; etc.). **8:** *Nakedness,* an allusion to both the

and there was no one to help her,
the foe looked on mocking
over her downfall.

8 Jerusalem sinned grievously,
so she has become a mockery;
all who honored her despise her,
for they have seen her nakedness;
she herself groans,
and turns her face away.

9 Her uncleanness was in her skirts;
she took no thought of her
future;
her downfall was appalling,
with none to comfort her.
"O LORD, look at my affliction,
for the enemy has triumphed!"

10 Enemies have stretched out
their hands
over all her precious things;
she has even seen the nations
invade her sanctuary,
those whom you forbade
to enter your congregation.

11 All her people groan
as they search for bread;
they trade their treasures for food
to revive their strength.
Look, O LORD, and see
how worthless I have become.

12 Is it nothing to you,[a] all you who
pass by?
Look and see
if there is any sorrow like my sorrow,
which was brought upon me,
which the LORD inflicted
on the day of his fierce anger.

13 From on high he sent fire;
it went deep into my bones;
he spread a net for my feet;
he turned me back;
he has left me stunned,
faint all day long.

14 My transgressions were bound[a] into
a yoke;
by his hand they were fastened
together;
they weigh on my neck,
sapping my strength;
the Lord handed me over
to those whom I cannot withstand.

15 The LORD has rejected
all my warriors in the midst of me;
he proclaimed a time against me
to crush my young men;
the Lord has trodden as in a
wine press
the virgin daughter Judah.

a Meaning of Heb uncertain

punishment of a prostitute (cf. Isa 47.3; Jer 13.22; Ezek 16.37; Nah 3.5) and her victimization. **9:** *Uncleanness . . . skirts,* perhaps menstruation, or a bloody discharge. *O LORD . . . ,* Zion herself voices this plea. **10:** *Precious things,* Temple treasures (cf. 2 Chr 36.10). *Invade,* elsewhere connotes sexual intercourse (Gen 6.4; 2 Sam 16.21; Ezek 23.44; Prov 6.29), suggesting rape. **11:** *Look . . . and see,* repeated in v. 12, joining the two halves of the poem, vv. 1–11 and 12–22.

1.12–22: The city's lament. Except in 1.17, the city itself speaks the second half of the poem. **12:** *Sorrow,* better, "pain." The Heb word translated weakly as *was brought,* properly conveys violence: torture or rape (1 Sam 31.4; Jer 38.19; Judg 19.25). *Day . . . anger,* i.e., "the Day of the LORD," when God comes in judgment against Judah itself (e.g., Am 5.18). **13:** *Left me stunned,* better, "ravished or desolated me," describing devastated lands (Lev 26.33; Isa 1.7; 54.3; Jer 12.11; Am 9.14) and the physical state of a raped woman (2 Sam 13.20). **14:** "Yoke," servitude (Deut 28.48; 1 Kings 12.4; Isa 47.6; Jer 28.1–17). *Lord* (Heb "adonai"), occurs fourteen times in Lamentations, while the proper name, LORD ("yhwh"), occurs thirty-two times. **15:** *In the midst of me* (lit. "the Lord in my midst"), God's presence, which typically means good things for Israel and Judah and bad things for their enemies (Deut 7.21; Josh 3.5; Isa 12.6; Jer 14.9; Zeph 3.15), here, ironically, spells disaster for Judah. *Virgin,* another common epithet applied to the goddess Anat in Ugaritic and to personified cities (Isa 23.12; Jer 31.4; Am 5.2; Lam 2.13b). **17:** *Filthy thing,* i.e., "menstruant," the ruined city as an arch-symbol of death and impurity (see

16 For these things I weep;
my eyes flow with tears;
for a comforter is far from me,
one to revive my courage;
my children are desolate,
for the enemy has prevailed.

17 Zion stretches out her hands,
but there is no one to comfort her;
the LORD has commanded against
Jacob
that his neighbors should become
his foes;
Jerusalem has become
a filthy thing among them.

18 The LORD is in the right,
for I have rebelled against his
word;
but hear, all you peoples,
and behold my suffering;
my young women and young men
have gone into captivity.

19 I called to my lovers
but they deceived me;
my priests and elders
perished in the city
while seeking food
to revive their strength.

20 See, O LORD, how distressed I am;
my stomach churns,
my heart is wrung within me,
because I have been very rebellious.
In the street the sword bereaves;
in the house it is like death.

21 They heard how I was groaning,
with no one to comfort me.
All my enemies heard of my trouble;
they are glad that you have done it.
Bring on the day you have
announced,
and let them be as I am.

22 Let all their evil doing come
before you;
and deal with them
as you have dealt with me
because of all my transgressions;
for my groans are many
and my heart is faint.

2 How the Lord in his anger
has humiliated[a] daughter Zion!
He has thrown down from heaven to
earth
the splendor of Israel;
he has not remembered his footstool
in the day of his anger.

2 The Lord has destroyed without
mercy
all the dwellings of Jacob;
in his wrath he has broken down
the strongholds of daughter Judah;
he has brought down to the ground in
dishonor
the kingdom and its rulers.

3 He has cut down in fierce anger
all the might of Israel;

a Meaning of Heb uncertain

Lev 15.16–24). **18:** *The LORD is in the right,* a double entendre constituting both a legal declaration of innocence (Ex 9.27; 1 Sam 24.18; 2 Kings 10.9) and a statement of the common expectation for divine and royal behavior (Isa 45.21; Jer 12.1; Ps 11.5,7). **20:** *Distressed,* in Hebrew, forms a pun with "adversary, foe," which appears five other times (1.5a,c,7d,10a,17b). *In the street . . . in the house,* see Deut 32.25. **21:** *They heard,* better "hear" (as in Syr, Gk), an imperative addressed to the LORD. **22:** *Deal with them as you have dealt with me,* correspondence between the wrong and the judgment (e.g., Ob 13; 1 Sam 15.33; Judg 1.7). The Heb word for *many* ("rabbot") is a form of the word translated "full" in v. 1, a device for marking closure as well as contrast: formerly, many people; now, many sighs.

2.1–8: The Lord battles against Jerusalem. The first eight verses focus on the Divine Warrior's battle against Jerusalem. **1:** *Splendor of Israel,* another common epithet of personified cities (cf. Lam 2.15c; Isa 13.19; 22.2; 23.7; Jer 48.2; Ezek 26.17; Nah 2.8a). *His footstool,* i.e., the ark of the covenant (Ps 99.5; 132.7; 1 Chr 28.2), by extension the Temple (Isa 60.13). *Day of his anger* (see 1.12n.) forms an inclusio with 2.22b. **3:** *Right hand,* divine protection (Ex 15.6,12; Isa 41.10; Ps 48.10; 89.13; 98.1; Job 40.14).

he has withdrawn his right hand from
them
in the face of the enemy;
he has burned like a flaming fire
in Jacob,
consuming all around.

4 He has bent his bow like an enemy,
with his right hand set like a foe;
he has killed all in whom we
took pride
in the tent of daughter Zion;
he has poured out his fury like
fire.

5 The Lord has become like an enemy;
he has destroyed Israel.
He has destroyed all its palaces,
laid in ruins its strongholds,
and multiplied in daughter Judah
mourning and lamentation.

6 He has broken down his booth like a
garden,
he has destroyed his tabernacle;
the LORD has abolished in Zion
festival and sabbath,
and in his fierce indignation has
spurned
king and priest.

7 The Lord has scorned his altar,
disowned his sanctuary;
he has delivered into the hand of the
enemy
the walls of her palaces;
a clamor was raised in the house of
the LORD
as on a day of festival.

8 The LORD determined to lay in ruins
the wall of daughter Zion;
he stretched the line;
he did not withhold his hand from
destroying;
he caused rampart and wall
to lament;
they languish together.

9 Her gates have sunk into the ground;
he has ruined and broken her bars;
her king and princes are among
the nations;
guidance is no more,
and her prophets obtain
no vision from the LORD.

10 The elders of daughter Zion
sit on the ground in silence;
they have thrown dust on their heads
and put on sackcloth;
the young girls of Jerusalem
have bowed their heads to
the ground.

11 My eyes are spent with weeping;

4: In the space of four couplets, the LORD is labeled an *enemy* three times (2.4a,b; 5a). *Tent,* archaism for the Temple. **6:** *Booth,* both a temporary shelter (Job 27.18; Jon 4.5) and the Temple (Ps 27.5). *Like a garden,* better, "as in a garden" (cf. Isa 1.8); the destroyed Temple is a dilapidated and abandoned harvest booth. **7:** *A clamor,* both the boisterous enemy celebrating as they loot, and the LORD's *clamor* of judgment (see 2 Sam 22.14; Joel 2.11; Am 1.2; Ps 18.13; 46.6). **8:** *He stretched the line,* i.e., "he measured with a measuring-line" (2 Kings 21.13; Isa 34.11; Zech 1.16; Job 38.5), as in a building project (Jer 31.39; Zech 1.16). Demolition also requires planning and measurement (see 2 Kings 24.13; Isa 34.11). *He did not withhold his hand* (Ex 15.12; Isa 5.25; Ezek 6.14; Zeph 1.4) parallels 2.3b. The image harshly answers the earlier petition when "Zion stretches out her hands" (1.17a). **9–10:** A transition between the presentation of the *LORD*'s assault on Jerusalem (vv. 1–8) and reaction to this assault, from the poet (vv. 11–19) and then from Zion (vv. 20–22). **9:** *Her gates have sunk into the ground,* either the battered doors lying in the dirt, or the ruined gate-towers (Jer 14.2). *Among the nations,* in exile.

2.11–19: Reactions to the suffering. The section moves from initial reaction to the horrors (vv. 11–12), to a statement of inability to assuage the hurt (v. 13), to a survey of other potential consolers (vv. 14–16), and finally to the improbable and ironic conclusion that Zion must turn to the LORD, the author of her suffering (v. 17), for consolation (vv. 18–19). **11:** The poet's words echo those of Zion in 1.20. *My people,* lit. "Daughter of My People," another of the city's epithets (cf. 3.48; 4.3,6,10). *Streets,* better,

my stomach churns;
my bile is poured out on the ground
because of the destruction of
my people,
because infants and babes faint
in the streets of the city.

12 They cry to their mothers,
"Where is bread and wine?"
as they faint like the wounded
in the streets of the city,
as their life is poured out
on their mothers' bosom.

13 What can I say for you, to what
compare you,
O daughter Jerusalem?
To what can I liken you, that I may
comfort you,
O virgin daughter Zion?
For vast as the sea is your ruin;
who can heal you?

14 Your prophets have seen for you
false and deceptive visions;
they have not exposed your iniquity
to restore your fortunes,
but have seen oracles for you
that are false and misleading.

15 All who pass along the way
clap their hands at you;
they hiss and wag their heads
at daughter Jerusalem;
"Is this the city that was called
the perfection of beauty,
the joy of all the earth?"

16 All your enemies
open their mouths against you;
they hiss, they gnash their teeth,
they cry: "We have devoured her!
Ah, this is the day we longed for;
at last we have seen it!"

17 The LORD has done what he
purposed,
he has carried out his threat;
as he ordained long ago,
he has demolished without pity;
he has made the enemy rejoice
over you,
and exalted the might of your foes.

18 Cry aloud[a] to the Lord!
O wall of daughter Zion!
Let tears stream down like a torrent
day and night!
Give yourself no rest,
your eyes no respite!

19 Arise, cry out in the night,
at the beginning of the watches!
Pour out your heart like water
before the presence of the Lord!
Lift your hands to him
for the lives of your children,
who faint for hunger
at the head of every street.

20 Look, O LORD, and consider!
To whom have you done this?
Should women eat their offspring,
the children they have borne?
Should priest and prophet be killed
in the sanctuary of the Lord?

21 The young and the old are lying

a Cn: Heb *Their heart cried*

"plazas" or "squares," broad open places near gates (Judg 19.15; Esth 4.6; 6.9; 2 Chr 32.6). **12:** The lives of innocent victims are poured out *on their mothers' bosom* where they should find succor (Ruth 4.16; cf. Ps 22.9; Job 3.12) and security (1 Kings 3.20). **15:** *Clap . . . hiss . . . wag,* gestures of derision and contempt. *Perfection of beauty* (see Ezek 16.14; 27.3; Ps 50.2); *joy of all the earth,* see Jer 51.41; Ps 48.2. **17:** The language intentionally alludes to 2.1–8. **18:** *Aloud* (lit. "heartily, from the heart," one of the centers of the emotions), cf. 1.20b; 2.19b. **19:** *Watches,* the night was divided into three watches (Ex 14.24; 1 Sam 11.11; Song 3.1–3; 5.7).

2.20–22: Zion's address is more accusation than petition. **20:** *To whom have you done this?* is not a question but a declaration. *Offspring* (lit. "fruit," see Gen 30.2; Deut 7.13), sharpening the reference to cannibalism (cf. Deut 28.53–57). **21:** *Day of your anger . . . slaughtering,* the sacrificial victims on the

on the ground in the streets;
my young women and my young men
have fallen by the sword;
in the day of your anger you have
killed them,
slaughtering without mercy.

22 You invited my enemies from
all around
as if for a day of festival;
and on the day of the anger of
the LORD
no one escaped or survived;
those whom I bore and reared
my enemy has destroyed.

3 I am one who has seen affliction
under the rod of God's[a] wrath;
2 he has driven and brought me
into darkness without any light;
3 against me alone he turns his hand,
again and again, all day long.

4 He has made my flesh and my skin
waste away,
and broken my bones;
5 he has besieged and enveloped me
with bitterness and tribulation;
6 he has made me sit in darkness
like the dead of long ago.

7 He has walled me about so that I
cannot escape;
he has put heavy chains on me;
8 though I call and cry for help,
he shuts out my prayer;
9 he has blocked my ways with hewn
stones,
he has made my paths crooked.

10 He is a bear lying in wait for me,
a lion in hiding;
11 he led me off my way and tore me to
pieces;
he has made me desolate;
12 he bent his bow and set me
as a mark for his arrow.

13 He shot into my vitals
the arrows of his quiver;
14 I have become the laughingstock
of all my people,
the object of their taunt-songs all
day long.
15 He has filled me with bitterness,
he has sated me with wormwood.

16 He has made my teeth grind
on gravel,
and made me cower in ashes;
17 my soul is bereft of peace;
I have forgotten what happiness is;
18 so I say, "Gone is my glory,
and all that I had hoped for from
the LORD."

a Heb *his*

Day of the Lord are usually enemies (Isa 34.6; Jer 12.3; Ezek 39.17), though here, as in Zeph 1.7–8, they are Judah and Jerusalem. **22:** *You invited . . . as if for a day of festival,* further play on the image of sacrifice.

3.1–18: The complaint of the *one who has seen affliction.* This counterpart to Zion's speech in 1.12–22 uses the language and motifs of the individual lament. **1:** *I am one* (lit. "I am the man"), counterbalancing Zion's feminine voice. **2:** *Driven and brought,* like a flock (e.g., Isa 40.11; Ps 78.52–53). The rod is a shepherd's tool (Mic 7.14; Ezek 20.37; Ps 23.4) also used for beatings (Ex 21.20; Prov 10.13). **4:** See Mic 3.1–3; Ps 38.3–4; Job 13.28. **6:** *Darkness,* the netherworld (Ps 88.18; cf. Job 10.21–22; Eccl 6.4). **7:** *Walled me about,* i.e., the destroyed city and Temple walls (Ezek 42.7,12; Mic 7.11) are rebuilt (Am 9.11) as a prison. **9:** The *hewn stones,* which should be used in relaying the foundation for the Temple (1 Kings 5.31; 1 Chr 22.2), are instead scattered in the road to block the man's path. **12–13:** The Divine Archer imagery (Deut 32.23–24; Ps 38.2; Job 16.12–13) carries over from one stanza to the next. Similar strategies for interlocking stanzas appear elsewhere in this poem, e.g., 3.27–28,28–36,48–50,53–55. *Vitals* (lit. "kidneys"), a seat of the emotions (Ps 16.7; Jon 19.27; Prov 23.16; cf. Lam 1.20; 2.11). **17:** *My soul,* a person's essential life force (1.11b,16b,19c; 2.12c,19c). **18:** For the first time in this chapter the LORD is explicitly named. **19–24:** Two transitional stanzas joined by the

19 The thought of my affliction and my homelessness
is wormwood and gall!
20 My soul continually thinks of it
and is bowed down within me.
21 But this I call to mind,
and therefore I have hope:

22 The steadfast love of the LORD never ceases,[a]
his mercies never come to an end;
23 they are new every morning;
great is your faithfulness.
24 "The LORD is my portion," says my soul,
"therefore I will hope in him."

25 The LORD is good to those who wait for him,
to the soul that seeks him.
26 It is good that one should wait quietly
for the salvation of the LORD.
27 It is good for one to bear
the yoke in youth,
28 to sit alone in silence
when the Lord has imposed it,
29 to put one's mouth to the dust
(there may yet be hope),
30 to give one's cheek to the smiter,
and be filled with insults.

31 For the Lord will not
reject forever.
32 Although he causes grief, he will have compassion
according to the abundance of his steadfast love;
33 for he does not willingly afflict
or grieve anyone.

34 When all the prisoners of the land
are crushed under foot,
35 when human rights are perverted
in the presence of the Most High,
36 when one's case is subverted
—does the Lord not see it?

37 Who can command and have it done,
if the Lord has not ordained it?
38 Is it not from the mouth of the Most High
that good and bad come?
39 Why should any who draw breath complain
about the punishment of their sins?

40 Let us test and examine our ways,
and return to the LORD.
41 Let us lift up our hearts as well as our hands
to God in heaven.
42 We have transgressed and rebelled,
and you have not forgiven.

a Syr Tg: Heb *LORD, we are not cut off*

refrain *therefore I have/will hope* (3.21,24). **22–23:** *Steadfast love, mercies, faithfulness,* the LORD's covenant loyalties, as in the divine promises to David (2 Sam 7.15; 1 Kings 8.23; Isa 55.3; Ps 89.2–4).

3.25–39: Sapiential consolation. The second major section contemplates reasons for hope in the face of adversity and suffering, drawing on wisdom traditions. **25:** *The LORD is good to those who wait* in hope; see Ps 25.3; Prov 20.22, but see 2.16c and 3.17. *The soul* recalls the earlier threefold use of this term (3.17,20,24), but here it is generic, i.e., "any soul." **26:** *Wait* (lit. "hope") *quietly,* cf. Ps 4.4; 37.7, but the speaking voices in these poems are far from quiet (Lam 2.10a). **27:** *To bear the yoke* implies a beneficial value to suffering (see Prov 13.24; 23.13–14), although 1.14b and 5.5 express the opposite sentiment. **28:** *Sit alone,* cf. 1.1a. **29:** *To put one's mouth to the dust,* in obeisance and humiliation (cf. Mic 7.17; Ps 72.9). **31:** Cf. 2.7a; 5.20,22. **32:** Cf. 2.2a,17b,21c. **33:** *Willingly,* lit. "from his heart." **36:** The translation *does the Lord not see it?* is conjectural. The words echo the claim expressed elsewhere: "The LORD does not see" (Ezek 8.12; 9.9; Ps 94.7). **39:** *Complain* (Num 11.1; Sir 10.25) here likely bears overtones of mourning.

3.40–47: Communal lament. This section is set apart by its use of "we." **40–41:** As if persuaded by 3.25–39, the speaker calls for self-examination, repentance, and contrition. **42:** The turning point in the poem. *We have transgressed and rebelled,* a confession of sin. But the penitence is short-lived. *And,* better,

43 You have wrapped yourself with
anger and pursued us,
killing without pity;
44 you have wrapped yourself with
a cloud
so that no prayer can pass through.
45 You have made us filth and rubbish
among the peoples.

46 All our enemies
have opened their mouths against
us;
47 panic and pitfall have come upon us,
devastation and destruction.
48 My eyes flow with rivers of tears
because of the destruction of
my people.

49 My eyes will flow without ceasing,
without respite,
50 until the LORD from heaven
looks down and sees.
51 My eyes cause me grief
at the fate of all the young women
in my city.

52 Those who were my enemies without
cause
have hunted me like a bird;
53 they flung me alive into a pit
and hurled stones on me;
54 water closed over my head;
I said, "I am lost."

55 I called on your name, O LORD,
from the depths of the pit;
56 you heard my plea, "Do not close
your ear
to my cry for help, but give
me relief!"
57 You came near when I called on you;
you said, "Do not fear!"

58 You have taken up my cause, O Lord,
you have redeemed my life.
59 You have seen the wrong done to me,
O LORD;
judge my cause.
60 You have seen all their malice,
all their plots against me.

61 You have heard their taunts, O LORD,
all their plots against me.
62 The whispers and murmurs of my
assailants
are against me all day long.
63 Whether they sit or rise—see,
I am the object of their taunt-songs.

"but," given the following statement's promised adversative sense. The speaker, having come to the brink of being consoled (cf. vv. 25–39), is finally crushed by the LORD's continued absence and silence and the persistence of suffering. **44:** *Wrapped yourself with a cloud,* as in 2.1a, recalls the radiant cloud (Ex 19.16) by which the LORD reveals himself, overwhelms enemies, and even, as here, hides himself (cf. Isa 45.15; Ps 55.1; 88.14).

3.48–66: Individual lament. The "I" returns, now a more inclusive "I" than in 3.1–18. The shift in voice reasserts the personal dimension of the suffering. **51:** *Cause me grief,* better, "assault my soul" (i.e., "my very being"). The verb is the same as found in 1.12b, 22a,b, and 2.20a. The eyes either are worn out from crying or are assaulted by terrible knowledge. **52:** See Ps 11.1; 124.7. **53:** *Pit,* the netherworld, Sheol (Isa 14.15; Ps 30.3; 88.4). **54:** *Water,* associated with Sheol (Jon 2.3–6; Ps 69.1–2,14–16; 88.6–7). *I am lost* (lit. "I am cut off"), i.e., dead (Isa 53.8; Ps 88.5). **55–56:** Many of the verbs translated as past tense throughout the remainder of the poem are to be understood as expressing a wish or request (cf. 1.21c; 4.22b). **55:** See Ps 88.10; 119.145–46. **56:** *My plea,* lit. "my voice." See Ps 130.2. **57:** *You came near . . . ,* better, "come near when I call you." *You said,* better, "say." **58:** *You have taken up,* better "take up (legally)." *Cause* is a legal term and recalls the imagery in 3.34–36. *You have redeemed,* better, "redeem." Redemption here denotes rescue from the speaker's current distress (see Ps 69.18), and more specifically from the powers of death (3.53–55; cf. Hos 13.14; Ps 103.4). **59–60:** *You have seen,* better, "see." *Malice,* lit. "vengeance, vindication," primarily associated with the LORD, prefiguring the vengeance called for in 3.64–66. **61:** *You have heard,* better, "hear." **63:** *I am* recalls the *I am* that began the poem, providing a sense of closure to the poem before it shifts to invective in the final stanza.

64 Pay them back for their deeds,
O LORD,
according to the work of their
hands!
65 Give them anguish of heart;
your curse be on them!
66 Pursue them in anger and
destroy them
from under the LORD's heavens.

4 How the gold has grown dim,
how the pure gold is changed!
The sacred stones lie scattered
at the head of every street.
2 The precious children of Zion,
worth their weight in fine gold—
how they are reckoned as
earthen pots,
the work of a potter's hands!

3 Even the jackals offer the breast
and nurse their young,
but my people has become cruel,
like the ostriches in the wilderness.

4 The tongue of the infant sticks
to the roof of its mouth for thirst;
the children beg for food,
but no one gives them anything.

5 Those who feasted on delicacies
perish in the streets;
those who were brought up in purple
cling to ash heaps.

6 For the chastisement[a] of my people
has been greater
than the punishment[b] of Sodom,
which was overthrown in a moment,
though no hand was laid on it.[c]

7 Her princes were purer than snow,
whiter than milk;
their bodies were more ruddy
than coral,
their hair[c] like sapphire.[d]

8 Now their visage is blacker than soot;
they are not recognized in
the streets.
Their skin has shriveled on
their bones;
it has become as dry as wood.

9 Happier were those pierced by
the sword
than those pierced by hunger,
whose life drains away, deprived
of the produce of the field.

10 The hands of compassionate women
have boiled their own children;
they became their food
in the destruction of my people.

11 The LORD gave full vent to his wrath;
he poured out his hot anger,
and kindled a fire in Zion
that consumed its foundations.

12 The kings of the earth did not believe,

a Or *iniquity* *b* Or *sin* *c* Meaning of Heb uncertain *d* Or *lapis lazuli*

3.64–66: Final invectives. Cf. 1.21–22; 4.21–22. The stanza is unified by the use of imperfect verb forms throughout. **64:** As in 1.22a,b, the LORD should deal out retribution in exact proportion to the crime.
4.1–16: The suffering of the population. 1: *Gold,* usually impervious to tarnishing, has *grown dim* and *changed,* emphasizing the severity of the suffering. *Sacred stones,* "jewels." **2:** *Earthen pots,* clay vessels, the most common of ancient artifacts, which when broken were simply discarded (Jer 18.1–12; 22.28; Hos 8.8; Ps 2.9). **3:** The personified city's actions are less humane even than that of the cruelest of animals, *jackals* (commonly associated with deserted ruins; see Isa 13.22; Mic 1.8) and *ostriches* (cf. Job 39.13–18). **6:** *Sodom*'s utter destruction was legendary (Gen 19.24–25; Deut 29.23). **7:** Light skin (*purer . . . whiter,* cf. 5.10; Ps 104.15; contrast Song 1.5) and a *ruddy* complexion (5.10; cf. 1 Sam 16.12; 17.42) were identified with health and vigor. *Hair like sapphire,* cf. Song 5.10–16. **8:** For associations of blackness with famine, see Job 30.30; Lam 5.10. **10:** See 2.20n. **12:** An allusion to the belief in Zion's inviolability; see Ps 48.3–8. **13–15:** Because of the sins of prophets and priests (v. 13), the larger

nor did any of the inhabitants
of the world,
that foe or enemy could enter
the gates of Jerusalem.

13 It was for the sins of her prophets
and the iniquities of her priests,
who shed the blood of the righteous
in the midst of her.

14 Blindly they wandered through
the streets,
so defiled with blood
that no one was able
to touch their garments.

15 "Away! Unclean!" people shouted
at them;
"Away! Away! Do not touch!"
So they became fugitives and
wanderers;
it was said among the nations,
"They shall stay here no longer."

16 The LORD himself has scattered
them,
he will regard them no more;
no honor was shown to the priests,
no favor to the elders.

17 Our eyes failed, ever watching
vainly for help;
we were watching eagerly
for a nation that could not save.

18 They dogged our steps
so that we could not walk in
our streets;
our end drew near; our days were
numbered;
for our end had come.

19 Our pursuers were swifter
than the eagles in the heavens;
they chased us on the mountains,
they lay in wait for us in the
wilderness.

20 The LORD's anointed, the breath of
our life,
was taken in their pits—
the one of whom we said, "Under his
shadow
we shall live among the nations."

21 Rejoice and be glad, O daughter
Edom,
you that live in the land of Uz;
but to you also the cup shall pass;
you shall become drunk and strip
yourself bare.

22 The punishment of your iniquity,
O daughter Zion, is
accomplished,
he will keep you in exile no longer;
but your iniquity, O daughter Edom,
he will punish,
he will uncover your sins.

community wanders blindly and bloodied through the streets. V. 15 alludes to the treatment of lepers (Lev 13.45–46). Judah as a community has become contaminated and isolated (cf. 1.17). **16:** *The LORD himself,* lit. "the face of the LORD," which elsewhere turns hostile or threatening (Lev 26.16; Ezek 14.8; Ps 34.16; 80.16). *He will regard them no more,* i.e., he withholds the benevolent look (Ezek 9.12) that these poems seek (1.9c,11c,20a; 2.20a; 3.59–60; 5.1).

4.17–22: Communal voice. A transition into the "we" of the community whose horrible plight has just been graphically depicted. **17:** *Watching vainly for help,* see Jer 34.21–22; 37.5–11. **20:** *The LORD's anointed* (1 Sam 24.7,11; 2 Sam 1.14,16), *the breath of our life* and *under his shadow* (Ps 17.8; 91.1) are all traditional royal epithets. **21–22:** *Edom* elsewhere in the exilic and postexilic literature comes in for special comment (Ezek 35; Ob 11; Ps 137.7). *Uz,* a country in northwestern Arabia (Jer 25.20; Job 1.1), often connected with Edom (Gen 36.28; 1 Chr 1.42). For the *cup* of wrath imagery, see Isa 51.17–22; Jer 25.15–29; Ezek 23.30–34; Hab 2.15–16; Ob 16; Job 21.20. *Drunk,* cf. Jer 51.7; Hab 2.15–16. *Strip yourself bare,* here personified Edom is to suffer the same abuse that personified Zion suffered (1.8–10). *Accomplished,* lit. "to be complete" (Heb "tam") begins the final ("taw") stanza and signals the conclusion or completion of the alphabetic acrostic portion of the sequence. Moreover, 4.22a forms the mirror image of 1.3a, underscoring the strong sense of closure.

5 Remember, O LORD, what has
befallen us;
look, and see our disgrace!
2 Our inheritance has been turned over
to strangers,
our homes to aliens.
3 We have become orphans, fatherless;
our mothers are like widows.
4 We must pay for the water we drink;
the wood we get must be bought.
5 With a yoke[a] on our necks we are
hard driven;
we are weary, we are given no rest.
6 We have made a pact with[b] Egypt
and Assyria,
to get enough bread.
7 Our ancestors sinned; they are
no more,
and we bear their iniquities.
8 Slaves rule over us;
there is no one to deliver us from
their hand.
9 We get our bread at the peril of
our lives,
because of the sword in the
wilderness.
10 Our skin is black as an oven
from the scorching heat of famine.
11 Women are raped in Zion,
virgins in the towns of Judah.
12 Princes are hung up by their hands;
no respect is shown to the elders.
13 Young men are compelled to grind,
and boys stagger under loads
of wood.
14 The old men have left the city gate,
the young men their music.
15 The joy of our hearts has ceased;
our dancing has been turned
to mourning.
16 The crown has fallen from our head;
woe to us, for we have sinned!
17 Because of this our hearts are sick,
because of these things our eyes
have grown dim:
18 because of Mount Zion, which
lies desolate;
jackals prowl over it.

a Symmachus: Heb lacks *With a yoke* *b* Heb *have given the hand to*

5.1: Address. The opening address to the LORD recalls the earlier appeals voiced by Zion and the man (1.9c,11c,20a; 2.20a; 3.59–61).

5.2–18: The complaint. 2: *Inheritance,* the land (Deut 4.38; 25.19; 26.1), and even the people themselves (Deut 4.20; 9.26,29; 32.9). **3:** See the image of widowed mother Zion in 1.1b. *Orphans* and *widows,* vulnerable groups who required special protection (e.g., Isa 1.23; Ps 68.5). **5:** The images of persecution (1.3c,6c; 3.43; 4.19), slavery (1.1c,14b; 3.27), weariness (1.6c,22c), and lack of rest (1.3b) all occur elsewhere in the book. **6:** *Egypt* and *Assyria,* the two traditionally dominant superpowers of the ancient Near East are commonly linked, even in later literature (e.g., Isa 52.4; Zech 10.10–11). **7:** Both a statement of fact (Ex 20.5) and a protest (cf. Jer 31.29; Ezek 18.2). The Heb word for *iniquities* can also mean "punishment." **8:** *Slaves rule over us,* a commonplace emphasizing the absence of normality and the dire nature of the situation (Prov 30.21–23; cf. Isa 3.4; Eccl 10.6–7). **11:** The imagery recalls the similar fate suffered by personified Zion (1.8–10). **12:** *Hung up,* either execution (e.g., Gen 40.19; Esth 2.23) by hanging or by being impaled on a stake, or exposure of the corpses (after execution) to degrade them and instill fear in the survivors (e.g., Deut 21.22; Josh 10.26–27; 1 Sam 31.10). *By their hands,* i.e., the hands of the enemy, the "slaves" of v. 8. **13:** Grinding was a menial task usually undertaken by women (Ex 11.5; Isa 47.2; Job 31.10) and slaves (Judg 16.21). **14:** *The old men,* i.e., the "elders" of v. 12, who would gather at the city gate to discuss matters and adjudicate disputes (Deut 22.15; Isa 29.21; Am 5.12,15; Job 5.4). **15:** *The joy of our hearts,* i.e., general happiness and well-being, but also an allusion to the city, "the joy of all the earth" (2.15c), whose existence has been brought to an ignominious end. **16:** The crenelated walls of Palestinian cities were often likened to a great crown adorning the head of the city (Isa 28.1–5; 54.11; Jer 13.18; Ezek 16.12; Mic 4.8). **17:** *Because of this . . . because of these* refers back to 5.2–16 and not just forward. *Dim,* lit. "dark or black"; see 2.1a; 4.8; 5.10; cf. Ps 69.23; Eccl 12.3. **18:** *Jackals,* or "foxes," proverbial inhabitants of ruined cities (see 4.3; Ezek 13.4; cf. Isa 34.11–17; Zeph 2.13–15).

19 But you, O Lord, reign forever;
your throne endures to all
generations.
20 Why have you forgotten us
completely?
Why have you forsaken us these
many days?
21 Restore us to yourself, O Lord,
that we may be restored;
renew our days as of old—
22 unless you have utterly rejected
us,
and are angry with us beyond
measure.

5.19–22: Conclusion. 19: Not a straightforward hymn of praise as in other communal laments (e.g., Ps 44.1–8; 74.12–17; 89.1–18). The Lord's eternal enthronement in heaven distances him from earthly and human misery and contrasts with his earthly throne, Jerusalem, "his footstool" (2.1c; cf. 1.10; 2.6a), which has been demolished and profaned. **20:** Cf. Ps 22.1; 44.24; 74.19. **21:** A short prayer for restoration (cf. Ps 14.7; 90.13; Jer 48.47; Zeph 3.14–20). **22:** *Unless*, the Heb is difficult. Perhaps "but instead" (as in Vg; cf. Num 24.22; 1 Sam 21.6; 2 Sam 13.33), underscoring the Lord's rejection and anger; or even more literally, "for if," in which case the conditional clause's apodosis has been intentionally withheld. Either sentiment runs contrary to the traditional concluding lines in communal laments and, when combined with the brevity of the prayer in v. 21, undoes whatever hopefulness inheres in the prayer. Therefore the poem, and the book, ends pessimistically, even tragically.

EZEKIEL

The prophecies in the book of Ezekiel are among the most fascinating and puzzling writings in the Bible. The prophet expresses his thought through a variety of literary forms—signs, visions, allegories, denunciations, and legal arguments, among others. He sometimes uses bizarre or extreme imagery and elaborates it to an almost excessive point. He has inspired fear, awe, and wonder in readers because he attempts not merely to name, but also to embody, God's sovereignty, holiness, and mystery in words that come close to the limits of expression.

At first this variety, intricacy, and elaboration can seem confusing. It is easy to get lost in Ezekiel's images and forget his larger concerns; it is easy as well to pick out striking passages and ignore the context of the book as a whole. But Ezekiel makes a coherent effort to deal with profound and difficult issues: Has God abandoned Jerusalem and the Temple? Does the suffering of the people of Judah have a purpose? How should the people understand their tragic history? And, perhaps most important, how can God now move on with God's people, in a transformed and renewed state? To understand how Ezekiel addresses these questions, we must consider not only the situation in which he found himself, but also the traditions and beliefs to which he looked for answers. The complexity of the book becomes clearer when we understand that it is the carefully written composition of one with a profound respect for the texts of his tradition, and that it has been carefully put together and preserved for the instruction of later readers.

Ezekiel wrote his prophecies, and his followers edited, expanded, and preserved them, in the sixth century BCE in Babylon, during the exile of the Judeans from their homeland. The exile thus forms the historical context of the book, and at several points, particularly in the allegory in 17.1–24, Ezekiel refers to the Babylonian subjugation of Judah.

The Babylonians under Nebuchadrezzar II (who ruled 605–562) defeated the Egyptians in 605. The Egyptians had allied with the great Assyrian Empire, which the Babylonians destroyed between 614 and 609. Although these victories made Babylon the leading political power in Syria-Palestine, including the territory of Judah, the Judeans, often acting in concert with other neighboring states, eventually rebelled. The Babylonians, in an escalating response to the continued efforts of the Judeans to throw them off, exiled the Judeans in two phases, spaced about a decade apart. They first besieged Jerusalem under Jehoiakim, who died before Jerusalem fell in 597. When the Babylonians took over the city, his son, Jehoiachin, along with most of the Judean ruling class, was exiled to Babylon. The Babylonians installed a puppet king, Zedekiah; when he, too, attempted to rebel, they destroyed Jerusalem and the Temple, deposed the rest of the rulers, and exiled much of the population except the poorest to Babylon in 586.

Ezekiel was among the first group of exiles, taken to Babylonia in 597. Even so, he remained well informed about events in Judah, and his prophecies concern both expatriates and those who remained behind. He could address both communities as a single entity, since they were in ready contact with each other, and both were passionately concerned about the fate of Jerusalem. Neither group accepted Ezekiel's indictment of their guilt or believed his prophecies about Jerusalem's coming destruction. After the destruction in fact took place, the prophet's words turned to themes of renewed hope and restoration.

Ezekiel and his school, the followers who edited and preserved his prophecies, were members of a specific lineage of priests in Israel known as the Zadokites (see 1.1–3n.; 44.15–31n.). At the time of Ezekiel's exile the Zadokites controlled the Israelite high priesthood and held power at the Jerusalem Temple. These Jerusalem priests were proponents of "Zion theology," the traditions that emphasized God's choice of Jerusalem as Zion, the holy city, and the protection for Jerusalem that resulted from this choice (see 2 Sam 7.4–17; Ps 46; 132). These traditions also stressed God's unconditional choice of the Davidic monarchy and of Abraham's descendants. (See the annotations for instances of Ezekiel's use of this theology.)

The exile of the Judean rulers and the destruction of Jerusalem directly challenged this theology, since they called into question God's eternal promises to Zion. Ezekiel answered these challenges with cosmic, eschatological, and apocalyptic visions of a rebuilt Zion that fulfilled the promises of God's eternal protection despite the fall of the earthly Jerusalem (see 1.22–25n., 26–28n.; 37.28n.; 38.12n.; 43.7n.; 48.35n.). In these visions particularly, Ezekiel anticipated much that was yet to come in the biblical writings, including later developments of apocalypticism (see esp. Dan 7–12, and, in the New Testament, the book of Revelation).

The specific language and laws of the priests and the traditions of the Temple heavily influenced Ezekiel as a Zadokite. A significant body of these laws, the so-called "Holiness Collection" (HC), can be found in the Pentateuch. HC is in the form of a vassal-covenant, a type of agreement in which guarantees on one side are specifically linked to responsibilities on the other. For Ezekiel this covenant form proved invaluable in interpreting the exile, since it allowed for the possibility that defilement, injustice, and covenant infidelity on Israel's part could lead to judgment and even exile without annulling God's eternal promises to Israel (Lev 26.42). The HC material stresses the unique sacredness of the people and land of Israel, in the midst of which the LORD dwells. This sacredness includes not only ritual and worship, but also morality and social justice.

The Holiness Collection extends beyond the confines of Lev 17–26 (known as the "Holiness Code"), and includes other parts of the Pentateuch often identified as belonging to the Priestly source (P). Authoritative, written traditions such as HC profoundly influenced Ezekiel, an influence that extended to the character of the book of Ezekiel itself.

The prophet and his followers composed the book in writing and preserved it for the specific purpose of instructing readers at a later time. The written composition and the careful preservation of Ezekiel contrast with much of the other prophetic literature in the Hebrew Bible, which was spoken directly to a contemporaneous audience. Many of the words of prophets such as Isaiah were only written down some considerable time after they had been spoken; therefore they could be, and often were, modified to adapt them to situations that arose in later times. In Ezekiel, however, there are clear indications of an originally written composition and of an early intention to preserve the text. For instance, the thoroughgoing chronological notations show that Ezekiel and his followers took great care to demonstrate the timeliness and veracity of Ezekiel's oracles, and thereby their authority as prophecy. This care for the written text and its accurate transmission, as well as for the preservation of authoritative traditions such as the HC material, mark a breakthrough in the development of written scripture in Israel, and therefore help us to understand the historical processes that created the biblical canon over the centuries.

Ezekiel's character as a literary text makes it a complex book to read and interpret. Much of the other prophetic literature, as oral literature, generally uses less elaborate forms; Ezekiel, however, is made up of intricate, deliberately composed literary creations. Although some scholarship has viewed such literary ornamentation and intricacy as indicating confused layers of literary growth, newer readings have discovered literary integrity in the texts, even when the final form has resulted from a process of transmission and editing. One of the characteristic features of the book is the frequent repetition of key words or phrases (e.g., "mortal" [lit. "son of man"], "for the sake of my holy name," "so that you/they will know that I am the LORD"). Important aspects of the theology of Ezekiel are reinforced by the repetition of these and other formulas.

The style of Ezekiel is often "non-mimetic": It does not always render reality by immediate representation. Instead, it probes behind or beyond observable things and events, using metaphors and mythic poetry to portray the underlying structure of existence or the transcendent realities beneath both plain sensory observation and historical records. The visions in Ezekiel show both inner and outer realities, abolishing or going beyond normal sensory and temporal bounds.

Because of these literary qualities, reading Ezekiel requires a sophisticated approach, in order to avoid mistaking some of the descriptions for historical events, observable behaviors, or factual reports. For example, some interpretations of Ezekiel's behavior take it as evidence of a disoriented or abnormal personality. But the descriptions of these acts—muteness, for example, or holding prolonged, agonizing postures—are not evidence of psychopathology but are instead literary images that have rich theological import (see 3.22–27n.; 4.4–8n.).

The book of Ezekiel is complex, but fortunately its organization and outline are agreeably simple. Chapters 1–24 are set before the fall of Jerusalem, and are largely prophecies of doom against the city and against Judah. An extended body of material on Ezekiel's call to prophesy begins this section in chs 1–3. Chapters 25–32 are prophecies against foreign nations, forming a bridge between Ezekiel's initial message of doom and his ultimate message of hope. The hope comes in the prophecies of restoration, chs 33–48, dating from the time after Jerusalem's fall. Clearly the capture and destruction of Jerusalem in 586 was the critical moment in Ezekiel's prophetic career. The prophecies of restoration include an apocalyptic passage (chs 38–39) and an extended blueprint for the restored Temple and land (chs 40–48).

1 In the thirtieth year, in the fourth
month, on the fifth day of the month, as
I was among the exiles by the river Chebar,
the heavens were opened, and I saw visions
of God. 2 On the fifth day of the month (it
was the fifth year of the exile of King Jehoi-
achin), 3 the word of the LORD came to the
priest Ezekiel son of Buzi, in the land of the
Chaldeans by the river Chebar; and the
hand of the LORD was on him there.
4 As I looked, a stormy wind came out
of the north: a great cloud with brightness

1.1–3.27: Part 1: The call of Ezekiel. 1.1–3: Superscription. Ezekiel was a Zadokite priest (v. 3; 44.15–31n.), steeped in the traditions of Jerusalemite royal theology (Zion theology; see Introduction). Despite his exile, he never loses his priestly role (cf. 43.12n.). *The thirtieth year,* probably Ezekiel's own age. At the age for assuming his duties at the Jerusalem Temple (Num 4.3), Ezekiel sought solitude outside his settlement (see 3.14–15) to reflect on what course his life might instead take in exile. *Fifth day* of the *fourth month . . . fifth year of the exile* would be July 31, 593 BCE. *Chebar,* a canal, flowing near Nippur, which is mentioned also in Babylonian documents. **3:** The name *Ezekiel* means "God strengthens." *Hand of the LORD* (3.14,22; 8.1; 33.22; 37.1; 40.1), Ezekiel undergoes the same types of divine compulsions and ecstatic trances experienced by Israel's early prophets, such as Elijah and Elisha (1 Kings 18.46; 2 Kings 3.15). *Chaldeans,* Babylonians.

1.4–28a: The throne-chariot vision. Cf. the imagery in 1 Kings 22.19–22; Isa 6.1–9. The first two-thirds of Ezekiel's vision of God merely describes the creatures and wheels below the platform supporting God's throne. In Ezekiel's theology of God's transcendence, God is clearly far removed from earthly perception. **4:** *Stormy wind . . . cloud . . .* and *fire* are phenomena often associated with the appearance of God in the Hebrew Bible (see Ps 18.8–12). *Out of the north,* because the shape of the Fertile Crescent meant that anything coming from Jerusalem arrived in Babylonia from the north. *Something like,* Ezekiel uses the word *like* to suggest the difference between his description and the transcendent reality itself.

around it and fire flashing forth continual-
ly, and in the middle of the fire, something
like gleaming amber. 5 In the middle of it
was something like four living creatures.
This was their appearance: they were of hu-
man form. 6 Each had four faces, and each
of them had four wings. 7 Their legs were
straight, and the soles of their feet were like
the sole of a calf's foot; and they sparkled
like burnished bronze. 8 Under their wings
on their four sides they had human hands.
And the four had their faces and their
wings thus: 9 their wings touched one an-
other; each of them moved straight ahead,
without turning as they moved. 10 As for
the appearance of their faces: the four had
the face of a human being, the face of a lion
on the right side, the face of an ox on the
left side, and the face of an eagle; 11 such
were their faces. Their wings were spread
out above; each creature had two wings,
each of which touched the wing of another,
while two covered their bodies. 12 Each
moved straight ahead; wherever the spirit
would go, they went, without turning as
they went. 13 In the middle of[a] the living
creatures there was something that looked
like burning coals of fire, like torches mov-
ing to and fro among the living creatures;
the fire was bright, and lightning issued
from the fire. 14 The living creatures darted
to and fro, like a flash of lightning.

15 As I looked at the living creatures, I
saw a wheel on the earth beside the living
creatures, one for each of the four of
them.[b] 16 As for the appearance of the
wheels and their construction: their appear-
ance was like the gleaming of beryl; and the
four had the same form, their construction
being something like a wheel within a
wheel. 17 When they moved, they moved in
any of the four directions without veering
as they moved. 18 Their rims were tall and
awesome, for the rims of all four were full
of eyes all around. 19 When the living crea-
tures moved, the wheels moved beside
them; and when the living creatures rose
from the earth, the wheels rose. 20 Wherev-
er the spirit would go, they went, and the
wheels rose along with them; for the spirit
of the living creatures was in the wheels.
21 When they moved, the others moved;
when they stopped, the others stopped; and
when they rose from the earth, the wheels
rose along with them; for the spirit of the
living creatures was in the wheels.

22 Over the heads of the living creatures
there was something like a dome, shining
like crystal,[c] spread out above their heads.
23 Under the dome their wings were
stretched out straight, one toward another;
and each of the creatures had two wings
covering its body. 24 When they moved, I
heard the sound of their wings like the
sound of mighty waters, like the thunder of
the Almighty,[d] a sound of tumult like the
sound of an army; when they stopped, they
let down their wings. 25 And there came a
voice from above the dome over their
heads; when they stopped, they let down
their wings.

26 And above the dome over their heads

a Gk OL: Heb *And the appearance of* *b* Heb *of their faces* *c* Gk: Heb *like the awesome crystal* *d* Traditional rendering of Heb *Shaddai*

5–14: *The living creatures* are identified as cherubim in a later vision (10.15,20), guardians of God's throne (see Ex 25.18–22; 1 Kings 6.23–28), namely winged, human-headed lions or bulls. Uncharacteristically, the creatures Ezekiel sees have four faces (v. 10; cf. Rev 4.7). **13:** *Torches,* cf. Gen 15.17. **15–21:** *The four . . . wheels* (compare the four faces of the creatures) to God's throne are a crucial element in Ezekiel's reconciling of his central priestly belief that God had elected and now dwelled in Zion with the earthly Zion's coming destruction by the Babylonians (see Introduction). Its wheels mean that the real, cosmic Zion-throne has omnidirectional mobility and is not tied down to earthly Jerusalem. See further 1.26–28n. **18:** *Full of eyes,* symbolic of omniscience (10.12; Zech 4.10; cf. Rev 4.6,8). **22–25:** *A dome,* referring to the cosmic firmament of Gen 1.6–8, which separates earth and heaven. Jerusalem and its Temple mount symbolize the cosmic mountain where heaven and earth intersect at the dome. **26–28:** Thus the LORD was still really enthroned atop the cosmos, even though Jerusalem, the symbol of God's cosmic dwelling (Ps 26.8; 63.2; 102.16), was to be destroyed by the Babylonians. On the *glory of the*

there was something like a throne, in ap-
pearance like sapphire;[a] and seated above
the likeness of a throne was something that
seemed like a human form. 27 Upward from
what appeared like the loins I saw some-
thing like gleaming amber, something that
looked like fire enclosed all around; and
downward from what looked like the loins
I saw something that looked like fire, and
there was a splendor all around. 28 Like the
bow in a cloud on a rainy day, such was the
appearance of the splendor all around. This
was the appearance of the likeness of the
glory of the LORD.

When I saw it, I fell on my face, and I
heard the voice of someone speaking.

2 He said to me: O mortal,[b] stand up on
your feet, and I will speak with you.
2 And when he spoke to me, a spirit entered
into me and set me on my feet; and I heard
him speaking to me. 3 He said to me, Mor-
tal, I am sending you to the people of Israel,
to a nation[c] of rebels who have rebelled
against me; they and their ancestors have
transgressed against me to this very day.
4 The descendants are impudent and stub-
born. I am sending you to them, and you
shall say to them, "Thus says the Lord
GOD." 5 Whether they hear or refuse to
hear (for they are a rebellious house), they
shall know that there has been a prophet
among them. 6 And you, O mortal, do not
be afraid of them, and do not be afraid of
their words, though briers and thorns sur-
round you and you live among scorpions;
do not be afraid of their words, and do not
be dismayed at their looks, for they are a
rebellious house. 7 You shall speak my
words to them, whether they hear or refuse
to hear; for they are a rebellious house.

8 But you, mortal, hear what I say to
you; do not be rebellious like that rebel-
lious house; open your mouth and eat what
I give you. 9 I looked, and a hand was
stretched out to me, and a written scroll
was in it. 10 He spread it before me; it had
writing on the front and on the back, and
written on it were words of lamentation
and mourning and woe.

3 He said to me, O mortal, eat what is
offered to you; eat this scroll, and go,
speak to the house of Israel. 2 So I opened
my mouth, and he gave me the scroll to eat.
3 He said to me, Mortal, eat this scroll that
I give you and fill your stomach with it.
Then I ate it; and in my mouth it was as
sweet as honey.

4 He said to me: Mortal, go to the house
of Israel and speak my very words to them.
5 For you are not sent to a people of obscure
speech and difficult language, but to the
house of Israel— 6 not to many peoples of

a Or *lapis lazuli* *b* Or *son of man*; Heb *ben adam* (and so throughout the book when Ezekiel is addressed) *c* Syr: Heb *to nations*

LORD, see 10.1–22n. *Appearance of the likeness,* the qualified language again emphasizes God's transcendence and cosmic power (see 1.4n.). God's self is three levels removed from Ezekiel's description of God.

1.28b–3.27: Ezekiel's commissioning. The sheer length of this section reflects the need to establish Ezekiel's authority in the factious milieu of his times. **1.28b–2.8a:** Ezekiel is commissioned in a series of addresses. **2.1:** The term *mortal* is literally "son of man" (textual note *b*), a Heb idiom designating a member of the category of "humanity." The traditions of Ezekiel's group stressed how God and the divine realm transcended this category (the idiom occurs ninety-three times in Ezekiel). **2:** *Spirit* (see 3.12,14,24), an empowerment that Ezekiel experiences as coming from God. **2.5:** *Rebellious house,* a phrase unique to Ezekiel that designates one of his major themes: Judah's ingrained defiance (ch 20). **6:** *Briers and thorns . . . scorpions,* though Ezekiel is a priestly official, his message will be met with hostility. **2.8b–3.3:** In conformity with the contemporary emergence of the concept of God's word as sacred text, Ezekiel is told to eat a *scroll* (cf. Zech 5.1–4; Rev 10.8–11). The scroll depicts the coming, fixed judgment of Judah. See 3.22–27n. **3.3:** Jeremiah's metaphor (Jer 15.16) becomes a concrete sensation in Ezekiel. Yielding to God's word is *sweet* (Ps 19.10), even when its contents involve pain. **3.4–9:** Preparation for resistance. **6–7:** *Obscure speech,* Isa 33.19. **8–9:** *Hard,* or "strong." Compare the meaning of Ezekiel's name, "God strengthens" (1.3n.). **10–11:** A final charge.

obscure speech and difficult language,
whose words you cannot understand. Sure-
ly, if I sent you to them, they would listen
to you. 7 But the house of Israel will not
listen to you, for they are not willing to
listen to me; because all the house of Israel
have a hard forehead and a stubborn heart.
8 See, I have made your face hard against
their faces, and your forehead hard against
their foreheads. 9 Like the hardest stone,
harder than flint, I have made your fore-
head; do not fear them or be dismayed at
their looks, for they are a rebellious house.
10 He said to me: Mortal, all my words that
I shall speak to you receive in your heart
and hear with your ears; 11 then go to the
exiles, to your people, and speak to them.
Say to them, "Thus says the Lord GOD";
whether they hear or refuse to hear.

12 Then the spirit lifted me up, and as
the glory of the LORD rose[a] from its place,
I heard behind me the sound of loud rum-
bling; 13 it was the sound of the wings of the
living creatures brushing against one an-
other, and the sound of the wheels beside
them, that sounded like a loud rumbling.
14 The spirit lifted me up and bore me away;
I went in bitterness in the heat of my spirit,
the hand of the LORD being strong upon
me. 15 I came to the exiles at Tel-abib, who
lived by the river Chebar.[b] And I sat there
among them, stunned, for seven days.

16 At the end of seven days, the word of
the LORD came to me: 17 Mortal, I have
made you a sentinel for the house of Israel;
whenever you hear a word from my mouth,
you shall give them warning from me. 18 If
I say to the wicked, "You shall surely die,"
and you give them no warning, or speak to
warn the wicked from their wicked way, in
order to save their life, those wicked per-
sons shall die for their iniquity; but their
blood I will require at your hand. 19 But if
you warn the wicked, and they do not turn
from their wickedness, or from their wick-
ed way, they shall die for their iniquity; but
you will have saved your life. 20 Again, if
the righteous turn from their righteousness
and commit iniquity, and I lay a stumbling
block before them, they shall die; because
you have not warned them, they shall die
for their sin, and their righteous deeds that
they have done shall not be remembered;
but their blood I will require at your hand.
21 If, however, you warn the righteous not
to sin, and they do not sin, they shall surely
live, because they took warning; and you
will have saved your life.

22 Then the hand of the LORD was upon
me there; and he said to me, Rise up, go out
into the valley, and there I will speak with
you. 23 So I rose up and went out into the
valley; and the glory of the LORD stood
there, like the glory that I had seen by the

a Cn: Heb *and blessed be the glory of the LORD*
b Two Mss Syr: Heb *Chebar, and to where they lived.* Another reading is *Chebar, and I sat where they sat*

3.12–15: Ezekiel returns to his people. 12: *Glory of the LORD*, see 10.1–22n. **14:** Ezekiel feels either God's anger at the people or his own distress over his difficult task. *The hand of the LORD*, see 1.3n. **15:** *Tel-abib*, a town near Nippur. *Chebar*, 1.1–3n.

3.16–21: The sentinel. Prophets as watchers (Jer 6.17; Hab 2.1) provide warnings. Ezekiel is assured that his personal responsibility is limited to delivering such warnings; it is the individuals of his audience who are accountable for their responses (18.1–32; see also 33.1–9).

3.22–27: Ezekiel's speechlessness. *The valley*, a specific site near Tel-abib (see 37.1n.). It was probably a low-lying area, perhaps with a spring. Ezekiel's *speechless* state has been a scholarly conundrum. It is best seen as one of the characteristic literary metaphors of the book, with a complex relationship to observable reality (Ezekiel is not literally speechless after this point; cf. 11.25). The metaphor's meaning is bound up with the growing significance of written, authoritative scripture in Ezekiel's time. In view of this development, Ezekiel's role as a prophet has changed. He must fall speechless, and let the scroll that he has swallowed (2.8b–3.3n.) have its fulfillment. The judgments of scripture (such as those of the book of Habakkuk) are thus now inevitable. The metaphor of speechlessness is also a major literary device that structures the book of Ezekiel. The judgments of the swallowed scroll play themselves out in the first half of Ezekiel, after which he regains his speech (24.25–27; 33.21–22).

river Chebar; and I fell on my face. 24 The
spirit entered into me, and set me on my
feet; and he spoke with me and said to me:
Go, shut yourself inside your house. 25 As
for you, mortal, cords shall be placed on
you, and you shall be bound with them, so
that you cannot go out among the people;
26 and I will make your tongue cling to the
roof of your mouth, so that you shall be
speechless and unable to reprove them; for
they are a rebellious house. 27 But when I
speak with you, I will open your mouth,
and you shall say to them, "Thus says the
Lord GOD"; let those who will hear, hear;
and let those who refuse to hear, refuse; for
they are a rebellious house.

4 And you, O mortal, take a brick and
set it before you. On it portray a city,
Jerusalem; 2 and put siegeworks against it,
and build a siege wall against it, and cast up
a ramp against it; set camps also against
it, and plant battering rams against it all
around. 3 Then take an iron plate and place
it as an iron wall between you and the city;
set your face toward it, and let it be in a
state of siege, and press the siege against it.
This is a sign for the house of Israel.

4 Then lie on your left side, and place
the punishment of the house of Israel upon
it; you shall bear their punishment for the
number of the days that you lie there. 5 For
I assign to you a number of days, three hun-
dred ninety days, equal to the number of
the years of their punishment; and so you
shall bear the punishment of the house of
Israel. 6 When you have completed these,
you shall lie down a second time, but on
your right side, and bear the punishment of
the house of Judah; forty days I assign you,
one day for each year. 7 You shall set your
face toward the siege of Jerusalem, and
with your arm bared you shall prophesy
against it. 8 See, I am putting cords on you
so that you cannot turn from one side to
the other until you have completed the days
of your siege.

9 And you, take wheat and barley, beans
and lentils, millet and spelt; put them into
one vessel, and make bread for yourself.
During the number of days that you lie on
your side, three hundred ninety days, you
shall eat it. 10 The food that you eat shall be
twenty shekels a day by weight; at fixed
times you shall eat it. 11 And you shall drink
water by measure, one-sixth of a hin; at
fixed times you shall drink. 12 You shall eat
it as a barley-cake, baking it in their sight
on human dung. 13 The LORD said, "Thus
shall the people of Israel eat their bread,
unclean, among the nations to which I will
drive them." 14 Then I said, "Ah Lord GOD!
I have never defiled myself; from my youth
up until now I have never eaten what died
of itself or was torn by animals, nor has
carrion flesh come into my mouth." 15 Then
he said to me, "See, I will let you have
cow's dung instead of human dung, on
which you may prepare your bread."

16 Then he said to me, Mortal, I am go-
ing to break the staff of bread in Jerusalem;
they shall eat bread by weight and with
fearfulness; and they shall drink water by

4.1–24.27: Part 2: Prophecies of doom against Judah and Jerusalem. 4.1–5.17: Symbolic actions describing the coming siege of Jerusalem. Like his speechlessness, these actions appear to be literary metaphors rather than observable performances (e.g., see 4.4–8n.). In Ezekiel, reality is more complex than the merely observable. **4.1–3:** A *brick* inscribed, before baking, with a drawing of Jerusalem. *An iron plate,* a baking griddle, symbolizing the barrier between the city and God. **4–8:** At one level the postures commanded of Ezekiel illustrate the coming siege of Jerusalem and its duration. They also depict both God's pre-siege punishments of Israel in the land (v. 5; see Lev 26.14–32) and God's post-siege punishment of Judah in exile (v. 6; cf. Num 14.34). **5–6:** The precise significance of the numbers is unclear. **9–17:** Coarse bread and rationing symbolize the rigors of the coming siege of Jerusalem (cf. Jer 19.9; Lam 4.10). **9:** The necessity of mixing grains indicates scarcity of foodstuffs. **10–11:** *Twenty shekels,* approximately 228 gr (8 oz). *One-sixth of a hin,* approximately .64 l (.67 qt). **12–13:** Siege symbolism again blurs into exile symbolism here. *Human dung,* considered unclean (Deut 23.13), represents the defiling effects of exile to an unclean land. Zech 3.3–5 shows how those in the tradition of Ezekiel came to terms with this defilement after the exile. Ezekiel was allowed to substitute dried "cow dung" (v. 15), common fuel measure and in dismay. 17 Lacking bread and water, they will look at one another in dismay, and waste away under their punishment.

5 And you, O mortal, take a sharp sword; use it as a barber's razor and run it over your head and your beard; then take balances for weighing, and divide the hair. 2 One third of the hair you shall burn in the fire inside the city, when the days of the siege are completed; one third you shall take and strike with the sword all around the city;[a] and one third you shall scatter to the wind, and I will unsheathe the sword after them. 3 Then you shall take from these a small number, and bind them in the skirts of your robe. 4 From these, again, you shall take some, throw them into the fire and burn them up; from there a fire will come out against all the house of Israel.

5 Thus says the Lord GOD: This is Jerusalem; I have set her in the center of the nations, with countries all around her. 6 But she has rebelled against my ordinances and my statutes, becoming more wicked than the nations and the countries all around her, rejecting my ordinances and not following my statutes. 7 Therefore thus says the Lord GOD: Because you are more turbulent than the nations that are all around you, and have not followed my statutes or kept my ordinances, but have acted according to the ordinances of the nations that are all around you; 8 therefore thus says the Lord GOD: I, I myself, am coming against you; I will execute judgments among you in the sight of the nations. 9 And because of all your abominations, I will do to you what I have never yet done, and the like of which I will never do again. 10 Surely, parents shall eat their children in your midst, and children shall eat their parents; I will execute judgments on you, and any of you who survive I will scatter to every wind. 11 Therefore, as I live, says the Lord GOD, surely, because you have defiled my sanctuary with all your detestable things and with all your abominations—therefore I will cut you down;[b] my eye will not spare, and I will have no pity. 12 One third of you shall die of pestilence or be consumed by famine among you; one third shall fall by the sword around you; and one third I will scatter to every wind and will unsheathe the sword after them.

13 My anger shall spend itself, and I will vent my fury on them and satisfy myself; and they shall know that I, the LORD, have spoken in my jealousy, when I spend my fury on them. 14 Moreover I will make you a desolation and an object of mocking among the nations around you, in the sight of all that pass by. 15 You shall be[c] a mockery and a taunt, a warning and a horror, to the nations around you, when I execute judgments on you in anger and fury, and with furious punishments—I, the LORD, have spoken— 16 when I loose against you[d] my deadly arrows of famine, arrows for destruction, which I will let loose to destroy you, and when I bring more and more famine upon you, and break your staff of bread. 17 I will send famine and wild animals against you, and they will rob you of your children; pestilence and bloodshed shall pass through you; and I will bring the sword upon you. I, the LORD, have spoken.

a Heb *it* *b* Another reading is *I will withdraw*
c Gk Syr Vg Tg: Heb *It shall be* *d* Heb *them*

in the Near East. **14:** Cf. Lev 17.10–16. **16:** *Staff of bread,* "food supply" (Lev 26.26). **5.1–17:** The *razor* symbolizes military defeat (Isa 7.20). The defeated people are then destroyed in three different ways. Even their remnant undergoes further judgment. **5:** *Center of the nations,* central priests, such as Ezekiel, viewed Jerusalem as the mythopoetic center of the earth (see 38.12, "center [lit. navel] of the earth"; 43.13–17n.). **10:** Cannibalism was a curse for breaking the "Holiness Collection" covenant (Lev 26.29). **12:** *Pestilence, famine,* and *sword* (also 6.11–12; 7.15; 12.16; 14.21) are also linked as modes of destruction in Lev 26.25–26 and in Jeremiah (e.g., Jer 14.12; 21.7). **13:** *They shall know . . . ,* 6.7n. **16:** *Staff of bread,* 4.16n. **17:** 14.21; Lev 26.22.

6 The word of the LORD came to me:
2 O mortal, set your face toward the
mountains of Israel, and prophesy against
them, 3 and say, You mountains of Israel,
hear the word of the Lord GOD! Thus says
the Lord GOD to the mountains and the
hills, to the ravines and the valleys: I, I my-
self will bring a sword upon you, and I will
destroy your high places. 4 Your altars shall
become desolate, and your incense stands
shall be broken; and I will throw down
your slain in front of your idols. 5 I will lay
the corpses of the people of Israel in front
of their idols; and I will scatter your bones
around your altars. 6 Wherever you live,
your towns shall be waste and your high
places ruined, so that your altars will be
waste and ruined,[a] your idols broken and
destroyed, your incense stands cut down,
and your works wiped out. 7 The slain shall
fall in your midst; then you shall know that
I am the LORD.
8 But I will spare some. Some of you
shall escape the sword among the nations
and be scattered through the countries.
9 Those of you who escape shall remember
me among the nations where they are car-
ried captive, how I was crushed by their
wanton heart that turned away from me,
and their wanton eyes that turned after
their idols. Then they will be loathsome in
their own sight for the evils that they have
committed, for all their abominations.
10 And they shall know that I am the LORD;
I did not threaten in vain to bring this disas-
ter upon them.
11 Thus says the Lord GOD: Clap your
hands and stamp your foot, and say, Alas
for all the vile abominations of the house of
Israel! For they shall fall by the sword, by
famine, and by pestilence. 12 Those far off
shall die of pestilence; those nearby shall
fall by the sword; and any who are left and
are spared shall die of famine. Thus I will
spend my fury upon them. 13 And you shall
know that I am the LORD, when their slain
lie among their idols around their altars, on
every high hill, on all the mountain tops,
under every green tree, and under every
leafy oak, wherever they offered pleasing
odor to all their idols. 14 I will stretch out
my hand against them, and make the land
desolate and waste, throughout all their
settlements, from the wilderness to Rib-
lah.[b] Then they shall know that I am the
LORD.

7 The word of the LORD came to me:
2 You, O mortal, thus says the Lord
GOD to the land of Israel:

An end! The end has come
upon the four corners of the land.
3 Now the end is upon you,
I will let loose my anger upon you;
I will judge you according to
your ways,
I will punish you for all your
abominations.
4 My eye will not spare you, I will have
no pity.

a Syr Vg Tg: Heb *and be made guilty* *b* Another reading is *Diblah*

6.1–14: Two prophecies against Israel's idolatry. 1–10: *The mountains of Israel,* the highlands, representing all Israel, are here associated with illegitimate worship and idolatry (v. 9; cf. 18.6). *High places* were ritual installations or shrines. Their destruction was a curse for breaking the "Holiness Collection" covenant (Lev 26.30). **4:** *Idols* translates Ezekiel's characteristic term "gillulim," found in Lev 26.30 and thirty-nine times in Ezekiel. **6:** *Towns shall be waste . . . ,* Lev 26.31. **7:** *You shall know . . . ,* one of over sixty similar closing declarations in Ezekiel (see vv. 10,13–14). Ezekiel prophesies that God's judging and saving acts will prove God's sovereign identity and result in human recognition of God. In general, the book of Ezekiel deemphasizes the prophet's human experience, focusing instead on God's desire to reveal the mystery of God's own self. **11–14:** A second prophecy of judgment, beginning with an expressive action. **14:** *From the wilderness* of south Judah *to Riblah* in central Syria was the maximum extent of Israelite territory.

7.1–27: Prophecies on the approaching end. 1–4: The theme, *the end,* is reminiscent of Am 8.2. **3:** Cf. Ps 78.49. **5–9:** The day (v. 7) of the end is "the day of the LORD" (Am 5.18–20; Isa 2.11–17; Joel

I will punish you for your ways,
while your abominations are among you.
Then you shall know that I am the LORD.
5 Thus says the Lord GOD:
Disaster after disaster! See, it comes.
6 An end has come, the end has come.
It has awakened against you; see, it comes!
7 Your doom[a] has come to you,
O inhabitant of the land.
The time has come, the day is near—
of tumult, not of reveling on the mountains.
8 Soon now I will pour out my wrath upon you;
I will spend my anger against you.
I will judge you according to your ways,
and punish you for all your abominations.
9 My eye will not spare; I will have no pity.
I will punish you according to your ways,
while your abominations are among you.
Then you shall know that it is I the LORD who strike.
10 See, the day! See, it comes!
Your doom[a] has gone out.
The rod has blossomed, pride has budded.
11 Violence has grown into a rod of wickedness.
None of them shall remain,
not their abundance, not their wealth;
no pre-eminence among them.[a]
12 The time has come, the day draws near;
let not the buyer rejoice, nor the seller mourn,
for wrath is upon all their multitude.
13 For the sellers shall not return to what
has been sold as long as they remain alive.
For the vision concerns all their multitude;
it shall not be revoked. Because of their in-
iquity, they cannot maintain their lives.[a]
14 They have blown the horn and made everything ready;
but no one goes to battle,
for my wrath is upon all their multitude.
15 The sword is outside, pestilence and famine are inside;
those in the field die by the sword;
those in the city—famine and pestilence devour them.
16 If any survivors escape,
they shall be found on the mountains
like doves of the valleys,
all of them moaning over their iniquity.
17 All hands shall grow feeble,
all knees turn to water.
18 They shall put on sackcloth,
horror shall cover them.
Shame shall be on all faces,
baldness on all their heads.
19 They shall fling their silver into the streets,
their gold shall be treated as unclean.
Their silver and gold cannot save them on
the day of the wrath of the LORD. They
shall not satisfy their hunger or fill their
stomachs with it. For it was the stumbling
block of their iniquity. 20 From their[b]
beautiful ornament, in which they took
pride, they made their abominable images,

a Meaning of Heb uncertain *b* Syr Symmachus: Heb *its*

1.15). **9:** See v. 4. **10–27: The end** spells dissolution of normal life. **10:** *The rod,* the term both connotes "discipline" and evokes a similar Heb word meaning "injustice." **12:** The joys and sorrows of daily life and commerce (Prov 20.14) are rendered moot by the approach of Jerusalem's end. **14:** The trumpet calls to the defense, but the people are too enfeebled to respond. **18:** Wearing coarse *sackcloth* and shaving the head (baldness) were both signs of mourning. **20:** *Beautiful ornament,* probably jewelry made of the gold and silver of v. 19. **22:** *My treasured place,* Jerusalem. **23a:** Perhaps a call to be chained for exile, but see their detestable things; therefore I will make of it an unclean thing to them.

21 I will hand it over to strangers
as booty,
to the wicked of the earth
as plunder;
they shall profane it.
22 I will avert my face from them,
so that they may profane my
treasured[a] place;
the violent shall enter it,
they shall profane it.
23 Make a chain![b]
For the land is full of bloody crimes;
the city is full of violence.
24 I will bring the worst of the nations
to take possession of their houses.
I will put an end to the arrogance of
the strong,
and their holy places shall be
profaned.
25 When anguish comes, they will seek
peace,
but there shall be none.
26 Disaster comes upon disaster,
rumor follows rumor;
they shall keep seeking a vision from
the prophet;
instruction shall perish from
the priest,
and counsel from the elders.
27 The king shall mourn,
the prince shall be wrapped
in despair,
and the hands of the people of the
land shall tremble.
According to their way I will deal
with them;
according to their own judgments I
will judge them.
And they shall know that I am the LORD.

8 In the sixth year, in the sixth month, on
the fifth day of the month, as I sat in my
house, with the elders of Judah sitting be-
fore me, the hand of the Lord GOD fell
upon me there. 2 I looked, and there was a
figure that looked like a human being;[c]
below what appeared to be its loins it was
fire, and above the loins it was like the ap-
pearance of brightness, like gleaming am-
ber. 3 It stretched out the form of a hand,
and took me by a lock of my head; and the
spirit lifted me up between earth and heav-
en, and brought me in visions of God to
Jerusalem, to the entrance of the gateway
of the inner court that faces north, to the
seat of the image of jealousy, which pro-
vokes to jealousy. 4 And the glory of the
God of Israel was there, like the vision that
I had seen in the valley.
5 Then God[d] said to me, "O mortal,
lift up your eyes now in the direction of the
north." So I lifted up my eyes toward the
north, and there, north of the altar gate, in
the entrance, was this image of jealousy.
6 He said to me, "Mortal, do you see what
they are doing, the great abominations that
the house of Israel are committing here, to
drive me far from my sanctuary? Yet you
will see still greater abominations."
7 And he brought me to the entrance of
the court; I looked, and there was a hole in
the wall. 8 Then he said to me, "Mortal, dig

a Or *secret* *b* Meaning of Heb uncertain
c Gk: Heb *like fire* *d* Heb *he*

textual note *b*. **23b:** Social ethics, as well as idolatry, concern Ezekiel (12.19; 28.16; cf. Gen 6.11). **24:** Human *arrogance* has no place in the theology of Zion borne by Ezekiel (see Introduction), which stresses God's sovereignty (Lev 26.19; Isa 13.11). **26:** Cf. 22.26–28; Jer 4.9; 18.18; Mic 3.11.

8.1–11.25: The Temple visions. 8.1–18: The vision of idolatry (September 17, 592 BCE). In his vision of wickedness in Jerusalem's Temple, Ezekiel saw beyond the observable offenses of his time into the ingrained, polluted essence of the shrine. **1:** *Elders,* in exile with the prophet, also his audience in 14.1; 20.1. *The hand of the LORD,* see 1.3n. **2:** The *figure* is described in terms similar to those in 1.26–27. **3:** *By a lock of my head,* cf. Bel 36. The *gateway* led north from the palace complex into the Temple precincts. The *image of jealousy* is probably the carved image of the goddess Asherah that King Manasseh set up in the Temple (2 Kings 21.7). Though removed in Josiah's reform (2 Kings 23.6), it stood out starkly in Ezekiel's transhistorical perception. **4:** See 3.22–23. On *the glory of the God of Israel,* see 10.1–22n. **7–13:** The elders of Judah with censers inside the secret gatehouse chamber perform the same

through the wall"; and when I dug through
the wall, there was an entrance. 9 He said to
me, "Go in, and see the vile abominations
that they are committing here." 10 So I went
in and looked; there, portrayed on the wall
all around, were all kinds of creeping
things, and loathsome animals, and all the
idols of the house of Israel. 11 Before them
stood seventy of the elders of the house
of Israel, with Jaazaniah son of Shaphan
standing among them. Each had his censer
in his hand, and the fragrant cloud of in-
cense was ascending. 12 Then he said to me,
"Mortal, have you seen what the elders of
the house of Israel are doing in the dark,
each in his room of images? For they say,
'The LORD does not see us, the LORD has
forsaken the land.'" 13 He said also to me,
"You will see still greater abominations
that they are committing."

14 Then he brought me to the entrance
of the north gate of the house of the LORD;
women were sitting there weeping for Tam-
muz. 15 Then he said to me, "Have you seen
this, O mortal? You will see still greater
abominations than these."

16 And he brought me into the inner
court of the house of the LORD; there, at
the entrance of the temple of the LORD,
between the porch and the altar, were
about twenty-five men, with their backs to
the temple of the LORD, and their faces to-
ward the east, prostrating themselves to the
sun toward the east. 17 Then he said to me,
"Have you seen this, O mortal? Is it not
bad enough that the house of Judah com-
mits the abominations done here? Must
they fill the land with violence, and pro-
voke my anger still further? See, they are
putting the branch to their nose! 18 There-
fore I will act in wrath; my eye will not
spare, nor will I have pity; and though they
cry in my hearing with a loud voice, I will
not listen to them."

9 Then he cried in my hearing with a loud
voice, saying, "Draw near, you execu-
tioners of the city, each with his destroying
weapon in his hand." 2 And six men came
from the direction of the upper gate, which
faces north, each with his weapon for
slaughter in his hand; among them was a
man clothed in linen, with a writing case at
his side. They went in and stood beside the
bronze altar.

3 Now the glory of the God of Israel had
gone up from the cherub on which it rested
to the threshold of the house. The LORD
called to the man clothed in linen, who had
the writing case at his side; 4 and said to
him, "Go through the city, through Jerusa-
lem, and put a mark on the foreheads of
those who sigh and groan over all the

sort of improper act as that described in the story of the rebellion in the wilderness in Num 16.2,17,35. Ezekiel views this scriptural story about ritual rebellion as prototypical, and it informs his assessment of the preexilic Temple's wickedness (see also 44.6–14n.). **10:** Cf. 23.14; Deut 4.17–18. **11:** The *seventy elders* here are in Jerusalem, and are not the same as those in v. 1. *Jaazaniah*'s father *Shaphan* was active in King Josiah's reform movement (2 Kings 22), and other members of the family protected Jeremiah against his enemies (Jer 26.24; 39.14). **14–15:** *Tammuz,* the Mesopotamian vegetation god; the weeping was for his descent into the underworld, coinciding with the annual decline of vegetation. Transtemporal perception is again suggested here, since Ezekiel sees the weeping rite in the sixth month (v. 1) and not in the fourth month (June-July), when it was normally practiced. **16–18:** The climactic abomination seen by Ezekiel was sun worship. Its practice in Israel is evidenced by texts such as 2 Kings 23.5,11 and by artifacts. The *branch* gesture may be an obscene expression. **18:** The judgment is irrevocable (see 14.12–23n.).

9.1–11: The punishment of the guilty. 1–2: From the upper gate (Jer 20.2) came the *executioners* (divine functionaries mustered to punish) and *a man clothed in linen,* who functioned as the LORD's scribe, as did Nabu among the seven Babylonian planetary deities (cf. Rev 8.2,6). *Linen,* a bleached fabric signifying purity, was worn by priests (Lev 6.10) and angels (Dan 10.5). **3:** On the departure of the *glory,* see 10.1–22n. *The cherub,* in the singular, is used of the inanimate pair of statues in the Temple (also 10.4). The actual living entities are referred to with the Heb plural, "cherubim." **4:** The *mark* was the Heb

abominations that are committed in it."
5 To the others he said in my hearing, "Pass
through the city after him, and kill; your
eye shall not spare, and you shall show no
pity. 6 Cut down old men, young men and
young women, little children and women,
but touch no one who has the mark. And
begin at my sanctuary." So they began with
the elders who were in front of the house.
7 Then he said to them, "Defile the house,
and fill the courts with the slain. Go!" So
they went out and killed in the city. 8 While
they were killing, and I was left alone, I fell
prostrate on my face and cried out, "Ah
Lord GOD! will you destroy all who remain
of Israel as you pour out your wrath upon
Jerusalem?" 9 He said to me, "The guilt of
the house of Israel and Judah is exceedingly
great; the land is full of bloodshed and the
city full of perversity; for they say, 'The
LORD has forsaken the land, and the LORD
does not see.' 10 As for me, my eye will not
spare, nor will I have pity, but I will bring
down their deeds upon their heads."
11 Then the man clothed in linen, with
the writing case at his side, brought back
word, saying, "I have done as you commanded me."

10 Then I looked, and above the dome
that was over the heads of the cherubim
there appeared above them something
like a sapphire,[a] in form resembling
a throne. 2 He said to the man clothed in
linen, "Go within the wheelwork underneath
the cherubim; fill your hands with
burning coals from among the cherubim,
and scatter them over the city." He went in
as I looked on. 3 Now the cherubim were
standing on the south side of the house
when the man went in; and a cloud filled
the inner court. 4 Then the glory of the
LORD rose up from the cherub to the
threshold of the house; the house was filled
with the cloud, and the court was full of the
brightness of the glory of the LORD. 5 The
sound of the wings of the cherubim was
heard as far as the outer court, like the
voice of God Almighty[b] when he speaks.
6 When he commanded the man clothed
in linen, "Take fire from within the wheelwork,
from among the cherubim," he went
in and stood beside a wheel. 7 And a cherub
stretched out his hand from among the
cherubim to the fire that was among the
cherubim, took some of it and put it into
the hands of the man clothed in linen, who
took it and went out. 8 The cherubim appeared
to have the form of a human hand
under their wings.
9 I looked, and there were four wheels
beside the cherubim, one beside each cherub;
and the appearance of the wheels was
like gleaming beryl. 10 And as for their appearance,
the four looked alike, something
like a wheel within a wheel. 11 When they
moved, they moved in any of the four directions
without veering as they moved; but in
whatever direction the front wheel faced,
the others followed without veering as they

a Or *lapis lazuli* *b* Traditional rendering of Heb *El Shaddai*

letter "taw," made like an X (cf. Rev 7.3–4). **6:** The *elders* are those of 8.16. **7:** Ezekiel's "Holiness Collection" traditions stressed that corpses defile (Lev 21.1; Num 5.2–3; 9.6; 19.11,13).

10.1–22 and **11.22–25: The departure of the LORD's glory from the Temple** is repeatedly described in each of three versions of Jerusalem's abandonment (9.3; 10.4; 11.22). *The glory of the LORD* is the objective overpowering majesty of God, not so much an attribute as an expression of God's presence (Lev 9.23; Num 20.6). The pattern of movement of the glory of the LORD is a major literary device structuring the book of Ezekiel. The glory has been present in Jerusalem, even when the city's inhabitants felt forsaken by it (8.4,12b). Because of their wickedness it departs, however, first to the doorway of the Temple (also 9.3), and then to the east gate of the Temple's outer court (10.18–19). The departure continues in 11.22–25, where the glory heads east over the Mount of Olives toward Babylon. It was in Babylonia that Ezekiel first saw the glory of the LORD (1.28; 3.22–23; cf. 8.4; 11.16). Eventually, the prophet envisions it returning to the restored Temple (43.2–5; 44.4). **10.1:** *Cherubim,* see 1.5–14n. **2:** *Burning coals,* cf. Isa 31.9; Ps 18.10–13; Rev 8.5. **3–4:** The throne-chariot comes to collect the glory of the LORD from the cherub statues (see 9.3n.). The *cloud* filling the Temple recalls Ex 16.10; 40.34–35. It both conceals and

moved. 12 Their entire body, their rims,
their spokes, their wings, and the wheels—
the wheels of the four of them—were full of
eyes all around. 13 As for the wheels, they
were called in my hearing "the wheel-
work." 14 Each one had four faces: the first
face was that of the cherub, the second face
was that of a human being, the third that of
a lion, and the fourth that of an eagle.

15 The cherubim rose up. These were
the living creatures that I saw by the river
Chebar. 16 When the cherubim moved, the
wheels moved beside them; and when the
cherubim lifted up their wings to rise up
from the earth, the wheels at their side did
not veer. 17 When they stopped, the others
stopped, and when they rose up, the others
rose up with them; for the spirit of the liv-
ing creatures was in them.

18 Then the glory of the LORD went out
from the threshold of the house and
stopped above the cherubim. 19 The cheru-
bim lifted up their wings and rose up from
the earth in my sight as they went out with
the wheels beside them. They stopped at
the entrance of the east gate of the house of
the LORD; and the glory of the God of Isra-
el was above them.

20 These were the living creatures that I
saw underneath the God of Israel by the
river Chebar; and I knew that they were
cherubim. 21 Each had four faces, each four
wings, and underneath their wings some-
thing like human hands. 22 As for what
their faces were like, they were the same
faces whose appearance I had seen by the
river Chebar. Each one moved straight
ahead.

11 The spirit lifted me up and brought
me to the east gate of the house of
the LORD, which faces east. There, at the
entrance of the gateway, were twenty-five
men; among them I saw Jaazaniah son of
Azzur, and Pelatiah son of Benaiah, offi-
cials of the people. 2 He said to me, "Mor-
tal, these are the men who devise iniquity
and who give wicked counsel in this city;
3 they say, 'The time is not near to build
houses; this city is the pot, and we are the
meat.' 4 Therefore prophesy against them;
prophesy, O mortal."

5 Then the spirit of the LORD fell upon
me, and he said to me, "Say, Thus says the
LORD: This is what you think, O house of
Israel; I know the things that come into
your mind. 6 You have killed many in this
city, and have filled its streets with the
slain. 7 Therefore thus says the Lord GOD:
The slain whom you have placed within it
are the meat, and this city is the pot; but
you shall be taken out of it. 8 You have
feared the sword; and I will bring the sword
upon you, says the Lord GOD. 9 I will take
you out of it and give you over to the hands
of foreigners, and execute judgments upon
you. 10 You shall fall by the sword; I will
judge you at the border of Israel. And you
shall know that I am the LORD. 11 This city
shall not be your pot, and you shall not be
the meat inside it; I will judge you at the
border of Israel. 12 Then you shall know
that I am the LORD, whose statutes you
have not followed, and whose ordinances
you have not kept, but you have acted ac-
cording to the ordinances of the nations
that are around you."

reveals the divine presence. **12:** Cf. 1.18; Zech 4.2,5,10b. **14:** *That of the cherub,* the bull face of 1.10 (some ancient cherubim were bovine). **15:** *Chebar,* 1.1–3n.

11.1–25: Judgment and promise. 11.1–13: A disputation over the city. *Jaazaniah* and *Pelatiah* are otherwise unknown *officials of the people* (a postexilic title). *Wicked counsel* perhaps refers to the plot between Egypt and Zedekiah's pro-Egyptian counselors against the Babylonian king Nebuchadrezzar (Jer 27.1–3; 37.5,7,11). **3:** Having a false confidence in Zion's ironclad invulnerability (*the pot*), they assure the populace of the city's security. They put off domestic construction, perhaps because they have now appropriated the houses of the slain (v. 6) and of the deportees (v. 15). Alternatively, they are urging that all construction be concentrated on fortifying Jerusalem for their planned rebellion. **5–13:** Ezekiel has formulated a far more sophisticated theology of Zion than their rather denuded conception (see 1.15–21n., 26–28n.). Accusing the leaders of gross violence (7.23; ch 22), he tells them that a morally complacent trust in Zion will not protect them (cf. 24.1–14), but that they will be judged *at the border*

13 Now, while I was prophesying, Pela-
tiah son of Benaiah died. Then I fell down
on my face, cried with a loud voice, and
said, "Ah Lord GOD! will you make a full
end of the remnant of Israel?"
14 Then the word of the LORD came to
me: 15 Mortal, your kinsfolk, your own kin,
your fellow exiles,[a] the whole house of Is-
rael, all of them, are those of whom the
inhabitants of Jerusalem have said, "They
have gone far from the LORD; to us this
land is given for a possession." 16 Therefore
say: Thus says the Lord GOD: Though I
removed them far away among the nations,
and though I scattered them among the
countries, yet I have been a sanctuary to
them for a little while[b] in the countries
where they have gone. 17 Therefore say:
Thus says the Lord GOD: I will gather you
from the peoples, and assemble you out of
the countries where you have been scat-
tered, and I will give you the land of Israel.
18 When they come there, they will remove
from it all its detestable things and all its
abominations. 19 I will give them one[c]
heart, and put a new spirit within them; I
will remove the heart of stone from their
flesh and give them a heart of flesh, 20 so
that they may follow my statutes and keep
my ordinances and obey them. Then they
shall be my people, and I will be their God.
21 But as for those whose heart goes after
their detestable things and their abomina-
tions,[d] I will bring their deeds upon their
own heads, says the Lord GOD.
22 Then the cherubim lifted up their
wings, with the wheels beside them; and the
glory of the God of Israel was above them.
23 And the glory of the LORD ascended from
the middle of the city, and stopped on the
mountain east of the city. 24 The spirit lifted
me up and brought me in a vision by the
spirit of God into Chaldea, to the exiles.
Then the vision that I had seen left me.
25 And I told the exiles all the things that the
LORD had shown me.

12 The word of the LORD came to me:
2 Mortal, you are living in the midst
of a rebellious house, who have eyes to see
but do not see, who have ears to hear but
do not hear; 3 for they are a rebellious
house. Therefore, mortal, prepare for your-
self an exile's baggage, and go into exile by
day in their sight; you shall go like an exile
from your place to another place in their
sight. Perhaps they will understand, though
they are a rebellious house. 4 You shall

a Gk Syr: Heb *people of your kindred* *b* Or *to some extent* *c* Another reading is *a new* *d* Cn: Heb *And to the heart of their detestable things and their abominations their heart goes*

of Israel (perhaps Riblah; see 2 Kings 25.7,18–21). **13:** Pelatiah's death is a prediction within the prophetic vision, not an actual event. Ezekiel's desperate question at the end of this verse receives a reassuring negative answer in vv. 14–21, an authentically early (pre-586 BCE, see v. 15) oracle of promise in Ezekiel.

11.14–21: The future lies with the exiles. This passage disputes the claim of those who remained in the land that the exiles were bearing God's punishment, and that their property thus now belonged to those who remained. Ezekiel warns them that God is with his exiled people and will restore them. It is the exile group that constitutes the true Israel (cf. 20.41–42). **15:** *Your fellow exiles,* see textual note *a;* the rare Heb noun translated "kindred" denotes people who, according to Lev 25.25–28, should be defended against the permanent alienation of their land. The Jerusalemites are violating "Holiness" traditions. **16:** *A sanctuary,* the Hebrew indicates that the glory of the LORD is now tabernacling with the exiles in Babylonia rather than with those who remained (v. 23). **17–21:** Promise of restoration to the exiles. **19:** New *heart,* see 36.26n. **20:** The new covenant, cf. 16.60; 36.27–28; 37.23,27. **24:** *Chaldea,* Babylonia.

11.22–25: Two reports conclude the Temple visions. **22–23:** See 10.1–22n. *The mountain east of the city* is the Mount of Olives.

12.1–20: Two symbolic actions. 12.1–16: First symbol, an exile's baggage. Ezekiel is commanded to symbolize the Jerusalemites' coming exile. Features within this text in time revealed themselves as stunningly applicable to events surrounding Zedekiah (the *prince,* v. 12), who left Jerusalem by night at the city's fall. The oracle was then revised to bring out this applicability. It now specifies how Zedekiah was captured (17.20), taken to Riblah, and blinded (*may not see,* vv. 6,12; 2 Kings 25.4,7; Jer 39.1–10). **3–4:**

bring out your baggage by day in their
sight, as baggage for exile; and you shall go
out yourself at evening in their sight, as
those do who go into exile. 5 Dig through
the wall in their sight, and carry the bag-
gage through it. 6 In their sight you shall lift
the baggage on your shoulder, and carry it
out in the dark; you shall cover your face,
so that you may not see the land; for I have
made you a sign for the house of Israel.
7 I did just as I was commanded. I
brought out my baggage by day, as baggage
for exile, and in the evening I dug through
the wall with my own hands; I brought it
out in the dark, carrying it on my shoulder
in their sight.
8 In the morning the word of the LORD
came to me: 9 Mortal, has not the house of
Israel, the rebellious house, said to you,
"What are you doing?" 10 Say to them,
"Thus says the Lord GOD: This oracle con-
cerns the prince in Jerusalem and all the
house of Israel in it." 11 Say, "I am a sign
for you: as I have done, so shall it be done
to them; they shall go into exile, into cap-
tivity." 12 And the prince who is among
them shall lift his baggage on his shoulder
in the dark, and shall go out; he[a] shall dig
through the wall and carry it through; he
shall cover his face, so that he may not see
the land with his eyes. 13 I will spread my
net over him, and he shall be caught in my
snare; and I will bring him to Babylon, the
land of the Chaldeans, yet he shall not see
it; and he shall die there. 14 I will scatter to
every wind all who are around him, his
helpers and all his troops; and I will un-
sheathe the sword behind them. 15 And they
shall know that I am the LORD, when I
disperse them among the nations and scat-
ter them through the countries. 16 But I will
let a few of them escape from the sword,
from famine and pestilence, so that they
may tell of all their abominations among
the nations where they go; then they shall
know that I am the LORD.
17 The word of the LORD came to me:
18 Mortal, eat your bread with quaking,
and drink your water with trembling and
with fearfulness; 19 and say to the people of
the land, Thus says the Lord GOD concern-
ing the inhabitants of Jerusalem in the land
of Israel: They shall eat their bread with
fearfulness, and drink their water in dis-
may, because their land shall be stripped of
all it contains, on account of the violence of
all those who live in it. 20 The inhabited
cities shall be laid waste, and the land shall
become a desolation; and you shall know
that I am the LORD.
21 The word of the LORD came to me:
22 Mortal, what is this proverb of yours
about the land of Israel, which says, "The
days are prolonged, and every vision comes
to nothing"? 23 Tell them therefore, "Thus
says the Lord GOD: I will put an end to this
proverb, and they shall use it no more as a
proverb in Israel." But say to them, The
days are near, and the fulfillment of every
vision. 24 For there shall no longer be any
false vision or flattering divination within
the house of Israel. 25 But I the LORD will
speak the word that I speak, and it will be
fulfilled. It will no longer be delayed; but in
your days, O rebellious house, I will speak
the word and fulfill it, says the Lord GOD.
26 The word of the LORD came to me:
27 Mortal, the house of Israel is saying,
"The vision that he sees is for many years
ahead; he prophesies for distant times."
28 Therefore say to them, Thus says the
Lord GOD: None of my words will be de-
layed any longer, but the word that I speak
will be fulfilled, says the Lord GOD.

a Gk Syr: Heb *they*

An exile's baggage, the essential food, clothing, and equipment that could be easily carried. **5:** *Dig through the wall,* imitating the actions of one escaping a besieged city. **14:** 5.2,12; 17.21; Lev 26.33. **15–16:** 14.21–23.

12.17–20: Second symbol, eating with trembling. The people's emotional breakdown at the approaching invasion (cf. Ps 80.5) is prophesied.

12.21–28: Disputations about prophecy. Ezekiel condemns the people's skepticism about prophecies of judgment (vv. 22,27; Jer 5.12; 17.15). **26–28:** Second disputation.

13 The word of the LORD came to me: 2 Mortal, prophesy against the prophets of Israel who are prophesying; say to those who prophesy out of their own imagination: "Hear the word of the LORD!" 3 Thus says the Lord GOD, Alas for the senseless prophets who follow their own spirit, and have seen nothing! 4 Your prophets have been like jackals among ruins, O Israel. 5 You have not gone up into the breaches, or repaired a wall for the house of Israel, so that it might stand in battle on the day of the LORD. 6 They have envisioned falsehood and lying divination; they say, "Says the LORD," when the LORD has not sent them, and yet they wait for the fulfillment of their word! 7 Have you not seen a false vision or uttered a lying divination, when you have said, "Says the LORD," even though I did not speak?

8 Therefore thus says the Lord GOD: Because you have uttered falsehood and envisioned lies, I am against you, says the Lord GOD. 9 My hand will be against the prophets who see false visions and utter lying divinations; they shall not be in the council of my people, nor be enrolled in the register of the house of Israel, nor shall they enter the land of Israel; and you shall know that I am the Lord GOD. 10 Because, in truth, because they have misled my people, saying, "Peace," when there is no peace; and because, when the people build a wall, these prophets[a] smear whitewash on it. 11 Say to those who smear whitewash on it that it shall fall. There will be a deluge of rain,[b] great hailstones will fall, and a stormy wind will break out. 12 When the wall falls, will it not be said to you, "Where is the whitewash you smeared on it?" 13 Therefore thus says the Lord GOD: In my wrath I will make a stormy wind break out, and in my anger there shall be a deluge of rain, and hailstones in wrath to destroy it. 14 I will break down the wall that you have smeared with whitewash, and bring it to the ground, so that its foundation will be laid bare; when it falls, you shall perish within it; and you shall know that I am the LORD. 15 Thus I will spend my wrath upon the wall, and upon those who have smeared it with whitewash; and I will say to you, The wall is no more, nor those who smeared it— 16 the prophets of Israel who prophesied concerning Jerusalem and saw visions of peace for it, when there was no peace, says the Lord GOD.

17 As for you, mortal, set your face against the daughters of your people, who prophesy out of their own imagination; prophesy against them 18 and say, Thus says the Lord GOD: Woe to the women who sew bands on all wrists, and make veils for the heads of persons of every height, in the hunt for human lives! Will you hunt down lives among my people, and maintain your own lives? 19 You have profaned me among my people for handfuls of barley and for pieces of bread, putting to death persons who should not die and keeping alive persons who should not live, by your lies to my people, who listen to lies.

20 Therefore thus says the Lord GOD: I am against your bands with which you

a Heb *they*   *b* Heb *rain and you*

13.1–23: Oracles against false prophecy. 1–16: A major challenge for Ezekiel was opposing false prophets, particularly ones advocating nationalistic hope. Such prophets gave the people a false security that robbed them of their chance to find life amidst the coming judgment. **4:** *Jackals among ruins* have no regard for their surroundings and actually contribute to their decay (Lam 5.18). **5:** True prophets would care enough about their people to go *up into the breaches* (like Moses, Ps 106.23), i.e., to risk their lives by arguing with God on their behalf (9.8; 11.13). **10–16:** *Whitewash,* better, "plaster." The false prophets' messages (Jer 23; 27–29), like mud-plaster that dissolves in a storm, were futile attempts to bolster the people, despite their ultimate defenselessness before God's inevitable, coming judgment.

13.17–23: Against sorceresses. For a meager fee (v. 19), some exiles safeguarded the wicked and attacked their enemies through magic. *Bands* and *veils* (perhaps "head clothes") were likely cloth charms used in Babylonian witchcraft to attack and defend, respectively. **18:** The hunting may have involved snatching victims' souls from their bodies.

hunt lives;[a] I will tear them from your
arms, and let the lives go free, the lives that
you hunt down like birds. 21 I will tear off
your veils, and save my people from your
hands; they shall no longer be prey in your
hands; and you shall know that I am the
LORD. 22 Because you have disheartened
the righteous falsely, although I have not
disheartened them, and you have encour-
aged the wicked not to turn from their
wicked way and save their lives; 23 therefore
you shall no longer see false visions or prac-
tice divination; I will save my people from
your hand. Then you will know that I am
the LORD.

14 Certain elders of Israel came to me
and sat down before me. 2 And the
word of the LORD came to me: 3 Mortal,
these men have taken their idols into their
hearts, and placed their iniquity as a stum-
bling block before them; shall I let myself
be consulted by them? 4 Therefore speak to
them, and say to them, Thus says the Lord
GOD: Any of those of the house of Israel
who take their idols into their hearts and
place their iniquity as a stumbling block
before them, and yet come to the prophet—
I the LORD will answer those who come
with the multitude of their idols, 5 in order
that I may take hold of the hearts of the
house of Israel, all of whom are estranged
from me through their idols.
6 Therefore say to the house of Israel,
Thus says the Lord GOD: Repent and turn
away from your idols; and turn away your
faces from all your abominations. 7 For any
of those of the house of Israel, or of the
aliens who reside in Israel, who separate
themselves from me, taking their idols into
their hearts and placing their iniquity as a
stumbling block before them, and yet come
to a prophet to inquire of me by him, I the
LORD will answer them myself. 8 I will set
my face against them; I will make them a
sign and a byword and cut them off from
the midst of my people; and you shall know
that I am the LORD.
9 If a prophet is deceived and speaks a
word, I, the LORD, have deceived that
prophet, and I will stretch out my hand
against him, and will destroy him from the
midst of my people Israel. 10 And they shall
bear their punishment—the punishment of
the inquirer and the punishment of the
prophet shall be the same— 11 so that the
house of Israel may no longer go astray
from me, nor defile themselves any more
with all their transgressions. Then they
shall be my people, and I will be their God,
says the Lord GOD.
12 The word of the LORD came to me:
13 Mortal, when a land sins against me by
acting faithlessly, and I stretch out my hand
against it, and break its staff of bread and
send famine upon it, and cut off from it
human beings and animals, 14 even if Noah,
Daniel,[b] and Job, these three, were in it,
they would save only their own lives by
their righteousness, says the Lord GOD.
15 If I send wild animals through the land to
ravage it, so that it is made desolate, and no

a Gk Syr: Heb *lives for birds* *b* Or, as otherwise read, *Danel*

14.1–11: A legal case involving consultation. Ezekiel uses the legal language of the "Holiness Collection" to indict unregenerate elders who try to consult God. Consultation is refused, since the words for the situation have already been inscribed as scripture (see 3.22–27n.). For now, there will be no negotiation, only performance (12.28). **5:** *Idols,* not necessarily false gods here, but an expression for any religious duplicity. **7:** *Aliens,* see 47.21–23n. **9–11:** Deceived prophets will be punished similarly to those inquiring of them.

14.12–23: The inevitability of God's judgment. Infamous Sodom might have been spared for a sufficient number of righteous people (Gen 18.22–33), but Jerusalem's impending punishment is inevitable (since it is already a matter of scriptural record, 2.8b–3.3n.). Under these circumstances, only righteous individuals themselves can be saved. **14:** Noah and Job are renowned in the Bible for their righteousness. Ezekiel's references to Daniel (also 28.3) suggest the Canaanite Danel (see textual note *b*) of the Ugaritic texts (ca. 1400 BCE), who is described as an ideally righteous ruler. **21:** See 5.16–17. **22–23:** *Console,* since their wicked behavior would prove the justice of God's judgment.

one may pass through because of the ani-
mals; 16 even if these three men were in it, as
I live, says the Lord GOD, they would save
neither sons nor daughters; they alone
would be saved, but the land would be des-
olate. 17 Or if I bring a sword upon that
land and say, "Let a sword pass through
the land," and I cut off human beings and
animals from it; 18 though these three men
were in it, as I live, says the Lord GOD, they
would save neither sons nor daughters, but
they alone would be saved. 19 Or if I send a
pestilence into that land, and pour out my
wrath upon it with blood, to cut off hu-
mans and animals from it; 20 even if Noah,
Daniel,[a] and Job were in it, as I live, says
the Lord GOD, they would save neither son
nor daughter; they would save only their
own lives by their righteousness.

21 For thus says the Lord GOD: How
much more when I send upon Jerusalem my
four deadly acts of judgment, sword, fam-
ine, wild animals, and pestilence, to cut off
humans and animals from it! 22 Yet, survi-
vors shall be left in it, sons and daughters
who will be brought out; they will come
out to you. When you see their ways and
their deeds, you will be consoled for the evil
that I have brought upon Jerusalem, for all
that I have brought upon it. 23 They shall
console you, when you see their ways and
their deeds; and you shall know that it was
not without cause that I did all that I have
done in it, says the Lord GOD.

15 The word of the LORD came to me:
2 O mortal, how does the wood
of the vine surpass all other
wood—
the vine branch that is among the
trees of the forest?
3 Is wood taken from it to make
anything?
Does one take a peg from it on
which to hang any object?
4 It is put in the fire for fuel;
when the fire has consumed both
ends of it
and the middle of it is charred,
is it useful for anything?
5 When it was whole it was used
for nothing;
how much less—when the fire has
consumed it,
and it is charred—
can it ever be used for anything!

6 Therefore thus says the Lord GOD:
Like the wood of the vine among the trees
of the forest, which I have given to the fire
for fuel, so I will give up the inhabitants of
Jerusalem. 7 I will set my face against them;
although they escape from the fire, the fire
shall still consume them; and you shall
know that I am the LORD, when I set my
face against them. 8 And I will make the
land desolate, because they have acted
faithlessly, says the Lord GOD.

16 The word of the LORD came to me:
2 Mortal, make known to Jerusalem
her abominations, 3 and say, Thus says the
Lord GOD to Jerusalem: Your origin and
your birth were in the land of the Canaan-
ites; your father was an Amorite, and your
mother a Hittite. 4 As for your birth, on the
day you were born your navel cord was not

a Or, as otherwise read, *Danel*

15.1–8: Analogy of the useless vine. The wood of the vine is good only when it is cultivated in a vineyard and produces; a wild vine of the forest is practically useless—its fruit may be poisonous (2 Kings 4.39–40), and it is unusable for woodworking. This metaphor for Jerusalem shows it has no autonomous worthiness. **7:** *They escape*d from total destruction back in 597 BCE, when the Babylonians first assailed Jerusalem.

16.1–63: The allegory of the unfaithful wife. 1–8: Jerusalem, the Foundling. 3: Jerusalem's historical ancestry here suggests a predisposition to apostasy. The *Canaanite*s and *Amorite*s were West Semitic ethno-linguistic groups. The *Hittite*s were an Indo-European people located in Asia Minor, some of whom are depicted living in Palestine with the Canaanites (Gen 23; 2 Sam 11.3). Israel often assimilated such residents (Josh 3.10) of Palestine, their practices, and their cities (e.g., Jerusalem). **4:** Rubbing the skin with salt was believed to make it firm and clean. **5–7:** By God's intervention, this abandoned and

cut, nor were you washed with water to
cleanse you, nor rubbed with salt, nor
wrapped in cloths. 5 No eye pitied you, to
do any of these things for you out of compassion for you; but you were thrown out
in the open field, for you were abhorred on
the day you were born.
6 I passed by you, and saw you flailing
about in your blood. As you lay in your
blood, I said to you, "Live! 7 and grow up[a]
like a plant of the field." You grew up and
became tall and arrived at full womanhood;[b]
your breasts were formed, and your hair had
grown; yet you were naked and bare.
8 I passed by you again and looked on
you; you were at the age for love. I spread
the edge of my cloak over you, and covered
your nakedness: I pledged myself to you
and entered into a covenant with you, says
the Lord GOD, and you became mine.
9 Then I bathed you with water and washed
off the blood from you, and anointed you
with oil. 10 I clothed you with embroidered
cloth and with sandals of fine leather; I
bound you in fine linen and covered you
with rich fabric.[c] 11 I adorned you with ornaments: I put bracelets on your arms, a
chain on your neck, 12 a ring on your nose,
earrings in your ears, and a beautiful crown
upon your head. 13 You were adorned with
gold and silver, while your clothing was of
fine linen, rich fabric,[c] and embroidered
cloth. You had choice flour and honey and
oil for food. You grew exceedingly beautiful, fit to be a queen. 14 Your fame spread
among the nations on account of your
beauty, for it was perfect because of my
splendor that I had bestowed on you, says
the Lord GOD.
15 But you trusted in your beauty, and
played the whore because of your fame,
and lavished your whorings on any passerby.[d] 16 You took some of your garments,
and made for yourself colorful shrines, and
on them played the whore; nothing like this
has ever been or ever shall be.[c] 17 You also
took your beautiful jewels of my gold and
my silver that I had given you, and made
for yourself male images, and with them
played the whore; 18 and you took your embroidered garments to cover them, and set
my oil and my incense before them. 19 Also
my bread that I gave you—I fed you with
choice flour and oil and honey—you set it
before them as a pleasing odor; and so it
was, says the Lord GOD. 20 You took your
sons and your daughters, whom you had
borne to me, and these you sacrificed to
them to be devoured. As if your whorings
were not enough! 21 You slaughtered my
children and delivered them up as an offering to them. 22 And in all your abominations and your whorings you did not remember the days of your youth, when you
were naked and bare, flailing about in your
blood.
23 After all your wickedness (woe, woe
to you! says the Lord GOD), 24 you built
yourself a platform and made yourself a
lofty place in every square; 25 at the head of

a Gk Syr: Heb *Live! I made you a myriad*
b Cn: Heb *ornament of ornaments* *c* Meaning of Heb uncertain *d* Heb adds *let it be his*

exposed infant grew into *full womanhood. Breasts* and pubic *hair* indicate sexual maturity. **8:** Covering a woman with a garment symbolized marriage (Ruth 3.9). *Covenant,* used of the marriage contract in Mal 2.14. **9–14: The beautiful bride. 9:** The *blood* may signify the breaking of the bride's hymen. (Divine procreation is assumed below, v. 20.) Alternatively, the birth blood of v. 6 may still be in mind (due to the time compression of the allegory). **15–34: Sexual betrayal.** The image of Israel as a sexually unfaithful wife was first popularized by Hosea, for whom the image had both literal reference to fertility rituals (Hos 4.10–14) and metaphorical reference to religious apostasy in general (Hos 2.13). Ezekiel adopts the image as a metaphor from Hosea and Jeremiah (Jer 3.1–13), intensifies it to shocking extremes, and expands it into a quasi-biography of Israel's infidelity. This biography will climax in Jerusalem's destruction. **20–22:** Children were offered as human sacrifices (20.26,31; 23.37; Jer 7.31), against the prohibitions of Lev 18.21; 20.2. **23–34:** The traditions of Zion (see Introduction), in which Ezekiel was steeped, advocated trust in God's exclusive sovereignty over geopolitics (cf. Isa 7.8–9). Given this divine prerogative, foreign alliances were a form of unfaithfulness. **26:** *Lustful neighbors,* the Hebrew denotes their oversized

every street you built your lofty place and
prostituted your beauty, offering yourself
to every passer-by, and multiplying your
whoring. 26 You played the whore with the
Egyptians, your lustful neighbors, multiply-
ing your whoring, to provoke me to anger.
27 Therefore I stretched out my hand
against you, reduced your rations, and gave
you up to the will of your enemies, the
daughters of the Philistines, who were
ashamed of your lewd behavior. 28 You
played the whore with the Assyrians, be-
cause you were insatiable; you played the
whore with them, and still you were not
satisfied. 29 You multiplied your whoring
with Chaldea, the land of merchants; and
even with this you were not satisfied.

30 How sick is your heart, says the Lord
GOD, that you did all these things, the
deeds of a brazen whore; 31 building your
platform at the head of every street, and
making your lofty place in every square!
Yet you were not like a whore, because you
scorned payment. 32 Adulterous wife, who
receives strangers instead of her husband!
33 Gifts are given to all whores; but you
gave your gifts to all your lovers, bribing
them to come to you from all around for
your whorings. 34 So you were different
from other women in your whorings: no
one solicited you to play the whore; and
you gave payment, while no payment was
given to you; you were different.

35 Therefore, O whore, hear the word
of the LORD: 36 Thus says the Lord GOD,
Because your lust was poured out and your
nakedness uncovered in your whoring with
your lovers, and because of all your abomi-
nable idols, and because of the blood of
your children that you gave to them,
37 therefore, I will gather all your lovers,
with whom you took pleasure, all those
you loved and all those you hated; I will
gather them against you from all around,
and will uncover your nakedness to them,
so that they may see all your nakedness. 38 I
will judge you as women who commit adul-
tery and shed blood are judged, and bring
blood upon you in wrath and jealousy. 39 I
will deliver you into their hands, and they
shall throw down your platform and break
down your lofty places; they shall strip you
of your clothes and take your beautiful ob-
jects and leave you naked and bare. 40 They
shall bring up a mob against you, and they
shall stone you and cut you to pieces with
their swords. 41 They shall burn your
houses and execute judgments on you in
the sight of many women; I will stop you
from playing the whore, and you shall also
make no more payments. 42 So I will satisfy
my fury on you, and my jealousy shall turn
away from you; I will be calm, and will be
angry no longer. 43 Because you have not
remembered the days of your youth, but
have enraged me with all these things;
therefore, I have returned your deeds upon
your head, says the Lord GOD.

Have you not committed lewdness be-
yond all your abominations? 44 See, every-
one who uses proverbs will use this proverb
about you, "Like mother, like daughter."
45 You are the daughter of your mother,
who loathed her husband and her children;
and you are the sister of your sisters, who
loathed their husbands and their children.
Your mother was a Hittite and your father
an Amorite. 46 Your elder sister is Samaria,
who lived with her daughters to the north
of you; and your younger sister, who lived
to the south of you, is Sodom with her
daughters. 47 You not only followed their

genitals (cf. 23.20). **27:** A probable reference to Judean territory having been given to the Philistine cities of Ashdod, Ekron, and Gaza by the Assyrian king Sennacherib in 701 BCE. **28:** Judah willingly became an Assyrian vassal in 734 BCE (see 2 Kings 16.7–8) and remained one, with only occasional exceptions, for the next century. **29:** *Chaldea,* Babylonia. **33:** *Gifts,* see 2 Kings 16.8. **35–43: The threat of punishment.** Foreign nations (her lovers) will turn against her. God will divorce her and expose her to be stoned (Lev 20.10). **44–58: Additional accusation.** This section elaborates the preceding theme, showing Jerusalem to be so much worse than *Samaria* (2 Kings 17) and *Sodom* (Gen 19), both of which were destroyed, that they appear righteous by comparison (Jer 3.11). **46:** *Elder sister,* better, "bigger sister" (which makes more sense historically). Likewise, Sodom is a "smaller" sister, not a *younger* one. **49:** The characteristic

ways, and acted according to their abomi-
nations; within a very little time you were
more corrupt than they in all your ways.
48 As I live, says the Lord GOD, your sister
Sodom and her daughters have not done as
you and your daughters have done. 49 This
was the guilt of your sister Sodom: she and
her daughters had pride, excess of food,
and prosperous ease, but did not aid the
poor and needy. 50 They were haughty, and
did abominable things before me; therefore
I removed them when I saw it. 51 Samaria
has not committed half your sins; you have
committed more abominations than they,
and have made your sisters appear righ-
teous by all the abominations that you have
committed. 52 Bear your disgrace, you also,
for you have brought about for your sisters
a more favorable judgment; because of
your sins in which you acted more abomi-
nably than they, they are more in the right
than you. So be ashamed, you also, and
bear your disgrace, for you have made your
sisters appear righteous.

53 I will restore their fortunes, the for-
tunes of Sodom and her daughters and the
fortunes of Samaria and her daughters, and
I will restore your own fortunes along with
theirs, 54 in order that you may bear your
disgrace and be ashamed of all that you
have done, becoming a consolation to
them. 55 As for your sisters, Sodom and her
daughters shall return to their former state,
Samaria and her daughters shall return to
their former state, and you and your
daughters shall return to your former state.
56 Was not your sister Sodom a byword in
your mouth in the day of your pride, 57 be-
fore your wickedness was uncovered? Now
you are a mockery to the daughters of
Aram[a] and all her neighbors, and to the
daughters of the Philistines, those all
around who despise you. 58 You must bear
the penalty of your lewdness and your
abominations, says the LORD.

59 Yes, thus says the Lord GOD: I will
deal with you as you have done, you who
have despised the oath, breaking the cove-
nant; 60 yet I will remember my covenant
with you in the days of your youth, and I
will establish with you an everlasting cove-
nant. 61 Then you will remember your
ways, and be ashamed when I[b] take your
sisters, both your elder and your younger,
and give them to you as daughters, but not
on account of my[c] covenant with you. 62 I
will establish my covenant with you, and
you shall know that I am the LORD, 63 in
order that you may remember and be con-
founded, and never open your mouth again
because of your shame, when I forgive you
all that you have done, says the Lord GOD.

17 The word of the LORD came to me:
2 O mortal, propound a riddle, and
speak an allegory to the house of Israel.
3 Say: Thus says the Lord GOD:

A great eagle, with great wings and
long pinions,
rich in plumage of many colors,
came to the Lebanon.
He took the top of the cedar,
4 broke off its topmost shoot;
he carried it to a land of trade,
set it in a city of merchants.
5 Then he took a seed from the land,
placed it in fertile soil;
a plant[d] by abundant waters,

a Another reading is *Edom* *b* Syr: Heb *you*
c Heb lacks *my* *d* Meaning of Heb uncertain

sin of Sodom is injustice toward the *poor and needy.* **53–58:** God will restore all three sisters, humiliating Jerusalem by putting it on the same footing as Samaria and Sodom. **57:** *Aram* should probably be read as "Edom" (see textual note *a;* cf. 36.5). **59–63: Jerusalem's restoration.** God will remember the covenant with the ancestors of the exiles, as was anticipated by Lev 26.43–45. **62:** *Will establish my covenant* (see also v. 60), this phrase is characteristic of the "Holiness Collection" (e.g., Gen 17.7; Ex 6.4; Lev 26.9).

17.1–24: The allegorical fable of the eagles. 1–10: The fable. *Great eagle,* the Babylonian king Nebuchadrezzar; *the top of the cedar,* house of David (Jer 22.23); *topmost shoot,* Jehoiachin, Judean king who was exiled to Babylon in 597 BCE (2 Kings 24.8–16); *land of trade,* Babylonia; *city of merchants,* Babylon; *seed from the land,* Zedekiah, the last king of Judah (597–586). **5:** *Placed it in fertile soil,* i.e., made him king (2 Kings 24.17). **7:** *Another great eagle,* Psammetichus II of Egypt (594–588 BCE), with whom

he set it like a willow twig.
6 It sprouted and became a vine
spreading out, but low;
its branches turned toward him,
its roots remained where it stood.
So it became a vine;
it brought forth branches,
put forth foliage.

7 There was another great eagle,
with great wings and much
plumage.
And see! This vine stretched out
its roots toward him;
it shot out its branches toward him,
so that he might water it.
From the bed where it was planted
8 it was transplanted
to good soil by abundant waters,
so that it might produce branches
and bear fruit
and become a noble vine.
9 Say: Thus says the Lord GOD:
Will it prosper?
Will he not pull up its roots,
cause its fruit to rot[a] and wither,
its fresh sprouting leaves to fade?
No strong arm or mighty army will
be needed
to pull it from its roots.
10 When it is transplanted, will it thrive?
When the east wind strikes it,
will it not utterly wither,
wither on the bed where it grew?

11 Then the word of the LORD came to
me: 12 Say now to the rebellious house: Do
you not know what these things mean? Tell
them: The king of Babylon came to Jerusa-
lem, took its king and its officials, and
brought them back with him to Babylon.
13 He took one of the royal offspring and
made a covenant with him, putting him un-
der oath (he had taken away the chief men
of the land), 14 so that the kingdom might
be humble and not lift itself up, and that by
keeping his covenant it might stand. 15 But
he rebelled against him by sending ambas-
sadors to Egypt, in order that they might
give him horses and a large army. Will he
succeed? Can one escape who does such
things? Can he break the covenant and yet
escape? 16 As I live, says the Lord GOD,
surely in the place where the king resides
who made him king, whose oath he de-
spised, and whose covenant with him he
broke—in Babylon he shall die. 17 Pharaoh
with his mighty army and great company
will not help him in war, when ramps are
cast up and siege walls built to cut off many
lives. 18 Because he despised the oath and
broke the covenant, because he gave his
hand and yet did all these things, he shall
not escape. 19 Therefore thus says the Lord
GOD: As I live, I will surely return upon his
head my oath that he despised, and my cov-
enant that he broke. 20 I will spread my net
over him, and he shall be caught in my
snare; I will bring him to Babylon and enter
into judgment with him there for the trea-
son he has committed against me. 21 All the
pick[b] of his troops shall fall by the sword,
and the survivors shall be scattered to every
wind; and you shall know that I, the LORD,
have spoken.

22 Thus says the Lord GOD:
I myself will take a sprig
from the lofty top of a cedar;
I will set it out.
I will break off a tender one

a Meaning of Heb uncertain *b* Another reading is *fugitives*

Zedekiah negotiated for assistance against Babylonia (Jer 37.5). **9–10:** Zedekiah will be unable to resist Nebuchadrezzar (*he,* v. 9; *the east wind,* v. 10) for long. **11–21: The interpretation. 13:** *Under oath,* 2 Chr 36.13. Nebuchadrezzar would have to punish Zedekiah for violating his oath of fealty (see v. 7n.). **17:** The original text read, "and not with a mighty army shall he [Nebuchadrezzar] deal with him" (as in v. 9b). The verse was revised after the siege of Jerusalem to reflect historical detail, thus bringing out the prophecy's correlation with its fulfillment. **19–21:** Just as Nebuchadrezzar will not overlook Zedekiah's breaking his oath of fealty, so also will God punish him for breaking the LORD's covenant with Israel (16.59). **22–24: The fable expanded,** a messianic allegory. For the messiah as a *twig* or branch, cf. Isa 11.1; Jer 23.5–6; 33.15; Zech 3.8; 6.12. *Lofty mountain,* Mount Zion (Isa 2.2).

from the topmost of its
young twigs;
I myself will plant it
on a high and lofty mountain.
23 On the mountain height of Israel
I will plant it,
in order that it may produce boughs
and bear fruit,
and become a noble cedar.
Under it every kind of bird will live;
in the shade of its branches
will nest
winged creatures of every kind.
24 All the trees of the field shall know
that I am the LORD.
I bring low the high tree,
I make high the low tree;
I dry up the green tree
and make the dry tree flourish.
I the LORD have spoken;
I will accomplish it.

18 The word of the LORD came to me:
2 What do you mean by repeating
this proverb concerning the land of Israel,
"The parents have eaten sour grapes, and
the children's teeth are set on edge"? 3 As I
live, says the Lord GOD, this proverb shall
no more be used by you in Israel. 4 Know
that all lives are mine; the life of the parent
as well as the life of the child is mine: it is
only the person who sins that shall die.
5 If a man is righteous and does what is
lawful and right— 6 if he does not eat upon
the mountains or lift up his eyes to the idols
of the house of Israel, does not defile his
neighbor's wife or approach a woman dur-
ing her menstrual period, 7 does not oppress
anyone, but restores to the debtor his
pledge, commits no robbery, gives his
bread to the hungry and covers the naked
with a garment, 8 does not take advance or
accrued interest, withholds his hand from
iniquity, executes true justice between con-
tending parties, 9 follows my statutes, and is
careful to observe my ordinances, acting
faithfully—such a one is righteous; he shall
surely live, says the Lord GOD.
10 If he has a son who is violent, a shed-
der of blood, 11 who does any of these
things (though his father[a] does none of
them), who eats upon the mountains, de-
files his neighbor's wife, 12 oppresses the
poor and needy, commits robbery, does not
restore the pledge, lifts up his eyes to the
idols, commits abomination, 13 takes ad-
vance or accrued interest; shall he then live?
He shall not. He has done all these abomi-
nable things; he shall surely die; his blood
shall be upon himself.
14 But if this man has a son who sees all
the sins that his father has done, considers,
and does not do likewise, 15 who does not
eat upon the mountains or lift up his eyes to
the idols of the house of Israel, does not
defile his neighbor's wife, 16 does not
wrong anyone, exacts no pledge, commits
no robbery, but gives his bread to the hun-
gry and covers the naked with a garment,
17 withholds his hand from iniquity,[b] takes
no advance or accrued interest, observes
my ordinances, and follows my statutes; he
shall not die for his father's iniquity; he
shall surely live. 18 As for his father, because
he practiced extortion, robbed his brother,
and did what is not good among his people,
he dies for his iniquity.

a Heb *he* *b* Gk: Heb *the poor*

18.1–32: Being accountable. 1–4: Sins and their punishments may involve long-term consequences for the corporate community, as 16.44; Ex 20.5 recognize. In the exiles' current situation, however, it is not appropriate for them to blame their ancestors for their misfortunes, as they were doing (Jer 31.29–30). Ezekiel's audience is far from an innocent generation. Nevertheless, individuals within the community can take responsibility, turn from sin, and choose life amidst the coming corporate (communal) punishment. **5–9:** First, righteous generation. The list includes both ritual and ethical provisions. **6:** *Eat upon the mountains,* idolatrous sacrifices at high places (6.1–14; Hos 4.13). *His neighbor's wife,* Lev 18.20. *Menstrual period,* Lev 18.19. **7:** *Oppress anyone,* Lev 25.17. *Restore to the debtor his pledge,* Ex 22.26. *Robbery,* Lev 19.13. **8:** *Interest,* Lev 25.36. *Executes true justice,* Lev 19.15; Zech 7.9. **10–13:** Second, wicked generation. *Shedder of blood,* 16.38; 22.3; 23.45; 33.25; Num 35.33–34. **14–18:** Third, righteous generation. Again a reversal. **19–20:** Summation: Neither the righteousness nor the wickedness of a

19 Yet you say, "Why should not the
son suffer for the iniquity of the father?"
When the son has done what is lawful and
right, and has been careful to observe all
my statutes, he shall surely live. 20 The per-
son who sins shall die. A child shall not
suffer for the iniquity of a parent, nor a
parent suffer for the iniquity of a child; the
righteousness of the righteous shall be his
own, and the wickedness of the wicked
shall be his own.
21 But if the wicked turn away from all
their sins that they have committed and
keep all my statutes and do what is lawful
and right, they shall surely live; they shall
not die. 22 None of the transgressions that
they have committed shall be remembered
against them; for the righteousness that
they have done they shall live. 23 Have I any
pleasure in the death of the wicked, says the
Lord GOD, and not rather that they should
turn from their ways and live? 24 But when
the righteous turn away from their righ-
teousness and commit iniquity and do the
same abominable things that the wicked
do, shall they live? None of the righteous
deeds that they have done shall be remem-
bered; for the treachery of which they are
guilty and the sin they have committed,
they shall die.
25 Yet you say, "The way of the Lord is
unfair." Hear now, O house of Israel: Is my
way unfair? Is it not your ways that are
unfair? 26 When the righteous turn away
from their righteousness and commit iniq-
uity, they shall die for it; for the iniquity
that they have committed they shall die.
27 Again, when the wicked turn away from
the wickedness they have committed and
do what is lawful and right, they shall save
their life. 28 Because they considered and
turned away from all the transgressions
that they had committed, they shall surely
live; they shall not die. 29 Yet the house of
Israel says, "The way of the Lord is un-
fair." O house of Israel, are my ways un-
fair? Is it not your ways that are unfair?
30 Therefore I will judge you, O house
of Israel, all of you according to your ways,
says the Lord GOD. Repent and turn from
all your transgressions; otherwise iniquity
will be your ruin.[a] 31 Cast away from you
all the transgressions that you have com-
mitted against me, and get yourselves a new
heart and a new spirit! Why will you die,
O house of Israel? 32 For I have no pleasure
in the death of anyone, says the Lord GOD.
Turn, then, and live.

19 As for you, raise up a lamentation
for the princes of Israel, 2 and say:

What a lioness was your mother
among lions!
She lay down among young lions,
rearing her cubs.
3 She raised up one of her cubs;
he became a young lion,
and he learned to catch prey;
he devoured humans.
4 The nations sounded an alarm against
him;
he was caught in their pit;
and they brought him with hooks
to the land of Egypt.
5 When she saw that she was thwarted,
that her hope was lost,
she took another of her cubs
and made him a young lion.
6 He prowled among the lions;
he became a young lion,
and he learned to catch prey;
he devoured people.

a Or *so that they shall not be a stumbling block of iniquity to you*

previous generation is transferable to the next. See Deut 24.16. **21–24:** Within one's life the same argument of non-extension pertains. **23:** God is squarely on the side of life (cf. 33.11). **25–29:** To object is to misunderstand God's justice; 33.17. **30–32:** The invitation to repentance is open. *New heart and a new spirit,* 11.19; 36.26n.; cf. Jer 32.39.

19.1–14: Two funeral dirges. 1–9: The *lioness* is Judah (Gen 49.9). The first cub is Jehoahaz, the king who was taken to Egypt (2 Kings 23.30–34; Jer 22.10–12). The second cub could be Jehoiachin (Jer 22.24–30; 2 Kings 24.8–16), but is more likely Zedekiah, likewise exiled to Babylon (2 Kings 25.7; Jer 39.7). If the latter, the two cubs would have the same literal mother, Hamutal (2 Kings 23.31; 24.18).

7 And he ravaged their strongholds,[a]
and laid waste their towns;
the land was appalled, and all in it,
at the sound of his roaring.
8 The nations set upon him
from the provinces all around;
they spread their net over him;
he was caught in their pit.
9 With hooks they put him in a
cage,
and brought him to the king
of Babylon;
they brought him into custody,
so that his voice should be heard
no more
on the mountains of Israel.
10 Your mother was like a vine in
a vineyard[b]
transplanted by the water,
fruitful and full of branches
from abundant water.
11 Its strongest stem became
a ruler's scepter;[c]
it towered aloft
among the thick boughs;
it stood out in its height
with its mass of branches.
12 But it was plucked up in fury,
cast down to the ground;
the east wind dried it up;
its fruit was stripped off,
its strong stem was withered;
the fire consumed it.
13 Now it is transplanted into
the wilderness,
into a dry and thirsty land.
14 And fire has gone out from its
stem,
has consumed its branches
and fruit,
so that there remains in it no strong
stem,
no scepter for ruling.

This is a lamentation, and it is used as a lamentation.

20 In the seventh year, in the fifth
month, on the tenth day of the
month, certain elders of Israel came to con-
sult the LORD, and sat down before me.
2 And the word of the LORD came to me:
3 Mortal, speak to the elders of Israel, and
say to them: Thus says the Lord GOD: Why
are you coming? To consult me? As I live,
says the Lord GOD, I will not be consulted
by you. 4 Will you judge them, mortal, will
you judge them? Then let them know the
abominations of their ancestors, 5 and say
to them: Thus says the Lord GOD: On the
day when I chose Israel, I swore to the off-
spring of the house of Jacob—making my-
self known to them in the land of Egypt—I
swore to them, saying, I am the LORD your
God. 6 On that day I swore to them that I
would bring them out of the land of Egypt
into a land that I had searched out for
them, a land flowing with milk and honey,
the most glorious of all lands. 7 And I said
to them, Cast away the detestable things
your eyes feast on, every one of you, and
do not defile yourselves with the idols of
Egypt; I am the LORD your God. 8 But they
rebelled against me and would not listen to
me; not one of them cast away the detest-
able things their eyes feasted on, nor did
they forsake the idols of Egypt.

Then I thought I would pour out my

a Heb *his widows* b Cn: Heb *in your blood*
c Heb *Its strongest stems became rulers' scepters*

19.10–14: The *vine* is Judah. The *strongest stem* is Zedekiah, who was dried up by *the east wind* (Nebuchadrezzar, 17.10) and *transplanted* (taken to Babylon).

20.1–44: Israel's pattern of rebellion. 1–4: Date: August 14, 591 BCE. All consultation of the LORD is prohibited (see v. 31n.; 14.1–11n.). **5–9:** Rebellion in Egypt. Already with these verses, this passage of Ezekiel exhibits a theological schematization of history. The passage is not intended as a chronological account but as a theological retelling of the people's essential behavior. The schematization repeats three times a pattern of rebellion despite God's self-revelation (vv. 5–9,10–17,18–26). The effect is to drive home how this same rebellious pattern is inevitable for the present generation (vv. 30–32). **6:** *A land flowing with milk and honey,* v. 15; Ex 3.8; Lev 20.24; Deut 6.3. **8:** Idolatrous worship in Egypt is not found in Pentateuchal traditions, but see Josh 24.14; Ezek 23.3,8. **9:** *For the sake of my name*

wrath upon them and spend my anger
against them in the midst of the land of
Egypt. 9 But I acted for the sake of my
name, that it should not be profaned in the
sight of the nations among whom they
lived, in whose sight I made myself known
to them in bringing them out of the land of
Egypt. 10 So I led them out of the land of
Egypt and brought them into the wilder-
ness. 11 I gave them my statutes and showed
them my ordinances, by whose observance
everyone shall live. 12 Moreover I gave them
my sabbaths, as a sign between me and
them, so that they might know that I the
LORD sanctify them. 13 But the house of Is-
rael rebelled against me in the wilderness;
they did not observe my statutes but reject-
ed my ordinances, by whose observance
everyone shall live; and my sabbaths they
greatly profaned.

Then I thought I would pour out my
wrath upon them in the wilderness, to
make an end of them. 14 But I acted for the
sake of my name, so that it should not be
profaned in the sight of the nations, in
whose sight I had brought them out.
15 Moreover I swore to them in the wilder-
ness that I would not bring them into the
land that I had given them, a land flowing
with milk and honey, the most glorious of
all lands, 16 because they rejected my ordi-
nances and did not observe my statutes,
and profaned my sabbaths; for their heart
went after their idols. 17 Nevertheless my
eye spared them, and I did not destroy them
or make an end of them in the wilderness.

18 I said to their children in the wilder-
ness, Do not follow the statutes of your
parents, nor observe their ordinances, nor
defile yourselves with their idols. 19 I the
LORD am your God; follow my statutes,
and be careful to observe my ordinances,
20 and hallow my sabbaths that they may be
a sign between me and you, so that you
may know that I the LORD am your God.
21 But the children rebelled against me; they
did not follow my statutes, and were not
careful to observe my ordinances, by whose
observance everyone shall live; they pro-
faned my sabbaths.

Then I thought I would pour out my
wrath upon them and spend my anger
against them in the wilderness. 22 But I
withheld my hand, and acted for the sake
of my name, so that it should not be pro-
faned in the sight of the nations, in whose
sight I had brought them out. 23 Moreover
I swore to them in the wilderness that I
would scatter them among the nations and
disperse them through the countries, 24 be-
cause they had not executed my ordi-
nances, but had rejected my statutes and
profaned my sabbaths, and their eyes were
set on their ancestors' idols. 25 Moreover I
gave them statutes that were not good and
ordinances by which they could not live.
26 I defiled them through their very gifts, in
their offering up all their firstborn, in order
that I might horrify them, so that they
might know that I am the LORD.

27 Therefore, mortal, speak to the house
of Israel and say to them, Thus says the
Lord GOD: In this again your ancestors
blasphemed me, by dealing treacherously
with me. 28 For when I had brought them
into the land that I swore to give them, then
wherever they saw any high hill or any
leafy tree, there they offered their sacrifices

(vv. 14,22,44; Ex 9.16; Lev 22.32–33), expresses prevenient grace; see 36.22–32n. Israel's deliverances from Egypt, from the wilderness, and eventually from the exile, were accomplished neither because of human initiative nor because of human intrinsic worth. **10–17:** Rebellion in the wilderness. **11:** Lev 18.5. **12–13:** Ezekiel is influenced by the emphasis on the sabbath in the "Holiness Collection" (Ex 31.13; Lev 19.30; 26.2). In this tradition, keeping the sabbath is a sign of the holiness and priestly service of all God's people. For a particular example of violation of the sabbath, see Ex 16.27–30. **13b–17:** Ex 32.9–14; Num 14.11–20; Deut 9.25–29. **18–26:** Rebellion of the next generation. **25–26:** The people must have been using the "law of the firstborn" (Ex 22.29; 34.19) to legitimate child sacrifice (16.20–22n.). Ezekiel interprets this turn of events as a "negative" use of God's law: God may use such laws to demonstrate people's rebelliousness and even to harden them in it. **27–32:** Application of the passage to Ezekiel's contemporaries. **29:** The word play here is explained by the textual note *a.* **31:** On making *children pass*

and presented the provocation of their
offering; there they sent up their pleasing
odors, and there they poured out their
drink offerings. 29 (I said to them, What is
the high place to which you go? So it is
called Bamah[a] to this day.) 30 Therefore
say to the house of Israel, Thus says the
Lord GOD: Will you defile yourselves after
the manner of your ancestors and go astray
after their detestable things? 31 When you
offer your gifts and make your children
pass through the fire, you defile yourselves
with all your idols to this day. And shall I
be consulted by you, O house of Israel? As
I live, says the Lord GOD, I will not be
consulted by you.

32 What is in your mind shall never hap-
pen—the thought, "Let us be like the na-
tions, like the tribes of the countries, and
worship wood and stone."

33 As I live, says the Lord GOD, surely
with a mighty hand and an outstretched
arm, and with wrath poured out, I will be
king over you. 34 I will bring you out from
the peoples and gather you out of the coun-
tries where you are scattered, with a mighty
hand and an outstretched arm, and with
wrath poured out; 35 and I will bring you
into the wilderness of the peoples, and
there I will enter into judgment with you
face to face. 36 As I entered into judgment
with your ancestors in the wilderness of the
land of Egypt, so I will enter into judgment
with you, says the Lord GOD. 37 I will make
you pass under the staff, and will bring you
within the bond of the covenant. 38 I will
purge out the rebels among you, and those
who transgress against me; I will bring
them out of the land where they reside as
aliens, but they shall not enter the land of
Israel. Then you shall know that I am the
LORD.

39 As for you, O house of Israel, thus
says the Lord GOD: Go serve your idols,
everyone of you now and hereafter, if you
will not listen to me; but my holy name you
shall no more profane with your gifts and
your idols.

40 For on my holy mountain, the moun-
tain height of Israel, says the Lord GOD,
there all the house of Israel, all of them,
shall serve me in the land; there I will ac-
cept them, and there I will require your
contributions and the choicest of your gifts,
with all your sacred things. 41 As a pleasing
odor I will accept you, when I bring you
out from the peoples, and gather you out of
the countries where you have been scat-
tered; and I will manifest my holiness
among you in the sight of the nations.
42 You shall know that I am the LORD,
when I bring you into the land of Israel, the
country that I swore to give to your ances-
tors. 43 There you shall remember your
ways and all the deeds by which you have
polluted yourselves; and you shall loathe
yourselves for all the evils that you have
committed. 44 And you shall know that I
am the LORD, when I deal with you for my
name's sake, not according to your evil
ways, or corrupt deeds, O house of Israel,
says the Lord GOD.

45[b] The word of the LORD came to me:
46 Mortal, set your face toward the south,
preach against the south, and prophesy
against the forest land in the Negeb; 47 say

a That is *High Place* *b* Ch 21.1 in Heb

through the fire, see 16.20–22n.; 23.37; Deut 18.10; 2 Kings 16.3; 17.17; 21.6. The end of the verse echoes v. 3, forming an "inclusio" (envelope) around the passage. Judgment on the people's faithless state is fixed: Ezekiel cannot intervene for them with God (see 3.22–27n.). **33–38: An oracle of promise,** but with an angry tone dating prior to Jerusalem's destruction in 586 BCE. God's irresistible (stubborn) grace will triumph with Israel, through force if necessary. As in the wilderness (Num 14.26–35), the unfaithful will be purged. **39–44: Final reconciliation.** After the new Exodus, God will restore the people to Zion, and their sacrifices will again be acceptable. **40:** Ezekiel's pro-Zion theology (cf. 5.5n.; 43.12; Zech 8.3; Joel 3.17).

20.45–21.32: Sword prophecies (Lev 26.25,33 ["Holiness Collection"]). **20.45–21.7: The sword against all flesh. 45–49:** A threat against the south. *South* and *Negeb* both stand for Judah and Jerusalem, which lie south of their attackers. **49:** The people cannot take a claim of Jerusalem's vulnerability seriously

to the forest of the Negeb, Hear the word
of the LORD: Thus says the Lord GOD, I
will kindle a fire in you, and it shall devour
every green tree in you and every dry tree;
the blazing flame shall not be quenched,
and all faces from south to north shall be
scorched by it. 48 All flesh shall see that I
the LORD have kindled it; it shall not be
quenched. 49 Then I said, "Ah Lord GOD!
they are saying of me, 'Is he not a maker of
allegories?' "

21 [a]The word of the LORD came to me:
2 Mortal, set your face toward Jeru-
salem and preach against the sanctuaries;
prophesy against the land of Israel 3 and say
to the land of Israel, Thus says the LORD: I
am coming against you, and will draw my
sword out of its sheath, and will cut off
from you both righteous and wicked. 4 Be-
cause I will cut off from you both righteous
and wicked, therefore my sword shall go
out of its sheath against all flesh from south
to north; 5 and all flesh shall know that I the
LORD have drawn my sword out of its
sheath; it shall not be sheathed again.
6 Moan therefore, mortal; moan with
breaking heart and bitter grief before their
eyes. 7 And when they say to you, "Why do
you moan?" you shall say, "Because of the
news that has come. Every heart will melt
and all hands will be feeble, every spirit will
faint and all knees will turn to water. See, it
comes and it will be fulfilled," says the
Lord GOD.

8 And the word of the LORD came to
me: 9 Mortal, prophesy and say: Thus says
the Lord; Say:

A sword, a sword is sharpened,
it is also polished;
10 it is sharpened for slaughter,
honed to flash like lightning!
How can we make merry?
You have despised the rod,
and all discipline.[b]
11 The sword[c] is given to be polished,
to be grasped in the hand;
it is sharpened, the sword is polished,
to be placed in the slayer's hand.
12 Cry and wail, O mortal,
for it is against my people;
it is against all Israel's princes;
they are thrown to the sword,
together with my people.
Ah! Strike the thigh!

13 For consider: What! If you despise the
rod, will it not happen?[b] says the Lord
GOD.

14 And you, mortal, prophesy;
strike hand to hand.
Let the sword fall twice, thrice;
it is a sword for killing.
A sword for great slaughter—
it surrounds them;
15 therefore hearts melt
and many stumble.
At all their gates I have set
the point[b] of the sword.
Ah! It is made for flashing,
it is polished[d] for slaughter.
16 Attack to the right!
Engage to the left!
—wherever your edge is directed.
17 I too will strike hand to hand,
I will satisfy my fury;
I the LORD have spoken.

18 The word of the LORD came to me:
19 Mortal, mark out two roads for the
sword of the king of Babylon to come; both
of them shall issue from the same land. And
make a signpost, make it for a fork in the
road leading to a city; 20 mark out the road
for the sword to come to Rabbah of the

a Ch 21.6 in Heb *b* Meaning of Heb uncertain
c Heb *It* *d* Tg: Heb *wrapped up*

(see 2.6n.; 3.7; 33.32). **21.1–5:** The preceding forest fire is interpreted as the sword of God. **6–7:** The message is reiterated through an expressive action.

21.8–17: Song of the sword. The sword is first polished (vv. 8–13), and then it will be engaged (vv. 14–17). **12:** *Strike the thigh,* a sign of mourning (Jer 31.19). **14:** *Strike hand to hand,* in vexation (also v. 17).

21.18–32: The sword of Nebuchadrezzar. 18–24: A symbolic act. **20:** *Rabbah* (modern Amman), capital of Ammon. **21:** Perhaps from Riblah (cf. 2 Kings 25.6), Nebuchadrezzar uses *divination* to deter-

Ammonites or to Judah and to[a] Jerusalem
the fortified. 21 For the king of Babylon
stands at the parting of the way, at the fork
in the two roads, to use divination; he
shakes the arrows, he consults the tera-
phim,[b] he inspects the liver. 22 Into his
right hand comes the lot for Jerusalem, to
set battering rams, to call out for slaughter,
for raising the battle cry, to set battering
rams against the gates, to cast up ramps, to
build siege towers. 23 But to them it will
seem like a false divination; they have
sworn solemn oaths; but he brings their
guilt to remembrance, bringing about their
capture.

24 Therefore thus says the Lord God:
Because you have brought your guilt to re-
membrance, in that your transgressions are
uncovered, so that in all your deeds your
sins appear—because you have come to re-
membrance, you shall be taken in hand.[c]

25 As for you, vile, wicked prince
of Israel,
you whose day has come,
the time of final punishment,
26 thus says the Lord God:
Remove the turban, take off
the crown;
things shall not remain as they are.
Exalt that which is low,
abase that which is high.
27 A ruin, a ruin, a ruin—
I will make it!
(Such has never occurred.)
Until he comes whose right it is;
to him I will give it.

28 As for you, mortal, prophesy, and
say, Thus says the Lord God concerning
the Ammonites, and concerning their re-
proach; say:

A sword, a sword! Drawn for
slaughter,
polished to consume,[d] to flash like
lightning.
29 Offering false visions for you,
divining lies for you,
they place you over the necks
of the vile, wicked ones—
those whose day has come,
the time of final punishment.
30 Return it to its sheath!
In the place where you were created,
in the land of your origin,
I will judge you.
31 I will pour out my indignation upon
you,
with the fire of my wrath
I will blow upon you.
I will deliver you into brutish hands,
those skillful to destroy.
32 You shall be fuel for the fire,
your blood shall enter the earth;
you shall be remembered no more,
for I the Lord have spoken.

22 The word of the Lord came to me:
2 You, mortal, will you judge, will
you judge the bloody city? Then declare to
it all its abominable deeds. 3 You shall say,
Thus says the Lord God: A city! Shedding
blood within itself; its time has come; mak-
ing its idols, defiling itself. 4 You have be-
come guilty by the blood that you have
shed, and defiled by the idols that you have

a Gk Syr: Heb *Judah in* b Or *the household gods*
c Or *be taken captive* d Cn: Heb *to contain*

mine which rebel to attack first: belomancy (i.e., casting of *arrows* inscribed with names of projected victims); necromancy (*teraphim* were religious images sometimes expected to convey messages to the living [see Zech 10.2]); and hepatoscopy (making predictions based on the configurations and markings of animal *livers*). **22:** The sword is about to fall—on Jerusalem! **23:** The results of the divination seem false to the Jerusalemites, since they believe Jerusalem invulnerable (20.49n.). **25–27:** The sword will strike Zedekiah, Judah's last king (Jer 21.7). *To him,* i.e., to Nebuchadrezzar. **28–32: A poem** addressing the Babylonian sword directly and telling it of its own eventual punishment. **28:** A prose introduction alerts the *Ammonites* (see v. 20) that their glee over the sword's work (25.3,6) will be short-lived. **29:** Divination (v. 21) has directed the sword's use. **30–31:** The ultimate end of Nebuchadrezzar, and of Babylon.

22.1–31: Prophecies of judgment. 22.1–16: A prophecy against Jerusalem, the bloody city. The indictment of vv. 6–12 contains a catalogue of sins based on the regulations in Lev 18–20. **13–16:** In scorn and

made; you have brought your day near, the
appointed time of your years has come.
Therefore I have made you a disgrace be-
fore the nations, and a mockery to all the
countries. 5Those who are near and those
who are far from you will mock you, you
infamous one, full of tumult.

6 The princes of Israel in you, everyone
according to his power, have been bent on
shedding blood. 7Father and mother are
treated with contempt in you; the alien re-
siding within you suffers extortion; the or-
phan and the widow are wronged in you.
8You have despised my holy things, and
profaned my sabbaths. 9In you are those
who slander to shed blood, those in you
who eat upon the mountains, who commit
lewdness in your midst. 10In you they un-
cover their fathers' nakedness; in you they
violate women in their menstrual periods.
11One commits abomination with his
neighbor's wife; another lewdly defiles his
daughter-in-law; another in you defiles his
sister, his father's daughter. 12In you, they
take bribes to shed blood; you take both
advance interest and accrued interest, and
make gain of your neighbors by extortion;
and you have forgotten me, says the Lord
GOD.

13 See, I strike my hands together at the
dishonest gain you have made, and at the
blood that has been shed within you. 14Can
your courage endure, or can your hands
remain strong in the days when I shall deal
with you? I the LORD have spoken, and I
will do it. 15I will scatter you among the
nations and disperse you through the coun-
tries, and I will purge your filthiness out of
you. 16And I[a] shall be profaned through
you in the sight of the nations; and you
shall know that I am the LORD.

17 The word of the LORD came to me:
18Mortal, the house of Israel has become
dross to me; all of them, silver,[b] bronze,
tin, iron, and lead. In the smelter they have
become dross. 19Therefore thus says the
Lord GOD: Because you have all become
dross, I will gather you into the midst of
Jerusalem. 20As one gathers silver, bronze,
iron, lead, and tin into a smelter, to blow
the fire upon them in order to melt them; so
I will gather you in my anger and in my
wrath, and I will put you in and melt you.
21I will gather you and blow upon you with
the fire of my wrath, and you shall be melt-
ed within it. 22As silver is melted in a smelt-
er, so you shall be melted in it; and you
shall know that I the LORD have poured
out my wrath upon you.

23 The word of the LORD came to me:
24Mortal, say to it: You are a land that is
not cleansed, not rained upon in the day of
indignation. 25Its princes[c] within it are
like a roaring lion tearing the prey; they
have devoured human lives; they have tak-
en treasure and precious things; they have
made many widows within it. 26Its priests
have done violence to my teaching and
have profaned my holy things; they have
made no distinction between the holy and
the common, neither have they taught the
difference between the unclean and the
clean, and they have disregarded my sab-
baths, so that I am profaned among them.
27Its officials within it are like wolves tear-
ing the prey, shedding blood, destroying
lives to get dishonest gain. 28Its prophets
have smeared whitewash on their behalf,
seeing false visions and divining lies for
them, saying, "Thus says the Lord GOD,"
when the LORD has not spoken. 29The peo-
ple of the land have practiced extortion and
committed robbery; they have oppressed
the poor and needy, and have extorted

a Gk Syr Vg: Heb *you* *b* Transposed from the end of the verse; compare verse 20 *c* Gk: Heb *indignation. 25A conspiracy of its prophets*

anger (*strike my hands together,* 21.14,17) God will wreak punishment upon this bloody city (18.10n.; Num 35.33–34).

22.17–22: Israel is dross. The judgment will be like a smelter in which base metals are removed.

22.23–31: All classes are corrupt. This oracle seems to come after Jerusalem's fall in 586 BCE (see v. 31) and describes Judah's sinfulness in retrospect. All classes of Judean society were corrupt, and all must be punished; cf. Jer 8.8–10; Zeph 3.3–4. **26:** 42.20; 44.23; Lev 10.10–11. **28:** 13.10n. **30:** 13.5n.

from the alien without redress. 30 And I
sought for anyone among them who would
repair the wall and stand in the breach be-
fore me on behalf of the land, so that I
would not destroy it; but I found no one.
31 Therefore I have poured out my indigna-
tion upon them; I have consumed them
with the fire of my wrath; I have returned
their conduct upon their heads, says the
Lord GOD.

23 The word of the LORD came to me:
2 Mortal, there were two women,
the daughters of one mother; 3 they played
the whore in Egypt; they played the whore
in their youth; their breasts were caressed
there, and their virgin bosoms were fon-
dled. 4 Oholah was the name of the elder
and Oholibah the name of her sister. They
became mine, and they bore sons and
daughters. As for their names, Oholah is
Samaria, and Oholibah is Jerusalem.

5 Oholah played the whore while she
was mine; she lusted after her lovers the
Assyrians, warriors[a] 6 clothed in blue, gov-
ernors and commanders, all of them hand-
some young men, mounted horsemen. 7 She
bestowed her favors upon them, the choic-
est men of Assyria all of them; and she de-
filed herself with all the idols of everyone
for whom she lusted. 8 She did not give up
her whorings that she had practiced since
Egypt; for in her youth men had lain with
her and fondled her virgin bosom and
poured out their lust upon her. 9 Therefore
I delivered her into the hands of her lovers,
into the hands of the Assyrians, for whom
she lusted. 10 These uncovered her naked-
ness; they seized her sons and her daugh-
ters; and they killed her with the sword.
Judgment was executed upon her, and she
became a byword among women.

11 Her sister Oholibah saw this, yet she
was more corrupt than she in her lusting
and in her whorings, which were worse
than those of her sister. 12 She lusted after
the Assyrians, governors and commanders,
warriors[a] clothed in full armor, mounted
horsemen, all of them handsome young
men. 13 And I saw that she was defiled; they
both took the same way. 14 But she carried
her whorings further; she saw male figures
carved on the wall, images of the Chalde-
ans portrayed in vermilion, 15 with belts
around their waists, with flowing turbans
on their heads, all of them looking like offi-
cers—a picture of Babylonians whose na-
tive land was Chaldea. 16 When she saw
them she lusted after them, and sent mes-
sengers to them in Chaldea. 17 And the Bab-
ylonians came to her into the bed of love,
and they defiled her with their lust; and
after she defiled herself with them, she
turned from them in disgust. 18 When she
carried on her whorings so openly and
flaunted her nakedness, I turned in disgust
from her, as I had turned from her sister.
19 Yet she increased her whorings, remem-
bering the days of her youth, when she
played the whore in the land of Egypt
20 and lusted after her paramours there,

a Meaning of Heb uncertain

23.1–49: **The allegory of the sisters, Oholah and Oholibah** (cf. ch 16). **1–4:** Introduction. **3:** *In Egypt,* Israel's apostasy was deep-rooted (20.5–9). **4:** The word play *Oholah,* "her [own] tent," (i.e., Samaria), and *Oholibah,* "my tent [is] in her" (i.e., Jerusalem), may suggest that though the Northern Kingdom had shrines to Yahweh, God's real dwelling (tent) was in Jerusalem, thus emphasizing the enormity of Judah's apostasy. Oholah/Samaria is a "bigger" sister, not an *elder* one (see 16.46n.). Ezekiel borrowed the image of the marrying of sisters from Jeremiah (Jer 3.6–11). **5–10:** Oholah. The Northern Kingdom is condemned for its alliances with Assyria (e.g., 2 Kings 15.19; 17.3). Like Isaiah (7.1–9), and Jeremiah (4.30; same rare word for "*lovers*" as in Ezek 23.5, 9), Ezekiel viewed foreign alliances as disloyalty to God. For Ezekiel, true realism had to do not with political pragmatism but with trusting in God's geopolitical prerogative. **10:** The fall of Samaria to Assyria in 722 BCE. **11–21:** Indictment of Oholibah. Judah had allied itself with Assyria (2 Kings 16.7–9) and then with Babylon ("Chaldea"; see 17.13; 2 Kings 24.1,17; cf. Isa 39.1–8). **17:** Judah swung to an anti-Babylonian policy (2 Kings 24.20; Jer 27.3). **19:** The passage moves to the contemporary event of Judah's alliance with Egypt (17.7,15). **20:** The reference is to oversized genitals and ejaculations; cf. 16.26n. Horses are proverbially oversexed (Jer 5.8). **22–35:** An-

whose members were like those of donkeys,
and whose emission was like that of stal-
lions. 21 Thus you longed for the lewdness
of your youth, when the Egyptians[a] fon-
dled your bosom and caressed[b] your
young breasts.
22 Therefore, O Oholibah, thus says the
Lord GOD: I will rouse against you your
lovers from whom you turned in disgust,
and I will bring them against you from
every side: 23 the Babylonians and all the
Chaldeans, Pekod and Shoa and Koa, and
all the Assyrians with them, handsome
young men, governors and commanders all
of them, officers and warriors,[c] all of them
riding on horses. 24 They shall come against
you from the north[d] with chariots and
wagons and a host of peoples; they shall set
themselves against you on every side with
buckler, shield, and helmet, and I will com-
mit the judgment to them, and they shall
judge you according to their ordinances.
25 I will direct my indignation against you,
in order that they may deal with you in
fury. They shall cut off your nose and your
ears, and your survivors shall fall by the
sword. They shall seize your sons and your
daughters, and your survivors shall be de-
voured by fire. 26 They shall also strip you
of your clothes and take away your fine
jewels. 27 So I will put an end to your lewd-
ness and your whoring brought from the
land of Egypt; you shall not long for them,
or remember Egypt any more. 28 For thus
says the Lord GOD: I will deliver you into
the hands of those whom you hate, into the
hands of those from whom you turned in
disgust; 29 and they shall deal with you in
hatred, and take away all the fruit of your
labor, and leave you naked and bare, and
the nakedness of your whorings shall be
exposed. Your lewdness and your whorings
30 have brought this upon you, because you
played the whore with the nations, and pol-
luted yourself with their idols. 31 You have
gone the way of your sister; therefore I will
give her cup into your hand. 32 Thus says
the Lord GOD:

You shall drink your sister's cup,
deep and wide;
you shall be scorned and derided,
it holds so much.
33 You shall be filled with drunkenness
and sorrow.
A cup of horror and desolation
is the cup of your sister Samaria;
34 you shall drink it and drain it out,
and gnaw its sherds,
and tear out your breasts;

for I have spoken, says the Lord GOD.
35 Therefore thus says the Lord GOD: Be-
cause you have forgotten me and cast me
behind your back, therefore bear the conse-
quences of your lewdness and whorings.
36 The LORD said to me: Mortal, will
you judge Oholah and Oholibah? Then de-
clare to them their abominable deeds. 37 For
they have committed adultery, and blood is
on their hands; with their idols they have
committed adultery; and they have even
offered up to them for food the children
whom they had borne to me. 38 Moreover
this they have done to me: they have defiled
my sanctuary on the same day and pro-
faned my sabbaths. 39 For when they had
slaughtered their children for their idols, on
the same day they came into my sanctuary
to profane it. This is what they did in my
house.
40 They even sent for men to come from
far away, to whom a messenger was sent,
and they came. For them you bathed your-
self, painted your eyes, and decked yourself
with ornaments; 41 you sat on a stately

a Two Mss: MT *from Egypt* *b* Cn: Heb *for the sake of* *c* Compare verses 6 and 12: Heb *officers and called ones* *d* Gk: Meaning of Heb uncertain

nouncements about Oholibah's punishment. **23:** Kindred allies of the *Babylonians* included *Pekod* (an east Aramean tribe), *Shoa,* and *Koa* (unknown tribes). *Assyrian* troops were coopted by their Babylonian conquerors. **32–34:** The poem of the cup of wrath (Jer 25.15–29; Hab 2.16; Ob 16) links Jerusalem's fate with Samaria's. **36–49: Subordinate oracle.** As adulterers are stoned (Lev 20.10), so the adultery (i.e., child sacrifice, profanation of the sabbath, foreign alliances) of Samaria and Judah has been and will be punished—with death. **37:** 16.20–22n. **40:** Cf. vv. 16–17.

couch, with a table spread before it on
which you had placed my incense and my
oil. 42 The sound of a raucous multitude
was around her, with many of the rabble
brought in drunken from the wilderness;
and they put bracelets on the arms[a] of the
women, and beautiful crowns upon their
heads.

43 Then I said, Ah, she is worn out with
adulteries, but they carry on their sexual
acts with her. 44 For they have gone in to
her, as one goes in to a whore. Thus they
went in to Oholah and to Oholibah, wan-
ton women. 45 But righteous judges shall
declare them guilty of adultery and of
bloodshed; because they are adulteresses
and blood is on their hands.

46 For thus says the Lord GOD: Bring up
an assembly against them, and make them
an object of terror and of plunder. 47 The
assembly shall stone them and with their
swords they shall cut them down; they shall
kill their sons and their daughters, and
burn up their houses. 48 Thus will I put an
end to lewdness in the land, so that all
women may take warning and not commit
lewdness as you have done. 49 They shall
repay you for your lewdness, and you shall
bear the penalty for your sinful idolatry;
and you shall know that I am the Lord
GOD.

24 In the ninth year, in the tenth
month, on the tenth day of the
month, the word of the LORD came to me:
2 Mortal, write down the name of this day,
this very day. The king of Babylon has laid
siege to Jerusalem this very day. 3 And utter
an allegory to the rebellious house and say
to them, Thus says the Lord GOD:

Set on the pot, set it on,
pour in water also;
4 put in it the pieces,
all the good pieces, the thigh and
the shoulder;
fill it with choice bones.
5 Take the choicest one of the flock,
pile the logs[b] under it;
boil its pieces,[c]
seethe[d] also its bones in it.

6 Therefore thus says the Lord GOD:
Woe to the bloody city,
the pot whose rust is in it,
whose rust has not gone out of it!
Empty it piece by piece,
making no choice at all.[e]
7 For the blood she shed is inside it;
she placed it on a bare rock;
she did not pour it out on the
ground,
to cover it with earth.
8 To rouse my wrath, to take
vengeance,
I have placed the blood she shed
on a bare rock,
so that it may not be covered.
9 Therefore thus says the Lord GOD:
Woe to the bloody city!
I will even make the pile great.
10 Heap up the logs, kindle the fire;
boil the meat well, mix in
the spices,
let the bones be burned.
11 Stand it empty upon the coals,
so that it may become hot, its
copper glow,
its filth melt in it, its rust
be consumed.
12 In vain I have wearied myself;[f]
its thick rust does not depart.

a Heb *hands* *b* Compare verse 10: Heb *the bones* *c* Two Mss: Heb *its boilings* *d* Cn: Heb *its bones seethe* *e* Heb *piece, no lot has fallen on it* *f* Cn: Meaning of Heb uncertain

24.1–14: The allegory of the pot is a disputation with those still quoting nationalistic slogans about Jerusalem being as inviolable as a metal cauldron (11.3). Ezekiel turns the cauldron image on its head by depicting it as a dirty pot about to be cleaned by overheating (like a modern self-cleaning oven; vv. 5,9) until the bones inside are burned (v. 10). **1:** January 15, 588 BCE, the day that the Babylonian siege of Jerusalem began. **5:** Jerusalem will be *boil*ed as its assailants heap siege equipment around it. **6–8:** Going beyond mere interpretation, these verses expand the image of the pot to provide reasons for Jerusalem's punishment. *Rust,* or alternatively, "encrusted gunk" (also vv. 11–12), represents injustice and bloodguilt (22.6–12).

To the fire with its rust![a]
13 Yet, when I cleansed you in your filthy lewdness,
you did not become clean from your filth;
you shall not again be cleansed
until I have satisfied my fury upon you.
14 I the LORD have spoken; the time is com-
ing, I will act. I will not refrain, I will not
spare, I will not relent. According to your
ways and your doings I will judge you, says
the Lord GOD.
15 The word of the LORD came to me:
16 Mortal, with one blow I am about to take
away from you the delight of your eyes; yet
you shall not mourn or weep, nor shall
your tears run down. 17 Sigh, but not aloud;
make no mourning for the dead. Bind on
your turban, and put your sandals on your
feet; do not cover your upper lip or eat the
bread of mourners.[b] 18 So I spoke to the
people in the morning, and at evening my
wife died. And on the next morning I did as
I was commanded.
19 Then the people said to me, "Will
you not tell us what these things mean for
us, that you are acting this way?" 20 Then I
said to them: The word of the LORD came
to me: 21 Say to the house of Israel, Thus
says the Lord GOD: I will profane my sanc-
tuary, the pride of your power, the delight
of your eyes, and your heart's desire; and
your sons and your daughters whom you
left behind shall fall by the sword. 22 And
you shall do as I have done; you shall not
cover your upper lip or eat the bread of
mourners.[b] 23 Your turbans shall be on
your heads and your sandals on your feet;
you shall not mourn or weep, but you shall
pine away in your iniquities and groan to
one another. 24 Thus Ezekiel shall be a sign
to you; you shall do just as he has done.
When this comes, then you shall know that
I am the Lord GOD.
25 And you, mortal, on the day when I
take from them their stronghold, their joy
and glory, the delight of their eyes and their
heart's affection, and also[c] their sons and
their daughters, 26 on that day, one who has
escaped will come to you to report to you
the news. 27 On that day your mouth shall
be opened to the one who has escaped, and
you shall speak and no longer be silent. So
you shall be a sign to them; and they shall
know that I am the LORD.

25 The word of the LORD came to me:
2 Mortal, set your face toward the
Ammonites and prophesy against them.
3 Say to the Ammonites, Hear the word of
the Lord GOD: Thus says the Lord GOD,
Because you said, "Aha!" over my sanctu-
ary when it was profaned, and over the
land of Israel when it was made desolate,
and over the house of Judah when it went
into exile; 4 therefore I am handing you

a Meaning of Heb uncertain *b* Vg Tg: Heb *of men*
c Heb lacks *and also*

24.15–27: The sign of the death of Ezekiel's wife. Ezekiel's symbolic action of mourning without outward expression shows the people that the loss of cherished persons and things at Jerusalem's fall would bring numbing, inexpressible grief. This deep, silent grief will signify the people's profound discernment of divine judgment (in contrast to their previous skepticism and enmity toward Ezekiel). **23:** Am 5.13. **25–27: The release from speechlessness predicted.** When word of the fall of Jerusalem reached Ezekiel (see 33.21–22), his tongue would be loosed (3.24–27), and he would proclaim a new message of restoration. At that time, Ezekiel's speechlessness will be transferred to and appropriated by the people (v. 23).

25.1–32.32: Part 3: Oracles against the nations. This part of Ezekiel is an effective bridge between the book's message of doom and its message of hope. Here, doom for Israel's antagonists spells hope for Israel itself. Seven nations (Ammon, Moab, Edom, Philistia, Tyre, Sidon, and Egypt) will be punished before Israel is restored (36.5–7).

25.1–17: Oracles against Ammon, Moab, Edom, and Philistia. 1–7: Against Ammon (21.28; Am 1.13–15; Jer 49.1–6). Ammon, which had maliciously gloated over Judah's fall (Lam 2.15–16), is to be occupied by *the people of the east* (v. 4; cf. Isa 11.14), i.e., nomadic Arab tribes. **5:** *Rabbah* (modern

over to the people of the east for a posses-
sion. They shall set their encampments
among you and pitch their tents in your
midst; they shall eat your fruit, and they
shall drink your milk. 5 I will make Rabbah
a pasture for camels and Ammon a fold for
flocks. Then you shall know that I am the
LORD. 6 For thus says the Lord GOD: Be-
cause you have clapped your hands and
stamped your feet and rejoiced with all the
malice within you against the land of Israel,
7 therefore I have stretched out my hand
against you, and will hand you over as
plunder to the nations. I will cut you off
from the peoples and will make you perish
out of the countries; I will destroy you.
Then you shall know that I am the LORD.
8 Thus says the Lord GOD: Because
Moab[a] said, The house of Judah is like all
the other nations, 9 therefore I will lay open
the flank of Moab from the towns[b] on its
frontier, the glory of the country, Beth-
jeshimoth, Baal-meon, and Kiriathaim. 10 I
will give it along with Ammon to the peo-
ple of the east as a possession. Thus Am-
mon shall be remembered no more among
the nations, 11 and I will execute judgments
upon Moab. Then they shall know that I
am the LORD.
12 Thus says the Lord GOD: Because
Edom acted revengefully against the house
of Judah and has grievously offended in
taking vengeance upon them, 13 therefore
thus says the Lord GOD, I will stretch out
my hand against Edom, and cut off from it
humans and animals, and I will make it
desolate; from Teman even to Dedan they
shall fall by the sword. 14 I will lay my ven-
geance upon Edom by the hand of my peo-

a Gk Old Latin: Heb *Moab and Seir* *b* Heb *towns from its towns*

Amman) was the Ammonite capital. **8–11: Against Moab.** Cf. Jer 48. **8:** Cf. 20.32. **9:** God will lay bare Moab's high tableland (*flank*) through the destruction of the three northern fortified cities named. **12–14: Against Edom.** Cf. Jer 49.7–22; Ob; Ps 137.7. **12:** *Vengeance,* Ob 10–14; Ps 137.7. **13:** Destruction will stretch from *Teman* to *Dedan,* localities also associated with Edom in Jer 49.7–8. **15–17: Against**

Chs 25–32: The oracles against the nations.

ple Israel; and they shall act in Edom according to my anger and according to my wrath; and they shall know my vengeance, says the Lord GOD.

15 Thus says the Lord GOD: Because with unending hostilities the Philistines acted in vengeance, and with malice of heart took revenge in destruction;
16 therefore thus says the Lord GOD, I will stretch out my hand against the Philistines, cut off the Cherethites, and destroy the rest of the seacoast.
17 I will execute great vengeance on them with wrathful punishments. Then they shall know that I am the LORD, when I lay my vengeance on them.

26 In the eleventh year, on the first day of the month, the word of the LORD came to me:
2 Mortal, because Tyre said concerning Jerusalem,

"Aha, broken is the gateway of the peoples;
it has swung open to me;
I shall be replenished,
now that it is wasted,"
3 therefore, thus says the Lord GOD:
See, I am against you, O Tyre!
I will hurl many nations against you,
as the sea hurls its waves.
4 They shall destroy the walls of Tyre
and break down its towers.
I will scrape its soil from it
and make it a bare rock.
5 It shall become, in the midst of the sea,
a place for spreading nets.
I have spoken, says the Lord GOD.
It shall become plunder for the nations,
6 and its daughter-towns in the country
shall be killed by the sword.
Then they shall know that I am the LORD.

7 For thus says the Lord GOD: I will bring against Tyre from the north King Nebuchadrezzar of Babylon, king of kings, together with horses, chariots, cavalry, and a great and powerful army.

8 Your daughter-towns in the country
he shall put to the sword.
He shall set up a siege wall against you,
cast up a ramp against you,
and raise a roof of shields against you.
9 He shall direct the shock of his battering rams against your walls
and break down your towers with his axes.
10 His horses shall be so many
that their dust shall cover you.
At the noise of cavalry, wheels, and chariots
your very walls shall shake,
when he enters your gates
like those entering a breached city.
11 With the hoofs of his horses
he shall trample all your streets.
He shall put your people to the sword,
and your strong pillars shall fall to the ground.
12 They will plunder your riches
and loot your merchandise;

Philistia. Cf. Jer 47. *Cherethites,* probably Cretans (the Philistines originally came from the islands of the Aegean Sea; cf. 1 Sam 30.14; Am 9.7; Zeph 2.5; Jer 47.4).

26.1–28.19: Oracles against Tyre. 26.1–21: Tyre is to be destroyed by Nebuchadrezzar. 1–6: Announcement of the judgment. Tyre is judged for gloating over the fall of Jerusalem, a commercial rival, and for looking forward to taking over the city's trade. **1:** Both the (partially preserved) Hebrew and Septuagint texts date the passage several months before Jerusalem's fall, anticipating it as having occurred already (v. 2). **7–14:** Nebuchadrezzar will besiege the island city, which lay a half-mile offshore from the mainland city, after destroying the outlying settlements on the mainland (*daughter-towns,* v. 8). In fact, Nebuchadrezzar besieged the island of Tyre (after the mainland fell) for thirteen years. Tyre lost the war, but it was not destroyed or pillaged (as prophesied, v. 12). This state of affairs is addressed in 29.17–21. Tyre finally fell to Alexander the Great in 332 BCE. **11:** *Strong pillars* probably refer to standing stones held to represent deities. **14:** Cf. vv. 4–5. **15–18:** Dirge of *the princes of the sea,* perhaps coastal cities

they shall break down your walls
and destroy your fine houses.
Your stones and timber and soil
they shall cast into the water.
13 I will silence the music of your songs;
the sound of your lyres shall be
heard no more.
14 I will make you a bare rock;
you shall be a place for
spreading nets.
You shall never again be rebuilt,
for I the LORD have spoken,
says the Lord GOD.

15 Thus says the Lord GOD to Tyre:
Shall not the coastlands shake at the sound
of your fall, when the wounded groan,
when slaughter goes on within you?
16 Then all the princes of the sea shall step
down from their thrones; they shall remove
their robes and strip off their embroidered
garments. They shall clothe themselves
with trembling, and shall sit on the ground;
they shall tremble every moment, and be
appalled at you.
17 And they shall raise a
lamentation over you, and say to you:

How you have vanished[a] from
the seas,
O city renowned,
once mighty on the sea,
you and your inhabitants,[b]
who imposed your[c] terror
on all the mainland![d]
18 Now the coastlands tremble
on the day of your fall;
the coastlands by the sea
are dismayed at your passing.

19 For thus says the Lord GOD: When I
make you a city laid waste, like cities that
are not inhabited, when I bring up the deep
over you, and the great waters cover you,
20 then I will thrust you down with those
who descend into the Pit, to the people of
long ago, and I will make you live in the
world below, among primeval ruins, with
those who go down to the Pit, so that you
will not be inhabited or have a place[e] in
the land of the living.
21 I will bring you to
a dreadful end, and you shall be no more;
though sought for, you will never be found
again, says the Lord GOD.

27 The word of the LORD came to me:
2 Now you, mortal, raise a lamenta-
tion over Tyre,
3 and say to Tyre, which sits
at the entrance to the sea, merchant of the
peoples on many coastlands, Thus says the
Lord GOD:

O Tyre, you have said,
"I am perfect in beauty."
4 Your borders are in the heart of the
seas;
your builders made perfect
your beauty.
5 They made all your planks
of fir trees from Senir;
they took a cedar from Lebanon
to make a mast for you.
6 From oaks of Bashan
they made your oars;
they made your deck of pines[f]
from the coasts of Cyprus,
inlaid with ivory.
7 Of fine embroidered linen from Egypt
was your sail,
serving as your ensign;

a Gk OL Aquila: Heb *have vanished, O inhabited one,*
b Heb *it and its inhabitants* *c* Heb *their*
d Cn: Heb *its inhabitants* *e* Gk: Heb *I will give beauty* *f* Or *boxwood*

in trade alliance with Tyre. **19–21:** The simile of the attack of the sea in v. 3 is here converted and heightened into mythic metaphor. The waters of the primordial *deep* (Gen 1.2) will cover the wasted city, which will *descend into the Pit* (Sheol, see 31.15–18; 32.17–32; Isa 14.15), the mythopoetic abode of the dead.

27.1–36: Dirge over the ship Tyre. Ezekiel's metaphorical language serves his need to push beyond the ordinarily observable and speak of ultimate realities. **1–25:** Tyre's glory. **2:** *Lamentation,* better, a funerary "dirge," in which present downfall is contrasted with past glory. **3:** *I am perfect in beauty* is supposed to be Jerusalem's epithet (16.14; Lam 2.15), not Tyre's. **5–9:** The text shifts directly into the ship metaphor. The good ship Tyre was constructed of the best materials. *Senir* is Mount Hermon (Deut 3.9). *Bashan* is east of the Sea of Galilee; *Elishah* is probably Cyprus. The ship's crew was from *Sidon, Arvad, Zemer* (textual note *a*), and *Gebal* (Byblos), Phoenician island and port cities. **10:** The ship's

blue and purple from the coasts
of Elishah
was your awning.
8 The inhabitants of Sidon and Arvad
were your rowers;
skilled men of Zemer[a] were
within you,
they were your pilots.
9 The elders of Gebal and its artisans
were within you,
caulking your seams;
all the ships of the sea with their
mariners were within you,
to barter for your wares.
10 Paras[b] and Lud and Put
were in your army,
your mighty warriors;
they hung shield and helmet in you;
they gave you splendor.
11 Men of Arvad and Helech[c]
were on your walls all around;
men of Gamad were at
your towers.
They hung their quivers all around
your walls;
they made perfect your beauty.

12 Tarshish did business with you out of
the abundance of your great wealth; silver,
iron, tin, and lead they exchanged for your
wares. 13 Javan, Tubal, and Meshech trad-
ed with you; they exchanged human beings
and vessels of bronze for your merchandise.
14 Beth-togarmah exchanged for your
wares horses, war horses, and mules. 15 The
Rhodians[d] traded with you; many coast-
lands were your own special markets; they
brought you in payment ivory tusks and
ebony. 16 Edom[e] did business with you be-
cause of your abundant goods; they ex-
changed for your wares turquoise, purple,
embroidered work, fine linen, coral, and
rubies. 17 Judah and the land of Israel trad-
ed with you; they exchanged for your mer-
chandise wheat from Minnith, millet,[f]
honey, oil, and balm. 18 Damascus traded
with you for your abundant goods—be-
cause of your great wealth of every kind—
wine of Helbon, and white wool. 19 Vedan
and Javan from Uzal[f] entered into trade
for your wares; wrought iron, cassia, and
sweet cane were bartered for your mer-
chandise. 20 Dedan traded with you in sad-
dlecloths for riding. 21 Arabia and all the
princes of Kedar were your favored dealers
in lambs, rams, and goats; in these they did
business with you. 22 The merchants of She-
ba and Raamah traded with you; they ex-
changed for your wares the best of all kinds
of spices, and all precious stones, and gold.
23 Haran, Canneh, Eden, the merchants of
Sheba, Asshur, and Chilmad traded with
you. 24 These traded with you in choice gar-
ments, in clothes of blue and embroidered
work, and in carpets of colored material,
bound with cords and made secure; in these
they traded with you.[g] 25 The ships of Tar-
shish traveled for you in your trade.

a Cn Compare Gen 10.18: Heb *your skilled men, O Tyre* *b* Or *Persia* *c* Or *and your army* *d* Gk: Heb *The Dedanites* *e* Another reading is *Aram* *f* Meaning of Heb uncertain *g* Cn: Heb *in your market*

warriors included those from Persia (textual note *b*), *Lud* (Lydia in western Asia Minor), and *Put* (Libya). **11:** Literal reality (Tyre as a city) momentarily intrudes into Ezekiel's ship metaphor. *Arvad,* see v. 8. *Helech,* possibly Cilicia, in southeastern Asia Minor. The *men of Gamad* are perhaps the Cimmerians or Cappadocians in eastern Asia Minor. **12–25:** A (mostly prose) description of the gallant ship's cargo of rich wares from many nations. Tyre's commercial empire is described first in its west and north zone (vv. 12–15): *Tarshish,* perhaps Tartessus in southern Spain or Sardinia; *Javan,* Ionians, i.e., the Greeks of the Aegean; *Tubal* and *Meshech,* peoples settled in Asia Minor; *Beth-togarmah,* in eastern Asia Minor (Armenia); *Rhodians* (see textual note *d*) from the Aegean Sea. The description then moves vertically from Tyre's south to its northeast (vv. 16–19): *Edom; Judah* and *Israel; Minnith,* an Ammonite city (Judg 11.33); *Damascus; Helbon,* a wine center north of Damascus. The Arabian region is treated next (vv. 20–22): *Dedan,* in northwest Arabia; *Kedar,* a tribal group of northern Arabia; *Sheba* and *Raamah,* in southwest Arabia. Several Mesopotamian cities conclude the list (v. 23): *Haran,* in northwest Mesopotamia; *Canneh,* a town near Haran; *Eden,* the Aramean state of Bit-Adini, south of Haran; *Asshur,* south of Nineveh; *Chilmad,* unidentified. **25:** *Ships of Tarshish,* see 1 Kings 10.22; 22.48; Ps 48.7; Isa 23.1.

So you were filled and heavily laden
in the heart of the seas.
26 Your rowers have brought you
into the high seas.
The east wind has wrecked you
in the heart of the seas.
27 Your riches, your wares, your
merchandise,
your mariners and your pilots,
your caulkers, your dealers in
merchandise,
and all your warriors within you,
with all the company
that is with you,
sink into the heart of the seas
on the day of your ruin.
28 At the sound of the cry of your pilots
the countryside shakes,
29 and down from their ships
come all that handle the oar.
The mariners and all the pilots
of the sea
stand on the shore
30 and wail aloud over you,
and cry bitterly.
They throw dust on their heads
and wallow in ashes;
31 they make themselves bald for you,
and put on sackcloth,
and they weep over you in bitterness
of soul,
with bitter mourning.
32 In their wailing they raise a
lamentation for you,
and lament over you:
"Who was ever destroyed[a] like Tyre
in the midst of the sea?
33 When your wares came from the seas,
you satisfied many peoples;
with your abundant wealth and
merchandise
you enriched the kings of the earth.
34 Now you are wrecked by the seas,
in the depths of the waters;
your merchandise and all your crew
have sunk with you.
35 All the inhabitants of the coastlands
are appalled at you;
and their kings are horribly afraid,
their faces are convulsed.
36 The merchants among the peoples
hiss at you;
you have come to a dreadful end
and shall be no more forever."

28 The word of the LORD came to me:
2 Mortal, say to the prince of Tyre,
Thus says the Lord GOD:
Because your heart is proud
and you have said, "I am a god;
I sit in the seat of the gods,
in the heart of the seas,"
yet you are but a mortal, and no god,
though you compare your mind
with the mind of a god.
3 You are indeed wiser than Daniel;[b]
no secret is hidden from you;
4 by your wisdom and your
understanding
you have amassed wealth
for yourself,
and have gathered gold and silver
into your treasuries.
5 By your great wisdom in trade
you have increased your wealth,
and your heart has become proud
in your wealth.
6 Therefore thus says the Lord GOD:
Because you compare your mind
with the mind of a god,

a Tg Vg: Heb *like silence* *b* Or, as otherwise read, *Danel*

26–36: With this section, the dirge shifts from picturing Tyre's past glory to describing its sudden end. As in 19.12, the east wind (sirocco) is an agent of destruction (cf. Ps 48.7). The sudden end of the great commercial city brings astonishment and fear, and grief to seafarers, merchants, and inhabitants of the coastlands.

28.1–10: Oracle against the leader of Tyre. 2: *Prince,* the Heb term means "leader" or "ruler" here. The leader, who represents the whole people of Tyre, is judged for his pride (a universal offense, Prov 16.5). Hubris leads to self-deification. Thus the prince of Tyre sat in *the seat of the gods* (cf. Isa 14.13–14). *Heart of the seas,* see 28.14n. **3:** In the Ugaritic tablets, *Danel* is the wise judge of widows and orphans (see 14.14n.). **6–10:** The leader will be slain by *the most terrible of the nations,* Babylonia

7 therefore, I will bring strangers
against you,
the most terrible of the nations;
they shall draw their swords against
the beauty of your wisdom
and defile your splendor.
8 They shall thrust you down to the Pit,
and you shall die a violent death
in the heart of the seas.
9 Will you still say, "I am a god,"
in the presence of those who
kill you,
though you are but a mortal, and no
god,
in the hands of those who
wound you?
10 You shall die the death of the
uncircumcised
by the hand of foreigners;
for I have spoken, says the
Lord God.

11 Moreover the word of the LORD
came to me: 12 Mortal, raise a lamentation
over the king of Tyre, and say to him, Thus
says the Lord GOD:

You were the signet of perfection,[a]
full of wisdom and perfect in
beauty.
13 You were in Eden, the garden of God;
every precious stone was your
covering,
carnelian, chrysolite, and moonstone,
beryl, onyx, and jasper,
sapphire,[b] turquoise, and emerald;
and worked in gold were your
settings
and your engravings.[a]
On the day that you were created
they were prepared.
14 With an anointed cherub as guardian
I placed you;[a]
you were on the holy mountain
of God;
you walked among the stones
of fire.
15 You were blameless in your ways
from the day that you were created,
until iniquity was found in you.
16 In the abundance of your trade
you were filled with violence, and
you sinned;
so I cast you as a profane thing from
the mountain of God,
and the guardian cherub drove you
out
from among the stones of fire.
17 Your heart was proud because of
your beauty;
you corrupted your wisdom for the
sake of your splendor.
I cast you to the ground;
I exposed you before kings,
to feast their eyes on you.
18 By the multitude of your iniquities,
in the unrighteousness of
your trade,
you profaned your sanctuaries.
So I brought out fire from within you;
it consumed you,

a Meaning of Heb uncertain *b* Or *lapis lazuli*

(30.10–11), and come to an ignominious end (*the death of the uncircumcised*) in *the Pit,* that is, Sheol, the abode of the dead (32.30). Like the Israelites, the Phoenicians practiced circumcision.

28.11–19: A dirge over the king of Tyre. The passage reworks 28.1–10 based on a primordial mythic figure, either human (cf. Gen 2–3) or celestial (cf. the Ugaritic myth of Athtar). Here, the judgment of Tyre's king serves as a concrete instance of the downfall of the primal being. The text of v. 14 is ambiguous as to whether this being was *with* a cherub, or, more likely, was a great cherub himself (also see v. 16b n.). With his *covering* of precious stones, compare the stones of the high priest's breastplate in Ex 28.17–20 (which itself must have held mythic significance). **13–14:** The garden paradise of *Eden* (v. 13) sat atop the mythic cosmic mountain. Rivers flow from God's mountain, watering the earth (47.1–12; Gen 2.10–14; Ps 46.4; Zech 14.8). **16–19:** The dirge moves from the primal being's past glory to an account of his downfall through hubris. **16a:** The actual referent (Tyre's corrupt trade) intrudes into the allegorical figure (the primal being's sin) here. **16b:** The NRSV follows the Septuagint (cf. Gen 3.23–24). The Hebrew reads, "I drove you out, O guardian cherub." For demotions of supernatural figures, cf. Ps 82.6–7; Isa 14.12.

and I turned you to ashes on
the earth
in the sight of all who saw you.
19 All who know you among the
peoples
are appalled at you;
you have come to a dreadful end
and shall be no more forever.

20 The word of the LORD came to me:
21 Mortal, set your face toward Sidon, and
prophesy against it, 22 and say, Thus says
the Lord GOD:

I am against you, O Sidon,
and I will gain glory in your midst.
They shall know that I am the LORD
when I execute judgments in it,
and manifest my holiness in it;
23 for I will send pestilence into it,
and bloodshed into its streets;
and the dead shall fall in its midst,
by the sword that is against it on
every side.
And they shall know that I am
the LORD.

24 The house of Israel shall no longer find a pricking brier or a piercing thorn among all their neighbors who have treated them with contempt. And they shall know that I am the Lord GOD.

25 Thus says the Lord GOD: When I
gather the house of Israel from the peoples
among whom they are scattered, and mani-
fest my holiness in them in the sight of the
nations, then they shall settle on their own
soil that I gave to my servant Jacob. 26 They
shall live in safety in it, and shall build
houses and plant vineyards. They shall live
in safety, when I execute judgments upon
all their neighbors who have treated them
with contempt. And they shall know that I
am the LORD their God.

29 In the tenth year, in the tenth
month, on the twelfth day of the
month, the word of the LORD came to me:
2 Mortal, set your face against Pharaoh
king of Egypt, and prophesy against him
and against all Egypt; 3 speak, and say,
Thus says the Lord GOD:

I am against you,
Pharaoh king of Egypt,
the great dragon sprawling
in the midst of its channels,
saying, "My Nile is my own;
I made it for myself."
4 I will put hooks in your jaws,
and make the fish of your channels
stick to your scales.
I will draw you up from your
channels,
with all the fish of your channels
sticking to your scales.
5 I will fling you into the wilderness,
you and all the fish of your
channels;
you shall fall in the open field,
and not be gathered and buried.
To the animals of the earth and to
the birds of the air
I have given you as food.
6 Then all the inhabitants of Egypt shall
know
that I am the LORD
because you[a] were a staff of reed
to the house of Israel;
7 when they grasped you with the hand,
you broke,

a Gk Syr Vg: Heb *they*

28.20–26: Oracle against Sidon, north of Tyre. **22:** A good example of Ezekiel's Priestly language (cf. Ex 14.17–18; Lev 10.3). **24–26:** Sidon's doom spells God's vindication. **24:** Cf. Num 33.55. **25–26:** Cf. 34.28; Lev 25.19.

29.1–32.32: Prophecies against Egypt. 29.1–16: Against Pharaoh (January 7, 587 BCE). **3:** *Dragon,* the Heb term may refer to a primeval monster of watery chaos (Job 7.12; Ps 74.13; Isa 51.9; cf. Isa 30.7) or to a crocodile of the Nile (Ex 7.8–12). The imagery of the mythical monster is more pronounced in 32.1–16 than it is here. God will cast this creature of the Nile on the land as carrion (32.1–8). *Its channels,* the Nile delta and canals. **4:** *Hooks,* cf. Isa 37.29; Job 41.2. *Fish of your channels,* the Egyptians and their mercenaries. **6b–9a:** *Staff of reed,* compare the Rabshakeh's similar belittlement of Egypt in 2 Kings 18.21; Isa 36.6. Pharaoh Hophra's attack against Nebuchadrezzar in the spring of 588 had failed to relieve Jerusalem (Jer 37.5–10). **10:** *Migdol to Syene,* northern and southern Egyptian localities, together

and tore all their shoulders;
and when they leaned on you,
you broke,
and made all their legs unsteady.[a]
8 Therefore, thus says the Lord GOD: I
will bring a sword upon you, and will cut
off from you human being and animal;
9 and the land of Egypt shall be a desolation
and a waste. Then they shall know that I
am the LORD.

Because you[b] said, "The Nile is mine,
and I made it," 10 therefore, I am against
you, and against your channels, and I will
make the land of Egypt an utter waste and
desolation, from Migdol to Syene, as far as
the border of Ethiopia.[c] 11 No human foot
shall pass through it, and no animal foot
shall pass through it; it shall be uninhabited
forty years. 12 I will make the land of Egypt
a desolation among desolated countries;
and her cities shall be a desolation forty
years among cities that are laid waste. I will
scatter the Egyptians among the nations,
and disperse them among the countries.

13 Further, thus says the Lord GOD: At
the end of forty years I will gather the
Egyptians from the peoples among whom
they were scattered; 14 and I will restore the
fortunes of Egypt, and bring them back to
the land of Pathros, the land of their origin;
and there they shall be a lowly kingdom.
15 It shall be the most lowly of the king-
doms, and never again exalt itself above the
nations; and I will make them so small that
they will never again rule over the nations.
16 The Egyptians[d] shall never again be the
reliance of the house of Israel; they will
recall their iniquity, when they turned to
them for aid. Then they shall know that I
am the Lord GOD.

17 In the twenty-seventh year, in the
first month, on the first day of the month,
the word of the LORD came to me: 18 Mor-
tal, King Nebuchadrezzar of Babylon made
his army labor hard against Tyre; every
head was made bald and every shoulder
was rubbed bare; yet neither he nor his
army got anything from Tyre to pay for
the labor that he had expended against it.
19 Therefore thus says the Lord GOD: I will
give the land of Egypt to King Nebuchad-
rezzar of Babylon; and he shall carry off its
wealth and despoil it and plunder it; and it
shall be the wages for his army. 20 I have
given him the land of Egypt as his payment
for which he labored, because they worked
for me, says the Lord GOD.

21 On that day I will cause a horn to
sprout up for the house of Israel, and I will
open your lips among them. Then they
shall know that I am the LORD.

30 The word of the LORD came to me:
2 Mortal, prophesy, and say, Thus
says the Lord GOD:
Wail, "Alas for the day!"
3 For a day is near,
the day of the LORD is near;
it will be a day of clouds,
a time of doom[e] for the nations.
4 A sword shall come upon Egypt,
and anguish shall be in Ethiopia,[c]

a Syr: Heb *stand* b Gk Syr Vg: Heb *he*
c Or *Nubia*; Heb *Cush* d Heb *It* e Heb lacks *of doom*

signifying all Egypt. **11:** *Forty years,* 4.6; Num 14.33. **13–16:** The only promise of Egyptian restoration in Ezekiel, though Egypt will be restored only as a *lowly kingdom,* not a great empire. **14:** *Pathros,* southern Egypt.

29.17–21: Egypt as "wages" for Nebuchadrezzar, instead of Tyre. Ezekiel's latest dated oracle, April 26, 571 BCE. This unique passage amends the Tyre prophecies (26.12) in light of subsequent events. Nebuchadrezzar will get sufficient booty from Egypt to compensate for his lack of booty from the siege of Tyre. The followers of Ezekiel thus understood "unfulfilled" prophecy as showing God's mysterious freedom, not as discrediting Ezekiel. **21:** *Horn* may refer to a reestablished Davidic monarch in Israel (Ps 132.17).

30.1–19: The doom of Egypt. 1–9: Since the time of Amos (Am 5.18–20) the Day of the LORD was God's judgment day (7.5–9n.; 13.5); later, as here, it became Israel's restoration day, but remained doomsday for the nations (38.18; 39.8). *Sword,* 7.15. *Put, and Lud,* see 27.10n. **6–9:** Egypt's allies will

when the slain fall in Egypt,
and its wealth is carried away,
and its foundations are torn down.
5 Ethiopia,[a] and Put, and Lud, and all Ara-
bia, and Libya,[b] and the people of the
allied land[c] shall fall with them by the
sword.

6 Thus says the LORD:
Those who support Egypt shall fall,
and its proud might shall
come down;
from Migdol to Syene
they shall fall within it by
the sword,
says the Lord GOD.
7 They shall be desolated among other
desolated countries,
and their cities shall lie among
cities laid waste.
8 Then they shall know that I am
the LORD,
when I have set fire to Egypt,
and all who help it are broken.
9 On that day, messengers shall go out
from me in ships to terrify the unsuspecting
Ethiopians;[d] and anguish shall come upon
them on the day of Egypt's doom;[e] for it is
coming!

10 Thus says the Lord GOD:
I will put an end to the hordes
of Egypt,
by the hand of King
Nebuchadrezzar of Babylon.
11 He and his people with him, the most
terrible of the nations,
shall be brought in to destroy
the land;
and they shall draw their swords
against Egypt,
and fill the land with the slain.
12 I will dry up the channels,
and will sell the land into the hand
of evildoers;
I will bring desolation upon the land
and everything in it
by the hand of foreigners;
I the LORD have spoken.

13 Thus says the Lord GOD:
I will destroy the idols
and put an end to the images
in Memphis;
there shall no longer be a prince in
the land of Egypt;
so I will put fear in the land
of Egypt.
14 I will make Pathros a desolation,
and will set fire to Zoan,
and will execute acts of judgment
on Thebes.
15 I will pour my wrath upon Pelusium,
the stronghold of Egypt,
and cut off the hordes of Thebes.
16 I will set fire to Egypt;
Pelusium shall be in great agony;
Thebes shall be breached,
and Memphis face adversaries
by day.
17 The young men of On and of
Pi-beseth shall fall by
the sword;
and the cities themselves[f] shall go
into captivity.
18 At Tehaphnehes the day shall
be dark,
when I break there the dominion of
Egypt,
and its proud might shall come to an
end;

a Or *Nubia*; Heb *Cush* *b* Compare Gk Syr Vg: Heb *Cub* *c* Meaning of Heb uncertain *d* Or *Nubians*; Heb *Cush* *e* Heb *the day of Egypt* *f* Heb *and they*

collapse. *Migdol to Syene,* see 29.10n. *Unsuspecting Ethiopians,* the enormity of the fall of great Egypt is emphasized by describing onlookers' reactions. **10–12**: Nebuchadrezzar is Egypt's destroyer. **13–19**: All Egypt will be destroyed. *Images* are condemned in Lev 19.4; 26.1. *Memphis,* south of Cairo, was the ancient capital of lower (northern) Egypt. *Pathros,* see 29.14n. *Zoan,* in the northeast delta region. *Thebes,* capital of upper Egypt, is present-day Karnak and Luxor. *Pelusium,* east of Zoan, in the delta region. *On* is Heliopolis, slightly northeast of Cairo. *Pi-beseth,* Bubastis, in the eastern delta. *Tehaphnehes,* Tahpanhes, on Egypt's northeastern frontier.

the city[a] shall be covered by
a cloud,
and its daughter-towns shall go
into captivity.
19 Thus I will execute acts of judgment
on Egypt.
Then they shall know that I am the
LORD.

20 In the eleventh year, in the first
month, on the seventh day of the month,
the word of the LORD came to me: 21 Mor-
tal, I have broken the arm of Pharaoh king
of Egypt; it has not been bound up for heal-
ing or wrapped with a bandage, so that it
may become strong to wield the sword.
22 Therefore thus says the Lord GOD: I am
against Pharaoh king of Egypt, and will
break his arms, both the strong arm and the
one that was broken; and I will make the
sword fall from his hand. 23 I will scatter
the Egyptians among the nations, and dis-
perse them throughout the lands. 24 I will
strengthen the arms of the king of Babylon,
and put my sword in his hand; but I will
break the arms of Pharaoh, and he will
groan before him with the groans of one
mortally wounded. 25 I will strengthen the
arms of the king of Babylon, but the arms
of Pharaoh shall fall. And they shall know
that I am the LORD, when I put my sword
into the hand of the king of Babylon. He
shall stretch it out against the land of
Egypt, 26 and I will scatter the Egyptians
among the nations and disperse them
throughout the countries. Then they shall
know that I am the LORD.

31 In the eleventh year, in the third
month, on the first day of the
month, the word of the LORD came to me:
2 Mortal, say to Pharaoh king of Egypt and
to his hordes:
Whom are you like in your greatness?
3 Consider Assyria, a cedar
of Lebanon,
with fair branches and forest shade,
and of great height,
its top among the clouds.[b]
4 The waters nourished it,
the deep made it grow tall,
making its rivers flow[c]
around the place it was planted,
sending forth its streams
to all the trees of the field.
5 So it towered high
above all the trees of the field;
its boughs grew large
and its branches long,
from abundant water in its shoots.
6 All the birds of the air
made their nests in its boughs;
under its branches all the animals of
the field
gave birth to their young;
and in its shade
all great nations lived.
7 It was beautiful in its greatness,
in the length of its branches;
for its roots went down
to abundant water.
8 The cedars in the garden of God
could not rival it,
nor the fir trees equal its boughs;
the plane trees were as nothing

a Heb *she* *b* Gk: Heb *thick boughs* *c* Gk: Heb *rivers going*

30.20–26: Pharaoh disarmed. April 29, 587 BCE. The body imagery of broken arms represents military defeat. Nebuchadrezzar had broken one arm of Hophra the year before (vv. 20–21; see 29.6b–9a n.). The next time, he will break both arms (vv. 22–26).

31.1–18: The comparison between Assyria and Egypt. Date, June 21, 587 BCE. Ezekiel uses the archetype of the cosmic tree to emphasize that, as with Assyria of late, the cause for Egypt's fall will be pride (hubris). **3a:** The fact of the downfall undergone by great Assyria, the superpower preceding Babylonia, supports the credibility of Ezekiel's judgments against Egypt. See Nah 3.8–10 for a similar comparison of Egypt and Assyria. Ezekiel's image of Assyria as a tree may have its source of inspiration in Isa 10.33–34. **3b–9:** A dirge for the cosmic tree begins by describing its former glory. **4:** *The deep* (Heb "tehom"), here, the world's subterranean sweet-waters (Gen 7.11), which nourished the tree so that it reached into the heavens and sheltered all life (cf. Dan 4). **7–9:** The splendor of the great cedar was incomparable (v. 18), surpassing those *in the garden of God* (thus rivaling God, Gen 2.9; 11.1–9). **10–18:**

compared with its branches;
no tree in the garden of God
was like it in beauty.
9 I made it beautiful
with its mass of branches,
the envy of all the trees of Eden
that were in the garden of God.

10 Therefore thus says the Lord GOD:
Because it[a] towered high and set its top
among the clouds,[b] and its heart was
proud of its height, 11 I gave it into the hand
of the prince of the nations; he has dealt
with it as its wickedness deserves. I have
cast it out. 12 Foreigners from the most ter-
rible of the nations have cut it down and
left it. On the mountains and in all the val-
leys its branches have fallen, and its boughs
lie broken in all the watercourses of the
land; and all the peoples of the earth went
away from its shade and left it.

13 On its fallen trunk settle
all the birds of the air,
and among its boughs lodge
all the wild animals.

14 All this is in order that no trees by the
waters may grow to lofty height or set their
tops among the clouds,[b] and that no trees
that drink water may reach up to them in
height.

For all of them are handed over
to death,
to the world below;
along with all mortals,
with those who go down to the Pit.

15 Thus says the Lord GOD: On the day
it went down to Sheol I closed the deep
over it and covered it; I restrained its rivers,
and its mighty waters were checked. I
clothed Lebanon in gloom for it, and all the
trees of the field fainted because of it. 16 I
made the nations quake at the sound of its
fall, when I cast it down to Sheol with those
who go down to the Pit; and all the trees of
Eden, the choice and best of Lebanon, all
that were well watered, were consoled in
the world below. 17 They also went down
to Sheol with it, to those killed by the
sword, along with its allies,[c] those who
lived in its shade among the nations.

18 Which among the trees of Eden was
like you in glory and in greatness? Now
you shall be brought down with the trees
of Eden to the world below; you shall lie
among the uncircumcised, with those who
are killed by the sword. This is Pharaoh
and all his horde, says the Lord GOD.

32 In the twelfth year, in the twelfth
month, on the first day of the
month, the word of the LORD came to me:
2 Mortal, raise a lamentation over Pharaoh
king of Egypt, and say to him:

You consider yourself a lion among
the nations,
but you are like a dragon in
the seas;
you thrash about in your streams,
trouble the water with your feet,
and foul your[d] streams.

3 Thus says the Lord GOD:
In an assembly of many peoples
I will throw my net over you;
and I[e] will haul you up in
my dragnet.
4 I will throw you on the ground,
on the open field I will fling you,

a Syr Vg: Heb *you* *b* Gk: Heb *thick boughs*
c Heb *its arms* *d* Heb *their* *e* Gk Vg: Heb *they*

The tree's two-phased disaster. God will have it cut down; the life it sheltered will be dispersed (vv. 10–14). Once felled, it will go down still farther, to *the Pit* (v. 14), or *Sheol,* the abode of the dead (vv. 15–18), where it will lie with those who died untimely, violent, or dishonorable deaths. **11:** *Prince of the nations,* Nabopolassar (626–605 BCE), founder of the Neo-Babylonian Empire, who, in alliance with the Medes, destroyed the Assyrian Empire in a series of battles between 614 and 609.

32.1–16: Dirge over Pharaoh. Date, March 3, 585 BCE. **2:** *Dragon,* the mythical chaos monster (see 29.3n.). In his hubris, Pharaoh aspires to rock the cosmos (*in the seas,* cf. Isa 27.1 and the watery chaos of Ps 46.3; 93.3). Vv. 2,13–14 show, however, that in reality he can only stir up a little local trouble, muddying the water with his feet. **3–8:** His punishment. Vv. 6–8 recall the Day of the LORD (see 30.1–9n.; Isa 13.10; Joel 2.2,30), in which God overcomes all opposing forces. They also echo the Exodus plagues against Egypt (Ex 7.17; 10.21–23). **9–10:** The nations' reactions (cf. 26.16; 27.35). **11–15:** The

and will cause all the birds of the air
to settle on you,
and I will let the wild animals of
the whole earth gorge
themselves with you.
5 I will strew your flesh on the
mountains,
and fill the valleys with your
carcass.[a]
6 I will drench the land with your
flowing blood
up to the mountains,
and the watercourses will be filled
with you.
7 When I blot you out, I will cover the
heavens,
and make their stars dark;
I will cover the sun with a cloud,
and the moon shall not give
its light.
8 All the shining lights of the heavens
I will darken above you,
and put darkness on your land,
says the Lord GOD.
9 I will trouble the hearts of many
peoples,
as I carry you captive[b] among the
nations,
into countries you have not known.
10 I will make many peoples appalled at
you;
their kings shall shudder because of
you.
When I brandish my sword before
them,
they shall tremble every moment
for their lives, each one of them,
on the day of your downfall.
11 For thus says the Lord GOD:
The sword of the king of Babylon
shall come against you.
12 I will cause your hordes to fall
by the swords of mighty ones,
all of them most terrible among the
nations.
They shall bring to ruin the pride of
Egypt,
and all its hordes shall perish.
13 I will destroy all its livestock
from beside abundant waters;
and no human foot shall trouble them
any more,
nor shall the hoofs of cattle trouble
them.
14 Then I will make their waters clear,
and cause their streams to run like
oil, says the Lord GOD.
15 When I make the land of Egypt
desolate
and when the land is stripped of all
that fills it,
when I strike down all who live in it,
then they shall know that I am the
LORD.
16 This is a lamentation; it shall
be chanted.
The women of the nations shall
chant it.
Over Egypt and all its hordes they
shall chant it,
says the Lord GOD.

17 In the twelfth year, in the first
month,[c] on the fifteenth day of the month,
the word of the LORD came to me:
18 Mortal, wail over the hordes
of Egypt,
and send them down,

a Symmachus Syr Vg: Heb *your height* *b* Gk: Heb *bring your destruction* *c* Gk: Heb lacks *in the first month*

sword of God (v. 10; 30.4; Lev 26.25,33) is concretely the Babylonians' sword (cf. 30.25). **14:** Reversing v. 2, God restores the Nile's natural state (cf. Lev 26.34–35).

32.17–32: Egypt in the underworld. The Septuagint's date (textual note *c*) is April 27, 586 BCE. Ezekiel imaginatively uses mythological images of a netherworld ("the Pit," "Sheol") to describe Egypt's consignment to the sphere of uncleanness and dishonor. Like Tyre (28.10), Egypt belongs in the section of the underworld reserved for the uncircumcised and those who are executed or who die violent or untimely deaths. They do not enjoy the status of the honored war dead, who were properly buried (v. 27). The Egyptians apparently practiced circumcision, as did the Edomites (v. 29) and the Sidonians (v. 30; cf. 28.10n.). Thus, their fate is to the disgrace of all three peoples. **22–30:** A roster. In its dishonorable

with Egypt[a] and the daughters of
majestic nations,
to the world below,
with those who go down to the Pit.
19 "Whom do you surpass in beauty?
Go down! Be laid to rest with the
uncircumcised!"
20 They shall fall among those who are
killed by the sword. Egypt[b] has been hand-
ed over to the sword; carry away both it
and its hordes. 21 The mighty chiefs shall
speak of them, with their helpers, out of the
midst of Sheol: "They have come down,
they lie still, the uncircumcised, killed by
the sword."
22 Assyria is there, and all its company,
their graves all around it, all of them killed,
fallen by the sword. 23 Their graves are set
in the uttermost parts of the Pit. Its compa-
ny is all around its grave, all of them killed,
fallen by the sword, who spread terror in
the land of the living.
24 Elam is there, and all its hordes
around its grave; all of them killed, fallen
by the sword, who went down uncircum-
cised into the world below, who spread ter-
ror in the land of the living. They bear their
shame with those who go down to the Pit.
25 They have made Elam[a] a bed among the
slain with all its hordes, their graves all
around it, all of them uncircumcised, killed
by the sword; for terror of them was spread
in the land of the living, and they bear their
shame with those who go down to the Pit;
they are placed among the slain.
26 Meshech and Tubal are there, and
all their multitude, their graves all around
them, all of them uncircumcised, killed by
the sword; for they spread terror in the land
of the living. 27 And they do not lie with the
fallen warriors of long ago[c] who went
down to Sheol with their weapons of war,
whose swords were laid under their heads,
and whose shields[d] are upon their bones;
for the terror of the warriors was in the
land of the living. 28 So you shall be broken
and lie among the uncircumcised, with
those who are killed by the sword.
29 Edom is there, its kings and all its
princes, who for all their might are laid
with those who are killed by the sword;
they lie with the uncircumcised, with those
who go down to the Pit.
30 The princes of the north are there, all
of them, and all the Sidonians, who have
gone down in shame with the slain, for all
the terror that they caused by their might;
they lie uncircumcised with those who are
killed by the sword, and bear their shame
with those who go down to the Pit.
31 When Pharaoh sees them, he will be
consoled for all his hordes—Pharaoh and
all his army, killed by the sword, says the
Lord GOD. 32 For he[e] spread terror in the
land of the living; therefore he shall be laid
to rest among the uncircumcised, with
those who are slain by the sword—Pharaoh
and all his multitude, says the Lord GOD.
33 The word of the LORD came to me:
2 O Mortal, speak to your people
and say to them, If I bring the sword upon
a land, and the people of the land take one
of their number as their sentinel; 3 and if the
sentinel sees the sword coming upon the
land and blows the trumpet and warns the

a Heb *it* *b* Heb *It* *c* Gk Old Latin: Heb *of the uncircumcised* *d* Cn: Heb *iniquities* *e* Cn: Heb *I*

demise Egypt will join others who were objects of God's wrath (Isa 14.9–11), such as *Assyria* (31.3–17), *Elam* (defeated by Assyria, its western neighbor), *Meshech* and *Tubal* (38.2–3), *Edom* (25.12–14), *princes of the north* (unnamed rulers in Phoenicia and Syria), and *Sidon* (28.20–26). **23:** The *uttermost parts of the Pit* constitute, in mythic poetry, a fate opposite to the goal of ascending to heaven (Isa 14.15).

33.1–39.29: Part 4: Prophecies of Israel's restoration. 33.1–20: Clarification of Ezekiel's role. The social setting is given in v. 10. The exiles are now resigned to their condemnation and to Jerusalem's destruction, but this resignation has led to an unanticipated, paralyzing hopelessness. Ezekiel delivers two responses to their demoralized state: God desires people to live, and sin is forgivable. **1–9:** God reminds Ezekiel of his commission as a *sentinel* (3.16–21). This metaphor had originally assuaged Ezekiel's personal reluctance about his calling. Here the prophet's role as sentinel is stressed again to explain how the intention behind Ezekiel's doom prophecy is not death but life, to call the people to repentance.

people; 4 then if any who hear the sound of
the trumpet do not take warning, and the
sword comes and takes them away, their
blood shall be upon their own heads. 5 They
heard the sound of the trumpet and did not
take warning; their blood shall be upon
themselves. But if they had taken warning,
they would have saved their lives. 6 But if
the sentinel sees the sword coming and does
not blow the trumpet, so that the people
are not warned, and the sword comes and
takes any of them, they are taken away in
their iniquity, but their blood I will require
at the sentinel's hand.

7 So you, mortal, I have made a sentinel
for the house of Israel; whenever you hear
a word from my mouth, you shall give
them warning from me. 8 If I say to the
wicked, "O wicked ones, you shall surely
die," and you do not speak to warn the
wicked to turn from their ways, the wicked
shall die in their iniquity, but their blood I
will require at your hand. 9 But if you warn
the wicked to turn from their ways, and
they do not turn from their ways, the wick-
ed shall die in their iniquity, but you will
have saved your life.

10 Now you, mortal, say to the house of
Israel, Thus you have said: "Our transgres-
sions and our sins weigh upon us, and we
waste away because of them; how then can
we live?" 11 Say to them, As I live, says the
Lord GOD, I have no pleasure in the death
of the wicked, but that the wicked turn
from their ways and live; turn back, turn
back from your evil ways; for why will you
die, O house of Israel? 12 And you, mortal,
say to your people, The righteousness of
the righteous shall not save them when they
transgress; and as for the wickedness of the
wicked, it shall not make them stumble
when they turn from their wickedness; and
the righteous shall not be able to live by
their righteousness[a] when they sin.
13 Though I say to the righteous that they
shall surely live, yet if they trust in their
righteousness and commit iniquity, none of
their righteous deeds shall be remembered;
but in the iniquity that they have commit-
ted they shall die. 14 Again, though I say to
the wicked, "You shall surely die," yet if
they turn from their sin and do what is law-
ful and right— 15 if the wicked restore the
pledge, give back what they have taken by
robbery, and walk in the statutes of life,
committing no iniquity—they shall surely
live, they shall not die. 16 None of the sins
that they have committed shall be remem-
bered against them; they have done what is
lawful and right, they shall surely live.

17 Yet your people say, "The way of the
Lord is not just," when it is their own way
that is not just. 18 When the righteous turn
from their righteousness, and commit iniq-
uity, they shall die for it.[b] 19 And when the
wicked turn from their wickedness, and do
what is lawful and right, they shall live by
it.[b] 20 Yet you say, "The way of the Lord is
not just." O house of Israel, I will judge all
of you according to your ways!

21 In the twelfth year of our exile, in the
tenth month, on the fifth day of the month,
someone who had escaped from Jerusalem
came to me and said, "The city has fallen."
22 Now the hand of the LORD had been
upon me the evening before the fugitive
came; but he had opened my mouth by the
time the fugitive came to me in the morn-
ing; so my mouth was opened, and I was no
longer unable to speak.

a Heb *by it* *b* Heb *them*

10–20: Repentance as the way to life. This oracle reemphasizes ch 18 and its stress on the moral autonomy of generations. Earlier this material had aimed to convict the exiles of their personal culpability. Here, Ezekiel's theme of taking responsibility is used to show that one's personal sinfulness is forgivable.

33.21–22: Release from speechlessness. *Escaped from Jerusalem,* escaped death by exile to Babylonia. The exiles from Jerusalem arrived in Babylonia on January 19, 585 BCE, about half a year after Jerusalem's fall. (See Ezra 7.9 for a comparable travel time.) Ezekiel's concurrent release from the speechlessness of 3.26–27 was predicted at 24.27. The event marks a watershed. The prophetic judgment on Jerusalem had been fulfilled, and now a message of promise was possible.

23 The word of the LORD came to me:
24 Mortal, the inhabitants of these waste
places in the land of Israel keep saying,
"Abraham was only one man, yet he got
possession of the land; but we are many;
the land is surely given us to possess."
25 Therefore say to them, Thus says the
Lord GOD: You eat flesh with the blood,
and lift up your eyes to your idols, and shed
blood; shall you then possess the land?
26 You depend on your swords, you commit
abominations, and each of you defiles his
neighbor's wife; shall you then possess the
land? 27 Say this to them, Thus says the
Lord GOD: As I live, surely those who are
in the waste places shall fall by the sword;
and those who are in the open field I will
give to the wild animals to be devoured;
and those who are in strongholds and in
caves shall die by pestilence. 28 I will make
the land a desolation and a waste, and its
proud might shall come to an end; and the
mountains of Israel shall be so desolate that
no one will pass through. 29 Then they shall
know that I am the LORD, when I have
made the land a desolation and a waste be-
cause of all their abominations that they
have committed.

30 As for you, mortal, your people who
talk together about you by the walls, and at
the doors of the houses, say to one another,
each to a neighbor, "Come and hear what
the word is that comes from the LORD."
31 They come to you as people come, and
they sit before you as my people, and they
hear your words, but they will not obey
them. For flattery is on their lips, but their
heart is set on their gain. 32 To them you are
like a singer of love songs,[a] one who has a
beautiful voice and plays well on an instru-
ment; they hear what you say, but they will
not do it. 33 When this comes—and come it
will!—then they shall know that a prophet
has been among them.

34 The word of the LORD came to me:
2 Mortal, prophesy against the shep-
herds of Israel: prophesy, and say to
them—to the shepherds: Thus says the
Lord GOD: Ah, you shepherds of Israel
who have been feeding yourselves! Should
not shepherds feed the sheep? 3 You eat the
fat, you clothe yourselves with the wool,
you slaughter the fatlings; but you do not
feed the sheep. 4 You have not strengthened
the weak, you have not healed the sick, you
have not bound up the injured, you have
not brought back the strayed, you have not
sought the lost, but with force and harsh-
ness you have ruled them. 5 So they were
scattered, because there was no shepherd;
and scattered, they became food for all the
wild animals. 6 My sheep were scattered,
they wandered over all the mountains and
on every high hill; my sheep were scattered
over all the face of the earth, with no one to
search or seek for them.

7 Therefore, you shepherds, hear the
word of the LORD: 8 As I live, says the Lord
GOD, because my sheep have become a
prey, and my sheep have become food for
all the wild animals, since there was no
shepherd; and because my shepherds have
not searched for my sheep, but the shep-
herds have fed themselves, and have not fed

a Cn: Heb *like a love song*

33.23–33: Resistance in the homeland and in exile. 23–29: Disputation over possession of homeland property. V. 24 reveals the social setting. Those who remained behind are repeating their earlier claim to the land (11.15). Vv. 25–26 indict them in terms echoing 18.1–20; 22.11; Lev 19.16,26. On the three punishments in v. 27, cf. 5.17; 14.21. **30–33:** With the fulfillment of his prophecy of Jerusalem's destruction, Ezekiel's popularity grew among the exiles. Unfortunately, the response of many exiles to Ezekiel's words was shallow, lacking in personal obedience. *Love songs,* the Hebrew indicates that Ezekiel's words were just erotic entertainment to them.

34.1–31: The shepherds of Israel. 1–10: Israel's kings are symbolized by herders, contracted by God to care for God's livestock, the people ("my sheep," v. 6). But they had abused their people and scattered them. The chapter combines Priestly ("Holiness Collection") and Jeremianic (Jer 10.21; 23.1–4) language. **5:** *Wild animals,* Judah's attackers, especially Babylonia. **7–10:** Punishment of the herders and rescue of the flock. **11–16: God is the good shepherd** (Isa 40.11; Jer 31.10) who will gather the entire my sheep; [9]therefore, you shepherds, hear the word of the LORD: [10]Thus says the Lord GOD, I am against the shepherds; and I will demand my sheep at their hand, and put a stop to their feeding the sheep; no longer shall the shepherds feed themselves. I will rescue my sheep from their mouths, so that they may not be food for them.

11 For thus says the Lord GOD: I myself will search for my sheep, and will seek them out. [12]As shepherds seek out their flocks when they are among their scattered sheep, so I will seek out my sheep. I will rescue them from all the places to which they have been scattered on a day of clouds and thick darkness. [13]I will bring them out from the peoples and gather them from the countries, and will bring them into their own land; and I will feed them on the mountains of Israel, by the watercourses, and in all the inhabited parts of the land. [14]I will feed them with good pasture, and the mountain heights of Israel shall be their pasture; there they shall lie down in good grazing land, and they shall feed on rich pasture on the mountains of Israel. [15]I myself will be the shepherd of my sheep, and I will make them lie down, says the Lord GOD. [16]I will seek the lost, and I will bring back the strayed, and I will bind up the injured, and I will strengthen the weak, but the fat and the strong I will destroy. I will feed them with justice.

17 As for you, my flock, thus says the Lord GOD: I shall judge between sheep and sheep, between rams and goats: [18]Is it not enough for you to feed on the good pasture, but you must tread down with your feet the rest of your pasture? When you drink of clear water, must you foul the rest with your feet? [19]And must my sheep eat what you have trodden with your feet, and drink what you have fouled with your feet?

20 Therefore, thus says the Lord GOD to them: I myself will judge between the fat sheep and the lean sheep. [21]Because you pushed with flank and shoulder, and butted at all the weak animals with your horns until you scattered them far and wide, [22]I will save my flock, and they shall no longer be ravaged; and I will judge between sheep and sheep.

23 I will set up over them one shepherd, my servant David, and he shall feed them: he shall feed them and be their shepherd. [24]And I, the LORD, will be their God, and my servant David shall be prince among them; I, the LORD, have spoken.

25 I will make with them a covenant of peace and banish wild animals from the land, so that they may live in the wild and sleep in the woods securely. [26]I will make them and the region around my hill a blessing; and I will send down the showers in their season; they shall be showers of blessing. [27]The trees of the field shall yield their fruit, and the earth shall yield its increase. They shall be secure on their soil; and they shall know that I am the LORD, when I break the bars of their yoke, and save them from the hands of those who enslaved them. [28]They shall no more be plunder for the nations, nor shall the animals of the land devour them; they shall live in safety, and no one shall make them afraid. [29]I will provide for them a splendid vegetation so that they shall no more be consumed with hunger in the land, and no longer suffer the insults of the nations. [30]They shall know that I, the LORD their God, am with them, and that they, the house of Israel, are my people, says the Lord GOD. [31]You are my sheep, the sheep of my pasture[a] and I am your God, says the Lord GOD.

a Gk OL: Heb *pasture, you are people*

dispersed flock. **12:** *Day of clouds,* see 30.1–9n.; 32.3–8n. **16:** The focus shifts to God's care for needy individuals within the flock and to God's judgment of particular sheep (not just their shepherds). **17–31: A new order for Israel. 17–24:** Sheep, good and bad, are found in the flock; the bad must be separated out (20.38). **23–24:** God will install a Davidic ruler over the people (37.22–25; Jer 23.3–6; 30.9; Zech 6.12). **25–31:** An announcement of future blessedness dependent on the "Holiness Collection": God will banish wild animals (Lev 26.6), bless the people from Mount Zion (*my hill*), and break the bars of their yoke (Lev 26.13). Thus, the people will live in safety (Lev 26.5–6). **29:** *Insults,* see 36.15.

35 The word of the LORD came to me:
2 Mortal, set your face against
Mount Seir, and prophesy against it, 3 and
say to it, Thus says the Lord GOD:
I am against you, Mount Seir;
I stretch out my hand against you
to make you a desolation and
a waste.
4 I lay your towns in ruins;
you shall become a desolation,
and you shall know that I am
the LORD.
5 Because you cherished an ancient enmity,
and gave over the people of Israel to the
power of the sword at the time of their ca-
lamity, at the time of their final punish-
ment; 6 therefore, as I live, says the Lord
GOD, I will prepare you for blood, and
blood shall pursue you; since you did not
hate bloodshed, bloodshed shall pursue
you. 7 I will make Mount Seir a waste and
a desolation; and I will cut off from it all
who come and go. 8 I will fill its mountains
with the slain; on your hills and in your
valleys and in all your watercourses those
killed with the sword shall fall. 9 I will make
you a perpetual desolation, and your cities
shall never be inhabited. Then you shall
know that I am the LORD.
10 Because you said, "These two na-
tions and these two countries shall be mine,
and we will take possession of them,"—al-
though the LORD was there— 11 therefore,
as I live, says the Lord GOD, I will deal with
you according to the anger and envy that
you showed because of your hatred against
them; and I will make myself known
among you,[a] when I judge you. 12 You
shall know that I, the LORD, have heard all
the abusive speech that you uttered against
the mountains of Israel, saying, "They are
laid desolate, they are given us to devour."
13 And you magnified yourselves against
me with your mouth, and multiplied your
words against me; I heard it. 14 Thus says
the Lord GOD: As the whole earth rejoices,
I will make you desolate. 15 As you rejoiced
over the inheritance of the house of Israel,
because it was desolate, so I will deal with
you; you shall be desolate, Mount Seir, and
all Edom, all of it. Then they shall know
that I am the LORD.

36 And you, mortal, prophesy to the
mountains of Israel, and say:
O mountains of Israel, hear the word of the
LORD. 2 Thus says the Lord GOD: Because
the enemy said of you, "Aha!" and, "The
ancient heights have become our posses-
sion," 3 therefore prophesy, and say: Thus
says the Lord GOD: Because they made you
desolate indeed, and crushed you from all
sides, so that you became the possession of
the rest of the nations, and you became an
object of gossip and slander among the
people; 4 therefore, O mountains of Israel,
hear the word of the Lord GOD: Thus says
the Lord GOD to the mountains and the
hills, the watercourses and the valleys, the
desolate wastes and the deserted towns,
which have become a source of plunder and
an object of derision to the rest of the na-
tions all around; 5 therefore thus says the

a Gk: Heb *them*

35.1–36.15: Oracle on behalf of the mountains of Israel.

35.1–15: Oracles against Edom. Edom has already been judged in Ezekiel's middle section (25.12–14). The present description of its grabbing of land belonging to Israel (v. 10; cf. 1 Esd 4.50) has been placed here as a foil for the restoration message of 35.1–36.15. Ezekiel's prophecies of restoration generally have as foils past wrongs, which they aim to reverse. **1–4:** First oracle. **2:** *Mount Seir* is the plateau in which Sela, the Edomite capital, was located. **5–9:** Second oracle. **5:** Cf. 25.12; Ob 10,14; Ps 137.7. **10–13:** Third oracle. **10:** *Two nations,* Israel and Judah. The LORD *was there* until the glory left (see 11.22–25n.); however, the glory will return (48.35). **14–15:** Fourth oracle. **15a:** As Edom rejoiced over Judah's fall (Ob 12), so the world will rejoice over Edom's fall. **36.1–12: Deliverance as "punishment."** *Mountains of Israel,* the highlands, representing all Israel, are here promised deliverance and blessing as a defiant response to the nations who desolated and slandered them. Though dispossessed by *Edom* (35.1–15) and surrounding nations (Neh 2.19), Israel will be restored to her heritage. This oracle reverses ch 6 (e.g., contrast v. 10 with 6.4–7). **5:** God's personal identification with the land of Israel is shown by the phrase

Lord GOD: I am speaking in my hot jealou-
sy against the rest of the nations, and
against all Edom, who, with wholehearted
joy and utter contempt, took my land as
their possession, because of its pasture, to
plunder it. 6 Therefore prophesy concerning
the land of Israel, and say to the mountains
and hills, to the watercourses and valleys,
Thus says the Lord GOD: I am speaking in
my jealous wrath, because you have suf-
fered the insults of the nations; 7 therefore
thus says the Lord GOD: I swear that the
nations that are all around you shall them-
selves suffer insults.

8 But you, O mountains of Israel, shall
shoot out your branches, and yield your
fruit to my people Israel; for they shall soon
come home. 9 See now, I am for you; I will
turn to you, and you shall be tilled and
sown; 10 and I will multiply your popula-
tion, the whole house of Israel, all of it; the
towns shall be inhabited and the waste
places rebuilt; 11 and I will multiply human
beings and animals upon you. They shall
increase and be fruitful; and I will cause
you to be inhabited as in your former times,
and will do more good to you than ever
before. Then you shall know that I am the
LORD. 12 I will lead people upon you—my
people Israel—and they shall possess you,
and you shall be their inheritance. No lon-
ger shall you bereave them of children.

13 Thus says the Lord GOD: Because
they say to you, "You devour people, and
you bereave your nation of children,"
14 therefore you shall no longer devour peo-
ple and no longer bereave your nation of
children, says the Lord GOD; 15 and no lon-
ger will I let you hear the insults of the
nations, no longer shall you bear the dis-
grace of the peoples; and no longer shall
you cause your nation to stumble, says the
Lord GOD.

16 The word of the LORD came to me:
17 Mortal, when the house of Israel lived on
their own soil, they defiled it with their
ways and their deeds; their conduct in my
sight was like the uncleanness of a woman
in her menstrual period. 18 So I poured out
my wrath upon them for the blood that
they had shed upon the land, and for the
idols with which they had defiled it. 19 I
scattered them among the nations, and they
were dispersed through the countries; in
accordance with their conduct and their
deeds I judged them. 20 But when they came
to the nations, wherever they came, they
profaned my holy name, in that it was said
of them, "These are the people of the
LORD, and yet they had to go out of his
land." 21 But I had concern for my holy
name, which the house of Israel had pro-
faned among the nations to which they
came.

22 Therefore say to the house of Israel,
Thus says the Lord GOD: It is not for your
sake, O house of Israel, that I am about to
act, but for the sake of my holy name,
which you have profaned among the na-
tions to which you came. 23 I will sanctify
my great name, which has been profaned
among the nations, and which you have

my land (cf. Lev 25.23). **9:** Lev 26.9. **10:** *All of it,* including the Northern Kingdom (37.21–22). **11:** See Gen 1.28; Lev 26.9. **12:** An editorial transition to vv. 13–15. **13–15: No more disgrace.** The land had been feared as a devouring land at least since the time that Israel first reconnoitered it (Num 13.32). In Ezekiel's new Exodus and settlement, there will be no place for such defamation.

36.16–38: God's honor as the cause of the restoration. 16–21: Historical prologue. According to the "Holiness Collection," when the homeland becomes defiled, it vomits out its inhabitants (Lev 18.25,28). This is what has happened to the exiled Israelites. **17:** *Uncleanness,* see Lev 15.19–30; 18.19. **20:** God's name was desecrated (cf. Lev 20.3; 22.2,32) either because the exile made God look powerless to protect the Israelites (NRSV's interpretation) or because God's people from God's own land prove to be depraved (alternate sense of the Hebrew). **22–32:** Vv. 22 and 32 form an envelope around this section by their parallel assertions that the restoration is not anything deserved. God's grace is unmerited by the people and even precedes their repentance. (According to v. 31, the people show remorse only after their restoration to the land. This chapter thus moves beyond texts such as Lev 26.40–42; Jer 31.18–20, where repentance is the driving motivation behind restoration.) **24:** A reversal of v. 19. **25:** God will *sprinkle*

profaned among them; and the nations
shall know that I am the LORD, says the
Lord GOD, when through you I display my
holiness before their eyes. 24 I will take you
from the nations, and gather you from all
the countries, and bring you into your own
land. 25 I will sprinkle clean water upon
you, and you shall be clean from all your
uncleannesses, and from all your idols I will
cleanse you. 26 A new heart I will give you,
and a new spirit I will put within you; and
I will remove from your body the heart of
stone and give you a heart of flesh. 27 I will
put my spirit within you, and make you
follow my statutes and be careful to ob-
serve my ordinances. 28 Then you shall live
in the land that I gave to your ancestors;
and you shall be my people, and I will be
your God. 29 I will save you from all your
uncleannesses, and I will summon the grain
and make it abundant and lay no famine
upon you. 30 I will make the fruit of the tree
and the produce of the field abundant, so
that you may never again suffer the dis-
grace of famine among the nations. 31 Then
you shall remember your evil ways, and
your dealings that were not good; and you
shall loathe yourselves for your iniquities
and your abominable deeds. 32 It is not for
your sake that I will act, says the Lord
GOD; let that be known to you. Be ashamed
and dismayed for your ways, O house of
Israel.
33 Thus says the Lord GOD: On the day
that I cleanse you from all your iniquities, I
will cause the towns to be inhabited, and
the waste places shall be rebuilt. 34 The land
that was desolate shall be tilled, instead of
being the desolation that it was in the sight
of all who passed by. 35 And they will say,
"This land that was desolate has become
like the garden of Eden; and the waste and
desolate and ruined towns are now inhabit-
ed and fortified." 36 Then the nations that
are left all around you shall know that I,
the LORD, have rebuilt the ruined places,
and replanted that which was desolate; I,
the LORD, have spoken, and I will do it.
37 Thus says the Lord GOD: I will also
let the house of Israel ask me to do this for
them: to increase their population like a
flock. 38 Like the flock for sacrifices,[a] like
the flock at Jerusalem during her appointed
festivals, so shall the ruined towns be filled
with flocks of people. Then they shall know
that I am the LORD.

37 The hand of the LORD came upon
me, and he brought me out by the
spirit of the LORD and set me down in the
middle of a valley; it was full of bones. 2 He
led me all around them; there were very
many lying in the valley, and they were very
dry. 3 He said to me, "Mortal, can these
bones live?" I answered, "O Lord GOD,
you know." 4 Then he said to me, "Proph-
esy to these bones, and say to them: O dry
bones, hear the word of the LORD. 5 Thus
says the Lord GOD to these bones: I will

a Heb *flock of holy things*

them (cf. Num 19.20) with water, cleansing them, inasmuch as human beings cannot make themselves clean. **26:** Ezekiel's calls to repentance have failed (see especially 18.31). A radical, new creation (see 11.19; 18.31; cf. Deut 30.1–6; Jer 31.31–34) will be needed to break the people's bondage to the cycles of sin and retribution of Israel's past (ch 20). The concept of engrafting a *new heart* goes beyond Jer 31.33 and Deut 30.1–6 and is in keeping with Ezekiel's focus on God's sovereignty in effecting salvation (20.33–34). **27:** God will place obedience to the covenant within each member of the community (Lev 26.3), so the restoration will be permanent. **29–30:** Lev 26.4. **33–36:** The skeptical nations (v. 20) will recognize Israel's transformation to a paradise as God's act. *Garden of Eden* (28.13; 47.1–12; Isa 51.3; see Gen 2–3). **37–38:** Note the reversal of 14.3; 20.3,31. Population growth is a blessing of the "Holiness Collection" covenant (Lev 26.9). *Like a flock,* see ch 34.

37.1–14: Vision of the valley of dry bones. 1: *A valley,* in Hebrew "the valley," suggesting that this is the same locale as in 3.22; 8.4. **3:** Ezekiel does not yet realize that this vision refers to the reestablishment of the exiles in their homeland. Thus, the hope of bodily resurrection was already a live possibility for Ezekiel (cf. 1 Kings 17.22; 2 Kings 4.35; 13.21). **4–8:** The first of two prophecies to the bones. As in Gen 2.7, life is generated here in two stages. **9–10:** Suspense builds, as a second prophesying within cause breath[a] to enter you, and you shall live. 6 I will lay sinews on you, and will cause flesh to come upon you, and cover you with skin, and put breath[a] in you, and you shall live; and you shall know that I am the LORD."

7 So I prophesied as I had been commanded; and as I prophesied, suddenly there was a noise, a rattling, and the bones came together, bone to its bone. 8 I looked, and there were sinews on them, and flesh had come upon them, and skin had covered them; but there was no breath in them. 9 Then he said to me, "Prophesy to the breath, prophesy, mortal, and say to the breath:[b] Thus says the Lord GOD: Come from the four winds, O breath,[b] and breathe upon these slain, that they may live." 10 I prophesied as he commanded me, and the breath came into them, and they lived, and stood on their feet, a vast multitude.

11 Then he said to me, "Mortal, these bones are the whole house of Israel. They say, 'Our bones are dried up, and our hope is lost; we are cut off completely.' 12 Therefore prophesy, and say to them, Thus says the Lord GOD: I am going to open your graves, and bring you up from your graves, O my people; and I will bring you back to the land of Israel. 13 And you shall know that I am the LORD, when I open your graves, and bring you up from your graves, O my people. 14 I will put my spirit within you, and you shall live, and I will place you on your own soil; then you shall know that I, the LORD, have spoken and will act, says the LORD."

15 The word of the LORD came to me: 16 Mortal, take a stick and write on it, "For Judah, and the Israelites associated with it"; then take another stick and write on it, "For Joseph (the stick of Ephraim) and all the house of Israel associated with it"; 17 and join them together into one stick, so that they may become one in your hand. 18 And when your people say to you, "Will you not show us what you mean by these?" 19 say to them, Thus says the Lord GOD: I am about to take the stick of Joseph (which is in the hand of Ephraim) and the tribes of Israel associated with it; and I will put the stick of Judah upon it,[c] and make them one stick, in order that they may be one in my hand. 20 When the sticks on which you write are in your hand before their eyes, 21 then say to them, Thus says the Lord GOD: I will take the people of Israel from the nations among which they have gone, and will gather them from every quarter, and bring them to their own land. 22 I will make them one nation in the land, on the mountains of Israel; and one king shall be king over them all. Never again shall they be two nations, and never again shall they be divided into two kingdoms. 23 They shall never again defile themselves with their idols and their detestable things, or with

a Or *spirit* *b* Or *wind* or *spirit* *c* Heb *I will put them upon it*

the vision is required in order to animate the bones. Heb "ruaḥ" can mean "spirit," "breath," or "wind"; thus there is a constant word play here. *Four winds* may refer to God's cosmic reach (1.17; Zech 6.5). *These slain,* the bones' identity is still unclear at this point, the assumption now being that Ezekiel is surveying an old battlefield. (The Heb word *multitude* in v. 10 commonly means "army.") **11–14:** The interpretation. V. 11 finally reveals the actual life setting of the prophecy by citing words from a lament: The exiles' *bones are dried,* a metaphor for a downcast spirit (Prov 17.22; 15.30). The metaphor of resurrection is the antidote to such despair. *Cut off,* a metaphor for being within the power of death (Ps 88.5; Lam 3.54). In vv. 12–14, the passage shifts to a metaphor of disinterment as an antidote to this complaint.

37.15–28: The symbolic action of the two sticks (Zech 11.7–14) envisions the reunification of the Southern ("Judah") and Northern ("Joseph/Ephraim/Israel") Kingdoms and the establishment of a united Israel, ruled by one king. Full restoration will then be realized (34.28; 36.10): law-abiding living (11.20) in the promised land (28.25) under the Davidic ruler (34.23–24) in a covenant of peace (34.25). At that time, God will permanently return to the central *sanctuary* (43.9). **25:** *Prince,* monarchic ruler (cf. 12.10;

any of their transgressions. I will save them
from all the apostasies into which they have
fallen,[a] and will cleanse them. Then they
shall be my people, and I will be their God.
24 My servant David shall be king over
them; and they shall all have one shepherd.
They shall follow my ordinances and be
careful to observe my statutes. 25 They shall
live in the land that I gave to my servant
Jacob, in which your ancestors lived; they
and their children and their children's chil-
dren shall live there forever; and my servant
David shall be their prince forever. 26 I will
make a covenant of peace with them; it
shall be an everlasting covenant with them;
and I will bless[b] them and multiply them,
and will set my sanctuary among them for-
evermore. 27 My dwelling place shall be
with them; and I will be their God, and they
shall be my people. 28 Then the nations
shall know that I the LORD sanctify Israel,
when my sanctuary is among them forever-
more.

38 The word of the LORD came to me:
2 Mortal, set your face toward Gog,
of the land of Magog, the chief prince of
Meshech and Tubal. Prophesy against him
3 and say: Thus says the Lord GOD: I am
against you, O Gog, chief prince of Me-
shech and Tubal; 4 I will turn you around
and put hooks into your jaws, and I will
lead you out with all your army, horses and
horsemen, all of them clothed in full armor,
a great company, all of them with shield
and buckler, wielding swords. 5 Persia,
Ethiopia,[c] and Put are with them, all of
them with buckler and helmet; 6 Gomer and
all its troops; Beth-togarmah from the re-
motest parts of the north with all its
troops—many peoples are with you.
7 Be ready and keep ready, you and all
the companies that are assembled around
you, and hold yourselves in reserve for
them. 8 After many days you shall be mus-
tered; in the latter years you shall go
against a land restored from war, a land
where people were gathered from many na-
tions on the mountains of Israel, which had
long lain waste; its people were brought out
from the nations and now are living in safe-
ty, all of them. 9 You shall advance, coming
on like a storm; you shall be like a cloud
covering the land, you and all your troops,
and many peoples with you.
10 Thus says the Lord GOD: On that
day thoughts will come into your mind,
and you will devise an evil scheme. 11 You
will say, "I will go up against the land of
unwalled villages; I will fall upon the quiet
people who live in safety, all of them living
without walls, and having no bars or
gates"; 12 to seize spoil and carry off plun-
der; to assail the waste places that are now
inhabited, and the people who were gath-

a Another reading is *from all the settlements in which they have sinned* *b* Tg: Heb *give* *c* Or *Nubia;* Heb *Cush*

34.24). **27:** *Dwelling place* (Lev 26.11), the "tabernacle" of the wilderness period: The restoration is to involve a new Exodus and settlement. **28:** Zion theology triumphs in the new age.

38.1–39.29: The Gog of Magog oracles are early apocalyptic literature, describing the imminent coming of a foe from the north (an embodiment of evil) against the promised land. After a cataclysmic, doomsday battle, God will be acknowledged by all nations as the undisputed victor (38.23; 39.21–29). As of this point in the book, Ezekiel's prophecies of restoration, which aim to reverse preceding judgments, have not yet reversed Israel's Babylonian destruction. The northern foe here is thus probably an end-time surrogate for Babylon, and for any superpower that has challenged the sovereignty of God. The followers of Ezekiel who recorded these apocalyptic oracles were central priests of their society. This undercuts the claims of those scholars who assert that all apocalyptic texts derive from peripheral groups. **38.1–9:** *Gog* (perhaps derived from Gyges, a seventh-century ruler of Lydia), king of *Magog,* is no symbol but a mythic-realistic entity: historically real, but of mythological proportions (cf. Rev 20.8). *Magog,* Gen 10.2. *Meshech, Tubal, . . . Put,* see 27.10n., 12–25n.; Gen 10.2. *Gomer,* the Cimmerians in Asia Minor (Gen 10.2–3), far north of Israel. *Beth-togarmah,* see 27.12–25n. **10–13:** The perspective shifts from God's external control (vv. 3–9) to Gog's interior motives. **12:** *Center,* see 5.5n. Ezekiel is affirming and revisioning Zion theology here. **13:** *Sheba* (27.22), *Dedan* (25.13; 27.20), and *Tarshish* (27.12) are all

ered from the nations, who are acquiring
cattle and goods, who live at the center[a] of
the earth. 13 Sheba and Dedan and the mer-
chants of Tarshish and all its young war-
riors[b] will say to you, "Have you come
to seize spoil? Have you assembled your
horde to carry off plunder, to carry away
silver and gold, to take away cattle and
goods, to seize a great amount of booty?"

14 Therefore, mortal, prophesy, and say
to Gog: Thus says the Lord GOD: On that
day when my people Israel are living se-
curely, you will rouse yourself[c] 15 and
come from your place out of the remotest
parts of the north, you and many peoples
with you, all of them riding on horses, a
great horde, a mighty army; 16 you will
come up against my people Israel, like a
cloud covering the earth. In the latter days
I will bring you against my land, so that the
nations may know me, when through you,
O Gog, I display my holiness before their
eyes.

17 Thus says the Lord GOD: Are you he
of whom I spoke in former days by my ser-
vants the prophets of Israel, who in those
days prophesied for years that I would
bring you against them? 18 On that day,
when Gog comes against the land of Israel,
says the Lord GOD, my wrath shall be
aroused. 19 For in my jealousy and in my
blazing wrath I declare: On that day there
shall be a great shaking in the land of Israel;
20 the fish of the sea, and the birds of the
air, and the animals of the field, and all
creeping things that creep on the ground,
and all human beings that are on the face of
the earth, shall quake at my presence, and
the mountains shall be thrown down, and
the cliffs shall fall, and every wall shall
tumble to the ground. 21 I will summon the
sword against Gog[d] in[e] all my mountains,
says the Lord GOD; the swords of all will be
against their comrades. 22 With pestilence
and bloodshed I will enter into judgment
with him; and I will pour down torrential
rains and hailstones, fire and sulfur, upon
him and his troops and the many peoples
that are with him. 23 So I will display my
greatness and my holiness and make myself
known in the eyes of many nations. Then
they shall know that I am the LORD.

39 And you, mortal, prophesy against
Gog, and say: Thus says the Lord
GOD: I am against you, O Gog, chief prince
of Meshech and Tubal! 2 I will turn you
around and drive you forward, and bring
you up from the remotest parts of the
north, and lead you against the mountains
of Israel. 3 I will strike your bow from your
left hand, and will make your arrows drop
out of your right hand. 4 You shall fall upon
the mountains of Israel, you and all your
troops and the peoples that are with you; I
will give you to birds of prey of every kind
and to the wild animals to be devoured.
5 You shall fall in the open field; for I have
spoken, says the Lord GOD. 6 I will send fire
on Magog and on those who live securely
in the coastlands; and they shall know that
I am the LORD.

7 My holy name I will make known
among my people Israel; and I will not let
my holy name be profaned any more; and
the nations shall know that I am the LORD,
the Holy One in Israel. 8 It has come! It has
happened, says the Lord GOD. This is the
day of which I have spoken.

9 Then those who live in the towns of

a Heb *navel* b Heb *young lions* c Gk: Heb *will you not know?* d Heb *him* e Heb *to* or *for*

mentioned in ch 27 as engaged in trade. **14–16:** God's motive is God's glory. **17:** Transition. **38.18–23** and **39.11–16:** A secondary development of the Gog oracles. The radical magnitude of the apocalyptic threat is clear from the cosmic collapse (cf. Joel 2.10,30; Zech 14.4–5) and from the *seven months* (39.12) required to remove the enemy dead to the region east of the Dead Sea. In keeping with the Ezekiel group's status as priests, increasing priestly concern accompanies the increased apocalyptic fervor: This section draws heavily on "Holiness Collection" traditions about the defiling effect of corpses (Lev 21.1; Num 5.2–3; 9.6; 19.11,13). **39.1–10:** Gog will be defeated both in the field (vv. 1–5) and back at home (v. 6). God's holy name will then be established (vv. 7–8; cf. 36.22). **9–10:** As in the holy wars of the biblical conquest narrative (Deut 7.2; 20.16–18; Josh 6.24), everything of the enemy's is burned as material de-

Israel will go out and make fires of the weapons and burn them—bucklers and shields, bows and arrows, handpikes and spears—and they will make fires of them for seven years. 10 They will not need to take wood out of the field or cut down any trees in the forests, for they will make their fires of the weapons; they will despoil those who despoiled them, and plunder those who plundered them, says the Lord GOD.

11 On that day I will give to Gog a place for burial in Israel, the Valley of the Travelers[a] east of the sea; it shall block the path of the travelers, for there Gog and all his horde will be buried; it shall be called the Valley of Hamon-gog.[b] 12 Seven months the house of Israel shall spend burying them, in order to cleanse the land. 13 All the people of the land shall bury them; and it will bring them honor on the day that I show my glory, says the Lord GOD. 14 They will set apart men to pass through the land regularly and bury any invaders[c] who remain on the face of the land, so as to cleanse it; for seven months they shall make their search. 15 As the searchers[c] pass through the land, anyone who sees a human bone shall set up a sign by it, until the buriers have buried it in the Valley of Hamon-gog.[b] 16 (A city Hamonah[d] is there also.) Thus they shall cleanse the land.

17 As for you, mortal, thus says the Lord GOD: Speak to the birds of every kind and to all the wild animals: Assemble and come, gather from all around to the sacrificial feast that I am preparing for you, a great sacrificial feast on the mountains of Israel, and you shall eat flesh and drink blood. 18 You shall eat the flesh of the mighty, and drink the blood of the princes of the earth—of rams, of lambs, and of goats, of bulls, all of them fatlings of Bashan. 19 You shall eat fat until you are filled, and drink blood until you are drunk, at the sacrificial feast that I am preparing for you. 20 And you shall be filled at my table with horses and charioteers,[e] with warriors and all kinds of soldiers, says the Lord GOD.

21 I will display my glory among the nations; and all the nations shall see my judgment that I have executed, and my hand that I have laid on them. 22 The house of Israel shall know that I am the LORD their God, from that day forward. 23 And the nations shall know that the house of Israel went into captivity for their iniquity, because they dealt treacherously with me. So I hid my face from them and gave them into the hand of their adversaries, and they all fell by the sword. 24 I dealt with them according to their uncleanness and their transgressions, and hid my face from them.

25 Therefore thus says the Lord GOD: Now I will restore the fortunes of Jacob, and have mercy on the whole house of Israel; and I will be jealous for my holy name. 26 They shall forget[f] their shame, and all the treachery they have practiced against me, when they live securely in their land with no one to make them afraid, 27 when I have brought them back from the peoples and gathered them from their enemies' lands, and through them have displayed my holiness in the sight of many nations. 28 Then they shall know that I am the LORD their God because I sent them into exile among the nations, and then gathered them into their own land. I will leave none of

a Or *of the Abarim* b That is, *the Horde of Gog*
c Heb *travelers* d That is *The Horde*
e Heb *chariots* f Another reading is *They shall bear*

voted to the LORD alone. The huge quantities of war material (enough *wood* for fuel for *seven years*) identify this as an apocalyptic, rather than a mundane victory. **11–16:** See 38.18–23n. **11:** *Valley of the Travelers,* possibly in the Abarim range (Num 27.12; see textual note *a*) east of the Dead Sea. Alternatively, the *Travelers* may be the departed, whose great numbers stop up passage to the underworld. **17–20:** An invitation to an apocalyptic, sacrificial feast (39.4b; cf. Isa 34.5–7; Zeph 1.7). **18:** *Bashan,* in northern Transjordan, was noted for its cattle. **21–29: Secondary summary and concluding oracles.** **25:** *Now I will restore,* a shift in focus to a stage before the end times. The victory and restoration are linked here

them behind; 29 and I will never again hide
my face from them, when I pour out my
spirit upon the house of Israel, says the
Lord GOD.

40 In the twenty-fifth year of our exile,
at the beginning of the year, on the
tenth day of the month, in the fourteenth
year after the city was struck down, on that
very day, the hand of the LORD was upon
me, and he brought me there. 2 He brought
me, in visions of God, to the land of Israel,
and set me down upon a very high moun-
tain, on which was a structure like a city to
the south. 3 When he brought me there, a
man was there, whose appearance shone
like bronze, with a linen cord and a mea-
suring reed in his hand; and he was stand-
ing in the gateway. 4 The man said to me,
"Mortal, look closely and listen attentively,
and set your mind upon all that I shall
show you, for you were brought here in
order that I might show it to you; declare
all that you see to the house of Israel."

5 Now there was a wall all around the
outside of the temple area. The length of
the measuring reed in the man's hand was
six long cubits, each being a cubit and a
handbreadth in length; so he measured the
thickness of the wall, one reed; and the
height, one reed. 6 Then he went into the
gateway facing east, going up its steps, and
measured the threshold of the gate, one
reed deep.[a] There were 7 recesses, and each
recess was one reed wide and one reed
deep; and the space between the recesses,
five cubits; and the threshold of the gate by
the vestibule of the gate at the inner end
was one reed deep. 8 Then he measured the
inner vestibule of the gateway, one cubit.
9 Then he measured the vestibule of the
gateway, eight cubits; and its pilasters, two
cubits; and the vestibule of the gate was at
the inner end. 10 There were three recesses
on either side of the east gate; the three
were of the same size; and the pilasters on
either side were of the same size. 11 Then he
measured the width of the opening of the
gateway, ten cubits; and the width of the
gateway, thirteen cubits. 12 There was a

a Heb *deep, and one threshold, one reed deep*

with the familiar language and narrative line of Ezekiel (5.8 [reversed]; 28.26; 34.28–30). **29:** Cf. 36.27; 37.9,14; Zech 12.10; Joel 2.28–29.

40.1–48.35: Part 5: Blueprint for the restored Temple and land. The blueprint that Ezekiel details here includes new ideal features that aim to prevent the wrongs of the past that led to the destruction of Solomon's Temple in 586 BCE from ever happening again. Thus, new Temple fortifications and new land boundaries will demarcate the holiness of the land and people (e.g., 42.20n.), with the Temple functioning as an organizing center of this holiness (43.12). In accordance with the "Holiness Collection," the plan provides for the settlements and entire people of Israel to be encompassed by the holiness of God, whose dwelling in their midst is now to be permanently safeguarded (43.7; 44.1–3; 48.35). This section of Ezekiel does not prophesy a literal future for the Temple; rather, it offers a Temple plan as an embodiment of the community's values. Though it has never actually been built, Ezekiel's "literary temple" has proved more enduring than the physical temples of both his predecessors and his successors.

40.1–42.20: The new Temple. The Temple complex is modeled on that built by Solomon, although the plan is more detailed than that given in 1 Kings 6 and 2 Chr 3. **1–27: The Temple area and gates. 1–5:** April 28, 573 BCE. On the twenty-fifth anniversary of his exile, Ezekiel is transported in a vision (cf. 8.2–3) to the Temple mountain (*very high mountain,* 17.22; Isa 2.2). **3:** *Appearance . . . like bronze,* an angelic figure (1.7). **5:** An outer wall surrounded the entire Temple area. The *long cubit* was about 52.5 cm (20.7 in); the ordinary cubit was about 44 cm (17.5 in). The *reed* was about 3.1m (10.3 ft) long. **6–16:** The outer court's east gate-tower was a massive, fortified complex consisting of a *threshold,* a long hallway with *recesses* (side rooms), a second threshold, and an *inner vestibule* room. Heavy *pilasters* (piers) with windows separated the recessed chambers, or guardrooms, inside the gate-tower (three on each side). This gate is treated further in 43.1–5; 44.1–3. The plan of the gate is similar to gateways excavated at Megiddo, Gezer, and Hazor that some scholars have dated to the time of Solomon, mid-tenth century BCE. **8:** *One cubit,* the Hebrew text is problematic here. **16:** *Palm trees* also decorated

barrier before the recesses, one cubit on ei-
ther side; and the recesses were six cubits
on either side. 13 Then he measured the gate
from the back[a] of the one recess to the
back[a] of the other, a width of twenty-five
cubits, from wall to wall.[b] 14 He mea-
sured[c] also the vestibule, twenty cubits;
and the gate next to the pilaster on every
side of the court.[d] 15 From the front of the
gate at the entrance to the end of the inner
vestibule of the gate was fifty cubits. 16 The
recesses and their pilasters had windows,
with shutters[d] on the inside of the gateway
all around, and the vestibules also had win-
dows on the inside all around; and on the
pilasters were palm trees.

17 Then he brought me into the outer
court; there were chambers there, and a
pavement, all around the court; thirty
chambers fronted on the pavement. 18 The
pavement ran along the side of the gates,
corresponding to the length of the gates;
this was the lower pavement. 19 Then he
measured the distance from the inner front
of[e] the lower gate to the outer front of the
inner court, one hundred cubits.[f]

20 Then he measured the gate of the
outer court that faced north—its depth and
width. 21 Its recesses, three on either side,
and its pilasters and its vestibule were of
the same size as those of the first gate; its
depth was fifty cubits, and its width
twenty-five cubits. 22 Its windows, its vesti-
bule, and its palm trees were of the same
size as those of the gate that faced toward
the east. Seven steps led up to it; and its
vestibule was on the inside.[g] 23 Opposite
the gate on the north, as on the east, was a
gate to the inner court; he measured from
gate to gate, one hundred cubits.

24 Then he led me toward the south,
and there was a gate on the south; and he
measured its pilasters and its vestibule; they
had the same dimensions as the others.
25 There were windows all around in it and
in its vestibule, like the windows of the oth-
ers; its depth was fifty cubits, and its width
twenty-five cubits. 26 There were seven
steps leading up to it; its vestibule was on
the inside.[g] It had palm trees on its pilas-
ters, one on either side. 27 There was a gate
on the south of the inner court; and he mea-
sured from gate to gate toward the south,
one hundred cubits.

28 Then he brought me to the inner
court by the south gate, and he measured
the south gate; it was of the same dimen-
sions as the others. 29 Its recesses, its pilas-
ters, and its vestibule were of the same size
as the others; and there were windows all
around in it and in its vestibule; its depth
was fifty cubits, and its width twenty-five
cubits. 30 There were vestibules all around,
twenty-five cubits deep and five cubits
wide. 31 Its vestibule faced the outer court,
and palm trees were on its pilasters, and its
stairway had eight steps.

32 Then he brought me to the inner
court on the east side, and he measured the
gate; it was of the same size as the others.
33 Its recesses, its pilasters, and its vestibule
were of the same dimensions as the others;
and there were windows all around in it
and in its vestibule; its depth was fifty cu-
bits, and its width twenty-five cubits. 34 Its
vestibule faced the outer court, and it had

a Gk: Heb *roof* *b* Heb *opening facing opening*
c Heb *made* *d* Meaning of Heb uncertain
e Compare Gk: Heb *from before* *f* Heb adds *the east and the north* *g* Gk: Heb *before them*

Solomon's Temple (1 Kings 6.29,35). **17–19:** The Temple area's outer courtyard. The thirty chambers around the court's periphery were probably for the use of the Levites and for people to meet and eat together (Jer 35.2; Neh 13.4–14). See also 46.21–24. **20–27:** The other two (northern and southern) gates of the outer courtyard were identical to the east gate-tower. That there were steps up to the gates (vv. 22,26) shows that the whole Temple platform was an elevated area. **28–46: The inner gate-towers.** Ezekiel is shown three gates (south, east, north) leading to the inner court corresponding to those leading to the outer court. Only priests could pass through these inner gates (42.14; 44.19; 46.3). **31:** *Eight steps,* the Temple was built on a succession of terraces, so that height demarcated gradations of holiness, just as did walled perimeters and gates (vv. 34,37). Holiness increased as one entered farther up and into the Temple. **38–43:** The vestibules of the inner gates contained facilities for the preparation of sacrifices.

palm trees on its pilasters, on either side;
and its stairway had eight steps.
35 Then he brought me to the north
gate, and he measured it; it had the same
dimensions as the others. 36 Its recesses, its
pilasters, and its vestibule were of the same
size as the others;[a] and it had windows all
around. Its depth was fifty cubits, and its
width twenty-five cubits. 37 Its vestibule[b]
faced the outer court, and it had palm trees
on its pilasters, on either side; and its stair-
way had eight steps.
38 There was a chamber with its door in
the vestibule of the gate,[c] where the burnt
offering was to be washed. 39 And in the
vestibule of the gate were two tables on
either side, on which the burnt offering and
the sin offering and the guilt offering were
to be slaughtered. 40 On the outside of the
vestibule[d] at the entrance of the north gate
were two tables; and on the other side of
the vestibule of the gate were two tables.
41 Four tables were on the inside, and four
tables on the outside of the side of the gate,
eight tables, on which the sacrifices were to
be slaughtered. 42 There were also four ta-
bles of hewn stone for the burnt offering, a
cubit and a half long, and one cubit and a
half wide, and one cubit high, on which the
instruments were to be laid with which the
burnt offerings and the sacrifices were
slaughtered. 43 There were pegs, one hand-
breadth long, fastened all around the in-
side. And on the tables the flesh of the
offering was to be laid.
44 On the outside of the inner gateway
there were chambers for the singers in the
inner court, one[e] at the side of the north
gate facing south, the other at the side of
the east gate facing north. 45 He said to me,
"This chamber that faces south is for the
priests who have charge of the temple,
46 and the chamber that faces north is for
the priests who have charge of the altar;
these are the descendants of Zadok, who
alone among the descendants of Levi may
come near to the LORD to minister to him."
47 He measured the court, one hundred cu-
bits deep, and one hundred cubits wide, a
square; and the altar was in front of the
temple.
48 Then he brought me to the vestibule
of the temple and measured the pilasters of
the vestibule, five cubits on either side; and
the width of the gate was fourteen cubits;
and the sidewalls of the gate were three cu-
bits[f] on either side. 49 The depth of the
vestibule was twenty cubits, and the width
twelve[g] cubits; ten steps led up[h] to it; and
there were pillars beside the pilasters on ei-
ther side.

41 Then he brought me to the nave,
and measured the pilasters; on each
side six cubits was the width of the pilas-
ters.[i] 2 The width of the entrance was ten
cubits; and the sidewalls of the entrance
were five cubits on either side. He mea-
sured the length of the nave, forty cubits,
and its width, twenty cubits. 3 Then he went
into the inner room and measured the pilas-

a One Ms: Compare verses 29 and 33: MT lacks *were of the same size as the others* *b* Gk Vg Compare verses 26, 31, 34: Heb *pilasters* *c* Cn: Heb *at the pilasters of the gates* *d* Cn: Heb *to him who goes up* *e* Heb lacks *one* *f* Gk: Heb *and the width of the gate was three cubits* *g* Gk: Heb *eleven* *h* Gk: Heb *and by steps that went up* *i* Compare Gk: Heb *tent*

Burnt, sin, and *guilt* offerings, see Lev 1.1–7.38. **44–46:** Priests' chambers. On the north and south sides of the inner court were buildings for the use of the priests. These may be small cells, different from the chambers in 42.1–14. **44:** *The singers,* Levitical priests (cf. 1 Chr 9.33). *East gate,* read "south gate" with the LXX. **46b:** An editorial clarification that only priests descended from *Zadok* (see 44.15–31n.), such as Ezekiel and his group, may sacrifice at the altar (43.19; 44.15–31n.). **40.47–41.4: The Temple proper.** The successive entrances to its three rooms become more narrow, symbolizing increasing holiness (40.48; 41.2; 41.3). According to the LXX (textual note *h*), the Temple was *ten steps* (about 3 m [10 ft]; see 41.8) above the level of the inner court. (Again, steps indicate increasing holiness; cf. vv. 22,31.) In front of the vestibule were freestanding *pillars* (1 Kings 7.15–22). *The vestibule* (40.48–49) was 10.5 m (34 ft) x 6.3 m (20.5 ft). *The nave* (41.1–2), which Ezekiel could enter as a Zadokite priest, was 21 m (69 ft) x 10.5 m (34 ft). The adytum (*inner room* or *most holy place,* 41.3–4), which Ezekiel did not enter (Lev 16), was

ters of the entrance, two cubits; and the
width of the entrance, six cubits; and the
sidewalls[a] of the entrance, seven cubits.
4 He measured the depth of the room, twen-
ty cubits, and its width, twenty cubits, be-
yond the nave. And he said to me, This is
the most holy place.
5 Then he measured the wall of the tem-
ple, six cubits thick; and the width of the
side chambers, four cubits, all around the
temple. 6 The side chambers were in three
stories, one over another, thirty in each sto-
ry. There were offsets[b] all around the wall
of the temple to serve as supports for the
side chambers, so that they should not be
supported by the wall of the temple. 7 The
passageway[c] of the side chambers widened
from story to story; for the structure was
supplied with a stairway all around the
temple. For this reason the structure be-
came wider from story to story. One as-
cended from the bottom story to the upper-
most story by way of the middle one. 8 I
saw also that the temple had a raised plat-
form all around; the foundations of the side
chambers measured a full reed of six long
cubits. 9 The thickness of the outer wall of
the side chambers was five cubits; and the
free space between the side chambers of the
temple 10 and the chambers of the court was
a width of twenty cubits all around the
temple on every side. 11 The side chambers
opened onto the area left free, one door
toward the north, and another door toward
the south; and the width of the part that
was left free was five cubits all around.
12 The building that was facing the tem-
ple yard on the west side was seventy cubits
wide; and the wall of the building was five
cubits thick all around, and its depth ninety
cubits.
13 Then he measured the temple, one
hundred cubits deep; and the yard and the
building with its walls, one hundred cubits
deep; 14 also the width of the east front of
the temple and the yard, one hundred cu-
bits.
15 Then he measured the depth of the
building facing the yard at the west, togeth-
er with its galleries[d] on either side, one
hundred cubits.
The nave of the temple and the inner
room and the outer[e] vestibule 16 were pan-
eled,[f] and, all around, all three had win-
dows with recessed[g] frames. Facing the
threshold the temple was paneled with
wood all around, from the floor up to the
windows (now the windows were covered),
17 to the space above the door, even to the
inner room, and on the outside. And on all
the walls all around in the inner room and
the nave there was a pattern.[h] 18 It was
formed of cherubim and palm trees, a palm
tree between cherub and cherub. Each cher-
ub had two faces: 19 a human face turned
toward the palm tree on the one side, and
the face of a young lion turned toward the
palm tree on the other side. They were
carved on the whole temple all around;
20 from the floor to the area above the door,
cherubim and palm trees were carved on
the wall.[i]
21 The doorposts of the nave were
square. In front of the holy place was some-
thing resembling 22 an altar of wood, three
cubits high, two cubits long, and two cubits
wide;[j] its corners, its base,[k] and its walls

a Gk: Heb *width* *b* Gk Compare 1 Kings 6.6: Heb *they entered* *c* Cn: Heb *it was surrounded* *d* Cn: Meaning of Heb uncertain *e* Gk: Heb *of the court* *f* Gk: Heb *the thresholds* *g* Cn Compare Gk 1 Kings 6.4: Meaning of Heb uncertain *h* Heb *measures* *i* Cn Compare verse 25: Heb *and the wall* *j* Gk: Heb lacks *two cubits wide* *k* Gk: Heb *length*

a square of 10.5 m (34 ft) per side (1 Kings 6.16; 7.50; 8.6; Ex 26.33–34). **41.5–15a: Annexes and surroundings.** The three tiers of thirty chambers per tier on the sides of the Temple (1 Kings 6.5–10) were probably for equipment for the Temple services, storage, and the Temple treasures (1 Kings 14.26; 2 Kings 14.14). **10:** *Chambers of the court,* 42.1–14. **12:** A very large auxiliary building stood west of the Temple; it may also have been intended for storage purposes. **15b–26: Wall decoration and interior furnishings.** The windows were like those in the gates (40.16); for the decorative motifs of *cherubim and palm trees,* see 1 Kings 6.29–30. **22:** The *table* in the nave was for the bread of the Presence; see Ex

were of wood. He said to me, "This is the
table that stands before the LORD." 23 The
nave and the holy place had each a double
door. 24 The doors had two leaves apiece,
two swinging leaves for each door. 25 On
the doors of the nave were carved cherubim
and palm trees, such as were carved on the
walls; and there was a canopy of wood in
front of the vestibule outside. 26 And there
were recessed windows and palm trees on
either side, on the sidewalls of the vesti-
bule.[a]

42 Then he led me out into the outer
court, toward the north, and he
brought me to the chambers that were op-
posite the temple yard and opposite the
building on the north. 2 The length of the
building that was on the north side[b] was[c]
one hundred cubits, and the width fifty cu-
bits. 3 Across the twenty cubits that be-
longed to the inner court, and facing the
pavement that belonged to the outer court,
the chambers rose[d] gallery[e] by gallery[e]
in three stories. 4 In front of the chambers
was a passage on the inner side, ten cubits
wide and one hundred cubits deep,[f] and
its[g] entrances were on the north. 5 Now
the upper chambers were narrower, for the
galleries[e] took more away from them than
from the lower and middle chambers in the
building. 6 For they were in three stories,
and they had no pillars like the pillars of
the outer[h] court; for this reason the upper
chambers were set back from the ground
more than the lower and the middle ones.
7 There was a wall outside parallel to the
chambers, toward the outer court, opposite
the chambers, fifty cubits long. 8 For the
chambers on the outer court were fifty cu-
bits long, while those opposite the temple
were one hundred cubits long. 9 At the foot
of these chambers ran a passage that one
entered from the east in order to enter them
from the outer court. 10 The width of the
passage[i] was fixed by the wall of the
court.

On the south[j] also, opposite the vacant
area and opposite the building, there were
chambers 11 with a passage in front of
them; they were similar to the chambers on
the north, of the same length and width,
with the same exits[k] and arrangements
and doors. 12 So the entrances of the cham-
bers to the south were entered through the
entrance at the head of the corresponding
passage, from the east, along the matching
wall.[e]

13 Then he said to me, "The north
chambers and the south chambers opposite
the vacant area are the holy chambers,
where the priests who approach the LORD
shall eat the most holy offerings; there they
shall deposit the most holy offerings—the
grain offering, the sin offering, and the guilt
offering—for the place is holy. 14 When the
priests enter the holy place, they shall not
go out of it into the outer court without
laying there the vestments in which they
minister, for these are holy; they shall put
on other garments before they go near to
the area open to the people."

15 When he had finished measuring the
interior of the temple area, he led me out by
the gate that faces east, and measured the
temple area all around. 16 He measured the
east side with the measuring reed, five hun-
dred cubits by the measuring reed. 17 Then
he turned and measured[l] the north side,
five hundred cubits by the measuring reed.
18 Then he turned and measured[l] the south

a Cn: Heb *vestibule. And the side chambers of the temple and the canopies* *b* Gk: Heb *door* *c* Gk: Heb *before the length* *d* Heb lacks *the chambers rose* *e* Meaning of Heb uncertain *f* Gk Syr: Heb *a way of one cubit* *g* Heb *their* *h* Gk: Heb lacks *outer* *i* Heb lacks *of the passage* *j* Gk: Heb *east* *k* Heb *and all their exits* *l* Gk: Heb *measuring reed all around. He measured*

25.23–30; Lev 24.5–9. **42.1–14: The priests' chambers.** Ezekiel first sees the north sacristy, which was behind (west of) the north gate-tower to the inner court. Similar chambers were on the Temple's south side (vv. 10–12). Perhaps the three stories of chambers were arranged terrace-fashion against the north and south walls retaining the inner court. A second, smaller, apartment building was opposite, on the outer-court side. **13:** On the sacrifices, see 40.38–39n.; 44.28–31; Lev 2.1–10; 7.7–10. **14:** See 44.19n. **15–20: The measuring completed.** The total Temple area was a square of 262 m (861 ft) per side. **20:**

side, five hundred cubits by the measuring
reed. 19 Then he turned to the west side and
measured, five hundred cubits by the mea-
suring reed. 20 He measured it on the four
sides. It had a wall around it, five hundred
cubits long and five hundred cubits wide, to
make a separation between the holy and
the common.

43 Then he brought me to the gate, the
gate facing east. 2 And there, the glo-
ry of the God of Israel was coming from
the east; the sound was like the sound of
mighty waters; and the earth shone with his
glory. 3 The[a] vision I saw was like the vi-
sion that I had seen when he came to de-
stroy the city, and[b] like the vision that I
had seen by the river Chebar; and I fell
upon my face. 4 As the glory of the LORD
entered the temple by the gate facing east,
5 the spirit lifted me up, and brought me
into the inner court; and the glory of the
LORD filled the temple.

6 While the man was standing beside
me, I heard someone speaking to me out of
the temple. 7 He said to me: Mortal, this is
the place of my throne and the place for the
soles of my feet, where I will reside among
the people of Israel forever. The house of
Israel shall no more defile my holy name,
neither they nor their kings, by their whor-
ing, and by the corpses of their kings at
their death.[c] 8 When they placed their
threshold by my threshold and their door-
posts beside my doorposts, with only a wall
between me and them, they were defiling
my holy name by their abominations that
they committed; therefore I have consumed
them in my anger. 9 Now let them put away
their idolatry and the corpses of their kings
far from me, and I will reside among them
forever.

10 As for you, mortal, describe the tem-
ple to the house of Israel, and let them mea-
sure the pattern; and let them be ashamed
of their iniquities. 11 When they are
ashamed of all that they have done, make
known to them the plan of the temple, its
arrangement, its exits and its entrances,
and its whole form—all its ordinances and
its entire plan and all its laws; and write it
down in their sight, so that they may ob-
serve and follow the entire plan and all its
ordinances. 12 This is the law of the temple:
the whole territory on the top of the moun-
tain all around shall be most holy. This is
the law of the temple.

13 These are the dimensions of the altar
by cubits (the cubit being one cubit and a
handbreadth): its base shall be one cubit
high,[d] and one cubit wide, with a rim of
one span around its edge. This shall be the
height of the altar: 14 From the base on the
ground to the lower ledge, two cubits, with
a width of one cubit; and from the smaller

a Gk: Heb *Like the vision* *b* Syr: Heb *and the visions* *c* Or *on their high places* *d* Gk: Heb lacks *high*

Marking boundaries of holiness, distinguishing between *the holy and the common,* was a central concern of Zadokites, such as Ezekiel (22.26; 44.23; Lev 10.10–11).

43.1–12: Return of the glory of the LORD. As God on the throne-chariot had forsaken the Temple by the east gate (10.18–19; 11.22–23), so God's glory returns through the same gate (40.6–16; 44.1–3) and dwells in the new Temple (Ex 40.34–38 ["Holiness Collection"]; 1 Kings 8.10–11). **2:** *Sound of mighty waters,* 1.24. **3:** *Chebar,* 1.1–3n. *Fell upon my face,* 1.28; 3.23. **6–12:** God warns against any more defiling of the Temple. The text particularly attacks the preexilic use of the Temple as a royal chapel and the practice of royal burials near the Temple (see 2 Kings 21.18,26; 23.30). **7:** Zion theology triumphs in the new age (37.28; 38.12; 48.35). **10–12:** Instructions and statement of purpose. The Temple plan of chs 40–42 provides for the holiness appropriate for God's eternal presence. **12:** *Law of the temple,* it was the priests, such as Ezekiel, who transmitted such law to people (44.23n.).

43.13–27: The altar of burnt offerings (40.47). The altar was built in three stepped layers (two ledges and a hearth) resting on a rimmed base. The altar symbolizes a mythic cosmic center (cf. 38.12n.): Its shape resembles the Babylonian ziggurats (see Gen 11.4n.), also cosmic centers. *The base on the ground* (v. 14) is literally "the bosom of the earth." The *altar hearth* (v. 15) in Hebrew is spelled like "the mountain of God." **13:** *Cubit,* see 40.5n. **15:** *Horns,* see 1 Kings 1.50n. **16:** *Hearth,* the altar's top layer,

ledge to the larger ledge, four cubits, with a
width of one cubit; 15 and the altar hearth,
four cubits; and from the altar hearth pro-
jecting upward, four horns. 16 The altar
hearth shall be square, twelve cubits long
by twelve wide. 17 The ledge also shall be
square, fourteen cubits long by fourteen
wide, with a rim around it half a cubit
wide, and its surrounding base, one cubit.
Its steps shall face east.

18 Then he said to me: Mortal, thus says
the Lord God: These are the ordinances for
the altar: On the day when it is erected for
offering burnt offerings upon it and for
dashing blood against it, 19 you shall give to
the levitical priests of the family of Zadok,
who draw near to me to minister to me,
says the Lord God, a bull for a sin offering.
20 And you shall take some of its blood, and
put it on the four horns of the altar, and on
the four corners of the ledge, and upon the
rim all around; thus you shall purify it and
make atonement for it. 21 You shall also
take the bull of the sin offering, and it shall
be burnt in the appointed place belonging
to the temple, outside the sacred area.

22 On the second day you shall offer a
male goat without blemish for a sin offer-
ing; and the altar shall be purified, as it was
purified with the bull. 23 When you have
finished purifying it, you shall offer a bull
without blemish and a ram from the flock
without blemish. 24 You shall present them
before the Lord, and the priests shall
throw salt on them and offer them up as a
burnt offering to the Lord. 25 For seven
days you shall provide daily a goat for a sin
offering; also a bull and a ram from the
flock, without blemish, shall be provided.
26 Seven days shall they make atonement
for the altar and cleanse it, and so conse-
crate it. 27 When these days are over, then
from the eighth day onward the priests
shall offer upon the altar your burnt offer-
ings and your offerings of well-being; and I
will accept you, says the Lord God.

44 Then he brought me back to the
outer gate of the sanctuary, which
faces east; and it was shut. 2 The Lord said
to me: This gate shall remain shut; it shall
not be opened, and no one shall enter by it;
for the Lord, the God of Israel, has entered
by it; therefore it shall remain shut. 3 Only
the prince, because he is a prince, may sit in
it to eat food before the Lord; he shall
enter by way of the vestibule of the gate,
and shall go out by the same way.

4 Then he brought me by way of the
north gate to the front of the temple; and I
looked, and lo! the glory of the Lord filled
the temple of the Lord; and I fell upon my
face. 5 The Lord said to me: Mortal, mark
well, look closely, and listen attentively to
all that I shall tell you concerning all the
ordinances of the temple of the Lord and
all its laws; and mark well those who may
be admitted to[a] the temple and all those
who are to be excluded from the sanctuary.
6 Say to the rebellious house,[b] to the house
of Israel, Thus says the Lord God: O house

a Cn: Heb *the entrance of*   *b* Gk: Heb lacks *house*

where sacrifices were burned. **17:** The height of the altar, over 5.2 m (17 ft), necessitated its having *steps* (contrast Ex 20.26). **43.18–27: The altar's consecration.** A ritual for the dedication of the altar, when it is completed. On the analogy of earlier consecratory rites (Ex 29.36–37; 40.1–38; Lev 8.14–15), the priests of Zadok (40.46n.; 44.15–31n.) are to dedicate the altar. **21:** Lev 4.11–12; 8.16–17.

44.1–3: The outer east gate. This gate-tower (40.6–14) remains closed, symbolizing its consecration by God's entrance (43.4) and God's permanent presence inside the Temple (43.7). Thus shut, the gate complex becomes a ceremonial room. As his sacral privilege, the *prince* was to enter it from the Temple's outer courtyard to eat his part of the sacrificial meal (43.27; Lev 7.15; 22.21). The book of Ezekiel presents differing pictures of Israel's monarchic leader, whom Ezekiel terms the *prince*. In 34.24 and 37.25, the prince is a Davidic figure who ushers in the era of salvation. Here, in chs 40–48, the prince is less a messianic figure than a civil ruler with immediate, concrete tasks.

44.4–31: Temple ordinances. 4–5: A renewed commission. **6–14:** Ezekiel's blueprint for the restored priesthood of Israel again redresses past wrongs. Under the influence of the "Holiness Collection," Ezekiel finds these particular past wrongs encapsulated in Num 16–18, a text about the rebellion of Levites

of Israel, let there be an end to all your
abominations 7 in admitting foreigners, un-
circumcised in heart and flesh, to be in my
sanctuary, profaning my temple when you
offer to me my food, the fat and the blood.
You[a] have broken my covenant with all
your abominations. 8 And you have not
kept charge of my sacred offerings; but you
have appointed foreigners[b] to act for you
in keeping my charge in my sanctuary.
9 Thus says the Lord GOD: No foreign-
er, uncircumcised in heart and flesh, of all
the foreigners who are among the people of
Israel, shall enter my sanctuary. 10 But the
Levites who went far from me, going astray
from me after their idols when Israel went
astray, shall bear their punishment. 11 They
shall be ministers in my sanctuary, having
oversight at the gates of the temple, and
serving in the temple; they shall slaughter
the burnt offering and the sacrifice for the
people, and they shall attend on them and
serve them. 12 Because they ministered to
them before their idols and made the house
of Israel stumble into iniquity, therefore I
have sworn concerning them, says the Lord
GOD, that they shall bear their punishment.
13 They shall not come near to me, to serve
me as priest, nor come near any of my sa-
cred offerings, the things that are most sa-
cred; but they shall bear their shame, and
the consequences of the abominations that
they have committed. 14 Yet I will appoint
them to keep charge of the temple, to do all
its chores, all that is to be done in it.
15 But the levitical priests, the descen-
dants of Zadok, who kept the charge of my
sanctuary when the people of Israel went
astray from me, shall come near to me to
minister to me; and they shall attend me to
offer me the fat and the blood, says the
Lord GOD. 16 It is they who shall enter my
sanctuary, it is they who shall approach my
table, to minister to me, and they shall keep
my charge. 17 When they enter the gates of
the inner court, they shall wear linen vest-
ments; they shall have nothing of wool on
them, while they minister at the gates of the
inner court, and within. 18 They shall have
linen turbans on their heads, and linen un-
dergarments on their loins; they shall not
bind themselves with anything that causes
sweat. 19 When they go out into the outer
court to the people, they shall remove the
vestments in which they have been minis-
tering, and lay them in the holy chambers;
and they shall put on other garments, so

a Gk Syr Vg: Heb *They* *b* Heb lacks *foreigners*

during Israel's wilderness wanderings after the Exodus. **7–8:** The primary reference is to a prototypical narrative: the Levites' encroachment on priestly prerogatives in Num 16–18 (Num 16.40; 18.4,7). The Levites are *foreigners*/"outsiders" with respect to the priestly obligations of the sanctuary and the altar. **10–14:** After their rebellion in the wilderness, the Levites were given circumscribed responsibilities. Here, the Levites are restored to these responsibilities in the new Temple, as Num 18.3–4 had specified them. **10:** *When Israel went astray,* Num 16.2,22,41. *Bear their punishment,* Num 18.23. **11:** The limitation of the slaughtering of sacrifices to the Levites, thus disenfranchising the general populace, is a new holiness stricture that goes beyond the priestly stipulations of Lev 1.5,11. *Attend . . . and serve,* Num 16.9. **13:** Num 18.3. **14:** Num 18.4. **15–31:** The Zadokite priesthood (see 40.46n.; 43.19; 48.11). The Zadokites, one of at least three major priestly lineages in ancient Israel, had been the central priests at Jerusalem's preexilic Temple. Their origins trace back to Solomon's elevation of *Zadok,* the founder of the Zadokite lineage, to be chief priest after Abiathar's banishment (2 Sam 20.25; 1 Kings 1.7–8,41–45; 2.26–27). Ezekiel and his group were themselves Zadokite priests. 1 Chr 6.50–53; 24.31 trace Zadok's ancestry back to Eleazar, Aaron's son. Here, vv. 15–16 refer to how Aaron and Eleazar had been faithful during the Levites' rebellion (Num 16.11,20–22,36–40,46–50). These priests were the ancestors of the Zadokites, and Ezekiel views the Zadokites as present "embryonically" in their actions. **15–16:** Num 18.7 (cf. Lev 16.14–15). **17–31: Priestly rules. 17:** *Linen vestments,* see 9.1–2n.; Ex 39.27–29. **19:** 42.14. *Communicate holiness,* cf. 46.20. Sanctity could sometimes be transmitted through direct contact with a sacred substance (see Lev 6.18,26–27). The goal here is to preserve gradations of sanctity. Failure in this regard was life-threatening (see Num 16.38). **20:** The care of the hair, Lev 21.5. **21:** No *wine* before

that they may not communicate holiness to
the people with their vestments. 20They
shall not shave their heads or let their locks
grow long; they shall only trim the hair of
their heads. 21No priest shall drink wine
when he enters the inner court. 22They
shall not marry a widow, or a divorced
woman, but only a virgin of the stock of the
house of Israel, or a widow who is the wid-
ow of a priest. 23They shall teach my peo-
ple the difference between the holy and the
common, and show them how to distin-
guish between the unclean and the clean.
24In a controversy they shall act as judges,
and they shall decide it according to my
judgments. They shall keep my laws and
my statutes regarding all my appointed fes-
tivals, and they shall keep my sabbaths
holy. 25They shall not defile themselves by
going near to a dead person; for father or
mother, however, and for son or daughter,
and for brother or unmarried sister they
may defile themselves. 26After he has be-
come clean, they shall count seven days for
him. 27On the day that he goes into the
holy place, into the inner court, to minister
in the holy place, he shall offer his sin offer-
ing, says the Lord GOD.

28 This shall be their inheritance: I am
their inheritance; and you shall give them
no holding in Israel; I am their holding.
29They shall eat the grain offering, the sin
offering, and the guilt offering; and every
devoted thing in Israel shall be theirs. 30The
first of all the first fruits of all kinds, and
every offering of all kinds from all your
offerings, shall belong to the priests; you
shall also give to the priests the first of your
dough, in order that a blessing may rest on
your house. 31The priests shall not eat of
anything, whether bird or animal, that died
of itself or was torn by animals.

45 When you allot the land as an inher-
itance, you shall set aside for the
LORD a portion of the land as a holy dis-
trict, twenty-five thousand cubits long and
twenty[a] thousand cubits wide; it shall be
holy throughout its entire extent. 2Of this,
a square plot of five hundred by five hun-
dred cubits shall be for the sanctuary, with
fifty cubits for an open space around it. 3In
the holy district you shall measure off a
section twenty-five thousand cubits long
and ten thousand wide, in which shall be
the sanctuary, the most holy place. 4It shall
be a holy portion of the land; it shall be for
the priests, who minister in the sanctuary
and approach the LORD to minister to him;
and it shall be both a place for their houses
and a holy place for the sanctuary. 5Anoth-
er section, twenty-five thousand cubits long
and ten thousand cubits wide, shall be for
the Levites who minister at the temple, as
their holding for cities to live in.[b]

6 Alongside the portion set apart as the
holy district you shall assign as a holding
for the city an area five thousand cubits
wide, and twenty-five thousand cubits
long; it shall belong to the whole house of
Israel.

7 And to the prince shall belong the land
on both sides of the holy district and the
holding of the city, alongside the holy dis-
trict and the holding of the city, on the west
and on the east, corresponding in length to
one of the tribal portions, and extending
from the western to the eastern boundary

a Gk: Heb *ten* *b* Gk: Heb *as their holding, twenty chambers*

service, Lev 10.9. **22:** Proper marriage, Lev 21.7,13–15. **23:** Teaching of the people, Lev 10.10–11; 2 Chr 17.9; Hag 2.10–13. **24:** *Judges,* 1 Chr 23.4; 2 Chr 19.11. **25:** Defilement by a corpse, see 39.11–16n.; Lev 21.1–3. **28:** No *inheritance,* 45.1–5; 48.8–14; Num 18.20–24. **29–30:** Eating sacrifices and *first fruits,* Num 18.9–13; Lev 2.3; 6.16,26; 7.6–7. *Every devoted thing,* Num 18.14. **31:** Lev 7.24; 22.8.

45.1–9: The distribution of land (continued in 47.13–48.35) is idealized. A *holy district* is to contain a northern section for the Levites and a southern section for the sacrificing priests. The latter includes the square section for the Temple area (42.15–20) plus an enclosure space (not mentioned earlier). The property of Jerusalem south of the holy district (v. 6) makes with the holy district (v. 1) a square area of ca. 13 km (8 mi) per side. The prince (see 44.1–3n.) is to hold the strips of land to the west and east of this square area.

8 of the land. It is to be his property in Isra-
el. And my princes shall no longer oppress
my people; but they shall let the house of
Israel have the land according to their
tribes.
9 Thus says the Lord GOD: Enough,
O princes of Israel! Put away violence and
oppression, and do what is just and right.
Cease your evictions of my people, says the
Lord GOD.
10 You shall have honest balances, an
honest ephah, and an honest bath.[a] 11 The
ephah and the bath shall be of the same
measure, the bath containing one-tenth of a
homer, and the ephah one-tenth of a ho-
mer; the homer shall be the standard mea-
sure. 12 The shekel shall be twenty gerahs.
Twenty shekels, twenty-five shekels, and
fifteen shekels shall make a mina for you.
13 This is the offering that you shall
make: one-sixth of an ephah from each ho-
mer of wheat, and one-sixth of an ephah
from each homer of barley, 14 and as the
fixed portion of oil,[b] one-tenth of a bath
from each cor (the cor,[c] like the homer,
contains ten baths); 15 and one sheep from
every flock of two hundred, from the pas-
tures of Israel. This is the offering for grain
offerings, burnt offerings, and offerings of
well-being, to make atonement for them,
says the Lord GOD. 16 All the people of the
land shall join with the prince in Israel in
making this offering. 17 But this shall be the
obligation of the prince regarding the burnt
offerings, grain offerings, and drink offer-
ings, at the festivals, the new moons, and
the sabbaths, all the appointed festivals of
the house of Israel: he shall provide the sin
offerings, grain offerings, the burnt offer-
ings, and the offerings of well-being, to
make atonement for the house of Israel.
18 Thus says the Lord GOD: In the first
month, on the first day of the month, you
shall take a young bull without blemish,
and purify the sanctuary. 19 The priest shall
take some of the blood of the sin offering
and put it on the doorposts of the temple,
the four corners of the ledge of the altar,
and the posts of the gate of the inner court.
20 You shall do the same on the seventh day
of the month for anyone who has sinned
through error or ignorance; so you shall
make atonement for the temple.
21 In the first month, on the fourteenth
day of the month, you shall celebrate the
festival of the passover, and for seven days
unleavened bread shall be eaten. 22 On that
day the prince shall provide for himself and
all the people of the land a young bull for
a sin offering. 23 And during the seven days
of the festival he shall provide as a burnt
offering to the LORD seven young bulls and
seven rams without blemish, on each of the
seven days; and a male goat daily for a
sin offering. 24 He shall provide as a grain
offering an ephah for each bull, an ephah
for each ram, and a hin of oil to each
ephah. 25 In the seventh month, on the fif-
teenth day of the month and for the seven
days of the festival, he shall make the same
provision for sin offerings, burnt offerings,
and grain offerings, and for the oil.
46 Thus says the Lord GOD: The gate
of the inner court that faces east
shall remain closed on the six working

a A Heb measure of volume *b* Cn: Heb *oil, the bath the oil* *c* Vg: Heb *homer*

45.10–17: Weights and measures for offerings. For present-day equivalents of ephah, bath, homer, shekel, gerah, and mina, see Table of Weights and Measures (pp. 534–535 ES). For the importance of *honest* measures, see Lev 19.35–36; Deut 25.13–16; Am 8.5; Mic 6.10–11. **13–17:** The people will bring gifts for the regular sacrifices to the prince, who, as their representative, will offer them to God. These offerings are in addition to the donations given to the priests of 44.30.

45.18–25: Festival regulations. 18–20: An annual ritual for purifying the Temple, otherwise unattested. **21–25:** Ezekiel's brief festival calendar highlights the *passover* (Ex 12; Lev 23.4–8) and the festival of booths (the *festival* of the *seventh month* in v. 25; see Lev 23.33–36; Num 29.12–38; Deut 16.13–15). It omits the Festival of Weeks (Pentecost; Lev 23.15–21). **24:** *Ephah* and *hin,* see Table of Weights and Measures (pp. 534–535 ES).

46.1–15: Gate regulations and the prince's minor offerings. 1–7: Both weekly and monthly, the *prince*

days; but on the sabbath day it shall be
opened and on the day of the new moon it
shall be opened. 2 The prince shall enter by
the vestibule of the gate from outside, and
shall take his stand by the post of the gate.
The priests shall offer his burnt offering
and his offerings of well-being, and he shall
bow down at the threshold of the gate.
Then he shall go out, but the gate shall not
be closed until evening. 3 The people of the
land shall bow down at the entrance of that
gate before the LORD on the sabbaths and
on the new moons. 4 The burnt offering
that the prince offers to the LORD on the
sabbath day shall be six lambs without
blemish and a ram without blemish; 5 and
the grain offering with the ram shall be
an ephah, and the grain offering with the
lambs shall be as much as he wishes to give,
together with a hin of oil to each ephah.
6 On the day of the new moon he shall offer
a young bull without blemish, and six
lambs and a ram, which shall be without
blemish; 7 as a grain offering he shall pro-
vide an ephah with the bull and an ephah
with the ram, and with the lambs as much
as he wishes, together with a hin of oil to
each ephah. 8 When the prince enters, he
shall come in by the vestibule of the gate,
and he shall go out by the same way.
9 When the people of the land come be-
fore the LORD at the appointed festivals,
whoever enters by the north gate to wor-
ship shall go out by the south gate; and
whoever enters by the south gate shall go
out by the north gate: they shall not return
by way of the gate by which they entered,
but shall go out straight ahead. 10 When
they come in, the prince shall come in with
them; and when they go out, he shall go
out.
11 At the festivals and the appointed
seasons the grain offering with a young bull
shall be an ephah, and with a ram an
ephah, and with the lambs as much as one
wishes to give, together with a hin of oil to
an ephah. 12 When the prince provides a
freewill offering, either a burnt offering or
offerings of well-being as a freewill offering
to the LORD, the gate facing east shall be
opened for him; and he shall offer his burnt
offering or his offerings of well-being as he
does on the sabbath day. Then he shall go
out, and after he has gone out the gate shall
be closed.
13 He shall provide a lamb, a yearling,
without blemish, for a burnt offering to the
LORD daily; morning by morning he shall
provide it. 14 And he shall provide a grain
offering with it morning by morning regu-
larly, one-sixth of an ephah, and one-third
of a hin of oil to moisten the choice flour,
as a grain offering to the LORD; this is the
ordinance for all time. 15 Thus the lamb and
the grain offering and the oil shall be pro-
vided, morning by morning, as a regular
burnt offering.
16 Thus says the Lord GOD: If the
prince makes a gift to any of his sons out of
his inheritance,[a] it shall belong to his sons,
it is their holding by inheritance. 17 But if he
makes a gift out of his inheritance to one of
his servants, it shall be his to the year of
liberty; then it shall revert to the prince;
only his sons may keep a gift from his in-
heritance. 18 The prince shall not take any

a Gk: Heb *it is his inheritance*

(see 44.1–3n.) shall bring offerings (vv. 4–7) into the inner east gate (40.32–34). He will stand by, while the priests offer the sacrifices on the altar directly ahead. Contrast preexilic practice, in which the king might perform priestly functions himself (1 Kings 8.63; 2 Kings 16.12–13). For the *sabbath* sacrifices, see Num 28.9–10; on Ezekiel's emphasis on the sabbath here, see 20.12–13n. For the *new moon* (i.e., monthly) sacrifices, see Num 28.11–15. **8–10:** Exit procedures. The great festival crowds require regulations for controlled egress. **11–15:** Further rules. **11:** See 45.24; 46.5,7. **12:** When the prince makes a *freewill offering* (Lev 22.18–23), the inner east gate (v. 1) may be opened. **13–15:** The prince must also provide for daily sacrifices (Num 28.3–8; Ex 29.38–42).

46.16–18: The prince's property. Crown property (45.7; 48.21–22) was to be inalienable from the royal line. When given to a nonrelative, it had to be returned on the *year of liberty* (jubilee year, Lev

of the inheritance of the people, thrusting
them out of their holding; he shall give his
sons their inheritance out of his own hold-
ing, so that none of my people shall be dis-
possessed of their holding.
19 Then he brought me through the en-
trance, which was at the side of the gate, to
the north row of the holy chambers for the
priests; and there I saw a place at the ex-
treme western end of them. 20 He said to
me, "This is the place where the priests
shall boil the guilt offering and the sin
offering, and where they shall bake the
grain offering, in order not to bring them
out into the outer court and so communi-
cate holiness to the people."
21 Then he brought me out to the outer
court, and led me past the four corners of
the court; and in each corner of the court
there was a court— 22 in the four corners of
the court were small[a] courts, forty cubits
long and thirty wide; the four were of the
same size. 23 On the inside, around each of
the four courts[b] was a row of masonry,
with hearths made at the bottom of the
rows all around. 24 Then he said to me,
"These are the kitchens where those who
serve at the temple shall boil the sacrifices
of the people."

47 Then he brought me back to the en-
trance of the temple; there, water
was flowing from below the threshold of
the temple toward the east (for the temple
faced east); and the water was flowing
down from below the south end of the
threshold of the temple, south of the altar.
2 Then he brought me out by way of the
north gate, and led me around on the out-
side to the outer gate that faces toward the
east;[c] and the water was coming out on
the south side.
3 Going on eastward with a cord in his
hand, the man measured one thousand cu-
bits, and then led me through the water;
and it was ankle-deep. 4 Again he measured
one thousand, and led me through the wa-
ter; and it was knee-deep. Again he mea-
sured one thousand, and led me through
the water; and it was up to the waist.
5 Again he measured one thousand, and it
was a river that I could not cross, for the
water had risen; it was deep enough to
swim in, a river that could not be crossed.
6 He said to me, "Mortal, have you seen
this?"
Then he led me back along the bank of
the river. 7 As I came back, I saw on the
bank of the river a great many trees on the
one side and on the other. 8 He said to me,
"This water flows toward the eastern re-
gion and goes down into the Arabah; and
when it enters the sea, the sea of stagnant
waters, the water will become fresh.
9 Wherever the river goes,[d] every living
creature that swarms will live, and there
will be very many fish, once these waters
reach there. It will become fresh; and every-
thing will live where the river goes. 10 Peo-
ple will stand fishing beside the sea[e] from
En-gedi to En-eglaim; it will be a place for
the spreading of nets; its fish will be of a
great many kinds, like the fish of the Great
Sea. 11 But its swamps and marshes will not
become fresh; they are to be left for salt.

a Gk Syr Vg: Meaning of Heb uncertain *b* Heb *the four of them* *c* Meaning of Heb uncertain
d Gk Syr Vg Tg: Heb *the two rivers go* *e* Heb *it*

25.8–17). **18:** Royal appropriation of others' property is prohibited; contrast 1 Kings 21.1–16; Isa 5.8; Mic 2.2.

46.19–24: Sacrificial kitchens. 19–20: Behind (west of) the priest's chambers (42.1–14) were priests' kitchens, for ritual preparation of offerings (42.13) for priestly consumption. *Communicate holiness,* see 42.14; 44.19n. **21–24:** Temple kitchens, for the Levites to prepare the common-meal sacrifices of the general populace, were in all four corners of the Temple's outer court (40.17–19).

47.1–12: The sacred river. From the throne of God (the Temple; 43.7) issue the waters of life, making the land a new paradise. This paradisiacal motif (see 28.14n.) is also found in Joel 3.18 and Zech 14.8 (both Zadokite apocalyptic texts that follow in the tradition of Ezekiel). **8:** *Arabah,* the Jordan valley, in which the Dead Sea is located. **10:** *En-gedi to En-eglaim,* two springs on the western side of the Dead Sea. *The Great Sea,* the Mediterranean. **11:** A source of salt would supply Temple rituals (43.24).

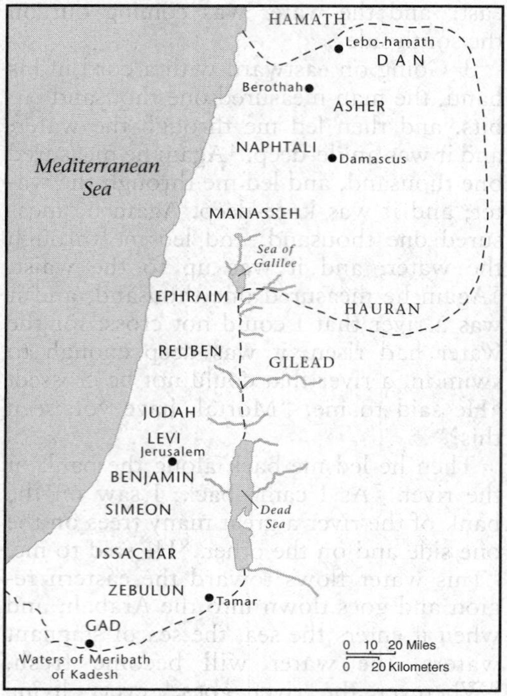

Chs 47–48: Tribal territories in the restored Israel.

12 On the banks, on both sides of the river,
there will grow all kinds of trees for food.
Their leaves will not wither nor their fruit
fail, but they will bear fresh fruit every
month, because the water for them flows
from the sanctuary. Their fruit will be for
food, and their leaves for healing."
13 Thus says the Lord GOD: These are
the boundaries by which you shall divide
the land for inheritance among the twelve
tribes of Israel. Joseph shall have two por-
tions. 14 You shall divide it equally; I swore
to give it to your ancestors, and this land
shall fall to you as your inheritance.
15 This shall be the boundary of the
land: On the north side, from the Great Sea
by way of Hethlon to Lebo-hamath, and on
to Zedad,[a] 16 Berothah, Sibraim (which
lies between the border of Damascus and
the border of Hamath), as far as Hazer-
hatticon, which is on the border of Hauran.
17 So the boundary shall run from the sea to
Hazar-enon, which is north of the border
of Damascus, with the border of Hamath
to the north.[b] This shall be the north side.
18 On the east side, between Hauran
and Damascus; along the Jordan between
Gilead and the land of Israel; to the eastern
sea and as far as Tamar.[c] This shall be the
east side.
19 On the south side, it shall run from
Tamar as far as the waters of Meribath-
kadesh, from there along the Wadi of
Egypt[d] to the Great Sea. This shall be the
south side.
20 On the west side, the Great Sea shall
be the boundary to a point opposite Lebo-
hamath. This shall be the west side.
21 So you shall divide this land among
you according to the tribes of Israel. 22 You
shall allot it as an inheritance for yourselves
and for the aliens who reside among you
and have begotten children among you.
They shall be to you as citizens of Israel;
with you they shall be allotted an inheri-
tance among the tribes of Israel. 23 In what-
ever tribe aliens reside, there you shall as-

a Gk: Heb *Lebo-zedad,* [16]*Hamath* *b* Meaning of Heb uncertain *c* Compare Syr: Heb *you shall measure* *d* Heb lacks *of Egypt*

47.13–48.29: A new holy land.

47.13–23: Boundary and allotment instructions. Ezekiel's new Exodus and settlement (cf. 20.33–38n.; 37.27n.) occasion a new allotment of the land. **14:** *I swore,* 20.6; 36.28. **15–20:** National boundaries. Several of the sites mentioned are unidentified. North border: roughly from the Mediterranean north of Tyre to Damascus (cf. Num 34.7–9). It is approximately the border of the Davidic empire (1 Kings 8.65). East border: along the *Jordan* River to *Tamar,* a site south of the Dead Sea (*eastern sea*) (Num 34.10–12). Territory in the Transjordan is not included in the new land (contrast Num 34.13–15). South border: from Tamar along the southern Negeb through Kadesh-barnea (*Meribath-kadesh*) to *the Wadi of Egypt* (1 Kings 8.65n.) and the Mediterranean (Num 34.3–5). West border: the Mediterranean Sea (Num 34.6). **21–23:** Allotment. Resident *aliens* and native Israelites should be treated alike (a widespread principle in the "Holiness Collection": Num 15.29; Lev 19.33–34; 24.22).

sign them their inheritance, says the Lord GOD.

48 These are the names of the tribes: Beginning at the northern border, on the Hethlon road,[a] from Lebo-hamath, as far as Hazar-enon (which is on the border of Damascus, with Hamath to the north), and[b] extending from the east side to the west,[c] Dan, one portion. 2 Adjoining the territory of Dan, from the east side to the west, Asher, one portion. 3 Adjoining the territory of Asher, from the east side to the west, Naphtali, one portion. 4 Adjoining the territory of Naphtali, from the east side to the west, Manasseh, one portion. 5 Adjoining the territory of Manasseh, from the east side to the west, Ephraim, one portion. 6 Adjoining the territory of Ephraim, from the east side to the west, Reuben, one portion. 7 Adjoining the territory of Reuben, from the east side to the west, Judah, one portion.

8 Adjoining the territory of Judah, from the east side to the west, shall be the portion that you shall set apart, twenty-five thousand cubits in width, and in length equal to one of the tribal portions, from the east side to the west, with the sanctuary in the middle of it. 9 The portion that you shall set apart for the LORD shall be twenty-five thousand cubits in length, and twenty[d] thousand in width. 10 These shall be the allotments of the holy portion: the priests shall have an allotment measuring twenty-five thousand cubits on the northern side, ten thousand cubits in width on the western side, ten thousand in width on the eastern side, and twenty-five thousand in length on the southern side, with the sanctuary of the LORD in the middle of it. 11 This shall be for the consecrated priests, the descendants[e] of Zadok, who kept my charge, who did not go astray when the people of Israel went astray, as the Levites did. 12 It shall belong to them as a special portion from the holy portion of the land, a most holy place, adjoining the territory of the Levites. 13 Alongside the territory of the priests, the Levites shall have an allotment twenty-five thousand cubits in length and ten thousand in width. The whole length shall be twenty-five thousand cubits and the width twenty[f] thousand. 14 They shall not sell or exchange any of it; they shall not transfer this choice portion of the land, for it is holy to the LORD.

15 The remainder, five thousand cubits in width and twenty-five thousand in length, shall be for ordinary use for the city, for dwellings and for open country. In the middle of it shall be the city; 16 and these shall be its dimensions: the north side four thousand five hundred cubits, the south side four thousand five hundred, the east side four thousand five hundred, and the west side four thousand five hundred. 17 The city shall have open land: on the north two hundred fifty cubits, on the south two hundred fifty, on the east two hundred fifty, on the west two hundred fifty. 18 The remainder of the length alongside the holy portion shall be ten thousand cubits to the east, and ten thousand to the west, and it shall be alongside the holy portion. Its produce shall be food for the workers of the city. 19 The workers of the city, from all the tribes of Israel, shall cultivate it. 20 The whole portion that you shall set apart shall be twenty-five thousand cubits

a Compare 47.15: Heb *by the side of the way* *b* Cn: Heb *and they shall be his* *c* Gk Compare verses 2-8: Heb *the east side the west* *d* Compare 45.1: Heb *ten* *e* One Ms Gk: Heb *of the descendants* *f* Gk: Heb *ten*

48.1–29: Tribal and holy-district allotments. All tribes receive equal allotments consisting of idealized strips of land. Ephraim and Manasseh ("Joseph," 47.13) receive a portion each, but Levi, the priestly tribe, is omitted, so that the tribal allotments number twelve in all. **1–7:** Seven tribes north of the central strip (vv. 8–22; 45.1–9). **1:** *Hethlon, Lebo-hamath,* sites on the land's northern border (47.15). **8–22:** The central strip. The description matches and expands on that in 45.1–9. **11:** See 44.6–14n.; 44.15–31n. **15:** *Ordinary* ["common" as opposed to "holy"] *use,* see 22.26; 42.20n.; 44.23; Lev 10.10. **16–17:** The area of Jerusalem, with the surrounding *open land,* was exactly one hundred times that of the Temple

square, that is, the holy portion together
with the property of the city.
21 What remains on both sides of the
holy portion and of the property of the city
shall belong to the prince. Extending from
the twenty-five thousand cubits of the holy
portion to the east border, and westward
from the twenty-five thousand cubits to the
west border, parallel to the tribal portions,
it shall belong to the prince. The holy por-
tion with the sanctuary of the temple in the
middle of it, 22 and the property of the Le-
vites and of the city, shall be in the middle
of that which belongs to the prince. The
portion of the prince shall lie between the
territory of Judah and the territory of Ben-
jamin.
23 As for the rest of the tribes: from the
east side to the west, Benjamin, one por-
tion. 24 Adjoining the territory of Benjamin,
from the east side to the west, Simeon, one
portion. 25 Adjoining the territory of Sime-
on, from the east side to the west, Issachar,
one portion. 26 Adjoining the territory of
Issachar, from the east side to the west,
Zebulun, one portion. 27 Adjoining the ter-
ritory of Zebulun, from the east side to the
west, Gad, one portion. 28 And adjoining
the territory of Gad to the south, the
boundary shall run from Tamar to the wa-
ters of Meribath-kadesh, from there along
the Wadi of Egypt[a] to the Great Sea.
29 This is the land that you shall allot as an
inheritance among the tribes of Israel, and
these are their portions, says the Lord GOD.
30 These shall be the exits of the city:
On the north side, which is to be four thou-
sand five hundred cubits by measure,
31 three gates, the gate of Reuben, the gate
of Judah, and the gate of Levi, the gates of
the city being named after the tribes of Isra-
el. 32 On the east side, which is to be four
thousand five hundred cubits, three gates,
the gate of Joseph, the gate of Benjamin,
and the gate of Dan. 33 On the south side,
which is to be four thousand five hundred
cubits by measure, three gates, the gate of
Simeon, the gate of Issachar, and the gate
of Zebulun. 34 On the west side, which is to
be four thousand five hundred cubits, three
gates,[b] the gate of Gad, the gate of Asher,
and the gate of Naphtali. 35 The circumfer-
ence of the city shall be eighteen thousand
cubits. And the name of the city from that
time on shall be, The LORD is There.

a Heb lacks *of Egypt*   *b* One Ms Gk Syr: MT *their gates three*

(42.20), i.e., a square of 2.6 km (1.6 mi) per side. **21–22:** The allotment of the prince is as described in 45.7. **23–29:** Five tribes south of the central strip. **28:** See 47.19.

48.30–35: The new Jerusalem. Three gates on each of the city's four sides, with each gate named after a tribe (cf. Rev 21.12–14). **35:** The new city receives a new name in keeping with a re-actualized Zion theology (Isa 1.26; 60.14; 62.2; Zech 8.3). The name *The LORD is There* (Heb "Yahweh-shammah") reverses 10.18–19.

DANIEL

The book of Daniel combines the humor of folktale with the mystery of apocalyptic to create a message of hope and encouragement. Daniel himself is as much a mystery as the symbols in the book that bears his name: The earliest reference to a figure named Daniel is that of a Ugaritic king who lived in the fourteenth century BCE. Ezekiel 14.14 associates this king with Noah and Job: three non-Jewish individuals known for belief in the face of danger, wisdom in the face of foolishness. According to Ezek 28.3, Daniel is one who knows secrets. The Daniel of this prophetic book is similar in knowledge, fidelity, and circumstances; he is, however, emphatically Jewish.

Blending theological emphasis on personal piety and divine intervention with staples of folktales such as wise courtiers, endangered heroes, and foolish kings, the first six chapters entertain and edify even as they provide encouragement to Jews living as a minority under foreign rule. The accounts of Daniel and his friends, Jewish youths taken into Babylonian captivity, reflect a time in which the imperial rule is ignorant and often dangerous rather than malevolent, and in which Jews can live at peace with their non-Jewish neighbors, though perhaps not with a complete sense of security. Consequently, the tales are most often regarded as products of the Persian (539–333 BCE) or early Hellenistic (333–168) periods. Like Joseph, Daniel succeeds in service to the ruler through his ability to interpret dreams; like Mordecai in the book of Esther, he succeeds in foreign political service despite challenges by rival politicians.

These stories contrast with the apocalyptic materials in chs 7–12, which depict extreme hostility to foreign governments and which underscore ongoing universal tribulation rather than temporary personal danger. In this second section, Daniel is not the interpreter of visions but the visionary himself, and he is now in need of an angel's interpretive skills. In a series of dreams, he learns of the history of the Near East and Egypt from the Babylonian Empire, through Persian rule, to the time of Alexander the Great, and finally to the attacks against Judaism and Jerusalem by the Syrian-Greek ruler Antiochus IV Epiphanes. The increasingly detailed descriptions of the period following the division of Alexander's empire up to the Hellenization crisis under Antiochus in 167 BCE suggest that the apocalyptic sections were composed on the eve of the Maccabean revolt against the assimilationist policies of Antiochus and his allies in Jerusalem's priestly circles (see 1 Macc 1). The author may well have been one of the "wise men" who promulgated a counsel of nonviolence together with the expectation that God would punish the wicked and redeem the faithful (Dan 12.3). That the visions are presented pseudonymously, that is, under the name of an ancient figure who "foresees" what is to come, is typical of apocalypses (so also 2 Esdras, 2 Baruch, and later Christian texts such as the *Apocalypse of Peter*).

Daniel 2.4b–7.28 is written in Aramaic, the common language of the Near East from the time of the Babylonian exile until the conquests of Alexander the Great; 1.1–2.4a and chs 8–12 are in Hebrew, which by then had become largely the language of worship, not of ordinary discourse, of the Jews. Complicating the linguistic history of the volume are the Septuagint and Old Greek translations. These texts contain additions to the story of Daniel: Susanna, the Prayer of Azariah and the Song of the Three, and Bel and the Dragon. In this Bible these additional texts appear in the Apocryphal/Deuterocanonical Books. Still more books within the Danielic corpus appear among the documents discovered in 1948 at Qumran, the so-called Dead Sea Scrolls. One text, the Prayer of Nabonidus (4QprNab), may represent an earlier version of Dan 4; that Nabonidus engaged in erratic behavior, and that he rather than Nebuchadnezzar was the father of Belshazzar (Dan 5.1) make this supposition particularly intriguing.

The wisdom of the Jewish courtiers in negotiating the difficulties of living under an often arbitrary and dangerous foreign rule is juxtaposed with a vision of wars, persecutions, and, finally, salvation under God's sovereignty; through these images the book of Daniel offers to its readers both advice and consolation. The folktales speak to all peoples persecuted as religious and ethnic minorities, especially under conditions of colonial rule. The apocalyptic materials, whose meanings would have been known to the author's own circle, have provided for over two thousand years occasion for speculation and, often, hope.

1 In the third year of the reign of King
Jehoiakim of Judah, King Nebuchad-
nezzar of Babylon came to Jerusalem and
besieged it. 2 The Lord let King Jehoiakim
of Judah fall into his power, as well as some
of the vessels of the house of God. These he
brought to the land of Shinar,[a] and placed
the vessels in the treasury of his gods.
3 Then the king commanded his palace
master Ashpenaz to bring some of the Isra-
elites of the royal family and of the nobility,
4 young men without physical defect and
handsome, versed in every branch of wis-
dom, endowed with knowledge and in-
sight, and competent to serve in the king's
palace; they were to be taught the literature
and language of the Chaldeans. 5 The king
assigned them a daily portion of the royal
rations of food and wine. They were to be
educated for three years, so that at the end
of that time they could be stationed in the
king's court. 6 Among them were Daniel,
Hananiah, Mishael, and Azariah, from the
tribe of Judah. 7 The palace master gave
them other names: Daniel he called Belte-
shazzar, Hananiah he called Shadrach,
Mishael he called Meshach, and Azariah he
called Abednego.
8 But Daniel resolved that he would not

a Gk Theodotion: Heb adds *to the house of his own gods*

1.1–21: The Babylonian exile. This first chapter introduces the young courtier Daniel, his companions in exile, and the difficulties they will face as Jews in the foreign court. **1:** *Third year of the reign of King Jehoiakim* is 606 BCE (see 2 Chr 36.5–7). Jehoiakim's son, Jehoiachin, ruled when Jerusalem was captured in 586. Nebuchadnezzar reigned 605–562 BCE (see Isa 46.1; Jer 24.1; 25.1,9), but did not invade Israel until after 605. The difficulties of the dating cannot be resolved; such chronological problems are, rather, typical of folktales (see Jdt 1.1). **2:** *Shinar,* an ancient (Gen 14.1,9; Isa 11.11; Zech 5.11) term for Babylon, is the site of the tower of Babel (Gen 11.2); both tower and Babylon fall through the sin of pride. *His gods,* Marduk, Babylon's tutelary god, and Nabu, the king's personal deity; cf. Isa 46.1n. *Vessels,* noted in 2 Chr 36.7,10, foreshadow Belshazzar's feast (Dan 5).

1.3–7: Courtiers in exile. 3: *Palace master* (lit. "chief eunuch"). Nobility from conquered kingdoms were typically brought into exile (see 2 Kings 24.14–16); educating their youth was thought to increase acceptance of foreign rule and minimize attempts at revolt. **4:** *Without physical defect* may suggest priests (Lev 21.17–23) as well as sacrificial animals (Lev 22.19–22), or may simply indicate attractive men (Absalom in 2 Sam 14.25; Song 4.7). *Versed in every branch of wisdom* also describes the heroes of the author's generation (11.33,35; 12.3). *Chaldeans* can refer either to Aramaic-speaking Neo-Babylonian people (Jer 24.5; Ezek 1.3; Dan 5.30; 9.1; Ezra 5.12) or, more specifically, to magicians and astrologers (Dan 2.2–5,10; 4.7; 5.7,11). **5:** *Three years* are cited by Persian texts as the time required for gaining knowledge of religious concerns. **6–7:** The names contain "el," meaning (the Jewish) "God." All four names occur in the book of Nehemiah (8.4; 10.3,7,24) though referring to different individuals. The new names refer to the Babylonian gods Bel (Marduk; see 1.2n.) and Nabu. Changing names was a well-known practice of kings (Gen 41.45; 2 Kings 24.17). Fidelity is marked when those whose names are changed preserve their ethnic and religious identity (such as Joseph, Daniel).

1.8–21: The first resistance. 8: *Defile himself* by eating non-kosher food (see Lev 11); in the postexilic period, diet was a major indication of Jewish identity (Tob 1.10–11; 1 Macc 1.62–63; Jdt 10.5; 12.1–4;

defile himself with the royal rations of food
and wine; so he asked the palace master to
allow him not to defile himself. 9 Now God
allowed Daniel to receive favor and com-
passion from the palace master. 10 The pal-
ace master said to Daniel, "I am afraid of
my lord the king; he has appointed your
food and your drink. If he should see you in
poorer condition than the other young men
of your own age, you would endanger my
head with the king." 11 Then Daniel asked
the guard whom the palace master had ap-
pointed over Daniel, Hananiah, Mishael,
and Azariah: 12 "Please test your servants
for ten days. Let us be given vegetables to
eat and water to drink. 13 You can then
compare our appearance with the appear-
ance of the young men who eat the royal
rations, and deal with your servants ac-
cording to what you observe." 14 So he
agreed to this proposal and tested them for
ten days. 15 At the end of ten days it was
observed that they appeared better and fat-
ter than all the young men who had been
eating the royal rations. 16 So the guard
continued to withdraw their royal rations
and the wine they were to drink, and gave
them vegetables. 17 To these four young
men God gave knowledge and skill in every
aspect of literature and wisdom; Daniel
also had insight into all visions and dreams.
18 At the end of the time that the king
had set for them to be brought in, the pal-
ace master brought them into the presence
of Nebuchadnezzar, 19 and the king spoke
with them. And among them all, no one
was found to compare with Daniel, Hana-
niah, Mishael, and Azariah; therefore they
were stationed in the king's court. 20 In ev-
ery matter of wisdom and understanding
concerning which the king inquired of
them, he found them ten times better than
all the magicians and enchanters in his
whole kingdom. 21 And Daniel continued
there until the first year of King Cyrus.

2 In the second year of Nebuchadnezzar's
reign, Nebuchadnezzar dreamed such
dreams that his spirit was troubled and his
sleep left him. 2 So the king commanded
that the magicians, the enchanters, the sor-
cerers, and the Chaldeans be summoned to
tell the king his dreams. When they came in
and stood before the king, 3 he said to them,
"I have had such a dream that my spirit is
troubled by the desire to understand it."
4 The Chaldeans said to the king (in Arama-
ic),[a] "O king, live forever! Tell your ser-
vants the dream, and we will reveal the
interpretation." 5 The king answered the

a The text from this point to the end of chapter 7 is in Aramaic

2 Macc 6–7; Esth 14.17). Leviticus does not forbid *wine;* perhaps Daniel's refusal of *food and wine* symbolizes a refusal to feast when Israel is in exile. However, Hos 9.3–4 (also Ezek 4.13) suggests Gentile food is impure. **10:** *The palace master,* Ashpenaz (1.3) is one of several sympathetic court functionaries (Gen 41.9–13; Esth 2.15; Achior of the book of Judith). **12:** *Test your servants* suggests trial by ordeal, a stock folktale motif. *Vegetables . . . and water* are also food of the poor. **17:** God grants the youths what Nebuchadnezzar had sought to teach them (1.4). *Visions and dreams* associates Daniel with Joseph, another handsome youth who faces temptation and danger in a foreign land (Gen 39–50), as well as Mordecai of the Greek Additions to Esther. **20:** *Magicians* appear in the sagas of Joseph (Gen 41.8,24) and Moses and Aaron (Ex 7.11,22; 8.3,14–15; 9.11). *Enchanters* are priests who make incantations (Dan 2.2; 4.7; 5.7). **21:** *First year of King Cyrus* is 539 BCE.

2.1–12: Nebuchadnezzar's test. 1: *Second year* is 603 BCE; the inconsistency with 1.1, which claims Nebuchadnezzar had been ruling three years before bringing Daniel to Babylon, suggests that the chapters were composed separately. *Dreams,* especially those of kings, were regarded as portents (Gen 15.12; 20.3; 28.10–2; 37.5–10; 41.1–32; 1 Sam 3.3–5; Mt 27.19; Artimedorus's *Oneirocritica*). *His spirit was troubled* also describes Pharaoh in Gen 41.8; Daniel in turn resembles Joseph in the foreign court. **2:** *Magicians* and *Chaldeans,* see 1.4,20n.; they are not depicted favorably in biblical accounts. **4:** The greeting begins the Aramaic section; the book shifts back to Hebrew at 8.1. **5:** Nebuchadnezzar's insistence that the magicians *tell . . . the dream* as well as its interpretation tests their abilities; this hint of distrust anticipates his later celebration of Daniel's God. *Torn limb from limb* suggests the king's volatility (see also 3.29;

Chaldeans, "This is a public decree: if you
do not tell me both the dream and its inter-
pretation, you shall be torn limb from limb,
and your houses shall be laid in ruins. 6 But
if you do tell me the dream and its interpre-
tation, you shall receive from me gifts and
rewards and great honor. Therefore tell me
the dream and its interpretation." 7 They
answered a second time, "Let the king first
tell his servants the dream, then we can give
its interpretation." 8 The king answered, "I
know with certainty that you are trying to
gain time, because you see I have firmly
decreed: 9 if you do not tell me the dream,
there is but one verdict for you. You have
agreed to speak lying and misleading words
to me until things take a turn. Therefore,
tell me the dream, and I shall know that
you can give me its interpretation." 10 The
Chaldeans answered the king, "There is no
one on earth who can reveal what the king
demands! In fact no king, however great
and powerful, has ever asked such a thing
of any magician or enchanter or Chaldean.
11 The thing that the king is asking is too
difficult, and no one can reveal it to the
king except the gods, whose dwelling is not
with mortals."

12 Because of this the king flew into a
violent rage and commanded that all the
wise men of Babylon be destroyed. 13 The
decree was issued, and the wise men were
about to be executed; and they looked for
Daniel and his companions, to execute
them. 14 Then Daniel responded with pru-
dence and discretion to Arioch, the king's
chief executioner, who had gone out to exe-
cute the wise men of Babylon; 15 he asked
Arioch, the royal official, "Why is the de-
cree of the king so urgent?" Arioch then
explained the matter to Daniel. 16 So Daniel
went in and requested that the king give
him time and he would tell the king the
interpretation.

17 Then Daniel went to his home and
informed his companions, Hananiah,
Mishael, and Azariah, 18 and told them to
seek mercy from the God of heaven con-
cerning this mystery, so that Daniel and his
companions with the rest of the wise men
of Babylon might not perish. 19 Then the
mystery was revealed to Daniel in a vision
of the night, and Daniel blessed the God of
heaven.

20 Daniel said:

"Blessed be the name of God from
age to age,
for wisdom and power are his.
21 He changes times and seasons,
deposes kings and sets up kings;

2 Macc 1.16); Ezra 6.11 depicts Darius's edict threatening destruction of *houses*. Under such a ruler, Daniel and his companions can never be assured of their own safety. **11:** The Chaldeans' admission coupled with their failure to pray to their own gods contrasts with Daniel's faith. **12:** Perhaps a hint of Nebuchadnezzar's later irrationality (Dan 4).

2.13–19: Daniel seeks divine aid. This section suggests that Daniel and his colleagues were not present at the earlier meeting with the king. **14:** *Arioch* is elsewhere unattested although his name appears in Gen 14.1; Jdt 1.6; like Ashpenaz (1.10), he is willing to disregard the king's orders to help Daniel. **16:** Daniel's access to Nebuchadnezzar contrasts with 2.24, where he requires Arioch's intervention. This discrepancy, coupled with the reintroduction of Daniel's companions in 2.17, suggests to some scholars that 2.13–23 is a later addition to the story. **17:** The companions are introduced in 1.6–7. **18:** *God of heaven* is a common phrase from the Persian and Hellenistic periods (Dan 2.19,37,44; Ezra 1.2; 5.11–12; 6.9–10; 7.12,21,23; Neh 1.4–5; 2.4,20; Jon 1.9; Tob 10.1; Jdt 5.8; 6.19; 11.17); its universalistic implications befit accounts set in exile. *Mystery* (2.19,27–30; 4.9), a term found frequently in the scrolls from Qumran (Dead Sea Scrolls), indicates a secret that can be learned through divine wisdom. **19:** Appropriately, Daniel receives a vision of the night (Dan 7.2; Gen 46.2; Zech 1.8) for interpreting Nebuchadnezzar's dream.

2.20–23: Daniel's doxology. This short psalm (see Ps 36.9; 41.13; 106.48; 139.11–12) emphasizes the divine as the repository of wisdom (see also Prov 2.6; Isa 60.19–20; Hab 3.4; Job 12.13). Hymns and prayers are frequently inserted into postexilic narratives (Esther [Gk], Judith, Tobit). **21:** *Deposes kings*, a traditional attribute (Job 12.9,22–23; Lk 1.47–55) in this context foreshadows the end of Nebuchad-

he gives wisdom to the wise
and knowledge to those who have
understanding.
22 He reveals deep and hidden things;
he knows what is in the darkness,
and light dwells with him.
23 To you, O God of my ancestors,
I give thanks and praise,
for you have given me wisdom
and power,
and have now revealed to me what
we asked of you,
for you have revealed to us what
the king ordered."

24 Therefore Daniel went to Arioch,
whom the king had appointed to destroy
the wise men of Babylon, and said to him,
"Do not destroy the wise men of Babylon;
bring me in before the king, and I will give
the king the interpretation."

25 Then Arioch quickly brought Daniel
before the king and said to him: "I have
found among the exiles from Judah a man
who can tell the king the interpretation."
26 The king said to Daniel, whose name was
Belteshazzar, "Are you able to tell me the
dream that I have seen and its interpreta-
tion?" 27 Daniel answered the king, "No
wise men, enchanters, magicians, or divin-
ers can show to the king the mystery that
the king is asking, 28 but there is a God in
heaven who reveals mysteries, and he has
disclosed to King Nebuchadnezzar what
will happen at the end of days. Your dream
and the visions of your head as you lay in
bed were these: 29 To you, O king, as you
lay in bed, came thoughts of what would be
hereafter, and the revealer of mysteries dis-
closed to you what is to be. 30 But as for me,
this mystery has not been revealed to me
because of any wisdom that I have more
than any other living being, but in order
that the interpretation may be known to
the king and that you may understand the
thoughts of your mind.

31 "You were looking, O king, and lo!
there was a great statue. This statue was
huge, its brilliance extraordinary; it was
standing before you, and its appearance
was frightening. 32 The head of that statue
was of fine gold, its chest and arms of sil-
ver, its middle and thighs of bronze, 33 its
legs of iron, its feet partly of iron and partly
of clay. 34 As you looked on, a stone was
cut out, not by human hands, and it struck
the statue on its feet of iron and clay and
broke them in pieces. 35 Then the iron, the
clay, the bronze, the silver, and the gold,
were all broken in pieces and became like
the chaff of the summer threshing floors;
and the wind carried them away, so that
not a trace of them could be found. But the
stone that struck the statue became a great
mountain and filled the whole earth.

36 "This was the dream; now we will
tell the king its interpretation. 37 You,

nezzar's reign. **23:** *God of my ancestors,* a traditional epithet (Deut 1.21; 6.3; 12.1) here emphasizes Daniel's continuity with his community even in exile.

2.24–30: Daniel approaches the king. 24–25: See 2.14–16. Arioch trusts Daniel's powers; perhaps readers are to recall the less extreme miracle of 1.12–15. **26:** *Belteshazzar,* see 1.7. **27:** Daniel distinguishes his powers from that of foreign wisdom (see Isa 44.25; 47.13 on Babylonian divination). **28:** *End of days* is here the distant future (Dan 10.14; Isa 2.2; Jer 23.20; Ezek 38.16; Hos 3.5). **29–30:** The true *revealer of mysteries* is God (cf. Gen 41.16). Daniel gives God full credit, but the effect of the revelation is nonetheless that Daniel will be promoted.

2.31–35: Nebuchadnezzar's dream. 31: Giant figures frequent ancient Near Eastern dream records; there were also several famous giant statues. **32–33:** The metals are of decreasing worth. The descent from the golden age through silver, bronze, and iron periods appears in Greek (Hesiod, *Works and Days*), Latin (Ovid, *Metamorphosis*) and Persian (*Bahman Yasht*) writing (see also 2 Esd 7.55–56). **33:** *Clay* is unexpected and potentially humorous, for this weakest substance is to support the weightier metals. **34:** *A stone was cut out, not by human hands* both indicates divine control of history and signals that precious metals will ultimately be of no value. **35:** *A great mountain* may suggest Sinai (Deut 32), Zion (Ps 36.6; Isa 8.14; 11.9–10; Ezek 17.22–24), or the covenant community; see also 2.45.

2.36–45: Daniel's first interpretation. 37–38: Elaborating Nebuchadnezzar's powers, Daniel actually

O king, the king of kings—to whom the
God of heaven has given the kingdom, the
power, the might, and the glory, 38 into
whose hand he has given human beings,
wherever they live, the wild animals of the
field, and the birds of the air, and whom he
has established as ruler over them all—you
are the head of gold. 39 After you shall arise
another kingdom inferior to yours, and yet
a third kingdom of bronze, which shall rule
over the whole earth. 40 And there shall be
a fourth kingdom, strong as iron; just as
iron crushes and smashes everything,[a] it
shall crush and shatter all these. 41 As you
saw the feet and toes partly of potter's clay
and partly of iron, it shall be a divided
kingdom; but some of the strength of iron
shall be in it, as you saw the iron mixed
with the clay. 42 As the toes of the feet were
part iron and part clay, so the kingdom
shall be partly strong and partly brittle.
43 As you saw the iron mixed with clay, so
will they mix with one another in mar-
riage,[b] but they will not hold together, just
as iron does not mix with clay. 44 And in
the days of those kings the God of heaven
will set up a kingdom that shall never be
destroyed, nor shall this kingdom be left to
another people. It shall crush all these king-
doms and bring them to an end, and it shall
stand forever; 45 just as you saw that a
stone was cut from the mountain not by
hands, and that it crushed the iron, the
bronze, the clay, the silver, and the gold.
The great God has informed the king what
shall be hereafter. The dream is certain, and
its interpretation trustworthy."

46 Then King Nebuchadnezzar fell on
his face, worshiped Daniel, and command-
ed that a grain offering and incense be of-
fered to him. 47 The king said to Daniel,
"Truly, your God is God of gods and Lord
of kings and a revealer of mysteries, for you
have been able to reveal this mystery!"
48 Then the king promoted Daniel, gave
him many great gifts, and made him ruler
over the whole province of Babylon and
chief prefect over all the wise men of Bab-
ylon. 49 Daniel made a request of the king,
and he appointed Shadrach, Meshach, and
Abednego over the affairs of the province
of Babylon. But Daniel remained at the
king's court.

3 King Nebuchadnezzar made a golden
statue whose height was sixty cubits

a Gk Theodotion Syr Vg: Aram adds *and like iron that crushes* *b* Aram *by human seed*

celebrates the rule of his God. **37:** *King of kings* is used for Nebuchadnezzar in Ezek 26.7. **38:** Interpreting the dream allegorically, Daniel equates Nebuchadnezzar, and by extension Babylon (probably indicating the Neo-Babylonian empire), with gold. **39–44:** The other kingdoms, although not named, are probably Media (silver), Persia (bronze), and Greece (iron and clay). This four-fold pattern of kingdoms appears also in *Sibylline Oracles* 4, Babylonian and Greek writings, and Qumran scrolls (4QPseudoDan). **41:** *A divided kingdom* is the division of Alexander the Great's empire among his four generals. Judea fell under Ptolemaic (Egyptian) control during 323–198 BCE, and then, until Maccabean rule in 163, under Seleucid (Syrian-Greek) control. **43:** *In marriage* (lit. "by human seed"), intermarriage between Ptolemaic and Seleucid dynasties in 252 and again in 194/93 BCE (see also Dan 11.6n.,17) did not prevent conflict. **44:** *A kingdom that shall never be destroyed* is Israel, the Jews, who retained their identity despite political changes. **45:** *Cut from the mountain* contrasts 2.35, where the stone became a mountain. The image of Israel as a stone occurs in Isa 51.1 (cf. 28.16); Ps 118.22; Christian interpretation will associate the stone with the Christ (Lk 20.18) and, later, the church.

2.46–49: Daniel's promotion. 46: *Worshiped,* along with offerings of grain and incense, suggests Nebuchadnezzar viewed Daniel as divine (see Dan 3.5–7,10,15; Isa 44.15–19; 46.6). **47:** *Your God,* Nebuchadnezzar respects Daniel's God, but he is not a convert. Compare the death-bed promises of Antiochus IV Epiphanes in 2 Macc 9.17. **48:** *Made him ruler* is reminiscent of Joseph (Gen 41.37–45; see also Esth 8.1–2). **49:** Daniel's concern for his colleagues anticipates 3.12.

3.1–7: The golden statue. 1: Free-standing, enormous golden statues are known from ancient Egypt and Mesopotamia; Herodotus (fifth century BCE) mentions a golden statue of Zeus (Bel?) in Babylon. Sixty cubits by 6 cubits (the Babylonians used a sexagesimal numerical system) is approximately

and whose width was six cubits; he set it up
on the plain of Dura in the province of Bab-
ylon. 2Then King Nebuchadnezzar sent for
the satraps, the prefects, and the governors,
the counselors, the treasurers, the justices,
the magistrates, and all the officials of the
provinces, to assemble and come to the
dedication of the statue that King Nebu-
chadnezzar had set up. 3So the satraps, the
prefects, and the governors, the counselors,
the treasurers, the justices, the magistrates,
and all the officials of the provinces, assem-
bled for the dedication of the statue that
King Nebuchadnezzar had set up. When
they were standing before the statue that
Nebuchadnezzar had set up, 4the herald
proclaimed aloud, "You are commanded,
O peoples, nations, and languages, 5that
when you hear the sound of the horn, pipe,
lyre, trigon, harp, drum, and entire musical
ensemble, you are to fall down and worship
the golden statue that King Nebuchadnez-
zar has set up. 6Whoever does not fall
down and worship shall immediately be
thrown into a furnace of blazing fire."
7Therefore, as soon as all the peoples heard
the sound of the horn, pipe, lyre, trigon,
harp, drum, and entire musical ensemble,
all the peoples, nations, and languages fell
down and worshiped the golden statue that
King Nebuchadnezzar had set up.

8 Accordingly, at this time certain Chal-
deans came forward and denounced the
Jews. 9They said to King Nebuchadnezzar,
"O king, live forever! 10You, O king, have
made a decree, that everyone who hears the
sound of the horn, pipe, lyre, trigon, harp,
drum, and entire musical ensemble, shall
fall down and worship the golden statue,
11and whoever does not fall down and
worship shall be thrown into a furnace of
blazing fire. 12There are certain Jews whom
you have appointed over the affairs of the
province of Babylon: Shadrach, Meshach,
and Abednego. These pay no heed to you,
O king. They do not serve your gods and
they do not worship the golden statue that
you have set up."

13 Then Nebuchadnezzar in furious
rage commanded that Shadrach, Meshach,
and Abednego be brought in; so they
brought those men before the king. 14Neb-
uchadnezzar said to them, "Is it true,
O Shadrach, Meshach, and Abednego, that
you do not serve my gods and you do not
worship the golden statue that I have set
up? 15Now if you are ready when you hear
the sound of the horn, pipe, lyre, trigon,
harp, drum, and entire musical ensemble to
fall down and worship the statue that I
have made, well and good.[a] But if you
do not worship, you shall immediately be
thrown into a furnace of blazing fire, and

a Aram lacks *well and good*

30 x 3 m, or 90 x 9 ft; ten times as high as wide, the statue was likely an obelisk or stele (if it could stand at all). The exaggerated dimensions may be an element of folktale style. *Dura* means "fortress" and need not suggest a specific place. **2–3:** Repetition of officers, a folkloric motif, indicates the (almost) universal acceptance of Nebuchadnezzar's order. **5:** The list of instruments, reprised in 3.7,10,15, echoes the hyperbole. Several of the terms are Greek loan words. *Pipes* may be peasant instruments and *lyres* instruments of the aristocracy; if so, Nebuchadnezzar's order crosses economic classes as well as ethnic groups. Jews faithful to their law could not obey the command. **6:** The *furnace,* or flames, was sometimes used for capital crimes (Jer 29.10; 2 Macc 13.4–8); it also functions as a symbol of testing and purifying (Deut 4.20; Isa 48.10). The folktale scenario anticipates the policies of Antiochus IV Epiphanes, one of the earliest instances of governmental persecution for refusing to worship the state's god.

3.8–15: The youths accused. 8: *Chaldeans,* see 1.4n. *Denounced,* lit. "ate the pieces of," indicates maliciousness and professional jealousy. **10:** The by-now humorous repetition decreases the threat of the story. **12:** Ethnic prejudice surfaces again in Esth 5.8. **13–15:** Nebuchadnezzar's questioning repeats the law, again. **15:** *Who is the god* may suggest that this story did not originally follow Dan 2, in which the king acknowledges the power of Daniel's God, or that Nebuchadnezzar is at best foolish; in either case, statements by foreign rulers of sympathy for Jews and their God are not seen to endure. See also 2 Kings 19.19,28–35; Isa 36.13–20; 37.8–13.

who is the god that will deliver you out of
my hands?"
16 Shadrach, Meshach, and Abednego
answered the king, "O Nebuchadnezzar,
we have no need to present a defense to you
in this matter. 17 If our God whom we serve
is able to deliver us from the furnace of
blazing fire and out of your hand, O king,
let him deliver us.[a] 18 But if not, be it
known to you, O king, that we will not
serve your gods and we will not worship
the golden statue that you have set up."
19 Then Nebuchadnezzar was so filled
with rage against Shadrach, Meshach, and
Abednego that his face was distorted. He
ordered the furnace heated up seven times
more than was customary, 20 and ordered
some of the strongest guards in his army to
bind Shadrach, Meshach, and Abednego
and to throw them into the furnace of blaz-
ing fire. 21 So the men were bound, still
wearing their tunics,[b] their trousers,[b]
their hats, and their other garments, and
they were thrown into the furnace of blaz-
ing fire. 22 Because the king's command was
urgent and the furnace was so overheated,
the raging flames killed the men who lifted
Shadrach, Meshach, and Abednego. 23 But
the three men, Shadrach, Meshach, and
Abednego, fell down, bound, into the fur-
nace of blazing fire.
24 Then King Nebuchadnezzar was as-
tonished and rose up quickly. He said to his
counselors, "Was it not three men that we
threw bound into the fire?" They answered
the king, "True, O king." 25 He replied,
"But I see four men unbound, walking in
the middle of the fire, and they are not hurt;
and the fourth has the appearance of a
god."[c] 26 Nebuchadnezzar then ap-
proached the door of the furnace of blazing
fire and said, "Shadrach, Meshach, and
Abednego, servants of the Most High God,
come out! Come here!" So Shadrach, Me-
shach, and Abednego came out from the
fire. 27 And the satraps, the prefects, the
governors, and the king's counselors gath-
ered together and saw that the fire had not
had any power over the bodies of those
men; the hair of their heads was not singed,
their tunics[b] were not harmed, and not
even the smell of fire came from them.
28 Nebuchadnezzar said, "Blessed be the
God of Shadrach, Meshach, and Abednego,
who has sent his angel and delivered his
servants who trusted in him. They dis-
obeyed the king's command and yielded up
their bodies rather than serve and worship
any god except their own God. 29 Therefore
I make a decree: Any people, nation, or lan-
guage that utters blasphemy against the
God of Shadrach, Meshach, and Abednego
shall be torn limb from limb, and their

a Or *If our God whom we serve is able to deliver us, he will deliver us from the furnace of blazing fire and out of your hand, O king.* *b* Meaning of Aram word uncertain *c* Aram *a son of the gods*

3.16–18: Resistance. 16: The refusal to respond continues the theme of Jewish resistance and Nebuchadnezzar's ultimate powerlessness. **17–18:** Anticipating later martyrs, the youths assert their loyalty regardless of their fate (1 Macc 1; 2; 7).

3.19–27: The furnace. 19: Nebuchadnezzar's response continues to indicate lack of control. **21:** Mention of clothing (the Aramaic has a rhythmic quality appropriate to folktales) foreshadows 3.27. **22:** The king's anger leads to his own soldiers' deaths; meanwhile, not only are the Jews saved, their clothes do not even smell of smoke (v. 27). **23:** The Septuagint, Eastern Orthodox, and Roman Catholic Bibles insert here the Prayer of Azariah and the Song of the Three; Protestant tradition places the text in the Old Testament Apocrypha. **25:** The king is first to see the mysterious fourth figure. *Has the appearance of a god* (lit. "son of God") implies an angel (Gen 6.2; Ex 14.19; 23.20; 1 Kings 22.10; Job 1.6; 38.7; Ps 148.2; see also the "men" who aided Judas Maccabeus in 2 Macc 10.29–31). **26:** *Most High God,* Nebuchadnezzar answers the question he posed in 3.15. **27:** The details enhance the miracle and evoke Isa 43.2.

3.28–30: Nebuchadnezzar's acknowledgment. 28: Ironically, the king celebrates that the youths *disobeyed the king's command.* His reaction, similar to those of 2.47; 4.37; and 6.26–27, is, in the context of the book, only temporarily good news. **29:** Historically unlikely, the decree follows official form (see Ezra 6.6–12). **30:** The Jews achieve political success; at this point, the three disappear from the story.

houses laid in ruins; for there is no other
god who is able to deliver in this way."
30 Then the king promoted Shadrach, Me-
shach, and Abednego in the province of
Babylon.

4 [a]King Nebuchadnezzar to all peoples,
nations, and languages that live
throughout the earth: May you have abun-
dant prosperity! 2 The signs and wonders
that the Most High God has worked for me
I am pleased to recount.

3 How great are his signs,
how mighty his wonders!
His kingdom is an everlasting
kingdom,
and his sovereignty is from
generation to generation.

4[b]I, Nebuchadnezzar, was living at ease
in my home and prospering in my palace. 5 I
saw a dream that frightened me; my fanta-
sies in bed and the visions of my head terri-
fied me. 6 So I made a decree that all the
wise men of Babylon should be brought be-
fore me, in order that they might tell me the
interpretation of the dream. 7 Then the ma-
gicians, the enchanters, the Chaldeans, and
the diviners came in, and I told them the
dream, but they could not tell me its inter-
pretation. 8 At last Daniel came in before
me—he who was named Belteshazzar after
the name of my god, and who is endowed
with a spirit of the holy gods[c]—and I told
him the dream: 9 "O Belteshazzar, chief of
the magicians, I know that you are en-
dowed with a spirit of the holy gods[c] and
that no mystery is too difficult for you.
Hear[d] the dream that I saw; tell me its
interpretation.

10[e]Upon my bed this is what I saw;
there was a tree at the center of the
earth,
and its height was great.
11 The tree grew great and strong,
its top reached to heaven,
and it was visible to the ends of the
whole earth.
12 Its foliage was beautiful,
its fruit abundant,
and it provided food for all.
The animals of the field found shade
under it,
the birds of the air nested in
its branches,
and from it all living beings
were fed.

13 "I continued looking, in the visions
of my head as I lay in bed, and there was a
holy watcher, coming down from heaven.
14 He cried aloud and said:

'Cut down the tree and chop off
its branches,
strip off its foliage and scatter
its fruit.
Let the animals flee from beneath it
and the birds from its branches.
15 But leave its stump and roots in the
ground,

a Ch 3.31 in Aram *b* Ch 4.1 in Aram *c* Or *a holy, divine spirit* *d* Theodotion: Aram *The visions of* *e* Theodotion Syr Compare Gk: Aram adds *The visions of my head*

4.1–3: Nebuchadnezzar's doxology. 4.1–37 is composed as a letter to the Babylonian Empire. **3:** The traditional doxology evokes the king's earlier (2.47; 3.28–29) confession. *His kingdom* contrasts Nebuchadnezzar's Babylon; *his sovereignty,* a frequent term in Dan 1–7, contrasts with Nebuchadnezzar's imminent removal from his throne.

4.4–18: The king's vision. 5: The *dream* recollects Dan 2; *visions* anticipates the apocalyptic passages of Dan 7–12. **7:** As in Dan 2, the non-Jewish courtiers are unable to solve mysteries. **8:** *Belteshazzar* probably derives from a Babylonian expression meaning "guard his life." The implicit connection to Bel and reference to the *holy gods* contrasts with the letter's opening praise of the "Most High God" (4.2). For Daniel's Babylonian name, see 1.7. **9:** See 1.20; 2.47. **10:** *A tree at the center of the earth* evokes cross-cultural myths of the center of the world and also symbolizes the king's self-image as the one who provides food and shelter (4.22; see also Ezek 17; 31). **11:** *Reached to heaven* suggests the Tower of Babel (see 1.2n.). **13:** *Holy watcher* (4.17,23; also Dan 8.13 as well as *Jubilees* and 1 Enoch) indicates an angel. **14:** *Animals* and *birds* likely represent the peoples of the empire. **15:** With *let him* the symbolism changes from tree to beast. **16:** The king becomes insane. *Seven times* probably means seven years (see Dan 7.25).

with a band of iron and bronze,
in the tender grass of the field.
Let him be bathed with the dew
of heaven,
and let his lot be with the animals
of the field
in the grass of the earth.
16 Let his mind be changed from that of
a human,
and let the mind of an animal be
given to him.
And let seven times pass over him.
17 The sentence is rendered by decree of
the watchers,
the decision is given by order of the
holy ones,
in order that all who live may know
that the Most High is sovereign
over the kingdom of mortals;
he gives it to whom he will
and sets over it the lowliest of
human beings.'

18 "This is the dream that I, King Nebu-
chadnezzar, saw. Now you, Belteshazzar,
declare the interpretation, since all the wise
men of my kingdom are unable to tell me
the interpretation. You are able, however,
for you are endowed with a spirit of the
holy gods."[a]
19 Then Daniel, who was called Belte-
shazzar, was severely distressed for a while.
His thoughts terrified him. The king said,
"Belteshazzar, do not let the dream or the
interpretation terrify you." Belteshazzar
answered, "My lord, may the dream be for
those who hate you, and its interpretation
for your enemies! 20 The tree that you saw,
which grew great and strong, so that its top
reached to heaven and was visible to the
end of the whole earth, 21 whose foliage
was beautiful and its fruit abundant, and
which provided food for all, under which
animals of the field lived, and in whose
branches the birds of the air had nests—
22 it is you, O king! You have grown great
and strong. Your greatness has increased
and reaches to heaven, and your sovereign-
ty to the ends of the earth. 23 And whereas
the king saw a holy watcher coming down
from heaven and saying, 'Cut down the tree
and destroy it, but leave its stump and roots
in the ground, with a band of iron and
bronze, in the grass of the field; and let him
be bathed with the dew of heaven, and let
his lot be with the animals of the field, until
seven times pass over him'— 24 this is the
interpretation, O king, and it is a decree of
the Most High that has come upon my lord
the king: 25 You shall be driven away from
human society, and your dwelling shall be
with the wild animals. You shall be made
to eat grass like oxen, you shall be bathed
with the dew of heaven, and seven times
shall pass over you, until you have learned
that the Most High has sovereignty over
the kingdom of mortals, and gives it to
whom he will. 26 As it was commanded to
leave the stump and roots of the tree, your
kingdom shall be re-established for you
from the time that you learn that Heaven is
sovereign. 27 Therefore, O king, may my
counsel be acceptable to you: atone for[b]
your sins with righteousness, and your iniq-
uities with mercy to the oppressed, so that
your prosperity may be prolonged."
28 All this came upon King Nebuchad-
nezzar. 29 At the end of twelve months he
was walking on the roof of the royal palace
of Babylon, 30 and the king said, "Is this not
magnificent Babylon, which I have built as

a Or *a holy, divine spirit*   *b* Aram *break off*

4.19–27: Daniel's second interpretation. 19: Whether Daniel is *distressed* because he is unsure of the interpretation or because he is shocked by it is not immediately clear. **20–22:** The repetition of the tree's greatness may indicate either sympathy or satire. **22:** For people symbolized by trees, see Ps 1.3; 37.35; Jer 17.8. **26:** *Heaven* as a circumlocution for God is common in the Apocrypha and the Gospel of Matthew, but appears only here in Hebrew and Aramaic biblical texts. **27:** Charity is an appropriate means of atoning for sins against humanity. Daniel thus becomes Nebuchadnezzar's spiritual adviser.

4.28–33: Nebuchadnezzar's punishment. 30: The king's prideful statements serve as a catalyst for his fall (see Ezek 31.10). **31:** The *voice . . . from heaven,* an increasingly common motif in the Second Temple

a royal capital by my mighty power and for
my glorious majesty?" 31 While the words
were still in the king's mouth, a voice came
from heaven: "O King Nebuchadnezzar, to
you it is declared: The kingdom has depart-
ed from you! 32 You shall be driven away
from human society, and your dwelling
shall be with the animals of the field. You
shall be made to eat grass like oxen, and
seven times shall pass over you, until you
have learned that the Most High has sover-
eignty over the kingdom of mortals and
gives it to whom he will." 33 Immediately
the sentence was fulfilled against Nebu-
chadnezzar. He was driven away from hu-
man society, ate grass like oxen, and his
body was bathed with the dew of heaven,
until his hair grew as long as eagles' feath-
ers and his nails became like birds' claws.
34 When that period was over, I, Nebu-
chadnezzar, lifted my eyes to heaven, and
my reason returned to me.

I blessed the Most High,
and praised and honored the one
who lives forever.
For his sovereignty is an everlasting
sovereignty,
and his kingdom endures from
generation to generation.
35 All the inhabitants of the earth are
accounted as nothing,
and he does what he wills with the
host of heaven
and the inhabitants of the earth.
There is no one who can stay
his hand
or say to him, "What are you
doing?"

36 At that time my reason returned to me;
and my majesty and splendor were restored
to me for the glory of my kingdom. My
counselors and my lords sought me out, I
was re-established over my kingdom, and
still more greatness was added to me.
37 Now I, Nebuchadnezzar, praise and ex-
tol and honor the King of heaven,
for all his works are truth,
and his ways are justice;
and he is able to bring low
those who walk in pride.

5 King Belshazzar made a great festival
for a thousand of his lords, and he was
drinking wine in the presence of the thou-
sand.

2 Under the influence of the wine, Bel-
shazzar commanded that they bring in the
vessels of gold and silver that his father
Nebuchadnezzar had taken out of the tem-
ple in Jerusalem, so that the king and his
lords, his wives, and his concubines might
drink from them. 3 So they brought in the
vessels of gold and silver[a] that had been
taken out of the temple, the house of God
in Jerusalem, and the king and his lords,
his wives, and his concubines drank from
them. 4 They drank the wine and praised
the gods of gold and silver, bronze, iron,
wood, and stone.
5 Immediately the fingers of a human

a Theodotion Vg: Aram lacks *and silver*

period, can offer either good or distressing news (Mt 3.17; Mk 1.11; Lk 3.22; many instances in rabbinic texts). **32–33:** Although no sources indicate the banishment of Nebuchadnezzar, the later Babylonian king, Nabonidus, inexplicably left Babylon to spend several years in north Arabia; from the Qumran scrolls, the Prayer of Nabonidus records the king's seven years of illness and his cure by a Jewish exorcist. **33:** Nebuchadnezzar's description may anticipate the human-like beasts of Daniel's apocalyptic visions (Dan 7–12).

4.34–37: Restoration. Vv. 34–35 echo and expand upon the opening doxology (4.3). See also 2.20–21; 6.26–27. This king's affirmation does not influence his "son," Belshazzar (5.2).

5.1–9: The handwriting on the wall. 1: *Belshazzar* was actually the son of Nabonidus, not Nebuchadnezzar. He served as regent during his father Nabonidus's absence (see 4.32–33n.). The banquet is a standard motif in Second Temple literature (see esp. Esther). **2:** Lacking a statue of Israel's God to symbolize their conquest, the Babylonians took ritual vessels (1.2; Ezra 5.14; 6.5). **4:** The scene is one of sacrilegious debauchery; the Greek historians Xenophon and Herodotus also describe such dissipation at the time of Babylon's fall. **5:** Although the writing appears in public, only Belshazzar is alarmed; cf. 3.25.

hand appeared and began writing on the plaster of the wall of the royal palace, next to the lampstand. The king was watching the hand as it wrote. 6 Then the king's face turned pale, and his thoughts terrified him. His limbs gave way, and his knees knocked together. 7 The king cried aloud to bring in the enchanters, the Chaldeans, and the diviners; and the king said to the wise men of Babylon, "Whoever can read this writing and tell me its interpretation shall be clothed in purple, have a chain of gold around his neck, and rank third in the kingdom." 8 Then all the king's wise men came in, but they could not read the writing or tell the king the interpretation. 9 Then King Belshazzar became greatly terrified and his face turned pale, and his lords were perplexed.

10 The queen, when she heard the discussion of the king and his lords, came into the banqueting hall. The queen said, "O king, live forever! Do not let your thoughts terrify you or your face grow pale. 11 There is a man in your kingdom who is endowed with a spirit of the holy gods.[a] In the days of your father he was found to have enlightenment, understanding, and wisdom like the wisdom of the gods. Your father, King Nebuchadnezzar, made him chief of the magicians, enchanters, Chaldeans, and diviners,[b] 12 because an excellent spirit, knowledge, and understanding to interpret dreams, explain riddles, and solve problems were found in this Daniel, whom the king named Belteshazzar. Now let Daniel be called, and he will give the interpretation."

13 Then Daniel was brought in before the king. The king said to Daniel, "So you are Daniel, one of the exiles of Judah, whom my father the king brought from Judah? 14 I have heard of you that a spirit of the gods[c] is in you, and that enlightenment, understanding, and excellent wisdom are found in you. 15 Now the wise men, the enchanters, have been brought in before me to read this writing and tell me its interpretation, but they were not able to give the interpretation of the matter. 16 But I have heard that you can give interpretations and solve problems. Now if you are able to read the writing and tell me its interpretation, you shall be clothed in purple, have a chain of gold around your neck, and rank third in the kingdom."

17 Then Daniel answered in the presence of the king, "Let your gifts be for yourself, or give your rewards to someone else! Nevertheless I will read the writing to the king and let him know the interpretation. 18 O king, the Most High God gave your father Nebuchadnezzar kingship, greatness, glory, and majesty. 19 And because of the greatness that he gave him, all peoples, nations, and languages trembled and feared before him. He killed those he wanted to kill, kept alive those he wanted to keep alive, honored those he wanted to honor, and degraded those he wanted to degrade. 20 But when his heart was lifted up and his spirit was hardened so that he acted proudly, he was deposed from his kingly

a Or *a holy, divine spirit* *b* Aram adds *the king your father* *c* Or *a divine spirit*

7: Like Nebuchadnezzar, Belshazzar summons Babylon's wise men; those familiar with the previous chapters can anticipate the magicians' failure and Daniel's success. *Rank third,* after the king and crown prince (see 2.48).

5.10–12: The queen's intervention. Like Ashpenaz (1.9) and Arioch (2.25), the queen—the only woman to speak in the book—recognizes Daniel's worth. The account may reflect knowledge of Nebuchadnezzar's wife who, according to Herodotus, had exceptional wisdom and political ability. She, as queen-mother, knows of Daniel's abilities and rank but Belshazzar does not (cf. Ex 1.8); Daniel, as representative of the Jews in exile, continually has to demonstrate the power of his God.

5.13–31: Deciphering the handwriting. 13: Reference to the *exile* makes a fitting start to a chapter that concludes with the fall of Babylon (5.30). **14:** *Spirit of the gods* shows Belshazzar's lack of familiarity with Daniel's faith. **17:** Daniel disdains the offer, although later he appears to accept it (5.29). **18–21:** Recollects 4.30–37. **22:** Belshazzar's memory is selective, as was Nebuchadnezzar's (Dan 3). **25:** *MENE* (Heb

throne, and his glory was stripped from
him. 21 He was driven from human society,
and his mind was made like that of an ani-
mal. His dwelling was with the wild asses,
he was fed grass like oxen, and his body
was bathed with the dew of heaven, until
he learned that the Most High God has sov-
ereignty over the kingdom of mortals, and
sets over it whomever he will. 22 And you,
Belshazzar his son, have not humbled your
heart, even though you knew all this!
23 You have exalted yourself against the
Lord of heaven! The vessels of his temple
have been brought in before you, and you
and your lords, your wives and your concu-
bines have been drinking wine from them.
You have praised the gods of silver and
gold, of bronze, iron, wood, and stone,
which do not see or hear or know; but the
God in whose power is your very breath,
and to whom belong all your ways, you
have not honored.
24 "So from his presence the hand was
sent and this writing was inscribed. 25 And
this is the writing that was inscribed: MENE,
MENE, TEKEL, and PARSIN. 26 This is the in-
terpretation of the matter: MENE, God has
numbered the days of[a] your kingdom and
brought it to an end; 27 TEKEL, you have
been weighed on the scales and found
wanting; 28 PERES,[b] your kingdom is divid-
ed and given to the Medes and Persians."
29 Then Belshazzar gave the command,
and Daniel was clothed in purple, a chain
of gold was put around his neck, and a
proclamation was made concerning him
that he should rank third in the kingdom.
30 That very night Belshazzar, the Chal-
dean king, was killed. 31 [c] And Darius the
Mede received the kingdom, being about
sixty-two years old.

6 It pleased Darius to set over the king-
dom one hundred twenty satraps, sta-
tioned throughout the whole kingdom,
2 and over them three presidents, including
Daniel; to these the satraps gave account,
so that the king might suffer no loss. 3 Soon
Daniel distinguished himself above all the
other presidents and satraps because an ex-
cellent spirit was in him, and the king
planned to appoint him over the whole
kingdom. 4 So the presidents and the sa-
traps tried to find grounds for complaint
against Daniel in connection with the king-
dom. But they could find no grounds for
complaint or any corruption, because he
was faithful, and no negligence or corrup-
tion could be found in him. 5 The men said,
"We shall not find any ground for com-
plaint against this Daniel unless we find it
in connection with the law of his God."
6 So the presidents and satraps con-
spired and came to the king and said to
him, "O King Darius, live forever! 7 All the
presidents of the kingdom, the prefects and
the satraps, the counselors and the gover-
nors are agreed that the king should estab-
lish an ordinance and enforce an interdict,
that whoever prays to anyone, divine or hu-

a Aram lacks *the days of* *b* The singular of *Parsin*
c Ch 6.1 in Aram

"mina") is a large weight and is related to the word "count"; *TEKEL* (Heb "shekel"), related to the word "weight," is one-sixtieth of a mene; *PARSIN* are two spheres, with one sphere (or *PERES*) equaling a half-shekel; it is interpreted as meaning "divide." **28:** The weights, which match the descending values of the metals in 2.32, symbolize Nebuchadnezzar's successors, from Belshazzar through the Medes and the Persians (see 2.39–44). **29:** Belshazzar appears oblivious to the fateful prediction: Did he think rewarding Daniel would forestall it? Jewish tradition (*b. Ned.* 62b) attributes Belshazzar's death to his profaning the Temple vessels. **31:** No such person as *Darius the Mede* is known to history, but there were three Persian kings named Darius. It was Cyrus the Persian who overthrew the Neo-Babylonian power in 539 BCE.

6.1–9: Persian plot against Daniel. 1: On *Darius,* see 5.31n. *One hundred twenty satraps* is the conventional number; see Esth 8.9. **2:** Like Joseph and Mordecai, Daniel advances in the foreign court; how Daniel impressed the Persian king is not recorded. **3:** Daniel distinguished himself, apparently by political acumen, not supernatural powers. **5:** The first reference to Jewish *law* in the book of Daniel. **7:** The plot resembles that of Dan 3. **8–9:** The unalterable law of the Medes and the Persians lies also behind man, for thirty days, except to you, O king, shall be thrown into a den of lions. 8 Now, O king, establish the interdict and sign the document, so that it cannot be changed, according to the law of the Medes and the Persians, which cannot be revoked." 9 Therefore King Darius signed the document and interdict.

10 Although Daniel knew that the document had been signed, he continued to go to his house, which had windows in its upper room open toward Jerusalem, and to get down on his knees three times a day to pray to his God and praise him, just as he had done previously. 11 The conspirators came and found Daniel praying and seeking mercy before his God. 12 Then they approached the king and said concerning the interdict, "O king! Did you not sign an interdict, that anyone who prays to anyone, divine or human, within thirty days except to you, O king, shall be thrown into a den of lions?" The king answered, "The thing stands fast, according to the law of the Medes and Persians, which cannot be revoked." 13 Then they responded to the king, "Daniel, one of the exiles from Judah, pays no attention to you, O king, or to the interdict you have signed, but he is saying his prayers three times a day."

14 When the king heard the charge, he was very much distressed. He was determined to save Daniel, and until the sun went down he made every effort to rescue him. 15 Then the conspirators came to the king and said to him, "Know, O king, that it is a law of the Medes and Persians that no interdict or ordinance that the king establishes can be changed."

16 Then the king gave the command, and Daniel was brought and thrown into the den of lions. The king said to Daniel, "May your God, whom you faithfully serve, deliver you!" 17 A stone was brought and laid on the mouth of the den, and the king sealed it with his own signet and with the signet of his lords, so that nothing might be changed concerning Daniel. 18 Then the king went to his palace and spent the night fasting; no food was brought to him, and sleep fled from him.

19 Then, at break of day, the king got up and hurried to the den of lions. 20 When he came near the den where Daniel was, he cried out anxiously to Daniel, "O Daniel, servant of the living God, has your God whom you faithfully serve been able to deliver you from the lions?" 21 Daniel then said to the king, "O king, live forever! 22 My God sent his angel and shut the lions' mouths so that they would not hurt me, because I was found blameless before him; and also before you, O king, I have done no wrong." 23 Then the king was exceedingly glad and commanded that Daniel be taken up out of the den. So Daniel was taken up out of the den, and no kind of harm was found on him, because he had trusted in his God. 24 The king gave a command, and those who had accused Daniel were

the plot of the book of Esther (Esth 1.19; 8.8). Like Ahasuerus in Esther, Darius acts, without thinking, on his courtiers' advice. Historically, however, Persian rulers supported the various religious beliefs and practices of those under imperial rule.

6.10–17: Daniel's defiance. 10: *Windows . . . open* indicates either happenstance or Daniel's deliberate flaunting of the edict (see Tob 3.8). *Toward Jerusalem,* the direction toward which Jews pray (1 Kings 8.35; 1 Esd 4.58). *Three times* a day for prayer became Jewish custom in early rabbinic (*Ber.* 4.1) and early Christian (Didache 8) times. **13:** *Exiles from Judah* shows ethnic antagonism: The courtiers remind Darius that Daniel is not "one of them." **14:** Sympathy for Darius may be compromised by his willingness to pronounce the edict that condemned Daniel (v. 9). V. 16 shows that Darius knew of Daniel's religious practices; in contrast, Nebuchadnezzar did not (3.15).

6.18–23: In the lions' den. 18–19: Darius appears more agitated than Daniel. **22:** *Sent his angel* recollects the fourth man in the furnace (3.25). *I have done no wrong,* Daniel subtly faults the king for endangering an innocent man.

6.24–28: Restitution. 24: *Children . . . wives* (see also Josh 7.24–26; Bel 21) indicate that the innocent, especially family members, suffer because of others' misdeeds. **25:** The letter and doxology resemble

brought and thrown into the den of lions—
they, their children, and their wives. Before
they reached the bottom of the den the li-
ons overpowered them and broke all their
bones in pieces.

25 Then King Darius wrote to all peo-
ples and nations of every language through-
out the whole world: "May you have abun-
dant prosperity! 26 I make a decree, that in
all my royal dominion people should trem-
ble and fear before the God of Daniel:

For he is the living God,
enduring forever.
His kingdom shall never be destroyed,
and his dominion has no end.
27 He delivers and rescues,
he works signs and wonders in
heaven and on earth;
for he has saved Daniel
from the power of the lions."

28 So this Daniel prospered during the reign
of Darius and the reign of Cyrus the Per-
sian.

7 In the first year of King Belshazzar of
Babylon, Daniel had a dream and vi-
sions of his head as he lay in bed. Then he
wrote down the dream:[a] 2 I,[b] Daniel, saw
in my vision by night the four winds of
heaven stirring up the great sea, 3 and four
great beasts came up out of the sea, differ-
ent from one another. 4 The first was like
a lion and had eagles' wings. Then, as I
watched, its wings were plucked off, and it
was lifted up from the ground and made to
stand on two feet like a human being; and
a human mind was given to it. 5 Another
beast appeared, a second one, that looked
like a bear. It was raised up on one side,
had three tusks[c] in its mouth among its
teeth and was told, "Arise, devour many
bodies!" 6 After this, as I watched, another
appeared, like a leopard. The beast had
four wings of a bird on its back and four
heads; and dominion was given to it. 7 After
this I saw in the visions by night a fourth
beast, terrifying and dreadful and exceed-
ingly strong. It had great iron teeth and was
devouring, breaking in pieces, and stamp-
ing what was left with its feet. It was differ-
ent from all the beasts that preceded it, and
it had ten horns. 8 I was considering the
horns, when another horn appeared, a lit-
tle one coming up among them; to make
room for it, three of the earlier horns were

a Q Ms Theodotion: MT adds *the beginning of the words; he said* *b* Theodotion: Aram *Daniel answered and said, I* *c* Or *ribs*

4.1–3,34–37. **28:** Cyrus the Persian (ruled 559–530 BCE) promulgated the edict in 538 BCE that permitted Jews in Babylon to return to Judea (Ezra 1.1–4; 6.3–5; Isa 44.28; 45.1; 48.14).

7.1–8: The first vision. Unlike Nebuchadnezzar's dreams and Belshazzar's visions, Daniel's apocalyptic revelations focus less on the dreamer's fate and more on international events. Also in contrast to the earlier scenes, Daniel is now himself in need of an interpreter. The history recorded in the visions suggests that they were composed sometime before 164 BCE, when Judas Maccabeus purified the Temple that Antiochus IV Epiphanes had profaned in 167. **2:** Daniel describes his dream in the first person. *The great sea* represents primeval chaos (Gen 1.2); the winds may be angels (as in 1 Enoch) or divine tools (Job 26.12–13; Ps 89.9–10). **3:** Four beasts symbolize kingdoms (7.17; Ps 68.30; 74.13; 87.4; Isa 27.1; Ezek 29.3; 32; see also Hos 13.7–8). These predatory kingdoms, arising from chaotic waters, no longer have even the possibility of goodness suggested earlier by Nebuchadnezzar and Darius. Cf. 2.31–45. **4:** The mixed natures of the beasts imply uncleanness (see Lev 11). The beast *like a human* reverses the image of Nebuchadnezzar (4.33). *Plucked* wings indicates both loss of power and transition to human form. *Human mind* may reflect Nebuchadnezzar's return to sanity in Dan 4.34–35. **5:** The *bear* is most likely to be identified with Media (cf. Jer 51.11 on the Medes' attacking Babylon). **6:** The *leopard* is Persia. **7:** The *fourth beast* is the Greek kingdom, in particular the Seleucid kingdom founded by Seleucus I, one of Alexander the Great's generals, in Syria and Mesopotamia after Alexander's death in 323 BCE. *Stamping* may suggest the elephant, part of the Greek war effort (1 Macc 1.17; 3.34; 6.28–47; 3 Macc 5.45). *Ten horns* a round number representing the kings of the Seleucid kingdom from Seleucus I until the time of Antiochus IV Epiphanes. **8:** The *little horn* is probably Antiochus IV Epiphanes (8.9; 1 Macc 1.41–50), who attempted to outlaw Jewish practices. *Three of the earlier horns,* Antiochus IV usurped the throne from plucked up by the roots. There were eyes like human eyes in this horn, and a mouth speaking arrogantly.

9 As I watched,
thrones were set in place,
and an Ancient One[a] took
his throne,
his clothing was white as snow,
and the hair of his head like
pure wool;
his throne was fiery flames,
and its wheels were burning fire.
10 A stream of fire issued
and flowed out from his presence.
A thousand thousands served him,
and ten thousand times ten
thousand stood attending him.
The court sat in judgment,
and the books were opened.
11 I watched then because of the noise of the arrogant words that the horn was speaking. And as I watched, the beast was put to death, and its body destroyed and given over to be burned with fire. 12 As for the rest of the beasts, their dominion was taken away, but their lives were prolonged for a season and a time. 13 As I watched in the night visions,
I saw one like a human being[b]
coming with the clouds of heaven.
And he came to the Ancient One[c]
and was presented before him.
14 To him was given dominion
and glory and kingship,
that all peoples, nations, and
languages
should serve him.
His dominion is an everlasting
dominion
that shall not pass away,
and his kingship is one
that shall never be destroyed.

15 As for me, Daniel, my spirit was troubled within me,[d] and the visions of my head terrified me. 16 I approached one of the attendants to ask him the truth concerning all this. So he said that he would disclose to me the interpretation of the matter: 17 "As for these four great beasts, four kings shall arise out of the earth. 18 But the holy ones of the Most High shall receive the kingdom and possess the kingdom forever—forever and ever."

19 Then I desired to know the truth con-

a Aram *an Ancient of Days* *b* Aram *one like a son of man* *c* Aram *the Ancient of Days* *d* Aram *troubled in its sheath*

his brother, Seleucus IV's heir Demetrius; Seleucus had been murdered by his own prime minister, Heliodorus, and Antiochus in turn got rid of Heliodorus.

7.9–14: The heavenly throneroom. See 1 Kings 22.19; Isa 6; Ezek 1.26–28; 3.22–24; 10.1; 1 Enoch 14. **9:** *Thrones,* although the other parts of the Hebrew Bible and other Jewish apocalypses refer to only a single throne in heaven, the multiple thrones of the court setting in Daniel 7 are reflected in early Christian texts (see Mt 19.28; Rev 4.2; 20.4). *Ancient One,* God. Although the depiction of God as an old man becomes common in later Jewish and Christian traditions, it is unusual in the Hebrew Bible. *White clothing,* Mt 28.3; Rev 3.5. *Fiery flames,* Ezek 1.4; *wheels,* Ezek 1.15–21; 10.2. **10:** *The books* in which human deeds are recorded become a common image for the divine court (Ps 56.9; Isa 65.6; Mal 3.16; 1 Enoch 90.20). **12:** *Prolonged for a season and a time,* although the first three empires are stripped of power, they are not destroyed as the fourth is. **13:** *One like a human being,* also translated "son of man," is probably the angel Michael, Israel's guardian (10.13,21; see also Rev 12). As the beasts represent foreign powers, Michael represents the Jews. Other modern identifications of this figure as Gabriel (see Dan 9.21), Judas Maccabeus, Daniel himself, etc. have also been suggested. Early Jewish (1 Enoch) and Christian (the canonical Gospels) literature contribute to the development of this figure; in the Gospels, the term is Jesus' preferred self-designation. **14:** Cf. 4.3,34; 6.26.

7.15–28: The interpretation. 15: *Spirit was troubled* is a typical reaction to revelatory visions (2.1; 4.1; 8.27; Gen 41.8). It is not clear whether Daniel has awakened or is still dreaming. **17:** The *four kings* are, traditionally, Babylon, Media, Persia, and Greece. **18:** *The holy ones* connotes members of the heavenly court (Deut 33.2; Job 5.1; 15.15; Ps 89.5,7; Zech 14.5). It may also refer to Jews persecuted by Antiochus. **22:** The prediction anticipates the reversal of fortune for the persecuted faithful, just as the

cerning the fourth beast, which was different from all the rest, exceedingly terrifying, with its teeth of iron and claws of bronze, and which devoured and broke in pieces, and stamped what was left with its feet;
20 and concerning the ten horns that were on its head, and concerning the other horn, which came up and to make room for which three of them fell out—the horn that had eyes and a mouth that spoke arrogantly, and that seemed greater than the others.
21 As I looked, this horn made war with the holy ones and was prevailing over them,
22 until the Ancient One[a] came; then judgment was given for the holy ones of the Most High, and the time arrived when the holy ones gained possession of the kingdom.

23 This is what he said: "As for the fourth beast,
there shall be a fourth kingdom
on earth
that shall be different from all the
other kingdoms;
it shall devour the whole earth,
and trample it down, and break it
to pieces.
24 As for the ten horns,
out of this kingdom ten kings
shall arise,
and another shall arise after them.
This one shall be different from the
former ones,
and shall put down three kings.
25 He shall speak words against the
Most High,
shall wear out the holy ones of the
Most High,
and shall attempt to change the
sacred seasons and the law;
and they shall be given into his power
for a time, two times,[b] and half a
time.
26 Then the court shall sit in judgment,
and his dominion shall be
taken away,
to be consumed and totally
destroyed.
27 The kingship and dominion
and the greatness of the kingdoms
under the whole heaven
shall be given to the people of the
holy ones of the Most High;
their kingdom shall be an everlasting
kingdom,
and all dominions shall serve and
obey them."

28 Here the account ends. As for me, Daniel, my thoughts greatly terrified me, and my face turned pale; but I kept the matter in my mind.

8 In the third year of the reign of King Belshazzar a vision appeared to me, Daniel, after the one that had appeared to
me at first. 2 In the vision I was looking and saw myself in Susa the capital, in the province of Elam,[c] and I was by the river
Ulai.[d] 3 I looked up and saw a ram standing beside the river.[e] It had two horns. Both horns were long, but one was longer than the other, and the longer one came up
second. 4 I saw the ram charging westward

a Aram *the Ancient of Days* *b* Aram *a time, times* *c* Gk Theodotion: MT Q Ms repeat *in the vision I was looking* *d* Or *the Ulai Gate* *e* Or *gate*

folktales of Dan 1–6 depict. **23–25:** The greater detail suggests a time closer to the author's own. The *fourth beast* and the *ten horns* see 7.7–8n. **25:** *Words against the Most High,* Antiochus IV Epiphanes was the first Hellenistic king to use divine self-designations on coinage. *Sacred seasons and the law* are those practices marking Jewish religious and cultural identity disrupted by Antiochus (1 Macc 1.45; 2 Macc 6.6). *A time, two times, and half a time* indicates three and a half years (see 4.36), approximately the time of Antiochus's persecution. **28:** *Kept the matter in my mind,* apocalyptic visions are typically kept secret until an opportune time (2 Esd 14.45–46).

8.1–14: The second vision. With this chapter, the book of Daniel reverts from Aramaic to Hebrew. **1:** The earlier vision is that of Dan 7. **2:** *Susa,* the royal city of Persia (Esth 1.2). *River Ulai,* Ulai is a river near Susa; visionary experiences are frequently associated with riverbank settings (Ezek 1.1). **3–4:** *Two horns* are Media and Persia. *The ram* may be an astrological symbol; 8.20 states it represents the kings of Media and Persia. **5:** *The goat* may also be a zodiacal sign; here it appears to symbolize Alexander's

and northward and southward. All beasts
were powerless to withstand it, and no one
could rescue from its power; it did as it
pleased and became strong.
5 As I was watching, a male goat ap-
peared from the west, coming across the
face of the whole earth without touching
the ground. The goat had a horn[a] between
its eyes. 6 It came toward the ram with the
two horns that I had seen standing beside
the river,[b] and it ran at it with savage
force. 7 I saw it approaching the ram. It was
enraged against it and struck the ram,
breaking its two horns. The ram did not
have power to withstand it; it threw the
ram down to the ground and trampled
upon it, and there was no one who could
rescue the ram from its power. 8 Then the
male goat grew exceedingly great; but at
the height of its power, the great horn was
broken, and in its place there came up four
prominent horns toward the four winds of
heaven.
9 Out of one of them came another[c]
horn, a little one, which grew exceedingly
great toward the south, toward the east,
and toward the beautiful land. 10 It grew as
high as the host of heaven. It threw down
to the earth some of the host and some of
the stars, and trampled on them. 11 Even
against the prince of the host it acted arro-
gantly; it took the regular burnt offering
away from him and overthrew the place of
his sanctuary. 12 Because of wickedness, the
host was given over to it together with the
regular burnt offering;[d] it cast truth to the
ground, and kept prospering in what it did.
13 Then I heard a holy one speaking, and
another holy one said to the one that spoke,
"For how long is this vision concerning the
regular burnt offering, the transgression
that makes desolate, and the giving over of
the sanctuary and host to be trampled?"[d]
14 And he answered him,[e] "For two thou-
sand three hundred evenings and mornings;
then the sanctuary shall be restored to its
rightful state."
15 When I, Daniel, had seen the vision,
I tried to understand it. Then someone ap-
peared standing before me, having the ap-
pearance of a man, 16 and I heard a human
voice by the Ulai, calling, "Gabriel, help
this man understand the vision." 17 So he
came near where I stood; and when he
came, I became frightened and fell pros-
trate. But he said to me, "Understand,
O mortal,[f] that the vision is for the time
of the end."

a Theodotion: Gk *one horn*; Heb *a horn of vision*
b Or *gate* *c* Cn Compare 7.8: Heb *one*
d Meaning of Heb uncertain *e* Gk Theodotion Syr Vg: Heb *me* *f* Heb *son of man*

army; 8.21 states that it is the king of Greece. *Across . . . the whole earth* suggests Alexander the Great's swift eastern campaign. **8:** The *great horn* is Alexander; *four prominent horns* are his generals who divided his empire. **9:** The little horn is, again (Dan 7.8), Antiochus IV Epiphanes. *The beautiful land* is Israel or, more specifically, Jerusalem (11.16,41; Jer 3.19; Ezek 20.6,15). **10–11:** See Isa 14.12–16; Antiochus's outrages have cosmic import. *Host of heaven* can refer either to stars or to heavenly beings. For *threw down* some of the host, see Rev 12.4. **11:** *Prince of the host* is God, although elsewhere *prince* is a term designating angels (10.13,20–21). *Took the . . . offering away,* Antiochus and his supporters replaced the Temple's offerings (Ex 29.38–42; Num 28–29; Ezra 3.5; Neh 10.34; Ezek 46.1–5) with sacrifices to Zeus (1 Macc 1.45,59; 2 Macc 5.5). **12:** *Truth* or true religion is, for Daniel, Judaism. **13:** *Holy ones,* see 7.18n. "*How long*" is a major question of penitential and apocalyptic literature (Ps 6.3; 79.5; 80.4; 90.13; Isa 6.11; Jer 12.4; Zech 1.12). *The transgression that makes desolate* is likely the image Antiochus IV erected in the Temple (1 Macc 1.54; 2 Macc 6.2); the Heb term ("shiqquts shomem") is a play on the expression "Baal Shamen," or "lord of heaven," an epithet of Zeus. **14:** The time of 1,150 days is less than three and a half years (7.25); *evenings and mornings* evokes the daily sacrifice.

8.15–27: Gabriel's interpretation. 15: *Appearance of a man* indicates an angel; see 7.13n. **16:** *Gabriel,* whose name means "man of God" or "God is my hero/warrior," serves as a divine messenger (Lk 1.19, 26). **17:** *Fell prostrate,* Daniel had not bowed to any Babylonian king or idol; the response is appropriate to an epiphany (10.9; Josh 5.14; Ezek 1.28; 3.23). *Time of the end* indicates the final judgment, restitution of the faithful, and punishment of the wicked (see Hab 2.3). **18:** *Trance* (lit. "deep sleep") is the same term

18 As he was speaking to me, I fell into
a trance, face to the ground; then he
touched me and set me on my feet. 19 He
said, "Listen, and I will tell you what will
take place later in the period of wrath; for
it refers to the appointed time of the end.
20 As for the ram that you saw with the two
horns, these are the kings of Media and
Persia. 21 The male goat[a] is the king of
Greece, and the great horn between its eyes
is the first king. 22 As for the horn that was
broken, in place of which four others arose,
four kingdoms shall arise from his[b] nation,
but not with his power.

23 At the end of their rule,
when the transgressions have
reached their full measure,
a king of bold countenance
shall arise,
skilled in intrigue.
24 He shall grow strong in power,[c]
shall cause fearful destruction,
and shall succeed in what he does.
He shall destroy the powerful
and the people of the holy ones.
25 By his cunning
he shall make deceit prosper under
his hand,
and in his own mind he shall
be great.
Without warning he shall
destroy many
and shall even rise up against the
Prince of princes.
But he shall be broken, and not by
human hands.

26 The vision of the evenings and the morn-
ings that has been told is true. As for you,
seal up the vision, for it refers to many days
from now."

27 So I, Daniel, was overcome and lay
sick for some days; then I arose and went
about the king's business. But I was dis-
mayed by the vision and did not under-
stand it.

9 In the first year of Darius son of Ahasu-
erus, by birth a Mede, who became
king over the realm of the Chaldeans— 2 in
the first year of his reign, I, Daniel, per-
ceived in the books the number of years
that, according to the word of the LORD to
the prophet Jeremiah, must be fulfilled for
the devastation of Jerusalem, namely, sev-
enty years.

3 Then I turned to the Lord God, to seek
an answer by prayer and supplication with
fasting and sackcloth and ashes. 4 I prayed
to the LORD my God and made confession,
saying,

"Ah, Lord, great and awesome God,
keeping covenant and steadfast love with
those who love you and keep your com-
mandments, 5 we have sinned and done
wrong, acted wickedly and rebelled, turn-
ing aside from your commandments and
ordinances. 6 We have not listened to your
servants the prophets, who spoke in your
name to our kings, our princes, and our
ancestors, and to all the people of the land.
7 "Righteousness is on your side,

a Or *shaggy male goat* *b* Gk Theodotion Vg: Heb *the* *c* Theodotion and one Gk Ms: Heb repeats (from 8.22) *but not with his power*

used for Adam's sleep (Gen 2.21). Touch conveys heavenly concern (9.21; 10.10,16,18; Isa 6.7; Jer 1.9). **23:** On *transgressions* that must reach a certain number, see Gen 15.16; 2 Macc 6.14; 2 Esd 4.36–37. **25:** *Without warning* may refer to the surprise attack against Jerusalem (1 Macc 1.29–30). *Prince of princes,* see 8.11n. *Not by human hands*, part of Daniel's counsel of pacifism (see 2.34); Antiochus IV Epiphanes actually died in battle in late 164 BCE. **26:** See 7.28n.; Isa 29.11.

9.1–19: Daniel's prayer. 1: An attempt to resolve the chronological problem of 5.31 (see note) and ch 6. **2:** Reading the scriptures is rarely noted in the biblical tradition; the reference is to Jer 25.11–12; 29.10–14. *Devastation,* Jerusalem was destroyed by the Babylonians in 586 BCE. **3:** *Fasting, sackcloth, and ashes* are traditional indications of mourning and penance, including in perilous times (Jer 49.28–33; Joel 2.5; Ezra 8.21–23; Esth 4.1–4; 1 Macc 3.44–46; 2 Macc 13.12); fasting also serves as preparation for visionary experiences (Ex 34.28; 1 Kings 19.8). **5:** Communal confession is typical of Jewish piety; even in cases where no sin is indicated, prayers begin with acknowledgment of guilt (see also 1 Kings 8.47; 2 Chr 6.37; Ps 106.6). **7:** *All Israel* includes the ten tribes dispersed with the destruction of the Northern

O Lord, but open shame, as at this day,
falls on us, the people of Judah, the inhabi-
tants of Jerusalem, and all Israel, those who
are near and those who are far away, in all
the lands to which you have driven them,
because of the treachery that they have
committed against you. 8 Open shame,
O LORD, falls on us, our kings, our offi-
cials, and our ancestors, because we have
sinned against you. 9 To the Lord our God
belong mercy and forgiveness, for we have
rebelled against him, 10 and have not
obeyed the voice of the LORD our God by
following his laws, which he set before us
by his servants the prophets.

11 "All Israel has transgressed your law
and turned aside, refusing to obey your
voice. So the curse and the oath written in
the law of Moses, the servant of God, have
been poured out upon us, because we have
sinned against you. 12 He has confirmed his
words, which he spoke against us and
against our rulers, by bringing upon us a
calamity so great that what has been done
against Jerusalem has never before been
done under the whole heaven. 13 Just as it is
written in the law of Moses, all this calami-
ty has come upon us. We did not entreat
the favor of the LORD our God, turning
from our iniquities and reflecting on his[a]
fidelity. 14 So the LORD kept watch over
this calamity until he brought it upon us.
Indeed, the LORD our God is right in all
that he has done; for we have disobeyed his
voice.

15 "And now, O Lord our God, who
brought your people out of the land of
Egypt with a mighty hand and made your
name renowned even to this day—we have
sinned, we have done wickedly. 16 O Lord,
in view of all your righteous acts, let your
anger and wrath, we pray, turn away from
your city Jerusalem, your holy mountain;
because of our sins and the iniquities of our
ancestors, Jerusalem and your people have
become a disgrace among all our neigh-
bors. 17 Now therefore, O our God, listen
to the prayer of your servant and to his
supplication, and for your own sake,
Lord,[b] let your face shine upon your deso-
lated sanctuary. 18 Incline your ear, O my
God, and hear. Open your eyes and look at
our desolation and the city that bears your
name. We do not present our supplication
before you on the ground of our righteous-
ness, but on the ground of your great mer-
cies. 19 O Lord, hear; O Lord, forgive;
O Lord, listen and act and do not delay!
For your own sake, O my God, because
your city and your people bear your
name!"

20 While I was speaking, and was pray-
ing and confessing my sin and the sin of my
people Israel, and presenting my supplica-
tion before the LORD my God on behalf of
the holy mountain of my God— 21 while I
was speaking in prayer, the man Gabriel,
whom I had seen before in a vision, came to
me in swift flight at the time of the evening
sacrifice. 22 He came[c] and said to me,
"Daniel, I have now come out to give you
wisdom and understanding. 23 At the begin-
ning of your supplications a word went
out, and I have come to declare it, for you
are greatly beloved. So consider the word
and understand the vision:

24 "Seventy weeks are decreed for your
people and your holy city: to finish the
transgression, to put an end to sin, and to
atone for iniquity, to bring in everlasting

a Heb *your* *b* Theodotion Vg Compare Syr: Heb *for the Lord's sake* *c* Gk Syr: Heb *He made to understand*

Kingdom of Israel by Assyria in 722 BCE. **11:** *Curse and the oath,* see Deut 28.15–45; Neh 10.29. **13:** For what was *written,* see Lev 26.14–22; Deut 30.1. **15:** The expressions echo Deuteronomy. **16:** Although in exile, Daniel's thoughts turn to Jerusalem. **17:** Reference to the *desolated sanctuary* would have particular meaning to those living during the Maccabean revolt (see 8.13; 11.29–31).

9.20–27: Gabriel's response. 21: See 8.16n. *Swift flight* indicates Gabriel's angelic nature. **24:** *Seventy weeks* Jeremiah's seventy years (see v. 2n.) are interpreted to mean seventy weeks of years (70 x 7) or four-hundred and ninety years (see Lev 25 on the Jubilee, which may also be reflected in this interpretation). The prediction of future peace echoes that of 7.26–27. The *most holy place* is the Temple. **25:** The

righteousness, to seal both vision and
prophet, and to anoint a most holy place.[a]
25 Know therefore and understand: from
the time that the word went out to restore
and rebuild Jerusalem until the time of an
anointed prince, there shall be seven weeks;
and for sixty-two weeks it shall be built
again with streets and moat, but in a trou-
bled time. 26 After the sixty-two weeks, an
anointed one shall be cut off and shall have
nothing, and the troops of the prince who is
to come shall destroy the city and the sanc-
tuary. Its[b] end shall come with a flood,
and to the end there shall be war. Desola-
tions are decreed. 27 He shall make a strong
covenant with many for one week, and for
half of the week he shall make sacrifice and
offering cease; and in their place[c] shall be
an abomination that desolates, until the de-
creed end is poured out upon the desola-
tor."

10 In the third year of King Cyrus of
Persia a word was revealed to Dan-
iel, who was named Belteshazzar. The
word was true, and it concerned a great
conflict. He understood the word, having
received understanding in the vision.

2 At that time I, Daniel, had been
mourning for three weeks. 3 I had eaten no
rich food, no meat or wine had entered my
mouth, and I had not anointed myself at
all, for the full three weeks. 4 On the
twenty-fourth day of the first month, as I
was standing on the bank of the great river
(that is, the Tigris), 5 I looked up and saw a
man clothed in linen, with a belt of gold
from Uphaz around his waist. 6 His body
was like beryl, his face like lightning, his
eyes like flaming torches, his arms and legs
like the gleam of burnished bronze, and the
sound of his words like the roar of a multi-
tude. 7 I, Daniel, alone saw the vision; the
people who were with me did not see the
vision, though a great trembling fell upon
them, and they fled and hid themselves. 8 So
I was left alone to see this great vision. My
strength left me, and my complexion grew
deathly pale, and I retained no strength.
9 Then I heard the sound of his words; and
when I heard the sound of his words, I fell
into a trance, face to the ground.

10 But then a hand touched me and
roused me to my hands and knees. 11 He
said to me, "Daniel, greatly beloved, pay
attention to the words that I am going to
speak to you. Stand on your feet, for I have
now been sent to you." So while he was
speaking this word to me, I stood up trem-
bling. 12 He said to me, "Do not fear, Dan-
iel, for from the first day that you set your
mind to gain understanding and to humble
yourself before your God, your words have
been heard, and I have come because of
your words. 13 But the prince of the king-
dom of Persia opposed me twenty-one

a Or *thing* or *one* *b* Or *His* *c* Cn: Meaning of Heb uncertain

Edict of Cyrus, sponsoring the restoration of *Jerusalem,* was promulgated in 538 BCE. The one *anointed* is likely Joshua the high priest (see Zech 4.14; also Ezra 2.2; 3.2; Hag 1.1–14). **26:** The deposed *anointed one* may be Onias III (see 2 Macc 4.23–28), murdered in 171 BCE. The *prince who is to come* is Antiochus IV Epiphanes. **27:** *Strong covenant,* Antiochus received support from Jason the high priest and various members of the Judean upper class (1 Macc 1.11). **27:** See 8.13n.

10.1–9: Daniel's visionary experience. The last three chapters of the book comprise a single vision. **1:** *Third year of King Cyrus* is 536 BCE. Reference to Daniel's Babylonian name (1.7; 5.12) connects the apocalypse with the earlier folktales. *Word,* accompanying the visual experience is auditory revelation. **3:** Daniel's regimen signals mourning. **4:** The dating indicates that Daniel fasted during the Passover, the feast of freedom. *On the bank of the . . . river,* see 8.2n. **5:** *Clothed in linen* suggests the Temple priesthood (see Ezek 9.2–7). The description of the "man"—probably the angel Gabriel—is reminiscent of Ezek 9.2–3,11; 10.2,6–7; see also Rev 1.13. **7:** *Alone saw the vision,* a similar experience occurs to Saul (Paul; Acts 9.7).

10.10–21: Gabriel's encouragement. 10: *Touch,* see 8.18n. **12:** *Do not fear* is standard exhortation for those receiving angelic revelation (10.19). **13:** War on earth is matched by war in heaven; *Michael* is chief of the angelic princes (see Rev 12.7) and guardian of Israel (12.1). *Prince of the kingdom of Persia*

days. So Michael, one of the chief princes,
came to help me, and I left him there with
the prince of the kingdom of Persia,[a]
14and have come to help you understand
what is to happen to your people at the end
of days. For there is a further vision for
those days."
15 While he was speaking these words
to me, I turned my face toward the ground
and was speechless. 16Then one in human
form touched my lips, and I opened my
mouth to speak, and said to the one who
stood before me, "My lord, because of the
vision such pains have come upon me that
I retain no strength. 17How can my lord's
servant talk with my lord? For I am shak-
ing,[b] no strength remains in me, and no
breath is left in me."
18 Again one in human form touched
me and strengthened me. 19He said, "Do
not fear, greatly beloved, you are safe. Be
strong and courageous!" When he spoke to
me, I was strengthened and said, "Let my
lord speak, for you have strengthened me."
20Then he said, "Do you know why I have
come to you? Now I must return to fight
against the prince of Persia, and when I
am through with him, the prince of Greece
will come. 21But I am to tell you what is
inscribed in the book of truth. There is
no one with me who contends against
these princes except Michael, your prince.
11 1As for me, in the first year of Dari-
us the Mede, I stood up to support
and strengthen him.
2 "Now I will announce the truth to
you. Three more kings shall arise in Persia.
The fourth shall be far richer than all of
them, and when he has become strong
through his riches, he shall stir up all
against the kingdom of Greece. 3Then a
warrior king shall arise, who shall rule with
great dominion and take action as he
pleases. 4And while still rising in power, his
kingdom shall be broken and divided to-
ward the four winds of heaven, but not to
his posterity, nor according to the domin-
ion with which he ruled; for his kingdom
shall be uprooted and go to others besides
these.
5 "Then the king of the south shall grow
strong, but one of his officers shall grow
stronger than he and shall rule a realm
greater than his own realm. 6After some
years they shall make an alliance, and the
daughter of the king of the south shall
come to the king of the north to ratify the
agreement. But she shall not retain her
power, and his offspring shall not endure.
She shall be given up, she and her atten-
dants and her child and the one who sup-
ported her.
"In those times 7a branch from her roots
shall rise up in his place. He shall come
against the army and enter the fortress of
the king of the north, and he shall take ac-
tion against them and prevail. 8Even their
gods, with their idols and with their pre-
cious vessels of silver and gold, he shall car-
ry off to Egypt as spoils of war. For some
years he shall refrain from attacking the

a Gk Theodotion: Heb *I was left there with the kings of Persia* *b* Gk: Heb *from now*

is Persia's patron angel; cf. Deut 32.8; Sir 17.17. **16:** *Human form,* see 7.13n. Touching the *lips* suggests Isa 6.7; Jer 1.9. **17:** Daniel's reluctance is common among those called to prophetic tasks (see Ex 3). **20:** Greece is either Alexander the Great's empire or specifically the rule of Antiochus IV. **21:** *The book of truth,* apparently different from the book of 12.1, describes the future; such determinism is typical of apocalyptic literature.

11.1–13: Succession of kings. 2: There were more than four kings of *Persia;* the numbers do not neatly match historical records. **3:** The *warrior king* is Alexander the Great. **4:** *Toward the four winds* see 8.8n. **5:** *King of the south* is Ptolemy I Soter of Egypt (satrap, 323–305; king, 305–282); the *officer* is Seleucus I Nicanor who established the Seleucid empire. **6:** *King of the north* is probably Antiochus II Theos of Syria, grandson of Seleucus, who married Berenice, the daughter of Ptolemy II Philadelphus, in 252 BCE. Berenice, her child, and her attendants were murdered. **7:** The *branch* is Berenice's brother, Ptolemy III Euergetes, who campaigned against the Seleucids. **8:** Ptolemy III captured many treasures from Egypt taken by the Persian king Cambyses in the fourth century and held in Babylon. **9:** The *latter* invader is

king of the north; 9 then the latter shall in-
vade the realm of the king of the south, but
will return to his own land.
10 "His sons shall wage war and assem-
ble a multitude of great forces, which shall
advance like a flood and pass through, and
again shall carry the war as far as his for-
tress. 11 Moved with rage, the king of the
south shall go out and do battle against the
king of the north, who shall muster a great
multitude, which shall, however, be defeat-
ed by his enemy. 12 When the multitude has
been carried off, his heart shall be exalted,
and he shall overthrow tens of thousands,
but he shall not prevail. 13 For the king of
the north shall again raise a multitude, larg-
er than the former, and after some years[a]
he shall advance with a great army and
abundant supplies.
14 "In those times many shall rise
against the king of the south. The lawless
among your own people shall lift them-
selves up in order to fulfill the vision, but
they shall fail. 15 Then the king of the north
shall come and throw up siegeworks, and
take a well-fortified city. And the forces
of the south shall not stand, not even his
picked troops, for there shall be no strength
to resist. 16 But he who comes against him
shall take the actions he pleases, and no one
shall withstand him. He shall take a posi-
tion in the beautiful land, and all of it shall
be in his power. 17 He shall set his mind to
come with the strength of his whole king-
dom, and he shall bring terms of peace[b]
and perform them. In order to destroy the
kingdom,[c] he shall give him a woman in
marriage; but it shall not succeed or be to
his advantage. 18 Afterward he shall turn to
the coastlands, and shall capture many. But
a commander shall put an end to his inso-
lence; indeed,[d] he shall turn his insolence
back upon him. 19 Then he shall turn back
toward the fortresses of his own land, but
he shall stumble and fall, and shall not be
found.
20 "Then shall arise in his place one
who shall send an official for the glory of
the kingdom; but within a few days he shall
be broken, though not in anger or in battle.
21 In his place shall arise a contemptible
person on whom royal majesty had not
been conferred; he shall come in without
warning and obtain the kingdom through
intrigue. 22 Armies shall be utterly swept
away and broken before him, and the
prince of the covenant as well. 23 And after
an alliance is made with him, he shall act

a Heb *and at the end of the times years* *b* Gk: Heb *kingdom, and upright ones with him* *c* Heb *it* *d* Meaning of Heb uncertain

Seleucus II Callinicus, whose invasion of Egypt in 242–240 BCE was unsuccessful. **10:** Callinicus's *sons* were Seleucus III Ceraunus (227–223 BCE) and Antiochus III the Great (223–187). **11:** Antiochus III campaigned against Ptolemy IV but was defeated by him at the Battle of Raphia in 217. **13:** *King of the north* is Antiochus III, who waged successful campaigns during 212–205.

11.14–20: Campaigns of Antiochus III. The Ptolemies and Seleucids continued to fight until, in 198 BCE at the battle of Paneas, the Seleucids defeated the Egyptian forces and gained control of Judea. **14:** *Lawless* among your own people (Ezek 7.22) may refer to the rivalry between the Tobiad family and the supporters of Onias III; both sought control of the Jerusalem Temple. **15–16:** The *well-fortified city* is Sidon; its fall resulted in Antiochus III's personally taking possession of Judea, *the beautiful land.* **17:** *Terms of peace* refers to the alliance formed when Antiochus III betrothed his daughter, Cleopatra I, to Ptolemy V Epiphanes, in 197 BCE. **18:** Defeated by the Romans at Thermopylae in 191 and at Magnesia in 190, Antiochus III incurred massive tribute debt. **19:** Antiochus III *stumbled and fell* at Elymais in 187, while attempting to plunder the temple of Bel in order to pay his debt to Rome. **20:** The *official* is the tribute-collector, Heliodorus, sent by Seleucus IV Philopator (187–175 BCE) who sought to plunder the Jerusalem Temple (2 Macc 3.1–40).

11.21–28: Antiochus IV. 21: The *contemptible person* is Antiochus IV Epiphanes (175–164 BCE). **22:** The *prince of the covenant* is Onias III, deposed by Antiochus and replaced by his assimilationist brother, Jason (see 9.26n.). **23:** The *small party* of Jews, supporting Hellenization, receive rewards from the king's plundering. **25–28:** Antiochus IV's successful first campaign against Egypt in 169 BCE. **26:** *Those who eat*

deceitfully and become strong with a small
party. 24 Without warning he shall come
into the richest parts[a] of the province and
do what none of his predecessors had ever
done, lavishing plunder, spoil, and wealth
on them. He shall devise plans against
strongholds, but only for a time. 25 He shall
stir up his power and determination against
the king of the south with a great army, and
the king of the south shall wage war with a
much greater and stronger army. But he
shall not succeed, for plots shall be devised
against him 26 by those who eat of the royal
rations. They shall break him, his army
shall be swept away, and many shall fall
slain. 27 The two kings, their minds bent on
evil, shall sit at one table and exchange lies.
But it shall not succeed, for there remains
an end at the time appointed. 28 He shall
return to his land with great wealth, but his
heart shall be set against the holy covenant.
He shall work his will, and return to his
own land.

29 "At the time appointed he shall re-
turn and come into the south, but this time
it shall not be as it was before. 30 For ships
of Kittim shall come against him, and he
shall lose heart and withdraw. He shall be
enraged and take action against the holy
covenant. He shall turn back and pay heed
to those who forsake the holy covenant.
31 Forces sent by him shall occupy and pro-
fane the temple and fortress. They shall
abolish the regular burnt offering and set
up the abomination that makes desolate.
32 He shall seduce with intrigue those who
violate the covenant; but the people who
are loyal to their God shall stand firm and
take action. 33 The wise among the people
shall give understanding to many; for some
days, however, they shall fall by sword and
flame, and suffer captivity and plunder.
34 When they fall victim, they shall receive a
little help, and many shall join them insin-
cerely. 35 Some of the wise shall fall, so
that they may be refined, purified, and
cleansed,[b] until the time of the end, for
there is still an interval until the time ap-
pointed.

36 "The king shall act as he pleases. He
shall exalt himself and consider himself
greater than any god, and shall speak hor-
rendous things against the God of gods. He
shall prosper until the period of wrath is
completed, for what is determined shall be
done. 37 He shall pay no respect to the gods
of his ancestors, or to the one beloved by
women; he shall pay no respect to any oth-
er god, for he shall consider himself greater
than all. 38 He shall honor the god of for-
tresses instead of these; a god whom his
ancestors did not know he shall honor with
gold and silver, with precious stones and
costly gifts. 39 He shall deal with the stron-
gest fortresses by the help of a foreign god.
Those who acknowledge him he shall make
more wealthy, and shall appoint them as
rulers over many, and shall distribute the
land for a price.

a Or *among the richest men* b Heb *made them white*

of the royal rations (see Dan 1) are Eulaeus and Lenaeus, Ptolemaic courtiers whose plots against Antiochus IV prompted him to invade Egypt. **28:** *Holy covenant* means either Antiochus's support in sponsoring anti-Jewish legislation or his attack on the Temple (1 Macc 1.20).

11.29–39: Attack against the Jews. 30: *Kittim* here represents Rome (cf. Gen 10.4), which forced Antiochus to withdraw from Egypt in 168 BCE during his second campaign. That same year, Antiochus desecrated the Jerusalem Temple. **31:** *Forces sent,* see 2 Macc 5.24. The *abomination* is an altar to Zeus Olympios set up in the Temple's holy of holies (see 8.13n.); this phrase reappears in early Christian literature (Mk 13.14). **32:** *People who are loyal* include the Maccabees and their supporters. **33–34:** The visionary regards himself as one of the *wise* (Heb "maskilim"); they are distinguished from those of *little help,* probably the Maccabees. On *sword and flame,* cf. 1 Macc 1.63. **35:** *Refining* is a testing and purifying process (Ps 17.3; Jer 6.29; 9.6; Zech 13.9; Sir 2.5). **37:** *Beloved by women* is Tammuz (Adonis), a Mesopotamian god (Ezek 8.14). **38:** *God of fortresses* is Zeus Olympios; the fortress is likely the citadel in Jerusalem (the Akra) where occupation troops were stationed.

40 “At the time of the end the king of
the south shall attack him. But the king of
the north shall rush upon him like a whirl-
wind, with chariots and horsemen, and
with many ships. He shall advance against
countries and pass through like a flood.
41 He shall come into the beautiful land,
and tens of thousands shall fall victim, but
Edom and Moab and the main part of the
Ammonites shall escape from his power.
42 He shall stretch out his hand against the
countries, and the land of Egypt shall not
escape. 43 He shall become ruler of the trea-
sures of gold and of silver, and all the riches
of Egypt; and the Libyans and the Ethiopi-
ans[a] shall follow in his train. 44 But reports
from the east and the north shall alarm
him, and he shall go out with great fury
to bring ruin and complete destruction to
many. 45 He shall pitch his palatial tents be-
tween the sea and the beautiful holy moun-
tain. Yet he shall come to his end, with no
one to help him.

12 “At that time Michael, the great
prince, the protector of your people,
shall arise. There shall be a time of anguish,
such as has never occurred since nations
first came into existence. But at that time
your people shall be delivered, everyone
who is found written in the book. 2 Many
of those who sleep in the dust of the earth[b]
shall awake, some to everlasting life, and
some to shame and everlasting contempt.
3 Those who are wise shall shine like the
brightness of the sky,[c] and those who lead
many to righteousness, like the stars forev-
er and ever. 4 But you, Daniel, keep the
words secret and the book sealed until the
time of the end. Many shall be running
back and forth, and evil[d] shall increase.”
5 Then I, Daniel, looked, and two others
appeared, one standing on this bank of the
stream and one on the other. 6 One of them
said to the man clothed in linen, who was
upstream, “How long shall it be until the
end of these wonders?” 7 The man clothed
in linen, who was upstream, raised his right
hand and his left hand toward heaven. And
I heard him swear by the one who lives
forever that it would be for a time, two
times, and half a time,[e] and that when the
shattering of the power of the holy people
comes to an end, all these things would be
accomplished. 8 I heard but could not un-
derstand; so I said, “My lord, what shall be
the outcome of these things?” 9 He said,
“Go your way, Daniel, for the words are to
remain secret and sealed until the time of
the end. 10 Many shall be purified, cleansed,
and refined, but the wicked shall continue
to act wickedly. None of the wicked shall
understand, but those who are wise shall
understand. 11 From the time that the regu-
lar burnt offering is taken away and the
abomination that desolates is set up, there
shall be one thousand two hundred ninety
days. 12 Happy are those who persevere and
attain the thousand three hundred thirty-
five days. 13 But you, go your way,[f] and
rest; you shall rise for your reward at the
end of the days.”

a Or *Nubians*; Heb *Cushites* b Or *the land of dust*
c Or *dome* d Cn Compare Gk: Heb *knowledge*
e Heb *a time, times, and a half* f Gk Theodotion:
Heb adds *to the end*

11.40–45: The end-time. 40: *The time of the end* moves into speculative material; no longer reporting what happened, the author envisions what will occur. **41–42:** *Edom, Moab,* and *Ammon* are ancient enemies of Israel. **45:** The ending is particularly ignoble. In fact, Antiochus died of illness in Persia in 164 BCE.

12.1–13: Michael's victory. 1: For the *book,* see 7.9–10n.; Ps 69.28; Isa 4.3; Mal 3.16–18; Rev 20.12,15; 21.27. *Michael* had been in battle with Persia and Greece (10.21–11.1). **2:** The first clear biblical reference to a resurrection, final judgment, and afterlife (see also Ezek 37; Hos 6.2; Isa 26.19). *Many* suggests not all will rise. **4:** *The book sealed,* see 7.28n.; 8.26n. **5–7:** *The man clothed in linen,* resembles priests (see 10.5n.) but speaks like angels. *Time, two, times and half a time,* see 7.25. **10:** *Purified,* see 11.35n. **11–12:** The numbers, perhaps from separate traditions and themselves different from that of 8.14, provide assurance that the end will come.

HOSEA

The book of Hosea stands first in that part of the latter prophets called the Book of the Twelve, also known as the minor prophets because of their relative brevity in comparison with Isaiah, Jeremiah, and Ezekiel. Along with his contemporary Amos, Hosea was the first of the "writing prophets," those prophets whose speeches were collected and edited as literary documents.

The book consists primarily of speeches critiquing the political, social, and, above all, religious life of the Northern Kingdom, Israel, in the final days before its conquest and destruction by the Assyrians in 722 BCE. Hosea refers to Israel under the titles of "Ephraim," its largest tribe, and "Samaria," its capital (see 4.16n.). Over the course of three decades (ca. 750–720), Hosea interpreted the unfolding disaster as a divine punishment—the Assyrians were merely God's tool—for violation of the exclusive demands of the LORD. With frequent allusions to Israelite historical traditions, Hosea portrayed Israel's entire history as a spiritual decline from an ideal time, its "youth" in the period of Moses (2.25; 11.1).

Hosea is best known for his metaphors, drawn from the natural world, agriculture, and, especially, kinship structures: Israel as the LORD's wife, Israel as the LORD's son. These familial metaphors are introduced in two narrative sections about the prophet's own life at the beginning of the book (1.2–2.1; 3.1–5). The prophet's personal life is presented as a paradigm of the relationship between the LORD and Israel.

Not all aspects of Hosea's life are clear, and it remains debatable whether one can deduce actual biographical facts from the descriptions in chs 1–3. But insofar as these chapters construct a biographical story for prophetic purposes, it can best be reconstructed that Hosea deals with Gomer as the LORD deals with Israel. Gomer is "a wife of whoredom," best understood as "a promiscuous woman." She bore three children, of whom Hosea was presumably not the father (2.4–5). After a period of marital separation, Hosea took her back (3.1–5). In a similar way, Israel, the LORD's unfaithful wife, will be separated from her husband and home but, just as Hosea bought back Gomer (3.2), the LORD will restore Israel. Hosea's image of Israel's sexual misconduct may be more than symbolic (e.g., 4.13–19; 9.1). Canaanite religious practice may have included sexual rites in imitation of the gods, who, presumably, generated terrestrial fertility through sexual intercourse.

Hosea began his career in the final days of Jeroboam II (1.1), whose reign capped a century of political stability and economic prosperity in the Northern Kingdom under the Jehu dynasty. Jeroboam died in 747 about the time that, in Assyria, Tiglath-pileser III came to power (745) and initiated a program of imperial expansion. A prolonged national crisis ensued, which ended with the demise of the Northern Kingdom. Israel floundered under the Assyrian onslaught: Of the six kings who reigned in the next two decades, four were assassinated as the nation veered between appeasement, at the cost of heavy tribute, and rebellion, seeking futile alliances with Syria and Egypt. We cannot be sure when Hosea's prophetic career ended, though his oracles appear to allude to events right up to the Assyrian siege of Samaria in 722 (13.10–11,16).

During this national crisis, Hosea issued an unrelenting critique of existing political and religious institutions. Through dynastic kingship, political alliances with other nations, and, above all, illicit religious practices, Israel had violated the divine claim upon it, forged in the time of Moses, for exclusive dependence upon and worship of the LORD. As divine punishment, Israel would be stripped of political and religious institutions too corrupt to be reformed and its land left desolate and barren. Israel would, in essence, find itself again in the wilderness.

The severity of the prophetic critique, however, is juxtaposed with the language of divine longing and compassion (11.1–11; 13.4–7). In the short term, Hosea presented the disintegration of the northern state as inevitable. Drawing, however, on a pattern discerned in Israel's sacred traditions, Hosea ultimately offered hope. In this new wilderness, as in the Sinai desert, Israel would recognize its dependence on the LORD and be restored to a harmonious state with God, and with the natural world (2.14–23).

After the destruction of Samaria, Hosea's words were preserved and transmitted in Judah. Some or all of the references to Judah may have been added in this era as Hosea's words were reinterpreted to address an analogous situation there (e.g., 1.7; 3.5; 11.12). At the same time, it is possible that Hosea himself, though a northern prophet, addressed Judah as well.

The book has two major sections, which appear to be roughly chronological. Chapters 1–3 contain the material about Hosea's marriage and can be understood against the background of the last days of Jeroboam II, since 1.4 announces the demise of the Jehu dynasty of which Jeroboam was the final ruler. The second major section, chs 4–14, consists entirely of prophetic speeches that seem to allude to the chaotic days following the demise of the house of Jehu and the prolonged Assyria crisis. Boundaries between individual speech units in this second section are hard to discern. It seems to fall into two parts (chs 4–11; 12–14), rhetorically couched as legal indictments of Israel for breach of covenant (4.1; 12.2), and ending with images of restoration (11.1–11; 14.1–7).

1 The word of the LORD that came to
Hosea son of Beeri, in the days of Kings
Uzziah, Jotham, Ahaz, and Hezekiah of Ju-
dah, and in the days of King Jeroboam son
of Joash of Israel.
2 When the LORD first spoke through
Hosea, the LORD said to Hosea, "Go, take
for yourself a wife of whoredom and have
children of whoredom, for the land com-
mits great whoredom by forsaking the
LORD." 3 So he went and took Gomer
daughter of Diblaim, and she conceived
and bore him a son.
4 And the LORD said to him, "Name

1.1: Superscription. *Word of the LORD,* the customary term for prophetic verbal revelation (Jer 18.18). For similar introductions to prophetic books, see Joel 1.1, Mic 1.1, Zeph 1.1, and Mal 1.1. *Hosea* (= Hoshea) is also the name for other persons in the Hebrew Bible (e.g., Num 13.8; 2 Kings 15.3; 1 Chr 27.20; Neh 10.23) and means "salvation" or "deliverance." *Days of Kings Uzziah . . . ,* these kings of Judah reigned in Jerusalem in the last half of the eighth century BCE. Uzziah was a contemporary of *Jeroboam* II, who ruled 788–747 in Samaria, the capital of the Northern Kingdom, and Ahaz was king in Judah when Samaria fell. Presumably Hosea prophesied late in Jeroboam's reign and after his death.

1.2–3.5: Hosea's family life as a symbolic vehicle for divine communication. The prophetic acts of Hosea, detailed in two sections (1.2–2.1; 3.1–5), exemplify God's relationship with Israel in allegorical fashion. Between the narrative sections, a prophetic speech (2.2–23) indicts Israel for unfaithfulness and offers hope for restoration after a period of punishment.

1.2–2.1: Hosea's marriage to Gomer, and the birth, naming, and renaming of their children as prophetic signs. The marital states of Jeremiah (Jer 16.1–2) and Ezekiel (Ezek 24) also took on prophetic significance; Isaiah gave children symbolic names (Isa 7.3,10,14; 8.1,3). **1.2:** *Wife of whoredom,* a promiscuous woman. *Children of whoredom,* children born of promiscuity. **4–8:** Birth of three children, each with symbolic names. **4:** *Jezreel* ("God sows"), the site where Jehu's bloody coup d'etat began (2 Kings 9–10). *House of Jehu,* the Israelite dynasty founded by Jehu in 842 BCE extended for a century, ending with Jeroboam II. **6:** *Lo-ruhamah,* "Not loved;" cf. Ezek 16.4–5. **7:** *Judah,* Hosea's prophecies, originally

him Jezreel;[a] for in a little while I will pun-
ish the house of Jehu for the blood of Jezre-
el, and I will put an end to the kingdom of
the house of Israel. 5 On that day I will
break the bow of Israel in the valley of Jez-
reel."
6 She conceived again and bore a daugh-
ter. Then the LORD said to him, "Name her
Lo-ruhamah,[b] for I will no longer have
pity on the house of Israel or forgive them.
7 But I will have pity on the house of Judah,
and I will save them by the LORD their
God; I will not save them by bow, or by
sword, or by war, or by horses, or by horse-
men."
8 When she had weaned Lo-ruhamah,
she conceived and bore a son. 9 Then the
LORD said, "Name him Lo-ammi,[c] for
you are not my people and I am not your
God."[d]
10[e] Yet the number of the people of Isra-
el shall be like the sand of the sea, which
can be neither measured nor numbered;
and in the place where it was said to them,
"You are not my people," it shall be said to
them, "Children of the living God." 11 The
people of Judah and the people of Israel
shall be gathered together, and they shall
appoint for themselves one head; and they
shall take possession of[f] the land, for great
shall be the day of Jezreel.

2 [g]Say to your brother,[h] Ammi,[i] and to
your sister,[j] Ruhamah.[k]

2 Plead with your mother, plead—
for she is not my wife,
and I am not her husband—
that she put away her whoring from
her face,
and her adultery from between her
breasts,
3 or I will strip her naked
and expose her as in the day she
was born,
and make her like a wilderness,
and turn her into a parched land,
and kill her with thirst.
4 Upon her children also I will
have no pity,
because they are children of
whoredom.
5 For their mother has played
the whore;
she who conceived them has acted
shamefully.
For she said, "I will go after
my lovers;
they give me my bread and
my water,
my wool and my flax, my oil and
my drink."
6 Therefore I will hedge up her[l] way
with thorns;
and I will build a wall against her,
so that she cannot find her paths.
7 She shall pursue her lovers,
but not overtake them;
and she shall seek them,
but shall not find them.
Then she shall say, "I will go

a That is *God sows* *b* That is *Not pitied* *c* That is *Not my people* *d* Heb *I am not yours* *e* Ch 2.1 in Heb *f* Heb *rise up from* *g* Ch 2.3 in Heb *h* Gk: Heb *brothers* *i* That is *My people* *j* Gk Vg: Heb *sisters* *k* That is *Pitied* *l* Gk Syr: Heb *your*

addressed to Israel (Ephraim), were subsequently extended to the Southern Kingdom, whether by the prophet or later followers. **8:** *Weaned* the child, probably at age three (1 Sam 1.22; 2 Chr 31.16). **9:** *Lo-ammi,* "No-kin-of-mine." *I am not your God* can also be read, "I am not I AM" (see note *d*), as if God now withdraws the intimacy extended to Moses through revelation of the divine name (Ex 3.14). **1.10–2.1:** Jezreel's exaltation (1.11) and the renaming of Lo-ruhamah (2.1, *Ruhamah,* "Loved") and Lo-ammi (2.1, *Ammi,* "My-kin") signal restoration. **1.10:** For *the sand of the sea,* see the divine promise to Abraham (Gen 22.17) and Jacob (Gen 32.12); cf. Gen 15.5; 16.10; 1 Kings 3.8.

2.2–23: A prophetic speech based on the preceding sign-acts. Israel wrongly attributed its agricultural fertility to Baal, a Canaanite god. For this infidelity, the LORD first initiates divorce against Israel, the promiscuous wife; then promises a rebetrothal. **2:** *Plead with,* take legal action against. **3:** Ezekiel 16 expands this image. **4:** *No pity,* a pun on Lo-ruhamah. **5:** *My lovers,* foreign gods. *Wool and . . . flax,* pastoral and agricultural products, respectively, used for clothing. **8:** The LORD, not Baal, is Israel's benefactor.

and return to my first husband,
for it was better with me then than
now."
8 She did not know
that it was I who gave her
the grain, the wine, and the oil,
and who lavished upon her silver
and gold that they used for Baal.
9 Therefore I will take back
my grain in its time,
and my wine in its season;
and I will take away my wool and my
flax,
which were to cover her nakedness.
10 Now I will uncover her shame
in the sight of her lovers,
and no one shall rescue her out of
my hand.
11 I will put an end to all her mirth,
her festivals, her new moons, her
sabbaths,
and all her appointed festivals.
12 I will lay waste her vines and her fig
trees,
of which she said,
"These are my pay,
which my lovers have given me."
I will make them a forest,
and the wild animals shall devour
them.
13 I will punish her for the festival days
of the Baals,
when she offered incense to them
and decked herself with her ring and
jewelry,
and went after her lovers,
and forgot me, says the LORD.

14 Therefore, I will now allure her,
and bring her into the wilderness,
and speak tenderly to her.
15 From there I will give her her
vineyards,
and make the Valley of Achor a
door of hope.
There she shall respond as in the days
of her youth,
as at the time when she came out
of the land of Egypt.
16 On that day, says the LORD, you will call
me, "My husband," and no longer will you
call me, "My Baal."[a] 17 For I will remove
the names of the Baals from her mouth, and
they shall be mentioned by name no more.
18 I will make for you[b] a covenant on that
day with the wild animals, the birds of the
air, and the creeping things of the ground;
and I will abolish[c] the bow, the sword,
and war from the land; and I will make you
lie down in safety. 19 And I will take you for
my wife forever; I will take you for my wife
in righteousness and in justice, in steadfast
love, and in mercy. 20 I will take you for my
wife in faithfulness; and you shall know the
LORD.
21 On that day I will answer, says
the LORD,
I will answer the heavens

a That is, *"My master"* *b* Heb *them* *c* Heb *break*

11: The seasonal agricultural festivals (Ex 34.21–24) and the customary occasions for worship (Num 29.6; Ex 20.8) were now diluted by elements of Baalism. **13:** *Offered incense,* incense itself was a lawful Israelite element of worship (Ex 30.7–8) but here, unlawfully, it is offered to other gods (cf. 1 Kings 22.44; Isa 65.3). *Decked herself,* cf. Isa 3.16–22. **14:** *Allure her,* courtship language. The *wilderness* signifies Israel's early years after the Exodus, remembered here, in terms of the marital metaphor, as a honeymoon (Jer 2.2). The wilderness can also be a place of judgment (Ezek 20.33–38). In both cases, the wilderness is a place for transformation. **15:** *Achor,* a site just east of the Dead Sea where Israel got into "trouble" (the meaning of "Achor") soon after leaving the wilderness (Josh 7.22–26). **16:** *My Baal,* in secular usage, "baal" could also mean "husband." In this word play, Israel is to address the LORD as "husband" (Heb "'ish"), not as "husband" (Heb "baal"). **18:** *Animals, birds . . . , creeping things,* the phrases recall Gen 1.27–31 and suggest a return to a state of blessing. See also Lev 26.6. **20:** *You shall know,* "knowledge" implies covenant faithfulness and, in terms of the marital metaphor employed, intimacy. **20–23:** A conclusion to chs 1–2: The renaming of the children (see 1.4,6,9n.; 2.1n.) follows the rebetrothal of the LORD and Israel. **21–22:** Human faithfulness (or lack thereof) to the LORD has implications for the natural world. **23:** Cf. Ex 6.7; Lev 26.12.

and they shall answer the earth;
22 and the earth shall answer the grain,
the wine, and the oil,
and they shall answer Jezreel;[a]
23 and I will sow him[b] for myself in
the land.
And I will have pity on
Lo-ruhamah,[c]
and I will say to Lo-ammi,[d] "You
are my people";
and he shall say, "You are my
God."

3 The LORD said to me again, "Go, love
a woman who has a lover and is an
adulteress, just as the LORD loves the peo-
ple of Israel, though they turn to other gods
and love raisin cakes." 2 So I bought her for
fifteen shekels of silver and a homer of bar-
ley and a measure of wine.[e] 3 And I said to
her, "You must remain as mine for many
days; you shall not play the whore, you
shall not have intercourse with a man, nor
I with you." 4 For the Israelites shall remain
many days without king or prince, without
sacrifice or pillar, without ephod or tera-
phim. 5 Afterward the Israelites shall return
and seek the LORD their God, and David
their king; they shall come in awe to the
LORD and to his goodness in the latter
days.

4 Hear the word of the LORD, O people
of Israel;
for the LORD has an indictment
against the inhabitants
of the land.
There is no faithfulness or loyalty,
and no knowledge of God in
the land.
2 Swearing, lying, and murder,
and stealing and adultery
break out;
bloodshed follows bloodshed.
3 Therefore the land mourns,
and all who live in it languish;
together with the wild animals
and the birds of the air,
even the fish of the sea are
perishing.

4 Yet let no one contend,

a That is *God sows* *b* Cn: Heb *her* *c* That is *Not pitied* *d* That is *Not my people* *e* Gk: Heb *a homer of barley and a lethech of barley*

3.1–5: The restoration of Hosea's marriage. In a like manner, the LORD's relationship to Israel will be restored. This section is in first person while 1.2–2.1 was in third. Gomer is not mentioned here by name. **1:** *Raisin cakes* were associated with illicit worship (Isa 16.7; Jer 7.18; 44.19). **2:** *Shekel,* ca. 11.5 g (.4 oz); *homer,* about 230 l (6.5 bu). From whom Hosea *bought her* is not indicated. **3–4:** A transitional period is announced during which, on one level, the marital partners forgo relations, and on another, the covenant partners lack their customary mediators (king, prince) and religious mediations. *Pillar,* see 10.2; Gen 31.45. *Ephod,* Ex 28.6–14; 39.2–7; Judg 8.24–28; 1 Sam 2.18. *Teraphim,* Gen 31.19; probably ancestor statues. **5:** *David their king,* the sole reference in Hosea to a specifically Judahite institution such as the Davidic dynasty, Jerusalem, or Zion; probably a later addition.

4.1–14.9: The prophetic speeches of Hosea indict Israel for unfaithfulness and announce the divine judgment, while offering hope of eventual restoration. The boundaries between individual speech units in the remainder of the book are unclear. This may in part reflect the style of the prophet and may in part be due to later editorial rearrangement.

4.1–12.1: The LORD has an indictment against Israel. 4.1: *Hear the word of the LORD,* an introduction in the prophetic style, which serves both the immediate speech and the remainder of the book. *Israel,* the primary referent here is the Northern Kingdom (also known as Ephraim) but, like all of Hosea's prophecies, after 722 the prophecy is transmitted in Judah; so the address is also to Israel in its broader sense. *Indictment* is a legal term: On God's behalf, the prophet files suit against the people for breach of covenant. *Faithfulness, loyalty* (steadfast love), and *knowledge of God* are major theological terms in Hosea (2.19–20; 4.6; 5.4,7; 6.3,6; 10.12; 11.3–4,12b; 12.6). **2:** *Swearing* . . . , a full five of the Ten Commandments are listed (Ex 20.7,13–16; Deut 5.11,17–20). **3:** See 2.21n.

4.4–19: An indictment of corrupt religious practices. 4–8: The corruption issues from the priests. **4:** Legally, there are no grounds for a counterclaim against God. **5–6:** The phrases *destroy your mother* and

and let none accuse,
for with you is my contention,
O priest.[a]
5 You shall stumble by day;
the prophet also shall stumble with you by night,
and I will destroy your mother.
6 My people are destroyed for lack of knowledge;
because you have rejected knowledge,
I reject you from being a priest to me.
And since you have forgotten the law of your God,
I also will forget your children.

7 The more they increased,
the more they sinned against me;
they changed[b] their glory into shame.
8 They feed on the sin of my people;
they are greedy for their iniquity.
9 And it shall be like people, like priest;
I will punish them for their ways,
and repay them for their deeds.
10 They shall eat, but not be satisfied;
they shall play the whore, but not multiply;
because they have forsaken the LORD
to devote themselves to
11 whoredom.

Wine and new wine
take away the understanding.
12 My people consult a piece of wood,
and their divining rod gives them oracles.
For a spirit of whoredom has led them astray,
and they have played the whore, forsaking their God.
13 They sacrifice on the tops of the mountains,
and make offerings upon the hills,
under oak, poplar, and terebinth,
because their shade is good.

Therefore your daughters play the whore,
and your daughters-in-law commit adultery.
14 I will not punish your daughters when they play the whore,
nor your daughters-in-law when they commit adultery;
for the men themselves go aside with whores,
and sacrifice with temple prostitutes;
thus a people without understanding comes to ruin.

15 Though you play the whore, O Israel,
do not let Judah become guilty.
Do not enter into Gilgal,
or go up to Beth-aven,
and do not swear, "As the LORD lives."
16 Like a stubborn heifer,

a Cn: Meaning of Heb uncertain *b* Ancient Heb tradition: MT *I will change*

forget your children build on the foundation of 1.2–3.5. **7:** *The more ... the more,* for a similar formulation, see 11.2. **8:** *They feed,* the priests depend on the sacrificial system for food. Since more sins require more sacrifices, Hosea accuses the priests of a debased relationship in their role in the process of atonement. **9–14:** The corruption, detailed here in terms of drunkenness, sexual activity, and divination, spreads from priests to the rest of Ephraimite society. **10:** Human fertility, also part of the divine blessing (Gen 1.28), is affected by human unfaithfulness. **12:** *Piece of wood, divining rod,* the exact referents are unknown. Trees or wooden symbols were associated with the worship of Asherah, a Canaanite goddess. **13:** A reference to high-place sanctuaries and their sacred groves (Deut 12.2). *Their shade,* note the contrast between this shade and that of 14.7. **14:** The term *temple prostitutes* simply means "sacred women," i.e., female cultic officials, a feature in Canaanite but not orthodox Israelite practice. **15–19:** An admonishment to Judah: Do not let the contamination spread to you. **15:** *Gilgal, Beth-aven* (i.e., Bethel; Am 5.5), the northern shrines closest to Judah. *Beth-aven* (lit. "house of worthlessness") is a pejorative name for Bethel ("house of God"). **16:** *Stubborn heifer,* see 10.11. **17:** *Ephraim* was the name

Israel is stubborn;
can the LORD now feed them
like a lamb in a broad pasture?

17 Ephraim is joined to idols—
let him alone.
18 When their drinking is ended, they
indulge in sexual orgies;
they love lewdness more than their
glory.[a]
19 A wind has wrapped them[b] in
its wings,
and they shall be ashamed because
of their altars.[c]

5 Hear this, O priests!
Give heed, O house of Israel!
Listen, O house of the king!
For the judgment pertains to you;
for you have been a snare at Mizpah,
and a net spread upon Tabor,
2 and a pit dug deep in Shittim;[d]
but I will punish all of them.

3 I know Ephraim,
and Israel is not hidden from me;
for now, O Ephraim, you have played
the whore;
Israel is defiled.
4 Their deeds do not permit them
to return to their God.
For the spirit of whoredom is within
them,
and they do not know the LORD.

5 Israel's pride testifies against him;
Ephraim[e] stumbles in his guilt;
Judah also stumbles with them.
6 With their flocks and herds they shall
go
to seek the LORD,
but they will not find him;
he has withdrawn from them.
7 They have dealt faithlessly with the
LORD;
for they have borne illegitimate
children.
Now the new moon shall devour
them along with their fields.

8 Blow the horn in Gibeah,
the trumpet in Ramah.
Sound the alarm at Beth-aven;
look behind you, Benjamin!
9 Ephraim shall become a desolation
in the day of punishment;
among the tribes of Israel
I declare what is sure.

a Cn Compare Gk: Meaning of Heb uncertain
b Heb *her* *c* Gk Syr: Heb *sacrifices*
d Cn: Meaning of Heb uncertain *e* Heb *Israel and Ephraim*

for the region surrounding Samaria. Though often used as a general term for the Northern Kingdom, its use here and Hosea's preference for it over Israel in the rest of the book could reflect a changed political situation. Israel gradually lost its territory in Transjordan, Galilee, and Jezreel in this period; in the end Ephraim was all that remained.

5.1–6.6: The people do not know the LORD. 5.1: *The judgment,* in a legal sense. *Mizpah,* a fortress city on the border between Judah and Israel (1 Kings 15.22), probably housed, like many border towns, a sanctuary. *Tabor,* a mountain in the north of Palestine, overlooking the Jezreel valley (Ps 89.12); probably the site of a sanctuary (Deut 33.18–19). **2:** *Shittim,* a border town in Transjordan; the final encampment of the Israelites before they crossed the Jordan; also site of an infamy (Num 25.1–9). **3–4:** Note the word play with "knowledge": The LORD *knows* (is aware of) *Ephraim* ('s deeds) but *they do not know* (demonstrate loyalty toward) the LORD. **5–7:** Because of their disloyalty, the LORD will not be available to the people at festivals. **5:** *Israel's pride,* also in 7.10. **6:** *They shall go,* in pilgrimage festivals. **7:** *New moon shall devour,* meaning obscure. **8–14:** In the day of punishment the LORD will become the enemy of Israel (Am 9.2–4). This section may refer to the Syro-Ephraimite War (2 Kings 15.27–30) in 735, when Israel under Pekah formed a coalition with Syria to force Judah to join a rebellion against Assyria. **8:** *Blow the horn,* the alarm signal used by sentinels. *Gibeah, Ramah,* Benjaminite towns just north of Jerusalem, situated on the path an invading army would take approaching from the south (Isa 10.28–32); *Beth-aven,* see 4.15n. This may refer to a Judahite counterattack after the Syro-Ephraimite initiative failed. **10–14:** There is no defense against God. **10:** *Remove the landmark,* a landmark is a boundary marker, defining

10 The princes of Judah have become
like those who remove the
landmark;
on them I will pour out
my wrath like water.
11 Ephraim is oppressed, crushed in
judgment,
because he was determined to go
after vanity.[a]
12 Therefore I am like maggots to
Ephraim,
and like rottenness to the house of
Judah.
13 When Ephraim saw his sickness,
and Judah his wound,
then Ephraim went to Assyria,
and sent to the great king.[b]
But he is not able to cure you
or heal your wound.
14 For I will be like a lion to Ephraim,
and like a young lion to the house
of Judah.
I myself will tear and go away;
I will carry off, and no one
shall rescue.
15 I will return again to my place
until they acknowledge their guilt
and seek my face.
In their distress they will beg
my favor:

6 "Come, let us return to the LORD;
for it is he who has torn, and he
will heal us;
he has struck down, and he will
bind us up.
2 After two days he will revive us;
on the third day he will raise us up,
that we may live before him.
3 Let us know, let us press on to know
the LORD;
his appearing is as sure as
the dawn;
he will come to us like the showers,
like the spring rains that water the
earth."
4 What shall I do with you,
O Ephraim?
What shall I do with you, O Judah?
Your love is like a morning cloud,
like the dew that goes away early.
5 Therefore I have hewn them by the
prophets,
I have killed them by the words of
my mouth,
and my[c] judgment goes forth as
the light.
6 For I desire steadfast love and not
sacrifice,
the knowledge of God rather than
burnt offerings.

7 But at[d] Adam they transgressed the
covenant;
there they dealt faithlessly with me.
8 Gilead is a city of evildoers,
tracked with blood.
9 As robbers lie in wait[e] for someone,
so the priests are banded together;[f]
they murder on the road to Shechem,
they commit a monstrous crime.
10 In the house of Israel I have seen a
horrible thing;
Ephraim's whoredom is there, Israel
is defiled.

a Gk: Meaning of Heb uncertain *b* Cn: Heb *to a king who will contend* *c* Gk Syr: Heb *your* *d* Cn: Heb *like* *e* Cn: Meaning of Heb uncertain *f* Syr: Heb *are a company*

the extent of property. See Deut 19.14; 27.17; Prov 22.28; 23.10. **13:** *Went to Assyria,* Hoshea, the final king in Samaria (732–722 BCE), sought to appease Assyria in the wake of Pekah's failed rebellion (2 Kings 16.3). **5.15–6.6:** God punishes not to annihilate but in order to inspire repentance. This section is in the form of a dialogue. **6.2:** The punishment is temporary. *Two days . . . third day,* idiomatic expression for a brief period of time. **3:** *Spring rains,* the latter (March-April) rains (Deut 11.14). **4–6:** A summary of the entire speech. **4:** See the similar questions in 11.8. **6:** A persistent theme of the prophets (Am 5.22–24; Mic 6.6–8).

6.7–11a: An unholy gazetteer. 7: *At Adam,* a town in central Transjordan, close to where the Israelites crossed the Jordan (Josh 3.16). **8:** Men from *Gilead* participated in the assassination of King Pekahiah (2 Kings 15.25). **9:** *Shechem,* a major Ephraimite town, 12 km (7 mi) southeast of Samaria.

11 For you also, O Judah, a harvest
is appointed.

When I would restore the fortunes of
my people,

7 1 when I would heal Israel,
the corruption of Ephraim is
revealed,
and the wicked deeds of Samaria;
for they deal falsely,
the thief breaks in,
and the bandits raid outside.
2 But they do not consider
that I remember all their
wickedness.
Now their deeds surround them,
they are before my face.
3 By their wickedness they make the
king glad,
and the officials by their treachery.
4 They are all adulterers;
they are like a heated oven,
whose baker does not need to stir the
fire,
from the kneading of the dough
until it is leavened.
5 On the day of our king the officials
became sick with the heat of wine;
he stretched out his hand with
mockers.
6 For they are kindled[a] like an oven,
their heart burns within them;
all night their anger smolders;
in the morning it blazes like a
flaming fire.
7 All of them are hot as an oven,
and they devour their rulers.
All their kings have fallen;
none of them calls upon me.

8 Ephraim mixes himself with
the peoples;
Ephraim is a cake not turned.
9 Foreigners devour his strength,
but he does not know it;
gray hairs are sprinkled upon him,
but he does not know it.
10 Israel's pride testifies against[b] him;
yet they do not return to the LORD
their God,
or seek him, for all this.

11 Ephraim has become like a dove,
silly and without sense;
they call upon Egypt, they go
to Assyria.
12 As they go, I will cast my net
over them;
I will bring them down like birds of
the air;
I will discipline them according to
the report made to their
assembly.[c]
13 Woe to them, for they have strayed
from me!
Destruction to them, for they have
rebelled against me!
I would redeem them,
but they speak lies against me.

14 They do not cry to me from
the heart,
but they wail upon their beds;
they gash themselves for grain
and wine;
they rebel against me.

a Gk Syr: Heb *brought near* *b* Or *humbles*
c Meaning of Heb uncertain

6.11b–7.7: A corrupt people and government. 7.1: The theme of healing again (5.13; 6.1). *Samaria,* the capital of the Northern Kingdom. **4:** The time between the kneading of the dough and its fermentation is apparently when the oven was hottest. **5:** *Day of our king,* perhaps at an enthronement. **7:** *Devour their rulers,* four Israelite kings were assassinated between 747 and 732.

7.8–16: Mixing, religious and political, is bad. 8–10: Ephraim is a half-baked cake. **10:** Cf. 5.5. **11:** The *dove* was considered *silly* because it was overly familiar with humans and easily captured. *Egypt* and *Assyria* are the "foreigners" of v. 9. For the historical background, see 2 Kings 15.19–20; 17.3–4. **14:** The contrast is between acceptable forms of prayer, *crying to me from the heart,* and those which were unacceptable, such as *wailing upon their beds* (Isa 57.8) and self-mutilation (*they gash themselves*) (Deut 14.1; 1 Kings 18.28). **15:** Cf. 11.3–4. **16:** *Babbling,* i.e., negotiations conducted in the Egyptian language.

15 It was I who trained and strengthened
their arms,
yet they plot evil against me.
16 They turn to that which does not
profit;[a]
they have become like a
defective bow;
their officials shall fall by the sword
because of the rage of their tongue.
So much for their babbling in the
land of Egypt.

8 Set the trumpet to your lips!
One like a vulture[b] is over the
house of the LORD,
because they have broken my
covenant,
and transgressed my law.
2 Israel cries to me,
"My God, we—Israel—know
you!"
3 Israel has spurned the good;
the enemy shall pursue him.

4 They made kings, but not
through me;
they set up princes, but without my
knowledge.
With their silver and gold they made
idols
for their own destruction.
5 Your calf is rejected, O Samaria.
My anger burns against them.
How long will they be incapable of
innocence?
6 For it is from Israel,
an artisan made it;
it is not God.
The calf of Samaria
shall be broken to pieces.[c]

7 For they sow the wind,
and they shall reap the whirlwind.
The standing grain has no heads,
it shall yield no meal;
if it were to yield,
foreigners would devour it.
8 Israel is swallowed up;
now they are among the nations
as a useless vessel.
9 For they have gone up to Assyria,
a wild ass wandering alone;
Ephraim has bargained for lovers.
10 Though they bargain with
the nations,
I will now gather them up.
They shall soon writhe
under the burden of kings
and princes.

11 When Ephraim multiplied altars
to expiate sin,
they became to him altars for
sinning.
12 Though I write for him the multitude
of my instructions,
they are regarded as a strange
thing.
13 Though they offer choice sacrifices,[a]
though they eat flesh,
the LORD does not accept them.
Now he will remember their iniquity,
and punish their sins;
they shall return to Egypt.
14 Israel has forgotten his Maker,
and built palaces;
and Judah has multiplied fortified
cities;

a Cn: Meaning of Heb uncertain *b* Meaning of Heb uncertain *c* Or *shall go up in flames*

8.1–14: For the crime of assimilating foreign political models and religious practices, the punishment is foreign domination. 1–3: A military alarm signals the approach of an enemy, the Assyrians, the vehicle of divine judgment against Israel. This section is in the form of a dialogue. **1:** *Vulture,* or eagle, a symbol of the Assyrian army (Jer 49.22). **4:** *They made kings . . . without my knowledge,* without endorsement from the prophet of the LORD. **5–6:** There were calf images at the northern shrines of Dan and Bethel (1 Kings 12.28); the singular *calf* here probably refers to that at Bethel (10.5), the shrine closest to the city Samaria. *An artisan,* see Isa 40.19–20. **7–10:** As punishment for political defection, Israel shall be subjugated by foreigners. **9:** The phrase *a wild ass . . . Ephraim . . .* plays on the Heb words for wild ass ("pere") and Ephraim ("eprayim"); cf. Jer 2.24. **11–14:** As punishment for religious defection, Israel shall return to Egypt (cf. 9.3,6; 11.5; Deut 17.16). **12:** *My instructions,* my "torahs," the legacy of Moses.

but I will send a fire upon
his cities,
and it shall devour his strongholds.

9 Do not rejoice, O Israel!
Do not exult[a] as other nations do;
for you have played the whore,
departing from your God.
You have loved a prostitute's pay
on all threshing floors.
2 Threshing floor and wine vat shall
not feed them,
and the new wine shall fail them.
3 They shall not remain in the land of
the LORD;
but Ephraim shall return to Egypt,
and in Assyria they shall eat
unclean food.

4 They shall not pour drink offerings of
wine to the LORD,
and their sacrifices shall not please
him.
Such sacrifices shall be like mourners'
bread;
all who eat of it shall be defiled;
for their bread shall be for their
hunger only;
it shall not come to the house of
the LORD.

5 What will you do on the day of
appointed festival,
and on the day of the festival of the
LORD?
6 For even if they escape destruction,
Egypt shall gather them,
Memphis shall bury them.
Nettles shall possess their precious
things of silver;[b]
thorns shall be in their tents.

7 The days of punishment have come,
the days of recompense have come;
Israel cries,[c]
"The prophet is a fool,
the man of the spirit is mad!"
Because of your great iniquity,
your hostility is great.
8 The prophet is a sentinel for my God
over Ephraim,
yet a fowler's snare is on all his ways,
and hostility in the house of
his God.
9 They have deeply corrupted
themselves
as in the days of Gibeah;
he will remember their iniquity,
he will punish their sins.

10 Like grapes in the wilderness,
I found Israel.

a Gk: Heb *To exultation* *b* Meaning of Heb uncertain *c* Cn Compare Gk: Heb *shall know*

9.1–6: Israel's festivals are condemned. 1: *Prostitute's pay,* Gen 38.17; Deut 23.17; Mic 1.7. *Threshing floors*, harvest festivals were an occasion for communal worship; in this case, illicit worship. They were also the site of sexual overtures (Deut 3). **3:** See Am 7.17. **4:** *Drink offerings* were not, in themselves, forbidden; cf. Gen 35.14. *Mourners' bread* was unclean because of association with the dead. **6:** *Memphis* was the capital of Lower (northern) Egypt. *Tents* here probably refers to festival structures.

9.7–9: A response to the prophet's critics. 7: *Man of the spirit,* that is, the prophet (see Isa 11.2; 61.1; Ezek 2.2; Mic 3.8). **8:** For the prophet as *sentinel* who sees at a distance and announces the divine approach, see Isa 21.6; Jer 6.17; Ezek 3.16–21; 33.6–8. **9:** *Gibeah,* the infamous episode there and its aftermath are detailed in Judg 19–21.

9.10–11.11: Before and after. This section consists of a series of four metaphors (Israel as grapes in the wilderness, a luxuriant vine, a heifer trained, a beloved child) used to characterize the people's former fidelity and health, and contrasted with their present corrupt state brought about by religious, social, and political misdeeds. As the first three metaphors unfold, the cumulative message appears to be that the covenant is irrevocably broken and Israel is to be abandoned (9.17; 10.10; 10.15). The fourth part, the culmination of the series and, for many, the culmination of the prophecies of Hosea, initially continues in this vein (11.1–7), but then dramatically shifts from an angry to a compassionate tone (11.8–11).

9.10–17: Israel, grapes in the wilderness found by God (v. 10), is now desiccated (v. 16). 10: *Baal-*

Like the first fruit on the fig tree,
in its first season,
I saw your ancestors.
But they came to Baal-peor,
and consecrated themselves to a
thing of shame,
and became detestable like the
thing they loved.
11 Ephraim's glory shall fly away like a
bird—
no birth, no pregnancy, no
conception!
12 Even if they bring up children,
I will bereave them until no one is
left.
Woe to them indeed
when I depart from them!
13 Once I saw Ephraim as a young palm
planted in a lovely meadow,[a]
but now Ephraim must lead out his
children for slaughter.
14 Give them, O LORD—
what will you give?
Give them a miscarrying womb
and dry breasts.

15 Every evil of theirs began at Gilgal;
there I came to hate them.
Because of the wickedness of
their deeds
I will drive them out of my house.
I will love them no more;
all their officials are rebels.

16 Ephraim is stricken,
their root is dried up,
they shall bear no fruit.
Even though they give birth,
I will kill the cherished offspring of
their womb.
17 Because they have not listened to him,
my God will reject them;
they shall become wanderers among
the nations.

10 Israel is a luxuriant vine
that yields its fruit.
The more his fruit increased
the more altars he built;
as his country improved,
he improved his pillars.
2 Their heart is false;
now they must bear their guilt.
The LORD[b] will break down
their altars,
and destroy their pillars.

3 For now they will say:
"We have no king,
for we do not fear the LORD,
and a king—what could he do
for us?"
4 They utter mere words;
with empty oaths they make
covenants;
so litigation springs up like poisonous
weeds
in the furrows of the field.
5 The inhabitants of Samaria tremble
for the calf[c] of Beth-aven.
Its people shall mourn for it,
and its idolatrous priests shall
wail[d] over it,
over its glory that has departed
from it.
6 The thing itself shall be carried to
Assyria
as tribute to the great king.[e]
Ephraim shall be put to shame,

a Meaning of Heb uncertain *b* Heb *he* *c* Gk Syr: Heb *calves* *d* Cn: Heb *exult* *e* Cn: Heb *to a king who will contend*

peor, the site of an incident of grave disloyalty during the wilderness period (see Num 25.1–18). **15:** *Gilgal,* a venerable Israelite shrine near Jericho (e.g., Josh 4.20; 10.43; 1 Sam 7.16); condemned here as the site of illicit worship (4.15; 12.11; Am 4.4; 5.5). Also, at Gilgal the LORD reluctantly acceded to the people's request for a king (1 Sam 10.14–11.25).

10.1–7: Israel, a luxuriant vine (v. 1), is now weedy (v. 4) and overrun with thorns (v. 8). 1–2: In Canaan Israel increased in sin (here adopting illicit religious practices) as it increased in prosperity; cf. Deut 6.10–15. **2:** *Pillars,* standing stones, condemned by Mosaic law (Ex 23.24); see 3.4. **4:** *Empty oaths,* Ex 20.7. **5:** *Calf,* 8.5n. *Beth-aven,* see 4.15n. **8:** *Aven,* 10.5n. *Mountains, Cover us . . . ,* this phrase

and Israel shall be ashamed of his
idol.[a]

7 Samaria's king shall perish
like a chip on the face of
the waters.
8 The high places of Aven, the sin
of Israel,
shall be destroyed.
Thorn and thistle shall grow up
on their altars.
They shall say to the mountains,
Cover us,
and to the hills, Fall on us.

9 Since the days of Gibeah you have
sinned, O Israel;
there they have continued.
Shall not war overtake them in
Gibeah?
10 I will come[b] against the wayward
people to punish them;
and nations shall be gathered
against them
when they are punished[c] for their
double iniquity.

11 Ephraim was a trained heifer
that loved to thresh,
and I spared her fair neck;
but I will make Ephraim break the
ground;
Judah must plow;
Jacob must harrow for himself.
12 Sow for yourselves righteousness;
reap steadfast love;
break up your fallow ground;
for it is time to seek the LORD,
that he may come and rain
righteousness upon you.

13 You have plowed wickedness,
you have reaped injustice,
you have eaten the fruit of lies.
Because you have trusted in
your power
and in the multitude of your
warriors,
14 therefore the tumult of war shall rise
against your people,
and all your fortresses shall
be destroyed,
as Shalman destroyed Beth-arbel on
the day of battle
when mothers were dashed in
pieces with their children.
15 Thus it shall be done to you,
O Bethel,
because of your great wickedness.
At dawn the king of Israel
shall be utterly cut off.

11 When Israel was a child, I loved
him,
and out of Egypt I called my son.
2 The more I[d] called them,
the more they went from me;[e]
they kept sacrificing to the Baals,
and offering incense to idols.

3 Yet it was I who taught Ephraim to
walk,
I took them up in my[f] arms;
but they did not know that I healed
them.
4 I led them with cords of human
kindness,
with bands of love.
I was to them like those

a Cn: Heb *counsel* *b* Cn Compare Gk: Heb *In my desire* *c* Gk: Heb *bound* *d* Gk: Heb *they* *e* Gk: Heb *them* *f* Gk Syr Vg: Heb *his*

will be reused in New Testament depictions of divine judgment (Lk 23.30; Rev 6.16). **9:** *Gibeah,* 9.9n.

10.11–15: Heifer Israel now plows wickedness. 11: *Trained heifer,* compare with 4.16. *Spared her . . . neck,* i.e., she was unyoked. **12:** *Break up your fallow ground,* Jer 4.3. *Rain* is a frequent prophetic symbol of divine restoration and blessing (Isa 44.3; 45.8; 55.10). **13:** Contrast Ps 20.7, 44.6, Isa 31.1. **14:** *Shalman . . . Beth-arbel,* the allusion is unknown.

11.1–11: Israel as God's wayward child. This speech employs the culminating, and most intimate, metaphor in the series: Israel as the LORD's child. It also ends this long section, which began in 4.1, on a hopeful note. Here, the divine mood shifts from anger to compassion. **1:** Cf. Ex 4.22. **3:** Cf. 7.15. **5:**

who lift infants to their cheeks.[a]
I bent down to them and fed them.

5 They shall return to the land of Egypt,
and Assyria shall be their king,
because they have refused to return to me.
6 The sword rages in their cities,
it consumes their oracle-priests,
and devours because of their schemes.
7 My people are bent on turning away from me.
To the Most High they call,
but he does not raise them up at all.[b]

8 How can I give you up, Ephraim?
How can I hand you over, O Israel?
How can I make you like Admah?
How can I treat you like Zeboiim?
My heart recoils within me;
my compassion grows warm and tender.
9 I will not execute my fierce anger;
I will not again destroy Ephraim;
for I am God and no mortal,
the Holy One in your midst,
and I will not come in wrath.[b]

10 They shall go after the LORD,
who roars like a lion;
when he roars,
his children shall come trembling from the west.
11 They shall come trembling like birds from Egypt,
and like doves from the land of Assyria;
and I will return them to their homes, says the LORD.

12[c] Ephraim has surrounded me with lies,
and the house of Israel with deceit;
but Judah still walks[d] with God,
and is faithful to the Holy One.

12 Ephraim herds the wind,
and pursues the east wind all day long;
they multiply falsehood and violence;
they make a treaty with Assyria,
and oil is carried to Egypt.
2 The LORD has an indictment against Judah,
and will punish Jacob according to his ways,
and repay him according to his deeds.
3 In the womb he tried to supplant his brother,
and in his manhood he strove with God.
4 He strove with the angel and prevailed,
he wept and sought his favor;
he met him at Bethel,

a Or *who ease the yoke on their jaws* *b* Meaning of Heb uncertain *c* Ch 12.1 in Heb *d* Heb *roams* or *rules*

Return to . . . Egypt, 8.13; 9.3. **8–9:** At the pivotal point of this soliloquy, divine compassion overcomes divine anger. *Admah, Zeboiim,* cities destroyed along with Sodom and Gomorrah (Gen 19; Deut 29.23). **10:** In contrast with 5.14, this lion's *roar* is not aggressive but is a summons to its mate or cubs. **11:** *Doves,* contrast 7.11. These doves exhibit a homing instinct. *Egypt* and *Assyria,* contrast 9.3.

11.12–12.1: The futility of foreign alliances. 11.12: *But Judah still . . . ,* perhaps a later addition. **12.1:** Cf. 8.7. *Treaty with Assyria,* see 2 Kings 15.19–20; 17.3. *Oil . . . to Egypt,* Samaria was renowned for its olive oil, used here as a commodity of tribute to Egypt, which produced little.

12.2–14.9: Rebellion and restoration. Another major division in the book (like 4.1–12.1), which begins with the announcement of an indictment and ends with an oracle of hope.

12.2–13.16: A divine lawsuit against Israel, which mixes historical retrospection with contemporary critique. For a historical summary with a similar tone, see Ps 106. **12.2:** *The LORD has an indictment,* cf. 4.1. **3:** Gen 25.26; 32.22–30. **4–5:** Gen 28.11–17; 35.5–8. **7:** See Am 8.5. **8:** As if prosperity were

and there he spoke with him.[a]
5 The LORD the God of hosts,
the LORD is his name!
6 But as for you, return to your God,
hold fast to love and justice,
and wait continually for your God.

7 A trader, in whose hands are false
balances,
he loves to oppress.
8 Ephraim has said, "Ah, I am rich,
I have gained wealth for myself;
in all of my gain
no offense has been found in me
that would be sin."[b]
9 I am the LORD your God
from the land of Egypt;
I will make you live in tents again,
as in the days of the appointed
festival.

10 I spoke to the prophets;
it was I who multiplied visions,
and through the prophets I will
bring destruction.
11 In Gilead[c] there is iniquity,
they shall surely come to nothing.
In Gilgal they sacrifice bulls,
so their altars shall be like
stone heaps
on the furrows of the field.
12 Jacob fled to the land of Aram,
there Israel served for a wife,
and for a wife he guarded sheep.[d]
13 By a prophet the LORD brought Israel
up from Egypt,
and by a prophet he was guarded.
14 Ephraim has given bitter offense,
so his Lord will bring his crimes
down on him
and pay him back for his insults.

13 When Ephraim spoke, there was
trembling;
he was exalted in Israel;
but he incurred guilt through Baal
and died.
2 And now they keep on sinning
and make a cast image for
themselves,
idols of silver made according to their
understanding,
all of them the work of artisans.
"Sacrifice to these," they say.[e]
People are kissing calves!
3 Therefore they shall be like the
morning mist
or like the dew that goes
away early,
like chaff that swirls from the
threshing floor
or like smoke from a window.

4 Yet I have been the LORD your God
ever since the land of Egypt;
you know no God but me,
and besides me there is no savior.
5 It was I who fed[f] you in the
wilderness,
in the land of drought.
6 When I fed[g] them, they were
satisfied;
they were satisfied, and their heart
was proud;
therefore they forgot me.
7 So I will become like a lion to them,
like a leopard I will lurk beside the
way.
8 I will fall upon them like a bear
robbed of her cubs,
and will tear open the covering
of their heart;
there I will devour them like a lion,

a Gk Syr: Heb *us* *b* Meaning of Heb uncertain *c* Compare Syr: Heb *Gilead* *d* Heb lacks *sheep* *e* Cn Compare Gk: Heb *To these they say sacrifices of people* *f* Gk Syr: Heb *knew* *g* Cn: Heb *according to their pasture*

proof of virtue. **9:** *Tents,* a customary feature of seasonal rites (Lev 23.34–43; Deut 16.13) and symbolic of the wilderness period, will be all that remains for Israel following the divine punishment. **11:** Cf. 6.8n.; 9.15n. **12:** Gen 29.1–30. **13:** *By a prophet,* the first reference is clearly to Moses; the second may be Moses as well, or Samuel (1 Sam 3.20) or Elijah (1 Kings 18.22). **13.1:** An allusion to Ephraim's relative prosperity during much of the Divided Monarchy. **2:** *Kissing calves,* see 8.5–6n. **3:** *Morning mist,* cf. 6.4. **5:** Cf. 11.4. **8:** *A bear robbed of her cubs,* a popular image for ferocity (2 Sam 17.8; Prov 17.12). **9–11:**

as a wild animal would
mangle them.

9 I will destroy you, O Israel;
who can help you?[a]
10 Where now is[b] your king, that he
may save you?
Where in all your cities are
your rulers,
of whom you said,
"Give me a king and rulers"?
11 I gave you a king in my anger,
and I took him away in my wrath.

12 Ephraim's iniquity is bound up;
his sin is kept in store.
13 The pangs of childbirth come for him,
but he is an unwise son;
for at the proper time he does not
present himself
at the mouth of the womb.

14 Shall I ransom them from the power
of Sheol?
Shall I redeem them from Death?
O Death, where are[c] your plagues?
O Sheol, where is[c] your
destruction?
Compassion is hidden from
my eyes.

15 Although he may flourish among
rushes,[d]
the east wind shall come, a blast
from the LORD,
rising from the wilderness;
and his fountain shall dry up,
his spring shall be parched.
It shall strip his treasury
of every precious thing.
16[e] Samaria shall bear her guilt,
because she has rebelled against her
God;
they shall fall by the sword,
their little ones shall be dashed in
pieces,
and their pregnant women
ripped open.

14 Return, O Israel, to the LORD
your God,
for you have stumbled because of
your iniquity.
2 Take words with you
and return to the LORD;
say to him,
"Take away all guilt;
accept that which is good,
and we will offer
the fruit[f] of our lips.
3 Assyria shall not save us;
we will not ride upon horses;
we will say no more, 'Our God,'
to the work of our hands.
In you the orphan finds mercy."

4 I will heal their disloyalty;
I will love them freely,
for my anger has turned from them.
5 I will be like the dew to Israel;

a Gk Syr: Heb *for in me is your help* *b* Gk Syr Vg: Heb *I will be* *c* Gk Syr: Heb *I will be* *d* Or *among brothers* *e* Ch 14.1 in Heb *f* Gk Syr: Heb *bulls*

This may refer to the deposing of Hoshea by the Assyrians in 723 (2 Kings 17.4). **10:** *King . . . may save,* read this in light of 13.4: The LORD alone is Israel's savior. **11:** *I gave . . . a king in my anger,* cf. 1 Sam 12. **13:** The pain of divine judgment is designed not to kill but to induce new life, yet Israel, *unwise,* refuses to budge. **14:** *Death* (Mot), the Canaanite deity of the underworld, is probably referred to here; cf. Job 18.13; Ps 49.14; Isa 28.15; Hab 2.5. *Sheol,* in this era, the abode of all dead, righteous and unrighteous. In this judgment speech, *compassion is hidden,* unlike 11.8. **15:** *Flourish among rushes,* alludes to political reliance on Egypt, which will be blown away by the "east wind," Assyria. *The east wind . . . a blast from the LORD,* contrast this with an earlier east wind, the vehicle of the LORD's deliverance of Israel at the Red Sea (Ex 14.21; 15.8). **16:** The ravages of conquering armies; cf. 10.14; 2 Kings 8.12; Ps 137.9; Am 1.13.

14.1–8: A final plea for repentance and a vision of restoration. 2–3: *Take words,* i.e., take these words: The prophet coaches Israel in repentance. **3:** *Mercy* or "pity," the same root as in Lo-ruhamah/Ruhamah (1.6; 2.1). **6:** This *fragrance* is of the aromatic Lebanese cedar forest; in the next verse, of Lebanese scented

he shall blossom like the lily,
he shall strike root like the forests
of Lebanon.[a]
6 His shoots shall spread out;
his beauty shall be like the
olive tree,
and his fragrance like that of
Lebanon.
7 They shall again live beneath
my[b] shadow,
they shall flourish as a garden;[c]
they shall blossom like the vine,
their fragrance shall be like the
wine of Lebanon.

8 O Ephraim, what have I[d] to do with
idols?
It is I who answer and look
after you.[e]
I am like an evergreen cypress;
your faithfulness[f] comes from me.
9 Those who are wise understand these
things;
those who are discerning
know them.
For the ways of the LORD are right,
and the upright walk in them,
but transgressors stumble in them.

a Cn: Heb *like Lebanon* *b* Heb *his* *c* Cn: Heb *they shall grow grain* *d* Or *What more has Ephraim* *e* Heb *him* *f* Heb *your fruit*

wine. **7–8:** *My shadow,* more common is the poetic image of the "shade" under God's wings (Ps 17.8; 36.8); uniquely here, God's shade is that of a great tree.

14.9: A postscript in the style of wisdom literature. For the first half of the verse, cf. Ps 107.43; Jer 9.12; for the second, Prov 10.29.

JOEL

Of the prophet Joel himself nothing is known except that he was the son of Pethuel (1.1). From his book it appears that he lived in Judah during the Persian period (539–331 BCE). Thus the book's placement between Hosea and Amos among the Minor Prophets is not chronological and is apparently based on thematic and verbal correspondences between the end of Joel and the beginning of Amos. Joel 3.16a and Amos 1.2a are identical, and the final chapter of Joel and the initial chapter of Amos contain oracles against Tyre and Philistia.

Joel is not only acquainted with the Temple at Jerusalem, but is so much interested in its priesthood and services that, like Haggai and Zechariah, he can be considered a "cultic prophet," that is, a prophet who could exercise his ministry within the life of the Temple, even using liturgical forms, and whose message may have been transmitted through priestly circles. As such, Joel helps to mark a notable change in prophecy in the Hebrew Bible. Taking the characteristic forms of classical prophecy, he expands their apocalyptic and liturgical dimensions.

The dates of Joel's career cannot be determined with precision. The majority of historical references in the book, the absence of any mention of the Assyrians or Babylonians, and the heavy borrowing from other prophets point to the period from about 400 to 350 BCE.

The book has two major sections, and the second builds on the first. Joel viewed a locust plague that ravaged the country—a plague that devastated both the human community and the natural world—as God's judgment on the people, and he called them to repentance (1.2–2.27). Using this catastrophe as a dire warning, Joel went on to depict the coming of the "Day of the LORD" and its final judgments and blessings (2.28–3.21).

1 The word of the LORD that came to Joel son of Pethuel:

2 Hear this, O elders,
give ear, all inhabitants of the land!
Has such a thing happened in your days,
or in the days of your ancestors?
3 Tell your children of it,
and let your children tell their children,
and their children another generation.

4 What the cutting locust left,
the swarming locust has eaten.
What the swarming locust left,
the hopping locust has eaten,

1.1: Superscription. *Joel* means "Yahweh is God."

1.2–2.27: The day of the locusts. The prophet discerns the transcendent significance of an ecological catastrophe: Judah devastated by a swarm of the desert locust, an insect distantly related to the American grasshopper that can multiply very rapidly and suddenly appear in huge, dense swarms that will devour all of the crops in a wide area.

1.2–14: A call to lament. The entire community is called upon to express grief ritually. **2:** The *elders* appear to be the chief leaders, as was the case in the postexilic era (Ezra 5.9; 6.8,14; 10.8,14). No king is mentioned. **4:** For other references to *locust* plagues, see Ex 10.22; Ps 78.46; 105.34–35; Am 4.9. For prophetic allusions to locust behavior, see Isa 33.4; Nah 3.15–16. **6:** Cf. Rev 9.7–8, which draws on the

and what the hopping locust left,
the destroying locust has eaten.

5 Wake up, you drunkards, and weep;
and wail, all you wine-drinkers,
over the sweet wine,
for it is cut off from your mouth.
6 For a nation has invaded my land,
powerful and innumerable;
its teeth are lions' teeth,
and it has the fangs of a lioness.
7 It has laid waste my vines,
and splintered my fig trees;
it has stripped off their bark and
thrown it down;
their branches have turned white.

8 Lament like a virgin dressed in
sackcloth
for the husband of her youth.
9 The grain offering and the drink
offering are cut off
from the house of the LORD.
The priests mourn,
the ministers of the LORD.
10 The fields are devastated,
the ground mourns;
for the grain is destroyed,
the wine dries up,
the oil fails.

11 Be dismayed, you farmers,
wail, you vinedressers,
over the wheat and the barley;
for the crops of the field are ruined.
12 The vine withers,
the fig tree droops.
Pomegranate, palm, and apple—
all the trees of the field are
dried up;
surely, joy withers away
among the people.

13 Put on sackcloth and lament,
you priests;
wail, you ministers of the altar.
Come, pass the night in sackcloth,
you ministers of my God!
Grain offering and drink offering
are withheld from the house of
your God.

14 Sanctify a fast,
call a solemn assembly.
Gather the elders
and all the inhabitants of the land
to the house of the LORD your God,
and cry out to the LORD.

15 Alas for the day!
For the day of the LORD is near,
and as destruction from the
Almighty[a] it comes.
16 Is not the food cut off
before our eyes,
joy and gladness
from the house of our God?

17 The seed shrivels under the clods,[b]
the storehouses are desolate;
the granaries are ruined
because the grain has failed.
18 How the animals groan!
The herds of cattle wander about
because there is no pasture for them;
even the flocks of sheep are
dazed.[c]

19 To you, O LORD, I cry.
For fire has devoured
the pastures of the wilderness,

a Traditional rendering of Heb *Shaddai* *b* Meaning of Heb uncertain *c* Compare Gk Syr Vg: Meaning of Heb uncertain

imagery of Joel (see also 2.4n., 2.11n.). **8:** *Sackcloth,* a mourning garment, woven from goat-hair, black in color. *A virgin . . . the husband,* the marriage betrothed but not consummated (cf. Deut 22.23). **9:** *Grain* and *drink offerings* accompanied sacrifices (see, e.g., Num 29.12–16). **12:** *Joy withers away,* in good times, harvests were occasions for festivals (Isa 9.3). **13:** *Withheld from the house of your God,* echoing 1.9, this refrain emphasizes the transcendent dimension of the crisis: Without grain and drink, a vital mediation, the daily offering is imperiled.

1.15–20: A lament. 15: *The day of the LORD,* i.e., Zeph 1.14–18; for the concept, see Introduction to

and flames have burned
all the trees of the field.
20 Even the wild animals cry to you
because the watercourses are dried up,
and fire has devoured
the pastures of the wilderness.

2 Blow the trumpet in Zion;
sound the alarm on my holy mountain!
Let all the inhabitants of the land tremble,
for the day of the LORD is coming,
it is near—
2 a day of darkness and gloom,
a day of clouds and thick darkness!
Like blackness spread upon the mountains
a great and powerful army comes;
their like has never been from of old,
nor will be again after them
in ages to come.

3 Fire devours in front of them,
and behind them a flame burns.
Before them the land is like the garden of Eden,
but after them a desolate wilderness,
and nothing escapes them.

4 They have the appearance of horses,
and like war-horses they charge.
5 As with the rumbling of chariots,
they leap on the tops of the mountains,
like the crackling of a flame of fire
devouring the stubble,
like a powerful army
drawn up for battle.
6 Before them peoples are in anguish,
all faces grow pale.[a]
7 Like warriors they charge,
like soldiers they scale the wall.
Each keeps to its own course,
they do not swerve from[b] their paths.
8 They do not jostle one another,
each keeps to its own track;
they burst through the weapons
and are not halted.
9 They leap upon the city,
they run upon the walls;
they climb up into the houses,
they enter through the windows
like a thief.

10 The earth quakes before them,
the heavens tremble.
The sun and the moon are darkened,
and the stars withdraw their shining.
11 The LORD utters his voice
at the head of his army;
how vast is his host!
Numberless are those who obey his command.
Truly the day of the LORD is great;
terrible indeed—who can endure it?

12 Yet even now, says the LORD,
return to me with all your heart,
with fasting, with weeping, and with mourning;

a Meaning of Heb uncertain *b* Gk Syr Vg: Heb *they do not take a pledge along*

Amos. **20:** *The wild animals cry to you,* Job 38.39–41. *The watercourses are dried up,* this will be reversed at the end of the book (3.18).

2.1–11: The locust plague, an act of God. 1: The priests blow the ram's horn (the "shophar") to warn of imminent danger (Hos 5.8; Am 3.6; Zeph 1.16). **2:** The image of the dense locust cloud (i.e., Ex 10.22) merges with that of the ominous qualities of God's approach (Deut 5.22–23; Am 5.18–20; Zeph 1.15). **3:** Cf. Ex 10.22; contrast Ezek 36.35. For *the garden of Eden,* see Gen 2.8–9. **4:** Rev 9.7. **6:** Nah 2.10. **10:** Again, traditional language about the awesome and terrifying aspects of the divine visitation is invoked to describe the approach of the locusts (Judg 4.5; Am 8.9; Hab 3.5–6). **11:** Rev 6.17.

2.12–17: A call to repent. A call to repentance, by which the total calamity may yet be averted. **12–13:** Joel prescribes outward expressions of repentance (*fasting, weeping, mourning*), which emerge from an inward reorientation, *all your heart* (Deut 30.10; Hos 3.5; Am 3.5). **13:** In this crisis, Joel stresses the

13 rend your hearts and not
your clothing.
Return to the LORD, your God,
for he is gracious and merciful,
slow to anger, and abounding in
steadfast love,
and relents from punishing.
14 Who knows whether he will not turn
and relent,
and leave a blessing behind him,
a grain offering and a drink offering
for the LORD, your God?

15 Blow the trumpet in Zion;
sanctify a fast;
call a solemn assembly;
16 gather the people.
Sanctify the congregation;
assemble the aged;
gather the children,
even infants at the breast.
Let the bridegroom leave his
room,
and the bride her canopy.

17 Between the vestibule and the altar
let the priests, the ministers of the
LORD, weep.
Let them say, "Spare your people,
O LORD,
and do not make your heritage a
mockery,
a byword among the nations.
Why should it be said among the
peoples,
'Where is their God?' "

18 Then the LORD became jealous for his
land,
and had pity on his people.
19 In response to his people the
LORD said:
I am sending you
grain, wine, and oil,
and you will be satisfied;
and I will no more make you
a mockery among the nations.

20 I will remove the northern army far
from you,
and drive it into a parched and
desolate land,
its front into the eastern sea,
and its rear into the western sea;
its stench and foul smell will rise up.
Surely he has done great things!

21 Do not fear, O soil;
be glad and rejoice,
for the LORD has done great things!
22 Do not fear, you animals of the field,
for the pastures of the wilderness
are green;
the tree bears its fruit,
the fig tree and vine give their full
yield.

23 O children of Zion, be glad
and rejoice in the LORD your God;
for he has given the early rain[a] for
your vindication,

a Meaning of Heb uncertain

merciful elements in this classic formulation of the divine personality (Ex 34.6–7; contrast Nah 1.3). **14:** Characteristically, Joel regards Temple offerings as *a blessing.* **15:** 1.14; 2.1. **17:** *Between the vestibule* (1 Kings 6.3), the entrance into the Temple building itself, *and the altar,* situated in the Temple's outer court (2 Chr 4.1): the customary site for priestly intercession (1 Kings 8.22; Ezek 8.16). *Why should it be said,* for other appeals to God's honor, see, e.g., Ps 79.10; 115.2.

2.18–27: An oracle of salvation. The turning point: God promises the remission of the plague (vv. 20,25), the return of fertility (vv. 19,21–24), the removal of *shame* (vv. 26–27), and the restoration of covenantal blessing (vv. 26–27). The horizon of God's direct address includes the *soil* (v. 21) and the *animals* (v. 22) in addition to the human community (*children of Zion;* v. 23). **18:** *Jealous for his land,* the kind of divine passion exhibited on the Day of the LORD (e.g., Zeph 1.18) is now directed toward their deliverance, not their destruction. **20:** The *army* here means the locusts, though the adjective *northern* recalls images of other enemies from Jeremiah (1.14–15) and Ezekiel (39.1–2). *The eastern sea,* the Dead Sea. *The western sea,* the Mediterranean. **23:** *The early rain* (in October-November) and *the later rain* (in March-April) were rewards of the covenant with the LORD (Deut 11.14). **27:** Isa 45.5–6.

he has poured down for you
abundant rain,
the early and the later rain,
as before.
24 The threshing floors shall be full
of grain,
the vats shall overflow with wine
and oil.

25 I will repay you for the years
that the swarming locust has
eaten,
the hopper, the destroyer, and the
cutter,
my great army, which I sent against
you.

26 You shall eat in plenty and be
satisfied,
and praise the name of the LORD
your God,
who has dealt wondrously with
you.
And my people shall never again be
put to shame.
27 You shall know that I am in the
midst of Israel,
and that I, the LORD, am your God
and there is no other.
And my people shall never again be
put to shame.

28[a] Then afterward
I will pour out my spirit on
all flesh;
your sons and your daughters shall
prophesy,
your old men shall dream dreams,
and your young men shall
see visions.
29 Even on the male and female slaves,
in those days, I will pour out
my spirit.

30 I will show portents in the heavens
and on the earth, blood and fire and col-
umns of smoke. 31 The sun shall be turned
to darkness, and the moon to blood, before
the great and terrible day of the LORD
comes. 32 Then everyone who calls on the
name of the LORD shall be saved; for in
Mount Zion and in Jerusalem there shall be
those who escape, as the LORD has said,
and among the survivors shall be those
whom the LORD calls.

3 [b]For then, in those days and at that
time, when I restore the fortunes of Ju-
dah and Jerusalem, 2 I will gather all the
nations and bring them down to the valley
of Jehoshaphat, and I will enter into judg-
ment with them there, on account of my
people and my heritage Israel, because they
have scattered them among the nations.
They have divided my land, 3 and cast lots

a Ch 3.1 in Heb *b* Ch 4.1 in Heb

2.28–3.21: The Day of the LORD. The stage expands as the prophet, still drawing on Day of the LORD traditions, turns a terrestrial drama into a cosmic one. The deliverance from the desert locusts portends Judah's ultimate vindication, described here in apocalyptic language.

2.28–32: The faithful are delivered. 28–29: The entire community will share the immediacy and intimacy with God characteristic of prophets, echoing (Jer 31.31–34; Ezek 37.14) and expanding (Isa 11.2–3) the grandest hopes of the prophetic tradition. The mention of *sons, daughters, old men, young men,* and *male and female slaves* both levels and exalts an entire society in harmony with God. **28:** For Joel, *all flesh* meant primarily the Judahites (3.2,17,19–21); in the reappropriation of this passage by Peter at Pentecost it included all nations (Acts 2.17). **30–31:** A description of judgment day; the imagery influences descriptions in the New Testament (Mk 13.24; Rev 6.12). **31:** Here *blood* indicates color. **32:** In the midst of a cosmic catastrophe, those who seek refuge in the LORD, on *Mount Zion* (Ob 17), will survive. *Everyone who calls on the name of the LORD shall be saved,* cited in the New Testament in Acts 2.21; Rom 10.13.

3.1–21: The nations are judged. 1–3: The day of judgment for the nations that have oppressed Israel. **2:** *Valley of Jehoshaphat* ("Yahweh judges"), called "the valley of decision" in v. 14, is probably symbolic, though some traditions locate it in the Kidron valley. **3:** *Cast lots,* for the distribution of the conquered (Ob 11; Nah 3.10).

for my people, and traded boys for prosti-
tutes, and sold girls for wine, and drunk it
down.
4 What are you to me, O Tyre and Si-
don, and all the regions of Philistia? Are
you paying me back for something? If you
are paying me back, I will turn your deeds
back upon your own heads swiftly and
speedily. 5 For you have taken my silver and
my gold, and have carried my rich treasures
into your temples.[a] 6 You have sold the
people of Judah and Jerusalem to the
Greeks, removing them far from their own
border. 7 But now I will rouse them to leave
the places to which you have sold them,
and I will turn your deeds back upon your
own heads. 8 I will sell your sons and your
daughters into the hand of the people of
Judah, and they will sell them to the Sabe-
ans, to a nation far away; for the LORD has
spoken.

9 Proclaim this among the nations:
Prepare war,[b]
stir up the warriors.
Let all the soldiers draw near,
let them come up.
10 Beat your plowshares into swords,
and your pruning hooks into
spears;
let the weakling say, "I am a
warrior."

11 Come quickly,[c]
all you nations all around,
gather yourselves there.
Bring down your warriors, O LORD.
12 Let the nations rouse themselves,
and come up to the valley of
Jehoshaphat;
for there I will sit to judge
all the neighboring nations.

13 Put in the sickle,
for the harvest is ripe.
Go in, tread,
for the wine press is full.
The vats overflow,
for their wickedness is great.

14 Multitudes, multitudes,
in the valley of decision!
For the day of the LORD is near
in the valley of decision.
15 The sun and the moon are darkened,
and the stars withdraw their
shining.

16 The LORD roars from Zion,
and utters his voice from Jerusalem,
and the heavens and the earth
shake.
But the LORD is a refuge for his
people,
a stronghold for the people of
Israel.

17 So you shall know that I, the LORD
your God,
dwell in Zion, my holy mountain.
And Jerusalem shall be holy,
and strangers shall never again pass
through it.

18 In that day
the mountains shall drip sweet wine,
the hills shall flow with milk,

a Or *palaces* *b* Heb *sanctify war* *c* Meaning of Heb uncertain

3.4–8: An oracle against Phoenicia and Philistia. Israel's coastal rivals, Tyre (Isa 23; Ezek 26.1–28.19; Am 1.9–10; Zech 9.3–4), *Sidon* (Ezek 28.20–26; Zech 9.2), and *Philistia* (Isa 14.29–31; Jer 47; Ezek 25.15–17; Am 1.6–8; Zeph 2.4–7; Zech 9.5–7) receive their ironic recompense. The LORD *will sell* (v. 8) into slavery those who, previously (v. 3), had *sold* others. **8:** *Sabeans,* an Arabian (Job 1.14–15) or African (Isa 45.14) group.

3.9–17: The LORD throws down the gauntlet to the nations. 10: *Plowshares into swords,* see Mic 4.3n. **13:** Israel's three major crops are contained in this metaphor: grain (harvested by *sickle*); grapes (trodden and pressed); and olive oil (in *vats*). For judgment as a harvest, see Isa 63.1–6. **14:** The *multitudes,* the melee of massed warriors; cf. Dan 11.10–12. **15–16:** 2.10–11. **16:** Am 1.2.

3.18–21: **The divine blessings** bestowed in that day include the paradisiacal fertility of the land, the

and all the stream beds of Judah
shall flow with water;
a fountain shall come forth from the
house of the LORD
and water the Wadi Shittim.

19 Egypt shall become a desolation
and Edom a desolate wilderness,
because of the violence done to the
people of Judah,
in whose land they have shed
innocent blood.
20 But Judah shall be inhabited forever,
and Jerusalem to all generations.
21 I will avenge their blood, and I will
not clear the guilty,[a]
for the LORD dwells in Zion.

a Gk Syr: Heb *I will hold innocent their blood that I have not held innocent*

destruction of Israel's ancient enemies, and the restoration of Judah. **18:** *Mountains shall drip sweet wine,* Am 9.13. *Wadi Shittim,* the precise location is unknown; it could be symbolic (cf. vv. 2,14; see Num 25.1). For the image of a great river issuing from Jerusalem, see Ezek 47.1–12; Zech 14.8.

AMOS

The book of Amos is a compilation of sayings attributed to the prophet Amos, who was active in the first half of the eighth century BCE, during the long and peaceful reign of Jeroboam II (788–747; Am 1.1). In this period, Israel attained a height of territorial expansion and national prosperity never again reached. At the same time, this prosperity led to gross inequities between urban elites and the poor. Through manipulation of debt and credit, wealthy landowners amassed capital and estates at the expense of small farmers. The smallest debt served as the thin end of a wedge that lenders could use to separate farmers from their patrimonial farms and personal liberty.

Into this scene stepped Amos, a native of a small village in the Southern Kingdom, Judah, and himself a farmer and herder, probably during the decade 760–750 BCE. Amos denounced the society of the Northern Kingdom, Israel, in vivid language, bitterly describing the decadent opulence, immorality, and smug piety of elites who "trampled the head of the poor into the dust of the earth." Amos's program, in contrast, called for "justice" and "righteousness" (5.7,24; 6.12), terms that connote social equality and concern for the disadvantaged (Isa 5.7; Mic 6.8).

Against the background of Israelite tradition about "the Day of the LORD," occasions celebrated from the past and eagerly anticipated in the future when the LORD dramatically intervenes in human affairs, Amos announced that such a day was imminent. This time, however, the fortified palaces and temples of Israel would be leveled along with those of Israel's rival nations (1.3–2.3) when God executed the divine version of "justice and righteousness." Israel's covenant with God (3.2) did not absolve it from this ethical standard, which Amos, in so many words, universalized (9.7–8). Though Amos affirmed the special quality of God's relationship with Israel (9.8), he stressed that it entails a special ethical responsibility (3.1). The agent of this divine punishment would be the Assyrian army (Isa 10.5–11). The frequent references to exile in Amos (e.g., 3.11; 6.7; 7.17) reflect a grim threat, the Assyrian imperial practice of deporting and transplanting conquered peoples.

The book contains a variety of material. Some of Amos's sayings are presented as messenger speech ("thus says the LORD"), others as visions ("This is what the LORD showed me"), especially in chs 7–9. Amos, in a legal style of indictment followed by punishment ("therefore . . ."), announced judgments (e.g., 1.3–2.16), delivered funeral orations (e.g., 5.1–2), and exhorted (e.g., 5.6). He rarely encouraged (see 9.11–15 and the notes there). In addition to the above types of prophetic sayings, the book contains three fragments from a hymn (4.13; 5.8–9; 9.5–6) and one narrative, about Amos's encounter with Amaziah, priest of the Northern Kingdom's royal sanctuary at Bethel (7.10–17).

That narrative and the superscription (1.1) yield the only portrait of the prophet. A native of the southern state of Judah who raised livestock and tended fruit trees, Amos prophesied to and in the northern state, Israel. At Bethel (7.13) his bitter invective, voiced as divine word ("I hate, I despise your festivals," 5.21) no doubt scandalized pilgrims from Samaria, capital of the Northern Kingdom. His confrontation with Amaziah (7.10–17) remains one of the unforgettable scenes in biblical prophecy. Expelled from the royal sanctuary and commanded not to prophesy there again, Amos perhaps returned to Judah where he, or like-minded scribes, wrote down the essence of his public preaching in substantially its present form.

Amos's prophetic career was roughly contemporaneous with that of Hosea, though Amos probably preceded him. Chronologically, then, Amos inaugurated the era of classical prophecy. In some ancient manuscript traditions (the Septuagint [LXX], the ancient Greek translation of the Hebrew Bible), the book of Amos directly follows Hosea. The traditional arrangement of the Book of the Twelve, however, is based not solely on chronology but often on specific verbal similarities that link the end of one book to the beginning of the next. Amos is linked to its predecessor Joel by identical phrases (see Joel 3.16a and Am 1.2a) and to its successor Obadiah by a similar subject (Edom in Am 9.12 and in Ob 1).

The book of Amos falls into three major parts: Chs 1–2 represent a single speech, an ethical tour of the region from the divine perspective, which climaxes in the indictment of Israel itself; chs 3–6 are the most variegated section and form a collection of short prophetic sayings indicting Israel for sin and injustice; chs 7–9 contain the visions of Amos, as well as the Amaziah narrative (7.10–17) and a final speech of comfort (9.11–15) addressed not to Israel but to Judah. The best approach for readers is to follow the sequence of the book itself.

The book of Amos begins and ends with references to an earthquake (1.1 and the images of shaking in 9.1–9). We do not know its exact year (760 has been proposed), but there is archaeological evidence of a catastrophe. Did this earthquake, so severe that it was recalled centuries later (Zech 14.5), offer cosmic validation of Amos's preaching? We cannot know. Still, even today we feel the aftershocks of Amos, the first in a brilliant succession of biblical prophets whose words, now preserved in written form, have left their indelible stamp on later thought about God and human history.

1 The words of Amos, who was among the shepherds of Tekoa, which he saw concerning Israel in the days of King Uzziah of Judah and in the days of King Jeroboam son of Joash of Israel, two years[a] before the earthquake.
2 And he said:
The LORD roars from Zion,
and utters his voice from Jerusalem;
the pastures of the shepherds wither,
and the top of Carmel dries up.

3 Thus says the LORD:
For three transgressions of Damascus,

a Or *during two years*

1.1: Superscription. *Amos* means "one supported" (by the LORD). *Among the shepherds,* the word translated "shepherds" probably denotes a herder or owner of large flocks rather than a hired worker; the same word is translated "sheepbreeder" in 2 Kings 3.4, its only other occurrence in the Bible. See also 7.14–15. *Tekoa* was a town in Judah, ca. 16 km (10 mi) south of Jerusalem. *He saw,* see Nah 1.1; visions were common among prophets from Judah (e.g., Isaiah and Ezekiel). *Uzziah* reigned over the Southern Kingdom 785–733 BCE. *Jeroboam* II reigned over the Northern Kingdom 788–747. The *earthquake,* mentioned again in Zech 14.5, cannot be precisely dated.

1.2–2.16: A speech against the nations. A common feature of Israelite prophecy was the indictment of foreign nations, which implied the LORD's universal sovereignty. In general, Amos indicts the neighboring peoples for ethical transgressions on the order of war crimes. Near the end of this section, when Amos addresses Judah and Israel, the ethical standard is more exacting. There is another way to look at the indictments directed toward these foreign nations. All the nations discussed were either subject to or allies of the Davidic and Solomonic monarchy, and therefore bound by treaties to which the LORD would have been a witness and now was acting as enforcer of the treaty curses. **1.2:** This introductory verse occurs in similar form in Joel 3.16 (cf. Jer 25.30). *The LORD roars,* Amos uses the image of God as lion again in 3.4,8. The sequence *from Jerusalem . . .* (to) *Carmel* traces the trajectory of the book as Amos, a southerner from the vicinity of Jerusalem, addresses the Northern Kingdom, whose northwest boundary was Mt. Carmel (see 9.3n.). **3,6,8, etc.:** *Thus says the LORD* and the conclusion *says the LORD* are standard

and for four, I will not revoke the
punishment;[a]
because they have threshed Gilead
with threshing sledges of iron.
4 So I will send a fire on the house
of Hazael,
and it shall devour the strongholds
of Ben-hadad.
5 I will break the gate bars of
Damascus,
and cut off the inhabitants from the
Valley of Aven,
and the one who holds the scepter
from Beth-eden;
and the people of Aram shall go
into exile to Kir,
says the LORD.

6 Thus says the LORD:
For three transgressions of Gaza,
and for four, I will not revoke the
punishment;[a]

a Heb *cause it to return*

formulas identifying prophetic oracles. The idiom *for three . . . and for four* indicates "more than enough" (Prov 30.18; Job 33.14).

1.3–5: Against Damascus (cf. Isa 17.1–3; Jer 49.23–27; Zech 9.1–4). *Damascus* was the capital of Syria (Aram). *They have threshed Gilead*, Gilead was Israelite territory in northern Transjordan, particularly vulnerable to Syrian aggression (2 Kings 10.32–33); threshing was often used to symbolize martial brutality (Isa 41.15; Mic 4.13). *Hazael* and *Ben-hadad* II were Syrian rulers (2 Kings 13.3). *The Valley of Aven* probably refers to the Beqa region between the Lebanon and Anti-Lebanon ranges. *Beth-eden*, known in Assyrian records as Bit-idini, was a city-state on the Euphrates, between the Lebanon and Anti-Lebanon ranges. *Kir* is the place of Syrian origins (9.7) and exile (2 Kings 16.9); its precise location is unknown.

1.6–8: Against Philistia. Four cities of the Philistine pentapolis (1 Sam 6.17) on the southeast coast of the Mediterranean are condemned for their slave traffic with Edom (2 Chr 21.16–17; Joel 3.4–8; Zeph 2.4–7).

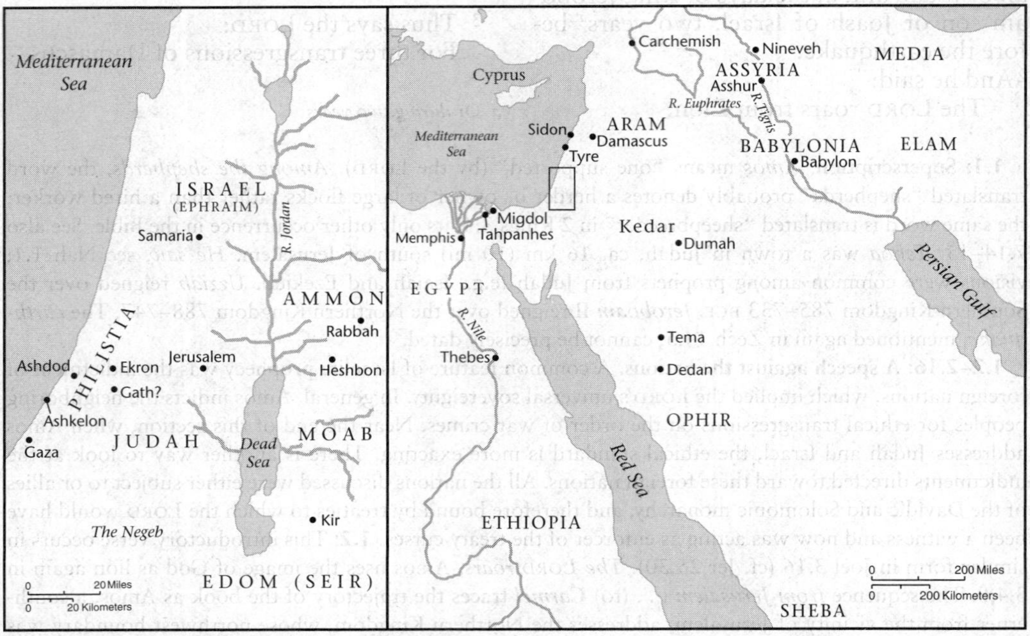

Chs 1–2: The oracles against the nations.

because they carried into exile entire
communities,
to hand them over to Edom.
7 So I will send a fire on the wall
of Gaza,
fire that shall devour its
strongholds.
8 I will cut off the inhabitants from
Ashdod,
and the one who holds the scepter
from Ashkelon;
I will turn my hand against Ekron,
and the remnant of the Philistines
shall perish,
says the Lord GOD.

9 Thus says the LORD:
For three transgressions of Tyre,
and for four, I will not revoke the
punishment;[a]
because they delivered entire
communities over to Edom,
and did not remember the covenant
of kinship.
10 So I will send a fire on the wall
of Tyre,
fire that shall devour its
strongholds.

11 Thus says the LORD:
For three transgressions of Edom,
and for four, I will not revoke the
punishment;[a]
because he pursued his brother with
the sword
and cast off all pity;
he maintained his anger perpetually,[b]
and kept his wrath[c] forever.
12 So I will send a fire on Teman,
and it shall devour the strongholds
of Bozrah.

13 Thus says the LORD:
For three transgressions of the
Ammonites,
and for four, I will not revoke the
punishment;[a]
because they have ripped open
pregnant women in Gilead
in order to enlarge their territory.
14 So I will kindle a fire against the wall
of Rabbah,
fire that shall devour its
strongholds,
with shouting on the day of battle,
with a storm on the day of the
whirlwind;
15 then their king shall go into exile,
he and his officials together,
says the LORD.

2 Thus says the LORD:
For three transgressions of Moab,
and for four, I will not revoke the
punishment;[a]
because he burned to lime
the bones of the king of Edom.
2 So I will send a fire on Moab,
and it shall devour the strongholds
of Kerioth,

a Heb *cause it to return* *b* Syr Vg: Heb *and his anger tore perpetually* *c* Gk Syr Vg: Heb *and his wrath kept*

1.9–10: Against Tyre (see Joel 3.4–8). Tyre was a Phoenician seaport north of Israel. *Covenant of kinship* (lit. "covenant of brothers"), cf. 1 Kings 5.12; 9.13.

1.11–12: Against Edom (Isa 34; Joel 3.19; Ezek 25.12). *Edom,* located south and east of the Dead Sea, was a perennial rival of neighboring Judah, especially in the exilic and postexilic era (Ps 137.7; Obadiah). The term *his brother,* i.e., Judah (Mal 1.2), draws on the ancient tradition of kinship between Jacob and Esau (Esau was "the father of Edom," Gen 36.43) and also connotes a treaty relationship (see vv. 9–10n.). *Teman,* a synonym for Edom. *Bozrah,* modern Buseirah, 40 km (25 mi) south of the Dead Sea.

1.13–15: Against Ammon (Zeph 2.8–11), which is condemned for atrocities against Israelites to its immediate north, in *Gilead. Rabbah,* the Ammonite capital (modern Amman).

2.1–3: Against Moab, Israel's neighbor and rival southeast of the Jordan (Isa 15.1–16.14). *Burned to lime,* for the practice of desecrating a corpse through disinterment and incineration, see 2 Kings 23.16–20; Isa 33.12. *Kerioth,* location uncertain; see Jer 48.24, 41.

and Moab shall die amid uproar,
amid shouting and the sound of the trumpet;
3 I will cut off the ruler from its midst,
and will kill all its officials with him,
says the LORD.

4 Thus says the LORD:
For three transgressions of Judah,
and for four, I will not revoke the punishment;[a]
because they have rejected the law of the LORD,
and have not kept his statutes,
but they have been led astray by the same lies
after which their ancestors walked.
5 So I will send a fire on Judah,
and it shall devour the strongholds of Jerusalem.

6 Thus says the LORD:
For three transgressions of Israel,
and for four, I will not revoke the punishment;[a]
because they sell the righteous for silver,
and the needy for a pair of sandals—
7 they who trample the head of the poor into the dust of the earth,
and push the afflicted out of the way;
father and son go in to the same girl,
so that my holy name is profaned;
8 they lay themselves down beside every altar
on garments taken in pledge;
and in the house of their God they drink
wine bought with fines they imposed.

9 Yet I destroyed the Amorite before them,
whose height was like the height of cedars,
and who was as strong as oaks;
I destroyed his fruit above,
and his roots beneath.
10 Also I brought you up out of the land of Egypt,
and led you forty years in the wilderness,
to possess the land of the Amorite.
11 And I raised up some of your children to be prophets
and some of your youths to be nazirites.[b]
Is it not indeed so, O people of Israel?
says the LORD.

12 But you made the nazirites[b] drink wine,
and commanded the prophets,
saying, "You shall not prophesy."

a Heb *cause it to return* b That is, *those separated* or *those consecrated*

2.4–5: Against Judah. Because of similarities between its language and that of the Deuteronomistic Reform (e.g., 2 Kings 17.15) in the late seventh century, many scholars consider this oracle a later addition, but it is consistent with Amos's view that all nations stand accountable before God.

2.6–16: Against Israel. Amos's ethical tour finally reaches home, where it surely shocked its audience. Here *Israel,* the counterpart of Judah (2.4), specifically refers to the Northern Kingdom; not to the nations as a whole, as in 3.1. Using the same literary form, Amos shows that Israel stands under divine judgment too, for oppression of the poor and for immorality. **6:** *They sell the righteous . . . and the needy* into debt slavery. **7:** *Same girl* probably does not refer to ritual prostitutes but to young unmarried women who, like the "needy" and the *poor,* were being exploited. **8:** *Garments taken in pledge,* see the prohibitions in Ex 22.25; Deut 24.17. The exploitation of the poor is especially odious when commodities gained unjustly, the above *garments* and *wine,* were paraded before the deity at the *altar* of *the house of their God.* **9:** *The Amorite . . . whose height,* pre-Israelite inhabitants of Canaan such as the Amorites (see Ezek 16.3) were often depicted as gigantic (Num 13.32–33). **11–12:** *Nazirites,* consecrated individuals who undertook vows, including abstinence from wine; Num 6.2; Judg 13.5. **13:** The entire

13 So, I will press you down in
your place,
just as a cart presses down
when it is full of sheaves.[a]
14 Flight shall perish from the swift,
and the strong shall not retain their
strength,
nor shall the mighty save their lives;
15 those who handle the bow shall
not stand,
and those who are swift of foot
shall not save themselves,
nor shall those who ride horses
save their lives;
16 and those who are stout of heart
among the mighty
shall flee away naked in that day,
says the LORD.

3 Hear this word that the LORD has spoken against you, O people of Israel,
against the whole family that I brought up
out of the land of Egypt:
2 You only have I known
of all the families of the earth;
therefore I will punish you
for all your iniquities.

3 Do two walk together
unless they have made an
appointment?
4 Does a lion roar in the forest,
when it has no prey?
Does a young lion cry out from
its den,
if it has caught nothing?
5 Does a bird fall into a snare on
the earth,
when there is no trap for it?
Does a snare spring up from
the ground,
when it has taken nothing?
6 Is a trumpet blown in a city,
and the people are not afraid?
Does disaster befall a city,
unless the LORD has done it?
7 Surely the Lord GOD does nothing,
without revealing his secret
to his servants the prophets.
8 The lion has roared;
who will not fear?
The Lord GOD has spoken;
who can but prophesy?

9 Proclaim to the strongholds
in Ashdod,
and to the strongholds in the land
of Egypt,
and say, "Assemble yourselves on
Mount[b] Samaria,
and see what great tumults are
within it,

a Meaning of Heb uncertain *b* Gk Syr: Heb *the mountains of*

Israelite army is defenseless: archers, infantry, and cavalry. **16:** *Naked,* unarmed and exposed; cf. Isa 20.1–6.

3.1–6.14: Judgment speeches against Israel come in three sections, each with the same opening (3.1; 4.1; 5.1).

3.1–2: A chosen people are held to a higher standard. 2: *You only have I known,* knowledge here refers to a relationship through covenant. The phrase *all the families of the earth* recalls traditions about divine promises to Abram (Gen 12.3) and Moses (Ex 19.4–6; Deut 7.6).

3.3–8: A series of rhetorical questions, which permit only a single response, build to an inescapable conclusion in v. 8b: The call to prophecy, unsolicited, cannot be resisted (7.14–15). Furthermore, the self-evident truths of vv. 1–8a render the audience susceptible to a truth in 8b it would naturally resist: Amos speaks on behalf of the LORD. **4:** *A lion roar,* see 1.2. **6:** *Trumpet,* the shofar, the ram's horn. **7:** *His secret to his servants the prophets,* for positive and negative illustrations of this principle, see, respectively, Gen 18.17–19 and 2 Kings 4.27; cf. 2 Kings 4.13. Because the phrase "his servants the prophets" is Deuteronomistic (see 2 Kings 21.10), and because the verse is in a different form, some scholars consider it a later addition (see 2.3–4n.).

3.9–15: Neighboring nations are invited to witness the LORD's complaint against the elites of Israelite society, who dwelt in *strongholds,* massive fortified palaces. **9:** *Ashdod,* see 1.8n. *Samaria,* the capital of the Northern Kingdom (1 Kings 16.23–24). **12:** As Amos, a pastoralist himself (7.14) knew, a *shepherd*

and what oppressions are in
its midst."
10 They do not know how to do right,
says the LORD,
those who store up violence and
robbery in their strongholds.
11 Therefore thus says the Lord GOD:
An adversary shall surround the
land,
and strip you of your defense;
and your strongholds shall be
plundered.

12 Thus says the LORD: As the shepherd
rescues from the mouth of the lion two legs,
or a piece of an ear, so shall the people of
Israel who live in Samaria be rescued, with
the corner of a couch and part[a] of a bed.

13 Hear, and testify against the house of
Jacob,
says the Lord GOD, the God
of hosts:
14 On the day I punish Israel for its
transgressions,
I will punish the altars of Bethel,
and the horns of the altar shall be cut
off
and fall to the ground.
15 I will tear down the winter house as
well as the summer house;
and the houses of ivory shall perish,
and the great houses[b] shall come to
an end,
says the LORD.

4 Hear this word, you cows of Bashan
who are on Mount Samaria,
who oppress the poor, who crush the
needy,
who say to their husbands, "Bring
something to drink!"
2 The Lord GOD has sworn by
his holiness:
The time is surely coming
upon you,
when they shall take you away with
hooks,
even the last of you with fishhooks.
3 Through breaches in the wall you
shall leave,
each one straight ahead;
and you shall be flung out into
Harmon,[a]
says the LORD.
4 Come to Bethel—and transgress;
to Gilgal—and multiply
transgression;
bring your sacrifices every morning,
your tithes every three days;
5 bring a thank offering of leavened
bread,

a Meaning of Heb uncertain *b* Or *many houses*

was absolved of blame for loss of livestock if there were even small remains, *legs, or a piece of an ear,* of a predator's attack. With sarcasm, Amos suggests that after the divine punishment, announced by the roar of a lion (1.2; 3.8), only scraps would remain from the palaces of Samaria. **14:** *Bethel* was near the southern border of the Northern Kingdom, ca. 18 km (11 mi) north of Jerusalem. For Bethel as a shrine, see 1 Kings 12.25–30; for Amos and *Bethel,* see 4.4; 5.5–6; 7.10–13. *The horns of the altar,* the projections at the corners of an altar had special significance; see Ex 21.14; 1 Kings 2.28–34. **15:** The LORD will raze the tokens of conspicuous Israelite consumption: *the winter house, the summer house,* and the *houses* decorated with carved *ivory* inlay, such as the royal palace in Samaria built by Ahab (1 Kings 22.39).

4.1–3: Israel's luxurious excesses. Wealthy and greedy women of Samaria would be punished along with their husbands. **1:** *Cows of Bashan,* Bashan was a fertile region in northern Transjordan renowned for its cattle (Ps 22.12). Israel's hold on this prize testifies to its prosperity in Amos's day. **3:** *Straight ahead,* with the city walls in ruins, the captives will be easily taken away.

4.4–5: Israel's piety is satirized. 4: *Bethel,* see 3.14n. *Gilgal,* a venerable Israelite shrine near Jericho (e.g., Josh 4.20; 10.43; 1 Sam 7.16), condemned by Amos (5.5) and his contemporary Hosea (Hos 4.15; 9.15; 12.11). The ritual practices listed here are prescribed elsewhere; for the morning sacrifice, see Ex 29.29; *tithes,* see Lev 27.30–32; Deut 14.28–29; *thank offering of unleavened bread,* see Lev 7.13; *freewill offerings*, see Num 15.3. Note the association of tithes with Bethel in Gen 28.22.

and proclaim freewill offerings,
publish them;
for so you love to do, O people
of Israel!
says the Lord GOD.

6 I gave you cleanness of teeth in all
your cities,
and lack of bread in all your
places,
yet you did not return to me,
says the LORD.

7 And I also withheld the rain from you
when there were still three months
to the harvest;
I would send rain on one city,
and send no rain on another city;
one field would be rained upon,
and the field on which it did not
rain withered;
8 so two or three towns wandered
to one town
to drink water, and were not
satisfied;
yet you did not return to me,
says the LORD.

9 I struck you with blight and mildew;
I laid waste[a] your gardens and
your vineyards;
the locust devoured your fig trees
and your olive trees;
yet you did not return to me,
says the LORD.

10 I sent among you a pestilence after
the manner of Egypt;
I killed your young men with
the sword;
I carried away your horses;[b]
and I made the stench of your
camp go up into your nostrils;
yet you did not return to me,
says the LORD.

11 I overthrew some of you,
as when God overthrew Sodom and
Gomorrah,
and you were like a brand snatched
from the fire;
yet you did not return to me,
says the LORD.

12 Therefore thus I will do to you,
O Israel;
because I will do this to you,
prepare to meet your God,
O Israel!

13 For lo, the one who forms the
mountains, creates the wind,
reveals his thoughts to mortals,
makes the morning darkness,
and treads on the heights of
the earth—
the LORD, the God of hosts, is
his name!

5 Hear this word that I take up over you
in lamentation, O house of Israel:
2 Fallen, no more to rise,
is maiden Israel;
forsaken on her land,
with no one to raise her up.
3 For thus says the Lord GOD:
The city that marched out a thousand
shall have a hundred left,

a Cn: Heb *the multitude of* b Heb *with the captivity of your horses*

4.6–13: Israel has ignored the divine warnings issued through plagues. These plagues typify the curses a treaty partner brought on itself through disobedience. Israel's covenantal documents contained such curses (Lev 26.14–39; Deut 28.15–68). **6:** *Cleanness of teeth,* i.e., famine. **10:** *A pestilence after the manner of Egypt,* Ex 9.3–7,15. *The stench* of unburied corpses, as in Isa 34.3. **11:** The verb *overthrew* here could refer to an earthquake, as it seems to in Gen 19.25,29, in which the destruction of *Sodom and Gomorrah* is described. **13:** The first of three doxologies interspersed throughout Amos (5.8–9; 9.5–6). These hymn-like sections emphasize that the God Israel encounters in judgment is the creator.

5.1–3: Lament for Israel. Among the forms of prophetic speech was the lament; hearing one's own funeral speech delivered by a prophet must have had a sobering effect (cf. Jer 9.17–22).

and that which marched out
a hundred
shall have ten left.[a]

4 For thus says the LORD to the house
of Israel:
Seek me and live;
5 but do not seek Bethel,
and do not enter into Gilgal
or cross over to Beer-sheba;
for Gilgal shall surely go into exile,
and Bethel shall come to nothing.

6 Seek the LORD and live,
or he will break out against the
house of Joseph like fire,
and it will devour Bethel, with no
one to quench it.
7 Ah, you that turn justice to
wormwood,
and bring righteousness to
the ground!

8 The one who made the Pleiades
and Orion,
and turns deep darkness into
the morning,
and darkens the day into night,
who calls for the waters of the sea,
and pours them out on the surface
of the earth,
the LORD is his name,
9 who makes destruction flash out
against the strong,
so that destruction comes upon the
fortress.

10 They hate the one who reproves
in the gate,
and they abhor the one who speaks
the truth.
11 Therefore because you trample on the
poor
and take from them levies of grain,
you have built houses of hewn stone,
but you shall not live in them;
you have planted pleasant vineyards,
but you shall not drink their wine.
12 For I know how many are your
transgressions,
and how great are your sins—
you who afflict the righteous, who
take a bribe,
and push aside the needy in
the gate.
13 Therefore the prudent will keep silent
in such a time;
for it is an evil time.

14 Seek good and not evil,
that you may live;
and so the LORD, the God of hosts,
will be with you,
just as you have said.
15 Hate evil and love good,
and establish justice in the gate;
it may be that the LORD, the God
of hosts,
will be gracious to the remnant of
Joseph.

a Heb adds *to the house of Israel*

5.4–7: A plea for repentance. Though the lament form was meant to convey a sense of inevitable judgment, there is yet time to *seek the LORD and live.* **5:** For *Bethel* and *Gilgal,* see 3.14n.; 4.4n. *Beer-sheba,* though in the Negeb to the far south, was a shrine associated with Israel's ancestors (Gen 21.25–31; 26.23; 46.1–4) and would have attracted pilgrims from the north. **6:** *House of Joseph,* i.e., the Northern Kingdom. **7:** The dried leaves of *wormwood* were aromatic and bitter; here, injustice leads to bitterness (see 6.12).

5.8–9: The second doxology (see 4.13n.). **8:** *Pleiades* and *Orion* also occur together in Job 9.9; 38.31. Though astral bodies could inspire illicit worship (e.g., 2 Kings 23.5), to the faithful they testified to God's power (e.g., Ps 8.3).

5.10–17: Amos condemns a corrupt legal system. 10–13: At the very site of legal proceedings, the city *gate,* the truth is rejected, the poor are plundered, and witnesses are bribed. **11:** A futility curse, in which the connections between actions and their expected effects are broken; cf. Deut 28.30–31,38–46; Mic 6.14–15; Zeph 1.13. **12:** Cf. 2.6–7. **14–15:** Another plea for repentance; see vv. 4–7. **16–17:** Staying

16 Therefore thus says the LORD, the
God of hosts, the Lord:
In all the squares there shall be
wailing;
and in all the streets they shall say,
"Alas! alas!"
They shall call the farmers to
mourning,
and those skilled in lamentation, to
wailing;
17 in all the vineyards there shall
be wailing,
for I will pass through the midst of
you,
says the LORD.

18 Alas for you who desire the day of
the LORD!
Why do you want the day of
the LORD?
It is darkness, not light;
19 as if someone fled from a lion,
and was met by a bear;
or went into the house and rested a
hand against the wall,
and was bitten by a snake.
20 Is not the day of the LORD darkness,
not light,
and gloom with no brightness in it?

21 I hate, I despise your festivals,
and I take no delight in your
solemn assemblies.
22 Even though you offer me your burnt
offerings and grain offerings,
I will not accept them;
and the offerings of well-being of
your fatted animals
I will not look upon.
23 Take away from me the noise of your
songs;
I will not listen to the melody of
your harps.
24 But let justice roll down like waters,
and righteousness like an
ever-flowing stream.

25 Did you bring to me sacrifices and
offerings the forty years in the wilderness,
O house of Israel? 26 You shall take up Sak-
kuth your king, and Kaiwan your star-god,
your images,[a] which you made for your-
selves; 27 therefore I will take you into exile
beyond Damascus, says the LORD, whose
name is the God of hosts.

a Heb *your images, your star-god*

with the images of village life and returning to the motif of lament (5.1–3), Amos depicts the divine punishment for injustice. **16:** *Skilled in lamentation,* professional mourners; see Jer 9.17–21; Ezek 32.16; Eccl 12.5; 2 Chr 35.25.

5.18–6.14: A series of "woe" sayings (5.18–25; 6.1–3; 6.4–14) complete the section of judgment speeches.

5.18–20: The Day of the LORD, in which Israelites expected to be vindicated against their enemies, will be, as depicted already in 1.1–2.16, a day when Israel too receives its judgment. Amos's profound reinterpretation of this popular concept is among his most significant contributions.

5.21–27: The LORD delights not in abundance of festivals and sacrifices but in justice and righteousness. V. 24 expresses a central message of the prophets; see also Mic 6.6–8. **21–23:** The language is harsh. *Festivals* refers to the three pilgrimage feasts (Ex 23.14–17; 34.18,22–23; Deut 16.16), as does *solemn assemblies* (Lev 23.36; Deut 16.8). The sacrifices in v. 22 were prescribed; see, e.g., Lev 7.8–14. *Songs* is often used of hymns (see 8.3), such as the psalms (e.g., see title of Ps 120). For a similar view, see Isa 1.11–17. **24:** An *ever-flowing stream* is a riverbed that never fails, as opposed to a wadi, common in Israel's landscape, which had run-off water only in the rainy season. **25:** As in Jeremiah (2.2–3) and Hosea (2.14–20; 9.10), the period in the wilderness after the Exodus is recalled as an ideal. Like Jer 7.21–23, the rhetorical question presumes that sacrifice was not a component of Israel's religious system immediately after the Exodus. This is inconsistent with other biblical traditions. **26:** *Sakkuth* and *Kaiwan* (Saturn) designate known Assyrian deities. *Sakkuth* may be the same as the "Succoth" whose cult the Babylonians established in Samaria after its fall (2 Kings 17.30). **27:** *Damascus,* 1.3–5n.

6 Alas for those who are at ease
in Zion,
and for those who feel secure on
Mount Samaria,
the notables of the first of the
nations,
to whom the house of Israel
resorts!
2 Cross over to Calneh, and see;
from there go to Hamath the
great;
then go down to Gath of the
Philistines.
Are you better[a] than these
kingdoms?
Or is your[b] territory greater than
their[c] territory,
3 O you that put far away the evil day,
and bring near a reign of violence?
4 Alas for those who lie on beds
of ivory,
and lounge on their couches,
and eat lambs from the flock,
and calves from the stall;
5 who sing idle songs to the sound
of the harp,
and like David improvise on
instruments of music;
6 who drink wine from bowls,
and anoint themselves with the
finest oils,
but are not grieved over the ruin of
Joseph!
7 Therefore they shall now be the first
to go into exile,
and the revelry of the loungers shall
pass away.

8 The Lord GOD has sworn by himself
(says the LORD, the God of hosts):
I abhor the pride of Jacob
and hate his strongholds;
and I will deliver up the city and all
that is in it.

9 If ten people remain in one house, they
shall die. 10 And if a relative, one who burns
the dead,[d] shall take up the body to bring
it out of the house, and shall say to some-
one in the innermost parts of the house, "Is
anyone else with you?" the answer will
come, "No." Then the relative[e] shall say,
"Hush! We must not mention the name of
the LORD."

11 See, the LORD commands,
and the great house shall be
shattered to bits,
and the little house to pieces.
12 Do horses run on rocks?
Does one plow the sea with
oxen?[f]
But you have turned justice
into poison
and the fruit of righteousness into
wormwood—
13 you who rejoice in Lo-debar,[g]

a Or *Are they better* b Heb *their* c Heb *your*
d Or *who makes a burning for him* e Heb *he*
f Or *Does one plow them with oxen* g Or *in a thing of nothingness*

6.1–7: An indictment of conspicuous consumption. 1: Amos targets elite classes of the capitals of both the South (*Zion,* i.e., Jerusalem) and the North (*Mount Samaria*). **2:** Cf. Isa 10.9–11. *Calneh* and *Hamath* were prosperous cities of Syria, conquered by the Assyrians in 738 BCE; the allusion to *Gath,* the only Philistine city unmentioned in 1.6–8, could refer to its defeat at the hands of Syria (2 Kings 12.18) or Judah (2 Chr 26.6), or its conquest by the Assyrians in 711. **4:** *Beds of ivory,* see 3.15n. Over 500 ivory fragments have been excavated from the site of Samaria. **5:** *David,* 1 Sam 16.23; 1 Chr 23.5; Neh 12.36. **6–7:** The elites of Samaria, accustomed to the choicest products, will be the first chosen for deportation by the Assyrians. **7:** The *revelry* (Heb "marzeah") was a social and funerary ritual banquet of Canaanite origin; cf. Jer 16.5.

6.8–14: Judgment on Israel. The *house of Israel,* both as a sociopolitical body and as representative of its palatial *strongholds,* is doomed. **10:** *Burns the dead* probably refers to practices employed to stop the spread of infection. In this extremity, the few survivors dare not *mention the name of the LORD,* out of fear of inviting their own destruction from a deity still intent on destruction. **12:** Israel's legal and moral machinations are a perversion bordering on the absurd. *Wormwood,* see 5.7n. **13:** *Lo-debar* and *Karnaim*

who say, "Have we not by our own
strength
taken Karnaim[a] for ourselves?"
14 Indeed, I am raising up against you a
nation,
O house of Israel, says the LORD,
the God of hosts,
and they shall oppress you from
Lebo-hamath
to the Wadi Arabah.

7 This is what the Lord GOD showed me:
he was forming locusts at the time the
latter growth began to sprout (it was the
latter growth after the king's mowings).
2 When they had finished eating the grass of
the land, I said,
"O Lord GOD, forgive, I beg you!
How can Jacob stand?
He is so small!"
3 The LORD relented concerning this;
"It shall not be," said the LORD.

4 This is what the Lord GOD showed
me: the Lord GOD was calling for a shower
of fire,[b] and it devoured the great deep and
was eating up the land. 5 Then I said,
"O Lord GOD, cease, I beg you!
How can Jacob stand?
He is so small!"
6 The LORD relented concerning this;
"This also shall not be," said the
Lord GOD.

7 This is what he showed me: the Lord
was standing beside a wall built with a
plumb line, with a plumb line in his hand.
8 And the LORD said to me, "Amos, what
do you see?" And I said, "A plumb line."
Then the Lord said,
"See, I am setting a plumb line
in the midst of my people Israel;
I will never again pass them by;
9 the high places of Isaac shall be made
desolate,
and the sanctuaries of Israel shall
be laid waste,
and I will rise against the house of
Jeroboam with the sword."

10 Then Amaziah, the priest of Bethel,
sent to King Jeroboam of Israel, saying,

a Or *horns* b Or *for a judgment by fire*

are two cities east of the Jordan recovered for Israel by Jeroboam II (2 Kings 14.25). The verse puns on the names of the cities, which mean "No-thing" and "Horns [i.e., strength]," respectively. **14:** *From Lebo-hamath to the Wadi Arabah,* the farthest limits of Israelite territory (see 2 Kings 14.25), from the Orontes Valley in Lebanon to the north to the Rift Valley in the southeast.

7.1–9.15: The visions of Amos. The final section of the book consists of accounts and interpretations of five visions (7.1–3; 7.4–6; 7.7–9; 8.1–3; 9.1–6), a biographical account about the prophet (7.10–17), and prophetic oracles (8.4–14; 9.5–15).

7.1–9: A series of three visions builds to a conclusion: Prophetic intercession will not deter God from punishing Israel. For classic examples of intercession, see Gen 18.17–33; Ex 32.7–14.

7.1–3: Judgment by locusts (cf. Joel 1.2–7). **1:** A locust plague at the time of *the latter growth* endangered the spring planting, just sprouting, after the harvest of the winter grains. **2:** The prophet appeals to God's sense of proportion: Israel (*Jacob*) is *so small* and, by implication, God is so big (cf. Job 7.20).

7.4–6: Judgment by fire. 4: *The great deep,* the cosmic waters under the earth and over the heavens (see Gen 1.2).

7.7–9: Israel falls short. The *plumb line* (2 Kings 21.13–15), a device for determining the true vertical line of a structure, reveals that Israel's religious and political institutions do not measure up and will be destroyed; here the prophet offers no intercessory protest or plea. *High places* were open-air *sanctuaries.* Though acceptable in earlier eras, Amos and Hosea (10.8) condemned them as places of illicit worship. *Isaac,* a rare designation for the Northern Kingdom (see v. 16). *House of Jeroboam,* the royal dynasty of Jeroboam II (788–747 BCE).

7.10–17: Amos and Amaziah. This piece, a narrative illustration of 2.12 in the form of a dramatic encounter between the royal priest and the prophet, the classic outsider, is placed at this point in the book

"Amos has conspired against you in the
very center of the house of Israel; the land
is not able to bear all his words. 11 For thus
Amos has said,

'Jeroboam shall die by the sword,
and Israel must go into exile
away from his land.' "

12 And Amaziah said to Amos, "O seer, go,
flee away to the land of Judah, earn your
bread there, and prophesy there; 13 but nev-
er again prophesy at Bethel, for it is the
king's sanctuary, and it is a temple of the
kingdom."

14 Then Amos answered Amaziah, "I
am[a] no prophet, nor a prophet's son; but
I am[a] a herdsman, and a dresser of syca-
more trees, 15 and the LORD took me from
following the flock, and the LORD said to
me, 'Go, prophesy to my people Israel.'

16 "Now therefore hear the word of the LORD.
You say, 'Do not prophesy against Israel,
and do not preach against the house of Isaac.'
17 Therefore thus says the LORD:
'Your wife shall become a prostitute in the city,
and your sons and your daughters shall fall by the sword,
and your land shall be parceled out by line;
you yourself shall die in an unclean land,
and Israel shall surely go into exile away from its land.' "

8 This is what the Lord GOD showed
me—a basket of summer fruit.[b] 2 He
said, "Amos, what do you see?" And I said,
"A basket of summer fruit."[b] Then the
LORD said to me,

"The end[c] has come upon my people Israel;
I will never again pass them by.
3 The songs of the temple[d] shall become wailings in that day,"
says the Lord GOD;
"the dead bodies shall be many,
cast out in every place. Be silent!"

4 Hear this, you that trample on the needy,
and bring to ruin the poor of the land,
5 saying, "When will the new moon be over
so that we may sell grain;

a Or *was* *b* Heb *qayits* *c* Heb *qets* *d* Or *palace*

perhaps because its reference to *King Jeroboam* (v. 10) fits well next to the phrase "house of Jeroboam" (v. 9). Amaziah was the official priest of the royal shrine at Bethel (see 3.14n.). **11:** *For thus Amos has said,* Amaziah does not attribute the prophet's words to God. The first utterance Amaziah cites (*Jeroboam shall die . . .*) is the rough but not exact equivalent of 7.9; the second phrase (*Israel must go . . .*) of 4.2–3; 5.5,26–27; 6.7; 9.4. **12:** *Earn your bread,* lit. "eat bread." **14:** Amos asserts that he is neither a professional prophet (1 Sam 9.6–10; Mic 3.5–8,11) nor a member of a prophetic guild (2 Kings 2.3; 1 Sam 10.5; 1 Kings 22.6). *Herdsman,* of large cattle (cf. 1.1n.); the word occurs only here in the Bible. *Dresser of sycamore trees,* the biblical sycamore was a type of fig tree whose fruit was gashed with knives to induce ripening. **15:** Cf. 2 Sam 7.8. **17:** A dreadful string of curses: May *your wife . . . become a prostitute;* may others acquire title to your land, i.e., *parcel* it *out* with a measuring *line. Israel shall surely go,* Amos closes his response to Amaziah by repeating the latter's words from v. 11.

8.1–9.15: Further visions and oracles. The final two chapters of Amos have a similar outline: Both begin with visions (8.1–3; 9.1–6), followed by oracles with many literary parallels (compare 8.8 with 9.5; 8.9 with 9.11; 8.11 with 9.13).

8.1–3: Fourth vision. A basket of ripe summer fruit symbolizes the immediacy of Israel's end. Note the pun in Hebrew between summer fruit, "qayits," and end, "qets." **3:** *Be silent,* see 6.10.

8.4–14: Judgment speeches against Israel akin to those in 3.1–6.14. **4–6:** Rapacious and fraudulent business practices victimize the poor. **5:** The merchants are impatient for the holy days to pass so they can resume their fraudulent business (Lev 19.35–36; Deut 25.13–16). *The new moon,* see Num 29.6. *Ephah small,* sell less than the apparent volume; an *ephah* was ca. 23 l (.66 bu). *Shekel great,* overcharge; a *shekel*

and the sabbath,
so that we may offer wheat
for sale?
We will make the ephah small and
the shekel great,
and practice deceit with false
balances,
6 buying the poor for silver
and the needy for a pair of sandals,
and selling the sweepings of
the wheat."

7 The LORD has sworn by the pride
of Jacob:
Surely I will never forget any of their
deeds.
8 Shall not the land tremble on
this account,
and everyone mourn who lives in it,
and all of it rise like the Nile,
and be tossed about and sink again,
like the Nile of Egypt?

9 On that day, says the Lord GOD,
I will make the sun go down
at noon,
and darken the earth in
broad daylight.
10 I will turn your feasts into mourning,
and all your songs into
lamentation;
I will bring sackcloth on all loins,
and baldness on every head;
I will make it like the mourning for
an only son,
and the end of it like a bitter day.

11 The time is surely coming, says the
Lord GOD,
when I will send a famine on
the land;
not a famine of bread, or a thirst for
water,
but of hearing the words of
the LORD.
12 They shall wander from sea to sea,
and from north to east;
they shall run to and fro, seeking the
word of the LORD,
but they shall not find it.

13 In that day the beautiful young
women and the young men
shall faint for thirst.
14 Those who swear by Ashimah
of Samaria,
and say, "As your god lives,
O Dan,"
and, "As the way of Beer-sheba
lives"—
they shall fall, and never rise again.

9 I saw the LORD standing beside[a] the
altar, and he said:
Strike the capitals until the thresholds
shake,
and shatter them on the heads of
all the people;[b]
and those who are left I will kill with
the sword;
not one of them shall flee away,
not one of them shall escape.

2 Though they dig into Sheol,
from there shall my hand
take them;

a Or *on* *b* Heb *all of them*

weighed ca. 11.5 gr (.4 oz). *False balances,* scales rigged in the merchant's favor. **6:** *Buying the poor* probably refers to outright slavery, as opposed to *selling the righteous* (2.6) into debt slavery. *Sweepings of the wheat,* they sell the chaff as wheat. **8:** *Like the Nile . . . tossed about and sink,* the annual inundation of the Nile (9.5; Jer 46.7–8). **9–10:** A solar eclipse portends divine punishment and elicits mourning rituals. *Sackcloth* and *baldness* were customary expressions of mourning associated with national disaster (e.g., Isa 22.12). *An only son,* Jer 6.26; Zech 12.10. **11:** 1 Sam 3.1. **13:** *Ashimah* (or "guilt") *of Samaria* could be a Syrian deity (2 Kings 17.30) or a disparaging reference ("the guilt") to the practice of treating the cosmic LORD merely as the patron of a local shrine, whether in the center of Israel (*Samaria*), the farthest north (*Dan*), or the farthest south (*Beer-sheba*).

9.1–6: Fifth vision. For other appearances of the LORD at shrines, see 1 Sam 3.1–18; Isa 6.1–13. **1:** Probably *the altar* at Bethel (3.14; 7.10) is intended. *Thresholds shake,* see Isa 6.4. **2:** *Sheol,* the place of

though they climb up to heaven,
from there I will bring them down.
3 Though they hide themselves on the top of Carmel,
from there I will search out and take them;
and though they hide from my sight at the bottom of the sea,
there I will command the sea-serpent, and it shall bite them.
4 And though they go into captivity in front of their enemies,
there I will command the sword, and it shall kill them;
and I will fix my eyes on them
for harm and not for good.

5 The Lord, GOD of hosts,
he who touches the earth and it melts,
and all who live in it mourn,
and all of it rises like the Nile,
and sinks again, like the Nile of Egypt;
6 who builds his upper chambers in the heavens,
and founds his vault upon the earth;
who calls for the waters of the sea,
and pours them out upon the surface of the earth—
the LORD is his name.

7 Are you not like the Ethiopians[a] to me,
O people of Israel? says the LORD.
Did I not bring Israel up from the land of Egypt,
and the Philistines from Caphtor
and the Arameans from Kir?
8 The eyes of the Lord GOD are upon the sinful kingdom,
and I will destroy it from the face of the earth
—except that I will not utterly destroy the house of Jacob,
says the LORD.

9 For lo, I will command,
and shake the house of Israel among all the nations
as one shakes with a sieve,
but no pebble shall fall to the ground.
10 All the sinners of my people shall die by the sword,
who say, "Evil shall not overtake or meet us."

11 On that day I will raise up

a Or *Nubians*; Heb *Cushites*

the dead (Job 10.19–22; Isa 14.11,15), which, Amos asserts, is within God's purview (Ps 139.7–12), though many feared it was not (e.g., Ps 6.6; 88.3–5). **3:** Mount *Carmel,* which juts into the Mediterranean at the northwestern border of Israel, reaches a summit of ca. 550 m (1,800 ft) above sea level and also boasts caves and forests for those who wish to *hide. Sea-serpent,* sea monsters, personifications of chaos, are at times cast as opponents of God (Ps 72.13); at other times, as here, as God's servants (Ps 104.25–26; Job 41). **5–6:** The third hymn-like passage (4.13; 5.8–9). **5:** See 8.8. **6:** *Upper chambers,* Ps 104.3. The vault is another name for the celestial barrier thought to separate the earth from the cosmic waters (Gen 1.6–8; Prov 8.27).

9.7–10: Israel has no claim to special privilege. Amos refutes the idea that Israel's relationship with God implies its superiority. This oracle suggests, positively, that God has enacted other exoduses at other times and places and, negatively, that Israel stands in judgment alongside the nations; see 3.2. **7:** *Like the Ethiopians,* even distant Nubia is within God's purview. *Philistines from Caphtor* (probably Crete) (Jer 47.4). *Kir,* see 1.5n.

9.11–15: An oracle of restoration. Prophetic collections often end on a similar, hopeful note; many, as above, refer to *that day* (Hos 14.1–7; Joel 3.18–21; Mic 7.11–20; Zeph 3.14–20; Hag 2.20; Zech 14.6,20; Mal 14.1–5). **11:** *Booth of David,* elsewhere in Amos, the fate of the Davidic dynasty, depicted here as in *ruins,* had not been a concern. This verse, at least, sounds like it stems from a later time, after the dynasty had *fallen.* The phrase "booth of David" suggests a more fragile structure than the more frequent "house of David" (cf. 2 Sam 7.11; Isa 1.8). **12:** *Edom* was a traditional rival of Judah, not

the booth of David that is fallen,
and repair its[a] breaches,
and raise up its[b] ruins,
and rebuild it as in the days of old;
12 in order that they may possess the remnant of Edom
and all the nations who are called by my name,
says the LORD who does this.

13 The time is surely coming, says the LORD,
when the one who plows shall overtake the one who reaps,
and the treader of grapes the one who sows the seed;
the mountains shall drip sweet wine,
and all the hills shall flow with it.
14 I will restore the fortunes of my people Israel,
and they shall rebuild the ruined cities and inhabit them;
they shall plant vineyards and drink their wine,
and they shall make gardens and eat their fruit.
15 I will plant them upon their land,
and they shall never again be plucked up
out of the land that I have given them,
says the LORD your God.

a Gk: Heb *their* *b* Gk: Heb *his*

Israel, so this is further evidence that part or all of this final oracle was added after the fall of Samaria in 722, at a time when the book was reinterpreted for Judahites. **13:** See Joel 3.18–21. *Shall overtake,* see Lev 26.5.

OBADIAH

Obadiah, the briefest book in the Hebrew Bible, is located between two eighth-century prophets, Amos and Micah. Though Obadiah contains no date formula, on the basis of its allusion to the fall of Jerusalem (586 BCE), it probably stems from the first half of the sixth century. Thus, its place in the sequence of the Minor Prophets is not based on chronology. It seems that thematic considerations govern its placement following Amos: The subject of Obadiah, divine judgment against the Edomites, can be associated with Am 9.12; the "Day of the LORD" is a central idea for both books. Nothing is known about the prophet Obadiah. Since the name itself means "servant of the LORD," it could simply be an appellation (see Introduction to Malachi).

The book consists of poetic declamations against the Edomites, Israel's southeastern neighbor. Many biblical passages testify to the fraternity (Gen 25; 27; 36; Num 20.14; Deut 2.4,8; 23.7; Am 1.11; Mal 1.2) between these neighboring peoples, as well as their enmity (Num 20.18–21; 1 Sam 14.47; 2 Sam 8.12–14; 1 Kings 11.14–22; Am 1.11; Mal 1.3). There are oracles against Edom throughout the prophetic corpus (Isa 21.11–12; 34; Jer 49.7–22; Ezek 35; Joel 3.19; Am 1.11–12; Mal 1.2–5). The strongest anti-Edomite invective stems from the time of the exile, when the Edomites, according to Ps 137.7; Lam 4.21; Ezek 35.5–6, abetted the Babylonian destruction of Jerusalem (see 1 Esd 4.45 for a later exaggeration of this theme).

Against the larger background of Edomite-Israelite hostility, Obadiah, similar to the above exilic writings, also focuses on Edom's complicity in the Babylonian conquest. Indeed, as indicated in the notes to the book, Obadiah's words of judgment bear striking similarities to this larger corpus of prophetic oracles against Edom.

In a book of only twenty-one verses, it is difficult and, perhaps, unnecessary to isolate subsections. There is a slight shift in subject matter from vv. 1–18, judgment directed against Edom, to 19–21, the vindication of Israel, which includes repatriation of its exiles and expansion into territories it had gradually lost to neighbors since the eighth century.

1 The vision of Obadiah.

Thus says the Lord GOD concerning
Edom:
We have heard a report from the LORD,
and a messenger has been sent
among the nations:
"Rise up! Let us rise against it
for battle!"
2 I will surely make you least among
the nations;
you shall be utterly despised.
3 Your proud heart has deceived
you,

1a: Introduction. *Vision,* see Isa 1.1; Nah 1.1.

1b–4: The divine judgment against Edom. Vv. 1b–4 are similar to Jer 49.12–16. **3–4:** For the theme of *proud* being humbled, see Isa 2.12–21. **3:** *Clefts of the rock,* the same Heb word means *rock* and Sela, an Edomite city perhaps to be identified with Umm el-Biyara, a site on a mountain within the later city of Petra. **4:** Cf. Isa 14.12–14.

you that live in the clefts of
the rock,[a]
whose dwelling is in the heights.
You say in your heart,
"Who will bring me down to
the ground?"
4 Though you soar aloft like the eagle,
though your nest is set among the
stars,
from there I will bring you down,
says the LORD.

5 If thieves came to you,
if plunderers by night
—how you have been destroyed!—
would they not steal only what they
wanted?
If grape-gatherers came to you,
would they not leave gleanings?
6 How Esau has been pillaged,
his treasures searched out!
7 All your allies have deceived you,
they have driven you to the border;
your confederates have prevailed
against you;
those who ate[b] your bread have
set a trap for you—
there is no understanding of it.
8 On that day, says the LORD,
I will destroy the wise out of Edom,
and understanding out of
Mount Esau.
9 Your warriors shall be shattered,
O Teman,
so that everyone from Mount Esau
will be cut off.
10 For the slaughter and violence done
to your brother Jacob,
shame shall cover you,
and you shall be cut off forever.
11 On the day that you stood aside,
on the day that strangers carried off
his wealth,
and foreigners entered his gates
and cast lots for Jerusalem,
you too were like one of them.
12 But you should not have gloated[c]
over[d] your brother
on the day of his misfortune;
you should not have rejoiced over the
people of Judah
on the day of their ruin;
you should not have boasted
on the day of distress.
13 You should not have entered the gate
of my people
on the day of their calamity;
you should not have joined in the
gloating over Judah's[e] disaster
on the day of his calamity;
you should not have looted his goods
on the day of his calamity.
14 You should not have stood at
the crossings
to cut off his fugitives;
you should not have handed over his
survivors
on the day of distress.

15 For the day of the LORD is near
against all the nations.
As you have done, it shall be done to
you;
your deeds shall return on your
own head.
16 For as you have drunk on my
holy mountain,

a Or *clefts of Sela* *b* Cn: Heb lacks *those who ate* *c* Heb *But do not gloat* (and similarly through verse 14) *d* Heb *on the day of* *e* Heb *his*

5–7: A taunt against Edom. 5–6: See Jer 49.9–10a. **5:** *Leave gleanings,* Deut 24.21. **6:** *Esau,* Jacob's twin, was the father of the Edomites (Gen 25.30; 36.1).

8–11: Doomsday for Edom. 8: *The wise out of Edom,* Jer 49.7. **9:** *Your warriors,* Jer 49.22. *Teman,* the northern region of Edom, here used simply as a synonym for Edom. **11:** Obadiah shares this bitterness against Edom with other writers of the sixth and fifth centuries BCE (Ps 137.7; Isa 35.5–7; 63.1–6; Lam 4.21; Ezek 25.12–14; Mal 1.2–5). *Cast lots,* see Joel 4.3.

12–14: An eight-fold indictment of Edom, cast in a repetitive style (*you should not . . .*). **13–14:** Ezek 35.5. **13:** *The gate of my people,* Mic 1.9. *The gloating,* e.g., Ps 137.7.

15–18: The Day of the LORD. 16: Jer 25.15–29; 49.12; Lam 4.21. **17:** Joel 2.32; 3.16–17. *Mount Zion,*

all the nations around you
shall drink;
they shall drink and gulp down,[a]
and shall be as though they had
never been.
17 But on Mount Zion there shall be
those that escape,
and it shall be holy;
and the house of Jacob shall take
possession of those who
dispossessed them.
18 The house of Jacob shall be a fire,
the house of Joseph a flame,
and the house of Esau stubble;
they shall burn them and
consume them,
and there shall be no survivor of
the house of Esau;
for the LORD has spoken.
19 Those of the Negeb shall possess
Mount Esau,
and those of the Shephelah the land
of the Philistines;
they shall possess the land of Ephraim
and the land of Samaria,
and Benjamin shall possess Gilead.
20 The exiles of the Israelites who are in
Halah[b]
shall possess[c] Phoenicia as far
as Zarephath;
and the exiles of Jerusalem who are in
Sepharad
shall possess the towns of
the Negeb.
21 Those who have been saved[d] shall go
up to Mount Zion
to rule Mount Esau;
and the kingdom shall be
the LORD's.

a Meaning of Heb uncertain *b* Cn: Heb *in this army* *c* Cn: Meaning of Heb uncertain *d* Or *Saviors*

the Temple mount in Jerusalem. **18:** *House of Jacob,* here southern Israel, Judah. *A fire,* Isa 10.17. *House of Joseph,* northern Israel. *Stubble, burn, consume,* for similar prophetic images, see Joel 2.5; Mal 4.1.

19–21: Israel's vindication. Israel will regain its lost territories. **19:** *Negeb* is the arid south; *Shephelah,* the western foothills. *Gilead* is in Transjordan. **20:** Exiles from the eighth-century Assyrian campaigns will return from *Halah,* a city in northern Mesopotamia (2 Kings 17.6). *Zarephath,* a city on the Phoenician coast, between Tyre and Sidon, represents the northwest border of an expanded Israel. *Sepharad,* location unknown; perhaps in Asia Minor. **21:** Joel 2.32.

JONAH

Jonah is unique among the prophetic books. Jonah himself is never called a prophet in the text. The book contains no collections of oracles in verse against Israel and foreign nations but presents a prose narrative about the prophet himself. Instead of portraying a prophet who is an obedient servant of the LORD, calling people to repentance, it features a recalcitrant prophet who tries to flee from God and his mission and sulks when his hearers repent.

The principal figure of this deceptively simple story is presumably based on an obscure Galilean prophet from Gath-hepher who counseled Jeroboam II (788–747 BCE) in a successful conflict with the Syrians (2 Kings 14.25). The author of the book of Jonah apparently drew upon legends that had collected about this prophet and put them to new use in a brief story that contains elements of folktale, fable, satire, and allegory. The two parts of the story, chs 1–2 and 3–4, are united by their central character (Jonah), a similar plot (the ironical conversion of foreigners to faith in the LORD), and an identical theme (the breadth of God's saving love). The influence of Jeremiah and Second Isaiah in the text suggests that the author probably lived in the postexilic period. Although the linguistic evidence is indecisive, a date in the fifth or fourth century BCE is plausible.

The book of Jonah is also uncharacteristic, when compared to other writings in the prophetic tradition, in its use of humor to make its points. Humorous qualities, such as exaggerated behavior (running away from God, 1.3); inappropriate actions (sleeping through a violent storm, 1.5); outlandish situations (offering a prayer of thanksgiving from inside a fish's belly, 2.1); ludicrous commands (animals must fast and wear sackcloth, 3.7–8); and emotions either contrary to expectation (anger at mercy, 4.1–2) or out of proportion (being angry enough to die because a plant has withered, 4.9) appear throughout the story. But all of these qualities serve to underline the book's themes.

Repentance and deliverance are the dominant themes in the story of Jonah, reflected in its use in the New Testament (Mt 12.38–41; Lk 11.29–32) and as the afternoon Prophetic Bible reading on the Jewish holy day of Yom Kippur (Day of Atonement). With skill and finesse this little book calls Israel to repentance and reminds it of God's extravagant mercy and forgiveness (Ex 34.6; Joel 2.13). In spirit, therefore, the book justifies its place in the Book of the Twelve Prophets.

1 Now the word of the LORD came to
Jonah son of Amittai, saying, 2 "Go at
once to Nineveh, that great city, and cry
out against it; for their wickedness has
come up before me." 3 But Jonah set out to
flee to Tarshish from the presence of the
LORD. He went down to Joppa and found
a ship going to Tarshish; so he paid his fare

1.1–16: Jonah's first call to preach to Nineveh (the capital of the Assyrians who destroyed Samaria in 722 BCE), although unheeded, results in the conversion of non-Israelite sailors. The story is told in concise folktale style. **1–3:** Jonah rebels against the divine commission and attempts to flee from God. **1:** *The word of the LORD,* the book begins like other prophetic books. Central to biblical prophecy is the belief that the prophet's inspiration and authority are not self-generated, but come from God, whose will is disclosed through the prophet (Ezek 2.3–5; 3.10–11; Am 3.7; Zech 1.6), whose personal agent the prophet is (Ex 4.15–16; Isa 6.8), and whom alone the prophet must obey (1 Kings 13; Am 7.14–17). *Jonah* means "dove." **2:** Gen 10.11 reports that Noah's great-grandson, Nimrod, built *Nineveh.* For other

and went on board, to go with them to
Tarshish, away from the presence of the
LORD.
4 But the LORD hurled a great wind
upon the sea, and such a mighty storm
came upon the sea that the ship threatened
to break up. 5 Then the mariners were
afraid, and each cried to his god. They
threw the cargo that was in the ship into
the sea, to lighten it for them. Jonah, mean-
while, had gone down into the hold of the
ship and had lain down, and was fast
asleep. 6 The captain came and said to him,
"What are you doing sound asleep? Get up,
call on your god! Perhaps the god will spare
us a thought so that we do not perish."
7 The sailors[a] said to one another,
"Come, let us cast lots, so that we may
know on whose account this calamity has
come upon us." So they cast lots, and the
lot fell on Jonah. 8 Then they said to him,
"Tell us why this calamity has come upon
us. What is your occupation? Where do
you come from? What is your country?
And of what people are you?" 9 "I am a
Hebrew," he replied. "I worship the LORD,
the God of heaven, who made the sea and
the dry land." 10 Then the men were even
more afraid, and said to him, "What is this
that you have done!" For the men knew
that he was fleeing from the presence of the
LORD, because he had told them so.
11 Then they said to him, "What shall
we do to you, that the sea may quiet down
for us?" For the sea was growing more and
more tempestuous. 12 He said to them,
"Pick me up and throw me into the sea;
then the sea will quiet down for you; for I
know it is because of me that this great
storm has come upon you." 13 Nevertheless
the men rowed hard to bring the ship back
to land, but they could not, for the sea grew
more and more stormy against them.
14 Then they cried out to the LORD, "Please,
O LORD, we pray, do not let us perish on
account of this man's life. Do not make us
guilty of innocent blood; for you, O LORD,
have done as it pleased you." 15 So they
picked Jonah up and threw him into the
sea; and the sea ceased from its raging.
16 Then the men feared the LORD even
more, and they offered a sacrifice to the
LORD and made vows.
17[b] But the LORD provided a large fish
to swallow up Jonah; and Jonah was in the
belly of the fish three days and three nights.

a Heb *They* *b* Ch 2.1 in Heb

divine judgments against the *wickedness* of Nineveh, see Nah 3; Zeph 2.13. The narrative echoes also the story of Sodom and Gomorrah (Gen 18.16–19.25). **3:** Prophets of judgment risk persecution and death. The port of *Joppa* was outside Israelite territory. Nineveh lay to the east, so Jonah heads for *Tarshish* (Isa 66.19; Ezek 27.12,25), probably the city of Tarsus on the southern coast of Turkey or Tartessus in southern Spain.

1.4–16: God stirs up a storm at sea to halt Jonah's flight (see Ps 48.7). **4:** *Wind,* especially the east wind (4.8) was a favorite weapon of the LORD (Ex 14.21; 15.10; Isa 27.8; Hos 13.15). The LORD controls the sea (Ps 65.7; 74.13; 107.23–32; Job 26.12; Isa 51.10; Hab 3.15). **5:** The *cargo* in *the sea* serves also as a sacrifice to the mariners' gods. **6:** The focus shifts from the mariners' ineffective gods to the God of Jonah. **7:** The LORD communicates by means of *lots,* a form of divination (Lev 16.8–10; 1 Sam 14.41). **9:** The term *Hebrew,* used to differentiate Israelites from non-Israelites (Gen 40.15; Ex 2.6–7), heightens the ironic contrast between Jonah and the conscientious foreign sailors who will soon acknowledge the LORD. **13:** Ezek 27.5–9 provides a likely description of the ship. The narrative betrays ignorance of seafaring; in storms ships must avoid land at all costs. **16:** *Feared . . . sacrificed . . . made vows,* multiple verbs highlight the non-Israelite sailors' new devotion to the LORD.

1.17–2.10: Jonah is miraculously saved and returned to *dry land* where he started. The *fish,* like the tempest, the east wind, the plant, and the worm, is an obedient agent of God's purpose. **1.17:** The hero swallowed by a fish is well-attested in folktales (Tob 6.3). The text uses the common Heb word for *fish; belly* is a general term for internal organs. Early Christian tradition compared Jesus' resurrection after three days in the tomb to Jonah's three days in the belly of the fish (Mt 12.38–41).

2 Then Jonah prayed to the LORD his
God from the belly of the fish, 2 saying,
"I called to the LORD out of my
distress,
and he answered me;
out of the belly of Sheol I cried,
and you heard my voice.
3 You cast me into the deep,
into the heart of the seas,
and the flood surrounded me;
all your waves and your billows
passed over me.
4 Then I said, 'I am driven away
from your sight;
how[a] shall I look again
upon your holy temple?'
5 The waters closed in over me;
the deep surrounded me;
weeds were wrapped around my head
6 at the roots of the mountains.
I went down to the land
whose bars closed upon me forever;
yet you brought up my life from the
Pit,
O LORD my God.
7 As my life was ebbing away,
I remembered the LORD;
and my prayer came to you,
into your holy temple.
8 Those who worship vain idols
forsake their true loyalty.
9 But I with the voice of thanksgiving
will sacrifice to you;
what I have vowed I will pay.
Deliverance belongs to the LORD!"
10 Then the LORD spoke to the fish, and it
spewed Jonah out upon the dry land.

3 The word of the LORD came to Jonah a
second time, saying, 2 "Get up, go to
Nineveh, that great city, and proclaim to it
the message that I tell you." 3 So Jonah set
out and went to Nineveh, according to the
word of the LORD. Now Nineveh was an
exceedingly large city, a three days' walk
across. 4 Jonah began to go into the city,
going a day's walk. And he cried out, "Forty days more, and Nineveh shall be overthrown!" 5 And the people of Nineveh be-
lieved God; they proclaimed a fast, and
everyone, great and small, put on sack-
cloth.
6 When the news reached the king of
Nineveh, he rose from his throne, removed

a Theodotion: Heb *surely*

2.1–10: Jonah's prayer and its answer. This psalm of thanksgiving (rather than the expression of penitence and cry for aid one might expect) is conventional and may have been originally independent of the prose narrative. Here, it simultaneously expresses Jonah's thanks for deliverance (v. 9), echoes the sailors' experience, and anticipates Nineveh's encounter with God's mercy (3.10). **1:** Ps 18.6; 120.1. According to the conventions of Hebrew poetry, the verbs in the poem may be translated in present or past tense. **2:** *Sheol* (or the *Pit,* v. 6) was the land of the dead (Ps 88.3–12). Jonah runs from God to the ends of the earth only to beseech God from the underworld. **3:** In poetry, the *deep* and the *flood* (lit. "river") refer to the mythic waters of chaos, which the LORD controls (Ex 15.8; Ps 24.2; 33.7; 135.6). **3a:** Ps 88.6. **3b:** Ps 42.7. **4a:** Ps 31.22. **5:** Lam 3.54; Ps 69.2. The *deep,* Heb "tehom," the primordial waters of creation (Gen 1.2). **6:** *Land,* of the dead, Sheol. *You brought up my life,* Jonah's downward trajectory, begun in 1.3, is reversed. **9:** Jonah's vow parallels the sailors' response in 1.16. **10:** *Spewed . . . out,* literally, "vomited," used to humorous effect.

3.1–4.11: Jonah's preaching to Nineveh. 3: Although Nineveh was indeed an *exceedingly large city,* the narrative exaggerates. Excavations at the site of Nineveh (Tell Nabi Yunus, "ruin of the Prophet Jonah"; the name reflects Muslim Jonah traditions) opposite the Iraqi city of Mosul have revealed a city about three miles long with a city wall eight miles around. By stressing the vast size of the city the author means to show the extent of Jonah's success and of God's mercy. **4:** The only explicit prophecy in the book. *Overthrown,* Jonah expects destruction, but this word can also refer to a "turn over" or change of heart. **5–10:** As in ch 1, foreigners acknowledge the LORD after encountering Jonah. The Heb text is full of clever, ironic word play. **6:** *Sackcloth* and *ashes,* traditional signs of mourning and repentance (2 Sam 3.31; Esth 4.3; Dan 9.3). Penitence is expressed internally by fasting, externally by wearing uncomfortable sackcloth. The title *king of Nineveh* is unknown in Assyrian texts. **7–10:** Contradicting Num 23.19;

his robe, covered himself with sackcloth,
and sat in ashes. [7]Then he had a proclama-
tion made in Nineveh: "By the decree of the
king and his nobles: No human being or
animal, no herd or flock, shall taste any-
thing. They shall not feed, nor shall they
drink water. [8]Human beings and animals
shall be covered with sackcloth, and they
shall cry mightily to God. All shall turn
from their evil ways and from the violence
that is in their hands. [9]Who knows? God
may relent and change his mind; he may
turn from his fierce anger, so that we do
not perish."
10 When God saw what they did, how
they turned from their evil ways, God
changed his mind about the calamity that
he had said he would bring upon them; and
he did not do it.

4 But this was very displeasing to Jonah,
and he became angry. [2]He prayed to
the LORD and said, "O LORD! Is not this
what I said while I was still in my own
country? That is why I fled to Tarshish at
the beginning; for I knew that you are a
gracious God and merciful, slow to anger,
and abounding in steadfast love, and ready
to relent from punishing. [3]And now,
O LORD, please take my life from me, for it
is better for me to die than to live." [4]And
the LORD said, "Is it right for you to be
angry?" [5]Then Jonah went out of the city
and sat down east of the city, and made a
booth for himself there. He sat under it in
the shade, waiting to see what would be-
come of the city.
6 The LORD God appointed a bush,[a]
and made it come up over Jonah, to give
shade over his head, to save him from his
discomfort; so Jonah was very happy about
the bush. [7]But when dawn came up the
next day, God appointed a worm that at-
tacked the bush, so that it withered. [8]When
the sun rose, God prepared a sultry east
wind, and the sun beat down on the head of
Jonah so that he was faint and asked that
he might die. He said, "It is better for me to
die than to live."
9 But God said to Jonah, "Is it right for
you to be angry about the bush?" And he
said, "Yes, angry enough to die." [10]Then
the LORD said, "You are concerned about
the bush, for which you did not labor and
which you did not grow; it came into being
in a night and perished in a night. [11]And
should I not be concerned about Nineveh,
that great city, in which there are more
than a hundred and twenty thousand per-
sons who do not know their right hand
from their left, and also many animals?"

a Heb *qiqayon*, possibly *the castor bean plant*

1 Sam 15.29, here God's plans are not always unalterable (cf. Gen 18.20–33; Ex 32.7–14); the reaction of the *king of Nineveh* is modeled on Jer 18.7–10. **8:** The intentionally humorous notion of animals in sackcloth makes a serious point: Mercy is not restricted to God's human creations (4.11). God's care for Nineveh and its cattle pointedly contrasts with God's lethal treatment of the Egyptians and their cattle in the Exodus plague of the firstborn (Ex 12.29).

4.1–11: God exposes Jonah's egotism and selfishness by word (disputation, reminiscent of Job 38–41) and deed (the fate of the bush). **1–4:** Jonah is angry and embarrassed; because his words (3.4) did not come true, he will be judged a false prophet (Deut 18.21–22). Unlike the LORD, Jonah is more concerned for his own credibility than for the lives of thousands of foreigners. **2:** *I knew that you are a gracious God . . .*, a traditional Israelite confession of faith (Ex 34.6; Neh 9.17; Ps 86.5; Joel 2.13). **3:** Jonah's death wish (also vv. 8–9) expresses frustration (Num 11.10–15; 1 Kings 19.2–4; Jer 20.14–18; Job 3). **7:** *Worm,* a general term for a destructive creeping creature (Isa 14.11; 66.24). **8:** *Wind,* see 1.4n. **10–11:** God uses classic rhetoric, linking a minor idea, concern (or "pity") for a plant, to a major one, concern for the helplessly ignorant inhabitants of Nineveh.

MICAH

The prophet Micah, active during the late eighth century BCE, was among the earliest of the Minor Prophets. According to 1.1, Micah prophesied in the days of Jotham, Ahaz, and Hezekiah, whose reigns spanned 759–687 BCE. Possible allusions to the fall of Samaria (1.6) and the campaign of Sennacherib (1.10–16) place the prophet in the final quarter of the eighth century. As such he was a younger contemporary of Isaiah of Jerusalem. The characteristics of the era in which Micah spoke were similar to those seen in Hosea, Amos, and Isaiah 1–39. Biblical accounts of this era are 1 Kings 16–19 and Isaiah 36–37. The prophetic scroll known as Micah may have material from later periods (e.g., 4.10 speaks of the Babylonian exile; 7.11 seems to reflect the postexilic period). Some suggest that chs 1–3 form the oldest core of the book; it is characterized by the judgmental tone for which Micah was most famous (Jer 26.18).

Micah offered a theological interpretation of the dizzying events near the end of the eighth century: the fall of Samaria, the expansion of Jerusalem fueled by emigrants from the north, and the international situation made unstable by an aggressive superpower, Assyria. Micah, from a small town southwest of Jerusalem, Moresheth-gath, had a populist message. He expressed disdain for the corruptions and pretensions of Jerusalem and its leaders. In an era of urbanization, he championed the traditions of early Israel (3.9–10; 6.3–5). Micah condemned religious practice untethered from ethical performance (6.6–8).

While Amos and Hosea condemned the high places, provincial shrines where the proper worship of the LORD was diluted by illicit elements, Micah called Jerusalem itself a high place (1.5) and announced its destruction (3.12), for which he was long remembered (Jer 26.18). At the same time, Micah never lost faith in the future. The middle section of the book, chs 4–5, contains images of a restored and glorious Zion to which the nations make pilgrimage, and of an ideal king (5.2–5).

In the organization of the Book of the Twelve, Micah follows Jonah, an arrangement apparently based on chronology since, according to 2 Kings 14.25, Jonah also lived in the eighth century. Micah is connected to the book of Nahum, which follows, by catchword; compare the final section of Micah (7.18–19) with the initial unit of Nahum (1.1–3).

The book may be divided into three sections: chs 1–3; 4–5; 6–7. Chs 1–3 mainly consist of oracles of judgment; chs 4–5 of oracles of hope. The final section, chs 6–7, begins with judgment and moves to hope. We do not know whether this alternation between judgment and hope conforms to some pattern in Micah's preaching or is an organizing device of later editors.

1 The word of the LORD that came to
Micah of Moresheth in the days of
Kings Jotham, Ahaz, and Hezekiah of Judah, which he saw concerning Samaria and Jerusalem.

2 Hear, you peoples, all of you;
listen, O earth, and all that is in it;
and let the Lord GOD be a witness
against you,
the Lord from his holy temple.
3 For lo, the LORD is coming out of his
place,
and will come down and tread
upon the high places of
the earth.
4 Then the mountains will melt under
him
and the valleys will burst open,
like wax near the fire,
like waters poured down a
steep place.
5 All this is for the transgression
of Jacob
and for the sins of the house
of Israel.
What is the transgression of Jacob?
Is it not Samaria?
And what is the high place[a]
of Judah?
Is it not Jerusalem?
6 Therefore I will make Samaria a heap
in the open country,
a place for planting vineyards.
I will pour down her stones into
the valley,
and uncover her foundations.
7 All her images shall be beaten
to pieces,
all her wages shall be burned with
fire,
and all her idols I will lay waste;
for as the wages of a prostitute she
gathered them,
and as the wages of a prostitute
they shall again be used.

8 For this I will lament and wail;
I will go barefoot and naked;
I will make lamentation like
the jackals,
and mourning like the ostriches.
9 For her wound[b] is incurable.
It has come to Judah;
it has reached to the gate of
my people,
to Jerusalem.

a Heb *what are the high places* b Gk Syr Vg: Heb *wounds*

1.1: Superscription. Among the Minor Prophets, this superscription is closest in form to those for Hosea (1.1), Amos (1.1), and Zephaniah (1.1). *Micah* is a short form of the name Micaiah (1 Kings 22), which means, "Who is like Yahweh?" *Moresheth,* a small town in southwest Judah (cf. 1.14), probably Tell el-Judeidah, 37 km (23 mi) southwest of Jerusalem. *Which he saw,* Judean prophecy often had a visionary quality (e.g., Isa 1.1; Ezek 1.1.; Am 1.1; Ob 1; Nah 1.1; Hab 1.1). *Jotham* reigned from ca. 759 to 743 BCE; *Ahaz* from 743/735 to 727/715; *Hezekiah* from 727/715 to 698/687 (the data are inconsistent for the reigns of Ahaz and Hezekiah).

1.2–3.12: Speeches condemning Judean society and its leaders. This collection of speeches begins with an indictment of Samaria, capital of the Northern Kingdom, and ends with an indictment of Jerusalem, capital of the Southern Kingdom. This first major section of Micah is dominated by judgment speeches.

1.2–7: The coming of the LORD: In grand style, the LORD descends from heaven to punish Samaria. This oracle is to be dated before 722 BCE, when Samaria fell to the Assyrians. **2:** Cf. Isa 1.2; Hab 2.20; and 1 Kings 22.28b. **3–4:** Judg 5.4; Ps 68.8; 97.1–5; Isa 26.21. **5:** *Jacob,* poetic synonym for Israel; cf. Gen 32.28. *High place* usually designates an open-air shrine, but seems to refer here to the Solomonic Temple. **7:** This destruction of images is consistent with Deuteronomic law (Deut 7.25; 12.3). The phrase *wages of a prostitute* recalls the imagery of Hosea (Hos 2.2–13).

1.8–16: A lament for Samaria, and Jerusalem too. 8: *Barefoot . . . naked,* conventional mourning behavior (2 Sam 15.30; Ezek 24.17,23), employed for effect by Micah's contemporary Isaiah (Isa 20.2). *Jackals* and *ostriches,* associated with desolation because they frequented ruins and produced eerie howls or cries; see also Job 30.29; Isa 34.13.

10 Tell it not in Gath,
weep not at all;
in Beth-leaphrah
roll yourselves in the dust.
11 Pass on your way,
inhabitants of Shaphir,
in nakedness and shame;
the inhabitants of Zaanan
do not come forth;
Beth-ezel is wailing
and shall remove its support
from you.
12 For the inhabitants of Maroth
wait anxiously for good,
yet disaster has come down from the
LORD
to the gate of Jerusalem.
13 Harness the steeds to the chariots,
inhabitants of Lachish;
it was the beginning of sin
to daughter Zion,
for in you were found
the transgressions of Israel.
14 Therefore you shall give parting gifts
to Moresheth-gath;
the houses of Achzib shall be
a deception
to the kings of Israel.
15 I will again bring a conqueror
upon you,
inhabitants of Mareshah;
the glory of Israel
shall come to Adullam.
16 Make yourselves bald and cut off
your hair
for your pampered children;
make yourselves as bald as the eagle,
for they have gone from you
into exile.

2 Alas for those who devise wickedness
and evil deeds[a] on their beds!
When the morning dawns, they
perform it,
because it is in their power.
2 They covet fields, and seize them;
houses, and take them away;
they oppress householder and house,
people and their inheritance.
3 Therefore thus says the LORD:
Now, I am devising against this
family an evil
from which you cannot remove
your necks;
and you shall not walk haughtily,
for it will be an evil time.
4 On that day they shall take up a
taunt song against you,
and wail with bitter lamentation,
and say, "We are utterly ruined;
the LORD[b] alters the inheritance of
my people;
how he removes it from me!
Among our captors[c] he parcels out
our fields."
5 Therefore you will have no one to
cast the line by lot
in the assembly of the LORD.

a Cn: Heb *work evil* *b* Heb *he* *c* Cn: Heb *the rebellious*

1.10–16: These towns in southwestern Judah lay along the path of the Assyrian king Sennacherib's campaign in 701 (2 Kings 18–19; Isa 36–37), although the specific locations of several are unknown. There is a pun in virtually every verse of this section, lost in translation. For the flavor in Hebrew, consider v. 12: "the inhabitants of Bitterness wait . . . for something sweet." **10:** *Gath,* one of the five Philistine cities on the coast; 2 Sam 1.20b. **13:** Sennacherib's siege of *Lachish,* an important city 45 km (28 mi) southwest of Jerusalem, is depicted in Assyrian records. **14:** *Moresheth-gath,* see 1.1n. **15:** *Mareshah,* later known as Marisa, is modern Tell Sandahanna, 5 km (3 mi) northeast of Lachish. **16:** *Make yourselves bald,* an extreme form of mourning behavior (e.g., Isa 15.2; Jer 7.29; 16.6; Am 8.10). *Pampered children* (better, "children of your delight") is not pejorative. It depicts the grief of parents bereft of exiled children. The *eagle,* more exactly, the griffon-vulture.

2.1–5: The LORD will punish the land barons. 1–2: Ps 36.4; Isa 5.8–12; 32.7. Micah condemns the injustice and inhumanity of creditors who, through manipulation of credit and courts, foreclose on family farms. **4:** *Taunt song,* cf. Num 21.27–30; Isa 23.15–16; Hab 2.6. **5:** *Cast the line by lot,* on a piece of land, thus acquiring title to it (Josh 18.6–10; Ps 16.6).

6 "Do not preach"—thus they preach—
"one should not preach of
such things;
disgrace will not overtake us."
7 Should this be said, O house
of Jacob?
Is the LORD's patience exhausted?
Are these his doings?
Do not my words do good
to one who walks uprightly?
8 But you rise up against my people[a]
as an enemy;
you strip the robe from the
peaceful,[b]
from those who pass by trustingly
with no thought of war.
9 The women of my people you
drive out
from their pleasant houses;
from their young children you
take away
my glory forever.
10 Arise and go;
for this is no place to rest,
because of uncleanness that destroys
with a grievous destruction.[c]
11 If someone were to go about uttering
empty falsehoods,
saying, "I will preach to you of
wine and strong drink,"
such a one would be the preacher
for this people!

12 I will surely gather all of you,
O Jacob,
I will gather the survivors of Israel;
I will set them together
like sheep in a fold,
like a flock in its pasture;
it will resound with people.
13 The one who breaks out will go up
before them;
they will break through and pass
the gate,
going out by it.
Their king will pass on before them,
the LORD at their head.

3 And I said:
Listen, you heads of Jacob
and rulers of the house of Israel!
Should you not know justice?—
2 you who hate the good and love
the evil,
who tear the skin off my people,[d]
and the flesh off their bones;
3 who eat the flesh of my people,
flay their skin off them,
break their bones in pieces,
and chop them up like meat[e] in a
kettle,
like flesh in a caldron.
4 Then they will cry to the LORD,
but he will not answer them;
he will hide his face from them at
that time,
because they have acted wickedly.

5 Thus says the LORD concerning
the prophets
who lead my people astray,
who cry "Peace"
when they have something to eat,

a Cn: Heb *But yesterday my people rose* *b* Cn: Heb *from before a garment* *c* Meaning of Heb uncertain *d* Heb *from them* *e* Gk: Heb *as*

2.6–11: The prophet responds to criticism. Micah, like other prophets (Isa 30.10; Jer 5.31; Am 2.12), realizes his uncompromising message is not one his audience wants to hear.

2.12–13: A shift to an oracle of encouragement. Against the background of exile, whether in 722 or 587, this oracle counters despair with images of the LORD as shepherd (v. 12) and victorious king (v. 13). **13:** *The one who breaks out:* i.e., the LORD; see Ex 19.22; 2 Sam 5.20; 6.8.

3.1–4: The LORD will punish the judicial leaders. Corrupt judges are described as cannibals; Ezekiel also used this image (Ezek 11.5–12; 24.1–14). **1:** *Listen,* lit. "Hear," as in 1.1; 3.9; 6.1; 6.9b, a common introduction to Micah's oracles. **2:** For comparison, Isa 5.20; for contrast, Am 5.15. **4:** Futile *cry to the LORD* (i.e., prayer), cf. Isa 1.15.

3.5–8: The LORD will punish the religious leaders. Micah's rival prophets are crowd pleasers (see also 2.11), inspired on commission (v. 5); by contrast, see Micah's source of inspiration in v. 8. **6:** A time

but declare war against those
who put nothing into their mouths.
6 Therefore it shall be night to you,
without vision,
and darkness to you, without
revelation.
The sun shall go down upon
the prophets,
and the day shall be black
over them;
7 the seers shall be disgraced,
and the diviners put to shame;
they shall all cover their lips,
for there is no answer from God.
8 But as for me, I am filled with power,
with the spirit of the LORD,
and with justice and might,
to declare to Jacob his transgression
and to Israel his sin.

9 Hear this, you rulers of the house of
Jacob
and chiefs of the house of Israel,
who abhor justice
and pervert all equity,
10 who build Zion with blood
and Jerusalem with wrong!
11 Its rulers give judgment for a bribe,
its priests teach for a price,
its prophets give oracles for money;
yet they lean upon the LORD and say,
"Surely the LORD is with us!
No harm shall come upon us."
12 Therefore because of you
Zion shall be plowed as a field;
Jerusalem shall become a heap
of ruins,
and the mountain of the house a
wooded height.

4 In days to come
the mountain of the LORD's house
shall be established as the highest of
the mountains,
and shall be raised up above
the hills.
Peoples shall stream to it,
2 and many nations shall come
and say:
"Come, let us go up to the mountain
of the LORD,
to the house of the God of Jacob;
that he may teach us his ways
and that we may walk in
his paths."
For out of Zion shall go forth
instruction,
and the word of the LORD
from Jerusalem.
3 He shall judge between many peoples,

without vision, 1 Sam 3.1. **7:** *Seers,* see 1 Sam 9.9. *Cover their lips,* a sign of mourning (Lev 13.45; Ezek 24.17,22). **8:** *Filled . . . with the spirit,* Isa 11.2; 61.1–3; Ezek 2.2.

3.9–12: Summary: Its leadership corrupt, Jerusalem is doomed. The first section ends with Micah's bold assertion that Jerusalem and the Temple itself shall be destroyed because of the corruption of its leaders. **10:** *Who build Zion,* following the collapse of the northern state, Jerusalem expanded as it absorbed refugees; Hab 2.12. **11–12:** Prophecy is inseparable from context: Here, hopes in Zion's inviolability are dashed; contrast Ps 46, where they are confirmed. *Heap of ruins,* Jerusalem's fate shall be similar to that of Samaria (1.6). This parallel reveals a key strategy of the preexilic Judean prophets: The fall of Samaria served as an example to Judah. **12:** This prophecy was quoted at the trial of Jeremiah (Jer 26.18).

4.1–5.15: Speeches promising divine restoration and exaltation of the people Israel and the city Jerusalem. A series of poems depicts an ideal age ("that day") when God reigns, Israel triumphs, and the nations are judged. Some scholars date this section to the exilic or postexilic period (see 4.10n.). Alternately, possible allusions to the Babylonian exile (e.g., 4.6,10) could stem from editors who recast Micah's oracles for a later audience.

4.1–8: The ideal age is depicted in three poems, the first of which (vv. 1–4) is nearly identical to Isaiah 2.2–4. **1–2:** There is a universal pilgrimage to Mt. Zion, to which cosmic significance is ascribed here as *the mountain of the LORD's house.* **1:** *Highest of the mountains,* claims for Mt. Zion's height (Ps 48.3; Ezek 40.2) were symbolic, not topographic. **2:** *Instruction,* Heb "torah." **3–4:** A classic articulation of the Israelite prophetic ideal: peace and a social equality rooted in family ownership of land. **3:** *Swords into plowshares* (or "plowpoints," a stick with a small metal point), i.e., the transition from war to peace, as

and shall arbitrate between strong
nations far away;
they shall beat their swords into
plowshares,
and their spears into pruning
hooks;
nation shall not lift up sword against
nation,
neither shall they learn war
any more;
4 but they shall all sit under their own
vines and under their own fig
trees,
and no one shall make them afraid;
for the mouth of the LORD of hosts
has spoken.

5 For all the peoples walk,
each in the name of its god,
but we will walk in the name of the
LORD our God
forever and ever.

6 In that day, says the LORD,
I will assemble the lame
and gather those who have been
driven away,
and those whom I have afflicted.
7 The lame I will make the remnant,
and those who were cast off, a
strong nation;
and the LORD will reign over them in
Mount Zion
now and forevermore.

8 And you, O tower of the flock,
hill of daughter Zion,
to you it shall come,
the former dominion shall come,
the sovereignty of daughter
Jerusalem.

9 Now why do you cry aloud?
Is there no king in you?
Has your counselor perished,
that pangs have seized you like a
woman in labor?
10 Writhe and groan,[a] O daughter
Zion,
like a woman in labor;
for now you shall go forth from
the city
and camp in the open country;
you shall go to Babylon.
There you shall be rescued,
there the LORD will redeem you
from the hands of your enemies.

11 Now many nations
are assembled against you,
saying, "Let her be profaned,
and let our eyes gaze upon Zion."
12 But they do not know
the thoughts of the LORD;
they do not understand his plan,
that he has gathered them as
sheaves to the threshing floor.
13 Arise and thresh,
O daughter Zion,
for I will make your horn iron
and your hoofs bronze;
you shall beat in pieces many peoples,
and shall[b] devote their gain to the
LORD,

a Meaning of Heb uncertain *b* Gk Syr Tg: Heb *and I will*

the militia man converts to farmer. For the opposite movement, see Joel 3.10. **4:** Zech 3.10; 1 Kings 4.25; 2 Kings 18.31 = Isa 36.16. **5:** Like its similarly worded parallel in Isa 2.5, this verse may have been read antiphonally, as an "Amen" to the visionary speech of 4.1–4 (= Isa 2.2–4). **6–7:** Cf. Zeph 3.19–20. **8:** *Tower of the flock,* an old epithet for Jerusalem (see "tower of Eder" in Gen 35.21; "Eder" means "flock").

4.9–10: The LORD will rescue the exiles. This speech, which describes the exiles' march to Babylon and promises their redemption, addresses the situation of the sixth century, not the eighth. *Like a woman in labor,* Isa 13.8; 26.17; Jer 4.31.

4.11–12: Israel will crush its enemies. The LORD has planned a stunning reversal. At the very place outside Jerusalem where hostile nations assemble, the city gate (also the site of threshing floors), Israel shall trample them. **13:** For Israel as bovine, see Hos 10.11. *Devote their gain,* Deut 20.16; Josh 6.18–19.

their wealth to the Lord of the
whole earth.

5 [a]Now you are walled around with
a wall;[b]
siege is laid against us;
with a rod they strike the ruler
of Israel
upon the cheek.

2 [c]But you, O Bethlehem of Ephrathah,
who are one of the little clans
of Judah,
from you shall come forth for me
one who is to rule in Israel,
whose origin is from of old,
from ancient days.
3 Therefore he shall give them up until
the time
when she who is in labor has
brought forth;
then the rest of his kindred shall
return
to the people of Israel.
4 And he shall stand and feed his flock
in the strength of the LORD,
in the majesty of the name of the
LORD his God.
And they shall live secure, for now he
shall be great
to the ends of the earth;
5 and he shall be the one of peace.

If the Assyrians come into our land
and tread upon our soil,[d]
we will raise against them seven
shepherds
and eight installed as rulers.
6 They shall rule the land of Assyria
with the sword,
and the land of Nimrod with the
drawn sword;[e]
they[f] shall rescue us from the
Assyrians
if they come into our land
or tread within our border.

7 Then the remnant of Jacob,
surrounded by many peoples,
shall be like dew from the LORD,
like showers on the grass,
which do not depend upon people
or wait for any mortal.
8 And among the nations the remnant
of Jacob,
surrounded by many peoples,
shall be like a lion among the animals
of the forest,
like a young lion among the flocks
of sheep,
which, when it goes through,
treads down
and tears in pieces, with no one to
deliver.
9 Your hand shall be lifted up over
your adversaries,
and all your enemies shall be
cut off.

10 In that day, says the LORD,

a Ch 4.14 in Heb *b* Cn Compare Gk: Meaning of Heb uncertain *c* Ch 5.1 in Heb *d* Gk: Heb *in our palaces* *e* Cn: Heb *in its entrances* *f* Heb *he*

5.1: *Strike . . . the cheek,* a gesture of insult; see 1 Kings 22.24; Job 16.10; Ps 3.7; Lam 3.30.

5.2–5a: A messianic poem. A new David shall arise, not from Jerusalem but from Bethlehem, David's place of birth, to rule in this ideal age. The New Testament interprets this poem as referring to the birth of Jesus (Mt 2.6; cf. Jn 7.40–43). **2:** *Bethlehem,* located 9 km (6 mi) south of Jerusalem; Gen 35.19; Ruth 4.11; 1 Sam 17.12. *Ephrathah,* the name of a Judahite clan and region; the latter includes the village of Bethlehem. The prophet Amos (9.11) also uses the phrase *of old* in reference to David. **3:** Isaiah of Jerusalem, a contemporary of Micah, also described the birth of an ideal king (7.14; 9.6).

5.5b–6: Assyria will be defeated. In the new age, Israel will not lack for leaders (contrast chs 2–3). **5:** *Seven . . . eight,* a sufficient number (see Am 1.3n). **6:** *Land of Nimrod,* Assyria; Gen 10.8–11 identifies Nimrod as a legendary warrior and king of Assyria.

5.7–9: Israel gains the upper hand. 7: *Dew,* the image is hostile; see 2 Sam 17.12.

5.10–15: But before reconstruction, demolition. The repetition of first-person verbs at the beginning of each line (*I will cut off,* four times; *I will uproot; I will execute vengeance*) sets the tone. **10:** *Cut off your*

I will cut off your horses from
among you
and will destroy your chariots;
11 and I will cut off the cities of
your land
and throw down all your
strongholds;
12 and I will cut off sorceries from your
hand,
and you shall have no more
soothsayers;
13 and I will cut off your images
and your pillars from among
you,
and you shall bow down no more
to the work of your hands;
14 and I will uproot your sacred poles[a]
from among you
and destroy your towns.
15 And in anger and wrath I will execute
vengeance
on the nations that did not obey.

6 Hear what the LORD says:
Rise, plead your case before
the mountains,
and let the hills hear your voice.
2 Hear, you mountains, the controversy
of the LORD,
and you enduring foundations of
the earth;
for the LORD has a controversy with
his people,
and he will contend with Israel.

3 "O my people, what have I done
to you?
In what have I wearied you?
Answer me!
4 For I brought you up from the land
of Egypt,
and redeemed you from the house
of slavery;
and I sent before you Moses,
Aaron, and Miriam.
5 O my people, remember now what
King Balak of Moab devised,
what Balaam son of Beor answered
him,
and what happened from Shittim
to Gilgal,
that you may know the saving acts
of the LORD."

6 "With what shall I come before
the LORD,
and bow myself before God
on high?
Shall I come before him with
burnt offerings,
with calves a year old?
7 Will the LORD be pleased with
thousands of rams,
with ten thousands of rivers of oil?
Shall I give my firstborn for my
transgression,
the fruit of my body for the sin of
my soul?"
8 He has told you, O mortal, what
is good;

a Heb *Asherim*

horses . . . and . . . chariots, Israel must rely on the LORD, not military force (Ps 20.17; 33.13–17; Zech 9.10). **11:** Jer 5.17; Hos 10.12–14. **12:** The precise forms these means of divination took are unknown; for the biblical prohibition, see Deut 18.10–11. **13–14:** *Pillars* and *sacred poles,* the equipment of Canaanite religion, banned for Israel (Ex 34.13). According to 2 Kings 18.4, King Hezekiah accomplished this.

6.1–7.20: A prophetic sampler moves from legal indictment of Israel's guilt to liturgical affirmation of God's mercy. The final section of Micah consists of four units, of different genres, which extend the themes of the first section (1.2–3.12).

6.1–8: A divine lawsuit. There are frequent shifts of speakers here, from the LORD (v. 1) to the prophet (v. 2) and back to the LORD (vv. 3–5), to a spokesperson for the community (vv. 6–7) and back to the prophet (v. 8), who delivers the punchline, the epitome of the entire Israelite prophetic tradition. **1–2:** The audience, in the style of ancient treaty witnesses, is the heavenly court. *Controversy,* lawsuit. **4:** Note the prominence of *Miriam* (Ex 15.20–21). **5:** *Balak, Balaam,* Num 22–24. **5:** *From Shittim* (Josh 3.1) *to Gilgal* (Josh 4.19) refers to the crossing of the Jordan. **6:** Cf. Ps 15.1; 24.3. **8:** In this single sentence the

and what does the LORD require of
you
but to do justice, and to love kindness,
and to walk humbly with
your God?

9 The voice of the LORD cries to
the city
(it is sound wisdom to fear
your name):
Hear, O tribe and assembly of
the city![a]
10 Can I forget[b] the treasures of
wickedness in the house of the
wicked,
and the scant measure that is
accursed?
11 Can I tolerate wicked scales
and a bag of dishonest weights?
12 Your[c] wealthy are full of violence;
your[d] inhabitants speak lies,
with tongues of deceit in
their mouths.
13 Therefore I have begun[e] to strike
you down,
making you desolate because of
your sins.
14 You shall eat, but not be satisfied,
and there shall be a gnawing
hunger within you;
you shall put away, but not save,
and what you save, I will hand over
to the sword.
15 You shall sow, but not reap;
you shall tread olives, but not
anoint yourselves with oil;
you shall tread grapes, but not
drink wine.
16 For you have kept the statutes
of Omri[f]
and all the works of the house
of Ahab,
and you have followed their
counsels.
Therefore I will make you a
desolation, and your[g]
inhabitants an object
of hissing;
so you shall bear the scorn of
my people.

7 Woe is me! For I have become like
one who,
after the summer fruit has
been gathered,
after the vintage has been gleaned,
finds no cluster to eat;
there is no first-ripe fig for which I
hunger.
2 The faithful have disappeared from
the land,
and there is no one left who
is upright;
they all lie in wait for blood,
and they hunt each other with nets.
3 Their hands are skilled to do evil;
the official and the judge ask for a
bribe,
and the powerful dictate what
they desire;
thus they pervert justice.[h]
4 The best of them is like a brier,
the most upright of them a
thorn hedge.

a Cn Compare Gk: Heb *tribe, and who has appointed it yet?* *b* Cn: Meaning of Heb uncertain
c Heb *Whose* *d* Heb *whose* *e* Gk Syr Vg: Heb *have made sick* *f* Gk Syr Vg Tg: Heb *the statutes of Omri are kept* *g* Heb *its* *h* Cn: Heb *they weave it*

prophet sums up a century of brilliant prophecy; see Am 5.21–24; Hos 6.6; Isa 1.11–17. *Kindness,* "ḥesed," covenant loyalty.

6.9–16: Jerusalem, the corrupt city, is cursed. Jerusalem, as wicked as Samaria (see v. 16), must be destroyed. This speech can be read as a separate oracle or as the judicial sentence following the indictment in 6.1–8. **14–16:** For other "futility curses" in which actions fail to produce normal and expected results, see Deut 28.30–31,38–46. **16:** *Omri, Ahab,* of the Northern Kingdom in the ninth century BCE; see 1 Kings 16.25–34. *Object of hissing,* Zeph 2.15.

7.1–7: A lament for a desperate society. 1: *Gleaned,* Lev 19.9–10; 23.22; Deut 24.19–21; Ruth 2–3. The *first-ripe fig* was the most delicious. **2:** Abraham (Gen 18.23–33), Jeremiah (Jer 5.1), and Ezekiel (Ezek 22.30) also searched for an honest man. **5:** Cf. Jer 9.4. **6:** Contrast Mal 4.6.

The day of their[a] sentinels, of their[a]
punishment, has come;
now their confusion is at hand.
5 Put no trust in a friend,
have no confidence in a loved one;
guard the doors of your mouth
from her who lies in your embrace;
6 for the son treats the father with
contempt,
the daughter rises up against
her mother,
the daughter-in-law against her
mother-in-law;
your enemies are members of your
own household.
7 But as for me, I will look to
the LORD,
I will wait for the God of my
salvation;
my God will hear me.

8 Do not rejoice over me, O my enemy;
when I fall, I shall rise;
when I sit in darkness,
the LORD will be a light to me.
9 I must bear the indignation of
the LORD,
because I have sinned against him,
until he takes my side
and executes judgment for me.
He will bring me out to the light;
I shall see his vindication.
10 Then my enemy will see,
and shame will cover her who said
to me,
"Where is the LORD your God?"
My eyes will see her downfall;[b]
now she will be trodden down
like the mire of the streets.

11 A day for the building of your walls!
In that day the boundary shall be
far extended.
12 In that day they will come to you
from Assyria to[c] Egypt,
and from Egypt to the River,
from sea to sea and from mountain
to mountain.
13 But the earth will be desolate
because of its inhabitants,
for the fruit of their doings.

14 Shepherd your people with your staff,
the flock that belongs to you,
which lives alone in a forest
in the midst of a garden land;
let them feed in Bashan and Gilead
as in the days of old.
15 As in the days when you came out of
the land of Egypt,
show us[d] marvelous things.
16 The nations shall see and be ashamed
of all their might;
they shall lay their hands on
their mouths;
their ears shall be deaf;
17 they shall lick dust like a snake,
like the crawling things of
the earth;
they shall come trembling out of their
fortresses;
they shall turn in dread to the
LORD our God,
and they shall stand in fear of you.

18 Who is a God like you, pardoning
iniquity
and passing over the transgression

a Heb *your* *b* Heb lacks *downfall* *c* One Ms: MT *Assyria and cities of* *d* Cn: Heb *I will show him*

7.8–20: A final liturgy. This final unit contains shifts in content, if not speakers, and may have been designed for worship. It begins with lament (vv. 8–10), followed by an oracle of encouragement (vv. 11–13) and prayer (vv. 14–17), before closing with hopeful affirmation of God's great mercy. **8–10:** The prophet speaks as Israel. **9:** Jer 10.19. **10:** *Shame will cover her,* Ob 10. *Mire of the streets,* Isa 10.6. **11–13:** The references to the (re)*building of your walls* (Neh 2.17) and the restoration of former boundaries (Isa 54.2–3) suggest that this oracle was probably written in the early postexilic period. **12:** *The River,* the Euphrates. **14:** *Bashan* and *Gilead* in northern Transjordan were known for their fertility. **18–19:** Cf. Ex 34.6–7; Ps 103.8–10; contrast Nah 1.2–3. **18:** The sentence *Who is a God like you* is reminiscent of the prophet's name (1.1n.). **20:** Gen 12.1–3; 17.6–8.

of the remnant of your[a]
possession?
He does not retain his anger forever,
because he delights in showing
clemency.
19 He will again have compassion upon
us;
he will tread our iniquities
under foot.
You will cast all our[b] sins
into the depths of the sea.
20 You will show faithfulness to Jacob
and unswerving loyalty to
Abraham,
as you have sworn to our ancestors
from the days of old.

a Heb *his* *b* Gk Syr Vg Tg: Heb *their*

NAHUM

Although Nahum does not begin with a date formula, its allusions to historical events allow us to date it to the middle or late seventh century BCE. Nahum refers to the fall of Thebes (3.8) which occurred in 663. The focus of the book, the fall of Nineveh (612), is either an imminent or recent event. Nahum's placement among the Minor Prophets thus seems to be chronological, directly following Micah, who was active in the late eighth century.

As is typical of Israelite prophecy, Nahum's words were prompted by the dramatic events of international history. The Assyrian Empire, whose power had for centuries been felt and feared from Mesopotamia to the Mediterranean, crumbled quickly after the death of Asshurbanipal (627 BCE). Under the combined assaults of the Medes from north of Persia and the Chaldeans from southern Babylonia, the ancient Assyrian capital city, Asshur, fell in 614. When the renowned Nineveh was destroyed in 612, Assyrian domination of the Near East was ended, though its imperial structures served as a template for subsequent empires.

The fervent reaction to the overthrow of Assyria, expressed by the peoples long subjected to its yoke, is nowhere seen more clearly than in Nahum. The core of the book is a superb, vivid poem (2.3–9; 3.1–3) extolling Nineveh's destruction. The prophet spells out the reason for the Assyrian downfall: It is the LORD's judgment against an oppressor.

This basic theme makes clear that Nahum's thought is passionately partisan. He asserts boldly that the LORD is the avenger of cruelty and immorality. Prophetic collections often include oracles against the nations (e.g., Isa 13–23; Jer 46–51). In essence, the brief book of Nahum, like that of Obadiah, consists entirely of this single genre. To that extent, it fails to indicate the consequences of this divine justice for Israel itself. The book and its sentiments toward Nineveh are often contrasted with those in the book of Jonah (contrast Nah 3.11 with Jon 4.11; Nah 1.2–3 with Jon 4.1–2).

The date of Nahum's triumphal ode lies close to the events it foretells (or describes), probably between 626 and 612 BCE. Its author is identified only by his name (which means "comforted"); even the location of his home, Elkosh (1.1), is unknown.

1 An oracle concerning Nineveh. The book of the vision of Nahum of Elkosh.

2 A jealous and avenging God is
the LORD,
the LORD is avenging and
wrathful;
the LORD takes vengeance on his
adversaries
and rages against his enemies.

1.1: Title. *Oracle* (lit. "burden") describes a kind of prophetic speech that responds to the questions of the community (Isa 13.1; Jer 23.33–40; Ezek 12.10; Hab 1.1; Zech 9.1; 12.1; Mal 1.1). Here the prophet attempts to clarify the divine role in the collapse of *Nineveh,* capital of the Neo-Assyrian empire. *The vision,* Ob 1. The location of *Elkosh* is unknown.

1.2–9: A hymn to the divine warrior. This paean to divine ferocity and retribution is presented in the form of a partial acrostic (most lines from vv. 2–8 begin with successive letters of the Hebrew alphabet). **2–3:** This variation on the classic formulation of the divine personality (Ex 34.6–7) emphasizes judgment,

3 The LORD is slow to anger but great
in power,
and the LORD will by no means
clear the guilty.

His way is in whirlwind and storm,
and the clouds are the dust of
his feet.
4 He rebukes the sea and makes it dry,
and he dries up all the rivers;
Bashan and Carmel wither,
and the bloom of Lebanon fades.
5 The mountains quake before him,
and the hills melt;
the earth heaves before him,
the world and all who live in it.

6 Who can stand before his
indignation?
Who can endure the heat of
his anger?
His wrath is poured out like fire,
and by him the rocks are broken in
pieces.
7 The LORD is good,
a stronghold in a day of trouble;
he protects those who take refuge in
him,
8 even in a rushing flood.
He will make a full end of his
adversaries,[a]
and will pursue his enemies into
darkness.
9 Why do you plot against the LORD?
He will make an end;
no adversary will rise up twice.
10 Like thorns they are entangled,
like drunkards they are drunk;
they are consumed like dry straw.

11 From you one has gone out
who plots evil against the LORD,
one who counsels wickedness.

12 Thus says the LORD,
"Though they are at full strength and
many,[b]
they will be cut off and pass away.
Though I have afflicted you,
I will afflict you no more.
13 And now I will break off his yoke
from you
and snap the bonds that bind you."

14 The LORD has commanded
concerning you:
"Your name shall be perpetuated
no longer;
from the house of your gods I will cut
off
the carved image and the
cast image.
I will make your grave, for you
are worthless."

15[c] Look! On the mountains the feet
of one
who brings good tidings,
who proclaims peace!
Celebrate your festivals, O Judah,
fulfill your vows,
for never again shall the wicked
invade you;
they are utterly cut off.

a Gk: Heb *of her place* b Meaning of Heb uncertain
c Ch 2.1 in Heb

in contrast to Jon 4.2 (also concerning Nineveh), which emphasizes mercy. **3b–5:** Cf. 2 Sam 22.8–16 = Ps 18.7–15. **3:** *Whirlwind and storm,* cf. Ex 19.16; Job 38.1; Isa 29.6; Jer 23.19; contrast 1 Kings 19.11–12. *Clouds are the dust of his feet,* 2 Sam 22.10–11; Ps 18.9–10; 68.4. **4:** *Bashan, Carmel,* and *Lebanon,* regions famous for their fertility, were situated between Judah and Syria.

1.10–2.2: Alternating oracles concerning Nineveh and Judah. The ominous words for Nineveh are, at the same time, good news for Judah. **10–11:** Addressed to Nineveh. **10:** *Consumed like dry straw,* cf. Isa 33.11–12. **11:** *Counsels wickedness,* alternate translation, "wicked counselor," which may refer to a specific person (the same word, "wicked," is used in v. 15), such as Sennacherib. **12–13:** Addressed to Judah. **13:** *Yoke,* a slave collar (Isa 58.6,9; Jer 28.10–12). **14:** Addressed to the king of Nineveh. **15:** Addressed to Judah. *One who brings good tidings,* 2 Sam 18.31; 1 Kings 1.42; Isa 40.9; 52.7. *Fulfill your*

2 A shatterer[a] has come up
against you.
Guard the ramparts;
watch the road;
gird your loins;
collect all your strength.

2 (For the LORD is restoring the majesty
of Jacob,
as well as the majesty of Israel,
though ravagers have ravaged them
and ruined their branches.)

3 The shields of his warriors are red;
his soldiers are clothed in crimson.
The metal on the chariots flashes
on the day when he musters them;
the chargers[b] prance.
4 The chariots race madly through the
streets,
they rush to and fro through
the squares;
their appearance is like torches,
they dart like lightning.
5 He calls his officers;
they stumble as they come forward;
they hasten to the wall,
and the mantelet[c] is set up.
6 The river gates are opened,
the palace trembles.
7 It is decreed[c] that the city[d]
be exiled,
its slave women led away,
moaning like doves
and beating their breasts.
8 Nineveh is like a pool
whose waters[e] run away.
"Halt! Halt!"—
but no one turns back.
9 "Plunder the silver,
plunder the gold!
There is no end of treasure!
An abundance of every precious
thing!"

10 Devastation, desolation, and
destruction!
Hearts faint and knees tremble,
all loins quake,
all faces grow pale!
11 What became of the lions' den,
the cave[f] of the young lions,
where the lion goes,
and the lion's cubs, with no one to
disturb them?
12 The lion has torn enough for
his whelps
and strangled prey for his lionesses;
he has filled his caves with prey
and his dens with torn flesh.

13 See, I am against you, says the LORD of hosts, and I will burn your[g] chariots in smoke, and the sword shall devour your young lions; I will cut off your prey from

a Cn: Heb *scatterer* *b* Cn Compare Gk Syr: Heb *cypresses* *c* Meaning of Heb uncertain *d* Heb *it* *e* Cn Compare Gk: Heb *a pool, from the days that she has become, and they* *f* Cn: Heb *pasture* *g* Heb *her*

vows, presumably vows made to God during the oppression in hopes of deliverance. **2.1:** Addressed to Nineveh. A *shatterer* (or *scatterer;* see translators' footnote *a*), the Medians and Babylonians who attacked Nineveh. **2:** This parenthetical observation suggests that the fall of Assyria inspired hope for the release and repatriation of the Ephraimites exiled in 722. *Jacob* here refers to the Northern Kingdom (Am 6.8; 8.7). *Ruined their branches,* for Israel as a vine, see Ps 80.8; Isa 5.1–7; Jer 5.10.

2.3–3.19: The sack of Nineveh. The remainder of the book, whether in third-person description (2.3–12; 3.1–3) or second-person address (2.13–3.19), directly concerns the collapse of the oppressive Assyrian Empire.

2.3–9: The assault. 3: *His warriors,* the attacking army. *Clothed in crimson,* the well-equipped attackers are uniformed. The *metal* refers to the steel hardware on wooden chariots and leather harnesses. *The chargers,* another possibility is "the cypresses" (see translators' footnote *b*), referring to the wooden frames of the chariots. **6:** *The river gates,* Nineveh was situated on the east bank of the Tigris River, whose tributary, the Khosr, flowed through the city. **8:** *Like a pool,* the city may have been flooded (see v. 6n.).

2.10–13: The taunt: Where is the lion now? 11: The lion was a popular symbol of the Assyrian court. **12–13:** Nineveh's treasures, plundered and extorted from its vassals, are likened to *prey.*

the earth, and the voice of your messengers
shall be heard no more.

3 Ah! City of bloodshed,
utterly deceitful, full of booty—
no end to the plunder!
2 The crack of whip and rumble
of wheel,
galloping horse and bounding
chariot!
3 Horsemen charging,
flashing sword and glittering spear,
piles of dead,
heaps of corpses,
dead bodies without end—
they stumble over the bodies!
4 Because of the countless debaucheries
of the prostitute,
gracefully alluring, mistress
of sorcery,
who enslaves[a] nations through her
debaucheries,
and peoples through her sorcery,
5 I am against you,
says the LORD of hosts,
and will lift up your skirts over
your face;
and I will let nations look on your
nakedness
and kingdoms on your shame.
6 I will throw filth at you
and treat you with contempt,
and make you a spectacle.
7 Then all who see you will shrink from
you and say,
"Nineveh is devastated; who will
bemoan her?"
Where shall I seek comforters
for you?

8 Are you better than Thebes[b]
that sat by the Nile,
with water around her,
her rampart a sea,
water her wall?
9 Ethiopia[c] was her strength,
Egypt too, and that without limit;
Put and the Libyans were her[d]
helpers.

10 Yet she became an exile,
she went into captivity;
even her infants were dashed in pieces
at the head of every street;
lots were cast for her nobles,
all her dignitaries were bound
in fetters.
11 You also will be drunken,
you will go into hiding;[e]
you will seek
a refuge from the enemy.
12 All your fortresses are like fig trees
with first-ripe figs—
if shaken they fall
into the mouth of the eater.
13 Look at your troops:
they are women in your midst.
The gates of your land
are wide open to your foes;
fire has devoured the bars of
your gates.

14 Draw water for the siege,
strengthen your forts;
trample the clay,
tread the mortar,
take hold of the brick mold!
15 There the fire will devour you,
the sword will cut you off.
It will devour you like the locust.

Multiply yourselves like the locust,
multiply like the grasshopper!

a Heb *sells* *b* Heb *No-amon* *c* Or *Nubia*; Heb *Cush* *d* Gk: Heb *your* *e* Meaning of Heb uncertain

3.1–3: A woe-oracle. The grim depiction of battle—here its aftermath—continues from 2.3–9.

3.4–19: A series of taunts. 4–7: Nineveh is portrayed as a disgraced prostitute, as were other cities in other prophetic indictments (e.g., Jerusalem in Ezek 16.1–43; Samaria and Jerusalem in Ezek 23.1–4); see also the portrayal of Babylon (Rome) in Rev 17.1–6; 18.1–24. **8:** The Egyptian capital *Thebes* (Jer 46.25; Ezek 30.14–16) had been captured by the Assyrians themselves in 663 BCE. **9:** *Ethiopia, Put,* and *Libya,* neighboring kingdoms which were allies of Egypt. **10:** Ps 137.8–9. **13:** *Your troops . . . are women,* Isa 19.16; Jer 30.6; 50.37; 51.30. **14–15:** Nahum's warnings are satirical; Nineveh is doomed. **16:** *The locust*

16 You increased your merchants
more than the stars of the
heavens.
The locust sheds its skin and
flies away.
17 Your guards are like grasshoppers,
your scribes like swarms[a]
of locusts
settling on the fences
on a cold day—
when the sun rises, they fly
away;
no one knows where they
have gone.

18 Your shepherds are asleep,
O king of Assyria;
your nobles slumber.
Your people are scattered on the
mountains
with no one to gather them.
19 There is no assuaging your hurt,
your wound is mortal.
All who hear the news about you
clap their hands over you.
For who has ever escaped
your endless cruelty?

a Meaning of Heb uncertain

sheds its skin, this may refer to the foreign *merchants* fleeing their stalls in the bazaars. **17:** *Your scribes,* diviners; the omen readers have seen the future and have fled. **18:** *Shepherds,* a common metaphor for rulers. **19:** *Clap their hands,* in derision (Lam 2.15; Job 27.23). *Your endless cruelty,* for a biblical example of Assyrian imperial rhetoric, see Isa 37.10–13.

HABAKKUK

Habakkuk, eighth in order among the twelve Minor Prophets, can be dated to the late seventh century BCE on the basis of the reference to the Chaldeans (1.6), whose domination of the Near East began around 612. Such a date makes the book roughly contemporaneous with its predecessor, Nahum, and successor, Zephaniah.

Although a Habakkuk legend appears in one of the additions to Daniel found in the Apocrypha (Bel 33–39), nothing is known about the life of the prophet, not even his father's name or his hometown. The book reflects the struggles of the Judahite community in the time between the death of King Josiah in 609 and the first deportation of exiles to Babylon in 597 (see 2 Kings 23.34–24.27).

At least three distinct literary forms can be recognized in Habakkuk. The section 1.2–2.4 is constructed as a dialogue between the prophet and God; the next section (2.5–20), consisting of five woes, is cast in classical prophetic style; and ch 3 is a lengthy poem, similar in structure to the Psalms. Despite their varied texture, the sections build on each other. In the opening dialogue, the prophet first laments the injustice of his society (1.2–4). The divine response is that the Chaldeans will serve as the instrument of judgment (1.5–11). The prophet questions the justice of this: "the wicked swallow those more righteous than they" (1.13). The LORD answers by urging the prophet to wait, faithfully, for an appointed time; this injustice will also be addressed (2.2–4).

The next section (2.5–20) is cast as the taunts addressed to Babylon by the very nations it had oppressed, once the cycle of divine judgment runs its full course ("The cup in the LORD's right hand will come around to you," 2.16). The final section, the song of Habakkuk (3.2–15), commemorates ancient triumphs of this God who comes in judgment. This psalm serves as the basis of the prophet's resilient hope in the face of calamity and deprivation (3.17–19) and also can be seen as a prayer (3.1) to arouse God to action (3.2).

Habakkuk was a contemporary of Jeremiah, who also contended that an invading foreign power would serve as the divine instrument of judgment against Judah (cf. Hab 1.6–11 with Jer 4.13; 5.15–17; 6.22–23), and furthermore that, in time, Babylon itself would come under divine judgment (Jer 50–51). At the same time, Habakkuk articulates on behalf of his community their searching question: Is this fair? To this perennial question the prophet receives an answer that is eternally valid: God is still sovereign, and in God's own way and at the proper time will deal with the wicked. In the meantime—in fact, at all times—the righteous shall live by their faith (2.4), a persistent, patient, and tenacious adherence to the instructions and promises of God.

1 The oracle that the prophet Habakkuk saw.

2 O LORD, how long shall I cry
for help,
and you will not listen?
Or cry to you "Violence!"
and you will not save?
3 Why do you make me see
wrongdoing
and look at trouble?
Destruction and violence are
before me;
strife and contention arise.
4 So the law becomes slack
and justice never prevails.
The wicked surround the righteous—
therefore judgment comes forth
perverted.

5 Look at the nations, and see!
Be astonished! Be astounded!
For a work is being done in
your days
that you would not believe if you
were told.
6 For I am rousing the Chaldeans,
that fierce and impetuous nation,
who march through the breadth of
the earth
to seize dwellings not their own.
7 Dread and fearsome are they;
their justice and dignity proceed
from themselves.
8 Their horses are swifter than
leopards,
more menacing than wolves
at dusk;
their horses charge.
Their horsemen come from far away;
they fly like an eagle swift
to devour.
9 They all come for violence,
with faces pressing[a] forward;
they gather captives like sand.
10 At kings they scoff,
and of rulers they make sport.
They laugh at every fortress,
and heap up earth to take it.
11 Then they sweep by like the wind;
they transgress and become guilty;
their own might is their god!

12 Are you not from of old,
O LORD my God, my Holy One?
You[b] shall not die.

a Meaning of Heb uncertain *b* Ancient Heb tradition: MT *We*

1.1: Title. *Oracle,* see Nah 1.1n. *The prophet . . . saw,* Isa 1.1; Am 1.1; Nah 1.1.

1.2–2.4: A dialogue in two cycles (1.2–11; 1.12–2.4) between the prophet and God, raising the question of the LORD's just governance of the world.

1.2–11: The first cycle. 2–4: In the form of a lament (cf. Ps 3.1; 12.1; 22.1–2), Habakkuk protests that God neither hears nor acts to address human corruption and injustice. Although the section could be directed against a foreign nation, it seems to refer to problems in the prophet's own society: *violence, strife, contention,* the perversion of *justice.* **2:** *How long,* Ps 13.1–2; 74.10. **3:** Jer 20.8. **4:** For similar prophetic complaints, see Isa 59.12–14; Jer 12.1–4. *The law becomes slack,* this could refer to the reign of Jehoiakim (608–598 BCE), when the reforms of his father Josiah languished (2 Kings 23.35–37; cf. Jer 2.8). The *law* (Heb "torah") formed the basis of Josiah's reforms. **5–11:** The LORD replies that the Chaldeans, wicked as they are, are the instrument of divine justice (Isa 10.5; 42.24; Jer 5.14–19; 27.6–7). **6:** *I am rousing,* Isa 9.11–12; 41.2–3. Properly a region in southern Mesopotamia, *Chaldea* is the biblical term (2 Kings 25.1–13; 2 Chr 36.17; Jer 21.4; Ezek 23.23) for the Neo-Babylonian empire (ca. 612–539 BCE).

1.12–2.4: The second cycle. 1.12–2.1: The prophet, hardly satisfied with the proposed solution to Judah's problems—Babylon's brutal and imperial interventions—again raises a protest. **12:** *Are you not from of old,* Ps 74.12. *Holy One* is a common epithet for God in Isaiah (1.4; 5.19,24; 10.20; etc.). *You shall not die,* as note *b* indicates, ancient scribes, uncomfortable with a statement that linked God and mortality, altered the Heb text to read "We shall not die." *O Rock,* as a metaphor for God, see Deut 32.4;

O LORD, you have marked them for
judgment;
and you, O Rock, have established
them for punishment.
13 Your eyes are too pure to behold evil,
and you cannot look on
wrongdoing;
why do you look on the treacherous,
and are silent when the wicked
swallow
those more righteous than they?
14 You have made people like the fish of
the sea,
like crawling things that have
no ruler.

15 The enemy[a] brings all of them up
with a hook;
he drags them out with his net,
he gathers them in his seine;
so he rejoices and exults.
16 Therefore he sacrifices to his net
and makes offerings to his seine;
for by them his portion is lavish,
and his food is rich.
17 Is he then to keep on emptying
his net,
and destroying nations without
mercy?

2 I will stand at my watchpost,
and station myself on the rampart;
I will keep watch to see what he will
say to me,
and what he[b] will answer
concerning my complaint.
2 Then the LORD answered me
and said:
Write the vision;
make it plain on tablets,
so that a runner may read it.
3 For there is still a vision for the
appointed time;
it speaks of the end, and does not
lie.
If it seems to tarry, wait for it;
it will surely come, it will
not delay.
4 Look at the proud!
Their spirit is not right in them,
but the righteous live by
their faith.[c]
5 Moreover, wealth[d] is treacherous;
the arrogant do not endure.
They open their throats wide
as Sheol;
like Death they never have enough.
They gather all nations for
themselves,
and collect all peoples as their own.

6 Shall not everyone taunt such people
and, with mocking riddles, say about them,
"Alas for you who heap up what is
not your own!"

a Heb *He* *b* Syr: Heb *I* *c* Or *faithfulness*
d Other Heb Mss read *wine*

2 Sam 23.3; Ps 95.1; Isa 30.29. **13:** The heart of Habakkuk's problem (see Ps 5.4–6). **2.1:** *Watchpost,* the prophet's role was often compared to sentry duty (Isa 21.6–12; 62.7; Ezek 3.17; 33.7; Hos 9.8). There may also be a connection to the priesthood, since *watchpost* was used to describe aspects of priestly "service" (Neh 13.14), including Temple guard duty (1 Chr 26.16). **2–4:** The LORD replies that divine justice will come in due time; for the meantime, see v. 4. **2–3:** The prophet is instructed to make a record of the divine response, eventually to be authenticated by events (cf. Isa 30.8). **2:** *Make it plain on tablets,* Deut 27.8; Isa 8.1. *A runner,* for the prophet as courier, see Jer 23.21 (for military and diplomatic runners, see 2 Sam 18.19–27; 2 Chr 30.6). **4:** The substance of the message: *The righteous* survive by remaining steadfast, reliable, faithful. Here the contrast is primarily between the oppressed Judahites (*the righteous*) and oppressing Chaldeans (*the proud*). Early Christian writers quoted the second part of the verse in various contexts (Rom 1.17; Gal 3.11; Heb 10.38–39).

2.5–20: The five woes (2.6b–8; 2.9–11; 2.12–14; 2.15–17; 2.18–19). Though a rapacious empire seeks to devour other nations, their respective fortunes are reversed in the end (cf. Isa 14.1–21). These nations get the last taunting word, delivered in the style of funeral laments (*Alas,* vv. 6,9,12,15,19; cf. 1 Kings 13.30; Jer 22.18). **5:** *Sheol,* the abode of the dead. **9:** *Evil gain,* cf. Jer 6.13. **14:** Isa 11.9. **15–16:** Gen

How long will you load yourselves
with goods taken in pledge?
7 Will not your own creditors suddenly
rise,
and those who make you tremble
wake up?
Then you will be booty for them.
8 Because you have plundered many
nations,
all that survive of the peoples shall
plunder you—
because of human bloodshed, and
violence to the earth,
to cities and all who live in them.

9 "Alas for you who get evil gain for
your house,
setting your nest on high
to be safe from the reach of harm!"
10 You have devised shame for
your house
by cutting off many peoples;
you have forfeited your life.
11 The very stones will cry out from the
wall,
and the plaster[a] will respond from
the woodwork.

12 "Alas for you who build a town by
bloodshed,
and found a city on iniquity!"
13 Is it not from the LORD of hosts
that peoples labor only to feed the
flames,
and nations weary themselves for
nothing?
14 But the earth will be filled
with the knowledge of the glory of
the LORD,
as the waters cover the sea.

15 "Alas for you who make your
neighbors drink,
pouring out your wrath[b] until they
are drunk,
in order to gaze on their
nakedness!"
16 You will be sated with contempt
instead of glory.
Drink, you yourself, and stagger![c]
The cup in the LORD's right hand
will come around to you,
and shame will come upon
your glory!
17 For the violence done to Lebanon will
overwhelm you;
the destruction of the animals will
terrify you—[d]
because of human bloodshed and
violence to the earth,
to cities and all who live in them.

18 What use is an idol
once its maker has shaped it—
a cast image, a teacher of lies?
For its maker trusts in what has been
made,
though the product is only an idol
that cannot speak!
19 Alas for you who say to the wood,
"Wake up!"
to silent stone, "Rouse yourself!"
Can it teach?
See, it is gold and silver plated,
and there is no breath in it at all.

20 But the LORD is in his holy temple;
let all the earth keep silence before
him!

3 A prayer of the prophet Habakkuk according to Shigionoth.

a Or *beam* *b* Or *poison* *c* Q Ms Gk: MT *be uncircumcised* *d* Gk Syr: Meaning of Heb uncertain

9.20–25; Jer 25.15–27; 51.7. **17:** *The violence done to Lebanon,* the Babylonians harvested the great Lebanese cedars (Isa 14.8). **18–19:** The worthlessness of idols is also a theme in Jer (10.1–10) and in Isaiah (40.18–20; 41.6–7; 44.9–20). **20:** Ps 11.4; Zeph 1.7; Zech 2.13.

3.1–19: Habakkuk's song. Whether composed in an archaic style or actually stemming from an earlier age, this psalm extolling God's triumphs is full of images from early Israelite poetry (Ex 15.1–18; Deut 33.2–5; Judg 5.4–5; Ps 18; 29). **1:** *Shigionoth,* a liturgical direction whose precise meaning is unknown (see Ps 7; other musical notations are in Hab 3.3,9,13,19). **3–7:** God appears from the south, marching

2 O LORD, I have heard of your
renown,
and I stand in awe, O LORD, of
your work.
In our own time revive it;
in our own time make it known;
in wrath may you remember mercy.
3 God came from Teman,
the Holy One from Mount Paran. *Selah*
His glory covered the heavens,
and the earth was full of his praise.
4 The brightness was like the sun;
rays came forth from his hand,
where his power lay hidden.
5 Before him went pestilence,
and plague followed close behind.
6 He stopped and shook the earth;
he looked and made the
nations tremble.
The eternal mountains were shattered;
along his ancient pathways
the everlasting hills sank low.
7 I saw the tents of Cushan under
affliction;
the tent-curtains of the land of
Midian trembled.
8 Was your wrath against the rivers,[a]
O LORD?
Or your anger against the rivers,[a]
or your rage against the sea,[b]
when you drove your horses,
your chariots to victory?
9 You brandished your naked bow,
sated[c] were the arrows at your
command.[d] *Selah*
You split the earth with rivers.
10 The mountains saw you, and writhed;
a torrent of water swept by;
the deep gave forth its voice.
The sun[e] raised high its hands;
11 the moon[f] stood still in its exalted
place,
at the light of your arrows speeding
by,
at the gleam of your flashing spear.
12 In fury you trod the earth,
in anger you trampled nations.
13 You came forth to save your people,
to save your anointed.
You crushed the head of the
wicked house,
laying it bare from foundation
to roof.[d] *Selah*
14 You pierced with their[g] own arrows
the head[h] of his warriors,[i]
who came like a whirlwind to
scatter us,[j]
gloating as if ready to devour the
poor who were in hiding.
15 You trampled the sea with
your horses,
churning the mighty waters.

16 I hear, and I tremble within;
my lips quiver at the sound.
Rottenness enters into my bones,
and my steps tremble[k] beneath me.
I wait quietly for the day of calamity

a Or *against River* *b* Or *against Sea* *c* Cn: Heb *oaths* *d* Meaning of Heb uncertain *e* Heb *It* *f* Heb *sun, moon* *g* Heb *his* *h* Or *leader* *i* Vg Compare Gk Syr: Meaning of Heb uncertain *j* Heb *me* *k* Cn Compare Gk: Meaning of Heb uncertain

northward, with dramatic effects on nature (Deut 33.2; Judg 5.4; Ps 68.7–8). **3:** *God,* the Heb word is "Eloah" (1.11), a term most often found in Job (e.g., 3.4; 40.2) and other poetic texts (e.g., Ps 18.31). *Teman, Mount Paran,* sites in southern Transjordan; see also Deut 33.2. **5:** *Pestilence* and *plague* are pictured here as divine attendants; cf. Lev 26.25; Deut 32.23–24; Ps 78.49–50. **6:** *He . . . shook the earth,* Judg 5.4–5; Ps 68.8. *The nations tremble,* Ex 15.14–15. *Mountains were shattered,* Ps 18.7. **7:** *Cushan,* location unknown, but presumably a synonym for *Midian,* which is in southern Transjordan. **8–15:** In full regalia, chariotry, *bow, arrows, spear,* the LORD defeats the divine enemies. **8:** *Wrath against the rivers, rage against the sea,* Ps 77.16–18; 114.3–6. *Rivers* and *sea* are terms used for the opponents of the divine warrior in Canaanite mythology. *Your horses, your chariots,* Ps 68.17–18. **9:** Ps 18.13–15. **10–11:** *Sun* and *moon* here are personified figures who defer to the LORD. **11:** *Arrows, spear,* lightning bolts. **13:** *Crushed the head,* Ps 68.21. **16–19:** Awed, and buoyed, by this account of God's power, the poet espouses

to come upon the people who
attack us.

17 Though the fig tree does not
blossom,
and no fruit is on the vines;
though the produce of the olive fails,
and the fields yield no food;
though the flock is cut off from
the fold,
and there is no herd in the stalls,
18 yet I will rejoice in the LORD;
I will exult in the God of my
salvation.
19 GOD, the Lord, is my strength;
he makes my feet like the feet of a
deer,
and makes me tread upon the
heights.[a]

To the leader: with stringed[b]
instruments.

a Heb *my heights* *b* Heb *my stringed*

the kind of faithful waiting evoked by the divine message of 2.4. **17:** *Fig tree, vines,* Isa 34.4. **19:** *To the leader . . . ,* see 3.1n.

ZEPHANIAH

Zephaniah's place in the canonical sequence is apparently chronological; along with its predecessors, Nahum and Habakkuk, it stems from the seventh century BCE. The superscription (1.1) traces Zephaniah's ancestry back to Hezekiah and dates his ministry to the reign of Josiah (640–609). Since the name Hezekiah is uncommon in the Hebrew Bible, this unusually long genealogical note probably refers to the famous Judean king (727/715–698/687).

Whether of royal descent or not, Zephaniah certainly was a Jerusalemite (1.10–11). His father's name, Cushi (1.1), could mean "the Cushite," and has prompted some speculation about African ancestry for the prophet (cf. 2.12; 3.10). Aside from his name (which means "Yahweh has protected") and these intriguing genealogical issues, nothing is known about the prophet.

Zephaniah's condemnation of practices prohibited by Deuteronomy (1.4–6,8–9,12; 3.1–13,7) suggests that he prophesied before Josiah's reforms of 621 BCE (2 Kings 23). The oracles thus can be dated, perhaps, to 630–620, and are roughly contemporaneous with those in Nahum.

The main motif of the collected oracles is the Day of the LORD. In the initial oracle (1.2–6), the Day of the LORD is described in terms of a global catastrophe brought on by worship of other deities (1.4–6). The next two oracles (or sections of the same oracle), 1.7–13; 1.14–2.3, maintain this tone of gloom. Invoking traditions about the ancient flood (see 1.2–3n.), for Zephaniah it is a case of "the fire next time" (1.18). Near the end of this section, the prophet gives a muted (*perhaps*, 2.3) call for repentance. The next section consists of oracles against Judah's rival nations (2.4–15), followed by the speeches that indict Jerusalem (3.1–8). Oracles of salvation (3.9–20) complete, and balance, the collection.

1 The word of the LORD that came to Zephaniah son of Cushi son of Gedaliah son of Amariah son of Hezekiah, in the days of King Josiah son of Amon of Judah.

2 I will utterly sweep away everything
from the face of the earth, says the LORD.
3 I will sweep away humans and animals;
I will sweep away the birds of the air
and the fish of the sea.
I will make the wicked stumble.[a]
I will cut off humanity
from the face of the earth, says the LORD.

a Cn: Heb *sea, and those who cause the wicked to stumble*

1.1: Superscription. For similar introductions, see Hos 1.1; Joel 1.1; Mic 1.1; Hag 1.1; Zech 1.1. *Cushi* means "Cushite"; "Cush" may refer to Ethiopia (2 Kings 19.9), to Midian (Hab 3.7), or to a region in Mesopotamia (Gen 2.13; 10.8–12). *Days of King Josiah,* ca. 640–609 BCE (2 Kings 22.1–23.30).

1.2–6: The threat of universal destruction. 2–3: The scope of the destruction and the echoes of Genesis (cf. 1.2 with Gen 7.23; the sequence *humans, animals, birds, fish* reverses the order of Gen 1.20–26) suggest the undoing of creation (cf. Jer 4.23–26). **4:** *Baal,* a Canaanite deity. **5:** *Bow down on the roofs,* 2 Kings 23.12; Jer 19.13; 32.29. *Host of the heavens,* astral deities; Deut 4.19; 2 Kings 21.3; Jer 8.2. *Milcom,* chief deity of Ammon.

4 I will stretch out my hand against
Judah,
and against all the inhabitants of
Jerusalem;
and I will cut off from this place
every remnant of Baal
and the name of the idolatrous
priests;[a]
5 those who bow down on the roofs
to the host of the heavens;
those who bow down and swear to
the LORD,
but also swear by Milcom;[b]
6 those who have turned back from
following the LORD,
who have not sought the LORD or
inquired of him.

7 Be silent before the Lord GOD!
For the day of the LORD is at hand;
the LORD has prepared a sacrifice,
he has consecrated his guests.
8 And on the day of the LORD's
sacrifice
I will punish the officials and the
king's sons
and all who dress themselves in
foreign attire.
9 On that day I will punish
all who leap over the threshold,
who fill their master's house
with violence and fraud.

10 On that day, says the LORD,
a cry will be heard from the
Fish Gate,
a wail from the Second Quarter,
a loud crash from the hills.
11 The inhabitants of the Mortar wail,
for all the traders have perished;
all who weigh out silver are cut off.
12 At that time I will search Jerusalem
with lamps,
and I will punish the people
who rest complacently[c] on
their dregs,
those who say in their hearts,
"The LORD will not do good,
nor will he do harm."
13 Their wealth shall be plundered,
and their houses laid waste.
Though they build houses,
they shall not inhabit them;
though they plant vineyards,
they shall not drink wine
from them.

14 The great day of the LORD is near,
near and hastening fast;
the sound of the day of the LORD
is bitter,
the warrior cries aloud there.
15 That day will be a day of wrath,
a day of distress and anguish,
a day of ruin and devastation,
a day of darkness and gloom,
a day of clouds and thick darkness,
16 a day of trumpet blast and
battle cry
against the fortified cities
and against the lofty battlements.

17 I will bring such distress upon people
that they shall walk like the blind;
because they have sinned against
the LORD,

a Compare Gk: Heb *the idolatrous priests with the priests* *b* Gk Mss Syr Vg: Heb *Malcam* (or, *their king*) *c* Heb *who thicken*

1.7–13: The Day of the LORD as a sacrifice. 7: *Be silent,* cf. Hab 2.20. *A sacrifice,* i.e., a slaughter of evildoers. **9:** *Leap over the threshold,* a Philistine rite (1 Sam 5.5). **10:** *Fish Gate* (Neh 3.1–6; 12.39), *Second Quarter* (2 Kings 22.14), and "the Mortar" are locales in Jerusalem. **11:** *Traders,* lit. "people of Canaan." **12:** *Who rest complacently on their dregs,* the Hebrew may mean "who become dull from (drinking) the wine that they have stored" (cf. Isa 25.6). **13:** A futility curse, i.e., one in which the connection between actions and their ordinary results is broken (cf. Deut 28.30–31).

1.14–23: The Day of the LORD as divine warfare. Zephaniah elaborates the preaching of Amos (Am 5.18–20; 8.9–14) that the *day of the LORD* will be dreadful for Israel as well as the nations. For similar descriptions, see Isa 13.9–13 and Joel 2.1–2. **18:** *End,* cf. Ezek 7.2–7.

their blood shall be poured out
like dust,
and their flesh like dung.
18 Neither their silver nor their gold
will be able to save them
on the day of the LORD's wrath;
in the fire of his passion
the whole earth shall be consumed;
for a full, a terrible end
he will make of all the inhabitants
of the earth.

2 Gather together, gather,
O shameless nation,
2 before you are driven away
like the drifting chaff,[a]
before there comes upon you
the fierce anger of the LORD,
before there comes upon you
the day of the LORD's wrath.
3 Seek the LORD, all you humble of the
land,
who do his commands;
seek righteousness, seek humility;
perhaps you may be hidden
on the day of the LORD's wrath.
4 For Gaza shall be deserted,
and Ashkelon shall become a
desolation;
Ashdod's people shall be driven out at
noon,
and Ekron shall be uprooted.
5 Ah, inhabitants of the seacoast,
you nation of the Cherethites!

a Cn Compare Gk Syr: Heb *before a decree is born; like chaff a day has passed away*

2.1–3: A muted call to repentance. The faithful, *perhaps* (v. 3), will be spared. **3:** *Seek*, Isa 55.6; Am 5.6–7. *Humble,* 3.12–13.

2.4–15: Against the nations. Prophetic collections often included speeches addressed to foreign nations (e.g., Isa 13–23; Jer 46–51; Am 1–2). **4–7:** An oracle against peoples to the west of Judah. **4:** Four of the five main Philistine cities (1 Sam 6.17) are named (cf. Jer 25.20; Am 1.6–8). **5:** *The Cherethites,* here and elsewhere, are identified with Philistines (Ezek 25.16). They probably originated in Crete. **8–11:** Oracles

Chs 2–15: The oracles against the nations.

The word of the LORD is against
you,
O Canaan, land of the Philistines;
and I will destroy you until no
inhabitant is left.
6 And you, O seacoast, shall be
pastures,
meadows for shepherds
and folds for flocks.
7 The seacoast shall become the
possession
of the remnant of the house
of Judah,
on which they shall pasture,
and in the houses of Ashkelon
they shall lie down at evening.
For the LORD their God will be
mindful of them
and restore their fortunes.

8 I have heard the taunts of Moab
and the revilings of the Ammonites,
how they have taunted my people
and made boasts against
their territory.
9 Therefore, as I live, says the LORD of
hosts,
the God of Israel,
Moab shall become like Sodom
and the Ammonites like Gomorrah,
a land possessed by nettles and
salt pits,
and a waste forever.
The remnant of my people shall
plunder them,
and the survivors of my nation
shall possess them.
10 This shall be their lot in return for
their pride,
because they scoffed and boasted
against the people of the LORD
of hosts.
11 The LORD will be terrible
against them;
he will shrivel all the gods of
the earth,
and to him shall bow down,
each in its place,
all the coasts and islands of
the nations.

12 You also, O Ethiopians,[a]
shall be killed by my sword.

13 And he will stretch out his hand
against the north,
and destroy Assyria;
and he will make Nineveh a
desolation,
a dry waste like the desert.
14 Herds shall lie down in it,
every wild animal;[b]
the desert owl[c] and the screech owl[c]
shall lodge on its capitals;
the owl[d] shall hoot at the window,
the raven[e] croak on the threshold;
for its cedar work will be laid bare.
15 Is this the exultant city
that lived secure,
that said to itself,
"I am, and there is no one else"?
What a desolation it has become,
a lair for wild animals!
Everyone who passes by it
hisses and shakes the fist.

3 Ah, soiled, defiled,
oppressing city!
2 It has listened to no voice;
it has accepted no correction.

a Or *Nubians*; Heb *Cushites* *b* Tg Compare Gk: Heb *nation* *c* Meaning of Heb uncertain *d* Cn: Heb *a voice* *e* Gk Vg: Heb *desolation*

against peoples to the east of Judah. **8:** *Moab, Ammon,* Transjordanian states. *How they have taunted my people,* probably refers to forms of ritual cursing, with origins in warfare; this very oracle serves as an Israelite example. **9:** *Like Sodom . . . Gomorrah,* Gen 19.24–28,30–38; Am 4.11; Jer 49.18; 50.40. **12:** An oracle against a nation to the south, *Ethiopia* (2 Kings 19.9; Isa 18; Am 9.7). *My sword,* Isa 34.6–7; Jer 47.6; Ezek 21.8–10. **13–15:** An oracle against a nation to the north, *Assyria;* see also Nahum. **15:** *Hisses,* to ward off a similar fate (Jer 18.16).

3.1–8: Against Jerusalem. As in Am 1–2, a sequence of judgment speeches against the nations ends at

It has not trusted in the LORD;
it has not drawn near to its God.

3 The officials within it
are roaring lions;
its judges are evening wolves
that leave nothing until
the morning.
4 Its prophets are reckless,
faithless persons;
its priests have profaned what
is sacred,
they have done violence to the law.
5 The LORD within it is righteous;
he does no wrong.
Every morning he renders his
judgment,
each dawn without fail;
but the unjust knows no shame.
6 I have cut off nations;
their battlements are in ruins;
I have laid waste their streets
so that no one walks in them;
their cities have been made desolate,
without people, without
inhabitants.
7 I said, "Surely the city[a] will fear me,
it will accept correction;
it will not lose sight[b]
of all that I have brought upon it."
But they were the more eager
to make all their deeds corrupt.

8 Therefore wait for me, says the LORD,
for the day when I arise as
a witness.
For my decision is to gather nations,
to assemble kingdoms,
to pour out upon them my
indignation,
all the heat of my anger;
for in the fire of my passion
all the earth shall be consumed.

9 At that time I will change the speech
of the peoples
to a pure speech,
that all of them may call on the name
of the LORD
and serve him with one accord.
10 From beyond the rivers of Ethiopia[c]
my suppliants, my scattered ones,
shall bring my offering.

11 On that day you shall not be put
to shame
because of all the deeds by which
you have rebelled against me;
for then I will remove from
your midst
your proudly exultant ones,
and you shall no longer be haughty
in my holy mountain.
12 For I will leave in the midst of you
a people humble and lowly.
They shall seek refuge in the name of
the LORD—
13 the remnant of Israel;
they shall do no wrong
and utter no lies,
nor shall a deceitful tongue
be found in their mouths.
Then they will pasture and lie down,
and no one shall make them afraid.

14 Sing aloud, O daughter Zion;
shout, O Israel!
Rejoice and exult with all your heart,
O daughter Jerusalem!
15 The LORD has taken away the
judgments against you,
he has turned away your enemies.
The king of Israel, the LORD, is in
your midst;
you shall fear disaster no more.

a Heb *it* *b* Gk Syr: Heb *its dwelling will not be cut off* *c* Or *Nubia*; Heb *Cush*

home. **1–2:** Cf. Isa 1.21–23. **3–5:** Cf. Ezek 22.25–28; Mic 3.1–12. **5:** *Every morning,* Hos 6.3; Lam 3.22–23. **6:** For other descriptions of ghost towns, see Isa 5.9; 6.11; Jer 9.11; 33.10; 46.19.

3.9–20: Oracles of salvation. 9–10: The *pure speech* removes the curse of Babel (Gen 11.9). For the theme of a universal pilgrimage, see, e.g., Ps 68.31 (with *Ethiopia*); Isa 2.2–4; 60.5–6,11; Mic 4.1–4. **11:** *You shall not be put to shame,* Isa 45.17. *My holy mountain,* Mt. Zion, site of the Temple. **14–18:** A song celebrating God's vindication of Israel (cf. Ps 47; 95; 97). **14:** Zech 9.9. **15:** *The LORD has taken away*

16 On that day it shall be said to
Jerusalem:
Do not fear, O Zion;
do not let your hands grow weak.
17 The LORD, your God, is in
your midst,
a warrior who gives victory;
he will rejoice over you with gladness,
he will renew you[a] in his love;
he will exult over you with
loud singing
18 as on a day of festival.[b]
I will remove disaster from you,[c]
so that you will not bear reproach
for it.
19 I will deal with all your oppressors
at that time.
And I will save the lame
and gather the outcast,
and I will change their shame
into praise
and renown in all the earth.
20 At that time I will bring you home,
at the time when I gather you;
for I will make you renowned
and praised
among all the peoples of the earth,
when I restore your fortunes
before your eyes, says the LORD.

a Gk Syr: Heb *he will be silent* *b* Gk Syr: Meaning of Heb uncertain *c* Cn: Heb *I will remove from you; they were*

the judgments against you, Isa 40.1–2. *In your midst,* Isa 12.6. **16:** Isa 41.10,13; 43.1,5. **17–18:** Isa 9.3–4. **17:** *A warrior,* Ex 15.3. *He will rejoice,* Isa 62.5. **18:** *I will remove disaster from you,* contrast with the beginning of the book, 1.2–3. **19–20:** Perhaps a late addition to the words of Zechariah. The major elements of postexilic eschatology are found here: destruction of the enemy (Ob 15–16; Mic 5.9; Zech 12.9), ingathering of the exiles (Isa 56.8; Mic 4.6–7; Zech 10.8–12), and return to Judah (Isa 62.10; Zech 8.7–8). **20:** *Make you renowned,* Isa 62.7.

HAGGAI

Following three prophetic books set in the late preexilic period, Haggai, along with the subsequent Zechariah and Malachi, is set in the postexilic period. When the Persian king Cyrus conquered Babylon, he not only published a decree (538 BCE) allowing the captive Jews to return to Judah but also encouraged them to rebuild the Temple at Jerusalem (Ezra 1.1–4), a policy confirmed by Darius (Ezra 5.17–6.5). It is possible that under Sheshbazzar, the leader of those who returned, rebuilding was immediately attempted (Ezra 1.8; 2.68; 5.14–16). By 520 BCE, however, no significant progress was evident (Ezra 3.1–7; 5.16). A successful effort was then begun, and the new Temple was completed in the spring of 515 BCE (Ezra 6.14–16).

Along with Zechariah (see Introduction to Zechariah), the man principally responsible for this major accomplishment was the prophet Haggai. Outside of references to him in Ezra 5.1 and 6.14, we know nothing about Haggai. The book bearing his name contains no biographical data, beyond confirming his pivotal role in inspiring the Jewish leadership and populace to complete reconstruction of the Temple, the ritual, economic, administrative, and symbolic center of their community.

Haggai exhorted Zerrubabel the governor and Joshua the high priest, the joint leaders of the Judean community, to assume official leadership in the reconstruction of the Temple, and urged the priests to purify the practices of worship. These twin projects were, first of all, urgent practical steps toward unifying the disrupted religious life of the community. But Haggai also saw them as necessary preparations for the ideal age.

The book is organized in five sections (1.1–11; 1.12–15a; 1.15b–2.9; 2.10–19; 2.20–23), each precisely dated from the sixth through the ninth months of 520 BCE. The precision of the date formulas is rivaled among the prophets only by those of his contemporary Zechariah (cf. Zech 1.1,7; 7.1). Four of these sections begin with date formulas and contain addresses of Haggai, and one (1.12–15a, in which the date formula is at the end rather than the beginning) records the response of Haggai's audience.

The initial section (1.1–11) is an oracle of judgment directed against the people for failing to complete the Temple. In the next section, 1.12–15a, the people respond favorably. The next two sections (1.15b–2.9; 2.10–19) are oracles encouraging the people in their efforts. The final section (2.10–23) is an oracle of salvation, promising that cosmic reversals, terrestrial justice, and national vindication will follow in the wake of the reconstruction of the Temple.

1 In the second year of King Darius, in
the sixth month, on the first day of the
month, the word of the LORD came by the
prophet Haggai to Zerubbabel son of She-
altiel, governor of Judah, and to Joshua son
of Jehozadak, the high priest: 2 Thus says
the LORD of hosts: These people say the
time has not yet come to rebuild the LORD's
house. 3 Then the word of the LORD came
by the prophet Haggai, saying: 4 Is it a time
for you yourselves to live in your paneled
houses, while this house lies in ruins?
5 Now therefore thus says the LORD of
hosts: Consider how you have fared. 6 You
have sown much, and harvested little; you
eat, but you never have enough; you drink,
but you never have your fill; you clothe
yourselves, but no one is warm; and you
that earn wages earn wages to put them
into a bag with holes.

7 Thus says the LORD of hosts: Consider
how you have fared. 8 Go up to the hills and
bring wood and build the house, so that I
may take pleasure in it and be honored,
says the LORD. 9 You have looked for
much, and, lo, it came to little; and when
you brought it home, I blew it away. Why?
says the LORD of hosts. Because my house
lies in ruins, while all of you hurry off to
your own houses. 10 Therefore the heavens
above you have withheld the dew, and the
earth has withheld its produce. 11 And I
have called for a drought on the land and
the hills, on the grain, the new wine, the oil,
on what the soil produces, on human be-
ings and animals, and on all their labors.

12 Then Zerubbabel son of Shealtiel,
and Joshua son of Jehozadak, the high
priest, with all the remnant of the people,
obeyed the voice of the LORD their God,
and the words of the prophet Haggai, as
the LORD their God had sent him; and the
people feared the LORD. 13 Then Haggai,
the messenger of the LORD, spoke to the
people with the LORD's message, saying, I
am with you, says the LORD. 14 And the
LORD stirred up the spirit of Zerubbabel
son of Shealtiel, governor of Judah, and the
spirit of Joshua son of Jehozadak, the high
priest, and the spirit of all the remnant of
the people; and they came and worked on
the house of the LORD of hosts, their God,
15 on the twenty-fourth day of the month,
in the sixth month.

2 In the second year of King Darius, 1 in
the seventh month, on the twenty-first
day of the month, the word of the LORD
came by the prophet Haggai, saying:
2 Speak now to Zerubbabel son of Shealtiel,
governor of Judah, and to Joshua son of

1.1–11: An oracle of judgment: While the Temple is in ruins, the people are cursed. 1: *Darius* was king of the Persian Empire from 522 to 486 BCE. *In the second year, sixth month, first day,* August 29, 520 BCE. *The first day of the month* was ordinarily a time of special religious observance; thus, a date when the dismal state of the Temple was even more apparent. *Haggai* means "(born on) the festival"; *Zerubbabel* (1 Chr 3.19; Ezra 2.2; 3.2,8; 5.2; Neh 12.1; Zech 4.6–10; Sir 49.11), the grandson of Jehoiachin (2 Kings 24.8–17; 1 Chr 3.16–19), was a descendant of David. *Son of Shealtiel,* cf. Ezra 3.2; contrast 1 Chr 3.19. *Joshua,* Zech 3.1–10; 6.11 (= *Jeshua* in Ezra 2–5; Sir 49.12). For this model of community leadership shared by a Davidic descendant and a *high priest,* see Zech 4.3n. **4:** The Temple had been plundered and burned in 586 (2 Kings 25.8–17). *Paneled* probably refers to "roofed" or completed houses, in contrast to the state of the Temple. **5–6:** The poor conditions in Judah were evidence of the people's disobedience to the covenant (Lev 26), and are presented here in the form of futility curses (cf. Deut 28.30–41). **9–11:** These verses are built around a Heb pun; as long as the Temple is in *ruins,* "ḥareb," the people will suffer *drought,* "ḥoreb." **11:** Contrast Hos 2.10.

1.12–15a: A favorable response: The people get to work. 12: The *remnant* probably refers to those who had recently returned from Babylon (Jer 43.5). **13:** For the prophet as a *messenger,* see Mal 1.1; 3.1; 2 Chr 36.15–16. **15:** September 21, 520 BCE.

1.15b–2.9: An oracle of encouragement: The new Temple will be more splendid than the old. 1.15b–2.1: October 17, 520 BCE. This date, the twenty-first day of the seventh month, would place this oracle during the festival of booths (Lev 23.33–36,39–42), which would make the reference to the Exodus

Jehozadak, the high priest, and to the rem-
nant of the people, and say, 3 Who is left
among you that saw this house in its former
glory? How does it look to you now? Is it
not in your sight as nothing? 4 Yet now take
courage, O Zerubbabel, says the LORD;
take courage, O Joshua, son of Jehozadak,
the high priest; take courage, all you people
of the land, says the LORD; work, for I am
with you, says the LORD of hosts, 5 accord-
ing to the promise that I made you when
you came out of Egypt. My spirit abides
among you; do not fear. 6 For thus says the
LORD of hosts: Once again, in a little while,
I will shake the heavens and the earth and
the sea and the dry land; 7 and I will shake
all the nations, so that the treasure of all
nations shall come, and I will fill this house
with splendor, says the LORD of hosts.
8 The silver is mine, and the gold is mine,
says the LORD of hosts. 9 The latter splen-
dor of this house shall be greater than the
former, says the LORD of hosts; and in this
place I will give prosperity, says the LORD
of hosts.

10 On the twenty-fourth day of the
ninth month, in the second year of Darius,
the word of the LORD came by the prophet
Haggai, saying: 11 Thus says the LORD of
hosts: Ask the priests for a ruling: 12 If one
carries consecrated meat in the fold of one's
garment, and with the fold touches bread,
or stew, or wine, or oil, or any kind of
food, does it become holy? The priests an-
swered, "No." 13 Then Haggai said, "If one
who is unclean by contact with a dead body
touches any of these, does it become un-
clean?" The priests answered, "Yes, it be-
comes unclean." 14 Haggai then said, So is
it with this people, and with this nation
before me, says the LORD; and so with ev-
ery work of their hands; and what they of-
fer there is unclean. 15 But now, consider
what will come to pass from this day on.
Before a stone was placed upon a stone in
the LORD's temple, 16 how did you fare?[a]
When one came to a heap of twenty mea-
sures, there were but ten; when one came to
the wine vat to draw fifty measures, there
were but twenty. 17 I struck you and all the
products of your toil with blight and mil-
dew and hail; yet you did not return to me,
says the LORD. 18 Consider from this day
on, from the twenty-fourth day of the ninth
month. Since the day that the foundation of
the LORD's temple was laid, consider: 19 Is
there any seed left in the barn? Do the vine,
the fig tree, the pomegranate, and the olive
tree still yield nothing? From this day on I
will bless you.

20 The word of the LORD came a second
time to Haggai on the twenty-fourth day of
the month: 21 Speak to Zerubbabel, gover-
nor of Judah, saying, I am about to shake
the heavens and the earth, 22 and to over-
throw the throne of kingdoms; I am about
to destroy the strength of the kingdoms of

a Gk: Heb *since they were*

(2.5) all the more appropriate. **2.3:** A few of the people present may have seen Solomon's Temple before its destruction. **4–6:** By using the style of war oracles (*take courage; I am with you; do not fear;* cf. Deut 31.7; Josh 1.9), the prophet rhetorically casts the building drive as nothing short of heroic. **4:** *Take courage . . . work,* in 1 Chr 28.10,20, David delivers a similar exhortation to Solomon, builder of the first Temple. *People of the land,* Haggai here may be addressing people who had not gone into exile and who resisted the efforts of the returning exiles (Ezra 4.1–5; Neh 4.7–8). **7:** Isa 60.5–16; 61.5–6.

2.10–19: An oracle of encouragement: Already, the curse is lifting. 10: December 18, 520 BCE. **12–13:** From a ritual point of view, the unclean is more "contagious" than the consecrated, or clean; see Num 19.11–16. **14:** *This people* may refer, as in 2.4n., to those who had remained, worshiping in a Temple that Haggai and the returnees considered defiled. **15–17:** Cf. Zech 8.9–13. **17:** Am 4.9. **18:** *From this day on,* the turning point, from cursed to blessed, was the day of ritual rededication when the foundation stone for the second Temple was set (Ezra 3.10–13; Zech 4.9).

2.20–23: An oracle of salvation: The ideal age is imminent. 21: Cf. 2.6; Joel 3.16. **22:** *Horses and their riders,* Ex 15.1,21; Job 39.18; Jer 51.21. **23:** Haggai hoped that *Zerubbabel* would fulfill hopes for a the nations, and overthrow the chariots and their riders; and the horses and their riders shall fall, every one by the sword of a comrade. 23 On that day, says the LORD of hosts, I will take you, O Zerubbabel my servant, son of Shealtiel, says the LORD, and make you like a signet ring; for I have chosen you, says the LORD of hosts.

restored Davidic messiah (cf. Zech 3.8n.; 6.9–15n.). Though the Temple was rebuilt and became the foundation of the Judean restoration, Zerubbabel disappears from the scene; his fate is unknown. *Signet ring,* a seal carved on a scarab or cylinder (Jer 22.24); when pressed into the seal on a document, it served as a guarantee of authenticity.

ZECHARIAH

The Book of Zechariah is the longest and most obscure of the Minor Prophets. Formally, it divides into two parts. The first, chs 1–8, consists of a series of vision reports. Often referred to as "First Zechariah," it is closely tied to the preceding book of Haggai by the date formulas in 1.1; 1.7; and 7.1 (cf. Hag 1.1; 2.1) and the references to Joshua, the high priest in Jerusalem, and Zerubbabel, its governor.

The second section, chs 9–14, is a collection of sayings organized in two parts under the title "An Oracle" (9.1; 12.1). "Second Zechariah," as it is sometimes called, is similar in form to the subsequent book, Malachi, which itself begins with the same title (Mal 1.1). These oracles cite neither specific dates nor contemporary persons. Their concerns are for "that day," the Day of the LORD (e.g., 9.16; 12.3; 13.1; 14.1), and for unnamed persons such as a king who enters Jerusalem on a donkey (9.9) and a "shepherd" stricken by a divine sword (13.7).

The prophecies in the first part date from 520–518 BCE. Zechariah, a contemporary of Haggai, prophesied in the early days of the restoration, when returning exiles joined with those who never left to rebuild Judahite society. There are no biographical details in the book itself, but Zechariah is mentioned, along with Haggai, in Ezra 5.1 and 6.14. He shared Haggai's zeal for a rebuilt Temple, a purified community, and the coming of an ideal age. But Zechariah differs from his contemporary in the form and presentation of his message. Zechariah speaks in the dialect of apocalyptic, with angelic interpreters and esoteric imagery. For his city, Zechariah had utopian expectations: The rebuilding of the Temple would inaugurate nothing short of the transformation of the world. For its leaders, Zechariah had messianic hopes (4.14). Yet despite the apocalyptic style, Zech 1–8 also has a down-to-earth focus on the rebuilding of the Temple, practical concerns such as fasting (7.1–14), and a given historical moment.

The second part of the book is more difficult to date, and its historical background is elusive. The reference to "Greece" (9.13) could suggest a date after Alexander the Great's campaigns (after ca. 330 BCE) but it is unwise to rely on a single datum. Though its oracles do not mention other-worldly interpreters, Zech 9–14 also contains an apocalyptic message. Conflicts in the restoration community are described against a cosmic backdrop (see the contrast between Judah and Jerusalem in 12.1–5). The ever present vulnerability of Judah to the parade of empires finds vivid expression: The nations attack Jerusalem but the LORD intervenes to defeat them and transform Jerusalem into a kind of Eden (14.1–11).

Zechariah is best read from start to finish: chs 1–8 in conjunction with Haggai; chs 9–14 in conjunction with Malachi. In terms of the development of apocalyptic literature in the Hebrew Bible, Zechariah stands between Ezekiel (e.g., chs 38–39) and Daniel (chs 7–12).

1 In the eighth month, in the second year
of Darius, the word of the LORD came
to the prophet Zechariah son of Berechiah
son of Iddo, saying: 2 The LORD was very
angry with your ancestors. 3 Therefore say
to them, Thus says the LORD of hosts: Re-
turn to me, says the LORD of hosts, and I
will return to you, says the LORD of hosts.
4 Do not be like your ancestors, to whom
the former prophets proclaimed, "Thus
says the LORD of hosts, Return from your
evil ways and from your evil deeds." But
they did not hear or heed me, says the
LORD. 5 Your ancestors, where are they?
And the prophets, do they live forever?
6 But my words and my statutes, which I
commanded my servants the prophets, did
they not overtake your ancestors? So they
repented and said, "The LORD of hosts has
dealt with us according to our ways and
deeds, just as he planned to do."
7 On the twenty-fourth day of the elev-
enth month, the month of Shebat, in the
second year of Darius, the word of the
LORD came to the prophet Zechariah son
of Berechiah son of Iddo; and Zechariah[a]
said, 8 In the night I saw a man riding on a
red horse! He was standing among the myr-
tle trees in the glen; and behind him were
red, sorrel, and white horses. 9 Then I said,
"What are these, my lord?" The angel who
talked with me said to me, "I will show you
what they are." 10 So the man who was
standing among the myrtle trees answered,
"They are those whom the LORD has sent
to patrol the earth." 11 Then they spoke to
the angel of the LORD who was standing
among the myrtle trees, "We have patrolled
the earth, and lo, the whole earth remains
at peace." 12 Then the angel of the LORD
said, "O LORD of hosts, how long will you
withhold mercy from Jerusalem and the cit-
ies of Judah, with which you have been an-
gry these seventy years?" 13 Then the LORD
replied with gracious and comforting
words to the angel who talked with me.
14 So the angel who talked with me said to
me, Proclaim this message: Thus says the
LORD of hosts; I am very jealous for Jerusa-
lem and for Zion. 15 And I am extremely
angry with the nations that are at ease; for
while I was only a little angry, they made
the disaster worse. 16 Therefore, thus says
the LORD, I have returned to Jerusalem
with compassion; my house shall be built in
it, says the LORD of hosts, and the measur-
ing line shall be stretched out over Jerusa-
lem. 17 Proclaim further: Thus says the
LORD of hosts: My cities shall again over-
flow with prosperity; the LORD will again

a Heb *and he*

1.1–8.23: Visions and oracles about the restoration of Jerusalem. This first major section of the book contains three parts, each introduced by a date formula (1.1; 1.7; 7.1).

1.1–6: Introduction: a call to repentance. 1: *Eighth month . . . second year,* mid-October to mid-November 520 BCE. *Darius* I reigned over the Persian Empire, which extended "from India to Ethiopia" (Esth 8.9), from 522 to 486. *Zechariah* means "the LORD has remembered." The phrase *son of Berechiah son of Iddo* is open to interpretation. Iddo could be the prophet's grandfather, although elsewhere in the Hebrew Bible Iddo alone is listed as Zechariah's father (Ezra 5.1; 6.14; Neh 12.16). There were several Zechariahs in the Bible (in this regard, note "Zechariah son of Jeberechiah" in Isa 8.2), and this may have led to scribal confusion (compare Mt 23.35 with 2 Chr 24.20–22). **3:** Cf. Mal 3.7. **4:** *The former prophets proclaimed,* e.g., Jer 18.11; 25.5; Ezek 33.11. **6:** *Overtake,* Deut 28.45. *So they repented and said,* see Lam 1.18; 3.40–42; 5.7. But see Zech 7.11.

1.6–6.15: The eight visions of Zechariah. Note the pattern: (a) vision, (b) question about its meaning, (c) angelic interpretation.

1.7–17: The first vision: divine horsemen patrol the earth. 7: Mid-January to mid-February 519. **8:** *The glen,* a deep hollow; no ordinary place. **9:** *My lord,* a term of respect for the angel. **11:** *Patrolled the earth,* see also Job 1.6–7; 2.2. *The whole earth remains at peace,* i.e., the nations have not yet received their judgment (cf. 1.15; Hag 2.6). **12:** *Seventy years,* the length of time since the destruction of Jerusalem was slightly less (586–519), but seventy years was a conventional term of punishment (Isa 23.15–17; Jer 25.11–12; 29.10). **13:** *Gracious and comforting words,* e.g., Isa 40.1–2; Jer 29.10; 33.14. **16:** *The*

comfort Zion and again choose Jerusalem.
18[a]And I looked up and saw four horns.
19I asked the angel who talked with me,
"What are these?" And he answered me,
"These are the horns that have scattered
Judah, Israel, and Jerusalem." 20Then the
LORD showed me four blacksmiths. 21And
I asked, "What are they coming to do?" He
answered, "These are the horns that scat-
tered Judah, so that no head could be
raised; but these have come to terrify them,
to strike down the horns of the nations that
lifted up their horns against the land of Ju-
dah to scatter its people."[b]

2 [c]I looked up and saw a man with a
measuring line in his hand. 2Then I
asked, "Where are you going?" He an-
swered me, "To measure Jerusalem, to see
what is its width and what is its length."
3Then the angel who talked with me came
forward, and another angel came forward
to meet him, 4and said to him, "Run, say to
that young man: Jerusalem shall be inhabit-
ed like villages without walls, because of
the multitude of people and animals in it.
5For I will be a wall of fire all around it,
says the LORD, and I will be the glory with-
in it."

6 Up, up! Flee from the land of the
north, says the LORD; for I have spread you
abroad like the four winds of heaven, says
the LORD. 7Up! Escape to Zion, you that
live with daughter Babylon. 8For thus said
the LORD of hosts (after his glory[d] sent
me) regarding the nations that plundered
you: Truly, one who touches you touches
the apple of my eye.[e] 9See now, I am going
to raise[f] my hand against them, and they
shall become plunder for their own slaves.
Then you will know that the LORD of hosts
has sent me. 10Sing and rejoice, O daughter
Zion! For lo, I will come and dwell in your
midst, says the LORD. 11Many nations shall
join themselves to the LORD on that day,
and shall be my people; and I will dwell in
your midst. And you shall know that the
LORD of hosts has sent me to you. 12The
LORD will inherit Judah as his portion in
the holy land, and will again choose Jerusa-
lem.

13 Be silent, all people, before the LORD;
for he has roused himself from his holy
dwelling.

3 Then he showed me the high priest
Joshua standing before the angel of the
LORD, and Satan[g] standing at his right

a Ch 2.1 in Heb *b* Heb *it* *c* Ch 2.5 in Heb
d Cn: Heb *after glory he* *e* Heb *his eye*
f Or *wave* *g* Or *the Accuser*; Heb *the Adversary*

measuring line, the first signs of new construction; see 2.1–5; Jer 31.38–39. **17:** Compare with 8.3; Isa 44.26; contrast with 2 Kings 23.27.

1.18–21: The second vision: four horns and four smiths. The four horns symbolize powerful nations (cf. Dan 2.36–40; 7.19–27) which the *blacksmiths* (the LORD's agents of destruction as in Isa 54.16; Ezek 21.31) will smash.

2.1–5: The third vision: a surveyor measures Jerusalem. This vision builds directly upon Ezekiel's vision of restoration (Ezek 40–48). **1:** *Measuring line,* Ezek 40.3–4. **4–5:** Jerusalem will rely on God, not a city wall, for defense (9.8; 14.11; Isa 4.5). The city walls, destroyed in 586 BCE, were not rebuilt until 445 (Neh 3.17–6.15). **4:** *The multitude,* following the exile, Jerusalem's population had dwindled from many thousand to mere hundreds. **5:** *Glory within it,* see Ezek 43.1–5.

2.6–13: A summons to the exiles. 6: Babylonia is *the land of the north* (6.6,8; Jer 3.18). **8:** *Apple of my eye,* the pupil; the most precious, the most fiercely defended part (Deut 32.10; Ps 17.8). **9:** For the role reversal between plunderer and plundered, see also Jer 30.16; Ezek 39.10. **10:** Isa 12.6; 54.1–3; 65.18–19; Ezek 43.6–9; Zeph 3.14–15. **11:** Jerusalem will be the site of a universal pilgrimage in the ideal age (8.20–23; Isa 2.2–4; 56.6–7; Mic 4.1–2). **12:** This is the only reference to Judah, or Israel, as *the holy land* in the Hebrew Bible (though see, in the Apocrypha, Wis 12.3; 2 Macc 1.7). **13:** Hab 2.20.

3.1–10: The fourth vision: Joshua and the Satan. 1: *Joshua,* high priest of Jerusalem (Hag 1.1; 2.2). The *Satan,* "the Adversary," here a member of the divine entourage who assays the virtue of mortals, a heavenly prosecutor (Job 1–2); only later, the arch-opponent of God and author of evil designs (1 Chr 21.1; 2 Cor 2.11). **2:** Joshua passes his heavenly trial. *Brand plucked from the fire,* Am 4.11. **5:** *Clean*

hand to accuse him. 2And the LORD said
to Satan,[a] "The LORD rebuke you,
O Satan![a] The LORD who has chosen Je-
rusalem rebuke you! Is not this man a
brand plucked from the fire?" 3Now Josh-
ua was dressed with filthy clothes as he
stood before the angel. 4The angel said to
those who were standing before him,
"Take off his filthy clothes." And to him he
said, "See, I have taken your guilt away
from you, and I will clothe you with festal
apparel." 5And I said, "Let them put a
clean turban on his head." So they put a
clean turban on his head and clothed him
with the apparel; and the angel of the LORD
was standing by.
6 Then the angel of the LORD assured
Joshua, saying 7"Thus says the LORD of
hosts: If you will walk in my ways and keep
my requirements, then you shall rule my
house and have charge of my courts, and I
will give you the right of access among
those who are standing here. 8Now listen,
Joshua, high priest, you and your col-
leagues who sit before you! For they are an
omen of things to come: I am going to bring
my servant the Branch. 9For on the stone
that I have set before Joshua, on a single
stone with seven facets, I will engrave its
inscription, says the LORD of hosts, and I
will remove the guilt of this land in a single
day. 10On that day, says the LORD of hosts,
you shall invite each other to come under
your vine and fig tree."

4 The angel who talked with me came
again, and wakened me, as one is wak-
ened from sleep. 2He said to me, "What do
you see?" And I said, "I see a lampstand all
of gold, with a bowl on the top of it; there
are seven lamps on it, with seven lips on
each of the lamps that are on the top of it.
3And by it there are two olive trees, one on
the right of the bowl and the other on its
left." 4I said to the angel who talked with
me, "What are these, my lord?" 5Then the
angel who talked with me answered me,
"Do you not know what these are?" I said,
"No, my lord." 6He said to me, "This is the
word of the LORD to Zerubbabel: Not by
might, nor by power, but by my spirit, says
the LORD of hosts. 7What are you, O great
mountain? Before Zerubbabel you shall be-
come a plain; and he shall bring out the top
stone amid shouts of 'Grace, grace to it!' "
8 Moreover the word of the LORD came
to me, saying, 9"The hands of Zerubbabel
have laid the foundation of this house; his
hands shall also complete it. Then you will
know that the LORD of hosts has sent me to
you. 10For whoever has despised the day of
small things shall rejoice, and shall see the
plummet in the hand of Zerubbabel.
"These seven are the eyes of the LORD,
which range through the whole earth."
11Then I said to him, "What are these two
olive trees on the right and the left of the
lampstand?" 12And a second time I said to
him, "What are these two branches of the
olive trees, which pour out the oil[b]

a Or *the Accuser*; Heb *the Adversary* *b* Cn: Heb *gold*

turban . . . the apparel, traditional priestly garb (Ex 28.4; Lev 8.1–9). **7:** *Access,* to the heavenly realm, to intercede on the people's behalf. **8:** *The Branch,* a Davidic figure who will usher in the new age (6.12; Isa 11.1; Jer 23.5; 33.15). Here Zerubbabel, the Davidic governor (Hag 1.1; 2.20–23), appears to be indicated (contrast with 6.9–12). **9:** *The stone,* perhaps an element in the priestly garb (whether that in Ex 28.9–12 or 28.36–38). **10:** See Mic 4.4n.

4.1–14: The fifth vision: a lampstand and two olive trees. 2: Ex 25.31–40. A normal lampstand (Heb "menorah"), a sign of God's presence, has seven lights; this lamp boasts forty-nine (seven times seven); symbolically, a surfeit of blessing. **3:** The *two olive trees* likely represent Joshua and Zerubbabel. The idea of shared leadership between a priest and royal figure, fundamental to Haggai and Zechariah, builds on Ezekiel's vision of the restoration (Ezek 40–48). **6–10:** With divine backing, Zerubbabel will complete the Temple (contrast with 6.12–13). **10:** *Eyes of the LORD,* see 2 Chr 16.9; cf. Job 34.21; Ps 66.7; Prov 15.3. **12:** *Oil,* the Hebrew has "gold," as in textual note *b*. Olive oil can have a golden hue. The olive trees then provide oil, here "gold," for the lamps. **14:** *Anointed* (lit. "sons of oil") is not the usual designation for an anointed priest or ruler.

through the two golden pipes?" 13He said
to me, "Do you not know what these are?"
I said, "No, my lord." 14Then he said,
"These are the two anointed ones who
stand by the Lord of the whole earth."

5 Again I looked up and saw a flying
scroll. 2And he said to me, "What do
you see?" I answered, "I see a flying scroll;
its length is twenty cubits, and its width ten
cubits." 3Then he said to me, "This is the
curse that goes out over the face of the
whole land; for everyone who steals shall
be cut off according to the writing on one
side, and everyone who swears falsely[a]
shall be cut off according to the writing on
the other side. 4I have sent it out, says the
LORD of hosts, and it shall enter the house
of the thief, and the house of anyone who
swears falsely by my name; and it shall
abide in that house and consume it, both
timber and stones."

5 Then the angel who talked with me
came forward and said to me, "Look up
and see what this is that is coming out." 6I
said, "What is it?" He said, "This is a bas-
ket[b] coming out." And he said, "This is
their iniquity[c] in all the land." 7Then a
leaden cover was lifted, and there was a
woman sitting in the basket![b] 8And he
said, "This is Wickedness." So he thrust her
back into the basket,[b] and pressed the
leaden weight down on its mouth. 9Then I
looked up and saw two women coming for-
ward. The wind was in their wings; they
had wings like the wings of a stork, and
they lifted up the basket[b] between earth
and sky. 10Then I said to the angel who
talked with me, "Where are they taking the
basket?"[b] 11He said to me, "To the land
of Shinar, to build a house for it; and when
this is prepared, they will set the basket[b]
down there on its base."

6 And again I looked up and saw four
chariots coming out from between two
mountains—mountains of bronze. 2The
first chariot had red horses, the second
chariot black horses, 3the third chariot
white horses, and the fourth chariot dap-
pled gray[d] horses. 4Then I said to the an-
gel who talked with me, "What are these,
my lord?" 5The angel answered me, "These
are the four winds[e] of heaven going out,
after presenting themselves before the Lord
of all the earth. 6The chariot with the black
horses goes toward the north country, the
white ones go toward the west country,[f]
and the dappled ones go toward the south
country." 7When the steeds came out, they
were impatient to get off and patrol the
earth. And he said, "Go, patrol the earth."
So they patrolled the earth. 8Then he cried
out to me, "Lo, those who go toward the

a The word *falsely* added from verse 4 *b* Heb *ephah* *c* Gk Compare Syr: Heb *their eye* *d* Compare Gk: Meaning of Heb uncertain *e* Or *spirits* *f* Cn: Heb *go after them*

5.1–4: The sixth vision: a flying scroll. 1: The scroll represents the divine message imparted to a prophet (Ezek 2.9–3.3; see Jer 36.1–3). **2:** The dimensions, in our terms, are ca. 9 m x 4 m (29 ft x 15 ft); gigantic for a scroll but precisely those of the porch of Solomon's Temple (1 Kings 6.3). **3–5:** The scroll contains curses for violators of ethical standards, as in the Decalogue (Ex 20.15–16; Deut 5.19–20; cf. Deut 27.15–26). *Shall be cut off,* better, "[those] who have gone unpunished." The scroll will fly through the city and settle all ethical accounts.

5.5–11: The seventh vision: a woman in a basket. Here, Judah becomes purified of and Babylon becomes polluted by a personified figure, "Wickedness." **11:** *Shinar,* Babylon (Gen 10.10; 11.2,9; Dan 1.2). *House* here means temple. *On its base,* as though the basket were a cultic image.

6.1–8: The eighth vision: four chariots. This vision, the last, has much in common with the first (1.7–17). In ch 1, the divine emissaries completed their patrol and returned to deliver a report to their lord; here they go out, not to gather information but, apparently, to initiate God's judgment upon the earth. **1–2:** Cf. Rev 6.2–8. *Two mountains,* in ancient Near Eastern thought, the sun rose from between two mountains at the edge of the world. **5:** *Four winds,* i.e., from all directions; Ps 104.3–4; Isa 66.15; Jer 4.13. *Presenting themselves,* 1.11n. **8:** *The north country,* Babylon, receives special attention; see 2.6n. *My spirit at rest,* note the contrast with 1.11,15: When the earth "remains at peace," the Lord is "angry"; when judgment is unleashed against the earth, the LORD's *spirit* is *at rest.*

north country have set my spirit at rest in
the north country."
9 The word of the LORD came to me:
10 Collect silver and gold[a] from the ex-
iles—from Heldai, Tobijah, and Jedaiah—
who have arrived from Babylon; and go the
same day to the house of Josiah son of
Zephaniah. 11 Take the silver and gold and
make a crown,[b] and set it on the head of
the high priest Joshua son of Jehozadak;
12 say to him: Thus says the LORD of hosts:
Here is a man whose name is Branch: for he
shall branch out in his place, and he shall
build the temple of the LORD. 13 It is he that
shall build the temple of the LORD; he shall
bear royal honor, and shall sit upon his
throne and rule. There shall be a priest by
his throne, with peaceful understanding be-
tween the two of them. 14 And the crown[c]
shall be in the care of Heldai,[d] Tobijah,
Jedaiah, and Josiah[e] son of Zephaniah, as
a memorial in the temple of the LORD.
15 Those who are far off shall come and
help to build the temple of the LORD; and
you shall know that the LORD of hosts has
sent me to you. This will happen if you
diligently obey the voice of the LORD your
God.
7 In the fourth year of King Darius, the
word of the LORD came to Zechariah
on the fourth day of the ninth month,
which is Chislev. 2 Now the people of Beth-
el had sent Sharezer and Regem-melech
and their men, to entreat the favor of the
LORD, 3 and to ask the priests of the house
of the LORD of hosts and the prophets,
"Should I mourn and practice abstinence in
the fifth month, as I have done for so many
years?" 4 Then the word of the LORD of
hosts came to me: 5 Say to all the people of
the land and the priests: When you fasted
and lamented in the fifth month and in the
seventh, for these seventy years, was it for
me that you fasted? 6 And when you eat and
when you drink, do you not eat and drink
only for yourselves? 7 Were not these the
words that the LORD proclaimed by the
former prophets, when Jerusalem was in-
habited and in prosperity, along with the
towns around it, and when the Negeb and
the Shephelah were inhabited?
8 The word of the LORD came to Zecha-
riah, saying: 9 Thus says the LORD of hosts:
Render true judgments, show kindness and
mercy to one another; 10 do not oppress the
widow, the orphan, the alien, or the poor;
and do not devise evil in your hearts against
one another. 11 But they refused to listen,
and turned a stubborn shoulder, and
stopped their ears in order not to hear.
12 They made their hearts adamant in order
not to hear the law and the words that
the LORD of hosts had sent by his spirit
through the former prophets. Therefore
great wrath came from the LORD of hosts.
13 Just as, when I[f] called, they would not

a Cn Compare verse 11: Heb lacks *silver and gold*
b Gk Mss Syr Tg: Heb *crowns* *c* Gk Syr: Heb *crowns* *d* Syr Compare verse 10: Heb *Helem*
e Syr Compare verse 10: Heb *Hen* *f* Heb *he*

6.9–15: The coronation. This section has difficulties, chiefly the absence of Zerubbabel. In 3.8, the Davidic term *Branch* seems to refer to Zerubbabel. In 4.1–14, two anointed ones, presumably Joshua and Zerubbabel, lead the community. In 4.9, Zerubbabel leads the Temple-rebuilding efforts. Here, however, Joshua alone is the *Branch* and Temple-builder. What happened to Zerubbabel? As textual note *b* indicates, the Hebrew of v. 11 has the plural *crowns.* Probably an earlier reference to Zerubbabel has been lost. **15:** In addition to the contributions of recent arrivals from Babylon (v. 10), those who are far off will also join the rebuilding efforts.

7.1–8.23: Various oracles. 7.1–14: The prophet responds to an inquiry about fasting. For the answer to the specific question about fasting, see 8.18–19. **1:** Mid-November to mid-December 518 BCE. **2:** *Bethel,* ca. 17 km (11 mi) north of Jerusalem. **3:** *Abstinence,* lit. "devotion." **5:** The Temple at Jerusalem was burned in *the fifth month* and Gedaliah the governor was murdered in *the seventh* (2 Kings 25.8–9,25). *These seventy years,* see 1.12n. **7–10:** An inquiry about fasting becomes an occasion for repeating a central message of *the former prophets* (e.g., Isa 1.16–17; Jer 7.5–7; Hos 6.6; Am 5.14–15,21–24; Mic 6.8). **7:** *The Negeb and the Shephelah,* the southern and western regions of Judah.

hear, so, when they called, I would not hear, says the LORD of hosts, 14 and I scattered them with a whirlwind among all the nations that they had not known. Thus the land they left was desolate, so that no one went to and fro, and a pleasant land was made desolate.

8 The word of the LORD of hosts came to me, saying: 2 Thus says the LORD of hosts: I am jealous for Zion with great jealousy, and I am jealous for her with great wrath. 3 Thus says the LORD: I will return to Zion, and will dwell in the midst of Jerusalem; Jerusalem shall be called the faithful city, and the mountain of the LORD of hosts shall be called the holy mountain. 4 Thus says the LORD of hosts: Old men and old women shall again sit in the streets of Jerusalem, each with staff in hand because of their great age. 5 And the streets of the city shall be full of boys and girls playing in its streets. 6 Thus says the LORD of hosts: Even though it seems impossible to the remnant of this people in these days, should it also seem impossible to me, says the LORD of hosts? 7 Thus says the LORD of hosts: I will save my people from the east country and from the west country; 8 and I will bring them to live in Jerusalem. They shall be my people and I will be their God, in faithfulness and in righteousness.

9 Thus says the LORD of hosts: Let your hands be strong—you that have recently been hearing these words from the mouths of the prophets who were present when the foundation was laid for the rebuilding of the temple, the house of the LORD of hosts. 10 For before those days there were no wages for people or for animals, nor was there any safety from the foe for those who went out or came in, and I set them all against one another. 11 But now I will not deal with the remnant of this people as in the former days, says the LORD of hosts. 12 For there shall be a sowing of peace; the vine shall yield its fruit, the ground shall give its produce, and the skies shall give their dew; and I will cause the remnant of this people to possess all these things. 13 Just as you have been a cursing among the nations, O house of Judah and house of Israel, so I will save you and you shall be a blessing. Do not be afraid, but let your hands be strong.

14 For thus says the LORD of hosts: Just as I purposed to bring disaster upon you, when your ancestors provoked me to wrath, and I did not relent, says the LORD of hosts, 15 so again I have purposed in these days to do good to Jerusalem and to the house of Judah; do not be afraid. 16 These are the things that you shall do: Speak the truth to one another, render in your gates judgments that are true and make for peace, 17 do not devise evil in your hearts against one another, and love no false oath; for all these are things that I hate, says the LORD.

18 The word of the LORD of hosts came to me, saying: 19 Thus says the LORD of hosts: The fast of the fourth month, and the fast of the fifth, and the fast of the seventh, and the fast of the tenth, shall be seasons of joy and gladness, and cheerful festivals for the house of Judah: therefore love truth and peace.

20 Thus says the LORD of hosts: Peoples shall yet come, the inhabitants of many cities; 21 the inhabitants of one city shall go to another, saying, "Come, let us go to entreat the favor of the LORD, and to seek the LORD of hosts; I myself am going." 22 Many

8.1–23: Ten sayings about Jerusalem (8.2; 8.3; 8.4–5; 8.6; 8.7–8; 8.9–13; 8.14–17; 8.18–19; 8.20–22; 8.23). **2:** Joel 2.18. **3:** Isa 1.26; 11.9; 62.11–12; Jer 31.23. **4–5:** Isa 65.19–20. Images of paradisiacal Jerusalem also close the second major section of Zechariah (14.6–11). **6:** *Though it seems impossible,* Gen 18.14; Jer 32.27. **8:** The covenant shall be reaffirmed (Ex 6.7; Jer 31.33); see also 13.9. **9:** Hag 1.6–11; 2.4–9,15–19. **13:** Jer 29.18; Gen 12.2–3. **16–17:** See 7.9–10. **19–20:** The answer to the inquiry of 7.3. These fasts of mourning for Jerusalem's fall and humiliation give way to feasts celebrating Jerusalem's recovery and exaltation. *The fourth month* was when the Babylonians breached the walls of Jerusalem and *the tenth,* when the Babylonians began their siege (2 Kings 25.1–4; Jer 39.2; 52.4–7). For *the fifth* and *seventh* months, see 7.5n. **20–23:** Cf. Isa 2.2–4; 45.14,24; Mic 4.1–3.

peoples and strong nations shall come to seek the LORD of hosts in Jerusalem, and to entreat the favor of the LORD.
23 Thus says the LORD of hosts: In those days ten men from nations of every language shall take hold of a Jew, grasping his garment and saying, "Let us go with you, for we have heard that God is with you."

9

An Oracle.

The word of the LORD is against the
land of Hadrach
and will rest upon Damascus.
For to the LORD belongs the capital[a]
of Aram,[b]
as do all the tribes of Israel;
2 Hamath also, which borders on it,
Tyre and Sidon, though they are
very wise.
3 Tyre has built itself a rampart,
and heaped up silver like dust,
and gold like the dirt of the
streets.
4 But now, the Lord will strip it
of its possessions
and hurl its wealth into the sea,
and it shall be devoured by fire.

5 Ashkelon shall see it and be afraid;
Gaza too, and shall writhe in
anguish;
Ekron also, because its hopes
are withered.
The king shall perish from Gaza;
Ashkelon shall be uninhabited;
6 a mongrel people shall settle
in Ashdod,
and I will make an end of the pride
of Philistia.
7 I will take away its blood from
its mouth,
and its abominations from between
its teeth;
it too shall be a remnant for our God;
it shall be like a clan in Judah,
and Ekron shall be like the
Jebusites.
8 Then I will encamp at my house as a
guard,
so that no one shall march to
and fro;
no oppressor shall again overrun
them,
for now I have seen with my
own eyes.

9 Rejoice greatly, O daughter Zion!
Shout aloud, O daughter Jerusalem!

a Heb *eye* *b* Cn: Heb *of Adam* (or *of humankind*)

9.1–14.21: The two burdens of Zechariah. The remainder of Zechariah, and the whole of the subsequent book of Malachi, can be divided into three units of comparable length, each introduced by the title, "An Oracle" (lit. "Burden") (Zech 9.1; 12.1; Mal 1.1).

9.1–11.17: The first burden. A collection of poetic speeches about the Day of the LORD (Joel 2.11; Isa 63.1–6) which ends, however, with an image of the community in disarray.

9.1–8: The LORD subdues Israel's neighbors. Note the geographic movement as the LORD moves from north to south, from Syria (v. 1) to *my house* (in Jerusalem, v. 8). **1–6:** These cities of Syria (*Aram*), Phoenicia, and Philistia fall within the maximal ideal limits of ancient Israel (Gen 15.18–21; Ex 23.31). **1:** *Hadrach,* a Syrian city-state north of Damascus. **2–3:** *Tyre* and *Sidon* were maritime Phoenician cities. For earlier oracles against Tyre, see Am 1.9–12; Ezek 27–28. **5–7:** Four of the five principal Philistine cities (1 Sam 6.17) are named, as in Am 1.6–8. Gath, which is missing, was probably destroyed by Sennacherib in the late seventh century. **7:** The Philistines will observe Jewish dietary laws (cf. Gen 9.4; Lev 11.2–47; Deut 14.3–21) and live as God's people. *Jebusites,* Jos 15.63; 2 Sam 5.6–9; 1 Chr 11.4–9.

9.9–10: The king of peace. A song celebrating the arrival of the king in Jerusalem (cf. Ps 72). **9–10:** The identity of the *king* is unclear. Some scholars identify him as the LORD himself (see Zeph 3.5), others as a historical individual (e.g., Alexander the Great), and still others as a future ruler in the Davidic line. **9:** *Donkey, colt,* in the style of Hebrew parallelism, a single animal (as in Gen 49.11; Jn 12.14–15) is meant here. In the New Testament, Mt 21.5–7 misunderstands and assumes two animals are meant. The choice of mount, *donkey* instead of *war-horse* (v. 10), indicates peaceful intentions. **10:** This description

Lo, your king comes to you;
triumphant and victorious is he,
humble and riding on a donkey,
on a colt, the foal of a donkey.
10 He[a] will cut off the chariot
from Ephraim
and the war-horse from Jerusalem;
and the battle bow shall be cut off,
and he shall command peace to the
nations;
his dominion shall be from sea to sea,
and from the River to the ends of
the earth.

11 As for you also, because of the blood
of my covenant with you,
I will set your prisoners free from
the waterless pit.
12 Return to your stronghold,
O prisoners of hope;
today I declare that I will restore to
you double.
13 For I have bent Judah as my bow;
I have made Ephraim its arrow.
I will arouse your sons, O Zion,
against your sons, O Greece,
and wield you like a
warrior's sword.

14 Then the LORD will appear
over them,
and his arrow go forth like
lightning;
the Lord GOD will sound the trumpet
and march forth in the whirlwinds
of the south.
15 The LORD of hosts will protect them,
and they shall devour and tread
down the slingers;[b]
they shall drink their blood[c]
like wine,
and be full like a bowl,
drenched like the corners of
the altar.
16 On that day the LORD their God
will save them
for they are the flock of his
people;
for like the jewels of a crown
they shall shine on his land.
17 For what goodness and beauty
are his!
Grain shall make the young
men flourish,
and new wine the young women.

10 Ask rain from the LORD
in the season of the spring rain,
from the LORD who makes the storm
clouds,
who gives showers of rain to
you,[d]
the vegetation in the field
to everyone.
2 For the teraphim[e] utter nonsense,
and the diviners see lies;
the dreamers tell false dreams,
and give empty consolation.
Therefore the people wander
like sheep;
they suffer for lack of a shepherd.

a Gk: Heb *I* *b* Cn: Heb *the slingstones*
c Gk: Heb *shall drink* *d* Heb *them*
e Or *household gods*

of universal peace is rich in biblical allusion (i.e., Ps 46.9; 72.8; 76.3; cf. 1 Kings 4.24). *The River,* the Euphrates in northern Syria.

9.11–17: The LORD liberates dispersed Israelites and leads them home. 11: *Blood of my covenant,* Ex 24.8. *Waterless pit,* a dungeon (Gen 37.24; cf. Isa 42.7; 49.8–9; 61.1). **12:** *Double,* Isa 40.2; 61.7; cf. Job 42.10. **13:** *Judah* and *Ephraim,* the preexilic Southern and Northern Kingdoms. *Greece,* Heb "yawan," could represent the people from Greek Asia Minor (Ionia) or Greece proper (Gen 10.2; Ezek 27.13; Joel 3.6); see Introduction. **14:** Cf. Hab 3.3–15. *Them,* i.e., Israel. **15:** See textual notes *b* and *c;* a banquet, not a bloodbath, is probably pictured, in which the victorious group shall eat (not *devour*), *tread down* their slingstones (not *the slingers*), and *drink . . . wine* (not *blood*).

10.1–2: An admonition to consult the LORD for the weather. 1: See 14.17; Job 38.25; Joel 2.23; Am 4.7–8. **2:** *Teraphim,* religious images sometimes used for prediction (Ezek 21.21 and note *e* there).

3 My anger is hot against the
shepherds,
and I will punish the leaders;[a]
for the LORD of hosts cares for his
flock, the house of Judah,
and will make them like his proud
war-horse.
4 Out of them shall come the
cornerstone,
out of them the tent peg,
out of them the battle bow,
out of them every commander.
5 Together they shall be like warriors in
battle,
trampling the foe in the mud of the
streets;
they shall fight, for the LORD is with
them,
and they shall put to shame the
riders on horses.

6 I will strengthen the house of Judah,
and I will save the house of Joseph.
I will bring them back because I have
compassion on them,
and they shall be as though I had
not rejected them;
for I am the LORD their God and I
will answer them.
7 Then the people of Ephraim shall
become like warriors,
and their hearts shall be glad as
with wine.
Their children shall see it and rejoice,
their hearts shall exult in the LORD.

8 I will signal for them and gather them
in,
for I have redeemed them,
and they shall be as numerous as
they were before.
9 Though I scattered them among
the nations,
yet in far countries they shall
remember me,
and they shall rear their children
and return.
10 I will bring them home from the land
of Egypt,
and gather them from Assyria;
I will bring them to the land of
Gilead and to Lebanon,
until there is no room for them.
11 They[b] shall pass through the sea of
distress,
and the waves of the sea shall be
struck down,
and all the depths of the Nile dried
up.
The pride of Assyria shall be laid low,
and the scepter of Egypt
shall depart.
12 I will make them strong in the LORD,
and they shall walk in his name,
says the LORD.

11 Open your doors, O Lebanon,
so that fire may devour
your cedars!
2 Wail, O cypress, for the cedar
has fallen,
for the glorious trees are ruined!
Wail, oaks of Bashan,
for the thick forest has been felled!
3 Listen, the wail of the shepherds,
for their glory is despoiled!
Listen, the roar of the lions,
for the thickets of the Jordan
are destroyed!

a Or *male goats* *b* Gk: Heb *He*

10.3–12: The LORD brings Israel home. 3: *Shepherds,* i.e., rulers. *Leaders,* lit. he-goats (textual note *a;* Isa 14.9). **4:** *Cornerstone,* the chief (Judg 20.2) or king (Ps 118.22; Isa 19.13). *Tent peg,* Isa 22.23–24. **6:** Isa 54.8. The Northern Kingdom of Israel, *the house of Joseph,* will be saved along with Judah; cf. 9.13; Ezek 37.15–28. **8–12:** Isa 43.1–7,14–21; Jer 23.3. **8:** *As numerous as they were before,* see 2.4n. **10–12:** A new Exodus. **10:** Deut 30.1–5; Hos 11.11. *Gilead,* northern Transjordan. **12:** Mic 4.5.

11.1–3: The fall of the tyrants. *Cedars, shepherds,* and *lions* refer to the rulers. **1:** Lebanon's *cedars* were proverbial symbols of strength (Ezek 31.2–9). **2:** *Oaks of Bashan,* Bashan, in northern Transjordan, was famous for its timber; see Isa 2.13; Ezek 27.6. **3:** The dense vegetation of the *Jordan* valley was a habitat of *lions;* see Jer 49.19.

4 Thus said the LORD my God: Be a
shepherd of the flock doomed to slaughter.
5 Those who buy them kill them and go
unpunished; and those who sell them say,
"Blessed be the LORD, for I have become
rich"; and their own shepherds have no
pity on them. 6 For I will no longer have
pity on the inhabitants of the earth, says the
LORD. I will cause them, every one, to fall
each into the hand of a neighbor, and each
into the hand of the king; and they shall
devastate the earth, and I will deliver no
one from their hand.
7 So, on behalf of the sheep merchants,
I became the shepherd of the flock doomed
to slaughter. I took two staffs; one I named
Favor, the other I named Unity, and I tend-
ed the sheep. 8 In one month I disposed of
the three shepherds, for I had become im-
patient with them, and they also detested
me. 9 So I said, "I will not be your shepherd.
What is to die, let it die; what is to be de-
stroyed, let it be destroyed; and let those
that are left devour the flesh of one anoth-
er!" 10 I took my staff Favor and broke it,
annulling the covenant that I had made
with all the peoples. 11 So it was annulled
on that day, and the sheep merchants, who
were watching me, knew that it was the
word of the LORD. 12 I then said to them,
"If it seems right to you, give me my wages;
but if not, keep them." So they weighed out
as my wages thirty shekels of silver. 13 Then
the LORD said to me, "Throw it into the
treasury"[a]—this lordly price at which I
was valued by them. So I took the thirty
shekels of silver and threw them into the
treasury[a] in the house of the LORD.
14 Then I broke my second staff Unity, an-
nulling the family ties between Judah and
Israel.
15 Then the LORD said to me: Take once
more the implements of a worthless shep-
herd. 16 For I am now raising up in the land
a shepherd who does not care for the per-
ishing, or seek the wandering,[b] or heal the
maimed, or nourish the healthy,[c] but de-
vours the flesh of the fat ones, tearing off
even their hoofs.

17 Oh, my worthless shepherd,
who deserts the flock!
May the sword strike his arm
and his right eye!
Let his arm be completely withered,
his right eye utterly blinded!

12

An Oracle.

The word of the LORD concerning Israel:
Thus says the LORD, who stretched out the
heavens and founded the earth and formed
the human spirit within: 2 See, I am about
to make Jerusalem a cup of reeling for all
the surrounding peoples; it will be against
Judah also in the siege against Jerusalem.
3 On that day I will make Jerusalem a heavy
stone for all the peoples; all who lift it shall
grievously hurt themselves. And all the na-
tions of the earth shall come together
against it. 4 On that day, says the LORD, I
will strike every horse with panic, and its
rider with madness. But on the house of
Judah I will keep a watchful eye, when I
strike every horse of the peoples with blind-
ness. 5 Then the clans of Judah shall say to

a Syr: Heb *it to the potter* *b* Syr Compare Gk Vg: Heb *the youth* *c* Meaning of Heb uncertain

11.4–17: The worthless shepherd. The prophet is commissioned as shepherd of the people (v. 4), but the mission fails (v. 8). Then the LORD raises for the people the shepherd they deserve (vv. 15–17). **5:** *Their own shepherds have no pity,* Jer 23.1–2; Ezek 34.1–6. **8:** The identification of *the three shepherds* is obscure. **13:** *Thirty shekels,* the price of a slave (Ex 21.32); in the New Testament this saying is attributed to Jeremiah (Mt 27.3–10; cf. Mt 26.15). *Lordly price* is ironic. **15–17:** See 11.5n. and Mic 3.1–7. The identification of the *worthless shepherd* is obscure.

12.1–14.21: The second burden.

12.1–13.6: Sayings about the coming Day of the LORD. 12.1: Isa 42.5. **2–3:** References to conflict between Jerusalem and Judah probably reflect tensions in the postexilic community. **2:** *Cup of reeling,* Ps 75.8; Isa 51.17–23; Jer 25.15–28. **8:** *Like the angel of the LORD,* 2 Sam 19.27. **9:** *All the nations*

themselves, "The inhabitants of Jerusalem
have strength through the LORD of hosts,
their God."
6 On that day I will make the clans of
Judah like a blazing pot on a pile of wood,
like a flaming torch among sheaves; and
they shall devour to the right and to the left
all the surrounding peoples, while Jerusa-
lem shall again be inhabited in its place, in
Jerusalem.
7 And the LORD will give victory to the
tents of Judah first, that the glory of the
house of David and the glory of the inhabi-
tants of Jerusalem may not be exalted over
that of Judah. 8 On that day the LORD will
shield the inhabitants of Jerusalem so that
the feeblest among them on that day shall
be like David, and the house of David shall
be like God, like the angel of the LORD, at
their head. 9 And on that day I will seek to
destroy all the nations that come against
Jerusalem.
10 And I will pour out a spirit of com-
passion and supplication on the house of
David and the inhabitants of Jerusalem, so
that, when they look on the one[a] whom
they have pierced, they shall mourn for
him, as one mourns for an only child, and
weep bitterly over him, as one weeps over a
firstborn. 11 On that day the mourning in
Jerusalem will be as great as the mourning
for Hadad-rimmon in the plain of Megid-
do. 12 The land shall mourn, each family by
itself; the family of the house of David by
itself, and their wives by themselves; the
family of the house of Nathan by itself, and
their wives by themselves; 13 the family of
the house of Levi by itself, and their wives
by themselves; the family of the Shimeites
by itself, and their wives by themselves;
14 and all the families that are left, each by
itself, and their wives by themselves.
13 On that day a fountain shall be
opened for the house of David and
the inhabitants of Jerusalem, to cleanse
them from sin and impurity.
2 On that day, says the LORD of hosts, I
will cut off the names of the idols from the
land, so that they shall be remembered no
more; and also I will remove from the land
the prophets and the unclean spirit. 3 And if
any prophets appear again, their fathers
and mothers who bore them will say to
them, "You shall not live, for you speak lies
in the name of the LORD"; and their fathers
and their mothers who bore them shall
pierce them through when they prophesy.
4 On that day the prophets will be ashamed,
every one, of their visions when they
prophesy; they will not put on a hairy man-
tle in order to deceive, 5 but each of them
will say, "I am no prophet, I am a tiller of
the soil; for the land has been my posses-
sion[b] since my youth." 6 And if anyone
asks them, "What are these wounds on

a Heb *on me* *b* Cn: Heb *for humankind has caused me to possess*

that come against Jerusalem, a conventional element in late prophetic eschatological scenarios (ch 14; Ezek 38.14–23; Joel 3.11–14). **10–14:** Compare this picture of Jerusalem mourning over a prophet or king whom it has martyred with Isa 52.12–53.12. **10:** The identification of *the one whom they have pierced* is uncertain. According to the Hebrew (see textual note *a*), it is apparently the putative speaker of the oracle, the LORD, but the text is difficult. Other proposals include some historical figure, such as a member of the Davidic line, a prophet (see 13.3), or a group; for the New Testament identification with Jesus, see Jn 19.37. *Only child,* Jer 6.26; Am 8.10. **11:** *Hadad-rimmon,* a Syrian storm god, also known as Baal, whose seasonal disappearance was mourned in the agriculturally fertile area around Megiddo; see 2 Kings 5.18. **12:** *Nathan,* perhaps David's son (2 Sam 5.14; 1 Chr 14.4), or the prophet with the same name (2 Sam 7.2; 1 Chr 9.29). **13:** *Shimeites,* descendants of Levi's grandson (Num 3.21; 1 Chr 6.17). **13.1:** *Fountain,* 14.8; Ps 46.4; Ezek 47.1–12; Joel 3.18. **2–6:** Prophecy is placed beside idolatry among the impurities that must be removed. For a negative glimpse of postexilic prophecy, see Neh 6.12–14. Though generally respected, prophets sometimes were mocked as "madmen" who "babble" (2 Kings 9.11). **2:** Hos 2.17; Zeph 1.4. **4:** *Hairy mantle,* an animal skin (Gen 27.15–27) often worn by prophets (1 Kings 19.13; 2 Kings 1.8; 2.8,13; Mk 1.6). **5:** Am 7.14. **6:** For self-laceration as part of prophetic activity, see 1 Kings 18.28.

your chest?"[a] the answer will be "The
wounds I received in the house of my
friends."

7 "Awake, O sword, against my
shepherd,
against the man who is my
associate,"
says the LORD of hosts.
Strike the shepherd, that the sheep
may be scattered;
I will turn my hand against
the little ones.
8 In the whole land, says the LORD,
two-thirds shall be cut off
and perish,
and one-third shall be left alive.
9 And I will put this third into the fire,
refine them as one refines silver,
and test them as gold is tested.
They will call on my name,
and I will answer them.
I will say, "They are my people";
and they will say, "The LORD is
our God."

14 See, a day is coming for the LORD,
when the plunder taken from you
will be divided in your midst. 2 For I will
gather all the nations against Jerusalem to
battle, and the city shall be taken and the
houses looted and the women raped; half
the city shall go into exile, but the rest of
the people shall not be cut off from the city.
3 Then the LORD will go forth and fight
against those nations as when he fights on
a day of battle. 4 On that day his feet shall
stand on the Mount of Olives, which lies
before Jerusalem on the east; and the
Mount of Olives shall be split in two from
east to west by a very wide valley; so that
one half of the Mount shall withdraw
northward, and the other half southward.
5 And you shall flee by the valley of the
LORD's mountain,[b] for the valley between
the mountains shall reach to Azal;[c] and
you shall flee as you fled from the earth-
quake in the days of King Uzziah of Judah.
Then the LORD my God will come, and all
the holy ones with him.
6 On that day there shall not be[d] either
cold or frost.[e] 7 And there shall be continu-
ous day (it is known to the LORD), not day
and not night, for at evening time there
shall be light.
8 On that day living waters shall flow
out from Jerusalem, half of them to the
eastern sea and half of them to the western
sea; it shall continue in summer as in win-
ter.
9 And the LORD will become king over
all the earth; on that day the LORD will be
one and his name one.
10 The whole land shall be turned into a
plain from Geba to Rimmon south of Jeru-
salem. But Jerusalem shall remain aloft on
its site from the Gate of Benjamin to the
place of the former gate, to the Corner
Gate, and from the Tower of Hananel to
the king's wine presses. 11 And it shall be
inhabited, for never again shall it be
doomed to destruction; Jerusalem shall
abide in security.
12 This shall be the plague with which

a Heb *wounds between your hands* *b* Heb *my mountains* *c* Meaning of Heb uncertain *d* Cn: Heb *there shall not be light* *e* Compare Gk Syr Vg Tg: Meaning of Heb uncertain

13.7–9: The stricken shepherd. A cryptic oracle that concerns an assault on a community leader which initiates a larger trial for the entire group, followed by restoration. **7:** For the *shepherd,* see 11.4–17. *Scattered,* 1 Kings 22.17. **8:** Ezek 5.1–12. **9:** *Refines,* Isa 1.25–26; 48.10. *My people . . . our God,* Hos 2.21–23.

14.1–21: The final battle. An eschatological description in which Jerusalem is attacked by all the nations (v. 2) before the LORD intervenes. **5:** *Azal,* location unknown. *Earthquake,* see Am 1.1n. *The holy ones,* angelic beings. **6–7:** Isa 24.23; 60.19–20. **8:** 13.1n. *Eastern sea,* the Dead Sea. *Western sea,* the Mediterranean (Joel 2.20). **9:** Deut 6.4; Ps 29.10; Ps 99.1–5. **10:** Jerusalem will be physically elevated above its environment (cf. Isa 2.2; Mic 4.1n.). *Geba,* located 10 km (6 mi) north-northeast of Jerusalem, and Rimmon, 60 km (37 mi) southwest of Jerusalem, represent the limits of Judah. **12–15:** 14.3; cf. other horrifying eschatological descriptions in Isa 66.24; Ezek 39.17–20. **16–19:** The remnants of the nations

the LORD will strike all the peoples that
wage war against Jerusalem: their flesh
shall rot while they are still on their feet;
their eyes shall rot in their sockets, and
their tongues shall rot in their mouths.
13 On that day a great panic from the LORD
shall fall on them, so that each will seize the
hand of a neighbor, and the hand of the one
will be raised against the hand of the other;
14 even Judah will fight at Jerusalem. And
the wealth of all the surrounding nations
shall be collected—gold, silver, and gar-
ments in great abundance. 15 And a plague
like this plague shall fall on the horses, the
mules, the camels, the donkeys, and what-
ever animals may be in those camps.

16 Then all who survive of the nations
that have come against Jerusalem shall go
up year after year to worship the King, the
LORD of hosts, and to keep the festival of
booths.[a] 17 If any of the families of the
earth do not go up to Jerusalem to worship
the King, the LORD of hosts, there will be
no rain upon them. 18 And if the family of
Egypt do not go up and present themselves,
then on them shall[b] come the plague that
the LORD inflicts on the nations that do not
go up to keep the festival of booths.[a]
19 Such shall be the punishment of Egypt
and the punishment of all the nations that
do not go up to keep the festival of
booths.[a]

20 On that day there shall be inscribed
on the bells of the horses, "Holy to the
LORD." And the cooking pots in the house
of the LORD shall be as holy as[c] the bowls
in front of the altar; 21 and every cooking
pot in Jerusalem and Judah shall be sacred
to the LORD of hosts, so that all who sacri-
fice may come and use them to boil the
flesh of the sacrifice. And there shall no
longer be traders[d] in the house of the
LORD of hosts on that day.

a Or *tabernacles*; Heb *succoth* *b* Gk Syr: Heb *shall not* *c* Heb *shall be like* *d* Or *Canaanites*

will make pilgrimages to Jerusalem; cf. 2.11n. **16:** *Festival of booths,* Sukkoth (Lev 23.33–36). **20–21:** Jerusalem itself becomes a virtual temple. **21:** *Traders,* see textual note *d.* The Hebrew Bible often uses the term "Canaanite" with the meaning of trader (see Zech 11.7,11; Job 41.6; Prov 31.24; Ezek 17.4; etc.). Various forms of economic activity were associated with temples. The absence of traders may suggest a heightened sense of the holiness of Jerusalem and the Temple.

MALACHI

The final book in the Minor Prophets is Malachi, whose placement following Haggai and Zechariah is probably based on a chronological principle, since the frequent allusions to Temple activity in the book presume the success of those prophets (e.g., Hag 1.7; Zech 6.15) in the restoration of the Temple. The superscription to Malachi ("an oracle," 1.1) further binds the book to its predecessor (cf. Zech 9.1; 12.1).

Nothing is known about the person of Malachi. Even his name, which means "my messenger," may be only an appellation, based on 3.1 (cf. 2.7). Though the book neither alludes to historical events nor includes date formulas, it seems to reflect the period of the fifth century BCE, since it presumes a completed Temple (which occurred in 515) and also shares many concerns with Ezra and Nehemiah, normally dated to the second half of the fifth century, including tithing (3.8–12; Neh 10.37–39; 13.10–14) and mixed marriages (2.10–12; Ezra 9–10; Neh 11.23–27).

This prophetic voice was devoted to the Temple and held a high view of the priesthood and its responsibilities. He speaks frequently of the covenant (2.4,5,8,10,14; 3.1) and shows great respect for the priestly "instruction" (*torah*, 2.6–9). Instead of adopting the poetic style used by earlier prophets, Malachi speaks in a more prosaic voice and adopts a question-and-answer method of stating his argument. Nevertheless, his emphases upon sin, judgment, and repentance, and upon an imminent day of reckoning (3.1–5,7; 4.1–3,6) mark him as a prophet, and he may be best understood as a "cultic prophet," like Joel.

The extravagant hopes of the restoration prophets had not materialized (Hag 2.6–9; Zech 8.1–5,20–23). The Temple had been rebuilt but the ideal age had not begun. Malachi probably spoke to a disheartened audience which questioned both the love (1.2) and justice (2.17) of God. Malachi reversed the discussion: God, he avers, has been faithful to the covenant (1.2; 2.5–7; and esp. 3.6, "For I the LORD do not change"); it is Judah that has been faithless (1.6; 2.8,14; 3.8). Furthermore, any lingering doubts about divine justice will be addressed and overcome, the prophet states, soon enough when the LORD comes in judgment (2.17–3.5; 3.16–4.6).

Following the superscription (1.1), the book contains six units that follow a similar pattern. The pattern is argumentative and disputational. The prophet makes a statement (e.g., "I have loved you, says the LORD," 1.2a), followed by a question voiced by the prophet but attributed to the audience (e.g., "But you say, 'How have you loved us?'" 1.2b), followed by the prophet's response. The six units are 1.2–5; 1.6–2.9; 2.10–16; 2.17–3.5; 3.6–12; 3.13–4.3. Two appendices (4.4; 4.5–6), probably added later, complete the book.

Overall, the book can be read as a single argument. Against a background of ennui (see the "weariness" of the people in 1.13; of God in 3.17), the prophet emphasizes God's reliability (1.2–5) and countercharges that it is the priests (1.6–2.9) and the larger society (2.10–16) who have been unfaithful. Nevertheless, divine judgment is imminent (2.17–3.5), so the people should return to God (3.6–12). In the end, the faithful remnant in the community will be vindicated (3.13–4.3).

In Jewish Bibles, Malachi ends the Book of the Twelve and the entire prophetic collection (see 4.4–6n.). In Christian Bibles it ends the Old Testament; its final words about Elijah as messenger, already in the Gospels and subsequently in Christian tradition, are traditionally interpreted to foreshadow Jesus as the Christ.

1 An oracle. The word of the LORD to
Israel by Malachi.[a]

2 I have loved you, says the LORD. But
you say, "How have you loved us?" Is not
Esau Jacob's brother? says the LORD. Yet I
have loved Jacob 3 but I have hated Esau; I
have made his hill country a desolation and
his heritage a desert for jackals. 4 If Edom
says, "We are shattered but we will rebuild
the ruins," the LORD of hosts says: They
may build, but I will tear down, until they
are called the wicked country, the people
with whom the LORD is angry forever.
5 Your own eyes shall see this, and you shall
say, "Great is the LORD beyond the borders
of Israel!"
6 A son honors his father, and servants
their master. If then I am a father, where is
the honor due me? And if I am a master,
where is the respect due me? says the LORD
of hosts to you, O priests, who despise my
name. You say, "How have we despised
your name?" 7 By offering polluted food on
my altar. And you say, "How have we pol-
luted it?"[b] By thinking that the LORD's ta-
ble may be despised. 8 When you offer blind
animals in sacrifice, is that not wrong? And
when you offer those that are lame or sick,
is that not wrong? Try presenting that to
your governor; will he be pleased with you
or show you favor? says the LORD of hosts.
9 And now implore the favor of God, that
he may be gracious to us. The fault is yours.
Will he show favor to any of you? says the
LORD of hosts. 10 Oh, that someone among
you would shut the temple[c] doors, so that
you would not kindle fire on my altar in
vain! I have no pleasure in you, says the
LORD of hosts, and I will not accept an
offering from your hands. 11 For from the
rising of the sun to its setting my name is
great among the nations, and in every place
incense is offered to my name, and a pure
offering; for my name is great among the
nations, says the LORD of hosts. 12 But you
profane it when you say that the Lord's
table is polluted, and the food for it[d] may
be despised. 13 "What a weariness this is,"
you say, and you sniff at me,[e] says the
LORD of hosts. You bring what has been
taken by violence or is lame or sick, and
this you bring as your offering! Shall I ac-
cept that from your hand? says the LORD.
14 Cursed be the cheat who has a male in
the flock and vows to give it, and yet sacri-
fices to the Lord what is blemished; for I
am a great King, says the LORD of hosts,
and my name is reverenced among the na-
tions.

2 And now, O priests, this command is
for you. 2 If you will not listen, if you
will not lay it to heart to give glory to my
name, says the LORD of hosts, then I will

a Or *by my messenger* *b* Gk: Heb *you*
c Heb lacks *temple* *d* Compare Syr Tg: Heb *its fruit, its food* *e* Another reading is *at it*

1.1: Superscription: Cf. Zech 9.1n., 12.1. *Oracle,* lit. "burden"; see Nahum 1.1n. *Malachi* means "my messenger"; see 2.7; 3.1.

1.2–5: Affirmation of God's faithfulness to Israel. 2–4: The implication is that the respective fortunes of these sibling cultures after the exile were evidence of divine favor or disfavor: Jerusalem and Judah were rebuilt; Edom was not. **2:** *I have loved you,* cf. Deut 7.7–10. *Esau, Jacob's* twin *brother,* was the ancestor of the Edomites (Gen 25.19–34; 36.1). For other anti-Edomite sentiments, see Isa 34; 63.1–6; Jer 49.7–22; Ezek 25.12–14; Am 1.11–12; Obadiah.

1.6–2.9: The priests have been unfaithful to their covenant. 1.6: Ex 20.12. **8:** *Blind* or *lame* animals were unacceptable for sacrifice (Lev 1.3; 22.17–25; Deut 15.21). **9:** *The favor* (lit. "face") *of God, that he may be gracious,* there are echoes here of the classic priestly blessing of Num 6.24–26. **10:** *Shut the temple doors* to halt unacceptable worship; cf. Isa. 1.13; Am 5.21–24. **11:** *Among the nations,* this may refer to Jewish worship in the Diaspora or to worship by Gentiles (cf. Ps 102.15). **2.3:** Ex 29.14; Nah 3.6.

send the curse on you and I will curse your
blessings; indeed I have already cursed
them,[a] because you do not lay it to heart.
3 I will rebuke your offspring, and spread
dung on your faces, the dung of your offer-
ings, and I will put you out of my pres-
ence.[b]
4 Know, then, that I have sent this com-
mand to you, that my covenant with Levi
may hold, says the LORD of hosts. 5 My
covenant with him was a covenant of life
and well-being, which I gave him; this
called for reverence, and he revered me and
stood in awe of my name. 6 True instruction
was in his mouth, and no wrong was found
on his lips. He walked with me in integrity
and uprightness, and he turned many from
iniquity. 7 For the lips of a priest should
guard knowledge, and people should seek
instruction from his mouth, for he is the
messenger of the LORD of hosts. 8 But you
have turned aside from the way; you have
caused many to stumble by your instruc-
tion; you have corrupted the covenant of
Levi, says the LORD of hosts, 9 and so I
make you despised and abased before all
the people, inasmuch as you have not kept
my ways but have shown partiality in your
instruction.
10 Have we not all one father? Has not
one God created us? Why then are we faith-
less to one another, profaning the covenant
of our ancestors? 11 Judah has been faith-
less, and abomination has been committed
in Israel and in Jerusalem; for Judah has
profaned the sanctuary of the LORD, which
he loves, and has married the daughter of a
foreign god. 12 May the LORD cut off from
the tents of Jacob anyone who does this—
any to witness[c] or answer, or to bring an
offering to the LORD of hosts.
13 And this you do as well: You cover
the LORD's altar with tears, with weeping
and groaning because he no longer regards
the offering or accepts it with favor at your
hand. 14 You ask, "Why does he not?" Be-
cause the LORD was a witness between you
and the wife of your youth, to whom you
have been faithless, though she is your
companion and your wife by covenant.
15 Did not one God make her?[d] Both flesh
and spirit are his.[e] And what does the one
God[f] desire? Godly offspring. So look to
yourselves, and do not let anyone be faith-
less to the wife of his youth. 16 For I hate[g]
divorce, says the LORD, the God of Israel,
and covering one's garment with violence,
says the LORD of hosts. So take heed to
yourselves and do not be faithless.

a Heb *it* *b* Cn Compare Gk Syr: Heb *and he shall bear you to it* *c* Cn Compare Gk: Heb *arouse* *d* Or *Has he not made one?* *e* Cn: Heb *and a remnant of spirit was his* *f* Heb *he* *g* Cn: Heb *he hates*

4: *Levi* was the priestly tribe (Num 3.45; 18.21–24; Deut 33.8–11). *Covenant with Levi,* Jer 33.21; Neh 13.29. **5:** *Covenant of life and well-being,* Num 25.10–13, where Heb "shalom" (here *well-being*) is translated "peace." **6–8:** *Instruction,* Heb "torah." **7:** Lev 10.11; Deut 21.5.

2.10–16: The people have been unfaithful to each other. On a literal level, this section concerns exogamous marriage (i.e., with outsiders) and divorce. It has also been read figuratively, that Judah has been faithless in its covenant with the LORD. **10:** *One father* probably refers to the LORD (Deut 32.6), though Abraham (Isa 51.2) and Jacob (3.6) were also father figures (*ancestors,* lit. "fathers"). *Covenant* may refer to Sinai (Ex 19.5; Deut 4.13) or to Ezra 10.3. **11:** *Abomination* usually refers to idolatry (e.g., Isa 44.19). *Daughter of a foreign god,* a foreign woman. There are several biblical prohibitions of exogamous marriage (e.g., Gen 24.3–4; Deut 7.3–4), a special concern of the postexilic period (Ezra 9–10; Neh 13.23–29; contrast with the story of Ruth, a Moabite). **13–14:** Since the LORD serves as a *witness* to human covenants including marriage (see Gen 31.50; Prov 2.17), divine sanctions were the consequences of *faithless* actions. **15:** The text is difficult and the translation uncertain (see the translators' notes). **2.16:** Though Mosaic law contains provision for divorce (Deut 24.1–4), the Bible generally considers marriage a sacred covenant (Gen 2.24; 31.50; Prov 2.17; Ezek 16.8; Hos 2.19; Mk 10.2–9; Eph 5.21–33).

17 You have wearied the LORD with
your words. Yet you say, "How have we
wearied him?" By saying, "All who do evil
are good in the sight of the LORD, and he
delights in them." Or by asking, "Where is
the God of justice?"

3 See, I am sending my messenger to pre-
pare the way before me, and the Lord
whom you seek will suddenly come to his
temple. The messenger of the covenant in
whom you delight—indeed, he is coming,
says the LORD of hosts. 2 But who can en-
dure the day of his coming, and who can
stand when he appears?

For he is like a refiner's fire and like ful-
lers' soap; 3 he will sit as a refiner and puri-
fier of silver, and he will purify the descen-
dants of Levi and refine them like gold and
silver, until they present offerings to the
LORD in righteousness.[a] 4 Then the offer-
ing of Judah and Jerusalem will be pleasing
to the LORD as in the days of old and as in
former years.

5 Then I will draw near to you for judg-
ment; I will be swift to bear witness against
the sorcerers, against the adulterers, against
those who swear falsely, against those who
oppress the hired workers in their wages,
the widow and the orphan, against those
who thrust aside the alien, and do not fear
me, says the LORD of hosts.

6 For I the LORD do not change; there-
fore you, O children of Jacob, have not
perished. 7 Ever since the days of your an-
cestors you have turned aside from my stat-
utes and have not kept them. Return to me,
and I will return to you, says the LORD of
hosts. But you say, "How shall we return?"

8 Will anyone rob God? Yet you are
robbing me! But you say, "How are we
robbing you?" In your tithes and offerings!
9 You are cursed with a curse, for you are
robbing me—the whole nation of you!
10 Bring the full tithe into the storehouse, so
that there may be food in my house, and
thus put me to the test, says the LORD of
hosts; see if I will not open the windows of
heaven for you and pour down for you an
overflowing blessing. 11 I will rebuke the lo-
cust[b] for you, so that it will not destroy the
produce of your soil; and your vine in the
field shall not be barren, says the LORD of
hosts. 12 Then all nations will count you
happy, for you will be a land of delight,
says the LORD of hosts.

13 You have spoken harsh words
against me, says the LORD. Yet you say,
"How have we spoken against you?"
14 You have said, "It is vain to serve God.
What do we profit by keeping his com-
mand or by going about as mourners be-
fore the LORD of hosts? 15 Now we count
the arrogant happy; evildoers not only
prosper, but when they put God to the test
they escape."

16 Then those who revered the LORD

a Or *right offerings to the LORD*   *b* Heb *devourer*

2.17–3.5: Judgment is coming. The prophet addresses doubts about divine justice (2.17) by announcing that God's approach is imminent (3.1) and, perhaps, more than they have bargained for (3.5). **2.17:** *All who do evil,* apparently, *are* reckoned as *good,* the people deduce, since these evildoers prosper (cf. Hab 1.13). *God of justice,* Gen 18.25; Isa 30.18. **3.1:** The identity of the *messenger,* one who announces the divine procession (Isa 40.3), is vague. Later in Malachi, the messenger is Elijah (4.5); in the New Testament, the messenger is identified as John the Baptist (Mt 11.10; Mk 1.2; Lk 1.17,76; 7.27). See 4.5n. **5:** Contrast with Isa 40.1–3, where the messenger announced news of comfort. The list of offenses is a common prophetic theme; see Isa 1.23; Jer 7.5–10; Ezek 22.7–13; Zech 7.9–10.

3.6–12: A call to repentance. 6: *I the LORD do not change,* another response to whether God is just or reliable (2.17); cf. Num 23.19. **7:** Zech 1.3. **8:** *Tithes,* a tenth of all agricultural produce (see Lev 27.30–32; Deut 14.28–29). *Offerings,* Num 18.25–32. **10–12:** Obedience brings the blessings of covenant (Deut 28.8–12). **10:** *Storehouse,* Neh 13.10–13. *Open the windows of heaven,* i.e., bring rain (Gen 7.11; 8.2). **11:** *Locust,* see Joel 1.4; 2.25. **12:** Isa 62.4.

3.13–4.3: The righteous and wicked receive their just deserts. 3.14: Isa 58.3. **15:** Cf. 2.17; Job 21.7–15. **16:** Unique in Malachi, this is a sentence of narration. *Book,* here the righteous constitute a select group (contrast with, e.g., Deut 7.6) whose identities are hidden in a heavenly scroll (Ex 32.32–34; Ps 69.28;

spoke with one another. The LORD took
note and listened, and a book of remem-
brance was written before him of those
who revered the LORD and thought on his
name. 17 They shall be mine, says the LORD
of hosts, my special possession on the day
when I act, and I will spare them as parents
spare their children who serve them.
18 Then once more you shall see the differ-
ence between the righteous and the wicked,
between one who serves God and one who
does not serve him.

4 [a]See, the day is coming, burning like an
oven, when all the arrogant and all evil-
doers will be stubble; the day that comes
shall burn them up, says the LORD of hosts,
so that it will leave them neither root nor
branch. 2 But for you who revere my name
the sun of righteousness shall rise, with
healing in its wings. You shall go out leap-
ing like calves from the stall. 3 And you
shall tread down the wicked, for they will
be ashes under the soles of your feet, on the
day when I act, says the LORD of hosts.

4 Remember the teaching of my servant
Moses, the statutes and ordinances that I
commanded him at Horeb for all Israel.

5 Lo, I will send you the prophet Elijah
before the great and terrible day of the
LORD comes. 6 He will turn the hearts of
parents to their children and the hearts of
children to their parents, so that I will not
come and strike the land with a curse.[b]

a Ch 4.1-6 are Ch 3.19-24 in Heb *b* Or *a ban of utter destruction*

87.6; Isa 4.3; 65.6; Dan 7.10; 12.1; Rev 20.12; 21.27); see also Esth 2.23; 6.1–3. **17:** *Special possession,* Ex 19.5; Deut 7.6; Ps 135.4. **4.1:** Cf. 3.2–5. **2:** *Sun . . . with healing in its wings,* the image is the winged sun-disk, a common motif in ancient Near Eastern art.

4.4–6: Two appendices. The first (v. 4) functions as a conclusion to the entire collection of prophetic writings which, in Hebrew, began with Joshua 1.1–2 (see *my servant Moses* there and here). The second (vv. 4–6) serves as a commentary on 3.1. **4:** *Teaching,* Heb "torah." *Horeb,* alternate name for Sinai, the site of the giving of the law to Moses (Deut 5.1–3) and of a revelation to Elijah (1 Kings 19.1–18). **5–6:** See 3.1n. For an expansion of this tradition in early Christian tradition, see Mt 11.7–15; 17.10–13; Mk 6.14–16; Lk 1.17; cf. Sir 48.10.

THE NEW TESTAMENT

THE NEW COVENANT COMMONLY CALLED
THE NEW TESTAMENT OF OUR LORD
AND SAVIOR JESUS CHRIST

New Revised Standard Version

INTRODUCTION
to the Gospels

THE LITERARY GENRE OF THE GOSPELS

THE OPENING OF Mark's Gospel, "The beginning of the good news [or "gospel"] of Jesus Christ, the Son of God" (1.1), uses the word "gospel" for the message about salvation through Jesus. The word "gospel" (Gk "euangelion"; NRSV: "good news") always refers either to the act of preaching (1 Thess 1.5, NRSV: "our message of the gospel") or its content (Acts 15.7, NRSV: "message of the good news"; 20.24, NRSV: "good news"). Outside the New Testament and other early Christian writings, the term was used for various happy announcements, such as a military victory, the birth of a son, or a wedding. An inscription from 9 BCE uses the noun (in the plural) to refer to the past event of the birth of the emperor Augustus: "the birthday of the god was for the world the beginning of 'joyful messages' which have gone forth because of him." The idea that an emperor's birth, coming of age, and ascent to the throne was "good news" for the world would have come to mind when Christian missionaries came preaching "good news." The noun is not used for a literary genre until the mid-second century CE (Justin Martyr, *Dialogue with Trypho* 10.2; Irenaeus, *Against the Heresies* 50.26.6).

The use of the word "gospel" in Mark's introduction presumably led to its being adopted as the designation for written accounts of the ministry, teaching, death, and resurrection of Jesus. Short formulas in Paul's letters show that the "good news" of the early mission focused on the death, resurrection, and exaltation of Jesus (1 Thess 1.9–10; Rom 1.2–4; 1 Cor 15.3–5). Mark has expanded this to include Jesus' own preaching of the kingdom of God (Mk 1.14–15). So far as we know, Mark was the first to create a distinctive literary form by combining the church's preaching about Jesus (his words and deeds) with a narrative account of Jesus' life and ministry. Writings that have been surmised to predate Mark are collections of sayings with little or no narrative framework.

By presenting a narrative about Jesus as the basis of Christian preaching (see Lk 1.1–4), the Gospel writers (evangelists) assume that the life of Jesus provides evidence for its claims. By providing an account of Jesus from his emergence on the public stage through his trial and death, Mark presents a "life" (Gk "bios") of his subject. The ancient "bios" should not be confused with a biography, which explicates the subject's origins, family, cultural influences, and character development, and tends to emphasize uniqueness and individuality. Ancient writers often characterized persons as types, and the narratives of their lives reflected a view that individuals had fixed characters from birth rather than personalities that developed through life.

Even granting such differences, scholars disagree over the extent to which the Gospels follow conventions of ancient biography. Because it concerns a figure with a crucial place in the history of God's relationship with Israel, the story of Jesus is closer to Jewish accounts of Moses or a prophet like Elijah than to the typical Greco-Roman biographies of rulers or philosophers (e.g., Xenephon, *Agesilaus*; Isocrates, *Evagoras*; Tacitus, *Agricola*; or Lucian, *Demonax*), which had a wider scope, including an account of the preliminary education of the subject of the biography. Greco-Roman biographies were addressed to a social and literary elite, which may explain why the Gospels, addressed to a much broader audience, do not match them very closely. Philo's *Life of Moses* adopts a Hellenistic-style laudatory biography for a Jewish subject. Echoes of the life of Moses as related in Exodus and other Jewish sources appear in Matthew's version of the birth and infancy of Jesus (Mt 1–2).

Since the genre "biography" emerged from Greek historical writing, the question of whether or not the Gospels belong to this genre often involves a prior judgment concerning their historical plausibility. Scholars who reject biography as a description of the Gospels often overemphasize the ideological or legendary elements found in the narratives. They prefer to read the Gospels as etiological legends that explain the emergence of a new religion or as ideological representations of the christology of particular early Christian communities. Such writings do not intend primarily to provide historical information about their subject. Rather, they operate like myths and symbols to support Christian beliefs and practices.

Second-century CE authors, on the other hand, both adherents of Christianity like Justin Martyr and opponents like Celsus, presumed that the evangelists intended to provide information. Justin Martyr's designation of the Gospels as "memoirs" (Gk "hypomnemata"; *1 Apology* 1.67.3) suggests something less than the full literary biography, and something more like a gathering of notes about the subject and his teaching. This perception may have been enhanced by the fact that early Christians disseminated their writings using the codex (similar to a bound book) rather than the scroll. Though modern readers often think of the codex as a technological advance over the scroll, the ancients did not. Serious literary works were copied onto scrolls. Notes, preliminary drafts, and all sorts of records were kept in codices. Thus their physical appearance would suggest to an ancient reader that the Gospels were something like educational handbooks, not examples of high literary art. Papias's comment that Mark is "not in order" (Eusebius, *History of the Church* 3.39.5) shows that even some Christian readers considered it an unfinished composition. Papias also noted that Matthew was a more polished work (Eusebius, *History of the Church* 3.39.16). Luke's prologue states that he intends to correct the deficiencies in earlier accounts (1.1–4). Such concerns indicate that Mark's earliest readers treated the Gospel as a rough life of Jesus. Such a biography invited the expansions in content and revisions of style that Matthew and Luke subsequently undertook.

THE SOURCES OF THE GOSPELS

A historical genre does not necessarily guarantee historical accuracy or reliability. Nor did the evangelists or their first readers engage in historical analysis. Their aim was to confirm Christian faith (Lk 1.4; Jn 20.31). Scholars generally agree that the Gospels were written forty to sixty years after the death of Jesus. They thus do not present an eyewitness or contemporary account of Jesus' life and teaching. Even the language has changed. Though Greek had become the common language used between groups whose primary languages were different in the eastern Roman Empire, and inscriptions and fragments of Greek translations of the Hebrew Bible show that Greek was used even among Jews within Judea, Jesus, his disciples, and the crowds would have spoken Aramaic. Despite scholarly efforts to detect an underlying Aramaic original for Mark or Matthew, it is probable that all the evangelists wrote in the common ("koine") Greek of their day. Further, the vast majority of Hebrew Bible citations in the New Testament follow the Greek translation of the Hebrew Bible (the Septuagint).

Large sections of Matthew, Mark, and Luke repeat the stories about and sayings of Jesus in nearly identical words. Hence these three Gospels are referred to as the "Synoptic" Gospels (from Gk "synoptikos," "view together"). At the linguistic level, both Luke and Matthew improve on Markan style, smoothing out inelegant expressions and repetitions. Luke eliminates Markan parataxis (one short phrase following another without indicating how they are related) by employing balancing particles and subordinating clauses. Matthew follows Mark's outline, though the insertion of considerable sections of discourse material may obscure that relationship for the casual reader. Luke knows most of Mark but has no parallels to Mk 6.45–8.26; whether Luke has chosen to omit this section or has a different version of Mark remains unclear. Detailed analysis of the traditions shared by Matthew, Mark, and Luke provides strong support for the view that Mark was the earliest

Gospel. But, given its rough, draft-like composition, both Matthew and Luke revised it extensively.

Further study of additional material shared by Matthew and Luke shows a number of close verbal parallels in passages such as the temptation of Jesus (Mt 4.2–11; Lk 4.2–13), the Beatitudes (Lk 6.20–23; Mt 5.3,6,4,11–12), the parable of the lost sheep (Lk 15.4–7; Mt 18.12–14), and the Lord's Prayer (Lk 11.2–4; Mt 6.9–13). These parallels include various types of sayings, controversy stories, and parables. Scholars have hypothesized that a collection of such material must have been circulating in the early churches, and have designated it with the symbol "Q," from the German "Quelle" ("source"). In 1945, a library of religious treatises in Coptic was discovered near Nag Hammadi in Egypt. They included just such a "sayings book," the *Gospel of Thomas*. Subsequently, sayings from a variant tradition of this Gospel in Greek were identified among Greek papyri. The *Gospel of Thomas* is not "Q": Some of its sayings and parables appear to have been taken from the Synoptic Gospels rather than from earlier oral tradition. But its discovery provides evidence that such sayings collections existed.

Scholars presume that the Gospel writers may have had other such notebook-like collections of items such as parables and miracle stories. Presumably additional items, such as genealogies, canticles, and other legends in the infancy narratives of Matthew and Luke, were not created by the evangelists but come from earlier tradition. Similarly, some of the material found only in Matthew or in Luke is not likely to be the author's creation. There may also have been a pre-Markan narrative of the passion and death of Jesus; some scholars think that most of Mark's narrative came from such a source, while others maintain that there is no evidence for such an account. The origin of the story of Jesus' passion is unclear, and some details may have been based on biblical descriptions of the suffering righteous one.

While the Synoptic Gospels have a close relationship based on the literary relationships between them, the Fourth Gospel, the Gospel of John, presents a much greater puzzle. Its chronology of Jesus' ministry is quite different, as are many narrative details. Jesus spends three years preaching, during which he journeys between Galilee and Jerusalem. (In the Synoptic Gospels he visits Jerusalem only once, at the end of a ministry that apparently lasted less than a year.) The episode denouncing the sellers in the Temple, which enrages the religious authorities and leads to his death in the Synoptics, occurs near the beginning of the three-year ministry in John (Jn 2.13–22). John claims that Jesus' popularity with Jerusalem crowds after he dramatically restored Lazarus to life awakened political fears for the safety of the nation (Jn 11.45–57; 12.9–11). John's account of the passion also differs markedly: There is no agony; conscious of his unity with the Father and the cross as his exaltation and return to pre-existent glory, Jesus controls all the events; he engages the Roman governor in an ironic discussion of kingship; and John has a disciple-witness, a Jerusalemite, who does not flee with the others. Is this unnamed "disciple whom Jesus loved" (Jn 21.7,20; cf. 19.26; 20.2) a symbolic creation of the Evangelist? Some scholars think so; others suggest that he was a historical individual, the source of much of the Fourth Gospel's unique tradition and theology, as the text alleges (19.35; 21.24). What led John to compose such a unique variant on an outline of Jesus' life that still has a recognizable similarity to Mark (and in some instances to Luke)? Some scholars would use the parallels as indications of a shorter sketch of Jesus' life known to both authors. Others suggest that the Gospels of Mark, and perhaps Luke, were already circulating in the Evangelist's area. He assumes that readers know some other account of Jesus' life and teaching, and formulates a different version of who Jesus is and what he taught based on the insight that Jesus of Nazareth was not just a miracle-worker, a prophet, or a charismatic Jewish teacher, but the incarnate Son of God. That claim constitutes the flash point between Jesus and the Jewish authorities throughout the narrative.

Readers may ask similar questions for each of the Synoptics. What are the special features in that

Evangelist's presentation of Jesus and of those who follow Jesus? Each author has done more than compile a notebook of traditions about Jesus. Rather, each has shaped the narrative to emphasize particular features of Jesus and his teaching. Scholars often use those elements as clues about the church setting in which each Gospel was written.

The Gospel According to MATTHEW

The Gospel of Matthew highlights the Jewish origin and identity of Jesus and his first followers more than any other piece of early Christian literature. In Matthew Jesus is God's anointed, or messiah, and the one who best envisions and interprets God's plan for God's people. Jesus is presented as a great teacher of Israel like Moses for the present age. Jesus speaks with wisdom and authority reminiscent of Moses, unlike the teachers of Matthew's day whom the author rejects (7.28–29; 23.2–3). The Gospel draws from Israel's history. Jesus' lineage is traced back to Abraham. The title of the Gospel is, "the account of the genealogy of Jesus the Messiah, the son of David, the son of Abraham" (1.1). There is little mistaking here the Jewishness of the author, of Jesus, and the audience envisaged in the Gospel. The author frequently uses biblical quotations to explain and validate the actions of Jesus. Many of these are introduced with a phrase indicating the fulfillment of a prophecy (1.22; 2.15; 2.17; 2.23; 4.14; 8.17; 12.17; 13.35; 21.4; 27.9). The formula citations help to ground Matthew's story within the history and heroes of ancient Israel.

In Matthew Jesus presents an understanding of ancient history and recent events, of the Torah, and of the future as the proper path for Israel. This counsel is expressed, for example, in the parables unique to Matthew in chs 20–22 and 25 and in the Sermon on the Mount (chs 5–7). Some of Matthew's contemporaries, however, disagreed with his understanding of Jewish history and his claims about Jesus. For this reason Matthew is also the most contentious and polemical of the Gospels. There was a struggle for leadership and direction following 70 CE in Israel. Matthew's community or church was in the midst of that struggle. This tension is a defining feature of the Gospel. The central opponents in Matthew are the Pharisees. They are characterized hyperbolically as "hypocrites," and teachers who "lock people out of the kingdom of heaven" (23.13,23,25). A contemporary of Matthew, the Jewish historian Josephus, provides another picture of the Pharisees (*Ant.* 13.297,399–417). He says Pharisees were popular with the people. They were admired for being "the most accurate interpreters of the law." And they played a central role in the formation of rabbinic Judaism, a coalition that ultimately provided for the survival of Judaism after the fall of the Temple in Jerusalem. Pharisees also developed legal interpretations called "the traditions of the elders" which were not recorded in the law of Moses. In Matthew's day serious tensions developed between various Jewish groups over which laws and traditions would govern Israel.

It is no surprise then that in Matthew we find Jesus arguing about tradition and interpretation to an extent we do not find in other Gospels. Jesus explicitly takes up the argument about "the tradition of the elders" with the Pharisees in 15.1–20. He has similar disputes with Pharisees over sabbath observance (12.1–8), divorce (19.1–9), taxes (22.15–22), and the greatest commandment (22.34–40). The competition between Matthew's community formed around Jesus and the group represented by the Pharisees builds as the Gospel unfolds, culminating in ch 23. Here Jesus elaborates at length on the inadequacies of the Pharisees, their influence, and their actions.

The occasionally highly charged language in Matthew is best understood in terms of an inter-Jewish conflict and should be interpreted against the backdrop of the instability characteristic of first-century Palestine. Failure to appreciate this feature of the Gospel's setting has led at times to unfortunate misunderstandings of certain key Matthean texts. A prominent example is the passage known as the "cry of all the people," associated with the trial of Jesus and found only in Matthew 27.25. Some within the Christian tradition have mistakenly taken this passage to mean "the Jews" as a race should perpetually be held accountable for killing Jesus. In fact, read in the context of Matthew's post–70 CE setting, 27.25 emerges as a charge which, while caustic, is nevertheless typical of a people or group divided against itself, as was the case in Matthew's day. Polemical passages in the Gospel should be understood within their proper social context and not as later Christian denunciations of all Jews.

This Gospel is a presentation of the life and teachings of Jesus intended for a particular community. Issues of local governance (18.6–20), ethics (chs 5–7), succession and leadership (16.18–20), how to handle conflict with opposing groups and authorities (17.15–21; 23.1–3), and how the community should face the future are examples of the advice given directly to Matthew's church. The author has written his story of Jesus mindful of the predicament and problems of his own community.

While the traditional place of origin for Matthew has been considered the city of Antioch in ancient western Syria, many now consider a southern Galilean city, Tiberias or Sepphoris, a more likely location for the writing of the Gospel. It was in Galilee that followers of a Pharisaic party and devoted Jewish followers of Jesus would have encountered and rivaled one another. The Gospel was written after the Gospel of Mark. All but sixty verses of the Gospel of Mark appear in Matthew. The author's modifications of Mark's story are easily identified. For example, Matthew's depiction of Jesus' disciples, of Jewish law, and of the community's relationship to those in power modify the earlier Gospel of Mark. Another major source used by Matthew is the collection of sayings of Jesus designated by scholars as "Q" (from the German word "Quelle," meaning "source"). Luke also used this source, as the many very close parallels found only in those two Gospels indicate.

Matthew was written following the first Jewish revolt against Rome and the destruction of the Temple in 70 CE by the Roman general and eventual emperor, Titus. This monumental historical event is most likely referred to in 21.43–44 and 22.7. In terms of Roman political history the Gospel belongs to the end of the Flavian dynasty or shortly thereafter. In terms of the social and religious developments in Israel, Matthew belongs to that fluid and uncertain period between the fall of the Jerusalem Temple in 70 and the emergence of rabbinic Judaism as the decisive force and voice in the land between 135 and 200. Matthew's Gospel then dates from the last decade of the first century to the early second century.

1 An account of the genealogy[a] of Jesus
the Messiah,[b] the son of David, the
son of Abraham.
2 Abraham was the father of Isaac, and
Isaac the father of Jacob, and Jacob the fa-
ther of Judah and his brothers, 3 and Judah
the father of Perez and Zerah by Tamar,
and Perez the father of Hezron, and Hezron
the father of Aram, 4 and Aram the father
of Aminadab, and Aminadab the father of
Nahshon, and Nahshon the father of Sal-
mon, 5 and Salmon the father of Boaz by
Rahab, and Boaz the father of Obed by
Ruth, and Obed the father of Jesse, 6 and
Jesse the father of King David.
And David was the father of Solomon by
the wife of Uriah, 7 and Solomon the father
of Rehoboam, and Rehoboam the father of
Abijah, and Abijah the father of Asaph,[c]
8 and Asaph[c] the father of Jehoshaphat,
and Jehoshaphat the father of Joram, and
Joram the father of Uzziah, 9 and Uzziah
the father of Jotham, and Jotham the father
of Ahaz, and Ahaz the father of Hezekiah,
10 and Hezekiah the father of Manasseh,
and Manasseh the father of Amos,[d] and
Amos[d] the father of Josiah, 11 and Josiah
the father of Jechoniah and his brothers, at
the time of the deportation to Babylon.
12 And after the deportation to Bab-
ylon: Jechoniah was the father of Salathiel,
and Salathiel the father of Zerubbabel,
13 and Zerubbabel the father of Abiud, and
Abiud the father of Eliakim, and Eliakim
the father of Azor, 14 and Azor the father of
Zadok, and Zadok the father of Achim,
and Achim the father of Eliud, 15 and Eliud
the father of Eleazar, and Eleazar the father
of Matthan, and Matthan the father of Ja-
cob, 16 and Jacob the father of Joseph the
husband of Mary, of whom Jesus was born,
who is called the Messiah.[e]
17 So all the generations from Abraham
to David are fourteen generations; and
from David to the deportation to Babylon,
fourteen generations; and from the depor-
tation to Babylon to the Messiah,[e] four-
teen generations.

18 Now the birth of Jesus the Messiah[b]
took place in this way. When his mother
Mary had been engaged to Joseph, but be-
fore they lived together, she was found to
be with child from the Holy Spirit. 19 Her
husband Joseph, being a righteous man and
unwilling to expose her to public disgrace,
planned to dismiss her quietly. 20 But just
when he had resolved to do this, an angel of
the Lord appeared to him in a dream and
said, "Joseph, son of David, do not be
afraid to take Mary as your wife, for the
child conceived in her is from the Holy
Spirit. 21 She will bear a son, and you are to
name him Jesus, for he will save his people
from their sins." 22 All this took place to

a Or *birth* *b* Or *Jesus Christ* *c* Other ancient authorities read *Asa* *d* Other ancient authorities read *Amon* *e* Or *the Christ*

1.1–17: Jesus' place in Israel's family tree (Lk 3.23–38). **1:** *Son of David, son of Abraham, Messiah,* titles and heroes that place Jesus and the Gospel within Israel's history. *Messiah,* Heb term for "anointed," Gk "Christos." **3–6:** Jesus' genealogy is largely patriarchal, but includes four women from the Hebrew Bible: *Tamar* (Gen 38), *Rahab* (Josh 2), *Ruth,* and Bathsheba, *the wife of Uriah* (2 Sam 11–12; 1 Kings 1), breaking with the tradition of reciting only the male forebears. Each acted independently, in some cases scandalously, at critical junctures in Israel's history to ensure the continuation of the Davidic line. **11:** *Deportation,* the exile (2 Kings 24.8–16). **17:** *Fourteen,* the numerical value of "David" in Hebrew; some names have been omitted (Ahaziah, Joash, and Amaziah, v. 8; see 1 Chr 3.11–12) to form the pattern, which is presumably created as a memory aid.

1.18–25: Jesus' conception and birth (Lk 1.26–2.40). **18:** Mary is a virgin, though pregnant (Lk 1.34). **19:** *Joseph,* only in Matthew's Gospel is the character and the role of Jesus' father developed. *Dismiss her quietly,* divorce her discreetly. **20:** Angels and dreams frequently communicate God's plan in Matthew. **21:** The first mention of the name *Jesus,* the Gk form of the Heb Joshua, "The LORD saves/helps." This highlights the mission and purpose of the child. **22–23:** Isa 7.14; the first of Matthew's fulfillment citations, which help explain that what is occurring is God's plan.

fulfill what had been spoken by the Lord
through the prophet:
23 "Look, the virgin shall conceive and
bear a son,
and they shall name him
Emmanuel,"
which means, "God is with us." 24 When
Joseph awoke from sleep, he did as the an-
gel of the Lord commanded him; he took
her as his wife, 25 but had no marital rela-
tions with her until she had borne a son;[a]
and he named him Jesus.

2 In the time of King Herod, after Jesus
was born in Bethlehem of Judea, wise
men[b] from the East came to Jerusalem,
2 asking, "Where is the child who has been
born king of the Jews? For we observed his
star at its rising,[c] and have come to pay
him homage." 3 When King Herod heard
this, he was frightened, and all Jerusalem
with him; 4 and calling together all the chief
priests and scribes of the people, he in-
quired of them where the Messiah[d] was to
be born. 5 They told him, "In Bethlehem of
Judea; for so it has been written by the
prophet:
6 'And you, Bethlehem, in the land
of Judah,
are by no means least among the
rulers of Judah;
for from you shall come a ruler
who is to shepherd[e] my
people Israel.' "
7 Then Herod secretly called for the
wise men[b] and learned from them the ex-
act time when the star had appeared. 8 Then
he sent them to Bethlehem, saying, "Go
and search diligently for the child; and
when you have found him, bring me word
so that I may also go and pay him hom-
age." 9 When they had heard the king, they
set out; and there, ahead of them, went the
star that they had seen at its rising,[c] until
it stopped over the place where the child
was. 10 When they saw that the star had
stopped,[f] they were overwhelmed with
joy. 11 On entering the house, they saw the
child with Mary his mother; and they knelt
down and paid him homage. Then, opening
their treasure chests, they offered him gifts
of gold, frankincense, and myrrh. 12 And
having been warned in a dream not to re-
turn to Herod, they left for their own coun-
try by another road.
13 Now after they had left, an angel of
the Lord appeared to Joseph in a dream
and said, "Get up, take the child and his
mother, and flee to Egypt, and remain there
until I tell you; for Herod is about to search
for the child, to destroy him." 14 Then Jo-
seph[g] got up, took the child and his moth-
er by night, and went to Egypt, 15 and re-
mained there until the death of Herod. This
was to fulfill what had been spoken by the
Lord through the prophet, "Out of Egypt I
have called my son."
16 When Herod saw that he had been
tricked by the wise men,[b] he was infuriat-
ed, and he sent and killed all the children in
and around Bethlehem who were two years
old or under, according to the time that he
had learned from the wise men.[b] 17 Then

a Other ancient authorities read *her firstborn son*
b Or *astrologers*; Gk *magi* *c* Or *in the East*
d Or *the Christ* *e* Or *rule* *f* Gk *saw the star*
g Gk *he*

2.1–12: The birth of Jesus and Herod the Great. 1: *The time of King Herod* places the birth of Jesus within a fixed time period and set of political realities. Herod, the client king of Judea, ruled 37–4 BCE; Augustus, the first Roman emperor, was his patron. *Wise men* (Gk "magoi"), literate, political officials in the courts of Parthia, Armenia, or regions east of Judea. Foreign regimes often sent emissaries to greet and give gifts to new kings or rulers. The visit highlights the conflict between the king of Israel chosen by God, Jesus, and the king of Israel chosen by the Romans, Herod. A similar account of "Magi" is in the Roman writers Dio 63:7 and Suetonius, *Life of Nero* 13. **2:** *Star,* Num 24.17. **5–6:** Mic 5.2. **11:** *Gold, frankincense, and myrrh,* Isa 60.6. Precious metals and costly, fragrant spices and resins are appropriate gifts for a king.

2.13–23: The flight to Egypt and return. 15: *Out of Egypt . . . ,* quoting Hos 11.1, Matthew explicitly compares Jesus to Moses. **16:** Herod's action recalls the command of the king of Egypt in Ex 1.16. **18:**

was fulfilled what had been spoken
through the prophet Jeremiah:
18 "A voice was heard in Ramah,
wailing and loud lamentation,
Rachel weeping for her children;
she refused to be consoled, because
they are no more."
19 When Herod died, an angel of the
Lord suddenly appeared in a dream to Jo-
seph in Egypt and said, 20 "Get up, take the
child and his mother, and go to the land
of Israel, for those who were seeking the
child's life are dead." 21 Then Joseph[a] got
up, took the child and his mother, and went
to the land of Israel. 22 But when he heard
that Archelaus was ruling over Judea in
place of his father Herod, he was afraid
to go there. And after being warned in a
dream, he went away to the district of Gali-
lee. 23 There he made his home in a town
called Nazareth, so that what had been
spoken through the prophets might be ful-
filled, "He will be called a Nazorean."

3 In those days John the Baptist appeared
in the wilderness of Judea, proclaiming,
2 "Repent, for the kingdom of heaven has
come near."[b] 3 This is the one of whom the
prophet Isaiah spoke when he said,
"The voice of one crying out in
the wilderness:
'Prepare the way of the Lord,
make his paths straight.' "
4 Now John wore clothing of camel's hair
with a leather belt around his waist, and his
food was locusts and wild honey. 5 Then
the people of Jerusalem and all Judea were
going out to him, and all the region along
the Jordan, 6 and they were baptized by
him in the river Jordan, confessing their
sins.
7 But when he saw many Pharisees and
Sadducees coming for baptism, he said to
them, "You brood of vipers! Who warned
you to flee from the wrath to come? 8 Bear
fruit worthy of repentance. 9 Do not pre-
sume to say to yourselves, 'We have Abra-
ham as our ancestor'; for I tell you, God is
able from these stones to raise up children
to Abraham. 10 Even now the ax is lying at
the root of the trees; every tree therefore
that does not bear good fruit is cut down
and thrown into the fire.
11 "I baptize you with[c] water for re-
pentance, but one who is more powerful
than I is coming after me; I am not worthy
to carry his sandals. He will baptize you
with[c] the Holy Spirit and fire. 12 His win-
nowing fork is in his hand, and he will clear

a Gk *he* *b* Or *is at hand* *c* Or *in*

Jer 31.15. *Rachel,* wife of Jacob, is buried near Bethlehem (Gen 35.16–20); in the quotation she stands for all Israelite mothers. **19:** *Herod died* in 4 BCE. **20:** Cf. Ex 4.19. **22:** Upon Herod's death his kingdom was divided into four parts. *Archelaus,* one of his sons who was almost as brutal as his father, ruled over the area of *Judea* in the south from 4 BCE to 6 CE. *Galilee* to the north was under the rule of Herod Antipas. **23:** This citation has no known source.

3.1–12: Preparing the way (Mk 1.2–8; Lk 3.1–18; Jn 1.19–28). John's role as precursor to Jesus is emphasized, and his message is described as one of repentance and preparation. Josephus provides a fuller description of John in *Ant.* 18.116. **2:** *The kingdom of heaven,* Matthew's usual circumlocution for "the kingdom of God"; such phrasing allowed speakers and writers to avoid the word "God." **3:** Isa 40.3. **4:** *Camel's hair . . . honey,* John's ascetic style is in keeping with that of traditional prophets (2 Kings 1.8; Zech 13.4). *Locusts* were allowable as food (Lev 11.20–23). **7–12:** *Pharisees and Sadducees,* two of the major groups in Judaism of the time; they differed about interpretation of the Torah. The Sadducees held to a strict view of the primacy of the Torah, the first five books of the Hebrew Bible; they therefore did not accept teachings, including resurrection, based upon the "oral law" or tradition that the Pharisees did accept. John's demeanor toward them evokes that of the Essenes, the third group (Josephus, *War* 2.119–66). The call to repentance may reflect belief in an imminent judgment and culmination of history. **8:** *Bear fruit,* one of the goals of life according to Jesus (7.16–20; 13.23,30). **11:** *Baptize . . . repentance,* in Mark baptism includes forgiveness (Mk 1.4). According to Josephus, John baptized those who had purified their souls (*Ant.* 18.17). *Fire,* an agent of purification, not destruction. **12:** A *winnowing fork* was

his threshing floor and will gather his
wheat into the granary; but the chaff he
will burn with unquenchable fire."
13 Then Jesus came from Galilee to
John at the Jordan, to be baptized by him.
14 John would have prevented him, saying,
"I need to be baptized by you, and do you
come to me?" 15 But Jesus answered him,
"Let it be so now; for it is proper for us in
this way to fulfill all righteousness." Then
he consented. 16 And when Jesus had been
baptized, just as he came up from the wa-
ter, suddenly the heavens were opened to
him and he saw the Spirit of God descend-
ing like a dove and alighting on him. 17 And
a voice from heaven said, "This is my Son,
the Beloved,[a] with whom I am well
pleased."

4 Then Jesus was led up by the Spirit into
the wilderness to be tempted by the
devil. 2 He fasted forty days and forty
nights, and afterwards he was famished.
3 The tempter came and said to him, "If you
are the Son of God, command these stones
to become loaves of bread." 4 But he an-
swered, "It is written,

'One does not live by bread alone,
but by every word that comes from
the mouth of God.' "

5 Then the devil took him to the holy
city and placed him on the pinnacle of the
temple, 6 saying to him, "If you are the Son
of God, throw yourself down; for it is writ-
ten,

'He will command his angels
concerning you,'
and 'On their hands they will bear
you up,
so that you will not dash your foot
against a stone.' "

7 Jesus said to him, "Again it is written, 'Do
not put the Lord your God to the test.' "
8 Again, the devil took him to a very
high mountain and showed him all the
kingdoms of the world and their splendor;
9 and he said to him, "All these I will give
you, if you will fall down and worship me."
10 Jesus said to him, "Away with you, Sa-
tan! for it is written,

'Worship the Lord your God,
and serve only him.' "

11 Then the devil left him, and suddenly an-
gels came and waited on him.

12 Now when Jesus[b] heard that John
had been arrested, he withdrew to Galilee.
13 He left Nazareth and made his home in
Capernaum by the sea, in the territory of
Zebulun and Naphtali, 14 so that what had
been spoken through the prophet Isaiah
might be fulfilled:
15 "Land of Zebulun, land of Naphtali,

a Or *my beloved Son* *b* Gk *he*

used to toss grain in the air to separate the *chaff* or husks from the seed. *Fire,* here destruction (of the wicked, 1 Enoch 48.9).

3.13–17: Jesus' baptism (Mk 1.9–11; Lk 3.21–22; Jn 1.31–34). **13–14:** The assertion of Jesus' superiority may reflect an early dispute between followers of the Baptist and Jesus (see 11.2–11; cf. Acts 19.1–5). *The Jordan* River is east and south of Nazareth. **15:** *Righteousness* or "justice," a crucial notion for Matthew, is something both Jesus and his followers must exhibit (5.20). **16:** *Dove,* symbol of the new creation after the flood (Gen 8.8–12; for the flood as the end of the age, Mt 24.38; 1 Pet 3.20–21). **17:** A combination of Ps 2.7 and Isa 42.1; see also Gen 22.2. The *voice* makes a public declaration; cf. Mk 1.11.

4.1–11: Jesus and the devil. 1: *To be tempted,* God tests the faith of the righteous (Gen 22.1; Deut 13.3; Ps 81.7). **2:** *Forty,* a conventional number for a lengthy period as well as Israel's sojourn in the wilderness (Ex 34.28; cf. Ex 24.18; 1 Kings 19.8). **3:** This is the first time Jesus is referred to as *Son of God,* a title by which the emperor Augustus was known (cf. the challenge put to Jesus on the cross, Mt 27.40–43). **4:** Deut 8.3. **5:** *Holy city,* Jerusalem. **6:** Ps 91.11–12. **7:** Deut 6.16. **10:** Deut 6.13.

4.12–25: The beginning of Jesus' ministry. 12–17: Mk 1.14–15; Lk 4.14–15. **12:** John's arrest serves as the stimulus for the beginning of Jesus' public ministry. **13:** Only Matthew has Jesus and his disciples living in *Capernaum,* on the northwest coast of the *sea* of Galilee. **15–16:** Isa 9.1–2. *Galilee of the Gentiles,* in both Isa 9 and 1 Macc 5.15, Galilee is referred to as under the control of non-Israelites.

on the road by the sea, across the
Jordan, Galilee of the
Gentiles—
16 the people who sat in darkness
have seen a great light,
and for those who sat in the region
and shadow of death
light has dawned."
17 From that time Jesus began to proclaim,
"Repent, for the kingdom of heaven has
come near."[a]

18 As he walked by the Sea of Galilee,
he saw two brothers, Simon, who is called
Peter, and Andrew his brother, casting a
net into the sea—for they were fishermen.
19 And he said to them, "Follow me, and I
will make you fish for people." 20 Immedi-
ately they left their nets and followed him.
21 As he went from there, he saw two other
brothers, James son of Zebedee and his
brother John, in the boat with their father
Zebedee, mending their nets, and he called
them. 22 Immediately they left the boat and
their father, and followed him.

23 Jesus[b] went throughout Galilee,
teaching in their synagogues and proclaim-
ing the good news[c] of the kingdom and
curing every disease and every sickness
among the people. 24 So his fame spread
throughout all Syria, and they brought to
him all the sick, those who were afflicted
with various diseases and pains, demoni-
acs, epileptics, and paralytics, and he cured
them. 25 And great crowds followed him
from Galilee, the Decapolis, Jerusalem, Ju-
dea, and from beyond the Jordan.

5 When Jesus[d] saw the crowds, he went
up the mountain; and after he sat
down, his disciples came to him. 2 Then he
began to speak, and taught them, saying:
3 "Blessed are the poor in spirit, for
theirs is the kingdom of heaven.
4 "Blessed are those who mourn, for
they will be comforted.
5 "Blessed are the meek, for they will
inherit the earth.
6 "Blessed are those who hunger and
thirst for righteousness, for they will be
filled.
7 "Blessed are the merciful, for they will
receive mercy.
8 "Blessed are the pure in heart, for they
will see God.
9 "Blessed are the peacemakers, for they
will be called children of God.
10 "Blessed are those who are persecut-
ed for righteousness' sake, for theirs is the
kingdom of heaven.
11 "Blessed are you when people revile
you and persecute you and utter all kinds of
evil against you falsely[e] on my account.
12 Rejoice and be glad, for your reward is
great in heaven, for in the same way they
persecuted the prophets who were before
you.
13 "You are the salt of the earth; but if

a Or *is at hand* *b* Gk *He* *c* Gk *gospel* *d* Gk *he*
e Other ancient authorities lack *falsely*

Matthew is concerned with a geographical designation, not its ethnic makeup. **17:** See 3.2. Jesus' preaching and John's are identical. **18–22:** Mk 1.16–20; Lk 5.1–11. **23:** The *synagogues* or public gathering places tended to be simple buildings where the town's business, politics, and religious discourse took place. **24–25:** *Syria,* province northwest of Galilee. *The Decapolis* was the federation of ten Hellenistic cities (see Map on p. 68 NT). They were east of the Jordan, except for Scythopolis (Beth-shan), just south of Galilee. The mention of the Decapolis shows that Jesus is becoming known among the Gentiles.

5.1–7.27: The Sermon on the Mount. The first of the five discourses (chs 5–7,10,13,18,23–25). A much shorter version is in Lk 6.17–38. **5.1–12: The Beatitudes. 1–2:** Jesus, like Moses (Ex 19.3), ascends a mountain to begin his teaching. **3–11:** *Blessed* means happy or satisfied (Ps 1.1). In these nine beatitudes Jesus describes the ideal characteristics of the members of the Matthean community. They promise God's comfort in the coming age (Isa 61.2). **5:** Ps 37.11. *Meek,* not "submissive" or "inconsequential" but aware of one's proper position in the kingdom; not overweening. **6, 10:** Justice, fairness, or *righteousness* are vital for disciples of Jesus (Ps 72.2; 1 Enoch 96.5). **8:** *Pure in heart,* sincere, free from mixed motives; Ps 24.4; 51.10. **11:** A saying that perhaps reflects the difficult context in which the later Matthean community found itself (10.18,39; 16.25). **12:** *Persecuted the prophets,* see 1 Kings 19.10; Neh 9.26.

salt has lost its taste, how can its saltiness
be restored? It is no longer good for any-
thing, but is thrown out and trampled un-
der foot.
14 "You are the light of the world. A
city built on a hill cannot be hid. 15 No one
after lighting a lamp puts it under the bush-
el basket, but on the lampstand, and it gives
light to all in the house. 16 In the same way,
let your light shine before others, so that
they may see your good works and give
glory to your Father in heaven.
17 "Do not think that I have come to
abolish the law or the prophets; I have
come not to abolish but to fulfill. 18 For
truly I tell you, until heaven and earth pass
away, not one letter,[a] not one stroke of a
letter, will pass from the law until all is
accomplished. 19 Therefore, whoever
breaks[b] one of the least of these command-
ments, and teaches others to do the same,
will be called least in the kingdom of heav-
en; but whoever does them and teaches
them will be called great in the kingdom of
heaven. 20 For I tell you, unless your righ-
teousness exceeds that of the scribes and
Pharisees, you will never enter the kingdom
of heaven.
21 "You have heard that it was said to
those of ancient times, 'You shall not mur-
der'; and 'whoever murders shall be liable
to judgment.' 22 But I say to you that if you
are angry with a brother or sister,[c] you
will be liable to judgment; and if you in-
sult[d] a brother or sister,[e] you will be lia-
ble to the council; and if you say, 'You
fool,' you will be liable to the hell[f] of fire.
23 So when you are offering your gift at the
altar, if you remember that your brother or
sister[g] has something against you, 24 leave
your gift there before the altar and go; first
be reconciled to your brother or sister,[g]
and then come and offer your gift. 25 Come
to terms quickly with your accuser while
you are on the way to court[h] with him, or
your accuser may hand you over to the
judge, and the judge to the guard, and you
will be thrown into prison. 26 Truly I tell
you, you will never get out until you have
paid the last penny.
27 "You have heard that it was said,
'You shall not commit adultery.' 28 But I
say to you that everyone who looks at a
woman with lust has already committed
adultery with her in his heart. 29 If your
right eye causes you to sin, tear it out and
throw it away; it is better for you to lose
one of your members than for your whole
body to be thrown into hell.[f] 30 And if
your right hand causes you to sin, cut it off
and throw it away; it is better for you to
lose one of your members than for your
whole body to go into hell.[f]
31 "It was also said, 'Whoever divorces
his wife, let him give her a certificate of
divorce.' 32 But I say to you that anyone
who divorces his wife, except on the
ground of unchastity, causes her to commit
adultery; and whoever marries a divorced
woman commits adultery.
33 "Again, you have heard that it was

a Gk *one iota* *b* Or *annuls* *c* Gk *a brother*; other ancient authorities add *without cause* *d* Gk *say Raca to* (an obscure term of abuse) *e* Gk *a brother* *f* Gk *Gehenna* *g* Gk *your brother* *h* Gk lacks *to court*

5.13–16: The disciple in the world. 13: *Salt,* a preservative as well as a flavoring agent. **15:** *Lamp,* a term in the Hebrew Bible for David and his descendants (1 Kings 11.36; Ps 132.17). The members of the community will fulfill God's plan for Israel (Isa 42.6; 49.6).

5.17–48: Jesus and the law. This section discusses the community's understanding of the Torah, or law. **17–19:** Jesus and his followers in Matthew fulfill the law through Jesus' teaching, though they were accused of neglecting the law (12.2). *Prophets,* the second division of the Hebrew Bible, including Joshua, Judges, Samuel, and Kings, as well as the prophetic books. **20:** *Scribes,* authoritative interpreters of the law. **21–48:** Jesus engages the ten commandments and other aspects of Mosaic law. His teaching reveals God's purpose in giving the law (19.3–9). **21:** Ex 20.13; Deut 5.17. *Judgment,* by a local court. **22:** *Council,* the Sanhedrin. **27:** Ex 20.14; Deut 5.18. **30:** 18.8–9; Mk 9.43–48. **31:** Deut 24.1–4. **32:** *Except . . . unchastity,* absent from the parallels in Mk 10.11–12 and Lk 16.18, but see 19.9n. **33–37:** Lev 19.12; Num 30.2; Deut 23.21. **35:** Isa 66.1; Ps 48.2. **38–42:** These verses form the core of the nonviolence

said to those of ancient times, 'You shall
not swear falsely, but carry out the vows
you have made to the Lord.' 34 But I say to
you, Do not swear at all, either by heaven,
for it is the throne of God, 35 or by the
earth, for it is his footstool, or by Jerusa-
lem, for it is the city of the great King.
36 And do not swear by your head, for you
cannot make one hair white or black. 37 Let
your word be 'Yes, Yes' or 'No, No'; any-
thing more than this comes from the evil
one.[a]

38 "You have heard that it was said, 'An
eye for an eye and a tooth for a tooth.'
39 But I say to you, Do not resist an evildo-
er. But if anyone strikes you on the right
cheek, turn the other also; 40 and if anyone
wants to sue you and take your coat, give
your cloak as well; 41 and if anyone forces
you to go one mile, go also the second mile.
42 Give to everyone who begs from you,
and do not refuse anyone who wants to
borrow from you.

43 "You have heard that it was said,
'You shall love your neighbor and hate
your enemy.' 44 But I say to you, Love your
enemies and pray for those who persecute
you, 45 so that you may be children of your
Father in heaven; for he makes his sun rise
on the evil and on the good, and sends rain
on the righteous and on the unrighteous.
46 For if you love those who love you, what
reward do you have? Do not even the tax
collectors do the same? 47 And if you greet
only your brothers and sisters,[b] what more
are you doing than others? Do not even the
Gentiles do the same? 48 Be perfect, there-
fore, as your heavenly Father is perfect.

6 "Beware of practicing your piety before
others in order to be seen by them; for
then you have no reward from your Father
in heaven.

2 "So whenever you give alms, do not
sound a trumpet before you, as the hypo-
crites do in the synagogues and in the
streets, so that they may be praised by oth-
ers. Truly I tell you, they have received their
reward. 3 But when you give alms, do not
let your left hand know what your right
hand is doing, 4 so that your alms may be
done in secret; and your Father who sees in
secret will reward you.[c]

5 "And whenever you pray, do not be
like the hypocrites; for they love to stand
and pray in the synagogues and at the street
corners, so that they may be seen by others.
Truly I tell you, they have received their
reward. 6 But whenever you pray, go into
your room and shut the door and pray to
your Father who is in secret; and your Fa-
ther who sees in secret will reward you.[c]

7 "When you are praying, do not heap
up empty phrases as the Gentiles do; for
they think that they will be heard because
of their many words. 8 Do not be like them,
for your Father knows what you need be-
fore you ask him.

9 "Pray then in this way:

Our Father in heaven,

a Or *evil* *b* Gk *your brothers* *c* Other ancient authorities add *openly*

associated with Jesus' teaching. **38:** Ex 21.23–24; Lev 24.19–20; Deut 19.21. **40:** To give the *cloak,* or outer garment, would leave a person naked. The law forbade keeping a poor person's cloak overnight (Ex 22.26–27; Deut 24.12–13). **41:** Soldiers could compel civilians to carry their baggage (27.32); going *the second mile* would perhaps spare another from such compulsion.

5.43–48: Love and wholeness. 43: *Love your neighbor* quotes Lev 19.18 (see Ex 23.4–5), but *hate your enemy* is not commanded there. **48:** *Perfect* (see 19.21), or "merciful" (Lk 6.36), reflects the command to complete obedience (Deut 18.13) and holiness (Lev 19.2).

6.1–8: On justice and prayer. 1: *Piety* is the term elsewhere translated "justice" or "righteousness." **2:** *Alms,* charitable gifts, were a prime religious obligation for Jews (Tob 4.7). *Hypocrites,* originally referred to actors (Aristotle, *Poetics* 1456a). It was used by moralists for those whose deeds did not match their words (Sir 1.29). **3–4:** Acts of justice, like prayer (vv. 5–6), are between the doer and God, not for public approval, in contrast to Roman philanthropy, which included the public display of good works.

6.9–15: The Lord's Prayer. Cf. Lk 11.2–4. Matthew's version is the better known. **9:** *Father,* Isa 63.16; 64.8. **10:** The prayer for the coming of God's *kingdom* is for God's rule, not that of foreign or false

hallowed be your name.
10 Your kingdom come.
Your will be done,
on earth as it is in heaven.
11 Give us this day our daily bread.[a]
12 And forgive us our debts,
as we also have forgiven
our debtors.
13 And do not bring us to the time of
trial,[b]
but rescue us from the evil one.[c]
14 For if you forgive others their trespasses,
your heavenly Father will also forgive you;
15 but if you do not forgive others, neither
will your Father forgive your trespasses.
16 "And whenever you fast, do not look
dismal, like the hypocrites, for they disfig-
ure their faces so as to show others that
they are fasting. Truly I tell you, they have
received their reward. 17 But when you fast,
put oil on your head and wash your face,
18 so that your fasting may be seen not by
others but by your Father who is in secret;
and your Father who sees in secret will re-
ward you.[d]
19 "Do not store up for yourselves trea-
sures on earth, where moth and rust[e] con-
sume and where thieves break in and steal;
20 but store up for yourselves treasures in
heaven, where neither moth nor rust[e] con-
sumes and where thieves do not break in
and steal. 21 For where your treasure is,
there your heart will be also.
22 "The eye is the lamp of the body. So,
if your eye is healthy, your whole body will
be full of light; 23 but if your eye is un-
healthy, your whole body will be full of
darkness. If then the light in you is dark-
ness, how great is the darkness!
24 "No one can serve two masters; for a
slave will either hate the one and love the
other, or be devoted to the one and despise
the other. You cannot serve God and
wealth.[f]
25 "Therefore I tell you, do not worry
about your life, what you will eat or what
you will drink,[g] or about your body, what
you will wear. Is not life more than food,
and the body more than clothing? 26 Look
at the birds of the air; they neither sow nor
reap nor gather into barns, and yet your
heavenly Father feeds them. Are you not of
more value than they? 27 And can any of
you by worrying add a single hour to your
span of life?[h] 28 And why do you worry
about clothing? Consider the lilies of the
field, how they grow; they neither toil nor
spin, 29 yet I tell you, even Solomon in all
his glory was not clothed like one of these.
30 But if God so clothes the grass of the
field, which is alive today and tomorrow is
thrown into the oven, will he not much
more clothe you—you of little faith?
31 Therefore do not worry, saying, 'What
will we eat?' or 'What will we drink?' or
'What will we wear?' 32 For it is the Gen-
tiles who strive for all these things; and in-

a Or *our bread for tomorrow* *b* Or *us into temptation* *c* Or *from evil.* Other ancient authorities add, in some form, *For the kingdom and the power and the glory are yours forever. Amen.* *d* Other ancient authorities add *openly* *e* Gk *eating* *f* Gk *mammon* *g* Other ancient authorities lack *or what you will drink* *h* Or *add one cubit to your height*

leaders. *On earth as it is in heaven* applies to the first three petitions; it expresses the community's desire to reflect God's priorities in its actions and relations. **11:** *Daily bread,* basic needs; if the meaning is *bread for tomorrow* (see note *a*), it may refer to the eschatological banquet. **12:** *Debts,* a metaphor for "sins" (see 18.23–35). **13:** The community is in a time of trial and opposition. **14–15:** Reciprocity is vital in the economy of God's kingdom.

6.16–18: Fasting. Jesus returns to the third example of pious deeds. *Fasting,* often associated with festivals and holy days of the Second Temple period, was adopted as a mark of individual piety (Mk 2.18–20; Lk 18.12).

6.19–34: Religion and possessions (Lk 12.33–34; 11.34–36; 16.13; 12.22–31). These verses form a unity devoted to the subject of possessions. **21:** *Heart,* the center of will. **22–24:** Undue focus on possessions can distort judgment. **25–32:** A warning against allowing concern for basic needs to supersede God's rule. **29:** *Solomon,* see 1 Kings 10. **33–34:** The Matthean summary of how to balance human needs and priorities with service to God illustrates the disciple's trust in God (6.11).

deed your heavenly Father knows that you
need all these things. 33 But strive first for
the kingdom of God[a] and his[b] righteous-
ness, and all these things will be given to
you as well.
34 “So do not worry about tomorrow,
for tomorrow will bring worries of its own.
Today’s trouble is enough for today.
7 “Do not judge, so that you may not be
judged. 2 For with the judgment you
make you will be judged, and the measure
you give will be the measure you get. 3 Why
do you see the speck in your neighbor’s[c]
eye, but do not notice the log in your own
eye? 4 Or how can you say to your neigh-
bor,[d] ‘Let me take the speck out of your
eye,’ while the log is in your own eye? 5 You
hypocrite, first take the log out of your own
eye, and then you will see clearly to take the
speck out of your neighbor’s[c] eye.
6 “Do not give what is holy to dogs; and
do not throw your pearls before swine, or
they will trample them under foot and turn
and maul you.
7 “Ask, and it will be given you; search,
and you will find; knock, and the door will
be opened for you. 8 For everyone who asks
receives, and everyone who searches finds,
and for everyone who knocks, the door will
be opened. 9 Is there anyone among you
who, if your child asks for bread, will give
a stone? 10 Or if the child asks for a fish,
will give a snake? 11 If you then, who are
evil, know how to give good gifts to your
children, how much more will your Father
in heaven give good things to those who
ask him!
12 “In everything do to others as you
would have them do to you; for this is the
law and the prophets.
13 “Enter through the narrow gate; for
the gate is wide and the road is easy[e] that
leads to destruction, and there are many
who take it. 14 For the gate is narrow and
the road is hard that leads to life, and there
are few who find it.
15 “Beware of false prophets, who come
to you in sheep’s clothing but inwardly are
ravenous wolves. 16 You will know them
by their fruits. Are grapes gathered from
thorns, or figs from thistles? 17 In the same
way, every good tree bears good fruit, but
the bad tree bears bad fruit. 18 A good tree
cannot bear bad fruit, nor can a bad tree
bear good fruit. 19 Every tree that does not
bear good fruit is cut down and thrown
into the fire. 20 Thus you will know them by
their fruits.
21 “Not everyone who says to me,
‘Lord, Lord,’ will enter the kingdom of

a Other ancient authorities lack *of God* *b* Or *its*
c Gk *brother’s* *d* Gk *brother* *e* Other ancient authorities read *for the road is wide and easy*

7.1–6: Making judgments within the community (Lk 6.37–42). **1–2:** Avoiding judgment among the members of the community is also stressed in ch 18. **6:** *What is holy,* meat from sacrifices. Such meat was to be consumed by the priest or the worshiper; giving it to *dogs* would be sacrilege. Both *dogs* (because of their shameless behavior) and *swine* (because the law forbade eating their meat) were deeply offensive images of unworthy or hostile outsiders. The verse is used later in the *Didache* 9.4, an early Jewish Christian work indebted to Matthew, as a rationale for keeping nonbelievers from partaking in the Eucharist.

7.7–29: Concluding the Sermon on the Mount. This final section contains practical advice for the community both now and in the future; cf. Lk 6.31,43–49; 11.9–13; 13.23–27. **7–11:** The community should not be overly concerned about material needs, but can ask to obtain them. **9–10:** The usual round loaf resembled a *stone,* and a dried *fish* might look like snakeskin. **12:** This “Golden Rule” calls for activity on behalf of others. A variation is attributed to Rabbi Hillel (first century BCE): “What is hateful to you do not do to your neighbor; that is the whole Torah . . . go and learn it” (*b. Shabb.* 31a); cf. Tob 4.15; *Didache* 1.2. *Prophets,* see 5.17–19n. **13–23:** Disciples should not be naïve, but wise, shrewd, and gentle (Mt 10.16). **13–14:** For the frequent metaphor of the two roads, see, e.g., Prov 7.27; 15.24; Jer 21.8. **15:** *False prophets,* teachers of false doctrine; *ravenous wolves,* cf. Ezek 22.27; Zeph 3.3. The remark reflects the early church’s situation. **17–20:** Cf. 3.8–10. **22:** *Prophesy in your name,* cf. Jer 14.14;

heaven, but only the one who does the will
of my Father in heaven. 22 On that day
many will say to me, 'Lord, Lord, did we
not prophesy in your name, and cast out
demons in your name, and do many deeds
of power in your name?' 23 Then I will de-
clare to them, 'I never knew you; go away
from me, you evildoers.'
24 "Everyone then who hears these
words of mine and acts on them will be like
a wise man who built his house on rock.
25 The rain fell, the floods came, and the
winds blew and beat on that house, but it
did not fall, because it had been founded
on rock. 26 And everyone who hears these
words of mine and does not act on them
will be like a foolish man who built his
house on sand. 27 The rain fell, and the
floods came, and the winds blew and beat
against that house, and it fell—and great
was its fall!"
28 Now when Jesus had finished saying
these things, the crowds were astounded at
his teaching, 29 for he taught them as one
having authority, and not as their scribes.

8 When Jesus[a] had come down from the
mountain, great crowds followed him;
2 and there was a leper[b] who came to him
and knelt before him, saying, "Lord, if
you choose, you can make me clean."
3 He stretched out his hand and touched
him, saying, "I do choose. Be made clean!"
Immediately his leprosy[b] was cleansed.
4 Then Jesus said to him, "See that you say
nothing to anyone; but go, show yourself to
the priest, and offer the gift that Moses
commanded, as a testimony to them."
5 When he entered Capernaum, a centu-
rion came to him, appealing to him 6 and
saying, "Lord, my servant is lying at home
paralyzed, in terrible distress." 7 And he
said to him, "I will come and cure him."
8 The centurion answered, "Lord, I am not
worthy to have you come under my roof;
but only speak the word, and my servant
will be healed. 9 For I also am a man under
authority, with soldiers under me; and I say
to one, 'Go,' and he goes, and to another,
'Come,' and he comes, and to my slave, 'Do
this,' and the slave does it." 10 When Jesus
heard him, he was amazed and said to
those who followed him, "Truly I tell you,
in no one[c] in Israel have I found such faith.
11 I tell you, many will come from east and
west and will eat with Abraham and Isaac
and Jacob in the kingdom of heaven,
12 while the heirs of the kingdom will be
thrown into the outer darkness, where
there will be weeping and gnashing of
teeth." 13 And to the centurion Jesus said,
"Go; let it be done for you according to
your faith." And the servant was healed in
that hour.
14 When Jesus entered Peter's house, he
saw his mother-in-law lying in bed with a
fever; 15 he touched her hand, and the fever
left her, and she got up and began to serve
him. 16 That evening they brought to him
many who were possessed with demons;
and he cast out the spirits with a word, and
cured all who were sick. 17 This was to

a Gk *he* *b* The terms *leper* and *leprosy* can refer to several diseases *c* Other ancient authorities read *Truly I tell you, not even*

27.15. **23:** *Go away . . . you evildoers,* quoting Ps 6.8. **24–28:** *Founded,* the Sermon on the Mount has been described as a "constitution" for Matthew's church. The conclusion, *When Jesus had finished . . .*, marks the end of the other discourses as well (11.1; 13.53; 19.1; 26.1).

8.1–34: Deeds of power and discipleship. Following his teaching, Jesus turns to healing. **1–4:** Mk 1.40–45; Lk 5.12–16. *Leper,* one suffering from a skin disease (see note *b*) that made him unclean (Lev 13.1–59; Num 5.1–4). *Clean,* able to rejoin the community. *Show . . . the priest,* Lev 14.2–32. *The gift,* Lev 14.10. **5–13:** Lk 7.1–10; 13.28–30. A *centurion* is in charge of a company of up to one hundred men in a Roman legion. **6:** *Servant,* or "child" (Gk "pais"); the usual term for servant, "doulos," is used in v. 9. **8–10:** The centurion believes that, as he can command servants and soldiers, Jesus can command or control disease. **11–12:** *East and west,* those outside the land of Israel, non-Jews; cf. Isa 59.19; Mal 1.11. *Eat . . . in the kingdom,* the messianic banquet; cf. 22.1–10. **14–17:** Mk 1.29–34; Lk 4.38–41. The circle of those being healed broadens as the day progresses. **17:** Isa 53.4; another fulfillment citation.

fulfill what had been spoken through the
prophet Isaiah, "He took our infirmities
and bore our diseases."
18 Now when Jesus saw great crowds
around him, he gave orders to go over to
the other side. 19 A scribe then approached
and said, "Teacher, I will follow you wher-
ever you go." 20 And Jesus said to him,
"Foxes have holes, and birds of the air have
nests; but the Son of Man has nowhere to
lay his head." 21 Another of his disciples
said to him, "Lord, first let me go and bury
my father." 22 But Jesus said to him, "Fol-
low me, and let the dead bury their own
dead."
23 And when he got into the boat, his
disciples followed him. 24 A windstorm
arose on the sea, so great that the boat was
being swamped by the waves; but he was
asleep. 25 And they went and woke him up,
saying, "Lord, save us! We are perishing!"
26 And he said to them, "Why are you
afraid, you of little faith?" Then he got up
and rebuked the winds and the sea; and
there was a dead calm. 27 They were
amazed, saying, "What sort of man is this,
that even the winds and the sea obey him?"
28 When he came to the other side, to
the country of the Gadarenes,[a] two demo-
niacs coming out of the tombs met him.
They were so fierce that no one could pass
that way. 29 Suddenly they shouted, "What
have you to do with us, Son of God? Have
you come here to torment us before the
time?" 30 Now a large herd of swine was
feeding at some distance from them. 31 The
demons begged him, "If you cast us out,
send us into the herd of swine." 32 And he
said to them, "Go!" So they came out and
entered the swine; and suddenly, the whole
herd rushed down the steep bank into the
sea and perished in the water. 33 The swine-
herds ran off, and on going into the town,
they told the whole story about what had
happened to the demoniacs. 34 Then the
whole town came out to meet Jesus; and
when they saw him, they begged him to
leave their neighborhood.
9 1 And after
getting into a boat he crossed the sea
and came to his own town.
2 And just then some people were carry-
ing a paralyzed man lying on a bed. When
Jesus saw their faith, he said to the paralyt-
ic, "Take heart, son; your sins are forgiv-
en." 3 Then some of the scribes said to
themselves, "This man is blaspheming."
4 But Jesus, perceiving their thoughts, said,
"Why do you think evil in your hearts?
5 For which is easier, to say, 'Your sins are
forgiven,' or to say, 'Stand up and walk'?
6 But so that you may know that the Son
of Man has authority on earth to forgive
sins"—he then said to the paralytic—

a Other ancient authorities read *Gergesenes*; others, *Gerasenes*

18–34: Jesus crosses the Sea of Galilee. **18–22:** Lk 9.57–60. **18:** *Other side,* the eastern shore. **19:** *Scribe,* one who was literate and probably trained in the law of Moses. **20:** *Son of Man,* a characteristic self-identification of Jesus. The title is ambiguous, and can be understood either as "human being" (cf. Ps 8.4; Ezek 2.1), i.e., as a circumlocution for "I," or as a reference to the apocalyptic figure of Dan 7.13–14. **22:** The primacy and immediacy of discipleship is captured in this hard and hyperbolic scenario (cf. the call of Elisha, 1 Kings 19.19–21). **23–27:** Mk 4.35–41; Lk 8.22–25. *Little faith,* whereas in Mark the disciples are criticized somewhat harshly for their lack of understanding and hardness of heart, Matthew's disciples are at worst people who need to grow further and learn more about the life of a follower. **27:** *Even the winds and the sea obey,* perhaps an allusion to Ps 107.29; cf. Ps 104.7; 106.9. **28–34:** Mk 5.1–20; Lk 8.26–39. Gadara, modern Umm Qeis, in northern Transjordan, one of the cities of the Decapolis, contained a famous healing sanctuary. **31–33:** The irony and humor of the scene with the pigs would not have been lost on Matthew's Jewish audience.

9.1–38: Acts of power and growing tension. 1: *His own town,* Capernaum, not Nazareth; see 4.13. Healing a paralytic; Mk 2.1–12; Lk 5.17–26. **2–8:** The tension between Jesus and local authorities builds, with the healings providing the occasion. *Faith,* or trust, prompts the healing in this instance, and the healing verifies the forgiveness. **6:** *Son of Man,* see 8.20n. *On earth,* Jesus claims this authority is operative here and now, not just in the final age (cf. 25.31–46). **9:** The call of *Matthew* the tax collector; Mk 2.14.

"Stand up, take your bed and go to your home." 7 And he stood up and went to his home. 8 When the crowds saw it, they were filled with awe, and they glorified God, who had given such authority to human beings.

9 As Jesus was walking along, he saw a man called Matthew sitting at the tax booth; and he said to him, "Follow me." And he got up and followed him.

10 And as he sat at dinner[a] in the house, many tax collectors and sinners came and were sitting[b] with him and his disciples. 11 When the Pharisees saw this, they said to his disciples, "Why does your teacher eat with tax collectors and sinners?" 12 But when he heard this, he said, "Those who are well have no need of a physician, but those who are sick. 13 Go and learn what this means, 'I desire mercy, not sacrifice.' For I have come to call not the righteous but sinners."

14 Then the disciples of John came to him, saying, "Why do we and the Pharisees fast often,[c] but your disciples do not fast?" 15 And Jesus said to them, "The wedding guests cannot mourn as long as the bridegroom is with them, can they? The days will come when the bridegroom is taken away from them, and then they will fast. 16 No one sews a piece of unshrunk cloth on an old cloak, for the patch pulls away from the cloak, and a worse tear is made. 17 Neither is new wine put into old wineskins; otherwise, the skins burst, and the wine is spilled, and the skins are destroyed; but new wine is put into fresh wineskins, and so both are preserved."

18 While he was saying these things to them, suddenly a leader of the synagogue[d] came in and knelt before him, saying, "My daughter has just died; but come and lay your hand on her, and she will live." 19 And Jesus got up and followed him, with his disciples. 20 Then suddenly a woman who had been suffering from hemorrhages for twelve years came up behind him and touched the fringe of his cloak, 21 for she said to herself, "If I only touch his cloak, I will be made well." 22 Jesus turned, and seeing her he said, "Take heart, daughter; your faith has made you well." And instantly the woman was made well. 23 When Jesus came to the leader's house and saw the flute players and the crowd making a commotion, 24 he said, "Go away; for the girl is not dead but sleeping." And they laughed at him. 25 But when the crowd had

a Gk *reclined* *b* Gk *were reclining* *c* Other ancient authorities lack *often* *d* Gk lacks *of the synagogue*

Capernaum, near the border between Galilee and Gaulanitis, was probably a tax center. In Luke this disciple is called Levi (Lk 5.27). **10–13:** Mk 2.15–17; Lk 5.29–32. **10:** *At dinner,* the food one ate, and one's table companions, were important aspects of defining one's group. *Tax collectors,* the Roman system, known as "tax farming," leased out the right to collect taxes (including customs fees) in a given area for a flat fee. The entrepreneur, usually a local aristocrat, who obtained this right would then try to collect more than the fee in order to profit by the arrangement, with obvious potential for abuse (Philo, *Leg. Gai.* 199). Actual collections were carried out by underlings, who would be under pressure to bring in as much as possible, and were despised by the populace; most of the references to tax collectors probably are to this class. **12–13:** Jesus' response reveals his understanding of his own purpose and mission. **13:** Hos 6.6, used twice by Matthew and by no other Gospel writer. The same passage is used by the rabbinic document *Avot Rabbi Nathan* to explain how sacrifice will be made after the destruction of the Temple. **14–17:** On fasting; Mk 2.18–22; Lk 5.33–39. The wedding feast is a frequent metaphor for the end time; see 22.2–14; 25.1–13; Isa 62.5; Rev 21.2. The two sayings in vv. 16–17, presented separately from the issue of fasting in Luke, stress the newness of the teaching of Jesus. **18–26:** Mk 5.21–43; Lk 8.40–56. A ruler approaches Jesus. The phrase *of the synagogue* is not present in the Greek; it has been added from Mk 5.22. He is simply an authority or leader. **20–22:** Here, following Mark (5.21–43), the story of the hemorrhaging woman is spliced into the healing of the ruler's daughter. *Hemorrhages* would have made the woman continuously unclean (Lev 15.25–30). **21:** *Made well,* lit. "saved." **23:** *Flute players* accompanied the dirge sung by mourners. **27–31:** Cf. 20.29–34. **27:** *Son of*

been put outside, he went in and took her
by the hand, and the girl got up. 26 And the
report of this spread throughout that dis-
trict.
27 As Jesus went on from there, two
blind men followed him, crying loudly,
"Have mercy on us, Son of David!"
28 When he entered the house, the blind
men came to him; and Jesus said to them,
"Do you believe that I am able to do this?"
They said to him, "Yes, Lord." 29 Then he
touched their eyes and said, "According to
your faith let it be done to you." 30 And
their eyes were opened. Then Jesus sternly
ordered them, "See that no one knows of
this." 31 But they went away and spread the
news about him throughout that district.
32 After they had gone away, a demoni-
ac who was mute was brought to him.
33 And when the demon had been cast out,
the one who had been mute spoke; and the
crowds were amazed and said, "Never has
anything like this been seen in Israel."
34 But the Pharisees said, "By the ruler of
the demons he casts out the demons."[a]
35 Then Jesus went about all the cities
and villages, teaching in their synagogues,
and proclaiming the good news of the king-
dom, and curing every disease and every
sickness. 36 When he saw the crowds, he
had compassion for them, because they
were harassed and helpless, like sheep with-
out a shepherd. 37 Then he said to his disci-
ples, "The harvest is plentiful, but the la-
borers are few; 38 therefore ask the Lord of
the harvest to send out laborers into his
harvest."

10 Then Jesus[b] summoned his twelve
disciples and gave them authority
over unclean spirits, to cast them out, and
to cure every disease and every sickness.
2 These are the names of the twelve apos-
tles: first, Simon, also known as Peter, and
his brother Andrew; James son of Zebedee,
and his brother John; 3 Philip and Bartholo-
mew; Thomas and Matthew the tax collec-
tor; James son of Alphaeus, and Thaddae-
us;[c] 4 Simon the Cananaean, and Judas
Iscariot, the one who betrayed him.
5 These twelve Jesus sent out with the
following instructions: "Go nowhere
among the Gentiles, and enter no town of
the Samaritans, 6 but go rather to the lost
sheep of the house of Israel. 7 As you go,
proclaim the good news, 'The kingdom of
heaven has come near.'[d] 8 Cure the sick,
raise the dead, cleanse the lepers,[e] cast out
demons. You received without payment;
give without payment. 9 Take no gold, or
silver, or copper in your belts, 10 no bag for
your journey, or two tunics, or sandals,
or a staff; for laborers deserve their food.
11 Whatever town or village you enter, find

a Other ancient authorities lack this verse *b* Gk *he*
c Other ancient authorities read *Lebbaeus*, or *Lebbaeus called Thaddaeus* *d* Or *is at hand*
e The terms *leper* and *leprosy* can refer to several diseases

David hearkens back to the genealogy at the start of the Gospel. **32–34:** Cf. 12.22–24. **34:** *By the ruler of the demons,* authorities discredit Jesus by accusing him of practicing magic (also 12.24). **35–38:** A narrative summation of Jesus' activities and ministry over the last five chapters. He is a teacher, healer, and a proclaimer of good news for all the people. *Like sheep without a shepherd,* a traditional image from the Hebrew Bible (Num 27.17; 1 Kings 22.17; Ezek 34.5). **37–38:** The saying (see Lk 10.2) suggests that Matthew's community is not engaged in mission, and serves as a preamble for ch 10.

10.1–42: Matthew's sending and instruction about mission. The second discourse (vv. 5–41) deals with mission and the realities the disciples will encounter in the world. **1–5:** The *twelve,* representing the twelve tribes, shows that Jesus' followers claim to be the remnant of the true Israel (a symbolic group of twelve leaders existed among the Essenes, 1QS 8.1–2). For the list of the twelve, cf. Mk 3.16–19; Lk 6.14–16. **6–15:** Mk 6.8–11; Lk 9.2–5. **5–6:** Only in Matthew does Jesus instruct the twelve to limit their mission to Israel. Matthew's community does concern itself with non-Israelites (28.19), but first speaks to Jews (cf. Acts 10.28). *Among the Gentiles,* treats the restriction as geographic, not ethnic. **5:** *The Samaritans* lived in Samaria, between Galilee and Judea. Most Jews regarded them with hostility, although the two groups had much in common (e.g., the Torah). **12:** *Greet it,* by saying, "Peace be to this house." **14:** *Dust*

out who in it is worthy, and stay there until
you leave. 12 As you enter the house, greet
it. 13 If the house is worthy, let your peace
come upon it; but if it is not worthy, let
your peace return to you. 14 If anyone will
not welcome you or listen to your words,
shake off the dust from your feet as you
leave that house or town. 15 Truly I tell you,
it will be more tolerable for the land of
Sodom and Gomorrah on the day of judg-
ment than for that town.

16 "See, I am sending you out like sheep
into the midst of wolves; so be wise as ser-
pents and innocent as doves. 17 Beware of
them, for they will hand you over to coun-
cils and flog you in their synagogues; 18 and
you will be dragged before governors and
kings because of me, as a testimony to them
and the Gentiles. 19 When they hand you
over, do not worry about how you are to
speak or what you are to say; for what you
are to say will be given to you at that time;
20 for it is not you who speak, but the Spirit
of your Father speaking through you.
21 Brother will betray brother to death, and
a father his child, and children will rise
against parents and have them put to death;
22 and you will be hated by all because of
my name. But the one who endures to the
end will be saved. 23 When they persecute
you in one town, flee to the next; for truly
I tell you, you will not have gone through
all the towns of Israel before the Son of
Man comes.

24 "A disciple is not above the teacher,
nor a slave above the master; 25 it is enough
for the disciple to be like the teacher, and
the slave like the master. If they have called
the master of the house Beelzebul, how
much more will they malign those of his
household!

26 "So have no fear of them; for nothing
is covered up that will not be uncovered,
and nothing secret that will not become
known. 27 What I say to you in the dark,
tell in the light; and what you hear whis-
pered, proclaim from the housetops. 28 Do
not fear those who kill the body but cannot
kill the soul; rather fear him who can de-
stroy both soul and body in hell.[a] 29 Are
not two sparrows sold for a penny? Yet not
one of them will fall to the ground apart
from your Father. 30 And even the hairs of
your head are all counted. 31 So do not be
afraid; you are of more value than many
sparrows.

32 "Everyone therefore who acknowl-
edges me before others, I also will acknowl-
edge before my Father in heaven; 33 but
whoever denies me before others, I also will
deny before my Father in heaven.

34 "Do not think that I have come to
bring peace to the earth; I have not come to
bring peace, but a sword.

35 For I have come to set a man against
his father,
and a daughter against her mother,
and a daughter-in-law against her
mother-in-law;
36 and one's foes will be members of
one's own household.

37 Whoever loves father or mother more
than me is not worthy of me; and whoever
loves son or daughter more than me is not
worthy of me; 38 and whoever does not take
up the cross and follow me is not worthy of
me. 39 Those who find their life will lose it,
and those who lose their life for my sake
will find it.

40 "Whoever welcomes you welcomes

a Gk *Gehenna*

from your feet, see Lk 10.11. **15:** *Sodom and Gomorrah,* Gen 18.16–19.29. **17–25:** Mk 13.9–13; Lk 21.12–17. **17:** *Councils* and *synagogues,* local judicial forums and public centers. *Flog,* as punishment for violating the Torah (Deut 25.1–3); cf. 20.19; 23.34. **18:** *Governors,* the title used of Pilate (27.2). **23:** *Before the Son of Man comes,* the time before judgment is short and the task is urgent. **24:** Cf. Jn 13.16; 15.20. **25:** A reminder of the earlier charge by the Pharisees (9.34). *Beelzebul,* originally a title of the Canaanite deity Baal (see 2 Kings 1.2n.), in the Gospels a designation of Satan (see 11.24). **26–33:** Lk 12.2–9. **27:** A denial of any secret or esoteric teaching. **34–39:** Lk 12.51–53; 14.26–27. Jesus' presence creates division also. Cf. Mic 7.6. **40–42:** Mutual support and provision is a hallmark of the communities gathered around Jesus. *Whoever welcomes a prophet,* the prophet is equivalent to God who sent him (Ex

me, and whoever welcomes me welcomes
the one who sent me. 41 Whoever welcomes
a prophet in the name of a prophet will
receive a prophet's reward; and whoever
welcomes a righteous person in the name of
a righteous person will receive the reward
of the righteous; 42 and whoever gives even
a cup of cold water to one of these little
ones in the name of a disciple—truly I tell
you, none of these will lose their reward."

11 Now when Jesus had finished in-
structing his twelve disciples, he
went on from there to teach and proclaim
his message in their cities.
2 When John heard in prison what the
Messiah[a] was doing, he sent word by his[b]
disciples 3 and said to him, "Are you the
one who is to come, or are we to wait for
another?" 4 Jesus answered them, "Go and
tell John what you hear and see: 5 the blind
receive their sight, the lame walk, the lep-
ers[c] are cleansed, the deaf hear, the dead
are raised, and the poor have good news
brought to them. 6 And blessed is anyone
who takes no offense at me."
7 As they went away, Jesus began to
speak to the crowds about John: "What did
you go out into the wilderness to look at? A
reed shaken by the wind? 8 What then did
you go out to see? Someone[d] dressed in
soft robes? Look, those who wear soft
robes are in royal palaces. 9 What then did
you go out to see? A prophet?[e] Yes, I tell
you, and more than a prophet. 10 This is the
one about whom it is written,

'See, I am sending my messenger
ahead of you,
who will prepare your way
before you.'
11 Truly I tell you, among those born of
women no one has arisen greater than John
the Baptist; yet the least in the kingdom of
heaven is greater than he. 12 From the days
of John the Baptist until now the kingdom
of heaven has suffered violence,[f] and the
violent take it by force. 13 For all the proph-
ets and the law prophesied until John came;
14 and if you are willing to accept it, he is
Elijah who is to come. 15 Let anyone with
ears[g] listen!
16 "But to what will I compare this gen-
eration? It is like children sitting in the mar-
ketplaces and calling to one another,
17 'We played the flute for you, and you
did not dance;
we wailed, and you did not mourn.'
18 For John came neither eating nor drink-
ing, and they say, 'He has a demon'; 19 the
Son of Man came eating and drinking, and
they say, 'Look, a glutton and a drunkard,
a friend of tax collectors and sinners!' Yet
wisdom is vindicated by her deeds."[h]
20 Then he began to reproach the cities

a Or *the Christ* *b* Other ancient authorities read *two of his* *c* The terms *leper* and *leprosy* can refer to several diseases *d* Or *Why then did you go out? To see someone* *e* Other ancient authorities read *Why then did you go out? To see a prophet?* *f* Or *has been coming violently* *g* Other ancient authorities add *to hear* *h* Other ancient authorities read *children*

16.8; 1 Sam 8.7). Jesus' disciples are like the prophets (5.12; 11.9; 13.17). *Little ones,* new or vulnerable disciples. See 18.6.

11.1–19: Jesus and John the Baptist (Lk 7.18–35). John was arrested for sedition and killed by Herod Antipas (Josephus, *Ant.* 18; Mt 14.1–12; Mk 6.14–29). **2:** *Messiah,* or *Christ* (note *a*), a number of groups expected some kind of messianic or redemptive figure in this period, such as the Qumran community which produced the Dead Sea Scrolls; several first-century popular leaders were understood as "messianic" figures. John's question to Jesus is understandable in this broader context. **4–6:** Isa 29.18–19; 35.5–6; 42.18; 61.1; cf. Lk 4.17–21. **10:** Mal 3.1 (similar to Isa 40.3). **13:** *The prophets and the law,* the first two divisions of the Jewish scriptures. **14:** *Elijah* as a precursor to the messianic day was a popular tradition during Second Temple Judaism (Mal 4.5). **19:** *Her deeds,* refers to "what the Messiah was doing" (11.2). Jesus is identified with wisdom in 11.28–30.

11.20–30: Denunciation and true discipleship. 20–24: Lk 10.13–15. The denunciation of the villages of Bethsaida, Chorazin, and Capernaum north of the Sea of Galilee (cf. Isa 14.14–15) and the extolling of the non-Israelite coastal cities of Tyre and Sidon emphasize Jesus' primary mission to Israel. Galilean

in which most of his deeds of power had
been done, because they did not repent.
21 "Woe to you, Chorazin! Woe to you,
Bethsaida! For if the deeds of power done
in you had been done in Tyre and Sidon,
they would have repented long ago in sack-
cloth and ashes. 22 But I tell you, on the day
of judgment it will be more tolerable for
Tyre and Sidon than for you. 23 And you,
Capernaum,
will you be exalted to heaven?
No, you will be brought down
to Hades.
For if the deeds of power done in you had
been done in Sodom, it would have re-
mained until this day. 24 But I tell you that
on the day of judgment it will be more tol-
erable for the land of Sodom than for you."

25 At that time Jesus said, "I thank[a]
you, Father, Lord of heaven and earth, be-
cause you have hidden these things from
the wise and the intelligent and have re-
vealed them to infants; 26 yes, Father, for
such was your gracious will.[b] 27 All things
have been handed over to me by my Father;
and no one knows the Son except the Fa-
ther, and no one knows the Father except
the Son and anyone to whom the Son
chooses to reveal him.

28 "Come to me, all you that are weary
and are carrying heavy burdens, and I will
give you rest. 29 Take my yoke upon you,
and learn from me; for I am gentle and
humble in heart, and you will find rest for
your souls. 30 For my yoke is easy, and my
burden is light."

12 At that time Jesus went through the
grainfields on the sabbath; his disci-
ples were hungry, and they began to pluck
heads of grain and to eat. 2 When the Phari-
sees saw it, they said to him, "Look, your
disciples are doing what is not lawful to do
on the sabbath." 3 He said to them, "Have
you not read what David did when he and
his companions were hungry? 4 He entered
the house of God and ate the bread of the
Presence, which it was not lawful for him
or his companions to eat, but only for the
priests. 5 Or have you not read in the law
that on the sabbath the priests in the temple
break the sabbath and yet are guiltless? 6 I
tell you, something greater than the temple
is here. 7 But if you had known what this
means, 'I desire mercy and not sacrifice,'
you would not have condemned the guilt-
less. 8 For the Son of Man is lord of the
sabbath."

a Or *praise* *b* Or *for so it was well-pleasing in your sight*

towns that were home to Jesus and his first mission were granted unusual opportunities to see what was happening (see 10.15). Yet people in towns and regions peripheral to Jesus' earliest work better apprehended its import. **25–27:** Lk 10.21–22. The nature of true wisdom is an important question in Matthew. Powerful and influential people form the opposition in Matthew's Gospel. Ironically, it is the younger students without influence, training, and power who have heard and understood the message. Wisdom is hidden from "the wise"; see Job 12.1,24–25; Isa 19.11–12; Jer 8.8–9; Prov 3.7. **28–30:** In the Septuagint, the Greek version of the Hebrew Bible which Matthew quotes, the image of the yoke entails obedience and submission, but also political allegiance, wisdom, and justice (2 Chr 10.4; Prov 11.1,16; Mic 6.11; Ezek 45.10). For the yoke as wise teaching, see Sir 51.23–27. *Come to me,* cf. Prov 9.5; Sir 24.19.

12.1–42: Jesus and the Pharisees. This section narrates the developing conflict with the local leaders represented by the Pharisees, known for their meticulous interpretation of the law (Josephus, *War* 2.162; *Life* 191).

12.1–8: Sabbath laws (Mk 2.23–28; Lk 6.1–5). This story demonstrates Jesus' authority and legal interpretation. **2:** Ex 20.8–11. **3–4:** 1 Sam 21.1–6. *Bread of the Presence,* twelve loaves placed in the Temple every sabbath as a thank offering (Lev 24.5–9). **5–6:** Matthew adds this denunciation of the priests in the Jerusalem Temple, possibly referring to Num 28.9–10. **7:** The second quotation of Hos 6.6 (see 9.13n.). When Jesus offers a legal interpretation, or is embroiled in a dispute with other religious leaders, he usually cites scripture to support his argument.

9 He left that place and entered their
synagogue; 10 a man was there with a with-
ered hand, and they asked him, "Is it lawful
to cure on the sabbath?" so that they might
accuse him. 11 He said to them, "Suppose
one of you has only one sheep and it falls
into a pit on the sabbath; will you not lay
hold of it and lift it out? 12 How much more
valuable is a human being than a sheep! So
it is lawful to do good on the sabbath."
13 Then he said to the man, "Stretch out
your hand." He stretched it out, and it was
restored, as sound as the other. 14 But the
Pharisees went out and conspired against
him, how to destroy him.

15 When Jesus became aware of this, he
departed. Many crowds[a] followed him,
and he cured all of them, 16 and he ordered
them not to make him known. 17 This was
to fulfill what had been spoken through the
prophet Isaiah:

18 "Here is my servant, whom I
have chosen,
my beloved, with whom my soul is
well pleased.
I will put my Spirit upon him,
and he will proclaim justice to the
Gentiles.
19 He will not wrangle or cry aloud,
nor will anyone hear his voice
in the streets.
20 He will not break a bruised reed
or quench a smoldering wick
until he brings justice to victory.
21 And in his name the Gentiles will
hope."

22 Then they brought to him a demoni-
ac who was blind and mute; and he cured
him, so that the one who had been mute
could speak and see. 23 All the crowds were
amazed and said, "Can this be the Son of
David?" 24 But when the Pharisees heard it,
they said, "It is only by Beelzebul, the ruler
of the demons, that this fellow casts out
the demons." 25 He knew what they were
thinking and said to them, "Every kingdom
divided against itself is laid waste, and no
city or house divided against itself will
stand. 26 If Satan casts out Satan, he is di-
vided against himself; how then will his
kingdom stand? 27 If I cast out demons by
Beelzebul, by whom do your own exor-
cists[b] cast them out? Therefore they will be
your judges. 28 But if it is by the Spirit of
God that I cast out demons, then the king-
dom of God has come to you. 29 Or how
can one enter a strong man's house and
plunder his property, without first tying up
the strong man? Then indeed the house can
be plundered. 30 Whoever is not with me is
against me, and whoever does not gather
with me scatters. 31 Therefore I tell you,
people will be forgiven for every sin and
blasphemy, but blasphemy against the Spir-
it will not be forgiven. 32 Whoever speaks a
word against the Son of Man will be forgiv-
en, but whoever speaks against the Holy
Spirit will not be forgiven, either in this age
or in the age to come.

33 "Either make the tree good, and its
fruit good; or make the tree bad, and its
fruit bad; for the tree is known by its fruit.

a Other ancient authorities lack *crowds* *b* Gk *sons*

12.9–14: A sabbath healing (Mk 3.1–6; Lk 6.6–11). The *synagogue,* a common Greek term for an informal public gathering place or structure where civic and political issues were discussed, not yet a formal religious institution. Jesus argues using the rhetorical technique "from the small to the great," popular in both classical rhetoric and early rabbinic legal debate. *Will you not . . . lift it out,* the ordinary practice in Jesus' day (but Essenes opposed this view, CD 11.13–14). This story concludes with the first mention of a plan to *destroy* Jesus.

12.15–21: Justice and healing for many. 17–21: Isa 42.1–4,9. The citation aims to answer the question of later followers: Why was Jesus not more widely known and why did he not attract more followers during his ministry? The response is that this was not part of God's plan. In addition, Jesus' ministry is for all people. *Gentiles,* possibly a reference to the nations rather than to non-Jews.

12.22–37: The relationship between words and deeds (Mk 3.23–30; Lk 11.17–23). This story of an exorcism provides the occasion for the Pharisees to attempt to discredit Jesus (9.34). **24:** *Beelzebul,* see 10.25n. **30:** Found also in Luke (11.23), but not Mark, and perhaps originally an independent saying.

34 You brood of vipers! How can you speak
good things, when you are evil? For out
of the abundance of the heart the mouth
speaks. 35 The good person brings good
things out of a good treasure, and the evil
person brings evil things out of an evil trea-
sure. 36 I tell you, on the day of judgment
you will have to give an account for every
careless word you utter; 37 for by your
words you will be justified, and by your
words you will be condemned."

38 Then some of the scribes and Phari-
sees said to him, "Teacher, we wish to see
a sign from you." 39 But he answered them,
"An evil and adulterous generation asks for
a sign, but no sign will be given to it except
the sign of the prophet Jonah. 40 For just as
Jonah was three days and three nights in
the belly of the sea monster, so for three
days and three nights the Son of Man will
be in the heart of the earth. 41 The people of
Nineveh will rise up at the judgment with
this generation and condemn it, because
they repented at the proclamation of Jonah,
and see, something greater than Jonah is
here! 42 The queen of the South will rise up
at the judgment with this generation and
condemn it, because she came from the
ends of the earth to listen to the wisdom of
Solomon, and see, something greater than
Solomon is here!

43 "When the unclean spirit has gone
out of a person, it wanders through water-
less regions looking for a resting place, but
it finds none. 44 Then it says, 'I will return
to my house from which I came.' When it
comes, it finds it empty, swept, and put in
order. 45 Then it goes and brings along sev-
en other spirits more evil than itself, and
they enter and live there; and the last state
of that person is worse than the first. So
will it be also with this evil generation."

46 While he was still speaking to the
crowds, his mother and his brothers were
standing outside, wanting to speak to him.
47 Someone told him, "Look, your mother
and your brothers are standing outside,
wanting to speak to you."[a] 48 But to the
one who had told him this, Jesus[b] replied,
"Who is my mother, and who are my
brothers?" 49 And pointing to his disciples,
he said, "Here are my mother and my
brothers! 50 For whoever does the will of
my Father in heaven is my brother and sis-
ter and mother."

13 That same day Jesus went out of the
house and sat beside the sea. 2 Such
great crowds gathered around him that he
got into a boat and sat there, while the
whole crowd stood on the beach. 3 And he
told them many things in parables, saying:
"Listen! A sower went out to sow. 4 And as
he sowed, some seeds fell on the path, and
the birds came and ate them up. 5 Other
seeds fell on rocky ground, where they did

a Other ancient authorities lack verse 47 *b* Gk *he*

31–32: Speaking *against the Holy Spirit* is attributing authority to something other than God's spirit. **33–37:** Speech as evidence of character renders persons liable to judgment (cf. 5.21–22).

12.38–45: Seeking a sign (Lk 11.29–32; 11.24–26). **39:** *Adulterous,* the Hebrew Bible's metaphor for unfaithfulness (Jer 3.8; Ezek 23.37; Hos 2.2–10). **40:** Jon 1.17. **41:** Jon 3.5. **42:** *Queen of the South,* the queen of Sheba (1 Kings 10.1–10). **43:** *Waterless regions,* or deserts, believed to be the home of demons (Lev 16.10; Isa 13.21–22; 34.14). **44:** *House,* the formerly possessed person. *Empty,* i.e., no good spirit has replaced the evil one.

12.46–50: Jesus' true family (Mk 3.31–35; Lk 8.19–25). Jesus' implicit rejection of his family in favor of his disciples is a radical challenge to traditional values.

13.1–52: Teaching in parables. In this third discourse, Matthew has grouped several parables about the kingdom's presence in a single chapter. **1:** *The sea,* of Galilee. **3:** *Parables,* (Heb "mashal") can refer to stories or fables (Ezek 24.2–5), proverbial sayings (1 Sam 24.13) or riddles (Ezek 17.2). Narrative parables involve analogy or comparison between the situation and the subject being discussed (2 Sam 12.1–7; Isa 5.1–7). **3–9:** The parable of the sower (Mk 4.3–9; Lk 8.5–8). *Seeds,* a metaphor for God's law (2 Esd 9.31) and individuals who receive it (2 Esd 8.41–44). *Some a hundredfold,* indicates an extraordinarily bountiful harvest (Gen 26.12; *Jub.* 24.15), which makes up for the lost seed. **14–15:** Isa 6.9–10.

not have much soil, and they sprang up
quickly, since they had no depth of soil.
6 But when the sun rose, they were
scorched; and since they had no root, they
withered away. 7 Other seeds fell among
thorns, and the thorns grew up and choked
them. 8 Other seeds fell on good soil and
brought forth grain, some a hundredfold,
some sixty, some thirty. 9 Let anyone with
ears[a] listen!"

10 Then the disciples came and asked
him, "Why do you speak to them in para-
bles?" 11 He answered, "To you it has been
given to know the secrets[b] of the kingdom
of heaven, but to them it has not been giv-
en. 12 For to those who have, more will be
given, and they will have an abundance;
but from those who have nothing, even
what they have will be taken away. 13 The
reason I speak to them in parables is that
'seeing they do not perceive, and hearing
they do not listen, nor do they understand.'
14 With them indeed is fulfilled the proph-
ecy of Isaiah that says:

'You will indeed listen, but never
understand,
and you will indeed look, but never
perceive.
15 For this people's heart has
grown dull,
and their ears are hard of hearing,
and they have shut their eyes;
so that they might not look with
their eyes,
and listen with their ears,
and understand with their heart and
turn—
and I would heal them.'

16 But blessed are your eyes, for they see,
and your ears, for they hear. 17 Truly I tell
you, many prophets and righteous people
longed to see what you see, but did not see
it, and to hear what you hear, but did not
hear it.

18 "Hear then the parable of the sower.
19 When anyone hears the word of the king-
dom and does not understand it, the evil
one comes and snatches away what is sown
in the heart; this is what was sown on the
path. 20 As for what was sown on rocky
ground, this is the one who hears the word
and immediately receives it with joy; 21 yet
such a person has no root, but endures only
for a while, and when trouble or persecu-
tion arises on account of the word, that
person immediately falls away.[c] 22 As for
what was sown among thorns, this is the
one who hears the word, but the cares of
the world and the lure of wealth choke the
word, and it yields nothing. 23 But as for
what was sown on good soil, this is the one
who hears the word and understands it,
who indeed bears fruit and yields, in one
case a hundredfold, in another sixty, and in
another thirty."

24 He put before them another parable:
"The kingdom of heaven may be compared
to someone who sowed good seed in his
field; 25 but while everybody was asleep, an
enemy came and sowed weeds among the
wheat, and then went away. 26 So when the
plants came up and bore grain, then the
weeds appeared as well. 27 And the slaves
of the householder came and said to him,
'Master, did you not sow good seed in your
field? Where, then, did these weeds come
from?' 28 He answered, 'An enemy has done
this.' The slaves said to him, 'Then do you
want us to go and gather them?' 29 But he
replied, 'No; for in gathering the weeds you
would uproot the wheat along with them.
30 Let both of them grow together until the
harvest; and at harvest time I will tell the
reapers, Collect the weeds first and bind
them in bundles to be burned, but gather
the wheat into my barn.' "

31 He put before them another parable:

a Other ancient authorities add *to hear*
b Or *mysteries* c Gk *stumbles*

18–23: Mk 4.13–20; Lk 8.11–15. The explanation for the disciples. **24–33:** Three parables of the hidden kingdom. **24–30:** The weeds and the wheat, a parable unique to Matthew, reminds the Matthean community that it is impossible to separate good and evil individuals (7.1–5,15–20). **30:** *Bundles to be burned,* the farmer outwits his enemies by using the weeds as fuel. See vv. 36–43. **31–32:** The parable of the mustard seed (Mk 4.30–32; Lk 13.18–19). *Birds of the air . . . branches,* alludes to the image of God's

"The kingdom of heaven is like a mustard
seed that someone took and sowed in his
field; 32 it is the smallest of all the seeds, but
when it has grown it is the greatest of
shrubs and becomes a tree, so that the birds
of the air come and make nests in its
branches."

33 He told them another parable: "The
kingdom of heaven is like yeast that a
woman took and mixed in with[a] three
measures of flour until all of it was leav-
ened."

34 Jesus told the crowds all these things
in parables; without a parable he told them
nothing. 35 This was to fulfill what had
been spoken through the prophet:[b]

"I will open my mouth to speak
in parables;
I will proclaim what has been
hidden from the foundation of
the world."[c]

36 Then he left the crowds and went
into the house. And his disciples ap-
proached him, saying, "Explain to us the
parable of the weeds of the field." 37 He
answered, "The one who sows the good
seed is the Son of Man; 38 the field is the
world, and the good seed are the children
of the kingdom; the weeds are the children
of the evil one, 39 and the enemy who sowed
them is the devil; the harvest is the end of
the age, and the reapers are angels. 40 Just
as the weeds are collected and burned up
with fire, so will it be at the end of the age.
41 The Son of Man will send his angels, and
they will collect out of his kingdom all
causes of sin and all evildoers, 42 and they
will throw them into the furnace of fire,
where there will be weeping and gnashing
of teeth. 43 Then the righteous will shine
like the sun in the kingdom of their Father.
Let anyone with ears[d] listen!

44 "The kingdom of heaven is like trea-
sure hidden in a field, which someone
found and hid; then in his joy he goes and
sells all that he has and buys that field.

45 "Again, the kingdom of heaven is
like a merchant in search of fine pearls;
46 on finding one pearl of great value, he
went and sold all that he had and bought it.

47 "Again, the kingdom of heaven is
like a net that was thrown into the sea and
caught fish of every kind; 48 when it was
full, they drew it ashore, sat down, and put
the good into baskets but threw out the
bad. 49 So it will be at the end of the age.
The angels will come out and separate the
evil from the righteous 50 and throw them
into the furnace of fire, where there will be
weeping and gnashing of teeth.

51 "Have you understood all this?"
They answered, "Yes." 52 And he said to
them, "Therefore every scribe who has
been trained for the kingdom of heaven is
like the master of a household who brings
out of his treasure what is new and what is
old." 53 When Jesus had finished these par-
ables, he left that place.

54 He came to his hometown and began
to teach the people[e] in their synagogue, so
that they were astounded and said, "Where
did this man get this wisdom and these

a Gk *hid in* *b* Other ancient authorities read *the prophet Isaiah* *c* Other ancient authorities lack *of the world* *d* Other ancient authorities add *to hear* *e* Gk *them*

rule over the kingdoms of the earth (Ezek 17.23–24). **33:** *Mixed in with,* Gk "hid in" (note *a*), an unusual twist in the baking metaphor emphasizes the kingdom in the world. *Three measures,* about 23 liters (2/3 bu); cf. Gen 18.16. **34–35:** Ps 78.2. *The prophet,* Asaph, given as the author of Ps 78, is called "the seer" in 2 Chr 29.30. **36–43:** Jesus provides an apocalyptic interpretation to the parable of the weeds and wheat (cf. 2 Bar 70.2). **37:** *Son of Man,* see 8.20n. **39:** *End of the age,* the decisive break between one era and the next, or the end of the world in judgment. **43:** Dan 12.3. **44–50:** Three more brief parables of the kingdom. The first two—the *treasure* and the *pearl*—depict the inestimable value of the kingdom. The third is another apocalyptic parable. **51–53:** *Scribe . . . trained for the kingdom,* may reflect the Evangelist's background. (For Christian scribes see 23.34.) *New,* Jesus' teaching; *old,* the Torah.

13.54–58: Jesus' rejection in Nazareth. The rejection of Jesus in *his hometown,* Nazareth, is a pivotal event in the Gospels (Mk 6.1–6; Lk 4.16–30; Jn 4.44). The tide is turning against Jesus and his movement in Galilee. Open hostility is not far off.

deeds of power? 55 Is not this the carpen-
ter's son? Is not his mother called Mary?
And are not his brothers James and Joseph
and Simon and Judas? 56 And are not all his
sisters with us? Where then did this man get
all this?" 57 And they took offense at him.
But Jesus said to them, "Prophets are not
without honor except in their own country
and in their own house." 58 And he did not
do many deeds of power there, because of
their unbelief.

14 At that time Herod the ruler[a] heard
reports about Jesus; 2 and he said to
his servants, "This is John the Baptist; he
has been raised from the dead, and for this
reason these powers are at work in him."
3 For Herod had arrested John, bound him,
and put him in prison on account of Hero-
dias, his brother Philip's wife,[b] 4 because
John had been telling him, "It is not lawful
for you to have her." 5 Though Herod[c]
wanted to put him to death, he feared the
crowd, because they regarded him as a
prophet. 6 But when Herod's birthday
came, the daughter of Herodias danced be-
fore the company, and she pleased Herod
7 so much that he promised on oath to grant
her whatever she might ask. 8 Prompted by
her mother, she said, "Give me the head of
John the Baptist here on a platter." 9 The
king was grieved, yet out of regard for his
oaths and for the guests, he commanded it
to be given; 10 he sent and had John behead-
ed in the prison. 11 The head was brought
on a platter and given to the girl, who
brought it to her mother. 12 His disciples
came and took the body and buried it; then
they went and told Jesus.

13 Now when Jesus heard this, he with-
drew from there in a boat to a deserted
place by himself. But when the crowds
heard it, they followed him on foot from
the towns. 14 When he went ashore, he saw
a great crowd; and he had compassion for
them and cured their sick. 15 When it was
evening, the disciples came to him and said,
"This is a deserted place, and the hour is
now late; send the crowds away so that
they may go into the villages and buy food
for themselves." 16 Jesus said to them,
"They need not go away; you give them
something to eat." 17 They replied, "We
have nothing here but five loaves and two
fish." 18 And he said, "Bring them here to
me." 19 Then he ordered the crowds to sit
down on the grass. Taking the five loaves
and the two fish, he looked up to heaven,
and blessed and broke the loaves, and gave
them to the disciples, and the disciples gave
them to the crowds. 20 And all ate and were
filled; and they took up what was left over
of the broken pieces, twelve baskets full.
21 And those who ate were about five thou-
sand men, besides women and children.

22 Immediately he made the disciples
get into the boat and go on ahead to the
other side, while he dismissed the crowds.
23 And after he had dismissed the crowds,
he went up the mountain by himself to

a Gk *tetrarch* *b* Other ancient authorities read *his brother's wife* *c* Gk *he*

14.1–12: The death of John the Baptist (Mk 6.14–29). The death of John is described in detail in Josephus, *Ant.* 18.109–19. Also according to Josephus, Herod's desertion of his wife to marry Herodias caused war between Herod and his erstwhile father-in-law, Aretas IV, king of Nabatea, a war that Herod lost. **1:** *Herod* Antipas, son of Herod the Great. *Ruler* or *tetrarch* (note *a*), Herod the Great's kingdom was divided into parts after his death, and Antipas ruled Galilee and Perea. **4:** Marrying a brother's wife is prohibited in Lev 18.16; 20.21. **6:** *Daughter,* Salome (Josephus, *Ant.* 18.136). **12:** The courage of John's disciples in claiming their teacher's body for burial contrasts with that of Jesus' followers (Mt 27.57 treats Joseph of Arimathea as a disciple).

14.13–21: The miraculous feeding (Mk 6.30–44; Lk 9.10–17; Jn 6.1–13; cf. Mt 15.32–39). Anticipation of the messianic banquet forces a diptych with Herod's party. **13:** John's death had a profound impact on Jesus. **19:** *Looked up to heaven, blessed, broke,* and *gave* suggest a communal, liturgical context from the early church. These actions appear again in the Last Supper in 26.26. **21:** *Five thousand men* refers to the way the Israelites were counted in the wilderness (Ex 12.37).

14.22–36: Jesus' dominion over nature (Mk 6.45–52; Jn 6.15–21). **25:** *Early in the morning,* Gk "in

pray. When evening came, he was there
alone, 24 but by this time the boat, battered
by the waves, was far from the land,[a] for
the wind was against them. 25 And early in
the morning he came walking toward them
on the sea. 26 But when the disciples saw
him walking on the sea, they were terrified,
saying, "It is a ghost!" And they cried out
in fear. 27 But immediately Jesus spoke to
them and said, "Take heart, it is I; do not
be afraid."

28 Peter answered him, "Lord, if it is
you, command me to come to you on the
water." 29 He said, "Come." So Peter got
out of the boat, started walking on the wa-
ter, and came toward Jesus. 30 But when
he noticed the strong wind,[b] he became
frightened, and beginning to sink, he cried
out, "Lord, save me!" 31 Jesus immediately
reached out his hand and caught him, say-
ing to him, "You of little faith, why did you
doubt?" 32 When they got into the boat, the
wind ceased. 33 And those in the boat wor-
shiped him, saying, "Truly you are the Son
of God."

34 When they had crossed over, they
came to land at Gennesaret. 35 After the
people of that place recognized him, they
sent word throughout the region and
brought all who were sick to him, 36 and
begged him that they might touch even the
fringe of his cloak; and all who touched it
were healed.

15 Then Pharisees and scribes came to
Jesus from Jerusalem and said,
2 "Why do your disciples break the tradi-
tion of the elders? For they do not wash
their hands before they eat." 3 He answered
them, "And why do you break the com-
mandment of God for the sake of your tra-
dition? 4 For God said,[c] 'Honor your fa-
ther and your mother,' and, 'Whoever
speaks evil of father or mother must surely
die.' 5 But you say that whoever tells father
or mother, 'Whatever support you might
have had from me is given to God,'[d] then
that person need not honor the father.[e]
6 So, for the sake of your tradition, you
make void the word[f] of God. 7 You hypo-
crites! Isaiah prophesied rightly about you
when he said:

8 'This people honors me with
their lips,
but their hearts are far from me;
9 in vain do they worship me,
teaching human precepts as
doctrines.' "

10 Then he called the crowd to him and
said to them, "Listen and understand: 11 it
is not what goes into the mouth that defiles
a person, but it is what comes out of the
mouth that defiles." 12 Then the disciples
approached and said to him, "Do you
know that the Pharisees took offense when
they heard what you said?" 13 He an-
swered, "Every plant that my heavenly Fa-
ther has not planted will be uprooted. 14 Let
them alone; they are blind guides of the
blind.[g] And if one blind person guides an-
other, both will fall into a pit." 15 But Peter
said to him, "Explain this parable to us."

a Other ancient authorities read *was out on the sea* *b* Other ancient authorities read *the wind* *c* Other ancient authorities read *commanded, saying* *d* Or *is an offering* *e* Other ancient authorities add *or the mother* *f* Other ancient authorities read *law*; others, *commandment* *g* Other ancient authorities lack *of the blind*

the fourth watch of the night," i.e., between 3 and 6 AM. **27:** *It is I,* lit. "I am," a reference to the divine name (Ex 3.14), and an identification of Jesus with God. **28–31:** Matthew inserts this episode concerning Peter into the traditional story. Peter's call for help echoes Ps 69.1–3. **31:** Cf. 8.26; 6.30. **34:** *Gennesaret,* a district on the northwestern shore of the Sea of Galilee (which was sometimes called the Lake of Gennesaret).

15.1–20: Conflict over tradition and authority (Mk 7.1–23). Jesus enters into a legal argument. Similar disputes continued into Matthew's day. **2:** *Tradition of the elders,* regulations not found in the written Torah (Josephus, *Ant.* 13.297). *Wash,* Mk 7.4; Lk 11.38. **4:** Ex 20.12; Deut 5.16; Ex 21.17; Lev 20.9. **5:** Latter rabbinic tradition agrees that need to support one's parents overrides such a vow (*m. Ned.* 9.1). **8–9:** Isa 29.13 (in the Septuagint). **11:** *Defiles,* makes unclean, and therefore unable to participate in worship in the Temple. Such unclean foods are listed in Lev 11. **13:** Isa 60.21. **15:** *Parable,* in the sense

16 Then he said, "Are you also still without
understanding? 17 Do you not see that
whatever goes into the mouth enters the
stomach, and goes out into the sewer?
18 But what comes out of the mouth pro-
ceeds from the heart, and this is what de-
files. 19 For out of the heart come evil inten-
tions, murder, adultery, fornication, theft,
false witness, slander. 20 These are what de-
file a person, but to eat with unwashed
hands does not defile."

21 Jesus left that place and went away to
the district of Tyre and Sidon. 22 Just then a
Canaanite woman from that region came
out and started shouting, "Have mercy on
me, Lord, Son of David; my daughter is
tormented by a demon." 23 But he did not
answer her at all. And his disciples came
and urged him, saying, "Send her away, for
she keeps shouting after us." 24 He an-
swered, "I was sent only to the lost sheep of
the house of Israel." 25 But she came and
knelt before him, saying, "Lord, help me."
26 He answered, "It is not fair to take the
children's food and throw it to the dogs."
27 She said, "Yes, Lord, yet even the dogs
eat the crumbs that fall from their masters'
table." 28 Then Jesus answered her, "Wom-
an, great is your faith! Let it be done for
you as you wish." And her daughter was
healed instantly.

29 After Jesus had left that place, he
passed along the Sea of Galilee, and he
went up the mountain, where he sat down.
30 Great crowds came to him, bringing with
them the lame, the maimed, the blind, the
mute, and many others. They put them at
his feet, and he cured them, 31 so that the
crowd was amazed when they saw the mute
speaking, the maimed whole, the lame
walking, and the blind seeing. And they
praised the God of Israel.

32 Then Jesus called his disciples to him
and said, "I have compassion for the
crowd, because they have been with me
now for three days and have nothing to eat;
and I do not want to send them away hun-
gry, for they might faint on the way."
33 The disciples said to him, "Where are we
to get enough bread in the desert to feed so
great a crowd?" 34 Jesus asked them, "How
many loaves have you?" They said, "Seven,
and a few small fish." 35 Then ordering the
crowd to sit down on the ground, 36 he
took the seven loaves and the fish; and after
giving thanks he broke them and gave them
to the disciples, and the disciples gave them
to the crowds. 37 And all of them ate and
were filled; and they took up the broken
pieces left over, seven baskets full. 38 Those
who had eaten were four thousand men,
besides women and children. 39 After send-
ing away the crowds, he got into the boat
and went to the region of Magadan.[a]

16 The Pharisees and Sadducees came,
and to test Jesus[b] they asked him to

a Other ancient authorities read *Magdala* or *Magdalan*
b Gk *him*

of "saying" or "precept." **19:** Jesus has already referred (v. 4) to the fifth of the ten commandments (Ex 20.12); here, after *evil intentions,* he alludes to the sixth (*murder,* Ex 20.13); seventh (*adultery, fornication,* Ex 20.14); eighth (*theft,* Ex 20.15); and ninth (*false witness, slander,* Ex 20.16).

15.21–28: The Canaanite woman and her daughter (Mk 7.24–30). **21:** *District of Tyre and Sidon,* Phoenicia, part of the Roman province of Syria. **22:** *Son of David,* a messianic title. Even though the woman is not Jewish, she addresses Jesus as the Jewish messiah. **24:** See 10.6n. **25–28:** The woman, through persistence and cleverness, persuades Jesus. *Dogs,* an insulting term; see 7.6n. *Let it be done,* as with the centurion's servant (8.5–13), Jesus heals Gentiles at a distance.

15.29–31: Further healings.

15.32–39: The second feeding. This story is a reiteration of the earlier feeding story in 14.13–21, with the same liturgical language. Such reiteration was a form of narrative emphasis. The two wilderness feedings echo the two accounts of the giving of food to the Israelites in the wilderness (Ex 16; Num 11). **39:** *Magadan,* an unknown place. *Magdala* (note *a*) was on the western shore of the Sea of Galilee; cf. Mk 8.10n.

16.1–12: Conflict with Pharisees and Sadducees (Mk 8.11–21). **1:** *Pharisees and Sadducees,* see 3.7n.

show them a sign from heaven. 2He an-
swered them, "When it is evening, you say,
'It will be fair weather, for the sky is red.'
3And in the morning, 'It will be stormy to-
day, for the sky is red and threatening.'
You know how to interpret the appearance
of the sky, but you cannot interpret the
signs of the times.[a] 4An evil and adulter-
ous generation asks for a sign, but no sign
will be given to it except the sign of Jonah."
Then he left them and went away.

5 When the disciples reached the other
side, they had forgotten to bring any bread.
6Jesus said to them, "Watch out, and be-
ware of the yeast of the Pharisees and Sad-
ducees." 7They said to one another, "It is
because we have brought no bread." 8And
becoming aware of it, Jesus said, "You of
little faith, why are you talking about hav-
ing no bread? 9Do you still not perceive?
Do you not remember the five loaves for
the five thousand, and how many baskets
you gathered? 10Or the seven loaves for the
four thousand, and how many baskets you
gathered? 11How could you fail to perceive
that I was not speaking about bread? Be-
ware of the yeast of the Pharisees and Sad-
ducees!" 12Then they understood that he
had not told them to beware of the yeast of
bread, but of the teaching of the Pharisees
and Sadducees.

13 Now when Jesus came into the dis-
trict of Caesarea Philippi, he asked his dis-
ciples, "Who do people say that the Son of
Man is?" 14And they said, "Some say John
the Baptist, but others Elijah, and still oth-
ers Jeremiah or one of the prophets." 15He
said to them, "But who do you say that I
am?" 16Simon Peter answered, "You are
the Messiah,[b] the Son of the living God."
17And Jesus answered him, "Blessed are
you, Simon son of Jonah! For flesh and
blood has not revealed this to you, but my
Father in heaven. 18And I tell you, you are
Peter,[c] and on this rock[d] I will build my
church, and the gates of Hades will not pre-
vail against it. 19I will give you the keys of
the kingdom of heaven, and whatever you
bind on earth will be bound in heaven, and
whatever you loose on earth will be loosed
in heaven." 20Then he sternly ordered the
disciples not to tell anyone that he was[e]
the Messiah.[b]

21 From that time on, Jesus began to
show his disciples that he must go to Jeru-
salem and undergo great suffering at the
hands of the elders and chief priests and
scribes, and be killed, and on the third day

a Other ancient authorities lack *2When it is . . . of the times* *b* Or *the Christ* *c* Gk *Petros* *d* Gk *petra* *e* Other ancient authorities add *Jesus*

3: *Signs of the times,* perhaps those of 15.29–31. **4:** 12.39–41; Jon 3.4–5. **5:** *Other side,* the eastern shore of the Sea of Galilee. **6:** *Yeast,* traditionally an image of spoilage and therefore of evil. Lev 2.11 prohibits the sacrifice of any grain contaminated with yeast. **9:** 14.15–21. **10:** 15.32–38.

16.13–20: Peter's confession at Caesarea Philippi (Mk 8.27–33; Lk 9.18–22). **13:** *Caesarea Philippi,* modern Banias, was built by Herod the Great at the northernmost extent of the Hulah Valley near the modern Israeli-Syrian border. At this city in the first century was a shrine to the god Pan and a temple to the Roman emperor, Augustus. *Son of Man,* see 8.20n. **14:** The disciples' response is that Jesus is viewed largely as a prophetic figure. **16:** Peter's answer combines a traditional Jewish title with a familiar Greek title. The Hebrew *Messiah* (*Christ,* note *b*) means "anointed" and is a royal title (1 Kings 1.39). *Son of . . . God* was a Greek title for a ruler or divine leader, a favorite, in particular, of the first Roman emperor Augustus, who was Herod the Great's patron. It is also, however, another Hebrew royal title (Ps 2.7). **17:** *Flesh and blood,* i.e., human agency in contrast to God (cf. Gal 1.17). **18:** *Peter . . . rock,* in Greek (see notes *c* and *d*) a clear play on words, which is even clearer in Aramaic ("kepha" in both instances). **19:** *Keys,* a symbol of authority (cf. Isa 22.22, "key of the house of David"). *Bind . . . loose,* judicial terms meaning "forbid" and "permit." The expression contrasts Peter's teaching authority with that of the scribes and Pharisees (see 23.13). In 18.18 the same authority is given to the disciples.

16.21–28: Jesus' rebuke of Peter and the nature of discipleship. Peter, representing the disciples, reveals they do not understand the challenge of discipleship (see 5.10–12). **21:** Jesus' first prediction of his own death in Matthew; cf. 17.22–23; 20.17–19. **22:** *Rebuke,* usually applied to demons and evil forces in the

be raised. 22 And Peter took him aside and
began to rebuke him, saying, "God forbid
it, Lord! This must never happen to you."
23 But he turned and said to Peter, "Get be-
hind me, Satan! You are a stumbling block
to me; for you are setting your mind not on
divine things but on human things."
24 Then Jesus told his disciples, "If any
want to become my followers, let them
deny themselves and take up their cross and
follow me. 25 For those who want to save
their life will lose it, and those who lose
their life for my sake will find it. 26 For
what will it profit them if they gain the
whole world but forfeit their life? Or what
will they give in return for their life?
27 "For the Son of Man is to come with
his angels in the glory of his Father, and
then he will repay everyone for what has
been done. 28 Truly I tell you, there are
some standing here who will not taste
death before they see the Son of Man com-
ing in his kingdom."

17 Six days later, Jesus took with him
Peter and James and his brother
John and led them up a high mountain, by
themselves. 2 And he was transfigured be-
fore them, and his face shone like the sun,
and his clothes became dazzling white.
3 Suddenly there appeared to them Moses
and Elijah, talking with him. 4 Then Peter
said to Jesus, "Lord, it is good for us to be
here; if you wish, I[a] will make three dwell-
ings[b] here, one for you, one for Moses,
and one for Elijah." 5 While he was still
speaking, suddenly a bright cloud over-
shadowed them, and from the cloud a voice
said, "This is my Son, the Beloved;[c] with
him I am well pleased; listen to him!"
6 When the disciples heard this, they fell to
the ground and were overcome by fear.
7 But Jesus came and touched them, saying,
"Get up and do not be afraid." 8 And when
they looked up, they saw no one except
Jesus himself alone.
9 As they were coming down the moun-
tain, Jesus ordered them, "Tell no one
about the vision until after the Son of Man
has been raised from the dead." 10 And the
disciples asked him, "Why, then, do the
scribes say that Elijah must come first?"
11 He replied, "Elijah is indeed coming and
will restore all things; 12 but I tell you that
Elijah has already come, and they did not
recognize him, but they did to him whatev-
er they pleased. So also the Son of Man is
about to suffer at their hands." 13 Then the
disciples understood that he was speaking
to them about John the Baptist.
14 When they came to the crowd, a man
came to him, knelt before him, 15 and said,
"Lord, have mercy on my son, for he is an
epileptic and he suffers terribly; he often
falls into the fire and often into the water.
16 And I brought him to your disciples, but
they could not cure him." 17 Jesus an-
swered, "You faithless and perverse gener-

a Other ancient authorities read *we*   *b* Or *tents*
c Or *my beloved Son*

Gospels. **23:** *Satan,* adversary and tempter. **24–28:** Mk 8.34–9.1; Lk 9.23–27; cf. Mt 10.33,38–39. **27:** *He will repay everyone,* Ps 62.12.

17.1–8: The Transfiguration (Mk 9.2–8; Lk 9.28–36). **1:** *Six days,* cf. Ex 24.16. *Peter, James,* and *John* are often an inner circle of the disciples. The *high mountain* may be Mount Hermon, in close proximity to Caesarea Philippi; the traditional identification is Mount Tabor, south of Nazareth. **2:** *Transfigured,* having a divine appearance. *Face shone,* like Moses' face (Ex 34.29) after encountering God on Mount Sinai. *Clothes . . . white,* like the "Ancient One" in Daniel's vision (Dan 7.9). **3:** *Moses, Elijah,* showing the continuity of Jesus and his teaching with Israel's lawgiver and the prophetic precursor of the messiah (Mal 4.5–6). **5:** The *voice* echoes the baptismal one (3.17), adding the command to obey Jesus' word (cf. Deut 18.15). **6:** *Fell to the ground,* cf. Dan 8.18; 10.9.

17.9–13: The importance of John the Baptist (Mk 9.9–13). The expectation that Elijah would precede the coming of the messiah (Mal 4.5–6) becomes in the Synoptic Gospels the belief that John the Baptist was that Elijah. His execution anticipates the suffering and death of the messiah (14.1–2).

17.14–21: Faith and acts of power (Mk 9.14–29; Lk 9.37–43). The healing of the boy with epilepsy instructs the community about the relationship between accomplishing great deeds and possessing even

ation, how much longer must I be with
you? How much longer must I put up with
you? Bring him here to me." 18 And Jesus
rebuked the demon,[a] and it[b] came out
of him, and the boy was cured instantly.
19 Then the disciples came to Jesus privately
and said, "Why could we not cast it out?"
20 He said to them, "Because of your little
faith. For truly I tell you, if you have faith
the size of a[c] mustard seed, you will say to
this mountain, 'Move from here to there,'
and it will move; and nothing will be impossible for you."[d]

22 As they were gathering[e] in Galilee,
Jesus said to them, "The Son of Man is
going to be betrayed into human hands,
23 and they will kill him, and on the third
day he will be raised." And they were greatly distressed.

24 When they reached Capernaum, the
collectors of the temple tax[f] came to Peter
and said, "Does your teacher not pay the
temple tax?"[f] 25 He said, "Yes, he does."
And when he came home, Jesus spoke of it
first, asking, "What do you think, Simon?
From whom do kings of the earth take toll
or tribute? From their children or from others?"
26 When Peter[g] said, "From others,"
Jesus said to him, "Then the children are
free. 27 However, so that we do not give
offense to them, go to the sea and cast a
hook; take the first fish that comes up; and
when you open its mouth, you will find a
coin;[h] take that and give it to them for you
and me."

18 At that time the disciples came to
Jesus and asked, "Who is the greatest in the kingdom of heaven?"
2 He called
a child, whom he put among them, 3 and
said, "Truly I tell you, unless you change
and become like children, you will never
enter the kingdom of heaven. 4 Whoever becomes humble like this child is the greatest
in the kingdom of heaven. 5 Whoever welcomes one such child in my name welcomes me.

6 "If any of you put a stumbling block
before one of these little ones who believe
in me, it would be better for you if a great
millstone were fastened around your neck
and you were drowned in the depth of the
sea. 7 Woe to the world because of stumbling blocks! Occasions for stumbling are
bound to come, but woe to the one by
whom the stumbling block comes!

8 "If your hand or your foot causes you
to stumble, cut it off and throw it away; it

a Gk *it* or *him* *b* Gk *the demon* *c* Gk *faith as a grain of* *d* Other ancient authorities add verse 21, *But this kind does not come out except by prayer and fasting* *e* Other ancient authorities read *living* *f* Gk *didrachma* *g* Gk *he* *h* Gk *stater*; the stater was worth two didrachmas

the smallest amount of faith. **17:** *Faithless and perverse generation,* Deut 32.5,20. **20:** *Mustard seed,* Lk 17.6. *Say to this mountain, 'Move,* was an "impossible thing" that only God could do.

17.22–23: Jesus' second prediction of betrayal and death (Mk 9.30–32; Lk 9.43–45). Cf. 16.21; 20.17–19. **22:** *Were gathering,* for the pilgrimage to Jerusalem for Passover. *Be betrayed,* the passive verb suggests that God permits Jesus' passion (cf. Isa 53.6,10).

17.24–27: The question of taxes. The first of two Matthean sections devoted to the problem of paying taxes (see also 22.17). A revolt against Rome broke out in Judea in 66 CE. Payment of tax or tribute to Rome was a precipitating factor in that revolt. **24:** *Temple tax,* each Jewish male was to pay a half-shekel annually in March (Ex 30.13) for support of the Temple. After the revolt against Rome, Jews were forced to pay this tax to support the temple of Jupiter Capitolinus in Rome (Josephus, *War* 7.218). **26:** *The children are free,* suggests Jesus believes payment of the tax is not required in Israel. **27:** *So that we do not give offense,* Matthew encourages Jewish Christians to maintain solidarity with the larger Jewish community.

18.1–35: The fourth discourse. 1–9: The question about genuine greatness (Mk 9.33–37,42–48; Lk 9.46–48; 17.1–2). **3:** *Become like children,* a child's social status was little better than that of a slave (Gal 4.1). **6:** *Stumbling block,* as an image for causing someone to sin (Sir 9.5; 25.21; 34.7; 1QS 2.12; *T. Reuben* 4.7). **8–9:** *Enter life maimed,* could refer to Jewish martyrs (2 Macc 7.11; 4 Macc 10.20). Also see 5.29–30.

is better for you to enter life maimed or lame than to have two hands or two feet and to be thrown into the eternal fire. 9 And if your eye causes you to stumble, tear it out and throw it away; it is better for you to enter life with one eye than to have two eyes and to be thrown into the hell[a] of fire.

10 "Take care that you do not despise one of these little ones; for, I tell you, in heaven their angels continually see the face of my Father in heaven.[b] 12 What do you think? If a shepherd has a hundred sheep, and one of them has gone astray, does he not leave the ninety-nine on the mountains and go in search of the one that went astray? 13 And if he finds it, truly I tell you, he rejoices over it more than over the ninety-nine that never went astray. 14 So it is not the will of your[c] Father in heaven that one of these little ones should be lost.

15 "If another member of the church[d] sins against you,[e] go and point out the fault when the two of you are alone. If the member listens to you, you have regained that one.[f] 16 But if you are not listened to, take one or two others along with you, so that every word may be confirmed by the evidence of two or three witnesses. 17 If the member refuses to listen to them, tell it to the church; and if the offender refuses to listen even to the church, let such a one be to you as a Gentile and a tax collector. 18 Truly I tell you, whatever you bind on earth will be bound in heaven, and whatever you loose on earth will be loosed in heaven. 19 Again, truly I tell you, if two of you agree on earth about anything you ask, it will be done for you by my Father in heaven. 20 For where two or three are gathered in my name, I am there among them."

21 Then Peter came and said to him, "Lord, if another member of the church[g] sins against me, how often should I forgive? As many as seven times?" 22 Jesus said to him, "Not seven times, but, I tell you, seventy-seven[h] times.

23 "For this reason the kingdom of heaven may be compared to a king who wished to settle accounts with his slaves. 24 When he began the reckoning, one who owed him ten thousand talents[i] was brought to him; 25 and, as he could not pay, his lord ordered him to be sold, together with his wife and children and all his possessions, and payment to be made. 26 So the slave fell on his knees before him, saying, 'Have patience with me, and I will pay you everything.' 27 And out of pity for him, the lord of that slave released him and forgave him the debt. 28 But that same slave, as he went out, came upon one of his fellow slaves who owed him a hundred denarii;[j] and seizing him by the throat, he said, 'Pay what you owe.' 29 Then his fellow slave fell down and pleaded with him, 'Have patience with me, and I will pay you.' 30 But he refused; then he went and threw him into prison until he would pay the debt.

a Gk *Gehenna* *b* Other ancient authorities add verse 11, *For the Son of Man came to save the lost* *c* Other ancient authorities read *my* *d* Gk *If your brother* *e* Other ancient authorities lack *against you* *f* Gk *the brother* *g* Gk *if my brother* *h* Or *seventy times seven* *i* A talent was worth more than fifteen years' wages of a laborer *j* The denarius was the usual day's wage for a laborer

18.10–35: Life and relationships within the church. 10: *Little ones,* socially inferior or more vulnerable members of the church. *Their angels,* it was believed that one's guardian represented one in heaven (Acts 12.15). **12:** *A shepherd,* a common image for a community leader (Num 27.17; Jer 3.15), must seek out even the lowliest person; cf. Lk 15.3–7. **15–17:** The process of disciplining a member of the church. A similar process was used by the Essenes (cf. 1QS 6 and CD 9). **16:** Deut 19.15. **17:** Matthew is the only Gospel writer to use the term *church* (Gk "ekklesia"). **18:** *Bind . . . loose,* see 16.16n. The authority to interpret Jesus' teaching extends to the community's judicial decisions. **21:** Forgiveness is the guiding principle in church relations and resolving conflict; for the numbers, cf. Gen 4.24; Lk 17.4. **23–35:** The parable of the debtors uses exaggeration to make its point about forgiveness. **24:** *Ten thousand talents* was an immense sum (see note *i*), impossible for the slave to pay back. **25:** *Sold,* in accordance with the law (Lev 25.39; 2 Kings 4.1). **28:** *A hundred denarii* would have been three or four months' wages. **34:**

31 When his fellow slaves saw what had
happened, they were greatly distressed, and
they went and reported to their lord all that
had taken place. 32 Then his lord sum-
moned him and said to him, 'You wicked
slave! I forgave you all that debt because
you pleaded with me. 33 Should you not
have had mercy on your fellow slave, as I
had mercy on you?' 34 And in anger his lord
handed him over to be tortured until he
would pay his entire debt. 35 So my heaven-
ly Father will also do to every one of you,
if you do not forgive your brother or sis-
ter[a] from your heart."

19 When Jesus had finished saying
these things, he left Galilee and
went to the region of Judea beyond the Jor-
dan. 2 Large crowds followed him, and he
cured them there.

3 Some Pharisees came to him, and to
test him they asked, "Is it lawful for a man
to divorce his wife for any cause?" 4 He an-
swered, "Have you not read that the one
who made them at the beginning 'made
them male and female,' 5 and said, 'For this
reason a man shall leave his father and
mother and be joined to his wife, and the
two shall become one flesh'? 6 So they are
no longer two, but one flesh. Therefore
what God has joined together, let no one
separate." 7 They said to him, "Why then
did Moses command us to give a certificate
of dismissal and to divorce her?" 8 He said
to them, "It was because you were so hard-
hearted that Moses allowed you to divorce
your wives, but from the beginning it was
not so. 9 And I say to you, whoever divorces
his wife, except for unchastity, and marries
another commits adultery."[b]

10 His disciples said to him, "If such is
the case of a man with his wife, it is better
not to marry." 11 But he said to them, "Not
everyone can accept this teaching, but only
those to whom it is given. 12 For there are
eunuchs who have been so from birth, and
there are eunuchs who have been made eu-
nuchs by others, and there are eunuchs who
have made themselves eunuchs for the sake
of the kingdom of heaven. Let anyone ac-
cept this who can."

13 Then little children were being
brought to him in order that he might lay
his hands on them and pray. The disciples
spoke sternly to those who brought them;
14 but Jesus said, "Let the little children
come to me, and do not stop them; for it is
to such as these that the kingdom of heaven
belongs." 15 And he laid his hands on them
and went on his way.

16 Then someone came to him and said,

a Gk *brother* *b* Other ancient authorities read *except on the ground of unchastity, causes her to commit adultery*; others add at the end of the verse *and he who marries a divorced woman commits adultery*

To be tortured, a tactic used by kings to extort money from the victim's family (Livy, *History* 3.13.8).

19.1–12: Continued legal debate with some of the Pharisees (Mk 10.1–12). **1:** *Galilee . . . Judea beyond the Jordan,* traveling directly south from Galilee to Judea meant going through Samaria, which Jews avoided if they could because of religious conflict with Samaritans (see 10.5n.). Jesus, too, avoids Samaria, traveling east across the Jordan into Perea and then south. **3:** *Divorce . . . cause,* the Torah allows for divorce (Deut 24.1) at the initiative of the husband, but does not specify the grounds. The grounds for divorce thus became a matter for debate among the rabbis. **4–6:** Gen 1.27; 2.24. An appeal to creation in order to establish the purpose of marriage is also found in Essene texts (CD 4.20–5.2; 11QTemple 56.18–19, prohibiting polygamy). **9:** In Matthew, unlike the parallel in Mark (10.2–11), Jesus allows for an exception (as in 5.32), here translated *unchastity,* which may refer to adultery or to marriages between close kin. Mt 1.19 assumes that a pious Jew would divorce an adulterer. **10:** *Better not to marry,* an unusual position in the Judaism of the time, which regarded marriage and procreation as an obligation (Gen 1.28). **11–12:** *Eunuchs,* castrated males abhorred by Jews (Josephus, *Apion* 2.270–71). Jesus accepts the possibility of voluntary celibacy, as did other pious Jews (Josephus, *Ant.* 18.21; cf. 1 Cor 7).

19.13–30: Questions pertaining to eternal life (Mk 10.13–31; Lk 18.15–30). **13–15:** *Little children,* repeats 18.1–5 and makes an implicit comment on the following incident. **16:** Lev 18.5. The question shows respect for Jesus as a religious teacher (*b. Ber.* 28b; Acts 2.37). **17:** *Only one . . . good,* Deut 6.4.

“Teacher, what good deed must I do to
have eternal life?” 17 And he said to him,
“Why do you ask me about what is good?
There is only one who is good. If you wish
to enter into life, keep the command-
ments.” 18 He said to him, “Which ones?”
And Jesus said, “You shall not murder;
You shall not commit adultery; You shall
not steal; You shall not bear false witness;
19 Honor your father and mother; also, You
shall love your neighbor as yourself.”
20 The young man said to him, “I have kept
all these;[a] what do I still lack?” 21 Jesus
said to him, “If you wish to be perfect, go,
sell your possessions, and give the money[b]
to the poor, and you will have treasure in
heaven; then come, follow me.” 22 When
the young man heard this word, he went
away grieving, for he had many posses-
sions.
23 Then Jesus said to his disciples, “Tru-
ly I tell you, it will be hard for a rich person
to enter the kingdom of heaven. 24 Again
I tell you, it is easier for a camel to go
through the eye of a needle than for some-
one who is rich to enter the kingdom of
God.” 25 When the disciples heard this,
they were greatly astounded and said,
“Then who can be saved?” 26 But Jesus
looked at them and said, “For mortals it is
impossible, but for God all things are possi-
ble.”
27 Then Peter said in reply, “Look, we
have left everything and followed you.
What then will we have?” 28 Jesus said to
them, “Truly I tell you, at the renewal of all
things, when the Son of Man is seated on
the throne of his glory, you who have fol-
lowed me will also sit on twelve thrones,
judging the twelve tribes of Israel. 29 And
everyone who has left houses or brothers or
sisters or father or mother or children or
fields, for my name’s sake, will receive a
hundredfold,[c] and will inherit eternal life.
30 But many who are first will be last, and
the last will be first.

20 “For the kingdom of heaven is like a
landowner who went out early in
the morning to hire laborers for his vine-
yard. 2 After agreeing with the laborers for
the usual daily wage,[d] he sent them into
his vineyard. 3 When he went out about
nine o’clock, he saw others standing idle
in the marketplace; 4 and he said to them,
‘You also go into the vineyard, and I will
pay you whatever is right.’ So they went.
5 When he went out again about noon and
about three o’clock, he did the same. 6 And
about five o’clock he went out and found
others standing around; and he said to
them, ‘Why are you standing here idle all
day?’ 7 They said to him, ‘Because no one
has hired us.’ He said to them, ‘You also go
into the vineyard.’ 8 When evening came,
the owner of the vineyard said to his man-
ager, ‘Call the laborers and give them their
pay, beginning with the last and then going
to the first.’ 9 When those hired about five
o’clock came, each of them received the
usual daily wage.[d] 10 Now when the first
came, they thought they would receive
more; but each of them also received the
usual daily wage.[d] 11 And when they re-
ceived it, they grumbled against the land-

a Other ancient authorities add *from my youth*
b Gk lacks *the money* *c* Other ancient authorities
read *manifold* *d* Gk *a denarius*

18–19: Ex 20.12–16; Deut 5.16–20; Lev 19.18. **21:** *To be perfect,* Mt 5.48. **22:** This hard word provides a glimpse into the difficult and austere life of the first followers of Jesus (6.24; 10.8–11). **24:** A proverbial expression of impossibility. **25–26:** The disciples miss the point: complete reliance upon God. *God . . . possible,* Gen 18.14; Jer 32.17. **28:** *On twelve thrones,* the disciples assume the role of the twelve patriarchs (*T. Jud.* 25.1–2). **30:** The priorities and economy of the kingdom of heaven are reversed as in the following parable.

20.1–16: The laborers in the vineyard. This parable, unique to Matthew, is a deliberate challenge to conventional views of just reward. **1:** *Early,* about 6 AM. **2:** *Usual daily wage* or *denarius* (note *d*), the amount was enough to provide one day’s food for a family. **8:** *Evening,* according to Jewish law (Lev 19.13; Deut 24.14–15) laborers were to be paid on the same day as they had worked, before sundown.

owner, 12 saying, 'These last worked only
one hour, and you have made them equal
to us who have borne the burden of the day
and the scorching heat.' 13 But he replied to
one of them, 'Friend, I am doing you no
wrong; did you not agree with me for the
usual daily wage?[a] 14 Take what belongs
to you and go; I choose to give to this last
the same as I give to you. 15 Am I not al-
lowed to do what I choose with what be-
longs to me? Or are you envious because I
am generous?'[b] 16 So the last will be first,
and the first will be last."[c]

17 While Jesus was going up to Jerusa-
lem, he took the twelve disciples aside by
themselves, and said to them on the way,
18 "See, we are going up to Jerusalem, and
the Son of Man will be handed over to the
chief priests and scribes, and they will con-
demn him to death; 19 then they will hand
him over to the Gentiles to be mocked and
flogged and crucified; and on the third day
he will be raised."

20 Then the mother of the sons of Zebe-
dee came to him with her sons, and kneel-
ing before him, she asked a favor of him.
21 And he said to her, "What do you
want?" She said to him, "Declare that these
two sons of mine will sit, one at your right
hand and one at your left, in your king-
dom." 22 But Jesus answered, "You do not
know what you are asking. Are you able to
drink the cup that I am about to drink?"[d]
They said to him, "We are able." 23 He said
to them, "You will indeed drink my cup,
but to sit at my right hand and at my left,
this is not mine to grant, but it is for those
for whom it has been prepared by my Fa-
ther."

24 When the ten heard it, they were an-
gry with the two brothers. 25 But Jesus
called them to him and said, "You know
that the rulers of the Gentiles lord it over
them, and their great ones are tyrants over
them. 26 It will not be so among you; but
whoever wishes to be great among you
must be your servant, 27 and whoever
wishes to be first among you must be your
slave; 28 just as the Son of Man came not to
be served but to serve, and to give his life a
ransom for many."

29 As they were leaving Jericho, a large
crowd followed him. 30 There were two
blind men sitting by the roadside. When
they heard that Jesus was passing by, they
shouted, "Lord,[e] have mercy on us, Son of
David!" 31 The crowd sternly ordered them
to be quiet; but they shouted even more
loudly, "Have mercy on us, Lord, Son of

a Gk *a denarius* *b* Gk *is your eye evil because I am good?* *c* Other ancient authorities add *for many are called but few are chosen* *d* Other ancient authorities add *or to be baptized with the baptism that I am baptized with?* *e* Other ancient authorities lack *Lord*

12: *Made them equal to us,* presumes that justice requires distributing society's goods in proportion to status and merit (see Aristotle, *Nichomachean Ethics* 5.3–4). **15:** *Allowed to do what I choose,* not a general statement of economic rights, but rather an assertion of permission to exceed conventional expectation. *Envious,* implies that the complaint is motivated by greed (Sir 14.8–10).

20.17–19: Jesus anticipates his death and resurrection (Mk 10.32–34; Lk 18.31–34). For the third and final time (cf. 16.21; 17.22–23) Jesus specifically informs his inner group of followers that his death is near. **19:** *Gentiles,* a general term, refers to the presence in Jerusalem of Roman military and legal authorities. *Flogged,* see 10.17n.

20.20–28: Service as greatness (Mk 10.35–45). In the parallel passage in Mark it is the two sons themselves who ask the question, not their mother. **22:** *Cup,* a metaphor for that which is allotted by God, whether blessing (Ps 16.5; 116.13) or judgment (Isa 51.17; Lam 4.21). It here refers to Jesus' suffering and death (see 26.39). **23:** Acts 12.2. **28:** *Ransom,* rescue or deliver. *Many,* the opposite of "few," i.e., as many as will avail themselves of the offer, up to and including all; cf. Isa 53.10–12.

20.29–34: Seeking help from the Son of David (Mk 10.46–52; Lk 18.35–43). In Matthew's version of this story there are two men in need of healing, not one. **29:** *Jericho,* in the Jordan valley 21 km (13 mi) east-northeast of Jerusalem. **30:** *Son of David,* a royal, kingly title also associated with healing in Matthew (9.27; 12.23).

David!" 32Jesus stood still and called them,
saying, "What do you want me to do for
you?" 33They said to him, "Lord, let our
eyes be opened." 34Moved with compas-
sion, Jesus touched their eyes. Immediately
they regained their sight and followed him.

21 When they had come near Jerusalem
and had reached Bethphage, at the
Mount of Olives, Jesus sent two disciples,
2saying to them, "Go into the village ahead
of you, and immediately you will find a
donkey tied, and a colt with her; untie them
and bring them to me. 3If anyone says any-
thing to you, just say this, 'The Lord needs
them.' And he will send them immediate-
ly.[a]" 4This took place to fulfill what had
been spoken through the prophet, saying,
5 "Tell the daughter of Zion,
Look, your king is coming to you,
humble, and mounted on a donkey,
and on a colt, the foal of
a donkey."
6The disciples went and did as Jesus had
directed them; 7they brought the donkey
and the colt, and put their cloaks on them,
and he sat on them. 8A very large crowd[b]
spread their cloaks on the road, and others
cut branches from the trees and spread
them on the road. 9The crowds that went
ahead of him and that followed were shout-
ing,
"Hosanna to the Son of David!
Blessed is the one who comes in the
name of the Lord!
Hosanna in the highest heaven!"
10When he entered Jerusalem, the whole
city was in turmoil, asking, "Who is this?"
11The crowds were saying, "This is the
prophet Jesus from Nazareth in Galilee."
12 Then Jesus entered the temple[c] and
drove out all who were selling and buying
in the temple, and he overturned the tables
of the money changers and the seats of
those who sold doves. 13He said to them,
"It is written,
'My house shall be called a house
of prayer';
but you are making it a den
of robbers."
14 The blind and the lame came to him
in the temple, and he cured them. 15But
when the chief priests and the scribes saw
the amazing things that he did, and heard[d]
the children crying out in the temple, "Ho-
sanna to the Son of David," they became
angry 16and said to him, "Do you hear
what these are saying?" Jesus said to them,
"Yes; have you never read,

a Or *'The Lord needs them and will send them back immediately.'* b Or *Most of the crowd* c Other ancient authorities add *of God* d Gk lacks *heard*

21.1–11: Jesus' entry into Jerusalem. 1: *Bethphage,* a village located just east of Jerusalem. *The Mount of Olives* is part of a ridge on the east side of Jerusalem. A tradition within Second Temple Judaism held that a battle would take place there at the end of the age (Zech 14.4; Josephus, *Ant.* 20.167–72). **5:** Unlike the parallels in Mk 11.1–10 and Lk 19.28–38, Matthew includes one of his fulfillment citations, quoting Isa 62.11 and Zech 9.9. The specification of two animals, *donkey* and *colt,* presents Jesus as one who literally fulfills Zech 9.9. The scene evokes images of a king or triumphant general's entry into a city (1 Kings 1.32–40; 1 Macc 5.45–54; Josephus, *War* 7.70–71). *Mounted on a donkey,* coming in peace (warriors rode on stallions). **8:** *Spread . . . cloaks . . . branches,* signs of honor (for branches, see 1 Macc 13.49–53). **9:** *Hosanna,* derived from Ps 118.26, means "O save!" It was a general cry of acclamation, not necessarily a specific request for salvation.

21.12–27: Jesus' confrontations in the Temple (Lk 19.45–46; Mk 11.15–19; Jn 2.13–17). The Temple in Jerusalem was an enormous structure and known throughout the Roman world. It had been rebuilt by Herod the Great beginning around 20 BCE in his most ambitious building project. (It was not completed until 63 CE.) The Temple contained many precincts, including places to buy and sell animals for sacrifice, places for foreign visitors to change money into the Temple currency, and offices for local and imperial authorities. **13:** Combining passages from Jer 7.11 and Isa 56.7, Jesus condemns those in the Temple by calling them robbers, the same term used to describe the men with whom Jesus is crucified in 27.38. **16:** Ps 8.2. **17:** *Bethany,* another village to the east of Jerusalem. **18–22:** Sandwiched between two accounts

'Out of the mouths of infants and
nursing babies
you have prepared praise for
yourself'?"
17 He left them, went out of the city to Beth-
any, and spent the night there.
18 In the morning, when he returned to
the city, he was hungry. 19 And seeing a fig
tree by the side of the road, he went to it
and found nothing at all on it but leaves.
Then he said to it, "May no fruit ever come
from you again!" And the fig tree withered
at once. 20 When the disciples saw it, they
were amazed, saying, "How did the fig tree
wither at once?" 21 Jesus answered them,
"Truly I tell you, if you have faith and do
not doubt, not only will you do what has
been done to the fig tree, but even if you say
to this mountain, 'Be lifted up and thrown
into the sea,' it will be done. 22 Whatever
you ask for in prayer with faith, you will
receive."
23 When he entered the temple, the chief
priests and the elders of the people came to

of conflict in the Temple is an enacted parable about a fig tree, a sign of judgment against the Temple (23.37–38; 24.2); cf. Mk 11.12–14. **21**: 17.20. **22**: 7.7. **23–27**: Mk 11.27–33; Lk 20.1–8. The second

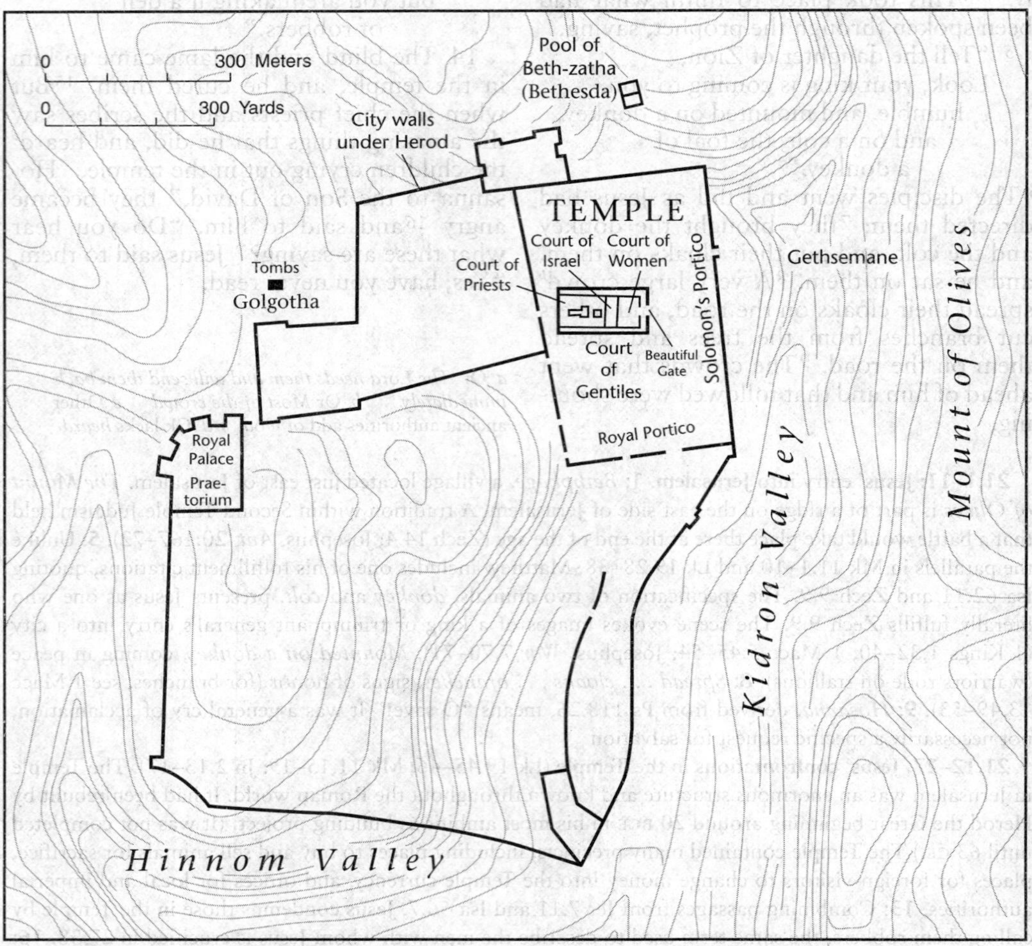

Chs 21–12: Jerusalem in the time of Jesus.

him as he was teaching, and said, "By what
authority are you doing these things, and
who gave you this authority?" 24 Jesus said
to them, "I will also ask you one question;
if you tell me the answer, then I will also
tell you by what authority I do these things.
25 Did the baptism of John come from heav-
en, or was it of human origin?" And they
argued with one another, "If we say, 'From
heaven,' he will say to us, 'Why then did
you not believe him?' 26 But if we say, 'Of
human origin,' we are afraid of the crowd;
for all regard John as a prophet." 27 So they
answered Jesus, "We do not know." And
he said to them, "Neither will I tell you by
what authority I am doing these things.

28 "What do you think? A man had two
sons; he went to the first and said, 'Son, go
and work in the vineyard today.' 29 He an-
swered, 'I will not'; but later he changed his
mind and went. 30 The father[a] went to the
second and said the same; and he answered,
'I go, sir'; but he did not go. 31 Which of the
two did the will of his father?" They said,
"The first." Jesus said to them, "Truly I tell
you, the tax collectors and the prostitutes
are going into the kingdom of God ahead
of you. 32 For John came to you in the way
of righteousness and you did not believe
him, but the tax collectors and the prosti-
tutes believed him; and even after you saw
it, you did not change your minds and be-
lieve him.

33 "Listen to another parable. There
was a landowner who planted a vineyard,
put a fence around it, dug a wine press in it,
and built a watchtower. Then he leased it
to tenants and went to another country.
34 When the harvest time had come, he sent
his slaves to the tenants to collect his pro-
duce. 35 But the tenants seized his slaves and
beat one, killed another, and stoned anoth-
er. 36 Again he sent other slaves, more than
the first; and they treated them in the same
way. 37 Finally he sent his son to them, say-
ing, 'They will respect my son.' 38 But when
the tenants saw the son, they said to them-
selves, 'This is the heir; come, let us kill him
and get his inheritance.' 39 So they seized
him, threw him out of the vineyard, and
killed him. 40 Now when the owner of the
vineyard comes, what will he do to those
tenants?" 41 They said to him, "He will put
those wretches to a miserable death, and
lease the vineyard to other tenants who will
give him the produce at the harvest time."

42 Jesus said to them, "Have you never
read in the scriptures:

'The stone that the builders rejected
 has become the cornerstone;[b]
this was the Lord's doing,
 and it is amazing in our eyes'?

43 Therefore I tell you, the kingdom of God
will be taken away from you and given to a
people that produces the fruits of the king-
dom.[c] 44 The one who falls on this stone

a Gk *He* b Or *keystone* c Gk *the fruits of it*

confrontation in the Temple is with Temple officials directly. **23:** *By what authority,* implies that Jesus is no more than a rabble rouser (Aristotle, *Politics* 3.6–7; Plutarch, *Moralia* 545C). **26:** *Afraid of the crowd,* 14.5; Josephus, *Ant.* 18.118. **27:** If the Temple officials will not acknowledge John's authority, it is useless to ask them to recognize Jesus' claims.

21.28–32: Tax collectors, prostitutes, and the kingdom of God. This parable about two sons addresses the subject of why those who are lax in observing the Mosaic law receive the kingdom of God. **31–32:** *Tax collectors,* see 9.10n. Along with *prostitutes* they were the members of a despised group. The parable serves to condemn Jesus' opponents for unbelief. (For use of a parable to accuse the powerful, see 2 Sam 12.1–15.)

21.33–46: The parable of the wicked tenants (Mk 12.1–12; Lk 20.9–19). See Isa 5.1–7. The *vineyard* was a traditional metaphor for Israel. **33–46:** The parable is an allegory, in which the vineyard is Jerusalem, the tenants the religious authorities (see v. 45), the slaves the prophets, and the son Jesus himself. **33:** *Planted . . . fence . . . wine press . . . watchtower,* almost a direct quotation of Isa 5.2. *Tenants* would contract to give the owner an agreed-upon portion of the crop, keeping for themselves what was left. **35–39:** The *tenants* hope to keep all of the produce. **41:** A prediction of the destruction of Jerusalem. *Other tenants,* the church or perhaps church leaders. **42:** Ps 118.22–23.

will be broken to pieces; and it will crush
anyone on whom it falls."[a]
45 When the chief priests and the Phari-
sees heard his parables, they realized that
he was speaking about them. 46 They want-
ed to arrest him, but they feared the
crowds, because they regarded him as a
prophet.

22 Once more Jesus spoke to them in
parables, saying: 2 "The kingdom of
heaven may be compared to a king who
gave a wedding banquet for his son. 3 He
sent his slaves to call those who had been
invited to the wedding banquet, but they
would not come. 4 Again he sent other
slaves, saying, 'Tell those who have been
invited: Look, I have prepared my dinner,
my oxen and my fat calves have been
slaughtered, and everything is ready; come
to the wedding banquet.' 5 But they made
light of it and went away, one to his farm,
another to his business, 6 while the rest
seized his slaves, mistreated them, and
killed them. 7 The king was enraged. He
sent his troops, destroyed those murderers,
and burned their city. 8 Then he said to his
slaves, 'The wedding is ready, but those in-
vited were not worthy. 9 Go therefore into
the main streets, and invite everyone you
find to the wedding banquet.' 10 Those
slaves went out into the streets and gath-
ered all whom they found, both good and
bad; so the wedding hall was filled with
guests.
11 "But when the king came in to see the
guests, he noticed a man there who was not
wearing a wedding robe, 12 and he said to
him, 'Friend, how did you get in here with-
out a wedding robe?' And he was speech-
less. 13 Then the king said to the attendants,
'Bind him hand and foot, and throw him
into the outer darkness, where there will
be weeping and gnashing of teeth.' 14 For
many are called, but few are chosen."
15 Then the Pharisees went and plotted
to entrap him in what he said. 16 So they
sent their disciples to him, along with the
Herodians, saying, "Teacher, we know that
you are sincere, and teach the way of God
in accordance with truth, and show defer-
ence to no one; for you do not regard peo-
ple with partiality. 17 Tell us, then, what
you think. Is it lawful to pay taxes to the
emperor, or not?" 18 But Jesus, aware of
their malice, said, "Why are you putting me
to the test, you hypocrites? 19 Show me the
coin used for the tax." And they brought
him a denarius. 20 Then he said to them,
"Whose head is this, and whose title?"
21 They answered, "The emperor's." Then
he said to them, "Give therefore to the em-
peror the things that are the emperor's, and
to God the things that are God's." 22 When
they heard this, they were amazed; and they
left him and went away.
23 The same day some Sadducees came

a Other ancient authorities lack verse 44

22.1–14: The wedding feast (Lk 14.16–24). This parable, like the previous one, concerns the refusal to enter the kingdom by those originally invited. **4:** *Again he sent,* traditionally the first two sendings (vv. 3–4) are allegorized as the prophets and the third (v. 10) as the Christian mission (Irenaeus, *Adv. haer.* 4.36.5). **7:** The destruction of Jerusalem by Roman legions in 70 CE (Josephus, *War* 6.353–408). **10:** The substitution of the Christians for Jesus' opponents. **11–14:** This may originally have been a separate parable dealing with preparedness, like the parables of judgment in chs 24–25. Otherwise, given the way in which the substitute guests have been gathered (vv. 9–10), this guest's lack of a *wedding robe* would be surprising. **13:** *Outer darkness . . . weeping . . . gnashing of teeth,* images of hell (1 Enoch 9–10).

22.15–46: A series of debates with the local leaders (Mk 12.13–37; Lk 20.20–44). **15:** The enmity between Jesus and his followers and local leaders is now overt. **16:** *The Herodians,* political supporters of the Herods; because of the origin of the Herodian family in Idumea, a non-Jewish area, many Jews did not regard the Herods as legitimate rulers of Israel. **17:** To approve of the tax would be offensive to Jewish nationalists; to disapprove would be treasonous. The poll tax provoked revolt in 66 CE (Josephus, *War* 2.118). **20:** *Whose head,* only coins from the imperial mint, probably silver denarii, had images and inscriptions honoring the emperor as divine. **23:** *Sadducees,* see 3.7–12n. They did not accept the *resurrec-*

to him, saying there is no resurrection;[a]
and they asked him a question, saying,
24 “Teacher, Moses said, ‘If a man dies
childless, his brother shall marry the wid-
ow, and raise up children for his brother.’
25 Now there were seven brothers among
us; the first married, and died childless,
leaving the widow to his brother. 26 The
second did the same, so also the third,
down to the seventh. 27 Last of all, the
woman herself died. 28 In the resurrection,
then, whose wife of the seven will she be?
For all of them had married her.”
29 Jesus answered them, “You are
wrong, because you know neither the scrip-
tures nor the power of God. 30 For in the
resurrection they neither marry nor are giv-
en in marriage, but are like angels[b] in
heaven. 31 And as for the resurrection of the
dead, have you not read what was said to
you by God, 32 ‘I am the God of Abraham,
the God of Isaac, and the God of Jacob’?
He is God not of the dead, but of the liv-
ing.” 33 And when the crowd heard it, they
were astounded at his teaching.
34 When the Pharisees heard that he had
silenced the Sadducees, they gathered to-
gether, 35 and one of them, a lawyer, asked
him a question to test him. 36 “Teacher,
which commandment in the law is the
greatest?” 37 He said to him, “ ‘You shall
love the Lord your God with all your heart,
and with all your soul, and with all your
mind.’ 38 This is the greatest and first com-
mandment. 39 And a second is like it: ‘You
shall love your neighbor as yourself.’ 40 On
these two commandments hang all the law
and the prophets.”
41 Now while the Pharisees were gath-
ered together, Jesus asked them this ques-
tion: 42 “What do you think of the Messi-
ah?[c] Whose son is he?” They said to him,
“The son of David.” 43 He said to them,
“How is it then that David by the Spirit[d]
calls him Lord, saying,
44 ‘The Lord said to my Lord,
“Sit at my right hand,
until I put your enemies under your
feet” ’?
45 If David thus calls him Lord, how can he
be his son?” 46 No one was able to give him
an answer, nor from that day did anyone
dare to ask him any more questions.

23 Then Jesus said to the crowds and
to his disciples, 2 “The scribes and
the Pharisees sit on Moses’ seat; 3 therefore,
do whatever they teach you and follow it;
but do not do as they do, for they do not
practice what they teach. 4 They tie up
heavy burdens, hard to bear,[e] and lay
them on the shoulders of others; but they
themselves are unwilling to lift a finger to
move them. 5 They do all their deeds to be
seen by others; for they make their phylac-

a Other ancient authorities read *who say that there is no resurrection* b Other ancient authorities add *of God* c Or *Christ* d Gk *in spirit* e Other ancient authorities lack *hard to bear*

tion, since it is not mentioned in the Torah. **24:** The law of levirate marriage (from Latin “levir,” brother-in-law), Deut 25.5. **26:** *Down to the seventh,* echoes Tob 3.7–10. **31–32:** Ex 3.6. (For Ex 3.6 as proof that the patriarchs were still living, see Philo, *Abraham* 50–55.) **35:** *A lawyer,* a scholar of the Law (the Torah), a scribe. **36:** Rabbi Hillel is said to have responded to this question in the Talmud, (*b. Shabb.* 31a), “What is hateful to you do not do to your neighbor; that is the whole Torah, the rest is commentary; go and learn it” (see 7.12n.). **37–39:** Jesus responds with the quotations from Deut 6.5 and Lev 19.18. **40:** *The law and the prophets,* the first two (of three) sections of the Hebrew Bible. **41–46:** Jesus turns the tables on his debate partners by asking them a question about the messiah. **43:** *David* was the traditional author of many of the Psalms. **44:** Ps 110.1. The first *Lord* is God; the second *Lord* is taken to be the messiah. The argument turns on the belief that the offspring cannot be greater than the progenitor.

23.1–25.46: The fifth discourse. 23.1–39: Cf. Lk 11.37–12.1. This entire chapter is devoted to Jesus’ critical judgment against the religious leadership. **2:** *Moses’ seat,* perhaps a metaphor for teaching authority. (On scribes and Pharisees teaching with Moses’ authority, see *m.’ Abot* 1.1.) **5:** *Phylacteries,* small leather boxes containing scripture quotations (e.g., Deut 6.4–9). They were tied onto the forehead and the left arm, in obedience to Deut 6.6,8. *Fringes,* blue twisted threads at the four corners of a garment, a reminder to teries broad and their fringes long. 6 They love to have the place of honor at banquets and the best seats in the synagogues, 7 and to be greeted with respect in the market-places, and to have people call them rabbi. 8 But you are not to be called rabbi, for you have one teacher, and you are all students.[a] 9 And call no one your father on earth, for you have one Father—the one in heaven. 10 Nor are you to be called instructors, for you have one instructor, the Messiah.[b] 11 The greatest among you will be your servant. 12 All who exalt themselves will be humbled, and all who humble themselves will be exalted.

13 "But woe to you, scribes and Pharisees, hypocrites! For you lock people out of the kingdom of heaven. For you do not go in yourselves, and when others are going in, you stop them.[c] 15 Woe to you, scribes and Pharisees, hypocrites! For you cross sea and land to make a single convert, and you make the new convert twice as much a child of hell[d] as yourselves.

16 "Woe to you, blind guides, who say, 'Whoever swears by the sanctuary is bound by nothing, but whoever swears by the gold of the sanctuary is bound by the oath.' 17 You blind fools! For which is greater, the gold or the sanctuary that has made the gold sacred? 18 And you say, 'Whoever swears by the altar is bound by nothing, but whoever swears by the gift that is on the altar is bound by the oath.' 19 How blind you are! For which is greater, the gift or the altar that makes the gift sacred? 20 So whoever swears by the altar, swears by it and by everything on it; 21 and whoever swears by the sanctuary, swears by it and by the one who dwells in it; 22 and whoever swears by heaven, swears by the throne of God and by the one who is seated upon it.

23 "Woe to you, scribes and Pharisees, hypocrites! For you tithe mint, dill, and cummin, and have neglected the weightier matters of the law: justice and mercy and faith. It is these you ought to have practiced without neglecting the others. 24 You blind guides! You strain out a gnat but swallow a camel!

25 "Woe to you, scribes and Pharisees, hypocrites! For you clean the outside of the cup and of the plate, but inside they are full of greed and self-indulgence. 26 You blind Pharisee! First clean the inside of the cup,[e] so that the outside also may become clean.

27 "Woe to you, scribes and Pharisees, hypocrites! For you are like whitewashed tombs, which on the outside look beautiful, but inside they are full of the bones of the dead and of all kinds of filth. 28 So you also on the outside look righteous to others, but inside you are full of hypocrisy and lawlessness.

29 "Woe to you, scribes and Pharisees, hypocrites! For you build the tombs of the prophets and decorate the graves of the righteous, 30 and you say, 'If we had lived in the days of our ancestors, we would not

a Gk *brothers* *b* Or *the Christ* *c* Other authorities add here (or after verse 12) verse 14, *Woe to you, scribes and Pharisees, hypocrites! For you devour widows' houses and for the sake of appearance you make long prayers; therefore you will receive the greater condemnation* *d* Gk *Gehenna* *e* Other ancient authorities add *and of the plate*

obey the commandments (Num 15.38–40). **13:** The seven woes (vv. 13,15,16,23,25,27,29) denounce empty religious observances; they should not be taken as an indictment of all Pharisees, nor of all Jews of the time. *Hypocrites,* a term derived from Greek theater referring to the role assumed by an actor. **16:** There is no evidence of this formula, but a similar phrase contrasting the Torah scroll and its words appears in *b. Ned.* 14b. **23:** *Tithe,* Lev 27.30. The point of the denunciation seems to be that in trying to carry out the law requiring tithes of produce even for such tiny herbs, the Pharisees miss the important requirements of the Law (see Mic 6.8). **24:** *Strain out a gnat,* an insect (which was unclean; Lev 11.20–23) that had fallen into wine. *Camel,* an unclean animal (Lev 11.4), proverbial example of a large animal (cf. 19.24). **27:** *Whitewashed tombs,* which were whitened so that pilgrims coming to Jerusalem to celebrate Passover would not touch them by mistake and so become ritually unclean. **30:** *Blood of the prophets,* 2 Chr 24.20–22. There were other accounts of prophets who were killed, but no others in the Hebrew Bible.

have taken part with them in shedding the
blood of the prophets.' 31 Thus you testify
against yourselves that you are descendants
of those who murdered the prophets. 32 Fill
up, then, the measure of your ancestors.
33 You snakes, you brood of vipers! How
can you escape being sentenced to hell?[a]
34 Therefore I send you prophets, sages, and
scribes, some of whom you will kill and
crucify, and some you will flog in your syn-
agogues and pursue from town to town,
35 so that upon you may come all the righ-
teous blood shed on earth, from the blood
of righteous Abel to the blood of Zechariah
son of Barachiah, whom you murdered be-
tween the sanctuary and the altar. 36 Truly
I tell you, all this will come upon this gener-
ation.

37 "Jerusalem, Jerusalem, the city that
kills the prophets and stones those who are
sent to it! How often have I desired to gath-
er your children together as a hen gathers
her brood under her wings, and you were
not willing! 38 See, your house is left to you,
desolate.[b] 39 For I tell you, you will not see
me again until you say, 'Blessed is the one
who comes in the name of the Lord.'"

24 As Jesus came out of the temple and
was going away, his disciples came
to point out to him the buildings of the
temple. 2 Then he asked them, "You see all
these, do you not? Truly I tell you, not one
stone will be left here upon another; all will
be thrown down."

3 When he was sitting on the Mount of
Olives, the disciples came to him privately,
saying, "Tell us, when will this be, and
what will be the sign of your coming and of
the end of the age?" 4 Jesus answered them,
"Beware that no one leads you astray. 5 For
many will come in my name, saying, 'I am
the Messiah!'[c] and they will lead many
astray. 6 And you will hear of wars and ru-
mors of wars; see that you are not alarmed;
for this must take place, but the end is not
yet. 7 For nation will rise against nation,
and kingdom against kingdom, and there
will be famines[d] and earthquakes in vari-
ous places: 8 all this is but the beginning of
the birth pangs.

9 "Then they will hand you over to be
tortured and will put you to death, and you
will be hated by all nations because of my
name. 10 Then many will fall away,[e] and
they will betray one another and hate one
another. 11 And many false prophets will
arise and lead many astray. 12 And because
of the increase of lawlessness, the love of
many will grow cold. 13 But the one who
endures to the end will be saved. 14 And this
good news[f] of the kingdom will be pro-
claimed throughout the world, as a testi-
mony to all the nations; and then the end
will come.

15 "So when you see the desolating sac-

a Gk *Gehenna* *b* Other ancient authorities lack *desolate* *c* Or *the Christ* *d* Other ancient authorities add *and pestilences* *e* Or *stumble* *f* Or *gospel*

33: See 3.7. **34:** *Flog,* see 10.17n. *Your synagogues,* an indication of the division that is already beginning to occur between Matthew's community and other Jewish groups in Matthew's setting. **35:** *Abel,* Gen 4.8–10. The identity of this *Zechariah* is uncertain; cf. 2 Chr 24.20–22; Zech 1.1. **37–39:** The concluding verses implicate these leadership groups in the most significant event of Matthew's era, the fall of Jerusalem, which was still a bitter and vivid memory at the time of the Gospel; cf. Lk 13.34–35; Jer 22.5. **39:** Ps 118.26, echoing 21.9.

24.1–51: Eschatological discourse (Mk 13.1–37; Lk 21.5–36). In this apocalyptic section Jesus teaches about the end of the age. Numerous writers, Jewish and Christian, and also Stoic philosophers, shared the belief that history was headed for some great transforming cataclysm. **1–2:** The destruction of the Jerusalem Temple in 70 CE by the Romans was seen as the beginning of the end. **3:** *Mount of Olives,* see 21.1n. **7:** *Nation will rise against nation,* better, "people will rise up against people, and kingdom against kingdom." The nation-state is a much later political idea not applicable to the time of the Gospels. **14:** See 28.19–20. **15:** *Desolating sacrilege,* the performance of non-Jewish religious observance, particularly idolatry and unclean sacrifice, in the Temple. The Seleucid king Antiochus IV perpetuated such acts in 167 BCE (1 Macc 1.54), provoking the Maccabean revolt; see Dan 9.27; 11.31; 12.11. *Daniel,* see

rilege standing in the holy place, as was
spoken of by the prophet Daniel (let the
reader understand), 16 then those in Judea
must flee to the mountains; 17 the one on
the housetop must not go down to take
what is in the house; 18 the one in the field
must not turn back to get a coat. 19 Woe to
those who are pregnant and to those who
are nursing infants in those days! 20 Pray
that your flight may not be in winter or on
a sabbath. 21 For at that time there will be
great suffering, such as has not been from
the beginning of the world until now, no,
and never will be. 22 And if those days had
not been cut short, no one would be saved;
but for the sake of the elect those days will
be cut short. 23 Then if anyone says to you,
'Look! Here is the Messiah!'[a] or 'There he
is!'—do not believe it. 24 For false messi-
ahs[b] and false prophets will appear and
produce great signs and omens, to lead
astray, if possible, even the elect. 25 Take
note, I have told you beforehand. 26 So, if
they say to you, 'Look! He is in the wilder-
ness,' do not go out. If they say, 'Look! He
is in the inner rooms,' do not believe it.
27 For as the lightning comes from the east
and flashes as far as the west, so will be the
coming of the Son of Man. 28 Wherever the
corpse is, there the vultures will gather.

29 "Immediately after the suffering of
those days

> the sun will be darkened,
> and the moon will not give its light;
> the stars will fall from heaven,
> and the powers of heaven will
> be shaken.

30 Then the sign of the Son of Man will
appear in heaven, and then all the tribes of
the earth will mourn, and they will see 'the
Son of Man coming on the clouds of heav-
en' with power and great glory. 31 And he
will send out his angels with a loud trumpet
call, and they will gather his elect from the
four winds, from one end of heaven to the
other.

32 "From the fig tree learn its lesson: as
soon as its branch becomes tender and puts
forth its leaves, you know that summer is
near. 33 So also, when you see all these
things, you know that he[c] is near, at the
very gates. 34 Truly I tell you, this genera-
tion will not pass away until all these things
have taken place. 35 Heaven and earth will
pass away, but my words will not pass
away.

36 "But about that day and hour no one
knows, neither the angels of heaven, nor
the Son,[d] but only the Father. 37 For as the
days of Noah were, so will be the coming of
the Son of Man. 38 For as in those days be-
fore the flood they were eating and drink-
ing, marrying and giving in marriage, until
the day Noah entered the ark, 39 and they
knew nothing until the flood came and
swept them all away, so too will be the
coming of the Son of Man. 40 Then two will
be in the field; one will be taken and one
will be left. 41 Two women will be grinding
meal together; one will be taken and one
will be left. 42 Keep awake therefore, for
you do not know on what day[e] your Lord
is coming. 43 But understand this: if the
owner of the house had known in what
part of the night the thief was coming, he
would have stayed awake and would not
have let his house be broken into. 44 There-

a Or *the Christ* *b* Or *christs* *c* Or *it* *d* Other ancient authorities lack *nor the Son* *e* Other ancient authorities read *at what hour*

Dan 9–12. *Let the reader understand,* an interpolation indicating that the audience for this passage is the later community. **20:** *Winter . . . sabbath,* when food could be scarce or unavailable. **21:** Dan 12.1; Joel 2.2. **24:** *False messiahs . . . prophets,* a reflection of competition between Jewish groups that were messianic in nature, like the Dead Sea Scrolls community or other popular movements like John the Baptist's. **27:** The *Son of Man,* an apocalyptic figure presaging the arrival of the end of the age (Dan 7); see 8.20n. **28:** *Corpse . . . vultures,* a proverbial expression (Job 39.30; Lk 17.37); the messiah will appear where needed, not at a preordained spot. **29:** Isa 13.10; Ezek 32.7. **30:** Dan 7.13. **31:** Isa 27.13; Zech 2.6; 1 Thess 4.16. **34:** *This generation,* the imminent end was a characteristic of early Christian preaching and teaching (1 Thess 4.17; 2 Thess 2). **35:** Cf. Isa 24.4; 40.8. **37:** *Days of Noah,* Gen 6–7. **45–51:** *Faithful and wise,*

fore you also must be ready, for the Son of
Man is coming at an unexpected hour.
45 "Who then is the faithful and wise
slave, whom his master has put in charge of
his household, to give the other slaves[a]
their allowance of food at the proper time?
46 Blessed is that slave whom his master will
find at work when he arrives. 47 Truly I tell
you, he will put that one in charge of all his
possessions. 48 But if that wicked slave says
to himself, 'My master is delayed,' 49 and he
begins to beat his fellow slaves, and eats
and drinks with drunkards, 50 the master of
that slave will come on a day when he does
not expect him and at an hour that he does
not know. 51 He will cut him in pieces[b] and
put him with the hypocrites, where there
will be weeping and gnashing of teeth.

25 "Then the kingdom of heaven will
be like this. Ten bridesmaids[c] took
their lamps and went to meet the bride-
groom.[d] 2 Five of them were foolish, and
five were wise. 3 When the foolish took
their lamps, they took no oil with them;
4 but the wise took flasks of oil with their
lamps. 5 As the bridegroom was delayed, all
of them became drowsy and slept. 6 But at
midnight there was a shout, 'Look! Here is
the bridegroom! Come out to meet him.'
7 Then all those bridesmaids[c] got up and
trimmed their lamps. 8 The foolish said to
the wise, 'Give us some of your oil, for our
lamps are going out.' 9 But the wise replied,
'No! there will not be enough for you and
for us; you had better go to the dealers and
buy some for yourselves.' 10 And while they
went to buy it, the bridegroom came, and
those who were ready went with him into
the wedding banquet; and the door was
shut. 11 Later the other bridesmaids[c] came
also, saying, 'Lord, lord, open to us.' 12 But
he replied, 'Truly I tell you, I do not know
you.' 13 Keep awake therefore, for you
know neither the day nor the hour.[e]
14 "For it is as if a man, going on a
journey, summoned his slaves and entrust-
ed his property to them; 15 to one he gave
five talents,[f] to another two, to another
one, to each according to his ability. Then
he went away. 16 The one who had received
the five talents went off at once and traded
with them, and made five more talents. 17 In
the same way, the one who had the two
talents made two more talents. 18 But the
one who had received the one talent went
off and dug a hole in the ground and hid his
master's money. 19 After a long time the
master of those slaves came and settled ac-
counts with them. 20 Then the one who had
received the five talents came forward,
bringing five more talents, saying, 'Master,
you handed over to me five talents; see, I
have made five more talents.' 21 His master
said to him, 'Well done, good and trust-
worthy slave; you have been trustworthy in
a few things, I will put you in charge of
many things; enter into the joy of your mas-
ter.' 22 And the one with the two talents
also came forward, saying, 'Master, you

a Gk *to give them* *b* Or *cut him off* *c* Gk *virgins*
d Other ancient authorities add *and the bride*
e Other ancient authorities add *in which the Son of Man is coming* *f* A talent was worth more than fifteen years' wages of a laborer

the final warning addresses leaders in the Christian community. **51:** *Cut him in pieces,* destroy him; Matthew has combined this image of punishment with another, *weeping and gnashing of teeth,* producing an incongruous image.

25.1–13: The parable of the ten maidens. An apocalyptic parable that exhorts the community not to lose hope or patience and to remain prepared. **1:** *Lamps,* to be carried in the procession. *Meet the bridegroom,* who would be coming from the house of the bride's parents to his own house. Everyone would take part in this procession. The omission of the phrase *and the bride* (note *d*) may indicate an effort to allegorize the *bridegroom* as the messiah. **5:** *Delayed,* an allusion to the postponement of the end-times. **11–12:** An addition about judgment, not preparedness. **13:** Cf. 24.42.

25.14–30: The parable of the talents (Lk 19.12–27). Also referred to as the parable of the hard master, this is the third in a series of parables dealing with attitudes and behavior in the face of the coming of the Son of Man. **15:** *Five talents,* equivalent to 30,000 denarii (a denarius was a day's wage for a laborer). The servants have the financial *ability* to manage the master's wealth. **29:** See 13.12.

handed over to me two talents; see, I have
made two more talents.' 23 His master said
to him, 'Well done, good and trustworthy
slave; you have been trustworthy in a few
things, I will put you in charge of many
things; enter into the joy of your master.'
24 Then the one who had received the one
talent also came forward, saying, 'Master, I
knew that you were a harsh man, reaping
where you did not sow, and gathering
where you did not scatter seed; 25 so I was
afraid, and I went and hid your talent in the
ground. Here you have what is yours.'
26 But his master replied, 'You wicked and
lazy slave! You knew, did you, that I reap
where I did not sow, and gather where I did
not scatter? 27 Then you ought to have in-
vested my money with the bankers, and on
my return I would have received what was
my own with interest. 28 So take the talent
from him, and give it to the one with the
ten talents. 29 For to all those who have,
more will be given, and they will have an
abundance; but from those who have noth-
ing, even what they have will be taken
away. 30 As for this worthless slave, throw
him into the outer darkness, where there
will be weeping and gnashing of teeth.'

31 "When the Son of Man comes in his
glory, and all the angels with him, then he
will sit on the throne of his glory. 32 All the
nations will be gathered before him, and he
will separate people one from another as
a shepherd separates the sheep from the
goats, 33 and he will put the sheep at his
right hand and the goats at the left. 34 Then
the king will say to those at his right hand,
'Come, you that are blessed by my Father,
inherit the kingdom prepared for you from
the foundation of the world; 35 for I was
hungry and you gave me food, I was thirsty
and you gave me something to drink, I was
a stranger and you welcomed me, 36 I was
naked and you gave me clothing, I was sick
and you took care of me, I was in prison
and you visited me.' 37 Then the righteous
will answer him, 'Lord, when was it that
we saw you hungry and gave you food, or
thirsty and gave you something to drink?
38 And when was it that we saw you a
stranger and welcomed you, or naked and
gave you clothing? 39 And when was it that
we saw you sick or in prison and visited
you?' 40 And the king will answer them,
'Truly I tell you, just as you did it to one of
the least of these who are members of my
family,[a] you did it to me.' 41 Then he will
say to those at his left hand, 'You that are
accursed, depart from me into the eternal
fire prepared for the devil and his angels;
42 for I was hungry and you gave me no
food, I was thirsty and you gave me noth-
ing to drink, 43 I was a stranger and you did
not welcome me, naked and you did not
give me clothing, sick and in prison and
you did not visit me.' 44 Then they also will
answer, 'Lord, when was it that we saw
you hungry or thirsty or a stranger or na-
ked or sick or in prison, and did not take
care of you?' 45 Then he will answer them,
'Truly I tell you, just as you did not do it to
one of the least of these, you did not do it
to me.' 46 And these will go away into eter-
nal punishment, but the righteous into eter-
nal life."

26 When Jesus had finished saying all
these things, he said to his disciples,
2 "You know that after two days the Pass-

a Gk *these my brothers*

25.31–46: The judgment. 31: *Son of Man,* see 24.27n. **32:** *All the nations,* the same phrase used at the close of the Gospel in 28.19. A better translation would be "all the people of the world." *Shepherd separates,* Ezek 34.17. **33:** *Right hand,* the hand with which a blessing would be given. **35–36:** *Hungry . . . prison,* the list of works of mercy ends with an unusual one, visiting prisoners, perhaps based on Isa 61.1. **41:** *Eternal fire,* 1 Enoch 10.13 refers to an "abyss of fire" in which evil ones will be shut up "for all eternity." **46:** Cf. Dan 12.2.

26.1–16: Approaching death and Judas's betrayal (Mk 14.1–11; Lk 22.1–6). The plot to kill Jesus starts to unfold. **2:** The death of Jesus is linked with the festival of *Passover,* a festival associated with sacrifice and liberation (Ex 12.1–20). Jesus' death is analogous to the Passover sacrifice (cf. Jn 19.36n.;

over is coming, and the Son of Man will be
handed over to be crucified."
3 Then the chief priests and the elders of
the people gathered in the palace of the
high priest, who was called Caiaphas, 4and
they conspired to arrest Jesus by stealth and
kill him. 5But they said, "Not during the
festival, or there may be a riot among the
people."
6 Now while Jesus was at Bethany in the
house of Simon the leper,[a] 7a woman
came to him with an alabaster jar of very
costly ointment, and she poured it on his
head as he sat at the table. 8But when the
disciples saw it, they were angry and said,
"Why this waste? 9For this ointment could
have been sold for a large sum, and the
money given to the poor." 10But Jesus,
aware of this, said to them, "Why do you
trouble the woman? She has performed a
good service for me. 11For you always have
the poor with you, but you will not always
have me. 12By pouring this ointment on
my body she has prepared me for burial.
13Truly I tell you, wherever this good
news[b] is proclaimed in the whole world,
what she has done will be told in remem-
brance of her."
14 Then one of the twelve, who was
called Judas Iscariot, went to the chief
priests 15and said, "What will you give me
if I betray him to you?" They paid him thir-
ty pieces of silver. 16And from that moment
he began to look for an opportunity to be-
tray him.
17 On the first day of Unleavened Bread
the disciples came to Jesus, saying, "Where
do you want us to make the preparations
for you to eat the Passover?" 18He said,
"Go into the city to a certain man, and say
to him, 'The Teacher says, My time is near;
I will keep the Passover at your house with
my disciples.'" 19So the disciples did as
Jesus had directed them, and they prepared
the Passover meal.
20 When it was evening, he took his
place with the twelve;[c] 21and while they
were eating, he said, "Truly I tell you, one
of you will betray me." 22And they became
greatly distressed and began to say to him
one after another, "Surely not I, Lord?"
23He answered, "The one who has dipped
his hand into the bowl with me will betray
me. 24The Son of Man goes as it is written
of him, but woe to that one by whom the
Son of Man is betrayed! It would have been
better for that one not to have been born."
25Judas, who betrayed him, said, "Surely
not I, Rabbi?" He replied, "You have
said so."
26 While they were eating, Jesus took a
loaf of bread, and after blessing it he broke
it, gave it to the disciples, and said, "Take,

a The terms *leper* and *leprosy* can refer to several diseases *b* Or *gospel* *c* Other ancient authorities add *disciples*

1 Cor 5.7n.; Rev 5.12). **3:** *Chief priests* and *elders* represent the local and regional authorities. These were mid-level bureaucrats who would need to appeal to a bona fide authority, like *Caiaphas* the *high priest,* to gain at least tacit approval to kill Jesus. Caiaphas held the office of high priest 18–36 CE. **5:** The possibility of a *riot* was a constant concern of Jerusalem officials during the holy days. **6:** *Bethany,* a village just east of Jerusalem. **13:** *In remembrance of her,* perhaps an indication of the important place of women early in the formation of the Christian church. **15:** *Thirty pieces of silver,* perhaps an allusion to the price of redeeming a person from a religious obligation (Lev 27.1–8) or to Zechariah's action indicting the Temple authorities for corruption by depositing tainted money in the treasury (Zech 11.12–13).

26.17–30: Preparation for the Passover and the Last Supper (Mk 14.12–26; Lk 22.7–39; cf. Jn 13). **17:** *The first day of Unleavened Bread,* though technically the day after Passover (Lev 23.6), the two feasts are equated in the Gospels (Mk 14.12; Lk 22.7; also Josephus, *Ant.* 18.29). **24:** *As it is written,* emphasizes that Jesus' death is part of God's plan (1 Cor 15.3). Isa 53.12 may be the text intended. **25:** Only Judas refers to Jesus directly as *Rabbi* in Matthew's Gospel. This Hebrew term, an honorific title meaning "teacher," does not become a technical term for an office within Judaism until the second century. **26–29:** Cf. 1 Cor 11.23–26. **28:** *Blood of the covenant,* Ex 24.8. For Matthew it is not a new *covenant* the

eat; this is my body." 27 Then he took a
cup, and after giving thanks he gave it to
them, saying, "Drink from it, all of you;
28 for this is my blood of the[a] covenant,
which is poured out for many for the for-
giveness of sins. 29 I tell you, I will never
again drink of this fruit of the vine until
that day when I drink it new with you in
my Father's kingdom."
30 When they had sung the hymn, they
went out to the Mount of Olives.
31 Then Jesus said to them, "You will
all become deserters because of me this
night; for it is written,
'I will strike the shepherd,
and the sheep of the flock will
be scattered.'
32 But after I am raised up, I will go ahead
of you to Galilee." 33 Peter said to him,
"Though all become deserters because of
you, I will never desert you." 34 Jesus said
to him, "Truly I tell you, this very night,
before the cock crows, you will deny me
three times." 35 Peter said to him, "Even
though I must die with you, I will not deny
you." And so said all the disciples.
36 Then Jesus went with them to a place
called Gethsemane; and he said to his disci-
ples, "Sit here while I go over there and
pray." 37 He took with him Peter and the
two sons of Zebedee, and began to be
grieved and agitated. 38 Then he said to
them, "I am deeply grieved, even to death;
remain here, and stay awake with me."
39 And going a little farther, he threw him-
self on the ground and prayed, "My Father,
if it is possible, let this cup pass from me;
yet not what I want but what you want."
40 Then he came to the disciples and found
them sleeping; and he said to Peter, "So,
could you not stay awake with me one
hour? 41 Stay awake and pray that you may
not come into the time of trial;[b] the spirit
indeed is willing, but the flesh is weak."
42 Again he went away for the second time
and prayed, "My Father, if this cannot pass
unless I drink it, your will be done."
43 Again he came and found them sleeping,
for their eyes were heavy. 44 So leaving
them again, he went away and prayed for
the third time, saying the same words.
45 Then he came to the disciples and said to
them, "Are you still sleeping and taking
your rest? See, the hour is at hand, and the
Son of Man is betrayed into the hands of
sinners. 46 Get up, let us be going. See, my
betrayer is at hand."
47 While he was still speaking, Judas,
one of the twelve, arrived; with him was a
large crowd with swords and clubs, from
the chief priests and the elders of the peo-
ple. 48 Now the betrayer had given them a
sign, saying, "The one I will kiss is the man;
arrest him." 49 At once he came up to Jesus
and said, "Greetings, Rabbi!" and kissed
him. 50 Jesus said to him, "Friend, do what
you are here to do." Then they came and
laid hands on Jesus and arrested him.
51 Suddenly, one of those with Jesus put his

a Other ancient authorities add *new* *b* Or *into temptation*

Supper initiates: Jesus' death and resurrection is the clear fulfillment of God's historic and ancient covenant with the people of Israel. The addition of the word "new" in some manuscripts (note *a*) was probably an attempt to make this passage harmonize with 1 Cor 11.25. **30:** *The hymn,* all or part of the Hillel Psalms (Ps 113–118), traditionally sung at the Passover seder.

26.31–56: Temptation, betrayal, and desertion (Mk 14.27–52; Lk 22.39–53; cf. Jn 18.1–12). **31:** Jesus predicts the disciples' desertion and cites Zech 13.7 as proof. **32:** This anticipates 28.10,16–17. **34:** *Before the cock crows,* before sunrise. **36:** *Gethsemane* means "oil press." This suggests it is on or near the Mount of Olives across the Kidron valley in Jerusalem. Lk 22.39 plainly states, "the Mount of Olives." **36–46:** Jesus' period of doubt and struggle begins here, prior to his trial and death sentence. **37:** *Peter and the two sons of Zebedee* (James and John) have constituted an inner circle of the disciples throughout the story. **38:** *I am,* lit. "my soul is." *Stay awake,* cf. 24.42; 25.13. **39:** *Cup,* see 20.22n. **47:** The crowd brought *swords and clubs,* indicating they expected violence or armed resistance. **48–49:** The authorities do not know Jesus well enough to recognize him in the garden. For examples of a deceitful *kiss,* see Jacob (Gen 27.27) and Joab (2 Sam 20.9–10). **51:** One of Jesus' followers does have a *sword.* To

hand on his sword, drew it, and struck the
slave of the high priest, cutting off his ear.
52 Then Jesus said to him, "Put your sword
back into its place; for all who take the
sword will perish by the sword. 53 Do you
think that I cannot appeal to my Father,
and he will at once send me more than
twelve legions of angels? 54 But how then
would the scriptures be fulfilled, which say
it must happen in this way?" 55 At that hour
Jesus said to the crowds, "Have you come
out with swords and clubs to arrest me as
though I were a bandit? Day after day I sat
in the temple teaching, and you did not ar-
rest me. 56 But all this has taken place, so
that the scriptures of the prophets may be
fulfilled." Then all the disciples deserted
him and fled.

57 Those who had arrested Jesus took
him to Caiaphas the high priest, in whose
house the scribes and the elders had gath-
ered. 58 But Peter was following him at a
distance, as far as the courtyard of the high
priest; and going inside, he sat with the
guards in order to see how this would end.
59 Now the chief priests and the whole
council were looking for false testimony
against Jesus so that they might put him
to death, 60 but they found none, though
many false witnesses came forward. At last
two came forward 61 and said, "This fellow
said, 'I am able to destroy the temple of
God and to build it in three days.' " 62 The
high priest stood up and said, "Have you
no answer? What is it that they testify
against you?" 63 But Jesus was silent. Then
the high priest said to him, "I put you un-
der oath before the living God, tell us if you
are the Messiah,[a] the Son of God." 64 Jesus
said to him, "You have said so. But I tell
you,

From now on you will see the
Son of Man
seated at the right hand of Power
and coming on the clouds
of heaven."

65 Then the high priest tore his clothes and
said, "He has blasphemed! Why do we still
need witnesses? You have now heard his
blasphemy. 66 What is your verdict?" They
answered, "He deserves death." 67 Then
they spat in his face and struck him; and
some slapped him, 68 saying, "Prophesy to
us, you Messiah![a] Who is it that struck
you?"

69 Now Peter was sitting outside in the
courtyard. A servant-girl came to him and
said, "You also were with Jesus the Gali-
lean." 70 But he denied it before all of them,
saying, "I do not know what you are talk-
ing about." 71 When he went out to the
porch, another servant-girl saw him, and
she said to the bystanders, "This man was
with Jesus of Nazareth."[b] 72 Again he de-
nied it with an oath, "I do not know the
man." 73 After a little while the bystanders
came up and said to Peter, "Certainly you
are also one of them, for your accent be-
trays you." 74 Then he began to curse, and
he swore an oath, "I do not know the
man!" At that moment the cock crowed.
75 Then Peter remembered what Jesus had
said: "Before the cock crows, you will deny

a Or *Christ* *b* Gk *the Nazorean*

some, Jesus and his followers look like rebels or bandits interested in the overthrow of the current Jerusalem government. **52:** *All who take the sword will perish by the sword,* similar to the prohibition against bloodshed in Gen 9.6 and reflects Jesus' teaching on nonretaliation (5.38–48). **53:** *Twelve legions,* compare the refusal to summon angels in 4.6–7. **54:** The events are in accordance with God's plan. **55:** Jesus explicitly addresses and denies the authorities' depiction of his movement as a seditious group.

26.57–75: Leveling charges against Jesus (Mk 14.53–72; Lk 22.54–71; cf. Jn 18.13–27). **59:** *Council,* the Sanhedrin, the official Jewish court, seventy scribes, priests, and elders, presided over by the high priest. **61–64:** Two charges serve as the pretext for sentencing Jesus: his words about tearing down the Temple (a misconstrual of Mt 24.2), and his evasive answer to Caiaphas's question. **64:** Dan 7.13; Ps 110.1. **66:** Cf. Lev 24.16. **67–68:** Borrowing this vignette from Mark, Matthew forgot to include the blindfolding of Jesus found in Mk 14.65, rendering the taunt to *prophesy* who it was that struck him less intelligible. **75:** See v. 34.

me three times." And he went out and wept
bitterly.

27 When morning came, all the chief
priests and the elders of the people
conferred together against Jesus in order to
bring about his death. 2 They bound him,
led him away, and handed him over to Pi-
late the governor.

3 When Judas, his betrayer, saw that
Jesus[a] was condemned, he repented and
brought back the thirty pieces of silver to
the chief priests and the elders. 4 He said, "I
have sinned by betraying innocent[b]
blood." But they said, "What is that to us?
See to it yourself." 5 Throwing down the
pieces of silver in the temple, he departed;
and he went and hanged himself. 6 But the
chief priests, taking the pieces of silver,
said, "It is not lawful to put them into the
treasury, since they are blood money." 7 Af-
ter conferring together, they used them to
buy the potter's field as a place to bury
foreigners. 8 For this reason that field has
been called the Field of Blood to this day.
9 Then was fulfilled what had been spoken
through the prophet Jeremiah,[c] "And they
took[d] the thirty pieces of silver, the price
of the one on whom a price had been set,[e]
on whom some of the people of Israel had
set a price, 10 and they gave[f] them for the
potter's field, as the Lord command-
ed me."

11 Now Jesus stood before the gover-
nor; and the governor asked him, "Are you
the King of the Jews?" Jesus said, "You say
so." 12 But when he was accused by the
chief priests and elders, he did not answer.
13 Then Pilate said to him, "Do you not
hear how many accusations they make
against you?" 14 But he gave him no an-
swer, not even to a single charge, so that
the governor was greatly amazed.

15 Now at the festival the governor was
accustomed to release a prisoner for the
crowd, anyone whom they wanted. 16 At
that time they had a notorious prisoner,
called Jesus[g] Barabbas. 17 So after they had
gathered, Pilate said to them, "Whom do
you want me to release for you, Jesus[g] Bar-
abbas or Jesus who is called the Messi-
ah?"[h] 18 For he realized that it was out of
jealousy that they had handed him over.
19 While he was sitting on the judgment
seat, his wife sent word to him, "Have
nothing to do with that innocent man, for
today I have suffered a great deal because
of a dream about him." 20 Now the chief
priests and the elders persuaded the crowds
to ask for Barabbas and to have Jesus
killed. 21 The governor again said to them,
"Which of the two do you want me to re-
lease for you?" And they said, "Barabbas."
22 Pilate said to them, "Then what should I
do with Jesus who is called the Messiah?"[h]
All of them said, "Let him be crucified!"
23 Then he asked, "Why, what evil has he

a Gk *he* *b* Other ancient authorities read *righteous*
c Other ancient authorities read *Zechariah* or *Isaiah*
d Or *I took* *e* Or *the price of the precious One*
f Other ancient authorities read *I gave* *g* Other ancient authorities lack *Jesus* *h* Or *the Christ*

27.1–31. The trial of Jesus (Mk 15.1–20; Lk 23.1–4,17–25; cf. Jn 18.28–19.16). In the Roman imperial system, not even Caiaphas, much less local leaders like elders of the people, scribes, or Pharisees, had final legal authority. They had to appeal to the regional Roman official, *the governor.* **2:** Pontius *Pilate* was the Roman governor of Judea 26–37 CE. His residence was in the city of Caesarea Maritima on the coast. Pilate was probably in Jerusalem for the Passover festival to help keep order. On other occasions Pilate's actions led to civic discord in Jerusalem (Josephus, *War* 2.169,177; *Ant.* 18.55,89). **3–10:** This account of Judas's death is found only in Matthew; for another legend about Judas's death, see Acts 1.18–20. **4:** A curse is pronounced upon anyone who betrays an innocent person for money (Deut 27.25). **9–10:** This citation is loosely based on Zech 11.12–13, though these verses also form a midrash on Jer 18–19. **11–14:** The governor's question to Jesus is different from that of Caiaphas. The latter was concerned with the Temple and with messianic claims. Pilate asks a purely political question: Are you guilty of sedition against the empire? **15:** There is no independent evidence for this custom. **16:** *Jesus Barabbas,* later manuscripts omit *Jesus* (note *g*) either to avoid confusion or because it had become a sacred name. **19:** Pilate's *wife,* like Joseph (1.19–23), learns the truth through a *dream.* **25:** This passage

done?" But they shouted all the more, "Let
him be crucified!"
24 So when Pilate saw that he could do
nothing, but rather that a riot was begin-
ning, he took some water and washed his
hands before the crowd, saying, "I am in-
nocent of this man's blood;[a] see to it your-
selves." 25 Then the people as a whole an-
swered, "His blood be on us and on our
children!" 26 So he released Barabbas for
them; and after flogging Jesus, he handed
him over to be crucified.
27 Then the soldiers of the governor
took Jesus into the governor's headquar-
ters,[b] and they gathered the whole cohort
around him. 28 They stripped him and put a
scarlet robe on him, 29 and after twisting
some thorns into a crown, they put it on his
head. They put a reed in his right hand and
knelt before him and mocked him, saying,
"Hail, King of the Jews!" 30 They spat on
him, and took the reed and struck him on
the head. 31 After mocking him, they
stripped him of the robe and put his own
clothes on him. Then they led him away to
crucify him.
32 As they went out, they came upon a
man from Cyrene named Simon; they com-
pelled this man to carry his cross. 33 And
when they came to a place called Golgotha
(which means Place of a Skull), 34 they of-
fered him wine to drink, mixed with gall;
but when he tasted it, he would not drink
it. 35 And when they had crucified him, they
divided his clothes among themselves by
casting lots;[c] 36 then they sat down there
and kept watch over him. 37 Over his head
they put the charge against him, which
read, "This is Jesus, the King of the Jews."
38 Then two bandits were crucified with
him, one on his right and one on his left.
39 Those who passed by derided[d] him,
shaking their heads 40 and saying, "You
who would destroy the temple and build it
in three days, save yourself! If you are the
Son of God, come down from the cross."
41 In the same way the chief priests also,
along with the scribes and elders, were
mocking him, saying, 42 "He saved others;
he cannot save himself.[e] He is the King of
Israel; let him come down from the cross
now, and we will believe in him. 43 He
trusts in God; let God deliver him now, if
he wants to; for he said, 'I am God's Son.'"
44 The bandits who were crucified with him
also taunted him in the same way.
45 From noon on, darkness came over
the whole land[f] until three in the after-
noon. 46 And about three o'clock Jesus
cried with a loud voice, "Eli, Eli, lema sa-
bachthani?" that is, "My God, my God,

a Other ancient authorities read *this righteous blood,* or *this righteous man's blood* *b* Gk *the praetorium* *c* Other ancient authorities add *in order that what had been spoken through the prophet might be fulfilled, "They divided my clothes among themselves, and for my clothing they cast lots."* *d* Or *blasphemed* *e* Or *is he unable to save himself?* *f* Or *earth*

has been erroneously employed over time to fuel anti-Jewish actions and attitudes. Guilt for killing the Lord's anointed is based on 2 Sam 1.16, where the reference is to the death of King Saul, God's anointed; cf. 1 Kings 2.23; Jer 26.15. *And on our children,* not all subsequent Jews, but the generation after Jesus' death who had to suffer through the destruction of Jerusalem in 70 CE. **26:** *Flogging* with a multi-thonged whip weakened the victim before execution. **27–31:** Jesus is mocked as a king by the crowd and soldiers. **31:** Crucifixion was a common Roman form of capital punishment for non-Roman citizens. It was regarded as particularly degrading, since it was a slow, painful method of death by suffocation that took place in public.

27.32–54: The crucifixion (Mk 15.21–39; Lk 23.26–48; cf. Jn 19.17–37). **32:** *Cyrene* was the capital of the north African district of Cyrenaica, on the southern Mediterranean coast west of Egypt. It had a large Jewish community. **33:** *Golgotha . . . Skull,* either the hill was shaped like a skull, or it was an unclean burial ground. **34:** *Gall,* any bitter substance. *Would not drink,* the wine would dull the pain, but Matthew (following Mark) wants to show that Jesus accepted the pain of his death fully. **37:** The charge, *King of the Jews,* specifies the crime for which Jesus was condemned: treason or sedition against Roman rule. **38:** He is crucified between *two bandits,* either common criminals or popular leaders viewed as a political threat. **46:** A citation from Ps 22.1, which the Gospel writers quote in Aramaic. **51:** The tearing

why have you forsaken me?" 47 When some
of the bystanders heard it, they said, "This
man is calling for Elijah." 48 At once one of
them ran and got a sponge, filled it with
sour wine, put it on a stick, and gave it to
him to drink. 49 But the others said, "Wait,
let us see whether Elijah will come to save
him."[a] 50 Then Jesus cried again with a
loud voice and breathed his last.[b] 51 At
that moment the curtain of the temple was
torn in two, from top to bottom. The earth
shook, and the rocks were split. 52 The
tombs also were opened, and many bodies
of the saints who had fallen asleep were
raised. 53 After his resurrection they came
out of the tombs and entered the holy city
and appeared to many. 54 Now when the
centurion and those with him, who were
keeping watch over Jesus, saw the earth-
quake and what took place, they were terri-
fied and said, "Truly this man was God's
Son!"[c]

55 Many women were also there, look-
ing on from a distance; they had followed
Jesus from Galilee and had provided for
him. 56 Among them were Mary Magda-
lene, and Mary the mother of James and
Joseph, and the mother of the sons of Zebe-
dee.

57 When it was evening, there came a
rich man from Arimathea, named Joseph,
who was also a disciple of Jesus. 58 He went
to Pilate and asked for the body of Jesus;
then Pilate ordered it to be given to him.
59 So Joseph took the body and wrapped it
in a clean linen cloth 60 and laid it in his
own new tomb, which he had hewn in the
rock. He then rolled a great stone to the
door of the tomb and went away. 61 Mary
Magdalene and the other Mary were there,
sitting opposite the tomb.

62 The next day, that is, after the day of
Preparation, the chief priests and the Phari-
sees gathered before Pilate 63 and said, "Sir,
we remember what that impostor said
while he was still alive, 'After three days I
will rise again.' 64 Therefore command the
tomb to be made secure until the third day;
otherwise his disciples may go and steal
him away, and tell the people, 'He has been
raised from the dead,' and the last decep-
tion would be worse than the first." 65 Pi-
late said to them, "You have a guard[d] of
soldiers; go, make it as secure as you
can."[e] 66 So they went with the guard and
made the tomb secure by sealing the stone.

28 After the sabbath, as the first day of
the week was dawning, Mary Mag-
dalene and the other Mary went to see the
tomb. 2 And suddenly there was a great
earthquake; for an angel of the Lord, de-
scending from heaven, came and rolled
back the stone and sat on it. 3 His appear-
ance was like lightning, and his clothing
white as snow. 4 For fear of him the guards
shook and became like dead men. 5 But the

a Other ancient authorities add *And another took a spear and pierced his side, and out came water and blood* b Or *gave up his spirit* c Or *a son of God* d Or *Take a guard* e Gk *you know how*

of the Temple *curtain* refers to an enormous tapestry that hung in front of the holy of holies, the innermost room of the Temple (see Ex 26.31–33). **54:** The confession of the *centurion* following the cosmic and natural phenomena at Jesus' death hints that Gentiles will come to believe in Jesus.

27.55–66: The burial (Mk 15.40–47; Lk 23.49–56; cf. Jn 19.28–42). **55:** The women who followed Jesus all the way from Galilee also ministered to and served Jesus. **57:** *Joseph* of *Arimathea* is mentioned by all four canonical Gospels as the person who takes the body and prepares it for burial. Such an act shows Joseph to be a pious Jew (cf. Tob 1.16–20; Josephus, *War* 4.317). **62–66:** Only Matthew includes these verses. They are presumably meant to counter a post-resurrection accusation that the *disciples* or someone else (see the anxiety voiced in Jn 20.2) had stolen the body.

28.1–20: Empty tomb, appearance, and commission. 1–8: Matthew follows Mk 16.1–8 in presenting women as the only witnesses to the empty tomb of Jesus (cf. Lk 24.1–11; contrast Jn 20.3–10). The story follows the pattern of an angelophany (cf. Dan 10.2–14). **1:** *Mary Magdalene . . . other Mary,* omits Mark's third witness, Salome, and the suggestion that the women intended to anoint the body. **2:** The *earthquake* is yet one more cosmic event that signals divine activity. Only Matthew includes this phenomenon. **3:** Cf. 17.2. **10:** The followers are told to gather in *Galilee,* their homeland and starting point

angel said to the women, "Do not be
afraid; I know that you are looking for
Jesus who was crucified. 6 He is not here;
for he has been raised, as he said. Come, see
the place where he[a] lay. 7 Then go quickly
and tell his disciples, 'He has been raised
from the dead,[b] and indeed he is going
ahead of you to Galilee; there you will see
him.' This is my message for you." 8 So they
left the tomb quickly with fear and great
joy, and ran to tell his disciples. 9 Suddenly
Jesus met them and said, "Greetings!" And
they came to him, took hold of his feet, and
worshiped him. 10 Then Jesus said to them,
"Do not be afraid; go and tell my brothers
to go to Galilee; there they will see me."

11 While they were going, some of the
guard went into the city and told the chief
priests everything that had happened. 12 Af-
ter the priests[c] had assembled with the el-
ders, they devised a plan to give a large sum
of money to the soldiers, 13 telling them,
"You must say, 'His disciples came by
night and stole him away while we were
asleep.' 14 If this comes to the governor's
ears, we will satisfy him and keep you out
of trouble." 15 So they took the money and
did as they were directed. And this story is
still told among the Jews to this day.

16 Now the eleven disciples went to
Galilee, to the mountain to which Jesus had
directed them. 17 When they saw him, they
worshiped him; but some doubted. 18 And
Jesus came and said to them, "All authority
in heaven and on earth has been given to
me. 19 Go therefore and make disciples of
all nations, baptizing them in the name of
the Father and of the Son and of the Holy
Spirit, 20 and teaching them to obey every-
thing that I have commanded you. And re-
member, I am with you always, to the end
of the age."[d]

a Other ancient authorities read *the Lord* *b* Other ancient authorities lack *from the dead* *c* Gk *they* *d* Other ancient authorities add *Amen*

of the movement. Thus their return is part of God's plan, not flight from Jerusalem. **11–15:** Only Matthew includes this detail of the guards being bribed, another detail created to stifle hostile rumors concerning Jesus' death and resurrection. *Story . . . to this day,* see 27.62–66n. **16:** *The mountain,* perhaps the same as in 17.1. **18–20:** Often referred to as "the great commission," this summarizes the ongoing ministry of the Matthean church. **19:** *All nations,* non-Jews as well as Jews. **20:** *Teaching* refers to the epitome of Jesus' teaching in the gospel. *I am with you always,* refers to the prophecy of Isaiah quoted in Mt 1.23, they shall name him "Emmanuel," which means, God is with us.

The Gospel According to MARK

Modern readers often take the Gospel according to Mark as a story of Christian discipleship, but it is much more than that. Mark is a story of conflict—or rather of multiple conflicts. That is why it is so exciting to read and why it has such a compelling message. In the dominant conflict that builds to a climax throughout the Gospel, Jesus' challenge to the high priestly rulers and their Roman imperial overlords escalates from his preaching and practice of the kingdom of God in the village gatherings of Galilee to his dramatic demonstration against the Temple and confrontation with the rulers in Jerusalem. That results in his torturous crucifixion by the Romans as an insurrectionary. In Jesus' exorcisms, moreover, God is winning the struggle with Satan and the demonic "unclean spirits" that have taken possession of the people like an occupying Roman legion. Surprisingly, however, a conflict between Jesus and the very disciples he designates as representative of the renewed people of Israel also develops in the course of the story. Although Jesus teaches them the mystery of the kingdom, they persistently fail to understand what he is teaching and doing, and at the end they betray, deny, and desert him. By contrast with the misunderstanding and faithless disciples, women, who play an increasingly prominent role in Mark's story, serve as models of faithfulness.

The Gospel story unfolds in an escalating series of steps. After Jesus' baptism by John, he proclaims the kingdom of God and manifests its miraculous power in the village gatherings of Galilee as the renewal of Israel, over against the Jerusalem priestly establishment and its representatives, the scribes and Pharisees (chs 1–3). In the first long speech of the Gospel, Jesus then teaches the mysterious plan of the kingdom in parables to his disciples and others in the movement (4.1–34). Jesus continues his program of the renewal of Israel in a sustained program of sea crossings, exorcisms, healings, and wilderness feedings reminiscent of the activities of Moses and Elijah (the great prophets of the past who, respectively, founded and renewed Israel), along with continuing disputes with the scribes and Pharisees (4.35–8.21). In the next step of the story, one framed by healings of blind men that highlights the disciples' misunderstanding, Jesus repeatedly makes clear that, besides being a new prophet equal in significance to Moses and Elijah in his restoration of covenantal Israel, it is necessary that he carry out the agenda of a martyr-messiah of Israel who must be condemned by the rulers, be killed, and rise again (8.22–10.52). After his dramatic messianic entry into Jerusalem and his provocative prophetic condemnation of the Temple, Jesus confronts the Jerusalem priestly establishment and their representatives (chs 11–12). In a second major speech, Jesus warns the disciples about fanatical misinterpretation of the coming political struggles (ch 13). In the final section of the Gospel, following Jesus' last meal with the disciples and his betrayal and arrest by the rulers' posse, he is accused of treason, blasphemy, and insurrection, condemned, and turned over to Pilate, the Roman governor, who orders him executed by crucifixion (chs 14–15). The Gospel then ends abruptly with the story of the empty tomb and the women's fear (16.1–8). Because the Gospel presents a sustained narrative of escalating conflicts, it should be read as a whole so components are understood in their connection with the overall story.

The Gospel of Mark presents Jesus' preaching and manifestation of the kingdom of God as a decisive new development in the history of Israel, not as the beginning of a new religion. Indeed, in this story religion is inseparable from the social, political, economic, even the physiological aspects of life. Throughout the Gospel, Jesus is portrayed and presented in terms of popular Israelite memories of the great prophets, especially Moses, who had led Israel's Exodus from subjection to alien rule in Egypt; Elijah, who had led the renewal of Israel in resistance to oppressive monarchs; and Jeremiah, who proclaimed God's judgment on the Temple and the rulers based there. At the beginning, in the middle, and especially toward the end, Mark also presents Jesus as a specially designated son of God, or king. Jesus, however, turns out to be a messiah (anointed one) who is also a martyr, in contrast to the disciples' expectations. And Jesus as both prophet and martyr-messiah is pointedly distinguished from the expectations of elite, scribal culture (see esp. 9.11–13; 12.35–37).

Although the Gospel is anonymous, an ancient tradition ascribes it to John Mark (mentioned in Acts 12.12; 15.37), who is supposed to have composed it at Rome as a summary of Peter's preaching (see 1 Pet 5.13). Modern scholars, however, find little evidence to support this tradition. Mark is by far the shortest of the four canonical Gospels and is generally thought to be the earliest, and to have been used in the composition of both Matthew and Luke. Because of the vague and indefinite references to the destruction of Jerusalem in Mark 13 (contrast Mt 22.7; Lk 19.43), the Gospel is thought to have been composed just prior to the widespread Jewish popular revolt that began in 66 CE and the Roman reconquest and destruction of Jerusalem and the Temple in 70 CE. The language of the Gospel is that of popular spoken Greek. Its style features rapid sequences of brief and vivid concrete episodes linked simply by "and" or "and immediately," often deleted in translation for less awkward reading in English. The narrative often shifts from the past tense into the present tense, enlivening the action. The contents of the Gospel consist mostly of stories about Jesus' actions and disputes with scribes and Pharisees, including some of Jesus' sayings, with two speeches (one mostly of parables) that interrupt the rapid flow of episodes. Mark appears to have drawn upon a rich variety of oral traditions of Jesus' actions and teachings, including chains of miracle stories, sets of parables, and stories of controversies with the Pharisees. The overall narrative weaves several sequences of episodes together into a complex plot with several interrelated themes and conflicts. In the earliest manuscripts, Mark ends abruptly at 16.8. This (apparently original) open ending invites the reader to continue the story of Jesus and the kingdom. In some later manuscripts Mark's story was "completed" with resurrection appearances of amalgamated elements from the other canonical Gospels, to make it conform to their common pattern.

1 The beginning of the good news[a] of Jesus Christ, the Son of God.[b]
2 As it is written in the prophet Isaiah,[c]
"See, I am sending my messenger
ahead of you,[d]
who will prepare your way;
3 the voice of one crying out in the
wilderness:

a Or *gospel* *b* Other ancient authorities lack *the Son of God* *c* Other ancient authorities read *in the prophets* *d* Gk *before your face*

1.1–13: Preparing the way of the Lord. 1: In the context of the Roman Empire, *the good news* (gospel) *of Jesus Christ,* i.e., Jesus the "anointed" king of Israel, a people subject to Rome, would have been understood over against the "gospel" of Caesar as the "Savior" who brought peace to the world. *Son of God* is missing in the earliest manuscripts.

1.2–8: John's baptism of repentance (Mt 3.1–12; Lk 3.1–20; Jn 1.6–15,19–28) preparing the *way* as the new Exodus and covenant renewal. **2–3:** See Ex 23.20; Mal 3.1 (cf. Mt 11.10; Lk 7.27); Isa 40.3. That this is not all a quotation from Isaiah suggests that it is rooted in a popular (non-scribal) oral conflation of "prophecies." It is not clear whether *my messenger ahead of you* refers to John sent ahead of Jesus, or Jesus sent ahead of the addressees. *"Prepare the way of the Lord"* proclaims a new Exodus, as in

'Prepare the way of the Lord,
make his paths straight,' "
4 John the baptizer appeared[a] in the wil-
derness, proclaiming a baptism of repen-
tance for the forgiveness of sins. 5 And peo-
ple from the whole Judean countryside and
all the people of Jerusalem were going out
to him, and were baptized by him in the
river Jordan, confessing their sins. 6 Now
John was clothed with camel's hair, with a
leather belt around his waist, and he ate
locusts and wild honey. 7 He proclaimed,
"The one who is more powerful than I is
coming after me; I am not worthy to stoop
down and untie the thong of his sandals. 8 I
have baptized you with[b] water; but he will
baptize you with[b] the Holy Spirit."
9 In those days Jesus came from Naza-
reth of Galilee and was baptized by John in
the Jordan. 10 And just as he was coming up
out of the water, he saw the heavens torn
apart and the Spirit descending like a dove
on him. 11 And a voice came from heaven,
"You are my Son, the Beloved;[c] with you
I am well pleased."
12 And the Spirit immediately drove
him out into the wilderness. 13 He was in
the wilderness forty days, tempted by Sa-
tan; and he was with the wild beasts; and
the angels waited on him.
14 Now after John was arrested, Jesus
came to Galilee, proclaiming the good
news[d] of God,[e] 15 and saying, "The time
is fulfilled, and the kingdom of God has
come near;[f] repent, and believe in the
good news."[d]

16 As Jesus passed along the Sea of Gali-
lee, he saw Simon and his brother Andrew

a Other ancient authorities read *John was baptizing*
b Or *in* c Or *my beloved Son* d Or *gospel*
e Other ancient authorities read *of the kingdom* f Or *is at hand*

Isa 40. The *wilderness,* also suggestive of a new Exodus, was a place where other popular prophets and movements often originated (e.g., Acts 5.36; cf. Josephus, *Ant.* 20.5.1). **4–5:** Acts 13.24. *Baptism of repentance for the forgiveness of sins,* John proclaims and performs a ritual of entrance into God's renewed covenant with Israel in which those ready to change their ways are baptized as forgiven for having broken the covenantal laws. **5:** *The whole Judean countryside and all the people of Jerusalem,* i.e., all the people of Israel, from the capital city as well as from the villages, were baptized. **6:** John's garb evokes an image of the prophet Elijah, as in 2 Kings 1.8; cf. 9.11–13. Jesus is also taken to be Elijah in 6.15; 8.28; 15.35–36. **7–8:** John also proclaims *one . . . more powerful* who will bring the enabling divine power of the *Holy Spirit.*

1.9–11: Jesus' baptism (Mt 3.13–17; Lk 3.21–22; Jn 1.29–34). Jesus himself is baptized into the renewal movement that began before him. *From Nazareth of Galilee,* a small village about 25 km (16 mi) west of the Sea of Galilee in the district now governed by "King" Herod Antipas (see 6.14), son of Herod the Great. **10–11:** *The heavens torn apart,* as the divine *Spirit* breaks through empowering Jesus as the anointed king of Israel. A traditional designation for the king was "son of God," as in 2 Sam 7.14; Ps 2.7; 89.26 (cf. Lk 9.35). *Beloved,* cf. Isa 42.1.

1.12–13: Jesus' testing (cf. the particular "temptations" added in Mt 4.1–11; Lk 4.1–13). Jesus undergoes a forty-day time of trial and testing in the wilderness for a prophet, such as Elijah in 1 Kings 19.8; cf. Ex 24.18. The battle against Satan (see 3.23–27) is already engaged.

1.14–3.35: Proclaiming and manifesting the kingdom of God as the renewal of Israel, over against the Jerusalem priestly rulers.

1.14–15: Jesus' opening proclamation of the kingdom of God (Mt 4.12–17; Lk 4.14–15). **14:** *John was arrested* (see 6.17) indicates the ominous situation as Jesus begins his mission centered in Galilee, a remote area of a country subjected to Rome. **15:** A summary of Jesus' program and of the Gospel according to Mark. At the right time, in fulfillment of long-standing yearnings and hopes, God is finally acting to reestablish his beneficent will for the people. *Repent,* return to God's way, in response to the good news of God's action.

1.16–20: Call of disciples (Mt 4.18–22; Lk 5.1–11; Jn 1.35–42). *Sea of Galilee* or the Lake of Gennesaret is a large lake in a deep basin mostly surrounded by high hills. *Simon,* also called Peter (3.16).

casting a net into the sea—for they were
fishermen. 17 And Jesus said to them, "Fol-
low me and I will make you fish for peo-
ple." 18 And immediately they left their nets
and followed him. 19 As he went a little far-
ther, he saw James son of Zebedee and his
brother John, who were in their boat mend-
ing the nets. 20 Immediately he called them;
and they left their father Zebedee in the
boat with the hired men, and followed him.
21 They went to Capernaum; and when
the sabbath came, he entered the synagogue
and taught. 22 They were astounded at his
teaching, for he taught them as one having
authority, and not as the scribes. 23 Just
then there was in their synagogue a man
with an unclean spirit, 24 and he cried out,
"What have you to do with us, Jesus of
Nazareth? Have you come to destroy us? I
know who you are, the Holy One of God."
25 But Jesus rebuked him, saying, "Be silent,
and come out of him!" 26 And the unclean
spirit, convulsing him and crying with a
loud voice, came out of him. 27 They were
all amazed, and they kept on asking one
another, "What is this? A new teaching—
with authority! He[a] commands even the
unclean spirits, and they obey him." 28 At
once his fame began to spread throughout
the surrounding region of Galilee.
29 As soon as they[b] left the synagogue,
they entered the house of Simon and An-
drew, with James and John. 30 Now Si-
mon's mother-in-law was in bed with a fe-
ver, and they told him about her at once.
31 He came and took her by the hand and
lifted her up. Then the fever left her, and
she began to serve them.
32 That evening, at sunset, they brought
to him all who were sick or possessed with
demons. 33 And the whole city was gathered
around the door. 34 And he cured many
who were sick with various diseases, and
cast out many demons; and he would not
permit the demons to speak, because they
knew him.
35 In the morning, while it was still very
dark, he got up and went out to a deserted
place, and there he prayed. 36 And Simon
and his companions hunted for him.
37 When they found him, they said to him,
"Everyone is searching for you." 38 He an-
swered, "Let us go on to the neighboring

a Or *A new teaching! With authority he* *b* Other ancient authorities read *he*

1.21–28: Exorcism and teaching with authority (Mt 7.28–29; Lk 4.33–37). **21–22:** *Capernaum,* a village at the north of the Lake, is the base of Jesus' activity in Galilee and the surrounding areas. *The synagogue* is the village assembly, here gathering on the sabbath (when Jesus performs the ensuing exorcism); at this time village assemblies apparently did not yet construct public buildings in which to gather. *His teaching* is inclusive of his healings and exorcisms, as the rest of this story indicates. *Authority,* the Greek word also means "power." *Scribes,* the literate elite of scholars-lawyers who represented the Jerusalem priestly rulers. **23:** *A man with an unclean spirit,* possessed by an alien force or demon. **24:** In Mark the unclean spirits immediately recognize who Jesus is, as again in 1.34; 3.11; 5.7. *Holy One of God,* a prophet possessed of divine power, as Elisha, 2 Kings 4.9. **25–26:** The actual exorcism involves a violent struggle. **27:** With v. 22 these exclamations frame Jesus' exorcism: In contrast to the scribal "authorities," Jesus teaches and acts with authority and power over the unclean spirits for the benefit of the people. In Jesus' struggle against the superhuman demonic spirits his political conflict with the rulers and their scribal representatives is also engaged. **28:** From his very first exorcism, Jesus' fame spreads rapidly throughout the region; see also 1.45; 3.7–8.

1.29–34: Healings and exorcisms (Mt 8.14–17; Lk 4.38–41). **30–31:** The first of several key healings of women in Mark; see 5.21–43. **32–34:** A Markan summary, cf. 1.39; 3.7–8. **33:** Mark often uses *city* with reference to a village. **34:** *Not permit the demons to speak,* Jesus commands the demons, who know who he is, not to make him known (see 3.12) and sometimes asks people who witness healings not to tell anyone (e.g., 1.44; 5.43; 7.36). Nevertheless, his fame spreads rapidly and widely (e.g., 1.37; 1.45; 3.7–8; 7.36). The readers of Mark, of course, like the demons, know who he is from the beginning (1.1).

1.35–39: Summary of Jesus' activity (Mt 4.23–25; Lk 4.42–44). A Markan summary of Jesus' program of proclaiming the kingdom of God and exorcism of demons throughout the villages of Galilee. **39:** *In*

towns, so that I may proclaim the message
there also; for that is what I came out to
do." 39 And he went throughout Galilee,
proclaiming the message in their syna-
gogues and casting out demons.
40 A leper[a] came to him begging him,
and kneeling[b] he said to him, "If you
choose, you can make me clean." 41 Moved
with pity,[c] Jesus[d] stretched out his hand
and touched him, and said to him, "I do
choose. Be made clean!" 42 Immediately the
leprosy[a] left him, and he was made clean.
43 After sternly warning him he sent him
away at once, 44 saying to him, "See that
you say nothing to anyone; but go, show
yourself to the priest, and offer for your
cleansing what Moses commanded, as a
testimony to them." 45 But he went out and
began to proclaim it freely, and to spread
the word, so that Jesus[d] could no longer go
into a town openly, but stayed out in the
country; and people came to him from ev-
ery quarter.

2 When he returned to Capernaum after
some days, it was reported that he was
at home. 2 So many gathered around that
there was no longer room for them, not
even in front of the door; and he was speak-
ing the word to them. 3 Then some people[e]
came, bringing to him a paralyzed man,
carried by four of them. 4 And when they
could not bring him to Jesus because of the
crowd, they removed the roof above him;
and after having dug through it, they let
down the mat on which the paralytic lay.
5 When Jesus saw their faith, he said to the
paralytic, "Son, your sins are forgiven."
6 Now some of the scribes were sitting
there, questioning in their hearts, 7 "Why
does this fellow speak in this way? It is
blasphemy! Who can forgive sins but God
alone?" 8 At once Jesus perceived in his
spirit that they were discussing these ques-
tions among themselves; and he said to
them, "Why do you raise such questions in
your hearts? 9 Which is easier, to say to the
paralytic, 'Your sins are forgiven,' or to
say, 'Stand up and take your mat and

a The terms *leper* and *leprosy* can refer to several diseases *b* Other ancient authorities lack *kneeling* *c* Other ancient authorities read *anger* *d* Gk *he* *e* Gk *they*

their synagogues, the Greek word means "assemblies." Jesus' proclamations, exorcisms, and healings take place largely in the village assemblies (see vv. 21–22n.).

1.40–45: Healing a leper (Mt 8.2–4; Lk 5.12–16). *Leper,* a person suffering from skin lesions of any sort, and interpreted in priestly sources (see Lev 13–14) as a channel of "unclean" contamination for individuals and society. **40–42:** The leper dares Jesus to declare him *clean,* and Jesus responds to the challenge, in defiance of the elaborate and costly procedures prescribed in biblical law. **41:** *Moved with pity,* some manuscripts have "with anger," i.e., at the Jerusalem priestly establishment and their institutionalized procedures and prescribed offering necessary for the "leper" to be declared free of the stigma (*clean*). **44:** Since Jesus has already made the man clean, his instructions must be intended either as a demonstrative *testimony* or "witness" against the priest and the costly offerings required by their code (Lev 14.10–32) or as a facetious remark (the now-clean man does pointedly disobey the instructions).

2.1–12: Healing paralysis and forgiveness of sins (Mt 9.1–8; Lk 5.17–26). This controversy story, which is also a healing story, begins a series of controversies in which the scribes (see 1.21–22n.) and Pharisees attack or question Jesus, whose sharp response is decisive. The scribes were the literate expert interpreters and guardians of the official law codes, the Pharisees a particular party or faction within the wider class of scribes. Both were based in the Jerusalem Temple (3.22; 7.1) and worked for and represented the priestly rulers in dealings with the people. **4:** Houses often had a flat roof consisting of mud plaster over a wood framework. **5–11:** Jesus equates the declaration *"Your sins are forgiven"* with *"Stand up . . . and walk."* The man's paralysis is believed to be due to his own sin (or that of his parents; see Ex 34.7; Jn 9.2). The scribes, the authorities who socially reinforced such self-blame for illness and misfortune, accuse Jesus of *blasphemy,* since forgiveness can be done by *God alone,* according to these his official interpreters. Again Jesus asserts his own prophetic authority and power over against the scribes, as in 1.22–27. *Son of Man* means either "human being" or refers to Jesus as an exalted figure representative of a finally restored Israel (derived from Dan 7.13), or both.

walk'? 10 But so that you may know that
the Son of Man has authority on earth to
forgive sins"—he said to the paralytic—
11 "I say to you, stand up, take your mat
and go to your home." 12 And he stood up,
and immediately took the mat and went
out before all of them; so that they were all
amazed and glorified God, saying, "We
have never seen anything like this!"

13 Jesus[a] went out again beside the sea;
the whole crowd gathered around him, and
he taught them. 14 As he was walking along,
he saw Levi son of Alphaeus sitting at the
tax booth, and he said to him, "Follow
me." And he got up and followed him.
15 And as he sat at dinner[b] in Levi's[c]
house, many tax collectors and sinners
were also sitting[d] with Jesus and his disci-
ples—for there were many who followed
him. 16 When the scribes of[e] the Pharisees
saw that he was eating with sinners and tax
collectors, they said to his disciples, "Why
does he eat[f] with tax collectors and sin-
ners?" 17 When Jesus heard this, he said to
them, "Those who are well have no need of
a physician, but those who are sick; I have
come to call not the righteous but sinners."
18 Now John's disciples and the Phari-
sees were fasting; and people[g] came and
said to him, "Why do John's disciples and
the disciples of the Pharisees fast, but your
disciples do not fast?" 19 Jesus said to them,
"The wedding guests cannot fast while the
bridegroom is with them, can they? As long
as they have the bridegroom with them,
they cannot fast. 20 The days will come
when the bridegroom is taken away from
them, and then they will fast on that
day.
21 "No one sews a piece of unshrunk
cloth on an old cloak; otherwise, the patch
pulls away from it, the new from the old,
and a worse tear is made. 22 And no one
puts new wine into old wineskins; other-
wise, the wine will burst the skins, and the
wine is lost, and so are the skins; but one
puts new wine into fresh wineskins."[h]
23 One sabbath he was going through
the grainfields; and as they made their way
his disciples began to pluck heads of grain.
24 The Pharisees said to him, "Look, why
are they doing what is not lawful on the
sabbath?" 25 And he said to them, "Have
you never read what David did when he
and his companions were hungry and in
need of food? 26 He entered the house of
God, when Abiathar was high priest, and
ate the bread of the Presence, which it is not
lawful for any but the priests to eat, and he
gave some to his companions." 27 Then he
said to them, "The sabbath was made for
humankind, and not humankind for the
sabbath; 28 so the Son of Man is lord even
of the sabbath."

a Gk *He* *b* Gk *reclined* *c* Gk *his*
d Gk *reclining* *e* Other ancient authorities read *and*
f Other ancient authorities add *and drink* *g* Gk *they*
h Other ancient authorities lack *but one puts new wine into fresh wineskins*

2.13–17: Eating with sinners (Mt 9.9–13; Lk 5.27–32). **14:** *Levi,* identified as "Matthew" in Mt 9.9, is a customs officer at Capernaum, a border village, working under an officer of Herod Antipas. **15–16:** *Eating with sinners and tax collectors* (or rather "toll collectors") would have entailed contact with impure people and social outcasts, according to *the scribes of the Pharisees.*

2.18–22: Fasting (Mt 9.14–17; Lk 5.33–39). **19:** A wedding feast, one of the principal times of celebration and feasting among peasants, was a traditional symbol of the future time of fulfillment, a time of justice and plenty; cf. Isa 62.5; Lk 17.22. **20:** *The bridegroom . . . taken away,* after the crucifixion when Jesus, understood as the bridegroom, is gone. **21–22:** With Jesus' preaching and manifestation of the kingdom something new has come, calling for suspension of old forms such as fasting.

2.23–28: The sabbath and hunger (Mt 12.1–8; Lk 6.1–5). **23–24:** The disciples' action may have violated the Pharisees' restrictions against travel as well as harvesting on the sabbath, meant to implement the fourth commandment (Ex 20.8–10). **25–26:** Jesus' reply summarizes a story about David commandeering food for his soldiers that appears in 1 Sam 21.1–6, in which Ahimelech, Abiathar's father, is the priest (cf. 2 Sam 15.35). The point of the story: David's men were *hungry,* a detail not found in

3 Again he entered the synagogue, and
a man was there who had a withered
hand. 2 They watched him to see whether
he would cure him on the sabbath, so that
they might accuse him. 3 And he said to the
man who had the withered hand, "Come
forward." 4 Then he said to them, "Is it
lawful to do good or to do harm on the
sabbath, to save life or to kill?" But they
were silent. 5 He looked around at them
with anger; he was grieved at their hardness
of heart and said to the man, "Stretch out
your hand." He stretched it out, and his
hand was restored. 6 The Pharisees went
out and immediately conspired with the
Herodians against him, how to destroy
him.

7 Jesus departed with his disciples to the
sea, and a great multitude from Galilee fol-
lowed him; 8 hearing all that he was doing,
they came to him in great numbers from
Judea, Jerusalem, Idumea, beyond the Jor-
dan, and the region around Tyre and Sidon.
9 He told his disciples to have a boat ready
for him because of the crowd, so that they
would not crush him; 10 for he had cured
many, so that all who had diseases pressed
upon him to touch him. 11 Whenever the
unclean spirits saw him, they fell down be-
fore him and shouted, "You are the Son of
God!" 12 But he sternly ordered them not to
make him known.

13 He went up the mountain and called
to him those whom he wanted, and they
came to him. 14 And he appointed twelve,
whom he also named apostles,[a] to be
with him, and to be sent out to proclaim
the message, 15 and to have authority to
cast out demons. 16 So he appointed the
twelve:[b] Simon (to whom he gave the
name Peter); 17 James son of Zebedee and
John the brother of James (to whom he
gave the name Boanerges, that is, Sons of
Thunder); 18 and Andrew, and Philip, and
Bartholomew, and Matthew, and Thomas,
and James son of Alphaeus, and Thaddae-
us, and Simon the Cananaean, 19 and Judas
Iscariot, who betrayed him.

Then he went home; 20 and the crowd
came together again, so that they could not
even eat. 21 When his family heard it, they
went out to restrain him, for people were
saying, "He has gone out of his mind."
22 And the scribes who came down from

a Other ancient authorities lack *whom he also named apostles* *b* Other ancient authorities lack *So he appointed the twelve*

1 Sam 21. **27:** Ex 23.12; Deut 5.14–15. **28:** *Son of Man,* even more clearly than in 2.10, could mean either "human being" or the future Jesus as an exalted figure representing a renewed Israel.

3.1–6: Healing on the sabbath (Mt 12.9–14; Lk 6.6–11). **1:** *Synagogue,* see 1.21–22n. **2–4:** Having already performed an exorcism on the sabbath (1.22–27), Jesus now pointedly performs a healing on the sabbath in the presence of the Pharisees, who remain silent. **5:** Juxtaposition of Jesus' anger and grief at the Pharisees' program and his compassion in curing the man's withered hand. **6:** In response to this and Jesus' previous actions, the Pharisees conspire with the *Herodians,* representatives of Herod Antipas, the ruler of Galilee, *to destroy him.*

3.7–12: Summary of Jesus' activity (Mt 4.24–25; 12.15–21; Lk 6.17–19; 4.41). A summary of Jesus' program and the burgeoning response it evokes. **8:** People flock to him in greater numbers and from a wider area, i.e., all Israel and even beyond (see Map on p. 68 NT), than they did to John the Baptist.

3.13–19a: Appointing the twelve (Mt 10.1–4; Lk 6.12–16). **13–14:** *Up the mountain . . . appointed twelve,* suggests a new Sinai, on which Jesus is constituting a renewed Israel symbolized by the twelve. **14–15:** The twelve are invested with the same proclamation (of the kingdom) and authority and power to exorcize demons as Jesus, an extension of his program.

3.19b–35: Defeat of Satan and the new community (Mt 12.22–27; Lk 11.14–23; 12.10; 16.43–45). In a repeated narrative technique, Mark "sandwiches" one story into another. **21:** To those who knew Jesus before he assumed the role of prophet or are concerned lest he be seized by the authorities, he appears to be *out of his mind* (cf. 6.1–3). **22–27:** Both Jesus and the scribes (see 1.21–22n.) think that current personal and social-political life is caught in the struggle for dominion between God and Satan.

Jerusalem said, "He has Beelzebul, and by
the ruler of the demons he casts out de-
mons." 23 And he called them to him, and
spoke to them in parables, "How can Satan
cast out Satan? 24 If a kingdom is divided
against itself, that kingdom cannot stand.
25 And if a house is divided against itself,
that house will not be able to stand. 26 And
if Satan has risen up against himself and is
divided, he cannot stand, but his end has
come. 27 But no one can enter a strong
man's house and plunder his property with-
out first tying up the strong man; then in-
deed the house can be plundered.
28 "Truly I tell you, people will be for-
given for their sins and whatever blasphe-
mies they utter; 29 but whoever blasphemes
against the Holy Spirit can never have for-
giveness, but is guilty of an eternal sin"—
30 for they had said, "He has an unclean
spirit."
31 Then his mother and his brothers
came; and standing outside, they sent to
him and called him. 32 A crowd was sitting
around him; and they said to him, "Your
mother and your brothers and sisters[a] are
outside, asking for you." 33 And he replied,
"Who are my mother and my brothers?"
34 And looking at those who sat around
him, he said, "Here are my mother and my
brothers! 35 Whoever does the will of God
is my brother and sister and mother."

4 Again he began to teach beside the sea.
Such a very large crowd gathered
around him that he got into a boat on the
sea and sat there, while the whole crowd
was beside the sea on the land. 2 He began
to teach them many things in parables, and
in his teaching he said to them: 3 "Listen! A
sower went out to sow. 4 And as he sowed,
some seed fell on the path, and the birds
came and ate it up. 5 Other seed fell on
rocky ground, where it did not have much
soil, and it sprang up quickly, since it had
no depth of soil. 6 And when the sun rose,
it was scorched; and since it had no root,
it withered away. 7 Other seed fell among
thorns, and the thorns grew up and choked
it, and it yielded no grain. 8 Other seed fell
into good soil and brought forth grain,
growing up and increasing and yielding
thirty and sixty and a hundredfold." 9 And
he said, "Let anyone with ears to hear lis-
ten!"
10 When he was alone, those who were
around him along with the twelve asked
him about the parables. 11 And he said to

a Other ancient authorities lack *and sisters*

22: The threatened scribes demonize Jesus' power: He is a witch! *Beelzebul,* possibly "Lord of the (divine) house" (cf. Mt 10.25), or "Baal, the prince," originally a title of the Canaanite storm and fertility god (2 Kings 1.2), later demonized into the chief power of evil. **23:** *In parables,* in extended metaphors or analogies; cf. 4.2,33. **24–26:** A kingdom was thought of as a household on a large scale, and both kingdom and household were metaphors for God's and Satan's power or control. Jesus argues both that the scribes' charge is absurd and that even assuming they are right, Satan's rule is at an end. **27:** By analogy, in his exorcism of demons Jesus (the "more powerful one," 1.7) has broken into Satan's house, tied up "the strong man," and "plundered his property." This further implies that God's is now the only kingdom left, by which Jesus is acting. **28–30:** From the Markan viewpoint, attacks on Jesus during his mission can be forgiven, but not attacks against the *Holy Spirit* acting in his movement. **31–35:** Not necessarily an attack on his family (but see v. 21), but rather an indication that within the Jesus-movement and its communities, those who do *the will of God* are Jesus' and each others' *brother and sister and mother.*

4.1–34: Teaching the mystery of the kingdom of God in parables (Mt 13; Lk 8.4–18; 13.18–21). **2:** *In parables,* in extended metaphors or analogies. **3–8:** Parable of the sower and the seeds. Despite all the obstacles, there is an absolutely amazing and unprecedented bumper crop (normal good yield was 7 to 1). **10:** The rest of the teaching is directed to the twelve (3.16–19) and other members of the movement. **11–12:** *The secret of the kingdom of God,* to them is disclosed the "mystery" or hidden plan of God (cf. Dan 2.28) for the fulfillment of history in the kingdom of God now being proclaimed and manifested. Since outsiders do not understand this "mystery" or "plan," the parables are opaque to them, just as them, "To you has been given the secret[a] of the kingdom of God, but for those outside, everything comes in parables; 12 in order that

'they may indeed look, but not perceive,
and may indeed listen, but not understand;
so that they may not turn again and be forgiven.' "

13 And he said to them, "Do you not understand this parable? Then how will you understand all the parables? 14 The sower sows the word. 15 These are the ones on the path where the word is sown: when they hear, Satan immediately comes and takes away the word that is sown in them. 16 And these are the ones sown on rocky ground: when they hear the word, they immediately receive it with joy. 17 But they have no root, and endure only for a while; then, when trouble or persecution arises on account of the word, immediately they fall away.[b] 18 And others are those sown among the thorns: these are the ones who hear the word, 19 but the cares of the world, and the lure of wealth, and the desire for other things come in and choke the word, and it yields nothing. 20 And these are the ones sown on the good soil: they hear the word and accept it and bear fruit, thirty and sixty and a hundredfold."

21 He said to them, "Is a lamp brought in to be put under the bushel basket, or under the bed, and not on the lampstand? 22 For there is nothing hidden, except to be disclosed; nor is anything secret, except to come to light. 23 Let anyone with ears to hear listen!" 24 And he said to them, "Pay attention to what you hear; the measure you give will be the measure you get, and still more will be given you. 25 For to those who have, more will be given; and from those who have nothing, even what they have will be taken away."

26 He also said, "The kingdom of God is as if someone would scatter seed on the ground, 27 and would sleep and rise night and day, and the seed would sprout and grow, he does not know how. 28 The earth produces of itself, first the stalk, then the head, then the full grain in the head. 29 But when the grain is ripe, at once he goes in with his sickle, because the harvest has come."

30 He also said, "With what can we compare the kingdom of God, or what parable will we use for it? 31 It is like a mustard seed, which, when sown upon the ground, is the smallest of all the seeds on earth; 32 yet when it is sown it grows up and becomes the greatest of all shrubs, and puts forth large branches, so that the birds of the air can make nests in its shade."

33 With many such parables he spoke the word to them, as they were able to hear it; 34 he did not speak to them except in parables, but he explained everything in private to his disciples.

35 On that day, when evening had come, he said to them, "Let us go across to

a Or *mystery* *b* Or *stumble*

Isaiah's contemporaries did not understand his prophecies (Isa 6.9–10). **13–20:** Explains the parable of the sower allegorically, with each principal symbol of the analogy standing for some aspect of the listeners' experiences of the effects of Jesus' preaching of the kingdom—and corresponding to later episodes in Mark. **15:** The struggle with Satan continues, as illustrated in Peter's misunderstanding in 8.29–33. **16–17:** Cf. 9.42–48; 13.19,24; 14.27,29. **18–19:** *The lure of wealth,* cf. 10.17–22,25. **21–23:** These sayings repeat and reinforce the message of 4.3–10,20; the kingdom, *hidden* now, will *come to light.* **24–25:** These sayings make most sense as a warning not to accept any cynical "realistic" advice that the established power-relations will inevitably continue. **26–29:** The kingdom of God will surely come to full fruition, just as the seed inevitably sprouts, grows, and produces a harvest (cf. Joel 3.13). **30–32:** The climax of the process by which the kingdom of God is growing is like the tiniest seed producing a large bush that provides homes for the birds. Note the modest metaphor, in contrast with the imperial metaphor of the cedar tree in Ezek 17; 31; Dan 4.

4.35–8.21: Continuing the prophetic renewal of Israel (and other peoples) despite opposition and the

the other side." 36 And leaving the crowd
behind, they took him with them in the
boat, just as he was. Other boats were with
him. 37 A great windstorm arose, and the
waves beat into the boat, so that the boat
was already being swamped. 38 But he was
in the stern, asleep on the cushion; and they
woke him up and said to him, "Teacher, do
you not care that we are perishing?" 39 He
woke up and rebuked the wind, and said to
the sea, "Peace! Be still!" Then the wind
ceased, and there was a dead calm. 40 He
said to them, "Why are you afraid? Have
you still no faith?" 41 And they were filled
with great awe and said to one another,
"Who then is this, that even the wind and
the sea obey him?"

5 They came to the other side of the sea,
to the country of the Gerasenes.[a] 2 And
when he had stepped out of the boat, im-
mediately a man out of the tombs with an
unclean spirit met him. 3 He lived among
the tombs; and no one could restrain him
any more, even with a chain; 4 for he had
often been restrained with shackles and
chains, but the chains he wrenched apart,
and the shackles he broke in pieces; and no
one had the strength to subdue him. 5 Night
and day among the tombs and on the
mountains he was always howling and
bruising himself with stones. 6 When he saw
Jesus from a distance, he ran and bowed
down before him; 7 and he shouted at the
top of his voice, "What have you to do with
me, Jesus, Son of the Most High God? I
adjure you by God, do not torment me."
8 For he had said to him, "Come out of the
man, you unclean spirit!" 9 Then Jesus[b]
asked him, "What is your name?" He re-
plied, "My name is Legion; for we are
many." 10 He begged him earnestly not to
send them out of the country. 11 Now there
on the hillside a great herd of swine was
feeding; 12 and the unclean spirits[c] begged
him, "Send us into the swine; let us enter
them." 13 So he gave them permission. And
the unclean spirits came out and entered
the swine; and the herd, numbering about
two thousand, rushed down the steep bank
into the sea, and were drowned in the sea.

14 The swineherds ran off and told it in
the city and in the country. Then people
came to see what it was that had happened.
15 They came to Jesus and saw the demoni-
ac sitting there, clothed and in his right
mind, the very man who had had the le-
gion; and they were afraid. 16 Those who
had seen what had happened to the demo-
niac and to the swine reported it. 17 Then
they began to beg Jesus[d] to leave their
neighborhood. 18 As he was getting into the

a Other ancient authorities read *Gergesenes*; others, *Gadarenes* *b* Gk *he* *c* Gk *they* *d* Gk *him*

disciples' misunderstanding. This section is organized around two sequences of Moses- and Elijah-like sea crossings, exorcisms, healings, and wilderness feedings.

4.35–41: First sea crossing (Mt 18.18,23–27; Lk 8.22–25). Emphasis falls on the disciples' lack of faith and their *great awe . . . "that even the wind and the sea obey him."* Control of the sea is a divine characteristic (see Ps 89.9; cf. Ps 89.25).

5.1–20: Exorcism of the demon whose name is "Legion" (Mt 8.28–34; Lk 8.26–39). This is the most embellished such episode in Mark. **1:** The territory of the city of Gerasa (modern Jerash) was in central Transjordan; its population was largely non-Jewish. Mt 8.28 situates this event in Gadara, southeast of the Sea of Galilee, a setting that fits the narrative somewhat better. **2–5:** The man's possession by the alien force generated such violence that his community had not been able to restrain him, even with chains. **7:** *Most High God* is not an Israelite but a Hellenistic name, found mainly in Luke-Acts. **9:** Once the unclean spirit is cast out, it is possible to find out its identity. A *legion* was a division (usually consisting of about five thousand troops) of the Roman military, who had conquered and, in effect, still occupied the country. **11–13:** Having entered the herd of pigs (which Jews were not permitted to eat, Lev 11.7; Deut 14.8), the Roman "legion" of unclean spirits, in a military image, charged into the sea and were destroyed, alluding to the destruction of Pharaoh's army in Israel's Exodus deliverance (Ex 15.4). Cf. the image of the (Temple-) mount "thrown into the sea," 11.23. **14–17:** The people were apprehensive that Jesus had disrupted their delicately balanced adjustment to the alien possession. **20:** The liberated man carried the

boat, the man who had been possessed by
demons begged him that he might be with
him. 19 But Jesus[a] refused, and said to him,
"Go home to your friends, and tell them
how much the Lord has done for you, and
what mercy he has shown you." 20 And he
went away and began to proclaim in the
Decapolis how much Jesus had done for
him; and everyone was amazed.

21 When Jesus had crossed again in the
boat[b] to the other side, a great crowd gath-
ered around him; and he was by the sea.
22 Then one of the leaders of the synagogue
named Jairus came and, when he saw him,
fell at his feet 23 and begged him repeatedly,
"My little daughter is at the point of death.
Come and lay your hands on her, so that
she may be made well, and live." 24 So he
went with him.

And a large crowd followed him and
pressed in on him. 25 Now there was a
woman who had been suffering from hem-
orrhages for twelve years. 26 She had en-
dured much under many physicians, and
had spent all that she had; and she was no
better, but rather grew worse. 27 She had
heard about Jesus, and came up behind him
in the crowd and touched his cloak, 28 for
she said, "If I but touch his clothes, I will
be made well." 29 Immediately her hemor-
rhage stopped; and she felt in her body that
she was healed of her disease. 30 Immediate-
ly aware that power had gone forth from
him, Jesus turned about in the crowd and
said, "Who touched my clothes?" 31 And
his disciples said to him, "You see the
crowd pressing in on you; how can you say,
'Who touched me?' " 32 He looked all
around to see who had done it. 33 But the
woman, knowing what had happened to
her, came in fear and trembling, fell down
before him, and told him the whole truth.
34 He said to her, "Daughter, your faith has
made you well; go in peace, and be healed
of your disease."

35 While he was still speaking, some
people came from the leader's house to say,
"Your daughter is dead. Why trouble the
teacher any further?" 36 But overhearing[c]
what they said, Jesus said to the leader of
the synagogue, "Do not fear, only believe."
37 He allowed no one to follow him except
Peter, James, and John, the brother of
James. 38 When they came to the house of
the leader of the synagogue, he saw a com-
motion, people weeping and wailing loud-
ly. 39 When he had entered, he said to them,
"Why do you make a commotion and
weep? The child is not dead but sleeping."
40 And they laughed at him. Then he put
them all outside, and took the child's father
and mother and those who were with him,
and went in where the child was. 41 He took
her by the hand and said to her, "Talitha
cum," which means, "Little girl, get up!"
42 And immediately the girl got up and be-
gan to walk about (she was twelve years
of age). At this they were overcome with
amazement. 43 He strictly ordered them
that no one should know this, and told
them to give her something to eat.

a Gk *he* *b* Other ancient authorities lack *in the boat*
c Or *ignoring*; other ancient authorities read *hearing*

good news about Jesus' actions into the wider *Decapolis,* the district of "ten cities" in the Jordan valley and in Transjordan. They were Hellenistic in character, with a largely non-Israelite population.

5.21–43: Healings of Jairus's daughter and the hemorrhaging woman (Mt 9.18–26; Lk 8.40–56). Again Mark has "sandwiched" one story into another. The healings of both the woman who had been hemorrhaging for twelve years and the almost dead twelve-year-old woman are also symbolic of Jesus' renewal of Israel. **22:** *Leaders of the synagogue,* i.e., of the village assembly. **25–26:** The woman is poverty-stricken from the worsening hemorrhaging that no physicians could stop. According to the purity code (Lev 15.25–30), she would also have been "unclean," although we do not know the degree to which that code affected village life. **27–33:** The initiative and action are entirely hers, Jesus being the passive conduit through which the healing power goes forth. **41:** The phrase *talitha cum* is Aramaic; cf. 7.34; 14.36; 15.34. **42:** The young woman, at twelve approaching marriage, appears to be dead, yet Jesus restores her to life and, presumably, the ability to reproduce new life in and of Israel.

6 He left that place and came to his
hometown, and his disciples followed
him. 2 On the sabbath he began to teach in
the synagogue, and many who heard him
were astounded. They said, "Where did
this man get all this? What is this wisdom
that has been given to him? What deeds of
power are being done by his hands! 3 Is not
this the carpenter, the son of Mary[a] and
brother of James and Joses and Judas and
Simon, and are not his sisters here with
us?" And they took offense[b] at him. 4 Then
Jesus said to them, "Prophets are not with-
out honor, except in their hometown, and
among their own kin, and in their own
house." 5 And he could do no deed of pow-
er there, except that he laid his hands on a
few sick people and cured them. 6 And he
was amazed at their unbelief.

Then he went about among the villages
teaching. 7 He called the twelve and began
to send them out two by two, and gave
them authority over the unclean spirits.
8 He ordered them to take nothing for their
journey except a staff; no bread, no bag, no
money in their belts; 9 but to wear sandals
and not to put on two tunics. 10 He said to
them, "Wherever you enter a house, stay
there until you leave the place. 11 If any
place will not welcome you and they refuse
to hear you, as you leave, shake off the dust
that is on your feet as a testimony against
them." 12 So they went out and proclaimed
that all should repent. 13 They cast out
many demons, and anointed with oil many
who were sick and cured them.

14 King Herod heard of it, for Jesus'[c]
name had become known. Some were[d]
saying, "John the baptizer has been raised
from the dead; and for this reason these
powers are at work in him." 15 But others
said, "It is Elijah." And others said, "It is a
prophet, like one of the prophets of old."
16 But when Herod heard of it, he said,
"John, whom I beheaded, has been raised."

17 For Herod himself had sent men who
arrested John, bound him, and put him in
prison on account of Herodias, his brother
Philip's wife, because Herod[e] had married
her. 18 For John had been telling Herod, "It
is not lawful for you to have your brother's
wife." 19 And Herodias had a grudge
against him, and wanted to kill him. But
she could not, 20 for Herod feared John,
knowing that he was a righteous and holy
man, and he protected him. When he heard
him, he was greatly perplexed;[f] and yet he

a Other ancient authorities read *son of the carpenter and of Mary* *b* Or *stumbled* *c* Gk *his* *d* Other ancient authorities read *He was* *e* Gk *he* *f* Other ancient authorities read *he did many things*

6.1–6a: Rejection in his hometown (Mt. 13.53–58; Lk 4.16–30). Those who knew Jesus from his early years, before he was called into service as a prophet mediating extraordinary powers, cannot respond in faith as others can; cf. 3.21. **5:** The powers that work through such a prophet are dependent on people's positive response with faith.

6.6b–13: Commissioning the twelve (Mt 10.1,9–11,14; Lk 9.1–6; cf. Lk 10.2–16). Jesus commissions the twelve, appointed as symbolic heads of the renewed Israel in 3.13–19, to expand his mission of proclamation, exorcism, and healing. They work in villages, staying in sympathetic households, building the renewal movement.

6.14–29: Herod's execution of John (Mt 14.1–12; Lk 9.7–9). **14–16:** *Herod,* Antipas, son of Herod the Great, technically appointed tetrarch, but popularly known as "King," ruled Galilee and part of Transjordan 4 BCE–39 CE. Clearly people were responding to and identifying Jesus out of their cultivation of popular tradition as "Elijah" or "one of the prophets." Herod, however, is anxiously superstitious because he had beheaded John. **17–29:** A popular tale of the decadent life at Herod's court and of the gruesome beheading of John that sounds an ominous note for Jesus' prophetic renewal of Israel over against the king appointed by Rome. **17–18:** Royal marriages were instruments of international politics. John's prophecy against Herod Antipas's marriage to his brother's wife, which alienated the Nabatean king Aretas IV, father of his first wife, was politically incendiary. **19–20:** Herod's and Herodias's respective feelings about John are reminiscent of Ahab's and Jezebel's stances toward Elijah in 1 Kings 18–19,21. **21:** *Leaders* is a misleading translation for "the first ones," i.e., high-ranking officials at court.

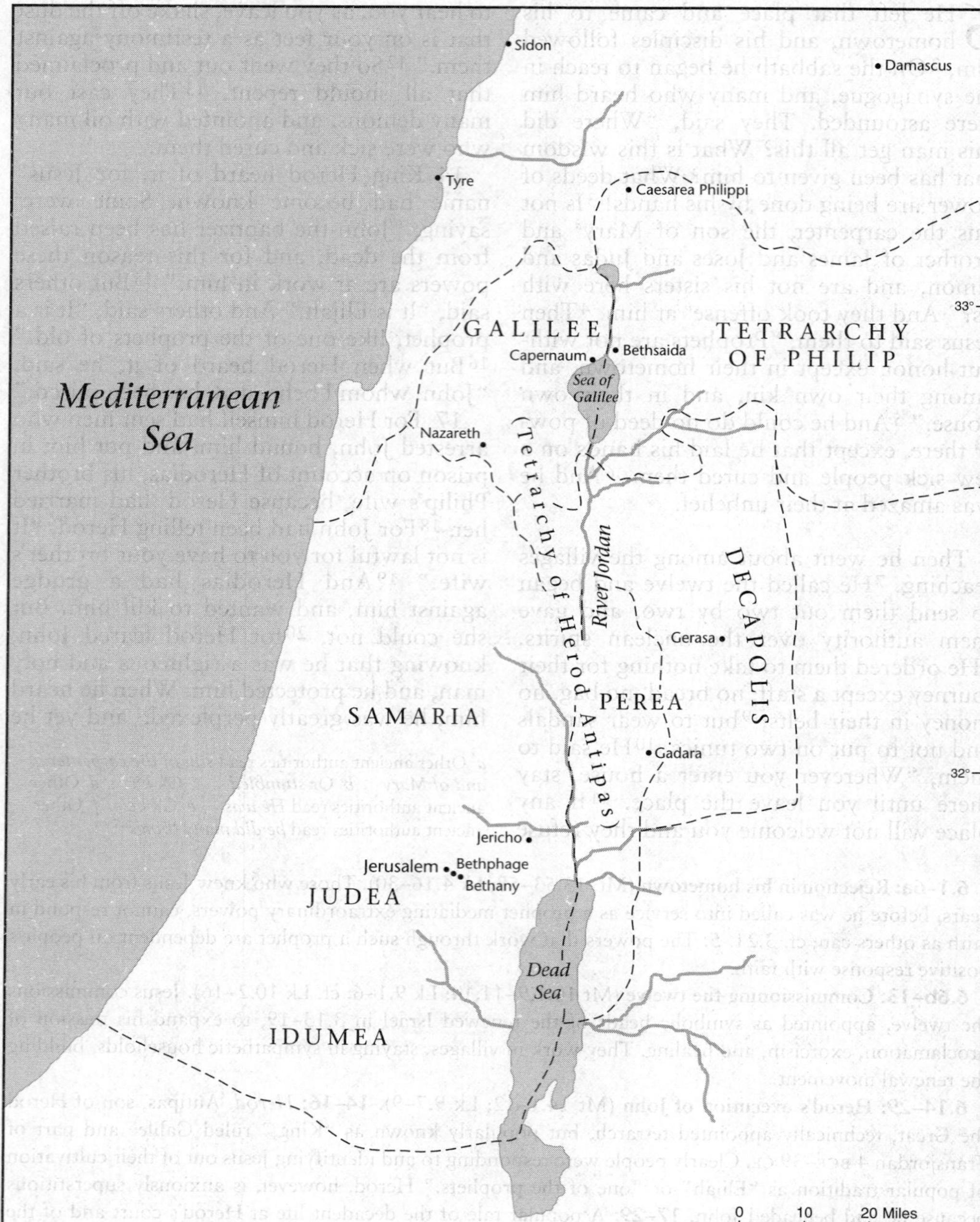

Chs 5–8: Sites of Jesus' travels in Galilee and vicinity.

liked to listen to him. 21 But an opportunity
came when Herod on his birthday gave a
banquet for his courtiers and officers and
for the leaders of Galilee. 22 When his
daughter Herodias[a] came in and danced,
she pleased Herod and his guests; and the
king said to the girl, "Ask me for whatever
you wish, and I will give it." 23 And he sol-
emnly swore to her, "Whatever you ask
me, I will give you, even half of my king-
dom." 24 She went out and said to her
mother, "What should I ask for?" She re-
plied, "The head of John the baptizer."
25 Immediately she rushed back to the king
and requested, "I want you to give me at
once the head of John the Baptist on a plat-
ter." 26 The king was deeply grieved; yet out
of regard for his oaths and for the guests,
he did not want to refuse her. 27 Immediate-
ly the king sent a soldier of the guard with
orders to bring John's[b] head. He went and
beheaded him in the prison, 28 brought his
head on a platter, and gave it to the girl.
Then the girl gave it to her mother. 29 When
his disciples heard about it, they came and
took his body, and laid it in a tomb.

30 The apostles gathered around Jesus,
and told him all that they had done and
taught. 31 He said to them, "Come away to
a deserted place all by yourselves and rest a
while." For many were coming and going,
and they had no leisure even to eat. 32 And
they went away in the boat to a deserted
place by themselves. 33 Now many saw
them going and recognized them, and they
hurried there on foot from all the towns
and arrived ahead of them. 34 As he went
ashore, he saw a great crowd; and he had
compassion for them, because they were
like sheep without a shepherd; and he be-
gan to teach them many things. 35 When it
grew late, his disciples came to him and
said, "This is a deserted place, and the hour
is now very late; 36 send them away so that
they may go into the surrounding country
and villages and buy something for them-
selves to eat." 37 But he answered them,
"You give them something to eat." They
said to him, "Are we to go and buy two
hundred denarii[c] worth of bread, and give
it to them to eat?" 38 And he said to them,
"How many loaves have you? Go and see."
When they had found out, they said, "Five,
and two fish." 39 Then he ordered them to
get all the people to sit down in groups
on the green grass. 40 So they sat down in
groups of hundreds and of fifties. 41 Taking
the five loaves and the two fish, he looked
up to heaven, and blessed and broke the
loaves, and gave them to his disciples to set
before the people; and he divided the two

a Other ancient authorities read *the daughter of Herodias herself* *b* Gk *his* *c* The denarius was the usual day's wage for a laborer

22: *His daughter,* called Salome by Josephus (*Ant.* 18.5.136). **29:** John also had disciples, and perhaps headed a prophetic movement parallel to that of Jesus.

6.30–44: Wilderness feeding of five thousand (Mt 14.13–21; Lk 9.10–17; Jn 6.1–13; cf. Mk 8.1–10). First of two wilderness feedings reminiscent of God's feeding early Israel in the wilderness through Moses (Ex 16; Num 11). **30–33:** In need of a temporary retreat from the rigors of their mission, Jesus and his apostles withdraw, but hordes of people clamor to them even in the wilderness. **34:** *Sheep without a shepherd,* a frequent image for a people without a prophet or king to lead them (see Num 27.17; 1 Kings 22.17; Ezek 34.8; Zech 10.2). Coming right after Herod's execution of John, it also alludes to the prophetic tradition of political criticism of predatory and exploitative kings who become rich by "fleecing" rather than caring for their people (see Ezek 34.2–5; Zech 11.4–17). **35–37:** The disciples' suggestion and protest both represent a misunderstanding of Jesus' program. That the villagers could no longer feed themselves from their own produce and had to become laborers to earn money to buy food is just the problem! **38–44:** One of the dreams of peasants, who are always economically marginal and therefore hungry, is a future good time when food is plentiful (cf. Lk 6.20–21). Both the multiplication of the food and the twelve baskets left over suggest that this story is reminiscent of Elijah-Elisha stories of feeding in times of famine (e.g., 1 Kings 4.42–44) and of their restoration of Israel symbolized in its twelve tribes. **41:** Christian readers usually find eucharistic overtones in Jesus' blessing and breaking of the loaves.

fish among them all. 42 And all ate and were
filled; 43 and they took up twelve baskets
full of broken pieces and of the fish.
44 Those who had eaten the loaves num-
bered five thousand men.

45 Immediately he made his disciples get
into the boat and go on ahead to the other
side, to Bethsaida, while he dismissed the
crowd. 46 After saying farewell to them, he
went up on the mountain to pray.

47 When evening came, the boat was
out on the sea, and he was alone on the
land. 48 When he saw that they were strain-
ing at the oars against an adverse wind, he
came towards them early in the morning,
walking on the sea. He intended to pass
them by. 49 But when they saw him walking
on the sea, they thought it was a ghost and
cried out; 50 for they all saw him and were
terrified. But immediately he spoke to them
and said, "Take heart, it is I; do not be
afraid." 51 Then he got into the boat with
them and the wind ceased. And they were
utterly astounded, 52 for they did not un-
derstand about the loaves, but their hearts
were hardened.

53 When they had crossed over, they
came to land at Gennesaret and moored the
boat. 54 When they got out of the boat, peo-
ple at once recognized him, 55 and rushed
about that whole region and began to bring
the sick on mats to wherever they heard he
was. 56 And wherever he went, into villages
or cities or farms, they laid the sick in the
marketplaces, and begged him that they
might touch even the fringe of his cloak;
and all who touched it were healed.

7 Now when the Pharisees and some of
the scribes who had come from Jerusa-
lem gathered around him, 2 they noticed
that some of his disciples were eating with
defiled hands, that is, without washing
them. 3 (For the Pharisees, and all the Jews,
do not eat unless they thoroughly wash
their hands,[a] thus observing the tradition
of the elders; 4 and they do not eat anything
from the market unless they wash it;[b] and
there are also many other traditions that
they observe, the washing of cups, pots,
and bronze kettles.[c]) 5 So the Pharisees and
the scribes asked him, "Why do your disci-
ples not live[d] according to the tradition of
the elders, but eat with defiled hands?" 6 He
said to them, "Isaiah prophesied rightly
about you hypocrites, as it is written,

'This people honors me with
their lips,
but their hearts are far from me;
7 in vain do they worship me,
teaching human precepts as
doctrines.'

8 You abandon the commandment of God
and hold to human tradition."

9 Then he said to them, "You have a
fine way of rejecting the commandment of

a Meaning of Gk uncertain *b* Other ancient authorities read *and when they come from the marketplace, they do not eat unless they purify themselves* *c* Other ancient authorities add *and beds* *d* Gk *walk*

6.45–52: Second sea crossing (Mt 14.22–33; Jn 6.15–21). **45:** *Bethsaida,* a village at the north of the Sea of Galilee, transformed into a small "city" by Herod Philip. **47–52:** Again the disciples are terrified, not only at the wind but also at the apparition. **50:** Mark compares Jesus to God, using the phrase "I am" (Gk "ego eimi"; cf. Ex 3.14). **51–52:** Yet the disciples not only lack faith, as in 4.40, but *their hearts were hardened,* as had occurred with enemies of God in earlier times (e.g., Ex 7.3,14; Deut 2.30; Josh 11.20; 1 Sam 6.6).

6.53–56: A summary passage highlighting the widening response to Jesus. Mt 14.34–36.

7.1–23: Traditions of the elders vs. the commandment of God (Mt 15.1–20). **1–5:** As representatives of the Jerusalem religious establishment, the Pharisees and scribes cultivated oral *traditions of the elders* supplementary to the law of Moses, in this story focused on purity codes for processing and eating food. **3–4:** The parenthetical explanation claims that "all the Judeans," not just the Pharisees, observed their hand-washing regulations. **6–8:** In reply, quoting Isa 29.13 (LXX), Jesus claims that the Pharisees in effect replace the basic Mosaic covenantal *commandment of God* with their merely *human tradition.* **9–13:** Jesus focuses the dispute in concrete economic terms on the *commandment of God* concerning *Honor your father and your mother* (cf. Ex 20.12; 21.17), which includes economic support in their declining years.

God in order to keep your tradition! 10 For
Moses said, 'Honor your father and your
mother'; and, 'Whoever speaks evil of fa-
ther or mother must surely die.' 11 But you
say that if anyone tells father or mother,
'Whatever support you might have had
from me is Corban' (that is, an offering to
God[a])— 12 then you no longer permit do-
ing anything for a father or mother, 13 thus
making void the word of God through your
tradition that you have handed on. And
you do many things like this."
14 Then he called the crowd again and
said to them, "Listen to me, all of you, and
understand: 15 there is nothing outside a
person that by going in can defile, but the
things that come out are what defile."[b]
17 When he had left the crowd and en-
tered the house, his disciples asked him
about the parable. 18 He said to them,
"Then do you also fail to understand? Do
you not see that whatever goes into a per-
son from outside cannot defile, 19 since it
enters, not the heart but the stomach, and
goes out into the sewer?" (Thus he declared
all foods clean.) 20 And he said, "It is what
comes out of a person that defiles. 21 For it
is from within, from the human heart, that
evil intentions come: fornication, theft,
murder, 22 adultery, avarice, wickedness,
deceit, licentiousness, envy, slander, pride,
folly. 23 All these evil things come from
within, and they defile a person."

24 From there he set out and went away
to the region of Tyre.[c] He entered a house
and did not want anyone to know he was
there. Yet he could not escape notice, 25 but
a woman whose little daughter had an un-
clean spirit immediately heard about him,
and she came and bowed down at his feet.
26 Now the woman was a Gentile, of Syro-
phoenician origin. She begged him to cast
the demon out of her daughter. 27 He said
to her, "Let the children be fed first, for it
is not fair to take the children's food and
throw it to the dogs." 28 But she answered
him, "Sir,[d] even the dogs under the table
eat the children's crumbs." 29 Then he said
to her, "For saying that, you may go—the
demon has left your daughter." 30 So she
went home, found the child lying on the
bed, and the demon gone.
31 Then he returned from the region of
Tyre, and went by way of Sidon towards
the Sea of Galilee, in the region of the De-
capolis. 32 They brought to him a deaf man
who had an impediment in his speech; and
they begged him to lay his hand on him.
33 He took him aside in private, away from
the crowd, and put his fingers into his ears,
and he spat and touched his tongue.
34 Then looking up to heaven, he sighed
and said to him, "Ephphatha," that is, "Be
opened." 35 And immediately his ears were
opened, his tongue was released, and he
spoke plainly. 36 Then Jesus[e] ordered them

a Gk lacks *to God* *b* Other ancient authorities add verse 16, *"Let anyone with ears to hear listen"*
c Other ancient authorities add *and Sidon*
d Or *Lord*; other ancient authorities prefix *Yes*
e Gk *he*

He claims that the Pharisees make it void with their *tradition* of *Corban,* encouraging people to dedicate the produce of their land to the Jerusalem Temple—thus siphoning off produce that otherwise could have been used to support parents. *Corban* is an Aramaic word meaning "offering." **14–19a:** Addresses purity codes with a touch of earthy humor regarding eating and resultant bodily functions. **17:** *Parable* here has the sense of "riddle." **19b:** Perhaps a later addition to the text. **20–23:** Shifts the focus from bodily functions to the inner motivations of "defiling," socially destructive behavior.

7.24–30: The Syrophoenician woman (Mt 15.21–28). **24–26:** In *the region of Tyre,* not in the city itself, a "Greek" woman intrudes with her plea on behalf of her possessed daughter. **27–28:** To Jesus' insistence that the manifestation of the kingdom (*food*) is primarily for Israelites (*children*), she gives a reply that wins the debate. **29–30:** The representative figure of the peoples surrounding Israel insists on receiving the benefits of the kingdom, and her insistence produces precisely that.

7.31–37: Healing the deaf (Mt 15.29–31). Healing the deaf-mute, which is symbolic of a more general restoration of hearing and speech, confirms that the kingdom of God and the movement of renewal has extended to the peoples round about Israel. **34:** The word *ephphatha* is Aramaic; see 5.41n.

to tell no one; but the more he ordered
them, the more zealously they proclaimed
it. 37 They were astounded beyond measure,
saying, "He has done everything well; he
even makes the deaf to hear and the mute
to speak."

8 In those days when there was again a
great crowd without anything to eat, he
called his disciples and said to them, 2 "I
have compassion for the crowd, because
they have been with me now for three days
and have nothing to eat. 3 If I send them
away hungry to their homes, they will faint
on the way—and some of them have come
from a great distance." 4 His disciples re-
plied, "How can one feed these people with
bread here in the desert?" 5 He asked them,
"How many loaves do you have?" They
said, "Seven." 6 Then he ordered the crowd
to sit down on the ground; and he took the
seven loaves, and after giving thanks he
broke them and gave them to his disciples
to distribute; and they distributed them to
the crowd. 7 They had also a few small fish;
and after blessing them, he ordered that
these too should be distributed. 8 They ate
and were filled; and they took up the bro-
ken pieces left over, seven baskets full.
9 Now there were about four thousand peo-
ple. And he sent them away. 10 And im-
mediately he got into the boat with his
disciples and went to the district of
Dalmanutha.[a]

11 The Pharisees came and began to ar-
gue with him, asking him for a sign from
heaven, to test him. 12 And he sighed deeply
in his spirit and said, "Why does this gener-
ation ask for a sign? Truly I tell you, no
sign will be given to this generation."
13 And he left them, and getting into the
boat again, he went across to the other side.

14 Now the disciples[b] had forgotten to
bring any bread; and they had only one loaf
with them in the boat. 15 And he cautioned
them, saying, "Watch out—beware of the
yeast of the Pharisees and the yeast of Her-
od."[c] 16 They said to one another, "It is
because we have no bread." 17 And becom-
ing aware of it, Jesus said to them, "Why
are you talking about having no bread? Do
you still not perceive or understand? Are
your hearts hardened? 18 Do you have eyes,
and fail to see? Do you have ears, and
fail to hear? And do you not remember?
19 When I broke the five loaves for the five
thousand, how many baskets full of broken
pieces did you collect?" They said to him,
"Twelve." 20 "And the seven for the four
thousand, how many baskets full of broken
pieces did you collect?" And they said to
him, "Seven." 21 Then he said to them, "Do
you not yet understand?"

22 They came to Bethsaida. Some peo-

a Other ancient authorities read *Mageda* or *Magdala*
b Gk *they* *c* Other ancient authorities read *the Herodians*

8.1–9: Wilderness feeding of four thousand (Mt 15.32–38; cf. 6.30–44). As he had fed the earlier crowd in the wilderness, implicitly composed of Jews, now Jesus also feeds the surrounding peoples in the wilderness. *Seven* is symbolic of the surrounding peoples, as twelve was of Israel (6.43). The two wilderness feedings echo the two accounts of the giving of food to the Israelites in the wilderness (Ex 16; Num 11).

8.10–12: No sign will be given (Mt 16.1–4; 12.28–39; Lk 11.29; 11.16; 12.54–56). This passage would make better sense if v. 10 were in one paragraph with vv. 11–12, and v. 13 were joined to the following paragraph (vv. 14–21). Blind to the sequences of Moses- and Elijah-like actions Jesus has just taken, the Pharisees again press Jesus, asking *for a sign from heaven, to test him,* which they do again in 10.2 and 12.15. **10:** *Dalmanutha,* the parallel in Mt 15.39 reads "Magadan" (see note there).

8.13–21: The disciples misunderstand (Mt 16.4–12; Lk 12.1). In a bridge to the next section, the disciples simply do not understand what is happening, either the scheming of the religious and political authorities seeking to destroy Jesus (cf. 3.6) or the renewal movement underway among the surrounding peoples as well as among Israelite villages. **17–18:** 4.9–12; 6.52. **19:** 6.41–44. **20:** 8.5–8.

8.22–10.52: Jesus confirms and continues his prophetic role in the renewal of Israel while announcing his agenda as martyr-messiah to the misunderstanding disciples.

ple[a] brought a blind man to him and
begged him to touch him. 23 He took the
blind man by the hand and led him out of
the village; and when he had put saliva on
his eyes and laid his hands on him, he asked
him, "Can you see anything?" 24 And the
man[b] looked up and said, "I can see peo-
ple, but they look like trees, walking."
25 Then Jesus[b] laid his hands on his eyes
again; and he looked intently and his sight
was restored, and he saw everything clear-
ly. 26 Then he sent him away to his home,
saying, "Do not even go into the village."[c]

27 Jesus went on with his disciples to the
villages of Caesarea Philippi; and on the
way he asked his disciples, "Who do people
say that I am?" 28 And they answered him,
"John the Baptist; and others, Elijah; and
still others, one of the prophets." 29 He
asked them, "But who do you say that I
am?" Peter answered him, "You are the
Messiah."[d] 30 And he sternly ordered them
not to tell anyone about him.
31 Then he began to teach them that the
Son of Man must undergo great suffering,
and be rejected by the elders, the chief
priests, and the scribes, and be killed, and
after three days rise again. 32 He said all this
quite openly. And Peter took him aside and
began to rebuke him. 33 But turning and
looking at his disciples, he rebuked Peter
and said, "Get behind me, Satan! For you
are setting your mind not on divine things
but on human things."

34 He called the crowd with his disci-
ples, and said to them, "If any want to be-
come my followers, let them deny them-
selves and take up their cross and follow
me. 35 For those who want to save their life
will lose it, and those who lose their life for
my sake, and for the sake of the gospel,[e]
will save it. 36 For what will it profit them
to gain the whole world and forfeit their
life? 37 Indeed, what can they give in return
for their life? 38 Those who are ashamed of
me and of my words[f] in this adulterous

a Gk *They* *b* Gk *he* *c* Other ancient authorities add *or tell anyone in the village* *d* Or *the Christ* *e* Other ancient authorities read *lose their life for the sake of the gospel* *f* Other ancient authorities read *and of mine*

8.22–26: Healing of a blind man (Jn 9.1–7). This restoration of a blind man's sight and that of Bartimaeus in 10.46–52 frame this part of Mark in which the disciples are "blind" to what is said and done.

8.27–33: Jesus' first announcement and Peter's misunderstanding (Mt 16.13–23; Lk 9.18–22). **27:** *The villages of Caesarea Philippi,* villages subject to Herod Philip in the northernmost area of (formerly) Israelite territory. **28:** Again, not surprisingly given his program, Jesus is popularly understood as Elijah, one of the prophets, or even John. **29–30:** There is very little evidence for expectations of "the messiah," which was hardly standardized at the time. The role and title *the Messiah* would fit Jesus' subsequent actions (e.g., in 11.2–10) and statements about him, but not his previous actions in Mark. **31:** The translation softens a key Greek term: "it is necessary that . . . ," i.e., in God's plan, given the historical situation. *The Son of Man,* meaning "human being" or the future figure representing a restored Israel, or both, is clearly Jesus' self-reference. This is the first of three clear announcements that "it is necessary" that he be condemned by the rulers, be killed, and rise again. **32–33:** Following Peter's rebuke (presumably about having to be killed), Jesus in turn rebukes Peter in startling terms, contrasting the purpose or will of God for human beings with the purposes those human beings would have for themselves. Jesus will be a martyr-messiah.

8.34–9.1: The cost of following Jesus (Mt 16.24–28; Lk 9.23–27; cf. Mt 10.28–33; Lk 12.4–9). Pointedly telling *the crowd* to join the disciples, Jesus warns that, like himself, his followers must also be prepared to suffer martyrdom for the gospel, the cause of the kingdom. **34:** *Take up their cross,* the Romans used crucifixion as a gruesome means of terrorizing subject peoples by hanging rebels and agitators from crosses for several days until they suffocated to death. They required condemned provincials to carry the crossbeam on which they were about to be hung. **38:** How the followers stand toward Jesus and his gospel when facing trial will determine how the Son of Man will stand toward them when, in God's final condemnation of the oppressive empire, he comes in judgment as well as restoration of

and sinful generation, of them the Son of
Man will also be ashamed when he comes
in the glory of his Father with the holy an-
9 gels." 1 And he said to them, "Truly I
tell you, there are some standing here
who will not taste death until they see that
the kingdom of God has come with[a]
power."

2 Six days later, Jesus took with him Pe-
ter and James and John, and led them up a
high mountain apart, by themselves. And
he was transfigured before them, 3 and his
clothes became dazzling white, such as no
one[b] on earth could bleach them. 4 And
there appeared to them Elijah with Moses,
who were talking with Jesus. 5 Then Peter
said to Jesus, "Rabbi, it is good for us to be
here; let us make three dwellings,[c] one for
you, one for Moses, and one for Elijah."
6 He did not know what to say, for they
were terrified. 7 Then a cloud overshad-
owed them, and from the cloud there came
a voice, "This is my Son, the Beloved;[d]
listen to him!" 8 Suddenly when they
looked around, they saw no one with them
any more, but only Jesus.

9 As they were coming down the moun-
tain, he ordered them to tell no one about
what they had seen, until after the Son of
Man had risen from the dead. 10 So they
kept the matter to themselves, questioning
what this rising from the dead could mean.
11 Then they asked him, "Why do the
scribes say that Elijah must come first?"
12 He said to them, "Elijah is indeed coming
first to restore all things. How then is it
written about the Son of Man, that he is to
go through many sufferings and be treated
with contempt? 13 But I tell you that Elijah
has come, and they did to him whatever
they pleased, as it is written about him."

14 When they came to the disciples, they
saw a great crowd around them, and some
scribes arguing with them. 15 When the
whole crowd saw him, they were immedi-
ately overcome with awe, and they ran for-
ward to greet him. 16 He asked them,
"What are you arguing about with them?"
17 Someone from the crowd answered him,
"Teacher, I brought you my son; he has a
spirit that makes him unable to speak;
18 and whenever it seizes him, it dashes him
down; and he foams and grinds his teeth
and becomes rigid; and I asked your disci-
ples to cast it out, but they could not do
so." 19 He answered them, "You faithless
generation, how much longer must I be
among you? How much longer must I put
up with you? Bring him to me." 20 And they
brought the boy[e] to him. When the spirit
saw him, immediately it convulsed the

a Or *in* *b* Gk *no fuller* *c* Or *tents* *d* Or *my beloved Son* *e* Gk *him*

the people (cf. Mk 13.26–27; 14.62; Dan 13.13–14). **9.1:** *The kingdom of God* will *come with power* already during their lifetime.

9.2–8: Transfiguration of Jesus (Mt 17.1–8; Lk 9.28–36). **2–4:** The mountain setting is reminiscent of Moses and the elders of Israel on Sinai (Ex 24). *Transfigured . . . dazzling white,* in the disciples' visionary experience, Jesus appears as a vindicated martyr (see Dan 11.36; Rev 3.5,18; 4.4; 6.9–11; 7.9,13–14), linked to what he had just told the disciples in 8.31. With him are Elijah and Moses, the prophetic restorer and founder of Israel, respectively, whose great actions of deliverance Jesus' actions, just performed in 4.35–8.26, resemble. **5–6:** Peter, mystified and *terrified,* addresses Jesus not as "messiah," but as *Rabbi,* as he does again in 11.21 when he is again mystified, and as Judas does in his betrayal, 14.45. **7:** Now Peter, James, and John hear the same voice that Jesus heard at his baptism in 1.11.

9.9–13: Correction of scribal teaching about Elijah (Mt 17.9–13). **9–11:** The disciples, still not understanding the necessity of his martyrdom, remain oriented toward the teachings of the Jerusalem scribes, as in Sir 48.10 (cf. Mal 4.4–5). **12–13:** First pointing to the obvious contradiction between the official scribal teaching and what he has just told them, mockingly couching it in scribal terms as scriptural, "it is written," he asserts that in fact Elijah has already come in John, and he was ignominiously killed.

9.14–29: Healing of epileptic child (Mt 17.14–21; Lk 9.37–42). Since Matthew and Luke have no parallels to sections of this unusually elaborate story in Mark (not to vv. 15–16,21–27), the text may have been much shorter originally.

boy,[a] and he fell on the ground and rolled
about, foaming at the mouth. 21 Jesus[b]
asked the father, "How long has this been
happening to him?" And he said, "From
childhood. 22 It has often cast him into the
fire and into the water, to destroy him; but
if you are able to do anything, have pity on
us and help us." 23 Jesus said to him, "If
you are able!—All things can be done for
the one who believes." 24 Immediately the
father of the child cried out,[c] "I believe;
help my unbelief!" 25 When Jesus saw that
a crowd came running together, he rebuked
the unclean spirit, saying to it, "You spirit
that keeps this boy from speaking and hear-
ing, I command you, come out of him, and
never enter him again!" 26 After crying out
and convulsing him terribly, it came out,
and the boy was like a corpse, so that most
of them said, "He is dead." 27 But Jesus
took him by the hand and lifted him up,
and he was able to stand. 28 When he had
entered the house, his disciples asked him
privately, "Why could we not cast it out?"
29 He said to them, "This kind can come
out only through prayer."[d]

30 They went on from there and passed
through Galilee. He did not want anyone to
know it; 31 for he was teaching his disciples,
saying to them, "The Son of Man is to be
betrayed into human hands, and they will
kill him, and three days after being killed,
he will rise again." 32 But they did not un-
derstand what he was saying and were
afraid to ask him.

33 Then they came to Capernaum; and
when he was in the house he asked them,
"What were you arguing about on the
way?" 34 But they were silent, for on the
way they had argued with one another who
was the greatest. 35 He sat down, called the
twelve, and said to them, "Whoever wants
to be first must be last of all and servant of
all." 36 Then he took a little child and put it
among them; and taking it in his arms, he
said to them, 37 "Whoever welcomes one
such child in my name welcomes me, and
whoever welcomes me welcomes not me
but the one who sent me."

38 John said to him, "Teacher, we saw
someone[e] casting out demons in your
name, and we tried to stop him, because he
was not following us." 39 But Jesus said,
"Do not stop him; for no one who does a
deed of power in my name will be able soon
afterward to speak evil of me. 40 Whoever is
not against us is for us. 41 For truly I tell
you, whoever gives you a cup of water to
drink because you bear the name of Christ
will by no means lose the reward.

42 "If any of you put a stumbling block
before one of these little ones who believe
in me,[f] it would be better for you if a great
millstone were hung around your neck and
you were thrown into the sea. 43 If your
hand causes you to stumble, cut it off; it is
better for you to enter life maimed than to
have two hands and to go to hell,[g] to the
unquenchable fire.[h] 45 And if your foot
causes you to stumble, cut it off; it is better

a Gk *him* *b* Gk *He* *c* Other ancient authorities add *with tears* *d* Other ancient authorities add *and fasting* *e* Other ancient authorities add *who does not follow us* *f* Other ancient authorities lack *in me* *g* Gk *Gehenna* *h* Verses 44 and 46 (which are identical with verse 48) are lacking in the best ancient authorities

9.30–37: Second announcement and misunderstanding (Mt 17.22–23; 18.1–5; Lk 9.43–48). Despite his teaching, again, that the Son of Man would be killed and rise again, the disciples still do not understand, as illustrated in their blithe discussion of *who was the greatest.* **36–37:** A *child* was the lowest-status person in a household.

9.38–41: Unknown exorcist (Lk 9.49–50). An allusion to the story in Num 11.27–29. The movement is not to be defensive or controlling.

9.42–50: Warning on discipline (Mt 18.6–9; 5.29–30; 5.13; Lk 17.1–2; 14.34–35). A series of warnings addressed not to the individual but to the movement and its communities about internal discipline: Whoever causes a member to stumble in whatever way must be disciplined (possibly expelled). **43:** *Hell,* lit. "Gehenna," the valley of the son of Hinnom (2 Kings 23.10; Jer 7.31), symbolizing the place of eternal punishment by fire. **48:** See Isa 66.24.

for you to enter life lame than to have two
feet and to be thrown into hell.[a,b] 47 And
if your eye causes you to stumble, tear it
out; it is better for you to enter the king-
dom of God with one eye than to have two
eyes and to be thrown into hell,[a] 48 where
their worm never dies, and the fire is never
quenched.

49 "For everyone will be salted with
fire.[c] 50 Salt is good; but if salt has lost its
saltiness, how can you season it?[d] Have
salt in yourselves, and be at peace with one
another."

10 He left that place and went to the
region of Judea and[e] beyond the
Jordan. And crowds again gathered around
him; and, as was his custom, he again
taught them.

2 Some Pharisees came, and to test him
they asked, "Is it lawful for a man to di-
vorce his wife?" 3 He answered them,
"What did Moses command you?" 4 They
said, "Moses allowed a man to write a cer-
tificate of dismissal and to divorce her."
5 But Jesus said to them, "Because of your
hardness of heart he wrote this command-
ment for you. 6 But from the beginning of
creation, 'God made them male and fe-
male.' 7 'For this reason a man shall leave
his father and mother and be joined to his
wife,[f] 8 and the two shall become one
flesh.' So they are no longer two, but one
flesh. 9 Therefore what God has joined to-
gether, let no one separate."

10 Then in the house the disciples asked
him again about this matter. 11 He said to
them, "Whoever divorces his wife and mar-
ries another commits adultery against her;
12 and if she divorces her husband and mar-
ries another, she commits adultery."

13 People were bringing little children to
him in order that he might touch them; and
the disciples spoke sternly to them. 14 But
when Jesus saw this, he was indignant and
said to them, "Let the little children come
to me; do not stop them; for it is to such as
these that the kingdom of God belongs.
15 Truly I tell you, whoever does not receive
the kingdom of God as a little child will
never enter it." 16 And he took them up
in his arms, laid his hands on them, and
blessed them.

17 As he was setting out on a journey,
a man ran up and knelt before him, and
asked him, "Good Teacher, what must I do
to inherit eternal life?" 18 Jesus said to him,
"Why do you call me good? No one is good
but God alone. 19 You know the command-
ments: 'You shall not murder; You shall
not commit adultery; You shall not steal;
You shall not bear false witness; You shall
not defraud; Honor your father and moth-
er.' " 20 He said to him, "Teacher, I have
kept all these since my youth." 21 Jesus,
looking at him, loved him and said, "You

a Gk *Gehenna* *b* Verses 44 and 46 (which are identical with verse 48) are lacking in the best ancient authorities *c* Other ancient authorities either add or substitute *and every sacrifice will be salted with salt* *d* Or *how can you restore its saltiness?* *e* Other ancient authorities lack *and* *f* Other ancient authorities lack *and be joined to his wife*

10.1–16: Marriage and children in the kingdom (Mt 19.1–15; Lk 18.15–17). **1:** Jesus moves into Israelite territory beyond Galilee, now concentrating on teaching. **2–12:** The first step in a series of covenantal instructions and exhortations focuses on (the commandment against) adultery, i.e., on marriage and divorce. **3–4:** See Deut 24.1–4; Jer 3.8. **5–9:** To the Pharisees' focus on divorce as a male prerogative, Jesus insists upon the equality of marriage intended in the creation stories, Gen 1.27; 2.24. **10–12:** Cf. Mt 5.31–32. The juxtaposition of vv. 2–9 and vv. 11–12 indicates that Jesus' restrictive interpretation of the commandment against adultery, allowing divorce but prohibiting remarriage, was grounded in creation. **13–16:** Not an idealization of childhood. Against the disciples' restriction of access to Jesus and his movement, Jesus uses children, who occupied the lowest status in society, as a symbol for how one should receive the kingdom.

10.17–31: Egalitarian economic relations in the kingdom (Mt 19.16–30; Lk 18.18–30). An exhortation for egalitarian covenantal economic relations. **17:** The man's address is flattering and his question unusual for Mark, in which the common people have more concrete concerns. **19:** Recitation of covenantal commandments, Ex 20.12–16, adding *defraud*. **21–22:** Jesus' test exposes him as adamantly attached

lack one thing; go, sell what you own, and
give the money[a] to the poor, and you will
have treasure in heaven; then come, follow
me." 22 When he heard this, he was
shocked and went away grieving, for he
had many possessions.

23 Then Jesus looked around and said
to his disciples, "How hard it will be for
those who have wealth to enter the king-
dom of God!" 24 And the disciples were
perplexed at these words. But Jesus said to
them again, "Children, how hard it is[b] to
enter the kingdom of God! 25 It is easier for
a camel to go through the eye of a needle
than for someone who is rich to enter the
kingdom of God." 26 They were greatly as-
tounded and said to one another,[c] "Then
who can be saved?" 27 Jesus looked at them
and said, "For mortals it is impossible, but
not for God; for God all things are possi-
ble."

28 Peter began to say to him, "Look, we
have left everything and followed you."
29 Jesus said, "Truly I tell you, there is no
one who has left house or brothers or sis-
ters or mother or father or children or
fields, for my sake and for the sake of the
good news,[d] 30 who will not receive a hun-
dredfold now in this age—houses, brothers
and sisters, mothers and children, and
fields, with persecutions—and in the age to
come eternal life. 31 But many who are first
will be last, and the last will be first."

32 They were on the road, going up to
Jerusalem, and Jesus was walking ahead of
them; they were amazed, and those who
followed were afraid. He took the twelve
aside again and began to tell them what
was to happen to him, 33 saying, "See, we
are going up to Jerusalem, and the Son of
Man will be handed over to the chief priests
and the scribes, and they will condemn him
to death; then they will hand him over to
the Gentiles; 34 they will mock him, and spit
upon him, and flog him, and kill him; and
after three days he will rise again."

35 James and John, the sons of Zebedee,
came forward to him and said to him,
"Teacher, we want you to do for us what-
ever we ask of you." 36 And he said to them,
"What is it you want me to do for you?"
37 And they said to him, "Grant us to sit,
one at your right hand and one at your left,
in your glory." 38 But Jesus said to them,
"You do not know what you are asking.
Are you able to drink the cup that I drink,
or be baptized with the baptism that I am

a Gk lacks *the money* *b* Other ancient authorities add *for those who trust in riches* *c* Other ancient authorities read *to him* *d* Or *gospel*

to his wealth, which (from the covenantal viewpoint) he might have gained by defrauding peasants by charging interest on loans, etc., thus also violating the commandment against stealing. **23–25:** Jesus consolidates the point just illustrated with a little proverbial peasant humor: It is impossible for a rich person to enter the kingdom of God. **26–27:** Jesus' reply to the disciples' incomprehension, although precisely how it connects with the previous discussion is unclear. **28–31:** To Peter's anxious plea, Jesus' reply is serious about the concrete restoration (houses, fields, families) but teasingly facetious as well. The obvious exaggeration about the degree is canceled out by the *persecutions,* and the promise of *eternal life in the age to come* is a throw-away line mocking the rich man's concern (v. 17).

10.32–45: Egalitarian social-political relations in the kingdom and the third announcement and misunderstanding (Mt 20.17–28; Lk 18.31–34, 22.24–27). Mark uses Jesus' third explanation to the disciples that the Son of Man will be condemned, killed, and rise again, combined with the disciples' stubborn misunderstanding, as a foil for exhortation on egalitarian social-political relations in the movement and its communities. **32–34:** The tone becomes ominous as they head toward Jerusalem and the climax of Jesus' escalating conflict with the rulers there, as explicitly dramatized in the details added to this third announcement of his destiny there. **35–37:** James and John's request indicates that they have completely misunderstood Jesus' mission and movement as well as refused to hear what Jesus has repeatedly told them. **38–40:** They claim they are prepared to follow the path of Jesus into martyrdom for the cause, which he promises will happen. But he rejects their request as presumptuous. On the metaphor of *cup,* see 14.24,36; Isa 51.17; Lam 4.21. **41–45:** The request for positions of power and privilege results in

baptized with?" 39 They replied, "We are
able." Then Jesus said to them, "The cup
that I drink you will drink; and with the
baptism with which I am baptized, you will
be baptized; 40 but to sit at my right hand or
at my left is not mine to grant, but it is for
those for whom it has been prepared."

41 When the ten heard this, they began
to be angry with James and John. 42 So
Jesus called them and said to them, "You
know that among the Gentiles those whom
they recognize as their rulers lord it over
them, and their great ones are tyrants over
them. 43 But it is not so among you; but
whoever wishes to become great among
you must be your servant, 44 and whoever
wishes to be first among you must be slave
of all. 45 For the Son of Man came not to be
served but to serve, and to give his life a
ransom for many."

46 They came to Jericho. As he and his
disciples and a large crowd were leaving
Jericho, Bartimaeus son of Timaeus, a blind
beggar, was sitting by the roadside.
47 When he heard that it was Jesus of Naza-
reth, he began to shout out and say, "Jesus,
Son of David, have mercy on me!" 48 Many
sternly ordered him to be quiet, but he cried
out even more loudly, "Son of David, have
mercy on me!" 49 Jesus stood still and said,
"Call him here." And they called the blind
man, saying to him, "Take heart; get up, he
is calling you." 50 So throwing off his cloak,
he sprang up and came to Jesus. 51 Then
Jesus said to him, "What do you want me
to do for you?" The blind man said to him,
"My teacher,[a] let me see again." 52 Jesus
said to him, "Go; your faith has made you
well." Immediately he regained his sight
and followed him on the way.

11 When they were approaching Jeru-
salem, at Bethphage and Bethany,
near the Mount of Olives, he sent two of
his disciples 2 and said to them, "Go into
the village ahead of you, and immediately
as you enter it, you will find tied there a
colt that has never been ridden; untie it and
bring it. 3 If anyone says to you, 'Why are
you doing this?' just say this, 'The Lord
needs it and will send it back here immedi-
ately.' " 4 They went away and found a colt
tied near a door, outside in the street. As
they were untying it, 5 some of the bystand-
ers said to them, "What are you doing, un-
tying the colt?" 6 They told them what Jesus
had said; and they allowed them to take it.
7 Then they brought the colt to Jesus and
threw their cloaks on it; and he sat on it.
8 Many people spread their cloaks on the
road, and others spread leafy branches that

a Aramaic *Rabbouni*

conflict among the disciples. But in contrast to the imperial practices of the nations, there will be no rulers in Jesus' movement or communities! Rather, would-be leaders must take the role of servants, following the paradigm of the Son of Man, Jesus, whose martyrdom will be a ransom (paid for redemption from slavery or indebtedness) of many.

10.46–52: Healing of the blind Bartimaeus (Mt 20.29–34; Lk 18.35–43). The second healing of a blind man that frames and completes this section focuses partly on the blindness of the disciples. **46:** *Jericho* is in the Jordan Valley ca. 21 km (13 mi) east-northeast of Jerusalem; a secondary road connected the two cities (see 11.1; Lk 10.30). *Bartimaeus* means *son of Timaeus* in Aramaic. **47–48:** Though blind, Bartimaeus nevertheless sees or knows that Jesus is the *Son of David.* In some circles a "son of David" was expected to restore the fortunes of Israel as king (2 Sam 5.1–5). In Mk 12.35–37 Jesus himself explains that the messiah is not the "son of David." **52:** After his sight is restored, he pointedly *followed* Jesus *on the way,* in striking contrast to the disciples.

11.1–13.2: Confronting the rulers and ruling institutions in Jerusalem.

11.1–11: A messianic demonstration (Mt 21.1–9; Lk 19.28–38; Jn 12.12–15). As Jesus and his followers enter into the capital city, they stage a "messianic" demonstration, in fulfillment of the prophecy of Zechariah (Zech 9.9–10) of a peasant king riding on a donkey (cf. 1 Kings 1.38), not in an imperial war-chariot. **1:** *Bethphage and Bethany,* villages just east of Jerusalem. **8:** *Spread their cloaks on the road,* before the messiah, the "anointed" king, just as was done when Elisha anointed Jehu to lead the rebellion

they had cut in the fields. 9 Then those who
went ahead and those who followed were
shouting,

"Hosanna!
Blessed is the one who comes in the
name of the Lord!
10 Blessed is the coming kingdom of
our ancestor David!
Hosanna in the highest heaven!"

11 Then he entered Jerusalem and went
into the temple; and when he had looked
around at everything, as it was already late,
he went out to Bethany with the twelve.

12 On the following day, when they
came from Bethany, he was hungry. 13 See-
ing in the distance a fig tree in leaf, he went
to see whether perhaps he would find any-
thing on it. When he came to it, he found
nothing but leaves, for it was not the season
for figs. 14 He said to it, "May no one ever
eat fruit from you again." And his disciples
heard it.

15 Then they came to Jerusalem. And he
entered the temple and began to drive out
those who were selling and those who were
buying in the temple, and he overturned the
tables of the money changers and the seats
of those who sold doves; 16 and he would
not allow anyone to carry anything
through the temple. 17 He was teaching and
saying, "Is it not written,

'My house shall be called a house of
prayer for all the nations'?
But you have made it a den
of robbers."

18 And when the chief priests and the
scribes heard it, they kept looking for a way
to kill him; for they were afraid of him,
because the whole crowd was spellbound
by his teaching. 19 And when evening came,
Jesus and his disciples[a] went out of the
city.

20 In the morning as they passed by,
they saw the fig tree withered away to its

[a] Gk *they*: other ancient authorities read *he*

against the oppressive Omride regime, 2 Kings 9.1–13. The *leafy branches* appear to have a similar significance; cf. the "palm branches" waved in victorious celebration (with hymns, etc.) of the newly established independence of Jerusalem and Judea in 1 Macc 13.51. **9:** The throng shouts a psalm of thanksgiving (Ps 118.25–26) for victory over Israel's enemies, one that was sung at the Passover festival. *Hosanna* means "Save us!" **10:** Added to the psalm, linking the festal demonstration with the hope of Israel's future restoration and independence led by the anointed "son of David," as in Bartimaeus's repeated cry in 10.48–49 that just preceded the demonstration. **11:** *Looked around,* after the messianic demonstration in seeming anticipation of the restoration of Israel, Jesus enters Jerusalem, but only to reconnoiter before launching his aggressive face-off with the rulers the next day.

11.12–25 [26]: Prophetic demonstration against the Temple (Mt 21.12–13,18–22; Lk 19.45–48). Mark again sandwiches one story into another, framing the prophetic demonstration against the Temple with the cursing of the fig tree (which is bearing no fruit), a figure for God's judgment in Israelite tradition. The Temple, the central religious and economic institution of the Jerusalem state, supported by the tithes and offerings of the people, had been rebuilt by the Judean ruling families upon return from exile in the sixth century BCE. Herod the Great had begun reconstruction of the Temple on a grand scale in 20 BCE, making it one of the wonders of the Roman imperial world and a center of Jewish pilgrimage. **15–16:** Jesus took forcible action against the sellers and buyers in the large Court of the Gentiles, the principal open public space in Jerusalem, where anyone—including non-Israelites—could go. Commerce, including money-changing, was necessary in connection with sacrifices and offerings in the semi-monetarized economy. **17:** Quoting Isa 56.7, and Jeremiah's prophecy against the first Temple (Jer 7.11), Jesus interprets his action as a prophetic demonstration of God's condemnation of the Temple. *Den of robbers* is better translated "bandits' stronghold," conveying more the original sense in Jeremiah that the rulers plunder the people like bandits and then seek refuge in the Temple. **18–19:** In response to Jesus' prophetic demonstration, the Jerusalem rulers intensify the long-standing scheme to kill him, known since 3.6. In preindustrial cities, rulers had to worry at festival times about touching off mob action by taking repressive measures against agitators, as indicated in 14.1–2. But Jesus and his disciples strategically withdraw from the city at evening. **20–24:** This astounding statement about the mount of the Temple upon which

roots. 21 Then Peter remembered and said
to him, "Rabbi, look! The fig tree that you
cursed has withered." 22 Jesus answered
them, "Have[a] faith in God. 23 Truly I tell
you, if you say to this mountain, 'Be taken
up and thrown into the sea,' and if you do
not doubt in your heart, but believe that
what you say will come to pass, it will be
done for you. 24 So I tell you, whatever you
ask for in prayer, believe that you have re-
ceived[b] it, and it will be yours.

25 "Whenever you stand praying, for-
give, if you have anything against anyone;
so that your Father in heaven may also for-
give you your trespasses."[c]

27 Again they came to Jerusalem. As he
was walking in the temple, the chief priests,
the scribes, and the elders came to him
28 and said, "By what authority are you do-
ing these things? Who gave you this author-
ity to do them?" 29 Jesus said to them, "I
will ask you one question; answer me, and
I will tell you by what authority I do these
things. 30 Did the baptism of John come
from heaven, or was it of human origin?
Answer me." 31 They argued with one an-
other, "If we say, 'From heaven,' he will
say, 'Why then did you not believe him?'
32 But shall we say, 'Of human origin'?"—
they were afraid of the crowd, for all re-
garded John as truly a prophet. 33 So they
answered Jesus, "We do not know." And
Jesus said to them, "Neither will I tell you
by what authority I am doing these things."

12 Then he began to speak to them in
parables. "A man planted a vine-
yard, put a fence around it, dug a pit for the
wine press, and built a watchtower; then he
leased it to tenants and went to another
country. 2 When the season came, he sent a
slave to the tenants to collect from them his
share of the produce of the vineyard. 3 But
they seized him, and beat him, and sent him
away empty-handed. 4 And again he sent
another slave to them; this one they beat
over the head and insulted. 5 Then he sent
another, and that one they killed. And so it
was with many others; some they beat, and
others they killed. 6 He had still one other,
a beloved son. Finally he sent him to them,
saying, 'They will respect my son.' 7 But
those tenants said to one another, 'This is

a Other ancient authorities read *"If you have*
b Other ancient authorities read *are receiving*
c Other ancient authorities add verse 26, *"But if you do not forgive, neither will your Father in heaven forgive your trespasses."*

Jesus has just demonstrated God's condemnation says, in effect, to trust God to do what has been prophesied. **25–[26]:** Early manuscripts omit v. 26, as does the NRSV translation. If original to Mark, it establishes mutual forgiveness (as in the Lord's Prayer, Lk 11.2–4) as the focus of prayer, now that the Temple, the official site for prayer and for obtaining divine forgiveness (see Lev 6.7), stands under God's condemnation.

11.27–33: Jesus' authority (Mt 21.23–27; Lk 20.1–8; cf. Jn 2.18–22). The first in a series of sharp charges and countercharges in the escalating conflict between Jesus and the Roman-backed Jewish priestly rulers and their representatives. **27–28:** *The chief priests, the scribes, and the elders,* authorized presumably by God as well as imperial Rome, challenge Jesus on the *authority* by which he acts and speaks, referring to the confrontation regarding "authority and power" with which the whole gospel story began in 1.22–28. **29–30:** In his counter question Jesus cleverly entraps them and exposes their lack of authority among the people, while avoiding any statement that might seem to justify his seizure by them.

12.1–12: Parable of the vineyard (Mt 21.33–46; Lk 20.9–19). Building on the traditional image of Israel as the vineyard of God in Isa 5.1–7, Jesus tells a parable that invites listeners to see the chief priests, who were themselves absentee landlords of estates with tenant labor, as well as tenants of God's vineyard. It also resonated with the resentment of indebted peasants who feared nothing more than becoming such share-cropping tenants on their own ancestral land and would have reveled at such role-reversal. In Mark the parable virtually passes over into allegory, with the landlord's "slaves" being analogous to the prophets God sent to "tenants" to demand the fruit of justice and the *beloved son* clearly being Jesus himself, as in 1.11 and 9.7, and the rejected *stone* becoming the *cornerstone* (citing Ps 118.22–23) of the new political-religious order that will replace the Temple establishment.

the heir; come, let us kill him, and the in-
heritance will be ours.' 8 So they seized him,
killed him, and threw him out of the vine-
yard. 9 What then will the owner of the
vineyard do? He will come and destroy the
tenants and give the vineyard to others.
10 Have you not read this scripture:
'The stone that the builders rejected
has become the cornerstone;[a]
11 this was the Lord's doing,
and it is amazing in our eyes'?"
12 When they realized that he had told
this parable against them, they wanted to
arrest him, but they feared the crowd. So
they left him and went away.
13 Then they sent to him some Pharisees
and some Herodians to trap him in what he
said. 14 And they came and said to him,
"Teacher, we know that you are sincere,
and show deference to no one; for you do
not regard people with partiality, but teach
the way of God in accordance with truth. Is
it lawful to pay taxes to the emperor, or
not? 15 Should we pay them, or should we
not?" But knowing their hypocrisy, he said
to them, "Why are you putting me to the
test? Bring me a denarius and let me see it."
16 And they brought one. Then he said to
them, "Whose head is this, and whose ti-
tle?" They answered, "The emperor's."
17 Jesus said to them, "Give to the emperor
the things that are the emperor's, and to
God the things that are God's." And they
were utterly amazed at him.
18 Some Sadducees, who say there is no
resurrection, came to him and asked him a
question, saying, 19 "Teacher, Moses wrote
for us that if a man's brother dies, leaving
a wife but no child, the man[b] shall marry
the widow and raise up children for his
brother. 20 There were seven brothers; the
first married and, when he died, left no
children; 21 and the second married the
widow[c] and died, leaving no children; and
the third likewise; 22 none of the seven left
children. Last of all the woman herself
died. 23 In the resurrection[d] whose wife
will she be? For the seven had married
her."
24 Jesus said to them, "Is not this the
reason you are wrong, that you know nei-
ther the scriptures nor the power of God?
25 For when they rise from the dead, they
neither marry nor are given in marriage,
but are like angels in heaven. 26 And as for
the dead being raised, have you not read in
the book of Moses, in the story about the
bush, how God said to him, 'I am the God
of Abraham, the God of Isaac, and the God
of Jacob'? 27 He is God not of the dead, but
of the living; you are quite wrong."

a Or *keystone* *b* Gk *his brother* *c* Gk *her*
d Other ancient authorities add *when they rise*

12.13–17: Paying taxes to the emperor (Mt 22.15–22; Lk 20.20–26). As in 3.6, the representatives of both the Jerusalem priestly establishment and Herod Antipas's regime conspire to entrap Jesus into giving some pretext to arrest and kill him. **14:** They preface the entrapping question with heavy, insincere flattery. *Is it lawful to pay taxes to the emperor?* A genuine dilemma. In the strict adherence to the law of Moses, supposedly advocated by the Pharisees themselves, it was not lawful because God was their exclusive sovereign. Yet the Romans treated nonpayment of tribute as rebellion. **16:** Turning the trick question back upon the questioners, Jesus exposes their own collaboration with the Romans by asking them to show him a coin—literally forcing their hand. **17:** Jesus ingeniously gives an ambiguous answer that does not literally advocate nonpayment of tribute to the emperor, but could be understood that way by those committed to the first commandment of the Mosaic covenant: *the things that are the emperor's,* i.e., nothing; *the things that are God's,* i.e., everything.

12.18–27: Dispute with the Sadducees (Mt 22.23–33; Lk 20.27–40). **18–23:** The Sadducees, the aristocratic priestly party of property, power, and privilege, denied that there could be a future resurrection of the dead. While their question took the form of academic casuistry, their focus on levirate marriage (Deut 25.5) hinted at their real agenda: the protection of property rights and power through patriarchal marriage that perpetuated the male lineage. **24–25:** Life after resurrection will not involve marriage. **26–27:** God's words to Moses (Ex 3.6) speak of Abraham, Isaac, and Jacob in the present tense, i.e., as *living* not *dead.*

28 One of the scribes came near and
heard them disputing with one another,
and seeing that he answered them well, he
asked him, "Which commandment is the
first of all?" 29 Jesus answered, "The first
is, 'Hear, O Israel: the Lord our God, the
Lord is one; 30 you shall love the Lord your
God with all your heart, and with all your
soul, and with all your mind, and with all
your strength.' 31 The second is this, 'You
shall love your neighbor as yourself.' There
is no other commandment greater than
these." 32 Then the scribe said to him, "You
are right, Teacher; you have truly said that
'he is one, and besides him there is no
other'; 33 and 'to love him with all the
heart, and with all the understanding, and
with all the strength,' and 'to love one's
neighbor as oneself,'—this is much more
important than all whole burnt offerings
and sacrifices." 34 When Jesus saw that he
answered wisely, he said to him, "You are
not far from the kingdom of God." After
that no one dared to ask him any question.

35 While Jesus was teaching in the temple, he said, "How can the scribes say that
the Messiah[a] is the son of David? 36 David
himself, by the Holy Spirit, declared,

'The Lord said to my Lord,
"Sit at my right hand,
until I put your enemies under your
feet."'

37 David himself calls him Lord; so how can
he be his son?" And the large crowd was
listening to him with delight.

38 As he taught, he said, "Beware of the
scribes, who like to walk around in long
robes, and to be greeted with respect in the
marketplaces, 39 and to have the best seats
in the synagogues and places of honor at
banquets! 40 They devour widows' houses
and for the sake of appearance say long
prayers. They will receive the greater condemnation."

41 He sat down opposite the treasury,
and watched the crowd putting money into
the treasury. Many rich people put in large
sums. 42 A poor widow came and put in
two small copper coins, which are worth a
penny. 43 Then he called his disciples and
said to them, "Truly I tell you, this poor
widow has put in more than all those who
are contributing to the treasury. 44 For all
of them have contributed out of their abundance; but she out of her poverty has put in
everything she had, all she had to live on."

13 As he came out of the temple, one of
his disciples said to him, "Look,

a Or *the Christ*

12.28–34: Love your neighbor (Mt 22.34–40; Lk 10.25–28). The polemic softens, but the argument sets up the sharp condemnation of the scribes in 12.38–44. **29–31:** Jesus satisfies the scribe by immediately reciting Deut 6.4, but he quickly insists that love of God means love of neighbor by reciting Lev 19.18 as well, which climaxes a series of prohibitions against exploiting and oppressing the poor (cf. Lev 19.9–17; Lk 6.27–36; Mt 5.38–48). **32–33:** The scribe admits that love of God and love of neighbor are more important than the elaborate sacrifices at the Temple, from which he draws his living. **34:** The scribe does not "resign" his position, and Jesus does not invite him into the movement. Jesus has outmaneuvered all segments of the Temple establishment in the series of attacks and counterattacks from 11.27.

12.35–37: How can the messiah be David's son? (Mt 22.41–46; Lk 20.41–44). This passage constitutes a rejection of any triumphalist restoration of the Davidic state (which Bartimaeus and the shouts of the crowd may have suggested; see 10.47–48n.; 11.10), reciting one of the imperial Davidic psalms (Ps 110.1) in the refutation.

12.38–44: Beware of the scribes (Mt 23.1,6; Lk 20.45–47; 21.1–4; 11.43; 14.7–11). **38–40:** Condemnation of the scribes, moving from their craving for honor to a concrete example of their exploitation of the poor. *Houses* refers to all their inheritance and resources. **41–44:** Illustrates how the scribes *devour widow's houses:* by inducing them to give their meager resources to the Temple. For this *they will receive the greater condemnation,* v. 40, confirmed by the immediately ensuing prophecy of the destruction of the Temple which they serve.

13.1–2: Destruction of Jerusalem and the Temple (Mt 24.1–3; Lk 21.5–7). This section of the Gospel,

Teacher, what large stones and what large
buildings!" 2 Then Jesus asked him, "Do
you see these great buildings? Not one
stone will be left here upon another; all will
be thrown down."
3 When he was sitting on the Mount of
Olives opposite the temple, Peter, James,
John, and Andrew asked him privately,
4 "Tell us, when will this be, and what will
be the sign that all these things are about to
be accomplished?" 5 Then Jesus began to
say to them, "Beware that no one leads you
astray. 6 Many will come in my name and
say, 'I am he!'[a] and they will lead many
astray. 7 When you hear of wars and ru-
mors of wars, do not be alarmed; this must
take place, but the end is still to come. 8 For
nation will rise against nation, and king-
dom against kingdom; there will be earth-
quakes in various places; there will be fam-
ines. This is but the beginning of the birth
pangs.
9 "As for yourselves, beware; for they
will hand you over to councils; and you will
be beaten in synagogues; and you will stand
before governors and kings because of me,
as a testimony to them. 10 And the good
news[b] must first be proclaimed to all na-
tions. 11 When they bring you to trial and
hand you over, do not worry beforehand
about what you are to say; but say whatev-
er is given you at that time, for it is not you
who speak, but the Holy Spirit. 12 Brother
will betray brother to death, and a father
his child, and children will rise against par-
ents and have them put to death; 13 and you
will be hated by all because of my name.
But the one who endures to the end will be
saved.
14 "But when you see the desolating
sacrilege set up where it ought not to be (let
the reader understand), then those in Judea
must flee to the mountains; 15 the one on
the housetop must not go down or enter the
house to take anything away; 16 the one in
the field must not turn back to get a coat.
17 Woe to those who are pregnant and to
those who are nursing infants in those
days! 18 Pray that it may not be in winter.
19 For in those days there will be suffering,
such as has not been from the beginning of
the creation that God created until now,
no, and never will be. 20 And if the Lord
had not cut short those days, no one would

a Gk *I am* *b* Gk *gospel*

which began with Jesus' prophetic demonstration against the Temple (11.15–17), ends with his prophecy of its destruction—also implicating those whose base of power it constituted.

13.3–37: Exhortation not to be distracted from the movement by distressing events (Mt 24.3–36; Lk 21.7–36). Jesus' second speech uses apocalyptic motifs in order to caution against an apocalyptic interpretation of historical crises of resistance, repression, and reconquest under Roman imperial rule, but to remain disciplined and vigilant in the struggle, despite persecution. The Israelite prophetic and Judean revelatory traditions are framed, balanced, and interpreted by the exhortation in vv. 5–6,9–13, and 28–37, particularly by the carefully positioned and repeated *beware/be alert* in vv. 5,9,23,33. Judging from v. 14, these paragraphs must be written from a viewpoint outside both Jerusalem and Judea. **3:** Addressed through Peter and other disciples to the whole movement. **4:** Despite this apparent link with the destruction of the Temple just prophesied in v. 2, nothing in the rest of ch 13 implies that the events prophesied have anything to do with Jerusalem. **6:** *I am he,* lit. "I am"; see 6.50n. **7–8:** Stereotypical phrases from Israelite prophetic and Judean revelatory literature. *Rumors of wars* may refer to the intense resistance to the order of Emperor Gaius Caligula (37–41 CE) to install his bust in the Temple. *Famines* may refer to the disastrous effects of the severe drought in the late 40s. **9–13:** Cf. Lk 12.2–12,51–53; Mk 8.34–38. Far from being distracted by wars and famines, the movement should expect repressions, but not worry, expect to be hated by all, but endure. **14a:** A shift from the past to the present and future, from the readers' standpoint. *The desolating sacrilege,* cf. Dan 9.27; 11.31; 12.11. In contrast to Mt 24.15, nothing in Mark's vague phrase or the literary context points to Jerusalem or the Temple, let alone its destruction. **14b–20:** Anticipation of events in Judea and Galilee, where political conflict escalated during the 50s and 60s, based on long experience of how the Romans reacted to actual or perceived resistance with severe repressive measures and "scorched earth" reconquest of the people. **21–22:** Other prophets

be saved; but for the sake of the elect,
whom he chose, he has cut short those
days. 21 And if anyone says to you at that
time, 'Look! Here is the Messiah!'[a] or
'Look! There he is!'—do not believe it.
22 False messiahs[b] and false prophets will
appear and produce signs and omens, to
lead astray, if possible, the elect. 23 But be
alert; I have already told you everything.
24 "But in those days, after that suffer-
ing,

the sun will be darkened,
and the moon will not give its light,
25 and the stars will be falling
from heaven,
and the powers in the heavens will
be shaken.

26 Then they will see 'the Son of Man com-
ing in clouds' with great power and glory.
27 Then he will send out the angels, and
gather his elect from the four winds, from
the ends of the earth to the ends of heaven.
28 "From the fig tree learn its lesson: as
soon as its branch becomes tender and puts
forth its leaves, you know that summer is
near. 29 So also, when you see these things
taking place, you know that he[c] is near, at
the very gates. 30 Truly I tell you, this gener-
ation will not pass away until all these
things have taken place. 31 Heaven and
earth will pass away, but my words will not
pass away.
32 "But about that day or hour no one
knows, neither the angels in heaven, nor
the Son, but only the Father. 33 Beware,
keep alert;[d] for you do not know when the
time will come. 34 It is like a man going on
a journey, when he leaves home and puts
his slaves in charge, each with his work,
and commands the doorkeeper to be on the
watch. 35 Therefore, keep awake—for you
do not know when the master of the house
will come, in the evening, or at midnight, or
at cockcrow, or at dawn, 36 or else he may
find you asleep when he comes suddenly.
37 And what I say to you I say to all: Keep
awake."

14 It was two days before the Passover
and the festival of Unleavened
Bread. The chief priests and the scribes
were looking for a way to arrest Jesus[e] by
stealth and kill him; 2 for they said, "Not
during the festival, or there may be a riot
among the people."
3 While he was at Bethany in the house
of Simon the leper,[f] as he sat at the table,
a woman came with an alabaster jar of very
costly ointment of nard, and she broke
open the jar and poured the ointment on

a Or *the Christ* *b* Or *christs* *c* Or *it* *d* Other ancient authorities add *and pray* *e* Gk *him*
f The terms *leper* and *leprosy* can refer to several diseases

and messiahs were already familiar features in Judea in particular, and more appeared around the mid-first century. **24–25:** Traditional prophetic portrayal of God's coming in judgment, drawn from Isa 13.10; 34.4; Ezek 32.7–8; Joel 2.10,31; 3.15. **26–27:** In contrast to Dan 7.13, where the "human-like one" symbolizes the elect generally, *the Son of Man* here presides over the gathering of the elect (cf. Zech 2.6; Deut 30.4). **28–31:** Reassurance that the resolution of the historical crisis is near, as symbolized by the impending coming of the Son of Man, and that Jesus' words are utterly credible. **28:** Reverses the image of the fig tree from 11.12–14, now symbolizing new blessing for the people. **30:** Cf. 9.1. **31:** Cf. Isa 51.6; 40.8. **32–37:** Since no one knows precisely when the crisis will be resolved, they must simply maintain discipline and *Keep awake!*

14.1–15.47: Jesus' death as martyr-messiah (Mt 26.1–27.66; Lk 22.1–23.56; Jn 18.1–19.42). **1–2:** *Passover and the festival of Unleavened Bread,* in March/April, celebrated Israel's deliverance from foreign rule in ancient Egypt. Repressive actions by rulers repeatedly touched off massive protest demonstrations at Passover.

14.3–8: Anointing for burial (Mt 26.6–13; Jn 12.1–8). As a prophet had poured oil on the head of (anointed, made a messiah of) David and other popular kings leading Israel, so *a woman . . . poured ointment on* Jesus' head, but to prepare his body for burial. In reply to strenuous objections, Jesus recognizes what she has done as part of the gospel itself. **3:** *Nard* was imported from the Himalayan mountains.

his head. 4 But some were there who said to
one another in anger, "Why was the oint-
ment wasted in this way? 5 For this oint-
ment could have been sold for more than
three hundred denarii,[a] and the money
given to the poor." And they scolded her.
6 But Jesus said, "Let her alone; why do you
trouble her? She has performed a good ser-
vice for me. 7 For you always have the poor
with you, and you can show kindness to
them whenever you wish; but you will not
always have me. 8 She has done what she
could; she has anointed my body before-
hand for its burial. 9 Truly I tell you, wher-
ever the good news[b] is proclaimed in the
whole world, what she has done will be
told in remembrance of her."
10 Then Judas Iscariot, who was one of
the twelve, went to the chief priests in order
to betray him to them. 11 When they heard
it, they were greatly pleased, and promised
to give him money. So he began to look for
an opportunity to betray him.
12 On the first day of Unleavened
Bread, when the Passover lamb is sacri-
ficed, his disciples said to him, "Where do
you want us to go and make the prepara-
tions for you to eat the Passover?" 13 So he
sent two of his disciples, saying to them,
"Go into the city, and a man carrying a jar
of water will meet you; follow him, 14 and
wherever he enters, say to the owner of the
house, 'The Teacher asks, Where is my
guest room where I may eat the Passover
with my disciples?' 15 He will show you a
large room upstairs, furnished and ready.
Make preparations for us there." 16 So the
disciples set out and went to the city, and
found everything as he had told them; and
they prepared the Passover meal.
17 When it was evening, he came with
the twelve. 18 And when they had taken
their places and were eating, Jesus said,
"Truly I tell you, one of you will betray me,
one who is eating with me." 19 They began
to be distressed and to say to him one after
another, "Surely, not I?" 20 He said to
them, "It is one of the twelve, one who is
dipping bread[c] into the bowl[d] with me.
21 For the Son of Man goes as it is written
of him, but woe to that one by whom the
Son of Man is betrayed! It would have been
better for that one not to have been born."
22 While they were eating, he took a
loaf of bread, and after blessing it he broke
it, gave it to them, and said, "Take; this is
my body." 23 Then he took a cup, and after
giving thanks he gave it to them, and all of
them drank from it. 24 He said to them,
"This is my blood of the[e] covenant, which
is poured out for many. 25 Truly I tell you,
I will never again drink of the fruit of the
vine until that day when I drink it new in
the kingdom of God."
26 When they had sung the hymn, they

a The denarius was the usual day's wage for a laborer
b Or *gospel* c Gk lacks *bread* d Other ancient authorities read *same bowl* e Other ancient authorities add *new*

14.10–11: Prediction of betrayal (Mt 26.14–16; Lk 22.3–6). It is from within the twelve, representatives of the renewed Israel, that the betrayal comes.

14.12–25: The Last Supper (Mt 26.17–29; Lk 22.7–20). **12–16:** Just as the chief priests and scribes had resorted to covert means *to arrest Jesus by stealth* (14.1), so Jesus and his disciples are now operating covertly, "underground," as indicated by Jesus' instructions for discreet movement inside the city and the carefully planned signal of a *man carrying a jar of water* (a task that a woman would usually have performed). **18:** Cf. Ps 41.9. **20:** *Dipping bread into the bowl with me,* the common meal was the most intimate form of fellowship. **22–25:** Mt 26.26–29; Lk 22.15–20; 1 Cor 11.23–26. Jesus' words at the Last Supper became the words of institution of the regularly celebrated Lord's Supper. **22:** *My body,* without "for you" as in 1 Cor 11.24, clearly a collective symbol of the community. **24:** *My blood of the covenant,* thus renewing the covenant between God and the people, alluding to the covenant ceremony on Sinai (Ex 24.4–8). *For many,* see Isa 53.12. **25:** The Supper is eaten in anticipation of celebrating it *new in the kingdom of God,* whereas in 1 Cor 11.25–26 it is eaten also in memory.

14.26–52: Agony and betrayal in Gethsemane (Mt 26.30–56; Lk 22.31–53). Jesus' prediction of the disciples' desertion and their actual desertion frames his agonized prayer over his impending martyrdom

went out to the Mount of Olives. 27 And
Jesus said to them, "You will all become
deserters; for it is written,

'I will strike the shepherd,
and the sheep will be scattered.'

28 But after I am raised up, I will go before
you to Galilee." 29 Peter said to him, "Even
though all become deserters, I will not."
30 Jesus said to him, "Truly I tell you, this
day, this very night, before the cock crows
twice, you will deny me three times." 31 But
he said vehemently, "Even though I must
die with you, I will not deny you." And all
of them said the same.

32 They went to a place called Gethsem-
ane; and he said to his disciples, "Sit here
while I pray." 33 He took with him Peter
and James and John, and began to be dis-
tressed and agitated. 34 And he said to
them, "I am deeply grieved, even to death;
remain here, and keep awake." 35 And go-
ing a little farther, he threw himself on the
ground and prayed that, if it were possible,
the hour might pass from him. 36 He said,
"Abba,[a] Father, for you all things are pos-
sible; remove this cup from me; yet, not
what I want, but what you want." 37 He
came and found them sleeping; and he said
to Peter, "Simon, are you asleep? Could
you not keep awake one hour? 38 Keep
awake and pray that you may not come
into the time of trial;[b] the spirit indeed is
willing, but the flesh is weak." 39 And again
he went away and prayed, saying the same
words. 40 And once more he came and
found them sleeping, for their eyes were
very heavy; and they did not know what to
say to him. 41 He came a third time and said
to them, "Are you still sleeping and taking
your rest? Enough! The hour has come; the
Son of Man is betrayed into the hands of
sinners. 42 Get up, let us be going. See, my
betrayer is at hand."

43 Immediately, while he was still
speaking, Judas, one of the twelve, arrived;
and with him there was a crowd with
swords and clubs, from the chief priests,
the scribes, and the elders. 44 Now the be-
trayer had given them a sign, saying, "The
one I will kiss is the man; arrest him and
lead him away under guard." 45 So when he
came, he went up to him at once and said,
"Rabbi!" and kissed him. 46 Then they laid
hands on him and arrested him. 47 But one
of those who stood near drew his sword
and struck the slave of the high priest, cut-
ting off his ear. 48 Then Jesus said to them,
"Have you come out with swords and clubs
to arrest me as though I were a bandit?
49 Day after day I was with you in the tem-
ple teaching, and you did not arrest me. But
let the scriptures be fulfilled." 50 All of them
deserted him and fled.

a Aramaic for *Father* *b* Or *into temptation*

and his enemies' surreptitious seizure of him. **26:** The Passover ended with the singing of Ps 115–118. **27:** Zech 13.7; Jn 16.32. See 6.34n. **28:** Although the disciples are all about to desert, the movement will continue as Jesus will go back to Galilee after his martyr's death; see 16.7. **29–31:** Cf. 8.34; 14.66–72; Jn 13.36–38; 18.15–18,25–27. **32:** *Gethsemane,* meaning "oil press," was an olive orchard or "garden" (Jn 18.1) on the slope of the Mount of Olives just east of Jerusalem. **33–35:** *Distressed and agitated . . . deeply grieved, even to death . . . threw himself on the ground.* The language and action are very strong, v. 34 echoing Ps 42.5,11; 43.5. **36:** *Abba,* Aramaic for "father" (see 5.41n.). *This cup,* refers to both vv. 23–24 and 10.39, implicating the disciples, especially James and John. **37–41:** The disciples are utterly incapable of doing what Jesus had emphasized in teaching about future crises; see 13.35–37. **43–50:** Emphasis is on the excessive force used by the Jerusalem rulers in their covert action to capture Jesus, as if Jesus were a violent bandit-chieftain. Jesus mocks their reluctance simply to seize him when he had been teaching in the Temple courtyard, which betrays their lack of "authority" and political impotence with the people. **45:** *Rabbi,* see 9.5–6n. **47:** In contrast to Mt 26.52–53, Lk 22.51, and John 18.10–11, Jesus in Mark does not rebuke the spontaneous violent response by *one of those who stood near* (not necessarily a disciple, although identified as Peter in Jn 18.10). **49:** *Let the scriptures be fulfilled,* Jesus' arrest, trial, and death in particular proceed "as written" in the scripture (vv. 21,27; etc.); *fulfilled,* only here and 1.15, marks a highly significant point in the overall gospel. **51–52:** *Young man . . . naked,*

51 A certain young man was following
him, wearing nothing but a linen cloth.
They caught hold of him, 52 but he left the
linen cloth and ran off naked.
53 They took Jesus to the high priest;
and all the chief priests, the elders, and the
scribes were assembled. 54 Peter had fol-
lowed him at a distance, right into the
courtyard of the high priest; and he was
sitting with the guards, warming himself at
the fire. 55 Now the chief priests and the
whole council were looking for testimony
against Jesus to put him to death; but they
found none. 56 For many gave false testimo-
ny against him, and their testimony did not
agree. 57 Some stood up and gave false testi-
mony against him, saying, 58 "We heard
him say, 'I will destroy this temple that is
made with hands, and in three days I will
build another, not made with hands.' "
59 But even on this point their testimony did
not agree. 60 Then the high priest stood up
before them and asked Jesus, "Have you no
answer? What is it that they testify against
you?" 61 But he was silent and did not an-
swer. Again the high priest asked him, "Are
you the Messiah,[a] the Son of the Blessed
One?" 62 Jesus said, "I am; and
'you will see the Son of Man
seated at the right hand of
the Power,'
and 'coming with the clouds
of heaven.' "
63 Then the high priest tore his clothes and
said, "Why do we still need witnesses?
64 You have heard his blasphemy! What is
your decision?" All of them condemned
him as deserving death. 65 Some began to
spit on him, to blindfold him, and to strike
him, saying to him, "Prophesy!" The
guards also took him over and beat him.
66 While Peter was below in the court-
yard, one of the servant-girls of the high
priest came by. 67 When she saw Peter
warming himself, she stared at him and
said, "You also were with Jesus, the man
from Nazareth." 68 But he denied it, saying,
"I do not know or understand what you are
talking about." And he went out into the
forecourt.[b] Then the cock crowed.[c]
69 And the servant-girl, on seeing him, be-
gan again to say to the bystanders, "This
man is one of them." 70 But again he denied
it. Then after a little while the bystanders
again said to Peter, "Certainly you are one

a Or *the Christ* b Or *gateway* c Other ancient authorities lack *Then the cock crowed*

presumably symbolic in the narrative, of the disciples now standing exposed as unfaithful deserters and of Jesus as defenseless before the rulers. The "young man" appears once more in the narrative in 16.5–7.

14.53–72: Jesus condemned by chief priests and council and Peter's denial (Mt 26.57–75; Lk 22.54–71). Jesus is condemned twice, first by the ruling chief priest and council (Gk "synedrion," Sanhedrin), then by the Roman governor. While the accounts are integral parts of the Gospel, not historical transcripts, they have historical plausibility against the background of Roman imperial rule in Judea. **53:** Convening the council at night would have been highly unusual, but by this point due process was hardly a concern of the Jerusalem rulers. **55–59:** Although Jesus had been speaking and acting in public (see v. 49), the council had no witnesses with credible testimony to justify his execution. The *false testimony* appears to be a confusing parody of Jesus' prophetic condemnation of the Temple and his renewal of Israel (the "house of God" "not made with hands"?) in opposition to the Temple (the "house of God" "made with hands"?). **61–62:** *The Messiah,* it is unclear whether this is a charge. *"I am"* would be an uncharacteristic answer for Jesus (but see 6.50n.). It stands in sharp contrast with his answer to Pilate in 15.2: "You say so," and both Mt 26.64 and Lk 22.70 have "You say (that I am)," which suggests that Mk 14.62 also originally read "You say so" or "Am I?" But in immediately confessing *the Son of Man . . . coming with the clouds of heaven* (quoting Dan 7.13 and Ps 110.1), Jesus gives the high priest all he needs for condemnation. **63–64:** *Blasphemy* would presumably refer to the confession of being the Son of Man, rather than his threat against the Temple. For the prescribed punishment, see Lev 24.16. **66–72:** Cf. v. 54. Peter's denial of Jesus is juxtaposed to and simultaneous with Jesus' confession and condemnation. Even the servants of the high priest share the prejudice against and contempt of Galileans such as Jesus, "the man from Nazareth," and Peter. **71:** Peter's third denial is very strong language. *I do not know*

of them; for you are a Galilean." 71 But he
began to curse, and he swore an oath, "I do
not know this man you are talking about."
72 At that moment the cock crowed for the
second time. Then Peter remembered that
Jesus had said to him, "Before the cock
crows twice, you will deny me three times."
And he broke down and wept.

15 As soon as it was morning, the chief
priests held a consultation with the
elders and scribes and the whole council.
They bound Jesus, led him away, and hand-
ed him over to Pilate. 2 Pilate asked him,
"Are you the King of the Jews?" He an-
swered him, "You say so." 3 Then the chief
priests accused him of many things. 4 Pilate
asked him again, "Have you no answer?
See how many charges they bring against
you." 5 But Jesus made no further reply, so
that Pilate was amazed.

6 Now at the festival he used to release
a prisoner for them, anyone for whom they
asked. 7 Now a man called Barabbas was in
prison with the rebels who had committed
murder during the insurrection. 8 So the
crowd came and began to ask Pilate to do
for them according to his custom. 9 Then he
answered them, "Do you want me to re-
lease for you the King of the Jews?" 10 For
he realized that it was out of jealousy that
the chief priests had handed him over.
11 But the chief priests stirred up the crowd
to have him release Barabbas for them in-
stead. 12 Pilate spoke to them again, "Then
what do you wish me to do[a] with the man
you call[b] the King of the Jews?" 13 They
shouted back, "Crucify him!" 14 Pilate
asked them, "Why, what evil has he done?"
But they shouted all the more, "Crucify
him!" 15 So Pilate, wishing to satisfy the
crowd, released Barabbas for them; and af-
ter flogging Jesus, he handed him over to be
crucified.

16 Then the soldiers led him into the
courtyard of the palace (that is, the gover-

a Other ancient authorities read *what should I do*
b Other ancient authorities lack *the man you call*

this man had double meaning: As indicated repeatedly throughout the Gospel, Peter indeed does not understand who Jesus is and what he is doing. **72:** See v. 30.

15.1–15: Jesus condemned by Pilate (Mt 27.1–2,11–26; Lk 23.1–5,18–25; Jn 18.28–40; 19.4–16). The second trial, before the Roman governor Pilate (26–37 CE). **1:** This further *consultation* suggests that the specific charge(s) against Jesus were still not clear, and that this continued in the hearing before Pilate (v. 3). **2:** It is the Roman governor who defines the charge as one of indigenous kingship in potential insurrection against the Roman order. The formulation of the question is that of outsiders to Israel, who viewed Galileans and others subject to Herodian rulers as "Judeans." It is surely significant also that the title *King of the Jews* (i.e., Judeans) occurs only in speech by Pilate or the Roman soldiers and the inscription on the cross presumably placed there by Pilate's order, in vv. 2,9,12,18,26, in contrast with "the Messiah, the King of Israel," used by the chief priests and scribes in v. 32. Thus Jesus' answer: "That is what *you* say." **4–5:** As in 14.60–61, Jesus is just "above it all," or is deliberately refusing to cooperate in his own interrogation. **6–15:** There is no evidence outside the New Testament of such a custom by Roman governors of Judea generally. Mark does not in any way suggest that "the Jews" demanded Jesus' death. The crowd is stirred up by the chief priests. Infamous in sources outside the New Testament for his tough stance, provocations, and violence as Roman governor, Pilate is portrayed as an experienced imperial official who understands both that Jesus is politically more dangerous to the Roman order than an anti-imperial assassin and how to mollify the crowd while manipulating them into a choice. On crucifixion as the intensely cruel Roman form of torture and execution for provincial rebels, see 8.34n. Beating was standard treatment of political prisoners, whether they were to be executed or not.

15.16–38: The crucifixion (Mt 27.27–48; Lk 23.18–43). **16–20:** Along with the *purple cloak* symbolizing royalty, the mockery, by the whole cohort, of Jesus as "King of the Judeans," includes several allusions to worship of the Roman emperor whom Jesus has the audacity to challenge: The crown of thorns suggests the laurel wreath crowning the emperor's head, the hailing suggests the acclamation of the emperor, and kneeling in homage suggests the prostration to the emperor. The mutual hostility between Mark's Jesus and the imperial army is unmistakably intense. **21:** *Simon of Cyrene,* a peasant

nor's headquarters[a]); and they called to-
gether the whole cohort. 17 And they
clothed him in a purple cloak; and after
twisting some thorns into a crown, they put
it on him. 18 And they began saluting him,
"Hail, King of the Jews!" 19 They struck his
head with a reed, spat upon him, and knelt
down in homage to him. 20 After mocking
him, they stripped him of the purple cloak
and put his own clothes on him. Then they
led him out to crucify him.

21 They compelled a passer-by, who
was coming in from the country, to carry
his cross; it was Simon of Cyrene, the father
of Alexander and Rufus. 22 Then they
brought Jesus[b] to the place called Golgo-
tha (which means the place of a skull).
23 And they offered him wine mixed with
myrrh; but he did not take it. 24 And they
crucified him, and divided his clothes
among them, casting lots to decide what
each should take.

25 It was nine o'clock in the morning
when they crucified him. 26 The inscription
of the charge against him read, "The King
of the Jews." 27 And with him they crucified
two bandits, one on his right and one on his
left.[c] 29 Those who passed by derided[d]
him, shaking their heads and saying, "Aha!
You who would destroy the temple and
build it in three days, 30 save yourself, and
come down from the cross!" 31 In the same
way the chief priests, along with the
scribes, were also mocking him among
themselves and saying, "He saved others;
he cannot save himself. 32 Let the Messi-
ah,[e] the King of Israel, come down from
the cross now, so that we may see and be-
lieve." Those who were crucified with him
also taunted him.

33 When it was noon, darkness came
over the whole land[f] until three in the af-
ternoon. 34 At three o'clock Jesus cried out
with a loud voice, "Eloi, Eloi, lema sabach-
thani?" which means, "My God, my God,
why have you forsaken me?"[g] 35 When
some of the bystanders heard it, they said,
"Listen, he is calling for Elijah." 36 And
someone ran, filled a sponge with sour
wine, put it on a stick, and gave it to him to
drink, saying, "Wait, let us see whether Eli-
jah will come to take him down." 37 Then
Jesus gave a loud cry and breathed his last.

a Gk *the praetorium* *b* Gk *him* *c* Other ancient authorities add verse 28, *And the scripture was fulfilled that says, "And he was counted among the lawless."* *d* Or *blasphemed* *e* Or *the Christ* *f* Or *earth* *g* Other ancient authorities read *made me a reproach*

coming in from the country, had perhaps moved back to Judea from the Diaspora Jewish community in Cyrene, west of Egypt; his sons apparently later joined the movement. This Simon in effect replaces Peter, whose original name was Simon, and who had just proven incapable of "taking up his cross" by denying Jesus instead of himself (8.34; 14.66–72). Perhaps they "compel" Simon to carry the cross because Jesus is already too weak from repeated beatings, 14.65; 15.15,19. Once hung on the cross he died more quickly than expected (vv. 44–45). **23:** Jesus declines the offer of a sedative to mitigate the pain. **24:** *Casting lots,* see Ps 22.18; the first of three allusions to this psalm. **26:** The inscription indicates the crime: As "King of the Judeans" Jesus threatened to bring about a rebellion against the law and order of the empire, which was maintained by such gruesome, terrorizing violence against subject peoples. **27:** *Two bandits,* perhaps actually ancient "Robin Hoods"; but the Romans used the term contemptuously to demean rebels against Roman rule. *On his right . . . on his left,* cf. 10.37–40; not James and John, but the two "bandits" undergo the baptism of death with Jesus. **29–30:** *Shaking their heads,* cf. Ps 22.7–8. The mocking passers-by would appear to be hostile, using the same terms as the false witnesses in 14.56–58. **31:** *He saved others; he cannot save himself.* Double meaning: cf. 8.34; 10.45. **33–38:** Mt 27.45–53; Lk 23.44–48. **33:** *Darkness came over the whole land,* crisis in the natural order indicating God coming in judgment (cf. Joel 2.2; Am 5.18–20; Zeph 1.15). **34:** *"Eloi, Eloi,"* Jesus crying out in abandonment in the words of Ps 22.1 in Aramaic (see 5.41n.). **35–36:** Voyeurs, misinterpreting the word "Eloi," suggest that he is calling for Elijah, and want to revive him, prolonging the ordeal, to see if Elijah comes. **37–38:** As Jesus dies, the curtain of the Temple (see Ex 26.33), separating but also protecting the people from the presence of God, is torn in two, in judgment on the Temple's mediation of the Holy but also opening access to God for the people; see also 1.10.

38 And the curtain of the temple was torn in
two, from top to bottom. 39 Now when the
centurion, who stood facing him, saw that
in this way he[a] breathed his last, he said,
"Truly this man was God's Son!"[b]
40 There were also women looking on
from a distance; among them were Mary
Magdalene, and Mary the mother of James
the younger and of Joses, and Salome.
41 These used to follow him and provided
for him when he was in Galilee; and there
were many other women who had come up
with him to Jerusalem.
42 When evening had come, and since it
was the day of Preparation, that is, the day
before the sabbath, 43 Joseph of Arimathea,
a respected member of the council, who
was also himself waiting expectantly for
the kingdom of God, went boldly to Pilate
and asked for the body of Jesus. 44 Then
Pilate wondered if he were already dead;
and summoning the centurion, he asked
him whether he had been dead for some
time. 45 When he learned from the centuri-
on that he was dead, he granted the body to
Joseph. 46 Then Joseph[c] bought a linen
cloth, and taking down the body,[d]
wrapped it in the linen cloth, and laid it in
a tomb that had been hewn out of the rock.
He then rolled a stone against the door of
the tomb. 47 Mary Magdalene and Mary
the mother of Joses saw where the body[d]
was laid.

16 When the sabbath was over, Mary
Magdalene, and Mary the mother
of James, and Salome bought spices, so that
they might go and anoint him. 2 And very
early on the first day of the week, when
the sun had risen, they went to the tomb.
3 They had been saying to one another,
"Who will roll away the stone for us from
the entrance to the tomb?" 4 When they
looked up, they saw that the stone, which
was very large, had already been rolled
back. 5 As they entered the tomb, they saw
a young man, dressed in a white robe, sit-
ting on the right side; and they were
alarmed. 6 But he said to them, "Do not be
alarmed; you are looking for Jesus of Naza-

a Other ancient authorities add *cried out and*
b Or *a son of God* *c* Gk *he* *d* Gk *it*

15.39–47: Jesus' burial (Mt 27.54–61; Lk 23.49–56). Three interrelated responses to Jesus' death: by a military representative of the Roman rulers, by a representative of the Jerusalem religious establishment, and by loyal women followers. **39:** Just as Jesus' other opponents earlier in the Gospel know who he is, so the Roman centurion (the equivalent of a company commander) presiding at his crucifixion recognizes that he was truly "a son of God." While neither a confession of faith (the centurion continues his duties in 15.44–45) nor the final resolution of the messianic secret, contrary to previous interpretations, Mark ironically has the officer who presides at Jesus' execution recognize his true identity. He also confirms to Pilate that Jesus is dead in 15.44–45. **40–41:** As the disciples, commissioned as the leaders of the movement, consistently misunderstood, women were healed by Jesus as symbolic of the renewal of Israel. Now, after the disciples had betrayed, denied, and abandoned Jesus, some of the many women who had followed him and provided for him stood by him, at a distance, throughout the ordeal. Neither of the two women named here has been mentioned earlier. Both will witness the burial site (v. 47) and the empty tomb (16.1). **42–46:** *Joseph of Arimathea,* a *member of the council* that had condemned Jesus (see 14.64), but like the scribe in 12.28–34, interested in the kingdom of God, asked for the body. Apparently eager to dispose of it *before the sabbath,* he *wrapped it,* and secured it in a rock tomb sealed with a heavy stone (cf. 16.3), without even a gesture of proper burial rites. **47:** Although the disciples, having completely disappeared, make no effort to afford Jesus proper burial (contrast John's disciples in 6.22), the two Marys witness *where the body was laid.*

16.1–8: The empty tomb, the call back to Galilee, and *they were afraid* (Mt 28.1–8a; Lk 24.1–11). **1:** The women go finally to perform proper rites of burial. **3:** The disk-shaped stone rolled in a groove to close the tomb's entry. **5:** The *young man* (cf. 14.51–52) is *dressed in a white robe,* as a martyr vindicated by God would be dressed (cf. Dan 11.35; Rev 7.9,13), reminiscent of Jesus' garments becoming "dazzling white" in the transfiguration, 9.3. **6:** The "young man" tells the women *He has been raised;*

reth, who was crucified. He has been raised; he is not here. Look, there is the place they laid him.
7 But go, tell his disciples and Peter that he is going ahead of you to Galilee; there you will see him, just as he told you."
8 So they went out and fled from the tomb, for terror and amazement had seized them; and they said nothing to anyone, for they were afraid.[a]

THE SHORTER ENDING OF MARK

⟦And all that had been commanded them they told briefly to those around Peter. And afterward Jesus himself sent out through them, from east to west, the sacred and imperishable proclamation of eternal salvation.[b]⟧

THE LONGER ENDING OF MARK

9 ⟦Now after he rose early on the first day of the week, he appeared first to Mary Magdalene, from whom he had cast out seven demons.
10 She went out and told those who had been with him, while they were mourning and weeping.
11 But when they heard that he was alive and had been seen by her, they would not believe it.

12 After this he appeared in another form to two of them, as they were walking into the country.
13 And they went back and told the rest, but they did not believe them.

14 Later he appeared to the eleven themselves as they were sitting at the table; and he upbraided them for their lack of faith and stubbornness, because they had not believed those who saw him after he had risen.[c]
15 And he said to them, "Go into all the world and proclaim the good news[d] to the whole creation.
16 The one who believes and is baptized will be saved; but the one who does not believe will be condemned.
17 And these signs will accompany those who believe: by using my name they will cast out demons; they will speak in new

a Some of the most ancient authorities bring the book to a close at the end of verse 8. One authority concludes the book with the shorter ending; others include the shorter ending and then continue with verses 9-20. In most authorities verses 9-20 follow immediately after verse 8, though in some of these authorities the passage is marked as being doubtful. *b* Other ancient authorities add *Amen* *c* Other ancient authorities add, in whole or in part, *And they excused themselves, saying, "This age of lawlessness and unbelief is under Satan, who does not allow the truth and power of God to prevail over the unclean things of the spirits. Therefore reveal your righteousness now"—thus they spoke to Christ. And Christ replied to them, "The term of years of Satan's power has been fulfilled, but other terrible things draw near. And for those who have sinned I was handed over to death, that they may return to the truth and sin no more, that they may inherit the spiritual and imperishable glory of righteousness that is in heaven."* *d* Or *gospel*

there was apparently no resurrection appearance in the original text of Mark that ended at 16.8. **7:** The risen Jesus is *going ahead . . . to Galilee* (cf. 14.28), where they *will see him,* in the same way as Jesus twice before said people would "see the Son of Man coming with the clouds of heaven," i.e., the standard symbol of the renewed Israel. Jesus is vindicated and his movement is to continue. Mark's Gospel is open-ended and must be completed by the hearers and readers of the Gospel. **8:** The narrative ends with the women terrified. Obviously, however, they eventually told the tale, or Mark's Gospel could not have been written.

16.9–20: Two attempts to provide a more satisfactory ending to the Gospel of Mark. The shorter ending. Although present in some manuscripts, this ending is clearly different from the rest of Mark in style and understanding of Jesus.

16.9–20: The longer ending. Possibly written in the early second century and appended to the Gospel later in the second century. These sentences borrow some motifs from the other Gospels and contain several unusual apocryphal elements. **9–10:** Mary is alone in Jn 20.1–2,11–19. *Seven demons,* Lk 8.2. **11:** Lk 24.11,22–25; Jn 20.19–29. **12–13:** Lk 24.12–35. **13:** Cf. Lk 24.34. **14–18:** Mt 28.19; Lk 24.47. **16:** Acts 2.37–42; 10.47–48; Rom 10.9. **17–18:** Exorcisms, Acts 8.6–7; 16.18; 19.11–20; *new tongues,* Acts 2.4–11n.; 10.46; 19.6; and possibly 1 Cor 12.10,28; 14.2–33; snakes and drinking poison lack New

tongues; 18 they will pick up snakes in
their hands,[a] and if they drink any deadly
thing, it will not hurt them; they will lay
their hands on the sick, and they will recover."
19 So then the Lord Jesus, after he had
spoken to them, was taken up into heaven
and sat down at the right hand of God.
20 And they went out and proclaimed the
good news everywhere, while the Lord
worked with them and confirmed the message by the signs that accompanied it.[b]]]

a Other ancient authorities lack *in their hands*
b Other ancient authorities add *Amen*

Testament parallels. **19–20:** Jesus' exaltation, Phil 2.9–11; Heb 1.3; *taken up,* Acts 1.2,11,22; *right hand of God,* Ps 110.1; Acts 7.55; Heb 1.3.

The Gospel According to LUKE

The Third Gospel, traditionally called the Gospel according to Luke, forms a unique literary and theological contribution to the New Testament story of Jesus Christ. Jesus is presented in an elegantly and deliberately crafted account so that readers perceive him to be "the Lord," God's Son who is the universal savior of humanity. Jesus himself is shown to inaugurate a mission to all humankind as the kingdom of God draws near to the earthly lives of people in Jesus' very person and work. Luke's telling of Jesus' story presents Jesus' coming among humanity—in birth, life, ministry, suffering, death, and resurrection—as a fulfillment of God's promises of salvation, which brings peace and wholeness of life in a decisive way. This saving event began the "final days" of God's dealings with humanity in anticipation of the "Last Day," "the Day of the Lord." Jesus himself and, in turn, his disciples call people to true repentance, which means a new relationship to God and to other human beings in a manner of life that embodies God's will for human existence.

In recounting this story, Luke reveals the ability to write in different literary styles. The initial four verses of the book are a single Greek sentence that forms a highly stylized introductory statement typically found in ancient historiographical writings. The Greek is formal and refined in a fashion that would have been familiar to well-educated citizens of the Greco-Roman era. After this distinctive start, however, the storytelling shifts into a style of Greek reminiscent of the Septuagint (the ancient Greek translation of the Hebrew Bible, with additional writings from Hellenistic Judaism). (In the annotations, places where Luke's quotations from the scriptures follow the Septuagint rather than the Hebrew are marked with the standard abbreviation for the Septuagint, LXX.) This Semitic-influenced form of Greek permeates the stories surrounding the birth and childhood of Jesus. Yet, the Septuagint-like style lightens into a more normal (and more typically secular) form of first-century Greek (called "koine") in the narrative that comprises the remainder of the Gospel. When situations shift in the story, the language of the account varies appropriately to suit the locale and characters in the narrative. Luke's appreciation of stylistic variation in narrative communication is apparent from his skilled employment of this technique. Indeed, it seems that the Gospel itself captures and communicates the universal significance of the story of God's salvation in and through Jesus Christ in the variety of ways that Luke styles the story. Readers from different religious, ethnic, and social backgrounds would find one level or another of the overall account to which they could relate and, thereby, find a point of identity and entry into the story of Jesus Christ.

The oldest traditions of the Christian church identify Luke, a physician who was a traveling companion and coworker with Paul (Philem 1.24; Col 4.14), as the author of the Gospel and its sequel, The Acts of the Apostles. At times the tradition further identifies Luke as a Syrian from Antioch, but practically nothing else is remembered of the writer of the Third Gospel. The earliest of these traditions about the identity of the author are from the late second century, and scholarly analysis of the Gospel and Acts raises critical questions about the accuracy of the attribution of the writings to the doctor, Luke, who was Paul's associate. The strongest argument in favor of the validity of identifying Luke the physician as the author of the Gospel and Acts is the relative obscurity of this particular figure from early Christianity. Yet, even defenders of the traditional identity of Luke recognize difficulties with that understanding. In particular, Luke's familiarity with Judaism is extensive, though he seems to have more book-knowledge than practical experience with particular rituals and beliefs. Similarly, Luke recalls detailed information about Palestinian locations and practices, though readers encounter a tendency toward giving the story an urban aura rather than presenting the predominantly non-urban reality that Jesus would have known. Above all, Luke never mentions in Acts that Paul wrote letters, and his account of the Gospel is quite clearly dependent on other earlier writings, especially the Gospel According to Mark. That Luke knew and used still other materials, both oral and written, in composing this Gospel is certain, if not demonstrable. In fact, Luke shares a body of material (probably written in form) with the author of the Gospel According to Matthew that accounts for approximately one-fifth of the overall Gospel story. Scholars designate this common material as "Q" (German "Quelle," "source"). Whether Luke had further written sources for his unique recital of Jesus' birth, childhood, certain parables, and the materials peculiar to Luke's account of Jesus' passion and resurrection is debated and at present beyond final determination. Yet, Luke's concern with sources—with acknowledging and using them profitably—is clear from his prologue to the Gospel (1.1–4).

The time and place of the writing of this Gospel are uncertain. Tradition identifies Luke's account with both Antioch and Rome (where Acts comes to its end), but no firm tradition or record locates the precise time and place of composition. Almost any major urban center in the Mediterranean would make a suitable location for such a document to be written and read. As for the time of the writing, all one can say with certainty is that Luke wrote this account after Mark composed his Gospel. The typical suggestion of scholars that Luke wrote around 85 CE is plausible, though the Gospel could have been completed five to fifteen years earlier or even five to ten years later. The available evidence from antiquity does not make precision possible in either locating or dating the origin of Luke's narrative.

In broad strokes, Luke tells the same basic story that one reads in the other three canonical Gospels: Jesus appears, ministers in Galilee, and moves to Judea and Jerusalem where he encounters deadly hostility that leads to his suffering, death, and resurrection. Yet, Luke's story of Jesus has logic and content that distinguish it among the four Gospels. The advent of Jesus in Judaism has a continuity and coherence with the history of Israel that presents it as the fulfillment of Israel's hopes. In Luke's remembrance of Jesus one finds the manifestation of divine compassion as Jesus reaches out to live and work among the marginal members of his society. Women, the less-than-pious, tax collectors, the poor, the sick, the oppressed, and even noble Pharisees are present and interact with Jesus more prominently in this account than in any other. As stated in Acts, "Jesus of Nazareth . . . went about doing good . . . for God was with him" (Acts 10.38). Both the coming of Jesus and his ministry of compassion are the direct results of God's anointing Jesus with the power of the Holy Spirit. That divine outpouring of the Spirit was neither unprecedented nor singular, however, for the same Spirit of God was active in the history of Israel, clearly present and active in the Gospel account prior to the conception and birth of Jesus, and later present and active in the account in Acts of the church at work among all the people of the known world.

The story told by Luke unfolds in a deliberate and seemingly logical way. The prologue prepares the readers for the significance of the story that follows, 1.1–4. The infancy and childhood of Jesus is told in a series of scenes that alternate with an account of the origins of John the Baptist; the result is that readers meet and understand the role of both these figures in God's bringing salvation to all humanity, though Jesus is clearly presented as the superior person in this arrangement (1.5–2.52). The adult Jesus prepares for his ministry through an encounter with the adult John (then, readers learn Jesus' genealogy) and he undergoes temptations by the devil (3.1–4.13); Jesus ministers in

Galilee, provoking controversy, calling disciples, preaching, working miracles, teaching, commissioning the initial ministry of his followers, and dealing compassionately with the masses of people (4.14–9.50). Jesus and his followers journey to Jerusalem and he ministers along the way (9.51–19.27). Jesus enters Jerusalem, working in the Temple area and teaching about the future (19.28–21.38). Jesus directs the Last Supper, suffers, dies, and is buried (22.1–23.56), and Jesus' empty tomb is found before he appears to the disciples and then ascends to heaven (24.1–53).

Luke's narrative starts with a clear beginning, but one also containing anticipations of the full story that follows and declarations that make the significance of the whole story explicit. The narrative unfolds naturally. Events occur as results of prior occurrences, and initial incidents are told in such a way that they anticipate later developments in the narrative. Readers who become actively involved with Luke's account will find hints and signals that provoke questions and expectations that are later answered and met in the reading of the whole story. In general, wondering about the nature of salvation, the character of the kingdom of God, the reality of repentance, and the person and work of Jesus as the Lord—God's messiah, Son, and Savior—will lead readers to ask about the depths of the story that Luke is intent upon communicating. Luke's primary concern is to inform the reader who Jesus of Nazareth was—and now, who he is as the suffering, crucified Savior and the risen, exalted Lord. Furthermore, in the wake of Luke's purposeful presentation of the person and work of Jesus Christ, there is another dimension of the story that preserves and communicates Jesus' teaching about what it means to be his follower. Discipleship is a secondary theme that is closely related to the primary theme of Jesus' identity and significance. Discipleship, however, is sometimes a difficult dimension of the story for contemporary readers to grasp, for discipleship is a way of life as a member of the repentant and saved people of God. For Luke, one is not a disciple alone, but one finds profound personal significance in becoming one of the people of God who live as citizens of God's kingdom in a manner consistent with God's intentions for the life of all humanity as brought and taught, shown and known in Jesus Christ, God's Son, the universal Savior of humankind.

1 Since many have undertaken to set
down an orderly account of the events
that have been fulfilled among us, 2 just as
they were handed on to us by those who
from the beginning were eyewitnesses and
servants of the word, 3 I too decided, after
investigating everything carefully from the
very first,[a] to write an orderly account for
you, most excellent Theophilus, 4 so that
you may know the truth concerning the
things about which you have been instructed.

5 In the days of King Herod of Judea,

a Or *for a long time*

1.1–4: The prologue (Mt 1.1; Mk 1.1). See Acts 1.1–2. Jn 20.30–31; 21.25 show similar awareness of sources used by the Gospel writers. This literary prologue resembles the openings of many classical or Hellenistic Greek works, particularly histories. Accordingly, Luke refers to previous early Christian writings, acknowledges sources, and explains the need or purpose of his own work. **3:** *Theophilus* means "friend of God" and may address a person of prominent social standing, since Theophilus is designated "most excellent," terminology typically applied to persons of high official or socioeconomic status. While the address may be to a particular person, the symbolic sense of the name may designate any ideal Christian, as it has been understood since the earliest interpretations of Luke's Gospel.

1.5–2.52: The infancy and childhood of Jesus.

1.5–25: The annunciation of the birth of John the Baptist. 5: *In the days of King Herod of Judea* refers broadly to 37–4 BCE. The specific time in view in this story is probably 7–6 BCE (see Mt 2.1,15). *The priestly order of Abijah* was the eighth of twenty-four divisions of priests (1 Chr 24.10) who served twice

there was a priest named Zechariah, who
belonged to the priestly order of Abijah.
His wife was a descendant of Aaron, and
her name was Elizabeth. [6]Both of them
were righteous before God, living blame-
lessly according to all the commandments
and regulations of the Lord. [7]But they had
no children, because Elizabeth was barren,
and both were getting on in years.

8 Once when he was serving as priest
before God and his section was on duty,
[9]he was chosen by lot, according to the cus-
tom of the priesthood, to enter the sanctu-
ary of the Lord and offer incense. [10]Now at
the time of the incense offering, the whole
assembly of the people was praying out-
side. [11]Then there appeared to him an an-
gel of the Lord, standing at the right side of
the altar of incense. [12]When Zechariah saw
him, he was terrified; and fear over-
whelmed him. [13]But the angel said to him,
"Do not be afraid, Zechariah, for your
prayer has been heard. Your wife Elizabeth
will bear you a son, and you will name him
John. [14]You will have joy and gladness,
and many will rejoice at his birth, [15]for he
will be great in the sight of the Lord. He
must never drink wine or strong drink;
even before his birth he will be filled with
the Holy Spirit. [16]He will turn many of the
people of Israel to the Lord their God.
[17]With the spirit and power of Elijah he
will go before him, to turn the hearts of
parents to their children, and the disobedi-
ent to the wisdom of the righteous, to make
ready a people prepared for the Lord."
[18]Zechariah said to the angel, "How will I
know that this is so? For I am an old man,
and my wife is getting on in years." [19]The
angel replied, "I am Gabriel. I stand in
the presence of God, and I have been sent
to speak to you and to bring you this
good news. [20]But now, because you did
not believe my words, which will be ful-
filled in their time, you will become mute,
unable to speak, until the day these things
occur."

21 Meanwhile the people were waiting
for Zechariah, and wondered at his delay in
the sanctuary. [22]When he did come out, he
could not speak to them, and they realized
that he had seen a vision in the sanctuary.
He kept motioning to them and remained
unable to speak. [23]When his time of service
was ended, he went to his home.

24 After those days his wife Elizabeth
conceived, and for five months she re-
mained in seclusion. She said, [25]"This is
what the Lord has done for me when he
looked favorably on me and took away the
disgrace I have endured among my peo-
ple."

26 In the sixth month the angel Gabriel
was sent by God to a town in Galilee called
Nazareth, [27]to a virgin engaged to a man
whose name was Joseph, of the house of
David. The virgin's name was Mary. [28]And
he came to her and said, "Greetings, fa-

annually, for one week at a time, in the Jerusalem Temple. These priests were Levites who served God both in behalf of and in the place of the firstborn males of all the tribes of Israel (Num 3.11–13). As *a descendant of Aaron,* Israel's first priest, Elizabeth was also from a priestly family. **5–7:** The mention of Elizabeth, the righteousness of the couple, their childlessness, and their advanced age all anticipate the appearance of the angel and are not directly related to Zechariah's Temple service. The description also echoes images and lines from the Hebrew Bible (Gen 15.3; 16.1; 25.2; 29.31; Judg 13.2–3; 1 Sam 1.2; Ex 30.6–8). **9:** The privilege of offering the incense was normally granted only once in a lifetime. **13:** The name *John* (Heb "J[eh]ohanan") means "God has shown favor." **15:** Num 6.1–4; Judg 13.4–5; 1 Sam 1.11 LXX. **17:** *He will go before him,* that is, he will be the forerunner of the messiah (Mal 4.5–6; Mt 11.14); on *Elijah,* see 1 Kings 17–19; 21. **19:** *Gabriel* means "God is my hero" and is one of two angels named in the Hebrew Bible (Dan 8.16; 9.21). **25:** Among Jews sterility was regarded as a sign of divine disfavor and therefore a *disgrace* (see Gen 16.2; 25.21; 30.23; 1 Sam 1.1–18; Lev 20.20–21; Ps 128.3; Jer 22.30).

1.26–38: The annunciation of Jesus' birth. 26: *In the sixth month,* after the conception of John. *Nazareth,* a small village (cf. Jn 1.46) in southern Galilee. **31:** *Jesus,* the Greek form of the Hebrew name

vored one! The Lord is with you."[a] 29 But
she was much perplexed by his words and
pondered what sort of greeting this might
be. 30 The angel said to her, "Do not be
afraid, Mary, for you have found favor
with God. 31 And now, you will conceive in
your womb and bear a son, and you will
name him Jesus. 32 He will be great, and
will be called the Son of the Most High,
and the Lord God will give to him the
throne of his ancestor David. 33 He will
reign over the house of Jacob forever, and
of his kingdom there will be no end."
34 Mary said to the angel, "How can this
be, since I am a virgin?"[b] 35 The angel said
to her, "The Holy Spirit will come upon
you, and the power of the Most High will
overshadow you; therefore the child to be
born[c] will be holy; he will be called Son of
God. 36 And now, your relative Elizabeth in
her old age has also conceived a son; and
this is the sixth month for her who was said
to be barren. 37 For nothing will be impossi-
ble with God." 38 Then Mary said, "Here
am I, the servant of the Lord; let it be with
me according to your word." Then the an-
gel departed from her.

39 In those days Mary set out and went
with haste to a Judean town in the hill
country, 40 where she entered the house of
Zechariah and greeted Elizabeth. 41 When
Elizabeth heard Mary's greeting, the child
leaped in her womb. And Elizabeth was
filled with the Holy Spirit 42 and exclaimed
with a loud cry, "Blessed are you among
women, and blessed is the fruit of your
womb. 43 And why has this happened to
me, that the mother of my Lord comes to
me? 44 For as soon as I heard the sound of
your greeting, the child in my womb leaped
for joy. 45 And blessed is she who believed
that there would be[d] a fulfillment of what
was spoken to her by the Lord."

46 And Mary[e] said,

"My soul magnifies the Lord,
47 and my spirit rejoices in God
my Savior,
48 for he has looked with favor on the
lowliness of his servant.
Surely, from now on all generations
will call me blessed;
49 for the Mighty One has done great
things for me,
and holy is his name.
50 His mercy is for those who fear him
from generation to generation.
51 He has shown strength with his arm;
he has scattered the proud in the
thoughts of their hearts.
52 He has brought down the powerful
from their thrones,
and lifted up the lowly;
53 he has filled the hungry with
good things,
and sent the rich away empty.
54 He has helped his servant Israel,
in remembrance of his mercy,
55 according to the promise he made to
our ancestors,
to Abraham and to his descendants
forever."

56 And Mary remained with her about
three months and then returned to her
home.

57 Now the time came for Elizabeth to

a Other ancient authorities add *Blessed are you among women* *b* Gk *I do not know a man* *c* Other ancient authorities add *of you* *d* Or *believed, for there will be* *e* Other ancient authorities read *Elizabeth*

Joshua, meaning "God has saved" (see Mt 1.21). **32:** *The Son of the Most High* implies both divinity (see Sir 4.10) and royal authority (see 2 Sam 7.13–16; cf. Lk 2.35,76; 6.35; 8.28; Acts 7.48; 16.17). **36:** *Elizabeth . . . conceived,* the angel offers Mary some corroboration, on which she acts (v. 39).

1.39–56: Mary and Elizabeth. 41: Elizabeth's being *filled with the Holy Spirit* may also acknowledge the presence and the power of the Holy Spirit at work in relation to the unborn John *in her womb.* **43:** Prior to his birth Jesus is designated *Lord.* **46–55:** These verses form the first of four "canticles" or "hymns" in the infancy narrative of Luke. This "song" is the "Magnificat" (so called from its first word in the Latin or Vulgate translation); compare the prayer of Hannah in 1 Sam 2.1–10, a passage to which these verses relate. **55:** Gen 17.7; 18.18; 22.17; Mic 7.20.

1.57–80: The birth and naming of John. 59: Lev 12.3; Gen 17.12; Lk 2.21. **65:** *Fear* (rendered "awe"

give birth, and she bore a son. 58 Her neigh-
bors and relatives heard that the Lord had
shown his great mercy to her, and they re-
joiced with her.
59 On the eighth day they came to cir-
cumcise the child, and they were going to
name him Zechariah after his father. 60 But
his mother said, "No; he is to be called
John." 61 They said to her, "None of your
relatives has this name." 62 Then they began
motioning to his father to find out what
name he wanted to give him. 63 He asked
for a writing tablet and wrote, "His name is
John." And all of them were amazed. 64 Im-
mediately his mouth was opened and his
tongue freed, and he began to speak, prais-
ing God. 65 Fear came over all their neigh-
bors, and all these things were talked about
throughout the entire hill country of Judea.
66 All who heard them pondered them and
said, "What then will this child become?"
For, indeed, the hand of the Lord was with
him.
67 Then his father Zechariah was filled
with the Holy Spirit and spoke this proph-
ecy:
68 "Blessed be the Lord God of Israel,
for he has looked favorably on his
people and redeemed them.
69 He has raised up a mighty savior[a]
for us
in the house of his servant David,
70 as he spoke through the mouth of his
holy prophets from of old,
71 that we would be saved from our
enemies and from the hand of
all who hate us.
72 Thus he has shown the mercy
promised to our ancestors,
and has remembered his
holy covenant,
73 the oath that he swore to our
ancestor Abraham,
to grant us 74 that we, being rescued
from the hands of our enemies,
might serve him without fear, 75 in
holiness and righteousness
before him all our days.
76 And you, child, will be called the
prophet of the Most High;
for you will go before the Lord to
prepare his ways,
77 to give knowledge of salvation to his
people
by the forgiveness of their sins.
78 By the tender mercy of our God,
the dawn from on high will break
upon[b] us,
79 to give light to those who sit in
darkness and in the shadow of
death,
to guide our feet into the way
of peace."
80 The child grew and became strong in
spirit, and he was in the wilderness until the
day he appeared publicly to Israel.

2 In those days a decree went out from
Emperor Augustus that all the world
should be registered. 2 This was the first
registration and was taken while Quirinius

a Gk *a horn of salvation* *b* Other ancient authorities read *has broken upon*

in 5.26) designates humble, reverent recognition of the limits of human understanding and power before God (2.9; 7.16; Acts 2.43,46–47; 5.5,11; 19.17). **67–79:** The second hymn, called the "Benedictus." **69:** *A mighty savior,* lit. "a horn of salvation," uses a biblical metaphor ("horn") for power (Ps 18.3; 75.5–6; 89.18; 112.9; 148.14) and here refers to one who will bring salvation; see Ps 92.10–11; 132.17–18. **76:** See 3.4. **80:** These words cover a period of approximately thirty years (see 3.23). *In the wilderness,* see 3.4.

2.1–7: The birth of Jesus (Mt 1.18–25). **1:** General censuses of Roman citizens are known from 28 BCE, 8 BCE, and 14 CE; but outside the New Testament this enrollment under Caesar *Augustus* is not attested. Caesar *Augustus* reigned 27 BCE–14 CE. His rule marked a time of peace, the *pax Augusta,* which caused the populace to hail him as lord and savior of the world. **2:** *Quirinius* was at this time legate or commissioner of *Augustus* in a war against a rebellious tribe, the Homonadenses. As such he was a military governor of Syria, while civil administration was in the hands of Varus. It is possible that *Quirinius* was affiliated with Syria as a governmental authority on two different occasions, 6–4 BCE and

was governor of Syria. 3 All went to their
own towns to be registered. 4 Joseph also
went from the town of Nazareth in Galilee
to Judea, to the city of David called Bethle-
hem, because he was descended from the
house and family of David. 5 He went to be
registered with Mary, to whom he was en-
gaged and who was expecting a child.
6 While they were there, the time came for
her to deliver her child. 7 And she gave birth
to her firstborn son and wrapped him in
bands of cloth, and laid him in a manger,
because there was no place for them in the
inn.

8 In that region there were shepherds
living in the fields, keeping watch over their
flock by night. 9 Then an angel of the Lord
stood before them, and the glory of the
Lord shone around them, and they were
terrified. 10 But the angel said to them, "Do
not be afraid; for see—I am bringing you
good news of great joy for all the people:
11 to you is born this day in the city of
David a Savior, who is the Messiah,[a] the
Lord. 12 This will be a sign for you: you will
find a child wrapped in bands of cloth and
lying in a manger." 13 And suddenly there
was with the angel a multitude of the heav-
enly host,[b] praising God and saying,

14 "Glory to God in the highest heaven,
and on earth peace among those
whom he favors!"[c]

15 When the angels had left them and
gone into heaven, the shepherds said to one
another, "Let us go now to Bethlehem and
see this thing that has taken place, which
the Lord has made known to us." 16 So they
went with haste and found Mary and Jo-
seph, and the child lying in the manger.
17 When they saw this, they made known
what had been told them about this child;
18 and all who heard it were amazed at
what the shepherds told them. 19 But Mary
treasured all these words and pondered
them in her heart. 20 The shepherds re-
turned, glorifying and praising God for all
they had heard and seen, as it had been told
them.

21 After eight days had passed, it was
time to circumcise the child; and he was
called Jesus, the name given by the angel
before he was conceived in the womb.

22 When the time came for their purifi-
cation according to the law of Moses, they
brought him up to Jerusalem to present him
to the Lord 23 (as it is written in the law of
the Lord, "Every firstborn male shall be
designated as holy to the Lord"), 24 and
they offered a sacrifice according to what is
stated in the law of the Lord, "a pair of
turtledoves or two young pigeons."

25 Now there was a man in Jerusalem
whose name was Simeon;[d] this man was
righteous and devout, looking forward to
the consolation of Israel, and the Holy Spir-
it rested on him. 26 It had been revealed to
him by the Holy Spirit that he would not

a Or *the Christ* b Gk *army* c Other ancient authorities read *peace, goodwill among people*
d Gk *Symeon*

6–9 CE. **7:** *Firstborn son* indicates nothing about Mary's subsequent childbearing; the word is more a technical term in reference to the child upon which God laid full claim (Num 3.11–13). *Bands of cloth* were normally used to bundle and provide warmth and comfort for infants.

2.8–20: Annunciation to shepherds and their visit (cf. Mt 2.1–12). **8:** That the shepherds were *living in the fields* indicates nothing about the season of Jesus' birth. **11:** Jesus is identified by three primary titles of Christian belief, *Savior, Messiah,* and *Lord* (see Mt 1.21; 16.16; Jn 4.42; Acts 2.36; 5.31; Phil 2.11). The designation of the newborn Jesus as Lord is striking (see 1.43), for that word in Greek ("kyrios") is the precise term used consistently throughout the LXX to translate the tetragrammaton, God's holy and personal name (Heb "yhwh"). **14:** The third hymn.

2.21–38: Jesus' circumcision and presentation. 22–23: Ex 13.2,12,15; Lev 5.11; 12.8. The phrase *their purification* is ambiguous and likely refers to the parents, though there was no rite of purification for the father (or the newborn). Luke's interest in this ritual is to recognize the occasion of the parents' taking Jesus to the Temple. **25–38:** *Simeon* and *Anna,* not otherwise known, acclaim Jesus as savior and redeemer. **29–32:** The fourth hymn, whose opening words in Latin are "Nunc dimittis." **30–31:** See 3.6.

see death before he had seen the Lord's
Messiah.[a] 27 Guided by the Spirit, Sime-
on[b] came into the temple; and when the
parents brought in the child Jesus, to do for
him what was customary under the law,
28 Simeon[c] took him in his arms and
praised God, saying,

29 "Master, now you are dismissing your
servant[d] in peace,
according to your word;
30 for my eyes have seen your salvation,
31 which you have prepared in the
presence of all peoples,
32 a light for revelation to the Gentiles
and for glory to your people
Israel."

33 And the child's father and mother
were amazed at what was being said about
him. 34 Then Simeon[e] blessed them and
said to his mother Mary, "This child is des-
tined for the falling and the rising of many
in Israel, and to be a sign that will be op-
posed 35 so that the inner thoughts of many
will be revealed—and a sword will pierce
your own soul too."

36 There was also a prophet, Anna[f] the
daughter of Phanuel, of the tribe of Asher.
She was of a great age, having lived with
her husband seven years after her marriage,
37 then as a widow to the age of eighty-
four. She never left the temple but wor-
shiped there with fasting and prayer night
and day. 38 At that moment she came, and
began to praise God and to speak about the
child[g] to all who were looking for the re-
demption of Jerusalem.

39 When they had finished everything
required by the law of the Lord, they re-
turned to Galilee, to their own town of
Nazareth. 40 The child grew and became
strong, filled with wisdom; and the favor of
God was upon him.

41 Now every year his parents went to
Jerusalem for the festival of the Passover.
42 And when he was twelve years old, they
went up as usual for the festival. 43 When
the festival was ended and they started to
return, the boy Jesus stayed behind in Jeru-
salem, but his parents did not know it.
44 Assuming that he was in the group of
travelers, they went a day's journey. Then
they started to look for him among their
relatives and friends. 45 When they did not
find him, they returned to Jerusalem to
search for him. 46 After three days they
found him in the temple, sitting among the
teachers, listening to them and asking them
questions. 47 And all who heard him were
amazed at his understanding and his an-
swers. 48 When his parents[h] saw him they
were astonished; and his mother said to
him, "Child, why have you treated us like
this? Look, your father and I have been
searching for you in great anxiety." 49 He
said to them, "Why were you searching for
me? Did you not know that I must be in my
Father's house?"[i] 50 But they did not un-
derstand what he said to them. 51 Then he
went down with them and came to Naza-
reth, and was obedient to them. His mother
treasured all these things in her heart.

52 And Jesus increased in wisdom and
in years,[j] and in divine and human favor.

3 In the fifteenth year of the reign of Em-
peror Tiberius, when Pontius Pilate was

a Or *the Lord's Christ* b Gk *In the Spirit, he*
c Gk *he* d Gk *slave* e Gk *Symeon* f Gk *Hanna*
g Gk *him* h Gk *they* i Or *be about my Father's interests?* j Or *in stature*

32: See Isa 49.6; 46.13. **33:** Luke calls Joseph the *father* of Jesus (notwithstanding 1.34–35) since he was Mary's husband and Jesus' legal father (cf. Mt 13.55; Lk 2.48; 3.23).

2.39–40: Jesus' childhood in Nazareth (Mt 2.22–23).

2.41–52: Young Jesus in the Temple. This story of Jesus' boyhood is unique to Luke among the canonical Gospels, though later legendary writings also show interest in this otherwise unknown period of Jesus' life. **41:** Ex 23.15; Deut 16.1–8. **49:** *My Father's house* recognizes the special relationship between Jesus and God and contrasts with Mary's reference to Joseph as "your father" (v. 48). **52:** 1 Sam 2.26; Lk 1.80; 2.40.

3.1–4.13: Jesus' preparation for ministry (Mt 3.1–4.11; Mk 1.2–13).

3.1–6: The appearance of John the Baptist (Mt 3.1–6; Mk 1.2–6). **1:** *Tiberius* Caesar succeeded

governor of Judea, and Herod was ruler[a]
of Galilee, and his brother Philip ruler[a] of
the region of Ituraea and Trachonitis, and
Lysanias ruler[a] of Abilene, 2 during the
high priesthood of Annas and Caiaphas,
the word of God came to John son of Zech-
ariah in the wilderness. 3 He went into all
the region around the Jordan, proclaiming
a baptism of repentance for the forgiveness
of sins, 4 as it is written in the book of the
words of the prophet Isaiah,

"The voice of one crying out in
the wilderness:
'Prepare the way of the Lord,
make his paths straight.
5 Every valley shall be filled,
and every mountain and hill shall
be made low,
and the crooked shall be made
straight,
and the rough ways made smooth;
6 and all flesh shall see the salvation of
God.' "

7 John said to the crowds that came out
to be baptized by him, "You brood of vi-
pers! Who warned you to flee from the
wrath to come? 8 Bear fruits worthy of re-
pentance. Do not begin to say to your-
selves, 'We have Abraham as our ancestor';
for I tell you, God is able from these stones
to raise up children to Abraham. 9 Even
now the ax is lying at the root of the trees;
every tree therefore that does not bear good
fruit is cut down and thrown into the fire."

10 And the crowds asked him, "What
then should we do?" 11 In reply he said to
them, "Whoever has two coats must share
with anyone who has none; and whoever
has food must do likewise." 12 Even tax col-
lectors came to be baptized, and they asked
him, "Teacher, what should we do?" 13 He
said to them, "Collect no more than the
amount prescribed for you." 14 Soldiers
also asked him, "And we, what should we
do?" He said to them, "Do not extort mon-
ey from anyone by threats or false accusa-
tion, and be satisfied with your wages."

15 As the people were filled with expec-
tation, and all were questioning in their
hearts concerning John, whether he might
be the Messiah,[b] 16 John answered all of
them by saying, "I baptize you with water;
but one who is more powerful than I is
coming; I am not worthy to untie the thong
of his sandals. He will baptize you with[c]
the Holy Spirit and fire. 17 His winnowing

[a] Gk *tetrarch* [b] Or *the Christ* [c] Or *in*

Augustus in 14 CE and ruled until 37. Thus, depending on the manner of reckoning years, sometime between 26 and 29 CE is indicated. *Pontius Pilate,* a Roman governor, held authority in *Judea,* Samaria, and Idumea 26–36 CE; see 23.1, etc. The remainder of the kingdom of Herod the Great had been divided between his sons *Herod* Antipas who ruled Galilee and Perea (23.6–7) and Philip (see Map on p. 68 NT). Initially another son, Herod Archelaus, had ruled Judea as ethnarch from 4 BCE, but he was deposed and banished for incompetence and replaced by a Roman official in 6 CE (see Mt 2.22). **2:** *Annas* was high priest 6–15 CE when the Romans deposed him. He was followed by relatives; initially by his son, Eleazar; then by his son-in-law *Caiaphas* (18–36 CE), and thereafter by four more sons. Because Jewish custom was for the high priest to serve for life, even when out of office, Annas's influence and authority continued to be recognized by the population. **3:** A summary statement of the shape and substance of John's ministry. Proclamation led to baptism, *a baptism of repentance,* a symbolic act of cleansing to indicate realignment with the will of God in forgiveness of the one baptized. **4–6:** Isa 40.3–5. **6:** *All flesh* refers to all humanity and emphasizes that God's salvation was universal in character; see 2.30–32; Acts 2.21.

3.7–9: John's call to repentance (Mt 3.7–10). **8:** The assertion to have *Abraham as . . . ancestor* was a claim to privileged standing with God through natural birth (see Jn 8.33,39; Rom 2.28–29). **9:** *Fire,* a symbol of judgment, often eschatological judgment (see 3.16; 16.24).

3.10–14: John's directions to the crowd. **11:** *Two coats,* lit. "two tunics," usually worn as undergarments.

3.15–18: John's heralding of the messiah (Mt 3.11–12; Mk 1.7–8). **16:** *He will baptize you with the Holy Spirit and fire,* a promise or prophecy fulfilled at Pentecost (Acts 2.1–4). **17:** *Winnowing fork,* a tool used in threshing grain.

fork is in his hand, to clear his threshing
floor and to gather the wheat into his gra-
nary; but the chaff he will burn with un-
quenchable fire."
18 So, with many other exhortations, he
proclaimed the good news to the people.
19 But Herod the ruler,[a] who had been re-
buked by him because of Herodias, his
brother's wife, and because of all the evil
things that Herod had done, 20 added to
them all by shutting up John in prison.
21 Now when all the people were bap-
tized, and when Jesus also had been bap-
tized and was praying, the heaven was
opened, 22 and the Holy Spirit descended
upon him in bodily form like a dove. And
a voice came from heaven, "You are my
Son, the Beloved;[b] with you I am well
pleased."[c]

23 Jesus was about thirty years old
when he began his work. He was the son
(as was thought) of Joseph son of Heli,
24 son of Matthat, son of Levi, son of Mel-
chi, son of Jannai, son of Joseph, 25 son of
Mattathias, son of Amos, son of Nahum,
son of Esli, son of Naggai, 26 son of Maath,
son of Mattathias, son of Semein, son of
Josech, son of Joda, 27 son of Joanan, son of
Rhesa, son of Zerubbabel, son of Shealti-
el,[d] son of Neri, 28 son of Melchi, son of
Addi, son of Cosam, son of Elmadam, son
of Er, 29 son of Joshua, son of Eliezer, son of
Jorim, son of Matthat, son of Levi, 30 son
of Simeon, son of Judah, son of Joseph, son
of Jonam, son of Eliakim, 31 son of Melea,
son of Menna, son of Mattatha, son of Na-
than, son of David, 32 son of Jesse, son of
Obed, son of Boaz, son of Sala,[e] son of
Nahshon, 33 son of Amminadab, son of Ad-
min, son of Arni,[f] son of Hezron, son of
Perez, son of Judah, 34 son of Jacob, son of
Isaac, son of Abraham, son of Terah, son of
Nahor, 35 son of Serug, son of Reu, son
of Peleg, son of Eber, son of Shelah, 36 son
of Cainan, son of Arphaxad, son of Shem,
son of Noah, son of Lamech, 37 son of Me-
thuselah, son of Enoch, son of Jared, son of
Mahalaleel, son of Cainan, 38 son of Enos,
son of Seth, son of Adam, son of God.

4 Jesus, full of the Holy Spirit, returned
from the Jordan and was led by the
Spirit in the wilderness, 2 where for forty
days he was tempted by the devil. He ate
nothing at all during those days, and when
they were over, he was famished. 3 The
devil said to him, "If you are the Son of
God, command this stone to become a loaf
of bread." 4 Jesus answered him, "It is writ-
ten, 'One does not live by bread alone.' "
5 Then the devil[g] led him up and
showed him in an instant all the kingdoms

a Gk *tetrarch* b Or *my beloved Son* c Other ancient authorities read *You are my Son, today I have begotten you* d Gk *Salathiel* e Other ancient authorities read *Salmon* f Other ancient authorities read *Amminadab, son of Aram*; others vary widely g Gk *he*

3.19–20: John's imprisonment by Herod. Herod Antipas had divorced the daughter of the Nabatean king in order to marry his niece, Herodias, who had been married to Antipas's brother, Herod Philip. In Luke, John's imprisonment is placed before the baptism of Jesus; cf. Mt 14.3–4; Mk 6.17–18.

3.21–22: The baptism of Jesus (Mt 3.13–17; Mk 1.9–11). **21:** Prayer is a regular activity of Jesus and a prominent theme in Luke's portrait (5.16; 6.12; 9.18,28; 11.1; 22.32,41–46). **22:** See Ps 2.7; Isa 42.1. The *voice* from heaven speaks again at the Transfiguration (9.35).

3.23–38: The genealogy of Jesus (Mt 1.1–17). Luke traces the lineage of Jesus back to Adam, the first human (Gen 5.1); linking Jesus' line with God's original creation shows Jesus' common humanity and establishes his credentials as the universal savior. **23–27:** The persons named from *Heli* to *Zerubbabel* are otherwise unknown. For the rest of the genealogy cf. Gen 5.3–32; 11.10–26; Ruth 4.18–22; 1 Chr 1.1–4,24–28; 2.1–15.

4.1–13: The temptation of Jesus (Mt 4.1–11; Mk 1.12–13). The order of the temptations differs from Matthew's, but the particular tests are the same. **2:** The mention of *forty days* in relation to the stay in the "wilderness" recalls the wilderness wanderings of Israel during the Exodus (Deut 8.2; see also Deut

of the world. 6 And the devil[a] said to him,
"To you I will give their glory and all this
authority; for it has been given over to me,
and I give it to anyone I please. 7 If you,
then, will worship me, it will all be yours."
8 Jesus answered him, "It is written,
'Worship the Lord your God,
and serve only him.' "
9 Then the devil[a] took him to Jerusa-
lem, and placed him on the pinnacle of the
temple, saying to him, "If you are the Son
of God, throw yourself down from here,
10 for it is written,
'He will command his angels
concerning you,
to protect you,'
11 and
'On their hands they will bear
you up,
so that you will not dash your foot
against a stone.' "
12 Jesus answered him, "It is said, 'Do not
put the Lord your God to the test.' "
13 When the devil had finished every test,
he departed from him until an opportune
time.

14 Then Jesus, filled with the power of
the Spirit, returned to Galilee, and a report
about him spread through all the surround-
ing country. 15 He began to teach in their
synagogues and was praised by everyone.
16 When he came to Nazareth, where he
had been brought up, he went to the syna-
gogue on the sabbath day, as was his cus-
tom. He stood up to read, 17 and the scroll
of the prophet Isaiah was given to him. He
unrolled the scroll and found the place
where it was written:
18 "The Spirit of the Lord is upon me,
because he has anointed me
to bring good news to the poor.
He has sent me to proclaim release to
the captives
and recovery of sight to the blind,
to let the oppressed go free,
19 to proclaim the year of the Lord's
favor."
20 And he rolled up the scroll, gave it back
to the attendant, and sat down. The eyes of
all in the synagogue were fixed on him.
21 Then he began to say to them, "Today
this scripture has been fulfilled in your
hearing." 22 All spoke well of him and were
amazed at the gracious words that came
from his mouth. They said, "Is not this Jo-
seph's son?" 23 He said to them, "Doubtless
you will quote to me this proverb, 'Doctor,
cure yourself!' And you will say, 'Do here
also in your hometown the things that we
have heard you did at Capernaum.' "
24 And he said, "Truly I tell you, no prophet
is accepted in the prophet's hometown.
25 But the truth is, there were many widows
in Israel in the time of Elijah, when the
heaven was shut up three years and six
months, and there was a severe famine over
all the land; 26 yet Elijah was sent to none of
them except to a widow at Zarephath in
Sidon. 27 There were also many lepers[b] in
Israel in the time of the prophet Elisha, and

a Gk *he* *b* The terms *leper* and *leprosy* can refer to several diseases

9.9; 1 Kings 19.8). **4:** Deut 8.3. **8:** Deut 6.13; 10.20. **10–11:** Ps 91.11–12. **12:** Deut 6.16. **13:** *Until an opportune time,* see 22.3,28,53.

4.14–9.50: Jesus' ministry in Galilee (Mt 4.12–18.35; Mk 1.14–9.50).

4.14–15: The beginning of the Galilean ministry (Mt 4.12–17; Mk 1.14–15). **14:** Luke mentions Jesus' fame repeatedly, see v. 37; 5.15; 7.17.

4.16–30: Jesus in Nazareth (Mt 13.53–58; Mk 6.1–6). Luke has transposed this incident to make it a frontispiece at the outset of Jesus' ministry. The parallel account in Mark 6.1–6 follows earlier appearances and work in Galilee; statements in Luke's version of this incident seem out of sequence because Jesus has not yet engaged in the specific ministry to which he refers in this speech (v. 23). The details given here of synagogue worship are the earliest accounts of them. **17:** *The scroll of . . . Isaiah was given to* Jesus by the "chazzan" or attendant of the synagogue (v. 20). Scrolls were kept in a special place in the synagogue and were given to readers by the attendant. **18–19:** Isa 61.1; 58.6; 61.2. **24–27:** Traditions of the prophets (1 Kings 17.8–16; 2 Kings 5.1–14) illustrate that foreigners sometimes experienced God's aid when Israel

none of them was cleansed except Naaman
the Syrian." 28 When they heard this, all in
the synagogue were filled with rage. 29 They
got up, drove him out of the town, and led
him to the brow of the hill on which their
town was built, so that they might hurl him
off the cliff. 30 But he passed through the
midst of them and went on his way.
31 He went down to Capernaum, a city
in Galilee, and was teaching them on the
sabbath. 32 They were astounded at his
teaching, because he spoke with authority.
33 In the synagogue there was a man who
had the spirit of an unclean demon, and
he cried out with a loud voice, 34 "Let us
alone! What have you to do with us, Jesus
of Nazareth? Have you come to destroy us?
I know who you are, the Holy One of
God." 35 But Jesus rebuked him, saying,
"Be silent, and come out of him!" When
the demon had thrown him down before
them, he came out of him without having
done him any harm. 36 They were all
amazed and kept saying to one another,
"What kind of utterance is this? For with
authority and power he commands the un-
clean spirits, and out they come!" 37 And
a report about him began to reach every
place in the region.
38 After leaving the synagogue he en-
tered Simon's house. Now Simon's mother-
in-law was suffering from a high fever, and
they asked him about her. 39 Then he stood
over her and rebuked the fever, and it left
her. Immediately she got up and began to
serve them.
40 As the sun was setting, all those who
had any who were sick with various kinds
of diseases brought them to him; and he
laid his hands on each of them and cured
them. 41 Demons also came out of many,
shouting, "You are the Son of God!" But
he rebuked them and would not allow them
to speak, because they knew that he was
the Messiah.[a]
42 At daybreak he departed and went
into a deserted place. And the crowds were
looking for him; and when they reached
him, they wanted to prevent him from leav-
ing them. 43 But he said to them, "I must
proclaim the good news of the kingdom of
God to the other cities also; for I was sent
for this purpose." 44 So he continued pro-
claiming the message in the synagogues of
Judea.[b]
5 Once while Jesus[c] was standing beside
the lake of Gennesaret, and the crowd
was pressing in on him to hear the word of
God, 2 he saw two boats there at the shore

a Or *the Christ* *b* Other ancient authorities read *Galilee* *c* Gk *he*

did not. **28:** The hostile reaction comes in response to Jesus' references to Gentiles (vv. 24–27), not to his apparent messianic claims (v. 21).

4.31–37: Jesus in the synagogue at Capernaum (Mt 4.13; 7.28–29; Mk 1.21–28). Demons were thought of as nonmaterial existences of a personal kind, hostile to human welfare and rebellious against God. The Gospels reflect widespread dread of demons and a general sense of helplessness before demonic activity. Jesus is portrayed here and elsewhere (11.20–22) as one who can deliver persons from demonic oppression and from Satan himself (see 13.16). **31:** This incident is the first of five sabbath healings or exorcisms by Jesus (4.31,38; 6.6; 13.10; 14.1).

4.38–39: The healing of Simon Peter's mother-in-law (Mt 8.14–15; Mk 1.29–31). While not stated explicitly, this incident is another "sabbath healing" (see 4.31n.). Simon Peter is more fully introduced in 5.1–11; 6.13–14.

4.40–41: Healings and exorcisms at sunset (Mt 8.16–17; Mk 1.32–34). With the sabbath ending at sundown, people began to present their problems and maladies to Jesus for attention and healing.

4.42–44: Departure and further preaching in Galilee (Mt 4.23; Mk 1.35–39). **44:** This is the only express mention outside the Fourth Gospel of Jesus' early Judean ministry (but compare the implication of Mt 23.37 and Lk 13.34). Here, however, Luke may simply employ *Judea* to refer to the broader Palestinian region as the land of the Jews.

5.1–11: The great catch of fish (Mt 13.1–3a; 4.18–22; Mk 4.1–2; 1.16–20). **1:** *Lake of Gennesaret,* Sea of Galilee.

of the lake; the fishermen had gone out of
them and were washing their nets. 3He got
into one of the boats, the one belonging to
Simon, and asked him to put out a little
way from the shore. Then he sat down and
taught the crowds from the boat. 4When he
had finished speaking, he said to Simon,
"Put out into the deep water and let down
your nets for a catch." 5Simon answered,
"Master, we have worked all night long but
have caught nothing. Yet if you say so, I
will let down the nets." 6When they had
done this, they caught so many fish that
their nets were beginning to break. 7So they
signaled their partners in the other boat to
come and help them. And they came and
filled both boats, so that they began to sink.
8But when Simon Peter saw it, he fell down
at Jesus' knees, saying, "Go away from me,
Lord, for I am a sinful man!" 9For he and
all who were with him were amazed at the
catch of fish that they had taken; 10and so
also were James and John, sons of Zebedee,
who were partners with Simon. Then Jesus
said to Simon, "Do not be afraid; from now
on you will be catching people." 11When
they had brought their boats to shore, they
left everything and followed him.

12 Once, when he was in one of the cit-
ies, there was a man covered with lepro-
sy.[a] When he saw Jesus, he bowed with his
face to the ground and begged him, "Lord,
if you choose, you can make me clean."
13Then Jesus[b] stretched out his hand,
touched him, and said, "I do choose. Be
made clean." Immediately the leprosy[a] left
him. 14And he ordered him to tell no one.
"Go," he said, "and show yourself to the
priest, and, as Moses commanded, make an
offering for your cleansing, for a testimony
to them." 15But now more than ever the
word about Jesus[c] spread abroad; many
crowds would gather to hear him and to
be cured of their diseases. 16But he would
withdraw to deserted places and pray.

17 One day, while he was teaching,
Pharisees and teachers of the law were sit-
ting near by (they had come from every vil-
lage of Galilee and Judea and from Jerusa-
lem); and the power of the Lord was with
him to heal.[d] 18Just then some men came,
carrying a paralyzed man on a bed. They
were trying to bring him in and lay him
before Jesus;[c] 19but finding no way to
bring him in because of the crowd, they
went up on the roof and let him down with
his bed through the tiles into the middle of
the crowd[e] in front of Jesus. 20When he
saw their faith, he said, "Friend,[f] your sins
are forgiven you." 21Then the scribes and
the Pharisees began to question, "Who is
this who is speaking blasphemies? Who can
forgive sins but God alone?" 22When Jesus
perceived their questionings, he answered
them, "Why do you raise such questions
in your hearts? 23Which is easier, to say,
'Your sins are forgiven you,' or to say,
'Stand up and walk'? 24But so that you
may know that the Son of Man has author-
ity on earth to forgive sins"—he said to the

a The terms *leper* and *leprosy* can refer to several diseases *b* Gk *he* *c* Gk *him* *d* Other ancient authorities read *was present to heal them* *e* Gk *into the midst* *f* Gk *Man*

5.12–16: The healing of a leper (Mt 8.1–4; Mk 1.40–45). **14:** Lev 13.2–3; 14.2–32. Jesus' touching this man countered the common religious assumption that such contact rendered a person unclean. The healing demonstrates the power of God in Jesus overcoming that which was deemed unclean.

5.17–26: Healing and forgiveness of sins (Mt 9.1–8; Mk 2.1–12). **17:** The *Pharisees* were lay persons who were part of a religious movement (a sectarian group within Judaism) that was devoted to strict and faithful observance of the law of Moses. The concern of the Pharisees was with both the written form of the law and the interpretation of the law offered and preserved in oral tradition. *The law* is the law of Moses or the Torah. **19:** *Through the tiles* is Luke's adjustment of Mark's story to present a tiled roof rather than the mud-plaster roof in which Mark's account says the people "dug" a hole through which to lower the paralytic. **20:** The connection here between forgiveness of sins and healing reflects an ancient belief that sickness resulted from sin (see Ex 34.7; Jn 9.2). **21:** *Scribes,* the group called "teachers of the law" at 5.17, were Jewish specialists in the law of Moses. Luke also refers to these persons as "lawyers," e.g., 7.30. **24:** *Son of Man,* Jesus' self-designation here and in other Gospel accounts is an ambiguous title

one who was paralyzed—"I say to you,
stand up and take your bed and go to your
home." 25 Immediately he stood up before
them, took what he had been lying on,
and went to his home, glorifying God.
26 Amazement seized all of them, and they
glorified God and were filled with awe, say-
ing, "We have seen strange things today."
27 After this he went out and saw a tax
collector named Levi, sitting at the tax
booth; and he said to him, "Follow me."
28 And he got up, left everything, and fol-
lowed him.
29 Then Levi gave a great banquet for
him in his house; and there was a large
crowd of tax collectors and others sitting at
the table[a] with them. 30 The Pharisees and
their scribes were complaining to his disci-
ples, saying, "Why do you eat and drink
with tax collectors and sinners?" 31 Jesus
answered, "Those who are well have no
need of a physician, but those who are sick;
32 I have come to call not the righteous but
sinners to repentance."
33 Then they said to him, "John's disci-
ples, like the disciples of the Pharisees, fre-
quently fast and pray, but your disciples eat
and drink." 34 Jesus said to them, "You
cannot make wedding guests fast while the
bridegroom is with them, can you? 35 The
days will come when the bridegroom will
be taken away from them, and then they
will fast in those days." 36 He also told
them a parable: "No one tears a piece from
a new garment and sews it on an old gar-
ment; otherwise the new will be torn, and
the piece from the new will not match the
old. 37 And no one puts new wine into old
wineskins; otherwise the new wine will
burst the skins and will be spilled, and the
skins will be destroyed. 38 But new wine
must be put into fresh wineskins. 39 And no
one after drinking old wine desires new
wine, but says, 'The old is good.' "[b]

6 One sabbath[c] while Jesus[d] was going
through the grainfields, his disciples
plucked some heads of grain, rubbed them
in their hands, and ate them. 2 But some of
the Pharisees said, "Why are you doing
what is not lawful[e] on the sabbath?"
3 Jesus answered, "Have you not read what
David did when he and his companions
were hungry? 4 He entered the house of
God and took and ate the bread of the Pres-
ence, which it is not lawful for any but the
priests to eat, and gave some to his com-
panions?" 5 Then he said to them, "The Son
of Man is lord of the sabbath."
6 On another sabbath he entered the
synagogue and taught, and there was a man
there whose right hand was withered. 7 The
scribes and the Pharisees watched him to
see whether he would cure on the sabbath,
so that they might find an accusation
against him. 8 Even though he knew what
they were thinking, he said to the man who
had the withered hand, "Come and stand
here." He got up and stood there. 9 Then
Jesus said to them, "I ask you, is it lawful
to do good or to do harm on the sabbath,
to save life or to destroy it?" 10 After look-
ing around at all of them, he said to him,
"Stretch out your hand." He did so, and his
hand was restored. 11 But they were filled

a Gk *reclining* b Other ancient authorities read *better*; others lack verse 39 c Other ancient authorities read *On the second first sabbath* d Gk *he* e Other ancient authorities add *to do*

that can be understood either to refer to Jesus as a human being among humans (e.g., Ps 8.4; Ezek 2.1) or to identify Jesus with the apocalyptic figure of Dan 7.13–14, who was often understood to be the coming messiah and deputy of God.

5.27–32: The call of Levi (Mt 9.9–13; Mk 2.13–17). **27:** *Levi* is identified by some as Matthew (6.15; cf. Mt 10.3).

5.33–39: Debate about fasting (Mt 9.14–17; Mk 2.18–22). **36:** *Parable,* memorable word-pictures or stories that captured and communicated in sometimes cryptic form the essence of Jesus' message concerning God and God's kingdom. **39:** Found only in Luke, this saying is difficult to interpret. It may be ironic, indicating that contentment with *the old* prevents openness to the *new.*

6.1–11: Eating and healing on the sabbath (Mt 12.1–14; Mk 2.23–3.6). **2:** Harvesting violated the sabbath rest (Ex 34.21). **3:** 1 Sam 21.1–6. **4:** Lev 24.5–9. **6:** See 4.31n.

with fury and discussed with one another
what they might do to Jesus.
12 Now during those days he went out
to the mountain to pray; and he spent the
night in prayer to God. 13 And when day
came, he called his disciples and chose
twelve of them, whom he also named apos-
tles: 14 Simon, whom he named Peter, and
his brother Andrew, and James, and John,
and Philip, and Bartholomew, 15 and Mat-
thew, and Thomas, and James son of Al-
phaeus, and Simon, who was called the
Zealot, 16 and Judas son of James, and Ju-
das Iscariot, who became a traitor.
17 He came down with them and stood
on a level place, with a great crowd of his
disciples and a great multitude of people
from all Judea, Jerusalem, and the coast of
Tyre and Sidon. 18 They had come to hear
him and to be healed of their diseases; and
those who were troubled with unclean spir-
its were cured. 19 And all in the crowd were
trying to touch him, for power came out
from him and healed all of them.
20 Then he looked up at his disciples
and said:
"Blessed are you who are poor,
for yours is the kingdom of God.
21 "Blessed are you who are
hungry now,
for you will be filled.
"Blessed are you who weep now,
for you will laugh.
22 "Blessed are you when people hate
you, and when they exclude you, revile
you, and defame you[a] on account of the
Son of Man. 23 Rejoice in that day and leap
for joy, for surely your reward is great in
heaven; for that is what their ancestors did
to the prophets.
24 "But woe to you who are rich,
for you have received your
consolation.
25 "Woe to you who are full now,
for you will be hungry.
"Woe to you who are laughing now,
for you will mourn and weep.
26 "Woe to you when all speak well of
you, for that is what their ancestors did to
the false prophets.
27 "But I say to you that listen, Love
your enemies, do good to those who hate
you, 28 bless those who curse you, pray for
those who abuse you. 29 If anyone strikes

a Gk *cast out your name as evil*

6.12–16: Jesus' selection of the twelve (Mt 10.1–4; Mk 3.13–19a). Other lists of the twelve occur at Mt 10.2–4; Mk 3.16–19; Acts 1.13; while there is variation, Peter is always named first and Judas Iscariot is always named last. **13:** "The twelve" (8.1; Acts 6.2; etc.) are a recognized and remembered group in early Christianity, and Luke designates the *twelve* to be *apostles* in such a way that the two titles are strictly equated. "Apostle" (from the Gk verb "apostellein," "to send") occurs in the New Testament to designate a Christian who was commissioned to preach the gospel, essentially as a missionary. **14:** The "name" *Peter* is a nickname, meaning "rock." **15:** Zealots were a distinct faction of revolutionaries in the Jewish war with Rome of 66–70 CE, but whether this designation indicates that this *Simon* was zealous in a political fashion is debatable since it is unlikely that a Zealot party existed during Jesus' life. **16:** *Iscariot* is a peculiar term that probably means "the man from Kerioth" (see Josh 15.25); if so, then this Judas was the only Judean among the twelve.

6.17–49: The Sermon on the Plain (Mt 5–7).

6.17–19: The occasion of the preaching (Mt 4.24–5.2; Mk 3.7–13a). **18:** *Unclean spirits* designates "spirits" that are contrary to God. "Clean" and "unclean" were religious terms, not strictly descriptions of sanitary conditions, and can be understood as categories of "holiness" or "sanctity."

6.20–23: The beatitudes (Mt 5.3–12). The focus is on economic and social conditions, not spiritual states.

6.24–26: The woes. These verses provide a point-by-point antithesis to the previous statements of blessing in vv. 20–23. Again, actual circumstances are the point of Jesus' statements. In Jesus' declarations of blessings and woes, the earthly status of those addressed will be reversed in the divinely determined future.

6.27–36: The love of enemies (Mt 5.38–48; 7.12). Jesus demands love and forbids spite or retaliation.

you on the cheek, offer the other also; and
from anyone who takes away your coat do
not withhold even your shirt. 30 Give to ev-
eryone who begs from you; and if anyone
takes away your goods, do not ask for them
again. 31 Do to others as you would have
them do to you.
32 "If you love those who love you,
what credit is that to you? For even sinners
love those who love them. 33 If you do good
to those who do good to you, what credit is
that to you? For even sinners do the same.
34 If you lend to those from whom you hope
to receive, what credit is that to you? Even
sinners lend to sinners, to receive as much
again. 35 But love your enemies, do good,
and lend, expecting nothing in return.[a]
Your reward will be great, and you will be
children of the Most High; for he is kind to
the ungrateful and the wicked. 36 Be merci-
ful, just as your Father is merciful.
37 "Do not judge, and you will not be
judged; do not condemn, and you will not
be condemned. Forgive, and you will be
forgiven; 38 give, and it will be given to you.
A good measure, pressed down, shaken to-
gether, running over, will be put into your
lap; for the measure you give will be the
measure you get back."
39 He also told them a parable: "Can a
blind person guide a blind person? Will not
both fall into a pit? 40 A disciple is not
above the teacher, but everyone who is ful-
ly qualified will be like the teacher. 41 Why
do you see the speck in your neighbor's[b]
eye, but do not notice the log in your own
eye? 42 Or how can you say to your neigh-
bor,[c] 'Friend,[c] let me take out the speck
in your eye,' when you yourself do not see
the log in your own eye? You hypocrite,
first take the log out of your own eye, and
then you will see clearly to take the speck
out of your neighbor's[b] eye.
43 "No good tree bears bad fruit, nor
again does a bad tree bear good fruit; 44 for
each tree is known by its own fruit. Figs are
not gathered from thorns, nor are grapes
picked from a bramble bush. 45 The good
person out of the good treasure of the heart
produces good, and the evil person out of
evil treasure produces evil; for it is out of
the abundance of the heart that the mouth
speaks.
46 "Why do you call me 'Lord, Lord,'
and do not do what I tell you? 47 I will show
you what someone is like who comes to me,
hears my words, and acts on them. 48 That
one is like a man building a house, who dug
deeply and laid the foundation on rock;
when a flood arose, the river burst against
that house but could not shake it, because
it had been well built.[d] 49 But the one who
hears and does not act is like a man who
built a house on the ground without a foun-
dation. When the river burst against it, im-
mediately it fell, and great was the ruin of
that house."

7 After Jesus[e] had finished all his sayings
in the hearing of the people, he entered
Capernaum. 2 A centurion there had a slave
whom he valued highly, and who was ill
and close to death. 3 When he heard about

a Other ancient authorities read *despairing of no one*
b Gk *brother's* c Gk *brother* d Other ancient authorities read *founded upon the rock* e Gk *he*

28: In Luke, Jesus gives an example of this on the cross in 23.34, if that verse is authentic. **34–35:** For Israelite laws concerning loans, see Ex 22.25; Lev 25.36–37; Deut 23.19–20. **36:** Cf. Mt 5.48; God's own actions and character provide the standard.

6.37–42: On judging others (Mt 7.1–5; 12.36–37; 15.14; Mk 4.24–25). **41–42:** The form of this teaching is hyperbole.

6.43–45: The sources of good and evil (Mt 7.15–20; 12.33–35). Cf. Jas 3.11–12.

6.46–49: The wise and the foolish builders (Mt 7.21–27). Cf. Jas 1.22–25.

7.1–10: The centurion's slave (Mt 8.5–13). This story parallels the account of Peter's conversion of the Gentile centurion Cornelius, who was also generous to the Jews; see Acts 10.2,34–35. **2:** *Centurion,* an officer in charge of a company of 100 soldiers. Clearly a Gentile, this particular centurion was either an employee of Herod Antipas, a member of the Roman police force, or an official attached to the customs service. **3:** *Elders,* leaders in the Jewish community. **6:** According to Acts 10.28, the house of a Gentile

Jesus, he sent some Jewish elders to him,
asking him to come and heal his slave.
4 When they came to Jesus, they appealed to
him earnestly, saying, "He is worthy of
having you do this for him, 5 for he loves
our people, and it is he who built our syna-
gogue for us." 6 And Jesus went with them,
but when he was not far from the house,
the centurion sent friends to say to him,
"Lord, do not trouble yourself, for I am not
worthy to have you come under my roof;
7 therefore I did not presume to come to
you. But only speak the word, and let my
servant be healed. 8 For I also am a man set
under authority, with soldiers under me;
and I say to one, 'Go,' and he goes, and to
another, 'Come,' and he comes, and to my
slave, 'Do this,' and the slave does it."
9 When Jesus heard this he was amazed at
him, and turning to the crowd that fol-
lowed him, he said, "I tell you, not even in
Israel have I found such faith." 10 When
those who had been sent returned to the
house, they found the slave in good health.

11 Soon afterwards[a] he went to a town
called Nain, and his disciples and a large
crowd went with him. 12 As he approached
the gate of the town, a man who had died
was being carried out. He was his mother's
only son, and she was a widow; and with
her was a large crowd from the town.
13 When the Lord saw her, he had compas-
sion for her and said to her, "Do not
weep." 14 Then he came forward and
touched the bier, and the bearers stood still.
And he said, "Young man, I say to you,
rise!" 15 The dead man sat up and began to
speak, and Jesus[b] gave him to his mother.
16 Fear seized all of them; and they glorified
God, saying, "A great prophet has risen
among us!" and "God has looked favor-
ably on his people!" 17 This word about
him spread throughout Judea and all the
surrounding country.

18 The disciples of John reported all
these things to him. So John summoned
two of his disciples 19 and sent them to the
Lord to ask, "Are you the one who is to
come, or are we to wait for another?"
20 When the men had come to him, they
said, "John the Baptist has sent us to you to
ask, 'Are you the one who is to come, or are
we to wait for another?'" 21 Jesus[c] had
just then cured many people of diseases,
plagues, and evil spirits, and had given
sight to many who were blind. 22 And he
answered them, "Go and tell John what
you have seen and heard: the blind receive
their sight, the lame walk, the lepers[d] are
cleansed, the deaf hear, the dead are raised,
the poor have good news brought to them.
23 And blessed is anyone who takes no of-
fense at me."

24 When John's messengers had gone,
Jesus[b] began to speak to the crowds about
John:[e] "What did you go out into the wil-
derness to look at? A reed shaken by the
wind? 25 What then did you go out to see?
Someone[f] dressed in soft robes? Look,
those who put on fine clothing and live in

a Other ancient authorities read *Next day* *b* Gk *he* *c* Gk *He* *d* The terms *leper* and *leprosy* can refer to several diseases *e* Gk *him* *f* Or *Why then did you go out? To see someone*

was considered unclean, and entering such a home defiled a Jew (see also *m. Oholot* 18.7). **9:** Though Luke lacks the climactic utterance of Mt 8.13, his intent is the same: The faith of a Gentile is acceptable to Jesus (4.27; 5.32).

7.11–17: The widow's son at Nain. Cf. 1 Kings 17.17–24; 2 Kings 4.32–37; see Lk 4.25–26. **11:** *Nain,* about 37 km (23 mi) southwest of Capernaum. **12:** Cemeteries were usually located outside a city or town. **16:** Apparently the similarity of Jesus' action to that of Elijah in raising the only son of a widow of Zarephath (1 Kings 17) elicits the reaction of the crowd.

7.18–35: Jesus and John the Baptist (Mt 11.2–19). **18:** *John* the Baptist was at this time in prison (see 2.9) at Machaerus, east of the Dead Sea. **19:** *Lord,* Luke's own title for Jesus. *The one who is to come,* the messiah. **22:** This verse contains phrases from Isa 29.18; 42.18; 26.19; see also Isa 35.5–6; 61.1; Lk 4.18–19. **24–30:** Jesus' statements concerning John indicate the nature of the relationship between them. John is Jesus' precursor, the messenger mentioned in Mal 3.1 and identified in Mal 3.23 as Elijah. John, then, is an Elijah-like figure, not Elijah reincarnated. **27:** Ex 23.20; Mal 3.1. **30:** *The Pharisees and the*

luxury are in royal palaces. 26 What then
did you go out to see? A prophet? Yes, I tell
you, and more than a prophet. 27 This is the
one about whom it is written,

'See, I am sending my messenger
ahead of you,
who will prepare your way
before you.'

28 I tell you, among those born of women
no one is greater than John; yet the least in
the kingdom of God is greater than he."
29 (And all the people who heard this, in-
cluding the tax collectors, acknowledged
the justice of God,[a] because they had been
baptized with John's baptism. 30 But by re-
fusing to be baptized by him, the Pharisees
and the lawyers rejected God's purpose for
themselves.)

31 "To what then will I compare the
people of this generation, and what are
they like? 32 They are like children sitting in
the marketplace and calling to one another,

'We played the flute for you, and you
did not dance;
we wailed, and you did not weep.'

33 For John the Baptist has come eating no
bread and drinking no wine, and you say,
'He has a demon'; 34 the Son of Man has
come eating and drinking, and you say,
'Look, a glutton and a drunkard, a friend
of tax collectors and sinners!' 35 Neverthe-
less, wisdom is vindicated by all her chil-
dren."

36 One of the Pharisees asked Jesus[b] to
eat with him, and he went into the Phari-
see's house and took his place at the table.
37 And a woman in the city, who was a sin-
ner, having learned that he was eating in
the Pharisee's house, brought an alabaster
jar of ointment. 38 She stood behind him at
his feet, weeping, and began to bathe his
feet with her tears and to dry them with her
hair. Then she continued kissing his feet
and anointing them with the ointment.
39 Now when the Pharisee who had invited
him saw it, he said to himself, "If this man
were a prophet, he would have known who
and what kind of woman this is who is
touching him—that she is a sinner."
40 Jesus spoke up and said to him, "Simon,
I have something to say to you." "Teach-
er," he replied, "speak." 41 "A certain cred-
itor had two debtors; one owed five hun-
dred denarii,[c] and the other fifty. 42 When
they could not pay, he canceled the debts
for both of them. Now which of them will
love him more?" 43 Simon answered, "I
suppose the one for whom he canceled the
greater debt." And Jesus[d] said to him,
"You have judged rightly." 44 Then turning
toward the woman, he said to Simon, "Do
you see this woman? I entered your house;
you gave me no water for my feet, but she
has bathed my feet with her tears and dried
them with her hair. 45 You gave me no kiss,
but from the time I came in she has not
stopped kissing my feet. 46 You did not
anoint my head with oil, but she has
anointed my feet with ointment. 47 There-
fore, I tell you, her sins, which were many,
have been forgiven; hence she has shown
great love. But the one to whom little is
forgiven, loves little." 48 Then he said to
her, "Your sins are forgiven." 49 But those
who were at the table with him began to
say among themselves, "Who is this who
even forgives sins?" 50 And he said to the
woman, "Your faith has saved you; go in
peace."

8 Soon afterwards he went on through
cities and villages, proclaiming and

a Or *praised God* *b* Gk *him* *c* The denarius was the usual day's wage for a laborer *d* Gk *he*

lawyers are specific, not simply all, members of their classes. **33:** *Demon* possession is offered as the explanation of unconventional behavior or attitudes that were deemed unacceptable or inappropriate.

7.36–50: Simon the Pharisee, Jesus, and the woman with the ointment (Mt 26.6–13; Mk 14.3–9; Jn 12.1–8). **37:** Houses seem to have been open to intrusion of this kind (cf. Mk 1.33; 2.2). **38:** Jesus reclined at the banquet table, stretching out his feet on a couch. The motivation for the woman's anointing Jesus' feet rather than his head, which was the normal action, is uncertain. **47:** *Hence she has shown great love,* her great love proving that her many sins had been forgiven. **50:** Cf. 5.20.

8.1–3: Jesus' tour and the ministering women. These verses recall the itinerant character of Jesus'

bringing the good news of the kingdom of
God. The twelve were with him, 2 as well as
some women who had been cured of evil
spirits and infirmities: Mary, called Magda-
lene, from whom seven demons had gone
out, 3 and Joanna, the wife of Herod's stew-
ard Chuza, and Susanna, and many others,
who provided for them[a] out of their re-
sources.

4 When a great crowd gathered and peo-
ple from town after town came to him, he
said in a parable: 5 "A sower went out to
sow his seed; and as he sowed, some fell on
the path and was trampled on, and the
birds of the air ate it up. 6 Some fell on the
rock; and as it grew up, it withered for lack
of moisture. 7 Some fell among thorns, and
the thorns grew with it and choked it.
8 Some fell into good soil, and when it grew,
it produced a hundredfold." As he said this,
he called out, "Let anyone with ears to hear
listen!"

9 Then his disciples asked him what this
parable meant. 10 He said, "To you it has
been given to know the secrets[b] of the
kingdom of God; but to others I speak[c] in
parables, so that

'looking they may not perceive,
and listening they may not
understand.'

11 "Now the parable is this: The seed is
the word of God. 12 The ones on the path
are those who have heard; then the devil
comes and takes away the word from their
hearts, so that they may not believe and be
saved. 13 The ones on the rock are those
who, when they hear the word, receive it
with joy. But these have no root; they be-
lieve only for a while and in a time of test-
ing fall away. 14 As for what fell among the
thorns, these are the ones who hear; but as
they go on their way, they are choked by
the cares and riches and pleasures of life,
and their fruit does not mature. 15 But as for
that in the good soil, these are the ones
who, when they hear the word, hold it fast
in an honest and good heart, and bear fruit
with patient endurance.

16 "No one after lighting a lamp hides it
under a jar, or puts it under a bed, but puts
it on a lampstand, so that those who enter
may see the light. 17 For nothing is hidden
that will not be disclosed, nor is anything
secret that will not become known and
come to light. 18 Then pay attention to how
you listen; for to those who have, more will
be given; and from those who do not have,
even what they seem to have will be taken
away."

19 Then his mother and his brothers
came to him, but they could not reach him

a Other ancient authorities read *him* *b* Or *mysteries*
c Gk lacks *I speak*

preaching, teaching, and healing. His entourage included the unusual combination of male and female followers. Given ancient Palestinian attitudes toward women, this association of these Galilean women with Jesus' ministry is remarkable, as is the mixture of the sexes among the followers. Many of those persons mentioned here later follow Jesus to Jerusalem and witness his arrest, crucifixion, death, burial, empty tomb, and resurrection appearances. **2:** *Mary, called Magdalene,* apparently came from Magdala on the western coast of the Sea of Galilee. There is no evidence to identify her with the woman in 7.36–50. See 23.49. **3:** Herod's *steward* was probably a domestic administrator. *Others,* i.e., other women.

8.4–8: Parable of the sower (Mt 13.1–9; Mk 4.1–9).

8.9–10: Jesus' explanation of parables (Mt 13.10–17; Mk 4.1–10). **10:** Paraphrase of Isa 6.9–10. See Mk 4.11; Mt 13.11; Jer 5.21; Ezek 12.2. The meaning of the statement is enigmatic and implies that parables deliberately created obscurity while actually revealing a message.

8.11–15: Interpretation of the parable of the sower (Mt 13.18–23; Mk 4.13–20). **15:** The words *honest and good,* here spoken of the heart (cf. Mk 7.21–23), echo the classical Greek description of the true gentleman.

8.16–18: On obedient listening (Mk 4.21–25).

8.19–21: Jesus' true relatives (Mt 12.46–50; Mk 3.31–35). **19:** *Brothers,* four names are given in Mk 6.3, and there is also a mention of sisters. A variety of explanations come from the early church, usually arguing that they were sons of Joseph by a previous marriage, or that they were cousins, or that they were

because of the crowd. 20 And he was told,
"Your mother and your brothers are stand-
ing outside, wanting to see you." 21 But he
said to them, "My mother and my brothers
are those who hear the word of God and
do it."

22 One day he got into a boat with his
disciples, and he said to them, "Let us go
across to the other side of the lake." So they
put out, 23 and while they were sailing he
fell asleep. A windstorm swept down on the
lake, and the boat was filling with water,
and they were in danger. 24 They went to
him and woke him up, shouting, "Master,
Master, we are perishing!" And he woke
up and rebuked the wind and the raging
waves; they ceased, and there was a calm.
25 He said to them, "Where is your faith?"
They were afraid and amazed, and said to
one another, "Who then is this, that he
commands even the winds and the water,
and they obey him?"

26 Then they arrived at the country of
the Gerasenes,[a] which is opposite Galilee.
27 As he stepped out on land, a man of the
city who had demons met him. For a long
time he had worn[b] no clothes, and he did
not live in a house but in the tombs.
28 When he saw Jesus, he fell down before
him and shouted at the top of his voice,
"What have you to do with me, Jesus, Son
of the Most High God? I beg you, do not
torment me"— 29 for Jesus[c] had com-
manded the unclean spirit to come out of
the man. (For many times it had seized him;
he was kept under guard and bound with
chains and shackles, but he would break
the bonds and be driven by the demon into
the wilds.) 30 Jesus then asked him, "What
is your name?" He said, "Legion"; for
many demons had entered him. 31 They
begged him not to order them to go back
into the abyss.

32 Now there on the hillside a large herd
of swine was feeding; and the demons[d]
begged Jesus[e] to let them enter these. So he
gave them permission. 33 Then the demons
came out of the man and entered the swine,
and the herd rushed down the steep bank
into the lake and was drowned.

34 When the swineherds saw what had
happened, they ran off and told it in the
city and in the country. 35 Then people
came out to see what had happened, and
when they came to Jesus, they found the
man from whom the demons had gone sit-
ting at the feet of Jesus, clothed and in his
right mind. And they were afraid. 36 Those
who had seen it told them how the one who
had been possessed by demons had been
healed. 37 Then all the people of the sur-

a Other ancient authorities read *Gadarenes*; others, *Gergesenes* *b* Other ancient authorities read *a man of the city who had had demons for a long time met him. He wore* *c* Gk *he* *d* Gk *they* *e* Gk *him*

the natural children of Joseph and Mary. **21:** Luke seems to soften Mark's version of Jesus' reply, not reporting items such as Mk 3.20–21,33, so that the natural family of Jesus is not rejected as Jesus highlights the importance of obedience to God as the essential criterion for intimacy and mutual concern among Jesus' followers.

8.22–25: Winds and water obey (Mt 8.23–27; Mk 4.35–41). Power over the elements is a divine capacity often celebrated in the Psalms and other texts (see Ps 107.28–30).

8.26–39: The Gerasene demoniac (Mt 8.28–34; Mk 5.1–20). **26:** *Gerasenes,* the territory of the city of Gerasa (modern Jerash) was in central Transjordan; its population was largely non-Jewish. Mt 8.28 situates this event in Gadara, southeast of the Sea of Galilee, a setting that fits the narrative somewhat better. **30:** The inquiry after the name of the demon-possessed man probably reflects the ancient idea that knowledge of the name of a supernatural power gave one an advantage over it. *Legion,* the technical term for a division of the Roman army, usually consisting of about five thousand troops; thus the name suggests a horde of demons (see 11.24–26). **31:** *Abyss,* a place of confinement for demonic forces which, though hostile to God, are ultimately under his control (Rev 9.1–11; 11.7; 17.8; 20.1–3). The words attribute a judicial authority to Jesus (as do Mt 7.21–23; 11.20–24). **32:** *Swine,* Jews were prohibited from eating pork (Lev 11.7; Deut 14.8), but the pigs were raised for the large Gentile population that lived in sections of Palestine.

rounding country of the Gerasenes[a] asked
Jesus[b] to leave them; for they were seized
with great fear. So he got into the boat and
returned. 38 The man from whom the de-
mons had gone begged that he might be
with him; but Jesus[c] sent him away, say-
ing, 39 "Return to your home, and declare
how much God has done for you." So he
went away, proclaiming throughout the
city how much Jesus had done for him.
40 Now when Jesus returned, the crowd
welcomed him, for they were all waiting for
him. 41 Just then there came a man named
Jairus, a leader of the synagogue. He fell at
Jesus' feet and begged him to come to his
house, 42 for he had an only daughter,
about twelve years old, who was dying.
As he went, the crowds pressed in on
him. 43 Now there was a woman who had
been suffering from hemorrhages for
twelve years; and though she had spent all
she had on physicians,[d] no one could cure
her. 44 She came up behind him and
touched the fringe of his clothes, and imme-
diately her hemorrhage stopped. 45 Then
Jesus asked, "Who touched me?" When all
denied it, Peter[e] said, "Master, the crowds
surround you and press in on you." 46 But
Jesus said, "Someone touched me; for I no-
ticed that power had gone out from me."
47 When the woman saw that she could not
remain hidden, she came trembling; and
falling down before him, she declared in the
presence of all the people why she had
touched him, and how she had been imme-
diately healed. 48 He said to her, "Daugh-
ter, your faith has made you well; go in
peace."
49 While he was still speaking, someone
came from the leader's house to say, "Your
daughter is dead; do not trouble the teacher
any longer." 50 When Jesus heard this, he
replied, "Do not fear. Only believe, and she
will be saved." 51 When he came to the
house, he did not allow anyone to enter
with him, except Peter, John, and James,
and the child's father and mother. 52 They
were all weeping and wailing for her; but
he said, "Do not weep; for she is not dead
but sleeping." 53 And they laughed at him,
knowing that she was dead. 54 But he took
her by the hand and called out, "Child, get
up!" 55 Her spirit returned, and she got up
at once. Then he directed them to give her
something to eat. 56 Her parents were as-
tounded; but he ordered them to tell no one
what had happened.

9 Then Jesus[c] called the twelve together
and gave them power and authority
over all demons and to cure diseases, 2 and
he sent them out to proclaim the kingdom
of God and to heal. 3 He said to them,
"Take nothing for your journey, no staff,
nor bag, nor bread, nor money—not even
an extra tunic. 4 Whatever house you enter,
stay there, and leave from there. 5 Wherever
they do not welcome you, as you are leav-
ing that town shake the dust off your feet as
a testimony against them." 6 They departed
and went through the villages, bringing the
good news and curing diseases everywhere.
7 Now Herod the ruler[f] heard about all

a Other ancient authorities read *Gadarenes*; others, *Gergesenes* *b* Gk *him* *c* Gk *he* *d* Other ancient authorities lack *and though she had spent all she had on physicians* *e* Other ancient authorities add *and those who were with him* *f* Gk *tetrarch*

8.40–56: Jairus's daughter and the hemorrhaging woman (Mt 9.18–26; Mk 5.21–43). **41:** *Leader of the synagogue,* one who held responsibility for overseeing and arranging the worship and life of the congregation. **43:** Cf. Lev 15.25–30. Since the exact nature of this issue of blood is not specified, precise diagnoses are speculative. **55:** Cf. 1 Kings 17.22.

9.1–6: Commissioning the twelve (Mt 10.1–14; Mk 6.6b–13). The sharing of power by Jesus with the disciples indicates their continuation and extension of his ministry as seen in the preceding stories. **3:** The command to *take nothing for [the] journey* forces the twelve to rely completely on God for their ministry. **5:** The act of shaking off dust was a graphic demonstration of renunciation of further responsibility for those who did not welcome the twelve; cf. 10.10–12.

9.7–9: Herod's curiosity about Jesus (Mt 14.1–2; Mk 6.14–16). *Herod* Antipas, son of Herod the Great; see 3.1n. Cf. 9.18–19. **9:** *John I beheaded,* see Mk 6.17–29.

that had taken place, and he was perplexed,
because it was said by some that John had
been raised from the dead, 8 by some that
Elijah had appeared, and by others that one
of the ancient prophets had arisen. 9 Herod
said, "John I beheaded; but who is this
about whom I hear such things?" And he
tried to see him.
10 On their return the apostles told
Jesus[a] all they had done. He took them
with him and withdrew privately to a city
called Bethsaida. 11 When the crowds found
out about it, they followed him; and he
welcomed them, and spoke to them about
the kingdom of God, and healed those who
needed to be cured.
12 The day was drawing to a close, and
the twelve came to him and said, "Send the
crowd away, so that they may go into the
surrounding villages and countryside, to
lodge and get provisions; for we are here in
a deserted place." 13 But he said to them,
"You give them something to eat." They
said, "We have no more than five loaves
and two fish—unless we are to go and buy
food for all these people." 14 For there were
about five thousand men. And he said to
his disciples, "Make them sit down in
groups of about fifty each." 15 They did so
and made them all sit down. 16 And taking
the five loaves and the two fish, he looked
up to heaven, and blessed and broke them,
and gave them to the disciples to set before
the crowd. 17 And all ate and were filled.
What was left over was gathered up, twelve
baskets of broken pieces.
18 Once when Jesus[b] was praying
alone, with only the disciples near him, he
asked them, "Who do the crowds say that
I am?" 19 They answered, "John the Bap-
tist; but others, Elijah; and still others, that
one of the ancient prophets has arisen."
20 He said to them, "But who do you say
that I am?" Peter answered, "The Messi-
ah[c] of God."
21 He sternly ordered and commanded
them not to tell anyone, 22 saying, "The Son
of Man must undergo great suffering, and
be rejected by the elders, chief priests, and
scribes, and be killed, and on the third day
be raised."
23 Then he said to them all, "If any
want to become my followers, let them
deny themselves and take up their cross
daily and follow me. 24 For those who want
to save their life will lose it, and those who
lose their life for my sake will save it.
25 What does it profit them if they gain the
whole world, but lose or forfeit themselves?
26 Those who are ashamed of me and of my
words, of them the Son of Man will be
ashamed when he comes in his glory and
the glory of the Father and of the holy an-
gels. 27 But truly I tell you, there are some

a Gk *him* *b* Gk *he* *c* Or *The Christ*

9.10–11: The apostles' return and the crowds' following Jesus (Mt 14.12–14; Mk 6.30–34). **10:** *Bethsaida,* located just north of the Sea of Galilee.

9.12–17: Feeding of the five thousand (Mt 14.15–21; Mk 6.35–44; Jn 6.5–14). The one story from the account of Jesus' ministry that occurs in all four canonical Gospels. **16:** The language of this sentence anticipates the account of the Last Supper in 22.17–20.

9.18–20: Peter's confession (Mt 16.13–19; Mk 8.27–29). *The Messiah of God,* translates Gk "ho christos tou theou," lit. "God's anointed one," a title that typically named a royal Davidic leader who would reconstitute the former political glory of Israel for the people and the nation.

9.21–22: Jesus' command to silence and first prediction of his death (Mt 16.20–21; Mk 8.30–31). Jesus' forceful direction to silence probably reflects his attempt to prevent misunderstandings of his "messianic" work. In turn, Luke's version of this first prediction does not include the attempt of Peter to redirect Jesus' thinking and commitments, so that Peter's previous confession (9.20) maintains more force in this version of the story than in Mark's account, in which Jesus sharply rebukes him (Mk 8.32–33).

9.23–27: The requirements of discipleship (Mt 16.24–28; Mk 8.34–9.1). *Take up their cross daily and follow me,* the Greek is not cast in the plural (*any . . . their*) but in the singular ("anyone . . . her/his"), so that the challenge is intensely personal. The temporal qualifier *daily* makes clear the ongoing character of discipleship.

standing here who will not taste death be-
fore they see the kingdom of God."
28 Now about eight days after these say-
ings Jesus[a] took with him Peter and John
and James, and went up on the mountain to
pray. 29 And while he was praying, the ap-
pearance of his face changed, and his
clothes became dazzling white. 30 Suddenly
they saw two men, Moses and Elijah, talk-
ing to him. 31 They appeared in glory and
were speaking of his departure, which he
was about to accomplish at Jerusalem.
32 Now Peter and his companions were
weighed down with sleep; but since they
had stayed awake,[b] they saw his glory and
the two men who stood with him. 33 Just as
they were leaving him, Peter said to Jesus,
"Master, it is good for us to be here; let us
make three dwellings,[c] one for you, one
for Moses, and one for Elijah"—not know-
ing what he said. 34 While he was saying
this, a cloud came and overshadowed them;
and they were terrified as they entered the
cloud. 35 Then from the cloud came a voice
that said, "This is my Son, my Chosen;[d]
listen to him!" 36 When the voice had spo-
ken, Jesus was found alone. And they kept
silent and in those days told no one any of
the things they had seen.
37 On the next day, when they had
come down from the mountain, a great
crowd met him. 38 Just then a man from the
crowd shouted, "Teacher, I beg you to look
at my son; he is my only child. 39 Suddenly
a spirit seizes him, and all at once he[e]
shrieks. It convulses him until he foams at
the mouth; it mauls him and will scarcely
leave him. 40 I begged your disciples to cast
it out, but they could not." 41 Jesus an-
swered, "You faithless and perverse gener-
ation, how much longer must I be with you
and bear with you? Bring your son here."
42 While he was coming, the demon dashed
him to the ground in convulsions. But Jesus
rebuked the unclean spirit, healed the boy,
and gave him back to his father. 43 And all
were astounded at the greatness of God.
While everyone was amazed at all that he
was doing, he said to his disciples, 44 "Let
these words sink into your ears: The Son of
Man is going to be betrayed into human
hands." 45 But they did not understand this
saying; its meaning was concealed from
them, so that they could not perceive it.
And they were afraid to ask him about this
saying.
46 An argument arose among them as to
which one of them was the greatest. 47 But
Jesus, aware of their inner thoughts, took a
little child and put it by his side, 48 and said

a Gk *he* *b* Or *but when they were fully awake* *c* Or *tents* *d* Other ancient authorities read *my Beloved* *e* Or *it*

9.28–36: The Transfiguration (Mt 17.1–9; Mk 9.2–10). This account recalls an intense religious experience, the exact nature of which is uncertain. The aura of unnatural brilliance is associated with mystical experiences elsewhere (Ex 34.29–35; Mt 17.9; Acts 9.3). **28:** *About eight days,* may merely indicate the passage of a week, but in the early church "the eighth day" became a designation for both the Lord's day and the day of Jesus' resurrection, the first day of a new creation. **30:** *Moses and Elijah,* two paragons of the faith of Israel: Moses was the lawgiver and Elijah the great prophet. **31:** *Departure,* lit. "exodus," probably referring to Jesus' death, resurrection, and ascension. **32:** The sleepy condition of the disciples may indicate that this event transpired at night, though not necessarily (cf. 22.45). **33:** Peter's suggestion concerning *three dwellings* demonstrates his desire to preserve the experience. **35:** The *voice* is clearly that of God (see 3.22), and the command, *listen to him,* focuses the attention and obedience of the disciples on Jesus above all others.

9.37–43a: Jesus heals an afflicted boy (Mt 17.14–21; Mk 9.14–29). The description of the boy's malady leads some scholars to conclude that the boy had epilepsy, but any diagnosis is speculative.

9.43b–45: A second prediction (Mt 17.22–23; Mk 9.30–32). Cf. 9.22; 18.31–33. **44:** 9.22; 18.31–34; 17.25. **45:** The comment is based on the view that (a) the messiah's death was not part of the disciples' Jewish faith, and (b) spiritual truth must be revealed (see 24.16).

9.46–48: True greatness (Mt 18.1–5; Mk 9.33–37). An acted parable rejecting sheer self-centered ambition. **47:** The reception of the *little child* requires generosity without expectation of gain.

to them, "Whoever welcomes this child in
my name welcomes me, and whoever wel-
comes me welcomes the one who sent me;
for the least among all of you is the great-
est."
49 John answered, "Master, we saw
someone casting out demons in your name,
and we tried to stop him, because he does
not follow with us." 50 But Jesus said to
him, "Do not stop him; for whoever is not
against you is for you."

51 When the days drew near for him to
be taken up, he set his face to go to Jerusa-
lem. 52 And he sent messengers ahead of
him. On their way they entered a village
of the Samaritans to make ready for him;
53 but they did not receive him, because his
face was set toward Jerusalem. 54 When his
disciples James and John saw it, they said,
"Lord, do you want us to command fire
to come down from heaven and consume
them?"[a] 55 But he turned and rebuked
them. 56 Then[b] they went on to another
village.
57 As they were going along the road,
someone said to him, "I will follow you
wherever you go." 58 And Jesus said to him,
"Foxes have holes, and birds of the air have
nests; but the Son of Man has nowhere to
lay his head." 59 To another he said, "Fol-
low me." But he said, "Lord, first let me go
and bury my father." 60 But Jesus[c] said to
him, "Let the dead bury their own dead;
but as for you, go and proclaim the king-
dom of God." 61 Another said, "I will fol-
low you, Lord; but let me first say farewell
to those at my home." 62 Jesus said to him,
"No one who puts a hand to the plow and
looks back is fit for the kingdom of God."

10 After this the Lord appointed seven-
ty[d] others and sent them on ahead
of him in pairs to every town and place
where he himself intended to go. 2 He said
to them, "The harvest is plentiful, but the
laborers are few; therefore ask the Lord of
the harvest to send out laborers into his
harvest. 3 Go on your way. See, I am send-
ing you out like lambs into the midst of
wolves. 4 Carry no purse, no bag, no san-
dals; and greet no one on the road. 5 What-
ever house you enter, first say, 'Peace to

a Other ancient authorities add *as Elijah did*
b Other ancient authorities read *rebuked them, and said, "You do not know what spirit you are of, 56for the Son of Man has not come to destroy the lives of human beings but to save them." Then*
c Gk *he*
d Other ancient authorities read *seventy-two*

9.49–50: The unknown exorcist (Mk 9.38–41). This incident records Jesus' repudiation of intolerance, though contrast the statement in 11.23, which indicates the necessity of aligning actions and concerns with Jesus' values and work.

9.51–19.27: Jesus' journey to Jerusalem with his followers (Mt 19.1–20.34; Mk 10.1–52). This section, most of which is found only in Luke, reports the ministry of Jesus in Samaria and Judea.

9.51: Jesus' resolve to go to Jerusalem (Mt 19.1–2; Mk 10.1). *To be taken up,* explicitly refers to the ascension, but probably also designates Jesus' suffering, death, and resurrection that led to his departure into heaven. *He set his face to go to Jerusalem,* states Jesus' resolve using a Semitic idiom (see Isa 50.7).

9.52–56: Samaritans' rejection of Jesus. 52–53: The Samaritans did not help pilgrims going to keep a feast at what they regarded as the wrong sanctuary (cf. Jn 4.20). **52:** *Samaritan* is a geographical designation used also to name an inhabitant of Samaria, which was originally the capital of the former Northern Kingdom that fell to the Assyrians ca. 722 BCE. *Samaritan* became a term for persons living between Judea and Galilee who came to be regarded as a distinct ethnic and religious group. Tensions existed between Samaritans and Jews after the return of the Jews from exile in Babylon and remained, as this story recognizes, in Jesus' day. **54:** Incorporates wordings parallel to 2 Kings 1.10–12. Elijah had called down fire from heaven on hostile troops (see 2 Kings 1.9–16).

9.57–62: The demands of following Jesus (Mt 18.18–22). **59:** From the statement that follows (v. 60), the man's father was almost certainly not yet dead; rather, the man used this responsibility to procrastinate complete commitment to discipleship. **60:** *Let the dead bury their own dead,* suggests that the spiritually dead should be left to bury the physically dead. **61:** See 1 Kings 19.20.

10.1–12: The mission of the seventy (Mt 9.37–38; 10.7–16). **1:** 9.1–5,51–52; Mk 6.7–11. **4:** *Greet no*

this house!' 6 And if anyone is there who
shares in peace, your peace will rest on that
person; but if not, it will return to you.
7 Remain in the same house, eating and
drinking whatever they provide, for the la-
borer deserves to be paid. Do not move
about from house to house. 8 Whenever you
enter a town and its people welcome you,
eat what is set before you; 9 cure the sick
who are there, and say to them, 'The king-
dom of God has come near to you.'[a] 10 But
whenever you enter a town and they do not
welcome you, go out into its streets and
say, 11 'Even the dust of your town that
clings to our feet, we wipe off in protest
against you. Yet know this: the kingdom of
God has come near.'[b] 12 I tell you, on that
day it will be more tolerable for Sodom
than for that town.

13 "Woe to you, Chorazin! Woe to you,
Bethsaida! For if the deeds of power done
in you had been done in Tyre and Sidon,
they would have repented long ago, sitting
in sackcloth and ashes. 14 But at the judg-
ment it will be more tolerable for Tyre and
Sidon than for you. 15 And you, Caper-
naum,

will you be exalted to heaven?
No, you will be brought down
to Hades.

16 "Whoever listens to you listens to
me, and whoever rejects you rejects me,
and whoever rejects me rejects the one who
sent me."

17 The seventy[c] returned with joy, say-
ing, "Lord, in your name even the demons
submit to us!" 18 He said to them, "I
watched Satan fall from heaven like a flash
of lightning. 19 See, I have given you au-
thority to tread on snakes and scorpions,
and over all the power of the enemy; and
nothing will hurt you. 20 Nevertheless, do
not rejoice at this, that the spirits submit to
you, but rejoice that your names are writ-
ten in heaven."

21 At that same hour Jesus[d] rejoiced in
the Holy Spirit[e] and said, "I thank[f] you,
Father, Lord of heaven and earth, because
you have hidden these things from the wise
and the intelligent and have revealed them
to infants; yes, Father, for such was your
gracious will.[g] 22 All things have been
handed over to me by my Father; and no
one knows who the Son is except the Fa-
ther, or who the Father is except the Son
and anyone to whom the Son chooses to
reveal him."

23 Then turning to the disciples, Jesus[d]
said to them privately, "Blessed are the eyes
that see what you see! 24 For I tell you that
many prophets and kings desired to see
what you see, but did not see it, and to hear
what you hear, but did not hear it."

25 Just then a lawyer stood up to test
Jesus.[h] "Teacher," he said, "what must I

a Or *is at hand for you* *b* Or *is at hand* *c* Other ancient authorities read *seventy-two* *d* Gk *he*
e Other authorities read *in the spirit* *f* Or *praise*
g Or *for so it was well-pleasing in your sight*
h Gk *him*

one, which might cause delay; thus underscoring the urgency of the mission. **5:** 1 Sam 25.6. **7:** Deut 24.15. **10–11:** Cf. 9.5n. **12:** Gen 19.24–28.

10.13–15: Woes to unrepentant cities (Mt 11.20–24). **13:** *Chorazin,* a town 3 km (2 mi) north of Capernaum. Tyre and Sidon were Gentile cities on the Mediterranean coast north of Galilee. *Sackcloth and ashes* recalls the repentance of Nineveh in Jon 3. **15:** The words echo Isa 14.13–15 (see v. 18).

10.16: Jesus' interpretation of the mission (Mt 10.40).

10.17–20: Return of the seventy (Mt 11.25–27). **17:** *Even the demons submit to us,* unlike the twelve (9.1), the seventy had not been promised this power. **18:** *I watched Satan fall from heaven,* alluding to the victory of the seventy over the demons; cf. Isa 14.15; Jn 12.31; Rev 12.7–12. **20:** Jesus did not regard exorcism in itself as a sign of God's kingdom (11.19). *Written in heaven,* Dan 12.1; Ps 69.28; Ex 32.32.

10.21–22: Jesus' thanksgiving to God (Mt 11.25–27). **21:** *In the Holy Spirit,* in communion with God.

10.23–24: Jesus' blessing of the disciples (Mt 13.16–17).

10.25–28: A lawyer's question (Mt 22.34–40; Mk 12.28–34; cf. Lk 18.9–14). **25:** *Lawyer,* an expert in the law of Moses, probably synonymous with "scribe" and likely affiliated with or belonging to the party of the Pharisees. **27:** Deut 6.5; Lev 19.18.

do to inherit eternal life?" 26 He said to
him, "What is written in the law? What do
you read there?" 27 He answered, "You
shall love the Lord your God with all your
heart, and with all your soul, and with all
your strength, and with all your mind; and
your neighbor as yourself." 28 And he said
to him, "You have given the right answer;
do this, and you will live."

29 But wanting to justify himself, he
asked Jesus, "And who is my neighbor?"
30 Jesus replied, "A man was going down
from Jerusalem to Jericho, and fell into the
hands of robbers, who stripped him, beat
him, and went away, leaving him half dead.
31 Now by chance a priest was going down
that road; and when he saw him, he passed
by on the other side. 32 So likewise a Levite,
when he came to the place and saw him,
passed by on the other side. 33 But a Samari-
tan while traveling came near him; and
when he saw him, he was moved with pity.
34 He went to him and bandaged his
wounds, having poured oil and wine on
them. Then he put him on his own animal,
brought him to an inn, and took care of
him. 35 The next day he took out two de-
narii,[a] gave them to the innkeeper, and
said, 'Take care of him; and when I come
back, I will repay you whatever more you
spend.' 36 Which of these three, do you
think, was a neighbor to the man who fell
into the hands of the robbers?" 37 He said,
"The one who showed him mercy." Jesus
said to him, "Go and do likewise."

38 Now as they went on their way, he
entered a certain village, where a woman
named Martha welcomed him into her
home. 39 She had a sister named Mary, who
sat at the Lord's feet and listened to what
he was saying. 40 But Martha was distract-
ed by her many tasks; so she came to him
and asked, "Lord, do you not care that my
sister has left me to do all the work by my-
self? Tell her then to help me." 41 But the
Lord answered her, "Martha, Martha, you
are worried and distracted by many things;
42 there is need of only one thing.[b] Mary
has chosen the better part, which will not
be taken away from her."

11 He was praying in a certain place,
and after he had finished, one of his
disciples said to him, "Lord, teach us to
pray, as John taught his disciples." 2 He
said to them, "When you pray, say:

Father,[c] hallowed be your name.
Your kingdom come.[d]
3 Give us each day our daily bread.[e]
4 And forgive us our sins,
for we ourselves forgive everyone
indebted to us.

a The denarius was the usual day's wage for a laborer
b Other ancient authorities read *few things are necessary, or only one*
c Other ancient authorities read *Our Father in heaven*
d A few ancient authorities read *Your Holy Spirit come upon us and cleanse us.* Other ancient authorities add *Your will be done, on earth as in heaven*
e Or *our bread for tomorrow*

10.29–37: Parable of the Good Samaritan. 29: *Justify himself* means to show himself to be righteous, acceptable to God. **30:** *Down from Jerusalem to Jericho,* about 30 km (18 mi) with a drop in elevation from about 760 m (2,500 ft) to about 250 m (820 ft) below sea level. The road between the cities was notoriously dangerous. **31–33:** The *priest* represented the highest religious leadership among the Jews; the *Levite* (v. 32) was the designated lay associate of the priest. In contrast, it was a *Samaritan* (see 9.52n.), a foreigner not expected to show sympathy to Jews, who was moved with pity. **34:** The *oil* served as a salve (see Isa 1.6) and the *wine* as an antiseptic. **35:** *Two denarii* would provide approximately two months of lodging in an ancient inn.

10.38–42: Martha and Mary. This enigmatic account affirms the importance of listening to Jesus and at the same time the account shows Jesus' openness to and acceptance of women among his followers. According to Jn 11.1, Martha and Mary were the sisters of Lazarus and lived in Bethany, just east of Jerusalem.

11.1–4: The Lord's Prayer (Mt 6.9–13). This model prayer appears in a more elaborate form in Matthew. In both Matthew and Luke there is an eschatological cast to the petitions. Yet the concerns registered are related to daily life.

And do not bring us to the time of
trial."[a]
5 And he said to them, "Suppose one of
you has a friend, and you go to him at mid-
night and say to him, 'Friend, lend me three
loaves of bread; 6 for a friend of mine has
arrived, and I have nothing to set before
him.' 7 And he answers from within, 'Do
not bother me; the door has already been
locked, and my children are with me in bed;
I cannot get up and give you anything.' 8 I
tell you, even though he will not get up and
give him anything because he is his friend,
at least because of his persistence he will get
up and give him whatever he needs.
9 "So I say to you, Ask, and it will be
given you; search, and you will find; knock,
and the door will be opened for you. 10 For
everyone who asks receives, and everyone
who searches finds, and for everyone who
knocks, the door will be opened. 11 Is there
anyone among you who, if your child asks
for[b] a fish, will give a snake instead of a
fish? 12 Or if the child asks for an egg, will
give a scorpion? 13 If you then, who are evil,
know how to give good gifts to your chil-
dren, how much more will the heavenly Fa-
ther give the Holy Spirit[c] to those who ask
him!"
14 Now he was casting out a demon
that was mute; when the demon had gone
out, the one who had been mute spoke, and
the crowds were amazed. 15 But some of
them said, "He casts out demons by Beelze-
bul, the ruler of the demons." 16 Others, to
test him, kept demanding from him a sign
from heaven. 17 But he knew what they
were thinking and said to them, "Every
kingdom divided against itself becomes a
desert, and house falls on house. 18 If Satan
also is divided against himself, how will his
kingdom stand?—for you say that I cast
out the demons by Beelzebul. 19 Now if I
cast out the demons by Beelzebul, by whom
do your exorcists[d] cast them out? There-
fore they will be your judges. 20 But if it is
by the finger of God that I cast out the
demons, then the kingdom of God has
come to you. 21 When a strong man, fully
armed, guards his castle, his property is
safe. 22 But when one stronger than he at-
tacks him and overpowers him, he takes
away his armor in which he trusted and
divides his plunder. 23 Whoever is not with
me is against me, and whoever does not
gather with me scatters.
24 "When the unclean spirit has gone
out of a person, it wanders through water-
less regions looking for a resting place, but
not finding any, it says, 'I will return to
my house from which I came.' 25 When it
comes, it finds it swept and put in order.
26 Then it goes and brings seven other spir-
its more evil than itself, and they enter and
live there; and the last state of that person
is worse than the first."
27 While he was saying this, a woman in
the crowd raised her voice and said to him,
"Blessed is the womb that bore you and the
breasts that nursed you!" 28 But he said,
"Blessed rather are those who hear the
word of God and obey it!"

a Or *us into temptation.* Other ancient authorities add *but rescue us from the evil one* (or *from evil*)
b Other ancient authorities add *bread, will give a stone; or if your child asks for*
c Other ancient authorities read *the Father give the Holy Spirit from heaven*
d Gk *sons*

11.5–8: Teaching about persistence (Mt 7.7–11). Cf. Lk 18.1–5.

11.9–13: A parabolic admonition and assurance concerning prayer (Mt 7.7–11).

11.14–23: The Beelzebul controversy (Mt 12.22–30; Mk 3.22–27). **15:** *Beelzebul, the ruler of the demons,* Satan (see v. 18); Beelzebul was originally a title of the Canaanite storm and fertility god Baal (see 2 Kings 1.2). **16:** The request for a sign comes almost immediately after Jesus restores the power of speech to one afflicted with muteness. **20:** Ex 8.19. *Finger* stands for God's power. *The kingdom of God has come to you* indicates Jesus' interpretation of the meaning of his ministry. **23:** Cf. 9.50. This statement registers the uncompromising demands of Jesus' call to discipleship, and in relation to the preceding parable the saying declares that in the struggle between Jesus and Beelzebul neutrality is not an option.

11.24–26: The return of unclean spirits (Mt 12.43–45).

11.27–28: True blessedness. Cf. 8.21.

29 When the crowds were increasing, he
began to say, "This generation is an evil
generation; it asks for a sign, but no sign
will be given to it except the sign of Jonah.
30 For just as Jonah became a sign to the
people of Nineveh, so the Son of Man will
be to this generation. 31 The queen of the
South will rise at the judgment with the
people of this generation and condemn
them, because she came from the ends of
the earth to listen to the wisdom of Solo-
mon, and see, something greater than Solo-
mon is here! 32 The people of Nineveh will
rise up at the judgment with this generation
and condemn it, because they repented at
the proclamation of Jonah, and see, some-
thing greater than Jonah is here!

33 "No one after lighting a lamp puts it
in a cellar,[a] but on the lampstand so that
those who enter may see the light. 34 Your
eye is the lamp of your body. If your eye is
healthy, your whole body is full of light;
but if it is not healthy, your body is full of
darkness. 35 Therefore consider whether the
light in you is not darkness. 36 If then your
whole body is full of light, with no part of
it in darkness, it will be as full of light as
when a lamp gives you light with its rays."

37 While he was speaking, a Pharisee in-
vited him to dine with him; so he went in
and took his place at the table. 38 The Phar-
isee was amazed to see that he did not first
wash before dinner. 39 Then the Lord said
to him, "Now you Pharisees clean the out-
side of the cup and of the dish, but inside
you are full of greed and wickedness.
40 You fools! Did not the one who made the
outside make the inside also? 41 So give for
alms those things that are within; and see,
everything will be clean for you.

42 "But woe to you Pharisees! For you
tithe mint and rue and herbs of all kinds,
and neglect justice and the love of God; it is
these you ought to have practiced, without
neglecting the others. 43 Woe to you Phari-
sees! For you love to have the seat of honor
in the synagogues and to be greeted with
respect in the marketplaces. 44 Woe to you!
For you are like unmarked graves, and peo-
ple walk over them without realizing it."

45 One of the lawyers answered him,
"Teacher, when you say these things, you
insult us too." 46 And he said, "Woe also to
you lawyers! For you load people with bur-
dens hard to bear, and you yourselves do
not lift a finger to ease them. 47 Woe to you!
For you build the tombs of the prophets
whom your ancestors killed. 48 So you are
witnesses and approve of the deeds of your
ancestors; for they killed them, and you
build their tombs. 49 Therefore also the
Wisdom of God said, 'I will send them
prophets and apostles, some of whom they
will kill and persecute,' 50 so that this gener-
ation may be charged with the blood of all
the prophets shed since the foundation of
the world, 51 from the blood of Abel to the

a Other ancient authorities add *or under the bushel basket*

11.29–32: The sign of Jonah (Mt 12.38–42; Mk 8.11–12). **29:** *The sign of Jonah* was given through Jonah's preaching to the Ninevites; here, Jesus is not referring to his resurrection. **30:** Jon 3.4. **31:** 1 Kings 10.1–10; 2 Chr 9.1–9.

11.33: Light and sight (Mt 5.15; Mk 4.21). Cf. 8.16.

11.34–36: The healthy eye (Mt 6.22–23).

11.37–54: Sayings against Pharisees and lawyers (Mt 15.1–9; Mk 7.1–9; Mt 23.1–36, in different order). **37:** 7.36; 14.1. **38:** *Wash before dinner,* ceremonial washing (lit. "baptize before dinner"; cf. Mk 7.1–5). **39–41:** Mt 23.25–26. Jesus turns back the Pharisees' criticism that the outside is unwashed by insisting that the inner life is equal in importance to the outer (v. 40), indeed, that it exercises a cleansing or corrupting power over the outer (v. 41; Mk 7.23). **42:** *Tithe,* see Deut 14.22–29. *Mint and rue* were common herbs of little value. **44:** Graves were carefully marked and even whitewashed (Mt 23.27) to prevent defilement through unintentional contact with the dead. **49:** *The Wisdom of God said,* introduces an apparent quotation, but from neither the Hebrew Bible nor the nonbiblical writings of Judaism. **51:** *Abel* is the first person murdered in the Bible (Gen 4.8), and *Zechariah* seems to be the person murdered in 2 Chr 24.20–22. **54:** Cf. 6.11; 19.47–48; 20.19–20; 22.2.

blood of Zechariah, who perished between
the altar and the sanctuary. Yes, I tell you,
it will be charged against this generation.
52 Woe to you lawyers! For you have taken
away the key of knowledge; you did not
enter yourselves, and you hindered those
who were entering."
53 When he went outside, the scribes
and the Pharisees began to be very hostile
toward him and to cross-examine him
about many things, 54 lying in wait for him,
to catch him in something he might say.

12 Meanwhile, when the crowd gath-
ered by the thousands, so that they
trampled on one another, he began to
speak first to his disciples, "Beware of the
yeast of the Pharisees, that is, their hypocri-
sy. 2 Nothing is covered up that will not be
uncovered, and nothing secret that will not
become known. 3 Therefore whatever you
have said in the dark will be heard in the
light, and what you have whispered behind
closed doors will be proclaimed from the
housetops.
4 "I tell you, my friends, do not fear
those who kill the body, and after that can
do nothing more. 5 But I will warn you
whom to fear: fear him who, after he has
killed, has authority[a] to cast into hell.[b]
Yes, I tell you, fear him! 6 Are not five spar-
rows sold for two pennies? Yet not one of
them is forgotten in God's sight. 7 But even
the hairs of your head are all counted. Do
not be afraid; you are of more value than
many sparrows.
8 "And I tell you, everyone who ac-
knowledges me before others, the Son of
Man also will acknowledge before the an-
gels of God; 9 but whoever denies me before
others will be denied before the angels of
God. 10 And everyone who speaks a word
against the Son of Man will be forgiven;
but whoever blasphemes against the Holy
Spirit will not be forgiven. 11 When they
bring you before the synagogues, the rulers,
and the authorities, do not worry about
how[c] you are to defend yourselves or what
you are to say; 12 for the Holy Spirit will
teach you at that very hour what you ought
to say."
13 Someone in the crowd said to him,
"Teacher, tell my brother to divide the fam-
ily inheritance with me." 14 But he said to
him, "Friend, who set me to be a judge
or arbitrator over you?" 15 And he said to
them, "Take care! Be on your guard against
all kinds of greed; for one's life does not
consist in the abundance of possessions."
16 Then he told them a parable: "The land
of a rich man produced abundantly. 17 And
he thought to himself, 'What should I do,
for I have no place to store my crops?'
18 Then he said, 'I will do this: I will pull
down my barns and build larger ones, and
there I will store all my grain and my
goods. 19 And I will say to my soul, Soul,
you have ample goods laid up for many
years; relax, eat, drink, be merry.' 20 But
God said to him, 'You fool! This very night

a Or *power* *b* Gk *Gehenna* *c* Other ancient authorities add *or what*

12.1: The yeast of the Pharisees (Mt 16.5–6; Mk 8.14–15).

12.2–9: Calls to fearless confession (Mt 10.26–33). **5:** *Him who . . . has authority to cast into hell,* God alone. *Hell* is "Gehenna," not Hades; Gehenna was a deep ravine to the south of Jerusalem. Human sacrifices were allegedly made there during the Judean monarchy (2 Kings 23.10), and it came to symbolize the place of eternal punishment. **6:** The *penny* ("assarion") was one-sixteenth of a denarius (see 12.59n.). **8–9:** Cf. Mk 8.38.

12.10: Blaspheming the Holy Spirit (Mt 12.31–32; Mk 3.28–30). Blasphemy *against the Holy Spirit* is attributing the genuine work of the Spirit to the forces of evil rather than to God.

12.11–12: Aid from the Holy Spirit (Mt 10.19–20; Mk 13.11).

12.13–15: Warning against greed. 13: According to Deut 21.17 the oldest son received double the younger's share. Jesus shows no interest in ensuring equitable division and subsequently warns against greed and material self-satisfaction.

12.16–21: Parable of the rich fool. 19: *Eat, drink, be merry,* see Eccl 8.15. **20:** Cf. Jer 17.11; Lk 12.33–34. The declaration by God in Greek is difficult, reading literally, "Fool! In this night your soul

your life is being demanded of you. And the
things you have prepared, whose will they
be?' 21 So it is with those who store up trea-
sures for themselves but are not rich to-
ward God."
22 He said to his disciples, "Therefore I
tell you, do not worry about your life, what
you will eat, or about your body, what you
will wear. 23 For life is more than food, and
the body more than clothing. 24 Consider
the ravens: they neither sow nor reap, they
have neither storehouse nor barn, and yet
God feeds them. Of how much more value
are you than the birds! 25 And can any of
you by worrying add a single hour to your
span of life?[a] 26 If then you are not able to
do so small a thing as that, why do you
worry about the rest? 27 Consider the lilies,
how they grow: they neither toil nor spin;[b]
yet I tell you, even Solomon in all his glory
was not clothed like one of these. 28 But if
God so clothes the grass of the field, which
is alive today and tomorrow is thrown into
the oven, how much more will he clothe
you—you of little faith! 29 And do not keep
striving for what you are to eat and what
you are to drink, and do not keep worry-
ing. 30 For it is the nations of the world that
strive after all these things, and your Father
knows that you need them. 31 Instead, strive
for his[c] kingdom, and these things will be
given to you as well.
32 "Do not be afraid, little flock, for it is
your Father's good pleasure to give you the
kingdom. 33 Sell your possessions, and give
alms. Make purses for yourselves that do
not wear out, an unfailing treasure in heav-
en, where no thief comes near and no moth
destroys. 34 For where your treasure is,
there your heart will be also.
35 "Be dressed for action and have your
lamps lit; 36 be like those who are waiting
for their master to return from the wedding
banquet, so that they may open the door
for him as soon as he comes and knocks.
37 Blessed are those slaves whom the master
finds alert when he comes; truly I tell you,
he will fasten his belt and have them sit
down to eat, and he will come and serve
them. 38 If he comes during the middle of
the night, or near dawn, and finds them so,
blessed are those slaves.
39 "But know this: if the owner of the
house had known at what hour the thief
was coming, he[d] would not have let his
house be broken into. 40 You also must be
ready, for the Son of Man is coming at an
unexpected hour."
41 Peter said, "Lord, are you telling this
parable for us or for everyone?" 42 And the
Lord said, "Who then is the faithful and
prudent manager whom his master will put
in charge of his slaves, to give them their
allowance of food at the proper time?
43 Blessed is that slave whom his master will
find at work when he arrives. 44 Truly I tell
you, he will put that one in charge of all his
possessions. 45 But if that slave says to him-
self, 'My master is delayed in coming,' and
if he begins to beat the other slaves, men
and women, and to eat and drink and get
drunk, 46 the master of that slave will come
on a day when he does not expect him and
at an hour that he does not know, and will
cut him in pieces,[e] and put him with the
unfaithful. 47 That slave who knew what
his master wanted, but did not prepare

a Or *add a cubit to your stature* *b* Other ancient authorities read *Consider the lilies; they neither spin nor weave* *c* Other ancient authorities read *God's* *d* Other ancient authorities add *would have watched and* *e* Or *cut him off*

they demand from you." The subject "they" may be a circumlocution for God, but more likely it is "the things" that now own the man and that claim his life.

12.22–32: Anxiety concerning life (Mt 6.25–34). **27:** See 1 Kings 10. **32:** *Flock* refers to the messiah's people (Ezek 34.23).

12.33–34: Treasure in heaven (Mt 6.19–21). Compare Mk 10.21; Lk 18.22; Acts 2.45; 4.32–35.

12.35–48: Sayings on watchfulness and faithfulness (Mt 24.42–51). **35:** *Dressed for action,* lit. "your loins girded"; see Ex 12.11. **37:** The language suggests the messianic banquet (13.29; 14.15; 22.16), to which a marriage feast served as an analogy. For the action of this master in serving the servants, see 17.7–8; cf. Jn 13.3–16; Lk 22.27. **48:** 8.18; 19.26.

himself or do what was wanted, will receive
a severe beating. 48 But the one who did not
know and did what deserved a beating will
receive a light beating. From everyone to
whom much has been given, much will be
required; and from the one to whom much
has been entrusted, even more will be de-
manded.
49 "I came to bring fire to the earth, and
how I wish it were already kindled! 50 I
have a baptism with which to be baptized,
and what stress I am under until it is com-
pleted! 51 Do you think that I have come to
bring peace to the earth? No, I tell you, but
rather division! 52 From now on five in one
household will be divided, three against
two and two against three; 53 they will be
divided:

father against son
  and son against father,
mother against daughter
  and daughter against mother,
mother-in-law against her
    daughter-in-law
  and daughter-in-law against
    mother-in-law."

54 He also said to the crowds, "When
you see a cloud rising in the west, you im-
mediately say, 'It is going to rain'; and so it
happens. 55 And when you see the south
wind blowing, you say, 'There will be
scorching heat'; and it happens. 56 You
hypocrites! You know how to interpret the
appearance of earth and sky, but why do
you not know how to interpret the present
time?
57 "And why do you not judge for your-
selves what is right? 58 Thus, when you go
with your accuser before a magistrate, on
the way make an effort to settle the case,[a]
or you may be dragged before the judge,
and the judge hand you over to the officer,
and the officer throw you in prison. 59 I tell
you, you will never get out until you have
paid the very last penny."

13 At that very time there were some
present who told him about the
Galileans whose blood Pilate had mingled
with their sacrifices. 2 He asked them, "Do
you think that because these Galileans suf-
fered in this way they were worse sinners
than all other Galileans? 3 No, I tell you;
but unless you repent, you will all perish
as they did. 4 Or those eighteen who were
killed when the tower of Siloam fell on
them—do you think that they were worse
offenders than all the others living in Jeru-
salem? 5 No, I tell you; but unless you re-
pent, you will all perish just as they did."
6 Then he told this parable: "A man had
a fig tree planted in his vineyard; and he
came looking for fruit on it and found
none. 7 So he said to the gardener, 'See here!
For three years I have come looking for
fruit on this fig tree, and still I find none.
Cut it down! Why should it be wasting the
soil?' 8 He replied, 'Sir, let it alone for one
more year, until I dig around it and put
manure on it. 9 If it bears fruit next year,
well and good; but if not, you can cut it
down.'"
10 Now he was teaching in one of the

a Gk *settle with him*

12.49–53: The controversial character of Jesus' mission (Mt 10.34–36). **49:** *Fire,* a symbol of judgment (Mt 3.11; 7.19; Mk 9.48; Lk 3.16). **50:** *Baptism,* Jesus' death. **53:** Incorporates phrases from Mic 7.6.

12.54–56: Interpreting the times (Mt 16.2–3). Winds from the west blew off the Mediterranean, those from the south off the desert. Jesus says there are signs of crisis that human beings neglect.

12.57–59: Settling with an accuser (Mt 5.25–26). **59:** *Penny,* Greek "lepton," the smallest Greek coin in circulation. There were two lepta to a quadrans ("penny" in Mt 5.26; Mk 12.42), eight to an assarion ("penny" in Lk 12.6), and one hundred twenty-eight to a denarius, the daily wage in Mt 20.2.

13.1–9: Parable of the unfruitful fig tree (compare Mt 21.18–19; Mk 11.12–14). **1:** The Galileans had been slain by the order of Pilate (see 3.1n.) while sacrificing in the Temple at Jerusalem. This incident is otherwise unattested. **2:** The reports carried with them questions of a deeper meaning. According to common Jewish belief, painful experiences were signs of God's judgments (see 5.20n.). Jesus issues a call to repentance lest catastrophe overtake his hearers. **4:** *Siloam,* in the southeast corner of Jerusalem, where the pool of Siloam (Isa 8.6; Neh 3.15; Jn 9.7) was located. **7:** See 3.9.

synagogues on the sabbath. 11 And just then
there appeared a woman with a spirit that
had crippled her for eighteen years. She was
bent over and was quite unable to stand up
straight. 12 When Jesus saw her, he called
her over and said, "Woman, you are set
free from your ailment." 13 When he laid
his hands on her, immediately she stood up
straight and began praising God. 14 But the
leader of the synagogue, indignant because
Jesus had cured on the sabbath, kept saying
to the crowd, "There are six days on which
work ought to be done; come on those days
and be cured, and not on the sabbath day."
15 But the Lord answered him and said,
"You hypocrites! Does not each of you on
the sabbath untie his ox or his donkey from
the manger, and lead it away to give it wa-
ter? 16 And ought not this woman, a daugh-
ter of Abraham whom Satan bound for
eighteen long years, be set free from this
bondage on the sabbath day?" 17 When he
said this, all his opponents were put to
shame; and the entire crowd was rejoicing
at all the wonderful things that he was do-
ing.

18 He said therefore, "What is the king-
dom of God like? And to what should I
compare it? 19 It is like a mustard seed that
someone took and sowed in the garden; it
grew and became a tree, and the birds of
the air made nests in its branches."

20 And again he said, "To what should
I compare the kingdom of God? 21 It is like
yeast that a woman took and mixed in
with[a] three measures of flour until all of it
was leavened."

22 Jesus[b] went through one town and
village after another, teaching as he made
his way to Jerusalem. 23 Someone asked
him, "Lord, will only a few be saved?" He
said to them, 24 "Strive to enter through the
narrow door; for many, I tell you, will try
to enter and will not be able. 25 When once
the owner of the house has got up and shut
the door, and you begin to stand outside
and to knock at the door, saying, 'Lord,
open to us,' then in reply he will say to you,
'I do not know where you come from.'
26 Then you will begin to say, 'We ate and
drank with you, and you taught in our
streets.' 27 But he will say, 'I do not know
where you come from; go away from me,
all you evildoers!' 28 There will be weeping
and gnashing of teeth when you see Abra-
ham and Isaac and Jacob and all the proph-
ets in the kingdom of God, and you your-
selves thrown out. 29 Then people will come
from east and west, from north and south,
and will eat in the kingdom of God. 30 In-
deed, some are last who will be first, and
some are first who will be last."

31 At that very hour some Pharisees
came and said to him, "Get away from
here, for Herod wants to kill you." 32 He
said to them, "Go and tell that fox for
me,[c] 'Listen, I am casting out demons and
performing cures today and tomorrow, and
on the third day I finish my work. 33 Yet
today, tomorrow, and the next day I must
be on my way, because it is impossible for
a prophet to be killed outside of Jerusalem.'

a Gk *hid in* *b* Gk *He* *c* Gk lacks *for me*

13.10–17: Healing of a crippled woman on the sabbath. A similar sabbath healing follows in 14.1–6; see 4.31n. **14:** Ex 20.9–10. **16:** Jesus relates the physical disorder of the woman to the work of Satan (cf. 11.14). Such afflictions conflict with God's purpose of salvation in his covenant with Abraham and are the concern of Jesus' ministry (4.18).

13.18–19: Parable of the mustard seed (Mt 13.31–32; Mk 4.30–32). **19:** The last phrase of this verse reflects the wording of Ps 104.12; Dan 4.12,21.

13.20–21: Parable of the yeast (Mt 13.33). This parable, like the preceding one (vv. 18–19), contrasts the future grandeur of the kingdom with the seemingly small start that was occurring in the ministry of Jesus.

13.22–30: The necessity of discipline for salvation (Mt 7.13–14,22–23; 8.11–12; 19.30; Mk 10.31). **27:** The wording of this verse bears similarities to Ps 6.9. **29:** Ps 107.3.

13.31–33: Report and reply concerning Herod. 31: *Here,* Herod's domain of Galilee and Perea (see 3.1n.). **32:** *Fox,* an unflattering metaphor. Jesus denies that Herod's intended opposition can hinder his

34 Jerusalem, Jerusalem, the city that kills
the prophets and stones those who are sent
to it! How often have I desired to gather
your children together as a hen gathers her
brood under her wings, and you were not
willing! 35 See, your house is left to you.
And I tell you, you will not see me until the
time comes when[a] you say, 'Blessed is the
one who comes in the name of the Lord.' "

14 On one occasion when Jesus[b] was
going to the house of a leader of the
Pharisees to eat a meal on the sabbath, they
were watching him closely. 2 Just then, in
front of him, there was a man who had
dropsy. 3 And Jesus asked the lawyers and
Pharisees, "Is it lawful to cure people on
the sabbath, or not?" 4 But they were silent.
So Jesus[b] took him and healed him, and
sent him away. 5 Then he said to them, "If
one of you has a child[c] or an ox that has
fallen into a well, will you not immediately
pull it out on a sabbath day?" 6 And they
could not reply to this.

7 When he noticed how the guests chose
the places of honor, he told them a parable.
8 "When you are invited by someone to a
wedding banquet, do not sit down at the
place of honor, in case someone more dis-
tinguished than you has been invited by
your host; 9 and the host who invited both
of you may come and say to you, 'Give this
person your place,' and then in disgrace
you would start to take the lowest place.
10 But when you are invited, go and sit
down at the lowest place, so that when
your host comes, he may say to you,
'Friend, move up higher'; then you will be
honored in the presence of all who sit at the
table with you. 11 For all who exalt them-
selves will be humbled, and those who
humble themselves will be exalted."

12 He said also to the one who had in-
vited him, "When you give a luncheon or a
dinner, do not invite your friends or your
brothers or your relatives or rich neighbors,
in case they may invite you in return, and
you would be repaid. 13 But when you give
a banquet, invite the poor, the crippled, the
lame, and the blind. 14 And you will be
blessed, because they cannot repay you, for
you will be repaid at the resurrection of the
righteous."

15 One of the dinner guests, on hearing
this, said to him, "Blessed is anyone who
will eat bread in the kingdom of God!"
16 Then Jesus[b] said to him, "Someone gave
a great dinner and invited many. 17 At the
time for the dinner he sent his slave to say
to those who had been invited, 'Come; for
everything is ready now.' 18 But they all
alike began to make excuses. The first said
to him, 'I have bought a piece of land, and
I must go out and see it; please accept my
regrets.' 19 Another said, 'I have bought five
yoke of oxen, and I am going to try them
out; please accept my regrets.' 20 Another
said, 'I have just been married, and there-
fore I cannot come.' 21 So the slave returned
and reported this to his master. Then the
owner of the house became angry and said
to his slave, 'Go out at once into the streets
and lanes of the town and bring in the
poor, the crippled, the blind, and the lame.'
22 And the slave said, 'Sir, what you or-
dered has been done, and there is still

a Other ancient authorities lack *the time comes when*
b Gk *he* *c* Other ancient authorities read *a donkey*

ministry, which has not reached its goal. **33:** *It is impossible* . . . , bitter irony that leads to the ensuing laments (see 13.34–35; 19.41–42).

13.34–35: Jesus' lament over Jerusalem (Mt 23.37–39). **35:** See Jer 22.5. The quotation is from Ps 118.26; see Lk 19.37–38.

14.1–6: Healing of a man with dropsy on the sabbath. This healing story forms the second part of a balanced pair with the foregoing account of Jesus' healing the crippled woman (13.1–16), exhibiting Luke's concern to show the inclusive nature of Jesus' ministry. **2:** *Dropsy,* swelling from abnormal fluid retention. **5:** The variant reading, "a donkey" instead of "a child" (see note *c*) was a scribal alteration to make this verse conform to the wording of 13.15.

14.7–14: Parable on humility. 8: Prov 25.6–7. **11:** See 13.30; 18.14; Mt 18.4; 23.12.

14.15–24: Parable of the great dinner (Mt 22.1–14). **24:** *You* is plural here, whereas the master in the

room.’ 23 Then the master said to the slave,
‘Go out into the roads and lanes, and com-
pel people to come in, so that my house
may be filled. 24 For I tell you,[a] none of
those who were invited will taste my din-
ner.’ ”
25 Now large crowds were traveling
with him; and he turned and said to them,
26 “Whoever comes to me and does not hate
father and mother, wife and children,
brothers and sisters, yes, and even life itself,
cannot be my disciple. 27 Whoever does not
carry the cross and follow me cannot be my
disciple. 28 For which of you, intending to
build a tower, does not first sit down and
estimate the cost, to see whether he has
enough to complete it? 29 Otherwise, when
he has laid a foundation and is not able to
finish, all who see it will begin to ridicule
him, 30 saying, ‘This fellow began to build
and was not able to finish.’ 31 Or what
king, going out to wage war against anoth-
er king, will not sit down first and consider
whether he is able with ten thousand to
oppose the one who comes against him
with twenty thousand? 32 If he cannot,
then, while the other is still far away, he
sends a delegation and asks for the terms of
peace. 33 So therefore, none of you can be-
come my disciple if you do not give up all
your possessions.
34 “Salt is good; but if salt has lost its
taste, how can its saltiness be restored?[b]
35 It is fit neither for the soil nor for the
manure pile; they throw it away. Let any-
one with ears to hear listen!”

15 Now all the tax collectors and sin-
ners were coming near to listen to
him. 2 And the Pharisees and the scribes
were grumbling and saying, “This fellow
welcomes sinners and eats with them.”
3 So he told them this parable: 4 “Which
one of you, having a hundred sheep and
losing one of them, does not leave the
ninety-nine in the wilderness and go after
the one that is lost until he finds it? 5 When
he has found it, he lays it on his shoulders
and rejoices. 6 And when he comes home,
he calls together his friends and neighbors,
saying to them, ‘Rejoice with me, for I have
found my sheep that was lost.’ 7 Just so, I
tell you, there will be more joy in heaven
over one sinner who repents than over
ninety-nine righteous persons who need no
repentance.
8 “Or what woman having ten silver
coins,[c] if she loses one of them, does not
light a lamp, sweep the house, and search
carefully until she finds it? 9 When she has
found it, she calls together her friends and
neighbors, saying, ‘Rejoice with me, for I
have found the coin that I had lost.’ 10 Just
so, I tell you, there is joy in the presence of

a The Greek word for *you* here is plural b Or *how can it be used for seasoning?* c Gk *drachmas*, each worth about a day's wage for a laborer

parable was speaking to only one servant (“you” singular). Thus, Jesus seems to have completed the parabolic form in v. 23 and, now, he speaks to the guests directly in this verse (v. 24) as a reply to the statement by the guest in v. 15. *My dinner* suggests the messianic banquet (see 12.37n.).

14.25–33: The costs of discipleship (Mt 10.37–38). A series of sayings declaring the necessity of the disciples' total devotion to following Jesus. **26:** Jn 12.25. *Hate* is vivid language; the parallel passage in Mt 10.37 reflects Jesus' plain meaning. **27:** See Mk 8.34. **31–32:** Possibly alludes to some contemporary event.

14.34–35: Saying about salt (Mt 5.13; Mk 9.49–50). This saying warns against lackadaisical discipleship. Ancient salt was not pure sodium chloride, so the other material in the salt could go bad and cause the salt to be no good.

15.1–7: Parable of the lost sheep (Mt 18.12–14). God is frequently called the shepherd, both of Israel (e.g., Ps 78.52; 80.1; 100.3) and of the individual (Ps 23); for the image of lost sheep, see Ps 119.176; Jer 50.6; Ezek 34.15–16. **6–7:** The mention of joy anticipates the declarations of joy in the following two parables, which share the theme of lost and found.

15.8–10: Parable of the lost coin. The woman sweeping and seeking the coin is freely cast in the parable to depict the activity of God. **8:** The coins are Greek drachmas; see note *c*.

the angels of God over one sinner who re-
pents."

11 Then Jesus[a] said, "There was a man
who had two sons. 12 The younger of them
said to his father, 'Father, give me the share
of the property that will belong to me.' So
he divided his property between them. 13 A
few days later the younger son gathered
all he had and traveled to a distant coun-
try, and there he squandered his property
in dissolute living. 14 When he had spent
everything, a severe famine took place
throughout that country, and he began to
be in need. 15 So he went and hired himself
out to one of the citizens of that country,
who sent him to his fields to feed the pigs.
16 He would gladly have filled himself
with[b] the pods that the pigs were eating;
and no one gave him anything. 17 But when
he came to himself he said, 'How many of
my father's hired hands have bread enough
and to spare, but here I am dying of hun-
ger! 18 I will get up and go to my father, and
I will say to him, "Father, I have sinned
against heaven and before you; 19 I am no
longer worthy to be called your son; treat
me like one of your hired hands." ' 20 So he
set off and went to his father. But while he
was still far off, his father saw him and was
filled with compassion; he ran and put his
arms around him and kissed him. 21 Then
the son said to him, 'Father, I have sinned
against heaven and before you; I am no lon-
ger worthy to be called your son.'[c] 22 But
the father said to his slaves, 'Quickly, bring
out a robe—the best one—and put it on
him; put a ring on his finger and sandals on
his feet. 23 And get the fatted calf and kill it,
and let us eat and celebrate; 24 for this son
of mine was dead and is alive again; he was
lost and is found!' And they began to cele-
brate.

25 "Now his elder son was in the field;
and when he came and approached the
house, he heard music and dancing. 26 He
called one of the slaves and asked what
was going on. 27 He replied, 'Your brother
has come, and your father has killed the
fatted calf, because he has got him back
safe and sound.' 28 Then he became angry
and refused to go in. His father came out
and began to plead with him. 29 But he
answered his father, 'Listen! For all these
years I have been working like a slave for
you, and I have never disobeyed your com-
mand; yet you have never given me even a
young goat so that I might celebrate with
my friends. 30 But when this son of yours
came back, who has devoured your proper-
ty with prostitutes, you killed the fatted calf
for him!' 31 Then the father[a] said to him,
'Son, you are always with me, and all that
is mine is yours. 32 But we had to celebrate
and rejoice, because this brother of yours
was dead and has come to life; he was lost
and has been found.' "

16 Then Jesus[a] said to the disciples,
"There was a rich man who had a

a Gk *he* *b* Other ancient authorities read *filled his stomach with* *c* Other ancient authorities add *Treat me like one of your hired servants*

15.11–32: Parable of the lost prodigal son. 12: On inheritance, see Deut 21.17. **15:** *Pigs,* see 8.32n. **22–24:** His place as son is freely restored, though his inheritance is gone. The parable illustrates God's grace toward those who rebel and return. **22:** *Robe,* a festal garment (not worn while working); *ring,* symbol of authority; *sandals,* slaves would have been barefooted. Cf. Gen 41.42; Zech 3.4. **23:** *Fatted calf,* a luxury; see 1 Sam 28.24; Am 6.4. **25–32:** Rivalry between brothers is a common biblical theme (see Gen 4.2–8; 25.27–34; 27.1–36; 37.1–4). Note the elder son's pique ("this son of yours," v. 30). **31:** See v. 12n.

16.1–9: Parable of the dishonest manager. The culmination of this enigmatic story appears to be v. 8, and Jesus' exposition follows in v. 9. The meaning of the story for those hearing Jesus' teaching is that the dishonest manager was prudent in using the things of this life to ensure the future, so believers should do the same. More generally, however, the probable sense of the story itself is that the steward was dishonest in his squandering of his master's estate. When confronted, he does not necessarily engage in dishonest behavior (in fact he is praised for his actions), but he calls in the debtors and reduces their bills by eliminating his own commission. Thus, he shrewdly uses material goods to win gratitude from his manager, and charges were brought to him that this man was squandering his property. 2 So he summoned him and said to him, 'What is this that I hear about you? Give me an accounting of your management, because you cannot be my manager any longer.' 3 Then the manager said to himself, 'What will I do, now that my master is taking the position away from me? I am not strong enough to dig, and I am ashamed to beg. 4 I have decided what to do so that, when I am dismissed as manager, people may welcome me into their homes.' 5 So, summoning his master's debtors one by one, he asked the first, 'How much do you owe my master?' 6 He answered, 'A hundred jugs of olive oil.' He said to him, 'Take your bill, sit down quickly, and make it fifty.' 7 Then he asked another, 'And how much do you owe?' He replied, 'A hundred containers of wheat.' He said to him, 'Take your bill and make it eighty.' 8 And his master commended the dishonest manager because he had acted shrewdly; for the children of this age are more shrewd in dealing with their own generation than are the children of light. 9 And I tell you, make friends for yourselves by means of dishonest wealth[a] so that when it is gone, they may welcome you into the eternal homes.[b]

10 "Whoever is faithful in a very little is faithful also in much; and whoever is dishonest in a very little is dishonest also in much. 11 If then you have not been faithful with the dishonest wealth,[a] who will entrust to you the true riches? 12 And if you have not been faithful with what belongs to another, who will give you what is your own? 13 No slave can serve two masters; for a slave will either hate the one and love the other, or be devoted to the one and despise the other. You cannot serve God and wealth."[a]

14 The Pharisees, who were lovers of money, heard all this, and they ridiculed him. 15 So he said to them, "You are those who justify yourselves in the sight of others; but God knows your hearts; for what is prized by human beings is an abomination in the sight of God.

16 "The law and the prophets were in effect until John came; since then the good news of the kingdom of God is proclaimed, and everyone tries to enter it by force.[c] 17 But it is easier for heaven and earth to pass away, than for one stroke of a letter in the law to be dropped.

18 "Anyone who divorces his wife and marries another commits adultery, and whoever marries a woman divorced from her husband commits adultery.

a Gk *mammon* *b* Gk *tents* *c* Or *everyone is strongly urged to enter it*

master's debtors. **8:** *His master,* lit. "the lord"; perhaps indicating a reference by Luke to Jesus ("the Lord") rather than being the words of Jesus' conclusion to the parable. *Children of light,* those who are spiritually enlightened; this phrase appears in Jn 12.36; Eph 5.8; 1 Thess 5.5, as well as in the Dead Sea Scrolls where it is contrasted with the phrase "children of darkness." **9:** *Wealth,* lit. "mammon," is the Greek transliteration of a Semitic word probably meaning "that in which one fully trusts."

16.10–18: A series of sayings. 10–12: Sayings on faithfulness. **11,13:** *Wealth,* see v. 9n. **13:** The impossibility of serving two masters (Mt 6.24; cf. Deut 6.13). **14–15:** Strong criticism of the Pharisees. **16–17:** Sayings concerning the law (Mt 11.12–13; 5.18; cf. Lk 21.33). **16:** Here, John the Baptist is presented as the figure through whom the fulfillment of God's promises began to appear. *The law and the prophets,* the first two parts of what became the three divisions of the Hebrew Bible, the Torah or "law" of Moses, and the prophets (the books of Joshua through 2 Kings; see the Prologue to Sirach; 2 Macc 15.9; Lk 16.29; 24.27,44). **18:** Saying concerning divorce (Mt 19.9; Mk 10.11–12). This statement may condemn the simultaneous actions of divorce and marrying another; in other words, a divorce that occurred to facilitate remarriage. Herod Antipas had done exactly that; see 3.19–20n.

16.19–31: Parable of the rich man and Lazarus. A clear emphasis of this parable (vv. 27–31) is that the Hebrew Bible speaks an urgent and sufficient call to repentance (v. 17). As a whole the story seems to illustrate vv. 10–15. **19:** The *rich man,* though unnamed, is commonly called "Dives," which is Latin

19 "There was a rich man who was
dressed in purple and fine linen and who
feasted sumptuously every day. 20 And at
his gate lay a poor man named Lazarus,
covered with sores, 21 who longed to satisfy
his hunger with what fell from the rich
man's table; even the dogs would come and
lick his sores. 22 The poor man died and
was carried away by the angels to be with
Abraham.[a] The rich man also died and
was buried. 23 In Hades, where he was be-
ing tormented, he looked up and saw Abra-
ham far away with Lazarus by his side.[b]
24 He called out, 'Father Abraham, have
mercy on me, and send Lazarus to dip the
tip of his finger in water and cool my
tongue; for I am in agony in these flames.'
25 But Abraham said, 'Child, remember that
during your lifetime you received your
good things, and Lazarus in like manner
evil things; but now he is comforted here,
and you are in agony. 26 Besides all this,
between you and us a great chasm has been
fixed, so that those who might want to pass
from here to you cannot do so, and no one
can cross from there to us.' 27 He said,
'Then, father, I beg you to send him to my
father's house— 28 for I have five broth-
ers—that he may warn them, so that they
will not also come into this place of tor-
ment.' 29 Abraham replied, 'They have Mo-
ses and the prophets; they should listen to
them.' 30 He said, 'No, father Abraham; but
if someone goes to them from the dead,
they will repent.' 31 He said to him, 'If they
do not listen to Moses and the prophets,
neither will they be convinced even if some-
one rises from the dead.' "

17 Jesus[c] said to his disciples, "Occa-
sions for stumbling are bound to
come, but woe to anyone by whom they
come! 2 It would be better for you if a mill-
stone were hung around your neck and you
were thrown into the sea than for you to
cause one of these little ones to stumble.
3 Be on your guard! If another disciple[d]
sins, you must rebuke the offender, and if
there is repentance, you must forgive. 4 And
if the same person sins against you seven
times a day, and turns back to you seven
times and says, 'I repent,' you must for-
give."

5 The apostles said to the Lord, "In-
crease our faith!" 6 The Lord replied, "If
you had faith the size of a[e] mustard seed,
you could say to this mulberry tree, 'Be up-
rooted and planted in the sea,' and it would
obey you.

7 "Who among you would say to your
slave who has just come in from plowing or
tending sheep in the field, 'Come here at
once and take your place at the table'?
8 Would you not rather say to him, 'Prepare
supper for me, put on your apron and serve
me while I eat and drink; later you may eat
and drink'? 9 Do you thank the slave for
doing what was commanded? 10 So you
also, when you have done all that you were
ordered to do, say, 'We are worthless
slaves; we have done only what we ought to
have done!' "

a Gk *to Abraham's bosom* *b* Gk *in his bosom* *c* Gk *He* *d* Gk *your brother* *e* Gk *faith as a grain of*

for "rich man." *Purple* was an expensive cloth dyed with the liquid obtained from a species of shellfish. **20:** The person named here is not to be identified with the Lazarus of Jn 11.1–44; 12.1,9. **21–22:** The moral character of Lazarus is passed over to illustrate the fatal deficiency in the life of the indifferent rich man and the impossibility of altering his condemnation. **22:** *With Abraham,* traditional terminology for a blessed condition in the afterlife; see 13.28–29. **29:** *Moses and the prophets,* see v. 16n. **31:** *Rises from the dead,* a clear reference to Jesus' resurrection (see 9.22) and the ensuing refusal of some to believe it.

17.1–3a: The peril of causing temptation (Mt 18.6–7; Mk 9.42). **2:** *Little ones,* disciples.

17.3b–4: Sayings concerning forgiveness (Mt 18.15,21–22).

17.5–6: Saying concerning faith (Mt 17.19–21; Mk 9.28–29). **6:** *The size of a mustard seed,* see Mk 4.31.

17.7–10: The obligation to obedience. For the apostles, obedience to God is a duty to be fulfilled and not an occasion for reward; yet, cf. 12.35–38.

11 On the way to Jerusalem Jesus[a] was
going through the region between Samaria
and Galilee. 12 As he entered a village, ten
lepers[b] approached him. Keeping their dis-
tance, 13 they called out, saying, "Jesus,
Master, have mercy on us!" 14 When he saw
them, he said to them, "Go and show your-
selves to the priests." And as they went,
they were made clean. 15 Then one of them,
when he saw that he was healed, turned
back, praising God with a loud voice. 16 He
prostrated himself at Jesus'[c] feet and
thanked him. And he was a Samaritan.
17 Then Jesus asked, "Were not ten made
clean? But the other nine, where are they?
18 Was none of them found to return and
give praise to God except this foreigner?"
19 Then he said to him, "Get up and go on
your way; your faith has made you well."

20 Once Jesus[a] was asked by the Phari-
sees when the kingdom of God was com-
ing, and he answered, "The kingdom of
God is not coming with things that can be
observed; 21 nor will they say, 'Look, here it
is!' or 'There it is!' For, in fact, the kingdom
of God is among[d] you."

22 Then he said to the disciples, "The
days are coming when you will long to see
one of the days of the Son of Man, and you
will not see it. 23 They will say to you,
'Look there!' or 'Look here!' Do not go, do
not set off in pursuit. 24 For as the lightning
flashes and lights up the sky from one side
to the other, so will the Son of Man be in
his day.[e] 25 But first he must endure much
suffering and be rejected by this generation.
26 Just as it was in the days of Noah, so too
it will be in the days of the Son of Man.
27 They were eating and drinking, and mar-
rying and being given in marriage, until the
day Noah entered the ark, and the flood
came and destroyed all of them. 28 Like-
wise, just as it was in the days of Lot: they
were eating and drinking, buying and sell-
ing, planting and building, 29 but on the day
that Lot left Sodom, it rained fire and sulfur
from heaven and destroyed all of them
30 —it will be like that on the day that the
Son of Man is revealed. 31 On that day,
anyone on the housetop who has belong-
ings in the house must not come down to
take them away; and likewise anyone in the
field must not turn back. 32 Remember
Lot's wife. 33 Those who try to make their
life secure will lose it, but those who lose
their life will keep it. 34 I tell you, on that
night there will be two in one bed; one will
be taken and the other left. 35 There will be
two women grinding meal together; one
will be taken and the other left."[f] 37 Then
they asked him, "Where, Lord?" He said to
them, "Where the corpse is, there the vul-
tures will gather."

18 Then Jesus[a] told them a parable
about their need to pray always and

a Gk *he* *b* The terms *leper* and *leprosy* can refer to several diseases *c* Gk *his* *d* Or *within* *e* Other ancient authorities lack *in his day* *f* Other ancient authorities add verse 36, *"Two will be in the field; one will be taken and the other left."*

17.11–19: The cleansing of ten lepers. 12: Lev 13.45–46. **14:** *Priests,* Lev 13.2–3; 14.2–32. **16:** *Samaritan,* see 9.52n. **17:** *The other nine* were, presumably, Jews. **18:** 7.9. **19:** 7.50; 8.48; 18.42. *Made you well,* lit. "saved you."

17.20–21: The coming of the kingdom of God. 20: 19.11; 21.7; Acts 1.6. **21:** The questioners had in mind a kingdom bringing material and political benefits. Jesus shifted the emphasis from future expectation to the observable presence of the kingdom in his ministry; see 11.20.

17.22–37: The day of the Son of Man (Mt 24.17–18,23,26–28,37–41; Mk 13.14–16,19–23). Mt 24 has similar teachings in a different order and setting. **24:** The coming will be sudden and discernible to all. **25:** 9.22. **26–27:** Gen 6.5–8; 7.6–24. **28–30:** Gen 18.16–19.28. **31:** *On the housetop,* a flat-top roof reached by an exterior staircase. **32:** Gen 19.26. **33:** 9.24. **[36]:** This verse is a scribal addition to Luke to incorporate a saying from Mt 24.20. **37:** Mt 24.28. The questioners wish to know *where* the messiah and his people will be located. Instead of answering them directly, Jesus warns: As surely as vultures find the carcass, so surely will divine judgment come; therefore always be ready!

18.1–8: Parable of the unjust judge and the persistent widow. 1: The aim is carefully stated (cf. 11.5–8), perhaps because the details are incongruous (as in 16.1–9). **3:** Cf. Deut 27.19.

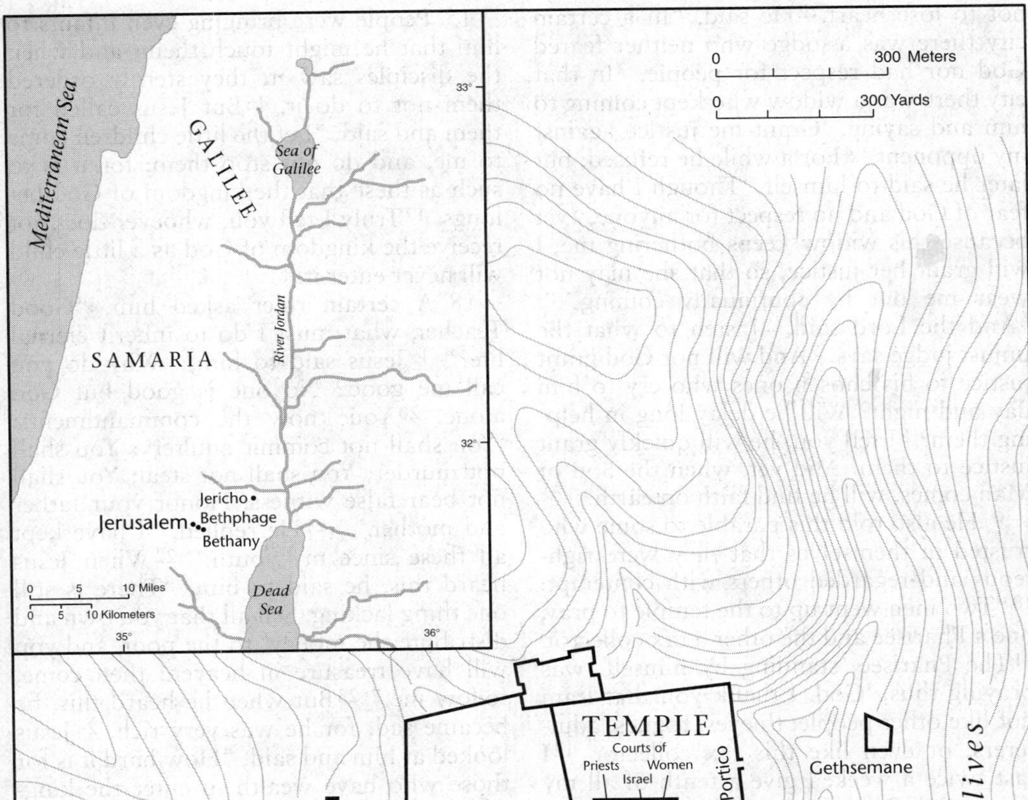

Chs 17–19: Sites of Jesus' journey to Jerusalem and within it.

not to lose heart. 2 He said, "In a certain
city there was a judge who neither feared
God nor had respect for people. 3 In that
city there was a widow who kept coming to
him and saying, 'Grant me justice against
my opponent.' 4 For a while he refused; but
later he said to himself, 'Though I have no
fear of God and no respect for anyone, 5 yet
because this widow keeps bothering me, I
will grant her justice, so that she may not
wear me out by continually coming.' "[a]
6 And the Lord said, "Listen to what the
unjust judge says. 7 And will not God grant
justice to his chosen ones who cry to him
day and night? Will he delay long in help-
ing them? 8 I tell you, he will quickly grant
justice to them. And yet, when the Son of
Man comes, will he find faith on earth?"
9 He also told this parable to some who
trusted in themselves that they were righ-
teous and regarded others with contempt:
10 "Two men went up to the temple to pray,
one a Pharisee and the other a tax collector.
11 The Pharisee, standing by himself, was
praying thus, 'God, I thank you that I am
not like other people: thieves, rogues, adul-
terers, or even like this tax collector. 12 I
fast twice a week; I give a tenth of all my
income.' 13 But the tax collector, standing
far off, would not even look up to heaven,
but was beating his breast and saying,
'God, be merciful to me, a sinner!' 14 I tell
you, this man went down to his home justi-
fied rather than the other; for all who exalt
themselves will be humbled, but all who
humble themselves will be exalted."

15 People were bringing even infants to
him that he might touch them; and when
the disciples saw it, they sternly ordered
them not to do it. 16 But Jesus called for
them and said, "Let the little children come
to me, and do not stop them; for it is to
such as these that the kingdom of God be-
longs. 17 Truly I tell you, whoever does not
receive the kingdom of God as a little child
will never enter it."
18 A certain ruler asked him, "Good
Teacher, what must I do to inherit eternal
life?" 19 Jesus said to him, "Why do you
call me good? No one is good but God
alone. 20 You know the commandments:
'You shall not commit adultery; You shall
not murder; You shall not steal; You shall
not bear false witness; Honor your father
and mother.' " 21 He replied, "I have kept
all these since my youth." 22 When Jesus
heard this, he said to him, "There is still
one thing lacking. Sell all that you own and
distribute the money[b] to the poor, and you
will have treasure in heaven; then come,
follow me." 23 But when he heard this, he
became sad; for he was very rich. 24 Jesus
looked at him and said, "How hard it is for
those who have wealth to enter the king-
dom of God! 25 Indeed, it is easier for a
camel to go through the eye of a needle
than for someone who is rich to enter the
kingdom of God."
26 Those who heard it said, "Then who

a Or *so that she may not finally come and slap me in the face* b Gk lacks *the money*

8: *Comes,* from heaven, in judgment (see Dan 7.13–14). This verse links the parable with 17.20–37.

18.9–14: Parable of the Pharisee and the tax collector. 9: *Righteous,* that is, acceptable to God because of their strict observance of the law. **11:** *Standing by himself, was praying thus,* more literally, "standing to himself these things prayed," a suggestively ambiguous statement. **12:** *Twice a week,* Mondays and Thursdays; such a practice was apparently voluntary rather than prescribed. **14:** *Justified* means "right with God" or "accepted by God." *All who exalt themselves . . . ,* see 14.11n.

18.15–17: Jesus and the little children (Mt 19.13–15; Mk 10.13–16). Located between the preceding parable and the subsequent incident with the rich ruler, this brief story with its sayings contrasts humility with self-righteousness and self-satisfaction.

18.18–30: The rich ruler, wealth, and salvation (Mt 19.16–30; Mk 10.17–31). **18:** 10.25. **20:** The order of the commandments, varying from the Hebrew Bible, follows the ancient Greek translation, the Septuagint (LXX); see Ex 20.12–16; Deut 5.16–20. **22:** *Treasure in heaven,* see 12.33–34. **26:** To be *saved* refers to the same spiritual experience as to *inherit eternal life* (v. 18), and to *enter the kingdom of God* (v. 25). **27:** Gen 18.14; Job 42.2; Jer 32.17; Lk 1.37. **28:** 5.1–11. **30:** *In this age, and in the age to*

can be saved?" 27He replied, "What is im-
possible for mortals is possible for God."
28 Then Peter said, "Look, we have left
our homes and followed you." 29And he
said to them, "Truly I tell you, there is no
one who has left house or wife or brothers
or parents or children, for the sake of the
kingdom of God, 30who will not get back
very much more in this age, and in the age
to come eternal life."

31 Then he took the twelve aside and
said to them, "See, we are going up to Jeru-
salem, and everything that is written about
the Son of Man by the prophets will be
accomplished. 32For he will be handed over
to the Gentiles; and he will be mocked and
insulted and spat upon. 33After they have
flogged him, they will kill him, and on the
third day he will rise again." 34But they
understood nothing about all these things;
in fact, what he said was hidden from them,
and they did not grasp what was said.
35 As he approached Jericho, a blind
man was sitting by the roadside begging.
36When he heard a crowd going by, he
asked what was happening. 37They told
him, "Jesus of Nazareth[a] is passing by."
38Then he shouted, "Jesus, Son of David,
have mercy on me!" 39Those who were in
front sternly ordered him to be quiet; but
he shouted even more loudly, "Son of Da-
vid, have mercy on me!" 40Jesus stood still
and ordered the man to be brought to him;
and when he came near, he asked him,
41"What do you want me to do for you?"
He said, "Lord, let me see again." 42Jesus
said to him, "Receive your sight; your faith
has saved you." 43Immediately he regained
his sight and followed him, glorifying God;
and all the people, when they saw it,
praised God.

19 He entered Jericho and was passing
through it. 2A man was there
named Zacchaeus; he was a chief tax col-
lector and was rich. 3He was trying to see
who Jesus was, but on account of the
crowd he could not, because he was short
in stature. 4So he ran ahead and climbed a
sycamore tree to see him, because he was
going to pass that way. 5When Jesus came
to the place, he looked up and said to him,
"Zacchaeus, hurry and come down; for I
must stay at your house today." 6So he
hurried down and was happy to welcome
him. 7All who saw it began to grumble and
said, "He has gone to be the guest of one
who is a sinner." 8Zacchaeus stood there
and said to the Lord, "Look, half of my
possessions, Lord, I will give to the poor;
and if I have defrauded anyone of anything,
I will pay back four times as much." 9Then
Jesus said to him, "Today salvation has
come to this house, because he too is a son
of Abraham. 10For the Son of Man came to
seek out and to save the lost."

a Gk *the Nazorean*

come, traditional apocalyptic language contrasting the present evil age and the age of God's kingdom or reign.

18.31–34: Jesus' third prediction of his death (Mt 20.17–19; Mk 10.32–34). Cf. 9.22,44–45; 17.25. The details of this prediction form an outline of the events in chs 22–23. **31:** *Everything that is written . . . by the prophets,* an allusion to passages such as Ps 22; Isa 53; Zech 13.7.

18.35–43: Healing of a blind man (Mt 20.29–34; Mk 10.46–52). **38:** *Son of David,* a phrase identifying Jesus with the messianic expectations associated with the house of David, probably indicating political and nationalistic aspirations. **42:** See 17.19n.

19.1–10: Zacchaeus's salvation. Although he is rich, Zacchaeus's response to Jesus is a striking contrast to that of the rich man in 18.18–23. **1:** Because of its location *Jericho* was an important customs center. **2:** As *chief tax collector* Zacchaeus had contracted with the Roman overlords for the right to collect revenues (lit. "tolls") in the district. His neighbors despised him for sharing in the Roman domination (v. 7). **7:** 5.29–30; 15.1–2. **8:** *I will give,* henceforth, a vow amounting to repentance. *Four times as much,* cf. Ex 22.1; Lev 6.5; Num 5.6–7. **9:** *Salvation,* or the kingdom of God, *has come* in Jesus' presence and message and evinces itself in Zacchaeus's transformation. **10:** A summary of Jesus' ministry in the entire Gospel; see ch 15.

11 As they were listening to this, he
went on to tell a parable, because he was
near Jerusalem, and because they supposed
that the kingdom of God was to appear
immediately. 12 So he said, "A nobleman
went to a distant country to get royal pow-
er for himself and then return. 13 He sum-
moned ten of his slaves, and gave them ten
pounds,[a] and said to them, 'Do business
with these until I come back.' 14 But the citi-
zens of his country hated him and sent a
delegation after him, saying, 'We do not
want this man to rule over us.' 15 When he
returned, having received royal power, he
ordered these slaves, to whom he had given
the money, to be summoned so that he
might find out what they had gained by
trading. 16 The first came forward and said,
'Lord, your pound has made ten more
pounds.' 17 He said to him, 'Well done,
good slave! Because you have been trust-
worthy in a very small thing, take charge of
ten cities.' 18 Then the second came, saying,
'Lord, your pound has made five pounds.'
19 He said to him, 'And you, rule over five
cities.' 20 Then the other came, saying,
'Lord, here is your pound. I wrapped it up
in a piece of cloth, 21 for I was afraid of you,
because you are a harsh man; you take
what you did not deposit, and reap what
you did not sow.' 22 He said to him, 'I will
judge you by your own words, you wicked
slave! You knew, did you, that I was a
harsh man, taking what I did not deposit
and reaping what I did not sow? 23 Why
then did you not put my money into the
bank? Then when I returned, I could have
collected it with interest.' 24 He said to the
bystanders, 'Take the pound from him and
give it to the one who has ten pounds.'
25 (And they said to him, 'Lord, he has ten
pounds!') 26 'I tell you, to all those who
have, more will be given; but from those
who have nothing, even what they have
will be taken away. 27 But as for these ene-
mies of mine who did not want me to be
king over them—bring them here and
slaughter them in my presence.' "

28 After he had said this, he went on
ahead, going up to Jerusalem.

29 When he had come near Bethphage
and Bethany, at the place called the Mount
of Olives, he sent two of the disciples,
30 saying, "Go into the village ahead of you,
and as you enter it you will find tied there
a colt that has never been ridden. Untie it
and bring it here. 31 If anyone asks you,
'Why are you untying it?' just say this, 'The
Lord needs it.' " 32 So those who were sent
departed and found it as he had told them.
33 As they were untying the colt, its owners
asked them, "Why are you untying the
colt?" 34 They said, "The Lord needs it."
35 Then they brought it to Jesus; and after
throwing their cloaks on the colt, they set
Jesus on it. 36 As he rode along, people kept
spreading their cloaks on the road. 37 As he
was now approaching the path down from
the Mount of Olives, the whole multitude
of the disciples began to praise God joyfully
with a loud voice for all the deeds of power
that they had seen, 38 saying,

"Blessed is the king
who comes in the name of
the Lord!

a The mina, rendered here by *pound,* was about three months' wages for a laborer

19.11–27: Parable of the ten pounds (Mt 25.14–30; Mk 13.34). The parable alludes to the journey of Archelaus to Rome in 4 BCE to assure his succession to his father Herod's throne; his mission was opposed by a delegation of leaders from Judea (Josephus *Ant.* 17.9.4; 17.10). **11:** 9.51; 13.22; 17.11; 18.31. **13:** *Ten pounds,* lit. "ten minas," golden coins, each of which equaled a hundred drachmas (see 15.8n.). **17:** 16.10. **26:** See 8.18.

19.28–21.38: Jesus' ministry in Jerusalem (Mt 21.1–24.36; Mk 11.1–13.37).

19.28–40: The entry into Jerusalem (Mt 21.1–9; Mk 11.1–10). Jn 12.12–18. **29:** *Bethphage and Bethany,* villages just east of Jerusalem. **32:** 22.13. **36:** Cf. 2 Kings 9.13. **37:** The road crossed a ridge into the Kidron valley. **38:** Incorporates a phrase from Ps 118.26; see Zech 9.9; Lk 13.35. This scene depicts a royal entry, naming Jesus as *king,* a title that will be used in the charges against Jesus before Pilate in 23.2. **39–40:** Hab 2.11.

Peace in heaven,
and glory in the highest heaven!"
39 Some of the Pharisees in the crowd said
to him, "Teacher, order your disciples to
stop." 40 He answered, "I tell you, if these
were silent, the stones would shout out."
41 As he came near and saw the city, he
wept over it, 42 saying, "If you, even you,
had only recognized on this day the things
that make for peace! But now they are hid-
den from your eyes. 43 Indeed, the days will
come upon you, when your enemies will set
up ramparts around you and surround you,
and hem you in on every side. 44 They will
crush you to the ground, you and your chil-
dren within you, and they will not leave
within you one stone upon another; be-
cause you did not recognize the time of
your visitation from God."[a]
45 Then he entered the temple and be-
gan to drive out those who were selling
things there; 46 and he said, "It is written,
'My house shall be a house of prayer';
but you have made it a den
of robbers."
47 Every day he was teaching in the tem-
ple. The chief priests, the scribes, and the
leaders of the people kept looking for a way
to kill him; 48 but they did not find anything
they could do, for all the people were spell-
bound by what they heard.

20 One day, as he was teaching the
people in the temple and telling the
good news, the chief priests and the scribes
came with the elders 2 and said to him,
"Tell us, by what authority are you doing
these things? Who is it who gave you this
authority?" 3 He answered them, "I will
also ask you a question, and you tell me:
4 Did the baptism of John come from heav-
en, or was it of human origin?" 5 They dis-
cussed it with one another, saying, "If we
say, 'From heaven,' he will say, 'Why did
you not believe him?' 6 But if we say, 'Of
human origin,' all the people will stone us;
for they are convinced that John was a
prophet." 7 So they answered that they did
not know where it came from. 8 Then Jesus
said to them, "Neither will I tell you by
what authority I am doing these things."
9 He began to tell the people this para-
ble: "A man planted a vineyard, and leased
it to tenants, and went to another country
for a long time. 10 When the season came,
he sent a slave to the tenants in order that
they might give him his share of the pro-
duce of the vineyard; but the tenants beat
him and sent him away empty-handed.
11 Next he sent another slave; that one also
they beat and insulted and sent away
empty-handed. 12 And he sent still a third;
this one also they wounded and threw out.
13 Then the owner of the vineyard said,
'What shall I do? I will send my beloved
son; perhaps they will respect him.' 14 But
when the tenants saw him, they discussed it
among themselves and said, 'This is the
heir; let us kill him so that the inheritance
may be ours.' 15 So they threw him out of
the vineyard and killed him. What then will
the owner of the vineyard do to them? 16 He
will come and destroy those tenants and
give the vineyard to others." When they
heard this, they said, "Heaven forbid!"
17 But he looked at them and said, "What
then does this text mean:

a Gk lacks *from God*

19.41–44: Weeping over Jerusalem. See 13.33–34; cf. 23.27–31. These verses may reflect historical knowledge of the actual destruction of Jerusalem in 70 CE. **43:** 21.20–24; 21.6; Isa 29.3; Jer 6.6; Ezek 4.2. *Your enemies,* the Roman army. *Ramparts,* palisade that would keep out all supplies of food. **44:** Ps 137.9; Hos 10.14; 13.16.

19.45–46: Cleansing of the Temple (Mt 21.12–13; Mk 11.15–17; Jn 2.13–17). In this display of authority in the Temple, Jesus dramatically acts out Mal 3.1–2. **45:** *Selling* the prescribed offerings, as in 2.24; Lev 1.14. **46:** Isa 56.7; Jer 7.11.

19.47–48: The religious leaders' hostility toward Jesus (Mk 11.18–19).

20.1–8: Questioning Jesus' authority (Mt 21.23–27; Mk 11.27–33; Jn 2.18–22).

20.9–19: Parable of the vineyard and tenants (Mt 21.33–46; Mk 12.1–12). **9:** Isa 5.1–7. **13:** The use of *beloved* (see 3.22) identifies the son with Jesus. **15:** The murder of the son outside the vineyard may

'The stone that the builders rejected
has become the cornerstone'?[a]
18 Everyone who falls on that stone will be
broken to pieces; and it will crush anyone
on whom it falls." 19 When the scribes and
chief priests realized that he had told this
parable against them, they wanted to lay
hands on him at that very hour, but they
feared the people.
20 So they watched him and sent spies
who pretended to be honest, in order to
trap him by what he said, so as to hand him
over to the jurisdiction and authority of the
governor. 21 So they asked him, "Teacher,
we know that you are right in what you say
and teach, and you show deference to no
one, but teach the way of God in accor-
dance with truth. 22 Is it lawful for us to pay
taxes to the emperor, or not?" 23 But he
perceived their craftiness and said to them,
24 "Show me a denarius. Whose head and
whose title does it bear?" They said, "The
emperor's." 25 He said to them, "Then give
to the emperor the things that are the em-
peror's, and to God the things that are
God's." 26 And they were not able in the
presence of the people to trap him by what
he said; and being amazed by his answer,
they became silent.
27 Some Sadducees, those who say there
is no resurrection, came to him 28 and asked
him a question, "Teacher, Moses wrote for
us that if a man's brother dies, leaving a
wife but no children, the man[b] shall marry
the widow and raise up children for his
brother. 29 Now there were seven brothers;
the first married, and died childless; 30 then
the second 31 and the third married her, and
so in the same way all seven died childless.
32 Finally the woman also died. 33 In the res-
urrection, therefore, whose wife will the
woman be? For the seven had married
her."
34 Jesus said to them, "Those who be-
long to this age marry and are given in mar-
riage; 35 but those who are considered wor-
thy of a place in that age and in the
resurrection from the dead neither marry
nor are given in marriage. 36 Indeed they
cannot die anymore, because they are like
angels and are children of God, being chil-
dren of the resurrection. 37 And the fact that
the dead are raised Moses himself showed,
in the story about the bush, where he
speaks of the Lord as the God of Abraham,
the God of Isaac, and the God of Jacob.
38 Now he is God not of the dead, but of the
living; for to him all of them are alive."
39 Then some of the scribes answered,
"Teacher, you have spoken well." 40 For
they no longer dared to ask him another
question.
41 Then he said to them, "How can they
say that the Messiah[c] is David's son?
42 For David himself says in the book of
Psalms,
'The Lord said to my Lord,
"Sit at my right hand,

a Or *keystone* *b* Gk *his brother* *c* Or *the Christ*

reflect Jesus' crucifixion outside the city of Jerusalem; see Jn 19.17; Heb 13.12; cf. Acts 7.52–53. **17:** Ps 118.22; see Isa 28.16; Acts 4.11. **18:** Isa 8.14–15. **19:** Lk 19.47.

20.20–26: Paying taxes to the emperor (Mt 22.15–22; Mk 12.13–17). **20:** *Honest* translates a Greek word that normally means "correct according to the law," i.e., "righteous." It is used here in the same sense of false pretense that it has in Mt 23.28. **22–25:** A falsified version of this incident lies behind the charge against Jesus before Pilate in 23.2. **24:** *Denarius,* a coin that had the head of the emperor on one side.

20.27–40: Question concerning resurrection (Mt 22.23–33; Mk 12.18–27). **27:** *Sadducees* were the elite class of landed Jerusalem gentry who operated the Temple and wielded power from that religious base of operations; cf. Acts 4.1–2; 23.6–10. **28:** The question reflects the practice of levirate marriage in Deut 25.5–10; see Gen 38.8. **34–36:** Human relations in marriage do not exist in the same way beyond death. Jesus distinguishes two ages and kinds of existence. Mortals are part of this age by their physical birth, and of the age to come by resurrection. **37:** Ex 3.6. **39:** Note the praise of Jesus by the *scribes,* affirmation that shows that all scribes were not simply aligned against Jesus.

20.41–44: A question about David's son (Mt 22.41–46; Mk 12.35–37a). **42–43:** Ps 110.1. **44:** King

43 until I make your enemies your
footstool.” ’
44 David thus calls him Lord; so how can he
be his son?”
45 In the hearing of all the people he
said to the[a] disciples, 46 “Beware of the
scribes, who like to walk around in long
robes, and love to be greeted with respect in
the marketplaces, and to have the best seats
in the synagogues and places of honor at
banquets. 47 They devour widows’ houses
and for the sake of appearance say long
prayers. They will receive the greater con-
demnation.”

21 He looked up and saw rich people
putting their gifts into the treasury;
2 he also saw a poor widow put in two
small copper coins. 3 He said, “Truly I tell
you, this poor widow has put in more than
all of them; 4 for all of them have contribut-
ed out of their abundance, but she out of
her poverty has put in all she had to
live on.”
5 When some were speaking about the
temple, how it was adorned with beautiful
stones and gifts dedicated to God, he said,
6 “As for these things that you see, the days
will come when not one stone will be left
upon another; all will be thrown down.”
7 They asked him, “Teacher, when will
this be, and what will be the sign that this
is about to take place?” 8 And he said, “Be-
ware that you are not led astray; for many
will come in my name and say, ‘I am he!’[b]
and, ‘The time is near!’[c] Do not go after
them.
9 “When you hear of wars and insurrec-
tions, do not be terrified; for these things
must take place first, but the end will not
follow immediately.” 10 Then he said to
them, “Nation will rise against nation, and
kingdom against kingdom; 11 there will be
great earthquakes, and in various places
famines and plagues; and there will be
dreadful portents and great signs from
heaven.
12 “But before all this occurs, they will
arrest you and persecute you; they will
hand you over to synagogues and prisons,
and you will be brought before kings and
governors because of my name. 13 This will
give you an opportunity to testify. 14 So
make up your minds not to prepare your
defense in advance; 15 for I will give you
words[d] and a wisdom that none of your
opponents will be able to withstand or con-
tradict. 16 You will be betrayed even by par-
ents and brothers, by relatives and friends;
and they will put some of you to death.
17 You will be hated by all because of my
name. 18 But not a hair of your head will
perish. 19 By your endurance you will gain
your souls.
20 “When you see Jerusalem surround-
ed by armies, then know that its desolation

a Other ancient authorities read *his* *b* Gk *I am*
c Or *at hand* *d* Gk *a mouth*

David was traditionally viewed as the author of most of the Psalms. The question is: How can the messiah be David’s descendant if David calls him *Lord*? Ps 110 was frequently referred to in early Christian writings; see Acts 2.34–35; 1 Cor 15.25; Heb 1.5.

20.45–47: Warning concerning the scribes (Mt 23.1–36; Mk 12.37b–40). **46:** 11.43.

21.1–4: The widow’s offering (Mk 12.41–44). **1:** *The treasury* refers here to a container (shaped like an inverted trumpet for protection against theft) to receive offerings; there were thirteen of these receptacles in “the court of the women” of the Temple; in Jn 8.20 the term refers to a room in the Temple. **2:** The *copper coin* (Gk “lepton”) was of little monetary value (see 12.59 n.) but of great cost to this giver.

21.5–6: Foretelling the destruction of the Temple (Mt 24.1–2; Mk 13.1–2). Jesus’ teachings in these and the following verses are related to the material in Mk 13, but Luke’s version of that eschatological discourse offers distinctive elements and perspectives. **6:** See 19.44n.

21.7–11: Sayings about end-time signs (Mt 24.3–8; Mk 13.3–8). **7:** 17.20; Acts 1.6. **10:** 2 Chr 15.6; Isa 19.2.

21.12–19: Foretelling the persecution of the disciples (Mt 24.9–14; Mk 13.9–13). These themes developed in the narrative of Acts. **18:** 12.7; Acts 27.34; 1 Sam 14.45.

21.20–24: The desolation of Jerusalem (Mt 24.15–22; Mk 13.14–20. See 19.41–44n.). **20–22:**

has come near.[a] 21 Then those in Judea must flee to the mountains, and those inside the city must leave it, and those out in the country must not enter it; 22 for these are days of vengeance, as a fulfillment of all that is written. 23 Woe to those who are pregnant and to those who are nursing infants in those days! For there will be great distress on the earth and wrath against this people; 24 they will fall by the edge of the sword and be taken away as captives among all nations; and Jerusalem will be trampled on by the Gentiles, until the times of the Gentiles are fulfilled.

25 "There will be signs in the sun, the moon, and the stars, and on the earth distress among nations confused by the roaring of the sea and the waves. 26 People will faint from fear and foreboding of what is coming upon the world, for the powers of the heavens will be shaken. 27 Then they will see 'the Son of Man coming in a cloud' with power and great glory. 28 Now when these things begin to take place, stand up and raise your heads, because your redemption is drawing near."

29 Then he told them a parable: "Look at the fig tree and all the trees; 30 as soon as they sprout leaves you can see for yourselves and know that summer is already near. 31 So also, when you see these things taking place, you know that the kingdom of God is near. 32 Truly I tell you, this generation will not pass away until all things have taken place. 33 Heaven and earth will pass away, but my words will not pass away.

34 "Be on guard so that your hearts are not weighed down with dissipation and drunkenness and the worries of this life, and that day does not catch you unexpectedly, 35 like a trap. For it will come upon all who live on the face of the whole earth. 36 Be alert at all times, praying that you may have the strength to escape all these things that will take place, and to stand before the Son of Man."

37 Every day he was teaching in the temple, and at night he would go out and spend the night on the Mount of Olives, as it was called. 38 And all the people would get up early in the morning to listen to him in the temple.

22 Now the festival of Unleavened Bread, which is called the Passover, was near. 2 The chief priests and the scribes were looking for a way to put Jesus[b] to death, for they were afraid of the people.

3 Then Satan entered into Judas called Iscariot, who was one of the twelve; 4 he went away and conferred with the chief

a Or *is at hand* b Gk *him*

19.41–44; 23.28–31; 17.31. **20:** *Armies,* the Roman forces. **22:** Cf. Isa 63.4; Jer 5.29; Hos 9.7. **24:** Isa 63.18; Dan 8.13. *The times of the Gentiles* may mean the divinely imposed limit on Roman dominance, or the extension of salvation to all people (20.16).

21.25–28: The coming of the Son of Man (Mt 24.29–31; Mk 13.24–27). **25–27:** These verses reflect language and elements of thought from Joel 3.3–4; Isa 24.19 (LXX); Ps 65.8; 46.4; 89.10; Wis 5.22; Jon 1.15. **25:** Isa 13.10; Joel 2.10; Zeph 1.15. **26:** Incorporates wording parallel to Isa 34.4. *The powers of the heavens* are likely the celestial bodies mentioned in v. 25. **27:** Incorporates wording parallel to Dan 7.13–14.

21.29–33: The lesson of the fig tree (Mt 24.32–36; Mk 13.28–32). **33:** 16.17.

21.34–36: Admonition to alertness (cf. Mt 24.43–51; 25.13; Mk 13.33–37). **34:** 8.14; 12.22; 1 Thess 5.6–7. **36:** 2 Cor 5.10.

21.37–38: Summary concerning Jesus' ministry in Jerusalem. 38: The story of the woman caught in adultery (Jn 8.1–11) appears after this verse in some ancient manuscripts; see Jn 8.11, note *c*.

22.1–23.56: The Last Supper and Jesus' trials, death, and burial (Mt 26.1–27.61; Mk 14.1–15.47; Jn 13.1–19.42).

22.1–6: The deadly conspiracy against Jesus. 1–2: Mt 26.2–5; Mk 14.1–2; Jn 11.47–53. The word "called" is a concession to the Gentile readers for whom Luke wrote. **3–6:** Mt 26.14–16; Mk 14.10–11; Jn 13.2. **3:** The entry of *Satan* into *Judas* (see 6.16n.) reintroduces the theme from 4.13.

priests and officers of the temple police
about how he might betray him to them.
5 They were greatly pleased and agreed to
give him money. 6 So he consented and be-
gan to look for an opportunity to betray
him to them when no crowd was present.
7 Then came the day of Unleavened
Bread, on which the Passover lamb had to
be sacrificed. 8 So Jesus[a] sent Peter and
John, saying, "Go and prepare the Passover
meal for us that we may eat it." 9 They
asked him, "Where do you want us to
make preparations for it?" 10 "Listen," he
said to them, "when you have entered the
city, a man carrying a jar of water will meet
you; follow him into the house he enters
11 and say to the owner of the house, 'The
teacher asks you, "Where is the guest
room, where I may eat the Passover with
my disciples?" ' 12 He will show you a large
room upstairs, already furnished. Make
preparations for us there." 13 So they went
and found everything as he had told them;
and they prepared the Passover meal.
14 When the hour came, he took his
place at the table, and the apostles with
him. 15 He said to them, "I have eagerly
desired to eat this Passover with you before
I suffer; 16 for I tell you, I will not eat it[b]
until it is fulfilled in the kingdom of God."
17 Then he took a cup, and after giving
thanks he said, "Take this and divide it
among yourselves; 18 for I tell you that from
now on I will not drink of the fruit of the
vine until the kingdom of God comes."
19 Then he took a loaf of bread, and when
he had given thanks, he broke it and gave it
to them, saying, "This is my body, which is
given for you. Do this in remembrance of
me." 20 And he did the same with the cup
after supper, saying, "This cup that is
poured out for you is the new covenant in
my blood.[c] 21 But see, the one who betrays
me is with me, and his hand is on the table.
22 For the Son of Man is going as it has been
determined, but woe to that one by whom
he is betrayed!" 23 Then they began to ask
one another which one of them it could be
who would do this.
24 A dispute also arose among them as
to which one of them was to be regarded as
the greatest. 25 But he said to them, "The
kings of the Gentiles lord it over them; and
those in authority over them are called
benefactors. 26 But not so with you; rather
the greatest among you must become like
the youngest, and the leader like one who
serves. 27 For who is greater, the one who is
at the table or the one who serves? Is it not
the one at the table? But I am among you as
one who serves.
28 "You are those who have stood by

a Gk *he* *b* Other ancient authorities read *never eat it again* *c* Other ancient authorities lack, in whole or in part, verses 19b-20 (*which is given . . . in my blood*)

22.7–13: Preparations for the Passover (Mt 26.17–19; Mk 14.12–16; Jn 13.1). **7:** Ex 12.18–20; Deut 16.5–8. **10:** The plans appear to rest on some prior arrangement; a man carrying a jar of water would be doing woman's work and would be easily noticeable. **11:** The identity of the householder is unknown. **12:** The *large room upstairs* was on the second floor, probably served by an outside staircase; such rooms were regularly available and rented to pilgrims to Jerusalem.

22.14–20: The Last Supper (Mt 26.26–29; Mk 14.22–25; cf. Jn 6.51–58). **14:** *The hour,* of the meal, after sundown. **15:** 12.49–50. **16:** Jesus thinks of the meal as pointing forward to the meal celebrating the fulfilling of God's kingdom (12.37n.; 13.28–29; 14.15; 22.28–30). **17:** Some Jewish meals included prayers over the cup of wine, and several such prayers might be offered during the meal (see v. 20). Luke's order of events may be related to this practice, or to a variation among early Christians in the way they remembered and observed the "Lord's supper." Jesus transformed a Jewish devotional meal into a continuing expression of association with himself in death and victory. **19:** 1 Cor 11.23–26. **21:** Ps 41.9; Jn 13.21–30.

22.21–23: The foretelling of the betrayal (Mt 26.21–25; Mk 14.18–21; Jn 13.21–30).

22.24–30: True discipleship (Mt 20.24–28; Mk 10.41–45). These verses and those of the two sections that follow (21.31–34,35–38) form a brief farewell discourse delivered by Jesus to his disciples. **24:** Jn 13.3–16. **25:** *Benefactors,* a title bestowed on Hellenistic kings. **27:** See 12.37n.

me in my trials; 29 and I confer on you, just
as my Father has conferred on me, a king-
dom, 30 so that you may eat and drink at
my table in my kingdom, and you will sit
on thrones judging the twelve tribes of Is-
rael.
31 “Simon, Simon, listen! Satan has de-
manded[a] to sift all of you like wheat,
32 but I have prayed for you that your own
faith may not fail; and you, when once you
have turned back, strengthen your broth-
ers.” 33 And he said to him, “Lord, I am
ready to go with you to prison and to
death!” 34 Jesus[b] said, “I tell you, Peter,
the cock will not crow this day, until you
have denied three times that you
know me.”
35 He said to them, “When I sent you
out without a purse, bag, or sandals, did
you lack anything?” They said, “No, not a
thing.” 36 He said to them, “But now, the
one who has a purse must take it, and like-
wise a bag. And the one who has no sword
must sell his cloak and buy one. 37 For I tell
you, this scripture must be fulfilled in me,
‘And he was counted among the lawless’;
and indeed what is written about me is
being fulfilled.” 38 They said, “Lord, look,
here are two swords.” He replied, “It is
enough.”
39 He came out and went, as was his
custom, to the Mount of Olives; and the
disciples followed him. 40 When he reached
the place, he said to them, “Pray that you
may not come into the time of trial.”[c]
41 Then he withdrew from them about a
stone’s throw, knelt down, and prayed,
42 “Father, if you are willing, remove this
cup from me; yet, not my will but yours be
done.” ⟦43 Then an angel from heaven ap-
peared to him and gave him strength. 44 In
his anguish he prayed more earnestly, and
his sweat became like great drops of blood
falling down on the ground.⟧[d] 45 When he
got up from prayer, he came to the disciples
and found them sleeping because of grief,
46 and he said to them, “Why are you sleep-
ing? Get up and pray that you may not
come into the time of trial.”[c]
47 While he was still speaking, suddenly
a crowd came, and the one called Judas,
one of the twelve, was leading them. He
approached Jesus to kiss him; 48 but Jesus
said to him, “Judas, is it with a kiss that
you are betraying the Son of Man?”
49 When those who were around him saw
what was coming, they asked, “Lord,
should we strike with the sword?” 50 Then
one of them struck the slave of the high
priest and cut off his right ear. 51 But Jesus
said, “No more of this!” And he touched
his ear and healed him. 52 Then Jesus said
to the chief priests, the officers of the tem-
ple police, and the elders who had come for
him, “Have you come out with swords and
clubs as if I were a bandit? 53 When I was
with you day after day in the temple, you
did not lay hands on me. But this is your
hour, and the power of darkness!”
54 Then they seized him and led him

a Or *has obtained permission* *b* Gk *He* *c* Or *into temptation* *d* Other ancient authorities lack verses 43 and 44

22.31–34: The foretelling of Peter’s denial (Mt 26.30–35; Mk 14.26–31; Jn 13.36–38). **31:** Job 1.6–12; Am 9.9. **32:** *You* in this verse is singular (contrast v. 31). **34:** See vv. 54–62.

22.35–38: Sayings about the coming crisis. 35: See 10.4; cf. 9.3. **36:** An example of Jesus’ fondness for striking metaphors, but the disciples take it literally (v. 38). **37:** Isa 53.12. **38:** An ironic rebuke.

22.39–46: Jesus’ prayer on the Mount of Olives (Mt 26.36–46; Mk 14.32–42; Jn 18.1–2). **40:** See 11.4. **42:** *Cup,* metaphor for that which is allotted by God, whether blessing (Ps 16.5; 116.13) or judgment (Isa 51.17; Lam 4.21). Here it refers to Jesus’ suffering and death. **43–44:** Important early manuscripts lack these verses, but they were known to Christian writers of the second century and reflect tradition concerning the suffering of Jesus. Whether they were a part of the original text is debatable.

22.47–53: The betrayal and arrest of Jesus (Mt 26.47–56; Mk 14.43–52; Jn 18.2–12). **52:** Isa 53.12. Only in Luke are the chief priests themselves present.

22.54–62: Peter’s denials (Mt 26.69–75; Mk 14.66–72; Jn 18.25–27). **54–55:** Jn 18.12–16. **56–62:** Jn 18.16–18,25–27. **61:** 22.34. Jesus’ turning to face Peter is a detail found only in Luke (cf. 7.13).

away, bringing him into the high priest's
house. But Peter was following at a dis-
tance. 55 When they had kindled a fire in
the middle of the courtyard and sat down
together, Peter sat among them. 56 Then a
servant-girl, seeing him in the firelight,
stared at him and said, "This man also was
with him." 57 But he denied it, saying,
"Woman, I do not know him." 58 A little
later someone else, on seeing him, said,
"You also are one of them." But Peter said,
"Man, I am not!" 59 Then about an hour
later still another kept insisting, "Surely
this man also was with him; for he is a
Galilean." 60 But Peter said, "Man, I do not
know what you are talking about!" At that
moment, while he was still speaking, the
cock crowed. 61 The Lord turned and
looked at Peter. Then Peter remembered
the word of the Lord, how he had said to
him, "Before the cock crows today, you
will deny me three times." 62 And he went
out and wept bitterly.

63 Now the men who were holding
Jesus began to mock him and beat him;
64 they also blindfolded him and kept ask-
ing him, "Prophesy! Who is it that struck
you?" 65 They kept heaping many other in-
sults on him.

66 When day came, the assembly of the
elders of the people, both chief priests and
scribes, gathered together, and they
brought him to their council. 67 They said,
"If you are the Messiah,[a] tell us." He re-
plied, "If I tell you, you will not believe;
68 and if I question you, you will not an-
swer. 69 But from now on the Son of Man
will be seated at the right hand of the pow-
er of God." 70 All of them asked, "Are you,
then, the Son of God?" He said to them,
"You say that I am." 71 Then they said,
"What further testimony do we need? We
have heard it ourselves from his own lips!"

23 Then the assembly rose as a body
and brought Jesus[b] before Pilate.
2 They began to accuse him, saying, "We
found this man perverting our nation,
forbidding us to pay taxes to the emperor,
and saying that he himself is the Messiah,
a king."[c] 3 Then Pilate asked him, "Are
you the king of the Jews?" He answered,
"You say so." 4 Then Pilate said to the chief
priests and the crowds, "I find no basis for
an accusation against this man." 5 But they
were insistent and said, "He stirs up the
people by teaching throughout all Judea,
from Galilee where he began even to this
place."

6 When Pilate heard this, he asked
whether the man was a Galilean. 7 And
when he learned that he was under Herod's
jurisdiction, he sent him off to Herod, who
was himself in Jerusalem at that time.
8 When Herod saw Jesus, he was very glad,
for he had been wanting to see him for a
long time, because he had heard about him
and was hoping to see him perform some
sign. 9 He questioned him at some length,
but Jesus[d] gave him no answer. 10 The
chief priests and the scribes stood by, vehe-
mently accusing him. 11 Even Herod with
his soldiers treated him with contempt and
mocked him; then he put an elegant robe

a Or *the Christ* *b* Gk *him* *c* Or *is an anointed king* *d* Gk *he*

22.63–65: The mockery of Jesus (Mt 26.67–68; 27.27–31a; Mk 14.65; 15.16–20a). See Jn 18.22–24. This scene in Luke's account is located differently in the sequence of the narrative from the parallels in the other Gospels.

22.66–71: Jesus before the council (Mt 27.1; 26.59–65; Mk 15.1; 14.55–63; Jn 18.13–14,19–23). **66:** *Council,* Gk "synedrion," Sanhedrin. **67:** The demand put to Jesus, *If you are the Messiah, tell us,* becomes an element of the charges against Jesus before Pilate in 23.2. **69:** See Ps 110.1; Dan 7.13.

23.1–5: Jesus before Pilate (Mt 27.1–14; Mk 15.1–5; Jn 18.28–38). **1:** *Pilate,* see 3.1n. **2:** Cf. 19.38; 20.25; see Acts 24.5. The charge is phrased to sound like treason. **4:** 23.14,22,41; Jn 19.4,6; Acts 13.28. Pilate refused to take religious ideas in a political sense. Here, and later, Pilate sought to free Jesus but then yielded to pressures.

23.6–12: Jesus before Herod. Only Luke reports this episode. *Herod* Antipas was a son of Herod the Great (see 3.1n.). **8:** 9.9; Acts 4.27–28. **11:** Jn 19.2–3.

on him, and sent him back to Pilate. 12 That
same day Herod and Pilate became friends
with each other; before this they had been
enemies.
13 Pilate then called together the chief
priests, the leaders, and the people, 14 and
said to them, "You brought me this man as
one who was perverting the people; and
here I have examined him in your presence
and have not found this man guilty of any
of your charges against him. 15 Neither has
Herod, for he sent him back to us. Indeed,
he has done nothing to deserve death. 16 I
will therefore have him flogged and release
him."[a]
18 Then they all shouted out together,
"Away with this fellow! Release Barabbas
for us!" 19 (This was a man who had been
put in prison for an insurrection that had
taken place in the city, and for murder.)
20 Pilate, wanting to release Jesus, ad-
dressed them again; 21 but they kept shout-
ing, "Crucify, crucify him!" 22 A third time
he said to them, "Why, what evil has he
done? I have found in him no ground for
the sentence of death; I will therefore have
him flogged and then release him." 23 But
they kept urgently demanding with loud
shouts that he should be crucified; and their
voices prevailed. 24 So Pilate gave his ver-
dict that their demand should be granted.
25 He released the man they asked for, the
one who had been put in prison for insur-
rection and murder, and he handed Jesus
over as they wished.
26 As they led him away, they seized a
man, Simon of Cyrene, who was coming
from the country, and they laid the cross on
him, and made him carry it behind Jesus.
27 A great number of the people followed
him, and among them were women who
were beating their breasts and wailing for
him. 28 But Jesus turned to them and said,
"Daughters of Jerusalem, do not weep for
me, but weep for yourselves and for your
children. 29 For the days are surely coming
when they will say, 'Blessed are the barren,
and the wombs that never bore, and the
breasts that never nursed.' 30 Then they will
begin to say to the mountains, 'Fall on us';
and to the hills, 'Cover us.' 31 For if they do
this when the wood is green, what will hap-
pen when it is dry?"
32 Two others also, who were criminals,
were led away to be put to death with him.
33 When they came to the place that is
called The Skull, they crucified Jesus[b]
there with the criminals, one on his right
and one on his left. ⟦34 Then Jesus said, "Fa-
ther, forgive them; for they do not know
what they are doing."⟧[c] And they cast lots
to divide his clothing. 35 And the people
stood by, watching; but the leaders scoffed
at him, saying, "He saved others; let him
save himself if he is the Messiah[d] of God,
his chosen one!" 36 The soldiers also
mocked him, coming up and offering him
sour wine, 37 and saying, "If you are the
King of the Jews, save yourself!" 38 There

a Here, or after verse 19, other ancient authorities add verse 17, *Now he was obliged to release someone for them at the festival* b Gk *him* c Other ancient authorities lack the sentence *Then Jesus . . . what they are doing* d Or *the Christ*

23.13–16 [17]: Pilate's declaration of Jesus' innocence. 14: Vv. 4,22,41. **16:** Jn 19.12–14. **[17]:** An addition to Luke's account from Mk 15.6; see note there.

23.18–25: The sentencing of Jesus to death (Mt 27.15–26; Mk 15.6–15; Jn 18.39–40; 19.16; see Acts 3.13–14).

23.26–31: On the way to the cross (Mt 27.31b–32; Mk 15.20b–21; Jn 19.17a). **26:** *Cyrene,* in Libya. *The cross,* i.e., the horizontal cross-beam. **28–32:** 21.23–24; 19.41–44. **30:** Incorporates wording parallel to Hos 10.8. **31:** Cf. Prov 11.31. This proverb may mean either that if the innocent Jesus meets such a fate, then a worse fate awaits the guilty Jerusalem, or that if such takes place with Jesus present and active, what will happen when he is no longer present? Cf. 1 Pet 4.17–18.

23.32: Two criminals with Jesus.

23.33–38: The scene of the crucifixion (Mt 27.33–43; Mk 15.22–32a; Jn 19.17b–27). **33:** *The Skull,* its Aramaic name, Golgotha, is found in the other Gospels. **34:** See note *c*; cf. Acts 7.60. The final phrase alludes to Ps 22.18. **36:** Ps 69.21.

was also an inscription over him,[a] "This is
the King of the Jews."
39 One of the criminals who were
hanged there kept deriding[b] him and say-
ing, "Are you not the Messiah?[c] Save
yourself and us!" 40 But the other rebuked
him, saying, "Do you not fear God, since
you are under the same sentence of con-
demnation? 41 And we indeed have been
condemned justly, for we are getting what
we deserve for our deeds, but this man has
done nothing wrong." 42 Then he said,
"Jesus, remember me when you come
into[d] your kingdom." 43 He replied, "Tru-
ly I tell you, today you will be with me in
Paradise."
44 It was now about noon, and darkness
came over the whole land[e] until three in
the afternoon, 45 while the sun's light
failed;[f] and the curtain of the temple was
torn in two. 46 Then Jesus, crying with a
loud voice, said, "Father, into your hands I
commend my spirit." Having said this, he
breathed his last. 47 When the centurion
saw what had taken place, he praised God
and said, "Certainly this man was inno-
cent."[g] 48 And when all the crowds who
had gathered there for this spectacle saw
what had taken place, they returned home,
beating their breasts. 49 But all his acquaint-
ances, including the women who had fol-
lowed him from Galilee, stood at a dis-
tance, watching these things.
50 Now there was a good and righteous
man named Joseph, who, though a member
of the council, 51 had not agreed to their
plan and action. He came from the Jewish
town of Arimathea, and he was waiting ex-
pectantly for the kingdom of God. 52 This
man went to Pilate and asked for the body
of Jesus. 53 Then he took it down, wrapped
it in a linen cloth, and laid it in a rock-hewn
tomb where no one had ever been laid. 54 It
was the day of Preparation, and the sab-
bath was beginning.[h] 55 The women who
had come with him from Galilee followed,
and they saw the tomb and how his body
was laid. 56 Then they returned, and pre-
pared spices and ointments.
On the sabbath they rested according to
the commandment.

24 But on the first day of the week, at
early dawn, they came to the tomb,
taking the spices that they had prepared.
2 They found the stone rolled away from

a Other ancient authorities add *written in Greek and Latin and Hebrew* (that is, *Aramaic*)
b Or *blaspheming* *c* Or *the Christ* *d* Other ancient authorities read *in* *e* Or *earth* *f* Or *the sun was eclipsed.* Other ancient authorities read *the sun was darkened* *g* Or *righteous* *h* Gk *was dawning*

23.39–43: The exchange between Jesus and the two criminals (Mt 27.44; Mk 15.32b). **41:** Vv. 4,14,22. **42:** The robber's appeal may be based on the charge against Jesus (vv. 2,3,38); he thinks in terms of 21.27–28. Jesus promises him more than he asked, intimating that God's kingly power is a present reality, not merely future. **43:** *Paradise,* originally a term for the garden of Eden (Gen 2.8–10), was a contemporary term for the lodging place of the righteous dead prior to the resurrection; cf. 16.22.

23.44–48: The death of Jesus (Mt 27.45–54; Mk 15.33–39; Jn 19.28–30). **45:** Ex 26.31–35. *The sun's light failed,* the translation is uncertain; see Am 8.9; Joel 2.31. **46:** Jesus' words quote Ps 31.6. **47:** In the context of Luke's Gospel, the centurion (see 7.2n.) declares Jesus to be "righteous" rather than merely *innocent.* **48:** The cause of this popular agitation is not clear (Zech 12.10), though compare 18.13–14 for a possible meaning of the crowd's reaction.

23.49: Jesus' acquaintances at the crucifixion (Mt 27.55–56; Mk 15.40–41; Jn 19.25–27). See 23.55; cf. 8.1–3; 24.10; Ps 38.11.

23.50–54: The burial of Jesus (Mt 27.57–60; Mk 15.42–46; Jn 19.38–42). **50:** *The council,* 22.66n. **54:** *The sabbath* began at sundown. Luke, perhaps having Gentile readers in mind, indicates the urgency of the burial in Jewish custom.

23.55–56: Women at the burial (Mt 27.61; Mk 15.47–16.1). **55:** Cf. 24.10. **56:** Ex 12.16; 20.10. *Spices and ointments* were applied to the corpse; see Mk 16.1; Jn 19.40.

24.1–53: The empty tomb and the resurrection (Mt 28.1–8; Mk 16.1–8; Jn 20.1–13,19–23).

24.1–12: The women at the tomb (Mt 28.1–8; Mk 16.1–8; Jn 20.1–13). **4:** The *two men* wear clothing

the tomb, 3 but when they went in, they did
not find the body.[a] 4 While they were per-
plexed about this, suddenly two men in
dazzling clothes stood beside them. 5 The
women[b] were terrified and bowed their
faces to the ground, but the men[c] said to
them, "Why do you look for the living
among the dead? He is not here, but has
risen.[d] 6 Remember how he told you, while
he was still in Galilee, 7 that the Son of Man
must be handed over to sinners, and be cru-
cified, and on the third day rise again."
8 Then they remembered his words, 9 and
returning from the tomb, they told all this
to the eleven and to all the rest. 10 Now it
was Mary Magdalene, Joanna, Mary the
mother of James, and the other women
with them who told this to the apostles.
11 But these words seemed to them an idle
tale, and they did not believe them. 12 But
Peter got up and ran to the tomb; stooping
and looking in, he saw the linen cloths by
themselves; then he went home, amazed at
what had happened.[e]

13 Now on that same day two of them
were going to a village called Emmaus,
about seven miles[f] from Jerusalem, 14 and
talking with each other about all these
things that had happened. 15 While they
were talking and discussing, Jesus himself
came near and went with them, 16 but their
eyes were kept from recognizing him.
17 And he said to them, "What are you dis-
cussing with each other while you walk
along?" They stood still, looking sad.[g]
18 Then one of them, whose name was Cle-
opas, answered him, "Are you the only
stranger in Jerusalem who does not know
the things that have taken place there in
these days?" 19 He asked them, "What
things?" They replied, "The things about
Jesus of Nazareth,[h] who was a prophet
mighty in deed and word before God and
all the people, 20 and how our chief priests
and leaders handed him over to be con-
demned to death and crucified him. 21 But
we had hoped that he was the one to re-
deem Israel.[i] Yes, and besides all this, it is
now the third day since these things took
place. 22 Moreover, some women of our
group astounded us. They were at the tomb
early this morning, 23 and when they did
not find his body there, they came back and
told us that they had indeed seen a vision of
angels who said that he was alive. 24 Some
of those who were with us went to the
tomb and found it just as the women had
said; but they did not see him." 25 Then he
said to them, "Oh, how foolish you are,
and how slow of heart to believe all that the
prophets have declared! 26 Was it not neces-
sary that the Messiah[j] should suffer these
things and then enter into his glory?"
27 Then beginning with Moses and all the
prophets, he interpreted to them the things
about himself in all the scriptures.

28 As they came near the village to
which they were going, he walked ahead as

a Other ancient authorities add *of the Lord Jesus*
b Gk *They* *c* Gk *but they* *d* Other ancient authorities lack *He is not here, but has risen*
e Other ancient authorities lack verse 12 *f* Gk *sixty stadia;* other ancient authorities read *a hundred sixty stadia* *g* Other ancient authorities read *walk along, looking sad?"* *h* Other ancient authorities read *Jesus the Nazorean* *i* Or *to set Israel free* *j* Or *the Christ*

that identifies them as angels, not ordinary humans (see v. 23), as do their sudden appearance and supernatural knowledge (vv. 5–7). **6:** 9.22; 13.32–33. *You* here suggests that Jesus' disciples as a group often included others in addition to those of the inner circle. **10:** 8.1–3; Jn 19.25; 20.2. **12:** This verse, though appearing in some ancient manuscripts, seems to be an addition to the original text of Luke based on Jn 20.3–10.

24.13–35: The Emmaus incident. 13: *Seven miles,* lit. "sixty stadia"; a stade was approximately 180 m (600 ft). The exact location of Emmaus is uncertain. **16:** The inability of these persons to recognize Jesus is typical of initial reactions to Jesus in resurrection stories (cf. 24.37). **19:** 7.16; 13.33; Acts 3.22; 10.38. **26:** *Necessary* because of God's divine plan (see 7.30; Acts 2.23; 13.36; 20.27). **27:** *Moses,* the traditional author of the first five books of the Bible. *The prophets,* a major section of the Jewish scriptures more extensive in scope than the prophetic works of the Hebrew Bible (see 16.16n; 24.44; Acts 28.23). **30:** *Took, blessed,* and *broke,* echo the actions of Jesus at the Last Supper (22.19) and the

if he were going on. 29 But they urged him
strongly, saying, "Stay with us, because it is
almost evening and the day is now nearly
over." So he went in to stay with them.
30 When he was at the table with them, he
took bread, blessed and broke it, and gave
it to them. 31 Then their eyes were opened,
and they recognized him; and he vanished
from their sight. 32 They said to each other,
"Were not our hearts burning within us[a]
while he was talking to us on the road,
while he was opening the scriptures to us?"
33 That same hour they got up and returned
to Jerusalem; and they found the eleven
and their companions gathered together.
34 They were saying, "The Lord has risen
indeed, and he has appeared to Simon!"
35 Then they told what had happened on
the road, and how he had been made
known to them in the breaking of the
bread.

36 While they were talking about this,
Jesus himself stood among them and said to
them, "Peace be with you."[b] 37 They were
startled and terrified, and thought that they
were seeing a ghost. 38 He said to them,
"Why are you frightened, and why do
doubts arise in your hearts? 39 Look at my
hands and my feet; see that it is I myself.
Touch me and see; for a ghost does not
have flesh and bones as you see that I
have." 40 And when he had said this, he
showed them his hands and his feet.[c]
41 While in their joy they were disbelieving
and still wondering, he said to them, "Have
you anything here to eat?" 42 They gave
him a piece of broiled fish, 43 and he took it
and ate in their presence.

44 Then he said to them, "These are my
words that I spoke to you while I was still
with you—that everything written about
me in the law of Moses, the prophets, and
the psalms must be fulfilled." 45 Then he
opened their minds to understand the scrip-
tures, 46 and he said to them, "Thus it is
written, that the Messiah[d] is to suffer and
to rise from the dead on the third day,
47 and that repentance and forgiveness of
sins is to be proclaimed in his name to all
nations, beginning from Jerusalem. 48 You
are witnesses[e] of these things. 49 And see,
I am sending upon you what my Father
promised; so stay here in the city until you
have been clothed with power from on
high."

50 Then he led them out as far as Betha-
ny, and, lifting up his hands, he blessed
them. 51 While he was blessing them, he
withdrew from them and was carried up
into heaven.[f] 52 And they worshiped him,
and[g] returned to Jerusalem with great joy;
53 and they were continually in the temple
blessing God.[h]

a Other ancient authorities lack *within us* *b* Other ancient authorities lack *and said to them, "Peace be with you."* *c* Other ancient authorities lack verse 40 *d* Or *the Christ* *e* Or *nations. Beginning from Jerusalem* 48*you are witnesses* *f* Other ancient authorities lack *and was carried up into heaven* *g* Other ancient authorities lack *worshiped him, and* *h* Other ancient authorities add *Amen*

multiplication of the loaves (9.16). **34:** 1 Cor 15.5. Peter's experience is not described. **35:** *Breaking of the bread,* see Acts 2.42; 20.7; 1 Cor 10.16.

24.36–43: Jesus' appearance to his disciples (Jn 20.19–23). See 1 Cor 15.5. The experience of Jesus, affirmed in v. 36, is tentatively interpreted in v. 37 as an encounter with the dead, but this explanation is rejected in v. 39. **42:** *Broiled fish,* cf. Jn 21.9–13.

24.44–53: Jesus' final words and withdrawal into heaven (cf. elements of the longer ending of Mark: Mk 16.15,19). **44:** Vv. 26–27; Acts 28.23. The Psalms formed the opening and the longest part of the third division of the Hebrew Bible; see 16.16n. **45:** 24.32. **46:** Hos 6.2; cf. 1 Cor 15.3–4. **47:** Acts 1.4–8; 5.31; 10.43; 13.38; 26.18. **49:** *Power from on high,* the words allude to the energy of the Spirit of God referred to in Joel 2.28–32 (cf. Acts 2.1–21). The new age has begun, but its power is not yet fully realized. **50:** *Bethany,* see 19.29n. **51:** Acts 1.9–11. **52–53:** Acts 1.12–14; 2.46–47.

The Gospel According to
JOHN

The prologue of the Fourth Gospel (1.1–18), long recognized as the introduction to and summary of the Gospel's main concerns and emphases, takes pains not only to acknowledge Jesus as a human being, but as a social being as well when it proclaims, "The Word became flesh and lived among us" (1.14). Any effort to understand the Fourth Gospel must take this central pronouncement as a major point of interpretive entry. For although it speaks in a mystical tone that is meant to convey the unique relationship to God and solitary grandeur of the person of Jesus, the Fourth Gospel treats with equal gravity the "fleshly" nature of Jesus as it critiques the social relations and structures of the world that Jesus confronts. Thus even as it presents Jesus as the incarnate Word of God, the Fourth Gospel is also the story of Jesus as flesh and blood. Indeed, a careful reading reveals its focus to be precisely the doings of the "flesh" in the "world" (1.10), that is, the activities of Jesus and the individual and collective responses to them.

In telling the story of Jesus the author symbolically uses a number of terms drawn from common experience—bread, water, light, life, word, shepherd, door, way—to make the significance of Jesus both clear and gripping. After the prologue (1.1–1.18), the Gospel presents the public ministry of Jesus as both the object of faith (1.19–4.54) and the object of persecution and unbelief (chs 5–12), depicts his ministry to the disciples in the upper room (chs 13–17), narrates his death and resurrection (chs 18–20), and concludes with an epilogue (ch 21). The following division is suggested by the Gospel itself: the prologue (1.1–18); the book of Jesus' signs that he is the revelation of the Father (1.19–12.50); the book of Jesus' glory as it is revealed through his crucifixion, resurrection, and ascension to those that accept him (13.1–20.31); the epilogue, which contains accounts of Jesus' post-resurrection appearances (21.1–25).

The major concerns of the Gospel are engendering faith in the person of Jesus (20.21) and discrediting the Temple-centered, hereditary religious authorities who present a collective obstacle to the acceptance of faith in Jesus (1.14; 9.22–23). Its attempts to engender faith in Jesus are seen in its presentation of him as the incarnate Word (1.1), the only begotten Son (3.16,18), the messiah (1.41), the Holy One of God (6.69), the King of Israel (1.49), its portrayal of him as totally in control in his life as well as in his death (18.12; 19.30), and its use as a term of self-description the Greek phrase "ego eimi" ("I am") without a predicate, which is reminiscent of God's self-reference in Ex 3.14; Isa 41.4; 43.10; 46.4. Its concern to discredit the religious authorities, whom it calls "the Jews," is effectuated by portraying them as mercenary and uncaring shepherds (10.12–13), as haughty and condescending to the people (7.15,49; 9.34), as being more concerned with worldly acclaim than divine favor (12.43), and as betrayers of Jesus (11.53). In addition to its usage as cited above, in many instances its repeated use of "ego eimi" with a predicate contrasts Jesus with the religious authorities ("I am") or portrays him as replacing some aspect of established first-century Judaism. Even further, it presents him as embodying basic elements of the natural world, such as light (8.12) and life itself (11.25). This replacement or embodying motif is employed in other instances, such as the depiction of Jesus as replacing the Temple and the Passover (6.1–4), and serves to strengthen the Gospel's emphasis on the incarnation.

Although its scathing portrayal of "the Jews" has opened it to charges of anti-Semitism, a careful reading of the Gospel reveals "the Jews" to be a class designation, not a religious or ethnic grouping; rather than denoting adherents to Judaism in general, the term primarily refers to the hereditary Temple religious authorities. The Gospel further acknowledges their influential status by including among "the Jews" those who have accepted the worldview and class interests of the hereditary religious authorities as their own. This larger group includes the Pharisees (1.19,24) and even the "crowd" of laypersons whose worth the religious authorities dismissed (7.49; cf. 6.22,41). Thus the rejection and persecution of Jesus by "the Jews" is seen to be not only the result of what he says and does, but because his healings, his pronouncements, and his earthly person lack the pedigree and imprimatur of the religious elite (7.15,48–49; cf. 9.34).

Several factors in the Fourth Gospel's attention to detail in the story of the fleshly Jesus suggest that it incorporates a much earlier tradition. Current scholarly consensus dates the final editing of the Gospel in 80–90 CE. The bitter and combative tone with which the Gospel discredits "the Jews" and its angry demonizing of them, as in 8.44, for instance, indicates opposition to a dominant group with the power to determine who is to be accepted in the Jewish community by anathematizing and expelling from Judaism those who challenge the dominant group's authority (9.22; 12.42). The powerful Temple hierarchy, in effect, ceased to exist in 70 CE with the destruction of the Jerusalem Temple. Moreover, the portrayal of Jesus as replacing the Temple may suggest that the Temple still stands as the center of Judaism (5.2), even as it repeats longstanding critiques of the Temple that prophesy its destruction (2.19; 4.21). Once the Temple and its hierarchy were no longer in existence, this polemic was transferred to local opponents of Christian believers. The "Jews" are equated with "the world" (16.1–4). Finally, recent archaeological finds indicate that the Fourth Gospel contains accurate details about the Jerusalem Temple and its environs prior to 70 CE (e.g., 9.7; 10.22–23; 19.13). Together these factors suggest a possible alternate date for the earliest version of the Gospel material before 70 CE. Although the theological complexity and high christology, especially in chs 14–17, could indicate a longer period of theological gestation and symbolic development (and this is the view of most scholars), similarly developed views are found in such early New Testament writings as Paul's letter to the Romans. Although some scholars deny any dependence of the Fourth Gospel upon the Synoptic Gospels, most scholars accept the Fourth Gospel's dependence upon the Synoptics; at the least, they hold that its writer was aware of them.

Who wrote this Gospel? Tradition says it was the apostle John. Scholarly opinion has long held that it was composed by a disciple of John who recorded his preaching. The epilogue speaks of an anonymous, loyal Jerusalem disciple of Jesus, called "the disciple whom Jesus loved" (20.2; see 13.23; 19.26; 21.7,20), as the source of this unique understanding of Jesus.

1 In the beginning was the Word, and the
Word was with God, and the Word was
God. 2 He was in the beginning with God.
3 All things came into being through him,
and without him not one thing came into
being. What has come into being 4 in him

1.1–18: The prologue signals the major concerns of the Gospel. **1–3:** The *Word* (Gk "logos") of God is more than speech; it is God's preeminent agent in the world, creating (Ps 33.6; Wis 9.1; Sir 43.26; cf. Gen 1.3, etc.), redeeming (Ps 107.19–20; Wis 18.15). The *Word* is eternally (*in the beginning*) and personally (*with* God) divine (*was* God). Jesus is this *Word* (v. 14). **3:** Using language derived from the depiction of Wisdom (Prov 8.27–30; Wis 9.9; Sir 24.9), Jesus is described as God's sole mediator of creation (see Col 1.16–17; Heb 1.2). **4:** Cf. Wis 7.26. **5:** The "Word" shone in the primal darkness of

was life,[a] and the life was the light of all
people. 5 The light shines in the darkness,
and the darkness did not overcome it.
6 There was a man sent from God,
whose name was John. 7 He came as a wit-
ness to testify to the light, so that all might
believe through him. 8 He himself was not
the light, but he came to testify to the light.
9 The true light, which enlightens everyone,
was coming into the world.[b]
10 He was in the world, and the world
came into being through him; yet the world
did not know him. 11 He came to what was
his own,[c] and his own people did not ac-
cept him. 12 But to all who received him,
who believed in his name, he gave power to
become children of God, 13 who were born,
not of blood or of the will of the flesh or of
the will of man, but of God.
14 And the Word became flesh and lived
among us, and we have seen his glory, the
glory as of a father's only son,[d] full of
grace and truth. 15 (John testified to him
and cried out, "This was he of whom I said,
'He who comes after me ranks ahead of me
because he was before me.' ") 16 From his
fullness we have all received, grace upon
grace. 17 The law indeed was given through
Moses; grace and truth came through
Jesus Christ. 18 No one has ever seen God.
It is God the only Son,[e] who is close to
the Father's heart,[f] who has made him
known.

19 This is the testimony given by John
when the Jews sent priests and Levites
from Jerusalem to ask him, "Who are
you?" 20 He confessed and did not deny it,
but confessed, "I am not the Messiah."[g]
21 And they asked him, "What then? Are
you Elijah?" He said, "I am not." "Are you
the prophet?" He answered, "No." 22 Then
they said to him, "Who are you? Let us
have an answer for those who sent us.
What do you say about yourself?" 23 He
said,

"I am the voice of one crying out
in the wilderness,
'Make straight the way of
the Lord,' "

as the prophet Isaiah said.
24 Now they had been sent from the
Pharisees. 25 They asked him, "Why then

a Or [3]*through him. And without him not one thing came into being that has come into being.* [4]*In him was life* *b* Or *He was the true light that enlightens everyone coming into the world* *c* Or *to his own home* *d* Or *the Father's only Son* *e* Other ancient authorities read *It is an only Son, God,* or *It is the only Son* *f* Gk *bosom* *g* Or *the Christ*

creation (Gen 1.2) and continues to shine (cf. Ps 18.28). **6–8:** Summary of John's role. John (the Baptist) was *sent* (commissioned by God; Isa 6.8; Jer 1.7; Mal 3.1) to be a witness to Jesus (vv. 19–34). **10:** The primary meaning of *world* in the Fourth Gospel is the fallible social systems and social relations created by humanity (see 12.31; 16.11), but it also denotes physical creation, including humanity. **11:** *His own people,* the Jews, who were uniquely God's own people (4.22; Ex 19.5; Rom 15.8). **12–13:** Membership in the household of God is determined not by hereditary claims of privileged status, such as those of the hereditary priesthood of Israel, but by God alone. In this context *will of man* (lit. "will of a man") could refer to religious officials. **14:** Jesus was fully human (*the Word became flesh*) and fully involved in human society (*and lived among us*). **15:** Jesus has both priority of status and priority in time, with regard to John (see vv. 2–3,30). **16:** His grace is inexhaustible (*grace upon grace*). **17:** God's earlier revelation of covenant faithfulness is brought to fulfillment in Jesus. **18:** Jesus' priority over Moses (Ex 34.18–20) is reinforced.

1.19–34: The testimony of John. 19: *The Jews,* the Temple religious authorities; also used for those who supported them (see v. 24n.). **21:** *Elijah* (2 Kings 2.11) was expected to return to prepare the messiah's way (Mal 4.5). *The prophet* was likewise an expected messianic forerunner (6.14; 7.40; see Deut 18.15). **23:** As a *voice* John fulfills a prophetic role announcing the messiah's coming (Isa 40.3). **24:** *The Pharisees,* along with the high priest and the chief priests, comprised "the Jews," the religious authorities. These terms are used interchangeably (see v. 19; 7.32,45; 11.47,57; 18.3,12). The Pharisees were an influential Jewish sect committed to extending priestly standards of purity to all Jews. **25:** John was challenged because he lacked a status recognized by the religious authorities and engaged in a ritual not

are you baptizing if you are neither the
Messiah,[a] nor Elijah, nor the prophet?"
26 John answered them, "I baptize with wa-
ter. Among you stands one whom you do
not know, 27 the one who is coming after
me; I am not worthy to untie the thong of
his sandal." 28 This took place in Bethany
across the Jordan where John was baptiz-
ing.
29 The next day he saw Jesus coming
toward him and declared, "Here is the
Lamb of God who takes away the sin of the
world! 30 This is he of whom I said, 'After
me comes a man who ranks ahead of me
because he was before me.' 31 I myself did
not know him; but I came baptizing with
water for this reason, that he might be re-
vealed to Israel." 32 And John testified, "I
saw the Spirit descending from heaven like
a dove, and it remained on him. 33 I myself
did not know him, but the one who sent me
to baptize with water said to me, 'He on
whom you see the Spirit descend and re-
main is the one who baptizes with the Holy
Spirit.' 34 And I myself have seen and have
testified that this is the Son of God."[b]
35 The next day John again was stand-
ing with two of his disciples, 36 and as he
watched Jesus walk by, he exclaimed,
"Look, here is the Lamb of God!" 37 The
two disciples heard him say this, and they
followed Jesus. 38 When Jesus turned and
saw them following, he said to them,
"What are you looking for?" They said
to him, "Rabbi" (which translated means
Teacher), "where are you staying?" 39 He
said to them, "Come and see." They came
and saw where he was staying, and they
remained with him that day. It was about
four o'clock in the afternoon. 40 One of the
two who heard John speak and followed
him was Andrew, Simon Peter's brother.
41 He first found his brother Simon and said
to him, "We have found the Messiah"
(which is translated Anointed[c]). 42 He
brought Simon[d] to Jesus, who looked at
him and said, "You are Simon son of John.
You are to be called Cephas" (which is
translated Peter[e]).
43 The next day Jesus decided to go to
Galilee. He found Philip and said to him,
"Follow me." 44 Now Philip was from
Bethsaida, the city of Andrew and Peter.
45 Philip found Nathanael and said to him,
"We have found him about whom Moses
in the law and also the prophets wrote,
Jesus son of Joseph from Nazareth." 46 Na-
thanael said to him, "Can anything good
come out of Nazareth?" Philip said to him,
"Come and see." 47 When Jesus saw Na-
thanael coming toward him, he said of him,
"Here is truly an Israelite in whom there
is no deceit!" 48 Nathanael asked him,
"Where did you get to know me?" Jesus

a Or *the Christ* *b* Other ancient authorities read *is God's chosen one* *c* Or *Christ* *d* Gk *him*
e From the word for *rock* in Aramaic (*kepha*) and Greek (*petra*), respectively

sanctioned by them. **27:** *Untie . . . sandal,* a slave's task. John's baptism is preparation for the appearance of the hidden messiah who is already in their midst. **28:** *Bethany across the Jordan,* precise location unknown. **29:** John identifies Jesus as the powerful Lamb who has come to change the sinful condition of society (see v. 10; Rev 5). The imagery of the Lamb is drawn from the Passover lamb (Ex 12; see Jn 19.36; 1 Cor 5.7) and from the depiction of the "servant" of the Lord in Isa 53.4–7. **30:** See v. 15n. **34:** *Son of God,* the expected messiah (v. 49; 11.27).

1.35–51: The testimony of Jesus' first disciples. 37: *They followed Jesus,* the first known disciples of Jesus, Andrew (v. 40) and possibly the beloved disciple (13.23; 19.26; 20.2; 21.7,20; see Introduction) or Philip (6.58; 12.21–22); cf. Mk 1.16–20. **42:** In Aramaic *Cephas* (Gk "Petros") means "rock"; cf. Mt 15.18. **44:** *Bethsaida,* on the northwestern shore of the Sea of Galilee. **45:** *Moses . . . prophets,* the Hebrew Bible is understood as having predicted Jesus. **46:** *Nazareth,* located about 25 km (16 mi) west of the Sea of Galilee, was a small village in the first century CE, thought too insignificant to be the place of the messiah's origin. **47–51:** *Nathanael* (Heb "God has given") may be a collective character (see note *a* in v. 51) representing those in Israel who have *no deceit,* i.e., none of the qualities of Jacob before he became Israel (Gen 27.35; 32.28). Because of their openness to Jesus they will see him in the fullness of his role as mediator between heaven and earth; cf. Gen 28.12. **49:** For the understanding of the *King of*

answered, "I saw you under the fig tree
before Philip called you." 49Nathanael re-
plied, "Rabbi, you are the Son of God! You
are the King of Israel!" 50Jesus answered,
"Do you believe because I told you that I
saw you under the fig tree? You will see
greater things than these." 51And he said to
him, "Very truly, I tell you,[a] you will see
heaven opened and the angels of God as-
cending and descending upon the Son of
Man."

2 On the third day there was a wedding
in Cana of Galilee, and the mother of
Jesus was there. 2Jesus and his disciples had
also been invited to the wedding. 3When
the wine gave out, the mother of Jesus said
to him, "They have no wine." 4And Jesus
said to her, "Woman, what concern is that
to you and to me? My hour has not yet
come." 5His mother said to the servants,
"Do whatever he tells you." 6Now stand-
ing there were six stone water jars for the
Jewish rites of purification, each holding
twenty or thirty gallons. 7Jesus said to
them, "Fill the jars with water." And they
filled them up to the brim. 8He said to
them, "Now draw some out, and take it to
the chief steward." So they took it. 9When
the steward tasted the water that had be-
come wine, and did not know where it
came from (though the servants who had
drawn the water knew), the steward called
the bridegroom 10and said to him, "Every-
one serves the good wine first, and then the
inferior wine after the guests have become
drunk. But you have kept the good wine
until now." 11Jesus did this, the first of his
signs, in Cana of Galilee, and revealed his
glory; and his disciples believed in him.
12 After this he went down to Caperna-
um with his mother, his brothers, and his
disciples; and they remained there a few
days.
13 The Passover of the Jews was near,
and Jesus went up to Jerusalem. 14In the
temple he found people selling cattle,
sheep, and doves, and the money changers
seated at their tables. 15Making a whip of
cords, he drove all of them out of the tem-
ple, both the sheep and the cattle. He also
poured out the coins of the money changers
and overturned their tables. 16He told
those who were selling the doves, "Take
these things out of here! Stop making my
Father's house a marketplace!" 17His disci-
ples remembered that it was written, "Zeal
for your house will consume me." 18The

a Both instances of the Greek word for *you* in this verse are plural

Israel as "Son of God," see 2 Sam 7.14; Ps 2.7; 89.26. **51:** *Son of Man,* a messenger from heaven (see Dan. 7.13) who makes God known (3.13) and is the final judge (5.27).

2.1–12: The wedding at Cana. 1: *On the third day,* Nathanael (and those he represents; see 1.47–51n.) did not have to wait long for the promise of "greater things" (1.50) to be fulfilled. *Cana,* a small village about 15 km (9 mi) north of Nazareth. *The mother of Jesus* is never named in John. **4:** *Woman,* a term of respect and affection (cf. 4.21; 8.10; 19.26; 20.13,15). The *hour* of Jesus' glory on the cross (see 12.23; 17.1) was not to be determined by his mother's desires. **6:** *Rites of purification* were ceremonial; unlike clay or wooden vessels, stone vessels would not become ceremonially unclean by contact with an unclean object or person. **8:** *Steward,* headwaiter or master of ceremonies. **11:** Jesus' miracles were not wonders to astound, but *signs* pointing to *his glory,* God's presence in him (see 1.14). **12:** *Capernaum,* on the northwestern shore of the Sea of Galilee.

2.13–25: The demonstration against corruption in the Temple (cf. Mt 21.17; Mk 11.15–19; Lk 19.45–48). **13:** *Passover* was celebrated in March-April. **14:** Animals were sold for sacrifice. Different currencies used by worshipers had to be changed to the official half-shekel of Tyre for the Temple tax (see Ex 30.11–16). Roman money was changed into Jewish money to pay the Temple tax. **15–16:** A public demonstration against the materialism that had become part of Temple worship services. Jesus' indignation was not toward those engaged in worship, but those detracting from it. **17:** Ps 69.9 (see Zech 14.21; Mal 3.1). **18:** *The Jews,* the Temple religious authorities. *What sign . . . ?* is less a question than an assertion by the religious authorities that only they have authority to make religious pronouncements (9.34). **19:** *Destroy this temple . . . ,* reflects a longstanding tradition of Temple critique (cf. 4.21;

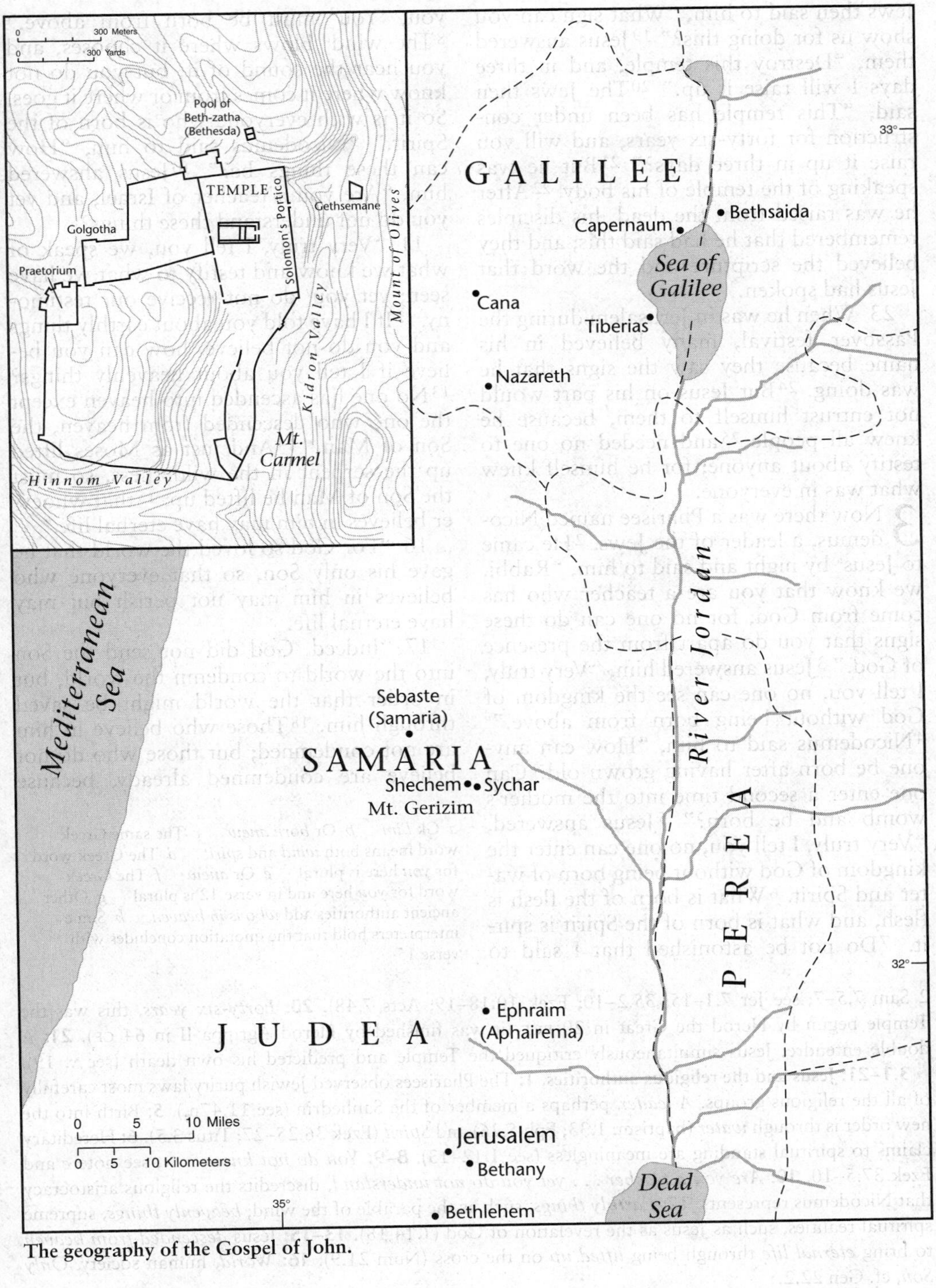

The geography of the Gospel of John.

Jews then said to him, "What sign can you
show us for doing this?" 19 Jesus answered
them, "Destroy this temple, and in three
days I will raise it up." 20 The Jews then
said, "This temple has been under con-
struction for forty-six years, and will you
raise it up in three days?" 21 But he was
speaking of the temple of his body. 22 After
he was raised from the dead, his disciples
remembered that he had said this; and they
believed the scripture and the word that
Jesus had spoken.

23 When he was in Jerusalem during the
Passover festival, many believed in his
name because they saw the signs that he
was doing. 24 But Jesus on his part would
not entrust himself to them, because he
knew all people 25 and needed no one to
testify about anyone; for he himself knew
what was in everyone.

3 Now there was a Pharisee named Nico-
demus, a leader of the Jews. 2 He came
to Jesus[a] by night and said to him, "Rabbi,
we know that you are a teacher who has
come from God; for no one can do these
signs that you do apart from the presence
of God." 3 Jesus answered him, "Very truly,
I tell you, no one can see the kingdom of
God without being born from above."[b]
4 Nicodemus said to him, "How can any-
one be born after having grown old? Can
one enter a second time into the mother's
womb and be born?" 5 Jesus answered,
"Very truly, I tell you, no one can enter the
kingdom of God without being born of wa-
ter and Spirit. 6 What is born of the flesh is
flesh, and what is born of the Spirit is spir-
it.[c] 7 Do not be astonished that I said to
you, 'You[d] must be born from above.'[e]
8 The wind[c] blows where it chooses, and
you hear the sound of it, but you do not
know where it comes from or where it goes.
So it is with everyone who is born of the
Spirit." 9 Nicodemus said to him, "How
can these things be?" 10 Jesus answered
him, "Are you a teacher of Israel, and yet
you do not understand these things?

11 "Very truly, I tell you, we speak of
what we know and testify to what we have
seen; yet you[f] do not receive our testimo-
ny. 12 If I have told you about earthly things
and you do not believe, how can you be-
lieve if I tell you about heavenly things?
13 No one has ascended into heaven except
the one who descended from heaven, the
Son of Man.[g] 14 And just as Moses lifted
up the serpent in the wilderness, so must
the Son of Man be lifted up, 15 that whoev-
er believes in him may have eternal life.[h]

16 "For God so loved the world that he
gave his only Son, so that everyone who
believes in him may not perish but may
have eternal life.

17 "Indeed, God did not send the Son
into the world to condemn the world, but
in order that the world might be saved
through him. 18 Those who believe in him
are not condemned; but those who do not
believe are condemned already, because

a Gk *him* *b* Or *born anew* *c* The same Greek word means both *wind* and *spirit* *d* The Greek word for *you* here is plural *e* Or *anew* *f* The Greek word for *you* here and in verse 12 is plural *g* Other ancient authorities add *who is in heaven* *h* Some interpreters hold that the quotation concludes with verse 15

2 Sam 7.5–7; see Jer 7.1–15; 35.2–10; Ezek 10.18–19; Acts 7.48). **20:** *Forty-six years,* this was the Temple begun by Herod the Great in 20 BCE (it was finished by Herod Agrippa II in 64 CE). **21:** A double entendre; Jesus simultaneously critiqued the Temple and predicted his own death (see v. 19).

3.1–21: Jesus and the religious authorities. 1: The Pharisees observed Jewish purity laws most carefully of all the religious groups. *A leader,* perhaps a member of the Sanhedrin (see 11.47n.). **5:** Birth into the new order is through *water* (baptism; 1.33; Eph 5.26) and *Spirit* (Ezek 36.25–27; Titus 3.5). **6:** Hereditary claims to spiritual standing are meaningless (see 1.12–13). **8–9:** *You do not know . . . ,* see note *c* and Ezek 37.5–10. **10:** *Are you a teacher . . . yet you do not understand,* discredits the religious aristocracy that Nicodemus represents. **12:** *Earthly things,* such as the parable of the wind; *heavenly things,* supreme spiritual realities, such as Jesus as the revelation of God (1.14,18). **13–15:** Jesus *descended from heaven* to bring *eternal life* through being *lifted up* on the cross (Num 21.9). **16:** *World,* human society. *Only Son,* cf. Gen 22.2.

they have not believed in the name of the
only Son of God. 19 And this is the judg-
ment, that the light has come into the
world, and people loved darkness rather
than light because their deeds were evil.
20 For all who do evil hate the light and do
not come to the light, so that their deeds
may not be exposed. 21 But those who do
what is true come to the light, so that it
may be clearly seen that their deeds have
been done in God."[a]

22 After this Jesus and his disciples went
into the Judean countryside, and he spent
some time there with them and baptized.
23 John also was baptizing at Aenon near
Salim because water was abundant there;
and people kept coming and were being
baptized 24—John, of course, had not yet
been thrown into prison.

25 Now a discussion about purification
arose between John's disciples and a Jew.[b]
26 They came to John and said to him,
"Rabbi, the one who was with you across
the Jordan, to whom you testified, here he
is baptizing, and all are going to him."
27 John answered, "No one can receive any-
thing except what has been given from
heaven. 28 You yourselves are my witnesses
that I said, 'I am not the Messiah,[c] but I
have been sent ahead of him.' 29 He who
has the bride is the bridegroom. The friend
of the bridegroom, who stands and hears
him, rejoices greatly at the bridegroom's
voice. For this reason my joy has been ful-
filled. 30 He must increase, but I must de-
crease."[d]

31 The one who comes from above is
above all; the one who is of the earth be-
longs to the earth and speaks about earthly
things. The one who comes from heaven is
above all. 32 He testifies to what he has seen
and heard, yet no one accepts his testimo-
ny. 33 Whoever has accepted his testimony
has certified[e] this, that God is true. 34 He
whom God has sent speaks the words of
God, for he gives the Spirit without mea-
sure. 35 The Father loves the Son and has
placed all things in his hands. 36 Whoever
believes in the Son has eternal life; whoever
disobeys the Son will not see life, but must
endure God's wrath.

4 Now when Jesus[f] learned that the
Pharisees had heard, "Jesus is making
and baptizing more disciples than John"
2—although it was not Jesus himself but
his disciples who baptized— 3 he left Judea
and started back to Galilee. 4 But he had to
go through Samaria. 5 So he came to a Sa-
maritan city called Sychar, near the plot of
ground that Jacob had given to his son Jo-
seph. 6 Jacob's well was there, and Jesus,
tired out by his journey, was sitting by the
well. It was about noon.

7 A Samaritan woman came to draw
water, and Jesus said to her, "Give me a
drink." 8 (His disciples had gone to the city
to buy food.) 9 The Samaritan woman said
to him, "How is it that you, a Jew, ask a
drink of me, a woman of Samaria?" (Jews
do not share things in common with Sa-
maritans.)[g] 10 Jesus answered her, "If you
knew the gift of God, and who it is that is
saying to you, 'Give me a drink,' you would
have asked him, and he would have given

a Some interpreters hold that the quotation concludes with verse 15 *b* Other ancient authorities read *the Jews* *c* Or *the Christ* *d* Some interpreters hold that the quotation continues through verse 36 *e* Gk *set a seal to* *f* Other ancient authorities read *the Lord* *g* Other ancient authorities lack this sentence

3.22–36: Further testimony of John (cf. 1.19–34). **23:** The exact locations of Aenon and Salim are uncertain. **24:** See Mk 6.14–29. **25:** *Purification,* Jewish ceremonial washing. **27–29:** John was only the *friend of the bridegroom,* leading Israel, the bride, to Jesus, the bridegroom. He *rejoices* in their union (cf. Mk 2.19–20). **32–34:** *No one,* a generalization about Israel (see 1.11).

4.1–42: Jesus and the Samaritans. 1–3: Jesus departs to avoid the opposition of the *Pharisees.* **4:** *Samaria,* between Judea and Galilee, was inhabited by remnants of the northern tribes of ancient Israel who worshiped the Lord God and used the Pentateuch. Jews did not acknowledge the authenticity of the Samaritan observances; see v. 9. **5:** *Sychar,* near ancient Shechem; see Gen 33.19; 48.22; Josh 24.32. **10:** *Living water,* i.e., flowing water, as in a spring or river; see Jer 2.14; 17.13. **13:** *Everyone who drinks,*

you living water." 11 The woman said to
him, "Sir, you have no bucket, and the well
is deep. Where do you get that living water?
12 Are you greater than our ancestor Jacob,
who gave us the well, and with his sons and
his flocks drank from it?" 13 Jesus said to
her, "Everyone who drinks of this water
will be thirsty again, 14 but those who drink
of the water that I will give them will never
be thirsty. The water that I will give will
become in them a spring of water gushing
up to eternal life." 15 The woman said to
him, "Sir, give me this water, so that I may
never be thirsty or have to keep coming
here to draw water."

16 Jesus said to her, "Go, call your hus-
band, and come back." 17 The woman an-
swered him, "I have no husband." Jesus
said to her, "You are right in saying, 'I have
no husband'; 18 for you have had five hus-
bands, and the one you have now is not
your husband. What you have said is true!"
19 The woman said to him, "Sir, I see that
you are a prophet. 20 Our ancestors wor-
shiped on this mountain, but you[a] say that
the place where people must worship is in
Jerusalem." 21 Jesus said to her, "Woman,
believe me, the hour is coming when you
will worship the Father neither on this
mountain nor in Jerusalem. 22 You worship
what you do not know; we worship what
we know, for salvation is from the Jews.
23 But the hour is coming, and is now here,
when the true worshipers will worship the
Father in spirit and truth, for the Father
seeks such as these to worship him. 24 God
is spirit, and those who worship him must
worship in spirit and truth." 25 The woman
said to him, "I know that Messiah is com-
ing" (who is called Christ). "When he
comes, he will proclaim all things to us."
26 Jesus said to her, "I am he,[b] the one who
is speaking to you."

27 Just then his disciples came. They
were astonished that he was speaking with
a woman, but no one said, "What do you
want?" or, "Why are you speaking with
her?" 28 Then the woman left her water jar
and went back to the city. She said to the
people, 29 "Come and see a man who told
me everything I have ever done! He cannot
be the Messiah,[c] can he?" 30 They left the
city and were on their way to him.

31 Meanwhile the disciples were urging
him, "Rabbi, eat something." 32 But he said
to them, "I have food to eat that you do not
know about." 33 So the disciples said to one
another, "Surely no one has brought him
something to eat?" 34 Jesus said to them,
"My food is to do the will of him who sent
me and to complete his work. 35 Do you not
say, 'Four months more, then comes the
harvest'? But I tell you, look around you,
and see how the fields are ripe for harvest-
ing. 36 The reaper is already receiving[d]
wages and is gathering fruit for eternal life,
so that sower and reaper may rejoice to-
gether. 37 For here the saying holds true,
'One sows and another reaps.' 38 I sent you
to reap that for which you did not labor.
Others have labored, and you have entered
into their labor."

39 Many Samaritans from that city be-
lieved in him because of the woman's testi-
mony, "He told me everything I have ever
done." 40 So when the Samaritans came to
him, they asked him to stay with them; and

a The Greek word for *you* here and in verses 21 and 22 is plural *b* Gk *I am* *c* Or *the Christ*
d Or 35. . . *the fields are already ripe for harvesting.* 36*The reaper is receiving*

cf. Sir 24.21. **14:** *Eternal life,* see 1.4. **17–18:** This is an observation, not a judgment against the woman, and divorce is not the only possible explanation of her past; cf. Gen 38. **19:** Jesus' accurate reading of her situation convinces the woman that he is a *prophet;* thus he should be able to settle the most burning issue between Jews and Samaritans. **20–21:** *This mountain,* i.e., Mount Gerizim, near Shechem, where the Samaritan temple had once stood (see 2 Macc 6.2). *Nor in Jerusalem,* the Jerusalem Temple has only a provisionally divine sanction and status; Jesus thus brings into question its legitimacy (cf. 2 Sam 7.5–7; Jer 35.2–9; Acts 7.48) and predicts its demise as the center of Jewish worship (cf. 2.13–16). **27:** Religious teachers avoided speaking to a *woman* in public. See v. 9n. **35:** Apparently a proverbial saying; see also v. 37. **36:** *Wages,* the harvest of believers; cf. Mt 9.37–38. **38:** Cf. Josh 24.13.

he stayed there two days. 41 And many
more believed because of his word. 42 They
said to the woman, "It is no longer because
of what you said that we believe, for we
have heard for ourselves, and we know that
this is truly the Savior of the world."
43 When the two days were over, he
went from that place to Galilee 44 (for Jesus
himself had testified that a prophet has no
honor in the prophet's own country).
45 When he came to Galilee, the Galileans
welcomed him, since they had seen all that
he had done in Jerusalem at the festival; for
they too had gone to the festival.
46 Then he came again to Cana in Gali-
lee where he had changed the water into
wine. Now there was a royal official whose
son lay ill in Capernaum. 47 When he heard
that Jesus had come from Judea to Galilee,
he went and begged him to come down and
heal his son, for he was at the point of
death. 48 Then Jesus said to him, "Unless
you[a] see signs and wonders you will not
believe." 49 The official said to him, "Sir,
come down before my little boy dies."
50 Jesus said to him, "Go; your son will
live." The man believed the word that Jesus
spoke to him and started on his way. 51 As
he was going down, his slaves met him and
told him that his child was alive. 52 So he
asked them the hour when he began to re-
cover, and they said to him, "Yesterday at
one in the afternoon the fever left him."
53 The father realized that this was the hour
when Jesus had said to him, "Your son will
live." So he himself believed, along with his
whole household. 54 Now this was the sec-
ond sign that Jesus did after coming from
Judea to Galilee.

5 After this there was a festival of the
Jews, and Jesus went up to Jerusalem.
2 Now in Jerusalem by the Sheep Gate
there is a pool, called in Hebrew[b] Beth-
zatha,[c] which has five porticoes. 3 In these
lay many invalids—blind, lame, and para-
lyzed.[d] 5 One man was there who had been
ill for thirty-eight years. 6 When Jesus saw
him lying there and knew that he had been
there a long time, he said to him, "Do you
want to be made well?" 7 The sick man an-
swered him, "Sir, I have no one to put me
into the pool when the water is stirred up;
and while I am making my way, someone
else steps down ahead of me." 8 Jesus said
to him, "Stand up, take your mat and
walk." 9 At once the man was made well,
and he took up his mat and began to walk.
Now that day was a sabbath. 10 So the
Jews said to the man who had been cured,
"It is the sabbath; it is not lawful for you to
carry your mat." 11 But he answered them,
"The man who made me well said to me,
'Take up your mat and walk.'" 12 They
asked him, "Who is the man who said to
you, 'Take it up and walk'?" 13 Now the
man who had been healed did not know
who it was, for Jesus had disappeared in[e]
the crowd that was there. 14 Later Jesus
found him in the temple and said to him,
"See, you have been made well! Do not sin

a Both instances of the Greek word for *you* in this verse are plural *b* That is, *Aramaic* *c* Other ancient authorities read *Bethesda*, others *Bethsaida* *d* Other ancient authorities add, wholly or in part, *waiting for the stirring of the water; 4for an angel of the Lord went down at certain seasons into the pool, and stirred up the water; whoever stepped in first after the stirring of the water was made well from whatever disease that person had.* *e* Or *had left because of*

4.43–54: Healing of the official's son. Cf. Mt 8.5–13; Lk 7.1–10. **44:** See Mk 6.4; Lk 4.24. **46:** *A royal official,* probably of Herod Antipas, tetrarch of Galilee (4 BCE–39 CE). *Capernaum* was about 30 km (18 mi) from Cana. **48–53:** *You* is plural here; the official is a representative figure exemplifying faith progressing from *signs* (v. 48), to individual faith (*the man believed,* v. 50), to collective faith (*with his whole household,* v. 53). **54:** *Second,* for the first see 2.1–11.

5.1–18: Healing the lame man on the sabbath. 2: *Sheep Gate,* see Neh 3.1. Excavations near the later church of St. Anne have uncovered evidence of a second-century CE healing sanctuary and pool with *five porticoes.* **3:** After *paralyzed* later manuscripts add an explanatory statement; see note *d.* **7–9:** *When the water is stirred up* is explained by the addition to v. 3, which attributes the movement to divine action. Faith is not a theme of this episode (cf. 4.48). **14:** The verse alludes to the traditional view that illness was

any more, so that nothing worse happens
to you." 15 The man went away and told
the Jews that it was Jesus who had made
him well. 16 Therefore the Jews started per-
secuting Jesus, because he was doing such
things on the sabbath. 17 But Jesus an-
swered them, "My Father is still working,
and I also am working." 18 For this reason
the Jews were seeking all the more to kill
him, because he was not only breaking the
sabbath, but was also calling God his own
Father, thereby making himself equal to
God.

19 Jesus said to them, "Very truly, I tell
you, the Son can do nothing on his own,
but only what he sees the Father doing; for
whatever the Father[a] does, the Son does
likewise. 20 The Father loves the Son and
shows him all that he himself is doing; and
he will show him greater works than these,
so that you will be astonished. 21 Indeed,
just as the Father raises the dead and gives
them life, so also the Son gives life to
whomever he wishes. 22 The Father judges
no one but has given all judgment to the
Son, 23 so that all may honor the Son just as
they honor the Father. Anyone who does
not honor the Son does not honor the Fa-
ther who sent him. 24 Very truly, I tell you,
anyone who hears my word and believes
him who sent me has eternal life, and does
not come under judgment, but has passed
from death to life.

25 "Very truly, I tell you, the hour is
coming, and is now here, when the dead
will hear the voice of the Son of God, and
those who hear will live. 26 For just as the
Father has life in himself, so he has granted
the Son also to have life in himself; 27 and
he has given him authority to execute judg-
ment, because he is the Son of Man. 28 Do
not be astonished at this; for the hour is
coming when all who are in their graves
will hear his voice 29 and will come out—
those who have done good, to the resurrec-
tion of life, and those who have done evil,
to the resurrection of condemnation.

30 "I can do nothing on my own. As I
hear, I judge; and my judgment is just, be-
cause I seek to do not my own will but the
will of him who sent me.

31 "If I testify about myself, my testimo-
ny is not true. 32 There is another who testi-
fies on my behalf, and I know that his testi-
mony to me is true. 33 You sent messengers
to John, and he testified to the truth. 34 Not
that I accept such human testimony, but I
say these things so that you may be saved.
35 He was a burning and shining lamp, and
you were willing to rejoice for a while in his
light. 36 But I have a testimony greater than
John's. The works that the Father has given
me to complete, the very works that I am
doing, testify on my behalf that the Father
has sent me. 37 And the Father who sent me
has himself testified on my behalf. You
have never heard his voice or seen his form,
38 and you do not have his word abiding in
you, because you do not believe him whom
he has sent.

39 "You search the scriptures because
you think that in them you have eternal life;
and it is they that testify on my behalf.
40 Yet you refuse to come to me to have life.
41 I do not accept glory from human beings.
42 But I know that you do not have the love

a Gk *that one*

a punishment for sin; see 9.2–3. **16:** *The Jews,* the religious authorities (see 1.24n.), opposed Jesus for his violation of the sabbath rules. **17:** Cf. Gen 2.3. **18:** *Equal,* see 10.30–33; Phil 2.6.

5.19–29: Jesus' relation to God. 21: See 11.1–44. **22:** On the Son as judge, see Mt 19.28; 25.31–46. **24:** *Anyone* who *believes* on the basis of Jesus' word *has* already *passed* into *eternal life;* see 11.26; 1 Jn 3.14. **25–30:** The voice of Jesus will signal the final *resurrection* in which all will meet *judgment* (cf. Dan 12.1–3; 1 Thess 4.13–18). **27:** *Son of Man,* see 1.51n.

5.31–40: Evidence of Jesus' relationship to God. 31: Jewish tradition (*m. Ketub.* 2.9; cf. Jn 8.13) regarded testimony on one's own behalf as invalid. **32:** *Another,* the Father (see v. 37). **33–40:** God witnesses to Jesus through the ministry of *John* the Baptist (vv. 33–35), through Jesus' *works* (v. 36), and through *the scriptures* (vv. 37–40).

5.41–47: Jesus rebukes those who refuse his offer. 42: Lacking the *love of God,* they *do not accept* (v. 43)

of God in[a] you. 43 I have come in my Fa-
ther's name, and you do not accept me; if
another comes in his own name, you will
accept him. 44 How can you believe when
you accept glory from one another and do
not seek the glory that comes from the one
who alone is God? 45 Do not think that I
will accuse you before the Father; your ac-
cuser is Moses, on whom you have set your
hope. 46 If you believed Moses, you would
believe me, for he wrote about me. 47 But if
you do not believe what he wrote, how will
you believe what I say?"

6 After this Jesus went to the other side of
the Sea of Galilee, also called the Sea of
Tiberias.[b] 2 A large crowd kept following
him, because they saw the signs that he was
doing for the sick. 3 Jesus went up the
mountain and sat down there with his dis-
ciples. 4 Now the Passover, the festival of
the Jews, was near. 5 When he looked up
and saw a large crowd coming toward him,
Jesus said to Philip, "Where are we to buy
bread for these people to eat?" 6 He said
this to test him, for he himself knew what
he was going to do. 7 Philip answered him,
"Six months' wages[c] would not buy
enough bread for each of them to get a lit-
tle." 8 One of his disciples, Andrew, Simon
Peter's brother, said to him, 9 "There is a
boy here who has five barley loaves and
two fish. But what are they among so many
people?" 10 Jesus said, "Make the people sit
down." Now there was a great deal of grass
in the place; so they[d] sat down, about five
thousand in all. 11 Then Jesus took the
loaves, and when he had given thanks, he
distributed them to those who were seated;
so also the fish, as much as they wanted.
12 When they were satisfied, he told his dis-
ciples, "Gather up the fragments left over,
so that nothing may be lost." 13 So they
gathered them up, and from the fragments
of the five barley loaves, left by those who
had eaten, they filled twelve baskets.
14 When the people saw the sign that he had
done, they began to say, "This is indeed the
prophet who is to come into the world."

15 When Jesus realized that they were
about to come and take him by force to
make him king, he withdrew again to the
mountain by himself.

16 When evening came, his disciples
went down to the sea, 17 got into a boat,
and started across the sea to Capernaum. It
was now dark, and Jesus had not yet come
to them. 18 The sea became rough because
a strong wind was blowing. 19 When they
had rowed about three or four miles,[e] they
saw Jesus walking on the sea and coming
near the boat, and they were terrified.
20 But he said to them, "It is I;[f] do not be
afraid." 21 Then they wanted to take him
into the boat, and immediately the boat
reached the land toward which they were
going.

22 The next day the crowd that had
stayed on the other side of the sea saw that
there had been only one boat there. They
also saw that Jesus had not got into the
boat with his disciples, but that his disciples

a Or *among* b Gk *of Galilee of Tiberias*
c Gk *Two hundred denarii*; the denarius was the usual day's wage for a laborer d Gk *the men*
e Gk *about twenty-five or thirty stadia* f Gk *I am*

the one God sent. **43–44:** The Jews (see v. 16n.) will not accept the testimony of anyone who is not one of them. **45:** See 9.28. **46–47:** *Moses . . . wrote about me,* see 1.45; cf. Lk 16.31; 24.27.

6.1–15: Feeding the five thousand; Jesus replaces the Passover. The only miracle recorded by all four Gospels (Mt 14.13–21; Mk 6.32–44; Lk 9.10–17). **1:** *The other side,* the eastern shore. *Sea of Tiberias,* so named after the city on the western shore, founded by Herod Antipas about 20 CE in honor of the Roman Emperor Tiberius. **4:** *Passover . . . of the Jews,* see 2.13n. **5:** The crowd goes to Jesus in Galilee for Passover instead of to the Temple in Jerusalem. **9:** *Barley,* the grain harvested at Passover. **10:** *Five thousand men* (see note *d*), the approximate size of a Roman military legion. **15:** *To make him king,* as a political messiah opposing Rome, but Jesus would not accept this (see 18.36).

6.16–21: Jesus walks on the sea (Mt 14.22–27; Mk 6.45–51). Jesus is more than an earthly ruler (v. 15); he is lord of creation (1.3). **20:** *It is I,* an assertion of divinity (see note *f;* 6.35n.).

6.22–71: Jesus, the bread of life. 22: *On the other side,* the eastern shore. **25:** *The other side,* the

had gone away alone. 23 Then some boats
from Tiberias came near the place where
they had eaten the bread after the Lord had
given thanks.[a] 24 So when the crowd saw
that neither Jesus nor his disciples were
there, they themselves got into the boats
and went to Capernaum looking for Jesus.
25 When they found him on the other
side of the sea, they said to him, "Rabbi,
when did you come here?" 26 Jesus an-
swered them, "Very truly, I tell you, you
are looking for me, not because you saw
signs, but because you ate your fill of the
loaves. 27 Do not work for the food that
perishes, but for the food that endures for
eternal life, which the Son of Man will give
you. For it is on him that God the Father
has set his seal." 28 Then they said to him,
"What must we do to perform the works of
God?" 29 Jesus answered them, "This is the
work of God, that you believe in him
whom he has sent." 30 So they said to him,
"What sign are you going to give us then,
so that we may see it and believe you?
What work are you performing? 31 Our an-
cestors ate the manna in the wilderness; as
it is written, 'He gave them bread from
heaven to eat.' " 32 Then Jesus said to them,
"Very truly, I tell you, it was not Moses
who gave you the bread from heaven, but it
is my Father who gives you the true bread
from heaven. 33 For the bread of God is that
which[b] comes down from heaven and
gives life to the world." 34 They said to him,
"Sir, give us this bread always."
35 Jesus said to them, "I am the bread of
life. Whoever comes to me will never be
hungry, and whoever believes in me will
never be thirsty. 36 But I said to you that
you have seen me and yet do not believe.
37 Everything that the Father gives me will
come to me, and anyone who comes to me
I will never drive away; 38 for I have come
down from heaven, not to do my own will,
but the will of him who sent me. 39 And this
is the will of him who sent me, that I should
lose nothing of all that he has given me, but
raise it up on the last day. 40 This is indeed
the will of my Father, that all who see the
Son and believe in him may have eternal
life; and I will raise them up on the last
day."
41 Then the Jews began to complain
about him because he said, "I am the bread
that came down from heaven." 42 They
were saying, "Is not this Jesus, the son of
Joseph, whose father and mother we
know? How can he now say, 'I have come
down from heaven'?" 43 Jesus answered
them, "Do not complain among yourselves.
44 No one can come to me unless drawn by
the Father who sent me; and I will raise that
person up on the last day. 45 It is written in
the prophets, 'And they shall all be taught
by God.' Everyone who has heard and
learned from the Father comes to me.
46 Not that anyone has seen the Father ex-
cept the one who is from God; he has seen
the Father. 47 Very truly, I tell you, whoever
believes has eternal life. 48 I am the bread of
life. 49 Your ancestors ate the manna in the
wilderness, and they died. 50 This is the
bread that comes down from heaven, so
that one may eat of it and not die. 51 I am
the living bread that came down from heav-

a Other ancient authorities lack *after the Lord had given thanks* *b* Or *he who*

crowd had crossed in boats (v. 24) to the western side. **26:** *Signs,* of Jesus' sonship. **27:** *Son of Man,* see 1.51n. *Seal,* God's authentication, perhaps at the baptism (1.32; cf. 3.33, note *e*). **28:** *Works,* 3.21. **29:** There is one *work* above all works (v. 28): to *believe* in Jesus, who reveals God. **30:** *See,* the crowd ties faith to the senses. **31:** The messiah was expected to reproduce the miracle of the giving of manna (Ex 16.4,15; Num 11.8; Ps 78.24; 105.40). Again the depth of Jesus' meaning is misunderstood (cf. 4.15). **35–40:** Jesus himself is God's gift of sustenance for time and eternity. No one who *comes* to Jesus, i.e., *believes* in him, will be rejected, but will have *eternal life* in the present and resurrection *on the last day.* **35:** *I am,* an expression of divinity and oneness with God (Ex 3.14; Jn 1.1–3; 6.20; 8.58). In Greek *I am* is emphatic, i.e., Jesus is *the bread of life.* **44–45:** *Unless drawn by the Father,* allow themselves to hear God's call through Jesus. *Prophets,* Isa 54.13; cf. Jer 31.34. **51–58:** In these verses the Fourth Evangelist (who does not include an account of the institution of the Lord's Supper) presents teachings that have

en. Whoever eats of this bread will live for-
ever; and the bread that I will give for the
life of the world is my flesh."
52 The Jews then disputed among them-
selves, saying, "How can this man give us
his flesh to eat?" 53 So Jesus said to them,
"Very truly, I tell you, unless you eat the
flesh of the Son of Man and drink his
blood, you have no life in you. 54 Those
who eat my flesh and drink my blood have
eternal life, and I will raise them up on the
last day; 55 for my flesh is true food and my
blood is true drink. 56 Those who eat my
flesh and drink my blood abide in me, and
I in them. 57 Just as the living Father sent
me, and I live because of the Father, so
whoever eats me will live because of me.
58 This is the bread that came down from
heaven, not like that which your ancestors
ate, and they died. But the one who eats
this bread will live forever." 59 He said
these things while he was teaching in the
synagogue at Capernaum.
60 When many of his disciples heard it,
they said, "This teaching is difficult; who
can accept it?" 61 But Jesus, being aware
that his disciples were complaining about
it, said to them, "Does this offend you?
62 Then what if you were to see the Son of
Man ascending to where he was before?
63 It is the spirit that gives life; the flesh is
useless. The words that I have spoken to
you are spirit and life. 64 But among you
there are some who do not believe." For
Jesus knew from the first who were the
ones that did not believe, and who was the
one that would betray him. 65 And he said,
"For this reason I have told you that no one
can come to me unless it is granted by the
Father."
66 Because of this many of his disciples
turned back and no longer went about with
him. 67 So Jesus asked the twelve, "Do you
also wish to go away?" 68 Simon Peter an-
swered him, "Lord, to whom can we go?
You have the words of eternal life. 69 We
have come to believe and know that you
are the Holy One of God."[a] 70 Jesus an-
swered them, "Did I not choose you, the
twelve? Yet one of you is a devil." 71 He
was speaking of Judas son of Simon Iscari-
ot,[b] for he, though one of the twelve, was
going to betray him.

7 After this Jesus went about in Galilee.
He did not wish[c] to go about in Judea
because the Jews were looking for an op-
portunity to kill him. 2 Now the Jewish fes-
tival of Booths[d] was near. 3 So his brothers
said to him, "Leave here and go to Judea so
that your disciples also may see the works
you are doing; 4 for no one who wants[e] to
be widely known acts in secret. If you do
these things, show yourself to the world."
5 (For not even his brothers believed in
him.) 6 Jesus said to them, "My time has
not yet come, but your time is always here.
7 The world cannot hate you, but it hates

a Other ancient authorities read *the Christ, the Son of the living God* *b* Other ancient authorities read *Judas Iscariot son of Simon;* others, *Judas son of Simon from Karyot* (Kerioth) *c* Other ancient authorities read *was not at liberty* *d* Or *Tabernacles* *e* Other ancient authorities read *wants it*

unmistakable eucharistic echoes. **51:** *The living bread . . . is my flesh,* Jesus became *flesh* (1.14) and offered himself to God in death, thus sacrificing his life *for the life of the world.* **60:** *This teaching is difficult* means it is offensive (see v. 61). Eating blood was forbidden because, as the life of any creature, it was sacred to God (Gen 9.4; Lev 17.15). **62–63:** Jesus' eventual ascension to divine glory will show that he was speaking of realities deeper than the actual eating of his earthly flesh (1.1–18). **64–65:** These truths can be discerned only by faith, which is God's gift, not human achievement. **66–71:** Jesus' emphasis on spiritual transformation rather than on political concerns alone causes the crowd to lose interest in him. **70:** *One of you is a devil* buttresses the Evangelist's claim of Jesus' omniscience (1.3). **71:** *Iscariot* probably identifies *Judas* as a man from Kerioth, a town in southern Judea.

7.1–52: The conflict between Jesus and the religious authorities escalates. 1: Jesus took precautions for his own safety. **2:** *Booths,* a festival that began on the fifteenth day of the seventh month (Sept.–Oct.), commemorating the wilderness wanderings (Lev 23.39–43; Deut 16.13–15). **6–9:** Unlike Jesus, who is following a divine strategy, his brothers (see Mk 6.3) move according to their own whim and judgment.

me because I testify against it that its works
are evil. 8 Go to the festival yourselves. I am
not[a] going to this festival, for my time has
not yet fully come." 9 After saying this, he
remained in Galilee.
10 But after his brothers had gone to the
festival, then he also went, not publicly but
as it were[b] in secret. 11 The Jews were
looking for him at the festival and saying,
"Where is he?" 12 And there was consider-
able complaining about him among the
crowds. While some were saying, "He is a
good man," others were saying, "No, he is
deceiving the crowd." 13 Yet no one would
speak openly about him for fear of the
Jews.
14 About the middle of the festival Jesus
went up into the temple and began to teach.
15 The Jews were astonished at it, saying,
"How does this man have such learning,[c]
when he has never been taught?" 16 Then
Jesus answered them, "My teaching is not
mine but his who sent me. 17 Anyone who
resolves to do the will of God will know
whether the teaching is from God or
whether I am speaking on my own.
18 Those who speak on their own seek their
own glory; but the one who seeks the glory
of him who sent him is true, and there is
nothing false in him.
19 "Did not Moses give you the law?
Yet none of you keeps the law. Why are
you looking for an opportunity to kill me?"
20 The crowd answered, "You have a de-
mon! Who is trying to kill you?" 21 Jesus
answered them, "I performed one work,
and all of you are astonished. 22 Moses gave
you circumcision (it is, of course, not from
Moses, but from the patriarchs), and you
circumcise a man on the sabbath. 23 If a
man receives circumcision on the sabbath
in order that the law of Moses may not be
broken, are you angry with me because I
healed a man's whole body on the sabbath?
24 Do not judge by appearances, but judge
with right judgment."
25 Now some of the people of Jerusalem
were saying, "Is not this the man whom
they are trying to kill? 26 And here he is,
speaking openly, but they say nothing to
him! Can it be that the authorities really
know that this is the Messiah?[d] 27 Yet we
know where this man is from; but when the
Messiah[d] comes, no one will know where
he is from." 28 Then Jesus cried out as he
was teaching in the temple, "You know me,
and you know where I am from. I have not
come on my own. But the one who sent me
is true, and you do not know him. 29 I know
him, because I am from him, and he sent
me." 30 Then they tried to arrest him, but
no one laid hands on him, because his hour
had not yet come. 31 Yet many in the crowd
believed in him and were saying, "When
the Messiah[d] comes, will he do more signs
than this man has done?"[e]
32 The Pharisees heard the crowd mut-

a Other ancient authorities add *yet* *b* Other ancient authorities lack *as it were* *c* Or *this man know his letters* *d* Or *the Christ* *e* Other ancient authorities read *is doing*

The world cannot hate his brothers, because by their disbelief they are part of it. **10–13:** Jesus visits the festival undercover to escape detection and arrest. Compare Jesus' *secret* journey with the public one in 12.12–15, and the reasons for both in v. 8 and 12.23. **14:** Jesus discards his clandestine posture. **15:** *Never been taught,* a statement of elitism by the religious authorities; the only interpretation they recognize as legitimate is their own (cf. 7.49). Also, they are surprised that a Galilean peasant could read (see note *c*). **18:** *Those who . . . seek their own glory,* an implicit indictment of the religious authorities (see 12.43). **19–24:** They are condemned not only because of their rejection of Jesus (see 5.46), but also because of their desire to *kill* him, ostensibly for healing on the sabbath (5.15–18), when the law enjoins circumcision even if the eighth day falls on a sabbath. If circumcision, why not healings? **20:** *Who is trying to kill you,* the crowd of pilgrims is unaware of the religious authorities' homicidal designs on Jesus (see v. 1). **25–31:** Because they are closer to the religious authorities, *the people of Jerusalem* know their intentions better than the pilgrims do. **26–27:** They deny the possibility of Jesus' messiahship because his origin is known; a popular belief was that the messiah's origin would be mysterious (see 1 Enoch 48.6; 2 Esd 13.51–52). **28:** Jesus' true origin is from God, who *sent* him. **32–33:** *The chief priests and Pharisees,* tering such things about him, and the chief priests and Pharisees sent temple police to arrest him. 33 Jesus then said, "I will be with you a little while longer, and then I am going to him who sent me. 34 You will search for me, but you will not find me; and where I am, you cannot come." 35 The Jews said to one another, "Where does this man intend to go that we will not find him? Does he intend to go to the Dispersion among the Greeks and teach the Greeks? 36 What does he mean by saying, 'You will search for me and you will not find me' and 'Where I am, you cannot come'?"

37 On the last day of the festival, the great day, while Jesus was standing there, he cried out, "Let anyone who is thirsty come to me, 38 and let the one who believes in me drink. As[a] the scripture has said, 'Out of the believer's heart[b] shall flow rivers of living water.' " 39 Now he said this about the Spirit, which believers in him were to receive; for as yet there was no Spirit,[c] because Jesus was not yet glorified.

40 When they heard these words, some in the crowd said, "This is really the prophet." 41 Others said, "This is the Messiah."[d] But some asked, "Surely the Messiah[d] does not come from Galilee, does he? 42 Has not the scripture said that the Messiah[d] is descended from David and comes from Bethlehem, the village where David lived?" 43 So there was a division in the crowd because of him. 44 Some of them wanted to arrest him, but no one laid hands on him.

45 Then the temple police went back to the chief priests and Pharisees, who asked them, "Why did you not arrest him?" 46 The police answered, "Never has anyone spoken like this!" 47 Then the Pharisees replied, "Surely you have not been deceived too, have you? 48 Has any one of the authorities or of the Pharisees believed in him? 49 But this crowd, which does not know the law—they are accursed." 50 Nicodemus, who had gone to Jesus[e] before, and who was one of them, asked, 51 "Our law does not judge people without first giving them a hearing to find out what they are doing, does it?" 52 They replied, "Surely you are not also from Galilee, are you? Search and you will see that no prophet is to arise from Galilee."

a Or *come to me and drink. 38The one who believes in me, as* b Gk *out of his belly* c Other ancient authorities read *for as yet the Spirit* (others, *Holy Spirit) had not been given* d Or *the Christ* e Gk *him*

the high priest who oversaw them, and those under their influence are collectively called "the Jews" (cf. v. 35; see 1.24n.). Their attempt to *arrest* Jesus (v. 33) leads him to speak of his death (*I am going to him who sent me*). **34–35:** Later *the Jews* will seek deliverance in the messiah, but *will not find* him, for he will have ascended to where they *cannot come* because of their unbelief (contrast 8.21 with 12.26; 17.24). They miss the point, thinking that he is going to the Jews of the *Dispersion,* those living outside Palestine among the *Greeks* (Gentiles). **37–39:** For seven days water was carried in a golden pitcher from the Pool of Siloam to the Temple as a reminder of the water from the rock in the desert (Num 20.2–13) and as a symbol of hope for the coming messianic deliverance (Isa 12.3). **37:** *Let anyone who is thirsty come to me,* Jesus is the true water; he embodies the actual power the festival only points to (Isa 44.3; see also Jn 4.10–14). "Tabernacles" (v. 2, note *d*) and "lived" in 1.14, (lit. "tented" or "tabernacled") come from the same Greek word, perhaps implying that Jesus replaces this festival. **38–39:** No biblical passage contains these exact words; for the general sense, see Prov 18.4; Isa 44.3; 58.11. Believers become channels of life to others, through Jesus' *Spirit* given at Pentecost after he was *glorified* (crucified, risen, ascended). The gift of the *Spirit* is a mark of the messianic age (Joel 2.28–29; Acts 2.14–21). An alternate reading (see note *b*) has Jesus give the Spirit (see Jn 19.34–35). **40–44:** *The prophet . . . the Messiah,* see 1.21n. **42:** *Descended from David,* 2 Sam 7.12–13; Ps 89.3–4; 132.11–12. *Bethlehem,* Mic 5.2. **49:** Describes the dismissive tone of the religious authorities toward the *crowd,* mostly provincial pilgrims, whose spiritual welfare they are supposed to serve. **50:** *Nicodemus,* see 3.1–21. **52:** *You are not also from Galilee,* the more rural Galileans were often looked down upon by Jerusalemites (cf. 1.46; Mt 26.73; Mk 14.70; Lk 22.59).

8 ⟦53 Then each of them went home,
1 while Jesus went to the Mount of Ol-
ives. 2 Early in the morning he came again
to the temple. All the people came to him
and he sat down and began to teach them.
3 The scribes and the Pharisees brought a
woman who had been caught in adultery;
and making her stand before all of them,
4 they said to him, "Teacher, this woman
was caught in the very act of committing
adultery. 5 Now in the law Moses com-
manded us to stone such women. Now
what do you say?" 6 They said this to test
him, so that they might have some charge
to bring against him. Jesus bent down and
wrote with his finger on the ground.
7 When they kept on questioning him, he
straightened up and said to them, "Let any-
one among you who is without sin be the
first to throw a stone at her." 8 And once
again he bent down and wrote on the
ground.[a] 9 When they heard it, they went
away, one by one, beginning with the el-
ders; and Jesus was left alone with the
woman standing before him. 10 Jesus
straightened up and said to her, "Woman,
where are they? Has no one condemned
you?" 11 She said, "No one, sir."[b] And
Jesus said, "Neither do I condemn you. Go
your way, and from now on do not sin
again."⟧[c]

12 Again Jesus spoke to them, saying, "I
am the light of the world. Whoever follows
me will never walk in darkness but will
have the light of life." 13 Then the Pharisees
said to him, "You are testifying on your
own behalf; your testimony is not valid."
14 Jesus answered, "Even if I testify on my
own behalf, my testimony is valid because
I know where I have come from and where
I am going, but you do not know where I
come from or where I am going. 15 You
judge by human standards;[d] I judge no
one. 16 Yet even if I do judge, my judgment
is valid; for it is not I alone who judge, but
I and the Father[e] who sent me. 17 In your
law it is written that the testimony of two
witnesses is valid. 18 I testify on my own
behalf, and the Father who sent me testifies
on my behalf." 19 Then they said to him,
"Where is your Father?" Jesus answered,
"You know neither me nor my Father. If
you knew me, you would know my Father
also." 20 He spoke these words while he
was teaching in the treasury of the temple,
but no one arrested him, because his hour
had not yet come.

21 Again he said to them, "I am going
away, and you will search for me, but you
will die in your sin. Where I am going, you
cannot come." 22 Then the Jews said, "Is he
going to kill himself? Is that what he means
by saying, 'Where I am going, you cannot
come'?" 23 He said to them, "You are from
below, I am from above; you are of this
world, I am not of this world. 24 I told you

a Other ancient authorities add *the sins of each of them* *b* Or *Lord* *c* The most ancient authorities lack 7.53—8.11; other authorities add the passage here or after 7.36 or after 21.25 or after Luke 21.38, with variations of text; some mark the passage as doubtful. *d* Gk *according to the flesh* *e* Other ancient authorities read *he*

7.53–8.11: The woman caught in adultery. This episode is not found in the most authoritative manuscripts. **8.1:** *Mount of Olives,* a prominent ridge east of Jerusalem; it is separated from the city by the Kidron valley. **5:** *In the law,* Lev 20.10; Deut 22.23–24. **3:** *The scribes,* mentioned only here in the Gospel of John, are often connected with the Pharisees and other religious groups opposed to Jesus in the Synoptic Gospels. **11:** *Do not sin again,* 5.14.

8.12–59: Jesus the light of life. Great golden lamps in the Temple court were lit during the "festival of Booths" (7.2). **12:** *Again,* picks up from 7.52. *I am the light of the world,* as in 7.37, Jesus announces that he embodies what the festival celebrates. **13–18:** Jesus does not need the approval of his self-witness from the religious authorities because: (a) in that he comes from the world above, he alone knows who he is; (b) the joint witness of the Father and the Son fulfills the requirement of *two* witnesses (Deut 19.15). See 5.31n. **20:** *In the treasury,* non-priests were not allowed in the treasury. This probably refers to the Court of the Women, which was adjacent to the treasury. In it were thirteen bronze chests for voluntary offerings and the Temple tax (see 2.14n.). **25–27:** An indirect claim to oneness with God (cf. 5.19–30). **28–29:**

that you would die in your sins, for you will
die in your sins unless you believe that I am
he."[a] 25 They said to him, "Who are you?"
Jesus said to them, "Why do I speak to you
at all?[b] 26 I have much to say about you
and much to condemn; but the one who
sent me is true, and I declare to the world
what I have heard from him." 27 They did
not understand that he was speaking to
them about the Father. 28 So Jesus said,
"When you have lifted up the Son of Man,
then you will realize that I am he,[a] and
that I do nothing on my own, but I speak
these things as the Father instructed me.
29 And the one who sent me is with me; he
has not left me alone, for I always do what
is pleasing to him." 30 As he was saying
these things, many believed in him.

31 Then Jesus said to the Jews who had
believed in him, "If you continue in my
word, you are truly my disciples; 32 and you
will know the truth, and the truth will
make you free." 33 They answered him,
"We are descendants of Abraham and have
never been slaves to anyone. What do you
mean by saying, 'You will be made free'?"

34 Jesus answered them, "Very truly, I
tell you, everyone who commits sin is a
slave to sin. 35 The slave does not have a
permanent place in the household; the son
has a place there forever. 36 So if the Son
makes you free, you will be free indeed. 37 I
know that you are descendants of Abra-
ham; yet you look for an opportunity to kill
me, because there is no place in you for my
word. 38 I declare what I have seen in the
Father's presence; as for you, you should
do what you have heard from the Fa-
ther."[c]

39 They answered him, "Abraham is
our father." Jesus said to them, "If you
were Abraham's children, you would be
doing[d] what Abraham did, 40 but now you
are trying to kill me, a man who has told
you the truth that I heard from God. This is
not what Abraham did. 41 You are indeed
doing what your father does." They said to
him, "We are not illegitimate children; we
have one father, God himself." 42 Jesus said
to them, "If God were your Father, you
would love me, for I came from God and
now I am here. I did not come on my own,
but he sent me. 43 Why do you not under-
stand what I say? It is because you cannot
accept my word. 44 You are from your fa-
ther the devil, and you choose to do your
father's desires. He was a murderer from
the beginning and does not stand in the
truth, because there is no truth in him.
When he lies, he speaks according to his
own nature, for he is a liar and the father of
lies. 45 But because I tell the truth, you do
not believe me. 46 Which of you convicts me
of sin? If I tell the truth, why do you not
believe me? 47 Whoever is from God hears
the words of God. The reason you do not
hear them is that you are not from God."

48 The Jews answered him, "Are we not
right in saying that you are a Samaritan and
have a demon?" 49 Jesus answered, "I do
not have a demon; but I honor my Father,
and you dishonor me. 50 Yet I do not seek
my own glory; there is one who seeks it and
he is the judge. 51 Very truly, I tell you,
whoever keeps my word will never see
death." 52 The Jews said to him, "Now we
know that you have a demon. Abraham
died, and so did the prophets; yet you say,
'Whoever keeps my word will never taste
death.' 53 Are you greater than our father
Abraham, who died? The prophets also

a Gk *I am* *b* Or *What I have told you from the beginning* *c* Other ancient authorities read *you do what you have heard from your father* *d* Other ancient authorities read *If you are Abraham's children, then do*

This oneness is based on obedience (5.30), of which the crucifixion is the final proof (12.32). *I am he,* (v. 28), see 6.35n. **31–38:** *The Jews,* refers both to the religious authorities and those under their influence (see 1.19n.). **32:** *Truth,* not general knowledge, but saving truth (14.6). *Free,* from the power of sin and its slavery (v. 34). **33:** We *have never been slaves,* an inaccurate claim (see Ex 13.3). **39–47:** Their desire to *kill* Jesus forfeits their claim to be heirs of Abraham's faith and true children of God. **43:** *Word,* teaching. **48:** *The Jews* turn to insult and calumny; unable to deny the miracles of Jesus, they attribute them to a *demon* (cf. Mk 3.20–30). **56:** Refusal to believe severs them from *Abraham* (see v. 39), who

died. Who do you claim to be?" 54 Jesus
answered, "If I glorify myself, my glory is
nothing. It is my Father who glorifies me,
he of whom you say, 'He is our God,'
55 though you do not know him. But I
know him; if I would say that I do not
know him, I would be a liar like you. But I
do know him and I keep his word. 56 Your
ancestor Abraham rejoiced that he would
see my day; he saw it and was glad."
57 Then the Jews said to him, "You are not
yet fifty years old, and have you seen Abra-
ham?"[a] 58 Jesus said to them, "Very truly,
I tell you, before Abraham was, I am." 59 So
they picked up stones to throw at him, but
Jesus hid himself and went out of the tem-
ple.

9 As he walked along, he saw a man blind
from birth. 2 His disciples asked him,
"Rabbi, who sinned, this man or his par-
ents, that he was born blind?" 3 Jesus an-
swered, "Neither this man nor his parents
sinned; he was born blind so that God's
works might be revealed in him. 4 We[b]
must work the works of him who sent me[c]
while it is day; night is coming when no one
can work. 5 As long as I am in the world, I
am the light of the world." 6 When he had
said this, he spat on the ground and made
mud with the saliva and spread the mud on
the man's eyes, 7 saying to him, "Go, wash
in the pool of Siloam" (which means Sent).
Then he went and washed and came back
able to see. 8 The neighbors and those who
had seen him before as a beggar began to
ask, "Is this not the man who used to sit
and beg?" 9 Some were saying, "It is he."
Others were saying, "No, but it is someone
like him." He kept saying, "I am the man."
10 But they kept asking him, "Then how
were your eyes opened?" 11 He answered,
"The man called Jesus made mud, spread it
on my eyes, and said to me, 'Go to Siloam
and wash.' Then I went and washed and
received my sight." 12 They said to him,
"Where is he?" He said, "I do not know."

13 They brought to the Pharisees the
man who had formerly been blind. 14 Now
it was a sabbath day when Jesus made the
mud and opened his eyes. 15 Then the Phar-
isees also began to ask him how he had
received his sight. He said to them, "He put
mud on my eyes. Then I washed, and now
I see." 16 Some of the Pharisees said, "This
man is not from God, for he does not ob-
serve the sabbath." But others said, "How
can a man who is a sinner perform such
signs?" And they were divided. 17 So they
said again to the blind man, "What do
you say about him? It was your eyes he
opened." He said, "He is a prophet."

18 The Jews did not believe that he had
been blind and had received his sight until
they called the parents of the man who had
received his sight 19 and asked them, "Is this
your son, who you say was born blind?
How then does he now see?" 20 His parents
answered, "We know that this is our son,
and that he was born blind; 21 but we do
not know how it is that now he sees, nor do
we know who opened his eyes. Ask him; he
is of age. He will speak for himself." 22 His

a Other ancient authorities read *has Abraham seen you?* *b* Other ancient authorities read *I* *c* Other ancient authorities read *us*

rejoiced (Gen 17.17) in the hope of the coming of the messiah (see Heb 11.17). God revealed the end-times to Abraham (see 2 Esd 2.14). **58:** *I am* (see 6.35n.), a claim to preexistence (cf. 1.1–3).

9.1–41: The healing of a man born blind. 1–3: Suffering was attributed to sin, either of the parents (Ex 20.5) or of the man before birth (*Gen. Rab.* 63: [39c] on Gen 25.22; Wis 8.19–20). Jesus denies this explanation and shifts attention from cause to purpose; this is an opportunity for God to act. **4:** *We must work,* Jesus includes his disciples in the fulfillment of his mission. **5:** See 6.35n.; 8.12. **6:** Jesus incorporates into his healing the ancient understanding of *saliva* as having medicinal value (Pliny, *Nat. Hist.* 28.4.7). **7:** *The pool of Siloam* (see 7.37–39n.; Isa 8.6; Neh 3.15) was in the southeast corner of the city. Symbolizes Jesus as "sent" from God to give light. **13–14:** *They,* neighbors and friends. The *Pharisees* considered making *mud* to be work, a violation of sabbath laws; cf. 5.9–18; 7.23. **17:** To the blind man the healing is proof that Jesus is sent from God. **18–23:** The parents are interrogated to avoid the possibility of mistaken identity. **22:** *Afraid of the Jews . . . put out of the synagogue,* clear indication that

parents said this because they were afraid
of the Jews; for the Jews had already agreed
that anyone who confessed Jesus[a] to be the
Messiah[b] would be put out of the syna-
gogue. 23 Therefore his parents said, "He is
of age; ask him."
24 So for the second time they called the
man who had been blind, and they said to
him, "Give glory to God! We know that
this man is a sinner." 25 He answered, "I do
not know whether he is a sinner. One thing
I do know, that though I was blind, now I
see." 26 They said to him, "What did he do
to you? How did he open your eyes?" 27 He
answered them, "I have told you already,
and you would not listen. Why do you
want to hear it again? Do you also want to
become his disciples?" 28 Then they reviled
him, saying, "You are his disciple, but we
are disciples of Moses. 29 We know that
God has spoken to Moses, but as for this
man, we do not know where he comes
from." 30 The man answered, "Here is an
astonishing thing! You do not know where
he comes from, and yet he opened my eyes.
31 We know that God does not listen to sin-
ners, but he does listen to one who wor-
ships him and obeys his will. 32 Never since
the world began has it been heard that any-
one opened the eyes of a person born blind.
33 If this man were not from God, he could
do nothing." 34 They answered him, "You
were born entirely in sins, and are you try-
ing to teach us?" And they drove him out.
35 Jesus heard that they had driven him
out, and when he found him, he said, "Do
you believe in the Son of Man?"[c] 36 He
answered, "And who is he, sir?[d] Tell me,
so that I may believe in him." 37 Jesus said
to him, "You have seen him, and the one
speaking with you is he." 38 He said,
"Lord,[d] I believe." And he worshiped him.
39 Jesus said, "I came into this world for
judgment so that those who do not see may
see, and those who do see may become
blind." 40 Some of the Pharisees near him
heard this and said to him, "Surely we are
not blind, are we?" 41 Jesus said to them,
"If you were blind, you would not have sin.
But now that you say, 'We see,' your sin
remains.

10 "Very truly, I tell you, anyone who
does not enter the sheepfold by the
gate but climbs in by another way is a thief
and a bandit. 2 The one who enters by the
gate is the shepherd of the sheep. 3 The
gatekeeper opens the gate for him, and the
sheep hear his voice. He calls his own sheep
by name and leads them out. 4 When he has
brought out all his own, he goes ahead of
them, and the sheep follow him because
they know his voice. 5 They will not follow
a stranger, but they will run from him be-
cause they do not know the voice of strang-
ers." 6 Jesus used this figure of speech with
them, but they did not understand what he
was saying to them.
7 So again Jesus said to them, "Very tru-

a Gk *him* *b* Or *the Christ* *c* Other ancient authorities read *the Son of God* *d* *Sir* and *Lord* translate the same Greek word

for the author the term *the Jews* denotes power as well as religion or ethnicity. *Put out,* excommunicated (v. 34). **24:** *Give glory to God,* a technical phrase adjuring the man to tell the truth (Josh 7.19). One who broke the sabbath must be a *sinner.* **25:** The man's concern was his recovered sight, not sabbath observance. **27:** *Do you also want to become his disciples,* a sarcastic remark betraying the healed man's disdain for his interrogators. **28:** The healed man's allegiance to Judaism is questioned (see 1.12–13n.). **31:** *We know,* from teachings in the Hebrew Bible (e.g., Ps 66.18; Prov 15.29). **34:** The haughty elitism of the religious authorities erupts again (cf. 7.49). *Drove him out,* seems to reflect the author's concern—or experience—that those in positions of religious control in his own setting might force Christian believers from community fellowship. **41:** The Pharisees' refusal to admit spiritual blindness demonstrates their *sin.*

10.1–42: Jesus, the shepherd who gives his life. 1–6: Jesus uses a *figure of speech* (v. 6) to describe his own role and the role of his opponents, the religious hierarchy. **3:** *Calls his own,* presumes a fold used by several shepherds. **7–10:** *I am* is emphatic, and shifts the metaphor to Jesus as the *gate* into God's fold, in contrast to those contending against him. For the metaphor, see Ps 118.20. **8:** *Thieves and bandits,*

ly, I tell you, I am the gate for the sheep.
8 All who came before me are thieves and
bandits; but the sheep did not listen to
them. 9 I am the gate. Whoever enters by me
will be saved, and will come in and go out
and find pasture. 10 The thief comes only to
steal and kill and destroy. I came that they
may have life, and have it abundantly.

11 "I am the good shepherd. The good
shepherd lays down his life for the sheep.
12 The hired hand, who is not the shepherd
and does not own the sheep, sees the wolf
coming and leaves the sheep and runs
away—and the wolf snatches them and
scatters them. 13 The hired hand runs away
because a hired hand does not care for the
sheep. 14 I am the good shepherd. I know
my own and my own know me, 15 just as
the Father knows me and I know the Fa-
ther. And I lay down my life for the sheep.
16 I have other sheep that do not belong to
this fold. I must bring them also, and they
will listen to my voice. So there will be one
flock, one shepherd. 17 For this reason the
Father loves me, because I lay down my
life in order to take it up again. 18 No one
takes[a] it from me, but I lay it down of my
own accord. I have power to lay it down,
and I have power to take it up again. I have
received this command from my Father."

19 Again the Jews were divided because
of these words. 20 Many of them were say-
ing, "He has a demon and is out of his
mind. Why listen to him?" 21 Others were
saying, "These are not the words of one
who has a demon. Can a demon open the
eyes of the blind?"

22 At that time the festival of the Dedi-
cation took place in Jerusalem. It was win-
ter, 23 and Jesus was walking in the temple,
in the portico of Solomon. 24 So the Jews
gathered around him and said to him,
"How long will you keep us in suspense?
If you are the Messiah,[b] tell us plainly."
25 Jesus answered, "I have told you, and
you do not believe. The works that I do in
my Father's name testify to me; 26 but you
do not believe, because you do not belong
to my sheep. 27 My sheep hear my voice. I
know them, and they follow me. 28 I give
them eternal life, and they will never perish.
No one will snatch them out of my hand.
29 What my Father has given me is greater
than all else, and no one can snatch it out
of the Father's hand.[c] 30 The Father and I
are one."

31 The Jews took up stones again to
stone him. 32 Jesus replied, "I have shown
you many good works from the Father. For
which of these are you going to stone me?"
33 The Jews answered, "It is not for a good
work that we are going to stone you, but
for blasphemy, because you, though only a
human being, are making yourself God."
34 Jesus answered, "Is it not written in your
law,[d] 'I said, you are gods'? 35 If those to
whom the word of God came were called
'gods'—and the scripture cannot be an-
nulled— 36 can you say that the one whom
the Father has sanctified and sent into the
world is blaspheming because I said, 'I am
God's Son'? 37 If I am not doing the works
of my Father, then do not believe me. 38 But
if I do them, even though you do not be-
lieve me, believe the works, so that you

a Other ancient authorities read *has taken* *b* Or *the Christ* *c* Other ancient authorities read *My Father who has given them to me is greater than all, and no one can snatch them out of the Father's hand* *d* Other ancient authorities read *in the law*

messianic pretenders. **10:** *Life . . . abundantly,* see 3.13–15n. **11:** *I am* is emphatic; contrasts with "hired hand" (v. 12). *Good shepherd,* Ezek 34.11–16; see also Gen 49.24; Ps 23; 78.52; 95.7; Isa 40.10–11. **12–13:** *Hired hand,* cf. Ezek 34.1–10, another attack on the leadership of Israel. **16:** *Other sheep,* Gentiles (17.20–23). *One flock,* the death of the *shepherd* is for the salvation of all humanity (3.16–17). **19–21:** See 8.48; 9.16. **22:** *Dedication,* or Hanukkah, commemorating the rededication of the Temple in 164 BCE after its desecration by Antiochus IV Epiphanes (1 Macc 4.52–59). **23:** *The portico of Solomon,* a cloister on the east side of the Temple buildings (Josephus, *War* 5.184; Acts 3.11). **24–30:** The religious authorities do not accept Jesus' oneness with God because their elitism makes them unable to *hear* him (cf. 7.15). **31:** Stoning was the penalty for blasphemy (Lev 29.16; *Sanhedrin* 7.4). **34–36:** Ps 82.6 discredits their charge of blasphemy; *your law,* here used for Jewish scripture in general. **37–39:** Jesus'

may know and understand[a] that the Fa-
ther is in me and I am in the Father."
39 Then they tried to arrest him again, but
he escaped from their hands.
40 He went away again across the Jor-
dan to the place where John had been bap-
tizing earlier, and he remained there.
41 Many came to him, and they were saying,
"John performed no sign, but everything
that John said about this man was true."
42 And many believed in him there.
11 Now a certain man was ill, Lazarus
of Bethany, the village of Mary and
her sister Martha. 2 Mary was the one who
anointed the Lord with perfume and wiped
his feet with her hair; her brother Lazarus
was ill. 3 So the sisters sent a message to
Jesus,[b] "Lord, he whom you love is ill."
4 But when Jesus heard it, he said, "This
illness does not lead to death; rather it is for
God's glory, so that the Son of God may be
glorified through it." 5 Accordingly, though
Jesus loved Martha and her sister and Laza-
rus, 6 after having heard that Lazarus[c] was
ill, he stayed two days longer in the place
where he was.
7 Then after this he said to the disciples,
"Let us go to Judea again." 8 The disciples
said to him, "Rabbi, the Jews were just
now trying to stone you, and are you going
there again?" 9 Jesus answered, "Are there
not twelve hours of daylight? Those who
walk during the day do not stumble, be-
cause they see the light of this world. 10 But
those who walk at night stumble, because
the light is not in them." 11 After saying
this, he told them, "Our friend Lazarus has
fallen asleep, but I am going there to awak-
en him." 12 The disciples said to him,
"Lord, if he has fallen asleep, he will be all
right." 13 Jesus, however, had been speak-
ing about his death, but they thought that
he was referring merely to sleep. 14 Then
Jesus told them plainly, "Lazarus is dead.
15 For your sake I am glad I was not there,
so that you may believe. But let us go to
him." 16 Thomas, who was called the
Twin,[d] said to his fellow disciples, "Let us
also go, that we may die with him."
17 When Jesus arrived, he found that
Lazarus[c] had already been in the tomb
four days. 18 Now Bethany was near Jerusa-
lem, some two miles[e] away, 19 and many
of the Jews had come to Martha and Mary
to console them about their brother.
20 When Martha heard that Jesus was com-
ing, she went and met him, while Mary
stayed at home. 21 Martha said to Jesus,
"Lord, if you had been here, my brother
would not have died. 22 But even now I
know that God will give you whatever you
ask of him." 23 Jesus said to her, "Your
brother will rise again." 24 Martha said to
him, "I know that he will rise again in the
resurrection on the last day." 25 Jesus said
to her, "I am the resurrection and the life.[f]
Those who believe in me, even though they
die, will live, 26 and everyone who lives and
believes in me will never die. Do you be-
lieve this?" 27 She said to him, "Yes, Lord,

a Other ancient authorities lack *and understand;* others read *and believe* *b* Gk *him* *c* Gk *he* *d* Gk *Didymus* *e* Gk *fifteen stadia* *f* Other ancient authorities lack *and the life*

works authenticate him, for they are the kind which God does. **40:** Jesus withdraws to Perea *across the Jordan* for safety (cf. 8.59). **41:** 1.26–36.

11.1–57: The raising of Lazarus is the crowning miracle or "sign" (12.17–18) that both reveals Jesus as the giver of life (5.25–29) and precipitates his death (11.53). **1:** *Lazarus,* a shortened form of the Hebrew name Eleazar. *Bethany,* see v. 18. *Mary and . . . Martha,* perhaps the same sisters who appear in Lk 10.38–42. **2:** 12.1–3. **4:** *God may be glorified,* see 9.3. **9:** His life would end when God willed; his enemies could not shorten it. **11:** Sleep is a frequent euphemism for death; see Ps 13.4; Acts 7.60 note *c;* 1 Cor 15.6 note *e;* 1 Thess 4.13 note *d.* **15:** The raising of Lazarus will confirm their faith. **16:** *Thomas,* one of the twelve (20.24; Mk 3.18; Acts 1.13). **17:** *Four days,* establishes the finality of Lazarus's death (*Gen. Rab.* 100 [64a]). **19:** *Many* came *to console them,* they become witnesses of Jesus' life-giving power (12.9–11). **20:** Cf. Lk 10.40. **24:** Belief in *the resurrection on the last day* was widespread among Jews in the Hellenistic and Roman periods (see Dan 12.1–3; 2 Macc 7.9). **25:** *I am,* see 6.35n. **25–26:** *Will never die,* Jesus is not only the agent of final resurrection, but gives eternal life now (5.24–26; 6.54). **27:**

I believe that you are the Messiah,[a] the
Son of God, the one coming into the
world."

28 When she had said this, she went
back and called her sister Mary, and told
her privately, "The Teacher is here and is
calling for you." 29 And when she heard it,
she got up quickly and went to him. 30 Now
Jesus had not yet come to the village, but
was still at the place where Martha had met
him. 31 The Jews who were with her in the
house, consoling her, saw Mary get up
quickly and go out. They followed her be-
cause they thought that she was going to
the tomb to weep there. 32 When Mary
came where Jesus was and saw him, she
knelt at his feet and said to him, "Lord, if
you had been here, my brother would not
have died." 33 When Jesus saw her weeping,
and the Jews who came with her also weep-
ing, he was greatly disturbed in spirit and
deeply moved. 34 He said, "Where have you
laid him?" They said to him, "Lord, come
and see." 35 Jesus began to weep. 36 So the
Jews said, "See how he loved him!" 37 But
some of them said, "Could not he who
opened the eyes of the blind man have kept
this man from dying?"

38 Then Jesus, again greatly disturbed,
came to the tomb. It was a cave, and a
stone was lying against it. 39 Jesus said,
"Take away the stone." Martha, the sister
of the dead man, said to him, "Lord, al-
ready there is a stench because he has been
dead four days." 40 Jesus said to her, "Did
I not tell you that if you believed, you
would see the glory of God?" 41 So they
took away the stone. And Jesus looked up-
ward and said, "Father, I thank you for
having heard me. 42 I knew that you always
hear me, but I have said this for the sake of
the crowd standing here, so that they may
believe that you sent me." 43 When he had
said this, he cried with a loud voice, "Laza-
rus, come out!" 44 The dead man came out,
his hands and feet bound with strips of
cloth, and his face wrapped in a cloth. Jesus
said to them, "Unbind him, and let
him go."

45 Many of the Jews therefore, who had
come with Mary and had seen what Jesus
did, believed in him. 46 But some of them
went to the Pharisees and told them what
he had done. 47 So the chief priests and the
Pharisees called a meeting of the council,
and said, "What are we to do? This man is
performing many signs. 48 If we let him go
on like this, everyone will believe in him,
and the Romans will come and destroy
both our holy place[b] and our nation."
49 But one of them, Caiaphas, who was
high priest that year, said to them, "You
know nothing at all! 50 You do not under-
stand that it is better for you to have one
man die for the people than to have the
whole nation destroyed." 51 He did not say
this on his own, but being high priest that
year he prophesied that Jesus was about to
die for the nation, 52 and not for the nation
only, but to gather into one the dispersed
children of God. 53 So from that day on
they planned to put him to death.

54 Jesus therefore no longer walked
about openly among the Jews, but went
from there to a town called Ephraim in
the region near the wilderness; and he re-
mained there with the disciples.

55 Now the Passover of the Jews was
near, and many went up from the country
to Jerusalem before the Passover to purify
themselves. 56 They were looking for Jesus
and were asking one another as they stood
in the temple, "What do you think? Surely
he will not come to the festival, will he?"
57 Now the chief priests and the Pharisees
had given orders that anyone who knew

a Or *the Christ* *b* Or *our temple*; Greek *our place*

A full confession of faith (cf. 1.29–51). **32:** The same response as v. 21, but without the subsequent expression of belief. **40:** *Glory of God,* see v. 4. **47:** *Council,* the Sanhedrin, the highest leadership in Jerusalem, presided over by the high priest. **48:** The First Jewish Revolt, begun in 67 CE, ended with the fall of Jerusalem to the Romans and the destruction of the Temple in 70 CE. **49:** *Caiaphas* was high priest 18–36 CE. **53:** After the raising of Lazarus, the religious authorities' desire to kill Jesus became strategic (12.10). **54:** *Ephraim,* about 20 km (12 mi) north-northeast of Jerusalem. **56:** Cf. 7.11.

where Jesus[a] was should let them know, so
that they might arrest him.

12 Six days before the Passover Jesus
came to Bethany, the home of Laza-
rus, whom he had raised from the dead.
2 There they gave a dinner for him. Martha
served, and Lazarus was one of those at the
table with him. 3 Mary took a pound of
costly perfume made of pure nard, anoint-
ed Jesus' feet, and wiped them[b] with her
hair. The house was filled with the fra-
grance of the perfume. 4 But Judas Iscariot,
one of his disciples (the one who was about
to betray him), said, 5 "Why was this per-
fume not sold for three hundred denarii[c]
and the money given to the poor?" 6 (He
said this not because he cared about the
poor, but because he was a thief; he kept
the common purse and used to steal what
was put into it.) 7 Jesus said, "Leave her
alone. She bought it[d] so that she might
keep it for the day of my burial. 8 You al-
ways have the poor with you, but you do
not always have me."

9 When the great crowd of the Jews
learned that he was there, they came not
only because of Jesus but also to see Laza-
rus, whom he had raised from the dead.
10 So the chief priests planned to put Laza-
rus to death as well, 11 since it was on ac-
count of him that many of the Jews were
deserting and were believing in Jesus.

12 The next day the great crowd that
had come to the festival heard that Jesus
was coming to Jerusalem. 13 So they took
branches of palm trees and went out to
meet him, shouting,

"Hosanna!
Blessed is the one who comes in
the name of the Lord—
the King of Israel!"

14 Jesus found a young donkey and sat on
it; as it is written:

15 "Do not be afraid, daughter of Zion.
Look, your king is coming,
sitting on a donkey's colt!"

16 His disciples did not understand these
things at first; but when Jesus was glorified,
then they remembered that these things had
been written of him and had been done to
him. 17 So the crowd that had been with
him when he called Lazarus out of the
tomb and raised him from the dead contin-
ued to testify.[e] 18 It was also because they
heard that he had performed this sign that
the crowd went to meet him. 19 The Phari-
sees then said to one another, "You see,
you can do nothing. Look, the world has
gone after him!"

20 Now among those who went up to
worship at the festival were some Greeks.
21 They came to Philip, who was from Beth-
saida in Galilee, and said to him, "Sir, we
wish to see Jesus." 22 Philip went and told
Andrew; then Andrew and Philip went and
told Jesus. 23 Jesus answered them, "The
hour has come for the Son of Man to be
glorified. 24 Very truly, I tell you, unless a
grain of wheat falls into the earth and dies,

a Gk *he* *b* Gk *his feet* *c* Three hundred denarii would be nearly a year's wages for a laborer *d* Gk lacks *She bought it* *e* Other ancient authorities read *with him began to testify that he had called. . .from the dead*

12.1–11: The anointing at Bethany. See Mk 14.3–11. Despite the plot against his life (11.53,57), Jesus returns to the vicinity of Jerusalem. **1:** *Bethany,* 11.18. **2:** *Martha served,* cf. Lk 10.40. **3:** A (Roman) *pound,* ca. 326 g (11.5 oz). *Nard* was imported from the Himalayan mountains. **4–6:** This is the fullest description of Judas in the New Testament. Judas is described in the same general way as the religious authorities: *one . . . about to betray him,* i.e., to commit actions that result in Jesus' death (v. 4; cf. 5.18; 7.1; 8.59; 10.31–33; 19.6); *thief* (v. 6; cf. 10.1,8; see 10.10n.); *he cared* not *about the poor* (v. 6; cf. 10.13). **5:** *Three hundred denarii,* see note *c.* **7:** Jesus foresees his death; anointing was part of the preparation of the corpse for burial (see Mt 26.12; Mk 16.2).

12.12–19: Jesus' triumphal entry into Jerusalem. Cf. Mt 21.1–9; Mk 11.1–10; Lk 19.28–38. **13:** See Ps 118.25–26. *Hosanna,* originally a Hebrew invocation to God, meaning "Save!" *In the name of,* with the authority of God. *King of Israel,* the messiah. **15:** Zeph 3.16; Zech 9.9.

12.20–50: The conclusion of Jesus' public ministry. **21–22:** *Philip* and *Andrew,* see 1.43–44. *Bethsaida,* see 1.44n. **23:** *The hour,* see 2.4n. **24:** See 1 Cor 15.36. **25–26:** Mt 10.39; Mk 8.35; Lk 9.24; 14.26.

it remains just a single grain; but if it dies,
it bears much fruit. 25 Those who love their
life lose it, and those who hate their life
in this world will keep it for eternal life.
26 Whoever serves me must follow me, and
where I am, there will my servant be also.
Whoever serves me, the Father will honor.
27 “Now my soul is troubled. And what
should I say—‘Father, save me from this
hour’? No, it is for this reason that I have
come to this hour. 28 Father, glorify your
name.” Then a voice came from heaven, “I
have glorified it, and I will glorify it again.”
29 The crowd standing there heard it and
said that it was thunder. Others said, “An
angel has spoken to him.” 30 Jesus an-
swered, “This voice has come for your
sake, not for mine. 31 Now is the judgment
of this world; now the ruler of this world
will be driven out. 32 And I, when I am lift-
ed up from the earth, will draw all people[a]
to myself.” 33 He said this to indicate the
kind of death he was to die. 34 The crowd
answered him, “We have heard from the
law that the Messiah[b] remains forever.
How can you say that the Son of Man must
be lifted up? Who is this Son of Man?”
35 Jesus said to them, “The light is with you
for a little longer. Walk while you have the
light, so that the darkness may not overtake
you. If you walk in the darkness, you do
not know where you are going. 36 While
you have the light, believe in the light, so
that you may become children of light.”
After Jesus had said this, he departed and
hid from them. 37 Although he had per-
formed so many signs in their presence,
they did not believe in him. 38 This was to
fulfill the word spoken by the prophet Isa-
iah:
“Lord, who has believed our message,
and to whom has the arm of the
Lord been revealed?”
39 And so they could not believe, because
Isaiah also said,
40 “He has blinded their eyes
and hardened their heart,
so that they might not look with their
eyes,
and understand with their heart
and turn—
and I would heal them.”
41 Isaiah said this because[c] he saw his glory
and spoke about him. 42 Nevertheless
many, even of the authorities, believed in
him. But because of the Pharisees they did
not confess it, for fear that they would be
put out of the synagogue; 43 for they loved
human glory more than the glory that
comes from God.
44 Then Jesus cried aloud: “Whoever
believes in me believes not in me but in him
who sent me. 45 And whoever sees me sees
him who sent me. 46 I have come as light
into the world, so that everyone who be-
lieves in me should not remain in the dark-
ness. 47 I do not judge anyone who hears
my words and does not keep them, for I
came not to judge the world, but to save the
world. 48 The one who rejects me and does
not receive my word has a judge; on the last
day the word that I have spoken will serve
as judge, 49 for I have not spoken on my
own, but the Father who sent me has him-
self given me a commandment about what
to say and what to speak. 50 And I know
that his commandment is eternal life. What
I speak, therefore, I speak just as the Father
has told me.”

a Other ancient authorities read *all things* *b* Or *the Christ* *c* Other ancient witnesses read *when*

27–30: *A voice . . . from heaven,* divine reassurance. *For your sake,* that the assembled “crowd” might believe that Jesus came from God. **31–33:** Reality reverses appearances: Jesus’ death judges the *world,* not him; it defeats Satan (*the ruler of this world*), not Jesus; draws, does not repel, *all people.* **34:** *The law,* see 10.34–36n. *The Messiah remains forever,* Ps 89.36–37. **36a:** *Children of light,* those who are spiritually enlightened. The phrase appears in Lk 16.8; Eph 5.8; 1 Thess 5.5; as well as the Dead Sea Scrolls (see 1QS 3.13–4.26), where it is contrasted with the “children of darkness.” **38:** Isa 53.1. **40:** Isa 6.10. **42:** *Many . . . authorities,* Nicodemus and Joseph of Arimathea are the only ones who have been named, cf. 7.48; Acts 15.5. *Fear . . . put out of the synagogue,* see 9.22n. **43:** A scathing indictment of the insincerity of the religious authorities (cf. 10.13). **44–50:** Summary of Jesus’ teaching; cf. 3.16–19.

13 Now before the festival of the Pass-
over, Jesus knew that his hour had
come to depart from this world and go to
the Father. Having loved his own who were
in the world, he loved them to the end.
2 The devil had already put it into the heart
of Judas son of Simon Iscariot to betray
him. And during supper 3 Jesus, knowing
that the Father had given all things into his
hands, and that he had come from God and
was going to God, 4 got up from the table,[a]
took off his outer robe, and tied a towel
around himself. 5 Then he poured water
into a basin and began to wash the disci-
ples' feet and to wipe them with the towel
that was tied around him. 6 He came to Si-
mon Peter, who said to him, "Lord, are you
going to wash my feet?" 7 Jesus answered,
"You do not know now what I am doing,
but later you will understand." 8 Peter said
to him, "You will never wash my feet."
Jesus answered, "Unless I wash you, you
have no share with me." 9 Simon Peter said
to him, "Lord, not my feet only but also my
hands and my head!" 10 Jesus said to him,
"One who has bathed does not need to
wash, except for the feet,[b] but is entirely
clean. And you[c] are clean, though not all
of you." 11 For he knew who was to betray
him; for this reason he said, "Not all of you
are clean."

12 After he had washed their feet, had
put on his robe, and had returned to the
table, he said to them, "Do you know what
I have done to you? 13 You call me Teacher
and Lord—and you are right, for that is
what I am. 14 So if I, your Lord and Teach-
er, have washed your feet, you also ought
to wash one another's feet. 15 For I have set
you an example, that you also should do as
I have done to you. 16 Very truly, I tell you,
servants[d] are not greater than their master,
nor are messengers greater than the one
who sent them. 17 If you know these things,
you are blessed if you do them. 18 I am not
speaking of all of you; I know whom I have
chosen. But it is to fulfill the scripture, 'The
one who ate my bread[e] has lifted his heel
against me.' 19 I tell you this now, before it
occurs, so that when it does occur, you may
believe that I am he.[f] 20 Very truly, I tell
you, whoever receives one whom I send
receives me; and whoever receives me re-
ceives him who sent me."

21 After saying this Jesus was troubled
in spirit, and declared, "Very truly, I tell
you, one of you will betray me." 22 The dis-
ciples looked at one another, uncertain of
whom he was speaking. 23 One of his disci-
ples—the one whom Jesus loved—was re-
clining next to him; 24 Simon Peter there-
fore motioned to him to ask Jesus of whom
he was speaking. 25 So while reclining next
to Jesus, he asked him, "Lord, who is it?"
26 Jesus answered, "It is the one to whom I
give this piece of bread when I have dipped
it in the dish."[g] So when he had dipped the
piece of bread, he gave it to Judas son of
Simon Iscariot.[h] 27 After he received the
piece of bread,[i] Satan entered into him.
Jesus said to him, "Do quickly what you
are going to do." 28 Now no one at the ta-
ble knew why he said this to him. 29 Some
thought that, because Judas had the com-
mon purse, Jesus was telling him, "Buy
what we need for the festival"; or, that he
should give something to the poor. 30 So,
after receiving the piece of bread, he imme-
diately went out. And it was night.

31 When he had gone out, Jesus said,
"Now the Son of Man has been glorified,

a Gk *from supper* *b* Other ancient authorities lack *except for the feet* *c* The Greek word for *you* here is plural *d* Gk *slaves* *e* Other ancient authorities read *ate bread with me* *f* Gk *I am* *g* Gk *dipped it* *h* Other ancient authorities read *Judas Iscariot son of Simon*; others, *Judas son of Simon from Karyot* (Kerioth) *i* Gk *After the piece of bread*

13.1–38: The footwashing and betrayal. Preparation for the teaching (chs 14–17) and events (chs 18–21) to follow. **1:** In John the *Passover* begins on Friday (see 19.14); contrast Mk 14.12–16; Lk 22.15. **2:** See 12.4–6n. **4–5:** Taking off his *outer robe* and tying a *towel around himself* underscores the humility of his action; cf. 1 Sam 25.41. **10:** *You are clean,* 15.3. **16:** Cf. Mt 10.24; Lk 6.40. **18:** Ps 41.9; see v. 26. **19:** *I am,* see note *f.* **20:** Cf. Mt 10.40. **21:** Cf. Mt 26.21; Mk 14.17. **23:** The first appearance of the "beloved disciple," the apparent narrator (see 19.25–27; 20.1–10; 21.1–14,20–24). **29:** See 12.6. **31–32:**

and God has been glorified in him. 32 If
God has been glorified in him,[a] God will
also glorify him in himself and will glorify
him at once. 33 Little children, I am with
you only a little longer. You will look for
me; and as I said to the Jews so now I say
to you, 'Where I am going, you cannot
come.' 34 I give you a new commandment,
that you love one another. Just as I have
loved you, you also should love one anoth-
er. 35 By this everyone will know that you
are my disciples, if you have love for one
another."
36 Simon Peter said to him, "Lord,
where are you going?" Jesus answered,
"Where I am going, you cannot follow me
now; but you will follow afterward." 37 Pe-
ter said to him, "Lord, why can I not follow
you now? I will lay down my life for you."
38 Jesus answered, "Will you lay down your
life for me? Very truly, I tell you, before the
cock crows, you will have denied me three
times.

14 "Do not let your hearts be troubled.
Believe[b] in God, believe also in me.
2 In my Father's house there are many
dwelling places. If it were not so, would I
have told you that I go to prepare a place
for you?[c] 3 And if I go and prepare a place
for you, I will come again and will take you
to myself, so that where I am, there you
may be also. 4 And you know the way to the
place where I am going."[d] 5 Thomas said
to him, "Lord, we do not know where you
are going. How can we know the way?"
6 Jesus said to him, "I am the way, and the
truth, and the life. No one comes to the
Father except through me. 7 If you know
me, you will know[e] my Father also. From
now on you do know him and have seen
him."
8 Philip said to him, "Lord, show us the
Father, and we will be satisfied." 9 Jesus
said to him, "Have I been with you all this
time, Philip, and you still do not know me?
Whoever has seen me has seen the Father.
How can you say, 'Show us the Father'?
10 Do you not believe that I am in the Father
and the Father is in me? The words that I
say to you I do not speak on my own;
but the Father who dwells in me does his
works. 11 Believe me that I am in the Father
and the Father is in me; but if you do not,
then believe me because of the works them-
selves. 12 Very truly, I tell you, the one who
believes in me will also do the works that I
do and, in fact, will do greater works than
these, because I am going to the Father. 13 I
will do whatever you ask in my name, so
that the Father may be glorified in the Son.
14 If in my name you ask me[f] for anything,
I will do it.
15 "If you love me, you will keep[g] my
commandments. 16 And I will ask the Fa-

a Other ancient authorities lack *If God has been glorified in him* *b* Or *You believe* *c* Or *If it were not so, I would have told you; for I go to prepare a place for you* *d* Other ancient authorities read *Where I am going you know, and the way you know* *e* Other ancient authorities read *If you had known me, you would have known* *f* Other ancient authorities lack *me* *g* Other ancient authorities read *me, keep*

The departure of Judas begins the events that will *glorify* Jesus. **33:** *Little children,* a self-designation used in Johannine circles, see 1 Jn 2.1,12,28; 3.7,18; 4.4; 5.21. **36–38:** Cf. Mk 14.29–30; Lk 22.33–34. It is not yet Peter's time to *follow* Jesus to his death; *afterward,* according to tradition, Peter himself was also crucified under Nero at Rome about 64–68 CE (*1 Clem* 4–6; Eusebius, *Hist. Eccl.* 2.25.6).

13.31–17.26: Jesus' farewell discourse and prayer. An interpretation of Jesus' completed work on earth and his relation both to believers and to the world after his glorification.

14.1–31: The believers' relation to the glorified Christ. 2–3: For him to *go,* through death and resurrection, was to *prepare a place* of permanent fellowship (13.33,36). *Dwelling places,* the resting places for the righteous (cf. 1 Enoch 39.4–5). **4–7:** Jesus is the gateway to God (10.9). *I am,* see 6.35n. **6:** Cf. Acts 4.12. **8–11:** God is revealed through the *words* and *works* of Jesus. See 10.30; 17.11,21. **12:** *Greater works* (5.20), Jesus' ascension to the Father opens up a global mission (17.20–24). **13–14:** Cf. 15.7,16; 16.23–26; Mt 21.22. **15:** Cf. Ex 20.6; Deut 7.9. **16–17:** *Advocate . . . Spirit of truth,* Jesus is the heavenly *Advocate* for Christians (1 Jn 2.1). The *Spirit of truth* as guide for the righteous may represent the angelic figure described in Qumran texts (see 1QS 3.18–21; *T. Jud.* 20,1–5). **20:** *On that*

ther, and he will give you another Advo-
cate,[a] to be with you forever. 17 This is the
Spirit of truth, whom the world cannot re-
ceive, because it neither sees him nor knows
him. You know him, because he abides
with you, and he will be in[b] you.
18 "I will not leave you orphaned; I am
coming to you. 19 In a little while the world
will no longer see me, but you will see me;
because I live, you also will live. 20 On that
day you will know that I am in my Father,
and you in me, and I in you. 21 They who
have my commandments and keep them
are those who love me; and those who love
me will be loved by my Father, and I will
love them and reveal myself to them." 22 Ju-
das (not Iscariot) said to him, "Lord, how
is it that you will reveal yourself to us, and
not to the world?" 23 Jesus answered him,
"Those who love me will keep my word,
and my Father will love them, and we will
come to them and make our home with
them. 24 Whoever does not love me does
not keep my words; and the word that you
hear is not mine, but is from the Father
who sent me.
25 "I have said these things to you while
I am still with you. 26 But the Advocate,[a]
the Holy Spirit, whom the Father will send
in my name, will teach you everything, and
remind you of all that I have said to you.
27 Peace I leave with you; my peace I give to
you. I do not give to you as the world gives.
Do not let your hearts be troubled, and do
not let them be afraid. 28 You heard me say
to you, 'I am going away, and I am coming
to you.' If you loved me, you would rejoice
that I am going to the Father, because the
Father is greater than I. 29 And now I have
told you this before it occurs, so that when
it does occur, you may believe. 30 I will no
longer talk much with you, for the ruler of
this world is coming. He has no power over
me; 31 but I do as the Father has command-
ed me, so that the world may know that I
love the Father. Rise, let us be on our way.
15 "I am the true vine, and my Father
is the vinegrower. 2 He removes ev-
ery branch in me that bears no fruit. Every
branch that bears fruit he prunes[c] to make
it bear more fruit. 3 You have already been
cleansed[c] by the word that I have spoken
to you. 4 Abide in me as I abide in you. Just
as the branch cannot bear fruit by itself un-
less it abides in the vine, neither can you
unless you abide in me. 5 I am the vine, you
are the branches. Those who abide in me
and I in them bear much fruit, because
apart from me you can do nothing. 6 Who-
ever does not abide in me is thrown away
like a branch and withers; such branches
are gathered, thrown into the fire, and
burned. 7 If you abide in me, and my words
abide in you, ask for whatever you wish,
and it will be done for you. 8 My Father is
glorified by this, that you bear much fruit
and become[d] my disciples. 9 As the Father
has loved me, so I have loved you; abide in
my love. 10 If you keep my commandments,
you will abide in my love, just as I have
kept my Father's commandments and abide
in his love. 11 I have said these things to you
so that my joy may be in you, and that your
joy may be complete.
12 "This is my commandment, that you

a Or *Helper* *b* Or *among* *c* The same Greek root refers to pruning and cleansing *d* Or *be*

day, the last day (Isa 2.11; 4.12). *I . . . in my Father, and you in me,* their relationship with the risen Jesus will reflect the union of the Son with the Father. **22:** *Judas,* see Lk 6.16; Acts 1.13. **25–27:** The *Holy Spirit* enables believers to remember and understand Jesus' words (see 12.16). **28–31:** *I am going to the Father,* Jesus' submission to crucifixion at the hands of *the ruler of this world* (see 12.31–33n.; 16.11), whose *power* is broken by Jesus' death and resurrection.

15.1–27: The pattern of the believer's life. 1–11: The believer's relation to Jesus: *abide.* **1:** *I am* is emphatic (see 6.35n.). *True vine,* true Israel, fulfilling the vocation that Israel had failed (Isa 5.1–7; Jer 2.21; Ezek 19.10–14; cf. Mk 12.1–12 par.). **3:** *Already . . . cleansed,* see note *c.* For those believing in him Jesus has replaced the priestly function of providing ritual purification from sin and uncleanness. **6:** Cf. Mt 3.10; 7.19. **12–17:** The relation of believers to one another: *love.* Jesus' sacrificial death is the

love one another as I have loved you. 13 No
one has greater love than this, to lay down
one's life for one's friends. 14 You are my
friends if you do what I command you. 15 I
do not call you servants[a] any longer, be-
cause the servant[b] does not know what
the master is doing; but I have called you
friends, because I have made known to you
everything that I have heard from my Fa-
ther. 16 You did not choose me but I chose
you. And I appointed you to go and bear
fruit, fruit that will last, so that the Father
will give you whatever you ask him in my
name. 17 I am giving you these commands
so that you may love one another.
18 "If the world hates you, be aware
that it hated me before it hated you. 19 If
you belonged to the world,[c] the world
would love you as its own. Because you do
not belong to the world, but I have chosen
you out of the world—therefore the world
hates you. 20 Remember the word that I
said to you, 'Servants[d] are not greater than
their master.' If they persecuted me, they
will persecute you; if they kept my word,
they will keep yours also. 21 But they will
do all these things to you on account of my
name, because they do not know him who
sent me. 22 If I had not come and spoken to
them, they would not have sin; but now
they have no excuse for their sin. 23 Whoev-
er hates me hates my Father also. 24 If I had
not done among them the works that no
one else did, they would not have sin. But
now they have seen and hated both me and
my Father. 25 It was to fulfill the word that
is written in their law, 'They hated me
without a cause.'
26 "When the Advocate[e] comes, whom
I will send to you from the Father, the Spirit
of truth who comes from the Father, he will
testify on my behalf. 27 You also are to testi-
fy because you have been with me from the
beginning.

16 "I have said these things to you to
keep you from stumbling. 2 They
will put you out of the synagogues. Indeed,
an hour is coming when those who kill you
will think that by doing so they are offering
worship to God. 3 And they will do this be-
cause they have not known the Father or
me. 4 But I have said these things to you so
that when their hour comes you may re-
member that I told you about them.
"I did not say these things to you from
the beginning, because I was with you. 5 But
now I am going to him who sent me; yet
none of you asks me, 'Where are you go-
ing?' 6 But because I have said these things
to you, sorrow has filled your hearts. 7 Nev-
ertheless I tell you the truth: it is to your
advantage that I go away, for if I do not go
away, the Advocate[e] will not come to you;
but if I go, I will send him to you. 8 And
when he comes, he will prove the world
wrong about[f] sin and righteousness and
judgment: 9 about sin, because they do not
believe in me; 10 about righteousness, be-
cause I am going to the Father and you will
see me no longer; 11 about judgment, be-
cause the ruler of this world has been con-
demned.
12 "I still have many things to say to
you, but you cannot bear them now.
13 When the Spirit of truth comes, he will
guide you into all the truth; for he will not
speak on his own, but will speak whatever
he hears, and he will declare to you the
things that are to come. 14 He will glorify
me, because he will take what is mine and
declare it to you. 15 All that the Father has
is mine. For this reason I said that he will
take what is mine and declare it to you.
16 "A little while, and you will no lon-
ger see me, and again a little while, and you

a Gk *slaves* *b* Gk *slave* *c* Gk *were of the world* *d* Gk *Slaves* *e* Or *Helper* *f* Or *convict the world of*

standard for love (v. 13). **15:** Cf. 13.13,16. **18–27:** The believer's relation to the *world*. **20:** See 13.16n. **25:** Ps 35.19; 69.4.

16.1–33: The believer's relation to the world. 1–4a: Forewarning of conflict. It is to be expected that the religious authorities and their adherents will persecute believers; cf. 9.22; 12.42. **4a:** *Hour,* see 5.25–30n. **4b–11:** The work of the *Advocate* (Holy Spirit). **16:** *A little while,* Isa 10.25; 29.17; Jer 51.33;

will see me." [17]Then some of his disciples
said to one another, "What does he mean
by saying to us, 'A little while, and you will
no longer see me, and again a little while,
and you will see me'; and 'Because I am
going to the Father'?" [18]They said, "What
does he mean by this 'a little while'? We
do not know what he is talking about."
[19]Jesus knew that they wanted to ask him,
so he said to them, "Are you discussing
among yourselves what I meant when I
said, 'A little while, and you will no longer
see me, and again a little while, and you
will see me'? [20]Very truly, I tell you, you
will weep and mourn, but the world will
rejoice; you will have pain, but your pain
will turn into joy. [21]When a woman is in
labor, she has pain, because her hour has
come. But when her child is born, she no
longer remembers the anguish because of
the joy of having brought a human being
into the world. [22]So you have pain now;
but I will see you again, and your hearts
will rejoice, and no one will take your joy
from you. [23]On that day you will ask noth-
ing of me.[a] Very truly, I tell you, if you ask
anything of the Father in my name, he will
give it to you.[b] [24]Until now you have not
asked for anything in my name. Ask and
you will receive, so that your joy may be
complete.

25 "I have said these things to you in
figures of speech. The hour is coming when
I will no longer speak to you in figures, but
will tell you plainly of the Father. [26]On
that day you will ask in my name. I do not
say to you that I will ask the Father on your
behalf; [27]for the Father himself loves you,
because you have loved me and have be-
lieved that I came from God.[c] [28]I came
from the Father and have come into the
world; again, I am leaving the world and
am going to the Father."

29 His disciples said, "Yes, now you are
speaking plainly, not in any figure of
speech! [30]Now we know that you know all
things, and do not need to have anyone
question you; by this we believe that you
came from God." [31]Jesus answered them,
"Do you now believe? [32]The hour is com-
ing, indeed it has come, when you will be
scattered, each one to his home, and you
will leave me alone. Yet I am not alone
because the Father is with me. [33]I have said
this to you, so that in me you may have
peace. In the world you face persecution.
But take courage; I have conquered the
world!"

17 After Jesus had spoken these words,
he looked up to heaven and said,
"Father, the hour has come; glorify your
Son so that the Son may glorify you, [2]since
you have given him authority over all peo-
ple,[d] to give eternal life to all whom you
have given him. [3]And this is eternal life,
that they may know you, the only true
God, and Jesus Christ whom you have sent.
[4]I glorified you on earth by finishing the
work that you gave me to do. [5]So now,
Father, glorify me in your own presence
with the glory that I had in your presence
before the world existed.

6 "I have made your name known to
those whom you gave me from the world.
They were yours, and you gave them to me,
and they have kept your word. [7]Now they
know that everything you have given me is
from you; [8]for the words that you gave to
me I have given to them, and they have
received them and know in truth that I
came from you; and they have believed that
you sent me. [9]I am asking on their behalf;
I am not asking on behalf of the world, but
on behalf of those whom you gave me, be-
cause they are yours. [10]All mine are yours,
and yours are mine; and I have been glori-

a Or *will ask me no question* b Other ancient authorities read *Father, he will give it to you in my name* c Other ancient authorities read *the Father* d Gk *flesh*

Hos 1.4. **20–22:** Cf. Isa 66.7–14. **23–26:** Prayer in Jesus' *name;* cf. 15.16. **25:** Cf. 10.1–6n. **31:** An expression of skepticism. **32:** Cf. Zech 13.7; Mt 26.31; Mk 14.27.

17.1–26: Jesus' final prayer. 1–5: Jesus' prayer for himself. *The hour has come* (see 2.4n.) for Jesus to manifest his eternal glory (see 1.1–3,14). **6–19:** Jesus' prayer for his disciples. There are echoes here of the "Lord's Prayer" (Mt 6.9–13; Lk 11.2–4); note "Father" (vv. 11,25), "sanctify" (vv. 17,19; translated

fied in them. 11 And now I am no longer in
the world, but they are in the world, and I
am coming to you. Holy Father, protect
them in your name that you have given me,
so that they may be one, as we are one.
12 While I was with them, I protected them
in your name that[a] you have given me. I
guarded them, and not one of them was
lost except the one destined to be lost,[b] so
that the scripture might be fulfilled. 13 But
now I am coming to you, and I speak these
things in the world so that they may have
my joy made complete in themselves.[c] 14 I
have given them your word, and the world
has hated them because they do not belong
to the world, just as I do not belong to the
world. 15 I am not asking you to take them
out of the world, but I ask you to protect
them from the evil one.[d] 16 They do not
belong to the world, just as I do not belong
to the world. 17 Sanctify them in the truth;
your word is truth. 18 As you have sent me
into the world, so I have sent them into the
world. 19 And for their sakes I sanctify my-
self, so that they also may be sanctified in
truth.

20 "I ask not only on behalf of these,
but also on behalf of those who will believe
in me through their word, 21 that they may
all be one. As you, Father, are in me and I
am in you, may they also be in us,[e] so that
the world may believe that you have sent
me. 22 The glory that you have given me I
have given them, so that they may be one,
as we are one, 23 I in them and you in me,
that they may become completely one,
so that the world may know that you
have sent me and have loved them even as
you have loved me. 24 Father, I desire that
those also, whom you have given me, may
be with me where I am, to see my glory,
which you have given me because you
loved me before the foundation of the world.

25 "Righteous Father, the world does
not know you, but I know you; and these
know that you have sent me. 26 I made your
name known to them, and I will make it
known, so that the love with which you
have loved me may be in them, and I in
them."

18 After Jesus had spoken these words,
he went out with his disciples across
the Kidron valley to a place where there
was a garden, which he and his disciples
entered. 2 Now Judas, who betrayed him,
also knew the place, because Jesus often
met there with his disciples. 3 So Judas
brought a detachment of soldiers together
with police from the chief priests and the
Pharisees, and they came there with lan-
terns and torches and weapons. 4 Then
Jesus, knowing all that was to happen to
him, came forward and asked them,
"Whom are you looking for?" 5 They an-
swered, "Jesus of Nazareth."[f] Jesus re-
plied, "I am he."[g] Judas, who betrayed
him, was standing with them. 6 When
Jesus[h] said to them, "I am he,"[g] they
stepped back and fell to the ground. 7 Again
he asked them, "Whom are you looking
for?" And they said, "Jesus of Nazareth."[f]
8 Jesus answered, "I told you that I am he.[g]
So if you are looking for me, let these men
go." 9 This was to fulfill the word that he
had spoken, "I did not lose a single one of
those whom you gave me." 10 Then Simon
Peter, who had a sword, drew it, struck the
high priest's slave, and cut off his right ear.

a Other ancient authorities read *protected in your name those whom* *b* Gk *except the son of destruction* *c* Or *among themselves* *d* Or *from evil* *e* Other ancient authorities read *be one in us* *f* Gk *the Nazorean* *g* Gk *I am* *h* Gk *he*

"hallowed" in Mt 6.9), and "the evil one" (v. 15). **12:** See 13.11,18,26; Acts 1.16. **20–26:** Jesus' prayer for future believers. **24:** *Before the foundation of the world,* see v. 5; 1.2,14.

18.1–19.42: Arrest, trial, crucifixion, and burial of Jesus (cf. Mt 26.30–27.61; Mk 14.26–15.47; Lk 22.39–23.56). **18.1:** *Kidron valley,* east of Jerusalem; see 8.1n. *A garden,* called Gethsemane in Mt 26.36; Mk 14.32. **2:** *Jesus often met there,* cf. Lk 21.37; 22.39. **3:** Roman *soldiers* and the Jewish religious authorities' *police* (see 7.32) collaborated on Jesus' arrest. *Lanterns and torches,* because it was night (13.30). **5:** *I am he,* Jesus' unexpected assertion of divinity awes the arresting party (v. 6; see 6.35n.). **9:** 6.39; 10.28; 17.12. **10:** *Simon Peter, Malchus,* both identified by name only in this Gospel. **11:** *Cup,*

The slave's name was Malchus. 11 Jesus said
to Peter, "Put your sword back into its
sheath. Am I not to drink the cup that the
Father has given me?"
12 So the soldiers, their officer, and the
Jewish police arrested Jesus and bound
him. 13 First they took him to Annas, who
was the father-in-law of Caiaphas, the high
priest that year. 14 Caiaphas was the one
who had advised the Jews that it was better
to have one person die for the people.
15 Simon Peter and another disciple fol-
lowed Jesus. Since that disciple was known
to the high priest, he went with Jesus into
the courtyard of the high priest, 16 but Peter
was standing outside at the gate. So the
other disciple, who was known to the high
priest, went out, spoke to the woman who
guarded the gate, and brought Peter in.
17 The woman said to Peter, "You are not
also one of this man's disciples, are you?"
He said, "I am not." 18 Now the slaves and
the police had made a charcoal fire because
it was cold, and they were standing around
it and warming themselves. Peter also was
standing with them and warming himself.
19 Then the high priest questioned Jesus
about his disciples and about his teaching.
20 Jesus answered, "I have spoken openly to
the world; I have always taught in syna-
gogues and in the temple, where all the
Jews come together. I have said nothing in
secret. 21 Why do you ask me? Ask those
who heard what I said to them; they know
what I said." 22 When he had said this, one
of the police standing nearby struck Jesus
on the face, saying, "Is that how you an-
swer the high priest?" 23 Jesus answered, "If
I have spoken wrongly, testify to the
wrong. But if I have spoken rightly, why do
you strike me?" 24 Then Annas sent him
bound to Caiaphas the high priest.
25 Now Simon Peter was standing and
warming himself. They asked him, "You
are not also one of his disciples, are you?"
He denied it and said, "I am not." 26 One of
the slaves of the high priest, a relative of the
man whose ear Peter had cut off, asked,
"Did I not see you in the garden with him?"
27 Again Peter denied it, and at that mo-
ment the cock crowed.
28 Then they took Jesus from Caiaphas
to Pilate's headquarters.[a] It was early in
the morning. They themselves did not enter
the headquarters,[a] so as to avoid ritual de-
filement and to be able to eat the Passover.
29 So Pilate went out to them and said,
"What accusation do you bring against this
man?" 30 They answered, "If this man were
not a criminal, we would not have handed
him over to you." 31 Pilate said to them,
"Take him yourselves and judge him ac-
cording to your law." The Jews replied,
"We are not permitted to put anyone to
death." 32 (This was to fulfill what Jesus
had said when he indicated the kind of
death he was to die.)
33 Then Pilate entered the headquar-
ters[a] again, summoned Jesus, and asked
him, "Are you the King of the Jews?"
34 Jesus answered, "Do you ask this on
your own, or did others tell you about

a Gk *the praetorium*

metaphor for that which God allots (Ps 16.5; Isa 51.17; Lam 4.21); cf. Mk 10.38–39 par.; 14.36 par. **13:** *Annas,* though deposed as high priest by the Romans in 15 CE, was still the leading influence among the religious authorities through his son-in-law Caiaphas (see 11.49n.) and five sons who succeeded him. **14:** See 11.49–50. **19–24:** An informal trial before Annas (here called "the high priest"; see v. 13n.). *Synagogues and . . . the temple,* are part of the *world* (see 1.10n.), not spiritual centers (see 2.15–16n.; 4.20–21n.). **27:** 13.38.

18.28–19.16a: Jesus and Pilate. 28: *They took Jesus,* the religious authorities (see v. 31). *Pilate's headquarters,* the Praetorium (see note *a* and Mk 15.16) was the official residence of Pontius Pilate, the Roman governor of Judea (ca. 26–37 CE). It was probably located on the west side of Jerusalem (see Map on p. 151 NT). *Defilement,* entering a Gentile's house might make them ceremonially unclean and unable to celebrate Passover. **29–31:** A humiliating exchange highlighting the powerlessness of the Jewish religious authorities to administer their own law (see Lev 24.16). **32:** Crucifixion (3.14; 12.32), rather than the Jewish method of stoning. **33–40:** This exchange is laced with sarcasm. **33:** *King of the Jews,* a charge me?" 35 Pilate replied, "I am not a Jew, am I? Your own nation and the chief priests have handed you over to me. What have you done?" 36 Jesus answered, "My kingdom is not from this world. If my kingdom were from this world, my followers would be fighting to keep me from being handed over to the Jews. But as it is, my kingdom is not from here." 37 Pilate asked him, "So you are a king?" Jesus answered, "You say that I am a king. For this I was born, and for this I came into the world, to testify to the truth. Everyone who belongs to the truth listens to my voice." 38 Pilate asked him, "What is truth?"

After he had said this, he went out to the Jews again and told them, "I find no case against him. 39 But you have a custom that I release someone for you at the Passover. Do you want me to release for you the King of the Jews?" 40 They shouted in reply, "Not this man, but Barabbas!" Now Barabbas was a bandit.

19 Then Pilate took Jesus and had him flogged. 2 And the soldiers wove a crown of thorns and put it on his head, and they dressed him in a purple robe. 3 They kept coming up to him, saying, "Hail, King of the Jews!" and striking him on the face. 4 Pilate went out again and said to them, "Look, I am bringing him out to you to let you know that I find no case against him." 5 So Jesus came out, wearing the crown of thorns and the purple robe. Pilate said to them, "Here is the man!" 6 When the chief priests and the police saw him, they shouted, "Crucify him! Crucify him!" Pilate said to them, "Take him yourselves and crucify him; I find no case against him." 7 The Jews answered him, "We have a law, and according to that law he ought to die because he has claimed to be the Son of God."

8 Now when Pilate heard this, he was more afraid than ever. 9 He entered his headquarters[a] again and asked Jesus, "Where are you from?" But Jesus gave him no answer. 10 Pilate therefore said to him, "Do you refuse to speak to me? Do you not know that I have power to release you, and power to crucify you?" 11 Jesus answered him, "You would have no power over me unless it had been given you from above; therefore the one who handed me over to you is guilty of a greater sin." 12 From then on Pilate tried to release him, but the Jews cried out, "If you release this man, you are no friend of the emperor. Everyone who claims to be a king sets himself against the emperor."

13 When Pilate heard these words, he brought Jesus outside and sat[b] on the judge's bench at a place called The Stone Pavement, or in Hebrew[c] Gabbatha. 14 Now it was the day of Preparation for the Passover; and it was about noon. He said to the Jews, "Here is your King!" 15 They cried out, "Away with him! Away with him! Crucify him!" Pilate asked them, "Shall I crucify your King?" The chief priests answered, "We have no king but the emperor." 16 Then he handed him over to them to be crucified.

So they took Jesus; 17 and carrying the cross by himself, he went out to what is called The Place of the Skull, which in He-

a Gk *the praetorium* b Or *seated him* c That is, Aramaic

constituting sedition. **39:** Such a *custom* is reported only in the New Testament. **40:** *Bandit* (Gk "lestes"), a term also connoting "insurrectionist." **19.1:** *Flogged,* possibly as an alternative to crucifixion (cf. vv. 4,6; 18.38b). **6–8:** See 18.31n.; 5.17–18; 10.30–39. *Afraid,* of incurring divine displeasure if Jesus was the *Son of God.* **12:** A threat of blackmail by accusing Pilate of permitting rebellion *against the emperor.* **13:** *Gabbatha,* occurring only here, probably means "the elevated (place)" in Aramaic (see note *c*) and designates an outdoor platform. It was probably near the Praetorium (see 18.28n.). **14:** *Day of Preparation . . . about noon,* the beginning of Passover activities (see 13.1n.). **15:** *No king but the emperor,* the ultimate betrayal of the religious authorities' divine trust and repudiation of the promise of the kingdom of God.

19.16b–37: The crucifixion. 17: *Cross,* not the entire cross, but the cross-beam upon which Jesus hung. *Skull,* a place of skull-like appearance just outside the city walls (v. 20) to the northwest (see Map on brew[a] is called Golgotha. 18 There they crucified him, and with him two others, one on either side, with Jesus between them. 19 Pilate also had an inscription written and put on the cross. It read, "Jesus of Nazareth,[b] the King of the Jews." 20 Many of the Jews read this inscription, because the place where Jesus was crucified was near the city; and it was written in Hebrew,[a] in Latin, and in Greek. 21 Then the chief priests of the Jews said to Pilate, "Do not write, 'The King of the Jews,' but, 'This man said, I am King of the Jews.' " 22 Pilate answered, "What I have written I have written." 23 When the soldiers had crucified Jesus, they took his clothes and divided them into four parts, one for each soldier. They also took his tunic; now the tunic was seamless, woven in one piece from the top. 24 So they said to one another, "Let us not tear it, but cast lots for it to see who will get it." This was to fulfill what the scripture says,

"They divided my clothes among
    themselves,
  and for my clothing they cast lots."

25 And that is what the soldiers did.

Meanwhile, standing near the cross of Jesus were his mother, and his mother's sister, Mary the wife of Clopas, and Mary Magdalene. 26 When Jesus saw his mother and the disciple whom he loved standing beside her, he said to his mother, "Woman, here is your son." 27 Then he said to the disciple, "Here is your mother." And from that hour the disciple took her into his own home.

28 After this, when Jesus knew that all was now finished, he said (in order to fulfill the scripture), "I am thirsty." 29 A jar full of sour wine was standing there. So they put a sponge full of the wine on a branch of hyssop and held it to his mouth. 30 When Jesus had received the wine, he said, "It is finished." Then he bowed his head and gave up his spirit.

31 Since it was the day of Preparation, the Jews did not want the bodies left on the cross during the sabbath, especially because that sabbath was a day of great solemnity. So they asked Pilate to have the legs of the crucified men broken and the bodies removed. 32 Then the soldiers came and broke the legs of the first and of the other who had been crucified with him. 33 But when they came to Jesus and saw that he was already dead, they did not break his legs. 34 Instead, one of the soldiers pierced his side with a spear, and at once blood and water came out. 35 (He who saw this has testified so that you also may believe. His testimony is true, and he knows[c] that he tells the truth.) 36 These things occurred so that the scripture might be fulfilled, "None of his bones shall be broken." 37 And again another passage of scripture says, "They will look on the one whom they have pierced."

38 After these things, Joseph of Arimathea, who was a disciple of Jesus, though a secret one because of his fear of the Jews, asked Pilate to let him take away the body of Jesus. Pilate gave him permission; so he came and removed his body. 39 Nicodemus, who had at first come to Jesus by night,

a That is, *Aramaic* *b* Gk *the Nazorean*
c Or *there is one who knows*

p. 151 NT). **20–22:** The ultimate irony; despite the best efforts of the religious authorities to discredit and destroy him, Jesus is declared *King of the Jews* in three languages. **23:** A Roman custom. *His clothes,* cloak or outer garment, belt, sandals. *Tunic,* undergarment. **24:** Ps 22.18. **25:** *His mother,* see 2.1n. *Mary the wife of Clopas,* probably the mother of James and Joses (Mk 15.40). *Clopas* may be a variant of Cleopas (Lk 24.18). **26–27:** As the new *son* of Jesus' *mother,* the *disciple* Jesus *loved* is given elevated status among the disciples (13.23; 21.7). **28:** *I am thirsty,* Ps 69.21. **29:** *Hyssop,* a wild shrub whose branches were used for sprinkling blood and water in religious ceremonies. **30:** *Finished,* all that God has sent him to accomplish (17.4). **31:** *A day of great solemnity,* especially holy since it fell on the first day of Passover; see Deut 21.23. **32:** *Broke the legs,* to hasten death. **34:** *Blood and water,* both literal (v. 35; see 1 Jn 5.6) and symbolic, perhaps denoting the Lord's Supper and baptism (3.5; 6.53–58). **36:** Jesus embodies the Passover lamb (Ex 12.46; see also Ps 34.20; Jn 1.29n.). **37:** Zech 12.10. **38:** *Joseph of Arimethea,* Mt

also came, bringing a mixture of myrrh and
aloes, weighing about a hundred pounds.
40 They took the body of Jesus and
wrapped it with the spices in linen cloths,
according to the burial custom of the Jews.
41 Now there was a garden in the place
where he was crucified, and in the garden
there was a new tomb in which no one had
ever been laid. 42 And so, because it was the
Jewish day of Preparation, and the tomb
was nearby, they laid Jesus there.

20 Early on the first day of the week,
while it was still dark, Mary Mag-
dalene came to the tomb and saw that the
stone had been removed from the tomb.
2 So she ran and went to Simon Peter and
the other disciple, the one whom Jesus
loved, and said to them, "They have taken
the Lord out of the tomb, and we do not
know where they have laid him." 3 Then
Peter and the other disciple set out and
went toward the tomb. 4 The two were run-
ning together, but the other disciple outran
Peter and reached the tomb first. 5 He bent
down to look in and saw the linen wrap-
pings lying there, but he did not go in.
6 Then Simon Peter came, following him,
and went into the tomb. He saw the linen
wrappings lying there, 7 and the cloth that
had been on Jesus' head, not lying with the
linen wrappings but rolled up in a place
by itself. 8 Then the other disciple, who
reached the tomb first, also went in, and he
saw and believed; 9 for as yet they did not
understand the scripture, that he must rise
from the dead. 10 Then the disciples re-
turned to their homes.

11 But Mary stood weeping outside the
tomb. As she wept, she bent over to look[a]
into the tomb; 12 and she saw two angels in
white, sitting where the body of Jesus had
been lying, one at the head and the other at
the feet. 13 They said to her, "Woman, why
are you weeping?" She said to them, "They
have taken away my Lord, and I do not
know where they have laid him." 14 When
she had said this, she turned around and
saw Jesus standing there, but she did not
know that it was Jesus. 15 Jesus said to her,
"Woman, why are you weeping? Whom
are you looking for?" Supposing him to be
the gardener, she said to him, "Sir, if you
have carried him away, tell me where you
have laid him, and I will take him away."
16 Jesus said to her, "Mary!" She turned
and said to him in Hebrew,[b] "Rabbouni!"
(which means Teacher). 17 Jesus said to her,
"Do not hold on to me, because I have not
yet ascended to the Father. But go to my
brothers and say to them, 'I am ascending
to my Father and your Father, to my God
and your God.'" 18 Mary Magdalene went
and announced to the disciples, "I have
seen the Lord"; and she told them that he
had said these things to her.

19 When it was evening on that day, the
first day of the week, and the doors of the
house where the disciples had met were
locked for fear of the Jews, Jesus came and
stood among them and said, "Peace be with
you." 20 After he said this, he showed them
his hands and his side. Then the disciples
rejoiced when they saw the Lord. 21 Jesus
said to them again, "Peace be with you. As
the Father has sent me, so I send you."
22 When he had said this, he breathed on
them and said to them, "Receive the Holy
Spirit. 23 If you forgive the sins of any, they

a Gk lacks *to look* *b* That is, *Aramaic*

27.57–60; Mk 15.43; Lk 23.50–53. **39:** *Nicodemus,* 3.1–15; 7.50–52. *Myrrh,* a resinous gum which, when mixed with crushed or pounded *aloes,* was used for embalming. A *hundred* (Roman) *pounds,* about 34 kg (75 lb). **40:** *Linen cloths,* cf. 11.44; contrast Mk 15.46.

20.1–31: The resurrection (cf. Mt 28; Mk 16; Lk 24). **1:** *First day,* Sunday. **2–3:** *The other disciple,* see 13.23n. *They,* perhaps grave robbers. **5:** *Wrappings lying there,* grave robbers would not have left the linen behind. **9:** *The scripture,* passages in the Hebrew Bible that were taken to pertain to Jesus' resurrection (cf. Lk 24.25–27,32,44–47; Acts 2.24–32; 1 Cor 15.4). **16:** *Rabbouni,* a variant of "Rabbi" (see 1.38). **19:** *The Jews,* see 1.24n. *Peace be with you,* a traditional Jewish greeting (see Tob 12.17). **20:** *Hands and . . . side,* to identify the marks of his crucifixion. The hands (forearms) had been nailed to the cross, and the side had been pierced (19.34). **22:** *He breathed on them,* cf. Gen 2.7. **23:** Cf. Mt 16.19;

are forgiven them; if you retain the sins of
any, they are retained."
24 But Thomas (who was called the
Twin[a]), one of the twelve, was not with
them when Jesus came. 25 So the other disci-
ples told him, "We have seen the Lord."
But he said to them, "Unless I see the mark
of the nails in his hands, and put my finger
in the mark of the nails and my hand in his
side, I will not believe."
26 A week later his disciples were again
in the house, and Thomas was with them.
Although the doors were shut, Jesus came
and stood among them and said, "Peace be
with you." 27 Then he said to Thomas, "Put
your finger here and see my hands. Reach
out your hand and put it in my side. Do not
doubt but believe." 28 Thomas answered
him, "My Lord and my God!" 29 Jesus said
to him, "Have you believed because you
have seen me? Blessed are those who have
not seen and yet have come to believe."
30 Now Jesus did many other signs in
the presence of his disciples, which are not
written in this book. 31 But these are writ-
ten so that you may come to believe[b] that
Jesus is the Messiah,[c] the Son of God, and
that through believing you may have life in
his name.

21 After these things Jesus showed
himself again to the disciples by the
Sea of Tiberias; and he showed himself in
this way. 2 Gathered there together were Si-
mon Peter, Thomas called the Twin,[a] Na-
thanael of Cana in Galilee, the sons of Zeb-
edee, and two others of his disciples.
3 Simon Peter said to them, "I am going
fishing." They said to him, "We will go
with you." They went out and got into the
boat, but that night they caught nothing.
4 Just after daybreak, Jesus stood on the
beach; but the disciples did not know that
it was Jesus. 5 Jesus said to them, "Chil-
dren, you have no fish, have you?" They
answered him, "No." 6 He said to them,
"Cast the net to the right side of the boat,
and you will find some." So they cast it,
and now they were not able to haul it in
because there were so many fish. 7 That dis-
ciple whom Jesus loved said to Peter, "It is
the Lord!" When Simon Peter heard that it
was the Lord, he put on some clothes, for
he was naked, and jumped into the sea.
8 But the other disciples came in the boat,
dragging the net full of fish, for they were
not far from the land, only about a hundred
yards[d] off.
9 When they had gone ashore, they saw
a charcoal fire there, with fish on it, and
bread. 10 Jesus said to them, "Bring some of
the fish that you have just caught." 11 So
Simon Peter went aboard and hauled the
net ashore, full of large fish, a hundred
fifty-three of them; and though there were
so many, the net was not torn. 12 Jesus said
to them, "Come and have breakfast." Now
none of the disciples dared to ask him,
"Who are you?" because they knew it was
the Lord. 13 Jesus came and took the bread
and gave it to them, and did the same with
the fish. 14 This was now the third time that
Jesus appeared to the disciples after he was
raised from the dead.
15 When they had finished breakfast,
Jesus said to Simon Peter, "Simon son of
John, do you love me more than these?" He
said to him, "Yes, Lord; you know that I
love you." Jesus said to him, "Feed my
lambs." 16 A second time he said to him,

a Gk *Didymus* b Other ancient authorities read *may continue to believe* c Or *the Christ* d Gk *two hundred cubits*

18.18. **30–31:** Purpose of the Gospel according to John; seems to indicate that this is the ending. *Other signs,* in addition to the miracles and post-resurrection appearances narrated in the *book.*

21.1–25: Epilogue. Most scholars consider this section a post-Johannine addendum (cf. Lk 5.1–11). A post-resurrection appearance in Galilee (*Sea of Tiberias,* see 6.1n.). **2–3:** Reflects continued camaraderie of the disciples. *Nathanael,* see 1.45–51. *Sons of Zebedee,* James and John; see Mk 1.19–20. **5:** *Children,* a colloquialism meaning "boys." **9–13:** *Bread and . . . fish* has eucharistic overtones (see 6.11). **11:** *A hundred fifty-three,* the meaning of the number is unclear. **14:** *The third time,* for the two previous appearances, see 20.19–23 and 26–29. **15–17:** *These,* the other disciples. The triple question recalls

"Simon son of John, do you love me?" He
said to him, "Yes, Lord; you know that I
love you." Jesus said to him, "Tend my
sheep." 17 He said to him the third time,
"Simon son of John, do you love me?" Pe-
ter felt hurt because he said to him the third
time, "Do you love me?" And he said to
him, "Lord, you know everything; you
know that I love you." Jesus said to him,
"Feed my sheep. 18 Very truly, I tell you,
when you were younger, you used to fasten
your own belt and to go wherever you
wished. But when you grow old, you will
stretch out your hands, and someone else
will fasten a belt around you and take you
where you do not wish to go." 19 (He said
this to indicate the kind of death by which
he would glorify God.) After this he said to
him, "Follow me."
20 Peter turned and saw the disciple
whom Jesus loved following them; he was
the one who had reclined next to Jesus at
the supper and had said, "Lord, who is it
that is going to betray you?" 21 When Peter
saw him, he said to Jesus, "Lord, what
about him?" 22 Jesus said to him, "If it is
my will that he remain until I come, what is
that to you? Follow me!" 23 So the rumor
spread in the community[a] that this disciple
would not die. Yet Jesus did not say to him
that he would not die, but, "If it is my will
that he remain until I come, what is that to
you?"[b]
24 This is the disciple who is testifying
to these things and has written them, and
we know that his testimony is true. 25 But
there are also many other things that Jesus
did; if every one of them were written
down, I suppose that the world itself could
not contain the books that would be writ-
ten.

a Gk *among the brothers* *b* Other ancient authorities lack *what is that to you*

Peter's triple denial (18.17,25–27). **18–19:** *Stretch out your hands,* see 13.36n. **20–21:** See 13.23–26. *What about him,* inquiry about the fate of *the disciple whom Jesus loved* (cf. vv. 18–19). **22:** *Until I come,* the second coming. **23:** The rumor that Jesus would return before the beloved disciple's death was erroneous. **24:** *We,* the Evangelist and all who believe. **25:** Cf. 20.30.

THE ACTS
of the Apostles

The book of Acts tells a dramatic story of the birth and expansion of the church from the time of the ascension of Jesus until the arrival of Paul in Rome. Written from the perspective of the late first century CE, Acts alone among the documents of the earliest Christian period offers a narrative sequel to the accounts of Jesus' words and deeds found in the Gospels. Its author, identified by tradition as Luke, had already produced the Gospel (1.1–2). His purpose in writing again was more than a matter of antiquarian interest, although Acts can be appropriately compared with other Hellenistic historical monographs. The account was intended to imbue Christians of his day with an unshakable confidence in their future through a didactic survey of their past. In carrying out that overarching purpose, it addresses and tries to solve potential and actual social and theological problems brought about by the church's relationship to its Jewish heritage and its Roman cultural and political environment. Luke sought to clarify both how the church was faithful to the God of the Bible and how Christianity was not incompatible with citizenship in the Roman Empire. Luke also devotes considerable attention to Paul, constructing for Christians of a post-Pauline era an image of this important figure consistent with and supportive of the stance taken on Jewish and Roman concerns in the book.

As a title, Acts of the Apostles is clearly a misnomer, since Peter is the only apostle who receives individualized portrayal. Nevertheless, it does capture one of the key concepts of the book, namely, that the apostles guarantee continuity with Jesus through their status as witnesses to everything that happened during his ministry (1.21–22); this testimony applies above all to his resurrection (10.39–41). The plot line of Acts begins with the ascension of Jesus, and the narrative first portrays the life and dynamic growth of the primitive community in Jerusalem, energized by the Spirit and led by Peter and the apostles up through the martyrdom of Stephen (chs 1–7). The persecution initiated upon Stephen's death results in mission activity outside Jerusalem highlighted by approaches to non-Jews (ch 8). After narrating the conversion of Saul/Paul (ch 9), Peter is represented as the individual through whom God establishes the inclusion of the Gentiles (10.1–11.18). Next the early missionary tour of Barnabas and Paul on behalf of Antioch is narrated (11.19–14.28), along with a story about Peter's miraculous escape from death (ch 12). The center of the book recounts the apostolic council's vindication of the efforts to free the Gentile mission from the requirements of Jewish ritual law (ch 15). Then Paul's further missionary travels are depicted (15.36–21.26) in Philippi, Thessalonica, Athens, Corinth, Ephesus, Miletus, Caesarea, and Jerusalem. Finally, the book portrays Paul's arrest, imprisonment, and trials in Jerusalem and Caesarea, and his transfer to Rome (21.27–28.31), closing with the uplifting image of Paul, while under house arrest, preaching and teaching without hindrance in the capital city of the empire.

For Luke, who was most likely a Gentile Christian, the fact that God's promises in scripture had been made to the ancient people of God required that the church stand in continuity with Israel. But the experience of unbelief among Jews and the abandonment of ritual observance in the mission to the Gentiles threatened to compromise the integrity of this history. Luke responds by depicting the earliest Christians as faithful Jews in Jerusalem until persecution pushes them out. Then, by means of multiple elaborations of the Cornelius episode (10.1–48; 11.1–18; 15.7–9) and of the story of Paul's conversion (9.1–19; 22.4–16; 26.9–18), he stresses that the entrance of Gentiles into the church is nothing less than an act of God, and so by definition in continuity with Israel's history. Nevertheless, Luke's ideal Gentile convert is one who continues to practice Jewish piety (10.2), and Gentile Christians are urged to adhere to behavior that would permit association with Jews (15.20). Luke's portrayal of Paul's constant visits to synagogues and his Jewish lifestyle serve to reinforce this maintenance of continuity with Jewish roots.

One consequence of Luke's larger narrative goals is that his understanding of Paul stands in considerable tension with biographical and theological details in Paul's own letters. This raises doubts about the traditional identification of Luke as a companion of Paul. That connection was based on speculation centered on the appearance of Luke's name in Philem 24 and some letters attributed to Paul (Col 4.14; 2 Tim 4.11) in combination with certain "clues" found in the text of Acts. Irenaeus (ca. 130–200 CE) found in the so-called "we" passages (16.10–17; 20.5–15; 21.1–18; 27.1–28.16) proof that Luke was Paul's inseparable collaborator. But it is far from clear that these curious first-person plural passages reveal any firsthand knowledge of Paul on the part of the author. Indeed, to raise only one of the numerous difficulties, Luke's denial of the status "apostle" to Paul in Acts is a bit of literary license almost unimaginable for an actual companion of "Paul the apostle" (Gal 1.1).

It is reasonable to date Acts sometime after Luke's Gospel, which may be placed around 85–95 CE. Luke's geographical location is uncertain. Ancient tradition placed him in Antioch, but his obvious attachment to Paul and the Pauline tradition could indicate his connection to one of the cities of the Pauline mission around the Aegean. Paul's image had already undergone revision by Luke's day (cf. the Pastoral epistles), and Luke did not hesitate to portray Paul as subject to the law in line with his understanding of the continuity of the history of Israel and the church. Moreover, according to Luke it is not Paul's theological argument but the conversion of Cornelius through Peter, ratified by the apostolic council, that establishes the freedom of Gentile Christians from the law. Discrepancies between the Paul of Acts and the Paul of the epistles have long been recognized. Such contradictions arise because Acts preserves an image of Paul from a period several decades after his death. Paul's role in Acts is thus dictated not only by the biographical details of his life but also by the needs of Luke's theology.

Luke offers no guidance concerning the origins of the information upon which the narrative presented in Acts is based. He appears to have relied on a mixture of traditional information uncovered by his own investigation (cf. Lk 1.3) and his imagination of how the founding events unfolded in Jerusalem. In line with the general practice of Hellenistic historians, Luke filled his narrative with speeches appropriate to significant occasions. These speeches, which amount to nearly one-third of the total text, are properly regarded as Luke's literary creations, inserted into the narrative to instruct and please the reader. They serve a subsidiary goal of demonstrating the substantial unity of the earliest Christian preaching, even as they embody Luke's own interpretation of the "events" surrounding the emergence of the church.

Apart from any value Acts has as a work of history, it is an important example of early Christian theology. Luke develops the idea of the church as a historical entity with its own distinctive period. Moreover, the earliest church, by being confined to Jerusalem, is set apart from the church of Luke's day. The ideal and unrepeatable structures of the early community are accounted for by the presence of the apostles and eyewitnesses. Luke's concern to highlight the continuity between Israel and the church is expressed by the continued observance of Jewish practices in the early period, implicitly in contrast to Luke's later situation. The gap between Luke's generation and the primitive time is bridged by the endorsement of the Gentile mission in the deliberations of the apostolic council and the promulgation of the apostolic decree (15.20,29; 21.25). The latter pronouncement may have been of practical value for Luke's community in particular, creating the conditions necessary to allow table fellowship between Jewish and Gentile Christians. Luke's portrayal of Christianity's close ties to Judaism also bolsters his appeal to Roman officials not to concern themselves with "internal theological disputes" (25.19,20). Acts portrays influential Romans expressing interest in Christianity (13.12; 19.31), or at least substantiating that it poses no threat to the state (18.15; 19.37; 23.29; 25.25; 26.32). In this way Luke demonstrates the nonsubversive nature of the church, possibly in an effort to convince Roman citizens of his own day that nothing stood in the way of their membership in the Christian community.

Key among the factors promoting continuity within the church itself throughout the narrative are the descriptions of the church's proclamation and teaching about Jesus and the constancy of the presence of the Spirit as the prime mover at the crucial junctures of early ecclesiastical history (e.g., 8.29; 10.19; 16.6–7). Yet in Acts it is God who occupies the dominant place. Jesus is described as a man whom God legitimated by mighty works, wonders, and signs (2.22). The view of Christ's death as atoning occurs only once in an expression taken over from the tradition (20.28). The focal point of salvation is the resurrection, which is marked as the crucial turning point of history. The combination of all of these forces allows Luke to portray the successful expansion of the early Christian mission throughout the Roman Empire under the direction of the Spirit according to the purpose of God.

1 In the first book, Theophilus, I wrote
about all that Jesus did and taught from
the beginning 2 until the day when he was
taken up to heaven, after giving instruc-
tions through the Holy Spirit to the apos-
tles whom he had chosen. 3 After his suffer-
ing he presented himself alive to them by
many convincing proofs, appearing to them
during forty days and speaking about the
kingdom of God. 4 While staying[a] with
them, he ordered them not to leave Jerusa-
lem, but to wait there for the promise of the
Father. "This," he said, "is what you have
heard from me; 5 for John baptized with
water, but you will be baptized with[b] the
Holy Spirit not many days from now."
6 So when they had come together, they
asked him, "Lord, is this the time when you
will restore the kingdom to Israel?" 7 He
replied, "It is not for you to know the times
or periods that the Father has set by his
own authority. 8 But you will receive power

a Or *eating* *b* Or *by*

1.1–14: Introduction and summary. The author (hereafter, "Luke") reprises information from *the first book,* the Gospel of Luke. **1:** *Theophilus,* "dear to God"; perhaps a patron sponsoring publication of the two books (note the respectful address "most excellent" in Lk 1.3), or symbolic for any ideal reader. An opening dedication and reference to previous work is a common pattern in ancient literature. **3:** Examples of the *many convincing proofs* are given in Lk 24.13–53. *Appearing to them during forty days,* note that Lk 24.50–53 seems to place the ascension on Easter; *forty,* an important symbolic number in biblical texts here signaling sacred time. *Kingdom of God* stands for the Christian proclamation (8.12; 19.8; 20.25) and indicates continuity with the teaching of Jesus. **4:** The Gk word translated *staying* means "to eat at the same table with" (see note *a*) and likely refers to Lk 24.30,31,35,41–43. *Jerusalem,* Luke locates all of the significant founding events in this holy city; the other Gospels report resurrection appearances in Galilee. **5:** *John* the Baptist, Lk 3.1–20. The *Holy Spirit* is one of the major characters of Acts. **6–11:** The ascension, cf. Lk 24.44–51. **6:** The apostles suppose that Jesus intends to *restore the kingdom to Israel* (Lk 22.28–30) and reestablish the dominion once enjoyed by David (Lk 1.32). **7:** The nationalistic tenor of the question is deflected. **8:** The theme of the apostles as *witnesses* (Lk 24.48) recurs often (1.22; 2.32; 3.15; 5.32; 10.39,41; 13.31). *Jerusalem . . . Judea . . . Samaria . . . the ends of the earth,* the plan of the book is given in geographical terms. **9:** Elsewhere in the New Testament the ascension is found only at

when the Holy Spirit has come upon you;
and you will be my witnesses in Jerusalem,
in all Judea and Samaria, and to the ends of
the earth." 9 When he had said this, as they
were watching, he was lifted up, and a
cloud took him out of their sight. 10 While
he was going and they were gazing up to-
ward heaven, suddenly two men in white
robes stood by them. 11 They said, "Men of
Galilee, why do you stand looking up to-
ward heaven? This Jesus, who has been
taken up from you into heaven, will come
in the same way as you saw him go into
heaven."

12 Then they returned to Jerusalem
from the mount called Olivet, which is near
Jerusalem, a sabbath day's journey away.
13 When they had entered the city, they
went to the room upstairs where they were
staying, Peter, and John, and James, and
Andrew, Philip and Thomas, Bartholomew
and Matthew, James son of Alphaeus, and
Simon the Zealot, and Judas son of[a]
James. 14 All these were constantly devoting
themselves to prayer, together with certain
women, including Mary the mother of
Jesus, as well as his brothers.

15 In those days Peter stood up among
the believers[b] (together the crowd num-
bered about one hundred twenty persons)
and said, 16 "Friends,[c] the scripture had to
be fulfilled, which the Holy Spirit through
David foretold concerning Judas, who be-
came a guide for those who arrested
Jesus— 17 for he was numbered among us
and was allotted his share in this ministry."
18 (Now this man acquired a field with the
reward of his wickedness; and falling head-
long,[d] he burst open in the middle and
all his bowels gushed out. 19 This became
known to all the residents of Jerusalem, so
that the field was called in their language
Hakeldama, that is, Field of Blood.) 20 "For
it is written in the book of Psalms,

'Let his homestead become desolate,
and let there be no one to live
in it';

and

'Let another take his position of
overseer.'

21 So one of the men who have accompa-
nied us during all the time that the Lord
Jesus went in and out among us, 22 begin-
ning from the baptism of John until the day
when he was taken up from us—one of
these must become a witness with us to his
resurrection." 23 So they proposed two, Jo-

a Or *the brother of* *b* Gk *brothers* *c* Gk *Men, brothers* *d* Or *swelling up*

Lk 24.51 (cf. Mk 16.19). **10:** *Two men in white robes,* angels (24.4; Jn 20.12); in Lk 9.30 the two men are Moses and Elijah. There are other parallels between Luke's Transfiguration account (Lk 9.28–36) and the ascension scene. **11:** *Will come in the same way,* note the cloud in v. 9; Lk 21.27; cf. Mk 14.62; Dan 7.13. **12:** *Olivet,* the Mount of Olives was just east of Jerusalem. *A sabbath day's journey,* about 1,000 meters (3,000 feet), the distance it was permissible for an observant Jew to walk on the sabbath (Tr. Eruvin) without breaking the command not to leave one's "place" on the sabbath (Ex 6.29). **13:** The same list as in Lk 6.14–16, but in a different order (and without Judas Iscariot). **14:** Jesus' family is incorporated into the church. *Brothers,* see Mt 13.55; Mk 6.3; James later appears as the leader of the Jerusalem church (12.17; 15.13; 21.18).

1.15–26: The restoration of the twelve. The sacred number, corresponding to the tribes of Israel, is restored. **16:** *Through David,* in the Psalms quoted in v. 20; King David was traditionally viewed as the author of the Psalms. **17:** *Us,* the apostles. **18:** Compare the gruesome death of Herod Agrippa in 12.23. According to Mt 27.5, Judas hanged himself. **19:** *Their language,* Aramaic, a dialect related to Hebrew; the information is clearly for Luke's Greek readers, not Peter's Aramaic-speaking audience. **20:** Scripture foresaw the situation (Ps 69.25) and dictates a course of action (Ps 109.8). In Acts citations from the Hebrew Bible are based on the Greek version, the Septuagint. **21:** The requirements stipulated here explain why Paul does not qualify as an apostle in Acts. **22:** *The baptism of John* marks the beginning of Jesus' ministry (10.37). To *become a witness . . . to* Jesus' *resurrection* in Acts means to become one of the twelve apostles, who function in a special sense as witnesses (v. 8; 2.32). **23:** Nothing else is known about Joseph (but see 15.22) and Matthias. **26:** *Cast lots,* allowing Jesus (the "Lord" of v. 24) to choose.

seph called Barsabbas, who was also
known as Justus, and Matthias. 24 Then
they prayed and said, "Lord, you know ev-
eryone's heart. Show us which one of these
two you have chosen 25 to take the place[a]
in this ministry and apostleship from which
Judas turned aside to go to his own place."
26 And they cast lots for them, and the lot
fell on Matthias; and he was added to the
eleven apostles.

2 When the day of Pentecost had come,
they were all together in one place.
2 And suddenly from heaven there came a
sound like the rush of a violent wind, and it
filled the entire house where they were sit-
ting. 3 Divided tongues, as of fire, appeared
among them, and a tongue rested on each
of them. 4 All of them were filled with the
Holy Spirit and began to speak in other
languages, as the Spirit gave them ability.

5 Now there were devout Jews from ev-
ery nation under heaven living in Jerusa-
lem. 6 And at this sound the crowd gathered
and was bewildered, because each one
heard them speaking in the native language
of each. 7 Amazed and astonished, they
asked, "Are not all these who are speaking
Galileans? 8 And how is it that we hear,
each of us, in our own native language?
9 Parthians, Medes, Elamites, and residents
of Mesopotamia, Judea and Cappadocia,
Pontus and Asia, 10 Phrygia and Pamphylia,
Egypt and the parts of Libya belonging to
Cyrene, and visitors from Rome, both Jews
and proselytes, 11 Cretans and Arabs—in
our own languages we hear them speaking
about God's deeds of power." 12 All were
amazed and perplexed, saying to one an-
other, "What does this mean?" 13 But oth-
ers sneered and said, "They are filled with
new wine."

14 But Peter, standing with the eleven,
raised his voice and addressed them, "Men
of Judea and all who live in Jerusalem, let
this be known to you, and listen to what I
say. 15 Indeed, these are not drunk, as you
suppose, for it is only nine o'clock in the
morning. 16 No, this is what was spoken
through the prophet Joel:

17 'In the last days it will be, God
declares,
that I will pour out my Spirit upon all
flesh,
and your sons and your daughters
shall prophesy,
and your young men shall see visions,
and your old men shall
dream dreams.

a Other ancient authorities read *the share*

Lots were widely used in the ancient world for religious and social decisions and are often mentioned in the Hebrew Bible (e.g., Lev 16.8; 1 Chr 25.8–9).

2.1–41: The day of Pentecost. The Feast of Weeks or Pentecost (Lev 23.15–21), the spring barley harvest, falls fifty days after Passover. Jewish tradition held that the law had been given on this day. **1–13:** The coming of the Holy Spirit. **2:** *Rush of a violent wind,* perhaps an allusion to Gen 1.2 ("while a mighty wind swept over the face of the waters" [alternate version]), though this and other features here are typical of theophanies—manifestations of God (Ex 19.16–19; 1 Kings 19.11; Isa 66.15). **3:** John the Baptist had predicted a baptism "with the Holy Spirit and fire" (Lk 3.16; Mt 3.11; cf. Mk 1.8; Jn 1.33). **4:** This baptism (1.5) or filling with the Spirit is clearly foundational for Acts but is not referred to elsewhere in the New Testament (but cf. Jn 20.22). **5:** *Devout Jews from every nation,* emphasizing the universal character of the Pentecost event. **6:** The *other languages* (v. 4) are foreign languages, not the "tongues" of 1 Cor 14.1–33. Perhaps the author thinks of a reversal of the confusion of languages at the tower of Babel (Gen 11.1–9). **9–11:** The list of countries and races, generally moving from east to west, suggests universal participation in the Pentecost event. **10:** *Proselytes,* full converts to Judaism. **13:** *Filled with new wine,* i.e., drunk (v. 15). **14–36:** Peter's sermon. Like other Hellenistic historians Luke provides characters with speeches appropriate to their circumstances. This does not exclude the use of traditional material but assures the presence of the author's concerns. The speeches share the pronounced biblical style in which Luke has composed the early chapters of Acts. **14:** *Peter* remains the spokesman for the apostles (1.15); individualized actions by the others are not portrayed in Acts. **16:** The event is interpreted as a fulfillment of scripture. **17:** *In the last days* is added to the beginning of the quotation of Joel 2.28–32. **22:** *A man,*

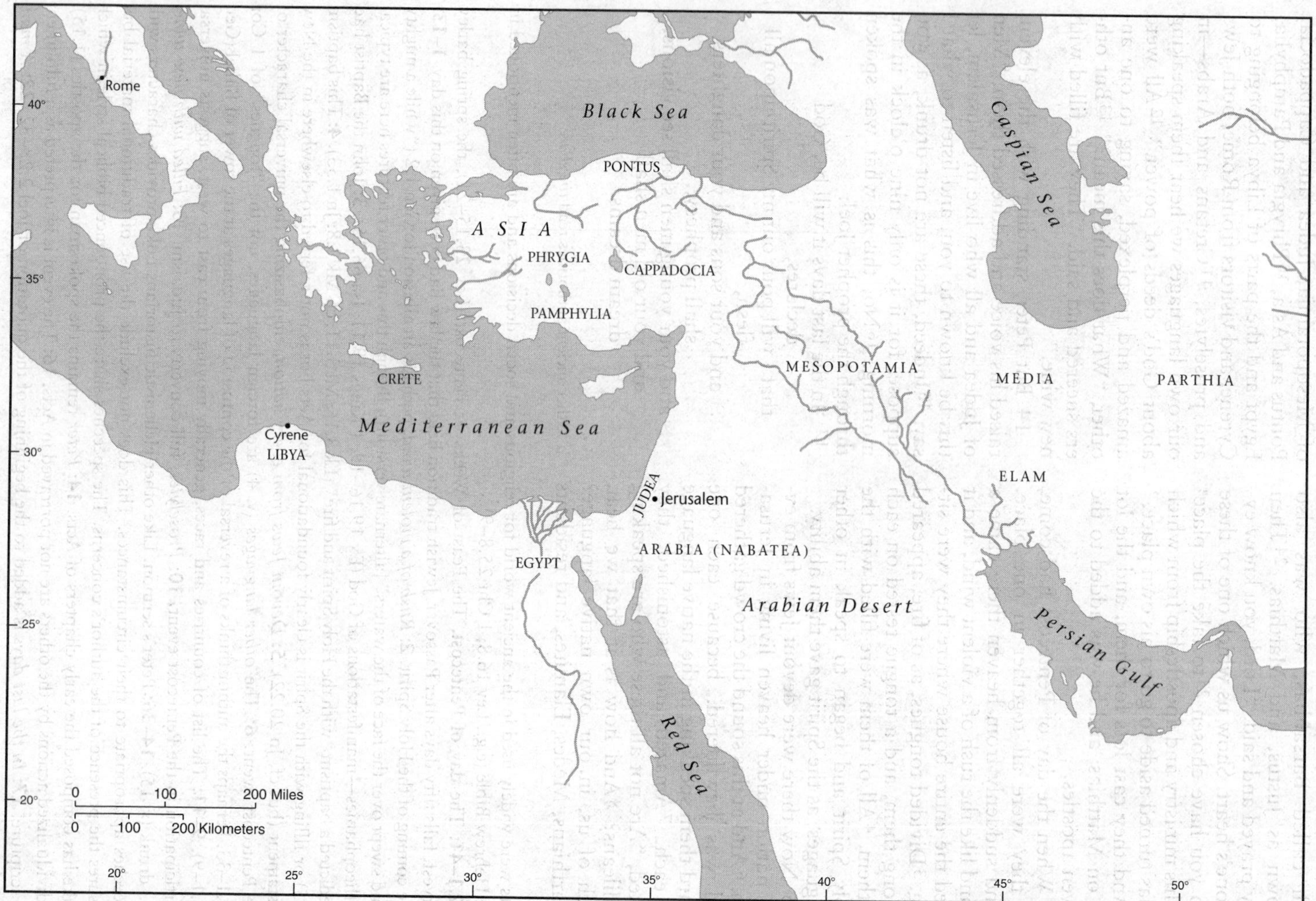

2.9–11: The native lands of Pentecost pilgrims.

18 Even upon my slaves, both men and
women,
in those days I will pour out
my Spirit;
and they shall prophesy.
19 And I will show portents in the
heaven above
and signs on the earth below,
blood, and fire, and smoky mist.
20 The sun shall be turned to darkness
and the moon to blood,
before the coming of the Lord's
great and glorious day.
21 Then everyone who calls on the name
of the Lord shall be saved.'
22 "You that are Israelites,[a] listen to
what I have to say: Jesus of Nazareth,[b] a
man attested to you by God with deeds of
power, wonders, and signs that God did
through him among you, as you yourselves
know— 23 this man, handed over to you
according to the definite plan and fore-
knowledge of God, you crucified and killed
by the hands of those outside the law.
24 But God raised him up, having freed him
from death,[c] because it was impossible for
him to be held in its power. 25 For David
says concerning him,
'I saw the Lord always before me,
for he is at my right hand so that I
will not be shaken;
26 therefore my heart was glad, and my
tongue rejoiced;
moreover my flesh will live in
hope.
27 For you will not abandon my soul to
Hades,
or let your Holy One experience
corruption.
28 You have made known to me the
ways of life;
you will make me full of gladness
with your presence.'
29 "Fellow Israelites,[d] I may say to you
confidently of our ancestor David that he
both died and was buried, and his tomb is
with us to this day. 30 Since he was a proph-
et, he knew that God had sworn with an
oath to him that he would put one of his
descendants on his throne. 31 Foreseeing
this, David[e] spoke of the resurrection of
the Messiah,[f] saying,
'He was not abandoned to Hades,
nor did his flesh experience
corruption.'
32 This Jesus God raised up, and of that all
of us are witnesses. 33 Being therefore exalt-
ed at[g] the right hand of God, and having
received from the Father the promise of the
Holy Spirit, he has poured out this that you
both see and hear. 34 For David did not as-
cend into the heavens, but he himself says,
'The Lord said to my Lord,
"Sit at my right hand,
35 until I make your enemies your
footstool." '
36 Therefore let the entire house of Israel
know with certainty that God has made
him both Lord and Messiah,[h] this Jesus
whom you crucified."
37 Now when they heard this, they were
cut to the heart and said to Peter and to the
other apostles, "Brothers,[d] what should
we do?" 38 Peter said to them, "Repent, and

a Gk *Men, Israelites* *b* Gk *the Nazorean* *c* Gk *the pains of death* *d* Gk *Men, brothers* *e* Gk *he* *f* Or *the Christ* *g* Or *by* *h* Or *Christ*

Luke does not think of the incarnation of a divine being. *Deeds of power, wonders, and signs,* biblical language (e.g., Deut 4.34; 6.22; 26.8) used often in Acts. **23:** The crucifixion of Jesus by Jews and Gentiles was part of a *plan,* see Lk 22.22; 24.26; Acts 4.27–28. **25:** Ps 16.8–11. *David,* see 1.16n. **29:** *His tomb,* see, e.g., Josephus, *Ant.* 7.392–394. **30:** 2 Sam 7.12–13; Ps 132.11. **31:** *The Messiah* is assumed to come from the line of *David* (cf. Rom 1.3). **32:** *Witnesses,* see 1.22n. **33:** *Exalted,* a reference to the ascension. *The promise,* i.e., Joel 2.28–32 in vv. 17–21. **34–35:** Ps 110.1, like Ps 16.8–11 (v. 25), here also refers not to *David* but to Jesus. It was widely used in early Christian thought about Jesus (Mk 12.36; 1 Cor 15.25; Heb 1.13). **36:** *Made him both Lord and Messiah,* apparently at the resurrection. This "adoptionist" christology appears to conflict with Luke's account of Jesus' baptism (Lk 3.21–22); see 10.38n. Such tensions in Acts may indicate the use of sources with contrasting viewpoints. **37–41:** The call to repentance. **37:** Lk 3.10. **38:** Here the gift of the *Spirit* follows baptism, but there is variety elsewhere (8.16;

be baptized every one of you in the name of
Jesus Christ so that your sins may be for-
given; and you will receive the gift of the
Holy Spirit. 39 For the promise is for you,
for your children, and for all who are far
away, everyone whom the Lord our God
calls to him." 40 And he testified with many
other arguments and exhorted them, say-
ing, "Save yourselves from this corrupt
generation." 41 So those who welcomed his
message were baptized, and that day about
three thousand persons were added.
42 They devoted themselves to the apostles'
teaching and fellowship, to the breaking of
bread and the prayers.

43 Awe came upon everyone, because
many wonders and signs were being done
by the apostles. 44 All who believed were
together and had all things in common;
45 they would sell their possessions and
goods and distribute the proceeds[a] to all,
as any had need. 46 Day by day, as they
spent much time together in the temple,
they broke bread at home[b] and ate their
food with glad and generous[c] hearts,
47 praising God and having the goodwill of
all the people. And day by day the Lord
added to their number those who were be-
ing saved.

3 One day Peter and John were going up
to the temple at the hour of prayer, at
three o'clock in the afternoon. 2 And a man
lame from birth was being carried in. Peo-
ple would lay him daily at the gate of the
temple called the Beautiful Gate so that he
could ask for alms from those entering the
temple. 3 When he saw Peter and John
about to go into the temple, he asked them
for alms. 4 Peter looked intently at him, as
did John, and said, "Look at us." 5 And he
fixed his attention on them, expecting to
receive something from them. 6 But Peter
said, "I have no silver or gold, but what I
have I give you; in the name of Jesus Christ
of Nazareth,[d] stand up and walk." 7 And
he took him by the right hand and raised
him up; and immediately his feet and an-
kles were made strong. 8 Jumping up, he
stood and began to walk, and he entered
the temple with them, walking and leaping
and praising God. 9 All the people saw him
walking and praising God, 10 and they rec-
ognized him as the one who used to sit and
ask for alms at the Beautiful Gate of the
temple; and they were filled with wonder
and amazement at what had happened to
him.

11 While he clung to Peter and John, all
the people ran together to them in the por-

a Gk *them* *b* Or *from house to house*
c Or *sincere* *d* Gk *the Nazorean*

10.44; 18.26; 19.5–6). **39:** Isa 57.19; Joel 2.32. *All who are far away,* the universal nature of the church is clear from the beginning (cf. Lk 2.32). **41:** *Three thousand persons were added,* illustrating the phenomenal success of Peter's speech.

2.42–47: Life in the first Christian community. 42: *The breaking of bread* (v. 46) describes both a common Christian meal (e.g., 20.7,11) and the Lord's Supper (27.33–38; cf. 1 Cor 11.17–34). **43–47:** Luke portrays life in the early Jerusalem community as a golden age. **43:** By performing *wonders and signs* the apostles fulfill Joel's prophecy (2.19) and imitate Jesus (2.22). **44–45:** The ideal use of possessions and money illustrates the proper response to the preaching of Jesus on this subject in the Gospel (see Lk 6.20; 12.13–21,33–34; 14.12–24,33). For community of goods in the Dead Sea scrolls, see 1QS 1.11–12; cf. Josephus, *War* 2.122 on the Essenes. **46:** Members of the growing Christian group are simultaneously devout Jews who remain close to *the temple.*

3.1–10: Peter's healing miracle in the Temple. An illustration of the apostles' "wonders and signs" (2.43). **1:** The apostles center their activity in *the temple* (see 2.46) and so imitate Jesus' practice in Jerusalem (note the distinctive portrayal in Lk 20–21). *John* appears here and elsewhere with *Peter* but with no individualized role. *Three o'clock in the afternoon,* when sacrifice was offered with prayer (Ex 29.39; Lev 6.20; Josephus, *Ant.* 14.65). **2:** *The Beautiful Gate,* perhaps the Nicanor Gate of Corinthian bronze on the east side of the Temple; see Josephus, *War* 5.201. **6:** *The name* is a key concept in Acts (v. 16; 2.21,38), as 4.7–12 will underline (see also 4.17,18,30; 10.43; 19.13).

3.11–26: Peter's explanation. In a second sermon Peter links Jesus with the patriarchs and Moses. **11:**

tico called Solomon's Portico, utterly as-
tonished. 12 When Peter saw it, he ad-
dressed the people, "You Israelites,[a] why
do you wonder at this, or why do you stare
at us, as though by our own power or piety
we had made him walk? 13 The God of
Abraham, the God of Isaac, and the God of
Jacob, the God of our ancestors has glori-
fied his servant[b] Jesus, whom you handed
over and rejected in the presence of Pilate,
though he had decided to release him.
14 But you rejected the Holy and Righteous
One and asked to have a murderer given to
you, 15 and you killed the Author of life,
whom God raised from the dead. To this
we are witnesses. 16 And by faith in his
name, his name itself has made this man
strong, whom you see and know; and the
faith that is through Jesus[c] has given him
this perfect health in the presence of all of
you.

17 "And now, friends,[d] I know that
you acted in ignorance, as did also your
rulers. 18 In this way God fulfilled what he
had foretold through all the prophets, that
his Messiah[e] would suffer. 19 Repent
therefore, and turn to God so that your sins
may be wiped out, 20 so that times of re-
freshing may come from the presence of the
Lord, and that he may send the Messiah[f]
appointed for you, that is, Jesus, 21 who
must remain in heaven until the time of uni-
versal restoration that God announced long
ago through his holy prophets. 22 Moses
said, 'The Lord your God will raise up for
you from your own people[d] a prophet like
me. You must listen to whatever he tells
you. 23 And it will be that everyone who
does not listen to that prophet will be utter-
ly rooted out of the people.' 24 And all the
prophets, as many as have spoken, from
Samuel and those after him, also predicted
these days. 25 You are the descendants of
the prophets and of the covenant that God
gave to your ancestors, saying to Abraham,
'And in your descendants all the families of
the earth shall be blessed.' 26 When God
raised up his servant,[b] he sent him first to
you, to bless you by turning each of you
from your wicked ways."

4 While Peter and John[g] were speaking
to the people, the priests, the captain
of the temple, and the Sadducees came to
them, 2 much annoyed because they were
teaching the people and proclaiming that in
Jesus there is the resurrection of the dead.
3 So they arrested them and put them in cus-
tody until the next day, for it was already
evening. 4 But many of those who heard the
word believed; and they numbered about
five thousand.

5 The next day their rulers, elders, and

a Gk *Men, Israelites* *b* Or *child* *c* Gk *him*
d Gk *brothers* *e* Or *his Christ* *f* Or *the Christ*
g Gk *While they*

Solomon's Portico, a colonnade located by Josephus (*War* 5.185; *Ant.* 20.221) on the east side of the Temple. **13:** The word *servant* recalls Isa 52.13 and the suffering servant of the Lord (4.27; 8.30–35). Roman responsibility for the death of Jesus is downplayed here as in Lk 23.4,14–16,20–25; contrast Acts 4.27. **14:** *A murderer,* Barabbas (Lk 23.18–19). **15:** *Author,* the word can mean "pioneer" or "founder" (of a new city); in 5.31 it is "leader" (cf. Heb 2.10; 12.2). The testimony of the *witnesses* is again emphasized (1.22n.). **16:** *Name,* see v. 6n. **17:** *You acted in ignorance,* an amelioration of the culpability emphasized in vv. 13–15 (see 4.10). Compare 14.16 and 17.30. **18:** The necessity that the *Messiah would suffer* was *foretold,* see Lk 24.25–27,46; Acts 17.2–3; 26.22–23. Recall the "plan" of 2.23. **19:** Lk 3.3. **22:** 7.37. Jesus is successor of Moses (Deut 18.15) as well as David. **23:** Deut 18.19; Lev 23.29. **24:** *These days,* i.e., the last days (2.17). **25:** Gen 12.3; 18.18; 22.18. **26:** *First to you,* implying the later turn to the Gentiles.

4.1–22: Arrest and release of Peter and John. The first of many incidents in which the apostles defend the faith before the authorities. **1–2:** *Captain of the temple,* the officer in charge of the Temple police. *Sadducees,* a circle composed of priestly and lay nobility who according to Luke denied the *resurrection of the dead* (23.6–8). **3:** It was not legal to hold a judicial inquiry at night. **4:** *Five thousand,* the rapid growth of the community of believers continues (see 2.41). This is a recurrent theme in Acts, typically in the face of opposition. **5–6:** Perhaps the *rulers* are priests; with the *elders and scribes* they made up the

scribes assembled in Jerusalem, 6 with An-
nas the high priest, Caiaphas, John,[a] and
Alexander, and all who were of the high-
priestly family. 7 When they had made the
prisoners[b] stand in their midst, they in-
quired, "By what power or by what name
did you do this?" 8 Then Peter, filled with
the Holy Spirit, said to them, "Rulers of the
people and elders, 9 if we are questioned to-
day because of a good deed done to some-
one who was sick and are asked how this
man has been healed, 10 let it be known to
all of you, and to all the people of Israel,
that this man is standing before you in
good health by the name of Jesus Christ of
Nazareth,[c] whom you crucified, whom
God raised from the dead. 11 This Jesus[d] is
'the stone that was rejected by you,
the builders;
it has become the cornerstone.'[e]
12 There is salvation in no one else, for there
is no other name under heaven given
among mortals by which we must be
saved."

13 Now when they saw the boldness of
Peter and John and realized that they were
uneducated and ordinary men, they were
amazed and recognized them as compan-
ions of Jesus. 14 When they saw the man
who had been cured standing beside them,
they had nothing to say in opposition. 15 So
they ordered them to leave the council
while they discussed the matter with one
another. 16 They said, "What will we do
with them? For it is obvious to all who live
in Jerusalem that a notable sign has been
done through them; we cannot deny it.
17 But to keep it from spreading further
among the people, let us warn them to
speak no more to anyone in this name."
18 So they called them and ordered them not
to speak or teach at all in the name of Jesus.
19 But Peter and John answered them,
"Whether it is right in God's sight to listen
to you rather than to God, you must judge;
20 for we cannot keep from speaking about
what we have seen and heard." 21 After
threatening them again, they let them go,
finding no way to punish them because of
the people, for all of them praised God for
what had happened. 22 For the man on
whom this sign of healing had been per-
formed was more than forty years old.

23 After they were released, they went
to their friends[f] and reported what the
chief priests and the elders had said to
them. 24 When they heard it, they raised
their voices together to God and said, "Sov-
ereign Lord, who made the heaven and the
earth, the sea, and everything in them, 25 it
is you who said by the Holy Spirit through
our ancestor David, your servant:[g]
'Why did the Gentiles rage,
and the peoples imagine vain
things?
26 The kings of the earth took their
stand,
and the rulers have gathered
together
against the Lord and against his
Messiah.'[h]
27 For in this city, in fact, both Herod and
Pontius Pilate, with the Gentiles and the
peoples of Israel, gathered together against

a Other ancient authorities read *Jonathan*
b Gk *them* *c* Gk *the Nazorean* *d* Gk *This*
e Or *keystone* *f* Gk *their own* *g* Or *child*
h Or *his Christ*

Sanhedrin, or council (v. 15), of which *the high priest* was head. *Annas* held this office from 6–14 CE; *Caiaphas* was his son-in-law (Jn 18.13) and became high priest in 18 CE (Lk 3.2); *John* may be Jonathan, the son of Annas who succeeded Caiaphas in 37 CE. **8–12:** A condensed version of the speeches in chs 2, 3, 10, and 13. The scene in v. 8 represents the fulfillment of Jesus' promise in Lk 12.12; compare the prediction of Lk 21.15. **11:** Ps 118.22 was popular in Christian arguments (Mt 21.42; Mk 12.10; Lk 20.17; 1 Pet 2.7). **12:** . *No other name* underlines the answer (v. 10) to the question posed (v. 7) about the name; see 3.6,16; 4.17–18,30. **13:** *Boldness,* this word and its cognates are used often in Acts and connote frank and courageous speech (e.g., 13.46; 18.26). *Uneducated and ordinary men,* lacking legal training. **19:** The reply here and in 5.29 is reminiscent of Socrates' famous words (Plato, *Apology* 29d).

4.23–31: Prayer of the community. 24: Ps 146.6. **25–26:** Ps 2.1–2. **27:** *Servant,* see 3.13n.; the same term is used of David in v. 25. *Herod and Pontius Pilate,* Lk 23.12; see Lk 3.1n. **28:** See 2.23n.; 3.18.

your holy servant[a] Jesus, whom you
anointed, 28 to do whatever your hand and
your plan had predestined to take place.
29 And now, Lord, look at their threats, and
grant to your servants[b] to speak your
word with all boldness, 30 while you stretch
out your hand to heal, and signs and won-
ders are performed through the name of
your holy servant[a] Jesus." 31 When they
had prayed, the place in which they were
gathered together was shaken; and they
were all filled with the Holy Spirit and
spoke the word of God with boldness.
32 Now the whole group of those who
believed were of one heart and soul, and no
one claimed private ownership of any pos-
sessions, but everything they owned was
held in common. 33 With great power the
apostles gave their testimony to the resur-
rection of the Lord Jesus, and great grace
was upon them all. 34 There was not a
needy person among them, for as many
as owned lands or houses sold them and
brought the proceeds of what was sold.
35 They laid it at the apostles' feet, and it
was distributed to each as any had need.
36 There was a Levite, a native of Cyprus,
Joseph, to whom the apostles gave the
name Barnabas (which means "son of en-
couragement"). 37 He sold a field that be-
longed to him, then brought the money,
and laid it at the apostles' feet.

5 But a man named Ananias, with the
consent of his wife Sapphira, sold a
piece of property; 2 with his wife's knowl-
edge, he kept back some of the proceeds,
and brought only a part and laid it at the
apostles' feet. 3 "Ananias," Peter asked,
"why has Satan filled your heart to lie to
the Holy Spirit and to keep back part of the
proceeds of the land? 4 While it remained
unsold, did it not remain your own? And
after it was sold, were not the proceeds at
your disposal? How is it that you have con-
trived this deed in your heart? You did not
lie to us[c] but to God!" 5 Now when Anani-
as heard these words, he fell down and
died. And great fear seized all who heard of
it. 6 The young men came and wrapped up
his body,[d] then carried him out and buried
him.
7 After an interval of about three hours
his wife came in, not knowing what had
happened. 8 Peter said to her, "Tell me
whether you and your husband sold the
land for such and such a price." And she
said, "Yes, that was the price." 9 Then Peter
said to her, "How is it that you have agreed
together to put the Spirit of the Lord to the
test? Look, the feet of those who have bur-
ied your husband are at the door, and they
will carry you out." 10 Immediately she fell
down at his feet and died. When the young
men came in they found her dead, so they
carried her out and buried her beside her
husband. 11 And great fear seized the whole
church and all who heard of these things.
12 Now many signs and wonders were
done among the people through the apos-
tles. And they were all together in Solo-
mon's Portico. 13 None of the rest dared to
join them, but the people held them in high
esteem. 14 Yet more than ever believers
were added to the Lord, great numbers of
both men and women, 15 so that they even

a Or *child* *b* Gk *slaves* *c* Gk *to men*
d Meaning of Gk uncertain

29: *Look at their threats,* a prayer to be shielded from harm. **31:** *The place . . . was shaken,* meaning that the prayer was heard (cf. 16.25–26).

4.32–5.11: The sharing of goods. 4.32–35: The ideal handling of possessions in the early Jerusalem community (see 2.43–47). **36–37:** *Barnabas,* who later appears as Paul's missionary companion in 13.1–14.28, embodies the response of the ideal believer. **5.1–11:** The negative example of *Ananias* and *Sapphira.* Compare the story of Achan in Josh 7. **3:** *Satan,* Lk 22.3. The apostles, or perhaps the church, represent *the Holy Spirit;* cf. 9.4; 15.28. **4:** The property was at Ananias's *disposal* (although this contradicts 4.32,34) until he pretended to dedicate all his goods.

5.12–16: Signs and wonders. 12: *Solomon's Portico,* see 3.11n. **13:** *None of the rest,* i.e., nonbelievers; the Christians now stand out as a clearly defined group. **16:** Compare Mk 1.32–34.

carried out the sick into the streets, and laid
them on cots and mats, in order that Peter's
shadow might fall on some of them as he
came by. 16 A great number of people
would also gather from the towns around
Jerusalem, bringing the sick and those tor-
mented by unclean spirits, and they were all
cured.

17 Then the high priest took action; he
and all who were with him (that is, the sect
of the Sadducees), being filled with jealou-
sy, 18 arrested the apostles and put them in
the public prison. 19 But during the night an
angel of the Lord opened the prison doors,
brought them out, and said, 20 "Go, stand
in the temple and tell the people the whole
message about this life." 21 When they
heard this, they entered the temple at day-
break and went on with their teaching.

When the high priest and those with him
arrived, they called together the council
and the whole body of the elders of Israel,
and sent to the prison to have them
brought. 22 But when the temple police
went there, they did not find them in the
prison; so they returned and reported,
23 "We found the prison securely locked
and the guards standing at the doors, but
when we opened them, we found no one
inside." 24 Now when the captain of the
temple and the chief priests heard these
words, they were perplexed about them,
wondering what might be going on. 25 Then
someone arrived and announced, "Look,
the men whom you put in prison are stand-
ing in the temple and teaching the people!"
26 Then the captain went with the temple
police and brought them, but without vio-
lence, for they were afraid of being stoned
by the people.

27 When they had brought them, they
had them stand before the council. The
high priest questioned them, 28 saying, "We
gave you strict orders not to teach in this
name,[a] yet here you have filled Jerusalem
with your teaching and you are determined
to bring this man's blood on us." 29 But
Peter and the apostles answered, "We must
obey God rather than any human authori-
ty.[b] 30 The God of our ancestors raised up
Jesus, whom you had killed by hanging him
on a tree. 31 God exalted him at his right
hand as Leader and Savior that he might
give repentance to Israel and forgiveness
of sins. 32 And we are witnesses to these
things, and so is the Holy Spirit whom God
has given to those who obey him."

33 When they heard this, they were en-
raged and wanted to kill them. 34 But a
Pharisee in the council named Gamaliel, a
teacher of the law, respected by all the peo-
ple, stood up and ordered the men to be put
outside for a short time. 35 Then he said to
them, "Fellow Israelites,[c] consider careful-
ly what you propose to do to these men.
36 For some time ago Theudas rose up,
claiming to be somebody, and a number of
men, about four hundred, joined him; but
he was killed, and all who followed him
were dispersed and disappeared. 37 After
him Judas the Galilean rose up at the time
of the census and got people to follow him;
he also perished, and all who followed him
were scattered. 38 So in the present case, I
tell you, keep away from these men and let
them alone; because if this plan or this un-

a Other ancient authorities read *Did we not give you strict orders not to teach in this name?* *b* Gk *than men* *c* Gk *Men, Israelites*

5.17–42: Second arrest of the apostles. The motif of obeying God rather than human beings is played out again before the council (cf. ch 4). **19:** *An angel . . . opened the prison doors,* see 12.6–11; cf. 16.25–26. **21:** *Body of the elders,* another word for *council* or Sanhedrin. **29:** See 4.19n. **30:** The reference to the *tree* (cross; 10.39; 13.29) recalls Deut 21.22–23, but it is not developed; cf. Gal 3.13. **31:** A concise summary of the theology of Acts. *Leader,* the same Gk word is translated "Author" in 3.15. *Savior,* a term widely used in the Hellenistic world (e.g., 11.19n.). **34:** *A Pharisee,* the famous Rabban *Gamaliel,* the Elder (see 15.5n.), later identified as Paul's teacher (22.3). **36–37:** The historical order of the figures referred to is reversed. *Theudas,* according to Josephus (*Ant.* 20.97–98), raised his revolt (ca. 44–46 CE) some years after Gamaliel's speech. *Judas the Galilean,* a revolutionary leader who in 6 or 7 CE

dertaking is of human origin, it will fail;
39 but if it is of God, you will not be able
to overthrow them—in that case you may
even be found fighting against God!"

They were convinced by him, 40 and
when they had called in the apostles, they
had them flogged. Then they ordered them
not to speak in the name of Jesus, and let
them go. 41 As they left the council, they
rejoiced that they were considered worthy
to suffer dishonor for the sake of the name.
42 And every day in the temple and at
home[a] they did not cease to teach and pro-
claim Jesus as the Messiah.[b]

6 Now during those days, when the disci-
ples were increasing in number, the
Hellenists complained against the Hebrews
because their widows were being neglected
in the daily distribution of food. 2 And the
twelve called together the whole communi-
ty of the disciples and said, "It is not right
that we should neglect the word of God
in order to wait on tables.[c] 3 Therefore,
friends,[d] select from among yourselves
seven men of good standing, full of the
Spirit and of wisdom, whom we may ap-
point to this task, 4 while we, for our part,
will devote ourselves to prayer and to serv-
ing the word." 5 What they said pleased the
whole community, and they chose Stephen,
a man full of faith and the Holy Spirit, to-
gether with Philip, Prochorus, Nicanor, Ti-
mon, Parmenas, and Nicolaus, a proselyte
of Antioch. 6 They had these men stand be-
fore the apostles, who prayed and laid their
hands on them.

7 The word of God continued to spread;
the number of the disciples increased great-
ly in Jerusalem, and a great many of the
priests became obedient to the faith.

8 Stephen, full of grace and power, did
great wonders and signs among the people.
9 Then some of those who belonged to the
synagogue of the Freedmen (as it was
called), Cyrenians, Alexandrians, and oth-
ers of those from Cilicia and Asia, stood up
and argued with Stephen. 10 But they could
not withstand the wisdom and the Spirit[e]
with which he spoke. 11 Then they secretly
instigated some men to say, "We have
heard him speak blasphemous words
against Moses and God." 12 They stirred up
the people as well as the elders and the
scribes; then they suddenly confronted him,
seized him, and brought him before the
council. 13 They set up false witnesses who
said, "This man never stops saying things
against this holy place and the law; 14 for
we have heard him say that this Jesus of
Nazareth[f] will destroy this place and will
change the customs that Moses handed on
to us." 15 And all who sat in the council

a Or *from house to house* *b* Or *the Christ*
c Or *keep accounts* *d* Gk *brothers* *e* Or *spirit*
f Gk *the Nazorean*

opposed the imposition of new taxes following *the census* of Quirinius (Lk 2.2). **40:** *Had them flogged,* to reinforce the warning.

6.1–7: Choice of the seven. The seven are identified as the first deacons by later tradition but hold no ecclesiastical office here. **1:** *The Hellenists,* Greek-speaking Jewish Christians; the *Hebrews,* Aramaic-speaking Jewish Christians. **2:** *The twelve* is used to designate the apostles only here in Acts. *To wait on tables,* i.e., to feed the hungry. **5:** *Stephen, Philip,* and the other names are Greek. *Proselyte,* a Gentile convert to Judaism, implying that the others were born Jews. **6:** *Laid . . . hands,* a ritual of consecration and appointment; see Num 8.10; 27.23; 1 Tim 4.14; 2 Tim 1.6 (13.3). **7:** Not all *priests* are hostile. Acts throughout reports the success (albeit partial) of the Christian movement among Jews (21.20n.; 28.24).

6.8–8.1a: Preaching and martyrdom of Stephen. Elements of Stephen's trial and death reflect the passion of Jesus. **6.8:** Stephen does *wonders and signs* like the apostles (2.43; 4.30; 5.12). **9:** Diaspora Jews *argued with Stephen. Freedmen,* former slaves, either Jews or proselytes; an inscription found in Jerusalem possibly refers to this *synagogue. Cyrenians,* from Cyrene in northern Africa (see 11.20n.). *Cilicia,* the southeastern portion of Asia Minor where Paul was from (21.39; 22.3; 23.34). *Asia,* the Roman province of that name in western Asia Minor. **10:** A fulfillment of Jesus' prediction in Lk 21.15. **13:** *False witnesses,* cf. Mk 14.55–57. **14:** *Jesus . . . will destroy this place,* Mk 14.58; Lk 21.6; Jn 2.19. The *change* in *customs* reported by Mk 7.15,19 is not recorded in Lk. These charges had not been made

looked intently at him, and they saw that
his face was like the face of an angel.

7 Then the high priest asked him, "Are
these things so?" 2 And Stephen replied:
"Brothers[a] and fathers, listen to me. The
God of glory appeared to our ancestor
Abraham when he was in Mesopotamia,
before he lived in Haran, 3 and said to him,
'Leave your country and your relatives and
go to the land that I will show you.' 4 Then
he left the country of the Chaldeans and
settled in Haran. After his father died, God
had him move from there to this country in
which you are now living. 5 He did not give
him any of it as a heritage, not even a foot's
length, but promised to give it to him as his
possession and to his descendants after
him, even though he had no child. 6 And
God spoke in these terms, that his descen-
dants would be resident aliens in a country
belonging to others, who would enslave
them and mistreat them during four hun-
dred years. 7 'But I will judge the nation
that they serve,' said God, 'and after that
they shall come out and worship me in this
place.' 8 Then he gave him the covenant of
circumcision. And so Abraham[b] became
the father of Isaac and circumcised him on
the eighth day; and Isaac became the father
of Jacob, and Jacob of the twelve patri-
archs.

9 "The patriarchs, jealous of Joseph,
sold him into Egypt; but God was with
him, 10 and rescued him from all his afflic-
tions, and enabled him to win favor and to
show wisdom when he stood before Phar-
aoh, king of Egypt, who appointed him rul-
er over Egypt and over all his household.
11 Now there came a famine throughout
Egypt and Canaan, and great suffering, and
our ancestors could find no food. 12 But
when Jacob heard that there was grain in
Egypt, he sent our ancestors there on their
first visit. 13 On the second visit Joseph
made himself known to his brothers, and
Joseph's family became known to Pharaoh.
14 Then Joseph sent and invited his father
Jacob and all his relatives to come to him,
seventy-five in all; 15 so Jacob went down
to Egypt. He himself died there as well as
our ancestors, 16 and their bodies[c] were
brought back to Shechem and laid in the
tomb that Abraham had bought for a sum
of silver from the sons of Hamor in She-
chem.

17 "But as the time drew near for the
fulfillment of the promise that God had
made to Abraham, our people in Egypt in-
creased and multiplied 18 until another king
who had not known Joseph ruled over
Egypt. 19 He dealt craftily with our race and
forced our ancestors to abandon their in-
fants so that they would die. 20 At this time
Moses was born, and he was beautiful be-
fore God. For three months he was brought
up in his father's house; 21 and when he was
abandoned, Pharaoh's daughter adopted
him and brought him up as her own son.
22 So Moses was instructed in all the wis-
dom of the Egyptians and was powerful in
his words and deeds.

23 "When he was forty years old, it
came into his heart to visit his relatives, the
Israelites.[d] 24 When he saw one of them
being wronged, he defended the oppressed
man and avenged him by striking down the
Egyptian. 25 He supposed that his kinsfolk

[a] Gk *Men, brothers* [b] Gk *he* [c] Gk *they*
[d] Gk *his brothers, the sons of Israel*

in the earlier examinations of the apostles. **7.2–50:** Stephen's speech contains some thirty citations from the Greek version of the Hebrew Bible (the Septuagint), which was the Bible of the early Christians. Accordingly, preaching often made reference to *Abraham* (v. 2), *Joseph* (v. 9), *Moses* (v. 20), and others (cf. 13.16–24; Heb 11.4–40). **3:** Gen 12.1; according to Gen 11.31 Abraham was already in Haran (against v. 2). **5:** Gen 12.7; 13.15; 17.8; 48.4. **6–7:** *Four hundred years,* see Gen 15.13–14; cf. Ex 12.40. **8:** Gen 17.10–13. **9:** Gen 37. **10–16:** Gen 39–50. **14:** *Seventy-five,* according to the Septuagint of Gen 46.27; Ex 1.5. **16:** *Shechem,* but according to Gen 50.13 Jacob was buried at Hebron. *Abraham,* but according to Gen 33.19 and Josh 24.32 it was Jacob who bought the tomb at Shechem. **17–19:** Ex 1–2. **20–22:** Ex 2.1–10. **20:** The importance of *Moses* is stressed by the amount of space devoted to him in the following verses. **23–29:** Ex 2.11–22. **29:** *Midian,* northwestern Arabia, on the east coast of the Gulf

would understand that God through him
was rescuing them, but they did not under-
stand. 26 The next day he came to some of
them as they were quarreling and tried to
reconcile them, saying, ‘Men, you are
brothers; why do you wrong each other?’
27 But the man who was wronging his
neighbor pushed Moses[a] aside, saying,
‘Who made you a ruler and a judge over
us? 28 Do you want to kill me as you killed
the Egyptian yesterday?’ 29 When he heard
this, Moses fled and became a resident alien
in the land of Midian. There he became the
father of two sons.

30 “Now when forty years had passed,
an angel appeared to him in the wilderness
of Mount Sinai, in the flame of a burning
bush. 31 When Moses saw it, he was
amazed at the sight; and as he approached
to look, there came the voice of the Lord:
32 ‘I am the God of your ancestors, the God
of Abraham, Isaac, and Jacob.’ Moses be-
gan to tremble and did not dare to look.
33 Then the Lord said to him, ‘Take off the
sandals from your feet, for the place where
you are standing is holy ground. 34 I have
surely seen the mistreatment of my people
who are in Egypt and have heard their
groaning, and I have come down to rescue
them. Come now, I will send you to Egypt.’

35 “It was this Moses whom they reject-
ed when they said, ‘Who made you a ruler
and a judge?’ and whom God now sent as
both ruler and liberator through the angel
who appeared to him in the bush. 36 He led
them out, having performed wonders and
signs in Egypt, at the Red Sea, and in the
wilderness for forty years. 37 This is the
Moses who said to the Israelites, ‘God will
raise up a prophet for you from your own
people[b] as he raised me up.’ 38 He is the
one who was in the congregation in the wil-
derness with the angel who spoke to him at
Mount Sinai, and with our ancestors; and
he received living oracles to give to us.
39 Our ancestors were unwilling to obey
him; instead, they pushed him aside, and
in their hearts they turned back to Egypt,
40 saying to Aaron, ‘Make gods for us who
will lead the way for us; as for this Moses
who led us out from the land of Egypt, we
do not know what has happened to him.’
41 At that time they made a calf, offered a
sacrifice to the idol, and reveled in the
works of their hands. 42 But God turned
away from them and handed them over to
worship the host of heaven, as it is written
in the book of the prophets:

‘Did you offer to me slain victims and
sacrifices
forty years in the wilderness,
O house of Israel?
43 No; you took along the tent
of Moloch,
and the star of your god Rephan,
the images that you made
to worship;
so I will remove you beyond
Babylon.’

44 “Our ancestors had the tent of testi-
mony in the wilderness, as God[c] directed
when he spoke to Moses, ordering him to
make it according to the pattern he had
seen. 45 Our ancestors in turn brought it in
with Joshua when they dispossessed the na-
tions that God drove out before our ances-
tors. And it was there until the time of
David, 46 who found favor with God and
asked that he might find a dwelling place
for the house of Jacob.[d] 47 But it was Solo-
mon who built a house for him. 48 Yet the

a Gk *him* *b* Gk *your brothers* *c* Gk *he*
d Other ancient authorities read *for the God of Jacob*

of Aqaba (Eilat). **30–34:** Ex 3.1–10. **30:** In Ex 3.1 the mountain is Horeb, not *Sinai.* **35:** Ex 2.14. **37:** *A prophet,* 3.22. **38:** In the Hebrew Bible God, not an *angel,* speaks to Moses and gives him the law (*living oracles*); cf. v. 53. **40:** Ex 32.1. **42–43:** Am 5.25–27 is quoted to support the charge of idolatry raised in vv. 40–42. The *book of the* (twelve minor) *prophets* (Hosea through Malachi) was thought of as a unit. **42:** *The host of heaven,* the stars (2 Kings 17.16). **43:** *Moloch,* a deity to whom children were offered as sacrifices (Jer 32.35). *Rephan,* an astral deity (Saturn). **44:** *The tent of testimony,* the tabernacle (Ex 27.21), is brought forward in the following verses as preferable to the Temple; compare the “true tent” of Heb 8.1–5. **45:** Josh 3.7–4.18. **46:** Ps 132.5; cf. 2 Sam 7.1–2. **47:** 1 Kings 6. **48:** Since *made with*

Most High does not dwell in houses made
with human hands;[a] as the prophet says,
49 'Heaven is my throne,
and the earth is my footstool.
What kind of house will you build for
me, says the Lord,
or what is the place of my rest?
50 Did not my hand make all these
things?'
51 "You stiff-necked people, uncircum-
cised in heart and ears, you are forever op-
posing the Holy Spirit, just as your ances-
tors used to do. 52 Which of the prophets
did your ancestors not persecute? They
killed those who foretold the coming of the
Righteous One, and now you have become
his betrayers and murderers. 53 You are the
ones that received the law as ordained by
angels, and yet you have not kept it."
54 When they heard these things, they
became enraged and ground their teeth at
Stephen.[b] 55 But filled with the Holy Spirit,
he gazed into heaven and saw the glory of
God and Jesus standing at the right hand of
God. 56 "Look," he said, "I see the heavens
opened and the Son of Man standing at the
right hand of God!" 57 But they covered
their ears, and with a loud shout all rushed
together against him. 58 Then they dragged
him out of the city and began to stone him;
and the witnesses laid their coats at the feet
of a young man named Saul. 59 While they
were stoning Stephen, he prayed, "Lord
Jesus, receive my spirit." 60 Then he knelt
down and cried out in a loud voice, "Lord,
do not hold this sin against them." When
8 he had said this, he died.[c] 1 And Saul
approved of their killing him.
That day a severe persecution began
against the church in Jerusalem, and all ex-
cept the apostles were scattered throughout
the countryside of Judea and Samaria. 2 De-
vout men buried Stephen and made loud
lamentation over him. 3 But Saul was ravag-
ing the church by entering house after
house; dragging off both men and women,
he committed them to prison.
4 Now those who were scattered went
from place to place, proclaiming the word.
5 Philip went down to the city[d] of Samaria
and proclaimed the Messiah[e] to them.
6 The crowds with one accord listened ea-
gerly to what was said by Philip, hearing
and seeing the signs that he did, 7 for un-
clean spirits, crying with loud shrieks, came
out of many who were possessed; and

a Gk *with hands* *b* Gk *him* *c* Gk *fell asleep*
d Other ancient authorities read *a city* *e* Or *the Christ*

human hands is language associated with idolatry in the Hebrew Bible (see Ps 115.4; Isa 2.8), its application to the Temple would be offensive to a Jewish audience. Cf. 17.24–25. **49–50:** Isa 66.1–2. **51:** *Stiff-necked people, uncircumcised in heart and ears,* see Ex 33.3,5; Lev 26.41; Jer 9.26; cf. Rom 2.29. **52:** The question is hyperbolic but recalls Lk 11.47–48. **53:** *The law,* being *ordained by angels* (cf. v. 38) is considered valid (Heb 2.2); but Paul used this Jewish tradition to argue that the law is secondary (Gal 3.19). **54–58a:** Here Stephen appears as the victim of a lynching. **55–56:** Lk 22.69. *Son of Man* in the Gospels often denotes Jesus as the glorified heavenly judge; elsewhere in the New Testament the term is found only here and in Rev 1.13; 14.14. **58b–8.1:** The presence of *witnesses,* who were legally required to cast the first stones at the offender (Deut 17.7), suggests not a lynching but a judicial execution. **58b:** *Saul,* Luke's dramatic introduction of Paul. His presence may have been suggested by 1 Cor 15.9 and Gal 1.13 but is not confirmed by these references. **59:** Lk 23.46. **60:** See Lk 23.34n.

8.1b–40: Spread of the gospel to Samaria and beyond. Christianity now first reaches non-Jewish regions. **1:** *Except the apostles,* although unrealistic, it is important for Luke that the apostles remain in *Jerusalem. Samaria,* between Galilee to the north and Judea to the south, was inhabited by remnants of the northern tribes who worshiped the Lord God and used the Pentateuch. Jews despised them (2 Kings 17.24–41; cf. Mt 10.5). **3:** *Saul was ravaging the church,* 9.1–2; cf. Gal 1.13. **4:** Ironically, severe persecution leads to *proclaiming the word* in new places. **5:** *Philip,* one of the seven mentioned in 6.5, is now active as an evangelist (21.8). All second-century references to this individual consider him to be one of the twelve apostles, but according to the idealized account of Acts the apostles remain in Jerusalem during this period. **9:** Acts displays great interest in distinguishing between *magic* and Christian signs (see

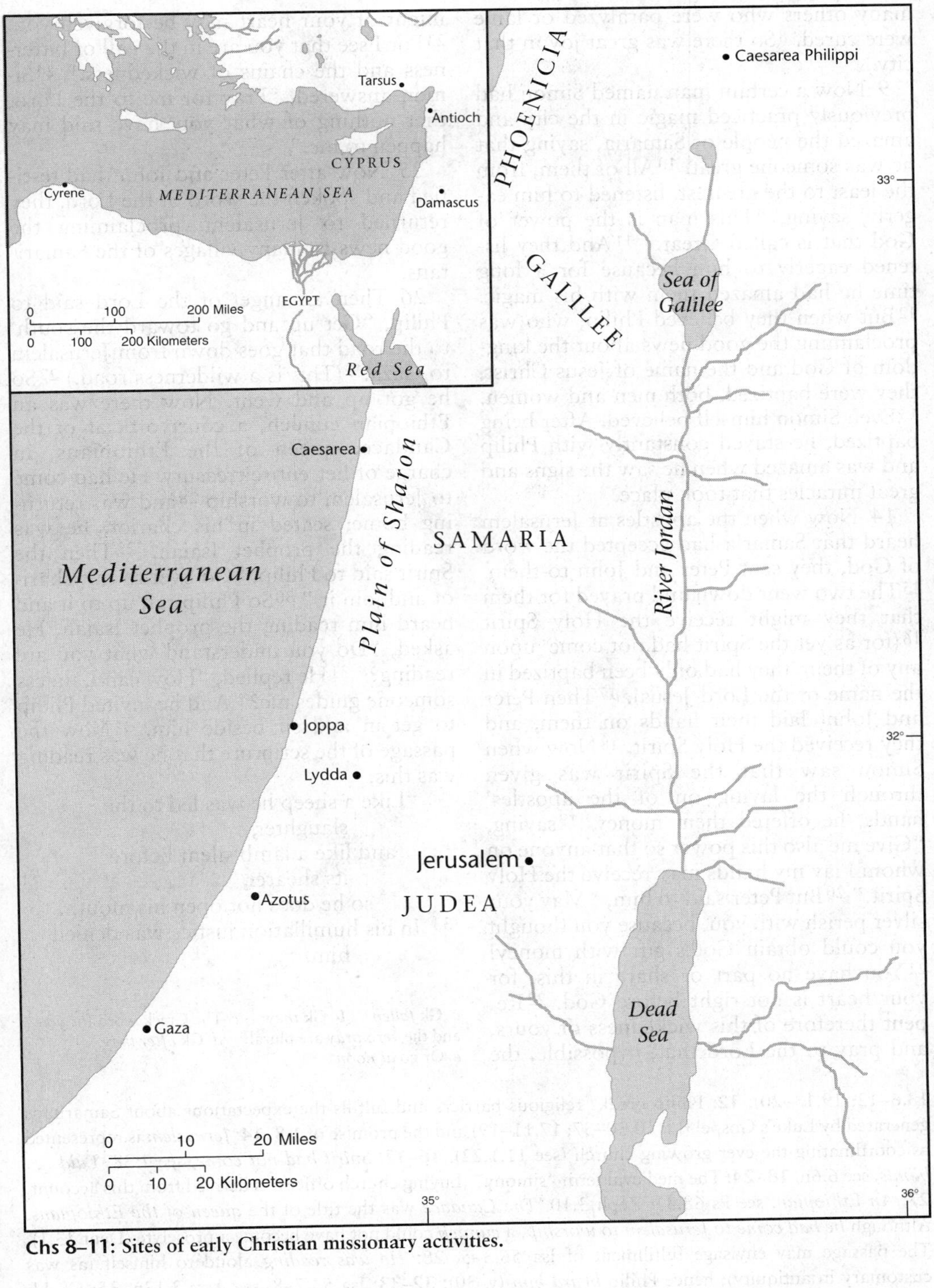

Chs 8–11: Sites of early Christian missionary activities.

many others who were paralyzed or lame
were cured. 8 So there was great joy in that
city.
9 Now a certain man named Simon had
previously practiced magic in the city and
amazed the people of Samaria, saying that
he was someone great. 10 All of them, from
the least to the greatest, listened to him ea-
gerly, saying, "This man is the power of
God that is called Great." 11 And they lis-
tened eagerly to him because for a long
time he had amazed them with his magic.
12 But when they believed Philip, who was
proclaiming the good news about the king-
dom of God and the name of Jesus Christ,
they were baptized, both men and women.
13 Even Simon himself believed. After being
baptized, he stayed constantly with Philip
and was amazed when he saw the signs and
great miracles that took place.
14 Now when the apostles at Jerusalem
heard that Samaria had accepted the word
of God, they sent Peter and John to them.
15 The two went down and prayed for them
that they might receive the Holy Spirit
16 (for as yet the Spirit had not come[a] upon
any of them; they had only been baptized in
the name of the Lord Jesus). 17 Then Peter
and John[b] laid their hands on them, and
they received the Holy Spirit. 18 Now when
Simon saw that the Spirit was given
through the laying on of the apostles'
hands, he offered them money, 19 saying,
"Give me also this power so that anyone on
whom I lay my hands may receive the Holy
Spirit." 20 But Peter said to him, "May your
silver perish with you, because you thought
you could obtain God's gift with money!
21 You have no part or share in this, for
your heart is not right before God. 22 Re-
pent therefore of this wickedness of yours,
and pray to the Lord that, if possible, the
intent of your heart may be forgiven you.
23 For I see that you are in the gall of bitter-
ness and the chains of wickedness." 24 Si-
mon answered, "Pray for me to the Lord,
that nothing of what you[c] have said may
happen to me."
25 Now after Peter and John[d] had testi-
fied and spoken the word of the Lord, they
returned to Jerusalem, proclaiming the
good news to many villages of the Samari-
tans.
26 Then an angel of the Lord said to
Philip, "Get up and go toward the south[e]
to the road that goes down from Jerusalem
to Gaza." (This is a wilderness road.) 27 So
he got up and went. Now there was an
Ethiopian eunuch, a court official of the
Candace, queen of the Ethiopians, in
charge of her entire treasury. He had come
to Jerusalem to worship 28 and was return-
ing home; seated in his chariot, he was
reading the prophet Isaiah. 29 Then the
Spirit said to Philip, "Go over to this chari-
ot and join it." 30 So Philip ran up to it and
heard him reading the prophet Isaiah. He
asked, "Do you understand what you are
reading?" 31 He replied, "How can I, unless
someone guides me?" And he invited Philip
to get in and sit beside him. 32 Now the
passage of the scripture that he was reading
was this:

"Like a sheep he was led to the
slaughter,
and like a lamb silent before
its shearer,
so he does not open his mouth.
33 In his humiliation justice was denied
him.

a Gk *fallen* *b* Gk *they* *c* The Greek word for *you* and the verb *pray* are plural *d* Gk *after they* *e* Or *go at noon*

13.6–12; 19.13–20). **12:** Philip breaks religious barriers and fulfills the expectations about Samaritans generated by Luke's Gospel (Lk 10.30–37; 17.11–19) and the promise of 1.8. **14:** *Jerusalem* is represented as coordinating the ever growing church (see 11.1,22). **16–17:** *Spirit had not come,* see 2.38. *Laid . . . hands,* see 6.6n. **18–24:** The medieval term "simony" (buying church offices) is derived from this account. **27:** *An Ethiopian,* see Ps 68.31; Zeph 3.10. *The Candace* was the title of the *queen of the Ethiopians.* Although *he had come to Jerusalem to worship,* a *eunuch* could not have become a proselyte (Deut 23.1). The passage may envisage fulfillment of Isa 56.3–5. **28:** *He was reading* aloud to himself (as was customary in antiquity); hence Philip *heard him* (v. 30). **32–33:** Isa 53.7–8; see Acts 3.13n. **35:** Cf. Lk

Who can describe his generation?
For his life is taken away from
the earth."
34 The eunuch asked Philip, "About whom,
may I ask you, does the prophet say this,
about himself or about someone else?"
35 Then Philip began to speak, and starting
with this scripture, he proclaimed to him
the good news about Jesus. 36 As they were
going along the road, they came to some
water; and the eunuch said, "Look, here is
water! What is to prevent me from being
baptized?"[a] 38 He commanded the chariot
to stop, and both of them, Philip and the
eunuch, went down into the water, and
Philip[b] baptized him. 39 When they came
up out of the water, the Spirit of the Lord
snatched Philip away; the eunuch saw him
no more, and went on his way rejoicing.
40 But Philip found himself at Azotus, and
as he was passing through the region, he
proclaimed the good news to all the towns
until he came to Caesarea.

9 Meanwhile Saul, still breathing threats
and murder against the disciples of the
Lord, went to the high priest 2 and asked
him for letters to the synagogues at Damas-
cus, so that if he found any who belonged
to the Way, men or women, he might bring
them bound to Jerusalem. 3 Now as he was
going along and approaching Damascus,
suddenly a light from heaven flashed
around him. 4 He fell to the ground and
heard a voice saying to him, "Saul, Saul,
why do you persecute me?" 5 He asked,
"Who are you, Lord?" The reply came, "I
am Jesus, whom you are persecuting. 6 But
get up and enter the city, and you will be
told what you are to do." 7 The men who
were traveling with him stood speechless
because they heard the voice but saw no
one. 8 Saul got up from the ground, and
though his eyes were open, he could see
nothing; so they led him by the hand and
brought him into Damascus. 9 For three
days he was without sight, and neither ate
nor drank.
10 Now there was a disciple in Damas-
cus named Ananias. The Lord said to him
in a vision, "Ananias." He answered,
"Here I am, Lord." 11 The Lord said to him,
"Get up and go to the street called Straight,
and at the house of Judas look for a man of
Tarsus named Saul. At this moment he is
praying, 12 and he has seen in a vision[c] a
man named Ananias come in and lay his

a Other ancient authorities add all or most of verse 37, *And Philip said, "If you believe with all your heart, you may." And he replied, "I believe that Jesus Christ is the Son of God."* *b* Gk *he* *c* Other ancient authorities lack *in a vision*

24.27. **38:** As in the case of the Samaritans, the baptism of an Ethiopian eunuch breaks social and ritual barriers (v. 12n.). Since in the ancient Mediterranean world Ethiopia was often considered to be located at the "ends of the earth" (e.g., *Odyssey* 1.22–23; Herodotus 3.25), this conversion proleptically fulfills the prediction of 1.8. **39:** *The Spirit of the Lord snatched Philip away,* cf. 1 Kings 18.12; 2 Kings 2.16. **40:** *Philip*'s evangelizing journey proceeds along the Mediterranean coast from Gaza (v. 26) through *Azotus* (ancient Ashdod, ca. 37 km [23 mi] north-northeast of Gaza) to *Caesarea* (ca. 90 km [55 mi] farther north). Caesarea was an important seaport and the headquarters of the Roman governor; see 10.1; 21.8.

9.1–19a: The conversion and call of Saul of Tarsus. Slightly different versions are found in 22.4–16; 26.9–18; Paul's own account is in Gal 1.13–17; see 1 Cor 15.8. Key narratives in Acts are stressed by repetition. **1–2:** Acts connects Paul with Jerusalem (7.58; 9.13,26), although Paul claimed he was unknown by sight in Judea (Gal 1.22–23). **2:** *The Way* stands for Christianity (18.25; 19.9,23; 22.4; 24.14,22), but its origin is uncertain. The closest parallels can be found in the Dead Sea Scrolls; cf. Isa 40.3. **3–9:** The passage incorporates various features of theophanies (e.g., 2 Macc 3; Acts 2.2n.) and stories of the call of prophets (e.g., Isa 6.1–13). **4–5:** In persecuting the disciples, he persecuted *Jesus* (cf. Mt 25.40). **10:** *Ananias,* evidently one of the leaders of the believers at *Damascus* (see 22.12). Acts does not record how or when Christians first arrived in Damascus. **11:** *The street called Straight,* commonly identified as Darb el-Mostakim, an east-to-west street in the Old City of Damascus. *Tarsus,* see

hands on him so that he might regain his
sight." 13 But Ananias answered, "Lord, I
have heard from many about this man,
how much evil he has done to your saints
in Jerusalem; 14 and here he has authority
from the chief priests to bind all who in-
voke your name." 15 But the Lord said to
him, "Go, for he is an instrument whom I
have chosen to bring my name before Gen-
tiles and kings and before the people of Is-
rael; 16 I myself will show him how much he
must suffer for the sake of my name." 17 So
Ananias went and entered the house. He
laid his hands on Saul[a] and said, "Brother
Saul, the Lord Jesus, who appeared to you
on your way here, has sent me so that you
may regain your sight and be filled with the
Holy Spirit." 18 And immediately some-
thing like scales fell from his eyes, and his
sight was restored. Then he got up and was
baptized, 19 and after taking some food, he
regained his strength.

For several days he was with the disciples
in Damascus, 20 and immediately he began
to proclaim Jesus in the synagogues, saying,
"He is the Son of God." 21 All who heard
him were amazed and said, "Is not this the
man who made havoc in Jerusalem among
those who invoked this name? And has he
not come here for the purpose of bringing
them bound before the chief priests?"
22 Saul became increasingly more powerful
and confounded the Jews who lived in Da-
mascus by proving that Jesus[b] was the
Messiah.[c]

23 After some time had passed, the Jews
plotted to kill him, 24 but their plot became
known to Saul. They were watching the
gates day and night so that they might kill
him; 25 but his disciples took him by night
and let him down through an opening in
the wall,[d] lowering him in a basket.

26 When he had come to Jerusalem, he
attempted to join the disciples; and they
were all afraid of him, for they did not be-
lieve that he was a disciple. 27 But Barnabas
took him, brought him to the apostles, and
described for them how on the road he had
seen the Lord, who had spoken to him, and
how in Damascus he had spoken boldly in
the name of Jesus. 28 So he went in and out
among them in Jerusalem, speaking boldly
in the name of the Lord. 29 He spoke and
argued with the Hellenists; but they were
attempting to kill him. 30 When the believ-
ers[e] learned of it, they brought him down
to Caesarea and sent him off to Tarsus.

31 Meanwhile the church throughout
Judea, Galilee, and Samaria had peace and
was built up. Living in the fear of the Lord
and in the comfort of the Holy Spirit, it
increased in numbers.

32 Now as Peter went here and there
among all the believers,[f] he came down
also to the saints living in Lydda. 33 There

a Gk *him* b Gk *that this* c Or *the Christ*
d Gk *through the wall* e Gk *brothers* f Gk *all of them*

v. 30n. **15:** Saul, like the prophets, was chosen for a special purpose (Jer 1.5; Gal 1.15). **17:** *Laid his hands,* see 6.6n.

9.19b–31: Saul's preaching in Damascus and first visit to Jerusalem. 20: *Immediately he began to proclaim Jesus in the synagogues,* this will be the consistent pattern followed by Paul in Acts; according to Paul himself, he went immediately to Arabia (Gal 1.17). *Son of God* occurs only here in Acts; cf. Gal 1.15–16. **24–25:** In 2 Cor 11.32–33 Paul flees the ethnarch of Aretas IV, king of the Nabateans. **26:** See vv. 1–2n. In Gal 1.18 Paul states that his first visit to Jerusalem was three years after his conversion. Luke associates Paul with Jerusalem from the beginning. **27–28:** *Barnabas* (see 4.36–37) intercedes with the *apostles* on Paul's behalf. Paul himself (Gal 1.18–19) claimed only to have seen Peter and James, the Lord's brother (not considered an apostle in Acts). **29:** Paul, from the Diaspora himself, contends with the *Hellenists,* namely, Stephen's Greek-speaking, Jewish opponents (6.9–14). **30:** *Tarsus,* Paul's home city according to 21.39 (see 11.25; cf. Gal 1.21), was in Cilicia on the southern coast of Asia Minor. **31:** The familiar note of growth. The persecution of 8.1 has apparently passed.

9.32–43: Peter in Lydda and Joppa. 32: *Lydda,* northwest of Jerusalem between Azotus and Caesarea (see 8.40n.), about 17 km (11 mi) southeast of Joppa (v. 36). There are already *believers* in both places,

he found a man named Aeneas, who had
been bedridden for eight years, for he was
paralyzed. 34 Peter said to him, "Aeneas,
Jesus Christ heals you; get up and make
your bed!" And immediately he got up.
35 And all the residents of Lydda and Shar-
on saw him and turned to the Lord.
36 Now in Joppa there was a disciple
whose name was Tabitha, which in Greek
is Dorcas.[a] She was devoted to good
works and acts of charity. 37 At that time
she became ill and died. When they had
washed her, they laid her in a room up-
stairs. 38 Since Lydda was near Joppa, the
disciples, who heard that Peter was there,
sent two men to him with the request,
"Please come to us without delay." 39 So
Peter got up and went with them; and when
he arrived, they took him to the room up-
stairs. All the widows stood beside him,
weeping and showing tunics and other
clothing that Dorcas had made while she
was with them. 40 Peter put all of them out-
side, and then he knelt down and prayed.
He turned to the body and said, "Tabitha,
get up." Then she opened her eyes, and see-
ing Peter, she sat up. 41 He gave her his
hand and helped her up. Then calling the
saints and widows, he showed her to be
alive. 42 This became known throughout
Joppa, and many believed in the Lord.
43 Meanwhile he stayed in Joppa for some
time with a certain Simon, a tanner.

10 In Caesarea there was a man named
Cornelius, a centurion of the Italian
Cohort, as it was called. 2 He was a devout
man who feared God with all his house-
hold; he gave alms generously to the people
and prayed constantly to God. 3 One after-
noon at about three o'clock he had a vision
in which he clearly saw an angel of God
coming in and saying to him, "Cornelius."
4 He stared at him in terror and said, "What
is it, Lord?" He answered, "Your prayers
and your alms have ascended as a memorial
before God. 5 Now send men to Joppa for a
certain Simon who is called Peter; 6 he is
lodging with Simon, a tanner, whose house
is by the seaside." 7 When the angel who
spoke to him had left, he called two of his
slaves and a devout soldier from the ranks
of those who served him, 8 and after telling
them everything, he sent them to Joppa.
9 About noon the next day, as they were
on their journey and approaching the city,
Peter went up on the roof to pray. 10 He
became hungry and wanted something to
eat; and while it was being prepared, he fell
into a trance. 11 He saw the heaven opened
and something like a large sheet coming
down, being lowered to the ground by its
four corners. 12 In it were all kinds of four-
footed creatures and reptiles and birds of

a The name Tabitha in Aramaic and the name Dorcas in Greek mean *a gazelle*

perhaps the result of Philip's activity (8.40). **34:** Lk 5.24–25. **35:** *Sharon,* the coastal plain between Joppa and Caesarea. **36–42:** Cf. Lk 8.41–42,49–56 (Mk 5.22–24,35–43); 2 Kings 4.33. **36:** *Joppa,* modern Jaffa, on the coast in the Plain of Sharon, ca. 50 km (30 mi) south of Caesarea. **39:** *Widows,* see 6.1; 1 Tim 5.3–16. **43:** Peter's lodging with *a tanner,* who would be ritually unclean, may suggest preparation for his encounter with Cornelius.

10.1–48: The conversion of Cornelius. This key narrative in which the inclusion of Gentiles is directed by God is essentially repeated in 11.1–18 and referred to in significant terms at 15.7–9. Luke ascribes to Peter the honor of converting the first Gentile; but recall the Ethiopian (8.26–39) and see 11.19–21. **1:** *Caesarea,* see 8.40n. *A centurion,* an officer in the Roman army. Luke may want to show that Roman citizenship was compatible with Christianity (13.7n.; 16.37–38n.; 18.14–15n.; 22.25–29n.; 23.27–30n.; 25.8n.). On "friendly" centurions, see 27.3,43. **2:** Cornelius was *devout* and *feared God,* i.e., worshiped him (see v. 22); although he had not adopted the Jewish religion (i.e., undergone circumcision), he practiced the characteristic acts of Jewish piety: almsgiving and prayer. The similar profile of the centurion in Lk 7.1–10 shows that Luke is particularly interested in Gentiles who practice Jewish piety (v. 35). **3:** *About three o'clock,* the time of afternoon prayer (3.1). Angels often appear in Acts in service of the divine will. **7:** *A devout soldier,* suggests that those with Cornelius shared his piety (see 16.15n.,33). **9:** *Noon,* the usual Roman time for luncheon. **14:** *Profane,* only some animals might be eaten (Lev 11). **15:** In

the air. [13]Then he heard a voice saying,
"Get up, Peter; kill and eat." [14]But Peter
said, "By no means, Lord; for I have never
eaten anything that is profane or unclean."
[15]The voice said to him again, a second
time, "What God has made clean, you must
not call profane." [16]This happened three
times, and the thing was suddenly taken up
to heaven.

17 Now while Peter was greatly puzzled
about what to make of the vision that he
had seen, suddenly the men sent by Cornel-
ius appeared. They were asking for Simon's
house and were standing by the gate.
[18]They called out to ask whether Simon,
who was called Peter, was staying there.
[19]While Peter was still thinking about the
vision, the Spirit said to him, "Look,
three[a] men are searching for you. [20]Now
get up, go down, and go with them without
hesitation; for I have sent them." [21]So Peter
went down to the men and said, "I am the
one you are looking for; what is the reason
for your coming?" [22]They answered, "Cor-
nelius, a centurion, an upright and God-
fearing man, who is well spoken of by the
whole Jewish nation, was directed by a
holy angel to send for you to come to his
house and to hear what you have to say."
[23]So Peter[b] invited them in and gave them
lodging.

The next day he got up and went with
them, and some of the believers[c] from Jop-
pa accompanied him. [24]The following day
they came to Caesarea. Cornelius was ex-
pecting them and had called together his
relatives and close friends. [25]On Peter's ar-
rival Cornelius met him, and falling at his
feet, worshiped him. [26]But Peter made him
get up, saying, "Stand up; I am only a mor-
tal." [27]And as he talked with him, he went
in and found that many had assembled;
[28]and he said to them, "You yourselves
know that it is unlawful for a Jew to associ-
ate with or to visit a Gentile; but God has
shown me that I should not call anyone
profane or unclean. [29]So when I was sent
for, I came without objection. Now may I
ask why you sent for me?"

30 Cornelius replied, "Four days ago at
this very hour, at three o'clock, I was pray-
ing in my house when suddenly a man in
dazzling clothes stood before me. [31]He
said, 'Cornelius, your prayer has been
heard and your alms have been remem-
bered before God. [32]Send therefore to Jop-
pa and ask for Simon, who is called Peter;
he is staying in the home of Simon, a tan-
ner, by the sea.' [33]Therefore I sent for you
immediately, and you have been kind
enough to come. So now all of us are here
in the presence of God to listen to all that
the Lord has commanded you to say."

34 Then Peter began to speak to them:
"I truly understand that God shows no par-
tiality, [35]but in every nation anyone who
fears him and does what is right is accept-
able to him. [36]You know the message he
sent to the people of Israel, preaching peace
by Jesus Christ—he is Lord of all. [37]That
message spread throughout Judea, begin-
ning in Galilee after the baptism that John
announced: [38]how God anointed Jesus of
Nazareth with the Holy Spirit and with
power; how he went about doing good and
healing all who were oppressed by the

a One ancient authority reads *two*; others lack the word *b* Gk *he* *c* Gk *brothers*

Mk 7.14–19 Jesus declared all foods clean, but this statement is not included in Luke's Gospel and Peter seems unaware of it. Some conditions regarding food will still apply at 15.20,29. **16:** *Three times,* for emphasis and warning. **19–20:** The *Spirit*'s message obliquely refers to Cornelius's vision and is reminiscent of the coordinated visions of Ananias and Paul in ch 9. **23:** *Invited them in,* Peter is prepared to associate with Gentiles. **28:** *You yourselves know,* the audience is aware that association with Gentiles can be a cause of defilement for Jews (the centurion in Lk 7.6–7 seems to be sensitive to this). *But God has shown me,* Peter now understands the vision about food (vv. 11–17) to refer allegorically to people—i.e., defilement is no longer an issue. **30:** See v. 3n. **34:** *No partiality,* lit. "God is no respecter of persons"; cf. Rom 2.10–11. **36–43:** A synopsis of Luke's Gospel. **36:** *Lord of all,* both Jews and Gentiles. **38:** *God anointed Jesus,* seems to refer to the baptism at Lk 3.22 (see also Lk 4.14); but note Lk 2.11; Acts 2.36n.; 3.20.

devil, for God was with him. 39 We are wit-
nesses to all that he did both in Judea and
in Jerusalem. They put him to death by
hanging him on a tree; 40 but God raised
him on the third day and allowed him to
appear, 41 not to all the people but to us
who were chosen by God as witnesses, and
who ate and drank with him after he rose
from the dead. 42 He commanded us to
preach to the people and to testify that he is
the one ordained by God as judge of the
living and the dead. 43 All the prophets tes-
tify about him that everyone who believes
in him receives forgiveness of sins through
his name."

44 While Peter was still speaking, the
Holy Spirit fell upon all who heard the
word. 45 The circumcised believers who had
come with Peter were astounded that the
gift of the Holy Spirit had been poured out
even on the Gentiles, 46 for they heard them
speaking in tongues and extolling God.
Then Peter said, 47 "Can anyone withhold
the water for baptizing these people who
have received the Holy Spirit just as we
have?" 48 So he ordered them to be baptized
in the name of Jesus Christ. Then they in-
vited him to stay for several days.

11 Now the apostles and the believ-
ers[a] who were in Judea heard that
the Gentiles had also accepted the word of
God. 2 So when Peter went up to Jerusalem,
the circumcised believers[b] criticized him,
3 saying, "Why did you go to uncircumcised
men and eat with them?" 4 Then Peter be-
gan to explain it to them, step by step, say-
ing, 5 "I was in the city of Joppa praying,
and in a trance I saw a vision. There was
something like a large sheet coming down
from heaven, being lowered by its four cor-
ners; and it came close to me. 6 As I looked
at it closely I saw four-footed animals,
beasts of prey, reptiles, and birds of the air.
7 I also heard a voice saying to me, 'Get up,
Peter; kill and eat.' 8 But I replied, 'By no
means, Lord; for nothing profane or un-
clean has ever entered my mouth.' 9 But a
second time the voice answered from heav-
en, 'What God has made clean, you must
not call profane.' 10 This happened three
times; then everything was pulled up again
to heaven. 11 At that very moment three
men, sent to me from Caesarea, arrived at
the house where we were. 12 The Spirit told
me to go with them and not to make a
distinction between them and us.[c] These
six brothers also accompanied me, and we
entered the man's house. 13 He told us how
he had seen the angel standing in his house
and saying, 'Send to Joppa and bring Si-
mon, who is called Peter; 14 he will give you
a message by which you and your entire
household will be saved.' 15 And as I began
to speak, the Holy Spirit fell upon them just
as it had upon us at the beginning. 16 And I
remembered the word of the Lord, how he
had said, 'John baptized with water, but
you will be baptized with the Holy Spirit.'
17 If then God gave them the same gift that

a Gk *brothers* *b* Gk lacks *believers* *c* Or *not to hesitate*

39: *We are witnesses,* also v. 41, see 1.8n.; 1.21–22; *tree,* 5.30n. **41:** Jesus was seen only by those *chosen* (Lk 24.48; Acts 1.8,22). *Ate and drank with him,* Lk 24.30–31,41–43. **42:** *Judge,* 17.31. **43:** *All the prophets,* Lk 24.25–27,44–47; *forgiveness of sins,* Lk 24.47; Acts 2.38; 13.26,39; *through his name,* 3.6. **44–48:** The *circumcised believers* knew by the *speaking in tongues* (2.4–11) that *the Holy Spirit* fell upon *the Gentiles* before baptism (see 2.38n.).

11.1–18: Peter's defense. The Jerusalem church requires an explanation for the baptism of Gentiles. **1:** News of the new development reaches Jerusalem, cf. 8.14; 11.22. **2:** Up to this point all believers were *circumcised* (see note *b;* at 10.45 the text says "circumcised believers," but the meaning is the same, as v. 18 makes clear). **3:** The question is framed in terms of association with Gentiles, not their entry into the church; cf. Gal 2.12. **4–17:** *Peter* answers by retelling 10.1–48 in abbreviated fashion. **12:** *Not to make a distinction,* clarifies "go . . . without hesitation" in 10.20. *Six,* replaces "some" in 10.23. **14:** Unlike 10.33, here it is made clear that Cornelius is expecting a *message* of salvation (4.12). **16:** See 1.5n. **17–18:** The "Gentile Pentecost" (v. 15; 10.47; 15.8) was an act of *God.* Although the issue of Gentile inclusion seems to be decisively settled, controversy will resurface in ch 15.

he gave us when we believed in the Lord
Jesus Christ, who was I that I could hinder
God?" 18 When they heard this, they were
silenced. And they praised God, saying,
"Then God has given even to the Gentiles
the repentance that leads to life."

19 Now those who were scattered be-
cause of the persecution that took place
over Stephen traveled as far as Phoenicia,
Cyprus, and Antioch, and they spoke the
word to no one except Jews. 20 But among
them were some men of Cyprus and Cyrene
who, on coming to Antioch, spoke to the
Hellenists[a] also, proclaiming the Lord
Jesus. 21 The hand of the Lord was with
them, and a great number became believers
and turned to the Lord. 22 News of this
came to the ears of the church in Jerusalem,
and they sent Barnabas to Antioch.
23 When he came and saw the grace of God,
he rejoiced, and he exhorted them all to
remain faithful to the Lord with steadfast
devotion; 24 for he was a good man, full of
the Holy Spirit and of faith. And a great
many people were brought to the Lord.
25 Then Barnabas went to Tarsus to look
for Saul, 26 and when he had found him, he
brought him to Antioch. So it was that for
an entire year they met with[b] the church
and taught a great many people, and it was
in Antioch that the disciples were first
called "Christians."

27 At that time prophets came down
from Jerusalem to Antioch. 28 One of them
named Agabus stood up and predicted by
the Spirit that there would be a severe fam-
ine over all the world; and this took place
during the reign of Claudius. 29 The disci-
ples determined that according to their
ability, each would send relief to the believ-
ers[c] living in Judea; 30 this they did, send-
ing it to the elders by Barnabas and Saul.

12 About that time King Herod laid
violent hands upon some who be-
longed to the church. 2 He had James, the
brother of John, killed with the sword. 3 Af-

a Other ancient authorities read *Greeks* *b* Or *were guests of* *c* Gk *brothers*

11.19–26: Mission to the Greeks in Antioch. The narrative now rejoins the mission initiated by the *persecution* following Stephen's death (8.1,4). **19:** *Antioch* on the Orontes River, capital of the Roman province of Syria, which included Galilee and Judea, and according to Josephus (*War* 3.29), the third largest city (after Rome and Alexandria) in the Roman Empire. Antioch was a popular city name in Syria and Asia Minor, reflecting the rule of Antiochus I (whose cult-name was "savior"), son of Seleucus I, one of the successors of Alexander the Great. **20:** *Cyrene,* a great North African city (2.10; 6.9; 13.1; Lk 23.26), had a large Jewish colony. *Hellenists* (unlike 6.1 and 9.29) here apparently refers to non-Jewish, Greek-speaking residents of *Antioch*. **22–24:** *Barnabas* came from Cyprus (4.36), and there were Cypriots in Antioch (v. 20). He investigates and expresses approval over the latest developments on behalf of *Jerusalem* (cf. 8.14–17; 11.1–18). Compare his description (v. 24) with that of Stephen (6.5). **25–26:** *Saul* was in *Tarsus* (9.30), cf. Gal 1.21. An extended collaboration with Barnabas is initiated (see Gal 2.1,9,13; 1 Cor 9.6). *Christians,* a Latin word meaning "partisans of Christ," perhaps at first a term of reproach. It occurs elsewhere in the New Testament only at 26.28 and 1 Pet 4.16.

11.27–30: Antioch aids Jerusalem. 27: *Prophets* (13.1; 15.32) were numerous in the early church and in Acts characterize the last days (2.17–18). Here they predict the future (see 21.10). According to 1 Cor 14.3–4,31 they teach and build up the church. **28:** *Agabus,* 21.10–11. The *famine . . . during the reign of Claudius* (41–54 CE) probably occurred in 47 CE; it was not worldwide (see Josephus, *Ant.* 20.51–53,101). **29:** The *relief* operation resembles the arrangements for Paul's collection (20.4n.; 1 Cor 16.2; 2 Cor 9.7); the days of selling all (2.44–45; 4.32–35) are gone. **30:** *Elders,* as leaders are first mentioned here ("old men" in 2.17 translates the same Gk word); their emergence may reflect synagogue practice. According to Gal 2.1–10, Paul's second visit to Jerusalem coincided with the discussion portrayed in Acts 15.1–29.

12.1–19: Persecution touches the apostles. 1: *Herod* Agrippa I, grandson of Herod the Great, nephew of Herod Antipas (4.27; 13.1; the Herod of Luke's Gospel), was made king of Judea by Claudius in 41 CE. **2:** An apostle, *James* the son of Zebedee, is martyred. No replacement is made (cf. 1.15–26). **3:** *Peter,* like

ter he saw that it pleased the Jews, he pro-
ceeded to arrest Peter also. (This was dur-
ing the festival of Unleavened Bread.)
4 When he had seized him, he put him in
prison and handed him over to four squads
of soldiers to guard him, intending to bring
him out to the people after the Passover.
5 While Peter was kept in prison, the church
prayed fervently to God for him.
6 The very night before Herod was go-
ing to bring him out, Peter, bound with two
chains, was sleeping between two soldiers,
while guards in front of the door were
keeping watch over the prison. 7 Suddenly
an angel of the Lord appeared and a light
shone in the cell. He tapped Peter on the
side and woke him, saying, "Get up quick-
ly." And the chains fell off his wrists. 8 The
angel said to him, "Fasten your belt and
put on your sandals." He did so. Then he
said to him, "Wrap your cloak around you
and follow me." 9 Peter[a] went out and fol-
lowed him; he did not realize that what was
happening with the angel's help was real;
he thought he was seeing a vision. 10 After
they had passed the first and the second
guard, they came before the iron gate lead-
ing into the city. It opened for them of its
own accord, and they went outside and
walked along a lane, when suddenly the an-
gel left him. 11 Then Peter came to himself
and said, "Now I am sure that the Lord has
sent his angel and rescued me from the
hands of Herod and from all that the Jew-
ish people were expecting."
12 As soon as he realized this, he went
to the house of Mary, the mother of John
whose other name was Mark, where many
had gathered and were praying. 13 When he
knocked at the outer gate, a maid named
Rhoda came to answer. 14 On recognizing
Peter's voice, she was so overjoyed that, in-
stead of opening the gate, she ran in and
announced that Peter was standing at the
gate. 15 They said to her, "You are out of
your mind!" But she insisted that it was so.
They said, "It is his angel." 16 Meanwhile
Peter continued knocking; and when they
opened the gate, they saw him and were
amazed. 17 He motioned to them with his
hand to be silent, and described for them
how the Lord had brought him out of the
prison. And he added, "Tell this to James
and to the believers."[b] Then he left and
went to another place.
18 When morning came, there was no
small commotion among the soldiers over
what had become of Peter. 19 When Herod
had searched for him and could not find
him, he examined the guards and ordered
them to be put to death. Then he went
down from Judea to Caesarea and stayed
there.
20 Now Herod[c] was angry with the
people of Tyre and Sidon. So they came to
him in a body; and after winning over Blas-
tus, the king's chamberlain, they asked for
a reconciliation, because their country de-
pended on the king's country for food.
21 On an appointed day Herod put on his
royal robes, took his seat on the platform,
and delivered a public address to them.

a Gk *He* *b* Gk *brothers* *c* Gk *he*

Jesus, is arrested at Passover season (v. 4), *the festival of Unleavened Bread* (v. 3). **4:** *Four squads of soldiers,* emphasizes the impossibility of escape (similarly v. 6). **6–11:** Cf. 5.17–23; 16.23–28. Miraculous escapes were a staple of ancient literature. **6:** *Bring him out,* for execution. **12:** *John . . . Mark* is connected with Peter elsewhere (1 Pet 5.13), and tradition credited him with authoring the second Gospel as Peter's interpreter (Eusebius, *Hist. eccl.* 3.39.15; 5.8.3). In 12.25–13.13 he travels with Paul and Barnabas. According to Col 4.10 he is Barnabas's cousin (see also Philem 24; 2 Tim 4.11). **13:** *Outer gate,* a significant house is suggested. **15:** A person's guardian *angel* (Mt 18.10) was thought to resemble the person protected. **17:** *James,* the brother of Jesus next in age (1.14n.), soon emerges as the leader of the Jerusalem church (15.13; see Gal 1.19; 2.12). Peter goes to *another place,* appearing one last time at the Jerusalem council (15.7–11).

12.20–23: Death of Herod Agrippa. Josephus (*Ant.* 19.343–353) gives a somewhat parallel account in which Herod is stricken by a fatal disease after flatterers addressed him as a god and dies after five days

22 The people kept shouting, "The voice of
a god, and not of a mortal!" 23 And imme-
diately, because he had not given the glory
to God, an angel of the Lord struck him
down, and he was eaten by worms and
died.
24 But the word of God continued to
advance and gain adherents. 25 Then after
completing their mission Barnabas and
Saul returned to[a] Jerusalem and brought
with them John, whose other name was
Mark.

13 Now in the church at Antioch there
were prophets and teachers: Barna-
bas, Simeon who was called Niger, Lucius
of Cyrene, Manaen a member of the court
of Herod the ruler,[b] and Saul. 2 While they
were worshiping the Lord and fasting, the
Holy Spirit said, "Set apart for me Barna-
bas and Saul for the work to which I have
called them." 3 Then after fasting and pray-
ing they laid their hands on them and sent
them off.
4 So, being sent out by the Holy Spirit,
they went down to Seleucia; and from there
they sailed to Cyprus. 5 When they arrived
at Salamis, they proclaimed the word of
God in the synagogues of the Jews. And
they had John also to assist them. 6 When
they had gone through the whole island as
far as Paphos, they met a certain magician,
a Jewish false prophet, named Bar-Jesus.
7 He was with the proconsul, Sergius Pau-
lus, an intelligent man, who summoned
Barnabas and Saul and wanted to hear the
word of God. 8 But the magician Elymas
(for that is the translation of his name) op-
posed them and tried to turn the proconsul
away from the faith. 9 But Saul, also known
as Paul, filled with the Holy Spirit, looked
intently at him 10 and said, "You son of the
devil, you enemy of all righteousness, full
of all deceit and villainy, will you not stop
making crooked the straight paths of the
Lord? 11 And now listen—the hand of the
Lord is against you, and you will be blind
for a while, unable to see the sun." Immedi-
ately mist and darkness came over him, and
he went about groping for someone to lead
him by the hand. 12 When the proconsul
saw what had happened, he believed, for he
was astonished at the teaching about the
Lord.

a Other ancient authorities read *from* *b* Gk *tetrarch*

of pain—but he acknowledges the false acclamation and accepts his fate. **23:** Herod's death in 44 CE occurred before the probable date of the famine mentioned at 11.28—Acts does not necessarily present all events in correct chronological sequence. *Died,* the Gk word here is used elsewhere in the New Testament only to describe the deaths of Ananias and Sapphira (5.5,10).

12.24–13.3: Commission at Antioch. 24: The attack on the church's leaders fails to stem growth. **25:** *Barnabas and Saul returned* from *Jerusalem* to Antioch (see note *a*) after the relief visit (11.29–30). **13.1:** *Prophets and teachers* were important leaders in the early church (see 11.27n.; 1 Cor 12.28; Eph 4.11). *Manaen,* Gk form of Heb Menahem. *Herod the ruler,* Herod Antipas (4.27; Lk 3.19; 8.3; 9.7,9; 13.31; 23.7–15), not Herod the king (12.1n.). **2:** As is usual in Acts *the Holy Spirit* initiates new developments. *Set apart,* cf. Rom 1.1; Gal 1.15. **3:** *Laid . . . hands,* see 6.6n.

13.4–12: Cyprus. 4: *Seleucia* Pieria, Antioch's seaport, about 20 km (12 mi) west at the mouth of the Orontes River. **5:** *Salamis,* important port and former capital city at the eastern end of Cyprus. *Synagogues,* there was a large Jewish population on Cyprus. According to Acts, Paul regularly begins mission work in a new place in the local synagogue (13.14; 14.1; 17.1,10,17; 18.4,19; 19.8; see 9.20n.; cf. Rom 1.16). *John,* see 12.12n. According to 11.19, missionaries had previously reached the island. **6:** *Paphos,* capital of Cyprus, located in the extreme west. *Magician,* see 8.9n. *Bar-Jesus,* "son of Jesus [or Joshua]." **7:** The island was a senatorial province ruled by a *proconsul. Sergius Paulus,* another Roman official favorable to Christianity (see 10.1n.). **8:** *Elymas* does not mean "Bar-Jesus." **9:** *Saul* was his Jewish name, used up to this point to stress his origin; *Paul* was his Roman name, the one he was generally known by, and is used from now on in Acts as missionary activity aims at both Jews and Gentiles. **10–11:** Compare Peter's rebuke of Simon (8.20–24).

13 Then Paul and his companions set sail from Paphos and came to Perga in Pamphylia. John, however, left them and returned to Jerusalem; [14]but they went on from Perga and came to Antioch in Pisidia. And on the sabbath day they went into the synagogue and sat down. [15]After the reading of the law and the prophets, the officials of the synagogue sent them a message, saying, "Brothers, if you have any word of exhortation for the people, give it." [16]So Paul stood up and with a gesture began to speak:

"You Israelites,[a] and others who fear

a Gk *Men, Israelites*

13.13–52: Journey to Antioch of Pisidia and Iconium. The focus now clearly shifts to Paul as his first work in inner Asia Minor is depicted. **13:** *Perga* is inland 13 km (8 mi) from Attalia (14.25), main seaport of *Pamphylia,* a small province south of the Taurus mountains, between Cilicia and Lycia. *John . . . left,* v. 5; see 15.38. **14:** Strictly, *Antioch* near *Pisidia,* a Roman city and colony (see 11.19n.). *Synagogue,* v. 5n. **15:** One lesson each from *the law and the prophets* was customary. **16:** *Gesture,* an orator's move. *Others who fear God,* here and v. 26 probably equivalent to "devout converts" to Judaism in v. 43

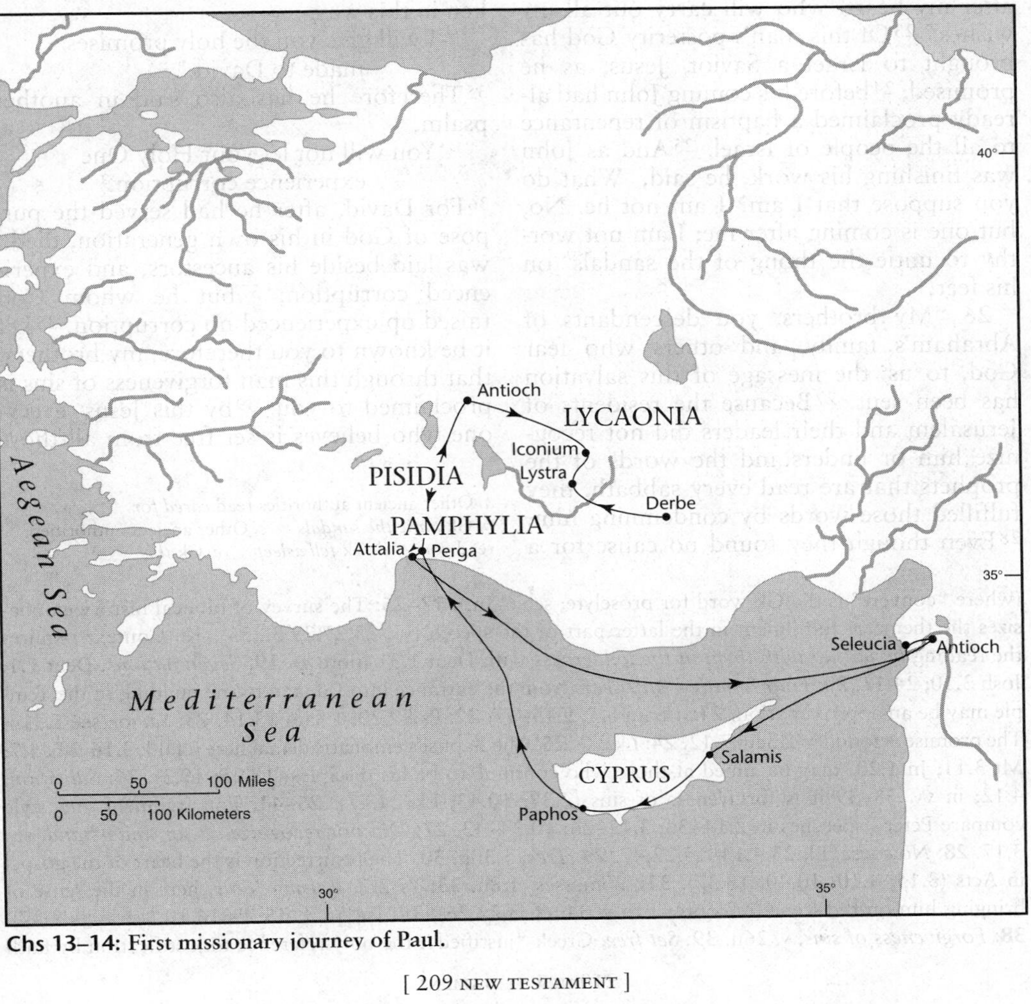

Chs 13–14: First missionary journey of Paul.

God, listen. 17 The God of this people Israel
chose our ancestors and made the people
great during their stay in the land of Egypt,
and with uplifted arm he led them out of it.
18 For about forty years he put up with[a]
them in the wilderness. 19 After he had de-
stroyed seven nations in the land of Ca-
naan, he gave them their land as an inheri-
tance 20 for about four hundred fifty years.
After that he gave them judges until the
time of the prophet Samuel. 21 Then they
asked for a king; and God gave them Saul
son of Kish, a man of the tribe of Benjamin,
who reigned for forty years. 22 When he
had removed him, he made David their
king. In his testimony about him he said, 'I
have found David, son of Jesse, to be a man
after my heart, who will carry out all my
wishes.' 23 Of this man's posterity God has
brought to Israel a Savior, Jesus, as he
promised; 24 before his coming John had al-
ready proclaimed a baptism of repentance
to all the people of Israel. 25 And as John
was finishing his work, he said, 'What do
you suppose that I am? I am not he. No,
but one is coming after me; I am not wor-
thy to untie the thong of the sandals[b] on
his feet.'

26 "My brothers, you descendants of
Abraham's family, and others who fear
God, to us[c] the message of this salvation
has been sent. 27 Because the residents of
Jerusalem and their leaders did not recog-
nize him or understand the words of the
prophets that are read every sabbath, they
fulfilled those words by condemning him.
28 Even though they found no cause for a
sentence of death, they asked Pilate to have
him killed. 29 When they had carried out
everything that was written about him,
they took him down from the tree and laid
him in a tomb. 30 But God raised him from
the dead; 31 and for many days he appeared
to those who came up with him from Gali-
lee to Jerusalem, and they are now his wit-
nesses to the people. 32 And we bring you
the good news that what God promised to
our ancestors 33 he has fulfilled for us, their
children, by raising Jesus; as also it is writ-
ten in the second psalm,

> 'You are my Son;
> today I have begotten you.'

34 As to his raising him from the dead, no
more to return to corruption, he has spo-
ken in this way,

> 'I will give you the holy promises
> made to David.'

35 Therefore he has also said in another
psalm,

> 'You will not let your Holy One
> experience corruption.'

36 For David, after he had served the pur-
pose of God in his own generation, died,[d]
was laid beside his ancestors, and experi-
enced corruption; 37 but he whom God
raised up experienced no corruption. 38 Let
it be known to you therefore, my brothers,
that through this man forgiveness of sins is
proclaimed to you; 39 by this Jesus[e] every-
one who believes is set free from all those

a Other ancient authorities read *cared for*
b Gk *untie the sandals* c Other ancient authorities read *you* d Gk *fell asleep* e Gk *this*

(where "convert" is the Gk word for proselyte; see 6.5n.). **17–25:** The survey of biblical history emphasizes the theme of fulfillment in the latter part of the speech (vv. 23,27,29,32,33). **18:** Context requires the reading *he put up with them in the wilderness* with Deut 1.31 (note *a*). **19:** *Seven nations,* Deut 7.1; Josh 3.10; 24.11. **20:** *Four hundred fifty years* from the entrance into Canaan to the building of the Temple may be an approximation. **21:** 1 Sam 8.5; 9.15–17. **22:** Ps 89.20; 1 Sam 13.14. **23:** *Savior,* see 5.31n. The promise is found in 2 Sam 7.12. **24:** Lk 3.3. **25:** The Baptist's emphatic denial here (cf. Lk 3.16; Mk 1.7; Mt 3.11; Jn 1.20) may be aimed at those who continue to be his disciples (18.25; 19.3). **26:** *Salvation,* 4.12; in vv. 38–39 it is forgiveness of sins (2.38; 10.43; Lk 24.47). **26–41:** For argument and style compare Peter's speeches in 2.14–36; 3.12–26; 10.34–43. **27:** *Did not recognize . . . or understand,* see 3.17. **28:** *No cause,* Lk 23.4,14–15,22,47. **29:** *Tree,* 5.30n. **30:** The resurrection is the heart of the gospel in Acts (3.15; 4.10; 10.40. 13.37). **31:** *Witnesses,* 1.8n. **33:** Ps 2.7. *Raising Jesus,* here in the sense of bringing him on the scene (in contrast to v. 34; cf. 3.22,26). **34:** Isa 55.3. **35:** Ps 16.10 (see Acts 2.27). **38:** *Forgiveness of sins,* v. 26n. **39:** *Set free,* Greek "justified"; the only reference to justification by faith

sins[a] from which you could not be freed by
the law of Moses. 40 Beware, therefore, that
what the prophets said does not happen to
you:
41 'Look, you scoffers!
Be amazed and perish,
for in your days I am doing a work,
a work that you will never believe,
even if someone tells you.' "
42 As Paul and Barnabas[b] were going
out, the people urged them to speak about
these things again the next sabbath.
43 When the meeting of the synagogue
broke up, many Jews and devout converts
to Judaism followed Paul and Barnabas,
who spoke to them and urged them to con-
tinue in the grace of God.
44 The next sabbath almost the whole
city gathered to hear the word of the
Lord.[c] 45 But when the Jews saw the
crowds, they were filled with jealousy; and
blaspheming, they contradicted what was
spoken by Paul. 46 Then both Paul and Bar-
nabas spoke out boldly, saying, "It was
necessary that the word of God should be
spoken first to you. Since you reject it and
judge yourselves to be unworthy of eternal
life, we are now turning to the Gentiles.
47 For so the Lord has commanded us, say-
ing,
'I have set you to be a light for
the Gentiles,
so that you may bring salvation to
the ends of the earth.' "
48 When the Gentiles heard this, they
were glad and praised the word of the
Lord; and as many as had been destined for
eternal life became believers. 49 Thus the
word of the Lord spread throughout the
region. 50 But the Jews incited the devout
women of high standing and the leading
men of the city, and stirred up persecution
against Paul and Barnabas, and drove them
out of their region. 51 So they shook the
dust off their feet in protest against them,
and went to Iconium. 52 And the disciples
were filled with joy and with the Holy
Spirit.

14 The same thing occurred in Iconi-
um, where Paul and Barnabas[b]
went into the Jewish synagogue and spoke
in such a way that a great number of both
Jews and Greeks became believers. 2 But the
unbelieving Jews stirred up the Gentiles
and poisoned their minds against the broth-
ers. 3 So they remained for a long time,
speaking boldly for the Lord, who testified
to the word of his grace by granting signs
and wonders to be done through them.
4 But the residents of the city were divided;
some sided with the Jews, and some with
the apostles. 5 And when an attempt was
made by both Gentiles and Jews, with their
rulers, to mistreat them and to stone them,
6 the apostles[b] learned of it and fled to Lys-
tra and Derbe, cities of Lycaonia, and to
the surrounding country; 7 and there they
continued proclaiming the good news.
8 In Lystra there was a man sitting who

a Gk *all* *b* Gk *they* *c* Other ancient authorities read *God*

in Acts fittingly appears on Paul's lips even if the sense is not fully that found in Paul's letters. **41:** Hab 1.5. **43:** *Devout converts to Judaism,* see v. 16n. **46:** The same dramatic announcement of turning to the *Gentiles* occurs in 18.5–6; 28.25–28. *Spoke out boldly,* 14.3; 18.26; 19.8; 26.26; see 4.13n. **47:** Isa 49.6; cf. Lk 2.32. **49:** A typical summary that makes it clear that Acts claims only to be a partial report of the spread of Christianity; cf. 9.10n. **50:** The scene depicted here (see 2 Tim 3.11) is repeated in subsequent accounts (see 14.2,19; 17.5,13). **51:** *They shook the dust off* (18.6) to show that their responsibility ended (Lk 9.5; 10.11; Mt 10.14). *Iconium,* modern Konya, ca. 120 km (75 mi) southeast of Antioch.

14.1–28: Ministry in the Iconium region and return to Antioch. 1: In spite of the announcement of 13.46, *Paul and Barnabas* again start at the *Jewish synagogue.* **2:** 13.50n. **4:** The Gk word *apostles* is used of Paul and Barnabas in Acts only here and in v. 14. Since the term otherwise is limited to the twelve, here the meaning may be "apostles (i.e., emissaries) of the church of Antioch," the church that sent them (13.2–3). **6:** *Lystra,* according to 16.1 the home of Timothy, was a Roman colony 40 km (24 mi) south-southwest of Iconium. *Derbe,* another town in Lycaonia 96 km (60 mi) southeast of Lystra. **7:** In Acts persecution always leads to new opportunities. **8–18:** Cf. 3.1–8. In this and other episodes in Acts

could not use his feet and had never
walked, for he had been crippled from
birth. 9 He listened to Paul as he was speak-
ing. And Paul, looking at him intently and
seeing that he had faith to be healed, 10 said
in a loud voice, "Stand upright on your
feet." And the man[a] sprang up and began
to walk. 11 When the crowds saw what Paul
had done, they shouted in the Lycaonian
language, "The gods have come down to us
in human form!" 12 Barnabas they called
Zeus, and Paul they called Hermes, because
he was the chief speaker. 13 The priest of
Zeus, whose temple was just outside the
city,[b] brought oxen and garlands to the
gates; he and the crowds wanted to offer
sacrifice. 14 When the apostles Barnabas
and Paul heard of it, they tore their clothes
and rushed out into the crowd, shouting,
15 "Friends,[c] why are you doing this? We
are mortals just like you, and we bring you
good news, that you should turn from these
worthless things to the living God, who
made the heaven and the earth and the sea
and all that is in them. 16 In past genera-
tions he allowed all the nations to follow
their own ways; 17 yet he has not left him-
self without a witness in doing good—giv-
ing you rains from heaven and fruitful sea-
sons, and filling you with food and your
hearts with joy." 18 Even with these words,
they scarcely restrained the crowds from
offering sacrifice to them.

19 But Jews came there from Antioch
and Iconium and won over the crowds.
Then they stoned Paul and dragged him out
of the city, supposing that he was dead.
20 But when the disciples surrounded him,
he got up and went into the city. The next
day he went on with Barnabas to Derbe.

21 After they had proclaimed the good
news to that city and had made many disci-
ples, they returned to Lystra, then on to
Iconium and Antioch. 22 There they
strengthened the souls of the disciples and
encouraged them to continue in the faith,
saying, "It is through many persecutions
that we must enter the kingdom of God."
23 And after they had appointed elders for
them in each church, with prayer and fast-
ing they entrusted them to the Lord in
whom they had come to believe.

24 Then they passed through Pisidia and
came to Pamphylia. 25 When they had spo-
ken the word in Perga, they went down to
Attalia. 26 From there they sailed back to
Antioch, where they had been commended
to the grace of God for the work[d] that they
had completed. 27 When they arrived, they
called the church together and related all
that God had done with them, and how he
had opened a door of faith for the Gentiles.
28 And they stayed there with the disciples
for some time.

15 Then certain individuals came down
from Judea and were teaching the

a Gk *he* *b* Or *The priest of Zeus-Outside-the-City*
c Gk *Men* *d* Or *committed in the grace of God to the work*

Paul replicates the experiences of Peter. **11–12:** According to a myth of this region, the gods *Zeus* and *Hermes* visited Baucis and Philemon *in human form* and rewarded their hospitality (Ovid, *Metamorphoses,* 8.618–724). Paul, *the chief speaker,* was hailed as the messenger of the gods, not the chief god. **14:** *Tore their clothes,* a sign of horror and dismay at what they looked upon as blasphemy (cf. Mk 14.63). **15–17:** Cf. 17.22–31; 1 Thess 1.9–10. Paul (v. 15), like Peter (10.26), rejects worship of himself. **19:** 13.50n. Paul tells of receiving a stoning in 2 Cor 11.25; see 2 Tim 3.11. **20:** Perhaps a miraculous recovery. **23:** In Acts, Paul's churches are ruled by *elders* (cf. 20.17). Their presence may reflect conditions in Luke's day read back into the earlier period (see 15.2n.). The word is not used in Paul's letters (but see 1 Timothy and Titus). See 11.30n. **25:** *Attalia,* the seaport of Perga (13.13n.). **26:** *Antioch,* their starting point for the *work* (13.2) now *completed.*

15.1–35: Jerusalem affirms the admission of Gentiles. 1: *Certain individuals,* cf. v. 5, Pharisees; Gal 2.4, "false believers." *Unless you are circumcised* and "keep the law" (v. 5), reopens issues seemingly settled with the approval of the "circumcised believers" (11.2n.,18) in 11.1–18. If the right of Gentile admission to the church was confirmed in ch 11, the present discussion may raise the issue of the conditions that might nevertheless apply. **2:** *Were appointed,* in Gal 2.2 Paul says he went "by revelation"

brothers, "Unless you are circumcised ac-
cording to the custom of Moses, you can-
not be saved." 2 And after Paul and Barna-
bas had no small dissension and debate
with them, Paul and Barnabas and some of
the others were appointed to go up to Jeru-
salem to discuss this question with the
apostles and the elders. 3 So they were sent
on their way by the church, and as they
passed through both Phoenicia and Samar-
ia, they reported the conversion of the Gen-
tiles, and brought great joy to all the believ-
ers.[a] 4 When they came to Jerusalem, they
were welcomed by the church and the apos-
tles and the elders, and they reported all
that God had done with them. 5 But some
believers who belonged to the sect of the
Pharisees stood up and said, "It is necessary
for them to be circumcised and ordered to
keep the law of Moses."

6 The apostles and the elders met to-
gether to consider this matter. 7 After there
had been much debate, Peter stood up and
said to them, "My brothers,[b] you know
that in the early days God made a choice
among you, that I should be the one
through whom the Gentiles would hear the
message of the good news and become be-
lievers. 8 And God, who knows the human
heart, testified to them by giving them the
Holy Spirit, just as he did to us; 9 and in
cleansing their hearts by faith he has made
no distinction between them and us.
10 Now therefore why are you putting God
to the test by placing on the neck of the
disciples a yoke that neither our ancestors
nor we have been able to bear? 11 On the
contrary, we believe that we will be saved
through the grace of the Lord Jesus, just as
they will."

12 The whole assembly kept silence, and
listened to Barnabas and Paul as they told
of all the signs and wonders that God had
done through them among the Gentiles.
13 After they finished speaking, James re-
plied, "My brothers,[b] listen to me. 14 Sime-
on has related how God first looked favor-
ably on the Gentiles, to take from among
them a people for his name. 15 This agrees
with the words of the prophets, as it is writ-
ten,

16 'After this I will return,
and I will rebuild the dwelling of
David, which has fallen;
from its ruins I will rebuild it,
and I will set it up,
17 so that all other peoples may seek the
Lord—
even all the Gentiles over whom my
name has been called.
Thus says the Lord, who has
been making these things
18 known from long ago.'[c]

19 Therefore I have reached the decision
that we should not trouble those Gentiles
who are turning to God, 20 but we should

a Gk *brothers* *b* Gk *Men, brothers* *c* Other ancient authorities read *things.* 18*Known to God from of old are all his works.'*

(Gal 2.2). *Elders* (11.30n.; 14.23n.) now appear with the *apostles* (vv. 4,6,22,23; 16.4n.) as leaders of the Jerusalem church under James (vv. 13,19). Peter is the only apostle named; the others function as a corporate symbol as they have throughout. **5:** In Acts *Pharisees* are portrayed as *believers* (26.5) or tolerant of Christianity (5.34), often in sharp contrast to Sadducees (4.1–2; 5.17; 23.6–9). **7–9:** Peter's second summary (see 11.1–18) of the events narrated in 10.1–48. *I should be the one,* contrast Gal 2.7–8. **10:** The *yoke* is that of the law (Lk 11.46); Paul's view (Rom 7.12; Phil 3.6) is different. **11:** Peter's words echo Paul's language (Rom 3.24). **12:** 14.27; 15.4. The contentious debate reported in Gal 2 is passed over in silence in Acts. **13:** *James,* see 12.17n. **14:** *Simeon,* the Semitic form of Peter's given name, emphasizing connections with Judaism even as the church is becoming a mixed group (v. 19) of Jews and Gentiles (see 14.1; 17.4,11–12; 18.4,8; 19.10). **16–18:** Am 9.11–12; Jer 12.15; Isa 45.21. **20:** *Things polluted by idols,* i.e., food sacrificed to them—prohibiting by extension idolatry itself (note Paul's more liberal stance in 1 Cor 10.27–29). *Whatever has been strangled,* i.e., meat not ritually butchered, which may mean the same thing as *blood* (omitted by some manuscripts), although the latter could mean murder. Suggested backgrounds for the items included in the "apostolic decree" include the so-called Noachian precepts (regulations to be observed by all peoples; see Gen 9.4–6) and the regulations for Gentiles living among Jews in

write to them to abstain only from things
polluted by idols and from fornication and
from whatever has been strangled[a] and
from blood. 21 For in every city, for genera-
tions past, Moses has had those who pro-
claim him, for he has been read aloud every
sabbath in the synagogues."
22 Then the apostles and the elders,
with the consent of the whole church, de-
cided to choose men from among their
members[b] and to send them to Antioch
with Paul and Barnabas. They sent Judas
called Barsabbas, and Silas, leaders among
the brothers, 23 with the following letter:
"The brothers, both the apostles and the
elders, to the believers[c] of Gentile origin in
Antioch and Syria and Cilicia, greetings.
24 Since we have heard that certain persons
who have gone out from us, though with
no instructions from us, have said things
to disturb you and have unsettled your
minds,[d] 25 we have decided unanimously
to choose representatives[e] and send them
to you, along with our beloved Barnabas
and Paul, 26 who have risked their lives for
the sake of our Lord Jesus Christ. 27 We
have therefore sent Judas and Silas, who
themselves will tell you the same things by
word of mouth. 28 For it has seemed good
to the Holy Spirit and to us to impose on
you no further burden than these essentials:
29 that you abstain from what has been sac-
rificed to idols and from blood and from
what is strangled[f] and from fornication. If
you keep yourselves from these, you will do
well. Farewell."

30 So they were sent off and went down
to Antioch. When they gathered the con-
gregation together, they delivered the letter.
31 When its members[g] read it, they rejoiced
at the exhortation. 32 Judas and Silas, who
were themselves prophets, said much to en-
courage and strengthen the believers.[c]
33 After they had been there for some time,
they were sent off in peace by the believ-
ers[c] to those who had sent them.[h] 35 But
Paul and Barnabas remained in Antioch,
and there, with many others, they taught
and proclaimed the word of the Lord.

36 After some days Paul said to Barna-
bas, "Come, let us return and visit the be-
lievers[c] in every city where we proclaimed
the word of the Lord and see how they are
doing." 37 Barnabas wanted to take with
them John called Mark. 38 But Paul decided
not to take with them one who had desert-
ed them in Pamphylia and had not accom-
panied them in the work. 39 The disagree-
ment became so sharp that they parted
company; Barnabas took Mark with him
and sailed away to Cyprus. 40 But Paul
chose Silas and set out, the believers[c] com-
mending him to the grace of the Lord. 41 He

a Other ancient authorities lack *and from whatever has been strangled* *b* Gk *from among them* *c* Gk *brothers* *d* Other ancient authorities add *saying, 'You must be circumcised and keep the law,'* *e* Gk *men* *f* Other ancient authorities lack *and from what is strangled* *g* Gk *When they* *h* Other ancient authorities add verse 34, *But it seemed good to Silas to remain there*

Lev 17–18. The list may have a more practical function (avoid non-kosher food and *fornication*) or stipulate matters beyond compromise (idolatry, murder, and incest). **21:** *In every city . . . Moses,* seems to explain the necessity of the decree (v. 20) in terms of the pervasiveness of the Jewish lifestyle, which continues to be practiced by Jewish Christians (cf. 21.20–25). **22:** *Judas called Barsabbas,* see 1.23. *Silas* may be the Silvanus of 2 Cor 1.19; 1 Thess 1.1; 2 Thess 1.1. He becomes a missionary companion of Paul at 15.40. **28:** *To the Holy Spirit and to us,* see 5.3n. *No further burden than these essentials,* cf. Gal 2.10. **32:** *Prophets,* 13.1n. **35:** 11.26; 14.28.

15.36–16.5: Paul revisits the churches of the previous mission. 37–38: *John called Mark . . . had deserted,* see 12.12n.; 13.13. **39:** Compare the *disagreement* here over John *Mark* with the report in Gal 2.11–13 that Barnabas disagreed with Paul over the legitimacy of Jews and Gentiles eating together. According to Acts, this problem had already been dealt with in 10.1–11.18, although the apostolic decree (15.20,29) may have been intended to make association over meals acceptable for Jewish Christians. Barnabas and Mark revisit *Cyprus* (13.4–12), which had been omitted on the return journey to Antioch described in 14.24–26. **40:** *Paul* now sets out as an "independent" missionary, accompanied by *Silas*

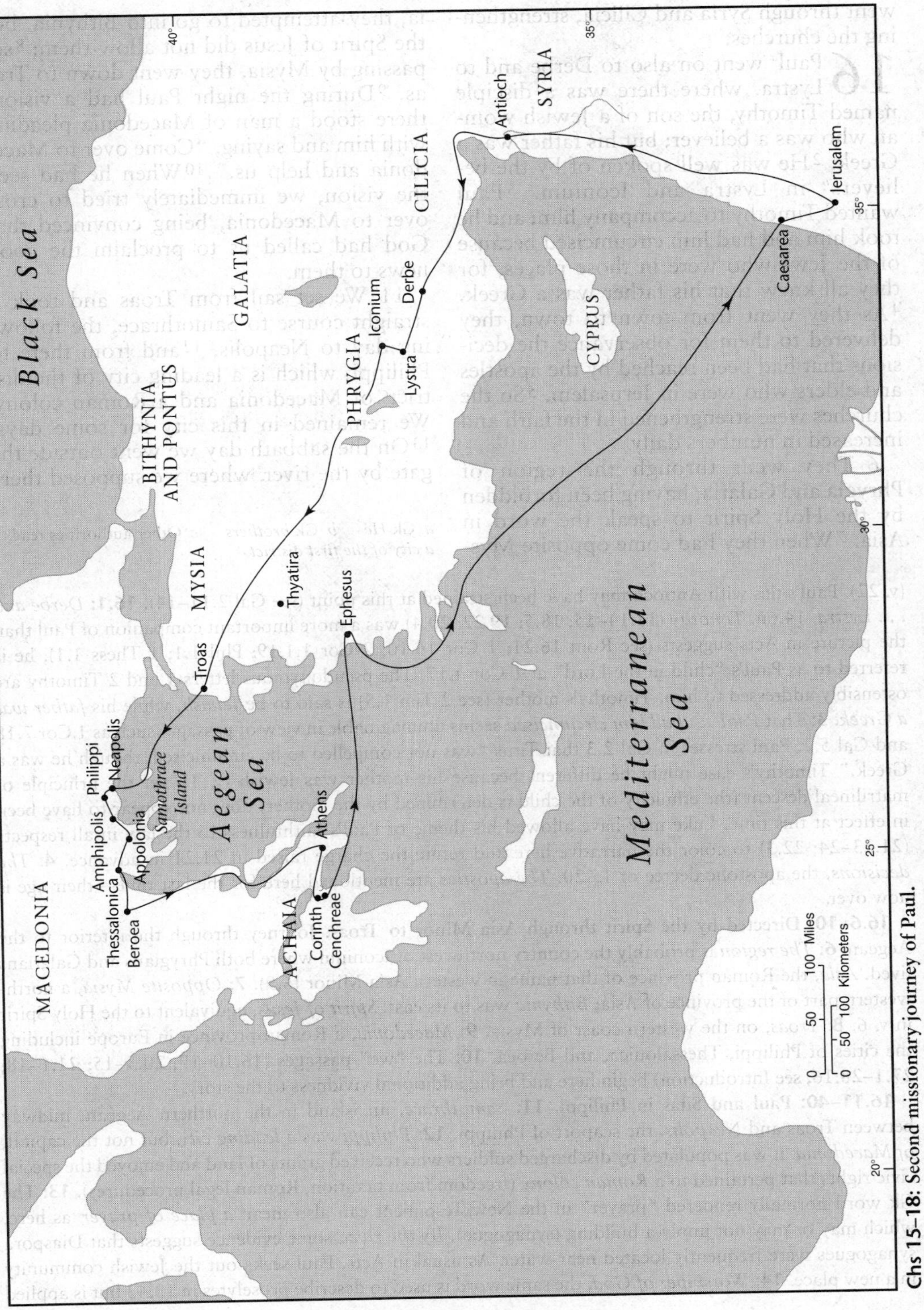

Chs 15–18: Second missionary journey of Paul.

went through Syria and Cilicia, strengthen-
ing the churches.
16 Paul[a] went on also to Derbe and to
Lystra, where there was a disciple
named Timothy, the son of a Jewish wom-
an who was a believer; but his father was a
Greek. 2 He was well spoken of by the be-
lievers[b] in Lystra and Iconium. 3 Paul
wanted Timothy to accompany him; and he
took him and had him circumcised because
of the Jews who were in those places, for
they all knew that his father was a Greek.
4 As they went from town to town, they
delivered to them for observance the deci-
sions that had been reached by the apostles
and elders who were in Jerusalem. 5 So the
churches were strengthened in the faith and
increased in numbers daily.
6 They went through the region of
Phrygia and Galatia, having been forbidden
by the Holy Spirit to speak the word in
Asia. 7 When they had come opposite Mys-
ia, they attempted to go into Bithynia, but
the Spirit of Jesus did not allow them; 8 so,
passing by Mysia, they went down to Tro-
as. 9 During the night Paul had a vision:
there stood a man of Macedonia pleading
with him and saying, "Come over to Mace-
donia and help us." 10 When he had seen
the vision, we immediately tried to cross
over to Macedonia, being convinced that
God had called us to proclaim the good
news to them.
11 We set sail from Troas and took a
straight course to Samothrace, the follow-
ing day to Neapolis, 12 and from there to
Philippi, which is a leading city of the dis-
trict[c] of Macedonia and a Roman colony.
We remained in this city for some days.
13 On the sabbath day we went outside the
gate by the river, where we supposed there

a Gk *He* *b* Gk *brothers* *c* Other authorities read *a city of the first district*

(v. 22). Paul's ties with Antioch may have been strained at this point (see Gal 2.11–14). **16.1:** *Derbe and . . . Lystra,* 14.6n. *Timothy* (17.14–15; 18.5; 19.22; 20.4) was a more important companion of Paul than the picture in Acts suggests (see Rom 16.21; 1 Cor 16.10; 2 Cor 1.1,19; Phil 1.1; 1 Thess 1.1); he is referred to as Paul's "child in the Lord" at 1 Cor 4.17. The pseudonymous letters 1 and 2 Timothy are ostensibly addressed to him. Timothy's mother (see 2 Tim 1.5) is said to be *Jewish,* while his *father was a Greek.* **3:** That *Paul . . . had him circumcised* seems unimaginable in view of passages such as 1 Cor 7.18 and Gal 5.2. Paul stresses in Gal 2.3 that Titus "was not compelled to be circumcised, though he was a Greek." Timothy's case might be different because his mother was Jewish (v. 1), yet the principle of matrilineal descent (the ethnicity of the child is determined by the mother) does not appear to have been in effect at this time. Luke may have allowed his theme of Paul's faithfulness to the law in all respects (21.23–24; 22.3) to color the narrative here and refute the charge raised in 21.21 in advance. **4:** *The decisions,* the apostolic decree of 15.20. *The apostles* are mentioned here for the last time—their age is now over.

16.6–10: Directed by the Spirit through Asia Minor to Troas. Journey through the interior to the Aegean. **6:** *The region* is probably the country northwest of Iconium where both Phrygians and Galatians lived. *Asia,* the Roman province of that name in western Asia Minor (6.9). **7:** *Opposite Mysia,* a northwestern part of the province of Asia; *Bithynia* was to its east. *Spirit of Jesus,* equivalent to the Holy Spirit in v. 6. **8:** *Troas,* on the western coast of Mysia. **9:** *Macedonia,* a Roman province in Europe including the cities of Philippi, Thessalonica, and Beroea. **10:** The "we" passages (16.10–17; 20.5–15; 21.1–18; 27.1–28.16; see Introduction) begin here and bring additional vividness to the story.

16.11–40: Paul and Silas in Philippi. 11: *Samothrace,* an island in the northern Aegean, midway between Troas and *Neapolis,* the seaport of Philippi. **12:** *Philippi* was *a leading city,* but not the capital, *of Macedonia.* It was populated by discharged soldiers who received grants of land and enjoyed the special civic rights that pertained to a *Roman colony* (freedom from taxation, Roman legal procedures). **13:** The Gk word normally rendered "prayer" in the New Testament can also mean *a place of prayer,* as here, which may or may not imply a building (synagogue). *By the river,* some evidence suggests that Diaspora synagogues were frequently located near water. As usual in Acts, Paul seeks out the Jewish community in a new place. **14:** *Worshiper of God,* the same word is used to describe proselytes in 13.43 but is applied

was a place of prayer; and we sat down and
spoke to the women who had gathered
there. 14 A certain woman named Lydia, a
worshiper of God, was listening to us; she
was from the city of Thyatira and a dealer
in purple cloth. The Lord opened her heart
to listen eagerly to what was said by Paul.
15 When she and her household were bap-
tized, she urged us, saying, "If you have
judged me to be faithful to the Lord, come
and stay at my home." And she prevailed
upon us.
16 One day, as we were going to the
place of prayer, we met a slave-girl who
had a spirit of divination and brought her
owners a great deal of money by fortune-
telling. 17 While she followed Paul and us,
she would cry out, "These men are slaves of
the Most High God, who proclaim to you[a]
a way of salvation." 18 She kept doing this
for many days. But Paul, very much an-
noyed, turned and said to the spirit, "I or-
der you in the name of Jesus Christ to come
out of her." And it came out that very hour.
19 But when her owners saw that their
hope of making money was gone, they
seized Paul and Silas and dragged them into
the marketplace before the authorities.
20 When they had brought them before the
magistrates, they said, "These men are dis-
turbing our city; they are Jews 21 and are
advocating customs that are not lawful for
us as Romans to adopt or observe." 22 The
crowd joined in attacking them, and the
magistrates had them stripped of their
clothing and ordered them to be beaten
with rods. 23 After they had given them a
severe flogging, they threw them into pris-
on and ordered the jailer to keep them se-
curely. 24 Following these instructions, he
put them in the innermost cell and fastened
their feet in the stocks.
25 About midnight Paul and Silas were
praying and singing hymns to God, and the
prisoners were listening to them. 26 Sudden-
ly there was an earthquake, so violent that
the foundations of the prison were shaken;
and immediately all the doors were opened
and everyone's chains were unfastened.
27 When the jailer woke up and saw the
prison doors wide open, he drew his sword
and was about to kill himself, since he sup-
posed that the prisoners had escaped. 28 But
Paul shouted in a loud voice, "Do not harm
yourself, for we are all here." 29 The jailer[b]
called for lights, and rushing in, he fell
down trembling before Paul and Silas.
30 Then he brought them outside and said,
"Sirs, what must I do to be saved?" 31 They
answered, "Believe on the Lord Jesus, and
you will be saved, you and your house-
hold." 32 They spoke the word of the
Lord[c] to him and to all who were in his
house. 33 At the same hour of the night he
took them and washed their wounds; then
he and his entire family were baptized with-
out delay. 34 He brought them up into the

a Other ancient authorities read *to us* *b* Gk *He*
c Other ancient authorities read *word of God*

to "women of high standing" in 13.50 in contradistinction to Jews. The term might simply describe *Lydia* as pious or suggest that she is a Jewish sympathizer. *Thyatira* (Rev 2.18–29), a city of Lydia, a country in western Asia Minor, was a center for the dyeing industry. **15:** *She and her household were baptized,* dependents followed the head of the household in religious matters (v. 31; 10.2; 1 Cor 1.16). **17:** In Lk 8.28 the Gerasene demoniac identifies Jesus as Son of *the Most High God.* The epithet is common for God in the Psalms of the Septuagint. The "we" passage (v. 10n.) stops here and resumes at 20.5. **19:** Acts frowns on *making money* by magical or supernatural means (see 8.18–24; 19.25n.). **20:** *Magistrates,* Gk "generals"; here probably not a military but a civic term (apparently to be distinguished from the "authorities," v. 19). **21:** It was *not lawful* for Jews to make converts of *Romans.* **22–23:** Cf. 2 Cor 11.23–25 ("imprisonments . . . floggings . . . beaten with rods"). **24:** The familiar motif of escape-proof security (5.19–20; 12.6). **26:** *An earthquake,* here a supernatural event (see 4.31). *Doors* open and bonds are loosened for Dionysus in Euripides' *Bacchae* 447–448; see also Ovid, *Metamorphoses* 15.669–671. See 12.6–11n. **27:** *Drew his sword,* a Roman jailer whose prisoner escaped was liable to forfeit his life (cf. 12.19; 27.42). **30:** The question is elicited by the supernatural circumstances. **33:** The entire household is *baptized* (v. 15). **35:** *Police,* lictors, officials who enforced the decisions of a magistrate. **37–38:**

house and set food before them; and he and
his entire household rejoiced that he had
become a believer in God.
35 When morning came, the magistrates
sent the police, saying, "Let those men go."
36 And the jailer reported the message to
Paul, saying, "The magistrates sent word to
let you go; therefore come out now and go
in peace." 37 But Paul replied, "They have
beaten us in public, uncondemned, men
who are Roman citizens, and have thrown
us into prison; and now are they going to
discharge us in secret? Certainly not! Let
them come and take us out themselves."
38 The police reported these words to the
magistrates, and they were afraid when
they heard that they were Roman citizens;
39 so they came and apologized to them.
And they took them out and asked them to
leave the city. 40 After leaving the prison
they went to Lydia's home; and when they
had seen and encouraged the brothers and
sisters[a] there, they departed.
17 After Paul and Silas[b] had passed
through Amphipolis and Apollonia,
they came to Thessalonica, where there was
a synagogue of the Jews. 2 And Paul went
in, as was his custom, and on three sabbath
days argued with them from the scriptures,
3 explaining and proving that it was neces-
sary for the Messiah[c] to suffer and to rise
from the dead, and saying, "This is the
Messiah,[c] Jesus whom I am proclaiming to
you." 4 Some of them were persuaded and
joined Paul and Silas, as did a great many
of the devout Greeks and not a few of the
leading women. 5 But the Jews became jeal-
ous, and with the help of some ruffians in
the marketplaces they formed a mob and
set the city in an uproar. While they were
searching for Paul and Silas to bring them
out to the assembly, they attacked Jason's
house. 6 When they could not find them,
they dragged Jason and some believers[a]
before the city authorities,[d] shouting,
"These people who have been turning the
world upside down have come here also,
7 and Jason has entertained them as guests.
They are all acting contrary to the decrees
of the emperor, saying that there is another
king named Jesus." 8 The people and the
city officials were disturbed when they
heard this, 9 and after they had taken bail
from Jason and the others, they let
them go.
10 That very night the believers[a] sent
Paul and Silas off to Beroea; and when they
arrived, they went to the Jewish synagogue.
11 These Jews were more receptive than
those in Thessalonica, for they welcomed
the message very eagerly and examined the
scriptures every day to see whether these
things were so. 12 Many of them therefore
believed, including not a few Greek women
and men of high standing. 13 But when the
Jews of Thessalonica learned that the word
of God had been proclaimed by Paul in Be-
roea as well, they came there too, to stir up
and incite the crowds. 14 Then the believ-

a Gk *brothers* *b* Gk *they* *c* Or *the Christ*
d Gk *politarchs*

With dramatic flair the reader suddenly learns that both *Paul* and Silas are *Roman citizens* protected by law against scourging (22.25; contrast 2 Cor 11.23–25). This increase in Paul's credentials strongly endorses the theme of the compatibility of Christianity with Roman life (see 10.1n.; 13.7n.).

17.1–15: From Thessalonica to Athens. Paul founds churches in Thessalonica and Beroea. **1:** *Amphipolis and Apollonia* were on the Via Egnatia between Philippi and *Thessalonica* (modern Saloniki), capital of the second district of Macedonia. **2:** *His custom,* the pattern of starting a new mission in a synagogue (vv. 1,10,17) is explicitly stated (see 13.5n.; 14.1n.). **3:** See 3.18n. **4:** *Devout Greeks,* see 16.14n. *Leading women,* v. 12; contrast 13.50. **5:** *Jealous,* 13.45. On the typical nature of the scene, see 13.50n.; cf. 1 Thess 2.14–16. **6–7:** *City authorities,* i.e., politarchs, a Macedonian title for non-Roman magistrates. Serious charges of activities that threaten Roman order are advanced; cf. Lk 23.2. **9:** *Had taken bail from Jason,* had made him financially and legally responsible for future good behavior. **10:** *Beroea,* a city of Macedonia, 58 km (36 mi) west-southwest of Thessalonica. **11–12:** *Jews* and Gentiles believe (15.14n.). *Greek women and men of high standing,* Christianity is attracting people with status (16.37–38n.). **14:** *To the coast,* where he would take a ship to Athens (v. 15).

ers[a] immediately sent Paul away to the
coast, but Silas and Timothy remained be-
hind. 15 Those who conducted Paul brought
him as far as Athens; and after receiving
instructions to have Silas and Timothy join
him as soon as possible, they left him.

16 While Paul was waiting for them in
Athens, he was deeply distressed to see that
the city was full of idols. 17 So he argued in
the synagogue with the Jews and the devout
persons, and also in the marketplace[b] ev-
ery day with those who happened to be
there. 18 Also some Epicurean and Stoic
philosophers debated with him. Some said,
"What does this babbler want to say?"
Others said, "He seems to be a proclaimer
of foreign divinities." (This was because he
was telling the good news about Jesus and
the resurrection.) 19 So they took him and
brought him to the Areopagus and asked
him, "May we know what this new teach-
ing is that you are presenting? 20 It sounds
rather strange to us, so we would like to
know what it means." 21 Now all the Athe-
nians and the foreigners living there would
spend their time in nothing but telling or
hearing something new.

22 Then Paul stood in front of the Are-
opagus and said, "Athenians, I see how
extremely religious you are in every way.
23 For as I went through the city and looked
carefully at the objects of your worship, I
found among them an altar with the in-
scription, 'To an unknown god.' What
therefore you worship as unknown, this I
proclaim to you. 24 The God who made the
world and everything in it, he who is Lord
of heaven and earth, does not live in shrines
made by human hands, 25 nor is he served
by human hands, as though he needed any-
thing, since he himself gives to all mortals
life and breath and all things. 26 From one
ancestor[c] he made all nations to inhabit
the whole earth, and he allotted the times
of their existence and the boundaries of the
places where they would live, 27 so that they
would search for God[d] and perhaps grope
for him and find him—though indeed he is
not far from each one of us. 28 For 'In him
we live and move and have our being'; as
even some of your own poets have said,

'For we too are his offspring.'

a Gk *brothers* *b* Or *civic center*; Gk *agora*
c Gk *From one*; other ancient authorities read *From one blood* *d* Other ancient authorities read *the Lord*

17.16–34: Paul at Athens. The apostle is portrayed as the first Christian philosopher, using Stoic and Jewish arguments. **16:** *Waiting . . . in Athens,* cf. 1 Thess 3.1–2. *Full of idols,* v. 22; cf. 1 Thess 1.9. **18:** *Epicurean and Stoic philosophers,* recognizable tenets from both groups are incorporated into Paul's speech in vv. 22–31. *Babbler,* a term of disparagement; the Gk word is literally used in reference to birds to mean "picking up seeds," of persons "one who makes a living by picking up scraps" (here implied: "of learning"). *Jesus and* Anastasis (the Gk word for *resurrection*) are mistaken for two *foreign divinities.* **19:** *Took him,* could either imply arrest or friendly conveyance, and *Areopagus* could refer either to arraignment before the Council of the Areopagus (essentially the chief Roman court in Athens) or the Areopagus hill west of the Acropolis. The request *"May we know . . . ?"* suggests a more relaxed setting for discussion, though allusions to Socrates before the Areopagus court are surely intended (see v. 34). **21:** The curiosity of *the Athenians* was proverbial. **22–31:** Contrast the approach to Gentiles attributed to Paul in this speech with Rom 1.18–31. **22:** *Extremely religious,* can be taken in a good or bad sense. It connects to "idols" in v. 16 and leads to v. 23. **23:** *To an unknown god,* such an inscription has not been found in Athens to date; the plural form is attested. The scene intends to illustrate the anxiety of the "extremely religious" (v. 22) lest the honor due to any deity be inadvertently omitted and gives Paul an opening to *proclaim* the Christian message. **24–25:** *God* as the creator (14.15) is an idea common to Jews (Gen 1.1) and Greeks (e.g., Plato, *Timaeus*). *Shrines made by human hands,* 7.48n. **26:** *From one ancestor,* Adam. **27:** God created "all nations" (v. 26) to *search for God* (cf. 14.17). That God was near to all people was a Stoic belief. **28:** Although the first quotation is sometimes attributed to Epimenides, its language is probably to be associated with Posidonius (based on Plato); the second quotation is from Aratus (*Phaenomena* 5), a Greek poet of Cilicia educated as a Stoic. In Paul's usage the original pantheistic sense of both "quotations" is reinterpreted. **30:** *Ignorance,* cf. 14.16. **31:** That the *world* will be *judged*

29 Since we are God's offspring, we ought
not to think that the deity is like gold, or
silver, or stone, an image formed by the art
and imagination of mortals. 30 While God
has overlooked the times of human igno-
rance, now he commands all people every-
where to repent, 31 because he has fixed a
day on which he will have the world judged
in righteousness by a man whom he has
appointed, and of this he has given assur-
ance to all by raising him from the dead."
32 When they heard of the resurrection
of the dead, some scoffed; but others said,
"We will hear you again about this." 33 At
that point Paul left them. 34 But some of
them joined him and became believers, in-
cluding Dionysius the Areopagite and a
woman named Damaris, and others with
them.

18 After this Paul[a] left Athens and
went to Corinth. 2 There he found a
Jew named Aquila, a native of Pontus, who
had recently come from Italy with his wife
Priscilla, because Claudius had ordered all
Jews to leave Rome. Paul[b] went to see
them, 3 and, because he was of the same
trade, he stayed with them, and they
worked together—by trade they were tent-
makers. 4 Every sabbath he would argue in
the synagogue and would try to convince
Jews and Greeks.
5 When Silas and Timothy arrived from
Macedonia, Paul was occupied with pro-
claiming the word,[c] testifying to the Jews
that the Messiah[d] was Jesus. 6 When they
opposed and reviled him, in protest he
shook the dust from his clothes[e] and said
to them, "Your blood be on your own
heads! I am innocent. From now on I will
go to the Gentiles." 7 Then he left the syna-
gogue[f] and went to the house of a man
named Titius[g] Justus, a worshiper of God;
his house was next door to the synagogue.
8 Crispus, the official of the synagogue, be-
came a believer in the Lord, together with
all his household; and many of the Corin-
thians who heard Paul became believers
and were baptized. 9 One night the Lord
said to Paul in a vision, "Do not be afraid,
but speak and do not be silent; 10 for I am
with you, and no one will lay a hand on
you to harm you, for there are many in this
city who are my people." 11 He stayed there

a Gk *he* b Gk *He* c Gk *with the word*
d Or *the Christ* e Gk *reviled him, he shook out his clothes* f Gk *left there* g Other ancient authorities read *Titus*

(10.42) *by a man,* i.e., Jesus (2.22,36), *appointed* by God has been guaranteed by the resurrection. **32:** *Some scoffed,* Greek thought made no provision for resurrection of the body (e.g., Aeschylus, *Eumenides,* 647–648; cf. 1 Cor 15.12,35), *but others* were intrigued. **34:** The conversion of *Dionysius,* a member of the Areopagus court, contributes to the theme of rulers attracted to Christianity. The note about *Damaris* conforms to a pattern found in both the Gospel (e.g., Lk 15.3–10) and Acts (e.g., 5.1–11) of juxtaposing characters of both genders.

18.1–17: Paul in Corinth. See 1 Cor 1–4 for Paul's own account. **1:** *Corinth,* the old city was famous but was razed in 146 BCE by the Romans. It was refounded as a colony in 44 BCE by Julius Caesar, became the capital of the senatorial province of Achaia in 27 BCE, and quickly emerged as an important commercial center owing to its location on the isthmus linking the Peloponnesus to mainland Greece with neighboring seaports to the east and west. **2:** *Pontus,* a Roman province of Asia Minor on the Black Sea. An edict issued by *Claudius* (see Suetonius, *Claudius* 25) expelling the *Jews* from *Rome* can probably be dated to 49 CE; this verse suggests that the trouble was connected with Jewish Christians. *Aquila* and *Priscilla* (or Prisca) worked with Paul, according to Rom 16.3–5. The fact that a church met in their house (Rom 16.5; 1 Cor 16.19) suggests that they were wealthy. In the epistles (including 2 Tim 4.19) their names appear in reverse order. **3:** *Same trade . . . tentmakers,* see 20.34. *He stayed with them,* possibly "lodged with them." **4:** *Synagogue,* 13.5n.; *Jews and Greeks,* 15.14n. **6:** 13.46n.,51n. *Your blood . . . ,* 2 Sam 1.16; Mt 27.25. **7:** *Worshiper of God,* 16.14n. **8:** *Crispus,* his baptism by Paul is mentioned as an exceptional case in 1 Cor 1.14. The conversion of the *official of the synagogue* (i.e., president; see 13.15) and his *household* (16.15n.) illustrates the continued success of Paul's mission among Jews (in spite of v. 6) in addition to Gentiles (*many of the Corinthians . . . became believers*). **12:** L. Junius *Gallio,* older

a year and six months, teaching the word of
God among them.
12 But when Gallio was proconsul of
Achaia, the Jews made a united attack on
Paul and brought him before the tribunal.
13 They said, "This man is persuading peo-
ple to worship God in ways that are con-
trary to the law." 14 Just as Paul was about
to speak, Gallio said to the Jews, "If it were
a matter of crime or serious villainy, I
would be justified in accepting the com-
plaint of you Jews; 15 but since it is a matter
of questions about words and names and
your own law, see to it yourselves; I do not
wish to be a judge of these matters." 16 And
he dismissed them from the tribunal.
17 Then all of them[a] seized Sosthenes, the
official of the synagogue, and beat him in
front of the tribunal. But Gallio paid no
attention to any of these things.
18 After staying there for a considerable
time, Paul said farewell to the believers[b]
and sailed for Syria, accompanied by Pris-
cilla and Aquila. At Cenchreae he had his
hair cut, for he was under a vow. 19 When
they reached Ephesus, he left them there,
but first he himself went into the synagogue
and had a discussion with the Jews.
20 When they asked him to stay longer, he
declined; 21 but on taking leave of them, he
said, "I[c] will return to you, if God wills."
Then he set sail from Ephesus.
22 When he had landed at Caesarea, he
went up to Jerusalem[d] and greeted the
church, and then went down to Antioch.
23 After spending some time there he de-
parted and went from place to place
through the region of Galatia[e] and Phryg-
ia, strengthening all the disciples.
24 Now there came to Ephesus a Jew
named Apollos, a native of Alexandria. He
was an eloquent man, well-versed in the
scriptures. 25 He had been instructed in the
Way of the Lord; and he spoke with burn-
ing enthusiasm and taught accurately the
things concerning Jesus, though he knew
only the baptism of John. 26 He began to
speak boldly in the synagogue; but when
Priscilla and Aquila heard him, they took
him aside and explained the Way of God
to him more accurately. 27 And when he
wished to cross over to Achaia, the believ-
ers[b] encouraged him and wrote to the dis-
ciples to welcome him. On his arrival he
greatly helped those who through grace
had become believers, 28 for he powerfully
refuted the Jews in public, showing by the
scriptures that the Messiah[f] is Jesus.

a Other ancient authorities read *all the Greeks*
b Gk *brothers* *c* Other ancient authorities read *I must at all costs keep the approaching festival in Jerusalem, but I* *d* Gk *went up* *e* Gk *the Galatian region* *f* Or *the Christ*

brother of the philosopher Seneca, *proconsul of Achaia* about 52 CE. The dating of Gallio's proconsulship is crucial for the chronological reconstruction of Paul's career. **13:** *The law,* could mean the Jewish law (as Gallio takes it in v. 15) or Roman law, i.e., charges of sedition similar to the complaints raised in 16.21 and 17.7 (the latter would make more sense to present before a proconsul). **14–15:** *Gallio* again voices one of the subthemes of the book: Christianity is not a cause of concern for Rome. Roman representatives tend either to be outwardly favorable (e.g., Cornelius, Sergius Paulus), or at worst indifferent to Christianity, suggesting that it need not be viewed as incompatible with Rome (see 10.1n.). **17:** *Sosthenes* may be the one mentioned in 1 Cor 1.1, but the name is common.

18.18–23: End of the second missionary journey and beginning of the third. Paul returns to Antioch and goes back to Asia Minor. **18:** Paul *had his hair cut* as a temporary nazirite *vow* (21.23–24; Num 6.1–21), but the rule was to cut the hair off at the end of the vow. *Cenchreae,* the eastern port of Corinth (Rom 16.1). **19:** *Ephesus,* on the Aegean coast, was the capital of the Roman province of Asia. **22:** *Caesarea,* see 8.40n. *Jerusalem* still appears as the mother church. *Antioch,* see 11.19n. **23:** *The region of Galatia and Phrygia,* see 16.6n.

18.24–28: Apollos in Ephesus. 25: *The Way,* see 9.2n. Although he *taught accurately,* he had not received Christian baptism (13.25n.). **26:** *Speak boldly,* 13.46n. It is not disclosed in what sense things were *explained . . . more accurately.* **27–28:** For his activity in Corinth, see 1 Cor 1.12; 3.1–9,21–23.

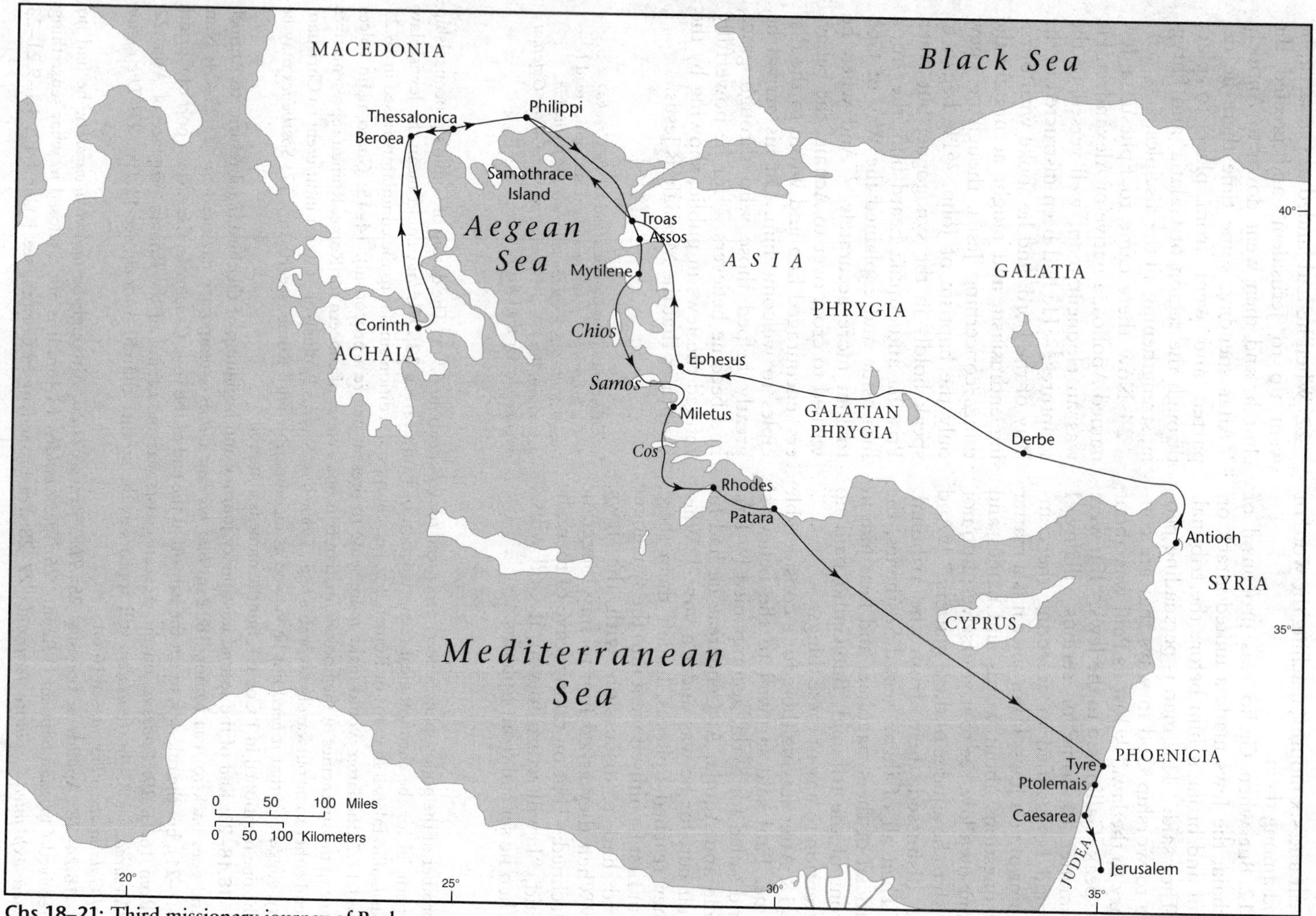

Chs 18–21: Third missionary journey of Paul.

19 While Apollos was in Corinth, Paul
passed through the interior regions
and came to Ephesus, where he found some
disciples. 2 He said to them, "Did you re-
ceive the Holy Spirit when you became be-
lievers?" They replied, "No, we have not
even heard that there is a Holy Spirit."
3 Then he said, "Into what then were you
baptized?" They answered, "Into John's
baptism." 4 Paul said, "John baptized with
the baptism of repentance, telling the peo-
ple to believe in the one who was to come
after him, that is, in Jesus." 5 On hearing
this, they were baptized in the name of the
Lord Jesus. 6 When Paul had laid his hands
on them, the Holy Spirit came upon them,
and they spoke in tongues and proph-
esied— 7 altogether there were about
twelve of them.

8 He entered the synagogue and for
three months spoke out boldly, and argued
persuasively about the kingdom of God.
9 When some stubbornly refused to believe
and spoke evil of the Way before the con-
gregation, he left them, taking the disciples
with him, and argued daily in the lecture
hall of Tyrannus.[a] 10 This continued for
two years, so that all the residents of Asia,
both Jews and Greeks, heard the word of
the Lord.

11 God did extraordinary miracles
through Paul, 12 so that when the handker-
chiefs or aprons that had touched his skin
were brought to the sick, their diseases left
them, and the evil spirits came out of them.
13 Then some itinerant Jewish exorcists
tried to use the name of the Lord Jesus over
those who had evil spirits, saying, "I adjure
you by the Jesus whom Paul proclaims."
14 Seven sons of a Jewish high priest named
Sceva were doing this. 15 But the evil spirit
said to them in reply, "Jesus I know, and
Paul I know; but who are you?" 16 Then the
man with the evil spirit leaped on them,
mastered them all, and so overpowered
them that they fled out of the house naked
and wounded. 17 When this became known
to all residents of Ephesus, both Jews and
Greeks, everyone was awestruck; and the
name of the Lord Jesus was praised. 18 Also
many of those who became believers con-
fessed and disclosed their practices. 19 A
number of those who practiced magic col-
lected their books and burned them public-
ly; when the value of these books[b] was
calculated, it was found to come to fifty
thousand silver coins. 20 So the word of the
Lord grew mightily and prevailed.

21 Now after these things had been ac-
complished, Paul resolved in the Spirit to
go through Macedonia and Achaia, and
then to go on to Jerusalem. He said, "After
I have gone there, I must also see Rome."

a Other ancient authorities read *of a certain Tyrannus, from eleven o'clock in the morning to four in the afternoon* *b* Gk *them*

19.1–41: Paul's long ministry in Ephesus. This period of more than two years (v. 10; cf. 20.31) forms the background of 1 and 2 Corinthians. **1:** *The interior regions* of Asia Minor (18.23). *Disciples* elsewhere in Acts means Christians. **2:** All who read the Jewish scriptures would know of *a Holy Spirit* (Ps 51.11; Isa 63.10,11). The reference may be to outward signs of the Spirit's presence (v. 6; 10.44–48n.). **3:** *John's baptism,* 13.25n. **5–6:** See 6.6n.; 8.17. **8:** *Synagogue,* 13.5n. *Kingdom of God,* 1.3n. **9:** *The Way,* v. 23; see 9.2n. *Tyrannus,* perhaps a local philosopher; the name appears in inscriptions in Ephesus. The hours mentioned in note *a* suggest the building was available to Paul during siesta time. **10:** During Paul's stay of *two years . . . all the residents of Asia* heard the word (note the churches of Rev 2–3). The mixed character of the audience (*Jews and Greeks*) continues to be noted (15.14n.). **12:** Compare 5.15; on parallels between Peter and Paul, see 14.8–18n. **13:** For *Jewish exorcists,* see Lk 11.19. For use of the *name* outside the circle of Jesus, see Mk 9.38–39. **14:** *Sceva,* a high priest by this name is not known. **15–16:** The story makes it clear that the name (v. 17; 3.6n.) does not belong to the realm of magic. On a number of occasions Acts attempts to distinguish Christian miracle working from the activities of religious charlatans and profiteers (8.18–24; 13.6–12; 16.16–19). **19:** Ephesus was such a noted center of *magic* that magical books were often called "Ephesian Scripts." **21:** *Must . . . see Rome,* 23.11; 27.24; cf. Rom 1.13–15; 15.22–29. **22:** A city treasurer named *Erastus* is mentioned at Rom 16.23; the city of

22 So he sent two of his helpers, Timothy and Erastus, to Macedonia, while he himself stayed for some time longer in Asia.

23 About that time no little disturbance broke out concerning the Way. 24 A man named Demetrius, a silversmith who made silver shrines of Artemis, brought no little business to the artisans. 25 These he gathered together, with the workers of the same trade, and said, "Men, you know that we get our wealth from this business. 26 You also see and hear that not only in Ephesus but in almost the whole of Asia this Paul has persuaded and drawn away a considerable number of people by saying that gods made with hands are not gods. 27 And there is danger not only that this trade of ours may come into disrepute but also that the temple of the great goddess Artemis will be scorned, and she will be deprived of her majesty that brought all Asia and the world to worship her."

28 When they heard this, they were enraged and shouted, "Great is Artemis of the Ephesians!" 29 The city was filled with the confusion; and people[a] rushed together to the theater, dragging with them Gaius and Aristarchus, Macedonians who were Paul's travel companions. 30 Paul wished to go into the crowd, but the disciples would not let him; 31 even some officials of the province of Asia,[b] who were friendly to him, sent him a message urging him not to venture into the theater. 32 Meanwhile, some were shouting one thing, some another; for the assembly was in confusion, and most of them did not know why they had come together. 33 Some of the crowd gave instructions to Alexander, whom the Jews had pushed forward. And Alexander motioned for silence and tried to make a defense before the people. 34 But when they recognized that he was a Jew, for about two hours all of them shouted in unison, "Great is Artemis of the Ephesians!" 35 But when the town clerk had quieted the crowd, he said, "Citizens of Ephesus, who is there that does not know that the city of the Ephesians is the temple keeper of the great Artemis and of the statue that fell from heaven?[c] 36 Since these things cannot be denied, you ought to be quiet and do nothing rash. 37 You have brought these men here who are neither temple robbers nor blasphemers of our[d] goddess. 38 If therefore Demetrius and the artisans with him have a complaint against anyone, the courts are open, and there are proconsuls; let them bring charges there against one another. 39 If there is anything further[e] you want to know, it must be settled in the regular assembly. 40 For we are in danger of being charged with rioting today, since there is no cause that we can give to justify this commotion." 41 When he had said this, he dismissed the assembly.

20 After the uproar had ceased, Paul sent for the disciples; and after en-

a Gk *they* *b* Gk *some of the Asiarchs* *c* Meaning of Gk uncertain *d* Other ancient authorities read *your* *e* Other ancient authorities read *about other matters*

his office is not named, but Romans was likely written in Corinth; the name also appears at 2 Tim 4.20 ("Erastus remained in Corinth"). A Corinthian inscription mentions a Roman official (an aedile) by this name. **24:** *Shrines,* apparently miniature temples for use in religious ceremonies or as souvenirs or amulets. *Artemis,* chief divinity of Ephesus; her temple was one of the seven wonders of the ancient world. **25:** *Wealth,* the story joins others in which gain by religious means is criticized (see vv. 15–16n.). **29:** The *theater* has been excavated and could seat at least 24,000. **31:** *Asiarchs* (in note *b*) held office in a league of the cities of Asia and promoted the emperor cult. They were *friendly to* Paul and so portray again the favorable disposition of high officials toward Christianity. The portrayal of such acceptance by high-status individuals suggested to Christian readers that social respectability was not beyond their grasp (16.37–38n.). **35:** *Temple keeper,* a designation assumed by Asiatic cities that had built a temple in honor of their patron god or the emperor. *The statue that fell from heaven,* apparently a meteorite. **36–40:** An argument that Christians were entitled to due process and that the actions taken thus far were unwarranted is put into the mouth of the town clerk.

20.1–6: The last visit to Greece. 2: *Through those regions,* revisiting the churches of Philippi, Thessalo-

couraging them and saying farewell, he left
for Macedonia. 2When he had gone
through those regions and had given the
believers[a] much encouragement, he came
to Greece, 3where he stayed for three
months. He was about to set sail for Syria
when a plot was made against him by the
Jews, and so he decided to return through
Macedonia. 4He was accompanied by So-
pater son of Pyrrhus from Beroea, by Aris-
tarchus and Secundus from Thessalonica,
by Gaius from Derbe, and by Timothy, as
well as by Tychicus and Trophimus from
Asia. 5They went ahead and were waiting
for us in Troas; 6but we sailed from Philip-
pi after the days of Unleavened Bread, and
in five days we joined them in Troas, where
we stayed for seven days.

7 On the first day of the week, when we
met to break bread, Paul was holding a dis-
cussion with them; since he intended to
leave the next day, he continued speaking
until midnight. 8There were many lamps in
the room upstairs where we were meeting.
9A young man named Eutychus, who was
sitting in the window, began to sink off into
a deep sleep while Paul talked still longer.
Overcome by sleep, he fell to the ground
three floors below and was picked up dead.
10But Paul went down, and bending over
him took him in his arms, and said, "Do
not be alarmed, for his life is in him."
11Then Paul went upstairs, and after he
had broken bread and eaten, he continued
to converse with them until dawn; then he
left. 12Meanwhile they had taken the boy
away alive and were not a little comforted.

13 We went ahead to the ship and set
sail for Assos, intending to take Paul on
board there; for he had made this arrange-
ment, intending to go by land himself.
14When he met us in Assos, we took him on
board and went to Mitylene. 15We sailed
from there, and on the following day we
arrived opposite Chios. The next day we
touched at Samos, and[b] the day after that
we came to Miletus. 16For Paul had decid-
ed to sail past Ephesus, so that he might not
have to spend time in Asia; he was eager to
be in Jerusalem, if possible, on the day of
Pentecost.

17 From Miletus he sent a message to
Ephesus, asking the elders of the church to
meet him. 18When they came to him, he
said to them:

"You yourselves know how I lived
among you the entire time from the first
day that I set foot in Asia, 19serving the
Lord with all humility and with tears, en-

a Gk *given them* *b* Other ancient authorities add *after remaining at Trogyllium*

nica, and Beroea (see 19.21). **3:** *Three months,* at Corinth (see 2 Cor 12.14; 13.1; the problems evident in 2 Corinthians are passed over in silence). *A plot . . . by the Jews,* 9.24; 20.19; 23.12. **4:** Paul's companions seem to be local representatives of churches that have contributed to the collection for Jerusalem organized by Paul (see 11.29n.) who are traveling with him to deliver it (Rom 15.25–29; 1 Cor 16.3–4). Apart from 24.17 there is no hint of this major project of Paul's in Acts. *Sopater,* perhaps the Sosipater of Rom 16.21. *Aristarchus,* 19.29; 27.2 (Col 4.10; Philem 24). A *Gaius* from Macedonia is mentioned in 19.29, but Derbe is in the same region as *Timothy*'s home (Lystra, see 16.1). *Tychicus,* Eph 6.21; Col 4.7; 2 Tim 4.12; Titus 3.12. *Trophimus,* 2 Tim 4.20. **5:** The "we" passages (16.10n.) resume here at Philippi, the city where the previous passage ended (16.17). **6:** *Days of Unleavened Bread,* 12.3.

20.7–38: The raising of Eutychus and the speech to the Ephesian elders. 7: *The first day of the week,* Sunday. *Break bread,* see 2.42n.; 27.36–37. **9:** *Eutychus,* a not uncommon name meaning "fortunate." *Three floors,* a tenement-style building is pictured. **10:** An understated miraculous resurrection (cf. 14.19–20). **13:** *Assos,* a port town on the coast, southwest of Troas, opposite the northern end of the island of Lesbos. **14:** *Mitylene,* capital city of Lesbos. **15:** *Chios,* an island south of Lesbos. *Samos,* an island southwest of Chios. *Miletus,* an important port on the western coast of Asia Minor at the mouth of the Meander. The "we" passages resume again at 21.1. **16:** *Sail past Ephesus,* while on route from Chios to Samos. *Pentecost,* see 2.1–41n. **17:** *Elders,* 14.23n. **18–35:** Paul's "farewell" address, the only speech in Acts explicitly addressed to Christians. It reviews Paul's accomplishments as depicted in Acts and looks forward to paint a picture of the church in Luke's day. **21:** Paul's mission has been consistently

during the trials that came to me through
the plots of the Jews. 20 I did not shrink
from doing anything helpful, proclaiming
the message to you and teaching you pub-
licly and from house to house, 21 as I testi-
fied to both Jews and Greeks about repen-
tance toward God and faith toward our
Lord Jesus. 22 And now, as a captive to the
Spirit,[a] I am on my way to Jerusalem, not
knowing what will happen to me there,
23 except that the Holy Spirit testifies to me
in every city that imprisonment and perse-
cutions are waiting for me. 24 But I do not
count my life of any value to myself, if only
I may finish my course and the ministry
that I received from the Lord Jesus, to testi-
fy to the good news of God's grace.

25 "And now I know that none of you,
among whom I have gone about proclaim-
ing the kingdom, will ever see my face
again. 26 Therefore I declare to you this day
that I am not responsible for the blood of
any of you, 27 for I did not shrink from de-
claring to you the whole purpose of God.
28 Keep watch over yourselves and over all
the flock, of which the Holy Spirit has
made you overseers, to shepherd the church
of God[b] that he obtained with the blood of
his own Son.[c] 29 I know that after I have
gone, savage wolves will come in among
you, not sparing the flock. 30 Some even
from your own group will come distorting
the truth in order to entice the disciples to
follow them. 31 Therefore be alert, remem-
bering that for three years I did not cease
night or day to warn everyone with tears.
32 And now I commend you to God and to
the message of his grace, a message that is
able to build you up and to give you the
inheritance among all who are sanctified.
33 I coveted no one's silver or gold or cloth-
ing. 34 You know for yourselves that I
worked with my own hands to support my-
self and my companions. 35 In all this I have
given you an example that by such work we
must support the weak, remembering the
words of the Lord Jesus, for he himself
said, 'It is more blessed to give than to re-
ceive.' "

36 When he had finished speaking, he
knelt down with them all and prayed.
37 There was much weeping among them
all; they embraced Paul and kissed him,
38 grieving especially because of what he
had said, that they would not see him
again. Then they brought him to the ship.

21 When we had parted from them and
set sail, we came by a straight course
to Cos, and the next day to Rhodes, and
from there to Patara.[d] 2 When we found
a ship bound for Phoenicia, we went on
board and set sail. 3 We came in sight of
Cyprus; and leaving it on our left, we sailed
to Syria and landed at Tyre, because the
ship was to unload its cargo there. 4 We
looked up the disciples and stayed there for
seven days. Through the Spirit they told
Paul not to go on to Jerusalem. 5 When our
days there were ended, we left and proceed-
ed on our journey; and all of them, with
wives and children, escorted us outside the
city. There we knelt down on the beach and
prayed 6 and said farewell to one another.

a Or *And now, bound in the spirit* *b* Other ancient authorities read *of the Lord* *c* Or *with his own blood*; Gk *with the blood of his Own* *d* Other ancient authorities add *and Myra*

portrayed as directed to both *Jews and Greeks.* **24–25:** *Finish my course . . . testify,* a premonition of martyrdom (2 Tim 4.6). **27:** *Purpose of God,* cf. 2.23; 4.28; 5.38–39; 13.36. **28:** *Overseers* (Gk "episkopoi"), used to designate officials in secular institutions; here it indicates those described as elders in v. 17. *Shepherd,* an image for leadership both in the Hebrew Bible (Jer 3.15; 23.1–4; Ezek 34.1–24) and in the nonbiblical world that also appears in the New Testament (Jn 21.15–17; Eph 4.11, "pastors"). At 1 Pet 5.1–4 elders are exhorted to "tend the flock of God." *With his own blood* (note *c*), understanding Jesus as a representative of God. Elsewhere in Luke-Acts, emphasis is placed on the resurrection, not the vicarious death of Christ. **29–30:** Mt 7.15; Mk 13.22; the Pastoral epistles. **34:** 18.3; 1 Cor 9.1–18. **35:** A saying of *Jesus* not found in the Gospels.

21.1–16: Journey to Jerusalem. 1: The "we" passages (16.10n.) resume. *Cos,* an island off the southwestern coast of Asia Minor. **4:** V. 12; 20.23. **7:** *Ptolemais,* a port town in Phoenicia (modern Akko, near

Then we went on board the ship, and they
returned home.
7 When we had finished[a] the voyage
from Tyre, we arrived at Ptolemais; and
we greeted the believers[b] and stayed with
them for one day. 8 The next day we left
and came to Caesarea; and we went into
the house of Philip the evangelist, one of
the seven, and stayed with him. 9 He had
four unmarried daughters[c] who had the
gift of prophecy. 10 While we were staying
there for several days, a prophet named Ag-
abus came down from Judea. 11 He came to
us and took Paul's belt, bound his own feet
and hands with it, and said, "Thus says the
Holy Spirit, 'This is the way the Jews in
Jerusalem will bind the man who owns this
belt and will hand him over to the Gen-
tiles.' " 12 When we heard this, we and the
people there urged him not to go up to Je-
rusalem. 13 Then Paul answered, "What are
you doing, weeping and breaking my
heart? For I am ready not only to be bound
but even to die in Jerusalem for the name of
the Lord Jesus." 14 Since he would not be
persuaded, we remained silent except to
say, "The Lord's will be done."
15 After these days we got ready and
started to go up to Jerusalem. 16 Some of
the disciples from Caesarea also came
along and brought us to the house of Mna-
son of Cyprus, an early disciple, with
whom we were to stay.
17 When we arrived in Jerusalem, the
brothers welcomed us warmly. 18 The next
day Paul went with us to visit James; and
all the elders were present. 19 After greeting
them, he related one by one the things that
God had done among the Gentiles through
his ministry. 20 When they heard it, they
praised God. Then they said to him, "You
see, brother, how many thousands of be-
lievers there are among the Jews, and they
are all zealous for the law. 21 They have
been told about you that you teach all the
Jews living among the Gentiles to forsake
Moses, and that you tell them not to cir-
cumcise their children or observe the cus-
toms. 22 What then is to be done? They will
certainly hear that you have come. 23 So do
what we tell you. We have four men who
are under a vow. 24 Join these men, go
through the rite of purification with them,
and pay for the shaving of their heads.
Thus all will know that there is nothing in
what they have been told about you, but
that you yourself observe and guard the
law. 25 But as for the Gentiles who have
become believers, we have sent a letter with
our judgment that they should abstain from
what has been sacrificed to idols and from
blood and from what is strangled[d] and
from fornication." 26 Then Paul took the
men, and the next day, having purified
himself, he entered the temple with them,
making public the completion of the days
of purification when the sacrifice would be
made for each of them.

a Or *continued* *b* Gk *brothers* *c* Gk *four daughters, virgins,* *d* Other ancient authorities lack *and from what is strangled*

Haifa), 35 km (22 mi) from Tyre. **8:** *Philip the evangelist* (8.5n.) had arrived in *Caesarea* (8.40n.) some time before. *One of the seven,* see 6.1–7. **9:** Philip's *daughters* became important figures in the church traditions of Hierapolis and Ephesus. **10–11:** *Agabus* (11.28), like Hebrew prophets (1 Kings 11.29–32; Isa 20.2–6), performs a symbolic act. The prediction is not strictly fulfilled in the chapters that follow. **12:** V. 4. **14:** Paul appears as a heroic figure.

21.17–26: Paul's conformity to Judaism. He takes a vow in order to allay suspicions. **16:** *An early disciple,* note Christianity in connection with *Cyprus* at 4.36; 11.19–20; 13.4–12. **17–20:** The *Jerusalem* church accepts Paul and his accomplishments as complementary to their own in a harmonious portrait of unity (cf. Gal 2). **18:** *James,* see 12.17n.; *the elders,* 11.30n. The "we" passage stops here. **20:** *Thousands of believers,* Acts represents the success of Christianity among *Jews* as phenomenal (cf. 6.7). *Zealous for the law,* see 11.2n.; 15.1n., 15.5n.; cf. Gal 2. **21:** The charge has been anticipated (16.3n.). The informants are not identified (see v. 28). **23–24:** Paul can demonstrate his faithfulness to the law by undergoing *purification* for uncleanness with some others and paying the expenses upon their release from a nazirite *vow* (18.18n.). **25:** He is told of the decree as though he had not heard of it (see 16.4).

27 When the seven days were almost
completed, the Jews from Asia, who had
seen him in the temple, stirred up the whole
crowd. They seized him, 28 shouting, "Fel-
low Israelites, help! This is the man who is
teaching everyone everywhere against our
people, our law, and this place; more than
that, he has actually brought Greeks into
the temple and has defiled this holy place."
29 For they had previously seen Trophimus
the Ephesian with him in the city, and they
supposed that Paul had brought him into
the temple. 30 Then all the city was aroused,
and the people rushed together. They seized
Paul and dragged him out of the temple,
and immediately the doors were shut.
31 While they were trying to kill him, word
came to the tribune of the cohort that all
Jerusalem was in an uproar. 32 Immediately
he took soldiers and centurions and ran
down to them. When they saw the tribune
and the soldiers, they stopped beating Paul.
33 Then the tribune came, arrested him, and
ordered him to be bound with two chains;
he inquired who he was and what he had
done. 34 Some in the crowd shouted one
thing, some another; and as he could not
learn the facts because of the uproar, he
ordered him to be brought into the bar-
racks. 35 When Paul[a] came to the steps, the
violence of the mob was so great that he
had to be carried by the soldiers. 36 The
crowd that followed kept shouting, "Away
with him!"

37 Just as Paul was about to be brought
into the barracks, he said to the tribune,
"May I say something to you?" The tri-
bune[b] replied, "Do you know Greek?
38 Then you are not the Egyptian who re-
cently stirred up a revolt and led the four
thousand assassins out into the wilder-
ness?" 39 Paul replied, "I am a Jew, from
Tarsus in Cilicia, a citizen of an important
city; I beg you, let me speak to the people."
40 When he had given him permission, Paul
stood on the steps and motioned to the peo-
ple for silence; and when there was a great
hush, he addressed them in the Hebrew[c]
language, saying:

22 "Brothers and fathers, listen to the
defense that I now make before
you."

2 When they heard him addressing them
in Hebrew,[c] they became even more quiet.
Then he said:

3 "I am a Jew, born in Tarsus in Cilicia,
but brought up in this city at the feet of
Gamaliel, educated strictly according to
our ancestral law, being zealous for God,
just as all of you are today. 4 I persecuted
this Way up to the point of death by bind-
ing both men and women and putting them
in prison, 5 as the high priest and the whole
council of elders can testify about me. From
them I also received letters to the brothers
in Damascus, and I went there in order to
bind those who were there and to bring
them back to Jerusalem for punishment.

6 "While I was on my way and ap-
proaching Damascus, about noon a great

a Gk *he* *b* Gk *He* *c* That is, *Aramaic*

21.27–40: Uproar in the Temple and arrest of Paul. Seized after a disturbance in the Temple, Paul tells of his conversion. **28:** It was a capital offense for non-Jews to pass beyond the Court of the Gentiles; an inscription stating this has been discovered (cf. Josephus, *War* 5.193–194; 6.125–126). **29:** *Trophimus,* 20.4; 2 Tim 4.20. **31:** A military *tribune* commanded a *cohort* (a detachment of 1,000 men); this would have been stationed in the citadel Antonia, which had access to the Temple courtyard (see Josephus, *War* 5.244). **33:** Paul's case came into the hands of Roman, not Jewish, authorities. **36:** *Away with him,* 22.22; cf. Lk 23.18. **38:** The question in Greek may be: "Are you not the Egyptian?" Concerning *the Egyptian,* a pseudo-messiah who, with thousands of followers, had planned to take Jerusalem from the Romans, see Josephus, *War* 2.261–263 (which puts the number at about 30,000); *Ant.* 20.169–172. **39:** *Paul* gives assurances that he is not the Egyptian. *Tarsus,* 9.30n.

22.1–29: Defense in the Temple and Roman custody. 1: *Defense* is the principal theme of the next chapters (24.10; 25.8,16; 26.1–2). It has a clear function at the level of the narrative and also allows Luke to defend Paul before readers who may have had questions about him. **3:** *Brought up,* educated. *Gamaliel,* see 5.34n. *Zealous,* 21.20; in Gal 1.14 as a self-description of Paul. **4–21:** Cf. 9.1–18; 26.9–18. **9:** In 9.7

light from heaven suddenly shone about
me. 7 I fell to the ground and heard a voice
saying to me, 'Saul, Saul, why are you per-
secuting me?' 8 I answered, 'Who are you,
Lord?' Then he said to me, 'I am Jesus of
Nazareth[a] whom you are persecuting.'
9 Now those who were with me saw the
light but did not hear the voice of the one
who was speaking to me. 10 I asked, 'What
am I to do, Lord?' The Lord said to me,
'Get up and go to Damascus; there you will
be told everything that has been assigned to
you to do.' 11 Since I could not see because
of the brightness of that light, those who
were with me took my hand and led me to
Damascus.
12 "A certain Ananias, who was a de-
vout man according to the law and well
spoken of by all the Jews living there,
13 came to me; and standing beside me, he
said, 'Brother Saul, regain your sight!' In
that very hour I regained my sight and saw
him. 14 Then he said, 'The God of our an-
cestors has chosen you to know his will, to
see the Righteous One and to hear his own
voice; 15 for you will be his witness to all
the world of what you have seen and heard.
16 And now why do you delay? Get up, be
baptized, and have your sins washed away,
calling on his name.'
17 "After I had returned to Jerusalem
and while I was praying in the temple, I fell
into a trance 18 and saw Jesus[b] saying to
me, 'Hurry and get out of Jerusalem quick-
ly, because they will not accept your testi-
mony about me.' 19 And I said, 'Lord, they
themselves know that in every synagogue I
imprisoned and beat those who believed in
you. 20 And while the blood of your witness
Stephen was shed, I myself was standing
by, approving and keeping the coats of
those who killed him.' 21 Then he said to
me, 'Go, for I will send you far away to the
Gentiles.' "
22 Up to this point they listened to him,
but then they shouted, "Away with such a
fellow from the earth! For he should not be
allowed to live." 23 And while they were
shouting, throwing off their cloaks, and
tossing dust into the air, 24 the tribune di-
rected that he was to be brought into the
barracks, and ordered him to be examined
by flogging, to find out the reason for this
outcry against him. 25 But when they had
tied him up with thongs,[c] Paul said to the
centurion who was standing by, "Is it legal
for you to flog a Roman citizen who is un-
condemned?" 26 When the centurion heard
that, he went to the tribune and said to
him, "What are you about to do? This man
is a Roman citizen." 27 The tribune came
and asked Paul,[b] "Tell me, are you a Ro-
man citizen?" And he said, "Yes." 28 The
tribune answered, "It cost me a large sum
of money to get my citizenship." Paul said,
"But I was born a citizen." 29 Immediately
those who were about to examine him
drew back from him; and the tribune also
was afraid, for he realized that Paul was a
Roman citizen and that he had bound him.
30 Since he wanted to find out what
Paul[d] was being accused of by the Jews,
the next day he released him and ordered
the chief priests and the entire council to
meet. He brought Paul down and had him
stand before them.

23 While Paul was looking intently at
the council he said, "Brothers,[e] up
to this day I have lived my life with a clear

a Gk *the Nazorean* b Gk *him* c Or *up for the lashes* d Gk *he* e Gk *Men, brothers*

the companions heard the voice but saw no one. **14–15:** What Ananias says here is roughly parallel to what the Lord tells him in 9.15. **17–21:** The report of the vision is not given in the other conversion accounts. Paul's commission to the Gentiles is significantly located in the *temple.* **20:** See 7.58. **24:** *Examined by flogging* to determine the truth of the matter (2 Cor 11.23). **25–29:** That Paul is *a Roman citizen* is disclosed at the last moment; see 16.37–38n. In the early part of Claudius's reign *citizenship* was often purchased for *a large sum.* The scene increases Paul's status for readers of Acts and reinforces the theme of the compatibility of Christianity and Roman life; there is nothing in Paul's letters to indicate that he was a Roman citizen.

22.30–23.11: Paul before the Sanhedrin. The tribune brings him before it to get evidence, not to try

conscience before God." 2 Then the high
priest Ananias ordered those standing near
him to strike him on the mouth. 3 At this
Paul said to him, "God will strike you, you
whitewashed wall! Are you sitting there to
judge me according to the law, and yet in
violation of the law you order me to be
struck?" 4 Those standing nearby said, "Do
you dare to insult God's high priest?" 5 And
Paul said, "I did not realize, brothers, that
he was high priest; for it is written, 'You
shall not speak evil of a leader of your peo-
ple.' "

6 When Paul noticed that some were
Sadducees and others were Pharisees, he
called out in the council, "Brothers, I am a
Pharisee, a son of Pharisees. I am on trial
concerning the hope of the resurrection[a] of
the dead." 7 When he said this, a dissension
began between the Pharisees and the Sad-
ducees, and the assembly was divided.
8 (The Sadducees say that there is no resur-
rection, or angel, or spirit; but the Pharisees
acknowledge all three.) 9 Then a great clam-
or arose, and certain scribes of the Phari-
sees' group stood up and contended, "We
find nothing wrong with this man. What if
a spirit or an angel has spoken to him?"
10 When the dissension became violent, the
tribune, fearing that they would tear Paul
to pieces, ordered the soldiers to go down,
take him by force, and bring him into the
barracks.

11 That night the Lord stood near him
and said, "Keep up your courage! For just
as you have testified for me in Jerusalem, so
you must bear witness also in Rome."

12 In the morning the Jews joined in a
conspiracy and bound themselves by an
oath neither to eat nor drink until they had
killed Paul. 13 There were more than forty
who joined in this conspiracy. 14 They went
to the chief priests and elders and said, "We
have strictly bound ourselves by an oath to
taste no food until we have killed Paul.
15 Now then, you and the council must no-
tify the tribune to bring him down to you,
on the pretext that you want to make a
more thorough examination of his case.
And we are ready to do away with him
before he arrives."

16 Now the son of Paul's sister heard
about the ambush; so he went and gained
entrance to the barracks and told Paul.
17 Paul called one of the centurions and
said, "Take this young man to the tribune,
for he has something to report to him."
18 So he took him, brought him to the tri-
bune, and said, "The prisoner Paul called
me and asked me to bring this young man
to you; he has something to tell you."
19 The tribune took him by the hand, drew
him aside privately, and asked, "What is it
that you have to report to me?" 20 He an-
swered, "The Jews have agreed to ask you
to bring Paul down to the council tomor-
row, as though they were going to inquire
more thoroughly into his case. 21 But do not
be persuaded by them, for more than forty
of their men are lying in ambush for him.
They have bound themselves by an oath
neither to eat nor drink until they kill him.
They are ready now and are waiting for
your consent." 22 So the tribune dismissed

a Gk *concerning hope and resurrection*

him. **22.30:** The tribune calls for an advisory meeting of the *council;* see 5.21n. **23.2:** *Ananias, high priest* in the reigns of Claudius and Nero, was murdered by rebels about 66 CE. **3:** *Whitewashed wall,* cf. Ezek 13.10–15; Mt 23.27. **5:** Ex 22.28. It is strange that Paul does not recognize the *high priest.* **6:** *Paul* as a *Pharisee* (26.5; Phil 3.5) realizes he can exploit a difference of opinion between *Sadducees* and *Pharisees* over the *resurrection* (see Josephus, *War* 2.163–165). **8:** *Sadducees* denied a *resurrection* (Mk 12.18). **9:** The *Pharisees* side with Paul (see 15.5n.). **10:** Paul is rescued from mob violence for a second time by an agent of Rome (21.33–36). **11:** A vision (cf. 18.9–10) provides assurance that martyrdom will not occur in Jerusalem (21.13).

23.12–35: A plot to kill Paul results in his transfer to Caesarea, the seat of the Roman governor. **12:** *Conspiracy,* 9.24; 20.19. **16:** There is no other extant information about Paul's family. Paul's education in Jerusalem (22.3) could suggest that other family members were there. **17–22:** The prisoner Paul's access to the commanders shows some favoritism. **23:** *Caesarea,* 8.40n. The number of *soldiers* emphasizes the

the young man, ordering him, "Tell no one
that you have informed me of this."
23 Then he summoned two of the centu-
rions and said, "Get ready to leave by nine
o'clock tonight for Caesarea with two hun-
dred soldiers, seventy horsemen, and two
hundred spearmen. 24 Also provide mounts
for Paul to ride, and take him safely to Felix
the governor." 25 He wrote a letter to this
effect:
26 "Claudius Lysias to his Excellency
the governor Felix, greetings. 27 This man
was seized by the Jews and was about to be
killed by them, but when I had learned that
he was a Roman citizen, I came with the
guard and rescued him. 28 Since I wanted to
know the charge for which they accused
him, I had him brought to their council. 29 I
found that he was accused concerning
questions of their law, but was charged
with nothing deserving death or imprison-
ment. 30 When I was informed that there
would be a plot against the man, I sent him
to you at once, ordering his accusers also to
state before you what they have against
him.[a]"
31 So the soldiers, according to their in-
structions, took Paul and brought him dur-
ing the night to Antipatris. 32 The next day
they let the horsemen go on with him, while
they returned to the barracks. 33 When they
came to Caesarea and delivered the letter to
the governor, they presented Paul also be-
fore him. 34 On reading the letter, he asked
what province he belonged to, and when he
learned that he was from Cilicia, 35 he said,
"I will give you a hearing when your accus-
ers arrive." Then he ordered that he be kept
under guard in Herod's headquarters.[b]

24 Five days later the high priest Ana-
nias came down with some elders
and an attorney, a certain Tertullus, and
they reported their case against Paul to the
governor. 2 When Paul[c] had been sum-
moned, Tertullus began to accuse him, say-
ing:
"Your Excellency,[d] because of you we
have long enjoyed peace, and reforms have
been made for this people because of your
foresight. 3 We welcome this in every way
and everywhere with utmost gratitude.
4 But, to detain you no further, I beg you to
hear us briefly with your customary gra-
ciousness. 5 We have, in fact, found this
man a pestilent fellow, an agitator among
all the Jews throughout the world, and a
ringleader of the sect of the Nazarenes.[e]
6 He even tried to profane the temple, and
so we seized him.[f] 8 By examining him
yourself you will be able to learn from him
concerning everything of which we accuse
him."
9 The Jews also joined in the charge by
asserting that all this was true.

a Other ancient authorities add *Farewell*
b Gk *praetorium* *c* Gk *he* *d* Gk lacks *Your Excellency* *e* Gk *Nazoreans* *f* Other ancient authorities add *and we would have judged him according to our law. 7But the chief captain Lysias came and with great violence took him out of our hands, 8commanding his accusers to come before you.*

danger faced. The Gk word translated *spearmen* is obscure. **24:** Antonius *Felix,* procurator of Judea (ca. 52–56 CE), brother of Pallas, a favorite freedman of Claudius. **26:** *His Excellency,* the word used in addressing Theophilus (Lk 1.3). **27–30:** The letter summarizes the preceding events and perhaps casts the tribune in a better light. As was the case with Jesus (Lk 23.4,14–16,20–25), Romans find no serious charges (v. 29; cf. 18.14–16). **31:** *Antipatris,* a city in the Plain of Sharon on the main road to Caesarea. **35:** *Herod's headquarters,* a palace built by Herod the Great and occupied by the Roman governors in Palestine.

24.1–27: Paul before Felix. The apostle denies the charges, and the governor postpones the case. **2–4:** *Tertullus* begins the prosecution with the customary method of opening a speech with praise that is intended to attract the attention and sympathy of the one being addressed. **5:** *Agitator,* a charge of political sedition (see 16.21; 17.7; 18.13) would be taken seriously by a Roman court. *Sect,* or party, is used in a bad sense here and at 24.14; 28.22; it is used of the Sadducees at 5.17. *Nazarenes,* the term otherwise used in the singular to identify Jesus (2.22; 3.6; 4.10; 6.14; 22.8) is here used in the plural to describe Christians. **6:** *Profane the temple,* 21.28. **10:** See 22.1n. **14:** *The Way* (see 9.2n.) is compatible

10 When the governor motioned to him to speak, Paul replied:

"I cheerfully make my defense, knowing that for many years you have been a judge over this nation. 11 As you can find out, it is not more than twelve days since I went up to worship in Jerusalem. 12 They did not find me disputing with anyone in the temple or stirring up a crowd either in the synagogues or throughout the city. 13 Neither can they prove to you the charge that they now bring against me. 14 But this I admit to you, that according to the Way, which they call a sect, I worship the God of our ancestors, believing everything laid down according to the law or written in the prophets. 15 I have a hope in God—a hope that they themselves also accept—that there will be a resurrection of both[a] the righteous and the unrighteous. 16 Therefore I do my best always to have a clear conscience toward God and all people. 17 Now after some years I came to bring alms to my nation and to offer sacrifices. 18 While I was doing this, they found me in the temple, completing the rite of purification, without any crowd or disturbance. 19 But there were some Jews from Asia—they ought to be here before you to make an accusation, if they have anything against me. 20 Or let these men here tell what crime they had found when I stood before the council, 21 unless it was this one sentence that I called out while standing before them, 'It is about the resurrection of the dead that I am on trial before you today.'"

22 But Felix, who was rather well informed about the Way, adjourned the hearing with the comment, "When Lysias the tribune comes down, I will decide your case." 23 Then he ordered the centurion to keep him in custody, but to let him have some liberty and not to prevent any of his friends from taking care of his needs.

24 Some days later when Felix came with his wife Drusilla, who was Jewish, he sent for Paul and heard him speak concerning faith in Christ Jesus. 25 And as he discussed justice, self-control, and the coming judgment, Felix became frightened and said, "Go away for the present; when I have an opportunity, I will send for you." 26 At the same time he hoped that money would be given him by Paul, and for that reason he used to send for him very often and converse with him.

27 After two years had passed, Felix was succeeded by Porcius Festus; and since he wanted to grant the Jews a favor, Felix left Paul in prison.

25 Three days after Festus had arrived in the province, he went up from Caesarea to Jerusalem 2 where the chief priests and the leaders of the Jews gave him a report against Paul. They appealed to him 3 and requested, as a favor to them against Paul,[b] to have him transferred to Jerusalem. They were, in fact, planning an ambush to kill him along the way. 4 Festus replied that Paul was being kept at Caesarea, and that he himself intended to go there shortly. 5 "So," he said, "let those of you who have the authority come down with me, and if there is anything wrong about the man, let them accuse him."

6 After he had stayed among them not more than eight or ten days, he went down

[a] Other ancient authorities read *of the dead, both of*
[b] Gk *him*

with the ancestral religion. **15:** *Resurrection,* here general belief in resurrection as common ground (also v. 21). **16:** *Clear conscience,* 20.20,27,33; 23.1. **17:** *To bring alms,* may connect to 21.23–26 but is reminiscent of Paul's plan in Rom 15.25–29 to deliver the collection (see 11.29n.; 20.4n.). **23:** *Custody,* perhaps protective custody. **24:** *Drusilla* was the sister of Herod Agrippa II and Bernice (25.13); she had left her husband Azizus, king of Emesa, to marry Felix. **25–26:** Cf. Mk 6.20. *Felix* embodies both positive and negative features, but ultimately his corruption means that Paul remains in prison. **27:** *After two years had passed,* either from Felix's appointment or Paul's arrest. *Porcius Festus,* appointed procurator of Judea by Nero in 60 CE.

25.1–12: Appeal to the emperor. Paul insists on a Roman trial, and Festus consents to send him to Rome. **3:** See 23.12. **6:** See 18.12. **8:** Paul maintains that he is both a good Jew and a good Roman citizen.

to Caesarea; the next day he took his seat on the tribunal and ordered Paul to be brought. 7 When he arrived, the Jews who had gone down from Jerusalem surrounded him, bringing many serious charges against him, which they could not prove. 8 Paul said in his defense, "I have in no way committed an offense against the law of the Jews, or against the temple, or against the emperor." 9 But Festus, wishing to do the Jews a favor, asked Paul, "Do you wish to go up to Jerusalem and be tried there before me on these charges?" 10 Paul said, "I am appealing to the emperor's tribunal; this is where I should be tried. I have done no wrong to the Jews, as you very well know. 11 Now if I am in the wrong and have committed something for which I deserve to die, I am not trying to escape death; but if there is nothing to their charges against me, no one can turn me over to them. I appeal to the emperor." 12 Then Festus, after he had conferred with his council, replied, "You have appealed to the emperor; to the emperor you will go."

13 After several days had passed, King Agrippa and Bernice arrived at Caesarea to welcome Festus. 14 Since they were staying there several days, Festus laid Paul's case before the king, saying, "There is a man here who was left in prison by Felix. 15 When I was in Jerusalem, the chief priests and the elders of the Jews informed me about him and asked for a sentence against him. 16 I told them that it was not the custom of the Romans to hand over anyone before the accused had met the accusers face to face and had been given an opportunity to make a defense against the charge. 17 So when they met here, I lost no time, but on the next day took my seat on the tribunal and ordered the man to be brought. 18 When the accusers stood up, they did not charge him with any of the crimes[a] that I was expecting. 19 Instead they had certain points of disagreement with him about their own religion and about a certain Jesus, who had died, but whom Paul asserted to be alive. 20 Since I was at a loss how to investigate these questions, I asked whether he wished to go to Jerusalem and be tried there on these charges.[b] 21 But when Paul had appealed to be kept in custody for the decision of his Imperial Majesty, I ordered him to be held until I could send him to the emperor." 22 Agrippa said to Festus, "I would like to hear the man myself." "Tomorrow," he said, "you will hear him."

23 So on the next day Agrippa and Bernice came with great pomp, and they entered the audience hall with the military tribunes and the prominent men of the city. Then Festus gave the order and Paul was brought in. 24 And Festus said, "King Agrippa and all here present with us, you see this man about whom the whole Jewish community petitioned me, both in Jerusalem and here, shouting that he ought not to live any longer. 25 But I found that he had done nothing deserving death; and when he appealed to his Imperial Majesty, I decided to send him. 26 But I have nothing definite to write to our sovereign about him. Therefore I have brought him before all of you, and especially before you, King Agrippa, so that, after we have examined him, I may

a Other ancient authorities read *with anything*
b Gk *on them*

9: *Favor,* 24.27. **10:** Paul fears being turned over to a Jewish court; therefore he insists on *the emperor's tribunal,* i.e., trial according to Roman law. **11–12:** Paul's *appeal* to the *emperor* becomes the mechanism that takes him to Rome (19.21; 23.11). Details of the law of appeals are unclear.

25.13–26.32: Paul's defense before Agrippa. Paul's speech is intended to present a model defense of Christianity and allows for the pronouncement of a symbolic Roman acquittal. **25.13:** *King Agrippa,* Herod Agrippa II (ruled 53–ca. 93 CE), sided with the Romans in the First Jewish Revolt. He and his sister *Bernice* were children of Herod Agrippa I (12.1n.). **16:** Roman judicial process is put in a good light. **18–20:** The *accusers* do not bring a *charge* of sedition (24.5). Cf. 18.13–16; but in this case Festus does not dismiss the charges. **25:** *Nothing deserving death* is the repeated verdict of the Roman authorities handling Paul's case (26.31; cf. Lk 23.4,15,22). *His Imperial Majesty,* lit. "Augustus," one of the imperial

have something to write— 27 for it seems to
me unreasonable to send a prisoner with-
out indicating the charges against him."

26 Agrippa said to Paul, "You have
permission to speak for yourself."
Then Paul stretched out his hand and began
to defend himself:

2 "I consider myself fortunate that it is
before you, King Agrippa, I am to make my
defense today against all the accusations of
the Jews, 3 because you are especially famil-
iar with all the customs and controversies
of the Jews; therefore I beg of you to listen
to me patiently.

4 "All the Jews know my way of life
from my youth, a life spent from the begin-
ning among my own people and in Jerusa-
lem. 5 They have known for a long time, if
they are willing to testify, that I have be-
longed to the strictest sect of our religion
and lived as a Pharisee. 6 And now I stand
here on trial on account of my hope in the
promise made by God to our ancestors, 7 a
promise that our twelve tribes hope to at-
tain, as they earnestly worship day and
night. It is for this hope, your Excellency,[a]
that I am accused by Jews! 8 Why is it
thought incredible by any of you that God
raises the dead?

9 "Indeed, I myself was convinced that I
ought to do many things against the name
of Jesus of Nazareth.[b] 10 And that is what
I did in Jerusalem; with authority received
from the chief priests, I not only locked up
many of the saints in prison, but I also cast
my vote against them when they were being
condemned to death. 11 By punishing them
often in all the synagogues I tried to force
them to blaspheme; and since I was so furi-
ously enraged at them, I pursued them even
to foreign cities.

12 "With this in mind, I was traveling to
Damascus with the authority and commis-
sion of the chief priests, 13 when at midday
along the road, your Excellency,[a] I saw a
light from heaven, brighter than the sun,
shining around me and my companions.
14 When we had all fallen to the ground, I
heard a voice saying to me in the Hebrew[c]
language, 'Saul, Saul, why are you perse-
cuting me? It hurts you to kick against the
goads.' 15 I asked, 'Who are you, Lord?'
The Lord answered, 'I am Jesus whom you
are persecuting. 16 But get up and stand on
your feet; for I have appeared to you for
this purpose, to appoint you to serve and
testify to the things in which you have seen
me[d] and to those in which I will appear to
you. 17 I will rescue you from your people
and from the Gentiles—to whom I am
sending you 18 to open their eyes so that
they may turn from darkness to light and
from the power of Satan to God, so that
they may receive forgiveness of sins and a
place among those who are sanctified by
faith in me.'

19 "After that, King Agrippa, I was not
disobedient to the heavenly vision, 20 but
declared first to those in Damascus, then in
Jerusalem and throughout the countryside
of Judea, and also to the Gentiles, that they
should repent and turn to God and do
deeds consistent with repentance. 21 For
this reason the Jews seized me in the temple
and tried to kill me. 22 To this day I have

a Gk *O king* b Gk *the Nazorean* c That is, Aramaic d Other ancient authorities read *the things that you have seen*

titles. **26.1:** The scene set for Paul's speech fulfills 9.15 and Lk 21.12–15. Compare Jesus' appearance before Herod Antipas (Lk 23.6–12). **2:** *Defense,* 22.1n. **3:** The narrative assumes that Agrippa was a practicing Jew. **4:** *Among my own people,* stresses Paul's thoroughly Jewish upbringing (22.3n.; Phil 3.5). **8:** *You,* i.e., the Jewish people. **9–20:** A third account of Paul's conversion (9.1–8; 22.4–16). **10:** *In Jerusalem,* according to 9.1–2 Paul's authorization concerned Damascus. **14:** Here *all* fall *to the ground* and the *voice* speaks *Hebrew,* quoting a common Greek proverb about the futility of resisting the divine will (cf. 9.4; 22.7); a goad is a pointed stick used to prod an ox or other animals. **16:** Only in this account does Paul's commission on the road come directly from Jesus (cf. Gal 1.1); there is no mention of Ananias or Paul's blindness. **20:** Paul's mission is universal, directed to both Jews and Greeks. **21:** *For this reason,* i.e., inclusion of the Gentiles. **22–23:** *The prophets and Moses . . . the Messiah must suffer,* 3.18n.; 10.43;

had help from God, and so I stand here,
testifying to both small and great, saying
nothing but what the prophets and Moses
said would take place: 23 that the Messiah[a]
must suffer, and that, by being the first to
rise from the dead, he would proclaim light
both to our people and to the Gentiles."
24 While he was making this defense,
Festus exclaimed, "You are out of your
mind, Paul! Too much learning is driving
you insane!" 25 But Paul said, "I am not out
of my mind, most excellent Festus, but I am
speaking the sober truth. 26 Indeed the king
knows about these things, and to him I
speak freely; for I am certain that none of
these things has escaped his notice, for this
was not done in a corner. 27 King Agrippa,
do you believe the prophets? I know that
you believe." 28 Agrippa said to Paul, "Are
you so quickly persuading me to become
a Christian?"[b] 29 Paul replied, "Whether
quickly or not, I pray to God that not only
you but also all who are listening to me
today might become such as I am—except
for these chains."
30 Then the king got up, and with him
the governor and Bernice and those who
had been seated with them; 31 and as they
were leaving, they said to one another,
"This man is doing nothing to deserve
death or imprisonment." 32 Agrippa said to
Festus, "This man could have been set free
if he had not appealed to the emperor."

27 When it was decided that we were
to sail for Italy, they transferred
Paul and some other prisoners to a centuri-
on of the Augustan Cohort, named Julius.
2 Embarking on a ship of Adramyttium that
was about to set sail to the ports along the
coast of Asia, we put to sea, accompanied
by Aristarchus, a Macedonian from Thes-
salonica. 3 The next day we put in at Sidon;
and Julius treated Paul kindly, and allowed
him to go to his friends to be cared for.
4 Putting out to sea from there, we sailed
under the lee of Cyprus, because the winds
were against us. 5 After we had sailed across
the sea that is off Cilicia and Pamphylia, we
came to Myra in Lycia. 6 There the centuri-
on found an Alexandrian ship bound for
Italy and put us on board. 7 We sailed slow-
ly for a number of days and arrived with
difficulty off Cnidus, and as the wind was
against us, we sailed under the lee of Crete
off Salmone. 8 Sailing past it with difficulty,
we came to a place called Fair Havens, near
the city of Lasea.
9 Since much time had been lost and
sailing was now dangerous, because even
the Fast had already gone by, Paul advised
them, 10 saying, "Sirs, I can see that the voy-
age will be with danger and much heavy
loss, not only of the cargo and the ship, but
also of our lives." 11 But the centurion paid
more attention to the pilot and to the own-
er of the ship than to what Paul said.
12 Since the harbor was not suitable for
spending the winter, the majority was in
favor of putting to sea from there, on the
chance that somehow they could reach

a Or *the Christ* b Or *Quickly you will persuade me to play the Christian*

Lk 24.25–27,44–47. **27:** See v. 3. **28:** *Christian,* see 11.25–26n. **31:** *Nothing to deserve death or imprisonment,* a further "acquittal" (25.25n.). **32:** See 25.11–12n.

27.1–44: Shipwreck. A dangerous winter voyage ends in shipwreck. **1:** The "we" passages (16.10n.) resume here. *The Augustan Cohort,* a unit of this name was stationed in Syria in the first century. **2:** *Adramyttium,* a seaport south of Troas (16.8). *Aristarchus,* 19.29; 20.4. *Thessalonica,* 17.1n. **3:** *Sidon,* a Phoenician seaport, north of Tyre. *Julius treated Paul kindly,* compare the centurions of Lk 7.1–10; 23.47; and of course Cornelius (10.1–2n.). *Friends,* i.e., Christians. **4:** *Under the lee of Cyprus,* apparently north of the island. **5–6:** *Myra* on the southern coast of Asia Minor was a regular stage in the route of Egyptian grain ships bound for Italy (see v. 38). **7:** *Cnidus,* on the mainland northwest of Rhodes. *Under the lee of Crete,* to its south for shelter from the *wind; Salmone* is at the northeast tip of the island. **8:** *Fair Havens,* a bay on the southern coast of Crete. *Lasea,* a city somewhat inland and east of Fair Havens. **9:** *Sailing was . . . dangerous* after September and ceased from mid-November until mid-March. *The Fast,* the Day of Atonement, in September or October. **16:** *Cauda,* south of Crete. *The ship's boat* (see

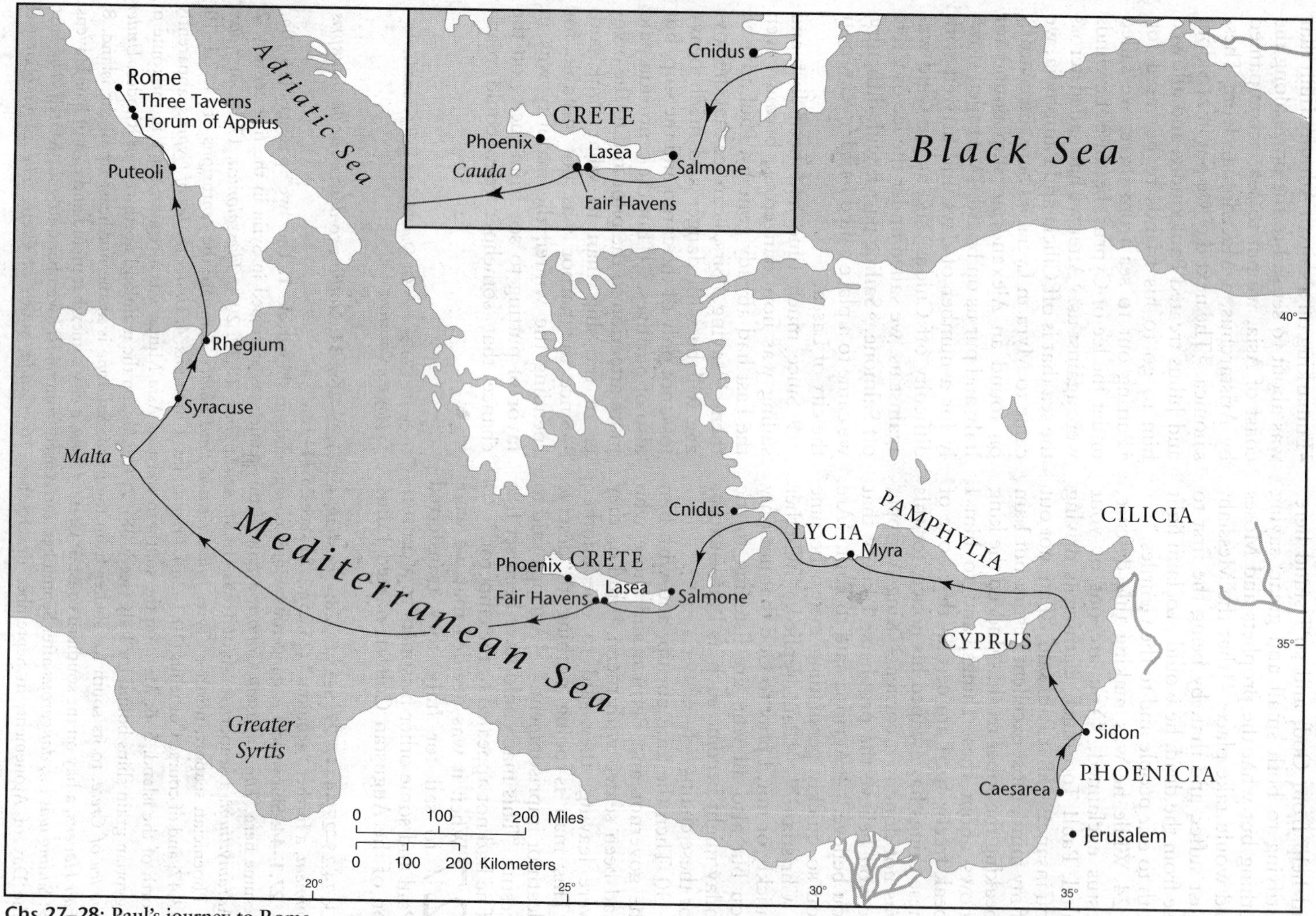

Chs 27–28: Paul's journey to Rome.

Phoenix, where they could spend the win-
ter. It was a harbor of Crete, facing south-
west and northwest.
13 When a moderate south wind began
to blow, they thought they could achieve
their purpose; so they weighed anchor and
began to sail past Crete, close to the shore.
14 But soon a violent wind, called the north-
easter, rushed down from Crete.[a] 15 Since
the ship was caught and could not be
turned head-on into the wind, we gave way
to it and were driven. 16 By running under
the lee of a small island called Cauda[b] we
were scarcely able to get the ship's boat
under control. 17 After hoisting it up they
took measures[c] to undergird the ship;
then, fearing that they would run on the
Syrtis, they lowered the sea anchor and so
were driven. 18 We were being pounded by
the storm so violently that on the next day
they began to throw the cargo overboard,
19 and on the third day with their own
hands they threw the ship's tackle over-
board. 20 When neither sun nor stars ap-
peared for many days, and no small tem-
pest raged, all hope of our being saved was
at last abandoned.
21 Since they had been without food for
a long time, Paul then stood up among
them and said, "Men, you should have lis-
tened to me and not have set sail from
Crete and thereby avoided this damage and
loss. 22 I urge you now to keep up your
courage, for there will be no loss of life
among you, but only of the ship. 23 For last
night there stood by me an angel of the God
to whom I belong and whom I worship,
24 and he said, 'Do not be afraid, Paul; you
must stand before the emperor; and indeed,
God has granted safety to all those who are
sailing with you.' 25 So keep up your cour-
age, men, for I have faith in God that it will
be exactly as I have been told. 26 But we will
have to run aground on some island."
27 When the fourteenth night had come,
as we were drifting across the sea of Adria,
about midnight the sailors suspected that
they were nearing land. 28 So they took
soundings and found twenty fathoms; a lit-
tle farther on they took soundings again
and found fifteen fathoms. 29 Fearing that
we might run on the rocks, they let down
four anchors from the stern and prayed for
day to come. 30 But when the sailors tried to
escape from the ship and had lowered the
boat into the sea, on the pretext of putting
out anchors from the bow, 31 Paul said to
the centurion and the soldiers, "Unless
these men stay in the ship, you cannot be
saved." 32 Then the soldiers cut away the
ropes of the boat and set it adrift.
33 Just before daybreak, Paul urged all
of them to take some food, saying, "Today
is the fourteenth day that you have been in
suspense and remaining without food, hav-
ing eaten nothing. 34 Therefore I urge you
to take some food, for it will help you sur-
vive; for none of you will lose a hair from
your heads." 35 After he had said this, he
took bread; and giving thanks to God in the
presence of all, he broke it and began to
eat. 36 Then all of them were encouraged
and took food for themselves. 37 (We were
in all two hundred seventy-six[d] persons in
the ship.) 38 After they had satisfied their
hunger, they lightened the ship by throwing
the wheat into the sea.
39 In the morning they did not recognize
the land, but they noticed a bay with a
beach, on which they planned to run the

a Gk *it* *b* Other ancient authorities read *Clauda*
c Gk *helps* *d* Other ancient authorities read
seventy-six; others, *about seventy-six*

vv. 30–32) was in tow. **17:** The *measures* undertaken by the crew are not clear. *The Syrtis,* a dangerous shoal west of Cyrene on the north coast of Africa. *Sea anchor,* a conjecture for the Gk word meaning "vessel" or "implement," i.e., a device to slow the ship. **18:** Jon 1.5; and numerous Greco-Roman parallels (e.g., Josephus, *War* 1.280). **22:** Cf. v. 10. **24:** 23.11; 25.11–12. **27:** The *sea of Adria* then included the central Mediterranean. **30:** *Escape* of the crew is a popular motif found in Greco-Roman novels. **35–36:** *He took bread,* gave *thanks,* and *broke it,* cf. Lk 22.19; 24.30,35 (see 2.42n.). The meal in which all partake has clear eucharistic overtones. **37:** *Two hundred seventy-six* people on board is

ship ashore, if they could. 40 So they cast off
the anchors and left them in the sea. At the
same time they loosened the ropes that tied
the steering-oars; then hoisting the foresail
to the wind, they made for the beach. 41 But
striking a reef,[a] they ran the ship aground;
the bow stuck and remained immovable,
but the stern was being broken up by the
force of the waves. 42 The soldiers' plan was
to kill the prisoners, so that none might
swim away and escape; 43 but the centuri-
on, wishing to save Paul, kept them from
carrying out their plan. He ordered those
who could swim to jump overboard first
and make for the land, 44 and the rest to
follow, some on planks and others on
pieces of the ship. And so it was that all
were brought safely to land.

28 After we had reached safety, we
then learned that the island was
called Malta. 2 The natives showed us un-
usual kindness. Since it had begun to rain
and was cold, they kindled a fire and wel-
comed all of us around it. 3 Paul had gath-
ered a bundle of brushwood and was put-
ting it on the fire, when a viper, driven out
by the heat, fastened itself on his hand.
4 When the natives saw the creature hang-
ing from his hand, they said to one another,
"This man must be a murderer; though he
has escaped from the sea, justice has not
allowed him to live." 5 He, however, shook
off the creature into the fire and suffered no
harm. 6 They were expecting him to swell
up or drop dead, but after they had waited
a long time and saw that nothing unusual
had happened to him, they changed their
minds and began to say that he was a god.

7 Now in the neighborhood of that
place were lands belonging to the leading
man of the island, named Publius, who re-
ceived us and entertained us hospitably for
three days. 8 It so happened that the father
of Publius lay sick in bed with fever and
dysentery. Paul visited him and cured him
by praying and putting his hands on him.
9 After this happened, the rest of the people
on the island who had diseases also came
and were cured. 10 They bestowed many
honors on us, and when we were about to
sail, they put on board all the provisions we
needed.

11 Three months later we set sail on a
ship that had wintered at the island, an Al-
exandrian ship with the Twin Brothers as
its figurehead. 12 We put in at Syracuse and
stayed there for three days; 13 then we
weighed anchor and came to Rhegium. Af-
ter one day there a south wind sprang up,
and on the second day we came to Puteoli.
14 There we found believers[b] and were in-
vited to stay with them for seven days. And
so we came to Rome. 15 The believers[b]
from there, when they heard of us, came as
far as the Forum of Appius and Three Tav-
erns to meet us. On seeing them, Paul
thanked God and took courage.

16 When we came into Rome, Paul was
allowed to live by himself, with the soldier
who was guarding him.

a Gk *place of two seas* *b* Gk *brothers*

quite possible. **41:** *A reef,* Gk "a place of two seas." **42:** The *soldiers* were responsible for the *prisoners* (see 12.19; 16.27). **43:** The "good" *centurion* intervenes (see v. 3n.; 10.1n.).

28.1–10: Paul on Malta. Unharmed though bitten by a viper, Paul heals the father of Publius. **1:** *Malta,* a significant island south of Sicily controlled by the Romans. **2:** *Natives* (lit. "barbarians"), used of non-Greek speakers. **4:** *Justice,* here a deity. **5:** Lk 10.19; Mk 16.18 (Ps 91.13). **7:** *Leading man,* a local official on Malta. **8–9:** Lk 4.38–40.

28.11–16: The journey to Rome. Paul goes by sea to Syracuse, Rhegium, and Puteoli, then by land to the capital. **11:** *Three months* (see 27.9n.) would be too soon to have set sail but is just an approximation. *The Twin Brothers,* the Dioscuri, Castor and Pollux, patron deities of sailors. **12:** *Syracuse,* capital city of the island of Sicily. **13:** *Rhegium,* port city on the Italian coast opposite Sicily. *Puteoli,* modern Pozzuoli, on the north side of the Bay of Naples. **14:** *Believers,* there are already Christians at Rome (see 18.2n.). **15:** The *Forum of Appius* was 65 km (40 mi) from Rome, and the *Three Taverns* 50 km (30 mi), both on the Via Appia. **16:** The "we" passages (16.10n.) end here. *By himself,* apparently in private quarters.

17 Three days later he called together
the local leaders of the Jews. When they
had assembled, he said to them, "Brothers,
though I had done nothing against our peo-
ple or the customs of our ancestors, yet I
was arrested in Jerusalem and handed over
to the Romans. 18 When they had examined
me, the Romans[a] wanted to release me,
because there was no reason for the death
penalty in my case. 19 But when the Jews
objected, I was compelled to appeal to the
emperor—even though I had no charge to
bring against my nation. 20 For this reason
therefore I have asked to see you and speak
with you,[b] since it is for the sake of the
hope of Israel that I am bound with this
chain." 21 They replied, "We have received
no letters from Judea about you, and none
of the brothers coming here has reported or
spoken anything evil about you. 22 But we
would like to hear from you what you
think, for with regard to this sect we know
that everywhere it is spoken against."

23 After they had set a day to meet with
him, they came to him at his lodgings in
great numbers. From morning until evening
he explained the matter to them, testifying
to the kingdom of God and trying to con-
vince them about Jesus both from the law
of Moses and from the prophets. 24 Some
were convinced by what he had said, while
others refused to believe. 25 So they dis-
agreed with each other; and as they were
leaving, Paul made one further statement:
"The Holy Spirit was right in saying to
your ancestors through the prophet Isaiah,

26 'Go to this people and say,
You will indeed listen, but never
understand,
and you will indeed look, but never
perceive.
27 For this people's heart has
grown dull,
and their ears are hard of hearing,
and they have shut their eyes;
so that they might not look with
their eyes,
and listen with their ears,
and understand with their heart and
turn—
and I would heal them.'

28 Let it be known to you then that this
salvation of God has been sent to the Gen-
tiles; they will listen."[c]

30 He lived there two whole years at his
own expense[d] and welcomed all who came
to him, 31 proclaiming the kingdom of God
and teaching about the Lord Jesus Christ
with all boldness and without hindrance.

a Gk *they* b Or *I have asked you to see me and speak with me* c Other ancient authorities add verse 29, *And when he had said these words, the Jews departed, arguing vigorously among themselves* d Or *in his own hired dwelling*

28.17–28: Paul and the Jews of Rome. 17: Even as a captive Paul sticks to the pattern of speaking to Jews first (9.20n.; 13.5n.; 17.2n.). **20:** The *hope of Israel* is now bound up with Christianity. **23:** *Kingdom of God,* 1.3n.; *the prophets,* 26.22–23n. **24:** The reception is mixed as it has been all along (17.11–12n.) as Israel is divided by the gospel. **26–27:** Isa 6.9–10 is used elsewhere to explain Jewish rejection of the gospel (see Mt 13.14–15; Jn 12.40; cf. Rom 9–11). **28:** The "turn to the *Gentiles*" of 13.46; 18.6 is repeated. It is no more a final rejection than the previous instances were but may indicate the social reality of Luke's day.

28.30–31: Conclusion. Though under house arrest (v. 16) Paul preached *without hindrance* for *two whole years.*

INTRODUCTION
to the Letters/Epistles in the New Testament

CLASSIFICATION AND AUTHORSHIP OF THE NEW TESTAMENT LETTERS

Letters are the earliest documents in the New Testament, and its most common literary form: Some scholars date 1 Thessalonians before 50 CE, twenty years before Mark's gospel, and there are twenty-one separate letters in the New Testament. Thirteen of these are from Paul or his missionary associates: Romans, 1 and 2 Corinthians, Ephesians, Philippians, Colossians, Galatians, 1 and 2 Thessalonians, 1 and 2 Timothy, Titus, and Philemon. When Hebrews was attributed to Paul, the number of Pauline letters in ancient manuscripts and lists came to be fourteen. Another seven letters, which appear to be pseudonymously attributed to other apostles, round out the group; 1 and 2 Peter, 1, 2, and 3 John, James, and Jude. The Greek word "epistole," "letter," originally referred to an oral communication sent by messenger (Herodotus, *Histories* 4.10.1). Even in the New Testament period, the letter-carrier might be entrusted with crucial information about a letter's content. Paul often makes a point of including missionary associates in the greeting of his letters (1 Cor 1.1; 2 Cor 1.1; Phil 1.1; Col 1.1; 1 Thess 1.1; Philem 1). He omits them in Galatians, where he has no future plans to visit the region, and in Romans, addressed to a church he did not found. Ephesians lacks a specific destination in the best manuscripts and may be a circular exhortation by a later disciple of Paul.

Several other Pauline epistles also differ in language and theological emphasis from the major Pauline letters. The so-called Pastorals (1 and 2 Timothy and Titus), addressed to his key assistants, treat them as youthful bishops of local churches. They look to a future in which Christians are established in the larger society. While both 1 and 2 Thessalonians have as their principal theme the return of the Lord Jesus in the end time, the second letter stresses living in the present, and this, as well as its warning against pseudo-Pauline writings, has led some scholars to the conclusion that it too was written by a later disciple of Paul. Since Paul had a number of close associates in his missionary activities, it would hardly be surprising if they used a familiar medium, the apostolic letter, to continue dealing with concrete issues in the churches of the Pauline mission. Although many of the letters unquestionably by Paul are considerably longer than ordinary private letters, they address concrete situations in the churches.

Ephesians, however, lacks not only an address but also references to specific individuals or problems. Among the non-Pauline letters, Hebrews and James also appear to be tractates or general exhortations, rather than letters to specific communities. Jude addresses a sharp apocalyptic warning to Christians in general. First John speaks to concrete problems in its church circles, but lacks the form of a letter; 2 and 3 John are both personal letters, though addressed to different problems. First Peter uses the letter form as exhortation for suffering Christians in Asia Minor. Finally, 2 Peter appears to be the latest epistle in the New Testament. It contains a possible allusion to the Gospel account of the Transfiguration (1.16–18; cf. Mk 9.2–8) and to Christians who misinterpret Paul's letters (3.15–16). Like 2 Timothy, 2 Peter is presented as the last testament of an apostle. It affirms the unity of apostolic teaching concerning the Day of the Lord against some who used Paul's authority to deny that God would end the world.

WRITING AND SENDING LETTERS IN ANTIQUITY

Letters from antiquity include imperial decrees addressed to subjects in a particular area, such as that by the emperor Claudius to "the city of Alexandria" in 41 CE concerning Jewish agitation for citizen rights; collections of philosophical letters by prominent figures like Cicero, Pliny, and Seneca; and hundreds of papyri from Egypt documenting the concerns of ordinary people. Royal diplomatic correspondence has its own formalities of language which are echoed in the so-called letters that the heavenly Christ addresses to the angels of the churches in Revelation 2–3. Philosophical letters often adopt a rhetorical formalism, which indicates that such letters were intended to be preserved for posterity. They are typically longer than private letters, which are generally described as "documentary" to distinguish them from such literary creations. Authors often retained copies of and revised literary correspondence before committing it to copying for posterity. Documentary letters existed only for the many purposes of the moment, such as dealing with problems at home, urging an absent husband or son to return, reporting on a military posting, pleading for legal redress, engaging in commerce, describing one's circumstances to family or friends, recommending the bearer of the letter to its recipient, and so on.

The existence of so many letters from private individuals does not imply a high rate of literacy among craftsmen, traders, or women. A letter could be dictated to a scribe who would be charged with the actual writing. Even those who could write often preferred to employ the services of a scribe (Rom 16.22; Gal 6.11). The letter-carrier or another party might read the letter at its destination and, depending upon the carrier's relationship to the sender, might also interpret the content of the letter. Some documentary letters in Egypt suggest that after the letter has been read in Greek, it will have to be translated into the local dialect so that the women in the sender's audience can understand it.

The formal parts of the ancient letter—to be distinguished from other rhetorical patterns authors of literary epistles might use—are straightforward. The opening or prescript identifies sender(s) and recipient(s) and concludes with a greeting or salutation. Epithets, information about geographical locations, and terms of endearment often expand on individuals named. Paul regularly shifts to a Semitic form of salutation, "grace and peace," expanded with reference to God and Christ Jesus (2 Cor 1.2). When his apostolic authority is an issue between himself and the recipients, that note may be attached as a self-designation (2 Cor 1.1; Rom 1.1–5, a community for which Paul is not an apostle founder). Ancient letters may follow the opening with a formal statement of the sender's wish for the health of the recipients. Such formulas may also be employed to close the letter. Another common formula expresses the sender's prayer to the gods or thanksgiving on behalf of the recipients. In the Pauline letter type, this conventional way of opening a letter commonly develops into a much longer thanksgiving or blessing section. That section often previews items from the body of the letter that follows.

After the opening formalities, the body of the letter states the actual business or request that is the reason for the letter. The sender may either give information about his own future travel plans or request it about others. Paul usually has such travel reports near the end of his letter-body. Various formulas can be used to conclude the letter. Often greetings are conveyed from or to others not mentioned in the letter-body.

Once the letter was written, the sender had to find a person to convey the letter to its recipient. Often the presence of someone who is on the way to the desired location provides an opportunity for writing. There was no guaranteed overnight global delivery in antiquity! Even letters entrusted to friends for delivery had an uncertain fate. Under the best of circumstances a response was weeks or months away. The sender would ordinarily have retained a copy, and some scholars have suggested that the first collection of Paul's letters was due to the apostle's own editing of his copies of Romans, 1 and 2 Corinthians, and Galatians. This hypothesis accounts for the start of the process of collecting and editing Pauline letters, but lacking any specific manuscript evidence, it remains speculative.

The Letter of Paul to the ROMANS

Although, because of its length, it is the first in the letters of the New Testament, Romans was probably the latest of Paul's undisputed letters to be written (see "Letters/Epistles in the New Testament). Romans also contains the longest and most complex sustained argument in any of Paul's letters even though it is addressed to Christians he has never met (1.13). For these reasons the letter, especially chs 1–8, has often been read as Paul's theological "last will and testament," a reflection on and a summary of the gospel of salvation in Christ. It was also intended to persuade the Christians of Rome to support Paul's prospective mission to Spain (15.23–24).

Paul wanted more from his readers, however. He meant to proclaim to the Christians of Rome the gospel, "the power of God for salvation" (1.15–16; 15.18–19), and thus to strengthen and encourage them (1.11–12). Romans is, like Paul's other letters, an instrument of moral instruction and exhortation (see 15.14–15).

The letter was occasioned in part by circumstances in Rome during the reign of the emperor Nero (54–68 CE). The greetings in ch 16 include Prisca and Aquila, known from Acts 18.2 as among the Jews expelled from Rome by the emperor Claudius around 49 CE. Their presence in Rome at the time Paul writes may reflect Nero's reversal of his predecessor's edict (Suetonius, *Life of Claudius* 25.3). The recent return of Jews to the imperial capital, including Jewish Christians like Prisca and Aquila, who had been driven out and probably lost property and community ties during their exile, may well have aroused tensions within Christian house groups in which Gentile believers had become predominant.

Paul's appeal to Gentile Christians in Rome not to "boast" over Jews (11.13–36) comes at the end of chs 9–11, the climax of the letter. Paul's argument responds to an incipient anti-Judaism, already rife among the Roman aristocracy and beginning to penetrate the Christian community as well. Given the recent horror of an anti-Jewish pogrom in Alexandria (38–41 CE), and even more recent tax riots that had turned deadly in nearby Puteoli, Paul is concerned to prevent in Rome the sort of civic disturbance in which the city's minority Jewish population might be especially vulnerable. This is at least one explanation for the notorious exhortation to "be subject to the governing authorities" (13.1–7n.). Similarly, Paul's admonitions regarding the "weak in faith," concerned with the observance of diet and special days (14.1–15.13), may address tensions between Jewish Christians, who would have had such observances, and Gentile Christians, who would not.

The theme of God's "righteousness" (1.17) or "justice" (3.5) resonates throughout the letter. At stake is God's faithfulness in the face of human faithlessness, as the rhetorical questions that punctuate the letter show (2.3–4,21–23; 3.3,5,7,9,27,29; 4.1; 6.1–3,15–16; 7.7,13; 9.14,19,30; 11.1,11). God's righteousness is manifest in the uncompromising judgment of all impiety and wickedness, and also in unwavering loyalty to the covenant with Israel. Paul wants the Christians of Rome to respect God's integrity in the salvation offered them through the faithful obedience of Jesus (5.6,18–19; see 3.22,26n.).

Paul is Christ's apostle, obligated to "bring about the obedience of faith among all the Gentiles," among whom he includes his Roman audience (1.1–6). He declares the gospel of God's salvation to all who believe, Jews and Greeks alike, but "to the Jew first" (1.16). The priority of the Jew in God's plan of salvation is an important theme in the letter (3.1–2; 9.1–4). Paul's mission to Gentiles should provoke his fellow Jews to jealousy (11.13–14), perhaps by convincing them that the last days prophesied by Isaiah were at hand (see 15.12). At last, Paul declares, "all Israel will be saved" (11.26), and all the nations will join Israel in the worship of the one true God (15.7–13).

As he writes, the apostle is about to present to his compatriots in Jerusalem both monetary aid from churches in his mission field (15.25–27) and an embassy of converts from paganism (1 Cor 16.3–4; on the eventual catastrophe of this mission, see Acts 21.27–30). Although the Roman Christians have not had the opportunity to contribute to this mission in tangible ways, Paul asks for their prayers (15.30–32). He also writes to safeguard the sanctity of the "offering of the Gentiles" (15.15–16) by exhorting the Christians of Rome to holy living (12.1–3; 15.7–9).

The underlying structure of Paul's exhortation resembles other letters written to congregations Paul had founded. By virtue of their baptism into Christ, Christians must no longer let sin have dominion over them (6.1–14). They are to live no longer as the pagan world does (1.18–32), but to give "spiritual worship" to God through sobriety of thought and bodily purity (12.1–3). Just so Paul had reminded the Corinthians, Galatians, and Thessalonians that they must no longer live as "the Gentiles who do not know God," having been sanctified by Christ (1 Cor 6.9–11; Gal 5.22–24; 1 Thess 4.1–5).

Universal accountability before God, Paul's theme throughout the early chapters of the letter, is more specifically applied in chs 12–16. Rather than being a treatise on Christian salvation, Romans is a sustained appeal for holy living, directed to Gentile Christians tempted to look down on their beleaguered Jewish neighbors, within the Christian congregations and without. The apostle's call to realize in common life the justice of God which the Christian congregation celebrates is the letter's enduring legacy.

1 Paul, a servant[a] of Jesus Christ, called
to be an apostle, set apart for the gospel
of God, 2 which he promised beforehand
through his prophets in the holy scriptures,
3 the gospel concerning his Son, who was
descended from David according to the
flesh 4 and was declared to be Son of God
with power according to the spirit[b] of holi-
ness by resurrection from the dead, Jesus
Christ our Lord, 5 through whom we have
received grace and apostleship to bring
about the obedience of faith among all the
Gentiles for the sake of his name, 6 includ-
ing yourselves who are called to belong to
Jesus Christ,

7 To all God's beloved in Rome, who
are called to be saints:

Grace to you and peace from God our
Father and the Lord Jesus Christ.

8 First, I thank my God through Jesus
Christ for all of you, because your faith is

a Gk *slave* *b* Or *Spirit*

1.1–7: Salutation. Ancient letters began with the names of sender and recipient and a short greeting (see Acts 23.26). Paul's expansion of this form reflects the liturgical context in which his letter would be read. **1:** A *servant . . . called . . . set apart,* the characteristic marks of Israel's prophets (Jer 1.5; Am 7.14). *Apostle,* lit. one "sent forth," i.e., by God (Isa 6.8; Jer 1.7; Ezek 2.3–4). **3:** *Gospel,* see 1.16n. *Descended from David,* messiah in David's royal lineage. **4:** *The spirit of holiness,* God's Spirit (see 8.2n.). The corresponding Heb phrase is translated "holy spirit" in Ps 51.11; Isa 63.10–11 (cf. 1QS 4.21; 8.16; 9.3; 1QH 7.6–7; 9.32). **5–6:** Despite greetings to Jews among his audience (16.3,7,11), Paul addresses the Roman Christians as Gentiles (1.13–15). **7:** *Saints,* lit. "holy ones."

1.8–17: Thanksgiving. Ancient letters continued with a prayer of thanksgiving. Paul's thanksgivings

proclaimed throughout the world. 9 For
God, whom I serve with my spirit by an-
nouncing the gospel[a] of his Son, is my wit-
ness that without ceasing I remember you
always in my prayers, 10 asking that by
God's will I may somehow at last succeed
in coming to you. 11 For I am longing to see
you so that I may share with you some spir-
itual gift to strengthen you— 12 or rather so
that we may be mutually encouraged by
each other's faith, both yours and mine. 13 I
want you to know, brothers and sisters,[b]
that I have often intended to come to you
(but thus far have been prevented), in order
that I may reap some harvest among you as
I have among the rest of the Gentiles. 14 I
am a debtor both to Greeks and to barbar-
ians, both to the wise and to the foolish
15 —hence my eagerness to proclaim the
gospel to you also who are in Rome.
16 For I am not ashamed of the gospel;
it is the power of God for salvation to ev-
eryone who has faith, to the Jew first and
also to the Greek. 17 For in it the righteous-
ness of God is revealed through faith for
faith; as it is written, "The one who is righ-
teous will live by faith."[c]
18 For the wrath of God is revealed
from heaven against all ungodliness and
wickedness of those who by their wicked-
ness suppress the truth. 19 For what can be
known about God is plain to them, because
God has shown it to them. 20 Ever since the
creation of the world his eternal power and
divine nature, invisible though they are,
have been understood and seen through the
things he has made. So they are without
excuse; 21 for though they knew God, they
did not honor him as God or give thanks to
him, but they became futile in their think-
ing, and their senseless minds were dark-
ened. 22 Claiming to be wise, they became
fools; 23 and they exchanged the glory of

a Gk *my spirit in the gospel* *b* Gk *brothers*
c Or *The one who is righteous through faith will live*

signal important themes in his letters. He describes his obligation to *proclaim the gospel* to the Romans as priestly service (v. 9; see 15.16,25), grounded in the revelation of God's righteousness (vv. 16–17). **10–13:** *By God's will . . . prevented,* apostolic obligations have delayed Paul's visiting the Romans (15.18–22). **11–13:** *Share . . . reap some harvest,* Paul seeks an active response from the Romans (15.14n). *Strengthen . . . encouraged,* 1 Thess 3.2. Polite circumspection dominates here and at 15.14–15. **14:** *To Greeks and . . . barbarians,* Paul describes the world as Roman orators saw it, divided into more or less civilized peoples (cf. 1.16n). *To you also,* the Romans stand within Paul's obligation as apostle to the Gentiles (15.14–19). **16–17:** Often taken as the "theme" of the letter, these verses explain Paul's eagerness to *proclaim the gospel* (v. 15) to the Romans. **16:** *I am not ashamed,* a confession of faith (cf. 4 Macc 5.34–38; 6.20; 9.2). Paul's "boast" in God's power is a recurrent theme in the letter (5.1–4,11; 15.17; cf. 1 Thess 1.5; 1 Cor 2.4). *The gospel,* "euangelion," in nonbiblical Greek, celebrated the triumph of a ruler; Paul announces God's triumph. Salvation is the result of the life-giving and right-making *power of God* (see 4.17; 5.11,12–21; 6.1–14; 8.1–4,10–11,21–25; 11.15,23; 15.18–19). *To the Jew first,* 2.9–10; 3.1–2; 9.4. *And also to the Greek,* Paul now describes the world from a Jewish point of view (cf. 1.14). **17:** *The righteousness of God,* or "justice" (as at 3.5). God's character as righteous, being *revealed* as God brings human beings into right relationship (see 3.21–26), is a sign of the last days (see 13.11–12). God's vindication before the nations is in view (Ps 98.2; Isa 51.5). *Through faith,* i.e., God's faithfulness (as at 3.3). *For faith,* God's faithfulness elicits human trust. *The one who . . . by faith,* Hab 2.4. Like other Jews, Paul may have read the citation as a messianic prophecy: The Righteous One, the messiah (Acts 3.14; 7.52; 22.14), will live on the basis of faithfulness (see 3.22n.).

1.18–32: An indictment of human wickedness and injustice. Paul argues in 1.18–3.20 that God's justice allows no impunity for any who willfully do wrong. **18:** *The wrath of God,* 2.5; 4.9. God's righteousness (1.17) requires that God no longer pass over sins with forbearance (see 3.25). *Wickedness,* lit. "injustice." **19–23:** Idolatry is an attempt to deny awareness of God, thus evading accountability for one's actions. Its opposite is the "spiritual worship" offered by renewed minds (12.1–2). **20:** *Without excuse,* 2.1; 3.19; compare Wis 13.1–9. **23:** *Images,* idolatry was condemned by the Torah (Ex 20.4–6) and ridiculed by the prophets (Isa 40.18–20; 42.17; 45.16,20; Jer 10.1–16). Like other Jews, Paul attributes the wicked-

the immortal God for images resembling
a mortal human being or birds or four-
footed animals or reptiles.
24 Therefore God gave them up in the
lusts of their hearts to impurity, to the de-
grading of their bodies among themselves,
25 because they exchanged the truth about
God for a lie and worshiped and served the
creature rather than the Creator, who is
blessed forever! Amen.
26 For this reason God gave them up
to degrading passions. Their women ex-
changed natural intercourse for unnatural,
27 and in the same way also the men, giving
up natural intercourse with women, were
consumed with passion for one another.
Men committed shameless acts with men
and received in their own persons the due
penalty for their error.
28 And since they did not see fit to ac-
knowledge God, God gave them up to a
debased mind and to things that should not
be done. 29 They were filled with every kind
of wickedness, evil, covetousness, malice.
Full of envy, murder, strife, deceit, crafti-
ness, they are gossips, 30 slanderers, God-
haters,[a] insolent, haughty, boastful, inven-
tors of evil, rebellious toward parents,
31 foolish, faithless, heartless, ruthless.
32 They know God's decree, that those who
practice such things deserve to die—yet
they not only do them but even applaud
others who practice them.
2 Therefore you have no excuse, whoever
you are, when you judge others; for in
passing judgment on another you condemn
yourself, because you, the judge, are doing
the very same things. 2 You say,[b] "We
know that God's judgment on those who
do such things is in accordance with truth."
3 Do you imagine, whoever you are, that
when you judge those who do such things
and yet do them yourself, you will escape
the judgment of God? 4 Or do you despise
the riches of his kindness and forbearance
and patience? Do you not realize that
God's kindness is meant to lead you to re-
pentance? 5 But by your hard and impeni-
tent heart you are storing up wrath for
yourself on the day of wrath, when God's

a Or *God-hated* *b* Gk lacks *You say*

ness characteristic of the pagan world to idolatry. A more irenic tone is attributed to Paul in Acts 17.22–23. **24–27:** *Impurity,* disordered thinking and behavior, to be left behind in baptism (6.6–14; 12.1). **24–25:** *God gave them up,* in a spiral of depravity, injustice leads mortals to suppress their awareness of truth and turn from God (vv. 18–23); God abandons them to increasing wickedness (vv. 24–32). *The Creator, who is blessed forever,* spontaneous praise to God (6.17; 7.25; 9.5; 11.33–36; 16.25–27). **26–27:** *Degrading passions,* while Torah forbids a male "lying with a male as with a woman" (Lev 18.22), Paul's Jewish contemporaries criticized a range of sexual behaviors common in the pagan world. Although widely read today as a reference to homosexuality, the language of *unnatural* intercourse was more often used in Paul's day to denote not the orientation of sexual desire, but its immoderate indulgence, which was believed to weaken the body (*the due penalty*). **28–31:** The spiraling descent into wickedness reaches its nadir in these vices, presented here in list form as elsewhere in the New Testament (e.g., Gal 5.19–21; 1 Tim 1.9–10; 1 Pet 4.3) and in Greek and Roman literature. *Full of envy, murder, strife,* the notorious perversity and brutality of emperors like Gaius (Caligula), or Paul's contemporary, Nero, come readily to mind. **32:** *They know God's decree,* they cannot plead ignorance as an excuse (see 1.20).

2.1–16: All are accountable before God for their works. 1: Paul attacks as hypocritical the presumption that God will have mercy on some by exempting them from punishment (2.4). **2:** *You say,* added to express one interpretation of this passage as a "trap" for "the Jew," who judges the pagan indicted in 1.18–32. Jews are not clearly addressed before 2.17. Here, any are condemned who *know that God's judgment . . . is in accordance with truth,* yet do *the very same things* they condemn in others (2.1,3). **4:** *Do you despise . . . kindness,* the question is rhetorical. Paul warns Christians not to presume God's grace in 6.1,15. **5:** *Day of wrath,* the time of divine judgment (see Isa 2.12n; 13.9,13; Lam 2.1; 1 Thess 1.10; etc.), understood in early Christian thought to be imminent and universal (e.g., 13.12; 2 Pet 3.10). God's punishment of sin coheres with God's righteousness (see 1.17–18). **6–11:** Judgment according to one's

righteous judgment will be revealed. 6 For
he will repay according to each one's deeds:
7 to those who by patiently doing good seek
for glory and honor and immortality, he
will give eternal life; 8 while for those who
are self-seeking and who obey not the truth
but wickedness, there will be wrath and
fury. 9 There will be anguish and distress
for everyone who does evil, the Jew first
and also the Greek, 10 but glory and honor
and peace for everyone who does good, the
Jew first and also the Greek. 11 For God
shows no partiality.

12 All who have sinned apart from the
law will also perish apart from the law, and
all who have sinned under the law will be
judged by the law. 13 For it is not the hear-
ers of the law who are righteous in God's
sight, but the doers of the law who will
be justified. 14 When Gentiles, who do not
possess the law, do instinctively what the
law requires, these, though not having the
law, are a law to themselves. 15 They show
that what the law requires is written on
their hearts, to which their own conscience
also bears witness; and their conflicting
thoughts will accuse or perhaps excuse
them 16 on the day when, according to my
gospel, God, through Jesus Christ, will
judge the secret thoughts of all.

17 But if you call yourself a Jew and rely
on the law and boast of your relation to
God 18 and know his will and determine
what is best because you are instructed in
the law, 19 and if you are sure that you are
a guide to the blind, a light to those who
are in darkness, 20 a corrector of the fool-
ish, a teacher of children, having in the law
the embodiment of knowledge and truth,
21 you, then, that teach others, will you not
teach yourself? While you preach against
stealing, do you steal? 22 You that forbid
adultery, do you commit adultery? You
that abhor idols, do you rob temples?
23 You that boast in the law, do you dishon-
or God by breaking the law? 24 For, as it is
written, "The name of God is blasphemed
among the Gentiles because of you."

25 Circumcision indeed is of value if you
obey the law; but if you break the law, your
circumcision has become uncircumcision.
26 So, if those who are uncircumcised keep
the requirements of the law, will not their
uncircumcision be regarded as circum-
cision? 27 Then those who are physically
uncircumcised but keep the law will con-
demn you that have the written code and
circumcision but break the law. 28 For a
person is not a Jew who is one outwardly,
nor is true circumcision something external

works: see 2 Cor 11.15; Jas 2.14–26, where the Gk word "erga," translated *deeds* here, is "works." **9–10:** The Jew is first in salvation (1.16; 3.1–2), therefore also in responsibility. *Anguish and distress,* eschatological woe (2 Cor 4.8). **11:** *No partiality,* Deut 10.17; 2 Chr 19.7. No discrimination compromises God's justice. **12:** *Apart from the law,* referring to Gentiles, just as *under the law* refers to Jews. **13:** *Hearers* and *doers,* Mt 7.21; Jas 1.22–25. *Doers of the law . . . will be justified,* see 3.20n. **14–15:** Ancient Judaism acknowledged righteous Gentiles who did "by nature" *what the law requires,* lit. "the work of the law." For Paul, those who walk according to the Spirit fulfill the law's *just requirement* (8.4). **15:** *Their own conscience also bears witness,* thus they acknowledge the validity of God's law. A similar argument appears in 7.14–22.

2.17–29: Does being a Jew relieve one from accountability to God? Paul makes his point through imaginary conversation with a Jew (the diatribe style). **17:** Although vv. 17–24 have often been read as an "indictment" of the Jew, Paul considers Israel's privileges real (see 3.1–9; 9.1–4). *Boast,* Paul warns repeatedly against groundless boasting before God (see 2.23; 3.27; 4.5; 5.1–3,11; 11.17–20). **21–23:** *Will you not teach yourself?* Paul interrogates an imaginary witness, whose testimony leads to the conclusions in vv. 25–29. Israel's covenantal privileges do not lessen accountability before God. **22:** *Do you rob temples?* While the Torah forbade idolatry, Jews in Paul's day were careful not to dishonor pagan shrines (Philo, *De Conf. Ling.* 163; Josephus, *Ag. Ap.* 269; *Ant.* 4.207). **23:** *Do you dishonor God?* A question in the earliest punctuated manuscript. **24:** Isa 52.5; cf. Ezek 36.20. **25–29:** These verses expand the principle that "all who have sinned under the law will be judged by the law" (v. 12). **26:** *The requirements of the law,* see v. 14; 8.1–4n. **29:** *Real circumcision . . . the heart,* Deut 10.16; 30.6,8; Jer 4.4; 9.26; Ezek 44.9.

and physical. 29 Rather, a person is a Jew
who is one inwardly, and real circumcision
is a matter of the heart—it is spiritual and
not literal. Such a person receives praise not
from others but from God.

3 Then what advantage has the Jew? Or
what is the value of circumcision?
2 Much, in every way. For in the first place
the Jews[a] were entrusted with the oracles
of God. 3 What if some were unfaithful?
Will their faithlessness nullify the faithful-
ness of God? 4 By no means! Although ev-
eryone is a liar, let God be proved true, as
it is written,

"So that you may be justified in your
words,
and prevail in your judging."[b]

5 But if our injustice serves to confirm the
justice of God, what should we say? That
God is unjust to inflict wrath on us? (I
speak in a human way.) 6 By no means!
For then how could God judge the world?
7 But if through my falsehood God's truth-
fulness abounds to his glory, why am I still
being condemned as a sinner? 8 And why
not say (as some people slander us by say-
ing that we say), "Let us do evil so that
good may come"? Their condemnation is
deserved!

9 What then? Are we any better off?[c]
No, not at all; for we have already charged
that all, both Jews and Greeks, are under
the power of sin, 10 as it is written:

"There is no one who is righteous,
not even one;
11 there is no one who has
understanding,
there is no one who seeks God.
12 All have turned aside, together they
have become worthless;
there is no one who shows
kindness,
there is not even one."
13 "Their throats are opened graves;
they use their tongues to deceive."
"The venom of vipers is under
their lips."
14 "Their mouths are full of cursing
and bitterness."
15 "Their feet are swift to shed blood;
16 ruin and misery are in their paths,
17 and the way of peace they have
not known."
18 "There is no fear of God before
their eyes."

19 Now we know that whatever the law
says, it speaks to those who are under the
law, so that every mouth may be silenced,
and the whole world may be held account-
able to God. 20 For "no human being will
be justified in his sight" by deeds prescribed
by the law, for through the law comes the
knowledge of sin.

a Gk *they* b Gk *when you are being judged*
c Or *at any disadvantage?*

3.1–9: God's integrity in the covenant with Israel. 1: The *advantage* of the Jew is real (9.1–4), but does not provide immunity from God's just judgment. **3:** The faithlessness of some Jews does not alter God's *faithfulness* to the covenant. **4:** Ps 116.11; 51.4. **5:** *The justice of God* (see 1.17n.) requires the judgment of injustice. **8:** *As some people slander us,* it is not clear who is slandering whom, but in 6.1,15, similar language refutes a possible misunderstanding of God's grace in Christ. **9:** *Are we any better off?* This translation echoes v. 2, yet reaches a different conclusion. The Gk may also be translated "Do we have a defense?"

3.10–20: The universality of God's judgment. These quotations from the Hebrew Bible insist that no one may claim to satisfy God's standards. **10–12:** Ps 14.1–2; 53.1–2. **13:** Ps 5.9; 140.3. **14:** Ps 10.7. **15–17:** Prov 1.16; Isa 59.7–8. **18:** Ps 36.1. **19:** The law holds everyone accountable before God (cf. 2.13). The previous scriptures emphasize sins of false speech (cf. 1.18). **20:** Ps 143.2. The lack of human righteousness is a theme throughout the Psalms and other Jewish writings (e.g., 1 Enoch 81.5; 1QH 8.20; 17.14–15). *By deeds prescribed by the law,* lit. "works of the law," is Paul's addition to the Psalm text (see 3.28n; Dan 9.18; 1QH 15.17). The "doers of the law" who "will be justified" (2.13) are not those who merely possess the law, but those who by God's Spirit fulfill its "just requirement" (8.4), by "doing," lit. working, "good" (2.7,10).

21 But now, apart from law, the righ-
teousness of God has been disclosed, and is
attested by the law and the prophets, 22 the
righteousness of God through faith in Jesus
Christ[a] for all who believe. For there is no
distinction, 23 since all have sinned and fall
short of the glory of God; 24 they are now
justified by his grace as a gift, through the
redemption that is in Christ Jesus, 25 whom
God put forward as a sacrifice of atone-
ment[b] by his blood, effective through
faith. He did this to show his righteousness,
because in his divine forbearance he had
passed over the sins previously committed;
26 it was to prove at the present time that he
himself is righteous and that he justifies the
one who has faith in Jesus.[c]

27 Then what becomes of boasting? It is
excluded. By what law? By that of works?
No, but by the law of faith. 28 For we hold
that a person is justified by faith apart from
works prescribed by the law. 29 Or is God
the God of Jews only? Is he not the God of
Gentiles also? Yes, of Gentiles also, 30 since
God is one; and he will justify the circum-
cised on the ground of faith and the uncir-
cumcised through that same faith. 31 Do we
then overthrow the law by this faith? By no
means! On the contrary, we uphold the
law.

4 What then are we to say was gained
by[d] Abraham, our ancestor according
to the flesh? 2 For if Abraham was justified
by works, he has something to boast about,
but not before God. 3 For what does the
scripture say? "Abraham believed God,
and it was reckoned to him as righteous-
ness." 4 Now to one who works, wages are
not reckoned as a gift but as something
due. 5 But to one who without works trusts
him who justifies the ungodly, such faith is
reckoned as righteousness. 6 So also David

a Or *through the faith of Jesus Christ* *b* Or *a place of atonement* *c* Or *who has the faith of Jesus*
d Other ancient authorities read *say about*

3.21–31: The revelation of God's justice. 21–22: *Apart from the law,* where no one might lay hold of the law as a defense from God's judgment. *Disclosed,* 1.17. The *righteousness of God* involves God's action in Christ to "justify" (make right) those who trust in God (see 6.1–23). **22:** The alternate translation in note *a, the faith of Jesus Christ,* is increasingly preferred. It conforms this phrase to identically structured phrases in 3.3 ("the faithfulness of God") and 4.12,16 ("the faith of . . . Abraham") and reflects the importance for Paul of Jesus' faithful obedience (5.19; Phil 2.8). **25–26:** Paul emphasizes God's integrity and justice, now "revealed" (1.17), not in putting up with sin but in dealing with it decisively through the *faith of Jesus* (see note *c*). *Sacrifice of atonement,* 4 Macc 17.22. The translation in note *b* (see Ex 25.17–22) is less likely. *Divine forbearance,* God has patiently withheld wrath, not to indulge sin but to lead sinners to repentance (2.4). **27:** *Boasting* is *excluded* by *the law of faith,* i.e., by the law rightly understood as eliciting trust in God's saving power (see 2.17n.; 4.5; 11.18n.; Deut 9.4–6; Dan 9.18). **28:** *We hold,* Paul's language resembles recently published Dead Sea Scroll fragments listing "works of the law" that will be "reckoned as righteousness" for those who perform them (4Q397, 398). Paul's point is that one is *justified by faith,* meaning either one's faithful obedience to God (see 1.5,16), God's faithfulness (as in 3.3), or Jesus' faithfulness (see 3.22,26n.). **29–31:** *God is one* (see Deut 6.4), judging Jew and Gentile alike on the basis of *faith,* i.e., faithful obedience (2.13–16), which will indeed *uphold the law* (7.7,12–16).

4.1–25: Abraham as a test case. Was Abraham reckoned righteous before God on any other basis than faithfulness? **1:** *Abraham . . . the flesh,* this translation implies Paul refers only to Jews. The Gk may also be translated "What shall we say: Have we found Abraham to be our ancestor according to the flesh?" which leads to the negative answer in 4.11–12,16 (cf. 9.6–9). **2–5:** Paul finds in Gen 15.6 proof that righteousness was *reckoned* to Abraham as a *gift,* not as *wages* paid as *something due* (6.23). God is free from any obligation to mortals (see 4.16). **5:** God *justifies the ungodly,* Paul shares his contemporaries' view that God had called Abraham out of idolatry (see Gen 12.1–4; 13.4; 17.9–14,23–27). Abraham's justification stands in contrast with the "ungodliness" of the pagan world (1.18) and provides the prototype for God's justification of the ungodly through Christ's death (5.6). **6–8:** Paul quotes Ps 32.1–2 (Gk) to bring in the theme of *blessedness* (Gen 12.2–3; Gal 3.8). **9–12:** Abraham was justified (Gen 15.6) *before*

speaks of the blessedness of those to whom
God reckons righteousness apart from
works:
7 "Blessed are those whose iniquities
are forgiven,
and whose sins are covered;
8 blessed is the one against whom the
Lord will not reckon sin."
9 Is this blessedness, then, pronounced
only on the circumcised, or also on the un-
circumcised? We say, "Faith was reckoned
to Abraham as righteousness." 10 How then
was it reckoned to him? Was it before or
after he had been circumcised? It was not
after, but before he was circumcised. 11 He
received the sign of circumcision as a seal of
the righteousness that he had by faith while
he was still uncircumcised. The purpose
was to make him the ancestor of all who
believe without being circumcised and who
thus have righteousness reckoned to them,
12 and likewise the ancestor of the circum-
cised who are not only circumcised but
who also follow the example of the faith
that our ancestor Abraham had before he
was circumcised.
13 For the promise that he would inherit
the world did not come to Abraham or to
his descendants through the law but
through the righteousness of faith. 14 If it is
the adherents of the law who are to be the
heirs, faith is null and the promise is void.
15 For the law brings wrath; but where
there is no law, neither is there violation.
16 For this reason it depends on faith, in
order that the promise may rest on grace
and be guaranteed to all his descendants,
not only to the adherents of the law but
also to those who share the faith of Abra-
ham (for he is the father of all of us, 17 as it
is written, "I have made you the father of
many nations")—in the presence of the
God in whom he believed, who gives life to
the dead and calls into existence the things
that do not exist. 18 Hoping against hope,
he believed that he would become "the fa-
ther of many nations," according to what
was said, "So numerous shall your descen-
dants be." 19 He did not weaken in faith
when he considered his own body, which
was already[a] as good as dead (for he was
about a hundred years old), or when he
considered the barrenness of Sarah's
womb. 20 No distrust made him waver con-
cerning the promise of God, but he grew
strong in his faith as he gave glory to God,
21 being fully convinced that God was able
to do what he had promised. 22 Therefore
his faith[b] "was reckoned to him as righ-
teousness." 23 Now the words, "it was
reckoned to him," were written not for his
sake alone, 24 but for ours also. It will be
reckoned to us who believe in him who
raised Jesus our Lord from the dead, 25 who

a Other ancient authorities lack *already*
b Gk *Therefore it*

he was circumcised (Gen 17.24), on account of his *faith,* therefore he could be ancestor of both circumcised (Gen 12.2; 15.13–14) and uncircumcised (Gen 17.5; see v. 17). **12:** *The faith that . . . Abraham had,* his faithful trust in God (vv. 5,17). **13–15:** God's promise comes through *the righteousness of faith,* or "faithful righteousness," like that of Abraham (vv. 16,20), not through the law. **14:** *The adherents of the law,* compare "hearers of the law" in 2.13. *Faith is null and the promise is void,* if God's blessing depended on the performance of those who possessed the law (3.3–4; 9.6–9). **15:** *The law brings wrath,* Paul may have in mind the solemn curses pronounced on the disobedient in Deut 28. *But where there is no law . . . violation,* Abraham did not stand under the law when he responded to God in faith.

4.16–25: The example of Abraham's faith. 16: *Not only . . . but also,* Jews and Gentiles alike inherit God's promise as they *share the faith of Abraham.* **17:** Gen 17.5. Abraham's faith in God's promise despite his own "dead" body (v. 19) is an example for all those who trust God *who raised Jesus . . . from the dead* (v. 24). God's power to *call into existence the things that do not exist* is a key theme (v. 24; 6.4–5,9–11; 8.11; 9.25–26; 11.5). Contrast Abraham's faith with those who refuse to acknowledge God through creation (1.20–22). **18:** Gen 15.5. *Hoping against hope,* see 8.24–25. **20–21:** God's ability *to do what he had promised* is at stake throughout Romans, especially regarding Israel (3.3–4; 9.6). *Gave glory to God,* again Abraham is contrasted with the ungodly of 1.21–24; see 15.9–12. **22–23:** Gen 15.6.

was handed over to death for our trespasses
and was raised for our justification.

5 Therefore, since we are justified by
faith, we[a] have peace with God
through our Lord Jesus Christ, 2 through
whom we have obtained access[b] to this
grace in which we stand; and we[c] boast in
our hope of sharing the glory of God. 3 And
not only that, but we[c] also boast in our
sufferings, knowing that suffering produces
endurance, 4 and endurance produces char-
acter, and character produces hope, 5 and
hope does not disappoint us, because God's
love has been poured into our hearts
through the Holy Spirit that has been given
to us.
6 For while we were still weak, at the
right time Christ died for the ungodly. 7 In-
deed, rarely will anyone die for a righteous
person—though perhaps for a good person
someone might actually dare to die. 8 But
God proves his love for us in that while we
still were sinners Christ died for us. 9 Much
more surely then, now that we have been
justified by his blood, will we be saved
through him from the wrath of God.[d]
10 For if while we were enemies, we were
reconciled to God through the death of his
Son, much more surely, having been recon-
ciled, will we be saved by his life. 11 But
more than that, we even boast in God
through our Lord Jesus Christ, through
whom we have now received reconcilia-
tion.
12 Therefore, just as sin came into the
world through one man, and death came
through sin, and so death spread to all be-
cause all have sinned— 13 sin was indeed in
the world before the law, but sin is not
reckoned when there is no law. 14 Yet death
exercised dominion from Adam to Moses,
even over those whose sins were not like
the transgression of Adam, who is a type of
the one who was to come.
15 But the free gift is not like the tres-
pass. For if the many died through the one
man's trespass, much more surely have the
grace of God and the free gift in the grace
of the one man, Jesus Christ, abounded for
the many. 16 And the free gift is not like the
effect of the one man's sin. For the judg-

a Other ancient authorities read *let us* *b* Other ancient authorities add *by faith* *c* Or *let us*
d Gk *the wrath*

5.1–21: The nature of justification in Christ. In light of the preceding argument, Paul declares that those justified in Christ may *boast* (vv. 2–3,11), not merely of being forgiven their sins (see vv. 8–10), but *much more surely,* of being saved from *wrath* (v. 9) and the *dominion* of *death* (vv. 14–17). This chapter prepares for the call to righteous living in ch 6. **1:** Being *justified by faith* (see 3.28n.) means entering God's life-giving and right-making *dominion* (v. 21), as ch 6 will make clear. Justification *by faith* may mean by the faith of Jesus, i.e., his obedience to God as shown in his death (v. 19). Thus Paul can speak of being justified *through Jesus Christ* (vv. 11,21), by Jesus' *blood* (v. 9), i.e., through his *death* (v. 10), or by his *obedience* (v. 19). **2–5:** *Hope* in the coming *glory of God,* see 8.16–25. **2:** *We boast* (or "let us boast," see v. 11), not in our own works (3.27; 4.2) but in God's power. **3:** *Sufferings,* see 8.18,35–36. **5:** *The Holy Spirit,* see 1.4n.; 8.2n. On the work of *the Spirit,* see 8.2–17,23–27. **6:** *While we were still weak,* God's grace preceded any human act that might constitute a claim to righteousness before God (see 3.27; 4.2; 9.11–12,16; regarding the Gentiles, 9.30). **9–11:** Paul stresses that God's saving purpose is *much more* than a reprieve from the punishment due for sins (vv. 15,17). **9–10:** *Justified by his blood . . . reconciled . . . through the death of his Son,* see v. 1n.

5.12–21: Adam and Christ. Christ's saving work surpasses even the effects of Adam's disobedience. (A different comparison of Christ and Adam is made in 1 Cor 15.21–23,45–49.) **12–14:** The catastrophe in Adam's transgression (Gen 3) is greater than the punishments reckoned for individual transgressions. It also introduced the *dominion* of sin (see v. 21; 6.6,12,14), and *much more,* allowed for *death* to invade creation (Gen 3.19,22–24). **14:** *To Moses,* until the law was given to Moses; see v. 20. *The one who was to come,* the messiah. **15–21: Salvation "much more" than forgiveness. 15–16:** Despite an apparent similarity between their effects on *the many,* Christ's obedience accomplished *much more* than to reverse the effects of Adam's sin. **17–18:** Christ's *act of righteousness* (see 8.1–4n.) brought the dominion of *life*

ment following one trespass brought con-
demnation, but the free gift following many
trespasses brings justification. 17If, because
of the one man's trespass, death exercised
dominion through that one, much more
surely will those who receive the abun-
dance of grace and the free gift of righ-
teousness exercise dominion in life through
the one man, Jesus Christ.

18 Therefore just as one man's trespass
led to condemnation for all, so one man's
act of righteousness leads to justification
and life for all. 19For just as by the one
man's disobedience the many were made
sinners, so by the one man's obedience the
many will be made righteous. 20But law
came in, with the result that the trespass
multiplied; but where sin increased, grace
abounded all the more, 21so that, just as
sin exercised dominion in death, so grace
might also exercise dominion through justi-
fication[a] leading to eternal life through
Jesus Christ our Lord.

6 What then are we to say? Should we
continue in sin in order that grace may
abound? 2By no means! How can we who
died to sin go on living in it? 3Do you not
know that all of us who have been baptized
into Christ Jesus were baptized into his
death? 4Therefore we have been buried
with him by baptism into death, so that,
just as Christ was raised from the dead by
the glory of the Father, so we too might
walk in newness of life.

5 For if we have been united with him in
a death like his, we will certainly be united
with him in a resurrection like his. 6We
know that our old self was crucified with
him so that the body of sin might be de-
stroyed, and we might no longer be en-
slaved to sin. 7For whoever has died is
freed from sin. 8But if we have died with
Christ, we believe that we will also live
with him. 9We know that Christ, being
raised from the dead, will never die again;
death no longer has dominion over him.
10The death he died, he died to sin, once
for all; but the life he lives, he lives to God.
11So you also must consider yourselves
dead to sin and alive to God in Christ Jesus.

12 Therefore, do not let sin exercise do-
minion in your mortal bodies, to make you
obey their passions. 13No longer present
your members to sin as instruments[b] of
wickedness, but present yourselves to God
as those who have been brought from death
to life, and present your members to God as
instruments[b] of righteousness. 14For sin
will have no dominion over you, since you
are not under law but under grace.

15 What then? Should we sin because
we are not under law but under grace? By
no means! 16Do you not know that if you

a Or *righteousness* *b* Or *weapons*

(6.13–14,23–24). **20:** The giving of the law is a minor episode, serving only to document sin's dominion through the increase of trespasses (7.7–11). The law could not bring that dominion to an end; God's powerful grace could (8.1–4; *Damascus Document* A 3.1–12).

6.1–23: Life in Christ requires obedience. 1: Compare other leading questions in 4.1; 6.15,21; 7.7,13. *Should we continue in sin?* (see v. 2; 3.8n.). Only if grace were simply a matter of being relieved of the punishment for trespasses. But it is "much more" (5.12–21). **2–6:** Baptism is a dying with Christ (v. 6; 7.6; Gal 2.19) to the power of sin, assuring that *we will also live with him* (v. 8). Contrast Eph 2.5–6; Col 2.12–13, where Christians are said already to be *raised* with Christ. **7–11:** *Whoever has died,* whether Christ, through his own death (v. 10), or Christians, by baptism (v. 14); see 7.1–6. **9–10:** The lethal collusion of sin and death are evident (see 5.12–14,21). The Gk word translated *has dominion* (5.21) is related to the word translated "lord" (see vv. 16–17n.). **12–13:** *Instruments of wickedness . . . of righteousness,* lit. "weapons of injustice" and "justice." Through martial imagery Paul calls Christians not to surrender themselves as sin's prisoners of war. **14–15:** If grace provided immunity from the law's verdict, then we might well "continue in sin" (see v. 1). **16–20:** An analogy from slavery. Since war captives were often enslaved, these verses may continue the imagery of vv. 13–14. **16–17:** *Slaves . . . obedient,* human existence is inevitably some form of obedience. Note that Paul refrains here from describing God as "Lord," lit. "master." **17:** *Obedient from the heart,* not in slavish obedience but with genuine intention (12.1–2).

present yourselves to anyone as obedient
slaves, you are slaves of the one whom you
obey, either of sin, which leads to death, or
of obedience, which leads to righteousness?
17 But thanks be to God that you, having
once been slaves of sin, have become obedi-
ent from the heart to the form of teaching
to which you were entrusted, 18 and that
you, having been set free from sin, have
become slaves of righteousness. 19 I am
speaking in human terms because of your
natural limitations.[a] For just as you once
presented your members as slaves to impu-
rity and to greater and greater iniquity, so
now present your members as slaves to
righteousness for sanctification.
20 When you were slaves of sin, you
were free in regard to righteousness. 21 So
what advantage did you then get from the
things of which you now are ashamed? The
end of those things is death. 22 But now that
you have been freed from sin and enslaved
to God, the advantage you get is sanctifica-
tion. The end is eternal life. 23 For the
wages of sin is death, but the free gift of
God is eternal life in Christ Jesus our Lord.
7 Do you not know, brothers and sis-
ters[b]—for I am speaking to those who
know the law—that the law is binding on a
person only during that person's lifetime?
2 Thus a married woman is bound by the
law to her husband as long as he lives; but
if her husband dies, she is discharged from
the law concerning the husband. 3 Accord-
ingly, she will be called an adulteress if she
lives with another man while her husband
is alive. But if her husband dies, she is free
from that law, and if she marries another
man, she is not an adulteress.
4 In the same way, my friends,[b] you
have died to the law through the body of
Christ, so that you may belong to another,
to him who has been raised from the dead
in order that we may bear fruit for God.
5 While we were living in the flesh, our sin-
ful passions, aroused by the law, were at
work in our members to bear fruit for
death. 6 But now we are discharged from
the law, dead to that which held us captive,
so that we are slaves not under the old writ-
ten code but in the new life of the Spirit.
7 What then should we say? That the
law is sin? By no means! Yet, if it had not
been for the law, I would not have known
sin. I would not have known what it is to
covet if the law had not said, "You shall
not covet." 8 But sin, seizing an opportunity
in the commandment, produced in me all
kinds of covetousness. Apart from the law
sin lies dead. 9 I was once alive apart from
the law, but when the commandment came,
sin revived 10 and I died, and the very com-

a Gk *the weakness of your flesh* b Gk *brothers*

18–20: "Not under law" (v. 15) does not imply freedom from moral obligation. **21:** *The things of which you now are ashamed,* 1.24–32.

7.1–25: A defense of the law. Paul relies on an analogy from marriage law. One is "free from the law" (v. 3) only when free from the circumstances to which the law rightly applies; here, free from the dominion of sin (6.6–11). Just as marriage law remains valid, so the Torah remains *holy* (v. 12), *spiritual* (v. 14), and *good* (v. 16). **1:** *Those who know the law,* i.e., marriage law. Paul does not presume specific knowledge of the Torah. **4:** The Christian has *died to the law,* and is thus "discharged" from it (v. 6). **5:** *Sinful passions, aroused by the law,* 5.20; 7.7–11. **6:** *That which held us captive,* the law, which bound us in our relationship to sin (6.15–23).

7.7–13: The law's poisonous interaction with sin. 7: Leading questions (see v. 13) express Paul's concern to exonerate the law. *I would not have known sin,* Paul is not speaking autobiographically (v. 9; Phil 3.6); some have suggested he refers to Adam (v. 10). More likely he presents a "speech in character," reflecting a typical human experience of the law. Although the law (here, Ex 20.17; Deut 5.21) aggravates the dominion of sin in one's members, the law itself remains valid. **8:** *Covetousness,* or "desire," was regarded by Paul's contemporaries as the root of all evil (see Jas 1.15; 4 Macc 2.4–6; Philo, *De spec. leg.* 4.84–94), even the source of Adam's sin (Philo, *Leg. all.* 3.115). *Sin lies dead,* cf. 5.13–14. **10:** *Promised life,* possibly an allusion to Lev 18.5, or to Deut 30.6–20; Paul juxtaposes those passages in 10.5–7 (Gal 3.21). **11:** *Sin . . . deceived me,* Gen 3.13. **13:** *That sin might be shown to be sin,* 5.13.

mandment that promised life proved to be
death to me. 11For sin, seizing an opportu-
nity in the commandment, deceived me and
through it killed me. 12So the law is holy,
and the commandment is holy and just and
good.
13 Did what is good, then, bring death
to me? By no means! It was sin, working
death in me through what is good, in order
that sin might be shown to be sin, and
through the commandment might become
sinful beyond measure.
14 For we know that the law is spiritual;
but I am of the flesh, sold into slavery un-
der sin.[a] 15I do not understand my own
actions. For I do not do what I want, but I
do the very thing I hate. 16Now if I do what
I do not want, I agree that the law is good.
17But in fact it is no longer I that do it, but
sin that dwells within me. 18For I know
that nothing good dwells within me, that is,
in my flesh. I can will what is right, but I
cannot do it. 19For I do not do the good
I want, but the evil I do not want is what
I do. 20Now if I do what I do not want, it
is no longer I that do it, but sin that dwells
within me.
21 So I find it to be a law that when I
want to do what is good, evil lies close at
hand. 22For I delight in the law of God in
my inmost self, 23but I see in my members
another law at war with the law of my
mind, making me captive to the law of sin
that dwells in my members. 24Wretched
man that I am! Who will rescue me from
this body of death? 25Thanks be to God
through Jesus Christ our Lord!
So then, with my mind I am a slave to the
law of God, but with my flesh I am a slave
to the law of sin.

8 There is therefore now no condemna-
tion for those who are in Christ Jesus.
2For the law of the Spirit[b] of life in Christ
Jesus has set you[c] free from the law of sin
and of death. 3For God has done what the
law, weakened by the flesh, could not do:
by sending his own Son in the likeness of
sinful flesh, and to deal with sin,[d] he con-
demned sin in the flesh, 4so that the just
requirement of the law might be fulfilled in
us, who walk not according to the flesh but
according to the Spirit.[b] 5For those who
live according to the flesh set their minds

a Gk *sold under sin* *b* Or *spirit* *c* Here the Greek word *you* is singular number; other ancient authorities read *me* or *us* *d* Or *and as a sin offering*

7.14–25: Even the disobedient acknowledge the rightness of the law's verdict. 14: *The flesh,* where *sin . . . dwells* (vv. 17–20); the Dead Sea Scrolls similarly speak of the "dominion" of sin in the flesh (e.g., 1QH 4.25), or of the "evil impulse" that prevents the fulfillment of God's law, until God intervenes (1QH 13.6). **15–16:** *I do not do what I want,* this is not Paul's view of Christian existence (see 12.1–2), but an illustration of the point made in 2.15: The law declares God's valid judgment on all human conduct. **18:** *I cannot do it,* 8.4,7–8. **25:** The "I" is hypothetical; Paul has already declared that those baptized into Christ are "no longer . . . enslaved to sin" (6.6).

8.1–39: Life in the Spirit. A turning point in the letter, summing up Paul's previous argument (*therefore,* v. 1) and serving as a foil for the dramatic appeal that follows. **1–4:** The inclination of human *flesh* (see 5.20n.) has prevented earlier generations—including those who received the law at Mt. Sinai—from fulfilling the *just requirement of the law* (2.14–15,26). The law is thus *weakened by the flesh* (v. 3). Now that Christ has satisfied that *just requirement* through his own "act of righteousness" (5.18, translating the same Gk word), those who are *in Christ* or *in the Spirit* (v. 9) likewise fulfill the law's *requirement,* in that they *walk . . . according to the Spirit* (v. 4). **2:** *The law of the Spirit of life* and *of death,* Paul speaks not of two different laws, but of God's law experienced under two opposing dominions, of sin and of righteousness (6.12–14; 7.6). *The Spirit of life,* capitalized to refer to the "Spirit of God" (vv. 9,11,14; "the Spirit that is from God," 1 Cor 2.14). Paul can use the word "spirit" indefinitely (e.g., "a spirit of slavery . . . a spirit of adoption," v. 15), or personally (vv. 26–27; 1 Cor 2.10–14). The latter use is capitalized in Christian convention, i.e., *the Holy Spirit* (5.5; 9.1; 1 Thess 4.8). **3:** *God has done what the law . . . could not do,* Jews in Paul's day regarded Israel's subjection to unjust powers as realizing God's curses on the disobedient (9.31; 10.3). Paul sees Israel's destiny as bound up with Christ's obedience (9.4–5). **5–17:** Life

on the things of the flesh, but those who
live according to the Spirit[a] set their minds
on the things of the Spirit.[a] 6 To set the
mind on the flesh is death, but to set the
mind on the Spirit[a] is life and peace. 7 For
this reason the mind that is set on the flesh
is hostile to God; it does not submit to
God's law—indeed it cannot, 8 and those
who are in the flesh cannot please God.

9 But you are not in the flesh; you are in
the Spirit,[a] since the Spirit of God dwells
in you. Anyone who does not have the Spir-
it of Christ does not belong to him. 10 But if
Christ is in you, though the body is dead
because of sin, the Spirit[a] is life because of
righteousness. 11 If the Spirit of him who
raised Jesus from the dead dwells in you, he
who raised Christ[b] from the dead will give
life to your mortal bodies also through[c]
his Spirit that dwells in you.

12 So then, brothers and sisters,[d] we
are debtors, not to the flesh, to live accord-
ing to the flesh— 13 for if you live according
to the flesh, you will die; but if by the Spirit
you put to death the deeds of the body, you
will live. 14 For all who are led by the Spirit
of God are children of God. 15 For you did
not receive a spirit of slavery to fall back
into fear, but you have received a spirit of
adoption. When we cry, "Abba![e] Father!"
16 it is that very Spirit bearing witness[f]
with our spirit that we are children of God,
17 and if children, then heirs, heirs of God
and joint heirs with Christ—if, in fact, we
suffer with him so that we may also be glo-
rified with him.

18 I consider that the sufferings of this
present time are not worth comparing with
the glory about to be revealed to us. 19 For
the creation waits with eager longing for
the revealing of the children of God; 20 for
the creation was subjected to futility, not of
its own will but by the will of the one who
subjected it, in hope 21 that the creation it-
self will be set free from its bondage to de-
cay and will obtain the freedom of the glory
of the children of God. 22 We know that the
whole creation has been groaning in labor
pains until now; 23 and not only the cre-
ation, but we ourselves, who have the first
fruits of the Spirit, groan inwardly while we
wait for adoption, the redemption of our
bodies. 24 For in[g] hope we were saved.
Now hope that is seen is not hope. For who
hopes[h] for what is seen? 25 But if we hope

a Or *spirit* *b* Other ancient authorities read *the Christ* or *Christ Jesus* or *Jesus Christ* *c* Other ancient authorities read *on account of* *d* Gk *brothers* *e* Aramaic for *Father* *f* Or *15a spirit of adoption, by which we cry, "Abba! Father!" 16The Spirit itself bears witness* *g* Or *by* *h* Other ancient authorities read *awaits*

in the Spirit and life in the flesh are contrasted. Paul thinks not of a sharp dualism of "spirit" or "mind" over body, but of different dispositions of the mind (vv. 5–7) corresponding to different ways of comporting one's body (6.12–19; 12.1–2). **7:** *Hostile to God,* 5.10. *Does not submit to God's law,* that is, to the law's "just requirement," which remains the standard of righteous living (v. 4; 2.14–15). **9–10:** Paul shifts from speaking of being "in Christ" (v. 1) or *in the Spirit* to having the Spirit or Christ dwell within oneself (6.22; 7.4). **11:** *He who raised Christ,* 4.17,24; 11.15. **13:** *Deeds of the body,* here Paul uses "body" interchangeably with *flesh.* See 6.6–8. **15–17:** *Adoption* by the Spirit: Those who live according to the Spirit (or by "faith," i.e., faithfulness, 4.12,16) are the *heirs* of the promises given to Abraham, even if not his descendants according to the flesh (4.1,11–14; Gal 4.5–7). **15:** *Abba,* an Aramaic word which Jesus may have used in his own prayer (Mk 14.36), was used in prayer by Gentile churches (Gal 4.6). **17:** *If . . . we suffer,* the tension between suffering and hope in the glory to come (5.3–5) is characteristic of the Christian life during "this present time" (v. 18; 12.12; 1 Cor 4.8–13).

8.18–39: Suffering, and hope in God's promise. God's purposes toward his children are much greater than the circumstances of *this present time* would indicate. This theme is crucial in chs 9–11. **19–22:** Paul shares an apocalyptic viewpoint that the present age is evil (see Gal 1.4), having been *subjected* by God to malevolent spiritual forces (v. 20; 1 Cor 15.20–28; Phil 3.21). **21:** Creation itself will participate in the liberation of the *children of God.* **22:** *Groaning in labor pains,* a frequent apocalyptic metaphor (2 Esd 4.42; 10.5–14; Mt 24.8; Mk 13.8; Jn 16.21–22). **23:** The inner testimony of the Spirit (vv. 16,26–27) is experienced as intense yearning and hope (5.1–5). *Adoption,* see 9.4n. **26–27:** If we "groan inwardly"

for what we do not see, we wait for it with
patience.
26 Likewise the Spirit helps us in our
weakness; for we do not know how to pray
as we ought, but that very Spirit inter-
cedes[a] with sighs too deep for words.
27 And God,[b] who searches the heart,
knows what is the mind of the Spirit, be-
cause the Spirit[c] intercedes for the saints
according to the will of God.[d]
28 We know that all things work togeth-
er for good[e] for those who love God, who
are called according to his purpose. 29 For
those whom he foreknew he also predes-
tined to be conformed to the image of his
Son, in order that he might be the firstborn
within a large family.[f] 30 And those whom
he predestined he also called; and those
whom he called he also justified; and those
whom he justified he also glorified.
31 What then are we to say about these
things? If God is for us, who is against us?
32 He who did not withhold his own Son,
but gave him up for all of us, will he not
with him also give us everything else?
33 Who will bring any charge against God's
elect? It is God who justifies. 34 Who is to
condemn? It is Christ Jesus, who died, yes,
who was raised, who is at the right hand
of God, who indeed intercedes for us.[g]
35 Who will separate us from the love of
Christ? Will hardship, or distress, or perse-
cution, or famine, or nakedness, or peril, or
sword? 36 As it is written,

"For your sake we are being killed all
day long;
we are accounted as sheep to be
slaughtered."

37 No, in all these things we are more than
conquerors through him who loved us.
38 For I am convinced that neither death,
nor life, nor angels, nor rulers, nor things
present, nor things to come, nor powers,
39 nor height, nor depth, nor anything else
in all creation, will be able to separate us
from the love of God in Christ Jesus our
Lord.

9 I am speaking the truth in Christ—I am
not lying; my conscience confirms it by
the Holy Spirit— 2 I have great sorrow and

a Other ancient authorities add *for us* *b* Gk *the one* *c* Gk *he* or *it* *d* Gk *according to God* *e* Other ancient authorities read *God makes all things work together for good*, or *in all things God works for good* *f* Gk *among many brothers* *g* Or *Is it Christ Jesus . . . for us?*

(v. 23), it is because of the Spirit at work in our prayers, interceding *for the saints.* This dramatic language is resumed in 9.1–3. **28–30:** The alternative translations in the footnote represent the reading in our earliest manuscript. Paul means, not that all circumstances of this life are good for us (the lament in 8.36 is genuine), but that amid *all* these *things* God's purpose prevails. *Those . . . who are called,* preeminently Israel (9.4; 11.2); also all those who are "the children of the promise," including Gentiles (9.8,23–26). *Conformed to the image of his Son,* Phil 3.21; 2 Cor 4.4. Christ the *firstborn,* 1 Cor 15.20; Col 1.18. **31–39:** Previous assurances of God's love (5.1–11) are reaffirmed; despite all present adversities, God's purpose will prevail. **34:** The heavenly Christ *intercedes for us,* as in vv. 26–27 the Spirit intercedes for the saints. **35–36:** *Hardship . . . or sword,* very real afflictions, as Israel's experience testifies; Ps 44.22 is quoted.

Chapters 9–11: The certainty of God's purposes toward Israel. The preceding argument reaches its climax in these extraordinary chapters, which combine earnest emotional appeal (9.1–5; 10.1–2), exegetical argument (9.6–13,25–29,33; 10.5–13,15–21; 11.2–4,8–10), the mock dialogue of the diatribe (9.14,19–21,30–32; 10.14,18; 11.1,4,7,11; see 2.17n.), and the stark pronouncement style of the prophets (11.25–27). The dramatic contrast in tone between chs 8 and 9, and the continuity of theme across chs 8–11, confirm Paul's overarching purpose. Despite present appearances, God has not abandoned promises made to Israel (9.6; 11.1,11–12,29). The same power that raised Jesus Christ from the dead (10.6–9) can restore Israel as well (11.15,23).

9.1–5: Paul's anguish for Israel is deeply personal—he speaks of his *own people* (v. 3)—yet also grounded in God's *promises* (v. 4). **1:** A solemn oath, confirmed by the Spirit (8.16,23,26–27). **2–3:** Paul's willingness to be *cut off from Christ* for the sake of Israel is especially poignant after the assurance

unceasing anguish in my heart. 3 For I could
wish that I myself were accursed and cut off
from Christ for the sake of my own peo-
ple,[a] my kindred according to the flesh.
4 They are Israelites, and to them belong the
adoption, the glory, the covenants, the giv-
ing of the law, the worship, and the prom-
ises; 5 to them belong the patriarchs, and
from them, according to the flesh, comes
the Messiah,[b] who is over all, God blessed
forever.[c] Amen.
6 It is not as though the word of God
had failed. For not all Israelites truly belong
to Israel, 7 and not all of Abraham's chil-
dren are his true descendants; but "It is
through Isaac that descendants shall be
named for you." 8 This means that it is not
the children of the flesh who are the chil-
dren of God, but the children of the prom-
ise are counted as descendants. 9 For this is
what the promise said, "About this time I
will return and Sarah shall have a son."
10 Nor is that all; something similar hap-
pened to Rebecca when she had conceived
children by one husband, our ancestor
Isaac. 11 Even before they had been born or
had done anything good or bad (so that
God's purpose of election might continue,
12 not by works but by his call) she was
told, "The elder shall serve the younger."
13 As it is written,

"I have loved Jacob,
but I have hated Esau."

14 What then are we to say? Is there in-
justice on God's part? By no means! 15 For
he says to Moses,

"I will have mercy on whom I
have mercy,
and I will have compassion on
whom I have compassion."

16 So it depends not on human will or exer-
tion, but on God who shows mercy. 17 For
the scripture says to Pharaoh, "I have
raised you up for the very purpose of show-
ing my power in you, so that my name may
be proclaimed in all the earth." 18 So then
he has mercy on whomever he chooses,
and he hardens the heart of whomever he
chooses.
19 You will say to me then, "Why then
does he still find fault? For who can resist
his will?" 20 But who indeed are you, a hu-
man being, to argue with God? Will what is
molded say to the one who molds it, "Why

a Gk *my brothers* *b* Or *the Christ* *c* Or *Messiah, who is God over all, blessed forever*; or *Messiah. May he who is God over all be blessed forever*

in 8.39. **4:** *To them belong the adoption,* lit. "sonship." The same Gk word appeared in 8.15,23. Paul's point is not that the people of Israel are more "naturally" God's children (vv. 6–9; 4.11–12), but that their "sonship" (see Ex 4.22–23; Hos 11.1) is prior to that of the Gentiles called in Christ (11.17–24). *The glory,* Ex 16.10; 24.16–17. *The covenants,* plural because several are recorded in scripture (Gen 15.8; 17.2,7,9; Ex 2.24). *Giving of the law,* Israel's privilege (2.17–20). *The worship,* Israel's covenant obligation (Ex 3.12; 4.23). *The promises,* of the land (see Gen 15.7; Ex 6.8), or more broadly "the world" (4.13). **5:** *The patriarchs,* Abraham, Isaac, and Jacob, see Ex 2.24. *According to the flesh,* see 1.3; 15.8–9. *Messiah . . . God blessed forever,* whether Christ is called God here depends on the punctuation inserted (see note *c*). Similar Gk phrases are translated as spontaneous praise to God in 1.25; 11.36; 16.25–27.

9.6–29: God's right to choose. Paul's concern to vindicate God's *purpose of election* (v. 11) runs throughout these verses, as rhetorical questions in vv. 14,19–24 and 30–32 show. **6:** Paul means not to restrict the number of those who are "truly Israel," but to insist that being "Abraham's children" (v. 7) has never been a matter of physical descent (v. 8). Because the promise came to Abraham through faith (4.13), his "true descendants" are "children of the promise." **7:** Though Abraham had other sons (Gen 25.2,12,19), only Isaac was his heir (Gen 21.2). **9:** God's promise was given to Sarah (Gen 18.10), not Hagar; Gal 4.21–31. **10–12:** God chose Jacob, not Esau (Gen 25.21,23), without regard to any human effort (v. 16). **13:** Mal 1.2–3. **14–29:** If election is not the result of human merit, is God unjust? Paul rejects this conclusion, not by appealing to moral principle, but by affirming God's sovereignty. **15:** Ex 33.19. **17–18:** God chose Pharaoh (Ex 9.16), not because of merit, but to show God's power (see 11.7–12). *Hardens the heart,* see Ex 4.21; Deut 2.30; Josh 11.20. **19–21:** Paul draws his conclusion in diatribe style, using biblical metaphors; see Isa 29.16; 45.9; Jer 18.6; Wis 15.7. **22–24:** *Objects of wrath,* sinners toward

have you made me like this?” 21 Has the
potter no right over the clay, to make out of
the same lump one object for special use
and another for ordinary use? 22 What if
God, desiring to show his wrath and to
make known his power, has endured with
much patience the objects of wrath that are
made for destruction; 23 and what if he has
done so in order to make known the riches
of his glory for the objects of mercy, which
he has prepared beforehand for glory—
24 including us whom he has called, not
from the Jews only but also from the Gen-
tiles? 25 As indeed he says in Hosea,

“Those who were not my people I
will call ‘my people,’
and her who was not beloved I will
call ‘beloved.’ ”
26 “And in the very place where it was
said to them, ‘You are not my
people,’
there they shall be called children
of the living God.”

27 And Isaiah cries out concerning Isra-
el, “Though the number of the children of
Israel were like the sand of the sea, only a
remnant of them will be saved; 28 for the
Lord will execute his sentence on the earth
quickly and decisively.”[a] 29 And as Isaiah
predicted,

“If the Lord of hosts had not left
survivors[b] to us,
we would have fared like Sodom
and been made like Gomorrah.”

30 What then are we to say? Gentiles,
who did not strive for righteousness, have
attained it, that is, righteousness through
faith; 31 but Israel, who did strive for the
righteousness that is based on the law, did
not succeed in fulfilling that law. 32 Why
not? Because they did not strive for it on
the basis of faith, but as if it were based on
works. They have stumbled over the stum-
bling stone, 33 as it is written,

“See, I am laying in Zion a stone that
will make people stumble, a
rock that will make them fall,
and whoever believes in him[c] will
not be put to shame.”

10 Brothers and sisters,[d] my heart’s
desire and prayer to God for them is
that they may be saved. 2 I can testify that
they have a zeal for God, but it is not en-
lightened. 3 For, being ignorant of the righ-
teousness that comes from God, and seek-
ing to establish their own, they have not
submitted to God’s righteousness. 4 For
Christ is the end of the law so that there
may be righteousness for everyone who be-
lieves.

5 Moses writes concerning the righ-
teousness that comes from the law, that
“the person who does these things will live

a Other ancient authorities read *for he will finish his work and cut it short in righteousness, because the Lord will make the sentence shortened on the earth*
b Or *descendants*; Gk *seed*
c Or *trusts in it*
d Gk *Brothers*

whom God has shown *patience,* as in 2.4–5; 3.25–26. Mortals may not presume God’s judgment on others, to vindicate or to condemn (see 8.1; 11.30–32; 14.3–4,10–13). **25–26:** Hosea spoke of the redemption of Israel (Hos 2.23; 1.10). Paul applies the passage to those God has called, *Jews* and *Gentiles* alike (v. 24). **27–29:** God’s preservation of *a remnant* in Israel (Isa 10.22; 1.9) shows God’s faithfulness (see 11.1–6). The word *only* does not appear in Gk.

9.30–11.12: What went wrong? Paul addresses the surprising circumstances of Israel and the Gentiles. **9.30–33:** A fixed footrace. The Greek “diokein” (“strive for”) can mean “chase after” as in a race. The Gentiles’ success and Israel’s failure to reach the goal or finish line have nothing to do with effort. Israel *stumbled over the stumbling stone,* tripped up, as it were, by God (v. 33; 11.7–8). **32:** Israel approached the law on the basis of *works* (3.20,27). Paul speaks here (and in 10.3) not of the desire to obey the law, but of the danger of boasting in one’s own righteousness (Deut 8.17; 9.4–5). **33:** Isa 8.14–15; 28.16. Other early Christians interpreted these verses in relation to Christ (1 Pet 2.6–8; Mt 21.42). For Paul, the *stone* laid *in Zion* may be the law itself. **10.1–3:** See 9.1–5. **3:** In Paul’s view, Israel was *ignorant* in failing to submit *to God’s righteousness,* i.e., the righteousness offered through the “faith of Jesus Christ” (see 3.22n.). **4:** *The end of the law* almost certainly means its goal, not its termination (3.31; 7.12,16,22; 9.30–32). **5–13:** Using a common Jewish technique, Paul interprets one passage of scripture (Lev 18.5)

by them." 6 But the righteousness that
comes from faith says, "Do not say in your
heart, 'Who will ascend into heaven?' "
(that is, to bring Christ down) 7 "or 'Who
will descend into the abyss?' " (that is, to
bring Christ up from the dead). 8 But what
does it say?

"The word is near you,
on your lips and in your heart"

(that is, the word of faith that we pro-
claim); 9 because[a] if you confess with your
lips that Jesus is Lord and believe in your
heart that God raised him from the dead,
you will be saved. 10 For one believes with
the heart and so is justified, and one con-
fesses with the mouth and so is saved.
11 The scripture says, "No one who believes
in him will be put to shame." 12 For there is
no distinction between Jew and Greek; the
same Lord is Lord of all and is generous to
all who call on him. 13 For, "Everyone who
calls on the name of the Lord shall be
saved."

14 But how are they to call on one in
whom they have not believed? And how are
they to believe in one of whom they have
never heard? And how are they to hear
without someone to proclaim him? 15 And
how are they to proclaim him unless they
are sent? As it is written, "How beautiful
are the feet of those who bring good news!"
16 But not all have obeyed the good news;[b]
for Isaiah says, "Lord, who has believed
our message?" 17 So faith comes from what
is heard, and what is heard comes through
the word of Christ.[c]

18 But I ask, have they not heard? In-
deed they have; for

"Their voice has gone out to all
the earth,
and their words to the ends of the
world."

19 Again I ask, did Israel not understand?
First Moses says,

"I will make you jealous of those who
are not a nation;
with a foolish nation I will make
you angry."

20 Then Isaiah is so bold as to say,

"I have been found by those who did
not seek me;
I have shown myself to those who
did not ask for me."

21 But of Israel he says, "All day long I have
held out my hands to a disobedient and
contrary people."

11 I ask, then, has God rejected his
people? By no means! I myself am
an Israelite, a descendant of Abraham, a
member of the tribe of Benjamin. 2 God has
not rejected his people whom he foreknew.
Do you not know what the scripture says of
Elijah, how he pleads with God against Is-
rael? 3 "Lord, they have killed your proph-
ets, they have demolished your altars; I

a Or *namely, that* b Or *gospel* c Or *about Christ*; other ancient authorities read *of God*

in light of others (Deut 30.11–14; cf. Ps 107.26). **5–7:** *The righteousness . . . from the law* and *from faith* are not opposed, since there is only "God's righteousness" (10.3). The promise of life to *the person who does these things* (Lev 18.5) requires not human effort to produce the messiah, but faith in the messiah whom God has sent. Such is Paul's christological reading of Deut 30.11–14. **9–13:** Salvation through "faith" (1.15–17). **11:** Isa 28.16. **12:** *No distinction,* see 3.22,29. **13:** Joel 2.32. Early Christians often applied to Jesus biblical references to the *Lord,* references which in their original context refer to God. **14–21:** God's faithfulness to Israel continues as *good news* is preached to them. **15:** Isa 52.17. **16:** Isa 53.1. *But not all have obeyed,* the disobedience of some in Israel does not alter God's faithfulness (see 3.3). *Good news,* the same word is elsewhere translated "gospel"; see 1.16n. **18:** Ps 19.4. **19:** Deut 32.21. Israel's disobedience does not indicate God's failure; to the contrary, God's purpose is to make Israel jealous. **20–21:** See 11.11–12. The Gentiles are the "foolish nation" (Deut 32.21), *those who did not seek me* (Isa 65.1–2). *All day long,* Paul emphasizes God's persistent faithfulness to a disobedient Israel.

11.1–12: God has preserved a remnant. Paul himself is evidence that *God has not rejected his people.* **2–5:** The *divine reply* to the prophet Elijah was a rebuke for presuming he *alone* was left (1 Kings 19.10,18). Similarly, the *remnant* in Paul's day does not exhaust God's gracious purpose (see vv. 12,15,25–27). **7–12:** Astonishingly, Paul concludes Israel *failed* (9.31–10.4) because they *were hard-*

alone am left, and they are seeking my life."
4 But what is the divine reply to him? "I
have kept for myself seven thousand who
have not bowed the knee to Baal." 5 So too
at the present time there is a remnant, cho-
sen by grace. 6 But if it is by grace, it is no
longer on the basis of works, otherwise
grace would no longer be grace.[a]

7 What then? Israel failed to obtain
what it was seeking. The elect obtained it,
but the rest were hardened, 8 as it is written,

"God gave them a sluggish spirit,
eyes that would not see
and ears that would not hear,
down to this very day."

9 And David says,

"Let their table become a snare
and a trap,
a stumbling block and a retribution
for them;
10 let their eyes be darkened so that they
cannot see,
and keep their backs forever bent."

11 So I ask, have they stumbled so as to
fall? By no means! But through their stum-
bling[b] salvation has come to the Gentiles,
so as to make Israel[c] jealous. 12 Now if
their stumbling[b] means riches for the
world, and if their defeat means riches for
Gentiles, how much more will their full in-
clusion mean!

13 Now I am speaking to you Gentiles.
Inasmuch then as I am an apostle to the
Gentiles, I glorify my ministry 14 in order to
make my own people[d] jealous, and thus
save some of them. 15 For if their rejection
is the reconciliation of the world, what will
their acceptance be but life from the dead!
16 If the part of the dough offered as first
fruits is holy, then the whole batch is holy;
and if the root is holy, then the branches
also are holy.

17 But if some of the branches were bro-
ken off, and you, a wild olive shoot, were
grafted in their place to share the rich
root[e] of the olive tree, 18 do not boast over
the branches. If you do boast, remember
that it is not you that support the root, but
the root that supports you. 19 You will say,
"Branches were broken off so that I might
be grafted in." 20 That is true. They were
broken off because of their unbelief, but
you stand only through faith. So do not
become proud, but stand in awe. 21 For if
God did not spare the natural branches,
perhaps he will not spare you.[f] 22 Note
then the kindness and the severity of God:
severity toward those who have fallen, but
God's kindness toward you, provided you
continue in his kindness; otherwise you

a Other ancient authorities add *But if it is by works, it is no longer on the basis of grace, otherwise work would no longer be work* *b* Gk *transgression* *c* Gk *them* *d* Gk *my flesh* *e* Other ancient authorities read *the richness* *f* Other ancient authorities read *neither will he spare you*

ened by God (9.18). **8:** Isa 29.10. **9:** Ps 69.22–23. **11–12:** Previous rhetorical questions concerned God's righteousness or faithfulness (3.3,29; 9.14,19); now Paul asks about God's faithfulness to the covenant with Israel. The obedience of the Gentiles will *make Israel jealous* (see 10.19–20). *Their full inclusion,* see vv. 15,26.

11.13–36: A warning to the Gentile Christians of Rome. The climax of chs 9–11, these verses reveal the heart of the letter's purpose. Paul is obliged as apostle to the Gentiles to address the Christians of Rome (see 1.1–13), and to pronounce the solemn warning that follows (see 15.14–16). **13:** *I glorify my ministry,* 15.18–21. **14:** *To make my own people jealous,* and thus, probably, to elicit their acceptance of the Christ (10.14–21). **15:** *Life from the dead,* see v. 23. **16:** The remnant preserved by God (see 9.27–29; 11.1–5), like a portion of *dough* offered in worship (Num 15.18–21) or the *root* of a tree (Jer 11.16–17), guarantees God's continuing care for the whole of Israel.

11.17–24: The metaphor of the olive tree. The tree, root and branches, is Israel (Jer 11.16; Hos 14.6); the *wild olive shoot* (v. 17) represents the Gentiles who believe in Christ. **17:** *Broken off,* the passive voice here and in vv. 19–20 reflects divine action (see v. 21). **18:** The ingrafting, "contrary to nature" (v. 24), of a *wild olive shoot* would give life to the shoot, but would not benefit the root. *Do not boast,* the tone of warning earlier (2.17n.) reaches its target here. **19–21:** Paul concedes the Gentile-Christian perception that *branches were broken off,* but warns against pride (see 12.3). **22:** *The kindness . . . severity,* 2.4–10.

also will be cut off. 23 And even those of
Israel,[a] if they do not persist in unbelief,
will be grafted in, for God has the power to
graft them in again. 24 For if you have been
cut from what is by nature a wild olive tree
and grafted, contrary to nature, into a culti-
vated olive tree, how much more will these
natural branches be grafted back into their
own olive tree.

25 So that you may not claim to be wiser
than you are, brothers and sisters,[b] I want
you to understand this mystery: a harden-
ing has come upon part of Israel, until the
full number of the Gentiles has come in.
26 And so all Israel will be saved; as it is
written,

"Out of Zion will come the Deliverer;
he will banish ungodliness
from Jacob."
27 "And this is my covenant with them,
when I take away their sins."

28 As regards the gospel they are enemies of
God[c] for your sake; but as regards election
they are beloved, for the sake of their an-
cestors; 29 for the gifts and the calling of
God are irrevocable. 30 Just as you were
once disobedient to God but have now re-
ceived mercy because of their disobedience,
31 so they have now been disobedient in or-
der that, by the mercy shown to you, they
too may now[d] receive mercy. 32 For God
has imprisoned all in disobedience so that
he may be merciful to all.

33 O the depth of the riches and wis-
dom and knowledge of God! How un-
searchable are his judgments and how in-
scrutable his ways!

34 "For who has known the mind of the
Lord?
Or who has been his counselor?"
35 "Or who has given a gift to him,
to receive a gift in return?"

36 For from him and through him and to
him are all things. To him be the glory for-
ever. Amen.

12 I appeal to you therefore, brothers
and sisters,[b] by the mercies of God,
to present your bodies as a living sacrifice,
holy and acceptable to God, which is your
spiritual[e] worship. 2 Do not be conformed
to this world,[f] but be transformed by the
renewing of your minds, so that you may
discern what is the will of God—what is
good and acceptable and perfect.[g]

3 For by the grace given to me I say to

a Gk lacks *of Israel* *b* Gk *brothers* *c* Gk lacks *of God* *d* Other ancient authorities lack *now* *e* Or *reasonable* *f* Gk *age* *g* Or *what is the good and acceptable and perfect will of God*

24: If ingrafting a *wild olive tree* is unusual, restoring branches that have been broken off is nothing less than miraculous (11.15,26; 4.17n.). *Natural branches,* deriving from the stock of Israel (9.6n.).

11.25–36: The hardening of Israel. A warning against Gentile-Christian arrogance, the heart of the letter (see 2.1–4; 3.27; 12.3). **25:** *I want you to understand,* such solemn disclosures indicate Paul's concerns in his letters (1 Cor 10.1–6; 12.1; 2 Cor 1.8; 1 Thess 4.13). *This mystery,* a truth revealed by God (Dan 2.18–30,47; 1 Cor 2.7; 13.2; 14.2). *A hardening,* vv. 7–8; 9.18. This hardening is temporary, until *the full number of the Gentiles,* those destined to trust in God, *has come in.* **26:** Isa 59.20–21; 27.9. *All Israel,* in view already in 11.16,23. *Saved,* delivered from *ungodliness* and forgiven their "sins." **28–32:** God's mysterious course of action fulfills the election of Israel (3.2; 9.6; 11.1) and precludes the possibility of human boasting (v. 32; 3.9–30). **34:** Isa 40.13. **35:** Job 35.7; 41.11. **36:** A doxology, as at 1.25; 9.5; 16.25–27.

12.1–15.13: Exhortation to holy living. On the basis of the argument in previous chapters, Paul now exhorts the Christians of Rome to right conduct. **12.1:** Holy living is *spiritual worship* (15.15–16), the opposite of "ungodliness" (1.21–28), made possible through baptism (6.12–23). Paul makes his "appeal" (the Gk phrase marks exhortations in his letters: 1 Cor 1.10; 2 Cor 10.1; 1 Thess 4.1; Philem 9) on the basis of *the mercies of God* (11.22–23,30–32) and the "grace given" to him as apostle (v. 3; 1.5; 15.15). **2:** Christians are to live no longer as belonging to *this world* (Gal 1.4; Phil 2.15; 1 Cor 7.29–31). The *renewing of . . . minds,* possible because of baptism (6.4), enables discerning *the will of God* (see Phil 1.9; 3.8–9). **3–8: A warning against arrogance. 3:** *I say,* direct speech echoes 11.1,11,13. *Not to think . . . more highly,* similar Gk phrases are translated "do not become proud" in 11.20, and "do not be haughty"

everyone among you not to think of your-
self more highly than you ought to think,
but to think with sober judgment, each ac-
cording to the measure of faith that God
has assigned. 4For as in one body we have
many members, and not all the members
have the same function, 5so we, who are
many, are one body in Christ, and individu-
ally we are members one of another. 6We
have gifts that differ according to the grace
given to us: prophecy, in proportion to
faith; 7ministry, in ministering; the teacher,
in teaching; 8the exhorter, in exhortation;
the giver, in generosity; the leader, in dili-
gence; the compassionate, in cheerfulness.
9 Let love be genuine; hate what is evil,
hold fast to what is good; 10love one anoth-
er with mutual affection; outdo one anoth-
er in showing honor. 11Do not lag in zeal,
be ardent in spirit, serve the Lord.[a] 12Re-
joice in hope, be patient in suffering, perse-
vere in prayer. 13Contribute to the needs of
the saints; extend hospitality to strangers.
14 Bless those who persecute you; bless
and do not curse them. 15Rejoice with
those who rejoice, weep with those who
weep. 16Live in harmony with one another;
do not be haughty, but associate with the
lowly;[b] do not claim to be wiser than you
are. 17Do not repay anyone evil for evil,
but take thought for what is noble in the
sight of all. 18If it is possible, so far as it
depends on you, live peaceably with all.
19Beloved, never avenge yourselves, but
leave room for the wrath of God;[c] for it is
written, "Vengeance is mine, I will repay,
says the Lord." 20No, "if your enemies are
hungry, feed them; if they are thirsty, give
them something to drink; for by doing this
you will heap burning coals on their
heads." 21Do not be overcome by evil, but
overcome evil with good.
13 Let every person be subject to the
governing authorities; for there is
no authority except from God, and those
authorities that exist have been instituted
by God. 2Therefore whoever resists author-
ity resists what God has appointed, and
those who resist will incur judgment. 3For
rulers are not a terror to good conduct, but
to bad. Do you wish to have no fear of the
authority? Then do what is good, and you
will receive its approval; 4for it is God's
servant for your good. But if you do what

a Other ancient authorities read *serve the opportune time* *b* Or *give yourselves to humble tasks*
c Gk *the wrath*

in v. 16. **4–8:** *Gifts* are given to nourish the community as *one body in Christ;* 1 Cor 12.4–31 provides a similar list.

12.9–21: Goodwill within the community and without. 9–10: *Love,* 13.8–10; 1 Cor 13. **12:** *Hope* and patience in *suffering,* see 5.3–5; 8.18–39. **13:** *Hospitality* was a crucial virtue in the early churches (see 16.1–2; Heb 13.2; 3 Jn 5–8). **14:** Here and in vv. 17,21, Paul may allude to sayings of Jesus (Mt 5.44). **16:** See v. 3n. *The lowly,* almost certainly people (despite the alternative in note *b*), as in Lk 1.52; Jas 1.9; the same Gk word is translated "humble" in Mt 11.29; Jas 4.6; 1 Pet 5.5. **17:** Mt 5.44. **19:** Deut 32.35. *Wrath,* see 2.5n. **20:** To *heap burning coals . . .* makes enemies feel ashamed and perhaps remorseful (Prov 25.21–22). **21:** Mt 5.39.

13.1–7: Subjection to governing authorities. Sometimes read as Paul's "theology of the state," these verses stand in tension with his view elsewhere of the "rulers of this age" (1 Cor 2.6–8; 15.24–26; 1 Thess 5.3–11), and with his own willingness to suffer punishment from civil authorities (2 Cor 11.23,25–27). This teaching is conventional (Wis 6.1–3; 1 Pet 2.13–17; 3.13), and there are other attitudes to civil authorities in the New Testament (Acts 5.29; Rev 13.2,5,11–18). These verses may have had a very specific application (see the Introduction). **1:** Empires rise and fall by the will of God (Isa 10.5–6; Jer 27.4–8,11; Dan 3.28–32). *Instituted,* lit. "put in their place"; the Gk word is related to the word translated *be subject.* **2:** Do not *resist* authority; contrast 12.2. *Resists what God has appointed,* 8.7; 9.19. **3–4:** The proper role of civil authorities; Paul was aware they could act otherwise. *God's servant,* Jer 27.6 (the Babylonian Nebuchadnezzar). The authority may punish; the individual Christian may not (12.19–21). *The sword,* a symbol of power over life and death (see 8.35). *Wrath,* elsewhere usually "the wrath of God" (1.18; 2.5; 5.9). **5–6:** Proper civil behavior is motivated both by fear of "wrath" (but

is wrong, you should be afraid, for the au-
thority[a] does not bear the sword in vain! It
is the servant of God to execute wrath on
the wrongdoer. 5 Therefore one must be
subject, not only because of wrath but also
because of conscience. 6 For the same rea-
son you also pay taxes, for the authorities
are God's servants, busy with this very
thing. 7 Pay to all what is due them—taxes
to whom taxes are due, revenue to whom
revenue is due, respect to whom respect is
due, honor to whom honor is due.

8 Owe no one anything, except to love
one another; for the one who loves another
has fulfilled the law. 9 The commandments,
"You shall not commit adultery; You shall
not murder; You shall not steal; You shall
not covet"; and any other commandment,
are summed up in this word, "Love your
neighbor as yourself." 10 Love does no
wrong to a neighbor; therefore, love is the
fulfilling of the law.

11 Besides this, you know what time it
is, how it is now the moment for you to
wake from sleep. For salvation is nearer to
us now than when we became believers;
12 the night is far gone, the day is near. Let
us then lay aside the works of darkness and
put on the armor of light; 13 let us live hon-
orably as in the day, not in reveling and
drunkenness, not in debauchery and licen-
tiousness, not in quarreling and jealousy.
14 Instead, put on the Lord Jesus Christ,
and make no provision for the flesh, to
gratify its desires.

14 Welcome those who are weak in
faith,[b] but not for the purpose of
quarreling over opinions. 2 Some believe in
eating anything, while the weak eat only
vegetables. 3 Those who eat must not de-
spise those who abstain, and those who ab-
stain must not pass judgment on those who
eat; for God has welcomed them. 4 Who are
you to pass judgment on servants of anoth-
er? It is before their own lord that they
stand or fall. And they will be upheld, for
the Lord[c] is able to make them stand.

5 Some judge one day to be better than
another, while others judge all days to be
alike. Let all be fully convinced in their own
minds. 6 Those who observe the day, ob-
serve it in honor of the Lord. Also those
who eat, eat in honor of the Lord, since
they give thanks to God; while those who
abstain, abstain in honor of the Lord and
give thanks to God.

7 We do not live to ourselves, and we do
not die to ourselves. 8 If we live, we live to
the Lord, and if we die, we die to the Lord;
so then, whether we live or whether we die,
we are the Lord's. 9 For to this end Christ
died and lived again, so that he might be
Lord of both the dead and the living.

10 Why do you pass judgment on your
brother or sister?[d] Or you, why do you
despise your brother or sister?[d] For we

a Gk *it* b Or *conviction* c Other ancient authorities read *for God* d Gk *brother*

see v. 3) and *conscience.* **6–7:** *Taxes,* the Roman tribute (as in Mt 22.21; Mk 12.17; Lk 20.25), from which Roman citizens were exempt. *Revenue,* commercial taxes. *Respect,* lit. "fear"; the same word is translated "terror" in v. 3. The one *to whom respect,* or fear, *is due* may be God alone (1 Pet 2.17).

13.8–14: Other exhortations. 8–10: *Love* fulfills *the law,* 2.14; 8.4; 12.9; Mt 22.39–40; Mk 12.31; Gal 5.14; Jas 2.8; 1 Jn 4.11. **9:** Ex 20.13–17; Deut 5.17–21; Lev 19.18. **11–14:** Imminent *salvation,* i.e., the return of Christ, makes it urgent to *wake* to holy and honorable living (1 Thess 5.1–11; Eph 5.8–18). **14:** *Put on the Lord Jesus,* an early Christian metaphor for baptism (Gal 3.27).

14.1–15.13: Exhortations regarding those who observe Torah. The observance of special days (vv. 5–6) and a kosher diet (vv. 2,14n.) are marks of Jewish observance. The Gentile Christians of Rome must not *despise* the observant (v. 3). **1–12: Tolerance for others' observance. 1–2:** Those who *eat only vegetables* are most likely keeping kosher by avoiding "unclean" meat (v. 14), or meat "sacrificed to idols" (Acts 15.29; 1 Cor 8.1; Dan 1.3–16; Esth 3.28; 14.17; Jdt 12.1–2). Paul calls them *weak in faith* (or "conviction"), not because they adhere to the Torah (see vv. 4,6; 7.12), but because they are scandalized by Gentile Christians who eat non-kosher food (vv. 13,15,20). **4:** *The Lord is able,* 11.23. **5–9:** Jews and Gentiles can, each in their own way, live *in honor of the Lord.* **11:** Isa 45.23. **13–23: Freedom is not**

will all stand before the judgment seat of
God.[a] 11 For it is written,
“As I live, says the Lord, every knee
shall bow to me,
and every tongue shall give praise
to[b] God.”
12 So then, each of us will be accountable to
God.[c]
13 Let us therefore no longer pass judg-
ment on one another, but resolve instead
never to put a stumbling block or hin-
drance in the way of another.[d] 14 I know
and am persuaded in the Lord Jesus that
nothing is unclean in itself; but it is unclean
for anyone who thinks it unclean. 15 If your
brother or sister[e] is being injured by what
you eat, you are no longer walking in love.
Do not let what you eat cause the ruin of
one for whom Christ died. 16 So do not let
your good be spoken of as evil. 17 For the
kingdom of God is not food and drink but
righteousness and peace and joy in the
Holy Spirit. 18 The one who thus serves
Christ is acceptable to God and has human
approval. 19 Let us then pursue what makes
for peace and for mutual upbuilding. 20 Do
not, for the sake of food, destroy the work
of God. Everything is indeed clean, but
it is wrong for you to make others fall by
what you eat; 21 it is good not to eat meat
or drink wine or do anything that makes
your brother or sister[e] stumble.[f] 22 The
faith that you have, have as your own con-
viction before God. Blessed are those who
have no reason to condemn themselves be-
cause of what they approve. 23 But those
who have doubts are condemned if they
eat, because they do not act from faith;[g]
for whatever does not proceed from faith[g]
is sin.[h]

15 We who are strong ought to put up
with the failings of the weak, and
not to please ourselves. 2 Each of us must
please our neighbor for the good purpose
of building up the neighbor. 3 For Christ
did not please himself; but, as it is written,
“The insults of those who insult you have
fallen on me.” 4 For whatever was written
in former days was written for our instruc-
tion, so that by steadfastness and by the
encouragement of the scriptures we might
have hope. 5 May the God of steadfastness
and encouragement grant you to live in
harmony with one another, in accordance
with Christ Jesus, 6 so that together you
may with one voice glorify the God and
Father of our Lord Jesus Christ.
7 Welcome one another, therefore, just
as Christ has welcomed you, for the glory
of God. 8 For I tell you that Christ has be-
come a servant of the circumcised on behalf
of the truth of God in order that he might
confirm the promises given to the patri-
archs, 9 and in order that the Gentiles might
glorify God for his mercy. As it is written,
“Therefore I will confess[i] you among
the Gentiles,
and sing praises to your name”;
10 and again he says,
“Rejoice, O Gentiles, with his
people”;
11 and again,
“Praise the Lord, all you Gentiles,
and let all the peoples praise him”;

a Other ancient authorities read *of Christ*
b Or *confess* *c* Other ancient authorities lack *to God* *d* Gk *of a brother* *e* Gk *brother* *f* Other ancient authorities add *or be upset or be weakened*
g Or *conviction* *h* Other authorities, some ancient, add here 16.25-27 *i* Or *thank*

license to give offense. 13: *Stumbling block . . . hindrance,* 9.32–33; 1 Cor 8.9. **14:** *Nothing is unclean in itself,* lit. “common,” as opposed to “clean” (v. 20; 1 Macc 1.47,62; Mk 7.19; Acts 10.14; 11.8). For the observant, however, non-kosher food *is unclean.* **17:** *The kingdom of God,* a rare phrase in Paul’s letters (1 Cor 4.20; 6.9–10). **19:** *Peace . . . mutual upbuilding,* 1 Cor 14.3–5,12,26. **20–23:** Faith does not allow one to violate the conscience of others, e.g., by encouraging them to act against their conscience. **15.1–13: Christ’s example. 1:** *Put up with the failings of the weak,* lit. “sustain the powerless in their weaknesses” (Gal 6.2). **2–3:** Ps 69.9 is read in terms of Christ’s humbling himself (Phil 2.5–8; 2 Cor 8.9). **4:** See 4.23–25; 1 Cor 9.10. **5–6:** The goal of Paul’s exhortation is that Gentiles and Jews should *with one voice glorify . . . God.* **8:** Christ came to *confirm the promises* given to Israel (9.3–5). **9:** Ps 18.49. **10:** Deut 32.43. **11:** Ps 117.1. **12:** Isa 11.10. (The Gk word for *Gentiles* in vv. 9–12 also means “nations.”)

12 and again Isaiah says,

"The root of Jesse shall come,
the one who rises to rule
the Gentiles;
in him the Gentiles shall hope."

13 May the God of hope fill you with all joy and peace in believing, so that you may abound in hope by the power of the Holy Spirit.

14 I myself feel confident about you, my brothers and sisters,[a] that you yourselves are full of goodness, filled with all knowledge, and able to instruct one another. 15 Nevertheless on some points I have written to you rather boldly by way of reminder, because of the grace given me by God 16 to be a minister of Christ Jesus to the Gentiles in the priestly service of the gospel of God, so that the offering of the Gentiles may be acceptable, sanctified by the Holy Spirit. 17 In Christ Jesus, then, I have reason to boast of my work for God. 18 For I will not venture to speak of anything except what Christ has accomplished[b] through me to win obedience from the Gentiles, by word and deed, 19 by the power of signs and wonders, by the power of the Spirit of God,[c] so that from Jerusalem and as far around as Illyricum I have fully proclaimed the good news[d] of Christ. 20 Thus I make it my ambition to proclaim the good news,[d] not where Christ has already been named, so that I do not build on someone else's foundation, 21 but as it is written,

"Those who have never been told of
him shall see,
and those who have never heard of
him shall understand."

22 This is the reason that I have so often been hindered from coming to you. 23 But now, with no further place for me in these regions, I desire, as I have for many years, to come to you 24 when I go to Spain. For I do hope to see you on my journey and to be sent on by you, once I have enjoyed your company for a little while. 25 At present, however, I am going to Jerusalem in a ministry to the saints; 26 for Macedonia and Achaia have been pleased to share their resources with the poor among the saints at Jerusalem. 27 They were pleased to do this, and indeed they owe it to them; for if the Gentiles have come to share in their spiritual blessings, they ought also to be of service to them in material things. 28 So, when I have completed this, and have delivered to them what has been collected,[e] I will set out by way of you to Spain; 29 and I know that when I come to you, I will come in the fullness of the blessing[f] of Christ.

30 I appeal to you, brothers and sisters,[a] by our Lord Jesus Christ and by the love of the Spirit, to join me in earnest prayer to God on my behalf, 31 that I may

a Gk *brothers* *b* Gk *speak of those things that Christ has not accomplished* *c* Other ancient authorities read *of the Spirit* or *of the Holy Spirit* *d* Or *gospel* *e* Gk *have sealed to them this fruit* *f* Other ancient authorities add *of the gospel*

15.14–32: The letter's argument brought to a close. 14–16: Despite confidence in the Romans (1.8,11,12), Paul has written *boldly,* compelled by the *grace given* him (1.5). **16:** *Minister . . . priestly service,* Paul will present a holy *offering* to God, i.e., the Gentile Christians themselves (1.9; 12.2). **17–32: The broader context of Paul's apostolate.** As at the letter's beginning (1.1–15), Paul links his letter to the Romans with his *work for God.* **19:** *Signs and wonders,* 1 Cor 12.10; 2 Cor 12.12; Gal 3.5. *Illyricum,* a Roman province on the east coast of the Adriatic Sea, mentioned only here. *Good news,* see 1.16n. **21:** Isa 52.15. **22–29:** Travel plans and further requests. **23:** *No further place,* Paul sees himself as a herald more than a pastor. **24:** Paul says nothing now of wishing to "proclaim the gospel" to the Romans (1.10–15); perhaps this letter has done that. **25–29:** The *ministry to the saints,* the collection mentioned in 1 Cor 16.1–4; 2 Cor 8–9; Gal 2.10. **26:** *Macedonia and Achaia,* Roman provinces in Greece. **30–33: Apprehensions regarding Jerusalem.** The Roman Christians may participate in the "offering of the Gentiles" (v. 16) through their own holiness (12.2) and their *earnest prayer* for Paul. The *unbelievers in Judea,* Jews who have not believed in Jesus (9.1–5; 10.1–2,14), are the ultimate targets of his work (11.13–14). On the fate of this *ministry to Jerusalem,* see Acts 21.7–28.31.

be rescued from the unbelievers in Judea,
and that my ministry[a] to Jerusalem may be
acceptable to the saints, 32 so that by God's
will I may come to you with joy and be
refreshed in your company. 33 The God of
peace be with all of you.[b] Amen.

16 I commend to you our sister Phoe-
be, a deacon[c] of the church at Cen-
chreae, 2 so that you may welcome her in
the Lord as is fitting for the saints, and help
her in whatever she may require from you,
for she has been a benefactor of many and
of myself as well.
3 Greet Prisca and Aquila, who work
with me in Christ Jesus, 4 and who risked
their necks for my life, to whom not only I
give thanks, but also all the churches of the
Gentiles. 5 Greet also the church in their
house. Greet my beloved Epaenetus, who
was the first convert[d] in Asia for Christ.
6 Greet Mary, who has worked very hard
among you. 7 Greet Andronicus and Ju-
nia,[e] my relatives[f] who were in prison
with me; they are prominent among the
apostles, and they were in Christ before I
was. 8 Greet Ampliatus, my beloved in the
Lord. 9 Greet Urbanus, our co-worker in
Christ, and my beloved Stachys. 10 Greet
Apelles, who is approved in Christ. Greet
those who belong to the family of Aristobu-
lus. 11 Greet my relative[g] Herodion. Greet
those in the Lord who belong to the family
of Narcissus. 12 Greet those workers in the
Lord, Tryphaena and Tryphosa. Greet the
beloved Persis, who has worked hard in the
Lord. 13 Greet Rufus, chosen in the Lord;
and greet his mother—a mother to me also.
14 Greet Asyncritus, Phlegon, Hermes, Pat-
robas, Hermas, and the brothers and sis-
ters[b] who are with them. 15 Greet Philolo-
gus, Julia, Nereus and his sister, and
Olympas, and all the saints who are with
them. 16 Greet one another with a holy kiss.
All the churches of Christ greet you.
17 I urge you, brothers and sisters,[h] to
keep an eye on those who cause dissensions
and offenses, in opposition to the teaching
that you have learned; avoid them. 18 For
such people do not serve our Lord Christ,
but their own appetites,[i] and by smooth
talk and flattery they deceive the hearts of
the simple-minded. 19 For while your obe-
dience is known to all, so that I rejoice over
you, I want you to be wise in what is good
and guileless in what is evil. 20 The God of
peace will shortly crush Satan under your
feet. The grace of our Lord Jesus Christ be
with you.[j]
21 Timothy, my co-worker, greets you;
so do Lucius and Jason and Sosipater, my
relatives.[f]

a Other ancient authorities read *my bringing of a gift* *b* One ancient authority adds 16.25-27 here *c* Or *minister* *d* Gk *first fruits* *e* Or *Junias*; other ancient authorities read *Julia* *f* Or *compatriots* *g* Or *compatriot* *h* Gk *brothers* *i* Gk *their own belly* *j* Other ancient authorities lack this sentence

16.1–23: A recommendation and greetings. 1: Some early manuscripts do not include 16.1–24; these verses nevertheless appear to be an authentic part of the letter (see also 16.25–27n.). **1–2:** Paul commends Phoebe, an officer of a nearby church, to the hospitality and support of the Roman Christians, thus honoring his obligations to her as his *benefactor.* On the early Christian office of *deacon,* see Phil 1.1; 1 Tim 3.8,12; Titus 1.9. **3–16:** A list of greetings shows Paul's personal connections with the Roman congregations. Most of the individuals named are mentioned only here. **3–4:** *Prisca and Aquila,* identified in Acts 18.2 as exiles from Rome, now returned (1 Cor 16.19; 2 Tim 4.19). **5:** Christian congregations first met in private homes (vv. 14,15; Philem 2). **7:** *Junia,* a woman; many manuscripts read "Junias," an otherwise unattested male Latin name; our earliest manuscript reads "Julia." *Relatives,* fellow Jews (vv. 11,21; 9.3). *The apostles,* Paul uses the term to mean more than the twelve (see 1 Cor 15.5,7; Phil 2.25). **13:** *A mother to me also,* an expression of affection. **16:** *A holy kiss,* a regular part of worship in the early church (1 Cor 16.20; 2 Cor 13.12; 1 Thess 5.26; 1 Pet 5.14).

16.17–20: A warning. *Those who cause dissensions,* otherwise unidentified, are clearly less central to the letter's purpose than those referred to in 1 Cor 5.1–13 or Gal 1.8–9; 6.17. *The teaching,* 6.17. **19:** 1.8. **20:** A concluding blessing (1 Cor 16.23; 1 Thess 5.28). **21:** *Timothy,* introduced in Acts 16.1–3. **22:**

22 I Tertius, the writer of this letter, greet you in the Lord.[a]
23 Gaius, who is host to me and to the whole church, greets you. Erastus, the city treasurer, and our brother Quartus, greet you.[b]

25 Now to God[c] who is able to strengthen you according to my gospel and the proclamation of Jesus Christ, according to the revelation of the mystery that was kept secret for long ages
26 but is now disclosed, and through the prophetic writings is made known to all the Gentiles, according to the command of the eternal God, to bring about the obedience of faith—
27 to the only wise God, through Jesus Christ, to whom[d] be the glory forever! Amen.[e]

a Or *I Tertius, writing this letter in the Lord, greet you* *b* Other ancient authorities add verse 24, *The grace of our Lord Jesus Christ be with all of you. Amen.* *c* Gk *the one* *d* Other ancient authorities lack *to whom.* The verse then reads, *to the only wise God be the glory through Jesus Christ forever. Amen.* *e* Other ancient authorities lack 16.25-27 or include it after 14.23 or 15.33; others put verse 24 after verse 27

Tertius wrote the letter as Paul dictated it; cf. 1 Pet 5.12. **23:** *Gaius,* perhaps the same person mentioned in 1 Cor 1.14.

16.25–27: A concluding blessing, appearing in different ancient manuscripts after 14.23 or 15.33, or missing altogether. Many consider these verses an addition by later scribes and editors. **25:** *My gospel,* 2.16. *The proclamation,* the Gk "kerygma" is another word for "gospel"; see 1 Cor 1.21–24. **25–26:** *Mystery,* 11.25–27. *The obedience of faith,* 1.5.

The First Letter of Paul to the CORINTHIANS

First Corinthians offers a fascinating window onto the struggles of one community of the movement that developed into Christianity. Paul's attempts to persuade them to see and do things his way reveals just how difficult it was for people rooted in the Hellenistic culture of a large metropolis such as Corinth to assimilate Paul's gospel of Christ and its implications for personal and community life and for their relations with the larger Roman imperial society.

The city of Corinth had been punitively destroyed by the Romans in 146 BCE, but then rebuilt in 44 BCE as a colony to which the Roman patricians sent the "dregs" of the surplus population from Rome itself, such as recently manumitted slaves and displaced peasants. Corinth quickly developed into a busy hub of east-west trade in the empire and the center of Roman imperial culture in Greece. Except for Antioch in Syria, where Paul was based at the very beginning of his mission to various peoples of the eastern Mediterranean, Corinth was the first major urban center to which Paul brought his mission. For eighteen months, with several coworkers such as Timothy and Silvanus, Prisca (Priscilla) and her husband Aquila, and Phoebe, leader of the community at nearby Cenchreae, he organized and taught in several house-assemblies of Corinthians who came together periodically as a "whole assembly" (church) to celebrate the Lord's Supper. After he moved across the Aegean Sea to work in the city of Ephesus, another missionary, Apollos, an eloquent Hellenistic Jew from Alexandria in Egypt, also taught in the community at Corinth.

In dictating 1 Corinthians (from Ephesus, 16.8), Paul was responding both to a letter from the Corinthians asking questions about several issues (see 7.1; 8.1; 12.1) and to news he had received through "Chloe's people" of some serious conflicts in the Corinthian community. The letter begins with the usual address, greeting, and opening thanksgiving (1.1–9) and ends with the standard closing exhortation, greetings, and grace (16.13–24). The body of the letter consists of a series of arguments on key issues over which the Corinthian community has come into conflict: divisions within the community connected with devotion to wisdom (1.10–4.21); how to deal with a man living with his stepmother (ch 5); on not taking disputes to the official courts (ch 6); on marriage and sexual relations (6.12–7.40); on eating food sacrificed to idols (8.1–11.1); on hair arrangement when prophesying (11.2–16); on procedure at celebration of the Lord's Supper (11.17–34); on the use of spiritual gifts, particularly "tongues" (chs 12–14); on the resurrection of the dead (ch 15); and finally on the collection for Jerusalem and Paul's travel plans (16.1–12).

The language Paul uses and the issues he deals with in 1 Corinthians are very different from those in his other letters. That suggests that the views he addresses in 1 Corinthians were distinctive to the Corinthians among the various communities Paul founded (and perhaps had something to do with Apollos's ministry in Corinth after Paul had gone to Ephesus). Indeed, it appears from the way Paul uses some of these distinctive terms that some of the Corinthians understood themselves as "spiritual" and "mature," as opposed to merely "unspiritual" or "physical" and "infants" (2.6,14–15; 3.1; 15.44,46) and as "wise," "powerful," "of noble birth," "rich," and "kings," as opposed to "fools," "weak," etc. (1.26; 4.8), apparently because of their possession of "wisdom" as the agent or substance of salvation, a religious self-understanding known from contemporary Jewish communities in Alexandria, where Apollos came from. Throughout 1 Corinthians Paul appears to be responding to what certain Corinthians were thinking and doing, and at several points in his major arguments he even uses their language and slogans.

Paul's arguments in 1 Corinthians were not immediately effective, as is evident from the continuing conflicts he had with the Corinthians in the various sections of 2 Corinthians (see Introduction to 2 Corinthians). Paul's arguments in 1 Corinthians, however, contain some of the earliest traditions of believers in Christ, such as the words of institution for the Lord's Supper (11.23–26) and the basic creed of Christ's crucifixion and resurrection (15.3–5). First Corinthians also contains Paul's most insistent emphasis on the cross of Christ (1.18–2.9), and his most extensive discussion of the resurrection of the dead (ch 15). Moreover, Paul's use of the Corinthians' language in attempting to persuade them to his viewpoint resulted in formulations that provided key bases for subsequent Christian belief and practices. In 1 Corinthians are the only statements among Paul's genuine letters in which Christ appears to be a preexistent figure (8.6; 10.4). Only in 1 Corinthians does Paul deal with issues such as sex and marriage and spiritual gifts such as glossolalia (speaking in "tongues"). Given the ways that subsequent generations of Christians have understood them, Paul's formulations in ch 7 in particular became a basis for Christian sexual asceticism and one of the texts used to legitimate the practice of slavery. Passages in 1 Corinthians (11.2–17; 14.34–36), moreover, became some of the principal bases on which women were subordinated in the patriarchal family and church. And it is in 1 Corinthians that Paul composes the famous "hymn to love" as part of his argument for solidarity of the community as the "body of Christ" (ch 13 as part of the argument in chs 12–14), and his almost ecstatic vision of the dramatic parousia, the coming of Christ and the resurrection of believers, "at the last trumpet" (15.51–55).

1 Paul, called to be an apostle of Christ
Jesus by the will of God, and our brother Sosthenes,
2 To the church of God that is in Corinth, to those who are sanctified in Christ
Jesus, called to be saints, together with all
those who in every place call on the name
of our Lord Jesus Christ, both their Lord[a]
and ours:
3 Grace to you and peace from God our
Father and the Lord Jesus Christ.
4 I give thanks to my[b] God always for
you because of the grace of God that has
been given you in Christ Jesus, 5 for in every
way you have been enriched in him, in
speech and knowledge of every kind—
6 just as the testimony of[c] Christ has been
strengthened among you— 7 so that you are
not lacking in any spiritual gift as you wait
for the revealing of our Lord Jesus Christ.

a Gk *theirs* *b* Other ancient authorities lack *my* *c* Or *to*

1.1–3: Salutation. Ancient Greek letters customarily began with the names of sender and recipient and a short greeting (cf. Acts 23.26). Paul expands this form to express his faith in Christ as well (see Rom 1.1–7). If he is the same person, *Sosthenes* plays a different role here from that in Acts 18.17. **2:** The *church of God* is the local community of the new worldwide movement or "assembly of God" and constitutes a pointed alternative to the official city "assembly" (Gk "ekklesia") of Corinth.

1.4–9: Thanksgiving. After the salutation in ancient letters there usually came a short prayer of thanksgiving or of petition for those addressed. This element Paul also expands in a characteristically Pauline way (see Rom 1.8–15). Paul mentions positively the eloquent speech, transcendent knowledge, and spiritual gifts valued by some Corinthians that he then discusses more critically in the body of the letter. But he emphasizes the future *revealing* or *day of our Lord Jesus Christ* at the *end,* the final time of judgment and fulfillment (elaborated in ch 15).

8 He will also strengthen you to the end, so
that you may be blameless on the day of
our Lord Jesus Christ. 9 God is faithful; by
him you were called into the fellowship of
his Son, Jesus Christ our Lord.
10 Now I appeal to you, brothers and
sisters,[a] by the name of our Lord Jesus
Christ, that all of you be in agreement and
that there be no divisions among you, but
that you be united in the same mind and the
same purpose. 11 For it has been reported to
me by Chloe's people that there are quar-
rels among you, my brothers and sisters.[b]
12 What I mean is that each of you says, "I
belong to Paul," or "I belong to Apollos,"
or "I belong to Cephas," or "I belong to
Christ." 13 Has Christ been divided? Was
Paul crucified for you? Or were you bap-
tized in the name of Paul? 14 I thank God[c]
that I baptized none of you except Crispus
and Gaius, 15 so that no one can say that
you were baptized in my name. 16 (I did
baptize also the household of Stephanas;
beyond that, I do not know whether I bap-
tized anyone else.) 17 For Christ did not
send me to baptize but to proclaim the gos-
pel, and not with eloquent wisdom, so that
the cross of Christ might not be emptied of
its power.
18 For the message about the cross is
foolishness to those who are perishing, but
to us who are being saved it is the power of
God. 19 For it is written,

"I will destroy the wisdom of
the wise,
and the discernment of the
discerning I will thwart."

20 Where is the one who is wise? Where is
the scribe? Where is the debater of this age?
Has not God made foolish the wisdom of
the world? 21 For since, in the wisdom of

a Gk *brothers* b Gk *my brothers* c Other ancient authorities read *I am thankful*

1.10–4.21: Paul's first major argument, for unity. Beginning with his appeal for *agreement* and *no divisions* among the Corinthians, the argument unfolds in five steps.

1.10–17: Divisions among the Corinthians. Speaking like a political leader of a city, Paul appeals for *agreement* or concord and *no divisions* among the Corinthians, who have divided at least in their loyalty to particular leaders or teachers, although not necessarily into different parties or factions. As indicated in 3.4–15, Paul believes the division is primarily between followers of *Apollos* and himself (cf. 3.22–23). *Cephas* (Peter) and particularly *Christ* are included here for rhetorical effect. *Apollos,* from Alexandria in Egypt, was known for his eloquence and knowledge of the scriptures (Acts 18.24–28). **11:** *Chloe* is not mentioned elsewhere. **14–17:** Not an attack on baptism itself, but on its connection with the Corinthians' attachment to particular leaders such as Apollos or himself. It is uncertain whether this is connected with some Corinthians' interest in "baptism for the dead," mentioned in 15.29. **14–16:** *Crispus* (see Acts 18.8), *Gaius,* and *Stephanas* were apparently heads of households prominent in the Corinthian assembly. The *household of Stephanas* may have included some slaves or freed-persons, perhaps including Fortunatas and Achaicus, who have typical slave names ("Lucky" and "the Greek"), included with Stephanas in the delegation visiting Paul in 16.15–18. **17:** Paul quickly identifies *wisdom* (Gk "sophia") and *eloquent wisdom* as the root of the divisiveness in the Corinthian assembly and hence a threat to the *power* of the *cross of Christ,* the content of his own *gospel.* For high valuation of eloquent words in connection with wisdom (among some Hellenistic Jews), see Wis 8.8,12,18. **1:18–2.5: The contrast of Christ crucified with wisdom.** In the second step of his argument for unity, Paul contrasts Christ crucified with wisdom and its eloquent communication by means of several plays on the words "wisdom," "foolishness," "power," and "weakness." **18–25:** In Paul's play on words, the meaning of the *cross/Christ crucified* remains stable, while that of *wisdom* shifts, from opposition to the cross and opposition by God (vv. 18–20) into apposition with the crucified Christ (and the power of God) and finally into identification as the *wisdom of God* (vv. 23–24). **19:** Isa 29.14 Gk (LXX). **21:** The *wisdom of God* apparently refers to God's plan for salvation (see Dan 2.27–30), in which Christ's crucifixion is the key event, as indicated by the "secret and hidden" wisdom of God in 2.7–8. By contrast, *wisdom* through which *the world did not know God* refers to the transcendent or heavenly wisdom so highly valued by some of the Corinthians (see esp. Wis 6.12–10.21), which Paul denigrates as *wisdom of the world* in 1.20. **23–24:**

God, the world did not know God through
wisdom, God decided, through the foolish-
ness of our proclamation, to save those
who believe. 22 For Jews demand signs and
Greeks desire wisdom, 23 but we proclaim
Christ crucified, a stumbling block to Jews
and foolishness to Gentiles, 24 but to those
who are the called, both Jews and Greeks,
Christ the power of God and the wisdom of
God. 25 For God's foolishness is wiser than
human wisdom, and God's weakness is
stronger than human strength.

26 Consider your own call, brothers and
sisters:[a] not many of you were wise by hu-
man standards,[b] not many were powerful,
not many were of noble birth. 27 But God
chose what is foolish in the world to shame
the wise; God chose what is weak in the
world to shame the strong; 28 God chose
what is low and despised in the world,
things that are not, to reduce to nothing
things that are, 29 so that no one[c] might
boast in the presence of God. 30 He is the
source of your life in Christ Jesus, who be-
came for us wisdom from God, and righ-
teousness and sanctification and redemp-
tion, 31 in order that, as it is written, "Let
the one who boasts, boast in[d] the Lord."

2 When I came to you, brothers and sis-
ters,[a] I did not come proclaiming the
mystery[e] of God to you in lofty words or
wisdom. 2 For I decided to know nothing
among you except Jesus Christ, and him
crucified. 3 And I came to you in weakness
and in fear and in much trembling. 4 My
speech and my proclamation were not with
plausible words of wisdom,[f] but with a
demonstration of the Spirit and of power,
5 so that your faith might rest not on human
wisdom but on the power of God.

6 Yet among the mature we do speak
wisdom, though it is not a wisdom of this

a Gk *brothers* *b* Gk *according to the flesh*
c Gk *no flesh* *d* Or *of* *e* Other ancient authorities
read *testimony* *f* Other ancient authorities read *the
persuasiveness of wisdom*

Crucifixion was an excruciatingly painful Roman form of torturous death by hanging on a pole or cross, reserved for the lower class, usually inflicted on slaves or rebels in subject provinces such as Judea. Thus (as in 1.18) the *cross* and *Christ crucified* would indeed have been *foolishness* to the dominant Roman and Greek culture. Paradoxically, the crucifixion had become the very *power of God* and *wisdom of God* to the members of the new movement of Christ-believers (cf. v. 17). **26–31:** Explains the paradox stated in vv. 18–25 by reference to the Corinthians' own call into the salvation now underway by God's power manifested in the crucifixion of Christ. The aristocratic qualities of being *wise, powerful,* and *of noble birth* (and "rich, kings," as in 4.8–10) were commonly used in a spiritualized sense both by Greek and by Hellenistic Jewish philosophers, particularly as the qualities gained by possession of wisdom (see Wis 6.20–21; 7.7–14; 8.3–5; 9.6; 10.11,14). **26:** Paul implies that, in contrast to their concrete social origins as poor common people, some of the Corinthians now claim to be spiritually powerful and nobly born. **27–28:** But precisely by calling them as poor, weak, "nothings" in the world, God is manifesting his purpose of overturning the established order, the dominance of the powerful, wise, and nobly born. (Overturning the dominance of the powerful is deeply rooted in biblical tradition, e.g., Ex 15.1–17,21; Judg 5; 1 Sam 2.1–10). **30:** Christ Jesus is now identified as the *wisdom from God,* which is relativized by association with God's other effects on believers, *righteousness and sanctification and redemption.* **31:** Therefore boasting should be *in the Lord,* not in one's spiritual mentor (as in 1.12–13). **2.1–5:** Provides a second illustration of the paradox stated in 1.18–25. Now Paul contrasts *lofty words or wisdom* not only with his message of the crucified Christ, but with *a demonstration of the Spirit and of power* as the effects of that message on the Corinthians. **1:** The alternative reading "testimony" (see note *e*) is to be preferred over *mystery,* which spoils the effect of "secret and hidden" (lit. "wisdom in a mystery") in 2.7. **4:** The alternative reading *the persuasiveness of wisdom* (see note *f*) is to be preferred to *plausible words of wisdom.* **5:** Recapitulates the argument from 1.18–2.4, repeating the main point from 1.18 and 1.23–24.

2.6–3.4: Spiritual wisdom is not for infants. In the third step of his argument for unity, Paul first declares that he does indeed *speak wisdom among the mature* or *spiritual* people, but that he could not do so among the Corinthians because they are still *infants* in their quarreling and attachments to spiritual mentors. His argument here is ironic, perhaps even sarcastic, as it takes a sharp turn from 2.6–16 to

age or of the rulers of this age, who are
doomed to perish. 7 But we speak God's
wisdom, secret and hidden, which God de-
creed before the ages for our glory. 8 None
of the rulers of this age understood this; for
if they had, they would not have crucified
the Lord of glory. 9 But, as it is written,
"What no eye has seen, nor
ear heard,
nor the human heart conceived,
what God has prepared for those who
love him"—
10 these things God has revealed to us
through the Spirit; for the Spirit searches
everything, even the depths of God. 11 For
what human being knows what is truly hu-
man except the human spirit that is within?
So also no one comprehends what is truly
God's except the Spirit of God. 12 Now we
have received not the spirit of the world,
but the Spirit that is from God, so that we
may understand the gifts bestowed on us by
God. 13 And we speak of these things in
words not taught by human wisdom but
taught by the Spirit, interpreting spiritual
things to those who are spiritual.[a]
14 Those who are unspiritual[b] do not
receive the gifts of God's Spirit, for they are
foolishness to them, and they are unable to
understand them because they are spiritual-
ly discerned. 15 Those who are spiritual dis-
cern all things, and they are themselves sub-
ject to no one else's scrutiny.
16 "For who has known the mind
of the Lord
so as to instruct him?"
But we have the mind of Christ.

3 And so, brothers and sisters,[c] I could
not speak to you as spiritual people, but
rather as people of the flesh, as infants in
Christ. 2 I fed you with milk, not solid food,
for you were not ready for solid food. Even
now you are still not ready, 3 for you are
still of the flesh. For as long as there is jeal-
ousy and quarreling among you, are you
not of the flesh, and behaving according to
human inclinations? 4 For when one says,
"I belong to Paul," and another, "I belong
to Apollos," are you not merely human?
5 What then is Apollos? What is Paul?
Servants through whom you came to be-
lieve, as the Lord assigned to each. 6 I plant-
ed, Apollos watered, but God gave the
growth. 7 So neither the one who plants nor
the one who waters is anything, but only
God who gives the growth. 8 The one who

a Or *interpreting spiritual things in spiritual language,* or *comparing spiritual things with spiritual*
b Or *natural* *c* Gk *brothers*

3.1–4. **6:** *The mature* or "perfect" are those who possess *wisdom,* as in Wis 6.15; 9.6. **7:** Paul quickly moves to identify the wisdom he speaks as *God's wisdom, secret and hidden,* with the term "mystery" (see 2.1n.) that refers to God's secret plan for the deliverance of the people of Israel from imperial domination, as in Dan 2.18–19,27–28. *The rulers of this age* are more likely the Roman rulers (see Rom 13.3; Acts 4.25–28) rather than demonic cosmic powers (as in Eph 6.12). **8:** As part of God's plan, in which the rulers "are doomed to perish," the Christ they crucified has been exalted as *the Lord of glory,* installed in heaven as the true ruler of the world (see 15.25). **9:** Perhaps from a Jewish writing that drew on Isa 64.4, cited as scripture. **10:** How the *Spirit* reveals the hidden wisdom which is the plan of God. **11–14:** Paul writes to the Corinthians in the language of the *spiritual* people who have received heavenly *wisdom,* which is identical with the *Spirit;* cf. Wis 17.7,22; 9.17. **14–15:** Perhaps quoting principles of the Corinthian spiritual people. **16:** Isa 40.13. **3.1–4:** Paul's irony or sarcasm becomes explicit in this sharp derogatory remark that reverses the seeming approval of special spiritual knowledge in 2.14–15. **1–2:** *Milk* and *solid food* are the foods appropriate to *infants* and "the mature" or "spiritual" people, respectively, in the complex metaphor that extends from 2.6 to 3.2; cf. Heb 5.12–14. **3:** Far from being "spiritual," the divisive Corinthians are still *of the flesh,* even lower in status than "unspiritual." **4:** Refers to where the argument started in 1.10–12.

3.5–23: Warnings about Apollos. In the fourth step in his argument for unity, Paul warns the Corinthians about the ministry of Apollos, which should have built on the foundation he laid. **5:** *Servants* (Gk "diakonoi") were leaders of the movement responsible for preaching and supervision of the assemblies, like Phoebe in nearby Cenchreae (Rom 16.1); cf. the "ruler" as a "servant of God" (Rom 13.4). **10–11:**

plants and the one who waters have a com-
mon purpose, and each will receive wages
according to the labor of each. 9 For we are
God's servants, working together; you are
God's field, God's building.

10 According to the grace of God given
to me, like a skilled master builder I laid a
foundation, and someone else is building
on it. Each builder must choose with care
how to build on it. 11 For no one can lay
any foundation other than the one that has
been laid; that foundation is Jesus Christ.
12 Now if anyone builds on the foundation
with gold, silver, precious stones, wood,
hay, straw— 13 the work of each builder
will become visible, for the Day will dis-
close it, because it will be revealed with fire,
and the fire will test what sort of work each
has done. 14 If what has been built on the
foundation survives, the builder will receive
a reward. 15 If the work is burned up, the
builder will suffer loss; the builder will be
saved, but only as through fire.

16 Do you not know that you are God's
temple and that God's Spirit dwells in
you?[a] 17 If anyone destroys God's temple,
God will destroy that person. For God's
temple is holy, and you are that temple.

18 Do not deceive yourselves. If you
think that you are wise in this age, you
should become fools so that you may be-
come wise. 19 For the wisdom of this world
is foolishness with God. For it is written,

"He catches the wise in their
craftiness,"

20 and again,

"The Lord knows the thoughts of the
wise,
that they are futile."

21 So let no one boast about human leaders.
For all things are yours, 22 whether Paul or
Apollos or Cephas or the world or life or
death or the present or the future—all be-
long to you, 23 and you belong to Christ,
and Christ belongs to God.

4 Think of us in this way, as servants of
Christ and stewards of God's mysteries.
2 Moreover, it is required of stewards that
they be found trustworthy. 3 But with me it
is a very small thing that I should be judged
by you or by any human court. I do not
even judge myself. 4 I am not aware of any-
thing against myself, but I am not thereby
acquitted. It is the Lord who judges me.
5 Therefore do not pronounce judgment be-
fore the time, before the Lord comes, who
will bring to light the things now hidden in
darkness and will disclose the purposes of
the heart. Then each one will receive com-
mendation from God.

6 I have applied all this to Apollos and
myself for your benefit, brothers and sis-
ters,[b] so that you may learn through us the
meaning of the saying, "Nothing beyond
what is written," so that none of you will
be puffed up in favor of one against anoth-
er. 7 For who sees anything different in

a In verses 16 and 17 the Greek word for *you* is plural
b Gk *brothers*

Paul insists that the Corinthian assembly is his own apostolic territory. He states later, in Rom 15.20, that he would "not build on someone else's foundation." **12–15:** *The Day* is clearly the day of judgment, complete with refining *fire.* **18–23:** Recapitulates the argument since 1.10. **18:** Again warning about presuming to be *wise.* **19–20:** Again denigrating *wisdom* as "in this age" and citing Job 5.13; Ps 94.11 as testimonies of how God opposes the *wise.* **21–23:** Referring to the slogans of 1.12, Paul reverses the possessive relationship, so that all of the "servants" along with *life or death,* etc. *belong to* the Corinthians, and then subordinates all to *Christ* and finally to *God.*

4.1–21: Paul's defense. In the final step of his argument for unity, Paul defends himself against Corinthian criticism and asserts his fatherly apostolic authority over the assembly. **1–5:** Using the language of a judicial proceeding, Paul insists that not the Corinthians, but the Lord will judge him. **1–2:** *Servants . . . and stewards* were responsible administrative officers of an estate or a political jurisdiction who worked under the authority of and had to be *trustworthy* to a lord or ruler (Christ). **6–7:** Applies the whole argument since 1.10 to the Corinthians by reference to himself and Apollos. **6:** *"Nothing beyond what is written"* must be aimed at members of the Corinthian community who "spiritualize" the interpretation of scripture, such as the "spiritual food, . . . drink, . . . and rock" in 10.3–4. **8–10:** *Already* is Paul's rhetorical

you?[a] What do you have that you did not
receive? And if you received it, why do you
boast as if it were not a gift?
8 Already you have all you want! Al-
ready you have become rich! Quite apart
from us you have become kings! Indeed, I
wish that you had become kings, so that we
might be kings with you! 9 For I think that
God has exhibited us apostles as last of all,
as though sentenced to death, because we
have become a spectacle to the world, to
angels and to mortals. 10 We are fools for
the sake of Christ, but you are wise in
Christ. We are weak, but you are strong.
You are held in honor, but we in disrepute.
11 To the present hour we are hungry and
thirsty, we are poorly clothed and beaten
and homeless, 12 and we grow weary from
the work of our own hands. When reviled,
we bless; when persecuted, we endure;
13 when slandered, we speak kindly. We
have become like the rubbish of the world,
the dregs of all things, to this very day.
14 I am not writing this to make you
ashamed, but to admonish you as my be-
loved children. 15 For though you might
have ten thousand guardians in Christ, you
do not have many fathers. Indeed, in Christ
Jesus I became your father through the gos-
pel. 16 I appeal to you, then, be imitators of
me. 17 For this reason I sent[b] you Timothy,
who is my beloved and faithful child in the
Lord, to remind you of my ways in Christ
Jesus, as I teach them everywhere in every
church. 18 But some of you, thinking that I
am not coming to you, have become arro-
gant. 19 But I will come to you soon, if the
Lord wills, and I will find out not the talk
of these arrogant people but their power.
20 For the kingdom of God depends not on
talk but on power. 21 What would you pre-
fer? Am I to come to you with a stick, or
with love in a spirit of gentleness?

5 It is actually reported that there is sexu-
al immorality among you, and of a kind
that is not found even among pagans; for a
man is living with his father's wife. 2 And
you are arrogant! Should you not rather
have mourned, so that he who has done
this would have been removed from among
you?
3 For though absent in body, I am
present in spirit; and as if present I have
already pronounced judgment 4 in the name

a Or *Who makes you different from another?*
b Or *am sending*

formulation, rooted in his own sense that salvation is not yet complete, and not an indication of the "spiritual" Corinthians' sense of "(over-) realized eschatology," which would have been an assertion that in them salvation had already been fully accomplished. *Rich . . . kings* and *strong . . . honor* are additional Corinthian terms for the exalted spiritual status attained by possession of wisdom, a spiritualized form of classical Greek aristocratic values (see 1.26n.). **9–13:** After mocking the "spiritual" Corinthian claims of exalted status, he contrasts his own experience as an apostle. **9:** The *spectacle* in which *God has exhibited us apostles . . . as though sentenced to death* refers either to the condemned thrown to wild beasts in the arena or to triumphal processions in which Roman generals displayed their captives. **13:** *The rubbish of the world, the dregs of all things,* concluding the list of the apostle's sufferings, are metaphors for what is most contemptible. **14–21:** Paul softens his argument before resuming a threatening tone at the very end. His authoritarian tone is rooted in the highly paternalistic social relations of Hellenistic-Roman antiquity. **15:** Contrasts himself as their *father,* with full authority over the family, with a myriad of *guardians* or "nannies" who were often slaves. **17:** *Timothy* had worked with Paul in Corinth, Acts 18.5 (cf. 16.10–11). Paul's *ways in Christ Jesus* include both his teachings and his behavior (cf. 3.3; 7.17; 12.31; Gal 5.16). **20:** This maxim summarizes the whole argument since 1.17–18. The offhand use of *kingdom of God* suggests that it was standard in Paul's vocabulary. **21:** This stern threatening plea both concludes the opening argument for unity and sets the tone for the subsequent arguments.

5.1–13: The need for community discipline. 1: Both Roman and Jewish law (Deut 22.20; 27.20; Lev 18.7–8) forbade marriage between a man and his stepmother. Is the man's action connected with the Corinthian principle cited in 6.12 and 10.23? **2:** Paul is shocked at the assembly's lack of discipline, which becomes the focus of his argument. **4:** Paul wants to proceed in conjunction with the community. His

of the Lord Jesus on the man who has done
such a thing.[a] When you are assembled,
and my spirit is present with the power of
our Lord Jesus, 5 you are to hand this man
over to Satan for the destruction of the
flesh, so that his spirit may be saved in the
day of the Lord.[b]
6 Your boasting is not a good thing. Do
you not know that a little yeast leavens the
whole batch of dough? 7 Clean out the old
yeast so that you may be a new batch, as
you really are unleavened. For our paschal
lamb, Christ, has been sacrificed. 8 There-
fore, let us celebrate the festival, not with
the old yeast, the yeast of malice and evil,
but with the unleavened bread of sincerity
and truth.
9 I wrote to you in my letter not to asso-
ciate with sexually immoral persons—
10 not at all meaning the immoral of this
world, or the greedy and robbers, or idola-
ters, since you would then need to go out of
the world. 11 But now I am writing to you
not to associate with anyone who bears the
name of brother or sister[c] who is sexually
immoral or greedy, or is an idolater, reviler,
drunkard, or robber. Do not even eat with
such a one. 12 For what have I to do with
judging those outside? Is it not those who
are inside that you are to judge? 13 God will
judge those outside. "Drive out the wicked
person from among you."

6 When any of you has a grievance
against another, do you dare to take it
to court before the unrighteous, instead of
taking it before the saints? 2 Do you not
know that the saints will judge the world?
And if the world is to be judged by you, are
you incompetent to try trivial cases? 3 Do
you not know that we are to judge angels—
to say nothing of ordinary matters? 4 If you
have ordinary cases, then, do you appoint
as judges those who have no standing in the
church? 5 I say this to your shame. Can it
be that there is no one among you wise

a Or *on the man who has done such a thing in the name of the Lord Jesus* *b* Other ancient authorities add *Jesus* *c* Gk *brother*

spirit is present in the same sense as Jesus would be present in cases of community discipline (see Mt 18.15–20), while *the power of our Lord Jesus* is the ultimately empowering authority of the judicial procedure of expulsion. **5:** *Flesh* for Paul does not refer to the human body, but the force that drives people into sinful behavior. Its *destruction* by *Satan* would be the ultimate effect of the man's expulsion from the protective sphere of the Spirit in the community, so that he might ultimately be saved at the Lord's coming. **6–8:** Paul apparently uses a popular proverb (see Gal 5.9; cf. Mk 8.15) as a warning about a corrupting influence in the community. But he then shifts the metaphor positively from the community as the unleavened bread to the community now celebrating the whole Passover festival of redemption by maintaining group discipline. During Passover (Gk "pascha") only unleavened bread was to be eaten; see Ex 12.15–20. **7:** *Our paschal lamb, Christ,* an image used only here by Paul; cf. Jn 19.36; Rev 5.12. **9:** Paul's earlier letter to the Corinthians is lost, but apparently dealt at least with community discipline. **10–11:** Addressing an apparent misunderstanding, he insists that the newly established people ("assembly") of God must keep open its contacts with *the immoral of this world* even while it maintains rigorous internal discipline. The tailor-made list of evildoers follows Jewish biblical tradition in closely associating immorality with idolatry and moves from sexual to economic matters such as theft and coveting. **13:** While *God will judge* outsiders, the community must discipline insiders, following the biblical instructions to *Drive out* . . . (Deut 13.5; 17.7; 19.9; 22.21–24).

6.1–11: Lawsuits. Paul is equally shocked that one member of the assembly is taking another into the civil court *instead of . . . before the saints.* In Paul's view of the imminent divine judgment, *the saints will judge the world* (cf. Dan 7.22 Gk [LXX]; Rev 20.4). He apparently understands the newly formed assembly of God as an alternative society to the dominant social-political order, one that must handle its own affairs in separation from the *unrighteous* and *unbelievers.* **2–3:** *The saints will judge the world . . . angels* is Paul's variation on a Jewish apocalyptic belief that the faithful righteous would participate in the divine judgment at the end of days. That they are to *judge the world* and *angels* is meant to jolt them into recognizing that they should handle their own *trivial . . . ordinary matters.* **5–6:** That Paul now does *say*

enough to decide between one believer[a]
and another, 6 but a believer[a] goes to court
against a believer[a]—and before unbeliev-
ers at that?
7 In fact, to have lawsuits at all with one
another is already a defeat for you. Why
not rather be wronged? Why not rather be
defrauded? 8 But you yourselves wrong and
defraud—and believers[b] at that.
9 Do you not know that wrongdoers
will not inherit the kingdom of God? Do
not be deceived! Fornicators, idolaters,
adulterers, male prostitutes, sodomites,
10 thieves, the greedy, drunkards, revilers,
robbers—none of these will inherit the
kingdom of God. 11 And this is what some
of you used to be. But you were washed,
you were sanctified, you were justified in
the name of the Lord Jesus Christ and in
the Spirit of our God.
12 "All things are lawful for me," but
not all things are beneficial. "All things are
lawful for me," but I will not be dominated
by anything. 13 "Food is meant for the
stomach and the stomach for food,"[c] and
God will destroy both one and the other.
The body is meant not for fornication but
for the Lord, and the Lord for the body.
14 And God raised the Lord and will also
raise us by his power. 15 Do you not know
that your bodies are members of Christ?
Should I therefore take the members of
Christ and make them members of a prosti-
tute? Never! 16 Do you not know that who-
ever is united to a prostitute becomes one
body with her? For it is said, "The two
shall be one flesh." 17 But anyone united
to the Lord becomes one spirit with him.
18 Shun fornication! Every sin that a person
commits is outside the body; but the forni-
cator sins against the body itself. 19 Or do
you not know that your body is a temple[d]
of the Holy Spirit within you, which you
have from God, and that you are not your
own? 20 For you were bought with a price;
therefore glorify God in your body.

7 Now concerning the matters about
which you wrote: "It is well for a man

a Gk *brother* *b* Gk *brothers* *c* The quotation may extend to the word *other* *d* Or *sanctuary*

this to your shame, having hesitated to shame them in his long opening argument (4.14), indicates how serious the issue is for him. **7–8:** The reference to being *defrauded* suggests that the litigant was pursuing an economic matter. **9–11:** A stern warning lest the Corinthians not attain the goal, the imminent *kingdom of God.* **9–10:** The Greek terms translated *male prostitutes* and *sodomites* do not refer to "homosexuals," as in inappropriate older translations; "masturbators" and *male prostitutes* might be a better translation. While continuing the emphasis on economic offenders, the list expands the sexual offenders (see 5.10–11n.), anticipating 6.12–20.

6.12–20: Sexual sins. The argument is about the relation of *the body* and *fornication,* as indicated in vv. 13,18, although it is not entirely clear what issue is addressed. **12–13:** As he does again in 7.1–2; 8.1, Paul proceeds first by quoting and then by qualifying or countering principles held by certain Corinthians, before stating his own main point in v.14 and explaining it in vv. 15–17. The claim that *all things are lawful* is rooted in the possession of enlightening theological knowledge (see 8.1), as is clear from its repetition in 10.23. For certain Corinthians it could have been an expression of liberation from cultural traditions such as dietary restrictions (as in 8.4,10) or the patriarchal subordination of wives (as perhaps in 7.1,4). **14–16:** Paul is warning of the logical implications of the Corinthians' principle, not necessarily their actual behavior. As becomes clearer in chs 8–10 and 12–14, Paul is insisting on what is "beneficial" (v. 12) to the whole community, as opposed to individual enlightenment. He focuses on the solidarity of *the Lord* with the believer's *body,* which Paul understood as integral to the person, even in resurrection (elaborated in 15.12–54), but which many Hellenistic people viewed as irrelevant to a person's soul or spiritual essence. **16:** Quoting Gen 2.24. **18:** *Shun fornication* is what Paul's argument has been leading to. **19–20:** *Your body is a temple of the Holy Spirit* again emphasizes the integral relationships with God, Christ, the Spirit, and one another in the newly formed assembly in order to counter an enlightened spiritual individualism.

7.1–40: Discussion of marriage and sexual relations. In contrast with his combative, authoritarian tone

not to touch a woman." 2But because of
cases of sexual immorality, each man
should have his own wife and each woman
her own husband. 3The husband should
give to his wife her conjugal rights, and
likewise the wife to her husband. 4For the
wife does not have authority over her own
body, but the husband does; likewise the
husband does not have authority over his
own body, but the wife does. 5Do not de-
prive one another except perhaps by agree-
ment for a set time, to devote yourselves to
prayer, and then come together again, so
that Satan may not tempt you because of
your lack of self-control. 6This I say by
way of concession, not of command. 7I
wish that all were as I myself am. But each
has a particular gift from God, one having
one kind and another a different kind.
8 To the unmarried and the widows I
say that it is well for them to remain un-
married as I am. 9But if they are not prac-
ticing self-control, they should marry. For
it is better to marry than to be aflame with
passion.
10 To the married I give this com-
mand—not I but the Lord—that the wife
should not separate from her husband
11(but if she does separate, let her remain
unmarried or else be reconciled to her hus-
band), and that the husband should not di-
vorce his wife.
12 To the rest I say—I and not the
Lord—that if any believer[a] has a wife who
is an unbeliever, and she consents to live
with him, he should not divorce her. 13And
if any woman has a husband who is an
unbeliever, and he consents to live with her,
she should not divorce him. 14For the un-
believing husband is made holy through his
wife, and the unbelieving wife is made holy
through her husband. Otherwise, your chil-
dren would be unclean, but as it is, they are
holy. 15But if the unbelieving partner sepa-
rates, let it be so; in such a case the brother
or sister is not bound. It is to peace that
God has called you.[b] 16Wife, for all you
know, you might save your husband. Hus-
band, for all you know, you might save
your wife.
17 However that may be, let each of you
lead the life that the Lord has assigned, to

a Gk *brother* *b* Other ancient authorities read *us*

elsewhere, Paul approaches marital and sexual relations with concessions more than commands. Also, in vv. 2–16 and 32–34 Paul addresses alternatively both women and men, unusual for ancient authors. Verses 2–31 follow the same pattern of argumentation, first enunciating a general rule (vv. 2–3, 8,10,12–13,17 [repeated 20 and 24],26–27) and then making an exception (vv. 5,9,11a, 15,21,28). **1–16:** Urges continuing marital relations rather than sexual abstinence *because of . . . immorality.* **1:** *Now concerning . . .*, indicates both a new topic and that Paul is responding to a letter from the Corinthians, as in 7.25; 8.1; 12.1; 16.1. The form of the ascetic principle of the Corinthians, *it is well for a man . . .* (i.e., focused on the man's behavior vis-à-vis a woman), suggests that Paul is addressing primarily women. The principle of sexual abstinence may be connected with certain Corinthians' attachment to Wisdom, to whom (as a personified heavenly figure) the wise person is exclusively devoted as a spiritual "life-mate" or spouse as in Wis 8.2,9,16–18. *Touch* is a euphemism for sexual intercourse. **4:** The husband's authority over his wife's body is patriarchal convention, but the wife's authority over her husband's body contradicts and challenges patriarchal forms of marriage. **5–6:** A limited exception to the general rule in vv. 3–4, and a *concession* to some people's desire to abstain from sexual relations. **7:** Perhaps because some were appealing to Paul's own unmarried and celibate status, he declares that celibacy is a special *gift from God.* **8–9:** *Practicing self-control* is likely a reference to certain Corinthians' celibacy. The memorable maxim, *It is better to marry . . .*, indicates how seriously Paul took the sex-drive. **10:** The *command* of *the Lord* appears to refer to the sayings in Mark 10.6–9,11–12 and Luke 16.18, one of only two times Paul cites Jesus' teachings (see 9.14; cf. 11.23–25). **12–13:** Although Paul gives his own opinion here, he appears to be applying the Lord's command against divorce in v. 10 to these special cases. **14:** The unbelieving spouse *is made holy through* the believing partner because the latter is separated from the world and sin in the new community of Christ and, Paul believes, in the mutually engaging bond of marriage the holy would be more powerful than the unholy. **17–24:** In the

which God called you. This is my rule in all
the churches. 18 Was anyone at the time of
his call already circumcised? Let him not
seek to remove the marks of circumcision.
Was anyone at the time of his call uncir-
cumcised? Let him not seek circumcision.
19 Circumcision is nothing, and uncircumci-
sion is nothing; but obeying the command-
ments of God is everything. 20 Let each of
you remain in the condition in which you
were called.
21 Were you a slave when called? Do
not be concerned about it. Even if you can
gain your freedom, make use of your
present condition now more than ever.[a]
22 For whoever was called in the Lord as a
slave is a freed person belonging to the
Lord, just as whoever was free when called
is a slave of Christ. 23 You were bought
with a price; do not become slaves of hu-
man masters. 24 In whatever condition you
were called, brothers and sisters,[b] there re-
main with God.
25 Now concerning virgins, I have no
command of the Lord, but I give my opin-
ion as one who by the Lord's mercy is trust-
worthy. 26 I think that, in view of the im-
pending[c] crisis, it is well for you to remain
as you are. 27 Are you bound to a wife? Do
not seek to be free. Are you free from a
wife? Do not seek a wife. 28 But if you mar-
ry, you do not sin, and if a virgin marries,
she does not sin. Yet those who marry will
experience distress in this life,[d] and I
would spare you that. 29 I mean, brothers

a Or *avail yourself of the opportunity*
b Gk *brothers* *c* Or *present* *d* Gk *in the flesh*

middle of his advice about marriage and sexual relations, Paul enunciates his general *rule in all the churches* (assemblies), in vv. 17,20,24, with two illustrations, one of which turns out to be an exception to the rule. Closely related to the principle is the baptismal formula cited in Gal 3.28. **17:** The translation *the life . . . to which God called you* is misleading; *to which* fits neither illustration, "slave-free" or "circumcised-uncircumcised." "In the condition in which you were called" in 7.20 gives a better sense: The statement is about the life situation of each believer at the time of God's call to join the new community, not a characterization of that life situation as God's calling. **18–19:** *Circumcision . . . and uncircumcision* then illustrates the "rule" (v. 17) intelligibly. **19:** *Obeying the commandments of God* indicates that for Paul the law was still valid as a guide for community life. **21:** The phrase *your present condition now more than ever* is not in the Greek, where the last, elliptical clause, *make use of [it]* or "rather use it," requires completion from the context, i.e., from the nearest noun, *freedom.* Thus the alternative translation in NRSV footnote *a* is to be preferred, with the sense being: "If you can gain your freedom, avail yourself of the opportunity!" Since the slave-free relation is not analogous to the male-female or the circumcised-uncircumcised relations, Paul makes an exception to his rule when it comes to slaves—following the pattern of the four preceding and one following sections of the argument, where he gives a general rule and then makes an exception. Slaves should seize any opportunity to become free. **22–23:** Explains the exception to the rule: Since both slaves and free were *bought with a price,* neither can be *slaves of human masters.* **25–40:** *Now concerning virgins* signals a new but related issue; see 7.1n. Abstention from sexual relations, an exception for the married, is the rule for *virgins.* Except for vv. 32–34, which is still in gender-balanced statements about both men and women, Paul now addresses not the virgins themselves but men engaged to virgins. The phrase *the unmarried woman* and *the virgin* in v. 34 indicates that throughout this section *virgins* refers to betrothed young women, not young unmarried women generally (see vv. 36–37n.). That Paul pointedly reassures the engaged men that *it is no sin* if you marry in vv. 28, 36 (a remarkable statement for a first-century Jew) indicates that someone in the Corinthian community was asserting that it was wrong for *virgins* to marry. **25:** Paul makes a point of having *no command of the Lord* but only his own *opinion* to offer in a relatively gentle attempt at persuasion that emphasizes context. **26:** Paul agrees with the ascetic principle of some of the Corinthians, formulated exactly like the quotation in 7.1b, that *it is well for you to remain as you are,* but offers his own reason: *in view of the impending crisis* (see v. 31; 15.51–55; 16.22n.). **29–35:** A lengthy explanation of the advice in vv. 26–28. **29–31:** *The appointed time has grown short* and *the present form of this world is passing away* in vv. 29 and 31 suggest how imminent in Paul's mind the fulfillment of history inaugu-

and sisters,[a] the appointed time has grown
short; from now on, let even those who
have wives be as though they had none,
30 and those who mourn as though they
were not mourning, and those who rejoice
as though they were not rejoicing, and
those who buy as though they had no pos-
sessions, 31 and those who deal with the
world as though they had no dealings with
it. For the present form of this world is
passing away.
32 I want you to be free from anxieties.
The unmarried man is anxious about the
affairs of the Lord, how to please the Lord;
33 but the married man is anxious about the
affairs of the world, how to please his wife,
34 and his interests are divided. And the un-
married woman and the virgin are anxious
about the affairs of the Lord, so that they
may be holy in body and spirit; but the
married woman is anxious about the affairs
of the world, how to please her husband.
35 I say this for your own benefit, not to put
any restraint upon you, but to promote
good order and unhindered devotion to the
Lord.
36 If anyone thinks that he is not behav-
ing properly toward his fiancée,[b] if his pas-
sions are strong, and so it has to be, let him
marry as he wishes; it is no sin. Let them
marry. 37 But if someone stands firm in his
resolve, being under no necessity but hav-
ing his own desire under control, and has
determined in his own mind to keep her as
his fiancée,[b] he will do well. 38 So then, he
who marries his fiancée[b] does well; and he
who refrains from marriage will do better.
39 A wife is bound as long as her hus-
band lives. But if the husband dies,[c] she is
free to marry anyone she wishes, only in the
Lord. 40 But in my judgment she is more
blessed if she remains as she is. And I think
that I too have the Spirit of God.

8 Now concerning food sacrificed to
idols: we know that "all of us possess

a Gk *brothers* *b* Gk *virgin* *c* Gk *falls asleep*

rated in the crucifixion and resurrection of Christ was. In vv. 29b–31a he offers five illustrations of how the economic system (private property, slavery, commerce) and basic social forms (patriarchal marriage), as well as the emotional aspects of life rooted in them, are about to disappear. Paul's operative principle of *as though . . . not* is a detachment from the dominant social forms and cultural values, while continuing to interact with unbelievers (see 5.9–10). **32–35:** Applies the *as though . . . [not]* stance to the question of marriage between virgins and those betrothed to them. The phrase *is anxious about* should be read consistently, and positively, throughout vv. 32–34. Because the married person's attention would thus be divided between the Lord and the spouse, the unmarried condition is the better one, as stated in vv. 26–28 and again in v. 38. **34:** *Holy in body and spirit* may reflect the Corinthian ascetics' concern for bodily purity for the sake of spiritual transcendence, or Paul's concern that body as well as spirit be kept holy. **36–37:** *Fiancée* appropriately interprets the Greek for "virgin," indicating that she is engaged (see vv. 25–40n.). **39:** Apparently addressing Corinthian women's ascetic separation from their husbands as the principal issue at hand, Paul reasserts the traditional Jewish stance on marriage. **40:** His own opinion comes closer to what the Corinthian ascetics probably wanted to hear. And like them he also has *the Spirit of God.*

8.1–11.1: Argument concerning food offered to idols. *Now concerning . . .* opens discussion of another issue about which the Corinthians had written (see 7.1n.): *food sacrificed to idols.* At several points Paul cites principles and formulations of some of the Corinthians, so that it is possible to discern both sides of the argument. The phrase *accustomed to idols until now* in 8.7 indicates that the weak in *conscience* (or, better, "consciousness") for whom Paul is concerned are Gentiles, not Jews or Jewish Christians. Paul's argument proceeds in five steps.

8.1–13: Eating food offered to idols. Paul begins his argument against eating idol-food in a temple, ending with a fundamental principle in v. 13. **1–6:** Paul first deals with the Corinthians' *knowledge,* in which their liberty is rooted, before directly addressing their liberty of eating idol-food in 8.7–13. **1:** *Food sacrificed to idols* refers to food sacrificed in the presence of an idol and eaten in the temple precincts. He uses a different term, "sacred food," "offered in sacrifice," when discussing eating dinner at a friend's house

knowledge." Knowledge puffs up, but love
builds up. 2 Anyone who claims to know
something does not yet have the necessary
knowledge; 3 but anyone who loves God is
known by him.

4 Hence, as to the eating of food offered
to idols, we know that "no idol in the
world really exists," and that "there is no
God but one." 5 Indeed, even though there
may be so-called gods in heaven or on
earth—as in fact there are many gods and
many lords— 6 yet for us there is one God,
the Father, from whom are all things and
for whom we exist, and one Lord, Jesus
Christ, through whom are all things and
through whom we exist.

7 It is not everyone, however, who has
this knowledge. Since some have become so
accustomed to idols until now, they still
think of the food they eat as food offered to
an idol; and their conscience, being weak, is
defiled. 8 "Food will not bring us close to
God."[a] We are no worse off if we do not
eat, and no better off if we do. 9 But take
care that this liberty of yours does not
somehow become a stumbling block to the
weak. 10 For if others see you, who possess
knowledge, eating in the temple of an idol,
might they not, since their conscience is
weak, be encouraged to the point of eating
food sacrificed to idols? 11 So by your
knowledge those weak believers for whom
Christ died are destroyed.[b] 12 But when
you thus sin against members of your fami-
ly,[c] and wound their conscience when it is
weak, you sin against Christ. 13 Therefore,

a The quotation may extend to the end of the verse
b Gk *the weak brother . . . is destroyed*
c Gk *against the brothers*

in 10.27–28. Paul cites with seeming approval a principle of the Corinthians: *All of us possess knowledge.* For some Hellenistic Jews "knowledge" was closely associated with wisdom, a virtual synonym for the content that heavenly Wisdom provided to her devotees, as in Wis 10.10. But Paul immediately objects that *Knowledge puffs up, but love builds up,* presumably meaning the community. **2–3:** The words *something, God,* and *by him* were missing in Paul's Greek text. **4:** *No idol* and *no God but one* are particular principles of the Corinthians' knowledge, which again have their background in Hellenistic Jewish theology, as in Wis 7.17; 13.1; 15.2–3. **5–6:** In a long, awkward sentence, Paul first appears to agree with the Corinthian principle, setting up the statement of faith in v. 6, but then bluntly asserts the reality of *many gods and many lords.* **6:** These statements do not follow from v. 5, fit poorly in context, and use formulaic language (cf. Rom 11.36) in connection with Christ that appears nowhere else in Paul, yet do appear in Hellenistic Jewish theological statements about heavenly Wisdom as the agent of creation and salvation (e.g., Wis 8.1,6; 9.10–18). Paul must be replacing Wisdom with Christ in formulas borrowed from the Corinthian theological knowledge, just as he argued that the real wisdom of God is the crucified Christ in 1.24. **7–13:** Moving from a gentle observation in v. 7 to an ominous warning in v. 12, Paul appeals to the enlightened Corinthians to cease eating food offered to idols. **7:** *Not everyone . . . has this knowledge* counters what he ostensibly accepted in 8.1. The Greek term translated *conscience* here and in 8.10,12; 10.25,27–29, means something more like "consciousness," which, when characterized as *defiled* because it is *weak,* makes more sense in this context. For the Corinthians, a "weak consciousness" stemmed from a lack of "knowledge." **8:** The whole verse is another quotation of Corinthian knowledge, and the second half would fit better with the first half if it were translated: "We are no better off if we do not eat and we are no worse off if we eat." **9–12:** The possible effect of the behavior of the enlightened Corinthians. **9:** *This liberty of yours,* gained from possession of "knowledge" (8.1,4), is their personal ethical authority or freedom (cf. 6.12; 10.23) to engage in actions such as eating food sacrificed to idols, contrary to traditional (Jewish) prohibitions about idolatry. Paul uses the same Greek term, translated "right," in 9.4–6,12,18, and the near synonym "free/freedom" in 9.1,19; 10.29. **10:** *You, who possess knowledge, eating in the temple . . . ,* this is what Paul sees as the concrete problem (as also in 10.19–21); at every level of the dominant society, from extended families and guilds to city celebrations and the imperial cult, sacrificial meals were instrumental in constituting the social structure. **13:** To conclude this opening of his argument against eating food offered to idols, Paul formulates a general ethical principle (focused on eating) that the criterion of personal behavior is its effect on others in the assembly.

if food is a cause of their falling,[a] I will
never eat meat, so that I may not cause one
of them[b] to fall.

9 Am I not free? Am I not an apostle?
Have I not seen Jesus our Lord? Are
you not my work in the Lord? 2 If I am not
an apostle to others, at least I am to you;
for you are the seal of my apostleship in the
Lord.
3 This is my defense to those who would
examine me. 4 Do we not have the right to
our food and drink? 5 Do we not have the
right to be accompanied by a believing
wife,[c] as do the other apostles and the
brothers of the Lord and Cephas? 6 Or is it
only Barnabas and I who have no right to
refrain from working for a living? 7 Who at
any time pays the expenses for doing mili-
tary service? Who plants a vineyard and
does not eat any of its fruit? Or who tends
a flock and does not get any of its milk?
8 Do I say this on human authority?
Does not the law also say the same? 9 For it
is written in the law of Moses, "You shall
not muzzle an ox while it is treading out
the grain." Is it for oxen that God is con-
cerned? 10 Or does he not speak entirely for
our sake? It was indeed written for our
sake, for whoever plows should plow in
hope and whoever threshes should thresh
in hope of a share in the crop. 11 If we have
sown spiritual good among you, is it too
much if we reap your material benefits? 12 If
others share this rightful claim on you, do
not we still more?
Nevertheless, we have not made use of
this right, but we endure anything rather
than put an obstacle in the way of the gos-
pel of Christ. 13 Do you not know that
those who are employed in the temple ser-
vice get their food from the temple, and
those who serve at the altar share in what is
sacrificed on the altar? 14 In the same way,
the Lord commanded that those who pro-
claim the gospel should get their living by
the gospel.
15 But I have made no use of any of
these rights, nor am I writing this so that
they may be applied in my case. Indeed, I
would rather die than that—no one will
deprive me of my ground for boasting! 16 If
I proclaim the gospel, this gives me no
ground for boasting, for an obligation is
laid on me, and woe to me if I do not pro-
claim the gospel! 17 For if I do this of my
own will, I have a reward; but if not of my
own will, I am entrusted with a commis-
sion. 18 What then is my reward? Just this:
that in my proclamation I may make the
gospel free of charge, so as not to make full
use of my rights in the gospel.
19 For though I am free with respect to

a Gk *my brother's falling* b Gk *cause my brother*
c Gk *a sister as wife*

9.1–27: Paul's rights and his freedom not to exercise them. Paul illustrates the principle in 8.13 from his nonuse of his apostolic freedom in his mission, in an emotionally charged self-defense of his apostolic conduct. **1:** *An apostle . . . seen Jesus our Lord,* see 15.8; Gal 1.1,11–16. **3:** See 4.3–4. **4–12a:** Paul first establishes his *right* or liberty as an apostle, purposely using the Corinthian term for enlightened individual "liberty" (see 8.9n.). **4–7:** Paul has the same right to economic support from the communities of the movement as do Cephas (Peter) and other apostles but, since his mission with Barnabas based in Antioch (see Acts 13–14), has not used it. **8–10:** The divine authority of *the law of Moses* (Deut 25.4) confirms his apostolic right to economic support. **12b–27:** Paul comes to the main point of his autobiographical illustration of the principle in 8.13 and his self-defense to the Corinthians who were examining him: He has not used his apostolic *right.* **14:** *The Lord commanded,* see 7.10n. **15:** Paul had followed the same practice in Thessalonica (1 Thess 2.7–9). **16–17:** *An obligation is laid on me . . . do this of my own will,* the terms in Greek are "necessity," the constraints of ordinary human affairs, which the enlightened Corinthians believe they have transcended in their "liberty," and "free will" to act without the constraints of necessity, which only the wise person possesses. Paul asserts that he was *entrusted with a commission,* like the biblical prophets. **18:** A paradoxical statement: His *reward* is to *make the gospel free of charge,* perhaps to make his gospel free of what would otherwise seem like patronage, which was increasingly common in the dominant society. **19–22:** He argues that the purpose of his nonuse of his apostolic right,

all, I have made myself a slave to all, so that
I might win more of them. 20 To the Jews I
became as a Jew, in order to win Jews. To
those under the law I became as one under
the law (though I myself am not under the
law) so that I might win those under the
law. 21 To those outside the law I became as
one outside the law (though I am not free
from God's law but am under Christ's law)
so that I might win those outside the law.
22 To the weak I became weak, so that I
might win the weak. I have become all
things to all people, that I might by all
means save some. 23 I do it all for the sake
of the gospel, so that I may share in its
blessings.

24 Do you not know that in a race the
runners all compete, but only one receives
the prize? Run in such a way that you may
win it. 25 Athletes exercise self-control in all
things; they do it to receive a perishable
wreath, but we an imperishable one. 26 So
I do not run aimlessly, nor do I box as
though beating the air; 27 but I punish my
body and enslave it, so that after proclaim-
ing to others I myself should not be disqual-
ified.

10 I do not want you to be unaware,
brothers and sisters,[a] that our an-
cestors were all under the cloud, and all
passed through the sea, 2 and all were bap-
tized into Moses in the cloud and in the sea,
3 and all ate the same spiritual food, 4 and
all drank the same spiritual drink. For they
drank from the spiritual rock that followed
them, and the rock was Christ. 5 Neverthe-
less, God was not pleased with most of
them, and they were struck down in the
wilderness.

6 Now these things occurred as exam-
ples for us, so that we might not desire evil
as they did. 7 Do not become idolaters as
some of them did; as it is written, "The
people sat down to eat and drink, and they
rose up to play." 8 We must not indulge in

a Gk *brothers*

i.e., to *win* or *save some*, is the opposite of the potential result of the enlightened Corinthians' use of their individual "liberty." **19:** His metaphor of self-enslavement is specific to this argument against the enlightened Corinthians' "liberty," not a general understanding of Christian life or discipleship. **20–21:** *To the Jews. . . . To those under the law. . . . To those outside the law . . .*, involves a more complex distinction than simply Jews and non-Jews (Greeks); perhaps Jews, others who observe the (Jewish) law, and (other) Gentiles/Greeks. **24–27:** The extended athletic metaphor alludes to the Isthmian and Imperial Games at Corinth.

10.1–13: Warning that the Corinthians are risking God's wrath (in eating food offered to idols). This step of his argument against eating food offered to idols is full of allusions to symbols and incidents from Israel's Exodus and wilderness traditions, but cites scripture only once, in v. 7. (Biblical versions of these incidents are in Ex 13.21; 14.22; 16.4–35; 17.6; Num 20.7–11.) **1–5:** That Paul uses the distinctively Corinthian terms of "spiritual" people and things in vv. 3–4 and then abruptly cites God's displeasure with those who consume "spiritual" food and drink in v. 5 suggests that he is again borrowing and countering Corinthian language. The enlightened Corinthians appear to have assimilated the tradition of interpreting Exodus and wilderness incidents such as *the cloud, and . . . the sea, and . . . spiritual food* (manna), *and . . . spiritual drink* (water) *from the spiritual rock* spiritually as symbols of heavenly Wisdom or the knowledge she provides (see Wis 10.17–18; 11.4; 16.20–22; 19.7). **2:** *Baptized . . . in the cloud and in the sea*, probably another symbol of immortality given by Wisdom, considering the Corinthian emphasis on "baptism for the dead" in 15.29, and Paul's de-emphasis on baptism in 1.14–17. **4:** *And the rock was Christ*, an intrusive, parenthetical comment by which again Paul attempts to replace the Corinthians' "Wisdom" with his own "Christ" as the agent of salvation (see 1.24 and 8.6). **5:** *Nevertheless, God was not pleased . . .*, the focus shifts from the "ancestors" to "God," and the tone from recitation of salvation to warning of judgment. **6–13:** Paul develops this warning in five exhortations of "We must not/Do not . . . as some of [the ancestors] did" in vv. 6b–10, framed in vv. 6a and 11 with parallel statements. (The biblical stories he alludes to are in Num 14.29–30; Ex 32.4–6; Num 25.1–9; Num 21.5–6; Num 16.13–14,41–49.) **7:** That Paul actually cites scripture (Ex 32.6) only in connection with idolatry indicates that this is his major

sexual immorality as some of them did, and
twenty-three thousand fell in a single day.
9 We must not put Christ[a] to the test, as
some of them did, and were destroyed by
serpents. 10 And do not complain as some
of them did, and were destroyed by the de-
stroyer. 11 These things happened to them
to serve as an example, and they were writ-
ten down to instruct us, on whom the ends
of the ages have come. 12 So if you think
you are standing, watch out that you do
not fall. 13 No testing has overtaken you
that is not common to everyone. God is
faithful, and he will not let you be tested
beyond your strength, but with the testing
he will also provide the way out so that you
may be able to endure it.

14 Therefore, my dear friends,[b] flee
from the worship of idols. 15 I speak as to
sensible people; judge for yourselves what I
say. 16 The cup of blessing that we bless, is
it not a sharing in the blood of Christ? The
bread that we break, is it not a sharing in
the body of Christ? 17 Because there is one
bread, we who are many are one body, for
we all partake of the one bread. 18 Consider
the people of Israel;[c] are not those who eat
the sacrifices partners in the altar? 19 What
do I imply then? That food sacrificed to
idols is anything, or that an idol is any-
thing? 20 No, I imply that what pagans sac-
rifice, they sacrifice to demons and not to
God. I do not want you to be partners with
demons. 21 You cannot drink the cup of the
Lord and the cup of demons. You cannot
partake of the table of the Lord and the
table of demons. 22 Or are we provoking
the Lord to jealousy? Are we stronger
than he?

23 "All things are lawful," but not all
things are beneficial. "All things are law-
ful," but not all things build up. 24 Do not
seek your own advantage, but that of the
other. 25 Eat whatever is sold in the meat
market without raising any question on the
ground of conscience, 26 for "the earth and
its fullness are the Lord's." 27 If an unbe-
liever invites you to a meal and you are
disposed to go, eat whatever is set before
you without raising any question on the
ground of conscience. 28 But if someone
says to you, "This has been offered in sacri-
fice," then do not eat it, out of consider-
ation for the one who informed you, and
for the sake of conscience— 29 I mean the
other's conscience, not your own. For why
should my liberty be subject to the judg-

a Other ancient authorities read *the Lord* *b* Gk *my beloved* *c* Gk *Israel according to the flesh*

concern; see v. 14. **12:** *Watch out . . . ,* completes the warning begun in v. 5. **13:** Perhaps realizing the severity of his criticism in vv. 5–12, Paul interrupts the flow of his argument with this reassurance.

10.14–22: Prohibition of eating food offered to idols. Beginning with a plea to "Flee idolatry" and ending with a blunt warning about the consequences of banqueting in temples, Paul comes to the point of the argument begun in 8.1–13. Picking up on 8.5, he now explicitly counters the Corinthian "knowledge" that "no idol/god in the world really exists" (8.4) by stressing the real communal relations involved when one dines in their temples, and he counters their claims about individual "authority/liberty" with a call for group solidarity in the new community centered on Christ. **16–17:** This interpretation of the bread in the sense of communal sharing is unique in the New Testament. In the main point of his argument, Paul combines *the body of Christ,* represented by the bread, with "body" as a standard political symbol of how the people of a city-state, though many, are united. **19–21:** Paul moves the focus from abstract principles of knowledge to concrete social practices—sacrificing and eating in temple banquets—and formulates his final prohibition in v. 21 in terms of the mutual exclusivity of solidarity with the Lord and solidarity with demons (gods/idols). **22:** These rhetorical questions allude to the warning historical examples given in vv. 6–12.

10.23–11.1: Responsibility to others. Paul begins and ends this final step of his argument against eating food sacrificed to idols by restating that one must seek the advantage of the other, not one's own, as he himself has tried to do (10.23–24; 10.31–11.1). In between he concedes ethical "liberty" on two matters that he views as relatively unimportant (vv. 25–27,28–29a). On *conscience,* see 8.7n. **29b–30:** Anticipation of possible objections.

ment of someone else's conscience? 30 If I
partake with thankfulness, why should I be
denounced because of that for which I give
thanks?
31 So, whether you eat or drink, or
whatever you do, do everything for the glo-
ry of God. 32 Give no offense to Jews or to
Greeks or to the church of God, 33 just as I
try to please everyone in everything I do,
not seeking my own advantage, but that of
11 many, so that they may be saved.
1 Be imitators of me, as I am of
Christ.

2 I commend you because you remem-
ber me in everything and maintain the tra-
ditions just as I handed them on to you.
3 But I want you to understand that Christ
is the head of every man, and the husband[a]
is the head of his wife,[b] and God is the
head of Christ. 4 Any man who prays or
prophesies with something on his head dis-
graces his head, 5 but any woman who
prays or prophesies with her head unveiled
disgraces her head—it is one and the same
thing as having her head shaved. 6 For if
a woman will not veil herself, then she
should cut off her hair; but if it is disgrace-
ful for a woman to have her hair cut off or
to be shaved, she should wear a veil. 7 For
a man ought not to have his head veiled,
since he is the image and reflection[c] of
God; but woman is the reflection[c] of man.
8 Indeed, man was not made from woman,
but woman from man. 9 Neither was man
created for the sake of woman, but woman
for the sake of man. 10 For this reason a
woman ought to have a symbol of[d] au-
thority on her head,[e] because of the an-
gels. 11 Nevertheless, in the Lord woman is
not independent of man or man indepen-
dent of woman. 12 For just as woman came
from man, so man comes through woman;
but all things come from God. 13 Judge for
yourselves: is it proper for a woman to pray
to God with her head unveiled? 14 Does not
nature itself teach you that if a man wears
long hair, it is degrading to him, 15 but if a
woman has long hair, it is her glory? For
her hair is given to her for a covering. 16 But
if anyone is disposed to be contentious—
we have no such custom, nor do the
churches of God.
17 Now in the following instructions I

a The same Greek word means *man* or *husband*
b Or *head of the woman* *c* Or *glory* *d* Gk lacks *a symbol of* *e* Or *have freedom of choice regarding her head*

11.2–16: Argument concerning hairstyles. (Because 11.3–16 interrupts an otherwise easy movement from 11.2 to 11.17–18, and because the vocabulary and content of the passage are strange for Paul, but resemble those of deutero-Pauline letters such as Colossians, Ephesians, and 1–2 Timothy, it may be a later interpolation.) **3:** The best understanding of *head* appears to be "source," rather than either "authority over" (excluded by "authority on her head" in v. 10) or an ontological subordination or "chain of being." This statement is very different from Paul's formulations elsewhere of the respective relationships involved (see 3.18; 15.20–28,49). **4–6:** In both Greek and Roman society, as portrayed on coins and statues, men normally had short hair and women long hair braided or wound up around their heads. Women let their hair down only for certain religious rites. The language of vv. 4–6 is ambiguous, but may have to do with hairstyles, rather than veils, as in the NRSV translation above. Thus v. 4 refers to a prophesying man's "hair down (around his) head" and vv. 5–6 to a prophesying woman "with head uncovered (by her bound-up hair)." Vv. 5–6a are sarcastic, as v. 6b indicates in making the main point. **7–12:** A new argument, in which the contrast begun in v. 7 is not completed until v. 10. **7:** See Gen 1.27. **8–9:** Two further points derived from the creation story; see Gen 2.18–20,23. **10:** *Because of the angels* is probably an allusion to women's claim that in their prophetic inspiration or ecstasy they have "authority" to let their hair flow freely, so that their head is "uncovered." **11–12:** Added to mitigate the severity of vv. 8–9, reminding men that they are interdependent with women *in the Lord.* **14–16:** The decisive argument is from *nature,* which is uncharacteristic of Paul, and from convention. **17–34:** This passage would fit readily after 11.2, if the preceding discussion of hairstyles were not in the original letter. In a manner typical of ancient arguments, Paul would then be commending the Corinthians for maintaining the traditions in general before admonishing them about the divisions at the Lord's Supper in particular.

do not commend you, because when you
come together it is not for the better but for
the worse. 18 For, to begin with, when you
come together as a church, I hear that there
are divisions among you; and to some ex-
tent I believe it. 19 Indeed, there have to be
factions among you, for only so will it be-
come clear who among you are genuine.
20 When you come together, it is not really
to eat the Lord's supper. 21 For when the
time comes to eat, each of you goes ahead
with your own supper, and one goes hun-
gry and another becomes drunk. 22 What!
Do you not have homes to eat and drink in?
Or do you show contempt for the church of
God and humiliate those who have noth-
ing? What should I say to you? Should I
commend you? In this matter I do not com-
mend you!

23 For I received from the Lord what I
also handed on to you, that the Lord Jesus
on the night when he was betrayed took a
loaf of bread, 24 and when he had given
thanks, he broke it and said, "This is my
body that is for[a] you. Do this in remem-
brance of me." 25 In the same way he took
the cup also, after supper, saying, "This
cup is the new covenant in my blood. Do
this, as often as you drink it, in remem-
brance of me." 26 For as often as you eat
this bread and drink the cup, you proclaim
the Lord's death until he comes.

27 Whoever, therefore, eats the bread or
drinks the cup of the Lord in an unworthy
manner will be answerable for the body
and blood of the Lord. 28 Examine your-
selves, and only then eat of the bread and
drink of the cup. 29 For all who eat and
drink[b] without discerning the body,[c] eat
and drink judgment against themselves.
30 For this reason many of you are weak
and ill, and some have died.[d] 31 But if we
judged ourselves, we would not be judged.
32 But when we are judged by the Lord, we
are disciplined[e] so that we may not be con-
demned along with the world.

33 So then, my brothers and sisters,[f]
when you come together to eat, wait for
one another. 34 If you are hungry, eat at
home, so that when you come together, it
will not be for your condemnation. About
the other things I will give instructions
when I come.

12 Now concerning spiritual gifts,[g]
brothers and sisters,[f] I do not want
you to be uninformed. 2 You know that
when you were pagans, you were enticed
and led astray to idols that could not speak.
3 Therefore I want you to understand that

a Other ancient authorities read *is broken for*
b Other ancient authorities add *in an unworthy manner,* *c* Other ancient authorities read *the Lord's body* *d* Gk *fallen asleep* *e* Or *When we are judged, we are being disciplined by the Lord*
f Gk *brothers* *g* Or *spiritual persons*

After rebuking the Corinthians for their divisions (vv. 17–22), he repeats the words of institution (23–26), then applies that tradition to their situation (vv. 27–32), and finally instructs them as to how they should proceed in the future (vv. 33–34). **17–20:** By repeating *when you come together* (vv. 17–18,20) he suggests that they are anything but "together." **18:** *As a church,* see 1.2n. *I hear,* see 1.11. **19:** *Factions,* more correctly "discriminations"; *genuine,* "distinguished." The sense is ironic, or even sarcastic. **21:** This may be rhetorical accusation, rather than an accurate picture of their procedure. Paul's real concern is that the communal celebration is lost (cf. Jude 12). **22:** The first rhetorical question indicates whom he is addressing: those who are well enough off to *have* (i.e., own) houses. **23–26:** Paul's tradition of the Lord's Supper is not in the context of a Passover meal, in contrast to Mk 14.12–25. The emphasis in both Mark's and Paul's traditions falls on the new covenant symbolized by the cup, following the original covenant on Sinai in which God and the people were also bound by blood, Ex 24.8. **27–32:** Picking up on "until [the Lord] comes" in v. 26 (see 1.7–8), Paul's application of the tradition is dominated by references to *judgment. Answerable for the body . . . ,* means that those who fail to *discern the body,* i.e., the community, *eat and drink judgment against themselves.*

Chapters 12–14: Discrimination among spiritual gifts. The introduction, 12.1–3, and the conclusion, 14.36–40, enclose three major steps in the argument.

12.1–3: Introduction. *Now concerning,* see 7.1n. In framing the ensuing argument, Paul sets Jesus as

no one speaking by the Spirit of God ever
says "Let Jesus be cursed!" and no one can
say "Jesus is Lord" except by the Holy
Spirit.
4 Now there are varieties of gifts, but
the same Spirit; 5 and there are varieties of
services, but the same Lord; 6 and there are
varieties of activities, but it is the same God
who activates all of them in everyone. 7 To
each is given the manifestation of the Spirit
for the common good. 8 To one is given
through the Spirit the utterance of wisdom,
and to another the utterance of knowledge
according to the same Spirit, 9 to another
faith by the same Spirit, to another gifts of
healing by the one Spirit, 10 to another the
working of miracles, to another prophecy,
to another the discernment of spirits, to an-
other various kinds of tongues, to another
the interpretation of tongues. 11 All these
are activated by one and the same Spirit,
who allots to each one individually just as
the Spirit chooses.
12 For just as the body is one and has
many members, and all the members of the
body, though many, are one body, so it is
with Christ. 13 For in the one Spirit we were
all baptized into one body—Jews or
Greeks, slaves or free—and we were all
made to drink of one Spirit.
14 Indeed, the body does not consist of
one member but of many. 15 If the foot
would say, "Because I am not a hand, I do
not belong to the body," that would not
make it any less a part of the body. 16 And
if the ear would say, "Because I am not an
eye, I do not belong to the body," that
would not make it any less a part of the
body. 17 If the whole body were an eye,
where would the hearing be? If the whole
body were hearing, where would the sense
of smell be? 18 But as it is, God arranged the
members in the body, each one of them, as
he chose. 19 If all were a single member,
where would the body be? 20 As it is, there
are many members, yet one body. 21 The
eye cannot say to the hand, "I have no need
of you," nor again the head to the feet, "I
have no need of you." 22 On the contrary,
the members of the body that seem to be
weaker are indispensable, 23 and those
members of the body that we think less
honorable we clothe with greater honor,
and our less respectable members are treat-
ed with greater respect; 24 whereas our
more respectable members do not need
this. But God has so arranged the body,
giving the greater honor to the inferior
member, 25 that there may be no dissension
within the body, but the members may
have the same care for one another. 26 If
one member suffers, all suffer together with
it; if one member is honored, all rejoice to-
gether with it.
27 Now you are the body of Christ and
individually members of it. 28 And God has
appointed in the church first apostles, sec-
ond prophets, third teachers; then deeds of
power, then gifts of healing, forms of assis-
tance, forms of leadership, various kinds of

Lord in authority over spiritual gifts and presents the confession *Jesus is Lord* as the criterion of being caught up in the Spirit, to which *Let Jesus be cursed* is Paul's rhetorical antithesis.

12.4–31: Variety in the community. In the long first step of the argument, Paul insists upon diversity in unity. **4–11:** A variety of gifts proceed from the same source, all given for the common good of the community. Paul makes these distinctions among spiritual gifts, which are listed only here in Paul's letters, to relativize the Corinthians' favorites with which he begins the list; the precise nature of each gift is not at issue. Paul returns to discussion of the last four on the list in ch 14. **12–26:** The well-known analogy between the human body and the body politic illustrates his argument for the diversity of the Spirit's manifestations for the common good. **10:** *Tongues,* see 14.1–33n. **15–20:** A separatist or individualistic attitude by one member of the body would not *make it any less a part of the body.* **21–26:** The argument opposes the "honor" values of hierarchical aristocratic Greek and imperial Roman culture, insisting on the solidarity of the interdependent and equally valued members. **27–31:** After v. 27 concludes this step of the argument, Paul adds two new twists. First, he now explicitly ranks the gifts, pointedly placing "tongues" last. Second, the series of rhetorical questions suggests that some are encouraging others to experience tongues. **31:** The first half of this verse is ironic, setting up the next step of the argument.

tongues. 29 Are all apostles? Are all proph-
ets? Are all teachers? Do all work miracles?
30 Do all possess gifts of healing? Do all
speak in tongues? Do all interpret? 31 But
strive for the greater gifts. And I will show
you a still more excellent way.

13 If I speak in the tongues of mortals
and of angels, but do not have love,
I am a noisy gong or a clanging cymbal.
2 And if I have prophetic powers, and un-
derstand all mysteries and all knowledge,
and if I have all faith, so as to remove
mountains, but do not have love, I am
nothing. 3 If I give away all my possessions,
and if I hand over my body so that I may
boast,[a] but do not have love, I gain noth-
ing.

4 Love is patient; love is kind; love is not
envious or boastful or arrogant 5 or rude. It
does not insist on its own way; it is not
irritable or resentful; 6 it does not rejoice in
wrongdoing, but rejoices in the truth. 7 It
bears all things, believes all things, hopes
all things, endures all things.

8 Love never ends. But as for proph-
ecies, they will come to an end; as for
tongues, they will cease; as for knowledge,
it will come to an end. 9 For we know only
in part, and we prophesy only in part;
10 but when the complete comes, the partial
will come to an end. 11 When I was a child,
I spoke like a child, I thought like a child,
I reasoned like a child; when I became an
adult, I put an end to childish ways. 12 For
now we see in a mirror, dimly,[b] but then
we will see face to face. Now I know only
in part; then I will know fully, even as I
have been fully known. 13 And now faith,
hope, and love abide, these three; and the
greatest of these is love.

14 Pursue love and strive for the spiri-
tual gifts, and especially that you
may prophesy. 2 For those who speak in a
tongue do not speak to other people but to
God; for nobody understands them, since
they are speaking mysteries in the Spirit.
3 On the other hand, those who prophesy
speak to other people for their upbuilding
and encouragement and consolation.
4 Those who speak in a tongue build up
themselves, but those who prophesy build
up the church. 5 Now I would like all of you
to speak in tongues, but even more to
prophesy. One who prophesies is greater
than one who speaks in tongues, unless
someone interprets, so that the church may
be built up.

6 Now, brothers and sisters,[c] if I come
to you speaking in tongues, how will I ben-
efit you unless I speak to you in some reve-
lation or knowledge or prophecy or teach-

a Other ancient authorities read *body to be burned*
b Gk *in a riddle* c Gk *brothers*

13.1–13: Praising love in contrast with the overvaluation of spiritual gifts that produces divisiveness. Paul's sudden shift into the high-blown style of formal, artful praise of a virtue may be a parody of those who are fond of rhetoric. **1–3:** Paul first mockingly exaggerates both the Corinthians' favorite spiritual gifts along with his own key values, then suddenly deflates them. On *tongues* (v. 1), see 14.1–33n. **4–7:** The positive qualities of love are the opposite of the Corinthians' behavior presented elsewhere in the letter. **8–13:** In these comparisons, Paul becomes more rhapsodic, no longer ironic, glorifying the qualities he most values—while still denigrating the Corinthians' most valued spiritual gifts. Against their sense of present transcendence, Paul emphasizes future fulfillment. **12:** To *now we see in a mirror, dimly,* compare Wisdom as "a spotless mirror of the working of God" in Wis 7.25–26.

14.1–33: Advocating prophecy that intelligibly edifies the community and devaluing tongues that do not. In the New Testament, detailed discussion of "speaking in tongues" is confined to this chapter; a related phenomenon is found in Acts 19.6; cf. Acts 2.4–18. The very phrase may be Paul's. In his characterization of "tongues" in the successive subsections of his argument against it—as personal speech to God (v. 2), as like the indistinct sound of a flute or harp (v. 7), as prayer in the spirit without the mind (vv. 14–15), and as apparent madness (v. 23)—it resembles ecstatic prophecy. **2–5:** While affirming the value of individual empowerment gained in tongues, he values prophecy for building up the assembly. **6–12:** In accordance with the analogies, their "spirits" should be channeled into intelligible forms of communication such as prophecy. **13–19:** Applying the analogies of vv. 6–12 to the meetings of the

ing? 7 It is the same way with lifeless
instruments that produce sound, such as
the flute or the harp. If they do not give
distinct notes, how will anyone know what
is being played? 8 And if the bugle gives an
indistinct sound, who will get ready for
battle? 9 So with yourselves; if in a tongue
you utter speech that is not intelligible, how
will anyone know what is being said? For
you will be speaking into the air. 10 There
are doubtless many different kinds of
sounds in the world, and nothing is without
sound. 11 If then I do not know the meaning
of a sound, I will be a foreigner to the
speaker and the speaker a foreigner to me.
12 So with yourselves; since you are eager
for spiritual gifts, strive to excel in them for
building up the church.

13 Therefore, one who speaks in a
tongue should pray for the power to inter-
pret. 14 For if I pray in a tongue, my spirit
prays but my mind is unproductive.
15 What should I do then? I will pray with
the spirit, but I will pray with the mind
also; I will sing praise with the spirit, but I
will sing praise with the mind also. 16 Oth-
erwise, if you say a blessing with the spirit,
how can anyone in the position of an out-
sider say the "Amen" to your thanksgiving,
since the outsider does not know what you
are saying? 17 For you may give thanks well
enough, but the other person is not built
up. 18 I thank God that I speak in tongues
more than all of you; 19 nevertheless, in
church I would rather speak five words
with my mind, in order to instruct others
also, than ten thousand words in a tongue.

20 Brothers and sisters,[a] do not be chil-
dren in your thinking; rather, be infants in
evil, but in thinking be adults. 21 In the law
it is written,

"By people of strange tongues
  and by the lips of foreigners
I will speak to this people;
  yet even then they will not listen to
    me,"

says the Lord. 22 Tongues, then, are a sign
not for believers but for unbelievers, while
prophecy is not for unbelievers but for be-
lievers. 23 If, therefore, the whole church
comes together and all speak in tongues,
and outsiders or unbelievers enter, will they
not say that you are out of your mind?
24 But if all prophesy, an unbeliever or out-
sider who enters is reproved by all and
called to account by all. 25 After the secrets
of the unbeliever's heart are disclosed, that
person will bow down before God and
worship him, declaring, "God is really
among you."

26 What should be done then, my
friends?[a] When you come together, each
one has a hymn, a lesson, a revelation, a
tongue, or an interpretation. Let all things
be done for building up. 27 If anyone speaks
in a tongue, let there be only two or at most
three, and each in turn; and let one inter-
pret. 28 But if there is no one to interpret, let
them be silent in church and speak to them-
selves and to God. 29 Let two or three
prophets speak, and let the others weigh
what is said. 30 If a revelation is made to
someone else sitting nearby, let the first
person be silent. 31 For you can all prophesy
one by one, so that all may learn and all be
encouraged. 32 And the spirits of prophets

a Gk *brothers*

assembly, Paul appeals to the Corinthians to move their experiences in the Spirit into intelligible interpretation by the mind. **16:** The context suggests that the word translated *an outsider* (Gk "idiotēs") is someone not adept at speaking in tongues. *Amen,* a Hebrew word meaning "certainly" or "let it be so," used in response to someone's statement and in liturgical settings; see Deut 27.14–16; 1 Chr 16.36; Neh 5.13; 8.6; 2 Cor 1.20. **20–25:** Not until vv. 23–25 is his argument clear, that while tongues are a counterproductive sign for outsiders, prophecy, because intelligible, will be productive on outsiders, by disclosing the secrets of their hearts. **21:** Not actually *in the law* but in Isa 28.11–12. **26–33:** Instructions for procedure with prophecy and tongues at assembly gatherings. Over against the spontaneous flow of "tongues," Paul insists on only a few speaking in turn and on intelligible interpretation. Instructions on prophecy are far less restrictive. Notably absent is any reference to guiding leadership or a chairperson. Emphasis is still on the common good. **34–35:** Since these statements silencing women in the assembly

are subject to the prophets, 33 for God is a
God not of disorder but of peace.
(As in all the churches of the saints,
34 women should be silent in the churches.
For they are not permitted to speak, but
should be subordinate, as the law also says.
35 If there is anything they desire to know,
let them ask their husbands at home. For
it is shameful for a woman to speak in
church.[a] 36 Or did the word of God origi-
nate with you? Or are you the only ones it
has reached?)
37 Anyone who claims to be a prophet,
or to have spiritual powers, must acknowl-
edge that what I am writing to you is a
command of the Lord. 38 Anyone who does
not recognize this is not to be recognized.
39 So, my friends,[b] be eager to prophesy,
and do not forbid speaking in tongues;
40 but all things should be done decently
and in order.

15 Now I would remind you, brothers
and sisters,[c] of the good news[d]
that I proclaimed to you, which you in turn
received, in which also you stand, 2 through
which also you are being saved, if you hold
firmly to the message that I proclaimed to
you—unless you have come to believe in
vain.
3 For I handed on to you as of first im-
portance what I in turn had received: that
Christ died for our sins in accordance with
the scriptures, 4 and that he was buried, and
that he was raised on the third day in accor-
dance with the scriptures, 5 and that he ap-
peared to Cephas, then to the twelve.
6 Then he appeared to more than five hun-
dred brothers and sisters[c] at one time,
most of whom are still alive, though some
have died.[e] 7 Then he appeared to James,
then to all the apostles. 8 Last of all, as to
one untimely born, he appeared also to me.
9 For I am the least of the apostles, unfit to
be called an apostle, because I persecuted
the church of God. 10 But by the grace of
God I am what I am, and his grace toward
me has not been in vain. On the contrary, I
worked harder than any of them—though
it was not I, but the grace of God that is
with me. 11 Whether then it was I or they,
so we proclaim and so you have come to
believe.
12 Now if Christ is proclaimed as raised
from the dead, how can some of you say
there is no resurrection of the dead? 13 If

a Other ancient authorities put verses 34-35 after verse 40 *b* Gk *my brothers* *c* Gk *brothers* *d* Or *gospel* *e* Gk *fallen asleep*

are found in two different places in the ancient manuscripts, between 14.33 and 14.36 and after 14.40, they may be a marginal gloss later interpolated into the text; similar wording occurs in 1 Tim 2.11–12. Moreover, nothing in these statements has to do with the manifestations of the Spirit in the community, and "all" in vv. 23–24,31 and "each one" in v. 26 imply that women as well as men pray and prophesy. If these statements are original to 1 Cor, then Paul must be addressing only married women. **36–40:** Paul bluntly asserts his authority, along with a threat against noncompliance, and then summarizes the argument of chs 12–14.

15.1–58: Arguments for the resurrection. The issue is not identified until v. 12: Some of the Corinthians are denying *the resurrection of the dead.* Paul's own term for the deceased is "those who have fallen asleep," in 7.39; 11.30; 15.6,18,20; 1 Thess 4.13. The recurrence of "dead," along with the prominence of the antitheses "mortal-immortal" and "perishable-imperishable," in Paul's arguments here suggests that, as people embedded in Hellenistic culture and influenced by the Alexandrian Jewish teacher Apollos, the skeptical Corinthians view their souls as separable from the bodies. Indeed, because they possessed wisdom their souls were immortal, so the resurrection of their "perishable" body, once it was "dead," made no sense. Paul proceeds in clear steps.

15.1–11: The proclamation of Christ's death and resurrection. Paul reminds the Corinthians of the movement's early creed, vv. 3–5, to establish common ground, and he expands the list of witnesses to the resurrection, including himself, to increase its credibility. **5:** In the pre-Pauline creed, in contrast to the Gospels, women are not among the earliest witnesses of Jesus' resurrection. *Cephas,* Peter. **7:** *James,* probably "the Lord's brother" (Gal 1.19). **9:** See Acts 9.4–5; 22.4–5; Gal 1.13.

there is no resurrection of the dead, then Christ has not been raised; 14 and if Christ has not been raised, then our proclamation has been in vain and your faith has been in vain. 15 We are even found to be misrepresenting God, because we testified of God that he raised Christ—whom he did not raise if it is true that the dead are not raised. 16 For if the dead are not raised, then Christ has not been raised. 17 If Christ has not been raised, your faith is futile and you are still in your sins. 18 Then those also who have died[a] in Christ have perished. 19 If for this life only we have hoped in Christ, we are of all people most to be pitied.

20 But in fact Christ has been raised from the dead, the first fruits of those who have died.[a] 21 For since death came through a human being, the resurrection of the dead has also come through a human being; 22 for as all die in Adam, so all will be made alive in Christ. 23 But each in his own order: Christ the first fruits, then at his coming those who belong to Christ. 24 Then comes the end,[b] when he hands over the kingdom to God the Father, after he has destroyed every ruler and every authority and power. 25 For he must reign until he has put all his enemies under his feet. 26 The last enemy to be destroyed is death. 27 For "God[c] has put all things in subjection under his feet." But when it says, "All things are put in subjection," it is plain that this does not include the one who put all things in subjection under him. 28 When all things are subjected to him, then the Son himself will also be subjected to the one who put all things in subjection under him, so that God may be all in all.

29 Otherwise, what will those people do who receive baptism on behalf of the dead? If the dead are not raised at all, why are people baptized on their behalf?

30 And why are we putting ourselves in danger every hour? 31 I die every day! That is as certain, brothers and sisters,[d] as my boasting of you—a boast that I make in Christ Jesus our Lord. 32 If with merely human hopes I fought with wild animals at Ephesus, what would I have gained by it? If the dead are not raised,

"Let us eat and drink,
for tomorrow we die."

33 Do not be deceived:
"Bad company ruins good morals."

34 Come to a sober and right mind, and sin no more; for some people have no knowledge of God. I say this to your shame.

a Gk *fallen asleep* *b* Or *Then come the rest*
c Gk *he* *d* Gk *brothers*

15.12–34: The reality of the resurrection of the dead. 12–19: A logical argument: If there is no resurrection of the dead, then Christ could not have been raised, which is the basis of salvation, so believers' faith would be in vain. **20–28:** Paul reasserts the reality of Christ's resurrection and, in a sweeping historical perspective since Adam (see Gen 3.19), the subsequent events in the completion of the fulfillment of history now underway since his resurrection. **23–28:** This passage should not be read as an elaborate sequence of final events, since *order* in v. 23 refers not to chronology but rank, with Christ, already resurrected, *coming* first, followed by the resurrection of *those who belong to Christ.* **24–26:** The very purpose of Christ's *kingdom* or reign, in which he had been established in his resurrection, was to destroy *every ruler and every authority and power,* i.e., the Roman imperial rulers and institutions, which indeed claimed to be superhuman in their power, and finally the last enemy, the power of *death.* **26:** On the personification of *death,* see vv. 54–55; Ps 49.14; Hos 13.14; Hab 2.5; Rom 5.14–17. **27:** Ps 8.6. **29–34:** Paul points out further that the reality of the resurrection of the dead constitutes the grounds for their own and his actions in three particular ways, explained in vv. 29, 30–32a, and 32b, respectively. **29:** The Corinthian practice of vicarious *baptism on behalf of the dead* reflects their apparent belief that baptism in the "cloud" and the "sea" (see 10.2) as symbols of Wisdom brought immortality to the soul. **32:** *Wild animals at Ephesus,* a metaphor. The following quotation is from Isa 22.13. **33–34:** Paul sharply shames the skeptical Corinthians, calling them to "Sober up!" and deriding those who are full of wisdom and knowledge as having *no knowledge of God.* The quotation in v. 33 is from the fourth-century BCE Greek poet Menander.

35 But someone will ask, "How are the
dead raised? With what kind of body do
they come?" 36 Fool! What you sow does
not come to life unless it dies. 37 And as for
what you sow, you do not sow the body
that is to be, but a bare seed, perhaps of
wheat or of some other grain. 38 But God
gives it a body as he has chosen, and to
each kind of seed its own body. 39 Not all
flesh is alike, but there is one flesh for hu-
man beings, another for animals, another
for birds, and another for fish. 40 There are
both heavenly bodies and earthly bodies,
but the glory of the heavenly is one thing,
and that of the earthly is another. 41 There
is one glory of the sun, and another glory of
the moon, and another glory of the stars;
indeed, star differs from star in glory.
42 So it is with the resurrection of the
dead. What is sown is perishable, what is
raised is imperishable. 43 It is sown in dis-
honor, it is raised in glory. It is sown in
weakness, it is raised in power. 44 It is sown
a physical body, it is raised a spiritual body.
If there is a physical body, there is also a
spiritual body. 45 Thus it is written, "The
first man, Adam, became a living being";
the last Adam became a life-giving spirit.
46 But it is not the spiritual that is first, but
the physical, and then the spiritual. 47 The
first man was from the earth, a man of
dust; the second man is[a] from heaven.
48 As was the man of dust, so are those who
are of the dust; and as is the man of heaven,
so are those who are of heaven. 49 Just as
we have borne the image of the man of
dust, we will[b] also bear the image of the
man of heaven.
50 What I am saying, brothers and sis-
ters,[c] is this: flesh and blood cannot inherit
the kingdom of God, nor does the perish-
able inherit the imperishable. 51 Listen, I
will tell you a mystery! We will not all
die,[d] but we will all be changed, 52 in a
moment, in the twinkling of an eye, at the
last trumpet. For the trumpet will sound,
and the dead will be raised imperishable,
and we will be changed. 53 For this perish-
able body must put on imperishability, and
this mortal body must put on immortality.
54 When this perishable body puts on im-
perishability, and this mortal body puts on
immortality, then the saying that is written
will be fulfilled:

"Death has been swallowed up
in victory."

a Other ancient authorities add *the Lord* *b* Other ancient authorities read *let us* *c* Gk *brothers* *d* Gk *fall asleep*

15.35–58: ***With what kind of body?*** For Paul the resurrection life would be social-political, requiring embodied people. **35–41:** He uses the analogy of a seed to establish the body as the principle of continuity from historical to resurrection life, and the analogy of heavenly bodies to imagine different kinds of bodies. **42–49:** Paul now uses antitheses that the Corinthians use for body versus soul or for contrasting levels of spiritual status to characterize the historical and resurrection bodies, respectively. That is, he characterizes the embodied resurrection life in the same terms they use with regard to the immortality of their souls and their exalted spiritual status. **42:** *Perishable . . . imperishable,* occur only here and in vv. 52–54 in Paul's letters. **43–44:** For *dishonor . . . glory, weakness . . . power, physical* (lit. "soul-like") *. . . spiritual,* see 1.26; 2.6–3.4; 4.8–10. **45–49:** Paul's pointed insistence that *the spiritual . . . man of heaven* is *second,* while *Adam, the physical* (lit. "soul-like") *. . . man . . . from the earth* was *the first man,* with quotation of Gen 2.7, suggests that he is borrowing and reversing a Corinthian interpretation of Gen 1.26–27 as the origin of the prototype (or perhaps "image") of the "spiritual" person and Gen 2.7 as the origin of the "physical/soul-like" person. **50–58:** In the final step of his argument—and of the whole body of the letter—Paul suddenly, in an almost ecstatic exclamation, launches into his own distinctive vision. As in 2.7–8, he identifies this as a *mystery,* the technical term in Jewish revelatory literature for God's plan of fulfillment of history. This "mystery" seems particularly appropriate to the Corinthian situation, with its emphasis on suddenness and the transformation when *the dead will be raised imperishable.* **52:** On the *last trumpet,* see Isa 27.3; Zech 9.14; 2 Esd 6.23; 1 Thess 4.16. **54–57:** An exclamation, by visionary anticipation, of the final victory over death (cf. v. 26), with thanksgiving to God. **54:** Quoting Isa 25.8

55 "Where, O death, is your victory?
Where, O death, is your sting?"
56 The sting of death is sin, and the power
of sin is the law. 57 But thanks be to God,
who gives us the victory through our Lord
Jesus Christ.
58 Therefore, my beloved,[a] be stead-
fast, immovable, always excelling in the
work of the Lord, because you know that
in the Lord your labor is not in vain.

16 Now concerning the collection for
the saints: you should follow the di-
rections I gave to the churches of Galatia.
2 On the first day of every week, each of
you is to put aside and save whatever extra
you earn, so that collections need not be
taken when I come. 3 And when I arrive, I
will send any whom you approve with let-
ters to take your gift to Jerusalem. 4 If it
seems advisable that I should go also, they
will accompany me.
5 I will visit you after passing through
Macedonia—for I intend to pass through
Macedonia— 6 and perhaps I will stay with
you or even spend the winter, so that you
may send me on my way, wherever I go. 7 I
do not want to see you now just in passing,
for I hope to spend some time with you, if
the Lord permits. 8 But I will stay in Ephe-
sus until Pentecost, 9 for a wide door for
effective work has opened to me, and there
are many adversaries.
10 If Timothy comes, see that he has
nothing to fear among you, for he is doing
the work of the Lord just as I am; 11 there-
fore let no one despise him. Send him on his
way in peace, so that he may come to me;
for I am expecting him with the broth-
ers.
12 Now concerning our brother Apol-
los, I strongly urged him to visit you with
the other brothers, but he was not at all
willing[b] to come now. He will come when
he has the opportunity.
13 Keep alert, stand firm in your faith,
be courageous, be strong. 14 Let all that you
do be done in love.
15 Now, brothers and sisters,[c] you
know that members of the household of
Stephanas were the first converts in Achaia,
and they have devoted themselves to the
service of the saints; 16 I urge you to put
yourselves at the service of such people,
and of everyone who works and toils with
them. 17 I rejoice at the coming of Stepha-
nas and Fortunatus and Achaicus, because
they have made up for your absence; 18 for
they refreshed my spirit as well as yours. So
give recognition to such persons.
19 The churches of Asia send greetings.
Aquila and Prisca, together with the church
in their house, greet you warmly in the
Lord. 20 All the brothers and sisters[c] send

a Gk *beloved brothers* b Or *it was not at all God's will for him* c Gk *brothers*

(LXX). **55:** Quoting Hos 13.14. **56:** *Sin . . . law,* see Rom 3.20; 7.7–8.2. **58:** The final encouraging exhortation that ends the body of the letter.

16.1–12: The collection, travel plans, and Apollos. 1–4: *Now concerning,* see 7.1n. *The collection for the saints* in Jerusalem from the Gentile assemblies indicates the economic dimension of this international movement. See Gal 2.10; 2 Cor 8–9; Rom 15.25–29. **5:** Acts 19.21. **8–9:** Acts 18.19–20; 19.8–10,20,23–27. **10:** *Timothy,* see 4.17n. **12:** Perhaps Paul and Apollos (see Introduction) had a tacit understanding that the latter would not return to Corinth very soon.

16.13–24: Conclusion. 15–18: This delegation from Corinth may have brought the Corinthians' letter to Paul or have been preparing to bring Paul's letter to Corinth. **16:** "Stephanas," see 1.14–16n. **17:** *Fortunatus and Achaicus* are elsewhere unmentioned. **19:** *Aquila and Prisca* (see Acts 18.2; Rom 16.3) had worked with Paul building the assembly in Corinth and were now working with him in Ephesus. **21:** Paul had clearly been dictating the letter. **22:** *Our Lord, come!* the eager yearning for the coming of Christ; cf. Rev 22.20. **24:** Having written sharply at several points, Paul sends his love in the last line, a closing unique to 1 Corinthians.

greetings. Greet one another with a holy
kiss.

21 I, Paul, write this greeting with my
own hand. 22 Let anyone be accursed who
has no love for the Lord. Our Lord,
come![a] 23 The grace of the Lord Jesus be
with you. 24 My love be with all of you in
Christ Jesus.[b]

a Gk *Marana tha*. These Aramaic words can also be read *Maran atha*, meaning *Our Lord has come* *b* Other ancient authorities add *Amen*

The Second Letter of Paul to the CORINTHIANS

First and Second Corinthians are not the only letters Paul wrote to Corinth, and an examination of the sequence of events behind these letters gives an indication of the tensions in the relationship between Paul and the Corinthian church. Although the exact events cannot all be recovered from the materials in the New Testament, they can reasonably be reconstructed as follows.

After Paul founded the church at Corinth (2 Cor 1.19; see also Acts 18.1–7, esp. v. 5), the congregation wrote to him at least once (1 Cor 7.1), and Paul also wrote them a letter, now lost, which is mentioned in 1 Cor 5.9. Then Paul wrote 1 Corinthians while he was in Ephesus (1 Cor 16.8). Some time after that, Paul sent Timothy to Corinth as his personal emissary (1 Cor 4.17 [see alternative translation]; 16.10–11), but Timothy returned with news that a group of Jewish-Christian missionaries had arrived at Corinth and might be undermining Paul's teaching and his apostolic authority. Paul refers to these missionaries ironically as "super-apostles" (2 Cor 11.5; 12.11), "false apostles" (11.13) and even "Satan's ministers" (11.15). This challenge to his missionary activity prompted Paul to visit Corinth a second time. The result was unfortunate: Evidently a member of the congregation offended him grievously (2.5–6); he later called this the "painful visit" (2.1; 7.2). After his bitter departure, Paul wrote what he called the "letter of tears" (2.4; 7.8), a letter that is now lost. Either despite or because of its severity, this letter evidently succeeded in persuading the majority of the church to Paul's position, as Titus reported when he met Paul in Macedonia (7.6–7). Paul, much relieved at the resolution of the conflict, wrote a conciliatory letter that may include 1.1–2.13; 7.5–16, and probably other parts, now lost. In addition, Paul sent two letters on the collection for the poor in the Jerusalem church (chs 8–9). Paul's confidence in the resolution was premature, however, for he later had to write a bitter polemical letter directed against the "super-apostles" (chs 10–13).

Thus, 2 Corinthians as it now stands seems to be a composite of fragments from different letters, though their precise extent and relative chronology are open to question (see notes on 2.13; 6.14–7.1; 8.1–9.15; 10.1–18). This disjointed character makes reading the letter difficult. After a standard salutation (1.1–2), Paul moves to a characteristic blessing of God and a thanksgiving for consoling his afflictions (1.3–7) and delivering him (1.8–11). He then dwells on his relationship with the Corinthians (1.12–2.13), but after a conciliatory passage and before he finishes recounting his travel plans (2.5–13) he enters into an argumentative discourse (2.14–5.21) that ends in an anxious appeal for reconciliation (6.1–13; 7.2–4 [6.14–7.1 appears to be parenthetical]). Thereafter the travelogue resumes, as does the earlier conciliatory theme, and Paul concludes by expressing his complete confidence in the Corinthians (7.5–16). Two chapters (8 and 9) on the collection for the poor in the Jerusalem church (1 Cor 16.1–4; see also Gal 2.10) may be two separate letters, one to Corinth and one to Achaia (compare 8.1 to 9.2). Finally, a highly charged polemical letter (10.1–13.10) ends with a farewell and Paul's fullest benediction (13.11–13).

Certain motifs run through the letter. The paradoxical relationship between affliction and consolation, first raised in 1.3–11, is the backbone of the arguments in 4.7–10; 4.16–5.10; and 12.7–10.

The twin themes of boasting and confidence intimated in 1.12–14 stand in the background in 3.4–18; 8.1–7,24; 9.1–5; and all of chs 10–13.

1 Paul, an apostle of Christ Jesus by the
will of God, and Timothy our brother,
To the church of God that is in Corinth,
including all the saints throughout Achaia:
2 Grace to you and peace from God our
Father and the Lord Jesus Christ.

3 Blessed be the God and Father of our
Lord Jesus Christ, the Father of mercies
and the God of all consolation, 4 who con-
soles us in all our affliction, so that we may
be able to console those who are in any
affliction with the consolation with which
we ourselves are consoled by God. 5 For
just as the sufferings of Christ are abundant
for us, so also our consolation is abundant
through Christ. 6 If we are being afflicted, it
is for your consolation and salvation; if we
are being consoled, it is for your consola-
tion, which you experience when you pa-
tiently endure the same sufferings that we
are also suffering. 7 Our hope for you is un-
shaken; for we know that as you share in
our sufferings, so also you share in our con-
solation.

8 We do not want you to be unaware,
brothers and sisters,[a] of the affliction we
experienced in Asia; for we were so utterly,
unbearably crushed that we despaired of
life itself. 9 Indeed, we felt that we had re-
ceived the sentence of death so that we
would rely not on ourselves but on God
who raises the dead. 10 He who rescued us
from so deadly a peril will continue to res-
cue us; on him we have set our hope that he
will rescue us again, 11 as you also join in
helping us by your prayers, so that many
will give thanks on our[b] behalf for the

a Gk *brothers* *b* Other ancient authorities read *your*

1.1–2.13: Opening.

1.1–2: Salutation. A standard part of Paul's letters; see 1 Cor 1.1; Phil 1.1; Philem 1. **1:** An *apostle* was a special emissary, but Paul reminds the Corinthians that he is sent *by the will of God.* Cf. Rom 1.1; 1 Cor 1.1; Gal 1.1. For Paul's self-understanding of his call to be an apostle, see Gal 1.10–17 but also Rom 1.1–6; 1 Cor 9; 15.7–11. *Timothy,* along with Silvanus, was with Paul at the founding of the Corinthian church (v. 19; Acts 18.5) and acted as Paul's representative when troubles broke out (1 Cor 4.17; 16.10–11; Acts 19.22). Elsewhere Paul calls Timothy "my beloved child" (1 Cor 4.17), but here he calls him *brother,* a sign of respect. Everywhere else in 2 Cor, the plural "churches" is used; the singular here, *church of God,* is a collective designation of all the congregations in Corinth. *Saints* refers not to an elite group of believers but to Christians being set apart by God. *Achaia,* the Roman senatorial province of which *Corinth* was the capital. **2:** *Grace to you and peace from God . . . ,* a standard Pauline greeting found in all his letters except 1 Thess 1.1, where a short form is used.

1.3–7: Paul blesses God for rescuing him and consoling his afflictions. Not the standard thanksgiving that reinforces Paul's relationship with the recipients (e.g., Phil 1.3–11; 1 Thess 1.2–10), but a blessing in the Jewish liturgical tradition that emphasizes the attributes of God. Paul chooses the latter, partly because his relationship with the Corinthians is strained, and partly because he wants to introduce the themes of *affliction* and *consolation,* which are repeated at key points in the letter (see Introduction). **3–4:** The designation of God as *Father of mercies* is common in Jewish worship; see Rom 12.1; Phil 2.1. *So that we may be able to console . . . ,* Paul asserts that whatever he experienced was for the sake of the Corinthians. **5–7:** Paul invites the Corinthians to be partners in suffering by noting the believer's identification with *the sufferings of Christ* which *are abundant for us;* see 4.10–11; Phil 3.10–11.

1.8–11: God delivers Paul. In recounting how God has delivered him from near death, Paul stresses the Corinthians' participation in his ministry. **8:** *Asia,* a Roman senatorial province in modern-day western Turkey that included Ephesus. **9:** There is no consensus on what this terrible ordeal was; possibilities include the imprisonment mentioned in Phil 1.19–24 or the event behind the cryptic phrase, "I fought with wild animals at Ephesus," in 1 Cor 15.32.

blessing granted us through the prayers of
many.
12 Indeed, this is our boast, the testimo-
ny of our conscience: we have behaved in
the world with frankness[a] and godly sin-
cerity, not by earthly wisdom but by the
grace of God—and all the more toward
you. 13 For we write you nothing other than
what you can read and also understand; I
hope you will understand until the end—
14 as you have already understood us in
part—that on the day of the Lord Jesus we
are your boast even as you are our boast.
15 Since I was sure of this, I wanted to
come to you first, so that you might have a
double favor;[b] 16 I wanted to visit you on
my way to Macedonia, and to come back
to you from Macedonia and have you send
me on to Judea. 17 Was I vacillating when I
wanted to do this? Do I make my plans
according to ordinary human standards,[c]
ready to say "Yes, yes" and "No, no" at
the same time? 18 As surely as God is faith-
ful, our word to you has not been "Yes and
No." 19 For the Son of God, Jesus Christ,
whom we proclaimed among you, Silvanus
and Timothy and I, was not "Yes and No";
but in him it is always "Yes." 20 For in him
every one of God's promises is a "Yes." For
this reason it is through him that we say the
"Amen," to the glory of God. 21 But it is
God who establishes us with you in Christ
and has anointed us, 22 by putting his seal
on us and giving us his Spirit in our hearts
as a first installment.
23 But I call on God as witness against
me: it was to spare you that I did not come
again to Corinth. 24 I do not mean to imply
that we lord it over your faith; rather, we
are workers with you for your joy, because
2 you stand firm in the faith. 1 So I made
up my mind not to make you another

a Other ancient authorities read *holiness* *b* Other ancient authorities read *pleasure* *c* Gk *according to the flesh*

1.12–2.13: Paul stresses his bond with the Corinthians. Paul recounts his past dealings with the Corinthians in hopes of cementing his relationship with them. **12–14:** Paul claims that his conduct toward the Corinthians is a basis of solidarity. **12:** *Boast* or confidence is a prominent theme in the Pauline letters (e.g., 1 Thess 2.19) but especially in the Corinthian correspondence; 2 Cor 1.15 "sure"; 3.4 "confidence"; 3.12 "boldness"; 6.11 "frankly"; 8.22; 9.3; 10.2 "boldness"; also 1 Cor 9.15. It is here used as a synonym of *conscience,* the human capacity for self-judgment. **13:** *Until the end* can also be translated as "completely," in contrast to "in part" in the next verse. **14:** *On the day of the Lord Jesus,* the Second Coming; see 1 Cor 5.5; Phil 1.6,10; 2.16. It is on that day when Paul's sincerity and conscience will be proven blameless, and that is his basis for boasting of his work done among the Corinthians.

1.15–2.13: Paul remembers the Corinthians as he travels to Macedonia. Paul's reference to his thoughts while traveling normally highlights his relationship to the congregation in spite of his absence (e.g., 1 Thess 2.17–3.3). Here he also responds to misunderstandings caused by his canceled visit. **15:** *Double favor* possibly refers to the two visits Paul would have made to Corinth to and from Macedonia. **16:** *Send me on,* to provide everything necessary for the journey (Rom 15.24; 1 Cor 16.6,11; Titus 3.13; 3 Jn 6), including finance, escorts (Acts 20.38; 21.5), letters of recommendation (2 Cor 3.1). *Macedonia,* the Roman province, here refers to Thessalonica and Philippi. *Judea,* not just southern Palestine but especially Jerusalem (Rom 15.31; Gal 1.22; cf. 1 Cor 16.3). **17:** *Vacillating,* lit. "trifling." Paul defends himself and his coworkers against the charge that they changed their minds frivolously and claims that his actions cannot be evaluated according to human standards. **18–19:** *"Yes and No,"* a sign of equivocating; see Mt 5.37; Jas 5.12. **19:** *Silvanus,* or Silas, accompanied Paul in Acts 15–18 and is mentioned here as cofounder of the Corinthian church with *Timothy;* see also 1.1n. **20:** *Amen,* a Hebrew word meaning "certainly" or "let it be so," used in response to someone's statement and in liturgical settings; see Deut 27.14–26; 1 Chr 16.36; Neh 5.13; 8.6; 1 Cor 14.16. **22:** The reception of the *Spirit* as *first installment* (same word translated as "guarantee" in 5.5) is proof that God's promises will be fulfilled (v. 20). **23:** *I did not come again* refers to the canceled double visit of vv. 15–16. **2.1:** Paul evidently made an unplanned *painful visit* to Corinth, his second, perhaps referred to in 13.2, during which some member of the congregation grievously offended him (see 2.5–11; 7.12). A third visit is anticipated in 12.14,21; 13.1. For sequence painful visit. 2 For if I cause you pain, who is there to make me glad but the one whom I have pained? 3 And I wrote as I did, so that when I came, I might not suffer pain from those who should have made me rejoice; for I am confident about all of you, that my joy would be the joy of all of you. 4 For I wrote you out of much distress and anguish of heart and with many tears, not to cause you pain, but to let you know the abundant love that I have for you.

5 But if anyone has caused pain, he has caused it not to me, but to some extent—not to exaggerate it—to all of you. 6 This punishment by the majority is enough for such a person; 7 so now instead you should forgive and console him, so that he may not be overwhelmed by excessive sorrow. 8 So I urge you to reaffirm your love for him. 9 I wrote for this reason: to test you and to know whether you are obedient in everything. 10 Anyone whom you forgive, I also forgive. What I have forgiven, if I have forgiven anything, has been for your sake in the presence of Christ. 11 And we do this so that we may not be outwitted by Satan; for we are not ignorant of his designs.

12 When I came to Troas to proclaim the good news of Christ, a door was opened for me in the Lord; 13 but my mind could not rest because I did not find my brother Titus there. So I said farewell to them and went on to Macedonia.

14 But thanks be to God, who in Christ always leads us in triumphal procession, and through us spreads in every place the fragrance that comes from knowing him. 15 For we are the aroma of Christ to God among those who are being saved and among those who are perishing; 16 to the one a fragrance from death to death, to the other a fragrance from life to life. Who is sufficient for these things? 17 For we are not peddlers of God's word like so many;[a] but in Christ we speak as persons of sincerity, as persons sent from God and standing in his presence.

a Other ancient authorities read *like the others*

of events, see Introduction. **3–4:** *I wrote as I did. . . . I wrote you . . . with many tears* (also v. 9), the "letter of tears," written shortly after the "painful visit"; see 7.8,12. The combination of *tears* and *joy* here recalls the twin themes of affliction and consolation in 1.3–11. This letter is probably lost. Some have argued that chs 10–13 might be a part of this letter, but it seems unlikely. An older view that it might be 1 Cor, with the immoral act condemned in ch 5, does not have many supporters today. See Introduction for sequence of events. **5–11:** The "letter of tears" was evidently well received. Paul pleads that the offender be forgiven now that the whole congregation has meted out appropriate punishment (v. 6). **6:** *Such a person,* his or her identity has never been ascertained; see also 7.12. **11:** *Satan,* Heb "accuser"; see also 11.14; 12.7. Elsewhere in 2 Cor this evil figure is called "the god of this world" (4.4), "Beliar" (6.15), and "serpent" (11.3). **12:** *Troas,* Roman colony in northwest modern Turkey, a short trip by sea to Philippi; see Acts 16.8–11. **13:** *Titus,* a coworker like Timothy and Silvanus, was likely the carrier of the "letter of tears" mentioned in 2.3–4; 7.8. The narrative at this point drops Paul's anxious wait for Titus and resumes in 7.5; see Introduction.

2.14–7.4: Real character of Paul's ministry.

2.14–4.6: The ministry of glory. God is the real author of Paul's ministry of glory.

2.14–17: God equips competent ministers. 14: The image is of God the victor leading Paul as captive in a Roman procession. *Fragrance,* and "aroma" (v. 15), could allude to the execution of prisoners at end of the procession, thus combining Roman customs with sacrificial language from the Hebrew Bible (e.g., Lev 1.9). It could also allude to the presence of divine wisdom (Sir 24.15). **15–16:** *Saved . . . perishing* describes the differing effects Paul's preaching of the gospel has on his hearers. *Sufficient,* or competent. The rhetorical question suggests that only God can equip competent ministers; see 3.5–6. **17:** Paul disdainfully calls his opponents *peddlers of God's word,* implying that their motive is personal gain. Paul possibly alludes to his own refusal to accept support from the Corinthians; see 11.8–9n. *Sincerity* anticipates the charges of falsehood and cunning (see 4.2).

3 Are we beginning to commend our-
selves again? Surely we do not need, as
some do, letters of recommendation to you
or from you, do we? 2 You yourselves are
our letter, written on our[a] hearts, to be
known and read by all; 3 and you show that
you are a letter of Christ, prepared by us,
written not with ink but with the Spirit of
the living God, not on tablets of stone but
on tablets of human hearts.
4 Such is the confidence that we have
through Christ toward God. 5 Not that we
are competent of ourselves to claim any-
thing as coming from us; our competence is
from God, 6 who has made us competent to
be ministers of a new covenant, not of letter
but of spirit; for the letter kills, but the Spir-
it gives life.
7 Now if the ministry of death, chiseled
in letters on stone tablets,[b] came in glory
so that the people of Israel could not gaze
at Moses' face because of the glory of his
face, a glory now set aside, 8 how much
more will the ministry of the Spirit come in
glory? 9 For if there was glory in the minis-
try of condemnation, much more does the
ministry of justification abound in glory!
10 Indeed, what once had glory has lost its
glory because of the greater glory; 11 for if
what was set aside came through glory,
much more has the permanent come in
glory!
12 Since, then, we have such a hope, we
act with great boldness, 13 not like Moses,
who put a veil over his face to keep the
people of Israel from gazing at the end of
the glory that[c] was being set aside. 14 But
their minds were hardened. Indeed, to this
very day, when they hear the reading of the
old covenant, that same veil is still there,
since only in Christ is it set aside. 15 Indeed,
to this very day whenever Moses is read, a
veil lies over their minds; 16 but when one
turns to the Lord, the veil is removed.
17 Now the Lord is the Spirit, and where
the Spirit of the Lord is, there is freedom.
18 And all of us, with unveiled faces, seeing
the glory of the Lord as though reflected in
a mirror, are being transformed into the
same image from one degree of glory to
another; for this comes from the Lord, the
Spirit.

4 Therefore, since it is by God's mercy
that we are engaged in this ministry, we
do not lose heart. 2 We have renounced the

a Other ancient authorities read *your* *b* Gk *on stones* *c* Gk *of what*

3.1–4.6: Ministers of the new covenant of Spirit. 1–6: Initial consideration of Paul's relationship to the Corinthians. **1:** *Letters of recommendation,* conventional introductions for itinerant missionaries to the writer's friends and wider circles; see Acts 18.27. Romans 16 is one such letter of recommendation for Phoebe. Paul's lack of such letters was seen as a deficiency; see also 5.12. **2–3:** Instead of producing a recommendation, Paul reminds the Corinthians that he was the founder of the Corinthian church and calls the church *our letter . . . of Christ.* Mention of *Spirit* recalls the Corinthians' conversion experience; see Gal 3.2–3. *Tablets of stone . . . tablets of human hearts* contrasts the Ten Commandments (Ex 20.1–17; 24.12; 31.18; 34.1) with the new covenant of Jer 31.31–33. **4:** *Confidence,* see v. 12 and 1.12–14n. **5–6:** *Competence,* see 2.15–16n. **7–11:** The controlling imagery is Moses' changed countenance in Ex 34.29–35, which Paul interprets using a rabbinic method of argumentation, from the lesser to the greater. **7:** *Ministry of death,* existence under the law of Moses. **12:** *Boldness,* see v. 4 and 1.12–14n. **13:** Paul interprets the *veil* of Moses as covering up the transitory nature of the *glory that was being set aside.* **14–15:** The *veil* becomes a metaphor for unenlightenment. *Old covenant* refers not to the Hebrew Bible in general but to the Sinai covenant (Ex 24.7) or to the law (2 Chr 34.30), see also *Moses* (2 Chr 25.4; Mk 12.26; Acts 15.21). **16–17:** Paul's reinterpretation of Ex 34.34, resulting in *the Spirit* removing *the veil,* with contrast to the veiled "minds" in vv. 14–15. **18:** *Glory of the Lord* parallels *the Lord, the Spirit* (also vv. 16–17). *Transformed,* see Rom 12.2; *image,* see Rom 8.29; 1 Cor 15.49; Col 3.10. *From one degree of glory to another* reflects belief in the Greco-Roman world that an encounter with the divine transforms the beholder into its image.

4.1–6: Climax of Paul's self-defense. Paul returns to the question of competence first raised in 2.16. **2–3:** Answers to charges; see 2.17. *Cunning,* see 11.3; 12.16 "crafty." *Conscience,* see 1.12n. **4:** *This*

shameful things that one hides; we refuse to
practice cunning or to falsify God's word;
but by the open statement of the truth we
commend ourselves to the conscience of ev-
eryone in the sight of God. 3 And even if our
gospel is veiled, it is veiled to those who are
perishing. 4 In their case the god of this
world has blinded the minds of the unbe-
lievers, to keep them from seeing the light
of the gospel of the glory of Christ, who is
the image of God. 5 For we do not proclaim
ourselves; we proclaim Jesus Christ as Lord
and ourselves as your slaves for Jesus' sake.
6 For it is the God who said, "Let light shine
out of darkness," who has shone in our
hearts to give the light of the knowledge of
the glory of God in the face of Jesus Christ.

7 But we have this treasure in clay jars,
so that it may be made clear that this ex-
traordinary power belongs to God and
does not come from us. 8 We are afflicted in
every way, but not crushed; perplexed, but
not driven to despair; 9 persecuted, but not
forsaken; struck down, but not destroyed;
10 always carrying in the body the death of
Jesus, so that the life of Jesus may also be
made visible in our bodies. 11 For while we
live, we are always being given up to death
for Jesus' sake, so that the life of Jesus may
be made visible in our mortal flesh. 12 So
death is at work in us, but life in you.

13 But just as we have the same spirit of
faith that is in accordance with scripture—
"I believed, and so I spoke"—we also be-
lieve, and so we speak, 14 because we know
that the one who raised the Lord Jesus will
raise us also with Jesus, and will bring us
with you into his presence. 15 Yes, every-
thing is for your sake, so that grace, as it
extends to more and more people, may in-
crease thanksgiving, to the glory of God.

16 So we do not lose heart. Even though
our outer nature is wasting away, our inner
nature is being renewed day by day. 17 For
this slight momentary affliction is prepar-
ing us for an eternal weight of glory beyond
all measure, 18 because we look not at what
can be seen but at what cannot be seen; for
what can be seen is temporary, but what
cannot be seen is eternal.

5 For we know that if the earthly tent we
live in is destroyed, we have a building
from God, a house not made with hands,
eternal in the heavens. 2 For in this tent we
groan, longing to be clothed with our heav-
enly dwelling— 3 if indeed, when we have
taken it off[a] we will not be found naked.
4 For while we are still in this tent, we groan
under our burden, because we wish not to
be unclothed but to be further clothed, so
that what is mortal may be swallowed up
by life. 5 He who has prepared us for this

a Other ancient authorities read *put it on*

world, see 1 Cor 3.19; 5.10; 7.31 (twice), a synonym in Paul for "the present age" (Gal 1.4) and "the present time" (Rom 3.26; 8.18; 11.5). *God of this world,* see "rulers of this age" (1 Cor 2.6,8; Eph 2.2) and 2.11n. **6:** A paraphrase of Gen 1.3; Ps 112.4; Isa 9.2.

4.7–5.10: Ministry of hardship. Affliction and consolation, first raised in 1.3–11, elaborated: Weakness points to God's empowering presence. **7:** *Clay jars,* once broken, cannot be mended but must be thrown away. The contrast with *treasure* demonstrates God's power. **8–9:** Catalogue of hardships formulated as antithetical pairs to show the incomparable power of God's glory. See also 6.4–10; 11.23–27; 12.10; Rom 8.35,38–39; 1 Cor 4.11–13; Phil 4.12. The Stoics used catalogues of hardship to demonstrate their indifference to adversity, but for Paul adversity demonstrates the unworthiness of the vessels, and the overcoming of adversity documents the surpassing power of God. **10–11:** *Carrying . . . the death of Jesus,* the death of Jesus is replicated in Paul's bodily sufferings, with the result that *the life of Jesus may be made visible;* cf. Gal 2.20. **13:** Ps 116.10. **4.16–5.10:** Paul uses the dualistic language current in Hellenistic thought to express the tension between present afflictions and ongoing renewal. **16:** *Lose heart,* see 4.1. The *outer nature* that is *wasting away* is that part that undergoes sufferings and hardships (vv. 8–9) and carries the death of Jesus (vv. 10–11). The *inner nature* is that part that *is being renewed* daily; cf. Rom 12.2. **18:** *Temporary* and *eternal* represent not consecutive but overlapping aeons. **5.1:** Paul continues the temporary-permanent contrast with one between *earthly tent,* a reference to the body (see Wis 9.15), and *building from God,* which is *eternal in the heavens.* **5:** *Guarantee,* see 1.22n. **6–8:**

very thing is God, who has given us the
Spirit as a guarantee.
6 So we are always confident; even
though we know that while we are at home
in the body we are away from the Lord—
7 for we walk by faith, not by sight. 8 Yes,
we do have confidence, and we would rath-
er be away from the body and at home with
the Lord. 9 So whether we are at home or
away, we make it our aim to please him.
10 For all of us must appear before the judg-
ment seat of Christ, so that each may re-
ceive recompense for what has been done in
the body, whether good or evil.
11 Therefore, knowing the fear of the
Lord, we try to persuade others; but we
ourselves are well known to God, and I
hope that we are also well known to your
consciences. 12 We are not commending
ourselves to you again, but giving you an
opportunity to boast about us, so that you
may be able to answer those who boast in
outward appearance and not in the heart.
13 For if we are beside ourselves, it is for
God; if we are in our right mind, it is for
you. 14 For the love of Christ urges us on,
because we are convinced that one has died
for all; therefore all have died. 15 And he
died for all, so that those who live might
live no longer for themselves, but for him
who died and was raised for them.
16 From now on, therefore, we regard
no one from a human point of view;[a] even
though we once knew Christ from a human
point of view,[a] we know him no longer in
that way. 17 So if anyone is in Christ, there
is a new creation: everything old has passed
away; see, everything has become new!
18 All this is from God, who reconciled us
to himself through Christ, and has given us
the ministry of reconciliation; 19 that is, in
Christ God was reconciling the world to
himself,[b] not counting their trespasses
against them, and entrusting the message of
reconciliation to us. 20 So we are ambassa-
dors for Christ, since God is making his
appeal through us; we entreat you on be-
half of Christ, be reconciled to God. 21 For
our sake he made him to be sin who knew
no sin, so that in him we might become the
righteousness of God.
6 As we work together with him,[c] we
urge you also not to accept the grace of
God in vain. 2 For he says,

a Gk *according to the flesh* b Or *God was in Christ reconciling the world to himself* c Gk *As we work together*

While . . . in the body we are away from the Lord, see Phil 1.21,23; the body is a barrier to being with Christ more perfectly. **10:** See Rom 14.10.

5.11–6.10: Ministry of reconciliation. 11–13: Paul recalls his relationship to the Corinthians. **11:** *Consciences,* see 1.12n.; 4.2. **12:** *Commending,* see 3.1n. *Boast,* see 1.12n. *Those who boast in outward appearance* likely refers to Paul's opponents; see 11.5–6,12–15; 12.11. **13:** Paul's opponents may have derided Paul for lack of ecstatic experiences (12.1,12), to which Paul answers by distinguishing between being *beside ourselves* (having an ecstatic experience), and being *in our right mind.* The former has to do with God; the latter has to do with his ministry with the Corinthians. Cf. 1 Cor 14.2–5,18–19,27–28. **14–17:** New existence in Christ. **14–15:** *Love of Christ,* Christ's love for us. *Those who live . . . was raised,* Christ's death enlivens all who by right should be dead, so that they owe their lives to him. See Gal 2.19–20; also Rom 7.4; 14.7–9. **17:** Being *in Christ* is an indication that the *new creation,* the cosmic reversal of the primordial fall, is now in process; the *old* way of looking from a human point of view *has passed away* and no longer has any validity. For new creation, see Gal 6.15; but also Eph 2.15; 2 Pet 3.13; Rev 21.1; for background, see Isa 43.18–19; 65.17; 66.22. **18–19:** As a result of Christ's undoing the damage caused by the primordial rebellion, *trespasses* are canceled (see Rom 4.8) and human beings are *reconciled* to God; Rom 5.10–11; Col 1.20. **21:** *Made him to be sin,* a difficult phrase that may refer to Christ's identification with humanity. Believers can be so embraced by God's reconciliation that *we might become the righteousness of God;* see Rom 1.17; 3.5,21–22,25–26; 10.3 (twice); Phil 3.9; also Mt 6.33; Jas 1.20; 2 Pet 1.1.

6.1–10: Summary of defense. 2: Isa 49.8. **4–5:** Catalogue of hardships; see 4.8–9n. **6–7:** Catalogue of

"At an acceptable time I have listened
to you,
and on a day of salvation I have
helped you."
See, now is the acceptable time; see, now is
the day of salvation! 3 We are putting no
obstacle in anyone's way, so that no fault
may be found with our ministry, 4 but as
servants of God we have commended our-
selves in every way: through great endur-
ance, in afflictions, hardships, calamities,
5 beatings, imprisonments, riots, labors,
sleepless nights, hunger; 6 by purity, knowl-
edge, patience, kindness, holiness of spirit,
genuine love, 7 truthful speech, and the
power of God; with the weapons of righ-
teousness for the right hand and for the left;
8 in honor and dishonor, in ill repute and
good repute. We are treated as impostors,
and yet are true; 9 as unknown, and yet are
well known; as dying, and see—we are
alive; as punished, and yet not killed; 10 as
sorrowful, yet always rejoicing; as poor, yet
making many rich; as having nothing, and
yet possessing everything.
11 We have spoken frankly to you Co-
rinthians; our heart is wide open to you.
12 There is no restriction in our affections,
but only in yours. 13 In return—I speak as
to children—open wide your hearts also.

14 Do not be mismatched with unbeliev-
ers. For what partnership is there between
righteousness and lawlessness? Or what fel-
lowship is there between light and dark-
ness? 15 What agreement does Christ have
with Beliar? Or what does a believer share
with an unbeliever? 16 What agreement has
the temple of God with idols? For we[a] are
the temple of the living God; as God said,
"I will live in them and walk among
them,
and I will be their God,
and they shall be my people.
17 Therefore come out from them,
and be separate from them, says the
Lord,
and touch nothing unclean;
then I will welcome you,
18 and I will be your father,
and you shall be my sons and
daughters,
says the Lord Almighty."

7 Since we have these promises, beloved,
let us cleanse ourselves from every de-
filement of body and of spirit, making holi-
ness perfect in the fear of God.

2 Make room in your hearts[b] for us; we
have wronged no one, we have corrupted
no one, we have taken advantage of no one.
3 I do not say this to condemn you, for I
said before that you are in our hearts, to die

a Other ancient authorities read *you* *b* Gk lacks *in your hearts*

virtues; see Gal 5.22–23; Phil 4.8. **8–10:** These seven contrasting pairs, *impostors, and yet are true . . . having nothing, and yet possessing everything,* are not paradoxes to show the imperturbability of an ideal sage (see the Stoics), but antitheses answering charges against Paul. This is a summary of his self-defense that began in 2.14. From a human point of view (5.16), Paul and his coworkers might be accused of being *impostors, unknown,* etc., but in the context of the new creation (5.17), they are really *true, known,* etc.

6.11–7.4: Final appeal to the Corinthians. 11–13: *Frankly,* see 1.12n. **6.14–7.1:** An abrupt interruption of Paul's appeal in the present context, since 7.2–4 more naturally follows 6.11–13. This passage contains many words used nowhere else by Paul; the stark dualism is also uncharacteristic of him. **14:** *Mismatched,* lit. "misyoked," used only here in the New Testament; see Lev 19.19. *Partnership,* used only here in the New Testament, *fellowship,* and "share" (v. 15) are synonyms meaning "association" in general. *Righteousness and lawlessness,* see Rom 6.19, "iniquity." *Light and darkness* (see Rom 2.19; 13.12; 1 Cor 4.5; 1 Thess 5.4–5) also undergirds the imagery of 4.3–6, where the same contrast between "believers" and *unbelievers* (v. 15) is also found. **15:** *Beliar,* another name for Satan; see 2.11n. **16a:** *Temple of the living God,* see 1 Cor 3.16. **16b–18:** A chain of citations from Lev 26.12; Ezek 37.27; Isa 52.11; 2 Sam 7.14; Isa 43.6 to show separation from defilement. **7.1:** *Defilement,* used only here in the New Testament. *Body* and *spirit* are not set in opposition here; contrast with Gal 5.16–26. *Fear of God,* see 5.11. **7.2–4:** Resumption of appeal in 6.11–13. **3:** *Die . . . live,* Paul reverses the traditional declaration of friendship,

together and to live together. 4 I often boast
about you; I have great pride in you; I am
filled with consolation; I am overjoyed in
all our affliction.
5 For even when we came into Macedo-
nia, our bodies had no rest, but we were
afflicted in every way—disputes without
and fears within. 6 But God, who consoles
the downcast, consoled us by the arrival of
Titus, 7 and not only by his coming, but
also by the consolation with which he was
consoled about you, as he told us of your
longing, your mourning, your zeal for me,
so that I rejoiced still more. 8 For even if I
made you sorry with my letter, I do not
regret it (though I did regret it, for I see that
I grieved you with that letter, though only
briefly). 9 Now I rejoice, not because you
were grieved, but because your grief led to
repentance; for you felt a godly grief, so
that you were not harmed in any way by us.
10 For godly grief produces a repentance
that leads to salvation and brings no regret,
but worldly grief produces death. 11 For see
what earnestness this godly grief has pro-
duced in you, what eagerness to clear your-
selves, what indignation, what alarm, what
longing, what zeal, what punishment! At
every point you have proved yourselves
guiltless in the matter. 12 So although I
wrote to you, it was not on account of the
one who did the wrong, nor on account of
the one who was wronged, but in order
that your zeal for us might be made known
to you before God. 13 In this we find com-
fort.
In addition to our own consolation, we
rejoiced still more at the joy of Titus, be-
cause his mind has been set at rest by all of
you. 14 For if I have been somewhat boast-
ful about you to him, I was not disgraced;
but just as everything we said to you was
true, so our boasting to Titus has proved
true as well. 15 And his heart goes out all the
more to you, as he remembers the obedi-
ence of all of you, and how you welcomed
him with fear and trembling. 16 I rejoice,
because I have complete confidence in you.

8 We want you to know, brothers and
sisters,[a] about the grace of God that
has been granted to the churches of Mace-
donia; 2 for during a severe ordeal of afflic-
tion, their abundant joy and their extreme
poverty have overflowed in a wealth of
generosity on their part. 3 For, as I can testi-

a Gk *brothers*

"live . . . die," to emphasize his bond with the Corinthians through identification with Christ's death and life. **4:** *Boast,* see 1.12–14n. *Consolation . . . affliction,* see 1.3–7n. All three themes are introduced in 1.3–14.

7.5–16: Resumption of travelogue (2.12–13). **5:** *Afflicted,* "consoles" (vv. 6,7,13), "boasting" (v. 14 twice), "confidence" (v. 16), introduced in 1.3–14, are recapitulated throughout this passage; see notes there, and also 7.4. **6–8:** *Titus* (see 2.13n.) brought news that Paul's *letter* (see 2.3–4n.) had been received favorably; see 2.5–11. **12:** *The one who did the wrong,* see 2.6n. *The one who was wronged,* Paul himself. **13–14:** *Titus,* see 2.13n. **16:** *Confidence* concludes the narrative of vv. 5–16 and anticipates the appeal for the collection in chs 8–9.

8.1–9.15: The collection for the Jerusalem church was meant not only to bring relief to its economic plight but also to show unity between it and the well-to-do, urban, largely Gentile churches in the Diaspora; see Gal 2.10; 1 Cor 16.1–4; Rom 15.25–27. Some have taken chs 8 and 9 as two separate letters to two different regions in Achaia; see 9.2n.

8.1–24: Letter of appeal to the Corinthians for the collection. 1–7: The Macedonian churches as an example of generosity. **1:** *Grace* (Gk "charis"), used ten times in chs 8–9 to describe the collection, translated in 8.4 as "privilege"; in 8.6,7,19 as "generous undertaking"; in 8.9 as "generous act"; in 8.16 as "thanks"; in 9.8 as "blessing"; in 9.15 as "thanks." Other words used in this connection: "bountiful" (Gk "eulogia"): 9.5 "bountiful gift" and "voluntary gift"; 9.6 twice; "ministry" (Gk "leitourgia"): 9.12; "sharing" (Gk "koinonia"): 8.4; 9.13. This attests to the rich theological significance Paul attaches to the collection. *Macedonia,* see 1.16n. Paul principally has the Philippian and Thessalonian churches in mind; but see 9.2. **2:** *Severe ordeal,* possibly the same event as in Phil 1.29–30. **4:** *Sharing* (Gk "koinonia"), used

fy, they voluntarily gave according to their
means, and even beyond their means, 4 beg-
ging us earnestly for the privilege[a] of shar-
ing in this ministry to the saints— 5 and
this, not merely as we expected; they gave
themselves first to the Lord and, by the will
of God, to us, 6 so that we might urge Titus
that, as he had already made a beginning,
so he should also complete this generous
undertaking[b] among you. 7 Now as you
excel in everything—in faith, in speech, in
knowledge, in utmost eagerness, and in our
love for you[c]—so we want you to excel
also in this generous undertaking.[b]

8 I do not say this as a command, but I
am testing the genuineness of your love
against the earnestness of others. 9 For you
know the generous act[d] of our Lord Jesus
Christ, that though he was rich, yet for
your sakes he became poor, so that by his
poverty you might become rich. 10 And in
this matter I am giving my advice: it is ap-
propriate for you who began last year not
only to do something but even to desire to
do something— 11 now finish doing it, so
that your eagerness may be matched by
completing it according to your means.
12 For if the eagerness is there, the gift is
acceptable according to what one has—not
according to what one does not have. 13 I
do not mean that there should be relief for
others and pressure on you, but it is a ques-
tion of a fair balance between 14 your
present abundance and their need, so that
their abundance may be for your need, in
order that there may be a fair balance. 15 As
it is written,

"The one who had much did not have
too much,
and the one who had little did not
have too little."

16 But thanks be to God who put in the
heart of Titus the same eagerness for you
that I myself have. 17 For he not only ac-
cepted our appeal, but since he is more ea-
ger than ever, he is going to you of his own
accord. 18 With him we are sending the
brother who is famous among all the
churches for his proclaiming the good
news;[e] 19 and not only that, but he has also
been appointed by the churches to travel
with us while we are administering this
generous undertaking[b] for the glory of the
Lord himself[f] and to show our goodwill.
20 We intend that no one should blame us
about this generous gift that we are admin-
istering, 21 for we intend to do what is right
not only in the Lord's sight but also in the
sight of others. 22 And with them we are
sending our brother whom we have often
tested and found eager in many matters,
but who is now more eager than ever be-
cause of his great confidence in you. 23 As
for Titus, he is my partner and co-worker
in your service; as for our brothers, they are
messengers[g] of the churches, the glory of
Christ. 24 Therefore openly before the
churches, show them the proof of your love
and of our reason for boasting about you.

9 Now it is not necessary for me to write
you about the ministry to the saints,
2 for I know your eagerness, which is the
subject of my boasting about you to the
people of Macedonia, saying that Achaia

a Gk *grace* *b* Gk *this grace* *c* Other ancient authorities read *your love for us* *d* Gk *the grace* *e* Or *the gospel* *f* Other ancient authorities lack *himself* *g* Gk *apostles*

here to describe the collection (as also in 9.13 and Rom 15.26), is a rich Pauline word referring also to participation in the Eucharist (1 Cor 10.16) and in Christ's suffering (Phil 3.10); see 8.1n. *Saints,* here and in 9.1,12, refers to the Jerusalem believers. **6:** *Titus,* see 2.13n.; 8.16–24. **8–15:** There should be a *fair balance* between those who have more and those who have less. **9:** *Though he was rich, . . . he became poor,* see Phil 2.6–8. **15:** *"The one . . . too little,"* Ex 16.18. **16–24:** The sending of Titus and two *brothers* (vv. 18,22–23) who remain nameless.

9.1–15: A second letter of appeal for the collection. 1: Ch 9 starts the appeal afresh as if ch 8 had not preceded it. **2:** *Macedonia,* in contrast to 8.1, now has to listen to Paul's boasting of the achievements of the Achaian churches; see also v. 4. *Achaia has been ready since last year,* in stark contrast to the unfinished state of the Corinthian collection (8.10–11). All this lends support to the view that ch 9 preserves a separate letter intended for another region in Achaia (see Introduction). **3:** *Brothers,* also v. 5,

has been ready since last year; and your
zeal has stirred up most of them. 3 But I
am sending the brothers in order that our
boasting about you may not prove to have
been empty in this case, so that you may be
ready, as I said you would be; 4 otherwise,
if some Macedonians come with me and
find that you are not ready, we would be
humiliated—to say nothing of you—in this
undertaking.[a] 5 So I thought it necessary to
urge the brothers to go on ahead to you,
and arrange in advance for this bountiful
gift that you have promised, so that it may
be ready as a voluntary gift and not as an
extortion.

6 The point is this: the one who sows
sparingly will also reap sparingly, and the
one who sows bountifully will also reap
bountifully. 7 Each of you must give as you
have made up your mind, not reluctantly or
under compulsion, for God loves a cheerful
giver. 8 And God is able to provide you with
every blessing in abundance, so that by al-
ways having enough of everything, you
may share abundantly in every good work.
9 As it is written,

"He scatters abroad, he gives to
the poor;
his righteousness[b] endures
forever."

10 He who supplies seed to the sower and
bread for food will supply and multiply
your seed for sowing and increase the har-
vest of your righteousness.[b] 11 You will be
enriched in every way for your great gener-
osity, which will produce thanksgiving to
God through us; 12 for the rendering of this
ministry not only supplies the needs of the
saints but also overflows with many
thanksgivings to God. 13 Through the test-
ing of this ministry you glorify God by your
obedience to the confession of the gospel of
Christ and by the generosity of your shar-
ing with them and with all others, 14 while
they long for you and pray for you because
of the surpassing grace of God that he has
given you. 15 Thanks be to God for his inde-
scribable gift!

10 I myself, Paul, appeal to you by the
meekness and gentleness of Christ—
I who am humble when face to face with
you, but bold toward you when I am
away!— 2 I ask that when I am present I
need not show boldness by daring to op-
pose those who think we are acting accord-
ing to human standards.[c] 3 Indeed, we live

a Other ancient authorities add *of boasting*
b Or *benevolence* c Gk *according to the flesh*

are possibly the same as those mentioned in 8.18,22–23, but there is no way of ascertaining their identities. **5:** *Bountiful gift* and *voluntary gift* both translate the Gk "eulogia"; see 8.1n. **7:** *God loves a cheerful giver,* Prov 22.8. **8:** Abundance carries with it the responsibility of sharing. *Enough,* see 1 Tim 6.6; Phil 4.11, where it is translated "content." The word connotes the Hellenistic philosophical ideal of self-sufficiency transcending all shortcomings and hardships. In contrast, Paul states that God is the basis for such sufficiency. See 12.9n. **9:** *"He scatters . . . forever,"* Ps 112.9. **10:** *Seed, food,* Isa 55.10. *Harvest of your righteousness,* Hos 10.12. **11–12:** One possible motive for Paul's working tirelessly on the collection is the apocalyptic vision of Gentiles pouring into Jerusalem, rendering overflowing *thanksgiving to God.*

10.1–13.13: Defense of apostolic authority.

10.1–18: Paul attacks his opponents. The ironic and polemical tone of chs 10–13 contrasts sharply with that of the preceding chapters. Paul no longer refers to his opponents indirectly (see 2.17n.; 5.12n.), but pointedly. For these reasons, many take chs 10–13 to be a fragment of another letter (see Introduction). **1–6:** His opponents criticize Paul for his obvious lack of power, but Paul insists on demonstrating power through weakness; see 4.7–12n.; 11.30 (summarizing 11.21b–29); 12.9–10 (summarizing 12.1–8); 1 Cor 1.17–25. **1:** *Meekness and gentleness of Christ,* the self-emptying state of Christ as depicted in 8.9; Phil 2.6–8. *I who am . . . when I am away,* alludes to the charge against him; see also v. 10. *Humble,* lit. "base" or "humiliated," see 11.7n. **2:** *Those who think . . . ,* the false apostles whom Paul addresses throughout the letter only in the third person; see 10.10–11,12; 11.5,12–15,22–23,26; 12.11. Paul appeals to the Corinthians directly and makes them choose between him and his opponents. **3–4:** *Not*

as human beings,[a] but we do not wage war
according to human standards;[b] 4 for the
weapons of our warfare are not merely hu-
man,[c] but they have divine power to de-
stroy strongholds. We destroy arguments
5 and every proud obstacle raised up against
the knowledge of God, and we take every
thought captive to obey Christ. 6 We are
ready to punish every disobedience when
your obedience is complete.

7 Look at what is before your eyes. If
you are confident that you belong to
Christ, remind yourself of this, that just as
you belong to Christ, so also do we. 8 Now,
even if I boast a little too much of our au-
thority, which the Lord gave for building
you up and not for tearing you down, I will
not be ashamed of it. 9 I do not want to
seem as though I am trying to frighten you
with my letters. 10 For they say, "His letters
are weighty and strong, but his bodily pres-
ence is weak, and his speech contemptible."
11 Let such people understand that what we
say by letter when absent, we will also do
when present.

12 We do not dare to classify or com-
pare ourselves with some of those who
commend themselves. But when they mea-
sure themselves by one another, and com-
pare themselves with one another, they do
not show good sense. 13 We, however, will
not boast beyond limits, but will keep with-
in the field that God has assigned to us, to
reach out even as far as you. 14 For we
were not overstepping our limits when we
reached you; we were the first to come all
the way to you with the good news[d] of
Christ. 15 We do not boast beyond limits,
that is, in the labors of others; but our hope
is that, as your faith increases, our sphere
of action among you may be greatly en-
larged, 16 so that we may proclaim the good
news[d] in lands beyond you, without boast-
ing of work already done in someone else's
sphere of action. 17 "Let the one who
boasts, boast in the Lord." 18 For it is not
those who commend themselves that are
approved, but those whom the Lord com-
mends.

11 I wish you would bear with me in a
little foolishness. Do bear with me!

a Gk *in the flesh* *b* Gk *according to the flesh*
c Gk *fleshly* *d* Or *the gospel*

merely human, but . . . divine power, Paul admits that he and those like him live as *human beings,* but his *weapons* have superhuman power. *We destroy arguments,* the opponents are characterized as debaters; see also 1 Cor 1.19–20. *Wage war, destroy,* and "take . . . captive" (v. 5), warfare imagery applied to the religious debate. **6:** Paul hopes that the Corinthians' *obedience* may be *complete.* Paul's threat of "punishment" here is in marked contrast to his commendation of the Corinthians in 7.15 for obedience at the receipt of that letter. This lends support to the view that chs 10–13 belong to a different letter. **7–11:** Paul answers specific charges. **7:** *Just as you belong to Christ, so also do we,* answers the opponents' boasting that they "belong to Christ." **8:** *Boast,* Paul normally boasts of the Corinthians; see 1.12n. Here he boasts of himself, but only by claiming authority as their founder. The proper content of one's boasting is a bone of contention in chs 10–13. **9–11:** *Letters* answers direct charges by the opponents (v. 10) that his personal appearances and speech, unlike his *weighty* letter, are unimpressive. *"His speech contemptible,"* see 11.6. **12–18:** The proper way to boast is within one's territory. **12:** *Classify or compare,* standard rhetorical device of calling attention to one's praiseworthy acts in comparison with persons of superiority. Paul denounces the practice here but parodies it later in his fool's speech; see 11.21b–12.10. **13:** The propriety of staying within one's own assigned territory (see Rom 15.20–21) and the carefully couched language in Rom 1.12–13. **14–15:** Paul reminds the Corinthians that they belong to his missionary territory. **16:** *In lands beyond you,* indication that Paul had hoped to use Corinth as a base for further missionary work; cf. Rom 15.23–24,28. **17:** Jer 9.23–24, also cited in 1 Cor 1.31.

11.1–12.10: A fool's speech. Paul parodies his opponents' penchant for comparison right after criticizing them for doing the same (10.12).

11.1–15: Appeal to the Corinthians as a fool. 1: *Foolishness* (Gk "aphrosyne") is the opposite of "moderation" or "sober-mindedness" (Gk "sophrosyne"); see "madman" (Gk "paraphronon"), 11.23. In contrast to "folly" (Gk "moria") or "foolishness" (Gk "moron") whose opposite is "wisdom" (Gk

2 I feel a divine jealousy for you, for I promised you in marriage to one husband, to present you as a chaste virgin to Christ. 3 But I am afraid that as the serpent deceived Eve by its cunning, your thoughts will be led astray from a sincere and pure[a] devotion to Christ. 4 For if someone comes and proclaims another Jesus than the one we proclaimed, or if you receive a different spirit from the one you received, or a different gospel from the one you accepted, you submit to it readily enough. 5 I think that I am not in the least inferior to these super-apostles. 6 I may be untrained in speech, but not in knowledge; certainly in every way and in all things we have made this evident to you.

7 Did I commit a sin by humbling myself so that you might be exalted, because I proclaimed God's good news[b] to you free of charge? 8 I robbed other churches by accepting support from them in order to serve you. 9 And when I was with you and was in need, I did not burden anyone, for my needs were supplied by the friends[c] who came from Macedonia. So I refrained and will continue to refrain from burdening you in any way. 10 As the truth of Christ is in me, this boast of mine will not be silenced in the regions of Achaia. 11 And why? Because I do not love you? God knows I do!

12 And what I do I will also continue to do, in order to deny an opportunity to those who want an opportunity to be recognized as our equals in what they boast about. 13 For such boasters are false apostles, deceitful workers, disguising themselves as apostles of Christ. 14 And no wonder! Even Satan disguises himself as an angel of light. 15 So it is not strange if his ministers also disguise themselves as ministers of righteousness. Their end will match their deeds.

16 I repeat, let no one think that I am a fool; but if you do, then accept me as a fool, so that I too may boast a little. 17 What I am saying in regard to this boastful confidence, I am saying not with the Lord's authority, but as a fool; 18 since many boast according to human standards,[d] I will also boast. 19 For you gladly put up with fools, being wise yourselves! 20 For you put up with it when someone makes slaves of you, or preys upon you, or takes advantage of you, or puts on airs, or gives you a slap in the face. 21 To my shame, I must say, we were too weak for that!

But whatever anyone dares to boast of—I am speaking as a fool—I also dare to boast of that. 22 Are they Hebrews? So am

a Other ancient authorities lack *and pure* *b* Gk *the gospel of God* *c* Gk *brothers* *d* Gk *according to the flesh*

"sophia"); see 1 Cor 1–3. **2:** *I promised you in marriage,* Paul presents himself as father of the bride, that is, he is the founder of the church; see 1.19. **3:** *Serpent,* Satan; see 2.11; 11.14; 1 Cor 7.5. *Deceived Eve,* Gen 3.13. In connection with "marriage" and "virginity" (v. 2), Paul is probably thinking of the Jewish tradition that Satan sexually seduced Eve (see *2 Enoch* 31.6). **4–5:** *Another Jesus, different spirit, different gospel,* reminiscent of language in Gal 1.6–9. This would support the view that the *super-apostles* were Jewish-Christian missionaries; see also 12.11. **6:** *Untrained in speech,* see 10.10. **7:** *Humbling myself,* lit. "debasing myself"; see also 12.21; Phil 4.12. The adjective is used in 10.1. Christ is said to be "debased" in Phil 2.8. Greco-Roman philosophers saw craftsmen as debased; Paul's use of the word may refer to his continual activity as a craftsman (see 1 Cor 4.12; 1 Thess 2.9) to support himself. **9:** *I did not burden anyone,* see 12.13; 1 Cor 9 for Paul's refusal to accept support from the Corinthians; see 1 Thess 2.9; Phil 4.16,18, for Macedonian support. In the Roman world, accepting support was to place the recipient (client) under the immediate obligation of the benefactor (patron). By not accepting Corinthian support, Paul is refusing the Corinthians the status and authority of patronage; by accepting Macedonian support, Paul could be seen as slighting the Corinthian congregation. **12–15:** Characterization of Paul's opponents. *Satan,* see 2.11n.

11.16–12.10: Paul compares himself to the false apostles. 16–33: Paul lists his hardships as validation of his apostolic authenticity. **16:** *Fool,* see 11.1n. **17–18:** *Boast according to human standards,* a different type of boasting from that of 1.12–14 and much closer to the boasting of 10.8. **22:** *Hebrews . . . Israelites*

I. Are they Israelites? So am I. Are they
descendants of Abraham? So am I. 23 Are
they ministers of Christ? I am talking like a
madman—I am a better one: with far great-
er labors, far more imprisonments, with
countless floggings, and often near death.
24 Five times I have received from the Jews
the forty lashes minus one. 25 Three times I
was beaten with rods. Once I received a
stoning. Three times I was shipwrecked; for
a night and a day I was adrift at sea; 26 on
frequent journeys, in danger from rivers,
danger from bandits, danger from my own
people, danger from Gentiles, danger in the
city, danger in the wilderness, danger at
sea, danger from false brothers and sis-
ters;[a] 27 in toil and hardship, through
many a sleepless night, hungry and thirsty,
often without food, cold and naked.
28 And, besides other things, I am under
daily pressure because of my anxiety for all
the churches. 29 Who is weak, and I am not
weak? Who is made to stumble, and I am
not indignant?

30 If I must boast, I will boast of the
things that show my weakness. 31 The God
and Father of the Lord Jesus (blessed be he
forever!) knows that I do not lie. 32 In Da-
mascus, the governor[b] under King Aretas
guarded the city of Damascus in order to[c]
seize me, 33 but I was let down in a basket
through a window in the wall,[d] and es-
caped from his hands.

12 It is necessary to boast; nothing is to
be gained by it, but I will go on to
visions and revelations of the Lord. 2 I
know a person in Christ who fourteen
years ago was caught up to the third heav-
en—whether in the body or out of the body
I do not know; God knows. 3 And I know
that such a person—whether in the body
or out of the body I do not know; God
knows— 4 was caught up into Paradise and
heard things that are not to be told, that no
mortal is permitted to repeat. 5 On behalf of
such a one I will boast, but on my own
behalf I will not boast, except of my weak-
nesses. 6 But if I wish to boast, I will not be
a fool, for I will be speaking the truth. But
I refrain from it, so that no one may think
better of me than what is seen in me or
heard from me, 7 even considering the ex-
ceptional character of the revelations.
Therefore, to keep[e] me from being too
elated, a thorn was given me in the flesh, a
messenger of Satan to torment me, to keep
me from being too elated.[f] 8 Three times I
appealed to the Lord about this, that it
would leave me, 9 but he said to me, "My
grace is sufficient for you, for power[g] is

a Gk *brothers* *b* Gk *ethnarch* *c* Other ancient authorities read *and wanted to* *d* Gk *through the wall* *e* Other ancient authorities read *To keep* *f* Other ancient authorities lack *to keep me from being too elated* *g* Other ancient authorities read *my power*

. . . *descendants of Abraham,* support the view that they were Jewish-Christian missionaries; see 11.4–5n. Paul is proud of his Jewish heritage, ready to declare it unflinchingly whenever the situation calls for it; see Rom 9.4; 11.1; Gal 1.13; Phil 3.5. **23a**: *Madman,* see 11.1n. **23b–27**: Catalogue of hardships used ironically to show the extreme afflictions and weakness of Paul, see notes on 1.3–7; 4.8–9; 10.1. Little is known about these hardships. **24**: *Forty lashes minus one,* see Deut 25.3. **32–33**: See Acts 9.23–25. *Damascus,* site of Paul's first contact with Christianity after his conversion. *Aretas* IV ruled the Nabateans from 9 BCE until his death ca. 41 CE. The Nabateans took control of Damascus in 37 CE, soon after which Paul escaped from the city *in a basket.*

12.1–10: Paul relates a mystical experience, since the false apostles have claimed such experiences as validation of their spiritual prowess; see 5.13n. **1**: *Visions and revelations,* extrasensory events; see v. 7; 1 Cor 9.1; 15.5–8; Gal 1.12; 2.1–2. **2–3**: *I know a person* (also v. 5), an oblique reference to himself; see vv. 7–9. *Third heaven,* i.e., *Paradise* (v. 4), where according to mystical Judaism one is granted a vision of the blessed. Some traditions posit seven levels of heavens. *In the body or out of the body,* an ecstatic experience. Nothing in the known life of Paul can be associated with this event. **4**: *Not to be told,* esoteric knowledge not to be divulged to the uninitiated. **5**: Cf. 5.13n. **7**: Nature of the *thorn* is unknown. **9**: *Sufficient* (Gk "arkein"), a different word from that of 2.6,16; 3.5–6 and a cognate of "enough" of 9.8 (see note there). Unlike the Hellenistic ideal of sufficiency that transcends hardships regardless of one's

made perfect in weakness." So, I will boast
all the more gladly of my weaknesses, so
that the power of Christ may dwell in me.
10 Therefore I am content with weaknesses,
insults, hardships, persecutions, and calam-
ities for the sake of Christ; for whenever I
am weak, then I am strong.
11 I have been a fool! You forced me to
it. Indeed you should have been the ones
commending me, for I am not at all inferior
to these super-apostles, even though I am
nothing. 12 The signs of a true apostle were
performed among you with utmost pa-
tience, signs and wonders and mighty
works. 13 How have you been worse off
than the other churches, except that I my-
self did not burden you? Forgive me this
wrong!
14 Here I am, ready to come to you this
third time. And I will not be a burden, be-
cause I do not want what is yours but you;
for children ought not to lay up for their
parents, but parents for their children. 15 I
will most gladly spend and be spent for
you. If I love you more, am I to be loved
less? 16 Let it be assumed that I did not bur-
den you. Nevertheless (you say) since I was
crafty, I took you in by deceit. 17 Did I take
advantage of you through any of those
whom I sent to you? 18 I urged Titus to go,
and sent the brother with him. Titus did
not take advantage of you, did he? Did we
not conduct ourselves with the same spirit?
Did we not take the same steps?
19 Have you been thinking all along
that we have been defending ourselves be-
fore you? We are speaking in Christ before
God. Everything we do, beloved, is for the
sake of building you up. 20 For I fear that
when I come, I may find you not as I wish,
and that you may find me not as you wish;
I fear that there may perhaps be quarreling,
jealousy, anger, selfishness, slander, gossip,
conceit, and disorder. 21 I fear that when I
come again, my God may humble me be-
fore you, and that I may have to mourn
over many who previously sinned and have
not repented of the impurity, sexual immo-
rality, and licentiousness that they have
practiced.
13 This is the third time I am coming to
you. "Any charge must be sustained
by the evidence of two or three witnesses."
2 I warned those who sinned previously and
all the others, and I warn them now while
absent, as I did when present on my second
visit, that if I come again, I will not be le-
nient— 3 since you desire proof that Christ
is speaking in me. He is not weak in dealing
with you, but is powerful in you. 4 For he
was crucified in weakness, but lives by the
power of God. For we are weak in him,[a]

[a] Other ancient authorities read *with him*

circumstance (see 9.8), Paul accepts these hardships as real, but they reveal the power of God; see 10.1n. **10:** Recapitulation of hardships but now stated in stark contrast to the exuberant experience of vv. 1–7a.

12.11–13: Conclusion of the fool's speech. 11: *Super-apostles,* see notes on 10.2; 11.5. *Commending,* see 3.1n. **12:** Paul is not above telling the Corinthians that he too has performed miracles. **13:** See 11.8–9n.

12.14–13.10: Paul prepares for a third visit. 14–18: Paul answers charges that he has been enriching himself through the collection (chs 8–9). **14:** *Third* visit (also v. 21; 13.1), see 2.1n. for the "painful visit," Paul's second to Corinth. *I will not be a burden,* see 11.9n. *Parents,* for Paul as father to his converts, see 11.2. **16:** *(You say) . . . I took you in by deceit,* some Corinthians evidently accused Paul of skimming the collection funds. **18:** *Titus* was sent to oversee the collection in 8.6,16,23; see also 2.13n. It is uncertain whether *the brother* is to be identified with one of the "brothers" in 8.18,22–23; 9.5. Paul mentions these people probably as witnesses; see 13.1. **19–21:** Paul warns the Corinthians to repent before his third visit. **19:** *Building you up,* see 10.8; 13.10. **20–21:** Catalogue of vices, see Rom 1.29–31; 13.13; 1 Cor 5.10–11; 6.9–10; Gal 5.19–21. **21:** Ironic use of *humble:* Paul fears God might humiliate him before the Corinthians, only because he might *mourn* for their unrepented sins. See 11.7n. **13.1–10:** Previously mentioned themes are collected to issue a severe warning of harsh discipline. **1:** *Third* visit, see 12.14n. *"Any . . . witnesses,"* Deut 19.15. **3–4:** *Christ . . . is not weak. . . but powerful,* the weakness-powerful paradox summarized. See 10.1n. **10:** Strong warning while *away,* so that Paul will not have to

but in dealing with you we will live with
him by the power of God.
5 Examine yourselves to see whether
you are living in the faith. Test yourselves.
Do you not realize that Jesus Christ is in
you?—unless, indeed, you fail to meet the
test! 6 I hope you will find out that we have
not failed. 7 But we pray to God that you
may not do anything wrong—not that we
may appear to have met the test, but that
you may do what is right, though we may
seem to have failed. 8 For we cannot do
anything against the truth, but only for the
truth. 9 For we rejoice when we are weak
and you are strong. This is what we pray
for, that you may become perfect. 10 So I
write these things while I am away from
you, so that when I come, I may not have to
be severe in using the authority that the
Lord has given me for building up and not
for tearing down.
11 Finally, brothers and sisters,[a] fare-
well.[b] Put things in order, listen to my
appeal,[c] agree with one another, live in
peace; and the God of love and peace will
be with you. 12 Greet one another with a
holy kiss. All the saints greet you.
13 The grace of the Lord Jesus Christ,
the love of God, and the communion of[d]
the Holy Spirit be with all of you.

a Gk *brothers* *b* Or *rejoice* *c* Or *encourage one another* *d* Or *and the sharing in*

resort to *severe* discipline, is precisely what the opponents accused Paul of doing (10.10–11). Paul reminds the Corinthians that this is so for the purpose of *building up,* not *tearing down;* see 10.8; 12.19.

13.11–13: Final benediction. 12: *Holy kiss,* see Rom 16.16; 1 Cor 16.20; 1 Thess 5.26. **13:** A full triadic benediction found nowhere else in the Pauline letters.

The Letter of Paul to the GALATIANS

By the middle of the first century CE, although the early Christian movement was still connected to Judaism, an increasing number of its members were Gentiles. The tireless missionary activity of Paul, who saw himself as the apostle to the Gentiles (1.16), had fostered this development. The relationship between these new, non-Jewish converts and Jewish Christians, and between the emerging Christian movement and Judaism, became an issue of burning importance. One crucial issue concerned the status of the law of Moses. Should Gentile Christians convert to Judaism in the process of becoming Christians? Were they required to observe the Jewish law, even in part? The Letter to the Galatians gives Paul's view of this controversy and states a position on the Jewish law that will have far-reaching consequences.

Paul does not, however, discuss the issue in the abstract. Instead, facing a concrete situation in a particular place, he argues passionately that his view is crucial both to the survival of his mission in Galatia and, more important, to that of Christianity generally. In his confrontation with Peter at Antioch, he had held that the demands of the Jewish law were an unnecessary burden for Gentiles when even Jewish Christians had ceased to observe them (2.11–14). Now he argues that the observance of the Jewish law by Gentiles is in itself incompatible with acceptance of the gospel (2.15–21). Paul does not directly address the question of whether Jewish Christians were still bound to keep the law. In his allegorical argument based upon the story of Hagar and Sarah (4.21–31) he seems to propose that the Sinai covenant and the community of Israel based upon the observance of the law is drastically at odds with the authentic Israel, the community united with the one true heir of Abraham, Jesus Christ (3.16). Previously Paul has talked about the law as a provisional measure, a means to discipline those who would inherit Abraham's promise during their religious infancy (3.24; cf. 4.1–6). The implication of these passages is that Judaism is redundant, perhaps even an obstacle to God's plan for human salvation. Paul does not draw this conclusion. Later, in Romans 9–11, he explicitly rebuts it. Paul accepts that Peter and James are "entrusted with the gospel to the circumcised" (2.7–8), and observance of the law was preserved at this time in Jewish Christian communities.

The exact date of the letter's composition is not known, but it was written presumably some time between the late forties and early fifties of the Common Era. Paul would develop his views on the law further in his Letter to the Romans. Although Galatians follows the form of a letter to specific Christian churches, there are no references to anyone in the community and little information about Paul's mission among them. The letter is rather Paul's defense of his Gentile mission as a whole and the particular understanding of the law on which it is based. The addressees of the letter are an unspecified number of "the churches in Galatia" (1.2), a Roman province in central Asia Minor where, according to Acts, Paul had preached (Acts 13.14–14.23; cf. 16.6; 18.23).

Prior to writing Galatians, Paul had been involved in discussions of Gentile observance of the law with the leaders of the Jerusalem church (2.1–10). This meeting may be identical with the council at Jerusalem, reported in Acts 15.1–29. Paul's account of his visit to Jerusalem is, however, very different from the account in Acts. In Galatians Paul is insistent that no demand was made for Gentiles to observe the law. A conflict in Antioch ensued over table fellowship of Jews and Gentiles (2.11–14). Paul names as his opponents in Antioch "certain people . . . from James" and "the circumcision faction," but it is unclear whether the two groups are the same. Nonetheless, they persuaded the rest of the Jews, including Peter and Barnabas, to break off table fellowship with Gentiles. Paul repeats his accusation against Peter that Peter himself no longer observed Jewish law and customs, yet wanted to impose them on Gentiles.

The context of Paul's formulations was his bitter struggle with opponents in Galatia. The content and sharp polemic of Galatians were worked out in reply to what Paul knew of his opponents' teaching and of their attacks upon him. We would have a better understanding of Paul's intentions if we knew more about them. Despite the best efforts of scholars to identify and reconstruct the arguments of Paul's opponents, they remain a shadowy group. Most commentators describe them as Judaizers because they insisted on circumcision. Whether they belonged to the same opposition that Paul had faced in Antioch or during his visit to the Jerusalem leaders (the "false believers" in 2.4) cannot be decided from Paul's letter. We also have no evidence that they were missionaries sent by the Jerusalem church and representing James, notwithstanding Paul's earlier conflict in Antioch. Nevertheless, the effect of their controversy with Paul is unmistakable. The opposition forced him to develop a defense of his mission to the Gentiles which would provide the basis for a Christianity independent of its Jewish roots.

The letter falls naturally into three parts. In the first, after a salutation (1.1–5), Paul reviews his life (1.6–2.14): his missionary relationship to the Galatians (1.6–12); his past, including his own call (1.13–24); and his relationship with the Jerusalem church and the other apostles (2.1–14). The second section (2.15–5.1) is a complex and densely argued presentation of Paul's vision of the gospel: the opposition faith and works of the law (2.15–21); the conversion of the Galatians (3.1–5); the promise to Abraham and his inheritance (3.6–18); the purpose of the law (3.19–25); baptism (3.26–29); the inheritance of the children of Christ (4.1–7); the danger of slipping back into bondage (4.8–11); the close relationship of Paul and the Galatians (4.12–20); and an allegorical argument based on the story of Hagar and Sarah (4.21–5.1). The third section (5.2–6.18) presents the practical application of Paul's view: reasons against the requirement of circumcision (5.2–12); true Christian liberty (5.13–26); moral exhortation (6.1–10); and a postscript (6.11–18).

1 Paul an apostle—sent neither by human commission nor from human authorities, but through Jesus Christ and God the Father, who raised him from the dead—
2 and all the members of God's family[a] who are with me,

To the churches of Galatia:
3 Grace to you and peace from God our Father and the Lord Jesus Christ, 4 who gave himself for our sins to set us free from

a Gk *all the brothers*

1.1–5: The salutation, in which Paul stresses his apostolic authority. **1:** *Apostle,* both a witness (Acts 1.22) and a proclaimer (1 Cor 12.28) of the resurrection of Jesus. Paul's apostleship results directly from his experience of the risen Christ. **2:** *Churches of Galatia,* the plural indicates that Paul was addressing several Christian communities. The location of these churches is uncertain. Current scholarly opinion favors the region named after and occupied by a people of Celtic origins (around modern Ankara in Turkey). The Roman province of Galatia extended to the south, however, to the cities of Iconium, Lystra, and Derbe, where Paul and Barnabas also founded churches (Acts 14.1–23). **3:** *Grace . . . peace,* the combined Greek and Hebrew greeting that Paul typically used (e.g., Rom 1.7; 1 Cor 1.3; 2 Cor 1.2). **4:** *Gave himself for our sins,* in sacrificial death (Mk 10.45) as a sin offering (Lev 4–5). Paul repeats this central early Christian tradition (see also 2.20; 1 Tim 2.6). The *present evil age* implies that there is

the present evil age, according to the will of
our God and Father, 5 to whom be the glory
forever and ever. Amen.

6 I am astonished that you are so quick-
ly deserting the one who called you in the
grace of Christ and are turning to a differ-
ent gospel— 7 not that there is another gos-
pel, but there are some who are confusing
you and want to pervert the gospel of
Christ. 8 But even if we or an angel[a] from
heaven should proclaim to you a gospel
contrary to what we proclaimed to you, let
that one be accursed! 9 As we have said be-
fore, so now I repeat, if anyone proclaims
to you a gospel contrary to what you re-
ceived, let that one be accursed!

10 Am I now seeking human approval,
or God's approval? Or am I trying to please
people? If I were still pleasing people, I
would not be a servant[b] of Christ.

11 For I want you to know, brothers
and sisters,[c] that the gospel that was pro-
claimed by me is not of human origin; 12 for
I did not receive it from a human source,
nor was I taught it, but I received it through
a revelation of Jesus Christ.

13 You have heard, no doubt, of my ear-
lier life in Judaism. I was violently persecut-
ing the church of God and was trying to
destroy it. 14 I advanced in Judaism beyond
many among my people of the same age,
for I was far more zealous for the traditions
of my ancestors. 15 But when God, who had
set me apart before I was born and called
me through his grace, was pleased 16 to re-
veal his Son to me,[d] so that I might pro-
claim him among the Gentiles, I did not
confer with any human being, 17 nor did I
go up to Jerusalem to those who were al-

a Or *a messenger* *b* Gk *slave* *c* Gk *brothers*
d Gk *in me*

another age, the "age to come" in Jewish apocalyptic thought (see also 2 Thess 2.7–8). Christ's death, therefore, cancels believers' sin and delivers them for this messianic era.

1.6–2.14: A recapitulation of Paul's life.

1.6–9: Paul rebukes the Galatians. Unlike Paul's other letters (Rom 1.8–15; 1 Cor 1.4–9), he does not offer thanksgiving for those addressed. Instead he immediately upbraids them for *deserting the one who called you*—not Paul here, but God or God through Christ. **7:** The new teaching that the Galatians have accepted is "a different gospel" and not compatible with Paul's instruction. **8–9:** Paul's opponents may have held that their teaching had been revealed by *an angel from heaven,* a common claim in Judaism (reflected in 3.19) and some other religions of antiquity. In any case, Paul's revelation comes from a higher source than any angel, Jesus Christ (1.11). *Accursed,* an anathema using a double curse for emphasis.

1.10–12: Paul states the defense of his gospel. His position is not based on expediency: He does not reject observance of the Jewish law by Gentiles as a means of winning more converts through lax requirements. **11–12:** Paul's gospel was directly revealed to him by Jesus Christ. Paul implies that the teaching of his opponents, unlike his *gospel,* is of *human origin.*

1.13–2.14: Paul recounts his background in Judaism, his calling as an apostle, and his mission to the Gentiles. The purpose of this autobiographical sketch is to state the facts, as Paul saw them, of how he became the apostle to the Gentiles.

1.13–24: Paul's conversion, early life in the church, and defense of his apostleship. 13–14: *Persecuting the church of God,* see Acts 8.3; 9.21; 22.4. Paul insists that he was an exemplary Jew (Acts 22.3; Phil 3.4–6) who was *zealous for the traditions of my ancestors,* i.e., for the Jewish law, including its oral traditions which were upheld in Pharisaic Judaism (Phil 3.5–6). **15–16:** Paul's conversion occurs as a direct result of divine intervention without human mediation in order to fulfill God's plan of revealing Christ to the Gentiles. *Set . . . born,* like a prophet in the Hebrew Bible (Isa 49.1; Jer 1.5). *To me* (lit. "in me"), links together the ideas that Christ is revealed to Paul and through Paul to the Gentiles. **17:** *Arabia,* the Nabataean kingdom, in Transjordan, of which the capital was Petra. *Damascus* is recorded in Acts

ready apostles before me, but I went away
at once into Arabia, and afterwards I re-
turned to Damascus.
18 Then after three years I did go up to
Jerusalem to visit Cephas and stayed with
him fifteen days; 19 but I did not see any
other apostle except James the Lord's
brother. 20 In what I am writing to you, be-
fore God, I do not lie! 21 Then I went into
the regions of Syria and Cilicia, 22 and I was
still unknown by sight to the churches of
Judea that are in Christ; 23 they only heard
it said, "The one who formerly was perse-
cuting us is now proclaiming the faith he
once tried to destroy." 24 And they glorified
God because of me.

9.8–25 as the place where Paul went immediately after his conversion; see also 2 Cor 11.32–33. **18:** It is unclear whether the *three years* are to be counted from Paul's call or from his return to Damascus. *Cephas* is the Aramaic equivalent of "Peter" (both names mean "rock") and the form of the name favored by Paul. **19:** *James* the brother of Jesus (Mk 6.3; Mt 13.55; 1 Cor 15.7) who became a leading member

Chs 1–2: Paul's journeys in Asia Minor.

2 Then after fourteen years I went up
again to Jerusalem with Barnabas, tak-
ing Titus along with me. 2 I went up in re-
sponse to a revelation. Then I laid before
them (though only in a private meeting
with the acknowledged leaders) the gospel
that I proclaim among the Gentiles, in or-
der to make sure that I was not running, or
had not run, in vain. 3 But even Titus, who
was with me, was not compelled to be cir-
cumcised, though he was a Greek. 4 But be-
cause of false believers[a] secretly brought
in, who slipped in to spy on the freedom we
have in Christ Jesus, so that they might en-
slave us— 5 we did not submit to them even
for a moment, so that the truth of the gos-
pel might always remain with you. 6 And
from those who were supposed to be ac-
knowledged leaders (what they actually
were makes no difference to me; God
shows no partiality)—those leaders con-
tributed nothing to me. 7 On the contrary,
when they saw that I had been entrusted
with the gospel for the uncircumcised, just
as Peter had been entrusted with the gospel
for the circumcised 8 (for he who worked
through Peter making him an apostle to the
circumcised also worked through me in
sending me to the Gentiles), 9 and when
James and Cephas and John, who were ac-
knowledged pillars, recognized the grace
that had been given to me, they gave to
Barnabas and me the right hand of fellow-
ship, agreeing that we should go to the
Gentiles and they to the circumcised.
10 They asked only one thing, that we re-
member the poor, which was actually what
I was[b] eager to do.
11 But when Cephas came to Antioch, I
opposed him to his face, because he stood
self-condemned; 12 for until certain people
came from James, he used to eat with the
Gentiles. But after they came, he drew back
and kept himself separate for fear of the

a Gk *false brothers* *b* Or *had been*

of the Jerusalem church (Acts 1.14; 15.13; 21.18–19). **21:** *Syria* had Antioch as its capital, and the chief city of *Cilicia* on the southeast coast of Asia Minor was Paul's hometown of Tarsus. **22–23:** Cf. Acts 9.26–30, which gives a different account of all these events.

2.1–10: Paul meets with the Jerusalem leaders. It is difficult to determine the relationship of Paul's and Barnabas's visit to Jerusalem, reported here, with the account of their visit in Acts 15.1–29. If the same events are being described, then we have two radically different versions. **1:** It is unclear whether the *fourteen years* are to be counted from his call or his first Jerusalem visit (1.18). *Barnabas,* a Jewish Christian and Paul's co-missionary, who participated in the mission to Antioch and brought Paul there (see Acts 4.36; 9.27; 11.22–30; 13.1–15.41). *Titus,* a Greek, possibly converted by Paul himself, who also becomes Paul's co-missionary. **2,6,9:** *Acknowledged,* the Gk means "seem, appear." Paul perhaps vacillates between the senses "seem [truly]" and "seem [falsely]." **3–5:** Paul's opponents, the *false believers,* both in this earlier conflict and in Galatia, claim that conversion to Judaism is a precondition for membership in the Christian community and therefore demand Titus's circumcision. **6–9:** *Uncircumcised . . . circumcised,* Gentiles and Jews. Paul asserts that the Jerusalem leaders agreed with him in distinguishing between their mission to their fellow Jews and his to the Gentiles, thus conceding his apostolic authority over the latter. The division of labor may not have been so sharply defined (Acts 10). *John,* probably the apostle (Acts 3–4). **10:** Paul organized a collection among the churches he founded to be sent to Jerusalem (Acts 11.29–30; 24.17; Rom 15.25–29; 1 Cor 16.1–3, 2 Cor 8.1–9.15). *The poor* may be a religious expression which identified the Jerusalem Christians as the righteous, humble ones of God (Lk 1.48; Mt 5.3; 1QpHab 12.2–6), or a reference to the physical neediness of the community after the famine of 46/48 CE (Josephus, *Ant.* 20.51).

2.11–14: Paul's confrontation with Peter at Antioch. The table fellowship of Jew and non-Jew was not forbidden by all interpretations of the Jewish law at the time of Paul. But refusal to eat Gentile food was a sign of loyal devotion to God (Dan 1.8–16; Tob 1.10–13; Jdt 10.5). Sharing, or not sharing, a meal was a strong indication of acceptance or nonacceptance (Acts 10.14; 11.3,8). **12:** The *people . . . from James,* messengers from the Jerusalem apostle who insisted on a stricter interpretation of the law, forbidding such table fellowship. **14:** Paul attacks Peter's behavior because it might *compel the Gentiles to live like Jews.*

circumcision faction. 13 And the other Jews
joined him in this hypocrisy, so that even
Barnabas was led astray by their hypocrisy.
14 But when I saw that they were not acting
consistently with the truth of the gospel, I
said to Cephas before them all, "If you,
though a Jew, live like a Gentile and not
like a Jew, how can you compel the Gen-
tiles to live like Jews?"[a]
15 We ourselves are Jews by birth and
not Gentile sinners; 16 yet we know that a
person is justified[b] not by the works of the
law but through faith in Jesus Christ.[c] And
we have come to believe in Christ Jesus,
so that we might be justified by faith in
Christ,[d] and not by doing the works of the
law, because no one will be justified by the
works of the law. 17 But if, in our effort to
be justified in Christ, we ourselves have
been found to be sinners, is Christ then a
servant of sin? Certainly not! 18 But if I
build up again the very things that I once
tore down, then I demonstrate that I am a
transgressor. 19 For through the law I died
to the law, so that I might live to God. I
have been crucified with Christ; 20 and it is
no longer I who live, but it is Christ who
lives in me. And the life I now live in the
flesh I live by faith in the Son of God,[e]
who loved me and gave himself for me. 21 I
do not nullify the grace of God; for if justi-
fication[f] comes through the law, then
Christ died for nothing.

3 You foolish Galatians! Who has be-
witched you? It was before your eyes
that Jesus Christ was publicly exhibited as
crucified! 2 The only thing I want to learn
from you is this: Did you receive the Spirit
by doing the works of the law or by believ-
ing what you heard? 3 Are you so foolish?
Having started with the Spirit, are you now
ending with the flesh? 4 Did you experience
so much for nothing?—if it really was for
nothing. 5 Well then, does God[g] supply
you with the Spirit and work miracles
among you by your doing the works of the
law, or by your believing what you heard?
6 Just as Abraham "believed God, and

a Some interpreters hold that the quotation extends into the following paragraph *b* Or *reckoned as righteous;* and so elsewhere *c* Or *the faith of Jesus Christ* *d* Or *the faith of Christ* *e* Or *by the faith of the Son of God* *f* Or *righteousness* *g* Gk *he*

Although the ban on table fellowship did not prohibit Gentiles from being members of the Christian community, it could have relegated those who did not choose full conversion to Judaism to second-class status.

2.15–5.1: Paul's gospel: faith in Christ frees us from law.

2.15–21: Jews and Gentiles are both justified through Christ. Paul states his basic principle: Trusting in Christ, including the sacrifice of his death, is what makes one righteous. **15:** *Gentile sinners,* Gentiles were sinners in Jewish eyes because they were idolators, i.e., adherents of non-Jewish religions. **16:** *Works of the law* refers to those practices (dietary laws, sabbath observance, etc.) that marked Jewish identity. *Faith in Jesus Christ* stresses the believer's trust in Christ. The alternative translation (notes *c* and *d*), *faith of Jesus Christ,* emphasizes the saving effect of Jesus' obedience, culminating in his death on the cross. **17:** Christ's exposure of our sinfulness, a consequence of bringing us to a righteous state, does not mean that Christ is carrying out the purpose of sin. **18:** *Things,* i.e., observance of the law as the only path to righteousness. **19:** *Crucified with Christ,* see 5.24; 6.14; Rom 6.5–11; 2 Cor 4.7–12. **20:** *Christ who lives in me,* see Rom 8.9–11; 2 Cor 13.5; Col 1.27. *Gave himself for me,* see 1.4n.

3.1–5: Paul's challenge to the Galatians. Paul asks the Galatians whether they received the gift of the Spirit through fulfilling practices required by Jewish law, or through accepting the gospel preached by Paul (*believing what you heard,* vv. 2,5). **3:** *Ending with the flesh,* an oblique reference to circumcision. The opposition of Spirit and flesh is an important theme in Paul (4.29; 5.16–25; 6.8; Rom 8.1–12; 1 Cor 3.1; 1 Cor 15.35–55; Phil 3.2–6). **5:** *Miracles* are associated with apostolic preaching and the presence of the Spirit (Rom 15.19; 1 Cor 12.10; 2 Cor 12.12).

3.6–14: Abraham the model for Christian faith. Paul contrasts the believer, whose exemplar is Abraham and who is justified by faith, with those who seek justification through performing the practices of the Jewish law. **6:** Gen 15.6; see also Rom 4.3. Paul again uses Abraham as a model of faith in Rom 4.

it was reckoned to him as righteousness,"
7 so, you see, those who believe are the de-
scendants of Abraham. 8 And the scripture,
foreseeing that God would justify the Gen-
tiles by faith, declared the gospel before-
hand to Abraham, saying, "All the Gentiles
shall be blessed in you." 9 For this reason,
those who believe are blessed with Abra-
ham who believed.
10 For all who rely on the works of the
law are under a curse; for it is written,
"Cursed is everyone who does not observe
and obey all the things written in the book
of the law." 11 Now it is evident that no one
is justified before God by the law; for "The
one who is righteous will live by faith."[a]
12 But the law does not rest on faith; on the
contrary, "Whoever does the works of the
law[b] will live by them." 13 Christ redeemed
us from the curse of the law by becoming a
curse for us—for it is written, "Cursed is
everyone who hangs on a tree"— 14 in or-
der that in Christ Jesus the blessing of
Abraham might come to the Gentiles, so
that we might receive the promise of the
Spirit through faith.
15 Brothers and sisters,[c] I give an ex-
ample from daily life: once a person's will[d]
has been ratified, no one adds to it or an-
nuls it. 16 Now the promises were made to
Abraham and to his offspring;[e] it does not
say, "And to offsprings,"[f] as of many; but
it says, "And to your offspring,"[e] that is,
to one person, who is Christ. 17 My point is
this: the law, which came four hundred
thirty years later, does not annul a cove-
nant previously ratified by God, so as to
nullify the promise. 18 For if the inheritance
comes from the law, it no longer comes
from the promise; but God granted it to
Abraham through the promise.
19 Why then the law? It was added be-
cause of transgressions, until the off-
spring[e] would come to whom the promise
had been made; and it was ordained
through angels by a mediator. 20 Now a me-
diator involves more than one party; but
God is one.
21 Is the law then opposed to the prom-
ises of God? Certainly not! For if a law had
been given that could make alive, then righ-
teousness would indeed come through the
law. 22 But the scripture has imprisoned all
things under the power of sin, so that what
was promised through faith in Jesus

a Or *The one who is righteous through faith will live* *b* Gk *does them* *c* Gk *Brothers* *d* Or *covenant* (as in verse 17) *e* Gk *seed* *f* Gk *seeds*

8: Gen 12.3; 18.18; 22.18. **10:** Deut 27.36. **11:** Hab 2.4; Rom 1.17. **12:** Lev 18.5; see also Rom 10.5. **13:** Deut 21.23 concerns execution by hanging but Paul takes *tree* as a reference to Jesus' cross.

3.15–18: The inheritance of Abraham. Paul argues that Christ is the one heir of Abraham and that what was promised Abraham cannot be inherited through the law. **15:** *Will,* the Gk means "covenant" as well as a person's document of bequest (note *d*). **16:** *Offspring,* lit. "seed" (notes *e* and *f*). Paul uses the same Greek word as the Septuagint text of God's promises to Abraham in Genesis (Gen 12.7; 15.5; 17.8; 22.17). Paul contrasts the singular *seed* in the text with the common (and in his view mistaken) interpretation of it as a plural, *seeds.* **17:** Paul follows the Septuagint, not the Hebrew, text of Ex 12.40 by including within the *four hundred thirty years* not only the Israelite sojourn in Egypt but also the earlier period in Canaan.

3.19–25: The purpose of the law of Moses. The law does not replace God's promise to Abraham but is a temporary means of discipline for God's people. **19:** *Added because of transgressions* allows several interpretations. It can mean to make aware of sin (Rom 3.20; 7.7). It can also carry the further sense of restraining transgressions (vv. 23–25). The phrase can also signify that the law provoked sin (Rom 5.20; 7.7–12). *Ordained through angels* reflects a later Jewish belief that the law was delivered on Sinai not directly from God but by angels; see Deut 33.2 (Septuagint); Acts 7.38,53; Heb 2.2. *A mediator,* Moses (see Lev 26.46; Num 36.13). **20:** An obscure verse that links monotheism with there being no need for a mediator of God's promise. **22:** *Faith in Jesus Christ* stresses the believer's faith as necessary for obtaining the promise, while the alternative, *faith of Jesus Christ* (note *a*), emphasizes Jesus' faith as that

Christ[a] might be given to those who be-
lieve.
23 Now before faith came, we were im-
prisoned and guarded under the law until
faith would be revealed. 24 Therefore the
law was our disciplinarian until Christ
came, so that we might be justified by faith.
25 But now that faith has come, we are no
longer subject to a disciplinarian, 26 for in
Christ Jesus you are all children of God
through faith. 27 As many of you as were
baptized into Christ have clothed your-
selves with Christ. 28 There is no longer Jew
or Greek, there is no longer slave or free,
there is no longer male and female; for all
of you are one in Christ Jesus. 29 And if you
belong to Christ, then you are Abraham's
offspring,[b] heirs according to the promise.

4 My point is this: heirs, as long as they
are minors, are no better than slaves,
though they are the owners of all the prop-
erty; 2 but they remain under guardians and
trustees until the date set by the father. 3 So
with us; while we were minors, we were
enslaved to the elemental spirits[c] of the
world. 4 But when the fullness of time had
come, God sent his Son, born of a woman,
born under the law, 5 in order to redeem
those who were under the law, so that we
might receive adoption as children. 6 And
because you are children, God has sent the
Spirit of his Son into our[d] hearts, crying,
"Abba![e] Father!" 7 So you are no longer a
slave but a child, and if a child then also an
heir, through God.[f]
8 Formerly, when you did not know
God, you were enslaved to beings that by
nature are not gods. 9 Now, however, that
you have come to know God, or rather to
be known by God, how can you turn back
again to the weak and beggarly elemental
spirits?[g] How can you want to be enslaved
to them again? 10 You are observing special
days, and months, and seasons, and years.
11 I am afraid that my work for you may
have been wasted.
12 Friends,[h] I beg you, become as I am,
for I also have become as you are. You have
done me no wrong. 13 You know that it was

a Or *through the faith of Jesus Christ* *b* Gk *seed* *c* Or *the rudiments* *d* Other ancient authorities read *your* *e* Aramaic for *Father* *f* Other ancient authorities read *an heir of God through Christ* *g* Or *beggarly rudiments* *h* Gk *Brothers*

which grants the promise; see 2.16n. **24–25:** *Disciplinarian,* the slave who accompanied a boy to school and who often harshly punished the boy for his behavior.

3.26–29: Baptism into Christ. Through baptism believers are incorporated into Christ, abolishing social distinctions, and are made with him the offspring of Abraham and heirs to the promise. **26–28:** Paul is likely here quoting from an early Christian baptismal formula. **26:** Christians are adopted children of God and therefore co-heirs with Christ (Rom 8.14–17). **27:** Baptism unites the believer with Christ (Rom 6.3–11). *Clothed . . . with Christ,* see Rom 13.14; Col 3.10. **28:** A similar erasure of social distinctions is proclaimed in 1 Cor 12.13; Col 3.11, where baptismal formulas also seem to be quoted, but without the phrase *male and female.* **29:** Christ alone is *Abraham's offspring* or *seed* (see 3.16n.) but now includes all those united in baptism with him.

4.1–7: Christ brings believers into their inheritance as adopted children of God. 1: *Minors,* like other members of a Roman family other than the father, had few rights. **3:** *Elemental spirits of the world* refers probably to cosmic powers that dominate human beings (see also 4.8; Col 2.8,20). The phrase (alternatively translated as *rudiments,* note *c*) can also denote the four elements (earth, air, fire, water), which in Paul's time were seen as controlling human destiny. The *rudiments* can additionally be the basic principles of a philosophy or code (see Heb 5.12). **4:** *Born of a woman, born under the law* stresses Jesus' human and Jewish birth, seen by Paul as the enslaved human condition, in contrast to the freedom Christ brings to those adopted as God's children. **6:** *Abba,* note *e* and Mk 14.36; Rom 8.15.

4.8–11: The Galatians slip back into bondage. Paul brands the Galatian observance of the law as a return to their pre-Christian enslavement. **9:** *Elemental spirits,* see 4.3n. **10:** The Galatians are observing the Jewish calendar.

4.12–20: Paul reminds the Galatians of their close relationship to him. 13: Paul may be alluding to one or both visits he made to Galatia as mentioned in Acts 16.6; 18.23. The *infirmity* is not known; efforts

because of a physical infirmity that I first
announced the gospel to you; 14 though my
condition put you to the test, you did not
scorn or despise me, but welcomed me as
an angel of God, as Christ Jesus. 15 What
has become of the goodwill you felt? For I
testify that, had it been possible, you would
have torn out your eyes and given them to
me. 16 Have I now become your enemy by
telling you the truth? 17 They make much of
you, but for no good purpose; they want to
exclude you, so that you may make much
of them. 18 It is good to be made much of
for a good purpose at all times, and not
only when I am present with you. 19 My
little children, for whom I am again in the
pain of childbirth until Christ is formed in
you, 20 I wish I were present with you now
and could change my tone, for I am perplexed about you.

21 Tell me, you who desire to be subject
to the law, will you not listen to the law?
22 For it is written that Abraham had two
sons, one by a slave woman and the other
by a free woman. 23 One, the child of the
slave, was born according to the flesh; the
other, the child of the free woman, was
born through the promise. 24 Now this is an
allegory: these women are two covenants.
One woman, in fact, is Hagar, from Mount
Sinai, bearing children for slavery. 25 Now
Hagar is Mount Sinai in Arabia[a] and corresponds to the present Jerusalem, for she is
in slavery with her children. 26 But the other
woman corresponds to the Jerusalem
above; she is free, and she is our mother.
27 For it is written,

"Rejoice, you childless one, you who
bear no children,
burst into song and shout, you who
endure no birth pangs;
for the children of the desolate
woman are more numerous
than the children of the one who is
married."

28 Now you,[b] my friends,[c] are children of
the promise, like Isaac. 29 But just as at that
time the child who was born according to
the flesh persecuted the child who was born
according to the Spirit, so it is now also.
30 But what does the scripture say? "Drive
out the slave and her child; for the child of
the slave will not share the inheritance with
the child of the free woman." 31 So then,
friends,[c] we are children, not of the slave

5 but of the free woman. 1 For freedom
Christ has set us free. Stand firm, therefore, and do not submit again to a yoke of
slavery.

2 Listen! I, Paul, am telling you that if

a Other ancient authorities read *For Sinai is a mountain in Arabia* *b* Other ancient authorities read *we* *c* Gk *brothers*

to identify it as eye trouble, based on v. 15, may be based on too literal a reading. The adverb *first* can also be translated as "formerly." **17:** *They,* i.e., Paul's opponents, may have threatened to exclude from the Christian community Gentiles who did not follow their example of observing the law. **19:** Paul uses as a metaphor of his apostolic activity a mother giving birth. Elsewhere Paul calls the members of the churches he founded his "children" (1 Cor 4.14; 2 Cor 6.13; 1 Thess 2.11).

4.21–5.1: The allegory of Hagar and Sarah. **21:** *The law* in the Hebrew Bible comprises the first five books, the Pentateuch or Torah. **22–23:** Gen 16.1–4,15; 21.1–7. **24:** *Allegory,* a method of reading a text that understands the characters, narrative, and other elements as speaking about another reality entirely. *These women are two covenants,* i.e., Hagar represents those descendants of Abraham who observe the law and Sarah those who through Christ are the true heirs to God's promise to Abraham. **25:** *Now Hagar is Mount Sinai in Arabia,* there are several variants of this text; see note *a*. Paul's identification of Hagar with Mount Sinai, where the law was given to Israel, is unparalleled. **26:** *The Jerusalem above . . . our mother,* Paul draws on the prophets' vision of the pilgrimage of the nations to the restored Jerusalem (Isa 51.2–6; ch 60; 62.1–2; Zech 2.10–12). Ps 86.5 (Septuagint) (cf. Ps 87.5) has the phrase "mother Zion." **27:** Isa 54.1; see also Isa 51.2–3. **29–30:** Gen 21.9–10. Genesis does not explicitly mention Ishmael persecuting Isaac, but the idea is found in interpretations of Gen 21.9.

5.2–6.10: Practical applications and exhortations.

5.2–12: Paul's case against circumcision. A Gentile, Paul argues, who accepts circumcision is seeking

you let yourselves be circumcised, Christ
will be of no benefit to you. 3 Once again I
testify to every man who lets himself be
circumcised that he is obliged to obey the
entire law. 4 You who want to be justified
by the law have cut yourselves off from
Christ; you have fallen away from grace.
5 For through the Spirit, by faith, we eagerly
wait for the hope of righteousness. 6 For in
Christ Jesus neither circumcision nor uncir-
cumcision counts for anything; the only
thing that counts is faith working[a]
through love.

7 You were running well; who prevent-
ed you from obeying the truth? 8 Such per-
suasion does not come from the one who
calls you. 9 A little yeast leavens the whole
batch of dough. 10 I am confident about
you in the Lord that you will not think oth-
erwise. But whoever it is that is confusing
you will pay the penalty. 11 But my
friends,[b] why am I still being persecuted if
I am still preaching circumcision? In that
case the offense of the cross has been re-
moved. 12 I wish those who unsettle you
would castrate themselves!

13 For you were called to freedom,
brothers and sisters;[b] only do not use your
freedom as an opportunity for self-
indulgence,[c] but through love become
slaves to one another. 14 For the whole law
is summed up in a single commandment,
"You shall love your neighbor as yourself."
15 If, however, you bite and devour one an-
other, take care that you are not consumed
by one another.

16 Live by the Spirit, I say, and do not
gratify the desires of the flesh. 17 For what
the flesh desires is opposed to the Spirit,
and what the Spirit desires is opposed to
the flesh; for these are opposed to each oth-
er, to prevent you from doing what you
want. 18 But if you are led by the Spirit, you
are not subject to the law. 19 Now the
works of the flesh are obvious: fornication,
impurity, licentiousness, 20 idolatry, sor-
cery, enmities, strife, jealousy, anger, quar-
rels, dissensions, factions, 21 envy,[d] drunk-
enness, carousing, and things like these. I
am warning you, as I warned you before:
those who do such things will not inherit
the kingdom of God.

22 By contrast, the fruit of the Spirit is
love, joy, peace, patience, kindness, gener-
osity, faithfulness, 23 gentleness, and self-
control. There is no law against such
things. 24 And those who belong to Christ
Jesus have crucified the flesh with its pas-
sions and desires. 25 If we live by the Spirit,
let us also be guided by the Spirit. 26 Let us
not become conceited, competing against
one another, envying one another.

a Or *made effective* *b* Gk *brothers* *c* Gk *the flesh*
d Other ancient authorities add *murder*

righteousness through the law, an act incompatible with faith in Christ. **4:** See 2.16; 3.10–12. **6:** *Neither circumcision nor uncircumcision,* 6.15; 1 Cor 7.19. The alternative *faith made effective through love* (note *a*) gives faith a passive sense. It is instigated through love, presumably God's love. **8:** *The one who calls you,* God through Christ, see 1.6n. **9:** Paul uses the same proverb in 1 Cor 5.6. He is concerned that his opponents will win over the whole Galatian community. **11:** Some of Paul's opponents may have alleged he was inconsistent in his position on Gentile circumcision, perhaps pointing out that he had Timothy circumcised (Acts 16.1–3). **12:** A negative and bitterly sarcastic allusion to circumcision; see Phil 3.2.

5.13–6.10: The behavior of those called in freedom to live by the Spirit. Paul presents a Christian ethic in reply to those demanding observance of the law from the Galatians.

5.13–26: Christian liberty. 13: See vv. 1,6. *Slaves to one another,* mutual submission is an important theme for Paul and his followers, see Eph 5.21; Phil 2.3. **14:** Lev 19.18; Mt 22.39; Rom 13.8–10. **16:** *Desires of the flesh,* the self-indulgence (lit. "flesh"; note *c*) warned against in v. 13; see Eph 2.3. **16–17:** The opposition of the Spirit to the flesh (3.3; Rom 8.1–17) leads to inner conflict (Rom 7.14–24). **18:** Rom 6.14. **19–23:** Catalogues of vices and virtues were a common form of ethical instruction in the Greco-Roman world (see Mk 7.21–22; Mt 15.19; Rom 1.29–31; 1 Cor 6.9–10; 2 Cor 6.6–7; 12.20–21; Phil 4.8; Col 3.5–14; 1 Tim 1.9–10; 6.11; 2 Tim 3.2–5; 1 Pet 2.1; 4.3; 2 Pet 1.5–7; Rev 21.8; 22.15).

6 My friends,[a] if anyone is detected in a
transgression, you who have received
the Spirit should restore such a one in a
spirit of gentleness. Take care that you
yourselves are not tempted. 2 Bear one an-
other's burdens, and in this way you will
fulfill[b] the law of Christ. 3 For if those who
are nothing think they are something, they
deceive themselves. 4 All must test their
own work; then that work, rather than
their neighbor's work, will become a cause
for pride. 5 For all must carry their own
loads.
6 Those who are taught the word must
share in all good things with their teacher.
7 Do not be deceived; God is not
mocked, for you reap whatever you sow.
8 If you sow to your own flesh, you will
reap corruption from the flesh; but if you
sow to the Spirit, you will reap eternal life
from the Spirit. 9 So let us not grow weary
in doing what is right, for we will reap at
harvest time, if we do not give up. 10 So
then, whenever we have an opportunity, let
us work for the good of all, and especially
for those of the family of faith.

11 See what large letters I make when I
am writing in my own hand! 12 It is those
who want to make a good showing in the
flesh that try to compel you to be circum-
cised—only that they may not be persecut-
ed for the cross of Christ. 13 Even the cir-
cumcised do not themselves obey the law,
but they want you to be circumcised so that
they may boast about your flesh. 14 May I
never boast of anything except the cross
of our Lord Jesus Christ, by which[c] the
world has been crucified to me, and I to the
world. 15 For[d] neither circumcision nor un-
circumcision is anything; but a new cre-
ation is everything! 16 As for those who will
follow this rule—peace be upon them, and
mercy, and upon the Israel of God.
17 From now on, let no one make trou-
ble for me; for I carry the marks of Jesus
branded on my body.
18 May the grace of our Lord Jesus
Christ be with your spirit, brothers and sis-
ters.[e] Amen.

a Gk *Brothers* *b* Other ancient authorities read *in this way fulfill* *c* Or *through whom* *d* Other ancient authorities add *in Christ Jesus* *e* Gk *brothers*

6.1–10: Paul offers the Galatians several maxims by which to judge their behavior. 2: *The law of Christ* may be a phrase Paul borrowed from his opponents; see also 1 Cor 9.21; Rom 8.2. The Spirit enables the believer to live out the principle of love, thus fulfilling the law without observing its requirements. **6:** Christian teachers are entitled to financial support from their church (1 Cor 9.14). **8:** Rom 8.5–8. **9:** *Not grow weary,* Paul uses the same Greek verb in 2 Cor 4.1,16 (translated as "not lose heart"); see also Lk 18.1. **10:** *The family of faith,* lit. "members of the household of faith"; compare the phrase "household of God" in Eph 2.19; 1 Tim 3.15; 1 Pet 4.17.

6.11–18: Postscript. 11: Paul had dictated this letter to a secretary, but writes the conclusion in his *own hand;* see 1 Cor 16; 2 Thess 3.17. **12–14:** *Boast about . . . flesh/boast* . . . about *the cross of our Lord Jesus Christ,* see also 1 Cor 1.29–31; Phil 3.2–4. *The flesh* may be a double reference to circumcision and his opponents' pride in the success of their mission. **15:** 3.28; 5.6. *New creation,* Rom 8.19–23; 2 Cor 5.17; also Rev 21.5. **16–18:** A two-part blessing. V. 16 has the form of a traditional Jewish benediction and is conditional, bestowed on those who follow Paul's teaching. As such it is the counterpart to the curse in 1.8. The address *brothers and sisters* in v. 18 does not appear in the final blessing of Paul's other letters and expresses the hope that the former warm relationship between the apostle and the community will be restored. **16:** *This rule* has been summarized in v. 15 but is in fact the standards of Christian faith and behavior Paul has advocated throughout the letter. *Israel of God,* a phrase unique to this verse, equivalent to the "true Israel," i.e., those who follow Paul's *rule* and not the teachings of his opponents. **17:** *Marks of Jesus,* the scars from injuries inflicted on Paul during his mission (2 Cor 6.4–5; 11.23–25). Paul may also be suggesting that his scars identify him as belonging to Christ like the brand marks on a slave.

The Letter of Paul to the EPHESIANS

In powerful poetic language drawn from early Christian hymns and the Jewish scriptures, the Letter to the Ephesians celebrates the author's vision of the church. According to God's eternal plan for humanity, Christ's death brought together both Jews and Gentiles into a new, unified community: The Jewish law, which previously distinguished and divided Jew from Gentile, was rendered irrelevant by the cross, and Christ thus reconciled both groups to each other and to God (2.14–16). According to Ephesians, human existence is beset by the malevolent influence of demonic beings. Christ has been given power over them, and through God's grace human beings may be freed from their immoral and deceitful influences. The new life of believers is one of knowledge and spiritual power, and thus there is the recurring contrast of the old life with the new (2.1–6, 11–13, 19; 4.22–24; 5.8). Another prominent theme is Paul's role as revealer of God's previously hidden plan (3.1–12). The church must recognize both Christ as its Lord and exemplar (4.12–16, 20–24; 5.1–2) and its own exalted status as a spirit-filled community that brings the power and presence of God to the world (1.22–23; 2.22; 3.10, 19; 4.24). Conflict with demonic forces continues (6.10–20), but the church looks forward to the complete reestablishment of God's sovereignty over the creation (1.10) and the perfection of the church as the body of Christ (4.12–16).

Ephesians begins with a salutation (1.1–2) and an introductory thanksgiving prayer (1.15–23) and ends with an epilogue (6.21–24), but it lacks many typical features of Paul's letters and is better classified as a homily. The text divides into two sections: theological teaching (chs 1–3) and ethical exhortation (chs 4–6). The first half focuses on the church as a new community in which Jews and Gentiles equally share in God's blessings. Tension between Jewish and Gentile believers persisted through the first century, and it is unclear whether Ephesians is intended to encourage Gentiles to recognize their position as full partners in the church or whether they are being admonished to respect their Jewish fellow believers more highly. The second half is an appeal for the church to maintain that new unity and press on toward complete maturity by rejecting former lifestyles and displaying Christian values of truth, love, forgiveness, and sexual purity. Rather than advocating a complete renewal of family relationships based on love, forgiveness, and mutual submission, however, the author's christology is used to justify the structure and duties of the ancient patriarchal family (5.22–6.9).

Some early manuscripts and early Christian writers make no reference to Ephesus in 1.1 (see note *a*), and Ephesians does not address problems specific to a single congregation. Some scholars conclude that Ephesians was originally a circular letter, distributed to a number of churches, perhaps in Asia Minor. Others, noting the text's similarities to Colossians, believe the original audience was the churches of Hierapolis and Laodicea (see Col 4.13, 16). The significant contrasts between Ephesians and the letters we can confidently ascribe to Paul raise questions about the identity of the author of Ephesians. Many important terms in Ephesians are not used by Paul elsewhere (e.g., heavenly places, dividing wall, fellow citizen), and some of Paul's characteristic terms and emphases either are given new meaning (e.g., mystery, church) or are completely absent (e.g., the Jews, justify). In addition, the verbose style of Ephesians, especially the use of complex, long sentences (many of which have been divided in the NRSV), is not characteristic of Paul. Theological differences, especially Ephesians' emphasis on believers' present salvation (1.3–12; 2.4–10) and the use of household rules (5.22–6.9), are also evident (see the Introduction to Colossians). As a result of the combined weight of these differences, many scholars hold that Ephesians was written in the late first century by a Jewish-Christian admirer of Paul who sought to apply Pauline thought to the situation of the church in his own day. A minority of scholars hold the author to be Paul, who was writing at the end of his career while imprisoned, probably in Rome; different theological emphases are attributed to developments in Paul's thinking and the particular situation addressed. There are, nevertheless, many verbal parallels between Ephesians and the Pauline letters, especially Colossians (see cross-references in the notes). If Paul was the author of both Ephesians and Colossians, they were probably written at the same time; if Ephesians was written by a later follower of Paul, he drew upon Colossians' established authority and modeled his work on it.

1 Paul, an apostle of Christ Jesus by the
will of God,
To the saints who are in Ephesus and are
faithful[a] in Christ Jesus:
2 Grace to you and peace from God our
Father and the Lord Jesus Christ.

3 Blessed be the God and Father of our
Lord Jesus Christ, who has blessed us in
Christ with every spiritual blessing in the
heavenly places, [4]just as he chose us in
Christ[b] before the foundation of the world
to be holy and blameless before him in love.
[5]He destined us for adoption as his chil-
dren through Jesus Christ, according to the
good pleasure of his will, [6]to the praise of
his glorious grace that he freely bestowed
on us in the Beloved. [7]In him we have re-
demption through his blood, the forgive-
ness of our trespasses, according to the
riches of his grace [8]that he lavished on us.
With all wisdom and insight [9]he has made
known to us the mystery of his will, accord-
ing to his good pleasure that he set forth in
Christ, [10]as a plan for the fullness of time,
to gather up all things in him, things in
heaven and things on earth. [11]In Christ we
have also obtained an inheritance,[c] having
been destined according to the purpose of
him who accomplishes all things according
to his counsel and will, [12]so that we, who
were the first to set our hope on Christ,
might live for the praise of his glory. [13]In
him you also, when you had heard the
word of truth, the gospel of your salvation,
and had believed in him, were marked with
the seal of the promised Holy Spirit;
[14]this[d] is the pledge of our inheritance to-

a Other ancient authorities lack *in Ephesus,* reading *saints who are also faithful* *b* Gk *in him* *c* Or *been made a heritage* *d* Other ancient authorities read *who*

1.1–2: Salutation (cf. Col 1.1–2). *Ephesus,* an important city on the west coast of Asia Minor, which Paul had visited (see Acts 18.19–21; 19; 1 Cor 16.8); see the Introduction. **2:** A common Pauline greeting drawing upon and transforming conventional Greek (*grace*) and Hebrew (*peace*) salutations.

1.3–14: Blessing of God for his blessings (cf. Rom 8.15–34). **3:** *In Christ,* a theme throughout this section, indicating Christ's mediation of divine blessings. *In the heavenly places,* heavenly benefits are a present reality for believers. **4–12:** God *chose us . . . as his children;* he provides forgiveness, wisdom, and an inheritance. **4:** See Col 1.15–17, 22–23. **5:** *Adoption,* see Rom 8.15; Gal 4.5. **6:** *Beloved,* a title for Christ; cf. "beloved son," Mk 1.11; Col 1.13. **7:** *His blood,* Christ's sacrificial death. **9:** *Mystery,* the previously hidden plan of God, which here encompasses all creation. **10:** *Fullness of time,* the culmination of human history. *To gather . . . earth,* the unification of the cosmos under and through Christ. **13:** *You,* the Gentiles (2.11; 3.1) have also been included in God's blessings. *Promised,* by the prophet Joel (Joel 2.28–32; Acts 2.14–21) or Jesus (Lk 24.49; Jn 14.26; Acts 1.4–5). **14:** *Pledge,* the same Gk word is translated "first installment" in 2 Cor 1.22.

ward redemption as God's own people, to
the praise of his glory.
15 I have heard of your faith in the Lord
Jesus and your love[a] toward all the saints,
and for this reason 16 I do not cease to give
thanks for you as I remember you in my
prayers. 17 I pray that the God of our Lord
Jesus Christ, the Father of glory, may give
you a spirit of wisdom and revelation as
you come to know him, 18 so that, with the
eyes of your heart enlightened, you may
know what is the hope to which he has
called you, what are the riches of his glori-
ous inheritance among the saints, 19 and
what is the immeasurable greatness of his
power for us who believe, according to the
working of his great power. 20 God[b] put
this power to work in Christ when he
raised him from the dead and seated him at
his right hand in the heavenly places, 21 far
above all rule and authority and power and
dominion, and above every name that is
named, not only in this age but also in the
age to come. 22 And he has put all things
under his feet and has made him the head
over all things for the church, 23 which is
his body, the fullness of him who fills all in
all.

2 You were dead through the trespasses
and sins 2 in which you once lived, fol-
lowing the course of this world, following
the ruler of the power of the air, the spirit
that is now at work among those who are
disobedient. 3 All of us once lived among
them in the passions of our flesh, following
the desires of flesh and senses, and we were
by nature children of wrath, like everyone
else. 4 But God, who is rich in mercy, out of
the great love with which he loved us 5 even
when we were dead through our trespasses,
made us alive together with Christ[c]—by
grace you have been saved— 6 and raised us
up with him and seated us with him in the
heavenly places in Christ Jesus, 7 so that in
the ages to come he might show the immea-
surable riches of his grace in kindness to-
ward us in Christ Jesus. 8 For by grace you
have been saved through faith, and this is
not your own doing; it is the gift of God—
9 not the result of works, so that no one
may boast. 10 For we are what he has made
us, created in Christ Jesus for good works,
which God prepared beforehand to be our
way of life.
11 So then, remember that at one time
you Gentiles by birth,[d] called "the uncir-
cumcision" by those who are called "the
circumcision"—a physical circumcision
made in the flesh by human hands— 12 re-
member that you were at that time without

a Other ancient authorities lack *and your love*
b Gk *He* *c* Other ancient authorities read *in Christ*
d Gk *in the flesh*

1.15–23: Thanksgiving prayer for wisdom and power (cf. Col 1.3–14). **18:** *Eyes of your heart enlightened,* in contrast to their former darkened understanding (4.18). **20:** *At his right hand,* a common early Christian description, dependent on Ps 110.1, of Christ's exaltation (Acts 2.34–35; Rom 8.34; Col 3.1; Heb 8.1). **21:** *Rule . . . dominion,* hostile spiritual powers subjected to Christ (1 Cor 15.20–28). *Name,* see Phil 2.9. **22:** *Head,* see Col 1.18. **23:** *Body,* see 4.11, 15–16; 1 Cor 12.12–13, 27. *The fullness,* the church expresses God's power and presence to the world or perhaps the church has been completed by Christ.

2.1–10: The old life contrasted with the new life (cf. Col 1.21–23). **1–5:** Both Gentile (*you*) and Jewish Christians (*all of us*) formerly engaged in a lifestyle of sin and lacked God's protection and blessings (*were dead/children of wrath*). **5, 8–9:** *By grace . . . saved,* deliverance to a new life is due solely to God's mercy and benevolence, and precludes any human boasting (Rom 3.21–30). **6:** *Raised . . . places,* believers have been exalted like Christ himself (1.20). **10:** *Good works . . . life,* a new, divinely designed lifestyle is the appropriate result of salvation.

2.11–22: The unity of Jews and Gentiles in the church. **11:** *The uncircumcision,* a derogatory label for Gentiles. *The circumcision,* the Jews, but often Jewish Christians who required all to obey the Mosaic law (Acts 10.45; Gal 2.12; Col 4.11; cf. Phil 3.3). **12–13:** *You were . . . But now . . . ,* another contrast of old and new, focused on the Gentiles' plight (cf. 2.1–5). **12:** *Covenants of promise,* God promised Abraham (Gen 15.18; 17.2–8), Israel/Jacob (Gen 28.13–15), and David (Ps 89) his presence and protection (see Ps

Christ, being aliens from the common-
wealth of Israel, and strangers to the cove-
nants of promise, having no hope and with-
out God in the world. 13 But now in Christ
Jesus you who once were far off have been
brought near by the blood of Christ. 14 For
he is our peace; in his flesh he has made
both groups into one and has broken down
the dividing wall, that is, the hostility be-
tween us. 15 He has abolished the law with
its commandments and ordinances, that he
might create in himself one new humanity
in place of the two, thus making peace,
16 and might reconcile both groups to God
in one body[a] through the cross, thus put-
ting to death that hostility through it.[b]
17 So he came and proclaimed peace to you
who were far off and peace to those who
were near; 18 for through him both of us
have access in one Spirit to the Father. 19 So
then you are no longer strangers and aliens,
but you are citizens with the saints and also
members of the household of God, 20 built
upon the foundation of the apostles and
prophets, with Christ Jesus himself as the
cornerstone.[c] 21 In him the whole structure
is joined together and grows into a holy
temple in the Lord; 22 in whom you also are
built together spiritually[d] into a dwelling
place for God.

3 This is the reason that I Paul am a pris-
oner for[e] Christ Jesus for the sake of
you Gentiles— 2 for surely you have al-
ready heard of the commission of God's
grace that was given me for you, 3 and how
the mystery was made known to me by rev-
elation, as I wrote above in a few words, 4 a
reading of which will enable you to per-
ceive my understanding of the mystery of
Christ. 5 In former generations this mys-
tery[f] was not made known to humankind,
as it has now been revealed to his holy
apostles and prophets by the Spirit: 6 that
is, the Gentiles have become fellow heirs,
members of the same body, and sharers in
the promise in Christ Jesus through the gos-
pel.

7 Of this gospel I have become a servant
according to the gift of God's grace that
was given me by the working of his power.
8 Although I am the very least of all the
saints, this grace was given to me to bring
to the Gentiles the news of the boundless
riches of Christ, 9 and to make everyone
see[g] what is the plan of the mystery hidden
for ages in[h] God who created all things;
10 so that through the church the wisdom of
God in its rich variety might now be made
known to the rulers and authorities in the
heavenly places. 11 This was in accordance
with the eternal purpose that he has carried
out in Christ Jesus our Lord, 12 in whom we
have access to God in boldness and confi-
dence through faith in him.[i] 13 I pray
therefore that you[j] may not lose heart
over my sufferings for you; they are your
glory.

a Or *reconcile both of us in one body for God* *b* Or *in him*, or *in himself* *c* Or *keystone* *d* Gk *in the Spirit* *e* Or *of* *f* Gk *it* *g* Other ancient authorities read *to bring to light* *h* Or *by* *i* Or *the faith of him* *j* Or *I*

105). **13:** *By the blood of Christ,* Christ's death inaugurated a new covenant. **14:** *Made both groups into one,* Jews and Gentiles are united under this new covenant. *Dividing wall,* the Jewish law, which distinguished Jew from Gentile (Acts 10.28) or perhaps the balustrade in the Jerusalem Temple, beyond which Gentiles were forbidden. **16:** *In one body,* the church. **17:** *Proclaimed peace,* see Isa 52.7. *Far off . . . near,* in relation to God (Isa 57.19). **20:** *Prophets,* early Christian prophets (3.5; 4.11; 1 Cor 14). *Cornerstone,* either the foundation (see Isa 28.16) or the capstone that completes a building. **21–22:** *A holy temple,* the church is the dwelling place of God.

3.1–13: Paul reveals God's plan (cf. Col 1.24–29). **1:** A prayer is interrupted by vv. 2–13 and resumed in v. 14. **3:** *Mystery,* see 1.9 n.; here God's plan is the uniting of Jews and Gentiles into a single community. *Above,* in 1.9–10 and 2.11–22 or perhaps "previously" and thus a reference to an earlier Pauline letter. **8:** *Least,* 1 Cor 15.8–9. **10:** *Wisdom of God . . . heavenly places,* the church in turn reveals God's plan (*wisdom*) to the spiritual powers. **13:** *Sufferings . . . glory,* imprisonment on behalf of the Gentiles (v. 1) has secured their life and future glorification (2 Cor 1.6; 4.12; Col 1.24).

14 For this reason I bow my knees be-
fore the Father,[a] 15 from whom every fami-
ly[b] in heaven and on earth takes its name.
16 I pray that, according to the riches of
his glory, he may grant that you may be
strengthened in your inner being with pow-
er through his Spirit, 17 and that Christ may
dwell in your hearts through faith, as you
are being rooted and grounded in love. 18 I
pray that you may have the power to com-
prehend, with all the saints, what is the
breadth and length and height and depth,
19 and to know the love of Christ that sur-
passes knowledge, so that you may be filled
with all the fullness of God.
20 Now to him who by the power at
work within us is able to accomplish abun-
dantly far more than all we can ask or
imagine, 21 to him be glory in the church
and in Christ Jesus to all generations, forev-
er and ever. Amen.

4 I therefore, the prisoner in the Lord,
beg you to lead a life worthy of the call-
ing to which you have been called, 2 with
all humility and gentleness, with patience,
bearing with one another in love, 3 making
every effort to maintain the unity of the
Spirit in the bond of peace. 4 There is one
body and one Spirit, just as you were called
to the one hope of your calling, 5 one Lord,
one faith, one baptism, 6 one God and Fa-
ther of all, who is above all and through all
and in all.
7 But each of us was given grace accord-
ing to the measure of Christ's gift. 8 There-
fore it is said,

"When he ascended on high he made
captivity itself a captive;
he gave gifts to his people."

9 (When it says, "He ascended," what does
it mean but that he had also descended[c]
into the lower parts of the earth? 10 He who
descended is the same one who ascended
far above all the heavens, so that he might
fill all things.) 11 The gifts he gave were that
some would be apostles, some prophets,
some evangelists, some pastors and teach-
ers, 12 to equip the saints for the work of
ministry, for building up the body of
Christ, 13 until all of us come to the unity of
the faith and of the knowledge of the Son
of God, to maturity, to the measure of the
full stature of Christ. 14 We must no longer
be children, tossed to and fro and blown
about by every wind of doctrine, by peo-
ple's trickery, by their craftiness in deceitful
scheming. 15 But speaking the truth in love,
we must grow up in every way into him
who is the head, into Christ, 16 from whom
the whole body, joined and knit together by
every ligament with which it is equipped, as
each part is working properly, promotes
the body's growth in building itself up in
love.
17 Now this I affirm and insist on in the
Lord: you must no longer live as the Gen-
tiles live, in the futility of their minds.
18 They are darkened in their understand-
ing, alienated from the life of God because
of their ignorance and hardness of heart.

a Other ancient authorities add *of our Lord Jesus Christ* *b* Gk *fatherhood* *c* Other ancient authorities add *first*

3.14–21: Prayer for the church's maturity in spiritual strength (v. 16), faith in Christ and love for each other (v. 17), and complete comprehension of Christ's fathomless love (v. 18–19). **14–15:** *Father . . . family,* a play on words in Greek ("pater," "patria," see note *b*); God is the Father (creator and ruler) of all nations and spiritual powers. **19:** *Fullness,* 1.23 n. **20–21:** A doxology celebrating God's ability to perfect the church through the Spirit.

4.1–6.20: Ethical implications.

4.1–16: Appeal for unity amid diversity. 3: *Unity* and *peace* are made possible by Christ (2.11–22), but must be consciously maintained. **4–6:** Seven bases of unity. **8:** Ps 68.18 is interpreted as Christ's exaltation over the spiritual powers (1.20–22) and distribution of gifts to the church. **9:** *Lower parts of the earth,* either the earth itself or Hades. **12:** The maturity of the church depends upon the activity of all Christians. **13, 15:** The perfected church is modeled on Christ himself.

4.17–5.21: Appeal for a changed lifestyle (cf. Col 3.5–17). **19:** *Licentiousness . . . impurity,* excessive

19They have lost all sensitivity and have
abandoned themselves to licentiousness,
greedy to practice every kind of impurity.
20That is not the way you learned Christ!
21For surely you have heard about him and
were taught in him, as truth is in Jesus.
22You were taught to put away your for-
mer way of life, your old self, corrupt and
deluded by its lusts, 23and to be renewed in
the spirit of your minds, 24and to clothe
yourselves with the new self, created ac-
cording to the likeness of God in true righ-
teousness and holiness.

25 So then, putting away falsehood, let
all of us speak the truth to our neighbors,
for we are members of one another. 26Be
angry but do not sin; do not let the sun go
down on your anger, 27and do not make
room for the devil. 28Thieves must give up
stealing; rather let them labor and work
honestly with their own hands, so as to
have something to share with the needy.
29Let no evil talk come out of your mouths,
but only what is useful for building up,[a] as
there is need, so that your words may give
grace to those who hear. 30And do not
grieve the Holy Spirit of God, with which
you were marked with a seal for the day of
redemption. 31Put away from you all bit-
terness and wrath and anger and wrangling
and slander, together with all malice, 32and
be kind to one another, tenderhearted, for-
giving one another, as God in Christ has
5 forgiven you.[b] 1Therefore be imitators
of God, as beloved children, 2and live
in love, as Christ loved us[c] and gave him-
self up for us, a fragrant offering and sacri-
fice to God.

3 But fornication and impurity of any
kind, or greed, must not even be mentioned
among you, as is proper among saints. 4En-
tirely out of place is obscene, silly, and vul-
gar talk; but instead, let there be thanksgiv-
ing. 5Be sure of this, that no fornicator or
impure person, or one who is greedy (that
is, an idolater), has any inheritance in the
kingdom of Christ and of God.

6 Let no one deceive you with empty
words, for because of these things the
wrath of God comes on those who are dis-
obedient. 7Therefore do not be associated
with them. 8For once you were darkness,
but now in the Lord you are light. Live as
children of light— 9for the fruit of the light
is found in all that is good and right and
true. 10Try to find out what is pleasing to
the Lord. 11Take no part in the unfruitful
works of darkness, but instead expose
them. 12For it is shameful even to mention
what such people do secretly; 13but every-
thing exposed by the light becomes visible,
14for everything that becomes visible is
light. Therefore it says,

"Sleeper, awake!
Rise from the dead,
and Christ will shine on you."

15 Be careful then how you live, not as
unwise people but as wise, 16making the
most of the time, because the days are evil.
17So do not be foolish, but understand
what the will of the Lord is. 18Do not get
drunk with wine, for that is debauchery;
but be filled with the Spirit, 19as you sing
psalms and hymns and spiritual songs
among yourselves, singing and making mel-
ody to the Lord in your hearts, 20giving
thanks to God the Father at all times and
for everything in the name of our Lord
Jesus Christ.

21 Be subject to one another out of rev-
erence for Christ.

22 Wives, be subject to your husbands
as you are to the Lord. 23For the husband
is the head of the wife just as Christ is the

a Other ancient authorities read *building up faith*
b Other ancient authorities read *us* *c* Other ancient authorities read *you*

and inappropriate sexual behavior. **22–24:** The *old* lifestyle, like worn-out clothing, must be replaced by a *new* lifestyle guided by one's knowledge of Christ. **25:** See Zech 8.16. **26–27:** Indulged anger (see Ps 4.4) is an opportunity for demonic influence (cf. v. 31). **30:** *Seal,* see 1.13. **4.32–5.2:** Christians must imitate God's (see Mt 5.48) and Christ's forgiveness and self-sacrificial actions. *Fragrant offering,* see Ex 29.18; Ezek 20.14; cf. Phil 4.18. **3–5:** Sexual sins are the primary focus in these verses. **8:** *Darkness/light,* apocalyptic imagery for the domains of the hostile spiritual powers and of God and Christ. **14:** *Sleeper*

head of the church, the body of which he is
the Savior. 24 Just as the church is subject to
Christ, so also wives ought to be, in every-
thing, to their husbands.
25 Husbands, love your wives, just as
Christ loved the church and gave himself
up for her, 26 in order to make her holy by
cleansing her with the washing of water by
the word, 27 so as to present the church to
himself in splendor, without a spot or wrin-
kle or anything of the kind—yes, so that
she may be holy and without blemish. 28 In
the same way, husbands should love their
wives as they do their own bodies. He who
loves his wife loves himself. 29 For no one
ever hates his own body, but he nourishes
and tenderly cares for it, just as Christ does
for the church, 30 because we are members
of his body.[a] 31 "For this reason a man will
leave his father and mother and be joined
to his wife, and the two will become one
flesh." 32 This is a great mystery, and I am
applying it to Christ and the church.
33 Each of you, however, should love his
wife as himself, and a wife should respect
her husband.
6 Children, obey your parents in the
Lord,[b] for this is right. 2 "Honor your
father and mother"—this is the first com-
mandment with a promise: 3 "so that it may
be well with you and you may live long on
the earth."
4 And, fathers, do not provoke your
children to anger, but bring them up in the
discipline and instruction of the Lord.
5 Slaves, obey your earthly masters with
fear and trembling, in singleness of heart,
as you obey Christ; 6 not only while being
watched, and in order to please them, but
as slaves of Christ, doing the will of God
from the heart. 7 Render service with enthu-
siasm, as to the Lord and not to men and
women, 8 knowing that whatever good we
do, we will receive the same again from the
Lord, whether we are slaves or free.
9 And, masters, do the same to them.
Stop threatening them, for you know that
both of you have the same Master in heav-
en, and with him there is no partiality.
10 Finally, be strong in the Lord and in
the strength of his power. 11 Put on the
whole armor of God, so that you may be
able to stand against the wiles of the devil.
12 For our[c] struggle is not against enemies
of blood and flesh, but against the rulers,
against the authorities, against the cosmic
powers of this present darkness, against the
spiritual forces of evil in the heavenly
places. 13 Therefore take up the whole ar-
mor of God, so that you may be able to
withstand on that evil day, and having
done everything, to stand firm. 14 Stand
therefore, and fasten the belt of truth
around your waist, and put on the breast-
plate of righteousness. 15 As shoes for your
feet put on whatever will make you ready
to proclaim the gospel of peace. 16 With all
of these,[d] take the shield of faith, with

a Other ancient authorities add *of his flesh and of his bones* *b* Other ancient authorities lack *in the Lord* *c* Other ancient authorities read *your* *d* Or *In all circumstances*

. . . *you,* perhaps a fragment of a baptismal hymn. **21:** This statement of mutual subjection is not used to challenge the subordination of wives, children, and slaves prescribed below.

5.22–6.9: Rules for household relationships (cf. Col 3.18–4.1). **22–33:** The subordination of *wives* to *husbands* is legitimized by analogy to Christ and the church. **23:** *Husbands* are to imitate Christ's self-sacrifice on behalf of the church (but cf. v. 28). **24:** *Wives* are to imitate not Christ (cf. 4.13–15; 4.32–5.2), but the church as the obedient recipient of Christ's blessings. **26:** Baptism is compared to the Jewish custom of a bride's prenuptial bath. **30–32:** *Mystery,* the unity of Christ and the church as revealed through exegesis of Gen 2.24. Note the scribal addition from Gen 2.23 (see note *a*). **6.1–4:** Relations between *children* and *fathers.* **2–3:** Ex 20.12; Deut 5.16. **5–9:** Relations between *slaves* and *masters.* Like wives, *slaves* are not to imitate Christ, but to obey their masters' divinely sanctioned authority; see Col 3.22–4.1; Titus 2.9–10. **9:** *Masters* must recognize their own subjection to God.

6.10–20: Appeal for strength in spiritual battle. 12: The Christian's enemies are not human (*blood and flesh*), but spiritual (1.21; 2.2). **13–17:** The *armor* of Israel's divine protector (Isa 11.4–5; 52.7; 59.17; Wis 5.17–20). **14:** *Righteousness,* appropriate Christian behavior. **17:** *Salvation,* deliverance from evil

which you will be able to quench all the
flaming arrows of the evil one. 17 Take the
helmet of salvation, and the sword of the
Spirit, which is the word of God.
18 Pray in the Spirit at all times in every
prayer and supplication. To that end keep
alert and always persevere in supplication
for all the saints. 19 Pray also for me, so that
when I speak, a message may be given to
me to make known with boldness the mys-
tery of the gospel,[a] 20 for which I am an
ambassador in chains. Pray that I may de-
clare it boldly, as I must speak.

21 So that you also may know how I am
and what I am doing, Tychicus will tell you
everything. He is a dear brother and a faith-
ful minister in the Lord. 22 I am sending him
to you for this very purpose, to let you
know how we are, and to encourage your
hearts.
23 Peace be to the whole community,[b]
and love with faith, from God the Father
and the Lord Jesus Christ. 24 Grace be with
all who have an undying love for our Lord
Jesus Christ.[c]

a Other ancient authorities lack *of the gospel*
b Gk *to the brothers* *c* Other ancient authorities
add *Amen*

spiritual powers. *The sword*, the only offensive weapon mentioned, is the proclamation of the gospel.
6.21–24: Epilogue (cf. Col 4.7–8). **21:** *Tychicus*, Paul's associate; see Acts 20.4; Col 4.7; 2 Tim 4.12.
23: *Whole community*, the Greek "brothers" (note *b*) includes both men and women.

The Letter of Paul to the PHILIPPIANS

Philippi was a major city of Macedonia and a Roman colony on the Via Egnatia, the Roman road linking Byzantium in the East to the western coast of Macedonia, from which ships could easily reach Italy. The Christian community in Philippi was the westernmost Pauline church at the time of its founding (Acts 16.11–13). The mutual affection between Paul and the Philippians is evident in the letter and stands in contrast to the problems he had with some other churches.

Paul writes from prison and is uncertain of the outcome for himself (1.12–26). The themes of opposition and the possibility of death are therefore prominent. Yet in the midst of suffering and uncertainty, the theme of joy emerges quite clearly and remarkably (1.4,18,25; 2.2,17–18,28; 4.4,10). The Philippians too are experiencing some kind of opposition (1.29), but Paul's major concern is to bring them together and thus to overcome the threat of internal disharmony. In keeping with that purpose, he uses the powerful hymnic passage that celebrates the self-emptying of Christ even to death, for which God bestowed on him the name of "Lord," the "name above all names" (2.6–11). The hymn was probably composed by a prior author and known both to Paul and the Philippians, perhaps as part of a baptismal liturgy. Here it is the prime example of why they should be willing also to empty themselves of their own opinions. The example of Paul himself follows and supports the argument (3.4–16). Paul offers both Christ and himself as examples of courage and self-surrender in the face of suffering and death. Thus he attempts to turn the Philippians from partisan interest to unity.

Except that Paul was in prison and awaiting trial at the time of writing (1.2–26), it is impossible to speak confidently of the time and place of the writing of this letter. Because of references to the imperial guard or praetorium (1.13) and to the emperor's household (4.22), and also because the situation reflected in the letter bears some resemblance to that described at the very end of the book of Acts, the traditional setting has been during the period of Paul's imprisonment at Rome (about 61–63 CE). The indications are by no means conclusive, however, and more recently it has been thought that the place of composition is perhaps Caesarea before Paul's arrival in Rome (Acts 24–26) or Ephesus at an earlier stage in Paul's career, especially because of the several goings and comings between Paul and Philippi implied in the letter (2.19,25–26; 4.10,18) put against the great distance from Philippi to Rome. The terms referring to the emperor's establishment were used also for provincial government centers and the imperial civil service outside Rome.

The immediate occasion of Paul's writing was the return to Philippi of Epaphroditus (2.25–30), who had been sent by the Philippian church with gifts for Paul (4.18), and who had been seriously ill while staying with him. Paul took this opportunity to thank them for their gifts, and to set their difficulties in a wider framework by describing his and their situation in light of the reality of Christ.

The letter follows the usual pattern of Paul's letters, but some seemingly abrupt changes of topic (especially between 3.1 and 2, and 4.3 and 4), in addition to the fact that an early Christian writer (Polycarp, *Philippians* 2.3), speaks of "letters" of Paul to the Philippians, has led some scholars to conclude that our present Philippians is composed of as many as three letters that Paul wrote to

Philippi. Many others, however, find that Philippians is a coherent whole as it stands. After the greeting (1.1–2) and thanksgiving (1.3–11), Paul lays out the situation (1.12–26) and exhorts the community to unity (1.27–4.3) with many arguments, including proposing Christ (2.5–11), Timothy and Epaphroditus (2.19–30), and himself (3.4–14) as models of self-giving for the good of the whole. He thanks them for their recent gift (4.10–20) and concludes the letter (4.21–23).

1 Paul and Timothy, servants[a] of Christ
Jesus,
To all the saints in Christ Jesus who are
in Philippi, with the bishops[b] and dea-
cons:[c]
2 Grace to you and peace from God our
Father and the Lord Jesus Christ.

3 I thank my God every time I remember
you, 4 constantly praying with joy in every
one of my prayers for all of you, 5 because
of your sharing in the gospel from the first
day until now. 6 I am confident of this, that
the one who began a good work among
you will bring it to completion by the day
of Jesus Christ. 7 It is right for me to think
this way about all of you, because you hold
me in your heart,[d] for all of you share in
God's grace[e] with me, both in my impris-
onment and in the defense and confirma-
tion of the gospel. 8 For God is my witness,
how I long for all of you with the compas-
sion of Christ Jesus. 9 And this is my prayer,
that your love may overflow more and
more with knowledge and full insight 10 to
help you to determine what is best, so that
in the day of Christ you may be pure and
blameless, 11 having produced the harvest
of righteousness that comes through Jesus
Christ for the glory and praise of God.
12 I want you to know, beloved,[f] that
what has happened to me has actually
helped to spread the gospel, 13 so that it has
become known throughout the whole im-
perial guard[g] and to everyone else that my
imprisonment is for Christ; 14 and most of
the brothers and sisters,[f] having been
made confident in the Lord by my impris-
onment, dare to speak the word[h] with
greater boldness and without fear.
15 Some proclaim Christ from envy and
rivalry, but others from goodwill. 16 These
proclaim Christ out of love, knowing that I
have been put here for the defense of the
gospel; 17 the others proclaim Christ out of
selfish ambition, not sincerely but intend-
ing to increase my suffering in my impris-
onment. 18 What does it matter? Just this,
that Christ is proclaimed in every way,
whether out of false motives or true; and in
that I rejoice.
Yes, and I will continue to rejoice, 19 for
I know that through your prayers and the
help of the Spirit of Jesus Christ this will
turn out for my deliverance. 20 It is my ea-
ger expectation and hope that I will not be
put to shame in any way, but that by my
speaking with all boldness, Christ will be
exalted now as always in my body, whether
by life or by death. 21 For to me, living is
Christ and dying is gain. 22 If I am to live in

a Gk *slaves* *b* Or *overseers* *c* Or *overseers and helpers* *d* Or *because I hold you in my heart* *e* Gk *in grace* *f* Gk *brothers* *g* Gk *whole praetorium* *h* Other ancient authorities read *word of God*

1.1–2: Salutation. 1: *Bishops and deacons,* the alternate translation *overseers and helpers* is preferable. These functions are not yet the church offices that they will later become.

1.3–11: Thanksgiving. A common feature of a Pauline letter. **5:** *Sharing,* "koinônia," an important Pauline concept (2.1; 3.10; 4.15). *From the first day,* when Paul first preached at Philippi (Acts 16.12). **6:** *The day of Jesus Christ,* when he will return and the present age will end (2.16; see 1 Cor 1.8; cf. 2 Thess 2.3 and 2 Pet 3.10). **10:** Rom 2.18.

1.12–26: Paul's situation in chains. 13: Paul is confined in some Roman administrative center, where he has had the opportunity to preach the gospel. **15–18:** Not all Christian preachers agreed with Paul or liked him; this is clear in Galatians and 1 and 2 Corinthians (especially 2 Cor 10–13), and here Paul questions their motives. **19:** Quoting Job 13.16. **21–24:** His life is not his own but is given over to Christ,

the flesh, that means fruitful labor for me;
and I do not know which I prefer. 23 I am
hard pressed between the two: my desire is
to depart and be with Christ, for that is far
better; 24 but to remain in the flesh is more
necessary for you. 25 Since I am convinced
of this, I know that I will remain and con-
tinue with all of you for your progress and
joy in faith, 26 so that I may share abun-
dantly in your boasting in Christ Jesus
when I come to you again.

27 Only, live your life in a manner wor-
thy of the gospel of Christ, so that, whether
I come and see you or am absent and hear
about you, I will know that you are stand-
ing firm in one spirit, striving side by side
with one mind for the faith of the gospel,
28 and are in no way intimidated by your
opponents. For them this is evidence of
their destruction, but of your salvation.
And this is God's doing. 29 For he has gra-
ciously granted you the privilege not only
of believing in Christ, but of suffering for
him as well— 30 since you are having the
same struggle that you saw I had and now
hear that I still have.

2 If then there is any encouragement in
Christ, any consolation from love, any
sharing in the Spirit, any compassion and
sympathy, 2 make my joy complete: be of
the same mind, having the same love, being
in full accord and of one mind. 3 Do noth-
ing from selfish ambition or conceit, but in
humility regard others as better than your-
selves. 4 Let each of you look not to your
own interests, but to the interests of others.
5 Let the same mind be in you that was[a] in
Christ Jesus,

6 who, though he was in the form
of God,
did not regard equality with God
as something to be exploited,
7 but emptied himself,
taking the form of a slave,
being born in human likeness.
And being found in human form,
8 he humbled himself
and became obedient to the point
of death—
even death on a cross.

9 Therefore God also highly
exalted him
and gave him the name
that is above every name,
10 so that at the name of Jesus
every knee should bend,
in heaven and on earth and under
the earth,
11 and every tongue should confess
that Jesus Christ is Lord,
to the glory of God the Father.

12 Therefore, my beloved, just as you
have always obeyed me, not only in my
presence, but much more now in my ab-
sence, work out your own salvation with
fear and trembling; 13 for it is God who is at
work in you, enabling you both to will and
to work for his good pleasure.

14 Do all things without murmuring
and arguing, 15 so that you may be blame-
less and innocent, children of God without
blemish in the midst of a crooked and per-
verse generation, in which you shine like
stars in the world. 16 It is by your holding
fast to the word of life that I can boast on
the day of Christ that I did not run in vain

a Or *that you have*

so that he is indifferent to the outcome of life or death; nevertheless, his death would mean loss to his churches.

1.27–4.4: Appeal to unity, to be followed by examples. 2.1–18: First example: self-emptying of Christ. 6: *In the form of God, equality with God,* may refer to divine status, or simply preexistence as a heavenly being (Dan 7.14), or Adam's original immortality (Wis 2.23–24), which Christ renounced by becoming subject to death. **7:** *But emptied himself,* the extreme limit of self-denial. **8:** Mt 26.39; Jn 10.18; Rom 5.19; Heb 5.8; 12.2. **9:** *Exalted,* in raising him from the dead. *The name . . . above every name* is Lord. **10–11:** Cf. Isa 45.23. **12:** *With fear and trembling,* a frequent biblical expression (Ex 15.16; Deut 2.25; Ps 2.11; Isa 19.6; 4 Macc 4.10) that had become a commonplace (1 Cor 2.3; 2 Cor 7.15; Eph 6.5). **15:**

or labor in vain. 17But even if I am being
poured out as a libation over the sacrifice
and the offering of your faith, I am glad
and rejoice with all of you— 18and in the
same way you also must be glad and rejoice
with me.
19 I hope in the Lord Jesus to send Tim-
othy to you soon, so that I may be cheered
by news of you. 20I have no one like him
who will be genuinely concerned for your
welfare. 21All of them are seeking their
own interests, not those of Jesus Christ.
22But Timothy's[a] worth you know, how
like a son with a father he has served with
me in the work of the gospel. 23I hope
therefore to send him as soon as I see how
things go with me; 24and I trust in the Lord
that I will also come soon.
25 Still, I think it necessary to send to
you Epaphroditus—my brother and co-
worker and fellow soldier, your messen-
ger[b] and minister to my need; 26for he has
been longing for[c] all of you, and has been
distressed because you heard that he was
ill. 27He was indeed so ill that he nearly
died. But God had mercy on him, and not
only on him but on me also, so that I would
not have one sorrow after another. 28I am
the more eager to send him, therefore, in
order that you may rejoice at seeing him
again, and that I may be less anxious.
29Welcome him then in the Lord with all
joy, and honor such people, 30because he
came close to death for the work of
Christ,[d] risking his life to make up for
those services that you could not give me.

3 Finally, my brothers and sisters,[e] re-
joice[f] in the Lord.

To write the same things to you is not
troublesome to me, and for you it is a safe-
guard.
2 Beware of the dogs, beware of the evil
workers, beware of those who mutilate the
flesh![g] 3For it is we who are the circum-
cision, who worship in the Spirit of God[h]
and boast in Christ Jesus and have no con-
fidence in the flesh— 4even though I, too,
have reason for confidence in the flesh.
If anyone else has reason to be confident
in the flesh, I have more: 5circumcised on
the eighth day, a member of the people of
Israel, of the tribe of Benjamin, a Hebrew
born of Hebrews; as to the law, a Pharisee;
6as to zeal, a persecutor of the church; as to
righteousness under the law, blameless.
7 Yet whatever gains I had, these I have
come to regard as loss because of Christ.
8More than that, I regard everything as loss
because of the surpassing value of knowing
Christ Jesus my Lord. For his sake I have
suffered the loss of all things, and I regard
them as rubbish, in order that I may gain
Christ 9and be found in him, not having a
righteousness of my own that comes from
the law, but one that comes through faith

a Gk *his* *b* Gk *apostle* *c* Other ancient authorities read *longing to see* *d* Other ancient authorities read *of the Lord* *e* Gk *my brothers* *f* Or *farewell* *g* Gk *the mutilation* *h* Other ancient authorities read *worship God in spirit*

Shine like stars, Dan 12.3. **16:** *Day of Christ,* see 1.6n. **17:** Paul's possible death is compared to a temple sacrifice.

2.19–3.1a: Second example: Timothy and Epaphroditus. 19: *Timothy,* Acts 16.1–3; 1 Cor 16.10–11. **24:** *I trust . . . that I will also come soon,* an argument against Rome as place of writing (see Rom 15.23–25). **25:** *Epaphroditus,* apostle and coworker of Paul who brought the gift from Philippi (4.18), now being sent home.

3.1b–3: A digression about those who preach the necessity of circumcision, requiring Christians to observe the laws of Judaism. They were Paul's bitter opponents elsewhere, especially in Galatia, and are introduced here as a negative example (cf. Gal 5.1–12). **3:** *The flesh,* emphasis on physical rituals.

3.4–4.1: Third example: Paul himself. 5: *Hebrew,* a more preferred self-designation than *Jew,* which was used more often by and for outsiders. *Pharisee,* member of the group most concerned with interpretation of the Jewish law. **6:** *A persecutor,* Acts 9.1–2; 1 Cor 15.9; Gal 1.13. *As to righteousness under the law, blameless,* Paul did not see himself as guilty or incomplete before his encounter with Christ. **8:** *Rubbish,* or excrement. **9:** *The righteousness from God based on faith,* a free gift bestowed by God

in Christ,[a] the righteousness from God
based on faith. 10 I want to know Christ[b]
and the power of his resurrection and the
sharing of his sufferings by becoming like
him in his death, 11 if somehow I may attain
the resurrection from the dead.
12 Not that I have already obtained this
or have already reached the goal;[c] but I
press on to make it my own, because Christ
Jesus has made me his own. 13 Beloved,[d] I
do not consider that I have made it my
own;[e] but this one thing I do: forgetting
what lies behind and straining forward to
what lies ahead, 14 I press on toward the
goal for the prize of the heavenly[f] call of
God in Christ Jesus. 15 Let those of us then
who are mature be of the same mind; and if
you think differently about anything, this
too God will reveal to you. 16 Only let us
hold fast to what we have attained.
17 Brothers and sisters,[d] join in imitat-
ing me, and observe those who live accord-
ing to the example you have in us. 18 For
many live as enemies of the cross of Christ;
I have often told you of them, and now I
tell you even with tears. 19 Their end is de-
struction; their god is the belly; and their
glory is in their shame; their minds are set
on earthly things. 20 But our citizenship[g] is
in heaven, and it is from there that we are
expecting a Savior, the Lord Jesus Christ.
21 He will transform the body of our humil-
iation[h] that it may be conformed to the
body of his glory,[i] by the power that also
enables him to make all things subject to

4 himself. 1 Therefore, my brothers and
sisters,[j] whom I love and long for, my
joy and crown, stand firm in the Lord in
this way, my beloved.
2 I urge Euodia and I urge Syntyche to
be of the same mind in the Lord. 3 Yes, and
I ask you also, my loyal companion,[k] help
these women, for they have struggled be-
side me in the work of the gospel, together
with Clement and the rest of my co-
workers, whose names are in the book of
life.
4 Rejoice[l] in the Lord always; again I
will say, Rejoice.[l] 5 Let your gentleness be
known to everyone. The Lord is near. 6 Do
not worry about anything, but in every-
thing by prayer and supplication with
thanksgiving let your requests be made
known to God. 7 And the peace of God,
which surpasses all understanding, will
guard your hearts and your minds in Christ
Jesus.

8 Finally, beloved,[m] whatever is true,
whatever is honorable, whatever is just,
whatever is pure, whatever is pleasing, what-
ever is commendable, if there is any ex-

a Or *through the faith of Christ* *b* Gk *him*
c Or *have already been made perfect* *d* Gk *Brothers*
e Other ancient authorities read *my own yet*
f Gk *upward* *g* Or *commonwealth* *h* Or *our humble bodies* *i* Or *his glorious body* *j* Gk *my brothers* *k* Or *loyal Syzygus* *l* Or *Farewell*
m Gk *brothers*

through the grace of Christ (Rom 1.16–4.25). **10–11:** Actually to know Christ as risen and living is to have power to suffer like him, and to possess the hope of rising and living with him. **12–14:** *The goal* and *the prize,* allusion to popular sports, the Greek foot races, their finishing post, and the award to the winner (see 2.16; 1 Cor 9.24–27). **18–19:** *Many live as enemies of the cross of Christ,* presumably professing Christians who cannot accept Paul's cross theology. **20:** *Our citizenship,* our ultimate political loyalty and real homeland, contrasting with the status of most of the Philippians as Roman citizens. **21:** Rom 8.23; 1 Cor 15.47–57; 2 Cor 5.1–5; Col 3.1–4. **1:** 1 Thess 2.19–20. A *crown* was often awarded to the winner of a race (see 3.12–14n.).

4.2–9: Heart of the problem. 2: *Euodia . . . Syntyche,* two women leaders in the Philippian church, most likely heads of house-churches and therefore among the overseers and helpers (1.1) whose disagreement has had a disastrous effect on the church; the factions into which they have broken are the major concern of the letter. **3:** *My loyal companion,* an unknown but influential figure who could serve as mediator between the two. Less likely, the Greek word for *companion* may be understood as a proper name, *Syzygus. Book of life,* a book kept by God containing names of those to be saved (Ps 69.28; Dan 12.1; Lk 10.20; Rev 3.5; etc.).

cellence and if there is anything worthy of
praise, think about[a] these things. 9 Keep
on doing the things that you have learned
and received and heard and seen in me, and
the God of peace will be with you.

10 I rejoice[b] in the Lord greatly that
now at last you have revived your concern
for me; indeed, you were concerned for me,
but had no opportunity to show it.[c] 11 Not
that I am referring to being in need; for I
have learned to be content with whatever I
have. 12 I know what it is to have little, and
I know what it is to have plenty. In any and
all circumstances I have learned the secret
of being well-fed and of going hungry, of
having plenty and of being in need. 13 I can
do all things through him who strengthens
me. 14 In any case, it was kind of you to
share my distress.

15 You Philippians indeed know that in
the early days of the gospel, when I left
Macedonia, no church shared with me in
the matter of giving and receiving, except
you alone. 16 For even when I was in Thes-
salonica, you sent me help for my needs
more than once. 17 Not that I seek the gift,
but I seek the profit that accumulates to
your account. 18 I have been paid in full and
have more than enough; I am fully satisfied,
now that I have received from Epaphrodi-
tus the gifts you sent, a fragrant offering, a
sacrifice acceptable and pleasing to God.
19 And my God will fully satisfy every need
of yours according to his riches in glory in
Christ Jesus. 20 To our God and Father be
glory forever and ever. Amen.

21 Greet every saint in Christ Jesus. The
friends[d] who are with me greet you. 22 All
the saints greet you, especially those of the
emperor's household.

23 The grace of the Lord Jesus Christ be
with your spirit.[e]

a Gk *take account of* b Gk *I rejoiced* c Gk lacks *to show it* d Gk *brothers* e Other ancient authorities add *Amen*

4.10–20: Acknowledgment of their gifts. 11: *Content,* Paul here expresses the Stoic ideal of indifference, but with new motivation because of Christ. **15–16:** *Macedonia, Thessalonica,* according to Acts 17.1, Paul had gone to Thessalonica immediately after his stay in Philippi. **15,17,18:** *Giving and receiving, profit . . . account, paid in full,* a series of business terms used metaphorically here and in other contexts of friendship. **18:** *Fragrant offering,* Gen 8.21; Ex 29.18; Ezek 20.41.

4.21–23: Conclusion. 22: *The emperor's household,* members of the imperial civil service who are believers where Paul is confined.

The Letter of Paul to the COLOSSIANS

The church in Colossae, a town on the Lycus river in the Roman province of Asia, was founded by a Colossian associate of Paul's named Epaphras (1.7–8; 4.12–13). The letter begins with a highly complimentary description of the Colossians' lives, but unnamed teachers, who observe Jewish rituals and pursue mystical experiences through ascetic practices (2.8–23), pose a threat to their faith. Unfortunately we possess no independent description of these teachings, and the polemical tone of this letter (for instance, "empty deceit, according to human tradition," 2.8) makes their precise identification difficult. The practices advocated are best understood as a form of Jewish apocalyptic mysticism, although others have preferred to see a synthesis of Judaism with proto-Gnostic thought, local Phrygian religious practices, or Hellenistic philosophy. The fact that these Jewish practices, which did not focus on Christ, were attractive to Christians reflects the continuing close connection of the synagogue and the church, as well as a typical first-century Christian ambivalence toward Judaism: A Jewish eschatological outlook and morality are central to the author's Christian vision, although many Jewish practices are simultaneously rejected as incompatible with Christ.

Colossians follows the basic structure of a Pauline letter, beginning with a salutation (1.1–2) and an introductory thanksgiving (1.3–8) and prayer (1.9–14), and ending with greetings and instructions (4.7–18). The body of the letter includes both a theological argument (2.6–23) and ethical instructions (3.1–4.6). The basis of the theological argument is laid in 1.12–2.5. In the elevated words of an early Christian hymn, Christ is praised as the supreme power over the cosmos and the church (1.15–20). Although demonic forces enslaved humanity in the past, Christians were freed from their influence, forgiven through Christ's death, and made full citizens of the kingdom of Christ, to whom they now owe complete allegiance and obedience (1.12–14, 21–23). Also emphasized is Christ's identity as the perfect revelation of God (1.19; 2.9–10) and as the singular source of wisdom about how to live rightly (1.9–10; 2.2–3). The main theological argument focuses on the significance of the cross and the change in believers' destiny achieved by it (2.9–15); the recurring contrasts of death and life (2.12–13, 20; 3.1–5), old and new (3.9–10), and past and present (1.12–14, 21–23) emphasize the fundamental psychological and moral reorientation demanded of the believer. Because Jewish rituals and mystical experiences of angelic worship do not foster allegiance to Christ and belong to the old order, they must be rejected as distractions from Christ's lordship and as threats to the church. The members of a true Christian community, rejecting their previous immoral lifestyle (3.5–11) and reorienting their entire lives around Christ as Lord (3.1–4), are to live in harmony with each other as they worship and give thanks to God and Christ (3.12–17). The Christian household, however, is only a mildly Christianized version of an ancient patriarchal family (3.18–4.1) rather than a complete renewal of family relationships based on the equality of all in the new community.

There are many similarities to the undisputed letters of Paul in the structure, theology, and even language of Colossians. However, Colossians lacks certain central Pauline terms, utilizes new theological vocabulary, and is written in a significantly different, liturgical style. Two theological contrasts stand out: first, the vision of believers' present lives as nearly completely transformed by Christ's death and resurrection, instead of Paul's usual tension between the only partly fulfilled present and the future resurrection and full enjoyment of Christ's benefits; second, the use of household rules, which is more characteristic of other post-Pauline literature (e.g., Ephesians and the Pastoral letters) than of Paul's own ethical instructions. The combined force of these differences has led some to conclude that Colossians was written in Paul's name by one of his disciples—either during Paul's own lifetime or a decade or two after his death—in order to lend authority to this application of Paul's thought to a new situation. Others, noting Colossians' close similarities to Philemon, think the letter was written by Paul himself while imprisoned (4.3,10,18) at Rome near the end of his life, and attribute the contrasts to developments in Paul's thinking and the particular situation addressed in the letter. Colossians also has significant similarities to Ephesians and was probably used as a model by the author of that letter (see the Introduction to Ephesians).

1 Paul, an apostle of Christ Jesus by the
will of God, and Timothy our brother,
2 To the saints and faithful brothers and
sisters[a] in Christ in Colossae:
Grace to you and peace from God our
Father.

3 In our prayers for you we always
thank God, the Father of our Lord Jesus
Christ, 4 for we have heard of your faith in
Christ Jesus and of the love that you have
for all the saints, 5 because of the hope laid
up for you in heaven. You have heard of
this hope before in the word of the truth,
the gospel 6 that has come to you. Just as it
is bearing fruit and growing in the whole
world, so it has been bearing fruit among
yourselves from the day you heard it and
truly comprehended the grace of God.
7 This you learned from Epaphras, our beloved
fellow servant.[b] He is a faithful minister
of Christ on your[c] behalf, 8 and he
has made known to us your love in the
Spirit.
9 For this reason, since the day we heard
it, we have not ceased praying for you and
asking that you may be filled with the
knowledge of God's[d] will in all spiritual
wisdom and understanding, 10 so that you
may lead lives worthy of the Lord, fully
pleasing to him, as you bear fruit in every
good work and as you grow in the knowledge
of God. 11 May you be made strong
with all the strength that comes from his
glorious power, and may you be prepared
to endure everything with patience, while
joyfully 12 giving thanks to the Father, who
has enabled[e] you[f] to share in the inheritance
of the saints in the light. 13 He has
rescued us from the power of darkness and
transferred us into the kingdom of his beloved
Son, 14 in whom we have redemption,
the forgiveness of sins.[g]
15 He is the image of the invisible God,
the firstborn of all creation; 16 for in[h] him

a Gk *brothers* *b* Gk *slave* *c* Other ancient authorities read *our* *d* Gk *his* *e* Other ancient authorities read *called* *f* Other ancient authorities read *us* *g* Other ancient authorities add *through his blood* *h* Or *by*

1.1–2: Salutation. 1: *Timothy,* Paul's fellow missionary and emissary (Philem 1; 2 Cor 1.1; Phil 1.1; 2.19–24). **2:** *Brothers and sisters,* see note *a* and Eph 6.23n. *Grace . . . peace,* see Eph 1.2n.

1.3–8: Thanksgiving for Colossians' obedience. 3–5: *Faith, love,* and *hope,* a summary of Christian virtues (1 Cor 13.13; 1 Thess 5.8). **6:** *The whole world,* hyperbole reflecting the numerous Christian communities in cities of the Roman empire; see also 1.23. **7:** *Epaphras,* founder of the church in Colossae, whose ministry the author endorses (4.12–13; Philem 23).

1.9–14: Prayer for Colossians' growth in knowledge (v. 9), moral maturity (v. 10), and endurance (v. 11). **12–14:** Perhaps a fragment of a baptismal hymn. **12–13:** *Light/darkness,* apocalyptic imagery for the domains of God and Christ and of malevolent spiritual beings (see 1.16n.; 1 Thess 5.5); believers have been rescued from the latter kingdom and transferred to the former. **14:** Release from slavery to the

all things in heaven and on earth were cre-
ated, things visible and invisible, whether
thrones or dominions or rulers or powers—
all things have been created through him
and for him. 17He himself is before all
things, and in[a] him all things hold togeth-
er. 18He is the head of the body, the
church; he is the beginning, the firstborn
from the dead, so that he might come to
have first place in everything. 19For in him
all the fullness of God was pleased to dwell,
20and through him God was pleased to
reconcile to himself all things, whether on
earth or in heaven, by making peace
through the blood of his cross.

21 And you who were once estranged
and hostile in mind, doing evil deeds, 22he
has now reconciled[b] in his fleshly body[c]
through death, so as to present you holy
and blameless and irreproachable before
him— 23provided that you continue se-
curely established and steadfast in the faith,
without shifting from the hope promised by
the gospel that you heard, which has been
proclaimed to every creature under heaven.
I, Paul, became a servant of this gospel.

24 I am now rejoicing in my sufferings
for your sake, and in my flesh I am com-
pleting what is lacking in Christ's afflic-
tions for the sake of his body, that is, the
church. 25I became its servant according to
God's commission that was given to me for
you, to make the word of God fully known,
26the mystery that has been hidden
throughout the ages and generations but
has now been revealed to his saints. 27To
them God chose to make known how great
among the Gentiles are the riches of the
glory of this mystery, which is Christ in
you, the hope of glory. 28It is he whom we
proclaim, warning everyone and teaching
everyone in all wisdom, so that we may
present everyone mature in Christ. 29For
this I toil and struggle with all the energy
that he powerfully inspires within me.

2 For I want you to know how much I am
struggling for you, and for those in La-
odicea, and for all who have not seen me
face to face. 2I want their hearts to be en-
couraged and united in love, so that they
may have all the riches of assured under-
standing and have the knowledge of God's
mystery, that is, Christ himself,[d] 3in
whom are hidden all the treasures of wis-
dom and knowledge. 4I am saying this so
that no one may deceive you with plausible

a Or *by* *b* Other ancient authorities read *you have now been reconciled* *c* Gk *in the body of his flesh* *d* Other ancient authorities read *of the mystery of God, both of the Father and of Christ*

demonic powers (*redemption*) comes from the forgiveness and reconciliation available through Christ's death (vv. 20,22).

1.15–20: The supremacy of Christ over the cosmos (vv. 15–17) and the church (vv. 18–20), taken from a hymn based on the figure of Wisdom (Prov 8; Sir 24; Wis 6–9; see also Jn 1.1–18; Phil 2.6–11). **15:** *Image,* the perfect, visible manifestation of God. *Firstborn* expresses priority and supremacy over all creation (v. 17). **16:** *Thrones . . . powers,* spiritual beings, probably hostile (1.13; 2.15; Eph 6.12). **18:** *Head,* ruling authority or originator; see Eph 1.22; 5.23. *The body, the church,* see Rom 12.4–5; 1 Cor 12.27. *Firstborn from the dead,* Christ is preeminent among the children of God (Rom 8.29; Rev 1.5), and his resurrection is the prelude to the final resurrection (1 Cor 15.23; Acts 26.23). **19:** *The fullness of God,* the power and presence of God (2.9–10). **20:** *Reconcile/making peace,* the enslavement of humanity to demonic powers is presupposed here (1.13; 2.15).

1.21–23: Assurance and warning. 22: *To present you . . . before him,* reconciliation culminates in Christ's approval at the eschatological judgment (v. 28). **23:** Continued allegiance to Christ alone, however, is necessary for eschatological salvation.

1.24–2.5: Paul's mission and pastoral commitment. 24: *Sufferings,* imprisonment (4.3,10,18) and hardships experienced while preaching the gospel (2 Cor 4.7–12; 11.23–28). *Completing . . . afflictions,* not a denigration of Christ's death, but a reflection of the apocalyptic belief that God's people must suffer before the culmination of history (1 Cor 4.9; Rev 6.9–11). **26–27:** *Mystery,* the previously hidden plan of God; here, the gospel proclaimed to Gentiles (2.2; 4.3; Rom 16.25–26; cf. Eph 1.10; 3.2–6). **2.1:** *Laodicea,* see 4.13n.

arguments. 5 For though I am absent in
body, yet I am with you in spirit, and I
rejoice to see your morale and the firmness
of your faith in Christ.
6 As you therefore have received Christ
Jesus the Lord, continue to live your lives[a]
in him, 7 rooted and built up in him and
established in the faith, just as you were
taught, abounding in thanksgiving.

8 See to it that no one takes you captive
through philosophy and empty deceit, ac-
cording to human tradition, according to
the elemental spirits of the universe,[b] and
not according to Christ. 9 For in him the
whole fullness of deity dwells bodily, 10 and
you have come to fullness in him, who is
the head of every ruler and authority. 11 In
him also you were circumcised with a spiri-
tual circumcision,[c] by putting off the body
of the flesh in the circumcision of Christ;
12 when you were buried with him in bap-
tism, you were also raised with him
through faith in the power of God, who
raised him from the dead. 13 And when you
were dead in trespasses and the uncircumci-
sion of your flesh, God[d] made you[e] alive
together with him, when he forgave us all
our trespasses, 14 erasing the record that
stood against us with its legal demands. He
set this aside, nailing it to the cross. 15 He
disarmed[f] the rulers and authorities and
made a public example of them, triumph-
ing over them in it.

16 Therefore do not let anyone con-
demn you in matters of food and drink or
of observing festivals, new moons, or sab-
baths. 17 These are only a shadow of what
is to come, but the substance belongs to
Christ. 18 Do not let anyone disqualify you,
insisting on self-abasement and worship of
angels, dwelling[g] on visions,[h] puffed up
without cause by a human way of think-
ing,[i] 19 and not holding fast to the head,
from whom the whole body, nourished and
held together by its ligaments and sinews,
grows with a growth that is from God.
20 If with Christ you died to the elemen-
tal spirits of the universe,[b] why do you live
as if you still belonged to the world? Why
do you submit to regulations, 21 "Do not
handle, Do not taste, Do not touch"? 22 All
these regulations refer to things that perish
with use; they are simply human com-
mands and teachings. 23 These have indeed
an appearance of wisdom in promoting
self-imposed piety, humility, and severe
treatment of the body, but they are of no
value in checking self-indulgence.[j]

a Gk *to walk* *b* Or *the rudiments of the world*
c Gk *a circumcision made without hands* *d* Gk *he*
e Other ancient authorities read *made us*; others, *made*
f Or *divested himself of* *g* Other ancient authorities
read *not dwelling* *h* Meaning of Gk uncertain
i Gk *by the mind of his flesh* *j* Or *are of no value,*
serving only to indulge the flesh

2.6–15: Instruction in Christ and the cross. 6–7: Thematic statement of the letter (see Introduction; 1.21–23; 3.1–4). **6:** *Received,* a technical term for the reception of oral tradition; here, that Jesus is Lord (Rom 10.9). **8:** *Philosophy* includes ethical and religious teachings. *Human tradition,* see 2.6n. *Elemental spirits,* spiritual entities or perhaps the four primal elements; they are associated with the Jewish law (Gal 4.1–5,9–10). **9:** See 1.19n. **11:** *Circumcision* marked membership in Israel; *spiritual circumcision* refers to baptism (v. 12). *By putting off . . . flesh,* a graphic description of Christ's death. **14:** *The record* of transgressions, using the metaphor of debt. **15:** *Rulers and authorities,* see 1.16n. *Made a public example,* as defeated enemies were displayed in a victorious general's parade.

2.16–23: Warnings against destructive religious practices. 16: *Matters of food and drink,* the observance of Jewish dietary laws. *Festivals, new moons, sabbaths,* summary of the Jewish religious calendar (e.g., 2 Chr 8.13; Neh 10.33). *New moons* mark the beginning of each lunar month. **17:** *Shadow/substance,* Platonic language indicating the superiority of Christ. **18:** *Insisting on . . . visions,* through rigorous asceticism (*self-abasement*) achieving a mystical ascent to heaven (*dwelling on visions*) and participating in the angelic worship of God. **19:** The church's (the *body*'s) growth depends solely upon adherence to Christ (*the head*); see 1.18n. **20:** *Died to the elemental spirits,* no longer under their authority (v. 8). **21:** Jewish purity regulations. **22:** See Mk 7.7,19.

3 So if you have been raised with Christ,
seek the things that are above, where
Christ is, seated at the right hand of God.
2 Set your minds on things that are above,
not on things that are on earth, 3 for you
have died, and your life is hidden with
Christ in God. 4 When Christ who is your[a]
life is revealed, then you also will be re-
vealed with him in glory.
5 Put to death, therefore, whatever in
you is earthly: fornication, impurity, pas-
sion, evil desire, and greed (which is idola-
try). 6 On account of these the wrath of
God is coming on those who are disobedi-
ent.[b] 7 These are the ways you also once
followed, when you were living that life.[c]
8 But now you must get rid of all such
things—anger, wrath, malice, slander, and
abusive[d] language from your mouth. 9 Do
not lie to one another, seeing that you have
stripped off the old self with its practices
10 and have clothed yourselves with the new
self, which is being renewed in knowledge
according to the image of its creator. 11 In
that renewal[e] there is no longer Greek and
Jew, circumcised and uncircumcised, bar-
barian, Scythian, slave and free; but Christ
is all and in all!
12 As God's chosen ones, holy and be-
loved, clothe yourselves with compassion,
kindness, humility, meekness, and patience.
13 Bear with one another and, if anyone has
a complaint against another, forgive each
other; just as the Lord[f] has forgiven you,
so you also must forgive. 14 Above all,
clothe yourselves with love, which binds
everything together in perfect harmony.
15 And let the peace of Christ rule in your
hearts, to which indeed you were called in
the one body. And be thankful. 16 Let the
word of Christ[g] dwell in you richly; teach
and admonish one another in all wisdom;
and with gratitude in your hearts sing
psalms, hymns, and spiritual songs to
God.[h] 17 And whatever you do, in word or
deed, do everything in the name of the Lord
Jesus, giving thanks to God the Father
through him.
18 Wives, be subject to your husbands,
as is fitting in the Lord. 19 Husbands, love
your wives and never treat them harshly.
20 Children, obey your parents in every-
thing, for this is your acceptable duty in the
Lord. 21 Fathers, do not provoke your chil-
dren, or they may lose heart. 22 Slaves, obey
your earthly masters[i] in everything, not
only while being watched and in order to
please them, but wholeheartedly, fearing

a Other authorities read *our* *b* Other ancient authorities lack *on those who are disobedient* (Gk *the children of disobedience*) *c* Or *living among such people* *d* Or *filthy* *e* Gk *its creator,* [11]*where*
f Other ancient authorities read *just as Christ*
g Other ancient authorities read *of God,* or *of the Lord* *h* Other ancient authorities read *to the Lord*
i In Greek the same word is used for *master* and *Lord*

3.1–4.6: Ethical implications.

3.1–4: Maintain a heavenly perspective. 1: *Raised,* 2.12. *Seated,* see Eph 1.20n. **1–2:** *Set your minds . . . above,* orient one's life around the heavenly reality of Christ's exaltation and authority. **3:** *Died,* see 2.20n. **3–4:** The new life is *hidden* from outsiders, but *will be revealed* to all at the eschatological judgment (1 Cor 2.6–16).

3.5–11: Reject sins of previous life. 5: *Put to death,* vehemently refuse to engage in. *Fornication . . . greed,* see Eph 4.19n. *Idolatry,* often linked with sexual sins in Jewish thought (Hos 4.12–19; Rom 1.23–27; 1 Cor 10.7–8). **6:** *Wrath,* God's eschatological judgment of sin (v. 4). **9–10:** See vv. 12,14; 2.11; Eph 4.22–24n. Christ, the *image* of God (1.15), is the model for *renewed* human beings (cf. Gen 1.26–27). **11:** In the church human distinctions and privileges of ethnicity and socioeconomic status are meaningless; cf. the abrogation of a gender hierarchy in Gal 3.28. *Greek,* i.e., Gentile.

3.12–17: Adopt virtues of the new life. A proper attitude toward oneself, genuine concern for others (v. 12), gracious forgiveness (v. 13; see Eph 4.32), and sacrificial love (v. 14) produce a harmonious and unified community (v. 15) that can worship God rightly (vv. 16–17).

3.18–4.1: Rules for household relationships. This passage idealizes the first-century patriarchal family as appropriate for a community dedicated to Christ as Lord; cf. the more extensive theological justification in Eph 5.22–6.9. **18–19:** *Wives* and *husbands. Never treat them harshly,* alternatively,

the Lord.[a] 23 Whatever your task, put
yourselves into it, as done for the Lord and
not for your masters,[b] 24 since you know
that from the Lord you will receive the in-
heritance as your reward; you serve[c] the
Lord Christ. 25 For the wrongdoer will be
paid back for whatever wrong has been
4 done, and there is no partiality. 1 Mas-
ters, treat your slaves justly and fairly,
for you know that you also have a Master
in heaven.

2 Devote yourselves to prayer, keeping
alert in it with thanksgiving. 3 At the same
time pray for us as well that God will open
to us a door for the word, that we may
declare the mystery of Christ, for which I
am in prison, 4 so that I may reveal it clear-
ly, as I should.

5 Conduct yourselves wisely toward
outsiders, making the most of the time.[d]
6 Let your speech always be gracious, sea-
soned with salt, so that you may know how
you ought to answer everyone.

7 Tychicus will tell you all the news
about me; he is a beloved brother, a faithful
minister, and a fellow servant[e] in the Lord.
8 I have sent him to you for this very pur-
pose, so that you may know how we are[f]
and that he may encourage your hearts; 9 he
is coming with Onesimus, the faithful and
beloved brother, who is one of you. They
will tell you about everything here.

10 Aristarchus my fellow prisoner greets
you, as does Mark the cousin of Barnabas,
concerning whom you have received in-
structions—if he comes to you, welcome
him. 11 And Jesus who is called Justus greets
you. These are the only ones of the circum-
cision among my co-workers for the king-
dom of God, and they have been a comfort
to me. 12 Epaphras, who is one of you, a
servant[e] of Christ Jesus, greets you. He is
always wrestling in his prayers on your be-
half, so that you may stand mature and
fully assured in everything that God wills.
13 For I testify for him that he has worked
hard for you and for those in Laodicea and
in Hierapolis. 14 Luke, the beloved physi-
cian, and Demas greet you. 15 Give my
greetings to the brothers and sisters[g] in La-
odicea, and to Nympha and the church in
her house. 16 And when this letter has been
read among you, have it read also in the
church of the Laodiceans; and see that you
read also the letter from Laodicea. 17 And
say to Archippus, "See that you complete
the task that you have received in the
Lord."

18 I, Paul, write this greeting with my
own hand. Remember my chains. Grace be
with you.[h]

a In Greek the same word is used for *master* and *Lord*
b Gk *not for men* *c* Or *you are slaves of*, or *be slaves of* *d* Or *opportunity* *e* Gk *slave* *f* Other authorities read *that I may know how you are*
g Gk *brothers* *h* Other ancient authorities add *Amen*

"do not be embittered against them." **20–21:** Relations between *children* and *fathers*. **3.22–4.1:** *Slaves* and *masters*. The impartial judgment of God should motivate both slaves and masters (4.1).

4.2–6: Final admonitions. 5–6: Conversation with non-Christians should be pleasant (*gracious*), interesting, and appropriate (*seasoned with salt*).

4.7–18: Final greetings and instructions. 7: *Tychicus*, Paul's associate (Acts 20.4; 2 Tim 4.12), commended like Epaphras (cf. 1.7). **9:** *Onesimus*, Philem 10–21. **10:** *Aristarchus*, Acts 20.4; 27.2; Philem 24. *Welcome him*, cf. Paul's earlier conflict with Mark (Acts 13.13; 15.37–39). **11:** *The circumcision*, the Jews. **12:** *Epaphras*, see 1.7n. **13:** *Laodicea, Hierapolis*, cities located 16 and 24 km (10 and 15 mi), respectively, northwest of Colossae. **14:** *Luke*, 2 Tim 4.11; Philem 24. Traditionally identified as the author of the Gospel of Luke and Acts (see Acts 16.10–17, etc.). *Demas*, 2 Tim 4.10; Philem 24. **15:** *Brothers and sisters*, see note *g* and Eph 6.23n. *Nympha*, not mentioned elsewhere, was probably an active leader of the church that met in her home (see Philem 1–2). **16:** *The letter from Laodicea*, a Pauline letter no longer extant, although some identify it with Ephesians. **17:** *Archippus*, Philem 2. **18:** A final word in the author's handwriting to authenticate the letter (cf. 1 Cor 16.21; Gal 6.11); the rest of the letter would have been dictated to a secretary (see Rom 16.22).

The First Letter of Paul to the THESSALONIANS

First Thessalonians is a friendly, exhortative letter of encouragement. Paul extends affectionate praise for the audience's steadfast hope (1.3) and consistent behavior (4.1,9). A stirring recounting of his separation from the community (2.17–3.7) reveals the community's affection for him. Allusions to family life such as "father" (1.1,3; 2.11; 3.11,13), "sons" (1.10; 5.5), and "brothers" (14 instances) also convey a friendly tone.

Yet, the numerous imperatives in chs 4 and 5 convey an exhortative tone as well. This tone also pervades the earlier chapters, for (as with other ancient letters of exhortation) the letter highlights the imitation of models (1.6; 2.14) and the remembrance of a teacher's previous words or deed (2.1–12; 3.4). With the friendly and exhortative tones, moreover, the letter encourages a community that is facing social pressures and perhaps outright persecution to maintain its apocalyptic vigilance.

Thessalonica, the capital of the Roman province of Macedonia, was strategically located on both sea and land routes. First Thessalonians, addressed to the congregation there, is Paul's earliest letter. After being mistreated at Phillipi (2.2; Acts 16.19–40), Paul went to Thessalonica where he established this congregation. After a painful separation (2.17) and the failure of repeated efforts to return (2.18), Paul dispatched Timothy to Thessalonica from Athens (3.1) while he later moved on to Corinth (Acts 18.1–17). From there, perhaps around 50 CE, he wrote this letter.

Commencing with a typical though simple Pauline opening (1.1) and ending with a typical Pauline closing (5.23–28), the letter offers repeated encouragement toward steadfastness. A thanksgiving acknowledges the congregation's growth, the gospel's power, and Paul's persistence in prayer (1.2–5). Next, Paul recalls the community's consistency in the reception, proclamation, and early work of the gospel despite ongoing opposition (1.6–2.16). Although 2.14–16 seems anti-Jewish and thus not characteristic of Paul, there is no evidence for a later addition here. Readers should remember that the polemics are directed to Jewish persecutors of the Judean churches, not all Jews. Such polemics, moreover, resonate with other "intra-Jewish" debates of Paul's day (see, for instance, Josephus *Antiquities,* 1.15.91; Philo *Cherubim,* 17). Then, when he recounts the deep anguish of the separation (2.17–3.13), Paul notes Timothy's mediation of comfort and his own prayer for a reunion with the congregation. A description of the sanctified life follows along with commendations toward apocalyptic vigilance despite the deaths of loved ones and the temptations of false forms of security (4.1–5.22).

1 Paul, Silvanus, and Timothy,
To the church of the Thessalonians in
God the Father and the Lord Jesus Christ:
Grace to you and peace.

2 We always give thanks to God for all
of you and mention you in our prayers,
constantly 3 remembering before our God
and Father your work of faith and labor of
love and steadfastness of hope in our Lord
Jesus Christ. 4 For we know, brothers and
sisters[a] beloved by God, that he has cho-
sen you, 5 because our message of the gos-
pel came to you not in word only, but also
in power and in the Holy Spirit and with
full conviction; just as you know what kind
of persons we proved to be among you for
your sake. 6 And you became imitators of
us and of the Lord, for in spite of persecu-
tion you received the word with joy in-
spired by the Holy Spirit, 7 so that you be-
came an example to all the believers in
Macedonia and in Achaia. 8 For the word
of the Lord has sounded forth from you not
only in Macedonia and Achaia, but in every
place your faith in God has become known,
so that we have no need to speak about it.
9 For the people of those regions[b] report
about us what kind of welcome we had
among you, and how you turned to God
from idols, to serve a living and true God,
10 and to wait for his Son from heaven,
whom he raised from the dead—Jesus, who
rescues us from the wrath that is coming.

2 You yourselves know, brothers and sis-
ters,[a] that our coming to you was not
in vain, 2 but though we had already suf-
fered and been shamefully mistreated at
Philippi, as you know, we had courage in
our God to declare to you the gospel of
God in spite of great opposition. 3 For our
appeal does not spring from deceit or im-
pure motives or trickery, 4 but just as we
have been approved by God to be entrusted
with the message of the gospel, even so we
speak, not to please mortals, but to please
God who tests our hearts. 5 As you know
and as God is our witness, we never came
with words of flattery or with a pretext for
greed; 6 nor did we seek praise from mor-
tals, whether from you or from others,
7 though we might have made demands as

a Gk *brothers* *b* Gk *For they*

1.1: Salutation. The simple epistolary opening here lacks Paul's later elaborations of the letter-sender and letter-recipient (cf. Phil 1.1–2). *Silvanus* is the Latin form of Silas, one of Paul's companions (Acts 15.22,40; 17.4). *Timothy,* one of Paul's emissaries, was also a traveling companion (Rom 16.21; 1 Cor 4.17; 16.10; Phil 2.19). *Church,* a term for the citizen assembly. *In God . . . and the Lord* indicates God's selection of the congregation as a holy (set apart) community. *Grace . . . and peace,* (see 2 Bar 78.2) is a variation of the Jewish greeting "mercy and peace."

1.2–5: Thanksgiving. Paul thanks God for evidence of the gospel's benefits in the congregation's life. **3:** *Faith . . . love . . . hope* is a typical Pauline triad (5.8; Rom 5.1–5; 1 Cor 13.13; Gal 5.5–6). **4:** *Beloved by God* (Deut 33.12) and chosen (Deut 4.37; 7.6–8; 10.14–15; 14.2) describe God's call of the congregation with expressions used in the Hebrew Bible to portray the special call of Israel. **5:** *Our . . . gospel* is not just words, but the saving power of God.

1.6–2.16: The gospel's effectiveness. An essential part of the gospel's effectiveness is the consistent character it creates in its recipients despite opposition. **6:** Paul and Silvanus's converts were subjected to much "persecution" (3.3,4,7), a term Paul uses for the apocalyptic horrors preceding Christ's end-time appearance, the "parousia." **7–8:** An indication of the gospel's effectiveness was its continuous spreading, as suggested by the Greek (perfect) tense of *sounded forth. Macedonia,* of which Thessolonica was the capital, and *Achaia* (Greece) were two of the Roman provinces of Paul's ministry. **9:** *Turned to God from idols* indicates (cf. Acts 17.1–4) the strictly Gentile background of Paul's Thessalonian converts (2.14). **10:** *Wrath* of God in judgment at the end-time. **2.1–12:** This self-description distances Paul from charlatans. It reveals the *opposition* Paul faced (2.2), as if Paul were in an athletic contest (cf. "agon" in Epictetus's *Dissertationes,* 1.24.1–2; 4 Macc 16.16); the continuous involvement of God *who tests our hearts* (Gal 5.16; Rom 13.13); and Paul's ministerial goal to help the congregation *lead a life worthy of God* (Gal 5.16; Rom 13.13). **2.13–16:** Another thanksgiving demonstrates Paul's persistent practice of

apostles of Christ. But we were gentle[a]
among you, like a nurse tenderly caring for
her own children. 8 So deeply do we care for
you that we are determined to share with
you not only the gospel of God but also our
own selves, because you have become very
dear to us.
9 You remember our labor and toil,
brothers and sisters;[b] we worked night and
day, so that we might not burden any of
you while we proclaimed to you the gospel
of God. 10 You are witnesses, and God also,
how pure, upright, and blameless our con-
duct was toward you believers. 11 As you
know, we dealt with each one of you like a
father with his children, 12 urging and en-
couraging you and pleading that you lead a
life worthy of God, who calls you into his
own kingdom and glory.
13 We also constantly give thanks to
God for this, that when you received the
word of God that you heard from us, you
accepted it not as a human word but as
what it really is, God's word, which is also
at work in you believers. 14 For you, broth-
ers and sisters,[b] became imitators of the
churches of God in Christ Jesus that are
in Judea, for you suffered the same things
from your own compatriots as they did
from the Jews, 15 who killed both the Lord
Jesus and the prophets,[c] and drove us out;
they displease God and oppose everyone
16 by hindering us from speaking to the
Gentiles so that they may be saved. Thus
they have constantly been filling up the
measure of their sins; but God's wrath has
overtaken them at last.[d]
17 As for us, brothers and sisters,[b]
when, for a short time, we were made or-
phans by being separated from you—in
person, not in heart—we longed with great
eagerness to see you face to face. 18 For we
wanted to come to you—certainly I, Paul,
wanted to again and again—but Satan
blocked our way. 19 For what is our hope or
joy or crown of boasting before our Lord
Jesus at his coming? Is it not you? 20 Yes,
you are our glory and joy!
3 Therefore when we could bear it no
longer, we decided to be left alone in
Athens; 2 and we sent Timothy, our brother
and co-worker for God in proclaiming[e]
the gospel of Christ, to strengthen and en-
courage you for the sake of your faith, 3 so
that no one would be shaken by these per-
secutions. Indeed, you yourselves know
that this is what we are destined for. 4 In
fact, when we were with you, we told you
beforehand that we were to suffer persecu-
tion; so it turned out, as you know. 5 For
this reason, when I could bear it no longer,
I sent to find out about your faith; I was
afraid that somehow the tempter had
tempted you and that our labor had been in
vain.
6 But Timothy has just now come to us
from you, and has brought us the good
news of your faith and love. He has told us
also that you always remember us kindly
and long to see us—just as we long to see
you. 7 For this reason, brothers and sis-
ters,[b] during all our distress and persecu-
tion we have been encouraged about you
through your faith. 8 For we now live, if
you continue to stand firm in the Lord.
9 How can we thank God enough for you in
return for all the joy that we feel before our
God because of you? 10 Night and day we

a Other ancient authorities read *infants*
b Gk *brothers* c Other ancient authorities read *their own prophets* d Or *completely* or *forever*
e Gk lacks *proclaiming*

giving thanks, a practice he will later commend (5.18; cf. 3.9). **2.16:** Perhaps the *wrath* of God is not an explicit occurrence (such as the expulsion of the Jews in 49 CE from Rome or the massacre of Jews in the Temple court in 49 CE [see Josephus, *War,* 2.12.1]), but simply God's justice (as in 1.10) in preventing opponents anywhere from destroying God's churches.

2.17–3.13: Separation and reunion. A moving account of the separation and its aftermath elucidates the congregation's survival and its affection for Paul. **2.18:** Though the separation's immediate cause is unstated, Paul recognizes in it the work of *Satan,* a deceiver (2 Cor 11.14), tempter (1 Cor 7.5; cf. 1 Thess 3.5), and adversary until the parousia (Rom 16.20). **19:** A *crown* is the laurel wreath won by an athletic victor. **3.8:** *Stand* is one of the letter's military terms. **11–13:** A prayer reminds the audience about the

pray most earnestly that we may see you
face to face and restore whatever is lacking
in your faith.
11 Now may our God and Father him-
self and our Lord Jesus direct our way to
you. 12 And may the Lord make you in-
crease and abound in love for one another
and for all, just as we abound in love for
you. 13 And may he so strengthen your
hearts in holiness that you may be blame-
less before our God and Father at the com-
ing of our Lord Jesus with all his saints.

4 Finally, brothers and sisters,[a] we ask
and urge you in the Lord Jesus that, as
you learned from us how you ought to live
and to please God (as, in fact, you are do-
ing), you should do so more and more.
2 For you know what instructions we gave
you through the Lord Jesus. 3 For this is the
will of God, your sanctification: that you
abstain from fornication; 4 that each one of
you know how to control your own body[b]
in holiness and honor, 5 not with lustful
passion, like the Gentiles who do not know
God; 6 that no one wrong or exploit a
brother or sister[c] in this matter, because
the Lord is an avenger in all these things,
just as we have already told you before-
hand and solemnly warned you. 7 For God
did not call us to impurity but in holiness.
8 Therefore whoever rejects this rejects not
human authority but God, who also gives
his Holy Spirit to you.
9 Now concerning love of the brothers
and sisters,[a] you do not need to have any-
one write to you, for you yourselves have
been taught by God to love one another;
10 and indeed you do love all the brothers
and sisters[a] throughout Macedonia. But
we urge you, beloved,[a] to do so more and
more, 11 to aspire to live quietly, to mind
your own affairs, and to work with your
hands, as we directed you, 12 so that you
may behave properly toward outsiders and
be dependent on no one.

13 But we do not want you to be unin-
formed, brothers and sisters,[a] about those
who have died,[d] so that you may not
grieve as others do who have no hope.
14 For since we believe that Jesus died and
rose again, even so, through Jesus, God will
bring with him those who have died.[d]
15 For this we declare to you by the word of
the Lord, that we who are alive, who are
left until the coming of the Lord, will by
no means precede those who have died.[d]
16 For the Lord himself, with a cry of com-
mand, with the archangel's call and with
the sound of God's trumpet, will descend
from heaven, and the dead in Christ will
rise first. 17 Then we who are alive, who are
left, will be caught up in the clouds together
with them to meet the Lord in the air; and
so we will be with the Lord forever.
18 Therefore encourage one another with
these words.

5 Now concerning the times and the sea-
sons, brothers and sisters,[a] you do not
need to have anything written to you. 2 For
you yourselves know very well that the day
of the Lord will come like a thief in the
night. 3 When they say, "There is peace and
security," then sudden destruction will

a Gk *brothers* b Or *how to take a wife for himself*
c Gk *brother* d Gk *fallen asleep*

parousia (3.13; cf. 2.19) and announces the themes of love (3.12; cf. 4.9–12), holiness (3.13; cf. 4.3), and the parousia (3.13; cf. 4.11; 5.11) to be developed in the next chapters. **13:** *Hearts* is not a synonym for feelings as in modern speech, but the center of knowledge and understanding. *Saints,* God's people.

4.1–5.22: Exhortation to maintain apocalyptic vigilance. 4.1: *To live,* literally "to walk" (or "to lead," 2.12; cf. 4.12), is to behave consistently within a distinctive path of living. **3:** Paul understands *sanctification* or the ongoing life of holiness to be God's will (3.13; 4.4; 5.23). **5:** *Who do not know God,* a typical slur against Gentiles (Ps 79.6; Jer 10.25). **4.13–5.11:** Paul commends vigilance in the face of death and false security claims. **4.16:** On *God's trumpet* as an end-time sign, see Isa 27.13; Joel 2.1; Zeph 1.14–16; and cf. Ex 19.16,19. **17:** *We who are alive,* Paul expects the end to come during his own life. *To meet the Lord* is to form a delegation to greet a ruler. **5.3:** *As labor pains . . . a pregnant woman* signifies the suddenness of the day of the Lord (cf. Mic 4.9). **5:** As here, *children of light* is also used in the Qumran literature

come upon them, as labor pains come upon
a pregnant woman, and there will be no
escape! 4 But you, beloved,[a] are not in
darkness, for that day to surprise you like a
thief; 5 for you are all children of light and
children of the day; we are not of the night
or of darkness. 6 So then let us not fall
asleep as others do, but let us keep awake
and be sober; 7 for those who sleep sleep at
night, and those who are drunk get drunk
at night. 8 But since we belong to the day,
let us be sober, and put on the breastplate
of faith and love, and for a helmet the hope
of salvation. 9 For God has destined us not
for wrath but for obtaining salvation
through our Lord Jesus Christ, 10 who died
for us, so that whether we are awake or
asleep we may live with him. 11 Therefore
encourage one another and build up each
other, as indeed you are doing.

12 But we appeal to you, brothers and
sisters,[a] to respect those who labor among
you, and have charge of you in the Lord
and admonish you; 13 esteem them very
highly in love because of their work. Be at
peace among yourselves. 14 And we urge
you, beloved,[a] to admonish the idlers, en-
courage the fainthearted, help the weak, be
patient with all of them. 15 See that none of
you repays evil for evil, but always seek to
do good to one another and to all. 16 Re-
joice always, 17 pray without ceasing,
18 give thanks in all circumstances; for this
is the will of God in Christ Jesus for you.
19 Do not quench the Spirit. 20 Do not de-
spise the words of prophets,[b] 21 but test
everything; hold fast to what is good; 22 ab-
stain from every form of evil.

23 May the God of peace himself sancti-
fy you entirely; and may your spirit and
soul and body be kept sound[c] and blame-
less at the coming of our Lord Jesus Christ.
24 The one who calls you is faithful, and he
will do this.

25 Beloved,[d] pray for us.

26 Greet all the brothers and sisters[a]
with a holy kiss. 27 I solemnly command
you by the Lord that this letter be read to
all of them.[e]

28 The grace of our Lord Jesus Christ be
with you.[f]

a Gk *brothers* *b* Gk *despise prophecies* *c* Or *complete* *d* Gk *Brothers* *e* Gk *to all the brothers* *f* Other ancient authorities add *Amen*

(1QS 1.9–10; 3.13) to distinguish the righteous from the nonrighteous ("children of the Darkness"). **8:** The believers' armor (Rom 13.12; 2 Cor 6.7; 10.4; cf. Isa 59.17; Wis 5.17–20), another military image, symbolizes vigilance. **12:** The persons who *have charge of you* are functionaries and perhaps patrons, but not officeholders. **14:** Perhaps influenced by 2 Thess 3.11, some scholars (including the NRSV translators) translate "ataktous" as *idlers,* but the expression means "disorderly ones."

5.23–28: Epistolary closing. The letter closing reminds the congregation of God's ongoing call (5.24; cf. 1.4; 2.12) and his role in their sanctification (5.23; cf. 3.13; 4.3,4,7,8) until the parousia (5.23, cf. 1.10; 2.19; 3.13). **23:** *Spirit and soul and body* refer to three distinctive vantage points for viewing the human person, not three distinctive parts of the human person. **24:** The word *calls,* a present participle, suggests God's ongoing call (cf. 2.12). **26:** As holiness is elsewhere commended (3.13; 4.3,4; 5.23), *a holy kiss* (Rom 16.16) symbolizes the congregation's distinctive love for the believers.

The Second Letter of Paul to the
THESSALONIANS

Like 1 Thessalonians, 2 Thessalonians is an exhortative letter of encouragement. As with other ancient letters of exhortation, this one accentuates imitation (3.7a,9) and remembrance of a teacher's words and deeds (2.5; 3.7b–10). Also, imperatives recur in chs 2 and 3, especially in the latter's disciplinary notices (3.6–15). Although the letter lacks the personal tone of 1 Thessalonians, 2 Thessalonians also encourages a community beset with opposition. Several forms of encouragement are evident: reports of the congregation's progress (1.3–4; 2.13); intercessory prayers (1.11–12; 2.16–17; 3.5,16); and apocalyptic narratives about the opposition's termination (1.5–10; 2.3–12).

The curiosity of several verbal and structural similarities between 1 and 2 Thessalonians—for example, simple letter openings (1 Thess 1.1; 2 Thess 1.2), repeated words of thanks (1 Thess 1.2; 2.13; 3.9; 2 Thess 1.3; 2.13), and repeated intercessory prayers (1 Thess 3.11; 2 Thess 2.16)—lead scholars to different conclusions about the authorship of 2 Thessalonians. One deduction from the similarities is that Paul wrote 2 Thessalonians shortly after writing 1 Thessalonians, in the early 50s. Another deduction, however, is that 2 Thessalonians is a conscious imitation of 1 Thessalonians written much later by someone else. Uncertainty remains, but a key argument against Paul's authorship is the letter's assumption of forgeries (or non-genuine letters, 2.1–2). Forgeries did not likely circulate while an author was alive (for their authorship could easily be disproved). As well, the letter's insistence that it contains a distinctive "mark" found in "every letter" (3.17) from Paul presupposes a time (probably in the late first century) when a body of Paul's letters had been collected.

First Thessalonians assumes, moreover, that Christ's appearance will be a surprise; we cannot know the time (1 Thess 5.1–11). In the opposite direction, 2 Thessalonians infers that at least we can know that the day of the Lord will not come at once; a dire struggle with evil must take place first, and even this is to be delayed for a time. The specifics of this apocalyptic story—the "rebellion" and the "lawless one" (2.3–4,8), and "the mystery of lawlessness" (2.7), as well as "what is now restraining [the lawless one]" (2.6) and "the one who restrains it" (2.7)—are references that may have been clear to the letter's recipients (2.6), but are not clear to us. The letter's emphasis on a delayed struggle prepared the church for a period of continued life in this world.

A typical, though simple, epistolary opening (1.1–2) begins the letter, and a typical epistolary ending (3.16–18) closes it. The rest offers encouragement through prayer forms, apocalyptic narratives, and exhortations (1.3–3.15). An initial thanksgiving prayer with praise for the congregation's steadfastness despite affliction (1.3–4) closes with an apocalyptic narrative that promises relief for beleaguered believers and reprisal for the opposition (1.5–10). Then, a brief intercessory prayer (1.11–12) acknowledges God's power in bringing the congregation's election to fruition. Two sets of exhortations follow: one (2.1–17) to refute apocalyptic enthusiasm and suggest instead an indefinite interim before the cataclysmic end of time; and a second (3.1–15) to steer the congregation toward practical pursuits during the interim. Both sets of admonitions, moreover, include prayer forms: a thanksgiving (2.13–14) to remind the congregation of its election and need for sanctification; a prayer request (3.1,2) for deliverance from evil persons; and an intercessory prayer (3.3) for God's aid in securing the congregation's steadfastness.

1 Paul, Silvanus, and Timothy,
To the church of the Thessalonians in
God our Father and the Lord Jesus Christ:
2 Grace to you and peace from God
our[a] Father and the Lord Jesus Christ.
3 We must always give thanks to God
for you, brothers and sisters,[b] as is right,
because your faith is growing abundantly,
and the love of everyone of you for one
another is increasing. 4 Therefore we our-
selves boast of you among the churches of
God for your steadfastness and faith during
all your persecutions and the afflictions
that you are enduring.
5 This is evidence of the righteous judg-
ment of God, and is intended to make you
worthy of the kingdom of God, for which
you are also suffering. 6 For it is indeed just
of God to repay with affliction those who
afflict you, 7 and to give relief to the afflict-
ed as well as to us, when the Lord Jesus is
revealed from heaven with his mighty an-
gels 8 in flaming fire, inflicting vengeance
on those who do not know God and on
those who do not obey the gospel of our
Lord Jesus. 9 These will suffer the punish-
ment of eternal destruction, separated from
the presence of the Lord and from the glory
of his might, 10 when he comes to be glori-
fied by his saints and to be marveled at on
that day among all who have believed, be-
cause our testimony to you was believed.
11 To this end we always pray for you, ask-
ing that our God will make you worthy of
his call and will fulfill by his power every
good resolve and work of faith, 12 so that
the name of our Lord Jesus may be glorified
in you, and you in him, according to the
grace of our God and the Lord Jesus Christ.

2 As to the coming of our Lord Jesus
Christ and our being gathered together
to him, we beg you, brothers and sisters,[b]
2 not to be quickly shaken in mind or
alarmed, either by spirit or by word or by
letter, as though from us, to the effect that
the day of the Lord is already here. 3 Let no

a Other ancient authorities read *the* *b* Gk *brothers*

1.1–2: Salutation. The epistolary opening is similar to the one in 1 Thess with the exception of a longer greeting. **1:** On *Silvanus* and *Timothy,* see 1 Thess 1.1.

1.3–10: A thanksgiving prayer with apocalyptic expectations. One long sentence in Greek, this thanksgiving prayer (cf. 2.13) relates the community's progress and concludes with an apocalyptic commentary on the vindication of the believers. **3–4:** 2 Thess, like 1 Thess (cf. 1 Thess 1.3n.), has a triad, but 2 Thess speaks of *faith, love,* and *steadfastness* (not hope). **4:** Both *persecutions* and *afflictions* refer to suffering, but the first, with a focus on external suffering, is more specific than the latter. **7–10:** Vivid descriptions first applied to God in the Hebrew Bible now communicate something about the end-time appearance of Jesus (cf. the *angels* in Zech 14.5; the *flaming fire* in Isa 66.15–16; *glorified* in Ps 89.7). **10:** The writer's allusion to *that day* anticipates 2.1–12, a refutation of the claim that the *day of the Lord* had already occurred.

1.11–12: God's election. In prayer form, the writer describes God's role in bringing to fruition a call in the believers' lives. **12:** Again, the writer draws on Isaiah (66.5), but avers that Jesus (not God, as in Isaiah) will be *glorified.*

2.1–17: Correction of apocalyptic enthusiasm. The writer refutes inaccurate views about the coming of Jesus. **1–15:** The refutation includes a statement about the delusion (vv. 1–2), a rebuttal of the delusion (vv. 3–12), and a thanksgiving prayer report revealing the difference between the fates of believers and unbelievers (vv. 13–15). Set against the false information, moreover, are comments about "truth" (v. 13) and about the writer's proclamation and the traditions in which the community should stand firm (vv. 14–15). **2:** False claims about the end-time were not uncommon, as the Synoptic tradition attests (Mk 13.5–6; Mt 24.4–5; Lk 21.8). **3:** Though the identity of the *lawless one* is unknown, some identify him as a false prophet or an emperor. **4:** Cf. Isa 14.13; Ezek 28.2; Dan 11.36. **6–7:** The person or thing

one deceive you in any way; for that day
will not come unless the rebellion comes
first and the lawless one[a] is revealed, the
one destined for destruction.[b] 4 He op-
poses and exalts himself above every so-
called god or object of worship, so that he
takes his seat in the temple of God, declar-
ing himself to be God. 5 Do you not remem-
ber that I told you these things when I was
still with you? 6 And you know what is now
restraining him, so that he may be revealed
when his time comes. 7 For the mystery of
lawlessness is already at work, but only un-
til the one who now restrains it is removed.
8 And then the lawless one will be revealed,
whom the Lord Jesus[c] will destroy[d] with
the breath of his mouth, annihilating him
by the manifestation of his coming. 9 The
coming of the lawless one is apparent in the
working of Satan, who uses all power,
signs, lying wonders, 10 and every kind of
wicked deception for those who are perish-
ing, because they refused to love the truth
and so be saved. 11 For this reason God
sends them a powerful delusion, leading
them to believe what is false, 12 so that all
who have not believed the truth but took
pleasure in unrighteousness will be con-
demned.

13 But we must always give thanks to
God for you, brothers and sisters[e] beloved
by the Lord, because God chose you as the
first fruits[f] for salvation through sanctifi-
cation by the Spirit and through belief in
the truth. 14 For this purpose he called you
through our proclamation of the good
news,[g] so that you may obtain the glory of
our Lord Jesus Christ. 15 So then, brothers
and sisters,[e] stand firm and hold fast to the
traditions that you were taught by us, ei-
ther by word of mouth or by our letter.

16 Now may our Lord Jesus Christ him-
self and God our Father, who loved us and
through grace gave us eternal comfort and
good hope, 17 comfort your hearts and
strengthen them in every good work
and word.

3 Finally, brothers and sisters,[e] pray for
us, so that the word of the Lord may
spread rapidly and be glorified everywhere,
just as it is among you, 2 and that we may
be rescued from wicked and evil people; for
not all have faith. 3 But the Lord is faithful;
he will strengthen you and guard you from
the evil one.[h] 4 And we have confidence in
the Lord concerning you, that you are do-
ing and will go on doing the things that
we command. 5 May the Lord direct your
hearts to the love of God and to the stead-
fastness of Christ.

6 Now we command you, beloved,[e] in

a Gk *the man of lawlessness*; other ancient authorities read *the man of sin* b Gk *the son of destruction* c Other ancient authorities lack *Jesus* d Other ancient authorities read *consume* e Gk *brothers* f Other ancient authorities read *from the beginning* g Or *through our gospel* h Or *from evil*

restraining the lawless one is also debated, though perhaps the purpose for mentioning both is to show that certain events must occur first before the day of the Lord occurs. **8:** *Breath of his mouth,* cf. Job 4.9; Isa 11.4. **9:** On *Satan,* see 1 Thess 2.18n. **13–14:** Another thanksgiving (cf. 1.3–10) indicates God's role in choosing the congregation and in sanctifying them. **15:** On *standing firm,* see 1 Thess 3.8n. **2.16–17:** The wish-prayer (cf. 1.11–12) introduces ideas that develop in subsequent parts of the letter, noting God's role in strengthening the community (2.17; cf. 3.3) and a concern about "work" (2.17; cf. 3.8–12). **17:** On *hearts,* see 1 Thess 3.13n.; cf. 2 Thess 3.5.

3.1–15: Correction of dissident behavior. Two sets of commands and general exhortative material (3.1–4 and 3.6–15), with a wish-prayer placed in between, direct the congregation to practical pursuits (3.5). **1:** In the face of afflictions, a prayer that the *word of the Lord may spread* suggests that the gaining of converts is one strategy for overcoming opposition. **3:** *The evil one,* see Mt 6.13. **5:** *Steadfastness of Christ* could mean endurance in following Christ or, as is more likely, Christ's own steadfastness. **6–15:** These verses, directed to the entire community (vv. 6–10, 13–15) and to the disorderly persons (vv. 11–12), offer aid in correcting the disobedient behavior. **6:** Some scholars translate the adverb "ataktos" here and in v. 11 as *in idleness,* though others translate it as "in disorderliness"; cf. 1 Thess 5.14n. Perhaps some believers wanted to stop working because they thought Christ had returned. **8–9:**

the name of our Lord Jesus Christ, to keep
away from believers who are[a] living in
idleness and not according to the tradition
that they[b] received from us. 7For you
yourselves know how you ought to imitate
us; we were not idle when we were with
you, 8and we did not eat anyone's bread
without paying for it; but with toil and la-
bor we worked night and day, so that we
might not burden any of you. 9This was
not because we do not have that right, but
in order to give you an example to imitate.
10For even when we were with you, we
gave you this command: Anyone unwilling
to work should not eat. 11For we hear that
some of you are living in idleness, mere
busybodies, not doing any work. 12Now
such persons we command and exhort in
the Lord Jesus Christ to do their work qui-
etly and to earn their own living. 13Broth-
ers and sisters,[c] do not be weary in doing
what is right.

14 Take note of those who do not obey
what we say in this letter; have nothing
to do with them, so that they may be
ashamed. 15Do not regard them as enemies,
but warn them as believers.[d]

16 Now may the Lord of peace himself
give you peace at all times in all ways. The
Lord be with all of you.

17 I, Paul, write this greeting with my
own hand. This is the mark in every letter
of mine; it is the way I write. 18The grace of
our Lord Jesus Christ be with all of you.[e]

a Gk *from every brother who is* b Other ancient authorities read *you* c Gk *Brothers* d Gk *a brother* e Other ancient authorities add *Amen*

The writer's own example of work models the way for others. **15:** Despite the stern warning against behavior, the goal for the writer is reclamation. **3.16–18: Epistolary closing.** As in 1 Thess, a peace wish begins the letter closing. Both 3.16 and 3.18 emphasize *all of you,* perhaps again suggesting the writer's desire to draw in the erring members. **17:** In light of 2.2, the expressions *with my own hand* (cf. 1 Cor 16.21) and *this is the mark in every letter of mine* suggest that the writer feels a need to authenticate his letter.

INTRODUCTION
to the Pastoral Epistles

THE TERM "Pastoral epistles" has been applied, since the eighteenth century, to the three letters from Paul to his two coworkers and envoys, Timothy and Titus. The name reflects the central concern in these three epistles for the internal life, governance, and behavior of Christian churches, as well as the individuals who comprise them. Scholars have long debated whether these letters were written by the apostle Paul himself, or by a loyal disciple who sought to provide Pauline answers for new times and places. While most scholars today regard them as pseudepigraphical (that is, ascribed to the authority of a major figure, but not actually written by him, a custom well attested both in ancient Jewish literature and in Greco-Roman philosophical and other texts), there is not complete unanimity on the question. The conclusion that these three epistles were not written by Paul is based upon literary, historical, and theological criteria. First and Second Timothy and Titus share a common Greek vocabulary and style which diverges in many ways from the rest of the Pauline epistles. Historically, the Pastoral epistles presume a situation marked by increasing institutionalization of the church and by heretical opposition, which perhaps better fits a period well after the death of Paul, at the beginning of the second century CE. And theologically these letters minimize or lack characteristic Pauline themes (such as justification by faith, or the church as the body of Christ) in favor of a new emphasis on adherence to tradition and regulation as signs of the Christian piety they seek to inculcate in their readers.

Recent challenges to the pseudepigraphical nature of all three letters have come from those who argue that each should be judged separately, that the letters contain fragments of original Pauline material, or that the very concept of "authorship" of a Pauline letter requires nuance, given that Paul used secretaries and served as a member of a cooperative missionary team. Neither is there scholarly unanimity about which other letters are certainly authentic, nor which parts of those are most tellingly "Pauline" for comparison with these epistles. Each reader should consider the evidence about the authorship of the Pastorals cumulatively, first as a question of historical fact—did Paul write them or not? Then, and separately, one should reflect on the hermeneutical and theological implications of such a decision, for the denial of Pauline authorship may or may not entail a loss of authoritative status for that document within a particular religious community.

Regardless of authorship, the Pastoral epistles share the same rhetorical strategy: Each is addressed to a single individual among Paul's coworkers, but also has in mind a wider circle of readers. In each the author presents himself as a Paul who speaks as an unambiguously authoritative figure of the past to church leaders and members of later generations who have not known him personally.

The First Letter of Paul to TIMOTHY

This letter from Paul to his "loyal child" Timothy (1.2) presents Paul as a wise and sure teacher who hands on to his student his deposit of tradition, his "sound teaching," so that his legacy will be handed down with fidelity to the next generation. The text presents a vision of household ethics that brings together instructions on Christian "godliness" (or "piety") for the individual, with a church order of regulations and qualifications for various roles in the church, designated "the household of God" (3.15). This advice is set in a dual context formed by the positively remembered relationship between Paul and Timothy, and, negatively, by the frequent allusions to purveyors of alternate teachings in or near Timothy's church in Ephesus. (For further information on Timothy, see the Introduction to 2 Timothy.)

The structure of this epistle is somewhat discursive, alternating sections containing contrast between true and false teaching with instruction for church order and governance. At times Timothy is directly addressed, but more often he recedes into the background, and the author speaks to a more universal audience. As ethical instruction (parenesis), 1 Timothy is cast in characteristic forms of Greco-Roman moral exhortation: letters between friends about progress in the ethical life, lists of virtues and vices, and contrasts between illustrious examples and notorious counterexamples. Likewise, the content is in many ways similar to contemporaneous moralizing literature: the emphasis on decorum and decency, on the hierarchical, orderly disposition of the patriarchal household, on reliable speech, and against accumulation of wealth. But the letter's theological universe, which is punctuated by shorthand terminology and quotations from established traditions, is distinctly Christian.

Although the author names two of his Christian opponents (1.20), exactly what they taught, and why, is only hazily sketched here, in vituperative terms (they have "deviated" from the truth [1.6]; they have "suffered shipwreck" [1.19]). Though no complete historical reconstruction is possible from these verbal assaults, it seems that these opponents have some connection with Judaism and Torah observance, "myths and endless genealogies" (1.4), and ascetic practices, such as preventing marriage and abstaining from certain foods (4.3). Recent research has connected the fellow Christians whom this author opposes with those who told and treasured the traditions found in the later apocryphal *Acts of Paul and Thecla*, which valorizes and authorizes women's ministries which, in their asceticism and renunciation of marriage, also claimed Paul as their champion.

The structure of 1 Timothy weaves between contrasting threads that are picked up, dropped, and then picked up again. After an epistolary prescript (1.1–2) the author launches (without the customary thanksgiving) into the body of the letter, which is roughly arranged with alternating sections of contrast between true and false teachers (1.3–2.15; 4.1–5.2; 6.2b–21a) and instructions for church order and governance, understood as the means for living in the church of God (3.1–16; 5.3–6.2a). The letter concludes with summary exhortations to Timothy to guard this tradition with which he has been entrusted (6.11–21). As with all Pauline letters a final benediction (6.21) seals the letter, perhaps in preparation for liturgical appropriation.

1 Paul, an apostle of Christ Jesus by the
command of God our Savior and of
Christ Jesus our hope,
2 To Timothy, my loyal child in the
faith:
Grace, mercy, and peace from God the
Father and Christ Jesus our Lord.

3 I urge you, as I did when I was on my
way to Macedonia, to remain in Ephesus so
that you may instruct certain people not to
teach any different doctrine, 4 and not to
occupy themselves with myths and endless
genealogies that promote speculations rath-
er than the divine training[a] that is known
by faith. 5 But the aim of such instruction is
love that comes from a pure heart, a good
conscience, and sincere faith. 6 Some people
have deviated from these and turned to
meaningless talk, 7 desiring to be teachers
of the law, without understanding either
what they are saying or the things about
which they make assertions.
8 Now we know that the law is good, if
one uses it legitimately. 9 This means under-
standing that the law is laid down not for
the innocent but for the lawless and disobe-
dient, for the godless and sinful, for the un-
holy and profane, for those who kill their
father or mother, for murderers, 10 fornica-
tors, sodomites, slave traders, liars, perjur-
ers, and whatever else is contrary to the
sound teaching 11 that conforms to the glo-
rious gospel of the blessed God, which he
entrusted to me.
12 I am grateful to Christ Jesus our
Lord, who has strengthened me, because he
judged me faithful and appointed me to his
service, 13 even though I was formerly a
blasphemer, a persecutor, and a man of vi-
olence. But I received mercy because I had
acted ignorantly in unbelief, 14 and the
grace of our Lord overflowed for me with
the faith and love that are in Christ Jesus.
15 The saying is sure and worthy of full ac-
ceptance, that Christ Jesus came into the
world to save sinners—of whom I am the
foremost. 16 But for that very reason I re-
ceived mercy, so that in me, as the fore-
most, Jesus Christ might display the utmost
patience, making me an example to those
who would come to believe in him for eter-
nal life. 17 To the King of the ages, immor-
tal, invisible, the only God, be honor and
glory forever and ever.[b] Amen.
18 I am giving you these instructions,
Timothy, my child, in accordance with the
prophecies made earlier about you, so that
by following them you may fight the good
fight, 19 having faith and a good conscience.
By rejecting conscience, certain persons
have suffered shipwreck in the faith;
20 among them are Hymenaeus and Alexan-

a Or *plan* *b* Gk *to the ages of the ages*

1.1–2: Epistolary prescript: sender, addressees, and salutation, following the typical form of a Pauline letter (see Philem 1.1–3), with the addition of *mercy* in the greeting (cf. 2 Tim 1.2).

1.3–2.15: The contrast of true and false teaching (part one).

1.3–11: Opening warning against false teachers, in place of a thanksgiving formula (cf. Philem 4–9), signaling the urgency of the problem, as the author sees it. **3:** *Instruct,* the author's main purpose (1.5,18; 4.11; 5.7; 6.13,17). **4:** *Myths and endless genealogies,* uncertain, but probably speculations on biblical texts (cf. 4.7; Titus 1.14; 3.9). *Divine training,* or "plan," or "stewardship." **5:** *Love . . . conscience . . . faith,* for Paul's usual triad of faith, love, and hope (1 Thess 1.3; 5.8; 1 Cor 13.13). **6:** *Deviated,* see 6.21n. **7:** *The law,* presumably the Torah. **9–10:** Implicitly, a stereotypical depiction of the false teachers as ethically depraved; cf. other catalogues of vice in Rom 1.29–31; 1 Cor 5.11; 6.9–10; Gal 5.19–21.

1.12–20: Contrasting portraits of faithfulness and faithlessness. 12–17: A portrait of Paul, the blasphemer transformed into the faithful proclaimer (cf. the different portrayals in Paul's letters [1 Cor 15.8–10; Gal 1.13–24; Phil 3.5–11], and in Acts 9). **15:** *The saying is sure,* a favored formula in the Pastorals (see 3.1; 4.9; 2 Tim 2.11; Titus 3.8). **17:** Theology cast as doxology (cf. 6.15–16). **18:** *Prophecies,* see 4.14. **19:** *Conscience,* the seat of self-awareness of guilt or innocence (a key theme; see 1.5; 3.9; 4.2; 2 Tim 1.3; Titus 1.15). **20:** *Hymenaeus* (unknown apart from here and 2 Tim 2.17) and *Alexander* (likely to be identified with "Alexander the coppersmith" in 2 Tim 4.14; perhaps Acts 19.33), characterized as blasphemers

der, whom I have turned over to Satan, so
that they may learn not to blaspheme.

2 First of all, then, I urge that supplications,
prayers, intercessions, and
thanksgivings be made for everyone, 2 for
kings and all who are in high positions, so
that we may lead a quiet and peaceable life
in all godliness and dignity. 3 This is right
and is acceptable in the sight of God our
Savior, 4 who desires everyone to be saved
and to come to the knowledge of the truth.
5 For

there is one God;
  there is also one mediator between
    God and humankind,
  Christ Jesus, himself human,
6 who gave himself a ransom for all

—this was attested at the right time. 7 For
this I was appointed a herald and an apostle
(I am telling the truth,[a] I am not lying),
a teacher of the Gentiles in faith and truth.

8 I desire, then, that in every place the
men should pray, lifting up holy hands
without anger or argument; 9 also that the
women should dress themselves modestly
and decently in suitable clothing, not with
their hair braided, or with gold, pearls, or
expensive clothes, 10 but with good works,
as is proper for women who profess reverence
for God. 11 Let a woman[b] learn in
silence with full submission. 12 I permit no
woman[b] to teach or to have authority over
a man;[c] she is to keep silent. 13 For Adam
was formed first, then Eve; 14 and Adam
was not deceived, but the woman was deceived
and became a transgressor. 15 Yet
she will be saved through childbearing,
provided they continue in faith and love
and holiness, with modesty.

3 The saying is sure:[d] whoever aspires to
the office of bishop[e] desires a noble
task. 2 Now a bishop[f] must be above reproach,
married only once,[g] temperate,
sensible, respectable, hospitable, an apt
teacher, 3 not a drunkard, not violent but
gentle, not quarrelsome, and not a lover of
money. 4 He must manage his own household
well, keeping his children submissive
and respectful in every way— 5 for if some-

a Other ancient authorities add *in Christ* *b* Or *wife* *c* Or *her husband* *d* Some interpreters place these words at the end of the previous paragraph. Other ancient authorities read *The saying is commonly accepted* *e* Or *overseer* *f* Or *an overseer* *g* Gk *the husband of one wife*

(cf. 1.13). *Turned over to Satan,* for correction or possibly for punishment (cf. 1 Cor 5.5). Satan or the devil is mentioned frequently in the Pastorals; see 3.6,7; 5.15; 2 Tim 2.26.

2.1–8: Instruction on prayer. 1–3: Accommodation with worldly authorities urged for the sake of peace for the church (see Rom 13.1–7). The irenic tone circumvents the difficult question of the limits of Christian acquiescence to an emperor who was honored as a god by daily worship and oaths of allegiance. *Godliness,* or "piety" ("eusebeia"), a predominant concern of the Pastorals (3.16; 4.7,8; 6.3,5,6; 2 Tim 3.5; Titus 1.1). **4:** Strong emphasis on God as universal savior (cf. 4.10). *Knowledge of the truth,* as found in the gospel proclamation (see 2 Tim 2.25; 3.7; Titus 1.1). **5:** *One God . . . one mediator,* a reformulation of the Shema (see Deut 6.4–9n.; cf. 1 Cor 8.6; Eph 4.5–6).

2.9–15: The proper demeanor of faithful women. The author objects to the current practice of women holding leadership and teaching positions because it threatens conventional domestic order (also 5.3–16). **9:** *Dress themselves modestly,* a standard concern of Stoic and other Hellenistic moralists. *And decently,* "sophrosune," "moderation," one of the four cardinal virtues of Greek philosophical thought. **11–12:** Very similar to the contested passage 1 Cor 14.34–35 (see note there). **13–14:** A "strong" reading of Gen 2–3 assigning all the blame to the woman (contrast Rom 5.12–21). **15:** *She will be saved through childbearing,* a soteriology (theology of salvation) at odds with Paul's justification by faith (Gal 2.16; Rom 1.16–17).

3.1–16: Living in the church of God (part one). Qualifications for prospective bishops (3.1–7) and deacons (3.8–13), already established ecclesial offices (contrast 1 Cor 12.28; Phil 1.1n.). **1,2:** *Bishop,* (Gk "episkopos"), "overseer," one who looks after church affairs (see note *e*). **5:** *God's church* (cf. v. 15, "the household of God"), the church is envisioned as an orderly patriarchal Greco-Roman household. **11:**

one does not know how to manage his own
household, how can he take care of God's
church? 6He must not be a recent convert,
or he may be puffed up with conceit and
fall into the condemnation of the devil.
7Moreover, he must be well thought of by
outsiders, so that he may not fall into dis-
grace and the snare of the devil.

8 Deacons likewise must be serious, not
double-tongued, not indulging in much
wine, not greedy for money; 9they must
hold fast to the mystery of the faith with a
clear conscience. 10And let them first be
tested; then, if they prove themselves
blameless, let them serve as deacons.
11Women[a] likewise must be serious, not
slanderers, but temperate, faithful in all
things. 12Let deacons be married only
once,[b] and let them manage their children
and their households well; 13for those who
serve well as deacons gain a good standing
for themselves and great boldness in the
faith that is in Christ Jesus.

14 I hope to come to you soon, but I am
writing these instructions to you so that,
15if I am delayed, you may know how one
ought to behave in the household of God,
which is the church of the living God, the
pillar and bulwark of the truth. 16Without
any doubt, the mystery of our religion is
great:

He[c] was revealed in flesh,
  vindicated[d] in spirit,[e]
    seen by angels,
  proclaimed among Gentiles,
    believed in throughout the world,
      taken up in glory.

4 Now the Spirit expressly says that in
later[f] times some will renounce the
faith by paying attention to deceitful spirits
and teachings of demons, 2through the hy-
pocrisy of liars whose consciences are
seared with a hot iron. 3They forbid mar-
riage and demand abstinence from foods,
which God created to be received with
thanksgiving by those who believe and
know the truth. 4For everything created by
God is good, and nothing is to be rejected,
provided it is received with thanksgiving;
5for it is sanctified by God's word and by
prayer.

6 If you put these instructions before the
brothers and sisters,[g] you will be a good
servant[h] of Christ Jesus, nourished on the
words of the faith and of the sound teach-
ing that you have followed. 7Have nothing
to do with profane myths and old wives'
tales. Train yourself in godliness, 8for,
while physical training is of some value,
godliness is valuable in every way, holding
promise for both the present life and the life
to come. 9The saying is sure and worthy of
full acceptance. 10For to this end we toil
and struggle,[i] because we have our hope
set on the living God, who is the Savior of
all people, especially of those who believe.

11 These are the things you must insist
on and teach. 12Let no one despise your
youth, but set the believers an example in
speech and conduct, in love, in faith, in pu-
rity. 13Until I arrive, give attention to the
public reading of scripture,[j] to exhorting,
to teaching. 14Do not neglect the gift that is

a Or *Their wives,* or *Women deacons* *b* Gk *be husbands of one wife* *c* Gk *Who;* other ancient authorities read *God;* others, *Which* *d* Or *justified* *e* Or *by the Spirit* *f* Or *the last* *g* Gk *brothers* *h* Or *deacon* *i* Other ancient authorities read *suffer reproach* *j* Gk *to the reading*

Women deacons (but see note *a* for the ambiguity), such as Phoebe (Rom 16.1). If women deacons are intended, the short treatment may be due to the author's anxiety about female leadership (see 2.9–15; 5.3–16). **14–15:** *I am delayed,* the letter takes Paul's place. **16:** Perhaps a quotation from an early Christian hymn.

4.1–5.2: The contrast of true and false teaching (part two). 1: The *later times* (see note *f*) were often associated with false teachings (Mk 13.21–23; 2 Thess 2.1–16; cf. 2 Tim 4.3–4). **3:** *They forbid marriage and demand abstinence from foods,* clearest statement of the opponents' ascetic practices. **6:** *The sound teaching,* the reliable tradition the Pastoral epistles pass on (1.10; 4.1,6,13,16; 5.17; 6.1,3; 2 Tim 1.13; 3.10,16; 4.3; Titus 1.9; 2.1,7,10). **7:** *Myths,* see 1.4n. **7–10:** The life of faith compared to training for an athletic contest (cf. 1 Cor 9.24–27; 2 Tim 2.5). **13:** A glimpse into the content of an early Christian in you, which was given to you through prophecy with the laying on of hands by the council of elders.[a] 15 Put these things into practice, devote yourself to them, so that all may see your progress. 16 Pay close attention to yourself and to your teaching; continue in these things, for in doing this you will save both yourself and your hearers.

5 Do not speak harshly to an older man,[b] but speak to him as to a father, to younger men as brothers, 2 to older women as mothers, to younger women as sisters—with absolute purity.

3 Honor widows who are really widows. 4 If a widow has children or grandchildren, they should first learn their religious duty to their own family and make some repayment to their parents; for this is pleasing in God's sight. 5 The real widow, left alone, has set her hope on God and continues in supplications and prayers night and day; 6 but the widow[c] who lives for pleasure is dead even while she lives. 7 Give these commands as well, so that they may be above reproach. 8 And whoever does not provide for relatives, and especially for family members, has denied the faith and is worse than an unbeliever.

9 Let a widow be put on the list if she is not less than sixty years old and has been married only once;[d] 10 she must be well attested for her good works, as one who has brought up children, shown hospitality, washed the saints' feet, helped the afflicted, and devoted herself to doing good in every way. 11 But refuse to put younger widows on the list; for when their sensual desires alienate them from Christ, they want to marry, 12 and so they incur condemnation for having violated their first pledge. 13 Besides that, they learn to be idle, gadding about from house to house; and they are not merely idle, but also gossips and busybodies, saying what they should not say. 14 So I would have younger widows marry, bear children, and manage their households, so as to give the adversary no occasion to revile us. 15 For some have already turned away to follow Satan. 16 If any believing woman[e] has relatives who are really widows, let her assist them; let the church not be burdened, so that it can assist those who are real widows.

17 Let the elders who rule well be considered worthy of double honor,[f] especially those who labor in preaching and teaching; 18 for the scripture says, "You shall not muzzle an ox while it is treading out the grain," and, "The laborer deserves to be paid." 19 Never accept any accusation against an elder except on the evidence of two or three witnesses. 20 As for those who persist in sin, rebuke them in the presence of all, so that the rest also may stand in fear. 21 In the presence of God and of Christ Jesus and of the elect angels, I warn you to keep these instructions without prejudice, doing nothing on the basis of partiality. 22 Do not ordain[g] anyone hastily, and do not participate in the sins of others; keep yourself pure.

a Gk *by the presbytery* *b* Or *an elder*, or *a presbyter* *c* Gk *she* *d* Gk *the wife of one husband* *e* Other ancient authorities read *believing man or woman*; others, *believing man* *f* Or *compensation* *g* Gk *Do not lay hands on*

worship service. **14:** *The laying on of hands,* a gesture marking the succession of ministerial authorization (see 5.22; 2 Tim 1.6; Acts 6.6). **15:** *Your progress,* "prokope," the Stoic concept of ethical advancement, which will be expressed negatively in 2 Tim 2.16; 3.9,13.

5.3–6.2a: Living in the church of God (part two). Three groups of persons are singled out for instructions: widows (vv. 3–16), elders (vv. 17–20), and slaves (6.1–2). **3–16:** *Real widows* (vv. 3,5,16), an attempt to legislate the practice of widowhood—women living on the support of the church while dedicating their time to a ministry of continual prayer—by insisting on the maintenance of the conventional patriarchal household. **9:** *Put on the list,* designated for communal support. **13:** Stereotypical caricature of idle women as busybodies. **14:** *The adversary,* see 3.7. **17–20:** *Elders* should be amply financially compensated, as supported by the same arguments as in 1 Cor 9.9 and 14. **18a:** Deut 25.4. **18b:** A saying of Jesus, according to Lk 10.7. **19:** *Two or three witnesses,* Deut 19.15; 2 Cor 13.1. **23:**

23 No longer drink only water, but take
a little wine for the sake of your stomach
and your frequent ailments.
24 The sins of some people are conspic-
uous and precede them to judgment, while
the sins of others follow them there. 25 So
also good works are conspicuous; and even
when they are not, they cannot remain hid-
den.

6 Let all who are under the yoke of slav-
ery regard their masters as worthy of all
honor, so that the name of God and the
teaching may not be blasphemed. 2 Those
who have believing masters must not be
disrespectful to them on the ground that
they are members of the church;[a] rather
they must serve them all the more, since
those who benefit by their service are be-
lievers and beloved.[b]

Teach and urge these duties. 3 Whoever
teaches otherwise and does not agree with
the sound words of our Lord Jesus Christ
and the teaching that is in accordance with
godliness, 4 is conceited, understanding
nothing, and has a morbid craving for con-
troversy and for disputes about words.
From these come envy, dissension, slander,
base suspicions, 5 and wrangling among
those who are depraved in mind and bereft
of the truth, imagining that godliness is a
means of gain.[c] 6 Of course, there is great
gain in godliness combined with content-
ment; 7 for we brought nothing into the
world, so that[d] we can take nothing out of
it; 8 but if we have food and clothing, we
will be content with these. 9 But those who
want to be rich fall into temptation and are
trapped by many senseless and harmful de-
sires that plunge people into ruin and de-
struction. 10 For the love of money is a root
of all kinds of evil, and in their eagerness to
be rich some have wandered away from the
faith and pierced themselves with many
pains.
11 But as for you, man of God, shun all
this; pursue righteousness, godliness, faith,
love, endurance, gentleness. 12 Fight the
good fight of the faith; take hold of the
eternal life, to which you were called and
for which you made[e] the good confession
in the presence of many witnesses. 13 In the
presence of God, who gives life to all
things, and of Christ Jesus, who in his testi-
mony before Pontius Pilate made the good
confession, I charge you 14 to keep the com-
mandment without spot or blame until the
manifestation of our Lord Jesus Christ,
15 which he will bring about at the right
time—he who is the blessed and only Sov-
ereign, the King of kings and Lord of lords.
16 It is he alone who has immortality and
dwells in unapproachable light, whom no
one has ever seen or can see; to him be
honor and eternal dominion. Amen.
17 As for those who in the present age
are rich, command them not to be haughty,
or to set their hopes on the uncertainty of
riches, but rather on God who richly pro-

a Gk *are brothers* *b* Or *since they are believers and beloved, who devote themselves to good deeds*
c Other ancient authorities add *Withdraw yourself from such people* *d* Other ancient authorities read *world—it is certain that* *e* Gk *confessed*

A little wine, in contrast to the asceticism of the opponents; see 4.3n. **6.1–2:** Reminiscent of the exhortations in Eph 6.5–9; Col 3.22–4.1, but lacking a reciprocal exhortation to the owners.

6.2b–21: The contrast of true and false teaching (part three). 3–5: A portrait of the unsound teacher, with many resonances to 1.3–11. **6–10:** The catchword *gain* leads to a favorite philosophical and biblical (Job 1.21; Eccl 5.15) commonplace about the false security of riches (taken up again in 6.17–19). **6:** *Contentment* (also v. 8), "autarkeia," a Stoic term meaning "self-sufficiency." **11–12:** *Fight the good fight,* compare 1.18 and 2 Tim 4.7. **13:** *Pontius Pilate,* the only New Testament reference to the Roman governor of Judea (see Mt 27.2; Lk 3.1) outside the Gospels and Acts. *The good confession,* see Jn 18.33–38, but cf. Mt 27.11–13. **14:** *Commandment,* a reference to the testimony in this letter, or perhaps the same as the "good confession" in v. 12, the vow Timothy made at his ordination. *Manifestation* (lit. "epiphany"), a reference to the Second Coming (a favored term in the Pastorals: 2 Tim 1.10; 4.1,8; Titus 2.13). **15–16:** A hymn to the sovereignty of God as all-powerful, immortal, and invisible (Ex 33.20; Rom 1.23; Col 1.15; Jn 1.18). **19:** *The treasure,* for the theme, see Mt 6.19–20; Lk 12.21; 2 Esd 7.77.

vides us with everything for our enjoyment.
18 They are to do good, to be rich in good
works, generous, and ready to share,
19 thus storing up for themselves the treasure of a good foundation for the future, so that they may take hold of the life that really is life.

20 Timothy, guard what has been entrusted to you. Avoid the profane chatter and contradictions of what is falsely called knowledge;
21 by professing it some have missed the mark as regards the faith.

Grace be with you.[a]

[a] The Greek word for *you* here is plural; in other ancient authorities it is singular. Other ancient authorities add *Amen*

6.20–21: Timothy the guardian of the true teaching. 20: *What has been entrusted to you* (lit. "the deposit"), the teachings in this letter, seen as a vaccination against false teaching. *What is falsely called knowledge,* perhaps a reference to Gnostics, religious persons who claimed sole possession of divine insight based on a complex dualistic cosmology, mythology, and anthropology. **21:** *Missed the mark,* a characterization of all opponents, which frames the letter (see also 1.6, "have deviated from," more literally, "being off the mark," and 2 Tim 2.18).

6.21b: Concluding benediction.

The Second Letter of Paul to
TIMOTHY

The second epistle addressed to Paul's "beloved child" Timothy, despite its similarities in address and diction, has a more personal tone than the first. (See the Introduction to The Pastoral Epistles preceding 1 Timothy.) Less concerned with general church order and roles, here Paul is portrayed as near death, in testamentary fashion handing on to his spiritual heir, Timothy, the wisdom and truth he has accumulated through a life of mission, ministry and, above all, suffering for the gospel. The letter is set within a carefully scripted historical circumstance marked by Paul's imminent death and Timothy's bereavement, at a time of distortions to the *sound doctrine* or "healthy teaching" received from the apostle.

Timothy is known from Paul's letters as one of his most loyal disciples (Phil 2.19–22), who acts as a delegate to churches (1 Cor 4.17; 16.10) and co-sender of six of the Pauline epistles (2 Cor 1.1; Phil 1.1; Col 1.1; 1 Thess 1.1; 2 Thess 1.1; Philem 1), as well as being the recipient of two. According to Acts 16, Timothy's mother was Jewish and his father Greek, which is why Paul circumcised him in the face of probable Jewish persecution (Acts 16.3, an event not corroborated by the epistles). This letter sketches Timothy's life only in broad strokes, from his early immersion in the scriptures (3.15) and matrilineal Christian pedigree (1.5), to his authorization for ministry by the laying on of Paul's hands (1.6), and his present ecclesiastical challenges. More prominent in the letter, however, is the detailed and passionate portrait of Paul, imprisoned for the gospel in Rome (1.8,16–17; 2.9), and forsaken by even his close friends (1.15; 4.10,16), yet empowered by his Lord not only to endure suffering and death, but to celebrate them as the fitting culmination of his life of ministry and service (4.6–8,17–18).

The theme of 2 Timothy is announced in 1.8: that Timothy and all who follow him should not be ashamed of the gospel or its representative, Paul, but should stand in fidelity to them, even to the point of suffering similarly. The structure of the letter reflects Timothy's alternatives, between Paul the prototypical example of faith, and the seductive, dangerous power of deceitful opposition. The letter implores Timothy to adhere to Paul's example of suffering for the gospel (1.12; 2.9–10; 3.11; 4.6–7,16–18), which he is called upon to imitate (2.3; 4.5), as are all believers (2.11–12).

Second Timothy follows a regular epistolary structure with prescript (1.1–2), thanksgiving (1.3–7), and body (1.8–4.18). Timothy is urged to suffer for the gospel through contemplating the positive example of Paul (1.8–14) and the negative one afforded by those who deserted Paul in time of need (1.15–18). The exhortation to Timothy to be strong and teach others rightly (2.1–13) is contrasted with false teachers who must be contended with (2.14–26), for, as expected at the end time, signs of their appearance are already here (3.1–9). But Timothy is to follow in Paul's footsteps (3.10–4.5). These exhortations build up to the depiction of Paul's death-bed reflections on his life and its imminent conclusion (4.6–8). But the letter ends on a more hopeful note as the imprisoned apostle exults in his divine deliverance (both past and future) and issues spirited directives for the ministry, including a future visit from Timothy (4.8–18).

1 Paul, an apostle of Christ Jesus by the
will of God, for the sake of the promise
of life that is in Christ Jesus,
2 To Timothy, my beloved child:
Grace, mercy, and peace from God the
Father and Christ Jesus our Lord.

3 I am grateful to God—whom I wor-
ship with a clear conscience, as my ances-
tors did—when I remember you constantly
in my prayers night and day. 4 Recalling
your tears, I long to see you so that I may
be filled with joy. 5 I am reminded of your
sincere faith, a faith that lived first in your
grandmother Lois and your mother Eunice
and now, I am sure, lives in you. 6 For this
reason I remind you to rekindle the gift of
God that is within you through the laying
on of my hands; 7 for God did not give us a
spirit of cowardice, but rather a spirit of
power and of love and of self-discipline.
8 Do not be ashamed, then, of the testi-
mony about our Lord or of me his prisoner,
but join with me in suffering for the gospel,
relying on the power of God, 9 who saved
us and called us with a holy calling, not
according to our works but according to
his own purpose and grace. This grace was
given to us in Christ Jesus before the ages
began, 10 but it has now been revealed
through the appearing of our Savior Christ
Jesus, who abolished death and brought life
and immortality to light through the gos-
pel. 11 For this gospel I was appointed a
herald and an apostle and a teacher,[a]
12 and for this reason I suffer as I do. But I
am not ashamed, for I know the one in
whom I have put my trust, and I am sure
that he is able to guard until that day what
I have entrusted to him.[b] 13 Hold to the
standard of sound teaching that you have
heard from me, in the faith and love that
are in Christ Jesus. 14 Guard the good trea-
sure entrusted to you, with the help of the
Holy Spirit living in us.
15 You are aware that all who are in
Asia have turned away from me, including
Phygelus and Hermogenes. 16 May the Lord
grant mercy to the household of Onesipho-
rus, because he often refreshed me and was
not ashamed of my chain; 17 when he ar-
rived in Rome, he eagerly[c] searched for me
and found me 18 —may the Lord grant that
he will find mercy from the Lord on that
day! And you know very well how much
service he rendered in Ephesus.

2 You then, my child, be strong in the
grace that is in Christ Jesus; 2 and what
you have heard from me through many wit-
nesses entrust to faithful people who will be
able to teach others as well. 3 Share in suf-
fering like a good soldier of Christ Jesus.
4 No one serving in the army gets entangled
in everyday affairs; the soldier's aim is to

a Other ancient authorities add *of the Gentiles*
b Or *what has been entrusted to me* *c* Or *promptly*

1.1–2: Salutation, following the typical form of a Pauline letter. 1.3–7 Thanksgiving for Timothy's faith. 5: Faith *lives* in Timothy (as does the Holy Spirit in 1.14). **6:** *I remind you,* memory plays a key role in the exhortation (also 2.8,14). *Laying on of my hands,* cf. 1 Tim 4.14n.

1.8–14: Theme: co-suffering, rather than shame, for the gospel and its apostle. 8: *Ashamed,* see also 1.12,16; 2.15; cf. Rom 1.16. **9–10:** Gospel proclamation in shorthand form, with characteristic themes. **9:** *Before the ages began,* see Titus 1.2; cf. Jn 1.2–3. **10:** *Appearing,* see 1 Tim 6.14n. *Abolished death,* cf. 1 Cor 15.26,54–57. **12:** *The one in whom I have put my trust,* Timothy, and each subsequent reader who stands in his place. *What I have entrusted to him* (lit. "the deposit"), as in 1.14; 1 Tim 6.20; cf. 2.2, a major theme of the Pastorals. *That day,* the Second Coming of Christ, the eschaton, see v. 18; 4.8; 2 Thess 1.10. **13:** *Sound teaching,* see 1 Tim 4.6n.

1.15–18: Examples, worthy and unworthy. 15: *Asia,* a Roman province in Asia Minor. *Phygelus and Hermogenes,* named only here. *Turned away from me,* Paul's abandonment is depicted again in 4.10,16. **16:** *Onesiphorus,* see 4.19; *my chain,* i.e., imprisonment; see 2.9. **18:** *That day,* see v. 12n.

2.1–13: Timothy's charge to suffer for the gospel. 2: *Entrust,* Timothy is to hand on the deposit he receives from Paul to the next generation. **4–6:** *Soldier, athlete, farmer,* commonplaces from three professions about the cost of securing divine favor. **8:** Another encapsulation of the gospel (cf. Rom 1.3). **11:**

please the enlisting officer. 5 And in the case
of an athlete, no one is crowned without
competing according to the rules. 6 It is the
farmer who does the work who ought to
have the first share of the crops. 7 Think
over what I say, for the Lord will give you
understanding in all things.
8 Remember Jesus Christ, raised from
the dead, a descendant of David—that is
my gospel, 9 for which I suffer hardship,
even to the point of being chained like a
criminal. But the word of God is not
chained. 10 Therefore I endure everything
for the sake of the elect, so that they may
also obtain the salvation that is in Christ
Jesus, with eternal glory. 11 The saying is
sure:

If we have died with him, we will
also live with him;
12 if we endure, we will also reign with
him;
if we deny him, he will also deny us;
13 if we are faithless, he remains
faithful—
for he cannot deny himself.

14 Remind them of this, and warn them
before God[a] that they are to avoid wran-
gling over words, which does no good but
only ruins those who are listening. 15 Do
your best to present yourself to God as one
approved by him, a worker who has no
need to be ashamed, rightly explaining the
word of truth. 16 Avoid profane chatter, for
it will lead people into more and more im-
piety, 17 and their talk will spread like gan-
grene. Among them are Hymenaeus and
Philetus, 18 who have swerved from the
truth by claiming that the resurrection has
already taken place. They are upsetting the
faith of some. 19 But God's firm foundation
stands, bearing this inscription: "The Lord
knows those who are his," and, "Let every-
one who calls on the name of the Lord turn
away from wickedness."
20 In a large house there are utensils not
only of gold and silver but also of wood
and clay, some for special use, some for
ordinary. 21 All who cleanse themselves of
the things I have mentioned[b] will become
special utensils, dedicated and useful to the
owner of the house, ready for every good
work. 22 Shun youthful passions and pursue
righteousness, faith, love, and peace, along
with those who call on the Lord from a
pure heart. 23 Have nothing to do with stu-
pid and senseless controversies; you know
that they breed quarrels. 24 And the Lord's
servant[c] must not be quarrelsome but
kindly to everyone, an apt teacher, patient,
25 correcting opponents with gentleness.
God may perhaps grant that they will re-
pent and come to know the truth, 26 and
that they may escape from the snare of the
devil, having been held captive by him to
do his will.[d]

3 You must understand this, that in the
last days distressing times will come.
2 For people will be lovers of themselves,

a Other ancient authorities read *the Lord* *b* Gk *of these things* *c* Gk *slave* *d* Or *by him, to do his* (that is, God's) *will*

The saying is sure, see 1 Tim 1.15n. **11–13:** A series of parallel clauses, suggesting to some scholars a quotation from a hymn. *Died with him . . . live with him,* Rom 6.5–11; 2 Cor 5.14–15. *Reign with him,* in glory at the end-time (1 Cor 4.8). *Deny him,* Mt 10.33; Mk 8.38; 1 Jn 2.22–23.

2.14–26: Strategies for proper combat with false teachers. 17: *Hymenaeus,* 1 Tim 1.20. *Philetus,* otherwise unknown. *Gangrene,* the opposite of "healthy" teaching (see 1.13n.). **18:** *Swerved from the truth,* see 1 Tim 6.21n. *The resurrection has already taken place,* a glimpse at the eschatology of the opponents, though not the theology behind it. They apparently spiritualized the future apocalyptic hope of resurrection, believing it to be a present reality. **19:** *God's firm foundation* (cf. 1 Tim 6.19), as known in scripture. *This inscription,* a quotation from Num 16.5; the second sentence has resonances with Isa 26.13; Job 36.10; Sir 17.26. **20–21:** *Utensils . . . some for special use, some for ordinary* (lit. "some for honor, some for dishonor"), contrast Rom 9.19–23. **26:** *Held captive,* "captured and kept alive" (the same verb is used in Lk 5.10).

3.1–9: End-time now: a close-up picture of the opposition. 1: *The last days* seen as both future and already present. **2–4:** Vice catalogue (see 1 Tim 1.9–10n.). **5:** *Godliness,* see 1 Tim 2.1–3n. **6:** *Captivate*

lovers of money, boasters, arrogant, abu-
sive, disobedient to their parents, ungrate-
ful, unholy, 3 inhuman, implacable, slan-
derers, profligates, brutes, haters of good,
4 treacherous, reckless, swollen with con-
ceit, lovers of pleasure rather than lovers of
God, 5 holding to the outward form of god-
liness but denying its power. Avoid them!
6 For among them are those who make their
way into households and captivate silly
women, overwhelmed by their sins and
swayed by all kinds of desires, 7 who are
always being instructed and can never ar-
rive at a knowledge of the truth. 8 As Jannes
and Jambres opposed Moses, so these peo-
ple, of corrupt mind and counterfeit faith,
also oppose the truth. 9 But they will not
make much progress, because, as in the
case of those two men,[a] their folly will be-
come plain to everyone.

10 Now you have observed my teaching,
my conduct, my aim in life, my faith, my
patience, my love, my steadfastness, 11 my
persecutions, and my suffering the things
that happened to me in Antioch, Iconium,
and Lystra. What persecutions I endured!
Yet the Lord rescued me from all of them.
12 Indeed, all who want to live a godly life
in Christ Jesus will be persecuted. 13 But
wicked people and impostors will go from
bad to worse, deceiving others and being
deceived. 14 But as for you, continue in
what you have learned and firmly believed,
knowing from whom you learned it, 15 and
how from childhood you have known the
sacred writings that are able to instruct you
for salvation through faith in Christ Jesus.
16 All scripture is inspired by God and is[b]
useful for teaching, for reproof, for correc-
tion, and for training in righteousness, 17 so
that everyone who belongs to God may be
proficient, equipped for every good work.

4 In the presence of God and of Christ
Jesus, who is to judge the living and the
dead, and in view of his appearing and his
kingdom, I solemnly urge you: 2 proclaim
the message; be persistent whether the time
is favorable or unfavorable; convince, re-
buke, and encourage, with the utmost pa-
tience in teaching. 3 For the time is coming
when people will not put up with sound
doctrine, but having itching ears, they will
accumulate for themselves teachers to suit
their own desires, 4 and will turn away from
listening to the truth and wander away to
myths. 5 As for you, always be sober, en-
dure suffering, do the work of an evange-
list, carry out your ministry fully.

6 As for me, I am already being poured
out as a libation, and the time of my depar-
ture has come. 7 I have fought the good
fight, I have finished the race, I have kept
the faith. 8 From now on there is reserved
for me the crown of righteousness, which
the Lord, the righteous judge, will give me

a Gk lacks *two men* b Or *Every scripture inspired by God is also*

silly women, common negative ancient caricature of women, employed as part of the invective against the opponents (cf. 1 Tim 2.11–12; 4.7). **7:** *Knowledge of the truth,* see 1 Tim 2.4n. **8:** *Jannes and Jambres,* the names of the Egyptian magicians who opposed Moses (Ex 7.11), according to postbiblical Jewish tradition.

3.10–4.5: Timothy's charge to steadfastness in his ministry. 11: *Antioch, Iconium, and Lystra,* Acts 13.14–14.23 recounts persecutions of Paul in these three cities in Asia Minor, in the same order (which may suggest knowledge of Acts by this author). **15–16:** *Sacred writings, scripture,* the Jewish scriptures (the Hebrew Bible in the ancient Greek version, the Septuagint, abbreviated LXX), which Christians will later call the Old Testament. **4.1:** *Appearing,* see 1 Tim 6.14n. *Kingdom,* also 4.18. **2:** A succinct list of the tasks of bishops. **3–4:** The false teachers as purveyors of myths (cf. 1 Tim 1.4; 4.7; Titus 1.14). **5:** *Evangelist,* Eph 4.11; Acts 21.8.

4.6–8: Paul's reflections on his impending death. 6–7: Sacrificial (Phil 2.17) and athletic (1 Cor 9.24–27; Phil 2.16; 1 Tim 6.12; Acts 20.24) metaphors applied to Paul's ministerial life. **8:** *Crown of righteousness,* the winner's prize, a symbol of positive judgment from the Lord at his Second Coming (1 Thess 2.19; 1 Cor 9.25; Phil 4.1).

4.8–18: An update from prison. 9: An abrupt shift from the previous indication of Paul's imminent

on that day, and not only to me but also to
all who have longed for his appearing.

9 Do your best to come to me soon,
10 for Demas, in love with this present
world, has deserted me and gone to Thessa-
lonica; Crescens has gone to Galatia,[a] Ti-
tus to Dalmatia. 11 Only Luke is with me.
Get Mark and bring him with you, for he is
useful in my ministry. 12 I have sent Tychi-
cus to Ephesus. 13 When you come, bring
the cloak that I left with Carpus at Troas,
also the books, and above all the parch-
ments. 14 Alexander the coppersmith did
me great harm; the Lord will pay him back
for his deeds. 15 You also must beware of
him, for he strongly opposed our message.
16 At my first defense no one came to
my support, but all deserted me. May it not
be counted against them! 17 But the Lord
stood by me and gave me strength, so that
through me the message might be fully pro-
claimed and all the Gentiles might hear it.
So I was rescued from the lion's mouth.
18 The Lord will rescue me from every evil
attack and save me for his heavenly king-
dom. To him be the glory forever and ever.
Amen.

19 Greet Prisca and Aquila, and the
household of Onesiphorus. 20 Erastus re-
mained in Corinth; Trophimus I left ill in
Miletus. 21 Do your best to come before
winter. Eubulus sends greetings to you, as
do Pudens and Linus and Claudia and all
the brothers and sisters.[b]
22 The Lord be with your spirit. Grace
be with you.[c]

a Other ancient authorities read *Gaul* *b* Gk *all the brothers* *c* The Greek word for *you* here is plural. Other ancient authorities add *Amen*

death (also 4.21). **10–11:** Paul's abandonment at the end (also 1.15; 4.16). **10–12:** *Demas, Luke, Mark,* mentioned together also in Philem 24 and Col 4.10–14. *Crescens,* mentioned only here. On *Titus,* see Introduction to Titus. **12:** *Tychicus,* see Col 4.7; cf. Eph 6.21–22; Acts 20.4; Titus 3.12. **13:** *Troas,* ancient Troy, the departure point from Asia to Europe (2 Cor 2.12–13; Acts 16.8–12). *Carpus* is mentioned only here. *The books, and above all the parchments,* a suggestive reference, but what is being referred to is unknown. **14:** *Alexander,* see 1 Tim 1.20n. **16:** *My first defense,* formal "apology" against judicial charges. **17:** *The Lord . . . gave me strength,* as he will Timothy (2.1; also 1 Tim 1.12). *Rescued from the lion's mouth,* Ps 21.22 (LXX); Dan 6.21; 1 Macc 2.60.

4.19–21: Epistolary Greetings. 19: *Prisca and Aquila,* prominent missionary team, who were close to Paul (Rom 16.3; 1 Cor 16.19; Acts 18.2,18). *Onesiphorus,* 1.16–17. **20:** *Erastus,* the city-treasurer of Corinth (Rom 16.23; cf. Acts 19.22). *Trophimus,* Acts 20.4; 21.29. **21:** All of these people who are with Paul (despite 4.11!) are found only here. *Come before winter,* while a sea voyage is possible.

4.22: Concluding benediction.

The Letter of Paul to TITUS

This epistle directed to Paul's envoy and coworker, Titus, bears many similarities to 1 Timothy. It is cast as a reminder and incitement to Titus to complete the things which remain to be done in his mission on Crete (1.5). Acts and the other Pauline letters make no mention of an apostolic mission to this, the largest of the Aegean islands, and home to a large Jewish community. Those who argue that the letter is genuine contend that such a mission could have taken place after Paul's imprisonment at Rome recounted in Acts 28, while those who regard it as pseudepigraphical (see Introduction to The Pastoral Epistles preceding 1 Timothy for the terms of the debate) think the author has chosen Crete simply as a locale representing quintessential disobedience (1.12), or because of a later tradition associating Titus with the island.

Although he is never mentioned in Acts, we are well informed about Titus from Paul's letters. According to Gal 2.3 he was a Gentile who accompanied Paul on his famous conference with the Jerusalem apostles, where he served as a kind of test case for the noncircumcision of Gentile converts. In the pastoral ministry to Corinth Titus played a crucial role, first as a key administrator of the collection for the saints in Jerusalem (2 Cor 8.6,16–17,23; 12.18), and later as Paul's diplomatic envoy who successfully brokered a reconciliation between the apostle and the church, which had harbored doubts about Paul's legitimacy and financial reliability (2 Cor 2.13; 7.6–7,13–16).

Paul delegates two tasks to Titus in this letter, under the heading of "putting things in order" (1.5): exhorting the faithful in sound teaching (1.9,13; 2.1–2,8), and refuting the opposition (2.2,15; cf. 1.9). The mainstay of sound teaching, as the author defines it, is strict maintenance of a patriarchal church order and the proper submission it demands (2.5,9; 3.1; contrast the characterization of the opponents as "insubordinate" or "rebellious" in 1.6,10). This logic of the "household code" as applied to the Christian house church reflects the wider cultural context of the Greco-Roman world in the Imperial period and is characteristic of the Pastoral epistles. The second task, the refutation of opponents (fellow Christians of Jewish background who adhere to the requirements of the laws of Moses, the Torah, such as dietary laws), is addressed by the author mostly in a negative fashion, through sharp invective and ridicule (1.10–16; 2.8; 3.9–11) rather than theological debate, which the author appears to eye largely with suspicion (1.13–14; 3.9–11).

Though short, this epistle is theologically packed, requiring readers to pause and reconstruct the underlying gospel narrative and theological concepts, which the author often invokes by terse shorthand. Passages such as 1.1–3; 2.11–14; 3.4–7 allow for instructive comparison with other tight Pauline formulations (such as Gal 4.1–11; Rom 3.21–26; 2 Tim 1.9–10), so the theology constructed here can be appreciated both for its distinctiveness and for its continuity with earlier traditions.

The epistle to Titus is framed as a commissioning letter for Paul's envoy to Crete. After the usual epistolary prescript (1.1–4, which is expanded with a theological creed), the body of the letter focuses on Titus's dual commission to correct things on Crete and appoint elders (1.5–16). The basis for his work follows in sections devoted to the submission expected of various roles in the church (2.1–10), the theological basis for pious living (2.11–15), and a final section bringing the two themes—of submission and good works—together (3.1–11). The epistle concludes with a discussion of travel plans (3.12–13), a final exhortation to good works (3.14), epistolary greetings (3.15a), and a benediction (3.15b).

1 Paul, a servant[a] of God and an apostle
of Jesus Christ, for the sake of the faith
of God's elect and the knowledge of the
truth that is in accordance with godliness,
2 in the hope of eternal life that God, who
never lies, promised before the ages be-
gan— 3 in due time he revealed his word
through the proclamation with which I
have been entrusted by the command of
God our Savior,

4 To Titus, my loyal child in the faith we
share:

Grace[b] and peace from God the Father
and Christ Jesus our Savior.

5 I left you behind in Crete for this rea-
son, so that you should put in order what
remained to be done, and should appoint
elders in every town, as I directed you:
6 someone who is blameless, married only
once,[c] whose children are believers, not
accused of debauchery and not rebellious.
7 For a bishop,[d] as God's steward, must
be blameless; he must not be arrogant or
quick-tempered or addicted to wine or vio-
lent or greedy for gain; 8 but he must be
hospitable, a lover of goodness, prudent,
upright, devout, and self-controlled. 9 He
must have a firm grasp of the word that is
trustworthy in accordance with the teach-
ing, so that he may be able both to preach
with sound doctrine and to refute those
who contradict it.

10 There are also many rebellious peo-
ple, idle talkers and deceivers, especially
those of the circumcision; 11 they must be
silenced, since they are upsetting whole
families by teaching for sordid gain what it
is not right to teach. 12 It was one of them,
their very own prophet, who said,

"Cretans are always liars, vicious
brutes, lazy gluttons."

13 That testimony is true. For this reason
rebuke them sharply, so that they may be-
come sound in the faith, 14 not paying at-
tention to Jewish myths or to command-
ments of those who reject the truth. 15 To
the pure all things are pure, but to the cor-
rupt and unbelieving nothing is pure. Their
very minds and consciences are corrupted.
16 They profess to know God, but they deny
him by their actions. They are detestable,
disobedient, unfit for any good work.

2 But as for you, teach what is consistent
with sound doctrine. 2 Tell the older
men to be temperate, serious, prudent, and
sound in faith, in love, and in endurance.

a Gk *slave* *b* Other ancient authorities read *Grace, mercy,* *c* Gk *husband of one wife* *d* Or *an overseer*

1.1–4: Salutation, with theological expansion reminiscent of Rom 1.2–6 (cf. 1 Cor 2.7; Col 1.26; 2 Tim 1.10). **2:** *God, who never lies,* cf. v. 12. *Before the ages began,* see 2 Tim 1.9; cf. Jn 1.2–3. **3:** *God our Savior* (also 2.10; 3.4; 1 Tim 1.1; 2.3; 4.10). **4:** *Christ Jesus our Savior* (also 2.13; 3.6; 2 Tim 1.10).

1.5–16: Titus's commission in Crete. 5–7: *Elders . . . bishop,* here apparently regarded as synonymous or at least overlapping categories (cf. 1 Tim 3.1–7; 5.17–20). **6:** *Rebellious,* lit. "insubordinate" (also 1.10). **7:** *Steward,* manager of the household (cf. 1 Cor 4.1–2). **9:** *Sound doctrine,* see 1 Tim 4.6n. **10:** *Those of the circumcision,* Jewish Christians who teach adherence to Torah, the law of Moses (see Gal 2.12), including dietary laws (see v. 15). **11:** *Upsetting whole families,* lit. "households," the basic unit of civic and church life. **12:** Invective against opponents supported by a hexameter from the Cretan poet Epimenides (ca. 600 BCE). **13:** *Sound in the faith,* having a "healthy" faith (also 2.2; see 1 Tim 4.6n.). **14:** *Jewish myths,* see 1 Tim 1.4n. **15:** Cf. Rom 14.14. **16:** *Good work,* see 2.7,14; 3.1,8,14 (also 3.8n.).

2.1–10: The proclamation of sound teaching in submission. A catalogue of virtues reflecting and inscribing the hierarchical order of the Greco-Roman household (v. 2, older men; vv. 3–5 women, older and younger; vv. 6–8 younger men; vv. 9–10, slaves). **5:** *Being submissive,* the author seeks to rein in the

3 Likewise, tell the older women to be
reverent in behavior, not to be slanderers or
slaves to drink; they are to teach what is
good, 4 so that they may encourage the
young women to love their husbands, to
love their children, 5 to be self-controlled,
chaste, good managers of the household,
kind, being submissive to their husbands,
so that the word of God may not be dis-
credited.
6 Likewise, urge the younger men to be
self-controlled. 7 Show yourself in all re-
spects a model of good works, and in your
teaching show integrity, gravity, 8 and
sound speech that cannot be censured; then
any opponent will be put to shame, having
nothing evil to say of us.
9 Tell slaves to be submissive to their
masters and to give satisfaction in every re-
spect; they are not to talk back, 10 not to
pilfer, but to show complete and perfect
fidelity, so that in everything they may be
an ornament to the doctrine of God our
Savior.
11 For the grace of God has appeared,
bringing salvation to all,[a] 12 training us to
renounce impiety and worldly passions,
and in the present age to live lives that are
self-controlled, upright, and godly, 13 while
we wait for the blessed hope and the mani-
festation of the glory of our great God and
Savior,[b] Jesus Christ. 14 He it is who gave
himself for us that he might redeem us from
all iniquity and purify for himself a people
of his own who are zealous for good deeds.
15 Declare these things; exhort and re-
prove with all authority.[c] Let no one look
down on you.

3 Remind them to be subject to rulers and
authorities, to be obedient, to be ready
for every good work, 2 to speak evil of no
one, to avoid quarreling, to be gentle, and
to show every courtesy to everyone. 3 For
we ourselves were once foolish, disobedi-
ent, led astray, slaves to various passions
and pleasures, passing our days in malice
and envy, despicable, hating one another.
4 But when the goodness and loving kind-
ness of God our Savior appeared, 5 he saved
us, not because of any works of righteous-
ness that we had done, but according to his
mercy, through the water[d] of rebirth and
renewal by the Holy Spirit. 6 This Spirit
he poured out on us richly through Jesus
Christ our Savior, 7 so that, having been
justified by his grace, we might become
heirs according to the hope of eternal life.
8 The saying is sure.
I desire that you insist on these things, so
that those who have come to believe in God
may be careful to devote themselves to
good works; these things are excellent and
profitable to everyone. 9 But avoid stupid
controversies, genealogies, dissensions, and
quarrels about the law, for they are unprof-
itable and worthless. 10 After a first and sec-

a Or *has appeared to all, bringing salvation* b Or *of the great God and our Savior* c Gk *commandment* d Gk *washing*

insubordinate (1.6,10) by calling for obedience to each one's superiors (also 2.9; 3.1) and for adherence to the model of Titus (v. 7).

2.11–15: The theological basis for present pious living. 11: *The grace of God has appeared* (lit. "been manifested"), in the life, death, and resurrection of Christ (cf. 3.4). **13:** *The manifestation* (see 1 Tim 6.14n.) *of our great God and Savior, Jesus Christ,* if translated this way (see note *b*), is one of the rare places in the New Testament where Christ may be referred to as God (Jn 1.18; 20.28; Rom 9.5). **14:** *Who gave himself,* Gal 1.4; 2.20; Eph 5.2; 1 Tim 2.6. *Redeem us,* buy back from slavery (Rom 3.24; 1 Cor 1.30; 6.20; 7.23; Eph 1.7; Col 1.14; cf. Mk 10.45). *A people of his own,* appropriation of the biblical promise to Israel (Deut 7.6–8; Ex 9.5–16); cf. 1 Pet 2.9.

3.1–11: Submission and good works are the marks of the saved. 1: *Subject to rulers and authorities,* advice for Christians to accommodate to the larger social order (similar to Rom 13.1–7; 1 Tim 2.1–3). **4–7:** A tight credal formulation, perhaps from an early hymn. **5:** *The water of rebirth and renewal,* baptism, as both promise of resurrection (Rom 6.3–5) and power for present transformation (Rom 12.2). **8:** *The saying is sure,* see 1 Tim 1.15n. *Good works,* as distinguished from "works of righteousness" in v. 5 (the works of the law); see 1.16n. **9–11:** Condemnatory attitude toward the opponents (cf. 1 Tim 6.3–5;

ond admonition, have nothing more to do
with anyone who causes divisions, 11 since
you know that such a person is perverted
and sinful, being self-condemned.
12 When I send Artemas to you, or
Tychicus, do your best to come to me at
Nicopolis, for I have decided to spend the
winter there. 13 Make every effort to send
Zenas the lawyer and Apollos on their way,
and see that they lack nothing. 14 And let
people learn to devote themselves to good
works in order to meet urgent needs, so
that they may not be unproductive.
15 All who are with me send greetings to
you. Greet those who love us in the faith.
Grace be with all of you.[a]

a Other ancient authorities add *Amen*

2 Tim 2.14–18), as contrasted with the gentler disposition of 1 Tim 2.4; 2 Tim 2.24–26. **9:** *Genealogies,* see 1 Tim 1.4n.

3.12–13: Travel plans. 12: *Artemas,* otherwise unknown. *Tychicus,* see 2 Tim 4.12n. **13:** *Zenas the lawyer,* named only here. *Apollos,* 1 Cor 1.12; 16.12; Acts 18.24. *See that they lack nothing,* providing hospitality for itinerant missionaries, as in Rom 16.2; 3 Jn 6. **3.14: Concluding exhortation to good works. 3.15a: Epistolary greetings. 3.15b: Concluding benediction.**

The Letter of Paul to
PHILEMON

This enigmatic text is a piece of the apostle Paul's business correspondence, a curious but intentional blend of personal and public appeal, addressed to three named recipients (Philemon, Apphia, and Archippus) and to the church that meets in one of their houses (v. 2). The letter shows Paul's epistolary style at its very best, and employs some of his most subtle rhetoric to make a request of one of the recipients—probably Philemon, because he is the first named. The exact nature of the request, however, is the basis for the enigma that the epistle to Philemon represents.

In order to interpret this brief epistle, one must reconstruct the situation it presupposes, but to do so the reader must largely depend upon the letter itself. Paul writes this letter while he is in prison (vv. 1,9–10, but the precise location is not specified), where he has been joined by a person named Onesimus, whom, Paul recounts, he has converted to the gospel while there (v. 10). This Onesimus, who is the slave of Philemon (v. 16), is the subject of the letter, and the object of Paul's appeal (v. 10). While the circumstances that led to Onesimus's encounter with Paul are not described in the letter itself, two quite different possibilities suggest themselves: Either Onesimus ran away from his master, perhaps after causing him some financial loss (vv. 15,18), or Onesimus was sent by his owner to serve Paul in prison (v. 13), much like Epaphroditus appears to have been sent to Paul in prison by the Philippians (Phil 2.25–30). The advantage of the latter possibility is that it explains how Onesimus came to be in prison with Paul, whereas the former option must explain why a slave would run away to a prison, though this can perhaps be overcome by the suggestion that Onesimus, according to legal precedent, sought out a friend of his master's to act as an intermediary for himself. The precise occasion of the letter is the moment of Paul's sending Onesimus back to his master (v. 12). The letter is intended to accompany Onesimus and register a plea on his behalf (v. 10). What exactly is Paul asking Philemon to do?

Because Paul formulates his request for Onesimus in intentionally vague and suggestively persuasive terms, a certain judgment is hard to make. Readers should try out at least three possible interpretations: (1) Paul is asking Philemon to receive Onesimus back into service and forgive his transgressions, whatever they might have been (vv. 17–18); (2) Paul is primarily asking Philemon to send Onesimus back to him to continue to serve his physical needs while in prison (vv. 13–14); (3) Paul is strongly hinting that Philemon should not only receive Onesimus back, but free him (vv. 16,21). Each of these options has some grounding in the text, and the choice of which the reader adopts depends upon which verses are thought to be the highlight of the argument, and upon how one assesses Paul's tone at various points. One thing, however, is certain about this letter: Paul engages in full-strength arm-twisting of Philemon to do his "good deed" (v. 14). But the final decision of what to do is left up to Philemon himself to decide—in the context of a range of on-lookers among his fellow Christians! One of the most remarkable things about this letter is that it was preserved at all, and ultimately incorporated in the canonical collection of Paul's letters, which perhaps gives us a hint about Philemon's ultimate decision.

This letter has played a role in the history of Christian social ethics disproportionate to its size.

The adequacy of Paul's attitude and actions toward the institution of slavery, both in his context and as a legacy for Christian social thought, continues to be debated.

The structure of Philemon is neatly exact. After the epistolary salutation (vv. 1–3) and thanksgiving (vv. 4–7), which praise Philemon for his past benefactions, in the epistolary body (vv. 8–22) Paul makes a fresh request for the present situation involving Onesimus through various forms of subtle and not-so-subtle appeal, ending with a forecast of his impending visit. He closes the letter with epistolary greetings from missionary coworkers that accent the public arena of Philemon's decision.

1 Paul, a prisoner of Christ Jesus, and
Timothy our brother,[a]
To Philemon our dear friend and co-
worker, 2 to Apphia our sister,[b] to Archip-
pus our fellow soldier, and to the church in
your house:
3 Grace to you and peace from God our
Father and the Lord Jesus Christ.
4 When I remember you[c] in my
prayers, I always thank my God 5 because I
hear of your love for all the saints and your
faith toward the Lord Jesus. 6 I pray that
the sharing of your faith may become effec-
tive when you perceive all the good that
we[d] may do for Christ. 7 I have indeed re-
ceived much joy and encouragement from
your love, because the hearts of the saints
have been refreshed through you, my
brother.
8 For this reason, though I am bold
enough in Christ to command you to do
your duty, 9 yet I would rather appeal to
you on the basis of love—and I, Paul, do
this as an old man, and now also as a pris-
oner of Christ Jesus.[e] 10 I am appealing to
you for my child, Onesimus, whose father
I have become during my imprisonment.
11 Formerly he was useless to you, but now
he is indeed useful[f] both to you and to me.
12 I am sending him, that is, my own heart,
back to you. 13 I wanted to keep him with
me, so that he might be of service to me in
your place during my imprisonment for the
gospel; 14 but I preferred to do nothing
without your consent, in order that your
good deed might be voluntary and not
something forced. 15 Perhaps this is the rea-
son he was separated from you for a while,
so that you might have him back forever,
16 no longer as a slave but more than a

a Gk *the brother* *b* Gk *the sister* *c* From verse 4 through verse 21, *you* is singular *d* Other ancient authorities read *you* (plural) *e* Or *as an ambassador of Christ Jesus, and now also his prisoner* *f* The name Onesimus means *useful* or (compare verse 20) *beneficial*

1–3: Salutation, with each sender and recipient carefully designated. **1:** *Timothy,* see Introduction to 2 Timothy. **2:** *Our sister,* fellow Christian. *Apphia,* named only here. *Archippus,* see Col 4.17. *And to the church in your house,* Paul puts Philemon's decision in a more public context.

4–7: Thanksgiving for Philemon's past good deeds. In vv. 4–22a Paul uses the singular address (*you*). Because he calls him "brother" in v. 20, it must refer either to Philemon or Archippus; tradition and current scholarship almost unanimously choose Philemon, on the grounds that he is the first named. **7:** *Hearts,* "splanchna," lit. "inner organs," refers to the emotional center of a person (see vv. 12,20).

8–22: Paul's appeal for another good deed from Philemon. **10:** *Whose father I have become,* lit. "whom I begot" to new life in the gospel (cf. 1 Cor 4.15). **11:** *Useful* ("eu-chrestos") is a double pun, referring both to Onesimus's name (see note *f*) and his identity in Christ ("eu-Christos" = "good in Christ"). **14:** *Voluntary,* Paul does not command (cf. v. 8), but prefers to persuade. **15:** *Was separated,* a perhaps deliberately vague reference to Onesimus's absence. **16:** *No longer as a slave,* finally the problem is stated: status dissonance (i.e., when a person occupies two or more social positions simultaneously). What happens when a slave of a Christian master becomes a Christian? Some scholars take Paul to mean the slave stops being a slave by becoming a brother, but others think Paul considers the new status of *brother* as relativizing, but not changing, the slave's station in the world. *In the flesh and in the Lord,* in the world and in the church. **17–19:** *Partner, charge . . . to my account, repay,* business terminology

slave, a beloved brother—especially to me
but how much more to you, both in the
flesh and in the Lord.
17 So if you consider me your partner,
welcome him as you would welcome me.
18 If he has wronged you in any way, or
owes you anything, charge that to my ac-
count. 19 I, Paul, am writing this with my
own hand: I will repay it. I say nothing
about your owing me even your own self.
20 Yes, brother, let me have this benefit
from you in the Lord! Refresh my heart in
Christ. 21 Confident of your obedience, I
am writing to you, knowing that you will
do even more than I say.
22 One thing more—prepare a guest
room for me, for I am hoping through your
prayers to be restored to you.
23 Epaphras, my fellow prisoner in
Christ Jesus, sends greetings to you,[a]
24 and so do Mark, Aristarchus, Demas,
and Luke, my fellow workers.
25 The grace of the Lord Jesus Christ be
with your spirit.[b]

a Here *you* is singular *b* Other ancient authorities add *Amen*

signaling Paul's financial obligations to Philemon. *Owing me even your own self,* Philemon's spiritual obligation to the one who converted him. **21:** *More than I say,* a mere commonplace or a diplomatically framed hint to release him from slavery? **22b:** *Your* prayers, in the plural. Paul here joins the co-recipients (v. 2) with him in registering his plea to Philemon.

23–24: **Greetings,** the same five people are named in Col 4.10–14. *Epaphras,* Col 1.7; 4.12. **25:** **Concluding benediction.**

The Letter to the HEBREWS

Traditionally known as "The Epistle of Paul to the Hebrews," this New Testament writing can best be understood as an anonymous sermon written to encourage an early Christian community to continued faith and hope in the face of hardship. In a manner unique among New Testament books, the sermon develops the image of Christ as the great high priest who fulfills and completes the Jewish system of sacrifice. In a sophisticated rhetorical style, the author alternates argument and exhortation. Although it concludes with greetings and other features of a letter (13.22–25), the work has no opening greeting and no identification of the author or of those addressed. Rather, the author refers to it as a "word of exhortation" (13.22) a phrase used in Acts 13.15 to describe a synagogue sermon of Paul.

When the New Testament was being formed, this anonymous sermon was attributed to Paul, presumably because of the growing authority of Paul's name and reputation as a letter writer. The early church leaders Origen, Clement, and Tertullian, however, recognized the differences in style and theology between Hebrews and Paul's letters. Clement argued that Luke translated Paul's Hebrew original into Greek and Origen suggested that a disciple of Paul wrote the letter based on Paul's notes. Modern interpreters have suggested other authors, including Apollos and Priscilla. There is not sufficient historical evidence, however, to prove that any person named in the New Testament was the author of Hebrews.

Like the name of the author, the precise date of Hebrews cannot be determined. Because the argument depends on description of the Temple sacrifice, some scholars argue that it must originate before the destruction of the Temple in 70 CE. Because the work deals with the exegesis of scriptural texts, however, the literal existence of Temple sacrifice is not necessary for the argument to be persuasive. The probable date of the work therefore falls somewhere in the range of 60 to 100 CE.

Despite the title "to the Hebrews," the audience probably consists of people of both Jewish and Gentile background. Evidence within the sermon for the identity of its audience suggests that the community has suffered hardship and persecution (10.32) and that some may have renounced their faith (2.3; 6.4–6; 12.25). The central role of interpretation of the Jewish scriptures (used by the author in their ancient Greek translation, the Septuagint [LXX]) in the argument of the sermon shows the continued importance of the Bible and of Jewish tradition for those who believed in Christ. The author seeks both to ground the argument in scripture and to argue that Jesus is superior to Jewish traditions. Within the audience were both Jewish Christians well versed in scripture and Gentile Christians who also would have found such arguments persuasive.

Because so many of the standard historical introductory questions about Hebrews are uncertain, Hebrews can best be read by leaving those questions open and exploring the work as a distinctive Christian writing. The work attempts to interpret the significance of Jesus Christ and his death in categories familiar to the author and audience. Its readers could appreciate the sophisticated rhetorical style, follow the repetition and development of images and vocabulary, and understand the logic of the author's argument in the context of Platonic and allegorical interpretation and of other early Christian language.

Hebrews is a document in which themes and motifs anticipate and reinforce each other. The sermon is organized into four main sections. Heb 1.1–4.13 explores the word of God spoken through the Son. Heb 4.14–10.31 interprets Jesus as the eternal high priest against the background of the Israelite priesthood. The third part, 10.32–12.29, describes faith as insight into a heavenly world of reality. Chapter 13 gives practical advice and greetings.

1 Long ago God spoke to our ancestors in
many and various ways by the proph-
ets, 2 but in these last days he has spoken to
us by a Son,[a] whom he appointed heir of
all things, through whom he also created
the worlds. 3 He is the reflection of God's
glory and the exact imprint of God's very
being, and he sustains[b] all things by his
powerful word. When he had made purifi-
cation for sins, he sat down at the right
hand of the Majesty on high, 4 having be-
come as much superior to angels as the
name he has inherited is more excellent
than theirs.
5 For to which of the angels did God
ever say,

"You are my Son;
today I have begotten you"?

Or again,

"I will be his Father,
and he will be my Son"?

6 And again, when he brings the firstborn
into the world, he says,

"Let all God's angels worship him."

7 Of the angels he says,

"He makes his angels winds,
and his servants flames of fire."

8 But of the Son he says,

"Your throne, O God, is[c] forever
and ever,
and the righteous scepter is the
scepter of your[d] kingdom.
9 You have loved righteousness and
hated wickedness;
therefore God, your God, has
anointed you
with the oil of gladness beyond
your companions."

10 And,

"In the beginning, Lord, you founded
the earth,
and the heavens are the work of
your hands;
11 they will perish, but you remain;
they will all wear out like clothing;
12 like a cloak you will roll them up,

a Or *the Son* b Or *bears along* c Or *God is your throne* d Other ancient authorities read *his*

1.1–4.13 Word of God spoken through the Son.

1.1–4: The prologue: God has spoken through a Son. The formal, rhythmic prologue contrasts God's mode of speaking in the past with God's mode of speaking *in these last days*. The contrast assumes that the one *Son* of the present is better than the many *prophets* of *long ago*. The relationship of the Son to God is elaborated in a hymn, similar to other Christological hymns in the New Testament (Phil 2.6–11; Col 1.15–20). **3:** The Son is described as participating in the creation and as one who *sustains all things. The reflection of God's glory and the exact imprint of God's very being*, language derived from Jewish wisdom speculation about the female figure of Wisdom, who was present at the time of creation (Prov 8.22–31; Wis 9.9), came to earth to dwell (Sir 24.8; Bar 3.37), and returned to her place in the heavens (1 Enoch 42.1–2). In Wis 7.26 wisdom is described as "a reflection . . . of God." See also Jn 1.1–3. When the Son accomplished the priestly work of *purification* (9.14,26–28), he sat down at God's right hand (Ps 110.1). **4:** *The name* may be "Son" or possibly "Lord" (Phil 2.9–11).

1.5–2.18: The superiority of the Son to the angels. *Angels*, thought to be mediators of God's word in the law of Israel and imagined to be in attendance at the enthronement of the Son, are inferior to the Son because their role is to serve (v. 14). Seven quotations from Jewish scripture are cited as speaking about or to Jesus. **5:** Ps 2.7; 2 Sam 7.14. **6:** Deut 32.43. **7:** Ps 104.4. **8:** Ps 45.6–7. **10–12:** Ps 102.25–27. **13:**

and like clothing[a] they will be
changed.
But you are the same,
and your years will never end."
13 But to which of the angels has he ever
said,
"Sit at my right hand
until I make your enemies a
footstool for your feet"?
14 Are not all angels[b] spirits in the divine
service, sent to serve for the sake of those
who are to inherit salvation?

2 Therefore we must pay greater atten-
tion to what we have heard, so that we
do not drift away from it. 2 For if the mes-
sage declared through angels was valid, and
every transgression or disobedience re-
ceived a just penalty, 3 how can we escape if
we neglect so great a salvation? It was de-
clared at first through the Lord, and it was
attested to us by those who heard him,
4 while God added his testimony by signs
and wonders and various miracles, and by
gifts of the Holy Spirit, distributed accord-
ing to his will.
5 Now God[c] did not subject the coming
world, about which we are speaking, to
angels. 6 But someone has testified some-
where,
"What are human beings that you are
mindful of them,[d]
or mortals, that you care for
them?[e]
7 You have made them for a little while
lower[f] than the angels;
you have crowned them with glory
and honor,[g]
8 subjecting all things under
their feet."
Now in subjecting all things to them, God[c]
left nothing outside their control. As it is,
we do not yet see everything in subjection
to them, 9 but we do see Jesus, who for a
little while was made lower[h] than the an-
gels, now crowned with glory and honor
because of the suffering of death, so that by
the grace of God[i] he might taste death for
everyone.
10 It was fitting that God,[c] for whom
and through whom all things exist, in
bringing many children to glory, should
make the pioneer of their salvation perfect
through sufferings. 11 For the one who
sanctifies and those who are sanctified all
have one Father.[j] For this reason Jesus[c] is
not ashamed to call them brothers and sis-
ters,[k] 12 saying,

a Other ancient authorities lack *like clothing*
b Gk *all of them* *c* Gk *he* *d* Gk *What is man that you are mindful of him?* *e* Gk *or the son of man that you care for him?* In the Hebrew of Psalm 8.4-6 both *man* and *son of man* refer to all humankind
f Or *them only a little lower* *g* Other ancient authorities add *and set them over the works of your hands* *h* Or *who was made a little lower* *i* Other ancient authorities read *apart from God* *j* Gk *are all of one* *k* Gk *brothers*

Ps 110.1. The author alludes to Ps 110.1 in 8.1; 10.12; 12.2. Ps 110.1 is interpreted messianically elsewhere in the New Testament (Acts 2.24; 1 Cor 15.25).

2.1–4: Exhortation not to fall away. The superiority of the Son to the angels makes it more necessary to obey the message of salvation he brought than the law of Moses, which came through the angels. **2:** *The message declared through angels,* see Acts 7.53; Gal 3.19; Josephus, *Ant.* 15.5.3. **3:** *Attested to us by those who heard,* the message has come to this community through an earlier generation. **4:** *Signs and wonders,* see Acts 2.43; 15.12; cf. Deut 6.22. *Miracles,* see Acts 8.13; 19.11; cf. Ps 105.27. *Gifts of the Holy Spirit,* see 1 Cor 12.4–11.

2.5–18: Jesus' exaltation through abasement. 6–9: Quoting Ps 8.4–6, the author interprets the verses as referring to Jesus, the human being. Unlike the original psalm which said that God created human beings "a little lower than the angels," the author understands that Jesus the human being is superior to angels but was made *for a little while lower* than them in his death (cf. Phil 2.6–11). **10–18:** Jesus shares humanity with all human beings (*children*). In order to liberate his *brothers and sisters* from *slavery* to the power of death, Jesus had to share their human experience *in every respect.* **10:** The expression, *make . . . perfect,* is characteristic of this letter (5.9; 7.19,28; 9.9; 10.1,14; 11.40; 12.23) and means "to make complete, to bring to maturity." Christ as *pioneer* goes before and points out the way to his followers (12.2); the same Gk word is translated "Author" (Acts 3.15) and "Leader" (Acts 5.31). **12:** Ps 22.22. **13:**

"I will proclaim your name to my
brothers and sisters,[a]
in the midst of the congregation I
will praise you."
13 And again,
"I will put my trust in him."
And again,
"Here am I and the children whom
God has given me."
14 Since, therefore, the children share
flesh and blood, he himself likewise shared
the same things, so that through death he
might destroy the one who has the power
of death, that is, the devil, 15 and free those
who all their lives were held in slavery by
the fear of death. 16 For it is clear that he
did not come to help angels, but the descen-
dants of Abraham. 17 Therefore he had to
become like his brothers and sisters[a] in ev-
ery respect, so that he might be a merciful
and faithful high priest in the service of
God, to make a sacrifice of atonement for
the sins of the people. 18 Because he himself
was tested by what he suffered, he is able to
help those who are being tested.

3 Therefore, brothers and sisters,[a] holy
partners in a heavenly calling, consider
that Jesus, the apostle and high priest of
our confession, 2 was faithful to the one
who appointed him, just as Moses also
"was faithful in all[b] God's[c] house." 3 Yet
Jesus[d] is worthy of more glory than Mo-
ses, just as the builder of a house has more
honor than the house itself. 4 (For every
house is built by someone, but the builder
of all things is God.) 5 Now Moses was
faithful in all God's[c] house as a servant, to
testify to the things that would be spoken
later. 6 Christ, however, was faithful over
God's[c] house as a son, and we are his
house if we hold firm[e] the confidence and
the pride that belong to hope.
7 Therefore, as the Holy Spirit says,
"Today, if you hear his voice,
8 do not harden your hearts as in
the rebellion,
as on the day of testing in the
wilderness,
9 where your ancestors put me to
the test,
though they had seen my works
10 for forty years.
Therefore I was angry with that
generation,
and I said, 'They always go astray in
their hearts,
and they have not known
my ways.'
11 As in my anger I swore,
'They will not enter my rest.' "
12 Take care, brothers and sisters,[a] that

a Gk *brothers* *b* Other ancient authorities lack *all*
c Gk *his* *d* Gk *this one* *e* Other ancient
authorities add *to the end*

Isa 8.17–18. **14:** See Wis 2.24; Rom 6.23. **17:** As *high priest* the Son is both *merciful* (cf. 5.2–3) and *faithful* (cf. 3.2,6), *to make a sacrifice of atonement* continually for *sins* that bring death and the fear of it to God's *people* (vv. 14–15). **18:** Jesus was *tested* by suffering (5.7–8); therefore he can help the community this sermon addresses, which is also being tested.

3.1–6: Comparison of Jesus and Moses. The author argues for Jesus' superiority to Moses, who, like the angels, is another intermediary of God's word or law. **1:** *Holy partners,* the readers or hearers are addressed in terms that remind them of their position and responsibility in sharing *in a heavenly calling,* as Jesus is in the heavens. As *apostle,* Jesus is the one sent by God to humankind; as *high priest,* he is their representative before God. **2:** The author first refers to what Jesus and Moses have in common: faithfulness to their respective tasks. *Was faithful in all God's house* alludes to the Septuagint version of Num 12.7–8. **3–5:** As to position, Christ (a "son," v. 6) is superior to Moses (a *servant* in God's house; Num 12.7). **6:** *We are his house,* the community of faithful believers. *That belong to hope,* hope is a key theme in the sermon (see 6.11,18; 7.19; 10.23).

3.7–4.13: Entering God's rest. The author makes an extended commentary on Ps 95.7–11 and applies it to the lives of the audience. **8:** *Rebellion* and *testing* are translations of the Hebrew names Meribah and Massah in Ps 95.8 (Ex 17.1–7; Num 20.1–13; Deut 33.8). **11:** *My rest,* the possession of the promised land of Canaan. **12:** Jer 17.5. **13:** *The deceitfulness of sin,* disobedience (Num 14.1–4,34,41), leading to

none of you may have an evil, unbelieving
heart that turns away from the living God.
13 But exhort one another every day, as
long as it is called "today," so that none of
you may be hardened by the deceitfulness
of sin. 14 For we have become partners of
Christ, if only we hold our first confidence
firm to the end. 15 As it is said,

"Today, if you hear his voice,
do not harden your hearts as in
the rebellion."

16 Now who were they who heard and yet
were rebellious? Was it not all those who
left Egypt under the leadership of Moses?
17 But with whom was he angry forty years?
Was it not those who sinned, whose bodies
fell in the wilderness? 18 And to whom did
he swear that they would not enter his rest,
if not to those who were disobedient? 19 So
we see that they were unable to enter be-
cause of unbelief.

4 Therefore, while the promise of enter-
ing his rest is still open, let us take care
that none of you should seem to have failed
to reach it. 2 For indeed the good news
came to us just as to them; but the message
they heard did not benefit them, because
they were not united by faith with those
who listened.[a] 3 For we who have believed
enter that rest, just as God[b] has said,

"As in my anger I swore,
'They shall not enter my rest,' "

though his works were finished at the foun-
dation of the world. 4 For in one place it
speaks about the seventh day as follows,
"And God rested on the seventh day from
all his works." 5 And again in this place it
says, "They shall not enter my rest." 6 Since
therefore it remains open for some to enter
it, and those who formerly received the
good news failed to enter because of dis-
obedience, 7 again he sets a certain day—
"today"—saying through David much lat-
er, in the words already quoted,

"Today, if you hear his voice,
do not harden your hearts."

8 For if Joshua had given them rest, God[b]
would not speak later about another day.
9 So then, a sabbath rest still remains for the
people of God; 10 for those who enter God's
rest also cease from their labors as God did
from his. 11 Let us therefore make every ef-
fort to enter that rest, so that no one may
fall through such disobedience as theirs.

12 Indeed, the word of God is living and
active, sharper than any two-edged sword,
piercing until it divides soul from spirit,
joints from marrow; it is able to judge the
thoughts and intentions of the heart. 13 And
before him no creature is hidden, but all are
naked and laid bare to the eyes of the one
to whom we must render an account.

14 Since, then, we have a great high
priest who has passed through the heavens,

a Other ancient authorities read *it did not meet with faith in those who listened* b Gk *he*

apostasy or renunciation of faith. **16–19:** A series of questions refers to Israel, *those who left Egypt under the leadership of Moses* and who did not *enter* the *rest*. The *unbelief* of the Israelites will be compared with the necessary faithfulness of the Christian community.

4.1–13: The faithfulness required of Christians. 1: God's promise, which must be fulfilled, remains for faithful Christians to inherit. **2:** *Those who listened,* Num 13.30–14.10. **3:** Ps 95.11. **4:** Gen 2.2. The meaning of "rest" is enlarged to include God's sabbath rest. **5:** Ps 95.11. **7–8:** *Today,* see 3.13. The possession of Canaan under Joshua was not the promised *rest,* otherwise *David,* understood to be the author of the psalm, would not have spoken centuries later of a rest still remaining (Ps 95.7–8). **9–10:** *Sabbath rest,* points back to God's rest after the work of creation (Gen 2.2), and forward to rest as the ultimate destiny of followers in heaven. **11–13:** The author exhorts the community to enter into the rest and concludes the opening section, which has explored the theme of God's speaking, with a statement about *the word of God* which is living. **13:** The Gk word translated *account* is "logos," the same word translated as "word" in v.12.

4.14–10.31: Jesus as the eternal high priest. 4.14–5.10: Christ as great high priest. The author understands Jesus' life, death, and present heavenly role through the category of "high priest" who perfects the ancient sacrificial system of Judaism. Having discussed Jesus' "faithfulness"(2.17; 3.1–6), the author

Jesus, the Son of God, let us hold fast to our
confession. 15 For we do not have a high
priest who is unable to sympathize with our
weaknesses, but we have one who in every
respect has been tested[a] as we are, yet
without sin. 16 Let us therefore approach
the throne of grace with boldness, so that
we may receive mercy and find grace to
help in time of need.

5 Every high priest chosen from among
mortals is put in charge of things pertaining to God on their behalf, to offer gifts
and sacrifices for sins. 2 He is able to deal
gently with the ignorant and wayward,
since he himself is subject to weakness;
3 and because of this he must offer sacrifice
for his own sins as well as for those of the
people. 4 And one does not presume to take
this honor, but takes it only when called by
God, just as Aaron was.

5 So also Christ did not glorify himself
in becoming a high priest, but was appointed by the one who said to him,

"You are my Son,
today I have begotten you";

6 as he says also in another place,

"You are a priest forever,
according to the order of
Melchizedek."

7 In the days of his flesh, Jesus[b] offered
up prayers and supplications, with loud
cries and tears, to the one who was able to
save him from death, and he was heard
because of his reverent submission. 8 Although he was a Son, he learned obedience
through what he suffered; 9 and having
been made perfect, he became the source
of eternal salvation for all who obey him,
10 having been designated by God a high
priest according to the order of Melchizedek.

11 About this[c] we have much to say
that is hard to explain, since you have become dull in understanding. 12 For though
by this time you ought to be teachers, you
need someone to teach you again the basic
elements of the oracles of God. You need
milk, not solid food; 13 for everyone who
lives on milk, being still an infant, is unskilled in the word of righteousness. 14 But
solid food is for the mature, for those
whose faculties have been trained by practice to distinguish good from evil.

6 Therefore let us go on toward perfection,[d] leaving behind the basic teach-

a Or *tempted* b Gk *he* c Or *him* d Or *toward maturity*

turns to reflect on his "mercy." **14:** *Through the heavens,* Jesus has passed through the series of heavens above the earth and entered into the highest where God dwells. His entry is the basis for the confidence and hope of Christians. **16:** *Approach the throne of grace,* the sermon's imagery shifts from holding fast (3.6,14; 4.14) to moving forward, an image that will be explored as the sermon proceeds. **5.1:** The author defines what a *high priest* is and shows how the definition fits Jesus. A priest is *chosen from among* human beings and represents them before God in sacrifices he offers. **2:** He can effectively represent them because he shares human *weakness.* **3:** See Lev 9.7. **4:** He is called by God to this office. *Aaron,* Ex 28.1. **5:** Citing Ps 2.7, the author demonstrates that Christ is *appointed* by God (cf. Lk 3.22). **6:** The author quotes Ps 110.4. *According to the order of Melchizedek* is interpreted to mean "like" Melchizedek. The sermon will return to this element in 7.1–22. **7–9:** The author refers to an example of Jesus' sharing human weakness and suffering in order to show how that makes him a source of salvation for human beings. **7:** Traditionally, this verse has been understood to refer to Gethsemane (Mk.14.32–42 and parallels). However, the description resembles the portrayal of the typical Jewish hero, such as Abraham or Moses, who prays loudly to God for deliverance (2 Macc 11.6; Philo, *Rer. div. her.* 19). **10:** *Melchizedek,* see 7.1–10n. Although simply called a "priest according to the order of Melchizedek" in the psalm citation, the author elaborates that Jesus is a "high priest according to the order of Melchizedek."

5.11–6.20: Exhortation to hope. The author's tone shifts from critical to complimentary in this hortatory passage. The community is encouraged to move forward, first *toward perfection* (6.1), then *to seize the hope set before us* (6.18). **12–14:** Common in Hellenistic rhetoric, the comparison between *milk* as rudimentary teaching and *solid food* as more advanced teaching is used to encourage the community to move beyond basic teachings (cf. 1 Cor 3.1–2). **6.1:** *Dead works,* "works that lead to death" or "sin."

ing about Christ, and not laying again the
foundation: repentance from dead works
and faith toward God, 2 instruction about
baptisms, laying on of hands, resurrection
of the dead, and eternal judgment. 3 And we
will do[a] this, if God permits. 4 For it is
impossible to restore again to repentance
those who have once been enlightened, and
have tasted the heavenly gift, and have
shared in the Holy Spirit, 5 and have tasted
the goodness of the word of God and the
powers of the age to come, 6 and then have
fallen away, since on their own they are
crucifying again the Son of God and are
holding him up to contempt. 7 Ground that
drinks up the rain falling on it repeatedly,
and that produces a crop useful to those for
whom it is cultivated, receives a blessing
from God. 8 But if it produces thorns and
thistles, it is worthless and on the verge of
being cursed; its end is to be burned over.

9 Even though we speak in this way, be-
loved, we are confident of better things in
your case, things that belong to salvation.
10 For God is not unjust; he will not over-
look your work and the love that you
showed for his sake[b] in serving the saints,
as you still do. 11 And we want each one of
you to show the same diligence so as to
realize the full assurance of hope to the very
end, 12 so that you may not become slug-
gish, but imitators of those who through
faith and patience inherit the promises.

13 When God made a promise to Abra-
ham, because he had no one greater by
whom to swear, he swore by himself, 14 say-
ing, "I will surely bless you and multiply
you." 15 And thus Abraham,[c] having pa-
tiently endured, obtained the promise.
16 Human beings, of course, swear by some-
one greater than themselves, and an oath
given as confirmation puts an end to all
dispute. 17 In the same way, when God de-
sired to show even more clearly to the heirs
of the promise the unchangeable character
of his purpose, he guaranteed it by an oath,
18 so that through two unchangeable
things, in which it is impossible that God
would prove false, we who have taken ref-
uge might be strongly encouraged to seize
the hope set before us. 19 We have this
hope, a sure and steadfast anchor of the
soul, a hope that enters the inner shrine
behind the curtain, 20 where Jesus, a fore-
runner on our behalf, has entered, having
become a high priest forever according to
the order of Melchizedek.

7 This "King Melchizedek of Salem,
priest of the Most High God, met Abra-

a Other ancient authorities read *let us do* *b* Gk *for his name* *c* Gk *he*

2: *Baptisms,* ritual washings used in both Jewish and Christian practice (see 9.10). *Laying on of hands* was a ritual of commissioning (see Acts 6.6; 8.17–19; 9.17; 13.3; 1 Tim 4.14; 2 Tim 1.6). Teaching about *resurrection of the dead* would have been accepted by both Jews and Christians. The author understands all these as "basic teaching," while the priesthood of Christ is the more advanced teaching explored by the sermon. **4–6:** Those who have *fallen away* cannot be restored to repentance; they therefore share in *crucifying . . . the Son of God.* These verses describe the dire consequence for one who loses hope and falls away. **9–12:** The author reassures the audience that they are not among those who are lost. **13–18:** As a basis for hope, the author refers to God's promise to Abraham that he would bless Abraham's descendants (Gen 22.16–18). The promise made to Abraham applies to all Christians. **18:** *Two unchangeable things,* God's promise and God's oath. **19–20:** The author summarizes the theme of *hope* and introduces the next topic: a *priest* like *Melchizedek* and the entry of the priest into the holy of holies. **19:** *The inner shrine,* the holy of holies (9.3) of the tabernacle, behind the *curtain* or veil (Ex 26.31–35), restricted to the high priest alone (Lev 16.2). **20:** As *forerunner,* however, Jesus goes ahead on behalf of human beings. *Melchizedek,* here the author picks up the argument of 5.10.

7.1–28: The priesthood of Melchizedek and the Levitical priesthood compared. Having referred to Ps 110.4 (see 5.6,10; 6.20), the author proceeds to show how Christ is a priest *according to the order of* ("like") *Melchizedek.* The Dead Sea Scrolls give evidence of Jewish speculation on Melchizedek as an angelic, heavenly figure who rescues the righteous (11QMelch). **1–10:** From Gen 14.17–20 the author deduces that the mysterious priest-king Melchizedek was greater than either Abraham or his descendent,

ham as he was returning from defeating the
kings and blessed him"; 2 and to him Abra-
ham apportioned "one-tenth of every-
thing." His name, in the first place, means
"king of righteousness"; next he is also
king of Salem, that is, "king of peace."
3 Without father, without mother, without
genealogy, having neither beginning of
days nor end of life, but resembling the Son
of God, he remains a priest forever.

4 See how great he is! Even[a] Abraham
the patriarch gave him a tenth of the spoils.
5 And those descendants of Levi who re-
ceive the priestly office have a command-
ment in the law to collect tithes[b] from
the people, that is, from their kindred,[c]
though these also are descended from
Abraham. 6 But this man, who does not
belong to their ancestry, collected tithes[b]
from Abraham and blessed him who had
received the promises. 7 It is beyond dispute
that the inferior is blessed by the superior.
8 In the one case, tithes are received by
those who are mortal; in the other, by one
of whom it is testified that he lives. 9 One
might even say that Levi himself, who re-
ceives tithes, paid tithes through Abraham,
10 for he was still in the loins of his ancestor
when Melchizedek met him.

11 Now if perfection had been attain-
able through the levitical priesthood—for
the people received the law under this
priesthood—what further need would
there have been to speak of another priest
arising according to the order of Melchize-
dek, rather than one according to the order
of Aaron? 12 For when there is a change in
the priesthood, there is necessarily a change
in the law as well. 13 Now the one of whom
these things are spoken belonged to anoth-
er tribe, from which no one has ever served
at the altar. 14 For it is evident that our
Lord was descended from Judah, and in
connection with that tribe Moses said noth-
ing about priests.

15 It is even more obvious when another
priest arises, resembling Melchizedek,
16 one who has become a priest, not
through a legal requirement concerning
physical descent, but through the power of
an indestructible life. 17 For it is attested of
him,

"You are a priest forever,
according to the order of
Melchizedek."

18 There is, on the one hand, the abrogation
of an earlier commandment because it was
weak and ineffectual 19 (for the law made
nothing perfect); there is, on the other
hand, the introduction of a better hope,
through which we approach God.

20 This was confirmed with an oath; for
others who became priests took their office
without an oath, 21 but this one became a
priest with an oath, because of the one who
said to him,

"The Lord has sworn
and will not change his mind,
'You are a priest forever' "—

22 accordingly Jesus has also become the
guarantee of a better covenant.

23 Furthermore, the former priests were
many in number, because they were pre-
vented by death from continuing in office;
24 but he holds his priesthood permanently,
because he continues forever. 25 Conse-
quently he is able for all time to save[d]
those who approach God through him,
since he always lives to make intercession
for them.

a Other ancient authorities lack *Even* *b* Or *a tenth* *c* Gk *brothers* *d* Or *able to save completely*

Levi. **3:** *Without father, without mother, without genealogy,* the Bible makes no mention of Melchizedek's ancestors, birth, and death. **5:** See Num 18.21–24; Deut 26.12. **8:** *Those who are mortal,* the Levitical priests (Num 18). One who *lives,* Melchizedek, whose death is not recorded.

7.11–25: The Levitical priesthood is inadequate because it is provisional and temporary (vv. 11–14). On the other hand, a priest resembling Melchizedek is eternal (Ps 110.4), and the office is neither inherited nor transmitted (vv. 15–19). Unlike the Levitical priests, Jesus was appointed with a divine oath (v. 17; Ps 110.4); furthermore, being immortal, Jesus holds his priesthood permanently (vv. 20–25). **14:** *From Judah,* Jesus, as a descendant of David, belonged to the tribe of Judah (1 Chr 2.3–15; Sir 45.25).

26 For it was fitting that we should have
such a high priest, holy, blameless, unde-
filed, separated from sinners, and exalted
above the heavens. 27 Unlike the other[a]
high priests, he has no need to offer sacri-
fices day after day, first for his own sins,
and then for those of the people; this he did
once for all when he offered himself. 28 For
the law appoints as high priests those who
are subject to weakness, but the word of
the oath, which came later than the law,
appoints a Son who has been made perfect
forever.

8 Now the main point in what we are
saying is this: we have such a high
priest, one who is seated at the right hand
of the throne of the Majesty in the heavens,
2 a minister in the sanctuary and the true
tent[b] that the Lord, and not any mortal,
has set up. 3 For every high priest is ap-
pointed to offer gifts and sacrifices; hence
it is necessary for this priest also to have
something to offer. 4 Now if he were on
earth, he would not be a priest at all, since
there are priests who offer gifts according
to the law. 5 They offer worship in a sanctu-
ary that is a sketch and shadow of the heav-
enly one; for Moses, when he was about to
erect the tent,[b] was warned, "See that you
make everything according to the pattern
that was shown you on the mountain."
6 But Jesus[c] has now obtained a more ex-
cellent ministry, and to that degree he is the
mediator of a better covenant, which has
been enacted through better promises. 7 For
if that first covenant had been faultless,
there would have been no need to look for
a second one.

8 God[d] finds fault with them when he
says:

"The days are surely coming, says the
Lord,
when I will establish a new
covenant with the house
of Israel
and with the house of Judah;
9 not like the covenant that I made
with their ancestors,
on the day when I took them by
the hand to lead them out
of the land of Egypt;
for they did not continue in
my covenant,
and so I had no concern for them,
says the Lord.
10 This is the covenant that I will make
with the house of Israel
after those days, says the Lord:
I will put my laws in their minds,
and write them on their hearts,
and I will be their God,
and they shall be my people.
11 And they shall not teach one another
or say to each other, 'Know
the Lord,'
for they shall all know me,
from the least of them to
the greatest.
12 For I will be merciful toward their
iniquities,

a Gk lacks *other* *b* Or *tabernacle* *c* Gk *he*
d Gk *He*

7.26–28: Summary of the merits of the high priest, Jesus the Son of God. The theme of perfection and completeness concludes this section (see also vv. 11,19). The law has been incapable of bringing the priesthood to perfection because the Israelite priests were mortal (vv. 23–24). The author has established the eternal character of Christ's priesthood.

8.1–6: Old and new ministry. The author asserts that Christians have an eternal high priest who has been exalted into heaven (1.3). Christ exercises his priestly ministry only in heaven, since on earth he is not a Levite, and therefore not a priest. **4–5:** The author refers to the scripture that describes these rituals rather than to the Jewish practice of his day. **5:** Ex 25.40. Popular Platonic ideas of the time held that true realities existed in the heavenly world, while earthly ones were copies or shadows of the real. The author argues that Christ's ministry is superior because it takes place in that true heavenly world.

8.7–13: Old and new covenant. The announcement of a "new covenant" in Jer 31.31–34 causes a comparison with the old covenant, with Moses on Mount Sinai. Jer 31.31–34 is quoted and commented upon here and in 9.15–20 and 10.9–18. **13:** The old covenant will be replaced by the new.

and I will remember their sins
no more."

13 In speaking of "a new covenant," he has made the first one obsolete. And what is obsolete and growing old will soon disappear.

9 Now even the first covenant had regulations for worship and an earthly sanctuary. 2 For a tent[a] was constructed, the first one, in which were the lampstand, the table, and the bread of the Presence;[b] this is called the Holy Place. 3 Behind the second curtain was a tent[a] called the Holy of Holies. 4 In it stood the golden altar of incense and the ark of the covenant overlaid on all sides with gold, in which there were a golden urn holding the manna, and Aaron's rod that budded, and the tablets of the covenant; 5 above it were the cherubim of glory overshadowing the mercy seat.[c] Of these things we cannot speak now in detail.

6 Such preparations having been made, the priests go continually into the first tent[a] to carry out their ritual duties; 7 but only the high priest goes into the second, and he but once a year, and not without taking the blood that he offers for himself and for the sins committed unintentionally by the people. 8 By this the Holy Spirit indicates that the way into the sanctuary has not yet been disclosed as long as the first tent[a] is still standing. 9 This is a symbol[d] of the present time, during which gifts and sacrifices are offered that cannot perfect the conscience of the worshiper, 10 but deal only with food and drink and various baptisms, regulations for the body imposed until the time comes to set things right.

11 But when Christ came as a high priest of the good things that have come,[e] then through the greater and perfect[f] tent[a] (not made with hands, that is, not of this creation), 12 he entered once for all into the Holy Place, not with the blood of goats and calves, but with his own blood, thus obtaining eternal redemption. 13 For if the blood of goats and bulls, with the sprinkling of the ashes of a heifer, sanctifies those who have been defiled so that their flesh is purified, 14 how much more will the blood of Christ, who through the eternal Spirit[g] offered himself without blemish to God, purify our[h] conscience from dead works to worship the living God!

15 For this reason he is the mediator of a new covenant, so that those who are called may receive the promised eternal inheritance, because a death has occurred that redeems them from the transgressions under the first covenant.[i] 16 Where a will[i] is involved, the death of the one who made it must be established. 17 For a will[i] takes effect only at death, since it is not in force as long as the one who made it is alive. 18 Hence not even the first covenant was inaugurated without blood. 19 For when every commandment had been told to all the people by Moses in accordance with the law, he took the blood of calves and

a Or *tabernacle* *b* Gk *the presentation of the loaves*
c Or *the place of atonement* *d* Gk *parable*
e Other ancient authorities read *good things to come*
f Gk *more perfect* *g* Other ancient authorities read *Holy Spirit* *h* Other ancient authorities read *your*
i The Greek word used here means both *covenant* and *will*

9.1–10: The earthly sanctuary. The author describes the wilderness tabernacle of Ex 25–26 and its ritual. **2:** *The bread of the Presence,* Lev 24.5. **3:** Ex 26.31–33. **4:** *The golden altar of incense* stood in the Holy Place (Ex 30.6). *Ark of the covenant,* the chest containing the tablets of the law (Ex 25.10–22). *Urn . . . manna,* Ex 16.32–34. *Aaron's rod,* Num 17.1–10. **7:** The ritual for the day of atonement (Yom Kippur), in which the high priest enters the holy of holies, is described; see Lev 16. **10:** *The time . . . to set things right,* the period of the new covenant, inaugurated by the death of Christ.

9.11–28: The sacrifice of Christ. The author applies the categories of priestly ministry, covenant, and sanctuary ritual to the saving death of Christ. Christ's death is interpreted as the one effective sacrifice that atones for the sins of humanity (vv. 14,26,28). **12–13:** The day of atonement ritual (Lev 16.1–19), the sacrifice of the red *heifer* (Num 19.1–10), and the sacrificial ratification of the Sinai covenant (Ex 24.3–8) all have to do with the shedding of blood and contribute to the imagery of this argument. **14:** *The eternal Spirit,* the spiritual aspects of Christ's sacrifice. **15:** See note *i.* Cf. Gal 3.15–18. **28:** *The sins*

goats,[a] with water and scarlet wool and
hyssop, and sprinkled both the scroll itself
and all the people, 20 saying, "This is the
blood of the covenant that God has or-
dained for you." 21 And in the same way he
sprinkled with the blood both the tent[b]
and all the vessels used in worship. 22 In-
deed, under the law almost everything is
purified with blood, and without the shed-
ding of blood there is no forgiveness of sins.

23 Thus it was necessary for the
sketches of the heavenly things to be puri-
fied with these rites, but the heavenly things
themselves need better sacrifices than these.
24 For Christ did not enter a sanctuary
made by human hands, a mere copy of the
true one, but he entered into heaven itself,
now to appear in the presence of God on
our behalf. 25 Nor was it to offer himself
again and again, as the high priest enters
the Holy Place year after year with blood
that is not his own; 26 for then he would
have had to suffer again and again since the
foundation of the world. But as it is, he has
appeared once for all at the end of the age
to remove sin by the sacrifice of himself.
27 And just as it is appointed for mortals to
die once, and after that the judgment, 28 so
Christ, having been offered once to bear the
sins of many, will appear a second time, not
to deal with sin, but to save those who are
eagerly waiting for him.

10 Since the law has only a shadow of
the good things to come and not the
true form of these realities, it[c] can never,
by the same sacrifices that are continually
offered year after year, make perfect those
who approach. 2 Otherwise, would they not
have ceased being offered, since the wor-
shipers, cleansed once for all, would no
longer have any consciousness of sin? 3 But
in these sacrifices there is a reminder of sin
year after year. 4 For it is impossible for the
blood of bulls and goats to take away sins.
5 Consequently, when Christ[d] came into
the world, he said,

"Sacrifices and offerings you have not
desired,
but a body you have prepared
for me;
6 in burnt offerings and sin offerings
you have taken no pleasure.
7 Then I said, 'See, God, I have come
to do your will, O God'
(in the scroll of the book[e] it is
written of me)."

8 When he said above, "You have neither
desired nor taken pleasure in sacrifices and
offerings and burnt offerings and sin offer-
ings" (these are offered according to the
law), 9 then he added, "See, I have come to
do your will." He abolishes the first in or-
der to establish the second. 10 And it is by
God's will[f] that we have been sanctified
through the offering of the body of Jesus
Christ once for all.

11 And every priest stands day after day
at his service, offering again and again the
same sacrifices that can never take away
sins. 12 But when Christ[g] had offered for
all time a single sacrifice for sins, "he sat
down at the right hand of God," 13 and
since then has been waiting "until his ene-
mies would be made a footstool for his
feet." 14 For by a single offering he has per-
fected for all time those who are sanctified.

a Other ancient authorities lack *and goats*
b Or *tabernacle* *c* Other ancient authorities read *they* *d* Gk *he* *e* Meaning of Gk uncertain
f Gk *by that will* *g* Gk *this one*

of many, Isa 53.12; Mk 10.45. *A second time,* a reference to the Second Coming of Christ is not wholly consistent with the understanding that Christ has entered into heaven and made salvation available in the present (v. 11).

10.1–18: Old and new sacrifice. The author summarizes the comparison between Christ's sacrifice and Israelite ritual. Evidence is found in scripture both for the limitations of the ritual and for the meaning of the word spoken in the Son. **1:** The *shadow* of the *law* is understood to be inferior to *the true form* that is in the future. **4–9:** The proof for the idea that it is *impossible* for animal sacrifices to *take away sins* is found in interpretation of Ps 40.6–8 (Septuagint) in which the speaker is understood to be Christ. **8:** 1 Sam 15.22; Ps 50.8–15; Isa 1.10–17; Jer 7.21–26; Hos 6.6. **10:** *Sanctified,* ceremonially cleansed and perfected through Christ's blood (10.29). **12–13:** Ps 110.1. **15–18:** The Holy Spirit is understood

15 And the Holy Spirit also testifies to us,
for after saying,
16 "This is the covenant that I will make
with them
after those days, says the Lord:
I will put my laws in their hearts,
and I will write them on
their minds,"
17 he also adds,
"I will remember[a] their sins and their
lawless deeds no more."
18 Where there is forgiveness of these, there
is no longer any offering for sin.
19 Therefore, my friends,[b] since we
have confidence to enter the sanctuary by
the blood of Jesus, 20 by the new and living
way that he opened for us through the cur-
tain (that is, through his flesh), 21 and since
we have a great priest over the house of
God, 22 let us approach with a true heart
in full assurance of faith, with our hearts
sprinkled clean from an evil conscience and
our bodies washed with pure water. 23 Let
us hold fast to the confession of our hope
without wavering, for he who has promised
is faithful. 24 And let us consider how to
provoke one another to love and good
deeds, 25 not neglecting to meet together, as
is the habit of some, but encouraging one
another, and all the more as you see the
Day approaching.
26 For if we willfully persist in sin after
having received the knowledge of the truth,
there no longer remains a sacrifice for sins,
27 but a fearful prospect of judgment, and a
fury of fire that will consume the adversar-
ies. 28 Anyone who has violated the law of
Moses dies without mercy "on the testimo-
ny of two or three witnesses." 29 How
much worse punishment do you think will
be deserved by those who have spurned the
Son of God, profaned the blood of the cov-
enant by which they were sanctified, and
outraged the Spirit of grace? 30 For we
know the one who said, "Vengeance is
mine, I will repay." And again, "The Lord
will judge his people." 31 It is a fearful thing
to fall into the hands of the living God.
32 But recall those earlier days when, af-
ter you had been enlightened, you endured
a hard struggle with sufferings, 33 some-
times being publicly exposed to abuse and
persecution, and sometimes being partners
with those so treated. 34 For you had com-
passion for those who were in prison, and
you cheerfully accepted the plundering of
your possessions, knowing that you your-
selves possessed something better and more
lasting. 35 Do not, therefore, abandon that
confidence of yours; it brings a great re-
ward. 36 For you need endurance, so that
when you have done the will of God, you
may receive what was promised. 37 For yet
"in a very little while,
the one who is coming will come
and will not delay;
38 but my righteous one will live
by faith.
My soul takes no pleasure in
anyone who shrinks back."
39 But we are not among those who shrink

a Gk *on their minds and I will remember*
b Gk *Therefore, brothers*

to be speaking a paraphrase of Jer 31.33–34. The new covenant assures full and final forgiveness of sins.

10.19–31: Exhortations and warnings. Compare the exhortation in 4.14–16. **20:** *That he opened for us through the curtain (that is, through his flesh),* perhaps the curtain symbolizes Jesus' physical existence, which separates the holy of holies from the outer sanctuary; or the physical existence of Jesus symbolizes the path of access to God. The *flesh* of Jesus is the means for approaching God. **22–25:** Three privileges and duties of Christians: *Let us approach* God in faith and worship (vv. 22,25); *let us hold fast* the public *confession of our hope* (v. 23); *let us consider* how we can help others in love (v. 24). **23:** *Confession of our hope,* the basic attitude of Christians. For Hebrews, faith undergirds hope (see 3.6; 6.11,18; 7.19). **25:** *The Day* of Christ's Second Coming, see 9.28n. **26:** Solemn warning about deliberate sin (see 5.2; 6.4–6). **28:** Deut 17.2–6. **30:** Deut 32.35–36.

10.39–12.29: The power of faith.

10.32–39: Living by faith. This transitional passage shifts from a focus on hope and confidence (vv. 35–36) to faith (vv. 38–39). **37:** Isa 26.20 (Septuagint). **37–38:** Hab 2.3–4 (cf. Rom 1.17; Gal 3.11).

back and so are lost, but among those who have faith and so are saved.

11 Now faith is the assurance of things hoped for, the conviction of things not seen. 2 Indeed, by faith[a] our ancestors received approval. 3 By faith we understand that the worlds were prepared by the word of God, so that what is seen was made from things that are not visible.[b]

4 By faith Abel offered to God a more acceptable[c] sacrifice than Cain's. Through this he received approval as righteous, God himself giving approval to his gifts; he died, but through his faith[d] he still speaks. 5 By faith Enoch was taken so that he did not experience death; and "he was not found, because God had taken him." For it was attested before he was taken away that "he had pleased God." 6 And without faith it is impossible to please God, for whoever would approach him must believe that he exists and that he rewards those who seek him. 7 By faith Noah, warned by God about events as yet unseen, respected the warning and built an ark to save his household; by this he condemned the world and became an heir to the righteousness that is in accordance with faith.

8 By faith Abraham obeyed when he was called to set out for a place that he was to receive as an inheritance; and he set out, not knowing where he was going. 9 By faith he stayed for a time in the land he had been promised, as in a foreign land, living in tents, as did Isaac and Jacob, who were heirs with him of the same promise. 10 For he looked forward to the city that has foundations, whose architect and builder is God. 11 By faith he received power of procreation, even though he was too old—and Sarah herself was barren—because he considered him faithful who had promised.[e] 12 Therefore from one person, and this one as good as dead, descendants were born, "as many as the stars of heaven and as the innumerable grains of sand by the seashore."

13 All of these died in faith without having received the promises, but from a distance they saw and greeted them. They confessed that they were strangers and foreigners on the earth, 14 for people who speak in this way make it clear that they are seeking a homeland. 15 If they had been thinking of the land that they had left behind, they would have had opportunity to return. 16 But as it is, they desire a better country, that is, a heavenly one. Therefore God is not ashamed to be called their God; indeed, he has prepared a city for them.

17 By faith Abraham, when put to the test, offered up Isaac. He who had received the promises was ready to offer up his only son, 18 of whom he had been told, "It is through Isaac that descendants shall be named for you." 19 He considered the fact that God is able even to raise someone from the dead—and figuratively speaking, he did receive him back. 20 By faith Isaac invoked blessings for the future on Jacob and Esau. 21 By faith Jacob, when dying, blessed each

a Gk *by this* *b* Or *was not made out of visible things* *c* Gk *greater* *d* Gk *through it* *e* Or *By faith Sarah herself, though barren, received power to conceive, even when she was too old, because she considered him faithful who had promised.*

11.1–12.2: A cloud of witnesses to faith. A series of examples of models of faith from the Hebrew Bible, culminating in the example of Jesus in 12.1–2. **1:** The Gk word translated *assurance* has an objective quality and might be translated "reality." Likewise, *conviction* has the connotation of "evidence." The people of faith who follow all possess insight into the reality of the invisible divine world. **3:** Ps 33.6; Wis 9.1. **4:** Gen 4.3–10. **5:** Gen 5.21–24. **6:** A general axiom referring to the existence and moral government of God. **7:** *Noah,* Gen 6.13–22. *Righteousness,* Gen 15.6. **8–9:** Gen 12.1–8. **10:** *The city,* the heavenly Jerusalem. *Foundations,* contrasted with tents (v. 9). **11:** In some manuscripts, Sarah is the subject of the sentence: "By faith, Sarah received the power of procreation . . ." Sarah's faith in the unseen is parallel to Abraham's, and she is one of the heroic people of faith. Gen 17.19; 18.11–14; 21.2. **12:** Gen 15.5–6; 22.17; 32.12; Rom 4.19. **16:** *A city,* see v. 10n. **17:** Gen 22.1–10. **18:** Gen 21.12. **19:** Abraham received Isaac back when he was told to offer a ram instead of his son (Gen 22.13). **20:** Gen 27.27–29,39–40. **21:** Gen 48; 47.31 (Septuagint). **22:** Gen 50.24–25; Ex 13.19. **23:** Ex 2.2; 1.22. **24–27:** Ex 2.10–15. **26:**

of the sons of Joseph, "bowing in worship
over the top of his staff." 22 By faith Joseph,
at the end of his life, made mention of the
exodus of the Israelites and gave instruc-
tions about his burial.[a]
23 By faith Moses was hidden by his
parents for three months after his birth, be-
cause they saw that the child was beautiful;
and they were not afraid of the king's
edict.[b] 24 By faith Moses, when he was
grown up, refused to be called a son of
Pharaoh's daughter, 25 choosing rather to
share ill-treatment with the people of God
than to enjoy the fleeting pleasures of sin.
26 He considered abuse suffered for the
Christ[c] to be greater wealth than the trea-
sures of Egypt, for he was looking ahead to
the reward. 27 By faith he left Egypt, un-
afraid of the king's anger; for he persevered
as though[d] he saw him who is invisible.
28 By faith he kept the Passover and the
sprinkling of blood, so that the destroyer of
the firstborn would not touch the firstborn
of Israel.[e]
29 By faith the people passed through
the Red Sea as if it were dry land, but when
the Egyptians attempted to do so they were
drowned. 30 By faith the walls of Jericho fell
after they had been encircled for seven
days. 31 By faith Rahab the prostitute did
not perish with those who were disobedi-
ent,[f] because she had received the spies in
peace.
32 And what more should I say? For
time would fail me to tell of Gideon, Barak,
Samson, Jephthah, of David and Samuel
and the prophets— 33 who through faith
conquered kingdoms, administered justice,
obtained promises, shut the mouths of li-
ons, 34 quenched raging fire, escaped the
edge of the sword, won strength out of
weakness, became mighty in war, put for-
eign armies to flight. 35 Women received
their dead by resurrection. Others were tor-
tured, refusing to accept release, in order to
obtain a better resurrection. 36 Others suf-
fered mocking and flogging, and even
chains and imprisonment. 37 They were
stoned to death, they were sawn in two,[g]
they were killed by the sword; they went
about in skins of sheep and goats, destitute,
persecuted, tormented— 38 of whom the
world was not worthy. They wandered in
deserts and mountains, and in caves and
holes in the ground.
39 Yet all these, though they were com-
mended for their faith, did not receive what
was promised, 40 since God had provided
something better so that they would not,
apart from us, be made perfect.

12 Therefore, since we are surrounded
by so great a cloud of witnesses, let
us also lay aside every weight and the sin
that clings so closely,[h] and let us run with
perseverance the race that is set before us,
2 looking to Jesus the pioneer and perfecter
of our faith, who for the sake of[i] the joy
that was set before him endured the cross,
disregarding its shame, and has taken his
seat at the right hand of the throne of God.
3 Consider him who endured such hos-

a Gk *his bones* *b* Other ancient authorities add *By faith Moses, when he was grown up, killed the Egyptian, because he observed the humiliation of his people* (Gk *brothers*) *c* Or *the Messiah* *d* Or *because* *e* Gk *would not touch them* *f* Or *unbelieving* *g* Other ancient authorities add *they were tempted* *h* Other ancient authorities read *sin that easily distracts* *i* Or *who instead of*

Abuse suffered for the Christ (cf. 13.13); see also Ps 89.52 where "the anointed one" refers to the people of God. **27:** *Him who is invisible,* Jn 1.18; Col 1.15; 1 Tim 1.17; 6.16. **28:** *Sprinkling of blood,* on the lintels and doorposts. See Ex 12.21–30. **29:** Ex 14.21–31. **30:** Josh 6.12–21. **31:** *Rahab,* Josh 2.1–21; 6.22–25. Rahab is referred to as a hero in Mt 1.5, Jas 2.25, *1 Clem* 12. **32:** *Gideon,* Judg 6–8; *Barak,* Judg 4–5; *Samson,* Judg 13–16; *Jephthah,* Judg 11–12; *David,* 1 Sam 16–30; 2 Sam 1–24; 1 Kings 1.1–2.11; *Samuel,* 1 Sam 1–12; 15.1–16.13. **33:** *Lions,* Dan 6. **34:** *Fire,* Dan 3. **35:** *Resurrection,* 1 Kings 17.17–24; 2 Kings 4.25–37; *tortured,* 2 Macc 7.9,14. **37:** 2 Chr 24.20–22; Jer 26.23; 2 Macc 5.27; 6.12–7.42. **38:** *Caves,* 2 Macc 6.11; 10.6.

12.1–2: Jesus, the ultimate example of faith. Jesus is the supreme model of faith in God and an example for those who follow him. **1:** *Witnesses,* those mentioned in ch 11. **2:** *Pioneer and perfecter,* see 2.10.

tility against himself from sinners,[a] so that
you may not grow weary or lose heart. 4In
your struggle against sin you have not yet
resisted to the point of shedding your
blood. 5And you have forgotten the exhor-
tation that addresses you as children—
"My child, do not regard lightly the
discipline of the Lord,
or lose heart when you are
punished by him;
6 for the Lord disciplines those whom
he loves,
and chastises every child whom he
accepts."
7Endure trials for the sake of discipline.
God is treating you as children; for what
child is there whom a parent does not disci-
pline? 8If you do not have that discipline in
which all children share, then you are ille-
gitimate and not his children. 9Moreover,
we had human parents to discipline us, and
we respected them. Should we not be even
more willing to be subject to the Father of
spirits and live? 10For they disciplined us
for a short time as seemed best to them, but
he disciplines us for our good, in order that
we may share his holiness. 11Now, disci-
pline always seems painful rather than
pleasant at the time, but later it yields the
peaceful fruit of righteousness to those who
have been trained by it.
12 Therefore lift your drooping hands
and strengthen your weak knees, 13and
make straight paths for your feet, so that
what is lame may not be put out of joint,
but rather be healed.
14 Pursue peace with everyone, and the
holiness without which no one will see the
Lord. 15See to it that no one fails to obtain
the grace of God; that no root of bitterness
springs up and causes trouble, and through
it many become defiled. 16See to it that no
one becomes like Esau, an immoral and
godless person, who sold his birthright for
a single meal. 17You know that later, when
he wanted to inherit the blessing, he was
rejected, for he found no chance to re-
pent,[b] even though he sought the bless-
ing[c] with tears.
18 You have not come to something[d]
that can be touched, a blazing fire, and
darkness, and gloom, and a tempest, 19and
the sound of a trumpet, and a voice whose
words made the hearers beg that not anoth-
er word be spoken to them. 20(For they
could not endure the order that was given,
"If even an animal touches the mountain, it
shall be stoned to death." 21Indeed, so ter-
rifying was the sight that Moses said, "I
tremble with fear.") 22But you have come
to Mount Zion and to the city of the living
God, the heavenly Jerusalem, and to innu-
merable angels in festal gathering, 23and to
the assembly[e] of the firstborn who are en-
rolled in heaven, and to God the judge of
all, and to the spirits of the righteous made
perfect, 24and to Jesus, the mediator of a
new covenant, and to the sprinkled blood

a Other ancient authorities read *such hostility from sinners against themselves* *b* Or *no chance to change his father's mind* *c* Gk *it* *d* Other ancient authorities read *a mountain* *e* Or *angels, and to the festal gathering* 23*and assembly*

12.3–17: The discipline of God. The author develops the metaphors of the athletic contest or race (vv. 1,12–13), the father disciplining his children (vv. 5–11), and the "bitter root" (v. 15). **5–8:** Prov 3.11–12. In the family structure of the ancient world, the father's (*parent*'s) obligation to punish sons (*children*) and so recognize their legitimacy is the background of the comparison between suffering and discipline from God. *Illegitimate* children were not disciplined. The author understands the scripture to be speaking to Christians as "sons" or "children" of the Father (cf. 5.8). *All . . . share,* namely, all children of God (v. 6). **9:** *Father of spirits,* God is traditionally understood to have power over the world of spirits (see Num 16.22; Rev 22.6). **12:** Isa 35.3. **14–17:** The necessity of *peace* and purity. **15:** *Root of bitterness,* Deut 29.18 (Septuagint). **16:** Gen 25.29–34. **17:** Gen 27.30–40.

12.18–29: Mount Sinai and Mount Zion contrasted. 18–19: *Something that can be touched,* Mount Sinai (Ex 19.12–22; 20.18–21; Deut 4.11–12; 5.22–27). **20:** Ex 19.12–13. **21:** Deut 9.19. **24:** Abel's *blood* cried for vengeance (11.4; Gen 4.10); the *sprinkled blood* of Jesus, which established the new

that speaks a better word than the blood of
Abel.
25 See that you do not refuse the one
who is speaking; for if they did not escape
when they refused the one who warned
them on earth, how much less will we es-
cape if we reject the one who warns from
heaven! 26 At that time his voice shook the
earth; but now he has promised, "Yet once
more I will shake not only the earth but
also the heaven." 27 This phrase, "Yet once
more," indicates the removal of what is
shaken—that is, created things—so that
what cannot be shaken may remain.
28 Therefore, since we are receiving a king-
dom that cannot be shaken, let us give
thanks, by which we offer to God an ac-
ceptable worship with reverence and awe;
29 for indeed our God is a consuming fire.

13 Let mutual love continue. 2 Do not
neglect to show hospitality to
strangers, for by doing that some have en-
tertained angels without knowing it. 3 Re-
member those who are in prison, as though
you were in prison with them; those who
are being tortured, as though you your-
selves were being tortured.[a] 4 Let marriage
be held in honor by all, and let the marriage
bed be kept undefiled; for God will judge
fornicators and adulterers. 5 Keep your lives
free from the love of money, and be content
with what you have; for he has said, "I will
never leave you or forsake you." 6 So we
can say with confidence,

"The Lord is my helper;
I will not be afraid.
What can anyone do to me?"

7 Remember your leaders, those who
spoke the word of God to you; consider the
outcome of their way of life, and imitate
their faith. 8 Jesus Christ is the same yester-
day and today and forever. 9 Do not be car-
ried away by all kinds of strange teachings;
for it is well for the heart to be strengthened
by grace, not by regulations about food,[b]
which have not benefited those who ob-
serve them. 10 We have an altar from which
those who officiate in the tent[c] have no
right to eat. 11 For the bodies of those ani-
mals whose blood is brought into the sanc-
tuary by the high priest as a sacrifice for sin
are burned outside the camp. 12 Therefore
Jesus also suffered outside the city gate in
order to sanctify the people by his own
blood. 13 Let us then go to him outside the
camp and bear the abuse he endured. 14 For
here we have no lasting city, but we are
looking for the city that is to come.
15 Through him, then, let us continually of-
fer a sacrifice of praise to God, that is, the
fruit of lips that confess his name. 16 Do not
neglect to do good and to share what you
have, for such sacrifices are pleasing to
God.
17 Obey your leaders and submit to
them, for they are keeping watch over your
souls and will give an account. Let them do
this with joy and not with sighing—for that
would be harmful to you.
18 Pray for us; we are sure that we have
a clear conscience, desiring to act honor-
ably in all things. 19 I urge you all the more

a Gk *were in the body* *b* Gk *not by foods*
c Or *tabernacle*

covenant (9.14; 13.20), *speaks . . . better* for forgiveness. **25:** Cf. 19.26–31. The theme of responding to the one who speaks recalls the beginning of the sermon. **26:** Hag 2.6. **29:** Deut 4.24; 9.3.

13.1–25: Practical instructions to the community and greetings.

13.1–17: The sermon concludes with specific ethical exhortation to show *mutual love.* **2:** *Entertained angels,* Gen 18.1–8; 19.1. **3:** Mt 25.35–46. **5:** Josh 1.5. **6:** Ps 118.6. **7:** *Your leaders,* former leaders who proclaimed God's word to the community in the past. **9:** Whether *regulations about food* refers to Jewish food laws or ritual dining practices is not clear. The author contrasts these to *grace,* which is effective. **11:** Lev 16.27. Cf. Col 2.16,20–23. **12:** As the sacrificed animals are burned outside the camp, so Jesus died outside the gate of Jerusalem (Jn 19.20). **14:** *The city . . . to come,* see 11.10. **15:** A sacrifice of thanksgiving (Lev 7.12; Ps 50.14,23; Hos 14.2). **17:** *Leaders,* those at the head of the community who protect people from harm.

13.18–25: Greetings, blessing, and postscript. 20–21: Blessing (see Isa 63.11). *Brought back,* lit. "led

to do this, so that I may be restored to you
very soon.
20 Now may the God of peace, who
brought back from the dead our Lord
Jesus, the great shepherd of the sheep, by
the blood of the eternal covenant, 21 make
you complete in everything good so that
you may do his will, working among us[a]
that which is pleasing in his sight, through
Jesus Christ, to whom be the glory forever
and ever. Amen.
22 I appeal to you, brothers and sis-
ters,[b] bear with my word of exhortation,
for I have written to you briefly. 23 I want
you to know that our brother Timothy has
been set free; and if he comes in time, he
will be with me when I see you. 24 Greet all
your leaders and all the saints. Those from
Italy send you greetings. 25 Grace be with
all of you.[c]

a Other ancient authorities read *you* *b* Gk *brothers*
c Other ancient authorities add *Amen*

up." The verb refers to the exaltation of Jesus to the right hand of God. **22**: *Word of exhortation,* a sermon, rather than a letter (see Acts 13.22); *for I have written to you briefly,* mention of the "briefness" of a letter is conventional in ancient letters. **23**: *Timothy* is referred to in Paul's letters and Acts of the Apostles as a companion to Paul (1 Cor 4.17; Acts 16.1–3).

The Letter of JAMES

This letter takes its name from the authority and tradition associated with James, the brother of Jesus (Mt 13.55; Mk 6.3; Gal 1.19), who eventually became the leader of the church in Jerusalem (Gal 2.9,12; Acts 12.17; 15.13; 21.18). Throughout the document, a consistent tone of moral authority (59 of 108 verses are in the imperative) determines its literary character as a series of moral instructions (parenesis or exhortation) and wisdom sayings, inspired by different parts of the Bible. The advice alludes both to the Hebrew Bible and to the Jesus tradition (particularly that of Matthew and Luke); there may also be references to Paul's teaching (2.14–26). The letter thereby combines pastoral, prophetic, and teaching moods appropriate to address the community crises. Its basic message is an urgent appeal for those who call themselves Christians to adopt a courageous faith that will help them cope effectively with the trials of life, and will produce in them heightened moral integrity and loving actions.

Directed to Jewish Christian congregations ("your assembly," lit. "synagogue," 2.2) toward the close of the first century, this letter was probably written in at least two stages. The original text was a sermon by James in the months prior to his martyrdom in the mid-60s. Then, someone skilled in Hellenistic rhetoric edited, expanded, and distributed the sermon in the form of a circular letter, probably in the late 80s or 90s. It went to Diaspora churches that were in disarray and needed to hear again the authoritative voice of the Jerusalem church's leader. Its aim was to instruct Jewish Christians experiencing tensions between their allegiance to the Torah and their newfound faith in Jesus. In this sense, James and Jude are the last New Testament echoes of Jewish Christianity.

In dealing with issues of concern to Jewish Christians, the letter (particularly in 2.14–26) appears to oppose the thinking of Paul on the issue of the relation between faith and works, and the means by which the believer attains "justification" or the state of right relationship with God. Paul and James each interpret a verse from the Hebrew Bible—"And he [Abraham] believed the LORD; and the LORD reckoned it to him as righteousness" (Gen 15.6)—to support his own view (Paul in Gal 3.6–14, James in Jas 2.21–24). For Paul, the believer's justification comes through faith, not works (Rom 4.16–5.2); for James, "faith by itself, if it has no works, is dead" (2.17). The conflict, however, is more apparent than real. For Paul, faith is primarily trust in God (Rom 4.5), a sense of the word that James also shares (1.5); but, in his critique of faith, James means by it essentially the assent to ideas about God without any personal relationship or commitment to inform them: "Even the demons believe" (2.19). James sees works as the acts that spring from the love of the believer for God (2.14), whereas for Paul works are the external observations of ritual, like circumcision, regarded in isolation from any connection to one's relationship to God.

The letter of James may strike the reader as having little in the way of unity and coherence, but rather as skipping from one topic to another without much connection. Its inherent unity, however, can be seen if one views the letter as a response to the situation in which these early Christians found themselves. The Christian assemblies were tiny minorities existing within large populations that were indifferent or hostile to their beliefs. The writer is concerned that these early Christian groups should not adopt, or fall back into, the values or the behavior of the surrounding population (4.4). From this comes the strategic mixture in the letter of the prophetic tradition (for instance, 2.5–7) and the wisdom tradition (for instance, 1.5–8). This combination is meant to help those who are struggling to live morally: the prophetic denunciations of arrogant wealth and immorality (2.6–7; 5.1–6) are strengthened and completed through the development of wisdom (3.13). Wisdom can serve both as a guide to behavior (for instance, guarding against malicious speech, 3.8–10; 4.11) and as an aid to discernment (seeing the joy that lies beyond present suffering, 3.17–18). The testing to which the faithful are subjected will help them learn and be transformed (1.12): it will show them what really matters, and it can be, if seen in the right way, a strengthening rather than a weakening ordeal. Thus, these communities will be built up through their sufferings (4.7–10), and their faith will be, not a substitute for acts of love (2.15–16), but rather a means to help them undertake such acts (1.22–27).

Martin Luther's cavalier assessment of James as "an epistle of straw" because it seemingly denigrated the Pauline doctrine of justification by faith (2.14–26) influenced its interpretation for many years. Yet as a witness to Jewish Christianity the letter of James constitutes "the second voice of Jesus," reminding Christians that a faith that fails to bear fruit in the moral life cannot save.

1 James, a servant[a] of God and of the
Lord Jesus Christ,
To the twelve tribes in the Dispersion:
Greetings.

2 My brothers and sisters,[b] whenever
you face trials of any kind, consider it noth-
ing but joy, 3 because you know that the
testing of your faith produces endurance;
4 and let endurance have its full effect, so
that you may be mature and complete,
lacking in nothing.
5 If any of you is lacking in wisdom, ask
God, who gives to all generously and un-
grudgingly, and it will be given you. 6 But
ask in faith, never doubting, for the one
who doubts is like a wave of the sea, driven
and tossed by the wind; 7, 8 for the doubter,
being double-minded and unstable in every
way, must not expect to receive anything
from the Lord.
9 Let the believer[c] who is lowly boast in
being raised up, 10 and the rich in being
brought low, because the rich will disap-
pear like a flower in the field. 11 For the sun
rises with its scorching heat and withers the
field; its flower falls, and its beauty per-
ishes. It is the same way with the rich; in the
midst of a busy life, they will wither away.

a Gk *slave* *b* Gk *brothers* *c* Gk *brother*

1.1: Salutation. *Servant of God* occurs elsewhere only in Titus 1.1. In the Hebrew Bible, "servant of the LORD" or "my servant" is applied to Moses (Deut 34.5; Josh 1.1), David (2 Sam 7.5; Ps 78.70), Daniel (Dan 6.20), and Israel (Isa 42.1; 49.3). *Dispersion,* Greek "diaspora," the scattering of Jews outside Palestine, here applied to Christians (see 1 Pet 1.1). *Twelve tribes,* the church as the new Israel. *Greetings,* a Hellenistic literary refinement (see Acts 15.23).

1.2–8: Faith that rejoices in trials. 2: *Trials,* or "temptations," "tests" (see Gen 22.1; Mt 4.1–14; Heb 4.15; 1 Pet 1.6). **3–4:** *Testing . . . endurance . . . complete,* a catena, or series of linked phrases, that builds to a climax; cf. Rom 5.3–4. *Mature and complete,* better "and perfect," recalling the teaching of Jesus (Mt 5.48). **5:** *Wisdom, ask God,* cf. 1 Kings 3. **6:** *Wave . . . sea . . . wind,* see also 3.4; cf. Isa 57.20. **8:** *Double-minded,* trying to hold two incompatible views; used in 4.8, and nowhere else in early Christian writings. The author's vocabulary includes other rare terms ("Father of lights" 1.17, "implanted word" 1. 21, "cycle of nature" 3.6).

1.9–11: A reversal of fortunes. 9–10: *Lowly . . . the rich,* wealthy people can be Christians; the issue is not social standing but unjust behavior; see 2.2–6; 5.1–6. **10:** *Like a flower,* see Ps 103.15; Isa 40.6–7. **11:** On the reversal of fortune, see 1 Sam 2.7; Lk 1.52–53; 6.20–26; 16.19–31.

12 Blessed is anyone who endures temp-
tation. Such a one has stood the test and
will receive the crown of life that the Lord[a]
has promised to those who love him. 13 No
one, when tempted, should say, "I am be-
ing tempted by God"; for God cannot be
tempted by evil and he himself tempts no
one. 14 But one is tempted by one's own
desire, being lured and enticed by it;
15 then, when that desire has conceived, it
gives birth to sin, and that sin, when it is
fully grown, gives birth to death. 16 Do not
be deceived, my beloved.[b]

17 Every generous act of giving, with
every perfect gift, is from above, coming
down from the Father of lights, with whom
there is no variation or shadow due to
change.[c] 18 In fulfillment of his own pur-
pose he gave us birth by the word of truth,
so that we would become a kind of first
fruits of his creatures.

19 You must understand this, my be-
loved:[b] let everyone be quick to listen,
slow to speak, slow to anger; 20 for your
anger does not produce God's righteous-
ness. 21 Therefore rid yourselves of all sor-
didness and rank growth of wickedness,
and welcome with meekness the implanted
word that has the power to save your souls.

22 But be doers of the word, and not
merely hearers who deceive themselves.
23 For if any are hearers of the word and
not doers, they are like those who look at
themselves[d] in a mirror; 24 for they look at
themselves and, on going away, immediate-
ly forget what they were like. 25 But those
who look into the perfect law, the law of
liberty, and persevere, being not hearers
who forget but doers who act—they will be
blessed in their doing.

26 If any think they are religious, and do
not bridle their tongues but deceive their
hearts, their religion is worthless. 27 Reli-
gion that is pure and undefiled before God,
the Father, is this: to care for orphans and
widows in their distress, and to keep one-
self unstained by the world.

2 My brothers and sisters,[e] do you with
your acts of favoritism really believe in

a Gk *he*; other ancient authorities read *God*
b Gk *my beloved brothers* *c* Other ancient authorities read *variation due to a shadow of turning*
d Gk *at the face of his birth* *e* Gk *My brothers*

1.12–18: God who rewards faithful endurance. 12: *Blessed* is reminiscent of the Beatitudes (Mt 5.3–11; Lk 6.20–22) and the refrain in the Psalms (e.g., 1.1). *The crown of life,* the only other occurrence is in Rev 2.10. A reiteration of vv. 2–3. *Promised to those who love him;* cf. Ex 20.6; Deut 5.10; Rom 8.28. **13–16:** Some Hellenistic Jews believed that each person has both an evil inclination and a good inclination; because God created both, the individual might blame God for moral lapses. James vigorously refutes this position (see Sir 15.11–20) without compromising a pastoral stance (*my beloved*). **17–18:** A return to the subject of God's generosity (v. 5). *Father of lights,* the title also occurs in CD 5.17–18; *Apocalypse of Moses* 36.5; *Testament of Abraham* 7.60; cf. Gen 1.15–16; Ps 136.7. *Gave us birth,* i.e., as Christians (cf. 1 Pet 1.23). *Word of truth,* i.e., the gospel (see Eph 1.13; Col 1.5). The Christian life thus constitutes a new creation.

1.19–25: Righteousness in word and deed. 19: A three-part wisdom saying (cf. Sir 5.11) alerts the reader to an important distinction between James and Paul. Paul (2 Cor 5.21) probably means a "righteousness found in God" but imparted to believers as a gift, whereas the Jewish Christian James means a standard of righteousness established by God to which the believer seeks to conform. **21:** *Implanted word,* a rare phrase meaning the same as "word of truth" in 1.18. **22–25:** Righteousness for James is a unity of word and deed. **22:** *Be doers of the word,* see Mt 7.24–27; cf. Rom 2.13. **25:** *Perfect law, the law of liberty,* enables Christians to become perfect (1.4; cf. Ps 18.8).

1.26–27: Religion that is personal and social. A summary focus on the outward practice of one's faith (cf. Acts 26.5; Wis 14.27; 1 Clem 62.1). **26:** *Bridle their tongues* refers to 1.13,19, but also anticipates the discussion of speech ethics in 3.2–12. **27:** *Orphans and widows* are wards of God the father (Deut 10–18; Ps 68.5) in whose *distress* believers are also to show mercy and love (cf. Sir 4.10).

2.1–13: Faith and acts of discrimination. The first of two large units in this chapter addresses the problem of discrimination based on social class. **1:** *Favoritism,* better, "acts of discrimination" or hurtful

our glorious Lord Jesus Christ?[a] 2 For if a
person with gold rings and in fine clothes
comes into your assembly, and if a poor
person in dirty clothes also comes in, 3 and
if you take notice of the one wearing the
fine clothes and say, "Have a seat here,
please," while to the one who is poor you
say, "Stand there," or, "Sit at my feet,"[b]
4 have you not made distinctions among
yourselves, and become judges with evil
thoughts? 5 Listen, my beloved brothers
and sisters.[c] Has not God chosen the poor
in the world to be rich in faith and to be
heirs of the kingdom that he has promised
to those who love him? 6 But you have dis-
honored the poor. Is it not the rich who
oppress you? Is it not they who drag you
into court? 7 Is it not they who blaspheme
the excellent name that was invoked over
you?
8 You do well if you really fulfill the
royal law according to the scripture, "You
shall love your neighbor as yourself." 9 But
if you show partiality, you commit sin and
are convicted by the law as transgressors.
10 For whoever keeps the whole law but
fails in one point has become accountable
for all of it. 11 For the one who said, "You
shall not commit adultery," also said, "You
shall not murder." Now if you do not com-
mit adultery but if you murder, you have
become a transgressor of the law. 12 So
speak and so act as those who are to be
judged by the law of liberty. 13 For judg-
ment will be without mercy to anyone who
has shown no mercy; mercy triumphs over
judgment.
14 What good is it, my brothers and sis-
ters,[c] if you say you have faith but do not
have works? Can faith save you? 15 If a
brother or sister is naked and lacks daily
food, 16 and one of you says to them, "Go
in peace; keep warm and eat your fill," and
yet you do not supply their bodily needs,
what is the good of that? 17 So faith by it-
self, if it has no works, is dead.
18 But someone will say, "You have
faith and I have works." Show me your
faith apart from your works, and I by my
works will show you my faith. 19 You be-
lieve that God is one; you do well. Even the
demons believe—and shudder. 20 Do you
want to be shown, you senseless person,
that faith apart from works is barren?
21 Was not our ancestor Abraham justified
by works when he offered his son Isaac on
the altar? 22 You see that faith was active
along with his works, and faith was

a Or *hold the faith of our glorious Lord Jesus Christ without acts of favoritism* *b* Gk *Sit under my footstool* *c* Gk *brothers*

partiality based solely on outward appearance and social position (see 2.9n.). *Our glorious Lord Jesus Christ,* a highly embellished phrase; perhaps an editorial flourish. **2–4:** A flagrant case of class discrimination. *Your assembly,* lit. "synagogue." Evidently, rich and poor participated in the worship services. **5:** *Has not God chosen the poor . . . to be rich in faith,* continues the theme of reversal begun in 1.9–10; cf. 1 Sam 2–8. Christians who show class prejudice are oppressing part of God's elect. **7:** *The excellent name,* that of Jesus Christ, *invoked* at the time of baptism. **8–13:** This segment discusses *partiality* as a matter of *law.* **8:** *The royal law,* a designation of Lev 19.18 that is unique to James. He attributes prominence to this precept because of its elevated status in the teachings of Jesus (Mt 22.39; Mk 12.31; Lk 10.27; cf. John 13.34 and Gal 5.14; Rom 13.9). **9:** Concern for impartiality in the assembly originated as part of the Hebrew Bible's social legislation (e.g., Deut 15 and Lev 19). **10–11:** Citing the Decalogue (Ex 20.13–14; Deut 5.17–18). Similar to the "law of solidarity" ("If a man does all things, but omits one, he is guilty of all," cf. Deut 27.26; 4 Macc 5.20; *T. Asher* 2.5–10). **12–13:** Cf. Mt 6.14–15.

2.14–26: The unity of faith and deeds. 14–17: The author again appeals to a flagrant example (see 2.2–4). **18:** The use of an imaginary interlocutor was a popular debating technique, called diatribe. James gives his view of the relationship between *faith* and *works,* probably from Pauline slogans (Rom 3.28; Gal 2.16). **18–26:** Faith demonstrated by acts: the examples of Abraham and Rahab. **19:** *God is one,* Deut 6.4. *Even the demons believe,* see Mk 1.24; 5.7. **21:** *Our ancestor Abraham,* a contrast to Paul's focus on Abraham's obedience and acceptance of God's promises (Rom 4.1–3; 9–13; Gal 3.6–9). James places the distinctive criterion for Abraham's righteousness on the willingness to sacrifice Isaac as a work (Gen brought to completion by the works. 23 Thus the scripture was fulfilled that says, "Abraham believed God, and it was reckoned to him as righteousness," and he was called the friend of God. 24 You see that a person is justified by works and not by faith alone. 25 Likewise, was not Rahab the prostitute also justified by works when she welcomed the messengers and sent them out by another road? 26 For just as the body without the spirit is dead, so faith without works is also dead.

3 Not many of you should become teachers, my brothers and sisters,[a] for you know that we who teach will be judged with greater strictness. 2 For all of us make many mistakes. Anyone who makes no mistakes in speaking is perfect, able to keep the whole body in check with a bridle. 3 If we put bits into the mouths of horses to make them obey us, we guide their whole bodies. 4 Or look at ships: though they are so large that it takes strong winds to drive them, yet they are guided by a very small rudder wherever the will of the pilot directs. 5 So also the tongue is a small member, yet it boasts of great exploits.

How great a forest is set ablaze by a small fire! 6 And the tongue is a fire. The tongue is placed among our members as a world of iniquity; it stains the whole body, sets on fire the cycle of nature,[b] and is itself set on fire by hell.[c] 7 For every species of beast and bird, of reptile and sea creature, can be tamed and has been tamed by the human species, 8 but no one can tame the tongue—a restless evil, full of deadly poison. 9 With it we bless the Lord and Father, and with it we curse those who are made in the likeness of God. 10 From the same mouth come blessing and cursing. My brothers and sisters,[d] this ought not to be so. 11 Does a spring pour forth from the same opening both fresh and brackish water? 12 Can a fig tree, my brothers and sisters,[e] yield olives, or a grapevine figs? No more can salt water yield fresh.

13 Who is wise and understanding among you? Show by your good life that your works are done with gentleness born of wisdom. 14 But if you have bitter envy and selfish ambition in your hearts, do not be boastful and false to the truth. 15 Such wisdom does not come down from above, but is earthly, unspiritual, devilish. 16 For where there is envy and selfish ambition, there will also be disorder and wickedness of every kind. 17 But the wisdom from above is first pure, then peaceable, gentle, willing to yield, full of mercy and good fruits, without a trace of partiality or hypocrisy. 18 And a harvest of righteousness is sown in peace for[f] those who make peace.

a Gk *brothers* *b* Or *wheel of birth* *c* Gk *Gehenna* *d* Gk *My brothers* *e* Gk *my brothers* *f* Or *by*

22.9–14; cf. Heb 11.17). **23:** Quoting Gen 15.6. *Friend of God,* see Isa 41.8; 2 Chr 20.7. **25:** *Rahab,* the prostitute of Jericho (Josh 2.1–21), is also a heroine of the faith in Heb 11.31.

3.1–12: Faithfulness through a disciplined tongue. This segment returns to personal speech-ethics (1.19–26). **1:** *We who teach,* James includes himself among those admonished for aspiring to the office of teacher. **2:** The comment on the human tendency to *make . . . mistakes,* appears to qualify the earlier insistence on the goal of perfection (1.4). **3–7:** A series of analogies develops the argument: *horses* (v. 3), *ships* (v. 4), *forest . . . fire* (v. 5), the peculiar reference (note *b*) to the *wheel of birth* (a Hellenistic philosophical concept for the transmigration of souls), and the survey of living creatures of air, land, and sea (v. 7). **8:** *Tame the tongue,* amplifying the pairing of "not bridling the tongue" and "deception" in 1.26, while intensifying the critique of those who disregard the need to control their speech (cf. Sir 5.10–14). **9–10:** *Bless the Lord and Father,* Jewish Christian phraseology; cf. 2.7, where blasphemy is presumably of Jesus Christ. *Likeness of God,* i.e., human beings (see Gen 1.26; 9.6). **11–12:** See Mt 7.16; Lk 6.44.

3.13–18: Two kinds of wisdom. **13:** *Wise and understanding,* the goal that will correct the "many mistakes" of the tongue (3.2–5); see also Deut 1.13. *Gentleness* recalls "meekness" in 1.21. **15:** *Earthly, unspiritual, devilish:* another progression (1.3–4n.), this time downward. The equation of *wisdom* that *is earthly* with what is *unspiritual* and *devilish* is similar to Paul's usage in Phil 3.19. James probably refers

4 Those conflicts and disputes among
you, where do they come from? Do
they not come from your cravings that are
at war within you? 2 You want something
and do not have it; so you commit murder.
And you covet[a] something and cannot ob-
tain it; so you engage in disputes and con-
flicts. You do not have, because you do not
ask. 3 You ask and do not receive, because
you ask wrongly, in order to spend what
you get on your pleasures. 4 Adulterers! Do
you not know that friendship with the
world is enmity with God? Therefore who-
ever wishes to be a friend of the world be-
comes an enemy of God. 5 Or do you sup-
pose that it is for nothing that the scripture
says, "God[b] yearns jealously for the spirit
that he has made to dwell in us"? 6 But he
gives all the more grace; therefore it says,
"God opposes the proud,
but gives grace to the humble."
7 Submit yourselves therefore to God. Re-
sist the devil, and he will flee from you.
8 Draw near to God, and he will draw near
to you. Cleanse your hands, you sinners,
and purify your hearts, you double-
minded. 9 Lament and mourn and weep.
Let your laughter be turned into mourning
and your joy into dejection. 10 Humble
yourselves before the Lord, and he will ex-
alt you.

11 Do not speak evil against one anoth-
er, brothers and sisters.[c] Whoever speaks
evil against another or judges another,
speaks evil against the law and judges the
law; but if you judge the law, you are not a
doer of the law but a judge. 12 There is one
lawgiver and judge who is able to save and
to destroy. So who, then, are you to judge
your neighbor?

13 Come now, you who say, "Today or
tomorrow we will go to such and such a
town and spend a year there, doing busi-
ness and making money." 14 Yet you do not
even know what tomorrow will bring.
What is your life? For you are a mist that
appears for a little while and then vanishes.
15 Instead you ought to say, "If the Lord

a Or *you murder and you covet* *b* Gk *He*
c Gk *brothers*

to the scene in 2.1–7. **18:** A wisdom proverb that forms the climax to James's argument by reiterating the importance of "doing" (1.19–27); cf. Isa 32.15–17; Phil 1.11; Heb 12.11.

4.1–6: Faithlessness in the community. These unadorned scoldings may be directed at recent converts who through *disputes and conflicts* have brought about a deplorable situation in the community. **2:** The violent rhetoric suggests that extreme socioeconomic disparities have caused Christians to lay aside their religious values. *Want . . . murder,* the awkward logical sequence recalls the progression in 1.15: "desire . . . sin . . . death." **4:** *Adulterers,* see Ex 20.3; Deut 5.7; 6.13; self-indulgence and greed at one level, but also idolatry (Hos 3.1). *Friendship with the world,* see Lk 16.13. **5:** The source of the quotation is unknown. God's "jealousy" is a prominent theme in the Hebrew Bible (e.g., Ex 20.5; Deut 4.24; Zech 8.2). James contrasts the frightful community jealousies with God's jealous seeking of their souls' salvation. **6:** Prov 3.34 (LXX); see also 1 Pet 5.5.

4.7–10: Corrective formulae: a call to repentance. The formulaic framework for this call to repentance recalls the original conversion of members of the community and their baptismal catechism. **7:** *Submit . . . resist . . .* is akin to 1.21 ("rid yourselves . . . welcome . . ."), but here reversed. **8:** *Double-minded,* see 1.8n. **10:** *Humble . . . exalt,* the exaltation of the humble recalls 1.9–11; see Mt 23.12; Lk 14.18; 18.14; 1 Pet 5.6.

4.11–12: Warning against improper speech. Continuing the theme of 1.26; 3.1–12. **11:** *Judges another,* see Mt 7.1–5; Lk 6.37–42; this also recalls Jas 2.2–4. *Doer of the law,* cf. "doers of the word" (1.22); this close identification of the word with the law of the Hebrew Bible places James with Jesus as bridges between the Torah and later Christianity. **12:** *One . . . judge,* cf. Rom 14.10.

4.13–17: Cautions to those who take God for granted. The tone of this passage, like 5.1–6, resembles a prophetic apostrophe; the concern about arrogant (boastful) merchants is placed within a lesson on the sovereignty of God (following up 4.12). It also recalls wisdom teaching on the uncertainty of life; see Prov 27.1.

wishes, we will live and do this or that."
16 As it is, you boast in your arrogance; all
such boasting is evil. 17 Anyone, then, who
knows the right thing to do and fails to do
it, commits sin.

5 Come now, you rich people, weep and
wail for the miseries that are coming to
you. 2 Your riches have rotted, and your
clothes are moth-eaten. 3 Your gold and sil-
ver have rusted, and their rust will be evi-
dence against you, and it will eat your flesh
like fire. You have laid up treasure[a] for the
last days. 4 Listen! The wages of the labor-
ers who mowed your fields, which you kept
back by fraud, cry out, and the cries of the
harvesters have reached the ears of the
Lord of hosts. 5 You have lived on the earth
in luxury and in pleasure; you have fat-
tened your hearts in a day of slaughter.
6 You have condemned and murdered the
righteous one, who does not resist you.

7 Be patient, therefore, beloved,[b] until
the coming of the Lord. The farmer waits
for the precious crop from the earth, being
patient with it until it receives the early and
the late rains. 8 You also must be patient.
Strengthen your hearts, for the coming of
the Lord is near.[c] 9 Beloved,[d] do not
grumble against one another, so that you
may not be judged. See, the Judge is stand-
ing at the doors! 10 As an example of suffer-
ing and patience, beloved,[b] take the
prophets who spoke in the name of the
Lord. 11 Indeed we call blessed those who
showed endurance. You have heard of the
endurance of Job, and you have seen the
purpose of the Lord, how the Lord is com-
passionate and merciful.

12 Above all, my beloved,[b] do not
swear, either by heaven or by earth or by
any other oath, but let your "Yes" be yes
and your "No" be no, so that you may not
fall under condemnation.

13 Are any among you suffering? They
should pray. Are any cheerful? They should
sing songs of praise. 14 Are any among you
sick? They should call for the elders of the
church and have them pray over them,
anointing them with oil in the name of the
Lord. 15 The prayer of faith will save the
sick, and the Lord will raise them up; and
anyone who has committed sins will be for-
given. 16 Therefore confess your sins to one
another, and pray for one another, so that
you may be healed. The prayer of the righ-

a Or *will eat your flesh, since you have stored up fire*
b Gk *brothers* c Or *is at hand* d Gk *Brothers*

5.1–6: Warnings to the rich. 1: *Come now,* the same imperative that introduces 4.13. James condemns the unjust rich, recalling the eschatological reversal in 1.9–11. **2–3:** *Moth-eaten . . . rusted,* Mt 6.19–21. As in 1.9–11, James speaks as if the judgment against the unjust rich has already begun. **4:** *Laborers . . . cry out,* a violation of standard social legislation in the Hebrew Bible (Deut 24.14–15). **6:** *The righteous one,* rather than a cryptic allusion to Jesus, this may be the editor's reference to James himself. The account of the crucifixion of Jesus, the stoning of Stephen (Acts 7.54–60), and the martyrdom of James (Josephus, *Ant.* 20.9.1; Eusebius, *Eccl. Hist.* 2.23.21) resemble one another in presenting the martyrs as innocent, prophetic, highly regarded by their followers, and killed without resisting by a sinful mob. Alternately, *the righteous one* may be the innocent laborer (v. 4) whose mistreatment is compared to murder; cf. Sir 34.24–26.

5.7–12: A word of consolation to the faithful. 7: *Beloved,* a resumption of the address from the beginning (1.2), "brothers," here translated *beloved* (vv. 7,9,10,12; "brothers," v. 19). **7–11:** *Patient . . . suffering . . . patience . . . endurance,* a return to the subject of 1.2–4. **8:** *Coming of the Lord,* the "parousia" or second coming of Jesus. **10:** *Prophets,* see Mt 5.12; Lk 6.23,26; Acts 7.52; cf. 1 Kings 19.10; 2 Chr 24.21; Jer 26.20–23. **11:** *Job,* see Job 1.20–22; 2.10; Testament of Job. **12:** *Above all,* the main point, closely aligned with Mt 5.33–37, and the culmination, stressing the importance of speech-ethics and moral integrity.

5.13–20: A closing litany of pastoral concerns. 14: *Oil,* a common medicinal remedy (Isa 1.6; Mk 6.13; Lk 10.34). Here it is invested with special significance through connection with the divine name. **15–16:** On the association of faith, forgiveness of sins, and healing, see Mt 9.2–6. *Confess your sins,* Mt 18.15–20. **17–18:** *Elijah,* see 1 Kings 17.1; 18.1,41–45; Lk 4.25. **20:** See Gal 6.1; 1 Pet 4.8.

teous is powerful and effective. 17 Elijah
was a human being like us, and he prayed
fervently that it might not rain, and for
three years and six months it did not rain
on the earth. 18 Then he prayed again, and
the heaven gave rain and the earth yielded
its harvest.
19 My brothers and sisters,[a] if anyone
among you wanders from the truth and is
brought back by another, 20 you should
know that whoever brings back a sinner
from wandering will save the sinner's[b]
soul from death and will cover a multitude
of sins.

a Gk *My brothers* *b* Gk *his*

The First Letter of PETER

The First Letter of Peter presents itself as a pastoral letter written by the apostle Peter from "Babylon," where he is accompanied by Silvanus (= Silas) and Mark (5.12–13), to churches in five provinces of Asia Minor (1.1). Some scholars continue to understand this as a literal description, with Silvanus often regarded as the actual writer at Peter's behest. The situation indirectly described by the letter, however, points to a time after Peter's death. The language, style, content, and thought world seem inappropriate to Peter the Galilean fisherman and missionary to the Jews (Gal 2.9). The excellent and sophisticated Greek, the lack of references to the life and teaching of the earthly Jesus, the christological emphasis on the cosmic Christ, and the address to Gentile Christians who had previously lived a sinful, idolatrous life (1.14,18,21; 2.1,9–11,25; 4.3) point to a disciple of Peter writing in the name of the revered apostle. Thus most critical scholars interpret the document as a letter from the last decade of the first century CE, written in Peter's name in order to claim that its teaching represented the apostolic faith. The letter itself indicates it was written by a presbyter (elder; 5.1) of the Roman church—the "Babylon" of 5.13 was a common cryptogram for Rome at the end of the first century (see, for instance, Rev 17.5,9; 18.2,10,21). The references to Silvanus and Mark, both known companions of Paul (1 Thess 1.1; Philem 24), are part of the fictive literary picture that combines elements of Pauline tradition with the figure of Peter, as is the Pauline letter form itself adopted by 1 Peter. The letter thus represents the combination of Pauline and Petrine traditions in the church of Rome at the end of the first century, set forth in Peter's name as a pastoral letter to churches struggling in a difficult social situation.

First Peter is a real letter, a united composition. It is not, as has often been thought, a baptismal homily or liturgy to which epistolary elements have been added secondarily. The letter addresses a critical situation in the lives of the addressees, who once participated in the social and cultural life of their communities, but since their conversion to Christ have become marginalized and abused. The society to which they once belonged now considers them an unwelcome, even dangerous sectarian movement (as in Acts 28.22—"the sect everywhere spoken against"). While Christians are called to suffer "for the name" (4.15–16), the abuse is mostly verbal (2.22–23; 3.9–12,16). The positive attitude toward the state (2.13–17) indicates there is as yet no overt government persecution, except perhaps for occasional arbitrary acts by subordinate officials. First Peter offers realistic encouragement and instruction to Christians attempting to live faithfully in such a situation.

The author does not present a theological essay, but the instructions he gives are based on deep theological reflection, expressed indirectly by the narrative world the letter projects: God created the world (4.19); God chose an elect people (2.9–10); God sent the Christ who was rejected by humans but exalted by God (2.4); God sent the Spirit and Christian evangelists who established a new people of God and converted the addressees (1.12); and God will send Christ in the near future to conduct the final judgment (1.7,13; 4.7). Christians live their lives in the time between Christ's resurrection and return. The christological pattern of suffering and exaltation is foundational for the ethic he commends: Just as Christ was misunderstood and suffered unjustly for the sake of others, so Christians are now called to follow "in his steps" (2.21). Just as all Christians are instructed to respect the government authorities (2.13–17), so the most vulnerable Christians, slaves of unbelieving masters and wives of unbelieving husbands, are instructed to fit uncomplainingly into the given structures of society as a testimony to the faith (2.18–3.6). Such behavior may convert the oppressor (3.1–2), but if not it is still following the example set by Christ and will be vindicated at the last judgment that is soon to come (4.5–7).

The structure of First Peter represents an adaptation of the Pauline letter form: epistolary greeting (1.1–2); thanksgiving (1.3–12); the body of the letter (1.13–5.11) portraying the new identity of the people of God (1.13–2.10), Christian conduct in the given structures of society (2.11–3.12), and responsible suffering in the face of society (3.13–5.11); epistolary conclusion (5.12–14).

1 Peter, an apostle of Jesus Christ,
To the exiles of the Dispersion in Pon-
tus, Galatia, Cappadocia, Asia, and Bithyn-
ia, 2 who have been chosen and destined by
God the Father and sanctified by the Spirit
to be obedient to Jesus Christ and to be
sprinkled with his blood:
May grace and peace be yours in abun-
dance.
3 Blessed be the God and Father of our
Lord Jesus Christ! By his great mercy he
has given us a new birth into a living hope
through the resurrection of Jesus Christ
from the dead, 4 and into an inheritance
that is imperishable, undefiled, and unfad-
ing, kept in heaven for you, 5 who are being
protected by the power of God through
faith for a salvation ready to be revealed in
the last time. 6 In this you rejoice,[a] even if
now for a little while you have had to suffer
various trials, 7 so that the genuineness of
your faith—being more precious than gold
that, though perishable, is tested by fire—
may be found to result in praise and glory
and honor when Jesus Christ is revealed.
8 Although you have not seen[b] him, you
love him; and even though you do not see
him now, you believe in him and rejoice
with an indescribable and glorious joy, 9 for
you are receiving the outcome of your faith,
the salvation of your souls.
10 Concerning this salvation, the proph-
ets who prophesied of the grace that was to
be yours made careful search and inquiry,
11 inquiring about the person or time that
the Spirit of Christ within them indicated
when it testified in advance to the suffer-
ings destined for Christ and the subsequent
glory. 12 It was revealed to them that they
were serving not themselves but you, in re-
gard to the things that have now been an-
nounced to you through those who brought
you good news by the Holy Spirit sent from
heaven—things into which angels long to
look!
13 Therefore prepare your minds for ac-
tion;[c] discipline yourselves; set all your

a Or *Rejoice in this* *b* Other ancient authorities read *known* *c* Gk *gird up the loins of your mind*

1.1–2: Salutation. The author adapts the Pauline form (see Rom 1.1–7n.). **1:** *Exiles of the Dispersion,* applying images of Israel to Christians (see Jas 1.1n.). **2:** A proto-Trinitarian formula. Obedience and being sprinkled with blood are covenant language (see Ex 24.3–8).

1.3–12: Thanksgiving. As in 2 Cor 1.3 and Eph 1.3, the customary thanksgiving (see Rom 1.8–15n.) becomes a doxological expression of praise that constitutes the theological basis of the imperatives to follow. **3:** *Hope* expresses the present confidence in the reality of future redemption founded on the *resurrection of Jesus Christ. New birth* is related to baptism (see 1.23; 2.2; 3.20–22; Jn 3.3–5). **5:** *Salvation* is *ready to be revealed* at the end-time. The present experience has a future consummation. The believer does not go "up" to heaven, but "forward" to the future reward to be revealed at the end-time. **12:** The readers' Christian lives, though beset with difficulties (1.6; 2.19–24; 3.14–15; 4.12–19; 5.10), represent the climax of God's plan for the ages, which even the prophets and the angels could only long to share.

1.13–5.11: Body of the letter, a united whole though incorporating elements of earlier Christian

hope on the grace that Jesus Christ will
bring you when he is revealed. 14 Like obe-
dient children, do not be conformed to the
desires that you formerly had in ignorance.
15 Instead, as he who called you is holy, be
holy yourselves in all your conduct; 16 for it
is written, "You shall be holy, for I am
holy."
17 If you invoke as Father the one who
judges all people impartially according to
their deeds, live in reverent fear during the
time of your exile. 18 You know that you
were ransomed from the futile ways inher-
ited from your ancestors, not with perish-
able things like silver or gold, 19 but with
the precious blood of Christ, like that of a
lamb without defect or blemish. 20 He was
destined before the foundation of the
world, but was revealed at the end of the
ages for your sake. 21 Through him you
have come to trust in God, who raised him
from the dead and gave him glory, so that
your faith and hope are set on God.
22 Now that you have purified your
souls by your obedience to the truth[a] so
that you have genuine mutual love, love
one another deeply[b] from the heart.[c]
23 You have been born anew, not of perish-
able but of imperishable seed, through the
living and enduring word of God.[d] 24 For
"All flesh is like grass
and all its glory like the flower
of grass.
The grass withers,
and the flower falls,
25 but the word of the Lord endures
forever."
That word is the good news that was an-
nounced to you.

2 Rid yourselves, therefore, of all malice,
and all guile, insincerity, envy, and all
slander. 2 Like newborn infants, long for
the pure, spiritual milk, so that by it you
may grow into salvation— 3 if indeed you
have tasted that the Lord is good.
4 Come to him, a living stone, though
rejected by mortals yet chosen and precious
in God's sight, and 5 like living stones, let
yourselves be built[e] into a spiritual house,
to be a holy priesthood, to offer spiritual
sacrifices acceptable to God through Jesus
Christ. 6 For it stands in scripture:
"See, I am laying in Zion a stone,
a cornerstone chosen and precious;
and whoever believes in him[f] will
not be put to shame."
7 To you then who believe, he is precious;
but for those who do not believe,
"The stone that the builders rejected
has become the very head of
the corner,"
8 and
"A stone that makes them stumble,
and a rock that makes them fall."

a Other ancient authorities add *through the Spirit*
b Or *constantly* c Other ancient authorities read *a pure heart* d Or *through the word of the living and enduring God* e Or *you yourselves are being built*
f Or *it*

tradition. **1.13–2.10: The new identity as the elect and holy people of God.** On the basis of the preceding indicative statements of God's mighty acts, imperatives are given for the Christian life. **13:** The first imperative (in Greek) in the letter is the command to live in the *hope* of Christ's triumphal appearance. **15:** The second imperative to *be holy* means to live a life set apart for God's service, though in the midst of the world. **16:** Quoting Lev 11.44–45; 19.2; 20.7. **17:** The third imperative is to *live in reverent fear* of God rather than the oppressive culture (cf. 2.17; 3.14). **19:** *Lamb without . . . blemish,* see Lev 23.12; Num 6.14; etc. **21:** Christian faith is theocentric, in God who has acted definitively in Christ. **22:** The fourth imperative is the command of *love,* unselfish caring for others (see Mt 22.34–40; Rom 13.8–10; 1 Cor 13). **24–25:** Isa 40.6–8.

2.1–10: The fifth imperative is to *long for* the means of spiritual nourishment so that they may *grow* (2.2). After the new birth comes nurture that leads to maturity. **3:** Ps 34.8. **4:** Ps 118.22; Isa 28.16; Mt 21.42. **5–8:** The imagery modulates from birth and growth to the construction of a *spiritual house* (temple) and then to a *holy priesthood.* The images of the Christian life are communal rather than individualistic. **6:** Isa 28.16. **7:** Ps 118.22. **8:** Isa 8.14–15. **9–10:** Hos 2.23; Ex 19.6. Language used for Israel in the Hebrew Bible is applied to the readers, who were formerly Gentiles (1.18).

They stumble because they disobey the
word, as they were destined to do.
9 But you are a chosen race, a royal
priesthood, a holy nation, God's own peo-
ple,[a] in order that you may proclaim the
mighty acts of him who called you out of
darkness into his marvelous light.

10 Once you were not a people,
but now you are God's people;
once you had not received mercy,
but now you have received mercy.

11 Beloved, I urge you as aliens and ex-
iles to abstain from the desires of the flesh
that wage war against the soul. 12 Conduct
yourselves honorably among the Gentiles,
so that, though they malign you as evildo-
ers, they may see your honorable deeds and
glorify God when he comes to judge.[b]
13 For the Lord's sake accept the au-
thority of every human institution,[c]
whether of the emperor as supreme, 14 or of
governors, as sent by him to punish those
who do wrong and to praise those who do
right. 15 For it is God's will that by doing
right you should silence the ignorance of
the foolish. 16 As servants[d] of God, live as
free people, yet do not use your freedom as
a pretext for evil. 17 Honor everyone. Love
the family of believers.[e] Fear God. Honor
the emperor.
18 Slaves, accept the authority of your
masters with all deference, not only those
who are kind and gentle but also those who
are harsh. 19 For it is a credit to you if, be-
ing aware of God, you endure pain while
suffering unjustly. 20 If you endure when
you are beaten for doing wrong, what cred-
it is that? But if you endure when you do
right and suffer for it, you have God's ap-
proval. 21 For to this you have been called,
because Christ also suffered for you, leav-
ing you an example, so that you should fol-
low in his steps.

22 "He committed no sin,
and no deceit was found in
his mouth."

23 When he was abused, he did not return
abuse; when he suffered, he did not threat-
en; but he entrusted himself to the one who
judges justly. 24 He himself bore our sins in
his body on the cross,[f] so that, free from
sins, we might live for righteousness; by his
wounds[g] you have been healed. 25 For you
were going astray like sheep, but now you
have returned to the shepherd and guardian
of your souls.

3 Wives, in the same way, accept the au-
thority of your husbands, so that, even
if some of them do not obey the word, they
may be won over without a word by their
wives' conduct, 2 when they see the purity
and reverence of your lives. 3 Do not adorn
yourselves outwardly by braiding your
hair, and by wearing gold ornaments or
fine clothing; 4 rather, let your adornment
be the inner self with the lasting beauty of
a gentle and quiet spirit, which is very pre-
cious in God's sight. 5 It was in this way
long ago that the holy women who hoped
in God used to adorn themselves by accept-
ing the authority of their husbands. 6 Thus
Sarah obeyed Abraham and called him
lord. You have become her daughters as

a Gk *a people for his possession* b Gk *God on the day of visitation* c Or *every institution ordained for human beings* d Gk *slaves* e Gk *Love the brotherhood* f Or *carried up our sins in his body to the tree* g Gk *bruise*

2.11–3.12: Christian existence and conduct in society. Cf. Col 3.18–4.1; Eph 5.22–6.9; Titus 2.1–10; 1 Tim 2–3; 5.1–3. The Roman Empire, the institution of slavery, and the patriarchal family are accepted as the present order of things that is soon to pass away (see 1.17; 2.11; 4.7). **11–12:** Christian conduct within social structures is a testimony to others. **13–17:** Instructions to all on attitude to God, the state, and each other. **14:** *Governors,* of provinces of the Roman Empire. **17:** Cf. Rom 13.7. **18–25:** Instructions to slaves, leading into a more general comment addressed to a wider audience (see note on 3.8–12). Though resembling the typical household codes of Hellenistic moralists, the author's instruction is based on the example of Christ who suffered unjustly, in words that reflect the suffering servant of Isa 53.5–12. **22:** Isa 53.9. **3.1–7:** Instructions to wives and husbands. **1:** Unbelieving husbands may be converted without preaching or argument by the Christian example of their wives; cf. 1 Cor 7.12–16. **6:** See Gen 18.12 (where NRSV translates the word "lord" as "husband"). **8–12:** Concluding instructions to all. The

long as you do what is good and never let
fears alarm you.
7 Husbands, in the same way, show con-
sideration for your wives in your life to-
gether, paying honor to the woman as the
weaker sex,[a] since they too are also heirs
of the gracious gift of life—so that nothing
may hinder your prayers.
8 Finally, all of you, have unity of spirit,
sympathy, love for one another, a tender
heart, and a humble mind. 9 Do not repay
evil for evil or abuse for abuse; but, on the
contrary, repay with a blessing. It is for this
that you were called—that you might in-
herit a blessing. 10 For

"Those who desire life
    and desire to see good days,
  let them keep their tongues from evil
    and their lips from speaking deceit;
11 let them turn away from evil and do
    good;
  let them seek peace and pursue it.
12 For the eyes of the Lord are on
      the righteous,
    and his ears are open to
      their prayer.
  But the face of the Lord is against
      those who do evil."

13 Now who will harm you if you are
eager to do what is good? 14 But even if you
do suffer for doing what is right, you are
blessed. Do not fear what they fear,[b] and
do not be intimidated, 15 but in your hearts
sanctify Christ as Lord. Always be ready to
make your defense to anyone who demands
from you an accounting for the hope that is
in you; 16 yet do it with gentleness and rev-
erence.[c] Keep your conscience clear, so
that, when you are maligned, those who
abuse you for your good conduct in Christ
may be put to shame. 17 For it is better to
suffer for doing good, if suffering should be
God's will, than to suffer for doing evil.
18 For Christ also suffered[d] for sins once
for all, the righteous for the unrighteous, in
order to bring you[e] to God. He was put to
death in the flesh, but made alive in the
spirit, 19 in which also he went and made
a proclamation to the spirits in prison,
20 who in former times did not obey, when
God waited patiently in the days of Noah,
during the building of the ark, in which a
few, that is, eight persons, were saved
through water. 21 And baptism, which this
prefigured, now saves you—not as a re-
moval of dirt from the body, but as an
appeal to God for[f] a good conscience,
through the resurrection of Jesus Christ,
22 who has gone into heaven and is at the
right hand of God, with angels, authorities,
and powers made subject to him.

4 Since therefore Christ suffered in the
flesh,[g] arm yourselves also with the
same intention (for whoever has suffered in
the flesh has finished with sin), 2 so as to
live for the rest of your earthly life[h] no
longer by human desires but by the will of

a Gk *vessel* b Gk *their fear* c Or *respect*
d Other ancient authorities read *died* e Other
ancient authorities read *us* f Or *a pledge to God
from* g Other ancient authorities add *for us*; others,
for you h Gk *rest of the time in the flesh*

more vulnerable members of the church, slaves and wives, are examples of the conduct required of the whole church, which is in a vulnerable position in a hostile society. **10–12:** Ps 34.12–16.

3.13–5.11: Responsible suffering in the face of hostility.

3.13–17: Suffering for doing good (= doing right). Following the example of Christ's unjust *suffering* does not mean passivity, but active doing of good. **15:** In word as well as action, Christians are to be able to give a *defense* ("apologia") for the Christian faith, here summarized as "hope" (1.2,13,21).

3.18–22: Christological grounding. *Put to death in the flesh* means that Jesus really died in the human sphere; *made alive in the spirit* does not refer to a "part" of Christ that survived death, but that God raised Christ to a new life in the divine realm (cf. 1.3; 2.4; 3.21–22). **19–20:** The precise meaning of this fragment of an ancient christological picture is unclear, but probably refers to Christ's preaching to the imprisoned evil spirits after his resurrection to announce his own victory (cf. Gen 6.1–4 as interpreted in 1 Enoch 10.4–6). The picture is unrelated to 4.6 and the "descent to the world of the dead" of the Apostles' Creed. **20:** *Noah*, see Gen 6–8. **22:** See Eph 1.20; Heb 1.3.

4.1–6: Application to the Christian life. 3: As in 2.9–10, the church is the continuing people of God,

God. 3 You have already spent enough time
in doing what the Gentiles like to do, living
in licentiousness, passions, drunkenness,
revels, carousing, and lawless idolatry.
4 They are surprised that you no longer join
them in the same excesses of dissipation,
and so they blaspheme.[a] 5 But they will
have to give an accounting to him who
stands ready to judge the living and the
dead. 6 For this is the reason the gospel
was proclaimed even to the dead, so that,
though they had been judged in the flesh as
everyone is judged, they might live in the
spirit as God does.

7 The end of all things is near;[b] there-
fore be serious and discipline yourselves for
the sake of your prayers. 8 Above all, main-
tain constant love for one another, for love
covers a multitude of sins. 9 Be hospitable
to one another without complaining.
10 Like good stewards of the manifold grace
of God, serve one another with whatever
gift each of you has received. 11 Whoever
speaks must do so as one speaking the very
words of God; whoever serves must do so
with the strength that God supplies, so that
God may be glorified in all things through
Jesus Christ. To him belong the glory and
the power forever and ever. Amen.

12 Beloved, do not be surprised at the
fiery ordeal that is taking place among you
to test you, as though something strange
were happening to you. 13 But rejoice inso-
far as you are sharing Christ's sufferings, so
that you may also be glad and shout for joy
when his glory is revealed. 14 If you are
reviled for the name of Christ, you are
blessed, because the spirit of glory,[c] which
is the Spirit of God, is resting on you.[d]
15 But let none of you suffer as a murderer,
a thief, a criminal, or even as a mischief
maker. 16 Yet if any of you suffers as a
Christian, do not consider it a disgrace, but
glorify God because you bear this name.
17 For the time has come for judgment to
begin with the household of God; if it be-
gins with us, what will be the end for those
who do not obey the gospel of God? 18 And

"If it is hard for the righteous
to be saved,
what will become of the ungodly
and the sinners?"

19 Therefore, let those suffering in accor-
dance with God's will entrust themselves to
a faithful Creator, while continuing to do
good.

5 Now as an elder myself and a witness of
the sufferings of Christ, as well as one
who shares in the glory to be revealed, I
exhort the elders among you 2 to tend the
flock of God that is in your charge, exercis-
ing the oversight,[e] not under compulsion
but willingly, as God would have you do
it[f]—not for sordid gain but eagerly. 3 Do
not lord it over those in your charge, but be
examples to the flock. 4 And when the chief
shepherd appears, you will win the crown
of glory that never fades away. 5 In the
same way, you who are younger must ac-
cept the authority of the elders.[g] And all of
you must clothe yourselves with humility in
your dealings with one another, for

"God opposes the proud,
but gives grace to the humble."

6 Humble yourselves therefore under
the mighty hand of God, so that he may

a Or *they malign you* b Or *is at hand* c Other ancient authorities add *and of power* d Other ancient authorities add *On their part he is blasphemed, but on your part he is glorified* e Other ancient authorities lack *exercising the oversight* f Other ancient authorities lack *as God would have you do it* g Or *of those who are older*

and outsiders are *Gentiles*. **6:** The *dead* are probably Christians who heard the gospel while they were alive.

4.7–11: Eschatological exhortation. 9: Cf. Heb 13.2; 3 Jn 5–8.

4.12–19: Suffering in joy and hope. Suffering is to be a witness to the truth of the faith, not the result of one's own antisocial behavior. *Fiery ordeal* refers to persecutions (1.6–7). On the name *Christian,* cf. Acts 11.26; 26.28. **18:** Prov 11.31.

5.1–11: Concluding exhortation. 1: *Elders,* church officials (Acts 14.23; 20.17–38; Jas 5.14; 2 Jn 1; 3 Jn 1). **5:** Prov 3.34.

exalt you in due time. 7 Cast all your anxi-
ety on him, because he cares for you. 8 Dis-
cipline yourselves, keep alert.[a] Like a roar-
ing lion your adversary the devil prowls
around, looking for someone to devour.
9 Resist him, steadfast in your faith, for you
know that your brothers and sisters[b] in all
the world are undergoing the same kinds of
suffering. 10 And after you have suffered for
a little while, the God of all grace, who has
called you to his eternal glory in Christ, will
himself restore, support, strengthen, and
establish you. 11 To him be the power forev-
er and ever. Amen.

12 Through Silvanus, whom I consider a
faithful brother, I have written this short
letter to encourage you and to testify that
this is the true grace of God. Stand fast in
it. 13 Your sister church[c] in Babylon, cho-
sen together with you, sends you greetings;
and so does my son Mark. 14 Greet one an-
other with a kiss of love.

Peace to all of you who are in Christ.[d]

a Or *be vigilant* *b* Gk *your brotherhood*
c Gk *She who is* *d* Other ancient authorities add *Amen*

5.12–14: Conclusion of the letter. *Silvanus* and *Mark* were companions of Paul (Acts 15.22; 2 Cor 1.19; Philem 24). *Babylon* was a cryptic name for Rome (Rev 17.1).

The Second Letter of PETER

The Second Letter of Peter follows the typical form of a letter, except that it lacks the customary final greeting. It also shares the characteristics of a testament (especially in 1.12–14), the final advice and warnings of a patriarch before his death (compare Paul's final address to the Ephesian elders in Acts 20.25–35). This combination of forms has resulted in the modification of each. Testaments are usually presented as a third-person report of the last spoken words of a patriarch to his sons before his death. Second Peter, however, is a first-person, written delivery of the last words of Peter to all who are of like faith (1.1). The writer makes use of a rich cultural heritage, including Hellenistic philosophical speculation, Jewish exegetical and apocalyptic traditions, the Hebrew Bible, traditions about Jesus, the Letter of Jude, and a collection of Paul's letters. The Greek style of 2 Peter is an example of the popular Greek rhetorical style of that age, characterized by grandiose, elaborate language.

There is little historical or literary evidence to connect the author of this letter either to Simon Peter or to the author of 1 Peter. The author wrote in the name of Peter, not to transmit a particular form of Petrine tradition, but to convey the common apostolic tradition of the church. Peter is chosen because of his reputation and his closeness to Jesus. Such pseudepigraphical attribution is frequent in the Bible and in other ancient literatures. The writer takes pains to appeal to the common apostolic teaching (3.2), explicitly including Paul (3.15–16). The letter was probably written from Rome around the end of the first century CE or the beginning of the second.

Second Peter is characterized by an apocalyptic vision of this world as corrupt because of lust (1.4) and bound for destruction. It urges the reader to escape by means of the knowledge of Christ and of God and by earnest moral striving that is grounded in the promises and gifts of God. The goal is to participate in the divine nature and to enter the eternal kingdom (1.11).

After a brief greeting, the letter opens with an ethical exhortation to pursue a chain of virtues based on the all-sufficient promises and gifts of God and achieved through knowledge and remembering (1.1–11). Three statements follow that establish the solemnity of the exhortation. The letter represents Peter's final "testament" (1.12–15); the heavenly voice guarantees the power and coming of Jesus (1.16–18); and the scripture is certain (1.19–21). Chapter 2 (much of which is adapted from Jude) is a warning against false teachers who want to exploit the unstable for the sake of greed and licentiousness. Their final destruction is as sure as is the final salvation of the godly. Those who are enticed by their empty promise of freedom are likewise doomed. Chapter 3 returns to the admonitions of chapter 1 and warns of the certainty of judgment. Just as the heaven and earth in Noah's time were destroyed through water, so the present heavens and earth will be destroyed through fire. Finally, there will be "new heavens and a new earth, where righteousness is at home" (3.13). Those who wait for these things should take Paul's advice and use the time that remains to repent. They should abstain from the defilement of the world, avoid being led astray by the error of the lawless, and grow in grace and knowledge.

1 Simeon[a] Peter, a servant[b] and apostle of Jesus Christ,

To those who have received a faith as precious as ours through the righteousness of our God and Savior Jesus Christ:[c]

2 May grace and peace be yours in abundance in the knowledge of God and of Jesus our Lord.

3 His divine power has given us everything needed for life and godliness, through the knowledge of him who called us by[d] his own glory and goodness. 4 Thus he has given us, through these things, his precious and very great promises, so that through them you may escape from the corruption that is in the world because of lust, and may become participants of the divine nature. 5 For this very reason, you must make every effort to support your faith with goodness, and goodness with knowledge, 6 and knowledge with self-control, and self-control with endurance, and endurance with godliness, 7 and godliness with mutual[e] affection, and mutual[e] affection with love. 8 For if these things are yours and are increasing among you, they keep you from being ineffective and unfruitful in the knowledge of our Lord Jesus Christ. 9 For anyone who lacks these things is short-sighted and blind, and is forgetful of the cleansing of past sins. 10 Therefore, brothers and sisters,[f] be all the more eager to confirm your call and election, for if you do this, you will never stumble. 11 For in this way, entry into the eternal kingdom of our Lord and Savior Jesus Christ will be richly provided for you.

12 Therefore I intend to keep on reminding you of these things, though you know them already and are established in the truth that has come to you. 13 I think it right, as long as I am in this body,[g] to refresh your memory, 14 since I know that my death[h] will come soon, as indeed our Lord Jesus Christ has made clear to me. 15 And I will make every effort so that after my departure you may be able at any time to recall these things.

16 For we did not follow cleverly devised myths when we made known to you the power and coming of our Lord Jesus Christ, but we had been eyewitnesses of his majesty. 17 For he received honor and glory from God the Father when that voice was conveyed to him by the Majestic Glory, saying, "This is my Son, my Beloved,[i] with whom I am well pleased." 18 We ourselves heard this voice come from heaven, while we were with him on the holy mountain.

19 So we have the prophetic message more fully confirmed. You will do well to be attentive to this as to a lamp shining in a dark place, until the day dawns and the

a Other ancient authorities read *Simon* *b* Gk *slave*
c Or *of our God and the Savior Jesus Christ*
d Other ancient authorities read *through*
e Gk *brotherly* *f* Gk *brothers* *g* Gk *tent*
h Gk *the putting off of my tent* *i* Other ancient authorities read *my beloved Son*

1.1–2: Salutation, see Rom 1.1–7n. **1:** *Simeon* is Peter's Hebrew name transliterated into Greek.

1.3–11: Opening exhortation. The major themes of the letter are introduced: *knowledge* of God and of Jesus, *effort* (variously translated as "be eager," "make every effort," or "strive"), stability (*confirm*), *godliness, corruption, lust,* and remembering. The readers should *escape from the corruption that is in the world because of lust* (cf. 2.20) and enter *into the eternal kingdom* by means of the knowledge of God, the promises of God, and earnest moral striving. **4:** *The divine nature* refers primarily to immortality, which is the opposite of *corruption.*

1.12–21: Three solemn appeals. The writer makes a solemn appeal to Peter's final words before his death, the Transfiguration of Jesus, and prophetic scripture to reinforce the reliability of the message. **12–15:** The reference to Peter's death transforms the letter into a kind of testament in which the speaker gives ethical exhortations and warnings about the future based on his own past experience. **16–18:** Peter's presence at the Transfiguration makes him an *eyewitness* of the voice from heaven, which confirms the apostolic testimony about Christ's *power and coming* (Mt 17.1–8; Mk 9.2–8; Lk 9.28–36). The wording of the heavenly voice differs slightly from that in the Gospels. The writer may be relying on oral tradition rather than a written gospel. **19:** *Morning star,* see Rev 22.16.

morning star rises in your hearts. 20 First
of all you must understand this, that no
prophecy of scripture is a matter of one's
own interpretation, 21 because no prophecy
ever came by human will, but men and
women moved by the Holy Spirit spoke
from God.[a]

2 But false prophets also arose among the
people, just as there will be false teach-
ers among you, who will secretly bring in
destructive opinions. They will even deny
the Master who bought them—bringing
swift destruction on themselves. 2 Even so,
many will follow their licentious ways, and
because of these teachers[b] the way of truth
will be maligned. 3 And in their greed they
will exploit you with deceptive words.
Their condemnation, pronounced against
them long ago, has not been idle, and their
destruction is not asleep.

4 For if God did not spare the angels
when they sinned, but cast them into hell[c]
and committed them to chains[d] of deepest
darkness to be kept until the judgment;
5 and if he did not spare the ancient world,
even though he saved Noah, a herald of
righteousness, with seven others, when he
brought a flood on a world of the ungodly;
6 and if by turning the cities of Sodom and
Gomorrah to ashes he condemned them to
extinction[e] and made them an example of
what is coming to the ungodly;[f] 7 and if he
rescued Lot, a righteous man greatly dis-
tressed by the licentiousness of the lawless
8 (for that righteous man, living among
them day after day, was tormented in his
righteous soul by their lawless deeds that he
saw and heard), 9 then the Lord knows how
to rescue the godly from trial, and to keep
the unrighteous under punishment until the
day of judgment 10—especially those who
indulge their flesh in depraved lust, and
who despise authority.

Bold and willful, they are not afraid to
slander the glorious ones,[g] 11 whereas an-
gels, though greater in might and power, do
not bring against them a slanderous judg-
ment from the Lord.[h] 12 These people,
however, are like irrational animals, mere
creatures of instinct, born to be caught and
killed. They slander what they do not un-
derstand, and when those creatures are de-
stroyed,[i] they also will be destroyed,
13 suffering[j] the penalty for doing wrong.
They count it a pleasure to revel in the day-
time. They are blots and blemishes, reveling
in their dissipation[k] while they feast with
you. 14 They have eyes full of adultery, insa-
tiable for sin. They entice unsteady souls.

a Other ancient authorities read *but moved by the Holy Spirit saints of God spoke* *b* Gk *because of them* *c* Gk *Tartaros* *d* Other ancient authorities read *pits* *e* Other ancient authorities lack *to extinction* *f* Other ancient authorities read *an example to those who were to be ungodly* *g* Or *angels*; Gk *glories* *h* Other ancient authorities read *before the Lord*; others lack the phrase *i* Gk *in their destruction* *j* Other ancient authorities read *receiving* *k* Other ancient authorities read *love-feasts*

2.1–22: Warnings against false teachers. Beginning with 2.1 the author borrows language from Jude 4–18 but modifies it extensively in order to accommodate a different polemic. The ethical condemnations are fairly standard polemical attacks: greed, licentiousness, and deception; the author adds disregard for authority (2.10). **1:** They *deny the Master* either by denying his future coming to judge (3.3–4) or by their immoral conduct (2.2,10,14,18). Jesus' death is understood as the purchase price for which he *bought* his followers as one buys a slave (either for freedom or for service). Cf. Jude 4. **4–10a:** Jude's examples (Jude 6–8) of judgment are rearranged, abbreviated, and supplemented to remove Jude's concern with falling from grace, to follow the order of the biblical events, and to introduce a balanced emphasis on judgment and salvation. See Sir 16.6–17 for a similar use of some of these examples. **4:** The *angels* who *sinned* are probably the "sons of God" of Gen 6.2 as popularized by the books of Enoch (see Jude 14–16n.). The allusive use of the Enochic traditions is in contrast with Jude's explicit quotation. *Tartaros* (*hell*) is the prison of the Titans of Greek myth. **5:** Gen 6.6–8; 8.18. **6:** Gen 19.24; cf. 3 Macc 2.5. **7:** Gen 19.16,29. **10b–11:** Jude 8–9. The *authority* that they despise may be either God's authority or angelic authorities. The *glorious ones* are probably angelic dignitaries. Jude's example of Michael's dispute with the devil (see Jude 9n.) is transformed into an example from contemporary angels, who refrain from bringing *a slanderous judgment from* (or *before*) *the Lord.* **12–13:** Jude 10,12. **15–16:** Jude 11; Num 22.7,21–35. The

They have hearts trained in greed. Accursed
children! 15 They have left the straight road
and have gone astray, following the road
of Balaam son of Bosor,[a] who loved the
wages of doing wrong, 16 but was rebuked
for his own transgression; a speechless don-
key spoke with a human voice and re-
strained the prophet's madness.
17 These are waterless springs and mists
driven by a storm; for them the deepest
darkness has been reserved. 18 For they
speak bombastic nonsense, and with licen-
tious desires of the flesh they entice people
who have just[b] escaped from those who
live in error. 19 They promise them free-
dom, but they themselves are slaves of cor-
ruption; for people are slaves to whatever
masters them. 20 For if, after they have es-
caped the defilements of the world through
the knowledge of our Lord and Savior Jesus
Christ, they are again entangled in them
and overpowered, the last state has become
worse for them than the first. 21 For it
would have been better for them never to
have known the way of righteousness than,
after knowing it, to turn back from the holy
commandment that was passed on to them.
22 It has happened to them according to the
true proverb,

"The dog turns back to its
own vomit,"

and,

"The sow is washed only to wallow
in the mud."

3 This is now, beloved, the second letter I
am writing to you; in them I am trying
to arouse your sincere intention by remind-
ing you 2 that you should remember the
words spoken in the past by the holy
prophets, and the commandment of the
Lord and Savior spoken through your
apostles. 3 First of all you must understand
this, that in the last days scoffers will come,
scoffing and indulging their own lusts 4 and
saying, "Where is the promise of his com-
ing? For ever since our ancestors died,[c] all
things continue as they were from the be-
ginning of creation!" 5 They deliberately ig-
nore this fact, that by the word of God
heavens existed long ago and an earth was
formed out of water and by means of wa-
ter, 6 through which the world of that time
was deluged with water and perished. 7 But
by the same word the present heavens and
earth have been reserved for fire, being kept
until the day of judgment and destruction
of the godless.
8 But do not ignore this one fact, be-
loved, that with the Lord one day is like a
thousand years, and a thousand years are
like one day. 9 The Lord is not slow about
his promise, as some think of slowness, but
is patient with you,[d] not wanting any to
perish, but all to come to repentance. 10 But

a Other ancient authorities read *Beor* *b* Other ancient authorities read *actually* *c* Gk *our fathers fell asleep* *d* Other ancient authorities read *on your account*

account of Balaam's sin, as in Jude, is taken directly from postbiblical Jewish traditions, which uniformly make Balaam a greedy villain. **17–18:** Jude 12–13,16. The seemingly excessive piling up of accusations functions as the necessary response to the challenge to God's honor. By publicly shaming those who have brought shame on God, the writer restores God's honor. **19:** *Slaves of corruption,* compare Rom 6.6,16; 8.21; John 8.34. **21:** Mt 12.45; Lk 11.26. **22:** Prov 26.11.

3.1–13: A defense of the expectation of the coming of Christ. The most troublesome of the false teachings is that the present world will continue without end. These scoffers were already predicted long ago by the prophets and by the Lord. Furthermore, from God's point of view, the delay is not long at all, and it is motivated by God's patience and desire for repentance. **1–3:** Jude 17–18. **3:** *Indulging their own lusts,* if there is no judgment, then one may do as one pleases. **4–13:** The flood destroyed the first world and made way for the present one. In the same way, fire will destroy the present world, and a third world will replace it. The destruction of the earth by fire is described in the language of Stoic philosophical speculation. **4:** *Our ancestors* are probably the biblical patriarchs since Adam. **5:** *They deliberately ignore* in contrast to the repeated exhortation to "remember" (1.9,12–15; 3.1–2,8). On creation by God's *word,* and an original watery state, see Gen 1.2,6–10; Ps 33.6–7. **6:** Gen 7.11. **8:** Ps 90.4. **10:** *Day of the Lord,* Am 5.18–20; Joel 2.2–32. *Like a thief* in the night, 1 Thess 5.2; Mt 24.43–44; Lk 12.39–40. The *elements*

the day of the Lord will come like a thief,
and then the heavens will pass away with a
loud noise, and the elements will be dis-
solved with fire, and the earth and every-
thing that is done on it will be disclosed.[a]
11 Since all these things are to be dis-
solved in this way, what sort of persons
ought you to be in leading lives of holiness
and godliness, 12 waiting for and hasten-
ing[b] the coming of the day of God, because
of which the heavens will be set ablaze and
dissolved, and the elements will melt with
fire? 13 But, in accordance with his promise,
we wait for new heavens and a new earth,
where righteousness is at home.
14 Therefore, beloved, while you are
waiting for these things, strive to be found
by him at peace, without spot or blemish;
15 and regard the patience of our Lord as
salvation. So also our beloved brother Paul
wrote to you according to the wisdom giv-
en him, 16 speaking of this as he does in all
his letters. There are some things in them
hard to understand, which the ignorant and
unstable twist to their own destruction, as
they do the other scriptures. 17 You there-
fore, beloved, since you are forewarned, be-
ware that you are not carried away with the
error of the lawless and lose your own sta-
bility. 18 But grow in the grace and knowl-
edge of our Lord and Savior Jesus Christ.
To him be the glory both now and to the
day of eternity. Amen.[c]

a Other ancient authorities read *will be burned up*
b Or *earnestly desiring* *c* Other ancient authorities lack *Amen*

(see also v. 12) are either earth, air, fire, and water or the heavenly bodies (possibly including the earth as well). **13:** Isa 65.17; 66.22; Rev 21.1.

3.14–17: Final exhortation. One ought to live blamelessly and take advantage of the opportunity to repent. **15–16:** Paul also taught that the delay of judgment is an opportunity to repent (Rom 2.4; 9.22), even though false teachers are likely to misinterpret him.

3.18: Doxology. Rom 16.25; Eph 3.20–21; Phil 4.20; 1 Tim 1.17; 2 Tim 4.18; Heb 13.21; 1 Pet 5.11; Jude 24–25; Rev 5.13. Only in Revelation and 2 Peter is glory ascribed explicitly to Jesus Christ.

The First Letter of JOHN

Though it lacks the formal features of an ancient letter—such as the opening greeting, designation of recipients and sender, reference to local persons, sender's plans, and concluding greeting (see 2 and 3 John)—1 John presents itself as an authoritative, written communication between the sender and its audience (1.4; 2.1,7–8, 12–14,21,26). The opening (1.1–4) echoes the prologue of the Fourth Gospel (Jn 1.1–18), including the testimony of a communal "we" to its belief in Jesus Christ (1.1; Jn 1.14). Where the Gospel emphasized the presence of the eternal Word of God in Jesus, the epistle focuses on the physical reality of the word of life.

The "we" of a group of authorized teachers provides a formal backdrop for the individual who writes these instructions to the community. In the rest of the letter, the author uses "we" to indicate the common faith that he shares with the readers (for example, 3.23–24). First John is the work of a single teacher, writing in the Johannine tradition. The opening "we" suggests that he belongs to a school of such teachers.

By the end of the second century, the author of 1 John had been identified with John, the evangelist (Eusebius, *Historia ecclesiastica* iii.39.17; *Muratorian Canon,* lines 26–31; Irenaeus, *Adversus Haereses* 3.16.5). Eventually, the Elder, author of 2 and 3 John, was also identified with John, the evangelist. Both theology and language, however, suggest that the Johannine letters were written ca. 100 CE by one or more teachers who are heirs to the evangelist's teaching, rather than by the evangelist himself.

First John often echoes phrases that remind readers of the Fourth Gospel. Yet such expressions also differ from the evangelist. Where the Gospel consistently speaks of Jesus as the light of the world (for example, Jn 1.4–5,7; 9.5; 12.46), in 1 John, "light" refers to God (1.5). "Walking in light" refers to belief in Jesus as revelation of God in the Gospel (Jn 8.12; 12.46) but to ethical conduct of life in 1 John 1.5–7. This ethical meaning for the image occurs in Jewish and other early Christian texts; 1 John often seems closer to those materials than to the Gospel's perspective that Jesus is the unique revelation of God. In the Gospel, belief in Jesus' relationship to the Father determines an individual's salvation (for example, Jn 3.35–36). The hostile confrontation with Jews over the Christian claims for Jesus, which dominates the ministry of Jesus in the Gospel (for instance, Jn 8.13–59), never appears in 1 John. Interpreters who conclude that 1 John reflects an earlier form of the Johannine tradition therefore have to account for the general lack of Jewish concerns in 1 John. In fact, only unbelieving pagans (1 Jn 5.21) and dissident Christians who have broken communion with the Johannine churches (2.18–21) threaten the faith of 1 John's readers.

The writer accuses the dissidents of denying that Jesus is the messiah, that is, denying the Father and Son (2.22–23). Early Christian sayings warn that those who deny Jesus will be rejected in the judgment (see, for instance, Mt 10.32–33 and its parallel at Lk 12.8–9). In the Gospel, denying the divinity of the Son is equivalent to denying the Father (for example, Jn 5.20–23). Since the author of 1 John writes to ensure that its readers will not be deceived by the doctrine of opposing teachers (2.26–27), it would hardly have been the case that the secessionists denied the Christian belief that

Jesus is the messiah or the Johannine insight that Jesus is identical with the Father. The link between christological belief and salvation is central to the Johannine tradition (5.1; Jn 1.12). The false teaching must have been one that introduced a subtle change into the tradition. First John 4.1–3 provides a clue: The opponents do not confess that Jesus has come "in the flesh." Combined with the opening stress on testimony to the physical reality of the word of life (1.1–4), this phrase suggests that their dispute concerned the humanity of Jesus.

Since 1 John does not argue against opposing views directly, interpreters often turn to other reports about dissident teachers in early Christianity. A close similarity to the views rejected in 1 John appears in references to the Gnostic heretic, Cerinthus (ca. 100 CE). He argued that the divine Christ descended upon the righteous man, Jesus, at his baptism. This gift of the Spirit enabled Jesus to work miracles and reveal the unknown Father-God, who is above the Jewish creator. Since the divine cannot suffer, the Christ separated from Jesus prior to his death on the cross (see Irenaeus, *Adversus Haereses* 1.26.1). First John hints that the dissidents taught that Jesus Christ came in water only, not in water and blood (5.6). They apparently denied any saving significance to the death of Jesus on the cross. Though the clues in 1 John suggest that the opponents held some views in common with Cerinthus, the evidence is not decisive. There are no traces of the typical Gnostic teaching about a Father God beyond the creator or hostility to the God of Genesis in 1 John. Perhaps the secessionists derived their views of Jesus and the Spirit from the portrayal of Jesus in the Gospel of John.

Since the Gospel highlights the unity of believers with Jesus and through him with God (for example, Jn 15.1–10; 17.6–19), schism threatened the promise of salvation at the heart of Johannine Christianity. First John charges the dissidents with breaking the commandment of love by which Jesus and the Father dwell with the community (2.9–11,20–21; 4.7–12; cf. Jn 14.15,21; 15.9–10). The appearance of such schismatics fulfills the prediction that false prophets and messiahs will attempt to deceive God's faithful (2.22; 4.1; cf. Mk 13.22). Because 1 John is so indirect in speaking about dissident teachers, one cannot determine whether all of the exhortation concerns them. Certainly questions concerning sin, judgment, mutual love among Christians, and confidence in prayer and in the redemptive death of Christ arose in other early Christian churches. Much of 1 John may reflect the ordinary style of preaching in the circle of Johannine teachers (for instance, 5.13–21). First John remains confident that the Spirit's presence in the community will enable readers to recognize this work as an expression of the truth revealed in Jesus (2.27; 4.6,13).

1 We declare to you what was from the
beginning, what we have heard, what
we have seen with our eyes, what we have
looked at and touched with our hands, con-
cerning the word of life— 2 this life was
revealed, and we have seen it and testify to
it, and declare to you the eternal life that
was with the Father and was revealed to
us— 3 we declare to you what we have seen
and heard so that you also may have fel-
lowship with us; and truly our fellowship
is with the Father and with his Son Jesus
Christ. 4 We are writing these things so that
our[a] joy may be complete.

a Other ancient authorities read *your*

1.1–4: Introduction. 1–2: *From the beginning* echoes the opening of John's Gospel (Jn 1.1–18) in which Jesus is the Word, life and light made flesh. Here, the phrase refers to the beginning of Christian faith. *We,* teachers in the Johannine community, charged with handing on the tradition. *Heard, seen, looked at, touched* insist on the human reality of the Son against false teachers (see Introduction). **3–4:** Fellowship with the Father and Son and abiding joy are two signs of genuine Christian community in the Johannine tradition (Jn 15.11; 17.13).

5 This is the message we have heard
from him and proclaim to you, that God is
light and in him there is no darkness at all.
6 If we say that we have fellowship with him
while we are walking in darkness, we lie
and do not do what is true; 7 but if we walk
in the light as he himself is in the light, we
have fellowship with one another, and the
blood of Jesus his Son cleanses us from all
sin. 8 If we say that we have no sin, we de-
ceive ourselves, and the truth is not in us.
9 If we confess our sins, he who is faithful
and just will forgive us our sins and cleanse
us from all unrighteousness. 10 If we say
that we have not sinned, we make him a
liar, and his word is not in us.

2 My little children, I am writing these
things to you so that you may not sin.
But if anyone does sin, we have an advocate
with the Father, Jesus Christ the righteous;
2 and he is the atoning sacrifice for our sins,
and not for ours only but also for the sins
of the whole world.
3 Now by this we may be sure that we
know him, if we obey his commandments.
4 Whoever says, "I have come to know
him," but does not obey his command-
ments, is a liar, and in such a person the
truth does not exist; 5 but whoever obeys
his word, truly in this person the love of
God has reached perfection. By this we may
be sure that we are in him: 6 whoever says,
"I abide in him," ought to walk just as he
walked.
7 Beloved, I am writing you no new
commandment, but an old commandment
that you have had from the beginning; the
old commandment is the word that you
have heard. 8 Yet I am writing you a new
commandment that is true in him and in
you, because[a] the darkness is passing away
and the true light is already shining. 9 Who-
ever says, "I am in the light," while hating
a brother or sister,[b] is still in the darkness.
10 Whoever loves a brother or sister[c] lives
in the light, and in such a person[d] there
is no cause for stumbling. 11 But whoever
hates another believer[e] is in the darkness,
walks in the darkness, and does not know
the way to go, because the darkness has
brought on blindness.

12 I am writing to you, little children,
because your sins are forgiven on
account of his name.
13 I am writing to you, fathers,
because you know him who is from
the beginning.
I am writing to you, young people,
because you have conquered
the evil one.
14 I write to you, children,

a Or *that* b Gk *hating a brother* c Gk *loves a brother* d Or *in it* e Gk *hates a brother*

1.5–10: Holiness in the community. 5: Light is a common symbol for the holiness and perfection of God (Ps 4.6; Isa 60.1–2). God's light is a guide for the righteous (Ps 27.1). **6–7:** No one can claim fellowship with God who does not follow God's commands (Jn 3.19; 1 Jn 2.11). Christians do not claim to be perfect. They receive forgiveness thanks to Jesus' death on the cross (cf. Rev 1.5; 5.9). **8–10:** The false teachers, who reject the saving death of Jesus (see Introduction), may have claimed that true believers did not sin. Such teaching makes God a liar (v. 10). False views about God and sin are typical of the wicked (Ps 53).

2.1–6: Christ, our advocate. 1–2: A similar image of the risen Christ interceding for Christians describes Christ as high priest in Heb 4.14–5.4. Here Christ is the *advocate,* one who defends the faithful in the divine court (for the Holy Spirit as *advocate* see Jn 14.15–16). **3–5:** Knowledge of God requires obedience to God's commandments (cf. Ezek 36.26–27). **6:** Jesus exemplifies the love which is God's commandment (Jn 13.1; 15.11–13).

2.7–11: The love commandment. 7: *I am writing you* repeats 2.1. Fidelity to Christ's *new commandment* to love one another (Jn 13.34) is freedom from sin and darkness. **8:** *The true light is already shining* picks up the portrayal of Jesus as light of the world from the Gospel (Jn 8.12; 9.5; 12.35–36).

2.12–17: Victory over evil. 12–14: A rhythmic series of phrases reminds all in the community from the youngest or newest members to the most senior (*little children . . . fathers . . . young people*) that they share Christ's victory over the world and its ruling power, *the evil one* (see Jn 12.31; 16.11,33b). **15–17:**

because you know the Father.
I write to you, fathers,
because you know him who is from
the beginning.
I write to you, young people,
because you are strong
and the word of God abides in you,
and you have overcome the
evil one.

15 Do not love the world or the things in
the world. The love of the Father is not in
those who love the world; 16 for all that is
in the world—the desire of the flesh, the
desire of the eyes, the pride in riches—
comes not from the Father but from the
world. 17 And the world and its desire[a] are
passing away, but those who do the will of
God live forever.

18 Children, it is the last hour! As you
have heard that antichrist is coming, so
now many antichrists have come. From this
we know that it is the last hour. 19 They
went out from us, but they did not belong
to us; for if they had belonged to us, they
would have remained with us. But by going
out they made it plain that none of them
belongs to us. 20 But you have been anoint-
ed by the Holy One, and all of you have
knowledge.[b] 21 I write to you, not because
you do not know the truth, but because you
know it, and you know that no lie comes
from the truth. 22 Who is the liar but the
one who denies that Jesus is the Christ?[c]
This is the antichrist, the one who denies
the Father and the Son. 23 No one who de-
nies the Son has the Father; everyone who
confesses the Son has the Father also. 24 Let
what you heard from the beginning abide
in you. If what you heard from the begin-
ning abides in you, then you will abide in
the Son and in the Father. 25 And this is
what he has promised us,[d] eternal life.

26 I write these things to you concerning
those who would deceive you. 27 As for
you, the anointing that you received from
him abides in you, and so you do not need
anyone to teach you. But as his anointing
teaches you about all things, and is true and
is not a lie, and just as it has taught you,
abide in him.[e]

28 And now, little children, abide in
him, so that when he is revealed we may
have confidence and not be put to shame
before him at his coming.

29 If you know that he is righteous, you
may be sure that everyone who does right
has been born of him.
3 1 See what love
the Father has given us, that we should
be called children of God; and that is what
we are. The reason the world does not
know us is that it did not know him. 2 Be-
loved, we are God's children now; what we

a Or *the desire for it* *b* Other ancient authorities read *you know all things* *c* Or *the Messiah* *d* Other ancient authorities read *you* *e* Or *it*

Though Jesus came to save the world (1 Jn 2.2), the world also represents the false love for wealth or honor and the passions that separate people from God and one another (3.17).

2.18–29: Victory over false teaching. 18–23: Since the secessionists are agents of the evil one, *antichrists* who are trying to deceive God's people, (v. 18; 4.1–3), a victory over evil means holding fast the true teaching (see Introduction). The appearance of false teachers who are able to deceive God's people signals the end of days, *the last hour* in apocalyptic texts (Mt 24.4–5,24; CD 5.20; *T. Moses* 7.4; Rev 20.10). The term *antichrist* only occurs in the Johannine letters. It appears to be a variant of the "false messiah" ("pseudochristos") in the Synoptic apocalypse (Mk 13.32; Mt 24.24). The figure of an opponent of God who arises in the last days combines the mythical chaos monster defeated by God's creative power (Isa 27.1; 51.9; Ps 74.13; Job 26.12), the figure of Satan as an angelic adversary (Job 1.6; Zech 3.1; Dan 12.1; *Jubilees* 1.20; 1 QS 1.18; 3.20–21), a human ruler who embodies evil (Dan 8.25; Ezek 38.1; 39.6; 2 Macc 9.12; 2 Esd 5.6–13), and the false prophet (Deut 13.2–6; 18.20). **24–27:** The presence of the Holy Spirit within the community enables Christians to distinguish true faith from lies about Jesus (cf. Jn 14.26; 16.13). **28–29:** *At his coming* refers to Christ coming in judgment. Those who remain true to their faith in Jesus have nothing to fear (cf. Jn 3.36).

3.1–10: God's children are holy. 1–3: As God's children, Christians become like Christ (Jn 1.12–13; 13.15–16; 17.16–19). **4–6:** Jesus' coming has taken away the sin of those who remain faithful (1.5–2.2).

will be has not yet been revealed. What we
do know is this: when he[a] is revealed, we
will be like him, for we will see him as he is.
3 And all who have this hope in him purify
themselves, just as he is pure.
4 Everyone who commits sin is guilty of
lawlessness; sin is lawlessness. 5 You know
that he was revealed to take away sins, and
in him there is no sin. 6 No one who abides
in him sins; no one who sins has either seen
him or known him. 7 Little children, let no
one deceive you. Everyone who does what
is right is righteous, just as he is righteous.
8 Everyone who commits sin is a child of the
devil; for the devil has been sinning from
the beginning. The Son of God was re-
vealed for this purpose, to destroy the
works of the devil. 9 Those who have been
born of God do not sin, because God's seed
abides in them;[b] they cannot sin, because
they have been born of God. 10 The chil-
dren of God and the children of the devil
are revealed in this way: all who do not do
what is right are not from God, nor are
those who do not love their brothers and
sisters.[c]
11 For this is the message you have
heard from the beginning, that we should
love one another. 12 We must not be like
Cain who was from the evil one and mur-
dered his brother. And why did he murder
him? Because his own deeds were evil and
his brother's righteous. 13 Do not be aston-
ished, brothers and sisters,[d] that the world
hates you. 14 We know that we have passed
from death to life because we love one an-
other. Whoever does not love abides in
death. 15 All who hate a brother or sister[c]
are murderers, and you know that murder-
ers do not have eternal life abiding in them.
16 We know love by this, that he laid down
his life for us—and we ought to lay down
our lives for one another. 17 How does
God's love abide in anyone who has the
world's goods and sees a brother or sister[e]
in need and yet refuses help?
18 Little children, let us love, not in
word or speech, but in truth and action.
19 And by this we will know that we are
from the truth and will reassure our hearts
before him 20 whenever our hearts condemn
us; for God is greater than our hearts, and
he knows everything. 21 Beloved, if our
hearts do not condemn us, we have bold-
ness before God; 22 and we receive from
him whatever we ask, because we obey his
commandments and do what pleases him.
23 And this is his commandment, that
we should believe in the name of his Son
Jesus Christ and love one another, just as
he has commanded us. 24 All who obey his
commandments abide in him, and he
abides in them. And by this we know that
he abides in us, by the Spirit that he has
given us.

4 Beloved, do not believe every spirit, but
test the spirits to see whether they are
from God; for many false prophets have

a Or *it* *b* Or *because the children of God abide in him* *c* Gk *his brother* *d* Gk *brothers* *e* Gk *brother*

7–8: Christians must take care not to be deceived about sin (2.1). **9–10:** *God's seed,* probably the Holy Spirit (2.26–27), and love for one another (Jn 13.35) distinguish God's children from others.

3.11–17: Moral examples. 11: See 2.7. **12:** Cain shows that hating a brother leads to murder (Gen 4.8). **13–14:** Even though they are righteous, like Abel, Christians can expect to be hated by the world (Jn 15.18–19). **15:** The phrase, *do not have eternal life abiding in them,* invites readers to apply this lesson to the secessionists. Though they claim to have faith, this break with the community is equivalent to murdering a brother (4.5; cf. Mt 5.21–22). **16–18:** Jesus' death is the supreme example of love (Jn 13.1; 15.9,13).

3.19–24: Love as confidence before God. 19–20: Love is the basis for God's judgment even if the false teachers have sown seeds of doubt (2.28). **21–22:** Jesus promised that God would answer his disciples' prayer (Jn 16.23–24). **23–24:** Belief in the Son and love establish a permanent relationship between believers and God (Jn 16.26–27).

4.1–6: Testing spirits. 1–3: Since false teachers can appear genuine (cf. Mt 7.15–23), Christians must *test* such claims by their belief in Jesus (cf. 1 Cor 12.1–3). The secessionists have modified the tradition

gone out into the world. 2 By this you know
the Spirit of God: every spirit that confesses
that Jesus Christ has come in the flesh is
from God, 3 and every spirit that does not
confess Jesus[a] is not from God. And this is
the spirit of the antichrist, of which you
have heard that it is coming; and now it is
already in the world. 4 Little children, you
are from God, and have conquered them;
for the one who is in you is greater than the
one who is in the world. 5 They are from the
world; therefore what they say is from the
world, and the world listens to them. 6 We
are from God. Whoever knows God listens
to us, and whoever is not from God does
not listen to us. From this we know the
spirit of truth and the spirit of error.

7 Beloved, let us love one another, be-
cause love is from God; everyone who loves
is born of God and knows God. 8 Whoever
does not love does not know God, for God
is love. 9 God's love was revealed among us
in this way: God sent his only Son into the
world so that we might live through him.
10 In this is love, not that we loved God but
that he loved us and sent his Son to be the
atoning sacrifice for our sins. 11 Beloved,
since God loved us so much, we also ought
to love one another. 12 No one has ever seen
God; if we love one another, God lives in
us, and his love is perfected in us.

13 By this we know that we abide in him
and he in us, because he has given us of his
Spirit. 14 And we have seen and do testify
that the Father has sent his Son as the Sav-
ior of the world. 15 God abides in those
who confess that Jesus is the Son of God,
and they abide in God. 16 So we have
known and believe the love that God has
for us.

God is love, and those who abide in love
abide in God, and God abides in them.
17 Love has been perfected among us in this:
that we may have boldness on the day of
judgment, because as he is, so are we in this
world. 18 There is no fear in love, but per-
fect love casts out fear; for fear has to do
with punishment, and whoever fears has
not reached perfection in love. 19 We love[b]
because he first loved us. 20 Those who say,
"I love God," and hate their brothers or
sisters,[c] are liars; for those who do not
love a brother or sister[d] whom they have
seen, cannot love God whom they have not
seen. 21 The commandment we have from
him is this: those who love God must love
their brothers and sisters[c] also.

5 Everyone who believes that Jesus is the
Christ[e] has been born of God, and ev-
eryone who loves the parent loves the child.
2 By this we know that we love the children
of God, when we love God and obey his
commandments. 3 For the love of God is
this, that we obey his commandments. And

a Other ancient authorities read *does away with Jesus* (Gk *dissolves Jesus*) *b* Other ancient authorities add *him*; others add *God* *c* Gk *brothers* *d* Gk *brother* *e* Or *the Messiah*

by denying that the Christ *has come in the flesh*. **4–6:** The Holy Spirit verifies that 1 John is witness to authentic tradition (Jn 16.13–14). **5:** *The world listens* may imply that the secessionist gospel enjoys greater success than the truth (cf. Jn 15.19).

4.7–21: God's love as the basis of salvation. 7–9: True Christians imitate the love that God has shown in sending the Son to give life to the world (3.16–22; Jn 3.16). **10–12:** God's love has been shown in the death of Jesus (Jn 13.1). It is the basis for the command to love others (Jn 15.12–13). **12:** See Jn 1.18; 6.46. **13–16a:** See 3.23–24. **14:** See Jn 4.42. **16b–18:** *God is love* (cf. Rom 8.32,39; 1 Cor 13.11). When Christian life corresponds to the nature of God (1 Jn 1.5–7), there is no reason to fear God's judgment (2.1–6,28; 3.18–20). **19:** 1 Jn 4.7,11. **20:** Love for others is the true evidence of our knowledge and love of God (2.3–11; 3.23–24). **21:** *Those who love God must love their brothers and sisters* represents the double commandment, to love God and neighbor (Mt 22.34–40, quoting Deut 6.5 and Lev 19.18) in the language of the Johannine tradition.

5.1–13: Concluding appeal to keep the true faith. 1–3: Belief in Jesus as the Christ (4.2–3; Jn 1.12–13; 20.31) and love for fellow believers (4.20–21; Jn 13.35) are the hallmarks of Johannine Christianity. **2:** *We know that we love the children of God, when we love God* appears to contradict 4.12. It serves as a polemic against the false teachers. Schism implies hating God's children (3.11–16). **4–5:** See 2.12–14; 4.4.

his commandments are not burdensome,
4 for whatever is born of God conquers the
world. And this is the victory that conquers
the world, our faith. 5 Who is it that con-
quers the world but the one who believes
that Jesus is the Son of God?

6 This is the one who came by water and
blood, Jesus Christ, not with the water only
but with the water and the blood. And the
Spirit is the one that testifies, for the Spirit
is the truth. 7 There are three that testify:[a]
8 the Spirit and the water and the blood,
and these three agree. 9 If we receive human
testimony, the testimony of God is greater;
for this is the testimony of God that he has
testified to his Son. 10 Those who believe in
the Son of God have the testimony in their
hearts. Those who do not believe in God[b]
have made him a liar by not believing in the
testimony that God has given concerning
his Son. 11 And this is the testimony: God
gave us eternal life, and this life is in his
Son. 12 Whoever has the Son has life; who-
ever does not have the Son of God does not
have life.

13 I write these things to you who be-
lieve in the name of the Son of God, so that
you may know that you have eternal life.

14 And this is the boldness we have in
him, that if we ask anything according to
his will, he hears us. 15 And if we know that
he hears us in whatever we ask, we know
that we have obtained the requests made of
him. 16 If you see your brother or sister[c]
committing what is not a mortal sin, you
will ask, and God[d] will give life to such
a one—to those whose sin is not mortal.
There is sin that is mortal; I do not say that
you should pray about that. 17 All wrong-
doing is sin, but there is sin that is not mor-
tal.

18 We know that those who are born of
God do not sin, but the one who was born
of God protects them, and the evil one does
not touch them. 19 We know that we are
God's children, and that the whole world
lies under the power of the evil one. 20 And
we know that the Son of God has come and
has given us understanding so that we may
know him who is true;[e] and we are in him
who is true, in his Son Jesus Christ. He is
the true God and eternal life.

21 Little children, keep yourselves from
idols.[f]

a A few other authorities read (with variations) 7*There are three that testify in heaven, the Father, the Word, and the Holy Spirit, and these three are one.* 8*And there are three that testify on earth:* *b* Other ancient authorities read *in the Son* *c* Gk *your brother* *d* Gk *he* *e* Other ancient authorities read *know the true God* *f* Other ancient authorities add *Amen*

6–8: *One who came by water and blood* refers to the death of Jesus as atonement for sin (1.7; 2.2; 4.10; Jn 1.29). The witnesses, *water, blood,* and *Spirit,* are evident in John's account of Jesus' death (Jn 19.34–35; for the water as Spirit, see Jn 7.38–39). **9–12:** The true faith is based not only on human testimony (1.1–4; Jn 1.7–8) but God's testimony as well (cf. Jn 5.31–38). **13:** *I write . . . that you have eternal life* echoes the ending in Jn 20.31.

5.14–21: Epilogue. Sin and forgiveness in the community. 14–15: God's children can be certain that God will hear their prayers (3.21–22; Jn 14.14–16; 15.16; 16.23–24; Mt 18.19–20). **16–17:** Communal prayer can elicit God's forgiveness and restore sinners (2.1–2; Mt 18.15–20; Jas 5.15b,19–20). *To those whose sin is not mortal* distinguishes a category of sin that cannot be forgiven. Elsewhere such sin is denying that God's Spirit is at work in Jesus (Mk 3.28–30) or apostasy from Christian faith (Heb 6.4–6). Here, the expression probably refers to the secessionists. Their break with the community means that they no longer dwell with God or have the Spirit (2.19–25). **18:** See 3.8–10. **19:** See 2.12–15; 5.4–5. **20:** *Him who is true* probably refers to knowledge of the true God as other manuscripts propose (Jn 1.18; 14.7,9–10). Knowledge of the *true God* (Father and Son) confers *eternal life* (Jn 17.3). **21:** In a general sense, *keep yourselves from idols* probably refers to the false gods of non-Christian neighbors (1 Cor 10.14). Traveling missionaries were to reject non-Christian hospitality (3 Jn 7). In this context, the phrase may refer to association with the secessionists and their teaching (2 Jn 7–9).

The Second Letter of
JOHN

Second John follows the structural conventions of an ancient letter: designation of sender and recipient (v. 1a); greeting formula, somewhat expanded (vv. 1b–3); wish or thanksgiving for well-being of recipient (v. 4); body of letter (vv. 5–11); concluding matters, travel plans (v. 12), and final greeting (v. 13). However, no concrete names, places, or details are specified. The expression "elect lady" (v. 1) may refer to one or more of the Johannine churches in Asia Minor. The author refers to himself as "the Elder," an expression which could indicate that he held the office of presbyter in a house church (cf. Acts 14.23; 20.17; 1 Pet 5.1; 1 Tim 5.17) or which may be a reminder of the respect due elders in the community (cf. 1 Pet 5.5; 1 Tim 5.2). Because the term is not used in 1 John, some scholars conclude that 2 John was composed by another person in the circle of Johannine teachers. However, its genre did not require that 1 John refer to either sender or addressee. The similarity in language and situation makes it more likely that the same individual composed both letters.

Use of an allusion to the love command and teaching held from the beginning (vv. 5–6; cf. 1 John 2.24; 3.11; 5.3) to bolster warnings against dissident teachers (v. 7; 1 John 4.3) shows that 2 John refers to the opponents refuted in 1 John. The Elder asks the recipients to exclude dissidents from any hospitality. To aid them would be to share in their diabolical work (vv. 8–11). Perhaps a copy of 1 John accompanied these instructions.

1 The elder to the elect lady and her chil-
dren, whom I love in the truth, and not
only I but also all who know the truth, 2 be-
cause of the truth that abides in us and will
be with us forever:
3 Grace, mercy, and peace will be with
us from God the Father and from[a] Jesus
Christ, the Father's Son, in truth and love.
4 I was overjoyed to find some of your
children walking in the truth, just as we
have been commanded by the Father. 5 But
now, dear lady, I ask you, not as though I
were writing you a new commandment, but
one we have had from the beginning, let us
love one another. 6 And this is love, that we
walk according to his commandments; this
is the commandment just as you have heard
it from the beginning—you must walk in it.
7 Many deceivers have gone out into the
world, those who do not confess that Jesus
Christ has come in the flesh; any such per-
son is the deceiver and the antichrist! 8 Be

a Other ancient authorities add *the Lord*

1–3: Letter opening. See Rom 1.1–7. *Elect lady* probably refers to the local church. *Love in the truth* sets out the author's vision of the church. Its members are united by Jesus' command to love one another (vv. 4–6; 1 Jn 2.22–23; 3.23). They reject false teaching about the Son (vv. 7–9). **4–11: Letter body.** The author's actual request comes at the end: Avoid extending any form of assistance or hospitality to false teachers (vv. 10–11). **4–6:** The *new commandment* to love one another has been an identifying mark of Johannine Christianity from its beginning (Jn 13.34–35; 1 Jn 2.7–10). **7–9:** The secessionists who do not *abide in the teaching of Christ* by denying that the human Jesus is the Christ (v. 7; see 1 Jn, Introduction) have shattered that fellowship (1 Jn 2.19). False teaching is a sign that the *antichrist* is at work in the world (1 Jn 2.18; 4.1–3). **7:** *Antichrist,* see 1 Jn 2.18–23. **10–11:** The severity of this demand, *do not*

on your guard, so that you do not lose what
we[a] have worked for, but may receive a
full reward. 9 Everyone who does not abide
in the teaching of Christ, but goes beyond
it, does not have God; whoever abides in
the teaching has both the Father and the
Son. 10 Do not receive into the house or
welcome anyone who comes to you and
does not bring this teaching; 11 for to wel-
come is to participate in the evil deeds of
such a person.

12 Although I have much to write to
you, I would rather not use paper and ink;
instead I hope to come to you and talk with
you face to face, so that our joy may be
complete.
13 The children of your elect sister send
you their greetings.[b]

a Other ancient authorities read *you* *b* Other ancient authorities add *Amen*

receive into the house (i.e., church) anyone connected with the secessionists, follows from the view that their activities are Satan's final effort against God's people. **12–13: Letter closing.** Ancient letters frequently end with a notice of the sender's future travel plans (Rom 15.22,33).

The Third Letter of JOHN

Third John has the form of a private letter from the Elder (see the Introduction to 2 Jn) to a certain Gaius, who is well known for showing hospitality to traveling missionaries (vv. 5–8). Because 3 John does not refer to the dissidents of 1 and 2 John, some interpreters hold that the Elder is not the same person who wrote those letters. However, the similarity of language in the conclusions to 2 John (vv. 12–13) and 3 John (vv. 13–15) makes it more likely that the same person is writing 3 John. Demetrius, whom the Elder recommends in v. 12, may have brought the letter to Gaius. The early Christian mission was dependent upon hospitality (Mt 10.40–42; Acts 16.14–15; Rom 16.1–2). However, the Elder is not writing to continue a relationship that is already well established. Verses 9–10 speak of a letter to a church in the region that was rejected. A certain Diotrephes not only refused hospitality to persons associated with the Elder, he even excluded others who did so from the church. Thus, 3 John appears to be seeking an alternate source of support in the region.

Has Diotrephes given the Elder a dose of the medicine prescribed in 2 John 8–11? Perhaps, though in that case one might suppose that the Elder would have distinguished his emissaries from dissident teachers. In the language of ancient diplomacy, refusing hospitality to someone's envoy implied rejecting the message he bears and the sender as well (cf. 1 Macc 14.21–23). The Gospel of John uses similar language about Jesus as God's emissary (John 13.20). Verses 9–10 indicate that the rift between Diotrephes and the Elder is serious, but provide no evidence about its cause.

1 The elder to the beloved Gaius, whom
I love in truth.
2 Beloved, I pray that all may go well
with you and that you may be in good
health, just as it is well with your soul. 3 I
was overjoyed when some of the friends[a]
arrived and testified to your faithfulness
to the truth, namely how you walk in the
truth. 4 I have no greater joy than this, to
hear that my children are walking in the
truth.
5 Beloved, you do faithfully whatever
you do for the friends,[a] even though they
are strangers to you; 6 they have testified to
your love before the church. You will do
well to send them on in a manner worthy of
God; 7 for they began their journey for the
sake of Christ,[b] accepting no support from
non-believers.[c] 8 Therefore we ought to
support such people, so that we may be-
come co-workers with the truth.
9 I have written something to the
church; but Diotrephes, who likes to put

a Gk *brothers* *b* Gk *for the sake of the name*
c Gk *the Gentiles*

1–2: Letter opening and health wish. This secular opening (contrast 2 Jn 1–3) indicates that this is a private letter from the Elder (of 2 Jn 1) to Gaius. *Beloved* (vv. 2,5,11) indicates the relationship of friendship and hospitality that this letter seeks to establish (see Introduction). **3–12: Letter body.** The Elder hopes that Gaius will provide a permanent base of support for traveling missionaries. **3–8:** Other missionaries have given a glowing report about Gaius, *testified to your love before the church* (v. 6). Traveling missionaries need to receive help from fellow Christians so that they will not have to turn to unbelievers (v. 7). **9–11:** The Elder is turning to Gaius because a prominent Christian in the region,

himself first, does not acknowledge our au-
thority. 10 So if I come, I will call attention
to what he is doing in spreading false
charges against us. And not content with
those charges, he refuses to welcome the
friends,[a] and even prevents those who
want to do so and expels them from the
church.

11 Beloved, do not imitate what is evil
but imitate what is good. Whoever does
good is from God; whoever does evil has
not seen God. 12 Everyone has testified fa-
vorably about Demetrius, and so has the
truth itself. We also testify for him,[b] and
you know that our testimony is true.

13 I have much to write to you, but I
would rather not write with pen and ink;
14 instead I hope to see you soon, and we
will talk together face to face.

15 Peace to you. The friends send you
their greetings. Greet the friends there, each
by name.

a Gk *brothers* *b* Gk lacks *for him*

Diotrephes, now refuses to have anything to do with missionaries sent by the Elder (vv. 9–10; see Introduction). *Does not acknowledge our authority* implies that Diotrephes refused to accept a previous letter from the Elder to the church in the region. However, a personal visit could heal the breach (v. 10). **12:** The Elder adds a recommendation for Demetrius (see Rom 16.1–2), who may have brought the letter to Gaius. **13–15: Letter Closing.** See 2 Jn 12–13.

The Letter of
JUDE

Although the addressees of the Letter of Jude are rather vaguely defined (v. 1), the emergency identified as its occasion (vv. 3–4) and the concrete descriptions of the opponents indicate that it was a real letter to particular recipients. The purpose of the letter is to encourage the addressees "to contend for the faith" against those who "pervert the grace of our God into licentiousness" (vv. 3–4). The date of composition is uncertain, except that it must be earlier than 2 Peter, which uses Jude. The reference to "the words spoken by the apostles" (v. 17) may indicate a period in the church when the apostles could be spoken of as a unified group from the past. If so, this may point to a date late in the first century CE. Others have dated Jude as early as the 50s.

Jude is the brother of James (Mt 13.55; Mk 6.3), who was the Lord's brother (Gal 1.19) and leader of the Jerusalem church. Only this James was prominent enough to have been sufficient identification for his brother. Attributing the authorship of a writing to a major figure is well attested in the Bible and in other ancient literature.

The letter is organized by an exhortation to "contend for the faith" (v. 3) and a closing exhortation to keep oneself "in the love of God" (v. 21) and have "mercy" on others who are erring (vv. 22–23). Between these two exhortations, a series of biblical and nonbiblical stories and prophecies are interpreted to show the error and eventual doom of the writer's opponents. They are an interpretation of selected judgments from Genesis and Exodus (vv. 5–8) with a note on Michael the archangel (vv. 9–10), an interpretation of selected errors from Genesis and Numbers (vv. 11–13), an application of the prophecy of 1 Enoch 1.9 to the opponents (vv. 14–16), and an application of apostolic prophecy (vv. 17–19). In each case the transition from citation to interpretation is marked by the word "these" as subject of the sentence: "these dreamers" (v. 8); "these people" (v. 10); "these" (vv. 12,16). The letter closes with an elaborate and beautiful doxology (vv. 24–25).

1 Jude,[a] a servant[b] of Jesus Christ and brother of James,

To those who are called, who are beloved[c] in[d] God the Father and kept safe for[d] Jesus Christ:

2 May mercy, peace, and love be yours in abundance.

3 Beloved, while eagerly preparing to write to you about the salvation we share, I find it necessary to write and appeal to you to contend for the faith that was once for all entrusted to the saints. 4 For certain intruders have stolen in among you, people who long ago were designated for this condemnation as ungodly, who pervert the grace of our God into licentiousness and

a Gk *Judas* *b* Gk *slave* *c* Other ancient authorities read *sanctified* *d* Or *by*

1–2: Salutation. See Rom 1.1–7n.
3–4: Occasion. The writer urges the readers to *contend for the faith* against certain *ungodly intruders* who have *perverted the* (inviolable, apostolic) *faith that was once for all entrusted to the saints.* Compare Gal 1.8–9 for similar sentiments. *Saints,* "holy ones," consecrated to God.

deny our only Master and Lord, Jesus
Christ.[a]

5 Now I desire to remind you, though
you are fully informed, that the Lord, who
once for all saved[b] a people out of the land
of Egypt, afterward destroyed those who
did not believe. 6 And the angels who did
not keep their own position, but left their
proper dwelling, he has kept in eternal
chains in deepest darkness for the judgment
of the great day. 7 Likewise, Sodom and
Gomorrah and the surrounding cities,
which, in the same manner as they, in-
dulged in sexual immorality and pursued
unnatural lust,[c] serve as an example by
undergoing a punishment of eternal fire.

8 Yet in the same way these dreamers
also defile the flesh, reject authority, and
slander the glorious ones.[d] 9 But when the
archangel Michael contended with the devil
and disputed about the body of Moses, he
did not dare to bring a condemnation of
slander[e] against him, but said, "The Lord
rebuke you!" 10 But these people slander
whatever they do not understand, and they
are destroyed by those things that, like irra-
tional animals, they know by instinct.
11 Woe to them! For they go the way of
Cain, and abandon themselves to Balaam's
error for the sake of gain, and perish in
Korah's rebellion. 12 These are blemishes[f]
on your love-feasts, while they feast with
you without fear, feeding themselves.[g]
They are waterless clouds carried along by
the winds; autumn trees without fruit,
twice dead, uprooted; 13 wild waves of the
sea, casting up the foam of their own
shame; wandering stars, for whom the
deepest darkness has been reserved forever.

14 It was also about these that Enoch, in
the seventh generation from Adam, proph-
esied, saying, "See, the Lord is coming[h]
with ten thousands of his holy ones, 15 to
execute judgment on all, and to convict ev-
eryone of all the deeds of ungodliness that
they have committed in such an ungodly
way, and of all the harsh things that ungod-
ly sinners have spoken against him."
16 These are grumblers and malcontents;

a Or *the only Master and our Lord Jesus Christ*
b Other ancient authorities read *though you were once for all fully informed, that Jesus* (or *Joshua*) *who saved*
c Gk *went after other flesh*
d Or *angels*; Gk *glories*
e Or *condemnation for blasphemy*
f Or *reefs*
g Or *without fear. They are shepherds who care only for themselves*
h Gk *came*

5–8: Three examples of judgment. Israelites who went out of Egypt with Moses (v. 5; see Num 14.20–23) and angels (v. 6; see Gen 6.1–4; 1 Enoch 6–16) were judged when they went astray, and Sodom and Gomorrah (Gen 19) were destroyed by fire for their *sexual immorality.* **8:** *These dreamers* will suffer a similar fate for their misdeeds. The intruders apparently claim to experience revelatory dreams. The *authority* that they despise may be either God's authority or angelic authorities. The *glorious ones* are probably angelic dignitaries.

9–10: A further example of the impropriety of slander. According to nonbiblical Jewish tradition, when the archangel Michael was about to bury the body of Moses, Satan accused Moses of being a murderer, not worthy of an honorable burial. Michael sent Satan off with the words, "May the Lord rebuke you" (Zech 3.2).

11–13: Three examples of error. *Cain* the murderer: Gen 4.9; Heb 11.4; 1 Jn 3.12. *Balaam* who prophesied for gain: Num 22; Rev 2.14 (see 2 Pet 2.15n.). *Korah* who rebelled: Num 16. Similarly, the opponents lead others to their doom by leading them astray for gain and rebelling against the (apostolic) leadership of the church. **12:** They are members of the group, participating in their *love-feasts* (see 1 Cor 11.20 – 21n.). Jude calls them intruders (v. 4) because their membership is illegitimate. They should *care . . . for* others (see note *g*), but they only *feed themselves* (see Ezek 34.2,10). *Waterless clouds,* see Hos 6.4. **13:** In the pseudepigraphical books of Enoch, *wandering stars* (planets) were understood to be disobedient angels. For Jude the phrase serves as a metaphor for the activity of the opponents.

14–16: A prophecy of judgment. 1 Enoch 1.9. 1 Enoch is a collection of apocalyptic writings dating from the third century BCE to the first century CE attributed to Enoch (Gen 5.21–24). Jude has a high regard for the authority of these writings, but it would be anachronistic to suppose that he considered them canonical.

they indulge their own lusts; they are bom-
bastic in speech, flattering people to their
own advantage.
17 But you, beloved, must remember the
predictions of the apostles of our Lord
Jesus Christ; 18 for they said to you, "In the
last time there will be scoffers, indulging
their own ungodly lusts." 19 It is these
worldly people, devoid of the Spirit, who
are causing divisions. 20 But you, beloved,
build yourselves up on your most holy
faith; pray in the Holy Spirit; 21 keep your-
selves in the love of God; look forward to
the mercy of our Lord Jesus Christ that
leads to[a] eternal life. 22 And have mercy on
some who are wavering; 23 save others by
snatching them out of the fire; and have
mercy on still others with fear, hating even
the tunic defiled by their bodies.[b]

24 Now to him who is able to keep you
from falling, and to make you stand with-
out blemish in the presence of his glory
with rejoicing, 25 to the only God our Sav-
ior, through Jesus Christ our Lord, be glo-
ry, majesty, power, and authority, before
all time and now and forever. Amen.

a Gk *Christ to* *b* Gk *by the flesh*. The Greek text of verses 22-23 is uncertain at several points

17–19: An apostolic prophecy. See 1 Tim 4.1; 2 Tim 3.1; 4.3; 2 Thess 2.3 for similar prophetic announcements.

20–23: Exhortations. 20–21: The promised encouragement "to contend for the faith" (v. 3) consists of traditional Christian ethical teaching. Jude incorporates a Trinitarian formula. **22–23:** The present text is probably a scribal expansion of an original exhortation to rescue some from *fire* (by getting them to repent; cf. Zech 3.24) but to *have mercy on* those who dispute *with fear* (of being corrupted).

24–25: Doxology. Rom 16.25; Eph 3.20–21; Phil 4.20; 1 Tim 1.17; 2 Tim 4.18; Heb 13–21; 1 Pet 5.11; 2 Pet 3.18; Rev 5.13.

THE REVELATION
to John

The book of Revelation, also known as the Apocalypse (from the Greek word meaning "disclosure," "unveiling," or "revelation") brings the canon of the New Testament to a close, appropriately so in view of its vivid visions of the consummation of God's plan of judgment and salvation. While the book presents itself as a work of prophecy (1.3; 22.10), it has given its name to a literary genre, the "apocalypse," found in a range of Jewish and Christian writings that first appeared about 250 BCE. Like other apocalyptic literature, the book of Revelation presents God's revelation to a human recipient. Unlike other apocalypses, which are pseudonymous, with their authors writing in the name of some revered figure from antiquity, the author of the book of Revelation identifies himself by his own name as John (1.1,4,9; 22.8). Although some ancient authorities (e.g., Justin, *Dialogue with Trypho* 81.4) have suggested that this is the apostle John, the son of Zebedee (see Mk 3.17), the internal evidence of the book itself is inconclusive. The author's acquaintance with the Jerusalem Temple and the rites conducted there, the depth of his knowledge of the Hebrew Bible (of the 404 verses in Revelation, some 275 include one or more allusions to passages in the Hebrew Bible, or to its Greek version, the Septuagint), as well as his adoption of a literary genre that was familiar in Palestinian Judaism, combine to suggest that John might have been a Palestinian Jewish Christian who fled to the Diaspora as a consequence of the First Jewish Revolt against the Romans (66–73 CE). His self-identification to the seven churches as "your brother who share with you in Jesus the persecution and the kingdom and the patient endurance" (1.9) suggests that he was well known to his audience, probably because he exercised a prophetic ministry among them (see 22.9). But he mentions the twelve apostles as figures from the past (21.14) and does not refer to himself as one of them. The traditional identification of the John of the book of Revelation with the apostle of the same name is thus questionable.

While it is likely that the book of Revelation draws on traditional material and on sources that were set in writing before the fall of Jerusalem in 70 CE (e.g., chs 11 and 12), it is probable that the book was composed toward the end of the reign of the emperor Domitian (81–96 CE). The book is addressed to "the seven churches that are in Asia" (1.4), Christian communities in the Roman proconsular province of Asia, located in the western portion of present-day Turkey. The book demonstrates its author's familiarity with the specific situation of each of the seven churches, beginning with Ephesus, the city that was the administrative capital of the province. The seven cities were complex and diverse in economic, social, political, and religious terms. Whether or not Christians faced organized and widespread persecutions sanctioned by Roman imperial authorities at the time the book was written, Christians in Asia were suffering serious oppression, facing the danger of being "slaughtered for the word of God and the testimony they had given" (6.9). One such martyr is Antipas, identified by name in the message to the church at Pergamum (2.13). John himself endured exile on the island of Patmos "because of the word of God and the testimony of Jesus" (1.9), and he reports that his visions took place there. A variety of voices and viewpoints competed for the attention of the late first-century Christians to whom the book of Revelation was originally addressed.

John exhorts them to stand firm in their convictions, to resist "with patient endurance" (2.2,19; 3.10) and at any cost the overwhelming pressures to yield to accommodation and compromise. The destruction of Jerusalem by the Romans in 70 CE gave John ample cause to identify Rome as Babylon, recalling the Babylonian destruction of Jerusalem in 586 BCE. The breadth and depth of Rome's political and economic power found expression in the widespread worship of the emperor in the province of Asia, with temples to the emperor and to Rome personified as the goddess Roma. The book of Revelation takes sides in a battle over sovereignty, where the Roman emperor competes with God and Christ in a contest for the allegiance of the faithful. Warning that those who worship the emperor, symbolized by "the beast" (13.1–10), will suffer ultimate defeat, the book urges believers to "hold fast to the faith of Jesus" (14.12) and to share in the paradoxical victory of his death and resurrection.

The book of Revelation is a work of extremes, ranging from soaring heights of hymnody inspired by Hebrew psalms and canticles to the gruesome language of plagues, warfare, and bloodshed. It uses the dualistic language characteristic of the apocalyptic genre to paint vivid portraits of the opposing sides in the eschatological conflict that will culminate in the victory of God and the final defeat of all evil. With its symbolic numbers and colors, animals, and angelic and demonic beings, and replete with echoes and images drawn from the literature of the ancient Near East, the Hebrew Bible, Greece, and Rome, the book of Revelation is so notoriously complex that the church father Jerome (345–420 CE) was led to remark that it contains as many mysteries as it contains words. Origen (185–254 CE) exclaimed, "Who can read the revelations granted to John without being amazed at the hidden depth of the ineffable mysteries, a depth apparent even to the person who does not understand what the text says?" (*On First Principles* 4.2.4). Many centuries later, the modern writer D.H. Lawrence wrote, "When we read Revelation, we feel at once there are meanings behind meanings." The symbolic visions of the book are by no means self-explanatory, and even John reports the need for the intervention of an angelic mediator to explain the meaning of the mystery disclosed to him (17.7). This characteristic, common in other works of the same genre, serves to emphasize that there are transcendent levels of meaning that must be discerned. The significance of events on earth is to be sought above and beyond what is immediately apparent, and it is ultimately to God that believers must turn to receive the meaning and guidance that strengthen their perseverance in the face of adversity. Over the centuries, the book of Revelation has been considered from a wide variety of interpretive strategies and approaches, ranging from literal readings of the book as predictive prophecy to readings that recognize in its utopian language the promise of hope in the midst of contemporary situations of suffering and oppression.

Although the structure of the book of Revelation is widely debated among scholars, there is general agreement that it involves a series of parallel, interconnected, and yet ever progressing sections. It begins with a prologue (1.1–3), an epistolary salutation (1.4–8) and an inaugural vision (1.9–20), which are followed by messages to each of the seven churches (2.1–3.22). Next (4.1–5.14) we find a vision of God enthroned and of Jesus depicted as a Lamb, who receives the seven sealed scrolls from the hand of God. A series of sevenfold visions commences at 6.1, beginning with the opening of each of the seven seals (6.1–8.5), followed by the sounding of each of seven trumpets (8.6–11.19). The sounding of the seventh trumpet is followed by the vision of the woman, the child, and the dragon (12.1–17), the vision of the two beasts (13.1–18), and a threefold vision of the victory and vindication of the faithful (14.1–20). These are followed by a final sevenfold series, the outpouring of the bowls of divine wrath (16.1–21). 17.1–18.24 presents the vision of the fall of Babylon, followed by the great doxology of 19.1–10 that also looks forward to the eschatological victory (19.11–21), the defeat of Satan (20.1–10), the last judgment (20.11–15), and the vision of the new Jerusalem (21.1–22.5). The book concludes with an epilogue (22.6–21).

1 The revelation of Jesus Christ, which
God gave him to show his servants[a]
what must soon take place; he made[b] it
known by sending his angel to his servant[c]
John, 2 who testified to the word of God
and to the testimony of Jesus Christ, even
to all that he saw.
3 Blessed is the one who reads aloud the
words of the prophecy, and blessed are
those who hear and who keep what is writ-
ten in it; for the time is near.

4 John to the seven churches that are in
Asia:
Grace to you and peace from him who is
and who was and who is to come, and from
the seven spirits who are before his throne,
5 and from Jesus Christ, the faithful wit-
ness, the firstborn of the dead, and the ruler
of the kings of the earth.
To him who loves us and freed[d] us from
our sins by his blood, 6 and made[b] us to be
a kingdom, priests serving[e] his God and
Father, to him be glory and dominion for-
ever and ever. Amen.
7 Look! He is coming with the clouds;
every eye will see him,
even those who pierced him;
and on his account all the tribes of
the earth will wail.
So it is to be. Amen.
8 "I am the Alpha and the Omega," says
the Lord God, who is and who was and
who is to come, the Almighty.

9 I, John, your brother who share with
you in Jesus the persecution and the king-
dom and the patient endurance, was on the
island called Patmos because of the word of
God and the testimony of Jesus.[f] 10 I was

a Gk *slaves* *b* Gk *and he made* *c* Gk *slave*
d Other ancient authorities read *washed*
e Gk *priests to* *f* Or *testimony to Jesus*

1.1–3: The prologue. This revelation came from God through Jesus Christ and was communicated to John by an angel (referred to again in 22.16). **1:** *Revelation* (Gk "apokalypsis"; see Dan 2.28–30,45), a literary form in which a vision from God, often under the guidance of an angel or other heavenly messenger, communicates in symbolic language God's hidden plan for the concluding period of history. Apocalypses also include visions of the heavenly world. **3:** *Blessed is . . .*, the first of seven beatitudes in Revelation (cf. 14.13; 16.15; 19.9; 20.6; 22.7, 14) is pronounced on the reader of this prophetic book and on those who hear it being read and who heed its message. In antiquity, texts were nearly always read *aloud.* The words *the time is near* (repeated in 22.10) provide a motive for obedience by announcing the imminence of the end-time.

1.4–8: Epistolary salutation to seven representative churches in the Roman province of Asia (in western Asia Minor). *Seven,* a number associated with heavenly realities, suggests the divine authority of the message delivered by John. **4:** *Grace . . . and peace* (2 Thess 1.2) combine the conventional Greek and Hebrew salutations, though John offers not his own greetings but those of God; *is . . . was . . . to come,* lit. "the being . . . the was . . . the coming." The *seven spirits* are either a symbolic reference to the manifold energies of the spirit of God (Isa 11.2), or a reference to the seven principal angels of God (Tob 12.15; 1 Enoch 20.1–8). Seven, the number of completion (of a ritual in Lev 4.6; of divine punishment in Lev 26.27–28) or wholeness, is the most important symbolic number in Revelation. **5:** *Faithful witness,* Jesus testifies to the truth (Jn 18.37) and is the model for Christians who died as "witnesses" (2.13; 11.7; 17.6). *Firstborn . . . ruler of the kings,* Ps 89.27. He *loves* continually; he *freed us* once for all by his death as a sacrifice (Rom 6.10; Heb 7.27). **6:** *Kingdom, priests,* the vocation promised to Israel (Ex 19.6; Isa 61.6) is extended to the church (1 Pet 2.9). *Glory and dominion,* Dan 7.14. **7:** Dan 7.13; Zech 12.10–12. *So it is to be. Amen,* a formal affirmation of this prophetic oracle announcing the coming of Christ. **8:** *Alpha* and *Omega,* the first and last letters of the Greek alphabet (like "A to Z" in English); hence, the beginning and end of all things (Isa 44.6; 48.12).

1.9–20: Inaugural vision and commission on *Patmos* (present-day Patino), a small island in the Aegean Sea where John had been exiled (see Introduction), ca. 90 km (55 mi) southwest of Ephesus (see Map on p. 424 NT). **10:** *In the spirit,* in a state of prophetic ecstasy, a state of altered consciousness (also 4.2; Ezek

in the spirit[a] on the Lord's day, and I
heard behind me a loud voice like a trum-
pet 11 saying, "Write in a book what you
see and send it to the seven churches, to
Ephesus, to Smyrna, to Pergamum, to Thy-
atira, to Sardis, to Philadelphia, and to La-
odicea."
12 Then I turned to see whose voice it
was that spoke to me, and on turning I saw
seven golden lampstands, 13 and in the
midst of the lampstands I saw one like the
Son of Man, clothed with a long robe and
with a golden sash across his chest. 14 His
head and his hair were white as white wool,
white as snow; his eyes were like a flame of
fire, 15 his feet were like burnished bronze,
refined as in a furnace, and his voice was
like the sound of many waters. 16 In his
right hand he held seven stars, and from his
mouth came a sharp, two-edged sword,
and his face was like the sun shining with
full force.
17 When I saw him, I fell at his feet as
though dead. But he placed his right hand
on me, saying, "Do not be afraid; I am the
first and the last, 18 and the living one. I was
dead, and see, I am alive forever and ever;
and I have the keys of Death and of Hades.
19 Now write what you have seen, what is,
and what is to take place after this. 20 As for
the mystery of the seven stars that you saw
in my right hand, and the seven golden
lampstands: the seven stars are the angels
of the seven churches, and the seven lamp-
stands are the seven churches.

2 "To the angel of the church in Ephesus
write: These are the words of him who
holds the seven stars in his right hand, who
walks among the seven golden lampstands:
2 "I know your works, your toil and
your patient endurance. I know that you
cannot tolerate evildoers; you have tested
those who claim to be apostles but are not,
and have found them to be false. 3 I also
know that you are enduring patiently and
bearing up for the sake of my name, and
that you have not grown weary. 4 But I have

a Or *in the Spirit*

2.2). *The Lord's day,* the weekly day of Christian worship, Sunday. **11:** *The seven churches,* see 2.1–3.22. **12–16:** In the midst of the churches (see v. 20) stands the exalted Christ, whose royalty, eternity, wisdom, and immutability are suggested by means of symbols; the effect is that of terrifying majesty (compare v. 17 with Isa 6.5). *Seven golden lampstands,* reminiscent of those that stood in the wilderness tabernacle and in the Jerusalem Temple (cf. Zech 4.1–14). *Son of Man* (cf. 14.14; Mk 2.10), a title Jesus used of himself, had two meanings: (1) a typical human being in accordance with a common extended meaning of "son of" (see Mt 5.45); (2) a reference to the heavenly figure of Dan 7.13–14 who was to embody God's rule over the nations. **13–15:** *Golden sash,* Dan 10.5; *white . . . snow,* Dan 7.10; *eyes . . . fire,* Dan 10.6; *feet . . . bronze,* Dan 10.6; *sound of many waters,* a frequent accompaniment of divine appearance; see Ps 29.3; 93.4; Ezek 1.24; 43.2; cf. Dan 10.6. The figure is a combination of attributes of the heavenly messenger from Dan 10 and the Ancient One from Dan 7. *From his mouth came a sharp, two-edged sword* (cf. 19.15,21), the word of God (Isa 49.2; cf. Heb 4.12). **18:** *Hades,* used here with its synonym *Death,* is the abode of the dead; Christ has *the keys* to release those confined within its gates (Mt 16.18; Jn 5.25–29). **20:** *Mystery,* hidden meanings that human beings cannot grasp without the assistance of divine revelation (Dan 2.29,45). Angel guardians are assigned to *the seven churches,* as also to nations (Dan 10.20–21; 12.1) and individuals (Dan 11.1).

2.1–3.22: The messages to the seven churches, each containing an address, a descriptive phrase referring to the risen Christ, a commendation or condemnation of the church addressed, an admonition, and a concluding promise and exhortation to the faithful. For the locations of the seven churches, see Map on p. 424 NT.

2.1–7: The first message is appropriately sent to *Ephesus,* a seaport city that was the administrative and commercial hub of the Roman province of Asia; Paul had labored here (Acts 19.8–10; 1 Cor 15.32; 16.8; cf. Eph 1.1). **1:** Christ *walks among* the churches (1.20). **2:** *Evildoers,* compare the warning to the Ephesian elders in Acts 20.29–30; cf. 2 Cor 11.13. **6:** To *hate* evil is the counterpart of the love of what

this against you, that you have abandoned
the love you had at first. 5 Remember then
from what you have fallen; repent, and do
the works you did at first. If not, I will
come to you and remove your lampstand
from its place, unless you repent. 6 Yet this
is to your credit: you hate the works of the
Nicolaitans, which I also hate. 7 Let anyone
who has an ear listen to what the Spirit is
saying to the churches. To everyone who
conquers, I will give permission to eat from
the tree of life that is in the paradise of
God.

8 "And to the angel of the church in
Smyrna write: These are the words of the
first and the last, who was dead and came
to life:

9 "I know your affliction and your pov-
erty, even though you are rich. I know the
slander on the part of those who say that
they are Jews and are not, but are a syna-

God approves (Isa 61.8; Zech 8.17; 1QS 1.4). The *Nicolaitans* (probably not connected with the Nicolaus of Acts 6.5, contrary to Irenaeus, *Adv. Haer.* 1.26.3) are also mentioned in the message to the church in Pergamum. It is not known what their *works* were, or what doctrines they taught, though they must have permitted some accommodation to pagan religious cults. **7:** *What the Spirit is saying,* speaking through Christ to John. *Conquers,* a military term, suggesting continuous vigilance. *Tree of life,* Gen 2.9; 3.24; cf. Rev 22.2,14.

2.8–11: The second message, sent to *Smyrna,* commends the church for its perseverance amid *affliction* and *poverty.* Smyrna (the modern Izmir) was a port city 50 km (30 mi) north of Ephesus. **8:** Isa 44.6; 48.12. **9:** *Rich,* in spiritual things. *Those who say that they are Jews and are not,* i.e., Jews whose anti-Christian arguments are causing suffering in the church. *Synagogue of Satan* reflects the tension between Jews and Jewish Christians (cf. Jn 8.44; 1QH 2.22, which refers to apostate Jews as "a

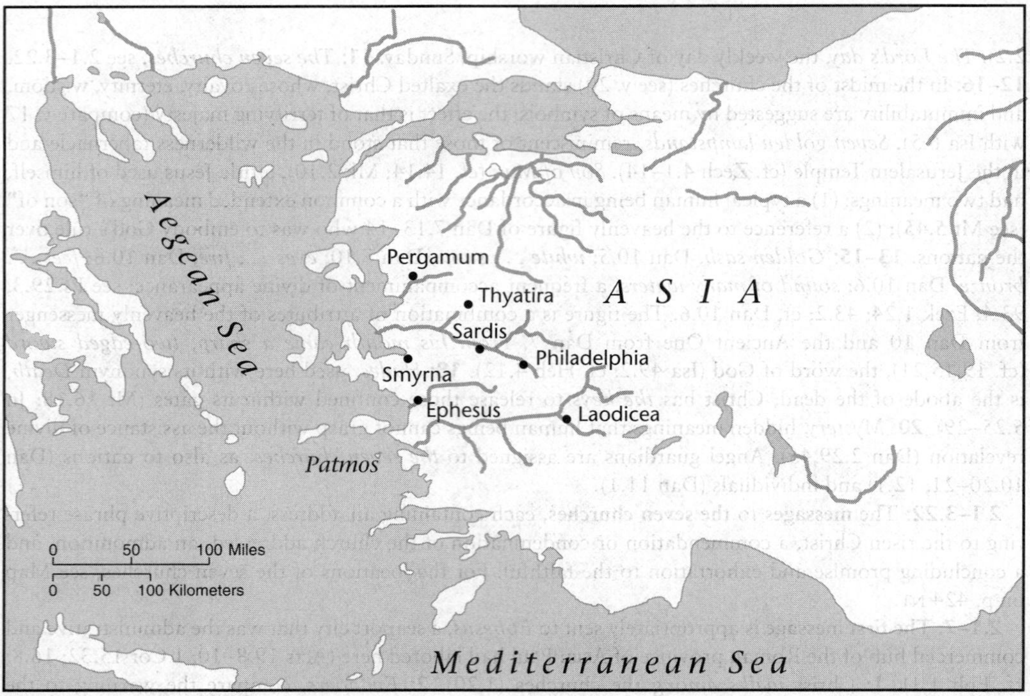

Chs 2–3: The seven churches.

gogue of Satan. 10 Do not fear what you are
about to suffer. Beware, the devil is about
to throw some of you into prison so that
you may be tested, and for ten days you
will have affliction. Be faithful until death,
and I will give you the crown of life. 11 Let
anyone who has an ear listen to what the
Spirit is saying to the churches. Whoever
conquers will not be harmed by the second
death.

12 "And to the angel of the church in
Pergamum write: These are the words of
him who has the sharp two-edged sword:
13 "I know where you are living, where
Satan's throne is. Yet you are holding fast
to my name, and you did not deny your
faith in me[a] even in the days of Antipas my
witness, my faithful one, who was killed
among you, where Satan lives. 14 But I have
a few things against you: you have some
there who hold to the teaching of Balaam,
who taught Balak to put a stumbling block
before the people of Israel, so that they
would eat food sacrificed to idols and prac-
tice fornication. 15 So you also have some
who hold to the teaching of the Nicolai-
tans. 16 Repent then. If not, I will come to
you soon and make war against them with
the sword of my mouth. 17 Let anyone who
has an ear listen to what the Spirit is saying
to the churches. To everyone who conquers
I will give some of the hidden manna, and
I will give a white stone, and on the white
stone is written a new name that no one
knows except the one who receives it.

18 "And to the angel of the church in
Thyatira write: These are the words of the
Son of God, who has eyes like a flame of
fire, and whose feet are like burnished
bronze:
19 "I know your works—your love,
faith, service, and patient endurance. I
know that your last works are greater than
the first. 20 But I have this against you: you
tolerate that woman Jezebel, who calls her-
self a prophet and is teaching and beguiling
my servants[b] to practice fornication and to
eat food sacrificed to idols. 21 I gave her
time to repent, but she refuses to repent of
her fornication. 22 Beware, I am throwing

a Or *deny my faith* *b* Gk *slaves*

congregation of Belial"). **10:** *Ten days,* a limited period of trial (Dan 1.12). *Crown of life,* the reward of eternal life (Jas 1.12; 1 Pet 5.4). **11:** *The second death,* the final condemnation of the unfaithful (20.14).

2.12–17: The third message is sent to *Pergamum,* a noted center of the Roman imperial cult ca. 80 km (60 mi) north of Smyrna. **12:** *Sharp two-edged sword,* 1.16n. **13:** *Where Satan's throne is,* in contrast to the throne of God in ch 4, this may be a reference either to the temple of the emperor Augustus or to the monumental altar of Zeus, both at Pergamum. *Antipas* is otherwise unknown; he is the only martyr named in the book. **14–15:** *The teaching of Balaam,* here the author vilifies an opponent by comparing him to the diviner Balaam of Num 22.5–24.25. After Balaam's oracles, the Israelites engaged in both sexual relations with outsiders and idolatry (see Num 25; 31.16). To *eat food sacrificed to idols* meant either to participate in ritual banquets or to purchase and consume meat that had been sacrificed in the temples of Pergamum (1 Cor 8; 10). *Practice fornication* here is meant metaphorically, with sexual misconduct symbolizing religious infidelity. **15:** *Nicolaitans,* see v. 6n. **17:** *Hidden manna,* eschatological nourishment from heaven (Ex 16.33–34; Ps 78.24). *White,* the color symbolizing victory and joy. *A new name,* Isa 62.2.

2.18–29: The fourth message is sent to *Thyatira,* a commercial center renowned for its many trade guilds, ca. 110 km (70 mi) north-northeast of Ephesus. Lydia, one of Paul's converts, was a dealer in purple cloth from Thyatira (Acts 16.14–15). **18:** Dan 10.6. **20:** *That woman Jezebel, who calls herself a prophet,* John's characterization of a female opponent at Thyatira, here identified contemptuously with the Phoenician wife of King Ahab, the queen who worshiped Baal and who opposed the prophet Elijah (1 Kings 16.31; 19.1–2). **22:** *I am throwing her on a bed,* punishment with serious sickness is threatened for the Thyatiran Jezebel. *Those who commit adultery with her* are those who are complicit in her idolatry. In the Hebrew Bible idolatry is often called *adultery,* with marital infidelity used as a metaphor for worship of other gods than the LORD (Deut 31.16; Judg 2.17; 1 Chr 5.25); see also vv. 14–15n.

her on a bed, and those who commit adul-
tery with her I am throwing into great dis-
tress, unless they repent of her doings;
23 and I will strike her children dead. And
all the churches will know that I am the one
who searches minds and hearts, and I will
give to each of you as your works deserve.
24 But to the rest of you in Thyatira, who
do not hold this teaching, who have not
learned what some call 'the deep things of
Satan,' to you I say, I do not lay on you any
other burden; 25 only hold fast to what you
have until I come. 26 To everyone who con-
quers and continues to do my works to the
end,

I will give authority over the nations;
27 to rule[a] them with an iron rod,
as when clay pots are shattered—
28 even as I also received authority from my
Father. To the one who conquers I will also
give the morning star. 29 Let anyone who
has an ear listen to what the Spirit is saying
to the churches.

3 "And to the angel of the church in Sar-
dis write: These are the words of him
who has the seven spirits of God and the
seven stars:

"I know your works; you have a name of
being alive, but you are dead. 2 Wake up,
and strengthen what remains and is on the
point of death, for I have not found your
works perfect in the sight of my God. 3 Re-
member then what you received and heard;
obey it, and repent. If you do not wake up,
I will come like a thief, and you will not
know at what hour I will come to you. 4 Yet
you have still a few persons in Sardis who
have not soiled their clothes; they will walk
with me, dressed in white, for they are wor-
thy. 5 If you conquer, you will be clothed
like them in white robes, and I will not blot
your name out of the book of life; I will
confess your name before my Father and
before his angels. 6 Let anyone who has an
ear listen to what the Spirit is saying to the
churches.

7 "And to the angel of the church in
Philadelphia write:

These are the words of the holy one,
the true one,
who has the key of David,
who opens and no one will shut,
who shuts and no one opens:

8 "I know your works. Look, I have set
before you an open door, which no one is
able to shut. I know that you have but little
power, and yet you have kept my word and
have not denied my name. 9 I will make
those of the synagogue of Satan who say
that they are Jews and are not, but are
lying—I will make them come and bow
down before your feet, and they will learn
that I have loved you. 10 Because you have
kept my word of patient endurance, I will
keep you from the hour of trial that is com-
ing on the whole world to test the inhabi-

a Or *to shepherd*

23: *Her children,* those who follow her teachings. **24:** *Deep things of Satan,* a sarcastic reference to heretical teachings (contrast 1 Cor 2.10). **26–27:** The conquerors will share in Christ's rule (Ps 2.8–9). **28:** *The morning star* is Christ himself (22.16). **29:** *Is saying,* in this revelation.

3.1–6: The fifth message is sent to *Sardis,* a prosperous city ca. 85 km (55 mi) northeast of Ephesus that had been the capital of the kingdom of Lydia. **1:** *Seven spirits,* see 1.4n. *Seven stars,* 1.20. *You have a name,* its Christianity was only nominal. **3:** *Received,* the gospel. *Like a thief,* just when unexpected (16.15; Mt 24.42–44; 1 Thess 5.2). **4–5:** *Soiled . . . white,* not impurity/purity, but surrender/conquest (see 2.17n.). *White robes* are a frequent image; see 3.18; 4.4; 6.11; 7.9; 19.14; cf. Zech 3.3–5. **5:** *Book of life,* the register of God containing the names of the redeemed (13.8; 17.8; 20.12,15; Ex 32.32; Ps 69.28; Dan 12.1; Mal 3.16; Lk 10.20).

3.7–13: The sixth message is sent to *Philadelphia,* a small town 50 km (80 mi) southeast of Sardis. **7:** *Key of David,* a symbol of authority (Isa 22.22). **8:** *An open door,* of opportunity (1 Cor 16.9; 2 Cor 2.12). **9:** *Synagogue of Satan,* see 2.9n. On conflict between Christians and Jews in Philadelphia see Ignatius, *Philad.* 6.1. *Bow down before your feet,* Isa 43.4; 60.14. **10:** Despite its weakness (v. 8), the Philadelphian church will be safeguarded during the eschatological tribulation. **11:** *I am coming soon,*

tants of the earth. 11 I am coming soon;
hold fast to what you have, so that no one
may seize your crown. 12 If you conquer, I
will make you a pillar in the temple of my
God; you will never go out of it. I will write
on you the name of my God, and the name
of the city of my God, the new Jerusalem
that comes down from my God out of
heaven, and my own new name. 13 Let any-
one who has an ear listen to what the Spirit
is saying to the churches.

14 "And to the angel of the church in
Laodicea write: The words of the Amen,
the faithful and true witness, the origin[a] of
God's creation:
15 "I know your works; you are neither
cold nor hot. I wish that you were either
cold or hot. 16 So, because you are luke-
warm, and neither cold nor hot, I am about
to spit you out of my mouth. 17 For you say,
'I am rich, I have prospered, and I need
nothing.' You do not realize that you are
wretched, pitiable, poor, blind, and naked.
18 Therefore I counsel you to buy from me
gold refined by fire so that you may be rich;
and white robes to clothe you and to keep
the shame of your nakedness from being
seen; and salve to anoint your eyes so that
you may see. 19 I reprove and discipline
those whom I love. Be earnest, therefore,
and repent. 20 Listen! I am standing at the
door, knocking; if you hear my voice and
open the door, I will come in to you and eat
with you, and you with me. 21 To the one
who conquers I will give a place with me on
my throne, just as I myself conquered and
sat down with my Father on his throne.
22 Let anyone who has an ear listen to what
the Spirit is saying to the churches."

4 After this I looked, and there in heaven
a door stood open! And the first voice,
which I had heard speaking to me like a
trumpet, said, "Come up here, and I will
show you what must take place after this."
2 At once I was in the spirit,[b] and there in
heaven stood a throne, with one seated on
the throne! 3 And the one seated there looks
like jasper and carnelian, and around the
throne is a rainbow that looks like an emer-
ald. 4 Around the throne are twenty-four
thrones, and seated on the thrones are
twenty-four elders, dressed in white robes,
with golden crowns on their heads. 5 Com-
ing from the throne are flashes of lightning,
and rumblings and peals of thunder, and
in front of the throne burn seven flaming

a Or *beginning* *b* Or *in the Spirit*

22.7,12,20. **12:** *A pillar,* steadfast and permanent (Gal 2.9). *New Jerusalem,* 21.2. *The name of my God,* marking the one inscribed as God's possession and as specially dedicated to God. *The name of the city of my God,* signifying citizenship in the new Jerusalem; see 21.2,10.

3.14–22: The seventh message is sent to *Laodicea,* a wealthy city near Colossae (Col 2.1; 4.13–16), 155 km (95 mi) east of Ephesus. **14:** *The Amen* is Jesus Christ (2 Cor 1.20). *The faithful and true witness,* 1.5. The list of titles may derive from a Greek translation of Isa 65.16. *The origin of God's creation,* Christ is the principle and source of all creation (Jn 1.3; Col 1.15,18). **15–16:** Their *lukewarm* Christianity is nauseating like the tepid water for which the city was known. **17:** Complacent and self-satisfied, they are spiritually poverty-stricken (Hos 12.8). **18:** *Buy from me gold refined by fire,* an idiom for removing sin from one's life (Job 13.10; Prov 27.21). A commercial transaction is here used as a metaphor for grasping salvation. *Eyes,* Laodicea was noted for its manufacture of a medication for ophthalmic disorders. **19:** God's chastening has beneficent motives (Prov 3.12; Heb 12.5–11). **20:** An invitation to participate in the messianic banquet in the coming age (cf. Mt 26.29). **21:** *A place with me,* a promise of reigning with Christ in glory (22.5; Lk 22.30).

4.1–5.14: Vision of God enthroned and of the Lamb. 4.1: *A door stood open,* Gen 28.17. *The first voice,* the voice of the exalted Christ mentioned in 1.10. *Come up,* John is invited to ascend to heaven, to behold visions of God (Ezek 3.12; 8.3; 11.1). **2:** *A throne,* Ezek 1.26–28; Dan 7.9. **3:** The glory of the divine presence is described in terms of precious gems; cf. Ex 24.10. **4:** *Twenty-four elders,* heavenly attendants around God's throne, probably symbolizing the twelve tribes of Israel and the twelve apostles. **5:** *Flashes of lightning,* expressive of the majesty of the Most High (Ex 19.16; Ezek 1.13; Rev 11.19). *Seven flaming*

torches, which are the seven spirits of God;
6 and in front of the throne there is some-
thing like a sea of glass, like crystal.

Around the throne, and on each side of
the throne, are four living creatures, full of
eyes in front and behind: 7 the first living
creature like a lion, the second living crea-
ture like an ox, the third living creature
with a face like a human face, and the
fourth living creature like a flying eagle.
8 And the four living creatures, each of
them with six wings, are full of eyes all
around and inside. Day and night without
ceasing they sing,

"Holy, holy, holy,
the Lord God the Almighty,
who was and is and is to come."

9 And whenever the living creatures give
glory and honor and thanks to the one who
is seated on the throne, who lives forever
and ever, 10 the twenty-four elders fall be-
fore the one who is seated on the throne
and worship the one who lives forever and
ever; they cast their crowns before the
throne, singing,

11 "You are worthy, our Lord and God,
to receive glory and honor
and power,
for you created all things,
and by your will they existed and
were created."

5 Then I saw in the right hand of the one
seated on the throne a scroll written on
the inside and on the back, sealed[a] with
seven seals; 2 and I saw a mighty angel pro-
claiming with a loud voice, "Who is worthy
to open the scroll and break its seals?"
3 And no one in heaven or on earth or under
the earth was able to open the scroll or to
look into it. 4 And I began to weep bitterly
because no one was found worthy to open
the scroll or to look into it. 5 Then one of
the elders said to me, "Do not weep. See,
the Lion of the tribe of Judah, the Root of
David, has conquered, so that he can open
the scroll and its seven seals."

6 Then I saw between the throne and the
four living creatures and among the elders
a Lamb standing as if it had been slaugh-
tered, having seven horns and seven eyes,
which are the seven spirits of God sent out
into all the earth. 7 He went and took the
scroll from the right hand of the one who
was seated on the throne. 8 When he had
taken the scroll, the four living creatures
and the twenty-four elders fell before the
Lamb, each holding a harp and golden
bowls full of incense, which are the prayers
of the saints. 9 They sing a new song:

"You are worthy to take the scroll
and to open its seals,
for you were slaughtered and by your
blood you ransomed for God
saints from[b] every tribe and
language and people
and nation;

[a] *Or written on the inside, and sealed on the back*
[b] *Gk ransomed for God from*

torches, Zech 4.2–3. *Seven spirits,* 1.4. **6:** *A sea of glass,* Ezek. 1.22. *Four living creatures,* heavenly beings representing humankind and all animals (Ezek 1.5,10). *Full of eyes,* symbolizing unceasing watchfulness (Ezek 1.18). **8:** *Six wings . . . Holy, holy, holy,* Isa 6.2–3. **10:** *Cast their crowns,* an act of homage and submission, acknowledging that all power comes from God. **11:** *Our Lord and God,* titles that were also attributed to the Roman emperor (Suetonius, *Domitian* 13). **5.1:** *A scroll,* containing the divine plan of judgment and salvation (Ezek 2.9–10). *Sealed,* therefore both unalterable and unknown to others (Dan 12.4). **3–5:** No created being is worthy to carry out God's plan; only the messiah can do so. *Lion of . . . Judah,* Gen 49.9–10. *Root of David,* Isa 11.1,10. *Has conquered,* the paradoxical victory of the cross and resurrection (Jn 16.33). **6–9:** The *Lamb . . . slaughtered,* the crucified messiah, a reference to Christ's sacrificial death, by which God's purposes contained in the scroll are accomplished (Isa 53.7; Jn 1.29,36; 1 Pet 1.19). *Seven horns,* fullness of power (Deut 33.17; Ps 89.17; Dan 7.7–8.24; 1 Enoch 80.6–12,37). *Seven eyes,* Zech 3.9; 4.10; 2 Chr 16.9. *Seven spirits,* 1.4. **8:** *Harp and golden bowls,* objects used in worship. *The prayers of the saints* on earth are joined with the worship rendered to the *Lamb* by the heavenly creatures. **9–10:** A *new song* is sung because Christ by his sacrifice has inaugurated a new era (14.3). New hymns of praise mark and celebrate special occasions (Ps 33.3; 40.3; 96.1; 98.1; 144.9; 149.1; Isa 42.10).

10 you have made them to be a kingdom
and priests serving[a] our God,
and they will reign on earth."
11 Then I looked, and I heard the voice
of many angels surrounding the throne and
the living creatures and the elders; they
numbered myriads of myriads and thou-
sands of thousands, 12 singing with full
voice,
"Worthy is the Lamb that was
slaughtered
to receive power and wealth and
wisdom and might
and honor and glory and blessing!"
13 Then I heard every creature in heaven
and on earth and under the earth and in the
sea, and all that is in them, singing,
"To the one seated on the throne and
to the Lamb
be blessing and honor and glory and
might
forever and ever!"
14 And the four living creatures said,
"Amen!" And the elders fell down and
worshiped.

6 Then I saw the Lamb open one of the
seven seals, and I heard one of the four
living creatures call out, as with a voice of
thunder, "Come!"[b] 2 I looked, and there
was a white horse! Its rider had a bow; a
crown was given to him, and he came out
conquering and to conquer.
3 When he opened the second seal, I
heard the second living creature call out,
"Come!"[b] 4 And out came[c] another
horse, bright red; its rider was permitted to
take peace from the earth, so that people
would slaughter one another; and he was
given a great sword.
5 When he opened the third seal, I heard
the third living creature call out,
"Come!"[b] I looked, and there was a black
horse! Its rider held a pair of scales in his
hand, 6 and I heard what seemed to be a
voice in the midst of the four living crea-
tures saying, "A quart of wheat for a day's
pay,[d] and three quarts of barley for a day's
pay,[d] but do not damage the olive oil and
the wine!"
7 When he opened the fourth seal, I
heard the voice of the fourth living creature
call out, "Come!"[b] 8 I looked and there
was a pale green horse! Its rider's name was
Death, and Hades followed with him; they
were given authority over a fourth of the
earth, to kill with sword, famine, and pesti-
lence, and by the wild animals of the earth.
9 When he opened the fifth seal, I saw

a Gk *priests to* *b* Or *"Go!"* *c* Or *went* *d* Gk *a denarius*

The Lamb is adored in terms similar to the adoration rendered to God (4.11). *A kingdom and priests,* see 1.6n. **11–12:** The sevenfold praise of *myriads* (Dan 7.10) in heaven honoring the sacrificial *Lamb.* **13:** Universal praise to God and to the *Lamb* as equal in majesty.

6.1–17: The opening of the first six seals of the scroll, and the enactment of what is written therein.

6.1–8: Four seals of destruction. 1: *Come!* Addressed successively to each of the four riders (Zech 6.1–8) who accomplish God's purposes. **2:** The *white horse* symbolizes a conquering power that none can resist (in 19.11–13 the reference is to Christ). The *crown* given to the rider as he is sent forth suggests a guarantee of victory. **4:** The *red horse* symbolizes war and bloodshed. *Permitted to take peace from the earth,* effectively annulling the "pax Romana," the self-congratulatory designation of Roman imperial rule as "the Roman peace." **5:** The *black horse* symbolizes famine, which follows upon war. **6:** *A quart of wheat . . . three quarts of barley,* sold at exorbitant prices because of war and famine. The prohibition against harming the *olive oil* and the *wine* (neither olive trees nor grape vines are newly planted each year) suggests that the famine is limited. **8:** The *pale green horse* symbolizes pestilence and death. *Hades,* the Greek god of the underworld; cf. 1.18. A *fourth* part indicates wide but not total devastation. *Pestilence,* Ex 9.3; 2 Sam 24.13; Ezek 5.12. *Wild animals,* Ezek 6.17; 29.5; 33.27.

6.9–8.1: Three seals of judgment.

6.9–11: The fifth seal describes the appeal for divine justice and retribution by the martyrs (v. 10), and the heavenly response to their plea (v. 11). **9:** The souls of the martyrs are said to be *under the altar* because they had been martyred for the sake of Christ (2.10; Mt 24.9; Phil 2.17; 2 Tim 4.6). **10:** *How*

under the altar the souls of those who had
been slaughtered for the word of God and
for the testimony they had given; 10 they
cried out with a loud voice, "Sovereign
Lord, holy and true, how long will it be
before you judge and avenge our blood on
the inhabitants of the earth?" 11 They were
each given a white robe and told to rest a
little longer, until the number would be
complete both of their fellow servants[a]
and of their brothers and sisters,[b] who
were soon to be killed as they themselves
had been killed.
12 When he opened the sixth seal, I
looked, and there came a great earthquake;
the sun became black as sackcloth, the full
moon became like blood, 13 and the stars of
the sky fell to the earth as the fig tree drops
its winter fruit when shaken by a gale.
14 The sky vanished like a scroll rolling it-
self up, and every mountain and island was
removed from its place. 15 Then the kings of
the earth and the magnates and the generals
and the rich and the powerful, and every-
one, slave and free, hid in the caves and
among the rocks of the mountains, 16 call-
ing to the mountains and rocks, "Fall on us
and hide us from the face of the one seated
on the throne and from the wrath of the
Lamb; 17 for the great day of their wrath
has come, and who is able to stand?"
7 After this I saw four angels standing at
the four corners of the earth, holding
back the four winds of the earth so that no
wind could blow on earth or sea or against
any tree. 2 I saw another angel ascending
from the rising of the sun, having the seal of
the living God, and he called with a loud
voice to the four angels who had been given
power to damage earth and sea, 3 saying,
"Do not damage the earth or the sea or the
trees, until we have marked the servants[a]
of our God with a seal on their foreheads."
4 And I heard the number of those who
were sealed, one hundred forty-four thou-
sand, sealed out of every tribe of the people
of Israel:
5 From the tribe of Judah twelve thou-
sand sealed,
from the tribe of Reuben twelve thou-
sand,
from the tribe of Gad twelve thousand,
6 from the tribe of Asher twelve thou-
sand,
from the tribe of Naphtali twelve
thousand,
from the tribe of Manasseh twelve
thousand,
7 from the tribe of Simeon twelve thou-
sand,
from the tribe of Levi twelve thousand,
from the tribe of Issachar twelve thou-
sand,
8 from the tribe of Zebulun twelve thou-
sand,
from the tribe of Joseph twelve thou-
sand,

a Gk *slaves* b Gk *brothers*

long? is a cry for divine vindication uttered by those who have suffered unbearable oppression (e.g., Ps 6.3; 13.2; 90.13; Zech 1.12–16). *Avenge our blood,* God is the one who takes up the cause of those killed for the sake of justice (Ps 78.1–10 [LXX]). **11:** *White robe,* see 2.17n.; 3.4–5n.; 7.9n.

6.12–17: The opening of the sixth seal unleashes *a great earthquake,* and its catastrophic effects on the cosmos and on human society are described. **12:** *Black as sackcloth . . . ,* Joel 2.30–31. **13–14:** *The stars . . . fell to the earth . . . ,* Isa 34.4; Mk 13.25. **15–17:** All classes of society seek to escape from the wrath of God (Isa 2.10,19). **16:** *Fall on us,* Hos 10.8; Lk 23.30. **17:** *The great day of their wrath,* the time of judgment (Joel 2.11).

7.1–17: An interlude between the sixth and seventh seals: two visions which provide the promise of divine protection for the faithful during the time of tribulation (vv. 1–8) and assurance of ultimate salvation (vv. 9–17). **1:** *The four winds* are destructive forces to be unleashed by God (Jer 49.36). They correspond to the four horsemen in 6.1–8 (see Zech 6.5). **3:** A *seal* (Ezek 9.4–6) marks those under God's protection. Seals were used to signify ownership or authorship. **4:** The symbolic number 144,000, which is the square of 12 multiplied by 1000, has been interpreted variously as a reference to: the faithful remnant of Israel; the church; the martyrs; the remnant of Christians who survive the eschatological

from the tribe of Benjamin twelve
thousand sealed.

9 After this I looked, and there was a
great multitude that no one could count,
from every nation, from all tribes and peo-
ples and languages, standing before the
throne and before the Lamb, robed in
white, with palm branches in their hands.
10 They cried out in a loud voice, saying,

"Salvation belongs to our God who is
seated on the throne, and to
the Lamb!"

11 And all the angels stood around the
throne and around the elders and the four
living creatures, and they fell on their faces
before the throne and worshiped God,
12 singing,

"Amen! Blessing and glory
and wisdom
and thanksgiving and honor
and power and might
be to our God forever and ever!
Amen."

13 Then one of the elders addressed me,
saying, "Who are these, robed in white,
and where have they come from?" 14 I said
to him, "Sir, you are the one that knows."
Then he said to me, "These are they who
have come out of the great ordeal; they
have washed their robes and made them
white in the blood of the Lamb.

15 For this reason they are before the
throne of God,
and worship him day and night
within his temple,
and the one who is seated on the
throne will shelter them.
16 They will hunger no more, and thirst
no more;
the sun will not strike them,
nor any scorching heat;
17 for the Lamb at the center of the
throne will be their shepherd,
and he will guide them to springs
of the water of life,
and God will wipe away every tear
from their eyes."

8 When the Lamb opened the seventh
seal, there was silence in heaven for
about half an hour. 2 And I saw the seven
angels who stand before God, and seven
trumpets were given to them.

3 Another angel with a golden censer
came and stood at the altar; he was given a
great quantity of incense to offer with the
prayers of all the saints on the golden altar
that is before the throne. 4 And the smoke
of the incense, with the prayers of the
saints, rose before God from the hand of
the angel. 5 Then the angel took the censer
and filled it with fire from the altar and
threw it on the earth; and there were peals
of thunder, rumblings, flashes of lightning,
and an earthquake.

6 Now the seven angels who had the
seven trumpets made ready to blow them.

turmoil; all the redeemed (14.1,3). *Every tribe,* but the tribes of Dan and Ephraim are not mentioned. **9:** *A great multitude,* in contrast with the 144,000 in v. 4 (5.9). *White* robes and *palm branches* symbolize righteousness and victory (see 3.4–5n.; Dan 11.35). **12:** A sevenfold ascription of praise to God. **14:** *The blood of the Lamb* cleanses from sin (Jn 1.29; 1 Jn 1.7); in the symbolism of the book, *blood* (sacrifice) can make *robes . . . white* (lead to victory). **15:** *Before the throne of God,* in God's presence because of their faithfulness. Their ceaseless *worship* takes place in God's temple in heaven. *Shelter them,* lit. "spread his tabernacle over them." **16:** Isa 49.10; Ps 121.6. **17:** A paradox: The *Lamb* is a *shepherd* (Ps 23.1–2; Ezek 34.23–24; Jn 10.11). *Springs of . . . life,* 21.6; 22.1,17; Jn 4.10; 7.37. *Wipe away every tear,* 21.4; Isa 25.8.

8.1–5: The seventh seal is opened. The opening of the last of the seven seals (5.1; 6.1) leads to an awesome and reverent *silence,* as response to divine judgment (Hab 3.3–6; Zech 2.13–3.2). A return to "primeval silence" prior to the judgment appears in 2 Esd 7.30. **2:** The seven angels *stand before God* ready to do God's will (Tob 12.15). **3:** *Incense . . . prayers,* Ps 141.2. **5:** Ezek 10.2. The *earthquake* announces the divine judgment about to be executed.

8.6–9.21: The first six trumpets unleash new convulsions of nature, patterned after the plagues inflicted on Egypt in the book of Exodus (Ex 7.14–10.23).

8.6–13: Four trumpets of destruction. 7: *Hail and fire,* Ex 9.23–25; both destroyers of crops. *A third,*

7 The first angel blew his trumpet, and
there came hail and fire, mixed with blood,
and they were hurled to the earth; and a
third of the earth was burned up, and a
third of the trees were burned up, and all
green grass was burned up.
8 The second angel blew his trumpet,
and something like a great mountain, burn-
ing with fire, was thrown into the sea. 9 A
third of the sea became blood, a third of the
living creatures in the sea died, and a third
of the ships were destroyed.
10 The third angel blew his trumpet, and
a great star fell from heaven, blazing like a
torch, and it fell on a third of the rivers and
on the springs of water. 11 The name of the
star is Wormwood. A third of the waters
became wormwood, and many died from
the water, because it was made bitter.
12 The fourth angel blew his trumpet,
and a third of the sun was struck, and a
third of the moon, and a third of the stars,
so that a third of their light was darkened;
a third of the day was kept from shining,
and likewise the night.
13 Then I looked, and I heard an eagle
crying with a loud voice as it flew in mid-
heaven, "Woe, woe, woe to the inhabitants
of the earth, at the blasts of the other trum-
pets that the three angels are about to
blow!"

9 And the fifth angel blew his trumpet,
and I saw a star that had fallen from
heaven to earth, and he was given the key
to the shaft of the bottomless pit; 2 he
opened the shaft of the bottomless pit, and
from the shaft rose smoke like the smoke of
a great furnace, and the sun and the air
were darkened with the smoke from the
shaft. 3 Then from the smoke came locusts
on the earth, and they were given authority
like the authority of scorpions of the earth.
4 They were told not to damage the grass of
the earth or any green growth or any tree,
but only those people who do not have the
seal of God on their foreheads. 5 They were
allowed to torture them for five months,
but not to kill them, and their torture
was like the torture of a scorpion when it
stings someone. 6 And in those days people
will seek death but will not find it; they
will long to die, but death will flee from
them.
7 In appearance the locusts were like
horses equipped for battle. On their heads
were what looked like crowns of gold; their
faces were like human faces, 8 their hair like
women's hair, and their teeth like lions'
teeth; 9 they had scales like iron breast-
plates, and the noise of their wings was like
the noise of many chariots with horses
rushing into battle. 10 They have tails like
scorpions, with stingers, and in their tails
is their power to harm people for five
months. 11 They have as king over them the
angel of the bottomless pit; his name in

the devastation wrought by the trumpet plagues is not total. **9:** Ex 7.20. **11:** *Wormwood,* a bitter herb, poisons the waters into which it falls (Jer 9.15; 23.15). It is associated with the constellation Scorpio. **12:** Ex 10.21–22; cf. Joel 3.15; Am 8.9. **13:** *An eagle* announces impending judgment. The threefold *woe* refers to the plagues unleashed at the sounding of the next three trumpets.

9.1–11.19: Three trumpets of woe.

9.1–12: The plague of monstrous locusts, which combine the terrors of evil spirits and of invading cavalry (probably Parthians). **1:** *A star . . . fallen from heaven,* a heavenly being, possibly an angel, identified by name in v. 11 (cf. Isa 14.12; Lk 10.18). The *bottomless pit* is the abyss, the underworld, from which the beast arises (11.7; 17.8). **3:** *Locusts,* Ex 10.12–15; cf. Joel 1.4. **4:** God's servants are not to be harmed (7.3). **5:** *Five months,* although this may be a reference to the life cycle of locusts, which are hatched in spring and live until the end of summer, the likely significance of this time period is symbolic, indicating the limited time span of this plague. **6:** *Will seek death,* in utter despair because of the torments (cf. Job 3.21). **7–10:** These are monstrous locusts, described in anthropomorphic terms (as in Joel 1 and 2), combining human features with the features of other creatures into a terrifying composite appearance. **11:** The name *Abaddon,* which means "Destruction," denotes the depths of Sheol (Job 26.6; see Prov 15.11; Sheol and *Abaddon* are the abode and state—destruction—of the dead).

Hebrew is Abaddon,[a] and in Greek he is
called Apollyon.[b]
12 The first woe has passed. There are
still two woes to come.
13 Then the sixth angel blew his trum-
pet, and I heard a voice from the four[c]
horns of the golden altar before God,
14 saying to the sixth angel who had the
trumpet, "Release the four angels who are
bound at the great river Euphrates." 15 So
the four angels were released, who had
been held ready for the hour, the day, the
month, and the year, to kill a third of hu-
mankind. 16 The number of the troops of
cavalry was two hundred million; I heard
their number. 17 And this was how I saw the
horses in my vision: the riders wore breast-
plates the color of fire and of sapphire[d]
and of sulfur; the heads of the horses were
like lions' heads, and fire and smoke and
sulfur came out of their mouths. 18 By these
three plagues a third of humankind was
killed, by the fire and smoke and sulfur
coming out of their mouths. 19 For the pow-
er of the horses is in their mouths and in
their tails; their tails are like serpents, hav-
ing heads; and with them they inflict harm.
20 The rest of humankind, who were
not killed by these plagues, did not repent
of the works of their hands or give up wor-
shiping demons and idols of gold and silver
and bronze and stone and wood, which
cannot see or hear or walk. 21 And they did
not repent of their murders or their sorcer-
ies or their fornication or their thefts.

10 And I saw another mighty angel
coming down from heaven,
wrapped in a cloud, with a rainbow over
his head; his face was like the sun, and his
legs like pillars of fire. 2 He held a little
scroll open in his hand. Setting his right
foot on the sea and his left foot on the land,
3 he gave a great shout, like a lion roaring.
And when he shouted, the seven thunders
sounded. 4 And when the seven thunders
had sounded, I was about to write, but I
heard a voice from heaven saying, "Seal up
what the seven thunders have said, and do
not write it down." 5 Then the angel whom
I saw standing on the sea and the land

raised his right hand to heaven
6 and swore by him who lives forever
and ever,

who created heaven and what is in it, the
earth and what is in it, and the sea and
what is in it: "There will be no more delay,
7 but in the days when the seventh angel is
to blow his trumpet, the mystery of God
will be fulfilled, as he announced to his ser-
vants[e] the prophets."
8 Then the voice that I had heard from
heaven spoke to me again, saying, "Go,

a That is, *Destruction* *b* That is, *Destroyer*
c Other ancient authorities lack *four* *d* Gk *hyacinth*
e Gk *slaves*

9.13–21: The plague of monstrous cavalry. 14: The *Euphrates* marked the eastern border of the Roman Empire, where invasion by its enemies the Parthians was feared. **16–19:** These fire-breathing, lion-headed, serpent-tailed monsters are composite creatures, like the Chimera of Greek and Roman mythology. Also see the description of conquering soldiers in Jer 46.2–23. **20–21:** The trumpet plagues fail to provoke the repentance that is their purpose. Compare the hardness of Pharaoh's heart despite the plagues (Ex 8.15,19). **20:** *Idols,* Dan 5.23. **21:** *Murders . . . thefts,* sins associated with idolatry, Wis 12.3–6.

10.1–11.13: An interlude between the sixth and seventh trumpets; two visions (10.1–11 and 11.1–13) present a renewal of John's prophetic commission (10.1–11) and describe what becomes of the two prophetic witnesses in the holy city (11.1–13).

10.1–11: The commission renewed. 1: *Another mighty angel,* in addition to the mighty angel in 5.2. **2:** The *little scroll* is distinct from the seven-sealed scroll in the right hand of God in 5.1. This scroll is in the angel's left hand, since in 10.5 he raises his right hand to heaven to swear an oath (Dan 12.7). *Sea* and *land* indicate the scope of the angel's authority. **4:** John is prohibited from disclosing what the *seven thunders have said,* but he "must prophesy again" (v. 11) after eating the little scroll. **6:** There will be *no more delay* in the accomplishment of God's will—the sounding of the seventh trumpet is imminent. **7:** *The mystery of God,* Rom 16.25–26; Eph 1.9; 3.3–9; Col 1.26–27. *His servants the prophets,* Am 3.7. **8–10:** Ezek 2.9–3.3. **10:** *Sweet,* because it contains God's words; *bitter* because it involves God's terrible

take the scroll that is open in the hand of
the angel who is standing on the sea and on
the land." 9 So I went to the angel and told
him to give me the little scroll; and he said
to me, "Take it, and eat; it will be bitter to
your stomach, but sweet as honey in your
mouth." 10 So I took the little scroll from
the hand of the angel and ate it; it was
sweet as honey in my mouth, but when I
had eaten it, my stomach was made bitter.
11 Then they said to me, "You must
prophesy again about many peoples and
nations and languages and kings."

11 Then I was given a measuring rod
like a staff, and I was told, "Come
and measure the temple of God and the
altar and those who worship there, 2 but do
not measure the court outside the temple;
leave that out, for it is given over to the
nations, and they will trample over the holy
city for forty-two months. 3 And I will
grant my two witnesses authority to proph-
esy for one thousand two hundred sixty
days, wearing sackcloth."
4 These are the two olive trees and the
two lampstands that stand before the Lord
of the earth. 5 And if anyone wants to harm
them, fire pours from their mouth and con-
sumes their foes; anyone who wants to
harm them must be killed in this manner.
6 They have authority to shut the sky, so
that no rain may fall during the days of
their prophesying, and they have authority
over the waters to turn them into blood,
and to strike the earth with every kind of
plague, as often as they desire.
7 When they have finished their testimo-
ny, the beast that comes up from the bot-
tomless pit will make war on them and con-
quer them and kill them, 8 and their dead
bodies will lie in the street of the great city
that is prophetically[a] called Sodom and
Egypt, where also their Lord was crucified.
9 For three and a half days members of the
peoples and tribes and languages and na-
tions will gaze at their dead bodies and re-
fuse to let them be placed in a tomb; 10 and
the inhabitants of the earth will gloat over
them and celebrate and exchange presents,
because these two prophets had been a tor-
ment to the inhabitants of the earth.
11 But after the three and a half days,
the breath[b] of life from God entered them,

a Or *allegorically*; Gk *spiritually* *b* Or *the spirit*

judgments (Ezek 2.10). **11:** *You must,* an inescapable obligation, in accord with the divine will, *prophesy again;* the second part of the book (chs 12–22) contains these prophecies. *Peoples and nations and languages and kings* (Dan 3.4,7 [LXX]; Rev 5.9; 7.9) suggests the broad range of John's prophetic activity.

11.1–13: The measuring of the temple and the two witnesses. 1: The symbolic act of the measurement of the sanctuary *and those who worship there* emphasizes the protection and preservation of the faithful who are within (as in Zech 2.1–5; cf. Ezek 40.3–42.20). **2:** *The court outside,* the court of the Gentiles. *The holy city,* Jerusalem (Mt 4.5; 27.53). *Forty-two months* = 1,260 days (v. 3) = 3 1/2 years, a number that symbolizes the period of eschatological tribulation (Dan 7.25; 9.27; 12.7,11–12). As half of seven, the number of completeness, it also symbolizes radical incompleteness. **3:** While the *two witnesses* are unnamed here, it has been suggested that they represent prophetic figures who were expected to return in the end-time, possibly Enoch (Gen 5.24) and Elijah (2 Kings 2.1–11; Mal 4.5) or Moses (Deut 18.15,18) and Elijah. They are clothed in *sackcloth,* a sign that their prophecy called for repentance. **4:** *Two olive trees,* supplying the lamps in the temple (Zech 4.3–14). **6:** *Shut the sky,* cause a drought, as did Elijah (1 Kings 17.1). *Authority over the waters . . . ,* as did Moses and Aaron (Ex 7.17–21). **7:** *The beast,* 13.1; 17.8. *The bottomless pit,* see 9.1n. *Will make war on them,* Dan 7.21. **8:** *The great city* is identified here *prophetically,* i.e., allegorically or spiritually rather than literally by its proper name. While the majority of scholars understand the city as Jerusalem, others suggest that the city is Rome, as is Babylon in 17.1–6. The name *Sodom,* applied to Jerusalem in Isa 1.10; Jer 23.14; Ezek 16.46–56, alludes to that city's legendary wickedness (Gen 18.16–19.29). *Egypt* is associated with idolatry and is the land from which God delivered the enslaved people of Israel. *Where also their Lord was crucified,* Jerusalem. **10:** The *prophets had been a torment,* preaching an unpopular message of repentance. **11–12:** The

and they stood on their feet, and those who
saw them were terrified. 12 Then they[a]
heard a loud voice from heaven saying to
them, "Come up here!" And they went up
to heaven in a cloud while their enemies
watched them. 13 At that moment there was
a great earthquake, and a tenth of the city
fell; seven thousand people were killed in
the earthquake, and the rest were terrified
and gave glory to the God of heaven.
14 The second woe has passed. The
third woe is coming very soon.
15 Then the seventh angel blew his
trumpet, and there were loud voices in
heaven, saying,

"The kingdom of the world has
become the kingdom of
our Lord
and of his Messiah,[b]
and he will reign forever and ever."

16 Then the twenty-four elders who sit
on their thrones before God fell on their
faces and worshiped God, 17 singing,

"We give you thanks, Lord
God Almighty,
who are and who were,
for you have taken your great power
and begun to reign.
18 The nations raged,
but your wrath has come,
and the time for judging the dead,
for rewarding your servants,[c]
the prophets
and saints and all who fear
your name,
both small and great,
and for destroying those who destroy
the earth."

19 Then God's temple in heaven was
opened, and the ark of his covenant was
seen within his temple; and there were
flashes of lightning, rumblings, peals of
thunder, an earthquake, and heavy hail.

12 A great portent appeared in heaven:
a woman clothed with the sun, with
the moon under her feet, and on her head a
crown of twelve stars. 2 She was pregnant
and was crying out in birth pangs, in the
agony of giving birth. 3 Then another por-
tent appeared in heaven: a great red drag-

a Other ancient authorities read *I* b Gk *Christ*
c Gk *slaves*

witnesses are resuscitated (cf. Ezek 37.5,10) and taken to heaven (2 Kings 2.11). **12:** *Come up here,* 4.1. **13:** *Gave glory to the God of heaven,* a positive outcome of the *great earthquake.*

11.14–19: The seventh trumpet announces (v. 15) the consummation of God's reign (10.7). **16:** *Elders,* 4.4n. **17–18:** A song of triumph. **19:** Divine self-revelation concludes the vision of the seven trumpets and introduces the vision of ch 12. *The ark of [the] covenant* was constructed according to divine instruction at Mount Sinai (Ex 25.10–16) and eventually installed in the innermost room of the Temple by Solomon (1 Kings 8.1–12). It was presumably destroyed when the Babylonians captured Jerusalem in 586 BCE (but see 2 Macc 2.4–8).

12.1–17: The vision of the woman, the child, and the dragon is rich in symbolism drawn from mythological traditions found in ancient Babylonia, Egypt, Greece, and Rome, as well as in the Hebrew Bible. One well-known version of the story tells of the goddess Leto, pregnant with Apollo, who is menaced by the dragon Python, who pursues her because he knows that Apollo is destined to kill him (Hyginus, *Fabulae* 140). Here this material is reinterpreted in terms of Jewish traditions and expectations as the story of the birth of the messiah. **1:** A *great portent,* a sign or omen *in heaven* that points to a momentous event on earth; see v. 3; 15.1; cf. Lk 21.11; *Didache* 16.6. The *woman* is unnamed, and her precise identity is uncertain. Many scholars understand her as the symbolic representation of Israel, from whom the messiah is born (v. 5); the *twelve stars* thus refer to the twelve tribes. Patristic and medieval Christian interpreters most often take her to be Mary, or sometimes to be the church. Elements of her description are characteristic of several ancient goddesses. **3:** The *dragon,* identified in v. 9 as "the Devil" and "Satan," is Leviathan, the great sea monster of Canaanite tradition and of the Hebrew Bible (Job 40.25; Isa 27.1), one specification of the primeval watery chaos. *Seven heads and ten horns,* 13.1; 17.3; cf. Ps 74.13–14. These details are probably drawn from Dan 7.1–8, where they represent various empires and rulers; it is unclear what they symbolize here; cf. 17.9–10. **4:** *A third of the stars,* a proportion analogous

on, with seven heads and ten horns, and
seven diadems on his heads. 4 His tail swept
down a third of the stars of heaven and
threw them to the earth. Then the dragon
stood before the woman who was about to
bear a child, so that he might devour her
child as soon as it was born. 5 And she gave
birth to a son, a male child, who is to rule[a]
all the nations with a rod of iron. But her
child was snatched away and taken to God
and to his throne; 6 and the woman fled
into the wilderness, where she has a place
prepared by God, so that there she can be
nourished for one thousand two hundred
sixty days.

7 And war broke out in heaven; Michael
and his angels fought against the dragon.
The dragon and his angels fought back,
8 but they were defeated, and there was no
longer any place for them in heaven. 9 The
great dragon was thrown down, that an-
cient serpent, who is called the Devil and
Satan, the deceiver of the whole world—he
was thrown down to the earth, and his an-
gels were thrown down with him.

10 Then I heard a loud voice in heaven,
proclaiming,

"Now have come the salvation and
the power
and the kingdom of our God
and the authority of his Messiah,[b]
for the accuser of our comrades[c] has
been thrown down,
who accuses them day and night
before our God.
11 But they have conquered him by the
blood of the Lamb
and by the word of their testimony,
for they did not cling to life even in
the face of death.
12 Rejoice then, you heavens
and those who dwell in them!
But woe to the earth and the sea,
for the devil has come down to you
with great wrath,
because he knows that his time
is short!"

13 So when the dragon saw that he had
been thrown down to the earth, he pur-
sued[d] the woman who had given birth to
the male child. 14 But the woman was given
the two wings of the great eagle, so that she
could fly from the serpent into the wilder-
ness, to her place where she is nourished for
a time, and times, and half a time. 15 Then
from his mouth the serpent poured water
like a river after the woman, to sweep her
away with the flood. 16 But the earth came
to the help of the woman; it opened its
mouth and swallowed the river that the

a Or *to shepherd* *b* Gk *Christ* *c* Gk *brothers*
d Or *persecuted*

to the destruction caused by the trumpet plagues (8.7–9.19; Dan 8.10). *Threw them to the earth,* Dan 8.20. **5:** *Rule . . . with a rod of iron,* an allusion to Ps 2.9, originally concerning the king of Israel, and interpreted as referring to a future anointed ruler or messiah (*Psalms of Solomon* 17.23–24). The messianic child is *snatched away and taken to God:* The resurrection and exaltation of Christ denies the demonic dragon victory over its prey. **6:** *The wilderness* is a place where God provides refuge and sustenance amidst adversity (e.g., Gen 21.14–21; Deut 8.15–16; 29.5; 32.10; 1 Kings 17.1–2). *One thousand, two hundred sixty days,* the equivalent of "a time, and times, and half a time" (v. 14), "forty-two months" (11.2; 13.5), amounts to three and a half years. This symbolic number suggests a period of time limited by divine design. **7–12:** The *war* in *heaven* and its outcome offers, in symbolic language, the reason for the persecution and oppression of believers (v. 17). **7:** *Michael,* an archangel and the champion of Israel (Dan 10.13,21; 12.1; Jude 9) engages in combat against *the dragon and his angels* (Dan 10.20). **8:** *Defeated . . . in heaven,* see 9.1–2. Both passages may allude to Isa 14.12–20. **9:** Lk 10.18. *That ancient serpent,* see 9.3n.; Gen 3.1–7; Isa 27.1. *Satan* means adversary, accuser (see Job 1.6–12; 2.1–7; Zech 3.1–2). The *deceiver,* 20.10. **10:** *The accuser,* Job 1.9–11. **11:** *They have conquered,* the paradoxical victory of the crucified Christ (see 5.6n.) and of the martyrs, who were faithful unto death. **12:** *Rejoice,* Ps 96.11; Isa 49.13. **14:** *Eagle,* Ex 19.4; Deut 32.11. **15:** *Water . . . flood,* the chaos of the primeval sea monster (Isa 27.1; Ps 74.13; see 12.3n.). **16:** *Earth* helps the woman, as in Ex 15.12 the earth swallows up the pursuing Egyptian armies. **17:** The frustrated *dragon* redirects its anger toward *the rest of* the woman's *children,* namely, those who *keep the commandments . . . and hold the testimony of Jesus* (14.12).

dragon had poured from his mouth.
17 Then the dragon was angry with the
woman, and went off to make war on the
rest of her children, those who keep the
commandments of God and hold the testi-
mony of Jesus.
18 Then the dragon[a] took his stand on
13 the sand of the seashore. 1 And I saw
a beast rising out of the sea, having
ten horns and seven heads; and on its horns
were ten diadems, and on its heads were
blasphemous names. 2 And the beast that I
saw was like a leopard, its feet were like
a bear's, and its mouth was like a lion's
mouth. And the dragon gave it his power
and his throne and great authority. 3 One of
its heads seemed to have received a death-
blow, but its mortal wound[b] had been
healed. In amazement the whole earth fol-
lowed the beast. 4 They worshiped the drag-
on, for he had given his authority to the
beast, and they worshiped the beast, say-
ing, "Who is like the beast, and who can
fight against it?"
5 The beast was given a mouth uttering
haughty and blasphemous words, and it
was allowed to exercise authority for forty-
two months. 6 It opened its mouth to utter
blasphemies against God, blaspheming his
name and his dwelling, that is, those who
dwell in heaven. 7 Also it was allowed to
make war on the saints and to conquer
them.[c] It was given authority over every
tribe and people and language and nation,
8 and all the inhabitants of the earth will
worship it, everyone whose name has not
been written from the foundation of the
world in the book of life of the Lamb that
was slaughtered.[d]
9 Let anyone who has an ear listen:
10 If you are to be taken captive,
into captivity you go;
if you kill with the sword,
with the sword you must be killed.
Here is a call for the endurance and faith of
the saints.
11 Then I saw another beast that rose
out of the earth; it had two horns like a
lamb and it spoke like a dragon. 12 It exer-
cises all the authority of the first beast on
its behalf, and it makes the earth and its
inhabitants worship the first beast, whose
mortal wound[e] had been healed. 13 It per-
forms great signs, even making fire come
down from heaven to earth in the sight of
all; 14 and by the signs that it is allowed to
perform on behalf of the beast, it deceives
the inhabitants of earth, telling them to
make an image for the beast that had been
wounded by the sword[f] and yet lived;
15 and it was allowed to give breath[g] to the
image of the beast so that the image of the
beast could even speak and cause those

a Gk *Then he*; other ancient authorities read *Then I stood* *b* Gk *the plague of its death* *c* Other ancient authorities lack this sentence *d* Or *written in the book of life of the Lamb that was slaughtered from the foundation of the world* *e* Gk *whose plague of its death* *f* Or *that had received the plague of the sword* *g* Or *spirit*

12.18–13.18: The two beasts. 13.1–10: The *beast* from *the sea* combines the powers of the four beasts of Dan 7 and represents the Roman Empire, incited by the *dragon* (v. 2) to oppress *the saints* (v. 7). **1–2:** Based on Dan 7.1–7. *The sea,* primeval chaos. *Blasphemous names,* Roman emperors were worshiped as gods. **3:** *Death-blow,* perhaps an allusion to the assassination of Julius Caesar in 44 BCE, or to the belief that the emperor Nero, who committed suicide in 68 CE, would be restored to life and rule (see 17.8n.). The *mortal wound* (to the beast as a whole) did not destroy the empire. *Amazement,* as of one astonished by a remarkable victory or portent (Jdt 11.16; 2 Esd 12.3, the destruction of Rome). **5:** The sovereignty of God, even amid the oppression of the faithful, is implied by the use of passive verbs here and in vv. 7,10,14,15 (cf. 6.4; see 17.17n.). *Forty-two months,* see 11.2n. **8:** *From the foundation of the world,* this phrase would most naturally qualify *slaughtered* (see note *d*). A *name* can be removed from *the book of life* (3.5n.); later, judgment seems to depend on one's conduct of life (20.12). The translation here is a harmonization with 17.8. **10:** Jer 15.2; 43.11; Mt 26.52. **11–18:** The *beast* from *the earth,* associated with the false prophet (16.13; 19.20), enforces emperor worship (v. 12) and produces *great signs* (v. 13) or portents to deceive the people (v. 14); cf. Mt 24.24; 2 Thess 2.9–10. **14:** The *image,* a statue of the deified emperor.

who would not worship the image of the
beast to be killed. 16 Also it causes all, both
small and great, both rich and poor, both
free and slave, to be marked on the right
hand or the forehead, 17 so that no one can
buy or sell who does not have the mark,
that is, the name of the beast or the number
of its name. 18 This calls for wisdom: let
anyone with understanding calculate the
number of the beast, for it is the number of
a person. Its number is six hundred sixty-
six.[a]

14 Then I looked, and there was the
Lamb, standing on Mount Zion!
And with him were one hundred forty-four
thousand who had his name and his Fa-
ther's name written on their foreheads.
2 And I heard a voice from heaven like the
sound of many waters and like the sound of
loud thunder; the voice I heard was like the
sound of harpists playing on their harps,
3 and they sing a new song before the
throne and before the four living creatures
and before the elders. No one could learn
that song except the one hundred forty-
four thousand who have been redeemed
from the earth. 4 It is these who have not
defiled themselves with women, for they
are virgins; these follow the Lamb wherever
he goes. They have been redeemed from hu-
mankind as first fruits for God and the
Lamb, 5 and in their mouth no lie was
found; they are blameless.

6 Then I saw another angel flying in
midheaven, with an eternal gospel to pro-
claim to those who live[b] on the earth—to
every nation and tribe and language and
people. 7 He said in a loud voice, "Fear God
and give him glory, for the hour of his judg-
ment has come; and worship him who
made heaven and earth, the sea and the
springs of water."

8 Then another angel, a second, fol-

a Other ancient authorities read *six hundred sixteen*
b Gk *sit*

16–17: *Marked* in imitation of the sealing of God's servants (7.2–4). The *mark* of the beast (also 14.9,11; 16.2; 19.20; 20.4) is different from the seal of God with which the faithful are identified (7.3; 9.4). Those who do not bear the mark of the beast suffer economic oppression. *Right hand . . . forehead,* phylacteries or "tephillin" were worn on the left arm and forehead (*Ep. Arist.* 159; Josephus, *Ant.* 4.213). Egyptian Jews were branded by Ptolemy IV (3 Macc 2.28–29). **18:** *This calls for wisdom,* Dan 12.10. *The number of a person* can be understood either as a number that stands for a specific person, or as a number that can be calculated by human beings, not a hidden number known only to God (cf. 21.17). In the ancient practice of gematria, the numerical equivalents of the letters of the Hebrew or Greek alphabets were added together, and the resulting sum was seen as giving a clue to the nature of the name. Thus *the number of the beast* (666) is the sum of the separate letters of its name. Of countless explanations, the most probable is "Neron Caesar" (in Hebrew letters), which, if spelled without the final "n", also accounts for the variant reading, 616 (see note *a*). The number six represents what falls short of the number of completeness, seven.

14.1–20: A series of three visions intended to reassure the faithful of ultimate victory and vindication. **1–5:** *The Lamb* and those redeemed from the earth; as in 7.4, the *one hundred forty-four thousand* is a symbolic expression. **1:** *Mount Zion,* Jerusalem, the center of God's eschatological reign (Heb 12.22). *Written on their foreheads,* 7.3n.; 22.4. **2:** *Many waters,* see 1.15n. **3:** *They,* the one hundred forty-four thousand. *New song,* 5.8–10. *Throne,* 4.2n. *Four living creatures,* 4.6n. **4:** *They are virgins,* a characterization of the 144,000 that should be understood metaphorically in terms of the sexual abstinence required before contact with the divine (Ex 19.15; Deut 23.10–14) and of warriors before battle (1 Sam 21.5; 2 Sam 11.9–13). *These follow the Lamb,* who is their shepherd (7.17). *First fruits,* Ex 23.19. *No lie,* cf. Zeph 3.13. **6–13:** Three angels announce the coming judgment. **6:** *Flying in midheaven,* 8.13. *Eternal gospel,* the message or proclamation that follows in v. 7, an announcement that God's judgment is imminent. **7:** *Fear God,* 15.4; Deut 10.12–15. *Judgment,* 16.7; 18.10; 19.2. *Worship* acknowledges God's cosmic sovereignty as Creator. **8:** *Fallen, fallen is Babylon* (Isa 21.9) *the great* (Dan 4.30), an anticipation of 18.2. *Babylon* is a symbolic name for Rome (2 Esd 3.1–2). The association of the two is

lowed, saying, "Fallen, fallen is Babylon
the great! She has made all nations drink of
the wine of the wrath of her fornication."
9 Then another angel, a third, followed
them, crying with a loud voice, "Those
who worship the beast and its image, and
receive a mark on their foreheads or on
their hands, 10 they will also drink the wine
of God's wrath, poured unmixed into the
cup of his anger, and they will be torment-
ed with fire and sulfur in the presence of
the holy angels and in the presence of the
Lamb. 11 And the smoke of their torment
goes up forever and ever. There is no rest
day or night for those who worship the
beast and its image and for anyone who
receives the mark of its name."
12 Here is a call for the endurance of the
saints, those who keep the commandments
of God and hold fast to the faith of[a] Jesus.
13 And I heard a voice from heaven say-
ing, "Write this: Blessed are the dead who
from now on die in the Lord." "Yes," says
the Spirit, "they will rest from their labors,
for their deeds follow them."
14 Then I looked, and there was a white
cloud, and seated on the cloud was one like
the Son of Man, with a golden crown on his
head, and a sharp sickle in his hand! 15 An-
other angel came out of the temple, calling
with a loud voice to the one who sat on the
cloud, "Use your sickle and reap, for the
hour to reap has come, because the harvest
of the earth is fully ripe." 16 So the one who
sat on the cloud swung his sickle over the
earth, and the earth was reaped.
17 Then another angel came out of the
temple in heaven, and he too had a sharp
sickle. 18 Then another angel came out from
the altar, the angel who has authority over
fire, and he called with a loud voice to him
who had the sharp sickle, "Use your sharp
sickle and gather the clusters of the vine of
the earth, for its grapes are ripe." 19 So the
angel swung his sickle over the earth and
gathered the vintage of the earth, and he
threw it into the great wine press of the
wrath of God. 20 And the wine press was
trodden outside the city, and blood flowed
from the wine press, as high as a horse's
bridle, for a distance of about two hundred
miles.[b]

15 Then I saw another portent in heav-
en, great and amazing: seven angels
with seven plagues, which are the last, for
with them the wrath of God is ended.
2 And I saw what appeared to be a sea
of glass mixed with fire, and those who had
conquered the beast and its image and the
number of its name, standing beside the sea
of glass with harps of God in their hands.

a Or *to their faith in* b Gk *one thousand six hundred stadia*

based on the destruction of Jerusalem by Babylon in 586 BCE and by Rome in 70 CE. *The wine of the wrath,* 18.3; Jer 51.7. **9–11:** The sentence pronounced against those who *worship the beast* will be worse than what is suffered by those who do not worship it or bear its *mark* (13.15–17). **10:** *Wine of God's wrath,* Jer 25.15–16; 51.7. *Unmixed,* not diluted and therefore more potent (see 3 Macc 5.2). Wine was mixed with water before being drunk. *Fire and sulfur* (19.20; 20.10; 21.8) are instruments of divine punishment (Gen 19.24; Ps 11.6; Ezek 38.22). *Holy angels,* Mk 8.38 **11:** *Smoke,* 18.9,18; 19.3. **12:** An exhortation to perseverance addressed to those against whom the dragon goes to make war in 12.17. **13:** *Blessed,* see 1.3n. A promise assured by *the Spirit. Their deeds,* 2.2,19; 3.1–2.15. **14–20:** The eschatological harvest, the final judgment of God (Joel 3.13), involves the ingathering of the saints by *one like the Son of Man* (vv. 14–16) and the assembling of the wicked for destruction (vv. 17–20; Isa 63.1–6). **14:** *White cloud . . . Son of Man,* Dan 7.13; Mt 24.30; Mk 14.62. **15–16:** A grain harvest. **18–20:** A vintage scene. **20:** Metaphorically, *wine* is frequently associated with *blood* (Gen 49.11; Deut 32.14; Sir 39.26; 1 Macc 6.34). Here the enormous quantity of blood suggests the vast extent of the divine judgment (cf. Isa 63.3–6). Mention of the *horse's bridle* here foreshadows the combat in 19.11–21.

15.1–16.21: The seven bowls of the wrath of God.

15.1–8: The preparation for judgment. 1: *Portent,* a third heavenly sign (see 12.1n.,3). *The wrath of God,* 14.10,19; 15.1,7; 16.1; 19.15. *Is ended,* accomplished or come to its fulfillment. **15.2–4:** Vision of the victorious martyrs in heaven (8.3–5). **2:** *Sea of glass,* see 4.6n. **3:** *Song of Moses,* Ex 15.1–18; Deut

3 And they sing the song of Moses, the servant[a] of God, and the song of the Lamb:
"Great and amazing are your deeds,
Lord God the Almighty!
Just and true are your ways,
King of the nations![b]
4 Lord, who will not fear
and glorify your name?
For you alone are holy.
All nations will come
and worship before you,
for your judgments have been
revealed."

5 After this I looked, and the temple of
the tent[c] of witness in heaven was opened,
6 and out of the temple came the seven an-
gels with the seven plagues, robed in pure
bright linen,[d] with golden sashes across
their chests. 7 Then one of the four living
creatures gave the seven angels seven gold-
en bowls full of the wrath of God, who
lives forever and ever; 8 and the temple was
filled with smoke from the glory of God
and from his power, and no one could enter
the temple until the seven plagues of the
seven angels were ended.

16 Then I heard a loud voice from the
temple telling the seven angels, "Go
and pour out on the earth the seven bowls
of the wrath of God."

2 So the first angel went and poured his
bowl on the earth, and a foul and painful
sore came on those who had the mark of
the beast and who worshiped its image.

3 The second angel poured his bowl into
the sea, and it became like the blood of a
corpse, and every living thing in the sea
died.

4 The third angel poured his bowl into
the rivers and the springs of water, and they
became blood. 5 And I heard the angel of
the waters say,
"You are just, O Holy One, who are
and were,
for you have judged these things;
6 because they shed the blood of saints
and prophets,
you have given them blood to
drink.
It is what they deserve!"
7 And I heard the altar respond,
"Yes, O Lord God, the Almighty,
your judgments are true and just!"

8 The fourth angel poured his bowl on
the sun, and it was allowed to scorch peo-
ple with fire; 9 they were scorched by the
fierce heat, but they cursed the name of
God, who had authority over these plagues,
and they did not repent and give him glory.

10 The fifth angel poured his bowl on
the throne of the beast, and its kingdom
was plunged into darkness; people gnawed
their tongues in agony, 11 and cursed the
God of heaven because of their pains and
sores, and they did not repent of their
deeds.

12 The sixth angel poured his bowl on
the great river Euphrates, and its water was
dried up in order to prepare the way for the
kings from the east. 13 And I saw three foul

a Gk *slave* *b* Other ancient authorities read *the ages* *c* Or *tabernacle* *d* Other ancient authorities read *stone*

32. **5:** *The temple . . . was opened,* cf. 11.19. On opening the heavenly gates as a prelude to judgment, see 3 Macc 6.18–19. In Rome, the "Temple of Janus" was opened as a prelude to war (Virgil, *Aeneid* 1.294). The heavenly counterpart of the tent of witness that accompanied Israel's journey through the desert (Num 9.15). **7:** *Golden bowls,* libation vessels used in religious rituals. **8:** *Smoke,* Ex 19.18; 40.34–35; Isa 6.1–4; cf. 1 Kings 8.10–11.

16.1–21: The pouring of the bowls (cf. chs 8–9, and the plagues inflicted on Egypt, Ex 7–12). **2:** A *foul and painful sore,* Ex 9.8–12. **3–4:** 8.8–9; Ex 7.14–24. **5–6:** A judgment doxology. **5:** *The angel* that has control *of the waters,* implying a worldview in which different angels preside over different elements of the cosmos (1 Enoch 60.10–22; Rev 7.1–2, winds; Rev 14.18, fire). **6:** Divine retribution (Isa 49.26). *Blood to drink,* cf. 17.6. **7:** *The altar,* 6.9–11. **10:** 8.12; Ex 10.21. *Throne of the beast,* 13.2. **12:** *Euphrates,* see 9.14n. *Kings from the east,* perhaps a reference to the Parthians, who would be led by Nero, restored to life; see 13.3n.; *Sib. Or.* 4.120,139. **13–14:** *Foul spirits like frogs,* Ex 8.1–15. **14:**

spirits like frogs coming from the mouth of
the dragon, from the mouth of the beast,
and from the mouth of the false prophet.
14 These are demonic spirits, performing
signs, who go abroad to the kings of the
whole world, to assemble them for battle
on the great day of God the Almighty.
15 ("See, I am coming like a thief! Blessed is
the one who stays awake and is clothed,[a]
not going about naked and exposed to
shame.") 16 And they assembled them at
the place that in Hebrew is called Harma-
gedon.
17 The seventh angel poured his bowl
into the air, and a loud voice came out of
the temple, from the throne, saying, "It is
done!" 18 And there came flashes of light-
ning, rumblings, peals of thunder, and a
violent earthquake, such as had not oc-
curred since people were upon the earth, so
violent was that earthquake. 19 The great
city was split into three parts, and the cities
of the nations fell. God remembered great
Babylon and gave her the wine-cup of the
fury of his wrath. 20 And every island fled
away, and no mountains were to be found;
21 and huge hailstones, each weighing
about a hundred pounds,[b] dropped from
heaven on people, until they cursed God for
the plague of the hail, so fearful was that
plague.

17 Then one of the seven angels who
had the seven bowls came and said
to me, "Come, I will show you the judg-
ment of the great whore who is seated on
many waters, 2 with whom the kings of the
earth have committed fornication, and with
the wine of whose fornication the inhabi-
tants of the earth have become drunk." 3 So
he carried me away in the spirit[c] into a
wilderness, and I saw a woman sitting on a
scarlet beast that was full of blasphemous
names, and it had seven heads and ten
horns. 4 The woman was clothed in purple
and scarlet, and adorned with gold and
jewels and pearls, holding in her hand a
golden cup full of abominations and the
impurities of her fornication; 5 and on her
forehead was written a name, a mystery:
"Babylon the great, mother of whores and
of earth's abominations." 6 And I saw that
the woman was drunk with the blood of
the saints and the blood of the witnesses to
Jesus.
When I saw her, I was greatly amazed.
7 But the angel said to me, "Why are you so
amazed? I will tell you the mystery of the
woman, and of the beast with seven heads
and ten horns that carries her. 8 The beast

a Gk *and keeps his robes* b Gk *weighing about a talent* c Or *in the Spirit*

Performing signs, 13.13. **15:** *Like a thief,* see 3.3n. *Blessed,* see 1.3n. **16:** *They,* the frog-like spirits, emissaries of the demonic trio, that is, the dragon, the beast, and the false prophet. *Harmagedon,* spelled variously in the manuscripts with "gg" and / or "dd"; also "Armagedon." This is perhaps an allusion to Megiddo, the site of several decisive battles in Israel's history (Judg 5.19; 2 Kings 9.27; 2 Chr 35.22); in Hebrew, "har Megiddo" means "the mountain of Megiddo." Here it is the symbolic assembly point of the forces hostile to God as they prepare for the eschatological battle. **19:** *The great city,* Rome. *Great Babylon,* 14.8. *Wine-cup,* 14.10. **21:** *Hail,* 8.7; Ex 9.13–35; Wis 5.22.

17.1–18.24: The fall of Babylon, which is Rome, the city on seven hills (17.9,18) and the archpersecutor of the saints (17.6).

17.1–18: The vision of the woman. 1: *The great whore,* a symbol that builds both on the fact that cities were grammatically constructed as feminine and on the Hebrew prophets' metaphorical references to cities and nations as brides, wives, or harlots (e.g., Tyre in Isa 23.17–18). **2:** Jer 51.7. *Fornication,* sexual misconduct applied metaphorically to the city's international commercial and political dealings, which are judged illicit and unjust. **3:** *In the spirit,* 1.10; 4.2; 21.10 (Ezek 2.2; 3.12,14,24). *Into a wilderness,* Isa 21.1–20. *Scarlet beast,* the Roman Empire (see 13.1n.). *Blasphemous names,* divine titles given to Roman emperors (see 13.1). **4:** *Gold and jewels and pearls,* 18.16. **5:** *On her forehead,* 13.16; 14.1; 20.4; 22.4. *A mystery,* indicating that the name is symbolic and that it requires interpretation, which the angel offers in vv. 7 – 18. *Mother of whores,* Hos 2.2 – 5. **6:** *Drunk with . . . blood,* Ezek 39.19. Persecution took the form of exile (1.9), jail (2.10), or death (2.10,13; 11.3). **8:** *The beast* now represents the Emperor Nero,

that you saw was, and is not, and is about
to ascend from the bottomless pit and go
to destruction. And the inhabitants of the
earth, whose names have not been written
in the book of life from the foundation of
the world, will be amazed when they see
the beast, because it was and is not and is
to come.
9 "This calls for a mind that has wis-
dom: the seven heads are seven mountains
on which the woman is seated; also, they
are seven kings, 10 of whom five have fallen,
one is living, and the other has not yet
come; and when he comes, he must remain
only a little while. 11 As for the beast that
was and is not, it is an eighth but it belongs
to the seven, and it goes to destruction.
12 And the ten horns that you saw are ten
kings who have not yet received a kingdom,
but they are to receive authority as kings
for one hour, together with the beast.
13 These are united in yielding their power
and authority to the beast; 14 they will make
war on the Lamb, and the Lamb will con-
quer them, for he is Lord of lords and King
of kings, and those with him are called and
chosen and faithful."
15 And he said to me, "The waters that
you saw, where the whore is seated, are
peoples and multitudes and nations and
languages. 16 And the ten horns that you
saw, they and the beast will hate the whore;
they will make her desolate and naked; they
will devour her flesh and burn her up with
fire. 17 For God has put it into their hearts
to carry out his purpose by agreeing to give
their kingdom to the beast, until the words
of God will be fulfilled. 18 The woman you
saw is the great city that rules over the
kings of the earth."

18 After this I saw another angel com-
ing down from heaven, having great
authority; and the earth was made bright
with his splendor. 2 He called out with a
mighty voice,

"Fallen, fallen is Babylon the great!
It has become a dwelling place
of demons,
a haunt of every foul spirit,
a haunt of every foul bird,
a haunt of every foul and
hateful beast.[a]
3 For all the nations have drunk[b]
of the wine of the wrath of her
fornication,
and the kings of the earth have
committed fornication
with her,
and the merchants of the earth have
grown rich from the power[c]
of her luxury."

4 Then I heard another voice from heav-
en saying,

"Come out of her, my people,
so that you do not take part in her
sins,
and so that you do not share in her
plagues;

a Other ancient authorities lack the words *a haunt of every foul beast* and attach the words *and hateful* to the previous line so as to read *a haunt of every foul and hateful bird* *b* Other ancient authorities read *She has made all nations drink* *c* Or *resources*

commonly expected to return to life and power (v. 11). *Was and is not and is to come,* a parody of the designation of God in 1.4,8. *Book of life,* see 3.5n. **9:** *This calls for a mind that has wisdom,* like the formula in 13.18, this expression introduces the interpretation of the symbolism of the preceding verses. The *seven mountains* are the seven hills of Rome. The *seven kings* are Roman emperors (cf. Dan 11.2; 2 Esd 12.22–26), which interpreters have sought to identify with emperors from Julius Caesar to Domitian. **12:** *Ten horns* represent subordinate or client rulers (Dan 7.7–8). **14:** The eschatological victory of Christ. *Lord of lords and king of kings,* 19.16. **16:** Ezek 23.26–29. **17:** The ten kings are unwitting instruments of God's will, fulfilling the divine plan (compare the passive verbs in 6.4; see 13.5n.). **18:** An explicit identification of the woman of v. 1 as *the great city,* i.e., Rome.

18.1–24: Dirge over the fallen city (Rome), with echoes from the taunt songs in Isa 23–24; 47; Jer 50–51; Ezek 26–27. **1–3:** Angelic announcement of judgment(14.8; Isa 21.9; Jer 50.39; 51.8). **1:** *The earth was made bright,* Ezek 43.2. **2:** *A dwelling place . . . a haunt,* Isa 13.21–22. **4–8:** Summons to God's people to leave the doomed city; cf. Jer 51.45; Mt 24.16. **5:** *High as heaven,* Jer 51.9. **6:** Jer 50.29; cf. Isa

5 for her sins are heaped high
as heaven,
and God has remembered
her iniquities.
6 Render to her as she herself
has rendered,
and repay her double for her deeds;
mix a double draught for her in the
cup she mixed.
7 As she glorified herself and lived
luxuriously,
so give her a like measure of
torment and grief.
Since in her heart she says,
'I rule as a queen;
I am no widow,
and I will never see grief,'
8 therefore her plagues will come in a
single day—
pestilence and mourning
and famine—
and she will be burned with fire;
for mighty is the Lord God who
judges her."
9 And the kings of the earth, who com-
mitted fornication and lived in luxury with
her, will weep and wail over her when they
see the smoke of her burning; 10 they will
stand far off, in fear of her torment, and
say,
"Alas, alas, the great city,
Babylon, the mighty city!
For in one hour your judgment
has come."
11 And the merchants of the earth weep
and mourn for her, since no one buys their
cargo anymore, 12 cargo of gold, silver, jew-
els and pearls, fine linen, purple, silk and
scarlet, all kinds of scented wood, all arti-
cles of ivory, all articles of costly wood,
bronze, iron, and marble, 13 cinnamon,
spice, incense, myrrh, frankincense, wine,
olive oil, choice flour and wheat, cattle and
sheep, horses and chariots, slaves—and hu-
man lives.[a]
14 "The fruit for which your soul longed
has gone from you,
and all your dainties and
your splendor
are lost to you,
never to be found again!"
15 The merchants of these wares, who
gained wealth from her, will stand far off,
in fear of her torment, weeping and mourn-
ing aloud,
16 "Alas, alas, the great city,
clothed in fine linen,
in purple and scarlet,
adorned with gold,
with jewels, and with pearls!
17 For in one hour all this wealth has
been laid waste!"
And all shipmasters and seafarers, sailors
and all whose trade is on the sea, stood far
off 18 and cried out as they saw the smoke
of her burning,
"What city was like the great city?"
19 And they threw dust on their heads, as
they wept and mourned, crying out,
"Alas, alas, the great city,
where all who had ships at sea
grew rich by her wealth!
For in one hour she has been
laid waste."
20 Rejoice over her, O heaven, you
saints and apostles and prophets! For God
has given judgment for you against her.
21 Then a mighty angel took up a stone
like a great millstone and threw it into the
sea, saying,
"With such violence Babylon the
great city
will be thrown down,
and will be found no more;
22 and the sound of harpists and
minstrels and of flutists and
trumpeters
will be heard in you no more;
and an artisan of any trade
will be found in you no more;

a Or *chariots, and human bodies and souls*

40.2. **9–20:** Lamentation of those who have been enriched through their dealings with the corrupt city: kings (vv. 9–10), merchants (vv. 11–16), and mariners (vv. 17–20; cf. Ezek 27.29–36). **20:** *Rejoice over her,* Jer 51.48. **21–24:** Symbolic action representing the total destruction of the city (Jer 51.63–64). **22:** *Sound of harpists,* Jer 25.10; Ezek 26.13. **24:** *Blood of prophets,* Mt 23.34–35; Lk 11.49–51; 13.33–34.

and the sound of the millstone
will be heard in you no more;
23 and the light of a lamp
will shine in you no more;
and the voice of bridegroom
and bride
will be heard in you no more;
for your merchants were the magnates
of the earth,
and all nations were deceived by
your sorcery.
24 And in you[a] was found the blood of
prophets and of saints,
and of all who have been
slaughtered on earth."

19 After this I heard what seemed to be
the loud voice of a great multitude
in heaven, saying,
"Hallelujah!
Salvation and glory and power
to our God,
2 for his judgments are true and just;
he has judged the great whore
who corrupted the earth with her
fornication,
and he has avenged on her the blood
of his servants."[b]
3 Once more they said,
"Hallelujah!
The smoke goes up from her forever
and ever."
4 And the twenty-four elders and the four
living creatures fell down and worshiped
God who is seated on the throne, saying,
"Amen. Hallelujah!"
5 And from the throne came a voice say-
ing,
"Praise our God,
all you his servants,[b]
and all who fear him,
small and great."
6 Then I heard what seemed to be the voice
of a great multitude, like the sound of many
waters and like the sound of mighty thun-
derpeals, crying out,
"Hallelujah!
For the Lord our God
the Almighty reigns.
7 Let us rejoice and exult
and give him the glory,
for the marriage of the Lamb
has come,
and his bride has made
herself ready;
8 to her it has been granted to
be clothed
with fine linen, bright and pure"—
for the fine linen is the righteous deeds of
the saints.
9 And the angel said[c] to me, "Write
this: Blessed are those who are invited to
the marriage supper of the Lamb." And he
said to me, "These are true words of God."
10 Then I fell down at his feet to worship
him, but he said to me, "You must not do
that! I am a fellow servant[d] with you and
your comrades[e] who hold the testimony of
Jesus.[f] Worship God! For the testimony of
Jesus[f] is the spirit of prophecy."

11 Then I saw heaven opened, and there
was a white horse! Its rider is called Faith-
ful and True, and in righteousness he
judges and makes war. 12 His eyes are like a
flame of fire, and on his head are many
diadems; and he has a name inscribed that

a Gk *her* b Gk *slaves* c Gk *he said* d Gk *slave*
e Gk *brothers* f Or *to Jesus*

19.1–10: Doxology giving praise to God for the destruction of Rome (vv. 1–5) and for the marriage of the Lamb (vv. 6–9). **3:** *Smoke . . . forever,* i.e., destruction never to be rebuilt. **4:** See 4.4,6. **5:** Ps 115.13. **7:** *His bride,* the new Jerusalem (21.2,9). **8:** *Fine linen,* in contrast to the attire of Babylon (17.4). **9:** *Blessed,* the fourth of seven beatitudes in the book; see 1.3n. **10:** God alone is the appropriate object of worship (cf. 22.8–9).

19.11–21: The victory of Christ and the heavenly armies over the beast and its cohorts. **11:** *Heaven opened,* Ezek 1.1. *In righteousness he judges,* Isa 11.4. **12:** *Many diadems,* in contrast to the diadems of the dragon (12.3). *A name . . . that no one knows,* because the name stands for a person, knowledge of a name confers power over the person. That his name is known only to himself implies that Christ's power is sovereign and unlimited (cf. 2.17). **13:** As revealer of God he is called *The Word of God* (Jn 1.1,14).

no one knows but himself. 13 He is clothed
in a robe dipped in[a] blood, and his name
is called The Word of God. 14 And the ar-
mies of heaven, wearing fine linen, white
and pure, were following him on white
horses. 15 From his mouth comes a sharp
sword with which to strike down the na-
tions, and he will rule[b] them with a rod of
iron; he will tread the wine press of the fury
of the wrath of God the Almighty. 16 On his
robe and on his thigh he has a name in-
scribed, "King of kings and Lord of lords."
17 Then I saw an angel standing in the
sun, and with a loud voice he called to all
the birds that fly in midheaven, "Come,
gather for the great supper of God, 18 to eat
the flesh of kings, the flesh of captains, the
flesh of the mighty, the flesh of horses and
their riders—flesh of all, both free and
slave, both small and great." 19 Then I saw
the beast and the kings of the earth with
their armies gathered to make war against
the rider on the horse and against his army.
20 And the beast was captured, and with it
the false prophet who had performed in its
presence the signs by which he deceived
those who had received the mark of the
beast and those who worshiped its image.
These two were thrown alive into the lake
of fire that burns with sulfur. 21 And the
rest were killed by the sword of the rider on
the horse, the sword that came from his
mouth; and all the birds were gorged with
their flesh.

20 Then I saw an angel coming down
from heaven, holding in his hand
the key to the bottomless pit and a great
chain. 2 He seized the dragon, that ancient
serpent, who is the Devil and Satan, and
bound him for a thousand years, 3 and
threw him into the pit, and locked and
sealed it over him, so that he would deceive
the nations no more, until the thousand
years were ended. After that he must be let
out for a little while.
4 Then I saw thrones, and those seated
on them were given authority to judge. I
also saw the souls of those who had been
beheaded for their testimony to Jesus[c] and
for the word of God. They had not wor-
shiped the beast or its image and had not
received its mark on their foreheads or their
hands. They came to life and reigned with
Christ a thousand years. 5 (The rest of the
dead did not come to life until the thousand
years were ended.) This is the first resurrec-

a Other ancient authorities read *sprinkled with*
b Or *will shepherd* *c* Or *for the testimony of Jesus*

14: *Armies,* the angelic host (see Lk 2.13 note *b*). *Fine linen,* 19.8. **15:** 1.16; 2.12,16; 19.21; Ps 2.9. **16:** 17.14; Deut 10.17. **17–18:** *An angel* summons the birds of prey (Ezek 39.4,17–20). **17:** *The great supper of God,* in gruesome contrast to the "marriage feast of the Lamb" (v. 9). **19–21:** The final battle between Christ and the beast (anticipated in 16.13–16). **20:** *The beast,* the first beast, introduced in 13.1–8. *The false prophet* is the second beast of 13.11–15. *The lake of fire,* see 14.10n.; 20.10,14–15; 21.8; Dan 7.11. *Sulfur* was well known in the ancient world as a noxious poison; it was used to render land infertile (Deut 29.23; Job 18.15), and burning sulfur symbolized God's judgment (Gen 19.24; Ps 11.6; Ezek 38.22). See 9.17; 14.10; 20.10; 21.8. **21:** *The sword of the rider . . . the sword that came from his mouth,* suggesting that the victory is won not by violence but by The Word of God (19.13).

20.1–10: The defeat of Satan.

20.1–6: The temporary imprisonment of Satan and the reign of Christ and the martyrs. **1:** *Chain,* 2 Pet 2.4; Jude 6. **2–3:** The period of a *thousand years* is symbolic both here and in vv. 4–7, suggesting a temporary time of righteousness and tranquility before the final eschatological consummation. Cf. Ps 90.4. **2:** *The dragon . . . serpent . . . Devil . . . Satan,* 12.9n. **3:** Satan is locked into the pit to prevent him from carrying out his demonic work as "the deceiver of the whole world" (12.9). After the *thousand years,* though, *he must be let out for a little while,* but even this limited period is under God's control (Dan 7.25). **4:** *Thrones* of judgment (Dan 7.9,22,27; Mt 19.28; Lk 22.30). *Those . . . beheaded for their testimony,* martyrs (in 6.9–10 the souls of the martyrs, under the altar, cry for vengeance). *Its mark,* 13.16–17; 14.9. *Reigned with Christ a thousand years,* this passage, which gave rise to Christian millenni-

tion. 6 Blessed and holy are those who share
in the first resurrection. Over these the sec-
ond death has no power, but they will be
priests of God and of Christ, and they will
reign with him a thousand years.
7 When the thousand years are ended,
Satan will be released from his prison 8 and
will come out to deceive the nations at the
four corners of the earth, Gog and Magog,
in order to gather them for battle; they are
as numerous as the sands of the sea. 9 They
marched up over the breadth of the earth
and surrounded the camp of the saints and
the beloved city. And fire came down from
heaven[a] and consumed them. 10 And the
devil who had deceived them was thrown
into the lake of fire and sulfur, where the
beast and the false prophet were, and they
will be tormented day and night forever
and ever.
11 Then I saw a great white throne and
the one who sat on it; the earth and the
heaven fled from his presence, and no place
was found for them. 12 And I saw the dead,
great and small, standing before the throne,
and books were opened. Also another book
was opened, the book of life. And the dead
were judged according to their works, as
recorded in the books. 13 And the sea gave
up the dead that were in it, Death and Ha-
des gave up the dead that were in them, and
all were judged according to what they had
done. 14 Then Death and Hades were
thrown into the lake of fire. This is the sec-
ond death, the lake of fire; 15 and anyone
whose name was not found written in the
book of life was thrown into the lake of
fire.

21 Then I saw a new heaven and a new
earth; for the first heaven and the
first earth had passed away, and the sea
was no more. 2 And I saw the holy city, the
new Jerusalem, coming down out of heaven
from God, prepared as a bride adorned for
her husband. 3 And I heard a loud voice
from the throne saying,

"See, the home[b] of God is among
mortals.
He will dwell[c] with them;
they will be his peoples,[d]
and God himself will be with them;[e]
4 he will wipe every tear from
their eyes.
Death will be no more;
mourning and crying and pain will be
no more,
for the first things have
passed away."

5 And the one who was seated on the
throne said, "See, I am making all things

a Other ancient authorities read *from God, out of heaven,* or *out of heaven from God* b Gk *the tabernacle* c Gk *will tabernacle* d Other ancient authorities read *people* e Other ancient authorities add *and be their God*

alism, suggests an interim messianic kingdom. **6:** *Blessed,* see 1.3n. *Priests,* 1.6; 5.10; Ex 19.6. *Second death,* see 2.11n.; 20.14; 21.8.

20.7–10: The release of Satan and the final conflict. *Gog and Magog,* Ezek 38–39. **9:** *The beloved city,* Jerusalem (Sir 24.11). *Fire,* Ezek 38.22; 39.6; 2 Kings 1.9–12. **10:** *Was thrown into the lake of fire,* the final overthrow of Satan.

20.11–15: The last judgment. 11: The *great white throne,* 4.2; 20.4. **12:** *Books* of deeds, ledgers that record what everyone has done (Dan 7.10). The *book of life* is distinguished from the books of deeds just opened (see 3.5n). *Judged according to their works,* Mt 16.27; Rom 2.6; 2 Cor 5.10. **13–14:** Personified *Death and Hades* (see 1.18n.; 6.8n.) are the last enemies to be defeated. **14:** *The second death,* see 2.11n.; Mt 25.41.

21.1–22.5: Vision of the new Jerusalem.

21.1–8: The renewal of creation: 1: *A new heaven and a new earth,* Isa 65.17; 66.22. All creation will be renewed, freed from imperfections, and transformed by God (Rom 8.19–21). *The sea,* the primeval force of turbulence and unrest (Gen 1.2; Ps 29.3,10). **2:** *New Jerusalem,* 21.9–10. *Coming down out of heaven,* 3.12. *Prepared as a bride,* 19.7–9; Isa 61.10. The image of the eschatological Jerusalem as a *bride* contrasts with the image of Rome as the whore Babylon in chs 17–18. **3:** Ezek 37.27. **4:** 7.16; Isa 25.8; 35.10. **5:** The speaker is God (1.8). **6:** *Alpha* and *Omega,* see 1.8n. *Water of life,* Isa 55.1; Jn 4.13; 7.37.

new." Also he said, "Write this, for these
words are trustworthy and true." 6 Then he
said to me, "It is done! I am the Alpha and
the Omega, the beginning and the end. To
the thirsty I will give water as a gift from
the spring of the water of life. 7 Those who
conquer will inherit these things, and I will
be their God and they will be my children.
8 But as for the cowardly, the faithless,[a]
the polluted, the murderers, the fornica-
tors, the sorcerers, the idolaters, and all li-
ars, their place will be in the lake that burns
with fire and sulfur, which is the second
death."

9 Then one of the seven angels who had
the seven bowls full of the seven last
plagues came and said to me, "Come, I will
show you the bride, the wife of the Lamb."
10 And in the spirit[b] he carried me away to
a great, high mountain and showed me the
holy city Jerusalem coming down out of
heaven from God. 11 It has the glory of God
and a radiance like a very rare jewel, like
jasper, clear as crystal. 12 It has a great, high
wall with twelve gates, and at the gates
twelve angels, and on the gates are in-
scribed the names of the twelve tribes of the
Israelites; 13 on the east three gates, on the
north three gates, on the south three gates,
and on the west three gates. 14 And the wall
of the city has twelve foundations, and on
them are the twelve names of the twelve
apostles of the Lamb.

15 The angel[c] who talked to me had a
measuring rod of gold to measure the city
and its gates and walls. 16 The city lies four-
square, its length the same as its width; and
he measured the city with his rod, fifteen
hundred miles;[d] its length and width and
height are equal. 17 He also measured its
wall, one hundred forty-four cubits[e] by
human measurement, which the angel was
using. 18 The wall is built of jasper, while
the city is pure gold, clear as glass. 19 The
foundations of the wall of the city are
adorned with every jewel; the first was jas-
per, the second sapphire, the third agate,
the fourth emerald, 20 the fifth onyx, the
sixth carnelian, the seventh chrysolite, the
eighth beryl, the ninth topaz, the tenth
chrysoprase, the eleventh jacinth, the
twelfth amethyst. 21 And the twelve gates
are twelve pearls, each of the gates is a sin-
gle pearl, and the street of the city is pure
gold, transparent as glass.

22 I saw no temple in the city, for its
temple is the Lord God the Almighty and
the Lamb. 23 And the city has no need of
sun or moon to shine on it, for the glory of
God is its light, and its lamp is the Lamb.
24 The nations will walk by its light, and the
kings of the earth will bring their glory into
it. 25 Its gates will never be shut by day—
and there will be no night there. 26 People
will bring into it the glory and the honor of
the nations. 27 But nothing unclean will en-
ter it, nor anyone who practices abomina-
tion or falsehood, but only those who are
written in the Lamb's book of life.

a Or *the unbelieving* *b* Or *in the Spirit* *c* Gk *He*
d Gk *twelve thousand stadia* *e* That is, almost
seventy-five yards

7: *Those who conquer,* compare the concluding words of each of the seven letters in chs 2 and 3. **8:** A list of vices. *The second death,* contrasted to the water of life in v. 6 (see 2.11n.).

21.9–27: The measuring of the city. Cf. Ezek 40–42. Both the city and its measurements (which are multiples of 12) are symbolic. **9:** *The seven bowls,* see ch 16. *The bride, the wife of the Lamb,* 19.7; 21.2. Israel is the bride of God in Isa 54.5; Hos 2.19–20. **10:** *In the spirit,* see 1.10n. *High mountain,* Ezek 40.2. *Jerusalem . . . out of heaven,* cf. Gal 4.26; Heb 11.10; 2 Esd 13.35–36. **11:** *Jasper,* 4.3. **12:** Ezek 48.30–34. **14:** *Apostles,* Eph 2.20. **15–18:** *The city* that *lies foursquare,* i.e., with streets that intersect at right angles, unlike the irregular walls of Palestinian cities (Ezek 42.20). The cube is a perfect square. The precious stones adorned the high priest's breastplate (Ex 28.17–21). **19:** Isa 54.11–12. **21:** *The street,* the paving of the streets enables them to reflect God's glory. **22–23:** *No temple . . . no . . . sun* are needed because the presence and glory of God pervade the entire community (Isa 24.23; 60.1,19; 2 Esd 7.39 – 42). *Its lamp is the Lamb,* Ps 132.17. **25:** City gates are closed at night and at the approach of enemies; perpetually open gates symbolize safety; see Isa 60.11; Zech 14.7; 1QM 12.13–15. **27:** *Book of life,* see 3.5n.

22 Then the angel[a] showed me the riv-
er of the water of life, bright as crys-
tal, flowing from the throne of God and of
the Lamb 2 through the middle of the street
of the city. On either side of the river is the
tree of life[b] with its twelve kinds of fruit,
producing its fruit each month; and the
leaves of the tree are for the healing of the
nations. 3 Nothing accursed will be found
there any more. But the throne of God and
of the Lamb will be in it, and his servants[c]
will worship him; 4 they will see his face,
and his name will be on their foreheads.
5 And there will be no more night; they need
no light of lamp or sun, for the Lord God
will be their light, and they will reign forev-
er and ever.

6 And he said to me, "These words are
trustworthy and true, for the Lord, the God
of the spirits of the prophets, has sent his
angel to show his servants[c] what must
soon take place."

7 "See, I am coming soon! Blessed is the
one who keeps the words of the prophecy
of this book."

8 I, John, am the one who heard and
saw these things. And when I heard and
saw them, I fell down to worship at the feet
of the angel who showed them to me; 9 but
he said to me, "You must not do that! I am
a fellow servant[d] with you and your com-
rades[e] the prophets, and with those who
keep the words of this book. Worship
God!"

10 And he said to me, "Do not seal up
the words of the prophecy of this book, for
the time is near. 11 Let the evildoer still do
evil, and the filthy still be filthy, and the
righteous still do right, and the holy still be
holy."

12 "See, I am coming soon; my reward
is with me, to repay according to every-
one's work. 13 I am the Alpha and the Ome-
ga, the first and the last, the beginning and
the end."

14 Blessed are those who wash their
robes,[f] so that they will have the right to
the tree of life and may enter the city by the
gates. 15 Outside are the dogs and sorcerers
and fornicators and murderers and idola-
ters, and everyone who loves and practices
falsehood.

16 "It is I, Jesus, who sent my angel to
you with this testimony for the churches. I
am the root and the descendant of David,
the bright morning star."

17 The Spirit and the bride say, "Come."
And let everyone who hears say,
"Come."
And let everyone who is thirsty come.
Let anyone who wishes take the water
of life as a gift.

18 I warn everyone who hears the words

a Gk *he* *b* Or *the Lamb.* [2]*In the middle of the street of the city, and on either side of the river, is the tree of life* *c* Gk *slaves* *d* Gk *slave* *e* Gk *brothers*
f Other ancient authorities read *do his commandments*

22.1–5: The river and the tree of life. 1: *The river,* cf. Gen 2.10; Ps 46.4; Ezek 47.1; Zech 14.8. **2:** *The tree,* a collective reference to many trees *on either side of the river* (Ezek 47.12; cf. 2.7n.). **3:** *The throne of God and of the Lamb* is one throne, 3.21. **4:** To *see* God's *face,* full awareness of God's immediate presence (Job 33.26; Ps 10.11; 42.2), an eschatological blessing (Ps 84.7; Mt 5.8; 1 Jn 3.2). *On their foreheads,* see 7.3n.; 14.1; contrast 13.16; 17.5. **5:** Those who *worship* God (v. 3) *will reign* with God in eternal triumph (Dan 7.18,27).

22.6–21: Epilogue, consisting of warnings and exhortations. **6:** *He said,* an angel (v. 8), perhaps the one referred to in 1.1. *These words,* the contents of this book. *The God of the spirits of the prophets,* the one who inspired the spirits of the prophets (*1 QH* 20.11–13). **7:** A parenthesis, reporting the words of Christ (cf. 16.15). *Blessed,* the seventh beatitude of the book; see 1.3n. **8–9:** 19.10. **10:** *Do not seal,* cf. Isa 8.16; Dan 12.4. This book is to remain unsealed because the end is imminent. **12:** *My reward is with me,* Isa 40.10; Jer 17.10. **13:** Christ applies God's title to himself (see 1.8n.). **14:** *Blessed,* see 1.3n. *Wash,* 7.14. *The city,* the heavenly Jerusalem. **15:** A list of those who are not permitted to enter the city, characterized generally as *everyone who loves and practices falsehood.* **16:** *Root . . . of David,* Isa 11.1,10; Mt 1.1. *Morning star,* see 2.28n. **17:** *The bride,* 21.2,9. *Come,* singular in Greek, is addressed to Jesus, as in v. 20.

of the prophecy of this book: if anyone
adds to them, God will add to that person
the plagues described in this book; 19 if any-
one takes away from the words of the book
of this prophecy, God will take away that
person's share in the tree of life and in the
holy city, which are described in this book.

20 The one who testifies to these things
says, "Surely I am coming soon."
Amen. Come, Lord Jesus!
21 The grace of the Lord Jesus be with
all the saints. Amen.[a]

a Other ancient authorities lack *all*; others lack *the saints*; others lack *Amen*

18–19: A solemn warning against altering the teachings of *this book* (cf. Deut 4.2; 12.21). **20:** *The one who testifies,* Jesus Christ; see 1.2. *Amen. Come, Lord Jesus,* a response, with liturgical echoes, to *surely I am coming soon.* **21:** An epistolary postscript.

ESSAYS

TABLES

BIBLIOGRAPHY

The Canons of the Bible

The contents of the Bible differ depending on the particular community in which it is in use. The major difference is between Christian Bibles, which include the New Testament, and the Jewish Bible, which does not. But there are also differences between the Hebrew Bible in Judaism and the Old Testament contents and order in Christianity, and there are differences among Christians about the contents of the Old Testament (see chart). The discussion below will explain, within the limits of what scholars now know, how these differences came about.

DEFINITIONS

"Canon," a Greek word meaning "reed," came to refer to any straight stick that could be used for measuring. This basic meaning was extended to refer to any rule or standard by which things could be compared or judged. The Alexandrian grammarians, classical Greek writers who were not simply grammarians but also what we would call literary critics, used "canon" as their term for the list of standard or classic authors who were worthy of attention and imitation. This was not a closed category, and there were disputes about adding or removing works from the list. Furthermore, inclusion on the list merely recognized a work's quality; it did not confer any new status. Nevertheless, a canon of writings came to denote those texts that were of central importance to a given group. When used in reference to the Bible, canon has an even stronger significance: Not only is a given set of texts included, but all other texts—no matter how worthy otherwise—are excluded. This sense is expressed in a rabbinic comment on Eccl 12.12. The biblical text reads:

> Of anything beyond these [Heb *mehemah*], my child, beware. Of making many books there is no end.

The rabbinic comment states:

> Those who bring more than twenty-four books [the standard number in the Hebrew Bible; see below] into their house introduce confusion [Heb *mehumah*] into their house (Qoh. Rab. 12.12).

This suggests not only that the works in the canon are important, but that they, along with their authoritative interpretation, are sufficient in and of themselves.

THE HEBREW BIBLE

It is extremely difficult to trace how this conception of canon developed, and how it is connected to related notions, such as the eventual stabilization of the biblical text. Until the mid-twentieth century, many scholars thought that the canon of the Hebrew Bible was established at Jabneh (Jamnia), a city near the Mediterranean coast, west of Jerusalem, that was a center of Jewish learning after the destruction of the Second Temple (70 CE). According to this theory, a group of rabbis met there in about 90 CE and voted on whether or not certain books are canonical; at the end of this meeting, the official contents of the Hebrew Bible were supposedly established. It is now acknowledged that this overly neat reconstruction is wrong and was based on a misunderstanding of rabbinic texts. Unfortunately, evidence is not available to offer a clear picture of how the canon of the Hebrew Bible was formed. Much of the material from early Jewish sources (for instance, the Dead Sea Scrolls, rabbinic texts, and the first-century CE historian Josephus) and Christian sources is ambiguous. Furthermore, many of the sources were written several centuries after the canon was clearly established, and are more interested in fostering a particular viewpoint than in presenting the facts objectively; they must, therefore, be used with great caution.

This much is clear: The canon of the Hebrew Bible did not develop at a single moment in time but rather in stages. There is general agreement that the Torah or Pentateuch was the first section of the Hebrew Bible to be canonized, that is, to be recognized as central by the community. Exactly when this happened is uncertain. Many scholars had associated this development with Ezra, and they saw the "law of your God" (Ezra 7.14), with which Ezra was entrusted in the fifth century BCE, as the Pentateuch. We now recognize, however, that this assertion goes beyond the evidence of the text. Though the Jewish community had recognized the Torah as central to its identity by the Persian period (sixth to fourth centuries), a conclusion suggested by citations of Torah material as authoritative in biblical books from this period (e.g., Chronicles, Ezra-Nehemiah), it is unclear exactly how this happened, or whether this development should be associated primarily with a single individual such as Ezra, or should be seen as part of a larger, more complicated process.

According to rabbinic tradition, the Torah is the first part of a tripartite (three-part) canon, followed by Nevi'im (prophets) and Ketubim (writings), forming a work that much later was known by the acronym Tanak(h), *T*orah, *N*evi'im, *K*etubim. Nevi'im is composed of Joshua, Judges, Samuel (seen as one book), Kings (seen as one book)—historical works known as "the former prophets"—and "the latter prophets," consisting of Isaiah, Jeremiah, Ezekiel, and the twelve minor prophets (Hosea through Malachi, seen as one book). The order of these eight books has been relatively stable. Ketubim is comprised of the following eleven books, which, by contrast, appear in a wide variety of orders in various book lists and biblical manuscripts: Psalms, Proverbs, Job; the "five scrolls," whose order has been especially variable, Ruth, Song of Solomon, Ecclesiastes, Lamentations, and Esther; Daniel, Ezra-Nehemiah (seen as one book), and Chronicles (seen as one book). The number of canonical books according to traditional Jewish sources is thus twenty-four (five in the Torah, eight in Nevi'im, eleven in Ketubim).

The origin of the tripartite canon has been a topic of recent dispute, with several scholars suggesting that a two-part canon, the Torah and other works, was the original form, and that only later was it divided into three parts. It is more likely, however, that the tripartite canon is primary, and evidence for it appears in such sources as Lk 24.44, which refers to "the law of Moses, the prophets, and the psalms," and in parallel expressions in the Dead Sea Scrolls. The tripartite canon likely reflects the gradual nature of the canonization process, with Nevi'im canonized before Ketubim. This would explain why the Ketubim contain the book of Daniel (dating from the second century BCE), and several late historical books, such as Ezra-Nehemiah and Chronicles, which would seem more appropriately to belong with similar works such as Joshua and Kings. The tripartite canon most likely suggests, therefore, that Torah was canonized in the Persian period, followed by the canonization of Nevi'im in the late Persian or early Greek period, while the Ketubim were canonized last, around the time of the destruction of the Second Temple (70 CE).

The tripartite order is not the only order known in antiquity, nor is the number of twenty-four books the only number mentioned in ancient Jewish sources. Josephus, the Jewish historian of the first century CE, refers to twenty-two biblical books (*Ag. Ap.* 1.42). It is not clear if he simply had a smaller canon or if, instead, his canon had the texts in a different order, combined in different ways. Some traditions put Ruth after Judges and Lamentations after Jeremiah, treating these smaller books as appendices to the ones they follow, rather than as independent works. Such an arrangement would yield twenty-two books, a number that conveniently corresponds to the number of letters in the Hebrew alphabet; some early Christian sources also cite this as the number of books in the Bible. The arrangement of Ruth and Lamentations mentioned above is that of the Septuagint, the Greek translation of the Bible begun in Alexandria, Egypt, in the second century BCE (see "The Greek Bible" below). According to this tradition, mentioned by some early church fathers and reflected in the arrangement of the earliest comprehensive Septuagint manuscripts (fourth century CE), the Hebrew Bible is divided into four parts: Torah, Histories, Poetical and Wisdom books, and Prophets (see the Introduction to the Poetical and Wisdom Books, p. 721 HB). This order continues to be used by Christians in their organization of the Hebrew Bible (Old Testament) materials. Older scholarship spoke of this four-part, twenty-two book arrangement as the Alexandrian canon, in contrast to the tripartite, twenty-four book Palestinian canon, but scholars now recognize that such a clear dichotomy never existed and therefore avoid the use of those terms.

Scholars also now recognize that even when canonization took place, the contents of the Bible did not absolutely freeze. This is true, first of all, about books whose status as scripture continued to be debated. The Bible had begun to stabilize significantly by the fourth century CE, with the development of explicit lists in the Christian community of books considered canonical (see the discussion below). Other groups, too, had their ideas about the canon; it is unlikely, for instance, that the Qumran community, most of whose texts date from the century or so immediately before and immediately after the Common Era, viewed Esther as canonical, since no clear biblical manuscript of that book has survived among the thousands of fragments discovered. In contrast, many manuscripts of *Jubilees,* a set of comments on Genesis and Exodus, have survived, and given this work's affinities with the practices of the Dead Sea community, it was probably a canonical text for them. Within rabbinic literature, the Wisdom of Jesus

CANONS OF THE HEBREW BIBLE

Jewish Canon

Torah (LAW)
Genesis
Exodus
Leviticus
Numbers
Deuteronomy

Nevi'im (PROPHETS)
FORMER PROPHETS
Joshua
Judges
Samuel (1 & 2)
Kings (1 & 2)

LATTER PROPHETS
Isaiah
Jeremiah
Ezekiel
The Twelve
  Hosea
  Joel
  Amos
  Obadiah
  Jonah
  Micah
  Nahum
  Habakkuk
  Zephaniah
  Haggai
  Zechariah
  Malachi

Ketubim (WRITINGS)
Psalms
Proverbs
Job
(Five Scrolls):
  Song of Solomon
  Ruth
  Lamentations
  Ecclesiastes
  Esther
Daniel
Ezra-Nehemiah
Chronicles (1 & 2)

There is no Apocrypha in the Hebrew Bible

Protestant Canon

PENTATEUCH
Genesis
Exodus
Leviticus
Numbers
Deuteronomy

HISTORIES
Joshua
Judges
Ruth
1 & 2 Samuel
1 & 2 Kings
1 & 2 Chronicles
Ezra
Nehemiah
Esther

POETICAL/WISDOM BOOKS
Job
Psalms
Proverbs
Ecclesiastes
Song of Solomon

PROPHETS
Isaiah
Jeremiah
Lamentations
Ezekiel
Daniel
Hosea
Joel
Amos
Obadiah
Jonah
Micah
Nahum
Habakkuk
Zephaniah
Haggai
Zechariah
Malachi

THE APOCRYPHA
1 & 2 Esdras
Tobit
Judith
Esther (with additions)
Wisdom of Solomon
Ecclesiasticus (Sirach)
Baruch
Letter of Jeremiah (Baruch ch 6)
Prayer of Azariah and Song of Three
Daniel and Susanna
Daniel, Bel, & Snake
Prayer of Manasseh
1 & 2 Maccabees

Roman Catholic/Orthodox Canon

PENTATEUCH
Genesis
Exodus
Leviticus
Numbers
Deuteronomy

HISTORIES
Joshua
Judges
Ruth
1 & 2 Samuel
1 & 2 Kings
1 & 2 Chronicles
Ezra
Nehemiah
Tobit
Judith
Esther
1 & 2 Maccabees

POETICAL/WISDOM BOOKS
Job
Psalms
Proverbs
Ecclesiastes
Song of Solomon
Wisdom of Solomon
Sirach

PROPHETS
Isaiah
Jeremiah
Lamentations
Baruch
Ezekiel
Daniel
Hosea
Joel
Amos
Obadiah
Jonah
Micah
Nahum
Habakkuk
Zephaniah
Haggai
Zechariah
Malachi

Orthodox Canons generally include
  1 & 2 Esdras
  Prayer of Manasseh
  Psalm 151
  3 Maccabees
  4 Maccabees (as an Appendix)

ben Sirach (Sirach or Ecclesiasticus) is sometimes cited with the same formula used for biblical texts and was thus, in some sense, canonical for some rabbis. Therefore, although we may speak of the canon as forming in the first century CE, there was a certain amount of flexibility or variability around the fringes.

This flexibility may also be seen in the extensive divergence with respect to the wording of the biblical text as shown in manuscripts from Qumran, in translations of the Hebrew Bible in the Septuagint and elsewhere, and to a lesser extent in early rabbinic citations. These differences are not just small, such as a variant spelling here or there, but are often major, and affect the meaning of the text. There are cases where the text is found in two or more different recensions—identifiably different versions, revisions, or critical texts, not merely two different copies of the same original with minor variants—which may simply vary the order of materials or may exhibit fundamentally different text-types (for example, short types versus expansive types, as with the text of Jeremiah; see the Introduction to Jeremiah). Early in the first millennium, however, these variations subsided as canonization and certain types of rabbinic exposition that paid a great deal of attention to the exact spelling of the individual word developed. This eventually brought about textual stability, though here too this was a gradual process, and the means by which it was accomplished are largely unknown.

The most basic question is why particular texts were canonized while others were not. Canonized texts within Jewish tradition were considered part of "the holy scriptures" or "that which is read" (to use rabbinic designations). Excluded texts in some cases had been translated in the Septuagint and were therefore canonized in the Christian community (see "The Greek Bible," below); others were lost, or survived as pseudepigrapha (writings falsely attributed to major biblical figures), or were preserved only in fragmentary form in the Dead Sea Scrolls. Some of these excluded texts date from after the Persian period (later than 332 BCE) and thus were seen as too recent to be eligible.

In various ways, canonical status for a book or group of books has to do with the community's views on their centrality, authority, sacredness, and inspiration. Over time these characteristics have become connected, inseparably so in some traditions; yet they are not identical, and though they overlap, they must still be viewed distinctly. The Song of Solomon, for instance, was originally an erotic love poem; by the early rabbinic period, it came to be interpreted allegorically as a love poem between God and Israel. It was also seen as the inspired composition of Solomon himself. Why was it canonized? Was it canonized before it was seen as a holy, allegorical text? In that case, its canonization might reflect a central role that it held in culture or ritual. Or was it canonized only after it was viewed as allegorical and as a composition of Solomon? In that case its significance, whether of authorship or of ideas, could have played a more important part. There is no way to judge between these two paths to canonization, and the resulting difficulty is characteristic of the problems in dealing with issues of canonization in general.

Despite such major uncertainties in our understanding of the process of canonization, however, several points seem fairly certain. First, it is likely that the final stages of canonization were a reaction to the destruction of the Second Temple in 70 CE. This crisis intensified a development which had begun over half a millennium earlier, with the destruction of the First Temple (586 BCE). Through this development Israel gradually became the people of the Book. Second, it is unlikely that canonization represents a purely top-down process, through which a small group of leaders (rabbis) determined the canon; instead, the designation of certain works as canonical was more like the official recognition of the works that a large segment of the community had already held to be central, holy, or authoritative. Finally, the act of canonization was remarkably inclusive, creating a body of works richly textured by a wide variety of genres, ideologies, and theologies. This is, fundamentally, a typical ancient Near Eastern process: Instead of creating a small, highly consistent text, as we perhaps would now do, those responsible for the process made efforts to include many of the viewpoints in ancient Israel, incorporating differing and even contradictory traditions into this single, and singular, book.

THE GREEK BIBLE

When Christian writings began to circulate, during the second half of the first century CE, the Bible that the early Christians used for reading and quotation was the Septuagint, the Greek translation and expansion of the Hebrew Bible that had been produced in Alexandria and other Diaspora communities for the use of Greek-speaking Jews. Probably as a result of the as yet unsettled matter of which works were canonical for the Jewish community, the Septuagint included further works: historical books (1 and 2 Maccabees, 1 Esdras); wisdom writings (The Wisdom of Solomon, The Wisdom of Jesus Ben Sirach); novels (Tobit, Judith); an apocalypse (2 Esdras); historical legend (3 Maccabees); philosophical diatribe (4 Maccabees); an addendum to Jeremiah (Baruch and the Letter of Jeremiah); and expansions to Esther, Daniel (the Prayer of Azariah and the Song of the Three Jews, Susanna, Bel and the Dragon), and Psalms (Prayer of Manasseh and Psalm 151). (For further details see the Introduction to the Apocryphal/Deuterocanonical Books and the introductions to the individual books.)

Greek-speaking Jews in the Diaspora granted this Greek Bible an authority equivalent to that of the Hebrew texts. The legend that God had directly inspired its seventy translators was familiar to Alexandrian Jews (Philo, *Life of Moses,* 2.40). Manuscripts discovered at Qumran include Greek texts as well as a Hebrew text closer to the Septuagint than to the Masoretic text (4QSam[a]; 4Q121 Num 3.30–4.14; see "Hebrew Bible: Texts and Versions," pp. 462–464 ES for information about the Masoretic Text). Toward the end of the first century BCE, some books of the Septuagint were revised in Palestine to bring them closer to the known Hebrew text. Some New Testament citations whose wordings are between the Greek and Hebrew texts that we have today may also reflect local revisions.

Evidently the various Jewish communities in the Greek-speaking Diaspora knew their Greek Bible in versions that differed from each other. Jewish revisions in the second century CE sought to bring the Greek text closer to the Hebrew and in some cases to replace terms that Christians had seized upon in disputes with Jews, such as "virgin" in Isa 7.14. The Theodotion version of the second century CE forms the text of most surviving manuscripts. Citations in Christian writers of the fourth century CE, as well as the Old Latin versions, suggest that there were Christian recensions of the Greek Bible during this period as well. The Septuagint, therefore, is really an anthology of translations and revisions.

Although some early Christians were aware that the Greek Bible they used was more extensive than the Hebrew Bible, its authority remained intact. Origen (185–254) recommended Judith, Tobit, and Wisdom to beginning Bible readers before the Gospels and Epistles. Athanasius (296–374) may also have shared this view: He includes Wisdom, as well as the Didache and the *Shepherd of Hermas* (two non-canonical early Christian writings) in his list of works to be used in the instruction of catechumens. Jerome (345–420) continued to cite the Greek Bible, though arguing for the superiority of the Hebrew text and canon. It was Jerome who first separated these additional works in the Greek Bible from those for which he had Hebrew originals, placing them at the end of the Old Testament.

The result of this history was that the Christian church ended up with a set of writings for its Old Testament that differed from those that for Jews formed the Hebrew Bible. Without definitive specification, Christians in the Western (Latin, later Roman) and Eastern (Greek, later Orthodox) churches used not only the works regarded as canonical by the Jewish community, but also those additional works, or a selection of them, included in the Septuagint. Most Christians naturally were unaware of the differences among the biblical books; most were illiterate, and of the literate, very few could read Hebrew, the language of the original texts. The Christian churches therefore entered the second millennium with an expanded Old Testament, in an order different from the Hebrew Bible.

The Protestant Reformation coincided with a greatly increased interest in the study of ancient languages other than Latin. Among the leaders of the Reformation churches there was, along with a desire to make the Bible itself the standard of theological inquiry, a heightened effort to go behind the Latin text to the original languages in which the Bible had been written, since the Bible alone, and not the Bible plus its traditional interpretation, was being given much more importance in Reformation thought. This effort reopened the issue of the status of those Old Testament books that were not accepted by the Jews and did not have original Hebrew texts. The result was a sharp demarcation between those texts in the Hebrew Bible and all the others, with the reformers granting clear privilege to the Hebrew texts—though retaining the order of the Septuagint for them. In Martin Luther's translation, the additional works were kept in their separate section, as Jerome had originally intended, between the Hebrew Bible (Old Testament) and the New Testament. Luther wanted these texts to be available for reading and meditation, but he did not regard them as scripture. Among the Calvinist reformers the position was even more definitive: None of these additional works were acceptable, and therefore they were excluded from the Bible entirely. The Anglican church, while retaining most of them (and using some in lectionary readings and services of prayer and worship), also held that though these additional books were valuable for reading and study, they could not be used to establish doctrine.

In response to this critique of their canonical status, the Roman Catholic Counter-Reformation position was to declare these works definitively a part of the Bible. The Catholic church to this day maintains the canonical status of Tobit, Judith, the longer version of Esther, 1 and 2 Maccabees, the Wisdom of Solomon, Sirach, Baruch (including the Letter of Jeremiah), and the Additions to Daniel. The Orthodox churches also maintained the canonical status of these works, and in addition regarded some or all of the following books as canonical: 1 Esdras, the Prayer of Manasseh, Psalm 151, 3 Maccabees, 2 Esdras, and (in an appendix) 4 Maccabees. The NRSV includes headings within the Apocryphal/Deuterocanonical Books calling attention to the varying canonical status of these works.

THE NEW TESTAMENT

As noted above, the early Christian community soon began to produce writings dealing with its own history, beliefs, and traditions. By the end of the first century CE and the beginning of the second, various gospels, narratives, letters, and didactic and apocalyptic writings were in circulation and were being used by one or more local Christian communities. The practice of reading from these works, along with selections from the Greek version of the Jewish Scriptures, soon arose in Christian worship, and this implicitly began the process of canonization of these Christian writings. When disputes broke out, as they inevitably would, about beliefs or traditions, the canonical or noncanonical status of the various Christian writings became important.

The later Christian tendency to equate "canonical" with "inspired" confuses the study of early Christianity, since official lists only appear in the fourth century CE as a consequence of theological polemics (see Athanasius, *Festal Letter* 39; Eusebius, *History of the Church* 3.3.5; 3.25.3–4). Christian canon lists remained fluid through the sixth century with such inclusions as the *Shepherd of Hermas* or the spurious *Epistle to the Laodiceans* among the Pauline letters. The Muratorian canon, whose date and provenance are disputed (second to fourth century CE), includes Wisdom of Solomon in the New Testament. Other collections omit Hebrews. (See the chart below for a comparison of three New Testament canon lists.)

Arguments over inspiration emerge as a consequence of second-century CE challenges to general Christian practice which set reading of the Gospels alongside the Jewish writings that had always been Scripture. Valentinus and other Gnostics—who taught an esoteric form of Christianity—asserted that the Jewish God was ignorant of the highest divine realms, and that therefore both the Jewish scriptures and Christian writings which accept them will mislead naïve believers. He and others stated that only the esoteric teaching found in Gnostic circles could unlock the truth. Such Gnostics produced a number of gospels and revelations said to demonstrate the apostolic origin of their teaching. Marcion sought to establish his own church on the basis of a Bible that excluded the Old Testament and whose New Testament comprised only a version of the Gospel of Luke and ten Pauline epistles that were purified of spurious passages contrary to what Marcion saw as Jesus' revelation of the Father. Some scholars credit him with the idea of a canon that cannot be expanded or altered. Against such developments, Irenaeus argued that the Spirit poured out on the Church enabled her to write scripture (*Against the Heresies* 3.21.3–4) and affirmed the unity of the Old Testament and New Testament (*Against the Heresies* 4.28.1–2). Tertullian refers to reading the "books of God" in Christian worship with no differentiation between Jewish and Christian writings (Apology 39.3).

Besides these disputes, in which different contents of a canonical collection of writings clearly reflected underlying differences of theology, there was the influence of the physical character of the texts themselves. From the beginning Christians used the codex (pl. codices) format—a bound volume of pages, similar to a present-day book—rather than the more traditional scroll for their writings. While the codex permits easier access than the scroll, codices were at the time the medium of early drafts, assembled notes, and the like. Finished literary works and sacred texts like the Torah would have been copied onto scrolls. Scholars disagree over whether the early Christian use of codices resulted from the predominantly lower to moderate socioeconomic status of most Christians, or whether the choice of this format was more conscious. Would they have agreed that their writ-

CANONS OF THE NEW TESTAMENT

The Muratorian Canon (second to fourth century)	The List of Eusebius (early fourth century)	The Canon of Athanasius (367 CE)
[Matthew][1]	Matthew	Matthew
[Mark]	Mark	Mark
Luke	Luke	Luke
John	John	John
Acts	Acts	Acts
1 & 2 Corinthians	Romans	James
Ephesians	1 & 2 Corinthians	1 & 2 Peter
Philippians	Ephesians	1, 2, & 3 John
Colossians	Philippians	Jude
Galatians	Colossians	Romans
1 & 2 Thessalonians	Galatians	1 & 2 Corinthians
Romans	1 & 2 Thessalonians	Galatians
Philemon	Philemon	Ephesians
Titus	Titus	Philippians
1 & 2 Timothy	1 & 2 Timothy	Colossians
Jude	[Hebrews][3]	1 & 2 Thessalonians
1 & 2 John[2]	1 Peter	Hebrews[5]
Wisdom of Solomon	1 John	1 & 2 Timothy
Revelation to John	[Revelation to John][4]	Titus
		Philemon
	Disputed books:	Revelation to John
	James	
	Jude	
	2 Peter	
	2 & 3 John	

1. The MS begins in the middle of a line, but the inclusion of Matthew and Mark is virtually certain. 2. Some scholars argue for a conjectural reading that would support inclusion of all three letters of John. 3. Elsewhere, Eusebius regards Hebrews as by Paul. 4. Also listed as "disputed." 5. Athanasius regards this as by Paul.

ings differed from the ancient authority of the Torah and the prophets? If the use of the codex originated with early collections of Paul's letters (seen as relatively informal writings compared, for instance, to formal histories) and with Gospel collections (seen as representative of the oral teaching of the apostles), then the codex would have been an appropriate form for such writings. The use of readings from the Gospels and prophets at the center of Christian worship, however, indicates that the Gospels enjoyed equal authority with the Torah and the prophets by the mid-second century (see Justin Martyr, *1 Apology* 67.3–5).

Scrolls were made of papyrus or leather pieces glued or sewn together, and lengthy ones became inconvenient to handle: The average length is about 6 to 8 meters (20–26 ft), though longer scrolls are known. The codex, however, does not suffer the same limitations and therefore can accommodate a much longer text. This meant that collections of books could be bound into one volume, and first the entire New Testament, finally the whole Bible, could appear in this way. This does not mean, however, that there was a uniform collection of books, or a uniform order in which they were placed. Individual Christian congregations may not have possessed copies of all writings included in canon lists. It would have been difficult to distinguish these texts from other early Christian writings also found in this form. Hence some Christians turned over apocryphal writings to imperial officials during the Diocletian persecution (303 CE). A confusion of unofficial and authorized scriptures in Christian worship persists into the mid-fourth century CE. Canon 59 of the Synod of Laodicea (360 CE) decreed, "Private psalms should not be read in church, neither uncanonized books, but only the canonical ones of the new and old covenant."

Origen's advice to those seeking to read scripture privately presumes that the educated, Christian elite would have copies of deuterocanonical writings, Gospels, epistles, psalms and the Torah. He proposes an order of reading designed to overcome the difficulties in such study. First, he suggests, Esther, Judith, Tobit, or Wisdom. Then, the Gospels, epistles and Psalms. Finally, the reader can tackle those which are difficult or seemingly without reward, Leviticus or Numbers (*Homilies on Numbers* 27.1). The great biblical codices of the fourth and fifth centuries CE include different selections of Jewish apocrypha. In Codex Sinaiticus one finds Tobit, Judith, Wisdom, Sirach, 1 and 4 Maccabees; in Codex Vaticanus, Baruch, Letter of Jeremiah, Wisdom, Sirach, Judith, Tobit; in Codex Alexandrinus, Psalms of Solomon, 3 and 4 Maccabees. Athanasius's Festal Letter 39 omits the deuterocanonical writings from the Old Testament but proposes that they be used as private reading. Though Athanasius includes all twenty-seven New Testament writings, the issue was clearly not settled. Gregory of Nazianzus (d. 389) omits Revelation from his verse catalogue as do the lectionaries of the Eastern church. Didymus of Alexandria omits 2 and 3 John but cites the apostolic fathers as authoritative. Such evidence indicates that although a group of Jewish and Christian writings was considered scripture, to be used in public worship, preaching, and instruction, regional variations persisted.

By the end of the fourth century, however, there was widespread agreement about which books had scriptural status. Among the large number of early Christian writings in a diversity of genres, including gospels, letters, acts, apocalypses, and didactic treatises, a smaller number had come to be widely accepted. The criteria that were implicitly, and sometimes explicitly, operative were apostolic authority—that a work was written by or attributed to one of the first generation of Christian leaders, especially Paul and the twelve apostles—and consistency with their teaching, especially as determined by ecclesiastical authorities whose power had grown in a number of centers. As a result, some of the writings that had come to be considered noncanonical were lost, and only rediscovered in the late nineteenth and twentieth centuries.

Textual Criticism

THE NEED FOR TEXTUAL CRITICISM

No original manuscript of any biblical book has survived. This situation, which may seem unusual to us, is actually quite normal for ancient writings, and even for those from only a few centuries ago. For instance, none of Shakespeare's plays is available in the original manuscript from Shakespeare's hand, and for most of them there are two or more early printed versions with many differences between them. For the biblical books, numerous copies or partial copies, varying greatly in age and quality, have been preserved in various parts of the world. Occasionally, as with the discovery of the Dead Sea Scrolls (the Qumran documents) in the mid-twentieth century, new copies turn up. Nevertheless, for the entire text of the Bible, scholars are faced with a situation in which they have multiple manuscripts that have been copied by hand so that each is a unique product, unlike a modern printed book, and therefore the copies differ among themselves in many places, some differences being trivial and some important. Given this situation, scholars have had to develop a methodology for deciding which wording should be followed in cases where the copies disagree. This methodology is called *textual criticism* because it is a way of assessing a text through critical comparison of its different copies.

Textual criticism is not used only on religious writings. Any important text where there is not a definitive, printed edition backed up with an author's manuscript or corrected by the author may need to undergo textual criticism. Typographical errors, omitted words, even graphic elements like incorrect indentions of poetic lines, can all mean that a text does not reflect the original author's intentions completely. The methods may have to be adapted to differing circumstances, but the principles have been developed over centuries and have been checked when manuscripts have been found that can confirm or refute reconstructions of a text. Most important, there is widespread agreement among textual scholars on the methods and procedures that should be used, even when the results in certain cases remain in dispute.

DEFINITIONS

Establishing a critical edition of the biblical text involves the collection of all the differences between manuscript copies of any text, and the publication of all significant ones. The manuscripts are in the form of collections of biblical books, usually bound leaves, called *codices* (the plural of *codex*); *scrolls*, or long strips of papyrus or parchment rolled up, of individual books, such as those found at Qumran near the Dead Sea; *lectionaries*, or passages excerpted from texts in order to be read in worship services; and *citations*, or quotations in ancient writers, such as the Dead Sea Scrolls, the rabbis, or early church theologians. These sources, taken all together, are called *witnesses* or *authorities*, and the differences among them are called *variant readings* or simply *variants*. Also important are ancient translations, or *versions*, of the Bible, which provide indirect evidence for the original text. More details on these different forms of the texts are given under the specific discussion of the texts for the Hebrew Bible, the Apocryphal/Deuterocanonical Books, and the New Testament.

REASONS FOR VARIANTS

Variants can be of several kinds. The copyist may have misseen or misheard a word, producing a simple spelling error, or perhaps a different word. For example, in Eph 4.32 (cf. 5.2), the variants alternate between the pronouns "us" and "you." In Greek these two words are quite close (*hemin* and *humin*), differing by only one letter, and when pronounced aloud they are almost indistinguishable. In other places, the copyist's eye may inadvertently have skipped a phrase or sentence, thereby leaving out a sequence of words. In Sir 30.11–12, for example, some manuscripts omit two lines ending ". . . in his youth," possibly because the immediately preceding line also ends ". . . in his youth" and the copyist picked up after the second occurrence, omitting what came in between. Conversely, the copyist may inadvertently have gone over a phrase twice, producing a repetition. Although it may be difficult to determine when these errors took place in particular instances, there is nothing complex about them, and many variants are of this kind.

Sometimes, however, copyists seem to have tried to improve the text they were reproducing. They might have done this in several ways. They may have tried to "correct" a word or phrase that was unacceptable for one reason or another by substituting a more acceptable word or phrase. At 1 Tim 5.16, for example, the text reads "believing woman," and the translators' note says that some manuscripts have "believing man or woman," others "believing man." Here the translators have chosen the variant that is the most unusual, assuming that a copyist would more likely expand the phrase, or substitute "man" for "woman," rather than the reverse, in a cultural context that tended to treat women as less important than men. Copyists might also have been aware of a similar passage in another biblical book, and tried to make the passage they were copying conform to that. For example, Lk 11.2, the beginning of the Lord's Prayer, has variant readings that are probably an effort to make it conform to Mt 6.9. Copyists might also have tried to make the text support a particular theological view or belief. For instance, at Deut 32.8, some manuscripts read "according to the number of the sons of God" (NRSV "the gods," a paraphrase), while others read "according to the number of the sons of Israel" (NRSV "Israelites"). There is general agreement that the second variant was introduced by a scribe trying to avoid a polytheistic wording. Copying a manuscript was not necessarily just a mechanical process, but could involve deliberate changes for a number of reasons.

ANCIENT TRANSLATIONS

These methods of trying to determine the correct reading do not always provide enough evidence, or it may be that none of the existing manuscripts seems to have preserved the exact wording of the original author. Another source of information that scholars turn to is very early translations of the Bible. These early translations are called *versions*, and they were in use among Jews or Christians whose primary languages were other than the ones used in the original writings. They include translations of the Hebrew Bible into Greek (for instance, the Septuagint), Syriac (the Peshitta), Aramaic (translations and paraphrases called Targums), and Latin (the Vulgate), and translations of part or all of the Christian scriptures into Syriac, Coptic, and Latin.

These versions are useful to translators because the early stage at which they were made provides insight into forms of the biblical text that may be closer to the original writings. They can therefore be consulted for help in determining what is more likely to be an original reading, or when the best manuscripts of the original language texts have gaps or obvious errors. In many translations, including the NRSV, these ancient versions are cited in the footnotes of the Hebrew Bible to explain where and why the translators have chosen an alternative reading or translated something other than the Hebrew text that has come down to us. For readers unfamiliar with the nomenclature of these ancient documents, however, such notes may not convey very much information. The versions are discussed in more detail in the section below on "The Hebrew Bible: Texts and Versions."

THE PROCESS OF TEXTUAL CRITICISM

In order to establish the best possible text, scholars must first collect all of the significant variants and information about the manuscripts in which they occur. As a practical matter, a *critical text*—one with a version of the Greek or Hebrew on the page and an *apparatus*, usually footnotes giving variants and their source manuscripts—is published. Scholars must then determine whether they will accept the readings in the text or adopt instead one of the alternatives.

They may first rely on external evidence. This would include matters such as the age of the manuscript in which the variant occurs, since older manuscripts are generally closer to the original than later ones; or whether the variant occurs in manuscripts from one region only or in those from widely different regions. They will also use internal evidence: In general, shorter readings are preferable to longer ones, since scribes are more likely to add to a text than to delete materials (though, in the case of offensive or theologically challenging texts, deletion must be considered); difficult readings, including awkward phrases, coarse words, and poor grammar, are preferable to smoother ones, since scribes might try to "correct" such difficulties; and stylistic considerations can help judgments about how a particular author would have written.

The task would be difficult enough if scholars could be sure that the original wording in any place with a variant reading was preserved in at least one manuscript; but even that is not necessarily the case. There are instances where no existing manuscript is likely to preserve the original wording: where none of the variants seem to be right, or where the original text does not make sense as far as current scholarship can determine. In such cases scholars must assume that the original wording of the text has been lost or distorted in the course of the copying process. They then have several options open to them. One (called *conjectural emendation*) is to conjecture, based on the text as it now stands, what the original wording might have been. This can often be based on a scholar's general knowledge of the ancient languages, just as an English speaker can notice, and mentally correct, a typographical error in a modern book without having access to the author's manuscript. Another possibility is to consult the ancient versions. Finally, scholars may have to admit defeat and acknowledge that, given the current state of our knowledge, it is impossible to determine what the original wording might have been. For instance, at 1 Sam 13.1, the translation shows, by the use of ellipsis, that a word (the age of Saul when he began to reign) is missing. The translators' note points out that this number is not in the Hebrew text, and that the obvious second place to look for it, the ancient Greek translation known as the Septuagint, does not include any part of the verse. It is therefore impossible to recover the original wording unless some other ancient manuscript source is discovered.

The translators' notes in the NRSV call attention to all of these matters, and many others as well. These notes, printed in italic type and keyed to the text by superscript letters, can be found at the bottom of the right-hand column of the translation on each page. The abbreviations used in these notes are given in the discussion below, and are listed on pp. xxv–xxvii.

THE HEBREW BIBLE: TEXTS AND VERSIONS

The Masoretic Text

The basic text for the Hebrew Bible today is called the *Masoretic Text* (MT), an edition of the Hebrew that was standardized in the fifth to tenth centuries CE by rabbinic scholars (called *masoretes*, from *massorah*, probably "what is handed down," that is, "tradition"). The Masoretic Text accomplished two things: It settled upon a *consonantal* text, that is, it established specific choices for the letters of the Hebrew words in the text; and it *pointed* those letters with a system of markings that indicated which vowels should be read with the Hebrew letters. This two-part decision was necessary because classical Hebrew writing was in effect a system of consonants, with only a few ways of indicating vowel sounds. Words with the same consonants but different vowels would look the same, as would the English words "untrained" and "interned" if they were both spelled "ntrnd." In the notes to the Hebrew Bible of the NRSV, "Heb" may refer to the consonantal (unpointed) Hebrew text, and MT to the same text with the vowel pointings included. The distinction is an important one, because the consonants are more likely to represent the original text than are the vowel sounds, which were added later, though based on older traditions. If the same consonants will make more sense with different vowels, the NRSV (and most other modern translations) will assume that those different vowels yield a word that is closer to the original text.

When scholars had gotten the Masoretic Text into its final form, it became the standard text-form and alternative text-traditions were lost. It was therefore the case that all copies of the Hebrew Bible that were known were based upon this Masoretic Text, and although there were variants among the different copies, there was no way to check independently on the textual basis of most of the Hebrew Bible. With a few exceptions, this remained the case until the discovery of the Dead Sea Scrolls (the documents of the Qumran community) in 1947. Among the scrolls were manuscripts of most books of the Hebrew Bible that were over a thousand years older than the oldest manuscripts available up to that point. These more ancient copies of the Hebrew text have shed light on some passages in the traditional form of the biblical text. For example, at 1 Sam 10.27–11.1 in the traditional text there is no indication of the background to the conflict between King Nahash of Ammon and the men of Jabesh-gilead. But in a Qumran manuscript of 2 Samuel there is a continuation of 10.27 and an opening phrase for 11.1 that explains the context, and the NRSV includes them.

Ancient Versions of the Hebrew Bible

In cases where no form of the Hebrew text gives a reading that is satisfactory, scholars can turn to the ancient versions. The assistance these ancient versions give to textual critics and translators is partly due to the situation with regard to the text of the Hebrew Bible explained above. These early translations were made from Greek or Hebrew texts that, for the most part, are earlier than those copies of the Masoretic Text that have survived to the present. They therefore can give guidance to scholars about the state of the text, and even choices of wording, that are not represented in existing manuscripts. They can also confirm certain readings as being more likely. Of course, these ancient translations are themselves preserved only in copies, so that all of the considerations that apply to the original language texts of the Bible also apply to them: It is necessary to establish a critical text for them by comparing variant readings. They must therefore be used with caution, and they cannot be relied upon absolutely. This is, of course, a standard of comparison at one remove from the text itself: Scholars must look at the Greek, for instance, in the Septuagint, and conjecture or assume what the Hebrew would have been in order to result in a particular rendition into Greek. Nevertheless, it is a valuable source of clues.

For example, at 1 Sam 10.1, the text of the Septuagint is longer than that of the Hebrew Bible. In examining the difference, scholars have theorized that a copyist of the Hebrew text inadvertently omitted part of the verse because the same phrase occurs twice in it, and the copyist went directly from one to the other, omitting what was in between.

Names and Character of the Ancient Versions

The ancient versions of the Bible are referred to in a variety of ways by scholars. Following is a list, by language, of the chief versions.

Greek: The most prominent Greek version, and the oldest surviving translation of the Hebrew Bible, is the Septuagint, which was translated for use of Jews who were living in the Diaspora in Alexandria, Egypt, and other places around the Mediterranean in the centuries after the conquests of Alexander the Great, and who therefore spoke Greek. The Septuagint, from a word meaning "seventy" because of a legend that seventy or seventy-two scholars worked on it, is abbreviated LXX (the Roman numerals for seventy) and, in the notes to the NRSV of the Hebrew text, is referred to as "Gk". Three later Greek versions—by Aquila, Symmachus, and Theodotion—were produced for the use of Jews after Christians had taken over the Septuagint and the increasing conflict between Jews and Christians about the interpretation of the Jewish scriptures had led Jews to stop using the Septuagint. These versions are also sometimes used by translators, but none of them has survived in its entirety.

Aramaic: The Aramaic language was the official language of the Persian Empire, and the Jewish people who lived under Persian domination spoke Aramaic, which eventually supplanted Hebrew as the ordinary language of Jews. Aramaic is a Semitic language, like Hebrew, and shares some vocabulary with it, but Aramaic speakers cannot easily understand Hebrew. It was therefore necessary to provide translations of the Hebrew Bible for Aramaic speakers. Read aloud in liturgical contexts, after the Hebrew had been read (see Neh 8.7 for an early example), these translations, called *Targums*, are often more paraphrases than literal translations. They nevertheless provide useful information about earlier forms of the Hebrew text. In the NRSV notes they are abbreviated "Tg".

Syriac: The Syriac language is a form of Aramaic and was spoken by Jews in northern Syria who translated their Bible into it. The *Peshitta* (which means "simple," that is, a plain translation without textual comments) was prepared for the use of Jews and later taken over by Syriac-speaking Christians, who added a Syriac version of the New Testament to it. In the NRSV notes it is abbreviated "Syr". There is also a Syriac translation of the Septuagint that was part of a *hexapla* or "sixfold" Bible; in the NRSV notes this is abbreviated "Syr H".

Latin: Two Latin translations are used by scholars. The first, the "Old Latin" version, was actually a Latin translation of the Septuagint and of the New Testament dating from before the fourth century CE. More useful is the Vulgate, the translation prepared in the fourth century by the great biblical scholar Jerome. Jerome, in translating his Old Testament, worked directly from the Hebrew text of the time, and his version therefore can be helpful in determining original readings in that text. In the NRSV notes the Old Latin version is abbreviated "OL," and the Vulgate is abbreviated "Vg".

THE APOCRYPHAL/DEUTEROCANONICAL BOOKS: TEXTS AND VERSIONS

For most of the Apocryphal/Deuterocanonical Books, the translational basis is the Septuagint text. Various manuscripts of the Septuagint have survived, and the complete text is available in a critical edition prepared by Alfred Rahlfs and published in 1935. A newer critical text is in process of publication—the Gottingen Septuagint project—but it is not yet complete. The NRSV has used the newer text when it is available, for example in Esther and Sirach. The translators used Theodotion's version for the Additions to Daniel. For the Wisdom of Jesus ben Sira (Sirach or Ecclesiasticus), Hebrew manuscripts of large parts of the text have been discovered, and the NRSV has therefore used the Hebrew text instead of the Greek when it seems to offer a better alternative; in addition, there are Syriac and Latin versions of this book that also shed light on the text. For 2 Esdras, scholars agree that the best text is the Latin; they also consult versions in Syriac, Ethiopic, Arabic, Armenian, and Georgian.

THE NEW TESTAMENT: TEXTS AND VERSIONS

New Testament Manuscripts

Text critics must evaluate the evidence of thousands of manuscripts in order to establish the wording of the Greek New Testament. (See the article on "The Process of Textual Criticism" above.) This is a very large number of surviving copies for a collection of ancient documents; many classical texts survive in only a few copies. The overwhelming majority of these New Testament manuscripts (ca. 2,400) contain full or partial Gospel texts, followed by texts containing all or portions of the Pauline epistles (ca. 800). Revelation survives in only 287 copies. The manuscripts consist of papyrus fragments (some of only a few pages, some even shorter, preserving only a few verses); *uncials*, very early manuscripts written in letters unconnected to each other and similar to upper-case letters; and *minuscules*, later manuscripts written in a script that connects the letters and in which lower-case letters predominate. In addition to manuscript evidence, citations in Christian writers, lectionaries (excerpted passages for liturgical reading), and translations into other languages may figure into judgments about the earliest wording of the text. With such a wealth of evidence, there is no phrase in the New Testament for which there is not some variant. Most involve issues of grammar, style, or copyists' corrections. Textual variants that affect the theological meaning of the text are fewer.

With such a wealth of information about the New Testament text, scholars have had to develop ways of classifying not only individual manuscripts but groups of copies so that they can more readily deal with all of the variants. If they can determine, for example, that a group of copies all descended from a common ancestor, they can assess the variants for that group together and compare them with other groups that descend from different early copies. Variants that occur in two or more of these "families" have a much higher probability of being original than variants that may have arisen within only one group, for instance.

Most of the known variants to the text of the New Testament originated in the first two centuries of its existence. As Christianity spread throughout the Mediterranean, different groups had their own copies of the various New Testament documents, in some cases excluding books that are now included, or including books that are now excluded. (See the essay on "The Canons of the Bible.") In addition, the Greek copies began to diverge, and they also began to translate the texts into other languages: Latin, Syriac, and Coptic. The Latin text, because of the dominance of the Latin language in the western Roman Empire, became the most prevalent, and the Greek text was used consistently only in the east, in the area around Constantinople (modern Istanbul). This Greek text, preserved and copied in the Orthodox churches of the east, became known as the *Byzantine* text, and for many centuries it was the only or main version of the Greek text available. Beginning in the seventeenth and eighteenth centuries, however, scholars began to discover other early texts. Early in the twentieth century, text-critics proposed families or text-types linked to the major regions of Christianity: Alexandria in Egypt, to the south; the east represented by Caesarea; and the west represented by Italy/Gaul and Africa. At first scholars assumed that the Byzantine text resulted from combinations of these types, but such an attempt to provide a genealogy of the various text-types could not accommodate the mixture of readings found in the papyri and the oldest surviving codices. The so-called *Alexandrian* tradition, texts from the area of Egypt that included many of the most ancient papyrus copies (preserved in the very dry climate of that area), became in the nineteenth century a favored basis for establishing original readings. But the complexity of variants has increasingly made this approach, too, untenable.

Since the papyri evidence from the earliest centuries represents copies of particular books of the New Testament, it is likely that the scribes who set out to produce codices containing the entire Bible in the fourth century would have had a variety of different text-types for the individual books. Any codex, therefore, is not of uniform reliability. Codex Alexandrinus (early fifth century CE) is, as it turns out, a poor witness for the Gospels, but many critics consider it the best text of Revelation, even superior to a third-century papyrus copy. The age of a manuscript, therefore, does not necessarily determine the value of its readings, although it is one factor among many that scholars need to take into account. Writings such as Revelation and the shorter catholic epistles (2 and 3 John; Jude; 2 Peter), which were not widely used as scripture until the fourth century, have a different textual tradition than the Gospels and the Pauline epistles.

Consequently, most text-critics do not begin with a particular manuscript tradition and correct it to establish the text. Instead, the wealth and diversity of manuscript evidence have enabled critics to produce a Greek text based on *eclectic* principles: choosing the best readings from a variety of manuscript sources. This range of choice has also meant that New Testament scholars do not need to make conjectural emendations of the text, a practice common in the editing of other ancient texts, including the Hebrew Bible, where few early manuscripts are available. The best text for a particular passage requires detailed study of all preserved variants. Internal principles of textual criticism include consideration of readings that are more likely to be scribal corrections or errors, that fit the theological biases of an author or later editors, or that could have given rise to the other known variants.

The NRSV translation is based on a modern eclectic edition of the Greek text, *Nestle-Aland* 26th edition (or the equivalent *United Bible Societies Greek New Testament* 3rd edition, but incorporating information from the 4th edition as well). Textual variants in wording, both stylistic and theologically significant, are indicated in the translators' notes as "other ancient authorities." In order to understand the basis for these alternative translations, readers would have to consult the text-critical notes in the Greek text or a commentary on the Greek text.

Versions of the New Testament

The early Christian orientation toward the written word led to translation of the Bible into other languages for converts who did not speak Greek. Evidence from Old Latin, Syriac, and Coptic translations from the late second and third centuries CE figures in text-criticism. Armenian (early fifth century), Ethiopic (mid-fourth century), and Old Slavonic (late ninth century) translations form a key moment in the cultural life of the people. Many of the apocryphal writings are preserved in Syriac, Coptic, and Armenian, thus providing a wider literature associated with the Bible.

Often manuscript evidence for the earliest translations is scanty or only derived from quotations. Tertullian's quotations appear to be his own translation into Latin, so the first evidence for the text appears in Cyprian (250 CE). Augustine and Jerome both complain about the large number of poor translations in circulation. Jerome was commissioned by Pope Damascus to produce a Latin Bible (ca. 383). His revised Gospels and translation of the Hebrew Bible were combined with other translations for the remaining books of the Old and New Testaments to produce a Latin version known as the Vulgate. The Vulgate enjoyed wide circulation from the seventh century CE and was officially promulgated as the text of the Roman Catholic Church by Pope Sixtus V (1590). A neo-Vulgate with alterations in the text, style, and corrections to bring the translation closer to the Greek text was promulgated by John Paul II (1979).

The earliest evidence for the Syriac New Testament comes from a harmony of the Gospels, *The Diatessaron*, composed by Tatian in the second century CE. It is the source of citations in the commentary by Ephraem (310–373 CE). Texts from Antioch contributed to revisions of the Syriac New Testament, the Peshitta or common version (earliest manuscripts from the mid-fifth century CE), and a translation by Philoxenus (507/508 CE). The oldest versions of the New Testament translated into the Sahidic dialect of Coptic emerge in the third century CE. In the fourth century the whole Bible was translated into the Bohairic dialect, which became the official language of Coptic Christianity. A number of manuscripts found in the twentieth century remain to be assembled, catalogued, and incorporated into editions of the Coptic text.

Translation of the Bible into English

PRINCIPLES OF TRANSLATION

Bible translation, though in principle the same as any other translation, is distinguished from it by two considerations: first, the reverence in which adherents of Judaism and Christianity hold the text, leading to concerns whenever a new translation is published that the text be treated with the respect it deserves; and second, the great popularity of the Bible, which has led to the proliferation of translations to meet every conceivable need and audience. In order to find one's way among the great variety of Bible translations available today, it is important to understand the principles underlying all efforts at translation.

In any translation from one language to another—the "source" language, or the original, and the "target" language, or the translation—two basic approaches define the limits at either end of a continuum of methods. The technical names for these "pure" translation approaches are *formal equivalence* and *dynamic equivalence*. Formal equivalence is usually explained as "word-for-word" translation, and dynamic equivalence as "sense-for-sense" or "meaning-for-meaning." In general, formal equivalence places more importance on the qualities of the source language, and dynamic equivalence is more concerned with the resulting readability in the target language.

Except where the source and the target languages are closely related, however, a purely word-for-word approach would be almost unreadable. Such is the case with translations of the Bible: ancient Greek, Hebrew, Aramaic, and Latin (the languages of the original texts) are very different from modern English. Here, for example, is Mt 6.9–10 in a word-for-word rendering:

> Father of us who in the heavens, be holy
> the name of you;
> come the kingdom of you;
> become the will of you as in heaven and
> upon earth.

While it would be possible to puzzle out some meaning from this, it is clear that it is not English, and that an entire Bible translated along these lines would never be read. Most translations, therefore, move in the direction of dynamic equivalence, at least far enough to make sure that their representation of the original text makes sense in English. Some are more strict, for example always trying to use the same English word to translate a given Greek or Hebrew word (a characteristic known as "consistency"); some are freer, trying to achieve a more colloquial English style and using what seems to be the best English word for a Greek or Hebrew word in each separate context, regardless of how the same Greek or Hebrew word might be translated elsewhere. The result is a great range of translation choices for the Bible in English, from those suited to close study to those designed for readability, and readers can usually find a translation that will make sense to them and fit their needs.

In the case of ancient documents, and especially those of religious significance like the Bible, there are further complicating factors. Translations must find ways to deal with cultural differences between the worlds of the ancient writers and modern readers; they often try to accommodate traditional phrasing or translations, especially in key passages; and they must take into account the actual uses to which the translation will be put, including uses on formal and significant occasions.

Cultural differences come into consideration when a passage to be translated presents, not a puzzle about the dictionary definition of a word, but one about the way the word was used in its original cultural environment. An example occurs in the following passages: "the two kidneys with the fat that is on them" (Lev 3.4); "He slashes open my kidneys" (Job 16.13); and "In the night also my heart instructs me" (Ps 16.7). The word translated "heart" in the Psalm and "kidneys" in Leviticus and Job is the same Hebrew word, *kelayot* (or *kilyotay*, "my kidneys"). Literally it means the bodily organs, and in the passage from Leviticus that is clearly its meaning: The passage is discussing which parts of an animal will be burnt as a sacrifice. As a metaphor, however, it means the inner life of the human person, and that meaning is represented in the Psalm. The verse from Job falls somewhere in between. In its context, it is part of a catalogue of images of physical torture, intended to express spiritual or psychological suffering, many of which cannot be taken literally. There is a question whether it should be translated literally here. An ancient Israelite listening to these passages would have differentiated among this range of meanings, just as we would differentiate among "stomach trouble" and "I have no stomach for that job," or "heart surgery," "My heart stood still," and "Have a heart." In the case of the Hebrew word, the translation has to make that distinction for us, since the literal rendering "kidneys" in the passage from Psalms would make no sense, or the wrong sense, to a modern reader.

A related problem sometimes arises when translators have to consider whether to add a word to the text to make something clear to a modern reader that the ancient audience would have understood without explanation. For example, in 2 Pet 2.14, the literal translation "children of a curse" is rendered in the NRSV as "Accursed children!" This conveys the correct meaning in idiomatic English, but it does not convey to the modern reader what ancient hearers would assume, that the curse is from God. The New English Bible translation does this effectively by adding a word to make this implicit meaning explicit: "God's curse is on them."

An example of a translation trying to accommodate traditional understanding occurs in Jn 1.18, where the NRSV translates a Greek phrase as "God the only Son," and a footnote calls attention to two other possibilities. The Greek in actuality has three variants: *monogenes theos*, "only God"; *ho monogenes theos*, "the only God"; and *ho monogenes huios*, "the only Son." The translators first must decide how to render the Greek adjective *monogenes*. Older versions translate it as "only-begotten," but it really means something like "only one of its kind," i.e., "unique." Then they must determine which noun—"God" or "Son"—this adjective is supposed to modify. The manuscript evidence tends to support "God," since that variant appears in two papyri from the early third century CE, and also in manuscripts and citations from the fourth century. The variant "Son" only appears in the fifth century, in Codex Alexandrinus, and in later manuscripts. Since "only God" is present earlier, closer to the original time of writing, and since it is awkward, whereas "only Son" could be an effort to smooth out the text, it would seem that "only God" is the original reading. The NRSV effort to combine the two phrases is probably not correct.

Variety of use affects Bible translation particularly because many translations are intended for audiences that are far beyond the classroom or the scholar's study. In particular, Bible translations are intended to be read aloud in worship services, and bearing this in mind, many translators will try to use an English style that is more formal or elevated than that in the underlying text. Passages from the Bible are used in ceremonies marking significant life events, like marriage; on important national occasions, like the inauguration of a President; and to help express and channel great communal emotions, as in the funeral of a national leader. A translation that is too colloquial could seem jarring in such contexts.

Translations, thus, rather than being static, fixed creations that plug in one word in English for one word in the original language, are dynamic mediations between different and sometimes opposing tendencies. Insofar as they take the original language seriously as a controlling factor, they will tend to be word-for-word renderings; insofar as they take English seriously, they will tend more toward a meaning-for-meaning approach. They will try to represent not just the language, but the thought and cultural background, of the original writers and audiences; but they must also be sensitive to, and aware of, the great variety of needs among contemporary readers.

ENGLISH VERSIONS OF THE BIBLE

Prior to the sixteenth century, translations of the Bible into English were made from the Latin Vulgate instead of from Hebrew or Greek, and existed only in manuscript copies. The first English versions of the entire Bible were the two associated with John Wycliffe, translated from the Vulgate between 1380 and 1397. Part of the work on the first version was done by Wycliffe himself, and the rest, including all of the second, by scholars who were his immediate associates. Nicholas Hereford was largely responsible for the first version, which was completed before Wycliffe's death. John Purvey, Wycliffe's secretary, was responsible for the second version, which was completed by 1397. In the "General Prologue" to the second version Purvey states that it is best "to translate after the sentence and not only after the words, so that the sentence be as open, or opener, in English as Latin"—that is, so that the meaning be as clear, or clearer.

The sixteenth century brought the Bible in English to the common people as a printed book. The first English version directly translated from the Hebrew and Greek was the work of William Tyndale: The New Testament was published in 1526, the Pentateuch in 1530, and Jonah in 1531. In 1534 and 1535 he published revised versions of the New Testament, which were the basis of all later revisions and the main source of the authorized versions of the New Testament in English. Tyndale was finally betrayed into the hands of his enemies, and in October 1536 was strangled and burned at the stake.

Miles Coverdale's translation appeared in 1535, the first complete Bible in English. It was not a direct translation from the original languages, but was based on two Latin versions and the translations by Tyndale into English, and by the European reformers Luther and Zwingli into German. In 1537 Matthew's Bible was published. "Thomas Matthew" was a pseudonym of John Rogers, a friend of Tyndale, who took Tyndale's manuscript translations of the books of the Old Testament from Joshua to 2 Chronicles, together with Tyndale's printed translations of the Pentateuch and the New Testament, and published them in this one volume, which he completed by adding Coverdale's version of the rest of the Old Testament and the Apocrypha. In 1539 Richard Taverner, a layman and a lawyer, published a revision of Matthew's Bible, one edition of which was issued in parts so that people who could not afford to purchase the whole Bible might buy one or more parts. He was a good Greek scholar, and made some changes in the translation of the New Testament that have been kept in later versions. Meanwhile at Paris, in early 1538, Miles Coverdale had begun a new revision of Matthew's Bible which had been commissioned by Sir Thomas Cromwell, Secretary to King Henry VIII and Vicar General. The Great Bible, as this was called, was published at London in 1539. It was the first authorized English version, and a copy was ordered to be placed in every church. Until very recently, the Psalms in the *Book of Common Prayer* were from this translation. A revision of the Great Bible under the auspices of the Anglican bishops, the Bishops' Bible, was published in 1568 and revised in 1572. This revised edition was to become the basis of the King James Version.

Under the Roman Catholic Queen Mary the printing of the English Bible ceased and its use in the churches was forbidden. Many English Protestants sought refuge on the Continent, and a group of these at Geneva undertook the revision of the English Bible. The Geneva version appeared in 1560. It was a convenient size instead of an unwieldy folio, and was the first English version to use numbered verses, each set off as a separate paragraph. The Geneva Bible was never authorized, but it became the household Bible of the English-speaking nations for three-quarters of a century. It was the Bible of Shakespeare, John Bunyan, and the Puritans.

In 1582 an English translation of the New Testament was published at Rheims, made from the Latin by Roman Catholic scholars led by Gregory Martin, who had been trained at Oxford University. A similar translation of the Old Testament was published at Douay in 1609.

On February 10, 1604, after a conference "for hearing and for the determining things pretended to be amiss in the church," King James I ordained: "That a translation be made of the whole Bible, as consonant as can be to the original Hebrew and Greek; and this to be set out and printed without any marginal notes, and only to be used in all churches of England in time of divine service." He appointed fifty-four translators, forty-eight of whom are named in the records that have come down. They worked in six companies, to each of which was assigned a section of the Bible. Two companies met at Oxford, two at Cambridge, and two at Westminster. Each company would consider the work of the other companies, and differences would be resolved by correspondence if possible, and if not, be referred to the general meeting at the end. This was a meeting at London of a committee of six, made up of two representatives from the companies at each of the three centers, which devoted nine months to final editing. Dr. Myles Smith, of Oxford University, wrote an informative preface, "The Translators to the Reader." This Bible, with a dedication to King James, was published in 1611.

An outstanding merit of the King James Version is the music of its cadences, the result of a sure instinct for what would sound well when read aloud. For example, here are the successive translations of Prov 3.17, in praise of wisdom, where Coverdale, the Great Bible, and the Bishops' Bible agree in reading: "Her wayes are pleasant wayes and all her paths are peaceable." The Geneva Bible has: "Her wayes are wayes of pleasure and all her pathes prosperitie." The King James Version gives to the verse a perfect melody: "Her wayes are wayes of pleasantnesse, and all her pathes are peace."

The English Bible owes more to William Tyndale than to anyone else because the basic structure of his translation has endured. It has been estimated that about sixty percent of the text of the English Bible achieved its final literary form before the King James Version appeared, and that in the King James Version at least one-third of the New Testament is worded exactly as in Tyndale's New Testament, while the sentences of the remaining two-thirds follow Tyndale's general pattern.

For two and a half centuries the King James Version maintained its place as the Authorized Version of the English-speaking peoples, without any serious consideration of its revision, but in 1870 the Convocation of the Province of Canterbury appointed a Committee to undertake a revision. The Revised Version of the New Testament was published in 1881, the Old Testament in 1885, and the Apocrypha in 1895. The American Standard Version, containing the renderings preferred by the American scholars who had cooperated in the work of revision, was published in 1901. In 1928 the copyright of the American Standard Version was acquired by the International Council of Religious Education, and thus passed into the ownership of the churches of the United States and Canada that were associated in this Council through their boards of education and publication. The Council appointed a committee of Protestant scholars to have charge of the text of the American Standard Version and to undertake inquiry as to whether further revision was necessary. After more than two years of study and experimental work, this committee decided that there was need for a thorough revision of the version of 1901, which would stay as close to the King James tradition as it could in the light of present knowledge of the Hebrew and Greek texts and their meaning on the one hand, and present usage of English on the other. In 1937 the revision was authorized by the Council. The Revised Standard Version of the New Testament was published in 1946, the Old Testament in 1952, and the Apocrypha in 1957. The Revised Standard Version took full account of the new knowledge of the history, geography, religions, and cultures of Bible lands, and of rich new resources for understanding the vocabulary, grammar, and idioms of the ancient languages. It also returned to the basic structure and more natural cadence of the Tyndale-King James tradition.

The second half of the twentieth century saw the publication of many translations and revisions of the English Bible. In fact, between 1952 and 1990, when the New Revised Standard Version was published, no fewer than twenty-six different renderings of the complete English Bible were issued, with twenty-five additional translations and revisions of the New Testament. Among these the following Jewish, Protestant, and Catholic translations are of special note.

In 1955 the Jewish Publication Society, whose first translation of the Hebrew Scriptures had appeared in 1917, initiated a new translation. *The Torah, The Five Books of Moses*, was published in 1962, *The Prophets (Nevi'im)* in 1978, and *The Writings (Kethuvim)* in 1982. These three volumes, with revisions, were brought together in 1985 under the title *Tanakh, A New Translation of the Holy Scriptures According to the Traditional Hebrew Text.* The *Tanakh* has useful footnotes of three kinds—textual, translational, and explanatory—and is notable for its perceptive handling of Hebrew vocabulary and syntax in contemporary English.

A newer rendering of the Hebrew Bible, still in process, is that of Everett Fox, which tries to preserve as much as possible of Hebrew idiom in its English style. Portions that have so far appeared are Genesis (In the Beginning), 1983; Exodus (Now These are the Names), 1986; Torah (The Five Books of Moses), 1995; 1–2 Samuel (Give Us a King! Samuel, Saul, and David), 1999.

In the year that the RSV New Testament was published (1946), British Protestant churches embarked on a totally new translation of the scriptures, The New English Bible; the New Testament appeared in 1961, and a revised New Testament, along with the Old Testament and Apocrypha, in 1970. At that time, C.H. Dodd, director of the enterprise and chairman of the New Testament translation panel, stated that this was "not another revision of an old version, but a genuinely new translation of the original, which should be frankly contemporary in vocabulary, idiom, style and rhythm—not to supersede the Authorized Version, but as a second version alongside it." The rendering is free and vigorous, tending at places to be periphrastic. Here and there the translators have rearranged the sequence of verses and sections of the text. A revision, under the chairmanship of W.D. McHardy, was published as the Revised English Bible in 1989.

The first English Bible made from the original Hebrew and Greek languages that received Roman Catholic approval was The Revised Standard Version Catholic Edition, of which the New Testament was published in 1965 and the complete Bible in 1966. In it the Deuterocanonical Books were placed among the Old Testament books in accord with the Catholic canon. It was prepared by the Catholic Biblical Association of Great Britain with the consent of the Revised Standard Version Bible Committee and the Division of Christian Education of the National Council of Churches of Christ in the U.S.A. There are no changes in the Old Testament text; the sixty-seven changes in the New Testament, made for liturgical and theological reasons, are carefully noted in an appendix. A significant further advance toward a Common Bible was achieved with the publication of the RSV without any changes whatever in the Oxford Annotated Bible with the Apocrypha (1966), to which Richard Cardinal Cushing of Boston granted the imprimatur.

The first English translation of the Bible made from the original languages by Catholic scholars was The Jerusalem Bible, published in 1966. With close comparison with the Hebrew and Greek, it is based on the French translation made under the direction of l'École Biblique of Jerusalem by a committee of scholars headed by Père Roland de Vaux, O.P., and popularly known as La Bible de Jérusalem. The English translation was made by a British Committee headed by Alexander Jones, L.S.S., of Christ's College, Liverpool. The translation is well done and has been warmly received. At the same time it must be acknowledged that occasionally the French idiom intrudes. "Yahweh" is used instead of the surrogate, the LORD. The volume is provided with useful introductions and notes, and "thee," "thou," and "thine" disappear from the text. A full revision was published in 1985 as *The New Jerusalem Bible* under the supervision of Henry Wansbrough of Ampleforth Abbey, York.

The New American Bible, a translation by members of the Catholic Biblical Association of America sponsored by the U.S. Bishops' Conference, was published in 1970. The completed work renders the text into modern American language. A revision, now in process, completed the New Testament in 1987.

For readers new to English, the American Bible Society issued "Good News for Modern Man," a translation of the New Testament by Robert G. Bratcher, in 1966. Also called Today's English Version, it uses simplified syntax and a limited vocabulary. The Old Testament, prepared by a committee, came out in 1976, and the Deuterocanonical/Apocryphal books in 1979. The popularity of the Good News Bible spurred the preparation of another modern-speech Bible. This is the New International Version, sponsored by the New York Bible Society (subsequently the New York International Bible Society). The New Testament was published in 1973 and the complete Bible in 1978. Less colloquial than Today's English Version, and more literal than the New English Bible, the version was prepared by twenty teams of translators from evangelical Protestant traditions in the United States, Canada, Australia, New Zealand, and Great Britain.

The ecumenicity of our times is in various degrees represented in these newer translations, but perhaps most of all in the New Revised Standard Version. The committee that produced the Revised Standard Version is a continuing committee, holding meetings at regular intervals and having charge of the RSV text, and it has become both international and ecumenical, with the appointment of Catholic and Protestant members from Great Britain, Canada, and the United States. Since 1946 an American Jewish scholar had been a member of the Old Testament section. More recently a Greek Orthodox scholar joined. In 1974 the Division of Christian Education of the National Council of Churches directed that the Committee undertake a revision of the RSV Bible with the Apocrypha, mandating that necessary changes be made (1) in paragraph structure and punctuation; (2) in the elimination of archaisms while retaining the flavor of the Tyndale-King James Bible tradition; (3) in attaining a greater degree of accuracy, clarity, and euphony; and (4) in eliminating masculine-oriented language relating to people, so far as this could be done without distorting passages that reflect the historical situation of ancient patriarchal culture. Within the constraints set by the original text and the mandates given by the Division, the committee followed the maxim, "As literal as possible, as free as necessary." As a consequence, the New Revised Standard Version (1990) remains essentially a literal translation. Paraphrastic renderings were adopted only sparingly, and then chiefly to compensate for the lack of a common-gender third-person singular pronoun. The NRSV contains all of the books that are regarded as authoritative by Protestant, Roman Catholic, and Eastern Orthodox churches.

THE INTERPRETATION OF THE BIBLE

The Hebrew Bible's Interpretation of Itself

Since the different books that make up the Bible were written and became authoritative at various times, later books refer in various ways to earlier ones. From the beginning of this process, whenever the Bible or any section that eventually became part of the Bible was read or recited, it was interpreted. This is a natural process; no text can be read purely in the abstract, since we all bring our lives and experiences to the text and often attempt to bring the text closer to our lives. It is thus not surprising that according to Neh 8.8, when sections of the biblical text were read to the postexilic community in the fifth century, "They read from the book, from the law of God, with interpretation. They gave the sense, so that the people understood the reading." Like any book, the Bible required interpretation. Since it was to them an authoritative book, the people needed to hear not only the text itself but also its correct interpretation because, like any literary work, the Bible is at some points ambiguous.

Since the covenant-making ceremony mentioned above occurred in the fall, it was likely that one reading from the Torah would have been Lev 23.33–43, which outlines the commemoration of the fall harvest festival of booths (Sukkot), beginning on the fifteenth day of the seventh month (counting from Nisan, in the spring, not Tishri, in the fall). According to v. 40, proper commemoration of the festival includes the following: "On the first day you shall take the fruit of majestic trees, branches of palm trees, boughs of leafy trees, and willows of the brook; and you shall rejoice before the LORD your God for seven days." This passage is ambiguous on at least two points: What should the worshipers do after they "take" these various greens? What is meant by "the fruit of majestic trees" and "boughs of leafy trees," which are interspersed with very specific tree names ("palm," "willow")?

The treatment of Lev 23.33–43 in the later passage in Neh. 8.14–15 shows how this postexilic community interpreted the text of Leviticus, resolving these ambiguities: "And they found it written in the law [Heb *torah*], which the LORD had commanded by Moses, that the people of Israel should live in booths during the festival of the seventh month, and that they should publish and proclaim in all their towns and in Jerusalem as follows, 'Go out to the hills and bring branches of olive, wild olive, myrtle, palm, and other leafy trees to make booths, as it is written.'" Thus, the term "take" from Lev 23.40 is interpreted in the context of the immediately following legislation (v. 42)—"You shall live in booths for seven days"—to mean "take" for the construction of "booths." Furthermore, the ambiguous trees are specified as olive trees and myrtles. The way in which this later text clarifies how the earlier text should be understood is not at all remarkable: The types of branches to be used are clarified and, naturally enough, the broader context of the fall festival laws of Lev 23 is used to explicate the purpose for which these branches are taken.

The process of inner-biblical interpretation, where we can see a later biblical text interpreting an earlier one, began early in the history of the development of the Bible. But it was certainly accelerated by the canonization of the Torah (see the essay "The Canons of the Bible" on p. 453 ES and the Introduction to the Pentateuch, p. 3 HB). It is especially obvious in Deuteronomy, which in both its legal and its narrative sections reuses and interprets earlier biblical traditions. One example from each genre will illustrate the pervasive interpretive nature of Deuteronomy.

The law of a Hebrew slave is found in Ex 21.2–11, the Covenant Collection, and in Deut 15.12–18 as part of the Deuteronomic Law Collection. A quick glance indicates that these two texts are closely related and interdependent. Moreover, biblical scholarship has ascertained that the Deuteronomic Law Collection (D) is later than the Covenant Code (C). It is thus significant that the words "without debt" from Ex 21.2 are missing in D's retelling of this law. Instead we find the following which, based on its placement and context, is most likely D's interpretation of C's "without debt": "And when you send a male slave out from you a free person, you shall not send him out empty-handed. Provide liberally out of your flock, your threshing floor, and your wine press, thus giving to him some of the bounty with which the LORD your God has blessed you" (Deut 15.13–14). The Deuteronomist has naturally subsumed the text of C into his own intellectual-theological framework, which includes the idea that the underprivileged must be looked after carefully. For the Deuteronomist, "without debt" could not be interpreted literally and narrowly; instead it suggested that the slave must be released with resources to enable him to be self-sufficient so that he will not immediately find himself in debt again; thus the slave must be provided for. While this is not an obvious interpretation of Exodus and is certainly not what the author of Exodus intended by the phrase, it offers a good example of how a word may be reinterpreted by a later writer to fit a later ideology.

In fact, this particular reinterpretation is mild when compared with other, more radical reworkings of the earlier law in Deuteronomy. Take, for example, the insistence that the same law applies to both male and female slaves, in contrast to Ex 21.2–6,7–11. Note that the ear-piercing ceremony, which transpires if the slave opts to stay with the master, must take place at the owner's house (Deut 15.17), while Exodus suggests that it happens "before God," namely at the local shrine (Ex 21.6). According to Deuteronomy, the local shrines were illegitimate, and worship was permitted only at the Jerusalem Temple. This suggests that later writers, facing differing circumstances, did not always feel bound by the letter of earlier laws and could "interpret" them into new laws which the earlier legislators would hardly have recognized.

These same tendencies may be seen in Deuteronomy's reinterpretation of earlier narratives. Both Ex 18 and Deut 1.9–18 narrate the establishment of a judicial system in ancient Israel so that Moses would not be responsible for all legal cases. The theme and vocabulary of the two stories are so similar that it is clear that Deuteronomy has created its story by "interpreting" Exodus. Some of this interpretation is quite reasonable; for example, Deut 1.17, "Any case that is too hard for you," clarifies the somewhat ambiguous "every important [lit. "great"] case" of Ex 18.22. However, the change of Ex 18.21, "able men . . . who fear God, are trustworthy, and hate dishonest gain" to Deut 1.13, "individuals who are wise, discerning, and reputable," is not based on a straightforward interpretation of the earlier text. It is as if the author of this passage thought: Is it reasonable that righteousness in religious observance is the most important quality of judges? Surely not. Surely he meant "wise" when he said "men who fear God"! There are other cases of radical revision in this interpretive passage in Deut 1. The Deuteronomist, for example, "ignores" the fact that this judicial system was set up at the instigation of Moses' father-in-law, and transfers the initiative to Moses. Like any reader, the Deuteronomist interprets the story within his own mental framework, even if this means that a "new" story quite distinct from the original is created.

The previous illustrations show how ambiguities in texts are resolved, and how a text can be (consciously or unconsciously) removed from its original context and reinterpreted within the framework of the later reader's context. They reflect cases where the later biblical interpreters are simply acting as readers of texts, and these readings, though at points radical, have parallels to the way contemporary readers might engage secular works. As a composite canonical text, however, the Bible presents challenges of interpretation which are quite different from contemporary literary works. In particular, the Bible contains diverse legal traditions that are ultimately incorporated into a single work and thus somehow need to be read together or reconciled. Additionally, particular parts of the Bible, especially from prophetic texts, present themselves as divine truths; when these seem not to have come true, they must be interpreted differently.

A simple case where laws are contradictory occurs in the legislation concerning the cooking of the Passover lamb. Exodus 12.8–9 notes, "They shall eat the lamb that same night; they shall eat it roasted over the fire with unleavened bread and bitter herbs. Do not eat any of it raw or boiled in water, but roasted over the fire, with its head, legs, and inner organs." Deuteronomy 16.7, however, insists, "You shall boil it [NRSV "cook it" reflects an incorrect attempt at harmonizing the various laws] and eat it at the place that the LORD your God will choose." These differences are not at all surprising within a source-critical model, which suggests that they reflect different practices of different groups of people at different times. But what are we to do when both texts enter the canonical Bible?

We are not the first to appreciate this problem; it was already felt, for example, in the postexilic book of Chronicles, for which the Torah (more or less in the form that we know it) was authoritative. The Chronicler depicts the Passover celebration under King Josiah (2 Chr 35.13): "They boiled the passover lamb with fire according to the ordinance" [a literal translation; NRSV is harmonistic and incorrect]. The Chronicler has thus reconciled the two traditions by choosing elements from both: The offering is "boiled," following Deut 16.7, but "with fire" reflects the "roasted over the fire" of Ex 12.8–9. Through the brilliant (but problematic) expression "boiled . . . with fire," the two variant authoritative traditions are retained, and in some sense reconciled.

The manner in which various problematic prophecies are already interpreted within the Bible, so that they become true, is quite remarkable. The clearest example of this is from one of the latest texts of the Hebrew Bible, Dan 9. The background of this text is the prophecy in Jer 25.11, which suggests that Babylon will be given dominion over the world for seventy years; Jer 29.10 builds upon that prophecy, suggesting that after these seventy years are completed, Israel will be restored. This presented a serious problem for the author of Dan 9, living during the reign of the (Seleucid) Greek king, Antiochus IV Epiphanes, who persecuted the Jews and forbade them to follow the most fundamental laws (see Introduction to Daniel). In this period, between 167 and 164 BCE, it seemed that Jeremiah's word, which claimed that a complete restoration would transpire, was false. But also by that time it is likely that Jeremiah was already considered a true prophet, whose book was canonical. How could this true prophet utter an oracle that was so patently and painfully false?

This explains why Daniel "intensively consulted [NRSV "perceived in" is incorrect] the books concerning the number of years that, according to the word of the LORD to the prophet Jeremiah, must be fulfilled for the devastation of Jerusalem, namely, seventy years" (9.2). Because Jeremiah's prophecy seemed not to be true, intensive consultation was needed, so that the real meaning, the proper interpretation of the seemingly unambiguous "seventy years" [Heb *shib ʿim shanah*] could be deciphered. The angel Gabriel (v. 21) finally offers Daniel the correct interpretation (v. 24): "Seventy weeks [Heb *shabu ʿim shib ʿim*] are decreed for your people and your holy city: to finish the transgression, to put an end to sin, and to atone for iniquity, to bring in everlasting righteousness, to seal both vision and prophet, and to anoint a most holy place." The consonants of Jeremiah's *shib ʿim*, seventy, are read twice, first as *shabu ʿim*, "weeks," then as expected, as *shib ʿim*, "seventy." (In the period when Daniel was written, Hebrew used consonants only, so the same word could be pronounced, and understood as, two different words with different vowels.) The result of this intensive consultation is that Jeremiah's seventy means seventy weeks of years: seventy times seven or four hundred and ninety years. Thus, Daniel updated the prophecy and gave Jeremiah a four-hundred-twenty-year extension so that his prophecy could still be true.

The author has here engaged in what one scholar has called (in reference to similar rabbinic texts) "creative philology," reading and interpreting words in a highly creative fashion. Here, as in later rabbinic texts, this is not frivolous but is done out of necessity, in order to maintain the status of Jeremiah and his prophecies. Closely related to "creative philology" is "creative historiography," where an interpreter rearranges or adds to earlier texts, thereby creating a fundamentally new historical tradition. This may be seen very often in Chronicles, which frequently and ingeniously rearranges or adds to its sources, typically the books of Samuel and Kings. A classic example of this type of interpretation through "creative historiography" may be seen in 2 Chr 8.2, which claims that "Solomon rebuilt the cities that Huram [a variant spelling of Hiram] had given to him, and settled the people of Israel in them." This is an imaginative revision of 1 Kings 9.11–12, which tells of cities that Solomon gave to Hiram! The Chronicler read his source within his own interpretive framework and theology, which included the notion that the righteous Solomon could not possibly give away cities from the holy land of Israel; 2 Chr 8.2 is an interpretive attempt to deal with this theological problem.

These examples illustrate how later biblical passages interpret earlier passages. Many other examples from almost every biblical book could be offered, including more subtle cases where the interpretation is accomplished through textual juxtaposition, or the interpretive tradition is not found in a separate text (like Chronicles), but has entered as a type of gloss in the original text that it is interpreting. The examples cited above are meant to illustrate the range of inner-biblical interpretations; some are rather straightforward, clarifying ambiguities, while others are remarkably radical, transforming legal or narrative traditions in a quite extreme fashion. Finally, when seen in combination with the following essay on the premodern Jewish interpretation of the Bible (pp. 478–484 ES), these illustrations highlight the continuity between inner-biblical interpretation and early rabbinic interpretation. This continuity should not be surprising; not only are the two historically contiguous, but both work within a canonical framework. As a result, both are beset by all the problems, as well as the opportunities, that the canonization of the Hebrew Bible presented.

THE INTERPRETATION OF THE BIBLE

The New Testament Interprets the Jewish Scriptures

SCRIPTURE IN THE NEW TESTAMENT

The second-century CE satirist Lucian of Samosata, in Asia Minor, attacked the early Christian movement in the person of a charlatan prophet, Peregrinus. Peregrinus feigned conversion, rose to the position of local bishop, and gained considerable prestige among his naïve coreligionists when he was imprisoned for the faith, before assuming another career. How did Peregrinus achieve his exalted position? According to Lucian, "He interpreted and explained some of their books and even composed many and they revered him as a god, made use of him as a lawgiver" (*On the Death of Peregrinus* 11). By the mid-second century CE, then, Christians could be mocked for their preoccupation with interpreting sacred texts as well as for composing their own writings. At least in part, such interpretation was understood to involve the promulgation of laws. Whether "a lawgiver" pronounced legal rulings on community discipline or codified ethical norms is not clear. From the point of view of the educated elite, Christians who followed such unlearned bishops could be duped because they, as well as their leaders, lacked the advanced rhetorical training required for the interpretation of texts.

Similar objections are given voice within the New Testament. Local Pharisees scorn the blind man's confession that Jesus is from God, not a sinner, on the grounds that he has no standing to interpret the Torah (Jn 9.24–34). Matthew insists that the scribe trained for the kingdom of heaven brings from his storehouse both new things and old ones (Mt 13.52). He defends Jesus' understanding of the Torah and the prophets as attending to the substantive matters—justice, mercy, and faithfulness—rather than making burdens of details about tithing as the Pharisees do (Mt 23.23–24). Paul insists that the true meaning of the law remains veiled, like Moses' face, from his fellow Israelites. They can only understand its meaning by turning to Christ (2 Cor 3.7–18).

Thus, most biblical interpretation in the New Testament serves a polemical or apologetic purpose: to defend Christian claims about Jesus. Neither the assertions themselves nor the presuppositions employed to derive them from scripture would be acceptable to those who did not share those presuppositions. Nevertheless, the interpretative methods used, especially by Matthew and Paul, have much in common with those used in early Jewish tradition.

Though Christians had begun to consider their own writings as sacred texts by the mid-second century CE, that was not yet true of the period during which the New Testament was being written. Only the latest of the New Testament texts, 2 Peter, suggests that a collection of Paul's letters was beginning to be regarded as authoritative (2 Pet 3.15–16). Thus, whenever a New Testament writer refers to or quotes scripture, he is interpreting texts so regarded by the Jewish community. The scriptures were known to these writers, however, not in their original Hebrew, but in Greek translation, the Septuagint (see "Hebrew Bible: Texts and Versions," p. 462 ES and "The Greek Bible," p. 456 ES). Since various text forms of the Septuagint were known in Judea itself, it was clearly used by Jews and not only by Gentile converts to Christianity. In many cases, the text that a New Testament author quotes or interprets differs from that found in a modern translation of the Hebrew Bible. We cannot claim that the author is quoting from memory, misquoting, or altering the text unless we have compared it with the Septuagint and not only with the Hebrew.

The writings that counted as scripture for the New Testament writers are those they held in common with Diaspora Jews: the Torah, prophets, Psalms, and assorted texts from the Writings. In frequency of quotation and allusion in the New Testament, Psalms and Isaiah predominate, followed by Deuteronomy and other passages from the Torah. Some are introduced with a formula such as "it is written" (Mt 2.5; Lk 20.17; Acts 15.15–18) or "it was said" (Mt 5.21). In other cases, the expression "that is" combined with application of the text to reading the community's experience as part of God's eschatological plan resembles the interpretation of prophetic passages in the interpretive commentaries ("pesharim") among the Dead Sea Scrolls from Qumran (Mt 3.3; 11.10; Jn 6.31,50; Acts 2.16; 4.11; Rom 9.7–9; 10.6–8; Heb 7.5; 1 Pet 1.24–25; see 1 QpHab 12.6; CD 7.14–15; 4Q174 1.11–14). Use of an adversative expression to correct a prior tradition of interpretation, as in Matthew's "you have heard . . . but I say" (Mt 5.21–22,27–28,31–32,33–34,38–39 43–44) resembles a rabbinic formula (*Midr. Pss.* 119.26). Matthew does not continue in the rabbinic mode, however, which would require that Jesus establish his interpretation by appealing to other texts from scripture.

CHRISTOLOGICAL READING OF SCRIPTURE

The primary focus of New Testament biblical interpretation is the belief that Jesus is God's messiah, the agent of God's eschatological salvation. Certain texts are repeatedly interpreted with a strong messianic meaning: Ps 2; 8; 110; Deut 18.15,18–19; and 2 Sam 7.14. Prophecies from Joel 2–3 (Acts 2.16–21), Zech 9–14 (Mark 11.1–2; Heb 10.19), Dan 7 (Mk 13.26), and Dan 12 (John 5.29) play a major role in understanding the risen and exalted Jesus as the one who has inaugurated the end-time. Daniel 7.13–14 lies behind the christological confession of Jesus as the Son of Man who will come in judgment (see Mk 14.62). In many cases, the reference to Daniel is not explicitly marked. Readers who do not recognize the allusion—or are not aided by the marginal notes found in a modern edition—may miss the use of allusions or partial quotations to support a claim about Jesus.

Even when the text being employed is evident, one cannot always determine whether the author is using the passage as an isolated prooftext or intends readers to incorporate elements from its larger biblical context into the interpretation. Among the Qumran texts, testimony collections gather biblical passages on a particular topic. Some combine references to a future prophet (4Q175: Deut 5.28–29; 18.18–19; 33.8–11; Num 24.15–17; 4Q174: 2 Sam 7.10–14; Ps 1.1; 2.1–2). If early Christians used such assemblages of individual texts on a theme, the larger context of any quotation (which would not have been given in the collection) is irrelevant. When the same texts are quoted in the same combination by different authors, such a source may well be behind all of them. Christ as the stumbling stone based on Isa 8.14; 28.16; and Ps 118.22 appears in several places (Mt 21.42; Acts 4.11; Eph 2.20; 1 Pet 2.6). Matthew's set of fulfillment quotations, which assert that events in the life of Jesus were foretold by the prophets (1.23 [Isa 7.14; 8.8]; 2.6 [Mic 5.2], 18 [Jer 31.15], 23 [source uncertain; see Judg 13.5,7; Isa 11.1; 53.2]; 4.14 [Isa 9.1–2]; 8.17 [Isa 53.4]; 12.17–21 [Isa 42.1–4]; 21.4–5 [Zech 9.9]) may have been taken from a collection of prooftexts. They exhibit the particular significance of Isaiah in early Christian understanding of the suffering and death of Jesus.

Christians, using the Septuagint translation, were able to read Isaiah's original reference to a young woman who will soon bear a child, as a reference to the miraculous birth of God's messiah from a virgin (Isa 7.14). When Matthew embedded this text into the story of Jesus' birth, he fixed its Christian interpretation in the imagination. A similar kind of reinterpretation arose in dealing with the end of Jesus' life: The necessity of explaining how Jesus' death fit into God's plan drew Christian attention to passages describing God's suffering righteous one. Early interpretation matched details in the story of

Jesus' passion to passages in Isaiah (for example, abuse of the prisoner from Isa 50.6 and 53.5; see Mt 27.67–68). Some scholars think that Jesus himself may have begun this process by applying texts concerning the suffering righteous one and the coming "son of man" (Dan 7.13–14) to his ministry.

Isaiah's prophecies about the salvation that is coming to Zion also play an important role in the Gospel narratives. The announcement of salvation to the suffering ones in Isa 61.1–3 has been embedded in an inaugural speech of Jesus (Lk 4.17–19). The same passage is reflected in Matthew's Beatitudes (Mt 5.3–12). Images of the day of salvation from Isaiah dominate the Christian liturgical celebrations of Advent, Christmas, Lent, and Easter. So firmly are these passages fixed within a christological interpretation tradition that many Christians find it impossible to imagine that they could refer to anything other than the coming of salvation in Jesus.

As Christians came to articulate claims about Jesus' identity as the unique Son of God, they used biblical texts to support this view in a more polemical way. Jesus is shown to prove his own superiority to the human descendants of David with a clever twist on Ps 110.1 (Mk 12.35–37): David himself (the presumed author of the Psalm) uses the title "Lord" of the messiah. Hebrews 1.5–14 attaches a number of other Psalm texts to Ps 2.7 as evidence that Jesus is God's Son and as such exalted above the angels. John 10.31–39 has Jesus cite Ps 82.6 in self-defense when he is accused of blasphemy for claiming to be the unique representative of God. In all of these examples, interpreting the Bible is not pursued for its own sake. Rather, Christian beliefs about Jesus are prior to the biblical passages produced to support them. The result, however, is that certain passages from the prophets and Psalms have become so embedded in the gospel narrative that for the Christian imagination they are the story of Jesus.

SCRIPTURE AND CHRISTIAN PRACTICE

Matthew 5.17–20 defends the teaching of Jesus against the charge of dissolving the Torah and the prophets. The Torah is identified with the exactitude of the written Hebrew scrolls, and Matthew affirms its divine authority in every particular. The Christian understanding represents the fulfillment of the Torah and prophets by establishing a righteousness superior to that taught by scribes and Pharisees. What principle underlies the adversative readings that follow in Mt 5.21–28? A common solution attributes to Jesus the authority of a messianic interpreter of the law. He can determine its intent with an authority greater than that of those Jewish interpreters who appeal to the oral tradition that was presumed to have been given by Moses. Disputed points are to be resolved once and for all based on the "prophet like Moses" of Deut 18.15–18 (see Jn 4.19,25). In what follows, Jesus and his followers are shown to do more, not less, than the Torah requires. The debate over divorce in Mt 19.3–13 employs a related argument. Though the Torah contains provisions for granting a divorce (Deut 21.1), Jesus claims that Moses introduced such stipulations as a concession. They do not reflect the will of God as revealed in Gen 1.27. The Genesis text also figures in a critique of social laxity about divorce in the Dead Sea Scrolls (see CD 4.19–21). Thus it was used to indicate God's intention concerning marriage prior to the time of the Qumran community (second century BCE through first century CE). The Qumran tradition, however, does not use it, as the New Testament does, to negate the legal standing of another text of the Torah. This passage from Matthew implies that the point of "messianic" interpretation is to restore the intention of the original lawgiver, namely God. Matthew 5.48 concludes on a similar note. Righteousness implies assimilation to God's own perfection.

New Testament authors do not interpret the details of legal traditions found in the Jewish scriptures. Rather a series of "summary principles" serves to demonstrate that the intention of the Torah has been realized in the Christian community. Matthew 7.12 uses the "golden rule" as such a summary, for instance. The most common Christian summary focuses on the injunction to love God and the neighbor, the love command (see Mk 12.28–34; Jn 13.34–35; Rom 13.8–10; Gal 5.14; Eph 5.1–2; 1 Thess 4.9–10; Heb 13.1; Jas 2.8). Matthew 23.23–24 employs the distinction between attention to observance of detailed precepts concerning tithing and the "weightier matters"—justice, mercy, and faithfulness. This passage has, apparently, been reformulated from Matthew's Jewish Christian perspective, since it presupposes the development of the law on tithing (Deut 14.22–29, later taken to include dill and cumin). The parallel in Lk 11.42 fits the more common New Testament pattern. Those condemned fail in justice and love of God, that is, the obligation to love God and neighbor. Though the text is not quoted exactly, Matthew's formula probably reflects Mic 6.8.

Christians presume that the stories concerning Israel provide instructional examples for their community. Tales of unfaithfulness or grumbling in the wilderness were particularly popular (see 1 Cor 10.1–13; Heb 3.7–4.13). Abraham serves as an example of the works (such as hospitality) appropriate to faith (Jas 2.21–26 includes Rahab as an example). The heading "faith" introduces a catalogue of biblical models in Heb 11.1–40, which serves as a summary of the biblical story from Abel through the prophets. Though "by faith" has been inserted into each example, the particular story which follows does not always represent faith, at least not in the same way. The christological exegesis by which Hebrews argued that Jesus as exalted Son of God was foreseen by the Psalms and prophets and that the sacrificial death of Jesus ended the need for Jewish sacrificial rituals (Heb 7.1–10.18) shapes this catalogue as well. Each of the heroes in the catalogue merits a promised reward for fidelity to God which has been deferred until the establishment of a heavenly people of God through Jesus (11.13–16).

SCRIPTURE IN CHRISTIAN POLEMIC

The Christian conviction that scripture spoke to and about their community even when it was made up largely of Gentiles (as in 1 Pet 1.10–23) resulted in polemical use of the biblical text against its literal meaning. The strategies employed in several of the more striking re-readings became fixed principles in early Christian exegesis: typology, allegory, and the distinction between the "spirit" and the "letter" of the text. Typology is a method of reading a text that sees characters, incidents, or themes within it as representing "types," or impressions, of a central form, the "antitype." When a coin or medallion was struck, the copies produced were called types, and the name therefore came to signify all of the related images based on one master design. Typological readings already occurred in the Hebrew Bible; the prophet known as Second Isaiah, for instance, interpreted the return from exile typologically as a second Exodus (Isa 48.20–21, alluding to Ex 17.1–7). In the New Testament, interpreting a biblical text typologically presumes that persons or events in the narrative provide a pattern of Christian experience; for instance, Israel's passage through the Red Sea and eating manna foreshadow Christian baptism and eucharist (1 Cor 10.1–4). In other cases, the relationship of the Christian person, idea, or event may be antithetical to the person, idea, or event found in scripture; for instance, Paul contrasts Adam and Christ (Rom 5.12–21), part of Paul's argument for faith rather than the law as the principle of salvation.

Paul's use of the Abraham story to defend the thesis moves into terrain foreign to the obvious meaning of the story. Genesis 15.6 is taken to mean that Abraham's righteousness depends only on faith (Rom 4.1–25). Some scholars call this type of argument "midrash," a traditional Jewish form of interpretation, in which one text is supplemented by others to extract a further meaning. Psalm 32.1–2 plays this role in Rom 4.7–8. John 6.30–51 contains a lengthy dispute in which the incarnate Christ is said to be the meaning of Exodus. Biblical references in the Fourth Gospel are notoriously indefinite. John 6.31 reflects some combination of Ex 16.4,15; Ps 78.24; and Wis 16.28. Such typologies do not deny that scripture refers to persons and events that belong to Israel's past. Their significance in God's plan of salvation, however, requires that they be recognized as prefiguring the Christian reality.

Paul's treatment of the Abraham story in Gal 4.21–31 moves beyond simple typology to a method of interpretation that becomes more prevalent in later Christian writers: allegory. Allegory in its pure sense is an extended comparison between two different levels, usually a narrative level and a psychological or spiritual level, in which the writer, speaking directly about the narrative incidents and characters, intends and is understood to mean to speak about the symbolic level. This kind of reading had already been adapted from Greek interpretive practice by the Jewish writer Philo of Alexandria (ca. 15 BCE–50 CE). In Galatians, the son born of a slave woman is rather shockingly associated with the Sinai covenant and all those who seek to be bound by it. Descendants of Isaac are not physical descendants of Abraham, but children of a promise. Paul concludes that since Gen 21.10 permits the slave woman and her son to be cast out, his audience should do the same to any Christians who insist upon belonging to Israel "according to the flesh." Even in what appears a blatant misreading of the Abraham story, Paul presumes that the text has a literal sense as well. Abraham, Isaac, Sarah, and Hagar are not merely symbolic figures representative of the two parties to the conflict in Galatia.

Later theories of allegorical meaning found support in Paul's distinction between "the letter that kills" and the life-giving "Spirit" in 2 Cor 3.6. The polemical context of this passage sets

Paul and his preaching over against what appear to have been Jewish Christian missionaries. Again Paul's version of Ex 34.28–35 in the argument which follows inverts the Jewish traditions of the Targums. The standard Jewish explanations of this passage assume that the splendor on Moses' face either remained permanently or increased. For Paul's Jewish contemporaries the glory on Moses' face and the eternity of the Sinai covenant are closely associated (see Pseudo-Philo, *Biblical Antiquities* 11.5; 19.10–16; 32.7; 1Q34 2.5–8). Israel's sin makes it impossible for the people to look upon the glory reflected in the face of Moses. Paul instead assumes that the veiling of Moses' face was a means of hiding the evidence of a fading glory, that is, an impermanent covenant. He asserts that he is the servant of a new, eternal covenant established through the Spirit (Jer 31.18,33; Ezek 36.26), not the letters carved on the tablets of stone.

With the Latin rendering of Greek *gramma* ("letter") as *littera*, its identification with the carved tablets of Torah gave way to "letter" as meaning the entire written text. Paul's antithesis of Spirit and letter was taken to be a hermeneutical principle rather than a polemical attack on the eternity of the law (also see Rom 2.27–29; 7.6). From this perspective, a literal reading of the text fails to convey its truth. Only the spiritual interpretation which associates scripture with the revelation of God in Christ conveys life. Israel may then stand for any persons who are trapped by the literal sense of the text and who therefore fail to interpret all of the scriptures in light of Christ.

THE INTERPRETATION OF THE BIBLE

Jewish Interpretation in the Premodern Era

There is a strong continuity of approaches between the inner-biblical interpretation of the Hebrew Bible (see above, p. 471 ES) and its interpretation in later Jewish tradition. The later interpreters faced the same issues as those from the end of the biblical period: the ambiguity of certain words, the desire to bring the text closer to Jewish life, and the fact that they now had to deal with these texts as canonical, that is, both authoritative and closed to further additions. Not surprisingly, they adopted and adapted many of the same solutions, especially the use of creative philology and creative historiography, in order to give the static text greater elasticity. Certain interpretive innovations appeared at particular periods, either as creative breakthroughs within the Jewish tradition or as a response to outside influences; among the latter were the use of the Old Testament in the Christian community for christological purposes and the study of Muslim interpreters of the Koran. By and large, however, continuity rather than discontinuity characterized the premodern interpretation of the Bible. The connection between early postbiblical interpretation and the preceding late inner-biblical interpretation was also uniform.

There is, however, major discontinuity in the genres through which the interpretations are expressed. Postbiblical interpretation recognizes the Bible as a canonical text, and it thus introduces the genre of commentary, in which a biblical passage is quoted with an introductory phrase separating the canonical text from its gloss or interpretation. This separation of text from commentary highlights the significance of the biblical text. It is fundamentally different from inner-biblical interpretation, in which the interpretive addition is often inserted into the text itself without differentiating text and commentary, or in which scripture is rewritten; for example, Deuteronomy rewrites sections of Exodus, or Chronicles rewrites Samuel-Kings (see above, pp. 472–474 ES). Although the practice of interpreting the text by rewriting it continued for a short period after the canonization of the Hebrew Bible, it was largely replaced by commentaries of various sorts. For clear theological reasons, these commentaries were interested in differentiating between the canonical biblical text and its interpretation.

TRANSLATION AS INTERPRETATION

The earliest postbiblical interpretive traditions, however, are found in another new genre, Bible translation. In the postexilic period, after the return from the Babylonian exile where the common language was Aramaic, many Jews were no longer fluent in Hebrew, and the Bible was for the first time translated into Aramaic. Though these earliest translations are no longer extant, we do have later translations of sections of the Bible that predate the destruction of the Second Temple (70 CE) from the Dead Sea community of Qumran, as well as a set of Aramaic translations, called Targums, that crystallized at a later date in both Babylon and Israel. In addition, the Bible was translated into Greek in Alexandria, Egypt, beginning in the third century BCE. This translation, called the Septuagint (the translation of the seventy), is of great value and is supplemented by a variety of other Greek translations, some of which were found at Qumran. (See "Hebrew Bible: Texts and Versions," pp. 462–464 ES.)

These translations illustrate the truism that all translations are interpretations. More particularly, they demonstrate the range of translation approaches, from literal interpretation to free paraphrase. (See the essay on "Translation of the Bible into English" for a discussion of translation approaches.) For example, the Septuagint and the Aramaic translation called Targum Onqelos are typically word-for-word, literal versions, as far as that is possible. Yet even these "literal" translations show nonliteral tendencies at certain points. For example, Onqelos was aware of the fact that the biblical verse, "You shall not boil a kid in its mother's milk" (Ex 23.19; 34.26; Deut 14.21), was generalized in early Jewish tradition and served as the basis for the prohibition of eating dairy products and meat together. For this reason, Onqelos translates the biblical text according to the rabbinic tradition, rendering it, "Do not eat meat with milk." The interpretive nature of the Septuagint is especially obvious in Psalms. Following an interpretive tendency that already existed in the Hebrew Bible, whereby several psalms were given historical superscriptions that contextualized them in the life of David (e.g., Ps 51, "To the leader. A Psalm of David, when the prophet Nathan came to him, after he had gone in to Bathsheba"), superscriptions were added to several additional psalms (e.g., Ps 27, introduced in the Septuagint with "A Psalm of David, before he was anointed"). Thus, a biblical model was followed, and new introductions, which provided new interpretive "Davidic" frameworks for these psalms, were composed.

In other cases, nonliteral translations were offered because the theology of the author and his community disagreed with what the text explicitly said; this is the philosophical equivalent of the translation by Onqelos of "You shall not boil a kid in its mother's milk" as "Do not eat meat with milk." For example, Num 12.8 says of Moses, "he beholds the form of the LORD," a notion that was very disturbing to the translator of the Septuagint, for whom the predominant image of Deuteronomy, that God has no form (see esp. Deut 4.12,15), was normative. The translator thus assimilated what the text explicitly says into his theology (and into the Priestly theology, which emphasizes the manifestation of God through his "glory"), and rendered this section of the verse as "and he saw the glory of the LORD." This was the same sort of change discussed above (p. 472 ES) when both Deuteronomy and Chronicles rewrote (rather than translated) earlier texts, changing them so that they conform to the later theology.

These cases of nonliteral, exegetical translations are rather tame when compared to some of the highly expansionistic translations seen in the Targums, especially those originating in Palestine. Most remarkable is the case where the Targums "translate" the *Akedah* or the binding of Isaac (Gen 22). In the biblical account, Isaac has a relatively minor role and is a character who is acted upon rather than one who acts. The Targums, however, interpret the story in such a way that Isaac now plays a major role. For example, Targum Pseudo-Jonathan glosses v. 10 as follows: "Abraham put forth his hand and took the knife to slaughter his son. Isaac spoke up and said to his father: 'Tie me well lest I struggle because of the anguish of my soul, with the result that a blemish will be found in your offering, and I will be thrust into the pit of destruction.' The eyes of Abraham were looking at the eyes of Isaac, and the eyes of Isaac were looking at the angels on high. Isaac saw them but Abraham did not see them. The angels on high exclaimed: 'Come, see two unique ones who are in the world; one is slaughtering, and one is being slaughtered; the one who slaughters does not hesitate, and the one who is being slaughtered stretches forth his neck'" (*Targum Pseudo-Jonathan: Genesis*, trans. Michael Maher. Collegeville, Minn: Liturgical, 1992, p. 79). (The translation in Targum Neofiti is similar.)

The Targum to Song of Solomon is even more remarkable in the way in which it assimilates the text to its general understanding that the book should be interpreted as a historical allegory. Thus, its "translation" of 1.2, "Let him kiss me with the kisses of his mouth! For your love is better than wine," reads as follows: "Solomon the prophet said: 'Blessed be the name of God who gave us the law via Moses the scribe, a law inscribed on two tablets of stone, and six orders of the Mishnah and the Talmud by oral tradition, and spoke to us face to face as a man kisses his companion, from the abundance of the love with which he loved us, more than the seventy nations'" (Marvin Pope, *Song of Songs* [*Anchor Bible*], New York: Doubleday, 1977, p. 299). A similar, very expansionistic translation of Genesis may also be seen in the much earlier Aramaic Genesis Apocryphon, found among the Dead Sea Scrolls.

PESHARIM

Though rabbinic interpretation is seen as the normative or mainstream type of premodern Jewish interpretation, that mode of interpretation is really not new, but shows much continuity with the postbiblical interpretation seen in the Dead Sea Scrolls and in Greek Jewish writing as well. The genre of Qumran literature called Pesher literature, in which a biblical text is first quoted, and then its interpretation is adduced, is structurally similar to rabbinic Midrash (see below) and medieval commentary. Pesher literature is distinct, however, from rabbinic literature (though not from the type of Jewish interpretation evidenced in much of the New Testament) in that it typically applies (mostly prophetic) texts to the author's current situation with the assumption that the biblical text, though written long ago, refers to the later author's time period. For example, Pesher Habakkuk quotes (in a slightly different form) the words of the seventh-century prophet Habakkuk (2.15), "Alas for you who make your neighbors drink, pouring out your wrath until they are drunk, in order to gaze on their nakedness," and then continues: "Its interpretation concerns the Wicked Priest who pursued the Teacher of Righteousness [the leader of the Qumran community] to consume him with the ferocity of his anger in the place of his banishment, in festival time, during the day of Atonement. He paraded in front of them, to consume them and make them fall on the day of fasting, the sabbath of their rest (trans. Florentino García Martínez and Elbert J.C. Tigchelaar, The Dead Sea Scrolls Study Edition, Leiden: Brill, 1977, vol. 1, pp. 19,21).

An example of (proto)rabbinic interpretation of legal material already found in this prerabbinic community is illustrated by the following interpretation from the Damascus Covenant, another key text of the Qumran community: "No one should do work on the sixth day, from the moment when the sun's disc is at a distance of its diameter from the gate [= the horizon], for this is what it says [Deut 5.12], 'Observe the sabbath day and keep it holy'" (CD X.15) (Dead Sea Scrolls Study Edition, ibid., pp. 567,569). This legal text is quoting the Decalogue from Deuteronomy, and is interpreting the first word, *shamor*, in a more literal sense as "guard"; it continues by suggesting that the way in which one guards the sabbath day is by ceasing from work a bit before the sabbath actually begins, the time when the sun is one diameter away from setting. This would, of course, help to prevent violation of the sabbath, which, according to the Bible, is a capital offense. Yet such stringent observance is never actually required by the biblical text; rather, it is "found" in the text through a slightly unusual reading, using (only mildly) creative philology on the Hebrew word *shamor*, "observe," which is understood as "guard."

CREATIVE HISTORIOGRAPHY

Prerabbinic texts are also useful in terms of tracing the notion of "creative historiography" from the late biblical through the early rabbinic periods. *Jubilees*, a pseudepigraphic book written in the second century BCE, at about the same time as Daniel, is filled with examples of creative historiography. For example, in retelling the creation story, *Jubilees* adds to the biblical text, noting among other additions that angels are fashioned on the first day of creation. Law is of paramount importance for this author, and he therefore retrojects many legal obligations from Exodus-Deuteronomy into his retelling of the book of Genesis, so that Genesis would not be "merely" a narrative work. (This shows, incidentally, that the emphasis on "law" was not a rabbinic or Pharisaic innovation.) In addition, because the Torah was canonical for the author of *Jubilees*, the two different creation stories, which critical scholars see as separate (Gen 1.1–2.4a; 2.4b–3.24), are read canonically as a single story by one divine author. As a result, the second (Yahwistic) story is used to fill in the details of the more laconic first (Priestly) story. There is nothing remarkable about this development: Once the Bible is read canonically and the existence of sources forgotten, it becomes natural to interpret the stories in this fashion.

Josephus, the Jewish historian of the first century CE, also offers many examples of creative historiography in his *Jewish Antiquities*. He often remolds biblical characters so that they better fit the ideals of his Greco-Roman audience. He also restructures biblical texts, so that problems inherent in the text as it is currently ordered are resolved. For example, Gen 10 contains a genealogical description of the nations of the world that recounts their dispersion. Yet this is followed by the Tower of Babel story, which begins with the geographical unity of humanity. Josephus brilliantly solves this problem by reversing the order of these chapters, putting the genealogies after the story of the Tower of Babel. This is an early example of what would later become a fundamental principle of Jewish interpretation, that the narrative order of the biblical text does not necessarily represent the chronological order of the events it is depicting.

Jubilees and Josephus are also important because they offer explicit justifications for their radical rewriting of earlier traditions. *Jubilees* presents itself as revealed to Moses on Sinai with the help of a mediating angel. Josephus notes in the introduction to *Antiquities*: "The precise details of our scripture will, then, be set forth, each in its place, as my narrative proceeds, that being the procedure that I have promised to follow throughout this work, neither adding nor omitting anything" (Josephus, *Jewish Antiquities*, Books I–IV, trans. Henry St. John Thackeray [Loeb Classical Library], Cambridge, Mass: Harvard University Press, 1967, p. 9). If these two ideas may be combined, we have much of the basis for the rabbinic interpretation of the Bible, which understood itself as (1) the legitimate (oral) law revealed to Moses on Sinai, which was passed down from generation to generation; and (2) the authoritative law, which might differ in word from the phraseology of the biblical text, but is, in reality, "neither adding nor omitting anything."

RABBINIC INTERPRETATION

There is a final, crucial assumption of the classical rabbinic world, which is best represented by the Mishnah (codified ca. 200 CE), the Babylonian Talmud (ca. 500), and the slightly earlier Talmud of the Land of Israel, as well as the various *Midrashim* (commentary or homily collections) from these periods: The Bible is divine speech, and as such should not be limited to the normal rules of human speech. The interpretation of Jer 25.11 in Dan 9 (see p. 473 ES) indicates that this idea, which would encourage extensively creative philology, did not first develop with the rabbis. Indeed, it was greatly fostered already by the creation from various sources of a "unified" Torah. How else but through the assumption that God-talk is fundamentally different from human-talk can we explain, for example, why the two versions of the Decalogue (Ex 20, Deut 5) are different? God, and only God, can speak two things simultaneously! How else can we explain the fact that there "seems" to be a contradiction between various texts concerning slavery, about whether a Hebrew slave may remain a slave forever, or must be released at the jubilee (see below)? Obviously, this apparent contradiction must be reconciled by creative reinterpretation, based on the assumption that God does not use words in the same way we do.

The rabbis, in expressing this assumption, typically insisted that there is a superconcentration of meaning in the Bible as divine word. This meant for them that it cannot be interpreted as a "normal" text which might have a stable meaning; rather, it has seventy (an indeterminate, but large, number of) faces or meanings. Interpretation for the rabbis is like striking a rock with a hammer: Many different types of pieces, each of which is a legitimate part of the whole, are broken off. Also, as divine speech superendowed with meaning, there are no extra words in the text; nor, for some, are there even extra letters—all is significant as the word of God.

Not all rabbis subscribed to these views to the same degree, and it might even be possible to isolate a group that saw the Bible as composed in more normal language. As a result, a tension developed between the desire to take the text at its face value and the desire to see it as overendowed with meaning. This tension continued throughout later Jewish interpretation. Yet all agreed that as a divine text, the Bible may not be interpreted just like any other text. This is true whether the rabbinic comments are found in a Midrash (plural: Midrashim), where they are organized around a particular text, or whether they are found in the Talmud and thus are organized (more or less) according to legal topics.

A particular interest of classical rabbinic interpretation was reconciling divergent legal traditions found in the Torah, and "expanding" the Torah through creative interpretation. This "expansion" allowed ambiguities to be clarified and the text to be contemporized despite its antiquated nature. For example, a Midrash to Ex 21.6, which states that the Hebrew slave under certain circumstances shall stay with his master "for life," is glossed "until the jubilee year." "Life" ordinarily means "forever," or at least until death; the Midrash, however, is "forced" into this reading, using creative philology, because Lev 25.40 says: "They shall serve with you until the year of the jubilee." The Torah, as the unified word of God, cannot contain different ideas of when a slave is released, so it is "obvious" that the "forever" of Ex 21.6 must "really mean" until the jubilee. Again, though this interpretation might seem forced to us, it is almost natural within the framework of a society that reads the Torah as a unified, divine work.

As noted earlier, the rabbis also often extend and clarify biblical laws. Thus, the biblical text states that "work" is prohibited on the sabbath day, and anyone who works has committed a capital offense (e.g., Ex 31.14–15). But what is work? The problem is the same as that discussed above in reference to the festival of booths, where Lev 23.40 says that you must "take" certain branches but does not explicitly say what is to be done with them (see p. 471 ES). In the case of the branches, the context was used to provide the answer, and thus Neh 8.15 suggested that the branches should be taken to build booths, most likely based on the fact that the booth legislation (Lev 23.42) immediately follows the branch legislation. Similarly, Ex 31.12–17, which concerns the general sabbath prohibition, is found immediately after the instruction to construct the tabernacle; the classical rabbis adduced from this juxtaposition that "work" is any type of labor involved with the construction of the tabernacle. This is a reasonable, though not fully compelling, interpretation, which takes the text in its final form very seriously. Not only is every letter significant, but even the juxtaposition of adjacent units yields meaning.

The vast literature of the classical rabbinic period is replete with examples of creative historiography, many of which are based on overly careful readings, what we might consider overreading the biblical text; but of course a divine text cannot be read too carefully. For example, the binding of Isaac opens with the phrase, "After these things God tested Abraham" (Gen 22.1). Modern, critical commentators might see the phrase "After these things" as a type of filler, or paragraph marker, but this was an unlikely choice within the rabbinic mindset. This created a problem, since Gen 22 is not obviously, causally related to the previous chapter. Thus, "these things" must be discovered through creative historiography. As is typical, there is no single rabbinic answer to what "these things" were. Various Midrashim, preserved both in Midrashic texts like Genesis Rabbah and in the Babylonian Talmud, create a dialogue between Isaac and Ishmael in which Ishmael boasts that he endured the pain of circumcision at the age of thirteen (Gen 17.25), while Isaac was circumcised at eight days; Isaac counters by saying that Ishmael just gave an organ to God, whereas he, Isaac, is willing to give all of his organs to God. It is, according to this view, "after these things," namely after Isaac expressed his willingness to be sacrificed, that God tested Abraham. Another view creates a dialogue between God and Satan, in which God says that Abraham would even be willing to sacrifice his son. This brings Genesis closer to the dialogue between God and the Satan (adversary) in Job 1–2; indeed, it is common for the rabbis to use one canonical story to fully explore the meaning of another. Finally, it is noteworthy that these two stories are not merely silly, nor do they simply "fill in" the details lacking in the story. They both help to explain the major problem of the text: How could a good God make such a request of Abraham?

Although the Midrashic inclination was deeply attuned to the text, its meaning as the Bible, and its connection to the life of community, it accomplished these goals with a certain amount of violence to the context of the text. Thus, many rabbinic interpretations concentrate on the meaning of the individual word and the significance of the single letter (for example, the comments in the Midrash Genesis Rabbah which explain why the Bible opened with a *bet*, the second letter of the Hebrew alphabet), so that the broader contextual story is often lost. The eleventh century saw a reaction against this type of interpretation in the development of the *peshat* school of interpretation.

MEDIEVAL COMMENTATORS

Peshat is a notoriously difficult term to define, and it seems to change meaning depending on the commentator involved. For Rabbi Solomon (Hebrew Shelomoh) son of Isaac, or Rashi, who lived in France from 1040 to 1105, *peshat* meant "contextual meaning." Rashi's commentary, covering almost the entire Hebrew Bible, is a type of medieval *Reader's Digest* of classical rabbinic interpretation. Very little in Rashi is original; his brilliance, and extreme popularity (Rashi on the Torah was the first Hebrew book printed, before the Torah itself!) lay in his ability to select and rework rabbinic traditions, largely ignoring the many rabbinic traditions which overly strained the context of the text and those which used the text as a type of peg on which to hang various ideas that are not at all connected to the context. More than that, the traditional

Midrashim were so atomistic and filled with diverse opinions that it is almost always impossible to answer a simple question of how the Midrash understood the text. Rashi, through his judicious selection process, chose Midrashim that were relatively close to the text, and were mutually reinforcing. Thus, we have *peshat* where the broader text, as well as each letter or word, has a clear meaning. This accomplishment was so significant that the commentary of Rashi, especially on the Torah, is one of the most significant Jewish postbiblical texts; its influence on Jewish understanding of the Bible, especially in European communities, as well as on medieval Christians, for whom Rashi epitomized Jewish exegesis, cannot be minimized.

The method of *peshat* was taken one step further by Rashi's son-in-law, Rabbi Samuel (Hebrew Shmuel) son of Meir, or Rashbam (1080–1174), who understood *peshat* in a more radical sense as the simple meaning of the text. Rashbam, though a leading scholar of Jewish law, felt free to offer interpretations of the text in his commentary on the Torah that disagreed with rabbinic law. For example, in contrast to his father-in-law Rashi who, following the rabbinic tradition, interprets the words "for life" concerning the Hebrew slave in Ex 21.6 as until the jubilee year, Rashbam glosses "according to the *peshat*, all the days of his life." It remains unclear how Rashbam would have reconciled this *peshat* with what he understood to be the requirements of rabbinic law. In any case, the type of very literal, non-Midrashic way of reading the text which characterized Rashbam found new followers.

Rashbam is also noteworthy for the way in which some of his comments are clearly the product of a reaction against the Christians, especially the persecution of Jews during the Crusades. Though anti-Christian polemic existed in Rashi as well, it was relatively mild; the Crusades, which marked a significant change in the status of the Jews in medieval Europe, would leave a deep impact on many commentators. Nevertheless, Jewish commentary should not be seen as predominantly reactive.

Much of the rest of medieval Jewish interpretation may be understood within the context provided above, as a continuum on which the classical atomistic Midrashim and the search for *peshat* existed as opposite poles. Several additional influences are noteworthy. Especially in countries where Arabic was spoken, a new serious study of the Hebrew language was begun, likely in an effort to counter the Muslim claim that the Arabic of the Koran is the most beautiful language. Arabic paradigms were applied to Hebrew by scholars in the Arab orbit (e.g., Sa'adya [882–942] in Babylon, Abraham ibn Ezra [1089–1164] in Spain and elsewhere), and commentaries that were more philological in nature, exploring the meaning of grammatical forms and lexical terms, developed. Spinoza offers a picture of ibn Ezra as a medieval radical, doubting the Mosaic authorship of several verses from the Torah. In reality, despite some atypical positions that include the suggestion that Isa 40–66, what scholars now call Second and Third Isaiah, are not by the same author as chs 1–39, ibn Ezra was quite traditional in his outlook, and deeply philological in his perspective. Rabbi David Kimchi (Radak), who lived in Provence from 1160 to 1235, systematized many of these interpretations, and his understanding of biblical grammar continues to have a major influence on the scientific study of Hebrew. More than any other medieval exegete, Radak also showed a deep interest in what would later be called textual criticism, namely deciding what the correct text of the Bible was, and many of his views in this area are remarkably modern.

The world of premodern interpretation is, of course, much richer than indicated here. There was a very significant strain of mystical interpretation of the text, exemplified in the Zohar (late thirteenth century), and in the commentary of Nachmanides, Rabbi Moses son of Nachman (active in the thirteenth century). Philosophical interpretations also developed; most notable are those found in *The Guide to the Perplexed* by Maimonides (1135–1204). With the Renaissance, Jewish scholars were influenced by the new science; this is especially seen in the extremely lengthy commentary by Don Isaac Abravanel (1437–1508), who also synthesizes and to an extent harmonizes the many commentators of all types and from various geographical locations who preceded him.

Postbiblical Jewish exegesis does not neatly divide into the schools through which medieval Christian interpretation is often defined. It is essentially different from much of the work of its Christian counterparts. Part of this is because they were studying different works: the Hebrew Bible studied alone, or in relation to rabbinic traditions, is fundamentally different from the Old Testament as part of the Bible, followed by the New Testament. The allegorical and especially the typological methods, which had a very significant role in Christian interpretation, played a much less weighty role in Jewish interpretation. Finally, direct access to the text in its original Hebrew typically distinguished Jewish biblical interpretation from that of the Christians. Despite these differences, which are very significant, most Jewish and Christian premodern interpretation shares a set of basic assumptions that make them fundamentally premodern. These include the idea that the Bible is an authoritative canonical work, which is revealed divine speech, and, as such, must be interpreted in a special way. Though set in history, it is in a sense timeless, speaking to every generation and to every individual. Although several medieval rabbis cast some small doubts on one aspect or another of these premises of interpretation, only in the seventeenth century would these shared assumptions begin to erode, and only then would we slowly move from premodern to modern biblical interpretation.

THE INTERPRETATION OF THE BIBLE

Christian Interpretation in the Premodern Era

As the article on New Testament interpretation of the Jewish Scriptures indicates, Christian interpretation of scripture has already begun in the New Testament writings. The New Testament writers developed two of the interpretive approaches that remained central to Christian biblical interpretation until the rise of modern historical criticism: (1) a christocentric focus, that is, a tendency to interpret Hebrew Bible texts, especially prophetic texts, as referring to Christ; and (2) typology, the recognition of a person or event in the Hebrew Bible as a type or figure of Christ or Christian salvation. A third approach, allegory, was also present in rudimentary form.

In order to understand the development of early Christian interpretation, it is important to consider the contexts within which and the purposes for which Christians interpreted the scriptures. Teaching and pastoral care of Christian communities was one important focus, and much early interpretation occurs in the context of sermons and pastoral letters (e.g., the letters of Ignatius [ca. 35–ca.107 CE] and the homilies of Melito [d. ca. 190]). Missionary activity and Christian apologetics (the defense of Christianity before pagan detractors) provided a quite different context. In this situation the biblical writings had to be interpreted to an audience which often found these texts crude and out of keeping with the intellectual tastes of Greek-speaking culture. Thus there was a strong impetus to interpret the scriptures in a way that would enhance their intellectual respectability. For this purpose Christian apologists used the tradition of allegorical interpretation that had been developed within Greek philosophical circles as a means of interpreting Homer and the other early Greek poets. Even before the rise of Christianity, the Jewish philosopher Philo of Alexandria (ca. 20 BCE–42 CE) had undertaken a detailed allegorical interpretation of Jewish scriptures, and Philo's influence upon the Alexandrian school of Christian interpreters was profound.

A third context for interpretation emerged from Christianity's attempts to define itself in comparison to Judaism. Since both religions laid claim to the same body of scripture (the Hebrew Bible for Jews, the Old Testament for Christians), Christian interpretation addressed itself to the competing interpretations made by Judaism and Christianity. The harshly polemical *Epistle of Barnabas* (early second century) rejects the claims of Judaism to the covenant and so does not even begin to struggle with the interpretive problem which engages other Christian writers of the early centuries, the problem of the nature of the relationship between the old and new covenants and the scriptures which witness to them. Much richer and more reflective is Justin Martyr's (ca. 100–165) *Dialogue with Trypho the Jew*. The work takes the form of a long conversation between Justin and Trypho, a learned rabbi, each of whom tries to persuade the other of the superiority of his claims and the interpretation of the scriptures upon which they are based. Justin attempts to establish a unity for the Old and New Testaments by arguing that the eternal Logos, fully revealed as Christ in the New Testament, was already the revealer of God's will to the prophets. Though the old covenant was valid, Justin claims that the Jewish scriptures themselves foresee its being superseded by a new covenant. Justin's approach, which anticipates the classic Christian understanding of the Old Testament, exhibits a historical perspective absent from Barnabas, but it is equally christocentric.

The fourth context of early Christian interpretation was provided by disputes among Christians. One challenge was posed by Marcion of Pontus (mid-second century), who rejected the Hebrew Bible entirely, claiming it was the revelation of an alien God, and accepted only the Gospel of Luke and ten Pauline epistles as the authentic "Gospel and apostle." Even these texts, he insisted, were corrupted by interpolations. To argue his case, Marcion invoked the principles of text criticism developed for the study of Greek poets. He also argued for a literal rather than an allegorical interpretation of the Old Testament (especially Genesis) in his attempts to discredit it as a crude and offensive book. Even more than the debate with Judaism, Marcion's claims required the church to articulate clearly its understanding of the revelatory significance of the Old Testament and its relationship to the New. A further challenge was posed by various Gnostic Christians. Like Marcion they also tended to reject the Old Testament, but in contrast to him, they engaged in a highly developed form of allegorical interpretation, which appealed strongly to one type of Hellenistic intellectualism.

Some of the liveliest of early Christian writings are those composed to refute Marcion and the Gnostics. The most notable is Irenaeus's (ca. 130–ca. 200) *Against All Heresies*. Irenaeus argues for the validity of the revelation of God in the Old Testament and its law but also claims that in the New Testament God is revealed in a new way. He demonstrates the unity of the scriptures by means of typology, so that the Old Testament serves as a witness to the New. Irenaeus also attacks the interpretive methods of his Gnostic opponents, objecting that they ignore the context of passages, overlooking the clear and obvious in favor of the obscure, and reading into the text their fanciful theories. Significantly, Irenaeus not only argues on the basis of interpretive principles but also invokes what comes to be known as "the rule of faith." As a defense against an anarchy of interpretation, there is a standard of correct interpretation, which Irenaeus claims is that which has been preserved in those churches which stand in the apostolic succession. Interpretation which differs from that of the apostolic churches cannot be deemed true.

The argument for the authoritative interpretation of the church was definitively established by Tertullian (ca. 160–ca. 225) in the early third century in *De praescriptione haereticorum*. In making orthodoxy the norm for the interpretation of scripture, Tertullian, the lawyer with no taste for philosophy, may have thought that he was establishing a narrow and simple standard. But even as the threat from heretical interpretation receded, more philosophically oriented Christian interpreters, such as Origen (ca. 185–ca. 254) and Augustine (354–430), developed more profound and supple understandings of the nature of interpretation and the relation of scripture to orthodox theology.

In addition to looking at early Christian biblical interpretation in the light of various contexts for interpretation, one should also take account of the two rival schools of interpretation that flourished in Alexandria and Antioch during the early Common Era. As noted above, the sophisticated intellectual environment of Alexandria was already home to a lively tradition of allegorical exegesis before the emergence of Christianity. Thus it was inevitable that Christians would adapt this method of interpretation to their scriptures. Among the most eminent of the Alexandrian school were Clement (ca. 150–ca. 215) and Origen. Allegorical interpretation reads a text as if the narrative incidents, characters, and other elements of its literal meaning are all intended to convey to the reader, by means of an extended comparison, another level of meaning entirely, usually a moral or spiritual one. Although many rather different types of interpretation may bear the name *allegory*, all share a conviction that the authoritative text being interpreted bears a deeper meaning than what appears on the surface by means of a literal reading. Thus allegory assumes that a text has multiple meanings, though interpreters may differ as to their worth. (Origen, for example, distinguished among literal, moral, and spiritual meanings.) Typically, allegorical interpretation shows little interest in meanings that are historically specific, preferring those that disclose timeless truths. Allegory is often invoked as an interpretive method when an ancient text that is undeniably authoritative has come to seem alien to the cultural sensitivities and intellectual values of a later age. Since the revered text must contain truth (which is often unconsciously equated with the highest and best values of the interpreter's own time), a method must be employed which will allow those truths to be found in the text. In this manner the Christian allegorists of the Alexandrian school interpreted those aspects of the scriptures which seemed morally offensive, obscure, or simply of little literal interest. Thus Origen could interpret the narrative of the Exodus as an allegory of the journey of the soul as it leaves the sensual world (Egypt) and journeys toward the promised land of blessedness (Canaan). Origen was the most sophisticated of the allegorists, and the one who first gave allegory its theoretical foundations. Moreover, he was the first Christian to compose what can properly be called a commentary on a biblical book, a mode of interpretation that flourished in the fourth and fifth centuries.

Despite the prestige which allegorical exegesis enjoyed in some circles, it was also the subject of strong criticism. In part it attracted suspicion because it was the method of interpretation favored by Gnostics. But allegory was also vulnerable to the charge that it was arbitrary and obscure. The strongest critique of the allegorical method favored by the Alexandrian school came from the rival tradition of biblical interpretation associated with the Syrian city of Antioch. Like Alexandria, Antioch was also heir to a long tradition of Hellenistic scholarship. But Antioch was influenced more by Aristotelian traditions and by Jewish rabbinic exegesis. Thus, even though the Antiochene interpreters sought a spiritual meaning in the text, understanding also required, in their view, a grasp of the historical context within which the texts were written, as well as an appreciation of the literal sense of the text. Diodore of Tarsus (d. ca. 390), for example, sought to arrange the Psalms in historical sequence, using information found internally and in the titles. He understood the Song of Songs as love poetry written by Solomon for the Queen of Sheba.

The most radical and most creative interpreter of the school of Antioch was Bishop Theodore of Mopsuestia (ca. 350–428). Theodore challenged the inspired character of several books of the canon, including Job, Song of Songs, Chronicles, and Ezra-Nehemiah, claiming that they reflected only human wisdom and learning. In reaction, the Second Council of Constantinople, in 553, ordered his exegetical works to be burned. In general, the Antiochene school aroused suspicion because several church leaders judged heretical, most notably Nestorius (d. ca. 451), were associated with it. Despite opposition to the more radical interpreters, however, many of the insights and understandings of the Antiochene approach were popularized by the influential sermon collections of the moderate John Chrysostom (ca. 347–407) and by the manuals of biblical interpretation written by Adrian (425) and Junilius Africanus (550).

The stance of the allegorists and that of the more literal-historical interpreters were not necessarily mutually exclusive. Many interpreters employed both methods. Jerome (347–420), the translator of the Vulgate, began as an allegorist in the style of Origen but increasingly came under the influence of the Antiochene approach. Even so, he never entirely abandoned allegory in his writings. Similarly, Augustine was troubled by the Manichean use of a literal-historical approach to discredit the Jewish scriptures on the grounds that they contained immoralities. He was unable to embrace Christianity until he saw how the allegorical method could provide a spiritual interpretation for such troubling passages. Like Jerome, however, Augustine moved beyond allegory to a more nuanced position that recognized the place of allegory but required the interpreter to distinguish between passages that can be understood in a literal and those requiring a figurative interpretation. Moreover, all interpretation must be guided by the rule of faith and the law of love: "If it seems to anyone that he has understood the divine scriptures, or any part of them, in such a way that by that understanding he does not build up that double love of God and neighbor, he has not yet understood" (*Confessions*, 5.11.21).

THE MIDDLE AGES

During the early Middle Ages scholars of the Bible mainly preserved and transmitted the understandings developed in earlier centuries. In the west most interpreters were no longer able to read Greek, the Irish scholar John Scotus Erigena (ca. 810–ca. 877) being a noteworthy exception. Moreover, there was no significant interchange with Jewish interpreters, such as had been possible at Antioch. The works of Jerome, Augustine, and other patristic writers, however, were widely studied. As in earlier centuries, both literal and allegorical exegesis was practiced. Most commonly, four senses of scripture were recognized: the literal or historical, the allegorical, the anagogical (a mystical sense signifying heaven, the afterlife, or communion with God), and the moral or tropological. Thus "Jerusalem" could signify, literally, the historical city; allegorically, the church; anagogically, the heavenly city; and morally, the human soul. The influence of this four-level interpretive method extended beyond scriptural interpretation; most notably, Dante deliberately constructed his *Divine Comedy* in order to allow, as far as possible, all four levels of interpretation to be applied to it.

The primary institutional context for the study of the Bible in the early medieval period was the monastery. Among the early monastic scholars the most prominent was the Venerable Bede (ca. 673–725), who composed commentaries and biblical aids as well as his influential *Ecclesiastical History*. An important impetus to the study of the Bible came from the religious and educational reforms sponsored by the Carolingian monarchs. Charlemagne (ca. 742–814) and his grandson Charles the Bald (d. 877) attracted the best scholars of the day, including Alcuin (ca. 735–804) and John Scotus Eriugena (ca. 810–ca. 877), to supervise education at the palace and cathedral schools. The growth of such schools created a demand for resources, and the scholars of the Carolingian renaissance produced an impressive number of biblical manuscripts, annotations and aids to study, commentaries, and historical work. These works were largely digests and compilations of glosses on the biblical text drawn from writings produced in late antiquity by the Latin fathers. The culmination of this type of scholarship was the production of the *Glossa ordinaria,* compiled by Anselm of Laon (d. 1117) in collaboration with other scholars.

The twelfth and thirteenth centuries saw the beginning of a more creative phase of medieval biblical scholarship, located first in the cathedral schools and subsequently in the universities. One important innovation was the division of the biblical books into chapters, first developed in England by Stephen Langton (d. 1228). (The numbering of the verses, or smaller units within the chapters, was developed in the fifteenth and sixteenth centuries by both Jewish and Christian scholars.) This system was used in another innovation, the production of concordances to the Bible, the most influential of which was that prepared by the Dominicans of St. Jacques in Paris, under the supervision of Hugo of St. Cher (ca. 1195–1263). Perhaps the most important of the cathedral schools was that of the Abbey of St. Victor, also in Paris, where a series of influential scholars taught during the twelfth century. The school, which was known for the rigor of study under the direction of its founder, Hugh of St. Victor (d. 1142), fostered both literal and allegorical (or mystical) exegesis. Later teachers tended to emphasize one or the other, Richard of St. Victor (d. 1173) developing allegorical interpretation, and Andrew of St. Victor (d. 1175) emphasizing the careful investigation of the literal and historical sense. Significantly, Andrew knew Hebrew and was influenced by Jewish scholars and traditions of Jewish exegesis. During the following centuries an appreciation of the importance of such knowledge became more common among Christian exegetes of the Bible. Although the presence of significant Jewish communities in the major medieval cities made the study of Hebrew and Jewish exegesis somewhat more accessible, such knowledge did not flourish among Christian biblical scholars until the Renaissance. Greek was still relatively little known at this time, although Robert Grosseteste (ca. 1175–1253) translated several works, including the *Testaments of the Twelve Patriarchs*, from Greek into Latin.

Along with the development of important schools in the twelfth century, there was also a shift in the form in which biblical study was presented. In contrast to the earlier compendia of glosses, which were organized as a running comment on the text of the Bible itself, in the twelfth century a different form of commentary developed, one that was organized according to theological topics and issues. This change in literary form both signaled and facilitated a closer relationship between the study of scripture and the development of theological doctrine. The most significant of these works, the *Sentences* of Peter Lombard (ca. 1100–1160), eventually became the standard theological textbook during the Middle Ages.

The establishment of universities in the thirteenth century marks an important shift in the social location of biblical study. In this context biblical interpretation became more specialized and was drawn even more closely into dialogue with theology and philosophy. Although some scholars continued to engage in allegorical exegesis, both the prominence of Aristotelian thought in the universities and the emphasis on doctrinal theology pushed biblical interpretation more strongly in the direction of literal exegesis. Albertus Magnus (1193–1280) and especially Thomas Aquinas (ca. 1225–1274) were the most eminent of these Aristotelian-influenced scholastic theologians and biblical interpreters. The harvest of this form of literal biblical exegesis can best be appreciated in the *Postilla literalis* of Nicholas of Lyra (ca. 1270–1349), which covers the entire Bible. Lyra's knowledge not only of biblical Hebrew, but also of the commentaries of Rashi (1040–1105) and other Jewish scholars (see "Jewish Interpretation in the Premodern Era"), gives his work a linguistic and exegetical precision that is lacking in many other medieval commentaries.

THE RENAISSANCE AND REFORMATION

The emphasis on original languages and a respect for the role of reason in interpretation, which had already become influential in late medieval scholarship, became the hallmarks of the new humanistic learning of the Renaissance. These values, however, which had previously been invoked in the service of scholastic theology in the Middle Ages, led in some rather different directions in the fifteenth and sixteenth centuries. The scholar Erasmus (ca. 1466–1536) is something of a transitional figure. Though he used his incomparable humanistic knowledge to produce a new critical edition of the Greek New Testament and drew on classical Roman rhetorical traditions in his interpretation of Ecclesiastes, he also defended allegorical interpretation of scripture and had a high regard for scholastic theology, Thomas Aquinas in particular. For the most part, the Christian humanist scholars did not set out to challenge the authority of the church. Yet in certain instances the claims of reason brought them into conflict with church authority and traditions. In 1440 Lorenzo Valla (1407–1457) published his *Declamation on the Donation of Constantine,* in which he used reason to argue that the so-called donation of Constantine, which had underwritten papal authority in Rome, was in fact a forgery. Similarly, he demonstrated that a letter supposedly written by Jesus to Abgar, king of Edessa, which had been considered genuine at least since the fourth century, was in fact spurious. His approach to such ancient documents, and to the New Testament itself in his other writings, anticipated the critical study of the Bible which was to develop in later centuries. The audience for such critical works on the text of the New Testament text was facilitated by the publication of several Greek grammars between 1495 and 1520.

Fueling the explosive growth in Renaissance scholarship was the new availability of texts and critical works made possible by the development of the printing press. Following the publication of Johannes Gutenberg's Latin Bible in 1454, a wide range of books became available, not only in Latin and vernacular languages, but in Greek and Hebrew as well. During the early sixteenth century several polyglot Bibles were published, that is, Bibles in which Greek, Latin, Hebrew, and Aramaic texts of the Bible were printed side by side to facilitate critical comparison.

The characteristic Renaissance interest in ancient languages and texts led some scholars, such as Giovanni Pico della Mirandola (1463–1494), Johannes Reuchlin (1455–1522), and Guillaume Postel (ca. 1510–1581), to explore the esoteric traditions of Jewish kabbalistic mysticism. Postel even translated the *Bahir* and the *Zohar* into Latin. These Christian kabbalists drew together elements of Jewish mysticism, Neoplatonic philosophy, Christian theology, and the Renaissance interest in the occult into a spiritual synthesis which, as one might expect, was condemned by church authorities. Reuchlin, however, can be called the father of Christian Renaissance study of Hebrew. He published an influential Hebrew grammar, based on the work of the medieval Jewish Rabbi David Kimchi (Radak) (see "Jewish Interpretation in the Premodern Era," p. 478 ES), and other aids that facilitated the increasing interest in the study of Hebrew by Christians. Reuchlin also played an important role in resisting some attempts by the church to suppress Jewish writings, including the Talmud.

With the Reformation, biblical interpretation increasingly took place within an intense debate about the role of scripture in relation to Christian faith. To a large extent, however, both the early Protestant reformers and the scholars who remained within the Catholic tradition incorporated the new linguistic and philological training in their interpretation of the Bible. Though Martin Luther (1483–1546) was not the first to argue that the Bible is the ultimate authority in matters of doctrine, the Protestant movement is distinctive in insisting that the Bible is the sole foundation for faith, doctrine, and church practices. In their refutation of the Protestants, Catholic scholars also appealed to biblical exegesis in support of the authority of the church and the papacy. Thus in the sixteenth century biblical interpretation reflects both the rich legacy of Renaissance humanism's linguistic and philological knowledge and a context of highly charged theological argument.

Although Protestant biblical interpreters in general rejected allegory in favor of the literal-historical sense, their interpretation of the Hebrew Bible was usually christological and typological. Luther, for example, attended both to the literal-historical sense and to the literal-prophetic sense of scripture (i.e., the typological meaning foreshadowed in the text). Thus, since David was considered to be a prophet, the Psalms referred not only to David's life and circumstances but also to Christ who was to come.

Luther's writings also reflect both continuity and discontinuity with the medieval tradition in his treatment of the tropological or moral meaning of scripture. Traditionally, this concern had been with the way in which the text addressed the nature and practice of the virtue of love. For Luther, the moral meaning is that aspect of the text that has to do with the nurture of faith, that is, trust in God's promises. Other Protestants, however, such as Zwingli and Bucer, follow Erasmus in understanding the moral meaning of scripture as providing paradigms for human behavior.

The issue of the relation of the two testaments also provoked a variety of responses among Protestant interpreters. Given Luther's theological distinction between law and gospel, his interpretation tends to posit a significant degree of tension between the testaments. In contrast, many other Protestant theologians saw an essential continuity between the testaments. Henrich Bullinger (1504–1575), for example, treated covenant as a hermeneutical principle which unifies the scriptures. Before the advent of Christ the sign of the covenant is circumcision; after the advent, baptism. But the covenant is one and the same, the New Testament only presenting it with greater clarity. The nature and extent of the canon of the Old Testament also became an issue of controversy between Protestants and the Roman Catholic Church. Like Jerome before them, the Protestant reformers argued that the church's Old Testament canon should be that of the Hebrew scriptures, that is, without the Apocrypha. At the Council of Trent (1546) the Roman Catholic church reaffirmed the inspired nature of some of these books, which were termed "deuterocanonical." The term does not denote a difference in status from the "protocanonical" books but signifies that their canonical status was clarified at a second stage. (See the essay, "The Canons of the Bible," pp. 453–460, and the introductions to individual books among the Apocryphal/Deuterocanonical Books for more details on the canonical status of particular books and the development of the differing canons of the Old Testament among the various Christian communities.)

Concern for historical context and for an understanding of biblical rhetoric was also prominent in early Protestant interpretation. The biblical interpretation of John Calvin (1509–1564), who had legal training, was influenced by Renaissance humanism's approach to clarifying ancient law by means of an appeal to the original historical contexts and the intentions of the authors. As Calvin observes in the dedicatory preface to his commentary on Romans, "almost [the commentator's] only task [is] to unfold the mind of the writer whom he has undertaken to expound." Calvin's interpretation thus tends to be contextual rather than atomistic and attends not only to history but also to the cultural institutions and background of biblical texts and to the rhetorical forms in which biblical language expresses itself. Indeed, a dispute over a proper understanding of biblical rhetoric lies at the heart of one of the most important doctrinal disputes within early Protestantism. Luther contended that the word *is* in the biblical phrase "this *is* my body" (Mt 26.26) is to be interpreted literally, whereas Zwingli (1484–1531) argued that its natural sense must be understood rhetorically as non-literal, "this *signifies* my body." Out of that interpretive dispute emerged two different theological understandings of the Eucharist.

Although Protestant theology's emphasis on scripture as the sole foundation of belief provided the impetus for intense interpretive activity, Roman Catholic scholars also produced a large amount of biblical scholarship, some provoked by controversies with Protestants and some not. Cardinal Cajetan (Thomas de Vio, 1469–1534) shared certain views with Protestants, such as the preference for the Hebrew text over the Vulgate, the advocacy of a shorter canon (excluding the Apocrypha), and a literal form of interpretation. But much of his exegetical work was devoted to demonstrating biblical support for papal authority and traditional church doctrine.

The spread of literacy, the increased availability of translations of the Bible into European languages, and the Protestant emphasis on the sufficiency of scripture alone contributed to the spread of biblical interpretation not only among those trained in theological institutions and having linguistic skills but also among laity with modest training or only a bare literacy. Thus in the sixteenth century and beyond one begins to see an increase in popular interpretations, often of a millenarian slant. Although Luther and the other reformers had believed that the Bible was so clear that all reasonable readers would agree as to its meaning, as matters actually developed the democratization of interpretation led to a bewildering array of readings of scripture, nowhere more so than in England in the late sixteenth century. From the ploughwright Matthew Hamond to the clerk John Hilton, those who claimed that the New Testament was "a mere fable" were seen as a threat to decency and social order. Later, during the English revolution and the period of the Commonwealth (1640–1660), biblical interpretation became a primary mode of political argument among partisans of all factions.

THE SEVENTEENTH AND EIGHTEENTH CENTURIES

At the same time that Protestant orthodoxy was developing a complex and minute exegesis of the Bible in support of various church doctrines, rationalists of various theological allegiances were developing ideas which many saw as challenging traditional understandings of the Bible. Both the new scientific discoveries and those resulting from the exploration of previously unknown lands raised questions about how this new knowledge was to be understood in relation to the Bible. The conflict between the astronomer Galileo Galilei (1564–1642) and the Catholic Church over the heliocentric view of the universe is only the most famous example. The perplexing problem of how to account for the existence of nations and peoples not mentioned by the Bible prompted the French reformer Isaac de la Peyrère (ca. 1596–1676) to suggest that Adam was not in fact the first human but was only the ancestor of the Israelites (*The Pre-Adamites . . . By which are prov'd that the first men were created before Adam*). At about the same time, along with others, the philosopher Thomas Hobbes in *Leviathan* (1651) questioned Moses' authorship of the entire Pentateuch and in general emphasized the human mediation between God's word and the scriptures as they are available to be read in the Bible. The French Catholic scholar Richard Simon (1638–1712), often called the father of modern biblical scholarship, wrote a *Critical History of the Old Testament* (1678), in which he discussed the various versions of the Bible with respect to their relationship and authority. Empirical in his approach, Simon also denied Moses' authorship of the Pentateuch and suggested that national archives preserved by prophets and scribes provided the sources from which the biblical books were composed long after the date of the events described in them. A similar rationalist criticism of the Bible was developed by the Jewish philosopher Baruch (Benedict) Spinoza (1632–1677).

Moral criticism of the Bible, which had in part given rise to the allegorical method of interpretation in antiquity, was also practiced. Pierre Bayle (1647–1706), a French Protestant, published a highly influential historical and critical dictionary which contained an article on David widely perceived as scandalous, since it drew attention to the themes of adultery, murder, treachery, and injustice in the story of the "man after God's own heart" (see 1 Sam 13.14). Both moral and rational criticism of the Bible, including a critique of the claims to miraculous events, is found to varying degrees in the Deists of the eighteenth century, some of the more radical of whom challenged even the resurrection of Christ. In France, Voltaire (1694–1778) popularized some of the more extreme notions concerning the Bible and its claims, and a similar radical stance was taken by the American Thomas Paine (1736–1809).

Although discussion and interpretation of the Bible was conducted by intellectuals of every stripe, as well as at a more popular level, the seventeenth and eighteenth centuries saw an enormous development of technical biblical scholarship, which was almost always related to theological and cultural debates. For instance, the controversy as to the date and origin of the vowel points in the traditional Hebrew text of the Bible was fueled largely by disputes concerning the inspiration of the Bible and the relative reliability of the Hebrew text versus the Septuagint and the Vulgate. The study of text criticism was significantly advanced by the publication of the London Polyglot (1655–1657), which included Hebrew, Greek, Vulgate, Syriac, Ethiopic, Arabic, and Persian versions, the Samaritan Pentateuch, and several Targums, along with a wealth of critical notes and aids. A large number of critical and historically oriented commentaries were published during the seventeenth century.

With the eighteenth century there developed what can be called modern criticism of the Bible. The theory of the composition of the Pentateuch from a number of still identifiable sources, an idea that has been central to modern criticism, was first advanced by French scholar Jean Astruc (1684–1766). In England Bishop and Oxford professor Robert Lowth (1710–1787) developed an analysis of the nature of Hebrew poetry which is still widely accepted. But it was German scholarship that systematized and gave a distinctively modern character to historical-critical study of the Bible. Two landmarks of this emergent discipline were J. D. Michaelis's (1717–1791) introduction to the New Testament and J. G. Eichhorn's (1752–1827) introduction to the Old Testament.

THE INTERPRETATION OF THE BIBLE
From the Nineteenth to the Mid-twentieth Centuries

THE HISTORICAL-CRITICAL METHOD

The philosophical developments of the seventeenth and eighteenth centuries had prompted an approach to the Bible that is often characterized as critical. It was critical not in a negative sense, although that would often seem to be the case, but in the sense that it was free of presuppositions, especially those derived from either theology or tradition. To fully understand the Bible, scholars increasingly adopted an inductive approach, interpreting the Bible in an almost secular way, setting aside received views of its authority and authorship. This critical approach, an outgrowth of attitudes fostered during the Enlightenment, was very much in the spirit of the times and was, like other legacies of the Enlightenment, influenced by larger intellectual currents, such as Romanticism and the theory of evolution.

The overriding goal was historical: to determine what had actually taken place, and to recover the actual persons and events of the Bible as they had been preserved in the various stages of biblical tradition. The nature and development of these stages were to be understood through critical scholarship. This was the aim of "higher criticism," as distinguished from "lower," or textual criticism, and this higher criticism was essentially the historical-critical method.

With its many subdisciplines, the historical-critical method dominated biblical interpretation through the mid-twentieth century and is still the basis from which newer criticisms begin, if only in opposition to it. The scholars whose work is surveyed in the following pages were immensely learned, often experts in a variety of fields, including philology, textual criticism, comparative literature, and the study of ancient cultures contemporaneous with the biblical traditions. Moreover, also in keeping with the intellectual mood of the nineteenth and early twentieth centuries, they were optimistic, in retrospect even overconfident, operating on the assured conviction that with sufficient data and careful analysis of the data an objective, accurate, and complete understanding of the Bible was possible.

SOURCE CRITICISM

The critical study of the Bible had been begun in the seventeenth century by Hobbes, Spinoza, and Richard Simon, and it continued to gain momentum during the Enlightenment. In many respects the conclusions of scholars working on the Hebrew Bible were paralleled by those who worked on the New Testament, and the methods and preoccupations of both were similar to those of classical scholarship. In all three disciplines there was a growing concentration upon history. And scholars in all three disciplines recognized that historical reconstruction needed to begin with a careful analysis of sources.

This was true first of all of the analysis of the Pentateuch into several literary strands. Jean Astruc had proposed in 1753 that the different names used for God in different parts of the book of Genesis were due to different sources that antedated the final composition of the book. Astruc's insight was elaborated and refined mainly by German scholars, especially W. M. L. de Wette and K. H. Graf, who extended the analysis of sources to the rest of the Pentateuch (and in some cases to the book of Joshua, leading to the term "Hexateuch"; see below).

The results of more than a century of this source criticism were brilliantly synthesized in 1878 by the German Old Testament scholar Julius Wellhausen in his book (*Prolegomena to*) *The History of Israel*. Wellhausen's goal was to write a history of ancient Israel, especially its religion, and he followed an evolutionary model. The religion of Israel, Wellhausen argued, had developed in three stages, from a primitive, spontaneous phase in the era before the monarchy, to its high point in an ethical monotheism, from which it degenerated into a sterile legalism. To support this reconstruction, he engaged in a careful analysis of the biblical traditions, and, drawing especially on the earlier work of de Wette and Graf, gave the classic formulation to what is called the Documentary Hypothesis. According to the Documentary Hypothesis as elaborated by Wellhausen, the Pentateuch was an unreliable source for reconstructing the history of the time periods it narrated, but the traditions that comprised it, identified as J, E, D, and P, were datable and important evidence for the periods in which they were compiled. (See further "Introduction to the Pentateuch," pp. 3–7 HB.) These "documents" were hypothetical, that is, they did not now exist, but they were the best explanation of the evidence—the parallels, repetitions, and inconsistencies in the final form of the Pentateuch.

Wellhausen's historical reconstruction is clearly a product of its time, and it reflects the biases of the late nineteenth century. His view of early Israel as a fresh, undefiled religious spirit has a Romantic flavor, and his characterization of postexilic Judaism as a decline into dead legalism has an anti-Semitic cast. But his formulation of the Documentary Hypothesis became a classic statement, the theory that subsequent scholars up to the present have built upon, accepted, modified, or rejected. Despite initial and continuing conservative opposition, and, in the case of Roman Catholics especially, institutional interdict, it was widely adopted by liberal Protestant scholars, and eventually by Roman Catholic and Jewish scholars as well, resulting in a large consensus that is still dominant.

Source criticism was not an end in itself, but a method to be used in historical reconstruction. It recognized the inherent complexity of biblical traditions, and attempted to disentangle the prior stages of their development. Among the many significant results of source criticism was the recognition that the book of Isaiah is a composite work. The isolated insights of earlier scholars, including Rabbi Ibn Ezra in the twelfth century, and J. G. Eichhorn and others in the eighteenth, were expanded and elaborated in the commentary on Isaiah by Bernhard Duhm in 1892. The book of Isaiah, Duhm argued, was in effect an anthology spanning several centuries. First Isaiah (chs 1–39) was a product of the preexilic period, and was itself a composite, including authentic oracles of the eighth-century BCE prophet Isaiah of Jerusalem, additions to those oracles and biographical materials added by his disciples, and historical narratives largely spliced in from 2 Kings. Chapters 40–55, Deutero-Isaiah or Second Isaiah, were a product of the mid-sixth century BCE, as the historical references in those chapters indicated. And the remainder of the book, chs 56–66, was to be dated a century or more later, despite similarities of language and themes to chs 40–55. In the Romantic spirit, Duhm was motivated to distinguish the genuine words of Isaiah himself, as well as those of the anonymous prophets responsible for the latter two divisions of the book, especially the author of the "Servant Songs" (Isa 42.1–4; 49.1–6; 50.4–9; 52.13–53.12).

Similar preoccupations and approaches characterized the study of the New Testament. Drawing on the work of earlier scholars, especially Simon (again!) and H. S. Reimarus, in 1835 David F. Strauss published his "life of Jesus critically examined," soon to be translated from German to English by George Eliot, in which he attempted to strip the Gospels of the miraculous and mythical in order to recover the real Jesus. This inaugurated a "quest" for the historical Jesus that continued in the work of Ernst Renan in the mid-nineteenth century and Albert Schweitzer at the beginning of the twentieth, and that remains unfulfilled, as the lack of consensus at the beginning of the twenty-first century demonstrates.

This quest was accompanied by a source-critical analysis of the Synoptic Gospels. While debate about which Gospel was written first was never fully resolved, the literary priority of Mark was argued by a succession of scholars in the nineteenth century. According to this view, held by a majority of New Testament scholars but by no means all of them, Mark was used as a source by both Matthew and Luke (or, more properly, the authors of the Gospels to whom those names are traditionally given). A large number of passages in Matthew and Luke other than those based on Mark also share a verbatim correspondence, and another source was hypothesized for them. Known as Q, from the German word *Quelle* ("source"), it consists almost entirely of sayings of Jesus and, though hypothetical, is the earliest source for the life of Jesus. This "Two-Source Hypothesis" was given classic formulation in English by B. H. Streeter in 1924. (See further "Introduction to the Gospels," p. 3–6 NT.)

Source criticism in the New Testament was also applied to the Gospel of John and the Acts of the Apostles. Careful analysis of the letters attributed to Paul led to the conclusion that some of them, especially the "Pastoral Epistles" (1 and 2 Timothy and Titus), and probably Ephesians and 2 Thessalonians as well, had not been written by Paul himself, and that others (such as 2 Corinthians) may be combinations of two or more originally distinct writings.

THE RECOVERY OF THE ANCIENT WORLD

The recovery of extensive written remains from the ancient Near East, and also to a lesser extent from the classical world, the latter especially in the form of papyri that document ordinary life, coincided with the development of the disciplines of anthropology and sociology. Both new data and new methods were applied to the biblical communities, resulting in works of extraordinary insight and, in retrospect, often of a certain naïveté. Biblical studies, however labeled, became a subject not just in denominational, seminary curriculums, but a discipline recognized in larger university contexts as well, often as part of religious studies or *Religionswissenschaft*.

The process of recovery began with the decipherment of ancient Egyptian hieroglyphic writing in the early nineteenth century, which was made possible when a member of Napoleon's army, in Egypt in 1799, discovered the Rosetta Stone. This opened up the vast literature of Egypt, including valuable historical texts that provided synchronisms with biblical data relating especially to the first millennium BCE, and provided the basis for what would eventually be a comprehensive absolute chronology of the ancient Near East. Egyptian literature also provided parallels to such biblical genres as love poetry and wisdom literature.

In the mid-nineteenth century, British and French explorers began to unearth hundreds of thousands of cuneiform texts in Mesopotamia, and these too were rapidly deciphered, giving access to the literature and written remains of ancient Babylon, Assyria, and Persia. Like the Egyptian texts, they could often be correlated with biblical history. But their impact on biblical studies was more profound. In 1872, George Smith, working in the British Museum, discovered on one of the tablets that had been sent to London a flood narrative remarkably similar to the account in Genesis. While some took this as a simple historical confirmation of the Flood, it soon became clear that the biblical account was a literary descendant of earlier Mesopotamian accounts. Further discoveries provided many other parallels between Babylonian and Israelite literature, law, institutions, and beliefs, and in most cases Babylon again appeared to be the source. Sparked by a series of lectures by the German Assyriologist Friedrich Delitzsch in 1902–1904, a heated controversy developed, pitting "Babel" against the Bible. Ultimately many of the simplistic conclusions concerning the priority, and the superiority, of the traditions of "Babel" were rejected, and in retrospect they seem clearly anti-Semitic. But the controversy not only marks the emergence of Assyriology (the study of the cultures of ancient Mesopotamia) as an independent discipline, but also established the importance of nonbiblical materials for the understanding of the Bible.

For the study of the New Testament, the most important discovery was that of the Oxyrhynchus Papyri, a large collection of documents dating to the early centuries of the Common Era. Among the thousands of mostly Greek texts excavated between 1897 and 1934 were fragments of very early manuscripts of parts of the New Testament, along with three collections of sayings of Jesus, some of which, though not found in the canonical Gospels, are apparently authentic. The latter were of considerable importance in the debate about the prehistory of the Gospels, that is, the reconstruction of the stages between Jesus himself and the earliest written traditions. The papyri also included hundreds of documents from ordinary life in Roman times, illuminating both the form of Greek used in the New Testament and the social world of its writers and audiences.

FORM CRITICISM

While source criticism became a dominant interpretive method, the influx of nonbiblical data prompted a more nuanced investigation of the prehistory of the written biblical traditions. The pioneer in this work was the German scholar Hermann Gunkel (1862–1932), perhaps the most influential biblical interpreter of the twentieth century. While accepting Wellhausen's analysis as valid, Gunkel incorporated evidence both from Babylonian literature and from comparative folklore to propose a shift in emphasis from history to the history of literature. Prior to the formation of the Pentateuchal "documents" there was discernible a long process of development and transmission of "forms," or genres, which both had parallels in nonbiblical sources, and, coincidentally, were vehicles for preserving very ancient traditions. These forms have their own history and chronological and cross-cultural continuity.

Central to form-critical method was the identification of the *Sitz im Leben* ("setting in life"), the original and subsequent contexts in which the forms were developed and used. Gunkel himself applied form criticism to the book of Genesis in his commentary first published in 1901, in which he isolated such forms as saga, legend, taunt, curse, hymn, etiology, and proverb. His studies on the Psalms (1928–1933) were also groundbreaking, setting the terms of the discussion for the rest of the century by his classification of the various genres (hymn, individual and communal laments, individual and communal thanksgivings, royal psalms, wisdom psalms, etc.). Although there is a kind of idealism about the definition of the forms, parallels from outside the Bible confirmed their applicability and enhanced the understanding of the particulars of biblical traditions.

Gunkel himself had not hesitated to apply his insights to the New Testament, as in his important monograph on creation and chaos as central themes in prophetic and especially apocalyptic literature, including the book of Revelation. Two of his students, Martin Dibelius and Rudolf Bultmann, applied the principles of form criticism more systematically to the Gospels. They refined the definitions of forms such as parables and miracle stories and, in Bultmann's case especially, identified similar forms in other ancient sources. Although the question of the historical Jesus was still an issue, New Testament form criticism moved beyond what could be hypothesized about the original setting in the life of Jesus himself and focused more on the role that the forms played in various settings in earliest Christianity.

ARCHAEOLOGY

Serious exploration of the Levant began in the early nineteenth century, and notable advances were made in mapping the region and in identifying ancient sites. In the decades before World War I extensive, and by the standards of the time scientific, excavations were undertaken by British, German, French, and American archaeologists. In Palestine, attention was focused on the major cities of ancient Israel, and Jerusalem, Samaria, Megiddo, Shechem, Jericho, Taanach, and Gezer were all partially excavated. An overriding preoccupation of the excavators was historical, even apologetic: to verify, by independent data, the historicity of biblical traditions.

In the 1920s and 1930s many more projects were initiated, and excavation techniques were improved. Greater accuracy in dating excavated remains was made possible through the refinement of ceramic typology, especially as elaborated by the American scholar W. F. Albright in his excavations at Tell Beit Mirsim. But very little of the vast amount of material that was excavated and published could be related directly to the Bible, and debates often ensued about how to synthesize archaeological and biblical data. When work resumed in the 1950s and 1960s, new projects were undertaken and many sites that had been earlier—and fortunately only partially—excavated were redug, especially by British, American, and Israeli archaeologists. In part because of the flood of material from periods long before and after biblical times or with little direct relevance to the Bible, archaeology began to develop as an independent discipline, as had already happened in the classical world. More attention was given to what archaeology actually produced, the material culture of the region in various periods, and in some circles there developed a theoretical tension between archaeology and biblical studies. Many earlier archaeologists were also biblical scholars. Now, more and more archaeologists were acquiring interest and expertise in periods and regions not directly relevant to biblical history. The result, by the late twentieth century, was that some archaeologists lacked sufficient expertise to connect what they excavated with the written sources, and many biblical scholars simply ignored the potential contributions of archaeology to the interpretation of the Bible. This was especially true in the case of the New Testament. Apart from continuing efforts since the late nineteenth century to identify sites associated with the life of Jesus, until the 1970s the study of the New Testament was largely restricted to texts, with little attention to the growing body of information about Palestine and the entire eastern Mediterranean world derived from archaeology.

ETHNOGRAPHY, SOCIOLOGY, AND ANTHROPOLOGY

As explorers and archaeologists began to make the ancient Near East known, they also observed those living there in the present. While many of the descriptions published were little more than naïve catalogues of perceived parallels between Arab customs and details of life in biblical times, there were serious works of scholarship, including W. Robertson Smith's *Lectures on the Religion of the Semites* (1889) and Gustaf Dalman's extensive survey of Palestinian social life and customs (*Arbeit* [work] *und Sitte* [customs] *in Palestina,* 1928–1939). At the same time, the disciplines of sociology and anthropology were becoming more sophisticated. An early sociological interpretation of the Hebrew Bible was Max Weber's *Ancient Judaism* (1917–1919), and there were sporadic applications of sociological method to early

Christianity as well. Not until the later twentieth century, however, would it become important in biblical interpretation.

Anthropological research had a more immediate impact. Typical of early efforts was the encyclopedic work of James G. Frazer. In *The Golden Bough: A Study in Comparative Religion* (1890; revised and abridged by Theodor Gaster in 1959) and subsequent works such as *Folk-lore in the Old Testament* (1919), Frazer organized a staggering amount of data in support of his understanding of the evolution of society from primitive beginnings to civilization. His principal focus was on myth and rituals, especially the essential role of the king in the welfare of the larger society, and he included both the Hebrew Bible and the New Testament in his analysis.

While Frazer's work was subsequently criticized for its failure to pay sufficient attention to specific cultural contexts and for his cavalier treatment of the data to fit his theories, his influence was considerable. In particular, both in Britain and in Scandinavia many scholars developed and refined his approach, developing what has been characterized as a "myth and ritual" school. The work of Sigmund Mowinckel of Norway is representative. Using form criticism as a method (he had been a student of Gunkel) and the function of the king as an organizing principle, and drawing heavily on Babylonian sources, his study of the Psalms (1921–1924) focused on their use in what he suggested was an annual enthronement festival of Yahweh, like the Babylonian New Year festival. He also identified the individual speaker in many of the psalms as the king himself, and found evidence for prophets giving oracular messages to the king or to the community as part of the New Year ceremony. In *He That Cometh* (1951), Mowinckel examined the reuse of these royal ritual traditions in postexilic Judaism and in the New Testament.

REDACTION CRITICISM

The impression left by source criticism was that the final forms of the Pentateuch and other biblical books or collections for which multiple sources were hypothesized were pedestrian compilations with little literary merit. Beginning in the 1930s, again mainly in Germany, attention began to be paid to the larger units as creative works in their own right. In a number of influential essays, and in his commentaries on Genesis and Deuteronomy, Gerhard von Rad argued that the Hexateuch (the Pentateuch plus Joshua) was itself a literary form. Its *Sitz im Leben* was the feast of weeks (see Deut 16.9; 26.1–2), where the key events of the nation's "salvation history"—the Exodus, the conquest of the land, and the covenant—were recited and reenacted. The Hexateuch is the final, literary product of a long development of such narrative creeds, earlier forms of which are found in such texts as Deut 26.5–9; Ps 136; Ex 15.

One reason that von Rad included the book of Joshua in his analysis was that the promise of the land, a central theme especially in J and P, was unfulfilled in the Pentateuch. Martin Noth took another approach. The original conclusion to the Pentateuch, he proposed, had been replaced by a "Deuteronomistic History." With the book of Deuteronomy as a kind of theological preface, the books of Joshua through 2 Kings comprised a carefully written history of Israel in the promised land. Since 2 Kings ended with the destruction of Jerusalem and the end of Israel's autonomy in the land, Noth argued that this history was an exilic composition which explained the catastrophe as the inevitable result of Israel's failure to live up to the obligations of its covenant with God as detailed in Deuteronomy. Subsequent scholars revised Noth's views, suggesting that while the final form of the Deuteronomistic History was, as he had suggested, a product of the mid-sixth century BCE, it had its own literary history and had existed in one or more editions during the monarchy before the exile. But his essential insight concerning the underlying unity of the books of Deuteronomy through 2 Kings remained the foundation for subsequent interpretation of the historical books.

Attention to larger units developed in the study of the New Testament as well, beginning in the 1950s. In important commentaries on Matthew and Mark, Gunther Bornkamm and Willi Marxsen understood those Gospels as creative literary works, with distinctive theologies and themes. In his study of the theology of Luke, Hans Conzelmann showed how the Gospel of Luke and the book of Acts together formed a carefully composed narrative, with thematic unity provided by an understanding of the life of Jesus as the center of history and Jerusalem as the geographical center of the story. Similar approaches were undertaken for the Gospel of John and the letters of Paul, and for both the Hebrew Bible and the New Testament, redaction criticism's focus on larger units anticipates the methods of literary criticism and canonical criticism later in the twentieth century.

DISCOVERIES OF TEXTS BETWEEN THE WORLD WARS

The discovery and decipherment of cuneiform texts of ancient Assyria and Babylon during the second half of the nineteenth century had profoundly changed the understanding of the Hebrew Bible. On the historical level, the repeated references especially in Assyrian annals to kings of Israel and Judah and to events mentioned in the Bible enabled the construction of a detailed chronology. But for the most part, connections between the cuneiform texts and biblical traditions were indirect. This is not surprising, given the distance and often the time that separated those Mesopotamian cultures from ancient Israel. And apart from a scattering of inscriptions in Hebrew, Phoenician, Aramaic, and Moabite, there were no significant written remains from Israel itself or its most immediate neighbors. That changed in the 1920s and 1930s, as excavations uncovered more collections of ancient texts, and further decipherment shed light on such groups as the Sumerians, the Hittites, and the Hurrians. While there were seldom direct correlations with the Bible, the tablets from Nuzi in northern Iraq and Mari and Ugarit in northern Syria were especially important in expanding the knowledge of the larger world to which ancient Israel belonged.

In many respects the mythological texts from Ugarit are the most important because of their geographical proximity to ancient Israel and the direct light they shed on the Hebrew Bible. Written in a previously unknown Semitic language belonging to the same subfamily as Hebrew, they are composed in poetry that is often remarkably close in diction and in form to biblical poetry. The myths feature gods and goddesses such as El, Baal, and Asherah, all frequently mentioned in the Bible but hitherto incompletely known, largely because of the biblical writers' antagonism toward gods other than Yahweh. Moreover, similar motifs—for example, the childless patriarch, the theophany of the storm god, the council of the gods, the sacred mountain—and innumerable smaller details illustrate the shared commonalties between the culture of Israel and those of its neighbors. Despite undeniable chronological and geographical discontinuities, the literary, religious, and institutional traditions of the Levant, including ancient Israel, are best understood as part of a cultural continuum that, allowing for local particularities, is remarkably consistent and pervasive.

THE DEAD SEA SCROLLS

Another discovery that sent scholarship in new directions was that of a cache of manuscripts in caves near Qumran at the northwest corner of the Dead Sea. Over the course of several years, beginning in 1947, the remains of hundreds of manuscripts were discovered, first by local Bedouin and subsequently by archaeologists. Some of the manuscripts were largely intact, including an almost complete scroll of the Hebrew text of the book of Isaiah, and others were preserved only in fragments. Written mostly in Hebrew and Aramaic, with a few in Greek, they are generally agreed to have been a library deposited in the caves for safekeeping during the First Jewish Revolt (66–73 CE) by the inhabitants of the nearby settlement. Most scholars identify these inhabitants as Essenes, one of the major groups within Judaism in the Roman period, according to the first-century CE Jewish historian Josephus. Among many important aspects of the scrolls, three may be highlighted here. First are the manuscripts of the Hebrew Bible, more than a thousand years older than any previously known, giving new impetus to text criticism (see pp. 460–464 ES). Second is their contribution to the understanding of both Hebrew and Aramaic in the Roman period. And third is the glimpse they provide—especially in what have been termed "sectarian documents," that is, various community regulations, hymns, eschatological texts, and biblical commentaries (*pesharim*; see p. 480 ES)—of one group within Judaism around the turn of the era. What had earlier been oversimplified as a kind of monolithic Judaism is now, on the basis of these texts and other sources reexamined in their light, understood rather as a complex spectrum of various "Judaisms," one of which was earliest Christianity. And while there are no direct links between the Dead Sea Scrolls and the New Testament, they do reveal a rich and complicated background for the emergence of Christianity as well as for the development of rabbinic Judaism after 70 CE.

THE NAG HAMMADI TEXTS

In 1945, at Nag Hammadi some 500 km (300 mi) south of Cairo, Egyptian peasants unearthed a large jar containing thirteen codices. Most of the texts contained within these volumes were Christian Gnostic texts, and although written in

Coptic many had been translated from Greek. One of the most important was *The Gospel of Thomas,* a collection of the sayings of Jesus perhaps originally compiled as early as the end of the first century CE. Fragments of *The Gospel of Thomas* had earlier been found among the Oxyrhynchus Papyri (see above). Less than half of the sayings attributed to Jesus in this text are paralleled in the New Testament, and the *Gospel of Thomas* thus provides both an important independent source and an example of how earliest Christian tradition was collected and expanded by a particular writer within a specific community, a process more and more recognized in the study of the canonical Gospels.

CONCLUSION

With few exceptions, until after World War II historical-critical scholarship was engaged in by Protestant scholars. With the promulgation of the papal encyclical *Divino Afflante Spiritu* in 1943, Roman Catholic scholars began to become practitioners as well. Likewise, both in the United States and in Israel, with the development there of the Hebrew University and later other institutions of higher education, Jewish scholars also made significant contributions. Facilities at major denominational graduate centers increasingly recruited scholars without regard to their affiliations. It is possible by the mid-twentieth century to speak of a consensus of interpretation: a general agreement on methods and results that largely transcended national and confessional differences. That consensus was evidenced in a number of ecumenical endeavors, especially in the United States, including several ongoing translation and commentary projects. Within the next several decades that consensus would begin to unravel.

Contemporary Methods in Biblical Study

In its development during the eighteenth and nineteenth centuries, biblical criticism was often in conversation with other disciplines, including linguistics, anthropology, the history of religion, sociology, philosophical hermeneutics, and literary aesthetics, as well as with theology. Yet as biblical studies became a discipline in its own right, it developed a set of classical methods and questions that set the parameters for research. These methods were largely concerned with the history of the text and of the cultures that produced the texts. The consensus that these were the relevant questions and the methods by which they should be pursued lasted until well after the middle of the twentieth century. Since the 1970s, however, many biblical scholars have questioned the adequacy of an almost exclusive orientation to questions with a historical focus. Also, in keeping with a trend characteristic of most of the humanities and social sciences, there has been a strong movement toward interdisciplinary conversation. Although it is difficult to give a simple overview of the proliferating approaches to biblical studies since the 1970s, they can be roughly grouped under the categories of literary, social-scientific, and cultural hermeneutical approaches.

LITERARY APPROACHES

A popular appreciation of the narrative art of the Bible has always existed. Its stories were represented in the sculpture and stained-glass windows of medieval churches, and Western literature has been profoundly influenced by its characters, themes, and symbols. In both Judaism and Christianity the reading and retelling of the stories in devotional and liturgical contexts made them deeply familiar. Yet even though biblical Hebrew poetry had been the subject of academic study since the eighteenth century (most notably in Bishop Robert Lowth's *Lectures on the Sacred Poetry of the Hebrews*), little attention had been paid to the poetics of biblical narrative. One impetus to the interest in biblical narrative that developed in the 1970s can be traced to a development in American higher education: the creation of departments of religious studies in nondenominational colleges and public universities in the 1960s and 1970s. In such contexts the study of the Bible "as literature" was deemed especially appropriate to a secular curriculum. Such interest was not restricted to scholars in secular contexts, however. In 1968 James Muilenberg, who for much of his career had been a professor at Union Theological Seminary, delivered a presidential address to the Society of Biblical Literature titled "Form Criticism and Beyond." In this lecture he called for a type of literary-theological approach to the poetry and prose of the Bible which he referred to as "rhetorical criticism." Giving further impetus to literary study of the Bible was the work of several scholars of English and comparative literature, who extended their expertise in the analysis of literature to biblical texts. Most prominent were Northrop Frye (*The Great Code: The Bible and Literature*), Robert Alter (*The Art of Biblical Narrative* and *The Art of Biblical Poetry*), and Frank Kermode (*The Genesis of Secrecy*, a study of the Gospel of Mark). Alter and Kermode later collaborated to edit *The Literary Guide to the Bible*.

This literary approach differed from historical study in significant ways. Whereas historical study tended to be concerned with the prehistory of the text (oral traditions and written source materials) and with its development through successive redactions, literary study focused on the final form of the text. Whereas historical study was interested in the world referred to *by* the text, literary study directed its attention to the world constructed *in* the text. Nevertheless, there were certain historical dimensions to this early work in biblical literature. Both Alter and Meir Sternberg attempted to isolate distinctive features of ancient Israelite narrative art (e.g., modes of characterization, the use of type-scenes, techniques of repetition, forms of plot development) which were not necessarily the same as the techniques used in modern Western narrative. Similarly, New Testament literary study has included a strong interest in the comparative analysis of Greco-Roman literary genres and techniques and those used in the Gospels, Acts, and early noncanonical Christian literature.

Much of the early literary study of the Bible was influenced by the "New Criticism," an approach that had dominated Anglo-American literary scholarship from the 1930s through the 1950s. In New Criticism the literary text was considered an autonomous work of art, to be studied independently of its author's intentions and of the sociopolitical currents of the time in which it was produced. New Criticism was a reaction both to a methodology arising out of the history of literature, in which new literary movements are seen as developing from those of previous eras, and to biographical criticism, which reads literary texts as expressions of the life experiences of the writers. The focus in New Criticism is rather on the way in which the text itself is structured so as to produce the observed or expected effects and understandings. Thus, the plot, characters, setting, point of view, and other aspects of the story's rhetoric are analyzed. As the literary study of the Bible was gaining ground, however, rapid changes were taking place in the larger field of literary study, changes that were quickly reflected in biblical studies.

Structuralism was the first of these new movements to make its impact. The origins of structuralism are in the work of the early twentieth-century linguist Ferdinand de Saussure, who attempted to analyze the system of relationships within a language that make acts of speech possible. In particular, he stressed that meanings are produced not so much by simple definition as by a network of contrasts (e.g., a tree is a woody plant that is *not* a bush or a shrub). The anthropologist Claude Lévi-Strauss argued that symbolic structures within human societies, including their kinship systems and their mythologies, could be analyzed in the same way, as systems of differences structured according to binary oppositions (e.g., life/death; male/female; hunting/farming; outside/inside). In a parallel development A. J. Greimas attempted to use Saussure's insights to develop a "grammar" of narrative in much the same way as Saussure attempted to develop a grammar of sentences. Biblical scholars, anthropologists, and literary theorists were quick to apply these approaches to the Bible. The mythic narratives and genealogical accounts of Genesis, the symbolic geography of the Gospel narratives, and even the theological vocabulary of Paul offered opportunities for analyzing the patterns of binary opposition that structuralists argued were the key to the meaning of the texts.

Even as structuralism was being adapted for the study of biblical literature, its assumptions and claims were being challenged in the wider world of philosophical and literary studies. Structuralism claimed that the binary oppositions that structure human thought are essentially universal and unaffected by culture or history. Though the surface features of texts might vary with different societies and over time, the underlying structures did not. Such claims proved difficult to sustain. Just as structuralism dispensed with history, so it also had no place for the reader in the production of meaning. Structuralism understood itself as a kind of scientific method. Yet different readers regularly reached different understandings of the same text. Finally, though structuralism seemed to lend itself well to myths, folktales, and highly formulaic narratives, it seemed unable to deal with more complex narratives.

Against the focus on a supposedly objective and stable text in narrative criticism and against structuralism's focus on impersonal and universal codes, reader-response criticism argued for the essential role of the reader in the process of making meaning. Structuralism tended to display its results in terms of charts, an implicitly spatial understanding of the text. But reader-response theory insisted that reading is essentially a temporal affair. In reading, one only gradually gathers information that is progressively organized and reorganized by the reader to produce meaning. Moreover, the text often contains "gaps" which the reader, consciously or unconsciously, fills in (e.g., details concerning characters, aspects of motivation or causality, connections between events). As the reader becomes actively involved in the process of reading, what the reader engages is not simply the issues of plot and character but also matters of norms and values, which the reader may embrace or resist. Reader-response criticism thus accounts for the different understandings of and reactions to the "same" text by different readers by claiming a necessary place for the subjective element in reading. Subjectivity is limited, however, by what the reader's community considers to be a plausible or implausible inference. Thus it is not so much individual readers as "interpretive communities" who set the parameters according to which interpretation takes place.

Although a number of reader-response studies of Hebrew Bible texts have been produced, the method found its most enthusiastic reception in the study of the New Testament Gospels. Yet it has been one of the most controversial of methods, challenged by historical critics for neglect of the intentions of the author and the horizon of the original audience, and by postmodern critics for its failure to break decisively with certain historical assumptions, such as the understanding of the text as a stable "object" opposed to the readerly "subject." One of the consequences of reader-response criticism's focus on the role of interpretive communities, however, has been a renewed appreciation for the forms of interpretation practiced by Jewish and Christian communities before the rise of modern biblical studies during the Enlightenment. Instead of seeing such traditional readings as naive or simply wrong, interpreters now ask about the assumptions and values that govern the reading practices of Christian typological and allegorical exegesis and of Rabbinic midrash. Midrash in particular has engaged contemporary literary scholars, because some of its interpretive practices bear an intriguing resemblance to forms of postmodern interpretation (for example, the acceptance of multiple, even contradictory, interpretations of the same text; the interpretation of one text by another without regard to historical influence).

If reader-response criticism represented one reaction to the limitations of traditional narratology and to structuralism, a more pervasive criticism emerged under the rubric of post-structuralism, or deconstruction. This movement, associated with the French philosopher Jacques Derrida, is above all a critique of the metaphysical assumptions of Western philosophy, and only secondarily an analysis of the nature of texts and the interpretive process. Derrida noted the attempt of philosophy to posit a central term (God, reason, the human being) in relation to which all of reality can be organized. This organization characteristically takes place by means of binary oppositions (e.g., rational/irrational, oral/written, presence/absence), in which the first term is accepted as superior to the second. Deconstruction attempts to dismantle such structures in order to show their artificiality and the inevitable ways in which any such structure of thought implicitly "decenters" its central term and undermines itself through internal inconsistency and contradiction. When applied to texts, deconstruction begins with the perception that language is inevitably incomplete and surprisingly fluid. It then analyzes how even a text's ostensible argument is rendered problematic and even self-contradictory by extraneous details or slippages in meaning which at first appear peripheral and unimportant. For deconstruction the point of reading is not to restate the meaning intended by the author but to engage the text in creative thought, often by means of punning play with the text. Deconstruction's very style serves to undermine the binary opposition serious/frivolous, for its aim is in part to uncover the ways in which various forms of thought attempt to inscribe power and privilege.

The perspectives of deconstruction have been combined with other intellectual currents (most notably Freudianism and Marxism) to produce a variety of related approaches that are often referred to comprehensively by the term postmodernism. Along with Derrida's deconstruction, Michel Foucault's study of the complex nature of power and truth and Fredric Jameson's neo-Marxist analysis of ideology have been deeply influential on postmodernism in biblical studies. For an overview of these trends as well as other forms of postmodernism, see *The Postmodern Bible* by The Bible and Culture Collective.

Since one of the features of postmodernism is its tendency to dissolve boundaries, it is scarcely surprising that its characteristic approaches have combined with a wide variety of other impulses within biblical studies, most notably feminist criticism, but also various forms of ideological criticism (see below under cultural hermeneutics). Similarly, postmodern analysis is not restricted to narrative but employed in relation to all sorts of texts. Indeed, the self-conscious study of the literary artistry of the Bible, such a controversial novelty in 1970, has been all but put aside in the rapidly shifting mix of methods and approaches that have been developed alongside the classical forms of biblical interpretation.

SOCIAL-SCIENTIFIC CRITICISM

Social-scientific criticism, another form of biblical criticism that has arisen in more recent years, applies insights and methods from the fields of sociology, anthropology, and ethnography to describe aspects of ancient social life manifested in the biblical texts and to reconstruct the social worlds behind the text. To a certain extent historical criticism has always had a social dimension, since the objects of its interest included nations, states, social groupings, and religious movements. Yet self-conscious social-scientific investigation, though not unknown in earlier stages of biblical studies, has come into its own since the 1960s.

As early as the Renaissance, students of the Bible were concerned to make cross-cultural comparisons between ancient Israel and the nations of the ancient Near East. With the development of critical biblical study in the nineteenth century, this interest in cross-cultural study focused particularly on the comparison between Israel and the pre-Islamic Bedouin Arabs, as well as with contemporary Bedouin society, especially in the work of Julius Wellhausen and William Robertson Smith. Similarly, Martin Noth compared Israel's premonarchical tribal confederacy with ancient Greek tribal leagues. In retrospect, these early attempts at social-scientific analysis were hampered by a lack of rigorous method, by erroneous assumptions about the economic and social organization of ancient Israel, and by an overly static model of ancient culture. More sophisticated was the work of the sociologist Max Weber, whose *Ancient Judaism* (compiled from lectures given in 1917–1919) attempted to incorporate the dimensions of historical and institutional change in his account of the social organization of ancient Israel. Sociological investigation was not as prominent in New Testament studies, although the Chicago school of social analysis (Shailer Mathews and Shirley Jackson Case) did investigate the social location of early Christians and attempted to account for the success of Christianity among Gentiles but not among Jews.

These early attempts at social-scientific criticism were largely displaced by interest in other questions and methods, and for almost forty years little was published in this field. By the 1960s and 1970s, however, interest in it revived. Since the issues posed by Hebrew Bible and New Testament materials are significantly different, each literature will be discussed separately. In studies concentrating on the Hebrew Bible, several areas have proven fruitful for analysis. The first issue to be examined, and one still sharply debated, is that of the socioeconomic and political nature of the formation of the Israelite tribal confederacy. Social historians rejected the conquest model of Israel's entry into Canaan as it is described in the biblical narrative. Both George Mendenhall and Norman Gottwald argued that Israel's origins were to be sought instead in a peasant revolt against urban Canaanite overlords. The peasant movement was a revolt against the hierarchical socioeconomic structure and developed as a retribalization along egalitarian lines in the central highlands. What differentiated Mendenhall and Gottwald, however, was Gottwald's explicit use of Marxist social theory. Although both of their proposals have been sharply criticized for reliance more on presupposed models than on textual or material evidence, they served to open the question of Israel's origins for fresh investigation. Since the 1970s archaeology has also generated increasing information concerning population patterns, forms of domestic architecture, agricultural practices, and trade patterns for the period preceding the monarchy. This information, together with a wider array of possible comparative models for the development of noncentralized peasant societies, has begun to generate new ways of understanding early Israel, though none has yet achieved consensus.

Similarly, attempts to understand the movement from a loose tribal confederation to the eventual formation of royal states has been aided by comparative social analysis. Social anthropologists have documented the development of chieftainships as an intermediate stage between these two forms of social organization. A chiefdom is a hierarchically organized society that lacks the strong central governmental apparatus characteristic of a true state. Though some aspects of the process are still debated, it is now generally thought that Saul's "kingship" and at least the early stages of David's rule should be thought of as chieftainships.

Prophecy is another area of Israel's religious and social life that has proven fruitful for social-scientific analysis. Apart from texts of prophetic oracles recovered from neighboring nations, archaeology does not contribute to this question. Rather, the biblical texts are analyzed in light of sociological models and comparative ethnographic evidence. Though the limited evidence makes many conclusions elusive, it has been possible to clarify to a certain extent the social location of the prophets and their relationship or nonrelationship to established religious institutions and to the monarchy. How a prophet secures legitimation, the role of ecstasy and other phenomena of abnormally heightened consciousness, and the relation of oral and written communication have all been examined in social-scientific perspective. The later development of apocalypticism and the question of its social location—whether it was, for example, an outgrowth of prophecy, a scribal phenomenon, or a movement of the social margins or of the priestly elite—has been debated as the biblical texts are reread in light of apocalyptic and millenarian movements in the medieval and modern periods.

The biblical text also contains significant information about purity laws and kinship and family patterns, topics that lend themselves to comparative social analysis. In the 1960s the anthropologist Mary Douglas pioneered such studies with her analysis of the food laws in Leviticus, interpreting them as a symbolic system for organizing the world and correlating purity laws in general with the social concern for boundaries. More recently the narratives in Genesis, the family laws in Deuteronomy, and the reports on the postexilic community in Ezra-Nehemiah have been investigated in an attempt to discern the basic structures of family organization, as well as changes over time in the patterns of family life. As modern interest in gender constructs and roles has grown, so has the investigation of such issues in ancient Israel. Although the resources are mainly the texts of the Hebrew Bible, attempts have been made to use the findings of archaeology to determine the patterns of life and activity characteristic of males and females in biblical times (see C. Meyers, *Discovering Eve: Ancient Israelite Women in Context*).

In the field of New Testament, insights from sociology were first used in the 1970s to analyze the nature of the early Christian movement. The anthropological study of millenarian movements and sociological typologies of sects were employed to clarify the dynamics of the Christian communities that emerged in the first two centuries of the era. One of the watersheds in the use of sociological and anthropological perspectives in New Testament studies was the publication of *The First Urban Christians* by Wayne Meeks, which was a comprehensive attempt to describe the social context and organization of the early Pauline communities. Also significant was the application to biblical texts of cultural anthropological studies of the roles of honor and shame in Mediterranean societies, and the functioning of patron-client forms of social relations. These studies not only illumined structural aspects of early Christian society and its context but also showed how aspects of discourse and categories of thought were organized in characteristic patterns that reflected these social values and assumptions. In such cases social-scientific and traditional theological investigation of the New Testament may converge, as the latter recognizes the need to understand the meaning and context of key terms by means of social-scientific analysis.

The rich comparative material available from the classical world has facilitated many types of sociological investigation. Slavery, as social phenomenon and as metaphor, has been an important topic, as has the role of prophets and prophecy, the practice of magic, and the class status of early converts to Christianity. As in the field of Hebrew Bible, the social study of family structures and gender roles has yielded important insights.

Although disputes concerning appropriate methodology for social analysis have not been absent in Hebrew Bible studies, they have been particularly prominent in New Testament studies. Even the terminology has been contested. Some scholars prefer to describe their work as social history, that is, as an extension of traditional historical criticism that is informed by categories and questions from sociology and cultural anthropology. Others have insisted that their work is social-scientific in the strong sense of the term, that is, as work guided by the correlation of models and data, as are more purely sociological and social-psychological studies. More significant than the disagreement over terminology, however, has been the issue of which sociological or anthropological methods and approaches are most suitable. Social conflict is a topic which has long been of interest to sociologists, though it has been studied from two quite different perspectives. Social functionalism examines the ways in which society, considered as an organism, attempts to contain and manage conflict, integrating disparate members and subgroups into the whole. This approach was used by Gerd Theissen to explore the earliest stages of the early Christian movement and its subsequent evolution. By contrast, conflict models in sociological theory emphasize the ways in which different groups in a society pursue their own interests and the ways in which different ideologies struggle with one another. More recent work in the sociology of early Christianity has favored conflict models over social functionalism. The nature of the textual sources has also influenced the choice of methods. Since much of the early Christian literature is self-consciously theological or ideological, cultural anthropology and the sociology of knowledge have proven particularly fruitful. Both of these approaches pay attention to the way in which societies create "symbolic universes" by which to negotiate issues of identity, legitimacy, and the creation or resolution of conflict. This focus on the social functions of language has drawn together literary and social criticism toward something of a convergence on what might be termed ideological criticism, an issue also central to the third methodological movement to be discussed, cultural hermeneutics.

CULTURAL HERMENEUTICS

Classical biblical studies, as it emerged from its Enlightenment roots, understood itself as a form of critical analysis that was objective, disinterested, and even "scientific." Though biblical theology might make normative claims, even those claims were based on a preliminary act of interpretation that was grounded in objective scholarship. In recent years the claim of classic biblical scholarship to be a quasi-scientific enterprise has been questioned by those who insist that the enterprise of historical criticism of the Bible is unconsciously shaped and informed by cultural assumptions specific to the time and place in which that method was developed. Pure objectivity is an illusion. In the interpretation of texts and cultures there is no "view from nowhere." All interpreters, whether or not they are aware of it, frame their questions and perceive the data from some perspective, which helps to shape their understanding of the text or culture in question. Rather than seeing the influence of the interpreter's social and cultural location as a problem, some have claimed it as a positive value. Thus the term "cultural hermeneutics" serves as an umbrella term for a variety of approaches to biblical interpretation (e.g., liberationist, feminist, post-colonial) in which the social location of the interpreter is not only made explicit but serves as a normative principle in interpretation. The primary categories that have figured in such interpretation are those of class, ethnicity, and gender.

The earliest and most methodologically self-conscious of these approaches is that of Latin American liberation theology, which emerged in the 1960s and 1970s. This approach did not begin as an academic perspective but rather emerged out of the concrete experience of the poor and of those pastors and other religious professionals who lived and worked with them. They insisted that the starting point for reading and interpreting the Bible must not be a stance of "objectivity" but rather the experience of the crushing poverty and oppression of the lowest social classes. Interpreted from the perspective of material poverty, the Bible discloses itself as a text of liberation and serves to further a revolutionary process of emancipation.

Much of the work of liberation hermeneutics took place in the Bible studies of Christian base communities, in which groups of the poor were encouraged to read and interpret the Bible for themselves, with the assistance of a priest or teacher. Although this oral interpretation was seldom recorded, Ernesto Cardenal's *The Gospel in Solentiname* provides an example. The interpretation developed in the base communities was paralleled by the work of theologians and biblical scholars, who articulated the principles of liberation hermeneutics in a series of important studies (see, especially, L. Boff and C. Boff, *Introducing Liberation Theology*; and J. Severino Croatto, *Biblical Hermeneutics: Toward a Theory of Reading in the Production of Meaning*). Liberation theology has tended to place special emphasis on certain portions of the Bible, notably the story of the Exodus, the social criticism of the prophets, the figure of Mary (as singer of the Magnificat, with its imagery of social transformation; Lk 1), Jesus' preaching of the kingdom of God in the Gospels, the depiction of the liberating Christian community in Acts, and the struggle against evil in its imperialist and cosmic guise in the book of Revelation.

In the wake of Latin American liberation hermeneutics, religious communities and academics in the various countries of Africa and Asia have developed analogous forms of biblical interpretation that work from the particular experiences of those nations. A related movement, which is indebted to liberation hermeneutics but which also draws on other sources, is post-colonial hermeneutics (see R. S. Sugirtharajah, ed., *Voices from the Margin: Interpreting the Bible in the Third World*). As European countries colonized various parts of the globe from the sixteenth to the nineteenth centuries, the Bible was an important aspect of the sometimes forced assimilation of indigenous peoples to European cultural values. The desire of European churches to spread Christianity meant that the Bible, as interpreted by Europeans, accompanied the colonizers. Where conversion took place, the Bible displaced indigenous traditions, even as it buttressed European dominance. In recent years biblical scholars in the Third World (and increasingly in Europe and North America) have examined this complex history and heritage. They have attempted to analyze the roles that the Bible and its interpretation have played in these colonized countries. Not only have the colonizers' interpretations been examined and critiqued (e.g., the use of the Exodus/Conquest story in North America and South Africa to justify the displacement of the indigenous peoples), but increasingly, attempts have been made to recover the forms of interpretation developed by the newly Christianized indigenous peoples themselves. Elements of "hybrid interpretation," that is, the mixing of indigenous traditions with Christian biblical narratives, are not only identified but often encouraged as a continuing creative practice. Thus part of the resistance to the effects of the colonization experience is to read the Bible along with rather than above other religious and cultural traditions.

Within North America several ethnic communities, including Hispanics, Asian-Americans, and Native Americans, have also developed self-conscious traditions of biblical interpretation. The earliest and most developed of these is African-American biblical hermeneutics. The Bible has played a particularly significant role in the African-American community, and popular forms of African-American biblical interpretation have been embedded in the songs and sermons of the community for centuries. In the 1960s and 1970s, as the Black Theology movement developed, African-American biblical scholars began to turn their attention both to the recovery and analysis of this traditional interpretation and to the development of a critical, academic form of African-American biblical interpretation (see C. H. Felder, ed., *Stony the Road We Trod: African-American Biblical Interpretation*). Afrocentric interpretation has drawn attention to the historical role played by African countries (especially Egypt and Ethiopia) and by Africans in the biblical text. But African-American biblical hermeneutics has also attended to texts and issues that have been important to the lives of the African-American community: for instance, the Exodus narratives, the place of slavery in Israelite and early Christian reflection, and the preaching of Jesus. African-American biblical studies has also been marked by a deep reflection on the nature of interpretation itself, especially the ways in which an oppressed community appropriates for its own liberation a text which also serves as the authorizing document of the society within which its members have been oppressed.

Whereas the various perspectives discussed so far under the rubric of cultural hermeneutics are distinctively Christian, the same cannot be said for feminist biblical hermeneutics. Here, although Christian feminist biblical interpretation emerged slightly earlier, Jewish and Christian feminist interpretation has largely developed in tandem, and the critical conversation between Jewish and Christian feminists has been one of the distinctive features of this movement. In the 1950s and 1960s Protestant seminaries began to admit women in significantly larger numbers than before, followed soon after by an increase in the number of Catholic and Jewish women pursuing theological education. The emergence of the women's movement in the 1960s and its criticism of the role of the Bible in the oppression of women posed a challenge to those who identified themselves as both Christian or Jewish and feminist. One early position, which still continues to be important in the Christian evangelical community, is to affirm that the Bible, when correctly interpreted, affirms women's full humanity. Other feminists, more critical of the Bible itself, have attempted to expose and analyze the patriarchal elements in the biblical text itself in order to show how the patriarchal values can be separated from the essentially liberating values that form its primary message. More radical feminists, however, have attempted to show that the biblical traditions are thoroughly and irredeemably antifeminist.

Feminist interpretation of the Bible has embraced a variety of methodologies. Some of it utilizes the approaches of historical-critical and sociological biblical scholarship, since it attempts to recover and reconstruct the historical reality of women's lives in ancient Israel and in the Greco-Roman world of early Christianity and early Judaism. Certain Christian feminists, in an attempt to make a case for the liberating nature of early Christianity, did so in ways that played off the egalitarian message of Jesus against his Jewish background. Jewish feminists challenged the accuracy of the representation of Judaism, and as a result considerably more nuanced pictures of gender relations in both early Christianity and Judaism have been developed.

Not all feminist interpretation has been concerned with historical reconstruction, however. A significant strand of feminism has used literary methods, exploring the ways in which biblical texts construct and represent an image of women that may function in the service of particular ideologies. In many instances this literary approach has involved reading against the grain of the text. For instance, a character whom the text treats as a subsidiary character may become for feminist analysis the central character of the text (e.g., Jephthah's daughter in Judg 11 or the Levite's concubine in Judg 19). Of particular concern to feminists has been the issue of women and violence, for many of the biblical texts do represent violence against women, and a smaller but significant number represent women engaged in violence. While much of this literary work has also had a historical focus, in that it has been concerned with how the ancient texts have represented women, increasingly attention has been drawn to what is called cultural studies, i.e., how Western traditions in art and, more recently, film have themselves depicted the biblical representations of women.

Since feminism made women aware of their own particular perspective as women in the process of interpretation, it is not surprising that feminism has also become aware that particular women occupy very different positions in society, depending on their social and economic class and their ethnicity. Consequently, it has become more problematic to refer to a single "feminist" movement, for women of color and Third World women have insisted that gender, class, and ethnicity must all be considered in their complex interrelationships. African-American women, for instance, have complicated the Anglo-European interpretation of the Abraham/Sarah narratives by focusing on the character of Hagar—the ethnic outsider, the slave, the surrogate wife—and her role in creating the narrative's moral complexity. Similarly, Latina, African, and Asian women have taken up the challenge of understanding the ways in which the practices of reading and interpreting the Bible serve to constrain or to emancipate women in their particular social and cultural contexts.

Finally, canonical criticism, which often describes itself as a theological mode of interpretation, may also be considered as a form of cultural hermeneutics, since it also puts the community context within which the text was created and from which it is to be read into the foreground. Though the forms of canonical criticism developed by its two major proponents, Brevard Childs and James Sanders, differ, one can identify common elements. Specifically, canonical criticism is concerned with how scripture's final form was created within a believing community and how the meanings created by that final form continue to guide the reading practices of the community. The canonical shaping of the Jewish Bible, for instance—which places the Writings in the final position and concludes with the call of 2 Chronicles for the exiles to go up to Jerusalem to rebuild the Temple—tells a different story from that produced by the shaping of the Christian Old Testament, which places the prophets last and concludes with Malachi's reference to the return of the prophet Elijah to announce the coming Day of the Lord.

In one sense canonical criticism is an extension of historical criticism's interest in the development of traditions. But in contrast to historical criticism's tendency to investigate the earliest stages of development, canonical criticism explicitly privileges the latest stage, the canon in its final form. This concern with reading the text of scripture in its final form gives canonical criticism some similarity to the literary approaches of the "New Criticism." Thus, where historical criticism, reading the book of Isaiah, tries to distinguish which materials come from the eighth-century prophet, the sixth-century prophet, and the fifth-century prophet, literary and canonical critics focus on how the final form of the book has created the context within which all of its materials are now to be read, as a movement from judgment to salvation. While canonical criticism's self-conscious attention to what it means to read scripture as a member of a religious tradition links it with cultural hermeneutics, it also differs from some of the other forms of cultural hermeneutics discussed above. Just as those forms of interpretation make repeated reference to the specific experience of the reader as a guide to interpretation, canonical hermeneutics finds the clues to a proper reading in the ways in which the text of scripture was shaped by the believing community at the time its canon was fixed.

If anything ties together the various strands of newly developing approaches to biblical interpretation, it is a concern for the relationship of language, meaning, and power. More historically oriented literary and social methods increasingly examine the ways in which issues of conflict and access to power can be traced in the texts of the Hebrew Bible and the New Testament. Cultural hermeneutics, though not uninterested in historical reconstruction, also focuses on the ways in which access to the power to interpret the text and construe its meaning serves to empower those who have traditionally been marginalized. And postmodernism has attempted to underscore the ironies of all such strategies, since in its view a stable and definitive meaning always eludes the interpreter.

The Geography of the Bible

The geographical territory encompassed by the Bible (if one includes all identifiable places that are at least mentioned) includes most countries that border the Mediterranean Sea as well as those to its east. The majority of the narratives of the Hebrew Bible and the Apocrypha, as well as the Gospels in the New Testament, are set in that subregion of the Middle East known as the Levant and now governed by Lebanon, Syria, Jordan, Israel, and the Palestinian Authority. Egypt to the southwest and Mesopotamia (largely modern Iraq) and Persia (Iran) to the northeast are also part of the biblical landscape.

In Mesopotamia—the Greek term for the region between the Euphrates and Tigris Rivers (see color Maps 6 and 14 at the end of this volume)—as in Egypt, urban civilization developed by the fourth millennium BCE in the river valleys that provided the essential water for a region where rainfall was at best seasonal and at worst, especially in the case of Egypt, insufficient for agriculture. The regular summer flooding of the Nile Valley enabled the early and continuous existence of a remarkably long-lasting culture in Egypt, which because of its proximity to the Middle East was an important player in that region's history, and the locale for a number of key episodes in biblical narrative, most notably the Exodus. In Mesopotamia the inhabitants had harnessed the two rivers to provide, by means of an elaborate irrigation system, sufficient water for agriculture as well as for consumption. The several successive imperial powers that originated in Mesopotamia were able to use this productive region as a base for expansion, especially to the west, over which they exercised control throughout most of the first millennium BCE, until the Hellenistic period.

Although surrounded by vast deserts, there is a narrow stretch of land where agriculture can flourish that extends from the Nile Valley around to the Persian Gulf. The western part of this "fertile crescent," the Levant, has the same environment as much of the rest of the region adjacent to the Mediterranean, which today as for the last several millennia is characterized by almost ideal growing conditions for grapes and olives and for raising sheep and goats; grains and legumes and other fruits can also be grown in much of the region. Its climate is moderate, without excessively high or low temperatures for the most part, and with abundant rainfall that occurs mainly during the winter months. Jerusalem, for example, receives on average about 550 mm (22 in) of rain annually, most of it falling between November and February, with January being the rainiest month. Higher elevations to the north receive still more rainfall, and the southern and easternmost regions considerably less.

Within the Levant itself, the primary focus of biblical narratives, there is a wide variety of environments, the result of the geological substructure of the region, which presents dramatic changes in a relatively small area. Moving from west to east, the Mediterranean coast is occupied by a coastal plain that is about 25 km (15 mi) wide in the south but narrows as one moves north. It is interrupted by Mount Carmel, which juts into it, and virtually disappears in northen Israel and Lebanon. The coast itself has several excellent harbors in the north, from which the Canaanites and their successors the Phoenicians conducted a flourishing maritime trade. Farther south, the coast is relatively even, and there are few natural harbors. Phoenician influence eventually extended to such port cities as Acco, Dor, Joppa, and Ashkelon, and in the late first century Herod the Great constructed an impressive artificial harbor at Caesarea. Along the coastal plain was a major route, known as "the way of the sea" (Isa 9.1), used by traders and by armies of conquest between Egypt and Damascus. This route ran to the point where the coast narrows below Mount Carmel, from which passes led from the coastal plain to the Jezreel (Esdraelon) Valley; from there, several routes could be taken to the northeast.

Adjacent to the coastal plain in the south is an uplift of smaller, gentler hills called "the Shephelah" ("lowland"). As the natural western boundary of the kingdom of Judah in the Iron Age, and of other entities in the same region before and after, it was protected by a number of important cities, including Lachish and Gezer. The Shephelah forms the foothills of the mountainous region immediately to its east. This is the "hill country" of the biblical writers, with higher elevations to the north. For example, Jerusalem, about 55 km (35 mi) east of the Mediterranean, is 760 m (2,500 ft) above sea level, and many mountains in northern Galilee have elevations of over 1,000 m (3,300 ft). The highest peak in the region is Mount Hermon, which is 2,800 m (9,200 ft) high and for that reason is snow-covered year-round. The hill country is the setting for many of the key locales in biblical narrative, including the relatively inaccessible sites of Jerusalem, the capital of the kingdom of Judah (later Judea), and Samaria, the capital of the Northern Kingdom of Israel and later of the province with the same name. This central mountainous ridge is bisected by the broad, fertile Jezreel Valley, the major route to the interior and hence the location of a number of important ancient cities, including Jokneam, Megiddo, Taanach, Ibleam, and Jezreel. Mount Tabor rises from the floor of the Jezreel Valley in splendid isolation to an elevation of 588 m (1,929 ft) above sea level. The village of Nazareth, home of Jesus, is in the hills immediately north of the valley.

To the north of the Jezreel Valley lies Galilee. Because of its abundant springs, Galilee was dotted by settlements from prehistoric times, but it plays little role in biblical narratives until the end of the first millennium BCE, when it is the setting both for some of the campaigns of the Maccabees and, in the early first century CE, of the ministry of Jesus in the Gospels.

Just east of this central mountainous region is the Rift Valley. This major depression in the earth's crust extends from southern Turkey into East Africa; in Israel and Jordan it is almost entirely below sea level. Included in it are the Huleh Basin in northern Galilee, 70 m (230 ft) above sea level, where the site of Hazor was a major fortified city from early in the second millennium BCE until its destruction by the Assyrians in 732 BCE. Some 20 km (12 mi) south of Lake Huleh is the Sea of Chinnereth, or the Sea of Galilee (also called the Sea of Tiberias), a large lake about 20 km (12 mi) long that fills the valley. It lies 210 m (700 ft) below sea level, and is fed by the Jordan River, which flows into it from the north. It is habitat to nearly two dozen species of fish, and the fishing industry has been an important part of the local economy since prehistoric times. Many of the events narrated in the Gospels are set in the many towns and cities near the lake, and the region was a center of resistance against the Romans during the First Jewish Revolt of 66–73 CE.

The Jordan River continues its flow south from the Sea of Galilee 105 km (65 mi) to the Dead Sea. The valley itself is about 20 km (12 mi) wide and is entirely below sea level, with a semi-tropical climate that produces lush vegetation, even though because of its low elevation it receives relatively little rain. Important cities in the valley include Beth-shan (later Scythopolis) in the north and Jericho in the south. The valley was an important subsidiary route, especially during the Roman period, when Jews often avoided the district controlled by the Samaritans between Galilee and Judea.

The Dead Sea, lying 400 m (1,300 ft) below sea level, is the lowest point on the land mass of the earth. Because of evaporation due to high temperatures (a record 51° C [124° F] was measured here), the composition of the water is about 25 percent salt and other minerals, making organic life impossible and giving this lake its ancient name, "the salt sea" (Num 34.3,12; NRSV "Dead Sea"). The desolate region that surrounds it is the narrative setting for the legendary cities of Sodom and Gomorrah. On its western shore are Qumran, where the Dead Sea Scrolls were found, and Masada, a palace constructed by Herod that was the last Jewish outpost to be captured in the First Jewish Revolt.

East of the Rift Valley there is a rapid rise to the relatively level Transjordanian plateau to the east, with the elevation of modern Amman (ancient Rabbah, later Philadelphia) at ca. 820 m (2,700 ft) about average. This region too receives sufficient rainfall to sustain agriculture, and moreover is watered by two tributaries of the Jordan, the Yarmuk and the Jabbok, and by the Arnon, which flows into the Dead Sea. The northern part of the plateau, biblical Bashan, was famous for its cattle and for its oak forests, and in the Hellenistic and Roman periods was the location of several of the cities of the Decapolis. Traversing the Transjordanian plateau from south to north is a major route, called in the Bible the "King's Highway" (Num 20.17), used throughout antiquity as a conduit for the incense and spice trade from Arabia to Damascus. East of the plateau is a vast desert region, a continuation of the Arabian desert that extends northward to the Euphrates Valley, and thus limits the Fertile Crescent on both east and west. Apart from a few oases, especially Tadmor (later Palmyra) northeast of Damascus, this desert was essentially uninhabited in historic times.

South of the hill country of Judah lies the Negeb, a region of limited rainfall and hence marginal agriculture. The city of Beer-sheba is located in the extreme northern Negeb, just south of the Judean hill country. The Negeb merges into the Sinai peninsula, which is formed by the two northern arms of the Red Sea, separating the Sinai from the North African desert to its west and the Arabian desert to its east.

The small size of this region is out of proportion to its importance in ancient times and to the importance of the biblical texts which are set in it. West of the Jordan, the traditional boundaries of ancient Israel were Dan in the north and Beer-sheba in the south, separated by a distance of about 240 km (150 mi). Between these two cities, and between the Mediterranean and the Rift Valley, is a region with an area approximately the same as that of the state of Vermont. From another perspective, Jerusalem is about 55 km (35 mi) east of the Mediterranean and 25 km (16 mi) west of the Dead Sea. In the right conditions, both bodies of water are visible from Jerusalem's hills.

CULTURAL CONTEXTS

The Ancient Near East and Ancient Israel to the Mid-first Millennium BCE

BEGINNINGS

By the time Israel appeared on the stage of the ancient Near East, civilization and the patterns of empires and of the larger shared culture of the Levant were already well established. Before the end of the fourth millennium BCE, full urbanization had developed in the great river valleys of Egypt and Mesopotamia. The development of sophisticated technology to exploit the flooding of the Nile and to channel the waters of the Euphrates and Tigris enabled the production of regular food supplies and led to regional hegemonies. In Egypt, oriented about the south-to-north direction of the Nile's flow, this culminated in the unification of Upper (southern) and Lower (northern) Egypt, at the onset of the Early Dynastic Period toward the end of the fourth millennium. In southern Mesopotamia the kings of Sumer ruled that region from a succession of dominant city-states beginning at about the same time.

The stages that had preceded urbanization are prehistoric in the sense that they antedate the development of writing. Archaeologists have been able to trace the slow, and often independent, progress from hunter-gatherer economies throughout the Near East to stable cultures that relied on domesticated crops and animals for their sustenance. Dependable supplies of food led to increases of population, and ultimately competition for resources. These factors combined to necessitate specialization of tasks, centralized control, and record-keeping. For these purposes, writing was invented, again toward the end of the fourth millennium, and once introduced, was widely adopted in different systems in Egypt and Mesopotamia. By 3000 BCE, then, written history may be said to have begun.

The result of nearly two centuries of discovery, excavation, and decipherment of ancient texts is that a detailed chronology of the ancient Near East has been established. While there are occasional gaps in the sequence of rulers for

Egypt and for the various Mesopotamian city-states, those sequences are relatively complete. For regions peripheral to the centers of power the historical record is more spotty, but still substantial. Allowing for minor scholarly disagreements, the chronology is secure and is the framework for the history of the entire ancient Near East, including Israel. Although there remain some small groups of undeciphered texts, including a few in what is apparently the Philistine language, and although much of cuneiform literature is still underground, it is unlikely that new discoveries will require substantial revision of our current understanding of the essential chronology of the ancient Near East.

Nor is the knowledge of the historical record restricted to kings and princes. Hundreds of thousands of nonelite texts have been found. These are not great myths and royal inscriptions, but mundane business and commercial records that shed valuable light on the lives of ordinary men and women and have begun to make possible a reconstruction of the social world of the ancient Near East.

Ancient cultures were as intrigued as we are by beginnings, and they constructed elaborate myths to explain their own prehistory. The establishment of the natural and social orders is typically presented in these myths as the work of a deity, usually the principal god or goddess of the political entity in which they were written. Both Egyptian and Mesopotamian literatures have a large number of such creation myths, many features of which have parallels in biblical traditions. Like their more powerful neighbors to the southwest and northeast, the ancient Israelites had their own accounts of origins, some of which were ultimately collected and edited in the book of Genesis. The early chapters of Genesis deal with prehistory and are largely mythical. In these Israelite expressions of the origins of the world, of society, and of civilization, the principal agent is the god of Israel. And, although intended as the prologue to a larger historical narrative, they are not historical in any modern sense; that is, they do not accurately represent what the archaeological record shows to have taken place, whether in terms of chronology, or the origin of species, or a universal flood.

Egypt and Mesopotamia have their own complex histories during the third millennium, now relatively well known thanks to textual and archaeological data. In the Levant this is the period known as the Early Bronze Age, when northern Syria was largely in the orbit of Mesopotamia, and Egypt exercised direct control over Palestine. For complex reasons not fully understood, toward the end of the third millennium Egypt experienced some internal disruption, reflected in the decline of city-states in Palestine but not in Syria farther to the north. By 2000 BCE, however, centralized control had been reestablished, and the textual and artifactual evidence is abundant. Trade flourished, as is indicated by both the archaeological record and commercial and diplomatic correspondence among larger urban centers, and between them and Mesopotamia and Egypt. The Levant was spanned by a cultural continuum, with Syria and northern Canaan being more closely linked with Mesopotamia, and southern Canaan with Egypt. Canaan itself had a relatively homogeneous culture, and its inhabitants, especially in rural and village settings, went about their lives with relatively few changes despite the struggles of the urban centers with each other. From as far back as the end of the fourth millennium, and into the first, there appears to have been continuity of population, whose patterns of material culture develop rather than being replaced by successive waves of invaders, as earlier historical reconstructions suggested.

It is in this larger context that Israel placed its own beginnings, centered on the lives of four generations of ancestors, the families of Abraham and Sarah, of Isaac and Rebekah, and of Jacob and Leah, Rachel, Bilhah, and Zilpah, and their offspring.

THE HISTORICITY OF THE ANCESTRAL NARRATIVES IN GENESIS

In the biblical account of the origins of Israel, narratives concerning Israel's ancestors in Gen 12–50 follow the mythic material in chs 1–11. The chronology of the narratives themselves is set in the early second millennium BCE, but there are no direct connections between the biblical traditions and nonbiblical sources. No person or event known from Egyptian, Mesopotamian, or other sources is even mentioned in the biblical narrative. At the relatively few points where the Bible does name rulers (as in Gen 14; 20.2; 26.8), none of them are found in any nonbiblical sources. Moreover, at many points in the narrative the Bible is tantalizingly vague. If the biblical writers had just named, for example, the pharaoh who took Sarah into his house (Gen 12.15), or the pharaoh in whose court Joseph rose to power (Gen 41), we would at least know when the biblical writers thought those events took place, and could correlate them with Egyptian chronology.

The biblical narratives themselves are the result of a lengthy and complicated process of formation, transmission, and editing (see "Introduction to the Pentateuch," pp. 3–7 HB). Although the reconstruction of that process is hypothetical, there is no doubt that the process itself has caused the inclusion of a large number of anachronisms. These reflect the times when the transmission and editing took place rather than the times in which the narratives are presumably set.

As a result of these factors, not surprisingly, scholars are divided on the question of historicity, with proposed dates for the ancestors of Israel, if in fact they even existed, spanning the entire second millennium BCE. A cautious positive assessment would be at best a convergence of possibilities. Allowing for anachronisms, the data are not inconsistent with the Middle to Late Bronze Ages (ca. 2000–1200), with some clues pointing to earlier rather than later in that time span. These clues are admittedly indirect, and include the forms of personal names used and the identification of the god of the ancestors as El (see Ex 6.3), also known in texts from Ugarit in northwest Syria as the head of the Canaanite pantheon from Ugarit. The account of Joseph's elevation to a position of prominence in the Egyptian court is not incompatible with the rise to power of the Hyksos, the Fifteenth Dynasty rulers of Semitic origin who controlled much of Lower Egypt at the end of the Middle Bronze Age (ca. 1650–1550).

Yet most of the details of the lives of the ancestors of Israel, both as pastoral semi-nomads and as periodically migrating to Egypt, fit not only the mid-second millennium but other times as well. Biblical writings probably do preserve some authentic historical memories, but these have been so refracted by the processes of transmission and the idealization of the ancestors that it is impossible to designate any of the individuals mentioned in Genesis as historical or to establish anything resembling a precise chronology.

THE HISTORICITY OF THE EXODUS FROM EGYPT

As with the ancestral narratives in Genesis, there is no direct connection between biblical traditions and other ancient sources. Egyptian records contain no mention of the major individuals and events of the narrative in Ex 1–15: Moses, Aaron, the plagues, and the defeat of the Egyptian army at the sea are completely absent from the extensive documentation we have for ancient Egypt. Again, the biblical sources are frustratingly unspecific. Neither the pharaoh "who did not know Joseph" (Ex 1.8) nor the pharaoh of the Exodus itself (Ex 5–15) is named. The only precise detail in the narrative is the store cities named in Ex 1.11, but both their precise location and the dates when they were founded and occupied are uncertain, and their inclusion could also be anachronistic. In addition, biblical chronology is both vague and inconsistent. Moreover, as with the ancestral narratives in Gen 12–50, the narrative has been shaped by centuries of transmission and redaction. Finally, although the importance of the Exodus is evident from the amount of space devoted to the generation of the Exodus (the books of Exodus through Deuteronomy), the narrative framework was supplemented by the attachment of large chunks of legal and ritual material from subsequent periods. Once again, then, it is hardly surprising that scholars have divergent views about the date and even the historicity of the Exodus and of its principal characters. And, again, we do best to speak of a convergence of probabilities based on indirect evidence.

The first fixed datum, one of great importance, is a victory stele of Pharaoh Merneptah (1213–1203). In it he claims to have defeated various enemies in Canaan, including the identifiable cities of Gezer, Yanoam, and Ashkelon, and in the same geographical region, a group identified as Israel. Whether or not the victory celebrated on the stela is as complete as claimed, it is clear that by the end of the thirteenth century the Egyptians knew of the existence of a geopolitical entity called Israel in the land of Canaan. Thus, the Exodus, or some movement of Hebrews out of Egypt, and their entry into Canaan, where they formed at least part of the group that called itself Israel, must have occurred before that date.

The biblical narrative is composite, and when critically analyzed suggests that what the Bible presents as a single episode may in fact have been several, and that more than one group of "Hebrews" eventually moved from Egypt to Palestine, probably entering it at several different places. Yet admittedly most of the details of the account of the forced labor of the Hebrews and of the glimpses of the Egyptian court that we get in the narratives would fit almost any period in ancient Egyptian history.

A majority of modern scholars, but by no means all, date the central episode, associated with Moses, to the thirteenth century, during the reign of Rameses II (1279–1213). An earlier date, toward the beginning of the Late Bronze Age, would link the Exodus with the expulsion of the Hyksos Dynasties from Egypt in the mid-sixteenth century, and better fits the chronology in the biblical text, which dates the Exodus to 480 years prior to the construction of the Solomonic Temple in the mid-tenth century (1 Kings 6.1). This correlation was first proposed by the first-century CE historian Josephus, and has many modern adherents. Among the arguments against it is the absence of any mention of Israel in the land of Canaan before the Merneptah inscription. This is especially true in the case of the Amarna Letters, which are diplomatic correspondence from the fourteenth century between the Egyptian court and the rulers of city-states in Canaan. Furthermore, the biblical accounts of the period after the entry into the land found in the books of Joshua and Judges (see further below) contain no hint of Egyptian presence in the land, although both archaeological and written sources indicate that it was significant throughout the Late Bronze Age. It thus seems more probable to most current scholars that the Exodus took place during the thirteenth century.

That some Exodus took place is a responsible inference, given the persistence of the Exodus tradition in the Bible and its presence in the earliest biblical poetry (notably Ex 15), and some smaller details, such as the Egyptian names of Moses, Aaron, and Phinehas. The event must have involved fewer people than the exaggerated biblical numbers (see Ex 12.37) indicate, and may have constituted little more than the escape of a relatively small group of Hebrews from forced labor in the eastern Nile delta. Given the lack of historical data it is impossible to say more.

That group, whatever its size, interpreted its escape as the direct intervention of the deity Yahweh on its behalf, to be celebrated in hymns and magnified in importance as it was told and retold. When the group eventually entered Canaan, at a time when there was no centralized power to oppose it, it joined with others and eventually became the twelve-tribe confederation of Israel.

THE EARLY HISTORY OF ISRAEL IN THE LAND OF CANAAN

Perhaps no period in the history of Israel is more controversial than the first two centuries of the Iron Age. The beginning and end of this era are framed by two synchronisms: the mention of Israel in the Merneptah Stele in the late thirteenth century (see above), and the campaign of the Pharaoh Shishak in Palestine in 925 (see below), an event documented both in Egyptian sources and in the Bible. During the intervening three centuries, according to the chronology accepted by the majority of scholars, Israel developed from a loose confederation of tribes into a relatively stable dynastic monarchy. But of the principal events and individuals that figure in biblical narratives, none occur in other sources. Once more, a historical reconstruction must be inferential.

One reconstruction of the beginning of this period that was dominant from the early to the mid-twentieth century is that of conquest. The book of Joshua describes how the large group of Israelites crossed the Jordan under the leadership of Joshua and in a series of swift and relentless campaigns defeated the kings of the major Canaanite cities and annihilated most of the indigenous population. This view seemed to be confirmed by the presence of destruction layers at key sites, all dated to the very end of the Late Bronze Age.

Reexcavation of many of those sites and more refined ceramic chronology, however, made it clear that some of the sites had not in fact been occupied at that time, and that the destructions were not all contemporaneous. Moreover, the opening chapters of the book of Judges presented a very different picture. While some Israelite tribes were apparently successful in defeating their Canaanite neighbors, many others coexisted alongside them. This is apparently confirmed even in the book of Joshua, where such Canaanite groups as the family of Rahab (Josh 6.25) and the Gibeonites (Josh 9) were incorporated into Israel. Thus the conquest model has largely been abandoned by scholars, but no other reconstruction has gained general acceptance.

One plausible scenario is to combine elements of various models to suggest that Israel as we know it emerged in the land of Canaan and was made up of diverse groups. One of these was the Exodus group, whose allegiance to the god who had brought them out of Egypt, Yahweh, would become the central religious tenet of the confederation. They were joined by others, some who were apparently their kin who had never gone down to Egypt, and some who may have been Canaanites disaffected from the centers of power. These disparate elements united in a confederation or league, whose primary principles of sole worship of Yahweh and mutual support were expressed in a social compact or covenant. The elements are called tribes, and they are associated with specific subregions in the land. While the number of twelve tribes is constant, both the names of the tribes and the territories with which they were associated shifted in response to historical vicissitudes. The religious symbol of the confederation was a moveable shrine, the ark of the covenant, which seems to have been based at different tribal centers at different times. The confederation was decentralized, with no overarching authority, and the tribes were relatively independent. In time of crisis, however, tribes were expected to come to the assistance of a beleaguered member, as in the very ancient poem in Judg 5, or to punish one of their own for breach of the compact, as in the account of the Benjaminite war in Judg 19–21. In situations like these a volunteer militia was mustered.

This reconstruction takes into account a variety of biblical data that are admittedly embedded in a later historical work, the Deuteronomistic History (see "Introduction to the Historical Books," pp. 309–313 HB). It also incorporates recent archaeological evidence, including both significant elements of cultural continuity between the Late Bronze Age and the Iron Age, and the proliferation of small rural settlements in the hill country both west and east of the Jordan. Not all of these settlements would have been Israelite, nor would tribal territory necessarily entail complete control. A number of urban centers remained outside the confederation, and Israel did not achieve total control of the promised land until the end of the eleventh century.

At the beginning of the Iron Age (ca. 1200 BCE), shortly after the likely date for the Exodus, another group had arrived in Canaan. These were the Philistines, one component of the "Sea Peoples" well documented in Egyptian sources and in the archaeological record. Of Aegean origin, they had repeatedly failed in their attempts to invade Egypt, and one or more of these Sea Peoples, including the Philistines, settled in Canaan. According to the biblical account, they formed a pentapolis in the five cities of Gaza, Ashkelon, Ashdod, Gath, and Ekron, and the four of these cities that have been securely identified (Gath is the exception) show a remarkably homogenous material culture at this time.

The biblical account, in Judg 13–16 and in 1 and 2 Samuel, and the archaeological record are in considerable agreement. The Philistines had a superior technology, especially in metallurgy (see 1 Sam 13.20) and military hardware, and a professional standing army. By the mid-eleventh century they had considerably expanded their territory to the north and east, and their presence is evident at important centers beyond it, including Beth-shan in the Jordan Valley, and at military outposts in the heart of Judah, the dominant southern tribe, and in the north as well. The Philistines and the Israelites were thus on a collision course, both vying for control of the same region, and Israel's survival was at stake.

THE UNITED MONARCHY (CA. 1020–928 BCE)

The emergence of Israel as a nation-state is part of a larger pattern of the development of regional geopolitical and ethnic entities throughout the region, such as those of the Edomites, Moabites, and Ammonites in Transjordan, the Arameans in Damascus and other centers in central and northern Syria, and the Phoenicians in Tyre. In the case of Israel, there was a particular stimulus. At least in part because of the Philistine threat, toward the end of the eleventh century Israel profoundly changed its form of government from a loose confederation of tribes to a monarchy. The first ruler, Saul, seems to have been more a military chief than a full-fledged king. And despite initial successes, he was unable to check the Philistine advance, and died in a battle with them deep in Israel's territory in the Jezreel Valley. He was succeeded by a former commander in his army, David, who moved swiftly to contain the Philistines within their original territory and to unite Israel around himself and a newly chosen capital, Jerusalem.

Biblical historians describe additional military successes, which enabled David, and his son and successor Solomon, to subject kingdoms adjacent to Israel to vassal status, including the Edomites, the Moabites, and the Ammonites in Transjordan and the Arameans in Damascus. Whether the extent of the territory controlled by David and Solomon is as large as biblical sources suggest is questionable. Clearly the biblical historians have magnified the period of the United Monarchy, the reigns of David and Solomon, viewing them in many respects as an ideal age, made possible by divine grant. Underlying the sometimes hyperbolic biblical accounts, however, is authentic historical memory of increasing centralized control and concomitant administrative complexity, a picture indirectly confirmed by the archaeological record. When textual and archaeological data are added to the synchronisms between the Israelite monarchy and those of its neighbors, beginning in the tenth century, there is little doubt that the outlines of the biblical narrative are essentially correct.

The most important of these synchronisms comes just after the death of Solomon. The Egyptian pharaoh Shishak (Sheshonq I) undertook a campaign in Western Asia in 925, a date based on established Egyptian chronology. Mentioned in 1 Kings 14.25–26 (cf. 2 Chr 12.2–9), this campaign is further documented in Egyptian sources and is confirmed by destruction layers at key cities in Israel. This synchronism is the basis for the chronology of the first three kings of Israel, Saul (ca. 1025–1005), David (1005–965), and Solomon (968–928, allowing for a coregency with David at the beginning of his reign).

To be sure, the biblical account of the reigns of these three kings, found in 1 and 2 Samuel and 1 Kings 1–11, is shaped by theological concerns, and also displays a pervading interest in the characters of the narrative—the tragically inadequate Saul, the heroic David, the ambitious but flawed Solomon—and in the intrigues of the royal court. But it is also significantly different from narratives about earlier periods in Israel's history. Divine intervention is minimal, with most events taking place largely on the human plane. Moreover, a careful reading of the biblical text discloses a myriad of archival and other details that can be correlated with the archaeological record and are consistent with the framework of events presupposed by the narrative. Thus, the skepticism of some modern historians, who argue that the biblical accounts of the United Monarchy are fictional retroversions from a later time, seems unwarranted.

David also seems to have initiated the transformation of the monarchy into a dynastic kingship which, consistent with other Near Eastern models, was promulgated as the result of divine choice. With the establishment of the monarchy came social and religious innovation. The older structures of the decentralized premonarchic confederation were now coopted by royal institutions. The ark of the covenant was enshrined in the Temple in Jerusalem built by Solomon, providing in effect divine sanction for the monarchy. Priests became royal appointees, and there was a growing movement toward centralization of worship in the capital. Yet this centralized administration formed a kind of overlay, a veneer, on the social systems of the nation as a whole. Individuals still identified themselves as members of a family, clan, and tribe, and disputes between them were usually settled at the local level. Apart from the requirement of paying taxes and providing personnel for royal projects and for the army, life in the villages probably proceeded much as it had for centuries.

The establishment of the monarchy, however, had entailed the formation of an elite, wealthy class. Life in the capital of Jerusalem, and after the split of the kingdom into two, in the northern capital of Samaria as well, was characterized by conspicuous consumption. This is evident in the accounts of Solomon's court (1 Kings 4.22–28; 10.14–22), and in the description of the Temple and royal palace complex he constructed (1 Kings 6–7). That the extravagances documented in these accounts are not entirely an exaggeration is evident from archaeological data at Samaria, and at royal cities such as Megiddo, Hazor, Gezer, and Dan. With the concentration of political power in the hands of a ruling aristocracy came abuse. One of the constants of the biblical traditions is opposition to the exploitation of the poorer classes. This opposition was frequently expressed in prophetic rebukes of the aristocracy, as in the admittedly legendary traditions concerning Elijah (2 Kings 20), and in the books of the prophets themselves. While their own relationship to the centers of power was not always antagonistic, prophets such as Amos, Isaiah, and Micah in the eighth century and Jeremiah in the late seventh to early sixth centuries were harsh in their denunciation of social injustice. In a sense they were conservatives, even perhaps reactionaries, insisting that the older premonarchic tradition of covenant was still binding, a tradition that commanded not only exclusive worship of Yahweh but also fair treatment of every Israelite.

THE DIVIDED MONARCHIES (CA. 928 TO THE LATE SEVENTH CENTURY BCE)

The union of north and south had been fragile, even during the United Monarchy, and it disintegrated at Solomon's death. The reason implied in 1 Kings 12 is the northerners' anger at the cost of the extravagances of the capital, and this must have been at least part of the motivation. Solomon's son and successor Rehoboam was unable to gain the allegiance of the ten northern tribes, who seceded and formed a separate kingdom. This inaugurates the period of the Divided Monarchy, the two kingdoms of Israel in the north and Judah in the south. The dynasty that David had established remained in power in Judah for nearly four centuries, while Israel was ruled by a succession of royal families, many of whose rulers came to power in military coups. The parts were less than their sum had been, and the two kingdoms had mixed relations, sometimes friendly, sometimes hostile. Neither was able to control effectively the regions that bordered them, and the Davidic empire, such as it was, ceased to exist.

Changes on the larger international scene would increasingly affect these two kingdoms. Pressure from a revived Egypt is already evident in the above-mentioned campaign of Shishak to the north in 925. Meanwhile, in northern Mesopotamia, the kingdom of Assyria had consolidated its control over Babylon in the south and adjacent regions to the north and east, and by the ninth century was poised to expand into the Levant. At this point the fairly complete Assyrian annals enable the construction of a relatively exact chronology and provide numerous synchronisms with biblical texts. Beginning with Ahab, king of Israel in the mid-ninth century, many of the rulers of both Israel and Judah are mentioned in Assyrian sources, an indication of the growing Assyrian interest in the region and a coincidence of ominous significance.

For the Assyrians were establishing an empire, a process that reached its zenith with the Assyrian king Esarhaddon's subjugation of Egypt in 671. They accomplished this by virtue of a technologically sophisticated army which in relatively rapid advance overwhelmed the smaller kingdoms of Syria and Palestine, usually incorporating their territories into the empire as provinces and deporting the elite of their populations to other regions. By the late eighth century this subjugation was virtually complete. The Syrian kingdoms had been taken, including that of the Arameans in Damascus in 732. In 722 Samaria fell, its ruling class was exiled to Assyria, and the Northern Kingdom of Israel became an Assyrian province. Judah's territory was curtailed, and in part because of the remote location of Jerusalem, was allowed to exist in vassal status. Toward the end of the eighth century the Judean king Hezekiah attempted to reassert Judean independence, but was ruthlessly quashed by the Assyrian king Sennacherib in a campaign (701) which is well documented in both biblical and Assyrian sources. Jerusalem avoided destruction only by payment of a heavy tribute, and the Davidic dynasty survived.

Beginning with Amos and Hosea in the mid-eighth century, the prophets, and the later authors of the Deuteronomistic History (Joshua–2 Kings), interpreted these events as a deserved punishment inflicted by Yahweh on his rebellious people. For them, the repeated experiences of attack, siege, and exile were ultimately caused not by the inexorable progress of the Assyrian armies, but by divine agency, imposing the fulfillment of the curses attached to the covenant.

THE END OF THE KINGDOM OF JUDAH (LATE SEVENTH TO EARLY SIXTH CENTURIES BCE)

By the late seventh century the Assyrian Empire was overextended, and was unable to prevent first independence and eventually overthrow by a resurgent Babylonia to its south. The Babylonians captured the Assyrian capital of Nineveh in 612, and in effect took over the Assyrian Empire. In the initial years, Egypt and Judah attempted to take advantage of the transfer of power by reasserting their independence. This was the time of the reign of the Judean king Josiah (640–609), whom biblical sources compare to David and whose accomplishments are magnified like those of his illustrious predecessor. While it seems likely that Judah was able to reestablish control over some of the territory to the north and west that had been under direct Assyrian rule, its autonomy, such as it was, was short-lived. After Josiah's death in battle at Megiddo in 609, in a failed attempt to prevent the Egyptians from moving north to reinforce the tottering Assyrians, Judah was again reduced to the status of a vassal, first to Egypt, and then, by the end of the seventh century, to Babylon. Caught between two greater powers, the Judean kings Jehoiakim and Zedekiah successively allied themselves with Egypt, which proved to be the weaker partner. Under Nebuchadrezzar (or Nebuchadnezzar) II, the Babylonians laid siege to Jerusalem in 597 and 586, in the second instance destroying the city and ending the Davidic dynasty.

It was the end of an era. Despite the extravagant propaganda of the royal establishment, neither the Davidic dynasty nor its capital city were impregnable. Jerusalem was destroyed, its dynastic Temple burned, and its population decimated by death and exile. Autonomous control of the promised land became only a memory.

And despite partial restoration later in the sixth century, exile in Babylon forever transformed the religion of Judah—Judaism. From this point on, a significant proportion of Jews would be living outside the promised land, without king, Temple, or priesthood.

CULTURAL CONTEXTS
The Persian and Hellenistic Periods

THE PERSIAN PERIOD (539–333 BCE)

The Babylonian exile and the period of Persian domination that followed was a time of great transformation for Judean institutions, religious practices, and culture, but it was equally a time in which the fundamental continuity with preexilic traditions was reaffirmed and secured. When Nebuchadnezzar put down the rebellion of Judah in 586 BCE, he exiled to Babylonia a portion of the population, including the ruling class and the skilled artisans. Most, however, remained in Judah, where a subsistence economy was soon reestablished. Although the system of regular sacrifices at the Temple was disrupted, the ruined Temple remained a focus for religious observances. The book of Lamentations may preserve liturgical poems used on days commemorating the destruction of Jerusalem and its Temple. Little is known about the circumstances of those who went into exile, although it appears that the exiles were settled in a number of local communities in Babylonia, where they were able to oversee their own internal and cultural affairs under the leadership of Jewish elders and prophets (see Ezekiel; Isa 40–55).

The conquest of Babylon by the Persian king Cyrus the Great in 539 BCE brought significant changes. In keeping with his policy of respecting the various deities worshiped throughout the empire, a decree by Cyrus in 538 (see Ezra 1.1–4; 6.1–5) authorized the rebuilding of the Temple in Jerusalem and the return of the Temple vessels captured by Nebuchadnezzar. In addition, Cyrus allowed any of the exiles who wished to return to Judah to do so. Within the exilic community in Babylon the anonymous prophet known as "Second Isaiah" (Isa 40–55) strongly supported Cyrus and urged the exiles to return to Judah. Although historical sources are few and not always easy to interpret, it appears that only a small minority of the exiles and their descendants returned to Judah, most choosing to remain in Babylonia. This latter group became the nucleus of a large and highly significant Jewish Diaspora community (Jews of "the dispersion," that is, living outside Palestine), which strongly influenced the development of Judaism and Jewish culture during the following centuries.

Despite the decree of Cyrus, the Temple in Jerusalem was not rebuilt until 520–515 BCE. The reasons for the delay were various. Persian control over the western territories may actually have been tentative until after the Persians conquered Egypt in 525. The economy of Yehud (the name by which the Persian province of Judah was known) was weak, and there appears to have been friction between the population that had remained in the land and the small but powerful group who returned from exile with the authorization and financial backing of the Persian king. Conflicts with the neighboring territories of Samaria and Geshur and Ammon in Transjordan also complicated the situation. Within the Bible the prophetic books of Haggai and Zechariah and portions of Ezra 1–6 refer to this period, but these sources have to be read and interpreted critically, for they are neither consistent with one another nor easy to understand on their own terms. At least during the early part of Persian rule the governors of Judah appear to have been prominent Jews from the Diaspora community, one of whom, Zerubbabel, was actually a member of the Davidic royal family. The province of Yehud itself was very small, consisting of Jerusalem and the territory surrounding it within a radius of about 24–32 km (15–20 mi).

Once the Temple was rebuilt, it became the nucleus of the restored community, and consequently a focus of conflict (Isa 56–66; Malachi). The high priestly family, which had also returned from the Diaspora, became very powerful, and at least on occasion was in conflict with the governor appointed by the Persian king. Although the details are often not clear, there appears to have been continuing conflict during the fifth century between those Jews whose ancestors had been in exile and those whose ancestors had remained in the land. Those who returned from the Diaspora styled themselves the "children of the exile" and referred rather contemptuously to the rest as "people of the land," as though their very status as Jews was in question. In fact, the question of the limits of the community was one of the most contentious issues of the period, reflected both in the controversy over mixed marriages between Jewish men and ethnically foreign women (Ezra 10; Neh 13) and also in conflicts within the Jewish community over who had the right to claim the traditional identity as descendants of "Abraham" and "Israel" (see Isa 63.16 and more generally "Third Isaiah," Isa 56–66). Although the conflicts between various contending groups in early Persian period Yehud are largely cast in religious terms, there is no question that they were also in part socioeconomic (see Neh 5). All of these conflicts and efforts toward redefinition of the community, however, took place within the reality of Persian imperial control. Thus it is not by accident that the two most prominent figures involved in various reforms of mid-fifth century Yehud, Ezra and Nehemiah, were Diaspora Jews of high standing, carrying out tasks that had been specifically authorized by the Persian kings.

Because this was a period of self-conscious reconstruction, it was also a time of immense literary activity, as traditional materials were collected, revised, and edited, and new works composed. Although much of the Pentateuch may have existed in various forms during the time of the monarchy, it was probably reworked during the Persian period into something close to its final form. Indeed, some have suggested that this revision may have been undertaken under the sponsorship of the Persian government, reflecting Persia's interest in achieving stability throughout its empire by means of religious and legal reforms in the provinces. Although a history of Israel and Judah known as the Deuteronomistic History (Deuteronomy through 2 Kings) had been composed during the latter years of the monarchy and updated during the exile, a new version of that history, 1–2 Chronicles, was prepared during the Persian period (ca. 350 BCE). It clearly reflects the concerns of the postexilic community, focusing almost exclusively on the history of Judah and giving particular emphasis to the institution of the Temple. The books of Ezra and Nehemiah interpret events from the decree of Cyrus in 538 until the late fifth century.

In addition to the prophetic books composed at this time (Isa 56–66, Haggai, Zechariah, Malachi, and perhaps Joel), there is evidence that the texts of older prophets were also edited and reinterpreted. Psalmody had been an important element of worship at the First Temple, but appears to have taken on an even more significant role in the Second Temple. Although the expansion and revision of the book of Psalms may have continued until well into the Hellenistic or even Roman period, an important shaping of the psalter, perhaps including its division into five "books," was part of Persian period activity. Wisdom writing, too, flourished during this time. The book of Job, parts of the book of Proverbs, and perhaps Ecclesiastes were likely composed then.

THE HELLENISTIC PERIOD (333–63 BCE)

The westward expansion of the Persian Empire into the area of Asia Minor had brought it into conflict with Greece, since many of the cities of Asia Minor which came under Persian control had been founded and populated by Greeks. Twice the Persians had even invaded the Greek mainland, but were defeated on both occasions. Eventually, Philip of Macedon developed a plan to free the Greek cities of Asia Minor from Persian domination. Although he died before he could undertake the campaign, it was taken up by his son Alexander the Great in 334 BCE. Alexander, however, did not stop with the accomplishment of that initial goal. In 333 he continued down the Phoenician coast, subduing any city that resisted, conquered Egypt, then turned to the Persian heartland, defeating Darius III, the last Persian emperor, in 331. Alexander continued his conquest into the eastern reaches of the Persian Empire before returning in 324 to Babylon, which he apparently intended to establish as the capital of the empire he now controlled. He died in 323, however, before he could successfully organize his enormous territory. After Alexander's death, his generals fought for control of portions of the empire. By 301 an agreement gave Egypt to Ptolemy and Mesopotamia and Syria-Palestine to Seleucus. Ptolemy, however, occupied Palestine and southern Syria. Through a series of five wars extending over more than a hundred years, the Ptolemaic kings managed to hold onto their Palestinian territory, finally losing it to the Seleucids in 198 BCE.

Jerusalem had surrendered to Alexander in 333 and was relatively undisturbed by the events of his conquest. Samaria, too, surrendered, but rebelled in 332 and was severely punished, its inhabitants killed or sold into slavery, and the city refounded as a Macedonian military colony. Documents belonging to a group of Samaritans who fled and were later tracked down and killed by Alexander's troops have been excavated from the Wadi Daliyeh in the Jordan Valley. In contrast to the relatively settled conditions following Alexander's conquest, however, the dispute between the Ptolemies and the Seleucids over control of Palestine had serious consequences for Jerusalem and Judea. Not only did the wars sometimes affect Judean territory, but the nation's leaders had to make difficult choices concerning which power to support. The conflict between pro-Ptolemaic and pro-Seleucid factions within the Judean community was a significant factor in internal politics during the third century BCE.

Although the high priest was the primary representative of the Judeans, the Ptolemaic system of government and taxation had significant effects on the power structure of the country. The Ptolemies considered their territories primarily as a source of revenue. Rather than collecting funds directly, they employed "tax farmers," often local persons who bought the right to collect taxes for a specified area. Their profit was the difference between the amount they raised and the amount they had pledged to the government. Some of these positions were quite lucrative. Moreover, the Ptolemies also engaged prominent landowners to keep the peace as the heads of locally organized military villages. The Jewish historian Josephus preserves a long account of the Tobiad family, which served the Ptolemaic government in both capacities. From his lively narrative one has a sense not only of the power and wealth such positions could afford but also of the dangers and conflict they often entailed.

Culturally, the most significant effect of Ptolemaic rule was the establishment of a large Jewish Diaspora community in Egypt, centered in the new city of Alexandria, founded by Alexander the Great. Jews had often migrated to Egypt during times of economic or political trouble (see Jer 42–44). In the fifth century a Jewish military colony in the service of the Persian army was established at Elephantine (near modern Aswan). They had their own temple, though they remained in correspondence with Jerusalem concerning various religious matters, including the proper celebration of Passover and assistance in securing Persian permission for the rebuilding of the Elephantine temple after it was destroyed by local Egyptians. The various Aramaic documents found there (letters, contracts, marriage documents, records of legal disputes, etc.) provide an important glimpse into the daily life of this Jewish community in Egypt. Among the papyri was a copy of the book of Ahikar, a legendary story about an official in the Assyrian court at the time of Sennacherib and Esarhaddon (late eighth to early seventh century). Although the story was not Jewish in origin, it became popular among the Jews. The book of Tobit in the Apocrypha makes reference to Ahikar, even calling him Tobit's nephew (Tob 1.21–22).

The Hellenistic era Egyptian Diaspora, however, was much larger and more influential than the previous small communities of Jews living in Egypt. Its origins are not clear, but during the initial Ptolemaic conquest of Palestine, Ptolemy I apparently captured Jerusalem and took many prisoners back to Egypt, where they settled. Later many other Jews migrated there, presumably for economic reasons. The community continued to grow, both in numbers and in prosperity, until in the Roman period the Jewish population numbered in the hundreds of thousands, including many wealthy and prominent families.

By the middle of the third century BCE the Jewish community in Egypt had translated the books of the Torah (Genesis–Deuteronomy) into Greek, and over the next century or so, the other books of the Hebrew Bible were also translated. A legendary account of this project is contained in the *Letter of Aristeas*. According to that narrative, the impetus for the project came from the king himself, Ptolemy II Philadelphus (285–246 BCE), who wished to have a copy for the library of Alexandria. Seventy-two Jewish translators were brought to Egypt from Jerusalem for the task; hence the translation came to be known as the Septuagint, from the Greek word for "seventy." Scholars largely reject this account as unhistorical and maintain that the translation was undertaken for the religious needs of a Jewish community that no longer understood Hebrew. (See the essays "The Canons of the Bible" and "Hebrew Bible: Texts and Versions" for more information about the Septuagint.)

In addition to the translation of the scriptures, the Jewish Diaspora in Egypt produced a rich and varied literature in Greek. One should not assume, however, that every Jewish writing in Greek originated in Alexandria, for during the Hellenistic period Greek became the most important international language. Educated Jews in Palestine and in the eastern Diaspora were nearly as likely to speak Greek as their counterparts in Egypt. Nevertheless, Alexandria remained unparalleled in the richness of its intellectual culture.

Throughout the Hellenistic world the increasing contact between different ethnic groups led to a new self-consciousness within communities about their own historical traditions and how these traditions related to those of other peoples. Thus historiographical writing, from the scholarly to the popular, became an important type of literary activity. In the late third century BCE an Alexandrian Jew named Demetrius investigated the chronologies of the biblical tradition, attempting to explain apparent contradictions and logical inconsistencies. A more entertaining work is Eupolemus's *Concerning the Kings in Judea*. A friend of Judas Maccabeus (see below), Eupolemus retold the biblical narrative with many embellishments and legendary details in an attempt to glorify Israel's traditions and accomplishments. In Eupolemus's history Moses appears as a culture-bringer, the inventor of the alphabet, which the Phoenicians and the Greeks later borrowed. Eupolemus particularly emphasizes the power and influence of the Israelite kingdom under David and Solomon, as well as the splendor of the Solomonic Temple. Not only was the Temple decorated with gifts from the kings of Tyre and Egypt, but Solomon reciprocated, sending a golden pillar to the temple of Zeus in Tyre.

The tendency to make connections between one's own traditions and those of other ethnic groups and to claim priority in the arts of civilization is reflected in the highly legendary history written in the second century BCE by an anonymous Samaritan. He identifies Enoch with Greek Atlas and claims that Abraham was the inventor of astrology, which he taught to the Egyptians when he sojourned there. A similar tendency is evident in the work of Artapanus. In his history Moses becomes the inventor of the technologies basic to civilization. Moreover, this Moses serves as a general in the Egyptian army, organizes Egyptian religion, and comes to be treated virtually as a god by the Egyptians, who identify him with Hermes (the Greek equivalent of the Egyptian god Thoth). The interest of Egyptian Jews in the biblical figure of Joseph is reflected in the romance, *Joseph and Asenath*, which tells the story of Joseph's marriage to the Egyptian noblewoman Asenath. She is depicted as a model convert to Judaism, and the story depicts some of the complications that attended Jewish-Gentile relations in Hellenistic Egypt.

Jewish poetic works composed in Greek also reflect a blending of cultural traditions. The Hellenistic genre of poetry praising cities and countries is represented in the work of Theodotus and Philo the Epic Poet, who wrote poems about Shechem and Jerusalem, respectively. Even more ambitious was the work of Ezekiel the Tragedian, whose play *The Exodus* retold the account of Ex 1–15 in a style influenced by the Greek dramatists Aeschylus and Euripedes.

Greek philosophy, too, left its imprint on Hellenistic Jewish culture. Already in the second century BCE an Alexandrian Jew named Aristobulus produced a philosophical commentary on the Torah in which he claimed that the law of Moses anticipated many of the fundamental tenets of Greek philosophy and that the Greek philosophers Pythagoras, Socrates, and Plato derived their ideas from the Jewish law. Written toward the end of the Hellenistic period, the Wisdom of Solomon continues the biblical tradition of wisdom books like Proverbs but incorporates many elements of Greek rhetoric, philosophy, and literary style.

Less is known about the Jews of the eastern Diaspora who remained under Seleucid control than about the Jews of Egypt and Palestine, but it appears that peoples of various ethnic groups had access to economic and political advancement within the Seleucid Empire. Several writings from this time—Tobit, Dan 1–6, and Esther—suggest something of the outlook of Jews in the eastern Diaspora. Written originally in Hebrew or Aramaic, and later enlarged when they were translated into Greek, these books are works of fiction, edifying entertainments that tell the stories of Jews who achieved high status in foreign courts, were threatened by jealous rivals, and yet succeeded in securing personal power and the good will of the king. Though the stories are all set in the pre-Hellenistic period (Tobit in the Assyrian Empire, Daniel in the Babylonian exile, and Esther in the Persian court) they were probably written during the Seleucid period. While they acknowledge that faithful Jews may be vulnerable because of their religion, on the whole these are optimistic stories with a positive view of the Gentile kings.

The eastern Diaspora was also the conduit for important religious developments that arose from the contact between Judaism and the religions of Babylon and Persia. This influence is most clearly seen in the development of apocalyptic literature. Parts of the book of *1 Enoch* composed in the third century BCE reflect astronomical lore and traditions about antediluvian sages that derive from Babylonian sources. Although it is more difficult to trace the path of influence in its earliest stages, the dualistic religious beliefs of Persian Zoroastrianism almost certainly contributed to the development of Jewish apocalyptic thought and to some of the ideas of the sectarians at Qumran.

The eventual triumph of the Seleucid kingdom over the Ptolemies in the fifth Syrian war (198 BCE) obviously had a greater significance for the Jews of Judea than for those of Egypt. The Seleucid ruler Antiochus III treated the Judeans generously in appreciation for the support he received from the pro-Seleucid faction, granting an allowance for the Temple and various tax concessions, as well as confirming the Judeans' right to live "according to the laws of their country." Although relations began well, the difference in the way the Seleucid Empire governed its territories set the stage for a terrible conflict. Unlike the Ptolemaic system of centralized government administered with the cooperation of local leaders, the Seleucid regime was more decentralized. It derived some unity, however, from a network of Greek cities established throughout the empire. These were not necessarily ethnically Greek but were cities that had received a charter to organize as a *polis*, the Greek form of city government. Cultural prestige and economic advantages often led the leadership of Near Eastern cities to request such a charter.

The events leading up to the conflict between Judea and the Seleucid king Antiochus IV Epiphanes (175–164 BCE) are complex and not fully understood. In part they involved a struggle for succession to the high priesthood and the attempts of various contenders to secure the support of the king by paying him large sums of money. The first of the contenders, Jason, also paid to have Jerusalem established as a Greek *polis*, Antioch at Jerusalem. Neither of these acts in itself seems to have aroused much opposition in Jerusalem. The conflict was not a cultural conflict between Judaism and Hellenism, for Palestinian Jews had already incorporated significant elements of Hellenistic culture, which they considered quite compatible with their religious identity.

The crisis was sparked by the attempt by another contender, Menelaus, to buy the office of high priest. When he promised the king more than he could pay, he attempted to raise the money by taking golden vessels from the Temple. At this, a riot broke out in Jerusalem. Subsequent fighting between the forces of Jason and Menelaus convinced Antiochus that Judea was in revolt, and he retook the city and plundered the Temple, either in 169 or 168. Sometime later there were further disturbances, and Antiochus sent Syrian troops, which remained garrisoned in Jerusalem. Whether the status of Jerusalem at this point was a *polis* or a military colony is uncertain, but in either case in 167 the Temple was reorganized to accommodate the religious needs of the Syrian troops. A dedication was made to Zeus Olympius, the Greek name for the Syrian god Baal Shamem, and an altar established for sacrifice. Though Menelaus continued to preside as high priest, most Jews considered these actions to have profaned the Temple. In addition, the traditional practice of Judaism was suppressed by Antiochus, perhaps with the cooperation of Menelaus. Since religious persecution was virtually unknown in antiquity, it is difficult to know how Antiochus understood this repression and what he hoped to accomplish by it. Its actual result was to ignite the resistance known as the Maccabean revolt.

The Hasmoneans, Mattathias and his sons Judas Maccabeus, Jonathan, Simon, John, and Eleazar, were the leaders of the revolt. Although Judas managed to retake control of the Temple in 164 (its rededication being the occasion for the institution of the festival of Hannukah), it was not until 142 that the last of the Seleucid army was expelled and actual independence was secured by Simon. From then until the Roman conquest of Judea in 63 BCE the small kingdom was ruled by the Hasmonean family, which in addition to ruling as kings also assumed the office of high priest.

Religious and cultural life in Judea during the Seleucid and Hasmonean periods was rich and varied, with a remarkable quantity of literature produced in Hebrew, Aramaic, and to some extent in Greek. Sirach (Ecclesiasticus), Jesus Ben Sira's book of wisdom teachings, was probably composed in Hebrew about 180 BCE. Though largely traditional, it embodies several innovations: Ben Sira's identification of wisdom with the law of Moses, his praise of the contemporary high priest Simon II, and his own explicit claim to authorship. Ben Sira disapproved of apocalyptic speculation, but the crisis under Antiochus IV produced an upsurge in apocalyptic writings, not only Dan 7–12, but also *1 Enoch* 83–90 and *The Testament of Moses*. After the establishment of the Hasmonean monarchy, a supporter of the dynasty composed an account of the war in Hebrew (1 Maccabees), modeling it after the earlier books of Kings and Chronicles. An Egyptian Jewish writer, Jason of Cyrene, also wrote a history of the war in Greek (2 Maccabees), which was strongly influenced by forms of Hellenistic history writing.

Our knowledge of the literature of this time has been greatly increased by the discovery of the Dead Sea Scrolls at Qumran. Although this library was the property of a sectarian religious group related to the Essenes, it contained many Hebrew and Aramaic texts that were not sectarian compositions. Several of these scrolls contain noncanonical psalms, blessings, and other liturgical material. There are also many examples of what is called "the rewritten Bible," fairly free retellings of parts of the biblical story, embellished with new narrative episodes, prayers, and other elements (e.g., *Jubilees, The Genesis Apocryphon, The Apocryphon of Joshua*). Some texts elaborate on the apocalyptic elements of the books of Ezekiel and Daniel or place apocalyptic pronouncements in the mouths of other biblical figures, such as Levi, Qahat, and Amram. A number of texts, often having to do with matters of religious law, purport to be discourses of Moses. Perhaps the most remarkable document is the Temple Scroll, which apparently takes the form of an address by God to Moses. Although it incorporates material from the books of Exodus through Deuteronomy, it also contains much new material, including detailed instructions for building the Temple.

These documents and others pertaining to the Qumran sect itself help to clarify a number of issues of religious controversy that shaped the period of Hasmonean rule. The Temple and the Torah were central institutions for Judaism, which made them focal points for conflict. The Qumran scrolls show that conflict over the proper calendar (i.e., a solar or lunar calendar) for the conduct of Temple sacrifices was a major issue dividing the Qumran Essenes from their rivals, the Pharisees. Though the Hasmoneans were not always on good terms with the Pharisees, they adopted the lunar calendar favored by them. Many other writings from Qumran also elaborate their understanding of disputed issues such as purity, marriage, and sabbath observance, concerning which they were at odds with the Pharisees. Although the Qumran community did not compose apocalypses (i.e., reports of revelatory visions), they were strongly influenced by apocalyptic ideas and considered themselves to be living in the last times, just before God would intervene to restore proper order to the world. They supported their ideas in part by writing commentaries (*pesharim*) on biblical texts, which they read as referring to themselves and their opponents.

In general, the Hellenistic period presents a picture of Judaism that is much more diverse than is often imagined. Not only did Jews live in a vast range of lands from Egypt to Parthia, they also creatively adapted many elements from the varied Hellenistic cultures of these lands. Nevertheless, important symbols and institutions, including the Temple in Jerusalem, the scriptures, and common religious practices based in the Torah, provided a sense of unity and common identity.

CULTURAL CONTEXTS
The Roman Period

The Roman conquest of Judea in 63 BCE was part of a centuries-long expansion of the power of Rome. The destruction of Carthage in North Africa in 146 BCE concluded the Punic Wars and secured the western Mediterranean, and the destruction of Corinth in the same year demonstrated Rome's control of Greece. In the next century, a series of conflicts with the successors of Alexander the Great in Asia and Egypt brought Roman rule to the entire eastern Mediterranean. The events that led to the replacement of the Roman republic by autocratic rule culminated with the installation of Julius Caesar's nephew Octavian (later Augustus) as the first emperor in 27 BCE, and included the conquest of Egypt. The Mediterranean was now, as it has aptly been called, "a Roman lake."

Within the Roman Empire, especially in the east, client states were allowed considerable autonomy as long as their rulers maintained order and paid tribute to Rome. In Judea, Herod the Great, king of Judea from 37 to 4 BCE, succeeded on both counts, and with Roman sanction his control eventually extended to all of the region west of the Jordan and over much of Transjordan. His successors were not so adept, and direct Roman rule of Judea itself began in 6 CE. Thus began an uneasy détente between a series of Roman governors and the leaders of the Jewish community, based in the Temple in Jerusalem. This broke down during the First Jewish Revolt (66–73), prompting the Roman destruction of Jerusalem in 70. A brief resurgence of Jewish nationalism in the Second Jewish Revolt (132–135) was easily crushed, and Jerusalem became Aelia Capitolina, a fully Hellenized city from which Jews were banned.

This is the historical setting for the life of Jesus and the development of earliest Christianity, one of several "Judaisms" that coexisted in Palestine before 70. For most of them the Temple was the primary place of worship and the locus of authority in religious and intracommunity issues. The priesthood in the Temple was hereditary, but from the time of Herod onward the high priest was appointed by a ruler or governor. The high priest was head of a council, called the Sanhedrin, which had jurisdiction in religious and, to a limited extent, in civic matters. Other groups that comprised Judaism, with boundaries not always sharply drawn, included the Sadducees, members of the priesthood whose social status was aristocratic and whose views were conservative. The Pharisees were a lay movement concerned with observance of the Torah and hence with its interpretation, often through local houses of assembly; these "synagogues," however, did not supplant the Temple as the place of sacrifice and pilgrimage. The Pharisees were forerunners of the rabbinic Judaism that developed after the Temple's destruction in 70. Outside of these groups, but still part of the broad spectrum of Judaism, were the Essenes, who had seceded from the Temple-based priesthood during the early Hasmonean period (mid-first century BCE), and the Samaritans, whose rejection of the Jerusalem Temple as the proper place for sacrificial worship had crystallized by the same time.

WITHIN THE ROMAN EMPIRE

Readers encounter two different cultural spaces within the New Testament: the village economy of agriculture and fishing in the Galilee, and the mobile economy of merchants and tradesmen in the urban centers of the empire. The first, the village economy, forms the context of Jesus' ministry and of the itinerant disciples who formulated the collections of sayings, stories, and miracles that underlie the Gospels. The second, the merchant economy, constitutes the world of Paul's missions as well as that of countless unknown disciples like those responsible for bringing the gospel message to Rome around 41 CE. This larger, urban world is that of the epistles and the book of Acts. It is also evident in the expansions and reformulations of Mark and "Q" that are found in Matthew and Luke. Both the village agriculturists and the traveling merchants view from below a third cultural space: that of the wealthy, educated elite who are responsible for most of the architectural, artistic, literary, legal, philosophical, and religious remains that represent the Roman world and its influence within Western history and culture.

The predominance of this third, elite world in its cultural influence creates a problem for historians. We must be cautious in using the productions of an elite minority to describe the religious or social world of ordinary people in ancient societies. Anthropologists, for instance, make a distinction between the high tradition of sacred texts, temple rites, and the learned commentary upon them that centers upon the great urban cultural milieu, and the humbler, smaller traditions of religious belief, story, and practice that villagers hand on to one another. The story of the young Jesus remaining in the Temple to debate the teachers (Lk 2.41–52) exemplifies this distinction. For the Galilean peasants, religious devotion is focused on, and expressed in, the act of pilgrimage to Jerusalem for Passover. For the religious elite, it rather consists of learned interpretation of the sacred texts. The thousands of papyri that have been found in the dry climate of Egypt are yielding new insights into the lives of ordinary people in ancient times. Scholars can also study texts for non-elite forms of storytelling, popular belief, and everyday life; these aspects of experience are reflected in novels, in expansions of the biblical text in the Targums (Aramaic paraphrases of the Hebrew Bible), in Jewish and Christian apocryphal writings, and within the New Testament itself, as well as in the remains of material culture recovered by archaeologists.

Roman rule constituted the overarching political reality for both the village agricultural society in the Gospels and the urban context of Acts and the epistles. Its most immediate impact within Palestine was the accession of the Idumean Herod as king. Rome, not the Jewish populace, established the terms of Herodian rule. Herod's massive building projects—including the city of Caesarea, his own mausoleum at Herodion, and the Temple complex in Jerusalem—followed Greek and Roman models. Further consequences of Herod's rule included the severing of ties between tenant farmers and landholders who were no longer local patrons (see Mk 12.1–9). The pressure on the tax system to meet Roman demands and to finance Herod's building projects must have been considerable; this, and the possibilities for corruption and extortion inherent in the system itself, resulted in the cultural disdain reflected in the phrase "tax collector and sinner" (Lk 15.1–2; Mt 18.17 uses the alternative, equally dismissive, "tax collector and Gentile"). The presence of Roman soldiers might mean that goods and services were extorted at random from the local populace (Mt 5.41), but retired centurions might also be valuable local patrons (Lk 7.1–10). Physicians who were attached to the army units could also serve the populace on the side (Mk 5.26).

Most of Galilee seems to have been a prosperous region of small landholders and grazing herds of sheep and goats. Families in the villages where Jesus preached were largely self-sufficient. Craftsmen, such as Jesus himself, may have worked in the cities that were being built in the region, like Tiberias and Sepphoris. Even the rebellion against Rome which zealots in Judea ignited in 66 CE had a short life in Galilee. Within a year its populace had given up and returned to everyday life. Further evidence for the general prosperity of the region emerges when one turns to the occupation of Jesus' core disciples, Peter, James, and John (Mk 1.16–20). The fishing industry around the Sea of Galilee was a flourishing one, as the archaeological remains of extensive harbor installations indicate. Fishing involved families or partners who owned the boats working with hired hands. Fish was salted, dried, smoked, or pickled, and packed in jars for export. Thus Jesus and his disciples were neither naïve isolated pastoralists nor poor peasants, but were engaged in economic enterprises crucial to Galilee's place in the larger world.

For Jerusalem, a city whose chief economic asset was its Temple, the crowds of pilgrims at major feasts and the massive new complex of buildings were both an economic boon and a source of civic pride. The major cities in the eastern Mediterranean, such as Antioch, Ephesus, Philippi, Corinth, and Thessalonica, also enjoyed increased prosperity as a consequence of Roman rule and the growing numbers of travelers on land and sea. Without the possibility of such routine travel, the Christian mission could not have taken place. It was also furthered by the existence of Jewish communities in those cities, which provided an initial network (e.g., see Acts 13.5; 14.1). Many of the peoples incorporated into the Roman Empire, Jew and non-Jew alike, would have shared positive sentiments toward its authority (see Rom 13.1–7; 1 Pet 2.13–17).

On the other hand, civic discord, rioting, and full-scale rebellion against Roman rule remained real possibilities. Alexandria in Egypt had a large Jewish population that included highly educated, cultured, and wealthy individuals like the philosopher and exegete Philo of Alexandria (d. ca. 50 CE). Yet non-Jewish residents rioted in 41 CE when the Jewish elite sought the same citizenship rights as the citizen descendants of the Greek founders. Despite the appeals of a delegation of prominent Jewish Alexandrians, the emperor Claudius refused to grant their request, and threatened severe punishment if further civil discord occurred. Claudius also expelled members of Rome's Jewish community for "rioting at the name of Chrestus," presumably local discord occasioned by Christian missionaries (see Acts 18.1–2). Nero, in 65, executed a number of the new sect of undesirables, the Christians—including, according to tradition, Peter and Paul—as scapegoats for a fire which destroyed blocks of wooden tenements in Rome. He became the focus of anti-Roman sentiment, the demonic persecutor of faithful Christians in later generations (see Rev 13.1–18).

Despite the counsel of moderate voices and the opposition of Agrippa, zealous leaders led Palestinian Jews to revolt against Rome in 66; by August of 70, Titus led Roman troops in burning and destroying the Temple. Christians living in Jerusalem appear to have fled the city prior to its fall. Jews living in the Diaspora did not support the rebellion; this did not keep the Romans from penalizing all Jews after the defeat. The Romans forced Jews who once paid a tax to support the Temple (see Mt 17.24–27) to pay instead an increased tax to the temple of Jupiter Capitolinus in Rome.

THE TYPICAL ROMAN CITY

A brief tour of Caesarea Maritima, the residence of the Roman governor of Judea (Acts 8.40; 9.30; 10.1,24; 11.11; 12.19–23; 18.22; 21.8;

23.23; 25.1–13), reveals the outline of an ancient city from the perspective of the rich. It was originally a small military settlement dating from the mid-third century BCE; Augustus gave it to Herod, who built a magnificent city of some 8,000 acres and a harbor to rival that of Alexandria. Two breakwaters created a sheltered harbor of 40 acres. An area with a temple, on a raised mound, dedicated to Rome and Augustus, faces the harbor at the south end of the forum that runs along the harborside. To the south of the city, a theater faces the sea, although the structure that has been unearthed is a later, rebuilt one. Among the discoveries there is a stone with an inscription referring to Pontius Pilate as prefect. There is also a large amphitheater similar to the Colosseum and a large racecourse (hippodrome).

An aqueduct supplied the city with water from springs on Mount Carmel and an elaborate sewer system under the city drained away waste. Walkways were decorated with mosaics, and promenades were lined with columns. Herod presumably spared no expense on his showcase; builders used imported marbles from Italy and Egypt and pink granite from Aswan. There were warehouses facing the harbor to store the goods that passed through the city from extensive maritime trade, which reached as far as south Asia. The residents of Palestine did not have to journey to Alexandria, Corinth, or Rome to see the world's riches on display for a wealthy elite.

Capernaum on the northern shore of the Sea of Galilee was the base for Jesus' preaching activities around Galilee. It lay on the Via Maris, the road that connected Caesarea and Ptolemais (Acco) on the coast with Damascus in Syria. Even if they never visited the new city of Caesarea, the traffic along the highway between the coast and Damascus would have alerted Jesus and his contemporaries to the cultural realities of Greco-Roman cities. Two other city foundations within Galilee itself, Sepphoris and Tiberias, contributed to the growth of urbanization. Herod Antipas, tetrarch of Galilee and Perea from 4 BCE to 39 CE, resided at Sepphoris, a mere 7 km (4 mi) from Nazareth, until he moved to the newly built Tiberias on the lake in 19–20 CE. The term *tekton* used for Joseph and his sons (Mk 6.3; Mt 13.55) is usually translated "carpenter," but there is no reason to assume that Jesus and his family were restricted to the carpenter's shop of a village. They are just as likely to have been employed in the building that occurred in Sepphoris and Tiberias. Jesus' view of the rich could have been shaped by such experiences, and his followers probably included some connected to the Herodian court (see Lk 8.3).

STATUS AND SOCIAL CLASS IN THE CITY

The artisans, manual laborers, and merchants who lived in a typical Roman city had little time for the pleasures of the city's main streets. Long days in cramped and often dark shops would have been more typical of Paul's life as a tentmaker, for instance (Acts 18.3; 2 Cor 6.5; 11.27). This trade involved creating the awnings, made of a rough, thick fabric like sailcloth, that provided cover from the sun in theaters and the forum, and in front of the booths from which goods were sold. When crowds thronged the city for a festival, such as the biennial Isthmian games outside Corinth in honor of Poseidon (see Dio Chrysostom, *Discourses* 8.9), there would be no shortage of work for tentmakers.

The members of the wealthy elite and the educated scribes, Pharisees, or philosophers who were attached to them despised such lowly occupations, as well as those who collected the taxes. The tensions between rich and poor that were evident in Corinth (1 Cor 11.17–34) show how difficult it could be to cross social divisions of class and status. Those in whose homes the community assembled would have thought it their right to provide a feast for the others who were from their own group; as for the rest—artisans who had to work from dawn to dusk, as well as slave members of the community—they should be glad for the meager rations provided for them. Similarly, the letter of James (2.1–13) excoriates Christians for showing deference to a rich man, giving him a comfortable seat and asking the poor to squat on the floor in the assembly. Although Paul's letters lack the sharp attacks on wealth found in the teaching of Jesus or in the letter of James, Paul does attack the privileges of social superiority to one's fellows when they surface in the Christian community.

Although most Christians did not belong to the local civic elite (1 Cor 1.26–30), a few individuals associated with the Corinthian church could claim such status. Acts 18.8 refers to Crispus (1 Cor 1.14) as *archisynagogos*, a title that he may have been accorded as a benefactor, perhaps by contributing funds for a synagogue building. Women can appear as patronesses and *archisynagogoi* as well. Paul recommends

Phoebe, a deaconess from the Corinthian port city Cenchrea (Rom 16.1–2). Such recommendations were a common letter form in the ancient world, in which patronage relationships were essential to success. Gaius (1 Cor 1.14) was wealthy enough to host all the Christians in Corinth at once (Rom 16.23).

Paul also conveys greetings from a certain Erastus, who is *oikonomos* of Corinth (1 Cor 16.23), the only convert who is known to have held a civic office. A pavement from the area between the north market and the theater bears an inscription stating that Erastus paved the area at his own expense in return for the office of *aedile* (one of the four magistrates who governed the city, and particularly the public officers in charge of the streets). Since the name is an unusual one (no other instances are known), scholars think it possible that it was the same person. The term that Paul uses is not the Greek equivalent for *aedile*, so it may therefore represent a lesser position in the municipal government that was an intermediate step on the way to becoming a magistrate.

Since Corinth had been refounded as a Roman colony under Julius Caesar less than a century before, and therefore would have had no long-entrenched ruling class, the opportunities it could offer for civic advancement may have encouraged competition. For other cities, the ranks of citizens—those enrolled who could hold various public offices—were strictly limited to a particular group of aristocratic families. Other residents, no matter how wealthy or influential, were excluded. Jews who sought to be included on the citizen rolls of Alexandria were rebuffed. Since Roman citizens and the Greek citizens of Alexandria were exempt from poll taxes levied by the Roman state, this status carried some economic advantage. Most Jews, who were laborers and artisans, would not have been eligible for enrollment in any case. Whether Jewish families succeeded in joining the citizen elite elsewhere in the Diaspora is less clear. Luke has Paul claim to be a citizen of Tarsus (Acts 21.39), but this may be mistaken or imprecise.

LITERACY AND EDUCATION

Scholars remain divided over how to assess the extent of literacy in the Greco-Roman period. Portraits showing girls holding the stylus and wax tablet of the student suggest that among the elite some level of education extended to women, but on the evidence of documentary papyri, far fewer women than men were able to sign their names, and women who were able to write often pointed out that fact explicitly. The cities and larger villages of Egypt had teachers who drilled children in the rudiments of reading and writing Greek as well as the study of classic texts. Further education would require sending each young person, accompanied by a family slave, off to Alexandria in search of a suitable tutor.

Even among those who could read, the difficulty of deciphering texts in which all the letters were run together (the standard way in which ancient texts are written) often made it preferable to listen to a slave who was trained to read such texts aloud. We can deduce which texts were most in demand by studying the literary papyri. Homeric texts are by far the most frequently found, with considerable numbers of texts by Demosthenes, Euripides, and Hesiod as well. Technical manuals on such subjects as medicine and astrology also show up in papyri fragments. Among the papyri that have been discovered are some that were orders to and from a book dealer in Oxyrhynchus: Outgoing orders seek dialogues of Plato and works of Homer, Menander, Euripides, and Aristophanes. The dealer acknowledges receipt of treatises on such edifying subjects as "On Training," "On Marriage," "On Freedom from Pain," "On the Uses of Parents," "On the Uses of Domestic Slaves," and Book 3 of a work by Poseidonios, "On Persuasion" (see *P. Oxy.* 1153; 2192). Apparently this dealer's clientele read for self-improvement or practical purposes as much as for entertainment or philosophical enlightenment.

The requirements of reading Torah may have made basic schooling even more necessary for Jewish boys, for whom the Bible would replace Homer as the text. Assimilated Jews in cities like Tarsus and Alexandria, however, saw to it that their sons received instruction in the classics as well. Philo defends the practice of sending Jewish students on to the more advanced instruction in arithmetic, geometry, music, and philosophy at the equivalent of a secondary school, the gymnasium (*Special Laws* 2.229–30). Educational centers like Alexandria and Tarsus had numerous schools of rhetoric to further a young man's ability to take his place in public affairs by training him to speak fluently and write persuasively. Although Paul insists that eloquence ("wisdom") is not needed to communicate the truth of the gospel (1 Cor 1.17) and disclaims any use of such methods (1 Cor 2.4; 2 Cor 11.6), both his opponents (2 Cor 10.10) and contemporary scholars notice a high degree of rhetorical art in his letters. Even his refusal to engage in the sort of rhetorical discourse that would please his audience exhibits familiarity with such arts (see the "fool's speech," 2 Cor 11.1–12.13).

It is more difficult to assess the kind of education received by boys growing up in the Galilean towns and villages. In an oral society, persons can be highly skilled and even have extensive cultural knowledge, such as Jesus' knowledge of Scripture, without being able to read or write. Luke 4.16 presumes that Jesus was literate, though Luke may be speaking from the perspective of an urban class that assumes literate habits as a normal part of education. The Jewish historian Josephus writing in the 90s CE makes no such assumption. Weekly Torah study can be accomplished orally: "He [Moses] appointed the Law to be most excellent and a necessary form of instructions, ordaining that it be heard not once or twice or several times, but that every week men should quit their other occupations and assemble to listen to the Law and obtain a thorough and accurate knowledge of it" (*Ag. Apion* 2.175).

The first-century CE synagogue building at Gamla in the Golan lacks the elaborate religious features of later synagogues like that at Capernaum. It consists of a central nave created by two rows of columns and four levels of stone benches set in steps along the walls. Without the ritual bath attached to the complex there would be nothing to distinguish it from an ordinary assembly hall. There is no evidence of a Torah shrine built into the walls, of a fixed elevated podium from which Torah was read, or of a seat of honor near the center; presumably Torah reading and instruction took place in the central area. The architectural space of the synagogue could serve a variety of community functions, from teaching and worship to legal proceedings and social gathering.

Another form of education required by Jesus and his disciples involves skills specific to their individual trades. Measuring, counting, and recording skills necessary to building or running a fishing business could have been taught on an apprentice basis. Tax collectors had to keep records of persons and amounts. Officials in the local Jewish community also had to collect the annual half-shekel paid to the Temple by all Jewish males (Ex 30.11–16; Mt 17.24–27). Such practical skills must have been taught, but little evidence of the process survives. Though not considered "education" by the literate, rhetorically trained elite of the Greco-Roman cities or by the literate scribes learned in Jewish Torah, such skills would distinguish Jesus and his disciples from others in their villages.

RELIGION, ASTROLOGY, AND MAGIC

When Herod the Great built Caesarea Maritima, he placed the temple to Rome and Augustus in a prominent place. The city was dedicated to the emperor; its civic life would include festive sacrifices in the ruler's honor. Herod's renovations to the Jerusalem Temple and his expansions of its surroundings were planned to enhance the prestige of the city. Other cities also had famous shrines and festivals that drew visitors from abroad. Acts 19.21–40 tells a story of a riot at Ephesus that occurred when those who sold silver models of its famous temple to the goddess Artemis (Diana) claimed that the effectiveness of Paul's preaching had cut into their business.

Christianity did not deliver the death blow to the established civic worship that Luke seems to suggest. Most of his readers lived in cities, and they could easily witness the ongoing enthusiasm for sacrifices and festivals. What individual residents actually believed about the gods was not an issue; their participation, not their internal assent, was the key, and that participation (or lack of it) was observed by the authorities. To join in sacrifices honoring the Roman emperor, for example, demonstrated that the city and its populace were loyal subjects of the empire. Jews refused to participate in these events, and this refusal often brought on them accusations of "hatred of humanity." At Alexandria some argued that Jews could never be admitted to the citizen rolls because they did not worship the city's gods. Nevertheless, through long-tolerated practice, Jews were not often persecuted for this failure to participate in civic rituals. When Christians who were not of Jewish origin began to withdraw from such public activities, however, it caused comment, suspicion, and even persecution. A story like that of Paul's deeds in Ephesus, leading some to abandon the worship of Artemis, would have highlighted the superiority of Christ to one of Asia Minor's most famous religious shrines and might increase Christian resolve to remain separate. Not all Christians would choose persecution, however. Some clearly followed the lead of educated pagans, who often did not believe in the real existence of the gods, or in their myths. They would join public religious activities as required by their social status or civic office, as a social bond rather than as a religious profession. When faced with

Christians who obstinately refused to participate, magistrates had no qualms about sentencing them to exile or death.

Astrologers, diviners, and magicians could be visited in the marketplace. Though such activities were frowned upon by those higher in the social scale, the large number of horoscopes, amulets, and magic spells recovered shows that these methods of making decisions, predicting the future, and bringing good luck (or guarding against bad) continued to be popular. Astrologers to the upper classes justified their practices with a philosophical veneer based on Stoic physical doctrines explaining the relations between earthly and heavenly bodies by means of an all-pervading "rational spirit." Christian insistence that the glorified and exalted Christ is above all the demonic powers and planetary forces (see Col 2.8–23; Eph 1.15–2.2; 6.12) did little to curb popular enthusiasm for these beliefs and practices. Biblical texts show up in Christian magical amulets. Jesus' exorcisms led to accusations that his powers were a consequence of an alliance with the leader of the demonic world (Mk 3.22–30), and Acts describes conflicts between Christian missionaries and local magicians (8.4–25; 13.4–12).

PHILOSOPHY AS HEALING THE SOUL

Unlike the monotheistic faith of Jews and Christians, which placed a high premium on hearing, interpreting, and acting on divine revelation preserved in sacred texts, Greco-Roman religions did not produce texts, legal and ethical codes, or theological doctrines. Those who sought teaching about the divine and its relationship to the observable cosmos, or moral guidance and advice about how to live a good life, turned to philosophy. Formal study of the philosophical systems that emerged from the schools of classical and Hellenistic Athens—especially Platonism, Stoicism, and Epicureanism—could only be pursued by the elite, who had the leisure time to devote to them. Luke's tale of Paul's visit to Athens (Acts 17.16–31) shows its first-century reputation as a destination for intellectuals, not the powerful center of commerce and art that it had been.

More ordinary citizens learned what they knew of philosophy from anthologies of moralistic tales, treatises on how to cope with various problems in life, public discourses offered by itinerant philosophical preachers, and the like. The philosopher-teacher saw himself as a physician for the soul. Under his guidance, people might be converted from the mindless, destructive pursuit of the passions, from fears about a future they could not control, even from superstitious belief in the gods. Some treatises, like Plutarch's "Advice on Marriage" (*Moralia* 12, 138–146) even recommend that the young husband share his knowledge with his wife. Such knowledge will protect her against the passion for luxuries, foolish behavior, and talk common among women. If she knows something of Plato, Xenophon, and astronomy, she will not be taken in by the common practices of magic or witchcraft. Such treatises also presume that in the properly ordered household the husband governs the life of his wife, his children, and his slaves in accordance with a reason that has been schooled by philosophical instruction. Similar kinds of assumptions appear in sections of the New Testament often referred to as "household codes" (Col 3.18–4.1; Eph 5.21–6.9; 1 Pet 2.18–3.7). They also inform the descriptions of requirements for leadership (1 Tim 3.1–11), including those that exclude women from teaching or supervising men (1 Tim 2.9–15; 1 Cor 14.34–36).

Scholars have become particularly interested in a movement of rough-spoken, anti-establishment street preachers called Cynics, from the Greek word for dog, originally a derogatory name that referred to their unrefined public behavior. Claiming as their inspiration Socrates, the impoverished stone mason who went about Athens challenging all its citizens, representatives of this movement could be found in the public marketplaces. They rejected the comforts that could be offered by wealthy patrons and lived on as little as possible. They were known for sharp sayings intended to wound an opponent, not persuasive speeches to soothe one into agreement. If the harsh medicine worked, the hearer might convert to a philosophical way of life. If not, he might become angry, even murderously so, as had Socrates's opponents. Some scholars think that this movement provides the best ancient analogy for the itinerant mission of Jesus and his disciples, as depicted in the Gospels. Others have proposed that Paul's description of himself as the solicitous nurse or the father to his fledgling converts (1 Thess 2.1–12) is analogous to the Cynics' relationship to their own followers. Although these cultural models may not have dictated the content of early Christian preaching, they provide a context for understanding what missionaries like Paul were doing in the cities that they visited, and how they would have appeared to their first hearers.

Timeline

DATE	PERIOD	EGYPT
Ca. 3300–2000 BCE	EARLY BRONZE AGE	
3300–3100	Early Bronze I	Earliest forms of writing
3100–2700	Early Bronze II	Political unification; Early Dynastic period
2700–2300	Early Bronze III	Old Kingdom; Dynasties 3–5
2300–2000	Early Bronze IV	First Intermediate Period
Ca. 2000–1550 BCE	MIDDLE BRONZE AGE	
2000–1650	Middle Bronze I–II	Middle Kingdom; Dynasties 11–12
1650–1550	Middle Bronze III	Second Intermediate/ Hyksos Period
Ca. 1550–1200 BCE	LATE BRONZE AGE	New Kingdom; Dynasties 18–19: Thutmose III (1479–1425), Akenhaten (1352–1336), Seti I (1294–1279), Rameses II (1279–1213), Merneptah (1213–1203); Sea Peoples (groups including Philistines) invasions begin
Ca. 1200–586 BCE	IRON AGE	
Ca. 1200–1025	Iron I	Rameses III (1184–1153)[1]
Ca. 1025–586	Iron II	
Ca. 1025–928	Iron IIA	
Ca. 928–722	Iron IIB	Shishak I invades Palestine (925)

1. For a more complete list of rulers, see "Chronological Table of Rulers," pp. 530–33 ES.

SYRIA-PALESTINE		MESOPOTAMIA, ASIA MINOR
		Earliest forms of writing; Full urbanization; Sumerian culture develops
In Egyptian sphere		High point of Sumerian culture
Flourishing city-states		Sargon of Akkad; Naram-Sin of Akkad; Gudea of Lagash
Decline/abandonment of city-states		Third Dynasty of Ur
Revival of urbanism; Invention of alphabet		Amorite kingdoms: Shamshi-Adad of Assyria (ca. 1813–1781); Hammurapi of Babylon (ca. 1792–1750); Rise of Hittites
In Egyptian sphere; Rise of Mitanni in north; Ugarit flourishes;		
Exodus of the Hebrews from Egypt;		Hittites challenge Egypt for control of Syria;
Collapse of city-states		Hittite empire collapses; Trojan War
Israel emerges in Canaan; Philistines settle on SW coast; Small city-states develop in Phoenicia, Syria, Transjordan		Resurgence of Assyria: Tiglath-pileser I (1114–1076)
United Monarchy in Israel: Saul (1025–1005); David (1005–965); Solomon (968–928)		
Divided Monarchy:		
JUDAH:	ISRAEL:	
Rehoboam (928–911)	Jeroboam I (928–907) Omri (882–871); Capital at Samaria Ahab (873–852)	Rise of Neo-Assyrian Empire Shalmaneser III (858–824); Battle of Qarqar (853)
Jehoshaphat (867–846)	Prophet Elijah (mid-ninth century) Prophet Elisha (mid- to late ninth century)	
Athaliah (842–836) Jehoash (836–798)	Jehu (842–814) Jehoash (800–788) Jeroboam II (788–747) Prophet Amos (mid-eighth century)	Adad-nirari III (811–783)
	Prophet Hosea (mid-eighth century)	Tiglath-pileser III (745–727); Assyrian conquest of the Levant
Ahaz (743/735–727/715)	Hoshea (732–722)	Shalmaneser V (727–722) Samaria captured (722)

DATE	PERIOD	EGYPT
Ca. 722–586	Iron IIC	Egypt conquered by Assyria (671) Psammetichus I (664–610) Neco II (610–595)
Ca. 586–539	NEO-BABYLONIAN	
		GREECE AND ROME
539–333	PERSIAN	Greeks repel Persian invasions Peloponnesian War (431–404)
333–63	HELLENISTIC	Alexander the Great (336–323); Defeats Persians at Issus (332); Occupies the Levant and Egypt Rome gains control over Greece (ca. 188–146); Sack of Carthage and Corinth (146)
63 BCE–330 CE	ROMAN	Julius Caesar named dictator (49); assassinated (44) Octavian (Augustus) defeats Antony at Actium (31); (Emperor 27 BCE–14 CE) Tiberius (14–37 CE) Gaius (Caligula) (37–41) Claudius (41–54) Nero (54–68) Vespasian (69–79) Titus (79–81) Domitian (81–96) Nerva (96–98) Trajan (98–117) Hadrian (117–138)

SYRIA-PALESTINE	MESOPOTAMIA
JUDAH:	
Prophet Isaiah (late eighth to early seventh centuries)	Sargon II (722–705)
Prophet Micah (late eighth century)	Sennacherib (705–681); Attack on Judah and seige of Jerusalem (701)
Hezekiah (727/715–698/687)	
Manasseh (698/687–642)	Esar-haddon (681–669)
Josiah (639–609)	Ashurbanipal (669–627)
Prophet Zephaniah (late seventh century)	
Prophet Jeremiah (late seventh to early sixth centuries)	Rise of Babylon
Jehoahaz (609)	Assyrian capital of Nineveh captured (612)
Jehoiakim (608–598)	
Jehoiachin (597)	Nebuchadrezzar II (604–562) of Babylon
Prophet Ezekiel (early sixth century)	
Zedekiah (597–586); Capture of Jerusalem (586)	
	Nabonidus (556–539)
EASTERN MEDITERRANEAN	
	Cyrus II (the Great) (559–530); Capture of Babylon
Some exiles return from Babylon (538)	Cambyses (530–522); Capture of Egypt (525)
Second Temple built (520–515)	Darius I (522–486)
Prophet Haggai (520); Prophet Zechariah (520–518)	Xerxes I (486–465)
Nehemiah governor of Judah (ca. 445–430)	Artaxerxes I (465–424)
Mission of Ezra the scribe (mid-fifth [or early fourth] century)	Artaxerxes II (405–359)
Seleucus I (312/311–281) controls Syria and Mesopotamia	
Ptolemy I (323–282) controls Egypt, Palestine, Phoenicia	
Antiochus III (223–187) gains control of southern Syria, Phoenicia, and Judea from Ptolemy IV (202–198)	
Ben Sira (Sirach) (early second century)	
Antiochus IV Epiphanes (175–164)	
Revolt of the Maccabees (167–164)	
HASMONEAN RULE OF JUDEA (165–37):	
John Hyrcanus (135–104); Alexander Janneus (103–76);	
Salome Alexandra (76–67)	
Pompey conquers the Levant (66–62); Enters Jerusalem (63)	
Herod the Great king of Judea (37–4); Rebuilds Second Temple	
(Herod) Antipas (4 BCE–39 CE)	
Life of Jesus of Nazareth (ca. 4 BCE–30 CE)	
Pontius Pilate governor of Judea (26–36)	
(Herod) Agrippa I (39–44)	
Missionary activity of Paul (mid-first century)	
(Herod) Agrippa II (53–93)	
First Jewish Revolt in Judea against Rome (66–73); Jerusalem is captured (70)	
Jewish revolts in Egypt, Libya, Cyprus (115–118)	
Second Jewish Revolt in Judea against Rome (132–135)	

Chronological Table of Rulers

DATE	EGYPT	ASSYRIA	BABYLONIA
1300 BCE	DYNASTY 19 (1295–1186): Seti I (1294–1279) Rameses II (1279–1213) Merneptah (1213–1203)		
1200	DYNASTY 20 (1186–1069)	Tiglath-pileser I (1114–1076)	
	DYNASTY 21 (1069–945)		
1000	DYNASTIES 22–24 (945–715): Shoshenq I (**Shishak**) (945–924)	Shalmaneser III (858–824) Shamshi-Adad V (824–811)	
	DYNASTY 25 (780–656):		
800		Adad-nirari III (811–783) Shalmaneser IV (783–773) Ashur-dan III (773–755) Ashur-nirari V (755–745) **Tiglath-pileser III (Pul)** (745–727) **Shalmaneser V** (727–722) **Sargon II** (722–705)	Marduk-apal-iddina II (**Merodach-baladan**) (721–710, 703)
700	Taharqa (**Tirhakah**) (690–664) DYNASTY 26 (664–525): Psammetichus I (664–610) **Neco II** (610–595) Psammetichus II (595–589) Apries (**Hophra**) (589–570) Amasis II (570–526) Psammetichus III (526–525)	**Sennacherib** (705–681) **Esar-haddon** (681–669) Ashurbanipal (669–627) Ashur-etil-ilani, Sin-shum-lishir, Sin-shar-ishkun (627–612) Ashur-uballit II (612–609)	Nabo-polassar (625–605) **Nebuchadrezzar II (Nebuchadnezzar)** (605–562) **Amel-Marduk (Evil-merodach)** (562–560) Neriglissar (560–556) Labashi-Marduk (556) **Nabonidus** (556–539) **Belshazzar** (coregent 553–543)
400			
325 BCE			

Note: Names in boldface occur in the Bible. Overlapping dates indicate coregencies. Date ranges are reigns, not lift spans.
1. The data are inconsistent for the dates of the reigns of Ahaz, Hezekiah, and Manasseh.

DATE	PERSIA	ISRAEL	
1300 BCE			
1200			
		UNITED MONARCHY: **Saul** (1025–1005); **David** (1005–965);	
1000		**Solomon (Yedidiah)** (968–928)	
		DIVIDED MONARCHY:	
		JUDAH:	ISRAEL:
		Rehoboam (928–911)	**Jeroboam** I (928–907)
		Abijam (Abijah) (911–908)	**Nadab** (907–906)
		Asa (908–867)	**Baasha** (906–883)
		Jehoshaphat (870–846)	**Elah** (883–882); **Zimri** (882)
			Omri (882–871)
		Jehoram (Joram) (851–843)	**Ahab** (873–852)
			Ahaziah (852–851)
		Ahaziah (Jehoahaz) (843–842)	**Jehoram (Joram)** (851–842)
		Athaliah (842–836)	**Jehu** (842–814)
800		**Jehoash (Joash)** (836–798)	**Jehoahaz** (817–800)
		Amaziah (798–769)	**Jehoash (Joash)** (800–784)
		Azariah (Uzziah) (785–733)	**Jeroboam** II (788–747)
			Zechariah (747); **Shallum** (747)
			Menahem (747–737)
			Pekahiah (737–735)
		Jotham (759–743)	**Pekah** (735–732)
		Ahaz (743/735–727/715)[1]	**Hoshea** (732–722)
		Hezekiah (727/715–698/687)[1]	
700			
		Manasseh (698/687–642)[1]	
		Amon (641–640)	
		Josiah (640–609)	
		Jehoahaz (Shallum) (609)	
		Jehoiakim (Eliakim) (608–598)	
		Jehoiachin (Jeconiah, etc.) (597)	
		Zedekiah (Mattaniah) (597–586)	
	Cyrus II (559–530)		
	Cambyses (530–522)		
	Darius I (522–486)		
	Xerxes I (**Ahasuerus**) (486–465)		
	Artaxerxes I (465–424)		
	Darius II (423–405)		
400	Artaxerxes II (405–359)		
	Artaxerxes III (359–338)		
	Artaxerxes IV (338–336)		
	Darius III (336–330)		
325 BCE			

DATE	EGYPT	SYRIA
	HELLENISTIC PERIOD	**Alexander** (the Great) (336–323)
300 BCE	Ptolemy I Soter (305–282)	**Seleucus I Nicator** (305–281)
	Ptolemy II Philadelphus (285–246)	Antiochus I Soter (281–261)
		Antiochus II Theos (261–246)
	Ptolemy III Euergetes (246–221)	Seleucus II Callinicus (246–225)
	Ptolemy IV Philopator (221–204)	Seleucus III Soter Ceraunos (225–223)
	Ptolemy V Epiphanes (204–180);	Antiochus III (the Great) (223–187)
	Cleopatra I (180–176)	**Seleucus** IV Philopator (187–175)
		Antiochus IV Epiphanes (175–164)
	Ptolemy VI Philometor (180–145);	**Antiochus** V **Eupator** (164–162)
	Cleopatra II (175–116)	**Demetrius** I Soter (162–150)
	Ptolemy VII Neos Philopator (145)	**Alexander Epiphanes** (Balas) (150–145)
	Ptolemy VIII Euergetes II Physcon (170–116)	**Demetrius** II Nicator (145–141 and 129–125)
		Antiochus VI Epiphanes (145–142)
		Trypho (142–138)
		Antiochus VII Sidetes (138–129)
		Cleopatra Thea (126–121)
		Antiochus VIII Grypus (125–121 and 121–96)
	Cleopatra III (116–101)	Seleucus V (125)
	Ptolemy IX Soter II (116–107 and 88–80)	Antiochus IX Cyzicenus (115–95)
100 BCE	Ptolemy X Alexander I (107–88)	Seleucus VI (95)
		Antiochus X Eusebes (95–83)
		Antiochus XI Philadelphus (95)
	Cleopatra Berenice (101–88)	Demetrius III Eukairos (95–88)
		Philip I Epiphanes Philadelphus (95–84)
	Ptolemy XI Alexander II (80)	Antiochus XII Dionysus Epiphanes (87–84)
		Philip II (67–66)
	Ptolemy XII Auletes (80–59 and 55–51)	Antiochus XIII Asiaticus (69–68 and 65–64)
50 BCE	Cleopatra VII (51–30)	
	Ptolemy XIII (51–47)	
	Ptolemy XIV (47–44)	
		ROMAN EMPIRE
		ROMAN EMPERORS:
		Octavian (**Augustus**) (27 BCE–14 CE)
25 CE		**Tiberius** (14–37)
		Gaius Caligula (37–41)
50 CE		**Claudius** (41–54)
		Nero (54–68)
		Galba (68–69); Otho (69); Vitellius (69)
		Vespasian (69–79)
		Titus (79–81)
100 CE		Domitian (81–96)
		Nerva (96–98)
		Trajan (98–117)
		Hadrian (117–138)

DATE	PALESTINE	
300 BCE		
	HASMONEAN RULERS	
	[Mattathias d. 166]	
	Judas Maccabeus, son of Mattathias (165–160)	
	Jonathan, son of Mattathias (160–142)	
	Simon, son of Mattathias (142–135)	
	John Hyrcanus I, son of Simon (135–104)	
	Judah Aristobulus I , son of John Hyrcanus (104–103)	
	Alexander Janneus, son of John Hyrcanus (103–76)	
100 BCE		
	Salome Alexandra, wife of Alexander Jannaeus (76–67)	
	Aristobulus II, son of Alexander Jannaeus and Salome Alexandra (67–63)	
	Hyrcanus II, son of Alexander Jannaeus and Salome Alexandra (63–40)	
	Mattathias Antigonus, son of Aristobulus II (40–37)	
50 BCE		
	HERODIAN DYNASTY	
	Herod the Great, king of the Jews (37–4)	
	Herod Archelaus, son of Herod the Great, ethnarch of Judea, Samaria, Idumea (4 BCE–6 CE)	**ROMAN GOVERNORS OF JUDEA**
	Herod Antipas, son of Herod the Great, tetrarch of Galilee and Perea (4 BCE–39 CE)	Coponius (6–8 CE) M. Ambivius (9–12)
	Herod **Philip,** son of Herod the Great, tetrarch of	Annius Rufus (12–15)
25 CE	Batanea, Trachonitis, Auranitis (4 BCE–34 CE)	Valerius Gratus (15–26) **Pontius Pilate** (26–36)
	Herod Agrippa I, grandson of Herod the Great, king of Batanea, Trachonitis, Aurantis (37–44) and of Judea, Galilee, and Perea (41–44)	Marcellus (36–37) Marullus (37–41)[2] Cuspius Fadus (44–46) Tiberius Julius Alexander (46–48)
50 CE		Ventidius Cumanus (48–52)
	Herod **Agrippa** II, son of Herod Agrippa I, king of Chalcis (50–53), king of Batanea, Trachonitis, Auranitis, Galilee, Perea (53–ca. 93)	M. Antonius **Felix** (52–60?) **Porcius Festus** (60?–62) Clodius Albinus (62–64) Gessius Florus (64–66)
100 CE		

2. In 41 Judea was made part of the kingdom of Herod Agrippa I, grandson of Herod the Great (see Herodian Dynasty, above). At his death in 44 it became a province again.

Weights and Measures

The modern equivalents for biblical measures and weights are presented in the following tables.

HEBREW WEIGHTS

HEBREW	NRSV	EQUIVALENCE	U.S. AVOIRDUPOIS	METRIC UNITS
kikkar	talent	60 minas	75.558 pounds	34.3 kilograms
maneh	mina	50 shekels	20.148 ounces	571.2 grams
sheqel	shekel	2 bekas	176.29 grains	11.42 grams
pim (or *payim*)	pim	.667 shekel	117.52 grains	7.61 grams
beqaʿ	beka, half a shekel	10 gerahs	88.14 grains	5.71 grams
gerah	gerah		8.81 grains	.57 gram

The practice of weighing unmarked ingots of metal used in commercial transactions prior to the invention of money explains that the names of the units of weight were used later as indications of value, and as names for monetary standards. There is, however, no direct relation between the shekel-weight and the weight of a shekel piece.

WEIGHTS IN THE NEW TESTAMENT

GREEK	NRSV	EQUIVALENCE	U.S. AVOIRDUPOIS	METRIC UNITS
talenton	talent	(Hebrew) talent	75.558 pounds	34.3 kilograms
mna	pound	(Hebrew) mina	20.148 ounces	571.2 grams
litra	pound	(Latin) libra	0.719 pound	326.4 grams

HEBREW MEASURES OF LENGTH

HEBREW	NRSV	EQUIVALENCE	U.S. MEASURES	METRIC UNITS
ʾammah	cubit	2 spans	17.49 inches	.443 meter
zeret	span	3 handbreadths	8.745 inches	.221 meter
topaḥ, tepaḥ	handbreadth	4 fingers	2.915 inches	.074 meter
ʾetsbaʿ	finger		0.728 inch	.019 meter

The cubit described in Ezekiel 40.5; 43.13 is equal to seven (not six) handbreadths, namely 20.405 inches.

MEASURES OF LENGTH IN THE NEW TESTAMENT

GREEK	NRSV	U.S. MEASURES	METRIC UNITS
pechus	cubit	about 1.5 feet	.456 meter
orguia	fathom	about 72.44 inches	1.839 meters
stadion	stadia, or the equivalent in miles	about 606 feet	184.7 meters
milion	mile	about 4,854 feet	1.482 kilometers

HEBREW MEASURES OF CAPACITY: LIQUID MEASURES

HEBREW	NRSV	EQUIVALENCE	U.S. MEASURES	METRIC UNITS
kor	measure, cor	10 baths	60.738 gallons	230 liters
bat	bath	6 hins	6.073 gallons	23 liters
hin	hin	3 kabs	1.012 gallons	3.829 liters
qab	kab	4 logs	1.4349 quarts	1.276 liters
log	log		0.674 pint	.32 liter

HEBREW MEASURES OF CAPACITY: DRY MEASURES

HEBREW	NRSV	EQUIVALENCE	U.S. MEASURES	METRIC UNITS
ḥomer	homer	2 lethechs	6.524 bushels	229.7 liters
kor	measure, cor	2 lethechs	6.524 bushels	229.7 liters
letek	lethech, measure	5 ephahs	3.262 bushels	114.8 liters
ʾepah	ephah, measure	3 seahs	20.878 quarts	22.9 liters
tseʾah	measure	3.33 omers	6.959 quarts	7.7 liters
ʿomer	omer	1.8 kabs	2.087 quarts	2.3 liters
ʿissaron	tenth part (of ephah)			
qab	kab		1.159 quarts	1.3 liters

MEASURES OF CAPACITY IN THE NEW TESTAMENT

HEBREW	NRSV	EQUIVALENCE	U.S. MEASURES	METRIC UNITS
batos	measure	(Hebrew) *bat*	6.073 gallons	23 liters
koros	measure	(Hebrew) *kor*	60.738 gallons or 6.524 bushels	230 liters
saton	measure	(Hebrew) *tseʾah*	6.959 dry quarts	7.71 liters
metretes	measure		10.3 gallons	39 liters
choinix	quart		0.98 dry quart	1.079 liters
modios	bushel	(Latin) modius	7.68 dry quarts	8.458 liters
xestes	pot	(Latin) sextarius	0.96 dry pint, or 1.12 fluid pints	.53 liter

Calendar

The year was composed of twelve lunar months (beginning on the day of the new moon), with an intercalary month added periodically (see perhaps 1 Kings 12.33). In some traditions, and perhaps originally, the year began in the fall, at the autumnal equinox (see Ex 23.16; 34.22). In others, following Babylonian practice, the new year was celebrated in the spring. The fall new year became standard in postbiblical Judaism.

Months in the Bible are usually identified by ordinal numbers, beginning with the spring new year. Some months (in boldface in the following list) are also designated with names derived either from a Canaanite calendar or, in postexilic texts, from a Babylonian one; the names of months not found in the Bible are known from other ancient sources.

	CANAANITE NAME	BABYLONIAN NAME	MODERN EQUIVALENT
First	**Abib**	**Nisan**	March–April
Second	**Ziv**	Iyyar	April–May
Third		**Sivan**	May–June
Fourth		Tammuz	June–July
Fifth		Ab	July–August
Sixth		**Elul**	August–September
Seventh	**Ethanim**	Tishri	September–October
Eighth	**Bul**	Marheshvan	October–November
Ninth		Chislev	November–December
Tenth		**Tebeth**	December–January
Eleventh		**Shebat**	January–February
Twelfth		**Adar**	February–March

Parallel Texts

Alongside the widespread evidence of alternative traditions in the Bible, in which two or more authors or traditions deal with the same general subjects (e.g., the two accounts of creation in Gen 1–3; the Gospel of John as compared with the first three Gospels), throughout the Bible there are also literary relationships between one book or part of a book and another. Sometimes the authors or editors of one book simply reproduced their sources verbatim; sometimes they were retouched. Often called "synoptic passages," because when viewed together their common elements can be seen, these texts are important in understanding the specific purposes and themes of a writer by analyzing what was included, added, omitted, revised, and rearranged. There follows a listing of the larger synoptic passages throughout the Bible. These texts have a demonstrable literary relationship with each other, either direct, where a source can be identified, or indirect, where a source that no longer survives but must be presumed is quoted at length and verbatim, or with only minor modifications in one or more places.

HEBREW BIBLE

	SYNOPTIC PASSAGES		SUBJECT MATTER
EXODUS	Ex 20.2–17	Deut 5.6–21	Ten Commandments
JOSHUA	Josh 21.1–39	1 Chr 6.54–81	Levitical cities
2 SAMUEL	2 Sam 22	Ps 18	Thanksgiving hymn
1 CHRONICLES	1 Chr 1.1–4	Gen 5	Descendants of Adam
	1 Chr 1.5–23	Gen 10.1–32	Descendants of Noah
	1 Chr 1.24–27	Gen 11.10–32	Descendants of Shem
	1 Chr 1.28–33	Gen 25.1–6,12–18	Descendants of Ishmael and Keturah
	1 Chr 1.34–54	Gen 36.1–43	Descendants of Esau
	1 Chr 3.1–9	2 Sam 3.2–5; 5.5,13–16	Sons of David
	1 Chr 6.54–81	Josh 21.1–39	Levitical cities
	1 Chr 10	1 Sam 31	Death of Saul
	1 Chr 11.1–9	2 Sam 5.1–10	David's early reign
	1 Chr 11.10–47	2 Sam 23.8–39	David's heroes
	1 Chr 13.5–14	2 Sam 6.1–11	David retrieves the ark
	1 Chr 14.1–17	2 Sam 5.11–25	David's reign in Jerusalem
	1 Chr 15.25–16.3	2 Sam 6.12–19	David brings the ark to Jerusalem
	1 Chr 16.8–36	Ps 105.1–15; 96.1–13; 106.1,47–48	Thanksgiving hymn
	1 Chr 17–21	2 Sam 7; 8; 10; 11.1; 12.26, 30–31; 21.18–22; 24	David's reign in Jerusalem
2 CHRONICLES	2 Chr 1.3–13	1 Kings 3.4–15	Solomon's prayer for wisdom
	2 Chr 1.14–17	1 Kings 10.26–29	Solomon's wealth
	2 Chr 2.1–18	1 Kings 5.1–18	Preparations for building Temple
	2 Chr 3.1–4	1 Kings 6.1–3	Temple dimensions
	2 Chr 4.1–5.1	1 Kings 7.23–26,39–51	Temple metalwork
	2 Chr 5.2–7.10	1 Kings 8	Dedication of the Temple
	2 Chr 7.11–9.29	1 Kings 9–10	Solomon's reign
	2 Chr 9.29–31	1 Kings 11.41–42	Solomon's death
	2 Chr 10.1–11.4	1 Kings 12.1–24	Rehoboam's accession
	2 Chr 12.2–16	1 Kings 14.25–31	Shishak's invasion
	2 Chr 15.16–17.1	1 Kings 15.17–24	Asa's reign
	2 Chr 18.2–34; 20.31–21.1	1 Kings 22	Jehoshaphat's reign

HEBREW BIBLE *(continued)*

	Synoptic Passages		Subject Matter
2 CHRONICLES	2 Chr 21.2–10	2 Kings 8.16–22	Jehoram's reign
	2 Chr 22.2–6	2 Kings 8.25–29	Ahaziah's reign
	2 Chr 22.10–23.21	2 Kings 11	Athaliah's reign
	2 Chr 24.1–14	2 Kings 12.1–14	Jehoash's reigh
	2 Chr 25.1–4,17–28; 26.1–2	2 Kings 14.1–22	Amaziah's reign
	2 Chr 26.3–4,21–23	2 Kings 15.1–7	Uzziah's reign
	2 Chr 27.1–9	2 Kings 15.32–38	Jotham's reign
	2 Chr 28.1–4,26–27	2 Kings 16.1–4,19–20	Ahaz's reign
	2 Chr 29.1–2; 32.1, 9–12,15	2 Kings 18.1–3,13,17–22, 29–30	Hezekiah's reign
	2 Chr 33.1–9,18–20	2 Kings 21.1–9,17–18	Manasseh's reign
	2 Chr 33.21–25	2 Kings 21.19–26	Amon's reign
	2 Chr 34.1–2,8–31; 35.20	2Kings 22.1–23.3,29	Josiah's reign
	2 Chr 36.1–4	2 Kings 23.30–34	Jehoahaz's reign
	2 Chr 36.5,6,8	2 Kings 23.36–37; 24.1,5	Jehoiakim's reign
	2 Chr 36.9	2 Kings 24.8	Jehoiakin's reign
	2 Chr 36.11–12	2 Kings 24.18–19	Zedekiah's reign
	2 Chr 36.22–23	Ezra 1.1–2	Decree of Cyrus
EZRA	Ezra 1.1–2	2 Chr 36.22–23	Decree of Cyrus
	Ezra 2.1–70	Neh 7.7–69	List of returning exiles
PSALMS	Ps 14	Ps 53	Lament
	Ps 18	2 Sam 22	Thanksgiving hymn
ISAIAH	Isa 2.2–4	Mic 4.1–3	Oracle of future age
	Isa 15–16	Jer 48.29–38	Oracle against Moab
	Isa 36–39	2 Kings 18.13–20.19	Events in Hezekiah's reign
JEREMIAH	Jer 39.1–10	2 Kings 25.1–12	The fall of Jerusalem
	Jer 48.29–38	Isa 16.6–10; 15.2–7; 16.11–12	Oracle against Moab
	Jer 49.9–10,14–16	Ob 5–6,1–4	Oracle against Edom
	Jer 52	2 Kings 24.18–25.30	The fall of Jerusalem
OBADIAH	Ob 1–6	Jer 49.14–16,9–10	Oracle against Edom
MICAH	Mic 4.1–3	Isa 2.2–4	Oracle of future age

APOCRYPHA

	Synoptic Passages		Subject Matter
1 ESDRAS	1 Esd 1.1–55	2 Chr 35.1–36.21	Last days of Judah
	1 Esd 2.1–15	Ezra 1.1–11	Cyrus's decree
	1 Esd 2.16–30	Ezra 4.7–24	Opposition to rebuilding Temple
	1 Esd 5.7–46	Ezra 2.1–70; Neh 7.7–69	List of returning exiles
	1 Esd 5.47–73	Ezra 3.1–4.5	Rebuilding Temple
	1 Esd 6.1–7.15	Ezra 4.24–6.22	Completion of Temple
	1 Esd 8.1–9.55	Ezra 7.1–10.44; Neh 7.73–8.12	Ezra's mission

NEW TESTAMENT

A majority of scholars think that the Gospel of Mark was independently used as a source by Matthew and Luke.

SYNOPTIC PASSAGES			SUBJECT MATTER
Mk 1.2–8	Mt 3.1–6,11–12	Lk 3.1–6,16	John the Baptist
Mk 1.9–11	Mt 3.13–17	Lk 3.21–22	Baptism of Jesus
Mk 1.12–13	Mt 4.1–2,11	Lk 4.1–2,13	Temptation of Jesus
Mk 1.16–20	Mt 4.18–22	(Lk 5.1–11)	Call of disciples
Mk 1.21–38	(Mt 7.28–29; 8.14–17)	Lk 4.31–43	Teaching and healing by Jesus
Mk 1.40–45	Mt 8.1–4	Lk 5.12–16	Healing of a leper
Mk 2.1–22	Mt 9.1–17	Lk 5.17–39	Events in Jesus' ministry
Mk 2.23–3.30	Mt 12.1–37; 10.1–4	Lk 6.1–19; 11.14–23; 12.10; 6.43–45	Events in Jesus' ministry
Mk 3.31–4.25	Mt 12.46–50; 13.1–13, 18–23	Lk 8.4–21	Sayings of Jesus
Mk 4.30–34	Mt 13.31–32,34–35	Lk 13.18–19	Sayings of Jesus
Mk 4.35–41	Mt 8.23–27	Lk 8.22–35	Stilling the storm
Mk 5.1–43	Mt 8.28–34; 9.18–26	Lk 8.26–56	Healings by Jesus
Mk 6.1–6	Mt 13.51–52		Rejection in Nazareth
Mk 6.7–14	Mt 10.1,9–11; 14.1–2	Lk 9.1–9	Events in Jesus' ministry
Mk 6.17–29	Mt 14.3–12		Death of John the Baptist
Mk 6.30–44	Mt 14.13–21	Lk 9.10–17	Feeding of five thousand
Mk 6.45–8.10	Mt 14.22–15.39		Events in Jesus' ministry
Mk 8.11–21	Mt 16.1–12	(Lk 11.29; 12.1)	Sayings of Jesus
Mk 8.27–9.48	Mt 16.13–17.23; 18.1–9	Lk 9.18–50; 17.1–2	Events in Jesus' ministry
Mk 12.28–31	Mt 22.34–40	Lk 10.25–38	Sayings of Jesus
Mk 10.1–12	Mt 19.1–12		On marriage
Mk 10.13–52	Mt 19.13–30; 20.17–34	Lk 18.15–43; 22.24–27	Sayings of Jesus
Mk 11.1–12.37	Mt 21.1–27,33–46; 22.15-46	Lk 19.28–38,45–48; 20.1–44; (10.25–28)	Jesus in Jerusalem
Mk 12.41–44		Lk 21.1–4	The poor widow
Mk 13.1–32	Mt 24.1–36	Lk 21.5–33	Sayings of Jesus about the end
Mk 14.1–15.47	Mt 26.1–27.2; 27.11–61	Lk 22.1–34,39–71; 23.1–5,18–55	Passion of Jesus
Mk 16.1–8	Mt 28.1–10	Lk 24.1–11	The empty tomb

A majority of scholars think that Matthew and Luke used a source that has not survived (known as "Q").

SYNOPTIC PASSAGES		SUBJECT MATTER
Mt 3.7–10,12	Lk 3.7–9,17	John the Baptist's preaching
Mt 4.3–10	Lk 3.3–12	Temptation of Jesus
Mt 5.3–12	Lk 6.20–23	Beatitudes
Mt 5.13–16	Lk 14.34–35; 11.33	Sayings of Jesus
Mt 5.21–26	Lk 12.57–59	Sayings of Jesus
Mt 5.38–48	Lk 6.27–36	Sayings of Jesus
Mt 6.9–15	Lk 11.2–4	Lord's Prayer
Mt 6.19–7.27	Lk 12.33–36; 16.13; 12.22–31; 6.37–38, 41–42; 11.9–13; 6.31; 13.23–24; 6.43–49	Sayings of Jesus
Mt 8.5–15	Lk 7.1–10	Healing of a centurion's servant
Mt 8.18–22	Lk 9.57–60	Sayings of Jesus
Mt 10.26–39	Lk 12.2–9,51–53; 14.26–27	Sayings of Jesus
Mt 11.2–19	Lk 7.18–35	On John the Baptist

NEW TESTAMENT *(continued)*

SYNOPTIC PASSAGES		SUBJECT MATTER
Mt 11.20–27	Lk 10.13–15,21–22	Sayings of Jesus
Mt 12.38–45	Lk 11.29–32; 11.24–26	Sayings of Jesus
Mt 13.16–17	Lk 10.23–24	Sayings of Jesus
Mt 13.33	Lk 13.20–21	Sayings of Jesus
Mt 18.10–14	Lk 15.3–7	Sayings of Jesus
Mt 22.1–4	Lk 14.16–22	Parable of the marriage feast
Mt 23.37–39	Lk 13.34–35	Lament over Jerusalem
Mt 24.37–51	Lk 17.26–35; 12.39–46	Sayings of Jesus about the end
Mt 25.14–30	Lk 19.12–27	Parable of the talents

Translations of Ancient Texts

ANCIENT NEAR EASTERN

Hallo, William W., and K. Lawson Younger, eds. *The Context of Scripture*. Vol. 1, *Canonical Compositions from the Biblical World*. Vol. 2, *Monumental Inscriptions from the Ancient World*. Leiden: E. J. Brill, 1997; 1999.

Parker, Simon B., ed. *Writings from the Ancient World*. A series produced by the Society of Biblical Literature (Atlanta, Ga.), with each volume devoted to a particular genre and language. Recent volumes include *Ugaritic Narrative Poetry* (ed. S. B. Parker; 1997); *Hittite Myths* (H. A. Hoffner, Jr.; 2d ed., 1998); *Law Collections from Mesopotamia and Asia Minor* (M. F. Roth; 2d ed., 1997).

Pritchard, James B., ed. *Ancient Near Eastern Texts Relating to the Old Testament*. Princeton, N.J.: Princeton University Press, 3d ed., 1969.

EARLY JEWISH

General

Bartlett, John R. *Jews in the Hellenistic World: Josephus, Aristeas, the Sibylline Oracles, Eupolemus*. Cambridge, Eng.: Cambridge University Press, 1985.

Maccoby, Hyam. *Early Rabbinic Writings*. Cambridge, Eng.: Cambridge University Press, 1988.

Dead Sea Scrolls

Abegg, Martin, Jr.; Peter Flint; and Eugene Ulrich, eds. *The Dead Sea Scrolls Bible: The Oldest Known Bible*. San Francisco: HarperSanFrancisco, 1999.

García Martínez, Florentino, ed. *The Dead Sea Scrolls Translated: The Qumran Texts in English*. Grand Rapids, Mich.: Eerdmans.

Vermes, Geza. *The Complete Dead Sea Scrolls in English*. New York: Penguin, 1997.

Apocrypha and Pseudepigrapha

Charles, R. H., ed. *The Apocrypha and Pseudepigrapha of the Old Testament*. 2 vols. Oxford: Clarendon, 1913.

Charlesworth, James H., ed. *The Old Testament Pseudepigrapha*. 2 vols. New York: Doubleday, 1983; 1985.

Josephus

Whiston, William, trans. *The Works of Josephus Complete and Unabridged*. 1736. New updated edition, Peabody, Mass.: Hendrickson, 1987.

Williamson, G. A., trans. *Josephus: The Jewish War*. New York: Penguin, 1984.

Loeb Classical Library

Philo of Alexandria

Williamson, Ronald. *Jews in the Hellenistic World: Philo*. Cambridge, Eng.: Cambridge University Press, 1989.

Yonge, C. D., trans. *The Works of Philo*. 1854. New updated edition, Peabody, Mass.: Hendrickson, 1993.

Loeb Classical Library

Mishnah

Neusner, Jacob. *The Mishnah: A New Translation*. New Haven: Yale University Press, 1988.

Talmud

Epstein, I. *The Babylonian Talmud*. 30 vols. London: Soncino, 1935–48.

Steinsaltz, Adin. *The Talmud*. New York: Random House, 1989– .

EARLY CHRISTIAN

General

Barrett, C. K. *The New Testament Background: Writings from Ancient Greece and the Roman Empire That Illuminate Christian Origins*. Rev. ed. San Francisco: HarperCollins, 1987.

Cartlidge, David R., and David L. Dungan, eds. *Documents for the Study of the Gospels*. Rev. ed. Minneapolis: Fortress, 1994.

Elliott, J. K. *The Apocryphal New Testament*. Oxford: Oxford University Press, 1994.

Richardson, Cyril D., ed. *Early Christian Fathers*. New York: Macmillan, 1970.

Staniforth, Maxwell, trans. *Early Christian Writings*. New York: Penguin, 1987.

Nag Hammadi

Layton, Bentley. *The Gnostic Scriptures: A New Translation*. Garden City, N.Y.: Doubleday, 1987.

Robinson, J. M., ed. *The Nag Hammadi Library in English*. 4th rev. ed. Leiden: E. J. Brill, 1996.

ANCIENT TRANSLATIONS OF THE BIBLE

Greek

Brenton, Lancelot C. L. *The Septuagint with Apocrypha: Greek and English*. 1851. Reprint, Peabody, Mass.: Hendrickson, 1986.

Aramaic

McNamara, Martin, et al. *The Aramaic Bible: The Targums*. Collegeville, Minn.: Liturgical, 1987– .

Classical Sources

Beard, Mary; Simon Price; and John North. *Religions of Rome*. Vol. 2: *A Sourcebook*. Cambridge, Eng.: Cambridge University Press, 1998.

Translations of the writings of most Greek and Roman authors are available in the Loeb Classical Library.

INDEX

Index to the Study Materials

The index is to the introductions, annotations, and essays, not to the biblical text. It therefore refers not to biblical citations but to page numbers, as follows: HB for the Hebrew Bible; AP for the Apocrypha; NT for the New Testament; ES for the essays immediately following the end of the New Testament. Readers of editions of this book that do not include the Apocrypha should disregard references preceded by AP.

B

D

H

J

Y

Z

Concordance

The following abbreviations are used for the Canonical Books:

1Ch	1 Chronicles	Ecc	Ecclesiastes	La	Lamentations
1Co	1 Corinthians	Eph	Ephesians	Lev	Leviticus
1Jn	1 John	Est	Esther	Lk	Luke
1Ki	1 Kings	Ex	Exodus	Mal	Malachi
1Pe	1 Peter	Eze	Ezekiel	Mic	Micah
1Sa	1 Samuel	Ezr	Ezra	Mk	Mark
1Th	1 Thessalonians	Gal	Galatians	Mt	Matthew
1Ti	1 Timothy	Ge	Genesis	Na	Nahum
2Ch	2 Chronicles	Hab	Habakkuk	Ne	Nehemiah
2Co	2 Corinthians	Hag	Haggai	Nu	Numbers
2Jn	2 John	Heb	Hebrews	Ob	Obadiah
2Ki	2 Kings	Hos	Hosea	Phm	Philemon
2Pe	2 Peter	Isa	Isaiah	Php	Philippians
2Sa	2 Samuel	Jas	James	Pr	Proverbs
2Th	2 Thessalonians	Jdg	Judges	Ps	Psalms
2Ti	2 Timothy	Jer	Jeremiah	Rev	Revelation
3Jn	3 John	Jn	John	Ro	Romans
Ac	Acts	Jnh	Jonah	Ru	Ruth
Am	Amos	Job	Job	SS	Song of Songs
Col	Colossians	Joel	Joel	Tit	Titus
Da	Daniel	Jos	Joshua	Zec	Zechariah
Dt	Deuteronomy	Jude	Jude	Zep	Zephaniah

The following abbreviations are used for the Deuterocanonical Books:

AdE	Additions to Esther	Jdt	Judith	4Mc	4 Maccabees
Aza	Prayer of Azariah	LtJ	Letter of Jeremiah	Pm	Psalm 151
Bar	Baruch	Man	Prayer of Manasseh	Sir	Sirach
Bel	Bel and the Dragon	1Mc	1 Maccabees	Sus	Susanna
1Es	1 Esdras	2Mc	2 Maccabees	Tob	Tobit
2Es	2 Esdras	3Mc	3 Maccabees	Wis	Wisdom

Other abbreviations and special symbols used:

S	Shorter ending of Mark
T	Psalm titles
Pr:	Sirach Prologue
*	Entries followed by an asterisk (e.g., ABBA*) contain every reference in the NRSV
†	A Dagger distinguishes LORD and GOD from Lord and God in Hebrew Bible references
➛	An arrow following an entry heading points to related words for additional study
=	An equals sign marks an alternate proper name for additional study (e.g., ISRAEL =JACOB)
[[ ]]	Contexts in double brackets are from passages that are similarly bracketed in the NRSV (e.g., John 7:53—8:11)

For further study consult *The Concise Concordance to the New Revised Standard Version* (Oxford University Press, 1993) and *The NRSV Concordance Unabridged* (Zondervan, 1991).—John R. Kohlenberger III

AARON

Genealogy (Ex 6:16-20; Jos 21:4, 10; 1Ch 6:3-15). Priesthood of (Ex 28:1; Nu 17; Heb 5:1-4; 7), vestments of (Ex 28; 39), consecration of (Ex 29), ordination of (Lev 8).

Spokesman for Moses (Ex 4:14-16, 27-31; 7:1-2). Supported Moses' hands in battle (Ex 17:8-13). Built golden calf (Ex 32; Dt 9:20). Spoke against Moses (Nu 12). Priesthood opposed (Nu 16); staff budded (Nu 17). Forbidden to enter the promised land (Nu 20:1-12). Death of (Nu 20:22-29; 33:38-39). Praise of (Sir 45:6-22).

ABANDON ➛ ABANDONED

Nu 32:15 will again a them in the wilderness;
Dt 4:31 will neither a you nor destroy you;
2Ch 15: 2 but if you a him, he will a you.
Mk 7: 8 You a the commandment of God
Ac 2:27 For you will not a my soul to Hades
Heb 10:35 Do not, therefore, a that confidence

ABANDONED ➛ ABANDON

Dt 29:25 they a the covenant of the LORD,
Jdg 2:13 a the LORD, and worshiped Baal
2Ch 12: 5 You a me, so I have a you
Isa 54: 7 For a brief moment I a you,
Sir 49: 4 for they a the law of the Most High;

ABBA*

Mk 14:36 "A, Father, for you all things are possible;
Ro 8:15 When we cry, "A! Father!"
Gal 4: 6 into our hearts, crying, "A! Father!"

ABEDNEGO* ➛ =AZARIAH

Deported to Babylon with Daniel (Da 1:1-6). Name changed from Azariah (Da 1:7). Refused defilement by food (Da 1:8-20). Refused idol worship (Da 3:1-12); saved from furnace (Da 3:13-30).

ABEL

Second son of Adam (Ge 4:2). Offered acceptable sacrifice (Ge 4:4; Heb 11:4; 12:24). Murdered by Cain (Ge 4:8; Mt 23:35; Lk 11:51; 1Jn 3:12).

ABHOR ➛ ABHORRENT

Lev 26:11 and I shall not a you.

ABHORRENT ➛ ABHOR
Dt 14: 3 You shall not eat any a thing.
18: 9 not learn to imitate the a practices

ABIATHAR
High priest in days of Saul and David (1Sa 22; 2Sa 15; 1Ki 1-2; Mk 2:26). Escaped Saul's slaughter of priests (1Sa 22:18-23). Supported David in Absalom's revolt (2Sa 15:24-29). Supported Adonijah (1Ki 1:7-42); deposed by Solomon (1Ki 2:22-35; cf. 1Sa 2:31-35).

ABIDE ➛ ABIDES, ABODE
Ge 6: 3 My spirit shall not a in mortals forever,
Ps 15: 1 O LORD, who may a in your tent?
91: 1 a in the shadow of the Almighty,
Jn 15: 4 A in me as I a in you.
1Co 13:13 faith, hope, and love a, these three;
1Jn 2:28 And now, little children, a in him,
Wis 3: 9 the faithful will a with him in love,

ABIDES ➛ ABIDE
Hag 2: 5 My spirit a among you; do not fear.
1Jn 3:14 Whoever does not love a in death.

ABIGAIL
1. Sister of David (1Ch 2:16-17).
2. Wife of Nabal (1Sa 25:30); pled for his life with David (1Sa 25:14-35). Became David's wife after Nabal's death (1Sa 25:36-42).

ABIHU
Son of Aaron (Ex 6:23; 24:1, 9); killed for offering illicit fire (Lev 10; Nu 3:2-4; 1Ch 24:1-2).

ABIJAH
1. Second son of Samuel (1Ch 6:28); a corrupt judge (1Sa 8:1-5).
2. An Aaronic priest (1Ch 24:10; Lk 1:5).
3. Son of Jeroboam I; died as prophesied by Ahijah (1Ki 14:1-18).
4. Son of Rehoboam, also called Abijam; king of Judah who fought Jeroboam I attempting to reunite Israel (1Ki 14:31-15:8; 2Ch 12:16-14:1).

ABILITY ➛ ABLE
Ex 31: 3 filled him with divine spirit, with a,
Mt 25:15 to each according to his a.
Ac 2: 4 as the Spirit gave them a.

ABIMELECH
1. King of Gerar who took Abraham's wife Sarah, believing her to be his sister (Ge 20). Covenanted with Abraham (Ge 21:22-33).
2. King of Gerar who took Isaac's wife Rebekah, believing her to be his sister (Ge 26:1-11). Covenanted with Isaac (Ge 26:12-31).
3. Son of Gideon (Jdg 8:31). Attempted to become king (Jdg 9).

ABIRAM
Sided with Dathan in rebellion against Moses and Aaron (Nu 16; 26:9; Dt 11:6; Sir 45:18).

ABISHAI
Son of Zeruiah, David's sister (1Sa 26:6; 1Ch 2:16). One of David's chief warriors (1Ch 11:15-21): against Edom (1Ch 18:12-13), Ammon (2Sa 10), Absalom (2Sa 18), Sheba (2Sa 20). Wanted to kill Saul (1Sa 26), killed Abner (2Sa 2:18-27; 3:22-39).

ABLE ➛ ABILITY
Ex 18:25 Moses chose a men from all Israel
Jos 1: 5 No one shall be a to stand against
23: 9 no one has been a to withstand you
Da 3:17 God whom we serve is a to deliver
Mt 9:28 "Do you believe that I am a to do
Mk 10:38 you a to drink the cup that I drink,
Ro 14: 4 the Lord is a to make them stand.
2Co 9: 8 God is a to provide you with every
Eph 6:11 a to stand against the wiles of the devil.
2Ti 1:12 he is a to guard until that day
Heb 2:18 a to help those who are being tested.
5: 2 is a to deal gently with the ignorant
7:25 he is a for all time to save
Rev 5: 3 a to open the scroll or to look into it.
Jdt 11:18 of them will be a to withstand you.

ABNER
Cousin of Saul and commander of his army (1Sa 14:50; 17:55-57; 26). Made Ish-Bosheth king after Saul (2Sa 2:8-10), but later defected to David (2Sa 3:6-21). Killed Asahel (2Sa 2:18-32), for which he was killed by Joab and Abishai (2Sa 3:22-39).

ABODE ➛ ABIDE
Ps 68:16 mount that God desired for his a,
Pr 3:33 but he blesses the a of the righteous.

ABOLISH ➛ ABOLISHED
Da 11:31 shall a the regular burnt offering
Mt 5:17 I have come not to a but to fulfill.

ABOLISHED ➛ ABOLISH
Eph 2:15 a the law with its commandments
2Ti 1:10 who a death and brought life

ABOMINABLE ➛ ABOMINATION
2Ch 28: 3 the a practices of the nations
Eze 7:20 they made their a images,
1Mc 1:48 to make themselves a by everything

ABOMINATION ➛ ABOMINABLE, ABOMINATIONS
Pr 6:16 seven that are an a to him:
Da 9:27 shall be an a that desolates,
Rev 21:27 anyone who practices a or falsehood
Sir 1:25 but godliness is an a to a sinner.
1Mc 6: 7 that they had torn down the a that

ABOMINATIONS ➛ ABOMINATION
Lev 18:27 committed all of these a,
1Ki 14:24 all the a of the nations that the LORD
Eze 44: 7 broken my covenant with all your a.
Rev 17: 5 mother of whores and of earth's a."

ABOUND ➛ ABOUNDED, ABOUNDING
Dt 28:11 LORD will make you a in prosperity,
Ro 6: 1 in sin in order that grace may a?

ABOUNDED ➛ ABOUND
Ro 5:20 sin increased, grace a all the more,

ABOUNDING ➛ ABOUND
Ex 34: 6 a in steadfast love and faithfulness,
Ps 86: 5 a in steadfast love to all who call on
Joel 2:13 to anger, and a in steadfast love,
Jnh 4: 2 to anger, and a in steadfast love,

ABOVE
Dt 4:39 the LORD is God in heaven a
Jn 3: 7 'You must be born from a.'
Php 2: 9 the name that is a every name,
Col 3: 2 Set your minds on things that are a,

ABRAHAM
Abram, son of Terah (Ge 11:26-27), husband of Sarah (Ge 11:29).
Covenant relation with the LORD (Ge 12:1-3; 13:14-17; 15; 17; 22:15-18; Ex 2:24; Ne 9:8; Ps 105; Mic 7:20; Lk 1:68-75; Ro 4; Heb 6:13-15).
Called from Ur, via Haran, to Canaan (Ge 12:1; Ac 7:2-4; Heb 11:8-10). Moved to Egypt, nearly lost Sarah to Pharoah (Ge 12:10-20). Divided the land with Lot; settled in Hebron (Ge 13). Saved Lot from four kings (Ge 14:1-16); blessed by Melchizedek (Ge 14:17-20; Heb 7:1-20). Declared righteous by faith (Ge 15:6; Ro 4:3; Gal 3:6-9; 1Mc 2:52). Fathered Ishmael by Hagar (Ge 16).
Name changed from Abram (Ge 17:5; Ne 9:7). Circumcised (Ge 17; Ro 4:9-12). Entertained three visitors (Ge 18); promised a son by Sarah (Ge 18:9-15; 17:16). Questioned destruction of Sodom and Gomorrah (Ge 18:16-33). Moved to Gerar; nearly lost Sarah to Abimelech (Ge 20). Fathered Isaac by Sarah (Ge 21:1-7; Ac 7:8; Heb 11:11-12); sent away Hagar and Ishmael (Ge 21:8-21; Gal 4:22-30). Covenant with Abimelech (Ge 21:22-32). Tested by offering Isaac (Ge 22; Heb 11:17-19; Jas 2:21-24). Sarah died; bought field of Ephron for burial (Ge 23). Secured wife for Isaac (Ge 24). Fathered children by Keturah (Ge 25:1-6; 1Ch 1:32-33). Death (Ge 25:7-11).
Called servant of God (Ge 26:24), friend of God (2Ch 20:7; Isa 41:8; Jas 2:23), prophet (Ge 20:7), father of Israel (Ex 3:15; Isa 51:2; Mt 3:9; Jn 8:39-58). Praised (Sir 44:19-45:1).

ABSALOM
Son of David by Maacah (2Sa 3:3; 1Ch 3:2). Killed Amnon for rape of his sister Tamar; banished by David (2Sa 13). Returned to Jerusalem; received by David (2Sa 14). Rebelled against David (2Sa 15-17). Killed (2Sa 18).

ABSENT
1Co 5: 3 a in body, I am present in spirit;
Col 2: 5 For though I am a in body,

ABUNDANCE ➛ ABUNDANTLY
Lk 6:45 a of the heart that the mouth speaks.
12:15 one's life does not consist in the a
2Co 9: 8 provide you with every blessing in a

ABUNDANTLY ➛ ABUNDANCE
Jn 10:10 that they may have life, and have it a.
Eph 3:20 to accomplish a far more than all

ABYSS
Lk 8:31 to order them to go back into the a.
Ro 10: 7 'Who will descend into the a?'"

ACCEPT ➛ ACCEPTABLE, ACCEPTED
Pr 19:20 Listen to advice and a instruction,
Jer 32:33 would not listen and a correction.
Mt 19:11 "Not everyone can a this teaching,
Jn 1:11 his own people did not a him.

ACCEPTABLE ➛ ACCEPT
Ps 19:14 meditation of my heart be a to you,
51:17 sacrifice a to God is a broken spirit;
Ro 12: 1 a living sacrifice, holy and a to God,

ACCEPTED ➛ ACCEPT
Ge 4: 7 If you do well, will you not be a?
Lk 4:24 no prophet is a in the prophet's hometown.

ACCESS
Ro 5: 2 we have obtained a to this grace
Eph 2:18 have a in one Spirit to the Father.

ACCOMPLISH ➛ ACCOMPLISHED
Isa 55:11 but it shall a that which I purpose,
Eze 17:24 I the LORD have spoken; I will a it.

ACCO7MPLISHED ➛ ACCOMPLISH
Mt 5:18 will pass from the law until all is a.

ACCORDING
Ps 28: 4 Repay them a to their work,
119: 9 By guarding it a to your word.
Mt 9:29 "A to your faith let it be done to you
Ro 8: 4 not a to the flesh but a to the Spirit.
Heb 2: 4 Holy Spirit, distributed a to his will.
1Jn 5:14 that if we ask anything a to his will,
Rev 20:12 dead were judged a to their works,
Sir 16:12 he judges a person a to one's deeds.

ACCOUNT ➛ ACCOUNTABLE
Mt 12:36 judgment you will have to give an a
Heb 4:13 to whom we must render an a.

ACCOUNTABLE ➛ ACCOUNT
Ro 14:12 each of us will be a to God.

ACCURSED ➛ CURSE
Ro 9: 3 I could wish that I myself were a
Rev 22: 3 Nothing a will be found there any

ACCUSATION ➛ ACCUSE
Lk 23: 4 no basis for an a against this man."

ACCUSE ➛ ACCUSATION, ACCUSER
Ps 103: 9 He will not always a,
Zec 3: 1 Satan standing at his right hand to a
Mt 12:10 so that they might a him.

ACCUSER ➛ ACCUSE
Jn 5:45 your a is Moses,
Rev 12:10 the a of our comrades has been thrown

ACHAN
Sinned at Jericho; stoned (Jos 7; 22:20; 1Ch 2:7).

ACHISH
King of Gath before whom David feigned insanity (1Sa 21:10-15). Later "ally" of David (2Sa 27-29).

ACKNOWLEDGE
Dt 4:35 you would a that the LORD is God;
Pr 3: 6 In all your ways a him,
Mt 10:32 I also will a before my Father in
Ro 1:28 since they did not see fit to a God,

ACT ➛ ACTED, ACTIVE, ACTS
Ps 37: 5 trust in him, and he will a.

Ro 14:23 because they do not a from faith;
Jas 1:25 hearers who forget but doers who a

ACTED ➛ ACT
Eze 20: 9 But I a for the sake of my name,
Ac 3:17 I know that you a in ignorance,
1Ti 1:13 mercy because I had a ignorantly

ACTIVE ➛ ACT
Heb 4:12 the word of God is living and a,
Jas 2:22 faith was a along with his works,

ACTS ➛ ACT
Ex 6: 6 outstretched arm and with mighty a
Ps 71:15 mouth will tell of your righteous a,
Mt 7:24 hears these words of mine and a

ADAM
First man (Ge 1:26-2:25; Ro 5:14; 1Ti 2:13; Tob 8:6). Sin of (Ge 3; Hos 6:7 [note]; Ro 5:12-21; 2Es 3:21; 7:70-140). Children of (Ge 4:1-5:5). Death of (Ge 5:5; Ro 5:12-21; 1Co 15:22).

ADD ➛ ADDED
Dt 4: 2 You must neither a anything
Pr 30: 6 Do not a to his words, or else
Lk 12:25 by worrying a a single hour to your

ADDED ➛ ADD
Ecc 3:14 nothing can be a to it, nor anything
Sir 42:21 Nothing can be a or taken away,

ADDICTED*
Tit 1: 7 or quick-tempered or a to wine

ADMONISH ➛ ADMONITION
Col 3:16 and a one another in all wisdom;

ADMONITION ➛ ADMONISH
Pr 15: 5 one who heeds a is prudent.

ADONIJAH
1. Son of David by Haggith (2Sa 3:4; 1Ch 3:2). Attempted to be king after David; killed at Solomon's order (1Ki 1-2).
2. Levite; teacher of the Law (2Ch 17:8).

ADOPTION
Ro 8:23 groan inwardly while we wait for a,
Gal 4: 5 that we might receive a as children.

ADORNED ➛ ADORNMENT
Lk 21: 5 how it was a with beautiful stones
Rev 17: 4 a with gold and jewels and pearls,
21: 2 as a bride a for her husband.

ADORNMENT ➛ ADORNED, ADORNS
Pr 3:22 for your soul and a for your neck.
1Pe 3: 4 let your a be the inner self with the

ADORNS ➛ ADORNMENT
Isa 61:10 as a bride a herself with her jewels.

ADULT* ➛ ADULTS
1Co 13:11 an a, I put an end to childish ways.

ADULTERERS ➛ ADULTERY
Jer 23:10 For the land is full of a;
1Co 6: 9 idolaters, a, male prostitutes,

ADULTERESS ➛ ADULTERY
Lev 20:10 the a shall be put to death.
Pr 2:16 from the a with her smooth words,

ADULTERY ➛ ADULTERERS, ADULTERESS
Ex 20:14 You shall not commit a.
Jer 3: 9 committing a with stone and tree.
Mt 5:28 committed a with her in his heart.
Lk 16:18 and marries another commits a,
Jn 8: 3 [[a woman who had been caught in a;]]

ADULTS* ➛ ADULT
1Co 14:20 infants in evil, but in thinking be a.

ADVANTAGE
Ecc 7:12 a of knowledge is that wisdom gives
Ro 3: 1 Then what a has the Jew?
1Co 10:24 Do not seek your own a, but that of

ADVERSARIES ➛ ADVERSARY
Dt 32:41 I will take vengeance on my a,
2Sa 22:49 you exalted me above my a,

ADVERSARY ➛ ADVERSARIES
1Ti 5:14 give the a no occasion to revile us.
1Pe 5: 8 roaring lion your a the devil prowls

ADVERSITY ➛ ADVERSARY
Dt 30:15 life and prosperity, death and a.
Isa 48:10 I have tested you in the furnace of a.

ADVICE ➛ ADVISERS
2Ch 10:13 rejected the a of the older men;
Ps 1: 1 do not follow the a of the wicked,
Pr 8:14 I have good a and sound wisdom;
Tob 4:18 Seek a from every wise person
Sir 37:11 pay no attention to any a they give.

ADVISERS ➛ ADVICE
Pr 15:22 but with many a they succeed.

ADVOCATE
Jn 14:26 But the A, the Holy Spirit,
15:26 the A comes, whom I will send
1Jn 2: 1 we have an a with the Father,

AFFLICT ➛ AFFLICTED, AFFLICTION, AFFLICTIONS, AFFLICTS
2Sa 7:10 evildoers shall a them no more,
La 3:33 for he does not willingly a
2Th 1: 6 repay with affliction those who a

AFFLICTED ➛ AFFLICT
Dt 26: 6 Egyptians treated us harshly and a
Na 1:12 Though I have a you, I will afflict
2Co 4: 8 are a in every way, but not crushed;

AFFLICTION ➛ AFFLICT
Dt 16: 3 bread with it—the bread of a—
Ps 25:18 Consider my a and my trouble,
Isa 30:20 of adversity and the water of a,
La 1: 9 "O Lord, look at my a,
2Co 4:17 this slight momentary a is preparing

AFFLICTIONS ➛ AFFLICT
Ps 34:19 Many are the a of the righteous,

AFFLICTS* ➛ AFFLICT
Tob 13: 2 For he a, and he shows mercy;

AFRAID ➛ FEAR
Ge 3:10 and I was a, because I was naked;
15: 1 not be a, Abram, I am your shield;
Ex 3: 6 his face, for he was a to look at God.
Lev 26: 6 and no one shall make you a;
Dt 20: 3 Do not lose heart, or be a,
Ps 3: 6 I am not a of ten thousands
27: 1 of whom shall I be a?
56:11 in God I trust; I am not a.
Isa 12: 2 I will trust, and will not be a,
Eze 2: 6 do not be a of their words,
Mt 10:31 So do not be a; you are of more
28:10 Jesus said to them, "Do not be a;
Lk 12:32 "Do not be a, little flock,
Heb 13: 6 Lord is my helper; I will not be a.

AGABUS*
A Christian prophet (Ac 11:28; 21:10).

AGAG
King of Amalekites; not killed by Saul (1Sa 15).

AGAIN
Job 14:14 If mortals die, will they live a?
Ecc 3:20 and all turn to dust a.
Mk 8:31 and after three days rise a.
Jn 14: 3 I will come a and will take you to
Heb 6: 6 they are crucifying a the Son of God
9:25 Nor was it to offer himself a and a,

AGE ➛ AGES
Ge 21: 2 bore Abraham a son in his old a,
Mt 28:20 with you always, to the end of the a."
Gal 1: 4 to set us free from the present evil a,

AGES ➛ AGE
Dt 4:32 For ask now about former a,
1Co 2: 7 decreed before the a for our glory.
Col 1:26 has been hidden throughout the a
1Ti 1:17 To the King of the a, immortal,

AGREE
Mt 18:19 if two of you a on earth about
Mk 14:56 and their testimony did not a.
1Jn 5: 8 and the blood, and these three a.

AGRIPPA
Descendant of Herod; king before whom Paul argued his case in Caesarea (Ac 25:13-26:32).

AHAB
1. Son of Omri; king of Israel (1Ki 16:28-22:40), husband of Jezebel (1Ki 16:31). Promoted Baal worship (1Ki 16:31-33); opposed by Elijah (1Ki 17:1; 18; 21), a prophet (1Ki 20:35-43), Micaiah (1Ki 22:1-28). Defeated Ben-Hadad (1Ki 20). Killed for failing to kill Ben-Hadad and for murder of Naboth (1Ki 20:35-21:40).
2. A false prophet (Jer 29:21-22).

AHASUERUS ➛ =ARTAXERXES
King of Persia (Ezr 4:6), husband of Esther. Deposed Vashti; replaced her with Esther (Est 1-2). Sealed Haman's edict to annihilate the Jews (Est 3). Received Esther without having called her (Est 5:1-8). Honored Mordecai (Est 6). Hanged Haman (Est 7). Issued edict allowing Jews to defend themselves (Est 8). Promoted Mordecai (Est 8:1-2, 15; 9:4; 10). Called Artaxerxes in the Additions to Esther.

AHAZ
Son of Jotham; king of Judah, (2Ki 16; 2Ch 28; Mt 1:9). Idolatry of (2Ki 16:3-4, 10-18; 2Ch 28:1-4, 22-25). Defeated by Aram and Israel (2Ki 16:5-6; 2Ch 28:5-15). Sought help from Assyria rather than the Lord (2Ki 16:7-9; 2Ch 28:16-21; Isa 7).

AHAZIAH ➛ =JEHOAHAZ
1. Son of Ahab; king of Israel (1Ki 22:51-2Ki 1:18; 2Ch 20:35-37). Made an unsuccessful alliance with Jehoshaphat (2Ch 20:35-37). Died for seeking Baal rather than the Lord (2Ki 1).
2. Son of Jehoram; king of Judah (2Ki 8:25-29; 9:14-29), also called Jehoahaz (2Ch 21:17-22:9; 25:23). Killed by Jehu while visiting Joram (2Ki 9:14-29; 2Ch 22:1-9).

AHEAD
Mt 11:10 sending my messenger a of you,
Php 3:13 straining forward to what lies a,
Heb 11:26 for he was looking a to the reward.

AHIJAH
1. Priest during Saul's reign (1Sa 14:3,18).
2. Prophet of Shiloh (1Ki 11:29-39; 14:1-18).

AHIKAM
Father of Gedaliah (2Ki 25:22), protector of Jeremiah (Jer 26:24).

AHIMAAZ
1. Father-in-law of Saul (1Sa 14:50).
2. Son of Zadok, the high priest, loyal to David (2Sa 15:27,36; 17:17-20; 18:19-33).

AHIMELECH
1. Priest who helped David in his flight from Saul (1Sa 21-22).
2. One of David's warriors (1Sa 26:6).

AHITHOPHEL
One of David's counselors who sided with Absalom (2Sa 15:12, 31-37; 1Ch 27:33-34); committed suicide when his advice was ignored (2Sa 16:15-17:23).

AI
Jos 7: 4 and they fled before the men of A.

AIR
Eph 2: 2 the ruler of the power of the a,
1Th 4:17 to meet the Lord in the a;
Rev 16:17 angel poured his bowl into the a,

ALARMED
Mk 13: 7 and rumors of wars, do not be a;
2Th 2: 2 to be quickly shaken in mind or a,

ALERT
Lk 12:37 slaves whom the master finds a
1Co 16:13 Keep a, stand firm in your faith,
Eph 6:18 keep a and always persevere
1Pe 5: 8 Discipline yourselves, keep a.

ALEXANDER
1Mc 1: 1 A son of Philip, the Macedonian,

ALIEN ➛ ALIENS
Ex 2:22 an a residing in a foreign land."
Lev 19:34 you shall love the a as yourself,
Dt 24:17 You shall not deprive a resident a

ALIENS ➛ ALIEN
Ge 15:13 your offspring shall be a in a land
Eph 2:19 you are no longer strangers and a,

1Pe 2:11 I urge you as a and exiles to abstain
1Mc 2: 7 the sanctuary given over to a?

ALIVE ➛ LIVE
Ge 6:19 to keep them a with you;
Dt 32:39 I kill and I make a; I wound and I heal;
Ac 1: 3 suffering he presented himself a
Ro 6:11 dead to sin and a to God
Eph 2: 5 made us a together with Christ—
1Th 4:17 Then we who are a, who are left,
Rev 1:18 I am a forever and ever;
19:20 were thrown a into the lake of fire

ALL
Ge 6:13 to make an end of a flesh,
Dt 6: 5 You shall love the LORD your God with a your heart, and with a your soul, and with a your might.
Ps 1: 3 In a that they do, they prosper.
Jer 29:13 if you seek me with a your heart,
Lk 10:27 love the Lord your God with a your
Ro 3:23 a have sinned and fall short of the
6:10 he died to sin, once for a;
1Co 6:12 "A things are lawful for me,"
15:51 not a die, but we will a be changed,
Eph 1:23 the fullness of him who fills a in a.
Php 4:13 I can do a things through him
2Ti 3:16 A scripture is inspired by God
2Pe 3: 9 but a to come to repentance.
Rev 21: 5 "See, I am making a things new."
Sir 7:29 With a your soul fear the Lord,

ALMIGHTY ➛ MIGHT
Ge 17: 1 "I am God A; walk before me,
Ex 6: 3 Isaac, and Jacob as God A,
Ps 91: 1 who abide in the shadow of the A,
Rev 1: 8 who was and who is to come, the A.
21:22 its temple is the Lord God the A
Bar 3: 1 O Lord A, God of Israel,
Man 1: 1 O Lord A, God of our ancestors,

ALMS
Mt 6: 2 "So whenever you give a,
Tob 12: 8 better to give a than to lay up gold.
Sir 7:10 do not neglect to give a.

ALONE ➛ LONELY
Ge 2:18 not good that the man should be a;
Dt 6: 4 The LORD is our God, the LORD a.
Isa 2:11 LORD a will be exalted in that day.
Mk 2: 7 Who can forgive sins but God a?
10:18 No one is good but God a.
Jas 2:24 justified by works and not by faith a

ALPHA
Rev 1: 8 "I am the A and the Omega,"
22:13 I am the A and the Omega,

ALTAR ➛ ALTARS
Ge 22: 9 Isaac, and laid him on the a,
Ex 27: 1 shall make the a of acacia wood,
30: 1 an a on which to offer incense;
Ezr 3: 2 to build the a of the God of Israel,
Mt 5:24 leave your gift there before the a
Heb 13:10 We have an a from which those
Jas 2:21 he offered his son Isaac on the a?
Rev 6: 9 I saw under the a the souls of those
Jdt 4:12 even draped the a with sackcloth
1Mc 1:54 a desolating sacrilege on the a of
4:47 built a new a like the former one.

ALTARS ➛ ALTAR
Ex 34:13 You shall tear down their a,
Nu 3:31 the table, the lampstand, the a,
1Mc 2:45 went around and tore down the a;

ALWAYS
Mt 28:20 And remember, I am with you a,
Lk 18: 1 to pray a and not to lose heart.
Php 4: 4 Rejoice in the Lord a; again I will

AMALEK
Ex 17: 8 Then A came and fought with Israel
1Sa 15: 3 attack A, and utterly destroy all

AMASA
Nephew of David (1Ch 2:17). Commander of Absalom's forces (2Sa 17:24-27). Returned to David (2Sa 19:13). Killed by Joab (2Sa 20:4-13).

AMAZED ➛ AMAZING
Mt 8:27 a, saying, "What sort of man is this,
Mk 6: 6 And he was a at their unbelief.
Ac 2: 7 A and astonished, they asked,

AMAZIAH
1. Son of Joash; king of Judah (2Ki 14; 2Ch 25). Defeated Edom (2Ki 14:7; 2Ch 25:5-13); defeated by Israel for worshiping Edom's gods (2Ki 14:8-14; 2Ch 25:14-24).
2. Idolatrous priest; opposed Amos (Am 7:10-17).

AMAZING ➛ AMAZED
Mk 12:11 and it is a in our eyes'?"
Rev 15: 3 "Great and a are your deeds,

AMBASSADOR* ➛ AMBASSADORS
Eph 6:20 for which I am an a in chains.

AMBASSADORS ➛ AMBASSADOR
2Co 5:20 So we are a for Christ,

AMBITION
Php 2: 3 Do nothing from selfish a or conceit
Jas 3:14 envy and selfish a in your hearts,

AMEN
Dt 27:15 people shall respond, saying, "A!"
2Co 1:20 through him that we say the "A,"
Rev 3:14 The words of the A, the faithful and

AMMONITE ➛ AMMONITES
Dt 23: 3 No A or Moabite shall be admitted

AMMONITES ➛ AMMONITE
Ge 19:38 the ancestor of the A to this day.
Jer 49: 6 I will restore the fortunes of the A,

AMNON
Firstborn of David (2Sa 3:2; 1Ch 3:1). Killed by Absalom for raping his sister Tamar (2Sa 13).

AMON
1. Son of Manasseh; king of Judah (2Ki 21:18-26; 1Ch 3:14; 2Ch 33:21-25).
2. Ruler of Samaria (1Ki 22:26; 2Ch 18:25).

AMORITES
Ge 15:16 iniquity of the A is not yet complete
Nu 21:31 Israel settled in the land of the A.

AMOS
Prophet from Tekoa (Am 1:1; 7:10-17; Tob 2:6).

ANANIAS
1. Early disciple; died for lying to God (Ac 5:1-11).
2. Disciple who baptized Saul (Ac 9:10-19).
3. High priest at Paul's arrest (Ac 22:30-24:1).

ANCESTOR ➛ ANCESTORS
Dt 26: 5 "A wandering Aramean was my a;
Mt 3: 9 'We have Abraham as our a';

ANCESTORS ➛ ANCESTOR
Ex 3:13 'The God of your a has sent me to
Dt 4:31 not forget the covenant with your a
La 5: 7 Our a sinned; they are no more,
Ac 5:30 The God of our a raised up Jesus,
Heb 1: 1 Long ago God spoke to our a in

ANCHOR
Heb 6:19 a sure and steadfast a of the soul,

ANCIENT
Ps 24: 7 and be lifted up, O a doors!
Jer 6:16 ask for the a paths, where the good
Da 7: 9 and an A One took his throne,
Mic 5: 2 origin is from of old, from a days.
Rev 20: 2 He seized the dragon, that a serpent,

ANDREW*
Apostle; brother of Simon Peter (Mt 4:18; 10:2; Mk 1:16-18, 29; 3:18; 13:3; Lk 6:14; Jn 1:35-44; 6:8-9; 12:22; Ac 1:13).

ANGEL ➛ ANGELS, ARCHANGEL, ARCHANGEL'S
Ge 22:11 the a of the LORD called to him
Ex 3: 2 the a of the LORD appeared to him
23:20 going to send an a in front of you,
Nu 22:22 the a of the LORD took his stand in
1Ch 21:15 sent an a to Jerusalem to destroy it;
Ps 34: 7 The a of the LORD encamps
Isa 37:36 the a of the LORD set out and struck
Da 3:28 who has sent his a and delivered
6:22 God sent his a and shut the lions'
Mt 1:20 an a of the Lord appeared to him in
Lk 1:26 In the sixth month the a Gabriel
Ac 5:19 during the night an a of the Lord
23: 8 say that there is no resurrection, or a,
2Co 11:14 Satan disguises himself as an a of light.
Gal 1: 8 if we or an a from heaven should
Tob 5: 4 the a Raphael standing in front of
Sir 48:21 and his a wiped them out.
LtJ 6: 7 For my a is with you,
Aza 1:26 But the a of the Lord came down
Sus 1:59 a of God is waiting with his sword
Bel 1:34 the a of the Lord said to Habakkuk,
1Mc 7:41 your a went out and struck
2Es 2:44 Then I asked an a, "Who are these,

ANGELS ➛ ANGEL
Ge 19: 1 The two a came to Sodom in the
28:12 a of God were ascending and
Ps 103:20 Bless the LORD, O you his a,
Mk 12:25 but are like a in heaven.
Lk 4:10 command his a concerning you,
Jn 1:51 and the a of God ascending and
Ro 8:38 that neither death, nor life, nor a,
1Co 6: 3 not know that we are to judge a—
Col 2:18 on self-abasement and worship of a,
Heb 2: 7 for a little while lower than the a;
1Pe 1:12 things into which a long to look!
2Pe 2: 4 not spare the a when they sinned,
Rev 1:20 stars are the a of the seven churches,
7: 1 After this I saw four a standing at
21:12 and at the gates twelve a,
Tob 11:14 and blessed be all his holy a.

ANGER ➛ ANGRY
Ex 32:19 the dancing, Moses' a burned hot,
34: 6 merciful and gracious, slow to a,
Dt 32:22 For a fire is kindled by my a,
Jdg 2:12 and they provoked the LORD to a.
1Ki 16:13 God of Israel to a with their idols.
Ps 30: 5 For his a is but for a moment;
Pr 12:16 Fools show their a at once,
Ecc 7: 9 Do not be quick to a,
Isa 48: 9 For my name's sake I defer my a,
Joel 2:13 slow to a, and abounding in
Jnh 4: 2 slow to a, and abounding in
Mk 3: 5 He looked around at them with a;
Eph 4:26 not let the sun go down on your a,
Jas 1:19 slow to speak, slow to a;
Rev 14:10 unmixed into the cup of his a,
Sir 5: 4 for the Lord is slow to a.

ANGRY ➛ ANGER
Ge 4: 5 So Cain was very a, and his
Jer 3:12 I will not be a forever.
Mt 5:22 that if you are a with a brother or

ANGUISH
Isa 53:11 Out of his a he shall see light;
Da 12: 1 There shall be a time of a,
Zep 1:15 a day of distress and a,
Lk 22:44 [[In his a he prayed more earnestly,]]

ANIMAL ➛ ANIMALS
Ge 2:19 God formed every a of the field
9: 2 dread of you shall rest on every a of
Ps 50:10 every wild a of the forest is mine,

ANIMALS ➛ ANIMAL
Ge 3:14 cursed are you among all a
Lev 26: 6 remove dangerous a from the land,
Ps 36: 6 save humans and a alike, O LORD.

ANNA
1. Prophetess; spoke of the child Jesus (Lk 2:36-38).
2. Wife of Tobit (Tob 1:20; 2:1, 11).

ANNAS*
High priest C.E. 6-15 (Lk 3:2; Jn 18:13, 24; Ac 4:6).

ANNOUNCED ➛ ANNOUNCING
Isa 48: 5 before they came to pass I a them
1Pe 1:25 the good news that was a to you.

ANNOUNCES ➛ ANNOUNCING
Isa 52: 7 feet of the messenger who a peace,

ANNOUNCING* ➛ ANNOUNCED, ANNOUNCES
Isa 63: 1 I, a vindication, mighty to save."
Ro 1: 9 serve with my spirit by a the gospel

ANNULLED
Jn 10:35 and the scripture cannot be a—

ANOINT ➛ ANOINTED, ANOINTING
Ex 30:30 You shall a Aaron and his sons,

1Sa 15: 1 "The LORD sent me to a you king
Ps 23: 5 you a my head with oil; my cup
Da 9:24 and to a a most holy place.

ANOINTED ➝ ANOINT
1Sa 2:10 and exalt the power of his a."
26: 9 raise his hand against the LORD's a,
1Ch 16:22 "Do not touch my a ones;
Ps 2: 2 against the LORD and his a, saying,
Isa 61: 1 because the LORD has a me;
Eze 28:14 With an a cherub as guardian
Da 9:26 an a one shall be cut off and
Zec 4:14 These are the two a ones who stand
Lk 4:18 he has a me to bring good news to
Jn 1:41 Messiah" (which is translated A).

ANOINTING ➝ ANOINT
Ex 30:25 it shall be a holy a oil.
Jas 5:14 a them with oil in the name of the Lord
1Jn 2:27 as his a teaches you about all things,

ANOTHER
Pr 27: 2 Let a praise you, and not your own
Isa 48:11 My glory I will not give to a.
Jn 14:16 and he will give you a Advocate,
Gal 1: 7 not that there is a gospel,

ANSWER ➝ ANSWERED
1Ki 18:37 A me, O LORD, a me,
Job 30:20 I cry to you and you do not a me;
Ps 65: 2 O you who a prayer!
Pr 15: 1 A soft a turns away wrath,
Isa 65:24 Before they call I will a,
Lk 23: 9 but Jesus gave him no a.

ANSWERED ➝ ANSWER
1Ch 21:26 and he a him with fire from heaven
Ps 118:21 I thank you that you have a me

ANT*
Pr 6: 6 Go to the a, you lazybones;

ANTICHRIST*
1Jn 2:18 As you have heard that a is coming,
2:22 the a, the one who denies the Father
4: 3 And this is the spirit of the a,
2Jn 1: 7 person is the deceiver and the a!

ANTIOCH
Ac 11:26 in A that the disciples were first called "Christians."
13: 1 the church at A there were prophets
Gal 2:11 But when Cephas came to A,

ANTIOCHUS
Antiochus IV Epiphanes, king of the Syrian Greeks B.C.E. 175-164 (1Mc 1:10-19). Plundered the temple in Jerusalem (1Mc 1:20-28). Attempted to force the Hellenization of the Jewish people (1Mc 1:41-53), including defiling the altar and holy place (1Mc 1:54-64). His policies sparked the Maccabean revolt.

ANXIETIES ➝ ANXIETY
1Co 7:32 I want you to be free from a.

ANXIETY ➝ ANXIETIES
Ecc 11:10 Banish a from your mind,
1Pe 5: 7 Cast all your a on him, because he

ANYTHING
Ge 18:14 Is a too wonderful for the LORD?
Jer 32:27 is a too hard for me?
Mt 18:19 if two of you agree on earth about a
Jn 16:23 if you ask a of the Father in my name,

APART ➝ PART
Jn 15: 5 a from me you can do nothing.
Ro 3:21 a from law, the righteousness of
Jas 2:20 that faith a from works is barren?

APOLLOS
Christian from Alexandria, learned in the Scriptures; instructed by Aquila and Priscilla (Ac 18:24-28). At Corinth (Ac 19:1; 1Co 1:12; 3; Tit 3:13).

APOSTASIES ➝ APOSTASY
Jer 2:19 and your a will convict you.
Eze 37:23 I will save them from all the a

APOSTASY* ➝ APOSTASIES
1Mc 2:15 officers who were enforcing the a

APOSTLE ➝ APOSTLES
Ro 11:13 as I am an a to the Gentiles,
1Co 9: 1 Am I not an a?
2Co 12:12 signs of a true a were performed
Heb 3: 1 a and high priest of our confession,

APOSTLES ➝ APOSTLE
See also Andrew, Bartholomew, Barnabas, James, John, Judas, Matthew, Matthias, Nathanael, Paul, Peter, Philip, Simon, Thaddaeus, Thomas.
Mt 10: 2 the names of the twelve a:
Ac 2:43 and signs were being done by the a.
1Co 12:28 has appointed in the church first a,
Eph 2:20 foundation of the a and prophets,
4:11 he gave were that some would be a,
Rev 21:14 are the twelve names of the twelve a

APPEAL
Mt 26:53 think that I cannot a to my Father,
Ac 25:11 I a to the emperor."
2Co 5:20 God is making his a through us;
Phm 1: 9 rather a to you on the basis of love
1Pe 3:21 an a to God for a good conscience,

APPEAR ➝ APPEARANCE, APPEARANCES, APPEARED, APPEARING
Mt 24:30 the sign of the Son of Man will a in
Mk 13:22 messiahs and false prophets will a
2Co 5:10 a before the judgment seat of Christ,
Heb 9:28 a a second time, not to deal with sin,

APPEARANCE ➝ APPEAR
Ex 24:17 Now the a of the glory of the LORD
1Sa 16: 7 not look on his a or on the height
2Co 5:12 those who boast in outward a
Jdt 11:23 You are not only beautiful in a,
AdE 2: 7 The girl was beautiful in a.
Sir 19:29 A person is known by his a,

APPEARANCES ➝ APPEAR
Jn 7:24 not judge by a, but judge with right

APPEARED ➝ APPEAR
Jn 21:14 that Jesus a to the disciples after he
1Co 15: 5 he a to Cephas, then to the twelve.
Heb 9:26 a once for all at the end of the age

APPEARING ➝ APPEAR
Ac 1: 3 a to them during forty days and
2Ti 4: 8 to all who have longed for his a.

APPETITES
Ro 16:18 our Lord Christ, but their own a,
Sir 18:30 base desires, but restrain your a.

APPLE
Dt 32:10 guarded him as the a of his eye.
Zec 2: 8 touches you touches the a of my eye

APPOINT ➝ APPOINTED
1Sa 8: 5 a for us, then, a king to govern us,
Isa 60:17 I will a Peace as your overseer

APPOINTED ➝ APPOINT
Lev 23: 2 the a festivals of the LORD
Ecc 3:17 for he has a a time for every matter,
Hab 2: 3 there is still a vision for the a time;
Mk 3:16 So he a the twelve: Simon (to whom
Ac 3:20 that he may send the Messiah a for
Heb 1: 2 whom he a heir of all things,
9:27 just as it is a for mortals to die once,

APPORTIONED ➝ PORTION
Dt 32: 8 When the Most High a the nations,
Jos 18:10 Joshua a the land to the Israelites,

APPROACH
Heb 4:16 a the throne of grace with boldness,
11: 6 whoever would a him must believe
Sir 1:28 do not a him with a divided mind.

APPROVAL ➝ APPROVED
Gal 1:10 I now seeking human a, or God's a?
Heb 11: 2 by faith our ancestors received a.
1Pe 2:20 and suffer for it, you have God's a.

APPROVED ➝ APPROVAL
1Th 2: 4 but just as we have been a by God
2Ti 2:15 to present yourself to God as one a

AQUILA*
Husband of Priscilla; co-worker with Paul, instructor of Apollos (Ac 18; Ro 16:3; 1Co 16:19; 2Ti 4:19).

ARABS
Ne 4: 7 and the A and the Ammonites
1Mc 5:39 also have hired A to help them,

ARAM ➝ ARAMAIC, ARAMEAN
Jdg 10: 6 the gods of A, the gods of Sidon,
2Ch 16: 7 you relied on the king of A,

ARAMAIC ➝ ARAM
2Ki 18:26 to your servants in the A language,
Ezr 4: 7 the letter was written in A and
Da 2: 4 Chaldeans said to the king (in A),

ARAMEAN ➝ ARAM
Dt 26: 5 "A wandering A was my ancestor;

ARARAT
Ge 8: 4 ark came to rest on the mountains of A.

ARAUNAH ➝ =ORNAN
2Sa 24:16 the threshing floor of A the Jebusite.

ARCHANGEL* ➝ ANGEL
Jude 1: 9 a Michael contended with the devil
2Es 4:36 the a Jeremiel answered and said,

ARCHANGEL'S* ➝ ANGEL
1Th 4:16 a call and with the sound of God's

ARCHITECT*
Heb 11:10 whose a and builder is God.

AREOPAGUS
Ac 17:22 Then Paul stood in front of the A

ARGUE ➝ ARGUES, ARGUMENT, ARGUMENTS
Job 13: 3 and I desire to a my case with God.
Isa 1:18 now, let us a it out, says the LORD:
Ac 18: 4 Every sabbath he would a in the
Ro 9:20 a human being, to a with God?

ARGUES* ➝ ARGUE
Job 40: 2 who a with God must respond."

ARGUMENT ➝ ARGUE
Lk 9:46 An a arose among them as to which
1Ti 2: 8 up holy hands without anger or a;

ARGUMENTS ➝ ARGUE
2Co 10: 4 destroy strongholds. We destroy a
Col 2: 4 may deceive you with plausible a.

ARIMATHEA
Jn 19:38 After these things, Joseph of A,

ARISE ➝ RISE
SS 2:10 "A, my love, my fair one, and
Isa 60: 1 A, shine; for your light has come,
Mt 24:11 false prophets will a and lead many
1Mc 14:41 until a trustworthy prophet should a,

ARK
Ge 6:14 Make yourself an a of cypress wood
Ex 25:10 shall make an a of acacia wood;
1Sa 4:11 The a of God was captured;
1Ki 8: 9 There was nothing in the a except
1Pe 3:20 during the building of the a,
Rev 11:19 the a of his covenant was seen
2Mc 2: 4 that the tent and the a should follow
2Es 10:22 the a of our covenant has been

ARM ➝ ARMIES, ARMOR, ARMS, ARMY
Ex 6: 6 redeem you with an outstretched a
Dt 7:19 mighty hand and the outstretched a
2Ch 32: 8 With him is an a of flesh;
Job 40: 9 Have you an a like God,
Ps 98: 1 his holy a have gotten him victory.
Isa 53: 1 the a of the LORD been revealed?
Jn 12:38 the a of the Lord been revealed?"

ARMIES ➝ ARM
1Sa 17:36 defied the a of the living God."
Lk 21:20 you see Jerusalem surrounded by a,
Rev 19:14 the a of heaven, wearing fine linen,

ARMOR ➝ ARM
1Sa 17:38 Saul clothed David with his a;
Ro 13:12 and put on the a of light;
Eph 6:11 Put on the whole a of God,
Wis 5:17 will take his zeal as his whole a,

ARMS ➝ ARM
Pr 31:17 and makes her a strong.
Hos 11: 3 I took them up in my a;
Mk 10:16 And he took them up in his a,

ARMY ➝ ARM
Ex 15: 4 and his a he cast into the sea;
Jos 5:14 as commander of the a of the LORD

Ps 27: 3 Though an a encamp against me,
Ps 33:16 A king is not saved by his great a;
Rev 19:19 rider on the horse and against his a.

AROMA
2Co 2:15 For we are the a of Christ to God

ARRESTED
Jer 37:14 and a Jeremiah and brought him to
Mt 14: 3 For Herod had a John, bound him,
26:50 and laid hands on Jesus and a him.
Ac 5:18 a the apostles and put them in the
28:17 yet I was a in Jerusalem and handed

ARROGANCE ➛ ARROGANT
Pr 8:13 Pride and a and the way of evil
Eze 7:24 put an end to the a of the strong,
Jdt 9:10 their a by the hand of a woman.
Sir 10: 7 A is hateful to the Lord and to
1Mc 1:24 much blood, and spoke with great a.

ARROGANT ➛ ARROGANCE
Ps 73: 3 For I was envious of the a;
Da 7:11 a words that the horn was speaking.
1Co 13: 4 love is not envious or boastful or a

ARROW ➛ ARROWS
Ps 64: 7 But God will shoot his a at them;
Isa 49: 2 he made me a polished a,

ARROWS ➛ ARROW
1Sa 20:20 I will shoot three a to the side of it,
Eph 6:16 quench all the flaming a of the evil

ARTAXERXES ➛ =AHASUERUS
1. King of Persia; allowed rebuilding of temple under Ezra (Ezr 4; 7), and of walls of Jerusalem under his cupbearer Nehemiah (Ne 2; 5:14; 13:6).
2. See Ahasuerus.

ARTEMIS
Ac 19:27 the temple of the great goddess A

ASA
King of Judah (1Ki 15:8-24; 1Ch 3:10; 2Ch 14-16). Godly reformer (2Ch 15); in later years defeated Israel with help of Aram, not the LORD (1Ki 15:16-22; 2Ch 16).

ASAHEL
Nephew of David, one of his warriors (2Sa 23:24; 1Ch 2:16; 11:26; 27:7). Killed by Abner (2Sa 2); avenged by Joab (2Sa 3:22-39).

ASAPH
1. Recorder to Hezekiah (2Ki 18:18, 37; Isa 36:3, 22).
2. Levitical musician (1Ch 6:39; 15:17-19; 16:4-7, 37), seer (2Ch 29:30). Sons of (1Ch 25; 2Ch 5:12; 20:14; 29:13; 35:15; Ezr 2:41; 3:10; Ne 7:44; 11:17; 12:27-47). Psalms of (2Ch 29:30; Ps 50; 73-83).

ASCEND ➛ ASCENDED, ASCENDING, ASCENTS
Ps 139: 8 If I a to heaven, you are there;
Isa 14:13 in your heart, "I will a to heaven;
Ac 2:34 David did not a into the heavens,
Ro 10: 6 'Who will a into heaven?'"
2Es 4: 8 neither did I ever a into heaven.'

ASCENDED ➛ ASCEND
2Ki 2:11 Elijah a in a whirlwind into heaven.
Jn 3:13 No one has a into heaven except

ASCENDING ➛ ASCEND
Ge 28:12 the angels of God were a and
Jn 1:51 the angels of God a and descending

ASCENTS ➛ ASCEND
Songs of ascents (Ps 120-134).

ASCRIBE
Dt 32: 3 a greatness to our God!
1Ch 16:29 A to the LORD the glory due his
Ps 68:34 A power to God,
Sir 39:15 A majesty to his name
Bar 2:17 not a glory or justice to the Lord;

ASHAMED ➛ SHAME
Ge 2:25 were both naked, and were not a.
Ps 6:10 All my enemies shall be a and
Isa 29:22 No longer shall Jacob be a,
Mk 8:38 who are a of me and of my words
Ro 1:16 For I am not a of the gospel;
2Ti 2:15 a worker who has no need to be a,

Heb 2:11 Jesus is not a to call them brothers
11:16 God is not a to be called their God;

ASHER
Son of Jacob by Zilpah (Ge 30:13; 35:26; 46:17; Ex 1:4; 1Ch 2:2). Tribe of blessed (Ge 49:20; Dt 33:24-25), numbered (Nu 1:40-41; 26:44-47), allotted land (Jos 10:24-31; Eze 48:2), failed to fully possess (Jdg 1:31-32), failed to support Deborah (Jdg 5:17), supported Gideon (Jdg 6:35; 7:23) and David (1Ch 12:36), 12,000 from (Rev 7:6).

ASHERAH ➛ ASHERAHS, ASTARTE
1Ki 18:19 and the four hundred prophets of A,
2Ch 15:16 made an abominable image for A.

ASHERAHS* ➛ ASHERAH
Jdg 3: 7 and worshiping the Baals and the A.

ASHES
Ge 18:27 I who am but dust and a.
Est 4: 1 and put on sackcloth and a,
Job 42: 6 and repent in dust and a."
Jnh 3: 6 himself with sackcloth, and sat in a.
Mt 11:21 long ago in sackcloth and a.
Jdt 4:11 the temple and put a on their heads
Sir 17:32 but all human beings are dust and a.

ASIA
Ac 16: 6 Holy Spirit to speak the word in A.
Rev 1: 4 to the seven churches that are in A:

ASIDE ➛ SIDE
Ex 32: 8 quick to turn a from the way that I
Dt 28:14 if you do not turn a from any of the
Jer 5:23 they have turned a and gone away.
Da 9: 5 turning a from your commandments
Ro 3:12 All have turned a, together they
Heb 12: 1 also lay a every weight and the sin

ASK
Ps 2: 8 A of me, and I will make the nations
Isa 65: 1 sought out by those who did not a,
Mt 6: 8 knows what you need before you a
7: 7 "A, and it will be given you;
Jn 16:24 A and you will receive,
Jas 4: 3 You a and do not receive, because you a wrongly,
1Jn 5:14 we a anything according to his will,

ASLEEP ➛ SLEEP
Jnh 1: 5 had lain down, and was fast a.
Mt 8:24 by the waves; but he was a.
1Th 5: 6 So then let us not fall a as others do,

ASSEMBLE ➛ ASSEMBLY
1Ki 18:19 all Israel a for me at Mount Carmel,
Zep 3: 8 to gather nations, to a kingdoms,
Rev 16:14 to a them for battle on the great day

ASSEMBLY ➛ ASSEMBLE
Ne 8: 2 Ezra brought the law before the a,
Ps 149: 1 his praise in the a of the faithful.
Heb 12:23 the a of the firstborn who are

ASSIGNED
Ro 12: 3 the measure of faith that God has a.
1Co 3: 5 as the Lord a to each.
7:17 lead the life that the Lord has a,

ASSURANCE
Dt 28:66 in dread, with no a of your life.
Heb 6:11 so as to realize the full a of hope
11: 1 faith is the a of things hoped for,

ASSYRIA
Ge 10:11 From that land he went into A,
2Ki 18:11 of A carried the Israelites away to A,
Jer 50:18 as I punished the king of A.

ASTARTE ➛ ASHERAH, ASTARTES
1Ki 11: 5 Solomon followed A the goddess

ASTARTES ➛ ASTARTE
Jdg 2:13 and worshiped Baal and the A.

ASTONISHED
Isa 52:14 there were many who were a at him
Lk 2:48 his parents saw him they were a;
Gal 1: 6 a that you are so quickly deserting

ASTRAY ➛ STRAY
Dt 30:17 are led a to bow down to other gods
Isa 53: 6 All we like sheep have gone a;
Jer 50: 6 their shepherds have led them a,

Mt 18:12 go in search of the one that went a?
1Pe 2:25 For you were going a like sheep,

ATE ➛ EAT
Ge 3: 6 she took of its fruit and a;
Ex 16:35 The Israelites a manna forty years,
Ps 78:25 Mortals a of the bread of angels;
Eze 3: 3 I a it; and in my mouth it was as
Mt 14:20 And all a and were filled;
15:37 And all of them a and were filled;
Rev 10:10 from the hand of the angel and a it;

ATHALIAH
Granddaughter of Omri; wife of Jehoram and mother of Ahaziah; encouraged their evil ways (2Ki 8:18, 27; 2Ch 22:2). At death of Ahaziah she made herself queen, killing all his sons but Joash (2Ki 11:1-3; 2Ch 22:10-12); killed six years later when Joash revealed (2Ki 11:4-16; 2Ch 23:1-15).

ATHLETE ➛ ATHLETES
2Ti 2: 5 And in the case of an a,

ATHLETES ➛ ATHLETE
1Co 9:25 A exercise self-control in all things;

ATONE ➛ ATONEMENT
Da 9:24 an end to sin, and to a for iniquity,
Sir 3: 3 who honor their father a for sins,

ATONED* ➛ ATONEMENT
Pr 16: 6 and faithfulness iniquity is a for,

ATONEMENT ➛ ATONE, ATONED, ATONING
Ex 29:36 a bull as a sin offering for a.
30:10 Aaron shall perform the rite of a
32:30 perhaps I can make a for your sin."
Lev 23:28 for it is a day of a,
Ro 3:25 God put forward as a sacrifice of a
Heb 2:17 to make a sacrifice of a for the sins

ATONING ➛ ATONEMENT
1Jn 2: 2 and he is the a sacrifice for our sins,
4:10 sent his Son to be the a sacrifice for
Sir 28: 5 will make an a sacrifice for his sins?

ATTAIN ➛ ATTAINED
Ps 139: 6 it is so high that I cannot a it.
Pr 8:12 and I a knowledge and discretion.
Da 12:12 those who persevere and a
Php 3:11 a the resurrection from the dead.

ATTAINED ➛ ATTAIN
Ro 9:30 not strive for righteousness, have a
Php 3:16 let us hold fast to what we have a.

ATTENTION
Nu 16:15 "Pay no a to their offering.
Job 24:12 yet God pays no a to their prayer.
Heb 2: 1 greater a to what we have heard,

ATTESTED
Ac 2:22 a man a to you by God with deeds
Ro 3:21 and is a by the law and the prophets,

AUTHOR*
Ac 3:15 and you killed the A of life,
Wis 13: 3 for the a of beauty created them.

AUTHORITIES ➛ AUTHORITY
Ro 13: 1 be subject to the governing a;
Col 2:15 He disarmed the rulers and a and

AUTHORITY ➛ AUTHORITIES
Ge 41:45 Thus Joseph gained a over the land
Pr 29: 2 When the righteous are in a,
Mk 1:27 A new teaching—with a!
Lk 5:24 Son of Man has a on earth to forgive
Ac 5:29 obey God rather than any human a.
Ro 13: 1 for there is no a except from God,
1Co 11:10 woman ought to have a symbol of a
Col 2:10 who is the head of every ruler and a.
1Ti 2:12 no woman to teach or to have a over
Rev 12:10 and the a of his Messiah,
20: 4 on them were given a to judge.

AVENGE ➛ VENGEANCE
Dt 32:43 he will a the blood of his children,
Joel 3:21 I will a their blood, and I will not
Ro 12:19 Beloved, never a yourselves,
Rev 6:10 and a our blood on the inhabitants
1Mc 2:67 a the wrong done to your people.

AVENGER ➛ VENGEANCE
Nu 35:12 shall be for you a refuge from the a,

Ps 8: 2 to silence the enemy and the **a.**
1Th 4: 6 the Lord is an **a** in all these things,

AVENGING → VENGEANCE
Na 1: 2 A jealous and **a** God is the LORD,

AVOID → AVOIDS
2Ti 2:16 **A** profane chatter, for it will lead
Tit 3: 9 But **a** stupid controversies,

AVOIDS → AVOID
Pr 16: 6 by the fear of the LORD one **a** evil.

AWAKE
Ps 44:23 **A,** do not cast us off forever!
57: 8 **A,** my soul! **A,** O harp and lyre!
Isa 51: 9 **A, a,** put on strength, O arm of the LORD!
Da 12: 2 in the dust of the earth shall **a,**
Mk 14:37 Could you not keep **a** one hour?
Eph 5:14 "Sleeper, **a!** Rise from the dead,
1Th 5: 6 but let us keep **a** and be sober;
Rev 16:15 Blessed is the one who stays **a** and

AWE → AWESOME
Ps 119:161 my heart stands in **a** of your words.
Isa 29:23 will stand in **a** of the God of Israel.
Mt 9: 8 saw it, they were filled with **a,**
Ac 2:43 **A** came upon everyone, because
Ro 11:20 do not become proud, but stand in **a.**

AWESOME → AWE
Ex 15:11 majestic in holiness, **a** in splendor,
Dt 6:22 before our eyes great and **a** signs
10:17 the great God, mighty and **a,**
Ne 1: 5 and **a** God who keeps covenant
Ps 47: 2 For the LORD, the Most High, is **a,**
65: 5 By **a** deeds you answer us with
68:35 **A** is God in his sanctuary,
Da 9: 4 saying, "Ah, Lord, great and **a** God,
Sir 43:29 **A** is the Lord and very great,

AX
2Ki 6: 5 his **a** head fell into the water;
Mt 3:10 Even now the **a** is lying at the root

AZARIAH → =ABEDNEGO, =UZZIAH
1. King of Judah; see Uzziah (2Ki 15:1-7).
2. Prophet (2Ch 15:1-8).
3. Opponent of Jeremiah (Jer 43:2).
4. Jewish exile; see Abednego (Da 1:6-19).

AZAZEL
Lev 16: 8 for the LORD and the other lot for **A.**

B

BAAL → BAALS
Nu 25: 3 Israel yoked itself to the **B** of Peor,
Jdg 2:13 and worshiped **B** and the Astartes.
1Ki 18:25 Elijah said to the prophets of **B,**
19:18 the knees that have not bowed to **B,**
Jer 2: 8 the prophets prophesied by **B,**
Hos 2:16 no longer will you call me, "My **B.**"
Ro 11: 4 not bowed the knee to **B.**"

BAALS → BAAL
Jdg 3: 7 worshiping the **B** and the Asherahs.
1Sa 7: 4 So Israel put away the **B** and the

BAASHA
King of Israel (1Ki 15:16-16:7; 2Ch 16:1-6).

BABEL → BABYLON
Ge 11: 9 Therefore it was called **B,**

BABES → BABIES
Ps 8: 2 Out of the mouths of **b** and infants
Isa 3: 4 and **b** shall rule over them.

BABIES → BABES
Mt 21:16 the mouths of infants and nursing **b**

BABYLON → BABEL
2Ki 24:15 into captivity from Jerusalem to **B.**
Ps 137: 1 By the rivers of **B**—there we sat
Isa 14: 4 this taunt against the king of **B:**
21: 9 he responded, "Fallen, fallen is **B;**
Jer 25:11 serve the king of **B** seventy years.
1Pe 5:13 Your sister church in **B,** chosen
Rev 14: 8 "Fallen, fallen is **B** the great!
Bel 1:36 he set him down in **B,**

BACK → BACKSLIDING
Ge 19:26 Lot's wife, behind him, looked **b,**
2Ki 20:11 he brought the shadow **b** the ten
Lk 9:62 puts a hand to the plow and looks **b**

BACKSLIDING* → BACK
Jer 8: 5 people turned away in perpetual **b?**

BAD
Pr 20:14 "**B, b,**" says the buyer, then goes
Mt 7:17 but the **b** tree bears **b** fruit.
1Co 15:33 "**B** company ruins good morals."

BALAAM
Prophet who attempted to curse Israel (Nu 22-24; Dt 23:4-5; 2Pe 2:15; Jude 11; Rev 2:14). Killed in Israel's vengeance on Midianites (Nu 31:8; Jos 13:22).

BALAK
Moabite king who hired Balaam to curse Israel (Nu 22-24; Jos 24:9; Mic 6:5).

BALANCE → BALANCES
Job 31: 6 let me be weighed in a just **b,**
Isa 40:12 in scales and the hills in a **b?**

BALANCES → BALANCE
Lev 19:36 shall have honest **b,** honest weights,
Pr 16:11 Honest **b** and scales are the LORD's;
Sir 28:25 make **b** and scales for your words.

BALM
Jer 8:22 Is there no **b** in Gilead?

BANDIT
Mt 26:55 to arrest me as though I were a **b?**
Jn 10: 1 in by another way is a thief and a **b.**

BANISH
Ecc 11:10 **B** anxiety from your mind,
Ro 11:26 he will **b** ungodliness from Jacob."

BANNER
Ex 17:15 and called it, The LORD is my **b.**

BAPTISM → BAPTIZE
Mk 1: 4 proclaiming a **b** of repentance for
10:38 be baptized with the **b** that I am
Lk 20: 4 the **b** of John come from heaven,
Ac 18:25 though he knew only the **b** of John.
19: 3 They answered, "Into John's **b.**"
Ro 6: 4 buried with him by **b** into death,
1Co 15:29 receive **b** on behalf of the dead?
Eph 4: 5 one Lord, one faith, one **b,**
Col 2:12 when you were buried with him in **b,**
1Pe 3:21 **b,** which this prefigured, now saves

BAPTISMS* → BAPTIZE
Heb 6: 2 about **b,** laying on of hands,
9:10 with food and drink and various **b,**

BAPTIST → BAPTIZE
Mt 3: 1 In those days John the **B** appeared
11:11 has arisen greater than John the **B;**
14: 8 the head of John the **B** here on a
16:14 they said, "Some say John the **B,**

BAPTIZE → BAPTISM, BAPTISMS, BAPTIST, BAPTIZED, BAPTIZING
Mt 3:11 "I **b** you with water for repentance,
Lk 3:16 He will **b** you with the Holy Spirit
1Co 1:17 For Christ did not send me to **b** but

BAPTIZED → BAPTIZE
Mt 3:13 to John at the Jordan, to be **b**
Ac 1: 5 John **b** with water, but you will be **b** with the Holy
2:38 "Repent, and be **b** every one of you
Ro 6: 3 **b** into Christ Jesus were **b** into his
1Co 10: 2 all were **b** into Moses in the cloud
12:13 one Spirit we were all **b** into one

BAPTIZING* → BAPTIZE
Mt 28:19 **b** them in the name of the Father
Jn 4: 1 "Jesus is making and **b** more

BARABBAS*
Prisoner released by Pilate instead of Jesus (Mt 27:16-26; Mk 15:7-15; Lk 23:18-19; Jn 18:40).

BARAK*
Judge who fought with Deborah against Canaanites (Jdg 4-5; 1Sa 12:11; Heb 11:32).

BARBARIAN → BARBARIANS
Col 3:11 circumcised and uncircumcised, **b,**

BARBARIANS* → BARBARIAN
Ro 1:14 am a debtor both to Greeks and to **b,**

BARBS*
Nu 33:55 let remain shall be as **b** in your eyes

BARE → BARED
Ps 18:15 were laid **b** at your rebuke,
Heb 4:13 all are naked and laid **b** to the eyes

BARED* → BARE
Isa 52:10 The LORD has **b** his holy arm

BARN → BARNS
Lk 12:24 they have neither storehouse nor **b,**

BARNABAS* → =JOSEPH
Disciple, originally Joseph (Ac 4:36), prophet (Ac 13:1), apostle (Ac 14:14). Brought Paul to apostles (Ac 9:27), Antioch (Ac 11:22-29; Gal 2:1-13), on the first missionary journey (Ac 13-14). Together at Jerusalem Council, they separated over John Mark (Ac 15). Later co-workers (1Co 9:6; Col 4:10).

BARNS* → BARN
Dt 28: 8 the blessing upon you in your **b,**
Ps 144:13 May our **b** be filled, with produce
Lk 12:18 pull down my **b** and build larger

BARREN → BARRENNESS
Ge 11:30 Now Sarai was **b;** she had no child.
Ex 23:26 No one shall miscarry or be **b** in
1Sa 2: 5 The **b** has borne seven, but she who
Ps 113: 9 He gives the **b** woman a home,
Isa 54: 1 Sing, O **b** one who did not bear;
Lk 1: 7 because Elizabeth was **b,**
Heb 11:11 too old—and Sarah herself was **b**—

BARRENNESS* → BARREN
Dt 7:14 neither sterility nor **b** among you
Ro 4:19 considered the **b** of Sarah's womb.

BARTHOLOMEW* → =NATHANAEL?
Apostle (Mt 10:3; Mk 3:18; Lk 6:14; Ac 1:13). Possibly also called Nathanael (Jn 1:45-49; 21:2).

BARUCH*
Jeremiah's secretary (Jer 32:12-16; 36; 43:1-6; 45:1-2). Deuterocanonical book ascribed to (Bar 1:1, 3, 8).

BARZILLAI
1. Gileadite who aided David during Absalom's revolt (2Sa 17:27; 19:31-39).
2. Son-in-law of 1. (Ezr 2:61; Ne 7:63).

BASED*
Ro 9:31 righteousness that is **b** on the law,
9:32 but as if it were **b** on works.
Php 3: 9 righteousness from God **b** on faith.

BASHAN
Nu 21:33 King Og of **B** came out against
Ps 22:12 strong bulls of **B** surround me;
Mic 7:14 let them feed in **B** and Gilead as in

BASIN
Ex 30:18 You shall make a bronze **b** with a
1Ki 7:30 four corners were supports for a **b.**
Jn 13: 5 **b** and began to wash the disciples'

BASIS
Lk 23: 4 "I find no **b** for an accusation
Phm 1: 9 rather appeal to you on the **b** of love

BASKET
Ex 2: 3 she got a papyrus **b** for him,
Mt 5:15 a lamp puts it under the bushel **b,**
Ac 9:25 in the wall, lowering him in a **b.**

BATHING
2Sa 11: 2 he saw from the roof a woman **b;**

BATHSHEBA*
Wife of Uriah; committed adultery with and married David (2Sa 11; Ps 51), mother of Solomon (2Sa 12:24; 1Ki 1-2; 1Ch 3:5).

BATTLE
1Sa 17:47 the **b** is the LORD's and he will give
2Ch 20:15 for the **b** is not yours but God's.
Ps 24: 8 and mighty, the LORD, mighty in **b.**
Ecc 9:11 nor the **b** to the strong, nor bread to
Rev 16:14 them for **b** on the great day of God
20: 8 Magog, in order to gather them for **b;**
1Mc 3:19 the army that victory in **b** depends,

BEAR → BEARS, BIRTH, BIRTHRIGHT, BORE, BORN, CHILDBEARING, FIRSTBORN
Ge 4:13 punishment is greater than I can **b!**
17:19 your wife Sarah shall **b** you a son,
Isa 7:14 is with child and shall **b** a son,

Mt 1:23 virgin shall conceive and **b** a son,
7:18 A good tree cannot **b** bad fruit,
Lk 11:46 load people with burdens hard to **b**,
Jn 15: 2 he prunes to make it **b** more fruit.
Gal 6: 2 **B** one another's burdens,
Col 3:13 **B** with one another and,
Heb 9:28 offered once to **b** the sins of many,
Rev 12: 4 woman who was about to **b** a child,

BEARS → BEAR
Ps 68:19 Blessed be the Lord, who daily **b** us
1Co 13: 7 It **b** all things, believes all things,

BEAST → BEASTS
Rev 11: 7 **b** that comes up from the bottomless pit
13:18 calculate the number of the **b**,
16: 2 who had the mark of the **b**
19:20 who had received the mark of the **b**

BEASTS → BEAST
Da 7: 3 four great **b** came up out of the sea,
Mk 1:13 and he was with the wild **b**;

BEAT → BEATEN, BEATING
Isa 2: 4 shall **b** their swords into plowshares,
Joel 3:10 **B** your plowshares into swords,
Lk 22:63 began to mock him and **b** him;

BEATEN → BEAT
2Co 11:25 Three times I was **b** with rods.
1Pe 2:20 If you endure when you are **b** for

BEATING → BEAT
Ex 2:11 He saw an Egyptian **b** a Hebrew,
1Co 9:26 nor do I box as though **b** the air;

BEAUTIFUL → BEAUTY
Ge 12:11 you are a woman **b** in appearance;
1Sa 25: 3 The woman was clever and **b**,
Est 2: 7 the girl was fair and **b**,
Job 42:15 no women so **b** as Job's daughters;
Ps 48: 2 **b** in elevation, is the joy of all
SS 1: 5 I am black and **b**, O daughters of
Isa 4: 2 the branch of the LORD shall be **b**
52: 7 How **b** upon the mountains are the
Ac 3: 2 the temple called the **B** Gate so that
Ro 10:15 **b** are the feet of those who bring
Tob 6:12 girl is sensible, brave, and very **b**,
Jdt 8: 7 She was **b** in appearance,
Wis 7:29 She is more **b** than the sun,
Sir 25: 1 and they are **b** in the sight of God
Sus 1: 2 very **b** woman and one who feared

BEAUTY → BEAUTIFUL
2Sa 14:25 so much for his **b** as Absalom;
Ps 27: 4 to behold the **b** of the LORD,
Pr 6:25 Do not desire her **b** in your heart,
31:30 Charm is deceitful, and **b** is vain,
1Pe 3: 4 with the lasting **b** of a gentle
Jdt 16: 9 her **b** captivated his mind,
Wis 13: 3 for the author of **b** created them.
Sir 9: 8 not gaze at **b** belonging to another;
Sus 1:56 **b** has beguiled you and lust has
1Mc 2:12 And see, our holy place, our **b**,

BED → BEDS
Ge 47:31 bowed himself on the head of his **b**.
Ps 139: 8 if I make my **b** in Sheol, you are
Lk 5:19 let him down with his **b** through the
Heb 13: 4 let the marriage **b** be kept undefiled;

BEDS → BED
Ps 36: 4 They plot mischief while on their **b**;
Mic 2: 1 and evil deeds on their **b**!

BEE* → BEES
Isa 7:18 the **b** that is in the land of Assyria.
Sir 11: 3 The **b** is small among flying

BEER-SHEBA
Ge 21:31 Therefore that place was called **B**;
1Sa 3:20 And all Israel from Dan to **B** knew

BEES → BEE
Jdg 14: 8 a swarm of **b** in the body of the lion,

BEFORE
Ex 20: 3 you shall have no other gods **b** me.
33: 2 I will send an angel **b** you,
Isa 43:10 **B** me no god was formed,
65:24 **B** they call I will answer,
Mal 3: 1 my messenger to prepare the way **b**
Mt 6: 8 Father knows what you need **b** you
Lk 22:61 "**B** the cock crows today,
Heb 12: 2 sake of the joy that was set **b** him

BEGGAR → BEGS
Mk 10:46 son of Timaeus, a blind **b**,
Jn 9: 8 who had seen him before as a **b**

BEGINNING
Ge 1: 1 In the **b** when God created the
Ps 111:10 fear of the LORD is the **b** of wisdom;
Pr 1: 7 The fear of the LORD is the **b** of
8:22 The LORD created me at the **b** of his
Ecc 7: 8 Better is the end of a thing than its **b**
Isa 40:21 Has it not been told you from the **b**?
Mt 24: 8 this is but the **b** of the birth pangs.
Jn 1: 1 In the **b** was the Word,
1Jn 1: 1 declare to you what was from the **b**,
2Jn 1: 6 as you have heard it from the **b**—
Rev 21: 6 and the Omega, the **b** and the end.
Wis 6:17 The **b** of wisdom is the most sincere
Sir 1:14 To fear the Lord is the **b** of wisdom;

BEGOTTEN
Ps 2: 7 You are my son; today I have **b** you.
Ac 13:33 are my Son; today I have **b** you.'
Heb 1: 5 are my Son; today I have **b** you"?
2Es 6:58 have called your firstborn, only **b**,

BEGS → BEG
Lk 6:30 Give to everyone who **b** from you;

BEHEADED → HEAD
Lk 9: 9 Herod said, "John I **b**;
Rev 20: 4 the souls of those who had been **b**

BEHEMOTH
Job 40:15 "Look at **B**, which I made just as I
2Es 6:49 the one you called **B** and the name

BEHIND
Isa 38:17 have cast all my sins **b** your back.
Mt 16:23 said to Peter, "Get **b** me, Satan!
Php 3:13 forgetting what lies **b** and straining

BEING
Ge 2: 7 and the man became a living **b**.
Nu 23:19 God is not a human **b**,
Da 7:13 one like a human **b** coming with the
Jn 1: 3 All things came into **b** through him,
1Co 15:45 Adam, became a living **b**";
Heb 1: 3 the exact imprint of God's very **b**,

BEL*
Babylonian deity (Isa 46:1; Jer 50:2; 51:44; LtJ 6:40; Bel 1:3-28).

BELIEF → BELIEVE
2Th 2:13 the Spirit and through **b** in the truth.

BELIEVE → BELIEF, BELIEVED, BELIEVER, BELIEVERS, BELIEVES, BELIEVING
Ex 4: 5 that they may **b** that the LORD,
Nu 14:11 long will they refuse to **b** in me,
2Ki 17:14 did not **b** in the LORD their God.
Ps 119:66 for I **b** in your commandments.
Pr 14:15 The simple **b** everything,
Jer 12: 6 do not **b** them, though they speak
Hab 1: 5 you would not **b** if you were told.
Mt 18: 6 one of these little ones who **b** in me,
24:23 or 'There he is!'—do not **b** it.
Mk 1:15 repent, and **b** in the good news."
9:24 "I **b**; help my unbelief!"
Lk 24:25 how slow of heart to **b** all that the
Jn 1: 7 so that all might **b** through him.
3:18 who **b** in him are not condemned;
5:46 believed Moses, you would **b** me,
6:29 you **b** in him whom he has sent."
10:38 you do not **b** me, **b** the works,
14: 1 **B** in God, **b** also in me.
17:20 will **b** in me through their word,
20:29 not seen and yet have come to **b**."
Ac 16:31 answered, "**B** on the Lord Jesus,
28:24 while others refused to **b**.
Ro 3:22 faith in Jesus Christ for all who **b**.
10: 9 **b** in your heart that God raised him
1Co 15: 2 unless you have come to **b** in vain.
Gal 3: 9 this reason, those who **b** are blessed
1Th 4:14 For since we **b** that Jesus died and
Heb 11: 6 would approach him must **b**
Jas 2:19 Even the demons **b**—and shudder.
1Pe 1: 8 you do not see him now, you **b**
1Jn 4: 1 Beloved, do not **b** every spirit,
Jude 1: 5 destroyed those who did not **b**.
Sir 19:15 so do not **b** everything you hear.

BELIEVED → BELIEVE
Ge 15: 6 And he **b** the LORD;
Ex 14:31 **b** in the LORD and in his servant
Isa 53: 1 Who has **b** what we have heard?
Jn 1:12 received him, who **b** in his name,
12:38 "Lord, who has **b** our message,
20: 8 also went in, and he saw and **b**;
Ac 2:44 All who **b** were together and had all
Ro 4: 3 "Abraham **b** God, and it was
10:16 "Lord, who has **b** our message?"
2Co 4:13 "I **b**, and so I spoke"—
Gal 3: 6 Just as Abraham "**b** God,
1Ti 3:16 **b** in throughout the world, taken up
Heb 4: 3 For we who have **b** enter that rest,
Jas 2:23 that says, "Abraham **b** God,
Jdt 14:10 had done, he **b** firmly in God.
1Mc 2:59 **b** and were saved from the flame.

BELIEVER → BELIEVE
1Co 6: 6 but a **b** goes to court against a **b**—
7:12 **b** has a wife who is an unbeliever,
2Co 6:15 Or what does a **b** share with an

BELIEVERS → BELIEVE
1Co 14:22 a sign not for **b** but for unbelievers,
Gal 2: 4 because of false **b** secretly brought
2Th 3: 6 keep away from **b** who are living in
1Pe 2:17 Love the family of **b**.

BELIEVES → BELIEVE
Jn 3:15 whoever **b** in him may have eternal
11:26 everyone who lives and **b** in me
Ro 9:33 whoever **b** in him will not be put to
10:10 **b** with the heart and so is justified,
1Co 13: 7 It bears all things, **b** all things,

BELIEVING → BELIEVE
Jn 20:31 through **b** you may have life in his
Gal 3: 5 or by your **b** what you heard?

BELLY
Ge 3:14 upon your **b** you shall go,
Lev 11:42 Whatever moves on its **b**,
Jnh 1:17 and Jonah was in the **b** of the fish
Mt 12:40 three days and three nights in the **b**
Php 3:19 is destruction; their god is the **b**;

BELONG → BELONGS
Dt 29:29 The secret things **b** to the LORD our God, but the revealed things **b** to us
Ps 82: 8 for all the nations **b** to you!
Da 9: 9 To the Lord our God **b** mercy and
Jn 10:16 sheep that do not **b** to this fold.
15:19 Because you do not **b** to the world,
Ro 9: 6 not all Israelites truly **b** to Israel,
1Co 3:23 you **b** to Christ, and Christ belongs
12:15 I do not **b** to the body,"
1Jn 2:19 out from us, but they did not **b** to us;

BELONGS → BELONG
Ps 22:28 For dominion **b** to the LORD,
62:11 I heard this: that power **b** to God,
Jnh 2: 9 Deliverance **b** to the LORD!"
Rev 7:10 "Salvation **b** to our God who is

BELOVED → LOVE
SS 2:16 My **b** is mine and I am his;
Mt 3:17 heaven said, "This is my Son, the **B**,
12:18 my **b**, with whom my soul is well
17: 5 "This is my Son, the **B**;
Col 3:12 As God's chosen ones, holy and **b**,
Rev 20: 9 camp of the saints and the **b** city.

BELSHAZZAR*
King of Babylon (Da 5; Bar 1:11-12).

BELT
1Sa 18: 4 his sword and his bow and his **b**.
Isa 11: 5 Righteousness shall be the **b** around
Mk 1: 6 with a leather **b** around his waist,
Eph 6:14 the **b** of truth around your waist,

BELTESHAZZAR → See DANIEL

BEN-HADAD*
1. King of Syria in time of Asa (1Ki 15:18-20; 2Ch 16:2-4).
2. King of Syria in time of Ahab (1Ki 20; 2Ki 6:24; 8:7-15).

3. King of Syria in time of Jehoahaz (2Ki 13:3, 24-25; Jer 49:27; Am 1:4).

BENAIAH
A commander of David's army (2Sa 8:18; 20:23; 23:20-30); loyal to Solomon (1Ki 1:8-2:46; 4:4).

BEND → BENT
Php 2:10 name of Jesus every knee should **b**,
Man 1:11 And now I **b** the knee of my heart,

BENEFICIAL → BENEFIT
1Co 6:12 but not all things are **b**.
10:23 lawful," but not all things are **b**.

BENEFIT → BENEFICIAL, BENEFITS
Gal 5: 2 Christ will be of no **b** to you.
Phm 1:20 have this **b** from you in the Lord!
Heb 4: 2 message they heard did not **b** them,

BENEFITS → BENEFIT
Ps 103: 2 and do not forget all his **b**—
1Co 9:11 if we reap your material **b**?

BENJAMIN → BENJAMINITE
Twelfth son of Jacob by Rachel (Ge 35:16-24; 46:19-21; 1Ch 2:2). Jacob refused to send him to Egypt, but relented (Ge 42-45). Tribe of blessed (Ge 49:27; Dt 33:12), numbered (Nu 1:37; 26:41), allotted land (Jos 18:11-28; Eze 48:23), failed to fully possess (Jdg 1:21), nearly obliterated (Jdg 20-21), sided with Ish-Bosheth (2Sa 2), but turned to David (1Ch 12:2, 29). 12,000 from (Rev 7:8).

BENJAMINITE → BENJAMIN
Jdg 3:15 the **B**, a left-handed man.
1Sa 9:21 Saul answered, "I am only a **B**,

BENT → BEND
Hos 11: 4 I **b** down to them and fed them.
Jn 8: 6 [[Jesus **b** down and wrote with his]]
20: 5 He **b** down to look in and saw

BEREAVE → BEREAVES
Lev 26:22 they shall **b** you of your children
Eze 36:12 No longer shall you **b** them of

BEREAVES* → BEREAVE
La 1:20 In the street the sword **b**;

BESIDES
Dt 32:39 there is no god **b** me.
Ps 18:31 And who is a rock **b** our God?—
Isa 45:21 There is no other god **b** me,
Wis 12:13 For neither is there any god **b** you,
Bel 1:41 there is no other **b** you!"

BEST → GOOD
Dt 33:21 He chose the **b** for himself,
Mk 12:39 the **b** seats in the synagogues and
2Ti 2:15 your **b** to present yourself to God

BETHANY
Mt 26: 6 Jesus was at **B** in the house of
Jn 11: 1 a certain man was ill, Lazarus of **B**,

BETHEL
Ge 12: 8 the east of **B**, and pitched his tent,
28:19 He called that place **B**;
1Sa 7:16 a circuit year by year to **B**, Gilgal,

BETHLEHEM
Ru 4:11 and bestow a name in **B**;
1Sa 17:12 David was the son of an Ephrathite of **B**
Mic 5: 2 But you, O **B** of Ephrathah,
Mt 2: 1 after Jesus was born in **B** of Judea,
Lk 2:15 "Let us go now to **B** and see this

BETRAY → BETRAYED
Mt 10:21 Brother will **b** brother to death,
Mk 14:11 to look for an opportunity to **b** him.
Jn 13:11 For he knew who was to **b** him;

BETRAYED → BETRAY
Lk 21:16 You will be **b** even by parents and
1Co 11:23 Jesus on the night when he was **b**

BETTER → GOOD
1Sa 15:22 Surely, to obey is **b** than sacrifice,
Ps 63: 3 your steadfast love is **b** than life,
Pr 15:16 **B** is a little with the fear of
27: 5 **B** is open rebuke than hidden love.
Ecc 2:24 There is nothing **b** for mortals than
9: 4 a living dog is **b** than a dead lion.
SS 1: 2 For your love is **b** than wine,
Da 1:20 he found them ten times **b** than all
Mt 5:29 it is **b** for you to lose one of your
Mk 14:21 It would have been **b** for that one
Jn 11:50 **b** for you to have one man die for
Ro 14: 5 Some judge one day to be **b** than
Php 1:23 and be with Christ, for that is far **b**;
2: 3 in humility regard others as **b** than
Heb 7:22 the guarantee of a **b** covenant.
9:23 need **b** sacrifices than these.
1Pe 3:17 For it is **b** to suffer for doing good,
Tob 12: 8 A little with righteousness is **b** than
Sir 40:26 the fear of the Lord is **b** than either.

BETWEEN
Ge 3:15 put enmity **b** you and the woman,
9:13 a sign of the covenant **b** me and
16: 5 the LORD judge **b** you and me!"
Isa 2: 4 He shall judge **b** the nations,
Eze 34:17 I shall judge **b** sheep and sheep, **b** rams and goats:
Jn 19:18 on either side, with Jesus **b** them.
Ro 10:12 no distinction **b** Jew and Greek;
Eph 2:14 dividing wall, that is, the hostility **b**
1Ti 2: 5 one mediator **b** God and humankind

BEWARE
Ecc 12:12 anything beyond these, my child, **b**.
Mt 6: 1 "**B** of practicing your piety before
Php 3: 2 **B** of the dogs, **b** of the evil workers,

BEYOND
Ps 147: 5 his understanding is **b** measure.
2Co 4:17 an eternal weight of glory **b** all
2Jn 1: 9 but goes **b** it, does not have God;
Sir 3:23 not meddle in matters that are **b** you

BEZALEL
Judahite craftsman in charge of building the tabernacle (Ex 31:1-11; 35:30-39:31).

BILDAD*
One of Job's friends (Job 2:11; 8; 18; 25; 42:9).

BILHAH
Servant of Rachel, mother of Jacob's sons Dan and Naphtali (Ge 30:1-7; 35:25; 46:23-25).

BIND → BINDS
Dt 6: 8 **B** them as a sign on your hand,
Pr 6:21 **B** them upon your heart always;
Isa 61: 1 to **b** up the brokenhearted,
Mt 16:19 whatever you **b** on earth will be

BINDS → BIND
Job 5:18 For he wounds, but he **b** up;
Col 3:14 **b** everything together in perfect

BIRD → BIRDS
Ge 1:21 and every winged **b** of every kind.
Lev 20:25 the unclean **b** and the clean;

BIRDS → BIRD
Ge 1:22 and let **b** multiply on the earth."
7: 3 and seven pairs of the **b** of the air
Ps 50:11 I know all the **b** of the air,
Jer 7:33 be food for the **b** of the air, and for
Mt 6:26 Look at the **b** of the air;
Rev 19:21 the **b** were gorged with their flesh.

BIRTH → BEAR
Dt 32:18 you forgot the God who gave you **b**.
Ps 22:10 On you I was cast from my **b**,
Mt 24: 8 is but the beginning of the **b** pangs.
Jas 1:18 he gave us **b** by the word of truth,
1Pe 1: 3 given us a new **b** into a living hope

BIRTHRIGHT → BEAR, RIGHT
Ge 25:34 Thus Esau despised his **b**.
Heb 12:16 who sold his **b** for a single meal.

BISHOP
1Ti 3: 1 whoever aspires to the office of **b**
Tit 1: 7 For a **b**, as God's steward, must be

BIT → BITE, BITS
Nu 21: 9 and whenever a serpent **b** someone,
Ps 32: 9 temper must be curbed with **b** and

BITE* → BIT
Gal 5:15 If, however, you **b** and devour one
Sir 21: 2 if you approach sin, it will **b** you.

BITS → BIT
Jas 3: 3 we put **b** into the mouths of horses

BITTER → BITTERNESS
Ex 1:14 made their lives **b** with hard service
12: 8 with unleavened bread and **b** herbs.
15:23 water of Marah because it was **b**.
Ru 1:13 it has been far more **b** for me than
Rev 8:11 the water, because it was made **b**.

BITTERNESS → BITTER
Nu 5:18 the water of **b** that brings the curse.
Pr 14:10 The heart knows its own **b**,
Ro 3:14 mouths are full of cursing and **b**."
Eph 4:31 Put away from you all **b** and wrath

BLACK
SS 1: 5 I am **b** and beautiful, O daughters
Zec 6: 2 the second chariot **b** horses,
Mt 5:36 cannot make one hair white or **b**.
Rev 6: 5 I looked, and there was a **b** horse!

BLAMELESS
Ge 17: 1 walk before me, and be **b**.
2Sa 22:26 with the **b** you show yourself **b**;
Job 1: 1 That man was **b** and upright,
Ps 37:18 The LORD knows the days of the **b**,
Pr 11:20 but those of **b** ways are his delight.
Eph 1: 4 holy and **b** before him in love.
Php 2:15 so that you may be **b** and innocent,
1Th 5:23 and **b** at the coming of our Lord
Tit 1: 7 bishop, as God's steward, must be **b**
Heb 7:26 **b**, undefiled, separated from sinners,
Rev 14: 5 mouth no lie was found; they are **b**.
1Mc 4:42 chose **b** priests devoted to the law,

BLASPHEME → BLASPHEMED, BLASPHEMER, BLASPHEMES, BLASPHEMIES, BLASPHEMOUS
Ac 26:11 I tried to force them to **b**;
1Ti 1:20 so that they may learn not to **b**.

BLASPHEMED → BLASPHEME
Eze 20:27 In this again your ancestors **b** me,
Mt 26:65 tore his clothes and said, "He has **b**!

BLASPHEMER → BLASPHEME
1Ti 1:13 even though I was formerly a **b**,
Sir 3:16 forsakes a father is like a **b**,

BLASPHEMES → BLASPHEME
Lev 24:16 One who **b** the name of the LORD
Lk 12:10 whoever **b** against the Holy Spirit

BLASPHEMIES → BLASPHEME
Mk 3:28 their sins and whatever **b** they utter;
Rev 13: 6 its mouth to utter **b** against God,
1Mc 2: 6 He saw the **b** being committed in

BLASPHEMOUS → BLASPHEME
Ac 6:11 "We have heard him speak **b** words
Rev 13: 1 and on its heads were **b** names.

BLAZING
Ex 3: 2 he looked, and the bush was **b**,
Dt 4:11 the mountain was **b** up to the very
Heb 12:18 a **b** fire, and darkness, and gloom,

BLEMISH → BLEMISHED
Ex 12: 5 Your lamb shall be without **b**,
Lev 22:20 not offer anything that has a **b**,
Eph 5:27 that she may be holy and without **b**.
Heb 9:14 offered himself without **b** to God,
1Pe 1:19 that of a lamb without defect or **b**.
Jude 1:24 to make you stand without **b** in the

BLEMISHED* → BLEMISH
Mal 1:14 yet sacrifices to the Lord what is **b**;
Sir 34:21 ill-gotten goods, the offering is **b**;

BLESS → BLESSED, BLESSING, BLESSINGS
Ge 12: 2 I will **b** you, and make your name
17:16 I will **b** her, and moreover I will
22:17 I will indeed **b** you, and I will make
26: 3 I will be with you, and will **b** you;
32:26 not let you go, unless you **b** me."
Ex 20:24 I will come to you and **b** you.
Nu 6:24 The LORD **b** you and keep you;
23:20 See, I received a command to **b**;
Dt 7:13 he will love you, **b** you,
30:16 the LORD your God will **b** you in
1Ch 29:20 "**B** the LORD your God."
Ps 5:12 For you **b** the righteous, O LORD;
29:11 the LORD **b** his people with peace!
34: 1 I will **b** the LORD at all times;
103: 1 **B** the LORD, O my soul,

Ps 109:28 Let them curse, but you will b.
Hag 2:19 From this day on I will b you.
Lk 6:28 b those who curse you, pray
Ro 12:14 B those who persecute you;
1Co 4:12 When reviled, we b;
Jas 3: 9 With it we b the Lord and Father,
Tob 4:19 At all times b the Lord God,
Sir 32:13 But above all b your Maker,

BLESSED ➝ BLESS
Ge 1:22 God b them, saying, "Be fruitful
2: 3 So God b the seventh day and
14:19 He b him and said, "B be Abram
Nu 24: 9 B is everyone who blesses you,
Job 1:21 b be the name of the LORD."
42:12 The LORD b the latter days
Ps 118:26 B is the one who comes in the name
Isa 30:18 b are all those who wait for him.
Jer 17: 7 B are those who trust in the LORD,
Mt 5: 3 "B are the poor in spirit,
Mk 10:16 laid his hands on them, and b them.
Lk 1:42 "B are you among women,
6:20 "B are you who are poor,
Jn 12:13 B is the one who comes in the name
20:29 B are those who have not seen and
Ac 20:35 It is more b to give than to receive.
Gal 3: 8 "All the Gentiles shall be b in you."
Eph 1: 3 who has b us in Christ
1Pe 3:14 for doing what is right, you are b.
Rev 1: 3 B is the one who reads aloud the
22: 7 B is the one who keeps the words of
Tob 3:11 she prayed and said, "B are you,
Jdt 13:17 one accord, "B are you our God,
Aza 1: 3 "B are you, O Lord, God of our
Sus 1:60 raised a great shout and b God,

BLESSING ➝ BLESS
Ge 12: 2 so that you will be a b.
22:18 the nations of the earth gain b for
27:36 now he has taken away my b."
Dt 11:26 before you today a b and a curse:
23: 5 your God turned the curse into a b
Ne 13: 2 our God turned the curse into a b.
Eze 34:26 they shall be showers of b.
Mal 3:10 for you an overflowing b.
Mk 14:22 of bread, and after b it he broke it,
Lk 24:51 While he was b them, he withdrew
1Co 10:16 The cup of b that we bless,
Gal 3:14 in Christ Jesus the b of Abraham
Eph 1: 3 every spiritual b in the heavenly
Rev 5:12 might and honor and glory and b!"
7:12 B and glory and wisdom and
Tob 8:15 you, O God, with every pure b;
Sir 34:20 he gives health and life and b.

BLESSINGS ➝ BLESS
Dt 28: 2 all these b shall come upon you
Jos 8:34 the words of the law, b and curses,
Ps 21: 6 You bestow on him b forever;
144:15 Happy are the people to whom such b
Pr 10: 6 B are on the head of the righteous,
Mal 2: 2 and I will curse your b;
Ro 15:27 come to share in their spiritual b,

BLIND ➝ BLINDED, BLINDNESS
Ex 4:11 mute or deaf, seeing or b?
Dt 27:18 misleads a b person on the road."
Ps 146: 8 the LORD opens the eyes of the b.
Isa 35: 5 the eyes of the b shall be opened,
42:19 Who is b but my servant,
Mt 11: 5 b receive their sight, the lame walk,
Lk 6:39 "Can a b person guide a b person?
Jn 9:25 though I was b, now I see."
Ro 2:19 sure that you are a guide to the b,
2Pe 1: 9 b, and is forgetful of the cleansing
Tob 2:10 until I became completely b.
LtJ 6:37 They cannot restore sight to the b;

BLINDED ➝ BLIND
Zec 11:17 withered, his right eye utterly b!
Jn 12:40 "He has b their eyes and hardened
2Co 4: 4 has b the minds of the unbelievers,

BLINDNESS ➝ BLIND
Ge 19:11 And they struck with b the men
Dt 28:28 will afflict you with madness, b,
1Jn 2:11 the darkness has brought on b.

BLOCK ➝ BLOCKS
Isa 44:19 I fall down before a b of wood?"
Eze 14: 7 their iniquity as a stumbling b
Mt 16:23 You are a stumbling b to me;
Ro 11: 9 a stumbling b and a retribution for
1Co 1:23 stumbling b to Jews and foolishness
Sir 31: 7 It is a stumbling b to those who are

BLOCKS ➝ BLOCK
Jer 6:21 before this people stumbling b
Mt 18: 7 the world because of stumbling b!

BLOOD ➝ BLOODSHED
Ge 4:10 your brother's b is crying out to me
9: 6 sheds the b of a human, by a human shall that person's b be shed;
Ex 7:17 and it shall be turned to b.
12:13 when I see the b, I will pass over
24: 8 the b of the covenant that the LORD
Lev 1: 5 the priests shall offer the b,
3:17 you must not eat any fat or any b.
17:11 it is the b that makes atonement.
Nu 35:33 for b pollutes the land,
Ps 72:14 and precious is their b in his sight.
Isa 1:11 I do not delight in the b of bulls,
Eze 33: 4 b shall be upon their own heads.
Joel 2:30 b and fire and columns of smoke.
Mt 27: 8 field has been called the Field of B
Mk 14:24 "This is my b of the covenant,
Lk 22:44 [[sweat became like great drops of b]]
Jn 1:13 who were born, not of b
6:53 of the Son of Man and drink his b,
19:34 and at once b and water came out.
Ac 2:20 to darkness and the moon to b,
Ro 5: 9 that we have been justified by his b,
1Co 11:25 cup is the new covenant in my b.
Eph 1: 7 we have redemption through his b,
6:12 not against enemies of b and flesh,
Heb 9:12 the b of goats and calves, but with his own b,
9:22 without the shedding of b there is no
1Jn 5: 6 the one who came by water and b,
Rev 1: 5 and freed us from our sins by his b,
5: 9 by your b you ransomed for God
6:12 the full moon became like b,
8: 9 A third of the sea became b,
12:11 conquered him by the b of the Lamb

BLOODSHED ➝ BLOOD, SHED
Isa 5: 7 he expected justice, but saw b;
Eze 35: 6 you did not hate b, b shall pursue
Hab 2: 8 because of human b, and violence

BLOSSOMS
Ex 25:33 three cups shaped like almond b,
Nu 17: 8 It put forth buds, produced b,

BLOT
Ge 6: 7 "I will b out from the earth
Ex 32:32 b me out of the book that you have
Ps 51: 1 mercy b out my transgressions.
Rev 3: 5 not b your name out of the book of

BLOW ➝ BLOWING
Joel 2: 1 B the trumpet in Zion; sound the
Rev 8: 6 the seven trumpets made ready to b

BOAST ➝ BOASTERS, BOASTFUL, BOASTING
Ps 34: 2 My soul makes its b in the LORD;
Pr 27: 1 Do not b about tomorrow,
Jer 9:24 but let those who b b in this,
Ro 2:23 You that b in the law,
1Co 1:31 the one who boasts, b in the Lord."
2Co 11:30 If I must b, I will b of the things that
Gal 6:14 never b of anything except the cross
Eph 2: 9 of works, so that no one may b.
Sir 25: 6 and their b is the fear of the Lord.

BOASTERS* ➝ BOAST
2Co 11:13 For such b are false apostles,
2Ti 3: 2 b, arrogant, abusive, disobedient to

BOASTFUL ➝ BOAST
Ps 5: 5 The b will not stand before your
1Co 13: 4 love is not envious or b or arrogant

BOASTING ➝ BOAST
1Co 5: 6 Your b is not a good thing.
1Th 2:19 or crown of b before our Lord Jesus

BOAZ
Bethlehemite who showed favor to Ruth (Ru 2), married her (Ru 4). Ancestor of David (Ru 4:18-22; 1Ch 2:12-15), Jesus (Mt 1:5-16; Lk 3:23-32).

BODIES ➝ BODY
Ro 12: 1 present your b as a living sacrifice,
1Co 6:15 that your b are members of Christ?
Heb 10:22 and our b washed with pure water.

BODILY ➝ BODY
Lk 3:22 upon him in b form like a dove.
Col 2: 9 the whole fullness of deity dwells b,

BODY ➝ BODIES, BODILY
2Sa 7:12 who shall come forth from your b,
Mic 6: 7 fruit of my b for the sin of my soul?
Mt 6:22 "The eye is the lamp of the b.
Mk 14:22 and said, "Take; this is my b."
Lk 12: 4 do not fear those who kill the b,
Jn 2:21 speaking of the temple of his b.
Ro 7:24 will rescue me from this b of death?
1Co 6:13 b is meant not for fornication but
15:44 It is sown a physical b, it is raised a spiritual b.
2Co 5: 8 from the b and at home with the Lord.
Eph 4: 4 There is one b and one Spirit,

BOLD ➝ BOLDNESS
Dt 31: 6 Be strong and b; have no fear
Pr 28: 1 but the righteous are as b as a lion.

BOLDNESS ➝ BOLD
Eph 3:12 whom we have access to God in b
Heb 4:16 approach the throne of grace with b,
1Jn 4:17 may have b on the day of judgment,

BONE ➝ BONES
Ge 2:23 "This at last is b of my bones and
Eze 37: 7 the bones came together, b to its b.

BONES ➝ BONE
Ex 12:46 and you shall not break any of its b.
Ps 34:20 He keeps all their b; not one of
Jn 19:36 "None of his b shall be broken."

BOOK ➝ BOOKS
Ex 17:14 "Write this as a reminder in a b and
Dt 31:24 writing down in a b the words of
Jos 1: 8 This b of the law shall not depart
Ps 69:28 be blotted out of the b of the living;
Rev 1:11 "Write in a b what you see and
21:27 who are written in the Lamb's b
1Mc 1:57 possessing the b of the covenant,

BOOKS ➝ BOOK
Ecc 12:12 Of making many b there is no end,
Da 7:10 in judgment, and the b were opened.
Jn 21:25 world itself could not contain the b
Rev 20:12 the throne, and b were opened.
1Mc 1:56 The b of the law that they found
2Es 14:44 ninety-four b were written.

BOOTHS
Lev 23:34 the festival of b to the LORD.
Ezr 3: 4 kept the festival of b, as prescribed,
Zec 14:16 and to keep the festival of b.

BORE ➝ BEAR
Isa 53:12 yet he b the sin of many,
Mt 8:17 our infirmities and b our diseases."
1Pe 2:24 He himself b our sins in his body

BORN ➝ BEAR
Ecc 3: 2 a time to be b, and a time to die;
Isa 9: 6 For a child has been b for us,
66: 8 Shall a land be b in one day?
Lk 2:11 is b this day in the city of David
Jn 3: 7 'You must be b from above.'
1Co 15: 8 Last of all, as to one untimely b,
1Pe 1:23 You have been b anew,
1Jn 4: 7 everyone who loves is b of God

BORROW ➝ BORROWER
Dt 28:12 to many nations, but you will not b.
Ps 37:21 The wicked b, and do not pay back,
Mt 5:42 anyone who wants to b from you.

BORROWER ➝ BORROW
Pr 22: 7 and the b is the slave of the lender.

BOUGHT ➝ BUY
1Co 6:20 For you were b with a price;
2Pe 2: 1 even deny the Master who b them—

BOW ➝ BOWED, RAINBOW
Ge 9:13 I have set my b in the clouds,
Ex 20: 5 You shall not b down to them or
Ps 95: 6 O come, let us worship and b down,

Isa 45:23 "To me every knee shall b,
Ro 14:11 every knee shall b to me,

BOWED ➛ BOW
Ps 146: 8 The LORD lifts up those who are b
Jn 19:30 he b his head and gave up his spirit.

BOWLS
Rev 16: 1 the seven b of the wrath of God."

BOY ➛ BOYS
Jer 1: 7 to me, "Do not say, 'I am only a b';
Lk 2:43 b Jesus stayed behind in Jerusalem,

BOYS ➛ BOY
Ex 1:18 and allowed the b to live?"
2Ki 2:24 and mauled forty-two of the b.

BRANCH ➛ BRANCHES
Isa 4: 2 On that day the b of the LORD shall
11: 1 and a b shall grow out of his roots.
Jer 23: 5 raise up for David a righteous B,
Zec 3: 8 going to bring my servant the B.
Jn 15: 2 every b in me that bears no fruit.

BRANCHES ➛ BRANCH
Ro 11:21 if God did not spare the natural b,

BREAD
Ge 3:19 sweat of your face you shall eat b
Ex 12: 8 with unleavened b and bitter herbs.
25:30 set the b of the Presence on the table
Dt 8: 3 that one does not live by b alone,
Ecc 11: 1 Send out your b upon the waters,
Mt 6:11 Give us this day our daily b.
Lk 4: 4 'One does not live by b alone.'"
Jn 6:35 Jesus said to them, "I am the b of life.
Ac 2:42 to the breaking of b and the prayers.
1Co 11:26 For as often as you eat this b and
Wis 16:20 from heaven with b ready to eat,
Sir 15: 3 will feed him with the b of learning,

BREAK ➛ BREAKING, BROKEN, BROKENHEARTED
Ps 2: 9 You shall b them with a rod of iron,
Mt 6:19 where thieves b in and steal;
Jn 19:33 they did not b his legs.

BREASTPIECE ➛ BREASTPLATE
Ex 28:15 You shall make a b of judgment,

BREASTPLATE ➛ BREASTPIECE
Isa 59:17 He put on righteousness like a b,
Eph 6:14 and put on the b of righteousness.
Wis 5:18 he will put on righteousness as a b,

BREATH
Ge 2: 7 into his nostrils the b of life;
6:17 all flesh in which is the b of life;
Job 7: 7 "Remember that my life is a b;
Ecc 12: 7 the b returns to God who gave it.
2Th 2: 8 will destroy with the b of his mouth,

BRIBE
Dt 16:19 for a b blinds the eyes of the wise
Pr 6:35 and refuses a b no matter how great.

BRIDE ➛ BRIDEGROOM
Isa 62: 5 the bridegroom rejoices over the b,
Rev 21: 9 the b, the wife of the Lamb."

BRIDEGROOM ➛ BRIDE
Mt 9:15 as long as the b is with them,
Jn 3:29 He who has the bride is the b.

BRIDLE
Ps 32: 9 must be curbed with bit and b,
Jas 3: 2 the whole body in check with a b.

BRIGHT ➛ BRIGHTNESS
Mt 17: 5 suddenly a b cloud overshadowed
Rev 15: 6 robed in pure b linen,
22:16 of David, the b morning star."

BRIGHTNESS ➛ BRIGHT
Da 12: 3 wise shall shine like the b of the sky
Am 5:20 not light, and gloom with no b in it?

BRING ➛ BRINGS, BROUGHT
Ge 6:19 b two of every kind into the ark,
Ecc 12:14 will b every deed into judgment,
Jer 24: 6 and I will b them back to this land.
Mt 10:34 not come to b peace, but a sword.
Ro 10:15 the feet of those who b good news!"

BRINGS ➛ BRING
1Sa 2: 6 The LORD kills and b to life;
Jas 5:20 that whoever b back a sinner

BROKE ➛ BREAK
Ex 32:19 tablets from his hands and b them
2Ch 36:19 b down the wall of Jerusalem,
Jer 31:32 a covenant that they b,
Mt 14:19 and blessed and b the loaves,
1Co 11:24 he b it and said, "This is my body
1Mc 3: 5 and pursued those who b the law;

BROKEN ➛ BREAK
Ne 1: 3 the wall of Jerusalem is b down,
Ps 51:17 acceptable to God is a b spirit;
Mt 15:37 they took up the b pieces left over,
Lk 20:18 who falls on that stone will be b
Ro 11:20 were b off because of their unbelief,

BROKENHEARTED ➛ BREAK, HEART
Ps 147: 3 He heals the b, and binds up their
Isa 61: 1 the oppressed, to bind up the b,

BRONZE
Nu 21: 9 look at the serpent of b and live.
Dt 28:23 The sky over your head shall be b,
Da 10: 6 legs like the gleam of burnished b,
Rev 1:15 his feet were like burnished b,

BROOD
Mt 3: 7 he said to them, "You b of vipers!
Lk 13:34 a hen gathers her b under her wings,

BROTHER ➛ BROTHER'S, BROTHER-IN-LAW, BROTHERS
Ge 4: 8 Cain rose up against his b Abel,
Mt 5:24 first be reconciled to your b or
10:21 B will betray b to death,

BROTHER'S ➛ BROTHER
Dt 25: 7 has no desire to marry his b widow,
Mk 6:18 lawful for you to have your b wife."

BROTHER-IN-LAW* ➛ BROTHER
Ge 38: 8 and perform the duty of a b to her;

BROTHERS ➛ BROTHER
Ge 9:25 lowest of slaves shall he be to his b.
37:11 So his b were jealous of him,
Mk 3:33 "Who are my mother and my b?"
Lk 22:32 turned back, strengthen your b."
Heb 2:11 not ashamed to call them b and

BROUGHT ➛ BRING
Ge 15: 7 b you from Ur of the Chaldeans,
Jdg 2: 1 "I b you up from Egypt, and b you into
2Ch 36:18 all these he b to Babylon.
Ezr 6: 5 b back to the temple in Jerusalem,
Ro 6:13 who have been b from death to life,
1Ti 6: 7 for we b nothing into the world,

BUILD ➛ BUILDER, BUILDERS, BUILDING, BUILDS, BUILT, REBUILD
Ge 11: 4 "Come, let us b ourselves a city,
Dt 6:10 fine, large cities that you did not b,
Ps 127: 1 those who b it labor in vain.
Isa 57:14 said, "B up, b up, prepare the way,
Mt 16:18 and on this rock I will b my church,
27:40 destroy the temple and b it in three
1Co 3:10 must choose with care how to b
10:23 are lawful," but not all things b up.

BUILDER ➛ BUILD
Heb 3: 4 but the b of all things is God.)
11:10 whose architect and b is God.

BUILDERS ➛ BUILD
Ps 118:22 The stone that the b rejected has
Mk 12:10 'The stone that the b rejected has
1Pe 2: 7 "The stone that the b rejected has

BUILDING ➛ BUILD
1Co 3: 9 you are God's field, God's b.
2Co 5: 1 we have a b from God,
Eph 4:12 for b up the body of Christ,

BUILDS ➛ BUILD
Ps 127: 1 Unless the LORD b the house,
Pr 14: 1 The wise woman b her house,
1Co 8: 1 Knowledge puffs up, but love b up.

BUILT ➛ BUILD
1Ki 6:14 Solomon b the house, and finished
Ne 7: 1 the wall had been b and I had set up
Pr 9: 1 Wisdom has b her house,
Da 9:25 sixty-two weeks it shall be b again
Eph 2:20 b upon the foundation of the

Tob 13:16 Jerusalem will be b as his house for
1Mc 4:47 b a new altar like the former one.

BULL ➛ BULLS
Ps 50: 9 will not accept a b from your house,

BULLS ➛ BULL
1Ch 29:21 a thousand b, a thousand rams,
Ps 22:12 b encircle me, strong b of Bashan
Isa 1:11 I do not delight in the blood of b,
Heb 10: 4 it is impossible for the blood of b

BURDEN ➛ BURDENS, BURDENSOME
Ps 55:22 Cast your b on the LORD,
Mt 11:30 my yoke is easy, and my b is light."
2Co 5: 4 in this tent, we groan under our b,

BURDENS ➛ BURDEN
Ex 6: 6 free you from the b of the Egyptians
Lk 11:46 you load people with b hard to bear,
Gal 6: 2 Bear one another's b, and

BURDENSOME ➛ BURDEN
1Jn 5: 3 And his commandments are not b,

BURIED ➛ BURY
Ro 6: 4 have been b with him by baptism
1Co 15: 4 he was b, and that he was raised on

BURN ➛ BURNED, BURNING, BURNT
Ex 21:25 b for b, wound for wound,
Ps 79: 5 Will your jealous wrath b like fire?
Jer 7:31 to b their sons and their daughters
Mal 4: 1 the day that comes shall b them up,
Lk 3:17 but the chaff he will b with

BURNED ➛ BURN
Ex 3: 3 and see why the bush is not b up."
Jn 15: 6 thrown into the fire, and b.
1Co 3:15 If the work is b up, the builder will

BURNING ➛ BURN
Lk 24:32 "Were not our hearts b within us

BURNT ➛ BURN
Ex 40: 6 You shall set the altar of b offering
Lev 1: 3 If the offering is a b offering from
1Sa 15:22 LORD as great delight in b offerings
Ps 51:16 if I were to give a b offering,
Da 8:11 it took the regular b offering away
Hos 6: 6 the knowledge of God rather than b
Mic 6: 6 Shall I come before him with b
Mk 12:33 more important than all whole b
1Mc 1:45 to forbid b offerings and sacrifices
4:56 and joyfully offered b offerings;

BURY ➛ BURIED
Lk 9:60 "Let the dead b their own dead;

BUSH
Ex 3: 2 he looked, and the b was blazing,
Jnh 4: 6 The LORD God appointed a b,

BUY ➛ BOUGHT, BUYS
Pr 23:23 B truth, and do not sell it;
Isa 55: 1 b wine and milk without money
Rev 3:18 to b from me gold refined by fire so

BUYS ➛ BUY
Pr 31:16 She considers a field and b it;
Mt 13:44 sells all that he has and b that field.

BYWORD ➛ WORD
Dt 28:37 and a b among all the peoples where
Job 17: 6 He has made me a b of the peoples,
Ps 44:14 made us a b among the nations,

C

CAESAREA
Mt 16:13 came into the district of C Philippi,
Ac 10: 1 C there was a man named Cornelius
25: 4 that Paul was being kept at C,

CAIAPHAS*
High priest at trial of Jesus (Mt 26:3, 57; Lk 3:2; Jn 11:49; 18:13-28); at trial of disciples (Ac 4:6).

CAIN*
Firstborn of Adam (Ge 4:1), murdered brother Abel (Ge 4:1-25; Heb 11:4; 1Jn 3:12; Jude 11; 4Mc 18:11).

CALAMITIES ➛ CALAMITY
1Sa 10:19 who saves you from all your c and
2Co 6: 4 in afflictions, hardships, c,
12:10 and c for the sake of Christ;

CALAMITY ➛ CALAMITIES
Pr 1:26 I also will laugh at your c;
Da 9:13 all this c has come upon us.
Hab 3:16 wait quietly for the day of c to come

CALEB
Judahite who spied out Canaan (Nu 13:6); allowed to enter land (Nu 13:30-14:38; Dt 1:36; Sir 46:7-9; 1Mc 2:56). Given Hebron (Jos 14:6-15:19).

CALF ➛ CALVES
Ex 32: 4 and cast an image of a c;
Lk 15:23 And get the fatted c and kill it,

CALL ➛ CALLED, CALLING
Dt 4:26 I c heaven and earth to witness
1Sa 3: 5 But he said, "I did not c; lie down
1Ki 18:24 you c on the name of your god and I will c on the name of the LORD;
1Ch 16: 8 thanks to the LORD, c on his name,
Ps 61: 2 From the end of the earth I c to you,
Pr 8: 1 Does not wisdom c, and does
Isa 65:24 Before they c I will answer,
Mt 9:13 to c not the righteous but sinners."
Lk 6:46 "Why do you c me 'Lord, Lord,'
Jn 15:15 I do not c you servants any longer,
Ro 10:12 and is generous to all who c on him.
Php 3:14 goal for the prize of the heavenly c

CALLED ➛ CALL
2Sa 22: 7 In my distress I c upon the LORD;
Isa 43: 1 I have c you by name, you are mine.
Mt 23: 8 But you are not to be c rabbi,
1Co 7:15 It is to peace that God has c you.
Eph 1:18 the hope to which he has c you,
1Jn 3: 1 that we should be c children of God;

CALLING ➛ CALL
Ro 11:29 and the c of God are irrevocable.
Eph 4: 1 lead a life worthy of the c to which

CALVES ➛ CALF
1Ki 12:28 and made two c of gold.
Mal 4: 2 go out leaping like c from the stall.

CAMEL
Mt 23:24 strain out a gnat but swallow a c!
Mk 10:25 c to go through the eye of a needle

CANA
Jn 2: 1 there was a wedding in C

CANAAN ➛ CANAANITE, CANAANITES
Ge 9:25 "Cursed be C; lowest of slaves
Nu 13: 2 "Send men to spy out the land of C,
1Ch 16:18 "To you I will give the land of C

CANAANITE ➛ CANAAN
Ge 28: 1 not marry one of the C women.
Mt 15:22 a C woman from that region came

CANAANITES ➛ CANAAN
Ex 33: 2 I will drive out the C, the Amorites,
Jdg 3: 5 So the Israelites lived among the C,

CAPERNAUM
Mt 4:13 and made his home in C by the sea,
Jn 6:59 was teaching in the synagogue at C.

CAPTIVE ➛ CAPTIVITY
2Ki 15:29 he carried the people c to Assyria.
24:16 king of Babylon brought c to
Ro 7:23 making me c to the law of sin
Eph 4: 8 he made captivity itself a c;

CAPTIVITY ➛ CAPTIVE
Dt 28:41 for they shall go into c.
Ezr 8:35 those who had come from c,

CARE ➛ CAREFUL, CARELESS, CARES, CARING
Ps 8: 4 mortals that you c for them?
Heb 2: 6 or mortals, that you c for them?
Jas 1:27 to c for orphans and widows in

CAREFUL ➛ CARE
Dt 4:23 So be c not to forget the covenant
Jos 1: 8 you may be c to act in accordance
Eph 5:15 Be c then how you live,

CARELESS* ➛ CARE
Pr 14:16 the fool throws off restraint and is c.
Mt 12:36 to give an account for every c word

CARES ➛ CARE
Lk 8:14 they are choked by the c and riches
1Pe 5: 7 on him, because he c for you.

CARMEL
1Ki 18:20 assembled the prophets at Mount C.

CARPENTER'S*
Mt 13:55 Is not this the c son?

CARRY
Ps 28: 9 their shepherd, and c them forever.
Isa 40:11 and c them in his bosom,
Lk 14:27 does not c the cross and follow me

CASE
Job 13: 3 and I desire to argue my c with God.
Isa 41:21 Set forth your c, says the LORD;
Lk 12:58 make an effort to settle the c,
Jn 18:38 "I find no c against him.

CAST
Ex 34:17 You shall not make c idols.
Est 9:24 Jews to destroy them, and had c Pur
Ps 22:18 and for my clothing they c lots.
55:22 C your burden on the LORD,
Pr 16:33 The lot is c into the lap,
Mk 3:23 "How can Satan c out Satan?
Jn 19:24 and for my clothing they c lots."
1Pe 5: 7 C all your anxiety on him,

CATTLE
Ge 1:25 and the c of every kind,
Ps 50:10 the c on a thousand hills.

CAUGHT
2Co 12: 2 was c up to the third heaven—
1Th 4:17 be c up in the clouds together with

CAUSE
Job 5: 8 and to God I would commit my c.
Ps 9: 4 For you have maintained my just c;
140:12 LORD maintains the c of the needy,
Jn 15:25 'They hated me without a c.'

CAVE
Ge 23: 9 he may give me the c of Machpelah,
1Sa 22: 1 and escaped to the c of Adullam;
24: 3 in the innermost parts of the c.
1Ki 18: 4 hid them fifty to a c,

CEASE
Ge 8:22 winter, day and night, shall not c."
Jer 31:36 If this fixed order were ever to c
1Co 13: 8 as for tongues, they will c;

CEDAR
2Sa 7: 2 See now, I am living in a house of c,
Ps 92:12 and grow like a c in Lebanon.

CELEBRATE
Lev 23:37 shall c as times of holy convocation,
1Co 5: 8 Therefore, let us c the festival,

CENSER
Lev 10: 1 Nadab and Abihu, each took his c,
Eze 8:11 Each had his c in his hand,
Rev 8: 3 Another angel with a golden c came

CENSUS
Nu 1: 2 Take a c of the whole congregation
2Sa 24: 2 and take a c of the people,

CENTURION
Mt 8: 5 he entered Capernaum, a c came to
Lk 23:47 the c saw what had taken place,
Ac 10: 1 a man named Cornelius, a c

CEPHAS* ➛ =PETER
Name given to the apostle Peter (Jn 1:42; 1Co 1:12; 3:22; 9:5; 15:5; Gal 1:18; 2:9, 11, 14).

CERTIFICATE
Dt 24: 1 and so he writes her a c of divorce,
Mt 5:31 let him give her a c of divorce.'
Mk 10: 4 a man to write a c of dismissal

CHAFF
Ps 1: 4 are like c that the wind drives away.
Lk 3:17 c he will burn with unquenchable

CHAINED* ➛ CHAINS
2Ti 2: 9 the point of being c like a criminal. But the word of God is not c.

CHAINS ➛ CHAINED
Eph 6:20 for which I am an ambassador in c.
Heb 11:36 and even c and imprisonment.
2Pe 2: 4 them to c of deepest darkness

CHALDEANS
Ge 15: 7 who brought you from Ur of the C,
Da 1: 4 the literature and language of the C.

CHANGE ➛ CHANGED, CHANGERS
Ex 32:12 c your mind and do not bring
Nu 23:19 a mortal, that he should c his mind.
1Sa 15:29 will not recant or c his mind;
Ps 46: 2 not fear, though the earth should c,
Jer 18: 8 I will c my mind about the disaster
Jas 1:17 is no variation or shadow due to c.

CHANGED ➛ CHANGE
1Co 15:51 will not all die, but we will all be c,
Heb 1:12 and like clothing they will be c.

CHANGERS ➛ CHANGE
Mk 11:15 overturned the tables of the money c
Jn 2:15 poured out the coins of the money c

CHARACTER
Ro 5: 4 endurance produces c, and c produces

CHARGE
Mt 25:21 I will put you in c of many things;
Mk 15:26 The inscription of the c against him
Ro 8:33 will bring any c against God's elect?
1Co 9:18 I may make the gospel free of c,

CHARIOT ➛ CHARIOTS
2Ki 2:11 a c of fire and horses of fire
Ps 104: 3 you make the clouds your c,

CHARIOTS ➛ CHARIOT
Ex 14:28 waters returned and covered the c
Zec 6: 1 and saw four c coming out from

CHARM
Pr 31:30 C is deceitful, and beauty is vain,
Sir 7:19 for her c is worth more than gold.
26:15 A modest wife adds c to c,

CHASTISEMENT ➛ CHASTISES
La 4: 6 the c of my people has been greater
Sir 16:12 Great as his mercy, so also is his c;

CHASTISES* ➛ CHASTISEMENT
Heb 12: 6 and c every child whom he accepts.

CHEEK
Ps 3: 7 you strike all my enemies on the c;
Mt 5:39 if anyone strikes you on the right c,

CHEERFUL
Pr 15:13 A glad heart makes a c countenance,
17:22 A c heart is a good medicine,
2Co 9: 7 for God loves a c giver.
Jas 5:13 Are any c? They should sing songs

CHEMOSH
1Ki 11: 7 Solomon built a high place for C
Jer 48: 7 C shall go out into exile,

CHERUB ➛ CHERUBIM
2Ch 3:11 touched the wing of the other c;
Ps 18:10 He rode on a c, and flew;
Eze 10:14 the first face was that of the c,
28:14 an anointed c as guardian I placed

CHERUBIM ➛ CHERUB
Ge 3:24 the garden of Eden he placed the c,
Ex 25:18 You shall make two c of gold;
Ps 80: 1 You who are enthroned upon the c,
Heb 9: 5 the c of glory overshadowing the

CHIEF
Ps 118:22 has become the c cornerstone.
Mk 15: 3 the c priests accused him of many
1Pe 5: 4 And when the c shepherd appears,

CHILD ➛ CHILDBEARING, CHILDISH, CHILDREN
Ge 17:17 c be born to a man who is a hundred
1Ki 3: 7 although I am only a little c;
Isa 11: 6 and a little c shall lead them.
49:15 Can a woman forget her nursing c,
Hos 11: 1 When Israel was a c, I loved him,
Mt 1:18 with c from the Holy Spirit.
Mk 10:15 the kingdom of God as a little c
Lk 2:12 you will find a c wrapped in bands
1Co 13:11 When I was a c, I spoke like a c,
Gal 4: 7 So you are no longer a slave but a c,
Rev 12: 4 that he might devour her c as soon

CHILDBEARING* ➛ CHILD, BEAR
Ge 3:16 greatly increase your pangs in c;
1Ti 2:15 Yet she will be saved through c,

CHILDISH* → **CHILD**
1Co 13:11 an adult, I put an end to c ways.

CHILDREN → **CHILD**
Ex 12:26 And when your c ask you,
Dt 6: 7 Recite them to your c and talk about
11:19 Teach them to your c, talking about
Pr 22: 6 Train c in the right way, and when
Mt 3: 9 stones to raise up c to Abraham.
Lk 18:16 "Let the little c come to me,
Jn 1:12 he gave power to become c of God,
Ro 8:14 by the Spirit of God are c of God.
1Co 14:20 do not be c in your thinking;
Eph 6: 4 do not provoke your c to anger,
Heb 12: 7 God is treating you as c;
1Jn 3:10 The c of God and the c of the devil
Sir 30: 1 CONCERNING C He who loves his son

CHOOSE → **CHOOSES, CHOSE, CHOSEN**
Dt 12:14 at the place that the LORD will c
30:19 C life so that you and your
Jos 24:15 c this day whom you will serve,
Jn 15:16 You did not c me but I chose you.

CHOOSES → **CHOOSE**
Ro 9:18 he has mercy on whomever he c,

CHOSE → **CHOOSE**
Dt 4:37 he c their descendants after them.
Ne 9: 7 God who c Abram and brought him
Mk 13:20 for the sake of the elect, whom he c,
1Co 1:27 God c what is foolish in the world

CHOSEN → **CHOOSE**
Isa 42: 1 my servant, whom I uphold, my c,
Mt 22:14 For many are called, but few are c."
Ro 11: 5 there is a remnant, c by grace.
1Pe 2: 6 a cornerstone c and precious;
2: 9 you are a c race, a royal priesthood,

CHRIST → **CHRIST'S, CHRISTIAN, CHRISTIANS, MESSIAH**
Jn 4:25 Messiah is coming" (who is called C).
Ro 5: 6 right time C died for the ungodly.
8:35 will separate us from the love of C?
10: 4 For C is the end of the law so that
1Co 1:23 but we proclaim C crucified,
3:11 that foundation is Jesus C.
11: 1 Be imitators of me, as I am of C.
15: 3 C died for our sins in accordance
Gal 5: 1 For freedom C has set us free.
Eph 4:15 into him who is the head, into C,
Php 1:21 to me, living is C and dying is gain.
2:11 should confess that Jesus C is Lord,
Col 1:27 C in you, the hope of glory.
Rev 20: 4 reigned with C a thousand years.

CHRIST'S → **CHRIST**
Col 1:24 what is lacking in C afflictions
1Pe 4:13 as you are sharing C sufferings,

CHRISTIAN* → **CHRIST**
Ac 26:28 persuading me to become a C?"
1Pe 4:16 Yet if any of you suffers as a C,

CHRISTIANS* → **CHRIST**
Ac 11:26 the disciples were first called "C."

CHURCH
Mt 16:18 and on this rock I will build my c,
Ac 8: 1 persecution began against the c
1Co 12:28 has appointed in the c first apostles,
14: 4 those who prophesy build up the c.
Col 1:18 He is the head of the body, the c;

CIRCUMCISE → **CIRCUMCISED, CIRCUMCISION**
Ge 17:11 shall c the flesh of your foreskins,
Dt 10:16 C, then, the foreskin of your heart,
Lk 1:59 the eighth day they came to c the
Jn 7:22 and you c a man on the sabbath.

CIRCUMCISED → **CIRCUMCISE**
Ge 17:10 Every male among you shall be c.
Ac 15: 1 c according to the custom of Moses,
Gal 6:13 c do not themselves obey the law,
Col 2:11 also you were c with a spiritual
1Mc 1:60 the women who had their children c,

CIRCUMCISION → **CIRCUMCISE**
Ro 2:29 and real c is a matter of the heart—
Gal 5: 6 For in Christ Jesus neither c

CISTERN
Pr 5:15 Drink water from your own c,
Jer 38: 6 Jeremiah and threw him into the c

CITIES → **CITY**
Ge 19:25 and he overthrew those c,
Jos 20: 2 'Appoint the c of refuge,
Rev 16:19 and the c of the nations fell.

CITIZENSHIP
Php 3:20 But our c is in heaven,

CITY → **CITIES**
1Ch 11: 7 it was called the c of David.
Ps 127: 1 Unless the LORD guards the c,
Pr 31:31 her works praise her in the c gates.
La 1: 1 lonely sits the c that once was full
Da 9:24 for your people and your holy c:
Mt 5:14 A c built on a hill cannot be hid.
Heb 12:22 Zion and to the c of the living God,
Rev 21: 2 I saw the holy c, the new Jerusalem,

CLAP
Ps 47: 1 C your hands, all you peoples;
Isa 55:12 all the trees of the field shall c their

CLAY
Isa 45: 9 Does the c say to the one who
Jer 18: 6 Just like the c in the potter's hand,
Da 2:33 its feet partly of iron and partly of c.
Ro 9:21 Has the potter no right over the c,
2Co 4: 7 But we have this treasure in c jars,
2Ti 2:20 and silver but also of wood and c,

CLEAN → **CLEANSE, CLEANSING**
Ge 7: 2 seven pairs of all c animals,
Lev 10:10 and between the unclean and the c;
Ps 51: 7 with hyssop, and I shall be c;
Mk 7:19 (Thus he declared all foods c.)
Jn 13:10 you are c, though not all of you."
Ac 10:15 "What God has made c,
Heb 10:22 with our hearts sprinkled c from

CLEANSE → **CLEAN**
Ps 51: 2 and c me from my sin.
1Jn 1: 9 c us from all unrighteousness.
Sir 38:10 and c your heart from all sin.

CLEANSING → **CLEAN**
Eph 5:26 by c her with the washing of water
2Pe 1: 9 and is forgetful of the c of past sins.

CLEAR → **CLEARING**
Ps 19: 8 the commandment of the LORD is c,
Na 1: 3 LORD will by no means c the guilty.
1Ti 3: 9 of the faith with a c conscience.
Rev 21:18 the city is pure gold, c as glass.

CLEARING* → **CLEAR**
Ex 34: 7 yet by no means c the guilty,

CLEFT
Ex 33:22 I will put you in a c of the rock,
Dt 14: 6 the hoof and has the hoof c in two,

CLINGS
Ge 2:24 and his mother and c to his wife,
Ps 119:25 My soul c to the dust;
Heb 12: 1 weight and the sin that c so closely,

CLOAK
Ex 4: 6 "Put your hand inside your c."
22:26 you take your neighbor's c in pawn,
1Sa 24: 4 cut off a corner of Saul's c.
Mk 15:17 And they clothed him in a purple c;
Heb 1:12 like a c you will roll them up,

CLOTH → **SACKCLOTH**
Isa 64: 6 righteous deeds are like a filthy c.
Lk 2: 7 and wrapped him in bands of c,

CLOTHE → **CLOTHED, CLOTHES, CLOTHING**
Col 3:14 Above all, c yourselves with love,
1Pe 5: 5 you must c yourselves with humility

CLOTHED → **CLOTHE**
2Co 5: 2 longing to be c with our heavenly
Gal 3:27 have c yourselves with Christ.
Rev 12: 1 a woman c with the sun,

CLOTHES → **CLOTHE**
Zec 3: 3 Joshua was dressed with filthy c as
Lk 8:44 and touched the fringe of his c,

CLOTHING → **CLOTHE**
Ps 22:18 and for my c they cast lots.
Mt 25:36 I was naked and you gave me c,
Jn 19:24 and for my c they cast lots."

CLOUD → **CLOUDS**
Ex 13:21 went in front of them in a pillar of c
1Ki 8:10 a c filled the house of the LORD,
18:44 a little c no bigger than a person's
Eze 10: 4 the house was filled with the c,
Mk 9: 7 Then a c overshadowed them,
Lk 21:27 'the Son of Man coming in a c'
Heb 12: 1 by so great a c of witnesses,
Rev 14:14 on the c was one like the Son of Man,

CLOUDS → **CLOUD**
Ge 9:13 I have set my bow in the c,
Da 7:13 being coming with the c of heaven.
Mt 24:30 'the Son of Man coming on the c of
1Th 4:17 be caught up in the c together with
Rev 1: 7 He is coming with the c;
2Es 13: 3 this man flew with the c of heaven;

CLUSTER
Nu 13:23 from there a branch with a single c

COALS
Ps 11: 6 On the wicked he will rain c of fire
Pr 25:22 will heap c of fire on their heads,
Ro 12:20 will heap burning c on their heads."

CODE*
Ro 2:27 condemn you that have the written c
7: 6 slaves not under the old written c

COIN*
Mt 17:27 open its mouth, you will find a c;
22:19 Show me the c used for the tax."
Lk 15: 9 I have found the c that I had lost.'

COLD
Zec 14: 6 that day there shall not be either c
Mt 24:12 the love of many will grow c.
Rev 3:16 lukewarm, and neither c nor hot,

COLLECTOR → **COLLECTORS**
Mt 10: 3 Thomas and Matthew the tax c;
Lk 18:10 one a Pharisee and the other a tax c.
19: 2 he was a chief tax c and was rich.

COLLECTORS → **COLLECTOR**
Mt 5:46 Do not even the tax c do the same?
11:19 a friend of tax c and sinners!'

COLT
Ge 49:11 his donkey's c to the choice vine,
Zec 9: 9 and riding on a donkey, on a c,
Jn 12:15 coming, sitting on a donkey's c!"

COME → **COMES, COMING**
Ps 144: 5 your heavens, O LORD, and c down;
Isa 59:20 And he will c to Zion as Redeemer,
Zec 14: 5 Then the LORD my God will c,
Mt 6:10 Your kingdom c. Your will be done,
Lk 7:20 'Are you the one who is to c,
Jn 6:37 the Father gives me will c to me,
1Co 16:22 Our Lord, c!
Rev 1: 4 who is and who was and who is to c,
22:20 Amen. C, Lord Jesus!

COMES → **COME**
Ps 118:26 one who c in the name of the LORD.
Lk 19:38 "Blessed is the king who c in the
Jn 14: 6 No one c to the Father except through

COMFORT → **COMFORTED, COMFORTER, COMFORTERS, COMFORTS**
Ps 23: 4 your rod and your staff—they c me.
Isa 40: 1 C, O c my people, says your God.

COMFORTED → **COMFORT**
Ps 86:17 LORD, have helped me and c me.
Isa 49:13 For the LORD has c his people,
Jer 31:15 she refuses to be c for her children,
Mt 5: 4 those who mourn, for they will be c.

COMFORTER* → **COMFORT**
La 1:16 for a c is far from me,

COMFORTERS → **COMFORT**
Job 16: 2 miserable c are you all.
Ps 69:20 and for c, but I found none.

COMFORTS → **COMFORT**
Isa 66:13 As a mother c her child, so I will

COMING → **COME**
Mal 3: 2 But who can endure the day of his c,

Heb 10:37 is c will come and will not delay;
2Pe 3: 4 "Where is the promise of his c?
Rev 22:20 "Surely I am c soon."

COMMAND ➛ COMMANDED, COMMANDING, COMMANDMENT, COMMANDMENTS
Ex 34:11 Observe what I c you today.
Dt 1:26 rebelled against the c of the LORD
Jdg 2: 2 But you have not obeyed my c.

COMMANDED ➛ COMMAND
Ge 7: 5 Noah did all that the LORD had c
Ex 40:32 as the LORD had c Moses.
Jos 1:16 "All that you have c us we will do,
Mt 28:20 to obey everything that I have c you.
Jn 14:31 but I do as the Father has c me,

COMMANDING ➛ COMMAND
Dt 4:40 c you today for your own well-being
30:11 c you today is not too hard for you,

COMMANDMENT ➛ COMMAND
Dt 6: 1 Now this is the c—the statutes
Ps 19: 8 c of the LORD is clear,
Mt 22:38 This is the greatest and first c.
Ro 7:12 and the c is holy and just and good.
Gal 5:14 law is summed up in a single c,
1Jn 3:23 this is his c, that we should believe

COMMANDMENTS ➛ COMMAND
Ex 20: 6 those who love me and keep my c.
Dt 4:13 to observe, that is, the ten c;
Ps 119:66 for I believe in your c.
Pr 10: 8 The wise of heart will heed c,
Ecc 12:13 Fear God, and keep his c;
Mt 22:40 On these two c hang all the law and
Jn 14:15 If you love me, you will keep my c.
1Co 7:19 obeying the c of God is everything.
1Jn 5: 3 And his c are not burdensome,
Rev 14:12 those who keep the c of God and
Sir 1:26 If you desire wisdom, keep the c,
1Mc 2:19 and have chosen to obey his c,

COMMENDABLE* ➛ COMMENDATION
Php 4: 8 whatever is pleasing, whatever is c,

COMMENDATION* ➛ COMMENDABLE, COMMENDED
1Co 4: 5 each one will receive c from God.

COMMENDED ➛ COMMENDATION
2Co 6: 4 but as servants of God we have c
Heb 11:39 though they were c for their faith,

COMMIT ➛ COMMITS
Dt 5:18 Neither shall you c adultery.
2Ki 17:21 and made them c great sin.
Ps 31: 5 Into your hand I c my spirit;
Pr 16: 3 C your work to the LORD,
Mt 5:27 'You shall not c adultery.'

COMMITS ➛ COMMIT
Jn 8:34 who c sin is a slave to sin.
Jas 4:17 to do and fails to do it, c sin.

COMMON
Lev 10:10 between the holy and the c,
Eze 22:26 between the holy and the c,
Ac 2:44 and had all things in c;
1Co 10:13 has overtaken you that is not c
12: 7 of the Spirit for the c good.

COMMUNION*
2Co 13:13 the c of the Holy Spirit be with all

COMPANY
1Co 15:33 "Bad c ruins good morals."

COMPARE ➛ COMPARING
Pr 8:11 all that you may desire cannot c
Isa 40:18 or what likeness c with him?
Lk 7:31 I c the people of this generation,

COMPARING* ➛ COMPARE
Ro 8:18 of this present time are not worth c

COMPASSION ➛ COMPASSIONATE
Dt 32:36 will vindicate his people, have c
Ps 103:13 As a father has c for his children,
Isa 54: 8 with everlasting love I will have c
Jer 12:15 I will again have c on them,
Hos 11: 8 my c grows warm and tender.
Mt 14:14 had c for them and cured their sick.
Ro 9:15 I will have c on whom I have c."
Col 3:12 clothe yourselves with c, kindness,
Sir 18:13 the c of the Lord is for every living

COMPASSIONATE ➛ COMPASSION
Ex 22:27 I will listen, for I am c.
Jas 5:11 how the Lord is c and merciful.
Sir 2:11 For the Lord is c and merciful;

COMPETE ➛ COMPETING, COMPETITION
Jer 12: 5 how will you c with horses?
1Co 9:24 that in a race the runners all c,

COMPETING* ➛ COMPETE
Gal 5:26 c against one another, envying one
2Ti 2: 5 is crowned without c according to

COMPLAIN ➛ COMPLAINING, COMPLAINT
Nu 14:27 shall this wicked congregation c
Jer 2:29 Why do you c against me?
1Co 10:10 And do not c as some of them did,

COMPLAINING ➛ COMPLAIN
Ex 16: 7 has heard your c against the LORD.
1Pe 4: 9 hospitable to one another without c.

COMPLAINT ➛ COMPLAIN
Job 10: 1 I will give free utterance to my c;
Ps 142: 2 I pour out my c before him;
Hab 2: 1 he will answer concerning my c.
Col 3:13 if anyone has a c against another,

COMPLETE ➛ COMPLETED, COMPLETION
Ge 15:16 iniquity of the Amorites is not yet c.
Lev 23: 3 seventh day is a sabbath of c rest,
Jn 4:34 him who sent me and to c his work.
Rev 6:11 until the number would be c

COMPLETED ➛ COMPLETE
Jer 25:12 Then after seventy years are c,
Da 11:36 until the period of wrath is c,

COMPLETION ➛ COMPLETE
Php 1: 6 work among you will bring it to c
Jas 2:22 faith was brought to c by the works.

CONCEALED
Lk 9:45 its meaning was c from them,
Sir 11: 4 his works are c from humankind.

CONCEIT ➛ CONCEITED
Php 2: 3 nothing from selfish ambition or c,
1Ti 3: 6 he may be puffed up with c and fall
Sir 3:24 For their c has led many astray,

CONCEITED* ➛ CONCEIT
Gal 5:26 Let us not become c, competing
1Ti 6: 4 is c, understanding nothing,

CONCEIVE ➛ CONCEIVED
Mt 1:23 the virgin shall c and bear a son,
Lk 1:31 you will c in your womb and bear

CONCEIVED ➛ CONCEIVE
1Co 2: 9 ear heard, nor the human heart c,
Jas 1:15 desire has c, it gives birth to sin,

CONDEMN ➛ CONDEMNATION, CONDEMNED
Job 10: 2 I will say to God, Do not c me;
Ps 109:31 save them from those who would c
Lk 11:31 of this generation and c them,
Jn 3:17 not send the Son into the world to c
Ro 8:34 Who is to c?
1Jn 3:21 Beloved, if our hearts do not c us,

CONDEMNATION ➛ CONDEMN
Mk 12:40 They will receive the greater c."
Ro 5:18 one man's trespass led to c for all,
1Ti 3: 6 fall into the c of the devil.
Jas 5:12 so that you may not fall under c.

CONDEMNED ➛ CONDEMN
Mt 12:37 and by your words you will be c."
Lk 24:20 handed him over to be c to death
Jn 3:18 Those who believe in him are not c;
16:11 the ruler of this world has been c.
1Co 11:32 disciplined so that we may not be c

CONDUCT
Eze 22:31 returned their c upon their heads,
Ro 13: 3 For rulers are not a terror to good c,
1Pe 1:15 be holy yourselves in all your c;
Tob 4:14 and discipline yourself in all your c.
Sir 37:17 The mind is the root of all c;

CONFESS ➛ CONFESSES, CONFESSION
Lev 5: 5 you shall c the sin that you have
16:21 c over it all the iniquities of the
Ps 38:18 c my iniquity; I am sorry for my sin.
Php 2:11 should c that Jesus Christ is Lord,
1Jn 1: 9 If we c our sins, he who is faithful
Rev 3: 5 will c your name before my Father
Sir 4:26 Do not be ashamed to c your sins,

CONFESSES ➛ CONFESS
Ro 10:10 c with the mouth and so is saved.
1Jn 2:23 who c the Son has the Father also.

CONFESSION ➛ CONFESS
Da 9: 4 to the LORD my God and made c,
1Ti 6:12 for which you made the good c in
Heb 4:14 let us hold fast to our c.

CONFIDENCE
Ps 118: 8 in the LORD than to put c in mortals.
Php 3: 3 and have no c in the flesh—
Heb 10:19 we have c to enter the sanctuary

CONFIRM ➛ CONFIRMED
2Sa 7:25 c it forever; do as you have
Ps 119:38 C to your servant your promise,
Ro 15: 8 that he might c the promises given

CONFIRMED ➛ CONFIRM
Ps 105:10 which he c to Jacob as a statute,
2Pe 1:19 the prophetic message more fully c.

CONFORMED*
Ro 8:29 predestined to be c to the image of
12: 2 Do not be c to this world,
Php 3:21 may be c to the body of his glory,
1Pe 1:14 do not be c to the desires that you

CONFUSE ➛ CONFUSION
Ge 11: 7 go down, and c their language there,

CONFUSION ➛ CONFUSE
Ex 23:27 and will throw into c all the people
Dt 28:28 blindness, and c of mind;
Ps 44: 7 and have put to c those who hate us.

CONGREGATION
Lev 4:13 c of Israel errs unintentionally
Nu 1: 2 a census of the whole c of Israelites,
Ps 1: 5 nor sinners in the c of the righteous;
Heb 2:12 the midst of the c I will praise you."

CONQUER ➛ CONQUERED, CONQUERORS, CONQUERS
Rev 17:14 and the Lamb will c them,
21: 7 who c will inherit these things,

CONQUERED ➛ CONQUER
Jn 16:33 take courage; I have c the world!"
Heb 11:33 who through faith c kingdoms,
1Jn 2:13 because you have c the evil one.
Rev 15: 2 who had c the beast and its image

CONQUERORS ➛ CONQUER
Ro 8:37 all these things we are more than c

CONQUERS ➛ CONQUER
1Jn 5: 4 victory that c the world, our faith.
Rev 2: 7 To everyone who c, I will give

CONSCIENCE
Ro 2:15 their own c also bears witness;
1Co 8: 7 and their c, being weak, is defiled.
1Ti 1: 5 a good c, and sincere faith.
Heb 9:14 purify our c from dead works to
1Pe 3:21 as an appeal to God for a good c,

CONSECRATE ➛ CONSECRATED
Ex 13: 2 C to me all the firstborn;
40: 9 and c it and all its furniture,

CONSECRATED ➛ CONSECRATE
Lev 8:30 Thus he c Aaron and his vestments,
2Ch 7:16 now I have chosen and c this house
Ne 3: 1 They c it and set up its doors;
1Mc 4:48 of the temple, and c the courts.

CONSIDER ➛ CONSIDERED
Ex 33:13 C too that this nation is your people.
1Sa 12:24 for c what great things he has done
Ps 107:43 and c the steadfast love of the LORD.
Lk 12:27 C the lilies, how they grow:
Ro 6:11 must c yourselves dead to sin
Jas 1: 2 of any kind, c it nothing but joy,

CONSIDERED ➛ CONSIDER
Pr 17:28 fools who keep silent are c wise;
Heb 11:11 he c him faithful who had promised.

CONSOLATION
Lk 2:25 looking forward to the c of Israel,
2Co 1: 3 of mercies and the God of all c,

CONSPIRACY → CONSPIRE
Isa 8:12 not call c all that this people calls c,

CONSPIRE → CONSPIRACY, CONSPIRED
Ps 2: 1 Why do the nations c,
83: 5 They c with one accord;

CONSPIRED → CONSPIRE
Da 6: 6 So the presidents and satraps c
Mt 26: 4 and they c to arrest Jesus by stealth

CONSULT → CONSULTED
1Sa 28: 8 And he said, "C a spirit for me,
Isa 31: 1 Holy One of Israel or c the LORD!
40:14 did he c for his enlightenment,
Sir 8:17 Do not c with fools, for they cannot

CONSULTED → CONSULT
1Ch 10:13 had c a medium, seeking guidance,
Eze 20: 3 Lord GOD, I will not be c by you.

CONSUME → CONSUMED, CONSUMING
Ex 32:12 c them from the face of the earth'?
Nu 16:21 so that I may c them in a moment.
Mt 6:19 where moth and rust c and where
Jn 2:17 "Zeal for your house will c me."

CONSUMED → CONSUME
Ex 3: 2 bush was blazing, yet it was not c.
Ps 69: 9 zeal for your house that has c me;
90: 7 For we are c by your anger;
Zep 3: 8 all the earth shall be c.
Gal 5:15 that you are not c by one another.

CONSUMING → CONSUME
Heb 12:29 for indeed our God is a c fire.

CONTAIN
2Ch 2: 6 even highest heaven, cannot c him?
Jn 21:25 world itself could not c the books

CONTEMPT
Da 12: 2 some to shame and everlasting c.
Mk 9:12 sufferings and be treated with c?
Heb 6: 6 and are holding him up to c.

CONTEND
Isa 49:25 I will c with those who c with you,
Jude 1: 3 to c for the faith that was once for

CONTENT → CONTENTMENT
2Co 12:10 Therefore I am c with weaknesses,
Php 4:11 learned to be c with whatever I have
Heb 13: 5 and be c with what you have;
Sir 29:23 Be c with little or much,

CONTENTMENT* → CONTENT
1Ti 6: 6 gain in godliness combined with c;

CONTINUE
1Ch 17:27 that it may c forever before you.
Jn 8:31 "If you c in my word,
Ac 13:43 urged them to c in the grace of God.
1Th 3: 8 if you c to stand firm in the Lord.
Heb 8: 9 for they did not c in my covenant,

CONTRARY
Gal 1: 8 a gospel c to what we proclaimed to
1Ti 1:10 else is c to the sound teaching

CONTRIBUTE* → CONTRIBUTING
Ro 12:13 C to the needs of the saints;

CONTRIBUTING* → CONTRIBUTE
Dt 16:10 c a freewill offering in proportion to
Mk 12:43 all those who are c to the treasury.

CONTRITE
Ps 51:17 broken and c heart, O God, you wil
Isa 57:15 who are c and humble in spirit,

CONVERT
Mt 23:15 sea and land to make a single c,
1Ti 3: 6 He must not be a recent c,

CONVICT → CONVICTION
Dt 19:15 to c a person of any crime
Jude 1:15 to c everyone of all the deeds of

CONVICTION → CONVICT
Heb 11: 1 the c of things not seen.

CONVINCE → CONVINCED, CONVINCING
Ac 28:23 and trying to c them about Jesus
2Ti 4: 2 c, rebuke, and encourage,

CONVINCED → CONVINCE
Lk 16:31 neither will they be c even if
Ro 8:38 For I am c that neither death, nor
2Co 5:14 we are c that one has died for all;

CONVINCING* → CONVINCE
Ac 1: 3 to them by many c proofs,

CONVOCATIONS
Lev 23: 2 that you shall proclaim as holy c,

COPPER
Lev 26:19 like iron and your earth like c.
Mk 12:42 and put in two small c coins,

COPY
Dt 17:18 he shall have a c of this law written
Heb 9:24 a mere c of the true one,

CORDS
2Sa 22: 6 the c of Sheol entangled me,
Hos 11: 4 led them with c of human kindness,

CORNELIUS*
First Gentile Christian (Ac 10).

CORNER → CORNERSTONE
Pr 1:21 At the busiest c she cries out;
1Pe 2: 7 has become the very head of the c,"

CORNERSTONE → CORNER, STONE
Ps 118:22 rejected has become the chief c.
Isa 28:16 a tested stone, a precious c, a sure
Zec 10: 4 Out of them shall come the c,
Lk 20:17 builders rejected has become the c'?
Eph 2:20 with Christ Jesus himself as the c.
1Pe 2: 6 laying in Zion a stone, a c chosen

CORRECT → CORRECTING, CORRECTION
Ps 141: 5 let the faithful c me.
Jer 10:24 C me, O LORD, but in just measure;
Sir 42: 8 Do not be ashamed to c the stupid

CORRECTING* → CORRECT
2Ti 2:25 c opponents with gentleness.

CORRECTION → CORRECT
Jer 5: 3 but they refused to take c.
2Ti 3:16 c, and for training in righteousness,

CORRUPT → CORRUPTION
Ge 6:11 Now the earth was c in God's sight,
Ac 2:40 yourselves from this c generation."
Eph 4:22 your old self, c and deluded

CORRUPTION → CORRUPT
Ac 2:31 nor did his flesh experience c.'
2Pe 1: 4 you may escape from the c

COST
1Ch 21:24 burnt offerings that c me nothing."
Lk 14:28 not first sit down and estimate the c,

COUNCIL → COUNCILS
Jer 23:18 who has stood in the c of the LORD
Mt 26:59 the whole c were looking for false

COUNCILS* → COUNCIL
Mk 13: 9 for they will hand you over to c;

COUNSEL → COUNSELOR, COUNSELORS
Job 38: 2 that darkens c by words without
Ps 2: 2 and the rulers take c together,
33:11 The c of the LORD stands forever,
Isa 28:29 he is wonderful in c, and excellent

COUNSELOR → COUNSEL
Isa 9: 6 and he is named Wonderful C,
Ro 11:34 Or who has been his c?"
Sir 42:21 and he needs no one to be his c.

COUNSELORS → COUNSEL
Pr 11:14 in an abundance of c there is safety.
24: 6 in abundance of c there is victory.

COUNT → COUNTED, COUNTS
Ge 13:16 if one can c the dust of the earth,
1Ch 21: 1 incited David to c the people of
Ps 90:12 So teach us to c our days

COUNTED → COUNT
Ecc 1:15 and what is lacking cannot be c.
Mt 10:30 even the hairs of your head are all c.

COUNTENANCE
Nu 6:26 the LORD lift up his c upon you,
Ps 89:15 O LORD, in the light of your c;
Pr 15:13 A glad heart makes a cheerful c,

COUNTRY
Ge 12: 1 "Go from your c and your kindred
Jer 31:17 shall come back to their own c.
Jn 4:44 has no honor in the prophet's own c).
Heb 11:16 they desire a better c, that is,

COURAGE → COURAGEOUS
1Ch 22:13 Be strong and of good c.
Jn 16:33 But take c; I have conquered

COURAGEOUS → COURAGE
Jos 1: 6 Be strong and c; for you shall put
Da 10:19 Be strong and c!"
1Co 16:13 stand firm in your faith, be c,
1Mc 2:64 be c and grow strong in the law,

COURT → COURTS
Ex 27: 9 shall make the c of the tabernacle.
Pr 25: 8 do not hastily bring into c;
Da 7:10 c sat in judgment, and the books
Mt 5:25 while you are on the way to c
1Co 6: 6 believer goes to c against a believer

COURTS → COURT
Ps 84:10 in your c is better than a thousand
96: 8 an offering, and come into his c.

COVENANT → COVENANTS
Ge 6:18 But I will establish my c with you;
9: 9 I am establishing my c with you
15:18 the LORD made a c with Abram,
Ex 2:24 remembered his c with Abraham,
19: 5 you obey my voice and keep my c,
24: 7 Then he took the book of the c,
40: 3 put in it the ark of the c,
Lev 26:42 will I remember my c with Jacob;
Jdg 2: 1 'I will never break my c with you.
1Ki 8:23 keeping c and steadfast love
Ezr 10: 3 now let us make a c with our God
Job 31: 1 "I have made a c with my eyes;
Ps 105: 8 He is mindful of his c forever,
Isa 61: 8 I will make an everlasting c with
Jer 31:31 when I will make a new c with
Eze 16:60 establish with you an everlasting c.
Da 9:27 a strong c with many for one week,
Mal 3: 1 The messenger of the c in whom
Lk 22:20 is the new c in my blood.
1Co 11:25 "This cup is the new c in my blood.
2Co 3: 6 be ministers of a new c, not of letter
Heb 7:22 become the guarantee of a better c.
12:24 the mediator of a new c,
Rev 11:19 the ark of his c was seen within his
Jdt 9:13 planned cruel things against your c,
Sir 28: 7 remember the c of the Most High,
1Mc 1:15 and abandoned the holy c.
2Es 3:15 You made an everlasting c with

COVENANTS → COVENANT
Ro 9: 4 the adoption, the glory, the c,
Gal 4:24 an allegory: these women are two c.

COVER
Ex 33:22 I will c you with my hand
Ps 139:11 "Surely the darkness shall c me,
Isa 11: 9 as the waters c the sea.
Jas 5:20 and will c a multitude of sins.

COVET
Ex 20:17 shall not c your neighbor's house;
Ro 7: 7 had not said, "You shall not c."
Jas 4: 2 you c something and cannot obtain

CRAFTINESS → CRAFTY
Ro 1:29 of envy, murder, strife, deceit, c,
1Co 3:19 "He catches the wise in their c,"

CRAFTY → CRAFTINESS
Ge 3: 1 serpent was more c than any other
2Co 12:16 (you say) since I was c, I took you

CRAVING*
Nu 11: 4 rabble among them had a strong c;
Ps 78:30 But before they had satisfied their c,

CREATE → CREATED, CREATION, CREATOR
Ps 51:10 C in me a clean heart, O God,
Isa 65:17 to c new heavens and a new earth;
Eph 2:15 c in himself one new humanity

CREATED → CREATE
Ge 1: 1 In the beginning when God c the
1:27 So God c humankind in his image,
Dt 32: 6 Is not he your father, who c you,
Pr 8:22 The LORD c me at the beginning of

Mal 2:10 Has not one God c us?
1Co 11: 9 Neither was man c for the sake of
Eph 2:10 c in Christ Jesus for good works,
Col 1:16 all things have been c through him
1Ti 4: 4 For everything c by God is good,
Rev 4:11 for you c all things, and by your will
Jdt 13:18 who c the heavens and the earth,
Wis 2:23 for God c us for incorruption,
Sir 1: 4 Wisdom was c before all other

CREATION ➛ CREATE
Ge 2: 3 all the work that he had done in c.
Mk 10: 6 But from the beginning of c,
Ro 8:19 the c waits with eager longing for
2Co 5:17 anyone is in Christ, there is a new c:
Col 1:15 invisible God, the firstborn of all c;
2Pe 3: 4 they were from the beginning of c!"

CREATOR ➛ CREATE
Ecc 12: 1 Remember your c in the days of
Ro 1:25 served the creature rather than the C
Col 3:10 according to the image of its c.
1Pe 4:19 to a faithful C,

CREATURE ➛ CREATURES
Ge 2:19 the man called every living c,
Ro 1:25 worshiped and served the c rather

CREATURES ➛ CREATURE
Lev 11: 2 these are the c that you may eat.
Ps 104:24 the earth is full of your c.
Eze 1: 5 was something like four living c.
Rev 4: 6 are four living c, full of eyes
19: 4 elders and the four living c fell

CREDIT ➛ CREDITED
Lk 6:33 what c is that to you?
1Pe 2:20 for doing wrong, what c is that?

CREDITED ➛ CREDIT
Lev 7:18 nor shall it be c to the one who

CREEPING
Ge 1:24 cattle and c things and wild animals
Ps 148:10 c things and flying birds!

CRIED ➛ CRY
Ex 2:23 under their slavery, and c out.
Nu 20:16 when we c to the LORD, he heard
Jdg 3: 9 the Israelites c out to the LORD,
Ps 22: 5 To you they c, and were saved;
Mt 27:46 Jesus c with a loud voice,

CRIMINAL ➛ CRIMINALS
Jn 18:30 "If this man were not a c,
2Ti 2: 9 the point of being chained like a c.
1Pe 4:15 suffer as a murderer, a thief, a c,

CRIMINALS ➛ CRIMINAL
Lk 23:32 Two others also, who were c,

CRIMSON
Ex 25: 4 purple, and c yarns and fine linen,
Lev 14: 4 cedarwood and c yarn and hyssop
Jos 2:21 she tied the c cord in the window.

CROOKED
Dt 32: 5 a perverse and c generation.
Ps 18:26 the c you show yourself perverse.
Ecc 1:15 What is c cannot be made straight,
Lk 3: 5 and the c shall be made straight,
Php 2:15 in the midst of a c and perverse

CROSS ➛ CROSSROADS
Dt 31: 3 your God himself will c over before
Mk 15:30 and come down from the c!"
Lk 14:27 the c and follow me cannot be my
1Co 1:18 the c is foolishness to those who are
Gal 6:14 never boast of anything except the c
Php 2: 8 of death—even death on a c.
Col 1:20 peace through the blood of his c.
Heb 12: 2 was set before him endured the c,

CROSSROADS* ➛ CROSS, ROAD
Pr 8: 2 at the c she takes her stand;
Jer 6:16 Stand at the c, and look, and ask for

CROW*
Lk 22:34 the cock will not c this day,

CROWD ➛ CROWDS
Mk 8: 2 "I have compassion for the c,
14:43 a c with swords and clubs,

CROWDS ➛ CROWD
Mt 7:28 c were astounded at his teaching,

CROWN ➛ CROWNED, CROWNS
Lev 8: 9 the golden ornament, the holy c,
Pr 4: 9 will bestow on you a beautiful c."
La 5:16 The c has fallen from our head;
Jn 19: 2 soldiers wove a c of thorns and put
Php 4: 1 my joy and c, stand firm in the Lord
2Ti 4: 8 there is reserved for me the c
1Pe 5: 4 the c of glory that never fades away.
Rev 6: 2 Its rider had a bow; a c was given
14:14 with a golden c on his head,
Sir 1:18 fear of the Lord is the c of wisdom,

CROWNED ➛ CROWN
Ps 8: 5 and c them with glory and honor.
2Ti 2: 5 no one is c without competing
Heb 2: 9 now c with glory and honor

CROWNS ➛ CROWN
Rev 4:10 they cast their c before the throne,

CRUCIFIED ➛ CRUCIFY
Mt 27:22 All of them said, "Let him be c!"
Lk 24: 7 c, and on the third day rise again."
Ac 4:10 whom you c, whom God raised
Ro 6: 6 We know that our old self was c
1Co 1:23 but we proclaim Christ c,
Gal 2:19 I have been c with Christ;

CRUCIFY ➛ CRUCIFIED, CRUCIFYING
Lk 23:21 they kept shouting, "C, c him!"
Jn 19:15 asked them, "Shall I c your King?"

CRUCIFYING* ➛ CRUCIFY
Heb 6: 6 they are c again the Son of God

CRUSH ➛ CRUSHED
Job 6: 9 that it would please God to c me,
Isa 53:10 it was the will of the LORD to c him
Da 2:40 it shall c and shatter all these.
Mt 21:44 it will c anyone on whom it falls."
Ro 16:20 will shortly c Satan under your feet.

CRUSHED ➛ CRUSH
Ps 34:18 and saves the c in spirit.
2Co 4: 8 afflicted in every way, but not c;

CRY ➛ CRIED, CRYING
Ex 2:23 Out of the slavery their c for help
Ps 5: 2 Listen to the sound of my c,
130: 1 Out of the depths I c to you,
Hab 1: 2 how long shall I c for help,
Mk 15:37 Then Jesus gave a loud c

CRYING ➛ CRY
Ge 4:10 your brother's blood is c out to me
Mk 1: 3 the voice of one c out in the
Rev 21: 4 c and pain will be no more,

CRYSTAL
Eze 1:22 shining like c, spread out above
Rev 22: 1 river of the water of life, bright as c,

CUP
Ps 23: 5 my head with oil; my c overflows.
Jer 25:15 my hand this c of the wine of wrath,
Mt 10:42 gives even a c of cold water to one
26:39 if it is possible, let this c pass from
Mk 10:38 you able to drink the c that I drink,
Lk 22:17 he took a c, and after giving thanks
1Co 11:25 c is the new covenant in my blood.
Rev 14:10 unmixed into the c of his anger,

CURE ➛ CURED
Hos 5:13 But he is not able to c you or heal

CURED ➛ CURE
Mt 8:16 and c all who were sick.
Ac 5:16 and they were all c.

CURSE ➛ ACCURSED, CURSED, CURSES
Ge 8:21 "I will never again c the ground
12: 3 and the one who curses you I will c;
Nu 22:12 not c the people, for they are blessed
Dt 21:23 hung on a tree is under God's c.
23: 5 God turned the c into a blessing
Job 2: 9 C God, and die."
Ps 109:28 Let them c, but you will bless.
Mal 4: 6 come and strike the land with a c.
Mk 14:71 he began to c, and he swore an oath,
Lk 6:28 bless those who c you, pray
Ro 12:14 bless and do not c them.
Gal 3:13 Christ redeemed us from the c of the law by becoming a c for us—
Sir 4: 5 and give no one reason to c you;

CURSED ➛ CURSE
Ge 3:17 c is the ground because of you;
9:25 "C be Canaan; lowest of slaves
27:29 C be everyone who curses you,
Nu 23: 8 can I curse whom God has not c?
Job 3: 1 Job opened his mouth and c the day
Mk 11:21 fig tree that you c has withered."
Gal 3:10 "C is everyone who does not
Heb 6: 8 and on the verge of being c;
Rev 16: 9 but they c the name of God,

CURSES ➛ CURSE
Lev 24:15 who c God shall bear the sin.
2Ch 34:24 all the c that are written in the book

CURTAIN
Ex 26:31 You shall make a c of blue, purple,
2Ch 3:14 And Solomon made the c of blue
Lk 23:45 the c of the temple was torn in two.
Heb 10:20 that he opened for us through the c

CUSTOM ➛ CUSTOMS
Est 9:23 Jews adopted as a c
Jn 18:39 But you have a c that I release

CUSTOMS ➛ CUSTOM
2Ki 17: 8 the c of the nations whom the LORD
Ac 16:21 advocating c that are not lawful for
1Mc 1:42 all should give up their particular c.

CUT
Ge 9:11 never again shall all flesh be c off
Ps 37: 9 For the wicked shall be c off,
Isa 53: 8 c off from the land of the living,
Da 2:45 a stone was c from the mountain
Mt 3:10 does not bear good fruit is c down
Mk 9:43 hand causes you to stumble, c it off;
Ro 11:22 otherwise you also will be c off.

CYMBAL* ➛ CYMBALS
1Co 13: 1 I am a noisy gong or a clanging c.

CYMBALS ➛ CYMBAL
2Sa 6: 5 tambourines and castanets and c.
Ne 12:27 and with singing, with c,
Ps 150: 5 Praise him with clanging c;

CYRUS
Persian king who allowed exiles to return (2Ch 36:22-Ezr 1:8), to rebuild temple (Ezr 5:13-6:14), as appointed by the LORD (Isa 44:28-45:13).

D

DAGON
Jdg 16:23 a great sacrifice to their god D,
1Sa 5: 2 and brought it into the house of D

DAILY ➛ DAY
Mt 6:11 Give us this day our d bread.
Lk 9:23 take up their cross d and follow me.

DAMASCUS
Ac 9: 3 was going along and approaching D,

DAN
1. Son of Jacob by Bilhah (Ge 30:4-6; 35:25; 46:23). Tribe of blessed (Ge 49:16-17; Dt 33:22), numbered (Nu 1:39; 26:43), allotted land (Jos 19:40-48; Eze 48:1), failed to fully possess (Jdg 1:34-35), failed to support Deborah (Jdg 5:17), possessed Dan (Jdg 18).
2. Northernmost city in Israel (Ge 14:14; Jdg 18; 20:1).

DANCE ➛ DANCED
Ps 150: 4 Praise him with tambourine and d;
Ecc 3: 4 a time to mourn, and a time to d;
Lk 7:32 the flute for you, and you did not d;

DANCED ➛ DANCE
2Sa 6:14 David d before the LORD with all
Mt 14: 6 the daughter of Herodias d before

DANIEL ➛ =BELTESHAZZAR
1. Hebrew exile to Babylon, name changed to Belteshazzar (Da 1:6-7). Refused to eat unclean food (Da 1:8-21). Interpreted Nebuchadnezzar's dreams (Da 2; 4), writing on the wall (Da 5). Thrown into lion's den (Da 6). Visions of (Da 7-12). In deuterocanonical books of Bel and the Dragon, Susanna.
2. Son of David (1Ch 3:1).

DARE
Mt 22:46 d to ask him any more questions.
Ro 5: 7 someone might actually d to die.

DARIUS
1. King of Persia (Ezr 4:5), allowed rebuilding of temple (Ezr 5-6).
2. Mede who conquered Babylon (Da 5:31).

DARK → DARKEST, DARKNESS
Ps 139:12 even the darkness is not d to you;
Lk 12: 3 whatever you have said in the d will
2Pe 1:19 as to a lamp shining in a d place,

DARKEST* → DARK
Ps 23: 4 though I walk through the d valley,

DARKNESS → DARK
Ge 1: 2 the earth was a formless void and d
Ex 10:22 was dense d in all the land of Egypt
Dt 5:23 you heard the voice out of the d,
Isa 9: 2 walked in d have seen a great light;
Joel 2:31 The sun shall be turned to d,
Zep 1:15 a day of d and gloom,
Mt 4:16 who sat in d have seen a great light,
6:23 light in you is d, how great is the d!
Jn 1: 5 light shines in the d, and the d did not
Eph 5: 8 For once you were d, but now in
Col 1:13 from the power of d and transferred
1Jn 1: 5 God is light and in him there is no d

DATHAN*
Involved in Korah's rebellion against Moses and Aaron (Nu 16:1-27; 26:9; Dt 11:6; Ps 106:17; Sir 45:18; 4Mc 2:17).

DAUGHTER → DAUGHTERS
Ex 2: 5 d of Pharaoh came down to bathe at
Est 2: 7 Mordecai adopted her as his own d.
Ps 9:14 and, in the gates of d Zion,
La 2: 1 in his anger has humiliated d Zion!
Mic 7: 6 the d rises up against her mother,
Zec 9: 9 Rejoice greatly, O d Zion!
Mt 14: 6 the d of Herodias danced before the
Lk 12:53 against d and d against mother,
Jdt 10:12 replied, "I am a d of the Hebrews,

DAUGHTERS → DAUGHTER
Ge 6: 4 of God went in to the d of humans,
19:36 the d of Lot became pregnant by their
Nu 27: 1 the d of Zelophehad came forward.
Dt 12:31 even burn their sons and their d in
Job 42:15 no women so beautiful as Job's d;
Joel 2:28 sons and your d shall prophesy,
Ac 2:17 sons and your d shall prophesy,
2Co 6:18 and you shall be my sons and d,
1Pe 3: 6 You have become her d as long

DAVID
Son of Jesse (Ru 4:17-22; 1Ch 2:13-15), ancestor of Jesus (Mt 1:1-17; Lk 3:31). Wives and children (1Sa 18; 25:39-44; 2Sa 3:2-5; 5:13-16; 11:27; 1Ch 3:1-9).
Anointed king by Samuel (1Sa 16:1-13). Musician to Saul (1Sa 16:14-23; 18:10). Killed Goliath (1Sa 17). Relation with Jonathan (1Sa 18:1-4; 19-20; 23:16-18; 2Sa 1). Disfavor of Saul (1Sa 18:6-23:29). Spared Saul's life (1Sa 24; 26). Among Philistines (1Sa 21:10-14; 27-30). Lament for Saul and Jonathan (2Sa 1).
Anointed king of Judah (2Sa 2:1-11). Conflict with house of Saul (2Sa 2-4). Anointed king of Israel (2Sa 5:1-4; 1Ch 11:1-3). Conquered Jerusalem (2Sa 5:6-10; 1Ch 11;4-9). Brought ark to Jerusalem (2Sa 6; 1Ch 13; 15-16). The LORD promised eternal dynasty (2Sa 7; 1Ch 17; Ps 132). Showed kindness to Mephibosheth (2Sa 9). Adultery with Bathsheba, murder of Uriah (2Sa 11-12). Son Amnon raped daughter Tamar; killed by Absalom (2Sa 13). Absalom's revolt (2Sa 14-17); death (2Sa 18). Sheba's revolt (2Sa 20). Victories: Philistines (2Sa 5:17-25; 21:15-22; 1Ch 14:8-17; 20:4-8), Ammonites (2Sa 10; 1Ch 19), various (2Sa 8; 1Ch 18). Mighty men (2Sa 23:8-39; 1Ch 11-12). Punished for numbering army (2Sa 24; 1Ch 21). Appointed Solomon king (1Ki 1:28-2:9). Prepared for building of temple (1Ch 22-29). Last words (2Sa 23:1-7). Death (1Ki 2:10-12; 1Ch 29:28).
Psalmist (Mt 22:43-45), musician (Am 6:5), prophet (2Sa 23:2-7; Ac 1:16; 2:30).
Psalms of: 2 (Ac 4:25), 3-32, 34-41, 51-65, 68-70, 86, 95 (Heb 4:7), 101, 103, 108-110, 122, 124, 131, 133, 138-145. Deuterocanonical Ps 151 ascribed to.

DAWN → DAWNS
Isa 14:12 from heaven, O Day Star, son of D!
Hos 6: 3 his appearing is as sure as the d;

DAWNS → DAWN
Ps 97:11 Light d for the righteous,
2Pe 1:19 until the day d and the morning star

DAY → DAILY, DAYS
Ge 1: 5 God called the light D, and
8:22 d and night, shall not cease."
Ex 13:21 of them in a pillar of cloud by d,
20: 8 Remember the sabbath d, and keep
Jos 1: 8 you shall meditate on it d and night,
Ps 1: 2 his law they meditate d and night.
118:24 is the d that the LORD has made;
Isa 66: 8 Shall a land be born in one d?
Joel 1:15 For the d of the LORD is near,
Zec 14: 1 See, a d is coming for the LORD,
Mal 3: 2 who can endure the d of his coming,
Mt 25:13 you know neither the d nor the hour.
Lk 11: 3 Give us each d our daily bread.
24:46 to rise from the dead on the third d,
Jn 6:40 I will raise them up on the last d."
Ro 14: 5 Some judge one d to be better than
2Co 6: 2 see, now is the d of salvation!
1Th 5: 2 very well that the d of the Lord
2Pe 3: 8 the Lord one d is like a thousand years,
3:10 d of the Lord will come like a thief,
1Jn 4:17 have boldness on the d of judgment,
Rev 1:10 I was in the spirit on the Lord's d,
16:14 for battle on the great d of God

DAYS → DAY
Ge 1:14 and for seasons and for d and years,
7: 4 rain on the earth for forty d and forty
Ex 24:18 on the mountain for forty d and
1Ki 19: 8 that food forty d and forty nights
Ps 90:10 The d of our life are seventy years,
Mk 1:13 He was in the wilderness forty d,
Eph 5:16 of the time, because the d are evil.
2Ti 3: 1 in the last d distressing times will
Heb 1: 2 last d he has spoken to us by a Son,
1Mc 4:56 dedication of the altar for eight d,
2Es 14:42 They sat forty d; they wrote

DEACON* → DEACONS
Ro 16: 1 a d of the church at Cenchreae,

DEACONS → DEACON
1Ti 3: 8 D likewise must be serious, not

DEAD → DEATH, DIE, DIED, DYING
Nu 16:48 stood between the d and the living;
Dt 18:11 or who seeks oracles from the d.
Ps 115:17 The d do not praise the LORD,
Ecc 9: 4 a living dog is better than a d lion.
Mt 8:22 and let the d bury their own d."
Mk 12:27 God not of the d, but of the living;
Lk 24: 5 look for the living among the d?
Ro 6:11 must consider yourselves d to sin
Eph 2: 1 You were d through the trespasses
Col 1:18 the firstborn from the d,
1Pe 4: 5 ready to judge the living and the d.
Rev 1: 5 witness, the firstborn of the d,
20:12 And the d were judged according to

DEAF
Ex 4:11 Who makes them mute or d,
Isa 29:18 On that day the d shall hear the
Lk 7:22 the lepers are cleansed, the d hear,

DEATH → DEAD
Dt 30:19 that I have set before you life and d,
Ru 1:17 if even d parts me from you!"
Ps 22:15 you lay me in the dust of d.
Pr 18:21 D and life are in the power of the
SS 8: 6 for love is strong as d,
Isa 25: 7 he will swallow up d forever.
Hos 13:14 O D, where are your plagues?
Mt 16:28 standing here who will not taste d
Lk 1:79 in darkness and in the shadow of d,
Jn 5:24 but has passed from d to life.
Ro 4:25 handed over to d for our trespasses
6:23 For the wages of sin is d,
1Co 15:55 "Where, O d, is your victory?
2Co 2:16 to the one a fragrance from d to d,
Heb 2:14 through d he might destroy the one who has the power of d,
1Jn 3:14 that we have passed from d to life
Rev 1:18 I have the keys of D and of Hades.
20:14 D and Hades were thrown into the lake
21: 4 D will be no more;
Sir 15:17 Before each person are life and d,

DEBAUCHERY
Ro 13:13 not in d and licentiousness,
Eph 5:18 drunk with wine, for that is d;

DEBORAH
Prophetess; led victory over Canaanites (Jdg 4-5).

DEBT → DEBTS, INDEBTED
Mt 18:27 released him and forgave him the d.

DEBTS → DEBT
Dt 15: 1 you shall grant a remission of d.
Mt 6:12 And forgive us our d, as we

DECEIT → DECEITFUL, DECEIVE, DECEIVED, DECEIVERS
Dt 32: 4 A faithful God, without d,
Isa 53: 9 and there was no d in his mouth.
Ro 1:29 Full of envy, murder, strife, d,
1Pe 2:22 and no d was found in his mouth."

DECEITFUL → DECEIT
Ps 35:20 but they conceive d words
Zep 3:13 nor shall a d tongue be found
1Ti 4: 1 by paying attention to d spirits

DECEIVE → DECEIT
Eph 5: 6 Let no one d you with empty words,
1Jn 1: 8 that we have no sin, we d ourselves,
Rev 20: 8 to d the nations at the four corners

DECEIVED → DECEIT
Gal 6: 7 Do not be d; God is not mocked,
1Ti 2:14 was not d, but the woman was d

DECEIVERS* → DECEIT
Tit 1:10 rebellious people, idle talkers and d,
2Jn 1: 7 Many d have gone out into the

DECISION
Pr 16:33 but the d is the LORD's alone.
Joel 3:14 multitudes, in the valley of d!

DECLARE → DECLARED
Ps 50: 6 The heavens d his righteousness,
Col 4: 3 that we may d the mystery of Christ,

DECLARED → DECLARE
Isa 41:26 Who d it from the beginning,
Mk 7:19 (Thus he d all foods clean.)
Ro 1: 4 and was d to be Son of God

DECREASE
Jn 3:30 He must increase, but I must d."

DECREE → DECREED, DECREES
Ps 2: 7 I will tell of the d of the LORD:
Lk 2: 1 d went out from Emperor Augustus

DECREED → DECREE
Da 9:24 "Seventy weeks are d for your

DECREES → DECREE
Dt 6: 2 and keep all his d and his
Ps 19: 7 the d of the LORD are sure,
119: 2 Happy are those who keep his d,

DEDICATED → DEDICATION
1Ki 8:63 all the people of Israel d the house
Lk 21: 5 beautiful stones and gifts d to God,

DEDICATION → DEDICATED
2Ch 7: 9 the d of the altar seven days and
Ezr 6:16 the d of this house of God with joy.
1Mc 4:56 the d of the altar for eight days,

DEED → DEEDS
Ecc 12:14 will bring every d into judgment,
Jer 32:10 I signed the d, sealed it,
Mt 19:16 good d must I do to have eternal life
Col 3:17 And whatever you do, in word or d,

DEEDS → DEED
Dt 3:24 in heaven or on earth can perform d
Ps 9: 1 I will tell of all your wonderful d.
Jer 50:29 Repay her according to her d;
Ob 1:15 your d shall return on your own
Lk 23:41 getting what we deserve for our d,
Ro 2: 6 repay according to each one's d:
Rev 15: 3 "Great and amazing are your d,
19: 8 the righteous d of the saints.

DEEP → DEPTH, DEPTHS
Ge 1: 2 darkness covered the face of the **d**,
7:11 the fountains of the great **d** burst
Ro 8:26 with sighs too **d** for words.

DEFECT
1Pe 1:19 like that of a lamb without **d** or

DEFEND
Ps 72: 4 May he **d** the cause of the poor of
Pr 31: 9 **d** the rights of the poor and needy.
Jdt 5:21 for their Lord and God will **d** them,

DEFILE → DEFILED
Lev 11:43 you shall not **d** yourselves
Nu 35:34 You shall not **d** the land
Mk 7:15 things that come out are what **d**."

DEFILED → DEFILE
Ps 79: 1 they have **d** your holy temple;
1Mc 1:37 they even **d** the sanctuary.

DEFRAUD*
Lev 19:13 You shall not **d** your neighbor;
Mk 10:19 You shall not **d**;
1Co 6: 8 you yourselves wrong and **d**—

DEITY
Col 2: 9 whole fullness of **d** dwells bodily,

DELAY
Dt 7:10 He does not **d** but repays
Ps 70: 5 my deliverer; O LORD, do not **d**!
Heb 10:37 will come and will not **d**;

DELIGHT → DELIGHTS
1Sa 15:22 "Has the LORD as great **d** in burnt
Ps 1: 2 but their **d** is in the law of the LORD,
40: 8 I **d** to do your will, O my God;
Pr 8:30 I was daily his **d**, rejoicing before
Ro 7:22 For I **d** in the law of God in my
Sir 1:27 fidelity and humility are his **d**.

DELIGHTS → DELIGHT
Ps 5: 4 not a God who **d** in wickedness;
Isa 42: 1 chosen, in whom my soul **d**;

DELILAH*
Philistine who betrayed Samson (Jdg 16:4-22).

DELIVER → DELIVERANCE, DELIVERED, DELIVERER, DELIVERS
Ex 3: 8 to **d** them from the Egyptians,
Dt 32:39 and no one can **d** from my hand.
Da 3:17 able to **d** us from the furnace
6:20 able to **d** you from the lions?"
Mt 27:43 let God **d** him now,

DELIVERANCE → DELIVER
Ex 14:13 and see the **d** that the LORD will
Est 4:14 **d** will rise for the Jews from another
Ps 3: 8 **D** belongs to the LORD;
Php 1:19 this will turn out for my **d**.
Jdt 8:17 while we wait for his **d**,

DELIVERED → DELIVER
Isa 66: 8 Shall a nation be **d** in one moment?
Da 12: 1 at that time your people shall be **d**,

DELIVERER → DELIVER
Ps 140: 7 O LORD, my Lord, my strong **d**,
Ro 11:26 "Out of Zion will come the **D**;

DEMON → DEMONIACS, DEMONIC, DEMONS
Mt 11:18 and they say, 'He has a **d**';
17:18 Jesus rebuked the **d**, and it came out
Jn 8:48 you are a Samaritan and have a **d**?"
10:21 not the words of one who has a **d**.
Tob 3: 8 the wicked Asmodeus had killed
6: 8 of a man or woman afflicted by a **d**

DEMONIACS → DEMON
Mt 4:24 **d**, epileptics, and paralytics, and he
8:28 two **d** coming out of the tombs met

DEMONIC* → DEMON
Rev 16:14 These are **d** spirits, performing signs

DEMONS → DEMON
Dt 32:17 They sacrificed to **d**, not God,
Ps 106:37 and their daughters to the **d**;
Lk 11:18 that I cast out the **d** by Beelzebul.
1Co 10:20 not want you to be partners with **d**.
1Ti 4: 1 deceitful spirits and teachings of **d**,
Jas 2:19 Even the **d** believe—and shudder.
Rev 9:20 their hands or give up worshiping **d**
Bar 4: 7 by sacrificing to **d** and not

DEN
Jer 7:11 a **d** of robbers in your sight?
Da 6: 7 shall be thrown into a **d** of lions.
Mk 11:17 you have made it a **d** of robbers."

DENARIUS
Mk 12:15 Bring me a **d** and let me see it."

DENIED → DENY
Mt 26:70 But he **d** it before all of them,
1Ti 5: 8 has **d** the faith and is worse than an
Rev 3: 8 my word and have not **d** my name.

DENIES → DENY
Lk 12: 9 but whoever **d** me before others
1Jn 2:22 the liar but the one who **d** that Jesus

DENY → DENIED, DENIES
Lev 16:29 you shall **d** yourselves,
23:27 you shall **d** yourselves
Mt 16:24 let them **d** themselves and take up
2Ti 2:12 if we **d** him, he will also **d** us;
2Pe 2: 1 **d** the Master who bought them—

DEPART → DEPARTED
Ge 49:10 The scepter shall not **d** from Judah,
Jos 1: 8 law shall not **d** out of your mouth;
Ps 34:14 **D** from evil, and do good;
Php 1:23 my desire is to **d** and be with Christ,

DEPARTED → DEPART
1Sa 4:21 "The glory has **d** from Israel,"

DEPRAVED → DEPRAVITY
1Ti 6: 5 among those who are **d** in mind
2Pe 2:10 who indulge their flesh in **d** lust,

DEPRAVITY → DEPRAVED
Lev 20:14 that there may be no **d** among you.

DEPRIVE
Dt 24:17 not **d** a resident alien or an orphan
1Co 7: 5 not **d** one another except perhaps

DEPTH → DEEP
Mt 13: 5 since they had no **d** of soil.
Ro 11:33 O the **d** of the riches and wisdom
Eph 3:18 and length and height and **d**,

DEPTHS → DEEP
Ps 130: 1 Out of the **d** I cry to you, O LORD.
1Co 2:10 even the **d** of God.

DESCENDANTS
Ge 15:18 saying, "To your **d** I give this land,
Dt 4:37 he chose their **d** after them.
Isa 44: 3 I will pour my spirit upon your **d**,
Ro 9: 7 Abraham's children are his true **d**;
Gal 3: 7 who believe are the **d** of Abraham.

DESCENDED → DESCENDING
Ex 34: 5 LORD **d** in the cloud and stood
Jn 3:13 except the one who **d** from heaven,
Eph 4: 9 does it mean but that he had also **d**

DESCENDING → DESCENDED
Ge 28:12 angels of God were ascending and **d**
Mk 1:10 and the Spirit **d** like a dove
Jn 1:51 the angels of God ascending and **d**

DESERT → DESERTED
Ps 106:14 and put God to the test in the **d**;
Isa 40: 3 make straight in the **d** a highway
Mk 8: 4 with bread here in the **d**?"

DESERTED → DESERT
Mt 26:56 all the disciples **d** him and fled.

DESERVE
Pr 14:14 and the good, what their deeds **d**.
Lk 23:15 he has done nothing to **d** death.
Ac 26:31 man is doing nothing to **d** death
Rev 2:23 give to each of you as your works **d**.

DESIRE → DESIRED, DESIRES
Ge 3:16 your **d** shall be for your husband,
Ps 20: 4 May he grant you your heart's **d**,
Pr 3:15 nothing you **d** can compare with her
Hos 6: 6 I **d** steadfast love and not sacrifice,
Mt 9:13 learn what this means, 'I **d** mercy,
Jas 1:14 But one is tempted by one's own **d**,
1Jn 2:16 the **d** of the flesh, the **d** of the eyes,

DESIRED → DESIRE
Ps 19:10 More to be **d** are they than gold,
Lk 22:15 I have eagerly **d** to eat this Passover

DESIRES → DESIRE
Ps 37: 4 he will give you the **d** of your heart.
Gal 5:16 do not gratify the **d** of the flesh.
1Ti 2: 4 who **d** everyone to be saved
2Ti 4: 3 teachers to suit their own **d**,
Sir 18:30 Do not follow your base **d**,

DESOLATE → DESOLATES, DESOLATING
Ex 23:29 or the land would become **d** and
Da 11:31 the abomination that makes **d**.
Mt 23:38 See, your house is left to you, **d**.
1Mc 1:39 sanctuary became **d** like a desert;

DESOLATES → DESOLATE
Da 9:27 shall be an abomination that **d**,

DESOLATING → DESOLATE
Mk 13:14 the **d** sacrilege set up where it ought
1Mc 1:54 erected a **d** sacrilege on the altar

DESPAIR → DESPAIRED
2Co 4: 8 perplexed, but not driven to **d**;

DESPAIRED* → DESPAIR
2Co 1: 8 crushed that we **d** of life itself.

DESPISE → DESPISED
Job 5:17 not **d** the discipline of the Almighty.
Ps 51:17 contrite heart, O God, you will not **d**
Pr 1: 7 fools **d** wisdom and instruction.
Lk 16:13 devoted to the one and **d** the other.

DESPISED → DESPISE
Isa 53: 3 He was **d** and rejected by others;
1Co 1:28 God chose what is low and **d** in the

DESTINED
Eph 1: 5 He **d** us for adoption as his children
1Th 5: 9 For God has **d** us not for wrath but
1Pe 1:11 to the sufferings **d** for Christ

DESTROY → DESTROYED, DESTROYER, DESTRUCTION
Ge 6:13 to **d** them along with the earth.
Est 3: 6 Haman plotted to **d** all the Jews,
Mt 10:28 rather fear him who can **d** both soul
Jn 10:10 comes only to steal and kill and **d**.
Jas 4:12 who is able to save and to **d**.
1Jn 3: 8 to **d** the works of the devil.

DESTROYED → DESTROY
Da 6:26 His kingdom shall never be **d**,
1Co 15:26 The last enemy to be **d** is death.
2Co 5: 1 if the earthly tent we live in is **d**,

DESTROYER → DESTROY
Ex 12:23 not allow the **d** to enter your houses
1Co 10:10 and were destroyed by the **d**.

DESTRUCTION → DESTROY
Pr 16:18 Pride goes before **d**, and a haughty
Mt 7:13 and the road is easy that leads to **d**,
Ro 9:22 objects of wrath that are made for **d**;
2Pe 3:16 and unstable twist to their own **d**,

DEVIL
Mt 4: 1 wilderness to be tempted by the **d**.
Lk 8:12 **d** comes and takes away the word
Jn 8:44 You are from your father the **d**,
Eph 4:27 and do not make room for the **d**.
6:11 to stand against the wiles of the **d**.
1Ti 3: 6 fall into the condemnation of the **d**.
Heb 2:14 the power of death, that is, the **d**,
Jas 4: 7 Resist the **d**, and he will flee from
1Pe 5: 8 lion your adversary the **d** prowls
1Jn 3: 8 to destroy the works of the **d**.
Jude 1: 9 Michael contended with the **d**
Rev 12: 9 who is called the **D** and Satan,
20: 2 that ancient serpent, who is the **D**

DEVOTED
Ps 86: 2 Preserve my life, for I am **d** to you;
Mt 6:24 **d** to the one and despise the other.

DEVOUR → DEVOURING
Gal 5:15 you bite and **d** one another,
1Pe 5: 8 looking for someone to **d**.
Rev 12: 4 that he might **d** her child

DEVOURING → DEVOUR
Ex 24:17 glory of the LORD was like a **d** fire
Dt 9: 3 crosses over before you as a **d** fire;

DEW
Jdg 6:37 if there is d on the fleece alone,

DICTATED*
Jer 36:18 "He d all these words to me,
2Es 14:42 and by turns they wrote what was d,

DIE → DEAD
Ge 2:17 eat of it you shall d."
3: 4 to the woman, "You will not d;
Ex 11: 5 firstborn in the land of Egypt shall d
Ru 1:17 Where you d, I will d—
Job 2: 9 Curse God, and d."
Pr 10:21 but fools d for lack of sense.
Ecc 3: 2 a time to be born, and a time to d;
Isa 22:13 eat and drink, for tomorrow we d."
Jer 31:30 But all shall d for their own sins;
Mt 26:35 "Even though I must d with you,
Jn 11:26 and believes in me will never d.
Ro 14: 8 if we d, we d to the Lord;
1Co 15:32 eat and drink, for tomorrow we d."
Heb 9:27 it is appointed for mortals to d once,

DIED → DEAD
Ro 5: 6 right time Christ d for the ungodly.
1Co 15: 3 Christ d for our sins in accordance
Gal 2:19 the law I d to the law,

DIFFERENT
2Co 11: 4 or a d gospel from the one you
Gal 1: 6 and are turning to a d gospel—

DIFFICULT
Da 4: 9 and that no mystery is too d
Jn 6:60 teaching is d; who can accept it?"

DILIGENCE → DILIGENTLY
Ro 12: 8 the leader, in d;
Heb 6:11 each one of you to show the same d

DILIGENTLY → DILIGENCE
Dt 4: 6 You must observe them d,
Pr 8:17 and those who seek me d find me.

DINAH*
Only daughter of Jacob, by Leah (Ge 30:21; 46:15). Raped by Shechem; avenged by Simeon and Levi (Ge 34).

DIRECT → DIRECTS
Ps 119:128 I d my steps by all your precepts;
2Th 3: 5 the Lord d your hearts to the love

DIRECTS → DIRECT
Pr 16: 9 but the LORD d the steps.
Jas 3: 4 wherever the will of the pilot d.

DISAPPOINT*
Ro 5: 5 and hope does not d us,

DISASTER
Ex 32:12 your mind and do not bring d
Dt 28:20 The LORD will send upon you d,
Jer 18: 8 I will change my mind about the d
Eze 7: 5 Thus says the Lord GOD: D after d!

DISCERNED → DISCERNMENT
1Co 2:14 because they are spiritually d.

DISCERNING → DISCERNMENT
Dt 4: 6 nation is a wise and d people!"
Pr 1: 5 in learning, and the d acquire skill,
1Co 1:19 discernment of the d I will thwart."
Sir 1:19 knowledge and d comprehension,

DISCERNMENT → DISCERNED, DISCERNING
1Ki 4:29 Solomon very great wisdom, d,
1Co 12:10 prophecy, to another the d of spirits,

DISCIPLE → DISCIPLES
Mt 10:24 "A d is not above the teacher,
Lk 14:26 even life itself, cannot be my d.

DISCIPLES → DISCIPLE
Isa 8:16 seal the teaching among my d.
Mt 26:56 all the d deserted him and fled.
28:19 therefore and make d of all nations,
Lk 6:13 he called his d and chose twelve of
Jn 8:31 in my word, you are truly my d;
Ac 11:26 the d were first called "Christians."

DISCIPLINE → DISCIPLINED
Job 5:17 not despise the d of the Almighty.
Ps 94:12 Happy are those whom you d,
Pr 5:23 They die for lack of d,
Jer 7:28 their God, and did not accept d;
Eph 6: 4 in the d and instruction of the Lord.
Heb 12: 5 not regard lightly the d of the Lord,
1Pe 5: 8 D yourselves, keep alert.
Sir 1:27 fear of the Lord is wisdom and d,

DISCIPLINED → DISCIPLINE
1Co 11:32 d so that we may not be condemned
Wis 3: 5 Having been d a little, they will

DISEASE → DISEASES
Mt 4:23 of the kingdom and curing every d
9:35 curing every d and every sickness.

DISEASES → DISEASE
Ex 15:26 d that I brought upon the Egyptians;
Ps 103: 3 your iniquity, who heals all your d,
Isa 53: 4 our infirmities and carried our d;
Mt 8:17 took our infirmities and bore our d."

DISGRACE
Jos 5: 9 I have rolled away from you the d
Pr 11: 2 When pride comes, then comes d;
Mt 1:19 unwilling to expose her to public d,
1Pe 4:16 do not consider it a d,
1Mc 4:58 the d brought by the Gentiles was

DISGUISES
2Co 11:14 Satan d himself as an angel of light.

DISHONEST
Jer 22:17 and heart are only on your d gain,
Lk 16:10 is d in a very little is d also in much.
Sir 5: 8 Do not depend on d wealth,

DISHONOR
Jn 8:49 I honor my Father, and you d me.
Ac 5:41 considered worthy to suffer d for
1Co 15:43 It is sown in d, it is raised in glory.

DISMAYED
Dt 1:21 do not fear or be d."
Jos 1: 9 do not be frightened or d,
Jer 17:18 them be d, but do not let me be d;

DISOBEDIENT → DISOBEY
Ne 9:26 they were d and rebelled
Ro 10:21 I have held out my hands to a d
11:30 as you were once d to God but have
Tit 3: 3 ourselves were once foolish, d, led

DISOBEY → DISOBEDIENT
Lev 26:27 But if, despite this, you d me,
1Pe 2: 8 stumble because they d the word,
Sir 1:28 Do not d the fear of the Lord;

DISPERSION
Jn 7:35 Does he intend to go to the D

DISQUALIFIED* → DISQUALIFY
1Co 9:27 to others I myself should not be d.

DISQUALIFY* → DISQUALIFIED
Col 2:18 Do not let anyone d you,

DISSENSION → DISSENSIONS
1Co 12:25 there may be no d within the body,
1Ti 6: 4 From these come envy, d, slander,

DISSENSIONS → DISSENSION
Gal 5:20 strife, jealousy, anger, quarrels, d,
Tit 3: 9 stupid controversies, genealogies, d,

DISTINCTION → DISTINCTIONS
Ex 8:23 I will make a d between my people
Lev 11:47 make a d between the unclean and
Eze 22:26 have made no d between the holy
Ro 3:22 For there is no d,

DISTINCTIONS* → DISTINCTION
Jas 2: 4 you not made d among yourselves,

DISTRESS → DISTRESSED
Dt 4:30 In your d, when all these things
Jdg 2:15 and they were in great d.
2Sa 22: 7 In my d I called upon the LORD;
Ps 81: 7 In d you called, and I rescued you;
Jer 30: 7 it is a time of d for Jacob;
Lk 21:23 For there will be great d on the earth
Ro 8:35 Will hardship, or d, or persecution,
Sir 2:11 and saves in time of d.

DISTRESSED → DISTRESS
La 1:20 See, O LORD, how d I am;

DISTRIBUTED
Jos 13:32 the inheritances that Moses d
Ps 112: 9 They have d freely,
Ac 4:35 it was d to each as any had need.
Heb 2: 4 gifts of the Holy Spirit, d according

DIVIDE → DIVIDED
Ex 14:16 your hand over the sea and d it,
Ps 22:18 d my clothes among themselves,
Lk 23:34 And they cast lots to d his clothing.

DIVIDED → DIVIDE
Lev 11: 3 Any animal that has d hoofs
Ps 136:13 who d the Red Sea in two,
Lk 11:18 If Satan also is d against himself,

DIVINATION → DIVINE
Dt 18:10 who practices d, or is a soothsayer,
1Sa 15:23 For rebellion is no less a sin than d,
2Ki 17:17 they used d and augury;

DIVINE → DIVINATION
Ro 1:20 his eternal power and d nature,
2Pe 1: 4 become participants of the d nature.

DIVORCE → DIVORCED
Dt 24: 1 so he writes her a certificate of d,
Isa 50: 1 Where is your mother's bill of d
Jer 3: 8 sent her away with a decree of d;
Mal 2:16 For I hate d, says the LORD,
Mt 5:31 let him give her a certificate of d.'
19: 3 a man to d his wife for any cause?"
1Co 7:11 the husband should not d his wife.
Sir 7:26 Do not d her;

DIVORCED → DIVORCE
Lev 21: 7 neither shall they marry a woman d
Mt 5:32 whoever marries a d woman

DOCTOR*
Lk 4:23 this proverb, 'D, cure yourself!'

DOCTRINE → DOCTRINES
Eph 4:14 blown about by every wind of d,
1Ti 1: 3 not to teach any different d,
2Ti 4: 3 people will not put up with sound d,
Tit 1: 9 able both to preach with sound d

DOCTRINES → DOCTRINE
Mk 7: 7 teaching human precepts as d.'

DOEG*
Edomite; Saul's chief shepherd; murdered 85 priests at Nob (1Sa 21:7; 22:6-23; Ps 52).

DOERS → DOES, DONE
Jas 1:22 But be d of the word,

DOES → DOERS
Ps 135: 6 Whatever the LORD pleases he d,
Ecc 3:14 whatever God d endures forever;
Mk 3:35 d the will of God is my brother

DOG → DOGS
Jdg 7: 5 as a d laps, you shall put to one side
Pr 26:11 Like a d that returns to its vomit
2Pe 2:22 "The d turns back to its own vomit,"

DOGS → DOG
Mt 7: 6 "Do not give what is holy to d;
15:26 children's food and throw it to the d
Php 3: 2 Beware of the d, beware of the evil
Rev 22:15 Outside are the d and sorcerers

DOMINION
Ge 1:26 and let them have d over
Ps 22:28 For d belongs to the LORD,
Da 7:14 His d is an everlasting d
Ro 6:14 For sin will have no d over you,
Rev 1: 6 to him be glory and d forever

DONE → DOERS
Mt 6:10 Your will be d, on earth as it is in
26:42 unless I drink it, your will be d."
Rev 16:17 from the throne, saying, "It is d!"
21: 6 Then he said to me, "It is d!

DONKEY
Nu 22:30 But the d said to Balaam,
Jdg 15:15 he found a fresh jawbone of a d,
Zec 9: 9 humble and riding on a d,
Mt 21: 5 humble, and mounted on a d,

DOOM → DOOMED
Dt 32:35 their d comes swiftly.
Ps 81:15 and their d would last forever.

DOOMED → DOOM
Ps 102:20 to set free those who were d to die;
1Co 2: 6 of this age, who are d to perish.

DOOR → DOORPOSTS
Mt 7: 7 knock, and the d will be opened for
Lk 13:24 Strive to enter through the narrow d
Rev 3:20 I am standing at the d, knocking;

DOORPOSTS → DOOR
Ex 12: 7 the blood and put it on the two d

DORCAS*
Disciple; raised from the dead (Ac 9:36-43).

DOUBLE → DOUBLE-TONGUED
Ex 22: 7 then the thief, if caught, shall pay d.
Dt 21:17 giving him a d portion of all that he
1Sa 1: 5 but to Hannah he gave a d portion,
2Ki 2: 9 me inherit a d share of your spirit."
Rev 18: 6 and repay her d for her deeds;

DOUBLE-TONGUED → DOUBLE, TONGUE
1Ti 3: 8 likewise must be serious, not d,
Sir 5:14 Do not be called d and do not

DOUBT → DOUBTED, DOUBTING
Mt 14:31 of little faith, why did you d?"
Jn 20:27 Do not d but believe."

DOUBTED* → DOUBT
Mt 28:17 they worshiped him; but some d.

DOUBTING* → DOUBT
Jas 1: 6 But ask in faith, never d,

DOUGH
Ex 12:39 d that they had brought out of Egypt
Gal 5: 9 yeast leavens the whole batch of d.

DOVE
Ge 8: 8 Then he sent out the d from him,
Mk 1:10 Spirit descending like a d on him.

DRAGON
Isa 27: 1 and he will kill the d that
Rev 12: 3 a great red d, with seven heads and
20: 2 seized the d, that ancient serpent,
Bel 1:23 in that place there was a great d,

DRANK → DRINK
Ex 24:11 beheld God, and they ate and d.
Mk 14:23 and all of them d from it.
1Co 10: 4 and all d the same spiritual drink.

DRAW
Jn 12:32 will d all people to myself."
Jas 4: 8 D near to God, and he will d near

DREAM → DREAMED, DREAMER, DREAMS
1Ki 3: 5 LORD appeared to Solomon in a d
Da 7: 1 Daniel had a d and visions of his
Joel 2:28 your old men shall d dreams,
Mt 1:20 of the Lord appeared to him in a d
Ac 2:17 and your old men shall d dreams.

DREAMED → DREAM
Ge 28:12 he d that there was a ladder set up
41: 1 Pharaoh d that he was standing by
Da 2: 1 Nebuchadnezzar d such dreams
2Es 13: 1 After seven days I d a dream in the

DREAMER* → DREAM
Ge 37:19 to one another, "Here comes this d.

DREAMS → DREAM
Nu 12: 6 I speak to them in d.
1Sa 28: 6 LORD did not answer him, not by d,
Sir 34: 7 For d have deceived many,

DRIED → DRY
Ge 8:13 the waters were d up from the earth;
Jos 5: 1 had d up the waters of the Jordan
Isa 51:10 Was it not you who d up the sea,

DRINK → DRANK, DRUNK, DRUNKARD, DRUNKENNESS
Ge 19:33 So they made their father d wine
Ex 32: 6 the people sat down to eat and d,
Ecc 9: 7 and d your wine with a merry heart;
Isa 22:13 eat and d, for tomorrow we die."
Mt 20:22 to d the cup that I am about to d?"
Jn 18:11 not to d the cup that the Father has
Ro 14:17 kingdom of God is not food and d
1Co 12:13 we were all made to d of one Spirit.
Rev 14:10 also d the wine of God's wrath,

DRIVE → DROVE
Ex 23:30 Little by little I will d them out
Nu 33:52 you shall d out all the inhabitants of
Jos 13:13 Yet the Israelites did not d out the
Mk 11:15 to d out those who were selling
Jn 6:37 comes to me I will never d away;

DROSS
Ps 119:119 wicked of the earth you count as d;
Isa 1:25 I will smelt away your d as with lye
Eze 22:18 house of Israel has become d to me;

DROVE → DRIVE
Jos 24:18 the LORD d out before us all the
Mk 1:12 Spirit immediately d him out into

DRUNK → DRINK
Ge 9:21 some of the wine and became d,
1Sa 1:13 therefore Eli thought she was d.
SS 5: 1 drink, and be d with love.
Jn 2:10 after the guests have become d.
Ac 2:15 these are not d, as you suppose,
Eph 5:18 Do not get d with wine,
Jdt 13: 2 on his bed, for he was dead d.

DRUNKARD → DRINK
Pr 23:21 for the d and the glutton will come
Mt 11:19 they say, 'Look, a glutton and a d,
1Co 5:11 is an idolater, reviler, d, or robber.
1Ti 3: 3 not a d, not violent but gentle,

DRUNKENNESS → DRINK
Ecc 10:17 for strength, and not for d!
Gal 5:21 d, carousing, and things like these.
Tob 4:15 to excess or let d go with you

DRY → DRIED
Ge 1: 9 and let the d land appear."
Ex 14:16 may go into the sea on d ground.
Jos 3:17 were crossing over on d ground,
Jdg 6:37 and it is d on all the ground,
Eze 37: 4 d bones, hear the word of the LORD.

DUE
1Ch 16:29 Ascribe to the LORD the glory d his
Ps 28: 4 render them their d reward.
Mal 1: 6 a father, where is the honor d me?
Ro 13: 7 Pay to all what is d them—

DULL
Isa 6:10 Make the mind of this people d,
59: 1 nor his ear too d to hear.
Mt 13:15 For this people's heart has grown d,

DUST
Ge 2: 7 LORD God formed man from the d
3:14 and d you shall eat all the days of
13:16 offspring like the d of the earth;
1Sa 2: 8 He raises up the poor from the d;
Ps 103:14 he remembers that we are d.
Ecc 3:20 from the d, and all turn to d again.
Na 1: 3 and the clouds are the d of his feet.
Mt 10:14 shake off the d from your feet
1Co 15:47 man was from the earth, a man of d;

DWELL → DWELLING, DWELLS
Ex 25: 8 so that I may d among them.
1Ki 8:27 But will God indeed d on the earth?
Ps 23: 6 and I shall d in the house of
Eph 3:17 that Christ may d in your hearts
Col 1:19 fullness of God was pleased to d,
Rev 21: 3 He will d with them as their God;

DWELLING → DWELL
Lev 26:11 I will place my d in your midst,
Dt 12:11 will choose as a d for his name:
Ps 90: 1 our d place in all generations.
Jn 14: 2 my Father's house there are many d
2Co 5: 2 to be clothed with our heavenly d—
Eph 2:22 spiritually into a d place for God.

DWELLS → DWELL
Jn 14:10 but the Father who d in me
Ro 7:17 but sin that d within me.
1Co 3:16 and that God's Spirit d in you?
Col 2: 9 the whole fullness of deity d bodily,

DYING → DEAD
2Co 6: 9 as d, and see—we are alive;
Php 1:21 living is Christ and d is gain.

E

EAGLE → EAGLES, EAGLES'
Eze 1:10 the left side, and the face of an e;
17: 3 A great e, with great wings and long
Rev 4: 7 fourth living creature like a flying e.
2Es 11: 1 an e that had twelve feathered wings

EAGLES → EAGLE
Isa 40:31 shall mount up with wings like e,

EAGLES' → EAGLE
Ex 19: 4 and how I bore you on e wings
Da 7: 4 like a lion and had e wings.

EAR → EARS
Isa 64: 4 has heard, no e has perceived,
Lk 22:51 he touched his e and healed him.
1Co 2: 9 "What no eye has seen, nor e heard,
Rev 2: 7 Let anyone who has an e listen

EARLY
Dt 11:14 the e rain and the later rain,
Lk 24:22 were at the tomb e this morning,
Jas 5: 7 receives the e and the late rains.

EARS → EAR
Dt 29: 4 or eyes to see, or e to hear.
Isa 35: 5 and the e of the deaf unstopped;
Mt 11:15 Let anyone with e listen!
2Ti 4: 3 sound doctrine, but having itching e,

EARTH → EARTHLY, EARTHQUAKE, EARTHQUAKES
Ge 1: 1 God created the heavens and the e,
6:11 the e was corrupt in God's sight,
Ex 19: 5 Indeed, the whole e is mine,
Ps 47: 2 a great king over all the e.
Isa 6: 3 the whole e is full of his glory."
65:17 to create new heavens and a new e;
Jer 23:24 Do I not fill heaven and e?
Mt 5: 5 the meek, for they will inherit the e.
24:35 Heaven and e will pass away,
Lk 5:24 has authority on e to forgive sins"—
2Pe 3:13 wait for new heavens and a new e,
Rev 21: 1 I saw a new heaven and a new e;
Sir 40:11 All that is of e returns to e,

EARTHLY → EARTH
Jn 3:12 If I have told you about e things
2Co 5: 1 if the e tent we live in is destroyed,

EARTHQUAKE → EARTH, QUAKE
1Ki 19:11 but the LORD was not in the e;
Mt 28: 2 And suddenly there was a great e;
Ac 16:26 Suddenly there was an e,
Rev 6:12 I looked, and there came a great e;
2Es 3:19 four gates of fire and e and wind

EARTHQUAKES → EARTH, QUAKE
Mt 24: 7 be famines and e in various places:
2Es 9: 3 there shall appear in the world e,

EASIER → EASY
Mt 9: 5 is e, to say, 'Your sins are forgiven,'
Lk 16:17 it is e for heaven and earth to pass
18:25 e for a camel to go through the eye

EAST
Ge 2: 8 planted a garden in Eden, in the e;
Ps 103:12 as far as the e is from the west,
Mt 2: 1 wise men from the E came to

EASY → EASIER
Mt 7:13 road is e that leads to destruction,
11:30 For my yoke is e, and my burden is

EAT → ATE, EATING, EATS
Ge 2:16 freely e of every tree of the garden;
Ex 12:11 This is how you shall e it:
Lev 3:17 not e any fat or any blood.
11: 4 you shall not e the following:
Ecc 2:24 nothing better for mortals than to e
Mt 26:26 to the disciples, and said, "Take, e;
Ac 10:13 "Get up, Peter; kill and e."
1Co 10:31 whether you e or drink, or whatever
Rev 3:20 I will come in to you and e with you

EATING → EAT
Lk 7:34 the Son of Man has come e and
Ro 14: 2 Some believe in e anything,
1Co 8: 4 as to the e of food offered to idols,

EATS → EAT
Jn 6:51 e of this bread will live forever;
1Co 11:27 e the bread or drinks the cup of the

EDEN
Ge 2: 8 a garden in E, in the east;
Isa 51: 3 and will make her wilderness like E,
Eze 28:13 You were in E, the garden of God;

EDOM → =ESAU
Ge 25:30 (Therefore he was called E.)

Nu 20:18 But E said to him, "You shall not
Ob 1: 1 says the Lord GOD concerning E:
Mal 1: 4 If E says, "We are shattered but we

EFFORT
Gal 2:17 in our e to be justified in Christ,
Eph 4: 3 every e to maintain the unity of the
Heb 4:11 make every e to enter that rest,
2Pe 1: 5 make every e to support your faith

EGYPT
Ge 12:10 So Abram went down to E to reside
37:28 And they took Joseph to E.
47:27 Thus Israel settled in the land of E,
Ex 1: 8 Now a new king arose over E,
12:40 in E was four hundred thirty years.
Jos 15:47 to the Wadi of E, and the Great Sea
Ne 9:18 God who brought you up out of E,'
Ps 78:51 He struck all the firstborn in E,
Hos 11: 1 and out of E I called my son.
Mt 2:15 "Out of E I have called my son."
Rev 11: 8 prophetically called Sodom and E,

EHUD
Judge of Israel (Jdg 3:12-30).

ELAH
1. Son of Baasha; king of Israel (1Ki 16:6-14).
2. Valley in which David fought Goliath (1Sa 17:2, 19; 21:9).

ELDER ➛ ELDERS
Ge 25:23 the e shall serve the younger."
Ro 9:12 "The e shall serve the younger."
1Ti 5:19 any accusation against an e except
1Pe 5: 1 as an e myself and a witness of the

ELDERS ➛ ELDER
Ex 24: 1 and seventy of the e of Israel,
Jdg 2: 7 days of the e who outlived Joshua,
Isa 3:14 enters into judgment with the e
Mt 27:12 accused by the chief priests and e,
Mk 7: 3 thus observing the tradition of the e;
1Ti 5:17 the e who rule well be considered
Jas 5:14 e of the church and have them pray
1Pe 5: 5 must accept the authority of the e.
Rev 4: 4 on the thrones are twenty-four e,
Sus 1:61 they took action against the two e,

ELEAZAR
1. Third son of Aaron (Ex 6:23-25). Succeeded Aaron as high priest (Nu 20:26; Dt 10:6). Allotted land to tribes (Jos 14:1). Death (Jos 24:33).
2. Brother of Judas Maccabeus (1Mc 2:5; 6:43-46).

ELECT ➛ ELECTION
Mt 24:22 sake of the e those days will be cut
Mk 13:22 to lead astray, if possible, the e.
Wis 4:15 grace and mercy are with his e,
2Es 16:73 Then the tested quality of my e

ELECTION* ➛ ELECT
Ro 9:11 God's purpose of e might continue,
11:28 but as regards e they are beloved,
2Pe 1:10 eager to confirm your call and e,

ELEMENTS
Heb 5:12 the basic e of the oracles of God.
2Pe 3:10 and the e will be dissolved with fire,

ELEVEN
Mt 28:16 Now the e disciples went to Galilee,
Ac 1:26 and he was added to the e apostles.

ELI
1. High priest in youth of Samuel (1Sa 1-4). Blessed Hannah (1Sa 1:12-18); raised Samuel (1Sa 2:11-26). Prophesied against because of wicked sons (1Sa 2:27-36). Death of Eli and sons (1Sa 4:11-22).
2. "Eli, Eli, lema sabachthani?" (Mt 27:46).

ELIAKIM ➛ =JEHOIAKIM
1. Original name of Jehoiakim (2Ki 23:34; 2Ch 36:4).
2. Hezekiah's palace administrator (2Ki 18:17-37; 19:2; Isa 36:1-22; 37:2).

ELIEZER
1. Servant of Abraham (Ge 15:2).
2. Son of Moses (Ex 18:4; 1Ch 23:15-17).

ELIHU
A friend of Job (Job 32-37).

ELIJAH
Prophet; predicted famine in Israel (1Ki 17:1; Jas 5:17). Fed by ravens (1Ki 17:2-6). Raised Sidonian widow's son (1Ki 17:7-24). Defeated prophets of Baal at Carmel (1Ki 18:16-46). Ran from Jezebel (1Ki 19:1-9). Prophesied death of Azariah (2Ki 1). Succeeded by Elishah (1Ki 19:19-21; 2Ki 2:1-18). Taken to heaven in whirlwind (2Ki 2:11-12; Sir 48:1-12; 1Mc 2:58).
Return prophesied (Mal 4:5-6); equated with John the Baptist (Mt 17:9-13; Mk 9:9-13; Lk 1:17). Appeared with Moses in transfiguration of Jesus (Mt 17:1-8; Mk 9:1-8).

ELIMELECH
Ru 1: 3 But E, the husband of Naomi, died,

ELIPHAZ
A friend of Job (Job 4-5; 15; 22; 42:7, 9).

ELISHA
Prophet; successor of Elijah (1Ki 19:16-21; Sir 48:12-14); inherited his mantle (2Ki 2:1-18). Purified bad water (2Ki 2:19-22). Cursed young men (2Ki 2:23-25). Aided Israel's defeat of Moab (2Ki 3). Provided widow with oil (2Ki 4:1-7). Raised Shunammite woman's son (2Ki 4:8-37). Purified food (2Ki 4:38-41). Fed 100 men (2Ki 4:42-44). Healed Naaman's leprosy (2Ki 5). Made axhead float (2Ki 6:1-7). Captured Arameans (2Ki 6:8-23). Political adviser to Israel (2Ki 6:24-8:6; 9:1-3; 13:14-19), Aram (2Ki 8:7-15). Death (2Ki 13:20).

ELIZABETH*
Mother of John the Baptist (Lk 1:5-58).

ELKANAH
Husband of Hannah, father of Samuel (1Sa 1-2).

EMMANUEL* ➛ =IMMANUEL
Mt 1:23 and they shall name him E,"

EMMAUS
Lk 24:13 were going to a village called E,

EMPEROR
Mt 22:17 Is it lawful to pay taxes to the e, or
Jn 19:12 you are no friend of the e.

EMPTIED ➛ EMPTY
1Co 1:17 cross of Christ might not be e of its
Php 2: 7 but e himself, taking the form of

EMPTY ➛ EMPTIED, EMPTY-HANDED
Ru 1:21 the LORD has brought me back e;
Isa 55:11 it shall not return to me e,
Mt 6: 7 do not heap up e phrases
Eph 5: 6 no one deceive you with e words,

EMPTY-HANDED ➛ EMPTY, HAND
Ex 23:15 No one shall appear before me e.
Ru 3:17 not go back to your mother-in-law e

EN-GEDI
1Sa 23:29 and lived in the strongholds of E.

ENCOURAGE ➛ ENCOURAGEMENT
1Th 4:18 e one another with these words.
1Pe 5:12 written this short letter to e you

ENCOURAGEMENT ➛ ENCOURAGE
Ac 4:36 Barnabas (which means "son of e").
Ro 15: 5 God of steadfastness and e grant
Php 2: 1 If then there is any e in Christ,

END ➛ ENDS
Ge 6:13 determined to make an e of all flesh,
Pr 14:12 but its e is the way to death.
Ecc 12:12 making many books there is no e,
Mt 24:13 But the one who endures to the e
28:20 always, to the e of the age."
Jn 13: 1 he loved them to the e.
Ro 10: 4 For Christ is the e of the law so that
Rev 22:13 the beginning and the e."

ENDOR*
1Sa 28: 7 "There is a medium at E."

ENDS ➛ END
Ps 2: 8 the e of the earth your possession.
Isa 40:28 the Creator of the e of the earth.
Ro 10:18 their words to the e of the world."
1Co 13: 8 Love never e. But as for prophecies,

ENDURANCE ➛ ENDURE
Lk 8:15 and bear fruit with patient e.
Ro 5: 3 knowing that suffering produces e,
1Ti 6:11 godliness, faith, love, e,
Heb 10:36 For you need e, so that when you
Jas 1: 3 the testing of your faith produces e;
2Pe 1: 6 and self-control with e, and e with
Rev 1: 9 and the kingdom and the patient e,

ENDURE ➛ ENDURANCE, ENDURED, ENDURES
Ps 89:29 his throne as long as the heavens e.
Mal 3: 2 who can e the day of his coming,
1Co 10:13 out so that you may be able to e it.
2Ti 2:12 if we e, we will also reign with him;

ENDURED ➛ ENDURE
Heb 12: 2 that was set before him e the cross,

ENDURES ➛ ENDURE
1Ch 16:41 for his steadfast love e forever.
Mt 13:21 but e only for a while,
Jn 6:27 for the food that e for eternal life,
1Co 13: 7 hopes all things, e all things.
1Pe 1:25 but the word of the Lord e forever."
Sir 40:17 and almsgiving e forever.
Bar 4: 1 the law that e forever.

ENEMIES ➛ ENEMY
Ex 23:22 be an enemy to your e and a foe to
Est 9: 5 the Jews struck down all their e
Ps 110: 1 until I make your e your footstool."
Mt 5:44 But I say to you, Love your e and
Lk 20:43 until I make your e your footstool."
Ro 5:10 For if while we were e,
12:20 "if your e are hungry, feed them;
Jdt 8:35 to take vengeance on our e."
1Mc 4:36 said, "See, our e are crushed;

ENEMY ➛ ENEMIES, ENMITY
Mt 13:39 the e who sowed them is the devil;
1Co 15:26 The last e to be destroyed is death.
Jas 4: 4 of the world becomes an e of God.

ENGAGED
Mt 1:18 mother Mary had been e to Joseph,

ENJOY ➛ ENJOYMENT
Ecc 3:22 that all should e their work,
9: 9 E life with the wife whom you love,

ENJOYMENT ➛ ENJOY
Ecc 8:15 So I commend e, for there is nothing
1Ti 6:17 with everything for our e.

ENLIGHTENED ➛ LIGHT
Ro 10: 2 have a zeal for God, but it is not e.
Eph 1:18 with the eyes of your heart e,
Heb 6: 4 those who have once been e,

ENLIGHTENS* ➛ LIGHT
Jn 1: 9 The true light, which e everyone,

ENMITY ➛ ENEMY
Ge 3:15 put e between you and the woman,
Jas 4: 4 with the world is e with God?

ENOCH
Walked with God and taken by him (Ge 5:18-24; Heb 11:5; Sir 44:16). Prophet (Jude 14).

ENSLAVE ➛ SLAVE
1Co 9:27 but I punish my body and e it,
Gal 2: 4 so that they might e us—

ENSLAVED ➛ SLAVE
Ro 6: 6 and we might no longer be e to sin.
Gal 4: 9 want to be e to them again?

ENTER ➛ ENTRY
Ex 40:35 Moses was not able to e the tent
Nu 20:24 not e the land that I have given to
Ps 95:11 I swore, "They shall not e my rest."
Mt 5:20 will never e the kingdom of heaven.
7:13 "E through the narrow gate;
Mk 10:15 as a little child will never e it."
Jn 3: 5 no one can e the kingdom of God
Heb 3:11 'They will not e my rest.'"
10:19 have confidence to e the sanctuary
Rev 21:27 But nothing unclean will e it,

ENTHRONED ➛ THRONE
1Ch 13: 6 the LORD, who is e on the cherubim,
Ps 9: 7 But the LORD sits e forever,

ENTRUST ➛ TRUST
Jn 2:24 Jesus on his part would not e
1Pe 4:19 e themselves to a faithful Creator,

ENTRUSTED → TRUST
- Lk 12:48 the one to whom much has been e,
- 2Ti 1:12 guard until that day what I have e to
- Jude 1: 3 the faith that was once for all e to

ENVY
- Pr 23:17 Do not let your heart e sinners,
- Mk 7:22 deceit, licentiousness, e, slander,
- Ro 1:29 Full of e, murder, strife, deceit,
- Jas 3:16 For where there is e and selfish

EPHOD
- Ex 28: 6 They shall make the e of gold,
- Jdg 8:27 Gideon made an e of it and put it in

EPHRAIM

1. Second son of Joseph (Ge 41:52; 46:20). Blessed as firstborn by Jacob (Ge 48). Tribe of numbered (Nu 1:33; 26:37), blessed (Dt 33:17), allotted land (Jos 16:4-9; Eze 48:5), failed to fully possess (Jos 16:10; Jdg 1:29).

2. Term for the Northern Kingdom (Isa 7:17; Hos 5).

EQUAL → EQUALITY
- Isa 40:25 you compare me, or who is my e?
- 46: 5 will you liken me and make me e,
- Jn 5:18 thereby making himself e to God.

EQUALITY* → EQUAL
- Php 2: 6 not regard e with God as something

ERROR
- Lev 5:18 for the e that you committed
- Ro 1:27 the due penalty for their e.
- 1Jn 4: 6 the spirit of truth and the spirit of e.
- Wis 1:12 Do not invite death by the e of your

ESAU → =EDOM

Firstborn of Isaac, twin of Jacob (Ge 25:21-26). Also called Edom (Ge 25:30). Sold Jacob his birthright (Ge 25:29-34); lost blessing (Gen 27). Married Hittites (Ge 26:34), Ishmaelites (Ge 28:6-9). Reconciled to Jacob (Gen 33). Genealogy (Ge 36). The LORD chose Jacob over Esau (Mal 1:2-3), but gave Esau land (Dt 2:2-12). Descendants eventually obliterated (Ob 1-21; Jer 49:7-22).

ESCAPE
- Ge 7: 7 went into the ark to e the waters of
- Ps 68:20 the Lord, belongs e from death.
- Ro 2: 3 you will e the judgment of God?
- 1Th 5: 3 and there will be no e!
- Heb 12:25 how much less will we e if we reject
- 2Pe 1: 4 you may e from the corruption

ESTABLISH → ESTABLISHED
- Ge 6:18 But I will e my covenant with you;
- Dt 28: 9 LORD will e you as his holy people,
- Ps 89: 4 'I will e your descendants forever,
- Eze 16:60 e with you an everlasting covenant.
- Ro 10: 3 and seeking to e their own,
- Heb 8: 8 when I will e a new covenant with

ESTABLISHED → ESTABLISH
- 2Sa 7:16 your throne shall be e forever.
- Ps 89: 2 your steadfast love is e forever;
- 103:19 The LORD has e his throne in the
- Jer 10:12 who e the world by his wisdom,
- 2Pe 1:12 you know them already and are e in

ESTHER

Jewess, originally named Hadassah, who lived in Persia; cousin of Mordecai (Est 2:7). Chosen queen of Xerxes (Est 2:8-18). Persuaded by Mordecai to foil Haman's plan to exterminate the Jews (Est 3-4). Revealed Haman's plans to Xerxes, resulting in Haman's death (Est 7), the Jews' preservation (Est 8-9), Mordecai's exaltation (Est 8:15; 9:4; 10). Decreed celebration of Purim (Est 9:18-32). See Additions to Esther.

ETERNAL → ETERNITY
- Mt 25:46 but the righteous into e life."
- Mk 10:17 what must I do to inherit e life?"
- Jn 3:16 may not perish but may have e life.
- 10:28 I give them e life, and they will
- Ro 5:21 e life through Jesus Christ our Lord.
- 2Co 4:17 an e weight of glory beyond all
- Heb 5: 9 the source of e salvation for all who
- 1Jn 5:13 may know that you have e life.

ETERNITY → ETERNAL
- Isa 57:15 high and lofty one who inhabits e,
- 2Pe 3:18 glory both now and to the day of e.
- Wis 2:23 made us in the image of his own e,
- Sir 42:21 he is from all e one and the same.

ETHIOPIANS
- Jer 13:23 Can E change their skin

EUNUCH → EUNUCHS
- Jer 38: 7 Ebed-melech the Ethiopian, a e
- Ac 8:27 Now there was an Ethiopian e,

EUNUCHS → EUNUCH
- Isa 56: 4 To the e who keep my sabbaths,
- Mt 19:12 made themselves e for the sake of the

EUPHRATES
- Ge 2:14 And the fourth river is the E.
- 15:18 Egypt to the great river, the river E,
- Rev 16:12 poured his bowl on the great river E

EUTYCHUS*
- Ac 20: 9 A young man named E,

EVANGELIST* → EVANGELISTS
- Ac 21: 8 went into the house of Philip the e,
- 2Ti 4: 5 do the work of an e, carry out your

EVANGELISTS* → EVANGELIST
- Eph 4:11 some e, some pastors and teachers,

EVE*
- Ge 3:20 The man named his wife E,
- 4: 1 Now the man knew his wife E,
- 2Co 11: 3 afraid that as the serpent deceived E
- 1Ti 2:13 For Adam was formed first, then E;
- Tob 8: 6 his wife E as a helper and support.

EVENING
- Ge 1: 5 there was e and there was morning,
- Ecc 11: 6 at e do not let your hands be idle;
- Zec 14: 7 for at e time there shall be light.

EVERLASTING → LAST
- Ge 9:16 remember the e covenant between
- Ps 90: 2 from e to e you are God.
- Isa 9: 6 God, E Father, Prince of Peace.
- 40:28 The LORD is the e God,
- Jer 31: 3 I have loved you with an e love;
- Da 4: 3 His kingdom is an e kingdom,

EVERY → EVERYTHING
- Ge 7:23 He blotted out e living thing that
- Ex 11: 5 E firstborn in the land of Egypt
- Dt 8: 3 e word that comes from the mouth
- Ecc 12:14 God will bring e deed into judgment
- Isa 45:23 "To me e knee shall bow,
- Mt 12:25 "E kingdom divided against itself
- Ro 14:11 e knee shall bow to me, and e tongue
- Php 2:10 at the name of Jesus e knee should
- 2Ti 3:17 equipped for e good work.
- 1Jn 4: 1 Beloved, do not believe e spirit,
- Rev 21: 4 he will wipe e tear from their eyes.

EVERYTHING → EVERY
- Ge 1:31 God saw e that he had made,
- Ex 19: 8 "E that the LORD has spoken we will
- Ecc 3: 1 For e there is a season,
- 1Co 10:31 do e for the glory of God.
- 1Ti 4: 4 For e created by God is good,
- 2Pe 1: 3 divine power has given us e needed

EVIDENCE
- Dt 17: 6 On the e of two or three witnesses
- Mt 18:16 by the e of two or three witnesses.
- Sus 1:43 men have given false e against me.

EVIL → EVILDOER, EVILDOERS
- Ge 2: 9 tree of the knowledge of good and e.
- 3: 5 be like God, knowing good and e."
- 6: 5 their hearts was only e continually.
- Ex 32:22 the people, that they are bent on e.
- Dt 13: 5 So you shall purge the e from your
- Jdg 2:11 Then the Israelites did what was e
- Ps 23: 4 the darkest valley, I fear no e;
- Pr 8:13 The fear of the LORD is hatred of e.
- Ecc 12:14 secret thing, whether good or e.
- Isa 5:20 you who call e good and good e,
- Mt 6:13 but rescue us from the e one.
- 12:35 e person brings e things out of an e
- Lk 11:13 who are e, know how to give good
- Jn 17:15 to protect them from the e one.
- Ro 12:17 Do not repay anyone e for e,
- Eph 5:16 of the time, because the days are e.
- 1Ti 6:10 of money is a root of all kinds of e,
- 1Pe 2:16 use your freedom as a pretext for e.
- 1Jn 5:18 and the e one does not touch them.
- 2Jn 1:11 to welcome is to participate in the e
- 3Jn 1:11 do not imitate what is e but imitate
- Tob 12: 7 Do good and e will not overtake
- Sir 7: 1 Do no e, and e will never overtake

EVILDOER → EVIL
- Ps 52: 6 and will laugh at the e, saying,
- Mt 5:39 But I say to you, Do not resist an e.

EVILDOERS → EVIL
- 2Sa 7:10 and e shall afflict them no more,
- Ps 34:16 The face of the LORD is against e,
- Lk 13:27 go away from me, all you e!'
- 1Pe 2:12 though they malign you as e,

EXALT → EXALTED, EXALTS
- Ex 15: 2 my father's God, and I will e him.
- Pr 4: 8 Prize her highly, and she will e you;
- Isa 25: 1 I will e you, I will praise your name;
- Lk 14:11 who e themselves will be humbled,
- Jas 4:10 before the Lord, and he will e you.

EXALTED → EXALT
- Ps 57: 5 Be e, O God, above the heavens.
- 97: 9 you are e far above all gods.
- Isa 2:11 the LORD alone will be e in that day.
- Php 2: 9 highly e him and gave him the name

EXALTS → EXALT
- Pr 14:34 Righteousness e a nation,
- Sir 7:11 for there is One who humbles and e.

EXAMINE
- 1Co 11:28 E yourselves, and only then eat of
- 2Co 13: 5 E yourselves to see whether you
- Sir 18:20 Before judgment comes, e yourself;

EXAMPLE → EXAMPLES
- Jn 13:15 For I have set you an e,
- Php 3:17 according to the e you have in us.

EXAMPLES → EXAMPLE
- 1Co 10: 6 these things occurred as e for us,
- 1Pe 5: 3 but be e to the flock.

EXCEL → EXCELLENCE, EXCELLENT
- 1Co 14:12 strive to e in them for building up
- Sir 33:23 E in all that you do;

EXCELLENCE → EXCEL
- Php 4: 8 if there is any e and if there is

EXCELLENT → EXCEL
- Isa 28:29 in counsel, and e in wisdom.
- 1Co 12:31 I will show you a still more e way.
- Heb 1: 4 the name he has inherited is more e

EXCEPT
- 2Sa 22:32 And who is a rock, e our God?
- Mt 11:27 no one knows the Son e the Father,
- Lk 11:29 be given to it e the sign of Jonah.
- Jn 14: 6 No one comes to the Father e

EXCHANGED
- Ps 106:20 They e the glory of God for the
- Ro 1:23 e the glory of the immortal God

EXCUSE
- Jn 15:22 but now they have no e for their sin.
- Ro 1:20 So they are without e;

EXHORT
- Tit 2:15 e and reprove with all authority.
- Heb 3:13 But e one another every day,

EXILE → EXILES
- 2Ki 25:11 carried into e the rest of the people
- Ezr 6:21 of Israel who had returned from e,

EXILES → EXILE
- 1Pe 2:11 I urge you as aliens and e

EXIST → EXISTED, EXISTS
- 1Co 8: 6 are all things and for whom we e,
- Heb 2:10 and through whom all things e,

EXISTED → EXIST
- 2Pe 3: 5 the word of God heavens e long ago
- Rev 4:11 by your will they e and were created

EXISTS → EXIST
- Ps 119:89 The LORD e forever;
- Heb 11: 6 that he e and that he rewards those

EXPECTING
- Lk 6:35 and lend, e nothing in return.
- Php 3:20 that we are e a Savior,

EXPLAIN ➛ EXPLAINED, EXPLAINING
2Ch 9: 2 Solomon that he could not e to her.
Da 5:12 to interpret dreams, e riddles,

EXPLAINED ➛ EXPLAIN
Mk 4:34 but he e everything in private to his

EXPLAINING ➛ EXPLAIN
2Ti 2:15 rightly e the word of truth.

EXPOSE ➛ EXPOSED
Mt 1:19 unwilling to e her to public disgrace
Eph 5:11 of darkness, but instead e them.

EXPOSED ➛ EXPOSE
Jn 3:20 so that their deeds may not be e.
Eph 5:13 everything e by the light becomes
Heb 10:33 sometimes being publicly e to abuse

EYE ➛ EYES, EYEWITNESSES
Ex 21:24 e for e, tooth for tooth,
Ps 17: 8 Guard me as the apple of the e;
Mt 5:29 If your right e causes you to sin,
5:38 An e for an e and a tooth for a tooth.
7: 3 see the speck in your neighbor's e,
Mk 10:25 to go through the e of a needle
1Co 15:52 in the twinkling of an e, at the last
Rev 1: 7 the clouds; every e will see him,

EYES ➛ EYE
Ge 3: 7 Then the e of both were opened,
Dt 29: 4 or e to see, or ears to hear.
2Ch 16: 9 e of the LORD range throughout the
Ps 121: 1 I lift up my e to the hills—
Pr 3: 7 Do not be wise in your own e;
22:12 The e of the LORD keep watch over
Isa 11: 3 He shall not judge by what his e see,
Jer 9: 1 and my e a fountain of tears,
Eze 1:18 rims of all four were full of e all
Da 10: 6 lightning, his e like flaming torches,
Zec 4:10 "These seven are the e of the LORD,
Mt 9:30 And their e were opened.
13:15 that they might not look with their e,
Lk 24:31 their e were opened, and they
Eph 1:18 with the e of your heart enlightened,
1Pe 3:12 e of the Lord are on the righteous,
1Jn 2:16 of the flesh, the desire of the e,
Rev 1:14 his e were like a flame of fire,
4: 6 full of e in front and behind:
21: 4 he will wipe every tear from their e.

EYEWITNESSES* ➛ EYE, WITNESS
Lk 1: 2 who from the beginning were e
2Pe 1:16 but we had been e of his majesty.

EZEKIEL
Priest called to be prophet to the exiles (Eze 1-3; Sir 49:8). Symbolically acted out destruction of Jerusalem (Eze 4-5; 12; 24).

EZRA
Priest and teacher of the Law who led a return of exiles to Israel to reestablish temple and worship (Ezr 7-8). Corrected intermarriage of priests (Ezr 9-10; 1Es 8-9). Read Law at celebration of Feast of Tabernacles (Ne 8; 1Es 9:37-55). Participated in dedication of Jerusalem's walls (Ne 12).

F

FACE ➛ FACES
Ge 1: 2 darkness covered the f of the deep,
32:30 saying, "For I have seen God f to f,
Ex 3: 6 Moses hid his f, for he was afraid to
34:30 the skin of his f was shining,
Nu 6:25 LORD make his f to shine upon you,
12: 8 With him I speak f to f—
Ps 4: 6 Let the light of your f shine on us,
Isa 54: 8 wrath for a moment I hid my f
Eze 39:29 I will never again hide my f from
Lk 9:29 the appearance of his f changed,
2Co 3: 7 not gaze at Moses' f because of the glory
Rev 1:16 his f was like the sun shining with

FACES ➛ FACE
Eze 1: 6 Each had four f, and each
2Co 3:18 And all of us, with unveiled f,
Rev 9: 7 their f were like human f,

FACTIONS*
1Co 11:19 there have to be f among you,
Gal 5:20 anger, quarrels, dissensions, f,

FADE ➛ FADES
Ps 37: 2 for they will soon f like the grass,
Isa 64: 6 We all f like a leaf,

FADES ➛ FADE
Isa 40: 7 The grass withers, the flower f,
1Pe 5: 4 crown of glory that never f away.

FAIL ➛ FAILED
Dt 31: 6 he will not f you or forsake you."
Jos 1: 5 I will not f you or forsake you.
Eze 47:12 will not wither nor their fruit f,
Mk 8:18 Do you have eyes, and f to see?

FAILED ➛ FAIL
Jos 23:14 pass for you, not one of them has f.
1Ki 8:56 not one word has f of all his good
Ro 9: 6 not as though the word of God had f

FAINT
Ps 142: 3 When my spirit is f, you know my
Isa 40:31 they shall walk and not f.

FAITH ➛ FAITHFUL, FAITHFULNESS, FAITHLESS
Ps 146: 6 in them; who keeps f forever;
Isa 7: 9 If you do not stand firm in f,
Hab 2: 4 but the righteous live by their f.
Mt 17:20 have f the size of a mustard seed,
Mk 2: 5 When Jesus saw their f, he said to
Lk 7:50 the woman, "Your f has saved you;
18: 8 comes, will he find f on earth?"
Ac 3:16 and the f that is through Jesus
Ro 1:17 one who is righteous will live by f."
3:28 that a person is justified by f apart
1Co 13:13 And now f, hope, and love abide,
Gal 3:11 one who is righteous will live by f."
Eph 4: 5 one Lord, one f, one baptism,
Php 3: 9 righteousness from God based on f.
1Ti 6:11 pursue righteousness, godliness, f,
2Ti 4: 7 finished the race, I have kept the f.
Heb 11: 1 f is the assurance of things hoped
12: 2 the pioneer and perfecter of our f,
Jas 2:17 f by itself, if it has no works, is dead
2Pe 1: 1 a f as precious as ours through the
1Jn 5: 4 that conquers the world, our f.
Jude 1: 3 the f that was once for all entrusted
Rev 2:13 and you did not deny your f in me
Sir 40:12 but good f will last forever.

FAITHFUL ➛ FAITH
Dt 32: 4 A f God, without deceit, just and
Ps 4: 3 LORD has set apart the f for himself;
116:15 is the death of his f ones.
Mic 7: 2 The f have disappeared from the
Zec 8: 3 Jerusalem shall be called the f city,
Mt 24:45 "Who then is the f and wise slave,
1Co 10:13 God is f, and he will not let you be
1Th 5:24 The one who calls you is f,
Heb 10:23 for he who has promised is f.
1Pe 4:19 to a f Creator,
1Jn 1: 9 is f and just will forgive us our sins
Rev 1: 5 f witness, the firstborn of the dead,
19:11 Its rider is called F and True,
Wis 3: 9 the f will abide with him in love,
Sir 4:16 If they remain f, they will inherit

FAITHFULNESS ➛ FAITH
Ex 34: 6 abounding in steadfast love and f,
Jos 24:14 and serve him in sincerity and in f;
Ps 26: 3 and I walk in f to you.
36: 5 to the heavens, your f to the clouds.
Pr 16: 6 By loyalty and f iniquity is atoned
Isa 11: 5 and f the belt around his loins.
Jer 31: 3 I have continued my f to you.
La 3:23 new every morning; great is your f.
Hos 4: 1 There is no f or loyalty, and no
Ro 3: 3 faithlessness nullify the f of God?
Gal 5:22 patience, kindness, generosity, f,

FAITHLESS ➛ FAITH
Jer 3:14 Return, O f children, says the LORD,
Mt 17:17 "You f and perverse generation,
2Ti 2:13 if we are f, he remains faithful—
Rev 21: 8 But as for the cowardly, the f,

FALL ➛ FALLEN, FALLING, FELL
Ps 91: 7 A thousand may f at your side,
Pr 16:18 and a haughty spirit before a f.
Lk 10:18 "I watched Satan f from heaven like
Ro 9:33 a rock that will make them f,
1Co 10:12 watch out that you do not f.
Heb 10:31 a fearful thing to f into the hands of
Sir 28:23 Those who forsake the Lord will f

FALLEN ➛ FALL
2Sa 1:19 How the mighty have f!
Isa 14:12 f from heaven, O Day Star,
21: 9 he responded, "F, f is Babylon;
Rev 9: 1 I saw a star that had f from heaven
18: 2 "F, f is Babylon the great!

FALLING ➛ FALL
Lk 22:44 [[like great drops of blood f down]]
Jude 1:24 him who is able to keep you from f,

FALSE
Dt 5:20 Neither shall you bear f witness
2Ki 17:15 went after f idols and became f;
Mt 7:15 "Beware of f prophets, who come to
Mk 13:22 F messiahs and f prophets will
Heb 6:18 impossible that God would prove f,
2Pe 2: 1 there will be f teachers among you,
Rev 16:13 and from the mouth of the f prophet.
20:10 where the beast and the f prophet
LtJ 6: 8 but they are f and cannot speak.
Sus 1:61 convicted them of bearing f witness;

FAMILIES ➛ FAMILY
Ac 3:25 all the f of the earth shall be blessed.
Tit 1:11 are upsetting whole f by teaching

FAMILY ➛ FAMILIES
Pr 6:19 and one who sows discord in a f.
Gal 6:10 especially for those of the f of faith.
Eph 3:15 from whom every f in heaven and
1Pe 2:17 Love the f of believers.

FAMINE
Ge 12:10 Now there was a f in the land.
41:27 They are seven years of f.
Ru 1: 1 there was a f in the land,
Ps 37:19 in the days of f they have abundance
Am 8:11 not a f of bread, or a thirst for water,
Ac 11:28 there would be a severe f over all
Ro 8:35 or distress, or persecution, or f,

FAR
Nu 16: 3 "You have gone too f!
1Sa 7:12 "Thus f the LORD has helped us."
Isa 57:19 Peace, peace, to the f and the near,
Jer 23:23 and not a God f off?
Mk 7: 6 but their hearts are f from me;
12:34 are not f from the kingdom of God."

FAST ➛ FASTED, FASTING
Isa 58: 5 Is such the f that I choose,
Mt 6:16 "And whenever you f,
Lk 18:12 I f twice a week; I give

FASTED ➛ FAST
Mt 4: 2 He f forty days and forty nights,

FASTING ➛ FAST
Mt 6:16 so as to show others that they are f.

FATHER ➛ FATHER'S
Ge 2:24 a man leaves his f and his mother
Ex 20:12 Honor your f and your mother,
21:15 Whoever strikes f or mother shall
2Sa 7:14 I will be a f to him, and he shall be
Ps 89:26 cry to me, 'You are my F, my God,
Pr 28:24 Anyone who robs f or mother and
Isa 8: 4 child knows how to call "My f" or
9: 6 Mighty God, Everlasting F, Prince
Jer 3:19 I thought you would call me, My F,
Mal 1: 6 If then I am a f, where is the honor
Mt 6: 9 Our F in heaven, hallowed be your
28:19 the name of the F and of the Son and
Lk 18:20 Honor your f and mother.'"
Jn 5:18 but was also calling God his own F,
8:44 You are from your f the devil,
14: 6 comes to the F except through me.
Ro 8:15 When we cry, "Abba! F!"
Gal 4: 6 into our hearts, crying, "Abba! F!"
Eph 6: 2 "Honor your f and mother"—
Heb 1: 5 be his F, and he will be my Son"?
12: 9 to be subject to the F of spirits
Jas 1:17 coming down from the F of lights,
Rev 3: 5 confess your name before my F
Wis 2:16 and boasts that God is his f.
Sir 3: 3 who honor their f atone for sins,

FATHER'S ➛ FATHER
Lk 2:49 that I must be in my F house?"
Jn 1:14 the glory as of a f only son,
2:16 making my F house a marketplace!"
10:29 can snatch it out of the F hand.
14: 2 F house there are many dwelling

FAULT
Ro 9:19 "Why then does he still find f?
Sir 11: 7 Do not find f before you investigate;

FAVOR ➛ FAVORITISM
Ge 6: 8 Noah found f in the sight of the
Ex 33:12 you have also found f in my sight.'
Ps 30: 5 his f is for a lifetime.
Isa 49: 8 In a time of f I have answered you,
Zec 11: 7 I named F, the other I named Unity,
Lk 4:19 proclaim the year of the Lord's f."

FAVORITISM* ➛ FAVOR
Jas 2: 1 with your acts of f really believe

FEAR ➛ AFRAID, FEARED, FEARFULLY, FEARS
Ge 22:12 for now I know that you f God,
Dt 6:13 The LORD your God you shall f;
Ps 19: 9 the f of the LORD is pure, enduring
23: 4 the darkest valley, I f no evil;
27: 1 and my salvation; whom shall I f?
Pr 1: 7 f of the LORD is the beginning of
Ecc 12:13 F God, and keep his commandments
Mt 10:28 rather f him who can destroy both
Mk 5:36 "Do not f, only believe."
Php 2:12 work out your own salvation with f
1Pe 3:14 Do not f what they f,
1Jn 4:18 but perfect love casts out f;
Rev 14: 7 "F God and give him glory,
Sir 1:11 The f of the Lord is glory

FEARED ➛ FEAR
Ex 14:31 the people f the LORD and believed
Job 1: 1 f God and turned away from evil.
Hag 1:12 and the people f the LORD.

FEARFULLY* ➛ FEAR
Ps 139:14 I am f and wonderfully made.

FEARS ➛ FEAR
Ps 34: 4 and delivered me from all my f.
Pr 31:30 a woman who f the LORD is to be
Jdt 16:16 whoever f the Lord is great forever.
Sir 15: 1 Whoever f the Lord will do this,

FED ➛ FEED
Dt 8:16 f you in the wilderness with manna
Ps 80: 5 have f them with the bread of tears,
Eze 34: 8 but the shepherds have f themselves,

FEED ➛ FED
Isa 40:11 He will f his flock like a shepherd;
65:25 wolf and the lamb shall f together,
Jn 21:15 Jesus said to him, "F my lambs."
Ro 12:20 "if your enemies are hungry, f them;

FEET ➛ FOOT
Ps 8: 6 you have put all things under their f,
119:105 Your word is a lamp to my f
Da 2:33 its f partly of iron and partly of clay.
Mt 22:44 I put your enemies under your f"?
Lk 24:39 Look at my hands and my f;
Jn 13: 5 and began to wash the disciples' f
Ro 16:20 shortly crush Satan under your f.
1Co 15:25 put all his enemies under his f.
Heb 1:13 enemies a footstool for your f"?
Rev 1:15 his f were like burnished bronze,

FELLOWSHIP
Ac 2:42 to the apostles' teaching and f,
2Co 6:14 Or what f is there between light and
1Jn 1: 3 and truly our f is with the Father and

FEMALE
Ge 1:27 male and f he created them.
Mk 10: 6 'God made them male and f.'
Gal 3:28 there is no longer male and f;

FESTIVAL ➛ FESTIVALS
Ex 23:14 in the year you shall hold a f for me.
1Co 5: 8 Therefore, let us celebrate the f,

FESTIVALS ➛ FESTIVAL
Lev 23: 2 are the appointed f of the LORD
Ne 10:33 the new moons, the appointed f,
Col 2:16 of food and drink or of observing f,

FEVER
Dt 28:22 will afflict you with consumption, f,
Mk 1:30 mother-in-law was in bed with a f,

FEW
Ps 105:12 When they were f in number,
Ecc 5: 2 therefore let your words be f.
Mt 22:14 many are called, but f are chosen."
Lk 13:23 "Lord, will only a f be saved?"

FIELD ➛ FIELDS
Pr 31:16 She considers a f and buys it;
Mt 6:28 Consider the lilies of the f, how
13:44 is like treasure hidden in a f,
24:40 Then two will be in the f;
1Co 3: 9 you are God's f, God's building.

FIELDS ➛ FIELD
Lk 2: 8 there were shepherds living in the f,
Jn 4:35 see how the f are ripe for harvesting.

FIG ➛ FIGS
Ge 3: 7 and they sewed f leaves together
Hab 3:17 Though the f tree does not blossom,
Mt 24:32 "From the f tree learn its lesson:
Lk 13: 6 "A man had a f tree planted in his

FIGHT ➛ FOUGHT
Ex 14:14 The LORD will f for you,
Ps 35: 1 f against those who f against me!
1Ti 1:18 you may f the good f,
2Ti 4: 7 I have fought the good f,

FIGS ➛ FIG
Jer 24: 1 LORD showed me two baskets of f
Lk 6:44 F are not gathered from thorns,

FILL ➛ FILLED, FULL, FULLNESS
Ge 1:28 and f the earth and subdue it;
9: 1 fruitful and multiply, and f the earth.
Ps 72:19 may his glory f the whole earth.
Jer 23:24 Do I not f heaven and earth?
Eph 4:10 so that he might f all things.)

FILLED ➛ FILL
Ex 1: 7 so that the land was f with them.
40:34 glory of the LORD f the tabernacle.
1Ki 8:11 glory of the LORD f the house of the
Eze 43: 5 the glory of the LORD f the temple.
Lk 1:15 he will be f with the Holy Spirit.
Ac 2: 4 were f with the Holy Spirit and
Eph 5:18 but be f with the Spirit,

FILTHY
Isa 64: 6 righteous deeds are like a f cloth.
Zec 3: 3 Joshua was dressed with f clothes
Rev 22:11 and the f still be f,

FIND ➛ FINDS, FOUND
Nu 32:23 and be sure your sin will f you out.
Dt 4:29 you will f him if you search after
Jer 29:13 you search for me, you will f me;
Mt 11:29 and you will f rest for your souls.
16:25 lose their life for my sake will f it.
Lk 11: 9 search, and you will f;

FINDS ➛ FIND
Pr 8:35 For whoever f me f life and obtains
18:22 He who f a wife f a good thing,

FINGER
Ex 8:19 "This is the f of God!"
Dt 9:10 tablets written with the f of God;
Mt 23: 4 themselves are unwilling to lift a f
Lk 11:20 if it is by the f of God that I cast out

FINISHED
Ge 2: 2 on the seventh day God f the work
Ex 40:33 So Moses f the work.
Jn 19:30 received the wine, he said, "It is f."
Sir 38: 8 God's works will never be f;

FIRE ➛ FIERY
Ex 3: 2 appeared to him in a flame of f out
13:21 and in a pillar of f by night, to give
Lev 9:24 F came out from the LORD and
Nu 11: 1 the f of the LORD burned against
Dt 4:24 the LORD your God is a devouring f,
1Ki 19:12 but the LORD was not in the f;
2Ki 2:11 a chariot of f and horses of f separated
2Ch 7: 1 f came down from heaven and
Isa 66:24 their f shall not be quenched,
Da 3:25 walking in the middle of the f,
Zec 2: 5 For I will be a wall of f all around it,
Mal 3: 2 For he is like a refiner's f and like
Mt 3:11 baptize you with the Holy Spirit and f.
Mk 9:43 to go to hell, to the unquenchable f.
Ac 2: 3 Divided tongues, as of f, appeared
1Co 3:13 the f will test what sort of work each
Heb 12:29 indeed our God is a consuming f.
Jas 3: 6 And the tongue is a f.
2Pe 3:10 elements will be dissolved with f,
Rev 20:14 the second death, the lake of f;
Sir 7:17 punishment of the ungodly is f and

FIRM ➛ FIRMLY
Ex 14:13 "Do not be afraid, stand f,
Isa 7: 9 If you do not stand f in faith,
2Co 1:24 because you stand f in the faith.
Eph 6:13 having done everything, to stand f.
Heb 3: 6 if we hold f the confidence

FIRMAMENT
Ps 19: 1 and the f proclaims his handiwork.
150: 1 praise him in his mighty f!

FIRMLY ➛ FIRM
Ps 119:89 your word is f fixed in heaven.
Ecc 12:11 like nails f fixed are the collected

FIRST ➛ FIRSTBORN
Ge 1: 5 and there was morning, the f day.
Nu 18:15 The f issue of the womb of all
Pr 8:22 the f of his acts of long ago.
Isa 41: 4 I, the LORD, am f,
Mt 6:33 But strive f for the kingdom of God
Mk 10:31 But many who are f will be last, and the last will be f."
16: 2 very early on the f day of the week,
Jn 2:11 Jesus did this, the f of his signs,
Ac 11:26 disciples were f called "Christians."
Ro 1:16 to the Jew f and also to the Greek.
1Co 15:45 it is written, "The f man, Adam,
1Th 4:16 and the dead in Christ will rise f.
1Jn 4:19 We love because he f loved us.
Rev 1:17 I am the f and the last,
20: 5 This is the f resurrection.
21: 1 the f heaven and the f earth

FIRSTBORN ➛ BEAR, FIRST
Ex 4:22 'Thus says the LORD: Israel is my f
12:29 the LORD struck down all the f
13: 2 Consecrate to me all the f;
Ps 78:51 He struck all the f in Egypt,
Zec 12:10 as one weeps over a f.
Lk 2: 7 And she gave birth to her f son and
Col 1:15 invisible God, the f of all creation;
Heb 1: 6 when he brings the f into the world,
Rev 1: 5 faithful witness, the f of the dead,
Sir 36:17 whom you have named your f,
2Es 6:58 whom you have called your f,

FISH
Ge 1:26 have dominion over the f of the sea,
Jnh 2: 1 his God from the belly of the f,
Mt 7:10 Or if the child asks for a f, will give
Jn 6: 9 has five barley loaves and two f.

FIVE
1Sa 17:40 chose f smooth stones from the wadi
Mt 14:19 Taking the f loaves and the two fish,
1Co 14:19 church I would rather speak f words

FLAME
Ex 3: 2 in a f of fire out of a bush;
Isa 10:17 and his Holy One a f;
Rev 19:12 His eyes are like a f of fire,
Aza 1:26 drove the fiery f out of the furnace,

FLED ➛ FLEE
Ex 2:15 But Moses f from Pharaoh.
1Sa 19:18 Now David f and escaped;
Mk 14:50 All of them deserted him and f.
Rev 12: 6 the woman f into the wilderness,
20:11 and the heaven f from his presence,

FLEE ➛ FLED
Ps 11: 1 "F like a bird to the mountains;
139: 7 where can I f from your presence?
Isa 30:17 A thousand shall f at the threat of
1Co 10:14 f from the worship of idols.
Jas 4: 7 Resist the devil, and he will f from

FLESH
Ge 2:23 is bone of my bones and f of my f;
2:24 and they become one f.

Job 19:26 then in my f I shall see God,
Eze 36:26 of stone and give you a heart of f.
Mt 16:17 For f and blood has not revealed this
26:41 but the f is weak."
Jn 1:14 the Word became f and lived among
3: 6 What is born of the f is f,
Ro 8: 4 to the f but according to the Spirit.
2Co 12: 7 a thorn was given me in the f,
Gal 5:19 Now the works of the f are obvious:
Eph 6:12 not against enemies of blood and f,
1Pe 1:24 "All f is like grass and all its glory
1Jn 4: 2 that Jesus Christ has come in the f

FLOCK
Isa 40:11 He will feed his f like a shepherd;
Eze 34:22 I will save my f, and they shall no
Mt 26:31 the sheep of the f will be scattered.'
Lk 12:32 "Do not be afraid, little f,
Jn 10:16 So there will be one f, one shepherd.
1Pe 5: 3 but be examples to the f.

FLOGGED
Jn 19: 1 Pilate took Jesus and had him f.
Ac 5:40 the apostles, they had them f.

FLOOD
Ge 7: 7 the ark to escape the waters of the f.
9:15 waters shall never again become a f
Ps 29:10 The LORD sits enthroned over the f;
2Pe 2: 5 a f on a world of the ungodly;
Sir 40:10 and on their account the f came.

FLOW ➛ FLOWING, FLOWS
Zec 14: 8 waters shall f out from Jerusalem,
Jn 7:38 'Out of the believer's heart shall f

FLOWER
Isa 40: 7 The grass withers, the f fades,
1Pe 1:24 The grass withers, and the f falls,

FLOWING ➛ FLOW
Ex 3: 8 a land f with milk and honey,
Jos 5: 6 a land f with milk and honey.
Eze 47: 1 water was f from below the
Rev 22: 1 f from the throne of God and

FOE
Ex 23:22 and a f to your foes.
Ps 60:11 O grant us help against the f,

FOLLOW ➛ FOLLOWED
Ex 16: 4 whether they will f my instruction
Dt 6:14 Do not f other gods, any of the gods
1Ki 18:21 If the LORD is God, f him;
Ps 23: 6 mercy shall f me all the days of my
Lk 9:23 take up their cross daily and f me.
Jn 10:27 I know them, and they f me.
Rev 14: 4 these f the Lamb wherever he goes.

FOLLOWED ➛ FOLLOW
Jdg 2:12 they f other gods, from among the
Jer 9:14 have stubbornly f their own hearts
Mk 1:18 they left their nets and f him.
Rev 13: 3 the whole earth f the beast.

FOLLY ➛ FOOL
Pr 13:16 but the fool displays f.
26: 4 not answer fools according to their f
Ecc 2:13 that wisdom excels f as light excels
Mk 7:22 envy, slander, pride, f.

FOOD ➛ FOODS
Ge 1:30 I have given every green plant for f.
9: 3 thing that lives shall be f for you;
Ps 136:25 who gives f to all flesh,
Mt 6:25 Is not life more than f,
Jn 6:55 for my flesh is true f and my blood
1Co 8: 8 "F will not bring us close to God."
1Mc 1:63 to die rather than to be defiled by f

FOODS ➛ FOOD
Mk 7:19 (Thus he declared all f clean.)
1Ti 4: 3 and demand abstinence from f,

FOOL ➛ FOLLY, FOOLISH, FOOLISHNESS, FOOLS
Pr 15: 5 A f despises a parent's instruction,
20: 3 but every f is quick to quarrel.
Mt 5:22 'You f,' you will be liable to the
2Co 11:21 I am speaking as a f—I also dare to

FOOLISH ➛ FOOL
Pr 17:25 F children are a grief to their father
Jer 5:21 O f and senseless people,
Mt 7:26 like a f man who built his house
25: 2 Five of them were f, and five were
1Co 1:20 Has not God made f the wisdom of
Gal 3: 1 f Galatians! Who has bewitched
Tit 3: 3 For we ourselves were once f,

FOOLISHNESS ➛ FOOL
1Co 1:18 cross is f to those who are perishing,
3:19 wisdom of this world is f with God.

FOOLS ➛ FOOL
Ps 14: 1 F say in their hearts, "There is no God."
Pr 1: 7 f despise wisdom and instruction.
10:21 but f die for lack of sense.
Ecc 5: 4 for he has no pleasure in f.
Ro 1:22 Claiming to be wise, they became f;
1Co 4:10 We are f for the sake of Christ,

FOOT ➛ FEET, FOOTSTOOL
Ps 91:12 will not dash your f against a stone.
Mt 18: 8 or your f causes you to stumble,
Lk 4:11 not dash your f against a stone.'"

FOOTSTOOL ➛ FOOT
Ps 110: 1 until I make your enemies your f."
Isa 66: 1 is my throne and the earth is my f;
Heb 10:13 until his enemies would be made a f

FORCES
Mt 5:41 and if anyone f you to go one mile,
Eph 6:12 spiritual f of evil in the heavenly

FOREHEAD ➛ FOREHEADS
Ex 13: 9 and as a reminder on your f,
1Sa 17:49 and struck the Philistine on his f;
Rev 13:16 marked on the right hand or the f,

FOREHEADS ➛ FOREHEAD
Eze 9: 4 and put a mark on the f of those
Rev 7: 3 of our God with a seal on their f."
20: 4 not received its mark on their f

FOREIGN ➛ FOREIGNER, FOREIGNERS
Jos 24:23 "Then put away the f gods that are
Ps 81: 9 you shall not bow down to a f god.

FOREIGNER ➛ FOREIGN
Ex 12:43 no f shall eat of it,
1Co 14:11 and the speaker a f to me.

FOREIGNERS ➛ FOREIGN
1Co 14:21 by the lips of f I will speak to this
Heb 11:13 were strangers and f on the earth,

FOREKNEW* ➛ KNOW
Ro 8:29 whom he f he also predestined to
11: 2 not rejected his people whom he f.

FORERUNNER* ➛ RUN
Heb 6:20 a f on our behalf, has entered,

FORESEEING* ➛ SEE
Ac 2:31 F this, David spoke of the
Gal 3: 8 f that God would justify the Gentiles

FORESKIN
Ge 17:14 circumcised in the flesh of his f
Dt 10:16 Circumcise, then, the f of your heart

FORETOLD ➛ TELL
Isa 43: 9 and f to us the former things?
Ac 3:18 this way God fulfilled what he had f

FOREVER
Ge 3:22 the tree of life, and eat, and live f"
6: 3 spirit shall not abide in mortals f,
Ex 3:15 This is my name f, and this my title
2Sa 7:13 the throne of his kingdom f.
1Ch 16:15 Remember his covenant f,
Ps 19: 9 fear of the LORD is pure, enduring f;
110: 4 "You are a priest f according to the
117: 2 faithfulness of the LORD endures f.
Ecc 3:14 that whatever God does endures f;
Isa 40: 8 the word of our God will stand f.
51: 6 but my salvation will be f,
Jn 6:51 eats of this bread will live f;
14:16 another Advocate, to be with you f.
Heb 5: 6 "You are a priest f, according to the
13: 8 the same yesterday and today and f.
1Pe 1:25 but the word of the Lord endures f."
Rev 1:18 I am alive f and ever;
11:15 and he will reign f and ever."
22: 5 and they will reign f and ever.
Wis 5:15 But the righteous live f,

FORFEIT
Mk 8:36 the whole world and f their life?

FORGAVE ➛ FORGIVE
Ps 32: 5 and you f the guilt of my sin.
85: 2 You f the iniquity of your people;
Col 2:13 when he f us all our trespasses,

FORGET ➛ FORGOT, FORGOTTEN
Dt 4:23 So be careful not to f the covenant
6:12 take care that you do not f the LORD,
Ps 137: 5 If I f you, O Jerusalem, let my right
Pr 4: 5 Get wisdom; get insight: do not f,
Isa 49:15 these may f, yet I will not f you.

FORGIVE ➛ FORGAVE, FORGIVEN, FORGIVENESS, FORGIVING
Ge 18:26 f the whole place for their sake."
Ex 32:32 But now, if you will only f their sin
Nu 14:20 the LORD said, "I do f,
1Ki 8:30 your dwelling place; heed and f.
Ne 9:17 But you are a God ready to f,
Ps 79: 9 and f our sins, for your name's sake.
Eze 16:63 when I f you all that you have done,
Da 9:19 O Lord, hear; O Lord, f;
Mt 6:12 And f us our debts, as we
Lk 5:24 has authority on earth to f sins"—
1Jn 1: 9 is faithful and just will f us our sins
Sir 5: 6 he will f the multitude of my sins,"
Man 1:13 f me, O Lord, f me!

FORGIVEN ➛ FORGIVE
Lev 4:20 for them, and they shall be f.
Ps 32: 1 are those whose transgression is f,
Mt 6:12 as we also have f our debtors.
12:31 against the Spirit will not be f.
Mk 2: 9 to the paralytic, 'Your sins are f,'
Ac 2:38 so that your sins may be f;
Ro 4: 7 are those whose iniquities are f,
Eph 4:32 as God in Christ has f you.

FORGIVENESS ➛ FORGIVE
Mk 1: 4 a baptism of repentance for the f
3:29 against the Holy Spirit can never have f,
Col 1:14 we have redemption, the f of sins.
Heb 9:22 the shedding of blood there is no f

FORGIVING ➛ FORGIVE
Ex 34: 7 f iniquity and transgression and sin,
Ps 86: 5 For you, O Lord, are good and f,
Eph 4:32 f one another, as God in Christ has

FORGOT ➛ FORGET
Dt 32:18 you f the God who gave you birth.
Jer 23:27 just as their ancestors f my name
Hos 2:13 and went after her lovers, and f me,
Bar 4: 8 You f the everlasting God,

FORGOTTEN ➛ FORGET
Ps 77: 9 Has God f to be gracious?
Isa 49:14 forsaken me, my Lord has f me."
Heb 12: 5 And you have f the exhortation

FORM ➛ FORMED, FORMLESS
Ex 20: 4 in the f of anything that is in heaven
Lk 3:22 descended upon him in bodily f

FORMED ➛ FORM
Ge 2: 7 the LORD God f man from the dust
Ps 139:13 you who f my inward parts;
Gal 4:19 until Christ is f in you,

FORMLESS* ➛ FORM
Ge 1: 2 the earth was a f void and darkness
Wis 11:17 created the world out of f matter,

FORNICATION ➛ FORNICATOR, FORNICATORS
Mk 7:21 that evil intentions come: f,
1Co 6:13 meant not for f but for the Lord,
Gal 5:19 works of the flesh are obvious: f,
Rev 19: 2 who corrupted the earth with her f,

FORNICATOR* ➛ FORNICATION
1Co 6:18 but the f sins against the body itself.
Eph 5: 5 that no f or impure person,
Sir 23:17 To a f all bread is sweet;

FORNICATORS ➛ FORNICATION
1Ti 1:10 f, sodomites, slave traders, liars,
Rev 22:15 and sorcerers and f and murderers

FORSAKE ➛ FORSAKEN
Dt 31: 6 he will not fail you or f you."

Jos 1: 5 I will not fail you or f you.
Jer 17:13 All who f you shall be put to shame;
Heb 13: 5 "I will never leave you or f you."

FORSAKEN → FORSAKE
Ps 9:10 O LORD, have not f those who seek
22: 1 my God, why have you f me?
Mt 27:46 my God, why have you f me?"
2Co 4: 9 persecuted, but not f;

FORTRESS
2Sa 22: 2 The LORD is my rock, my f, and my
Ps 71: 3 for you are my rock and my f.

FORTUNES
Dt 30: 3 LORD your God will restore your f
Jer 32:44 I will restore their f, says the LORD.

FORTY
Ge 7: 4 rain on the earth for f days and f
Nu 14:34 f days, for every day a year,
1Ki 19: 8 f days and f nights to Horeb
Jnh 3: 4 And he cried out, "F days more,
Mt 4: 2 He fasted f days and f nights,
Heb 3:17 with whom was he angry f years?
2Es 14:42 They sat f days; they wrote

FOUGHT → FIGHT
Jos 10:42 the LORD God of Israel f for Israel.
2Ti 4: 7 I have f the good fight,
Rev 12: 7 and his angels f against the dragon.

FOUND → FIND
Isa 55: 6 Seek the LORD while he may be f,
65: 1 be f by those who did not seek me.
Lk 15:24 he was lost and is f!'
Ro 10:20 f by those who did not seek me;
Rev 20:15 not f written in the book of life was

FOUNDATION → FOUNDATIONS
1Ki 6:37 f of the house of the LORD was laid,
Ezr 3: 6 f of the temple of the LORD was not
Isa 28:16 See, I am laying in Zion a f stone,
1Co 3:11 that f is Jesus Christ.
Eph 2:20 built upon the f of the apostles and
2Ti 2:19 But God's firm f stands,

FOUNDATIONS → FOUNDATION
Heb 11:10 looked forward to the city that has f,
Rev 21:14 the wall of the city has twelve f,

FOUNTAIN
Ps 36: 9 For with you is the f of life;
Pr 16:22 Wisdom is a f of life to one who
Jer 9: 1 and my eyes a f of tears,
Joel 3:18 a f shall come forth from the house
Zec 13: 1 a f shall be opened for the house of

FOUR
Eze 1: 5 something like f living creatures.
10:14 Each one had f faces:
Rev 4: 6 are f living creatures,

FOXES
Jdg 15: 4 went and caught three hundred f,
Lk 9:58 Jesus said to him, "F have holes,

FRAGRANCE → FRAGRANT
2Co 2:14 spreads in every place the f

FRAGRANT → FRAGRANCE
Ex 25: 6 anointing oil and for the f incense,
Eph 5: 2 a f offering and sacrifice to God.

FRANKINCENSE → INCENSE
Isa 60: 6 They shall bring gold and f,
Mt 2:11 gifts of gold, f, and myrrh.

FREE → FREED, FREEDOM, FREEWILL
Ex 21: 2 in the seventh he shall go out a f
Ps 146: 7 The LORD sets the prisoners f;
Jn 8:32 and the truth will make you f."
Ro 6:23 but the f gift of God is eternal life
1Co 9:21 not f from God's law but am under
Gal 3:28 there is no longer slave or f,
Eph 6: 8 whether we are slaves or f.

FREED → FREE
Ac 2:24 having f him from death,
Rev 1: 5 f us from our sins by his blood,

FREEDOM → FREE
2Co 3:17 the Spirit of the Lord is, there is f.
Gal 5: 1 For f Christ has set us free.
1Pe 2:16 not use your f as a pretext for evil.

FREEWILL → FREE, WILL
Ex 35:29 as a f offering to the LORD.
Ps 54: 6 With a f offering I will sacrifice to

FRIEND → FRIENDS, FRIENDSHIP
Ex 33:11 as one speaks to a f.
Pr 17:17 A f loves at all times,
18:24 but a true f sticks closer than one's
Mt 11:19 a f of tax collectors and sinners!'
Jas 2:23 and he was called the f of God.
4: 4 a f of the world becomes an enemy
Sir 7:18 Do not exchange a f for money,

FRIENDS → FRIEND
Job 2:11 when Job's three f heard of all
Jn 15:13 to lay down one's life for one's f.
Sir 6:15 Faithful f are beyond price;

FRIENDSHIP → FRIEND
Ps 25:14 The f of the LORD is for those who
Jas 4: 4 know that f with the world is enmity

FRINGES*
Nu 15:38 to make f on the corners of their
Mt 23: 5 phylacteries broad and their f long.

FRUIT → FRUITFUL, FRUITLESS, FRUITS
Ge 3: 6 she took of its f and ate;
Dt 28: 4 Blessed shall be the f of your womb,
Ps 1: 3 which yield their f in its season,
Pr 8:19 My f is better than gold,
Eze 47:12 will not wither nor their f fail,
Hos 14: 2 and we will offer the f of our lips.
Mt 3: 8 Bear f worthy of repentance.
Lk 6:44 for each tree is known by its own f.
Jn 15: 2 branch that bears f he prunes to make it bear more f.
Col 1:10 as you bear f in every good work
Heb 13:15 the f of lips that confess his name.
Rev 22: 2 tree of life with its twelve kinds of f,

FRUITFUL → FRUIT
Ge 1:22 Be f and multiply and fill the waters
9: 1 said to them, "Be f and multiply,
Ex 1: 7 the Israelites were f and prolific;

FRUITS → FRUIT
Ex 23:16 of the first f of your labor,
Pr 3: 9 with the first f of all your produce;
Mt 7:16 You will know them by their f.
Ro 8:23 who have the first f of the Spirit,
1Co 15:23 in his own order: Christ the first f,
Rev 14: 4 as first f for God and the Lamb,

FULFILL → FULFILLED, FULFILLING
Ps 20: 5 May the LORD f all your petitions.
Ecc 5: 4 F what you vow.
Mt 5:17 I have come not to abolish but to f.
Gal 6: 2 way you will f the law of Christ.
Jas 2: 8 really f the royal law according to

FULFILLED → FULFILL
Mk 1:15 "The time is f, and the kingdom
Lk 24:44 prophets, and the psalms must be f."
Ro 8: 4 requirement of the law might be f

FULFILLING → FULFILL
Ro 9:31 did not succeed in f that law.
13:10 love is the f of the law.

FULL → FILL
Isa 6: 3 the whole earth is f of his glory."
Eze 10:12 were f of eyes all around.
37: 1 it was f of bones.
Mt 6:22 your whole body will be f of light;
Jn 1:14 f of grace and truth.
Rev 4: 6 f of eyes in front and behind:
Sir 42:16 work of the Lord is f of his glory.

FULLNESS → FILL
Jn 1:16 From his f we have all received,
1Co 10:26 "the earth and its f are the Lord's."
Gal 4: 4 But when the f of time had come,
Eph 3:19 may be filled with all the f of God.
Col 1:19 in him all the f of God was pleased

FURNACE
Isa 48:10 have tested you in the f of adversity.
Da 3: 6 be thrown into a f of blazing fire."
Mt 13:42 will throw them into the f of fire,
Aza 1:26 of the Lord came down into the f

FURNITURE
Ex 25: 9 the tabernacle and of all its f,

FURY
Ps 2: 5 and terrify them in his f,
La 2: 4 he has poured out his f like fire.
Ro 2: 8 there will be wrath and f.
Rev 16:19 the wine-cup of the f of his wrath.

FUTILE
Ro 1:21 but they became f in their thinking,
1Co 3:20 thoughts of the wise, that they are f.

FUTURE
Pr 24:20 for the evil have no f;
Jer 31:17 hope for your f, says the LORD:
1Co 3:22 life or death or the present or the f—
1Ti 6:19 of a good foundation for the f,

G

GABRIEL*
Angel who interpreted Daniel's visions (Da 8:16-26; 9:20-27); announced births of John (Lk 1:11-20), Jesus (Lk 1:26-38).

GAD
1. Son of Jacob by Zilpah (Ge 30:9-11; 35:26; 1Ch 2:2). Tribe of blessed (Ge 49:19; Dt 33:20-21), numbered (Nu 1:25; 26:18), allotted land east of the Jordan (Nu 32; 34:14; Jos 18:7; 22), west (Eze 48:27-28), 12,000 from (Rev 7:5).
2. Prophet; seer of David (1Sa 22:5; 2Sa 24:11-19; 1Ch 29:29).

GAIN
Ecc 1: 3 What do people g from all the toil
Lk 9:25 if they g the whole world,
Php 1:21 living is Christ and dying is g.
3: 8 in order that I may g Christ
1Ti 6: 5 that godliness is a means of g.

GALILEAN → GALILEE
Mt 26:69 "You also were with Jesus the G."

GALILEANS → GALILEE
Ac 2: 7 not all these who are speaking G?

GALILEE → GALILEAN, GALILEANS
Isa 9: 1 beyond the Jordan, G of the nations.
Mt 4:15 across the Jordan, G of the Gentiles
Jn 7:41 the Messiah does not come from G,

GAMALIEL
Pharisee (Ac 5:34-39), teacher of Paul (Ac 22:5).

GARDEN
Ge 2: 8 the LORD God planted a g in Eden,
Eze 28:13 You were in Eden, the g of God;
Jn 19:41 and in the g there was a new tomb

GARMENT → GARMENTS
Ge 39:12 she caught hold of his g,
Dt 22: 5 nor shall a man put on a woman's g;
Ps 102:26 they will all wear out like a g.
Lk 5:36 a new g and sews it on an old g;

GARMENTS → GARMENT
Ge 3:21 the LORD God made g of skins for
Isa 61:10 clothed me with the g of salvation,

GATE → GATES
Mt 7:13 "Enter through the narrow g;
Jn 10: 7 I am the g for the sheep.
Heb 13:12 Jesus also suffered outside the city g

GATES → GATE
Ge 24:60 offspring gain possession of the g
Dt 6: 9 of your house and on your g.
Ps 100: 4 Enter his g with thanksgiving,
Mt 16:18 and the g of Hades will not prevail
Rev 21:21 And the twelve g are twelve pearls,

GATH
1Sa 17: 4 Goliath, of G, whose height was six
2Sa 1:20 Tell it not in G, proclaim it not in

GATHER → GATHERED, INGATHERING
Ex 16: 4 and g enough for that day.
Ru 2: 7 and g among the sheaves behind
Isa 11:12 and g the dispersed of Judah from
Mt 12:30 does not g with me scatters.
Lk 13:34 to g your children together as

GATHERED → GATHER
Mt 18:20 two or three are g in my name,
2Th 2: 1 Christ and our being g together
Rev 14:19 and g the vintage of the earth,

GAVE ➛ GIVE
Ge 28: 4 land that God g to Abraham."
Ex 31:18 he g him the two tablets of the
1Ki 4:29 God g Solomon very great wisdom,
Ne 9:15 you g them bread from heaven,
Ecc 12: 7 the breath returns to God who g it.
Mt 25:35 for I was hungry and you g me food,
Jn 1:12 g power to become children of God,
3:16 loved the world that he g his only Son,
Ro 8:32 but g him up for all of us,
Eph 4:11 The gifts he g were that some would
1Ti 2: 6 who g himself a ransom

GEDALIAH
Governor of Judah (2Ki 25:22-26; Jer 39-41).

GEHAZI*
Servant of Elisha (2Ki 4:12-5:27; 8:4-5).

GENEALOGIES ➛ GENEALOGY
1Ch 9: 1 So all Israel was enrolled by g;
Ne 7:64 among those enrolled in the g,

GENEALOGY ➛ GENEALOGIES
Mt 1: 1 of the g of Jesus the Messiah,

GENERATION ➛ GENERATIONS
Ge 15:16 come back here in the fourth g;
Ex 20: 6 steadfast love to the thousandth g
34: 7 to the third and the fourth g."
Da 4:34 his kingdom endures from g to g.
Mt 12:39 evil and adulterous g asks for a sign,
Lk 21:32 this g will not pass away

GENERATIONS ➛ GENERATION
Isa 51: 8 and my salvation to all g.
Lk 1:48 now on all g will call me blessed;

GENEROSITY ➛ GENEROUS
Ro 12: 8 the giver, in g;
Gal 5:22 joy, peace, patience, kindness, g,

GENEROUS ➛ GENEROSITY
Ro 10:12 and is g to all who call on him.
Jas 1:17 Every g act of giving,

GENTILE ➛ GENTILES
Mt 18:17 as a G and a tax collector.
Gal 2:14 live like a G and not like a Jew,
1Mc 1:14 according to G custom,

GENTILES ➛ GENTILE
Lk 21:24 until the times of the G are fulfilled.
Ac 15:19 those G who are turning to God,
Ro 3:29 Is he not the God of G also?
Gal 3: 8 God would justify the G by faith,
Eph 4:17 must no longer live as the G live,
Tob 1:11 from eating the food of the G.
1Mc 1:11 and make a covenant with the G
2Es 4:23 Israel has been given over to the G

GENTLE ➛ GENTLENESS
Pr 15: 4 A g tongue is a tree of life,
Mt 11:29 for I am g and humble in heart,
1Pe 3: 4 with the lasting beauty of a g

GENTLENESS ➛ GENTLE
Gal 5:23 g, and self-control. There is no law
Php 4: 5 Let your g be known to everyone.
1Ti 6:11 godliness, faith, love, endurance, g.

GETHSEMANE
Mk 14:32 They went to a place called G;

GHOST
Mt 14:26 were terrified, saying, "It is a g!"
Lk 24:39 for a g does not have flesh and

GIANT ➛ GIANTS
Sir 47: 4 In his youth did he not kill a g,

GIANTS ➛ GIANT
1Ch 20: 4 was one of the descendants of the g;
Sir 16: 7 He did not forgive the ancient g

GIBEON
Jos 10:12 "Sun, stand still at G, and Moon, in
1Ki 3: 5 G the LORD appeared to Solomon

GIDEON ➛ =JERUBBAAL
Judge, also called Jerubbaal; freed Israel from Midianites (Jdg 6-8; Heb 11:32). The fleece (Jdg 8:36-40).

GIFT ➛ GIFTS
Nu 18: 7 I give your priesthood as a g;
Ecc 5:19 this is the g of God.
Mt 5:23 So when you are offering your g at
Jn 4:10 "If you knew the g of God,
Ac 2:38 will receive the g of the Holy Spirit.
Ro 6:23 but the free g of God is eternal life
1Co 7: 7 each has a particular g from God,
Jas 1:17 with every perfect g, is from above,
Rev 21: 6 the thirsty I will give water as a g

GIFTS ➛ GIFT
Dt 12: 6 and your donations, your votive g,
Mt 2:11 offered him g of gold, frankincense,
Lk 11:13 how to give good g to your children,
Ro 11:29 for the g and the calling of God are
1Co 12: 1 Now concerning spiritual g,
Eph 4: 8 he gave g to his people."
Sir 32:13 who fills you with his good g.

GILGAL
Jos 5: 9 so that place is called G to this day.
1Sa 7:16 a circuit year by year to Bethel, G,

GIRL
Ex 1:16 but if it is a g, she shall live."
Mk 5:41 which means, "Little g, get up!"

GIVE ➛ GAVE, GIVEN, GIVER, GIVES
Ge 9: 3 the green plants, I g you everything.
12: 7 your offspring I will g this land."
1Ki 3: 5 said, "Ask what I should g you."
Pr 25:21 If your enemies are hungry, g them
30:15 leech has two daughters; "G, g,"
Eze 36:26 A new heart I will g you,
Mt 6:11 G us this day our daily bread.
7: 6 "Do not g what is holy to dogs;
Mk 10:45 to g his life a ransom for many."
Jn 10:28 I g them eternal life, and they will
Ac 20:35 more blessed to g than to receive.'"
Tob 12: 9 who g alms will enjoy a full life,
Sir 7:10 do not neglect to g alms.

GIVEN ➛ GIVE
Mt 7: 7 "Ask, and it will be g you;
Mk 4:25 to those who have, more will be g;
Lk 22:19 "This is my body, which is g for
Ro 5: 5 the Holy Spirit that has been g to us.
Sir 35:12 Give to the Most High as he has g

GIVER ➛ GIVE
Ro 12: 8 the g, in generosity;
2Co 9: 7 for God loves a cheerful g.

GIVES ➛ GIVE
2Co 3: 6 the letter kills, but the Spirit g life.
Jas 4: 6 But he g all the more grace;

GLAD ➛ GLADNESS
Ps 16: 9 Therefore my heart is g, and my
90:15 Make us g as many days as you
Pr 10: 1 A wise child makes a g father,
Mt 5:12 and be g, for your reward is great in
Ac 2:26 heart was g, and my tongue rejoiced

GLADNESS ➛ GLAD
Ps 100: 2 Worship the LORD with g;
Pr 10:28 The hope of the righteous ends in g,
Isa 16:10 Joy and g are taken away from the
Jer 31:13 and give them g for sorrow.
Zep 3:17 he will rejoice over you with g,
Heb 1: 9 has anointed you with the oil of g

GLASS
Rev 4: 6 there is something like a sea of g,
21:18 the city is pure gold, clear as g.

GLEAN
Dt 24:21 do not g what is left;
Ru 2: 2 Let me go to the field and g among

GLOOM
Isa 9: 1 there will be no g for those who
Joel 2: 2 a day of darkness and g,
Heb 12:18 and darkness, and g, and a tempest,

GLORIFIED ➛ GLORY
Lev 10: 3 before all the people I will be g.'"
Jn 13:31 "Now the Son of Man has been g,
17: 4 g you on earth by finishing the work
Ac 3:13 has g his servant Jesus,
Ro 8:30 those whom he justified he also g.

GLORIFY ➛ GLORY
Ps 86:12 and I will g your name forever.
Jn 17: 1 g your Son so that the Son may g you,
1Co 6:20 therefore g God in your body.
2Co 9:13 you g God by your obedience to
Rev 15: 4 who will not fear and g your name?
Sir 43:30 G the Lord and exalt him as much

GLORIOUS ➛ GLORY
Jas 2: 1 in our g Lord Jesus Christ?
Jdt 16:13 O Lord, you are great and g,
Aza 1: 3 and g is your name forever!

GLORY ➛ GLORIFIED, GLORIFY, GLORIOUS
Ex 24:16 The g of the LORD settled on Mount
33:18 Moses said, "Show me your g,
40:34 g of the LORD filled the tabernacle.
1Sa 4:21 "The g has departed from Israel,"
1Ki 8:11 g of the LORD filled the house of the
Ps 8: 5 crowned them with g and honor.
19: 1 heavens are telling the g of God;
24: 7 that the King of g may come in.
Isa 6: 3 the whole earth is full of his g."
40: 5 the g of the LORD shall be revealed,
Eze 11:23 g of the LORD ascended from the
44: 4 g of the LORD filled the temple of
Hos 4: 7 they changed their g into shame.
Mt 25:31 the Son of Man comes in his g,
Lk 2:14 "G to God in the highest heaven,
Jn 1:14 and we have seen his g,
12:41 Isaiah said this because he saw his g
Ro 3:23 sinned and fall short of the g of God;
8:18 not worth comparing with the g
9: 4 the g, the covenants, the giving of
1Co 10:31 do everything for the g of God.
2Co 4:17 for an eternal weight of g beyond
Heb 1: 3 reflection of God's g and the exact
2Pe 1:17 conveyed to him by the Majestic G,
Rev 4:11 to receive g and honor and power,
21:23 for the g of God is its light,
Sir 1:11 The fear of the Lord is g and
Bar 5: 4 "Righteous Peace, Godly G."
1Mc 1:40 dishonor now grew as great as her g

GLUTTON
Pr 23:21 and the g will come to poverty,
Mt 11:19 they say, 'Look, a g and a drunkard,

GNASHING
Mt 8:12 will be weeping and g of teeth."
25:30 will be weeping and g of teeth.'

GNAT*
Mt 23:24 strain out a g but swallow a camel!

GO
Ex 5: 1 the God of Israel, 'Let my people g,
Jos 1: 9 God is with you wherever you g."
Ru 1:16 Where you g, I will g;
Mt 28:19 G therefore and make disciples of
Jn 14: 3 if I g and prepare a place for you,

GOAT ➛ GOATS
Lev 16: 9 Aaron shall present the g on which
Da 8:21 The male g is the king of Greece,

GOATS ➛ GOAT
Ps 50:13 or drink the blood of g?
Mt 25:32 separates the sheep from the g,
Heb 10: 4 for the blood of bulls and g

***GOD ➛ GOD'S, GODDESS, GODLESS, GODLINESS, GODLY, GODS**
Ge 1: 1 In the beginning when G created
1:27 So G created humankind in his image,
3: 5 be like G, knowing good and evil."
6: 2 sons of G saw that they were fair;
17: 1 and said to him, "I am G Almighty;
Ex 3: 4 G called to him out of the bush,
15: 2 this is my G, and I will praise him,
20: 5 I the LORD your G am a jealous G,
34: 6 a G merciful and gracious, slow to
Nu 23:19 G is not a human being,
Dt 4: 7 a g so near to it as the LORD our G
6: 5 love the LORD your G with all your
Jos 22:34 between us that the LORD is G."
1Sa 2: 2 there is no Rock like our G.
1Ki 8:27 will G indeed dwell on the earth?
18:24 the g who answers by fire is indeed G.
2Ki 17: 7 sinned against the LORD their G,
2Ch 2: 5 for our G is greater than other gods.
Ezr 6:16 the dedication of this house of G
Ne 8:18 read from the book of the law of G.

Ps 19: 1 heavens are telling the glory of G;
Ps 22: 1 My G, my G, why have you forsaken
46: 1 G is our refuge and strength,
46:10 "Be still, and know that I am G!
47: 7 For G is the king of all the earth;
53: 1 Fools say in their hearts, "There is no G."
68:20 Our G is a G of salvation,
90: 2 everlasting to everlasting you are G.
136: 2 O give thanks to the G of gods,
145: 1 I will extol you, my G and King,
Ecc 12:13 Fear G, and keep his
Isa 9: 6 Wonderful Counselor, Mighty G,
12: 2 Surely G is my salvation;
40:28 The LORD is the everlasting G,
44: 6 besides me there is no g.
Jer 10:10 But the LORD is the true G;
Eze 28: 2 proud and you have said, "I am a g;
Hos 12: 6 But as for you, return to your G,
Am 4:12 prepare to meet your G,
Mic 6: 8 and to walk humbly with your G?
Hab 3:18 I will exult in the G of my salvation.
Mal 2:10 Has not one G created us?
Mt 1:23 which means, "G is with us."
4: 4 that comes from the mouth of G.'"
4: 7 not put the Lord your G to the test.'
4:10 written, 'Worship the Lord your G,
6:24 You cannot serve G and wealth.
27:40 If you are the Son of G,
Mk 1: 1 news of Jesus Christ, the Son of G.
2: 7 Who can forgive sins but G alone?"
10: 9 what G has joined together, let no
12:30 the Lord your G with all your heart,
Lk 2:14 "Glory to G in the highest heaven,
18:19 No one is good but G alone.
22:70 "Are you, then, the Son of G?"
Jn 1: 1 was with G, and the Word was G.
1:18 It is G the only Son,
3:16 G so loved the world that he gave his only Son,
5:18 calling G his own Father, thereby making himself equal to G.
20:28 "My Lord and my G!"
Ac 5:29 "We must obey G rather than any
Ro 4: 3 "Abraham believed G, and it was
6:23 gift of G is eternal life in Christ
8:31 If G is for us, who is against us?
1Co 10:31 do everything for the glory of G.
2Co 4: 4 Christ, who is the image of G.
6:16 we are the temple of the living G;
Eph 4: 6 one G and Father of all,
Php 2: 6 though he was in the form of G,
Col 1:19 fullness of G was pleased to dwell,
Tit 2:13 of our great G and Savior, Jesus
Heb 4:12 the word of G is living and active,
10:31 to fall into the hands of the living G.
12:29 indeed our G is a consuming fire.
Jas 2:23 "Abraham believed G,
4: 8 Draw near to G, and he will draw
1Jn 1: 5 G is light and in him there is no
4:16 G is love, and those who abide
5: 2 love G and obey his commandments
Jude 1:21 keep yourselves in the love of G;
Rev 4: 8 "Holy, holy, holy, the Lord G
19:13 his name is called The Word of G.
22: 5 for the Lord G will be their light,
Tob 4:19 At all times bless the Lord G,
Sir 32:14 seeks G will accept his discipline,
Bar 4: 8 You forgot the everlasting G,
Bel 1: 4 But Daniel worshiped his own G.
Man 1: 1 Lord Almighty, G of our ancestors,
2Es 16:67 Indeed, G is the judge; fear him!

†GOD ➛ †LORD
Ge 15: 2 But Abram said, "O Lord G,
2Sa 7:18 "Who am I, O Lord G,
Isa 25: 8 Lord G will wipe away the tears
61: 1 The spirit of the Lord G is upon me,

GOD'S ➛ *GOD
Mt 27:43 for he said, 'I am G Son.'"
27:54 "Truly this man was G Son!"
Ro 2: 4 that G kindness is meant to lead you
1Co 3: 9 you are G field, G building.
3:16 you are G temple and that G Spirit
Heb 1: 3 reflection of G glory and the exact imprint of G
1Jn 3: 2 Beloved, we are G children now;

GODDESS ➛ *GOD
1Ki 11: 5 Astarte the g of the Sidonians,
Ac 19:27 the temple of the great g Artemis

GODLESS ➛ *GOD
Job 8:13 the hope of the g shall perish.
Ps 119:122 do not let the g oppress me.
1Ti 1: 9 for the g and sinful,
2Pe 3: 7 judgment and destruction of the g.

GODLINESS ➛ *GOD
1Ti 4: 7 Train yourself in g,
6: 5 imagining that g is a means of gain.
2Ti 3: 5 outward form of g but denying its
Tit 1: 1 truth that is in accordance with g,
2Pe 1: 3 everything needed for life and g,
Wis 10:12 g is more powerful than anything

GODLY ➛ *GOD
Mal 2:15 the one God desire? G offspring.
2Co 7:10 For g grief produces a repentance
2Ti 3:12 to live a g life in Christ Jesus will
Tit 2:12 are self-controlled, upright, and g,
2Pe 2: 9 how to rescue the g from trial,
Sir 37:12 But associate with a g person
Bar 5: 4 "Righteous Peace, G Glory."

GODS ➛ *GOD
Ge 31:19 stole her father's household g.
Ex 12:12 g of Egypt I will execute judgments:
20: 3 you shall have no other g before me.
Jdg 2:17 they lusted after other g and bowed
2Ki 17: 7 They had worshiped other g
Jn 10:34 in your law, 'I said, you are g'?
1Co 8: 5 so-called g in heaven or on earth—

GOG
Eze 38:18 G comes against the land of Israel,
Rev 20: 8 G and Magog, in order to gather

GOLD
Ex 20:23 make for yourselves gods of g.
25:17 shall make a mercy seat of pure g;
25:31 shall make a lampstand of pure g.
28: 6 They shall make the ephod of g, of
32:31 have made for themselves gods of g.
1Ki 6:21 the inside of the house with pure g,
Job 28:15 It cannot be gotten for g,
Ps 119:127 love your commandments more than g,
Isa 60:17 Instead of bronze I will bring g,
Ac 3: 6 Peter said, "I have no silver or g,
1Pe 1: 7 being more precious than g that,
Rev 21:21 and the street of the city is pure g,
Tob 12: 8 better to give alms than to lay up g.
Sir 31: 5 who loves g will not be justified;

GOLGOTHA
Mt 27:33 G (which means Place of a Skull),

GOLIATH
Giant killed by David (1Sa 17; 21:9; Sir 47:4).

GOMORRAH
Ge 19:24 LORD rained on Sodom and G sulfur
Isa 1: 9 like Sodom, and become like G.
Jude 1: 7 Sodom and G and the surrounding

GOOD ➛ BEST, BETTER, GOODNESS
Ge 1:31 and indeed, it was very g.
2: 9 tree of the knowledge of g and evil.
3:22 become like one of us, knowing g
50:20 to me, God intended it for g,
Dt 6:18 Do what is right and g in the sight
2Ch 7: 3 "For he is g, for his steadfast love
Ps 14: 1 there is no one who does g.
34: 8 O taste and see that the LORD is g;
84:11 No g thing does the LORD withhold
Pr 18:22 He who finds a wife finds a g thing,
Ecc 12:14 every secret thing, whether g or evil.
Isa 52: 7 who brings g news, who announces
Mt 5:45 his sun rise on the evil and on the g,
13: 8 Other seeds fell on g soil and
25:21 'Well done, g and trustworthy slave;
Mk 10:18 No one is g but God alone.
Lk 2:10 I am bringing you g news of great
6:43 "No g tree bears bad fruit,
Jn 10:11 "I am the g shepherd.
Ro 7:16 I agree that the law is g.
12: 2 is g and acceptable and perfect.
12:21 but overcome evil with g.
Eph 2:10 created in Christ Jesus for g works,
1Ti 4: 4 For everything created by God is g,
Heb 10: 1 the law has only a shadow of the g
1Pe 3:17 For it is better to suffer for doing g,
Tob 4: 9 laying up a g treasure for yourself
Aza 1:67 to the Lord, for he is g,

GOODNESS ➛ GOOD
Ex 33:19 will make all my g pass before you,
Ps 23: 6 Surely g and mercy shall follow me
Heb 6: 5 tasted the g of the word of God and
2Pe 1: 5 support your faith with g, and g

GOSHEN
Ge 45:10 You shall settle in the land of G,
Ex 8:22 day I will set apart the land of G,

GOSPEL
Mk 8:35 and for the sake of the g,
Ro 1:16 For I am not ashamed of the g;
1Co 9:16 woe to me if I do not proclaim the g
2Co 4: 3 And even if our g is veiled,
Gal 1: 6 and are turning to a different g—
Php 1:27 life in a manner worthy of the g
Rev 14: 6 an eternal g to proclaim to those

GOSSIP
Pr 11:13 A g goes about telling secrets,
2Co 12:20 selfishness, slander, g, conceit,

GRACE ➛ GRACIOUS
Jn 1:14 father's only son, full of g and truth.
1:16 we have all received, g upon g.
Ac 15:11 that we will be saved through the g
Ro 3:24 are now justified by his g as a gift,
6: 1 in sin in order that g may abound?
6:14 you are not under law but under g.
11: 6 otherwise g would no longer be g.
2Co 12: 9 "My g is sufficient for you,
Gal 5: 4 you have fallen away from g.
Eph 2: 5 by g you have been saved—
2Th 2:16 through g gave us eternal comfort
Tit 2:11 For the g of God has appeared,
Heb 4:16 approach the throne of g with
Jas 4: 6 But he gives all the more g;
1Pe 5:10 the God of all g,
Jude 1: 4 who pervert the g of our God into
Rev 22:21 The g of the Lord Jesus be with all
Wis 3: 9 g and mercy are upon his holy ones,
2Es 2:32 and my g will not fail."

GRACIOUS ➛ GRACE
Ex 34: 6 the LORD, a God merciful and g,
Nu 6:25 to shine upon you, and be g to you;
Ezr 8:22 of our God is g to all who seek him,
Ne 9:31 for you are a g and merciful God.
Ps 77: 9 Has God forgotten to be g?
116: 5 G is the LORD, and righteous;
Col 4: 6 Let your speech always be g,

GRAFTED
Ro 11:17 were g in their place to share the

GRAIN
Lev 2: 1 presents a g offering to the LORD,
Dt 25: 4 an ox while it is treading out the g.
Mk 2:23 disciples began to pluck heads of g.
1Ti 5:18 an ox while it is treading out the g,"

GRAPES
Nu 13:23 a branch with a single cluster of g,
Isa 5: 2 to yield g, but it yielded wild g.
Jer 31:29 "The parents have eaten sour g,
Mt 7:16 Are g gathered from thorns, or figs
Rev 14:18 vine of the earth, for its g are ripe."

GRASS
Isa 40: 6 All people are g, their constancy is
Mt 6:30 if God so clothes the g of the field,
1Pe 1:24 "All flesh is like g and all its glory

GRATIFY*
Ro 13:14 for the flesh, to g its desires.
Gal 5:16 do not g the desires of the flesh.

GRAVE ➛ GRAVES
Ps 49:14 straight to the g they descend,
Isa 53: 9 They made his g with the wicked

GRAVES ➛ GRAVE
Eze 37:12 and bring you up from your g,
Lk 11:44 For you are like unmarked g,

GRAY
Pr 16:31 G hair is a crown of glory;
Sir 6:18 g hair you will still find wisdom.

HARD → HARD-HEARTED, HARDEN, HARDENED, HARDENING, HARDSHIP, HARDSHIPS
Ex 1:14 made their lives bitter with **h** service
Jer 32:17 Nothing is too **h** for you.
Mt 7:14 the road is **h** that leads to life,
19:23 **h** for a rich person to enter the

HARD-HEARTED* → HARD, HEART
Dt 15: 7 do not be **h** or tight-fisted toward
Pr 28:14 one who is **h** will fall into calamity.
Mt 19: 8 you were so **h** that Moses allowed

HARDEN → HARD
Ex 4:21 but I will **h** his heart,
Ps 95: 8 Do not **h** your hearts, as at Meribah,
Heb 3: 8 not **h** your hearts as in the rebellion,

HARDENED → HARD
Ex 10:20 But the LORD **h** Pharaoh's heart,
Mk 8:17 Are your hearts **h**?
Ro 11: 7 elect obtained it, but the rest were **h**,
2Co 3:14 But their minds were **h**.

HARDENING* → HARD
Ro 11:25 a **h** has come upon part of Israel,

HARDSHIP → HARD
Ro 8:35 Will **h**, or distress, or persecution,

HARDSHIPS → HARD
2Co 12:10 content with weaknesses, insults, **h**,

HARM
Ge 50:20 though you intended to do **h** to me,
Ne 6: 2 But they intended to do me **h**.
Pr 12:21 No **h** happens to the righteous,
Jer 29:11 plans for your welfare and not for **h**,
1Pe 3:13 who will **h** you if you are eager

HARP → HARPS
Ps 150: 3 praise him with lute and **h**!
Rev 5: 8 each holding a **h** and golden bowls

HARPS → HARP
1Ch 15:16 on **h** and lyres and cymbals,
Ne 12:27 with cymbals, **h**, and lyres.
Ps 137: 2 the willows there we hung up our **h**.

HARSHLY
Dt 26: 6 When the Egyptians treated us **h**
Col 3:19 your wives and never treat them **h**.
1Ti 5: 1 Do not speak **h** to an older man,

HARVEST → HARVESTING
Ge 8:22 the earth endures, seedtime and **h**,
Ex 23:16 You shall observe the festival of **h**,
Mt 13:39 **h** is the end of the age, and the
Lk 10: 2 He said to them, "The **h** is plentiful,
Rev 14:15 the **h** of the earth is fully ripe."

HARVESTING* → HARVEST
Jn 4:35 and see how the fields are ripe for **h**.

HASTENING*
Zep 1:14 day of the LORD is near, near and **h**
2Pe 3:12 and **h** the coming of the day of God,

HATE → HATED, HATING
Ps 45: 7 righteousness and **h** wickedness.
97:10 The LORD loves those who **h** evil;
Pr 13: 5 The righteous **h** falsehood,
Ecc 3: 8 a time to love, and a time to **h**;
Am 5:15 **H** evil and love good, and establish
Mal 2:16 For I **h** divorce, says the LORD,
Mt 5:43 your neighbor and **h** your enemy.'
Lk 6:27 do good to those who **h** you,
Jn 7: 7 The world cannot **h** you, but it hates
Ro 7:15 but I do the very thing I **h**.

HATED → HATE
Jn 15:18 aware that it **h** me before it **h** you.
Ro 9:13 loved Jacob, but I have **h** Esau."

HATES → HATE
Dt 16:22 things that the LORD your God **h**.
Pr 6:16 six things that the LORD **h**,
Jn 15:23 Whoever **h** me **h** my Father also.
Sir 15:13 The Lord **h** all abominations;

HAUGHTY
Pr 6:17 **h** eyes, a lying tongue, and hands
16:18 and a **h** spirit before a fall.
1Ti 6:17 command them not to be **h**,

HAY*
1Co 3:12 precious stones, wood, **h**, straw—

HEAD → BEHEADED, HEADS
Isa 59:17 and a helmet of salvation on his **h**;
Mt 8:20 of Man has nowhere to lay his **h**."
Mk 6:28 brought his **h** on a platter,
1Co 11: 3 Christ is the **h** of every man, and the husband is the **h** of his wife,
Eph 1:22 has made him the **h** over all things

HEADS → HEAD
Eze 11:21 bring their deeds upon their own **h**,
Rev 12: 3 a great red dragon, with seven **h**

HEAL → HEALED, HEALING, HEALS, HEALTH, HEALTHY
Dt 32:39 and I make alive; I wound and I **h**;
Ecc 3: 3 a time to kill, and a time to **h**;
Isa 57:19 says the LORD; and I will **h** them.
Jer 3:22 I will **h** your faithlessness.
Hos 14: 4 I will **h** their disloyalty; I will love
Jn 12:40 and turn—and I would **h** them."

HEALED → HEAL
Isa 6:10 their minds, and turn and be **h**."
53: 5 and by his bruises we are **h**.
Hos 11: 3 but they did not know that I **h** them.
Jas 5:16 one another, so that you may be **h**.
1Pe 2:24 by his wounds you have been **h**.

HEALING → HEAL
Pr 12:18 but the tongue of the wise brings **h**.
Eze 47:12 for food, and their leaves for **h**."
Mal 4: 2 shall rise, with **h** in its wings.
1Co 12: 9 another gifts of **h** by the one Spirit,
Rev 22: 2 leaves of the tree are for the **h** of
Sir 38: 2 gift of **h** comes from the Most High,

HEALS → HEAL
Ex 15:26 for I am the LORD who **h** you."
Ps 103: 3 iniquity, who **h** all your diseases,
Wis 16:12 your word, O Lord, that **h** all people

HEALTH → HEAL
3Jn 1: 2 and that you may be in good **h**,
Sir 30:15 **H** and fitness are better than any

HEALTHY → HEAL
Lk 11:34 If your eye is **h**, your whole body

HEAR → HEARD, HEARERS, HEARING, HEARS
Dt 6: 4 **H**, O Israel: The LORD is our God,
31:13 may **h** and learn to fear the LORD
1Ki 8:30 O **h** in heaven your dwelling place;
Isa 59: 1 nor his ear too dull to **h**.
Jer 5:21 who have ears, but do not **h**.
Eze 37: 4 dry bones, **h** the word of the LORD.
Mt 13:17 to **h** what you **h**, but did not **h** it.
Mk 12:29 answered, "The first is, '**H**, O Israel:
Lk 7:22 the lepers are cleansed, the deaf **h**,
Heb 3: 7 says, "Today, if you **h** his voice,
Sir 5:11 Be quick to **h**, but deliberate in

HEARD → HEAR
Isa 40:21 not known? Have you not **h**?
1Co 2: 9 "What no eye has seen, nor ear **h**,
1Jn 1: 3 to you what we have seen and **h** so
Rev 22: 8 I, John, am the one who **h** and saw

HEARERS → HEAR
Ro 2:13 For it is not the **h** of the law who
Jas 1:22 merely **h** who deceive themselves.

HEARING → HEAR
Pr 18:13 one gives answer before **h**,
Am 8:11 but of **h** the words of the LORD.
1Co 12:17 If the whole body were **h**,

HEARS → HEAR
Ps 69:33 For the LORD **h** the needy,
Pr 15:29 but he **h** the prayer of the righteous.
Mt 7:24 then who **h** these words of mine
Jn 5:24 I tell you, anyone who **h** my word
1Jn 5:14 according to his will, he **h** us.
Rev 22:18 I warn everyone who **h** the words

HEART → BROKENHEARTED, HARD-HEARTED, HEART'S, HEARTLESS, HEARTS, TENDERHEARTED
Ge 6: 6 and it grieved him to his **h**.
Ex 4:21 but I will harden his **h**,
14: 4 I will harden Pharaoh's **h**,
Dt 6: 5 the LORD your God with all your **h**,
30:14 in your mouth and in your **h** for you
Jos 22: 5 all your **h** and with all your soul."
1Sa 16: 7 but the LORD looks on the **h**."
Ps 19:14 meditation of my **h** be acceptable to
51:10 Create in me a clean **h**, O God,
Pr 3: 5 Trust in the LORD with all your **h**,
7: 3 write them on the tablet of your **h**.
Jer 9:26 of Israel is uncircumcised in **h**.
Eze 36:26 A new **h** I will give you,
Mt 5: 8 "Blessed are the pure in **h**, for they
5:28 adultery with her in his **h**.
Mk 12:30 the Lord your God with all your **h**,
Lk 12:34 treasure is, there your **h** will be also.
Ro 2:29 circumcision is a matter of the **h**—
10: 9 believe in your **h** that God raised
Heb 10:22 let us approach with a true **h** in full
Sir 1:12 The fear of the Lord delights the **h**,
Aza 1:16 Yet with a contrite **h** and
Man 1:11 And now I bend the knee of my **h**,

HEART'S → HEART
Ps 20: 4 May he grant you your **h** desire,
Ro 10: 1 my **h** desire and prayer to God for

HEARTLESS* → HEART
Ro 1:31 foolish, faithless, **h**, ruthless.

HEARTS → HEART
Ps 95: 8 not harden your **h**, as at Meribah,
Jer 31:33 and I will write it on their **h**;
Mk 7: 6 but their **h** are far from me;
Jn 14: 1 "Do not let your **h** be troubled.
Ro 2:15 law requires is written on their **h**,
Eph 3:17 Christ may dwell in your **h** through
Col 3:15 the peace of Christ rule in your **h**,
Heb 3: 8 do not harden your **h** as in the
10:16 I will put my laws in their **h**,
2Pe 1:19 and the morning star rises in your **h**.
1Jn 3:20 for God is greater than our **h**,
Rev 2:23 the one who searches minds and **h**,

HEAVEN → HEAVENLY, HEAVENS
Ge 14:19 by God Most High, maker of **h** and
28:12 the top of it reaching to **h**;
Ex 16: 4 "I am going to rain bread from **h**
Dt 30:12 "Who will go up to **h** for us,
31:28 and call **h** and earth to witness
1Ki 8:27 **h** and the highest **h** cannot contain
Job 16:19 now, in fact, my witness is in **h**,
Ecc 3: 1 and a time for every matter under **h**:
Isa 14:12 you are fallen from **h**, O Day Star,
Jer 23:24 Do I not fill **h** and earth?
Mt 3: 2 "Repent, for the kingdom of **h** has
6: 9 Father in **h**, hallowed be your name.
24:35 **H** and earth will pass away,
26:64 and coming on the clouds of **h**."
Mk 10:21 and you will have treasure in **h**;
Lk 10:18 "I watched Satan fall from **h** like a
19:38 Peace in **h**, and glory in the highest **h**!"
24:51 and was carried up into **h**.
Jn 3:13 No one has ascended into **h** except the one who descended from **h**,
Ac 1:11 same way as you saw him go into **h**.
Ro 10: 6 'Who will ascend into **h**?'"
2Co 12: 2 was caught up to the third **h**—
Php 3:20 But our citizenship is in **h**,
1Th 1:10 to wait for his Son from **h**,
Heb 9:24 but he entered into **h** itself,
2Pe 1:18 heard this voice come from **h**,
Rev 4: 1 and there in **h** a door stood open!
21: 1 I saw a new **h** and a new earth;

HEAVENLY → HEAVEN
Mt 5:48 as your **h** Father is perfect.
2Co 5: 2 longing to be clothed with our **h**
Eph 1: 3 spiritual blessing in the **h** places,
Heb 3: 1 holy partners in a **h** calling,

HEAVENS → HEAVEN
Ge 1: 1 when God created the **h** and
11: 4 and a tower with its top in the **h**,
Dt 10:14 the heaven of **h** belong to the LORD
Ps 57: 5 Be exalted, O God, above the **h**.
115:16 The **h** are the LORD's **h**,
Isa 65:17 to create new **h** and a new earth;
Jer 10:11 The gods who did not make the **h**
Eph 4:10 who ascended far above all the **h**,
Heb 4:14 priest who has passed through the **h**,
2Pe 3:10 the **h** will pass away with a loud

HEAVY
Mt 23: 4 They tie up **h** burdens, hard to bear,
Mk 14:40 for their eyes were very **h;**

HEBREW ➛ HEBREWS
Jnh 1: 9 "I am a **H**," he replied.
Jn 19:20 and it was written in **H**, in Latin,
Php 3: 5 of Benjamin, a **H** born of Hebrews;

HEBREWS ➛ HEBREW
Ex 3:18 The LORD, the God of the **H**, has
2Co 11:22 Are they **H**? So am I.
Jdt 10:12 "I am a daughter of the **H**,

HEBRON
Ge 13:18 the oaks of Mamre, which are at **H**;
2Sa 2:11 The time that David was king in **H**

HEEL
Ge 3:15 your head, and you will strike his **h**.
25:26 with his hand gripping Esau's **h;**
Ps 41: 9 has lifted the **h** against me.
Jn 13:18 has lifted his **h** against me.'

HEIGHT ➛ HIGH
Ro 8:39 nor **h**, nor depth, nor anything else
Eph 3:18 and length and **h** and depth,

HEIGHTS ➛ HIGH
Ps 148: 1 the heavens; praise him in the **h**!
Hab 3:19 and makes me tread upon the **h**.

HEIR ➛ HEIRS
Ge 15: 4 "This man shall not be your **h;**
Gal 4: 7 then also an **h**, through God.
Heb 1: 2 whom he appointed **h** of all things,

HEIRS ➛ HEIR
Ro 8:17 **h, h** of God and joint **h** with Christ—
Eph 3: 6 the Gentiles have become fellow **h**,
1Pe 3: 7 also **h** of the gracious gift of life—

HELL
Mt 10:28 both soul and body in **h**.
Mk 9:43 to have two hands and to go to **h**,
2Pe 2: 4 cast them into **h** and committed
2Es 2:29 so that your children may not see **h**.

HELMET
Isa 59:17 and a **h** of salvation on his head;
Eph 6:17 Take the **h** of salvation, and the

HELP ➛ HELPED, HELPER, HELPS
Ex 18: 4 "The God of my father was my **h**,
Ps 33:20 he is our **h** and shield.
46: 1 a very present **h** in trouble.
Mk 9:24 "I believe; **h** my unbelief!"
Heb 2:18 able to **h** those who are being tested.
4:16 receive mercy and find grace to **h**
Jdt 6:21 called on the God of Israel for **h**.
Sir 2: 6 Trust in him, and he will **h** you;

HELPED ➛ HELP
1Sa 7:12 "Thus far the LORD has **h** us."
Ps 118:13 I was falling, but the LORD **h** me.
Isa 49: 8 on a day of salvation I have **h** you;

HELPER ➛ HELP
Ge 2:18 I will make him a **h** as his partner."
Ps 30:10 O LORD, be my **h**!"
Heb 13: 6 Lord is my **h;** I will not be afraid.
Tob 8: 6 Eve as a **h** and support.

HELPS ➛ HELP
Ps 37:40 The LORD **h** them and rescues them;
Ro 8:26 the Spirit **h** us in our weakness;

HERBS
Ex 12: 8 with unleavened bread and bitter **h**.

HERMON
Dt 3: 8 from the Wadi Arnon to Mount **H**
Ps 133: 3 It is like the dew of **H**,

HEROD ➛ HERODIANS
1. King of Judea; tried to kill Jesus (Mt 2; Lk 1:5).
2. Son of 1. Tetrarch of Galilee who arrested and beheaded John the Baptist (Mt 14:1-12; Mk 6:14-29; Lk 3:1, 19-20; 9:7-9); tried Jesus (Lk 23:6-15).
3. Grandson of 1. King of Judea who killed James (Ac 12:2); arrested Peter (Ac 12:3-19). Death (Ac 12:19-23).

HERODIANS ➛ HEROD
Mk 3: 6 immediately conspired with the **H**
12:13 some **H** to trap him in what he said.

HERODIAS*
Wife of Herod the Tetrarch who persuaded her daughter to ask for John the Baptist's head (Mt 14:1-12; Mk 6:14-29; Lk 3:19).

HEWN
Ex 20:25 do not build it of **h** stones;
Mk 15:46 laid it in a tomb that had been **h**

HEZEKIAH
King of Judah (Sir 48:17-25). Restored the temple and worship (2Ch 29-31). Sought the LORD for help against Assyria (2Ki 18-19; 2Ch 32:1-23; Isa 36-37). Illness healed (2Ki 20:1-11; 2Ch 32:24-26; Isa 38). Judged for showing Babylonians his treasures (2Ki 20:12-21; 2Ch 32:31; Isa 39).

HID ➛ HIDE
Ge 3: 8 and his wife **h** themselves from the
Ex 2: 2 a fine baby, she **h** him three months.
3: 6 Moses **h** his face, for he was afraid
Jos 6:17 live because she **h** the messengers
1Ki 18:13 **h** a hundred of the LORD's prophets
Isa 49: 2 in the shadow of his hand he **h** me;
54: 8 wrath for a moment I **h** my face
Mt 25:25 and **h** your talent in the ground.

HIDDEN ➛ HIDE
Ps 19:12 Clear me from **h** faults.
Pr 2: 4 and search for it as for **h** treasures—
Isa 40:27 "My way is **h** from the LORD,
Mt 13:44 is like treasure **h** in a field,
Mk 4:22 nothing **h**, except to be disclosed;
Col 3: 3 your life is **h** with Christ in God.
Rev 2:17 the **h** manna, and I will give a white
Sir 42:20 and nothing is **h** from him.

HIDE ➛ HID, HIDDEN
Dt 31:17 I will forsake them and **h** my face
Ps 13: 1 How long will you **h** your face
17: 8 **h** me in the shadow of your wings,

HIGH ➛ HEIGHT, HEIGHTS, HIGHER, HIGHEST, HIGHLY
Ge 14:18 he was priest of God Most **H**.
1Ki 3: 2 were sacrificing at the **h** places,
Ps 91: 1 live in the shelter of the Most **H**,
Mt 4: 8 a very **h** mountain and showed him
17: 1 and led them up a **h** mountain,
Mk 5: 7 Jesus, Son of the Most **H** God?
Eph 4: 8 "When he ascended on **h** he made
Heb 2:17 a merciful and faithful **h** priest
7:26 that we should have such a **h** priest,

HIGHER ➛ HIGH
Ps 61: 2 Lead me to the rock that is **h** than I;
Isa 55: 9 so are my ways **h** than your ways

HIGHEST ➛ HIGH
1Ki 8:27 the **h** heaven cannot contain you,
Mt 21: 9 Hosanna in the **h** heaven!"
Lk 2:14 "Glory to God in the **h** heaven,

HIGHLY ➛ HIGH
Ps 47: 9 to God; he is **h** exalted.
Ro 12: 3 not to think of yourself more **h** than

HILL ➛ HILLS
Ps 15: 1 Who may dwell on your holy **h**?
Isa 40: 4 every mountain and **h** be made low;
Mt 5:14 A city built on a **h** cannot be hid.
Lk 3: 5 mountain and **h** shall be made low,

HILLS ➛ HILL
1Ki 20:23 "Their gods are gods of the **h**,
Ps 50:10 the cattle on a thousand **h**.

HINDER
1Sa 14: 6 nothing can **h** the LORD from saving
Isa 43:13 I work and who can **h** it?
1Pe 3: 7 so that nothing may **h** your prayers.

HIP
Ge 32:25 Jacob's **h** was put out of joint

HIRAM
King of Tyre; helped David build his palace (2Sa 5:11-12; 1Ch 14:1); helped Solomon build the temple (1Ki 5; 2Ch 2) and his navy (1Ki 9:10-27; 2Ch 8).

HITTITE ➛ HITTITES
Ge 23:10 Ephron the **H** answered Abraham
2Sa 11: 3 the wife of Uriah the **H**."

HITTITES ➛ HITTITE
Dt 20:17 **H** and the Amorites, the Canaanites
Ezr 9: 1 Canaanites, the **H**, the Perizzites,

HOLD ➛ HOLDS
Ps 73:23 you **h** my right hand.
Isa 41:13 I, the LORD your God, **h** your right
Jn 20:17 Jesus said to her, "Do not **h** on to
Col 1:17 and in him all things **h** together.

HOLDS ➛ HOLD
Ps 37:24 for the LORD **h** us by the hand.
Rev 2: 1 who **h** the seven stars in his right
Wis 1: 7 which **h** all things together

HOLES
Hag 1: 6 to put them into a bag with **h**.
Mt 8:20 Jesus said to him, "Foxes have **h**,

HOLINESS ➛ HOLY
Ex 15:11 Who is like you, majestic in **h**,
Dt 32:51 by failing to maintain my **h** among
Ps 89:35 and for all I have sworn by my **h;**
Ro 1: 4 according to the spirit of **h** by
2Co 6: 6 kindness, **h** of spirit, genuine love,
1Ti 2:15 continue in faith and love and **h**,
Heb 12:14 **h** without which no one will see the

HOLOFERNES
Assyrian general (Jdt 2:4). Beguiled and beheaded by Judith (Jdt 10-13).

HOLY ➛ HOLINESS
Ex 3: 5 which you are standing is **h** ground.
20: 8 the sabbath day, and keep it **h**.
26:33 the **h** place from the most **h**.
29:37 the altar shall be most **h;**
Lev 11:44 and be **h**, for I am **h**.
Jos 5:15 for the place where you stand is **h**."
1Sa 2: 2 "There is no **H** One like the LORD,
Ps 2: 6 set my king on Zion, my **h** hill."
11: 4 The LORD is in his **h** temple;
Isa 6: 3 "**H, h, h** is the LORD of hosts;
40:25 who is my equal? says the **H** One.
Da 9:24 and to anoint a most **h** place.
Mt 1:18 to be with child from the **H** Spirit.
3:11 baptize you with the **H** Spirit and
24:15 sacrilege standing in the **h** place,
Mk 1:24 who you are, the **H** One of God."
3:29 against the **H** Spirit can never have
Lk 3:22 the **H** Spirit descended upon him in
11:13 heavenly Father give the **H** Spirit
Jn 14:26 But the Advocate, the **H** Spirit,
Ac 2: 4 were filled with the **H** Spirit and
2:27 your **H** One experience corruption.
5: 3 your heart to lie to the **H** Spirit
Ro 12: 1 living sacrifice, **h** and acceptable to
Eph 1: 4 to be **h** and blameless
4:30 do not grieve the **H** Spirit of God,
Heb 6: 4 and have shared in the **H** Spirit,
1Pe 1:16 "You shall be **h**, for I am **h**."
1Jn 2:20 have been anointed by the **H** One,
Jude 1:14 with ten thousands of his **h** ones,
Rev 4: 8 **H, h, h**, the Lord God the Almighty
21: 2 I saw the **h** city, the new Jerusalem,
Wis 4:15 he watches over his **h** ones.
1Mc 1:15 and abandoned the **h** covenant.
2Es 14:22 send the **h** spirit into me,

HOME ➛ HOMELESS, HOMETOWN
Dt 6: 7 when you are at **h** and when you
Ps 68: 6 God gives the desolate a **h**
Jn 14:23 to them and make our **h** with them.
2Co 5: 8 the body and at **h** with the Lord.

HOMELESS* ➛ HOME
Isa 58: 7 the **h** poor into your house;
1Co 4:11 poorly clothed and beaten and **h**,

HOMETOWN ➛ HOME, TOWN
Mk 6: 4 not without honor, except in their **h**,

HONEST
Lev 19:36 have **h** balances, **h** weights,
Pr 16:11 **H** balances and scales are the

HONEY
Ex 3: 8 a land flowing with milk and **h**,
Jdg 14: 8 bees in the body of the lion, and **h**.
1Sa 14:26 honeycomb, the **h** was dripping out;
Ps 19:10 sweeter also than **h**, and drippings
Mt 3: 4 and his food was locusts and wild **h**.

HONOR ➤ HONORABLE, HONORED, HONORS
Dt 5:16 **H** your father and your mother,
1Ch 29:12 Riches and **h** come from you,
Ps 8: 5 and crowned them with glory and **h.**
Ecc 10: 1 little folly outweighs wisdom and **h.**
Isa 29:13 and **h** me with their lips,
Mal 1: 6 a father, where is the **h** due me?
Mt 13:57 not without **h** except in their own
15: 4 For God said, '**H** your father and
Jn 12:26 serves me, the Father will **h.**
Ro 13: 7 **h** to whom **h** is due.
Eph 6: 2 "**H** your father and mother"—
1Ti 5:17 considered worthy of double **h,**
Heb 2: 7 crowned them with glory and **h,**
Rev 4:11 to receive glory and **h** and power,
Tob 4: 3 **H** your mother and do not

HONORABLE ➤ HONOR
Php 4: 8 whatever is true, whatever is **h,**

HONORED ➤ HONOR
Hag 1: 8 I may take pleasure in it and be **h,**
1Co 12:26 if one member is **h,** all rejoice

HONORS ➤ HONOR
Mal 1: 6 A son **h** his father, and servants
Mt 15: 8 'This people **h** me with their lips,

HOOFS
Lev 11: 3 Any animal that has divided **h**

HOOK ➤ HOOKS
Mt 17:27 go to the sea and cast a **h;**

HOOKS ➤ HOOK
Isa 2: 4 and their spears into pruning **h;**
Joel 3:10 and your pruning **h** into spears;

HOPE ➤ HOPED, HOPES
Job 17:15 where then is my **h?**
Ps 62: 5 for my **h** is from him.
146: 5 whose **h** is in the LORD their God,
Pr 23:18 and your **h** will not be cut off.
Isa 8:17 and I will **h** in him.
Jer 14: 8 O **h** of Israel, its savior in time of
La 3:21 and therefore I have **h:**
Mt 12:21 in his name the Gentiles will **h."**
Ro 5: 5 and **h** does not disappoint us,
12:12 Rejoice in **h,** be patient in suffering,
1Co 13:13 And now faith, **h,** and love abide,
Col 1:27 Christ in you, the **h** of glory.
1Th 5: 8 and for a helmet the **h** of salvation.
Heb 6:19 this **h,** a sure and steadfast anchor
7:19 the introduction of a better **h,**
1Pe 1: 3 a living **h** through the resurrection
1Jn 3: 3 all who have this **h** in him purify
Sir 34:15 their **h** is in him who saves them.
Sus 1:60 who saves those who **h** in him.

HOPED ➤ HOPE
Heb 11: 1 faith is the assurance of things **h** for,
1Pe 3: 5 the holy women who **h** in God

HOPES ➤ HOPE
1Co 13: 7 believes all things, **h** all things,

HOREB ➤ =SINAI
Ex 3: 1 came to **H,** the mountain of God.
Dt 5: 2 God made a covenant with us at **H.**
1Ki 19: 8 forty days and forty nights to **H**

HORN ➤ HORNS
Ps 18: 2 and the **h** of my salvation,
Da 7: 8 when another **h** appeared,
8: 5 The goat had a **h** between its eyes.

HORNS ➤ HORN
Ge 22:13 caught in a thicket by its **h.**
Ex 27: 2 make **h** for it on its four corners;
Da 7: 7 that preceded it, and it had ten **h.**
8: 3 Both **h** were long, but one
Zec 1:18 And I looked up and saw four **h.**
Rev 5: 6 having seven **h** and seven eyes,
9:13 from the four **h** of the golden altar
17: 3 and it had seven heads and ten **h.**

HORSE ➤ HORSES
Ex 15: 1 **h** and rider he has thrown into the
Ps 33:17 The war **h** is a vain hope for victory,
Zec 1: 8 I saw a man riding on a red **h!**
Rev 6: 2 I looked, and there was a white **h!**
19:11 and there was a white **h!**

HORSES ➤ HORSE
2Ki 2:11 a chariot of fire and **h** of fire
Ps 20: 7 pride in chariots, and some in **h,**
Joel 2: 4 They have the appearance of **h,**
Rev 9: 7 appearance the locusts were like **h**
19:14 following him on white **h.**

HOSANNA
Mk 11:10 **H** in the highest heaven!"
Jn 12:13 went out to meet him, shouting, "**H!**

HOSEA
Prophet whose wife and family pictured the unfaithfulness of Israel (Hos 1-3).

HOSHEA ➤ =JOSHUA
1. Original name of Joshua (Nu 13:8, 16).
2. Last king of Israel (2Ki 15:30; 17:1-6).

HOSPITABLE* ➤ HOSPITALITY
1Ti 3: 2 temperate, sensible, respectable, **h,**
Tit 1: 8 but he must be **h,** a lover
1Pe 4: 9 Be **h** to one another without

HOSPITALITY* ➤ HOSPITABLE
Ro 12:13 of the saints; extend **h** to strangers.
1Ti 5:10 has brought up children, shown **h,**
Heb 13: 2 not neglect to show **h** to strangers,

HOST ➤ HOSTS
Dt 4:19 all the **h** of heaven,
2Ki 17:16 worshiped all the **h** of heaven
Lk 2:13 angel a multitude of the heavenly **h,**

HOSTILE ➤ HOSTILITY
Ro 8: 7 that is set on the flesh is **h** to God;
Col 1:21 once estranged and **h** in mind,

HOSTILITY ➤ HOSTILE
Eph 2:14 the dividing wall, that is, the **h**
Heb 12: 3 Consider him who endured such **h**

HOSTS ➤ HOST
1Sa 1: 3 and to sacrifice to the LORD of **h**
Ps 46: 7 The LORD of **h** is with us;
Isa 48: 2 the LORD of **h** is his name.

HOT
Rev 3:15 you are neither cold nor **h.**

HOUR
Mt 6:27 by worrying add a single **h** to your
24:36 about that day and **h** no one knows,
Jn 2: 4 My **h** has not yet come."
17: 1 "Father, the **h** has come;
Rev 3:10 I will keep you from the **h** of trial
14: 7 for the **h** of his judgment has come;

HOUSE ➤ HOUSEHOLD, HOUSES, HOUSETOP, HOUSETOPS, STOREHOUSE
Ex 20:17 shall not covet your neighbor's **h;**
2Sa 7:11 that the LORD will make you a **h.**
1Ch 22: 1 "Here shall be the **h** of the LORD
Ezr 1: 5 rebuild the **h** of the LORD in
Ps 69: 9 zeal for your **h** that has consumed
127: 1 Unless the LORD builds the **h,**
Pr 9: 1 Wisdom has built her **h,** she has
Isa 56: 7 my **h** shall be called a **h** of prayer
Mt 7:24 like a wise man who built his **h**
21:13 'My **h** shall be called a **h** of prayer';
Mk 3:25 And if a **h** is divided against itself,
Jn 2:17 "Zeal for your **h** will consume me."
14: 2 In my Father's **h** there are many
1Pe 2: 5 be built into a spiritual **h,**

HOUSEHOLD ➤ HOUSE
Jos 24:15 and my **h,** we will serve the LORD."
Mic 7: 6 enemies are members of your own **h**
Mt 10:36 will be members of one's own **h.**
1Ti 3: 4 He must manage his own **h** well,
Tit 2: 5 good managers of the **h,** kind,
1Pe 4:17 judgment to begin with the **h** of God

HOUSES ➤ HOUSE
Ex 12:27 passed over the **h** of the Israelites in
Mt 19:29 everyone who has left **h** or brothers

HOUSETOP ➤ HOUSE
Mt 24:17 the one on the **h** must not go down

HOUSETOPS ➤ HOUSE
Mt 10:27 whispered, proclaim from the **h.**

HULDAH*
Prophetess inquired by Hilkiah for Josiah (2Ki 22; 2Ch 34:14-28).

HUMAN ➤ HUMANKIND
Ge 6: 7 blot out from the earth the **h** beings
Ps 8: 4 are **h** beings that you are mindful
Da 2:34 a stone was cut out, not by **h** hands,
5: 5 the fingers of a **h** hand appeared
Hos 11: 4 I led them with cords of **h** kindness,
Mt 15: 9 teaching **h** precepts as doctrines.'"
Ac 5:29 obey God rather than any **h**
1Co 2:13 in words not taught by **h** wisdom
Php 2: 7 being born in **h** likeness.
Rev 4: 7 with a face like a **h** face,
Jdt 8:16 for God is not like a **h** being,

HUMANKIND ➤ HUMAN
Ge 1:26 "Let us make **h** in our image,
Mk 2:27 "The sabbath was made for **h,**
1Ti 2: 5 one mediator between God and **h,**

HUMBLE ➤ HUMBLED, HUMBLY, HUMILITY
Nu 12: 3 Now the man Moses was very **h,**
Dt 8:16 to **h** you and to test you,
Ps 25: 9 He leads the **h** in what is right,
149: 4 he adorns the **h** with victory.
Isa 57:15 to revive the spirit of the **h,**
Zep 2: 3 Seek the LORD, all you **h** of the land
Mt 11:29 for I am gentle and **h** in heart,
21: 5 **h,** and mounted on a donkey,
Jas 4:10 **H** yourselves before the Lord,
1Pe 5: 5 but gives grace to the **h."**
Sir 3:20 but by the **h** he is glorified.

HUMBLED ➤ HUMBLE
Ps 119:71 It is good for me that I was **h,**
Lk 14:11 all who exalt themselves will be **h,**
Php 2: 8 he **h** himself and became obedient

HUMBLY* ➤ HUMBLE
Mic 6: 8 and to walk **h** with your God?

HUMILITY ➤ HUMBLE
Pr 15:33 and **h** goes before honor.
Zep 2: 3 seek righteousness, seek **h;**
Php 2: 3 but in **h** regard others as better than
Col 3:12 with compassion, kindness, **h,**
1Pe 5: 5 must clothe yourselves with **h**
Sir 1:27 fidelity and **h** are his delight.

HUNDRED
Ge 17:17 born to a man who is a **h** years old?
Isa 65:20 one who dies at a **h** years will be
Ro 4:19 (for he was about a **h** years old),

HUNG
Dt 21:23 **h** on a tree is under God's curse.
Ps 137: 2 the willows there we **h** up our harps.
Mk 9:42 if a great millstone were **h** around

HUNGER ➤ HUNGRY
Dt 8: 3 He humbled you by letting you **h,**
Mt 5: 6 "Blessed are those who **h** and thirst
Rev 7:16 will **h** no more, and thirst no more;

HUNGRY ➤ HUNGER
Ps 50:12 "If I were **h,** I would not tell you,
146: 7 who gives food to the **h.**
Pr 25:21 If your enemies are **h,** give them
Mt 12: 1 his disciples were **h,** and they began
Jn 6:35 comes to me will never be **h,**
Ro 12:20 "if your enemies are **h,** feed them;

HUSBAND ➤ HUSBANDS
Ge 3: 6 and she also gave some to her **h,**
3:16 yet your desire shall be for your **h,**
Pr 31:28 her **h** too, and he praises her:
Isa 54: 5 For your Maker is your **h,**
Jer 31:32 they broke, though I was their **h,**
Hos 2:16 the LORD, you will call me, "My **h,"**
1Co 7:10 wife should not separate from her **h**
Eph 5:23 **h** is the head of the wife just as
Rev 21: 2 as a bride adorned for her **h.**
Sir 26: 1 Happy is the **h** of a good wife;

HUSBANDS ➤ HUSBAND
Jn 4:18 for you have had five **h,**
Eph 5:25 **H,** love your wives, just as Christ
Col 3:18 Wives, be subject to your **h,**
Tit 2: 4 the young women to love their **h,**
1Pe 3: 7 **H,** in the same way, show

HUSHAI
Wise man of David; foiled Absalom's revolt (2Sa 15:32-37; 16:15-17:16).

HYMN → HYMNS
Mt 26:30 When they had sung the **h**,
Sir 44: 1 H IN HONOR OF OUR ANCESTORS

HYMNS → HYMN
Eph 5:19 psalms and **h** and spiritual songs
Col 3:16 in your hearts sing psalms, **h**,
Aza 1: 1 singing **h** to God and blessing the

HYPOCRISY → HYPOCRITE, HYPOCRITES
Mt 23:28 but inside you are full of **h** and
Mk 12:15 knowing their **h**, he said to them,
Lk 12: 1 of the Pharisees, that is, their **h**.
Jas 3:17 without a trace of partiality or **h**.

HYPOCRITE → HYPOCRISY
Lk 6:42 You **h**, first take the log out of your
Sir 1:29 Do not be a **h** before others,

HYPOCRITES → HYPOCRISY
Mt 6: 5 you pray, do not be like the **h**;
23:13 to you, scribes and Pharisees, **h**!
Mk 7: 6 prophesied rightly about you **h**,

HYSSOP
Ex 12:22 a bunch of **h**, dip it in the blood that
Nu 19: 6 The priest shall take cedarwood, **h**,
Ps 51: 7 Purge me with **h**, and I shall be
Jn 19:29 full of the wine on a branch of **h**

I

I AM
Ex 3:14 God said to Moses, "**I AM WHO I AM**."
Isa 44: 6 **I am** the first and **I am** the last;
Mt 28:20 **I am** with you always, to the end of
Mk 8:29 "But who do you say that **I am**?"
Jn 6:35 to them, "**I am** the bread of life.
8:12 "**I am** the light of the world.
8:58 before Abraham was, **I am**."
9: 5 **I am** the light of the world."
10: 7 **I am** the gate for the sheep.
10:11 "**I am** the good shepherd.
11:25 "**I am** the resurrection and the life.
14: 6 "**I am** the way, and the truth, and
15: 1 "**I am** the true vine, and my Father
Rev 1: 8 "**I am** the Alpha and the Omega,"
22:20 "Surely **I am** coming soon."

IDLE
Ecc 11: 6 evening do not let your hands be **i**;
2Th 3: 7 were not **i** when we were with you,

IDOL → IDOLS
Ex 20: 4 shall not make for yourself an **i**,
Isa 40:19 An **i**?—A workman casts it,
1Co 10:19 or that an **i** is anything?

IDOLS → IDOL
Ex 34:17 You shall not make cast **i**.
2Ki 17:15 went after false **i** and became false;
Ps 115: 4 Their **i** are silver and gold,
1Co 8: 1 concerning food sacrificed to **i**:
1Mc 1:43 they sacrificed to **i** and profaned the

IGNORANCE → IGNORANT
Ac 17:30 overlooked the times of human **i**,
1Pe 2:15 silence the **i** of the foolish.

IGNORANT → IGNORANCE
Heb 5: 2 He is able to deal gently with the **i**
2Pe 3:16 the **i** and unstable twist to their own

ILL → ILLNESS
1Co 11:30 many of you are weak and **i**,

ILLEGITIMATE
Jn 8:41 said to him, "We are not **i** children;
Heb 12: 8 then you are **i** and not his children.

ILLNESS → ILL
Dt 7:15 will turn away from you every **i**;
Ps 41: 3 their **i** you heal all their infirmities.

IMAGE → IMAGES
Ge 1:26 "Let us make humankind in our **i**,
Dt 27:15 who makes an idol or casts an **i**,
1Co 15:49 the **i** of the man of heaven.
Col 1:15 He is the **i** of the invisible God,
Rev 20: 4 not worshiped the beast or its **i** and
Sir 17: 3 and made them in his own **i**.

IMAGES → IMAGE
Nu 33:52 destroy all their cast **i**,
Ps 97: 7 All worshipers of **i** are put to shame,

IMITATE → IMITATORS
Heb 13: 7 their way of life, and **i** their faith.
3Jn 1:11 not **i** what is evil but **i** what is good.

IMITATORS → IMITATE
1Co 11: 1 Be **i** of me, as I am of Christ.
Eph 5: 1 be **i** of God, as beloved children,

IMMANUEL* → =EMMANUEL
Isa 7:14 bear a son, and shall name him **I**.
8: 8 fill the breadth of your land, O **I**.

IMMORAL → IMMORALITY
1Co 5: 9 not to associate with sexually **i**
Heb 12:16 an **i** and godless person,

IMMORALITY → IMMORAL
2Co 12:21 sexual **i**, and licentiousness
Jude 1: 7 indulged in sexual **i** and pursued
Sir 41:17 Be ashamed of sexual **i**,

IMMORTAL → IMMORTALITY
Ro 1:23 the glory of the **i** God for images
1Ti 1:17 To the King of the ages, **i**, invisible,

IMMORTALITY → IMMORTAL
1Co 15:53 and this mortal body must put on **i**.
1Ti 6:16 It is he alone who has **i** and dwells

IMPERISHABLE
1Co 9:25 a perishable wreath, but we an **i** one.
15:52 and the dead will be raised **i**,
1Pe 1: 4 and into an inheritance that is **i**,

IMPORTANCE* → IMPORTANT
1Co 15: 3 of first **i** what I in turn had received:

IMPORTANT → IMPORTANCE
Mk 12:33 much more **i** than all whole burnt

IMPOSSIBLE
Zec 8: 6 should it also seem **i** to me,
Mt 17:20 and nothing will be **i** for you."
Mk 10:27 "For mortals it is **i**, but not for God;
Heb 11: 6 without faith it is **i** to please God,

IMPURE* → IMPURITY
Eph 5: 5 that no fornicator or **i** person,
1Th 2: 3 not spring from deceit or **i** motives

IMPURITY → IMPURE
Zec 13: 1 to cleanse them from sin and **i**.
Gal 5:19 fornication, **i**, licentiousness,
1Th 4: 7 did not call us to **i** but in holiness.

INCENSE → FRANKINCENSE
Ex 25: 6 anointing oil and for the fragrant **i**,

INCLINATION
Ge 6: 5 and that every **i** of the thoughts
Ecc 11: 9 Follow the **i** of your heart and

INCREASE → INCREASED
Ge 3:16 greatly **i** your pangs in childbearing;
Lk 17: 5 said to the Lord, "**I** our faith!"
Jn 3:30 He must **i**, but I must decrease."

INCREASED → INCREASE
Ro 5:20 but where sin **i**, grace abounded all

INDEBTED* → DEBT
Lk 11: 4 forgive everyone **i** to us.

INDEPENDENT*
1Co 11:11 not **i** of man or man **i** of woman.

INFANTS
Ps 8: 2 Out of the mouths of babes and **i**
Mt 21:16 'Out of the mouths of **i** and nursing
1Co 14:20 **i** in evil, but in thinking be adults.

INFIRMITIES
Isa 53: 4 borne our **i** and carried our diseases;
Mt 8:17 took our **i** and bore our diseases."

INGATHERING → GATHER
Ex 23:16 You shall observe the festival of **i**

INHERIT → INHERITANCE
Lev 20:24 You shall **i** their land,
Ps 37:11 But the meek shall **i** the land,
Zec 2:12 The LORD will **i** Judah as his portion
Lk 10:25 "what must I do to **i** eternal life?"
1Co 6: 9 wrongdoers will not **i** the kingdom
Heb 1:14 sake of those who are to **i** salvation?

INHERITANCE → INHERIT
Ex 34: 9 and take us for your **i**."
Eph 1:11 In Christ we have also obtained an **i**,
Heb 9:15 the promised eternal **i**,

INIQUITIES → INIQUITY
Lev 16:22 goat shall bear on itself all their **i**
Ps 103:10 nor repay us according to our **i**.
Isa 53:11 and he shall bear their **i**.
Ro 4: 7 are those whose **i** are forgiven,
Rev 18: 5 and God has remembered her **i**.

INIQUITY → INIQUITIES
Ex 34: 7 forgiving **i** and transgression and sin
Ps 103: 3 who forgives all your **i**,
Isa 53: 6 LORD has laid on him the **i** of us all.
Tit 2:14 that he might redeem us from all **i**

INJURY
Lev 24:20 the **i** inflicted is the **i** to be suffered.

INJUSTICE
Hos 10:13 wickedness, you have reaped **i**,
Ro 9:14 Is there **i** on God's part?

INN*
Lk 2: 7 there was no place for them in the **i**.
10:34 brought him to an **i**, and took care

INNER → INWARDLY
Mt 24:26 He is in the **i** rooms,' do not believe
2Co 4:16 our **i** nature is being renewed day
1Pe 3: 4 let your adornment be the **i** self

INNOCENCE → INNOCENT
Ps 26: 6 I wash my hands in **i**,
Hos 8: 5 long will they be incapable of **i**?

INNOCENT → INNOCENCE
Pr 6:17 tongue, and hands that shed **i** blood,
Mt 10:16 be wise as serpents and **i** as doves.
27:24 "I am **i** of this man's blood;

INQUIRE → INQUIRED
Dt 12:30 do not **i** concerning their gods,

INQUIRED → INQUIRE
Zep 1: 6 not sought the LORD or **i** of him.

INSCRIBED → INSCRIPTION
Da 10:21 what is **i** in the book of truth.
Rev 19:12 he has a name **i** that no one

INSCRIPTION → INSCRIBED
Mk 15:26 The **i** of the charge against him read,
2Ti 2:19 foundation stands, bearing this **i**:

INSIGHT
Pr 3: 5 and do not rely on your own **i**.
Eph 1: 8 With all wisdom and **i**
Sir 6:37 It is he who will give **i** to your mind,

INSPIRED
Ex 35:34 And he has **i** him to teach,
2Ti 3:16 All scripture is **i** by God and is

INSTITUTED → INSTITUTION
Ro 13: 1 that exist have been **i** by God.

INSTITUTION* → INSTITUTED
Nu 10: 8 this shall be a perpetual **i** for you
1Pe 2:13 the authority of every human **i**,

INSTRUCT → INSTRUCTED, INSTRUCTION, INSTRUCTOR
Dt 17:10 observing everything they **i** you.
Ne 9:20 You gave your good spirit to **i** them,
Ro 15:14 and able to **i** one another.
1Co 14:19 in order to **i** others also,

INSTRUCTED → INSTRUCT
Isa 40:13 or as his counselor has **i** him?
Jn 8:28 these things as the Father **i** me.

INSTRUCTION → INSTRUCT
Pr 8:10 Take my **i** instead of silver,
Mic 4: 2 For out of Zion shall go forth **i**,
Ro 15: 4 in former days was written for our **i**,
1Ti 1: 5 But the aim of such **i** is love
Sir 51:26 and let your souls receive **i**;

INSTRUCTOR → INSTRUCT
Mt 23:10 for you have one **i**, the Messiah.

INSULTS
Ps 69: 9 the **i** of those who insult you have
Lk 22:65 heaping many other **i** on him.
2Co 12:10 I am content with weaknesses, **i**,

INTEGRITY
Job 27: 5 until I die I will not put away my i
Pr 14:32 the righteous find a refuge in their i.
Tit 2: 7 and in your teaching show i, gravity,

INTELLIGENCE ➛ INTELLIGENT
Pr 8: 5 acquire i, you who lack it.
Sir 22:11 fool, for he has left i behind.

INTELLIGENT ➛ INTELLIGENCE
Pr 11:12 but an i person remains silent.
Ecc 9:11 nor riches to the i,

INTENDED ➛ INTENTIONS
Ge 50:20 i to do harm to me, God i it for good,
Jer 18:10 the good that I had i to do to it.

INTENTIONS ➛ INTENDED
Mk 7:21 the human heart, that evil i come:
Heb 4:12 judge the thoughts and i of the heart.

INTERCEDES ➛ INTERCESSION
Ro 8:26 Spirit i with sighs too deep for

INTERCESSION* ➛ INTERCEDES
1Sa 2:25 against the LORD, who can make i?"
Isa 53:12 and made i for the transgressors.
Heb 7:25 he always lives to make i for them.

INTERMARRY ➛ MARRIAGE
Dt 7: 3 Do not i with them, giving your

INTERPRET ➛ INTERPRETATION, INTERPRETATIONS
Ge 41:15 no one who can i it.
Mt 16: 3 cannot i the signs of the times.
1Co 12:30 Do all speak in tongues? Do all i?

INTERPRETATION ➛ INTERPRET
Da 2: 4 and we will reveal the i."
1Co 12:10 to another the i of tongues.
2Pe 1:20 scripture is a matter of one's own i,
2Es 12:10 "This is the i of this vision

INTERPRETATIONS ➛ INTERPRET
Ge 40: 8 to them, "Do not i belong to God?

INVADE ➛ INVADED
La 1:10 the nations i her sanctuary,
Na 1:15 never again shall the wicked i you;

INVADED ➛ INVADE
2Ki 17: 5 the king of Assyria i all the land

INVISIBLE
Col 1:15 He is the image of the i God,
1Ti 1:17 To the King of the ages, immortal, i,

INVITE ➛ INVITED, INVITES
Lk 14:13 when you give a banquet, i the poor,

INVITED ➛ INVITE
Rev 19: 9 Blessed are those who are i to

INVITES ➛ INVITE
1Co 10:27 If an unbeliever i you to a meal
Sir 13: 9 When an influential person i you,

INVOKE
Ex 23:13 Do not i the names of other gods;
1Pe 1:17 If you i as Father the one who

INWARDLY ➛ INNER
Ro 2:29 a person is a Jew who is one i,
8:23 groan i while we wait for adoption,

IRON
Ps 2: 9 shall break them with a rod of i,
Pr 27:17 I sharpens i, and one person
Da 2:33 its legs of i, its feet partly of i
Rev 19:15 he will rule them with a rod of i;

IRREVOCABLE
Ro 11:29 gifts and the calling of God are i.

ISAAC
Son of Abraham by Sarah (Ge 17:19; 21:1-7; 1Ch 1:28). Abrahamic covenant perpetuated with (Ge 17:21; 26:2-5). Offered up by Abraham (Ge 22; Heb 11:17-19). Rebekah taken as wife (Ge 24). Inherited Abraham's estate (Ge 25:5). Father of Esau and Jacob (Ge 25:19-26; 1Ch 1:34). Nearly lost Rebekah to Abimelech (Ge 26:1-11). Covenant with Abimelech (Ge 26:12-31). Tricked into blessing Jacob (Ge 27). Death (Ge 35:27-29). Father of Israel (Ex 3:6; Dt 29:13; Ro 9:10).

ISAIAH
Prophet to Judah (Isa 1:1). Called by the LORD (Isa 6). Announced judgment to Ahaz (Isa 7), deliverance from Assyria to Hezekiah (2Ki 19; Isa 36-37), deliverance from death to Hezekiah (2Ki 20:1-11; Isa 38). Chronicler of Judah's history (2Ch 26:22; 32:32).

ISCARIOT
Mt 10: 4 Judas I, the one who betrayed him.
Lk 22: 3 Satan entered into Judas called I,

ISHBAAL*
Son of Saul; would-be king (2Sa 2:8-4:12).

ISHMAEL
Son of Abraham by Hagar (Ge 16; 1Ch 1:28). Blessed, but not son of covenant (Ge 17:18-21; Gal 4:21-31). Sent away by Sarah (Ge 21:8-21). Children (Ge 25:12-18; 1Ch 1:29-31). Death (Ge 25:17).

ISRAEL ➛ ISRAELITE, ISRAELITES, =JACOB
1. Name given to Jacob (Ge 32:28; 35:10).
2. Corporate name of Jacob's descendants; often specifically Northern Kingdom.
Ge 49:28 All these are the twelve tribes of I,
Ex 28:11 with the names of the sons of I;
Nu 24:17 and a scepter shall rise out of I;
Dt 6: 4 Hear, O I: The LORD is our God,
Ps 125: 5 Peace be upon I!
Jer 31:31 a new covenant with the house of I
Hos 11: 1 When I was a child, I loved him,
Mt 2: 6 who is to shepherd my people I.'"
Mk 12:29 answered, "The first is, 'Hear, O I:
Lk 22:30 judging the twelve tribes of I.
Ac 1: 6 you will restore the kingdom to I?"
Ro 9: 6 not all Israelites truly belong to I,
Heb 8: 8 a new covenant with the house of I
Rev 7: 4 out of every tribe of the people of I:
Sir 17:17 but I is the Lord's own portion.

ISRAELITE ➛ ISRAEL
Jn 1:47 an I in whom there is no deceit!"
Ro 11: 1 I myself am an I, a descendant of

ISRAELITES ➛ ISRAEL
Ex 2:23 The I groaned under their slavery,
29:45 I will dwell among the I, and I will

ISSACHAR
Son of Jacob by Leah (Ge 30:18; 35:23; 1Ch 2:1). Tribe of blessed (Ge 49:14-15; Dt 33:18-19), numbered (Nu 1:29; 26:25), allotted land (Jos 19:17-23; Eze 48:25), assisted Deborah (Jdg 5:15), 12,000 from (Rev 7:7).

ITCHING
2Ti 4: 3 sound doctrine, but having i ears,

J

JACOB ➛ =ISRAEL
1. Son of Isaac, younger twin of Esau (Ge 26:21-26; 1Ch 1:34). Bought Esau's birthright (Ge 26:29-34); tricked Isaac into blessing him (Ge 27:1-37). Fled to Haran (Ge 28:1-5). Abrahamic covenant perpetuated through (Ge 28:13-15; Mal 1:2). Vision at Bethel (Ge 28:10-22). Served Laban for Rachel and Leah (Ge 29:1-30). Children (Ge 29:31-30:24; 35:16-26; 1Ch 2-9). Flocks increased (Ge 30:25-43). Returned to Canaan (Ge 31). Wrestled with God; name changed to Israel (Ge 32:22-32). Reconciled to Esau (Ge 33). Returned to Bethel (Ge 35:1-15). Favored Joseph (Ge 37:3). Sent sons to Egypt during famine (Ge 42-43). Settled in Egypt (Ge 46). Blessed Ephraim and Manasseh (Ge 48). Blessed sons (Ge 49:1-28; Heb 11:21). Death (Ge 49:29-33). Burial (Ge 50:1-14).
2. Corporate name of Jacob's descendants; often specifically Northern Kingdom.
Ps 135: 4 the LORD has chosen J for himself,
Mic 7:20 You will show faithfulness to J
Ro 9:13 "I have loved J,
1Mc 1:28 house of J was clothed with shame.

JAEL*
Woman who killed the Canaanite general, Sisera (Jdg 4:17-22; 5:6, 24-27).

JAIRUS
Synagogue ruler whose daughter Jesus raised (Mk 5:22-43; Lk 8:41-56).

JAMES
1. Apostle; brother of John (Mt 4:21-22; 10:2; Mk 3:17; Lk 5:1-10). At transfiguration (Mt 17:1-13; Mk 9:1-13; Lk 9:28-36). Killed by Herod (Ac 12:2).
2. Apostle (Mt 10:3; Mk 3:18; Lk 6:15).
3. Brother of Jesus (Mt 13:55; Mk 6:3; Lk 24:10; Gal 1:19) and Judas (Jude 1). With believers before Pentecost (Ac 1:13). Leader of church at Jerusalem (Ac 12:17; 15; 21:18; Gal 2:9, 12). Author of epistle (Jas 1:1).

JAPHETH
Son of Noah (Ge 5:32; 1Ch 1:4-5). Blessed (Ge 9:18-28). Sons of (Ge 10:2-5).

JAR ➛ JARS
1Ki 17:14 The j of meal will not be emptied
Mk 14: 3 alabaster j of very costly ointment
Lk 22:10 man carrying a j of water will meet

JARS ➛ JAR
Jn 2: 6 there were six stone water j for
2Co 4: 7 But we have this treasure in clay j,

JEALOUS
Ex 34:14 whose name is J, is a j God).
Dt 4:24 God is a devouring fire, a j God.
32:16 They made him j with strange gods,
Eze 39:25 and I will be j for my holy name.
Ro 10:19 "I will make you j of those

JEBUSITES
Ex 3: 8 the Perizzites, the Hivites, and the J.
Jos 15:63 Judah could not drive out the J,

JECONIAH ➛ See JEHOIACHIN

JEHOAHAZ
1. Son of Jehu; king of Israel (2Ki 13:1-9).
2. Son of Josiah; king of Judah (2Ki 23:31-34; 2Ch 36:1-4).

JEHOASH ➛ =JOASH
1. Son of Ahaziah, king of Judah (2Ki 12). See Joash, 1.
2. Son of Jehoahaz; king of Israel. Defeat of Aram prophesied by Elisha (2Ki 13:10-25). Defeated Amaziah in Jerusalem (2Ki 14:1-16). See Joash, 2.

JEHOIACHIN ➛ =CONIAH, =JECONIAH
Son of Jehoiakim; king of Judah exiled by Nebuchadnezzar (2Ki 24:8-17; 2Ch 36:8-10; Eze 1:2). Status improved (2Ki 25:27-30; Jer 52:31-34).

JEHOIADA
Priest who sheltered Joash from Athaliah (2Ki 11-12; 2Ch 22:11-24:16).

JEHOIAKIM ➛ =ELIAKIM
Son of Josiah; made king of Judah by Nebuchadnezzar (2Ki 23:34-24:6; 2Ch 36:4-8; Jer 22:18-23). Burned scroll of Jeremiah's prophecies (Jer 36).

JEHORAM ➛ =JORAM
1. Son of Jehoshaphat; king of Judah. Prophesied against by Elijah; killed by the LORD (2Ch 21). See Joram, 1.
2. Son of Ahab; king of Israel (2Ch 22:5). Joined Jehoshaphat against Moab (2Ki 3). See Joram, 2.

JEHOSHAPHAT
1. Son of Asa; king of Judah. Strengthened his kingdom (2Ch 17). Joined with Ahab against Aram (2Ki 22; 2Ch 18). Established judges (2Ch 19). Joined Joram against Moab (2Ki 3; 2Ch 20).
2. Valley of judgment (Joel 3:2, 12).

JEHU
1. Prophet against Baasha (2Ki 16:1-7).
2. King of Israel. Anointed by Elijah to obliterate house of Ahab (1Ki 19:16-17); anointed by servant of Elisha (2Ki 9:1-13). Killed Joram and Ahaziah (2Ki 9:14-29; 2Ch 22:7-9), Jezebel (2Ki 9:30-37), relatives of Ahab (2Ki 10:1-17; Hos 1:4), ministers of Baal (2Ki 10:18-29). Death (2Ki 10:30-36).

JEPHTHAH
Judge from Gilead who delivered Israel from Ammon (Jdg 10:6-12:7). Made rash vow concerning his daughter (Jdg 11:30-40).

JEREMIAH
Prophet to Judah (Jer 1:1-3). Called by the LORD (Jer 1). Put in stocks (Jer 20:1-3). Threatened for

prophesying (Jer 11:18-23; 26). Opposed by Hananiah (Jer 28). Scroll burned (Jer 36). Imprisoned (Jer 37). Thrown into cistern (Jer 38). Forced to Egypt with those fleeing Babylonians (Jer 43).

JERICHO

Jos 6: 2 "See, I have handed J over to you,
1Ki 16:34 In his days Hiel of Bethel built J;
Lk 18:35 As he approached J, a blind man

JEROBOAM

1. Official of Solomon; rebelled to become first king of Israel (1Ki 11:26-40; 12:1-20; 2Ch 10). Idolatry (1Ki 12:25-33; Tob 1:5; Sir 47:23); judgment for (1Ki 13-14; 2Ch 13).

2. Son of Jehoash; king of Israel (1Ki 14:23-29).

JERUSALEM

2Sa 5: 5 and at J he reigned over all Israel
15:29 carried the ark of God back to J,
2Ki 25:10 broke down the walls around J.
Ezr 2: 1 they returned to J and Judah,
Ne 2:17 Come, let us rebuild the wall of J,
Isa 40: 2 Speak tenderly to J,
La 1: 8 J sinned grievously, so she has
Da 9:25 went out to restore and rebuild J
Joel 3: 1 I restore the fortunes of Judah and J,
Mic 4: 2 and the word of the LORD from J.
Zec 1:14 I am very jealous for J and for Zion.
14: 8 living waters shall flow out from J,
Mt 23:37 "J, J, the city that kills the prophets
Lk 4: 9 Then the devil took him to J,
Gal 4:25 corresponds to the present J,
Heb 12:22 of the living God, the heavenly J,
Rev 21: 2 And I saw the holy city, the new J,
1Mc 1:29 and he came to J with a large force.

JESSE

Father of David (Ru 4:17-22; 1Sa 16; 1Ch 2:12-17).

JESUS

1. Jesus the Messiah.

LIFE: Genealogy (Mt 1:1-17; Lk 3:21-37). Birth announced (Mt 1:18-25; Lk 1:26-45). Birth (Mt 2:1-12; Lk 2:1-40). Escape to Egypt (Mt 2:13-23). As a boy in the temple (Lk 2:41-52). Baptism (Mt 3:13-17; Mk 1:9-11; Lk 3:21-22; Jn 1:32-34). Temptation (Mt 4:1-11; Mk 1:12-13; Lk 4:1-13). Ministry in Galilee (Mt 4:12-18:35; Mk 1:14-9:50; Lk 4:14-13:9; Jn 1:35-2:11; 4; 6), Transfiguration (Mt 17:1-8; Mk 9:2-8; Lk 9:28-36), on the way to Jerusalem (Mt 19-20; Mk 10; Lk 13:10-19:27), in Jerusalem (Mt 21-25; Mk 11-13; Lk 19:28-21:38; Jn 2:12-3:36; 5; 7-12). Last supper (Mt 26:17-35; Mk 14:12-31; Lk 22:1-38; Jn 13-17). Arrest and trial (Mt 26:36-27:31; Mk 14:43-15:20; Lk 22:39-23:25; Jn 18:1-19:16). Crucifixion (Mt 27:32-66; Mk 15:21-47; Lk 23:26-55; Jn 19:28-42). Resurrection and appearances (Mt 28; Mk 16; Lk 24; Jn 20-21; Ac 1:1-11; 7:56; 9:3-6; 1Co 15:1-8; Rev 1:1-20).

MIRACLES. *Healings:* official's son (Jn 4:43-54), demoniac in Capernaum (Mk 1:23-26; Lk 4:33-35), Peter's mother-in-law (Mt 8:14-17; Mk 1:29-31; Lk 4:38-39), leper (Mt 8:2-4; Mk 1:40-45; Lk 5:12-16), paralytic (Mt 9:1-8; Mk 2:1-12; Lk 5:17-26), cripple (Jn 5:1-9), shriveled hand (Mt 12:10-13; Mk 3:1-5; Lk 6:6-11), centurion's servant (Mt 8:5-13; Lk 7:1-10), widow's son raised (Lk 7:11-17), demoniac (Mt 12:22-23; Lk 11:14), Gadarene demoniacs (Mt 8:28-34; Mk 5:1-20; Lk 8:26-39), woman's bleeding and Jairus' daughter (Mt 9:18-26; Mk 5:21-43; Lk 8:40-56), blind man (Mt 9:27-31), mute man (Mt 9:32-33), Canaanite woman's daughter (Mt 15:21-28; Mk 7:24-30), deaf man (Mk 7:31-37), blind man (Mk 8:22-26), demoniac boy (Mt 17:14-18; Mk 9:14-29; Lk 9:37-43), ten lepers (Lk 17:11-19), man born blind (Jn 9:1-7), Lazarus raised (Jn 11), crippled woman (Lk 13:11-17), man with dropsy (Lk 14:1-6), two blind men (Mt 20:29-34; Mk 10:46-52; Lk 18:35-43), Malchus' ear (Lk 22:50-51). *Other Miracles:* water to wine (Jn 2:1-11), catch of fish (Lk 5:1-11), storm stilled (Mt 8:23-27; Mk 4:37-41; Lk 8:22-25), 5,000 fed (Mt 14:15-21; Mk 6:35-44; Lk 9:10-17; Jn 6:1-14), walking on water (Mt 14:25-33; Mk 6:48-52; Jn 6:15-21), 4,000 fed (Mt 15:32-39; Mk 8:1-9), money from fish (Mt 17:24-27), fig tree cursed (Mt 21:18-22; Mk 11:12-14), catch of fish (Jn 21:1-14).

MAJOR TEACHING: Sermon on the Mount (Mt 5-7; Lk 6:17-49), to Nicodemus (Jn 3), to Samaritan woman (Jn 4), Bread of Life (Jn 6:22-59), at Feast of Tabernacles (Jn 7-8), woes to Pharisees (Mt 23; Lk 11:37-54), Good Shepherd (Jn 10:1-18), Olivet Discourse (Mt 24-25; Mk 13; Lk 21:5-36), Upper Room Discourse (Jn 13-16).

PARABLES: Sower (Mt 13:3-23; Mk 4:3-25; Lk 8:5-18), seed's growth (Mk 4:26-29), wheat and weeds (Mt 13:24-30, 36-43), mustard seed (Mt 13:31-32; Mk 4:30-32), yeast (Mt 13:33; Lk 13:20-21), hidden treasure (Mt 13:44), valuable pearl (Mt 13:45-46), net (Mt 13:47-51), house owner (Mt 13:52), good Samaritan (Lk 10:25-37), unmerciful servant (Mt 18:15-35), lost sheep (Mt 18:10-14; Lk 15:4-7), lost coin (Lk 15:8-10), prodigal son (Lk 15:11-32), dishonest manager (Lk 16:1-13), rich man and Lazarus (Lk 16:19-31), persistent widow (Lk 18:1-8), Pharisee and tax collector (Lk 18:9-14), payment of workers (Mt 20:1-16), tenants and the vineyard (Mt 21:28-46; Mt 12:1-12; Lk 20:9-19), wedding banquet (Mt 22:1-14), faithful servant (Mt 24:45-51), ten virgins (Mt 25:1-13), talents (Mt 25:1-30; Lk 19:12-27).

DISCIPLES see APOSTLES. Call (Jn 1:35-51; Mt 4:18-22; 9:9; Mk 1:16-20; 2:13-14; Lk 5:1-11, 27-28). Named Apostles (Mk 3:13-19; Lk 6:12-16). Twelve sent out (Mt 10; Mk 6:7-11; Lk 9:1-5). Seventy sent out (Lk 10:1-24). Defection of (Jn 6:60-71; Mt 26:56; Mk 14:50-52). Final commission (Mt 28:16-20; Jn 21:15-23; Ac 1:3-8).

Ac 9: 5 "I am J, whom you are persecuting.
1Co 8: 6 and one Lord, J Christ,
Php 2:10 name of J every knee should bend,
2Th 2: 1 the coming of our Lord J Christ
1Ti 1:15 J came into the world to save
Heb 12: 2 to J the pioneer and perfecter of our
13: 8 J Christ is the same yesterday and
1Jn 1: 7 the blood of J his Son cleanses us
Rev 1: 1 The revelation of J Christ,
22:20 Amen. Come, Lord J!

2. Disciple, also called Justus (Col 4:11).

3. Writer of Sirach (Sir Pr:1; 50:27; 51:1).

JETHRO

Father-in-law and adviser of Moses (Ex 3:1; 4:18; 18). Also known as Reuel (Ex 2:18).

JEW → JEWS, JUDAISM

Est 10: 3 Mordecai the J was next in rank to
Zec 8:23 shall take hold of a J,
Ro 1:16 to the J first and also to the Greek.
2:29 a person is a J who is one inwardly,
1Co 9:20 To the Jews I became as a J,
Col 3:11 there is no longer Greek and J,

JEWEL → JEWELS

Pr 20:15 by knowledge are a precious j.
Rev 21:19 of the city are adorned with every j;

JEWELS → JEWEL

Pr 3:15 She is more precious than j,
Isa 54:12 your gates of j, and all your wall
Rev 17: 4 adorned with gold and j and pearls,

JEWS → JEW

Ne 4: 1 enraged, and he mocked the J.
Est 3:13 to kill, and to annihilate all J,
Mt 2: 2 who has been born king of the J?
27:11 "Are you the King of the J?"
Jn 4:22 for salvation is from the J.
Ro 3:29 Or is God the God of J only?

JEZEBEL*

Sidonian wife of Ahab (1Ki 16:31). Promoted Baal worship (1Ki 16:32-33). Killed prophets of the LORD (1Ki 18:4, 13). Opposed Elijah (1Ki 19:1-2). Had Naboth killed (1Ki 21). Death (1Ki 21:17-24; 2Ki 9:30-37). Metaphor of immorality (Rev 2:20).

JEZREEL

2Ki 10: 7 in baskets and sent them to him at J.
Hos 1: 4 the LORD said to him, "Name him J;

JOAB

Nephew of David (1Ch 2:16). Commander of his army (2Sa 8:16). Victorious over Ammon (2Sa 10; 1Ch 19), Rabbah (2Sa 11; 1Ch 20), Jerusalem (1Ch 11:6), Absalom (2Sa 18), Sheba (2Sa 20). Killed Abner (2Sa 3:22-39), Amasa (2Sa 20:1-13). Numbered David's army (2Sa 24; 1Ch 21). Sided with Adonijah (1Ki 1:17, 19). Killed by Benaiah (1Ki 2:5-6, 28-35).

JOASH → =JEHOASH

1. Son of Ahaziah; king of Judah. Sheltered from Athaliah by Jehoiada (2Ki 11; 2Ch 22:10-23:21). Repaired temple (2Ch 24). See Jehoash, 1.

2. Son of Jehoahaz, king of Israel (2Ki 13; 2Ch 25:17-25). See Jehoash, 2.

JOB

Wealthy man from Uz; feared God (Job 1:1-5). Integrity tested by disaster (Job 1:6-22), personal affliction (Job 2). Maintained innocence in debate with three friends (Job 3-31), Elihu (Job 32-37). Rebuked by the LORD (Job 38-41). Vindicated and restored to greater stature by the LORD (Job 42). Example of righteousness (Eze 14:14, 20; Sir 49:9).

JOEL

1. Son of Samuel (1Sa 8:2; 1Ch 6:28).

2. Prophet (Joel 1:1; Ac 2:16).

JOHANAN

1. First high priest in the temple (1Ch 6:9-10).

2. Jewish leader who tried to save Gedaliah from assassination (Jer 40:13-14); took Jews, including Jeremiah, to Egypt (Jer 40-43).

JOHN

1. Son of Zechariah and Elizabeth (Lk 1). Called the Baptist (Mt 3:1-12; Mk 1:2-8). Witness to Jesus (Mt 3:11-12; Mk 1:7-8; Lk 3:15-18; Jn 1:6-35; 3:27-30; 5:33-36). Doubts about Jesus (Mt 11:2-6; Lk 7:18-23). Arrest (Mt 4:12; Mk 1:14). Execution (Mt 14:1-12; Mk 6:14-29; Lk 9:7-9). Ministry compared to Elijah (Mt 11:7-19; Mk 9:11-13; Lk 7:24-35).

2. Apostle; brother of James (Mt 4:21-22; 10:2; Mk 3:17; Lk 5:1-10). At transfiguration (Mt 17:1-13; Mk 9:1-13; Lk 9:28-36). Desire to be greatest (Mk 10:35-45). Leader of church at Jerusalem (Ac 4:1-3; Gal 2:9). Elder who wrote epistles (2Jn 1; 3Jn 1). Prophet who wrote Revelation (Rev 1:1; 22:8).

3. Cousin of Barnabas, co-worker with Paul, (Ac 12:12-13:13; 15:37; see Mark).

4. Son of Simon Maccabeus (1Mc 13:53; 16).

JOIN → JOINED

Eze 37:17 and j them together into one stick,
2Ti 1: 8 j with me in suffering for the gospel

JOINED → JOIN

Mt 19: 6 what God has j together, let no one
Eph 2:21 the whole structure is j together and

JOINT → JOINTS

Ge 32:25 and Jacob's hip was put out of j
Ps 22:14 and all my bones are out of j;
Ro 8:17 heirs of God and j heirs with Christ

JOINTS → JOINT

Heb 4:12 soul from spirit, j from marrow;

JONAH

Prophet in days of Jeroboam II (2Ki 14:25). Called to Nineveh; fled to Tarshish (Jnh 1:1-3). Cause of storm; thrown into sea (Jnh 1:4-16). Swallowed by fish (Jnh 1:17). Prayer (Jnh 2). Preached to Nineveh (Jnh 3). Attitude reproved by the LORD (Jnh 4). Sign of (Mt 12:39-41; Lk 11:29-32).

JONATHAN

1. Son of Saul (1Sa 13:16; 1Ch 8:33). Valiant warrior (1Sa 13-14). Relation to David (1Sa 18:1-4; 19-20; 23:16-18). Killed at Gilboa (1Sa 31). Mourned by David (2Sa 1).

2. Brother and successor of Judas Maccabeus (1Mc 2:5; 9:28-31).

JOPPA

Jnh 1: 3 down to J and found a ship going
Ac 9:43 he stayed in J for some time with

JORAM → =JEHORAM

1. Son of Jehoshaphat; king of Judah (2Ki 8:16-24). See Jehoram, 1.

2. Son of Ahab; king of Israel. Killed with Ahaziah by Jehu (2Ki 8:25-29; 9:14-26; 2Ch 22:5-9). See Jehoram, 2.

JORDAN

Ge 13:10 the plain of the J was well watered
Nu 34:12 the boundary shall go down to the J,

Jos 3:17 dry ground in the middle of the J,
Mt 3: 6 were baptized by him in the river J,

JOSEPH ➛ =BARNABAS, =BARSABBAS

1. Son of Jacob by Rachel (Ge 30:24; 1Ch 2:2). Favored by Jacob, hated by brothers (Ge 37:3-4). Dreams (Ge 37:5-11). Sold by brothers (Ge 37:12-36). Served Potiphar; imprisoned by false accusation (Ge 39). Interpreted dreams of Pharaoh's servants (Ge 40), of Pharaoh (Ge 41:4-40). Made greatest in Egypt (Ge 41:41-57). Sold grain to brothers (Ge 42-45). Brought Jacob and sons to Egypt (Ge 46-47). Sons Ephraim and Manasseh blessed (Ge 48). Blessed (Ge 49:22-26; Dt 33:13-17). Death (Ge 50:22-26; Ex 13:19; Heb 11:22). 12,000 from (Rev 7:8).

2. Husband of Mary mother of Jesus (Mt 1:16-24; 2:13-19; Lk 1:27; 2; Jn 1:45).

3. Disciple from Arimathea; buried Jesus in his tomb (Mt 27:57-61; Mk 15:43-47; Lk 24:50-52).

4. Original name of Barnabas (Ac 4:36).

JOSHUA ➛ =HOSHEA, =JESHUA

1. Son of Nun; name changed from Hoshea (Nu 13:8, 16; 1Ch 7:27). Fought Amalekites under Moses (Ex 17:9-14). Servant of Moses on Sinai (Ex 24:13; 32:17). Spied Canaan (Nu 13). With Caleb, allowed to enter land (Nu 14:6, 30). Succeeded Moses (Dt 1:38; 31:1-8; 34:9).

Charged Israel to conquer Canaan (Jos 1). Crossed Jordan (Jos 3-4). Circumcised sons of wilderness wanderings (Jos 5). Conquered Jericho (Jos 6), Ai (Jos 7-8), five kings at Gibeon (Jos 10:1-28), southern Canaan (Jos 10:29-43), northern Canaan (Jos 11-12). Defeated at Ai (Jos 7). Deceived by Gibeonites (Jos 9). Renewed covenant (Jos 8:30-35; 24:1-27). Divided land among tribes (Jos 13-22). Last words (Jos 23). Death (Jos 24:28-31).

2. High priest during rebuilding of temple (Hag 1-2; Zec 3:1-9; 6:11). See Jeshua.

JOSIAH

Son of Amon; king of Judah (2Ki 21:26; 1Ch 3:14). Prophesied (1Ki 13:2). Book of the Law discovered during his reign (2Ki 22; 2Ch 34:14-31). Reforms (2Ki 23:1-25; 2Ch 34:1-13; 35:1-19; Sir 49:1-4). Killed in battle (2Ki 23:29-30; 2Ch 35:20-27).

JOTHAM

1. Son of Gideon (Jdg 9).

2. Son of Azariah (Uzziah); king of Judah (2Ki 15:32-38; 2Ch 26:21-27:9).

JOY ➛ JOYFUL

Ne 8:10 the j of the LORD is your strength."
Job 20: 5 j of the godless is but for a moment?
Ps 51:12 Restore to me the j of your salvation
Pr 21:15 When justice is done, it is a j to the
Isa 12: 3 With j you will draw water from
35:10 everlasting j shall be upon their
La 2:15 of beauty, the j of all the earth?"
Mt 28: 8 tomb quickly with fear and great j,
Mk 4:16 they immediately receive it with j.
Lk 1:44 the child in my womb leaped for j.
2:10 bringing you good news of great j
Jn 16:22 no one will take your j from you.
Ro 14:17 but righteousness and peace and j in
Gal 5:22 the fruit of the Spirit is love, j,
Php 4: 1 I love and long for, my j and crown,
Heb 12: 2 j that was set before him endured
Jas 1: 2 consider it nothing but j,
Tob 13:17 Jerusalem will sing hymns of j,
Bar 5: 9 For God will lead Israel with j,

JOYFUL ➛ JOY

Ps 98: 4 Make a j noise to the LORD,
Jdt 14: 9 and made a j noise in their town.

JUBILEE

Lev 25:10 It shall be a j for you:
Nu 36: 4 when the j of the Israelites comes,

JUDAH ➛ JUDEA

1. Son of Jacob by Leah (Ge 29:35; 35:23; 1Ch 2:1). Did not want to kill Joseph (Ge 37:26-27). Among Canaanites, fathered Perez by Tamar (Ge 38). Tribe of blessed as ruling tribe (Ge 49:8-12; Dt 33:7), numbered (Nu 1:27; 26:22), allotted land (Jos 15; Eze 48:7), failed to fully possess (Jos 15:63; Jdg 1:1-20).

2. Name used for Southern Kingdom.

2Sa 2: 4 David king over the house of J.
La 1: 3 J has gone into exile with suffering
Joel 3: 1 when I restore the fortunes of J and
Mic 5: 2 who are one of the little clans of J,
Mt 2: 6 least among the rulers of J;
Heb 7:14 our Lord was descended from J,
Rev 5: 5 See, the Lion of the tribe of J,

JUDAISM ➛ JEW

Ac 13:43 devout converts to J followed Paul
Gal 1:13 no doubt, of my earlier life in J.

JUDAS ➛ =BARSABBAS, =JUDE, =THADDAEUS, MACCABEUS

1. Apostle; son of James (Lk 6:16; Jn 14:22; Ac 1:13). Probably also called Thaddeus (Mt 10:3; Mk 3:18).

2. Brother of James and Jesus (Mt 13:55; Mk 6:3), also called Jude (Jude 1).

3. Christian prophet (Ac 15:22-32).

4. Apostle, also called Iscariot, who betrayed Jesus (Mt 10:4; 26:14-56; Mk 3:19; 14:10-50; Lk 6:16; 22:3-53; Jn 6:71; 12:4; 13:2-30; 18:2-11). Suicide of (Mt 27:3-5; Ac 1:16-25).

5. Leader of the Maccabean revolt (1Mc 2:4, 66). Recaptured Jerusalem and rededicated the temple and altar (1Mc 4:36-61). Death of (1Mc 9).

JUDE ➛ See JUDAS, 2

JUDEA ➛ JUDAH

Mt 2: 1 Jesus was born in Bethlehem of J,
Lk 3: 1 Pontius Pilate was governor of J,
Ac 1: 8 my witnesses in Jerusalem, in all J

JUDGE ➛ JUDGED, JUDGES, JUDGMENT, JUDGMENTS

Ge 16: 5 the LORD j between you and me!"
Ex 2:14 made you a ruler and j over us?
1Sa 2:10 LORD will j the ends of the earth;
Ps 96:13 for he is coming to j the earth.
Isa 11: 3 He shall not j by what his eyes see,
Jer 11:20 O LORD of hosts, who j righteously,
Eze 34:17 I shall j between sheep and sheep,
Lk 6:37 not j, and you will not be judged;
Jn 7:24 Do not j by appearances,
18:31 "Take him yourselves and j him
Ac 4:19 rather than to God, you must j;
Ro 3: 6 then how could God j the world?
1Co 6: 2 that the saints will j the world?
2Ti 4: 1 who is to j the living and the dead,
Heb 12:23 and to God the j of all,
Jas 5: 9 See, the J is standing at the doors!
Rev 20: 4 on them were given authority to j.
Sir 35:15 for the Lord is the j,

JUDGED ➛ JUDGE

Mt 7: 1 not judge, so that you may not be j.
1Co 11:31 if we j ourselves, we would not be j.
Jas 3: 1 know that we who teach will be j
Rev 20:12 dead were j according to their works

JUDGES ➛ JUDGE

Jdg 2:16 Then the LORD raised up j,
Lk 11:19 Therefore they will be your j.
Jas 4:11 evil against the law and j the law;
Rev 19:11 righteousness he j and makes war.
Sir 16:12 j a person according to one's deeds.

JUDGMENT ➛ JUDGE

Ex 6: 6 arm and with mighty acts of j.
Ps 1: 5 wicked will not stand in the j,
119:66 Teach me good j and knowledge,
Ecc 12:14 God will bring every deed into j,
Jer 25:31 he is entering into j with all flesh,
Da 7:22 j was given for the holy ones of the
Mal 3: 5 Then I will draw near to you for j;
Mt 11:24 day of j it will be more tolerable for
Jn 16:11 about j, because the ruler
Ro 14:10 we will all stand before the j seat of
2Co 5:10 all of us must appear before the j
Heb 9:27 to die once, and after that the j,
10:27 but a fearful prospect of j,
Jas 2:13 mercy triumphs over j.
1Pe 4:17 for j to begin with the household of
1Jn 4:17 may have boldness on the day of j,
Rev 18:10 For in one hour your j has come."
Wis 12:12 Or will resist your j?
Sir 18:20 Before j comes, examine yourself;
2Es 7:70 the things that pertain to the j.

JUDGMENTS ➛ JUDGE

Ps 119:75 LORD, that your j are right,
Ro 11:33 How unsearchable are his j and
Rev 19: 2 for his j are true and just;

JUDITH

Virtuous widow and heroine of the deuterocanonical book of Judith (Jdt 8-16).

JUST ➛ JUSTICE, JUSTIFICATION, JUSTIFIED, JUSTIFY

Ge 18:25 Judge of all the earth do what is j?"
Dt 32: 4 without deceit, j and upright is he;
Ps 111: 7 works of his hands are faithful and j
Eze 33:17 "The way of the Lord is not j,"
Ro 7:12 the commandment is holy and j and
1Jn 1: 9 he who is faithful and j will forgive
Rev 15: 3 J and true are your ways, King of
Tob 3: 2 O Lord, and all your deeds are j;
Sir 18: 2 the Lord alone is j.

JUSTICE ➛ JUST

Ex 23: 6 not pervert the j due to your poor
1Ki 7: 7 pronounce judgment, the Hall of J,
Job 19: 7 I call aloud, but there is no j.
37:23 he is great in power and j,
Ps 33: 5 He loves righteousness and j;
106: 3 Happy are those who observe j,
Pr 21:15 j is done, it is a joy to the righteous,
Isa 30:18 For the LORD is a God of j;
42: 4 until he has established j in the earth
Jer 9:24 I act with steadfast love, j,
Hos 12: 6 to your God, hold fast to love and j,
Am 5:24 But let j roll down like waters,
Mal 2:17 by asking, "Where is the God of j?"
Lk 11:42 and neglect j and the love of God;

JUSTIFICATION ➛ JUST

Ro 4:25 trespasses and was raised for our j.
2Co 3: 9 more does the ministry of j abound
Gal 2:21 for if j comes through the law,

JUSTIFIED ➛ JUST

Job 32: 2 he j himself rather than God;
Mt 12:37 for by your words you will be j,
Ro 3:24 they are now j by his grace as a gift,
5: 1 Therefore, since we are j by faith,
10:10 believes with the heart and so is j,
Gal 2:16 that we might be j by faith in Christ,
Jas 2:24 is j by works and not by faith alone.

JUSTIFY ➛ JUST

Ro 3:30 and he will j the circumcised on the
Gal 3: 8 that God would j the Gentiles

K

KADESH ➛ KADESH-BARNEA

Nu 20: 1 and the people stayed in K.
Dt 1:46 you had stayed at K as many days

KADESH-BARNEA ➛ KADESH

Nu 32: 8 sent them from K to see the land.

KEEP ➛ KEEPER, KEEPS, KEPT

Ge 17: 9 for you, you shall k my covenant,
Ex 19: 5 obey my voice and k my covenant,
Nu 6:24 The LORD bless you and k you;
Dt 5:10 love me and k my commandments.
Ne 1: 5 love him and k his commandments;
Pr 7: 2 k my commandments and live,
Ecc 3: 6 time to k, and a time to throw away;
12:13 Fear God, and k his commandments
Lk 17:33 those who lose their life will k it.
Jude 1:24 Now to him who is able to k you
Rev 22: 9 those who k the words of this book.
Sir 1:26 wisdom, k the commandments,

KEEPER ➛ KEEP

Ge 4: 9 am I my brother's k?"
Ps 121: 5 The LORD is your k;

KEEPS ➛ KEEP

Ps 121: 3 he who k you will not slumber.
Jas 2:10 whoever k the whole law but fails

KEPT ➛ KEEP

Mt 19:20 said to him, "I have k all these;
Jn 17: 6 and they have k your word.
2Ti 4: 7 finished the race, I have k the faith.

KEY ➛ KEYS

Isa 22:22 on his shoulder the k of the house
Lk 11:52 taken away the k of knowledge;
Rev 3: 7 true one, who has the k of David,

KEYS* → KEY
Mt 16:19 you the k of the kingdom of heaven,
Rev 1:18 I have the k of Death and of Hades.

KIDNAPS*
Ex 21:16 Whoever k a person, whether

KIDRON
2Sa 15:23 the king crossed the Wadi K,
Jn 18: 1 his disciples across the K valley

KILL → KILLED, KILLS
Ex 4:23 now I will k your firstborn son.'"
Ecc 3: 3 a time to k, and a time to heal;
Mt 10:28 not fear those who k the body but cannot k the soul;
Mk 14: 1 to arrest Jesus by stealth and k him;

KILLED → KILL
Mk 9:31 after being k, he will rise again."
Ac 3:15 and you k the Author of life,
Ro 7:11 deceived me and through it k me.
2Co 6: 9 as punished, and yet not k;

KILLS → KILL
1Sa 2: 6 The LORD k and brings to life;
2Co 3: 6 the letter k, but the Spirit gives life.

KIND → KINDNESS, KINDS
Ge 6:20 two of every k shall come in to you,
Ps 145:17 and k in all his doings.
1Co 13: 4 Love is patient; love is k;
Eph 4:32 and be k to one another,

KINDNESS → KIND
Pr 31:26 teaching of k is on her tongue.
Hos 11: 4 I led them with cords of human k,
Ro 2: 4 k is meant to lead you to repentance
Gal 5:22 joy, peace, patience, k, generosity,

KINDS → KIND
Lev 19:19 not sow your field with two k of
1Co 12:10 to another various k of tongues,
1Ti 6:10 of money is a root of all k of evil,

KING → KINGDOM, KINGS
Ex 1: 8 Now a new k arose over Egypt,
Dt 17:14 and you say, "I will set a k over me,
1Sa 8: 7 rejected me from being k over them.
2Sa 2: 4 there they anointed David k over
Ps 2: 6 set my k on Zion, my holy hill."
10:16 The LORD is k forever and ever;
Isa 6: 5 have seen the K, the LORD of hosts!
Jer 10:10 living God and the everlasting K.
Mt 2: 2 who has been born k of the Jews?
27:37 "This is Jesus, the K of the Jews."
Lk 19:38 "Blessed is the k who comes in the
Jn 1:49 You are the K of Israel!"
1Ti 1:17 To the K of the ages, immortal,
Rev 19:16 "K of kings and Lord of lords."
Tob 10:13 Lord of heaven and earth, K over all
Jdt 9:12 K of all your creation,

KINGDOM → KING
Ex 19: 6 you shall be for me a priestly k and
2Sa 7:12 and I will establish his k.
1Ki 11:31 "See, I am about to tear the k
Ps 145:13 Your k is an everlasting k,
Da 4: 3 His k is an everlasting k,
Mt 4:17 "Repent, for the k of heaven has
5: 3 for theirs is the k of heaven.
6:10 Your k come. Your will be done,
13:24 "The k of heaven may be compared
Mk 6:23 I will give you, even half of my k."
10:24 how hard it is to enter the k of God!
12:34 You are not far from the k of God."
13: 8 and k against k;
Lk 17:21 in fact, the k of God is among you."
22:16 not eat it until it is fulfilled in the k
Jn 18:36 "My k is not from this world.
Ac 1: 6 you will restore the k to Israel?"
Ro 14:17 the k of God is not food and drink
1Co 6: 9 wrongdoers will not inherit the k
Eph 5: 5 any inheritance in the k of Christ
Col 1:13 transferred us into the k of his
1Th 2:12 calls you into his own k and glory.
Heb 12:28 receiving a k that cannot be shaken,
2Pe 1:11 entry into the eternal k of our Lord
Rev 11:15 world has become the k of our Lord
Wis 10:10 she showed him the k of God,

KINGS → KING
Ge 17: 6 and k shall come from you.
Ps 2: 2 The k of the earth set themselves,
138: 4 All the k of the earth shall praise
Pr 8:15 By me k reign, and rulers decree
Isa 52:15 k shall shut their mouths because of
Da 7:24 of this kingdom ten k shall arise,
Ac 4:26 The k of the earth took their stand,
1Ti 6:15 the King of k and Lord of lords.
Rev 19:16 "King of k and Lord of lords."
Sir 51:12 *Give thanks to the King of the k of k,*

KISS
Ps 2:12 k his feet, or he will be angry,
SS 1: 2 Let him k me with the kisses of his
Mt 26:48 "The one I will k is the man; arrest
2Co 13:12 Greet one another with a holy k.

KNEE → KNEES
Isa 45:23 "To me every k shall bow,
Ro 14:11 says the Lord, every k shall bow to
Php 2:10 at the name of Jesus every k should

KNEEL → KNELT
Ps 95: 6 let us k before the LORD, our Maker

KNEES → KNEE
1Ki 19:18 the k that have not bowed to Baal,
Eph 3:14 I bow my k before the Father,

KNELT → KNEEL
2Ch 6:13 he k on his knees in the presence of
Lk 22:41 about a stone's throw, k down,

KNEW → KNOW
Dt 34:10 whom the LORD k face to face.
Jer 1: 5 I formed you in the womb I k you,
Mt 7:23 will declare to them, 'I never k you;
Ro 1:21 they k God, they did not honor him

KNOCK → KNOCKING
Lk 11: 9 k, and the door will be opened for

KNOCKING → KNOCK
Rev 3:20 I am standing at the door, k;

KNOW → FOREKNEW, KNEW, KNOWING, KNOWLEDGE, KNOWN, KNOWS
Ge 22:12 for now I k that you fear God,
Ex 6: 7 k that I am the LORD your God,
1Ki 8:39 only you k what is in every human
Job 19:25 For I k that my Redeemer lives,
Ps 46:10 "Be still, and k that I am God!
Ecc 8:16 I applied my mind to k wisdom,
Isa 1: 3 Israel does not k, my people do not
Jer 31:34 "K the LORD," for they shall all k
Mt 6: 3 left hand k what your right hand is
24:42 do not k on what day your Lord is
Lk 11:13 k how to give good gifts to your
22:34 denied three times that you k me."
Jn 10:14 I k my own and my own k me,
13:35 will k that you are my disciples,
21:24 and we k that his testimony is true.
Ac 1: 7 k the times or periods that the
Ro 8:28 We k that all things work together
1Co 8: 2 Anyone who claims to k something
13:12 I k only in part; then I will k fully,
Eph 3:19 k the love of Christ that surpasses
Php 3:10 to k Christ and the power of his
Tit 1:16 profess to k God, but they deny him
Heb 8:11 'K the Lord,' for they shall all k me,
1Jn 2: 4 Whoever says, "I have come to k
3:16 k love by this, that he laid down his
Rev 3: 3 not k at what hour I will come to

KNOWING → KNOW
Ge 3:22 like one of us, k good and evil;
Jn 18: 4 Jesus, k all that was to happen to
Php 3: 8 surpassing value of k Christ Jesus
Heb 13: 2 have entertained angels without k it.

KNOWLEDGE → KNOW
Ge 2: 9 the tree of the k of good and evil.
Job 21:22 Will any teach God k,
Pr 1: 7 of the LORD is the beginning of k;
8:10 and k rather than choice gold;
Ecc 1:18 who increase k increase sorrow.
Isa 11: 2 spirit of k and the fear of the LORD.
Hos 4: 6 people are destroyed for lack of k;
Lk 11:52 you have taken away the key of k;
Ro 11:33 riches and wisdom and k of God!
1Co 8: 1 K puffs up, but love builds up.
Eph 3:19 the love of Christ that surpasses k,
Col 2: 3 the treasures of wisdom and k.
1Ti 6:20 of what is falsely called k;
2Pe 1: 5 goodness, and goodness with k,
1Jn 2:20 and all of you have k.
Sir 3:25 without k there is no wisdom.

KNOWN → KNOW
Ps 139: 1 you have searched me and k me.
Lk 6:44 for each tree is k by its own fruit.
Jn 1:18 Father's heart, who has made him k.
Ro 7: 7 I would not have k sin.
1Co 2:16 For who has k the mind of the Lord
Eph 1: 9 made k to us the mystery of his will,

KNOWS → KNOW
Ps 94:11 The LORD k our thoughts,
103:14 For he k how we were made;
Mt 6: 8 your Father k what you need before
24:36 about that day and hour no one k,
Ro 8:27 k what is the mind of the Spirit,
2Ti 2:19 "The Lord k those who are his,"
1Jn 4: 7 loves is born of God and k God.
Sir 42:18 Most High k all that may be known;

KORAH → KORAHITES
Levite; led rebels against Moses (Nu 16; Jude 11).

KORAHITES → KORAH
Psalms of: Pss 42; 44-49; 84; 85; 87; 88.

L

LABAN
Brother of Rebekah (Ge 24:29), father of Rachel and Leah (Ge 29:16). Received Abraham's servant (Ge 24:29-51). Provided daughters as wives for Jacob in exchange for Jacob's service (Ge 29:1-30). Provided flocks for Jacob's service (Ge 30:25-43). Pursued and covenanted with Jacob (Ge 31).

LABOR → LABORER
Ex 1:11 to oppress them with forced l.
20: 9 Six days you shall l and do all your
Jn 4:38 reap that for which you did not l.

LABORER → LABOR
Lev 19:13 the wages of a l until morning.
Lk 10: 7 for the l deserves to be paid.
1Ti 5:18 and, "The l deserves to be paid."

LACKED → LACKING
Dt 2: 7 with you; you have l nothing."

LACKING → LACKED
Ecc 1:15 and what is l cannot be counted.
Lk 18:22 "There is still one thing l.
Col 1:24 completing what is l in Christ's

LADDER
Ge 28:12 that there was a l set up on the earth,

LAID → LAY
Isa 53: 6 the LORD has l on him the iniquity
Mk 16: 6 Look, there is the place they l him.
1Jn 3:16 that he l down his life for us—

LAKE
Rev 19:20 were thrown alive into the l of fire
20:14 This is the second death, the l of fire

LAMB → LAMBS
Ge 22: 8 "God himself will provide the l for
Ex 12:21 and slaughter the passover l.
Isa 53: 7 like a l that is led to the slaughter,
Mk 14:12 when the Passover l is sacrificed,
Jn 1:29 L of God who takes away the sin of
1Co 5: 7 For our paschal l, Christ, has been
1Pe 1:19 like that of a l without defect or
Rev 5:12 the L that was slaughtered to
21:23 and its lamp is the L.

LAMBS → LAMB
Isa 40:11 he will gather the l in his arms,
Jn 21:15 Jesus said to him, "Feed my l."

LAME
Isa 35: 6 then the l shall leap like a deer,
Zep 3:19 And I will save the l and gather the
Mt 11: 5 the l walk, the lepers are cleansed,

LAMENTATION
La 2: 5 in daughter Judah mourning and l.

LAMP → LAMPS, LAMPSTAND, LAMPSTANDS
1Ki 11:36 servant David may always have a l

Ps 18:28 It is you who light my l;
119:105 Your word is a l to my feet and a
Mt 5:15 lighting a l puts it under the bushel
6:22 "The eye is the l of the body.
Rev 22: 5 they need no light of l or sun,

LAMPS ➝ LAMP
Ex 25:37 You shall make the seven l for it;
Mt 25: 1 Ten bridesmaids took their l and

LAMPSTAND ➝ LAMP
Ex 25:31 You shall make a l of pure gold.
Zec 4: 2 And I said, "I see a l all of gold,
1Mc 4:50 and lit the lamps on the l,

LAMPSTANDS ➝ LAMP
Rev 1:20 the seven l are the seven churches.
11: 4 the two l that stand before the Lord

LAND
Ge 1:10 God called the dry l Earth,
12: 7 your offspring I will give this l."
Ex 3: 8 a l flowing with milk and honey,
20: 2 brought you out of the l of Egypt,
Nu 13: 2 to spy out the l of Canaan,
Jos 11:23 So Joshua took the whole l,
Jdg 1:27 Canaanites continued to live in that l
2Ki 17: 5 the king of Assyria invaded all the l
25:21 So Judah went into exile out of its l.
2Ch 7:14 will forgive their sin and heal their l.
Ps 37:11 But the meek shall inherit the l,
Jer 22:29 O l, l, l, hear the word of the LORD!
Da 11:41 He shall come into the beautiful l,
Mal 4: 6 come and strike the l with a curse.

LANGUAGE
Ge 11: 9 LORD confused the l of all the earth;
Ac 2: 6 speaking in the native l of each.

LAP
Jdg 7: 5 who l the water with their tongues,
Pr 16:33 The lot is cast into the l,

LASHES
Dt 25: 3 Forty l may be given but not more;
2Co 11:24 from the Jews the forty l minus one.

LAST ➝ EVERLASTING
2Sa 23: 1 Now these are the l words of David:
Isa 44: 6 I am the first and I am the l;
Mt 19:30 first will be l, and the l will be first.
Mk 9:35 first must be l of all and servant of
1Co 15:26 l enemy to be destroyed is death.
15:52 twinkling of an eye, at the l trumpet.
2Ti 3: 1 that in the l days distressing times
Heb 1: 2 l days he has spoken to us by a Son,
1Jn 2:18 Children, it is the l hour!
Rev 1:17 I am the first and the l,

LAUGH ➝ LAUGHINGSTOCK, LAUGHTER
Ge 18:13 said to Abraham, "Why did Sarah l,
Ecc 3: 4 a time to weep, and a time to l;
Lk 6:21 you who weep now, for you will l.

LAUGHINGSTOCK ➝ LAUGH
Ps 44:14 the nations, a l among the peoples.
La 3:14 have become the l of all my people,

LAUGHTER ➝ LAUGH
Ps 126: 2 Then our mouth was filled with l,
Jas 4: 9 Let your l be turned into mourning

LAW ➝ LAWFUL, LAWLESSNESS
Dt 1: 5 Moses undertook to expound this l
31: 9 Then Moses wrote down this l,
Jos 1: 8 book of the l shall not depart out of
Ps 1: 2 their delight is in the l of the LORD,
119:97 Oh, how I love your l!
Jer 31:33 I will put my l within them,
Mt 5:17 come to abolish the l or the prophets
23:23 the weightier matters of the l:
Lk 24:44 written about me in the l of Moses,
Jn 1:17 l indeed was given through Moses;
Ro 6:14 you are not under l but under grace.
10: 4 For Christ is the end of the l so that
Gal 2:19 through the l I died to the l,
Heb 10: 1 Since the l has only a shadow of the
Jas 2:10 For whoever keeps the whole l but
1Mc 2:48 They rescued the l out of the hands

LAWFUL ➝ LAW
Mt 12:12 So it is l to do good on the sabbath."
1Co 6:12 "All things are l for me,"
10:23 "All things are l," but

LAWLESSNESS ➝ LAW
2Th 2: 7 the mystery of l is already at work,
1Jn 3: 4 commits sin is guilty of l; sin is l.
Sir 21: 3 All l is like a two-edged sword;

LAY ➝ LAID
Mt 8:20 of Man has nowhere to l his head."
28: 6 Come, see the place where he l.
Jn 10:15 And I l down my life for the sheep.
1Co 3:11 no one can l any foundation other

LAZARUS*
1. Poor man in Jesus' parable (Lk 16:19-31).
2. Brother of Mary and Martha whom Jesus raised from the dead (Jn 11:1-12:19).

LAZY
Ex 5:17 He said, "You are l, l;
Pr 13: 4 The appetite of the l craves,

LEAD ➝ LEADER, LEADERS, LEADS, LED
Ex 32:34 l the people to the place
Ps 61: 2 L me to the rock that is higher than
Isa 11: 6 and a little child shall l them.
Mk 13:22 to l astray, if possible, the elect.
Ro 2: 4 meant to l you to repentance?

LEADER ➝ LEAD
1Ch 28: 4 for he chose Judah as l,
Ro 12: 8 the l, in diligence;

LEADERS ➝ LEAD
Isa 3:12 O my people, your l mislead you,
Lk 19:47 the l of the people kept looking for
Heb 13: 7 Remember your l, those who spoke

LEADS ➝ LEAD
Ps 23: 2 he l me beside still waters;
Mk 13: 5 "Beware that no one l you astray.
Ro 6:16 obedience, which l to righteousness

LEAH
Wife of Jacob (Ge 29:16-30); bore six sons and one daughter (Ge 29:31-30:21; 34:1; 35:23; Ru 4:11).

LEAPING
1Ch 15:29 and saw King David l and dancing;
Ac 3: 8 walking and l and praising God.

LEARN ➝ LEARNED, LEARNING
Dt 4:10 that they may l to fear me as long as
Isa 1:17 l to do good; seek justice,
1Ti 2:11 Let a woman l in silence with full

LEARNED ➝ LEARN
Jn 6:45 l from the Father comes to me.
Php 4:11 I have l to be content with whatever

LEARNING ➝ LEARN
Jn 7:15 "How does this man have such l,
Ac 26:24 Too much l is driving you insane!"

LEAST ➝ LESS
Mt 2: 6 are by no means l among the rulers
5:19 called l in the kingdom of heaven;
Lk 9:48 l among all of you is the greatest."

LEAVE ➝ LEFT
Nu 11:20 'Why did we ever l Egypt?'"
Mk 10: 7 this reason a man shall l his father
Jn 14:18 not l you orphaned; I am coming to
Heb 13: 5 said, "I will never l you or forsake

LEAVEN ➝ LEAVENS
Ex 12:15 on the first day you shall remove l

LEAVENS ➝ LEAVEN
Gal 5: 9 A little yeast l the whole batch of

LEAVES
Ge 3: 7 and they sewed fig l together
Eze 47:12 and their l for healing."
Rev 22: 2 l of the tree are for the healing of

LEBANON
Dt 11:24 from the wilderness to the L and
Isa 40:16 L would not provide fuel enough,

LED ➝ LEAD
Isa 53: 7 like a lamb that is l to the slaughter,
Jer 50: 6 their shepherds have l them astray,
Hos 11: 4 I l them with cords of human
Mt 4: 1 Then Jesus was l up by the Spirit
27:31 they l him away to crucify him.

Lk 21: 8 "Beware that you are not l astray;
Ro 8:14 For all who are l by the Spirit

LEFT ➝ LEAVE
Dt 28:14 either to the right or to the l,
Mt 6: 3 your l hand know what your right
25:33 his right hand and the goats at the l.
Lk 17:34 one will be taken and the other l.

LEGION
Lk 8:30 He said, "L"; for many demons

LEGS
Da 10: 6 l like the gleam of burnished bronze
Jn 19:33 they did not break his l.
Rev 10: 1 and his l like pillars of fire.

LENDER
Pr 22: 7 the borrower is the slave of the l.

LEPER ➝ LEPROUS
Mt 8: 2 and there was a l who came to him
26: 6 in the house of Simon the l,

LEPERS ➝ LEPROUS
Lk 7:22 the lame walk, the l are cleansed,

LEPROUS ➝ LEPER, LEPERS
Ex 4: 6 he took it out, his hand was l,
Nu 12:10 Miriam had become l,

LESS ➝ LEAST
Ex 30:15 and the poor shall not give l,
Ezr 9:13 punished us l than our iniquities

LETTER
Mt 5:18 not one l, not one stroke of a l,
2Co 3: 6 the l kills, but the Spirit gives life.

LEVI ➝ LEVITES, LEVITICAL, =MATTHEW
1. Son of Jacob by Leah (Ge 29:34; 46:11; 1Ch 2:1). With Simeon avenged rape of Dinah (Ge 34). Tribe of blessed (Ge 49:5-7; Dt 33:8-11), chosen as priests (Nu 3-4), numbered (Nu 3:39; 26:62), given cities, but not land (Nu 18; 35; Dt 10:9; Jos 13:14; 21), land (Eze 48:8-22), 12,000 from (Rev 7:7).
2. See Matthew.

LEVIATHAN
Job 41: 1 you draw out L with a fishhook,
Ps 74:14 You crushed the heads of L;
2Es 6:49 and the name of the other L.

LEVITES ➝ LEVI
Nu 1:53 L shall camp around the tabernacle
Jos 14: 4 no portion was given to the L in the
Ne 8: 9 L who taught the people said to all

LEVITICAL ➝ LEVI
Heb 7:11 attainable through the l priesthood

LIAR ➝ LIE
Pr 19:22 and it is better to be poor than a l.
Jn 8:44 for he is a l and the father of lies.
Ro 3: 4 Although everyone is a l,
1Jn 2:22 l but the one who denies that Jesus

LIARS ➝ LIE
1Ti 1:10 sodomites, slave traders, l, perjurers,
Rev 21: 8 the sorcerers, the idolaters, and all l,

LIBERTY
Lev 25:10 shall proclaim l throughout the land
Isa 61: 1 to proclaim l to the captives,
1Co 8: 9 this l of yours does not somehow

LICENTIOUSNESS
Mk 7:22 avarice, wickedness, deceit, l, envy,
Gal 5:19 fornication, impurity, l,
Jude 1: 4 pervert the grace of our God into l

LIE ➝ LIAR, LIARS, LIES, LYING
Nu 23:19 that he should l, or a mortal,
Ps 23: 2 makes me l down in green pastures;
Isa 11: 6 leopard shall l down with the kid,
Ac 5: 3 your heart to l to the Holy Spirit
1Jn 2:21 know that no l comes from the truth.

LIES ➝ LIE
Ps 5: 6 You destroy those who speak l;
Php 3:13 forgetting what l behind and straining forward to what l ahead,

LIFE ➝ LIVE
Ge 2: 7 into his nostrils the breath of l;
2: 9 the tree of l also in the midst of the
9: 5 require a reckoning for human l.

Ex 21:23 then you shall give l for l,
Dt 12:23 for the blood is the l,
30:19 Choose l so that you and your
Ps 34:12 Which of you desires l, and covets
Pr 18:21 Death and l are in the power of the tongue,
Ecc 7:12 that wisdom gives l to the one who
Isa 53:10 you make his l an offering for sin,
Da 12: 2 shall awake, some to everlasting l,
Mt 7:14 and the road is hard that leads to l,
10:39 Those who find their l will lose it,
20:28 to give his l a ransom for many."
Mk 10:30 and in the age to come eternal l.
Lk 12:25 a single hour to your span of l?
Jn 1: 4 in him was l, and the l was the light
3:15 believes in him may have eternal l.
6:35 said to them, "I am the bread of l.
11:25 "I am the resurrection and the l.
14: 6 "I am the way, and the truth, and the l.
Ac 3:15 and you killed the Author of l,
Ro 5:21 eternal l through Jesus Christ our
8:38 convinced that neither death, nor l,
2Co 3: 6 the letter kills, but the Spirit gives l.
Eph 4: 1 to lead a l worthy of the calling
Php 4: 3 whose names are in the book of l.
1Jn 3:14 that we have passed from death to l
5:20 He is the true God and eternal l.
Rev 2: 8 who was dead and came to l:
20: 4 came to l and reigned with Christ
20:12 book was opened, the book of l.
22: 2 the tree of l with its twelve kinds
Sir 4:12 Whoever loves her loves l,
2Es 8:52 the tree of l is planted,

LIFTED
Isa 52:13 he shall be exalted and l up,
Jn 3:14 so must the Son of Man be l up,

LIGHT → ENLIGHTENED, ENLIGHTENS, LIGHTS
Ge 1: 3 "Let there be l"; and there was l.
Ex 13:21 pillar of fire by night, to give them l,
Ps 27: 1 The LORD is my l and my salvation;
Pr 4:18 the path of the righteous is like the l
Ecc 2:13 that wisdom excels folly as l excels
Isa 9: 2 in darkness have seen a great l;
42: 6 as a covenant to the people, a l
60: 1 Arise, shine; for your l has come,
Mt 4:16 in darkness have seen a great l,
5:14 "You are the l of the world.
11:30 my yoke is easy, and my burden is l.
Jn 1: 9 true l, which enlightens everyone,
8:12 saying, "I am the l of the world.
Ro 13:12 and put on the armor of l;
2Co 11:14 Satan disguises himself as an angel of l.
1Pe 2: 9 of darkness into his marvelous l.
1Jn 1: 7 walk in the l as he himself is in the l
Rev 22: 5 for the Lord God will be their l,

LIGHTNING
Ex 19:16 third day there was thunder and l,
Da 10: 6 body was like beryl, his face like l,
Lk 10:18 from heaven like a flash of l.
Rev 4: 5 from the throne are flashes of l,

LIGHTS → LIGHT
Ge 1:16 God made the two great l—
Jas 1:17 coming down from the Father of l,

LIKE → LIKENESS
Ge 3: 5 be l God, knowing good and evil."
Ex 15:11 "Who is l you, O LORD, among the
2Sa 7:22 for there is no one l you,
Ps 113: 5 Who is l the LORD our God,
Isa 46: 9 I am God, and there is no one l me,
Jer 10: 6 There is none l you, O LORD;
Lk 13:18 "What is the kingdom of God l?
1Co 13:11 When I was a child, I spoke l a child
Rev 1:13 I saw one l the Son of Man,
10: 1 his face was l the sun,
16:15 ("See, I am coming l a thief!

LIKENESS → LIKE
Ge 1:26 in our image, according to our l;
Ro 8: 3 his own Son in the l of sinful flesh,
Php 2: 7 of a slave, being born in human l.

LILIES
Lk 12:27 Consider the l, how they grow:

LINE
Isa 28:10 l upon l, l upon l, here a little,
Am 7: 7 with a plumb l in his hand.

LINEN
Ex 26: 1 with ten curtains of fine twisted l,
Da 10: 5 and saw a man clothed in l,
Rev 19: 8 for the fine l is the righteous deeds

LION → LION'S, LIONS
1Sa 17:34 and whenever a l or a bear came,
Ecc 9: 4 a living dog is better than a dead l.
Isa 11: 7 and the l shall eat straw like the ox.
Da 7: 4 first was like a l and had eagles'
Rev 4: 7 the first living creature like a l,
5: 5 See, the L of the tribe of Judah,

LION'S → LION
2Ti 4:17 So I was rescued from the l mouth.

LIONS → LION
Da 6:20 able to deliver you from the l?"

LIPS
Dt 23:23 Whatever your l utter you must
Job 2:10 Job did not sin with his l.
Isa 6: 5 am lost, for I am a man of unclean l,
Mt 15: 8 with their l, but their hearts are far
Heb 13:15 the fruit of l that confess his name.

LISTEN → LISTENS
Ex 23:22 But if you l attentively to his voice
2Ki 17:40 They would not l, however,
Ps 5: 2 L to the sound of my cry, my King
Pr 4: 1 L, children, to a father's instruction,
Ecc 5: 1 l is better than the sacrifice offered
Mk 9: 7 my Son, the Beloved; l to him!"
Lk 16:31 'If they do not l to Moses and the
Ac 3:22 You must l to whatever he tells you.
Jas 1:19 be quick to l, slow to speak,
Sir 11: 8 Do not answer before you l,

LISTENS → LISTEN
Jn 18:37 Everyone who belongs to the truth l
1Jn 4: 6 Whoever knows God l to us,

LITTLE
Ex 16:18 who gathered l had no shortage;
Ps 8: 5 have made them a l lower than God,
Pr 15:16 Better is a l with the fear of
Mt 8:26 "Why are you afraid, you of l faith?
19:14 "Let the l children come to me,
2Co 8:15 one who had l did not have too l."
Gal 5: 9 A l yeast leavens the whole batch of
Rev 10: 2 He held a l scroll open in his hand.
Sir 29:23 Be content with l or much,

LIVE → ALIVE, LIFE, LIVED, LIVES, LIVING
Ge 3:22 and eat, and l forever"—
Ex 1:16 but if it is a girl, she shall l."
33:20 for no one shall see me and l."
Lev 18: 5 by doing so one shall l:
Dt 8: 3 one does not l by bread alone,
Ps 91: 1 l in the shelter of the Most High,
Hab 2: 4 but the righteous l by their faith.
Mt 4: 4 'One does not l by bread alone,
Jn 11:25 even though they die, will l,
Ro 1:17 one who is righteous will l by faith."
14: 8 If we l, we l to the Lord,
2Co 5:15 those who l might l no longer for
Gal 3:12 does works of the law will l
Wis 5:15 But the righteous l forever,
Sir 34:14 those who fear the Lord will l,

LIVED → LIVE
Ro 14: 9 to this end Christ died and l again,

LIVES → LIVE
Job 19:25 For I know that my Redeemer l,
Ps 18:46 The LORD l! Blessed be my rock,
Jn 11:26 and everyone who l and believes
Ro 6:10 but the life he l, he l to God.
1Jn 3:16 to lay down our l for one another.
Rev 15: 7 of God, who l forever and ever;
Tob 13: 1 "Blessed be God who l forever,

LIVING → LIVE
Ge 2: 7 and the man became a l being.
3:20 because she was the mother of all l.
6:19 And of every l thing, of all flesh,
Dt 5:26 the voice of the l God speaking out
Jer 2:13 forsaken me, the fountain of l water,
Zec 14: 8 that day l waters shall flow out from
Mt 16:16 the Messiah, the Son of the l God."
Jn 4:10 he would have given you l water."
6:51 I am the l bread that came down
Ro 12: 1 present your bodies as a l sacrifice,
2Co 6:16 For we are the temple of the l God;
Heb 4:12 the word of God is l and active,
1Pe 2: 4 l stone, though rejected by mortals

LOAVES
Mk 6:41 Taking the five l and the two fish,
8: 6 and he took the seven l,

LOCK
Mt 23:13 you l people out of the kingdom of

LOCUST → LOCUSTS
2Ch 6:28 if there is plague, blight, mildew, l,
Joel 2:25 years that the swarming l has eaten,

LOCUSTS → LOCUST
Ex 10: 4 I will bring l into your country.
Mt 3: 4 and his food was l and wild honey.
Rev 9: 3 from the smoke came l on the earth,

LOG
Mt 7: 3 do not notice the l in your own eye?

LONELY → ALONE
Ps 25:16 for I am l and afflicted.
La 1: 1 How l sits the city that once was full

LONG → LONGING
Ex 20:12 that your days may be l in the land
Ps 13: 1 How l, O LORD?
Pr 3:16 L life is in her right hand;
1Co 11:14 that if a man wears l hair,
1Pe 1:12 things into which angels l to look!
2: 2 Like newborn infants, l for the pure,
Rev 6:10 how l will it be before you judge

LONGING → LONG
Ro 8:19 the creation waits with eager l for
2Co 5: 2 l to be clothed with our heavenly

LOOK → LOOKED, LOOKS
Ex 3: 6 for he was afraid to l at God.
Ps 8: 3 When I l at your heavens,
80:14 l down from heaven, and see;
Lk 24:39 L at my hands and my feet;

LOOKED → LOOK
Ge 19:26 But Lot's wife, behind him, l back,
Ex 2:25 God l upon the Israelites,
Sir 16:29 Then the Lord l upon the earth,

LOOKS → LOOK
1Sa 16: 7 but the LORD l on the heart."
Ps 14: 2 The LORD l down from heaven
Mt 5:28 who l at a woman with lust

***LORD → *LORD'S, LORDS**
Ge 18:27 take it upon myself to speak to the L
Ex 4:10 Moses said to the LORD, "O my L,
Dt 10:17 God is God of gods and L of lords,
Ps 16: 2 I say to the LORD, "You are my L;
110: 1 The LORD says to my l,
Isa 6: 1 I saw the L sitting on a throne, high
Da 2:47 God is God of gods and L of kings
Mic 1: 2 the L from his holy temple.
Mt 7:22 many will say to me, 'L, L,
9:38 the L of the harvest to send out
12: 8 the Son of Man is l of the sabbath."
Mk 1: 3 'Prepare the way of the L,
12:29 the L our God, the L is one;
Lk 2:11 who is the Messiah, the L.
10:27 "You shall love the L your God
19:38 who comes in the name of the L!
Jn 13:13 You call me Teacher and L—
20:28 "My L and my God!"
Ac 2:34 'The L said to my L, "Sit at my
Ro 4:24 in him who raised Jesus our L
10:12 the same L is L of all and
1Co 2:16 who has known the mind of the L
8: 6 and one L, Jesus Christ,
2Co 3:17 Now the L is the Spirit,
Eph 4: 5 one L, one faith, one baptism,
Php 2:11 that Jesus Christ is L, to the glory
4: 5 The L is near.
Col 3:13 just as the L has forgiven you,
1Th 4:15 are left until the coming of the L,
1Ti 6:15 the King of kings and L of lords.
Heb 12:14 without which no one will see the L.
Jas 4:10 Humble yourselves before the L,

1Pe 3:15 in your hearts sanctify Christ as L.
2Pe 3: 9 The L is not slow about his promise,
Jude 1: 4 and deny our only Master and L,
Rev 4: 8 "Holy, holy, holy, the L God
19:16 "King of kings and L of lords."
22:20 Amen. Come, L Jesus!
Jdt 6:19 L God of heaven, see their
Wis 8: 3 and the L of all loves her.
Sir 1: 1 All wisdom is from the L,
Aza 1:35 Bless the L, all you works of the L;
Sus 1: 2 and one who feared the L.

†LORD ➛ †GOD, †LORD'S
Ge 2: 7 L God formed man from the dust of
6: 6 the L was sorry that he had made
13: 4 Abram called on the name of the L.
18:14 Is anything too wonderful for the L?
22:14 that place "The L will provide";
Ex 3:15 shall say to the Israelites, 'The L,
5: 2 But Pharaoh said, "Who is the L,
6: 7 know that I am the L your God,
15: 3 The L is a warrior; the L is his name.
34: 6 and proclaimed, "The L, the L,
Lev 19: 2 for I the L your God am holy.
Nu 6:24 The L bless you and keep you;
14:18 'The L is slow to anger,
Dt 6: 4 The L is our God, the L alone.
Jos 24:15 my household, we will serve the L."
1Sa 2: 2 "There is no Holy One like the L,
1Ki 8:11 of the L filled the house of the L.
18:21 If the L is God, follow him;
1Ch 16:11 Seek the L and his strength,
Ezr 7:10 his heart to study the law of the L,
Ne 8:10 the joy of the L is your strength."
Job 1:21 the L gave, and the L has taken
42:12 The L blessed the latter days
Ps 1: 2 their delight is in the law of the L,
10:16 The L is king forever and ever;
18: 1 I love you, O L, my strength.
23: 1 The L is my shepherd, I shall not
33:12 Happy is the nation whose God is the L
84:11 For the L God is a sun and shield;
110: 1 The L says to my lord,
113: 5 Who is like the L our God,
125: 2 so the L surrounds his people,
128: 1 Happy is everyone who fears the L,
145:18 The L is near to all who call on him,
150: 6 that breathes praise the L!
Pr 1: 7 fear of the L is the beginning of
3: 5 Trust in the L with all your heart,
19:23 The fear of the L is life indeed;
21: 2 but the L weighs the heart.
Isa 2:11 L alone will be exalted in that day.
6: 3 "Holy, holy, holy is the L of hosts;
33:22 the L is our judge, the L is our ruler,
53: 6 the L has laid on him the iniquity
64: 8 Yet, O L, you are our Father;
Jer 4: 4 Circumcise yourselves to the L,
31:34 "Know the L," for they shall all
32:27 I am the L, the God of all flesh;
La 3:25 The L is good to those who wait for
Eze 3:23 and the glory of the L stood there,
10:18 the glory of the L went out from
37: 4 O dry bones, hear the word of the L.
44: 4 glory of the L filled the temple
48:35 time on shall be, The L is There.
Hos 14: 1 Return, O Israel, to the L your God,
Joel 1:15 For the day of the L is near,
Am 5: 6 Seek the L and live,
Ob 1:15 the day of the L is near against all
Na 1: 3 The L is slow to anger but great in
Zep 1:14 The great day of the L is near,
Zec 14: 9 the L will be one and his name one.
Mal 3: 6 For I the L do not change;
4: 5 and terrible day of the L comes.

***LORD'S ➛ *LORD**
Mk 12:11 was the L doing, and it is amazing
Lk 4:19 to proclaim the year of the L favor."
Ro 14: 8 or whether we die, we are the L.
1Co 10:26 the earth and its fullness are the L."
Sir 17:17 but Israel is the L own portion.

†LORD'S ➛ †LORD
Nu 11:23 "Is the L power limited?
Dt 32: 9 the L own portion was his people,
Ps 24: 1 The earth is the L and all that is in it
Isa 59: 1 the L hand is not too short to save,
Ob 1:21 and the kingdom shall be the L.

LORDS ➛ *LORD
Dt 10:17 God is God of gods and Lord of l,
Ps 136: 3 O give thanks to the Lord of l,
1Co 8: 5 there are many gods and many l—
Rev 19:16 "King of kings and Lord of l."

LOSE ➛ LOSS, LOST
Mk 8:35 who l their life for my sake,
Jn 12:25 Those who love their life l it,
2Co 4: 1 in this ministry, we do not l heart.
Heb 12: 3 you may not grow weary or l heart.
2Jn 1: 8 do not l what we have worked for,

LOSS ➛ LOSE
1Co 3:15 burned up, the builder will suffer l;
Php 3: 8 I regard everything as l because of
Sir 32:24 who trusts the Lord will not suffer l.

LOST ➛ LOSE
Ps 119:176 I have gone astray like a l sheep;
Jer 50: 6 My people have been l sheep;
Eze 34:16 I will seek the l, and I will bring
Mt 10: 6 to the l sheep of the house of Israel.
Lk 15: 6 I have found my sheep that was l.'
19:10 came to seek out and to save the l."

LOT ➛ LOT'S, LOTS
1. Nephew of Abraham (Ge 11:27; 12:5). Chose to live in Sodom (Ge 13). Rescued from four kings (Ge 14). Rescued from Sodom (Ge 19:1-29; 2Pe 2:7). Fathered Moab and Ammon (Ge 19:30-38).
2. Object cast to make decisions.
Nu 33:54 You shall apportion the land by l
Est 3: 7 they cast Pur—which means "the l"
Pr 16:33 The l is cast into the lap,
Jnh 1: 7 cast lots, and the l fell on Jonah.
Ac 1:26 and the l fell on Matthias;

LOT'S ➛ LOT, 1
Ge 19:26 L wife, behind him, looked back,
Lk 17:32 Remember L wife.

LOTS ➛ LOT, 2
Ps 22:18 and for my clothing they cast l.
Mt 27:35 among themselves by casting l;

LOVE ➛ BELOVED, LOVED, LOVER, LOVERS, LOVES
Ex 20: 6 but showing steadfast l to the
34: 6 and abounding in steadfast l and
Lev 19:18 shall l your neighbor as yourself:
Nu 14:18 and abounding in steadfast l,
Dt 6: 5 You shall l the LORD your God
2Sa 7:15 not take my steadfast l from him,
1Ki 11: 2 Solomon clung to these in l.
2Ch 6:42 Remember your steadfast l
Ezr 3:11 his steadfast l endures forever
Ne 1: 5 steadfast l with those who l him
Ps 18: 1 I l you, O LORD, my strength.
86: 5 abounding in steadfast l to all who
116: 1 I l the LORD, because he has heard
119:97 Oh, how I l your law!
136: 1 for his steadfast l endures forever.
Pr 5:19 you be intoxicated always by her l.
8:17 I l those who l me,
19: 8 To get wisdom is to l oneself;
Ecc 3: 8 a time to l, and a time to hate;
SS 1: 2 For your l is better than wine,
8: 6 for l is strong as death,
Isa 54: 8 but with everlasting l I will have
La 3:22 steadfast l of the LORD never ceases,
Da 9: 4 steadfast l with those who l you
Hos 6: 4 Your l is like a morning cloud,
11: 4 of human kindness, with bands of l.
14: 4 heal their disloyalty; I will l them
Joel 2:13 and abounding in steadfast l,
Jnh 4: 2 and abounding in steadfast l,
Mt 5:44 L your enemies and pray
6:24 either hate the one and l the other,
Mk 12:31 shall l your neighbor as yourself.'
Lk 6:32 For even sinners l those who l them.
10:27 "You shall l the Lord your God
Jn 12:25 Those who l their life lose it,
13:34 new commandment, that you l one
14:15 "If you l me, you will keep my
15:13 No one has greater l than this,
21:16 "Simon son of John, do you l me?"
Ro 5: 8 But God proves his l for us in that
12: 9 Let l be genuine; hate what is evil,
13: 8 anything, except to l one another;
1Co 8: 1 Knowledge puffs up, but l builds up.
13: 4 L is patient; l is kind;
13:13 and the greatest of these is l.
Gal 5: 6 is faith working through l.
5:22 the fruit of the Spirit is l, joy,
Eph 3:19 l of Christ that surpasses knowledge
5:25 Husbands, l your wives,
Col 3:14 Above all, clothe yourselves with l,
1Th 5: 8 put on the breastplate of faith and l,
1Ti 6:10 For the l of money is a root of all
Tit 2: 2 in faith, in l, and in endurance.
Heb 10:24 provoke one another to l and good
13: 5 your lives free from the l of money,
Jas 2: 8 shall l your neighbor as yourself."
1Pe 1: 8 you have not seen him, you l him;
2Pe 1: 7 and mutual affection with l.
1Jn 2:15 not l the world or the things in the
3: 1 See what l the Father has given us,
3:16 We know l by this, that he laid
5: 3 For the l of God is this,
2Jn 1: 6 And this is l, that we walk according
Jude 1:21 keep yourselves in the l of God;
Rev 2: 4 abandoned the l you had at first.
Sir 2:15 and those who l him keep his ways.
7:30 With all your might l your Maker,
Bel 1:38 have not forsaken those who l you."
1Mc 4:33 with the sword of those who l you,

LOVED ➛ LOVE
Dt 4:37 And because he l your ancestors,
Jer 31: 3 have l you with an everlasting love;
Hos 11: 1 When Israel was a child, I l him,
Mal 1: 2 I have l you, says the LORD.
Jn 3:16 God so l the world that he gave his
13: 1 he l them to the end.
15: 9 the Father has l me, so I have l you;
15:12 love one another as I have l you.
Gal 2:20 who l me and gave himself for me.
Eph 5: 2 Christ l us and gave himself up for
1Jn 4:19 We love because he first l us.

LOVER ➛ LOVE
Ps 99: 4 Mighty King, l of justice,
Ecc 5:10 l of money will not be satisfied with
1Ti 3: 3 quarrelsome, and not a l of money.

LOVERS ➛ LOVE
Jer 3: 1 have played the whore with many l;
La 1: 2 all her l she has no one to comfort
Hos 2: 5 For she said, "I will go after my l;
Lk 16:14 Pharisees, who were l of money,
2Ti 3: 2 For people will be l of themselves,

LOVES ➛ LOVE
Ps 33: 5 He l righteousness and justice;
Pr 3:12 for the LORD reproves the one he l,
17:17 A friend l at all times,
Mt 10:37 Whoever l father or mother more
Lk 7:47 to whom little is forgiven, l little."
Ro 13: 8 who l another has fulfilled the law.
Eph 5:28 He who l his wife l himself.
Heb 12: 6 Lord disciplines those whom he l,
1Jn 4: 7 who l is born of God and knows
Rev 1: 5 who l us and freed us from our sins
Wis 8: 3 and the Lord of all l her.
Sir 4:12 Whoever l her l life,

LOW ➛ LOWER, LOWLY
Ps 136:23 who remembered us in our l estate,
Isa 40: 4 every mountain and hill be made l;
Lk 3: 5 mountain and hill shall be made l,

LOWER ➛ LOW
Ps 8: 5 have made them a little l than God,
Heb 2: 7 made them for a little while l than

LOWLY ➛ LOW
Pr 16:19 It is better to be of a l spirit
Lk 1:52 their thrones, and lifted up the l;
Ro 12:16 but associate with the l;
Jdt 9:11 But you are the God of the l,

LOYAL ➛ LOYALTY
2Sa 22:26 With the l you show yourself l;
Da 11:32 who are l to their God

LOYALTY ➛ LOYAL
Dt 7: 9 God who maintains covenant l
Ru 3:10 this last instance of your l

Ps 101: 1 I will sing of l and of justice;
Hos 4: 1 There is no faithfulness or l,

LUKE*
Associate of Paul (Col 4:14; 2Ti 4:11; Phm 24).

LUKEWARM*
Rev 3:16 because you are l, and neither cold

LUST → LUSTS
Mt 5:28 looks at a woman with l has already
2Pe 1: 4 that is in the world because of l,

LUSTS → LUST
Ro 1:24 gave them up in the l of their hearts
Eph 4:22 old self, corrupt and deluded by its l
2Pe 3: 3 scoffing and indulging their own l

LYDIA
Ac 16:14 named L, a worshiper of God,

LYING → LIE
1Ki 22:23 a l spirit in the mouth of all these
Pr 6:17 a l tongue, and hands that shed
Hos 4: 2 Swearing, l, and murder,
Wis 1:11 and a l mouth destroys the soul.

LYRE
1Sa 18:10 while David was playing the l,
Ps 33: 2 Praise the LORD with the l;
Da 3: 5 pipe, l, trigon, harp, drum,

M

MACCABEUS → JUDAS
1Mc 2:66 Judas M has been a mighty warrior

MACEDONIA
Ac 16: 9 a man of M pleading with him and

MADE → MAKE
Ge 1:31 God saw everything that he had m,
2:22 he m into a woman and brought her
3:21 the LORD God m garments of skins
6: 6 was sorry that he had m humankind
15:18 the LORD m a covenant with Abram,
Ex 20:11 For in six days the LORD m heaven
36: 8 the workers m the tabernacle with
Ps 8: 5 have m them a little lower than God
118:24 This is the day that the LORD has m;
139:14 I am fearfully and wonderfully m.
Jer 27: 5 outstretched arm have m the earth,
Mk 2:27 "The sabbath was m for humankind,
Ac 2:36 that God has m him both Lord and
Eph 2: 5 m us alive together with Christ—
Rev 14: 7 and worship him who m heaven
Sir 43:33 For the Lord has m all things,

MADNESS
Dt 28:28 The LORD will afflict you with m,
Ecc 9: 3 m is in their hearts while they live,

MAGDALENE
Mt 27:56 Among them were Mary M,

MAGICIANS
Ex 7:11 and they also, the m of Egypt,
Da 2: 2 So the king commanded that the m,

MAGNIFIES* → MAGNIFY
Lk 1:46 Mary said, "My soul m the Lord,

MAGNIFY → MAGNIFIES
Ps 34: 3 O m the LORD with me,

MAJESTIC → MAJESTY
Ex 15:11 Who is like you, m in holiness,
Ps 8: 1 how m is your name in all the earth!
2Pe 1:17 conveyed to him by the M Glory,

MAJESTY → MAJESTIC
1Ch 29:11 the glory, the victory, and the m;
Ps 93: 1 The LORD is king, he is robed in m;
Isa 53: 2 or m that we should look at him,
Heb 1: 3 sat down at the right hand of the M
2Pe 1:16 we had been eyewitnesses of his m.

MAKE → MADE, MAKER
Ge 1:26 "Let us m humankind in our image,
2:18 will m him a helper as his partner."
12: 2 I will m of you a great nation,
Ex 20: 4 You shall not m for yourself an idol,
32: 1 "Come, m gods for us, who shall go
Nu 6:25 LORD m his face to shine upon you,
Isa 61: 8 I will m an everlasting covenant
66:22 and the new earth, which I will m,
Jer 31:31 when I will m a new covenant with
Mt 28:19 and m disciples of all nations,
Mk 1:17 and I will m you fish for people."

MAKER → MAKE
Ge 14:19 God Most High, m of heaven and
Job 4:17 beings be pure before their M?
Ps 95: 6 kneel before the LORD, our M!
Isa 54: 5 For your M is your husband,
Sir 7:30 With all your might love your M,

MALACHI*
Post-exilic prophet (Mal 1:1; 2Es 1:40).

MALE
Ge 1:27 m and female he created them.
17:10 m among you shall be circumcised.
Lev 20:13 If a man lies with a m as with a
Mt 19: 4 'made them m and female,'
Rev 12: 5 she gave birth to a son, a m child,

MALICE
Ro 1:29 wickedness, evil, covetousness, m.
1Co 5: 8 the old yeast, the yeast of m and

MAN → MEN
Ge 2: 7 LORD God formed m from the dust
2:18 not good that the m should be alone;
32:24 m wrestled with him until daybreak.
1Sa 13:14 sought out a m after his own heart;
Mt 9: 6 Son of M has authority on earth to
Lk 6: 5 The Son of M is lord of the sabbath.
Jn 9:35 "Do you believe in the Son of M?"
1Co 11: 3 that Christ is the head of every m,
Rev 1:13 I saw one like the Son of M,
14:14 cloud was one like the Son of M,

MANAGE → MANAGERS
1Ti 3: 4 He must m his own household well,
5:14 children, and m their households,

MANAGERS* → MANAGE
Tit 2: 5 chaste, good m of the household,

MANASSEH
1. Firstborn of Joseph (Ge 41:51; 46:20). Blessed by Jacob but not as firstborn (Ge 48). Tribe of blessed (Dt 33:17), numbered (Nu 1:35; 26:34), half allotted land east of Jordan (Nu 32; Jos 13:8-33), half west (Jos 16; Eze 48:4), failed to fully possess (Jos 17:12-13; Jdg 1:27), 12,000 from (Rev 7:6).
2. Son of Hezekiah; king of Judah (2Ki 21:1-18; 2Ch 33:1-20). Judah exiled for his detestable sins (2Ki 21:10-15). Repented (2Ch 33:12-19; Man 1-15).

MANGER
Lk 2:12 in bands of cloth and lying in a m."

MANNA
Ex 16:31 The house of Israel called it m;
Jos 5:12 The m ceased on the day they ate
Jn 6:49 ate the m in the wilderness,
Rev 2:17 I will give some of the hidden m,

MANNER
1Co 11:27 cup of the Lord in an unworthy m
Php 1:27 life in a m worthy of the gospel

MANTLE
1Ki 19:19 and threw his m over him.
2Ki 2: 8 Elijah took his m and rolled it up,

MANY
Isa 53:12 yet he bore the sin of m,
Mt 22:14 m are called, but few are chosen."
Mk 10:45 and to give his life a ransom for m."
Jn 20:30 Now Jesus did m other signs in the
Ro 12: 5 who are m, are one body in Christ,

MARAH
Ex 15:23 That is why it was called M.

MARK → MARKED, MARKS
1. Cousin of Barnabas (Ac 12:12; 15:37-39; Col 4:10; 2Ti 4:11; Phm 24; 1Pe 5:13), see John.
2. Brand or symbol:
Ge 4:15 And the LORD put a m on Cain,
Eze 9: 6 but touch no one who has the m.
Rev 14: 9 receive a m on their foreheads or
19:20 who had received the m of the beast

MARKED → MARK
Hab 1:12 you have m them for judgment;
Eph 1:13 m with the seal of the promised

MARKET → MARKETPLACE
Mk 7: 4 not eat anything from the m unless
1Co 10:25 Eat whatever is sold in the meat m

MARKETPLACE → MARKET
Jn 2:16 Stop making my Father's house a m

MARKS → MARK
1Co 7:18 to remove the m of circumcision.
Gal 6:17 I carry the m of Jesus branded on
1Mc 1:15 and removed the m of circumcision,

MARRIAGE → INTERMARRY, MARRIED, MARRIES
Mt 22:30 are given in m, but are like angels
Heb 13: 4 Let m be held in honor by all,
Rev 19: 7 for the m of the Lamb has come,

MARRIED → MARRIAGE
Mal 2:11 has m the daughter of a foreign god.
Mk 12:23 For the seven had m her."
1Ti 3: 2 be above reproach, m only once,
Tit 1: 6 m only once, whose children are

MARRIES → MARRIAGE
Mk 10:11 and m another commits adultery
Ro 7: 3 if she m another man, she is not an
1Co 7:28 and if a virgin m, she does not sin.

MARTHA*
Sister of Mary and Lazarus (Lk 10:38-42; Jn 11; 12:2).

MARVELOUS
Ps 98: 1 for he has done m things.
131: 1 things too great and too m for me.
Sir 39:20 and nothing is too m for him.

MARY
1. Mother of Jesus (Mt 1:16-25; Lk 1:27-56; 2:1-40). With Jesus at temple (Lk 2:41-52), at the wedding in Cana (Jn 2:1-5), questioning his sanity (Mk 3:21), at the cross (Jn 19:25-27). Among disciples (Ac 1:14).
2. Magdalene; former demoniac (Lk 8:2). Helped support Jesus' ministry (Lk 8:1-3). At the cross (Mt 27:56; Mk 15:40; Jn 19:25), burial (Mt 27:61; Mk 15:47). Saw angel after resurrection (Mt 28:1-10; Mk 16:1-9; Lk 24:1-12); also Jesus (Jn 20:1-18).
3. Sister of Martha and Lazarus (Jn 11). Washed Jesus' feet (Jn 12:1-8).
4. Mother of James and Joses; witnessed crucifixion (Mt 27:56; Mk 15:40) and empty tomb (Mk 16:1; Lk 24:10).

MASTER → MASTERS, TASKMASTERS
Ge 4: 7 desire is for you, but you must m it.
Mal 1: 6 if I am a m, where is the respect due
Mt 25:21 enter into the joy of your m.'
Jn 15:20 Servants are not greater than their m
2Pe 2: 1 deny the M who bought them—

MASTERS → MASTER
Mt 6:24 "No one can serve two m;

MATTANIAH → See ZEDEKIAH

MATTATHIAS
Priest who started the Maccabean revolt (1Mc 2).

MATTER
Ecc 3: 1 a time for every m under heaven:
12:13 end of the m; all has been heard.

MATTHEW* → =LEVI
Apostle; former tax collector (Mt 9:9-13; 10:3; Mk 3:18; Lk 6:15; Ac 1:13). Also called Levi (Mk 2:14-17; Lk 5:27-32).

MATTHIAS
Disciple chosen to replace Judas (Ac 1:23-26).

MATURE → MATURITY
1Co 2: 6 among the m we do speak wisdom,
Php 3:15 who are m be of the same mind;
Col 4:12 you may stand m and fully assured
Heb 5:14 But solid food is for the m,

MATURITY → MATURE
Eph 4:13 to m, to the measure of the full

MEAN → MEANING, MEANS
Ex 12:26 What do you m by this observance?
Jos 4: 6 'What do those stones m to you?'

MEANING → MEAN
Ge 40: 5 and each dream with its own m.
Dt 6:20 "What is the m of the decrees

MEANS ➛ MEAN
Mt 9:13 learn what this **m**, 'I desire mercy,
1Co 9:22 that I might by all **m** save some.

MEASURE
Dt 25:15 have only a full and honest **m**,
Mk 4:24 **m** you give will be the **m** you get,
Lk 6:38 A good **m**, pressed down, shaken
Jn 3:34 for he gives the Spirit without **m**.

MEAT
Ex 16:12 'At twilight you shall eat **m**,
Ro 14:21 not to eat **m** or drink wine or do

MEDIA
Da 8:20 these are the kings of **M** and Persia.

MEDIATOR
Gal 3:19 ordained through angels by a **m**.
1Ti 2: 5 **m** between God and humankind,
Heb 8: 6 he is the **m** of a better covenant,

MEDICINE
Pr 17:22 A cheerful heart is a good **m**,
Sir 6:16 Faithful friends are life-saving **m**;

MEDITATE ➛ MEDITATION
Jos 1: 8 you shall **m** on it day and night,
Ps 1: 2 on his law they **m** day and night.
119:15 I will **m** on your precepts,
Wis 12:22 we may **m** upon your goodness,
Sir 6:37 and **m** at all times on his

MEDITATION ➛ MEDITATE
Ps 19:14 of my mouth and the **m** of my heart
119:97 It is my **m** all day long.

MEDIUM
Lev 20:27 A man or a woman who is a **m**
1Ch 10:13 moreover, he had consulted a **m**,

MEEK ➛ MEEKNESS
Ps 37:11 But the **m** shall inherit the land,
Mt 5: 5 "Blessed are the **m**, for they will

MEEKNESS ➛ MEEK
Col 3:12 kindness, humility, **m**, and patience.
Jas 1:21 with **m** the implanted word

MEET ➛ MEETING
Ex 30:36 tent of meeting where I shall **m** with
Am 4:12 prepare to **m** your God,
1Th 4:17 together with them to **m** the Lord

MEETING ➛ MEET
Ex 27:21 In the tent of **m**, outside the curtain
40:34 the cloud covered the tent of **m**,

MELCHIZEDEK
Ge 14:18 King **M** of Salem brought out bread
Ps 110: 4 forever according to the order of **M**."
Heb 7: 1 This "King **M** of Salem, priest of

MELT
Dt 1:28 made our hearts **m** by reporting,
Ps 97: 5 The mountains **m** like wax before
2Pe 3:12 and the elements will **m** with fire?

MEMBERS
Ro 7:23 I see in my **m** another law at war
1Co 6:15 that your bodies are **m** of Christ?
12:18 God arranged the **m** in the body,

MEMORIAL
Lev 5:12 a handful of it as its **m** portion,
Jos 4: 7 stones shall be to the Israelites a **m**

MEN ➛ MAN
Ge 18: 2 and saw three **m** standing near him.
Da 3:25 "But I see four **m** unbound,
Mt 2: 1 wise **m** from the East came to
Lk 9:30 they saw two **m**, Moses and Elijah,
Sir 44: 1 now sing the praises of famous **m**,

MENAHEM*
King of Israel (2Ki 15:14-23).

MENE
Da 5:25 inscribed: M, M, TEKEL, and PARSIN.

MEPHIBOSHETH
Son of Jonathan shown kindness by David (2Sa 4:4; 9; 21:7). Accused of siding with Absalom (2Sa 16:1-4; 19:24-30).

MERCIES ➛ MERCY
La 3:22 his **m** never come to an end;
2Co 1: 3 the Father of **m** and the God of all

MERCIFUL ➛ MERCY
Dt 4:31 the LORD your God is a **m** God,
Ps 111: 4 the LORD is gracious and **m**.
Jer 3:12 not look on you in anger, for I am **m**
Mt 5: 7 "Blessed are the **m**, for they will
Lk 6:36 Be **m**, just as your Father is **m**.
Heb 2:17 be a **m** and faithful high priest
Sir 2:11 the Lord is compassionate and **m**;

MERCY ➛ MERCIES, MERCIFUL
Ex 25:17 make a **m** seat of pure gold;
1Ch 21:13 of the LORD, for his **m** is very great;
Ps 40:11 Do not, O LORD, withhold your **m**
Da 9: 9 To the Lord our God belong **m**
Hab 3: 2 in wrath may you remember **m**.
Zec 1:12 will you withhold **m** from Jerusalem
Mt 9:13 learn what this means, 'I desire **m**,
23:23 of the law: justice and **m** and faith.
Ro 9:15 "I will have **m** on whom I have **m**,
Eph 2: 4 But God, who is rich in **m**,
1Ti 1:13 **m** because I had acted ignorantly
Tit 3: 5 had done, but according to his **m**,
Heb 4:16 so that we may receive **m** and find
Jas 2:13 **m** triumphs over judgment.
Sir 2:17 for equal to his majesty is his **m**,

MERIBAH
Ex 17: 7 He called the place Massah and **M**,
Ps 95: 8 Do not harden your hearts, as at **M**,

MESHACH ➛ =MISHAEL
Hebrew exiled to Babylon; name changed from Mishael (Da 1:6-7). Refused defilement by food (Da 1:8-20). Refused to worship idol (Da 3:1-18); saved from furnace (Da 3:19-30).

MESSAGE ➛ MESSENGER
Jn 12:38 "Lord, who has believed our **m**,
1Co 1:18 the **m** about the cross is foolishness
2Co 5:19 entrusting the **m** of reconciliation to

MESSENGER ➛ MESSAGE
Isa 42:19 or deaf like my **m** whom I send?
Mt 11:10 I am sending my **m** ahead of you,
2Co 12: 7 a **m** of Satan to torment me,

MESSIAH ➛ CHRIST, MESSIAHS
Mt 16:16 Peter answered, "You are the **M**,
Lk 2:11 a Savior, who is the **M**, the Lord.
Ac 2:36 God has made him both Lord and **M**
Ro 9: 5 according to the flesh, comes the **M**,
Rev 11:15 kingdom of our Lord and of his **M**,
2Es 7:28 For my son the **M** shall be revealed

MESSIAHS ➛ MESSIAH
Mk 13:22 False **m** and false prophets will

MICAH
1. Idolater from Ephraim (Jdg 17-18).
2. Prophet from Moresheth (Jer 26:18-19; Mic 1:1).

MICAIAH
Prophet of the LORD who spoke against Ahab (1Ki 22:1-28; 2Ch 18:1-27).

MICHAEL
Archangel (Jude 9); warrior in angelic realm, protector of Israel (Da 10:13, 21; 12:1; Rev 12:7).

MICHAL*
Daughter of Saul, wife of David (1Sa 14:49; 18:20-28). Warned David of Saul's plot (1Sa 19). Saul gave her to Paltiel (1Sa 25:44); David retrieved her (2Sa 3:13-16). Criticized David for dancing before the ark (2Sa 6:16-23; 1Ch 15:29).

MIDDLE
Ge 3: 3 tree that is in the **m** of the garden,
Rev 22: 2 the **m** of the street of the city.

MIDIAN ➛ MIDIANITES
Ex 18: 1 Jethro, the priest of **M**, Moses'

MIDIANITES ➛ MIDIAN
Ge 37:36 the **M** had sold him in Egypt to
Nu 31: 2 "Avenge the Israelites on the **M**;

MIDWIVES
Ex 1:17 But the **m** feared God; they did not

MIGHT ➛ ALMIGHTY, MIGHTY
2Ch 6:41 you and the ark of your **m**.
20: 6 In your hand are power and **m**,
Ps 54: 1 and vindicate me by your **m**.
Ecc 9:10 hand finds to do, do with your **m**;
Zec 4: 6 **m**, nor by power, but by my spirit,
Sir 7:30 With all your **m** love your Maker,

MIGHTY ➛ MIGHT
Ge 49:24 by the hands of the **M** One of Jacob,
Ex 6: 1 by a **m** hand he will let them go;
Dt 5:15 a **m** hand and an outstretched arm;
2Sa 1:19 How the **m** have fallen!
Ps 99: 4 **M** King, lover of justice, you have
Isa 9: 6 Wonderful Counselor, **M** God,
Lk 1:49 the **M** One has done great things
Rev 18: 8 for **m** is the Lord God who judges

MILE
Mt 5:41 one **m**, go also the second **m**.

MILK
Ex 3: 8 a land flowing with **m** and honey,
Heb 5:12 You need **m**, not solid food;
1Pe 2: 2 long for the pure, spiritual **m**,

MILLSTONE ➛ STONE
Lk 17: 2 better for you if a **m** were hung

MIND ➛ MINDFUL, MINDS
Nu 23:19 mortal, that he should change his **m**.
1Ch 28: 9 for the LORD searches every **m**,
Ps 110: 4 sworn and will not change his **m**,
Jnh 3: 9 God may relent and change his **m**;
Mt 22:37 all your soul, and with all your **m**.'
Ro 1:28 God gave them up to a debased **m**
8: 6 but to set the **m** on the Spirit is life
1Co 2:16 who has known the **m** of the Lord
Php 2: 5 same **m** be in you that was in Christ
Heb 7:21 sworn and will not change his **m**,
Sir 37:17 The **m** is the root of all conduct;

MINDFUL ➛ MIND
Ps 8: 4 beings that you are **m** of them,
111: 5 he is ever **m** of his covenant.
Heb 2: 6 beings that you are **m** of them,

MINDS ➛ MIND
2Co 4: 4 blinded the **m** of the unbelievers,
Eph 4:23 be renewed in the spirit of your **m**,
Php 4: 7 guard your hearts and your **m**

MINISTER ➛ MINISTERS, MINISTRY
Ex 28:43 to **m** in the holy place;
Ps 101: 6 that is blameless shall **m** to me.

MINISTERS ➛ MINISTER
2Co 3: 6 to be **m** of a new covenant,
11:15 if his **m** also disguise themselves as **m**

MINISTRY ➛ MINISTER
2Co 5:18 has given us the **m** of reconciliation;
Eph 4:12 equip the saints for the work of **m**,
Heb 8: 6 now obtained a more excellent **m**,

MIRACLES ➛ See also JESUS: MIRACLES
Ps 78:11 and the **m** that he had shown them.
Ac 19:11 did extraordinary **m** through Paul,
1Co 12:29 Are all teachers? Do all work **m**?
Heb 2: 4 signs and wonders and various **m**,

MIRIAM
Sister of Moses and Aaron (Nu 26:59). Led dancing at Red Sea (Ex 15:20-21). Struck with leprosy for criticizing Moses (Nu 12). Death (Nu 20:1).

MIRROR
1Co 13:12 For now we see in a **m**, dimly,
2Co 3:18 as though reflected in a **m**,
Jas 1:23 who look at themselves in a **m**;

MISHAEL ➛ See MESHACH

MISUSES
Ex 20: 7 not acquit anyone who **m** his name.

MOAB ➛ MOABITE
Ge 19:37 bore a son, and named him **M**;
Ru 1: 1 went to live in the country of **M**,
Isa 15: 1 An oracle concerning **M**.

MOABITE ➛ MOAB
Dt 23: 3 **M** shall be admitted to the assembly

MOCK ➛ MOCKED
Ps 22: 7 All who see me **m** at me;
Mk 10:34 they will **m** him, and spit upon him,

MOCKED ➛ MOCK
1Ki 18:27 At noon Elijah **m** them, saying,
Gal 6: 7 God is not **m**, for you reap

MOLECH
Lev 18:21 to sacrifice them to **M**,

MOMENT → MOMENTARY
Ex 33: 5 single **m** I should go up among you,
Ps 30: 5 For his anger is but for a **m**;
Isa 54: 7 For a brief **m** I abandoned you,
66: 8 a nation be delivered in one **m**?
1Co 15:52 in a **m**, in the twinkling of an eye,

MOMENTARY* → MOMENT
2Co 4:17 this slight **m** affliction is preparing

MONEY
Ecc 10:19 and **m** meets every need.
Mk 11:15 the tables of the **m** changers
1Ti 3: 3 quarrelsome, and not a lover of **m**.
6:10 love of **m** is a root of all kinds
Heb 13: 5 your lives free from the love of **m**,

MONTH
Ex 12: 2 be the first **m** of the year for you.
Eze 47:12 they will bear fresh fruit every **m**,
Rev 22: 2 producing its fruit each **m**;

MOON → MOONS
Ge 37: 9 the sun, the **m**, and eleven stars
Dt 17: 3 the sun or the **m** or any of the host
Jos 10:13 sun stood still, and the **m** stopped,
Joel 2:31 to darkness, and the **m** to blood,
Ac 2:20 to darkness and the **m** to blood,
Rev 6:12 the full **m** became like blood,
21:23 no need of sun or **m** to shine on it,

MOONS → MOON
2Ch 8:13 the new **m**, and the three annual
Col 2:16 or of observing festivals, new **m**,

MORALS*
1Co 15:33 "Bad company ruins good **m**."

MORDECAI
Benjamite exile who raised Esther (Est 2:5-15). Exposed plot to kill Xerxes (Est 2:19-23). Refused to honor Haman (Est 3:1-6; 5:9-14). Charged Esther to foil Haman's plot against the Jews (Est 4). Xerxes forced Haman to honor Mordecai (Est 6). Mordecai exalted (Est 8-10). Established Purim (Est 9:18-32). See also Additions to Esther.

MORE → MOST
Ps 19:10 **M** to be desired are they than gold,
69:31 will please the LORD **m** than an ox
Ecc 6:11 The **m** words, the **m** vanity,
Mk 4:25 to those who have, **m** will be given;
Lk 12:23 For life is **m** than food,
Ro 8:37 things we are **m** than conquerors
1Co 12:31 a still **m** excellent way.
Jas 4: 6 But he gives all the **m** grace;
Rev 7:16 will hunger no **m**, and thirst no **m**;
21: 4 Death will be no **m**;

MORIAH*
Ge 22: 2 you love, and go to the land of **M**,
2Ch 3: 1 the LORD in Jerusalem on Mount **M**,

MORNING
Ge 1: 5 and there was **m**, the first day.
Ps 30: 5 but joy comes with the **m**.
La 3:23 every **m**; great is your faithfulness.
Lk 24:22 They were at the tomb early this **m**,
2Pe 1:19 the day dawns and the **m** star rises
Rev 22:16 of David, the bright **m** star."

MORTAL
Nu 23:19 **m**, that he should change his mind.
1Sa 15:29 **m**, that he should change his mind."
1Co 15:53 **m** body must put on immortality.
2Co 5: 4 is **m** may be swallowed up by life.

MOSES
Levite; brother of Aaron (Ex 6:20; 1Ch 6:3). Put in basket into Nile; discovered and raised by Pharaoh's daughter (Ex 2:1-10). Fled to Midian after killing Egyptian (Ex 2:11-15). Married to Zipporah, fathered Gershom (Ex 2:16-22).

Called by the LORD to deliver Israel (Ex 3-4). Pharaoh's resistance (Ex 5). Ten plagues (Ex 7-11). Passover and Exodus (Ex 12-13). Led Israel through Red Sea (Ex 14). Song of deliverance (Ex 15:1-21). Brought water from rock (Ex 17:1-7). Raised hands to defeat Amalekites (Ex 17:8-16). Delegated judges (Ex 18; Dt 1:9-18).

Received Law at Sinai (Ex 19-23; 25-31; Jn 1:17). Announced Law to Israel (Ex 19:7-8; 24; 35). Broke tablets because of golden calf (Ex 32; Dt 9). Saw glory of the LORD (Ex 33-34). Supervised building of tabernacle (Ex 36-40). Set apart Aaron and priests (Lev 8-9). Numbered tribes (Nu 1-4; 26). Opposed by Aaron and Miriam (Nu 12). Sent spies into Canaan (Nu 13). Announced forty years of wandering for failure to enter land (Nu 14). Opposed by Korah (Nu 16). Forbidden to enter land for striking rock (Nu 20:1-13; Dt 1:37). Lifted bronze snake for healing (Nu 21:4-9; Jn 3:14). Final address to Israel (Dt 1-33). Succeeded by Joshua (Nu 27:12-23; Dt 34). Death and burial by God (Dt 34:5-12). Praise of (Sir 45).

Law of (1Ki 2:3; Ezr 3:2; Mk 12:26; Lk 24:44). Book of (2Ch 25:12; Ne 13:1). Song of (Ex 15:1-21; Rev 15:3). Prayer of (Ps 90).

MOST → MORE
Ge 14:18 he was priest of God **M** High.
Ex 26:33 the holy place from the **m** holy.
Ps 91: 1 live in the shelter of the **M** High,
Mk 5: 7 Jesus, Son of the **M** High God?
Col 4: 5 making the **m** of the time.
Jude 1:20 yourselves up on your **m** holy faith;

MOTH
Ps 39:11 consuming like a **m** what is dear to
Mt 6:19 where **m** and rust consume and

MOTHER → MOTHER'S, MOTHERS
Ge 2:24 a man leaves his father and his **m**
3:20 because she was the **m** of all living.
Ex 20:12 Honor your father and your **m**,
Jdg 5: 7 Deborah, arose as a **m** in Israel.
Pr 31: 1 An oracle that his **m** taught him:
Isa 66:13 As a **m** comforts her child, so I will
Mt 10:37 loves father or **m** more than me is
Lk 14:26 and does not hate father and **m**,
Jn 19:27 to the disciple, "Here is your **m**."
Eph 5:31 a man will leave his father and **m**
Rev 17: 5 **m** of whores and of earth's
Tob 4: 3 Honor your **m** and do not abandon
Sir 3: 6 who honor their **m** obey the Lord;

MOTHER'S → MOTHER
Job 1:21 "Naked I came from my **m** womb,
Pr 1: 8 and do not reject your **m** teaching;
Jn 3: 4 a second time into the **m** womb and

MOTHERS → MOTHER
Pr 15:20 but the foolish despise their **m**.
Mk 10:30 brothers and sisters, **m** and children,

MOUNT → MOUNTAIN, MOUNTAINS
Ge 22:14 "On the **m** of the LORD it shall be
Ex 19:20 the LORD descended upon **M** Sinai,
Dt 11:29 blessing on **M** Gerizim and the curse
Ps 78:68 **M** Zion, which he loves.
Mic 4: 7 will reign over them in **M** Zion
Zec 14: 4 the **M** of Olives shall be split in two
Mk 13: 3 he was sitting on the **M** of Olives
Heb 12:22 But you have come to **M** Zion and
Rev 14: 1 the Lamb, standing on **M** Zion!

MOUNTAIN → MOUNT
Ex 3: 1 and came to Horeb, the **m** of God.
24:18 on the **m** for forty days and forty
Isa 2: 2 the **m** of the LORD's house shall be
Da 2:45 saw that a stone was cut from the **m**
Mt 4: 8 a very high **m** and showed him all
17:20 you will say to this **m**, 'Move from
2Pe 1:18 we were with him on the holy **m**.

MOUNTAINS → MOUNT
Ge 7:20 the waters swelled above the **m**,
Ps 125: 2 As the **m** surround Jerusalem,
Isa 52: 7 beautiful upon the **m** are the feet of
1Co 13: 2 have all faith, so as to remove **m**,
Rev 16:20 and no **m** were to be found;

MOURN → MOURNFUL, MOURNING
Ecc 3: 4 a time to **m**, and a time to dance;
Zec 12:10 they shall **m** for him,
Mt 5: 4 "Blessed are those who **m**,
Sir 7:34 but **m** with those who **m**.

MOURNING → MOURN
Ps 30:11 You have turned my **m** into dancing
Isa 61: 3 the oil of gladness instead of **m**,
Rev 21: 4 **m** and crying and pain will be no

MOUTH → MOUTHS
Ex 4:12 Now go, and I will be with your **m**
Dt 8: 3 that comes from the **m** of the LORD.
Ps 19:14 Let the words of my **m** and
Ecc 5: 2 Never be rash with your **m**,
Isa 49: 2 He made my **m** like a sharp sword,
Mt 4: 4 every word that comes from the **m**
15:11 it is not what goes into the **m**
Jas 3:10 From the same **m** come blessing and
Rev 19:15 From his **m** comes a sharp sword
Sir 28:25 and a bolt for your **m**.

MOUTHS → MOUTH
Ps 115: 5 They have **m**, but do not speak;
Da 6:22 sent his angel and shut the lions' **m**

MUCH
Ps 19:10 they than gold, even **m** fine gold;
Ecc 12:12 **m** study is a weariness of the flesh.
Lk 12:48 to whom **m** has been given, **m** will be required;
Jn 12:24 but if it dies, it bears **m** fruit.
1Jn 4:11 since God loved us so **m**,

MUD
Jn 9: 6 and spread the **m** on the man's eyes,
2Pe 2:22 washed only to wallow in the **m**."

MULTIPLY
Ge 1:28 to them, "Be fruitful and **m**,
9: 7 And you, be fruitful and **m**,
Dt 6: 3 that you may **m** greatly in a land

MULTITUDE → MULTITUDES
Jas 5:20 and will cover a **m** of sins.
1Pe 4: 8 for love covers a **m** of sins.

MULTITUDES → MULTITUDE
Joel 3:14 **M**, **m**, in the valley of decision!
Rev 17:15 are peoples and **m** and nations

MURDER → MURDERER, MURDERERS
Ex 20:13 You shall not **m**.
Hos 4: 2 lying, and **m**, and stealing and
Mt 5:21 of ancient times, 'You shall not **m**';

MURDERER → MURDER
Nu 35:16 the **m** shall be put to death.
Jn 8:44 He was a **m** from the beginning

MURDERERS → MURDER
1Jn 3:15 who hate a brother or sister are **m**,
Rev 21: 8 the faithless, the polluted, the **m**,

MUSIC
1Sa 19: 9 while David was playing **m**.
Ps 92: 3 to the **m** of the lute and the harp,

MUSTARD
Mt 17:20 have faith the size of a **m** seed,
Mk 4:31 It is like a **m** seed, which,

MUTUAL
Ro 12:10 love one another with **m** affection;
Heb 13: 1 Let **m** love continue.

MYRRH
Mt 2:11 gifts of gold, frankincense, and **m**.
Mk 15:23 offered him wine mixed with **m**;

MYSTERY
Da 2:19 **m** was revealed to Daniel in a vision
Ro 11:25 I want you to understand this **m**:
1Co 15:51 Listen, I will tell you a **m**!
Eph 3: 4 my understanding of the **m** of Christ
1Ti 3: 9 must hold fast to the **m** of the faith
Rev 17: 5 a name, a **m**: "Babylon the great,

MYTHS
2Pe 1:16 did not follow cleverly devised **m**

N

NAAMAN
Aramean general whose leprosy was cleansed by Elisha (2Ki 5; Lk 4:27).

NABAL
Wealthy Carmelite the LORD killed for refusing to help David (1Sa 25). David married Abigail, his widow (1Sa 25:39-42).

NABOTH
Jezreelite killed for his vineyard (1Ki 21). Ahab's family punished (1Ki 21:17-24; 2Ki 9:21-37).

NADAB
1. Firstborn of Aaron (Ex 6:23); killed with Abihu for offering unauthorized fire (Lev 10; Nu 3:4).
2. Son of Jeroboam I; king of Israel (1Ki 15:25-32).

NAHUM
Prophet against Nineveh (Na 1:1; Tob 14:4).

NAILING* ➛ NAILS
Col 2:14 He set this aside, **n** it to the cross.

NAILS ➛ NAILING
Ecc 12:11 like **n** firmly fixed are the collected
Jn 20:25 put my finger in the mark of the **n**

NAKED ➛ NAKEDNESS
Ge 2:25 the man and his wife were both **n**,
Job 1:21 "**N** I came from my mother's womb, and **n** shall
2Co 5: 3 taken it off we will not be found **n**.

NAKEDNESS ➛ NAKED
Ro 8:35 or persecution, or famine, or **n**,

NAME ➛ NAME'S, NAMES
Ge 2:19 every living creature, that was its **n**.
4:26 people began to invoke the **n** of
12: 2 bless you, and make your **n** great,
Ex 3:15 my **n** forever, and this my title
20: 7 wrongful use of the **n** of the LORD
34: 5 and proclaimed the **n**, "The LORD."
Nu 17: 2 Write each man's **n** on his staff,
Dt 12:11 as a dwelling for his **n**:
Ps 9:10 know your **n** put their trust in you,
Pr 18:10 The **n** of the LORD is a strong tower;
Isa 42: 8 I am the LORD, that is my **n**;
Eze 20: 9 But I acted for the sake of my **n**,
Joel 2:32 on the **n** of the LORD shall be saved;
Zec 14: 9 the LORD will be one and his **n** one.
Mt 1:21 a son, and you are to **n** him Jesus,
6: 9 Father in heaven, hallowed be your **n**.
28:19 baptizing them in the **n** of the Father
Jn 1:12 received him, who believed in his **n**,
20:31 believing you may have life in his **n**.
Ac 4:12 for there is no other **n** under heaven
Php 2: 9 gave him the **n** that is above every **n**
Rev 13:17 **n** of the beast or the number of its **n**.
19:13 his **n** is called The Word of God.
22: 4 and his **n** will be on their foreheads.
Sir 2:17 and equal to his **n** are his works.

NAME'S ➛ NAME
Ps 23: 3 in right paths for his **n** sake.

NAMES ➛ NAME
Ge 2:20 The man gave **n** to all cattle,
Ex 28: 9 engrave on them the **n** of the sons
Mt 10: 2 are the **n** of the twelve apostles:
Rev 21:14 the twelve **n** of the twelve apostles

NAOMI*
Wife of Elimelech, mother-in-law of Ruth (Ru 1:2, 4). Left Bethlehem for Moab during famine (Ru 1:1). Returned a widow, with Ruth (Ru 1:6-22). Advised Ruth to seek marriage with Boaz (Ru 2:17-3:4). Cared for Ruth's son Obed (Ru 4:13-17).

NAPHTALI
Son of Jacob by Bilhah (Ge 30:8; 35:25; 1Ch 2:2). Tribe of blessed (Ge 49:21; Dt 33:23), numbered (Nu 1:43; 26:50), allotted land (Jos 19:32-39; Eze 48:3), failed to fully possess (Jdg 1:33), supported Deborah (Jdg 4:10; 5:18), David (1Ch 12:34), 12,000 from (Rev 7:6).

NARROW
Lk 13:24 "Strive to enter through the **n** door;

NATHAN
Prophet and chronicler of Israel's history (1Ch 29:29; 2Ch 9:29). Announced the Davidic covenant (2Sa 7; 1Ch 17). Denounced David's sin with Bathsheba (2Sa 12). Supported Solomon (1Ki 1).

NATHANAEL ➛ =BARTHOLOMEW?
Apostle (Jn 1:45-49; 21:2). Probably also called Bartholomew (Mt 10:3).

NATION ➛ NATIONS
Ge 12: 2 I will make of you a great **n**, and
Ex 32:10 and of you I will make a great **n**."
Ps 33:12 Happy is the **n** whose God is the LORD
Pr 14:34 Righteousness exalts a **n**,
Isa 2: 4 **n** shall not lift up sword against **n**,
66: 8 a **n** be delivered in one moment?
Mt 24: 7 For **n** will rise against **n**,
1Pe 2: 9 a holy **n**, God's own people,

NATIONS ➛ NATION
Ge 18:18 the **n** of the earth shall be blessed in
2Ki 17:15 followed the **n** that were around
Ps 47: 8 God is king over the **n**;
Isa 2: 2 all the **n** shall stream to it.
42: 1 he will bring forth justice to the **n**.
Am 9:12 and all the **n** who are called
Mt 28:19 and make disciples of all **n**,
Mk 11:17 a house of prayer for all the **n**'?
Ro 4:18 become "the father of many **n**,"
Rev 22: 2 the tree are for the healing of the **n**.

NATURAL ➛ NATURE
Nu 16:29 If these people die a **n** death,
Ro 11:21 if God did not spare the **n** branches,

NATURE ➛ NATURAL
Ro 1:20 his eternal power and divine **n**,
2Pe 1: 4 become participants of the divine **n**.

NAZARETH
Mt 2:23 made his home in a town called **N**,
Jn 1:46 Can anything good come out of **N**?
19:19 "Jesus of **N**, the King of the Jews."

NAZIRITE
Nu 6: 2 make a special vow, the vow of a **n**,
Jdg 13: 5 boy shall be a **n** to God from birth.

NEAR ➛ NEARSIGHTED
Dt 4: 7 has a god so **n** to it as the LORD
30:14 No, the word is very **n** to you;
Isa 55: 6 call upon him while he is **n**;
Zep 1:14 The great day of the LORD is **n**,
Lk 10: 9 'The kingdom of God has come **n**
Jas 4: 8 Draw **n** to God, and he will draw **n** to
Rev 22:10 of this book, for the time is **n**.

NEARSIGHTED* ➛ NEAR, SEE
2Pe 1: 9 lacks these things is **n** and blind,

NEBUCHADNEZZAR
Babylonian king, also spelled Nebuchadrezzar. Subdued and exiled Judah (2Ki 24-25; 2Ch 36; Jer 39). Dreams interpreted by Daniel (Da 2; 4). Worshiped God (Da 3:28-29; 4:34-37).

NECK ➛ STIFF-NECKED
Pr 3:22 your soul and adornment for your **n**.
Mt 18: 6 were fastened around your **n**

NECO
Pharaoh who killed Josiah (2Ki 23:29-30; 2Ch 35:20-22), deposed Jehoahaz (2Ki 23:33-35; 2Ch 36:3-4).

NEED ➛ NEEDY
Mt 6: 8 for your Father knows what you **n**
1Co 12:21 to the hand, "I have no **n** of you,"
Heb 4:16 and find grace to help in time of **n**.
1Jn 2:27 you do not **n** anyone to teach you.

NEEDLE
Lk 18:25 a camel to go through the eye of a **n**

NEEDY ➛ NEED
1Sa 2: 8 he lifts the **n** from the ash heap,
Job 29:16 I was a father to the **n**,
Ps 113: 7 and lifts the **n** from the ash heap,

NEGLECT
Lk 11:42 and **n** justice and the love of God;
1Ti 4:14 Do not **n** the gift that is in you,
Heb 2: 3 escape if we **n** so great a salvation?

NEHEMIAH
Cupbearer of Artaxerxes (Ne 2:1); governor of Israel (Ne 8:9). Returned to Jerusalem to rebuild walls (Ne 2-6). With Ezra, reestablished worship (Ne 8). Prayer confessing nation's sin (Ne 9). Dedicated wall (Ne 12). Story of the miraculous fire (2Mc 1).

NEIGHBOR
Lev 19:18 shall love your **n** as yourself:
Dt 5:20 bear false witness against your **n**.
Mt 19:19 You shall love your **n** as yourself."
Jas 2: 8 "You shall love your **n** as yourself."

NESTS
Mt 8:20 and birds of the air have **n**;
Lk 13:19 made **n** in its branches."

NEVER
Ps 15: 5 do these things shall **n** be moved.
La 3:22 steadfast love of the LORD **n** ceases,
Da 2:44 will set up a kingdom that shall **n**
Mt 7:23 will declare to them, 'I **n** knew you;
Jn 10:28 eternal life, and they will **n** perish.
1Co 13: 8 Love **n** ends. But as for prophecies,
Heb 13: 5 he has said, "I will **n** leave you or

NEW
Ex 1: 8 Now a **n** king arose over Egypt,
Ps 33: 3 Sing to him a **n** song;
Ecc 1: 9 there is nothing **n** under the sun.
Isa 43:19 I am about to do a **n** thing;
65:17 create **n** heavens and a **n** earth;
Jer 31:31 I will make a **n** covenant with the
La 3:23 they are **n** every morning;
Eze 36:26 A **n** heart I will give you,
Mt 9:17 is **n** wine put into old wineskins;
Mk 1:27 A **n** teaching—with authority!
Lk 22:20 is the **n** covenant in my blood.
Jn 13:34 I give you a **n** commandment,
2Co 3: 6 to be ministers of a **n** covenant,
Col 3:10 clothed yourselves with the **n** self,
Heb 8: 8 when I will establish a **n** covenant
1Pe 1: 3 mercy he has given us a **n** birth into
2Pe 3:13 we wait for **n** heavens and a **n** earth,
1Jn 2: 7 writing you no **n** commandment,
Rev 21: 1 I saw a **n** heaven and a **n** earth;
21: 2 I saw the holy city, the **n** Jerusalem,
21: 5 "See, I am making all things **n**."

NEWS
Isa 52: 7 who brings good **n**, who announces
Mt 11: 5 the poor have good **n** brought to
Mk 1:15 repent, and believe in the good **n**."

NICODEMUS
Pharisee who visted Jesus at night (Jn 3). Argued for fair treatment of Jesus (Jn 7:50-52). With Joseph, prepared Jesus for burial (Jn 19:38-42).

NIGHT ➛ NIGHTS
Ge 1: 5 and the darkness he called **N**.
Ex 13:21 a pillar of fire by **n**, to give them
Jos 1: 8 you shall meditate on it day and **n**,
Mt 24:43 part of the **n** the thief was coming,
1Th 5: 2 Lord will come like a thief in the **n**.
Rev 22: 5 And there will be no more **n**;

NIGHTS ➛ NIGHT
Ge 7:12 on the earth forty days and forty **n**.
Ex 24:18 mountain for forty days and forty **n**.
1Ki 19: 8 of that food forty days and forty **n**
Jnh 1:17 of the fish three days and three **n**.
Mt 4: 2 He fasted forty days and forty **n**,
12:40 for three days and three **n** the Son

NILE
Ex 7:17 will strike the water that is in the **N**,

NINEVEH
Jnh 1: 2 "Go at once to **N**, that great city,
Na 1: 1 An oracle concerning **N**.
Mt 12:41 The people of **N** will rise up at the

NOAH
Righteous man (Eze 14:14, 20) called to build ark (Ge 6-8; Heb 11:7; 1Pe 3:20; 2Pe 2:5). God's covenant with (Ge 9:1-17). Drunkenness of (Ge 9:18-23). Blessed sons, cursed Canaan (Ge 9:24-27). Praised (Sir 44:17-18).

NOISE
Ex 32:17 "There is a **n** of war in the camp."
Ps 66: 1 Make a joyful **n** to God, all the earth
2Pe 3:10 will pass away with a loud **n**,

NOON
Am 8: 9 I will make the sun go down at **n**,
Mk 15:33 When it was **n**, darkness came over

NORTH
Jer 4: 6 I am bringing evil from the **n**,
Da 11: 6 come to the king of the **n** to ratify

NOTHING
Ecc 1: 9 there is **n** new under the sun.
Jer 32:17 **N** is too hard for you.

Mt 17:20 and n will be impossible for you."
Jn 15: 5 apart from me you can do n.
1Co 13: 2 but do not have love, I am n.
Sir 39:20 and n is too marvelous for him.

NULLIFY
Ro 3: 3 n the faithfulness of God?
Gal 2:21 I do not n the grace of God;

NUMBER ➛ NUMBERED, NUMEROUS
Nu 1:45 So the whole n of the Israelites,
26:51 the n of the Israelites enrolled:
Ro 11:25 until the full n of the Gentiles has
Rev 13:18 Its n is six hundred sixty-six.

NUMBERED ➛ NUMBER
2Sa 24:10 because he had n the people.

NUMEROUS ➛ NUMBER
Ge 17: 2 and will make you exceedingly n."
Ex 1: 9 the Israelite people are more n
Zec 10: 8 shall be as n as they were before.

NURSING
Isa 49:15 Can a woman forget her n child,

O

OATH
Dt 7: 8 and kept the o that he swore to your
Ne 13:25 them take an o in the name of God,
Ps 132:11 a sure o from which he will not turn
Heb 7:20 This was confirmed with an o;

OBADIAH
1. Believer who sheltered 100 prophets from Jezebel (1Ki 18:1-16).
2. Prophet against Edom (Ob 1; 2Es 1:39).

OBEDIENCE ➛ OBEY
Ro 5:19 so by the one man's o the many will
Heb 5: 8 learned o through what he suffered;

OBEDIENT ➛ OBEY
Ex 24: 7 spoken we will do, and we will be o.
Php 2: 8 and became o to the point of death

OBEY ➛ OBEDIENCE, OBEDIENT, OBEYED
Ex 19: 5 if you o my voice and keep my
Dt 12:28 Be careful to o all these words that
Jos 24:24 we will serve, and him we will o."
Mt 28:20 o everything that I have commanded
Ac 5:29 "We must o God rather than any
Eph 6: 1 Children, o your parents in the Lord,
1Jn 5: 3 love of God is this, that we o his

OBEYED ➛ OBEY
Jer 3:13 have not o my voice, says the LORD.
Heb 11: 8 By faith Abraham o when he was

OBSERVE
Lev 20: 8 Keep my statutes, and o them;
Ps 119: 8 I will o your statutes;

OBSTACLE
1Co 9:12 o in the way of the gospel of Christ.
2Co 6: 3 are putting no o in anyone's way,

OBTAIN ➛ OBTAINED
Ro 11: 7 Israel failed to o what it was seeking
2Ti 2:10 that they may also o the salvation

OBTAINED ➛ OBTAIN
Php 3:12 Not that I have already o this
Heb 8: 6 Jesus has now o a more excellent

ODOR
Ge 8:21 the LORD smelled the pleasing o,
Ex 29:18 it is a pleasing o, an offering

OFFENSE
Mk 6: 3 And they took o at him.
Gal 5:11 o of the cross has been removed.

OFFER ➛ OFFERING, OFFERINGS
Ps 4: 5 O right sacrifices, and put your trust
Hos 14: 2 and we will o the fruit of our lips.
Heb 9:25 Nor was it to o himself again and

OFFERING ➛ OFFER
Ge 4: 4 LORD had regard for Abel and his o,
22: 8 will provide the lamb for a burnt o,
2Ch 7: 1 heaven and consumed the burnt o
Ps 40: 6 Sacrifice and o you do not desire,
Da 11:31 shall abolish the regular burnt o
Eph 5: 2 a fragrant o and sacrifice to God.
Heb 10:14 For by a single o he has perfected
1Mc 4:44 what to do about the altar of burnt o,

OFFERINGS ➛ OFFER
1Sa 15:22 the LORD as great delight in burnt o
Hos 6: 6 of God rather than burnt o.
Mk 12:33 important than all whole burnt o
1Mc 1:45 to forbid burnt o and sacrifices

OFFSPRING
Ge 3:15 and between your o and hers;
12: 7 "To your o I will give this land."
2Sa 7:12 I will raise up your o after you,

OHOLIAB
Craftsman who worked on the tabernacle (Ex 31:6; 35:34; 36:1-2; 38:23).

OIL
Ex 25: 6 o for the lamps, spices for the anointing o
Dt 14:23 your wine, and your o, as well
Ps 23: 5 you anoint my head with o;
Heb 1: 9 with the o of gladness beyond your
Jas 5:14 anointing them with o in the name

OLD
Ge 21: 7 I have borne him a son in his o age."
Ps 74:12 Yet God my King is from of o,
Mk 2:22 puts new wine into o wineskins;
Ro 4:19 he was about a hundred years o),
Eph 4:22 your o self, corrupt and deluded by

OLIVE ➛ OLIVES
Zec 4: 3 And by it there are two o trees,
Ro 11:17 and you, a wild o shoot,
Rev 11: 4 two o trees and the two lampstands

OLIVES ➛ OLIVE
Zec 14: 4 Mount of O shall be split in two
Mt 24: 3 he was sitting on the Mount of O,

OMEGA
Rev 1: 8 "I am the Alpha and the O,"

OMRI
King of Israel (1Ki 16:21-26).

ONCE ➛ ONE
Ex 30:10 O a year Aaron shall perform the
Ro 6:10 he died, he died to sin, o for all;
Heb 7:27 this he did o for all when he offered
9:27 it is appointed for mortals to die o,

ONE ➛ FIRST, ONCE
Ge 2:24 and they become o flesh.
Zec 14: 9 the LORD will be o and his name o.
Mk 12:29 the Lord our God, the Lord is o;
Jn 10:30 The Father and I are o."
1Co 12:13 For in the o Spirit we were all baptized
Eph 4: 5 o Lord, o faith, o baptism,

ONLY
Ge 22: 2 "Take your son, your o son Isaac,
1Ki 18:22 "I, even I o, am left a prophet
Jn 1:14 the glory as of a father's o son,
3:16 that he gave his o Son,
1Ti 1:17 the o God, be honor and glory
1Jn 4: 9 God sent his o Son into the world so

OPEN ➛ OPENED, OPENS
Isa 53: 7 so he did not o his mouth.
Rev 5: 2 "Who is worthy to o the scroll

OPENED ➛ OPEN
Ge 3: 7 Then the eyes of both were o,
Da 7:10 in judgment, and the books were o.
Zec 13: 1 a fountain shall be o for the house
Lk 11: 9 knock, and the door will be o for
Heb 10:20 new and living way that he o for us
Rev 20:12 book was o, the book of life.

OPENS ➛ OPEN
Rev 3: 7 who o and no one will shut,

OPPORTUNITY
Mt 26:16 began to look for an o to betray him.
Gal 5:13 not use your freedom as an o for

OPPRESSED ➛ OPPRESSION
Ge 15:13 shall be o for four hundred years;
Ex 1:12 But the more they were o,
Ps 146: 7 who executes justice for the o;
Isa 53: 7 He was o, and he was afflicted,
Jdt 9:11 God of the lowly, helper of the o,

OPPRESSION ➛ OPPRESSED
Jer 9: 6 O upon o, deceit upon deceit!
Eze 45: 9 Put away violence and o,

ORACLES
Ro 3: 2 entrusted with the o of God.

ORDAIN ➛ ORDINANCE, ORDINANCES
Ex 29: 9 shall then o Aaron and his sons.
1Ti 5:22 Do not o anyone hastily,

ORDER
Ps 110: 4 according to the o of Melchizedek."
Heb 5:10 according to the o of Melchizedek.

ORDINANCE ➛ ORDAIN
Ex 12:17 your generations as a perpetual o.
29: 9 shall be theirs by a perpetual o.

ORDINANCES ➛ ORDAIN
Ps 19: 9 o of the LORD are true and righteous

ORIGIN
Mt 21:26 But if we say, 'Of human o,'
Ac 5:38 or this undertaking is of human o,

ORNAMENTS
Ex 33: 6 stripped themselves of their o,
1Pe 3: 3 by wearing gold o or fine clothing;

ORPHAN ➛ ORPHANED, ORPHANS
Ex 22:22 You shall not abuse any widow or o.
Hos 14: 3 In you the o finds mercy."

ORPHANED ➛ ORPHAN
Jn 14:18 will not leave you o; I am coming

ORPHANS ➛ ORPHAN
Jas 1:27 to care for o and widows in their
Sir 4:10 Be a father to o, and be like a

OTHER ➛ OTHERS
Ex 20: 3 you shall have no o gods before me.
Jdg 2:19 following o gods,
2Ki 17: 7 They had worshiped o gods
Isa 45: 5 I am the LORD, and there is no o;
Mt 6:24 to the one and despise the o.

OTHERS ➛ OTHER
Lk 6:31 Do to o as you would have them do
Php 2: 3 but in humility regard o as better

OTHNIEL
Nephew of Caleb (Jos 15:15-19; Jdg 1:12-15). Judge who freed Israel from Aram (Jdg 3:7-11).

OUTSIDE
Lk 11:39 Pharisees clean the o of the cup and
Heb 13:12 Jesus also suffered o the city gate in
Rev 22:15 O are the dogs and sorcerers and

OUTSTRETCHED ➛ STRETCH
Ex 6: 6 I will redeem you with an o arm
Ps 136:12 an o arm, for his steadfast love
Jer 27: 5 by my great power and my o arm

OUTWARD
1Sa 16: 7 they look on the o appearance,
2Co 5:12 those who boast in o appearance
2Ti 3: 5 the o form of godliness but denying

OVERCOME
Jn 1: 5 and the darkness did not o it.
Ro 12:21 Do not be o by evil, but o evil with
1Jn 2:14 and you have o the evil one.

OVERSHADOW* ➛ OVERSHADOWED
Lk 1:35 power of the Most High will o you;

OVERSHADOWED ➛ OVERSHADOW
Lk 9:34 a cloud came and o them;

OWE ➛ OWES
Mt 18:28 he said, 'Pay what you o.'
Ro 13: 8 O no one anything, except to love

OWN
Isa 53: 6 we have all turned to our o way,
Jer 31:30 But all shall die for their o sins;
Jn 1:11 He came to what was his o, and his o people did not accept him.
10:18 but I lay it down of my o accord.
1Co 6:19 and that you are not your o?

OX ➛ OXEN
Dt 25: 4 not muzzle an o while it is treading
Isa 65:25 the lion shall eat straw like the o;
Eze 1:10 the face of an o on the left side,

1Ti 5:18 not muzzle an o while it is treading
Rev 4: 7 the second living creature like an o,

P

PAGANS
1Co 5: 1 that is not found even among p;
12: 2 You know that when you were p,

PAIN ➛ PAINS
Ge 3:16 in p you shall bring forth children,
1Pe 2:19 endure p while suffering unjustly.
Rev 21: 4 and crying and p will be no more,

PAINS ➛ PAIN
Ro 8:22 creation has been groaning in labor p
1Th 5: 3 as labor p come upon a pregnant

PALM ➛ PALMS
Jn 12:13 So they took branches of p trees
Rev 7: 9 robed in white, with p branches in

PALMS ➛ PALM
Isa 49:16 I have inscribed you on the p of my

PANGS
Ge 3:16 increase your p in childbearing;
Mk 13: 8 but the beginning of the birth p.
Rev 12: 2 and was crying out in birth p,

PARABLE ➛ PARABLES
Ps 78: 2 I will open my mouth in a p;
Mt 13:18 "Hear then the p of the sower.

PARABLES ➛ PARABLE; See also JESUS: PARABLES
Mt 13:35 I will open my mouth to speak in p;
Sir 39: 2 penetrates the subtleties of p;

PARADISE
Lk 23:43 today you will be with me in P."
2Co 12: 4 was caught up into P and heard
Rev 2: 7 tree of life that is in the p of God.
2Es 8:52 for you that p is opened,

PARALYTIC ➛ PARALYZED
Mt 9: 2 saw their faith, he said to the p,

PARALYZED ➛ PARALYTIC
Jn 5: 3 many invalids—blind, lame, and p.
Ac 8: 7 who were p or lame were cured.

PARCHMENTS*
2Ti 4:13 also the books, and above all the p.

PARDON
Ex 34: 9 p our iniquity and our sin,
Isa 55: 7 our God, for he will abundantly p.

PARENT ➛ PARENTS
Dt 8: 5 that as a p disciplines a child
Eze 18:20 nor a p suffer for the iniquity of a

PARENTS ➛ PARENT
Mal 4: 6 turn the hearts of p to their children
Lk 1:17 turn the hearts of p to their children,
Eph 6: 1 Children, obey your p in the Lord,
Sir 48:10 turn the hearts of p to their children,

PART ➛ APART
1Co 13: 9 For we know only in p, and we prophesy only in p;

PARTAKE
1Co 10:17 for we all p of the one bread.

PARTIALITY
Dt 16:19 distort justice; you must not show p;
Pr 24:23 P in judging is not good.
Ro 2:11 For God shows no p.
Jas 3:17 without a trace of p or hypocrisy.
Sir 35:15 and with him there is no p.

PARTICIPANTS ➛ PARTICIPATE
2Pe 1: 4 may become p of the divine nature.

PARTICIPATE* ➛ PARTICIPANTS
1Ti 5:22 and do not p in the sins of others;
2Jn 1:11 for to welcome is to p in the evil

PARTNER ➛ PARTNERS, PARTNERSHIP
Pr 2:17 who forsakes the p of her youth
1Co 7:15 But if the unbelieving p separates,

PARTNERS ➛ PARTNER
1Co 10:20 not want you to be p with demons.
Heb 3: 1 holy p in a heavenly calling,

PARTNERSHIP* ➛ PARTNER
2Co 6:14 p is there between righteousness

PASHHUR
Priest; opponent of Jeremiah (Jer 20:1-6).

PASS ➛ PASSED, PASSING
Ex 12:13 when I see the blood, I will p over
33:19 make all my goodness p before you,
Am 5:17 I will p through the midst of you,
Mt 24:35 Heaven and earth will p away, but my words will not p
2Pe 3:10 then the heavens will p away

PASSED ➛ PASS
Ge 15:17 torch p between these pieces.
Ex 12:27 he p over the houses of the Israelites
33:22 with my hand until I have p by;
2Co 5:17 everything old has p away;
1Jn 3:14 that we have p from death to life
Rev 21: 4 for the first things have p away."

PASSING ➛ PASS
1Co 7:31 present form of this world is p away
1Jn 2:17 the world and its desire are p away,

PASSIONS
Gal 5:24 have crucified the flesh with its p
2Ti 2:22 Shun youthful p and pursue

PASSOVER
Ex 12:11 It is the p of the LORD.
Dt 16: 1 the month of Abib by keeping the p
Mk 14:12 when the P lamb is sacrificed,

PASTORS*
Eph 4:11 evangelists, some p and teachers,

PASTURE ➛ PASTURES
Ps 100: 3 his people, and the sheep of his p.
Jer 50: 7 the LORD, the true p, the LORD,

PASTURES ➛ PASTURE
Ps 23: 2 He makes me lie down in green p;

PATH ➛ PATHS
Ps 16:11 You show me the p of life.
119:105 lamp to my feet and a light to my p.
Mt 13: 4 he sowed, some seeds fell on the p,

PATHS ➛ PATH
Ps 23: 3 in right p for his name's sake.
Pr 3: 6 and he will make straight your p.
Mt 3: 3 of the Lord, make his p straight.'"
Heb 12:13 and make straight p for your feet,

PATIENCE ➛ PATIENT
Mic 2: 7 Is the LORD's p exhausted?
Ro 2: 4 his kindness and forbearance and p?
Gal 5:22 fruit of the Spirit is love, joy, peace, p,
2Pe 3:15 regard the p of our Lord as salvation

PATIENT ➛ PATIENCE
Lk 8:15 and bear fruit with p endurance.
Ro 12:12 Rejoice in hope, be p in suffering,
1Co 13: 4 Love is p; love is kind;
2Pe 3: 9 as some think of slowness, but is p

PATTERN
Ex 25:40 make them according to the p for
Heb 8: 5 make everything according to the p

PAUL ➛ =SAUL
Also called Saul (Ac 13:9). Pharisee from Tarsus (Ac 9:11; Php 3:5). Apostle (Gal 1). At stoning of Stephen (Ac 8:1). Persecuted Church (Ac 9:1-2; Gal 1:13). Vision of Jesus on road to Damascus (Ac 9:4-9; 26:12-18). In Arabia (Gal 1:17). Preached in Damascus; escaped death through the wall in a basket (Ac 9:19-25). In Jerusalem; back to Tarsus (Ac 9:26-30).

Brought to Antioch by Barnabas (Ac 11:22-26). First missionary journey to Cyprus and Galatia (Ac 13-14). Stoned at Lystra (Ac 14:19-20). At Jerusalem council (Ac 15). Split with Barnabas over Mark (Ac 15:36-41).

Second missionary journey with Silas (Ac 16-20). Called to Macedonia (Ac 16:6-10). Freed from prison in Philippi (Ac 16:16-40). In Thessalonica (Ac 17:1-9). Speech in Athens (Ac 17:16-33). In Corinth (Ac 18). In Ephesus (Ac 19). Return to Jerusalem (Ac 20). Farewell to Ephesian elders (Ac 20:13-38). Arrival in Jerusalem (Ac 21:1-26). Arrested (Ac 21:27-36). Addressed crowds (Ac 22), Sanhedrin (Ac 23:1-11). Sent to Caesarea (Ac 23:12-35). Trial before Felix (Ac 24), Festus (Ac 25:1-12). Before Agrippa (Ac 25:13-26:32). Voyage to Rome; shipwreck (Ac 27). Arrival in Rome (Ac 28).

PAVEMENT
Ex 24:10 his feet there was something like a p
Jn 19:13 bench at a place called The Stone P,

PAY ➛ REPAY
Ex 22: 4 the thief shall p double.
Dt 24:15 You shall p them their wages daily
Mt 22:17 lawful to p taxes to the emperor, or
Ro 13: 7 P to all what is due them—

PEACE ➛ PEACEMAKERS
Lev 26: 6 And I will grant p in the land,
Ps 122: 6 Pray for the p of Jerusalem:
Isa 26: 3 in p because they trust in you.
57:19 P, p, to the far and the near,
57:21 no p, says my God, for the wicked.
Jer 6:14 saying, "P, p," when there is no p.
Mic 5: 5 and he shall be the one of p.
Lk 2:14 on earth p among those whom he
Jn 14:27 P I leave with you; my p I give
Ro 16:20 God of p will shortly crush Satan
1Co 14:33 is a God not of disorder but of p.
Gal 5:22 the fruit of the Spirit is love, joy, p,
Eph 4: 3 unity of the Spirit in the bond of p.
Php 4: 7 the p of God, which surpasses all
2Ti 2:22 righteousness, faith, love, and p,

PEACEMAKERS* ➛ PEACE
Mt 5: 9 "Blessed are the p, for they will be

PEARL* ➛ PEARLS
Mt 13:46 on finding one p of great value,
Rev 21:21 each of the gates is a single p,

PEARLS ➛ PEARL
Mt 7: 6 do not throw your p before swine,

PEKAH*
King of Israel (2Ki 15:25-31; 2Ch 28:6; Isa 7:1).

PEKAHIAH*
Son of Menahem; king of Israel (2Ki 15:22-26).

PENALTY
Ro 1:27 in their own persons the due p
2Pe 2:13 suffering the p for doing wrong.

PENTECOST
Ac 2: 1 When the day of P had come,

PEOPLE ➛ PEOPLES
Ex 5: 1 the God of Israel, 'Let my p go,
33:13 that this nation is your p."
Dt 4:20 a p of his very own possession,
32: 9 the LORD's own portion was his p,
Ru 1:16 your p shall be my p,
2Sa 5: 2 shall be shepherd of my p Israel,
Ps 29:11 the LORD bless his p with peace!
125: 2 so the LORD surrounds his p,
Isa 40: 1 Comfort, O comfort my p, says
42: 6 given you as a covenant to the p,
53: 8 for the transgression of my p.
Jer 50: 6 My p have been lost sheep;
La 1: 1 sits the city that once was full of p!
Da 9:24 "Seventy weeks are decreed for your p
Zec 13: 9 I will say, "They are my p";
Mt 1:21 he will save his p from their sins."
Jn 11:50 the p than to have the whole nation
18:14 to have one person die for the p.
Ro 9:25 not my p I will call 'my p,'
Heb 8:10 their God, and they shall be my p.
1Pe 2: 9 a holy nation, God's own p,

PEOPLES ➛ PEOPLE
Ge 17:16 kings of p shall come from her."
Dt 7: 7 for you were the fewest of all p.
Ps 117: 1 Extol him, all you p!
Rev 21: 3 they will be his p, and God himself

PERFECT ➛ PERFECTED, PERFECTER, PERFECTION
Lev 22:21 to be acceptable it must be p;
2Sa 22:31 This God—his way is p;
Ps 19: 7 The law of the LORD is p, reviving
Mt 5:48 Be p, therefore, as your heavenly Father is p.
Ro 12: 2 what is good and acceptable and p.
2Co 12: 9 for power is made p in weakness."
Heb 7:19 (for the law made nothing p);
1Jn 4:18 in love, but p love casts out fear;

PERFECTED → PERFECT
Heb 10:14 For by a single offering he has p
1Jn 4:12 God lives in us, and his love is p in

PERFECTER* → PERFECT
Heb 12: 2 Jesus the pioneer and p of our faith,

PERFECTION → PERFECT
Heb 6: 1 Therefore let us go on toward p,
1Jn 2: 5 the love of God has reached p.

PERISH → PERISHABLE
Lev 26:38 You shall p among the nations,
Jos 23:13 until you p from this good land that
Est 4:16 and if I p, I p."
Ps 1: 6 but the way of the wicked will p.
Lk 21:18 But not a hair of your head will p.
Jn 3:16 who believes in him may not p
2Pe 3: 9 with you, not wanting any to p,

PERISHABLE → PERISH
1Co 9:25 they do it to receive a p wreath,
15:42 What is sown is p, what is raised is
1Pe 1:23 not of p but of imperishable seed,

PERMANENT → PERMANENTLY
2Co 3:11 much more has the p come in glory!

PERMANENTLY* → PERMANENT
Heb 7:24 but he holds his priesthood p,

PERSECUTE → PERSECUTED, PERSECUTION
Mt 5:44 and pray for those who p you,
Ac 9: 4 "Saul, Saul, why do you p me?"
Ro 12:14 Bless those who p you; bless

PERSECUTED → PERSECUTE
Ps 119:86 I am p without cause; help me!
Jn 15:20 they p me, they will persecute you;
2Co 4: 9 p, but not forsaken; struck down,
2Ti 3:12 godly life in Christ Jesus will be p.

PERSECUTION → PERSECUTE
Mt 13:21 or p arises on account of the word,
Ro 8:35 Will hardship, or distress, or p, or
Heb 10:33 publicly exposed to abuse and p,

PERSEVERANCE* → PERSEVERE
Heb 12: 1 let us run with p the race that is set

PERSEVERE → PERSEVERANCE
Da 12:12 Happy are those who p
Ro 12:12 be patient in suffering, p in prayer.

PERSIA → PERSIANS
Ezr 1: 1 the spirit of King Cyrus of P
Da 8:20 these are the kings of Media and P.

PERSIANS → PERSIA
Da 6:15 a law of the Medes and P that

PESTILENCE
Dt 32:24 burning consumption, bitter p.
Ps 91: 6 or the p that stalks in darkness,

PETER → =CEPHAS, =SIMON
Apostle, brother of Andrew, also called Simon (Mt 10:2; Mk 3:16; Lk 6:14; Ac 1:13), and Cephas (Jn 1:42). Confession of Christ (Mt 16:13-20; Mk 8:27-30; Lk 9:18-27). At transfiguration (Mt 17:1-8; Mk 9:2-8; Lk 9:28-36; 2Pe 1:16-18). Caught fish with coin (Mt 17:24-27). Denial of Jesus predicted (Mt 26:31-35; Mk 14:27-31; Lk 22:31-34; Jn 13:31-38). Denied Jesus (Mt 26:69-75; Mk 14:66-72; Lk 22:54-62; Jn 18:15-27). Commissioned by Jesus to shepherd his flock (Jn 21:15-23).

Speech at Pentecost (Ac 2). Healed beggar (Ac 3:1-10). Speech at temple (Ac 3:11-26), before Sanhedrin (Ac 4:1-22). In Samaria (Ac 8:14-25). Sent by vision to Cornelius (Ac 10). Announced salvation of Gentiles in Jerusalem (Ac 11; 15). Freed from prison (Ac 12). Inconsistency at Antioch (Gal 2:11-21). At Jerusalem Council (Ac 15).

PHARAOH → PHARAOH'S
Ge 41:14 Then P sent for Joseph,
Ex 3:11 "Who am I that I should go to P,
14:17 I will gain glory for myself over P
Ro 9:17 For the scripture says to P,

PHARAOH'S → PHARAOH
Ex 7: 3 But I will harden P heart,
Heb 11:24 refused to be called a son of P

PHARISEE → PHARISEES
Lk 11:37 a P invited him to dine with him;
Jn 3: 1 a P named Nicodemus,
Ac 5:34 a P in the council named Gamaliel,
Php 3: 5 as to the law, a P;

PHARISEES → PHARISEE
Mt 5:20 that of the scribes and P,
16: 6 beware of the yeast of the P and
23:13 "But woe to you, scribes and P,

PHILEMON*
Phm 1: 1 To P our dear friend and co-worker,

PHILIP
1. Apostle (Mt 10:3; Mk 3:18; Lk 6:14; Jn 1:43-48; 14:8; Ac 1:13).
2. Deacon (Ac 6:1-7); evangelist in Samaria (Ac 8:4-25), to Ethiopian (Ac 8:26-40).

PHILISTINE → PHILISTINES
1Sa 17:37 save me from the hand of this P."
Pm 151: 6 I went out to meet the P,

PHILISTINES → PHILISTINE
Ge 26: 1 Gerar, to King Abimelech of the P.
1Sa 5: 1 the P captured the ark of God,
17: 1 the P gathered their armies for battle
2Sa 8: 1 David attacked the P and subdued
Am 1: 8 the remnant of the P shall perish,

PHILOSOPHERS* → PHILOSOPHY
Ac 17:18 Epicurean and Stoic p debated with

PHILOSOPHY → PHILOSOPHERS
Col 2: 8 no one takes you captive through p

PHINEHAS
1. Grandson of Aaron (Ex 6:25; Jos 22:30-32). Zeal for the LORD (Nu 25:7-13; Ps 106:30).
2. A wicked priest (1Sa 1:3; 2:12-17; 4:1-19).

PHOEBE*
Ro 16: 1 I commend to you our sister P,

PHYSICAL
1Co 15:44 It is sown a p body, it is raised a
1Ti 4: 8 while p training is of some value,

PHYSICIAN → PHYSICIANS
Mt 9:12 who are well have no need of a p,
Col 4:14 Luke, the beloved p, and Demas

PHYSICIANS → PHYSICIAN
Job 13: 4 all of you are worthless p.
Mk 5:26 had endured much under many p,

PIECES
Ge 15:17 torch passed between these p.
Mt 14:20 what was left over of the broken p,
15:37 they took up the broken p left over,
Lk 20:18 on that stone will be broken to p;

PIERCED
Zec 12:10 look on the one whom they have p,
Jn 19:37 look on the one whom they have p."
Rev 1: 7 even those who p him;

PIG
Dt 14: 8 the p, because it divides the hoof

PILATE
Governor of Judea. Questioned Jesus (Mt 27:1-26; Mk 15:15; Lk 22:66-23:25; Jn 18:28-19:16); sent him to Herod (Lk 23:6-12); consented to his crucifixion when crowds chose Barabbas (Mt 27:15-26; Mk 15:6-15; Lk 23:13-25; Jn 19:1-10).

PILLAR → PILLARS
Ge 19:26 back, and she became a p of salt.
Ex 13:21 and in a p of fire by night,

PILLARS → PILLAR
Jdg 16:29 Samson grasped the two middle p
1Ki 7:15 He cast two p of bronze.
Pr 9: 1 she has hewn her seven p.

PIONEER*
Heb 2:10 make the p of their salvation perfect
12: 2 Jesus the p and perfecter of our faith

PIT
Rev 20: 3 into the p, and locked and sealed it
Sir 21:10 but at its end is the p of Hades.

PITY
Dt 7:16 showing them no p;
Hos 1: 6 for I will no longer have p
2:23 And I will have p on Lo-ruhamah,

PLACE → PLACES
Ge 28:16 "Surely the LORD is in this p—
Ex 26:33 shall separate for you the holy p
Ps 24: 3 And who shall stand in his holy p?
32: 7 You are a hiding p for me;
Jn 14: 3 And if I go and prepare a p for you,

PLACES → PLACE
Lev 26:30 I will destroy your high p
Ps 78:58 him to anger with their high p;

PLAGUE → PLAGUES
Ex 32:35 the LORD sent a p on the people,
Nu 25: 8 So the p was stopped among the
Zec 14:12 the p with which the LORD will
Rev 11: 6 strike the earth with every kind of p,

PLAGUES → PLAGUE
Hos 13:14 O Death, where are your p?
Rev 15: 1 seven angels with seven p, which
22:18 God will add to that person the p

PLAIN
Ge 13:12 among the cities of the P and
Isa 40: 4 and the rough places a p.

PLANNED
Ex 32:14 his mind about the disaster that he p
Isa 46:11 I have p, and I will do it.

PLANT → PLANTED
Ge 1:29 I have given you every p yielding
Ecc 3: 2 time to p, and a time to pluck up

PLANTED → PLANT
Ge 2: 8 the LORD God p a garden in Eden,
Ps 1: 3 like trees p by streams of water,
1Co 3: 6 I p, Apollos watered, but God gave

PLEA
1Ki 8:28 your servant's prayer and his p,
La 3:56 heard my p, "Do not close your ear

PLEASE → PLEASED, PLEASES, PLEASING, PLEASURE
Ps 69:31 will p the LORD more than an ox
Ro 8: 8 who are in the flesh cannot p God.
15: 3 For Christ did not p himself;
1Co 10:33 as I try to p everyone in everything
1Th 4: 1 how you ought to live and to p God
Heb 11: 6 without faith it is impossible to p God,
Sir 2:16 Those who fear the Lord seek to p

PLEASED → PLEASE
Ps 40:13 Be p, O LORD, to deliver me;
Mic 6: 7 Will the LORD be p with thousands
Mt 3:17 Beloved, with whom I am well p."
Col 1:19 the fullness of God was p to dwell,
2Pe 1:17 Beloved, with whom I am well p."

PLEASES → PLEASE
Ps 115: 3 the heavens; he does whatever he p.
1Jn 3:22 commandments and do what p him.

PLEASING → PLEASE
Ps 104:34 May my meditation be p to him,
Eph 5:10 to find out what is p to the Lord.
Php 4:18 a sacrifice acceptable and p to God.

PLEASURE → PLEASE
Pr 21:17 Whoever loves p will suffer want;
Eze 18:32 I have no p in the death of anyone,
Eph 1: 5 according to the good p of his will,
2Ti 3: 4 lovers of p rather than lovers of God

PLENTIFUL → PLENTY
Lk 10: 2 He said to them, "The harvest is p,

PLENTY → PLENTIFUL
Php 4:12 and I know what it is to have p.

PLOT → PLOTTED
Ps 2: 1 and the peoples p in vain?
Na 1: 9 Why do you p against the LORD?

PLOTTED → PLOT
Est 9:24 p against the Jews to destroy them,

PLOWSHARES
Isa 2: 4 they shall beat their swords into p,
Joel 3:10 Beat your p into swords, and your

PLUNDER
Ex 3:22 and so you shall p the Egyptians."
Est 9:10 but they did not touch the p.
Eze 39:10 and p those who plundered them,

POISON
Ps 69:21 They gave me p for food,
Jas 3: 8 a restless evil, full of deadly p.

POLE → POLES
Nu 21: 8 poisonous serpent, and set it on a p;
Dt 16:21 not plant any tree as a sacred p

POLES → POLE
2Ki 17:10 for themselves pillars and sacred p

POLLUTED → POLLUTES
Ac 15:20 from things p by idols and from
Rev 21: 8 the cowardly, the faithless, the p,

POLLUTES* → POLLUTED
Nu 35:33 blood p the land, and no expiation

POOR → POVERTY
Ex 23: 6 not pervert the justice due to your p
1Sa 2: 8 He raises up the p from the dust;
Ps 113: 7 He raises the p from the dust,
Pr 19:22 and it is better to be p than a liar.
Mt 5: 3 "Blessed are the p in spirit,
Mk 10:21 own, and give the money to the p,
12:42 p widow came and put in two small
Jn 12: 8 You always have the p with you,
2Co 6:10 as p, yet making many rich;
8: 9 yet for your sakes he became p,
Jas 2: 5 Has not God chosen the p in the

PORTION → APPORTIONED
Dt 32: 9 the LORD's own p was his people,
Jos 18: 7 The Levites have no p among you,
Ps 142: 5 my p in the land of the living."
La 3:24 "The LORD is my p," says my soul,
Sir 17:17 Israel is the Lord's own p.

POSSESS → POSSESSED, POSSESSION, POSSESSIONS
Dt 28:21 the land that you are entering to p.
Ezr 9:11 that you are entering to p is a land
Isa 60:21 they shall p the land forever.

POSSESSED → POSSESS
Mt 8:16 many who were p with demons;
Heb 10:34 you yourselves p something better

POSSESSION → POSSESS
Ex 19: 5 treasured p out of all the peoples.
Jos 1:11 to go in to take p of the land that
Ps 2: 8 and the ends of the earth your p.

POSSESSIONS → POSSESS
Lk 12:15 not consist in the abundance of p."
1Co 13: 3 If I give away all my p,

POSSIBLE
Mt 19:26 but for God all things are p."
26:39 if it is p, let this cup pass from me;

POTIPHAR*
Egyptian who bought Joseph (Ge 37:36; 39:1-6), sent him to prison (Ge 39:7-30).

POTTER → POTTER'S
Isa 64: 8 we are the clay, and you are our p;
Ro 9:21 Has the p no right over the clay,
Sir 33:13 Like clay in the hand of the p,

POTTER'S → POTTER
Jer 18: 2 go down to the p house,
Mt 27: 7 to buy the p field as a place to bury

POUR → POURED
Dt 12:16 p it out on the ground like water.
Isa 44: 3 I will p my spirit upon your
Eze 39:29 I p out my spirit upon the house of
Joel 2:28 I will p out my spirit on all flesh;
Ac 2:17 I will p out my Spirit upon all flesh,
Rev 16: 1 p out on the earth the seven bowls

POURED → POUR
Mt 26:28 is p out for many for the forgiveness
Ac 2:33 he has p out this that you both see
Tit 3: 6 This Spirit he p out on us richly

POVERTY → POOR
Pr 30: 8 give me neither p nor riches;
Mk 12:44 out of her p has put in everything
2Co 8: 9 by his p you might become rich.
Sir 11:14 p and wealth, come from the Lord.

POWER → POWERFUL, POWERS
Ex 9:16 show you my p, and to make
15: 6 right hand, O LORD, glorious in p—
1Ch 29:11 O LORD, are the greatness, the p,
Ps 68:34 Ascribe p to God, whose majesty is
Pr 18:21 and life are in the p of the tongue,
Isa 40:29 He gives p to the faint,
Zec 4: 6 by might, nor by p, but by my spirit,
Mt 22:29 the scriptures nor the p of God.
Mk 13:26 coming in clouds' with great p and
Ro 1:20 creation of the world his eternal p
1Co 1:17 might not be emptied of its p.
15:24 and every authority and p.
Eph 1:19 the immeasurable greatness of his p
Php 3:10 Christ and the p of his resurrection
2Ti 3: 5 form of godliness but denying its p.
2Pe 1: 3 divine p has given us everything
Rev 19: 1 and glory and p to our God,
20: 6 these the second death has no p,
Jdt 9:14 the God of all p and might,
Sir 39:18 and none can limit his saving p.

POWERFUL → POWER
Mk 1: 7 one who is more p than I is coming
1Co 1:26 not many were p,
Heb 1: 3 he sustains all things by his p word.

POWERS → POWER
Ro 8:38 present, nor things to come, nor p,
Eph 6:12 against the cosmic p of this present

PRACTICE → PRACTICES
Mt 23: 3 for they do not p what they teach.
Sir 50:29 For if they put them into p,

PRACTICES → PRACTICE
Ex 23:24 or worship them, or follow their p,
Col 3: 9 stripped off the old self with its p

PRAISE → PRAISED, PRAISES
Ex 15: 2 this is my God, and I will p him,
Dt 10:21 He is your p; he is your God,
Ps 56: 4 whose word I p, in God I trust;
150: 6 that breathes p the LORD!
Pr 27: 2 Let another p you, and not your own
31:31 let her works p her in the city gates.
Mt 21:16 nursing babies you have prepared p
1Co 14:15 but I will sing p with the mind also.
Rev 19: 5 "P our God, all you his servants,
Tob 12: 6 Bless and sing p to his name.
Sir 24: 1 THE P OF WISDOM Wisdom praises

PRAISED → PRAISE
Ps 48: 1 is the LORD and greatly to be p
Lk 23:47 what had taken place, he p God and

PRAISES → PRAISE
Ps 47: 6 Sing p to God, sing p;

PRAY → PRAYED, PRAYER, PRAYERS
1Sa 12:23 against the LORD by ceasing to p
2Ch 7:14 humble themselves, p, seek my face
Ps 5: 2 King and my God, for to you I p.
122: 6 P for the peace of Jerusalem:
Jer 7:16 As for you, do not p for this people,
Mt 5:44 and p for those who persecute you,
6: 5 you p, do not be like the hypocrites;
Lk 11: 1 teach us to p, as John taught his
Ro 8:26 do not know how to p as we ought,
1Co 14:15 but I will p with the mind also;
1Th 5:17 p without ceasing,
Jas 5:16 and p for one another, so that you
Sir 37:15 But above all p to the Most High

PRAYED → PRAY
Mk 1:35 to a deserted place, and there he p.
14:35 threw himself on the ground and p

PRAYER → PRAY
Ps 6: 9 the LORD accepts my p.
Pr 15:29 but he hears the p of the righteous.
Isa 56: 7 house shall be called a house of p
Mt 21:13 house shall be called a house of p';
Mk 11:24 I tell you, whatever you ask for in p,
Ro 12:12 patient in suffering, persevere in p.
Jas 5:16 The p of the righteous is powerful

PRAYERS → PRAY
Mk 12:40 the sake of appearance say long p.
Heb 5: 7 Jesus offered up p and supplications
Rev 5: 8 which are the p of the saints.

PREACH → PREACHING
Tit 1: 9 able both to p with sound doctrine

PREACHING → PREACH
1Ti 5:17 those who labor in p and teaching;

PRECEPT → PRECEPTS
Isa 28:10 For it is p upon p, p upon p,

PRECEPTS → PRECEPT
Ps 19: 8 the p of the LORD are right,
119:15 I will meditate on your p,
Mt 15: 9 teaching human p as doctrines.'"

PRECIOUS
Ps 72:14 and p is their blood in his sight.
Pr 3:15 She is more p than jewels,
Isa 28:16 a tested stone, a p cornerstone,
1Pe 1:19 but with the p blood of Christ,
2: 6 a cornerstone chosen and p;
2Pe 1: 1 received a faith as p as ours

PREDESTINED
Ro 8:30 those whom he p he also called;

PREDICTION* → PREDICTIONS
Isa 44:26 and fulfills the p of his messengers;

PREDICTIONS* → PREDICT
Jude 1:17 the p of the apostles of our Lord

PREPARE → PREPARED
Ps 23: 5 You p a table before me in the
Mal 3: 1 sending my messenger to p the way
Mt 3: 3 'P the way of the Lord, make his
Jn 14: 2 I have told you that I go to p a place

PREPARED → PREPARE
Lk 1:17 make ready a people p for the Lord.
1Co 2: 9 God has p for those who love him"

PRESENCE → PRESENT
Ex 25:30 the bread of the P on the table
33:14 He said, "My p will go with you,
Ps 51:11 Do not cast me away from your p,
139: 7 Or where can I flee from your p?
Jn 17: 5 with the glory that I had in your p
Heb 9:24 now to appear in the p of God

PRESENT → PRESENCE
Ro 6:13 but p yourselves to God as
1Co 3:22 or death or the p or the future—
Eph 5:27 p the church to himself in splendor,
2Ti 2:15 p yourself to God as one approved

PRESS → PRESSED
Php 3:14 I p on toward the goal for the prize

PRESSED → PRESS
Lk 6:38 A good measure, p down, shaken
Php 1:23 I am hard p between the two:

PREVAIL → PREVAILED
1Sa 2: 9 for not by might does one p.

PREVAILED → PREVAIL
Ge 32:28 God and with humans, and have p."
Hos 12: 4 He strove with the angel and p,

PRICE
Mt 27: 9 the one on whom a p had been set,
1Co 6:20 For you were bought with a p;

PRIDE → PROUD
Ps 20: 7 our p is in the name of the LORD
Pr 16:18 P goes before destruction,
Mk 7:22 licentiousness, envy, slander, p,
1Jn 2:16 the desire of the eyes, the p in riches
Sir 10:13 For the beginning of p is sin,

PRIEST → PRIESTHOOD, PRIESTS
Ge 14:18 he was p of God Most High.
Ex 2:16 p of Midian had seven daughters.
Ne 8: 9 and Ezra the p and scribe,
Ps 110: 4 "You are a p forever according to
Mk 14:63 Then the high p tore his clothes and
Heb 3: 1 apostle and high p of our confession
7: 3 the Son of God, he remains a p
10:21 since we have a great p over the

PRIESTHOOD → PRIEST
Ex 29: 9 the p shall be theirs by a perpetual
Heb 7:24 but he holds his p permanently,
1Pe 2: 5 a holy p, to offer spiritual sacrifices

PRIESTS → PRIEST
Ex 28: 1 the Israelites, to serve me as p—
Dt 31: 9 this law, and gave it to the p,
Mic 3:11 its p teach for a price, its prophets
Mk 15: 3 the chief p accused him of many
Heb 7:27 Unlike the other high p, he has no
Rev 20: 6 they will be p of God and of Christ,

PRINCE ➛ PRINCES
Isa 9: 6 Everlasting Father, P of Peace.
Eze 37:25 David shall be their p forever.
Da 10:21 princes except Michael, your p.

PRINCES ➛ PRINCE
1Sa 2: 8 to make them sit with p and inherit
Da 8:25 even rise up against the Prince of p.

PRISCILLA*
Wife of Aquila, also called Prisca; co-worker with Paul (Ac 18; Ro 16:3; 1Co 16:19; 2Ti 4:19); instructor of Apollos (Ac 18:24-28).

PRISON ➛ PRISONER, PRISONERS
Ge 39:20 he remained there in p.
Mt 14:10 and had John beheaded in the p.
Ac 12: 5 While Peter was kept in p,
16:26 foundations of the p were shaken;

PRISONER ➛ PRISON
Mk 15: 6 at the festival he used to release a p
Eph 3: 1 that I Paul am a p for Christ Jesus

PRISONERS ➛ PRISON
Ps 146: 7 The LORD sets the p free;
Isa 61: 1 to the captives, and release to the p;

PRIZE
1Co 9:24 but only one receives the p?
Php 3:14 the p of the heavenly call of God in

PROCLAIM ➛ PROCLAIMED
Ex 33:19 p before you the name, 'The LORD';
Ps 97: 6 The heavens p his righteousness;
Mt 10:27 whispered, p from the housetops.
Lk 4:19 to p the year of the Lord's favor."
Ro 10: 8 the word of faith that we p);

PROCLAIMED ➛ PROCLAIM
Mk 13:10 the good news must first be p to all
Col 1:23 which has been p to every creature

PRODUCE ➛ PRODUCES
Nu 18:12 choice p that they give to the LORD,
Jos 5:11 they ate the p of the land,
Pr 3: 9 with the first fruits of all your p;

PRODUCES ➛ PRODUCE
2Co 7:10 For godly grief p a repentance that
Jas 1: 3 testing of your faith p endurance;

PROFANE
Lev 22:32 You shall not p my holy name,
1Mc 1:45 to p sabbaths and festivals,

PROFIT
Mt 16:26 For what will it p them if they gain
Sir 29:11 and it will p you more than gold.

PROMISE ➛ PROMISED, PROMISES
Ps 105:42 For he remembered his holy p,
Ac 2:39 the p is for you, for your children,
Eph 2:12 and strangers to the covenants of p,
1Ti 4: 8 holding p for both the present life
2Pe 3: 9 The Lord is not slow about his p,

PROMISED ➛ PROMISE
Dt 1:11 and bless you, as he has p you!
2Sa 7:28 p this good thing to your servant;
Lk 24:49 sending upon you what my Father p
Ac 13:23 to Israel a Savior, Jesus, as he p;
Eph 1:13 with the seal of the p Holy Spirit;
Heb 10:23 for he who has p is faithful.

PROMISES ➛ PROMISE
Jos 21:45 the good p that the LORD had made
Ps 12: 6 p of the LORD are p that are pure,
2Co 1:20 every one of God's p is a "Yes."
Heb 8: 6 has been enacted through better p.

PROOFS* ➛ PROVE
Isa 41:21 bring your p, says the King of Jacob
Ac 1: 3 to them by many convincing p,

PROPHECIES ➛ PROPHESY
1Co 13: 8 as for p, they will come to an end;

PROPHECY ➛ PROPHESY
Ac 21: 9 daughters who had the gift of p.
1Co 12:10 to another p, to another
2Pe 1:20 that no p of scripture is a matter
Rev 22:18 who hears the words of the p

PROPHESY ➛ PROPHECIES, PROPHECY, PROPHET, PROPHETS
Joel 2:28 sons and your daughters shall p,
Mt 7:22 Lord, did we not p in your name,
1Co 13: 9 only in part, and we p only in part;
Rev 11: 3 my two witnesses authority to p

PROPHET ➛ PROPHESY
Ex 7: 1 your brother Aaron shall be your p.
Dt 18:18 a p like you from among their own
Mal 4: 5 the p Elijah before the great and
Lk 4:24 no p is accepted in the prophet's
20: 6 are convinced that John was a p."
Rev 16:13 and from the mouth of the false p.
20:10 where the beast and the false p were
1Mc 4:46 until a p should come to tell what

PROPHETS ➛ PROPHESY
Nu 11:29 that all the LORD's people were p,
1Ki 18:40 said to them, "Seize the p of Baal;
Ps 105:15 anointed ones; do my p no harm."
Mt 5:17 come to abolish the law or the p;
22:40 hang all the law and the p."
Lk 24:44 p, and the psalms must be fulfilled."
1Co 12:28 the church first apostles, second p,
Eph 2:20 the foundation of the apostles and p,
4:11 some p, some evangelists,
Rev 11:10 these two p had been a torment to
18:20 you saints and apostles and p!
1Mc 9:27 that p ceased to appear among them.

PROSPER ➛ PROSPERING, PROSPERITY, PROSPEROUS
Ge 39: 3 LORD caused all that he did to p
Ps 1: 3 In all that they do, they p.
Isa 53:10 the will of the LORD shall p.

PROSPERING ➛ PROSPER
Dt 30: 9 will again take delight in p you,

PROSPERITY ➛ PROSPER
Dt 30:15 have set before you today life and p,
Ps 73: 3 I saw the p of the wicked.
Isa 48:18 your p would have been like a river,

PROSPEROUS ➛ PROSPER
Jos 1: 8 For then you shall make your way p

PROSTITUTE ➛ PROSTITUTES
Ex 34:15 they p themselves to their gods
Jos 2: 1 a p whose name was Rahab,
1Co 6:15 and make them members of a p?
Heb 11:31 By faith Rahab the p did not perish

PROSTITUTES ➛ PROSTITUTE
Mt 21:31 the p are going into the kingdom of
1Co 6: 9 idolaters, adulterers, male p,
Sir 9: 6 Do not give yourself to p,

PROTECT ➛ PROTECTS
Ps 91:14 I will p those who know my name.
Jn 17:11 p them in your name that you have

PROTECTS ➛ PROTECT
Ps 116: 6 The LORD p the simple;
Jdt 9:14 no other who p the people of Israel

PROUD ➛ PRIDE
Ps 94: 2 give to the p what they deserve!
Pr 21: 4 Haughty eyes and a p heart—
Jas 4: 6 God opposes the p, but gives grace
Sir 10: 9 How can dust and ashes be p?

PROVE ➛ PROOFS, PROVED
Heb 6:18 impossible that God would p false,

PROVED ➛ PROVE
Ro 3: 4 let God be p true,

PROVERBS
1Ki 4:32 He composed three thousand p,
Pr 1: 1 The p of Solomon son of David,
Ecc 12: 9 and studying and arranging many p.
Sir 39: 3 seeks out the hidden meanings of p

PROVIDE ➛ PROVIDES
Ge 22: 8 "God himself will p the lamb for
1Co 10:13 testing he will also p the way out

PROVIDES ➛ PROVIDE
Ps 111: 5 He p food for those who fear him;
1Ti 6:17 who richly p us with everything

PROVOKE ➛ PROVOKED
Dt 32:21 p them with a foolish nation.
Jer 25: 6 not p me to anger with the work of
Heb 10:24 how to p one another to love

PROVOKED ➛ PROVOKE
Ps 78:41 and p the Holy One of Israel.

PROWLS*
1Pe 5: 8 your adversary the devil p around,

PRUNES
Jn 15: 2 he p to make it bear more fruit.

PSALM ➛ PSALMS
Ps 47: 7 sing praises with a p.
Jdt 16: 1 Raise to him a new p;

PSALMS ➛ PSALM
Lk 24:44 and the p must be fulfilled."
Eph 5:19 you sing p and hymns and spiritual

PUBLIC
Mt 1:19 to expose her to p disgrace,
Col 2:15 and made a p example of them,
1Ti 4:13 to the p reading of scripture,

PUFFED ➛ PUFFS
Col 2:18 p up without cause by a human way
1Ti 3: 6 or he may be p up with conceit

PUFFS* ➛ PUFFED
1Co 8: 1 Knowledge p up, but love builds up.

PUNISH ➛ PUNISHING, PUNISHMENT
Ex 32:34 I will p them for their sin."
2Sa 7:14 I will p him with a rod such as
Jer 21:14 I will p you according to the fruit of
1Pe 2:14 by him to p those who do wrong

PUNISHING ➛ PUNISH
Dt 5: 9 p children for the iniquity of parents
Joel 2:13 in steadfast love, and relents from p.

PUNISHMENT ➛ PUNISH
Ge 4:13 "My p is greater than I can bear!
Isa 53: 5 was the p that made us whole,
Mt 25:46 these will go away into eternal p,
1Jn 4:18 for fear has to do with p,

PURE ➛ PURIFICATION, PURIFIED, PURIFY, PURITY
2Sa 22:27 with the p you show yourself p,
Ps 19: 9 the fear of the LORD is p, enduring
119: 9 can young people keep their way p?
Hab 1:13 Your eyes are too p to behold evil,
Mt 5: 8 "Blessed are the p in heart, for they
Php 4: 8 whatever is p, whatever is pleasing,
Tit 1:15 To the p all things are p,
1Jn 3: 3 purify themselves, just as he is p.

PURIFICATION ➛ PURE
Jn 2: 6 water jars for the Jewish rites of p,
Heb 1: 3 When he had made p for sins,

PURIFIED ➛ PURE
Da 12:10 Many shall be p, cleansed, and
1Pe 1:22 p your souls by your obedience to

PURIFY ➛ PURE
Tit 2:14 p for himself a people of his own
Heb 9:14 p our conscience from dead works

PURIM
Est 9:26 are called P, from the word Pur.

PURITY ➛ PURE
2Co 6: 6 by p, knowledge, patience, kindness
1Pe 3: 2 the p and reverence of your lives.

PURPLE
Ex 25: 4 p, and crimson yarns and fine linen,
Mk 15:17 And they clothed him in a p cloak;

PURPOSE
Ps 57: 2 to God who fulfills his p for me.
Isa 46:10 saying, "My p shall stand,
Ro 8:28 who are called according to his p.
Eph 3:11 was in accordance with the eternal p
2Ti 1: 9 works but according to his own p

PURSUE ➛ PURSUED, PURSUES
Ps 34:14 and do good; seek peace, and p it.
Ro 14:19 Let us then p what makes for peace
1Ti 6:11 p righteousness, godliness, faith,
Sir 27: 8 If you p justice, you will attain it

PURSUED ➛ PURSUE
Ex 14:23 Egyptians p, and went into the sea
Ps 18:37 I p my enemies and overtook them;

PURSUES ➛ PURSUE
Pr 21:21 Whoever p righteousness
Sir 31: 5 p money will be led astray by it.

PUT
Isa 42: 1 I have p my spirit upon him;
Eze 36:27 I will p my spirit within you,
Mt 12:18 I will p my Spirit upon him,
Eph 6:11 P on the whole armor of God,

Q

QUAILS
Ex 16:13 In the evening q came up
Nu 11:31 and it brought q from the sea and

QUARRELED ➛ QUARRELSOME
Ex 17: 7 the Israelites q and tested the LORD,
Nu 20: 3 The people q with Moses and said,

QUARRELSOME ➛ QUARRELED
1Ti 3: 3 not q, and not a lover of money.
2Ti 2:24 the Lord's servant must not be q

QUEEN
1Ki 10: 1 the q of Sheba heard of the fame of
Est 2:17 and made her q instead of Vashti.
Mt 12:42 The q of the South will rise up at
Rev 18: 7 in her heart she says, 'I rule as a q;

QUESTIONS
2Ch 9: 1 to Jerusalem to test him with hard q,
Mt 22:46 anyone dare to ask him any more q.

QUICK ➛ QUICKLY
Jas 1:19 be q to listen, slow to speak,
Sir 5:11 Be q to hear, but deliberate

QUICKLY ➛ QUICK
Jn 13:27 "Do q what you are going to do."
Ro 9:28 execute his sentence on the earth q
Gal 1: 6 so q deserting the one who called

QUIET
1Ti 2: 2 q and peaceable life in all godliness
1Pe 3: 4 beauty of a gentle and q spirit,

QUIVER
Ps 127: 5 Happy is the man who has his q full of
Isa 49: 2 in his q he hid me away.

R

RABBI
Mt 23: 8 But you are not to be called r,
Jn 1:38 "R" (which translated means Teacher),

RACE
Ecc 9:11 the sun the r is not to the swift,
1Co 9:24 that in a r the runners all compete,
Heb 12: 1 let us run with perseverance the r
1Pe 2: 9 But you are a chosen r, a royal

RACHEL
Daughter of Laban (Ge 29:16); wife of Jacob (Ge 29:28); bore two sons (Ge 30:22-24; 35:16-24; 46:19). Stole Laban's gods (Ge 31:19, 32-35). Death (Ge 35:19-20).

RAHAB
Prostitute who hid Israelite spies (Jos 2; 6:22-25; Heb 11:31; Jas 2:25). Mother of Boaz (Mt 1:5).

RAIN ➛ RAINBOW, RAINED, RAINS
Ge 7: 4 For in seven days I will send r on
1Ki 17: 1 neither dew nor r these years,
Isa 45: 8 let the skies r down righteousness;
Mt 5:45 sends r on the righteous and on the
Rev 11: 6 so that no r may fall during the days

RAINBOW ➛ BOW
Rev 4: 3 the throne is a r that looks like an

RAINED ➛ RAIN
Ge 19:24 r on Sodom and Gomorrah sulfur
Ex 9:23 LORD r hail on the land of Egypt;

RAINS ➛ RAIN
Lev 26: 4 I will give you your r in their season
Jas 5: 7 receives the early and the late r.

RAISE ➛ RISE
Dt 18:15 God will r up for you a prophet
Jn 2:19 and in three days I will r it up."
2Co 4:14 who raised the Lord Jesus will r us

RAISED ➛ RISE
Mt 17:23 and on the third day he will be r."
Ac 2:24 God r him up, having freed him
Ro 4:25 and was r for our justification.
1Co 15: 4 r on the third day in accordance

RAM ➛ RAMS
Ge 22:13 and took the r and offered it up as
Ex 29:22 (for it is a r of ordination),
Da 8: 3 saw a r standing beside the river.

RAMS ➛ RAM
1Sa 15:22 and to heed than the fat of r.

RANSOM ➛ RANSOMED
Ps 49: 8 For the r of life is costly, and can
Mt 20:28 and to give his life a r for many."
1Ti 2: 6 who gave himself a r for all

RANSOMED ➛ RANSOM
Isa 35:10 And the r of the LORD shall return,
Rev 5: 9 by your blood you r for God saints

RAVENS
1Ki 17: 6 r brought him bread and meat in
Lk 12:24 Consider the r: they neither sow

READ ➛ READING
Ex 24: 7 and r it in the hearing of the people;
Jos 8:34 he r all the words of the law,
Ne 8: 8 they r from the book, from the law
Lk 4:16 as was his custom. He stood up to r,
2Co 3:15 this very day whenever Moses is r,

READING ➛ READ
Ac 8:30 you understand what you are r?"

READY
Lk 1:17 r a people prepared for the Lord."
Rev 19: 7 and his bride has made herself r;

REAP
Gal 6: 7 for you r whatever you sow.
Rev 14:15 for the hour to r has come,

REBEKAH
Sister of Laban, secured as bride for Isaac (Ge 24). Mother of Esau and Jacob (Ge 25:19-26). Taken by Abimelech as sister of Isaac; returned (Ge 26:1-11). Encouraged Jacob to trick Isaac out of blessing (Ge 27:1-17).

REBEL ➛ REBELLED, REBELLION
Ex 23:21 do not r against him, for he will
1Sa 12:14 not r against the commandment

REBELLED ➛ REBEL
Nu 20:24 because you r against my command
Ne 9:26 they were disobedient and r

REBELLION ➛ REBEL
1Sa 15:23 For r is no less a sin than divination,
2Th 2: 3 the r comes first and the lawless one

REBUILD ➛ BUILD
Ezr 1: 3 and r the house of the LORD,
Ne 2:17 let us r the wall of Jerusalem,
Da 9:25 went out to restore and r Jerusalem
Ac 15:16 and I will r the dwelling of David,

REBUKE
Ps 6: 1 O LORD, do not r me in your anger,
Pr 27: 5 Better is open r than hidden love.
Zec 3: 2 said to Satan, "The LORD r you,
Mk 8:32 Peter took him aside and began to r
2Ti 4: 2 convince, r, and encourage,

RECEIVE ➛ RECEIVED
Jn 16:24 Ask and you will r, so that your joy
Ac 2:38 you will r the gift of the Holy Spirit.
20:35 'It is more blessed to give than to r.'
Rev 4:11 to r glory and honor and power,

RECEIVED ➛ RECEIVE
Mt 6: 2 I tell you, they have r their reward.
Jn 1:12 But to all who r him, who believed
1Co 11:23 I r from the Lord what I also handed

RECKONED ➛ RECKONING
Ge 15: 6 LORD r it to him as righteousness.
Ro 4: 3 it was r to him as righteousness."

RECKONING ➛ RECKONED
Ge 9: 5 I will require a r for human life.
Sir 2:14 you do when the Lord's r comes?

RECONCILE ➛ RECONCILED, RECONCILIATION
Ac 7:26 were quarreling and tried to r them,
Col 1:20 God was pleased to r to himself all

RECONCILED ➛ RECONCILE
Mt 5:24 first be r to your brother or sister,
1Co 7:11 let her remain unmarried or else be r

RECONCILIATION ➛ RECONCILE
Ro 5:11 whom we have now received r.
2Co 5:18 and has given us the ministry of r;

RED
Ex 15: 4 officers were sunk in the R Sea.
Mt 16: 3 for the sky is r and threatening.'
Rev 12: 3 a great r dragon, with seven heads

REDEEM ➛ REDEEMED, REDEEMER, REDEMPTION
Ex 6: 6 I will r you with an outstretched
2Sa 7:23 whose God went to r it as a people,
Gal 4: 5 to r those who were under the law,

REDEEMED ➛ REDEEM
Dt 15:15 and the LORD your God r you;
Ps 107: 2 Let the r of the LORD say so,

REDEEMER ➛ REDEEM
Job 19:25 For I know that my R lives,
Ps 19:14 O LORD, my rock and my r.
Isa 48:17 Thus says the LORD, your R,

REDEMPTION ➛ REDEEM
Lk 21:28 because your r is drawing near."
Eph 1: 7 In him we have r through his blood,
Heb 9:12 own blood, thus obtaining eternal r.

REFINE ➛ REFINED
Jer 9: 7 I will now r and test them,
Zec 13: 9 r them as one refines silver,

REFINED ➛ REFINE
Da 12:10 shall be purified, cleansed, and r,

REFLECTED ➛ REFLECTION
2Co 3:18 though r in a mirror,

REFLECTION ➛ REFLECTED
1Co 11: 7 since he is the image and r of God;
Heb 1: 3 He is the r of God's glory

REFUGE
Nu 35:11 select cities to be cities of r for you,
Ps 2:12 Happy are all who take r in him.
Pr 30: 5 a shield to those who take r in him.
Jer 16:19 my r in the day of trouble,

REFUSE
Ex 8: 2 If you r to let them go,
Eze 3:27 and let those who r to hear, r;
Heb 12:25 do not r the one who is speaking;

REGARD
Isa 8:13 of hosts, him you shall r as holy;
Php 2: 6 did not r equality with God as
3: 7 these I have come to r as loss
Heb 12: 5 not r lightly the discipline of the

REGULATIONS
Col 2:20 Why do you submit to r,
Heb 9:10 r for the body imposed until the

REHOBOAM
Son of Solomon (1Ki 11:43; 1Ch 3:10). Harsh treatment of subjects caused divided kingdom (1Ki 12:1-24; 14:21-31; 2Ch 10-12).

REIGN ➛ REIGNS
Ex 15:18 The LORD will r forever and ever."
Ps 146:10 The LORD will r forever,
1Co 15:25 r until he has put all his enemies
2Ti 2:12 we will also r with him;
Rev 11:15 and he will r forever and ever."
22: 5 and they will r forever and ever.

REIGNS ➛ REIGN
Isa 52: 7 who says to Zion, "Your God r."
Rev 19: 6 the Lord our God the Almighty r.

REJECT ➛ REJECTED
Ex 20: 5 generation of those who r me,
Isa 30:12 Because you r this word,

REJECTED ➛ REJECT
1Sa 8: 7 but they have r me from being king
Ps 60: 1 O God, you have r us, broken our
118:22 The stone that the builders r
Isa 53: 3 He was despised and r by others;
Mt 21:42 'The stone that the builders r
1Pe 2: 4 though r by mortals yet chosen and

REJOICE ➛ REJOICING
Ps 5:11 But let all who take refuge in you r;
118:24 let us r and be glad in it.
Isa 62: 5 so shall your God r over you.

Zep 3:17 he will r over you with gladness,
Lk 6:23 R in that day and leap for joy,
Php 4: 4 R in the Lord always; again I will say, R.

REJOICING ➛ REJOICE
2Sa 6:12 to the city of David with r;
Ne 8:17 And there was very great r.
2Co 6:10 as sorrowful, yet always r;

RELEASE
Isa 61: 1 liberty to the captives, and r to
Mt 27:15 the governor was accustomed to r

RELENT ➛ RELENTED
Eze 24:14 I will not spare, I will not r.
Joel 2:14 whether he will not turn and r,
Jnh 3: 9 God may r and change his mind;

RELENTED ➛ RELENT
1Ch 21:15 LORD took note and r concerning
Jer 4:28 I have not r nor will I turn back.

RELIGION
Jas 1:27 R that is pure and undefiled before

RELY
2Ch 14:11 O LORD our God, for we r on you,
Pr 3: 5 and do not r on your own insight.
Gal 3:10 all who r on the works of the law
Sir 5: 1 Do not r on your wealth,

REMAIN ➛ REMAINS
1Co 7:20 Let each of you r in the condition
Heb 1:11 they will perish, but you r;

REMAINS ➛ REMAIN
Jos 13: 2 This is the land that still r:
Heb 7: 3 Son of God, he r a priest forever.
10:26 there no longer r a sacrifice for sins,

REMEMBER ➛ REMEMBERED, REMEMBRANCE
Ge 9:15 I will r my covenant that is between
Ex 20: 8 R the sabbath day, and keep it holy.
Dt 8:18 But r the LORD your God,
Job 10: 9 R that you fashioned me like clay;
Ecc 12: 1 R your creator in the days of your
Jer 31:34 and r their sin no more.
2Ti 2: 8 R Jesus Christ, raised from the dead
Heb 8:12 and I will r their sins no more."
Sir 23:18 The Most High will not r sins."

REMEMBERED ➛ REMEMBER
Ex 2:24 God r his covenant with Abraham,
Ps 78:35 They r that God was their rock,
106:45 For their sake he r his covenant,
Rev 16:19 God r great Babylon and gave her

REMEMBRANCE ➛ REMEMBER
Lk 22:19 Do this in r of me."

REMNANT
Ge 45: 7 before you to preserve for you a r
Isa 10:21 A r will return, the r of Jacob,
Jer 50:20 will pardon the r that I have spared.
Ro 9:27 only a r of them will be saved;

REMOVE
Eze 36:26 r from your body the heart of stone
Lk 22:42 if you are willing, r this cup from

RENEW ➛ RENEWAL, RENEWED, RENEWING
Isa 40:31 for the LORD shall r their strength,
La 5:21 r our days as of old—

RENEWAL ➛ RENEW
Mt 19:28 I tell you, at the r of all things,
Col 3:11 In that r there is no longer Greek

RENEWED ➛ RENEW
2Co 4:16 inner nature is being r day by day.
Eph 4:23 to be r in the spirit of your minds,

RENEWING* ➛ RENEW
Ro 12: 2 transformed by the r of your minds,

REPAY ➛ PAY
Ps 28: 4 R them according to their work,
Isa 59:18 to their deeds, so will he r;
Ro 12:17 Do not r anyone evil for evil,
Rev 18: 6 and r her double for her deeds;

REPENT ➛ REPENTANCE
1Ki 8:47 r, and plead with you in the land
Job 42: 6 and r in dust and ashes."
Mt 3: 2 "R, for the kingdom of heaven has
Ac 2:38 "R, and be baptized every one of
Rev 16: 9 they did not r and give him glory.
Sir 18:21 and when you have sinned, r.

REPENTANCE ➛ REPENT
Mk 1: 4 a baptism of r for the forgiveness
Lk 3: 8 Bear fruits worthy of r.
Ro 2: 4 kindness is meant to lead you to r?
2Co 7:10 r that leads to salvation and brings
2Pe 3: 9 any to perish, but all to come to r.

REPROVE
Pr 19:25 r the intelligent, and they will gain
Tit 2:15 exhort and r with all authority.
Rev 3:19 r and discipline those whom I love.

REQUIRE
Dt 10:12 does the LORD your God r of you?
Mic 6: 8 the LORD r of you but to do justice,

RESCUE ➛ RESCUED, RESCUES
Ps 22: 8 him r the one in whom he delights!"
Mt 6:13 but r us from the evil one.
2Pe 2: 9 the Lord knows how to r the godly

RESCUED ➛ RESCUE
Col 1:13 has r us from the power of darkness
Sir 51:12 and r me in time of trouble.

RESCUES ➛ RESCUE
Ps 37:40 The LORD helps them and r them;
Da 6:27 and r, he works signs and wonders
1Th 1:10 Jesus, who r us from the wrath that

RESIST
Mt 5:39 I say to you, Do not r an evildoer.
Ro 9:19 For who can r his will?"
Jas 4: 7 R the devil, and he will flee from

RESPECT
Mal 1: 6 if I am a master, where is the r due
Ro 13: 7 r to whom r is due,

REST ➛ RESTED, RESTS
Ex 31:15 seventh day is a sabbath of solemn r
2Sa 7:11 give you r from all your enemies.
Ps 95:11 swore, "They shall not enter my r."
Mt 11:28 and I will give you r.
Heb 4:10 those who enter God's r also cease

RESTED ➛ REST
Ge 2: 2 he r on the seventh day from all the
Ex 20:11 all that is in them, but r the seventh

RESTORE ➛ RESTORES
Dt 30: 3 LORD your God will r your fortunes
Ps 51:12 R to me the joy of your salvation,
Da 9:25 the word went out to r and rebuild
Mt 17:11 "Elijah is indeed coming and will r

RESTORES ➛ RESTORE
Ps 23: 3 he r my soul. He leads me in right

RESTS ➛ REST
Ps 16: 9 my body also r secure.
Pr 19:23 one r secure and suffers no harm.

RESURRECTION
Mt 22:30 For in the r they neither marry nor
Mk 12:18 Sadducees, who say there is no r,
Jn 11:25 said to her, "I am the r and the life.
1Co 15:12 you say there is no r of the dead?
Php 3:10 know Christ and the power of his r
Rev 20: 5 This is the first r.
2Es 2:23 will give you the first place in my r.

RETURN
Ge 3:19 you are dust, and to dust you shall r.
Dt 30: 2 and r to the LORD your God,
Ps 116:12 What shall I r to the LORD
Hos 14: 1 R, O Israel, to the LORD your God,
Mal 3: 7 R to me, and I will r to you,

REUBEN
Firstborn of Jacob by Leah (Ge 29:32; 46:8; 1Ch 2:1). Attempted to rescue Joseph (Ge 37:21-30). Lost birthright for sleeping with Bilhah (Ge 35:22; 49:4). Tribe of blessed (Ge 49:3-4; Dt 33:6), numbered (Nu 1:21; 26:7), allotted land east of Jordan (Nu 32; 34:14; Jos 13:15), west (Eze 48:6), failed to help Deborah (Jdg 5:15-16), supported David (1Ch 12:37), 12,000 from (Rev 7:5).

REVEAL ➛ REVEALED, REVELATION, REVELATIONS
Mt 11:27 to whom the Son chooses to r him.

REVEALED ➛ REVEAL
Isa 40: 5 the glory of the LORD shall be r,
Mt 16:17 flesh and blood has not r this to you
Lk 17:30 on the day that the Son of Man is r.
Ro 1:17 in it the righteousness of God is r
2Th 1: 7 the Lord Jesus is r from heaven
1Jn 3: 2 we do know is this: when he is r,

REVELATION ➛ REVEAL
1Co 14: 6 some r or knowledge or prophecy
Eph 3: 3 was made known to me by r,
Rev 1: 1 The r of Jesus Christ, which God

REVELATIONS ➛ REVEAL
2Co 12: 1 but I will go on to visions and r of

REVERE ➛ REVERENCE
Jos 24:14 "Now therefore r the LORD,
Mal 4: 2 But for you who r my name the sun
Tob 4: 5 "R the Lord all your days,

REVERENCE ➛ REVERE
Eph 5:21 subject to one another out of r for
1Pe 3: 2 see the purity and r of your lives.

REVILE ➛ REVILED
Ex 22:28 You shall not r God, or curse
Mt 5:11 people r you and persecute you

REVILED ➛ REVILE
1Co 4:12 When r, we bless;
1Pe 4:14 If you are r for the name of Christ,

REWARD ➛ REWARDED
Ps 19:11 in keeping them there is great r.
Isa 40:10 r is with him, and his recompense
Mt 6: 5 I tell you, they have received their r.
Lk 6:23 for surely your r is great in heaven;
Heb 11:26 for he was looking ahead to the r.
Rev 22:12 I am coming soon; my r is with me,

REWARDED ➛ REWARD
2Sa 22:21 The LORD r me according to my

RIB
Ge 2:22 r that the LORD God had taken from

RICH ➛ RICHES
Pr 23: 4 Do not wear yourself out to get r;
Mt 19:23 hard for a r person to enter the
Lk 12:21 but are not r toward God."
2Co 8: 9 by his poverty you might become r.
Eph 2: 4 But God, who is r in mercy,
1Ti 6:18 to do good, to be r in good works,
Jas 1:10 and the r in being brought low,

RICHES ➛ RICH
Ps 62:10 if r increase, do not set your heart
Pr 30: 8 give me neither poverty nor r;
Lk 8:14 they are choked by the cares and r
Ro 11:33 O the depth of the r and wisdom
1Jn 2:16 the desire of the eyes, the pride in r
Sir 13:24 R are good if they are free from sin;

RID
Col 3: 8 But now you must get r of all such
1Pe 2: 1 R yourselves, therefore, of all

RIDER ➛ RIDES, RIDING
Rev 19:11 Its r is called Faithful and True,

RIDES ➛ RIDER
Dt 33:26 r through the heavens to your help,
Ps 68: 4 a song to him who r upon the clouds

RIDING ➛ RIDER
Zec 9: 9 humble and r on a donkey,

RIGHT ➛ BIRTHRIGHT
Ex 15: 6 Your r hand, O LORD, glorious in
Dt 6:18 Do what is r and good in the sight
Job 42: 7 have not spoken of me what is r,
Ps 110: 1 says to my lord, "Sit at my r hand
Pr 14:12 a way that seems r to a person,
Mt 25:33 sheep at his r hand and the goats at
Ac 2:34 said to my Lord, "Sit at my r hand,
Heb 1:13 "Sit at my r hand until I make your
1Pe 3:14 if you do suffer for doing what is r,

RIGHTEOUS ➛ RIGHTEOUSNESS
Ge 18:23 "Will you indeed sweep away the r
Job 4:17 'Can mortals be r before God?

Ps 11: 7 For the LORD is r; he loves r deeds;
Pr 10: 6 Blessings are on the head of the r,
11:23 desire of the r ends only in good;
15:29 but he hears the prayer of the r.
Jer 23: 5 I will raise up for David a r Branch,
Eze 3:20 if the r turn from their righteousness
Hab 2: 4 but the r live by their faith.
Mt 5:45 rain on the r and on the unrighteous.
Mk 2:17 come to call not the r but sinners."
Ro 1:17 one who is r will live by faith."
5:19 the many will be made r.
Heb 10:38 but my r one will live by faith.
1Jn 2: 1 with the Father, Jesus Christ the r;
Rev 19: 8 the fine linen is the r deeds of the
Wis 5:15 r live forever, and their reward
Sir 35:22 and does justice for the r,

RIGHTEOUSNESS ➛ RIGHTEOUS
Ge 15: 6 the LORD reckoned it to him as r.
Ps 9: 8 He judges the world with r;
Pr 12:28 In the path of r there is life,
Ecc 7:15 people who perish in their r,
Isa 11: 5 R shall be the belt around his waist,
Jer 23: 6 be called: "The LORD is our r."
Da 9:24 to bring in everlasting r,
12: 3 and those who lead many to r,
Hos 10:12 Sow for yourselves r; reap steadfast
Mt 5: 6 those who hunger and thirst for r,
Jn 16: 8 about sin and r and judgment:
Ro 5:18 act of r leads to justification
10: 4 be r for everyone who believes.
Gal 3: 6 and it was reckoned to him as r,"
Eph 6:14 and put on the breastplate of r.
1Pe 2:24 free from sins, we might live for r;
2Pe 3:13 heavens and a new earth, where r is
Rev 19:11 and in r he judges and makes war.

RIPE
Joel 3:13 Put in the sickle, for the harvest is r.
Jn 4:35 how the fields are r for harvesting.
Rev 14:15 the harvest of the earth is fully r."

RISE ➛ ARISE, RAISE, RAISED, ROSE
Nu 24:17 and a scepter shall r out of Israel;
Ps 94: 2 R up, O judge of the earth;
Da 12:13 shall r for your reward at the end of
Mal 4: 2 the sun of righteousness shall r,
Mt 27:63 'After three days I will r again.'
Eph 5:14 R from the dead, and Christ will
1Th 4:16 and the dead in Christ will r first.

RIVER ➛ RIVERS
Ps 46: 4 a r whose streams make glad the
Isa 48:18 prosperity would have been like a r,
Eze 47:12 On the banks, on both sides of the r,
Mt 3: 6 baptized by him in the r Jordan,
Rev 22: 1 showed me the r of the water of life,

RIVERS ➛ RIVER
Ps 137: 1 By the r of Babylon—there we sat
Rev 8:10 it fell on a third of the r and on the

ROAD ➛ CROSSROADS
Mt 7:13 and the r is easy that leads to

ROAR ➛ ROARING, ROARS
Ps 46: 3 though its waters r and foam,
Jer 25:30 The LORD will r from on high,

ROARING ➛ ROAR
1Pe 5: 8 a r lion your adversary the devil

ROARS ➛ ROAR
Hos 11:10 the LORD, who r like a lion;
Joel 3:16 The LORD r from Zion,

ROB ➛ ROBBER, ROBBERS
Mal 3: 8 anyone r God? Yet you are robbing

ROBBER ➛ ROB
1Co 5:11 an idolater, reviler, drunkard, or r.

ROBBERS ➛ ROB
Jer 7:11 become a den of r in your sight?
Mt 21:13 but you are making it a den of r."

ROBE ➛ ROBED, ROBES
Ge 37: 3 had made him a long r with sleeves.
Ex 28: 4 a breastpiece, an ephod, a r,
Jn 19: 5 crown of thorns and the purple r.
Rev 6:11 They were each given a white r and
19:13 He is clothed in a r dipped in blood,

ROBED ➛ ROBE
Ps 93: 1 LORD is king, he is r in majesty;
Rev 15: 6 r in pure bright linen,

ROBES ➛ ROBE
Mk 12:38 who like to walk around in long r,
Rev 22:14 Blessed are those who wash their r,

ROCK
Ex 17: 6 Strike the r, and water will come
Nu 20: 8 you shall bring water out of the r
1Sa 2: 2 there is no R like our God.
Ps 19:14 O LORD, my r and my redeemer.
Isa 44: 8 There is no other r; I know not one.
Mt 16:18 and on this r I will build my church,
Mk 15:46 that had been hewn out of the r.
1Pe 2: 8 and a r that makes them fall."

ROD
2Sa 7:14 I will punish him with a r such as
Ps 2: 9 shall break them with a r of iron,
23: 4 your r and your staff—they comfort
Pr 13:24 who spare the r hate their children,
Heb 9: 4 and Aaron's r that budded,
Rev 2:27 to rule them with an iron r,

ROLL
Am 5:24 But let justice r down like waters,
Mk 16: 3 "Who will r away the stone for us

ROOF
Jos 2: 6 to the r and hidden them
2Sa 11: 2 he saw from the r a woman bathing;
Mk 2: 4 they removed the r above him;

ROOM
Mk 14:15 He will show you a large r upstairs,
Ro 12:19 but leave r for the wrath of God;
Eph 4:27 and do not make r for the devil.

ROOT ➛ ROOTED
Isa 11:10 On that day the r of Jesse
53: 2 and like a r out of dry ground;
Ro 15:12 "The r of Jesse shall come,
1Ti 6:10 For the love of money is a r of all
Rev 5: 5 the tribe of Judah, the R of David,

ROOTED ➛ ROOT
Eph 3:17 are being r and grounded in love.

ROSE ➛ RISE
SS 2: 1 I am a r of Sharon, a lily
1Th 4:14 believe that Jesus died and r again,

ROUGH
Isa 40: 4 and the r places a plain.
Lk 3: 5 and the r ways made smooth;

ROYAL
Jas 2: 8 if you really fulfill the r law
1Pe 2: 9 are a chosen race, a r priesthood,

RUBBISH
1Co 4:13 have become like the r of the world,
Php 3: 8 and I regard them as r,

RUIN ➛ RUINS
Eze 21:27 A r, a r, a r—I will make it!
Zep 1:15 a day of r and devastation,

RUINS ➛ RUIN
Ezr 9: 9 the house of our God, to repair its r,
Ne 2:17 Jerusalem lies in r with its gates
Ac 15:16 from its r I will rebuild it,
1Co 15:33 "Bad company r good morals."
1Mc 3:43 "Let us restore the r of our people,

RULE ➛ RULER, RULER'S, RULERS, RULES
Ge 3:16 husband, and he shall r over you."
Ps 110: 2 R in the midst of your foes.
Eph 1:21 far above all r and authority and
Col 3:15 the peace of Christ r in your hearts,
Rev 19:15 he will r them with a rod of iron;

RULER ➛ RULE
Ex 2:14 made you a r and judge over us?
Mt 2: 6 a r who is to shepherd my people
1Co 15:24 after he has destroyed every r
Rev 1: 5 and the r of the kings of the earth.

RULER'S ➛ RULE
Ge 49:10 the r staff from between his feet,

RULERS ➛ RULE
Ps 2: 2 and the r take counsel together,
Isa 40:23 makes the r of the earth as nothing.
Eph 6:12 against the r, against the authorities,

RULES ➛ RULE
Ps 66: 7 who r by his might forever,
Isa 40:10 and his arm r for him;
2Ti 2: 5 competing according to the r.

RUMORS
Mt 24: 6 you will hear of wars and r of wars;

RUN ➛ FORERUNNER, RUNNERS
Isa 40:31 they shall r and not be weary,
Gal 2: 2 or had not r, in vain.
Heb 12: 1 let us r with perseverance the race

RUNNERS* ➛ RUN
1Co 9:24 that in a race the r all compete,

RUST
Mt 6:19 where moth and r consume
LtJ 6:12 cannot save themselves from r

RUTH
Moabitess; widow who went to Bethlehem with mother-in-law Naomi (Ru 1). Gleaned in field of Boaz; shown favor (Ru 2). Proposed marriage to Boaz (Ru 3). Married (Ru 4:1-12); bore Obed, ancestor of David (Ru 4:13-22), Jesus (Mt 1:5).

S

SABBATH
Ex 20: 8 Remember the s day, and keep it holy.
2Ch 36:21 the days that it lay desolate it kept s,
Mt 12: 1 through the grainfields on the s;
Mk 2:28 Son of Man is lord even of the s."
1Mc 1:43 to idols and profaned the s.

SACKCLOTH ➛ CLOTH
Da 9: 3 supplication with fasting and s and
Mt 11:21 would have repented long ago in s

SACRED
Ex 28: 2 You shall make s vestments for
34:13 and cut down their s poles

SACRIFICE ➛ SACRIFICED, SACRIFICES
Ex 12:27 'It is the passover s to the LORD,
Lev 3: 1 If the offering is a s of well-being,
1Sa 15:22 Surely, to obey is better than s,
Ps 40: 6 S and offering you do not desire,
Pr 15: 8 s of the wicked is an abomination
Da 9:27 he shall make s and offering cease;
Hos 6: 6 For I desire steadfast love and not s,
Mt 9:13 this means, 'I desire mercy, not s.'
Ro 3:25 put forward as a s of atonement
Php 4:18 a s acceptable and pleasing to God.
Heb 13:15 let us continually offer a s of praise
1Jn 2: 2 and he is the atoning s for our sins,

SACRIFICED ➛ SACRIFICE
1Co 5: 7 our paschal lamb, Christ, has been s.
8: 1 Now concerning food s to idols:

SACRIFICES ➛ SACRIFICE
Mk 12:33 all whole burnt offerings and s."
Heb 7:27 has no need to offer s day after day,

SADDUCEES
Mt 16: 6 the yeast of the Pharisees and S."
Mk 12:18 S, who say there is no resurrection,

SAFE ➛ SAFETY
Ps 37:28 righteous shall be kept s forever,
Pr 18:10 the righteous run into it and are s.

SAFETY ➛ SAFE
Dt 12:10 around so that you live in s,
Eze 34:28 they shall live in s,

SAINTS
Ps 31:23 Love the LORD, all you his s.
Ro 8:27 the Spirit intercedes for the s
1Co 6: 2 that the s will judge the world?
Eph 4:12 equip the s for the work of ministry,
Rev 5: 9 by your blood you ransomed for God s

SALT
Ge 19:26 back, and she became a pillar of s.
Mt 5:13 "You are the s of the earth;

SALVATION ➛ SAVE
Ex 15: 2 and he has become my s;
Ps 27: 1 The LORD is my light and my s;
51:12 Restore to me the joy of your s,

Isa 12: 3 draw water from the wells of s.
52: 7 brings good news, who announces s,
La 3:26 one should wait quietly for the s
Hab 3:18 I will exult in the God of my s.
Lk 3: 6 all flesh shall see the s of God.'"
Ac 4:12 There is s in no one else,
2Co 6: 2 see, now is the day of s!
Php 2:12 work out your own s with fear
Heb 2: 3 escape if we neglect so great a s?
2Pe 3:15 regard the patience of our Lord as s.
Rev 19: 1 S and glory and power to our God,
Bar 4:29 everlasting joy with your s.

SAMARIA → SAMARITAN
1Ki 16:24 and called the city that he built, S,
2Ki 17: 6 the king of Assyria captured S;
Jn 4: 4 But he had to go through S.
Ac 1: 8 in all Judea and S, and to the ends

SAMARITAN → SAMARIA
Lk 10:33 But a S while traveling came near
Jn 4: 7 A S woman came to draw water,

SAME
Ro 10:12 the s Lord is Lord of all
1Co 12: 4 varieties of gifts, but the s Spirit;
Heb 13: 8 Jesus Christ is the s yesterday and

SAMSON*
Danite judge. Birth promised (Jdg 13). Married a Philistine, but his wife given away (Jdg 14). Vengeance on the Philistines (Jdg 15). Betrayed by Delilah (Jdg 16:1-22). Death (Jdg 16:23-31). Feats of strength: killed lion (Jdg 14:6), 30 Philistines (Jdg 14:19), 1,000 Philistines with jawbone (Jdg 15:13-17), carried off gates of Gaza (Jdg 16:3), pushed down temple of Dagon (Jdg 16:25-30; Heb 11:32).

SAMUEL
Ephraimite judge and prophet (Heb 11:32). Birth prayed for (1Sa 1:10-18). Dedicated to temple by Hannah (1Sa 1:21-28). Raised by Eli (1Sa 2:11, 18-26). Called as prophet (1Sa 3). Led Israel to victory over Philistines (1Sa 7). Asked by Israel for a king (1Sa 8). Anointed Saul as king (1Sa 9-10). Farewell speech (1Sa 12). Rebuked Saul for sacrifice (1Sa 13). Announced rejection of Saul (1Sa 15). Anointed David as king (1Sa 16). Protected David from Saul (1Sa 19:18-24). Death (1Sa 25:1). Returned from dead to condemn Saul (1Sa 28).

SANCTIFICATION → SANCTIFY
Ro 6:19 as slaves to righteousness for s.
1Th 4: 3 For this is the will of God, your s:

SANCTIFIED → SANCTIFY
Ex 29:43 and it shall be s by my glory;
Jn 17:19 so that they also may be s in truth.
1Co 6:11 But you were washed, you were s,

SANCTIFY → SANCTIFICATION, SANCTIFIED
Lev 11:44 s yourselves therefore, and be holy,
Heb 13:12 to s the people by his own blood.

SANCTUARY
Ex 25: 8 And have them make me a s,
1Ch 22:19 build the s of the LORD God
Eze 37:26 and will set my s among them
Da 9:26 shall destroy the city and the s.
Heb 9:24 Christ did not enter a s made by
1Mc 1:21 He arrogantly entered the s
4:36 cleanse the s and dedicate it."

SAND
Ge 22:17 as the stars of heaven and as the s
Hos 1:10 Israel shall be like the s of the sea,
Mt 7:26 foolish man who built his house on s.

SANDALS
Ex 3: 5 Remove the s from your feet,
Mt 3:11 I am not worthy to carry his s.

SARAH
Wife of Abraham, originally named Sarai; barren (Ge 11:29-31; 1Pe 3:6). Taken by Pharaoh as Abraham's sister; returned (Ge 12:10-20). Gave Hagar to Abraham; sent her away in pregnancy (Ge 16). Name changed; Isaac promised (Ge 17:15-21; 18:10-15; Heb 11:11). Taken by Abimelech as Abraham's sister; returned (Ge 20). Isaac born; Hagar and Ishmael sent away (Ge 21:1-21; Gal 4:21-31). Death (Ge 23).

SAT → SIT
Heb 10:12 "he s down at the right hand of God,
Rev 3:21 and s down with my Father

SATAN
1Ch 21: 1 S stood up against Israel,
Job 1: 6 and S also came among them.
Zec 3: 2 "The LORD rebuke you, O S!
Mt 4:10 Jesus said to him, "Away with you, S!
12:26 If S casts out S, he is divided
16:23 said to Peter, "Get behind me, S!
2Co 11:14 S disguises himself as an angel of light.
Rev 12: 9 who is called the Devil and S,
20: 7 S will be released from his prison

SATISFIED → SATISFY
Ps 17:15 I shall be s, beholding your likeness.
Joel 2:26 You shall eat in plenty and be s,

SATISFY → SATISFIED
Isa 55: 2 labor for that which does not s?
Jer 31:25 I will s the weary, and all who are

SAUL → =PAUL
1. Benjamite; anointed by Samuel as first king of Israel (1Sa 9-10). Defeated Ammonites (1Sa 11). Rebuked for offering sacrifice (1Sa 13:1-15). Defeated Philistines (1Sa 14). Rejected as king for failing to annihilate Amalekites (1Sa 15). Soothed from evil spirit by David (1Sa 16:14-23). Sent David against Goliath (1Sa 17). Jealousy and attempted murder of David (1Sa 18:1-11). Gave David Michal as wife (1Sa 18:12-30). Second attempt to kill David (1Sa 19). Anger at Jonathan (1Sa 20:26-34). Pursued David: killed priests at Nob (1Sa 22), went to Keilah and Ziph (1Sa 23), life spared by David at En Gedi (1Sa 24) and in his tent (1Sa 26). Rebuked by Samuel's spirit for consulting witch at Endor (1Sa 28). Wounded by Philistines; took his own life (1Sa 31; 1Ch 10). Lamented by David (2Sa 1:17-27). Children (1Sa 14:49-51; 1Ch 8).
2. See Paul.

SAVE → SALVATION, SAVED, SAVIOR
Ps 54: 1 S me, O God, by your name,
Isa 59: 1 LORD's hand is not too short to s,
Jer 15:20 for I am with you to s you
Mt 1:21 he will s his people from their sins."
16:25 who want to s their life will lose it,
Lk 19:10 came to seek out and to s the lost."
Heb 7:25 to s those who approach God

SAVED → SAVE
Isa 45:22 Turn to me and be s,
Joel 2:32 on the name of the LORD shall be s;
Mt 10:22 who endures to the end will be s.
Mk 15:31 He s others; he cannot save himself.
Lk 13:23 "Lord, will only a few be s?"
Ac 2:21 on the name of the Lord shall be s.'
16:30 "Sirs, what must I do to be s?"
Ro 10:13 on the name of the Lord shall be s."
Eph 2: 8 For by grace you have been s

SAVIOR → SAVE
Ps 106:21 They forgot God, their S,
Isa 49:26 know that I am the LORD your S,
Hos 13: 4 and besides me there is no s.
Lk 2:11 this day in the city of David a S,
Ac 13:23 to Israel a S, Jesus, as he promised;
1Ti 4:10 who is the S of all people,
Tit 2:13 of the glory of our great God and S,
2Pe 3:18 knowledge of our Lord and S Jesus

SCARLET
Isa 1:18 your sins are like s, they shall be
Mt 27:28 stripped him and put a s robe on him

SCATTER → SCATTERED
Dt 4:27 LORD will s you among the peoples;
Jer 9:16 I will s them among nations that

SCATTERED → SCATTER
Dt 30: 3 the LORD your God has s you.
Jer 31:10 "He who s Israel will gather him,
Mk 14:27 the shepherd, and the sheep will be s.'

SCEPTER
Ge 49:10 The s shall not depart from Judah,
Nu 24:17 and a s shall rise out of Israel;
Heb 1: 8 righteous s is the s of your kingdom.

SCOFFED → SCOFFERS
Lk 23:35 but the leaders s at him, saying,

SCOFFERS → SCOFFED
Ps 1: 1 or sit in the seat of s;
Pr 19:29 Condemnation is ready for s,
2Pe 3: 3 that in the last days s will come,

SCRIBES
Mt 7:29 having authority, and not as their s.
23:13 "But woe to you, s and Pharisees,

SCRIPTURE → SCRIPTURES
Lk 4:21 "Today this s has been fulfilled in
Jn 10:35 and the s cannot be annulled—
1Ti 4:13 attention to the public reading of s,
2Ti 3:16 All s is inspired by God and is useful

SCRIPTURES → SCRIPTURE
Mt 22:29 know neither the s nor the power
Lk 24:45 their minds to understand the s,
Jn 5:39 "You search the s because you think
1Co 15: 3 our sins in accordance with the s,

SCROLL
Lk 4:17 the s of the prophet Isaiah was given
Rev 5: 2 to open the s and break its seals?"

SEA
Ge 1:26 have dominion over the fish of the s,
Ex 15: 1 and rider he has thrown into the s.
Dt 30:13 Neither is it beyond the s, that you
Ps 95: 5 The s is his, for he made it,
Da 7: 3 great beasts came up out of the s,
Mic 7:19 all our sins into the depths of the s.
Rev 4: 6 there is something like a s of glass,
13: 1 a beast rising out of the s having
21: 1 and the s was no more.

SEAL → SEALS
Da 8:26 As for you, s up the vision,
2Co 1:22 by putting his s on us and giving us
Eph 1:13 the s of the promised Holy Spirit;
Rev 7: 3 our God with a s on their foreheads.
22:10 not s up the words of the prophecy

SEALS → SEAL
Rev 5: 2 to open the scroll and break its s?"

SEARCH → SEARCHES
Dt 4:29 if you s after him with all your heart
Ps 139:23 S me, O God, and know my heart;
Eze 34:11 I myself will s for my sheep,

SEARCHES → SEARCH
Ro 8:27 And God, who s the heart,
1Co 2:10 the Spirit s everything,

SEASON → SEASONS
Ps 1: 3 which yield their fruit in its s,
Ecc 3: 1 For everything there is a s,

SEASONS → SEASON
Ge 1:14 let them be for signs and for s and
Gal 4:10 and months, and s, and years.
1Th 5: 1 Now concerning the times and the s,

SEAT → SEATED
Ex 25:17 make a mercy s of pure gold;
Ps 1: 1 or sit in the s of scoffers;
Ro 14:10 stand before the judgment s of God.
2Co 5:10 must appear before the judgment s

SEATED → SEAT
Lk 22:69 the Son of Man will be s at the right
Eph 1:20 and s him at his right hand
Rev 4: 4 s on the thrones are twenty-four elders,
19: 4 and worshiped God who is s on

SECOND → TWO
Mt 22:39 And a s is like it:
Rev 20:14 This is the s death, the lake of fire;

SECRET
Dt 29:29 The s things belong to the LORD
Ro 2:16 will judge the s thoughts of all.

SECURITY → SECURE
Pr 12: 3 No one finds s by wickedness,
1Th 5: 3 they say, "There is peace and s,"

SEE → FORESEEING, NEAR-SIGHTED, SEEN, SEES, SIGHT
Ex 12:13 when I s the blood, I will pass over
33:20 for no one shall s me and live."
Ps 115: 5 eyes, but do not s.
Jn 9:25 that though I was blind, now I s."

1Co 13:12 we s in a mirror, dimly,
1Jn 3: 2 for we will s him as he is.
Rev 1: 7 the clouds; every eye will s him,

SEED → SEEDS, SEEDTIME
Isa 6:13 The holy s is its stump.
Mt 17:20 have faith the size of a mustard s,
1Pe 1:23 of perishable but of imperishable s,

SEEDS → SEED
Mt 13: 8 Other s fell on good soil
Mk 4:31 the smallest of all the s on earth;

SEEK
1Ch 28: 9 If you s him, he will be found by
Ps 34:10 those who s the LORD lack no good
119:10 With my whole heart I s you;
Isa 55: 6 S the LORD while he may be found,
65: 1 found by those who did not s me.
Lk 19:10 came to s out and to save
Heb 11: 6 that he rewards those who s him.
Sir 2:16 who fear the Lord s to please him,

SEEMS
Pr 16:25 there is a way that s to be right,
Heb 12:11 discipline always s painful rather

SEEN → SEE
Jn 1:18 No one has ever s God.
14: 9 Whoever has s me has s the Father.
20:29 Blessed are those who have not s
1Pe 1: 8 you have not s him, you love him;

SELF-CONTROL → SELF-CONTROLLED
1Co 7: 5 tempt you because of your lack of s.
2Pe 1: 6 with s, and s with endurance,

SELF-CONTROLLED → SELF-CONTROL
Tit 1: 8 prudent, upright, devout, and s.
2: 5 to be s, chaste, good managers

SELFISH → SELFISHNESS
Ps 119:36 to your decrees, and not to s gain.
Php 1:17 proclaim Christ out of s ambition,
Jas 3:14 if you have bitter envy and s

SELFISHNESS* → SELFISH
2Co 12:20 anger, s, slander, gossip, conceit,

SELL
Pr 23:23 Buy truth, and do not s it;
Mk 10:21 s what you own, and give the money

SEND → SENT
Ex 33: 2 I will s an angel before you,
Isa 6: 8 And I said, "Here am I; s me!"
Jn 3:17 God did not s the Son into the world to
14:26 whom the Father will s in my name,

SENNACHERIB
Assyrian king; siege of Jerusalem was overthrown by the LORD following prayer of Hezekiah and Isaiah (2Ki 18:13-19:37; 2Ch 32:1-21; Isa 36-37).

SENT → SEND
Ex 3:14 'I AM has s me to you.'"
Lk 10:16 rejects me rejects the one who s me.
Jn 17:18 As you have s me into the world,
20:21 the Father has s me, so I send you."
1Jn 4:10 and s his Son to be the atoning

SEPARATE → SEPARATED
Mt 19: 6 joined together, let no one s."
Ro 8:35 will s us from the love of Christ?
1Co 7:10 wife should not s from her husband

SEPARATED → SEPARATE
Lev 20:24 I have s you from the peoples.
Heb 7:26 s from sinners, and exalted above

SERPENT → SERPENTS
Ge 3: 1 the s was more crafty than any other
Nu 21: 9 Moses made a s of bronze,
2Co 11: 3 the s deceived Eve by its cunning,
Rev 20: 2 He seized the dragon, that ancient s,

SERPENTS → SERPENT
Mt 10:16 wise as s and innocent as doves.

SERVANT → SERVANTS
Ps 19:11 Moreover by them is your s warned;
Isa 42: 1 Here is my s, whom I uphold,
43:10 and my s whom I have chosen,
53:11 my s, shall make many righteous,
Zec 3: 8 going to bring my s the Branch.
Lk 1:38 "Here am I, the s of the Lord;
Ac 3:13 has glorified his s Jesus,
2Ti 2:24 Lord's s must not be quarrelsome
Heb 3: 5 faithful in all God's house as a s,

SERVANTS → SERVANT
2Ki 17:23 as he had foretold through all his s
Jn 15:15 I do not call you s any longer,
1Pe 2:16 As s of God, live as free people,
Rev 7: 3 marked the s of our God with a seal

SERVE
Jos 24:15 my household, we will s the LORD."
1Sa 12:20 but s the LORD with all your heart;
Mt 6:24 You cannot s God and wealth.
Mk 10:45 Son of Man came not to be served but to s,
1Pe 4:10 s one another with whatever gift

SETH
Ge 4:25 she bore a son and named him S,

SETTLE
Ge 26: 2 s in the land that I shall show you.
Nu 33:53 possession of the land and s in it,

SEVEN → SEVENTH
Ge 7: 2 with you s pairs of all clean animals,
Ex 25:37 You shall make the s lamps for it;
Jos 6: 4 march around the city s times,
Da 9:25 prince, there shall be s weeks;
Mt 18:22 "Not s times, but, I tell you, seventy-seven
Rev 1:12 turning I saw s golden lampstands,
5: 1 and on the back, sealed with s seals;
8: 2 I saw the s angels who stand before
12: 3 a great red dragon, with s heads and
15: 1 s angels with s plagues,

SEVENTH → SEVEN
Ge 2: 2 on the s day God finished the work
Ex 20:10 the s day is a sabbath to the LORD
23:11 but the s year you shall let it rest
Heb 4: 4 God rested on the s day from all his

SEVENTY → SEVENTY-SEVEN
Ge 46:27 who came into Egypt were s.
2Ch 36:21 it kept sabbath, to fulfill s years.
Jer 25:12 Then after s years are completed,
Da 9:24 S weeks are decreed for your people

SEVENTY-SEVEN → SEVENTY
Mt 18:22 "Not seven times, but, I tell you, s

SEXUAL
1Co 10: 8 not indulge in s immorality as some

SHADOW
2Ki 20:11 brought the s back the ten intervals,
Ps 17: 8 hide me in the s of your wings,
91: 1 who abide in the s of the Almighty,
Mt 4:16 and s of death light has dawned."
Col 2:17 are only a s of what is to come,

SHADRACH → =HANANIAH
Hebrew exiled to Babylon; name changed from Hananiah (Da 1:6-7). Refused defilement by food (Da 1:8-20). Refused to worship idol (Da 3:1-18); saved from furnace (Da 3:19-30).

SHALLUM
King of Israel (2Ki 15:10-16).

SHALMANESER
King of Assyria; conquered and deported Israel (2Ki 17:3-4; 18:9; Tob 1:2).

SHAME → ASHAMED, SHAMEFUL
Ps 69: 6 who hope in you be put to s because
Eze 39:26 They shall forget their s, and all
Da 12: 2 some to s and everlasting contempt.
1Co 1:27 foolish in the world to s the wise;
Heb 12: 2 endured the cross, disregarding its s,
1Jn 2:28 be put to s before him at his coming.

SHAMEFUL → SHAME
2Co 4: 2 We have renounced the s things
Eph 5:12 For it is s even to mention

SHAMGAR*
Judge; killed 600 Philistines (Jdg 3:31; 5:6).

SHARE
Nu 18:20 I am your s and your possession
Lk 3:11 "Whoever has two coats must s
Ro 15:27 for if the Gentiles have come to s
Col 1:12 to s in the inheritance of the saints
Heb 12:10 in order that we may s his holiness.
Jude 1: 3 to you about the salvation we s,

SHARP → SHARPENS, SHARPER
Pr 5: 4 s as a two-edged sword.
Rev 19:15 a s sword with which to strike down

SHARPENS → SHARP
Pr 27:17 Iron s iron, and one person s

SHARPER* → SHARP
Heb 4:12 s than any two-edged sword,

SHEBA
1. Benjamite; rebelled against David (2Sa 20).
2. Queen of Sheba (1Ki 10; 2Ch 9; Mt 12:42; Lk 11:31).

SHECHEM
1. Raped Jacob's daughter Dinah; killed (Ge 34).
2. City where Joshua renewed the covenant (Jos 24). Abimelech as king (Jdg 9).

SHED → BLOODSHED, SHEDDING
Ge 9: 6 shall that person's blood be s;
Pr 6:17 and hands that s innocent blood,
Mt 23:35 may come all the righteous blood s
Rev 16: 6 s the blood of saints and prophets,

SHEDDING → SHED
Heb 9:22 without the s of blood there is no
12: 4 resisted to the point of s your blood.

SHEEP
1Ki 22:17 like s that have no shepherd;
Ps 100: 3 people, and the s of his pasture.
Isa 53: 6 All we like s have gone astray;
Eze 34:15 myself will be the shepherd of my s,
Zec 13: 7 shepherd, that the s may be scattered;
Mt 9:36 like s without a shepherd.
Lk 15: 4 a hundred s and losing one of them,
Jn 10: 7 I am the gate for the s.
10:15 And I lay down my life for the s.
Heb 13:20 the great shepherd of the s,
1Pe 2:25 For you were going astray like s,

SHELTER
Ps 91: 1 who live in the s of the Most High,
Rev 7:15 is seated on the throne will s them.

SHEM
Son of Noah (Ge 5:32; 6:10). Blessed (Ge 9:26). Descendants (Ge 10:21-31; 11:10-32; Lk 3:36).

SHEOL
Nu 16:30 and they go down alive into S,
Job 26: 6 S is naked before God,
Ps 139: 8 if I make my bed in S, you are there.
Isa 28:15 and with S we have an agreement;
Hos 13:14 O S, where is your destruction?

SHEPHERD → SHEPHERDS
2Sa 7: 7 whom I commanded to s my people
Ps 23: 1 The LORD is my s, I shall not want.
Ecc 12:11 sayings that are given by one s.
Isa 40:11 He will feed his flock like a s;
Mt 2: 6 ruler who is to s my people Israel.'"
26:31 strike the s, and the sheep of the flock
Jn 10:11 "I am the good s.
Heb 13:20 the great s of the sheep,
1Pe 5: 4 And when the chief s appears,

SHEPHERDS → SHEPHERD
Eze 34: 2 prophesy against the s of Israel:
Lk 2: 8 there were s living in the fields,

SHIELD
Ge 15: 1 I am your s; your reward shall be
Ps 7:10 God is my s, who saves the upright
Eph 6:16 With all of these, take the s of faith,

SHILOH
1Sa 1:24 to the house of the LORD at S;

SHIMEI
Cursed David (2Sa 16:5-14); spared (2Sa 19:16-23). Killed by Solomon (1Ki 2:8-9, 36-46).

SHINE → SHINES, SHINING
Nu 6:25 LORD make his face to s upon you,
Ps 4: 6 light of your face s on us, O LORD!"
Isa 60: 1 s; for your light has come,

Da 12: 3 Those who are wise shall s like the
Mt 5:16 let your light s before others,
Eph 5:14 the dead, and Christ will s on you."

SHINES → SHINE
Jn 1: 5 The light s in the darkness,

SHINING → SHINE
2Pe 1:19 to this as to a lamp s in a dark place,
1Jn 2: 8 and the true light is already s.

SHORT
Isa 59: 1 the LORD's hand is not too s to save,
Mt 24:22 if those days had not been cut s,
Ro 3:23 sinned and fall s of the glory of God;

SHOUT
Ps 47: 1 s to God with loud songs of joy.
Zec 9: 9 S aloud, O daughter Jerusalem!
Lk 19:40 were silent, the stones would s out."

SHOW → SHOWED
Ge 12: 1 to the land that I will s you.
Ex 33:18 Moses said, "S me your glory,
Ps 85: 7 S us your steadfast love, O LORD,
Jn 14: 8 said to him, "Lord, s us the Father,
1Co 12:31 will s you a still more excellent way
Rev 4: 1 I will s you what must take place

SHOWED → SHOW
Dt 34: 1 the LORD s him the whole land:
Jn 20:20 he s them his hands and his side.

SHOWERS
Dt 32: 2 rain on grass, like s on new growth.
Eze 34:26 they shall be s of blessing.

SHUT
Isa 22:22 he shall open, and no one shall s;
Da 6:22 God sent his angel and s the lions'
Rev 3: 7 who opens and no one will s,

SICK → SICKNESS
Mt 8:16 and cured all who were s.
9:12 of a physician, but those who are s.
Jas 5:14 Are any among you s?

SICKLE
Joel 3:13 Put in the s, for the harvest is ripe.
Rev 14:14 and a sharp s in his hand!

SICKNESS → SICK
Ex 23:25 I will take s away from among you.
Mt 4:23 and curing every disease and every s

SIDE → ASIDE
Ps 91: 7 A thousand may fall at your s,
124: 1 the LORD who was on our s
Jn 19:34 soldiers pierced his s with a spear,

SIFT
Isa 30:28 to s the nations with the sieve of
Lk 22:31 Satan has demanded to s all of you

SIGHT → SEE
Ge 6:11 the earth was corrupt in God's s,
Ps 72:14 and precious is their blood in his s.
Mt 11: 5 blind receive their s, the lame walk,
2Co 5: 7 for we walk by faith, not by s.
1Pe 3: 4 which is very precious in God's s.

SIGN → SIGNS
Ge 9:12 the s of the covenant that I make
17:11 a s of the covenant between me
Isa 7:14 the Lord himself will give you a s.
Mt 24: 3 the s of your coming and of the end
Mk 8:12 does this generation ask for a s?

SIGNS → SIGN
Ge 1:14 be for s and for seasons and for days
Ex 7: 3 I will multiply my s and wonders in
Da 6:27 he works s and wonders in heaven
Mt 16: 3 cannot interpret the s of the times.
Jn 20:30 Jesus did many other s in the
1Co 1:22 Jews demand s and Greeks desire
Rev 16:14 demonic spirits, performing s,

SILAS
Prophet (Ac 15:22-32); co-worker with Paul on second missionary journey (Ac 16-18; 2Co 1:19). Co-writer with Paul (1Th 1:1; 2Th 1:1); Peter (1Pe 5:12).

SILENT
Isa 53: 7 a sheep that before its shearers is s,
Zep 1: 7 Be s before the Lord GOD!
Mk 14:61 But he was s and did not answer.
1Co 14:34 women should be s in the churches.

SILVER
Ps 66:10 you have tried us as s is tried.
Pr 8:10 Take my instruction instead of s,
Isa 48:10 I have refined you, but not like s;
Zec 13: 9 refine them as one refines s,
Mt 26:15 They paid him thirty pieces of s.
Ac 3: 6 But Peter said, "I have no s or gold,
1Co 3:12 on the foundation with gold, s,

SIMEON → =SIMON
1. Son of Jacob by Leah (Ge 29:33; 35:23; 1Ch 2:1). With Levi killed Shechem for rape of Dinah (Ge 34:25-29). Held hostage by Joseph in Egypt (Ge 42:24-43:23). Tribe of blessed (Ge 49:5-7), numbered (Nu 1:23; 26:14), allotted land (Jos 19:1-9; Eze 48:24), 12,000 from (Rev 7:7).
2. Godly Jew who blessed the infant Jesus (2:25-35).
3. See Peter (Ac 15:14; 2Pe 1:1).

SIMON → =PETER, =SIMEON
1. See Peter.
2. Apostle; the Zealot (Mt 10:4; Mk 3:18; Lk 6:15; Ac 1:13).
3. Samaritan sorcerer (Ac 8:9-24).

SIMPLE
Ps 19: 7 are sure, making wise the s;
Pr 1:22 O s ones, will you love being s?
14:15 The s believe everything,

SIN → SINFUL, SINNED, SINNER, SINNERS, SINS
Ge 4: 7 not do well, s is lurking at the door;
Ex 32:32 if you will only forgive their s—
Nu 32:23 and be sure your s will find you out.
1Ki 8:46 "If they s against you—
2Ch 7:14 forgive their s and heal their land.
Ps 119:11 so that I may not s against you.
Isa 53:12 yet he bore the s of many,
Mt 5:29 If your right eye causes you to s,
Jn 1:29 who takes away the s of the world!
Ro 6:23 For the wages of s is death,
2Co 5:21 made him to be s who knew no s,
Heb 4:15 tested as we are, yet without s.
1Jn 1: 7 Jesus his Son cleanses us from all s.
Tob 12:10 but those who commit s
Wis 10:13 but delivered him from s.
Sir 3:30 so almsgiving atones for s.

SINAI → =HOREB
Ex 19:20 the LORD descended upon Mount S,
Ps 68:17 the Lord came from S into the holy
Gal 4:25 Now Hagar is Mount S in Arabia

SINFUL → SIN
Lk 5: 8 from me, Lord, for I am a s man!"
Ro 8: 3 Son in the likeness of s flesh,
1Mc 1:10 From them came forth a s root,

SING → SINGERS, SONG, SONGS, SUNG
Ex 15: 1 "I will s to the LORD,
Ps 47: 6 S praises to God, s praises;
Isa 5: 1 s for my beloved my love-song
1Co 14:15 I will s praise with the spirit,
Col 3:16 gratitude in your hearts s psalms,
Rev 5: 9 They s a new song:
Jdt 16:13 I will s to my God a new song:
Aza 1:35 s praise to him and highly exalt him

SINGERS → SING
1Ch 15:16 to appoint their kindred as the s
Ezr 2:70 and the s, the gatekeepers,

SINGLE
Mt 6:27 worrying add a s hour to your span
Rev 21:21 each of the gates is a s pearl,

SINNED → SIN
Nu 14:40 LORD has promised, for we have s."
Ps 51: 4 Against you, you alone, have I s,
La 5: 7 Our ancestors s; they are no more,
Ro 3:23 all have s and fall short of the glory of God;
1Jn 1:10 If we say that we have not s,
Sir 18:21 and when you have s, repent.

SINNER → SIN
Lk 15: 7 over one s who repents than
Jas 5:20 that whoever brings back a s

SINNERS → SIN
Ps 1: 1 or take the path that s tread,
Pr 23:17 Do not let your heart envy s,
Lk 6:33 For even s do the same.
Ro 5: 8 we still were s Christ died for us.
1Ti 1:15 Jesus came into the world to save s

SINS → SIN
1Sa 2:25 but if someone s against the LORD,
Ps 103:10 not deal with us according to our s,
Isa 1:18 your s are like scarlet, they shall be
Eze 18: 4 only the person who s that shall die.
Mic 7:19 cast all our s into the depths of the
Mt 9: 6 has authority on earth to forgive s"—
Mk 1: 5 the river Jordan, confessing their s.
Lk 11: 4 forgive us our s, for we ourselves
Ac 3:19 to God so that your s may be wiped
1Co 15: 3 Christ died for our s in accordance
Heb 9:28 offered once to bear the s of many,
1Jn 1: 9 If we confess our s, he who is faithful
Rev 1: 5 loves us and freed us from our s
Sir 2:11 he forgives s and saves

SISTER
Ge 12:13 Say you are my s, so that it may go
20: 2 of his wife Sarah, "She is my s."
Pr 7: 4 Say to wisdom, "You are my s,"
Mk 3:35 the will of God is my brother and s

SIT → SAT, SITS
Ps 1: 1 or s in the seat of scoffers;
110: 1 says to my lord, "S at my right hand
Jer 33:17 never lack a man to s on the throne
Mt 20:23 to s at my right hand and at my left,
Heb 1:13 "S at my right hand until I make

SITS → SIT
Ps 2: 4 He who s in the heavens laughs;
Isa 28: 6 to the one who s in judgment,

SIX
Ex 20: 9 S days you shall labor and do all
Pr 6:16 are s things that the LORD hates,
Isa 6: 2 above him; each had s wings:
Rev 4: 8 each of them with s wings,

SKILL
Ex 28: 3 whom I have endowed with s,
1Ki 7:14 he was full of s, intelligence,

SKIN
Job 2: 4 Satan answered the LORD, "S for s!
19:26 after my s has been thus destroyed,
Jer 13:23 Can Ethiopians change their s

SKULL
2Ki 9:35 they found no more of her than the s
Mt 27:33 Golgotha (which means Place of a S)

SKY
Dt 28:23 s over your head shall be bronze,
Mt 16: 3 to interpret the appearance of the s,
Rev 6:14 The s vanished like a scroll rolling

SLANDER → SLANDERED
Ps 15: 3 who do not s with their tongue,
Pr 10:18 and whoever utters s is a fool.
Mt 15:19 fornication, theft, false witness, s.
1Pe 2: 1 all guile, insincerity, envy, and all s.

SLANDERED → SLANDER
1Co 4:13 when s, we speak kindly.

SLAUGHTER → SLAUGHTERED
Pr 7:22 and goes like an ox to the s,
Isa 53: 7 like a lamb that is led to the s,
Zec 11: 4 a shepherd of the flock doomed to s.
Ac 8:32 "Like a sheep he was led to the s,

SLAUGHTERED → SLAUGHTER
Rev 5: 6 a Lamb standing as if it had been s,
6: 9 who had been s for the word of God

SLAVE → ENSLAVE, ENSLAVED, SLAVERY, SLAVES
Ge 21:10 Cast out this s woman with her son;
Mk 10:44 first among you must be s of all.
Jn 8:34 who commits sin is a s to sin.
Gal 3:28 there is no longer s or free,

SLAVERY → SLAVE
Ex 20: 2 out of the house of s;
Ro 7:14 of the flesh, sold into s under sin.
Gal 5: 1 do not submit again to a yoke of s.

SLAVES → SLAVE
Ro 6:16 are s of the one whom you obey,
2Pe 2:19 people are s to whatever masters

SLEEP → ASLEEP, SLEEPER, SLEEPING
Ge 2:21 God caused a deep s to fall upon
15:12 a deep s fell upon Abram,
Ps 121: 4 keeps Israel will neither slumber nor s.
Da 12: 2 Many of those who s in the dust of

SLEEPER → SLEEP
Eph 5:14 "S, awake! Rise from the dead,

SLEEPING → SLEEP
Mt 9:24 for the girl is not dead but s."
26:40 to the disciples and found them s;

SLING
1Sa 17:50 over the Philistine with a s and a stone,

SLIP
Dt 32:35 for the time when their foot shall s;
Ps 37:31 their steps do not s.

SLOW → SLOWNESS
Ex 34: 6 merciful and gracious, s to anger,
Nu 14:18 'The LORD is s to anger,
Ps 145: 8 s to anger and abounding in
Na 1: 3 The LORD is s to anger but great in
Lk 24:25 and how s of heart to believe all that
2Pe 3: 9 The Lord is not s about his promise,
Tob 12: 6 Do not be s to acknowledge him.
Sir 5: 4 for the Lord is s to anger.

SLOWNESS → SLOW
2Pe 3: 9 think of s, but is patient with you,

SMALL → SMALLEST
Jas 3: 5 So also the tongue is a s member,

SMALLEST → SMALL
Mk 4:31 is the s of all the seeds on earth;

SMOKE → SMOKING
Ex 19:18 Now Mount Sinai was wrapped in s,
Isa 6: 4 and the house filled with s.
Joel 2:30 blood and fire and columns of s.
Rev 15: 8 with s from the glory of God and

SMOKING → SMOKE
Ge 15:17 s fire pot and a flaming torch passed
Ex 20:18 of the trumpet, and the mountain s,

SNAKE
Ex 4: 3 and it became a s; and Moses drew
Lk 11:11 will give a s instead of a fish?

SNARE
Ex 23:33 it will surely be a s to you.
Jdg 2: 3 their gods shall be a s to you."

SNOW
Ps 51: 7 and I shall be whiter than s.
Isa 1:18 sins are like scarlet, they shall be like s;
Da 7: 9 his clothing was white as s,
Rev 1:14 as white wool, white as s;

SOBER
1Th 5: 6 but let us keep awake and be s;
2Ti 4: 5 always be s, endure suffering,

SODOM
Ge 19:24 rained on S and Gomorrah sulfur
Isa 1: 9 we would have been like S,
Lk 10:12 it will be more tolerable for S than
Rev 11: 8 city that is prophetically called S

SOLDIERS
Mt 28:12 give a large sum of money to the s,
Jn 19:23 When the s had crucified Jesus,

SOLID
1Co 3: 2 I fed you with milk, not s food,
Heb 5:14 But s food is for the mature,

SOLOMON
Son of David by Bathsheba; king of Judah (2Sa 12:24; 1Ch 3:5, 10). Appointed king by David (1Ki 1); adversaries Adonijah, Joab, Shimei killed by Benaiah (1Ki 2). Asked for wisdom (1Ki 3; 2Ch 1). Judged between two prostitutes (1Ki 3:16-28). Built temple (1Ki 5-7; 2Ch 2-5); prayer of dedication (1Ki 8; 2Ch 6). Visited by Queen of Sheba (1Ki 10; 2Ch 9). Wives turned his heart from God (1Ki 11:1-13). Jeroboam rebelled against (1Ki 11:26-40). Death (1Ki 11:41-43; 2Ch 9:29-31).
Proverbs of (1Ki 4:32; Pr 1:1; 10:1; 25:1); psalms of (Ps 72; 127); song of (SS 1:1).

SON → SONS
Ge 21: 2 conceived and bore Abraham a s
Ex 4:23 now I will kill your firstborn s.'"
2Sa 7:14 and he shall be a s to me.
Ps 2: 7 He said to me, "You are my s;
Isa 7:14 is with child and shall bear a s,
Mt 1:23 virgin shall conceive and bear a s,
2:15 "Out of Egypt I have called my s."
3:17 from heaven said, "This is my S,
12: 8 the S of Man is lord of the sabbath."
16:16 the Messiah, the S of the living God."
Mk 10:45 S of Man came not to be served but to
Lk 1:35 he will be called S of God.
20:44 so how can he be his s?"
Jn 1:34 testified that this is the S of God."
3:16 loved the world that he gave his only S,
Ro 8:29 be conformed to the image of his S,
1Th 1:10 to wait for his S from heaven,
Heb 1: 2 last days he has spoken to us by a S,
1: 5 my S; today I have begotten you"?
2Pe 1:17 saying, "This is my S, my Beloved,
1Jn 4: 9 God sent his only S into the world
Rev 12: 5 she gave birth to a s, a male child,
14:14 the cloud was one like the S of Man,
Sir 4:10 be like a s of the Most High,
2Es 13:32 then my S will be revealed,

SONG → SING
Ex 15: 1 sang this s to the LORD:
Dt 31:21 s will confront them as a witness,
Ps 40: 3 He put a new s in my mouth,
Rev 5: 9 They sing a new s: "You are worthy
15: 3 and the s of the Lamb:

SONGS → SING
1Ki 4:32 his s numbered a thousand and five.
Ps 137: 3 "Sing us one of the s of Zion!"
Col 3:16 hymns, and spiritual s to God.

SONS → SON
Ge 6: 2 the s of God saw that they were fair;
35:22 Now the s of Jacob were twelve.
Dt 7: 3 giving your daughters to their s
Ac 2:17 s and your daughters shall prophesy,
2Co 6:18 you shall be my s and daughters,

SOON
Isa 56: 1 for s my salvation will come,
Rev 22:20 says, "Surely I am coming s."

SORCERERS → SORCERY
Rev 22:15 Outside are the dogs and s and

SORCERY → SORCERERS
Gal 5:20 s, enmities, strife, jealousy, anger,
Rev 18:23 all nations were deceived by your s.

SORROW → SORROWFUL
Est 9:22 turned for them from s into gladness
Ecc 1:18 who increase knowledge increase s.
Isa 35:10 and s and sighing shall flee away.

SORROWFUL → SORROW
2Co 6:10 as s, yet always rejoicing;

SOUL → SOULS
Dt 6: 5 all your s, and with all your might.
Jos 22: 5 all your heart and with all your s."
Ps 16: 9 heart is glad, and my s rejoices;
25: 1 To you, O LORD, I lift up my s.
42: 1 so my s longs for you, O God.
Mic 6: 7 fruit of my body for the sin of my s?"
Mt 10:28 fear him who can destroy both s and
Heb 4:12 piercing until it divides s from spirit
Jas 5:20 will save the sinner's s from death
3Jn 1: 2 just as it is well with your s.
Sir 7:29 With all your s fear the Lord,

SOULS → SOUL
Jer 6:16 walk in it, and find rest for your s.
Mt 11:29 and you will find rest for your s.
1Pe 2:25 the shepherd and guardian of your s.

SOUND
Eze 1:24 like the s of mighty waters,
1Co 15:52 For the trumpet will s, and the dead
2Ti 4: 3 will not put up with s doctrine,
Tit 1: 9 able both to preach with s doctrine
Rev 1:15 voice was like the s of many waters.

SOUR
Jer 31:29 "The parents have eaten s grapes,
Mk 15:36 filled a sponge with s wine,

SOVEREIGN → SOVEREIGNTY
1Ki 4:21 Solomon was s over all the
Rev 6:10 "S Lord, holy and true, how long

SOVEREIGNTY → SOVEREIGN
Da 4:34 For his s is an everlasting s,

SOW → SOWED, SOWS
Ex 23:10 For six years you shall s your land
Ecc 11: 6 In the morning s your seed,
Hos 10:12 S for yourselves righteousness;
Mt 13: 3 A sower went out to s.
1Co 15:36 s does not come to life unless it dies.

SOWED → SOW
Mt 13:24 to someone who s good seed
Lk 13:19 took and s in the garden;

SOWS → SOW
Jn 4:37 'One s and another reaps.'
2Co 9: 6 who s sparingly will also reap

SPAN
Isa 40:12 marked off the heavens with a s,
Mt 6:27 add a single hour to your s of life?

SPARE
Ro 11:21 perhaps he will not s you.
2Pe 2: 4 if God did not s the angels when

SPARROWS
Lk 12: 7 you are of more value than many s.

SPEAK → SPEAKING, SPEECH, SPOKE
Ge 18:27 take it upon myself to s to the Lord,
Nu 12: 8 With him I s face to face—
Dt 18:20 presumes to s in my name a word
Job 13: 3 But I would s to the Almighty,
Ecc 3: 7 time to keep silence, and a time to s;
Mt 13:13 The reason I s to them in parables is
Ac 2: 4 began to s in other languages,
1Co 12:30 Do all s in tongues?
Jas 1:19 be quick to listen, slow to s,
Sir 4:25 Never s against the truth,

SPEAKING → SPEAK
1Co 14:39 and do not forbid s in tongues;
Eph 4:15 But s the truth in love,

SPEAR → SPEARS
1Sa 19:10 to pin David to the wall with the s;
Jn 19:34 the soldiers pierced his side with a s,

SPEARS → SPEAR
Joel 3:10 and your pruning hooks into s;
Mic 4: 3 and their s into pruning hooks;

SPECK
Mt 7: 4 'Let me take the s out of your eye,'

SPECTACLE
1Co 4: 9 we have become a s to the world,

SPEECH → SPEAK
Ex 4:10 I am slow of s and slow of tongue."
Ps 19: 3 There is no s, nor are there words;
1Ti 4:12 set the believers an example in s
1Jn 3:18 let us love, not in word or s,
Sir 4:29 Do not be reckless in your s,

SPICES
Ex 25: 6 s for the anointing oil and for
Jn 19:40 wrapped it with the s in linen cloths,

SPIES → SPY
Nu 13:32 we have gone through as s
Jos 2: 1 two men secretly from Shittim as s,

SPIRIT → SPIRITS, SPIRITUAL
Ge 6: 3 My s shall not abide in mortals forever,
Nu 11:25 s rested upon them, they prophesied.
2Ki 2: 9 inherit a double share of your s."
Ne 9:20 You gave your good s to instruct
Job 33: 4 The s of God has made me,
Ps 31: 5 Into your hand I commit my s;
51:17 acceptable to God is a broken s;
Pr 16:18 and a haughty s before a fall.
Isa 42: 1 I have put my s upon him;
Eze 36:26 and a new s I will put within you;
Joel 2:28 I will pour out my s on all flesh;
Mt 1:18 to be with child from the Holy S.

5: 3 "Blessed are the poor in s,
12:31 against the S will not be forgiven.
26:41 the s indeed is willing, but the flesh
Mk 1: 8 will baptize you with the Holy S."
Jn 3: 5 without being born of water and S.
4:24 God is s, and those who worship him must worship in s and truth."
6:63 It is the s that gives life;
14:26 But the Advocate, the Holy S,
Ac 2: 4 of them were filled with the Holy S
Ro 8: 9 not in the flesh; you are in the S,
8:26 the S helps us in our weakness;
1Co 6:19 your body is a temple of the Holy S
12: 4 are varieties of gifts, but the same S;
2Co 3: 6 the letter kills, but the S gives life.
Gal 5:22 the fruit of the S is love, joy, peace,
Eph 1:13 the seal of the promised Holy S;
4:30 do not grieve the Holy S of God,
5:18 but be filled with the S,
1Th 5:19 Do not quench the S.
Heb 4:12 piercing until it divides soul from s,
1Pe 3: 4 lasting beauty of a gentle and quiet s
1Jn 4: 1 Beloved, do not believe every s,
Rev 1:10 I was in the s on the Lord's day,

SPIRITS ➤ SPIRIT
Nu 16:22 the God of the s of all flesh,
Dt 18:11 or who consults ghosts or s,
Lk 4:36 power he commands the unclean s,
1Co 12:10 to another the discernment of s,
Gal 4: 3 we were enslaved to the elemental s
Rev 1: 4 seven s who are before his throne,

SPIRITUAL ➤ SPIRIT
Ro 7:14 For we know that the law is s;
1Co 2:13 interpreting s things to those who are s.
12: 1 Now concerning s gifts,
14: 1 Pursue love and strive for the s gifts,
15:46 the s that is first, but the physical,
Eph 1: 3 every s blessing in the heavenly
Col 1: 9 of God's will in all s wisdom
1Pe 2: 2 infants, long for the pure, s milk,
2: 5 yourselves be built into a s house,

SPIT
Mk 14:65 began to s on him, to blindfold him,
Rev 3:16 am about to s you out of my mouth.

SPLENDOR
1Ch 16:29 Worship the LORD in holy s;
Eph 5:27 to present the church to himself in s,

SPOKE ➤ SPEAK
Mk 4:33 many such parables he s the word
1Co 13:11 When I was a child, I s like a child,
Heb 1: 1 Long ago God s to our ancestors in
2Pe 1:21 moved by the Holy Spirit s from

SPOT
Eph 5:27 without a s or wrinkle or anything
2Pe 3:14 at peace, without s or blemish;

SPRING
Isa 45: 8 earth open, that salvation may s up,
Jn 4:14 a s of water gushing up to eternal life."
Rev 21: 6 from the s of the water of life.

SPRINKLE ➤ SPRINKLED
Nu 8: 7 s the water of purification on them,
Eze 36:25 I will s clean water upon you,

SPRINKLED ➤ SPRINKLE
Lev 8:11 He s some of it on the altar seven
Heb 10:22 with our hearts s clean from an evil
1Pe 1: 2 and to be s with his blood:

SPY ➤ SPIES
Nu 13: 2 men to s out the land of Canaan,
Jos 6:25 whom Joshua sent to s out Jericho.

STAFF
Ge 49:10 the ruler's s from between his feet,
Ex 4: 4 and it became a s in his hand—
Nu 17: 6 the s of Aaron was among theirs.
Ps 23: 4 your rod and your s—they comfort me.
Zec 11:10 I took my s Favor and broke it,

STAND ➤ STANDING
Ex 14:13 "Do not be afraid, s firm,
Job 19:25 at the last he will s upon the earth;
Ps 1: 5 wicked will not s in the judgment,
Isa 7: 9 If you do not s firm in faith,
Mt 12:25 house divided against itself will s.
Ro 14: 4 for the Lord is able to make them s.
14:10 all s before the judgment seat of God.
Eph 6:11 may be able to s against the wiles of

STANDARDS
Jn 8:15 You judge by human s; I judge no
1Co 1:26 of you were wise by human s,

STANDING ➤ STAND
1Co 10:12 So if you think you are s,
Jas 5: 9 See, the Judge is s at the doors!
Rev 3:20 I am s at the door, knocking;

STAR ➤ STARS
Nu 24:17 a s shall come out of Jacob,
Isa 14:12 are fallen from heaven, O Day S,
Mt 2: 2 For we observed his s at its rising,
2Pe 1:19 day dawns and the morning s rises
Rev 9: 1 saw a s that had fallen from heaven
22:16 of David, the bright morning s."

STARS ➤ STAR
Ge 1:16 to rule the night—and the s.
Job 38: 7 when the morning s sang together
Ps 148: 3 praise him, all you shining s!
Da 12: 3 like the s forever and ever.
Php 2:15 you shine like s in the world.
Rev 1:16 In his right hand he held seven s,
12: 4 a third of the s of heaven and threw

STATUE
Da 2:31 there was a great s.

STATUTE ➤ STATUTES
Lev 16:29 This shall be a s to you forever:
Nu 19:21 It shall be a perpetual s for them.

STATUTES ➤ STATUTE
Ge 26: 5 commandments, my s, and my laws.
Dt 4: 1 give heed to the s and ordinances
Ne 9:13 good s and commandments,
Ps 119: 8 I will observe your s;

STEADFAST
Ex 34: 6 abounding in s love and faithfulness
Nu 14:18 and abounding in s love,
2Sa 7:15 I will not take my s love from him,
Ps 57: 7 My heart is s, O God, my heart is s.
136: 1 for his s love endures forever.
Heb 6:19 a sure and s anchor of the soul,
1Pe 5: 9 Resist him, s in your faith,

STEAL
Ex 20:15 You shall not s.
Mt 6:19 and where thieves break in and s;
Jn 10:10 The thief comes only to s and kill

STEPHEN*
Early church leader (Ac 6:5). Arrested (Ac 6:8-15). Speech to Sanhedrin (Ac 7). Stoned (Ac 7:54-60; 8:2; 11:19; 22:20).

STEPS
Pr 16: 9 but the LORD directs the s.
1Pe 2:21 so that you should follow in his s.

STIFF-NECKED ➤ NECK
Ex 32: 9 "I have seen this people, how s
Ac 7:51 "You s people, uncircumcised in

STILL
Ex 14:14 and you have only to keep s."
Jos 10:13 sun stood s, and the moon stopped,
Ps 46:10 "Be s, and know that I am God!
Mk 4:39 said to the sea, "Peace! Be s!"
Ro 5: 8 we s were sinners Christ died for us.
Heb 11: 4 but through his faith he s speaks.

STING
1Co 15:55 Where, O death, is your s?"

STONE ➤ CORNERSTONE, MILLSTONE, STONED, STONES
Ge 28:18 the s that he had put under his head
Ex 28:10 six of their names on the one s,
31:18 tablets of s, written with the finger of
1Sa 17:50 the Philistine with a sling and a s,
Ps 118:22 The s that the builders rejected has
Isa 28:16 in Zion a foundation s, a tested s,
Eze 36:26 from your body the heart of s
Mt 4: 6 will not dash your foot against a s.'"
Mk 12:10 'The s that the builders rejected has
16: 3 "Who will roll away the s for us
Ro 9:32 have stumbled over the stumbling s,
2Co 3: 3 not on tablets of s but on tablets
1Pe 2: 4 living s, though rejected by mortals
Rev 2:17 and I will give a white s,

STONED ➤ STONE
2Ch 24:21 by command of the king they s him
Ac 14:19 Then they s Paul and dragged him
Heb 11:37 s to death, they were sawn in two,

STONES ➤ STONE
Ex 28:21 twelve s with names corresponding
Jos 4: 3 'Take twelve s from here out of the
1Sa 17:40 chose five smooth s from the wadi,
Mt 3: 9 God is able from these s to raise
Lk 19:40 were silent, the s would shout out."
1Co 3:12 precious s, wood, hay, straw—
1Pe 2: 5 like living s, let yourselves be built

STORE ➤ SHOREHOUSE, STORING
Pr 7: 1 and s up my commandments
Mt 6:19 Do not s up for yourselves treasures

STOREHOUSE ➤ HOUSE, STORE
Dt 28:12 LORD will open for you his rich s,
Mal 3:10 Bring the full tithe into the s,

STORING* ➤ STORE
Ro 2: 5 you are s up wrath for yourself
1Ti 6:19 s up for themselves the treasure of

STRAIGHT
Pr 3: 6 and he will make s your paths.
Isa 40: 3 s in the desert a highway for our God.
Mt 3: 3 way of the Lord, make his paths s.'"
Ac 9:11 Get up and go to the street called S,
Sir 2: 6 make your ways s, and hope in him.

STRANGE ➤ STRANGER, STRANGERS
Dt 32:16 They made him jealous with s gods,
1Co 14:21 "By people of s tongues and by the

STRANGER ➤ STRANGE
Dt 10:19 You shall also love the s,
Mt 25:35 I was a s and you welcomed me,

STRANGERS ➤ STRANGE
Dt 10:19 for you were s in the land of Egypt.
Ro 12:13 extend hospitality to s.
Eph 2:12 and s to the covenants of promise,
Heb 11:13 They confessed that they were s

STRAW
Ex 5:10 says Pharaoh, 'I will not give you s.
1Co 3:12 precious stones, wood, hay, s—

STRAY ➤ ASTRAY
Ps 119:10 not let me s from your commandments.
Pr 22: 6 and when old, they will not s.

STREAM ➤ STREAMS
Isa 2: 2 all the nations shall s to it.
Am 5:24 righteousness like an ever-flowing s

STREAMS ➤ STREAM
Ps 1: 3 like trees planted by s of water,
42: 1 As a deer longs for flowing s,

STREET
Pr 1:20 Wisdom cries out in the s;
Mt 6: 5 the synagogues and at the s corners,
Rev 21:21 and the s of the city is pure gold,

STRENGTH ➤ STRONG
Ex 15: 2 The LORD is my s and my might,
1Ch 16:11 Seek the LORD and his s,
Ne 8:10 for the joy of the LORD is your s."
Ps 46: 1 God is our refuge and s,
Pr 31:25 S and dignity are her clothing,
Isa 40:31 for the LORD shall renew their s,
Mk 12:30 all your mind, and with all your s.'
1Co 1:25 God's weakness is stronger than human s.
Jdt 9:11 your s does not depend on numbers,
1Mc 3:19 but s comes from Heaven.

STRENGTHEN ➤ STRONG
Jdg 16:28 and s me only this once, O God,
Ps 119:28 s me according to your word.
Lk 22:32 have turned back, s your brothers."
Heb 12:12 hands and s your weak knees,

STRENGTHENS ➤ STRONG
Isa 40:29 to the faint, and s the powerless.
Php 4:13 do all things through him who s me.

STRETCH → OUTSTRETCHED, STRETCHED
Ex 14:16 and s out your hand over the sea
Mk 3: 5 to the man, "S out your hand."

STRETCHED → STRETCH
2Sa 24:16 angel s out his hand toward Jerusalem
Isa 5:25 and his hand is s out still.

STRIFE → STRIVE
Pr 23:29 Who has sorrow? Who has s?
Ro 1:29 Full of envy, murder, s, deceit,
Gal 5:20 enmities, s, jealousy, anger,

STRIKE
Ge 3:15 he will s your head, and you will s
Ex 17: 6 S the rock, and water will come out
Zec 13: 7 S the shepherd, that the sheep may
Mal 4: 6 come and s the land with a curse.
Mk 14:27 'I will s the shepherd, and the sheep
Rev 19:15 to s down the nations,

STRIVE → STRIFE
Mt 6:33 But s first for the kingdom of God
1Co 12:31 But s for the greater gifts.
2Pe 3:14 s to be found by him at peace,

STRONG → STRENGTH, STRENGTHEN, STRENGTHENS, STRONGHOLD
Dt 31: 6 Be s and bold; have no fear
Jos 1: 6 Be s and courageous; for you shall
Ps 140: 7 O LORD, my Lord, my s deliverer,
Pr 18:10 The name of the LORD is a s tower;
Ecc 9:11 nor the battle to the s, nor bread to
SS 8: 6 for love is s as death, passion fierce
Ro 15: 1 We who are s ought to put up with
1Co 1:27 in the world to shame the s;
2Co 12:10 whenever I am weak, then I am s.
Eph 6:10 be s in the Lord and in the strength

STRONGHOLD → STRONG
Ps 9: 9 The LORD is a s for the oppressed,
Na 1: 7 a s in a day of trouble;

STRUGGLE
Eph 6:12 our s is not against enemies of
Heb 12: 4 In your s against sin you have not yet

STUBBORN
Dt 9: 6 for you are a s people.
Hos 4:16 Like a s heifer, Israel is s;

STUDY
Ezr 7:10 Ezra had set his heart to s the law
Ecc 12:12 much s is a weariness of the flesh.

STUMBLE → STUMBLING
Ps 37:24 we s, we shall not fall headlong,
Pr 4:12 and if you run, you will not s.
Mt 18: 9 And if your eye causes you to s,
Ro 9:33 a stone that will make people s,
1Pe 2: 8 s because they disobey the word,

STUMBLING → STUMBLE
Eze 14: 3 placed their iniquity as a s block
Mt 16:23 You are a s block to me;
Ro 11: 9 a s block and a retribution for them;
1Co 8: 9 not somehow become a s block to

STUMP
Isa 6:13 The holy seed is its s.
11: 1 shall come out from the s of Jesse,

SUBDUE
Ge 1:28 and fill the earth and s it;
1Ch 17:10 and I will s all your enemies.

SUBJECT → SUBJECTED
Ro 13: 1 be s to the governing authorities;
Gal 4:21 who desire to be s to the law,
Eph 5:21 s to one another out of reverence

SUBJECTED → SUBJECT
Ro 8:20 for the creation was s to futility,
1Co 15:28 When all things are s to him,

SUBMISSION* → SUBMIT
1Ti 2:11 a woman learn in silence with full s.
Heb 5: 7 was heard because of his reverent s.

SUBMISSIVE → SUBMIT
1Ti 3: 4 keeping his children s and respectful
Tit 2: 5 kind, being s to their husbands,

SUBMIT → SUBMISSION, SUBMISSIVE
Ps 81:11 Israel would not s to me.
Gal 5: 1 do not s again to a yoke of slavery.
Heb 13:17 Obey your leaders and s to them,

SUCCEED → SUCCESS, SUCCESSFUL
Pr 15:22 but with many advisers they s.
Ecc 10:10 but wisdom helps one to s.

SUCCESS → SUCCEED
Ps 118:25 O LORD, we beseech you, give us s!
Sir 10: 5 Human s is in the hand of the Lord,

SUCCESSFUL → SUCCEED
Jos 1: 7 that you may be s wherever you go.

SUDDENLY
Mal 3: 1 Lord whom you seek will s come to
Mk 13:36 find you asleep when he comes s.

SUFFER → SUFFERED, SUFFERING, SUFFERINGS, SUFFERS
Lk 22:15 this Passover with you before I s;
24:46 the Messiah is to s and to rise from
Heb 9:26 then he would have had to s again
1Pe 3:17 For it is better to s for doing good,

SUFFERED → SUFFER
Php 3: 8 For his sake I have s the loss of all
1Pe 2:21 because Christ also s for you,

SUFFERING → SUFFER
Job 2:13 they saw that his s was very great.
Isa 53: 3 a man of s and acquainted with
Mk 8:31 Son of Man must undergo great s,
Ro 12:12 Rejoice in hope, be patient in s,

SUFFERINGS → SUFFER
Ro 8:18 the s of this present time are not
1Pe 4:13 insofar as you are sharing Christ's s,

SUFFERS → SUFFER
1Co 12:26 If one member s, all suffer together

SUFFICIENT
2Co 12: 9 "My grace is s for you,

SULFUR
Ge 19:24 rained on Sodom and Gomorrah s
Ps 11: 6 he will rain coals of fire and s;
Rev 21: 8 in the lake that burns with fire and s,

SUMMED*
Ro 13: 9 commandment, are s up in this word
Gal 5:14 the whole law is s up in a single

SUN
Jos 10:13 And the s stood still,
Ps 84:11 For the LORD God is a s and shield;
Ecc 1: 9 there is nothing new under the s.
Joel 2:31 The s shall be turned to darkness,
Mal 4: 2 the sof righteousness shall rise,
Mt 5:45 he makes his s rise on the evil and
Ac 2:20 The s shall be turned to darkness
Rev 1:16 his face was like the s shining with
19:17 I saw an angel standing in the s,
22: 5 they need no light of lamp or s,

SUPERIOR
Heb 1: 4 having become as much s to angels
7: 7 that the inferior is blessed by the s.

SUPPER
Lk 22:20 he did the same with the cup after s,
Rev 19: 9 to the marriage s of the Lamb."

SUPPLICATION → SUPPLICATIONS
Ps 6: 9 The LORD has heard my s;
Zec 12:10 a spirit of compassion and s
Eph 6:18 at all times in every prayer and s.

SUPPLICATIONS → SUPPLICATION
1Ti 2: 1 then, I urge that s, prayers,
Heb 5: 7 Jesus offered up prayers and s,

SUPPORT
Ps 18:18 but the LORD was my s.
Ro 11:18 that it is not you that s the root,

SURE
Nu 32:23 and be s your sin will find you out.
Ps 19: 7 the decrees of the LORD are s,
Isa 28:16 a s foundation: "One who trusts
Heb 6:19 a s and steadfast anchor of the soul,

SURPASSES → SURPASSING
Eph 3:19 the love of Christ that s knowledge,
Php 4: 7 the peace of God, which s all
Sir 25:11 Fear of the Lord s everything;

SURPASSING → SURPASSES
Ps 150: 2 according to his s greatness!
2Co 9:14 pray for you because of the s grace

SURPRISE → SURPRISED
1Th 5: 4 for that day to s you like a thief;

SURPRISED → SURPRISE
1Pe 4:12 do not be s at the fiery ordeal that is

SURROUNDED → SURROUNDS
Lk 21:20 you see Jerusalem s by armies,
Heb 12: 1 s by so great a cloud of witnesses,
Rev 20: 9 of the earth and s the camp of

SURROUNDS → SURROUNDED
Ps 89: 8 Your faithfulness s you.
125: 2 so the LORD s his people,

SURVIVORS
Isa 1: 9 of hosts had not left us a few s,
Eze 14:22 Yet, s shall be left in it,

SUSA
Ne 1: 1 while I was in S the capital,
Est 1: 2 his royal throne in the citadel of S,

SUSANNA
Righteous woman wrongly accused of immorality (Sus 1:1-44); vindicated by Daniel (Sus 1:45-64).

SUSTAINS
Ps 3: 5 for the LORD s me.
Heb 1: 3 he s all things by his powerful word.

SWALLOW → SWALLOWED
Jnh 1:17 provided a large fish to s up Jonah;
Mt 23:24 You strain out a gnat but s a camel!

SWALLOWED → SWALLOW
Ge 41: 7 The thin ears s up the seven plump
Nu 16:32 earth opened its mouth and s them
1Co 15:54 "Death has been s up in victory."

SWEAR → SWORE, SWORN
Dt 10:20 and by his name you shall s.
Ps 24: 4 and do not s deceitfully.
Mt 5:34 Do not s at all, either by heaven,

SWEAT
Ge 3:19 By the s of your face you shall eat
Lk 22:44 [[s became like great drops of blood]]

SWEET → SWEETER
Ex 15:25 the water, and the water became s.
Ps 119:103 How s are your words to my taste,
Eze 3: 3 in my mouth it was as s as honey.
Rev 10:10 it was s as honey in my mouth,

SWEETER → SWEET
Jdg 14:18 "What is s than honey?
Ps 19:10 s also than honey, and drippings of

SWIFT
Ecc 9:11 the race is not to the s, nor the battle
2Pe 2: 1 bringing s destruction on themselves

SWINE
Mt 7: 6 do not throw your pearls before s,
Mk 5:12 "Send us into the s;
1Mc 1:47 sacrifice s and other unclean animals,

SWORD → SWORDS
Ge 3:24 and a s flaming and turning to guard
1Sa 17:47 LORD does not save by s and spear;
1Ch 21:30 he was afraid of the s of the angel
Isa 2: 4 shall not lift up s against nation,
49: 2 He made my mouth like a sharp s,
Hos 2:18 and I will abolish the bow, the s,
Mt 10:34 not come to bring peace, but a s.
Eph 6:17 the s of the Spirit, which is the word
Heb 4:12 sharper than any two-edged s,
Rev 1:16 mouth came a sharp, two-edged s,
19:15 a sharp s with which to strike down
Sir 21: 3 All lawlessness is like a two-edged s

SWORDS → SWORD
Isa 2: 4 shall beat their s into plowshares,
Joel 3:10 Beat your plowshares into s,

SWORE → SWEAR
Ex 6: 8 the land that I s to give to Abraham,
32:13 how you s to them by your own self,
Ps 132:11 The LORD s to David a sure oath
Heb 6:13 by whom to swear, he s by himself,

SWORN → SWEAR
Ge 22:16 "By myself I have s, says the LORD:
Ps 110: 4 The LORD has s and will not change
Heb 7:21 "The Lord has s and will not change

SYMPATHIZE* → SYMPATHIZE
Heb 4:15 unable to s with our weaknesses,

SYMPATHY → SYMPATHIZE
Php 2: 1 any compassion and s,
1Pe 3: 8 all of you, have unity of spirit, s,

SYNAGOGUE → SYNAGOGUES
Lk 4:16 he went to the s on the sabbath day,
8:41 man named Jairus, a leader of the s.
Ac 18:26 He began to speak boldly in the s;

SYNAGOGUES → SYNAGOGUE
Mt 4:23 teaching in their s and proclaiming
Jn 18:20 always taught in s and in the temple,

T

TABERNACLE
Ex 25: 9 concerning the pattern of the t
40:34 the glory of the LORD filled the t.
1Ch 6:48 for all the service of the t of the house

TABITHA* → See DORCAS

TABLE → TABLES
Ex 25:23 You shall make a t of acacia wood,
Ps 23: 5 a t before me in the presence of my

TABLES → TABLE
Mk 11:15 overturned the t of the money changers

TABLET → TABLETS
Pr 3: 3 write them on the t of your heart.

TABLETS → TABLET
Ex 31:18 gave him the two t of the covenant,
2Co 3: 3 not on t of stone but on t of human hearts.

TAKE → TAKEN, TAKES
Dt 12:32 do not add to it or t anything from
Mt 11:29 T my yoke upon you, and learn
Mk 8:34 deny themselves and t up their cross

TAKEN → TAKE
Ecc 3:14 added to it, nor anything t from it;
Heb 11: 5 By faith Enoch was t so that he did
Sir 44:16 Enoch pleased the Lord and was t

TAKES → TAKE
Jn 1:29 t away the sin of the world!
10:18 No one t it from me,
Rev 22:19 if anyone t away from the words of

TALENT
Mt 25:25 and hid your t in the ground.

TAMAR
1. Wife of Judah's sons Er and Onan (Ge 38:1-10). Children by Judah (Ge 38:11-30; Mt 1:3).
2. Daughter of David, raped by Amnon (2Sa 13).

TASTE → TASTED
Ps 34: 8 O t and see that the LORD is good;
Mt 16:28 not t death before they see the Son
Col 2:21 not handle, Do not t, Do not touch"?

TASTED → TASTE
Heb 6: 4 and have t the heavenly gift,
1Pe 2: 3 you have t that the Lord is good.

TAUGHT → TEACH
Isa 40:14 Who t him knowledge,
Jn 6:45 'And they shall all be t by God.'

TAX → TAXES
Mt 11:19 a friend of t collectors and sinners!'
Lk 18:10 Pharisee and the other a t collector.

TAXES → TAX
Mt 22:17 Is it lawful to pay t to the emperor,
Ro 13: 7 t to whom t are due,

TEACH → TAUGHT, TEACHER, TEACHERS, TEACHING
Dt 6: 1 to t you to observe in the land that
Ps 90:12 So t us to count our days that we
Jer 31:34 No longer shall they t one another,
Jn 14:26 will t you everything,
Col 3:16 t and admonish one another in all
1Ti 2:12 I permit no woman to t or
1Jn 2:27 so you do not need anyone to t you.

TEACHER → TEACH
Ecc 1: 1 words of the T, the son of David,
Mt 10:24 "A disciple is not above the t,
Jn 1:38 "Rabbi" (which translated means T)
1Ti 3: 2 respectable, hospitable, an apt t,

TEACHERS → TEACH
Ps 119:99 more understanding than all my t,
1Co 12:28 second prophets, third t;
Eph 4:11 evangelists, some pastors and t,
Jas 3: 1 Not many of you should become t,

TEACHING → TEACH
Mk 1:27 A new t—with authority!
Tit 1:11 by t for sordid gain what it is not right
2Jn 1: 9 who does not abide in the t of Christ,

TEAR → TORN
Mk 2:21 from the old, and a worse t is made.
Rev 7:17 God will wipe away every t from

TEETH → TOOTH
Mt 8:12 will be weeping and gnashing of t."

TEKEL
Da 5:27 T, you have been weighed on the scales

TELL → FORETOLD
Ps 50:12 "If I were hungry, I would not t you,
105: 2 t of all his wonderful works.
1Co 15:51 Listen, I will t you a mystery!

TEMPERATE
1Ti 3: 2 married only once, t, sensible,
Tit 2: 2 Tell the older men to be t, serious,

TEMPLE
1Sa 3: 3 Samuel was lying down in the t of the
2Ch 2:12 who will build a t for the LORD,
Ps 11: 4 The LORD is in his holy t;
Mt 4: 5 placed him on the pinnacle of the t,
12: 6 something greater than the t is here.
Jn 2:21 was speaking of the t of his body.
1Co 3:16 you are God's t and that God's Spirit
Eph 2:21 and grows into a holy t in the Lord;
Rev 21:22 its t is the Lord God the Almighty and
1Mc 4:48 sanctuary and the interior of the t,

TEMPTATION* → TEMPTED, TEMPTER
1Ti 6: 9 who want to be rich into t and
Jas 1:12 Blessed is anyone who endures t.

TEMPTED → TEMPTATION
Mk 1:13 wilderness forty days, t by Satan;
Gal 6: 1 care that you yourselves are not t.

TEMPTER* → TEMPTATION
Mt 4: 3 The t came and said to him,
1Th 3: 5 that somehow the t had tempted you

TEN → TENTH
Ex 34:28 the covenant, the t commandments.
Da 7:24 out of this kingdom t kings shall arise,
Mt 25: 1 T bridesmaids took their lamps and
Rev 17:12 the t horns that you saw are t kings

TENDER → TENDERHEARTED
Hos 11: 8 my compassion grows warm and t.
Lk 1:78 By the t mercy of our God,

TENDERHEARTED* → HEART, TENDER
Eph 4:32 t, forgiving one another,

TENT
Ex 27:21 the t of meeting, outside the curtain
2Sa 7: 2 but the ark of God stays in a t."
2Co 5: 1 the earthly t we live in is destroyed,

TENTH → TEN
Ge 14:20 Abram gave him one t of everything
Isa 6:13 Even if a t part remain in it,

TERROR
Ex 23:27 I will send my t in front of you,
Ps 91: 5 You will not fear the t of the night,
Ro 13: 3 rulers are not a t to good conduct,

TEST → TESTED, TESTING
Dt 6:16 not put the LORD your God to the t,
Lk 4:12 not put the Lord your God to the t.'
10:25 then a lawyer stood up to t Jesus.
2Co 13: 5 indeed, you fail to meet the t!
1Jn 4: 1 t the spirits to see whether they are
Sir 37:27 My child, t yourself while you live;

TESTED → TEST
Ge 22: 1 After these things God t Abraham.
Ps 78:41 They t God again and again,
Heb 4:15 been t as we are, yet without sin.

TESTIFIED → TESTIFY
Jn 1:15 (John t to him and cried out,
1Pe 1:11 it t in advance to the sufferings

TESTIFIES → TESTIFY
1Jn 5: 6 Spirit is the one that t,

TESTIFY → TESTIFIED, TESTIFIES, TESTIMONY
Jn 15:26 he will t on my behalf.
1Jn 5: 7 There are three that t:

TESTIMONY → TESTIFY
Nu 35:30 put to death on the t of a single
Mk 14:59 on this point their t did not agree.
Rev 1: 9 the word of God and the t of Jesus.

TESTING → TEST
1Co 10:13 No t has overtaken you that is not
Jas 1: 3 t of your faith produces endurance;

THADDAEUS* → =JUDAS
Apostle (Mt 10:3; Mk 3:18); probably also known as Judas son of James (Lk 6:16; Ac 1:13).

THANK → THANKS, THANKSGIVING
2Ch 29:31 bring sacrifices and t offerings to
Ps 52: 9 I will t you forever,
Sir 35: 4 gives alms sacrifices a t offering.

THANKS → THANK
1Ch 16: 8 give t to the LORD, call on his name,
Ps 107: 1 O give t to the LORD, for he is good;
Ro 1:21 not honor him as God or give t to
1Co 11:24 and when he had given t,
2Co 9:15 T be to God for his indescribable
Rev 4: 9 give glory and honor and t to

THANKSGIVING → THANK
Lev 7:12 If you offer it for t,
Ps 50:14 Offer to God a sacrifice of t,
Php 4: 6 with t let your requests be made known
Rev 7:12 glory and wisdom and t and honor

THEFT → THIEF
Mt 15:19 fornication, t, false witness, slander.

THEFTS* → THIEF
Rev 9:21 or their fornication or their t.

THIEF → THEFT, THEFTS, THIEVES
Ex 22: 1 The t shall make restitution,
Jn 10:10 The t comes only to steal and kill
1Th 5: 2 day of the Lord will come like a t in
Rev 16:15 ("See, I am coming like a t!

THIEVES → THIEF
Mt 6:19 and where t break in and steal;
Eph 4:28 T must give up stealing;

THINK → THINKING, THOUGHT, THOUGHTS
Ro 12: 3 not to t of yourself more highly than
1Co 10:12 So if you t you are standing,

THINKING → THINK
Ro 1:21 but they became futile in their t,
1Co 14:20 infants in evil, but in t be adults.

THIRD → THREE
Hos 6: 2 on the t day he will raise us up,
Mt 26:44 and prayed for the t time,
Lk 18:33 and on the t day he will rise again."
2Co 12: 2 was caught up to the t heaven—

THIRST → THIRSTY
Mt 5: 6 who hunger and t for righteousness,
Rev 7:16 will hunger no more, and t no more;

THIRSTY → THIRST
Mt 25:35 I was t and you gave me something
Jn 6:35 believes in me will never be t.
Rev 22:17 And let everyone who is t come.

THOMAS*
Apostle (Mt 10:3; Mk 3:18; Lk 6:15; Jn 11:16; 14:5; 21:2; Ac 1:13). Doubted resurrection (Jn 20:24-28).

THORN ➛ THORNS
2Co 12: 7 a t was given me in the flesh,

THORNS ➛ THORN
Ge 3:18 t and thistles it shall bring forth for
Mt 13: 7 Other seeds fell among t,
Jn 19: 2 the soldiers wove a crown of t and

THOUGHT ➛ THINK
1Co 13:11 I spoke like a child, I t like a child,
2Co 10: 5 take every t captive to obey Christ.

THOUGHTS ➛ THINK
Isa 55: 8 For my t are not your t,
1Co 3:20 "The Lord knows the t of the wise,
Heb 4:12 judge the t and intentions of the heart.

THOUSAND ➛ THOUSANDS
Ps 50:10 the cattle on a t hills.
90: 4 t years in your sight are like yesterday
2Pe 3: 8 one day is like a t years, and a t years
Rev 20: 4 and reigned with Christ a t years.

THOUSANDS ➛ THOUSAND
1Sa 18: 7 has killed his t, and David his ten t."
Da 7:10 A thousand t served him,
Rev 5:11 myriads of myriads and t of t,

THREE ➛ THIRD
Ge 18: 2 and saw t men standing near him.
Ex 23:14 T times in the year you shall hold a
Mt 18:20 two or t are gathered in my name,
26:34 you will deny me t times."
Mk 8:31 be killed, and after t days rise again.
2Co 12: 8 T times I appealed to the Lord
1Jn 5: 7 There are t that testify:

THRONE ➛ THRONES
2Sa 7:13 the t of his kingdom forever.
Ps 45: 6 Your t, O God, endures forever
Isa 6: 1 I saw the Lord sitting on a t, high
Jer 33:21 not have a son to reign on his t,
Mt 19:28 the Son of Man is seated on the t
Heb 4:16 approach the t of grace with boldness,
12: 2 his seat at the right hand of the t
Rev 4:10 they cast their crowns before the t,
20:11 I saw a great white t and the one

THRONES ➛ THRONE
Da 7: 9 t were set in place,
Rev 4: 4 Around the throne are twenty-four t,

THROW ➛ THROWN
Ex 1:22 Hebrews you shall t into the Nile,
Mt 7: 6 do not t your pearls before swine,

THROWN ➛ THROW
Ex 15: 1 horse and rider he has t into the sea.
Da 3:21 t into the furnace of blazing fire.
6:12 shall be t into a den of lions?"
Rev 20:10 t into the lake of fire and sulfur,

THUMMIM
Ex 28:30 you shall put the Urim and the T,

THUNDER ➛ THUNDERS
Ex 9:23 and the LORD sent t and hail,
Rev 4: 5 and rumblings and peals of t,

THUNDERS ➛ THUNDER
Rev 10: 3 he shouted, the seven t sounded.

TIBNI*
King of Israel (1Ki 16:21-22).

TIE
Pr 6:21 t them around your neck.
Mt 23: 4 t up heavy burdens, hard to bear,

TIME ➛ TIMES
Est 4:14 dignity for just such a t as this."
Ecc 3: 1 a t for every matter under heaven:
Da 7:25 for a t, two times, and half a t.
Ro 5: 6 the right t Christ died for the ungodly.
2Co 6: 2 See, now is the acceptable t;
Gal 4: 4 when the fullness of t had come,
Col 4: 5 making the most of the t.
Rev 12:14 for a t, and times, and half a t.
22:10 of this book, for the t is near.

TIMES ➛ TIME
Jos 6: 4 march around the city seven t,
Mt 16: 3 cannot interpret the signs of the t.
18:22 seven t, but, I tell you, seventy-seven t.
Mk 14:30 you will deny me three t."
Sir 20:12 but pay for it seven t over.

TIMOTHY
Believer from Lystra (Ac 16:1). Joined Paul on second missionary journey (Ac 16-20). Sent to settle problems at Corinth (1Co 4:17; 16:10). Led church at Ephesus (1Ti 1:3). Co-writer with Paul (1Th 1:1; 2Th 1:1; Phm 1).

TITHE
Dt 12:17 the t of your grain, your wine, and
Mal 3:10 Bring the full t into the storehouse,

TITUS
Gentile co-worker of Paul (Gal 2:1-3; 2Ti 4:10); sent to Corinth (2Co 2:13; 7-8; 12:18), Crete (Tit 1:4-5).

TOBIAH
Enemy of Nehemiah (Ne 2:10-19; 4; 6; 13:4-9).

TOBIT
Tob 1: 1 This book tells the story of T

TODAY
Dt 30:15 set before you t life and prosperity,
Ps 2: 7 my son; t I have begotten you.
Lk 23:43 t you will be with me in Paradise."
Heb 1: 5 my Son; t I have begotten you"?
13: 8 Christ is the same yesterday and t and

TOGETHER
Mt 19: 6 God has joined t, let no one separate."
Eph 2: 5 made us alive t with Christ—

TOLA
A judge of Israel (Jdg 10:1-2).

TOMB
Mk 15:46 laid it in a t that had been hewn out
Lk 24: 2 the stone rolled away from the t,

TOMORROW
Isa 22:13 "Let us eat and drink, for t we die."
Mt 6:34 "So do not worry about t,
Jas 4:14 do not even know what t will bring.

TONGUE ➛ DOUBLE-TONGUED, TONGUES
Ex 4:10 I am slow of speech and slow of t."
Ps 139: 4 before a word is on my t, O LORD,
Pr 18:21 Death and life are in the power of the t,
Isa 45:23 shall bow, every t shall swear."
1Co 14:19 than ten thousand words in a t.
Php 2:11 every t should confess that Jesus Christ
Jas 3: 8 but no one can tame the t—
Sir 20:18 is better than a slip of the t;
23: 7 DISCIPLINE OF THE T

TONGUES ➛ TONGUE
Ac 2: 3 Divided t, as of fire, appeared
1Co 12:10 of t, to another the interpretation of t.
14: 5 in t, unless someone interprets,

TOOTH ➛ TEETH
Ex 21:24 t for t, hand for hand, foot for foot,
Mt 5:38 'An eye for an eye and a t for a t.'

TORCHES
Da 10: 6 lightning, his eyes like flaming t,
Rev 4: 5 of the throne burn seven flaming t,

TORMENTED
Rev 20:10 they will be t day and night forever

TORN ➛ TEAR
1Sa 28:17 has t the kingdom out of your hand,
Lk 23:45 curtain of the temple was t in two.

TORTURED
Mt 18:34 handed him over to be t until
Heb 11:35 were t, refusing to accept release,

TOUCH
Ge 3: 3 nor shall you t it, or you shall die.'"
Mt 9:21 only t his cloak, I will be made well.
Lk 24:39 T me and see;
Col 2:21 not handle, Do not taste, Do not t"?

TOWER
Ge 11: 4 and a t with its top in the heavens,
Pr 18:10 The name of the LORD is a strong t;

TRADITION
Mt 15: 2 disciples break the t of the elders?
Col 2: 8 empty deceit, according to human t,

TRAIN ➛ TRAINING
Pr 22: 6 T children in the right way, and
1Ti 4: 7 T yourself in godliness,

TRAINING ➛ TRAIN
1Ti 4: 8 while physical t is of some value,
2Ti 3:16 and for t in righteousness,

TRAITOR
Lk 6:16 and Judas Iscariot, who became a t.

TRANSFIGURED
Mt 17: 2 And he was t before them,

TRANSFORM* ➛ TRANSFORMED
Php 3:21 will t the body of our humiliation

TRANSFORMED ➛ TRANSFORM
Ro 12: 2 be t by the renewing of your minds,
2Co 3:18 are being t into the same image

TRANSGRESSION ➛ TRANSGRESSIONS, TRANSGRESSORS
Ex 23:21 for he will not pardon your t;
Da 9:24 to finish the t, to put an end to sin,
Gal 6: 1 if anyone is detected in a t,

TRANSGRESSIONS ➛ TRANSGRESSION
Ps 103:12 so far he removes our t from us.
Isa 53: 5 But he was wounded for our t,

TRANSGRESSORS ➛ TRANSGRESSION
Ps 51:13 Then I will teach t your ways,
Isa 53:12 and was numbered with the t;

TRAP
Lk 20:20 in order to t him by what he said,
Ro 11: 9 their table become a snare and a t,

TREAD ➛ TREADING
Mic 7:19 he will t our iniquities under foot.
Rev 19:15 he will t the wine press of the fury

TREADING ➛ TREAD
Dt 25: 4 not muzzle an ox while it is t out
1Co 9: 9 not muzzle an ox while it is t out

TREASURE ➛ TREASURED, TREASURES
Ps 119:11 I t your word in my heart,
Mt 6:21 where your t is, there your heart
2Co 4: 7 But we have this t in clay jars,
2Ti 1:14 Guard the good t entrusted to you,

TREASURED ➛ TREASURE
Ex 19: 5 be my t possession out of all the

TREASURES ➛ TREASURE
Col 2: 3 are hidden all the t of wisdom

TREE ➛ TREES
Ge 3:24 to guard the way to the t of life.
Dt 21:23 hung on a t is under God's curse.
Mt 12:33 for the t is known by its fruit.
Ac 5:30 had killed by hanging him on a t.
Ro 11:24 grafted back into their own olive t.
Rev 22: 2 the t of life with its twelve kinds

TREES ➛ TREE
Ps 96:12 all the t of the forest sing for joy
Zec 4:11 "What are these two olive t on the
Rev 11: 4 two olive t and the two lampstands

TREMBLE ➛ TREMBLED, TREMBLING
Ps 114: 7 T, O earth, at the presence of the LORD
Hab 3: 6 he looked and made the nations t.

TREMBLED ➛ TREMBLE
Ex 20:18 they were afraid and t and stood at

TREMBLING ➛ TREMBLE
Ps 2:11 Serve the LORD with fear, with t
Php 2:12 your own salvation with fear and t;

TRESPASS ➛ TRESPASSES
Ro 5:15 But the free gift is not like the t.

TRESPASSES ➛ TRESPASS
Mt 6:14 For if you forgive others their t,
2Co 5:19 not counting their t against them,

TRIAL ➛ TRIALS
Lk 11: 4 do not bring us to the time of t."
2Pe 2: 9 knows how to rescue the godly from t,
Rev 3:10 I will keep you from the hour of t

TRIALS ➛ TRIAL
Jas 1: 2 whenever you face t of any kind,
1Pe 1: 6 you have had to suffer various t,

TRIBE ➛ TRIBES
Nu 1: 4 A man from each t shall be with you

Ps 78:68 but he chose the t of Judah,
Rev 5: 5 See, the Lion of the t of Judah,

TRIBES ➛ TRIBE
Ge 49:28 All these are the twelve t of Israel,
Ex 24: 4 to the twelve t of Israel.
Mt 19:28 judging the twelve t of Israel.
Rev 21:12 inscribed the names of the twelve t

TRIUMPH ➛ TRIUMPHAL, TRIUMPHS
Ps 112: 8 they will look in t on their foes.
Pr 28:12 the righteous t, there is great glory,

TRIUMPHAL* ➛ TRIUMPH
2Co 2:14 Christ always leads us in t procession,

TRIUMPHS ➛ TRIUMPH
Jas 2:13 mercy t over judgment.

TROUBLE ➛ TROUBLED
Job 14: 1 few of days and full of t,
Ps 9: 9 a stronghold in times of t.
Pr 11: 8 The righteous are delivered from t,
Isa 33: 2 our salvation in the time of t.
Mt 6:34 Today's t is enough for today.
Sir 51:10 do not forsake me in the days of t,

TROUBLED ➛ TROUBLE
Jn 14: 1 "Do not let your hearts be t.

TRUE ➛ TRUTH
Ps 119:151 and all your commandments are t.
Jn 1: 9 The t light, which enlightens
21:24 and we know that his testimony is t.
Ro 3: 4 everyone is a liar, let God be proved t,
1Jn 5:20 He is the t God and eternal life.
Rev 3:14 the Amen, the faithful and t witness,
19:11 Its rider is called Faithful and T,
22: 6 "These words are trustworthy and t,

TRUMPET ➛ TRUMPETS
Ex 19:16 a blast of a t so loud that all the
Joel 2:15 Blow the t in Zion; sanctify a fast;
1Co 15:52 twinkling of an eye, at the last t.
1Th 4:16 and with the sound of God's t,

TRUMPETS ➛ TRUMPET
Nu 10: 2 Make two silver t; you shall make
Rev 8: 2 and seven t were given to them.

TRUST ➛ ENTRUST, ENTRUSTED, TRUSTED, TRUSTEES, TRUSTS, TRUSTWORTHY
Ps 9:10 know your name put their t in you,
37: 3 T in the LORD, and do good;
119:42 for I t in your word.
Pr 3: 5 T in the LORD with all your heart,
Isa 12: 2 Surely God is my salvation; I will t,
Jer 17: 7 Blessed are those who t in the LORD,
Heb 2:13 And again, "I will put my t in him."
Sir 2: 6 T in him, and he will help you;

TRUSTED ➛ TRUST
Ps 22: 4 they t, and you delivered them.
Da 3:28 delivered his servants who t in him.
6:23 because he had t in his God.
Sus 1:35 for her heart t in the Lord.

TRUSTS ➛ TRUST
Ps 86: 2 save your servant who t in you.
Mt 27:43 He t in God; let God deliver him

TRUSTWORTHY ➛ TRUST
Ps 111: 7 and just; all his precepts are t.
Rev 22: 6 "These words are t and true,
1Mc 14:41 until a t prophet should arise,

TRUTH ➛ TRUE
Ps 25: 5 Lead me in your t, and teach me,
119:142 and your law is the t.
Pr 23:23 Buy t, and do not sell it;
Jn 1:17 grace and t came through Jesus Christ.
4:23 worship the Father in spirit and t,
8:32 and the t will make you free."
14: 6 "I am the way, and the t, and the life.
14:17 This is the Spirit of t,
Eph 4:15 But speaking the t in love,
2Ti 2:15 rightly explaining the word of t.
Tob 3: 2 all your ways are mercy and t;

TUNIC
Lk 9: 3 nor money—not even an extra t.
Jn 19:23 t was seamless, woven in one piece

TURN ➛ TURNED
Ex 32:12 T from your fierce wrath;
Jos 1: 7 do not t from it to the right hand or
Isa 6:10 and t and be healed."
45:22 T to me and be saved,
Mal 4: 6 He will t the hearts of parents to their
Lk 1:17 t the hearts of parents to their children

TURNED ➛ TURN
Dt 23: 5 your God t the curse into a blessing
Isa 53: 6 we have all t to our own way,
Ro 3:12 All have t aside, together they have

TWELVE
Ge 49:28 All these are the t tribes of Israel,
Ex 24: 4 the mountain, and set up t pillars,
Jos 4: 3 'Take t stones from here out of the
Mt 10: 1 Jesus summoned his t disciples
Lk 9:17 t baskets of broken pieces.
Rev 21:12 inscribed the names of the t tribes
22: 2 tree of life with its t kinds of fruit,

TWINKLING*
1Co 15:52 in the t of an eye, at the last trumpet

TWO ➛ TWICE, TWO-EDGED
Ge 1:16 God made the t great lights—
6:19 bring t of every kind into the ark,
Ex 31:18 the t tablets of the covenant,
Dt 17: 6 of t or three witnesses the death
Mt 6:24 "No one can serve t masters;
19: 5 and the t shall become one flesh'?

TWO-EDGED ➛ TWO
Heb 4:12 sharper than any t sword,
Rev 1:16 his mouth came a sharp, t sword,

TYRE
1Ki 5: 1 King Hiram of T sent his servants to
Eze 28:12 a lamentation over the king of T,
Mt 11:22 be more tolerable for T and Sidon

U

UNBELIEF ➛ UNBELIEVER, UNBELIEVERS
Mk 6: 6 And he was amazed at their u.
9:24 cried out, "I believe; help my u!"
Ro 11:20 were broken off because of their u,
1Ti 1:13 because I had acted ignorantly in u,

UNBELIEVER ➛ UNBELIEF
1Co 10:27 If an u invites you to a meal and
2Co 6:15 does a believer share with an u?

UNBELIEVERS ➛ UNBELIEF
2Co 6:14 Do not be mismatched with u.
2Es 15: 4 For all u shall die in their unbelief.

UNCHASTITY*
Mt 5:32 except on the ground of u,
19: 9 divorces his wife, except for u,

UNCIRCUMCISED ➛ UNCIRCUMCISION
Ex 12:48 But no u person shall eat of it;
Ac 7:51 people, u in heart and ears,
Ro 4:11 he had by faith while he was still u.
Col 3:11 circumcised and u, barbarian,
1Mc 1:48 and to leave their sons u.

UNCIRCUMCISION ➛ UNCIRCUMCISED
1Co 7:19 Circumcision is nothing, and u is
Gal 5: 6 neither circumcision nor u counts

UNCLEAN ➛ UNCLEANNESS
Lev 5: 2 when any of you touch any u thing
Isa 52:11 Touch no u thing;
Mk 3:11 Whenever the u spirits saw him,
Rev 21:27 But nothing u will enter it,

UNDER
Ps 8: 6 you have put all things u their feet,
Ac 4:12 for there is no other name u heaven
Ro 6:14 since you are not u law but u grace.
Eph 1:22 And he has put all things u his feet

UNDERSTAND ➛ UNDERSTANDING
Job 42: 3 I have uttered what I did not u,
Pr 2: 5 then you will u the fear of the LORD
Hos 14: 9 Those who are wise u these things;
Mt 13:15 and u with their heart and turn—
Lk 24:45 opened their minds to u the scriptures,
Ac 8:30 "Do you u what you are reading?"
Eph 5:17 but u what the will of the Lord is.

UNDERSTANDING ➛ UNDERSTAND
Ex 36: 1 has given skill and u to know how
Pr 2: 6 from his mouth come knowledge and u
Isa 40:14 and showed him the way of u?
Lk 2:47 heard him were amazed at his u
Php 4: 7 peace of God, which surpasses all u,
2Ti 2: 7 Lord will give you u in all things.

UNEXPECTED
Mt 24:44 Son of Man is coming at an u hour.

UNFAITHFUL ➛ UNFAITHFULNESS
Ro 3: 3 What if some were u?

UNFAITHFULNESS ➛ UNFAITHFUL
1Ch 9: 1 exile in Babylon because of their u.

UNGODLY
Ro 5: 6 the right time Christ died for the u.
2Pe 2: 6 example of what is coming to the u;
Sir 12: 5 but do not give to the u;

UNINTENTIONALLY
Lev 4: 2 When anyone sins u in any of
Nu 15:22 if you u fail to observe all these

UNITY
Ps 133: 1 when kindred live together in u!
Eph 4: 3 to maintain the u of the Spirit in the

UNJUST
Ro 3: 5 That God is u to inflict wrath on us?
Heb 6:10 For God is not u; he will

UNLEAVENED
Ex 12:17 shall observe the festival of u bread,
Mt 26:17 first day of U Bread the disciples

UNPRODUCTIVE*
1Co 14:14 my spirit prays but my mind is u.
Tit 3:14 so that they may not be u.

UNRIGHTEOUS ➛ UNRIGHTEOUSNESS
Mt 5:45 rain on the righteous and on the u.
2Pe 2: 9 u under punishment until the day

UNRIGHTEOUSNESS ➛ UNRIGHTEOUS
Ps 92:15 and there is no u in him.
1Jn 1: 9 and cleanse us from all u.

UPHOLD
Isa 42: 1 my servant, whom I u, my chosen,
Ro 3:31 On the contrary, we u the law.

UPRIGHT
Job 1: 1 That man was blameless and u,
Ps 7:10 God is my shield, who saves the u
Tit 1: 8 a lover of goodness, prudent, u,

UR
Ge 15: 7 LORD who brought you from U of

URIAH
Hittite husband of Bathsheba, killed (2Sa 11).

URIM
Ex 28:30 of judgment you shall put the U

USE ➛ USEFUL
Ex 20: 7 not make wrongful u of the name of
Gal 5:13 only do not u your freedom as an
2Ti 2:20 for special u, some for ordinary.

USEFUL ➛ USE
Eph 4:29 but only what is u for building up,
2Ti 3:16 scripture is inspired by God and is u

UZZIAH ➛ =AZARIAH
Son of Amaziah; king of Judah also known as Azariah (2Ki 15:1-7; 1Ch 6:24; 2Ch 26). Struck with leprosy because of pride (2Ch 26:16-23).

V

VAIN ➛ VANITY
Lev 26:16 You shall sow your seed in v,
Ps 2: 1 and the peoples plot in v?
Mt 15: 9 in v do they worship me,
Php 2:16 that I did not run in v or labor in v.

VALLEY
Ps 23: 4 through the darkest v, I fear no evil;
Isa 40: 4 Every v shall be lifted up,
Joel 3:14 multitudes, in the v of decision!
Lk 3: 5 Every v shall be filled, and every

VALUE
Mt 13:46 on finding one pearl of great v,
Ro 3: 1 Or what is the v of circumcision?
1Ti 4: 8 while physical training is of some v,

VANITY ➛ VAIN
Ecc 1: 2 v of vanities! All is v.
12: 8 V of vanities, says the Teacher; all is v.

VASHTI
Persian queen replaced by Esther (Est 1-2; AdE 1-2).

VEIL
Ex 34:33 he put a v on his face;
2Co 3:15 a v lies over their minds;

VENGEANCE ➛ AVENGE, AVENGER, AVENGING
Ps 94: 1 O LORD, you God of v,
Isa 34: 8 For the LORD has a day of v,
Na 1: 2 the LORD takes v on his adversaries

VICTORY
Pr 21:31 but the v belongs to the LORD.
1Co 15:54 Death has been swallowed up in v."
1Jn 5: 4 the v that conquers the world, our faith.

VINDICATE ➛ VINDICATED
Ps 26: 1 V me, O LORD, for I have walked
135:14 For the LORD will v his people,

VINDICATED ➛ VINDICATE
Job 13:18 I know that I shall be v.
Mt 11:19 Yet wisdom is v by her deeds."
1Ti 3:16 He was revealed in flesh, v in spirit,

VINE ➛ VINEYARD
Ps 80: 8 You brought a v out of Egypt;
Jer 2:21 Yet I planted you as a choice v,
Jn 15: 1 "I am the true v, and my Father is
Rev 14:18 gather the clusters of the v of the

VINEYARD ➛ VINE
1Ki 21: 1 Naboth the Jezreelite had a v in
Isa 5: 1 had a v on a very fertile hill.
Mt 21:33 a landowner who planted a v,

VIOLENCE ➛ VIOLENT
Ge 6:11 and the earth was filled with v.
Isa 53: 9 although he had done no v,
Hab 2:17 because of human bloodshed and v

VIOLENT ➛ VIOLENCE
1Ti 3: 3 not v but gentle, not quarrelsome,
Tit 1: 7 or addicted to wine or v or greedy

VIPERS
Mt 23:33 You snakes, you brood of v!
Ro 3:13 venom of v is under their lips."

VIRGIN
Jer 31:21 Return, O v Israel, return to these
Mt 1:23 the v shall conceive and bear a son,
Lk 1:34 "How can this be, since I am a v?"
2Co 11: 2 present you as a chaste v to Christ.

VISION ➛ VISIONS
Isa 22: 1 oracle concerning the valley of v.
Da 8:26 As for you, seal up the v,
Ac 26:19 not disobedient to the heavenly v,

VISIONS ➛ VISION
Nu 12: 6 make myself known to them in v;
Eze 1: 1 were opened, and I saw v of God.
Da 1:17 Daniel also had insight into all v
Joel 2:28 and your young men shall see v.
Ac 2:17 and your young men shall see v,

VOICE
Isa 40: 3 A v cries out: "In the wilderness
Jn 1:23 v of one crying out in the wilderness
10: 3 and the sheep hear his v.
Heb 3: 7 says, "Today, if you hear his v,
Rev 3:20 if you hear my v and open the door,

VOID
Ge 1: 2 the earth was a formless v
Mt 15: 6 you make v the word of God.

VOW ➛ VOWS
Ecc 5: 4 Fulfill what you v.
Sir 18:23 Before making a v, prepare yourself

VOWS ➛ VOW
Ps 22:25 my v I will pay before those who fear

W

WAGES
Ro 6:23 For the w of sin is death,

WAIT ➛ WAITS
Ps 27:14 W for the LORD; be strong,
La 3:26 should w quietly for the salvation of
Hab 2: 3 If it seems to tarry, w for it;
Ro 8:23 while we w for adoption,
1Th 1:10 to w for his Son from heaven,
Sir 2: 7 fear the Lord, w for his mercy;

WAITS ➛ WAIT
Ps 130: 6 my soul w for the Lord more than
Ro 8:19 the creation w with eager longing

WALK ➛ WALKED
Ge 17: 1 w before me, and be blameless.
Dt 10:12 to w in all his ways, to love him,
Ps 23: 4 I w through the darkest valley, I fear no
Isa 2: 5 let us w in the light of the LORD!
40:31 they shall w and not faint.
Jer 6:16 w in it, and find rest for your souls.
Jn 8:12 follows me will never w in darkness
2Co 5: 7 for we w by faith, not by sight.
Rev 21:24 The nations will w by its light,

WALKED ➛ WALK
Ge 5:24 Enoch w with God; then he was no

WALL
Jos 6:20 shout, and the w fell down flat;
Ne 2:17 let us rebuild the w of Jerusalem,
Zec 2: 5 I will be a w of fire all around it,
Eph 2:14 has broken down the dividing w,

WANT ➛ WANTING
Ps 23: 1 LORD is my shepherd, I shall not w.
Php 3:10 I w to know Christ and the power

WANTING ➛ WANT
2Pe 3: 9 not w any to perish, but all to come to

WAR ➛ WARRIOR, WARS
Ecc 3: 8 a time for w, and a time for peace.
Da 9:26 and to the end there shall be w.
Ro 7:23 in my members another law at w
Rev 19:11 righteousness he judges and makes w.

WARRIOR ➛ WAR
Ex 15: 3 LORD is a w; the LORD is his name.

WARS ➛ WAR
Mt 24: 6 you will hear of w and rumors of w;

WASH ➛ WASHED
Ps 51: 7 w me, and I shall be whiter than snow.
Jn 13: 5 and began to w the disciples' feet
Rev 22:14 Blessed are those who w their robes,

WASHED ➛ WASH
1Co 6:11 you were w, you were sanctified,
2Pe 2:22 sow is w only to wallow in the mud.

WATCH ➛ WATCHES
Lk 2: 8 keeping w over their flock by night.
Heb 13:17 they are keeping w over your souls

WATCHES ➛ WATCH
Ps 1: 6 LORD w over the way of the righteous,
Wis 3: 9 and he w over his elect.

WATER ➛ WATERS
Ex 17: 1 no w for the people to drink.
Nu 20: 2 there was no w for the congregation;
Jer 2:13 the fountain of living w,
Eze 36:25 I will sprinkle clean w upon you,
Mk 1: 8 I have baptized you with w;
Jn 2: 9 tasted the w that had become wine,
3: 5 without being born of w and Spirit.
4:10 he would have given you living w."
1Jn 5: 6 the one who came by w and blood,
Rev 22: 1 showed me the river of the w of life,

WATERS ➛ WATER
Ge 7: 7 the ark to escape the w of the flood.
Ex 14:21 dry land; and the w were divided.
Ecc 11: 1 Send out your bread upon the w,
Isa 55: 1 who thirsts, come to the w;

WAVERING
Heb 10:23 confession of our hope without w,
Jude 1:22 have mercy on some who are w;

WAY ➛ WAYS
Ps 1: 6 watches over the w of the righteous,
86:11 Teach me your w, O LORD,
Pr 12:15 Fools think their own w is right,
22: 6 Train children in the right w,
Isa 40: 3 wilderness prepare the w of the LORD,
Mal 3: 1 sending my messenger to prepare the w
Mt 3: 3 'Prepare the w of the Lord,
Jn 14: 6 "I am the w, and the truth, and the life.
Ac 9: 2 found any who belonged to the W,
1Co 12:31 show you a still more excellent w.
Heb 10:20 the new and living w that he opened

WAYS ➛ WAY
Dt 10:12 to walk in all his w, to love him,
Hos 14: 9 For the w of the LORD are right,
Rev 15: 3 Just and true are your w, King of
Sir 2:15 who love him keep his w.

WEAK ➛ WEAKNESS, WEAKNESSES
Mt 26:41 indeed is willing, but the flesh is w."
Ro 14: 1 Welcome those who are w in faith,
1Co 1:27 God chose what is w in the world
2Co 12:10 whenever I am w, then I am strong.

WEAKNESS ➛ WEAK
Ro 8:26 the Spirit helps us in our w;
1Co 15:43 It is sown in w, it is raised in power.

WEAKNESSES ➛ WEAK
2Co 12:10 I am content with w, insults,
Heb 4:15 to sympathize with our w,

WEALTH
Ps 49: 6 those who trust in their w and boast
Pr 19: 4 W brings many friends,
Mt 13:22 and the lure of w choke
Rev 5:12 receive power and w and wisdom
Sir 5: 1 Do not rely on your w,

WEAPONS
Ecc 9:18 Wisdom is better than w of war,
2Co 6: 7 the w of righteousness for the right

WEAR
Isa 51: 6 the earth will w out like a garment,
Mt 6:31 or 'What will we w?'

WEARY
Isa 40:31 they shall run and not be w,
Heb 12: 3 you may not grow w or lose heart.

WEDDING
Jn 2: 1 there was a w in Cana of Galilee,

WEEKS
Ex 34:22 You shall observe the festival of w,
Lev 23:15 you shall count off seven w;
Da 9:24 "Seventy w are decreed for your

WEEP ➛ WEEPING
Ecc 3: 4 a time to w, and a time to laugh;
Ro 12:15 w with those who w.

WEEPING ➛ WEEP
Ps 30: 5 W may linger for the night,
Mt 2:18 Rachel w for her children;
8:12 will be w and gnashing of teeth."

WEIGHED
1Sa 2: 3 and by him actions are w.
Da 5:27 you have been w on the scales

WELL
Dt 6: 3 so that it may go w with you,
Mt 3:17 with whom I am w pleased."
17: 5 I am w pleased; listen to him!"
2Pe 1:17 with whom I am w pleased."

WEST
Ps 103:12 as far as the east is from the w,
Isa 43: 5 and from the w I will gather you;

WHEAT
Mt 13:25 and sowed weeds among the w,
Lk 22:31 demanded to sift all of you like w,
Jn 12:24 grain of w falls into the earth and dies,

WHIRLWIND ➛ WIND
2Ki 2:11 Elijah ascended in a w into heaven.
Na 1: 3 His way is in w and storm,

WHITE ➛ WHITER
Da 7: 9 his clothing was w as snow,
Mt 5:36 cannot make one hair w or black.
Rev 1:14 his hair were w as w wool, w as snow;
20:11 a great w throne and the one who sat

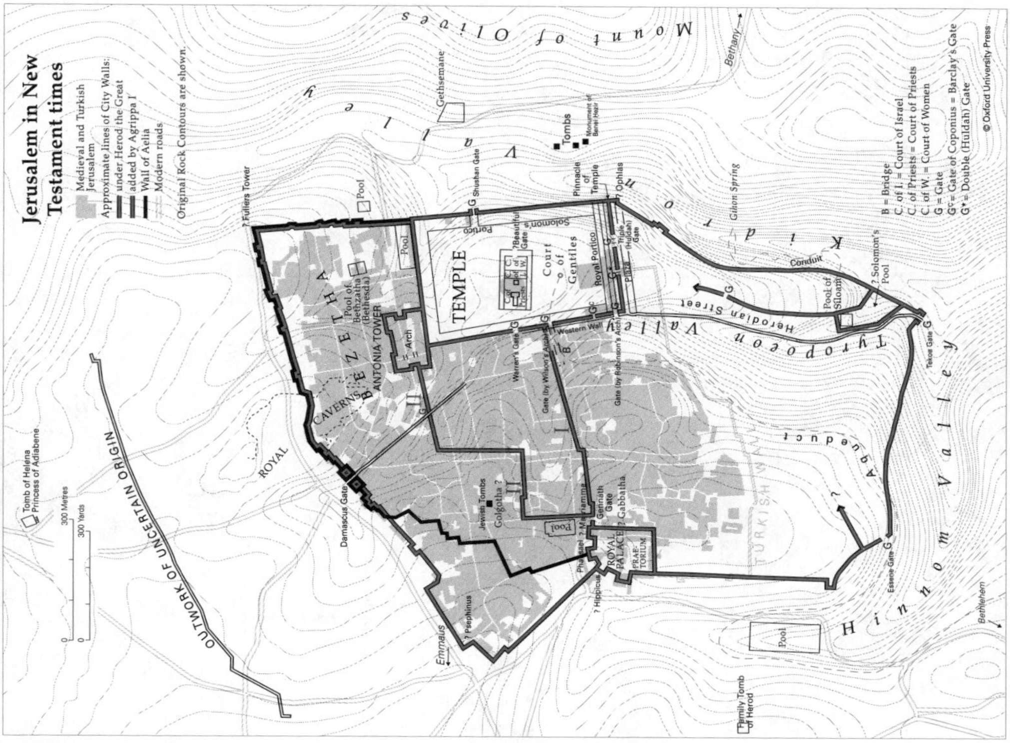

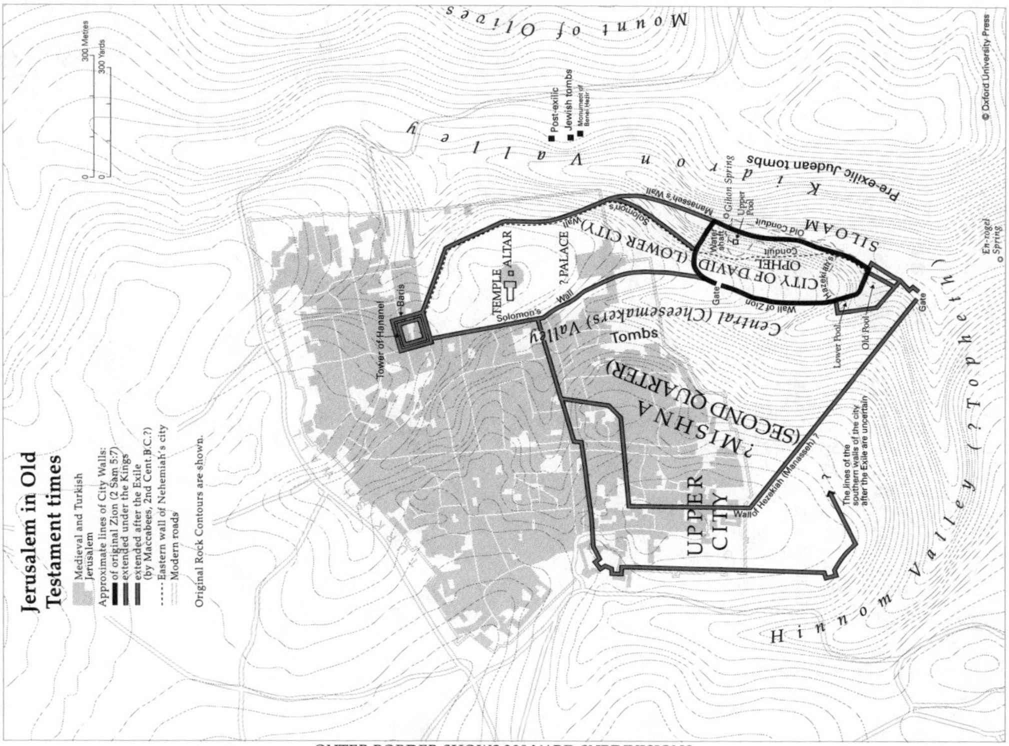

OUTER BORDER SHOWS 200 YARD SUBDIVISIONS

Prepared by Oxford Cartographers
and based on the Oxford Bible Atlas

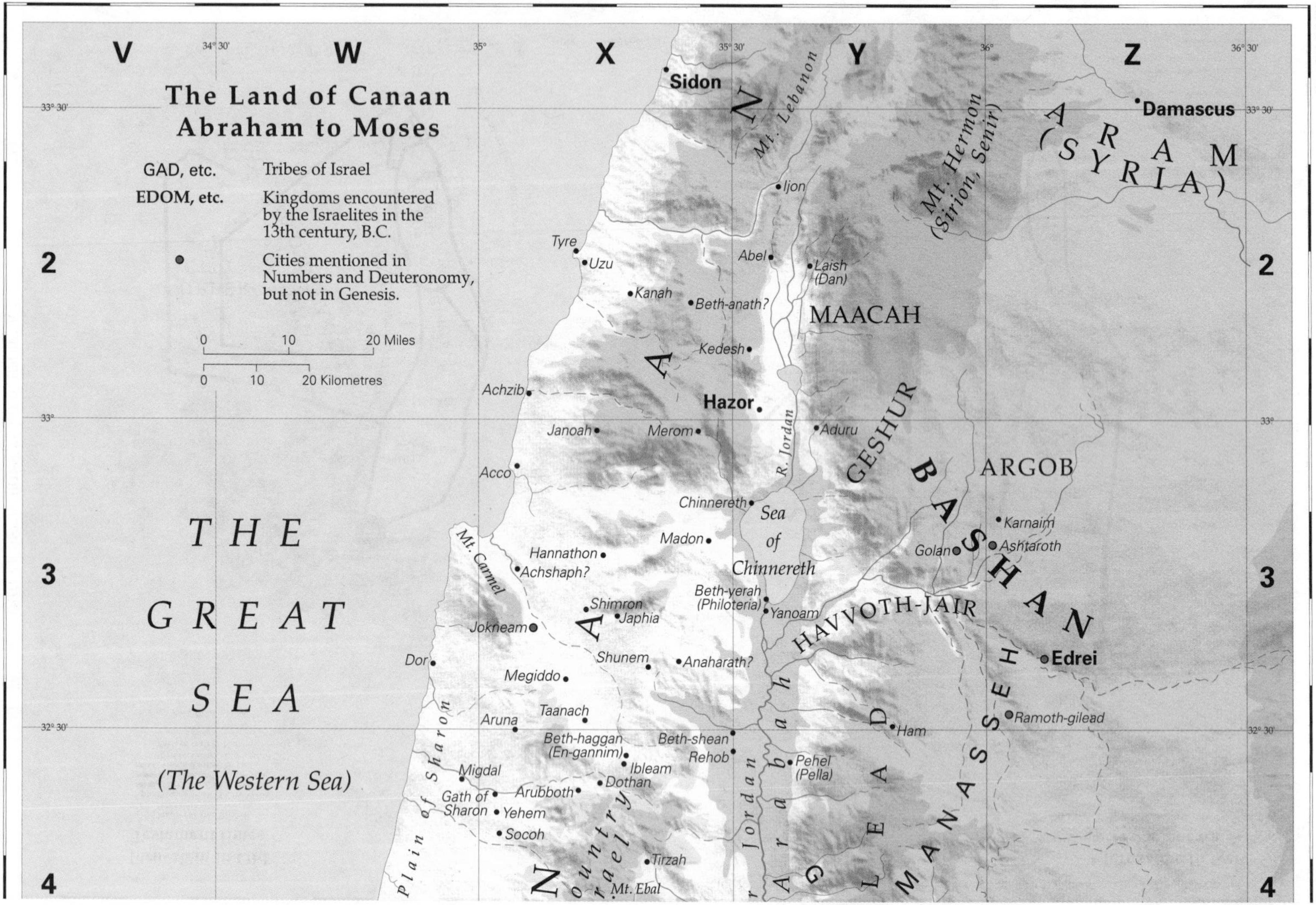

The Land of Canaan
Abraham to Moses
GAD, etc. Tribes of Israel
EDOM, etc. Kingdoms encountered by the Israelites in the 13th century, B.C.
Cities mentioned in Numbers and Deuteronomy, but not in Genesis.
0 10 20 Miles
0 10 20 Kilometres
V
W
X
Y
Z
2
3
4
THE GREAT SEA
(The Western Sea)
Sidon
Damascus
ARAM (SYRIA)
Mt. Lebanon
Mt. Hermon (Sirion, Senir)
Ijon
Tyre
Uzu
Abel
Laish (Dan)
Kanah
Beth-anath?
MAACAH
Kedesh
Achzib
Hazor
Janoah
Merom
Aduru
GESHUR
R. Jordan
ARGOB
Acco
BASHAN
Chinnereth
Sea of Chinnereth
Karnaim
Madon
Hannathon
Golan
Ashtaroth
Achshaph?
Mt. Carmel
Beth-yerah (Philoteria)
Yanoam
Shimron
Japhia
HAVVOTH-JAIR
Jokneam
Dor
Shunem
Anaharath?
Edrei
Megiddo
Taanach
Aruna
Ramoth-gilead
Ham
Beth-haggan (En-gannim)
Beth-shean
Rehob
Ibleam
Pehel (Pella)
Migdal
Dothan
Gath of Sharon
Arubboth
Yehem
Socoh
Tirzah
Mt. Ebal
Plain of Sharon
CANAAN
Hill Country of Israel
Jordan
Arabah
GILEAD
MANASSEH

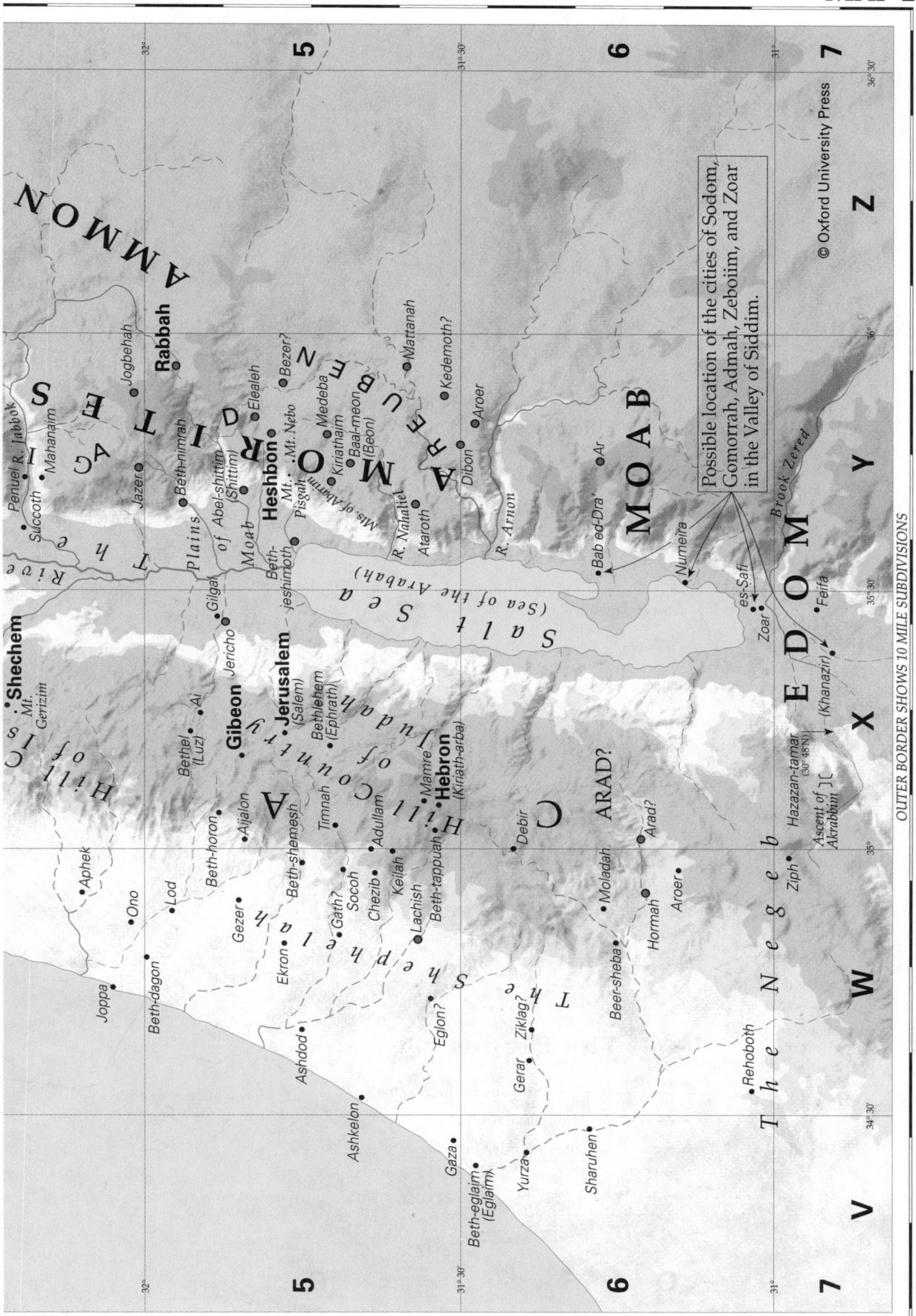
AMMON
Rabbah
Jogbehah
GADITES
Penuel
R. Jabbok
Mahanaim
Succoth
Jazer
Beth-nimrah
Abel-shittim
(Shittim)
Plains of Moab
The River
AMORITES
REUBEN
Heshbon
Elealeh
Bezer?
Medeba
Mt. Nebo
Baal-meon
(Beon)
Kiriathaim
Mts. of Abarim
Pisgah
Mattanah
Kedemoth?
Aroer
Dibon
Ataroth
R. Nahaliel
R. Arnon
Ar
Bab ed-Dra'
MOAB
Numeira
Possible location of the cities of Sodom, Gomorrah, Admah, Zeboiim, and Zoar in the Valley of Siddim.
Brook Zered
es-Safi
Zoar
Feifa
EDOM
(Khanazir)
© Oxford University Press
Beth-jeshimoth
Salt Sea
(Sea of the Arabah)
Shechem
Mt. Gerizim
Hill Country of Judah
Hill of Is...
Jericho
Gilgal
Ai
Bethel
(Luz)
Gibeon
Jerusalem
(Salem)
Bethlehem
(Ephrath)
Mamre
Hebron
(Kiriath-arba)
Timnah
Adullam
Keilah
Beth-tappuah
Debir
ARAD?
Arad?
Hazazan-tamar
(30° 48'N)
Ascent of Akrabbim
Aphek
Ono
Lod
Beth-horon
Aijalon
Gezer
Beth-shemesh
Socoh
Chezib
Lachish
Gath?
Ekron
The Shephelah
Moladah
Hormah
Aroer
Ziph
The Negeb
Joppa
Beth-dagon
Ashdod
Eglon?
Ziklag?
Beer-sheba
Gerar
Rehoboth
Ashkelon
Gaza
Beth-eglaim
(Eglaim)
Yurza
Sharuhen
V
W
X
Y
Z
5
6
7
32°
31° 30'
31°
34° 30'
35°
35° 30'
36°
36° 30'
OUTER BORDER SHOWS 10 MILE SUBDIVISIONS

MAP 3

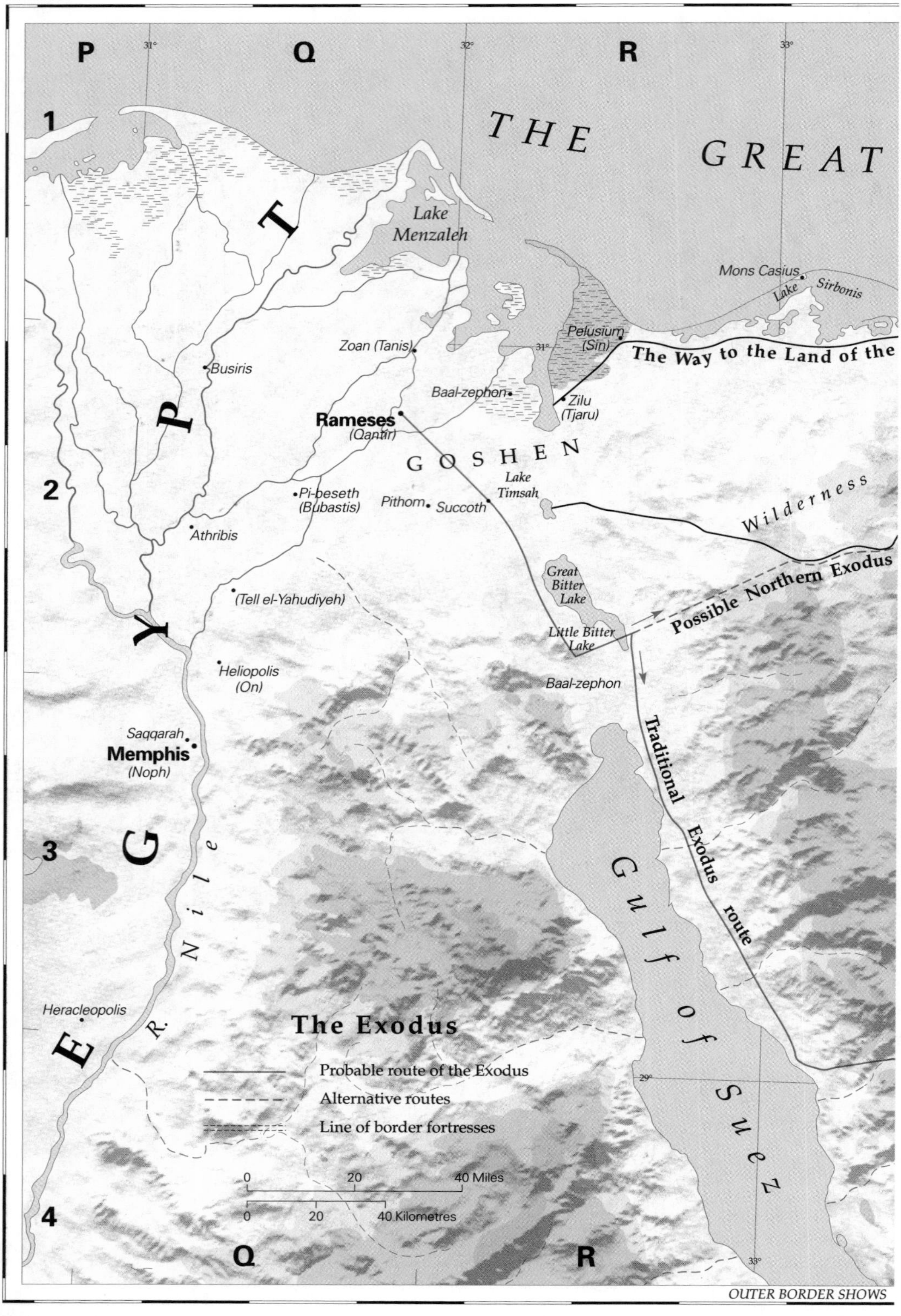

OUTER BORDER SHOWS

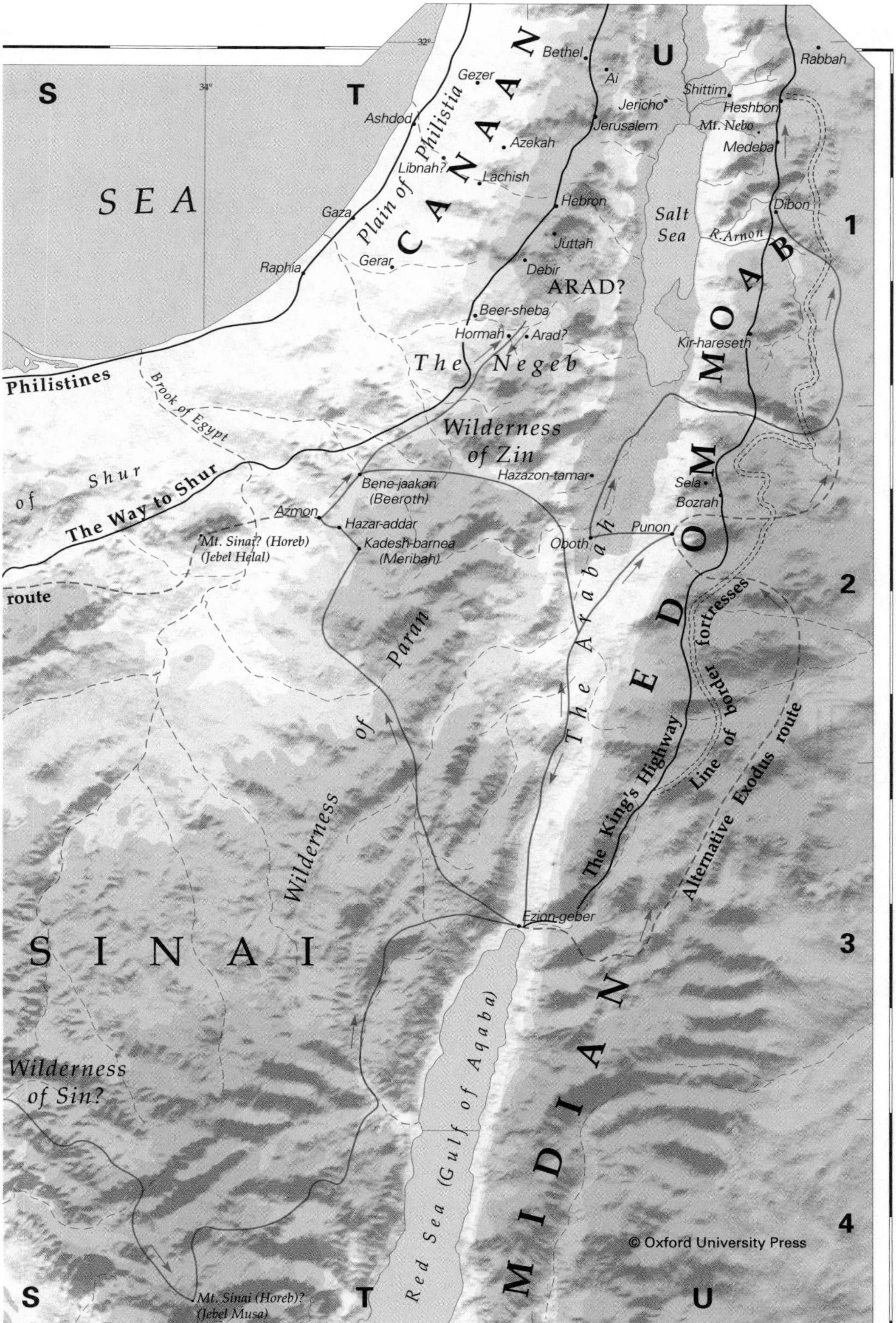

20 MILE SUBDIVISIONS

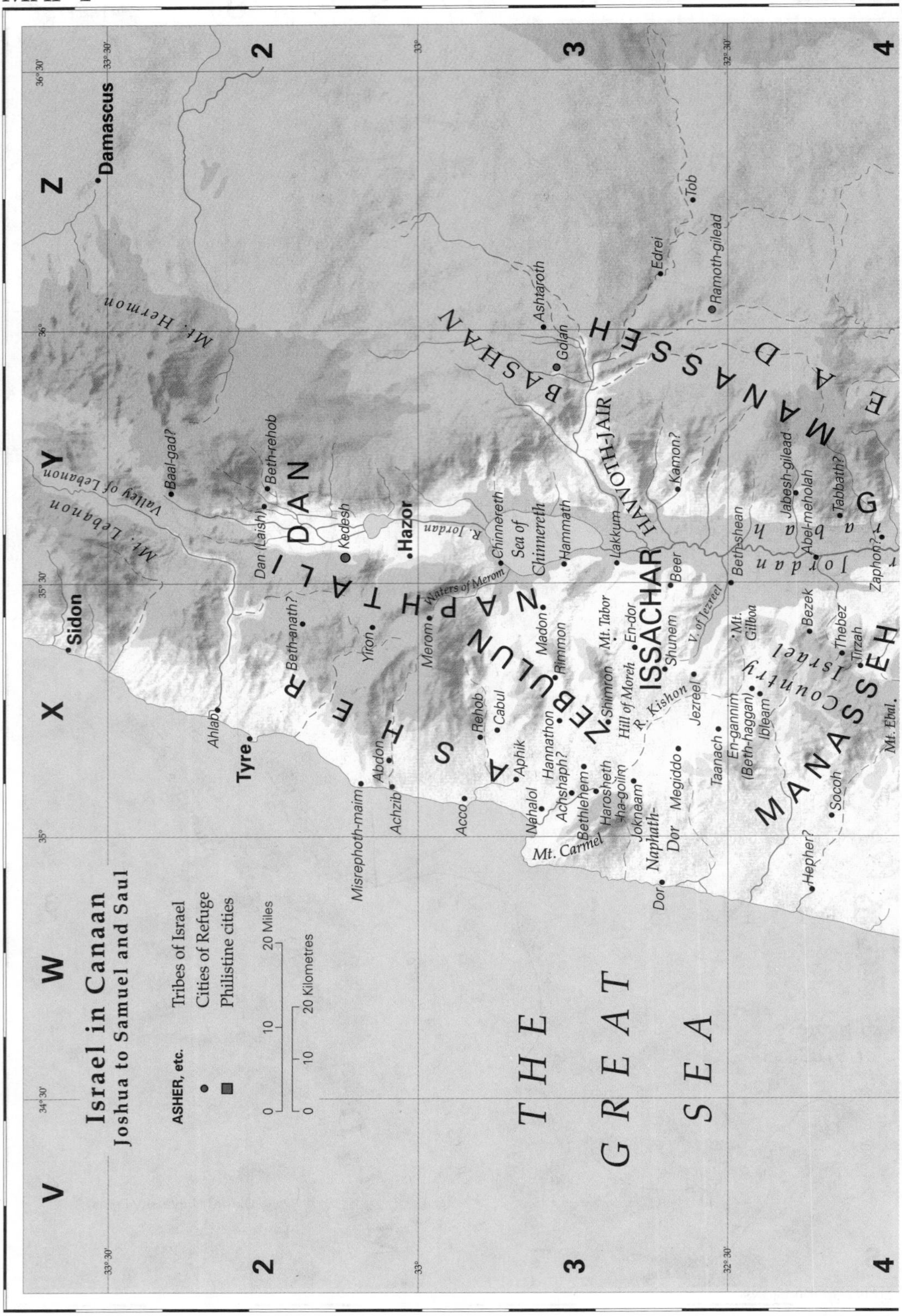
Israel in Canaan
Joshua to Samuel and Saul
ASHER, etc. Tribes of Israel
Cities of Refuge
Philistine cities
0 10 20 Miles
0 10 20 Kilometres
V
W
X
Y
Z
2
3
4
34° 30'
35°
35° 30'
36°
36° 30'
33° 30'
33°
32° 30'
THE GREAT SEA
Damascus
Mt. Hermon
Valley of Lebanon
Mt. Lebanon
Baal-gad?
Beth-rehob
Sidon
Ahlab
Tyre
Misrephoth-maim
Achzib
Abdon
Acco
Aphik
Rehob
Cabul
Beth-anath?
Yiron
Merom
Waters of Merom
Dan (Laish)
Kedesh
Hazor
R. Jordan
Chinnereth
Sea of Chinnereth
Hammath
Lakkum
DAN
NAPHTALI
ASHER
ZEBULUN
ISSACHAR
Madon
Rimmon
Hannathon
Shimron
Mt. Tabor
En-dor
Hill of Moreh
Shunem
R. Kishon
Jezreel
V. of Jezreel
Achshaph?
Bethlehem
Nahalol
Harosheth ha-goiim
Jokneam
Megiddo
Taanach
Naphath-Dor
Dor
Mt. Carmel
En-gannim (Beth-haggan)
Ibleam
Mt. Gilboa
Beth-shean
Beer
Bezek
Thebez
Tirzah
Israel
Country
Mt. Ebal
Socoh
Hepher?
MANASSEH
Jordan
Zaphon?
Abel-meholah
Jabesh-gilead
Tabbath?
Kamon?
HAVVOTH-JAIR
BASHAN
Golan
Ashtaroth
Edrei
Tob
Ramoth-gilead
GAD
MANASSEH

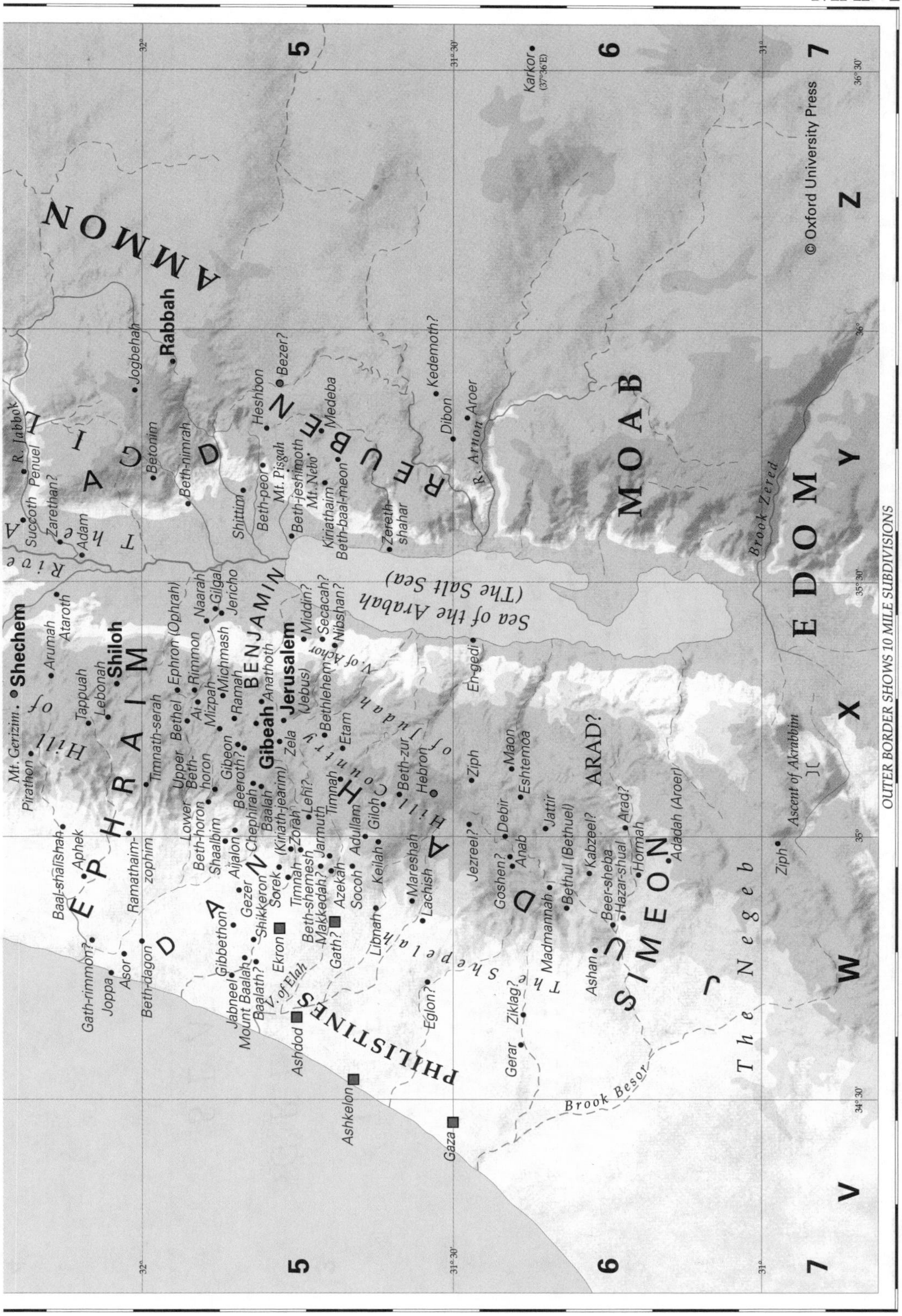
AMMON
MOAB
EDOM
REUBEN
GAD
The Hill Country of Judah
The Shephelah
The Negeb
PHILISTINES
DAN
EPHRAIM
Hill of Ephraim
BENJAMIN
JUDAH
SIMEON
ARAD?
River Jordan
Sea of the Arabah
(The Salt Sea)
R. Jabbok
R. Arnon
Brook Zered
Brook Besor
V. of Elah
V. of Achor
Ascent of Akrabbim
Rabbah
Jogbehah
Shechem
Shiloh
Jerusalem
(Jebus)
Gibeah
Mt. Gerizim
Karkor
(37°36'E)
Heshbon
Bezer?
Medeba
Dibon
Aroer
Kedemoth?
Mt. Pisgah
Mt. Nebo
Beth-jeshimoth
Beth-peor
Shittim
Beth-nimrah
Betonim
Penuel
Succoth
Zarethan?
Adam
Kiriathaim
Beth-baal-meon
Zereth-shahar
Ataroth
Arumah
Tappuah
Lebonah
Pirathon
Timnath-serah
Bethel
Ephron (Ophrah)
Ai
Rimmon
Naarah
Gilgal
Jericho
Michmash
Mizpah
Ramah
Anathoth
Gibeon
Beeroth?
Upper Beth-horon
Lower Beth-horon
Zela
Bethlehem
Etam
Middin?
Secacah?
Nibshan?
En-gedi
Baal-shalishah
Aphek
Ramathaim-zophim
Gath-rimmon?
Joppa
Asor
Beth-dagon
Shaalbim
Aijalon
Chephirah
Baalah
(Kiriath-jearim)
Lehi?
Timnah
Zorah
Beth-shemesh
Makkedah?
Jarmuth
Azekah
Socoh
Adullam
Keilah
Giloh
Beth-zur
Hebron
Ziph
Maon
Eshtemoa
Carmel
Jattir
Debir
Anab
Goshen?
Jezreel?
Mareshah
Lachish
Libnah
Gath?
Ekron
Sorek
Gezer
Shikkeron
Gibbethon
Jabneel
Mount Baalah
Baalath?
Ashdod
Ashkelon
Gaza
Eglon?
Ziklag?
Gerar
Madmannah
Bethul (Bethuel)
Kabzeel?
Beer-sheba
Hazar-shual
Arad?
Hormah
Adadah (Aroer)
Ashan
Ziph
© Oxford University Press
OUTER BORDER SHOWS 10 MILE SUBDIVISIONS
V W X Y Z
5 6 7
32°
31° 30'
31°
34° 30'
35°
35° 30'
36°
36° 30'

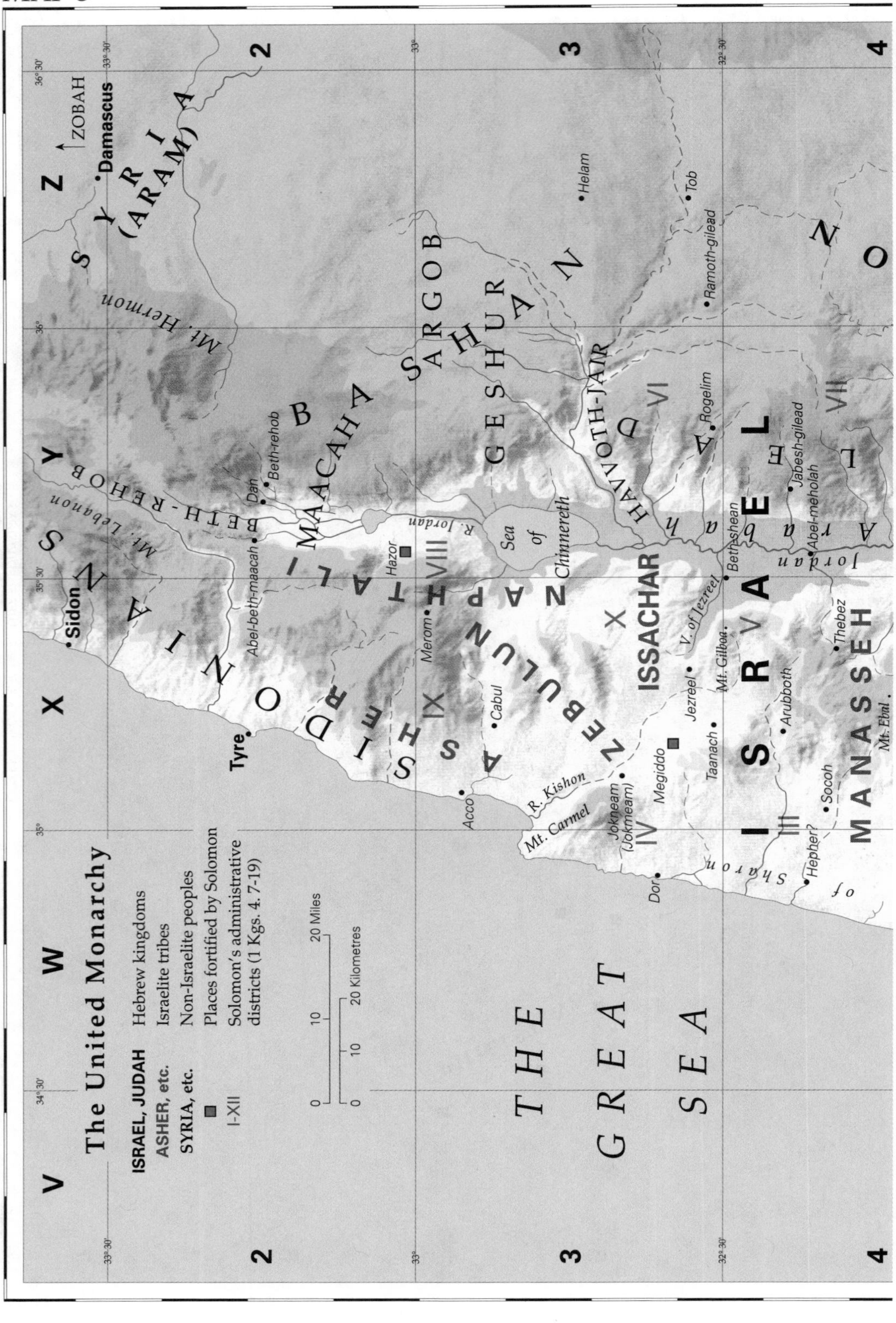
The United Monarchy
ISRAEL, JUDAH Hebrew kingdoms
ASHER, etc. Israelite tribes
SYRIA, etc. Non-Israelite peoples
Places fortified by Solomon
I-XII Solomon's administrative districts (1 Kgs. 4.7-19)
0 10 20 Miles
0 10 20 Kilometres
V
W
X
Y
Z
2
3
4
34° 30'
35°
35° 30'
36°
36° 30'
33° 30'
33°
32° 30'
THE GREAT SEA
SIDONIANS
Sidon
Tyre
Mt. Lebanon
BETH-REHOB
Mt. Hermon
ZOBAH
Damascus
SYRIA (ARAM)
Beth-rehob
Dan
Abel-beth-maacah
MAACAH
ARGOB
BASHAN
GESHUR
HAVVOTH-JAIR
GAD
Helam
Tob
Ramoth-gilead
Rogelim
Jabesh-gilead
Abel-meholah
GILEAD
AMMON
NAPHTALI
Hazor
Merom
R. Jordan
Sea of Chinnereth
ASHER
Cabul
Acco
ZEBULUN
ISSACHAR
V. of Jezreel
Beth-shean
Jezreel
Mt. Gilboa
Arabah
Jordan
ISRAEL
Mt. Carmel
R. Kishon
Jokneam (Jokmeam)
Megiddo
Taanach
Arubboth
Thebez
Dor
Sharon
Socoh
Hepher?
Mt. Ebal
MANASSEH
I
II
III
IV
V
VI
VII
VIII
IX
X

OUTER BORDER SHOWS 10 MILE SUBDIVISIONS

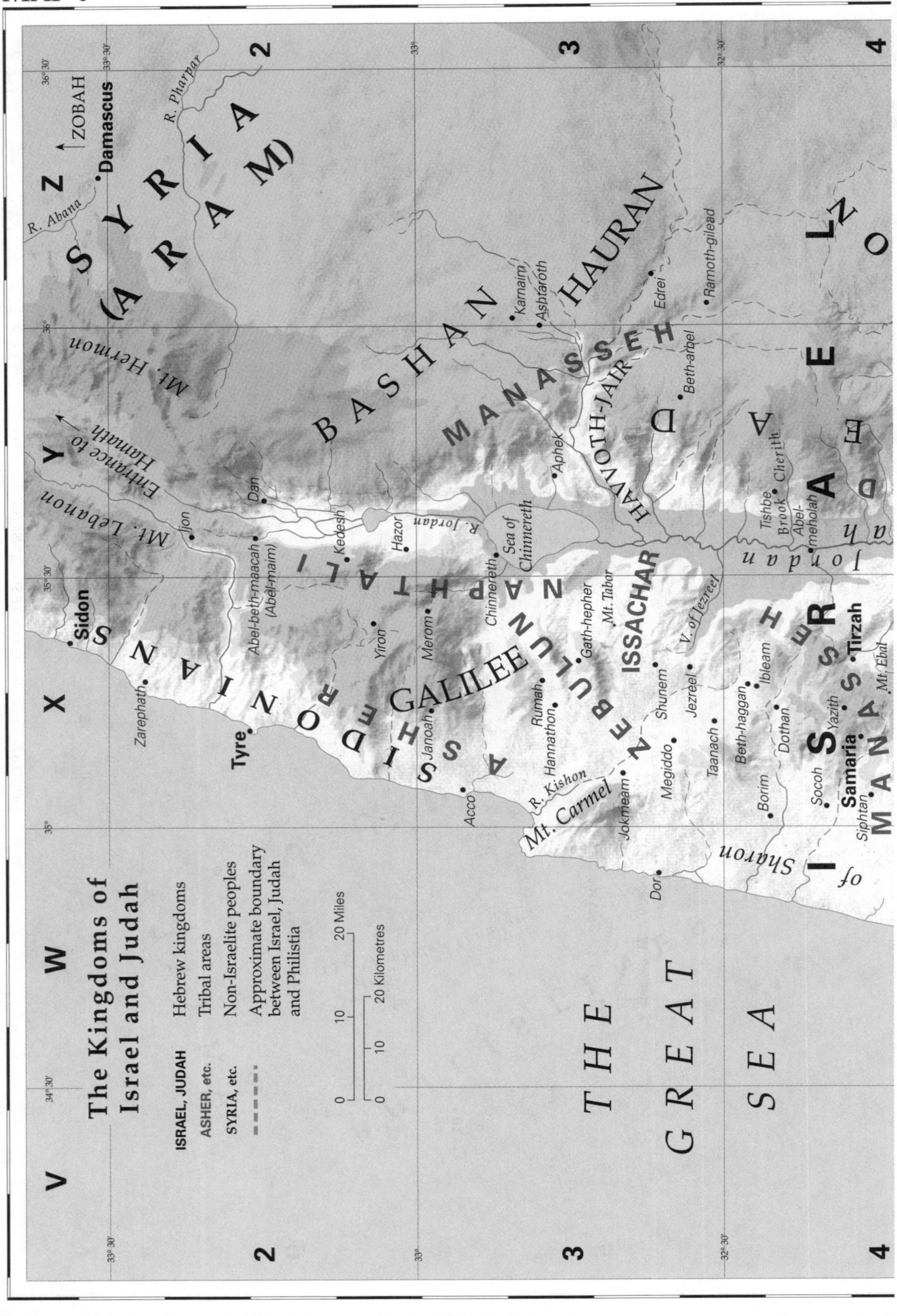
The Kingdoms of Israel and Judah
ISRAEL, JUDAH Hebrew kingdoms
ASHER, etc. Tribal areas
SYRIA, etc. Non-Israelite peoples
Approximate boundary between Israel, Judah and Philistia
0 10 20 Miles
0 10 20 Kilometres
V
W
X
Y
Z
2
3
4
34° 30'
35°
35° 30'
36°
36° 30'
33° 30'
33°
32° 30'
THE GREAT SEA
SYRIA (ARAM)
ZOBAH
Damascus
R. Abana
R. Pharpar
Mt. Hermon
Mt. Lebanon
Entrance to Hamath
BASHAN
HAURAN
MANASSEH
HAVOTH-JAIR
GAD
Karnaim
Ashtaroth
Edrei
Ramoth-gilead
Beth-arbel
Aphek
Dan
Ijon
Abel-beth-maacah (Abel-maim)
Kedesh
Hazor
R. Jordan
Sea of Chinnereth
Chinnereth
NAPHTALI
ZEBULUN
ISSACHAR
ASHER
SIDONIANS
GALILEE
Sidon
Zarephath
Tyre
Acco
Yiron
Merom
Janoah
Rumah
Hannathon
Gath-hepher
Mt. Tabor
V. of Jezreel
Shunem
Jezreel
R. Kishon
Mt. Carmel
Jokmeam
Megiddo
Taanach
Beth-haggan
Ibleam
Dothan
Dor
Borim
Socoh
Samaria
Siphtan
Yazith
Tirzah
Mt. Ebal
Plain of Sharon
Tishbe
Brook Cherith
Abel-meholah
Jordan
ISRAEL
MANASSEH
EDOM

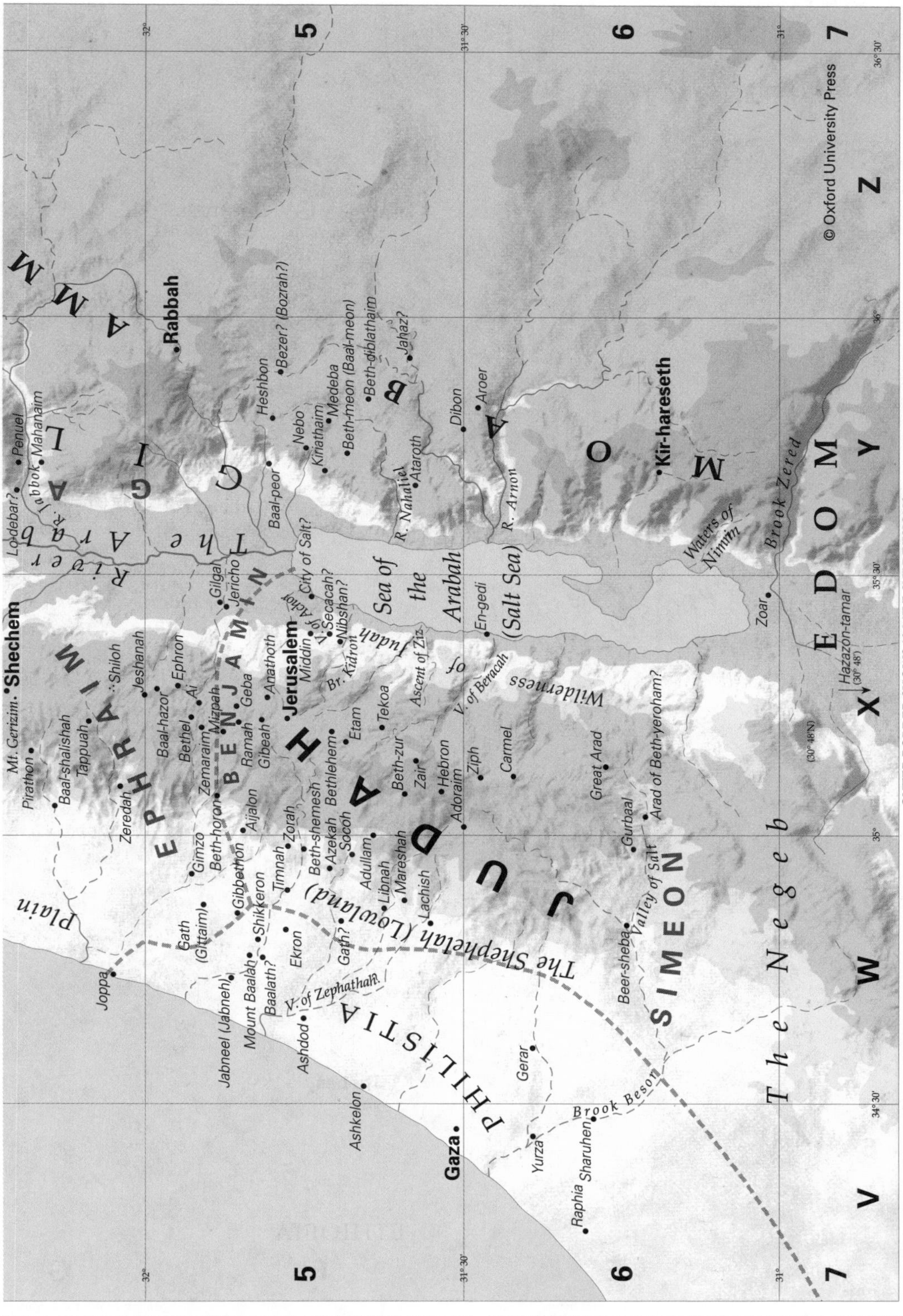

V W X Y Z
5 6 7
32°
31° 30'
31°
34° 30'
35°
35° 30'
36°
36° 30'
OUTER BORDER SHOWS 10 MILE SUBDIVISIONS
© Oxford University Press
AMMON
GILEAD
EPHRAIM
BENJAMIN
JUDAH
MOAB
EDOM
PHILISTIA
SIMEON
The Negeb
The Arabah
River Jabbok
Plain
The Shephelah (Lowland)
Sea of the Arabah (Salt Sea)
Wilderness of Judah
Shechem
Rabbah
Jerusalem
Kir-hareseth
Gaza
Lodebar?
Penuel
Mahanaim
Heshbon
Bezer? (Bozrah?)
Medeba
Beth-meon (Baal-meon)
Beth-diblathaim
Jahaz?
Nebo
Kiriathaim
Baal-peor
R. Nahaliel
Ataroth
Dibon
Aroer
R. Arnon
Waters of Nimrim
Brook Zered
Zoar
Hazazon-tamar (30° 48')
(30° 48'N)
Mt. Gerizim
Pirathon
Baal-shalishah
Tappuah
Shiloh
Jeshanah
Ephron
Baal-hazor
Bethel
Ai
Zemaraim
Mizpah
Ramah
Geba
Gibeah
Anathoth
Gilgal
Jericho
City of Salt?
V. of Achor
Secacah?
Middin
Nibshan?
Br. Kidron
Etam
Tekoa
Ascent of Ziz
V. of Beracah
En-gedi
Bethlehem
Beth-zur
Zair
Hebron
Ziph
Carmel
Adoraim
Great Arad
Gurbaal
Arad of Beth-yeroham?
Zeredah
Gimzo
Beth-horon
Aijalon
Zorah
Beth-shemesh
Timnah
Azekah
Socoh
Adullam
Libnah
Mareshah
Lachish
Gibbethon
Gath (Gittaim)
Shikkeron
Ekron
Gath?
Joppa
Jabneel (Jabneh)
Mount Baalah
Baalath?
V. of Zephathah
Ashdod
Ashkelon
Gerar
Beer-sheba
Valley of Salt
Brook Beson
Yurza
Sharuhen
Raphia

MAP 7

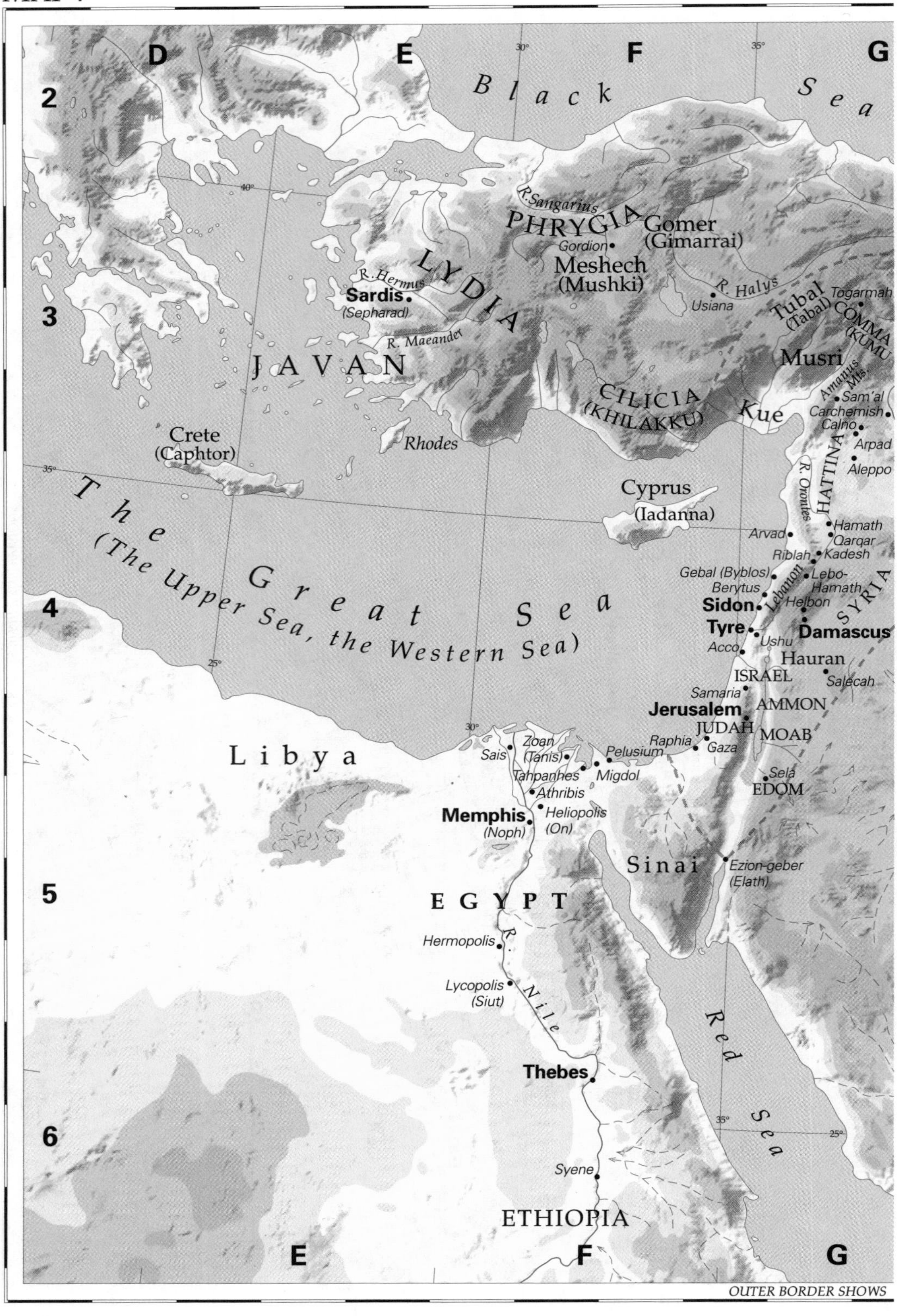
D
E
F
G
2
3
4
5
6
Black Sea
R. Sangarius
PHRYGIA
Gomer
(Gimarrai)
Gordion
Meshech
(Mushki)
LYDIA
R. Hermus
Sardis
(Sepharad)
R. Maeander
R. Halys
Usiana
Tubal
(Tabal)
Togarmah
COMMA
(KUMU)
Musri
JAVAN
Amanus Mts.
Sam'al
Carchemish
Calno
Arpad
Aleppo
HATTINA
CILICIA
(KHILAKKU)
Kue
Crete
(Caphtor)
Rhodes
Cyprus
(Iadanna)
R. Orontes
The Great Sea
(The Upper Sea, the Western Sea)
Hamath
Qarqar
Kadesh
Riblah
Arvad
Gebal (Byblos)
Berytus
Lebanon
Lebo-Hamath
Helbon
SYRIA
Sidon
Tyre
Ushu
Acco
Damascus
Hauran
Salecah
ISRAEL
Samaria
AMMON
Jerusalem
JUDAH
MOAB
Raphia
Gaza
Libya
Zoan
(Tanis)
Sais
Pelusium
Tahpanhes
Migdol
Athribis
Sela
EDOM
Memphis
(Noph)
Heliopolis
(On)
Sinai
Ezion-geber
(Elath)
EGYPT
Hermopolis
R. Nile
Lycopolis
(Siut)
Red Sea
Thebes
Syene
ETHIOPIA
E
F
G
OUTER BORDER SHOWS

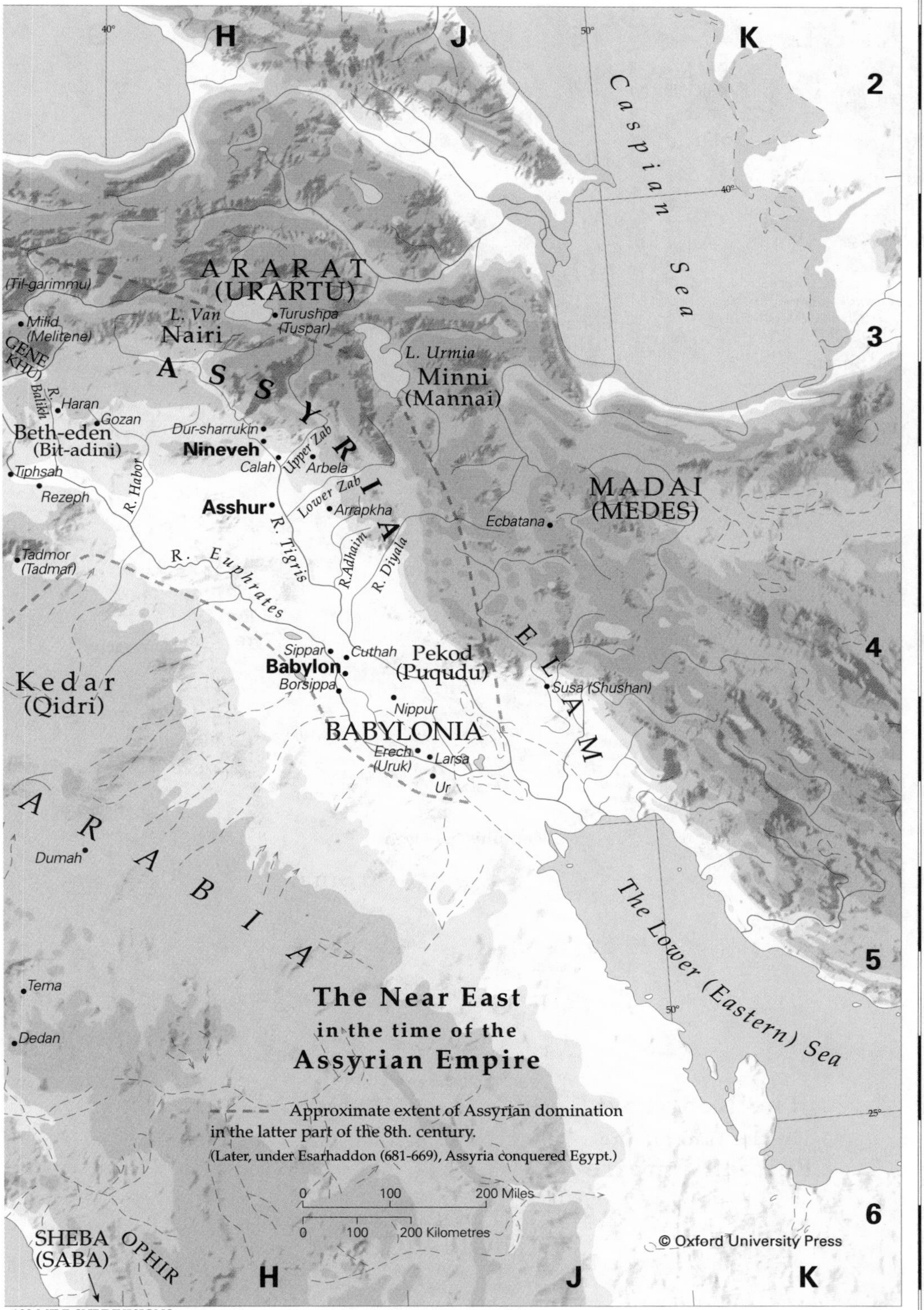

The Near East in the time of the Assyrian Empire
Approximate extent of Assyrian domination in the latter part of the 8th. century.
(Later, under Esarhaddon (681-669), Assyria conquered Egypt.)
0 100 200 Miles
0 100 200 Kilometres
© Oxford University Press
H
J
K
2
3
4
5
6
40°
50°
25°
ARARAT
(URARTU)
(Til-garimmu)
Milid
(Melitene)
GENE KHU
L. Van
Nairi
Turushpa
(Tuspar)
L. Urmia
Minni
(Mannai)
ASSYRIA
R. Balikh
Haran
Gozan
Beth-eden
(Bit-adini)
Dur-sharrukin
Nineveh
Calah
Upper Zab
Arbela
Tiphsah
Rezeph
R. Habor
Asshur
Lower Zab
Arrapkha
R. Tigris
R. Adhaim
R. Diyala
Tadmor
(Tadmar)
R. Euphrates
MADAI
(MEDES)
Ecbatana
Caspian Sea
ELAM
Sippar
Cuthah
Babylon
Borsippa
Pekod
(Puqudu)
Susa (Shushan)
Nippur
BABYLONIA
Erech
(Uruk)
Larsa
Ur
Kedar
(Qidri)
ARABIA
Dumah
Tema
Dedan
The Lower (Eastern) Sea
SHEBA
(SABA)
OPHIR

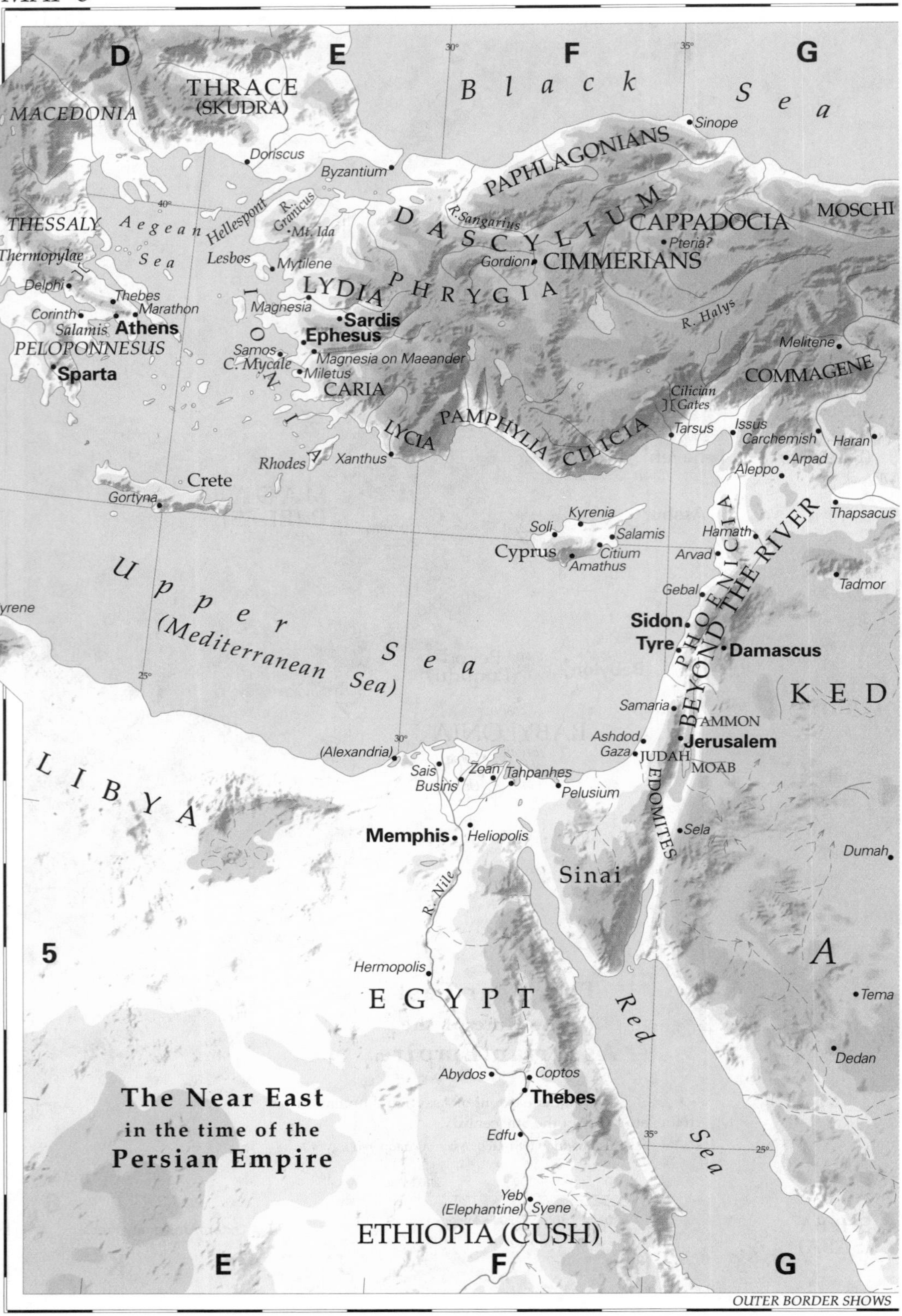
The Near East in the time of the Persian Empire
D
E
F
G
3
4
5
E
F
G
30°
35°
40°
25°
Black Sea
THRACE (SKUDRA)
MACEDONIA
Doriscus
Byzantium
Sinope
PAPHLAGONIANS
MOSCHI
THESSALY
Aegean Sea
Hellespont
R. Granicus
Mt. Ida
DASCYLIUM
R.Sangarius
CAPPADOCIA
Pteria?
Thermopylae
Lesbos
Mytilene
Gordion
CIMMERIANS
Delphi
Thebes
Marathon
LYDIA
PHRYGIA
Corinth
Salamis
Athens
Magnesia
Sardis
R. Halys
PELOPONNESUS
Samos
Ephesus
IONIA
Melitene
Sparta
C. Mycale
Magnesia on Maeander
Miletus
CARIA
COMMAGENE
Cilician Gates
LYCIA
PAMPHYLIA
CILICIA
Tarsus
Issus
Carchemish
Haran
Rhodes
Xanthus
Arpad
Aleppo
Crete
Gortyna
Thapsacus
Kyrenia
Soli
Salamis
Hamath
Cyprus
Citium
Amathus
Arvad
PHOENICIA
BEYOND THE RIVER
Tadmor
Upper Sea (Mediterranean Sea)
Cyrene
Gebal
Sidon
Tyre
Damascus
KED
Samaria
AMMON
Ashdod
Jerusalem
Gaza
JUDAH
MOAB
LIBYA
(Alexandria)
Sais
Busiris
Zoan
Tahpanhes
Pelusium
EDOMITES
Memphis
Heliopolis
Sela
Dumah
Sinai
R. Nile
A
Hermopolis
EGYPT
Red Sea
Tema
Dedan
Abydos
Coptos
Thebes
Edfu
Yeb (Elephantine)
Syene
ETHIOPIA (CUSH)
OUTER BORDER SHOWS

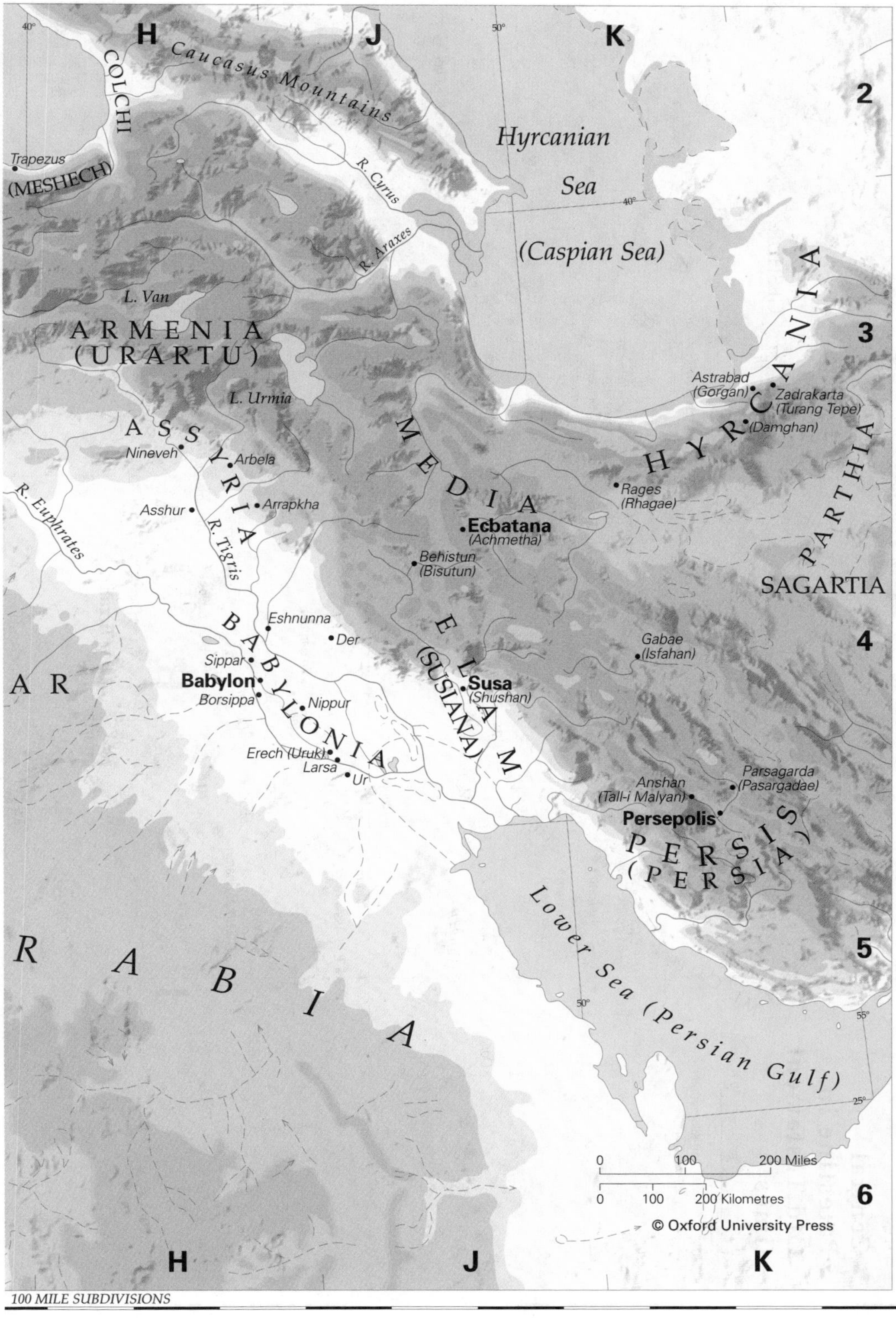

100 MILE SUBDIVISIONS

Central Palestine in Old Testament times

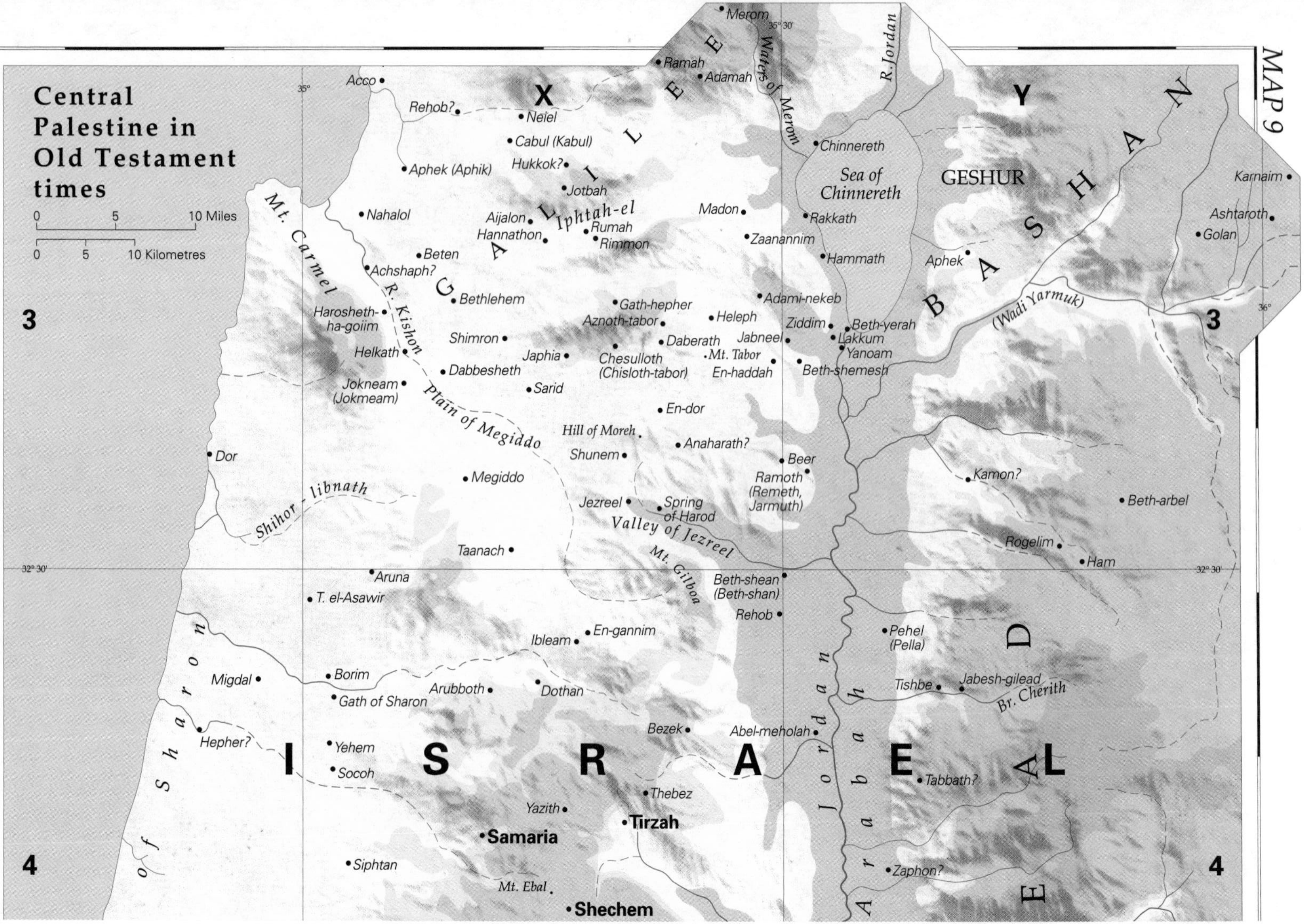

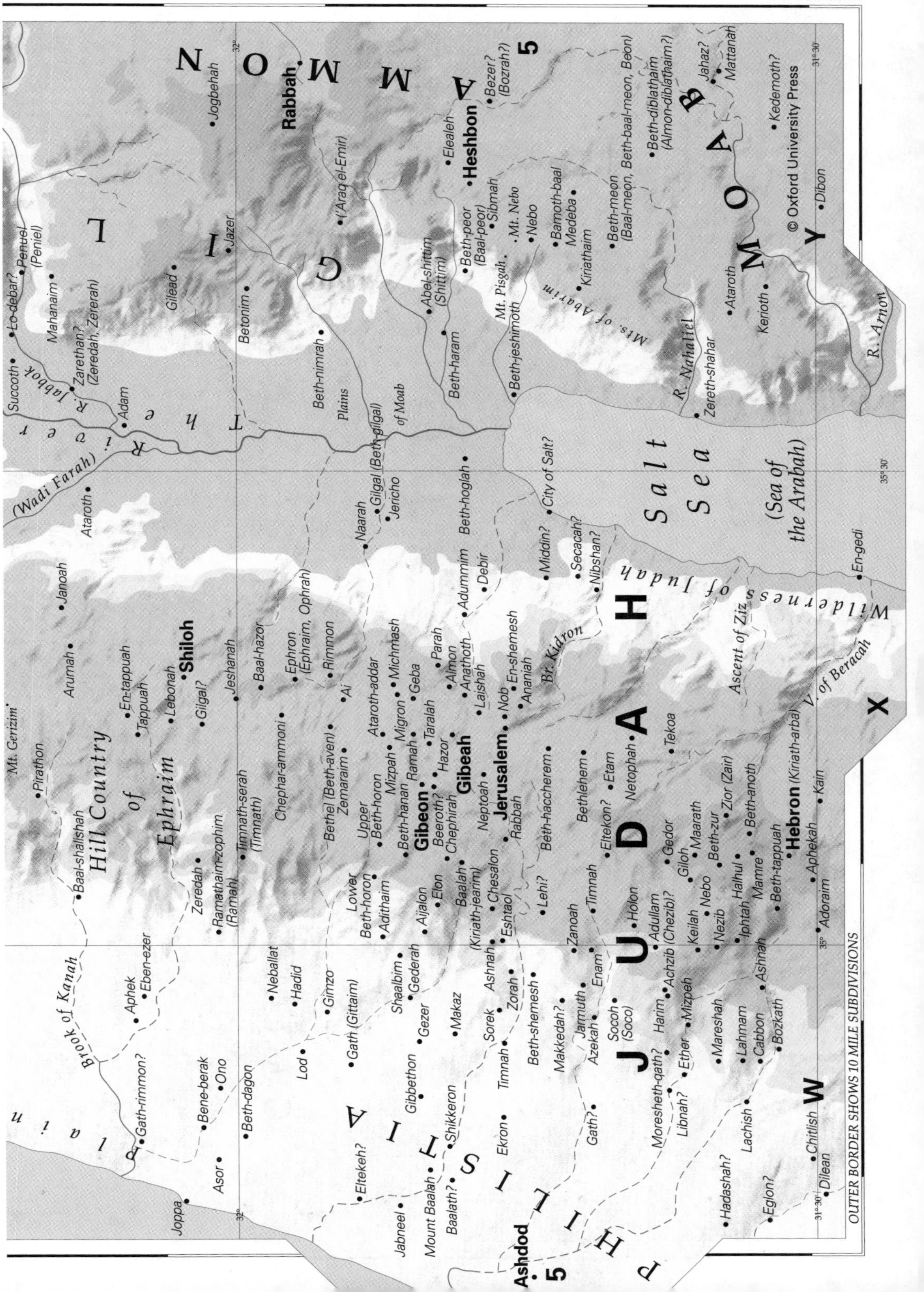

OUTER BORDER SHOWS 10 MILE SUBDIVISIONS
© Oxford University Press
Hill Country of Ephraim
Mts. of Abarim
Wilderness of Judah
Salt Sea (Sea of the Arabah)
Plains of Moab
R. Jabbok
R. Arnon
R. Nahaliel
Br. Kidron
Brook of Kanah
(Wadi Farah)
The River
Plain
Ascent of Ziz
V. of Beracah
Mt. Gerizim
Mt. Pisgah
Mt. Nebo
PHILISTIA
JUDAH
GILEAD
AMMON
MOAB
Jerusalem
Gibeah
Gibeon
Hebron (Kiriath-arba)
Shiloh
Heshbon
Rabbah
Ashdod
Joppa
Jericho
Gilgal (Beth-gilgal)
Bethlehem
Tekoa
En-gedi
Lachish
Ekron
Timnah
Gezer
Lod
Ono
Aphek
Eben-ezer
Bethel (Beth-aven)
Ai
Mizpah
Ramah
Anathoth
Michmash
Geba
Jabneel
Mount Baalah
Baalath?
Shikkeron
Eltekeh?
Gibbethon
Gath (Gittaim)
Gimzo
Hadid
Neballat
Beth-dagon
Bene-berak
Gath-rimmon?
Asor
Pirathon
Baal-shalishah
Zeredah
Ramathaim-zophim (Ramah)
Timnath-serah (Timnath)
Tappuah
En-tappuah
Lebonah
Gilgal?
Jeshanah
Arumah
Janoah
Baal-hazor
Ephron (Ephraim, Ophrah)
Rimmon
Chephar-ammoni
Zemaraim
Upper Beth-horon
Lower Beth-horon
Adithaim
Aijalon
Elon
Beth-hanan
Beeroth?
Chephirah
Baalah (Kiriath-jearim)
Chesalon
Eshtaol
Zorah
Ashnah
Sorek
Beth-shemesh
Shaalbim
Gederah
Makaz
Neptoah
Rabbah
Nob
Laishah
Ananiah
En-shemesh
Almon
Parah
Adummim
Debir
Hazor
Taralah
Migron
Ataroth-addar
Beth-haccherem
Lehi?
Zanoah
Timnah
Eltekon?
Etam
Netophah
Holon
Adullam
Achzib (Chezib)?
Enam
Jarmuth
Azekah
Socoh (Soco)
Makkedah?
Gath?
Moresheth-gath?
Harim
Mizpeh
Ether
Libnah?
Keilah
Nebo
Nezib
Mareshah
Giloh
Gedor
Maarath
Beth-zur
Zior (Zair)
Halhul
Mamre
Iphtah
Ashnah
Lahmam
Cabbon
Bozkath
Beth-anoth
Beth-tappuah
Aphekah
Adoraim
Kain
Hadashah?
Eglon?
Chitlish
Dilean
Ataroth
Naarah
Beth-hoglah
Middin?
Secacah?
Nibshan?
City of Salt?
Succoth
Adam
Zarethan? (Zeredah, Zererah)
Lo-debar?
Penuel (Peniel)
Mahanaim
Gilead
Jazer
Jogbehah
Betonim
Beth-nimrah
('Araq el-Emir)
Abel-shittim (Shittim)
Beth-haram
Beth-jeshimoth
Beth-peor (Baal-peor)
Sibmah
Elealeh
Nebo
Barnoth-baal
Medeba
Kiriathaim
Beth-meon (Baal-meon, Beth-baal-meon, Beon)
Beth-diblathaim (Almon-diblathaim?)
Bezer? (Bozrah?)
Jahaz?
Mattanah
Kedemoth?
Dibon
Ataroth
Kerioth
Zereth-shahar
W
X
Y
5
32°
31° 30'
35° 30'
36°

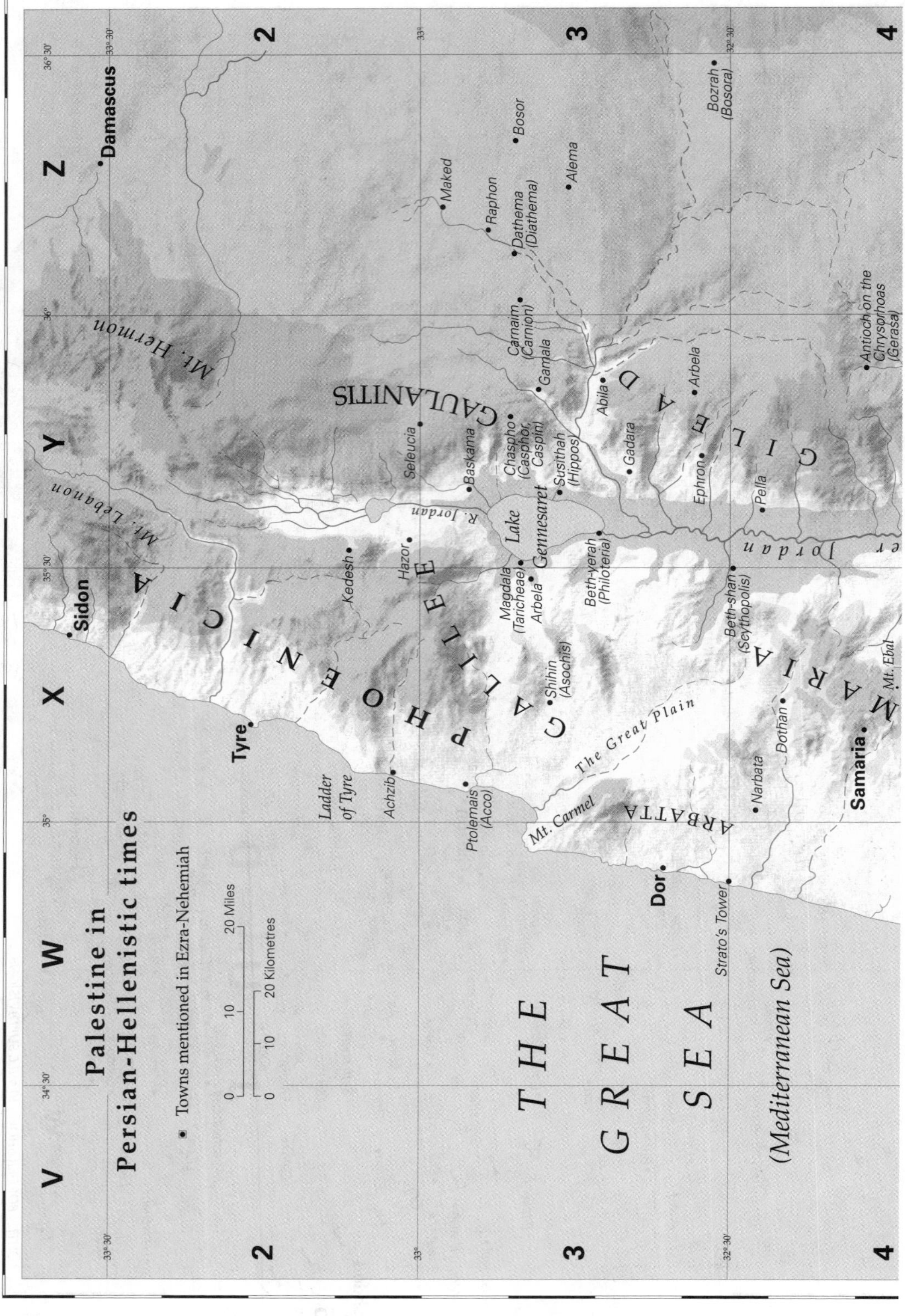
Palestine in
Persian-Hellenistic times
Towns mentioned in Ezra-Nehemiah
0 10 20 Miles
0 10 20 Kilometres
V
W
X
Y
Z
2
3
4
34° 30'
35°
35° 30'
36°
36° 30'
33° 30'
33°
32° 30'
THE
GREAT
SEA
(Mediterranean Sea)
PHOENICIA
GALILEE
GAULANITIS
GILEAD
SAMARIA
ARBATTA
Mt. Lebanon
Mt. Hermon
Mt. Carmel
Mt. Ebal
The Great Plain
Ladder of Tyre
R. Jordan
Jordan
Lake Gennesaret
Damascus
Sidon
Tyre
Achzib
Ptolemais (Acco)
Dor
Strato's Tower
Samaria
Narbata
Dothan
Shihin (Asochis)
Kedesh
Hazor
Seleucia
Baskama
Magdala (Taricheae)
Arbela
Beth-yerah (Philoteria)
Beth-shan (Scythopolis)
Chaspho (Casphor, Caspin)
Susithah (Hippos)
Gadara
Ephron
Pella
Abila
Arbela
Gamala
Carnaim (Carnion)
Dathema (Diathema)
Raphon
Maked
Alema
Bosor
Bozrah (Bosora)
Antioch on the Chrysorhoas (Gerasa)

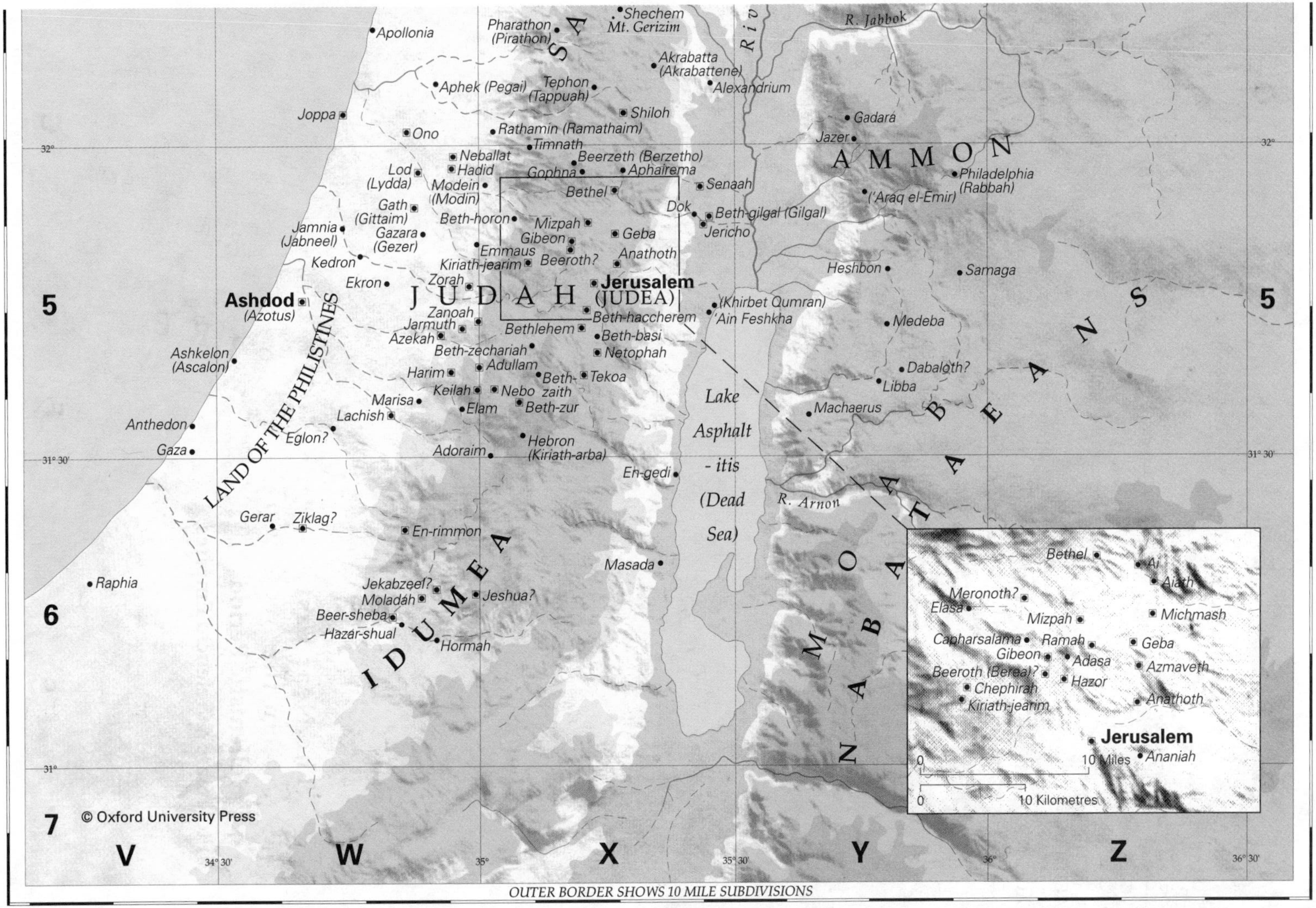
Shechem
Mt. Gerizim
Apollonia
Pharathon (Pirathon)
SA
R. Jabbok
Riv
Akrabatta (Akrabattene)
Aphek (Pegai)
Tephon (Tappuah)
Alexandrium
Shiloh
Joppa
Gadara
Ono
Rathamin (Ramathaim)
Jazer
Timnath
Neballat
Beerzeth (Berzetho)
AMMON
Hadid
Lod (Lydda)
Gophna
Aphairema
Philadelphia (Rabbah)
Modein (Modin)
Bethel
Senaah
Gath (Gittaim)
Dok
('Araq el-Emir)
Beth-horon
Mizpah
Beth-gilgal (Gilgal)
Jamnia (Jabneel)
Gazara (Gezer)
Gibeon
Geba
Jericho
Emmaus
Kedron
Kiriath-jearim
Beeroth?
Anathoth
Heshbon
Samaga
Ekron
Zorah
Jerusalem (JUDEA)
JUDAH
Ashdod (Azotus)
(Khirbet Qumran)
'Ain Feshkha
Zanoah
Beth-haccherem
Jarmuth
Bethlehem
Medeba
Azekah
Beth-basi
Beth-zechariah
Netophah
Ashkelon (Ascalon)
LAND OF THE PHILISTINES
Adullam
Dabaloth?
Harim
Beth-zaith
Tekoa
Libba
Keilah
Nebo
Lake Asphaltitis (Dead Sea)
Marisa
Elam
Beth-zur
Machaerus
Lachish
NABATAEANS
Anthedon
Eglon?
Hebron (Kiriath-arba)
Gaza
Adoraim
En-gedi
R. Arnon
Gerar
Ziklag?
En-rimmon
Masada
Raphia
Jekabzeel?
Moladah
Jeshua?
MOAB
IDUMEA
Beer-sheba
Hazar-shual
Hormah
Bethel
Ai
Aiath
Meronoth?
Elasa
Mizpah
Michmash
Capharsalama
Ramah
Geba
Gibeon
Adasa
Azmaveth
Beeroth (Berea)?
Hazor
Chephirah
Kiriath-jearim
Anathoth
Jerusalem
Ananiah
0
10 Miles
0
10 Kilometres
32°
31° 30'
31°
34° 30'
35°
35° 30'
36°
36° 30'
5
6
7
V
W
X
Y
Z
OUTER BORDER SHOWS 10 MILE SUBDIVISIONS

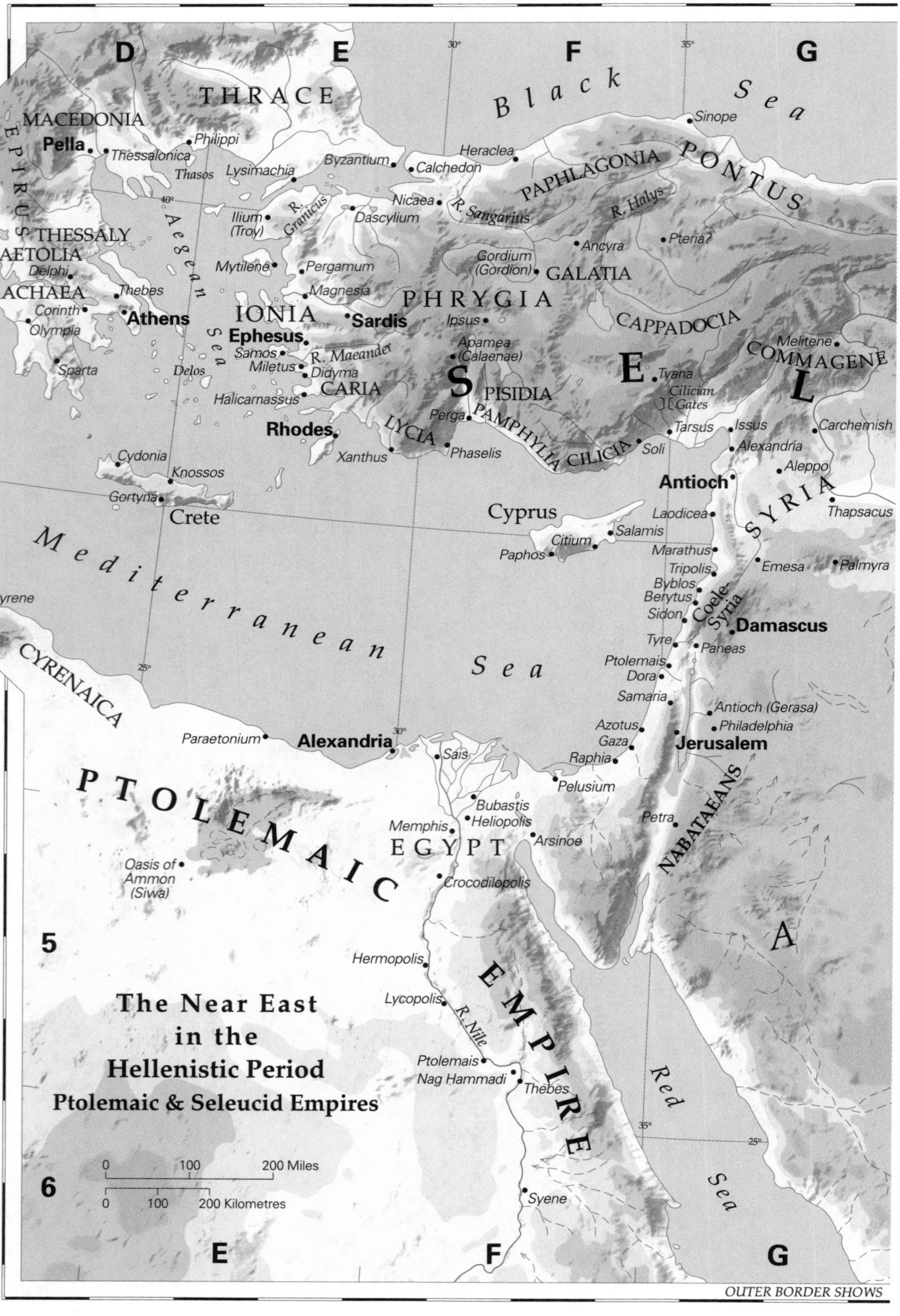
The Near East in the Hellenistic Period
Ptolemaic & Seleucid Empires
D
E
F
G
3
4
5
6
Black Sea
THRACE
MACEDONIA
EPIRUS
Pella
Philippi
Thessalonica
Thasos
Lysimachia
Byzantium
Calchedon
Heraclea
Sinope
PAPHLAGONIA
PONTUS
Nicaea
R. Sangarius
R. Halys
Ilium (Troy)
R. Granicus
Dascylium
THESSALY
AETOLIA
Delphi
Aegean Sea
Ancyra
Pteria?
Mytilene
Pergamum
Gordium (Gordion)
GALATIA
ACHAEA
Thebes
Magnesia
PHRYGIA
Corinth
Athens
IONIA
Sardis
Ipsus
CAPPADOCIA
Olympia
Ephesus
Samos
R. Maeander
Apamea (Calaenae)
Melitene
COMMAGENE
Sparta
Delos
Miletus
Didyma
SELEUCID EMPIRE
Tyana
Cilician Gates
CARIA
PISIDIA
Halicarnassus
Perga
PAMPHYLIA
Tarsus
Issus
Carchemish
Rhodes
LYCIA
CILICIA
Soli
Alexandria
Cydonia
Xanthus
Phaselis
Aleppo
Knossos
Antioch
SYRIA
Gortyna
Crete
Cyprus
Laodicea
Thapsacus
Salamis
Citium
Paphos
Marathus
Mediterranean Sea
Tripolis
Emesa
Palmyra
Cyrene
Byblos
Berytus
Coele-Syria
Sidon
Damascus
Tyre
Paneas
CYRENAICA
Ptolemais
Dora
Samaria
Antioch (Gerasa)
Azotus
Philadelphia
Paraetonium
Alexandria
Gaza
Jerusalem
Sais
Raphia
PTOLEMAIC EMPIRE
Pelusium
Bubastis
Heliopolis
NABATAEANS
Petra
Memphis
Arsinoe
EGYPT
Oasis of Ammon (Siwa)
Crocodilopolis
ARABIA
Hermopolis
Lycopolis
R. Nile
Ptolemais
Nag Hammadi
Thebes
Red Sea
Syene
0 100 200 Miles
0 100 200 Kilometres
30°
35°
40°
25°
OUTER BORDER SHOWS

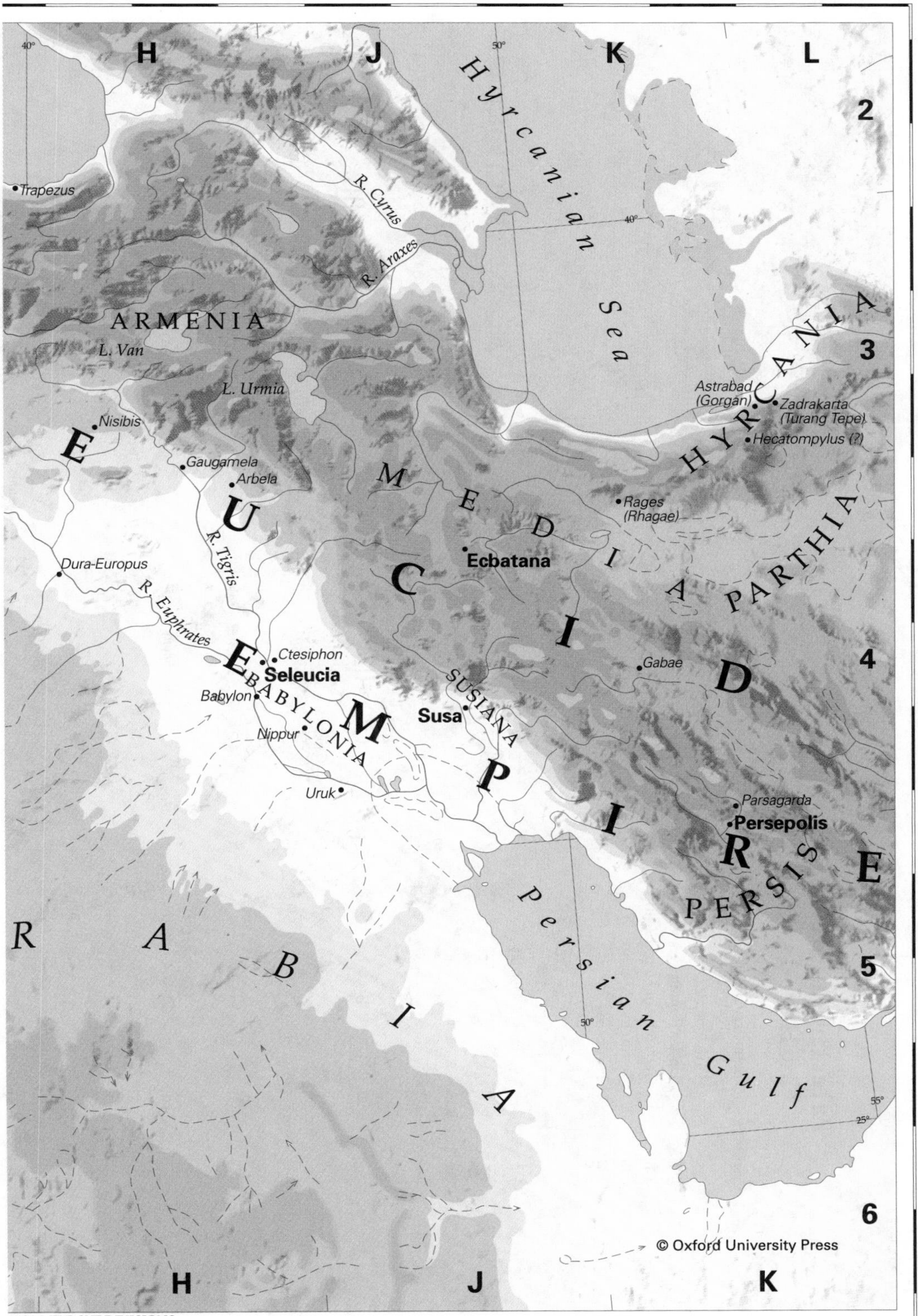
H
J
K
L
2
3
4
5
6
40°
50°
55°
25°
Hyrcanian Sea
R. Cyrus
R. Araxes
Trapezus
ARMENIA
L. Van
L. Urmia
Nisibis
Gaugamela
Arbela
R. Tigris
Dura-Europus
R. Euphrates
Ctesiphon
Seleucia
Babylon
BABYLONIA
Nippur
Uruk
SUSIANA
Susa
MEDIA
Ecbatana
Rages
(Rhagae)
HYRCANIA
Astrabad
(Gorgan)
Zadrakarta
(Turang Tepe)
Hecatompylus (?)
PARTHIA
Gabae
Parsagarda
Persepolis
PERSIS
SELEUCID EMPIRE
ARABIA
Persian Gulf
© Oxford University Press
H
J
K
100 MILE SUBDIVISIONS

MAP 12

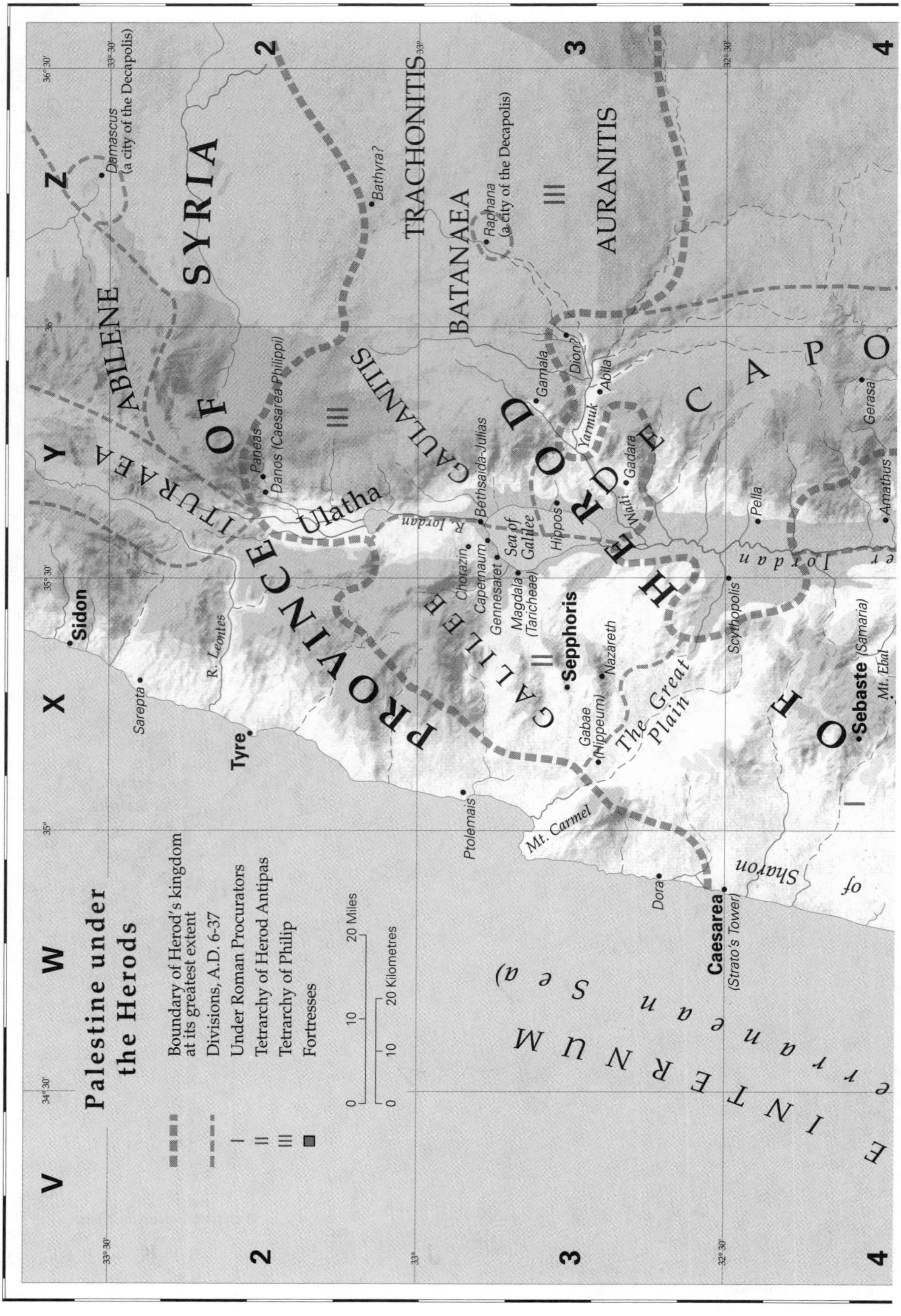

Palestine under the Herods
Boundary of Herod's kingdom at its greatest extent
Divisions, A.D. 6-37
I Under Roman Procurators
II Tetrarchy of Herod Antipas
III Tetrarchy of Philip
Fortresses
0 10 20 Miles
0 10 20 Kilometres
V
W
X
Y
Z
2
3
4
33° 30'
33°
32° 30'
34° 30'
35°
35° 30'
36°
36° 30'
PROVINCE OF SYRIA
ABILENE
ITURAEA
TRACHONITIS
BATANAEA
AURANITIS
GAULANITIS
GALILEE
DECAPOLIS
HEROD
Damascus (a city of the Decapolis)
Bathyra?
Raphana (a city of the Decapolis)
Sidon
Sarepta
R. Leontes
Tyre
Paneas
Danos (Caesarea Philippi)
Ulatha
R. Jordan
Bethsaida-Julias
Chorazin
Capernaum
Gennesaret
Magdala (Taricheae)
Sea of Galilee
Hippos
Gamala
Dion?
Abila
Yarmuk
Gadara
Wadi
Pella
Gerasa
Amathus
Jordan
Scythopolis
Sepphoris
Nazareth
The Great Plain
Gabae (Hippeum)
Ptolemais
Mt. Carmel
Dora
Caesarea (Strato's Tower)
Sharon
Sebaste (Samaria)
Mt. Ebal
INTERNUM Mediterranean Sea

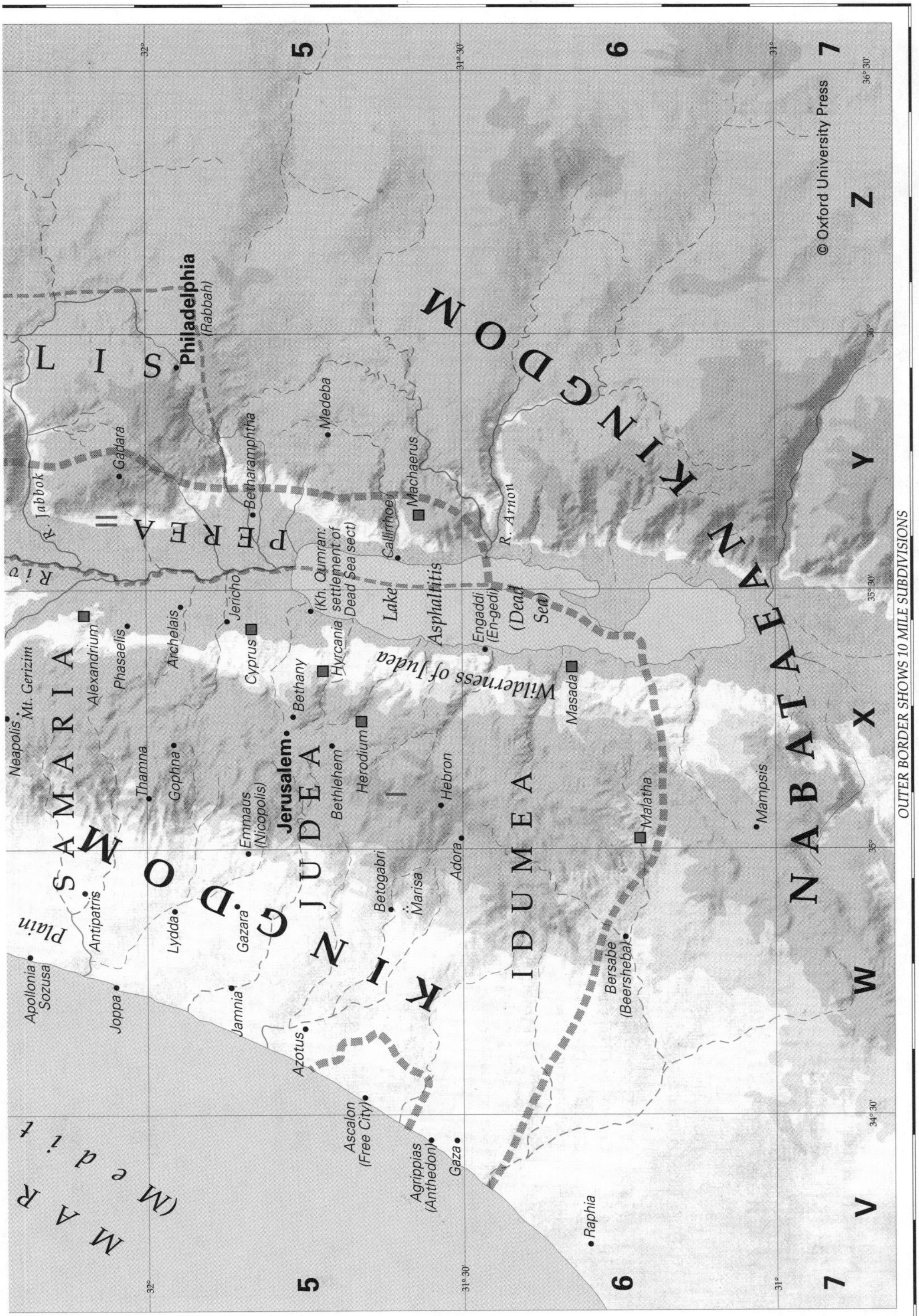
MARE (Medit
SAMARIA
JUDEA
IDUMEA
PEREA
KINGDOM
NABATAEAN KINGDOM
LIS
Philadelphia
(Rabbah)
Gadara
Betharamphtha
Medeba
Machaerus
Callirhoe
R. Jabbok
R. Arnon
Rio
Neapolis
Mt. Gerizim
Alexandrium
Phasaelis
Archelais
Jericho
Cyprus
(Kh. Qumran: settlement of Dead Sea sect)
Hyrcania
Bethany
Jerusalem
Bethlehem
Herodium
Hebron
Lake Asphaltitis
(Dead Sea)
Engaddi
(En-gedi)
Wilderness of Judea
Masada
Malatha
Mampsis
Thamna
Gophna
Emmaus
(Nicopolis)
Adora
Betogabri
Marisa
Antipatris
Lydda
Gazara
Plain
Apollonia
Sozusa
Joppa
Jamnia
Azotus
Ascalon
(Free City)
Agrippias
(Anthedon)
Gaza
Raphia
Bersabe
(Beersheba)
V
W
X
Y
Z
5
6
7
32°
31° 30'
31°
34° 30'
35°
35° 30'
36°
36° 30'
OUTER BORDER SHOWS 10 MILE SUBDIVISIONS

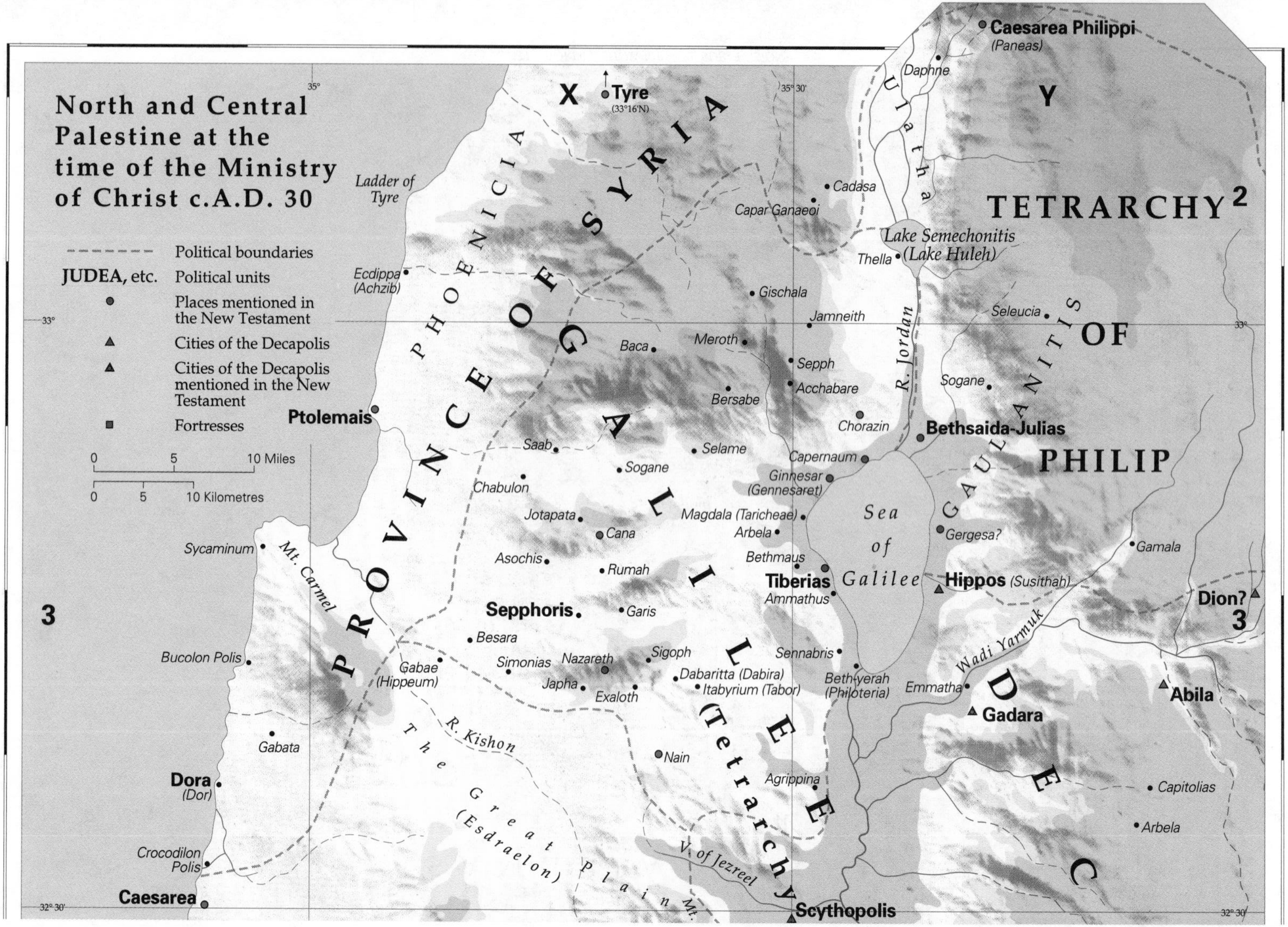
North and Central Palestine at the time of the Ministry of Christ c.A.D. 30
Political boundaries
JUDEA, etc. Political units
Places mentioned in the New Testament
Cities of the Decapolis
Cities of the Decapolis mentioned in the New Testament
Fortresses
0 5 10 Miles
0 5 10 Kilometres
35°
35° 30'
33°
32° 30'
2
3
PROVINCE OF SYRIA
PHOENICIA
GALILEE (Tetrarchy)
TETRARCHY OF PHILIP
GAULANITIS
DECAPOLIS
X
Y
Ulatha
Caesarea Philippi
(Paneas)
Daphne
Tyre
(33°16'N)
Ladder of Tyre
Ecdippa (Achzib)
Ptolemais
Cadasa
Capar Ganaeoi
Lake Semechonitis (Lake Huleh)
Thella
Gischala
Jamneith
Meroth
Baca
Sepph
Acchabare
Bersabe
Chorazin
R. Jordan
Seleucia
Sogane
Bethsaida-Julias
Saab
Selame
Sogane
Capernaum
Ginnesar (Gennesaret)
Chabulon
Jotapata
Cana
Magdala (Taricheae)
Arbela
Sea of Galilee
Gergesa?
Gamala
Asochis
Rumah
Bethmaus
Tiberias
Ammathus
Hippos (Susithah)
Dion?
Sycaminum
Mt. Carmel
Sepphoris
Garis
Besara
Sigoph
Sennabris
Wadi Yarmuk
Bucolon Polis
Gabae (Hippeum)
Simonias
Nazareth
Japha
Exaloth
Dabaritta (Dabira)
Itabyrium (Tabor)
Beth-yerah (Philoteria)
Emmatha
Abila
Gadara
R. Kishon
Gabata
Nain
The Great Plain (Esdraelon)
Dora (Dor)
Agrippina
Capitolias
Arbela
Crocodilon Polis
V. of Jezreel
Mt.
Caesarea
Scythopolis

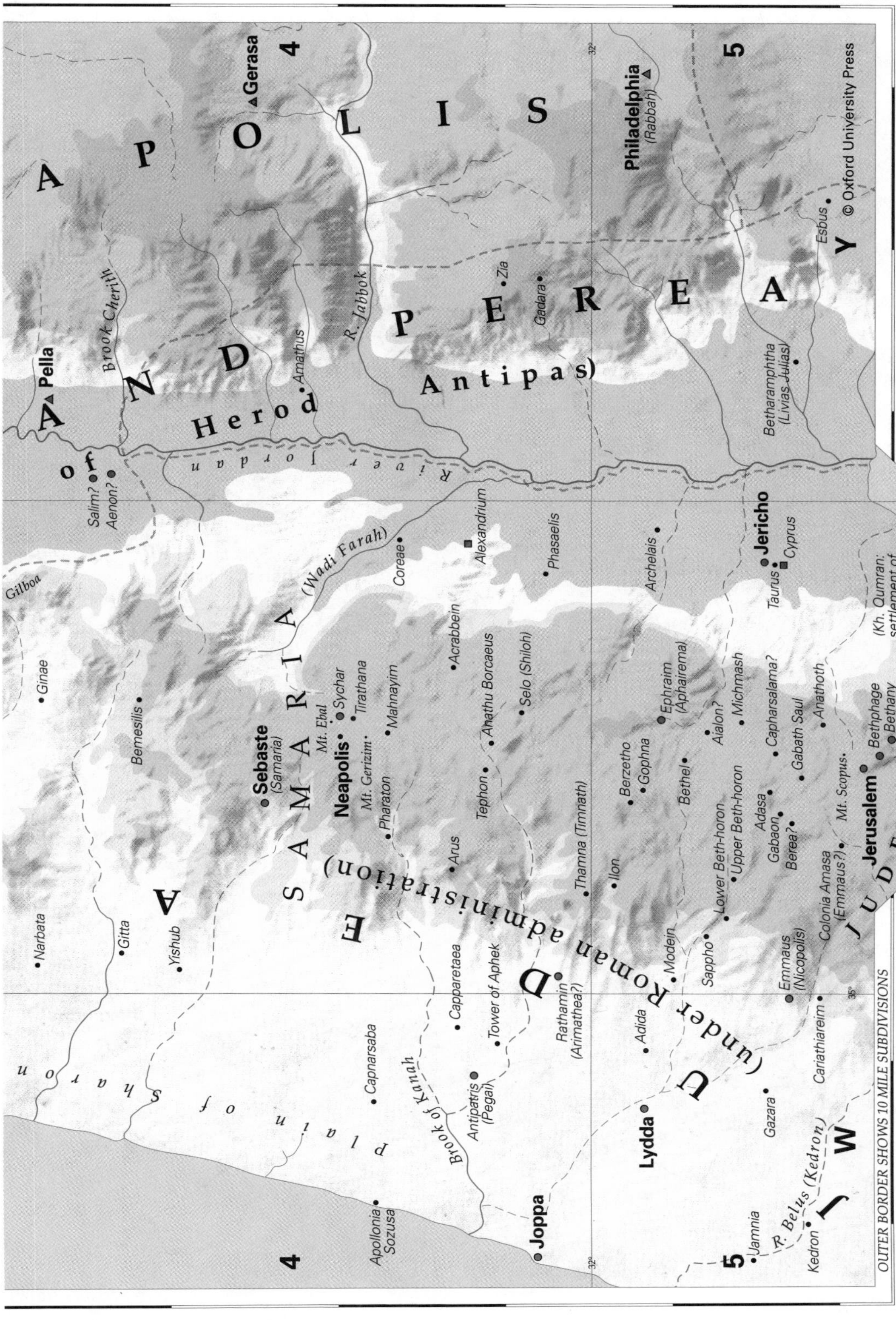
DECAPOLIS
PEREA
(of Herod Antipas)
SAMARIA
JUDEA
(under Roman administration)
Gerasa
Pella
Philadelphia
(Rabbah)
Brook Cherith
Amathus
R. Jabbok
Zia
Gadara
Esbus
Betharamphtha
(Livias Julias)
River Jordan
Salim?
Aenon?
Alexandrium
Phasaelis
Archelais
Jericho
Cyprus
Taurus
(Kh. Qumran: settlement of Dead Sea sect)
Gilboa
(Wadi Farah)
Coreae
Acrabbein
Ginae
Bemesilis
Mt. Ebal
Sychar
Tirathana
Mahnayim
Sebaste
(Samaria)
Neapolis
Mt. Gerizim
Pharaton
Anathu Borcaeus
Selo (Shiloh)
Tephon
Arus
Ephraim
(Aphairema)
Michmash
Aialon?
Capharsalama?
Gabath Saul
Anathoth
Bethphage
Bethany
Berzetho
Gophna
Bethel
Thamna (Timnath)
Ilon
Lower Beth-horon
Upper Beth-horon
Adasa
Gabaon
Berea?
Mt. Scopus
Jerusalem
Colonia Amasa
(Emmaus?)
Emmaus
(Nicopolis)
Sappho
Modein
Narbata
Gitta
Yishub
Capparetaea
Tower of Aphek
Rathamin
(Arimathea?)
Adida
Capnarsaba
Antipatris
(Pegai)
Brook of Kanah
Plain of Sharon
Lydda
Gazara
Cariathiareim
Apollonia
Sozusa
Joppa
Jamnia
R. Belus (Kedron)
Kedron
32°
35°
35° 30'
4
5
© Oxford University Press
OUTER BORDER SHOWS 10 MILE SUBDIVISIONS

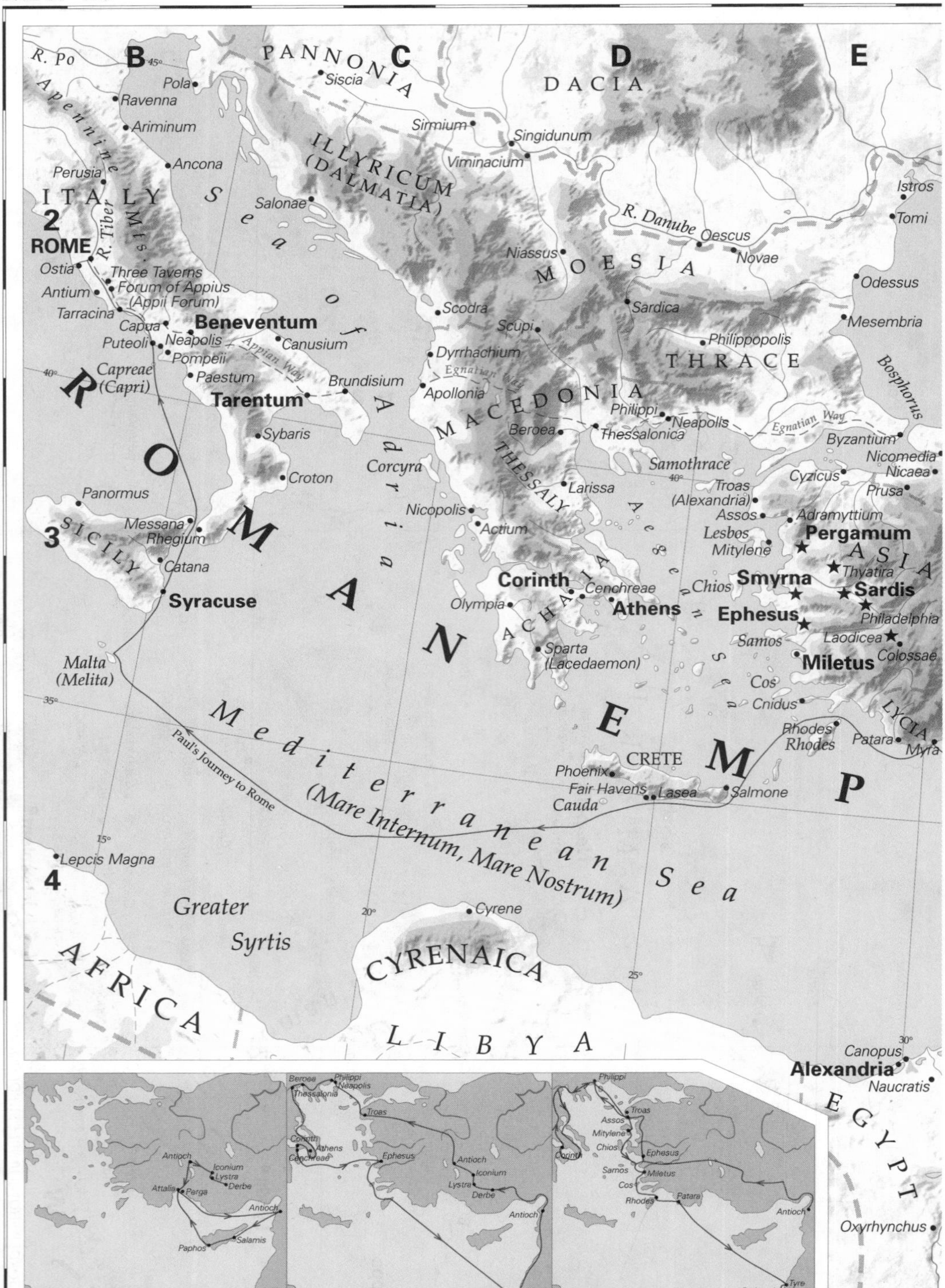

OUTER BORDER SHOWS